MW01152077

Who's Who in Hell

A Handbook and International Directory
for Humanists, Freethinkers, Naturalists,
Rationalists, and Non-Theists

Who's Who in Hell

A Handbook and International Directory for Humanists, Freethinkers, Naturalists, Rationalists, and Non-Theists

Warren Allen Smith

New York, New York
www.barricadebooks.com

Barricade Books
150 Fifth Ave. Ste 700
New York, NY 10011
www.barricadebooks.com

Who's Who in Hell: A Handbook and International Directory for Humanists, Freethinkers, Naturalists, Rationalists, and Non-Theists.

First Printing

Inquiries may be addressed <wasm@idt.net>

Library of Congress Cataloguing-in-Publication data
Who's Who in Hell: A Handbook and International Directory for Humanists, Freethinkers, Naturalists, Rationalists, and Non-Theists. / compiled by Warren Allen Smith

p. cm.
Includes bibliographical references and index
ISBN 1-56980-158-4

I. 1. Rationalists--Biography--Dictionaries. 2. Atheists--Biography--Dictionaries. I Smith, Warren Allen.

BL2785 . W55 2000
211'6'0922--dc21
[B] 99-055376

For

. . . Pierre Sylvain Maréchal (1750—1803)
author of *Dictionnaire des athées* (1798),
the first biographical dictionary of non-theists

. . . Fernando Rodolfo de Jesus Vargas Zamora (1928—1989)
my severest critic for forty years,
a non-believer and studio engineer
who recorded Liza Minnelli's first demo record

and for

. . . innumerable non-believers,
who may never before have suspected
they were amongst such inspiring company
as will be found herein.

CONTENTS

Note:

- the contents of most interest to freethinkers is in bold face and size 10 font
- that which is of marginal interest to freethinkers is in smaller size 9 font
- other items of related interest, but better researched elsewhere, are in size 7 font
- All listed individuals and subjects mentioned are important.
  The size of the entries is not an indication of a person's or a subject's importance.

Warren Allen Smith has compiled an engaging, impressive, and unique survey of those bold individuals and essential ideas that are relevant to critical thought and free inquiry.

This two-volume reference work humanizes the ongoing quest for truth and, as such, it is a must-read for all enlightened readers.

H. James Birx, Ph. D., D. Sci.
Professor of Anthropology,
Canisius College, Buffalo, NY
Visiting Scholar, Harvard University, 1997-1998

Who's Who in Hell is a remarkably comprehensive listing of freethinkers, past and present, freethought organizations, and freethought journals. The entries are not only informative but also frequently amusing. The work should be of special value to librarians and historians of free thought.

Religious fanatics will hate it.

Paul Edwards, Ph. D.
Editor-in-Chief
The Encyclopedia of Philosophy
New York City

Thank you for your tireless efforts at getting together a compendium of most of the infidels in the world in one place!

Babu Gogineni
Executive Director
International Humanist and Ethical Union
London

Mingling humour and wit, Warren Allen Smith is able to see the sunny side of unbelief. This book blazes a new trail for future rationalists. Its vast coverage from the Greeks to the present provides a broad canvas with kaleidoscopic depths. Future generations will find it an eye-opener with its details about the fraudulent and vicious propaganda of theologians and fundamentalists.

Who's Who in Hell is a unique attempt to place unbelievers in a proper perspective.

Innaiah Narisetti, Ph. D.
Vice President, Rationalist Association of India
Hyderabad, Andhra Pradesh, India.

FOREWORD

Mark Twain is reputed to have said, "Heaven for the climate, Hell for the company."

The company you will meet herein is guaranteed to keep your rapt attention. *Who's Who in Hell* is a kaleidoscope of contentious individuals: poets and philosophers, royalty and revolutionaries, secular saints and reprobates, all sharing one trait in common—a desire to think for themselves rather than to follow time-honored strictures or divine commandments. Many suffered greatly for their lack of conventional beliefs, and all demonstrate the defiant stance of the mythical Prometheus, who shook his fist at the gods and stole fire from them to benefit humankind. They have turned upside down the traditional view that questioning the divine will cause one to suffer eternal damnation. In the stirring words of John Stuart Mill, "I will call no Being good who is not what I mean when I apply that epithet to my fellow creatures; and if such a Being can sentence me to Hell for not so calling Him, to Hell I will go."

Warren Allen Smith is a wonderful guide to this potpourri of blasphemy. I have many times taken his personal walking tour of Greenwich Village, where he has long resided. He seems to know the history of every home, the celebrities who lived there, and the scandals that occurred therein. He brings this same eye for detail to *Who's Who in Hell*. He has pored through numerous reference works related to unbelief and has unearthed a wealth of material that otherwise likely would be lost to posterity. No dry recitation of names and dates, this work is a labor of love, sprinkled throughout with witticisms, arch comments, and pithy sayings. The individuals listed come to life in his descriptions—the only type of resurrection freethinkers would accept.

His chronicle of freethought goes back to his days as an undergraduate at the University of Northern Iowa. In 1948, as a graduate student at Columbia University, he founded a humanist club, receiving a one-dollar membership fee from the then ninety-one-year-old John Dewey (a check never cashed; one hopes that Dewey had no difficulty balancing his checkbook because of this!). Under the auspices of Lionel Trilling, writing a master's thesis on "Humanism Surveyed: A Study and Compilation of Books and Articles Pertaining to Humanism," he received personal statements from dozens of leading public figures, whose responses are included herein. Since that time, he has kept track of references pertaining to individuals espousing humanist viewpoints and has consulted with leading figures in the humanist movements.

It is important for any movement that it maintains a sense of its own history, especially a movement as fractious as that of humanism. Like the *philosophes* who compiled the famous *Encyclopédie* and helped to spark the Enlightenment, Warren Allen Smith has systematically arranged a body of work that will benefit anyone interested in learning about this history. The work reminds me most, though, of Pierre Bayle's *Historical and Critical Dictionary* (1697), another work done by a single author, which greatly influenced the *philosophes* and which contained one of the strongest defenses of the need for historians to be as impartial as possible. Bayle wrote,

> Every historian ought only to be concerned for the interest of truth, to which his duty obliges him to sacrifice the resentment of an injury, the remembrance of a favour, and even the love of his country. . . . If he be asked, "Of what country you are?" he ought to answer, "I am neither a Frenchman, nor a German, nor an Englishman, nor a Spaniard. I am an inhabitant of the world, neither engaged in the service of the Emperor, nor of the King of France, but only in that of truth: she is my sole Queen, and I have taken no oath of allegiance to any besides her."

This truly captures the cosmopolitan attitude that is at the heart of humanism. Yet these words are easily overlooked, for they are buried in a long entry entitled "Usson," which details with glee the outrageous sexual behavior of Queen Margot. In similar fashion, the following work mingles the salacious and sagacious in the true spirit of the Enlightenment.

I am honored to be listed in *Who's Who in Hell*, and I recognize that my own work on behalf of freedom of thought could not have happened were it not for the bravery and wisdom of so many of the people whose lives you will soon explore. I urge you to first read the entry on "Hell," in case you might think the title of this work is more than metaphorical. Most of the cast of characters found within would wholeheartedly concur with Robert Ingersoll's statement, "This world is enough." It is my expectation that you will find *Who's Who in Hell* to be a heavenly read.

Dr. Timothy J. Madigan
Chairman, Editorial Board of *Free Inquiry*

PREFACE

It is the author's expectation that the present work will be consulted in the years to come as a record of one editor's overview of the state of freethought at the end of the 20th Century. In many respects, the work has been inspired by **Pierre Sylvain Maréchal**'s *Dictionnaire des athées* (1798); **Joseph Mazzini Wheeler**'s *Biographical Dictionary of Freethinkers of All Ages and Nations* (1889); **John M. Robertson**'s two-volume *Short History of Freethought, Ancient and Modern* (1914); and **Joseph McCabe's** *A Rationalist Encyclopaedia, A Book of Reference on Religion, Philosophy, Ethics, and Science* (1948).

A listing of non-theists and a handbook for freethinkers is quite a different project from that of writing an autobiography. However, the present listing of non-theists is, in essence, a collection of personal notes on subjects that have been collected during a lifetime of searching for meanings. Rather than aiming to be solely encyclopedic, the present work combines objectivity with occasional touches (sometimes humorous, sometimes autobiographical) of subjectivity. The research includes extensive correspondence and personal discussions.

I have corresponded about theism with the following:

Swami Akhilananda, Faith Baldwin, Paul de Kruif, Alan Dowling, G. C. A. Gaskin, Lynn Harold Hough, Denise Levertov, E. L. Mayo, Howard A. Murphy, Reinhold Niebuhr, J. B. Priestley, Dorothy Sayers, Paul Scherer, Karl Shapiro, Russell Henry Stafford, and Richard Wilbur.

I have talked in person about freethought with the following:

Norm Allen, Shulami Aloni, Isaac Asimov, Janet Asimov, Hector Avalos, Enrique Bernain, H. James Birx, Margaret Bourke-White, Vern Bullough, Paul Cadmus, Marco Castillo Rojas, Pablo Cevallos Estarellas, Matt Cherry, Brock Chisholm, Alex Cox, Paul Edwards, Fred Edwords, Jan and Lee Eisler, Albert Ellis, Royston Ellis, Hugo Estrella, James T. Farrell, Tom W. Flynn, Levi Fragell, Erich Fromm, Annie Laurie Gaylor, Babu Gogineni, Alexeii Gostev, Emily Hahn, Jim Herrick, Julian Huxley, Horace Kallen, William Heard Kilpatrick, Hope Knutsson, Paul Kurtz, Valerii Kuvakin, Beth Lamont, Corliss Lamont, Gerald Larue, Helen Lockwood, Patricia López Zaragoza, Vashti McCollum, Butterfly McQueen, Tim Madigan, R. Lester Mondale, Mary and Lloyd Morain, Harley Myler, Innaiah Narisetti, Taslima Nasrin, Jerome Nathanson, Ricardo Otárola Pacheco, Kenneth Patton, Jean-Claude Pecker, Skipp Porteous, Charles Francis Potter, Jesus Puertas Fuentes, James Randi, Priscilla Robertson, Harry Ruja, Alan Ryan, Charles Smith, Gordon Stein, Barbara Stockers, Harry Stopes-Roe, Rob Tielman, Herbert Tonne, Norman L. Torrey, Gopi Uprety, Sir Peter Ustinov, Fernando Rolando de Jesus Vargas, Gore Vidal, Eva Ingersoll Wakefield, Sherman Wakefield, Ibn Warraq, Gerald Wendt, Glenway Wescott, Jane Wynne Willson, and Edwin H. Wilson.

I have corresponded with or talked about philosophic matters with the following:

James Truslow Adams, Conrad Aiken, Van Meter Ames, Maxwell Anderson, George Axtelle, John Cage, Arthur C. Clarke, George Counts, Norman Cousins, E. E. Cummings, John Dewey, Royston Ellis, Ian Franckenstein, Robert Frost, George Raymond Geiger, Allen Ginsberg, Robert Graves, Nat Henthoff, Sinclair Lewis, Walter Lippmann, Archibald MacLeish, Thomas Mann, Cesar Pelli, Kenneth Pobo, Allen Walker Read, Ned Rorem, Lord Bertrand Russell, George Santayana, Albert Schweitzer, Kurt Vonnegut Jr., and William Carlos Williams

To make the material more accessible, I purposely have omitted the endless scholarly footnotes and other minutiae. The reader is urged to use the present work as but an appetizer, then to proceed to the main course: the primary sources and other materials. Internet addresses change even more often than postal addresses. If e-mail addresses are no longer valid, users will need to consult the various internet search engines.

The present work refers not to hell but to Hell, the imaginary domain invented by theologians.

"The good life is one inspired by love and guided by knowledge," remarked Bertrand Russell. Many, but not all, of the freethinking individuals listed herein exemplify that outlook.

Warren Allen Smith
Greenwich Village, New York City, 31 December 1999

INTRODUCTION

The present compilation includes many researchers' listings of humanists and non-believers, individuals who over the centuries have listened to the evidence supplied by orthodox "believers" and have rejected such evidence for a variety of reasons, always because of their own critical intelligence. Rather than having a "faith" in the sometimes anti-human, anti-science, and anti-freedom tenets of others, these dissidents have developed through skepticism and reason a philosophic outlook that is secular, freethinking, rationalistic, naturalistic, humanistic, or a combination. (Milton placed such individuals in Circle #1 of Hell's Limbus.) The work originally started solely for my own edification, certainly not for possible submission to a publisher. Admittedly subjective, the listing purports to survey names of not-so-well-known as well as well-known non-believers. Readers will want to use this directory as a starting point for their own further research.

It must be emphasized that much of the information herein is taken *directly* or closely paraphrased from the sources named, particularly from standard reference books. *The Columbia Encyclopedia* has been used extensively to check dates of birth and death as well as to quote, definitively, appropriate technical or explanatory materials. Many definitions are taken directly, without specific attribution, from *The American Heritage Dictionary of the English Language, Webster's Third New International Dictionary*, or works cited at the ends of listings. Like Samuel Johnson I have striven for accuracy but, like him, will surely have made mistakes. "Ignorance, madam, pure ignorance," he told a lady who questioned why he had defined "pastern" as the "knee" of a horse. Unlike Johnson, I have been allowed to supply a final draft using the publisher's own QuarkXPress and am, therefore, clearly responsible for all errors herein.

A number of conservative, older Unitarians and Universalists are included herein. Their views today can be considered quasi-theistic, but in their day they were decidedly unorthodox. Included, for example, are deists like Benjamin Franklin who spoke of "a Supreme Architect" and transcendentalists like Ralph Waldo Emerson who wrote about "the Oversoul." Although borderline non-believer/freethinkers, they nevertheless were integral in helping lead the successful transition from theism to the various assortments of non-theism found today.

Unitarianism, which is creedless, attracts such a variety of thinkers that it is difficult to determine whether to exclude some because of their "religiosity." Or others because documentation of their membership is difficult to prove. Or whether to list them even if they appear to be theistic. No definitive European or American work on Unitarianism attempts so to label the membership. Some works named herein have cited individuals as being Unitarian; they may, however, just have been unitarian or attended Unitarian meetings to discuss their own viewpoints as freethinking inquirers. Such individuals point up the obvious limitations of labeling. One of the first Unitarians I ever met believed that butterflies, as well as humans, will have an afterlife; I forget if some supreme force was supposed to feed them all, but she made an excellent argument, and half-convinced me, that Heaven would just not be Heaven without butterflies.

It will be noted that interspersed throughout the listings is correspondence from various individuals (e.g., poet Witter Bynner, one of the many whose response is published for the first time). I specifically asked them whether they were theists or non-theists. If theists, they were encouraged to volunteer their religious affiliation. If non-theists, they were encouraged to suggest a label that described their outlook; e.g., agnostic, Unitarian, secular humanist, rationalist, freethinker, and so forth. Typical of individuals who declined is musician George Walker—in the year he was inducted into the American Academy of Arts and Letters, he wrote, "I have never discussed my religious beliefs with anyone." While many were aghast at self-labeling, others did not hesitate (e.g., "I am a theist; I know at all times that God exists and is good," responded poet Richard Wilbur. "All that is left to me, forced back from any knowledge except the report of the senses, is a humanistic naturalism, lit by the lightnings which play about the minds of saints and sinners," responded fellow poet William Carlos Williams).

Finally, many names, birthdates, telephone numbers, and addresses were valid at some point up to mid-1999. Readers are urged to forward suggested corrections or changes for inclusion in a second edition. It is hoped that readers, using these data decades hence, will have gained a better general view of the freethought scene at the end of the twentieth century.

Note: (1) Rather than use quotation marks and footnotes, as in orthodox research, the present unorthodox compilation often quotes word-for-word from the sources documented within the braces { }.

(2) The size of the individual entries is definitely **not** an indication of a person's importance.

KEY TO BIBLIOGRAPHICAL REFERENCES

(See bibliography at the end for an alphabetical listing by authors)

AA	*Alyson Almanac*
AAH	Allen, Norman R. Jr., ed. *African-American Humanism: An Anthology*
ACK	Ackerman, Diane. *A Natural History of Love*
AF	Flew, Antony. *A Dictionary of Philosophy*
BDF	Wheeler, J. M. *Biographical Dictionary of Freethinkers*
CA	"Celebrity Atheists" on the Internet
CB	Weil, Tom, *The Cemetery Book*
CE	*The Columbia Encyclopedia, 5th Edition, 1993*
CL	Lamont, Corliss. *The Philosophy of Humanism*, 6th Edition
DCL	*Dictionary of Cultural Literacy*
E	Reed Esay, "Celebrity Atheists, Agnostics, and Non-Theists," on the World Wide Web
EG	Gillis, Elizabeth. *People Like Us, Stories About Unitarian Universalists*
EP	Edwards, Paul, ed. *Encyclopedia of Philosophy*
ER	Ferm, Vergilius, ed. *Encyclopedia of Religion*
ESDM	Slater, Scott, and Alec Solomita. *Exits, Stories of Dying Moments and Parting Words*
EU	Stein, Gordon, ed. *Encyclopedia of Unbelief*
EW	Wilson, Edwin H. *The Genesis of a Humanist Manifesto*
FAF	Whitehead, Fred and Merle Muhrer, eds. *Freethought on the American Frontier*
FD	Briars, David. *Freethinker's Directory*
FI	*Free Inquiry, An International Journal of Secular Humanism*
FUK	Stein, Gordon. *Freethought in the United Kingdom and the Commonwealth*
FUS	Stein, Gordon and Marshall G. Brown. *Freethought in the United States*
GS	Stein, Gordon. *God Pro and Con*
HAB	Berman, David. *A History of Atheism in Britain, From Hobbes to Russell*
HM1	Humanist Manifesto I (first appeared in *The New Humanist*, May-June 1933, vol. VI, no. 3)
HM2	Humanist Manifesto II (first appeared in *The Humanist*, Sep-Oct 1973, vol. XXXIII, no. 5)
HNS	Morain, Lloyd and Mary Morain. *Humanism as the Next Step*
HWP	Russell, Bertrand. *A History of Western Philosophy*
ILP	*Index Librorum Prohibitorum*
IM	Edwards, Paul, ed. *Immortality*
ISL	*Intimate Sex Lives of Famous People*, edited by Irving Wallace, Amy Wallace, David Wallechinsky, and Sylvia Wallace
JHG	Groden, Michael and Martin Kreiswirth. *The Johns Hopkins Guide to Literary Theory and Criticism*
JM	McCabe, Joseph. *A Biographical Dictionary of Ancient, Medieval, and Modern Freethinkers*
JMR	Robertson, John M. *A Short History of Freethought, Ancient and Modern*
JMRH	Robertson, John M. *A History of Freethought, Ancient and Modern to the Period of the French Revolution*
LEE	Leedom, Tim C., ed. *The Book Your Church Doesn't Want You To Read*
OCAL	Hart, James D. *The Oxford Companion to American Literature*
OCP	Honderich, Ted, ed. *The Oxford Companion to Philosophy*
OEL	*Oxford Companion to English Literature, 5th Edition*
PA	Wallechinsky, David and Irving Wallace. *People's Almanac*
PA2	Wallechinsky, David *and* Irving Wallace, eds. *People's Almanac #2*
PE	Edwards, Paul. *Reincarnation: A Critical Examination*
PGA	Fitts, Dudley. *Poems from the Greek Anthology*

PK	Kurtz, Paul, ed., *The Humanist Alternative: Some Definitions of Humanism*
PUT	Putnam, Samuel P. *400 Years of Freethought*
QBR	Eisler, Lee. *The Quotable Bertrand Russell*
RAT	McCabe, Joseph. *Biographical Dictionary of Modern Rationalists*
RE	McCabe, Joseph. *A Rationalist Encyclopedia: A Book of Reference on Religion, Philosophy, Ethics, and Science*
RSR	Royle, Edward. *Radicals, Secularist and Republicans: Popular Freethought in Britain, 1866—1915*
SAU	Underwood, Sara A. *Heroines of Freethought*
SHD	*Secular Humanist Declaration*, 1980
SWW	Dahlitz, Ray. *Secular Who's Who: A Biographical Collection of Australasian Humanists, Rationalists, Secularists, and Freethinkers*
TRI	Tribe, David. *100 Years of Freethought*
TSV	Vernon, Thomas S. *Great Infidels*
TYD	Haught, James A. *2000 Years of Disbelief: Famous People with the Courage to Doubt*
U	"Unitarian Universalist Religious Education Calendar, 1992"
UU	Lange, Fred E. Jr. "Famous Unitarians / Universalists"
U&U	Robinson, David. *The Unitarians and the Universalists*
VI	Royle, Edward. *Victorian Infidels*
VOL	*A Philosophical Dictionary from the French of M. De Voltaire with Additional Notes, Both Critical and Argumentative*
VU	Gaskin, J. C. A., ed. *Varieties of Unbelief: From Epicurus to Sartre*
WAS	Smith, Warren Allen. "Humanists on Humanism," personal correspondence received
WIN	Winokur, Jon, Ed. *The Portable Curmudgeon*
WRF	Nass, Herbert E. *Wills of the Rich and Famous*
WSS	Smith, Warren Sylvester. *The London Heretics, 1870—1914*
WWTCL	Seymour-Smith, Martin. *Who's Who in Twentieth-Century Literature*

No one dies . . . so long as someone still remembers.

Key to the Entries

(For a key to references, see pages xii to xiii.)

Aakjaer, Jeppe (1866—1930)
Names in bold-faced type are humanists, agnostics, freethinkers, rationalists, secularists, non-theists, or Unitarians as well as others whose outlook was progressive during their era

ABANDONMENT
Capital letters refer to subjects.

Abbott of Unreason
Listings in 7-point font refer to people, terms related to theism, or items of only peripheral interest to non-believers

Acton, John Emerich
Names in regular print are cited for the reasons indicated within the entry

B.C.E.
Before the Common Era (analogous to the Christians' B.C., Before Christ)

B.P.
Before the Present (e.g., "A cave campsite was occupied as long ago as 11,200 years B.P.)

C.E.
The Common Era (analogous to the Christians' A.D., *anno Domini*)

Items within braces { } refer to entries in the bibliography or to materials and ideas described therein; the author's actual wording may be included, without quotation marks, from, for example,

{AF} signifies Antony Flew's *A Dictionary of Philosophy*
{CE} signifies material from *The Columbia Encyclopedia* (1993)
{CL) signifies Corliss Lamont's *The Philosophy of Humanism*
{EP} signifies material from *The Encyclopedia of Philosophy* edited by Paul Edwards
{EU} signifies material from *The Encyclopedia of Unbelief* edited by Gordon Stein
{HM2} signifies a signer of Humanist Manifesto II
{OCP} signifies *The Oxford Companion to Philosophy*

Aag: See entry for Zyp.

AAH EXAMINER

The *AAH Examiner*, PO Box 664, Buffalo, NY 14226, is a quarterly newsletter published by African Americans for Humanism.

E-mail: <cfiflynn@aol.com>.

Aakjaer, Jeppe (1866—1930)

Aakjaer was a Danish non-theist. (See entry for Scandinavian Unbelievers.)

AASH: See entry for Agnostics, Atheists, and Secular Humanists Who Are Infected/Affected with AIDS/HIV Illness.

ABANDONMENT

Inasmuch as God does not exist, say the atheistic existentialists, no outside authority is now or has ever been present to account for any meaning to human existence. Thus, mankind has been abandoned only in the sense that previously God had been credited for providing a meaning to life. Now, mankind must take *all* responsibility for providing a rational meaning for our existence. {AF; OCP}

Abano, Petrus de (1250—1320)

A learnèd Italian physician, Petrus denied the existence of spirits and ascribed all miracles to natural causes. Cited before the Inquisition in 1306 as a heretic, a magician, and an atheist, he ably defended himself and was acquitted. Petrus was accused a second time but, while the trial was preparing, he died. He was condemned after death, his body was disinterred and burned, and he was burned in effigy in the public square of Padua. {BDF}

Abauzit, Fiermin (1679—1774)

Abauzit was a French writer, descended from an Arabian family that settled in the south of France early in the ninth century. An acquaintance of Bayle, he was consulted by Voltaire and Rousseau. In an essay on the Apocalypse, Abauzit questioned the authority of that work. E. Harwood translated his *Miscellanies* into English in 1774. Abauzit's deistic views are expressed in his *Réflexions impartiales sur les évangiles* (1774). {BDF; JMRH; RAT}

Abbagnano, Nicola (1901—)

A philosophic naturalist, Abbagnano was a chief exponent of existentialism in Italy. He liked the work of John Dewey and wrote *Possibilità e libertà* (1956). {AF}

Abbe, Ernst (1840—1905)

Abbe was an intimate friend of Haeckel, sharing his monism. A distinguished German physicist, he was one of the most famous inventors on the staff of Carl-Zeiss optical works at Jena, of which in 1888 he became sole owner. He reorganized the firm on a cooperative basis, created a noncontributory pension fund, and introduced other advanced ideas that have been influential in shaping thought on the conditions of labor. He invented the Abbe refractometer for determining the refractive index of substances and improved photographic and microscopic lenses.

Leonard Abbott in his life of Ferrer wrote that Abbe had "just the same ideas and aims as Ferrer." {CE; JM; RAT}

Abbe, Karen (20th Century)

Abbe is associated with Atheists and Other Freethinkers, a Sacramento, California, group that serves hungry people, not for the purpose of informing people about atheism but merely to provide a service for people in need. {*Secular Nation*, Fall 1994}

Abbot, Abiel (Born 1765)

A Unitarian minister, Abbot is said to have originated the idea of a free, tax-supported public library. {U}

Abbott, Francis Ellingwood (1836—1903)

A leader in the dissent from moderate Unitarianism in the mid-nineteenth century, Abbott was an evolutionist. In 1870 he began agitating for organization of an American Secular Union through his Toledo, Ohio, paper entitled *The Index*. His appeals resulted in the preliminary organization of a few local chapters. He was active in the formation of the Free Religious Association and edited their newsletter. In 1872, he wrote *Impeachment of Christianity. Scientific Theism* (1885) was based upon idealist and intuitionist philosophy and attempted to replace the old religious radicalism of the Transcendentalists with realism and science. He thought the theory of evolution would throw new light on religion and, in a way, he anticipated process philosophy. Abbott's work, considered liberal in his day, is, today, admittedly dated and elementary.

Darwin, reading one of Abbott's 1871 tracts that spoke of "the extinction of faith in the Christian confession" and the development of a humanistic free religion, wrote of Abbott's views, "I admire them from my inmost heart, and I agree to almost every word."

In 1876 the Liberal Congress assembled in Philadelphia, and he was chosen president. The second congress was held in Syracuse in 1878 at a time when Anthony Comstock, the anti-obscenity extremist, had just had D. M. Bennett arrested. The Liberals of New York started a petition for repeal of the Comstock Law, which the *Truth Seeker* urged Liberals to sign in order to put a stop to Comstock's national witch-hunts. Abbott, however, took a stand that the law should be amended, not repealed. As a result, Elizur Wright was elected president and Abbot withdrew.

W. Creighton Peden has written a biography of Abbott called *The Philosopher of Free Religion*. In it he describes how Abbot's "free religion" was a sort of quasi-theism on the fringe of the freethought movement. He was the first President of the American National Liberal League. {BDF; FUS; PUT; RAT; TRI; U; U&U}

Abbott, George Frederick (20th Century)

Abbott, a Hellenist, wrote *Philosophy of a Don* (1911), a work which contains caustic and rationalist views. He deprecates aggressiveness on the genial ground that "the actual Ruler of the Universe compares very favourably with some of his predecessors." {RAT}

Abbott, Jan (20th Century)

Abbott is Vice President of Atheists of Northern Colorado. E-mail: <jan@tesser.com>.

Abbott, John Emery (1793—1819)

Abbott, a Unitarian minister who died when only twenty-six, believed that "rational" religion should be complemented by an intensely devotionist piety. {U&U}

Abbott, Leonard Dalton (Born 1878)

An American journalist born in Liverpool, England, Abbott was President of the Thomas Paine National Historical Association (1910) and one of the founders of the Rand School of Social Science. He edited the American memorial volume *Francisco Ferrer* (1910). {RAT}

Abbott, Ruth T. (20th Century)

Abbott, a published poet, was a humanist activist in North Wilbraham, Massachusetts. To the *Humanist Newsletter* (September-October 1953), she wrote, "I have written a card to Station WBZA, Springfield, Massachusetts, protesting substitution for our Dr. [Horace] Kallen broadcast this morning–instead, we had a Methodist bishop! I admire Kallen's humanism from my inmost heart, and I agree to almost every word."

ABBOT OF UNREASON

During the Middle Ages, McCabe states, annual festivals were held which included blasphemous parodies of the Mass in the cathedrals and churches, often in monasteries and convents, even including indecent revels on the streets. One of these was the Abbot of Unreason (also called the Abbot of Misrule, the Abbot of Joy, or the Pope of Fools), during which a layman was hilariously elected and robed as abbot for the express purpose of suspending for a day all rules of discipline and decency. Scott, in *The Abbot*, describes how the feast was held in Scotland. The clerical as well as civic dignitaries commonly took part, and the occasional zealots who protested were powerless. The details are often obscene, states McCabe, who documents the Feast of the Ass and other such feasts by citing Du Cange's *Glossarium mediae et infimae Latinitatis* (1678) and Du Tilliot's *Mémoires* (1741). Historians, he adds, have always appeared reticent to include such matters. (See entry for Ass, Feast Of.) {RE}

Abd ar-Rahman III (891—961)

Called by McCabe "the greatest of the Moslem Arab Caliphs," Abd ar-Rahman is said to have "raised Spain from a state of profound demoralization to one of unprecedented prosperity, culture, and brilliance while Christian Europe lay in the darkest phase of the Dark Age." He built up a strong army and navy, waging war successfully against the Fatimids in North Africa and the Christian kings of León. Abd ar-Rahman III made Córdoba one of the greatest cities in the West. Not only was he an atheist but also he defied the Koran (Qur'an) throughout his lifetime. {CE; JM; RE}

ABDUCTION BY SPACE ALIENS

Supernaturalists are often prone to belief in the paranormal, New Age, channeling, and the like. In the latter half of the twentieth century, not only were books published about the alleged abduction of humans by space aliens but also the *Journal of Regression Therapy* (October 1990) reviewed favorably a work by Edith Fiore, *Encounters* (1989):

> I feel that the discovery of visits to our planet Earth by beings from other worlds and their interactions with humans is the most exciting and significant happening of the twentieth century.

Two American journals, *Skeptic* and *Skeptical Inquirer*—both entirely naturalistic in their approach—are devoted to investigating such non-scientific allegations and other follies. {PE}

Abel, Lionel (1910—)

At the time he signed Humanist Manifesto II, Abel was a professor of English at the State University of New York at Buffalo. He wrote *The Intellectual Folies* (1984) and *Important Nonsense* (1987). {HM2}

Abel, Reuben (1911—1997)

Abel, a naturalistic humanist who reviewed Buchler's *Nature and Judgment* for *The Humanist* in the 1950s, is author of *The Pragmatic Humanism of F. C. S. Schiller* (1955) and *Man Is The Measure* (1976). In 1966, he edited *Humanistic Pragmatism*. Abel taught for forty years in the Graduate Faculty of Political and Social Science and in other divisions of City College in New York City. He was versed in eight modern and classical languages, sang with the Dessorf Choirs, and was noted for writing letters to editors about philosophic subjects. Editors of Webster's *New International Dictionary* credited Abel with calling to their attention the need to add the word *cathect* as a verb which described Freud's meaning, "to invest with libidinal energy." {Wolfgang Saxon, *The New York Times*, 14 August 1997}

Abelev, Garry I. (20th Century)

Abelev, of the N. N. Blokhin Cancer Research Center in Russia, signed Humanist Manifesto 2000.

Abel-Smith, Brian (1926—1996)

Abel-Smith, an educator and professor of social administration at the University of London, wrote with R. Titmuss *The Cost of the National Health Service in England and Wales* (1956); *A History of the Nursing Profession* (1960); *British Doctors at Home and Abroad* (1964); and *Legal Problems and the Citizen* (1973), among other works. In a *Guardian* tribute to Abel-Smith, Professor Julian Le Grand, of the London School of Economics, quoted Thomas Paine's "my country is the world and my religion is to do good." Paine could have been writing about Abel-Smith, Prof. Le Grand stated. {*Freethinker*, June 1996}

Abell, George, O(gden) (1927—1983)

Numerous star clusters, planetary nebulae, clusters of galaxies, and three comets have been discovered by Abell, a professor of astronomy at the University of California at Los Angeles. In 1980, he signed the Secular Humanist Declaration. He is author of *Realm of the Universe* (1984) and *Exploration of the Universe* (1991). Abell is a Laureate in the Council for Secular Humanism's Academy of Humanism. {SHD}

Abelard, Peter (1079—1142)

Abelard, a French philosopher renowned for being loved by the celebrated Heloise, was accused of teaching erroneous opinions about the Creation and the Trinity. At the instigation of St. Bernard, he was condemned by councils at Soissons in 1121 and Sens in 1140. Hired by Heloise, the niece of the canon of Notre Dame, to be her tutor, Abelard fell in love at forty with the seventeen-year-old and their affair inspired works of literature, particularly when she gave birth to a son and a secret marriage was arranged by her Uncle Fulbert. The monstrous revenge that followed was described by Abelard:

> . . . One night as I lay sleeping in my chamber, one of my servants, corrupted by gold, delivered me to their vengeance, which the world would learn of to its stupefaction: they cut off those parts of my body with which I had committed the offense they deplored. Then they fled.

In shame, he retreated to the Abbey of St. Denis, ordered Heloise to become a nun and spend the rest of her life in celibacy, and was shocked that in her letters she confided that she loved him more than she did God. However, he was accused of heresy and excommunicated, lost an appeal to the Pope, and spent the last year of his life as a monk at Cluny. He and Heloise are buried together in Paris's Père Lachaise, but rumor has it that when her body was being placed there his arms fell open to embrace her. Hallam observed that Abelard "was almost the first who awakened mankind, in the age of darkness, to a sympathy with intellectual excellence." McCabe lists Abelard as a freethinker, citing his first principle, "Reason precedes faith."

One Greenwich Village wag has noted that those who jocularly refer to priests as "having no balls" are probably oblivious to the Abelard tale. {BDF; JM; RE}

Abell, Theodore Curtis (1891—1960)

According to Sherman Wakefield, Abell in 1929 founded the first Humanist society independent of any church, the second being that of Charles Francis Potter in New York City. Abell's was the Hollywood (California) Humanist Society, which he led until 1934. In the 1950s, he was minister of the Sacramento Unitarian Church.

Edwin H. Wilson has described Abell as "a creative innovator and organizational guide of early religious humanism," founder of the oldest affiliate of the American Humanist Association. Wilson and Raymond Bragg had not asked Abell to be a signer of the Humanist Manifesto because they thought it not improbable "that Theodore Abell adopted an attitude that one often encounters among the 'prima donnas' of any movement: in this case *L'humanisme c'est moi!* (roughly translated, this means, 'Humanism is mine' or 'I am humanism.')." Wilson said Abell also was not happy that *The New Humanist* had purloined the name of his publication, *The Humanist*, adding that relations with Abell "were not improved in 1941 when our publication changed its name from *The New Humanist* to *The Humanist*. However, Wilson considered Abell "a real humanist pioneer." {EW; HNS}

THE ABERRANT

The Aberrant is a free thought journal (PO Box 621746, Littleton, Colorado 80162-1746) edited by Paul D. Roasberry. The work contains fiction and essays that in the main have been written by members of Mensa, the high IQ association. Its first 1994 issue had an article "There Is No God" by Fred Woodworth.

Abgar

The alleged letters of Jesus and Abgar, states McCabe, "are such clumsy forgeries, quoting gospels which no one claims to have existed until forty years later, that even the *Catholic Encyclopaedia* rejects them." They first appeared in the fourth century in Bishop Eusebius's *Ecclesiastical History*. McCabe cites Eusebius as "a diligent collector of fairy-tales about the early Church." {RE}

ABIOGENESIS

Abiogenesis is theory that living things are, or once were, developed from inanimate matter by what used to be called "spontaneous generation," or by natural chemical processes. Spontaneous generation has been discredited; for example, nonliving rotten meat cannot give rise to maggots—without a live fly to lay an egg, the rotten meat stays dead meat. However, Dr. Louis Lerman, a geophysicist at Lawrence Berkeley Laboratory in California, theorizes that bubbles forming on the surface of primordial seas collected chemicals and concentrated them for synthesis into complex molecules. According to his theory, through multistage reactions, constantly repeated by uncounted generations of bubbles, the molecules grow in size and complexity, ready for the transition to living, reproducing cells.

McCabe in 1950 said that the position of the rationalist is, like that of biologists generally, that the attempt to show that "life" or "vitality" is an immaterial something which *could not* have been evolved from matter has failed and it would therefore be absurd to suppose that, while our million species of advanced organisms are the outcome of evolution, the earliest and most primitive of all were not evolved. {CE; RE}

ABORTION

Until the early years of the present century, some Muslim peasant women in Upper Egypt reportedly believed it was possible to terminate an unwanted pregnancy by lying face down on the railroad tracks and allowing the next scheduled train to pass over them. Conversely, a woman who had difficulty conceiving would lie on her back on the tracks and pray that the passing train would impregnate her.

The Catechism of the Catholic Church (1994) states that, since the first century,

> . . . the Church has affirmed the moral evil of every procured abortion. This teaching has not changed and remains unchangeable. . . . Formal cooperation in an abortion constitutes a grave offense. The Church attaches the canonical penalty of excommunication to this crime against human life. . . . A person who procures a completed abortion incurs excommunication *latae sententiae*, by the very commission of the offense, and is subject to the conditions provided by Canon Law. The Church does not thereby intend to restrict the scope of mercy. Rather, she makes clear the gravity of the crime committed, the irreparable harm done to the innocent who is put to death, as well as to the parents and the whole of society.

In the 1990s, anti-abortionists have satirically taken the stand that enemies of abortion have every right to inflict the death penalty on everyone who is not pro-life. However, in 1994, an ex-Christian minister who murdered Dr. John Bayard Britton was himself sentenced to death for the crime.

"If men could get pregnant, abortion would be a sacrament," said Florynce Kennedy, a black American freethinker whose television programs frequently support Bill Baird and the cause of independent abortion clinics. (See entries for James Barrett, John Bayard Britton, and Florynce Kennedy.) {OCP}

Abousenna, Mona (20th Century)

An Egyptian who teaches English at Ain Shams University, Abousenna spoke about the future of fairness for motherhood at the 1996 Humanist World Congress held in Mexico City. She is editor of *Averroës Today*.

About, Edmond François Valentin (1826—1885)

A French novelist and dramatist, About wrote *Germaine* (1857) and other novels. In *Figaro*, he wrote under the name of Valentin de Quevilly and produced several plays. He was a friend of Prince Jerome Bonaparte, who was equally anti-clerical. In 1884 About was named to the French Academy.

His drastic rejection of all religious beliefs is seen in his *Question romaine* (1859), an exposure of what McCabe describes as "the foul condition of the Papal States before 1870," adding, "and its style moved Shérer to describe the author as 'the grandson of Voltaire.' "

According to About, an act of faith is "to close one's eyes in order to see better." {RAT}

Abraham

No proof is available that such a person as Abraham ever existed. But no one questions that the ancestors of the Hebrews may have come from a certain region or that the final "redactors" of *Genesis* lived, or had lived, in Babylonia. {RE}

Abrahams, J. (20th Century)

Abrahams is on the editorial Committee of *The New Zealand Rationalist and Humanist*.

Abrams, Sol (20th Century)

Abrams taught thirty-two years as a teacher and assistant principal in New York City. A retiree in Florida, he is active with Humanists of the Palm Beaches.

Abse, Leo (1917—)

A Labour MP and freethinker, Abse proposed a bill in England to free blackmail victims and make the consent of the Director of Public Prosecutions obligatory in all cases of private homosexual acts. His bill was defeated in the House of Commons, 213 to 99. Abse is author of *Margaret, Daughter of Beatrice: A Politician's Psycho-Drama of Margaret Thatcher* (1989).

ABSOLUTE, THE

In its broadest meaning, the absolute denotes a reality postulated in metaphysics (not proved to exist) which is not related to other realities or definable in terms of them: the ultimate, all-embracing, all-unifying reality. The assumption does not imply that it is a personality or is the cause (or creator) of the realities of which we have experience. But especially in Hegel's system, it is Mind or Spirit and excludes the existence of material things.

Absolutism in philosophy is the opposite of relativism. It means unlimited, unconditioned, or free of any relation; perfect, complete, or total; permanent, inherent, or ultimate; independent, or valid without reference to a perceiving subject.

In epistemology, *absolute* means certain or indubitable as opposed to probable or hypothetical. Theologically, it is synonymous with, or characteristic of, God. Philosophically, it may be considered as the unknowable, the thing-in-itself; as the ultimate nonrelative that is the basis of all relation; as the ultimate, all-comprehensive principle in which all differences and distinctions are merged.

In orthography, a "q" *absolutely* must be followed by a "u." Relativists, however, point out that even in spelling there are exceptions to absolute rules; e.g., faqir, qaid, qanat, qat, qindar, qindarka, qintar, qoph, tranq, Qantas Airlines. {AF; CE; OCP; RE}

ABSURDISM

• Absurdity, n. A statement or belief manifestly inconsistent with one's own opinion.

—**Ambroce Bierce**
The Devil's Dictionary

Absurdism, a philosophy that has affected the various arts, holds that humans live in a meaningless, irrational universe. It then follows that any attempt to search for order can only result in an absurd, pointless conflict with such a universe. John Simon has observed, "True absurdism is not *less* but *more* real than reality."

Although the concept has appealed to Samuel Beckett, Friedrich Dürrenmatt, Eugene Ionesco, Edward Albee, Harold Pinter, and others, secular humanists are not absurdists, except as appreciators of some of the absurdist creators' artistic endeavors. Although they find absurdism and irrationality abound, humanists are more involved in practical matters, working out meaningful possibilities for human welfare and developing rational solutions to humanity's various problems.

Abu Abd'allah Muhammad ibn Massara al Jabali (881—921)

An Arabian pantheist, Abu lived at Córdova, Spain, and studied the works of Empedocles and other Greek philosophers. Accused of impiety, he left Spain and traveled throughout the East, returned to Spain and collected disciples whom he led to skepticism. He was the most eminent predecessor of Ibn Rushd, or Averroës. His works were publicly burned at Seville. {BDF}

Abu Bakr Ibn Al-Tufail (Died 1185)

Abu J'afar, as Abu Bakr Ibn Al-Tufail was also known, was a Spanish-Arabian philosopher who wrote a pantheistic romance, *Hai Ibn Yakdan* (translated as *The Improvement of Human Reason* in 1771). He died in Morocco. {BDF}

Abu Tahir (Died 943)

Abu Tahir al Karmatti, the chief of a freethinking sect at Bahrain on the Persian Gulf, captured Mecca (930) with a small number of followers, taking away a revered black stone. He also imprisoned Abissaj, the head of 30,000 men whom the caliph had sent against him. {BDF}

Abu'l-ala-al-Ma'aari (Abu al-Ala al-Maarri) (973—1057)

A Syrian poet, Abu'l-ala-al-Ma'aari observed, "The world holds two classes of men–intelligent men without religion, and religious men without intelligence." Blinded by childhood smallpox, he called himself "the doubly imprisoned captive," an allusion to his seclusion and loss of sight. He took no pains to conceal that he believed in no revealed religion. For example, he wrote a parody of the Koran (Qur'an), deriding all religions as absurd.

Curiously, he was never persecuted by Islamic officials. Perhaps it was because he was eccentric: He opposed parenthood, he declared that to bring a child into the world was to add to the sum of suffering, and he was an ardent vegetarian. His work denies a resurrection, and he is incredulous of any divine revelation. For him, religion "is a product of the human mind, in which men believe through force of habit and education, never stopping to consider whether it is true." Concerning creeds, he wrote

Now this religion happens to prevail
Until by that one it is overthrown;
Because men will not live with men alone,
But always with another fairy-tale.

Robertson reported that Abu'l-ala-al-Ma'aari has been pronounced "incomparably greater" than Omar Khayyám "both as a poet and as an agnostic."

On his tomb he ordered written, "I owe this to the fault of my father: none owe the like to mine." {BDF; CE; JMR; JMRH}

Abu-Fazil [Abu al Fadhl Ibn Mubarak] (Died 1604)

Abu-Fazil, called *Al Hindi*, was vizier to the Emperor Akbar from 1572. Although born a Muslim, he was tolerant of all sects. His chief work, *Ayin Akbary*, was a statistical account of the Indian Empire. He was assassinated in 1604. {BDF}

Abu-Zaid, Nasr Hamid (20th Century)

An Egyptian intellectual, Abu-Zaid in 1995 was branded by his country's courts as a religious heretic. Legally declared a heretic, he had to flee with his wife to the Netherlands because under Egyptian religious law a heretic cannot be married to a believer. What outraged Islamic militants was the Cairo University professor's twelve books, in some of which he argued that Muslims must understand the Koran and Islam's other sacred texts historically. He held that certain Koranic references are not to be taken literally but as metaphors. "I am," he retorted from Leiden, "a Muslim. It is the militants who are betraying our faith by raising the banner of Islam for their own political project. They are hijacking Islam. My sin is recommending an enlightened view of Islamic thought."

Abul-Abbas-Abdallah III (786—833)

Al Mamoun was the seventh Abbasside, caliph, the son of Haroun al Rashid. He was a patron of science and literature, collected Greek and Hebrew manuscripts, and invited scholars of all nations to his capital. Born in Baghdad, he died in a war near Tarsus. {BDF}

Abulafia, Abraham Ben Semuel (1240— c. 1291)

Born in Spain, Abulafia in 1260 searched for a mythical ruler in Israel. Although he gained a large following eager to believe that redemption was at hand, he is illustrative of a fanatic and zealot. {LEE}

ABULCASIS: See the entry for dentistry.

ACADEMY

Plato's *Akademia*, a word that refers to "the olive grove of Academe," continued for over forty years after its founding in 386 until Plato's death in 340 B.C.E. Philosophical schools following its model continued to flourish in Greece and Rome for nine centuries until they were abolished, along with other "pagan" schools, by Emperor Justinian in 529.

In 1462 at Careggi, near Florence, the Academy of Florence under the guidance of Ficino was instrumental in encouraging the Platonic revival in Renaissance Europe.

In 1582, the ***Accademia della Crusca***, literally the academy of the chaff, was founded as an Italian literary society. Its purpose included maintaining the purity of the language. Leonardo Salviati, Pietro Bembo, and the poet Grazzini formed the group, which later joined two other academies and is still in existence.

In 1635, the ***Academie Française*** was formed to insure "the purification of the French language." It is supported by the government, and its forty members promote literary excellence. Among its eminent members have been Montesquieu, Corneille, Voltaire, Condorcet, La Fontaine, and Racine.

In 1666, the French ***Academie des Sciences*** began when a group of French scientists–Descartes, Pascal, Gassendi–began meeting. They were later joined by Colbert and Huygens, and under the patronage of Louis XIV the Academy was formally established.

In 1713, ***La Real Academia Española*** was founded in Spain. Like the French Academy, the Spanish Academy serves as an authority concerning what is and is not "correct" in the language. Its motto states that the academy "cleanses, fixes, and adds splendor" to Spanish, protecting it from debasing infiltrators. Although the academy has branches in most Latin American countries, they are subordinate to Madrid.

Although not an *academy*, the American Philosophical Society in 1743 was founded by Benjamin Franklin to "promote useful knowledge" and is the oldest scientific association in the United States. David Rittenhouse and Thomas Jefferson were his immediate successors.

In 1863, the National Academy of Sciences, a private organization of leading American scientists and engineers, was founded. Its approximately

2,000 members advise the Federal government on matters of science and technology. Separate sections represent all of the physical and biological sciences and many of the social sciences.

In 1904, the American Academy of Arts and Letters was founded and consists of the 250 major artists, writers, composers, and humanists in the nation. The National Institute of Arts and Letters, founded in 1898, served as the parent body for the American Academy, and in 1976 the two were amalgamated.

Today, "academy" refers to a society of learned persons organized to advance the arts, science, or literature, and some academics are devoted to archaeology, history, the social sciences, medicine and surgery, and the fine arts. Academies are found in various nations throughout the world. (See entries for the American Academy, French Academy, Greek Academy, and *Real Academia Española.*) {CE}

ACADEMY OF HUMANISM: See entry for International Academy of Humanism.

Acharya, N. K. (1923—)

Acharya, a member of the Andhra Pradesh Rationalist Association in Hyderabad, India, was secretary of the Indian Rationalist Association from 1967 to 1971. A retired lecturer in physics, he was editor of *Indian Rationalist* from 1967 to 1971.

Achelis, Thomas (1850—1909)

Achelis was a German ethnologist, an editor of *Archiv für Religionswissenschaft*. He wrote biographies of several German rationalists, held a high position in his science in Germany, and although called a Protestant wrote *Adolf Bastian* (1892), in which he entirely agrees with Bastian, an eminent and thorough rationalist. {RAT}

ACHILLES AND THE TORTOISE

Zeno of Elea (c. 490—430 B.C.E.) developed a paradox of motion. If Achilles races a tortoise and the tortoise is given a head start, Achilles can never win, Zeno argued. For wherever Achilles reaches the point that the tortoise has reached, the tortoise will have moved ahead to a new point. And when Achilles reaches that point, the tortoise will have moved to yet a new point, and so on, indefinitely. As Achilles closes a previous gap, the tortoise has moved on.

How Zeno explained the paradox is not known, but it is clear he questioned common-sense notions of time and space. {AF; CE; OCP}

Achillino, Alessandro (1463— 1545)

Achillini was an Italian physician, a philosopher who expounded the doctrines of Averroës and wrote largely upon astronomy. {BDF; PUT}

Ackermann, Louise Victorine (1813—1890)

A French poet, Ackermann exhibited in her work that she was a philosophic pessimist and atheist. Her husband, Paul, also an atheist, was a teacher for Prince Frederick William, who became Frederick III. Both Ackermanns were friends of Proudhon. "God is dethroned," said M. Caro of one of her 1874 poems. She professed a hatred of Christianity as well as its interested professors, and Sainte Beuve called her "the learned solitary of Nice." "Religions," she wrote, "impose antiquated and narrow beliefs which are entirely unsuitable for a being who knows nothing and can affirm nothing." McCabe said Ackermann was "very resolutely Agnostic, without using that word in her *Pensées d'une solitaire*, and she wrote a poem for her tombstone which begins: 'I do not know.' In the strict sense she was an atheist." {BDF; JM; RAT}

Ackley, Sheldon (20th Century)

Ackley, who was fired for atheism from teaching philosophy at Gettysburg College, was recruited by Joseph Blau as the highly successful first Leader of the Long Island Society of Ethical Culture (1950—1959). A university administrator and educator, Ackley was cited by Lamont as being a humanist. In 1982, after early retirement from teaching, he became a "Secular Humanist Leader" in New York. (See entry for Ethical Culture.)

Acollas, Pierre Antoine Rene Paul Emile (1826—1891)

Acollas was a French *juris-consult* and political writer. Mrs. Besant translated his monograph, *Les Droits de l'Homme* (*The Idea of God in the Revolution*). In 1871 the Communal Government at Paris made him Dean of the Faculty of Law, but he declined. Later, he was appointed Inspector-General of Prisons and was admitted to the Legion of Honour. {BDF; RAT}

Acontius, Jacobus (Died 1566?)

Giacomo Aconzio, who was born at Trent early in the sixteenth century, became an ordained priest, then relinquished the faith and fled to Switzerland in 1557. Subsequently he went to England, serving Queen Elizabeth as a military engineer and dedicating his *Stratagems of Satan* (1565) to her. A latitudinarian work, it was listed in the Catholic *Index*. Milton is said to have read the work. {BDF}

Acord, Gary (20th Century)

Acord is author of *Heaven on Earth: A Bold Affirmation of Humanist Faith* (1977). {GS}

ACOSMISM

Acosmism is the disbelief in the existence of a material world. Berkeley, Hume, Sir James Jeans, and Sir Arthur Eddington toyed with the idea. Materialists, however, are not believers in acosmism. {RE}

Acosta Urquidi, Mariclaire (20th Century)

Acosta, president of the Mexican Commission for the Defense and Promotion of Human Rights, has documented in "Under the Volcano" (*The Humanist*, November-December 1994) the fact that as many as 88% of all people who are detained in Mexico are tortured, this despite Mexico's having an excellent constitution which allegedly is disregarded by the executive branch.

Acosta, Uriel (1591—1647)

Son of a Christianized Jew and brought up a Christian, Acosta rejected that faith and in Holland published *Examen Traditorum Philosophicarum ad legem Scriptam*, a work that equally criticizes Moses and Jesus. Excommunicated by the synagogue and imprisoned by the Amsterdam authorities, he suffered many indignities from Jews as well as Christians. In 1647, Acosta the deist committed suicide. His pathetic experience of orthodox charity is recorded in his autobiography, *Exemplar Humanae Vitae*. {BDF; RAT}

ACTION FOR HUMANISM

Action for Humanism (Box 91, Ilisan Remo, Ogun State, Nigeria; or c/o C. D. Brobbey, Nestle [Ghana] Ltd., PO Box 8350, Yema, Ghana) publishes a newsletter, *The Sunrays*. The group is affiliated with African Americans for Humanism, and its president is Emmanuel Kofi Mensah.

Acton, John Emerich Edward Dalberg-Acton [1st Baron] (1834—1902)

Although Lord Acton was a nominal Catholic, this Cambridge University teacher of history had two of his books added to the Catholic Index *Librorum Prohibitorum* in 1871: *Z ur Geschichts des vaticanischen Concils* and *Sendschreiben einen deutschen Bischof des vaticanischen Concils*. By opposing Pius IX's Syllabus of Errors, Acton illustrated his distaste for all forms of absolutism. However, rather than risk excommunication he accepted the dogma of papal infallibility.

Secular humanists, who are against all forms of religious absolutism, often quote Lord Acton's 1887 statement to Bishop Mandell Creighton, "Power tends to corrupt; absolute power corrupts absolutely." They also cite his statement, "The principle of the Inquisition was murderous. . . . The popes were not only murderers in the great style, but they also made murder a legal basis of the Christian Church and a condition of salvation." {CE; ILP; RE; TYD}

ACTS OF GOD

An "act of God" is generally understood to include any extraordinary interruption of human life by a natural cause (such as an earthquake, perils of the sea, tornadoes, a severe flood) which, even with care, could not have been avoided. On the contrary, if events can be foreseen (that, for example, rain will leak through a defective roof and do considerable damage), failure to take the necessary precautions constitutes "negligence." Legal cases may arise if a fire in a building with lightning rods has been caused by lightning, in which case insurance companies may claim that the fire was caused by an act of God and is, therefore, not indemnifiable.

Arkansas Gov. Mike Huckabee, a leading Baptist minister, objected in 1997 to language describing such natural phenomena as tornadoes and floods as "acts of God." "I feel that I have indeed witnessed many 'acts of God,' but I see His actions in the miraculous sparing of life, the sacrifice and selfless spirit in which so many responded to the pain of others," he explained. State Representative Shane Broadway, who is aware that the term has been in insurance policies for ages and insists that the term be continued and included, retorted, "I'm just as much a Baptist as the Governor is."

Historically, theists have not complained about the expression. Survivors of events involving an Act of God, such as a hurricane, often respond with "thanks to God" that they were saved, overlooking Who it is analogously that they are blaming for killing the others or else implying that God wreaks havoc without reason. As for those unfortunates who were hurt or killed, shamans or other divines are quick to declare that God is punishing man for something specific, and various explanations are offered as to how now to regain God's love.

Freethinkers, who have no need for such an expression, use the scientific method to elucidate such occurrences. {CE}

ACTS OF GOD, EXAMPLES

Governor Mike Huckabee of Arkansas wants legal or insurance documents that refer to floods, hurricanes, and earthquakes no longer to be referred to as "acts of God." A Baptist minister, he wants the phrase to be replaced by, or used in tandem with, "natural disasters." "Acts of a supremely indifferent and meaningless universe" was rejected: it's unnecessarily existential. Recent Acts of God involving Muslims include the following:

- 1980: A Pakistani airliner caught fire and crashed after taking off from Jeddah, killing 301;
- 1987: In Mecca, when security forces clashed with Iranians demonstrating against the United States, 402 were killed and 649 were wounded;
- 1990: Pilgrims numbering 1,426 were killed in a stampede;
- 1991: An air crash killed 98;
- 1991: In another stampede, 270 pilgrims died as worshippers surged forward for the ritual "stoning the devil";
- 1997: More than 200 were killed and 1,000 injured as fire engulfed an encampment outside the holy city.

Voltaire, commenting on the Lisbon earthquake of 1755 in which 30,000 perished, many of them in their churches, wrote, "Unhappy mortals! Dark and mourning earth! / A frighted gathering of human kind!/ Eternal lingering of useless pain! . . . . God holds the chain: is not himself enchained. . . . Under a just God, no one is miserable who has not deserved misery. . . . Why suffer we, then, under one so just. . . . " He then asks, ". . . how conceive a God supremely good / Who heaps his favours on the sons he loves,/Yet scatters evil with so large a hand?" {*Chemistry and Industry*, 8 April 1997; *The Freethinker*, June 1997}

Acuna, Rosario de (19th Century)

Acuna was a Spanish writer and lecturer. She contributed to *Las Dominicales* of Madrid, wrote *The Doll's House*, and completed other educational works. {BDF}

ACUPUNCTURE

"The scientific evidence for acupuncture remains as weak as ever," according to Gary P. Posner in *Mensa Bulltin* (June 1999). He commented upon hearing that the Food and Drug Administration in Washington, D.C., which previously classified acupuncture needles as unapproved devices, recently approved them for use by licensed acupuncturists.

A physician and national Coordinator of the "Skeptic" M-to-M Service, Dr. Posner adds, however, that sticking the needles does serve "as a counterirritant for localized superficial pain." He also holds that "the evidence for therapeutic touch appears entirely illusory." E-mail: <garypos@aol.com>.

ADAM (Born some time after 9 a.m., 23 October 4004 B.C.E., according to Bishop James Ussher)

"To condemn all mankind for the sin of Adam and Eve," wrote W. K. Clifford, "to let the innocent suffer for the guilty, to keep anyone alive in torture forever and ever: These actions are simply magnified copies of what bad men do. No juggling with 'divine justice and mercy' can make them anything else. This must be said to all kinds and conditions of men: That if He has visited upon the innocent the punishment of the guilty, if He is to torture any single soul for ever, then it is wrong to worship Him."

If Adam's sin was that of having eaten of the fruit of knowledgein the Garden of Eden (and many believers mistakenly think the fruit was an apple), the symbolism is provocative in light of Edward O. Wilson's contemporary and dour view of mankind as a group which has reduced animal life in lakes, rivers, and even the open ocean. As a result, he observed, "The human species is, in a word, an environmental abnormality. It is possible that intelligence in the wrong kind of species was foreordained to be a fatal combination for the biosphere. Perhaps a law of evolution is that intelligence usually extinguishes itself." However, as an eminent sociobiologist, Wilson is a philosophic naturalist. What disturbs him is that humans appear to be suicidally programmed by their genetic heritage "to be so selfish that a sense of global responsibility will come too late," that "their genes also predispose them to plan ahead for one or two generations at most." (See entry for Bishop James Ussher, who determined from Biblical sources that Creation was completed in seven days, 4004 years before the birth of Jesus the Christ. Also see entry for Hermaphrodite, which Adam might have been.) {HAB; CE; ER; RE}

A.D.

A.D., which Christians use to denote *anno Domini,* the year of the birth of Jesus, was a term invented by a sixth-century monk named Dionysius Exiguus (or Dennis the Short, not a reference to what some might think but, rather, to his height). "Little" Dennis's calendar system started with Year One, for Western mathematics had not yet developed the concept of zero. Thus, the first century lasted from 1 through 100, the second from 101 through 200, and so forth until the twentieth century from 1901 through 2000. We must, therefore, remind ourselves that years like 1900 are in the nineteenth century whereas 1901 is in the 20th.

Moreover, Herod is now considered to have died in 4 B.C., for Little Dennis failed to get the starting point right. Or, at any rate, biblical stories of Herod's fear at the birth of Jesus, the tale of the Three Wise Men, and the Slaying of the Innocents would mean that Jesus must have been born in 4 B.C. or earlier.

Freethinkers use C.E. to signify "the common era" and B.C.E. to signify "before the common era." {Stephen Jay Gould, *USA Weekend*, 19—21 September 1997}

AD HOMINEM ARGUMENT

An *ad hominem* (literally, to the person) argument attacks by appealing to feelings rather than to intellect. For an example: "An atheist who teaches philosophy has to be an immoral individual" (but the argument fails to explain the individual's immorality and, instead, is an *ad hominem* attack on someone who is disliked).

Adagio, Affie (20th Century)

Adagio is editor in New South Wales of *Humanist Viewpoints*, newsletter of the Humanist Society in Australia.

ADAM AND EVE

- Conversation between Adam and Eve must have been difficult at times because they had nobody to talk about.

—Agnes Repplier

- Adam blamed Eve. Eve blamed the serpent. And the serpent hadn't a leg to stand on.

—Anonymous

Adam, Charles (Born 1857)

A French philosopher, Adam taught in several universities and became rector of the Nancy Academy and a Chevalier of the Legion of Honour. He edited works of Descartes and in his *La Philosophie en France* (1894) wrote, "Philosophy and politics leave theses to theology, which digs them up from a remote past, and are modestly content with hypotheses." {RAT}

ADAMASTOR

Phallocentrists are intrigued by Adamastor, whose penis was so monstrously huge that he and the nymph Thetis were unable to have sex. Rabelais's Gargantua *and Pantagruel* (1532—1562) makes mention of Adamastor, as does *Lusiads* by the Portuguese poet Luis de Camoens (1540—1580).

In 1993, South African novelist André Brink wrote *Cape of Storms: The First Life of Adamastor*, in which he uses the character to symbolize the inability of his nation's black majority to engage in peaceful and social intercourse with its white minority. The work was denounced by a British reviewer as being sexist and phallocentric. Similarly, orthodox religionists have publicly proclaimed their shock at Brink's having written about such matters.

Meanwhile, *The New York Times Book Review* front-paged the novel's revew. Reviewer Mario Vargas Llosa noted that, although it is not an anthropological essay, it is a wonderfully entertaining work of fiction: "Brink's beautiful mythological re-creation leaves us anguished over what appear to be its predictions regarding a society where, after a bloody past of injustice and institutionalized racism, different races and cultures are finally preparing to try coexistence under conditions of equality."

Adamic, Louis (1899—1951)

Adamic, a Yugoslav, wrote of his early move to the United States in *Laughing in the Jungle* (1932). When he proposed that European-Americans be returned to their homelands to educate Europeans in democracy, the scheme led to his conference with Franklin D. Roosevelt and Winston Churchill, which he described in *Dinner at the White House* (1946).

Adamic's freethought shows in *The Truth about Aimee Semple McPherson* (1926) and *The World of Satan in the Bible* (1928). {GS; TYD}

ADAMITES

The term *Adamites* refers to a radical group of Hussites, heretics who in the fifteenth century rebelled against the Catholic Church. They were said to have gone naked, believing that because their spirits were free they were in a sinless state. The Adamites attacked priests and organized religion. (See entry for John Hus.)

Adams, Abigail (1744—1818)

Adams, wife of President John Adams and mother of President John Quincy Adams, was a letter-writer of note whose detailed descriptions provided a vivid source of social history. Some of her letters can be found in *The Adams-Jefferson Letters*. As the first First Lady to live in the newly constructed White House in Washington, she found the place unfinished and remarked,

> I had much rather live in the house at Philadelphia. Not one room or chamber is finished of the whole. It is habitable by fires in every part, thirteen of which we are obliged to keep daily, or sleep in wet and damp places. . . . We have not the least fence, yard, or other convenience, without; and the great unfinished audience-room [now the East Room used for receptions and concerts] I make a drying room of, to hang up the clothes in.

Adams was a member of the Unitarian Church in Quincy, Massachusetts. (In Leonard Bernstein's Broadway musical, "1600 Pennsylvania Avenue," Abigail and her husband chose a black gentleman—Gilbert Price, on Broadway—to be the caretaker, and this person with his offspring continued to be caretaker of the place during a succession of presidents. Price, visiting the White House during the show's performances in Washington, joked to President Jimmy Carter of his having had a job there long before Carter. Carter, who said he was a great admirer of the Adamses, joked that Price who had lived in the Broadway White House had earned a nomination for an Antoinette Perry Award, an honor White House resident Carter had never received.) {CE; EG; U; numerous conversations with Gilbert Price}

Adams, Charles Francis (1807—1886)

Charles Francis Adams was an American statesman, diplomat, and son of John Quincy Adams. Both were Unitarians, members of the United First Parish in Quincy, Massachusetts. His *Life and Letters* (1886) shows him to be an agnostic of the Leslie Stephen school. After being President of Union Pacific Railroad (1884—1890), Adams wrote *Three Episodes of Massachusetts History* (1892). {JM; PUT; RAT; U; UU}

Adams, Clark Davis (20th Century)

Adams is an atheist activist in Mississippi. Reared a Roman Catholic who attended a Catholic boarding school, he is moderator of *alt.atheism.moderate* (an Internet newsgroup) and is the public relations director of Internet Infidels. On the Web: <www.dnaco.net/~rwdaniel/ex-tian/Clark.Davis.Adams.html>. E-mail: <cadams@infidels.org>.

Adams, Dale (20th Century)

Adams is Vice-Chair of the American Ethical Union's Membership Committee. E-mail: <dalepadams@juno.com>.

Adams, Douglas (1952-)

A British comic writer, Adams wrote a mock science-fiction series known collectively as *The Hitchhiker's Guide to the Galaxy* (1980-1990).

Although raised in a religious household, he once listened to a street preacher and realized he was hearing utter nonsense. Asked by *American Atheist*(1998-1999) if it was accurate that he had been described as a "radical atheist," Adams responded,

> Yes, I think I use the term "radical" rather loosely, just for emphasis. If you describe yourself as "atheist," some people will say, "Don't you mean 'agnostic'?" I have to reply that I really do mean atheist, I really do not believe that there is a god; in fact, I am convinced that there is not a god (a subtle difference), I see not a shred of evidence to suggest that there is one . . . etc., etc. It's easier to say that I am a radical atheist, just to signal that I really mean it, have thought about it a great deal, and that it's an opinion I hold seriously.

An article about Richard Dawkins in *The New Yorker* (9 September 1996), stated that "Douglas Adams, a friend of Dawkins's . . . found the experience of reading [*The Selfish Gene*] 'one of those absolutely shocking moments of revelation when you understand that the world is fundamentally different from what you thought it was.' He adds, 'I'm hesitating to use the word, but it's almost like a religious experience.' " That book was a key event in leading Adams to his position of atheism. {CA}

Adams, E(lie) M(aynard) (1919—)

Adams is author of *Philosophy and Cultural Freedom* (1985) and *Religion and Cultural Freedom* (1993). He explores the contradictions among biblical religions, democratic liberalism, and modern science, showing how religious beliefs over the ages have been reinterpreted in response to cultural conflicts.

Adams suggests that a humanistic revolution is at hand, one that will result in a fully accountable and intellectually credible religion.

Adams, Francis William Lauderdale (1862—1893)

An Australian poet, Adams wrote novels and poetry. A severe critic of Christianity but an ardent idealist, he wrote in "Mass of Christ" and other of his works about "the bastard God" of the churches. {RAT}

Adams, George (19th Century)

In 1842, Adams was sentenced in Bristol, England, to one month of imprisonment for having sold Thomas Paine's *Oracle of Reason*.

A cabinet maker as well as a radical bookseller, Adams was married to **Harriet Adams**, also a freethinker. {BDF; TYD; VI}

Adams, Hannah (1755—1831)

A View of Religions (1784) by Adams was the first objective analysis of world religions. She is the first American known to have supported herself through writing. A Unitarian, she provided the basis for later scholarship in the study of comparative religion. {U}

Adams, Henry (1838—1918)

An eminent historian and the grandson and great-grandson of presidents John Adams and John Quincy Adams, Adams wrote the following after the death of his sister:

> The idea that any personal deity could find pleasure or profit in torturing a poor woman, by accident, with a fiendish cruelty known to man only in perverted and insane temperaments, could not be held for a moment. For pure blasphemy, it made pure atheism a comfort.

His *The Education of Henry Adams* (1906) fails to mention his wife's suicide.

Adams, J. D. (19th Century)

Adams became a Unitarian, then a follower of William Johnson Fox of the South Place Ethical Society in London. He was a supporter of Charles Bradlaugh.

Adams, J. P. (19th Century)

A well-known London freethinker, Adams with Charles Bradlaugh and Charles Watts helped launch a drive to raise £10,000 to build a new lecture hall, which failed but another hall was built in 1868. Adams supported the *National Reformer*, which ceased after J. M. Robertson's editorship following Bradlaugh's death. Adams contributed to Hypatia Bradlaugh Bonner's publication, the *Reformer*. {RSR}

Adams, James Luther (1901—1994)

Son of a Baptist country preacher, Adams became attracted to John H. Dietrich's "scientific humanism." He then studied with Irving Babbitt, the Harvard "neo-humanist," but upon becoming a Unitarian minister Adams emphasized social engagement in "Taking Time Seriously" (*Christian Century*, September, 1939). A social ethicist, he has been ranked with Henry W. Bellows and William Ellery Channing as among the three greatest leaders of Unitarianism. In 1965 when his *Paul Tillich's Philosophy of Culture, Science, and Religion* was published, he was cited as one of the leading Tillich experts in addition to being an authority on ethics. Adams showed bravery in the time of McCarthyism, by protesting the Vietnam War and by taking part in civil rights struggles.

Adams once wrote:

> Very often the person who revolts against fundamentalism or orthodoxy only sets up a new orthodoxy. There are two principal reasons why the critical spirit and freedom of thought are in perennial danger. These reasons may be epitomized in two words: ignorance and idolatry. . . . Perhaps the greatest danger to the liberal spirit, however, is idolatry, the submission to some idea or ideology that is revered as an absolute and exclusive loyalty. . . . The average religious man is one who is hot for certainties, and though the answers he gets are dusty answers, he is inclined to view them as infallible. He wants an infallible Truth, a divine book true from cover to cover, a divine Founder for his religion, a divinely instituted Church outside which there can be no salvation. . . .
>
> What the orthodox overlooks, however, is this: The most pretentious pride of all is that of the man who thinks himself capable of recognizing infallibility, for he must himself claim to be infallible in order to identify infallibility. He may accuse those who do not accept his "divine" and infallible truths of being proud and of lacking humility. But he forgets that he claims to be infallible when he says he can *select* an infallible guide. How otherwise can he assert with assurance that he knows the infallible when he sees it?
>
> It is true that much religion in the world is a racket; and it is absolutely necessary to identify and attack that sort of religion. Indeed, the great enemy of religion is not anti-religion; it is pseudo-religion. It is not materialism; it is pseudo-spirituality, pseudo-idealism. That is why atheism and hostility to "religion" are often of great value and may even be a necessity.

{U; U&U}

Adams, James Truslow (1878—1949)

Adams, the Pulitzer Prize-winning historian, author of *Henry Adams* (1933), when asked about humanism, responded to the present author: "I make no pretense of being a specialist in Humanism and have not followed such shifts as Existentialism." {WAS, 26 March 1949}

Adams, John [President] (1735—1826)

"There is no doubt," wrote Corliss Lamont, "that George Washington, a rather indifferent member of the Episcopal Church, and John Adams, second President of the United States and sympathetic to Unitarianism, were strongly influenced by Deism, both through their colleagues and as a result of the general intellectual atmosphere. . . . It was President Adams, not President Washington, who in 1797 confirmed and signed the Treaty between the United States and Tripoli in which appears the significant statement, '. . . the Government of the United States of America is not in any sense founded on the Christian Religion.' "

In the Continental Congress, Adams was the delegate from Massachusetts, a leading advocate of American independence. As chairman of the committee to draft the Declaration of Independence, he assigned the actual writing to Virginia's delegate Thomas Jefferson. Upon becoming President, he steered a lonely course between Alexander Hamilton's Federalists, who strongly favored the British, and the opposition Republicans led by Jefferson, who favored the French. Less interested in immediate changes, he designed checks and balances to make change take place slowly and sensibly. When he lost to Jefferson in the 1800 elections, he was so upset he fled the capital before his successor was sworn in, the only sitting president who did not attend his successor's inauguration. He justified this for a decade, eventually reconciling with Jefferson in 1812. Adams was not a feminist, but he treated intellectually able women as his equals. He opposed slavery, correctly predicting that eventually it could lead to civil war, and he opposed the Missouri Compromise of 1820, which allowed slavery to spread beyond the borders of the South. For many, Adams represents an inspiring individual who can be judged by what he does, not by what he says he believes.

McCabe holds that Adams was not a very firm Deist, that in one letter to Jefferson (12 May 1820), he wrote that the Unitarians' "crowd of skepticisms" kept him awake at night. He defined God (17 January 1820) as "an essence that we know nothing of" and says that the attempts of philosophers to get beyond this are "games of push-pin." The Incarnation is called an "awful blasphemy," and he admitted he had no proof of a personal immortality. Further examples: "The question is whether the god of nature will govern the world by his own laws or whether priests and kings shall rule it by fictitious miracles"; and "I almost shudder at the thought of alluding to the most fatal example of the abuses of grief which the history of humankind has preserved—the Cross. Consider what calamities that engine of grief has produced!"

Adams is buried at the First Unitarian Church in Quincy, Massachusetts, which he had joined on 3 January 1773. In 1815 he had written to a Dr. Marsh, "Sixty-five years, my own minister the Rev. Lemuel Briant . . . and Dr. Jonathan Mayhew . . . were Unitarians." In 1816, writing to F. A. Van der Kamp, he wrote, "As

I understand the Christian religion, it was, and is, a revelation. But how has it happened that millions of fables, tales, legends have been blended with both Jewish and Christian revelation that have made them the most bloody religion that ever existed?" In 1817 he wrote that he often was "tempted to think that this would be the best of all possible worlds if there was no religion in it." On the day of his death, according to his biographer Page Smith, Adams's last words were, "This is the last of earth. I am content." {CL; CE; FUS; JMR; RAT; RE; TRI; TYD; U; UU}

Adams, John Quincy [President] (1767—1848)

John Quincy Adams was the sixth U. S. President, the first to be photographed. A conservative, he disliked Andrew Jackson, calling him "a hero, a murderer, an adulterer . . . who in his last days of his life belied and slandered me before the world and died." By post, Adams's mother had once lectured her son that death was preferable to vice.

He is said to have risen often at 4 a.m. to read the Bible and to have advised his son, George Washington Adams, to "Spurn the deadly draught of pleasure." He is also known to have swum naked in the Potomac River, to have written a book on weights and measures, to have been an exponent of the sciences, to have been an ambassador, secretary of state, and U. S. Senator, and to have been outspoken not only against slavery but also against the Southern politicians who defended slavery.

Adams's best-known achievement, as President James Madison's Secretary of State, was the Monroe Doctrine (1823). Although his presidency was somewhat of a disappointment, Adams was instrumental in the setting up of the Smithsonian Institution.

Gore Vidal has called Adams the hero of the *Armistad* affair, a reference to his part in an incident involving the kidnapping of several hundred West Africans by Portuguese slavers for shipment to the slave markets of Cuba. Adams aided Joseph Cinqué, a twenty-five-year-old from Sierra Leone who had led a mutiny and refused to become a slave. Vidal has suggested that Congress should, in light of Adams's accomplishments, hire sculptors with sandblasters "and let them loose on Mt. Rushmore so that they can turn the likeness of the war lover Theodore Roosevelt into that of a true hero, John Quincy Adams."

A conservative Unitarian, Adams deplored his father's and Jefferson's deistic views. He was a member of the United First Parish (Unitarian) in Quincy, Massachusetts, as were his son Charles Francis and his father, John.

Paul C. Nagel's *John Quincy Adams: A Public Life, a Private Life* (1997), points out that Adams's mother was a carrier of an alcoholic gene; Adams's two brothers and, later, his two sons were all to die of acute alcoholism. Adams, however, remained a political activist, "the acutest, the astutest, the archest enemy of Southern slavery," according to one Virginia congressman. Although he suffered a stroke and weakened, he continued to go to the House. In fact, he was a key figure in the *Amistad* case, in which he argued before the House and the Supreme Court concerning the rights of mutinous slaves.

On 21 February 1848 he cast his last vote, a "no" in regard to the war upon Mexico. Then, motioning to the chair that he wanted to speak, he rose but staggered, being caught by another member before he hit the floor. Two days later, he drifted in and out of consciousness. "This is the last of earth," he was then heard to murmur. "I am composed."

Vidal's evaluation: "Final words. Articulate to the end." {CE; Gore Vidal, *The New Yorker*, 10 November 1997; Paul C. Nagel, *John Quincy Adams* (1997); TYD; U; UU}

Adams, Mary (Born 1898)

Adams was an agnostic who headed the Council for the Unmarried Mother. She also was deputy chairman of the Consumers Association. {TRI}

Adams, Philip Andrew (1939—)

Adams is an Australian humanist, iconoclast, author, columnist, broadcaster, and filmmaker. His books include *Adams with Added Enzymes*, *Uncensored Adams*, and *Adams versus God* (1985).

His films include *The Naked Bunyip* and *The Getting of Wisdom*. Adams, active in Amnesty International, is a supporter of the Voluntary Euthanasia Society, has two orders of Australia (AO and AM), and was 1987 Humanist of the Year. He signed Humanist Manifesto 2000.

"I've spent a life-time attacking religious beliefs," Adams has written, "and have not wavered from a view of the universe that many would regard as bleak. Namely, that it is a meaningless place devoid of deity." {CA; SWW}

Adams, Robert Chamblett (1839—1902)

A Canadian freethought leader, Adams evidenced his rationalism in *Pioneer Pith: The Gist of Lectures on Rationalism* (1899) and *Good Without God* (1902). He guided the influential Pioneer Freethought Club in Canada until early in the 20th century. In 1884, Adams was elected President of the Canadian Secular Union. He helped challenge the ban by customs officials on such freethought works as Paine's *Age of Reason* and to secure the Dominion Oaths Act of 1893. {BDF; EU, A. Brian McKillop; FUK; FUS; PUT; RAT; RSR}

Adams, Sarah Flowers (Born 1805)

Adams, an English Unitarian, wrote poetry and sermons. She wrote "Nearer My God To Thee." {U}

Adams, Thomas (19th Century)

Adams, born a Congregationalist, was a master baker who became a secularist in the 1860s. {RSR}

Adams, William (18th Century)

A friend of Dr. Samuel Johnson, Adams was told by the dying Johnson of his fear of being considered damned. According to W. Jackson Bate's *Samuel Johnson* (1998), Adams asked what was meant and, in the words of biographer James Boswell, Johnson "passionately and loudly" replied, "Sent to Hell, Sir, and punished everlastingly." Adams told his friend he did not believe in Hell, and Johnson abruptly ended the discussion, saying, "I'll have no more on't." {Derek Jarrett, *The New York Review of Books*, 18 March 1999}

Adams, William Edwin (1832—1906)

A freethinker, Adams wrote *Tyrannicide: Is It Justifiable?* (1858). {VI}

Adamson, Robert (1852—1902)

Described by the *Cambridge History of Modern Literature* as being "the most learned of contemporary philosophers," Adamson was an outspoken agnostic and a utilitarian in ethics. In his *Ethical Democracy* (1900), Adamson wrote that even the most pretentious proofs of the existence of God are "intellectually unrepresentable" and that "the world conquered Christianity" instead of the other way about. {JM; RAT; RE}

Adcock, Arthur St. John (1864—1930)

Adcock, who became acting editor of the *Bookman*, was a poet and novelist. He wrote *Famous Houses and Literary Shrines of London* (1929). In 1920 he contributed to the Rationalist Press Association's annual journal. {RAT}

Addams, Jane (1860—1935)

Addams, winner in 1931 of the Nobel Peace Prize, founded Chicago's Hull House. In view of her prominent position, McCabe notes, "Miss Addams, who was the aunt of the late Marcet Haldeman-Julius, had to be reticent about religion, but her biographer F. W. Linn says that she never departed from the Rationalism which her father had taught her and 'just joined the Congregational Church as she might join a labor-union.' " She was active in the women's suffrage and pacifist movements. Although she attended All Souls' Unitarian Church in Chicago and was briefly an interim lecturer at Chicago's Ethical Culture Society, she retained a membership in a Presbyterian congregation.

Malcolm Bush has written that Addams "was the original secular humanist, rejecting Christianity and socialism alike as formal beliefs though she took inspiration from both." Strongly supported by John Haynes Holmes and the intellectual Unitarians of her day, Addams has been called, if not a Unitarian, certainly a unitarian. Her funeral, by her direction, was unsectarian. (See entry for Frank Lloyd Wright) {CE; *Free Inquiry*, Fall, 1993; HNS2; JM; RE; TSV; WWS}

Addis, Don (20th Century)

Addis is a freethinker and a cartoonist whose work appears in *Free Inquiry* and St. Petersburg *Times.*

Addison, Joseph (1672—1719)

The recognized master of the English essay, Addison advocated reason and moderation in life. In 1729, his *Remarks on Several Parts of Italy* were added by the Vatican to its list of prohibited books. However, according to his biographers, although he was called by some a Deist, basically he was a Christian. He once did write, however, "Atheist is an old-fashioned word. I am a freethinker."

Addison was interested in how Augustus, Cato, Seneca, and Thomas More had behaved at their deaths, feeling one should die with a kind of fortitude. When he suspected his own death was near, Addison called for his stepson and announced, somewhat dramatically, "See with what peace a Christian can die," whereupon he died. Observed Horace Walpole of Addison's death, "Unluckily, he died of brandy. Nothing makes a Christian die in peace like being maudlin." {CE; ILP; JMRH}

Addison, William (20th Century)

Addison of Yorkshire in England, was a lecturer in the early 1900s for the British Secular League in Bolton. {RSR}

Adickes, Erich (1866—1928)

A German philosopher, Adickes was a critical empiricist, or moderate Kantian, and he wrote important works on Kant, including in 1895 a Kantian bibliography in German. An opponent of Haeckel, Adickes in his *Kant contra Haeckel* wrote, "I have no more belief than he in a personal extra-mundane God, a creation of the world by him, or an immaterial soul separated from the body." {RAT}

Adler, Felix (1851—1933)

Adler, the founder in 1876 of the Society for Ethical Culture of New York, was a teacher of philosophy at Columbia University. Influenced by Emerson's idea of a purely moral religion, he was for a time (1877—1891) president of the Free Religious Association. Radest, in *The Encyclopedia of Unbelief,* has described how Adler built the Ethical Culture Society, with its schools, obtaining $400,000 from John D. Rockefeller Jr. Adler was a philosophic idealist, and the Society he founded was a religion based on ethics rather than creed and theology.

As described by Wolfgang Saxon, "Dr. Adler saw a pragmatic faith without God, a belief in the infinite worth of the individual, the centrality of ethical principles, and the urgency to redeem the democratic promise by improving the lot of the poor and fighting privilege. This, he thought, offered a reasoned approach that reached out to those wanting an attractive alternative to Christianity and Judaism." The platform he supplied spread to other parts of the nation and continues to inspire those interested in social ethics and free religion. (See the entry for Ethical Culture in which James F. Hornback supplies historical details of Adler's accomplishments. Also see entry for Walter Sheldon.) {BDF; CE; CL; ER; EU, Howard B. Radest; FUK; FUS; HNS2; JMR; TRI; WSS; RAT; RE}

Adler, Margot (20th Century)

Adler, a National Public Radio correspondence since 1979, is the author of *Drawing Down the Moon* (1995), a study of contemporary paganism and goddess spirituality, and *Heretic's Heart: A Journey Through Spirit and Revolution* (1997). She is a member of the Unitarian Church of All Souls in New York City. {*World,* November-December 1998}

ADMD-L BULLETIN (Right To Die With Dignity)

A quarterly *ADMD-L Bulletin,* is a quarterly of the *Association pour le Droit de Mourir dans la Dignité,* 50 Boulevard J. F. Kennedy, L-4170 Esch-Alzette, Luxembourg.

Admiraal, Aart (1833—1878)

Admiraal was a Dutch writer who, first a schoolmaster, became director of the telegraph bureau at Schoonhoven. From 1856 and for many years, he wrote using the anagram "Aramaldi" in *De Dageraad.* In 1867 he published *The Religion of the People* under the pseudonym "Bato van der Maas," a name he also used when writing in other periodicals.

Admiraal, Pieter (20th Century)

An anesthetist in the Netherlands, Admiraal is a Humanist Laureate in the Council for Secular Humanism's International Academy of Humanism. In 1995 at Delphi, Greece, Admiraal spoke at the first International Multidisciplinary Conference on Human Behaviour and the Meaning of Modern Humanism. He signed Humanist Manifesto 2000.

Dr. Admiraal has received from the International Humanist and Ethical Union (IHEU) a Humanist Award for his pioneer work in the field of euthanasia. In accepting, he gave a moving description of the last months of one of his favorite patients, an elderly man with cancer, whom he helped to die. After describing the details, Dr. Admiraal revealed that the man was his own father. "It is on behalf of *this* patient," he said proudly, "that I accept the Award." {BDF}

Ado-Dwanka, Niitse Akufo Awuku (20th Century)

Ado-Dwanka, a nuclear physicist who spent much of his professional career in Europe, is a member of a rationalist group in his native Ghana.

ADONIS

Adonis was the Greek form of the Syrian word *Adon* (Lord), a title given to the ancient Babylonian vegetation-god Tammuz. His cult, which spread westward to Egypt and Greece, was one of the chief sources of the Christian myth of the Resurrection, according to McCabe. {RE}

Adonis, Byron (19th Century)

In 1879, Adonis was editor in San Francisco of the *Pacific Coast Free-Thinker.*

ADULTERY

- It shall be considered adultery to offer presents to a married woman, to romp with her, to touch her dress or ornaments, or to sit with her on a bed.

—"Code of Manu," Hindu law scripture (600 B.C.E-300 C.E.)

- I have perfumed my bed with myrrh, aloes, and cinnamon. Come, let us take our fill of love until the morning: let us solace ourselves with loves. For the good man is not at home, he is gone a long journey.

—*Book of Proverbs* (c. 500 B.C.E.

- When cheated, wife or husband feels the same.

—**Euripides**, *Andromache* (c. 426 B.C.E.)

• A man may commit adultery with a woman knowing well who she is, but not of free choice, because he is under the influence of passion. In that case he is not an unjust man, though he acts unjustly.

—Aristotle, "The Nicomachean Ethics" (c. 340 B. C. E.)

• One should reflect deeply before having relations with married women. If it works, what do I risk? Is success possible without taking too many risks? When I have possessed her, what are the risks for the reputation of either of us?

—"Jayamangala," a 12th century commentary on the Kama Sutra by Yashodhara, an Indian writer

• He that is robb'd, not knowing what is stolen, / Let him not know it, and he's not robbed at all.

—William Shakespeare, *Othello* (1664); Othello is responding to rumors of his wife's infidelity.

• Adultery is an evil only inasmuch as it is a theft; but we do not steal that which is given to us.

Voltaire, *Philosophical Dictionary* (1764)

• What we call adultery, like what we call heresy, comes as a natural right.

—**Victor Hugo** (1802-1885), *Pierres*

• Young men want to be faithful, and are not; old men want to be faithless, and cannot.

—Oscar Wilde, *The Picture of Dorian Gray* (1891)

• The psychology of adultery has been falsified by conventional morals, which assume, in monogamous countries, that attraction to one person cannot coexist with a serious affection for another. Everyone knows that this is untrue.

—**Bertrand Russell**, *Marriage and Morals* (1929)

• The Tasmanians, who never committed adultery, are now extinct.

—**Somerset Maugham**, *The Breadwinner* (1930)

The Catechism of the Catholic Church (1994) states that "adultery refers to marital infidelity. When two partners, of whom at least one is married to another party, have sexual relations—even transient ones—they commit adultery. Christ condemns even adultery of mere desire. The sixth commandment and the New Testament forbid adultery absolutely. The prophets denounce the gravity of adultery; they see it as an image of the sin of idolatry."

Matthew 5:28 describes how looking lustfully at a woman constitutes adultery, the subject of Nathaniel Hawthorne's 1850 novel, *The Scarlet Letter*. Religious law ordinarily terms the married participant an *adulterer* and the single one merely a *fornicator*. Any offspring from such unions were called *adulterini*.

Freethinkers without a zipper problem are often amused that most accused adulterers are said by the adulterers themselves to be theists. (See entry for Lust.) {Alexander Green, *The New York Times*, 27 December 1998}

ADVENT

Christians think of the Advent as the coming of Jesus at the Incarnation, a complex theological view that the Son of God was somehow conceived in the womb of Mary, that her husband was not involved, and that Jesus is both the true God and also a true man.

Humanists use the word in the sense that we live in the time of "the advent of personal computers."

ADVERTISING, RELIGIOUSLY SATIRICAL

• [Virgin Mary, wearing denims]: Pure virginal 100% cotton. Soft yet miraculously strong. Our jeans are cut from superior denim, then carefully assembled by devoted Diesel followers. The finest denim clothing. This is our mission.

—an ad for Diesel Jeans, in *Sky*

• Nine out of ten saviours prefer Dazzle®, with added Radiance®, to any other washing powder.

• Saving souls can often be a grubby business—but I cannot afford to have my robes looking anything other than whiter than white at all times. When I took the Dazzle® challenge I was Godsmacked—"Jesus Christ," I exclaimed, "that's what I call *white*!" JC, Nazareth

—above two adverts which might one day be seen *The Freethinker*, May 1999

ADVOCATE, THE DEVIL'S

The Devil's Advocate is the Vatican official who is, in Papal law, styled the Promoter of the Faith (established 1587). His function is, in theory, to find objections against the character or the orthodoxy of those whom the Church proposes to declare "Blessed" or "Saint." In modern times, the motive is generally political, stated McCabe, and is done to conciliate the country to which the "saint" belongs or involves fees (as much as £10,000). As a result, the office is a mere formality. {RE}

Aenesidemus (1st Century B.C.E.)

Aenesidemus of Crete taught in Alexandria and overthrew the doctrines on probability advocated by Carneades. Reverting to the earliest of skeptical forms, he wrote "Arguments Against Belief in a God," in which he stated, "We skeptics follow in practice the way of the world, but without holding any opinion about it. We speak of the gods as existing and offer worship to the gods and say that they exercise providence, but in saying this we express no belief, and avoid the rashness of the dogmatizers." Aenesidemus noted that some think of God as corporeal, while others think of God as incorporeal. Since we cannot know His attributes, the existence of God is not self-evident and therefore needs proof."

He also held, states Bertrand Russell in *History of Philosophy*, that "those who affirm positively that God exists cannot avoid falling into an impiety. For if they say that God controls everything, they make Him the author of evil things; if, on the other hand, they say that He controls some things only, or that He controls nothing, they are compelled to make God either grudging or impotent, and to do that is quite obviously an impiety." The thinking of Aenesidemus influenced Lucian, in the 2nd century of the Christian Era. {BDF; CE; JMRH}

AEROBIOSIS

Aerobiosis is a mode of life that requires oxygen. What many do not realize is that for early forms of life oxygen was a poison, as is the case today for bacteria known as obligatory anaerobes, which survive only in the absence of oxygen. Life in the absence of oxygen is termed anaerobiosis, which is described by the Belgian bio-chemist Christian De Duve, a sharer of the 1974 Nobel Prize, in *Vital Dust, Life as a Cosmic Imperative* (1995). When oxygen first made its appearance, De Duve has written, "life had no defense against these poisons, and a major holocaust threatened. Fortunately, the process was slow and there was plenty of time for the main strategies of evolutionary adaptation to come into play. Victims probably were legion, but a few survivors emerged to people the world with new forms of life, thus turning an impending catastrophe into a major source of innovation." The concept is important in discussions as to whether life exists in other parts of the galaxy.

Aeschylus (525—456 B.C.E.)

Aeschylus, the Athenian tragic poet, implicitly challenged the popular faith of his time. But, as pointed out by Robertson, Aeschylus dwelt on the gods, the struggles of the gods, and on destiny, whereas Sophocles dwelt on man. {CE; HNS2; JMR; JMRH}

Aesop (6th Century B.C.E.)

Herodotus wrote that Aesop, a legendary Greek fabulist, was a slave who lived in Samos and was eventually set free by his master. Others hold that Aesop was the first major African writer and one of the first literary moralists. His fables, stories about animals which illustrate a moral lesson, include "The Tortoise and the Hare," "The Fox and the Grapes," and "The Boy Who Cried 'Wolf.' "

Contrary to what is found in numerous sophomore essays, according to one Manhattan wag, the fables were not written by Aesophogus.

In 1998, in their new translation of the fables, Olivia and Robert Temple wrote that "the fables are not the pretty purveyors of Victorian morals that we have been led to believe. They are instead savage, coarse, brutal, lacking in all mercy or compassion." Examples:

THE CAMEL WHO SHAT IN THE RIVER

A camel was crossing a swiftly flowing river. He shat and immediately saw his own dung floating in front of him, carried by the rapidity of the current.

"What is that there?" he asked himself. "That which was behind me I now see pass in front of me."

This applies to a situation where the rabble and the idiots hold sway rather than the eminent and the sensible.

THE BEAVER

The beaver is a four-footed animal who lives in pools. A beaver's genitals serve, it is said, to cure certain ailments. So when the beaver is spotted and pursued to be mutilated—since he knows why he is being hunted—he will run for a certain distance, and he will use the speed of his feet to remain intact. But when he sees himself about to be caught, he will bite off his own parts, throw them, and thus save his own life.

Among men also, those are wise who, if attacked for their money, will sacrifice it rather than lose their lives.

{*Harper's Magazine*, June 1998; CE; DCL}

AESTHETICS

Aesthetics is a branch of philosophy dealing with the subject of beauty, art, and taste. Aesthetic questions include "What is art?" and "What is meant when we say something is beautiful?" Philosophic naturalists who have written about aesthetics include Brand Blanshard, John Dewey, John Hospers, Horace Kallen, and George Santayana. Bertrand Russell, according to Blanshard, did not write about aesthetics because "I didn't know anything about it . . . although this is not a very good excuse, for my friends tell me it has not deterred me from writing on other subjects." (See entry for Beauty.) {CE; ER}

AFFIRMATIONS OF HUMANISM

The Council for Secular Humanism has a statement of principles containing the following affirmations:

- We are committed to the application of reason and science to the understanding of the universe and to the solving of human problems.
- We deplore efforts to denigrate human intelligence, to seek to explain the world in supernatural terms, and to look outside nature for salvation.
- We believe that scientific discovery and technology can contribute to the betterment of human life.
- We believe in an open and pluralistic society and that democracy is the best guarantee of protecting human rights from authoritarian élites and repressive majorities.
- We are committed to the principle of the separation of church and state.
- We cultivate the arts of negotiation and compromise as a means of resolving differences and achieving mutual understanding.
- We are concerned with securing justice and fairness in society and with eliminating discrimination and intolerance.
- We believe in supporting the disadvantaged and the handicapped so that they will be able to help themselves.
- We attempt to transcend divisive parochial loyalties based on race, religion, gender, nationality, creed, class, sexual orientation, or ethnicity, and strive to work together for the common good of humanity.
- We want to protect and enhance the earth, to preserve it for future generations, and to avoid inflicting needless suffering on other species.
- We believe in enjoying life here and now and in developing our creative talents to their fullest.
- We believe in the cultivation of moral excellence.
- We respect the right to privacy. Mature adults should be allowed to fulfill their aspirations, to express their sexual preferences, to exercise reproductive freedom, to have access to comprehensive and informed health-care, and to die with dignity.
- We believe in the common moral decencies: altruism, integrity, honesty, truthfulness, responsibility. Humanist ethics is amenable to critical, rational guidance. There are normative standards that we discover together. Moral principles are tested by their consequences.
- We are deeply concerned with the moral education of our children. We want to nourish reason and compassion.
- We are engaged by the arts no less than by the sciences.
- We are citizens of the universe and are excited by discoveries still to be made in the cosmos.
- We are skeptical of untested claims to knowledge, and we are open to novel ideas and seek new departures in our thinking.
- We affirm humanism as a realistic alternative to theologies of despair and ideologies of violence and as a source of rich personal significance and genuine satisfaction in the service to others.
- We believe in optimism rather than pessimism, hope rather than despair, learning in the place of dogma, truth instead of ignorance, joy rather than guilt or sin, tolerance in the place of fear, love instead of hatred, compassion over selfishness, beauty instead of ugliness, and reason rather than blind faith or irrationality.
- We believe in the fullest realization of the best and noblest that we are capable of as human beings.

AFRICA: See K. Anthony Appiah's "Africa: The Hidden History," a review of John Reader's *Africa: A Biography of the Continent* (1998). No satisfactory history of the continent has been written to date by an African.

AFRICA, HUMANISM AND FREETHOUGHT IN: See entries for individual countries, such as Algeria, Gambia, Ghana, Guinea, Nigeria, South Africa, Uganda, and Zaire. Also see entries for René Depestre (Haiti), Frantz Fanon (Algeria), Kenneth Kaunda (Zambia), Kwame Nkrumah (Ghana), Jacques Roumain (Haiti), Léopold Sédar Senghor (Senegal), and Ahmed Sékou Touré (Guinea).

AFRICAN AMERICAN

Citizens of the United States whose ancestors were Africans are referred to as blacks, Negroes, or African Americans. Afro-American, an earlier term, is not widely used today.

The two words, when hyphenated as a noun, imply that such "African-Americans" just stepped off a slave ship in the seventeenth century or perhaps arrived from Ghana and received citizenship last week. Many find it illogical for native Americans whose parents and even grandparents were born in the United States to be called "African-Americans." Analogous usages include Native Americans, Chinese Americans, Irish Americans, Polish Americans, etc. Many African Americans, however, dislike being described as Negroes. *Negress* is both antiquated and pejorative, in a category with *Jewess* or *actress*.

The adjectival use, however, takes a hyphen; e.g., an African-American parade. {*Guidelines for Bias-Free Writing*, 1995; Margaret Shertzer, ed., *The Elements of Grammar*, 1986}

AFRICAN AMERICANS FOR HUMANISM

African Americans for Humanism (AAH), POB 664, Amherst, New York 14226, was formed by Norm Allen to bring the ideals of humanism to the African American community. (See entry for Norm Allen.)

AFRICAN AMERICANS, RELIGIOSITY OF

In 1960, 82% of 2,000 blacks surveyed said they pray on a regular basis, whether in times of plenty or need. By 1990, only 68% maintained the habit. The latter tended to disbelieve they were actually being heard, different from the 1960s counterpart. Only 62% believe today (1995) that prayer can effect real changes in their lives. Of those with two years of college, 30% said they were skeptical that prayers they heard their grandmother pray aloud did any positive good for their families or the state of blacks in America. With the passage of each decade, black churches experience a 10% decrease in membership and at least that many more lose faith that a universal good exists at all. (See entries for Norm Allen and Wendall Potter.) {*Secular Nation*, Fall 1995}

AFRICAN EVE: See the entry for Martin G. Bernal.

AFRICAN HUMANISM

Wole Soyinka has pointed out that the Bible, the Koran, the Bhagavad-Gita, and other so-called "sacred" books do not expressly state that, for *all* human beings, human rights should exist. They do in part, "but always in curtailed form, relativist, patriarchal, always subject to the invisible divine realms whose interpreters are mortals with distinct, secular agendas, usually allied to the very arbitrary controls that are a contradiction to such ideas."

He cites Ifa, the corpus of Yoruban spiritual precepts and secular philosophy, which although its origins are lost in antiquity, preserves the human rights concept through Orunmila, the god of divination:

> *Dandan enia l'ayan ko mu ire lo s'aye . . . Ipo rere naa ni aye-amotan ohungbogbo, ayo nnigbagbogbo, igbesi laisi ominu tabi iberua ota.*
>
> Certainly, it is the human being that was elected to bring values to the world . . . and his place of good is the knowledge of all things, joy at all times, freedom from anxiety and freedom rom fear of the enemy. [Irosu Wori]

{Wole Soyinka, *The New York Times Magazine*, 18 April 1999}

AFRO-ASIAN PHILOSOPHY ASSOCIATION

In Egypt, the Afro-Asian Philosophy Association became an Associate Member in 1998 of the International Humanist and Ethical Union.

AFROCENTRISM

Some Afrocentrists claim that Greek civilization was actually created by black Africans in Egypt. Particularly in the latter quarter of the twentieth century, scholars argued about Martin G. Bernal's *Black Athena: The Afroasiatic Roots of Classical Culture* (1987), which sought to "lessen European cultural arrogance" by questioning the extent of the Greeks' achievements to non-European cultures. His and others' attempts to accept in full the ancient traditions of Greek indebtedness to Phoenicia and Egypt, and then to enlarge them, according to Glen Bowersock of the Institute for Advanced Study, "provoked a storm of protest unprecedented in modern classical scholarship in North America."

Now, he continued, "Mary Lefkowitz's *Not Out of Africa* is the definitive statement on the whole controversy and its implications. Her book illustrates why a subject that might seem academic and innocuous turns out to be so explosive. America watchers in Europe have found themselves bewildered by the Bernal phenomenon, even though some of them have been caught up in it." Meanwhile, it is claimed that Ms. Lefkowitz "systematically demolishes Afrocentric contentions about ancient history."

Bowersock summarized his scholarly evaluation by stating,

> Neither Mr. Bernal nor the Afrocentrists seem interested in asking why Egyptian origins or influences should be linked with Africans at all, except in the simple-minded geographical sense that Egypt is part of North Africa. Ancient Egyptians did not consider themselves Africans or blacks, and they consciously dissociated themselves from the blacks of Nubia to the south. The Greeks noticed that Egyptian complexions were darker than theirs, but they never confused Egyptians with the blacks they generically called Ethiopians.
>
> Even if there was a parallel goddess to Athena in Egypt, there is not the slightest reason to think she was represented as black. Mr. Bernal, whose intelligence and erudition are as formidable as his judgment is flawed, should have known better.

As for Ms. Lefkowitz, Bowersock remarks,

> Her impassioned defense of the Greeks arises from the racial politics of our time. The achievement of the Greeks is not going to go away, whatever the nature and extent of their indebtedness to other cultures. The paradoxical conclusion to be drawn from Mary Lefkowitz's polemic is that the Greek legacy remains today so rich and attractive that even the most ardent foes of European civilization want to claim it for themselves.

(For a review of Mary K. Lefkowitz's *Not Out of Africa: How Afrocentrism Became an Excuse to Teach Myth as History* (1996), see the entry for Martin Bernal; for Paul Kurtz's negative criticism, see entry for Consilience.) {Glen Bowersock, "Rescuing the Greeks, *New York Times Book Review*, 25 February 1996}

AFTERLIFE

The Egyptians were among the first to invent the concept of an afterlife, as exemplified by their burial customs and rites. The concept was taken up later by the ancient Hebrews. Paul Johnson's *The Quest for God: A Personal Pilgrimage* (1996) speculates that the first hell in people's minds may have been on Jerusalem's south side, where the city's garbage burned day and night and resulted in unpleasant aromas. James E. Alock's "Pseudoscience and the Soul" (*Essence* 5:1) suggests a reason individuals search for "proof" of an afterlife: "Intellectually capable of foreseeing that they will one day die, yet emotionally too frail to accept that physical death may indeed be the end of their existence, human beings have long clung to the idea that life continues beyond the grave."

Freethinkers generally hold that the mythology of an afterlife, which serves as a denial of death, provides little comfort either for the survivors or for the dying. (See entries for Heaven and Hell. Also note the entry for Epiphenomenalism, a theory that human beings do not survive the death of their bodies in any form whatsoever.) {PE; OCP}

AFTERLIFE, SPECULATIONS ABOUT

Camille Sweeney collected some people's ideas about the afterlife (*The New York Times Magazine*, 7 December 1997), which 74% of all Americans, according to the National Opinion Research Center in Chicago, believe in:

> • I don't believe in an afterlife. I don't even believe in *this* life. I'm completely unspiritual. If there is an afterlife, I guess I'd use it to return phone calls.
>
> —**Fran Lebowitz**, writer
>
> • I want to be ground up and have my assistants mix my ashes in a vat of oil paint and medium that they'll disperse into 10 little jars. Then they'll distribute the mixture to my 10 favorite painters, who'll use the mixture, me in the paint, to make art that'll hang in a group show–held in my honor. That'll be my afterlife, a group show.
>
> —**Ross Bleckner**, artist
>
> • The afterlife's going to be a life of activity. We won't be sitting around on clouds strumming on harps all day–although, come to think of it, that would be pretty strenuous. Heaven's going to look like a big city by a lake, something like Chicago, not at all like Manhattan.
>
> —Andrew M. Greeley, author, ordained Roman Catholic priest
>
> • I hope something *does* happen. Anything. Any kind of consciousness. My fear is that nothing will. I don't believe in reincarna-

tion–there's no control in that, and I'm much too ambitious. And a hereafter? I'm not sure what a Heaven would be like, but Hell, Hell might be interesting–a lot like the news business.

—Geraldo Rivera, talk-show host, who lists himself as a Jew in *Who's Who in America*

• If, at the end, we rejoice in what we did right and regret what we did wrong and wish we could do it all over and better, we earn peacefulness. That's Heaven. Not caring how we lived is to accept oblivion. That's Hell.

—Ex-Governor Mario Cuomo, New York State, a Catholic

• My hereafter is here. I am where I'm going, for I am mulch. It's a great comfort to know that in my mulch-hood I may nourish a row of parsnips.

—**Frank McCourt**, writer

• I used to believe there was an afterlife, that we'll all be reincarnated. Then I had my kids and realized that they're my afterlife. They are how a little bit of me is going to survive. My brother still believes in reincarnation. He's going to be born over and over and over again. He really hopes it happens. Not me. He's still trying to get it right, and I'm trying to get it over with.

—**Tommy Smothers**, comedian

Agarkar, Gopal Ganesh (1856—1895)

Agarkar, a social revolutionary, joined with Tilak and Chiplunkar to found the New English School in Pune, the Deccan Education Society, and subsequently Fergusson College. Agarkar is known in India not as a hedonist but as a humanist and secularist.

Agassiz, Elizabeth Cabot Cary (1822—1907)

According to Louise Hall Tharp's *Adventurous Alliance: The Story of the Agassiz Family of Boston* (1959), the Agassiz family attended King's Chapel (Unitarian). With her husband Louis, the famed Swiss-American zoologist and geologist, she started a boarding school for young ladies who wanted to study high school level subjects. Her experience led her to become one of the founders and the first president (1894—1903) of Radcliffe College. {CE; EG}

Agathias (Ancient Greece)

The ancient Greeks, unlike the Hebrews, wrote of earthy matters such as Agathias did in the following dialogue, as translated by Dudley Fitts:

A: Why that alarming sigh?
B: I'm in love.
A: With a boy or a girl?
B: With a girl
A: Attractive?
B: I think so!
A: Where did you meet her?
B: Last night at a dinner-party.
A: I see. And you think you've a chance with her?
B: I'm sure of it; but it's got to be kept a secret, friend.
A: Ah. Then you mean that you are not contemplating holy matrimony?
B: That isn't it. I mean that I've learned she hasn't a penny in the world.
A: You've "learned"!
Liar, liar, you're not in love!
The heart struck silly by Love's shaft
Forgets its arithmetic!

And this manifesto:

Let Aphroditê herself, let all the company of Love
Curse me, shrivel my sick heart with their hate,
If ever I turn to the love of boys.
O Goddess,
From sliding error and perversion guard me!
To sin with girls is sin enough:
Pittalakos may have the rest.

AGE

• The women of Greece counted their age from their marriage, not from their birth.

—Homer

• The best years are the forties; after fifty a man begins to deteriorate, but in the forties he is at the maximum of his villainy.

—**H. L. Mencken**

• Women deserve to have more than 12 years between the ages of 28 and 40.

—**James Thurber**

AGE OF ATHEISM

A quarterly published by the Atheist Society of India, *Age of Atheism* is at Pithani Dibba, Visakhapatnam 530 002, Andhra Pradesh, India.

AGNOSTIC CELEBRITIES

According to the Internet homepage for Celebrity Atheists and Agnostics, the following might be atheists but, tentatively and without further documentation, are listed as agnostics:

Margaret Atwood, novelist; Richard Avedon, photographer; George Clooney, actor; Alan Dershowitz, lawyer; Phyllis Diller, actress and comedian; David Duchovny, actor; Carrie Fisher, actress; Candace Gingrich, gay rights activist; Mikhail Gorbachev, former President of the USSR; Stephen Jay Gould, paleontologist; Matt Groening, cartoonist and producer of "The Simpsons"; Bob Guccione, publisher; Stephen Hawking, theoretical physicist; Robert Heilbroner, economist; Sir Edmund Hillary; John Irving, novelist; Molly Ivins, journalist; Robert Jastrow, astrophysicist; Bill Joel, recording artist; Jack Kevorkian, right-to-dieactivist; Larry King, television talk host; Barry Manilow, recording artist; Henry Morgentaler, Canadian abortion rights activist; Iris Murdoch, British philosopher; John Passmore, Australian philosopher; Sean Penn, actor-director; W. V. Quine, philosopher; Geraldo Rivera, television show host; Andy Rooney, television commentator; Neil Simon, playwright; Rod Steiger, actor; Howard Stern, radio personality; Uma Thurman, actress; Ted Turner, media mogul; Gene Wilder, actor; Bruce Willis, actor; Edward O. Wilson, entomologist; Rabbi Sherwin T. Wine, founder of the Society for Humanistic Judaism.

More individuals are listed at <http:///www.primenet.com/~lippard/atheistcelebs>. {See entries herein for individuals.}

AGNOSTICISM

Some hold that the agnostic is committed to believing in neither the existence nor non-existence of god, God, or supernatural entities. Others hold that the agnostic finds that any ultimate reality–God, gods, supernatural existences–is unknown and unknowable.

According to the *Catechism of the Catholic Church* (1994),

Agnosticism assumes a number of forms. In certain cases the agnostic refrains from denying God; instead he postulates the existence of a transcendent being which is incapable of revealing itself, and about which nothing can be said. In other cases, the agnostic makes no judgment about God's existence, declaring it impossible to prove, or even to affirm or deny. Agnosticism can sometimes include a certain search for God, but it can equally express indifferentism, a flight from the ultimate question of existence, and a sluggish moral conscience. Agnosticism is all too often equivalent to practical atheism.

T. H. Huxley, who coined the word in 1869, used it to indicate that, while his contemporaries seemed to have definite knowledge (*gnosis*), positive or negative, about ultimate realities and might be described as Gnostics, he had no such knowledge. Following the principles of Hume and Kant, Huxley held that the mind cannot attain to any truth beyond the phenomenal universe or the world of experience. Hence the original meaning is that man cannot know the truth about God and immortality, and must leave the issues open.

As Paul Edwards has pointed out, the position Huxley called "agnosticism" was much older and had usually gone under the name of "skepticism."

Individuals when asked if God exists often respond they are agnostic, adding that believers think He does.

Individuals when asked if Pink Elephants exist could respond they are agnostic, adding that many drunkards believe They do. Asked why *They* is capitalized, they retort, "Why is God capitalized?" (See the entries for atheism, atheistic humanism, and Japanese agnosticism, with corresponding definitions, and definitions by Edgar Sheffield Brightman and T. H. Huxley; also, see the entries for Aristippus, Comte, Spencer, and Kant.) {CE; Paul Edwards, *Free Inquiry*, Fall 1998; RE}

AGNOSTICS, ATHEISTS, AND SECULAR HUMANISTS INFECTED/AFFECTED WITH AIDS/HIV ILLNESS (AASH)

Agnostics, Atheists, and Secular Humanists Who Are Infected/Affected with AIDS/HIV Illness (AASH) was founded in 1992 by Larry Gutenburg, Randy Wicker, and the pseudonymous Allen Windsor. It commenced as an action group within the Secular Humanist Society of New York chapter. Unofficially, it was formed in memory of Fernando Vargas and friends of Gutenburg and Wicker who had died of the disease. However, when the secular humanist chapter's board of directors appeared uncomfortable with the association, Windsor pulled the group out and, simultaneously, resigned as editor of *Pique*, the society's newsletter.

Gutenburg, who had been president in 1990—1991 of People With AIDS (PWA), arranged for the group to meet in a Greenwich Village Episcopal meeting room which formerly PWA had been allowed to use without compensation. As many as thirty individuals attended different meetings until, upon Gutenberg's death, the group was disbanded in 1995.

Except for Wicker and Windsor, the members were HIV-positive and exchanged information about drugs they were or were not using, hospitals they preferred, wills, living will proxies, and health care proxies. AASH arranged visits to hospitalized members and get-togethers at brunches and dinners.

The Secular Humanist Bulletin (Summer 1995) and *Free Inquiry* carried items about the unusual group. AASH held secular memorials for Michael Callen, the lead singer of the Flirtations; for author Paul Monette; for Father Andrew DeMasi (who was a Jesuit-trained priest-turned-atheist); for businessman Luke Stanton; and for radio notable Larry Gutenburg. (See entries for Andrew DeMasi, Larry Gutenburg, Wayne Larsen, Luke Stanton, Randy Wicker, and Allen Windsor.)

AGUA BUENA HUMAN RIGHTS

Triangulo Rosa, a "pink triangle" association founded with help by ASIBEHU in Costa Rica, was funded with money from the International Humanist and Ethical Union (IHEU). Richard Stern was instrumental in its working with HIV-positives and people with AIDS under the direction of Guillermo Murillo. In 1998, because of problems within the association, the two founded *Asociación Agua Buena Pro Defensa de Los Derechos Humanos y Minorias* (The Agua Buena Human Rights Association, Apartado 366-2200, Coronado, Costa Rica.).

Agung, Ide Anak Agung Gde (1921—)

The Raja of Bali is a traditional Hindu leader, concerned that his island will be changed by the tourist trade into a commercialized Waikiki Beach. To counter such a tendency, in 1992 he arranged a royal cremation ceremony for his late wife and mother. The ceremony was not to mourn their deaths but, rather, to rejoice over the liberation of their souls and the ascent of those souls into the heavens. Heaven, the older Balinese hold, is a destination much like their earthly idyllic island home. "We believe," said the Raja, "that on the day of the cremation, the soul is freed and begins its journey to Nirvana." The raja, who is the 10th head of the House of Gianyar, is one of the traditional Hindu leaders of Bali, now a province of the mostly Muslim nation of Indonesia. During the ceremony, according to *The New York Times* reporter Philip Shenon, "thousands watched as massive wooden sarcophagi in the shape of sacred cattle were set ablaze. Six high priests shot wooden arrows, tipped with jasmine petals instead of a blade, into the air to direct the souls heavenward." Inasmuch as such practices wherever followed in the world are unscientific and contribute to a belief in superstition, they are held by non-believers to be of negative value.

AHA: See entry for American Humanist Association.

Ahlquist, Keith (20th Century)

Ahlquist in Britain is active with the Greater Manchester Humanists.

Ahlstrom, Sidney E. (20th Century)

Ahlstrom in 1951 wrote his Harvard Ph. D. thesis on the subject of the rationalism of Francis Ellingwood Abbott, a Unitarian. In 1987, he wrote *The Scientific Theist.* {FUS}

Ahrens, Heinrich (1808—1874)

Ahrens was a German jurist, a pantheist interested in the work of K. F. C. Krause. He lectured on German philosophy at Paris, taught in Brussels, and was appointed Deputy to the Frankfort Parliament in 1848, where he was prominent among the liberals. {RAT}

AHRIMAN

Ahriman, or Angra Mainyu the son of Zuruam, is the personified principle of evil, the one opposed to Orzmazd, in the Zoroastrian religion. Some scholars believe Ahriman and the dualism of evil and good were Judaism's inspiration for Satan. (See entry for Satan.) {ER; LEE}

AHURA MAZDAH

Ahura Mazdah, or Ormazd, was a god in the Zoroastrian religion. (See entry for Zoroaster.) {ER; JMRH}

AIDS

HIV (Human Immuno-deficiency Virus), which is believed to be the cause of the disease of AIDS (Acquired Immune Deficiency Syndrome), is the twentieth century's plague, one which has killed and continues to kill millions of human beings throughout the world. By the end of 1999, over sixteen million had died.

Nature (February 1998) reported that HIV is a virus that has hopped over the "species barrier" and into mankind from another animal. It was thought that the virus crossed from chimpanzees to humans in the late 1940s or early 1950s in Congo. Not until 1999 was it confirmed that the source of HIV-1 is almost certainly a subspecies of chimpanzee called Pan troglodytes troglodytes. The simian immunodeficiency virus (SIV) that affects monkeys and apes closely resembles HIV-1. Another virus, not that closely related and known as HIV-2, comes from a monkey called the sooty mangabey. According to a team of researchers led by Dr. Beatrice Hahn from the University of Alabama, this central African subspecies carries a simian version of HIV-1. Other than sexual contact, the only way to transmit these viruses is via blood. The supposition is that it was transmitted to humans who had butchered or handled chimpanzee meat.

A Bantu man in 1959, living in what was then the Belgian Congo and now is the Democratic Republic of Congo, gave a blood sample that is the first known incident, according to *Poz* (June 1998). According to *Nature*, Andre Nahmias of Emory University in Atlanta found that the form of AIDS now spreading worldwide was a "hop" which took place only once, implying that there was a true "patient zero," not necessarily the Bantu who had given a blood sample to some American physicians but certainly not the previously rumored gay airline steward who had been thought to have spread the disease unknowingly during his wide travels.

By the end of 1998, AIDS virus infections worldwide had risen ten percent over the previous year. Overall, the number of people infected with HIV, the human immuno-deficiency virus that causes acquired immune deficiency syndrom (AIDS), had risen to an estimated forty-seven million.

All but five percent of the infections occurred in Asia, Africa, and Eastern Europe. In five of India's states, more than one percent of pregnant women in urban areas had become infected. In Botswana, Namibia, Swaziland, and Zimbabwe, from twenty to twenty-six percent of people from the ages fifteen to thirty-nine had become infected. Asked why they had not used an available condom, Zimbabwans have been known to respond, "Would you eat a sweet with its wrapper on?" Some young Ugandan women have been told that without male sperm they will not grow up to be beautiful. Despite such staggering rates, many countries' officials refused to discuss the situation or even admit it existed, a major reason for the disease's continuation. In Kenya, as a protest Christian and Islamic groups have burned anti-AIDS leaflets and condoms, explaining that their aim was to reduce promiscuity.

In Senegal, forty percent of women under the ages of twenty-five, and sixty-five percent of men, used condoms in non-monogamous sexual relations in 1997, compared with fewer than five percent for both sexes at the start of the decade. Such a shift was attributed to educational programs.

United Nations observers in 1998 reported that AIDS had become the number one, malaria the number two, and tuberculosis the number three killer of human beings. An estimated 5,500 AIDS funerals were held daily in sub-Saharan Africa. Observed *The Economist* (7 February 1998), "an anonymous African who somehow and in some manner that will probably remain forever unknown, tangled with a chimpanzee and came away with more than he bargained for." In 1999, evidence existed that some individuals might have become infected with the simian strain, known as SIV.cpz, through exposure to blood in hunting and dressing meat. Unexplained is where that simian strain came from. Edward Hooper, in an overly wordy *The River: A Journey Back to the Source of HIV and AIDS* (1999), suggested that CHAT, a vaccine to treat chimpanzee polio, is somehow connected and that samples at Wistar Institute in Philadelphia need to be tested to see if somehow a link exists between vaccine workers and a Belgian Congo chimpanzee-research station. (See entries for Priests—who are dying at a rate four times higher than the general population—and Plague.) {*The Economist*, 13 November 1999; NY Review of Books, *2 December 1999*}

Aiken, Conrad (1889—1973)

A Pulitzer Prize-winning poet, Aiken when asked about humanism responded to the present author:

> Yes, I suppose I'm a naturalistic humanist, if I'm anything–that, and an evolutionist–I am against all forms of supernaturalism, dogma, myth, church–primarily I believe in the evolution of consciousness as something we're embarked on willy-nilly, the evolution of *mind,* and that devotion to this is all the devotion we need. You will find these and other pertinent views in the prefaces to the individual poems in my collected "symphonies," *The Divine Pilgrim*, Georgia University Press, 1949.

{CL; CE; HNS; WAS, 30 March 1951}

Aiken, Wayne (20th Century)

Aiken, who introduced the American Atheist Forum on North Carolina cable access television, was recipient of the Outreach Award by American Atheists, Inc. E-mail: <waiken@atheists.org>

Aikenhead, Thomas (1678—1697)

A Scottish undergraduate of Edinburgh University, Aikenhead was a martyr of freethought. McCabe notes that, brooding over his bible, Aikenhead came to the conclusion that it was "a rhapsody of ill-contrived nonsense" and said so. After a travesty of a trial, the eighteen-year-old was condemned and hanged for calling the Old Testament "Ezra's Fables," ridiculing the doctrines of the Trinity and the Incarnation, and expressing the hope and belief that Christianity would be extinct within a century. He had no counsel at the trial, and the only witnesses were those of the prosecutor. Found guilty, he reluctantly retracted what he had said. But Lord Advocate Stewart "called for blood" and the clergy, afraid William III might offer clemency, successfully pressed for Aikenhard's death. He became the last person executed for blasphemy in Britain, 12 January 1697, in Edinburgh. {JM; JMRH; RAT; RE}

Ainsbury, Len (20th Century)

Ainsbury in Britain is active with the Worcestershire Humanist Group.

AIR

Along with water, air is one of Earth's treasures. Both water and air are shockingly taken for granted by most. Air is colorless, odorless, and tasteless. It envelops Earth. It is a gaseous mixture, mainly nitrogen (approximately 78%) and oxygen (approximately 21%), with lesser amounts of argon, carbon dioxide, hydrogen, neon, helium, and other gases. Freethinker Joseph Priestley (1733-1804) in 1774 was the first to announce that he had isolated oxygen; however, Carl Wilhelm Scheele (1742-1786) had discovered oxygen in 1772 but not publicized his findings. The fact that the gas is a component of the atmosphere was finally and definitely established by Antoine Laurent Lavoisier (1743-1794)—he disproved the earlier theory of phlogiston, and his *Traité él'mentaire de chimie* (1789) contained the ideas which set chemistry on its modern path. Most aquatic animals use a respiratory organ called a gill to obtain oxygen by breathing water. Most other animals use a nose. In Australia, scientists have found that a newborn mouse—a marsupial called the Julia Creek dunnart—gets its oxygen through its skin. Its offspring are among the smallest newborn mammals known, about one-sixth of an inch long and weighing slightly more than half an ounce. The young mouse's skin is hairless and rich in blood, providing a convenient means for gas exchange. For mice up to about four ounces in weight, respiration through the skin exceeded that through the lungs. But as the mice grew more, the lungs took over. (CE; *Nature*, March 1999)

Airoldi, J. (Born 1829)

An Italian lawyer, Airoldi was a Swiss-born freethinker who wrote poetry. {BDF}

Airy, George Biddell (Sir) (1801—1892)

Airy, the Astronomer Royal and director of the Royal Greenwich Observatory from 1835 to 1881, made discoveries in theoretical and practical optics, including the cylindrical lens for correcting astigmatisms, an eye defect he himself possessed. His *Notes on the Earlier Hebrew Scriptures* (1876) rejects revelation and miracles. McCabe notes that Airy "was a Theist but assured the public that he regarded 'the ostensible familiarity of the biblical historian with the counsels of the Omnipotent as merely oriental allegories.' " {BDF; JM; RAT; RE}

Aithen, Martha Chapman (19th Century)

Aithen was ordained as Unitarian minister in 1894, one of the early graduates of Meadville/Lombard Theological School. {*World*, May-June 1995}

Aitzema, Lieuwe van (1600—1669)

A nobleman of Friesland and author of a suppressed history of the Netherlands, Aitzema was an atheist. He represented the Hanseatic towns at the Hague from 1645 until his death and was noted for his scholarship and integrity. {BDF; RAT}

Ajnat, Surendra (1948—)

Ajnat is author of *Critique on Vedas, An Atheist View* (1977), *Old Testament of Indian Atheism* (1977), and *Hindu Epics* (c. 1977). {GS}

Akbar (1542—1605)

Jalal-ed-din Muhammad, called the greatest of the emperors of India, was famous for his efficient administration and improvement of the empire. He showed toleration alike to

Christians, Muslims, and to all forms of the Hindu faith. Raised a Muslim, Akbar the Great became a theist, rejected the Islamic religion, acknowledged but one God, and rejected all other dogmas. His Grand Vizier had the same views. Muslims and Jesuits may have called him an atheist, but "If this is the definition of an atheist, the more we have of them the better," commented India's Jawaharlal Nehru. {BDF; JM}

AKDITI

Akditi in India is known as the mother of gods. {LEE}

Akerley, Ben Edward (20th Century)

Akerley, an atheist, wrote *The X-Rated Bible* (1985). The Christian Bible, he found, was filled with stories about rape, incest, murder, adultery, husband-swapping, misogyny, and perversions of various kinds. Web: <www.FeralHouse.com>.

AKH: See entry for Resurrection.

Akhenaton (14th Century B.C.E.): See entry for Ikhnaton, King of Ancient Egypt.

Akhilananda [Swami] (20th Century)

Swami Akhilananda, of the Ramakrishna Vedanta Society of Massachusetts, reviewed in *The Humanist* the translation by Swami Prabhavananda and Christopher Isherwood of *Bhagavad-Gita* (1954). A popularization of the teachings of the Upanishads, the work is one of the basic sources of Hindu religion and philosophy. In it, Krishna gives equal place to unselfish humanitarian work, the path of love, and the path of rationalism, meditation, or knowledge. He also tells that only immature persons make a differentiation among these paths or methods, as every one of them can lead to the realization of the ultimate Truth or Reality. In this respect Buddhism, which is regarded as ethical idealism, shows also that if anyone lives according to the Eightfold Path of right living, et cetera, he can know "the Truth." Saying the Gita has a non-sectarian attitude which emphasizes that any kind of worship, unselfish work, or any other method can lead one to the state of illumination, the swami adds that a person can have "peace of mind and abiding happiness, whether he is a humanist, agnostic, dualist, qualified monist, or monist." {WAS, 22 February 1954}

Akkermans, Tony (20th Century)

Akkermans writes for the British secular humanist monthly, *The Freethinker*. He has cited John Toland (1670—1722) as the first Irishman on record as a sceptic and a philosopher. In just four decades, he wrote in *Gay & Lesbian Humanist* (Spring, 1998), the Dutch Humanist Association has gained considerable status. The prime minister and half the cabinet attended its 40th anniversary celebrations. Humanist counselors are found in prisons, hospitals, and the armed forces. Voluntary euthanasia is widely available. Schoolgirl pregnancies are the lowest in Europe. Furthermore, sixty percent of the population now says it has no religion. {*The Freethinker*, June 1997}

ALABAMA FREETHINKERS and HUMANISTS

- *Alabama Freethinker*, PO Box 447, Ariton, AL 36311
- Alabama Freethought Association, PO Box 571, Tallaadego, Alabama 35161 (256) 362-8729. They publish a newsletter edited by Temy R. Beal. (See entry for Roger Cleveland.)
- The Freethought Forum meets in Huntsville, Alabama, and can be reached at (205) 828-9135. A University of Alabama student, Adam Butler <abutler@uab.edu>, maintains the group's homepage <http://www.mindspring.com/~alfreethought/>.
- O. Andrews Ferguson is coordinator for the American Humanist Association, Mid Atlantic Region (AHA), A-140, 1 College Row, Brevard, North Carolina 28712.
- University of Alabama's Birmingham Freethought Society is found on the Web: <www.secularhumanism.org/cfa/orgs.html>.
- University of South Alabama's humanists: <http://www.secularhumanism.org/cfa/orgs.html>.

Alain: See entry for Émile Auguste Chartier.

ALASKA ATHEISTS

Clyde Baxley is President of Atheists of Alaska, 3713 Deborah Lane, Anchorage, AK 99504. {FD}

Al Azim, Sadik (20th Century)

Al Azim, in Damascus, Syria, signed Humanist Manifesto 2000.

Albaida, Don Jose M. Orense [Marquis] (19th Century)

Albaida, one of the founders of Spain's Republican Party, was expelled for his principles. Upon returning to Spain, he became president of the Cortes in 1869. {BDF}

Albee, Edward (1928—)

The American playwright Albee is best known for his *Who's Afraid of Virginia Woolf* (1962; film 1966). The play is about an all-night drinking bout in which a middle-aged professor and his wife verbally lacerate each other. Albee has consistently denied that he originally had two males in mind rather than the married couple, but he has made no secret of his own homosexuality.

Abandoned at birth by his natural parents, he was adopted by millionaires Frances and Reed Albee who, according to Mel Gussow's biography, paid $133.30 for him. A rebellious child, he was expelled from three prep schools and a military academy before graduating from Choate. Albee won Pulitzer Prizes for *A Delicate Balance* (1967) and *Seascape* (1975).

In 1996 he was feted by President Bill Clinton in the White House and received the 1996 National Medal of Arts Award. Salman Rushdie has written that when he performed as an actor on Pakistani TV in Albee's *The Zoo Story* (1959), he had to cut a line about God's being a colored queen who wears a kimono, plucks His eyebrows, and indifferently files His nails.

Albee is said by Tribe to be an avowed freethinker. In partial confirmation, Albee told the present author that he is a nominal Quaker who admires the group's pacificism, that he thinks Jesus lived, that he is interested in Jesus's outlook, that he does not know about secular humanism, and that although he likes Christianity he does not accept "all that divinity stuff." {AA; CE; TRI; TYD; WAS, 10 December 1996}

Albee, John (1833—1915)

Albee was an American writer who abandoned the orthodox theology in which he had been trained for the liberal theism or pantheism of Emerson. In *Remembrances of Emerson* (1903), Albee wrote, "Growth ends with the birth of creeds." {RAT}

Alberdi, Juan Bautista (1810—1884)

Alberdi was an Argentine political philosopher, patriot, and diplomat. Because of his opposition to Manuel de Rosas, Alberdi spent years of exile in Uruguay, Chile, and in Europe. When Rosas was overthrown by Justo José de Urquiza in 1852, Alberdi returned and served on a number of diplomatic missions. He major work was *Bases y puntos de partida para la organización de la república argentina* (1852). Many of his suggestions were incorporated into the Argentine constitution of 1853.

After Urquiza was defeated in 1861, Alberdi moved to Paris and wrote political tracts against Bartolomé Mitre and Domingo Faustino Sarmiento. He and President Sarmiento, however, were both anticlerical and were opposed to the Catholic Church in Argentina. {CE; EU; WAS, conversations with Hugo Estrella.}

Alberger, John (19th Century)

Alberger, an American, wrote *Monks, Popes, and Their Political Intrigues* (1871) and *Antiquity of Christianity* (1874). {BDF}

Albert, John (20th Century)

Albert, an atheist in Phoenix, Arizona, wrote "The Perception of the Prevalence of Belief" in *Secular Nation* (April-June 1998).

ALBIGENSIANS, MASSACRE OF THE (1211—1215)

Innocent III deliberately ordered and directed the brutal slaughter of at least 100,000 men, women, and children, but probably a quarter of a million more, according to McCabe. They were heretics in the central part of the principality of Toulouse. Both Catholic and Protestant historians have failed to report objectively what happened.

In an extant letter, according to McCabe, "the Pope instructed his Legates to disarm the

Count of Toulouse by lying, and to the end he treated that prince with the gravest injustice. As the 'Crusaders' slew 20,000 (including babes in arms) in the first city they took—it is here that the Monk-Legate is reported to have said, 'Slay all, the Lord will know his own,' which is at least what they did—and the slaughter continued for three years; its monstrous proportions may be imagined." (See entry for Catharism, which held that Jesus did not die on a cross, that he married Mary Magdalen. The Albigenses were a branch of the Cathari. A summary of their doctrine of salvation is in the 18th century hymn "Eternal Light, Eternal Light.") {RE}

Albini, Giuseppe (1863—1933)

An Italian physiologist and freethinker, Albini wrote on embryology and other physiological subjects. {BDF}

Alboum, Marty (20th Century)

Alboum is secretary of the Humanists of New Jersey.

ALCHEMY

Alchemy, with its seemingly magical power or process of transmuting, has over the centuries attracted believers in the supernatural. Once a medieval chemical philosophy, it aimed at transmuting base metals into gold, the discovery of the panacea, and the preparation of the elixir of longevity.

Although it fell into disrepute, the searching quests of the alchemists led eventually to the scientific quests of chemists.

Alchindus (Died c. 864)

Yakub Ibn Is'hak Ibn Subbah (Abú Yúsuf) was an Arab physician and philosopher. Called Al Kindi, he was the great grandson of one of the companions of Muhammad, the prophet.

A rationalist in religion, he was denigrated as a magician because of his scientific studies. {BDF}

Alciati, Giovanni Paolo (Died 1570)

A Milanese of noble family, Alciati at first was a Romanist. He resigned that faith for Calvinism but gradually advanced to anti-trinitarianism, which he defended in two letters (1564 and 1565) to Gregorio Pauli.

Although Beza claimed Alciadi became a Muslim, Bayle takes pains to disprove this. {BDF}

Alcock, James (20th Century)

Alcock, a professor of psychology at York University in Toronto, Canada, is on the Executive Council of the Committee for the Scientific Investigation of Claims of the Paranormal, which publishes *Skeptical Inquirer*.

He is author of *Parapsychology, Science or Magic* (1981) and *Science and Supernatural* (1990).

ALCOHOL

- Alcohol is Satan's starter fluid.

Anonymous,
but likely said by a preacher who was absent at seminary when
served the Holy Eucharist (the administering of bread
and wine to thank God for the work of Christ)

- I feel sorry for people who don't drink, because when they get up in the morning, that's as good as they're going to feel all day.

—Frank Sinatra,
noted singer and Catholic

Alcott, Abigail May (1800—1877)

Alcott, wife of social reformer and transcendentalist Bronson Alcott, was mother of novelist Louisa May Alcott. She was a member of King's Chapel, her father having been one of the leaders that changed that church from the faith of the Church of England to become the first Unitarian church in the United States. {EG}

Alcott, (Amos) Bronson (1799—1888)

Alcott was an American educational and social reformer who founded the Temple School in Boston. He was a leading exponent of transcendentalism, although he differed with others by being opposed to any doctrine of individualism. His philosophy, mediating between the extreme idealistic and materialistic positions, was summed up in the term Personalism. A Unitarian, he believed that all seemingly separate minds are linked together by a common relation to a central Mind—that is, as he said, "all souls have a Personal identity with God and abide in Him."

Carlyle looked upon him indulgently as a man "bent on saving the world by a return to acorns and the golden age." Emerson said, "As pure intellect I have never seen his equal." Thoreau agreed, adding that Alcott was "the sanest man I ever knew." In 1859, Alcott became superintendent and reformed the Concord, Massachusetts, schools, introducing the teaching of singing, dancing, reading aloud, and such novel subjects as physiology. His work in education culminated in the Concord School of Philosophy (1879—1888), which had a profound influence on education through his disciple W. T. Harris and others. Although he lived much of his life in poverty, he was supported by his daughter, Louisa May Alcott, who in 1868 earned money by publishing *Little Women*, a work based on her family life. {CE; FUS; OCAL; RAT}

Alcott, Louisa May (1832—1888)

The author of *Little Women* (1868)—the daughter of educationalist and transcendentalist Bronson Alcott, a friend of Emerson, and a women's suffrage activist—was a nominal Unitarian. Alcott is said to have had a lifelong fear of one day going mad, and it is possible that she did suffer from deep anxiety and may once have had a nervous breakdown at the time of her Civil War nursing service. Recovering from typhoid, which she contracted while working in a Washington hospital, she often dreamed she had married a handsome Spaniard who whispered to her, "Lie still my dear!" The experience likely led to the creation of one of her fictional characters, Philip Tempest, a modern villain in mid-nineteenth century dress: "I seem a brute, but it is my love which drives me to such harsh measures," he moans.

Her publisher may have thought *Little Women* was boring, as she once was quoted as believing, but the work was a publishing success and continues to be her best known. In it, Professor Bhaer lectures her, the one of four sisters who aspires to be a writer, about the sensational tales she wrote for journals. "I would more rather give my boys gunpowder to play with than this bad trash," the priggish and repulsive man tells her. Alcott observed later, "I almost wish I hadn't any conscience; it's so inconvenient." And, as noted by novelist Stephen King, her reflections are followed "by what is surely the most horrible sentence in *Little Women*, the one that finishes 'and Jo corked up her ink-stand.' "

King also liked her *A Long Fatal Love Chase* (1866), in which Rose, the heroine, disguises herself as a boy and a nun, stays in an asylum (called a madhouse in those days), discovers that Baptiste is a notorious escaped criminal, and in many heated pages arranges a chaste romance with a priest.

The work, King noted, "ends on a darker note than any modern editor would be comfortable with, I suspect, but one in chilling harmony with any contemporary newspaper's front-page story of domestic abuse escalating into madness and murder. Dying by his own hand, Phillip gathers Rose's sodden corpse in his arms and voices the novel's creepy last line: 'Mine first–mine last–mine even in the grave!' " King notes that "this is quite a distance from the sunny sensibilities and high moral tone of *Little Women*."

Marylynne Diggs has written about the homoeroticism in two of Alcott's stories. In *Work: A Story of Experience* (1873), Christie and Rachel's romantic friendship involves a "vaguely described sin." And in *An Old-*

Fashioned Girl (1870), Rebecca and Lizzie are "mannish and rough," a "different race of creatures."

Unlike Emerson, Alcott believed in a personal God, even had paranormal experiences. When her sister Lizzie died, she wrote, "A few moments after the last breath came, as Mother and I sat silently watching the shadow fall on the dear little face, I saw a light mist rise from the body, and float up and vanish in the air. Mother's eyes followed mine, and when I said, 'What did you see?' she described the same light mist."

Grief-stricken, she went to Theodore Parker's church after her sister's death. Alcott was greatly influenced by Parker and by Henry David Thoreau. (One would be hard put now, a hundred years later, to find a Unitarian who has seen light mists rise from the deceased.)

Yet, Alcott did not believe in the Christian Trinity. E. D. Walker's *Reincarnation: A Study of Forgotten Truth* (1888) quotes Alcott as saying, "I must have been masculine (in my previous life) because my love is all for girls." According to a biography by Katharine Anthony in 1938, "The Alcott family were what is known among the orthodox as without religious affiliation." Mrs. Alcott "clung to her old King's Chapel faith. . . . The family had no orthodox church."

Alcott is buried on a rising ground called Authors' Ridge at Sleepy Hollow Cemetery in Concord, Massachusetts. Nearby are the remains of Henry David Thoreau and Ralph Waldo Emerson. (See entry for Bronson Alcott.) {CE; Marylynne Diggs, "Romantic Friendship, Female," GL; EG; Stephen King, "Blood and Thunder in Concord," *The New York Times Book Review*, 10 September 1995; PE; PUT; TYD; U; UU}

Alder, Rodger (1947—1997)

Alder, a Labour Party supporter, became deputy leader in England of the Northampton Borough Council and chairman of its planning committee. Alder was a senior lecturer in industrial archaeology at Northampton's Nene College. A trustee of the Pink Triangle Trust, Alder died of cancer. His Humanist funeral ceremony was held in the Great Hall of Northampton's Guildhall.

Aldergrove, John Romney (20th Century)

Aldergrove wrote *Enemies: The Rationalist View of Human Nature* (1998). A Canadian, he is critical of religion, politics, and sex, and shows why matters are the way they are. His concern is that rational individuals often remain silent instead of speaking out against irrationality. His book is not about the conflict between religion and rationality, for he accepts the nonexistence of gods as a given, then proceeds. He is negatively critical of psychiatry, the jury system, circumcision, the alleged existence of a "soul," and other controversial subjects. Aldergrove is aware that both Islam and Christianity may have originated as a consequence of hallucinations accompanying epileptic fits. {*The American Rationalist*, November-December 1998}

Aldred, Guy Alfred (1886—1963)

Aldred was an English atheist and anarchist, the subject of John Taylor Caldwell's biography entitled *Come Dungeons Dark*. Royle says Aldred settled in Glasgow "to propagate communism and the views of Richard Carlile."

In 1940 Aldred wrote *Dogmas Discarded* (1940) and in 1941 *Armageddon Incorporated, the True Story of the Jehovah's Witnesses*. {FUK; GS; RSR}

Aldridge, Alfred Owen (1915—)

An English language educator, Aldridge was professor of comparative literature at the University of Buffalo. From 1986—1987 he held the Will and Ariel Durant chair at St. Peter's College in Jersey City, New Jersey. He has taught at Pennsylvania State University as well as in Korea, France, Brazil, Japan, Kuwait, and Taiwan.

Aldridge in 1959 wrote *Man of Reason, the Life of Thomas Paine*. In 1987 he wrote *Benjamin Franklin and Nature's God*. Starting in 1963, Aldridge edited the *Journal of Comparative Literary Studies*. {FUK}

Aleiri, Vittorio [Count] (1749—1802)

Aleiri, a leading Italian tragedian of the eighteenth century, wrote works that ran to twenty-two volumes. In a two-volume work on despotism, *Della Tyrannide*, Aleiri rejects all religion and says that "the heretics are as stupid as the Catholics." {JM}

d'Alembert, Jean le Rond (1717—1783)

The illegitimate son of the chevalier Destouches and a famous hostess, Mme. de Tencin, Alembert was named for the St. Jean le Rond church where he had been found on the steps. Diderot in approximately 1746 made him co-editor of the *Encyclopédie*, for which he wrote mathematical, literary, and philosophical articles. Because of his unorthodox views, however, he withdrew from the staff. Just the same, he was secretary of the French Academy (1772) and a leading representative of the Enlightenment.

His treatise on dynamics (1743) enunciated what is called d'Alembert's Principle. He wrote an important history of the Academy (1787). *Pensées philosophiques* shows his freethought, as does his book on the Jesuits, *Sur la destruction des Jésuites en France* (1765), and the general rationalism of his Preliminary Discourse to the *Encyclopédie*. Alembert was one of Voltaire's staunchest friends, and his work successfully made the *Index Librorum Prohibitorum*.

"As for the existence of a supreme intelligence," he wrote to Frederick the Great, "I think that those who deny it advance far more than they can prove, and skepticism is the only reasonable course." He goes on to say, however, that experience invincibly proves the materiality of the "soul."

McCabe notes that d'Alembert "preferred to call himself a skeptic rather than an atheist, thinking that the latter implied an express denial of the existence of God . . . and he is convinced that the soul or mind is merely a function of the brain."

D'Alembert's last days were spent conversing with friends. He liked to hear others' views as well as tell stories of his own. Said Condorcet, "He only was able to think of other subjects than himself, and to give himself to gaiety and amusement." {BDF; CE; FO; ILP; JM; JMR; JMRH; PUT; RAT ; RE; TRI}

Alexander VI [Rodrigo de Borja, Spanish; Rodrigo Borgia, Italian] (1431?—1503)

Pope Alexander VI, the successor to Pope Innocent VIII, allegedly was the father of ten illegitimate children, four while he was Cardinal Borgia. One of his children, Lucrezia Borgia, inspired Victor Hugo's drama and Donizetti's opera. His youngest son, Cesare, was an important figure of the Italian Renaissance. His mother's brother, Alfonso, was Pope Calixtus III. The lax moral tone of Renaissance Rome has made Alexander's name symbolic of the worldly irreligion of Renaissance popes. Although he is known as a political strategist and church administrator, Alexander VI was severely criticized by Girolamo Savonarola. His name has become a symbol of the Renaissance popes' worldly irreligion.

According to McCabe, "Official documents establishing the birth of six of his children were published from the archives of the Duke of Ossuna, and the Vatican then admitted that it had copies of the same documents (birth-certificates, etc.), so that even Catholic writers have yielded."

William Manchester, in *A World Lit Only by Fire: The Medieval Mind and the Renaissance*, has described some of the Pope's parties:

> Once he became Pope Alexander VI, Vatican parties already wild, grew wilder. . . . As guests approached the papal palace, they were excited by the spectacle of living statues: naked, guilded young men and women in erotic poses. . . . After the banquet dishes had been cleared away, the city's fifty most beautiful whores danced with guests, "first clothed, then naked" [According to the diarist Johann Burchard]. The dancing over, the "ballet" began, with the pope and two of his children in the best seats.
>
> Candelabra were set up on the floor; scattered among them were chestnuts, "which," Burchard writes, "the courtesans had to pick up, crawling between the candles." Then the serious sex started. Guests stripped and ran out on the floor, where they mounted, or were mounted by, the prostitutes. "The coupling took place," according to Burchard, "in front of everyone present." Servants kept score of each man's orgasms, for the pope greatly admired virility and measured a man's machismo by his ejaculative capacity. After everyone was exhausted, His Holiness distributed prizes—cloaks, boots, caps, and fine silken tunics. The winners, the diarist wrote, were those "who made love with those courtesans the greatest number of times."

{CE; JMRH; RE}

Alexander, Charles and **Ezra** (18th Century)

Charles and Ezra Alexander, both of whom signed the Mecklenburg Declaration of Independence, were freethinkers. (See entry for North Carolina Freethinkers.)

Alexander, David (20th Century)

Alexander is owner of Centerline Press and, from 1990—1992, was editor of *The Humanist*. Both in the US and in Europe, he has noted, of the estimated 150,000 Unitarians in the US, 75% identify themselves as secular and/or religious humanists. In short, he implies that these people join the Unitarians rather than the humanist groups. Under his editorship he published an extensive interview with Gene Roddenberry and another with Dan Rather (the latter, a television notable, not being a secular humanist). Alexander, whose biography of Roddenberry is *"Star Trek" Creator* (1994), is a member of the Council for Secular Humanism's Faith-Healing Investigation Project, and he writes for *The Freethinker*.

Alfieri, Vittorio [Count] (1749—1802)

Alfieri in his poetry and drama attacked Catholicism as well as Christianity. "Born among a people slavish, ignorant, and already entirely subjugated by priests," he wrote, "the Christian religion knows only how to enjoin the blindest obedience and is unacquainted even with the name of liberty." His *Saul* has been prohibited on the English stage, according to Wheeler. {BDF; JMRH; RAT}

Alfonso X [King] (1223—1284)

Alfonso X the Wise, King of Castille and of Leon, was a patron of science and a lover of astronomy. Because of his independence shown toward the Pope and his free disposal of the clerical revenues, he was stigmatized as an atheist. To him is attributed the well-known remark that had he been present at the creation of the world, he would have proposed some improvements. {BDF; JMRH}

Algarotti, Francesco [Count] (1712—1761)

An Italian writer on science, history, and philosophy, Algarotti won high favor with Frederick the Great, Augustus of Saxony, and even (at first) Pope Clement XIV, who pronounced him "one of those rare men whom one would fain love even beyond the grave." A friend of Voltaire and a deist, Algarotti had a monument erected to him by Frederick the Great. {JM; JMRH; RAT}

ALGEBRA

The branch of mathematics concerned with operations on sets of numbers or other elements that are often represented by symbols was developed by medieval Islamic scholars and was named algebra (after *al-jabr*, an Arabic word meaning the reduction, the removing of an equation's negative terms). *Jabr wa-al-Muqabalah* (The Book of al-Jabr and al-Muqabalah), written approximately in 825 by the Persian mathematician al-Khwarizmi (*algorithm* is taken from his name), contains word problems, because Arabic numerals had not yet been introduced, so numbers were represented by symbols. {CE; DGC}

ALGEMEEN HUMANISTISCH TREPUNT

Algemeen Humanistisch Trefpunt, POB 1045, 2340 BA Oegstgeest, Netherlands, is an active Dutch humanist group.

Alger, Horatio Jr. (1832—1899)

Author of *Ragged Dick* (1867–1868), Alger was reared by strict Puritan parents, but in 1864 he became a Unitarian minister in the Cape Cod town of Brewster, Massachusetts.

However, accused of "the abominable and revolting crime of unnatural familiarity with boys," namely fifteen-year-old John Clark and his thirteen-year-old friend, Thomas Crocker, Alger left town for New York City. Concentrating upon his writing although allegedly "adopting" several youngsters "informally" without any scandals, he wrote popular novels, over twenty million copies of which have been sold. The 130 titles were based on the principle that if a boy struggles against poverty and temptation, he will eventually achieve wealth and fame.

His father, **Horatio Alger Sr.**, was a Unitarian minister in several small Massachusetts areas. Alger is buried at Glenwood Cemetery, ten miles southwest of Boston in South Natick. The pallbearers included seven respected citizens, all former orphan boys whom Alger had befriended. {CE; U; UU}

Alger, William Rounseville (1822—1905)

Alger was a Unitarian clergyman who wrote *Critical History of the Doctrine of a Future Life*. In 1990, Gary Scharnhorst wrote *A Literary Biography of William R. Alger, A Neglected Member of the Concord Circle* showing Alger's connections with Emerson and the elder Henry James.

Although Henry James Sr. alleged that Horatio Alger wrote a biography of Edwin Forrest, it was William, his cousin, who had done so. William, not Alger, had had a breakdown and been at an asylum in Somerville, Massachusetts. Part of the confusion is related to Henry James's alleged changing of dates, suppression of facts, and rewriting of passages from other people's letters. {Louis Menand, "William James & the Case of the Epileptic Patient," *The New York Review of Books*, 17 December 1998} {BDF}

Algeri, Pomponio (Died 1566)

A youth of Nola who studied at Padua, Algeri was accused of heresy and atheism. In 1566 Algeri was burned alive in a cauldron of boiling oil, pitch, and turpentine, courtesy of his loving Christian neighbors. {BDF}

ALGERIAN HUMANISM: See entry for Frantz Fanon. Also see entry for Lounes Matoub, who was murdered in 1998 "for his freethinking and his defiant mountain music."

Algie, William (19th Century)

In Canada, Algie was president from 1885 to 1889 of the Canadian Secular Union. In 1884, small societies were reported in Welland, St. Thomas, and Aylmer, Gananoque, Belleville, and Ottawa. The Toronto Freethought Society changed its name to Secular in the 1880s, and in Ottawa the Pioneer Freethought Club was formed in 1880. {RSR}

Aliabadi, Ali (20th Century)

In 1995, Aliabadi and Brie Waters founded the Atheist Students' Association (ASA) at the University of Maryland in College Park. He also was one of the founders of the Campus Freethought Alliance. {*International Humanist News*, December 1996}

Alice, Maud Mary [Princess] (1843—1878)

The daughter of Queen Victoria of England, Alice was a skeptic. So was her sister, the Empress Frederic. Alice was a friend of D. F. Strauss, the leading anti-Christian writer in Germany, who read his study of Voltaire to her in manuscript and was permitted to dedicate it to her. Prince von Bülow in his *Memoirs* wrote, "The Grand Duchess Alice was as liberal in politics, and especially in religion, as her sister the Crown Princess." In 1937, the editor of the *Literary Guide* revealed that it was Princess Alice who had translated the article by Haeckel that appeared in the first issue of the *Agnostic Annual*, which he also edited. {RE}

ALIEN ABDUCTIONS

"[S]leep paralysis accompanying a waking dream may well be a major factor in convincing some 'abductees' they have been examined by aliens," wrote Joe Nickell (*Skeptical Inquirer*, May-June-1998). Nickell does not doubt the financial benefits of writing about having been abducted, however, noting "abduction promoters have books to offer. Let the buyer beware."

Susan Blackmore, a Bristol psychologist, wrote in the same issue that the best explanation for nearly four million Americans' saying they had certain "indicator" experiences and therefore had probably been abducted by aliens "is that they are elaborations of the experience of sleep paralysis." In a typical sleep paralysis episode, a person wakes up paralyzed, senses a presence in the room, feels fear or even terror, and may hear buzzing and humming noises or see strange lights.

ALIENS FROM OUTER SPACE

Voltaire was among the first to describe "aliens from outer space," doing so in his *Micromegas*. The aliens came from Saturn and from a planet in the solar system of the star Sirius. Unlike humans with their five or six senses, the Saturnians had seventy-two. The Sirians had a thousand.

Contemporary naturalists, who are openly skeptical about all accounts of sightings, cite the negative findings of the Committee for the Scientific Investigation of Claims of the Paranormal, which is headed by philosopher Paul Kurtz. (See entry for Voltaire.)

Alkemade, A. de Mey van (19th Century)

Alkemade was a Dutch nobleman who contributed to *De Dageraad* and also published a work in 1862 containing many Bible contradictions. In 1859 he wrote a work on the Bible but used the pen name "Alexander de M." {BDF}

Al-Kindi (c. 800-c. 870)

Al-Kindi was an Arab philosopher who was born in Kufa, Iraq. Known as "the philosopher of the Arabs," he was among the first to spread Greek thought in the Arab world, synthesizing Aristotle's and other Greeks' views, with Islamic doctrine.

Al-Kurdi, Husayn (20th Century)

Al-Kurdi, describing the Christian Right in San Diego County, California, laments that homophobia is a central facet of the Christian rightist worldview.

In Alpine, California, he reports, gay men's sexual habits are discussed at the County Board of Supervisors meetings. One individual has publicly proclaimed his obsessions with "homosexuals who stick their penis in another man's anus" and then "want to shake your hand when you don't know where that hand has been."

He also laments the anti-Mexican, the anti-Islam, and the anti-feminist feelings that the Christian right has fostered in its successful goal of sweeping over sixty candidates into local offices in 1990 in San Diego County.

ALL SAINTS DAY

All Saints Day has no relevance to freethinkers. (See Entry for Humanist Holidays.)

ALLAH, OR AL-ILAH: See entry for God. Of interest is that the word is singular and has no plural.

Allais, Giovanni (Born 1847)

Allais was an Italian physician and freethinker. {BDF}

Allan, Don (20th Century)

Allan, in "Spiritual Atheism" (*Secular Nation*, April-June 1998), argues that love, creativity, and the human spirit are atheistic values, adding, "Let us assume our rightful place as atheistic educators and celebrate the human spirit and its triumph over the darkness of superstition and illusion." He lives in St. Paul, Minnesota.

Allan, James (20th Century)

Allan is a senior lecturer in law in the faculty of law at the University of Otago, New Zealand. He is author of *A Sceptical Theory of Morality and Law* (1998), which includes a defense of a sceptical moral theory that owes much to the views of David Hume.

Allbutt, Henry A. (20th Century)

Allbutt was a Leeds secularist who published a popular *Wife's Handbook* (1884 or 1885) which reached a forty-fifth printing by 1913 and by 1929 had sold half a million copies. Although not prosecuted for its obscenity, he was struck off the register of the General Medical Council. Allbutt's sin was not only that he advocated birth control but that he advocated it at a cost of sixpence. {RSR}

Allbutt, Thomas Clifford [Sir] (1826—1925)

Allbutt was one of the most distinguished British physicians of his time. His works on medicine and the Middle Ages are valuable. He openly criticized the Church for opposing and retarding the progress of science in *Historical Relations of Medicine and Surgery* (1905). In his Harveian Oration, Allbutt professed Agnosticism: "I wonder if we are glad that the riddle of the origin and issues of being, which tormented their eager hearts, is not solved but proved insoluble." {JM; JMRH; RAT; RE}

Allegro, John (1923—1988)

Allegro, an eminent Dead Sea Scrolls scholar, edited some of the most important of the Essene documents, including the biblical commentaries. He is author in *The Dead Sea Scrolls and the Christian Myth* (1984), in which he states that the Catholic Church deleted, changed, or suppressed large amounts of the newly found material. The Church also tried to hide the Nag Hammadi library materials discovered in Egypt, because of the Gnostic writings which helped undermine the entire basis of Christian beliefs. *John* 8:44 is one example of the Gnostic influence, and other Gnostic writings describe homosexual overtones in a particular form of baptism which Jesus knew about but which the Church sought to hide. In the 1984 work, Allegro wrote

> Unlike the Jewish Talmudist or "fundamentalist" Christian, the old-time Bible-thumper, we cannot seek in any traditional revelation a detailed code of rules of conduct; we are in the last resort thrown back upon our own inadequate selves for our authoring.

Michael Baigent and Richard Leigh, in *The Dead Sea Scrolls Deception* (1992), point out that Allegro, of the original team members, was the only disinterested scholar of religion. The others were Roman Catholic theologians. Chosen because he was one of Britain's foremost authorities on Middle Eastern languages, Allegro soon found he was denied access to some materials and was not allowed to attend important conferences.

After Allegro published material stating that "the origins of some Christian ritual and doctrines can be seen in the documents of an extremist Jewish sect that existed for more than 100 years before the birth of Jesus Christ," he was discredited by his colleagues, was called anti-Christian, and was removed from the project.

He insisted, however, that the ancient myths were being misrepresented as historical fact by the church. Baigent and Leigh, similarly, imply that despite the team's international character it was highly influenced by the Vatican from the beginning.

Allegro was ridiculed for his theory, expressed in *The Sacred Mushroom and the Cross* (1970), that Western religions were based on mushroom worship. The volume studied the nature and origins of Christianity within the fertility cults of the ancient Near East, and he contended that Judaism and Christianity were products of an ancient sex-and-mushroom cult.

"The bearing of the phallus was a marked feature of the Dionysiac processionals," he wrote, "but as we now know, it had more than a purely physiological significance. The penis was not only the sign of human generation but within the mushroom cult it symbolized the sacred fungus itself, the "phallus of God."

The book contains color photos of the mushroom, *Amanita muscaria,* and after 205 pages it appends 150 pages of notes in various languages, illustrating his erudition and interest in philology.

S. Levin, commenting upon Allegro's suspicion that the whole Paul-Jesus story was somehow tied up with a fungus tale, a mushroom hallucinatory story, has written of *The End of a Road* (1971) that "in complex philosophical philandering around semen, penis and vulva, he mushroomed everything and everybody into a fungus yarn. Peter was *pitriya* (Hebrew for fungus), Jonah's overhanging bush was a mushroom, and so was Jesus. (Allegro) was rightly attacked as way off the historical mark."

However, Levin adds that "Christianity began somewhere in those Greek regions [Ephesus, Tarsus, etc.], and as a consequence of a rumour heard by Paul, and fleshed into brilliance by the effects of LSD." {*Free Inquiry*, Fall 1984; *New Humanist*, February 1996; TRI}

Allen, Charles Grant Blairfindie (1848—1899)

Allen, the son of an Irish Protestant minister and notable scholar, was born near Kingston, Ontario, Canada. He enthusiastically taught the views on evolution of Darwin and Spencer, writing *Charles Darwin* (1885) and *The Evolution of the Idea of God: An Inquiry into the Origins of Religion* (1897). Using the pseudonym Cecil Power, he wrote a three-volume novel, *Philistia*, and in 1888 he wrote *The Devil's Die*. When George Bedborough was brought to court for selling a copy of Havelock Ellis's *Sexual Inversion,* Allen, along with G. W. Foote, George Holyoake, George Bernard Shaw, Edward Carpenter, and J. M. Robertson, formed a Free Press Defence Committee on his behalf.

Allen espoused the cause of "free love," a controversial topic in his day. He agreed with Herbert Spencer concerning the origin of religion, writing, "I believe I had made it tolerably clear that the vast mass of existing gods or divine persons, when we come to analyze them, do actually turn out to be dead and deified human beings. . . . I believe that corpse worship is the protoplasm of religion." {BDF; RAT}

Allen, Christ (20th Century)

Allen is a contact for American Atheists, Inc., in Utah. E-mail: <callen@atheists.org>.

Allen, David (1961-)

Allen, a writer in Washington, D.C., is an Advisory Board Member of African Americans for Humanism.

Allen, Don (19th Century)

Allen wrote *The Resurrection of Jesus, An Agnostic's View* (1893). {GS}

Allen, Ethan [Colonel] (1738—1789)

A hero of the American Revolution, Allen in 1784 wrote, "I have generally been denominated a Deist, the reality of which I have never disputed, being conscious that I am no Christian, except mere infant baptism makes me one; and as to being a Deist, I know not, strictly speaking, whether I am one or not." He found trinitarianism "destitute of foundation, and tends manifestly to superstition and idolatry." His deistic views were similar to those of Franklin and Jefferson (and to rituals of the Masonic Lodge) as shown in his *Reason the Only Oracle of Man* (1784). Like a watchmaker, the deists hypothesized, the Supreme Architect created his work, then moved on. Analogously, people who have a watch care little who designed their watch and have no way of determining who actually made it; it is to their benefit to keep the watch repaired and working well–life's purpose is therefore not to find out which individual or committee made an object, deists explained. They rejected claims of supernatural revelation and of formal religion.

With such a philosophy, they skirted the need for a Church of America (inasmuch as the enemy George III could hardly continue to be accepted as God's representative on earth) and wrote a Constitution placing the onus on *man*, not outside forces, to rule himself under law.

Reason the Only Oracle of Man was the first openly anti-Christian book published in North America, and Allen credited many of its ideas to his fellow nonconformist in religious thought, Dr. Thomas Young. The two planned upon writing the book together, but Young died before they could finish it. The book was widely used by Universalists. Shortly after the printing, a fire broke out in the printer's warehouse and the fearful printer would not agree to publishing any further freethought books. "Ethan Allen's Bible," as the book was called among his neighbors, although it may in part have been written by Young, hit hard at Calvinist theology. Allen "in the name of the Great Jehovah and the Continental Congress" defeated the British at Fort Ticonderoga, and he was a popular contributor to the secularization and dechristianizing of early American intellectual thought.

The story is told by Valery Countryman, a St. Louis author, that Allen defied a state statute that prohibited smallpox inoculations because they were said to be "a sin against God." At a local tavern Allen convinced his physician, Thomas Young, to publicly inoculate him. Allen was then quickly arrested for the crime of blasphemy. During the trial he cursed the judge by saying, "May (you) be in Hell a thousand years and every little insipid Devil shall come by and ask why."

Ms. Countryman also describes Allen's decision to remarry after the death of his estranged spouse. "Do you promise to live in agreement to God's law?" the officiating judge inquired. "Hold on!" Allen complained. "Whose god are you talking about?" The judge eventually was persuaded to amend the offending phrase to "laws as written in the Book of Nature."

A little-known section of *Israel Potter* (1855) by Herman Melville describes Allen during his period of captivity by the British, when he was displayed in the port of Falmouth, "Samson Among the Philistines":

> Like some baited bull in the ring, crouched the Patagonian-looking captive, handcuffed as before; the grass of the green trampled, and gored up all about him, both by his own movements and those of the people around. Except some soldiers and sailors, these seemed

> mostly townspeople, collected here out of curiosity. The stranger was outlandishly arrayed in the sorry remains of a half-Indian, half-Canadian sort of dress, consisting of a fawnskin jacket–the fur outside and hanging in ragged tufts–a half-rotten, bark-like belt of wampum; aged breeches of sagathy; bedarned worsted stockings to the knee; old moccasins riddled with holes, their metal tags yellow with salt-water rust; a faded red woolen bonnet, not unlike a Russian night-cap, or a portentous, ensanguined full-moon, all soiled, and stuck about with bits of half-rotted straw. He seemed just broken from the dead leaves in David's outlawed Cave of Adullam. Unshaven, beard and hair matted, and profuse as a cornfield beaten down by hailstorms, his whole marred aspect was that of some wild beast; but of a royal sort, and unsubdued by the cage.

According to legend, Allen's wife called for a preacher as he lay dying. The man, although he knew Allen had once stated, "That Jesus Christ was not God is evident from his own words," attempted to persuade Allen to pray. "Angels are waiting for you," Allen was told. "Waiting, are they?" Allen retorted. "Well, God damn them, let them wait!"

Vermont eventually erected a forty-two-foot high granite memorial topped by an eight-foot angel decades after Allen's death and at a site where no one was sure where the body lay. A previous marker had been blasted away by lightning sixty-six years earlier. {BDF; CE; EG; EU, Darline Gay Levy and Gordon Stein; FUS; JM; JMRH; PUT; RAT; TYD; U}

Allen, Evelyn (20th Century)

In 1995 Allen became secretary of the Northeast Atheist Association.

Allen, Frank (20th Century)

Allen wrote *In Jesus' Name* (1933). {GS}

Allen, Gina (20th Century; Deceased)

Allen, a signer of Humanist Manifesto II, was on the editorial board of *The Humanist* and was a secretary of the American Humanist Association. She addressed the Tenth International Humanist and Ethical Union (IHEU) World Congress held in Buffalo (1988). A Unitarian, she wrote *Prairie Children* (1941), *On the Oregon Trail* (1942), and *Sod-House Days* (1945). She was a Humanist counsellor. {HM2}

Allen, Grant (1848—1899)

Allen wrote *The Evolution of the Idea of God* (published 1931). In a *Fortnightly Review* article entitled "The New Hedonism" (1894), Allen wrote, "It is our duty to think as far as we can think; to get rid of all dogmas, preconceptions and prejudices; to make sure we are not tied by false fears or vague terms; to examine all faiths, all beliefs, all fancies, all shibboleths, political, religious, social, moral. . . . We should each of us arrive at a consistent theory of the universe for ourselves, and of our own place in it."

Allen was a respected figure in the group of late-Victorian agnostics, a member of the Free Press Defence Committee along with George Bernard Shaw, Edward Carpenter, Hyndman, Foote, Frank Podmore, W. M. Thompson, Truelove, Holyoake, Robertson, and Herbert Burrows. {*Freethinker*, December, 1996; FUK; RSR; RE}

Allen, John (1771—1843)

Allen, a physician and writer, practiced and lectured at Edinburgh until 1801, then accompanied Lord Holland and his family to Spain for a four-year position. At Holland House, he was known as "Lady Holland's Atheist" and was "a complete sceptic," doubting if Christ had ever existed. From 1820 to 1843, Allen was master at Dulwich College. {RAT}

Allen, Leslie H. (Born 1887)

Allen edited *Bryan and Darrow at Dayton*. {FUS}

Allen, Norm R. Jr. (1957-)

Allen edited *African American Humanism, An Anthology* (1991) and is Executive Director of the Council for Secular Humanism's African Americans for Humanism.

An editorial associate for *Free Inquiry*, and that magazine's director of public relations, Allen speaks on behalf of the secular humanist movement not only in the United States but also abroad. He is a Secular Humanist Mentor of the Council for Secular Humanism.

At the 1994 Toronto conference of the Coalition for Secular Humanism, Atheism, and Freethought (CSHAFT), Allen spoke on "What Is the Good Life? A Humanist Perspective." At the 1996 Humanist World Congress held in Mexico City, Allen spoke on the subject of global humanism and human rights.

Allen wrote "Religion and the New African American Intellectuals" in a University of Minnesota publication, *Nature, Society, and Thought, A Journal of Dialectical and Historical Materialism* (1996). The editor of the *African Americans for Humanism Examiner*, Allen signed Humanist Manifesto 2000.

Allen, Ralph Edward (1895—1971)

Allen, an Australian rationalist and medical practitioner, was a director in 1938 of the Rationalist Association of Australia Ltd.

Allen, Steve (1921—)

Allen, a noted American humorist, musician, and television star, is author of *"Dumbth!" And 81 Ways to Make Americans Smarter* (1989). He also has written thirty-five other books, including *Meeting of Minds* (1989) and *Steve Allen on the Bible, Religion, and Morality* (1990), in the latter of which he states that he is a theist but cannot believe that a just God would have committed all the crimes listed therein. Allen, who was a Catholic during his childhood, is one of the Council for Secular Humanism's laureates in the International Academy of Humanism, and at the 1988 Tenth Humanist World Congress he was presented with the Distinguished Humanist Award.

In *"Dumbth!"*, however, Allen wrote as follows:

> Although my own bias on this question (as to the existence of God) ought to be essentially irrelevant to you, I will satisfy your curiosity on the point that I am among the majority who assume that a God does exist.

Then why, some secular humanists have asked, is he a Humanist Laureate? Why is he not better categorized as a being a theistic humanist or a humanistic theist? His response is found in *Steve Allen on the Bible, Religion, and Morality*,

> I am, as a result of the present study, now of the firm opinion that to the extent that the total goodness of God can be defended as a philosophical proposition, the last place to which the devout believer should turn for supporting evidence is the Bible. There is better evidence in Nature herself–in the inherent order, enormous scale, largesse of air, water, food, sunlight, breathtaking beauty, in the human capacity for love and virtue–than in the familiar accounts of assorted slaughters, sex crimes, atrocities, murders of infants, torture, and other abominations we read about in the Old Testament.
>
> If all such crimes were committed by men the scriptural authors pointed to as evil, if they were condemned in some manner, some enlightening moral might be drawn. But a great many, the

devout believer is told, are performed either by God himself or by esteemed leaders and kings on his personal, clear-cut instruction!

Although I, like most believers, interpret the word *God* as implying perfection, it is more than understandable that atheists such as Kai Nielsen, professor of philosophy at the University of Calgary, [would not, whereupon he lists others such as Sidney Hook, Paul Edwards, Michael Scriven, Walter Kaufmann, Sigmund Freud, Erich Fromm. John Dewey, and Bertrand Russell].

I *assume* that existence of a Supreme Being; therefore, on grounds that will no doubt seem peculiar to some rigorous scholars, belief in God seems to me slightly less preposterous than its opposite.

He continues that *if* there is a God,

it is nothing more than a convenience of common speech to refer to that divine being as a masculine entity. Perfectly orthodox theologians invariably describe God as pure spirit. It is obvious that such a spirit can have no physical characteristics whatever, and since masculinity and femininity are physical characteristics, that would seem to settle the question.

When in the 1970s his son Brian joined a cult, Allen described in *Beloved Son: A Story of the Jesus Cults* (1982) the effect upon the family.

Allen is, although he does not use such labels and tries to avoid all such labels, a borderline deist-pantheist, close to being a religious humanist of the quasi-Unitarian variety. He has strongly supported efforts by the Council for Secular Humanism and was their co-chairman for raising funds to build in Buffalo, New York, a headquarters which has the world's largest freethought library. He helped dedicate the new Center for Inquiry 9 June 1995. He signed Humanist Manifesto 2000.

Martin Gardner in 1990 wrote that Allen, like Thomas Paine, stirs up opposition by his books, concluding that a careful reading of the Bible by people "to find out for themselves whether every absurdity and horror Allen refers to is really there . . . may even lead a few away from their narrow biblicism and back to God." Gardner, himself a deist, therefore categorizes Allen as a theist, not a humanist. Some classify both men as deists with a strong link to the secular humanists. {HNS2}

Allen, Woody (1935—)

Allen Stewart Konigsberg (a/k/a Woody Allen) is a comic, an actor, a writer, and an internationally known film director. His humorous responses to serious questions are a model of secular wit. Although of Hebrew lineage, when asked if he is a practicing Jew, he has responded, "I'm a practicing heterosexual." As for God, "Why is man unable to find God, or a plumber, on weekends?"

As for logic, "Bisexuality immediately doubles your chances for a date on Saturday night." As to whether or not he would want to know exactly when he would die, "I would definitely like to know the time and place of my death and if a necktie is required."

As for choosing between being popular while alive or immortal after death, "Rather than live on in the hearts and minds of an adoring public, I'd rather live on in my apartment."

The films he directs focus often on urban characters preoccupied with sex, death, and psychiatry. These include *Take the Money and Run* (1969), *Play It Again, Sam* (1972), *Love and Death* (1977), and *Manhattan* (1979).

In the autobiographical movie, *Stardust Memories*, his character is called an atheist. "To you, I'm an atheist," the character states. "To God, I'm the loyal opposition."

To Simon Hattenstone in *The Guardian Weekend* (29 March 1997), Allen said,

I am a Jew only in the sense that I was born into a Jewish family. I have no interest in the organized religions beyond a certain cerebral historical curiosity. They are all nonsense to me in their basic premises. . . . I'm agnostic, but I have one foot in atheism.

{*The Freethinker*, May 1997}

Allenby, Edmund Henry Hynman [1st Viscount] (1861—1936)

A British field marshal in World War I, Allenby was a member of the British Rationalist Press Association. In the course of an appeal for peace (*Allenby's Last Message*) at his inauguration as Rector of Edinburgh University shortly before his death, the Viscount ruled out religion as a help. He had waged the last of the great cavalry campaigns by invading Palestine, capturing Jerusalem, and ending Turkish resistance after the battle of Megiddo (1918). From 1919 to 1925, he served as British high commissioner for Egypt and the Sudan. Allenby was a member of the Rationalist Press Association, and his Rectorial Address to Edinburgh University, "World Police for World Peace," is said by McCabe "to be one of the noblest appeals for peace and progress ever made by a soldier." {CE; JM; RE}

Allende Gossens, Salvador [President] (1908—1973)

Allende, the president of Chile (1970—1973), was founder of the Chilean Socialist party (1933). He was the first freely elected Marxist leader in the Americas. In 1971, Corliss Lamont met Allende in the Palacio de la Moneda (the Government Palace). Allende escorted him into his office, talked about being attacked by hostile newspapers throughout South America, then pointed to a picture with the caption, "President Allende receiving the Order of Lenin from a Soviet General."

Asked if he was perhaps a naturalistic humanist in his philosophy, Allende said he did not go in much for labels but that, since he was a Marxist, he was also a naturalist and that his administration was doing many things of a humanist nature. Lamont was then given a copy of *The Political Thoughts of Salvador Allende*, which was inscribed, "To my friend C. L. from *companero Presidente* with hearty affection and faith in the victory of the peoples." In 1973, Allende was overthrown, and he was either murdered or committed suicide when the presidential palace was attacked. Thereupon, a conservative military junta led by Augusto Pinochet took over.

Alley, Robert Sutherland (1932—)

Alley, a professor emeritus at the University of Richmond, is on the Council for Secular Humanism's Committee for the Scientific Examination of Religion. He also is a contributing editor of *Free Inquiry*. Alley, who wrote *James Madison on Religious Liberty* (1989) and *School Prayer* (1993), is executive director of the James Madison Memorial Committee. He is a Secular Humanist Mentor of the Council for Secular Humanism and a member of Americans United's Board of Trustees.

Upon reading work by the Texas-based Religious Right propagandist David Barton, he researched some of the quotations that Barton was making and fundamentalists were quoting. Alley specifically found the following "Christian Nation" statements questionable, if not outright dishonest:

- It is impossible to rightly govern the world without God and the Bible.

—George Washington (questionable)

• I have always said and always will say that the studious perusal of the Sacred Volume will make us better citizens.

—Thomas Jefferson (questionable)

• We have staked the whole future of American civilization, not upon the power of government, far from it. We have staked the future of all of our political institutions upon the capacity of each and all of us to govern ourselves . . . according to the Ten Commandments of God.

—James Madison (questionable)

• It cannot be emphasized too strongly or too often that this great nation was founded, not by religionists, but by Christians; not on religions, but on the gospel of Jesus Christ!

—Patrick Henry (questionable)

• Whosoever shall introduce into the public affairs the principles of primitive Christianity will change the face of the world.

—Benjamin Franklin (questionable)

• A general dissolution of principles and manners will more surely overthrow the liberties of America than the whole force of the common enemy. While the people are virtuous they cannot be subdued; but when once they lose their virtue they will be ready to surrender their liberties to the first external or eternal invader.

—Samuel Adams (questionable)

• The principles of all genuine liberty, and of wise laws and administrations, are to be drawn from the Bible and sustained by its authority. The man therefore who weakens or destroys the divine authority of that book may be accessory [*sic*] to all the public disorders which society is doomed to suffer.

—Noah Webster (questionable)

• There are two powers only which are sufficient to control men, and secure the rights of individuals and a peaceable administration; these are the combined force of religion and law, and the force or fear of the bayonet.

—Noah Webster (questionable)

• The philosophy of the school room in one generation will be the philosophy of government in the next.

—Abraham Lincoln (questionable)

• The only assurance of our nation's safety is to lay our foundation in morality and religion.

—Abraham Lincoln (questionable)

• America is great because she is good, and if America ever ceases to be good, she will cease to be great.

—Alexis de Tocqueville
(This definitely is **not** in *Democracy in America.*)

• Our laws and our institutions must necessarily be based upon and embody the teachings of the Redeemer of mankind. It is impossible that it should be otherwise. In this sense and to this extent, our civilizations and our institutions are emphatically Christian.

—*Holy Trinity v U.S.*
(entirely false.)

At least nine of the twelve statements were included in Barton's *The Myth of Separation* (1989). In 1995, however, Barton's group, WallBuilders, issued a one-page document titled "Questionable Quotes," admitting the alleged statements are false. Embarrassed, Barton revised his earlier book and called it *Original Intent.*

Alley, however, finds that the revision cites sources with inaccurate material. Meanwhile, he continues to speak around the country at Christian Coalition meetings, attacking separation of church and state and advocating union between religion and government.

Alley, commenting upon the daunting task of proving that a quotation does not exist, laments that Barton and others are anti-historical. "We likely have not heard the last of this nonsense," he added, "but it is important to press the new media frauds to document what they claim. Because they cannot do so in most instances, time may ultimately discredit the lot of them." {*Church and State*, July-August 1996}

Allgeier, Elizabeth Rice (20th Century)

A professor of psychology at Bowling Green State University, Allgeier has written for *Free Inquiry*. She addressed the Tenth International Humanist and Ethical Union (IHEU) World Congress held in Buffalo in 1988. Allgeier is author of *Sexual Interactions* (1991). {*Free Inquiry*, Summer 1991}

ALLIANCE OF FREETHOUGHT CAMPUS GROUPS: See entry for Campus Freethought Alliance.

Allibaco, W. A. (19th Century)

Allibaco is author of *The Philosophic and Scientific Ultimatum* (1864). {GS}

Allingham, William (1824—1889)

Allingham was an Irish poet and close friend of Froude, Tennyson, Rossetti, and others whose conversations with him on religion are recorded in his *Diary* (1907). All were skeptics, he shows. Allingham professed to be an atheist, adding that "we cannot in the least comprehend or even think of Deity."

He also wrote, "I will have nothing to do with . . . any form of Christianity." At his secular funeral, a friend read his words, "Body to purifying flame,/Soul to the Great Deep whence it came,/Leaving a song on earth below,/An urn of ashes white as snow." {JM; RAT}

Allman, George Johnston (1824—1904)

Allman was a professor at Queen's College, Galway, 1853 to 1893. A positivist, he was unable to take part in the positivist movement because of the academic position he held. {RAT}

Allsop, Thoms (1794—1880)

Allsop was "the favorite disciple of Coleridge" and a friend of Robert Owen and the Chartists. He was implicated in the attempt of Orsini against Napoleon III. Allsop's freethought views are found in his *Letters, Conversations, and Recollections of Samuel Taylor Coleridge*. With Holyoake he attended the funeral of Owen.

But, when it turned out to be a religious ceremony, Allsop complained of this "mummery of an outworn creed" over the remains of a man who had spent a life freeing his fellows from "the degradation of superstition." {BDF; RAT}

Allston, Washington (1779—1843)

Allston, a painter who was one of S. F. B. Morse's teachers and was himself a student of Gilbert West, believed that a painting should tell a story as well as contain sentiment. A friend of Coleridge, Wordsworth, and Southey, Allston was one of the first recognized portrait painters.

Allston's first marriage was to Ann, sister of William Ellery Channing. According to Jared B. Flagg's *The Life and Letters of Washington Allston* (1892), "Mrs. Merriam . . . censured [Allston] for leaving the Episcopal Church, of which he was a member, and going with his wife to the Congregational Church to which she belonged. . . . 'I am neither an Episcopalian nor a Congregationalist. I endeavor to be a Christian. . . . Catholic in the largest sense of the word.' "

Some Unitarians claim he was a Unitarian in his outlook. {EG; UU}

Allwood, Martin S. (1916—)

Allwood translated numerous Scandinavian works. His *Marginal Man* (1937) includes a humanistic poem, "Occidental Nightmare":

My God my God I am my own God
My God I am my God
My own God my God
I am my own God
I am my own

Own God my God
I am my—God
I am my strange
I am my
Own God—
God!

I? God? Strange?
I. God. Strange.

Am I. Am I? Am I.
God—am I God?

God. Own. My own. Strange.
I am my own God?
My own God
Am I.

Asked about his views concerning humanism, Allood responded to the present author:

> I am a psychoanalytically oriented sociologist, and I take my starting point in the concept of *freedom*. As I conceive of freedom as a secular derivative of salvation, I am naturally suspicious of any concept of freedom limited by *nature*, human or physical. The freedom which can be achieved within the closed system of causality of any "nature" seems to me to be too predictable to be really worthy of the name of freedom. In science, we use the concept of *nature* mainly to afford a closed system of cause and effect, within which prediction is possible. This does not satisfy my observations regarding the actual freedom of human thought, action, and personality. This actual freedom is such that the future is "open" (to genuine new creation) rather than "closed," as it would have to be under a system of perfect prediction, i.e., perfect knowledge of cause and effect in social and human nature.
>
> A naturalistic humanism is, therefore, to my mind, a contradiction in terms. Naturalism can rest on the earlier 19th Century conception of science as having stable, much unchanging units. Copper is copper is copper . . . and copper cannot achieve freedom from its copper-nature. Therefore, we can predict the behavior of copper. Copper cannot have *insight* into the fact that it is copper. Human beings can have insight into the fact that they are human. Psychoanalysis is admirable because of its iron determinism, because of its scientifically "closed" system. But the end result of analysis is not slavery to nature but, rather, a profound insight into the nature of our nature. The *truth* makes human beings free in the sense of insight into the "human condition." Perhaps I should add, unless this is already apparent, that I am a Protestant in the sense of a firm belief in free thought, "free love," and freedom from infantile fixations to any authority or authority symbol. At the same time, I realize the possibility of Luciferian motives for the quest of freedom.
>
> {WAS, 2 March 1951}

Allyn, C. Fannie (19th Century)

Allyn was a representative of the rational Spiritualistic movement of the 1890s. A secularist, she worked on behalf of freedom and advancement of the world's humanity. Like Paine, she said, she hoped for "happiness beyond this life." {PUT}

Alma-Tadema, Laurence [Sir] (1836—1912)

Sir Laurence was an English painter who studied in Belgium, where he lived until 1869. Upon going to England and becoming a citizen, he became well known for his paintings of life in ancient Greece and Rome. According to the Hon. John Collier, his intimate, Alma-Tadema had no religious beliefs whatsoever. McCabe confirms that Alma-Tadema's closest friends said he was an agnostic. {JM; RE}

Almquist, Herman (Born 1839)

Almquist, a Swedish orientalist and professor of philology at the University of Uppsala, was an active defender of new ideas and freethought. {BDF}

Aloni, Shulamit (20h Century)

Aloni is a lawyer who was culture minister during the Rabin regime, a member of the Israeli Knesset, and Minister of Science during the Peres regime. She heads the Citizen's Rights Movement and is a secularist. In 1980, she signed the Secular Humanist Declaration.

In 1996 she was elected a Laureate in the Council for Secular Humanism's International Academy of Humanism. Also in 1996 while a participant at the Humanist World Congress held in Mexico City, she discussed the nature of secular humanism in Israel. As for the myth of Adam and Eve, Aloni noted jocularly that the story shows Eve's intelligence: "Eve really *enjoyed* eating of that fruit of knowledge." {HNS2; SHD}

Alpert, John (20th Century)

Alpert, a freethinker in Phoenix, Arizona, has written for *Secular Nation* (October-December 1998).

Alpharabius (Died 950)

Muhammad ibn Muhammad ibn Tarkhan (Abu Nasr), called *Al Farabi*, has been termed by Ibn Khallikan "the greatest philosopher the Moslems ever had." But he is said to have taught the eternity of the world and denied the permanent individuality of the soul. Rénan adds that Al Farabi expressly rejected all supernatural revelation. {BDF}

Al-Rawandi, Ibn (20th Century)

Al-Rawandi, in "Esoteric Evangelicals: Islam and the Traditionalists" (*New Humanist*, May 1994), discusses the tendency for some Westerners to convert to Islam and describes an influential group who have justified this move on the grounds of a traditionalist and autocratic approach. His conclusion is that the traditionalist dream, even if it were true, "would never overcome or replace the pathetic human need for cultural identity and group loyalty that religion so readily fulfills. Indeed, in the end we can see that traditionalism is itself just one more example of the same phenomenon. Esoteric, Autocratic, Intellectual, *The Truth*, set over against the rest–the exoterics, the democrats, the rationalists, *the infidel*."

Al-Rawandi finds it surprising that Westerners are sometimes so tolerant of religion. They overlook, he has written, "the wholly human origin of the Qur'an, the moral and intellectual inadequacies of Muhammad, the wholly tendentious and invented character of the *hadith*, the sexually-obsessed and anti-feminine nature of the *sharia*, the Arab empire spread by the sword and maintained by terror, the persecution of religious and intellectual minorities in that empire in the name of Islam, the incapacity of Muslims for any kind of critical or self-critical thought, and the abject intellectual and moral poverty of Islam vis-à-vis the modern secular West."

Despite the way apologists depict it, he has observed,

> Islam *was* spread by the sword and has been maintained by the sword throughout its history, not to mention the scourge and the cross. In truth it was the Arab empire that was spread by the sword and it is as an Arab empire that Islam is maintained to this day in the form a religion largely invented to hold that empire together and subdue native populations. An unmitigated cultural disaster parading as God's will. Religious minorities were always second-class citizens in this empire and were only tolerated on sufferance and in abject deference to their Arab/Muslim masters; for polytheists and unbelievers there was no tolerance at all; it was conversion or death.
>
> {*New Humanist*, December 1995}

Alsaaty, Faith (20th Century)

In 1972, Alsaaty was on the advisory board of the Humanist Society of Greater New York.

Alt, Ludwig (20th Century)

Alt edited a freethought journal, *Free Humanist* (1959—1963). It later became *American Atheist* with Madalyn Murray (later O'Hair) as its editor. {FUS}

Altman, Morris (1837—1876)

Altman, the founder of the Altman's department stores, came from a wealthy Jewish family and served as a trustee of Paine Hall in Boston where freethinkers met. His house was sometimes used as a meeting place for visiting religious liberals.

Before his death at the age of thirty-nine, Altman had given a large amount of money to D. M. Bennett to assure publication of several of the large volumes that Bennett had written. {Gordon Stein, "Freethought Financiers," *Truth Seeker* #123:1}

Altizer, Thomas J. (20th Century)

Altizer is a theologian who co-authored with William Hamilton *Radical Theology and the Death of God.* "Only by accepting and even willing the death of God in our experience," he has written, "can we be liberated from a transcendent beyond, an alien beyond which has been emptied and darkened by God's self-alienation in Christ."

Altmeyer, Jean Jacques (1804—1877)

Luxembourg-born Altmeyer became a professor at the University of Brussels, where he wrote an *Introduction to the Philosophical Study of the History of Humanity* (1836) and other historical works. Thc King of Denmark honored his rationalistic work with a gold medal. {BDF; RAT}

ALTRUISM

Antony Flew holds that altruism, as a philosophic term, is in opposition to (ethical) egoism. Altruism is defined as an unselfish regard for or devotion to the welfare of others, whereas egoism is a doctrine that individual self-interest is the valid end of all actions. (See entry for Egotism. Also, see the *Encyclopedia of Philosophy*, Volume 2.) {AF}

Alvarez, A(lfred) (1929-)

A British novelist, essayist, and critic, Alvarez had an unusual childhood, during which both of his parents attempted suicide. He entered Corpus Christi College at Oxford, founded a Critical Society, and later pursued his critical interests as a visiting fellow at Princeton (1953-1954) and elsewhere.

His novels include *Hers* (1974), about a loveless marriage; *Hunt* (1978), about a woman the protagonist discovers unconscious on Hampstead Heath; *Day of Atonement* (1991), a psychological thriller; and *Night: Night Life, Night Language, Sleep and Dreams* (1998).

In a critique of three books about death, including Jessica Mitford's *The American Way of Death Revisited*, Alvarez commented:

> Because I don't believe in God or an afterlife, it is the finality of death—the deadness of the dead—that matters most to me at funerals. That, too, becomes part of my memory of them.
>
> For the irreligious, in other words, death is strictly the concern of the living, and that means the living person who is about to die as well as those who survive the death.
>
> {*The New York Review of Books*, 24 September 1998}

Amador, Jorge González (1954—)

A Costa Rican humanist, Amador was one of the founders of *Iconoclasta*, the publication of *La Asociación Ético Humanista Costarricense* (ASEHUCO). Although his training is that of a lawyer, Amador is known for his aestheticism.

Amalric of Bene (Died c. 1206)

Amalric, a follower of the condemned theologian Joachim of Floris, was a heretic who was accused of being a pantheist. His followers are said to have believed that "the Father was incarnate in Abraham, the Son in Mary, the Holy Spirit is daily made incarnate in us. . . . All things are one, for whatever is, is God." {ER}

Amari, Michele (1806—1889)

Amari was a Sicilian historian and orientalist. In 1832 he produced a version of Scott's *Marmion*. He wrote a standard *History of the Musulmen in Sicily*. After the landing of Garibaldi, Amari was made head of public instruction for the island, and he took part in the anti-clerical council of 1869. {BDF; RAT}

Amaury de Chartres (13th Century)

Amalric de Chartres, or Amaury, was a heretic of the thirteenth century. A teacher of logic, he wrote *Physion*, which was condemned by a bull of Pope Innocent III (1204). Amaury is said to have taught a kind of pantheism and held that the reign of the Father and Son must give place to that of the Holy Spirit. He maintained that the sacraments were useless and that there is no other heaven than the satisfaction of doing right, nor is there any other hell than ignorance and sin. Ten of his disciples were burned in Paris in 1210, and his own bones were exhumed and thrown into the flames. {BDF}

Ambedkar, B. R. (20th Century)

Ambedkar, who was born into an "untouchable" family, converted to Buddhism. He is an architect of the Indian Constitution.

AMBEDKAR MISSION PATRIKA

Ambedkar Mission Patrika is a humanistic monthly journal in Hindi. Its address is Chitkohara P.O., Anishabad, Patna 800 002 India. (For information about Ambedkar, see entry for Ramendra.)

Amberley, John Russell [Viscount] (1843—1876)

Amberley, a viscount and eldest son of Earl Russell, entered Parliament in 1866 as a Radical member for Nottingham. In his heretical *Analysis of Religious Belief* (1876), he examines, compares, and criticizes the various faiths of the world. Viscount Amberley lived and died a Freethinker.

According to Foote's "Infidel Deathbeds," his will, which stipulated that Bertrand Russell, his son, should be educated by a skeptical friend, was set aside by Earl Russell, "the law of England being such that Freethinkers are denied the parental rights which are enjoyed by their Christian neighbors. Lady Frances Russell, who signs with her initials the Preface to Lord Amberley's book, which was published after his death, writes, 'Ere the pages now given to the public had left the press, the hand that had written them was cold, the heart—of which few could know the loving depths—had ceased to bat, the far-ranging mind was forever still, the fervent spirit was at rest. Let this be remembered by those who read, and add solemnity to the solemn purpose of the book.' " {BDF; FO; FUK; TRI}

AMBIGUITY

Something is ambiguous if it is capable of being understood in two or more possible senses or ways. Aristotle illustrated ambiguity by using the word "healthy." Today, a family may have a son who is healthier than a daughter. Living in a high-rent area of Athens may be healthier than living near the Athens garbage dump. However, it does not follow that the son is healthier than the high-rent area of Athens.

Bertrand Russell sent the following response to individuals who sent him boring material:

> Thank you for your recent communication.
> I shall lose no time reading it.
>
> {AF; *Russell: the Journal of the Bertrand Russell Archives*, Vol. 15, #1, Summer 1995}

AMEN

A word of Hebrew origin, *'amen* means certainly or verily. Believers often utter the word at the ends of prayers or statements with which they want to show they are in agreement.

Freethinkers are amused that no analogous word exists to show disapproval during services.

Amenhotep III [King] (14th Century B.C.E.)

One of the oldest individuals listed as a "heretic," Amenhotep III succeeded his father, Thutmose IV, to the ancient Egyptian throne approximately in 1411 B.C.E. and ruled until 1372 B.C.E. He built extensively at Karnak, Thebes, and Luxor.

His wife, Queen Tiy, had deserted the gods of Egypt for the solar deity of the Mitanni, an Aryan people of Asia Minor, and she persuaded her son, Ikhnaton (who ruled 1375—1358 B.C.E.), to adopt it. Ikhnaton, five centuries before the first prophet appeared in Judea, therefore embraced monotheism, a fact overlooked by those Hebrews who claim it was the Hebrews who were the first monotheists. For Ikhnaton (whose original name had been Akhenaton), the sun, Aton, was god and god alone, and he was Aton's physical son. The solar monotheism was absolute, and in his fanaticism Ikhnaton defaced every monument on which appeared the name of Amon, the previous greatest god of Egypt. His subjects and priests were outraged by his destruction of their traditions, and polytheism returned. Amenhetep IV has been called "the Heretic King," but McCabe and others speak of several rulers at that time as being "heretics." (See entry for Egyptian Religion.) {CE; RE}

AMERICA

Parents in the United States who teach their children that Heaven is up and Hell is down are likely also to teach that stars shoot and that Columbus discovered America. Meteors shoot up in the heavens, but it remains to be seen who first "discovered" America. The actual discoverers of America were prehistoric hunters who may have come from Asia (via the Bering Strait), Europe (via Iceland), Australia (unlikely, but Thor Heyerdahl proposed this), or possibly Africa. Leif Ericsson and other Norse seafarers reached the Americas in the decades after 1000 C.E. Natives from Asia, now variously called American Indians or Native Indians, had preceded Leif Ericcson.

In 1996 near the Columbia River in Kennewick, Washington, a man estimated to be 9,000 years old was found. The Kennewick Man's skeleton was missing only a few tiny bones. Scientists determined that his was a diet high in marine food and that he may have died from having drowned.

"On the physical characteristics alone, he could fit on the streets of Stockholm without causing any kind of notice," said James Chatters, a forensic anthropologist, implying the individual was not Asian. The bones constitute part of a growing quantity of evidence that Caucasoids, not Asians, were the earliest Americans. In 1997, however, differing theories were being expressed.

Eventually, a different and more accurate name might be substituted for the lands of the Western Hemisphere–North America, Middle (or Central) America, and South America. An acronymic name which Samuel Butler used to describe the country between Canada and the United States of Mexico is Usonia, its citizens being Usonians. Such a suggestion does not address how the continents may be re-named, or if citizens of the United States of Mexico will then be called Middle (or Central) Usonians. (See entries for Columbus and Usonia. Also, see entry for Man in Early America, a reference to the finding of a Caucasian skull in Washington that pre-dates "Native Americans.") {Douglas Preston, "The Lost Man," *The New Yorker*, 16 June 1997; John Noble Wilford, *The New York Times*, 9 Nov 99}

AMERICAN ACADEMY

The American Academy of Arts and Letters, founded in 1898 as the National Institute of Arts and Letters and limited to 250 members, was an offspring of the American Social Science Association. The original members, chosen by a committee of the Association, included such creative humanists as Henry Adams, Daniel Chester French, Childe Hassam, William Dean Howells, William and Henry James, John La Farge, Edward MacDowell, Augustus Saint-Gaudens, Mark Twain, and two future presidents—Theodore Roosevelt and Woodrow Wilson. Upon the death of a member, the remaining members choose a replacement. In 1904 the American Academy of Arts and Letters was founded as an inner body of the Institute, with membership limited to fifty persons chosen for special distinction from the membership of the Institute. The first seven chosen were William Dean Howells, Augustus Saint-Gaudens, Edmund Clarence Stedman, John La Farge, Mark Twain, John Hay, and Edward MacDowell. Henry James was the first of the eight to be selected by this initial group.

The Institute was incorporated by an Act of Congress signed by President Taft in 1913, and the Academy was similarly incorporated in 1916 under President Wilson. In 1923 a joint headquarters was established at 633 West 155th Street in New York City in a new building donated by Archer Milton Huntington. (Ezra Pound, who was inducted in 1938, once referred to the Institute in a 1950 letter to William Carlos Williams as "the Institute of Farts and Stutters.")

In 1976, after seventy-two years of separate though related existence, the two groups voted for a merger that made them one institution with a single Board of Directors. In 1992 the Institute dissolved and united into a single body of 250 members, which began 1993 as the American Academy of Arts and Letters. The Academy also elects seventy-five distinguished foreign artists, writers, and composers as Honorary Members. Other nations have a national academy. For example, the French Academy dates to the 1630s and has a fixed membership of forty.

A large number of Academy members are listed herein. {CE}

AMERICAN ASSOCIATION FOR THE ADVANCEMENT OF ATHEISM (AAAA): See the entry for California Atheists, Humanists.

AMERICAN ATHEIST

The *American Atheist* is a quarterly of American Atheists, PO Box 140195, Austin, Texas 78714-0195. E-mail: <fzindler@atheists.org>. On the Web: <www.americanatheist.org/>.

AMERICAN ATHEIST GENERAL HEADQUARTERS: See entry for Madalyn Murray O'Hair.

AMERICAN ATHEIST NEWSLETTER

The *American Atheist Newsletter* is published by American Atheists, Inc. (PO Box 140195, Austin, Texas 78714-0195). E-mail: <aanews@atheists.org>; and <editor@atheists.org>.

On the Web: <http://www.atheists.org> and <ftp.atheists.org/pub/>

AMERICAN ATHEISTS

On the Web, American Atheists is at: <http://www.atheists.org/>. See entries for Ron Barrier and Ellen Johnson.

AMERICAN ATHEISTS, INC.

Madalyn Murray O'Hair's American Atheists Inc. association was a family-held corporation that published books, a newsletter, and *American Atheist*. When in the early 1990s she disbanded most of the local chapters and seized their bank accounts and mailing lists, the Atheist Alliance was formed in San Mateo, California. Jon G. Murray became president of American Atheists, Inc. (POB 140195, Austin, Texas 78714), but according to journalist Mimi Swartz, "Many knew [Jon] lacked the smarts and charisma to keep the organization going, but O'Hair was ill and tired."

In 1995, Mrs. O'Hair, who had been in ill health, mysteriously disappeared along with her son and granddaughter. The newsletter was published in 1996, and it stated that the new group that had taken over from the O'Hairs "has gone to considerable lengths" to find the missing principals of the organization but that no new clues had turned up. Dennis Middlebrooks, among others, has lamented the "dirty name" atheists have been given in our time by Stalinist communism and Mrs. O'Hair.

The group's new president is Ellen Johnson, and Spike Tyson is a director. Although she resents "the media's fixation with numbers," Johnson told a *New York Times* reporter that the current membership is 2,500. In November 1998 the Atheist Community of Austin, Texas, rejected affiliation with American Atheists, citing the group's corporate structure, its lack of democracy, its financial secrecy, its future direction, and an alleged lack of real benefits from affiliation. Johnson, however, has justified the group's leaders for having taken over the organization after the Murrays and O'Hairs vanished.

American Atheists Inc.'s headquarters in Cranford on Christiani Street is at Box 5733, Parsippany, New Jersey 07054-6733. On the Web: <http://www.atheists.org>. (See entries for Ron Barrier, Ellen Johnson, and Madalyn Murray O'Hair.) {FD; *Freethought Observer*, November-December 1996}

AMERICAN BAPTIST CHURCHES IN THE USA

The American Baptist Churches in the USA, organized in 1907, are at PO Box 851, Valley Forge, PA 19482. Web: <http://www.abc-usa.org>.

AMERICAN CIVIL LIBERTIES UNION

The American Civil Liberties Union (ACLU) is a nonpartisan organization devoted to the preservation and extension of the basic rights set forth in the U. S. Constitution. It was founded (1920) by such prominent figures as Jane Addams, Helen Keller, Judah Magnus, and Norman Thomas.

The ACLU has participated directly or indirectly in almost every major civil liberties case contested in American courts. Included among these are the so-called Scopes "monkey trial" in Tennessee (1925), the Sacco-Vanzetti case (1920s), the Federal court test (1933) that ended the censorship of James Joyce's *Ulysses*, and the landmark *Brown v. Board of Education* (1954) school desegregation case.

On the Web: <http://www.aclu.org/> {CE}

AMERICAN ETHICAL UNION (AEU)

The American Ethical Union, a member of the International Humanist and Ethical Union, is at 2 West 64th Street, New York, NY 10023. Its thirteen-member Board is elected nationally. Currently, its president is Ellen McBride. On the Web: <http://miso.wwa.com/~jej/ves.html>. Also on the Web: <http://www.aeu.org/aeulists.html>.

E-mail: <aeuoffice@aeu.org>.

AMERICAN FREEMAN

The American Freeman was a freethought newspaper and journal of opinion published by Emanuel Haldeman-Julius. Upon his death, it ceased publication in November 1951. At the beginning it was a socialist paper that favored Eugene V. Debs, who was imprisoned for protesting World War I. While in jail he received one million votes while still running for the office of President, and partly because of Haldeman-Julius's efforts, Debs was freed.

The Appeal to Reason, begun in 1895 by J. A. Wayland, moved from Kansas City, Missouri, to Girard, Kansas. Haldeman-Julius took the paper over in 1919, calling it *The New Appeal* and in 1919 changing the title to *The Appeal To* Reason. In 1929 the paper again changed its name to *The American Freeman*. Originally a weekly, in June 1933 it became a monthly until its demise. During the Depression years of 1932-1933, the journal had a circulation of 30,000. {Hal Verb, *Freethought Today*, June-July 1998}

AMERICAN GAY AND LESBIAN ATHEISTS (AGLA)

The *American Gay and Lesbian Atheist* newsletter ceased in 1995 when Don Sanders died. In his will, Sanders wrote,

> It grieves me a great deal to know that so little concern has been shown by American Gay Atheists Inc.'s board of directors that not one of them is willing to take over the helm of the gay and lesbian community's most important movement. Therefore, I want none of my estate or property to be rendered unto anyone associated with American Gay Atheists Inc. for fear that it will simply be used to enrich individuals and not to further the cause of Atheism in the lesbian and gay community.

AMERICAN HUMANIST ASSOCIATION (AHA)

In 1935, a newly organized Humanist Press Association (HPA) became the first organized national association of humanism in the United States. It was originally inspired by the Rationalist Press Association and, on the suggestion of Curtis W. Reese, reorganized later as the American Humanist Association (AHA). In 1941, the association was incorporated and became the principal organization representing humanism in the United States.

Under the leadership of Edwin H. Wilson, one of its founders, the AHA was headquartered in Yellow Springs, Ohio, in the 1930s. It currently is at 7 Harwood Drive, Amherst, New York 14226, and publishes *The Humanist*, a bi-monthly which since 1951 has presented a nontheistic, secular, and naturalistic approach to philosophy, science, and broad areas of personal and social concern. It focuses on humanistic ideas, developments, and revolutions. In pursuit of free and open dialogue, the magazine strives to air opinions that may not necessarily reflect those of the editors or the publisher, which is the American Humanist Association. The AHA moved its offices to San Francisco after some years in Yellow Springs, then in 1978 moved to Amherst, New York.

In 1986 James F. Hornback wrote the following memories of his sixty-seven years of acquaintances within the Unitarian, Ethical Culture, and humanist groups:

> Though the American Humanist Association, as such, was incorporated as late as 1943, it was preceded by the Humanist Manifesto of 1933, the Humanist Press Association of 1927 with its *New Humanist* published by A. Eustace Haydon students Edwin Wilson, Harold Buschman, and Raymond B. Bragg, and the whole array of consciously (and unconsciously) Humanist sermons and books by Unitarian ministers of the Western ("Ethical Basis") Conference from 1875 on, and by such philosophers as John Dewey, Roy Wood Sellars, and Max Otto.
>
> (See Corliss Lamont's *Humanism as a Philosophy*, 1949, for the classic overview, and such books as Stow Persons's *Free Religion: An American Faith*, 1947, and Charles H. Lyttle's *Freedom Moves West: A History of the Western Unitarian Conference*, 1952, for early organizational details. John Dewey's *A Common Faith*, 1934, although an otherwise admirable philosophic statement, to my mind gave Humanism a so-far-fatal setback by offering otherwise promising ministers and teachers a provisional definition of God as "the uniting of the ideal and the actual," which kept thousands of them happy in the perpetuation of the traditional religions and the God-language.)
>
> Edwin Wilson performed much the same sacrificial role in the organization of the AHA that George O'Dell (1913—1947) and Burns Weston before him performed in the American Ethical Union. He carried the AHA at the expense of Unitarian pastorates in Schenectady and Salt Lake City, until the AHA set him up professionally in Yellow Springs.
>
> His successor as executive director, Toby McCarroll, at first promising, soon led the AHA down the primrose path of Humanistic Psychology (named "Humanistic" or "Third Force" only because of its opposition to Freudianism and Behaviorism). Toby, a speaker in St. Louis and a fellow traveler to the International Humanist and Ethical Union, was soon telling me of the advantages of appealing to priests, preachers, and rabbis. He is Brother Toby again, the head of a Catholic monastery.
>
> But many of the same erroneous ideas of pop psychology and mystic humanism (e.g., it's all in your head, or your head is a model of the universe, so downplay reason and science) are now plentiful in the AHA as well as in the AEU. The AEU always left itself open to such varied beliefs, as did the Unitarians. But the AHA? I had hoped for better.

> As a veteran of many interrelations between Humanism and Ethical Culture, I have valued the difference: the AHA for rigorous scientific, naturalistic ethics, derived from an ideal projection of real, felt human values and its testing in experience; and the AEU for "the larger humanism" of being ethical in a congregational fellowship, for whatever philosophy you may care to espouse. Philosophically, the differences are important. Structurally, believe me, they are insurmountable.

In addition to Edwin Wilson, the editors of *The Humanist* have included Priscilla Robertson, Gerald Wendt, Paul Kurtz, Tolbert H. McCarroll, Lloyd Morain, Don Page, Rick Szykowny, Gerry O'Sullivan, and Fred Edwords.

As of 1995, the editorial board consisted of Andre Bacard, Joseph E. Barnhart, H. J. Blackham, Bette Chambers, Edd Doerr, Beverley Earles, Albert Ellis, Edward L. Ericson, James Farmer, Betty Friedan, Edna Ruth Johnson, Marty Klein, Marvin Kohl, Jean S. Kotkin, Gerald Larue, Lester Mondale, Lloyd Morain, Mary Morain, Maxine Negri, Suzanne Paul, Howard B. Radest, James Randi, and Ward Tabler.

The late Corliss Lamont was always a key figure in the movement of naturalistic humanism, and he was instrumental in contributing financially to the success of the AHA as well as encouraging *The Humanist* to emphasize a nontheistic metaphysic and to assist in the formation of humanist chapters around the country. The American Humanist Association is a full member of the International Humanist and Ethical Union.

E-mail: <ap818@freenet.buffalo.edu> and on the Web: <http://www.infidels.org/org/aha/>.

The American Humanist Bookstore is on the Web: <http://www.imall.com>. (See entries Corliss Lamont, Paul Kurtz, Priscilla Robertson, and Edwin H. Wilson.)

AMERICAN INDIANS [NATIVE AMERICANS]

> • Indian reservations are a parcel of land set aside forIndians, surrounded by thieves.
>
> **General William Sherman** in 1865

The indigenous peoples of both North and South America, as well as their descendants, are variously called American Indians or Native Americans. Although once popular, the terms *Amerind* and *Amerindian* are now seldom used. Some do refer to themselves as Indian people, and aboriginal Canadians who are not Aleut or Inuks sometimes call themselves Indians.

Rather than using the umbrella terms, many humanists prefer using the names of the specific peoples: the Iowas, Crees, Iroquois, Cherokees, etc. Offensive are terms such as red, redskins, braves, bucks, half-breeds, papooses, squaws, wampum, warpath, etc. (See entry for Native American Religion.) {*Guidelines for Bias-Free Writing*, 1995}

AMERICAN RATIONALIST

The American Rationalist (PO Box 994, St. Louis, Missouri 63188) is published bi-monthly. A scholarly publication, the magazine was edited until his death in 1996 by Gordon Stein.

Kaz Dziamka is its current editor (PO Box 80182, Albuquerque, New Mexico 87198-0182); C. Lee Hubbell, associate editor; Barbara Stocker, managing editor; A. J. Mattill Jr. and Marge Mignacca, contributing editors; Judith Hayes, Walter Hoops, Frank Mortyn, Bernard Katz, and Eric Rajala, senior writers. E-mail: <rsslbarb@aol.com>. On the Web: <http://www.infidels.org/org/ar>.

AMERICAN SOCIETY OF FREETHINKERS

The American Society of Freethinkers, POB 984, Troy, Michigan, is led by Dick Mellen. {FD}

AMERICAN UNITARIAN ASSOCIATION (AUA)

The American Unitarian Association was organized in 1825. The Universalist Church of America dates back to 1793. In 1961 the two denominations, both liberal alternatives to more dogmatic forms of Christianity, merged. Their outlook is based on individual freedom of belief, therefore including agnostics, atheists, humanists, liberal Christians, and unitarian theists. Over the past decade feminist theology has made an impact, the hymn books are gender-inclusive, and half the settled ministers are women.

In 1998 there were 1,039 congregations, 1,296 ministers, and 150,413 members.

The Unitarian Universalist Association is at 25 Beacon Street, Boston, Massachusetts 02108. On the Web: <http://www.uua.org>. E-mail for the Rev. Kenneth Torquil MacLean, who is the special assistant to the President for Interfaith and International Relations, is <kmaclean@uua.org>. (See entry for Unitarian Universalist Association.)

AMERICANS FOR RELIGIOUS LIBERTY

Americans for Religious Liberty, POB 6656, Silver Springs, Maryland 20916, publishes *Voice of Reason*. It is dedicated to preserving the American tradition of religious, intellectual, and personal freedom in a secular democratic state. In 1995 the group published *The Case Against School Vouchers* by Edd Doerr, Albert J. Mendendez, and John M. Swomley. {FD}

AMERICANS UNITED FOR SEPARATION OF CHURCH AND STATE

Americans United for Separation of Church and State, 8120 Fenton Street, Silver Spring, Maryland 20910, was started in 1947. It is not sponsored by any freethought or humanistic organizations and is strictly nonsectarian.

On the Web: <www.netplexgroup.com>.

Ames, Charles G. (20th Century)

A Unitarian minister, Ames once stated, "We are not obliged to choose between a false religion and no religion at all; our choice is rather between the false and the true, or between the lower and the higher. Nor did harm ever come to the man who lets go a creed which he can no longer retain with honesty; such harm may come from heartless conformity and insincere profession."

Ames, Daniel T. (20th Century)

A freethinker, Ames wrote *Biblical Myths* (1922). {GS}

Ames, Edward Scribner (20th Century)

Ames, who taught at the University of Chicago, wrote *The Psychology of Religious Experience* (1919), *Away With God and Christianity* (1935), and *Religion* (1949). According to Edwin H. Wilson, Ames was a naturalist but one who used traditional theistic terms. He once explained, in a brochure entitled "Humanism,"

> (Religious) humanists are naturalistic, experimental, behavioristic, humanitarian. They accept the evolutionary doctrine. . . . This sphere (here and now) of human interests and accomplishments is the proper concern of many, according to these humanists. . . .
>
> [A] chief point of attack of the humanist upon the old beliefs is the existence of God, and in general the conception of the supernatural which runs through those beliefs. . . . They emphasize the function of scientific knowledge as a means of realizing a better and happier life.

Ames described the literary humanists of the 1930s as "violently opposed not only to Rousseau but to Francis Bacon and John Dewey." As for the gods, "The gods are not separate from men but are of one nature with them. Gods and men constitute one living organism, one kinship group." Because of his views on God, however, he was not invited to sign Humanist Manifesto I. For him to have signed, in Wilson's view, would have opened "the door to a flood of theist apologists."

In his old age, after he retired, his legs were both amputated and he told Wilson, "Here I sit, literally footless, wondering what it would be like if—as I do not believe—it were possible for me to rejoin the wife of my years in an existence other than this." {EW; GS}

Ames, Fanny Baker (1840—1931)

A leader of the Unitarian Women's Auxiliary Conference, Ames was a suffragist and charity organizer.

Ames, Van Meter (Born 1898)

Ames, a professor of philosophy, University of Cincinnati, and author of *André Gide* (1947) and *Prayers and Meditations* (1970), wrote of the word humanism: "I doubt if I could say anything more or better on the subject of my naturalistic humanism than I did in *The Humanist* (Issue 1, 1951)."

In *The Journal of Aesthetics and Art Criticism* (March 1952), Ames wrote "The Humanism of Thomas Mann." He found that "from first to last Thomas Mann thinks in terms of a conflict between unconscious nature and conscious spirit. Yet the discussions between the Jesuit Naphta and the humanist Settembrini in *The Magic Mountain* introduce something new: in considering science as a possible escape from the verbal squirrel cage." Ames finds that the work scarcely seems to be a tribute to science, unless obliquely, by letting the reader see the inadequacy of unscientific attitudes and the danger of pseudo-science.

Ames also found that, for Mann,

> God is the personification of value as found in human experience, refined by the thought and feeling of such men as Ikhnaton, Abraham, Isaac, and Jacob—and Joseph. God becomes remote, with a mysterious plan that overrides human feelings, when Mann reverts to a dualism that not only reverses the novel's drift but is anachronistic in attributing to ancient Israel the divorce of nature and spirit, practical life and religion, which came to be assumed by medieval Jews and Christians. Assertion of this divorce makes one wonder how far Mann has come toward the coalescence of the sacred and secular in scientific humanism.

{CL; HNS; WAS, 23 Sep 1956}

AMHERST COLLEGE ATHEISTS, AGNOSTICS, RATIONALISTS, AND GODLESS HUMANISTS:

Atheists at the Massachusetts college, Amherst, are found on the Web: <www.secularhumanism.org/cfa/orgs.html>.

Amicis, Edmonde de (1846—1908)

Amicis was a leading Italian who served in the army against the Pope's troops and then became, said the *Athenaeum*, "one of the most extensively read Italian authors of the last three-quarters of a Century." Amicis professed agnosticism in his *Memorie* and reported that he was "fascinated and tormented by the vast mystery of life." {JM}

AMISH: See entry for Mennonites.

Amiel, Henri Frédéric (1821—1881)

A Swiss poet and philosopher, descendant of an exiled Huguenot family, Amiel was professor of aesthetics and moral philosophy at Geneva Academy. His *Journal Intime* (1883—1884) is an expression of a mind that rejected Christianity with pain and regret. "We are always making God our accomplice," he wrote, "so that we may legalize our own inequities. Every successful massacre is consecrated by a *Te Deum*, and the clergy have never been wanting in benedictions for any victorious enormity."

Amiel remained theistic and mystic, yet his skepticism was profound. "The apologies of Pascal, Leibnitz, and Secretan," he wrote, "seem to me to prove no more than those of the Middle Ages." {RAT; TYD}

Amis, Kingsley (1922—1995)

Amis, an English novelist known for a satire on academic life, *Lucky Jim* (1953), was never involved with the freethought movement. However, according to Nicolas Walter, Amis wrote a poem, "New Approach Needed," and an article, "On Christ's Nature," which contained devastating criticisms of Christianity.

Amman, Hans Jacob (1586—1658)

Amman was a German surgeon and traveler who wrote *Voyage in the Promised Land.* {BDF}

Ammianus, Marcellinus (4th Century)

A Roman soldier-historian, Ammianus served under Julian. He compared the rancor of the Christians of the period to that of wild beasts. Gibbon called him "an accurate and faithful guide." Ammianus died approximately 395 C.E. {BDF}

Ammonius (3rd Century)

Surnamed Saccas or the porter, Ammonius was born of Christian parents in Alexandria but turned pagan and opened a school of philosophy. Among his pupils were Origen, Longinus, and Polotinus. Ammonius is thought to have originated the neo-Platnoic movement, which formed the most serious opposition to Christianity in its early times. Ammonius died in 243 C.E. {BDF}

Ammons, A(rchie) R(andolph) (1926—)

Ammons, a poet on the English department faculty of Cornell University in New York State, when asked if he found any of the categories of humanism described his viewpoint, replied to the present author, "None of the above. I'm not a humanist. I believe in the way things work, a naturalistic dynamics that includes man and the ways he works." {WAS, 3 June 1992}

AMNESTY INTERNATIONAL NETWORK

Amnesty International is a major group with concerns about human rights. On the Web: <http://www.derechos.org/amnesty/aigroups.html>

AMON (Amon Re)

Amon, in Egypt, was said to have become king of all the gods. {LEE}

AMORALITY

That which is amoral is neither moral nor immoral. A baby is amoral. An amoral choice is to prefer Beethoven to Brahms, cherries to strawberries, or blondes to brunettes. Some, however, incorrectly refer to extreme immorality as wickedness—these individuals mistakenly claim that anyone who does not understand what is generally considered moral or decent is therefore amoral.

Amos, Tori (20th Century)

Amos, the daughter of a Methodist minister, had a hit song, "God," in her 1990s album, *Under the Pink.* It is forthright in its rejection of Christianity's patriarchal presumptions. "God," the song goes, "sometimes you just don't come through. Do you need a woman to look after you?" Her general work is, however, "spiritual."

Amram, David (Werner) (1930-)

Amram is a composer, conductor, and musician. He was the first composer-in-residence of the New York Philharmonic Orchestra (1966-1967); composed incidental music for the New York Shakespeare Festival (1956-1967); wrote a Holocaust opera, "The Final Ingredient"; and composed music for such films as "The Manchurian Candidate" and "Splendor in the Grass." Accomplished on the French horn, he also plays piano, guitar, numerous flutes and whistles, combining symphony, jazz, and folk music with audience participation.

For Paddy Chayevsky's "Joseph D" on Broadway, he was a one-person symphony as well as choir, performing almost all the instruments and singing the soprano as well as the bass voices.

Amram's autobiography is *Vibrations: Adventures and Musical Times of David Amram* (1968). In it and elsewhere he has described having worked with Dizzy Gillespie, Lionel Hampton, Leonard Bernstein, and all the major Beatnick writers. He was musical accompanist at the historic 1957 first-ever Jazz-Poetry reading in New York with Jack Kerouac. Broadcast Music Incorporated has cited him as "one of twenty most performed composers of concern music in the United States." He is acknowledged as a pioneer member of world music and multi-cultural symphonic programming.

Asked his outlook about humanism and religion, Amram, one of the best-known of the Beat Generation, responded to the present author:

> I'm a hyperactive member of the Jewish faith, in the grand tradition of the wandering Klezmer-philosophers, who rejoiced in the beauty of each new day and walked humbly on God's great Mother Earth. All good things in life celebrate the spirit. I believe I'll be reincarnated as an eggplant, which is why I'm becoming a vegetarian again, to prepare my new career.

{WAS, 5 May 1998}

AMULETS

Objects called amulets were designed to ward off the power of any harmful influences. Like talismans, fetishes, or charms, they are thought to have apparently magical qualities for averting evil and ensuring good fortune. The Jewish mezuzah and phylactery are amulets. Christians have used a cross, others have used the rabbit's foot, and still others use magic squares, abracadabra, the wheel of the sun god, the swastika, or other devices to dispel evil and bring good luck.

The harmful influences are said to come from the Devil, who to Jews and Christians is the personal supreme spirit of evil as well as the ruler of Hell. They might also come from some evil spirit or from a zombie, one who has been raised from the grave by a houngan (sorcerer) or hounsie, then tries to enslave you, forcing you to perform evil acts.

Amulets or charms, found in commercially successful shops around the world, are popular in santería, voodoo, obeah, candomblé (in Brazil), and similar faiths, all of which state they are on the side of good over bad. {ER}

ANAGRAMS

To the religious zealots who object to *Santa* because it is an anagram of *Satan*, the nonsuperstitious point out that *evangelist* is an anagram for *evil's agent*.

Anaimuthu, V. (1925—)

Anaimuthu edits *Sinthanayaian*, a freethought Tamil publication in India. In 1976 he was a contributor to *The Progress of Atheism*. {FUK; GS}

ANALOG

With the advent of the computer, analog devices (e.g., hands on the clock's face) were complemented by digital devices (e.g., numbers such as 12:35 to show the time). An analog piano has strings whereas a digital piano operates electrically. Luddites are more apt to prefer the analog. Anyone with a noisy neighbor playing church music prefers listening to the digital piano with the pianist's earphones being used. (See entry for Digital.)

Anastos, M. Elizabeth (20th Century)

With David Marshak, Anastos wrote *Philosophy-Making for Unitarian Universalist Growth and Learning: A Process Guide* (1983).

Anaxagoras (c. 500—428 B.C.E.)

A personal friend of Pericles, Anaxagoras was found guilty of impiety for asserting that the sun is "a mass of red-hot metal . . . larger than the Peloponnesus," thus conflicting with current religious thought.

Robertson calls him "the first freethinker historically known to have been legally prosecuted and condemned for his freethought." (Philolaos was prosecuted but not condemned.)

According to Robertson, he taught that the moon is a fiery (or earthy) solid body having in it plains and mountains and valleys, "this while asserting that infinite mind was the source and introducer of all the motion in the infinite universe; infinite is extent and infinitely divisible." He also taught that the mythical personages of the poets were mere abstractions invested with name and gender. Athenians saw no blasphemy in his saying that Gê (Gaia) or Dêmeter was the earth, for to them the earth was a goddess. But Anaxagoras challenged the *divinity* of the sun. The trouble, then, lay rather in his negative than in his positive assertion. He is reputedly the first Greek who wrote a book in prose. Although Anaxagoras was a freethinker according to Robertson, he was cited as being a theist in Shelley's "A Refutation of Deism."

McCabe notes that Anaxagoras "found—not unnaturally at that time—that the materialistic philosophy of the Ionic School was not satisfying and he introduced Reason or Mind (Nous) into the Universe. This was the beginning of the 'Design Argument' for the existence of God, which Socrates and Plato developed and modern theists have used so extensively, but Anaxagoras did not mean a personal God. The irony of his life is that in spite of this service to mysticism he was under the protection of Pericles, for impiety; and the particular impiety that annoyed the Athenians was to say that the stars were white-hot material bodies, not the abodes of spirits." {BDF; CE; CL; ER; JM; JMR; JMRH; RE; TYD}

Anaxandrides (Ancient Greece)

Gore Vidal has quoted the little known Anaxandrides as having said, "We are all dullards in divinity; we know nothing."

Anaximandros (610—547 B.C.E.)

A pupil as well as companion of Thales, Anaximandros was, like him, an astronomer, geographer, and physicist, seeking for a first principle (for which he may or may not have invented the name). He rejected the idea of a single primordial element, such as water. He affirmed an infinite material cause, without beginning and indestructible, with an infinite number of worlds. And, showing a Chaldean impulse, he speculated on the ascent of man from something aquatic, as well as on the form and motion of the earth (figured by him as a cylinder), the nature and motions of the solar system, and thunder and lightning.

His doctrine of evolution, remarked Robertson, "stands out for us today like the fragment of a great ruin, hinting obscurely of a line of active thinkers." Further, he believed that only in the Mesopotamian world could the early evolution have taken place. According to Diogenes, Anaximandros invented the gnomon, the first map and globe, and one of the first clocks. {CE; JMR; JMRH}

Anaximenes (c. 548 B.C.E.)

Possibly a pupil but at least a follower of Anaximandros, Anaximenes made his infinite and first principle the air. He conceived the earth as suspended. He theorized on the rainbow, earthquakes, and the revolution of the heavenly bodies, mistakenly supposing the earth to be broad and flat. He affirmed the eternity of motion as well as the perishability of the earth. He needed no dogma of divine creation. According to Robertson, Anaximenes "cannot have anticipated the chemical conception of the reduction of all solids to gases: The thesis was framed either a priori or in adaptation of priestly claims for the deities of the elements; and others were to follow with the guesses of earth and fire and heat and cold. Still, the speculation is that of bold and far-grasping thinkers, and for these there can have been no validity in the ordinary God-ideas of polytheism." {CE; JMR; JMRH}

ANCESTOR WORSHIP

An element of religious expression, ancestor worship in Africa and Asia is often a form of respect shown to the deceased. The Pacific Confucianist Chinese burn incense, offer food, and speak to their ancestors as a sign of filial piety. (See entry for Shaman.) {DGC}

ANCIENT GREEK RELIGION: See entry for Greek Religion.

ANCIENT HUMANISM

It could be said that in all its various forms, humanism is merely the natural and to-be-expected by-product of mankind's progression from savage primitivism to an increasingly advanced form of civilization and culture. As the human species has developed, it has become progressively more self-reliant, self-confident, and self-assertive. The early priestly kingdoms allowed people almost no initiative or individuality, and the later feudal and military governments were little or no improvement. From the days of Sargon of Akkad, who united Babylonia approximately 2525 B.C.E., to those of the empires of the Assyrians, Hittites, Persians, Tartars, and Turks, little progress was made concerning betterment of the welfare of mankind or the encouragement of science. However, with the development in the ancient Hellenistic culture of the city-states or *polis*, a degree of stable civilization came into being and humane government might be considered to have entered into its childhood stage, at least from a Eurocentric point of view.

From this Hellenic civilization came a philosophical concept developed by Sophists which held that man was not just another part of the universe, as was believed by earlier Greek philosophers, but that he was the center. Protagoras of Abdera, ancient anticipator of pragmatism and believer in the relativity of truth, accented this change of thought by his maxim, "Man is the measure of all things; of the being of things that are, and of the non-being of things that are not."

Such a concept that man is the measure, that he is capable, within limits, of mastering his own fate, is one which is basic to ancient humanism. It helped turn the study of nature to the study of man and his social relationships; as a result, man came to think of mankind as being capable of changing the universe–in order to improve mankind's own lot, and as a gesture of the mastery men and women held over their own fate.

"Man" in Old English or Anglo-Saxon was universal and referred to all humans equally. *Waepman* was the word for a male human, *wifman* for the female human. Although some contemporary feminists object to the use of "man" to include women as well as men, the translation of Protagoras's "man" is meant to be gender-free. The newly coined pronoun "(s)he" is considered by many to be redundant.

In common with many contemporary humanists, the Sophists emphasized the spirit of free inquiry into all knowledge, displayed a marked interest in social legislation and public affairs, and created a furor over their questionings of religion and outright agnosticism. Protagoras, for instance, was banned from Athens on grounds of impiety for having said, "Concerning the gods I am unable to say whether they exist or not, nor, if they do, what they are like." However, the Sophists insisted that a person's religious beliefs are entirely his own; and included among their later numbers were such theists as Gorgias, Scopelian, and Julian the Apostate, the last of whom was known for his inconstant adherence to Christianity. Julian, in fact, tried unsuccessfully to reform paganism and reestablish it in the Empire.

The Stoics were also ancient humanists. Stoicism, in fact, was a blend of humanism and supernaturalism. However, the Stoics rejected the superstitious and anthropomorphic elements of religion and substituted allegorical explanations in their stead. Believing that reason was the vital principle of the universe, they taught that "all men are of one blood, of one family, and all and each are sacred to one another. Harmony with nature and oneself is the ideal life," wrote Willystine Goodsell in *Conflict of Naturalism and Humanism* (1910), a masterful study of ancient humanism. Their synonyms for "God" were Zeus, Providence, the Universal Law, and Nature. Their system of ethics was man-centered. They were concerned not only with making the individual more self-sufficient and independent of externals, but also with making the individual a good member of society and a citizen of the world. In the time of a caste-ridden world, they helped further the cause of humanitarian legislation.

The Epicureans were also ancient humanists. Although Epicureanism has been attacked vigorously in the past, scholars today are reinterpreting the philosophy and feel that it offers much more of a positive outlook than formerly had been admitted. The Epicureans were humanists in that they taught men to look to themselves rather than to gods, for they believed the gods were not interested in human affairs. Contrary to popular opinion, Epicurus's ethical system was not simply one of eating, drinking, and being merry. He taught that one should lead a simple life with few desires, that friendship is the most valuable feature of living, and that prudence is a cardinal virtue. Because he believed that there is nothing evil about death since the dead have no feelings and that for the living death exists not and therefore is not to be feared, he deduced that we should concentrate upon present happiness. His attitude toward fun and merriment has been the most contested of his ideas; however, he did not advocate the complete satisfaction of physical appetites–rather, he stressed the "lasting pleasures of the mind." Epicurus was the first to have brought forward the philosophical concept of chance in the universe, and he taught that there exist no deities nor is there any immortality. His most important link to contemporary humanists is his calling upon the natural sciences to serve human needs.

Also, Epicurus proclaimed that the sole value of knowledge is in relation to action. "Therefore," he reasoned, "the supreme purpose of philosophy should be to introduce tranquillity and happiness into human life." His was an outlook that was meant to sweep away the chimeras and religious scruples and superstitions that enchain man and destroy their happiness.

Plato stands apart as one who did not agree with Protagoras that man is the measure of all things. He believed that God is the measure of all things in the highest degree—a degree much higher than any mere man of whom the followers of Protagoras talk.

Siddhartha Gautama (the Buddha) as well as K'ung Fu-Tzu (Confucius), Socrates, and Sophocles are among the other ancient humanists. As non-Eurocentric scholars expand their studies, more and more sages can be expected to be added to the list of ancient humanists. {CE; ER}

Andersen, S. M. (20th Century)

In the 1950s, Andersen was a correspondent (Denmark) for *The Humanist.*

Anderson, David (20th Century)

Anderson is Secretary of Rationalists United for Secular Humanism.

Anderson, David Daniel (1924—)

Anderson wrote *Robert Ingersoll* (1972). A writer, educator, and editor, he has taught at Michigan State University. {FUS}

Anderson, Edward B. (20th Century)

Anderson, minister of the Second Congregational Meeting House Society (Unitarian-Universalist) in Nantucket, Massachusetts, was asked in 1992 his views about religion. He responded to the present author:

> Whatever New Age enthusiasts maintain, gnostics, shamans, and druids will not be the wave of the future. They will, however, be part of its inspiration. The impulse to study ancient religions long ago rejected and replaced is a sign that people are seeking new inspiration, new expressions of belief. This means they already believe differently from what traditional religions teach.
>
> Cover-up, secrecy, propaganda have taught us to be skeptical of those who govern, even of government itself. Such skepticism is healthy. It protects our ideas. Without skepticism, those ideals would perish. In the process we have become skeptical of all institutions, law, medicine, education, religion, and those who manage them. We suspect cover-up, secrecy, propaganda everywhere. Our suspicions are well-founded. The impetus to reject dishonesty and hypocrisy contributes to the movement to re-evaluate what establishment liars and hypocrites rejected centuries ago. This means taking a fresh look at gnosticism, shamanism, animism, witches, Albigensians, Manicheans, pagans, and druids. It is a good time to be a heretic, because heresy has been given the edge of idealism.

(See entry for Jon Andersson) {WAS, 5 March 1992}

Anderson, George (1824—1913)

Anderson was a generous contributor to the Rationalist Press Association and the National Secular Society. When he tired in 1899 of G. W. Foote's *Freethinker*, Anderson demanded back his loans and took Foote through the bankruptcy court. {RAT; RE; TRI}

Anderson, John (1893—1962)

Anderson, a Scottish freethinker whose socialist and anti-cleric father had a profound influence upon him, was appointed to Challis Chair of Philosophy, the University of Sydney, Australia, where he taught from 1927 to 1958. A pluralist, he claimed one can never know anything completely, that everything–religion, censorship, patriotism, social conventions–should be critically approached.

He founded the Sydney University Freethought Society, circulated the banned James Joyce *Ulysses* with a cover inscribed "A Book of Common Prayer," and held that religious influences should be hounded out of education. {SWW; TRI}

Anderson, John C. (1909—)

A humanist counselor, Anderson signed Humanist Manifesto II. {HM2}

Anderson, Marie (Born 1842)

A Dutch freethinker, Anderson wrote for *De Dageraad* and was an editor of *De Twintigste Eeuw* (*The Twentieth Century*). She wrote novels and in some of her works used the pen names of "Meirouw Quarlè" and "Dr. Al. Dondorf." {BDF}

Anderson, Maxwell (1888—1959)

Asked about humanism, Anderson, the journalist and dramatist who wrote *Winterset*, replied, "I don't know what I think about humanism, and I doubt that what I think is important." He had, however, once written, "The gods of men are sillier than their kings and queens, and emptier and more powerless." {TYD; WAS, 15 May 1956}

Anderson, Maybanke Sussanah (1845—1927)

Anderson, whose name formerly was Wolstenholme, was an early Australian secularist. A feminist and educationalist, she published and edited a fortnightly paper, *The Woman's Voice*, which in 1894 she described as "democratic but not revolutionary; womanly but not weak; fearless without effrontery; liberal without license." She published articles by Mary Wollstonecraft and Annie Besant. In 1899, she married Sir Frances Anderson. {SWW}

Anderson, Peter O. (20th Century)

When he signed Humanist Manifesto II, Anderson was an assistant professor at Ohio State University. {HM2}

Anderson, Robert [Sir] (19th Century)

Anderson, a freethinker, wrote *Christianized Rationalism and the Higher Criticism* (1903) and *A Doubter's Doubts About Science and Religion* (1899). {GS}

Anderson, William F. (20th Century)

Anderson, when he signed Humanist Manifesto II, was a humanist counselor. {HM2}

Andersson, Jon (20th Century)

Andersson, an accomplished musician and brother of Unitarian minister Edward B. Anderson, is the long-time freethinking companion-model of Paul Cadmus. (See entry for Paul Cadmus).

Andhazi, Federico (1964—)

Andhazi is a Freudian psychoanalyst of Hungarian descent. In Argentina, he wrote *El Anatomista* (The Anatomist, 1997) about Mateo Colón, said to have been the first man to discover the female organ. However, when the donor of the $15,000 prize, Amalia Lacroze de Fortabat, learned that the clitoris, and its discovery, were the center of the book's plot, the Cement Queen, as she has been described, abruptly called off a prize ceremony. Andahazi received the money in a check anonymously pushed under his door.

He fictionalized Colón's life, describing how university anatomists used dead bodies. When necrophilia was whispered about and the anatomists were rumored to be having sex with the bodies, local Italian peasant women were said to pretend to be dead after covering themselves with blankets and lying on body carts. One physician, caught with a body that suddenly squirmed with delight was described as running off while shouting, "It's a miracle," and declaring that his semen had brought her to life. The work received negative reviews by Catholic officials. {*World Press Review*, September 1997}

Andrade, David Alfred (1859—1928)

Andrade was an early Australian secularist. An anarchist, bookseller, and magician, he was honorary secretary of the Australasian Secular Association (ASA) in 1884. {SWW}

Andrade, William Charles (1863—1939)

Andrade was an Australian anarchist, illusionist, bookseller, and publisher. With his brother David, he opened in 1898 Melbourne's first book shop specializing in radical literature, freethought, marriage and sex education. With his manager, Percy Laidler, Andrade became the leading Australian first-editions publisher of left-wing, Marxist, and revolutionary books. He described himself as "the name that means magic in Australia." {SWW}

Andre-Nuytz, Louis (19th Century)

Andre-Nuytz wrote *Positivism For All*, an elementary exposition of philosophic positivism, for which Littré wrote a preface in 1868. {BDF}

Andrew, John Albion (1818—1867)

Andrew was the Civil War governor of Massachusetts (1861—1866). An anti-slavery advocate, he was one of the organizers of the Free-Soil party and, later, of the Republican party.

While a student at Bowdoin, which required attendance at chapel, Andrew asked permission to attend the Unitarian church, allegedly because the sermons were shorter, and he later became a member in Boston of the Church of the Disciples (Unitarian), whose minister was James Freeman Clarke. {CE; EG}

Andrews, Dana (1909—1992)

Andrews, a distinguished motion picture actor, supported various humanist causes and was on the editorial board of *The Humanist.* A suave Southern leading man, Andrews starred in 1940s classics like *Laura* and *The Best Years of Our Lives.*

Andrews, James (20th Century)

A professor of mathematics at Florida State University, Andrews is an Advisory Board Member of African Americans for Humanism.

Andrews, Jane (1833-1887)

Andrews, a Unitarian, was an educator and children's author.

Andrews, John Arthur (1865—1903)

"Jack" Andrews was an Australian anarchist, poet, journalist, and editor. Attracted to the ideas of Peter Kropotkin and Elisée Reclus, he lived a poverty-stricken lifestyle by choice. Author of *A Handbook of Anarchy* (1894), he was jailed for having failed to include a sufficient address as the printer. He was a co-editor of *Reason* (1896) and editor of *Tocsin*, and *The Bulletin* in 1895 published his poem, "Invicta Spes," which included the lines

> To drivel no religious consolation
> Take I the pen; no gods or creeds I own,
> No ghostly faith supplies my inspiration,
> No metaphysic lore of things unknown. . . .

{SWW}

Andrews, Richard (20th Century)

Andrews founded the Utah Chapter of American Atheists in 1979, serving as its director or co-director until the chapter closed in 1993. In this capacity he led fights against church tax exemption and prayer in government meetings. Also, he produced a Dial-An-Atheist service. In 1993, he was recognized as Atheist of the Year. He serves on the board of directors for the Society of Separationists and other atheist organizations. E-mail: <rich123@aol.com>

Andrews, Stephen Pearl (1812—1886)

An American sociologist and social reformer, Andrews wrote *The Basic Outline of Universology* (1871) and *The Church and Religion of the Future* (1886). He was vice-president of the Liberal Club of New York and a contributor to the New York *Truthseeker*. McCabe reported that Andrews may have known thirty-two languages, that he invented a universal language and a universal (non-theistic) religion. He agitated for making Texas a free state, and he spoke out on behalf of Abolitionism. In 1843, however, he was mobbed, driven from his Texas home in the middle of the night, and given the warning that he would be hanged if he was found in the city limits within an hour. (See entry for Lilian Leland, who married his son.) {BDF; *Freethought History #15*, 1995; JM; PUT; RAT}

Andrieu, Jean (20th Century)

Andrieu addressed the International Humanist and Ethical Union's (IHEU's) Second Moral Education Conference held in Brussels (1985).

Andrieux, Louis (Born 1840)

A French deputy, Andrieux took part in the Freethought Conference at Naples in 1869 and, in 1870, was imprisoned three months for his attack on the Empire. In 1879 he became Prefect of Police at Paris, after which he wrote *Souvenirs of a Prefect of Police* (1885).

Andrysek, Oldrich (20th Century)

At the Tenth International Humanist and Ethical Culture (IHEU) World Congress held in Buffalo (1988), Andrysek addressed the group. He lived in what then was Czechoslovakia. Andrysek is a senior officer of Refugee Policy with the International Federation of Red Cross and Red Crescent Societies in Switzerland.

Anellis, Irving H. (20th Century)

Anellis is on the board of directors of the Bertrand Russell Society. He wrote *Van Heijenoort: Logic and Its History in the Works of Jean Van Heijenoort* (1994).

Angela, Alberto (1962-) and Piero Angela (1928—)

Italian paleoanthropologists Alberto and Piero Angela wrote *The Extraordinary Story of Human Origins* (1993, translation by Gabriele Tonne). Our species, they report after focusing on fossils and artifacts of hominid evolution in central East Africa, is a recent product of, necessarily dependent upon, and totally within organic evolution. {H. James Birx, *Free Inquiry*, Summer 1994}

Angeles, Peter A(dam) (1931—)

Formerly a professor of philosophy at Santa Barbara City College in California, Angeles is author of *Critiques of God* (1976). With Corliss Lamont and David A. Law, Angeles wrote "Dewey's Idea of the Religious–Critical Evaluations" in *Religious Humanism* (Winter 1968).

As the editor of *Critiques of God: Making the Case Against Belief in God* (1997), Angeles included rejections of the view that moral values and human purpose require divine sanction. The volume was written by Dewey, Freud, Fromm, Hook, Lamont, Nagel, Russell, and others. {FUS}

Angell, Norman [Sir] (1872?—1967)

Sir Norman's given name was Ralph Norman Angell Lane, and he came to fame with *The Great Illusion* (1910), in which he detailed the futility of war inasmuch as the common interests of nations made war economically undesirable. In *Peace with the Dictators?* (1938), he attacked the British Conservative party's policies, and following World War II he urged unity among the Western democracies.

Knighted in 1931, Angell was awarded the 1933 Nobel Peace Prize. "Entreat for peace not of deified thunder-clouds," Sir Norman wrote, "but of every man, woman, and child thou shalt meet." {CE; JM; RE}

ANGELS

- Angels are just Prozac for poor people.

—**Paul Rudnick**
a line in the off-Broadway show,
"The Most Fabulous Story Ever Told"

Angels, the immortal spirits which in the Holy Bible visited Abraham, Lot, Jacob, and Tobit, are accepted in the traditional belief of Judaism, Christianity, Zoroastrianism, Islam, and other religions.

Judaism has no fixed ordering of the classes of angels. However, St. Dionysius the Areopagite, in *The Celestial Hierarchy* (5th Century C.E.), codified the classes. In his descending order, the ranks of angels are as follows: seraphim, cherubim, thrones, dominations, virtues, powers, principalities, arch-angels, and angels. Satan (or Lucifer), upon being cast out of heaven for leading a revolt, became an "angel of Hell," a dark angel, a devil, the evil counterpart of the heavenly host. (Presumably, St. Dionysius checked with God before making public his codification.)

Angels have figured conspicuously in medieval Christian art. However, Protestant leaders and the Enlightenment discredited them, relegating them to the domain of poetic fancy. In poetry, John Milton's *Paradise Lost* and Dante's *Divine Comedy* have elaborated upon the concept.

The Zoroastrians have *yazatas*, which as described in their sacred book, *Avesta*, are minor deities or "worshipful beings." Subordinate to Ahura Mazda and his angels, and mentioned in early hymns of praise such as the *Yashts*, *yazatas* are not mentioned in the *Gathas*, the oldest part of the *Avesta*, which consists of seventeen hymns arranged into five gathas according to meter. The various gathas are said to be the most authentic of the teachings of Zoroaster, who lived as far back as 1000 B.C.E. The entire concept of angels allegedly was "borrowed" by Judaism, Christianity, and Islam from the Zoroastrians.

Islam has four archangels—Jibrail, Mikail, Israfil, and Izrail (the Angel of Death)—who often act in place of Allah. Two recording angels, the Kiram al-Katibin, according to popular tradition, act as scribes for every individual, the one on the right recording a person's good deeds, the one on the left recording all the bad deeds. A lower order of angels they call the jinn.

Winged guardians or angelic messengers are found in Babylonian, Assyrian, Hittite, and Egyptian mythology as well as on their monuments and sculpture.

The British geneticist J. B. S. Haldane, however, once made a scientific calculation: "An angel who developed no more power weight for weight than those of an eagle or a pigeon would require a breast projecting for about four feet to house the muscles engaged in working its wings, while to economise in weight its legs would have to be reduced to mere stilts." {CE; ER}

Angelucci, Teodoro (1549—1600)

An Italian poet and philosopher, Angelucci advocated Aristotle against F. Patrizi and was banished from Rome. One of the first emancipators of modern thought in Italy, Angelucci made a much-praised translation of *The Aeneid*. {BDF}

Angiulli, Andrea (1837—1890)

Angiulli was an Italian positivist, a professor of anthropology at Naples in 1876. He edited a philosophical review starting in 1881 in Naples. In *La Filosofia e la Ricerca Positiva* (1869), Angiulli wrote, "The new religious consciousness will be superior to Catholicism, Protestantism, and Christianity, because it will be the Religion of Humanity." {BDF; RAT}

Angle, Paul M. (1900—1975)

Angle was director of the Chicago Historical Society. With Carl Sandburg, he wrote *Mary Lincoln, Wife and Widow* (1932). His *Herndon's Life of Lincoln* (1961) is cited often because of its clarification of Lincoln's religious outlook. Asked his own view of humanism, Angle responded to the present author, "One of the few things I've learned is to keep my mouth shut on subjects about which I know nothing." {WAS, 1 May 1956}

ANGLICAN COMMUNION

The group of churches that "are in communion" with the Church of England is called the Anglican Communion. This includes regional, provincial, and separate groups bound together by mutual loyalty as expressed in the Lambeth Conference of 1930. In 1992 an estimated seventy million members were members who worshipped in a liturgical fashion regulated by the *Book of Common Prayer*.

Historically, Henry VIII repudiated papal authority by abolishing it. Although his divorce was the pretext, it was not the cause of the Reformation in England. By abolishing the papal jurisdiction and reducing clerical privilege and property, Henry VIII proclaimed the royal supremacy even in the church. In so doing he found strong national support, and although many considered him an unscrupulous ruler he generally was known—according to Canadian theologian Gerald R. Cragg—as one with unusual political perception. He had wanted some kind of papal title like *Rex Christianissimus* (France) and *Res Catholicus* (Spain). In recognition of a work on the seven sacraments against Luther, in 1532 Leo X dubbed him *Fidei Defensir* (Defender of the Faith). The 1534 Acts of Supremacy declared Henry VIII "only supreme head in earth of the Church of England," legislation repealed in 1554 by Queen Mary but revived under Elizabeth I. Among prominent individuals who were executed for their opposition was former chancellor Sir Thomas More, whose moral idea expressed the reasonableness and open-mindedness of humanism. What the king had started as a period of enlightenment fast became one of bloody suppression.

In 1607 the first Anglican church in America held services in Jamestown, Virginia. When Americans could no longer accept the enemy George III as God's representative, they avoided setting up a Church of America. Instead, they established a separate ecclesiastical body in 1789.

Although the British and American groups have somewhat close ties today, the senior warden of St. Philip's Episcopal Church in Tucson, Arizona, wrote the following to *The New York Times* (11 August 1998):

> The bishops of the Anglican Communion had a rare opportunity to teach Christian compassion at [this year's] Lambeth Conference. But these would-be apostles instead chose to heap scorn on 600 million of God's children who are gay and lesbian. The bishops chose the way of ignorance and arrogance. Surely they remember that Jesus inspired his disciples by offering unqualified love to the persecuted, the despised and the nonconformists of his day.
>
> Many American Episcopalians and their churches are determined to welcome homosexual sisters and brothers and support their ordination. The bishops' pronouncement at the Lambeth Conference can only stiffen that resolve.
>
> Anglicans in America flourished for 178 years, from 1607 to 1785, without one bishop. We could do it again if we had to. Then we could give the money we now spend on Lambeth Conferences to the poor, as Christ taught us.

{CE; ER}

Angoff, Charles (20th Century)

Using the pseudonym Richard W. Hinton, Angoff wrote *Arsenal for Skeptics* (1934), a sampler of freethought. {FUS}

ANGST

Kierkegaard introduced the term *angst* (or dread) to illustrate that it is to our benefit to take the leap of faith and believe in God. Other existentialists, however, use the term to illustrate man's not knowing what the future holds, that life's emptiness is therefore filled by deliberately choosing actions, albeit granting that we do not understand our reason, if any, for existence.

ANIMAL

An animal is distinguishable from a plant by the ways in which it obtains food. As a member of Kingdom Animalia, it differs from members of Kingdom Plantae in its capacity for locomotion, nonphotosynthetic metabolism, pronounced response to stimuli, restricted growth, and fixed bodily structure.

Philosophically, humanists and freethinkers are aware that they are a fellow animal, not a "lord" over other animals. They also recognize that their species has evolved, as have other species of the animal kingdom. The scientific study of animals is called zoology, and the study of their relation to their environment and of their distribution is animal ecology.

The largest and heaviest of contemporary animals is the blue whale, which weighs about 150 tons—as much as 1,750 average American men. It is nearly 100 feet long, about the length of a basketball court. The very largest was a female blue whale caught in 1947—it weighed 209 tons and was 90 feet, 6 inches long. Blue whales can eat about eight tons of krill, a tiny shrimp, each day. The largest land animal is the African bull elephant, which weighs about six tons. The largest was a bull African elephant shot in Angola in 1974, one that weighed 13.5 tons and was thirteen feet tall.

Bruce Bagemihl's *Biological Exuberance: Animal Homosexuality and Natural Diversity* (1999) showed that animal sexuality is diverse, that animals are sometimes heterosexual, homosexual, bisexual, and transgendered. "Gay" or "lesbian," he found, are terms not suitable for non-human animals inasmuch as they carry cultural, psychological, historical, and/or political connotations. Bagemihl cites research indicating same-sex behavior in reptiles/amphibians, fishes, insects, and other invertebrates and domesticated animals. For example, he found some same-sex behavior in bedbugs, red ants, and fruit flies; in sheep, goats, horses, donkeys, pigs, cats, dogs, rabbits, rats, mice, turkeys, and chickens; in apes, dolphins, whales, seals, deer, giraffes, geese, swans, ducks, sparrows, and hummingbirds. "Over the years," he found, "some scientists have used double standards when observing sexual behavior in animals. If they couldn't tell the gender or genders of the animals involved, they would assume the pair were of opposite sexes. When observed, homosexuality has been dismissed as aberrant, unnatural, even criminal. To the contrary, Bagemihl found homosexual behavior in more than 450 species of mammals, birds, reptiles, and insects in his deconstruction of the all-heterosexual Noah's Ark myth. {CE}

ANIMAL RIGHTS

In December 1997, French actress Brigitte Bardot called Muslims "manic throat-cutters." At a court hearing in Paris where she was accused of inciting racial hatred, she retorted that she is proud of writing that Muslims "cut the throats of women and children, our monks, our officials. They will cut our throats one day and it will serve us right." She was cheered by animal rights activists who also oppose ritual sacrifice of sheep by Muslims. (See entry for People for the Ethical Treatment of Animals.)

ANIMISM

Religion is said to be based in the main on animism, the ancient view that within all objects dwells an individual spirit, a force which governs those objects. Early humankind did not distinguish between the animate and the inanimate or between the physical and the mental. Each item had its own individuality, whether it was a stone, a woman, a dog, a tree. So did emotions, such as love, hate, ideas, dreams. Among the Melanesians of the South Seas is the idea of mana, a spirit pervading everything, a spirit responsible for the universe's good as well as the universe's evil. Some inanimate objects, called fetishes, were thought to possess magical power and included physical pieces: feathers, animal claws, shells, wood carvings, for example.

A truly powerful fetish, one which if possessed could ward off evil, was a taboo (a Polynesian word which originally applied to the sacred or to the dangerous, unclean, and forbidden). Taboos could be placed on any object, person, place, or word believed to have extraordinary powers. A taboo was often placed on a totem, or ancestral guardian. If a taboo were broken, the offender would need to arrange some kind of ceremonial purification, lest he or she suffer punishment, even death, through fear of its powers. A taboo could include destroying objects which had been in contact with a corpse, in which case it was taboo to touch such items unless a purification ceremony was performed. Strangers were taboo until made safe by some kind of ritual. Blood of menstruation or childhood was dangerous, demanding rites of purification. Early taboos were commonsense steps or caution signs taken by a group to guard against things or actions which inherently are dangerous. It made sense not to eat putrefying food, for example, so that was taboo. Later, however, religious ceremonies were devised and these provided appropriate ceremonies over which shamans or priests presided.

Psychiatrists believe fetish objects often have phallic qualities, pointing to the deformed feet of Chinese upper-class women from the Sung dynasty until the present century. Animistic idols, treated as though alive, might be fed, bathed, clothed, even provided with a sexual partner.

Some individuals without a religious orientation are looking at animism in a new, environmental way. "The earliest indigenous peoples of the world," a letter writer to *The New York Times* has stated, "treated the earth as a living, breathing organism that created and sustained life. They did not 'rape' the earth as modern civilizations do, but gave back in equal measure to their taking and were true 'shepherds' of the earth. This is because most if not all early peoples practiced animism—the belief that *everything* has a soul: people, animals, plants, rocks, trees, water, etc. Inherent in this 'pre-modern' belief is love and respect for the earth and all of its life and beauty." {CE; ER; RE}

ANIS

ANIS is an organization in India which is devoted to exposing "god-men and their tricks." (See entry for Govind Deodhekar.)

Anneke, Mathile Franziska Giesler (1817—1884)

Anneke was a freethought editor, educator, and woman's rights advocate. She met Karl Marx and Michael Bakunin, fought in the German revolutions of 1848 and 1849, and in 1865 co-founded the Milwaukee Tochter Institut, a German-language girls' school.

"There does not exist a man-made doctrine," she said at an 1869 national Equal Rights Association in New York, "fabricated expressly for us, and which we must learn by heart, that shall henceforth be our law. Nor shall the authority of old traditions be a standard for us–be this authority called Veda, Talmud, Koran, or Bible. No. Reason, which we recognize as our highest and only law-giver, commands us to be free." {WWS}

Annet, Peter (1693—1769)

A prominent deist in his time, Annet wrote *An Examination of the History and Character of St. Paul* (1747). The apostle, he declared, had become a Christian for financial reasons and was, in fact, a liar and a hypocrite. In the same year, he wrote *Supernaturals Examined*, which E. Graham Waring has described as being "a simpler form of David Hume's argument that evidence on the side of the regularity of natural law must always be greater than evidence on the side of the exceptions to the law."

In 1749, he was made a victim of the then strengthened spirit of persecution, according to Robertson, "being sentenced to stand thrice in the pillory with the label 'For Blasphemy,' and to suffer a year's hard labour. Nevertheless, he was a popular enough freethinker to start a school on his release," having invented a system of shorthand. In 1761, Annet began publishing *Free Enquirer*, a publication for which he was tried for blasphemy, convicted, and imprisoned at Newgate. {BDF; EU, E. Graham Waring; FUK; JMR; JMRH; RAT; RE; VI}

ANNULMENT OF MARRIAGE

In the Catholic Church, which does not recognize divorce, the church allows Catholics to be free to marry again by declaring the marriage invalid in the first place.

Sheila Rauch Kennedy, in *Shattered Faith: A Woman's Struggle to Stop the Catholic Church From Annulling Her Marriage* (1997), describes how as an Episcopalian married to a prominent Catholic, Massachusetts Representative Joseph P. Kennedy II, she found the practice called annulment "hypocrisy" and "nonsense." The two, she described, were married in a Catholic church by his family's priest, they previously had attended Catholic premarital counseling, and "both of us understood the principles on which we started our life together." She had not, she added, considered divorce a moral problem in itself, that it simply is a recognition that a marriage has broken down. "But annulment says you were never married in the first place, at least in the eyes of God," and it is this which she found immoral.

Although in 1968 American church tribunals granted fewer than six hundred marriage annulments, in recent years they have granted almost sixty thousand. (See entries for Joseph P. Kennedy II and for Marriage.)

Annunzio, Gabriele: See entry for Gabriele D'Annunzio.

[Anonymous] (Died 1539)

An English chronicler has described one of the 16th century French atheists:

> 1539. This yeare, in October, died in the Universitie of Parris, in France, a great doctor, which said their was no God, and had bene of that opinion synce he was twentie yeares old, and was above fouerscore yeares olde when he died. And all that tyme had kept his error secrett, and was esteamed for one of the greatest clarkes in all the Universitie of Parris, and his sentence was taken and holden among the said students as firme as scripture, which shewed, when he was asked why he had not shewed his opinion till his death, he answered that for feare of death he durst not, but when he knew that he should die he said their was no lief to come after this lief, and so died miserably to his great damnation.
>
> {JMR}

ANONYMOUS: For books written by anonymous authors, consult Gordon Stein's *God Pro and Con* (1990). Many freethinkers have feared writing under their own names, afraid that they would be charged with blasphemy or attacked by righteous religionists.

Ansah, Freda Amarkye (20th Century)

A member of the Rational Centre of Ghana, Ansah laments the tribal customs that practice female circumcision to reduce promiscuity and promote fidelity. She also laments the superstitious view that an early marriage is desirable. One of the leaders of a feminist movement in Ghana, she feels women must embark upon vast programs of education to enlighten Africans about the way taboos and superstitions hamper progress and development in society in general and in the lives of African women in particular. {AAH; *Free Inquiry*, Fall 1990}

Ansbacher, H(einz) L(udwig) (20th Century)

Ansbacher, who was a member of the psychology department of the University of Vermont, wrote the present author concerning humanism: "I am much in sympathy with the humanistic orientation in psychology which, fortunately, has been gaining ground in recent years. Allport, Fromm, Horney, and Maslow are all colleagues whose work I very much appreciate." {WAS, 29 September 1956}

Anshen, Ruth Nanda (20th Century)

Anshen was editor of Harper & Brothers' World Perspective series and author of *The Reality of the Devil: Evil In Man* (1972). Asked her view of humanism, she responded to the present author:

> It seems to me that there is a fundamental error in the attempt to create various categories of humanism. In my opinion there is only one humanism—that humanism which is the spiritual, moral, and intellectual universe in which humanity moves and has its being. It bestows upon the past unity and upon the present meaning. Romans such as Varro and Cicero proclaimed the lasting truth of humanism and denied that it was exclusively an affair of the Greeks and a transitory historical phenomenon.
>
> The original meaning of tradition which is embodied in humanism has been buried in the miasma of the prejudices and mores of an established but obsolescent social order. The pristine sense of humanism cries out for the re-articulation of the genuine spiritual and moral heritage of the human race. This heritage is not a dead weight, a heritage that supine acceptance may subdue rather than liberate our minds. Instead its very concept and essence imply the transmission of all of mankind's sacred possessions, the consciousness of the fundamental achievements of man's life which have assumed their classical form and corporealization in the works of the greatest sons of the human race. Such works can never perish. Their symbol is the flame of the inextinguishable burning torch which one champion passes on to the next in the pilgrimage for the most sublime reward of human life. Such works teach us as Dante said, "*Come l'uom' s'eterna.*" There is a divine fire which works in each of us, though we may not be aware of it. It reveals itself, in the historical life of man, in the rhythm of coming-to-be and passing-away of new individual phenomena analogous to the never-ending flux of Heraclitus. Only within the flux there is contained the unchanging, the permanent, the logos.
>
> One cannot step into the same river twice, declared Heraclitus, but he added, "In change is rest." Apart from the repose of death, change gives us the consciousness of permanescence that we could not have in a static, frozen, congealed world. We are able to have an awareness of change only because of the permanence ever-present in the substructural modes and patterns, rhythms, and recurrences.
>
> Humanism thus offers us the spectacle of the constancy of basic forms and ideas throughout a process of continuous social change and intellectual development. And the original form maintains itself through *transformation*. For the new must contain the older form and preserve it on another level.
>
> {WAS, 16 May 1956}

Anstey, Francis (Frank) George (1865—1940)

Anstey was a London-born freethinker, politician, and orator, who stowed away and arrived in Australia in 1876. A foundation member of the Melbourne Anarchist Club in 1877, he was elected to the Victorian Legislative Assembly and in 1910 was the member for the Federal House of Representatives for the following twenty-four years.

At the time of his death, he had become disillusioned and disappointed with the parliamentary process. For his funeral Anstey directed that at the cremation there be no "followers or flowers, or praise, prayers, or preachers." {SWW}

Anston, Oscar (20th Century)

A freethinker, Anston wrote *Jesus, the Son of Nobody* (1949). {GS}

ANTENNE

A Flemish quarterly, *Antenne* is by Unie Vrijzinnige Verenigingen at Brand Whitlocklaan 50, 1200 Sint-Lambrechts-Woluwe, Belgium.

Anthero de Quental: See entry for Quental.

Anthony, Brenda (20th Century)

Anthony is a freethinker and rap artist. She has written,

> We don't glorify bloodshed, gangbanging, or any violence in our music. . . . In our "Unleash the Beast" (meaning, "let go of the lie"), we bring a message of peace in the "hood," without God the Bloodshedder. . . . My group, RAZEN KANE, raps about a day of atonement with ourselves and our neighbors, and about stopping the violence and leaving the "spookism alone." We rap about stopping racism by not pointing fingers and blaming the white man but by checking the man or woman in the mirror.
>
> We're humanists, we're artists, we're positive, and we're proud freethinkers. We're tired of being stepped on by these God-loving, God-fearing record companies. We notice all of the rappers screaming "Lord, Lord" while their killing, killing is paying off. The record companies are at fault here. They promote violence, God, and death.
>
> {*Freethought Observer*, Jan-Feb 1996}

Anthony, Piers (20th Century)

Anthony, a science fiction and fantasy author, stated at the end of his *For Love of Evil* that he is an agnostic. {CA}

Anthony, Susan Brownell (1820—1906)

A major feminist, Anthony is author of *History of Woman Suffrage* (1881—1902). With Elizabeth Cady Stanton, she secured the first laws in New York guaranteeing York guaranteeing women's rights over their children and control of property and wages. She once called marriage an institution of "legalized prostitution," and she actively supported the abolitionist movement. Chided by a prominent male abolitionist that "you are not married; you have no business discussing marriage," she retorted, "and you are not a slave. Suppose you quit lecturing on slavery."

Many hold that Susan, who met the beautiful Anna Dickinson during her anti-slavery work, developed a close and probably a sexual relationship with her. Another of her close friends, Amelia Bloomer, supplied her with a kind of puritanical garment, a kind of pants that then came to be called "bloomers."

An agnostic, Anthony was associated with various liberal religious causes and was a friend of Robert G. Ingersoll. In the presidential election of 1872, she was fined $100 for casting a vote, and she continued her efforts for women's suffrage until her death. Although nominally a Quaker, Anthony sometimes attended Unitarian churches both in Rochester, New York, and in San Francisco.

The Bible, she complained is a " 'He-book' from beginning to end. It has a He-God, a He-Christ, He-angels. Woman has no glory anywhere in the pages of the Bible. Jesus said to his own mother: 'Woman, what have I to do with thee?' " Anthony further observed, "They never seem to think we have any feelings to be hurt when we have to sit under their reiteration of orthodox cant and dogma. The boot is all on one foot with the dear religious bigots."

Traveling home from a National Suffrage Convention in Baltimore, Anthony fell ill and died of pneumonia three weeks later at her home in Rochester. Aware that she was dying, she bequeathed her total estate to the suffrage movement.

To her sister, she said in her final days, "To think that I have had more than sixty years of hard struggle for a little liberty, and then to die without it seems so cruel." It took another thirteen years before the 19th Amendment was passed to guarantee women the right to vote. She was buried at Mt. Hope Cemetery, Rochester, New York, the epitaph reading, "Liberty, Humanity, Justice, Equality."

What Anthony never could have guessed is that she would be the first woman ever to appear depicted on United States currency. {BDF; CE; EG; JM; EU, Gordon Stein; PUT; RAT; RE; TRI; U; UU; WWS

ANTHROPOLOGY

Anthropology [Greek *anthropos*, human being; *ology*, study of the] is the scientific study of the origin, the behavior, and the physical, social, and cultural development of human beings. Differing from sociology and certain other sciences, it emphasizes data from nonliterate peoples and archaeological exploration. It is linked with the philosophical speculations of the Enlightenment about the origins of human society and the sources of myth. It focuses on problems of human evolution, including physical and cultural anthropology, human paleontology, the study of race, the methods of anthropometry, genetics, physiology, ecology, ethnology.

For freethinkers, an understanding of anthropology is a key part in the development of one's personal philosophy. With new anthropological findings, the humanist is eager to change his or her outlook. In contrast, absolutists who "believe" the "sacred" bibles, upon learning new anthropological findings that are controversial, resort to apologetics. {CE}

ANTHROPOMORPHISM

Anthropomorphism ascribes human feelings to something that is not human. A horse that talks in movies; actors dressed to symbolize war or death who speak their characters' lines; a river that rushes "angrily"; a laughing Mickey Mouse—all such examples ascribe human forms and characteristics to non-human entities. A statue at the front of and on the face of St. John's Cathedral in New York City depicts God as an elderly male figure with a beard. He has two eyes, a head with which he presumably thinks (presumably on a superior level to that of creatures he has created), ears for listening to petitionary prayers, and arms. Polytheists justify anthropomorphism, explaining that there is a need for visual presentation of the gods.

Anthropopathism, according to John Ruskin's "pathetic fallacy," is a term used to discredit any such analogy, however remote, between man and the non-human. Ruskin held that it is illogical to ascribe human traits to things other than man. {CE; ER}

ANTHROPOSOPHY

Rudolf Steiner (1861—1925) was a German ocultist and social philosopher, leader in the founding of the German Theosophic Association. Abandoning theosophy, he developed what he called anthroposophy, a philosophy that tried to explain the world in terms of man's spiritual nature, of thinking independent of the senses. (See entry for Crucifix.) {CE}

ANTICHRIST

Literally, an anti-Christ is one who denies Christ. Specifically, the Antichrist is a great antagonist who is expected to fill the world with wickedness but who will be defeated by Christ at his "second coming." The concept likely was borrowed from the Zoroastrians, whose similar conflict was between Ahriman and Ahura Mazda. Most recently in Christian thinking, Antichrist has been identified with the Roman empire or emperors (especially Nero); with Muhamad; and not infrequently, for example by Wycliffe and Luther, with the Roman popes. The *Catechism of the Catholic Church* (1994) states that "the supreme religious deception is that of the Antichrist, a pseudo-messianism by which man glorifies himself in place of God and of his Messiah come in the flesh."

Robert Fuller, in *Naming the Antichrist: The History of an American Obsession* (1996), concludes that when apocalypticism takes the form of "projecting . . . anxiety onto a mythic villain" it is likely to arise among groups who feel a "curtailed sense of agency." This, according to Andrew

Delbanco, author of *The Death of Satan: How Americans Have Lost the Sense of Evil*, leads to the following: "What all these self-appointed sentries have in common, in other words, is a sense that the world is arrayed against them, that they have been denied and deprived, that the old neighborhood has been turned into an occupied zone. Since more and more Americans seem to feel this way, and since 'fear of separation, powerlessness, loneliness, and failing' are rampant features of modern life, there is reason to worry that the Antichrist will come back soon, and with a vengeance."

"Proof" advanced was that the idea is not a thing of the past. In Colombia on 6-6-1996 (the sixth day of the sixth month of a year that ended in six, feared as a sign of Satan), Archbishop Pedro Rubiano, head of the Roman Catholic Church, ordered priests to forfeit any money they received for performing mass baptisms during a scare about the Antichrist. "Serious harm has been done to the church because of the actions of some priests," he said. "They have distorted the true image of the church." However, a wave of baptisms had taken place because of rumors that the Antichrist would put the "mark of the beast" on any child who had not been baptized. Journalists were unable to find how much money had been collected.

Further "proof" was shown in the following:

Given: Barney is a cute purple dinosaur.
Prove: Barney is Satan

1. Start with the given: CUTE PURPLE DINOSAUR
2. Change all U's to Latin V's: CVTE PVRPLE DINOSAVR
3. Extract Roman Numerals: C V V L D I V
4. Convert into Arabic Values: 100 5 5 50 500 1 5
5. Total those numbers: 666
6. Ergo, Barney is the Antichrist!

The Rev. Jerry Falwell, in a 1999 televised speech about the concern people have expressed over the new millennium, said the Antichrist is probably alive and here today: "Because when he appears during the Tribulation period he will be a full-grown counterfeit of Christ. Of course he'll be Jewish. Of course he'll pretend to be Christ. And if in fact the Lord is coming soon, and he'll be an adult at the presentation of himself, he must be alive somewhere today." That Antichrist, Falwell assured his followers, will spread universal evil before the end of the world but finally will be conquered at the second coming of Christ. No, he was not intending his prediction to be anti-Jewish, Falwell added, saying he meant only that the Antichrist must be Jewish because Jesus Christ was a Jew and "If he's going to be the counterfeit of Christ, he has to be Jewish."

{Associated Press, 15 January 1999; CE; ER; Internet}

ANTI-HUMANISM: See entry for Postmodernist Criticism of Humanism.

Antill, W. J. (19th Century)

Antill was an undertaker who, when English freethinkers had no other place to meet or were too far from the Hall of Science, allowed them to meet in his cellar workshop. The audience sat on planks spread between coffins while the speaker stood on the trolley used to carry corpses. W. S. Ross (Saladin), when he referred to disreputable secularists, rather unfairly called them "plank-and-coffinites." {RSR}

ANTINOMENCLATURISM: See entry for Labels.

Antipater of Sidon (Died 319 B.C.E.)

Antipater, the Macedonian general who was the ablest lieutenant of Philip II and a supporter of Alexander the Great, is remembered for his humanistic list of "the seven wonders of the world." (See entry for Man.)

ANTIPEDABAPTISM

Antipedabaptists, such as Joshua Toulmin, opposed the Christian practice of baptizing babies.

ANTI-SEMITISM

In 1969, Bertrand Russell wrote, "Though I know it is not considered the right thing to say—anti-Semitism came in with Christianity; before that there was very, very much less. The moment the Roman government became Christian, it became anti-Semitic. [This was] because they said that the Jews killed Christ, and so it became a justification for hating the Jews. I have no doubt that there really were economic motives, but that was the justification."

Ben Zion Bokser, a rabbi who lectured at the Institute of Religious Studies of the Jewish Theological Seminary, wrote this explanation: "In ancient times, the Jews like the Christians, were charged with disloyalty to the Roman Empire for refusal to conform to the emperor cult as idolatrous. In the Middle Ages, Jews were condemned for persisting as a religious minority. In modern times anti-Semitism has been fostered by various fascist states which have found Jewish universalism inconsistent with their own tribal nationalism. Anti-Semitism has been condemned by the leading ecclesiastical representatives of both Catholicism and Protestantism, as is well summarized in Jacques Maritain's *A Christian Looks at the Jewish Question* (1939) and *Protestants Answer Anti-Semitism*, edited by Beatrice Jenney (1941)."

Dagobert Runes, whose mother was killed by Nazis, wrote in *The War Against the Jews* (1968), "Everything Hitler did to the Jews, all the horrible, unspeakable misdeeds, had already been done to the smitten people before by the Christian churches. . . . The isolation of Jews into ghetto camps, the wearing of the yellow spot, the burning of Jewish books, and finally the burning of the people—Hitler learned it all from the church. . . . Wherever there are Christian churches, there is anti-Semitism."

In 1991 Pat Robertson, a religious broadcaster known as one of America's leading Christian conservatives, wrote *The New World Order*. In the book he speculated about biblical prophecy and weaved theories of broad conspiracy against American interests by "European bankers" and others (citing Paul Warburg, Jacob Schiff, and the Rothschild family). The Jewish Anti-Defamation League of B'nai B'rith claimed this was a veiled reference to Jews and their alleged conspiracy to control world finance. The book sold an estimated 500,000 hardback copies and was on *The New York Times* best-seller list. Responding to criticism, Robertson said he was arguing against allowing the United Nations to influence American foreign policy and was warning that an international coalition like the one assembled against Iraq in 1990 could one day be turned against Israel. Therefore, "The whole thing was pro-Israel and pro-Jewish," Robertson reasoned.

The Secret Relationship Between Blacks and Jews (1993), a book published by the Nation of Islam but which has no listed author, received much publicity when at Wellesley College it was assigned to students by Prof. Tony Martin. The book's theme is that Jews played a dominant role in the slave trade. Martin also published *The Jewish Onslaught: Despatches from the Wellesley Battlefront* (1993), which contains accusations of a conspiracy against blacks. He explains, "Jews, now the richest group in the United States, with one-third of the country's billionaires as of 1992 (and less than three percent of the population), have made a conscious decision to defend their privileged white status in what they might perceive of as the time-honored way, mainly by scapegoating black folk." Further, "It may be that the Jewish establishment has concluded that a prostrate African-American population, to be oppressed or paternalized as the times warrant, will continue to be its insurance against a Euro-American reversion to European anti-Jewish activities."

Louis Farrakham, a noted minister of the Nation of Islam, has called Jews "hook-nosed" and "bagel-eatin'." In 1993, his aide Khalid Abdul Muhammad made a lecture in which he lashed out at Jews, calling them the "blood suckers of the black nation" who control the country's financial system, including the Federal Reserve. Note that the "Gold"-steins and the "Silver"-steins are appropriately named as sellers of "jew"-elry, he stated, adding phrases such as "Columbia Jewniversity" and "Jew York City." He labeled the Pope a "no-good cracker" [white] and urged black South Africans to kill all whites. The Anti-Defamation League of B'nai B'rith condemned such sentiment, saying that anti-Semitism is a hideous form of racial hatred and bigotry, a virulent strand of racism that must not go unchallenged.

Khalid Abdul Muhammad not only attacked individuals of other religions but also attacked a fellow African-American, Bayard Rustin, a key organizer in the civil rights movement, who was termed a "boot-licking, butt-licking, butt-dancing, bamboozled, half-baked, half-fried, sissified, punkified, pasteurized, homogenized nigger." In 1994, he blamed the death of Jesus on the Jews: "It was the white so-called Jews that set up a kangaroo court to charge Jesus with heresy and accepted a thief and a robber named Barabbas over the good black man Jesus (sic), and under a system of capital punishment ordered the death penalty for Jesus, the black revolutionary Messiah." As for anti-Semitism, Muhammad said, "I want to see my enemy on his back, whining, crying, on his back begging for mercy. No mercy here. If you give the cracker mercy and you turn your back, he will take you out. Don't give the cracker no mercy. Never will I say I am not an anti-Semite. Whatever he is, God damn it, I'm against him. I pray for my enemy all the time—I pray that God will kill my enemy and take him off the face of the planet Earth."

Skipp Porteous, alarmed at what he found in 1994 as the prevalence of anti-Semitism within the Christian Right, named their anti-abortion movement which lists "Jewish doctors" as the leading performers of abortion. He noted that Christian Right leaders link humanism with Judaism, citing Gary North's *The Judeo-Christian Tradition* (1989) that "Judaism grew out of the rejection of Jesus Christ and steadily became humanism." *The Sunday* (Hackensack, New Jersey) *Record* (21 June 1981) cites the Rev. Bailey Smith, a Christian leader, as saying, "I don't know why God chose the Jew. They have such funny noses." *The Washington Star* (3 July 1980) cited the Rev. Jerry Falwell: "A few of you don't like the Jews and I know why. He [sic] can make more money accidentally than you can make on purpose." Porteous, estimating that 500,000 children are being taught by Christians at home or in their private schools (*Freedom Writer*, May 1994), believes anti-Semitism within conservative Christianity will not only continue as a long-term problem but will escalate sharply. As an example of the continued problem, in 1995 at Swarthmore, the Quaker-founded school in Pennsylvania, several members of the college's chorus refused to sing Bach's "St. John Passion," saying it smacks of anti-Semitism with its tale of Jewish demands for Jesus' crucifixion. However, the most recent *Catechism of the Catholic Church* specifically eliminates the demeaning and prejudiced descriptions of Jews and Judaism found in the previous book used by generations of Catholics. Pope John Paul II has issued pronouncements against the Holocaust and anti-Semitism. Some rabbis, however, believe the catechism could have helped increase Catholic understanding of Jews had it included specific mentions of anti-Semitism, the Holocaust, and the modern state of Israel.

A revisionist version as to the cause of anti-Semitism is found in *The Origins of the Inquisition in 15th-Century Spain* (1995), by Benzion Netanyahu, a professor emeritus at Cornell University and the father of Benjamin Netanyahu, a leader of Israel's Likud Party. Netanyahu holds that the Spanish Jews who had been forced to convert had, indeed, assimilated with the Catholics and were "devoutly Christian." "Jew hatred," he then stated, was not started by Christians but can be traced back to ancient Egypt where in 525 B.C.E. the Persian conquerors of the Egyptians enlisted Jews as allies. This led to the Egyptian priest Manetho's publishing in Greek a 270 B.C.E. *History of Egypt* which Netanyahu called "the first written anti-Semitic piece to come down to us from antiquity." Furthermore, the work created a model of "the most atrocious lies and the most absurd libels" which became an idée fixe in the culture of Christendom. The Spaniards in the 15th Century defined the Jews not religiously, but racially, and this inspired others to treat the Jews as an evil race of men, worthy of, in Netanyahu's words, "a large-scale bloodbath, mass extermination, or, to use the language of our time, genocide." Indeed, 30,000 converted Jews during the 14th and 15th centuries were burned at the stakes of the Inquisition. (See entries for Pedro Arbués, Charles Lindbergh, Khallid Abdul Muhammad, and Meyer Rothschild.) {*Bertrand Russell Speaks His Mind*; ER; David Gonzalez, "Jews See Signs of Change in New Catholic Teachings, "*The New York Times*, 25 February 1995; for the role of the Jews in modern capitalism, see *The House of Rothschild* by Niall Ferguson (1999).}

ANTI-SEMITISM, THE ANTHROPOLOGY OF: See entry for Hyam Maccoby.

Antisthenes (444?—371 B.C.E.)

Antisthenes, founder in Greece of the Cynics and a follower of Socrates, held that cultivating virtue for its own sake leads to happiness. Shun pleasure, live in poverty, disagree with social conventions, and happiness can be achieved in this lifetime, he taught, not in Plato's next world. Virtue is the only good (not, as Socrates asserted, the highest good), and virtue means a simple lifestyle and an enjoyment of worldly pleasures.

Repudiating polytheism, Antisthenes believed in one god but described that god as something unlike anything else man has known. {CE; JMRH}

Antoine, Nicolas (17th Century)

A martyr, Antoine denied the messiahship and divinity of Jesus. As a result he was strangled, then burned at Geneva in 1632. {BDF}

Anton, John (1920—)

When he signed Humanist Manifesto II, Anton was a professor of philosophy at Emory University. In 1980, he signed the Secular Humanist Declaration.

His works include *Critical Humanism as a Philosophy of Culture* (1981), *Essays in Ancient Greek Philosophy* (1972), and *Philosophy and the Civilizing Arts, Essays Presented to Herbert W. Schneider* (1974). {HM2; SHD}

Antonelle, Pierre Antoine (1747—1817)

Antonelle was a French political economist who embraced the revolution with ardor. An article in the *Journal des Hommes Libres* occasioned his arrest, but he was acquitted. When he died at Arles, the clergy declined to give him the Christian burial, which his relatives desired. {BDF; RAT}

Antony [Father] (20th Century)

Father Antony was the name of a Franciscan priest who now is known by his secular name. (See entry for Joseph McCabe.)

Antony, P. M. (20th Century)

A playwright and rationalist, Antony was winner of the Kerala Literary Academy Award and author of *The Sixth Holy Wound of Christ*. When he was imprisoned for being accused (incorrectly) of murder and having written the controversial play, the Indian Rationalist Association appealed and after one decade Antony was released in 1996.

The work was inspired by Nikos Kasantsakis's *The Last Temptation of Christ*. It presents the story of Jesus as a depressed suicidal maniac, whom Judas, the hero, makes a willing martyr to provoke an uprising of the Roman slaves against the clergy. The Catholic Church called the work blasphemous, and the Rationalist Press Association stepped in to publish the work.

ANUS

The anus is a part of the body that, admittedly, is not a subject for conversation at a Puritan's annual family reunion banquet. Anyone for whom it is taboo to mention certain areas of the anatomy will hesitate to speak about the waste that passes into the rectum and is then expelled as bowel movements through the anus. Smut, filth, pornography, obscenity, naughty: such accusations arise at the mention of anything anal.

Some claim to be unaware, in fact, that the anus can be a point of sexual penetration (*paedicatio*, when done by Latins), let alone sexual pleasure. They find incredulous the statistics reported by popular magazines such as *Playboy* and *Playgirl* concerning erotic uses of the anus. Meanwhile, artists such as Mapplethorpe and Serrano have photographed various items being injected into or ejected from the body's seventh (for some, the lucky seventh) opening, which some but certainly not all individuals find enjoyable. (Knowing their audience's probable reactions, comedians enjoy pronouncing the seventh planet from the sun *yur-AYN-us*, which was named as the earliest supreme god, a personification of the sky, the son and consort of Gaea and the father of the Cyclopes and Titans. Freethinkers find even funnier, however, their telling bibliolaters, "You seem to know more about your Ezekiel than about Uranus.)

For those who enjoy "taking the Lord's name in vain" and tire of using religious references—e.g., "Goddammit, Hell no, for Chrisake!"—suitable alternatives do abound: "No, you arsehole, you ass bandit! You're no longer my asshole buddy." However, from the viewpoint of a rationalist, such denigration of a key part of the human anatomy is negatively discriminatory and borders on the oligrophrenic.

APARTHEID

The South African racial policy known as apartheid (from an Afrikaans word for "apartness" and having a last syllable that rhymes with "hate") was an ultimate form of inhumanism: a social and political policy of racial segregation and discrimination enforced by white minority governments from 1948 to 1994. With Nelson Mandela's election as the nation's first black president, the last vestiges of the apartheid system were legislatively eliminated. {DGC}

APE

Mike Howgate is the founder-member of the Association for the Protection of Evolution (APE). He has spoken to the Coventry and Warwickshire Humanists in England.

APHRODITE

Aphrodite, the ancient Greek goddess of fertility, love, and beauty, was designated by Homer as the child of Zeus and Dione. Hesiod held that Aphrodite rose from the foam of the sea where Uranus's genitals had fallen after he had been mutilated by Kronus. She was inseminated by many: Area, for whom she bore Harmonia; Hermes, for whom she bore Hermaphroditus; and the shepherd Anchises, by whom she bore Aeneas. The Romans identified Aphrodite with Venus. She was similar in many of her attributes to the Oriental goddesses Astarte and Ishtar. (See entry for Beauty.) {CE}

APOLOGETICS

Apologetics is a branch of theology that concerns itself with defending or proving the truth of religious doctrines.

If, for example, "and He rested on the seventh day from all His work which He had made" is a seemingly unscientific account in the revealed-from-God *Genesis* story, it follows that God had a different concept of "day" from that of us mere mortals.

APOLOGY

- Apologize, v.i. To lay the foundation for a future offence.

—Ambrose Bierce
The Devil's Dictionary

An apology is a literary work that defends, justifies, or clarifies an author's ideas or point of view. The literary use neither implies that wrong has been done nor expresses regret, although in everyday usage a person who gives an apology says he is sorry about something.

Plato's *Apology* (3rd Century B.C.E.) presents Socrates's defense of himself at his trial before the Athenian government. Sir Philip Sidney's *Apologie for Poetrie* and *Defense of Poesie*, both written in 1850, examined the art of poetry and its condition in England. The two works were written to justify the poet's craft after it had been attacked by critics.

In 1864, Cardinal Newman wrote a spiritual autobiography, *Apologia pro Vita sua*, which attempted to clarify his views after they had been misrepresented in an essay by Charles Kingsley.

In popular usage, true love means you never have to say you are sorry, the implication being that apologies involve specific wrongs and that, ideally, "true" lovers would never do wrong.

A POSTERIORI

A posteriori reasoning is derived inductively, by reasoning from observed facts. For example, one cannot prove the existence of gods by using a posteriori reasoning. One *can* deduce—contrary to what had been assumed up to the 1980s— that insects evolved 120 million years before plants, as revealed by 1993 studies made by Dr. Conrad C. Labandeira of the Smithsonian Institution in Washington, D.C., and Dr. J. John Sepkoski Jr., a paleontologist at the University of Chicago. (See entry for *a priori*.)

A PRIORI

A priori reasoning is derived from what are believed to be self-evident propositions; for example, theists and deists use *a priori* arguments to prove the existence of God, or the Supreme Architect of the universe.

"Only the sort of knowledge that is called *a priori*—especially logic and mathematics—can be possibly supposed to exist in every one independently of experience," Bertrand Russell wrote, adding, "In fact, this is the only sort of knowledge (apart from mystic insight) that Plato admits to be really knowledge."

However, as objected to by Russell and detailed in basic source books, including *A Modern Introduction to Philosophy* (1973) by Paul Edwards and Arthur Pap, philosophers question whether we have any a priori knowledge of matters of fact at all. For example, to those who claim that the principles of mathematics and logic are a priori, is this the case or is our knowledge of these principles not really based on experience?

For Russell,

> Mathematical knowledge, it is true, is not obtained by induction from experience; our reason for believing that 2 and 2 are 4 is not that we have so often found, by observation, that one couple and another couple together make a quartet.
>
> In this sense mathematical knowledge is still not empirical. But it is also not a priori knowledge about the world. It is, in fact, merely verbal knowledge. "3" means "2 + 1," and "4" means the same as "2 + 2." Thus mathematical knowledge ceases to be mysterious. It is all of the same nature as the "great truth" that there are three feet in a yard.

(See entries for *A Posteriori*, Plato, and Aristotle.)

Apelt, Ernst Friedrich (1812—1859)

Apelt, a German philosopher, criticized the philosophy of religion from the viewpoint of reason and wrote works on metaphysics. He became known as the leader of the aesthetic rationalist school, which on the religious side connotes a liberal theism. {BDF; RAT}

APOCALYPTICISM

Apocalypticism is a belief in the imminent destruction of the world. It also involves, once goodness triumphs over evil, the foundation of a new world order. Paul Edwards, in *Reincarnation: A Critical Examination* (1996), devastatingly attacks such nonsense concerning forecasts about the destruction of Japan as well as various American states. {PE}

APOCRYPHA, OLD TESTAMENT

The Apocrypha of the Old Testament contains fourteen books commonly found in the Greek Bible (the Septuagint) and the Latin Vulgate in excess over the Hebrew Bible. Catholics refer to the books as "deuterocanonical," reserving the name Apocrypha for other quasi-scriptural books in excess over those of the Vulgate to which Protestants give the name Pseudepigraphs. Generally speaking, the books in the Apocrypha have not been included by Protestants, who doubt their authenticity. For a table of those books of the Old Testament which are in the Roman Catholic Canon, the Protestant Canon, the Jewish Scripture, or the Protestant Apocypha, see the entry for Bible in most standard dictionaries. {CE; ER; RE}

APOLOGETICS

Apologetics, once called "a science of the defence of Christian truth," is a branch of theology which defends (the Greek root, *apologetikos*, means defend) the doctrine of the divine origin and authority, particularly within Christianity. Unlike polemics, the practice of theological controversy to refute errors of doctrine, apologetics is felt to be so fundamental to the Christian faith that argument with professing Christians is not anticipated. But attacks by non-Christians—Jews and pagans, particularly—were anticipated, so the apologists' efforts were made to defend Christianity by using evidence and sound reasoning. According to Edgar J. Goodspeed, who had been a professor of Biblical and Patristic Greek at the University of Chicago, *The Preaching of Peter*, which was written early in the second century, attacked both Greek and Jewish ways of worship and described the Christians as "a third race." Quadratus in 125 or 129 CE wrote a second apology which was to be presented to Hadrian in order to obtain more lenient treatment for the Christians. Aristides in 138 or 147 CE addressed a defense of the new faith to the emperor Antoninus, one which attacks Chaldean, Greek, Egyptian, and Jewish forms of worship, in contrast with Christian worship and morals. {ER}

APOSTROPHE

Humanists are aware that only one word in English contains three apostrophes, the manuscript sign ('). (See entry for Forecastle.)

APOTHEOSIS

Apotheosis is the ascribing of divine power to a human being. Alexander the Great, for example, obtained his first apotheosis at the oracle of Amon in Egypt. Originally, such ascriptions were only for deceased emperors but then became observed for living ones. Ancestor worship is related. (See entries for Shaman and Emperor Worship.) {CE; ER}

APPLE

"Some religious fundamentalists," stated the editor of *Pique*, newsletter of the Secular Humanist Society of New York, "still will not eat an apple, believing that Adam and Eve were expelled from Eden because they ate such. But the Biblical words are that the two were evicted from Paradise for having eaten 'the fruit of the tree which is in the midst of the garden.' Anyone who thinks a specific fruit is mentioned," stated the editor, "is full of applesauce."

Appleby, J. K. (19th Century)

Appleby, a Unitarian minister, influenced George William Foote to give up Anglicanism and adopt a Unitarian position early on in his youth. {RSR}

Appleman, Philip (1926—)

A poet and professor emeritus of English at Indiana University, Appleman is editor of the *Norton Critical Edition Darwin* (1979) and author of *Darwin's Ark* (1984), *Apes and Angels* (1989), and *New and Selected Poems 1956—1996.*

He lectures on humanistic subjects and is a member of the Secular Humanist Society of New York. In 1994, Appleman was named the Humanist Arts Awardee by the American Humanist Association. In 1996, he was a featured speaker at the national convention of the Freedom From Religion Foundation in Madison, Wisconsin.

Aquila (2nd Century)

Aquila, a Jew of Pontus, became a proselyte to Christianity, then left that religion. He published a Greek version of the Hebrew scriptures to show that the prophecies did not apply to Jesus. Justinian forbade the Jews to read Aquila's version of the Scriptures. {BDF}

AR RAZI CIRCLE

Ar Razi Circle (ARC), an institute for the promotion of secularism in the Islamic world, endorses the Universal Declaration of Human Rights and the International Covenants on Human Rights. It is committed to the ideas of democratic society and to a total separation between the state and religion. (See entries for Ar Razi and for Islamic Women, Rights Of.) {*International Humanist News*, December 1997}

ARABIC

"Arabic" refers to language. There are Arabic-speaking Jews, Arabic-speaking Christians, and Arabic-speaking Arabs. Arabic is spoken throughout the Arabian peninsula and also in Iraq, Syria, Jordan, Lebanon, Israel, Morocco, Tunisia, Algeria, Libya, Egypt, Sudan, Mauritania, and Chad. It is the mother tongue of more than 150 million in Africa and Asia.

The Qur'an (still called the Koran by some in the West) was written in Arabic and for religious reasons is said not to be translatable inasmuch as it is verbatim the Word of God. Neither must it be modified. In it, God speaks in the first person. Within Arab nations, disbelief is severely punished, with the tacit implication that Allah approves of the meting out of pain, tears, and suffering. {CE}

ARABS

Although originally "Arabs" referred to the Semitic peoples of the Arabian Peninsula, it now refers to those persons whose primary language is Arabic; i.e., most of the population of Algeria, Bahrain, Egypt, Iraq, Jordan, Kuwait, Lebanon, Libya, Morocco, Oman, Quatar, Saudi Arabia, Suday, Syria, Tunisia, the United Arab Emirates, the People's Democratic Republic of Yemen, and Yemen. The term does not usually include Arabic-speaking Jews (such as those in North Africa and formerly also in Yemen and Iraq), Kurds, Berbers, Copts, and Druses, but it does include Arabic-speaking Christians (such as those found in Syria, Lebanon, Israel, and Jordan).

Arab and Arabian are terms that are not interchangeable with Muslim. Not all Muslims are Arab, and not all Arabs are Muslim.

Freethinkers point out that it was the Arabs who introduced Europe to the Greek philosophers, whose writings they had already translated into Arabic. (See entry for Fons Elders, who has written that Arab humanism from the eighth to the twelfth century was essential to the development of the Renaissance.) (CE)

Arago, Dominique François Jean (1786—1853)

Arago's early work in mathematics and astronomy was so brilliant that the French Academy, against its own rules, admitted him at the age of twenty-three. Other European academies also honored him. He was equally distinguished in physics, in manuals of which his name still occurs.

An outspoken atheist and republican even under Napoleon (who esteemed him) and Louis Napoleon, Arago at the age of sixty-two fought at the barricades in the Revolution of 1848. In his published correspondence with Baron von Humboldt, who called him a "zealous defender of the interests of Reason," Arago often attacked religion. The French *Grande Encyclopédie* termed Arago "one of the most illustrious savants of the nineteenth century."

His son, **François Victor Emmanuel** (1812—1896), was a distinguished lawyer who took part in the Revolution of 1848, afterwards joining the advanced anti-clerical group which attacked the clerical policy of the Government in the Chambre. He sat in the National Assembly from 1871 to 1876, then was in the Senate from 1880 to 1894. From 1880 to 1894 he was French ambassador to Switzerland.

His brother **Étienne Vincent Aragao** (1802—1892), a distinguished dramatist, also attacked religion. During the fourth Revolution, Arago was Mayor of Paris during the siege. {BDF; JM; RAT; RE}

Aragon, Augustin (20th Century)

From 1901 to 1914, Aragon edited *Revista Positiva* in Mexico City.

Aragon, Louis (1897—1982)

Aragon, a French poet, wrote in *Treatise on Style* (1928), "Of all the possible sexual perversions, religion is the only one to have ever been scientifically systematized." {TYD}

Aramalla, Purnachandra (20th Century)

Originally from Andhra Pradesh State in India, Aramalla has long been active in Indian rationalist and humanist circles. He is author of *Nature, Life, and Man* (*Prakruti, Jeevamu, Manavudu*,1984); *What the Modern Science Tells Us?* (*Aadhunika Vijnanam Emi Cheputondi?*, 1993); and numerous articles. Before coming to New York in 1984, he taught at Andhra University in India for several years and currently is owner of two pharmacies in New York City.

Aramalla is the son of a popular teacher, history lecturer, and rationalist: Koti Reddi Aramalla (1923-). {WAS, interview}

Aranda, Pedro Pablo Abarca de Bolea [Count] (1718—1799)

A Spanish statesman, Count Aranda was a soldier and ambassador to Poland. He was inspired by the ideas of the Encyclopedists and contributed to the expulsion of the Jesuits from Spain in 1767. The clergy and monks conspired against him, drove him from office, and dragged Spain back to its medieval condition, states McCabe.

The Inquisition threatened him but, because of his reputation and because he neared the age of eighty, did not venture to take action. In 1792 he was elected Spanish minister to France but, then recalled, was later exiled to Aragon, where he died. Like his friend Voltaire, Aranda was a deist. {BDF; JM; RAT; RE}

Araujo, Derek Carl (20th Century)

Araujo, the founding president of the Campus Freethought Alliance, organized a humanist group at Harvard University in 1996 and served until 1999, leaving to teach physics in New York City. In 1998 he was a signer of the Alliance's "Bill of Rights for Unbelievers." Araujo is author of "Student Freethought Group Embarks on Productive Path" in *Free Inquiry* (Winter 1996—1997). He was a signer of Humanist Manifesto 2000.

E-mail: <derek@jackbruce.com> and <JBruceFan@aol.com>. {*International Humanist News*, December 1996}

Arbués, Pedro (1441—1485)

Arbués is also known as Saint Peter Arbués. According to Charles Lee in *History of the Inquisition*, Arbués said, "Innocent or not, let the Jew be fried." Ferdinand V had made him the chief Spanish Inquisitor in 1484. The following year while he was at prayer, Arbués was stabbed, allegedly at the instigation of nobles whom he was threatening. In 1664, he was beatified, and in 1867 he was canonized.

Arbuthnot, Forster (1883—1901)

On his return to England after being in the Indian Civil Service (1853—1878), Arbuthnot joined Burton in the Kama Shastra Society for the issue of unexpurgated translations of Eastern works. He initiated the Oriental Translation Fund (1891). Arbuthnot was an agnostic. {RAT}

Arcesilaus (c. 315—241 B.C.E.)

Arcesilaus and Carneades, teachers in Plato's Academy, started with the Delphic oracle's telling Socrates that he was the wisest of the Athenians. He realized he was, because he alone was aware that he knew nothing. If nothing can be known by our senses or our reason, there is no way to distinguish true or real perceptions from illusory ones, Arcesilaus taught. No certain criterion was known. Therefore, one has to suspend judgment on all that knowledge claims about any reality beyond our immediate experience.

What we possess is reasonable or probable information that may, or may not, actually be true. This idea—that probabilities are sufficient to guide us through life—gave birth to the academic skepticism that later would be discussed by Cicero and Diogenes Laertius. St. Augustine attempted to refute such an idea.

However, Bertrand Russell in *History of Philosophy* lauds Arcesilaus for his advocacy of skepticism though still professing to follow Plato. Arcesilaus "maintained no thesis," Russell explains,

> . . . but would refute any thesis set up by a pupil. Sometimes he would himself advance two contradictory propositions on successive occasions, showing how to argue convincingly in favour of either. A pupil sufficiently vigorous to rebel might have learnt dexterity and the avoidance of fallacies; in fact, none seem to have learnt anything except cleverness and indifference to truth. So great was the influence of Arcesilaus that the Academy remained skeptical for about two hundred years.

{CE; EU, Richard H. Popkin}

ARCHAEOLOGY

• An archeologist is the best husband any woman can have because the older she gets the more he is interested in her.

—Agatha Christie

• Let the believers be tricked by the Adam and Eve of "sacred" scriptures. Meanwhile, the humanists' "sacred" facts are dug up by freethinking archaeologists.

—Anonymous

Archaeology [Greek *arkhaio* + *log-ia*, study of beginnings] is a branch of anthropology that documents past human life and culture by studying such evidence as graves, buildings, tools, pottery, and human remains. Italians in the 15th century excavated ancient Greek sculpture. Later, Johann Winckelmann and Ennio Visconti advanced the study of the Greek and Roman past, and Heinrich Schliemann at Troy, Arthur Evans at Crete, Michael Ventris in his deciphering of the Minoan script—all helped advance the study. Today, archaeologists study New World as well as Old World sites, making such exciting findings as those of Louis Leakey, who located the skeletel remains of humans in East Africa dating back 1.7 million years.

As just one tantalizing illustration of the findings of archaeologists, the 1984 discovery of the body of a young man in a bog in Cheshire, England, led to the determination that he had been violently struck on the head, his throat had been cut, and this had happened during the 1st or 2nd century according to radiocarbon dating. The manner in which he had been killed was similar to that of the way others had been killed in Grauballe and Tollund in Denmark, indicating all had been ritually sacrificed. {CE}

ARCHBISHOP

• Archbishop: a Christian ecclesiastic of a rank superior to that attained by Christ.

—**H. L. Mencken**

Archelaos (5th Century B.C.E.)

The most important disciple of Anaxagoras, Archelaos of Miletos was the first systematic teacher of Ionic physical science in Athens. He taught about the universe's infinity, and he grasped the nature of sound. Archelaos is said to have been the master of Socrates. {JMR; JMRH}

Archer, Jeff (20th Century)

Archer wrote "Runs, Hits, and Prayers" (*Secular Nation*, Fall 1995), in which he tells some experiences he has had as a referee. One was calling a technical foul on a team that was praying too long, for which he received catcalls from fans and players alike. He laments the fact that in the "good old days" religion did not mix with sports but that Americans, unlike Europeans, have been increasingly mixing sports and religion.

Archer, who is editor of *The Alternative*, wrote *Strike Four: Adventures in European Baseball* (1995). In 1996, he became leader of San Diego's Atheist Coalition.

Archer, William (1856—1924)

Archer was a Scottish-born freethinker, author, critic, and translator of Ibsen's plays. To him, the god-idea was a noxious fallacy. For *The World*, Archer was a theatre critic in 1884, continuing for twenty-one years. He was opposed to any censorship and, when Shelley's "The Cenci" was banned in 1886, Archer insisted that "the English nation should be allowed to judge for itself as to whether the works of its great poets are fit or unfit for the stage."

" 'Theocracy,' " Archer wrote, "has always been the synonym for a bleak and narrow, if not a fierce and blood-stained, tyranny." A translator of "A Doll's House" and "Hedda Gabler," in which as co-director he starred his mistress, Elizabeth Robins, Archer was a friend of Henrik Ibsen as well as of George Bernard Shaw. Shaw, when Archer died, wrote that he felt that "he took a piece of me with him." Peter Whitebrook, in a biography, points out that Archer wrote for *Progress* and was an atheist and combative speaker.

He also contributed to the *Literary Guide*, the monthly organ of the Rationalist Press Association and to the *Rationalist Annual*. Archer wrote *The Life, Trial, and Death of Francisco Ferrer*, who was executed for advocating freethought at the *Esaula Moderna* in Barcelona; and *God and Mr. Wells*, which was a reply to Wells's *God the Invisible King*.

Joseph McCabe remarked that Archer "seems to have been lenient to Spiritualist claims," a reference to his having lost a son in World War I and had consulted a number of mediums in the hope of learning something definite. Whatever the reason, he "abruptly ceased" visits to mediums in 1920.

Archer will be remembered, not for recommending that blacks in the American South have their own separate state, but for his having introduced Ibsen to Britain, guided the early career of Shaw, and encouraged Pinero, Wilde, Galsworthy, and Granville Barker. {RAT; RE; TRI; TYD}

Archibald, Charles (20th Century)

Archibald is a board member of the American Humanist Association.

Archilochus (c. 700 or 650 B.C.E.)

Fragments of Archilochus's poetry survive. Isaiah Berlin liked the Greek poet's lines, "The fox knows many things but the hedgehog knows one big thing," turning the idea into his own observation that thinkers include those who contribute a number of unrelated but valuable insights and those who develop a unified vision or universal principle. {CE; Paul Johnson, *The New York Times*, 12 November 1997}

Ardell, Donald B. (20th Century)

Ardell publishes the *Ardell Wellness Reports* and hosts an internet wellness show at <www.yourhealth.com>. The author of *The Book of Wellness: A Secular Approach to Spirituality, Meaning, and Purpose*, he holds "that a satisfactory sense of meaningful work and a purposeful life are certain prerequisites for a continuing sense of happiness in life." E-mail: <donardell@earthlink.net>. {*Free Inquiry*, Summer 1998}

Ardigó, Roberto (1828—1920)

At the age of forty-three, Ardigó gave up being a Catholic priest. He then became a major figure in the movement of Italian positivism, teaching against idealism at the University of Padua and taking the position that human knowledge originates in sensation. He wrote the twelve-volume *Opere filosofiche* (1882—1918) and *La scienza della educacazione* (1909, 3rd edition). {BDF}

Ardila, Ruben (1942—)

A professor of psychology at the Universidad de Colombia, Ardila is one of the Humanist Laureates in the Council for Secular Humanism's International Academy of Humanism and is a signer of Humanist Manifesto 2000. Ardila is author of *La Psicologia en America Latina: Pasado, Presente, y Futur* (1993) and, with Mario Bunge, *The Philosophy of Psychology* (1987).

Arendt, Hannah (1906—1975)

Arendt, a German-American political theorist, was not a believer in God. In her *Origins of Totalitarianism* (1951), she traced Nazism and Communism to nineteenth-century imperialism and anti-Semitism. Her other works include *The Human Condition* (1958), *Eichmann in Jerusalem* (1963), and *The Life of the Mind* (1977). The 1968 work was controversial in its exploration of the complicity of the European nations in the destruction of the Jews and of what she termed the "eerie banality of the Nazi evil." (For a description of her intellectual as well as physical attraction to Heidegger, see the entry for Martin Heidegger. The two had a sexual relationship despite his never expressing regret about the Holocaust and his not helping his Jewish students, although he did not actively harass or persecute them.) {Paul Edwards, "Heidegger's Quest for Being," *Journal of Philosophy* 64:437-470, 1989; DGC}

Arents, John (Stephen) (1926—)

Although his parents were religiously conservative and he was a child gospel singer, he retired at age six because of ill health, never resuming that career. A Brooklyn-born chemist whose research has been in quantum chemistry, Arents taught and did graduate work at Columbia University from 1950 to 1956, then was a lecturer and professor at The City College of the City University of New York (CCNY) from 1956 until his retirement in 1991.

With Chester B. Kremer he co-authored *Theory and Problems of Modern General Chemistry* (1965) and, with Leonard C. Labowitz, *Physical Chemistry: Problems and Solutions* (1969). With F. Brescia, H. Meislich, and A. Turk, he was co-author of *General Chemistry* (5 editions with various titles, 1966—1988).

Arents is a fiercely independent thinker, as critical of liberal and humanist irrationality as of any other kind. E-mail: <jarents@best-web.net>.

Areschoug, F. W. C. (1830—1908)

Areschoug, a Swedish botanist, was an unbeliever. (See entry for Scandinavian Unbelievers.)

Aretino, Pietro (1492—1556)

The "scourge of princes," Aretino was an Italian satirist whose derisive wit helped him become wealthy, wealthy because those who feared he would write about them paid him not to. A writer of comedies and letters filled with satire, Aretino was a subject for one of Titian's portraits. In *I Raggionamenti (The Conversations)*, Aretino writes of an abbot who, according to Charles Rosen, "dallies with a girl in one hand and a boy with the other while simultaneously screwing a nun and being sodomized by a novice priest (all their simultaneous cries of delight skillfully orchestrated by the author)." {CE}

Arey, Lisa T. (20th Century)

In the 1950s, Arey was a director of the Humanist Fellowship of Boston, a group affiliated with the American Humanist Association.

Argens, Jean Baptiste de Boyer [Marquis] (1704—1771)

The Marquis d'Argens was a military man who became one of Frederick the Great's chamberlains. He translated Julian's discourse against Christianity and Ocellus Lucanus on the Eternity of the World. Wheeler says Argens took Bayle as his model but was inferior to that philosopher. Although clerical writers stated that he was "converted" before death, Argens's widow refuted the charge. {BDF; RAT}

Argenson, Marc Pierre de Voyer de Paulmy d' [Count] (1696—1764)

A French statesman who at one time was Governor of Paris and Minister of War, Argenson was a friend of Voltaire and the Encyclopedists. Largely owing to Voltaire's protection, the two were able to work in Paris during an age of despotic bigotry, and the dictionary was dedicated to him. Count Argenson shared their deistic views, as did his brother, **René Louis de Voyer de Paulmy** (1694—1757), the Marquis d'Argenson, Councillor of State and Minister of Foreign Affairs (1744—1747). {JM; RAT; RAT; RE}

Argental, Charles Augustin de Ferriol (1700—1788)

Count d'Argental was a French diplomat, a nephew of Mme. de Tencin, the mother of D'Alembert. A close friend of Voltaire, Argental wrote *Memoirs du Comte de Comminge* and *Anecdotes de la cour d'Edouard.* {BDF; RAT}

ARGENTINE FREETHINKERS, HUMANISTS

Hugo Estrella has completed a thorough study of the struggle of freethinkers in Argentina. In the first two of three parts, published in *International Humanist News* (Dec 1997 and Oct 1998), he claimed that the contributions of Juan José Castelli, Bernardo Monteagudo, Mariano Moreno, Domingo Sarmiento, Bartolomé Mitre, Esteban Echeverria, and Bernardino Rivadavia "were whispered with respect by every free thinking person in the country." The group's journal is *El Desorden* (Caseros 636 C.P. 5000, Córdoba). On the Web: <www.humanistarg.org>. (See entries for Juan Alberdi, Hugo Estrella, and Domingo Sarmiento.)

ARGENTINE UNITARIANS

Lilian Burlando, a retired clinical psychologist, leads a Unitarian group at Sanchez de Caballero 2030, (9410) Ushuaia, Tierre del Fuego, Argentina.

Argilleres, Antoine (16th Century)

Argilleres at first was a Jacobin monk and afterwards a Protestant preacher. For having eight years previously taken the part of Servetus against Calvin at Pont-de-Veyle in Bresse, Argilleres was tortured several times, was then decapitated, and his head was nailed to a gibbet at Geneva (1562). {BDF}

Argow, Waldemar (1916—1996)

A minister of the People's Church (Unitarian) in Cedar Rapids, Iowa, Argow was a naturalistic humanist who wrote reviews for *The Humanist* in the 1950s. He is author of *What Do Religious Liberals Believe?* (1950). He also served as minister in Toledo, Ohio, and Palm Beach, Florida.

ARGUMENT FROM DESIGN

Theologians who argue from design do so by appealing for the existence of God based on the hypothesis of an ultimate design, intention, or purpose in the universe. "Why do people believe in God?" Richard Dawkins has asked. He answered, "For most people the answer is still some version of the ancient Argument from Design." In "The Improbability of God" (*Free Inquiry*, Summer 1998), he tackled that subject using a scientist's reasoning, concluding after detailing the improbabilities of the design argument that "There is no reason for believing that any sort of gods exist and quite good reason for believing that they do not exist and never have." (See entry for Goldwin J. Emerson.) (For other types of arguments, see the *Encyclopedia of Philosophy*, Antony Flew's *Dictionary of Philosophy* or the *Oxford Companion to Philosophy*.)

ARGUMENTATION: See entry for Elenchus, the method Socrates used to refute the thinking of others.

ARGUMENTUM AD POPULUM

In logic, an *argumentum ad populum* is a fallacious argument, which holds that a hypothesis or belief is true if it is held by many people. If, for example, most people believe that they will go to Heaven when they die, then—using such an argument—Heaven exists.

Similarly, if most individuals in the State of Utah believe a half-literate seventeen-year-old named Joseph Smith was told by angels that golden plates bearing a history of ancient America were buried near his father's farm, then it is true that angels exist and that they supplied Smith with the information.

American advertisers utilize the concept to good commercial advantage.

ARIANISM: See the entries for Arius, Christianity, Origen, and William Whiston.

Arion, Frank Martinus (1936—)

Arion, a writer and poet who lives part-time in Curaçao and part-time in the Netherlands, founded the first humanist primary school of Curaçao, which allows teaching in the native language of Papiamento.

Arisian, Khoren (20th Century)

Arisian has been on the board of Leaders of Ethical Culture Societies in Boston (1966—1968) and New York (1968—1979; 1999—). He then became minister of the Minneapolis Unitarian society, a traditionally humanistic group. He has been an associate editor of *The Humanist* (USA) and in 1973 wrote *The New Wedding: Creating Your Own Marriage Ceremony.* In 1980, he signed the Secular Humanist Declaration, and he was a signer of Humanist Manifesto 2000.

The American Humanist Association in 1995 presented him with their Humanist Pioneer of the Year Award, citing his "devotion to the advancement of ethical humanism and service to the liberal religious community." He is editor of *Religious Humanism.* Institute. {HM2; HNS2; EU, Howard B. Radest; PK; SHD}

Aristarchus of Samos (c. 310—230 B.C.E.)

Aristarchus is the Greek astronomer credited with being the first to propose a heliocentric theory of the universe. Archimedes and Copernicus cited Aristarchus as believing that the earth moves around the sun and that the sun is at rest, also concluding that the sun is larger than the earth and that seasons are caused by the earth's axis being inclined to the plane of the ecliptic. Only his treatise, "The Sizes and Distances of the Sun and Moon," remains.

According to Julian Kane, professor of geology at Hofstra University, "the burning of the Great Library at Alexandria in the year 391 was considered an unsuccessful attempt by Christian zealots to destroy all records of Aristarchus, discoveries that the Church considered contrary to its dogma."

It was not Copernicus who first proposed the movements of the planets around the Sun; it was Aristarchus, 1800 years earlier. (See entry for Galileo.) {CE}

Aristarchus of Samothrace (c. 217—145 B.C.E.)

Aristarchus is the innovator of scientific scholarship. A Greek scholar, he succeeded his teacher, Aristophanes of Byzantium, as librarian at Alexandria. Without his expert revising of Homer's writings, those works would not have been passed down.

Although it is said that Aristarchus wrote over 800 volumes, few of his critiques of Alcaeus, Anacreon, Hesiod, Pindar, and the tragedians remain. {CE}

Aristippus (c. 435 B.C.E.—360 B.C.E.)

Aristippus was founder of the Cyrenaic School of Greek philosophy. A pupil of Socrates, he turned to the Skeptics and held that no knowledge beyond common human experience is possible. In contemporary terminology, McCabe states, Aristippus was an agnostic. Aristippus came from Cyrene, in a part of Africa now known as Libya and which then was a populous region, the Florida of the Greek world. He did not advocate surrender to sensual pleasure, often abstaining for a long period to show that he was master of himself and his pleasures. But his doctrines comprised the first coherent exposition of hedonism and opposed those of the Cynics, although the two groups drew upon Socratic philosophy.

"It is better to be impoverished than uneducated," he stated. "The one lacks wealth, the other lacks humanity." {CE; MC; RE}

Aristophanes (c. 448—388 B.C.E.)

The greatest of the ancient authors of comedy, Aristophanes wrote more than fifty plays, only eleven of which have survived Little, however, is known of his life. A satirist, he exposed not only the political and social evils of the age but also the philosophers, the gods, and the theology of the people. *The Clouds* (423) satirized the Sophists and Socrates. *Lysistrata* (411) amusingly suggested a way to stop war—women should simply withhold sex from their husband-soldiers. *The Women at Demeter's Festival* (411) conspire to ruin Euripides because of his misogyny. *Thesmophoriazusae*, a hilarious work, involves cross-dressing. Women, in *The Ecclesiazusae*, take over the government. In *Plutus* (388), the blind god of wealth recovers his eyesight and distributes the gifts of fortune more equitably. Plato is said to have died with Aristophanes's works under his pillow.

In the *Symposium*, Plato has Aristophanes defend male love, stating that male love was superior to that of love for females because it was "more masculine" and was more suitable for political leadership.

Aristophanes introduced the longest word ever penned in the history of literature, 172 letters long in Greek and 182 letters in its English transliteration. The word—which means a fricassee of sweet and sour ingredients including mullet, honey, brains, pickles, vegetable marrow, vinegar, and the Greek drink *ouzo*—is

> *Lopadotemachoselachogaleokranioleipsanodrimhypotrimmatosilphioparaomelitokatakechynokichlepikossyphophattperisteralektryonoptekephalliokigklopeleiolagoiosiraiobaphetraganopterygon.*

{BDF; CE; GL; JMRH; PA; TYD}

Aristotle (384—322 B.C.E.)

Called by Corliss Lamont "the first great naturalist in the history of philosophy," Aristotle codified the laws of logic. However, he thought man had a soul and body, spoke of "God" as the Prime Mover, or Unmoved Magnet, and, Lamont added, "marred the purity of his Naturalism by indulging in a confusing redefinition of supernaturalist concept [which] made it easier for the Catholic Church many centuries later to incorporate his thought with seeming logic into its theology."

Aristotle also believed in slavery and in the natural inferiority of women but apparently did not believe in an after-existence. During the French Revolution, Maréchal cited Aristotle as seeming to be an atheist only from the standpoint of the strictest religious orthodoxy.

According to Robertson, Aristotle was an unbeliever in the popular and Platonic religion. He was a monotheist, but a monotheist with no practical religion. What was worst in his thinking, states Robertson, "was its tendency to a priorism, which made it in a later age so adaptable to the purposes of the Roman Catholic Church. Thus his doctrines of the absolute levity of fire and of nature's abhorrence of a vacuum set up a hypnotizing verbalism, and his dictum that the earth is the center of the universe was fatally helpful to Christian obscurantism."

"The common idea that [Aristotle] and Plato are the two typical thinkers of ancient Greece," wrote McCabe, "is very far astray." Plato's spiritualism had few followers; Aristotle's rejection of the idea of spirit and his inventing the idea of the immaterial, got a few more followers. They were attracted to his idea that man's mind is not material but could exist only in an intimate union with matter. This did great harm to the evolutionary materialistic science of the Ionic School and introduced the metaphysical method. Another difference, says McCabe, is that he had red blood in his veins, that he "was very fond of his pretty mistress Herpyllis."

Aristotle's influence upon succeeding generations is not to be overlooked, for he was an albatross around the neck of science for fifteen hundred years. His dogmas, observed Harry Elmer Barnes in *An Intellectual and Cultural History of the Western World*, "held back the development of both physics and chemistry and were not finally obliterated until the time of Boyle and Stahl in the seventeenth century."

Asimov observed that Aristotle's views about the geography of Earth prevailed until the time of Columbus, and, as Ackerman points out, many still judge someone's character by their looks: "Aristotle claimed that if a person looked at all like an animal he shared that animal's essential nature. Someone with a beaky nose and angular face would be eaglelike—bold, brave, and egotistical. Someone with a horsey face would be loyal and proud. A broad face indicated stupidity, a small face trustworthiness, and so on."

Bertrand Russell found Aristotle to have been the first to write like a professor, not as an inspired prophet. A professional teacher, Aristotle was "not passionate, or in any sense religious." Saying Aristotle practically invented logic, Russell warns that traditional formal logic is analogous to Ptolemaic astronomy: Both are antiquated, a waste of time except to understand those historical periods. It has taken almost 2000 years, unfortunately, to break the hold that Aristotle has had on logic, and Russell blamed the Catholic Church's insistence upon teaching an antiquated logic instead of pursuing the discoveries of modern logic. (See entry for *a priori*.) {CE; CL; EU, Aram Vartanian; HNS2; Bernard Katz, *The American Rationalist*, July-August 1998; JM; JMR; JMRH; RE; TYD}

Arius (c. 250 — 336)

When Arius, a presbyter, asserted that Jesus was not part of the Trinity but of a different substance from God, the Council of Nicaea outlawed his views and affirmed the Nicene Creed: "God is a Trinity of Father, Son, and Holy Spirit." For Arius, God the Father was "uncreated" and was the first principle from which all else, including the Son and the Holy Ghost, was derived. As such, he taught that although the Father is eternal, the Son was created at some point and therefore is not eternal. Lamont states Arianism "never died out in Christian circles and for centuries had its secret adherents." Charles W. Lowry Jr. of the Virginia Theological Seminary has written that the Arian Controversy began in 318 when Arius openly opposed his Bishop Alexander on the eternity of the Son: "Against this Arius insisted that the Father must be older than the Son and that 'there was when the Son was not.' After his excommunication by Alexander, Arius found many allies, and 'in a short time the whole Eastern Church became a metaphysical battlefield.' The climax of the controversy was the Council of Nicaea (Nice) called in 325 by the Emperor Constantine."

Here Arius's views were condemned, and the famous anti-Arian Creed of Nicaea was promulgated. Its most important phrase, "of one being (or substance) with the Father," survives in the Creed commonly called the Nicene and used in many of the Liturgies of Christendom. (See entry for Origen.) {CE; CL; EH; ER; JMR; JMRH}

ARIZONA ATHEISTS, FREETHINKERS, AND HUMANISTS

• American Atheists, Inc., PO Box 64702, Phoenix, AZ 85082-4702. Pat Wilkinson, the state director, is at <pwikinson@atheists.org>.

• Arizona Secular Humanists are at PO Box 3738, Scottsdale, Arizona 85271 (602) 230-5328. E-mail: <103217.260@compuserve.com>. Contact is Tom Vincent.

• Dial-An-Atheist has been available at (602) 623-3861.

• Humanist Community of Tucson, contact: Hedy Simpson, P.O. Box 86014, Tucson, AZ 85754-6014; (520) 743-7804. Email: <75247.223@compuserve.com>.

• Humanist Society of Greater Phoenix (ASHS), 10540 East Firewheel Drive, Scottsdale, AZ 85249 <aztec.asu.edu/hsgp>.

• Humanists of Prescott, Jim Powers, chair, P.O. Box 10642, Prescott, AZ 86304-0642; Phone: (502) 776-1552.

ARKANSAS FREETHINKERS AND HUMANISTS

• Arkansas Society of Freethinkers, 13912 Willow Pond Road, Little Rock, Arkansas 77206. (501) 888-9333.

• Humanists of the Mid-South (AHA), address of which is Route 2 B-376A, Benton, Arkansas 72015, are led by Charles Dixon and J. J. Dixon.

ARMAGEDDON

Judeo-Christians make much of the Biblical Armageddon, an entirely unscientific concept which involves a belief about "the end of the world," at which time the forces of good and evil will indulge in a catastrophic battle. The idea is particularly popular at the end of any century, with some claiming that Armageddon will arrive, for example, precisely at midnight on 31 December 1999. Many were disappointed on 31 December 1899, 31 December 1799, et cetera.

Armellini, Carlo (1777—1863)

Armellini was an Italian statesman. Pope Pius VII made him a Consistorial Advocate at the Papal Court, but in 1848 Armellini joined the Anti-Papals. After the flight of Pius IX, Armellini became Minister of the Interior.

Mazzini made him a member of the Executive Committee of the Roman Republic, and he formed the Triumvirate with Saliceti and Montecchi, and afterwards with Saffi and Mazzini. At the restoration of the Pope by the French, Armellini retired to Belgium. {RAT}

ARMINIANISM: See entry for Jacobus Arminius.

Arminius, Jacobus (James) (1560—1609)

Arminius, a mild-mannered University of Leyden professor, was a Dutch Reformed theologian (whose name originally was Jacob Harmensen). He tried to defend the Calvinist doctrine of predestination but upon reflection concluded such a doctrine was wrong. He then tried to convince the Dutch Reformed Church that Calvin was wrong about the doctrine of irresistible grace, ending with a view similar to that of the Roman Catholic Council of Trent. His opponents held that God elects certain persons for salvation, denying the privilege to others. Furthermore, because God wills it so, therefore it is just. Disagreeing, Arminius held that "He cannot will to do . . . that which He cannot do of right. For His will is restricted by justice." God has foreknowledge, and He can see foresee the purely contingent—in other words, God knows in advance that a man will sin by free choice, but he does not will nor predestine the man to do so. Further, he held, man's freedom stands in contrast to compulsion, to necessity, and to spontaneity.

As explained by Walter Edwin Roush, a professor of Old Testament Language and Interpretation at the Bonebrake Theological Seminary in Dayton, Ohio, "Even in the desire for happiness, which is spontaneous, man is not free. Freedom exists only where there is the power of alternate choice. Man faces alternate choice and is actually free. . . . The Arminians [as his followers were called] held that grace is not irresistible, but that those who are ready for the conflict, and desire Christ's help, and are not inactive, will be kept from falling."

Arminius's influence spread widely and included such ministers as Ebenezer Gay (1696—1787), Charles Chainey (1705—1787), Jonathan Mayhew (1720—1766), William Bentley (1759—1819), and James Freeman (1759—1835). It was adopted by the Methodist and related movements in the 18th century, and its viewpoint promoted a spirit of tolerance. Rather than speculative theology, Arminianism led to an emphasis upon human duties. (CE; ER)

Armitage, Andrew (20th Century)

Armitrage, of Hebron, has reviewed books for England's *Gay and Lesbian Humanist.*

Armstrong, David Malet (1926—)

Armstrong is an Australian philosopher and atheist. He has been the Challis Professor of Philosophy at Sydney since 1964. His publications include *A Materialist Theory of the Mind* (1968) and *Belief, Truth, and Knowledge* (1973). (See entry for Richard C. Vitzthum.) {SWW}

Armstrong, Henry Edward (1848—1937)

Armstrong, recognized as one of the most distinguished organic chemists in Europe, was a humanitarian and an outspoken Agnostic. He closed an article in the *Humanist* (1918) with Swinburne's defiant line, "Glory to Man in the Highest." In the Rationalist Press Association *Annual* (1919), he professed his materialism. {RAT; RE}

Armstrong, Jesse L. (20th Century)

Armstrong has been active in the American Humanist Association. {HNS}

Armstrong, Rebecca (20th Century)

Armstrong is on the Board of Governors of The Humanist Institute.

Arnason, Wayne (20th Century)

Arnason is American president of the Unitarian Universalist Ministers' Association.

Arnesen, Liv (20th Century)

In 1994 Arnesen became the first woman to ski solo to the South Pole. A Norwegian newspaper, *Aftenposten* (23 August 1998), reported her [in translation] as saying

> I know many people who believe in God, and I expected to find Him on my way to the South Pole if He exists. My religious experiences were very different, however, [only] involving myself, nature, and the universe.

{CA}

Arnheim, Michael (20th Century)

Arnheim, professor of ancient history at the University of Witwatersrand (South Africa), is on the Council for Secular Humanism's Committee for the Scientific Examination of Religion. He is author of *Is Christianity True?* (1984) and *South Africa After Vorster* (1979).

Arnink, Dale E. (20th Century)

Arnink is minister to the Unitarian Church of Los Alamos in New Mexico. He is on the board of directors of the Unitarian Universalist Service Committee.

Arnold of Brescia (c. 1090—1155)

Said to have been a student of Peter Abelard, Arnold was an Italian monk, the prototype of an intellectual who questions and becomes a charismatic spiritual leader. Only secular powers should own property, he held, because he accused the church of being too temporal and its clergy unwilling to imitate Jesus, owning nothing. Ordered to come to Rome, he complied but expressed disgust at the clerical opulence and corruption which he found. Pope Adrian IV, the one English Pope, had Arnold, who throughout remained a strictly religious and ascetic monk, hanged, strangled with a garrote, and his body burned and thrown into the river. {BDF; EH; RE}

Arnold, Edwin [Sir] (1832—1904)

Arnold was a British poet who, during years of service in India, conceived an immense admiration of Buddhism, which he thought superior to Christianity. His *Light of Asia*, on the life of the Buddha, did much to broaden the public mind.

McCabe writes that Arnold's view about God is obscure, but Sir Edwin rejected the belief in personal immortality in *Death and Afterwards*. Sir Edwin rejected the idea of a future life and the Christian creed or "any extant religion." {JM; RAT; RE}

Arnold, Gipson (20th Century)

Arnold has been Treasurer and President of the Atheist Network and is a writer for its newsletter, the *Atheist Network Journal*. In *American Atheist* (May 1990), he wrote about the first atheist radio show, "Radio's Finest Hour."

Arnold, a practical person, has observed the following concerning toilet etiquette of the gods:

> • You shall have a place outside the camp and you shall go out to it; and you shall have a stick with your weapons; and when you sit down outside, you shall dig a hole with it, and turn your back and cover up your excrement.
>
> —*Deuteronomy* 23:12
>
> • Then he (God) said unto me, Lo, I have given thee cow's dung for man's dung, and thou shalt prepare thy bread therewith.
>
> —*Ezekiel* 4:15
>
> • Therefore, behold, I (God) will bring evil upon the house of Jeroboam, and will cut off from Jeroboam him that pisseth against the wall.
>
> —*I Kings* 14:10
>
> • Behold, I (God) will corrupt your seed, and spread dung upon your faces, even the dung of your solemn feasts.
>
> —*Malachi* 2:3
>
> • "The ear, the skin, the two eyes, the tongue, the nose, the two feet, the two hands, the speech, the genital organ and the anus: these verily are the ten sacrificial priests. Sound, touch, color, taste, smell, words, actions, motion, and the discharge of seed, urine, and excretions are the ten oblations (sacrifices).
>
> —*The Mahabbharata*
>
> • When defecating or urinating, one must squat in such a way as neither to face Mecca nor to turn one's back upon it. . . . It is not necessary to wipe one's anus with three stones or three pieces of fabric: a single stone or piece of fabric is enough.
>
> But if one wipes it with a bone, or any sacred object, such as, for example, a paper with the name of God on it, one may not say his prayers while in this state. . . . It is preferable, for urinating and defecating, to squat down in an isolated place; it is also preferable to go into this place with the left foot first; it is recommended that one keep his head covered while evacuating, and have the weight of his body carried by the left foot.
>
> —Ayatollah Ruhallah Khomeni,
> *Sayings of the Ayatollah Khomeni* (1980)

{FD; *Freethought History #9*, 1994}

Arnold, Madison (20th Century)

Arnold, an actor, in *Freethought Today* (March 1989), wrote that

> I never accepted religion, so I had nothing to reject as such. The history of "Christiansanity" (my own coinage of which I am proud!) is so brutal of mind, emotions, freedom, progress, science, and all that I hold precious, that by an standards of justice its leaders in almost any given period would be incarcerated for life, or worse! {CA}

Arnold, Matthew (1822—1888)

Arnold's father, Thomas, was immortalized in *Tom Brown's Schooldays* and in Lytton Strachey's portrait in *Eminent Victorians*. An earnest administrator, he stood for a profound Christian ethic. Matthew, his second child, became an inspector of schools for thirty-five years, continuing even after his poetry and criticism made him famous. His antipathy for what he considered the new middle classes' unthinking materialism is illustrated by his view of the Atlantic telegraph, "that great rope with a Philistine at each end of it talking inutilities." A deeply immersed classicist, he became professor of poetry at Oxford, where he claimed that the role of the critic was "simply to know the best that is known and thought in the world." *The Economist* dubbed him a "staunch Liberal," a "reactionary in some of his views," and an "almost socialist in others. Any pomposity was tempered with a vivacity and sense of humour, and behind his superior airs was a modest and playful man, if somewhat egotistical."

Corliss Lamont has stated that "the agnostically inclined Matthew Arnold vigorously attacked religious superstition and upheld the idea that Jesus was not God but a great teacher and oracle of 'sweet reasonableness.' " Although he liked Cardinal Newman's sermons at Oxford, they did not persuade him. Lamont lauds Arnold's minimal definition of God: "a Power not ourselves that makes for righteousness." However, most humanists are averse to using the word "God," relegating it to what believers generally mean by the term.

Often amusing in the way he expressed his views, Arnold wrote about the settling of New England:

> Notwithstanding the mighty results of the Pilgrim Fathers' voyage, they and their standard of perfection are rightly judged when we figure to ourselves Shakespeare or Virgil–souls in whom sweetness and light, and all that in human nature is most humane, were eminent–accompanying them on their voyage, and think what intolerable company Shakespeare and Virgil would have found them!

Known for his romantic pessimism, at a time torn between religion and science, Arnold described his feelings of spiritual isolation in "Dover Beach" and "Isolation: To Marguerite." Concerning religion, he penned *St. Paul and Protestantism* (1870), *Literature and Dogma* (1873), and *Last Essays on Church and Religion* (1877). "All the biblical miracles will at last disappear with the progress of science," he wrote. What Arnold looked forward to was a culture that would incorporate all the best that ever has been thought and said in the world, a goal much like that of contemporary teachers of the humanities. Arnold disbelieved in a future life and Christianity, but he remained a churchgoer. Religion he defined as "morality tinged with emotion." God, he once defined, is "the stream of tendency by which all things seek to fulfill the law of their being." (See entries for Arthur Hugh Clough and D. H. Lawrence.) {BDF; CE; CL; ER; FUK; HAB; JM; JMR; JMRH; RAT; RE; *The Economist*, 20 July 1996; TSV; TYD}

Arnoldson, Klas Pontus (1844—1916)

A Swedish reformer and author of *Hope for the Centuries, A Book on World Peace* (1900), Arnoldson was not a wealthy person but spent much of his money in the cause of peace. He opposed the war with Norway in 1906. In 1908, with Fredrik Bajer, he was awarded the Nobel Peace Prize. Arnoldson worked energetically for freethought causes in Sweden. {JM; RAT; RE}

Arnould, Arthur (1833—1895)

A French novelist, Arnould wrote *Bérenger* (2 volumes, 1864). His *Histoire de l'Inquisition* (1869) was a fiery criticism of the clergy under Napoleon III. For this, Arnould was prosecuted several times. His work is aggressively rationalist, and he wrote many dramas as well as plays. {RAT}

Arnould, Victor (1838—1894)

A Belgian, Arnould organized the freethought movement at Anvers and inaugurated a system of popular conferences. In Brussels, he was president of Brussels and also the president of the National Freethought Federation from 1875 to 1878 and from 1887 to 1888.

In 1869 he was elected delegate to the Freethought Congress at Naples. Arnauld wrote *History of the Church* (1878) and *Philosophy of Liberalism* (1877). From 1868 to 1873 he edited *La Liberté*, a freethought publication. {BDF; PUT; RAT}

Arnow, Harriette Simpson (1908—1986)

Arnow, author of a novel, *Dollmaker*, when asked about humanism, responded to the present author:

> It should be so simple to sit down and write a sentence or so saying what I do or do not believe. However, it isn't. It seems sometimes that for most of my life I have been on a long pondering.
>
> I grew up in the Christian Church; that was in the South where the Christian Church was the name of a Protestant faith promulgated by Alexander Campbell and known by various names in various places. We were a very religious people, but early doubt troubled me; one of my mother's cousins was a missionary to China, and I wondered if it were wise to destroy the belief of the Chinese in order to put another in its place; and then I was troubled being certain the devil would get me for such thoughts; and then I was comforted for God had given me a mind and it was up to me to use it; and so I began to go round and round and have been going ever since.
>
> I don't think I am a humanist. I sometimes think I am closer akin to some of the early settlers in Tennessee, Watauga for example; they said little of religion, didn't apparently have much, but believed that man was bigger than anything made by man, including his religion and political system, but now it would seem that we live in an age where all forces combine to belittle the individual; he exists less as an entity than as a part of something held as of much more importance than himself—his religion, politics, firm, etc.
>
> Time and again I go back to the Jesuit Relations; on one side all educated Frenchmen of one faith, on the other all ignorant savages, but so often the great hardships they endured together makes suffering men, individuals of them all.

{WAS, 22 November 1954}

Arnstein, Walter (20th Century)

Arnstein's *The Bradlaugh Case: Atheism, Sex, and Politics Among the Late Victorians* (1965) focused on government policy and Westminster debates. For six years in the 1880s, a major issue in British politics was whether Bradlaugh, an atheist, political radical, and advocate of birth control, should be allowed to take his seat in Parliament. {*Freethought History* #18, 1996}

Aron, Raymond (1905—1983)

Aron was the editor in London of *Le France Libre* (1940—1944), a columnist for *Figuro* (1947—1983), and a professor in the faculty of letters at Paris University (1955—1983).

In 1965 he was a Cornell University professor at large. He wrote *Introduction to the Philosophy of History* (1938), *Century of Total War* (1951), and *Opium of the Intellectuals* (1955).

Aron addressed both the First International Congress on Humanism and Ethical Culture held in Amsterdam (1952) and the 1962 Congress held in Oslo.

Aronson, M. J. (20th Century)

In the 1940s, Aronson was on the advisory board of Charles Francis Potter's First Humanist Society of New York.

Arouet, François: See entry for Voltaire.

Arpe, Peter Friedrich (1682—1740)

Arpe, a philosopher born in Kiel, Holstein, wrote an apology for Vanini in 1712. A reply to La Monnoye's treatise on *De Tribus Impostoribus* is attributed to him. {BDF}

Arreola, J. A. (20th Century)

Arreola is editor of *The Alternate Approach*, the newsletter of the Secular Humanist Association of San Antonio, Texas.

Arrhenius, Svante August (1859—1927)

A Swedish chemist and Nobel Prize winner, Arrhenius was a prominent member of the Monist League–the German equivalent of England's Rationalist Press Association–and an agnostic. He discovered the process of electrolytic dissociation. Arrhenius held that "conceptions of an all-embracing Nature and of freedom and manhood advance and recede together." {RAT; RE}

Arriaga. Manoel, José d' [President] (1839—1917)

Arriaga, who became President of the Portuguese Republic, was disinherited by his father, who claimed to be of royal blood, for becoming a freethinker and a republican at the university. Turning to law and politics, he had such a brilliant success that after the Revolution of 1911 he was appointed President. An atheist, Arriaga was both humanitarian and anti-clerical in the legislation he passed. {JM; RAT}

ART

- Art is a lie that enables us to realize the truth.

—Pablo Picasso

A branch of learning, art is one of the humanities. It is a form of creativity that goes back at least to works found in France's Chauvet Cave which has been dated as approximately 32,410 B.P. (plus or minus 720) for Chauvet and 27,100 B.P. (before the present) for the tracing of a hand at Cosquer near Marseilles.

Basically, artists are those creative individuals who transmute the personal into the supra-personal. (For a description of how one artist used elephant dung to create "The Holy Virgin Mary," see the entry for Chris Ofili.) {See "The Miracle at Chauvet" by E. H. Gombrich in *The New York Review of Books*, 14 November 1996}

Arthur, John (Died 1792)

Maréchal's *Dictionnaire des Athies* lists Arthur as a mechanic, as repairers of tools were called then, from near Birmingham, one who took a prize in Paris. Julian Hibbert also included him in his *Chronological Tables of Anti-Superstitionists*. {BDF}

Arthur, William (19th Century)

Arthur, an atheist, wrote *God Without Religion* (1887) and *Religion Without God* (1888). {GS}

ARTIFICIAL INTELLIGENCE

In the world of computer science, artificial intelligence refers to a machine's ability to perform activities normally thought to require human intelligence. Dr. Robert J. White, a professor of neuro-surgery at Case Western Reserve, has observed that

> While artificial-intelligence scientists are being forced to design miniaturized circuitry for their "think machines" that replicate the brain's cellular format, all of this research has a fundamental flaw. Artificial-intelligence investigation is based on advanced solid-state physics, whereas the humble human brain is a viable, semiliquid system! Have no fear. The artificial human mind is not here, nor will it be.

(See entry for Marvin Minsky) {*The New York Times*, 26 March 1998}

Aruoba, Oruc (20th Century)

In Turkey, Aruoba is a corresponding member of The Hume Society, a group engaged in scholarly activity concerning David Hume.

Arvin, Newton (1900—1963)

Arvin, who in 1952 became a member of the Institute of Arts and Letters of the American Academy, when asked about humanism replied to the present author,

> I more and more dislike labels and shibboleths, and shy away even from "naturalistic humanism" if that phrase is to take on or be given a cultic or sectarian connotation like Ethical Culture, New Thought, Unity, or what not; nevertheless, some such phrase comes as near as any to the philosophical position which seems to me the only tenable one for the contemporary mind to take.

Arvin, whose critical biography of Herman Melville won the National Book Award in 1951, also wrote scholarly biographies of Hawthorne, Longfellow, and Whitman.

When a senior at Harvard, he sent unsolicited reviews to Van Wyck Brooks, who encouraged him by writing "You are a critic by nature." However, he added that to succeed he needed to experience life more, not just remain in an ivory tower. In 1922 Arvin became a freshman-composition instructor at Smith.

The economic depression during his youth led him to speak out against social injustice—in 1932 he pledged to vote Communist, as did Lincoln Steffens, John Dos Passos, Sherwood Anderosn, and Theodore Dreiser. That same year he married Mary Garrison, said to have been a great Valkyrian figure. Their eight-year marriage was an unhappy one.

Barry Werth is one of many who has written about Arvin's homosexuality. Arvin kept a journal most of his life, describing an early recognition that he was "certainly a girlish small boy, not a virile one, even in promise, and the world of boys being what it is, I was not long in being made aware of this," particularly when taunted for his lack of skill in sports. He had a love affair for three years with Truman Capote in the late 1940s, but friends said Arvin's sexual outlet consisted of masturbating and collecting gay pornography.

In a notable invation of privacy, three state troopers, a federal postal inspector, and a local policeman raided his home in 1960 after he hesitantly let them enter. They confiscated large quantities of homosexual erotica as well as journals that documented his sexual activities. Arvin was charged with possessing "obscene pictures" and of "lewdness," offenses that could have landed him in jail for five years and a fine of twenty-five thousand dollars. Taken to the local police station, he regretably gave up the names of fifteen other men who collected similar erotica. Upon pleading guilty to the charges, he received a one-year suspended sentence.

Arvin was admitted several times to Northampton State Hospital for psychiatric treatment. Although not fired by Smith College, Arvin was forcibly retired and never returned to the classroom after his arrest made national headlines. Sylvia Plath had earned extra money in 1958 grading exams for him.

Arvin suffered, after prostate surgery, from painful incontinence. In early 1962 after finishing the Longfellow work, he was found to have pancreatic cancer. But he lived to read Edmund Wilson's glowing *The New Yorker* review that included, "Among the writers who have really devoted their lives to the study of our literature . . . I can think of only two who can themselves be called first-rate writers: Van Wyck Brooks and Newton Arvin." In the weeks before his death Arvin excised with a razor many of his journals' embarrassing passages, evidence to the end that he had been successfully taunted because of his sexual orientation.

In 1996 the first Truman Capote Lifetime Achievement Award in Literary Criticism, worth $100,000 and given by the author's estate, was awarded to Alfred Kazin. But, following Capote's instructions, the awards are made in honor of Arvin. At the inaugural award ceremony, Kazin said that he had taught at Smith when Arvin was there and, ironically, Arvin had not thought very highly of him. {WAS, 8 February 1951; Barry Werth, "The Scarlet Professor," *The New Yorker*, 5 October 1998}

ARYAN

Archaeological evidence corroborates the text of the Veda by placing the invasion of India by the Aryans at around 1500 B.C.E. Aryans are members of the people who spoke the parent language of the Indo-European languages. In Adolph Hitler's Nazi regime, however, an Aryan was a Caucasian Gentile especially of the Nordic type. (As to whether Aditya was the first known Aryan, see the entry for Hindu Skeptic.) {CE}

Asbury, Herbert (20th Century)

A freethinker, Asbury wrote *Up From Methodism* (1926). {FUS}

Ascarate, Gumezindo de (19th Century)

Ascarate, a Spanish professor of law at the University of Madrid, was a Republican deputy. An able Radical parliamentary orator, he wrote *Social Studies, Self- Government and Monarchy* and other political works. In philosophy, he was a follower of Krause. {BDF}

ASCESIS

Ascesis (from the Greek *askesis*, exercise) is the philosophic concept that by rigorous training in the activity of thought one can–through self-discipline–modify one's way of being. Foucault illustrated this by studying ancient dietary and sexual regimens.

As described by Parisian philosopher Richard Shusterman, Foucault's "experiments with drugs and S/M were somatic analogues of philosophy's textual disciplines of exploratory self-fashioning for better self-care," not just a way of discovering who one is. {*The Nation*, 30 June 1997}

ASCETICISM

Some ascetics, believing that a simple way of life allows one to concentrate upon the task at hand, believe that by self-denial and austerity they will release the soul from bondage to the body, permitting "union with the divine." Asceticism and contemplation often go hand-in-hand or, as used in context by Stringfellow Barr, "For the Catholic asceticism of poverty, the Protestant substituted the asceticism of work."

Humanists, such as admirers of Thoreau at Walden Pond, find the ascetic lifestyle one that downplays telephones, television programs, public programs, and extreme socializing.

ASEHUCO

The Costa Rican Ethical Humanist Association is *Asociación Ético Humanista Costarricense* (ASEHUCO). Commenced in 1989, its president is Marco Castillo Rojas. The group can be contacted on the Web: <http://idt.net/~wasm/asibehu>.

Asgill, John (18th Century)

Asgill wrote *Mr. Asgill's Defense Upon His Expulsion from the House of Commons of Great Britain in 1707* (published 1881). He was a rationalist whose religious doubts made him unpopular with the Establishment. {GS}

Ashby, Robert (20th Century)

In 1995, Ashby was appointed Executive Director of the British Humanist Association. In a speech at the South Place Ethical Society annual reunion, he mentioned that humanism has reached maturity through Corliss Lamont, Paul Kurtz, and others.

"The BHA," he said, "is moving away from the reinforcement of one popular image of secular people–that generally incorrect picture of a band of aggressive god-haters with a desire for vengeance. Instead we aim to present humanism as the positive outlook that it is, in today's terms. We should ensure that humanism today provides the basis for future civilisation." E-mail: <robert@humanism.org.uk> {*International Humanist News*, October 1995}

Ashurst, William H. (1792—1855)

Ashurst, a secularist like his son **William H. Ashurst Jr.** (1818—1879), was a friend of Garibaldi and Mazzini. As a youth, he joined the "freethinking Christians," but in later life he "ceased to be a member of any sect." {RAT; VI}

Ashman, Charles R. (20th Century)

Ashman wrote *The Gospel According to Billy* (1977), an exposé of William (Billy) Franklin Graham, the fiery and persuasive evangelist who has been the friend of several United States Presidents and who has been an international figure in Protestantism.

ASHS

The Alliance of Secular Humanist Societies is a network created for mutual support among local and regional societies of secular humanists. A Director of Humanist Community Development arranges the addition of many national chapters. Joan Mooney, however, in 1998 did not accept New York's FANNY (Freethinking Activist Nonbelieving New Yorkers). Snail-mail: PO Box 664, Amherst, NY 14226-0664; (716) 636-7571.

ASIA

Asia, the largest continent in the world, to the Assyrians was *asu*, a word meaning "where the sun sets." (See entry for Europe.)

ASIAN RATIONALIST FEDERATION

In 1996 at the World Atheist Conference held in India, the Asian Rationalist Federation was formed.

ASIBEHU

In 1994, the Ibero-American Ethical Humanist Association (ASIBEHU) commenced as an organization for Spanish-speaking humanists and freethinkers (*los librepensadors*) from South, Central, and North America as well as the Caribbean. On the World Wide Web: <http://idt.net/~wasm/asibehu>. (See entry for *Asociación Iberoamericana Ético Humanista* [ASIBEHU].)

Asimov, Isaac (1920—1992)

An internationally known science fiction author, Asimov was President of the American Humanist Association at the time of his death. He was on the editorial board of *The Humanist*, was a signer of Humanist Manifesto II, and was a Humanist Laureate of the Council for Secular Humanism's Academy of Humanism. In 1980, he signed the Secular Humanist Declaration. In 1984, the American Humanist Association named him Humanist of the Year.

His first 100 books took him 237 months. His second took 113 months. His third 100 took only 69 months. Asimov wrote at least 467 books, typing away on an Underwood 5 and researching a wide range of subjects: pre-school material as well as college textbooks. He also wrote mysteries as well as books about the Bible, astronomy, limericks, humor, sociology, mathematics, science, Shakespeare, ancient and modern history, and philosophy.

Asimov has been quoted as saying he usually awoke at 6 a.m., sat down at the typewriter by 7:30 a.m., and worked until 10 p.m. Asked by Barbara Walters what he would do if advised by a physician that he had only six months to live, he replied, "I'd type faster."

To the Secular Humanist Society of New York, of which he was an honorary member, he said that he disliked traveling far from his 33rd floor apartment on Central Park West in New York City. At one Manhattan lecture, he sang all the verses of a Tom Lehrer ditty.

In 1938 the teenaged Asimov left his father's Brooklyn candy store to take a story to John W. Campbell Jr., publisher of *Astounding Science Fiction.* Within a few days he received a rejection letter with several pages of positive criticism. A few weeks later he returned to deliver a new story, inspired by Campbell's advice if not his cigarette smoke. Again, a rejection letter arrived shortly afterwards. Asimov was later to note that acceptance letters usually just contained money but that reject letters contained something more valuable: advice.

It was on one such trip to Campbell's office, Oliver Morton wrote in *The New Yorker* (17 May 1999), that Asimov came up with the idea of a galactic empire. The "Foundation" stories that resulted always involved faster-than-light travel, "for an Empire that takes thousands of years to traverse will not remain an empire for long." The best ships have to be those of the Imperial Navy "or of the smugglers and/or traders who outflank them." Planets must play the role of the smallest administrative units "and are often oddly one-dimensional in their climate—one finds whole worlds of glacier, of desert, of swamp. There is a metropolitan world of tall towers, vast domes, and unbridled splendor amid the close-packed suns of the core—Asimov called his Trantor. There is a government loosely based on a historical model. The Roman is most common, but the Chinese dynasties have had their influence, as has Victorian England."

Of his 467 titles, the "Foundation" series detailed a complex future of humankind and robots, in which were detailed the three-part "law of robotics":

- A robot may not injure a human, or through inaction allow a human to come to harm.
- A robot must obey the orders given it by humans, except when such orders would conflict with the first law.
- A robot must protect its own existence as long as such protection does not conflict with the first or second law.

Asimov took the somewhat scientifically inaccurate script of the movie "Fantastic Voyage" and wrote a novelization. He noted, however, that the microscopic characters that were injected into the bloodstream of a dying man in the script were so small that even a molecule of oxygen would have been too big for them to breathe.

Asimov, said fellow scientist-author Carl Sagan, was "one of the master explainers of the age. I think millions of people owe their knowledge of science, their familiarity with some scientific fact, to reading either the fact or fiction of Isaac Asimov."

"I've never been particularly careful about what label I placed on my beliefs," Asimov has written.

> I believe in the scientific method and the rule of reason as a way of understanding the natural universe. I don't believe in the existence of entities that can not be reached by such a method and that are therefore "supernatural." I certainly don't believe in the mythologies, in heaven and hell, in God and angels, in Satan and demons. I've thought of myself as an "atheist," but that simply described what I didn't believe, not in what I did. Gradually, though, I became aware that there was a movement called "humanism," which used that name because, to put it most simply, humanists believe that human beings produced the progressive advance of human society and also the ills that plague it. They believe that if the ills are not to be alleviated, it is humanity that will have to do the job.

As to why humanists should fight with religionists when so outnumbered, Asimov observed, "Because we must. Because we have the call. Because it is nobler to fight for rationality without winning than to give up in the face of continued defeats. Because whatever true progress humanity makes is through the rationality of the occasional individual and because any one individual we may win for the cause may do more for humanity than a hundred thousand who hug superstition to their breasts."

And did he believe in life after death? No, of course not, said the son of Judah and Anna Rachel Berman Asimov. As a matter of fact, two months before his death he told a group of writers and artists that a recent bout with prostate problems made him, yes, wish for the end of conscious thought: This, from one whom the *Guiness Book of World Records* cites as being the American author with the most titles to his name. He explained, "I don't have to worry about death, because there isn't an idea I've ever had that I haven't put down on paper."

Asimov's memorial was held in the Ethical Culture Society, his wife Janet's choice, not far from the apartment he did not like to leave. His last book, written partly while he was hospitalized, was *I, Asimov* (1994). {CE; HM2; HNS2; SHD; TYD; WAS, 1991}

Asimov, Janet (20th Century)

Now a retired psychiatrist and psychoanalyst, Isaac Asimov's wife Janet has been a published writer since 1966. She has written stories, articles, and twenty books (eleven for children). Her bi-weekly science column, "Asimov on Science," for the Los Angeles Times Syndicate results in fan mail from around the world. Of Scandinavian lineage (one-quarter Danish, one-quarter English, one-half Swedish), she received her B.A. from Stanford University, her M. D. from the New York University College of Medicine in 1952, and in 1960 she graduated from the William Alanson White Institute of Psychoanalysis. She is a member of the Ethical Culture Society and of Freethinking Activist Non-believing New Yorkers.

The two Asimovs decided at the age of eleven to become writers but, being children of the Great Depression,

> Isaac and I were preoccupied with the problems of making a living. Since writers—especially now—have a hard time making ends meet, we both went to graduate school. It was important to have an advanced degree and professional status, while continuing to write on the side. Fortunately both of us liked our respective professions. He enjoyed teaching, and my brother (in the last medical school class that Isaac taught) affirms the fact that he gave great lectures.
>
> Isaac had more confidence and talent, becoming a published writer at the age of eighteen. I stopped writing during the rigors of medical school and residency and started again after I graduated from analytic school.
>
> I was never an official member of any religion until middle age, when I joined the New York Society for Ethical Culture. Isaac and I were married by an Ethical Culture Leader. I belong to the American Humanist Association.
>
> I think both Humanism and Ethical Culture could do more to emphasize human beings as part of Nature. For instance, we are irrevocably affected by what happens to Earth's atmosphere, ozone layer, oceans, etc. When I applied to become a student at the White Institute, one of the interviewers asked me what I thought my position was in Nature. Off the top of my head came something like "I am an animal living on planet Earth, in a Solar System, in a great big Universe." Simplistic, but then I didn't realize that many years later I'd be trying to simplify science for the laymen.
>
> {WAS, 20 August 1998}

Asklepiades (Ancient Greece)

Unlike the Hebrews, the Greeks, as illustrated by Asklepiades (in a Dudley Fitts translation), addressed, among other homely subjects, their mistresses:

> You deny me: and to what end?
> There are no lovers, dear, in the under world,
> No love but here; only the living know
> The sweetness of Aphrodite–but below,
> But in Acheron, careful virgin, dust and ashes
> Will be our only lying down together.

Asklepiades also offered humanistic advice:

> Drink down the strong wine: dawn's but the span of a finger,
> And shall we wait for the lamp that brings *Good night*?
> Drink, drink to joy, dear friend: for soon we'll have
> A lonely night for sleeping, and that's for ever.

Askenasy, Hans (20th Century)

Askenasy was born in Frankfurt, Germany, in 1930 and emigrated to the United States in 1949. He is a psychologist and the author of *Are We All Nazis?*, among other works on the Holocaust. He was critical of Daniel Jonah Goldhagen's *Hitler's Willing Executioners* in *Free Inquiry* (Winter 1996-1997).

Asma, Stephen T. (20th Century)

Asma, who holds a doctorate in philosophy, teaches humanities at Columbia College in Chicago, Illinois. In "Abortion and the Embarrassing Saint" (*The Humanist*, May/June 1994), Asma notes that "the discrepancy between classical and contemporary Catholic theories of fetal development is enough to make the pope cringe. What Christians really want," he added, "is to have their visceral responses and intuitional moral impressions stamped onto the gavel of state authority." Asma wrote *Following Form And Function* (1996).

ASOCIACIÓN IBERO-AMERICANA ÉTICO HUMANISTA (ASIBEHU)

An association of Spanish-speaking ethical humanists in South, Central, and North America, *Asociación Ibero-Americana Ético Humanista* (ASIBEHU, Apartado 1057, 2050 San Pedro, Costa Rica) was commenced in 1994 in San José, Costa Rica. It was made possible by a generous grant from the International Humanist and Ethical Union (IHEU) and by the efforts of Rob Tielman, Matt Cherry, Paul Kurtz, Tim Madigan, and Warren Allen Smith. ASIBEHU's first president was Alexander Cox Alvarado. Its webmaster and executive director is Ricardo Otárola. On the World Wide Web: <http://idt.net/~wasm/asibehu>

ASOCIACION MEXICANA ÉTICA RACIONALISTA (AMER)

In 1995, the *Asociacion Mexicana Ética Racionalista* published the first issue of a quarterly, *Razonamientos*. On its editorial board are humanists from Argentina, Canada, Colombia, Mexico, the Netherlands, Peru, Spain, and the United States of America. E-mail: <mendezm@spin.com.mx>.

Asoka (300 B.C.E.—232 B.C.E.)

H. G. Wells says of Asoka, the famous Hindu monarch, that in the world-list of kings, "the name of Asoka shines, and shines almost alone, a star." Asoka became a zealous Buddhist in mid-life and did wonders for the vast empire he had inherited. His moral code was severe and dogmatic, but it did not interfere with the ingenuous sexual freedom that then ruled in India. Vincent Smith, an authority on Hindu history, says that Asoka "ignored, without denying, the existence of a Supreme Deity." As such, Asoka embraced Buddhism in its pure atheistic form, giving the world an example of "the fruits of atheism." {JM; RE}

Asp, Mathilda (19th Century)

Asp founded Sweden's first nonbelievers' organization in 1887. (See entry for Scandinavian Unbelievers.)

ASP

ASP is short for Angle-Saxon Protestants. The expression often has negative and clique-like connotations, as does WASP (except that the W for white is considered redundant).

Aspasia (Mid-5th Century B.C.E.)

Pericles's unwedded wife, Aspasia, "was likely enough to be a freethinker" who shared her famous husband's opinions and ideals, according to Robertson. But when a comic playwright, Hermippos, brought a charge of impiety against her, Pericles, who had not taken the risk of letting Anaxagoras come to trial, himself defended Aspasia before the dicastery, or place where the courts sat.

The most famous woman of the ancient world, and one of the

most beautiful, Aspasia had come from Asia Minor (Ionia) and, being a foreigner and non-Athenian, was not eligible under Athenian law for Pericles to marry. One of the Hetairai, which McCabe says means *pals* or *companions*, "not courtesans as is often said," she was put on trial for irreligion. Pericles therefore defended her, obtaining her acquittal. According to some, she became adviser of Pericles after he divorced his wife in 445 B.C.E. Xenophon wrote favorably about Aspasia. {CE; JM; JMR; JMRH; RE; TYD}

Aspland, Lindsey Middleton (19th Century)

Aspland, a freethinker, wrote *Law of Blasphemy* (1884). {GS}

Aspland, Robert (19th Century)

Aspland, a freethinker, wrote *An Inquiry into the Nature of the Sin of Blasphemy* (1817). {GS}

ASS, BURIDAN'S

Jean Buridan (c. 1295—1356) was a French nominalist philosopher who, like Aristotle, wrote about a hungry ass. To its right was a haystack, and to its left was a haystack. Both haystacks appeared to be equally good and equidistant, but, unable to decide which to choose, the ass died of starvation. The illustration indicates the dilemma everyone has in choosing something when no evident reason exists for making one choice over another. {AF; OCP}

ASS, FEAST OF THE

During the Christmas season in the ninth century and following, an annual religious ceremony was held in parts of Europe. An ass, often ridden by a beautiful girl, was led through the city by the clergy and placed near the altar during Mass (higher as well as lower clerics assisting); and the priests he-hawed instead of making the usual responses, leading the body of people present to join in the braying. People then sang (sometimes coarse popular songs) and danced around the ass. {RE}

Asseline, Louis (1829—1878)

A French writer, Asseline established *La Libre Pensée*, a weekly journal of scientific materialism. He wrote *Diderot and the Nineteenth Century*. After the revolution of 1870, he was elected mayor of the fourteenth arrondissement of Paris. {BDF; RAT}

ASSEMBLY OF FREETHINKERS

The Assembly of Freethinkers (IHEU) is at House No. 258, Road No. 1, Dhanmondi R/A, Dhaka 1205, Bangladesh.

Assezat, Jules (1832—1876)

A French writer, Assezat was secretary of the Paris Society of Anthropology. He edited the complete works of Diderot. {BDF; RAT}

ASSIMILATION

• We should just keep fucking each other until we're all the same color.

—Warren Beatty, in the movie "Bulworth" (1998)

• It's good that there are yellow Frenchmen, black Frenchmen, brown Frenchmen. They show that France is open to all races—but so long as they remain a small minority. Otherwise France would no longer be France.

—Charles deGaulle in 1959;
a view that is usually branded as a racist statement

The Population Association of America has found that blacks and whites in the United States are not much more likely to intermarry in 1990 than they were thirty years prior. A total of 97.6% of black women were found to have husbands who are black, down from 99.1% in 1960. The odds of a black woman having a black husband are over nine thousand times the odds of a non-black woman having a black husband. Fewer than 40% of American Indian women, however, married another Indian, compared with 786% in 1960.

According to *The Economist* (20 June 1998), sociologists consider intermarriage to be the "litmus test" of assimilation. High rates of intermarriage signal a breakdown in barriers between racial or ethnic groups. Such marriages then speed that breakdown along by building family ties across groups. Intermarriage also produces children who are less clearly identified with a particular race or ethnic group. Golfer Tiger Woods, son of a Thai woman and a black man, was cited as an example. (See entry for Jew, Who Is A?)

ASSOCIATION FOR HUMANISM

The Association for Humanism in Poland is c/o Prof. Dolowy, UL. Rackowiecka 39A M 10, 02-521 Warsaw, Poland.

ASSOCIATION "HUMANIST CONSCIENCE"

Association "Humanist Conscience," Vesuviusstraat 2, Willemstad, is a humanist group in Curacao, the Netherlands Antilles. {FD}

ASSOCIATION LAÏQUE HUMANISTISCHE PRÄSENZ

The *Association Laïque Humanistische Präsenz* was formed in 1988 to work in nine German-speaking communes of Belgium.

ASSOCIATION OF CITIZENS WITHOUT RELIGION

The Association of Citizens Without Religion is led by Prof. RN Dr. Frantisek Fabian, C Sc., Volsinach 2012, CZ-100 00 Praha 10, Czech Republic

ASSOCIATION OF IRISH HUMANISTS

The Association of Irish Humanists is at 25 Wolf Tone Square West, Bray, County Wicklow, Ireland. The newsletter of the Association of Irish Humanists is at 5 Ailesbury Gardens, Ballsbridge, Dublin 4, Ireland.

Assollant, Jean Baptiste Alfred (Born 1827)

Larousse wrote that Assollant has all the skepticism of Voltaire in his novels. {BDF; RAT}

Ast, Georg Anton Friedrich (1778—1841)

A German Platonist, Ast was professor of classical literature at Landshut and Munich. He wrote *Elements of Philosophy* (1809). {BDF}

ASTROLOGY

Freethinkers and Catholics agree on astrology, the belief that star movements can be interpreted to predict human events. Both agree as to its unfortunate appeal to the uneducated. Specifically, the *Catechism of the Catholic Church* (1994) says, "All forms of divination are to be rejected: recourse to Satan or demons, conjuring up the dead or other practices falsely supposed to 'unveil' the future. Consulting horoscopes, astrology, palm reading, interpretation of omens and lots, the phenomena of clairvoyance, and recourse to mediums all conceal a desire for power over time, history, and, in the last analysis, other human beings, as well as a wish to conciliate hidden powers. They contradict the honor, respect, and loving fear that we owe to God alone." The last sentence, of course, is as meaningless to freethinkers as is astrology.

The Dutch Society of Skeptics in 1996 checked the competence of 44 astrologers by using two lists, one containing the place and date of birth of seven people, the other with extensive information about each of the seven. Asked to match the two, one-half did not even get one correct answer. None correctly matched more than three. However, the terms of the challenge had been set by the astrologers.

"What's your sign?" ask the astrologers.
"I don't carry one," respond the freethinkers.

{*American Rationalist*, May-June 1997}

ASTRONOMY

In the ancient Greek astronomer Ptolemy's view, the Earth was at the center of the universe, with the sun, moon, planets, and stars revolving around it. Fifteen hundred years later, Copernicus showed that the sun, not the earth, is at the center. Church authorities, meanwhile, had forced Galileo to declare belief in the Earth-centered universe.

Freethinkers and other non-theists build their philosophic outlooks on facts supplied by astronomers, not on beliefs guessed through theological divination. Rather than spending time on the "ontological argument" (an argument for the existence of God based upon the meaning of the term *God*), they spend their time investigating reality: quarks, black holes, or the "Great Attractor" which in the 1990s was found to be a huge region of matter that is drawing in the Milky Way galaxy with its gravitational pull.

"The Hubble constant" is still much discussed. For example, Allan Sandage, a Hubble pupil who holds that the universe is from 14 to 18 billion years old, used the Hubble telescope to check the distance to a galaxy called NGC 4639. "He managed," reported *The Economist* (9 March 1996), "to discover 20 cepheids in it and used them to calculate that it is 82 million light years away. With this value he was able to confirm that the luminosity of a supernova that was seen in NGC 4639 in 1990 matched expectations, yielding a Hubble constant of 57. Such supernovae ought, therefore, to be a reliable way of measuring the distances to galaxies too far away for their cepheids to be seen." Dr. Wendy Freedman of the Carnegie Institution in Pasadena, disagreed. Using the Hubble telescope to look at 20 cepheids in a galaxy called M100, she found that the galaxy, part of a nearby group known as the Virgo cluster, "is closer to the earth than previously realised. The result, when combined with M100's red shift, gave a value for the Hubble constant of 80. This, in turn, suggested that the universe is 12 billion years old at most. As to why she received such different results with her cepheids, *The Economist* suggested that one possibility "is that the Virgo cluster is simply too near. Though the Big Bang predicts that galaxies are moving apart more or less uniformly, it does allow for a bit of local jiggling. It may be that the Virgo galaxies are receding from the Milky Way that fast, not because of any general expansion but because of such local turbulence. Dr. Sandage reckons that cepheid distances to a dozen or so Virgo galaxies will be needed for a reliable result." Noting that Sandage is an Iowa-born theist, some freethinkers tend to look upon his findings with suspicion, particularly because he has made some unusual statements about a supernatural force "out there." Freethinkers are in the forefront of holding that the astronomers' findings and disagreements are far preferable to metaphysical extrapolations concerning the number of angels that can dance on a pinhead.

Astronomers using the Keck Telescope in Hawaii and the Hubble Space Telescope combined efforts in 1997 to discover the most distant object ever seen, a galaxy some 13 billion light years from the Earth. Formally named "Red Arc in CL1358+62," it contains small but intensely bright knots, each apparently a region where many stars are forming.

Astronomers at the very end of the 20th century were ecstatic upon finding that the solar system is not alone as an array of planets orbiting in the gravitational embrace of a shining star. Three large planets were found around Upsilon Andromedae, a solar-type star forty-four light-years away. As to the philosophical significance, they could only guess, according to *The New York Times* reporter John Noble Wilford (16 April 1999). (See entries for John D. Barrow, Christian deDuve, Edwin Powell Hubble, Sir Martin Reese, and Joseph Silk.) {*The New York Times*, 31 July 1997}

Astruc, Jean (1684—1766)

Astruc was a French physician and founder of Biblical criticism. He taught anatomy at Toulouse (1710), then at Montpellier, and later of medicine at Paris. In 1753, he published *Conjectures sur les mémoires originaux dont il parait que Moise s'est servi pour composer le livre de Genèse*, which for the first time divided the Mosaic narrative into Jahvist and Elohist documents. Astruc died "without the sacraments." {RAT}

Aszo y del Rio, Ignacio Jordan de (1742—1814)

A Spanish jurist, Aszo was a naturalist who wrote many scientific works. In his political works, he advocated the abolition of ecclesiastical power. {BDF; RAT}

ATARAXIA

Ataraxia, Greek for tranquility of mind, was the goal as well as the inspiration of the Greek Sceptics. When contentious issues arose, one achieved ataraxia by remaining calm and suspending one's judgment until the argument was clearly comprehended. {AF}

Atatürk, Mustafa Kemal (1881—1938)

Atatürk, the founder of modern Turkey, in reforming the country made secularism an indispensable pillar of the Republic. In 1923 he abolished the caliphate and established the republic, secularizing education. He dismantled the system of Islamic law which had prevailed during the long centuries of Ottoman rule.

Atatürk (the word means father of the Turks) introduced new laws based on Swiss and Italian civil codes. He banned the fez as a symbol of backwardness, outlawed the use of Arabic in the Muezzin's call to prayer, and gave women the vote. In the 1930s, tribunals tried people for wearing head-dress associated with Islam, the religion of ninety-nine percent of Turkey's people. All convents run by religious sects were banned, and primary school education was made compulsory. In 1928 the Arabic script was discarded, replaced by the Latin alphabet. "Islam" and "religion" were replaced in the constitution by "secular" and "democratic."

Among political leaders, Atatürk stands as one of the inspiring secularists of the century. As evidence of his opposition, Muslim students who attended a private Qur'an school were shown in a 1997 video lining up to file past, and to spit on, a bust of Atatürk. "I swear by Allah," the students vowed in unison, "to strive to create a state based on religion and Islamic law in Turkey and to devote myself to the war against Mustafa Kemal atheism." News reports indicated that militants were using schools to try to impose an Islamic-based political order, one that would supplant the government's secularism.

More than 100,000 Muslims protested against secularism in a May 1997 march within Istanbul. Onlookers were concerned about possible fateful results of the conflict.

Critics point out that during his mature years, Atatürk abandoned all religious belief, writing a civics manual that was anti-Islamic. "He described Mohammed," Andrew Mango has written in *Atatürk: The Rebirth of a Nation* (1997), "as a carrier of Arab nationalism and said that as for Turks, their religion had always been 'a religion of nature.' In the late 1920's he told an English journalist: 'I have no religion. I wish all religions at the bottom of the sea.' "

McCabe wrote, "They gave him the name Atatürk for his wonderful work. Like so many great theistic rulers he showed that personal asceticism is no more required of the head of a state than belief in the spiritual." McCabe later describes Atatürk as "a complete sceptic, protesting that his only ideal was the good of his country."

In 1998 when a movie about him was proposed by Tarquin Olivier, son of actor Laurence Olivier, some Greek-Americans complained that Atatürk was unworthy of favorable portrayal. Although small in numbers and allegedly motivated by a negative feeling toward Turkey in general, the group described him as a "savage maniac" who was also "a child molester of both sexes, a mass murderer, a destroyer of Greek civilization, and in general a disgrace to human civilization as we know it." Andrew Mango's *Atatürk* (1999) added, after describing his subject, "He was a man of the Enlightenment, and the Enlightenment was not made by saints."

In 1998 when an eight-pronged tower was constructed, commemorating the life of Turgut Ozal, the country's leader for most of the 1980s, its architect Yilmaz Sanli commented that the crescent on the top was a reminder that their former leader was a believer in Islam. In Ankara, however, Atatürk's resting-place is part shrine and part museum, entirely devoid of any religious imagery. {CE; *Free Inquiry*, Fall, 1991; *The Economist*, 2 May 1998; JM; RE}

ATEN

Aten, in early Egypt, was considered the God of the Sun. {LEE}

ATEO (ITALY)

The Italian atheistic publication, *Ateo, Trimestrale di cultura laica*, is at C.P. 989, I-35100, Padova PD, Italy. E-mail: <uaarpd@tin.it>.

ATHEISM

• I was a freethinker before I knew how to think.

—George Bernard Shaw

• Atheism: Historically a vague and contentious term meaning lack of belief in god(s) or impiety toward the god(s). Abandoned in favor of "unbelief" [in the present book].

—J. C. A. Gaskin
Varieties of Unbelief From Epicurus to Sartre (1989)

Atheists point out that all humans are born atheists. Linguistically, atheism (a + theism) is a disbelief in the existence of God, gods, and of any supernatural existence. Few avowed atheists wrote of their disbelief until the nineteenth century, at which time a popular belief in a conflict between religion and science was highlighted by the writings of such individuals as Robert G. Ingersoll and, in the twentieth century, Bertrand Russell and Madalyn Murray O'Hair, the latter of whom gave the word a bad name.

Atheism differs from agnosticism, which holds that the existence of God, gods, and the supernatural cannot be proved.

According to the *Catechism of the Catholic Church* (1994), "Since it rejects or denies the existence of God, atheism is a sin against the first commandment." Further:

> • Atheism must be regarded as one of the most serious problems of our time. The name "atheism" covers many very different phenomena. One common form is the practical materialism which restricts its needs and aspirations to space and time. Atheistic humanism falsely considers man to be "an end to himself, and the sole maker, with supreme control, of his own history." Another form of contemporary atheism looks for the liberation of man through economic and social liberation. It holds that religion, of its very nature, thwarts such emancipation by raising man's hopes in a future life, thus both deceiving him and discouraging him from working for a better form of life on earth.
>
> • Since it rejects or denies the existence of God, atheism is a sin against the virtue of religion. The imputability of this offense can be significantly diminished in virtue of the intentions and the circumstances. Believers can have more than a little to do with the rise of atheism. To the extent that they are careless about their instruction in the faith, or present its teaching falsely, or even fail in their religious, moral, or social life, they must be said to conceal rather than to reveal the true nature of god and of religion.
>
> • Atheism is often based on a false conception of human autonomy, exaggerated to the point of refusing any dependence on God. Yet, to acknowledge God is in no way to oppose the dignity of man, since such dignity is grounded and brought to perfection in God. . . . For the Church knows full well that her message is in harmony with the most secret desires of the human heart.

Gordon Stein, in *The American Rationalist* (Sep-Oct 1994), listed what he considered are the top ten books that have been "the most powerful in refuting the existence of God and truth of Christianity" (listed alphabetically):

The Bible (both Old and New Testament)
Cohen, Chapman, *Theism or Atheism*
Holbach, Paul Henri Thiry, Baron d', *The System of Nature*
Ingersoll, Robert G., *Some Mistakes of Moses*
Martin, Michael, *Atheism: A Philosophical Justification*
Martin, Michael, *The Case Against Christianity*
Paine, Thomas, *The Age of Reason*
Palmer, Elihu, *Principles of Nature*
Scott, Richard, *A Game of Chess*
Smith, George H., *Atheism: The Case Against God*

"Unbelief" is generally the preferred term, not "atheism," by many freethinkers and unbelievers. Meanwhile, to the cognoscenti, "Atheism is a non-prophet organization." (See entry for Humanism, Per Curtis Reese.)

ATHEISM, ANCIENT

"In Ancient Greece," Finngeir Hiorth has written, "there were not many atheists. The word 'atheist' comes from Greek, and about 10-15 persons in ancient Greece were called 'atheists.' But most of these believed in one or more gods, and about the others not much is known. In ancient China atheism was no real option. In ancient India there were some atheists, but their names are not known."

Atheism, Hiorth found, is a relatively new phenomenon, not more than three hundred years old. Those individuals who *were* atheistic, such as Karl Marx, Friedrich Nietzsche, Arthur Schopenhauer, and Ludwig Feuerbach, did not elaborate on their views, developed philosophies which were largely independent of atheism, or dressed their outlook in a profound but also an obscure philosophy of religion. {*New Humanist*, December 1998}

ATHEISMUSSTRICT

Atheismusstrict was a controversy in Germany toward the end of the eighteenth century. It concerned allegedly subversive philosophical views of Johann G. Fichte (1762—1814) and Friedrich C. Forberg (1770—1848). (See *Encyclopedia of Philosophy*, Vol. 3.)

ATHEISM, INTERNATIONAL: See entries for individual countries.

THE ATHEIST

Founded by Gora, *The Atheist* is at Benz Circle, Vijayawada, India 520 006. E-mail: <rajatha@VMM.XEEVGA.XEEMAIL>. ems.vsnl.net.in>.

ATHEIST ALLIANCE

The Atheist Alliance, the Democratic Alliance of Autonomous Atheist Societies (PO Box 5296, San Mateo, CA 94402) published their first quarterly, *Secular Nation*, in 1994. It was edited by Howard Kreisner. The founding president was John B. Massen. The co-presidents were Christos Tzanetakos and Marie Castle.

Their stated aims are to help develop a strong, democratic, atheist society; to assist fledgling groups; to make atheism a respected viewpoint in discussions of public policy; and to develop liaison with similar groups.

Castle in 1995 declined to be nominated again and was replaced by Lee Baker. The group held its first annual Atheist Alliance Convention, in North Hollywood, California.

Member societies include the following:

Arizona Secular Humanists, Phoenix-Scottsdale, Box 3738, Scottsdale, AZ 85271 (602) 230-5328 <103665.3310@com puserve.com>

Atheist Alliance, the nationwide coalition of atheist groups: <talkeetna@aol.com> Box 6261, Minneapolis, Minnesota 55406 <http://www.atheistalliance.org>
President: Marie Alena Castle,
5146 Newton Ave. North, Minneapolis, MN 55430 (612) 588-1597; <mac@mtn.org>

Atheist Centre, Benz Circle, Vijayawada, India 520006 (+91) 866-472330

Atheist Coalition (San Diego) (619) 622-1892 <atheistcoalition@hotmail.com>

Atheist Community of Austin, Texas, Box 3798, Austin, TX 78764 (512) 478-2116 or (512) 892-3188 <tankgirl@swbell.net> and <donrodz@swbell.net>

Atheist Network: <atheism@wally.hti.net>

Atheist Outreach (at-large membership), 278 Orchard Dr., Oregon, WI 53575 (608) 835-7937 <zemel@atheistalliance.org> or <slferoe@aol.com>

Atheists and Agnostics of Wisconsin, 278 Orchard Drive, Oregon, WI 53575 (608) 835-7937 <mwbookrevw@aol.com>

Atheists and Other Freethinkers, Box 15182, Sacramento, CA 95851; (916) 920-7834 <hkocol@hotmail.com> and <frethnkr@inforum.net> <www.rthoughtsrfree.org/aof/aof/htm>.

Atheists of Colorado, Box 391, Colorado Springs, CO (303) 530-0392 <slferoe@aol.com>

Atheists of Florida, Box 3893, Ft. Pierce, FL (305) 936-0210 <athalfle@aol.com> and <schisler@earthlink.net> <http://www.execpc.com/~aai/florida>.

Atheists of Northern Colorado, Box 2555, Loveland, CO (970) 577-0015 <vgmccoy@juno.com>

Atheists of San Francisco Region, Box 421815, San Francisco, CA 94142 (415) 647-9309 <jackmassen@aol.com> and <ray75511@aol.com>

Atheists United, Box 57435, Sherman Oaks, CA 94142 (818) 785-1743 <bkirkhart@aol.com>

Freethought Society of Greater Philadelphia, Pocopson, PA 19366 (610) 793-2737 <downey1@cris.com>

Metroplex Atheists, 6 Ft. Worth Ct., Mansfield, TX 76063 (817) 473-8213 <metroatheists@star-telegram.com>

Minnesota Atheists, Box 6261, Minneapolis, MN 55406 (612) 588-7031 <mac@mtn.org> and <august@mtn.org>

Rationalist Society of St. Louis, Box 2931, St. Louis, MO 63130 (314) 664-4424 <rsslbarb@aol.com> or <reover@juno.com>

Shasta Atheists & Freethinkers, 1544, Shasta Lake, CA 96019 (530) 244-3731 <spresz@snowcrest.net>

Society Against Religion (Commack, New York) <nogod1@aol.com>

Southeast Michigan Chapter FFRF, 414k91 Bellridge Blvd #12, Belleville, MI 48111 (734) 699-7232 <vipressverity@ameritech.net.org> or <slferoe@aol.com>

In 1998, at the time of their Fourth Annual Atheist Alliance Convention held in St. Louis, Missouri, the officers were Marie Castle, President; Jim Cox, Vice President; Richard Russell, Secretary; Ed Golly, Assistant Secretary; Shirley Moll, Treasurer; and Jack Massen, Assistant Treasurer. The 1999 national convention was held in Austin, Texas.

On the Net: <http://www.execpc.com/~aai> and <http://www.mnatheists.org/alliance.html>. (See entry for John B. Massen.)

ATHEIST AMATEUR RADIO NETWORK

Ray C. Beckett, A-2, 2003 Logan, Hamilton, Ohio 45015, has a ham radio station W90E that promotes an active network. {FD}

ATHEIST CELEBRITIES

According to an Internet homepage, the following are well-known individuals who may not be so well-known as atheists:

> Woody Allen, director; Russell Baker, columnist; Ingmar Bergman, film director; Pierre Boulez, composer-conductor; Marlon Brando, actor; Warren Buffett, financier; George Carlin, comedian; Noam Chomsky, linguist; Sir Arthur C. Clarke, author; Alexander Cockburn, columnist; Michael Crichton, author; Francis Crick, Nobel Laureate and biophysicist; Quentin Crisp, author; Richard Dawkins, author; Amanda Donohoe, actress; Paul Edwards, philosopher and editor; Barbara Ehrenreich, columnist; Albert Ellis, psychologist; Harlan Ellison, author; Harvey Fierstein, actor; Antony Flew, philosopher; Larry Flynt, publisher of *Hustler*; Dario Fo, Nobel Laureate and dramatist; James Forman, civil rights activist; Jodie Foster, actress; John Fowles, novelist; Bill Gates, Microsoft co-founder and CEO; Sir John Gielgud, actor; Jean Luc Godard, Director; Al Goldstein, publisher of *Screw*; Alan Hale, astronomer; Nat Hentoff, columnist; Katharine Hepburn, actress; Christopher Hitchens, columnist; Derek Humphry, euthanasia campaigner; Penn Jillette, magician; Wendy Kaminer, journalist; Neil Kinnock, European commissioner and former leader of the British Labour Party; W. P. Kinsella, novelist; Michael Kinsley, columnist; Paul Krassner, editor and comedian; Stanley Kubrick, director; Ring Lardner Jr., screenwriter; Richard Leakey, paleontologist; Alexander I. Lebed, Russian politician; Tom Lehrer, satirist; Sir Ian McKellen, actor; Arthur Miller, playwright; Marvin Minsky, artificial intelligence researcher; Desmond Morris, zoologist; Taslima Nasrin, Bangladeshi author; Ted Nelson, author; Randy Newman, recording artist; Jack Nicholson, actor; Camille Paglia, author; Roman Polanski, director; Katha Pollitt, editor; Vladimir Pozner, commentator; Jean-Pierre Rampal, flautist; James Randi, conjurer; Ron Reagan Jr., talk host; Christopher Reeve, actor; Richard Rorty, philosopher; Salman Rushdie, novelist; Dan Savage, sex advice columnist; George Soros, financier; Mira Sorvino, actress; Teller, magician; Gore Vidal, author; Max von Sydow, actor; Kurt Vonnegut Jr., author.

On the Web: <www.primenet.com/~lippard/atheistcelebs>. [See entries, herein, for individuals.]

ATHEIST CENTRE

The oldest existing atheist organization in India is the Atheist Centre (Benz Circle, Vijayawada 520 010, India). It was founded in 1940 by Gora and Saraswathi Gora, and its current president is Gora's son, Lavanam.

In 1996, the center was co-host with the Periyar Rationalist Movement of India of the fourth World Atheist Conference. Delegates were told of the center's large projects and facilities, including economic development, education, health, disaster relief, and social transformation. One of the programs serves 200,000 people in 150 villages.

Describing the conference, Jerry Rauser of Minnesota commented that upon visiting in Madras the one-day State Rationalist Conference that followed, the foreign delegates were impressed by the dynamism of the Indian non-theists.

At the statue of Periyar, they read aloud, even screamed, the saying on the base: "There is no God. There is no God. There is no God at all. He who invented God is a fool. He who propagates God is a scoundrel. He who worships God is a barbarian."

The Centre conducts intercaste marriages, criticizes religious taboos, organizes beef and pork suppers at which both Hindu and Muslim supporters can be challenged, acts to help child prostitutes, and opposes child marriages. It also conducts a campaign to promote the scientific outlook and rational thinking. Witchcraft and sorcery, which survive in rural life, are exposed with the cooperation of the Indian Medical Association.

An associated organization—the Arthik Aamata Mandal (Association for Economic Equality)—is devoted to comprehensive rural development. (See entries for Gora and Lavanam.) {FD; *New Humanist*, February 1996; HNS2}

ATHEIST COALITION

Atheist Coalition, a monthly of the Atheist Coalition, is at P. O. Box 4786, San Diego, CA 92164-4786. Their E-mail is <latheist-coalition@hotmail.com>.

ATHEIST CONTACTS PAGE

On the Web the Atheists Contact Page is found at <http://www.sdmst.edu/caa-bin/contact>.

ATHEIST NATION

Atheist Nation (PO Box 3217, Chicago, Illinois 60654) is a monthly newsletter found on the Web: <http://www.atheistnation.com>. The e-mail address of its publisher, J. L. Jaxon, is <jaxonpub@aol.com>.

ATHEIST NETWORK

Atheist Network is at POB 130898, Houston, Texas 77219 and, on the Web Atheist Network is found at <http://www.keith.com/~rkblack/tna.html>. {FD}

ATHEIST STUDENTS' ASSOCIATION (ASA)

The Atheist Students' Association (ASA) was founded in 1995 at the University of Maryland in College Park by Ali Aliabadi and Brie Waters. Its secretary, an Internet Infidel, is Keith Augustine.

ATHEIST THOUGHT

Eric Stockton's Atheist Thought is on the Web: <http://www.orknet.co.uk/godiva/at/index.htm>.

ATHEIST TV OUTREACH PROJECT (ATVOP)

Co-directors of the Atheist TV Outreach Project are Dwayne Walker and Brett Welch. Their e-mail: <mac@mtn.org>. Their phone: (612) 588-1597.

ATHEIST VIEWPOINT: See entry for Ellen Johnson.

ATHEISTIC HUMANISM

Theos and *atheos*, or some such similar terms, have always stimulated the imaginations of people interested in religion. Of the two, the former term has undoubtedly attracted more numerical adherents because of the affirmation, optimism, and proselytizing that have accompanied it. In contrast, the latter has carried with it a connotation of abnegation, pessimism, iconoclasm, and negativism. As an entity in itself, atheism has enjoyed relatively few wholehearted disciples, not even of most individuals in the Union of Socialist Soviet Republics where it was the "state religion" in the twentieth century.

Yet there is that logical position of atheism, and it not only serves as an opposite in one's mind to theism but also helps round out the logician's fancy syllogisms. By *atheism* is meant the denial of *any* god, regardless of the definition of "god" that may be offered. To define it otherwise, to define it in such a fashion that one can conclude there really are no atheists, is both illogical and non-constructive.

There are, however, those who call atheists *all* persons who deny a personal god or gods, or who deny a personal god or gods that have been particularly defined by some specific creed; e.g., the Trinitarian, the Calvinistic, the Catholic. President Theodore Roosevelt, for example, erroneously called the deist Thomas Paine "a filthy little atheist."

In his attempt to define atheism, Bradlaugh in *Plea for Atheism* (1864) wrote, "The atheist does not say, 'There is no God,' but he says, 'I know not what you mean by God; I am without idea of God; the word *God* is to me a sound conveying no clear or distinct affirmation. I do not deny God, because I cannot deny that of which I have no conception.'" Richard Carlile, however, simply said that not only is there no such being as a God but also there is no such place as Heaven in which God could dwell. Meanwhile, Charles Watts in 1898 offered the following: "I am a pronounced Atheist–that is, I have no belief in the existence of any 'God'; I am an Agnostic–that is, I know nothing of the alleged supernatural, or a future life. Further, I am a Secularist–that is, I believe in making the best, physically, morally, and intellectually, of what is known, leaving conjectures as to the unknown to those imaginative individuals who prefer to indulge in speculations, rather than in the realities of life."

Those who hold the atheistic position have so frequently been attacked because of their views that many have chosen alternate terms, such as freethinker, to describe their positions, thereby escaping what they fear will be adverse publicity. "The oldest freethought paper in the world," for example, is *The Truth Seeker*, the official organ of the National Liberal League and an atheistic journal which was first founded in 1873. Since its formation, the magazine has believed "in the right of everyone to pursue happiness in his own way, so long as he does not injure others." Although it favors "democracy and individual liberty," its editorial policy has at times been negativistic. Some have objected to its various editors' stands on secular as well as theological matters, but in general *The Truth Seeker*'s outlook has been that of atheistic humanism.

Although atheistic humanism has never enjoyed popularity in the United States, Jean-Paul Sartre in France developed a similar set of beliefs in which he not only admitted his atheistic negativism and pessimism but also endorsed this to others. Sartre has appealed to many disappointed god-seekers with his statement,

> Man is anguish. . . . He lives forlornly in a world without God. He has nothing to cling to within himself, nor without.

Rather than emphasizing the negation of God, however, Sartre claimed to have developed a religion of man, something more than just a plain rejection of natural or supernatural religion: "The doctrine I am presenting is the very opposite of quietism, since it declares that there is no reality except in action. It goes further and adds that Man is nothing else than his plan; he exists only to the extent that he fulfills himself; he is therefore nothing else than his life."

To some, this was not such pessimistic reasoning. After all, if man exists only to the extent that he fulfills himself, he must therefore do something positive to achieve such ends. Sartre continued: "Existentialism is nothing else than an attempt to draw all the consequences of a coherent atheistic position. [It] isn't trying to plunge man into despair. It declares that even if God did exist that would change nothing. Not that we believe God exists, but we think that the problem of His existence is not the point. In this sense Existentialism is optimistic, a doctrine of action. Man cannot start making excuses for himself. There is no determinism. Man is free. The coward makes himself cowardly. The hero makes himself heroic. What counts is total involvement."

Michael Valle, founder and president of University of Minnesota Atheists and Unbelievers, has offered some current definitions of agnosticism and atheism which, he stated, have been influenced by the writings of Michael Martin and Michael Scriven:

- **Negative atheism** refers to the literal definition. The negative atheist does not necessarily deny the existence of a god, but simply lacks a belief. Some negative atheists, such as the *logical positivists*, contend that the concept of god is factually meaningless, and so to affirm or deny its existence is to say nothing. They thus lack a belief in a god.

- **Positive atheism** refers to an actual denial of the existence of a god, whether that denial be a dogmatic assurance that there is no god or a more moderate assurance that it is more likely than not that there is no god. This definition conflicts with common usage, for the atheism most people refer to is the *dogmatic positive* variety.

- **Negative agnosticism** neither affirms nor denies the existence of a god. Negative agnostics have no opinion in the matter because of a lack of knowledge or interest in the subject.

- **Positive agnosticism** makes the claim that it is actually impossible to know whether there is a god or not. Such an agnostic has a substantial position, unlike the negative agnostic.

Valle continued, "Insofar as an agnostic lacks a belief in a god or gods, that agnostic is at least a negative atheist. The current meaning of agnosticism is perfectly compatible with negative atheism. It appears that agnosticism does not denote any concept that atheism does not cover–other than the positive agnostic's position that it is impossible to know whether there is a god. Thus, it appears that negative agnostics are generally uninterested negative atheists, and positive agnostics are negative atheists who think positive atheism can never be justified." He concluded, "Philosophically, it seems that agnostics and atheists are far more related than either might like to admit."

By "atheism," Theodore M. Drange means positive atheism. He uses "nontheism" to mean "negative atheism." All atheists, he notes, are nontheists, but not vice versa. Some nontheists are agnostics, withholding judgment one way or another on God's existence, possibly maintaining that neither judgment can be supported. Some other nontheists make the more forceful claim that both theism and atheism are mistaken or misguided regarding the nature of discourse about God. He calls such discourse "God-talk." Examples of noncognitivists who regard God-talk to be meaningless (or unintelligible) are A. J. Ayer, Antony Flew, Paul Edwards, and Kai Nielsen. Examples of those who claim that God-talk is noncognitive but not meaningless are philosophers such as R. B. Braithwaite, Ludwig Wittgenstein, and D. Z. Phillips. Although he feels some in the latter category might call themselves "theists," he regards them as nontheists.

Gaskin, preferring "unbelief" to atheism, used the following definition:

Unbelief: At least
(a) lack of belief in any supernatural agents and, by implication,
(b) lack of belief in miracles, and often, but connected with (a) and (b) only contingently,
(c) lack of belief in personal survival after death.

(See entry for Hell, and definition for Hell by Edgar Sheffield Brightman. Also, see entry for Hippo, the first atheist in Greek antiquity. McCabe's *A Rationalist Encyclopedia*. contains a discussion of atheism.)
{CE; ER; JMRH}

ATHEISTIC MUSIC: See entry for Freethought Music.

A-THEISTS AS CLASSIFIED BY A MANHATTAN WAG

- **Adolescent atheist**: Since I am a teenager, I know everything, and I know there is no God. So, like, the fact that many adults think that there is a God, like, proves my case.

- **Campus atheist**: I need attention, I need to feel important, and I can get these things by being obnoxious about the non-existence of God.

- **Closet atheist**: There are no good reasons for believing in God, but what harm can there be?

- **Evangelical atheist**: It is not sufficient that there is no God. We must do our best to make sure that nobody even thinks about believing that there is one.

- **Fundamentalist atheist**: There is no God, and anyone who thinks there is a God is a misguided, dangerous fool.

- **Lethargic atheist**: Religion is such a hassle. Why bother!

- **Nihilistic atheist**: Life as well as anything else has no point, and the existence of a god would invalidate this, so it is obviously not true.

- **Paranoid atheist**: Religion—sounds like another conspiracy, along with the aliens, the dolphins, and the CIA—they're all out to get me!

- **Philosophical atheist**: I don't believe, therefore I am.

- **Politically correct atheist**: God has a consistent history of discrimination on gender, sexual orientation, feminist, racial, and cultural grounds, therefore must be banned from existing.

- **Puritanical atheist**: We shall smite all evil believers in nonsense and shall continue our purge until not one damned theist is left alive.

- **Scientific atheist**: There is no God because I cannot create a falsifiable hypothesis concerning His existence.

- **Social atheist**: Well, everyone I know and respect is an atheist, so there must be something to it.

- **Theological atheist**: The principles of logic demonstrate the absence of any omnipotent and omniscient being in the universe.

{From the Internet}

ATHEISTS AND OTHER FREETHINKERS

Atheists and Other Freethinkers (AOF) publishes a monthly newsletter, *AOF News & Views* (PO Box 15182, Sacramento, California 95851).

ATHEISTS IN FOXHOLES

A granite memorial, "Atheists in Foxholes," was dedicated at Lake Hypatia, Alabama, on 4 July 1999. Freedom From Religion Foundation President Anne Gaylor envisioned such a monument, which features the insignia of all United States military branches, is made of Georgia granite, and was built at Fearn Park. Its wording is as follows:

IN MEMORY OF ATHEISTS IN FOXHOLES
AND THE COUNTLESS FREETHINKERS
WHO HAVE SERVED THIS COUNTRY WITH HONOR AND DISTINCTION.
PRESENTED BY THE NATIONAL FREEDOM FROM RELIGION FOUNDATION
WITH HOPE THAT IN THE FUTURE HUMANKIND MAY LEARN
TO AVOID ALL WAR

ATHEISTS OF FLORIDA

Ed Golly is Secretary of Atheists of Florida (PO Box 3893, Ft. Pierce, Florida 33948). The group is "dedicated to freedom of thought and expression and to the mandate of the First Amendment for complete separation of State and Church." Kyoko Brogdon was the original incorporator along with the late John Diamond. Jan Eisler was the first to become a life member in 1996, followed by Charles Schisler.

ATHEISTS WHO CONVERTED TO CHRISTIANITY

Antonio Casao Ibanez, writing from Spain, has cited several examples of famous atheists who later changed to Christianity: Jacques Maritain and his wife, both philosophers; Charles Foucault; André Frossard, son of a former Secretary of the French Communist Party; Vittorio Messori, the interviewer and collaborator of John Paul II's *Crossing the Threshold of Hope*; Max Jacob, the Jewish poet and friend of Picasso; Evelyn Waugh; and Sheldon Vanauken, a Virginia professor of history. {*The Skeptical Review*, January-February 1997}

ATHEISTS: For an estimate of the number of atheists in the world, see entry for Hell.

ATHEISTS, RELIGIOUS: See entry for Faith Atheism (Faitheism).

ATHEISTS' BELIEFS

"Atheists believe there is no God."

"No," retorts Brian Templeton in Des Moines, Washington, "all atheism says is the simple and obvious fact that there is no evidence for the existence of supernatural beings, whether they be gods or tooth fairies." {*Skeptical Inquirer*, March-April 1999}

Athelstan (Aesthelstan) (Died 939)

Athelstan, English son and successor of Edward the Elder, was king of Wessex (924—939) and grandson of Alfred. After a victory over his enemies at Brunanburn in 937, Athelstan became overlord of all England. In 960, he ruled that shops must be closed on the Christian Sabbath.

That religious stranglehold on Sunday ended in August 1994 when Queen Elizabeth II gave the Royal Assent to the Sunday Trading Bill. The bill allows shops to be open from 10 AM to 6 PM on Sunday, except that large shops and certain others including small shops under 3,000 square feet may open all hours on Sundays if they choose. England's National Secular Society and *The Freethinker* played a significant role in the victory.

ATHENS

The largest city in Greece, Athens according to tradition was governed until about 1,000 B.C.E by Ionian kings. Afterwards, it was governed by its aristocrats through an archontate. Solon in 594 B.C.E. abolished serfdom, modified the extreme laws attributed to Draco (who had governed Athens c. 621 B.C.E.), and gave power to the propertied classes, thus establishing a limited democracy.

The Persian Wars (500-449 B.C.E.) made it the strongest Greek city-state, and during the rule of Pericles (443-429 B.C.E.) the city reached the height of its cultural and imperial achievement. Socrates, Aeschylus, Sophocles, and Euripides were major figures of the time. The Peloponnesian War resulted in the city's losing to Sparta, its population humbled and halved. C. M. Bowra, Russell Meiggs, W. S. Ferguson, and Donald Kagan have documented the ancient Athenian humanism.

Secular humanists in the West, unlike the various religionists, wish that Europe had followed the philosophers of Athens and Ionia, not the theologians of Constantinople and Rome and Geneva. (See entry for Sparta.) {CE; *New Humanist*, October 1998}

ATHLETICS: See entry for Sports.

Atkins, Peter Williams (1940—)

Atkins is professor of chemistry at the University of Oxford and Fellow of Lincoln College. A writer for *Ethical Record* and *New Humanist*, he is author of *Creation Revisited* (1992), *The Creation* (1993), and *Concepts of Physical Chemistry* (1995). He has written,

> The scientific account of cosmogenesis cannot stop when it has accounted for the universe springing from a seed the size of a Sun, nor when it has arrived at a seed the size of a pea. Nor can it stop at any smaller seed. A seed the size of a proton implies that that seed had to be manufactured, placed there by some cosmic pre-existing gardener. Science will be forced to admit defeat if it has to stop at a seed of any size. That is the severity of the criterion that science sets for itself. If we are to be honest, then we have to accept that science will be able to claim complete success only if it achieves what many might think impossible: accounting for the emergency of everything from absolutely nothing. Not almost nothing, not a subatomic dustlike speck, but absolutely nothing. Nothing at all. Not ever empty space.

"My aim," he wrote in *The Creation*, is to argue that the universe can come into existence without intervention, and that there is no need to invoke the idea of a Supreme Being in one of its numerous manifestations."

"There is certainly no justification for asserting that the powers of science are circumscribed and that beyond the boundary the only recourse to comprehension is God," he wrote in *Chemistry and Industry* (20 January 1997). "To say that 'God made the world," he was quoted by *Electronic Telegraph* (11 September 1996) as saying during a debate held by the British Association for the Advancement of Science, "is simply a more or less sophisticated way of saying that we don't understand how the universe originated. A god, in so far as it is anything, is an admission of ignorance."

In 1993, Atkins was named an Honorary Associate of the Rationalist Press Association. He explained in *New Humanist* (February 1994) that he had been brought up "in a largely unthinking home and was banished to church on Sunday morning. In slightly later life I even summoned the faithful by ringing the bells. It was not until I entered the benign and encouraging environment of a university (Leicester, in fact) to study chemistry, that I began to think for myself, and soon discarded the remnants of belief in written authority."

In *Free Inquiry* (Spring, 1998), Atkins wrote that "Science reveals where religion conceals. Where religion purports to explain, it actually resorts to tautology." Atkins laments the fact that science respects the power of the human intellect whereas religion belittles it. {CA}

Atkinson, Alice (20th Century)

Atkinson, a Glasgwegian, once was an air hostess with what was then OAC, landing on the rivers and lakes of Africa in flying boats and touching down from Egypt to South America. Married to an ex-wartime Spitfire pilot, Atkinson is the film critic for *Humanism Scotland*.

Atkinson, Arthur (20th Century)

Atkinson in England is active with the Ealing Humanist Group. A naturalist, he is author of *The Approach to Humanism* (1997).

Atkinson, Henry George (1818—1884)

Atkinson was a philosophic writer. Interested in mesmerism, he wrote in the *Zoist*. He was a frequent contributor to the *National Reformer* and other secular journals. Harriet Martineau served as one of his philosophic guides. {BDF; RAT; RSR}

Atkinson, Sam (20th Century)

A freethinker, Atkinson wrote *Science and the Priest, the Emancipation of Women* and *Free Love Explained* (1910?). {GS}

ATON: See entry for Ikhnaton.

Attenborough, David Frederick (1926—)

In the James Herrick revision of Margaret Knight's *Humanist Anthology*, Attenborough is included as a humanist author. A broadcaster and naturalist, he is the younger brother of Richard Attenborough. "Zoo Quest" (1954—1964) was a program that allowed him to undertake zoological and ethnographic expeditions to remote parts of the world. He wrote *Trials of Life* (1990), *The First Eden* (1987), *The Living Planet* (1984), and *Life on Earth* (1979).

ATTENUATED DEISM

Attenuated deism is, according to J. C. A. Gaskin's *Varieties of Unbelief from Epicurus to Sartre* (1989), "[a]cknowledgment of the possibility of some inconceivably remote and unknowable creator-god who is neither concerned with nor of concern to the human race, nor thinkably like a human person."

Atwood, Isaac Morgan (1838—1917)

Atwood converted from his Baptist faith to Universalism and served two decades as the head of the theological school at St. Lawrence in Canton, New York, resigning there to become the first general superintendent of the Universalist church. He wrote *Revelation* (1889). {U&U}

Atwood, John Murray (1869—1951)

A professor of sociology and ethics, Atwood followed in his father's (Isaac's) footsteps by becoming Universalist dean of St. Lawrence Theological School. He once wrote, "The fact that in the Bible so-called history (temporary truth) is inaccurate often, does not subtract from its worth as a book of religious culture. Some stories like Jonah or Job or the parables of Jesus are plainly fiction, but of imperishable value, for they declare what is as true today as when first composed. . . . So a story may be historically false but morally and spiritually true. . . . There is no need of a church or a creed to tell a man what is truth. He can apprehend that for himself." {U; U&U; UU}

Atwood, Margaret (1939—)

In *The Handmaid's Tale* (1986), which has been made into a film by Volker Schlondorff, Canadian novelist Atwood "shows a humanist belief in the power of the survival of the deepest human feelings," according to Jim Herrick (*New Humanist*, December, 1990). The plot shows an American state of Gilead, following a catastrophe, in which a monotheistic autocracy rules. Fundamentalism takes over, women are not allowed to read or own property, and because of widespread infertility some women are chosen as submissive breeders, handmaids. As "two-legged wombs," women face the future in this time when "the Eyes of God run over all the earth." Herrick notes, "A witty addendum 200 years later demonstrates in the proceedings of a group of historians that the state of Gilead was part of the sectarian wars and had not survived."

Saying the was brought up by a doctrinaire agnostic, Atwood explained:

> A doctrinaire agnostic is different from someone who doesn't know what they believe. A doctrinaire agnostic believes quite passionately that there are certain things that you cannot know, and therefore ought not to make pronouncements about. In other words, the only things you can call *knowledge* are things that can be scientifically tested.

In 1987 Atwood was the Canadian and also the American Humanist Association's Humanist of the Year. {CA; HNS2}

Aubrey, Edwin E. (20th Century)

Aubrey wrote *Secularism A Myth* (1954). {GS}

AUCKLAND UNIVERSITY ATHEISTS

In New Zealand, the Auckland University Atheists (originally the Auckland University Freethinkers) was founded in 1990, formed as a reaction "to a wave of loathsome sectarian fundamentalist Christian interlopers who appeared to be hell-bent on dominating the social atmosphere of the campus." Its goals:

- to promote alternatives to religion on campus (and beyond, where possible)
- to provide fellowship for unbelievers in religious dogma
- to emphasize the superiority of reason over religious superstition

Its officers have been Bryce Boland, president; Oscar Martin, vice president; Alex Clark, treasurer; and Conrad Inskip, publicity.

The group's humorous Web homepage shows four creatures—homo Ignoramus, homo Hallucinatus, homo Religiosus, and finally homo Atheistus. Slowly, they advance ever upwards, ever onwards. On the Web: <http://crash.ihug.co.nz/~remk/fnz/aua/index.html> and <http://www.secularhumanism.org/cfa/orgs.html>.

Auclair, Walter (20th Century)

Auclair is an editor of the newsletter of the Capital District Humanist Society, PO Box 2148, Scotia, New York 12302.

Audebert, Louise (19th Century)

Audebert wrote *Romance of a Freethinker* and *Reply of a Mother to the Bishop of Orleans* (1868).

Auden, W(ystan) H(ugh) (1907—1973)

Auden, the Anglo-American poet who was a major literary figure in his time, wrote about politics and psychology as well as Christianity and homosexuality. He received the Pulitzer for *The Age of Anxiety* (1947) and completed numerous critical essays and opera librettos. Auden's father was a highly educated physician, his mother a highly religious Anglo-Catholic.

Auden wrote that his youthful Sundays were spent with "music, candles, and incense." When sent away to a prep school, he met the future novelist Christopher Isherwood, who became one of his closest friends. In 1925 he went to Oxford to study science but switched to English, during which time he read widely and wrote poetry. In 1930 his "Poems" were published by Faber & Faber, one of whose editors was T. S. Eliot, and Auden became a leader of such left-wing poets as Cecil Day-Lewis, Louis MacNeice, and Stephen Spender. Although never a member of the party, Auden was called by one critic a communist "with a love for England." Thomas Hardy, however, rated higher in his estimation than any of the political writers.

John Maynard Keynes described Auden as being "very dirty but a genius," for he wore ragged clothing and had sandy-colored hair which often fell over his forehead. Auden's face was noted for being etched with wrinkles. According to Dr. Douglas Model of Eastbourne, England, the condition had been caused by his excessive smoking. Facial wrinkles were deeply ingrained. He smoked non-stop, bit his fingernails, and in a self-description wrote, "The way he dresses / reveals an angry baby,/ howling to be dressed." His self-criticism included the admission that he felt embarrassed being near anyone who was not in some respect superior: "It may be a large cock, it may be sanctity," he explained.

During his last years, after having been a United States citizen and resident from 1939 to 1946, he lived and traveled in England, Italy, Austria, China, Spain, Belgium, Iceland, and New York. Other literary expatriates were Conrad, Eliot, James, Joyce, Pound, and Stein, so his exile was not particularly unusual. Upon moving to New York, he completed an elegy for William Butler Yeats, who had just died, in which he mourned also for his missing the England in which he had grown up and leaving the readership he had developed. Some readers never forgave him. For example, upon his death Anthony Powell read the news account to Kingsley Amis "No more Auden." Amis regretted hearing this, but Powell retorted, "I'm *delighted* that *shit* has gone. . . . Scuttling off to America in 1939 with his boyfriend."

Auden's love for Chester Kallman, stepson of Dorothy Farnan who wrote *Auden in Love* (1984), has been described by many, including the biographer Richard Davenport-Hines, author of *Auden* (1995). "Our first impression of Auden, slovenly in rumpled tweed, were of disbelief," remembered Harold Norse, Kallman's boyfriend at the time. "His shirt was unpressed, heavy woolen socks bunched limply around his thick ankles, and untied shoelaces flopped over his shoes." But Kallman, whom Auden described as being "a Roumanian-Latvian-American Jew," and he became lovers "mad with happiness." The love had its ups and downs. Kallman wrote to Norse that on a 1939 trip he had "almost precipitated a domestic crisis by groping a boy sitting next to me between Jacksonville and Tallahassee. . . . Wystan was quite rightly exasperated." Since first meeting, Kallman had been unfaithful to Auden and, in 1941, he informed an enraged Auden that he would never again sleep with him. Auden in a rage squeezed Kallman's throat, but the two were to remain together on and off in a sexless relationship.

When Thomas Mann's daughter, Erika Mann, asked him to marry her for passport purposes so she could escape from Nazi Germany, he complied. "What else are buggers for?" asked Auden, who was asked similarly by others. Isherwood noted that Auden once lamented that "no one would ever love him, that he would never have any sexual success," a fact related to his usually being attracted to teenagers, the critic Nicholas Jenkins wrote in an authoritative *New Yorker* (1 April 1996) article.

During the Spanish Civil War, Auden was aghast upon seeing how the Republicans treated clergy and destroyed their buildings, coming to believe that religion was a necessary good even if he was not religious. Same-sex relations were sinful, he felt, but not so sinful as dishonesty, greed, and violence.

In what has been described as self-chastisement, he held that humanity was thoroughly sinful and in 1940 he started going to church again, in Brooklyn Heights, returning to orthodox Episcopalianism.

The poet Alfred Corn has written that Auden's late poems, like "A Summer Night," "In Praise of Limestone," and Ischia" are political poems, "not only because of ironic touches in them about negative attitudes or actions, but also because they present a vision of happiness on earth, which Auden, as a proponent of incarnational theology, regarded as fundamental. To hold out that vision as an alternative to human cruelty and bigotry was the obligation, indeed, one of the chief exhilarations, of the poet."

Auden, however, was not quite that explicit, believing as he did "That love, or truth in any serious sense, / Like orthodoxy, is a reticence."

Auden died of a heart attack and complications of alcoholism. Stephen M. Silverman in *Where There's a Will* (1991) said the estate of approximately $857,000 in 1990 dollars was left to Kallman, who squandered much of the money. Kallman's will would have left everything to Auden, so Kallman's father became his heir. Auden's papers ended up at the New York Public Library. (See entry for Chester Kallman, an atheist.) {AA; CE; *The New York Times*, 19 June 1996}

Audifferent, Georges (Born 1823)

A positivist, Audifferent was executor to Auguste Comte. Born in Martinique, he settled in Marseilles and wrote several medical and scientific works. {BDF}

Auer, J. A. C. Fagginer (20th Century)

Auer, one of the signers of Humanist Manifesto I, wrote *Humanism States Its Case* (1933) and, with Julian Hart, *Humanism vs. Theism* (1951). The important part he played in the writing of the manifesto has been described in detail by Edwin H. Wilson in *The Genesis of a Humanist Manifesto* (1995). Dr. Auer was described as being a Harvard professor who was a "meticulous church historian." {FUS; HM1; HNS}

Auerbach, Berthold (1812—1882)

Auerbach was a German novelist, a Jew devoted to Spinoza. In 1841 he published a life of the philosopher along with a translation of his works. {BDF; RAT}

Augustine, Keith (20th Century)

Augustine, a philosophy major, is secretary of the Atheist Students' Association (ASA) at the University of Maryland at College Park. Also, he was one of the founding members of Campus Freethought Alliance. {*International Humanist News*, December 1996}

Augustine, Saint (Aurelius Augustinus) (354—430)

During the French Revolution Maréchal cited St. Augustine as holding the opposite views of an atheist. His *Confessions* is considered a classic of Christian mysticism. For Augustine, the world is God's inscrutable riddle, and the Bible is our guide for understanding God's inscrutability.

For evidence of St. Augustine's lack of humanism, consider the following:

- Intercourse with even a lawful wife is unlawful and wicked if the conception of off spring be prevented;
- Nothing is so much to be shunned as sex relations *(Soliloquies)*;
- Second marriages are lawful, but holy widowhood is better (*On the Good of Widowhood*);
- Cursed is everyone who places his hope in man (*Confessions*).
- If a man leaves his wife and she marries another, she commits adultery. . . Marriage is not good, but it is good in comparison with fornication (*On the Good of Marriage*).

{CE; ER; EU, Aram Vartarian; RE}

Aulard, François Victor Alphonse (1849—1928)

One of the most learned historians of France, Aulard taught at the Sorbonne (Paris University) and wrote *Culte de la Raison* (1892), in which he exposed the falseness of such legends as that of the Goddess of Reason. Aulard was a militant anti-clerical and an agnostic. {RAT; RE}

AURA: See entry for Spiritism.

Aurelius, Marcus: See entry for Marcus Aurelius.

Aureol, Pierre (Petrus Aureolus) (Died 1321)

William of Occam had been influenced by Aureol, whose Realism included the view that what the mind perceives are not realities but *formae speculares*. {JMR}

Aury, Dominique (1908—1998)

"The most ardent love letter any man has ever received": Jean Paulhan, one of the members of the French Academy, described *The Story of O* (1954) with those words.

A critic on a level in France with Edmund Wilson in the United States or Cyril Connolly in Britain, Paulhan did not reveal the rest. For the work had been written expressly for him by Aury, a woman who feared that he might end their long affair, an affair which spanned three decades, during war and peace, occupation and liberation, and through Paulhan's long second marriage.

In an interview (*The New Yorker*, 1 Aug 1994) with John de St. Jorre, the eighty-six-year-old explained that the novel had been written under the pen name of Pauline Réage, that it was the first explicitly erotic novel to have been written by a woman and published in the modern era. To the police or anyone who asked if she had been the author, Aury always responded, "That is a question to which I never respond."

But she had written the work, and it was only for an audience of one, M. Paulhan, who was then in his late sixties and she in her mid-forties. The work was, she said, a private document of their passion and *une entreprise de séduction* by which she hoped to "ensnare" a highly sophisticated man. "What else could I do? I couldn't paint, I couldn't write poetry. What could I do to make him sit up?"

The work sold millions of copies and in 1955 won the Deux-Magots Prize, then became a movie in 1975. The freethinking Aury read de Sade, and her novel, which was daringly published by the Olympia Press, includes sadism and masochism as well as sexual abuse and enslavement. Readers in 1954 were not accustomed to reading such as the following:

> They made her kneel down . . . with her bust on an ottoman, her hands still tied behind her, with her hips higher than her torso. Then one of the men, holding her with both his hands on her hips, plunged into her belly. He yielded to a second. The third wanted to force his way into the narrower passage and, driving hard, made her scream. When he let her go, sobbing and befouled by tears beneath her blindfold, she slipped to the floor, only to feel someone's knees against her face, and she realized that her mouth was not to be spared.

And . . .

> What O missed was not, properly speaking, Jacqueline, but the use of a girl's body, with no restrictions attached. If Natalie had not been declared off-limits to her, she would have taken Natalie, and the only reason she had not violated the restriction was her certainty that Natalie would be given to her at Roissy in a few weeks' time, and that, some time previously, Natalie would be handed over in her presence, by her, and thanks to her.

Clericals reacted with shock. Freethinkers inquired about a sequel.

Austin, Benjamin Fish (20th Century)

Austin, a freethinker, wrote *Conundrums for the Orthodox Clergy* (1924) and *The Devil* (1924).

Austin, Charles (1790—1874)

A lawyer and disciple of Bentham, Austin influenced J. S. Mill. The Hon. L. A. Tollemache wrote that in his heretical opinions Austin "inclined to Darwinism, because as he said, it is so antecedently probable; but, long before this theory broke the back of final causes, he himself had given them up." {BDF; RAT}

Austin, Dorothy (20th Century)

Austin is a chapter contact for the *Humanist Quest of Milwaukee, Wisconsin, Newsletter*.

Austin, John (1790—1850)

A jurist and brother of Charles Austin, John Austin was a friend of James Mill, Grote, and Bentham, whose opinions he shared. Austin wrote profound works on jurisprudence, and his lectures on the philosophy of law according to Oxford's Prof. John Finnis "gave wide and long-lasting currency to Bentham's legal positivism." {BDF; OCP}

Austin, Kate Cooper (1864-1902)

Austin, a freethinker and a Universalist, was a feminist, writer, and anarchist.

Austin, Sarah (1793—1867)

Austin was a writer who lived in the Mill-Bentham circle for many years. She translated French and German authors (including Goethe and Ranke). She disclaimed the title of Unitarian and was an impersonal theist. To Victor Cousin she wrote, "It is vain to try to uphold religion; her own ministers are her assassins." {RAT}

AUSTRALASIAN UNBELIEVERS

In 1925, the Rationalist Association of Australia was founded in Melbourne, the same year of the founding of the Rationalist Society of Australia. In 1927 the Auckland Rationalist Association was founded, the prime mover being A. E. Carrington. This was renamed the New Zealand Rationalist Association and Sunday Freedom League and was supported by Harry H. Pearce. From the 1930s on, a number of secular, atheist, freethinker, skeptic, and atheist organizations were formed. Those which are still active and the year of their founding are: The Humanist Society of Western Australia (1959); the Humanist Society of New South Wales (1964); the Humanist Society of Victoria (1961); the Humanist Society of South Australia (1962); the Humanist Society of Canberra (1964); the Council of Australian Humanists (1965); the Humanist Society of New Zealand (1967); the Humanist Society of Queensland (1968); the Atheist Foundation of Australia (1971); and Australian Skeptics (1981). (See entry for the Council of Australian Humanist Organizations.){FUK}

AUSTRALIA

• Australia, where everyone is a mate . . . and where, therefore, the leader must be a prime mate.

—Anonymous Australian

AUSTRALIA AND NEW ZEALAND UNITARIAN ASSOCIATION

The Australia and New Zealand Unitarian Association (ANZUA), formerly headed by Ms. Gayle Feeney, now has John Maindonald as its President. ANZUA was formed in 1974 to promote fellowship and communication between Unitarian and other liberal groups. Congregations in Adelaide, Melbourne, and Sydney were founded in the 1850s by Unitarians who emigrated from Britain. The Auckland Congregation was founded in 1898, but services had been held in New Zealand as early as 1863. By 1901 there were 468 recorded as Unitarians. ANZUA's address is Stat Dept., University of Newcastle, Callaghan, NSW 2308. E-mail: <john@maths.newcastle.edu.au>.

The Rev. Max Landau Moss is at 157 Schnapper Rock Road, Albany 1331, New Zealand. {*International Humanist News*, June 1995; *World*, November-December 1995}

AUSTRALIAN AND NEW ZEALAND HUMANISTS

In 1991 at an Adelaide Humanist Convention, it was resolved to achieve a number of aims by the year 2000. Among the aims were the legalization of voluntary euthanasia, the decriminalization of prostitution, and the decriminalization of certain drugs including marijuana. In 1995, in the Northern Territory, the first aim was achieved after a fourteen hours debate. Fifteen of the twenty-five members of the Northern Territory parliament voted for the so-called Terminally Ill Bill.

AUSTRALIAN HUMANIST

A quarterly, the *Australian Humanist* is at 138-B Princess Street, Kew, Victoria 3101, Australia.

AUSTRALIAN HUMANISTS, FREETHINKERS

The five humanist societies in Australia are situated in the five capital cities but are named after the five states: New South Wales, Queensland, South Australia, Victoria, and Western Australia. The five elect the Council of Australian Humanist Societies (CAHS) who are responsible for the *Australian Humanist* and for the running of "Australia 2000."

Ray Dahlits is President of the Council of Australian Humanist Societies, 4 Alandale Ave., Balwyn, Victoria 3103, Australia. Rosslyn Ives is Secretary. E-mail: <rayday@vic.bigpond.net.au> and <rosslyn@netspace.net.au>. James Gerrand formerly was the Council's secretary and the editor of *Australian Humanist.* His e-mail: "JamesGerrand"<ingroup@vicnet.net.au>.

• The Atheist Foundation of Australia is found on the Web at <http://www.users.bigpond.com/Atheist_Australia/index.htm>.

• *The Australian Humanist* is published quarterly at 138 B Princess Street, Kew, Victoria 3101. One member, Tony Lee, has jocularly questioned how Noah managed to get to Australia to pick up a couple of Koalas, plus sufficient eucalyptus trees of a certain species upon which they feed exclusively.

• *Humanist Viewpoints*, which John Tendy edits, is published monthly at Humanist House, 10 Shepherd Street, Chippendale, NSW 2008. <jtendys@triode.net.au>.

• New South Wales's humanist society is on the web: <http://sydney.dialix.oz.au/~hsnsw/index.html>.

• *Queensland Humanist* is at GPO Box 2041, Brisbane 4001. Contact is David Fisher at <humanist@petrie.starway.net.au>.

• Rationalist Society of Australia is headed by Peter Hanna: <rational@mail.mpx.com.au>.

• *South Australia Humanist Post* is a monthly. Its address is GPO Box 177, Adelaide, 5001 <rmc@adelaide.on.net>. Dick Clifford is President of the Humanist Society of South Australia, and in addition he is that group's webmaster: <http://www.users.on.net/rmc/hsofsa.htm>.

• *Victorian Humanist*, published ten times per year, is at GPO Box 1555 P, Melbourne, Victoria 3001 E-mail: <leeman@connexus.apana.org.au>. The homepage of Victoria's humanist society is at <http://home.vicnet.net.au/~humanist/>.

• *Western Australia-Humanist News* is at GPO Box T1799, Perth 6001, Western Australia. Contact is Robyn Edwards at <robyned@ozemail.com.au>.

{See article by David Tribe about Australasian unbelievers in the *Encyclopediaof Unbelief.*}

AUSTRALIAN SKEPTICS

Although not all skeptics are freethinkers or secular humanists, many are. The Australian skeptics are on the Web: <www.skeptics.com.au/>.

AUSTRIAN FREETHINKERS

Franz Sertl's *Die Freidenkerbewegung in Österreich im zwanzigsten jarhundert (*Freethought in 20th-Century Austria, 1995) describes the start of the "free religious" movement from 1848 to 1851 until the present. Freethinkers trace their history to 1887 when the *Vereinder Konfessionslosen* changed its name into *Verein der Fredenker.* In 1996 the freethinkers are organized under the name of *Freidenkerbund Österreichs* (Postfach 54, A-1153 Vienna, Austria). The chairman is Wolfgang Soos and the group's quarterly is called *Der Freidenker, Geist and Geselleschaft*, which has the e-mail <szanya@via-at>. Although the number of organized Austrian freethinkers hardly exceeded one thousand in 1989, there were 23,000 organized freethinkers in 1910 and a maximum of 100,000 members in 1925. The organization was prohibited from 1933 to 1945.

Martin Panosch, of Freidenkerbund Oesterreichs, can be reached at <mpan@fc.alpin.or.at>. {*Freethought History* #20, 1996}

Autissier, Isabelle (20th Century)

Autissier was the first woman to compete in Vendée Globe Challenge, a solo, nonstop, around-the-world sailing race. "I don't believe in heaven or God," she has stated, "and I want for this one life to be as rich in experience as possible." {*The New York Times*, 10 November 1996}

AUTOPSY

Although some religious groups and individuals do not allow autopsies, the Catholic Church has decreed that they can "be morally permitted for legal inquests or scientific research. The free gift of organs after death is legitimate and can be meritorious. The Church permits cremation, provided that it does not demonstrate a denial of faith in the resurrection of the body."

Freethinkers and humanists ordinarily have no objections to autopsy or cremation, leaving the decisions entirely up to the individual or the executor of the individual's estate. Fernando Vargas, asked by his executor if he would object to an autopsy, responded, "Surprise me!"

Avalos, Hector (1958—)

An assistant professor in the department of philosophy and religion at Iowa State University in Ames, Avalos was awarded that university's title, "1996 Professor of the Year." He is author of "Mary at Medjugorje" (*Free Inquiry*, Spring 1994), a critical inquiry into the supposed 1980s appearance of Jesus's mother in a little town in Bosnia-Herzegovina (formerly Yugoslavia). More Marian devotees showed up than appeared during the Jesus apparition stories of early Christianity, he found.

Avalos received his master's degree from the Harvard Divinity School and his doctoral degree from Harvard's Graduate School of Arts and Sciences. Born in Mexico, he became in 1968 a child preacher who gave the keynote sermon at the age of nine before hundreds at the Territorial Convention of the Church of God in Glendale, Arizona. He railed against the ascendant sexual revolution, rock music, long hair on men, mini-skirts, and other ideas that were anathema to his Pentecostal church.

By his early teens, he was a zealous believer, willing to go anywhere, to suffer any sacrifice, to preach the word of salvation to the "pagan" masses. He prayed for the sick, many of whom said that God had healed them through his prayers.

In high school he began a program of self-study which encompassed the study of Greek, Hebrew, Aramaic, Akkadian, Near Eastern history, philosophy, and theology. But, reading about chemistry, physics, biology, astronomy, and the Apollo mission, he decided in his first year in college that there might not be a God as defined by traditional Christianity.

"The logical consequence of this realization," Avalos has written, "was that miracles went down the drain." Finding that the God-myth was not necessary for a fulfilling and constructive life, he became a biblical scholar and an agnostic/atheist/secular humanist. The two philosophers he came most to admire were Spinoza and Hume.

In 1979, he developed a life-threatening illness called Wegner's Granulomatosis, which is a chronic condition in which the immune system attacks its own tissues as though they are foreign implants. A form of vasculitis, it is an extremely rare disorder that attacks the respiratory tract, the nasal sinuses, and the kidney in a progressively destructive process. Avalos has also suffered from a painful, systemic arthritis that is part of the disease.

His interest in biblical studies and in his physical condition led him to write *Illness and Health Care in the Ancient Near East: The Role of the Temple in Greece, Mesopotamia, and Israel* (1995). A work in medical anthropology, it compares the temples of Asclepius in Greece, the temples of Gula/Ninisina in Mesopotamia, and the temples of Yahweh to explain the socio-religious features that led Israel to develop its own ideas about the role of the temple in health care.

In 1996 Avalos was appointed executive director of the Committee for the Scientific Examination of Religion. Also in 1996 at the Humanist World Congress held in Mexico City, Avalos spoke about the failure of the theology of liberation. {"How Bible Study Made An Unbeliever Out of Me," *Freethought Today*, August 1991; WAS, interviews}

AVANT-GARDE

In the arts, to be in the avant-garde is to be in the vanguard. C. Carr (*Village Voice*, 22 September 1998) has listed some early examples:

- 1863: Artists assumed the task of *épater le bourgeois* when early modernists challenged academic painting at a *Salon des Refusés*. Harold Rosenberg observed that "Vanguard art must be synonymous with *rejected* art—not because advanced art desires to fail but for the deeper reason that only art officially cast aside can arouse in the spectator authentic feelings uncoerced by vested authority."
- 1873: Arthur Rimbaud stopped writing poetry at the age of nineteen.
- 1896: Alfred Jarry's *Ubu Roi* opened with the word *merde*, introducing obscenity to the stage and prompting a riot at Paris's *Théâtre Nouveau*.
- 1907: Picasso's first Cubist painting, *Les Demoiselles d'Avignon*, created an artistic stir.
- 1909: The first Futurist manifesto promised to destroy all museums, moralisms, and cowardice.
- 1910: Wassily Kandinsky created the first completely nonrepresentational painting.
- 1913: Stravinsky's *Rite of Spring* provoked such an outcry during its first performance that the dancers onstage could not hear the orchestra.
- 1914: Marcel Duchamp bought a bottle rack and signed it as an artwork, thus becoming the first conceptualist.
- 1916: Hugo Ball recited phonetic poems (no real words) while dressed in a cardboard costume at his Cabaret Voltaire.
- 1916: Dadaists embraced nonsense and negation, attacking all art, past, present, and future; their tracts defined Dada as "soft-boiled happiness" and "nothing, nothing, nothing."

An innovator in the 1960's avant-garde was Richard Higgins, a seminal figure in developing what he called Happenings. His 1969 book of essays, *foew&ombwhnw* (an acronym for "freaked out electronic wizard and other marvelous bartenders who have no wings") included theoretical essays, plays, poems, word scores, musical scores, graphic music notions, and performance piece instructions. The volume was bound like a prayer book, in leather, with a ribbon bookmark. His creative output has been called a forerunner of multi-media installation art. (See entries for Beat Generation, John Cage, Dada, Allen Ginsberg, Richard Higgins, Jack Kerouac, and William Burroughs. During the victory or V-Day celebration at the conclusion of World War II in Europe, a French girl, a Russian soldier who previously had been a Nazi prisoner-of-war, and the present writer, marched arm-in-arm as the three leaders of a parade that wended through the streets of Reims—they were before (*avant*) the flag-bearers and drummers (*le garde*) and the hundreds who then followed to mark the defeat of the Nazis immediately after General Jodl surrendered to General Ike Eisenhower at the city's Little Red Schoolhouse.)

AVATAR

An avatar is an embodiment, as of a concept or a philosophy, or an incarnation in human form. In Hinduism, the Buddha is thought of as an avatur of the god Vishnu. Non-believers seldom use the concept except in the sense of describing someone, for example a hypocritical religious leader, as "the very avatar of cunning."

Avebury, John Lubbock [Baron the Right Honorable] (1834—1913)

Avebury, a British banker who studied and wrote with authority on many branches of science, particularly anthropology, was termed by *Nature* in his obituary the "President General of his Age." One of his works, *The Pleasures of Life* sold a half million copies and was translated into forty languages.

A vague deist, according to McCabe, Baron Avebury admitted a "Divine Power" but was impatient "at all the assertions under the name of mystery." {JM; RAT; RE}

Avedon, Richard (1923—)

A master photographer, Avedon has been voted one of the world's ten greatest photographers by *Popular Photography* (1958). In 1989 he received the Lifetime Achievement Award of the Council of Fashion Designers of America. In a 1996 television profile, he stated that although he is Jewish and has had a "religious experience" of some sort, he is a total agnostic. {CA; E}

Aveling, Edward Bibbins (1849—1898)

An English freethought teacher, Aveling, according to Stein, "was one of the very few people associated with the freethought movement in the past two hundred years about whom the balance of opinion is negative. Aveling's weaknesses were women, toward whom he was thoroughly unprincipled, and money, which he had a fine knack of spending, especially when it was borrowed."

George Bernard Shaw once described him: "If it came to giving one's life for a cause one could rely on Aveling even if he carried all our purses with him to the scaffold."

In 1880 Aveling had delivered over a hundred freethought lectures and was made a National Secular Society vice-president. But Bradlaugh lent him money, which was not repaid, and Aveling although he had taken over Foote's publications during his imprisonment and Wheeler's illness lost the respect of his fellow freethinkers. Shaw implied that Aveling not only appropriated a microscope belonging to Mary Reed, one of the most promising pupils in the freethinkers' Science School, but probably seduced her as well.

Aveling was willed money by Eleanor Marx, daughter of Karl Marx. He had agreed to marry her when his former marriage could be dissolved. Instead, he married Eva Frye, a twenty-two-year old actress. Eleanor, in a duplication of the suicide of Emmy in *Madame Bovary*, drank prussic acid, which she had obtained by sending her maid to a chemist with "Dr." Aveling's card. Assuming Aveling was a medical doctor, the pharmacist gave the poison to the maid. {EU, Gordon Stein; FUK; RAT; RSR; TRI; WSS}

Aveling, Eleanor (1855—1898)

Aveling, who was Karl Marx's daughter, translated Flaubert's *Madame Bovary* (1886) and Ibsen's *The Lady from the Sea* (1891). She wrote *The Working-Class Movement in America* (1888) and, in conjunction with Dr. E. B. Aveling, with whom she lived, *The Woman Question* (1888). {RAT}

Avempace (12th Century)

Avempace, the Arabian philosopher and poet who was one of the teachers of Averroës, was called by Al-Fath Ibn Khakan "an infidel and atheist." He is said to have suffered imprisonment for his heterodoxy. {BDF}

Avenarius, Richard (1843—1896)

Avenarius was a German philosopher, the joint editor of the *Vierteljahrschrift für wissenschaftliche Philosophie*. He was a critical empiricist, relying upon experience purified of all metaphysics and rejecting the dualism of body and mind as well as all creeds based on that belief. {RAT}

Avenel, Georges (1828—1876)

A French writer, one of the promoters of the *Encyclopédie Générale*, Avenel edited some of Voltaire's work and, by his express wish, was buried without religious ceremony. {BDF; RAT}

Averroës (Ibn Roshd) (1126—1198)

During the French Revolution, Maréchal cited Averroës as being a "possible atheist." The Spanish-Arabian philosopher was influential in the West because use of his commentaries on Aristotle. He believed that philosophic truth derives not from faith but from reason, which positions him opposite St. Thomas Aquinas.

Robertson points out that he was the least mystical and the most rational of the thinkers of his circle. "At nearly all vital points he oppugns [challenges] the religious view of things, denying bodily resurrection, which he treats (here following all his predecessors in heretical Arab philosophy) as a vulgar fable; and making some approach to a scientific treatment of the problem of 'Freewill' as against, on the one hand, the ethic-destroying doctrine of the Motecallemin, who made God's will the sole standard of right, and affirmed predestination (Jabarism); and against, on the other hand, the anti-determinism of the Kadarites." Of all the tyrannies, Averroës boldly declared, the worst is that of priests.

Still, he remained a nominal Muslim. McCabe explains why, saying the Arabs had the quaint custom of choosing the most learned men for high political positions, and Averroës was Governor of Seville for twenty years. When the Moorish fanatics got him imprisoned, Averroës possibly disguised his atheism by referring to a belief in a vague pantheistic "World Soul," instead of Aristotle's (impersonal) God, thereby throwing them off the track.

Averroës and the Enlightenment, The First Humanist/Muslim Dialogue (1996) was edited by Mourad Wahba and Mona Abousenna. It contained comments by thirty-four scholars from eighteen countries on five continents who had met in Cairo in 1994 and Buffalo in 1995 to discuss the ideals of the Enlightenment and secularism while celebrating the approaching 800th anniversary of the noted Islamic philosopher. (See entry for Avicenna.) {BDF; CE; ER; EU, Aram Vartarian; JM; PUT; JMRH; RE}

AVERROÉS TODAY

A semi-annual publication in English and Arabic, *Averroés Today* is at PO Box 5101, Heliopolis West, Cairo, 11771, Egypt. (See entry for Averroës.)

Avery, Milton Clark (1893—1965)

Avery, an American painter, used bold massing of forms as shown in his "Poetry Reading" (1957). His "Green Sea" (1954) verges on complete abstraction and is said to be in the tradition of Matisse. Avery's memorial service was at New York's Society for Ethical Culture. {CE}

AVESTA, THE

The Avesta is the oldest part (the Gathas) of the sacred book of the Persians. McCabe points out that Christians obtained many of their ideas from the Persians, including the concept that the souls of all men one day will be summoned to judgment, the wicked punished, the good rewarded. The dogma of judgment was a fundamental part of the Persian view for at least six centuries before the Christ. {RE}

Avey, Albert E. (1886—1963)

Avey, a philosopher at Ohio State University, responded to the present author as follows:

> My position is theistic "superhumanism," but not "supernaturalism." Nature seems to have no limits, hence I do not know where the supernatural begins. This is not a useful distinction. But I believe the idea of God is valid when rightly reinterpreted. A form of pantheism, similar to that of Whitehead and Hartshorne, seems most adequate to present-day thinking. Man is certainly only a part of the scheme of things and not always the most significant. Yet I do not find myself torn by the inner struggles that the existentialists suffer from. I find myself sympathetic with recent neo-Kantianism, and Fichte appeals to me.
>
> {WAS, 3 August 1954}

Avicenna (980—1037)

Husain Ibn Abdallah, called Ibn Sina or Sind, was an Arabian physician and philosopher. A sovereign authority in medical science until the days of Harvey, he had a philosophy that was pantheistic in tone, with an attempt at compromise with theology. McCabe calls Avicenna the second of the two greatest scholars of the Arab-Persian civilization, the other being Averroës. Unlike Averroës, who is said to have studied far into every night except his wedding night, Avicenna was boisterously sensual and a frequenter of taverns. He wrote not only on medicine but also on theology, philosophy, philology, mathematics, astronomy, geology, physics, and music. To baffle the fanatics, McCabe states, Avicenna "professed a sort of Pantheism. Tradition ascribed to him the saying that 'the world is divided into men who have wit and no religion and men who have religion and no wit.' " {BDF; JM; RE}

Avila Camacho, Manuel [President] (20th Century)

While President of Mexico in the 1940s, Avila signed a decree stating that the rites of religious creeds do not conform with the dignity of the military uniform and insignia, nor with the martial personality of military men." As a result, soldiers in uniform were not permitted to attend religious services. It is likely that he and his Subsecretary of National Defense, Francisco L. Uraquizo, were nonbelievers. {CE}

Avoine, C. L. D. (1875—1945)

Avoine edited *Reason*, the official journal of the Rationalist Association of India. In 1934 he was accused of blasphemy, or according to the Indian Penal Code, of hurting the religious susceptibilities of His Majesty's subjects. At issue was an article he wrote, "Religion and Morality," but he was acquitted and hailed in the press as one who had triumphed for freedom of expression.

Avula, Gopala Krishnamurthy (20th Century)

Avula, a founding member of the Indian Rationalist Association, was its vice-president from 1955 to 1966.

Awbrey, Frank (20th Century)

In 1995 Awbrey, a biology professor at San Diego State University, was honored by the American Humanist Association for his valiant defense of biology against biblical creationism. Awbrey wrote *Evolutionists Confront Creationists* (1984).

Axelrod, Jacob (20th Century)

Axelrod wrote *Philip Freneau, Champion of Democracy* (1967). {FUS}

Axtelle, George Edward (1893—1974)

A professor emeritus at Southern Illinois University when he signed Humanist Manifesto II, Axtelle was active in New York humanist circles. Following his trip to Northeast Africa, he became interested in the effect of religious orthodoxy upon Egyptian culture and civilization. In 1954, he spoke on "Priesthood in Ancient Egypt" to the New York chapter of the American Humanist Association. In *Religious Humanism* (Summer 1967), he wrote, "John Dewey's Concept of 'The Religious.' " Axtelle was President of the American Humanist Association from 1959 to 1961. {HM2; HNS}

Ayer, Alfred J(ules) [Sir] (1910—1989)

Ayer, a British philosopher who was a first vice-president of the British Humanist Association and from 1965 to 1970 its president, edited *The Humanist Outlook* (1968). In 1980, he signed the Secular Humanist Declaration. To the present author, he wrote about humanism:

> I do not know how you wish to draw the distinction between atheistic humanism and naturalistic humanism. Is it that the atheistic humanists dramatize the fact that there is no God, whereas the naturalistic humanists assume it without being emotionally impressed by it? Or would you include theists and agnostics among your naturalistic humanists so long as their main interest was in the fortunes and activities of human beings independently of any matters of religious belief or disbelief? If that is the criterion of naturalistic humanism then I should classify myself as a naturalistic humanist, although I am in fact also an atheist.

In 1988, while Ayer was in the United States, his heart stopped. His thoughts on a rationalist's experience of "death" are written up as an article, "That Undiscovered Country" (*New Humanist*, May, 1989), in which he states, "My recent experiences have slightly weakened my conviction that my genuine death, which is due fairly soon, will be the end of me, though I continue to hope that it will be. They have not weakened my conviction that there is no god. I trust that my remaining an atheist will allay the anxieties of my fellow supporters of the British Humanist Association, the Rationalist Press Association and the South Place Ethical Society."

Ayer was concise in his writing, attacking racism in sport and the harassment of homosexuals. "There was something pathological about his pursuit of women," *The Economist* (19 June 1999) noted:

> He started soon after his first marriage, encouraged by the attentions of a dance-hall hostess in Vienna, and did not let up until he died approaching 80. When ill and old and about to remarry his second wife, Dee, he was still capable of planning to go off with a woman less than half his age. Women to him were like sweets to a greedy little boy. In general, he was not so much autistic as childlike, artlessly pleased with himself, insistent on being the centre of attention. He never really grew up.

A Fellow of the British Academy, Ayer was knighted in 1970. His works include *Foundation of Empirical Knowledge* (1940), *Philosophical Essays* (1954), and *Concept of a Person* (1963).

At the 1996 conference of the Humanist Society of Scotland, Ayer said that humanists think

- that this world is all we have and can provide all we need;
- that we should try to live full and happy lives ourselves and, as part of this, help others to do the same;
- that all situations and people deserve to be judged on their merits, by standards of reason and humanity; and
- that individual and social cooperation are equally important.

Observers were quick to notice that Ayer made no mention of religion. (An essay by Paul Edwards, in which Ayer is called the leading exponent of logical positivism in Great Britain, is found in the *Encyclopedia of Unbelief.* Edwards's *Immortality* includes supporting material which confirms Ayer's disbelief in any kind of survival after death.) {CE; CL; EU, Paul Edwards; HM2; *Humanist in Canada*, Summer 1997; SHD; TRI; TYD; WAS, 15 March 1951}

Aymon, Jean (1661—1734)

A French writer, Aymon abjured Catholicism at Geneva and married at the Hague. He published *Metamorphoses of the Romish Religion.* Aymon's *La vie et L'Esprit de M. Benoit Spinoza* (1719) was afterwards issued under the title of *Treatise of Three Impostors.* {BDF; RAT}

Ayres, A. P. (19th Century)

Ayres, a secularist, wrote *A Secular Funeral and Marriage Handbook* (1885?). {GS}

Ayres, C(larence) E(dwin) (1891—1972)

Ayres, when he reviewed books for *The Humanist* in the 1950s, taught economics at the University of Texas. {HNS}

Arton, William (1847—1908)

Ayrton was a physicist and engineer, one of Lord Kelvin's pupils at Glasgow. He made many discoveries and was one of the first to advocate the transmission of power from generating stations. An agnostic, Ayrton had a secular burial. {RAT}

AYUDH (The Weapon)

An Indian freethought quarterly, *Ayudh* is at 276 Telang Road, Matunga, Bombay 400 019, India.

Azaña Díaz, Manuel [President] (1880—1940)

Azana, the son of a Catholic Alcalde, discarded his creed and became a graduate of Madrid University in Spain. He was awarded the 1926 National Prize for Literature. An anti-clerical Republican, he became Minister of War during the Revolution of 1931, was imprisoned in Barcelona by the right-wing government in 1934, and later was named Premier. Azana was behind a series of laws which secularized Spain. In 1936, he became President of Spain and, when the Italians and Germans crushed the Republic, Azana fled to England and never returned to Spain.

His political and moral stand on freedom, as illustrated in his commentaries in *La velada en Benicarló*, illustrated his insistence on the need to liberalize Spain. His biggest battle was against the narrowness, hypocrisy, and dominance of the Catholic Church. This is shown in his first novel, *El jardín de los frailes*. A lover of art, music, and literature, he was said by Daniel de Bois-Juzan in *Celui qui fut Pedro Muñoz* to have had, possibly, a male lover in addition to his wife. The Azañas were childless. {GL; RE}

Azm, Sadik al (20th Century)

Azm, a professor of philosophy at the University of Damascus in Syria, signed Humanist Manifesto 2000.

AZTEC HUMAN SACRIFICE: See entry for Human Sacrifice

BA: See entry for Resurrection.

BAAL

Baal was the Canaanite god of weather and fertility. At Ugarit in present-day Syria the Canaanite *Poem of Baal*, which dates to well before the 14th Century B.C.E., was recently unearthed. Parts of Joel and Zephaniah satirize Canaanite myth and ritual, and in *Isaiah* Yahweh (Hebrew for "God") is credited with slaying the dragon of the oceans, a feat similar to that of Baal. The triumvirate of Air, Water, and Earth—Baal, Yam, and Mot—align closely with Zeus, Poseidon, and Hades. {DGC}

Baba, Satya Raju (1926—)

Satya Narayana Raju was born in Puttaparthi, India, of Easwaramma and her illiterate husband, Pedda Venkappa Raju. Suspected of mental illness when fifteen, and despite being a troublesome student in school, Raju cited a 1918 prediction of Sai Baba of Shirdi, that eight years after leaving the Shirdi body he would be reborn in Puttaparthi. Claiming to be that predicted individual and revealing his avatarhood to the world, the Sai Baba with a new name [*satya* means truth, which he considered an improvement on the previous *shirdi*, a place name) set about to prove his supernatural powers. In 1971, "He" allegedly resurrected Walter Cowan, who had been declared dead due to cardiac failure. He also allegedly created out of nowhere a copy of the Bhagavadgita (although, as G. R. R. Babu has pointed out, "even the Lord is not immune to orthographic error"). He is said to have converted water into petrol by dipping His finger into water. He is capable of bilocation, appearing in two places at the same time. And He claims that He never sleeps. To all who would listen, he declared,

> I, the Lord, was incarnated at Puttaparthi. Buddha, Christ, Mohammed and others were not avatars. They had some divine power. My power is infinite. My Truth is inexplicable, even unfathomable. My task is the regeneration of humanity by Truth and Love.

In the year 2022 He claims that He will be reborn as Prema Sai in Mandya district of Karnataka. Many eminent Indians deny the godman's claims. These include representatives of the World Union of Free Thinkers; Dr. H. Narasimhaiah, an Indian rationalist who formerly was vice-chancellor of the Bangalore University; Dr. Abraham T. Kovoor, a person who successfully galvanized public opinion—he was a Sri Lankan, the most famous rationalist of the land; and B. Premanand, a magician, former devotee of Baba, and today a well-known Indian skeptic who disproved the Walter Cowan resurrection story. They have expertly pointed out the various weaknesses in each of Baba's claims and lament that lesser educated individuals are being fooled by the godman.

In 1993, six inmates of Prashanti Nilayam were murdered in Baba's bedroom, all of whom had been part of the inner circle. As of 1997 the Supreme Court of India , which included one of the Satya Sai inner circle, Y. V. Anjaneyulu, had not found Baba guilty of anything. Anjaneyulu allowed the argument that Babu's "materializing" gold ornaments to be given to devotees did not violate the Gold Control Act. Articles which have come about through spiritual powers, he ruled, cannot be said to have been manufactured, prepared, or processed. (See G. R. R. Babu, "Sex, Lies, and Video Tape: Retelling the Satya Sai Baba Story.")

Babbitt, Irving: See entry for Neo-Classical Humanism.

Babe, M. A. (20th Century)

Babe, a member of the Indian Parliament, spoke in 1995 at the Indian Rationalist Association's conference in Bombay. He said he was happy to be associated with that group's campaign for freedom of speech, adding there should be the right to expose fraud and superstition but not to impose ideas on others. Babe had reservations about provocative attacks on religion, but he endorsed the need to counter an intolerable growth of intolerance. {*New Humanist*, February 1996}

Babcock, M. (19th Century)

Babcock, a freethinker, wrote *Superstition: The Religion of "Believe or Be Damned" (c. 1880) and Why Don't God Kill the Devil?* (1891). {GS}

Babeuf, François Noel (1764—1797)

Babeuf was a French economist, an atheist who founded *Société des Égaux*. He was a single-taxer who, at the outbreak of the Revolution, took the name of Caius Gracchus and edited a series of ephemeral papers advocating complete equality. Condemned to death for plotting against the Directorate, Babeuf committed suicide in court. {RAT}

BABI YAR

At Babi Yar, near Kiev, more than 150,000 Jews, Gypsies, and Soviet prisoners of war were killed by Nazi SS squads between 1941 and 1943. Yevgeny Yevtushenko's *Babi Yar* (1961), set to music by Dmitri Shostakovich, was a powerful humanistic statement condemning the Soviet government for having sanctioned anti-Semitism. {DCG}

Babic, Jovan (20th Century)

Babic, who chairs the Faculty of Philosophy at the Unviersity of Belgrade in Yugoslavia, signed Humanist Manifesto 2000.

Babinski, Edward T. (20th Century)

Babinski is the editor of *Cretinism or Evilution* (109 Burwood Drive, Simpsonville, SC 29681), a newsletter that is pro-Darwinian and anti-creationism. He is on the staff at the J. B. Duke Library at Furnam University. In *Leaving the Fold: Testimonies of Former Fundamentalists* (1995), Babinski relates religious odysseys of those who left fundamentalism in favor of atheism or agnosticism as well as those who remained Christians but backed away from the pull of fundamentalism. (See entry for South Carolina Humanists.) {FD}

Babu: See entry for Gogineni.

Bacard, Andre (20th Century)

Bacard is editor of *Affirmist Newsletter* and has written for *Free Inquiry*. He is on the editorial board of *The Humanist* and is author of *Hunger for Power Who Rules the World and How* (1986). {*Free Inquiry*, Winter 1984—1985}

Baccelli, Guido (1832—1916)

Baccelli was an Italian statesman who, after the fall of the Papacy, entered the Camera (1875) and sat with the Anti-Clericals. He was four times Minister of Public Instruction, and to him is due the reorganization of Italian education, which the Popes had left in a disgraceful state. Baccelli was a prominent Freemason and a rationalist. {RAT}

BACCHUS

- Bacchus, n. A convenient deity invented by the ancients as an excuse for getting drunk.

—Ambrose Bierce
The Devil's Dictionary

In mythology, Bacchus (also called Dionysus) was related to orgiastic religion, an indication that practices of some religionists have not changed dramatically over the centuries. In addition to being a god of fertility, Bacchus was also god of vegetation and wine.

Priestesses and followers of Bacchus were called Bacchae. A bacchanal is a drunken or riotous celebration. A bacchanalia is a boisterous festivity, like the Bacchanalia that was a festival in honor of Bacchus.

A Christian seaman, according to one drunken sailor, defined Bacchus as "a port in every woman." But that sailor knew wittily well, according to the storyteller, that Bacchus is a Roman and Greek, not a Christian, god.

BACHELORS

- Bachelors should be heavily taxed: it is not fair that some men should be happier than others.

—Oscar Wilde

- A bachelor's virtue depends upon his alertness; a married man's depends upon his wife's.

—H. L. Mencken

Bachrach, Fabian (20th Century)

The name of Bachrach is indelibly associated with portrait photography. Started in 1868 by Fabian Bachrach's grandfather in Baltimore, the Bachrach studios have photographed every United States President since Andrew Johnson. Bachrach is a lifelong member of the First Unitarian Society in Newton, Massachusetts.

Backus, E(dwin) Burdette (1888—1955)

A Unitarian minister, Backus signed Humanist Manifesto I. He was President of the American Humanist Association from 1944 to 1946. "One of the basic needs of men in this catastrophic period, as always, is for a religion, a philosophy of life, which provides them with the guidance, the incentives, the methods which shall enable them to attain the deepest desires of their hearts," he observed. Wilson has described Backus's considerable efforts in helping with the editing of Humanist Manifesto I. {EW; FUS; HM1; HNS}

Bacon, Francis [Sir] (1561—1626)

Bacon was no philosophic materialist and his metaphysics never rejected Christian supernaturalism. But his rejecting of the a priori method of medieval scholasticism led to the application of the inductive method of modern science. In his time, he was criticized for failing to keep up-to-date on scientific findings and for not carrying his investigations to their logical conclusions.

During the French Revolution, Maréchal cited Bacon as one who seems to be an atheist only from the standpoint of the strictest religious orthodoxy. This was in part because Bacon believed that there must be an absolute separateness of "divinity" and philosophy, adding "that men should not unwisely mingle or confound these learnings together."

"It were better," Bacon wrote, "to have no opinion of God at all than such an opinion as is unworthy of him. . . . And, as the contumely is greater towards God, so the danger (of superstition) is greater towards man. . . . Atheism did never perturb states, and we see that the times enclined to Atheism (as the time of Augustus Caesar) were civil times." McCabe comments that the quotation shows Bacon was a theist "though probably not more, but it is useful to remember that in Elizabethan England in spite of the skepticism of the Queen herself, atheism was a dangerous creed to admit."

However, Bacon in "Of Superstition" did write, "Atheism leaves a man to sense, to philosophy, to natural piety, to laws, to reputation: all of which may be guides to an outward moral virtue, though religion were not; but superstition dismounts all these and erecteth an absolute monarchy in the minds of men." (As for his mingling with other men, see A. L. Rowse, *Homosexuals in History* [1977]. Or Graham Hammill's chapter in Jonathan Goldberg's *Queering the Renaissance* [1994], in which Bacon's intimacy with male servants, his use of enemas, and his being accused of sodomy are discussed in academic detail. Also, see the entry for E. O. Wilson.). {CE; CL; EU, Aram Vartanian; JM; JMR JMRH; PUT}

Bacon, Francis (1909?—1992)

Bacon has been called "the greatest British painter since Turner," a figurative painter in a sea of abstract and conceptual artists, one who has given a new dimension to contemporary figurative painting. Known for his owl-like appearance, as illustrated in 1979 photos taken in Paris by Richard Avedon, the Dublin-born painter is famous for his strange obsessive art. Particularly controversial were three 1933 abstract works called *Crucifixion* and a 1951 exhibition of *The Screaming Popes*. John Russell, in *Francis Bacon* (1979), has explained that a " 'crucifixion' [in Bacon's painting] is not a descriptive title, and still less is it a reference to an actual event. It is, rather, a generic name for an environment in which bodily harm is done to one or more persons and one or more persons gather to watch." The latter work shows a pope wearing a white lace—trimming skirt suggestive of transvestism. Although an avowed atheist, Bacon turned out a number of works using the crucifixion theme or portraying religious subjects, including some inspired by Velázquez's portrait of Pope Innocent X.

"My figures are not twisted or tortured by torture," he told a French magazine in 1971. "I do not deform bodies for the pleasure of it, rather in order to transmit the reality of the image in its most poignant phase. Perhaps it is not the best way, but it is the only way I know of to get to something that is as close as possible to life." His comment was in reference to the howling mouths or silent screams that are found in his 1950's works.

A credible account of Bacon's personal life has been described by David Plante in *The New Yorker* (1 November 1993). When George Dyer, a minor criminal, broke into Bacon's house, Bacon greeted him with, "Not much of a burglar, are you?" Whereupon the two men became lovers and shared a sexual life together for years until Dyer committed suicide in 1971. Plante recalls talking one time with Bacon and Stephen Spender: "I can't remember who started talking about Christianity–perhaps it was Francis, when he said, repeatedly, that *Macbeth* showed that Shakespeare was not Christian. When Stephen said, 'Well, I think I'm Christian, at least in believing we must help one another,' it was as though he had become responsible for all the worst aspects of Christianity." Bacon reacted quite angrily, said Plante, exclaiming "that this was rubbish, and Bacon got very angry, more angry than the circumstances in any way justified, repeating again and again, 'Rubbish.' Stephen went silent, as I did, and I thought I saw behind Francis the depth of his hard darkness." Plante, who confirmed Bacon's being a nonbeliever, has detailed Bacon's life of gambling, alcoholism, and homosexuality.

"I've had a very hypnotic and curious [life]—being homosexual I have lived with the most marvelously disastrous people," Bacon once told *Time*.

In 1999 England's High Court ruled that Marlborough Fine Art, the gallery that had managed Bacon for virtually his entire career, could no longer do so. The court appointed Brian Clarke, an architectural artist who was a friend of Bacon and of John Edwards, the painter's closest friend, to whom Bacon willed his entire estate and who now would inherit Bacon's fortune. {CE}

Bacon, Roger (c.1214— 1294?)

A Franciscan scholastic philosopher and scientist, Bacon read Hebrew, Greek, and possibly Arabic texts in the original languages. Erroneously credited with inventing gunpowder, he was an alchemist and a natural scientist whose formula for gunpowder appeared in a work attributed to him. The Germans credited such an invention to an alchemist-monk by the name of Berthold Schwarz, but it is now held that as early as the 9th century the Chinese were making firecrackers, and that gunpowder was introduced to Europe in the 14th Century. Three of Bacon's works were written for Pope Clement IV in one year (1267—1268).

However, when Clement died Bacon wrote *Compendium Philosophiae* (1271), which according to Robertson "argued that the Christians were incomparably inferior to pagans in morals, and therefore in science; that there was more truth in Aristotle's few chapters on laws than in the whole *corpus juris*; that the Christian religion, as commonly taught, was not free of errors; and that philosophy truly taught, and not as in the schools, was perhaps the surer way to attain both truth and salvation." As a result, he was brought to trial and imprisoned for 14 years.

Bacon's *Imago Majus* was translated by Peter de Alliaco in 1410 and contained quotations from Aristotle, Pliny, and Seneca, all arguing for the possibility of reaching India by sailing westward. One who read *Imago Majus* was Christopher Columbus, according to a letter Columbus sent from Jamaica to Ferdinand and Isabella.

According to Donald Keene, Columbus also was impressed by Marco Polo's tales of all the gold in Japan, a further reason for his desire to reach the Orient. Scientists today find Bacon's faith in astrology was unwarranted, and philosophers find his ideas in theology were of a previous era.

Nevertheless, Bacon was in advance of his times in natural science, despite his interest in magic. McCabe held that, except for the article in the *Dictionary of National Biography*, no unbiased, reliable work on Bacon and the influence of Arab science has ever been completed. {CE; FUK; HNS2; JMR; JMRH; RE}

Bacrac, Norman (20th Century)

Bacrac is President of London's South Place Ethical Society. He edits *Ethical Record* and is a director of the National Secular Society.

Baden, Michael M. (1934—)

Baden is an educator and pathologist. He has been a lecturer for the Drug Enforcement Administration of the Department of Justice since 1973 and a professor of pathology at Albert Einstein School of Medicine since 1975. He wrote *Alcohol, Other Drugs, and Violent Death* (1978) and *Unnatural Death* (1989). Baden is a member of New York City's Unitarian Church of All Souls.

Bagdoyan, Bagsar Manoog (19th Century?)

Bagdoyan, a freethinker, wrote *Atheism! and the Dream of the Bridge of Upward Flowing Waters*. The work was published in California. {GS}

Bage, Robert (1728—1801)

Bage, who at the age of seven knew Latin, decided against being part of his father's business of papermaking. For four years (1775—1779), he was a partner with Erasmus Darwin in a large iron enterprise. When it failed, Bage took to writing novels. *Mount Henneth* (1781) was not successful, but his later stories earned a high reputation. Bage left the Society of Friends and became a deist. His pious and intimate friend Hutton said Bage "laid no stress upon revelation" and was "barely a Christian." {RAT}

Bagehot, Walter (1826—1877)

Bagehot, a British economist and editor of the *Economist*, was a Unitarian. "Great and terrible systems of divinity and philosophy lie round about us, which, if true," he wrote, "might drive a wise man mad." In *Physics and Politics* (1872), a series of essays on the volution of society, Bagehot applies Darwinism to politics.

Wheeler cites him as being "a bold, clear, and very original thinker who rejected historic Christianity." As for religion, Bagehot wrote,

> Few cultivated persons willingly think on the special dogmas of distinct theology. . . . They do not question the existence of Kamschatka, but they have no call to busy themselves with Kamschatka.

{BDF; RAT; UU}

Baggeson, Jens Immanuel (1764—1826)

A Danish poet, Baggeson married the grand-daughter of the Swiss scientist, Albrecht von Haller. An admirer of Voltaire, he wrote *Adam and Eve* (1826), a humorous mock epic. {BDF; RAT}

Bagot, Susan (20th Century)

Bagot became "certified" for Ethical Culture Leadership in 1983 and has served in a society in Northern Virginia. (See entry for Ethical Culture.)

Bahadur Singh, Raja Jai Prithvi (20th Century)

Bahadur in Bangalore founded in 1928 a Humanistic Club and wrote *Humanism* (1930). In addition, he edited a monthly journal, *The Humanist.*

BAHA'I

A Persian-derived universalist religion, Baha'i was founded by the Persian mirza Hoseyn Ali Nuri (1817—1892), known as "Baha' U'llah" (Arabic for "Glory of God"). The church advocates an international government and language, urges daily prayer, has no clergy, no sacraments, and no initiation ceremony. Because of its desire to abolish competition among religions and discrimination based upon race, gender, or class, it has grown greatly in Africa. At the same time, it has provoked severe repression from fundamentalist religious authorities, particularly in Iran. The world headquarters is in Israel.

Address is 536 Sheridan Road, Wilmette, Illinois 60091. On the Web: <http://www.us.bahai.org>. (For an estimate of the number of Bahai's in the world, see entry for Hell. {DGC}

Baham, Donald (20th Century)

Baham resigned in 1996 as president of the Humanists of the Portland/Vancouver Metro Area (HPVMA) in Oregon.

Bahm, Archie J(ohn) (Born 1907)

A professor of philosophy emeritus at the University of New Mexico, Bahm signed Humanist Manifesto II. He has been an editor for *The Humanist* and a contributing editor to *Religious Humanism.* In the former, he wrote "A Religious Affirmation" (March-April 1953). Three of Bahm's works are *The Heart of Confucius* (1969), *Metaphysics* (1974), and *Computocracy* (1985).

Bahm in 1933 contributed "A Religious Affirmation" to *The New Humanist*, listing items that "a person should":

1. Be creedless; that is, be intelligent enough to make adaptations without dependence upon some formula.
2. Be self-reliant; that is, be not dependent upon supernatural agency for intellectual support or moral guidance.
3. Be critical; that is, question assumptions and seek certitude scientifically.
4. Be tolerant; that is, be open-minded and hold conclusions tentatively.
5. Be active; that is, live today and grow by exercising his capacities.
6. Be efficient; that is, accomplish the most with the lease effort.
7. Be versatile; that is, vary his interests to attain a variety of interesting thoughts.
8. Be cooperative; that is, find some of his satisfactions in social activities.
9. Be appreciative; that is, make the present enjoyable by his attitude.
10. Be idealistic; that is, create and live by ideals which he finds inspiring.

{EW; HM2; HNS}

Bahnsen, Julius Friedrich August (Born 1830)

Bahnsen was a pessimist, an independent follower of Schopenhauer and Hartmann. A German, he joined monism to the idealism of Hegel. Among other works he wrote *The Philosophy of History* (1872) and a two-volume *Contradiction Between the Knowledge and the Nature of the World* (1880—1882). {BDF; RAT}

Bahrdt, Carl Friedrich (1741—1792)

Termed "much more notorious than any other German deist of his time," Bahrdt has been described by Robertson as "a kind of raw Teutonic Voltaire and the most popularly influential German freethinker of his age." His *New Revelations of God in Letters and Tales* (1773) was a kind of expurgated Bible, arousing Protestant hostility, and the second edition of his translation of the New Testament aroused Catholic hostility. He regarded Jesus as a great teacher, "like Moses, Confucius, Socrates, Semler, Luther, and myself."

He was called "the Theodore Parker of Germany," a reference to the American Unitarian. As to how a preacher like himself could have become a rationalist, he said he had asked himself "how Three Persons could be One God," this while believing devoutly in revelation, miracles, the divinity of Jesus, and the Atonement.

Wheeler comments, "The writings of this *enfant terrible* of the German Aufklarung fill 120 volumes." Bahrdt in 1788 suffered a year in prison for the controversial deism of his writings. {BDF; JMR; JMRH; RAT}

Baier, Annette (20th Century)

Baier, the wife of Kurt Baier, is a noted philosopher and a David Hume scholar.

Baier, Kurt Erich (1917—)

A professor emeritus of philosophy at the University of Pittsburgh, the Vienna-born Baier is a humanist laureate in the Council for Secular Humanism's International Academy of Humanism. He is author of *The Moral Point of View: A Rational Basis of Ethics* (1958, *Values and the Future* (1969), and *Rational and the Moral Order: The Social Roots of Reason and Morality* (1995).

In 1993 Baier delivered the prestigious Prometheus Lectures on the subject of naturalistic philosophy. He is a contributing editor of *Philo* and a signer of Humanist Manifesto 2000.

Baigent, Michael (20th Century)

Baigent, with Richard Leigh and Henry Lincoln, wrote *Holy Blood, Holy Grail* (1983).

Bailey, Eliza (1844-1920)

Bailey was a Universalist minister.

Bailey, Gillian (20th Century)

In Britain, Bailey is secretary of Humanist Holidays, a group formed in 1965 to organize holidays together for humanists at the festive times of year and in the summer.

Bailey, James Napier (19th Century)

Bailey was a Socialist who edited the *Model Republic* (1843) and wrote *Sophistry Unmasked* (1842). {BDF}

Bailey, Jesse (20th Century)

Bailey, an atheist activist in Birmingham, Alabama, regards himself as a logical positivist. He has written for *Freethought History #9* (1994) and *Freethought Perspective* (May 1998).

Bailey, Richard (20th Century)

Bailey is a lecturer at the Department of Education, Christ Church College, in Canterbury, England. In a December 1995 *New Humanist,* he described the formative years of Karl Popper, finding that although it is often thought that Popper was never active in politics or social reform, he had taken part in political reforms and social reform. "He worked, wrote, and protested," Bailey described, "fighting for reform and democracy, against the growing powers of the Fascist right and the Austrian Catholic Church.

His efforts, it turned out, were largely in vain; the social reforms were curtailed by the sweeping reaction by supporters of the Closed Society. Dejected and feeling betrayed, Popper took the opportunity to abandon his work in educational and social reform, in favour of the world of academia. Nevertheless, the effects of his early, revolutionary period can be seen in his approach to philosophical and political problems."

Bailey, Samuel (1791—1870)

An English philosophical writer, Bailey held that man is not responsible for his opinions because they are independent of his will, that opinions should not be the subject of punishment. An acquaintance of both James and John Stuart Mill, he shared in most of the views of the philosophical radicals of the period.

One of his freethought works was *Letters from an Egyptian Kaffir on a Visit to England in Search of Religion,* a work that shocked his townspeople because of its contempt for their Christian beliefs. Nevertheless, upon his death, he left £90,000. to his native town of Sheffield. Bailey was a deist, a determinist, and a utilitarian. {BDF; RE}

Bailey, William Shreeve (1806—1886)

Bailey, who edited the Nashville, Tennessee, *Liberal,* was an atheist who, in a slave-holding state, was an earnest advocate of abolition. His opinions were greeted with hostility. Upon Bailey's death, Photius Fisk erected a monument to his memory in Nashville. {BDF}

Baillie, George (1784—1873)

Baillie, a Scottish philanthropist, gave substantial prizes for the writing of rationalist works on deistic lines. In 1863 he offered his entire fortune (£18,000) to the Glasgow faculty on condition that they allow the interest to accumulate for twenty-one years, then build an institute for the education of the workers.

Baillie's Institution was opened in 1887 but, notes McCabe, "as in the case of all such Rationalist charities, the views of the founder are not obtruded." {RAT; RE}

Baillière, Gustave-Germer (Born 1837)

A French scientific publisher, Baillière published the *Library of Contemporary Philosophy*. He was an anti-clerical member of the Municipal Council of Paris. {BDF}

Bain, Alexander (1818—1903)

A Scottish philosopher, Bain discussed John Stuart Mill's *Logic* with him when it was in manuscript. A teacher of logic in the University of Aberdeen, he was considered obnoxious by the orthodox and was said to provoke disorder among the students. In 1881 Bain was elected for the first of two times Lord Rector of the university. In discussing free will, he favored physiological over metaphysical explanations and pointed to reflexes as evidence that a form of will, independent of consciousness, inheres in a person's limbs. Bain founded *Mind*, the first psychological journal, in 1886. Although sometimes wrongly described as a positivist, according to McCabe, Bain was an agnostic who merely agreed with Comte in the rejection of theology. {BDF; RAT; RE}

Bain, Force (20th Century)

Bain, a freethinker, wrote *Decadence of the Orthodox Church* (1920). {GS}

Bain, Read (1920—1962)

In the 1950s, Bain, who taught sociology at Miami University in Oxford, Ohio, was poetry editor of *The Humanist.* (See David T. Lewis's *The Published Works of Read Bain* (1962.) {HNS}

Bainbridge, William (20th Century)

Bainbridge, a sociologist, has referred to himself as "personally incapable of religious faith." He collaborated with Rodney Stark to write *A Theory of Religion.* (See entry for Rodney Stark) {CA}

Bainham, James (Died 1532)

A martyr, Bainham married the widow of Simon Fish, author of the *Supplycacion of Beggars*, an attack upon the clergy of the period. He was accused of heresy in 1531, having denied transubstantiation, the confessional, and "the power of the keys." It was asserted that he had said he would as lief pray to his wife as to "our lady," and that Christ was but a man. For such heresy, he was burned in 1532. {BDF}

Bainton, Roland H. (1894—1984)

Bainton is author of *Hunted Heretic* (1953), a biographical study of Michael Servetus (Miguel Serveto).

Baird, Bill (1932—)

A pioneering crusader for abortion rights, Baird in 1933 received from the American Humanist Association their Pioneer Movement award. Originally raised in a strict Lutheran family, he left Protestantism and became a Unitarian. Speaking to a group at a time when his grandson was severely ill, he was told by a member of the audience, "I know why your grandson got cancer. God's punishing you." To a *New York Times* reporter (14 April 1993), Baird said that the Christian's accusation "went through me like a knife. Believe it or not, I wake up in the night and think, 'Could I be wrong and everyone else is right? Could I be the Devil?' Then I realize, as I awaken, that I will not allow myself to be victimized by the hate propaganda of the anti-abortionists. I then recall those who tell me I am a good person whose life has benefited countless people nationally. It may sound corny, but sometimes you feel like death is on your shoulder." To the accuser and others, Baird replied, "I told them if there was a God, what kind of God would give a baby cancer?"

In 1967 after a speech at Boston University, he was arrested on charges of having exhibited obscene objects (abortion devices, diaphragms, condoms, etc.), thus challenging a Massachusetts "chastity" statute that barred giving of such materials to unmarried couples. In a 1972 case, *Baird v. Eisenstadt*, that the Supreme Court of the United States at first declined to hear, Justice William O. Douglas wrote, "The teachings of Baird and Galileo may be of a different order, but the suppression of either is equally repugnant." The case led to the national legalization of birth control for single people. The following year in *Roe v. Wade* (1973), a landmark ruling that made abortion legal, the majority opinion cited "bear or beget" six times Justice William J. Brennan Jr.'s words in the Baird case: "It is the right of the individual, married or single, to be free from unwarranted governmental intrusion into matters so fundamentally affecting a person as the decision whether to bear or beget a child."

Baird, saying he is estranged from his wife and five children, has explained, "They became quite conservative, very religious. They talk to me about Jesus Christ and tell me he is my savior. I tell them I don't know any saviors. I've lost my children: They talk to me, but they don't want to hear about their father and his wars. My life is sad. I wish I could tell you it's happy." His despondency has been compared with that of his friend Abbie Hoffman, who took his own life. Although some feminists claim Baird is self-serving, he counters that the major feminist leaders are remiss in not having more successfully pushed their cause. He ponders as to how he can be accused of being self-serving when such leaders have never paid the price that he has: of being jailed in five states for merely lecturing on reproductive rights, of being firebombed, chemically bombed, shot at, assaulted, and forced into debt after incurring tens of thousands of dollars in legal fees for his efforts to improve women's rights.

On 25 July 1993, the 25th anniversary of the Catholic Church's order banning artificial birth control, a videotaped message by Mother Teresa in Calcutta, India, was played in Omaha, Nebraska. The eighty-three-year-old Roman Catholic nun and winner of the Nobel Prize for peace said contraception is a selfish act and "the same selfishness that wants to prevent the child by contraception will grow until it wants to kill the child already conceived. We must fight selfishness with a true, generous, and sacrificing love."

Meanwhile, and exactly twenty-six years after his 1967 picketing at the same location, Baird stood in front of St. Patrick's Cathedral in New York City, protesting Pope Paul VI's 1968 *Humanae Vitae* Encyclical, that he said involves "Vatican roulette," a reference to the rhythm method of birth control. In the 1993 demonstration, Baird was joined by the present author and twenty supporters, some from Unitarian and Catholic churches, others who were atheists and secular humanists, all carrying signs opposing the Pope's ban on birth control. As churchgoers filed out, Baird delivered a note to be given to Cardinal O'Connor, pleading with him to help "free women from the cross of oppression" and influence present Catholic leaders at a summit meeting to overturn the 1968 encyclical. To the press, Baird added, "This cardinal has no right to tell me–a Unitarian–what I can believe. I suggest to him that he clean up his house of priests, who have sex with little boys, before he tells us we're immoral for using birth control."

In 1998 at a Brown University lecture, Baird said his three decades of fighting for abortion rights had left him penniless, adding, "I'm living on Social Security. You try to live on $14,000 a year. At the age of sixty-five I'm tired, you can tell, and I'm flat broke. I need you to fight. It's your life we're talking about. It's your freedom we're talking about. If you won't stand up, who will?" He denounced the Catholic Church several times, noting in passing that "three of my [abortion] patients were nuns." {U}

Baissac, Jules (Born 1827)

A French *littérateur*, Baissac published *Les Origines de la Religion* (1878), that merited being placed on the Catholic *Index*. In *Histoire de la Diablerie Chrétienne* (1882), he devoted the first part to the person and "personnel" of the devil. {BDF}

Baker, Celia (20th Century)

Baker signed Humanist Manifesto II. {HM2}

Baker, Daniel (19th Century)

A prosperous steel-pen manufacturer, Baker supported building a hall for Birmingham secularists to meet in the 1860s and 1870s. {RSR}

Baker, Don (20th Century)

Baker is treasurer of the National Secular Society.

Baker, Ernest (20th Century)

An associate professor at the University of the Pacific, Baker signed Humanist Manifesto II. {HM2}

Baker, G. Dawson (19th Century)

Writing in the *Freethinker* in 1898, Baker likened the difference between the English Ethical Culture and secularist movements as "the difference between church and chapel." {RSR}

Baker, George Jr.: See entry for Divine, which describes "Father Divine, God Almighty."

Baker, George Fisher (1840—1931)

A financier and philanthropist, once called the third richest man in the world, Baker was a member of the New York Unitarian Church of All Souls. He had been one of the founders (1863) of the First National Bank of New York and became its president (1877) and chairman of its board of directors (1909). Closely associated with the house of Morgan, Baker helped finance James J. Hill in building a railroad empire and became a leading figure in the world of railroad organization and finance. Among his various philanthropic bequests were $6 million to found and support the Harvard graduate school of business administration; $2 million to Cornell University; $1 million to build the Baker Memorial Library at Dartmouth; and the money for Baker Field of Columbia University. {CE}

Baker, I. Newton (20th Century)

Baker wrote *An Intimate View of Robert G. Ingersoll* (1920).

Baker, Jane (20th Century)

Baker has been production manager of *Religious Humanism*, the quarterly published by the Fellowship of Religious Humanists.

Baker, Jesse (20th Century)

A freethinker in Birmingham, Alabama, Baker has written for *Freethought Perspective* (June 1999).

Baker, Lee (20th Century)

Baker, of Atheist TV Outreach Project, is on the Web: <lbaker4989@aol.com>.

Baker, Marjorie S. (20th Century)

When she was president of the Humanist Community of San Francisco, California, Baker signed Humanist Manifesto II. {HM2}

Baker, Richard L. (Born 1827)

Baker, whose parents were of English stock and among the early settlers of New Brunswick, moved to Maine when young. At the age of twenty-four after a careful reading of the Bible he concluded that religion was the foe of mental liberty, that the church was the invention of priests. He organized the Fort Fairfield Liberal League. {PUT}

Baker, Robert A. (20th Century)

A professor of psychology at the university of Kentucky, Baker signed Humanist Manifesto 2000.

Baker, Rose (20th Century)

Baker in 1972 was treasurer of the Humanist Society of Greater New York.

Baker, Russell Wayne (1925—)

Baker, a noted newspaper columnist, humorist, and member of the American Academy of Arts and Letters, has written,

> One of the many burdens of the person professing Christianity has always been the odium likely to be heaped upon him by fellow Christians quick to smell out, denounce, and punish fraud, hypocrisy, and general unworthiness among those who assert the faith. In ruder days, disputes about what constituted a fully qualified Christian often led to sordid quarrels in which the disputants tortured, burned, and hanged each other in the conviction that torture, burning, and hanging were Christian things to do.

He lost his faith when he was five and his father died, he wrote in his Pulitzer Prize-winning memoir *Growing Up*. "After that I never cried with any real conviction, nor expected much of anyone's God except indifference, nor loved deeply without fear that it would cost me dearly in pain. At the age of five I had become a skeptic and began to sense that any happiness that came my way might be the prelude to some grim cosmic joke." {CA; E; TYD}

Baker, (Sara) Josephine (1873-1945)

A Unitarian, Baker was a physician, a health administrator, and a health reformer.

Baker, W. W. (19th Century)

Baker edited a freethought periodical, *The Delaware Free Press*, from 1830 to 1833. {FUS}

Baksh, S. A. (20th Century)

Baksh was a Vice President of the Andhra Pradesh Chapter of the Indian Radical Humanist Association.

Bakunin, Mikhail (1814—1876)

A revolutionist imprisoned by the Czar for years and author of *God and the State* (1916), Bakunin once stated, reversing Voltaire's phrase, "Even if God existed it would be necessary to abolish him." He also wrote: "Theology is the science of the divine lie"; "Religion is a collective insanity"; and "People go to church for the same reasons they go to a tavern: to forget their misery, to imagine themselves, for a few minutes anyway, free and happy." Bakunin was clear about his outlook: "We are materialists and atheists, and we glory in the fact."

Will Self, in *Cock and Bull* (1992), takes a novelist's, not a historian's, crack at Henry James and Mikhail Bakunin. Of the revolutionist, Self wrote, "[T]hat's the other great nineteenth-century non-cocksman that springs and then comes to mind," having just alleged that James lost half his penis in an accident while chasing after a fire engine:

> Bakunin at the barricades of 1848, rapier in hand. Bakunin at the inaugural meeting of the First International, striking the board and severing the working movement for all eternity; whilst all the time it wasn't a proud manhood that bumped for emphasis against the wooden lectern–but nothing at all. "*Die Lust der Zerstörung ist zugleiche eine schaffende Lust!*" Now there, there, dear, of course it is. And you know there's a pun there somewhere, but I'll be buggered if I'll grope for it . . . drink?

{BDF; CE; JM; PA; PUT; RAT; TRI; TYD}

Balaam, Diesel (20th Century)

"I am a post-gay humanist," Balaam has declared. Finding that "gay" is dead and "anti-gay" is a dead end because of "its hard-bitten cynicism and misplaced faith in the flexibility of the heterosexual hegemony," he says homosexuals need now to look forward to a post-gay period. Balaam, who works in the television industry, is co-author of *Black Confetti*, a book of short stories for gay men.

{*Gay and Lesbian Humanist*, Winter 1997-1998}

Balasuriya, Tissa (1924—)

A Roman Catholic Sri Lankan priest, Father Balasuriya was excommunicated at the end of 1996 because of his heresy. A sociologist in addition to being a priest, he argued in several books that Catholic dogma should adjust itself to the social and cultural realities of Asia. *Mary and Human Liberation* (1990), which sold fewer than one thousand copies, complemented *Jesus and Human Liberation* and *The Eucharist and Human Liberation*, a trilogy which led to his excommunication. "I firmly state that I have not committed any form of heresy, deviation from any doctrine of the Catholic faith," Balasuriya objected. But the formal notification of his heresy was issued by the Vatican's Congregation for the Doctrine of the Faith and carried "the weight and force of a papal act" since its findings were explicitly approved by Pope John Paul II.

His books challenged the traditional Catholic image of the mother of Jesus, saying it was too docile, even "dehydrated." He criticized the "Hail Mary," which he said lacks "a socially liberative dynamic" and thus has played a role in "tranquilizing Catholics." He also questioned the dogma of original sin, saying, "In our countries, the idea of humans being born alienated from the Creator would seem an abominable concept." In reporting about the case from Rome, journalist Celestine Bohlen noted that a Catholic scholar who disagreed with much of what the Sri Lankan priest said, and insisted upon his anonymity, observed that "What the Vatican is doing is making a personage out of this man. They are making a somebody out of a nobody."

In 1998 in a surprise development, the excommunicated priest was reunited with the Vatican. "There was no retraction because they have not proved any error," Father Balasuriya reported. Observers noted that for somebody to be excommunicated, then unexcommunicated, is indeed rare. Meanwhile, although his supporters claimed he was not cowed by the Holy Office, he did agree to submit future writings on faith and morals to his superiors for review, an obvious victory for the Vatican. {*The New York Times*, 15 January 1997; 5 March 1998}

Balch, Emily Greene (1867—1961)

An American economist and sociologist, Balch was international secretary of the Women's International League for Peace and Freedom (1919—1922) and shared with John R. Mott the 1946 Nobel Peace Prize. She was a member of the first class to graduate from Bryn Mawr College.

Although she was a member of the First Church, Unitarian Universalist, in Jamaica Plain, Massachusetts, she became disillusioned by Unitarian support for the war and joined the London Quaker Meeting in 1920. According to the Rev. Terry Burke, minister of First Church, Balch continued to identify as a "unitarian" with a "small *u*." {*World*, January-February 1997}

Baldwin, Faith: See the entry for Theism.

Baldwin, James (1924—1987)

Born James Arthur Jones in New York City's Harlem Hospital, Baldwin was an illegitimate child who never knew his biological father. In 1927 his mother married a Baptist preacher, David Baldwin, and together they reared eight other children. In *No Name in the Street* (1972), Baldwin wrote that his mother "scarcely belonged to us: she was always in the hospital, having another baby." As for his stepfather, a Baptist minister "with his unreciprocated love for the Great God Almighty, it is no wonder our father went mad."

Young Baldwin read everything he could get his hands on "except the Bible, probably because it was the only book I was encouraged to read." When fourteen, he had a religious conversion and began preaching as a Pentecostal minister. But, as he wrote in *The Devil Finds Work* (1976), "At this time of my life, Emile was the only friend I had who knew to what extent my ministry tormented me." So he left home and worked at a New Jersey defense plant, then at a Manhattan meat-packing plant, all the time enduring intolerable racism. By the age of nineteen he had become a Trotskyist, finding it useful because he "learned that it may be impossible to indoctrinate me." Moving to Greenwich Village in Manhattan, Baldwin became a bohemian and upon meeting Richard Wright got a job editing material for a publisher. He also wrote reviews for *Nation*

In 1948 he used money from a literary fellowship to go to Paris, where Richard Wright was helpful in finding contacts for him and where he happily found little or no racism. *Go Tell It On the Mountain* (1953) relates how John at the age of thirteen is "saved" in the Baptist church where his father preaches and where the hero suffers from his blackness and his gayness:

> His father had always said his face was the face of Satan—and was there not something in the lift of the eyebrow, in the way his rough hair formed a V on his brow—that bore witness to his father's words. In the eye there was a light that was not the light of Heaven, and the mouth trembled, lustful and lewd, to drink deep in the winds of Hell.

As pointed out by Hilton Als, "John cannot understand why his father despises him, because the fact that the father despises himself does not occur to John. Nor can John imagine being able to escape him: there will never be any reprieve from the memory of his cruelty and its effect."

Baldwin's work includes *Giovanni's Room* (1956), in which he described his homosexuality; *Another Country* (1962, *Notes of a Native Son* (1955), and *Just Above my Head* (1979). Baldwin was a leader not only in the black civil rights movement but also a strong supporter of gay rights. Americans, he felt, were "still trapped in a history they do not understand," that they needed to break out of their false view of reality. The myth of white superiority was in Baldwin's mind the most important, and most destructive, of the many myths that informed American culture. He did not dislike whites, however, preferring them as lovers. A Swiss, Lucien Happesberger, was his great lover but was primarily attracted to women, adding to Baldwin's feelings of the "love withheld" he had experienced throughout his childhood.

The Fire Next Time (1963), wrote Als,

> detailed Baldwin's evangelical upbringing and his views on Christianity as a form of slavery forced on and then embraced by blacks: oppression as the condition of black American life. In order to escape "the ghetto mentality" and be a "truly" moral human being, it was necessary for anyone, white or black, to first "divorce himself from all the

prohibitions, crimes, and hypocrisies of the Christian church. If the concept of God has any validity or any use, it can only be to make us larger, freer, and more loving. If God cannot do this, then it is time we got rid of Him."

Eldridge Cleaver called Baldwin "the white man's most valuable tool in oppressing other blacks." Norman Mailer found Baldwin "too charming a writer to be major." But by 1962, upon publication of his *Another Country* and the essay collection *Nobody Knows My Name*, Baldwin was his nation's leading black literary star.

"But in the end," Als described, "Baldwin could not distinguish between writing sermons and making art. He eventually returned to the pulpit—just where his stepfather had always wanted him to be." Unpublished work will reveal more of Baldwin, Als stated while lamenting that Baldwin's relatives are still sensitive about his homosexuality and are reluctant to reclaim wholly their bastard relative. {AA; Hilton Als, *The New Yorker*, 16 February 1998; DGC; TRI; TYD}

Baldwin, James Mark (1861—1934)

An American psychologist, Baldwin taught successively on the staff at Toronto, Princeton, Johns Hopkins, and Mexico universities. In his *Fragments of Philosophy and Science* (1903), his agnosticism is expressed and he disavows the creeds and accepted God only as "a construction of the imagination" (based on reality) or "the ideal self." {JM; RAT; RE}

Baldwin, Maria (1856-1922)

A Unitarian, Baldwin was an educator, a reformer, and the first African American woman principal.

Baldwin, Roger Nash (1884—1981)

Baldwin, an American civil libertarian, helped found in 1920 the American Civil Liberties Union. He was its director until 1950. His grandfather had been president of Boston's Young Men's Christian Union, named "union" because as a Unitarian he wanted Unitarians not to be excluded because of their belief that Jesus was a man, not a god. Unlike the Young Men's Christian Association, the "Union" welcomed all, not just Christians. During World War I, he asked to be a conscientious objector and, as a result, spent a year in prison despite the fact that the war ended on the day he left for prison.

Baldwin and Corliss Lamont had their political differences and, asked about humanism by the present author, Baldwin perhaps with Lamont in mind replied, "I am afraid I know too little about humanism to be of any service." However, reviewing Lamont's *Freedom Is As Freedom Does* for *The Humanist*, Baldwin concluded, "While Lamont addresses his book to liberals, radicals, and conservatives alike, his conservative audience, if any, will dismiss it, not without evidence, as just another case of special pleading."

Baldwin taught at the New School for Social Research in New York (1938—1942) and the University of Puerto Rico (1966—1974). In 1973, he wrote *Memorandum on the Origins of the ACLU*, that emphasizes his view that no matter how offensive one's ideas may appear to the majority those ideas are and must continue to be protected by the Bill of Rights. {EG; U; WAS, 3 May 1956}

BALI: See entry for Agung regarding a royal cremation ceremony.

Ball, Peter B. (20th Century)

Ball's "Are Humanists Atheists or Agnostics?" was published in the *Gay and Lesbian Humanist* (Summer 1990). His "Are Mormons Mad?" is a critique of the cult from which he escaped after many years. Web: <www.geocities.com/WestHollywood/Heights/5073>.

Ball, William Platt (1844—1917)

Ball, an English schoolmaster who retired rather than teach religious doctrines, joined the staff of the *Freethinker* in 1881. Approximately in the year 1883, he wrote *Christian Murderers*. Ball contributed Biblical contradictions and absurdities to G. W. Foote's *The Bible Handbook*, which became a classic in the 1900s because it provided freethinkers adequate replies to Christians who applied epithets to them. {BDF; FUK; GS; RAT; RSR; TRI}

Ballance, John (1839—1893)

Ballance was an Australian freethinker, reformer, and legislator. Son of a Primitive Methodist and a unitarian Quaker, he became a strict Anglican, then a Presbyterian, then an agnostic. Influenced by the ideas of Robert Owen and the secularist movement, he wrote for Robert Stout's freethought journal, the *Echo*, and helped form the Wanganui Freethought Association. From 1883 to 1885, he edited the monthly *Freethought Review* in Wanganui. Ballance was New Zealand's first Liberal Prime Minister (1891—1893), and he introduced many social reforms. The Honorable John Ballance openly professed and worked for atheism, rationalism, or agnosticism. {BDF; EU, D. A. Hamer; FUK; JM; SWW; RAT; RE; TRI}

Ballinger, J. F. (19th Century)

Ballinger, a freethinker, wrote *Nudis Verbis: Or The Bible and Real Truths* (1893). {GS}

BALLOONS

The fascination of mankind with flying has led to the successful invention of different kinds of aircraft. A balloon is a lighter-than-air craft without a propulsion system. By inflating containers with a gas lighter than air, or with heated air, the balloon lifts. As early as the 13th Century, balloons were envisaged.

An atheist, Joseph Montgolfier—with his brother, Jacques Étienne Montgolfier—was the first to get an actual balloon off the ground, causing a linen bag about 100 feet (30 meters) in diameter to rise in the air. That same year the Frenchman Pilatre de Rozier made one of the first balloon ascents by man, rising to a height of 84 feet (26 meters). Numbers of balloons and balloonists have since successfully broken various speed, height, and distance records. In 1999 pilots Dr. Bertrand Piccard of Switzerland and Brian Jones of England—in the British-made *Breitling Orbiter 3*—were the first to make a manned balloon, non-stop flight around Earth, doing so in three weeks and landing in Egypt after flying 29,055 miles. {CE}

Ballou, Adin (1803—1890)

A Universalist minister, Ballou organized the Hopedale community farm project in 1842. His views on pacifism greatly affected Universalist doctrines. He was critical of Hosea Ballou's view that there would be no future punishment for sinning, fearing such might invite moral laxity. He wrote the *Autobiography of Adin Ballou* (1896), mentioning that he was a distant relative of Hosea Ballou. {CE; U; U&U; UU}

Ballou, Hosea (1771—1852)

Ballou, an eminent Universalist minister, challenged the dogma of the Trinity. A kindly individual, he was not dogmatic. Once, a heckler challenged his view concerning universal salvation, saying, "What would you do with a man who died reeking in sin and crime?" Ballou responded, "I think it would be a good plan to bury him."

Ballou and John Murray had differing theological positions, but Universalism grew during their time. Citing Scripture, he preached that a loving God would not condemn humankind to eternal punishment, feeling instead that the consequences of sin are spiritual, psychological, and physical. *A Treatise on Atonement* (1805) was the first book published in America that openly rejected the doctrine of the Trinity. {CE; ER; EU, 696-701, Paul H. Beattie; FUS; U; U&U; UU}

Ballou, Hosea 2nd (1796—1861)

The grandnephew of Hosea Ballou, Hosea Ballou 2nd wrote *The Ancient History of Universalism* (1829), in which he argued that the doctrines of endless punishment were largely the product of Augustine's influence on early Christian thinking, that they were not original tenets of the early church. {CE; ER; U; U&U}

Ballou, Peter (20th Century)

Ballou is active in the Humanist Club of Long Beach (AHA). (See entry for California Atheists, Humanists.) {FD}

Balmaceda, José [President] (1840—1891)

Although educated in the Jesuit College at Santiago, Chile, Balmaceda became an atheist and joined the anti-clerical Liberals in the fight against the Church. From 1886 to 1890, he was President of Chile, but his policy was harsh, autocratic, and unparliamentary. In 1891 a disastrous civil war broke out, Balmaceda took refuge in the Argentine legation, and rather than surrender for a trial he committed suicide. {CE; JM; RAT; RE}

Balmworth, Owen (19th Century)

Balmworth, a second generation freethinker, was leader of the Huddersfield secularists in England. {RSR}

Baltzer, Wilhelm Eduard (1814—1887)

Baltzer, a German rationalist, founded at Nordhausen in 1847 a free community. He wrote a history of religion and numerous other works, including a translation of the life of Apollonius of Tyana. {BDF; RAT}

Balzac, Honoré de (1799-1850)

Great as he was, Balzac (the "de" he added to give his name something of an aristocratic touch) was never elected a member of the French Academy. Of the world's great works, Balzac's forty-seven volume collection of novels and short stories, the *Human Comedy*, stands out. At least 3,500 characters which he portrayed led Baudelaire, in awe, to observe that even Balzac's door-keepers have genius. Skepticism pervades the *Comédie humaine* as well as Balzac's twenty-four other novels. He also wrote a caustic history of the Jesuits; *Eugénie Grandet* (1833); *Père Goriot* (1835); and *Cousin Bette* (1847). They have been criticized as moralizing and tending toward melodrama, but the works are vividly imaginative and illustrate his powers of observation. In *Madame Bovary*, the pharmacist is given these lines:

> I have a religion, my religion, and I even have more than all the others with their mummeries and their juggling. . . . I believe in the Supreme Being, in a Creator, whatever he may be. I care little who has placed us here below to fulfill our duties as citizens and parents; but I don't need to go to church to kiss silver plates, and fatten, out of my pocket, a lot of good-for-nothings who live better than we do. For one can know him as well in a wood, in a field, or even contemplating the ethereal heavens like the ancients. My God is the God of Socrates, of Franklin, of Voltaire, and of Beranger! I support the *Profession du Foi du Vicaire Savoyard* and the immortal principles of '89. And I can't admit of an old boy God who takes walks in his garden with a cane in his hand, who lodges his friends in the belly of whales, dies uttering a cry, and rises again after three days; things absurd in themselves, and completely opposed, moreover, to all physical laws, which proves to us, by the way, that priests have always wallowed in squalid ignorance, and tried to drag whole nations down after them.

Starting in 1841 and continuing until 1864, the Vatican prohibited all his works from being read because of their implied negativism toward the church. "Today," Balzac wrote, "the writer has replaced the priest." He also wrote, "After a woman gets too old to be attractive to men, she turns to God."

Graham Robb, in *Balzac: A Life* (1994), mentions that Balzac could improvise stories at the drop of a pen, turning out in one night the 14,000 words (at 33.3 words per minute) of "The Illustrious Gaudissart." Although not physically attractive (or at least he was once described as a short, bulgy man who looked "like an army major in need of a haircut"), Balzac had a long string of romantic affairs and was father of several "illegitimate" children. He wrote about every category of human beings—in fact, Robb implies that Balzac's feminine aspects have been 'traditionally ignored," that he had a succession of young male secretaries and wrote with knowledge about the life of the homosexual Jacques Collin (alias Vautrin, alias Abbé Carlos Herrera).

More than two thousand characters are found in *The Human Comedy*. As a writer, one who wore a monk's robe while working, Balzac ran to excess in everything—in eating, sex, writing, spending. How, he illustrated, can there ever be too much of a good thing! Yet, he sometimes slept only two hours a night and, fearing that digestion might slow his mental processes, avoided solid food but drank gallons of coffee.

Balzac is buried in Père Lachaise, the Paris cemetery named after the Jesuit friar François d'Aix de la Chaize, who had been confessor to Louis XIV from 1675 to 1709.

On his monument is sculptor David d'Angers's large bust of the author. Although Balzac may have been known for his anticlericalism, a priest was present at the funeral, as described by Victor Hugo in his *Chose Vues*:

> The procession crossed Paris and went by way of the boulevards to Pére Lachaise. Rain was falling as we left the church and when we reached the cemetery. It was one of those days when the heavens seemed to weep. We walked the whole distance. I was at the head of the coffin on the right, holding one of the silver tassels of the pall. Alexandre Dumas was on the other side. . . . The coffin was lowered into the grave. . . . The priest said a last prayer and I a few words. While I was speaking the sun went down. All Paris lay before me, afar off, in the splendid mists of the sinking orb, the glow of which seemed to fall into the grave at my feet, as the dull sounds of the sods dropping on the coffin broke in upon my last words.

{CE; GL; ILP; JM; PUT; RAT; RE; TRI; TYD}

Balzac, Ralph (20th Century)

Balzac is an ethical humanist, active in the American Ethical Union. His e-mail: <balzacr@acpub.duke.edu>.

Ban, Stephen (20th Century)

Ban, while a student at McGill University in Montreal, Quebec, Canada, was one of the founders of Campus Freethought Alliance. {*International Humanist News*, December 1996}

Bancel, François Désiré (1822—1871)

A French politician elected to the Legislative Assembly in 1849, Bancel translated the work on rationalism by Ausonio Franchi. His own freethought views are found in his *Les Harangues de l'Exit* (3 volumes, 1863). Bancel wrote *La Revue Critique*. {BDF; RAT}

Bancroft, George (1800—1891)

A diplomat, the author of *History of the United States* (1834—1874), Bancroft was at one time a member of All Soul's Church (Unitarian) in Washington, D.C. However, his funeral was at St. John's (Episcopal). According to M. A. DeWolfe Howe's *The Life and Letters of George Bancroft* (1908), "Upon his own relations to the outward expressions of religion, the testimony is somewhat conflicting. . . . As early as 1854 his beliefs could hardly be reconciled with those of the Unitarian branch of New England Congregationalism, in which he was reared. It is related that in Washington Mrs. Bancroft took a pew in All Souls (Unitarian) Church, and that when her husband visited it and found her name on the silver plate at its entrance, he had his own substituted.

When he received notice in 1888 of his election to the Unitarian Club of Boston, he wrote in reply, "I pray you not to include me in the club you are forming. I was brought up a Congregationalist, and am not willing at this time to adopt any other name." . . . To the minister [of All Souls] in which he paid for but rarely occupied the pew . . . he once declared, "I am not an Episcopalian! I am a Congregationalist!." Although he complained about being labeled, Bancroft appears not to have been an orthodox believer, as was the case of other Congregationalist-Unitarians of his time. (See American Antiquarian Society Proceedings, 1891, p. 252). {CE; EG; RAT; UU}

Bancroft, Hubert Howe (1832—1918)

Bancroft, a historian and authority on Western America—he wrote thirty-nine volumes and had a library of sixty thousand volumes—expresses an uncompromising deism and scorn of the churches. "There is but little religion in the Churches," he wrote in *Retrospect* (1913), "and that little graft is strangling." {JM; RAT}

Banes, Warren C. (20th Century)

Banes, a freethinker, wrote *Self Contradictions of the Bible*, a rationalist tract, and *Short Talks on Free Thought* (1911). {GS}

BANGLADESH FREETHOUGHT

The Humanist and Ethical Association of Bangladesh (IHEU), is at 55/D, Dhaka U. Staff Quart, Dhaka 1000, Bangladesh. The Assembly of Freethinkers is at House No. 25B, Road No. 1, Dhanmondi R/A, Dhaka 1205, Bangladesh. A freethought movement commenced in Bangladesh in the 1920s but has remained weak.

This is the country that forced Taslima Nasrin—a noted critic of Islam as, in her opinion, it is being falsely practiced—to flee for her life. Freethought in any form is dangerous to express in Bangladesh. (See entries for Taslima Nasrin and for Nehal Karim. *Human Rights and Development Review*, an annual publication in English, is available at 68 Dhaka University Market, Sonargon Road, Kantabon, Dhaka-1000, Bangladesh. Also, see Gordon Stein's *Freethought in the United Kingdom and the Commonwealth*.)

Banko, Frank (20th Century)

Banko, who was raised a Catholic, became a Grand Rapids, Michigan, businessman and a member of the Freedom from Religion Foundation, "a human free from religion." A Vietnam veteran, he devised a plastic-coated Peace Poster that urged peace among religions. It contained symbols for twelve organized religions and the declaration, in eighteen languages, that "There will be peace on earth when there is peace among the world religions." When in 1992 he sent one to the televangelist Pat Robertson, the religious fundamentalist wrote back, "There can be no unity between

Christianity and the other religions listed, because they do not believe that Jesus Christ is 'the truth' and the *only* way to be reconciled with God." {*Freethought Today*, June-July 1995}

Banks, Iain [M.] (20th Century)

Banks, who was born in Dunfermline, Scotland, is noted for *Wasp Factory* (1984) and other works with a dark, absurdist portrayal of "crowded isolation." His fifteenth novel, *Whit* (1996), recounts the pilgrimage of Isis, "Elect to God" in a bizarre Scottish cult, as he is sent out into the techno-cursed world of the Unsaved to win back a wayward member. *The Crow Road* was dramatized on BBC TV and is available on video.

From his base in Fife, he writes fiction under the name Iain Banks but science fiction under Iain M. Banks (the M, he explains, is for Menzies which is "pronounced Ming-iss by those wishing to be excruciatingly correct").

Banks in 1999 became an honorary associate of the National Secular Society. He calls himself an "evangelical atheist" and, in an interview with the *Daily Telegraph* in 1996, said

> I want to proselytise about the badness of religion, and to say that faith is wrong, belief without reason and question is just evil. Within the next two or three generations everything will be explicable in scientific terms. What's left for mysticism or religion?

{CA; E; *Freethinker*, March 1999; Ra Page, *New Humanist*, December 1996}

Banks, Trevor (1934-1999)

Banks was a British educator, public speaker, and actor whose stage monologue, "Bertie," was a dramatization of the life of Bertrand Russell. He appeared as Russell in England at the South Place Ethical Society and the Leicester Secular Society; in Florida at the Humanist Association of St. Petersburg; in New York at the Humanist Association of New York City; and elsewhere in Canada and the United States. He dressed as if Russell and performed "Bertie" for members of the Bertrand Russell Society in Madison, New Jersey, and Buffalo, New York. He spoke about Russell at Bertrand Russell Society conferences at the universities of South Florida and Monmouth, New Jersey.

Banks, who lived in Ottawa, was formerly on the editorial committee of *Humanists in Canada*, for which he wrote six articles including "The Inhumane Society" (Spring 1998).

He died unexpectedly of a heart attack while riding his grey speed bike, an ending the man who helped found the National Capital Marathon and National Capital Running Association would have approved. "He feared more than anything else the idea of growing old and living on life support, with people praying over him, and not being able to choose when to pull the plug," said a friend, Madeline Weld, at the time of Banks's death. (See entry for Russell, Bertrand—Humor of.)

BANNED BOOKS

The American Library Association's *Banned Books* (1998) includes the following

Butler, William, *The Butterfly Revolution*—the book suggests "dislike of the Bible and belief in atheism."
Darwin, Charles R., *On the Origin of Species*—promotes evolution
Fast, Howard, *Citizen Tom Paine*—totalitarian; withdrawn from USIA libraries
Faulkner, William, *As I Lay Dying*—the book "questions the existence of God."
Fitzhugh, Louise, *The Long Secret*—the book "pokes fun at religion."
Gibbon, Edward, *History of the Decline and Fall of the Roman Empire*—the book contradicts official church history.
Greene, Bette, *I Know You, Al*—the book does not uphold the principles of the United States which were "established on the moral principles of the Bible."
Hall, Elizabeth, *Possible Impossibilities*—the book "would lead children to believe ideas contrary to the teadchings of the Bible."
Herbert, Frank, *Soul Catcher*—the book "is a mockery of Christianity and very much anti-God."
Howe, Norman, *God, the Universe, and Hot Fudge Sundaes*—the book "pushes several items of the humanist agenda: death education, anti-God, pro-evolution, anti-Bible, anti-Christian, and logic over faith."
Kesey, Ken, *One Flew Over the Cuckoo's Nest*—the book promotes "secular humanism."
Lawrence, Jerome, *Inherit the Wind*—its "anti-religious nature"
Lightner, A. M., *Gods or Demons?*—the book "promotes a secular-humanistic belief in evolution and portrays the 'Bible as myth'."
Lockridge, Ross Jr., *Raintree County*—"1066 pages of blasphemy and sacrilege inimical to faith and morals and within the prohibition of the Catholic Index."
Paine, Thomas, *The Age of Reason*—promotes use of reason
Paterson, Katherine, *The Great Gilly Hopkins*—"Christians are portrayed as being dumb and stupid."
Peck, Robert, *A Day No Pigs Would Die*—the book "is bigoted against Baptists."
Russell, Bertrand, *What I Believe*—author is a freethinker.
Starkey, Marion, *The Tall Man From Boston*—"would lead children to believe ideas contrary to the teachings of the Bible."
Vonnegut, Kurt Jr., *Slaughterhouse Five*—the book was burned, banned, challenged, and restricted for this sentence among others: "The gun made a ripping sound like the opening of the fly of God Almighty."
Walker, Barbara, *The Woman's Encyclopedia of Myths and Secrets*—the book "is of no benefit to anyone."

BANNED BOOKS WEEK

Freethinkers sometimes celebrate the week of September 26th to October 3rd as Banned Books Week, recommending it as a special ocassion to read a banned book.

BANNING OF BOOKS: Book banning was begun in 1491 by the Catholic Church. Trials under the Inquisition extended from 1547 to 1730, according to George H. Putnam's *Books and Their Makers During the Middle Ages*. See entries for Books, Censorship of and Censorship.

Bantock, Granville [Sir] (20th Century)

Bantock, an English musician, was an avowed freethinker. (See David Brock's *Sir Granville Bantock*.) {TRI}

BAPTISM

> • Baptism, n. A sacred rite of such efficacy that he who finds himself in heaven without having undergone it will be unhappy forever. It is performed with water in two ways—by immersion or plunging, and by aspersion, or sprinkling.
>
> —**Ambrose Bierce**
> *The Devil's Dictionary*

Baptism, for non-believers, is a curious sacrament in which water is used in a rite which involves petitioning God to cleanse the individual of Original Sin in order to "effect a union of the believer with Christ." The Bible makes no mention of the baptism of Jesus—in the practice of Jesus himself, according to the University of Chicago's Shirley Jackson Case, "baptism is never made a condition of discipleship." From the second century of the Christian Era on, baptism was supposed to be performed only once, "since it meant forgiveness of sins and regeneration." Post-baptismal forgiveness was questionable, which led some to postpone baptizing their children. Contemporary Christians differ in the ceremony. Some entirely immerse individuals, as for example the Baptists and the Dunkards, the latter of whom use a "trine immersion" which involves three successive dunkings "in the name of the Father and of the Son and of the Holy Spirit." Some symbolically "sprinkle" with water, first when the individual is a child and later when a teenager allegedly is old enough to understand the rite. Some believe that unbaptized infants who die will be saved in the life to come, whether baptized or not. Others believe that parents of unbaptized infants risk the possibility that their children will end not in Heaven but in Limbo, excluded from the vision of God in Heaven.

The mystery religions (Eleusinian, Orphic, Mithraic, Egyptian, Syrian) required baptism, according to the University of Chicago's A. Eustace Haydon, "for the washing away of moral evil as a preparation for the rites of communion with the deity whose mastery of death assured immortality to the initiates. These baptisms sometimes symbolized dying to the old life and rising again to the new. The same idea underlies the baptism by immersion which was part of the initiation of proselytes to Judaism."

Tibetan Buddhists are known to use a threefold immersion, and other non-Christian believers also use water as a cleansing fluid, according to Haydon, "as a means of removing the contagion acquired by contact with dangerous potencies (blood, death, things tabooed), and then by extension, the contagion of moral failure or sin."

Around the first century of the Christian Era in Corinth, St. Paul reported in *I Corinthians* 15:29 that baptisms were arranged on behalf of friends or relatives who had died without benefit of prior baptism. In the second century, the Marcionites and Montanists continued the practice, and it survives today among Latter Day Saints, whose genealogical library tracks by computer who was and was not baptized; the Salt Lake City, Utah, library is, as a result, the greatest in the world for checking any individual's ancestry. If it were possible, the Mormons would list *every* human who is presently alive (five billion, going on six) and as many who have died as can be verified.

In 1925, "Believe It Or Not" George Ripley estimated that there had been 302,231,454,657,293,676,543 human beings (302 quintillion, using the American system) who had been born by that time. Although his calculations were partly tongue-in-cheek and he erroneously explained that humanity's pool increases exponentially as one goes back in time (whereas the opposite is the case), diligent designers of computer programs believe it is theoretically possible for the Mormons to carry out their, or what they believe is their God's, plan.

In 1996, Dr. Kirby Godsey, the president of Mercer University in Macon, Georgia, wrote *When We Talk About God . . . Let's Be Honest,* in which he rejected the belief that every word of the Bible is literally true and suggested that salvation may not depend on one's acceptance of Christ as a personal savior. Inasmuch as Mercer is second in size only to Baylor in Baptist-affiliated universities, he was asked by the university's trustees to "prayerfully reconsider his theological convictions." The faculty supported him, but he has had to fight to avoid the heresy accusation. Nearly one hundred years ago, William Whitsitt was expelled as president of the Southern Baptist Theological Seminary in Louisville, Kentucky, after writing a book that questioned the long-held belief that the Baptist practice of immersing the faithful dated from the time of Jesus. Historians later demonstrated that Whitsitt was right, that the practice had not begun until the 17th century. (See entries for Debaptism and Unbaptism.) {CE; ER}

Barabas

Marlowe's *The Jew of Malta* (performed about 1592, published around 1633) is a drama in blank verse. The Grand Seignior of Turkey demands a tribute of Malta, the governor of Malta decides it has to be paid by the Jews of the island, and a rich Jew by the name of Barabas when resisting the edict has his wealth impounded and his house turned into a nunnery.

Barabas, a prototype for unscrupulous Machiavellian villains in later Elizabethan and Jacobean dramas, praises gold and precious stones as "Infinite riches in a little roome."

For revenge, Barabas indulges in an orgy of slaughter, killing some nuns in addition to his daughter and her lover. At the end, after tricking his way into becoming the Governor of Malta, he is betrayed and falls through a collapsible floor—it had been meant to destroy the Turkish commander and his aides at a banquet—into a cauldron where he dies. {OEL}

Barabbas

In the New Testament, Barabbas was the bandit held in jail along with Jesus. Pontius Pilate annually released one prisoner at Passover and, when he offered to free Jesus, the multitudes demanded he release Barabbas instead.

Pär Lagerkvist achieved international fame with his novel, *Barabbas* (1950), a psychoogical study of the criminal's journey. In 1953 he adapted the work into a two-act play. (See entries for Antisemitism and Pär Lagerkvist.) {CE}

Baraka, Imamu Amiri (1934—)

"God," wrote the African American author who changed his name from LeRoi Jones, "has been replaced, as he has all over the West, with respectability and air conditioning." {TYD}

Barbauld, Anna Laetitia Aiken (1743-1825)

Barbauld was a British Unitaian, a poet and an activist.

Barber, Benjamin R. (1939—)

Barber, a professor of political philosophy at Rutgers University, is author of *Jihad vs. McWorld: How the Planet is Both Falling Apart and Coming Together and What This Means for Democracy* (1995). He shows his discomfort with capitalism as well as with Christian, Muslim, and any other kind of religious fundamentalism.

Far to the political left, Barber stubbornly attacks the lack of positive political and the economic leadership that he sees in the world of democratic capitalism.

Barbier d'Aucour, Jean (1642—1694)

Barbier d'Aucour was a French critic and academician whose writings are directed against the Jesuits. {BDF}

Barbier, Edmond (Died 1883)

Barbier was the French translator of the works of Darwin, Lubbock, and Tyler. {BDF}

Barbour, Brian M. (1943—)

Barbour edited *American Transcendentalism,* an anthology of criticism, and *Benjamin Franklin, A Collection of Critical Essays* (1979).

Bard, Martin L. (20th Century)

Bard, an atheist, is author of *The Peril of Faith* (1982). He has written for the *American Atheist* on whether or not atheism is best prepared to lead humans to fruitful relationships. Bard affirms that it is.

BARDOLATRY

Freethinkers, who would gladly substitute bardolatry for christianity, find Harold Bloom's comment in *Shakespeare: The Invention of the Human* (1999) quite apropos:

> The more one reads and ponders the plays of Shakespeare, the more one realizes that the accurate stance toward them is one of awe. . . . Bardolatry, the worship of Shakespeare, ought to be even more a secular religion than it already is. The plays remain the outward limit of human achievement: aesthetically, cognitively, in certain ways morally, even spiritually.

Baretti, Giuseppe Marc Antonio (1719—1789)

Baretti was an Italian writer who migrated to London in 1751 and became a friend of Dr. Johnson. He wrote an Italian dictionary but because of his advanced views received opposition in Italy, forcing him to stay in England. Baretti abandoned Catholicism but adopted no other church's doctrines. {RAT}

Barker, Clive (1952—)

Barker is an English-born artist, screenwriter, director, and producer. He wrote the play, "Incarnations (Frankenstein in Love, History of the Devil, Colossus)"; the novel *The Damnation Game* (1985); and the screenplays "Hellraiser II: Hellbound" (1980), "Candyman II: Farewell to the Flesh" (1985); and "Lord of Illusions" (1995).

"Now, I don't believe in God," Barker has stated on his Web Site. "I think that God is [a] creation of men, by men, and for men. . . . I think that God that we have created and allowed to shape our culture, through essentially Christian theology, is a pretty villainouis creature." {CA; E}

Barker, Dan (1949—)

A fundamentalist minister turned freethought activist, Barker is author of *Just Pretend, A Freethought Book for Children* (1988) and *Maybe Yes, Maybe No, A Guide For Young Skeptics* (1991). In a 1992 debate with evangelist Cliffe Knechtl at the University of Wisconsin on the resurrection of Jesus, Barker quipped, "Next week will we debate, 'Did Minerva emerge from the brain of Jupiter?'" Barker is production assistant for *Freethought Today,* of which his wife Annie Laurie Gaylor is editor.

His *Losing Faith in Faith: From Preacher to Atheist* (1992) shows how, in moving from the position of a Christian to that of an atheist, he "threw out all the bath water" only to discover that "there is no baby there" and that he has no regrets whatsoever. Barker is a popular speaker who appears on television and addresses groups throughout the United States, often providing his own musical accompaniment.

Inasmuch as Barker travels widely and is well informed about non-theism, he is one of the best-known of contemporary freethinkers. (See entry for Freedom From Religion Foundation.)

Barker, John (1847—1937)

Barker was an early Australian secularist. {FUK; SWW}

Barker, Joseph (1806—1875)

Barker was an editor of *National Reformer,* a London publication from 1860 to 1893. In 1854 at the Hartford Bible Convention, he defied anyone present to prove the authority of the Bible. "It is not a book of divine authority," he challenged. Baker wrote *Atheism: What Can It Say For Itself?* (1858). {FUK; PUT; VI}

Barley, Keith Percival John (1926—1975)

Barley, a New Zealand-born humanist and agronomist, co-founded with Bruce Muirden the Humanist Society of South Australia as well as Keep Our State Schools Secular (KOSSS).

Barlow, Connie (20th Century)

Barlow, a science editor and writer specializing in evolutionary biology, is a Unitarian Universalist. She serves on the board of the Epic of Evolution Society and is editor of its publication. "The Way of Science and the Epic of Evolution," taken from her *Green Space, Green Time* (1997), was featured in *World* (November-December 1998).

Barlow, George (Born 1847)

Barlow, an English poet, included many freethought sentiments in his *Under the Dawn* and *Poems, Real and Ideal.* {BDF; RAT}

Barlow, Jane (1860—1917)

An Irish poet and novelist, Barlow was the daughter of the Rev. J. W. Barlow, Vice-Provost of Trinity College. In 1894 she translated the *Batrachomyomachia* of Homer.

Her agnosticism is found in *Between Doubt and Darin* g (1916), the first poem of which closes, "Be to the great Dark gathered man and brute." Barlow, according to McCabe, "took a warm interest in the work of the Rationalist Press Association." {RAT}

Barlow, Joel (1754—1812)

One of the Hartford (Connecticut) Wits, an informal group of Yale students and rectors, Barlow was a diplomat as well as American humorist. Although raised a Puritan and was a Congregationalist minister and chaplain in the War of Independence, he was influenced by Thomas Paine and other freethinkers.

While Paine was in a Paris jail, Barlow looked after details of the publication of his *The Age of Reason.* His own book, *The Hasty Pudding* (1796), is a mock epic that he claimed was inspired by his being homesick for New England and its corn mush. His *Vision of Columbus* and his being American ambassador to France made him well-known in Europe and America.

His biographer, James Woodress, notes that in his *Advice to the Privileged Orders,*

> Barlow makes a clear distinction between the state church as an ally of authoritarian government and plain religion. He argues that the wedding of church and state is a great evil and points to the blessings enjoyed by the United States without a state church. As a result, he asserts, "in no country are the people more religious."

The clergy attacked him, citing his translation of Volney's *Ruins,* and accusing him of being an atheist.

While negotiating a commercial treaty with Napoleon I, Barlow died from exposure, caught in the disastrous retreat of the armies from Moscow. {BDF; CE; EU, William F. Ryan; FUS; JM; RAT}

Barlow, John Perry (20th Century)

Barlow, co-founder of the Electronic Frontier Foundation, is a member of the WELL Board of Directors and a former lyricist for the Grateful Dead. He is a descendant of Thomas Paine's friend, Joel Barlow. A graduate of Wesleyan University in Connecticut, he received an honors degree in Comparative Religion (1969). With Mitchell Kapor, he promotes freedom of expression in digital media. *Utne Reader* has listed him among "100 Visionaries Who Could Change Your Life," according to *Truth Seeker,* for which he has written. Barlow's website is <http://www.eff.org/~barlow>. {CA}

Barmby, John Goodwyn (1820—1881)

Barmby, a Unitarian minister, edited *The Promethean.* {GS}

Barnaby, C(harles) F(rank) (20th Century)

Barnaby of the United Kingdom addressed the International Humanist and Ethical Union's (IHEU's) International Peace Conference in Zutphen (1983). He is author of *Man and the Atom* (1971), *Arms Controlled* (1975), and *Nuclear Proliferation and the South African Threat* (1977).

Barnard, Henry (1811—1900)

Barnard, the reformer who in conjunction with Horace Mann created the American school-system, was married to a strict Catholic. As a result and for the family's peace, he abstained from discussing religion. Barnard was a member of the Connecticut legislature, edited the *Connecticut Common School Journal,* was chancellor of the University of Wisconsin, and was nationally known as a major educator. Challenged to make a declaration of Christian faith, Barnard refused.

According to McCabe, Barnard's freethinking views were well-known to others. {JM}

Barnaud, Nicolas (16th Century)

Barnaud traveled in France, Spain, and Germany, and to him is attributed the authorship of *Le Cabinet du Roy de France,* that is largely directed against the clergy. {BDF}

Barnave, Antoine Pierre Joseph Marie (1761—1793)

Barnave was a French politician, author of a deistic *Dictionnaire de Pensées.* He accepted the principles of the Revolution and in 1790 became President of the National Assembly. Barnave has been described as "one of the greatest figures of the French Revolution," whose moderation and integrity brought him to the guillotine 30 November 1793. {RAT}

Barnes, Albert (1872—1951)

Barnes had a factory that made Argyrol, a product that had antiseptic powers without the burning quality of nitrate. A disciple first of William James, then of Dewey, he established a six-hour day for employees and had a mid-day one hour seminar during which James, Dewey, Bertrand Russell, and Santayana were discussed. At times, Barnes was known to have disagreed with Russell as well as with Alexander Woollcott.

Barnes also disagreed with philosopher Barrows Dunham and wanted him to be fired from Temple University because he felt he was a Communist. He got John Dewey to retract a favorable statement about Dunham's *Man Against Myth.* Later, when Dunham refused to answer questions of the House Un-American Committee, Dunham was suspended from his professorship.

Barnes's first Picasso cost $10, his first Matisse $50. As an art collector, he amassed a distinctive collection said to have been the finest privately owned collection in the country. Once, he invited Dewey to attend a lecture of art with him at the Louvre. In the late 1940s, now an extremely rich man, he took one of Dewey's classes at Columbia University, and Dewey said he never met Barnes's equal for "sheer brain power." Like Dewey, Barnes was a naturalist in philosophy.

Barnes was killed immediately in 1951 when his car was struck by a ten-ton trailer truck, and his body was hurled forty feet into a nearby field. No funeral services were held, and his body was cremated.

Barnes, Harry Elmer (1888—1968)

An eminent historian and naturalistic humanist, Barnes in the 1950s was on the advisory board of Charles Francis Potter's First Humanist Society of New York. An admirer of liberals, he found in 1955 they are "a fast disappearing race. Only a few–such as John

Haynes Holmes, Roger Baldwin, Norman Thomas, and the like–still survive, and they are getting old."

Barnes wrote *The Twilight of Christianity* (1929) and *Freeing the Human Mind* (1931). His connection with the formulating of Humanist Manifesto I has been described by Edwin H. Wilson in *The Genesis of a Humanist Manifesto* (1995). {CE; CL; EW; FUS; HM1; HNS; TRI}

Barnes, J. Edmestone (Born 1857)

After entering the ministry in Jamaica of the African Methodist Church, Barnes perceived the errors of Christian theology and became a land surveyor and civil engineer. He practiced in the British West Indies and South America and then was appointed Surveyor General to the Republic of Liberia. Also, he worked in South Africa and became managing director of a mining syndicate in Sierra Leone. An accomplished linguist, he wrote *The Economy of Life*, in which his rationalist views are expressed. Barnes was a member of the Rationalist Press Association. {RAT}

Barnes, Jimmie (20th Century)

Barnes is President of the Secular Humanist Association of San Antonio, Texas (PO Box 160881, San Antonio, Texas 78280-3081).

Barnes, Ken (20th Century)

Barnes is Treasurer of the Thomas Paine Pennsylvania Memorial Committee (Box 242, Pocopson, PA 19366).

Barnes, Lucy (1780—1809)

Barnes was a noted Universalist writer and poet. {U}

Barnes, Nigel (20th Century)

In Britain, Barnes is active in the Hampstead Humanist Society.

Barnet, Vern (20th Century)

Barnet, a Unitarian Universalist minister in Kansas, is author of *Love Without Desire* (1992), a collection of sonnets that proclaim his love for the many men in his life. He is the religion columnist for the *Kansas City Star* and minister-in-residence at the World Faiths Center for Religious Experience and Study.

Barnhart, Joe Edward (1931—)

A professor of philosophy and religious studies at the University of North Texas, Barnhart is on the National Advisory Board of the Council for Secular Humanism. He is on the editorial board of *The Humanist* as well as *Free Inquiry*. He is on the Council for Secular Humanism's Committee for the Scientific Examination of Religion and is one of its Secular Humanist Mentors. Barnhart signed Humanist Manifesto 2000.

A provocative speaker, Barnhart combines profound scholarliness with a positive sense of humor. At the Tenth International Humanist and Ethical Union (IHEU) World Congress held in Buffalo (1988), he addressed the group. Barnhart is author of *A Naturalist View of Religious Conversion* (1981) and *Jim and Tammy*, about the televangelist couple who were involved in scandals that resulted in Jim Bakker's imprisonment. (Bakker's *I Was Wrong* (1997) was followed by Tammy Faye Bakker Messner's *Tammy: Tell It My Way* (1997), both embarrassing confessionals.) {HNS2}

Barnhart, Mary Ann (20th Century)

Barnhart, a licensed professional counselor and a licensed marriage and family therapist, writes for various publications concerning gerontological problems. She is the wife of Joe Barnhart.

Barni, Jules Romains (1818—1878)

Barni was a French philosophic writer who translated the works of Kant into French. "Rationalism is my only religion," he once wrote. {BDF; RAT}

Barnout, Hippolyte (Born 1816)

A French architect and writer, Barnout published a *Rational Calendar* (1859) and *L'Athé*, that the clerical journals declared drew God's vengeance upon France. {BDF}

Barnum, Phineas Taylor (1810—1891)

Barnum, whose circus became Barnum and Bailey Circus, was a member of the Universalist Church on New York City's Central Park West. He became famous not only for his sideshows of freaks but also for his sign, "EGRESS," that pointed unsuspecting ticket purchasers to an exit, thereby forcing them to purchase another ticket in order to return. A Connecticut Yankee from Bethel and Bridgeport, he earned $285,000 by booking the "Swedish Nightingale," Jenny Lind, on an extensive US tour–she earned but $177,000. He introduced the 3-ring circus as well as found the means to transport his entire group by railroad.

"The orthodox faith," Barnum observed, "painted God as a revengeful being, and yet people talk about loving such a being." "The people," he concluded, "like to be humbugged," a reference to the small fee his museum charged to see hoaxes. His statement was misquoted as "There's a sucker born every minute."

Curious as to what his obituary would state, Barnum asked the *New York Evening News* to print his obituary prior to his death and at a time he was seriously ill and dying. The newspaper obliged with the headline: GREATEST AND ONLY BARNUM. HE WANTED TO READ HIS OBITUARY. HERE IT IS. Barnum died two weeks later. His body was preserved on ice for two days and was then taken to the largest church in Bridgeport, South Congregational, where a public ceremony was conducted. Barnum was buried at the Bridgeport, Connecticut, Mountain Grove Cemetery. Overlooking his own grave was that of Tom Thumb (whose real name was Charles S. Stratton), who had died in 1883 and whose memorial Barnum had constructed. It was a 40' high marble shaft, atop which was the midget's life-size 2' 11" statue.

His will provided money for printing and distributing two pamphlets: "213 Questions Without Answers" and "Universalism, What It Is and What It's Good For." (Tom Thumb married Lavinia Warren, a 21-year-old Massachusetts schoolteacher who was 2' 8", before an overflow crowd of dignitaries in New York City's Grace Church.) {CE; PA; TYD; U; UU}

Baron, Joseph L. (1894—1960)

Baron, a rabbi, declined to sign Humanist Manifesto I, taking exception to some of its conclusions. "Your manifesto ignores some personal effects of the old forms of piety which are a vital need in the life of many members of the Jewish group," he complained, "to say nothing of the Christian, whose arrogant, vulgar, and selfish reaction to the conditions of our environment makes it necessary that we follow a conservative and not a radical process in changing the meaning of holiness." {EW}

Barot, François Odysse (Born 1830)

A French writer, Barot wrote for several Radical papers, was secretary to Gustave Flourens, and published a work on the *Birth of Jesus* (1864). Barot was anti-clerical in his *L'Agonie de la Papauté* (1868) and was an authority on English literature. He translated Carlyle's *French Revolution*. {BDF; RAT}

Barr, Alfred Hamilton (1902—1981)

Barr, an American art historian, was the first director of the Museum of Modern Art in New York City. He organized more than 100 museum exhibitions and wrote a number of standard art history texts including *Cubism and Abstract Art* (1936), *Picasso* (1946), *Matisse* (1951), and *Painting and Sculpture in the Museum of Modern Art, 1929—1967* (1977). Barr was liked by Philip Johnson, whom he had appointed to head MOMA's department of architecture.

At the end of his life, suffering from Alzheimer's disease, Barr lost his mind and, according to his daughter, died a hideous death. The son of a Presbyterian minister but said to have been a freethinker, Barr was buried without fanfare. {CE; FI}

Barr, Margaret A. (1897?-1972))

Barr, a British Unitarian, is known for her social work in India. A friend of Gandhi and an educator and administrator, she helped create the Unitarian church movement in Khasi Hills, India. {U}

Barratt, Alfred (20th Century)

Barratt, author of *Physical Metempiric* (1883), was an ethicist interested in positivism.

Barrett, James H. (1920—1994)

Barrett flew in northern Africa in World War II, in Korea and in Vietnam, and after twenty-eight years of service retired as a lieutenant colonel in the Air Force. In the 1950s, one of his responsibilities was to discharge homosexuals from military service in accordance with official policy. He then taught in Texas and Maryland, finally retiring to Pensacola, Florida. After the death of his stepson from AIDS complications in 1993, however, he became a supporter of AIDS causes and told friends he was deeply bothered by his past activities against homosexuals in the military.

When an abortion doctor, David Gunn, was shot to death in Pensacola, he became so angry that he volunteered to be an escort for the doctor's replacement. Several dozen others, many military retirees, also volunteered to assume the risks of escorting women and health-care workers into the clinics. Having fought in three wars on foreign soil, the seventy-four-year-old Barrett was not to survive a fourth. He was killed along with the new doctor, John B. Britton, by a former Presbyterian minister and abortion opponent, Paul J. Hill. Barrett's wife, June, was wounded in the arm.

When Hill was convicted on Federal charges of killing Barrett and Britton and wounding Mrs. Barrett, the National Organization for Women's president, Patricia Ireland, warned, "It is a strong message to those who would be deterred by normal things, but many like Paul Hill want to be martyred and those people will not be deterred by this."

Illustrating this fear, Donna Bray, the founder of Defenders of the Defenders of Life, a Maryland-based group, reacted as follows: "Paul Hill laid down his life to defend innocent unborn children, and I thank him." Hill, also, did not budge, stating, "This Government is unjust because it does not protect human life. To the extent that we take part in this evil, we will answer to God, and may God have mercy on us all."

The memorial services, at which over four hundred heard his son describe his father, "He was a real 'neat' guy," were held at Pensacola's Unitarian Universalist Fellowship. (See "Fighting the Right on Abortion Clinic Access," *The World*, January/February 1995.)

Barrett, Stanley R. (20th Century)

Barrett, professor of anthropology at the University of Guelph, Ontario, has spoken and written about Canada's far right. {*Humanist in Canada*, Summer 1996}

Barrett, Stephen (1933—)

Barrett, a physician-psychiatrist and consumer health advocate, is on the Council for Secular Humanism's Faith-Healing Investigation Project. One of his forty-four articles and books is *Health, Sickness, Scams, and Frauds* (1990). Dr. Barrett is editor of *Nutrition Forum*.

Barrett, Thomas Squire (Born 1842)

The son of Quaker parents, both grandfathers being ministers of that body, Barrett published an acute examination of Gillespie's argument, *à priori,* for the existence of God (1869). He was a member of the British Rationalist Press Association. {BDF; RAT}

Barrier, F. M. (Died 1870)

A French Fourierist, Barrier became a professor of medicine at Lyons and wrote *Catechism of Liberal and Rational Socialism*, an abridgment of *Principles of Sociology* (1867). {BDF}

Barrier, Ron (20th Century)

Barrier, an active members of American Atheists Inc., has a talk show, "Atheist Viewpoint," with Ellen Johnson. (See entry for Ellen Johnson.)

Barrington, Denis (20th Century)

Barrington created the symbol called "the Happy Human," one used by many humanist organizations.

Barrington, Judith (20th Century)

British-born Barrington lives in Oregon, where she has written two books of poetry. Also, she is author of *Writing the Memoir: From Truth to Art* (1997) and is co-director of a summer writing workshop for women, The Flight of the Mind. Her many awards include the Freedom of Expression Award from the American Civil Liberties Union of Oregon.

Barrios, Ervin (20th Century)

Barrios is a Unitarian Universalist minister whose members are Spanish-speaking. (See entry for *Unitarios Universalistas de Habla Hispana*.)

Barrister, A. (19th Century)

Barrister, a freethinker, wrote *Notes on Bishop Magee's Pleadings for Christ* (c. 1875). {GS}

Barrow, Blake W. (20th Century)

Barrow wrote *Freethought in Texas: J. D. Shaw and the Independent Pulpit*, his 1983 master's thesis at Baylor University. {*Freethought History #15,* 1995}

Barrow, John D. (1952—)

Barrow, professor of astronomy at the University of Sussex, England, is author of *The Anthropic Cosmological Principle* (with Frank Tiper), *Pi in the Sky*, and *The Left Hand of Creation* (1994). In the latter, he and Joseph Silk of the University of California tell about the English clergyman John Michell, whose ideas about gravity pre-dated the discovery of black holes by American physicist John Wheeler some two centuries later. The work explains some of the current advances in cosmology. {*Secular Nation*, Fall 1994}

Barrow, R(uth) Nita [Dame] [Governor-General] (1916–1995)

Barrow, the first woman to serve as Governor-General of Barbados, was one of the Humanist Laureates in the Council for Secular Humanism's Academy of Humanism. She founded the Jamaica Nurses' Association and was a member of the International Peace Academy (1986–1990). She wrote "Some Issues on the Global Agenda of the 1990s" (1989).

Knighted by Queen Elizabeth II in 1980, Barrow had served as the Barbados representative at the United Nations and was president of the World YWCA. Dame Nita was the older sister of the late Prime Minister Errol Barrow, who led Barbados to independence from Britain in 1966. She was a member of the Council for Secular Humanism's International Academy of Humanism.

Barry, Gerald [Sir] (Born 1899)

Barry was vice president of the National Council for Civil Liberties. A freethinker, he supported the cause of legal abortions in his *News Chronicle*. {TRI}

Barry, Howard P. (20th Century)

Barry, who once was president of the largest local union in the United States, has taught labor relations in government at the St. Francis Xavier Labor School. He is a freethinker who retired in Florida.

Barry, John (1975-)

Barry, a computer specialist who works for Symbol Technologies, has said that, like George Carlin, he was a Christian before he reached the age of Reason. He is a strong believer "that communism would work if it didn't deal with greedy humans." Basically an infidel, Barry was born in San Antonio, Texas. E-mail: <kingCrimson@starcraft.org>. {WAS, 6 May 1999}

Barry, John Vincent William [Sir] (1903—1969)

Sir John Barry was a rationalist, civil libertarian, and in 1947 Justice of the Supreme Court of Victoria in Australia. He helped pave the way for no-fault divorce, and for years was the only absentee from the legal-ecclesiastical Opening of the Legal Year when other faithful judges wended their way into various church ceremonies. He co-wrote *An Introduction to Criminal Law in Australia* (1948) and was a contributor to *Pioneers in Criminology* (1960). A rationalist and unbeliever, Barry was cremated without a service. {SWW}

Barry, Matthew (20th Century)

Barry, an activist for state-church separation, lives in Washington. He has written for *Freethought Today* (March 1998) about faith healers who prey on the weaknesses, hopes, and superstitions of worshippers who all want "a quick fix."

Barrymore, John (1882—1942)

A matinee idol for playgoers and movie fans who liked his dashing nature and good looks, Barrymore in 1922 electrified the public with his portrayal of Hamlet. He was married four times, stunned people by revealing the intimate details of his lovemaking techniques, boozed during much of his waking hours, once vomiting into the footlights during a scene, and on his deathbed continued to shock. A priest, called to give him the last rites, asked, "Is there anything else you wish to tell me?" Barrymore replied, "Father, I have carnal thoughts." "About whom?" the startled priest asked. Knowing he was about to die, having been inculcated with the doctrine that it is a sin to lust, and mindful that he believed he soon would see and be judged by Saint Peter and God Himself, the legendary actor and playboy Barrymore looked across the room to a nurse. "Her," he replied. {Michael O'Regan, New York *Daily News*, 14 April 1996}

Barth, Ferdinand (1828—1850)

An Austrian, Barth attained a reputation in 1848 as orator to working men, and he took part in the revolution. When Vienna was retaken, Barth went to Leipzig and Zurich, where he died professing to be a freethinker. {BDF}

Barth, Joseph Nicholas (1906—)

A Unitarian minister, Barth defined God as "a word that will stand in speech, in a shorthand way, for all reality in which we live and move and have our being. . . . The God I believe in is a naturalistically conceived God." Barth has been an influential spokesman in contemporary liberal religion. {U&U}

Barth, Karl (1886-1968)

A leading 20th-century Protestant, Barth was a Swiss whose fundamental concern was that the word of God and God's revelation in Christ is the only means God has for Self-revelation. Such a theological position is related to less strict views by Emil Brunner, Friedrich Gogarten, and Rudolf Bultmann. {CE}

Barthélemy-Saint-Hilaire, Jules (1805—1895)

Like Cousin, Barthélemy-Saint-Hilaire was a liberal non-Christian theist. He translated all Aristotle's works (17 volumes) into French and wrote many philosophical works. {RAT}

Barthez, Paul (1734—1806)

Barthez, a French physician and friend of D'Alembert, was once shown by the Archbishop of Sens a number of works relating to the rites of his see. Barthez reportedly and wittily observed, "These are the Sens ceremonies, but can you show me the *sens* [sense] of ceremonies?" {BDF; RAT}

Bartle, Richard (20th Century)

Bartle is the co-creator of MUD, which starting in 1979 on the Internet became a popular multi-player interactive game. It is like a real-time chat forum with structure, one with multiple "locations" like an adventure game and could include combat, traps, puzzles, magic, and a simple economic system.

Interviewed in 1996 by Zedd the Wizard, known at the time as Asterix the arch-wizard, Bartle when asked what would be an appropriate epitaphy for his gravestone responded

> Since I'm an atheist and have no belief whatsoever in life after death, I couldn't care less—it's not like it'll have any impact on me, since by definition I will be completely extinguished. I guess if someone twisted my arm and forced me to provide an epitaph, it would be "Don't forget." Sound advice.
>
> {CA}

Bartlett, Willart (20th Century)

Bartlett, a freethinker, wrote *King Solomon's Goat* (c. 1918). {GS}

Bartley, Robert F. (Born 1890)

Bartley, a freethinker, wrote *The Star Studded Hoax of Christianity With Its Allied Gods* (1969). {FUS; GS}

Bartocci, Gianni (20th Century)

Bartocci, a professor of languages and literatures at the University of Guelph in Canada, is an honorary associate of the New Zealand Association of Rationalists and Humanists.

Bartók, Bela (1881—1945)

Bartók, a Hungarian composer, collected and published Hungarian, Transylvanian, Romanian, and other folk tales. Also, he wrote stage and other classical works. His last years were spent in poverty and neglect in New York City, but his music is revered today for its atonality and distinctiveness.

Early on, he felt that nature is self-sufficiently divine, that as humans we control our destinies. He once signed a letter, "Greetings from AN UNBELIEVER (who is more honest than a great many believers)." Were he ever to cross himself, he added, "it would be in the name of Nature, Art, and Science." Bartók was a member of the Budapest Unitarian Church in Hungary.

Ann Bartók, his wife, was a member also and served on a committee to choose its new church organist. {CE; Jay Gabler, Humanist Association of Massachusetts; U; UU}

Bartol, Cyrus A. Jr. (1813—1900)

Bartol was a Unitarian minister, one who liked the transcendentalist movement and who helped in the founding of the Free Religious Association, that he refused to head. He has been described as being an "intuitionist" rather than a "scientist" in his approach to Free Religion. In 1854, his *Grains of Gold or Select Thoughts on Sacred Themes* became the first book published under American Unitarian Association imprint. {U; U&U}

Bartoli, Hector Alexandre (1820—1883)

A Corsican rationalist, Bartoli was a professor of pathology at Marseilles. A leader of the Corsican liberals, he entered the Chambre in 1876 and 1881. A zealous worker for the divorce law, Bartoli was an anti-clerical. {RAT}

Barton, Bruce (20th Century)

In *The Man Nobody Knows: A Discovery of the Real Jesus* (1920), Barton illustrated how capitalist ideology embodied Christian precepts. Jesus, for example, was an exemplary CEO, or chief executive officer, a charismatic leader who "picked up twelve men from the bottom ranks of business and forged them into an organisation that conquered the world." A salesman, he put himself in step with his prospects. And when he left, the new CEO was blocked in his attempts to go global by internal politics and a lack of ability. It was a time when the potential Gentile market was in danger of being saturated by Mithraism, Barton explained, so a franchise was granted to Paul. He simplified the product and marketing mix and proved skillful in setting up independent subfranchises. In fact, Paul emerged as the organization's international marketing manager.

Barton, himself an advertising executive, noted that the Muslims also were adept in business—the Prophet's first wife was a businessperson who, even before they married, was employed as business manager. In 1926, Barton's humorous work was a non-fiction bestseller in New Zealand.

Barton, Clara (1821—1912)

Founder of the American Red Cross, famed Clara Barton was raised a Universalist. During the Civil war, the five-foot farmer's daughter who weighed scarcely one hundred pounds heroically set up a supply service, was a nurse in army camps, worked for the International Red Cross, and organized the American Red Cross, heading it until 1904. During the war, "the angel of the battlefield" worshipped in Washington, according to the Universalist National Memorial Church there. Her parents had helped establish the Oxford Meeting House, one of the first Universalist churches.

According to *The Dictionary of American Biography*, Barton "was brought up in the Universalist Church, but was never a Church member." However, in 1905 she wrote to a Mrs. Norman S. Thrasher: "Your 'belief that I am a Universalist' is as correct as your greater *belief* in being one yourself. A belief in which all who are privileged to possess it, rejoice. In my case, it was a great gift, for, like St. Paul, I 'was born free'. . . . I look anxiously for a time in the near future when the busy world will let me once more become a living part of its people, praising God for the advance in the liberal faith of the religious world of today, so largely due to the teachings of this belief."

McCabe labels Barton a rationalist and a theist, one opposed to Christianity. She is buried in Oxford, Massachusetts, the insignia of the Red Cross adorning her tombstone. In North Oxford, Barton's home is the site of a Unitarian Universalist camp for diabetic children. {CE; EG; JM; U; UU; RE}

Bartosek, Theodor (Born 1877)

A Moravian lawyer, Bartosek was a Socialist who took an active part in the rationalist movement and was conspicuous at the International Congresses in 1906 and 1907. Bartosek edited the *Volné Skola*. {RAT}

Bartram, John (1699—1777)

A pioneer American botanist, whose father had been killed by Indians in 1711, Bartram without formal schooling planted the first botanical garden in the United States. It still exists as part of the Philadelphia park system. Exchanging specimens with European botanists, Bartram introduced some American plants into Europe and introduced some European plants to America. *Observations* (1751) and *The Travels and Other Writings of William Bartram* (1996) describe his various ventures.

In 1758 he was disowned by his Quaker community for denying the divinity of Christ, but he continued attending the Meeting with his family. His son, **William Bartram** (1739—1823) was also a naturalist whose descriptions of the American wilderness influenced the works of Wordsworth, Coleridge, Chateaubriand, and others. {CE; *The New York Review of Books* (17 October 1996)}

Bartrina (1852—1880)

Bartrina was a Spanish atheistic poet, according to Wheeler. {BDF}

Baryshnikov, Mikhail (1948—)

Although his mother was religious and had him secretly baptized as a child, Baryshnikov, the Latvian-born ballet dancer, is not a believer. Asked by the Latvian theatre critic Normunds Naumanis about his views, the world-famous ballet dancer said he is not a religious person but that onstage he found what people seek in religion: "some approximation to exaltation, inner purification, self-discovery."

He has acted onstage, starred in motion pictures, and been a guest artist with leading ballet companies throughout the world. He wrote *Baryshnikov at Work*: Mikhail Baryshnikov Discusses His Roles *(1976)* and *Baryshnikov in Color* (1980). His *Who's Who in America* entry ends, "The dancer who would grow in his art must seek to explore and develop new phases of his talent, and to expand his performing horizons in terms of both the new and existing repertoire." {*The New Yorker*, 19 January 1998}

Barzelotti, Giacomo (Born 1844)

A professor of philosophy, Barzelotti has been described as "a sort of Italian Cousin, attracted by Taine and Spencer to the positive school." His *David Lazzretti*, which Renan admired, is on the *Index Prohibitorum*. {RAT}

Barzun, Jacques (1907—)

Barzun, the French-born American scholar, once a dean at Columbia, cares little for any categorization of humanism suggested herein. In 1989, he responded to the present author:

> It is not surprising that the word Humanism means so many different things, some of which contradict each other, since the root idea is Man, and in this generic sense Man contains everything that has been or may be conceived. It is the human habit of trying to corner what is good that has led to the attempts by successive groups to claim the ism for their particular outlook or endeavor. This situation requires, first of all, a distinction between, on the one hand, the label affixed by history to the Renaissance scholars, and on the other all the other labels. The only tolerable extension of that original humanism is to someone who nowadays teaches the Humanities in a humanistic spirit, that is, looking in works of literature for whatever they say about Man.
>
> All the other humanisms and humanists need an adjective, and perhaps a further identification. One can imagine a Diabolic Humanism that would find Man's highest self-expression in witchcraft, the black mass, and other fiendishnesses. I use this in all sorts of ways, which can be grouped in systems to form all sorts of Humanisms.

In 1992, he explained further:

> The only meanings I, as a student of history, attach to the term Humanism are those given in your definitions number 2 and 3; that is, the two historical definitions. The rest suffer from vagueness in both contents and coverage; they belong to the language of partisanship and polemic, rather than to definition proper. As such, they have their importance, but their use by an historian or critic requires research and explanation before they can be said to denote anything. I should perhaps add that in current talk about the academic humanities, the name "humanist" is given to someone who teaches those subjects and conveys their spirit, but that spirit and those subjects should not be called Humanism.

{WAS, 6 March 1989 and 2 June 1992}

Basayne, Henry S. (20th Century)

When he signed Humanist Manifesto II, Basayne was Associate Executive Officer of the Association for Humanistic Psychology. {HM 2}

Basedow, Johann Bernhard (1723—1790)

Basedow, a German rationalist and educational reformer, wrote *Philalethea, the Grounds of Religion* and other heterodox works that, according to Wheeler, "excited so much prejudice that he was in danger of being stoned." His followers were called Philanthropinists. {BDF; RAT}

Bashkirtseff, Marie (1860—1894)

A Russian artist, Bashkirtseff in *Journal* expresses her skepticism. She died young of consumption. {RAT}

Basil, Robert (1959—)

An editor at Prometheus Books and a *Free Inquiry* editorial associate, Basil is one of the editors of *On the Barricades: Religion and Free Inquiry in Conflict* (1990).

Baskerville, John (1706—1775)

Baskerville, a famous printer to Cambridge University in 1758, wrote a will that expressed the utmost contempt for Christianity. The monumental urn over his tomb reads, "Stranger, beneath this cone is unconsecrated ground a friend to the liberties of mankind directed his body to be inurned. May the example contribute to emancipate thy mind from the idle fears of superstition and wicked arts of priesthood."

His will, according to Leslie Stephen, "professed open contempt for Christianity, and the biographers who reproduce the document always veil certain passages with lines of stars as being far too indecent for repetition," covering the word "irreverent," for example. {BDF; RAT; TYD}

BASKETBALL

God is omnipresent, freethinkers note, and therefore could not have played basketball. "In light of His always being omnipresent," one freethinker noted, "He would, uh, always be out of bounds."

Bassus (1st Century)

Bassus, an Epicurean philosopher and friend of Seneca, was praised by Seneca for his patience and courage in the presence of death. {BDF}

BASTARDS: See entries for Miriam Allen deFord; Illegitimacy; and Patricia Thompson.

Bastian, Adolf (1837—1915)

A leading German anthropologist, Bastian was President of the Berlin Geographical Society (1871—1873) and professor at the Museum of Anthropology. In *Der Mensch in der Geschichte* (1860, 3 volumes), he states that "we no longer fear when a mighty foe [science] shakes our protector [God] from the heaven, to sink with him into an abyss of annihilation." Bastian was an agnostic. {RAT; RE}

Bastian, Henry Charlton (1837—1915)

Bastian was a physician who in 1871 championed "spontaneous generation" against Pasteur and Tyndall. His conclusions were not accepted, but Bastian was an uncompromising rationalist. {RAT}

Bastiat, Frédéric (1801—1850)

Bastiat was a French economist whose chief works are *Sophismes Économiques* (2 volumes, 1847—1848) and *Harmonies Économiques* (1850), in which his rationalism is expressed. A Deputy to the Legislative Assembly at the time of the Revolution of February 1848, he explained each socialist fallacy as it appeared and wrote that socialism must inevitably degenerate into communism, points that most of his fellow countrymen ignored. {RAT}

Bate, Frederick (19th Century)

Bate, a socialist, wrote *The Student* (1842, a drama in which his skeptical views are put forward. Bate was one of the founders of the social experiment at New Harmony, an Owenite scheme of community. {BDF}

Bates, Ernest Sutherland (1879—1939)

Bates, who was literary editor of the *Dictionary of American Biography*, taught at the University of Oregon (1915—1925). He wrote *The Friend of Jesus* (1928) and numerous other books. In *American Faith* (1940), Bates summarized the deist movement in the United States.

Bates, Henry Charlton (1837—1915)

Bates was a physician, a professor at London University (1867—1887) and Censor of the Royal College of Physicians. In spite of his position, Bastian was an aggressive materialist, as shown in his *Brain as the Organ of Mind* (1881). {RAT; RE}

Bates, Henry Walter (1825—1892)

A naturalist, Bates sailed with Wallace to South America, left him in 1850 and continued to travel in the upper Amazons. At Darwin's suggestion, Bates wrote *Naturalist on the Amazons* (1863).

Bates, an agnostic, was President of the Entomological Society in 1869 and 1878 and was a Chevalier of the Brazilian Order of the Rose. {RAT}

Bates, John (19th Century)

A basketmaker turned news agent, Bates kept a shop in The Drapery and was one of the leaders of Northampton, England, secularists. {RSR}

Bates, Marston (1906—1974)

Bates, who is the author of *The Prevalence of People* (1955), was a zoologist who has taught at the University of Michigan. He wrote *The Forest and the Sea* (1960).

Bates, Sanford (20th Century)

Edwin H. Wilson has written that in the late 1910s he "heard Unitarian Sanford Bates, the U.S. prison commissioner (as I recall), state that 'there is not one belief that I hold that I would not change on five minutes' notice if I ran into a new fact.' " {EW}

Battelli, Angelo (Born 1862)

A vigorous rationalist and anti-clerical, Battelli was an Italian physicist. He taught at the universities of Cagliari, Padua, and Pisa and was a Socialist Deputy for Pisa, then Urbino, in the Italian Parliament. {RAT}

Battaglia, Anthony

Battaglia has written in *The Secular Humanist Bulletin* (Winter 1998-1999) that although monks appear to be chanting overtime, secular music now comprises 99.9% of all the great music ever recorded. However, inasmuch as one of every seven radio stations in 1997 had a Christian radio format (1,648 stations) and reach an estimated twenty million listeners, he holds that humanists should fill a needed vacuum and enter the broadcasting field.

Batz, Philipp: See entry for Mainlaender.

Baudelaire, Charles Pierre (1821—1867)

Baudelaire, the French poet who influenced western poetry so greatly, is known for his religious mysticism and feelings of inner despair. He came from a Catholic aristocratic family but became a revolutionary who fought at the barricades in 1848. Baudelaire developed symbolism, symbolic correspondences among sensory images such as colors, sounds, and scents. *Les Fleurs du mal* (*The Flowers of Evil*, 1857, enlarged in 1861 and 1868) was the only book of his published while he lived, and its appearance shocked the public and was condemned particularly by religionists. It included "*Les Litanies de Satan*."

Beauty and corruption, he held, are inseparable, and such a theme combined with the alleged obscenity of his work led to his further condemnation. He did succeed as a critic, translating Edgar

Allan Poe and bringing him to an accepting French public. Baudelaire's criticism was published posthumously as *Curiosités esthétiques* (1868) and *L'Art romantique* (1869). His poetic prose pieces also were published posthumously as *Petits Poèmes en prose* (1869).

"In Charles Baudelaire's poetry," writes Thweatt, "the cult of grief and of the satanic alternates with a dream of absolute purity. Art itself also becomes an absolute." In his portrayal of the Devil, Baudelaire included touches of ancient beauty.

As for supernaturalism, he teasingly reasoned, "Even if God did not exist, religion would still be holy and divine. . . . God is the only being who does not have to exist in order to reign." Some cite such a passage when calling Baudelaire a mystic, others call him an atheist, and still others are content to call him a rationalist who introduced symbolism. Edna St. Vincent Millay translated his *Flowers of Evil* (1936).

While in his twenties and at a time when he contracted syphilis, the venereal disease that killed him later, Baudelaire composed his own epitaph:

> Here lies, for having too much dwelled
> in street girls' holes,
> A young fellow who now inhabits
> the kingdom of moles.

Although a cenotaph by de Charmoy is found in Paris's Montparnasse cemetery, Baudelaire is buried elsewhere next to his mother and stepfather. His final epitaph contains only the death date, 31 August 1867. {BDF; CE; EU, Vivien Thweatt; JM; JMR; RAT; TRI; TYD}

Baudissin, Wilhelm Friedrich von [Count] (Born 1847)

Baudissin was a German theological writer who, in *Adonis und Esmun* (1911), discusses with frankness the sources of the resurrection-myth. Rejecting the characteristic Christian doctrines, Baudissin discusses the characteristics of Jehovan and of Christ in Syrian mythology. {RAT}

Baudon, P. L. (19th Century)

A French author, Baudon wrote *Christian Superstition* (1862) and dedicated it to Bishop Dupanloup under the pseudonym of "Aristide." {BDF}

Baudrillart, Henri (1821—1892)

Baudrillart was a French economist who in 1855 became editor of the *Journal des Économistes*. In 1863 he was elected to the Academy. Besides important works on economics, he published a panegyric of Voltaire (*Discours sur Voltaire* (1844). {RAT}

Bauer, Bruno (1809—1882)

Bauer was a German theologian whose work Albert Schweitzer called "the ablest and most complete collection of the difficulties of the life of Jesus which is anywhere to be found." His criticism of the Bible resulted in his being dismissed by Prussian authorities from a university post in theology at Bonn in 1842. Wells in *Encyclopedia of Unbelief* describes Bauer's view that the principal letters ascribed to Paul are 2nd century forgeries. After he was expelled from teaching on the university level, Bauer according to Robertson "was a freelance, doing some relatively valid work on the Pauline problem, but pouring out his turbid spirit in a variety of political writings, figuring by turns as an anti-Semite (1843), a culture-historian, and a pre-Bismarckian imperialist, despairing of German unity, but looking hopefully to German absorption in a vast empire of Russia." At the time of his death, he was convinced that all educated men—at least in Germany—had ceased to believe in miracles and the supernatural, however they might appear as conforming to orthodoxy. Bauer's brother, Edgar, collaborated in some of his works. Edgar's *The Strife of Criticism with Church and State* (1843) resulted in his being imprisoned for four years. {BDF; EU, G. A. Wells; JMR; JMRH; RAT}

Bauer, Edgar (1820—1886)

Bauer, who was brother of Bruno Bauer, collaborated in some of his works. The police seized his brochure entitled "Bruno Bauer and His Opponents" (1842), and he was imprisoned for four years for his next publication, *The Strife of Criticism with Church and State* (1843). He took part in the revolutionary movement of 1848–1849 and was obliged to quit Germany. {BDF; RAT}

Bauer, Renate (20th Century)

Bauer was secretary of the West German Freethinkers and is on the editorial board of the *International Humanist*. She addressed the Seventh International Humanist and Ethical Union (IHEU) World Congress held in London (1978) and the Tenth held in Buffalo (1988). E-mail: <bauerpsy@aol.com>. {*Free Inquiry*, Summer 1988}

Bauer, Yehuda (20th Century)

Bauer is an honorary president of the International Federation of Secular Humanistic Jews.

Baulieu, Etienne (20th Century)

Baulieu, the French discoverer of RU486, signed Humanist Manifesto 2000.

Baum, L(yman) Frank (1856—1919)

An American journalist, Baum is best known for *The Wonderful Wizard of Oz* (1900) and thirteen other related books. In *The New York Times* (20 Dec 1991), his biographer, Michael Patrick Hearn, has written,

> Although raised in a strict Methodist family, Baum early rejected the Christian teachings of his childhood. Except for a brief period in Aberdeen, South Dakota, where he joined the local Episcopal church, he did not belong to any organized religion. He joined the Aberdeen church for its social, not its religious opportunities, and there is no record he ever attended services.
>
> Baum and his wife, Maud, did not have any of their children baptized and did not send them to church, but they did say that the children could choose any religion they wanted once they were old enough to decide for themselves. The only reference to a church in any of Baum's Oz books in Chapter 20 of *The Wizard of Oz*, and here it is "smashed . . . all to pieces" by the Cowardly Lion.
>
> The Rev. E. P. Ryland, a friend of Baum in Hollywood, who spoke at Baum's funeral, explained that the author of *The Wizard of Oz* "wasn't a denominationalist. When he went to church at all in Hollywood," Mr. Ryland said, "he attended mine, but he wasn't a member of it. He had a gospel of his own, and he preached it through his books, although you certainly couldn't call them religious either."
>
> The Judeo-Christian tradition had failed Baum. He once wrote, "When the priests acknowledge their fallibility; when they abolish superstition, intolerance and bigotry; when they abhor the thought of a vindictive and revengeful God; when they are able to reconcile reason and religion, and fear not to let the people think for themselves, then, and then only, will the church regain its old power and be able to draw to its pulpits the whole people." L. Frank Baum was a skeptic. After all, the Great and Terrible Wizard of Oz proves at the end to be a humbug.

However, Maud and her husband joined the Theosophists in 1896, held seances in their home and consulted with clairvoyants and astrologers. They both believed in the transmigration of souls and were certain that they had been together in past lives and would be in future ones. (See entry for *Wizard of Oz*, the message of which is entirely secular and humanistic.) {CE}

Baume-Desdossat, Jacques François (1705—1756)

Baume-Desdossat wrote *La Christiade* (1753), a satire on the gospels in which Jesus is tempted by Mary Magdalene. The work was suppressed by the French Parliament and the author was fined. {BDF}

Baumer, Erica S. (20th Century)

Baumer is secretary of Atheists and Agnostics of Wisconsin. On the web: <esbaumer@students.wisc.edu>.

Baumer, Franklin C. (20th Century)

Baumer, a freethinker, wrote *Religion and the Rise of Skepticism* (1960). {FUS}

Baumgardner, Raymond C. (20th Century)

In the 1950s, Baumgardner was a director of the American Humanist Association. {HNS}

Baur, Ferdinand Christian von (1792—1860)

Baur was a distinguished theological critic and professor of church history. His teachings and writings subverted all the fundamental positions of Christianity. A Hegelian pantheist, Baur acknowledged only four of the epistles of *Paul* and the *Revelation* as genuine products of the apostolic age, and he showed how very far from simplicity were the times and doctrines of primitive Christianity. {BDF}

Bautz, Yngve (20th Century)

If, as believers hold, God is both good and almighty, how can one rationally believe in such an entity that would allow a Holocaust or other such negative acts? Bautz declared this and his opposition to "new Christianity" or to the idea that God is a conscious being in *Freethinker* (June 1999).

Bax, Ernest Belfort (1854—1918)

A philosophic and social writer, Bax with William Morris founded the English Socialist League. For a time he was joint editor of the *Commonwealth* and, later, of *Justice*. He translated Kant's *Prolegomena* (1883). In his *Problems of Men, Mind, and Morals* (1912), Bax remarks that "for those who accept Socialism . . . it is scarcely possibly to conscientiously describe themselves as Christians, or even Theists." Bax preferred atheist to agnostic. {RAT}

Baxendell, Cedric Harold (1922—)

"Tup" Baxendell is an Australian rationalist and humanist. In 1968 he joined the Rationalist Society of Queensland, that in 1968 changed its name to the Humanist Society of Queensland, of which he is a life member. {SWW}

Baxendell, Margaret Dorothy (1922—)

Mrs. Cedric Baxendell, like her husband, was once a Congregational Sunday School teacher, which is where they originally met. She is a foundation member of Abortion Law Reform, now called Children by Choice. She was a member of Save Our Sons (SOS), a group opposing conscription in Australia for the Vietnam War. In addition, she is secretary of Australians for a Sustainable Population; the Union of Australian Women; and the May Belle Association, a domestic violence service organization. The building that houses Humanist headquarters has been named "Baxendell House." {SWW}

Baxley, Clyde (20th Century)

Baxley is president of Atheists of Alaska. (See entry for Alaska Atheists.)

Baxley, William Warren (20th Century)

Baxley wrote *Pitchfork Smith, Texas Liberal* as his master's thesis at the University of Texas in 1944. It draws upon memories of those who knew him personally. {*Freethought History #15*, 1995}

Baxter, Delia (20th Century)

In Britain, Mrs. Baxter is active in the Fylde Humanist Group.

Baxter, George E. (19th Century)

Baxter, of Perth Amboy, New Brunswick, was a contributor to *Truth Seeker, Secular Thought*, and other liberal publications. He lectured several times at Canada's Fort Fairfield Liberal League and expressed the view that "there are no national lines in Freethought." {PUT}

Bayle, Pierre (1647—1706)

An important 17th-century French skeptic, Bayle was persecuted for his views, for being first a Protestant, then a Catholic, then a Protestant. Voltaire liked him, believing he was secretly an atheist while appearing to be a Calvinist. Gibbon acknowledged his indebtedness to the "celebrated writer," calling him "the indefatigable Bayle." In one of his early works, Bayle wrote that a society of atheists could be as moral as or more moral than a society of Christians. During the French Revolution, Maréchal cited Bayle as being only a "possible atheist." Robertson, however, believes that no greater service was rendered in that age to the spread of rational views than that embodied in his grand *Dictionnaire Historique et Critique* (1697), in which he wrote that "in matters of religion, it is very easy to deceive a man, and very hard to undeceive him." Chased from France because of his freethinking, and persecuted even in Rotterdam, Bayle through his consummate scholarship produced, according to Robertson, "a virtual encyclopedia for freethinkers in his incomparable Dictionary, baffling hostility by the Pyrrhonian impartiality with which he handled all religious questions."

Berman describes Bayle's rather curious *ad hominem* argument:

> The most evil and depraved being is the most complete practical atheist. But if such a being believes firmly in the existence of God (and probably also has an adequate understanding of God), then there can hardly be a necessary connection, or any firm link, between theoretical and practical atheism. And these conditions are indeed fulfilled, since Satan is the most complete practical theist, but he is also a convinced believer in God.

Bayle's attempt to break down the connection between theoretical beliefs and practical consequences, Berman holds, "is derived from an essentially empiricist source." In 1953, Arnold Toynbee in *An Historian's Approach to Religion*, reprinted Bayle's "If Christian Theology is True, God is a Monster." Elisabeth LaBrousse, his biographer, has written that Bayle became a kind of tourist attraction during the last years of his life. He greeted his visitors affably and with a loquacity unheard of in his younger days. He assured the Abbé de Polignac that he was "a good Protestant" inasmuch as he was in the habit of protesting "against everything anyone says or does." Des Maiseaux is quoted as saying that Bayle "saw death approaching without either fearing or desiring it." Two months before his death, Bayle wrote to Lord Shaftesbury, "I should have thought that a dispute with Divines would put me out of humor, but I find by experience that it serves as an amusement for me in the solitude to which I have reduced myself."

According to *Nouvelle Biographic Générale*, "He died in his clothes, and as it were pen in hand." A friend, M. Seers, said Bayle died "with great tranquillity and without anybody with him. At nine o'clock in the morning his landlady entered his chamber; he asked her, but with a dying voice, if his fire was kindled, and died a moment after, without M. Basnage (author of the first *History of the Jews*) or me, or any of his friends with him."

Freethought History (#24, 1997) notes material about Bayle: <http://www.cisi.unito.it/progetti/bayle/index.html>. {BDF; CE; EU, Richard Popkin and Aram Vartanian; FUK; HAB; JM; JMR; JMRH; RAT; RE}

Baylee, Joseph (20th Century)

Baylee, a freethinker, wrote *God, Man, and the Bible* (191—?). {GS}

Bayley, John (20th Century)

Bayley wrote *Iris: A Memoir of Iris Murdoch* (1998) about his eventful life with his wife, how she was more concerned with the people around her than with her ego, and how at the end she developed Alzheimer's and went "sailing into darkness." Bayley and Murdoch were described by Jim Herrick as being "broadly humanist." {*New Humanist*, October 1998, and December 1999}

Bayrhoffer, Karl Theodor (1812—1888)

Bayrhoffer was a German philosopher who wrote *The Idea and History of Philosophy* (1838). A participant in the 1848 revolution, he then emigrated to America, where he wrote many polemical works. {BDF}

Bays, Jack (20th Century)

Bays, a freethinker, wrote *The Good Book* and *The Sadist God.* {GS}

Baysinger, Jeff (20th Century)

Baysinger is director of the chapter in Denver, Colorado, of the Freedom from Religion Foundation (FFRF). He is also on the FFRF board of directors.

Bazaz, Gauri Malik Bazaz (20th Century)

Bazaz, the daughter of Prem Nath Bazaz, is secretary of the Indian Renaissance Institute. A radical humanist, she is a physician.

Bazaz, Prem Nath (Died 1976)

Bazaz was a radical humanist and a freedom fighter for Kashmir. He wrote *A Critique of Gita* and *Secular Democracy.*

B.C.: See entries for B.C.E. and A.D.

B.C.E.

Lady Katie Magnus was the first to write B.C.E. (Before the Common Era), a more accurate description according to freethinkers, rather than B.C. (Before Christ). (See entry for A. D.) {William Safire, *The New York Times*, 17 August 1997}

Beach, Joseph Warren (1880—1957)

A scholar at the University of Minnesota and author of *American Fiction 1920—1940* and *The Twentieth- Century Novel*, Beach in 1956 just before his death wrote the present author:

> Of the various brands of humanism, the one that best fits my way of thinking is naturalistic humanism. Humanism is for me a handy way of designating the view that the values we most cherish in ethics have originated in human minds in a natural manner, and that they make up the ideal of a good life to which we owe allegiance individually and as members of the community. For me it implies a naturalistic philosophy, without reference to theological sanctions or supernatural assumptions as to the origin and 'ultimate' nature of the universe of which we are a part. As for the origins of our moral sense, it seems a reasonable hypothesis that it is traceable to our experience as men under the conditions of family life and of larger social units, and may have its psychological motivation in the feelings we have for the members of our family and our community, and above all in the need we have to maintain the esteem and love of our fellows. Along with this goes the natural instinct to avoid what is harmful to us, to prize what is helpful, and to wish to have prevail in society those types of behavior that make for the general well-being. In this sense our moral ideals are a natural development out of the ego.
>
> Such a naturalistic philosophy enables us to make a more rational analysis of our ideals and obligations and to construct a more systematic and coherent system of values than any theological philosophy, which brings in considerations from the outside, not subject to critical examination and tending to introduce confusion into our thinking. Obviously religion, itself a product of the human mind, has been closely associated with our ideas of good and bad, and has often been a vehicle for diffusing and enforcing many of our finest ideals. But it is also regrettably true that the great historical religions have had a negligible effect in preventing national and commercial rivalries and wars, and in many instances have been the cause of tragic divisions among men. And I feel that most religions as they are now professed tend to keep men from maturing intellectually and emotionally; and that there is a great wastage of energy in each generation as men go through the painful process of throwing off the religious teachings of their childhood. I realize, however, that for great populations the entire structure of their mores is bound up closely with the churches to which they belong, and that for them to be abruptly deprived of their religious faith might well have disastrous effects on their personal and social character. It seems a pity that so powerful an agent for good as is the church community should have so largely failed to adjust itself to a world-mentality dominated by the naturalistic and critical spirit associated with scientific thinking. One wishes to be associated with others in the group affirmation of a common faith. But for many decades I have been kept almost altogether away from churches by the sense that intellectual and moral integrity requires that one should not pretend to beliefs that one's mind rejects. The most nearly congenial to my way of thinking are the Unitarian and Universalist churches. But even with them I am made uneasy by vestiges in the service of a "mythology" which it is hard to reconcile with the critical spirit of their humanism.
>
> Of ancient philosophers, the Stoics and Epicureans are most congenial to me; but a combination of the two seems requisite for an adequate humanism. The Epicureans are admirable for building up a philosophy in naturalistic terms, and for stressing happiness (or the finer satisfactions) as the ultimate end of human activity. The Stoics depend too much on the notion of a transcendental moral order of the universe, for which we have no evidence; but they add to Epicurean ethics their important emphasis on the social order among men and the necessity for the individual to make sacrifices to this ideal. Perhaps the finest picture of the virtues peculiar to man is given by Aristotle in his Nichomachean Ethics. But his stress is rather too heavy on the individual freeman and too light on what we owe to the social body; and he writes within the framework of a slave state.
>
> In modern English literature, where I am most at home, the writers who have most influenced me in my impressionable years are probably Matthew Arnold (in his effort to divest religion of *Aberglaube* and to refine our critical sense and our social values and manners), and George Meredith, who in his poetry and fiction gave a fine representation of a naturalist system of ethics in theory and practice. But our English and American novelists almost from the start have been essentially humanists. They have been concerned with those qualities in the individual that make for the good life in society; and they have been pretty free from a more than conventional reference to theological assumptions. Among those who stand highest in these respects are George Eliot, Henry James, Thackeray, Dickens, and Hardy.
>
> Our poets have been more handicapped by religious commitments, though Tennyson and Browning, as well as the early Wordsworth, made a valiant effort at "liberalism." Shelley was, of course, a queer combination of eighteenth-century rationalism and Platonic mysticism. Many of our recent poets have failed to meet the challenge of modern thought. They are too much haunted by the notion of "original sin," which, to my thinking, is as false an assumption as the Rousseauistic premise of the "natural goodness of man." Man is a naturally selfish animal, but with great capacities for social behavior when properly trained and motivated. Many of our modern poets are also under the impression that they cannot do business without a large allowance of "mythology," and they don't trust men to stand up to the problems of life without constant appeal to their *Urvater*. The war years and the great depression have been more than they could take, and when the socialist ideal seemed to fail them they were readily discouraged and too often simply "gave up the game." Literary men and young men tend to be impatient; they live in great hopes for the immediate future; and when their hopes are not realized within a generation, they tend to turn cynical and religious. A stable philosophy must have a longer range.
>
> The Babbitt-and-More "new humanism" was provincial and puritan; it relied altogether on the "inner check," as we all must; but the inner check was too much conceived of as a check on all natural impulse, and the positive impulses were strangled with the negative.

Their literary criticism was a witch-hunt. In contemporary Germany and France Existentialism (à la Heidegger and Sartre) seems to me the most vital philosophy. German existentialism (in Pastor Bultmann) promises to be a good solvent for "mythology" in Lutheranism. But there is (in Jaspers) too much reliance on "transcendentals" and too much suspicion of the positive empiricism of science. The Sartre existentialism has one radical defect. It seems to imply that every man must go it alone and make a completely fresh start; there seems to be no general system of ethics available; whereas the humanistic ideal and set of values (owing much to the teachings of Jesus) have a long and august history. This may not be so clear in France as in English-speaking countries, where Protestantism has done so much to break down the all-or-nothing complex.

With us, humanism is available to the well-informed. But it does lack organization, and is at a disadvantage in comparison with organized religion. It is bound to make headway in a world permeated with the critical spirit of science. But it suffers from the widespread notion promoted in every pulpit that, unless the world is purposeful and benevolently directed by an intelligent spirit, we have no stable grounds for our moral idealism. It suffers from the aversion of numerous creative writers today who feel that our humanism has no room for the "soul," the will, or the imagination. What we need is a prophetic voice with the literary genius of an Emerson, but an Emerson not pledged to a transcendentalist view of the universe.

(For a contrary view concerning Heidegger, see the statement of Paul Edwards in the entry for Heidegger.) {WAS, 2 July 1956}

Beadnell, Charles Marsh (Born 1872)

From 1914 to 1917 Beadnell was Fleet Surgeon on H.M.S. *Shannon*, and he retired from the Navy in 1926. In 1940 he became President of the Rationalist Press Association in 1940. {FUK; RAT; RE}

Beadnell, Louise Myfanwy (1907—1988)

"Miffy" Beadnell, who was born in Scotland, had as role models her geologist father and a rationalist, surgeon uncle. She was a founding member and secretary of the Humanist Society of Victoria in Australia, and she was editor of the *Victorian Humanist*. Once asked her belief, Beadnell replied that it consisted of just nine words: "I do not believe that there is a god." {FUK; SWW}

Beal, Temy (20th Century)

Beal is editor of the Alabama Freethought Association newsletter (255 Lake Joan Circle, Munford, Alabama 36258).

Beam, Ben (20th Century)

Beam, who has held positions with the Universalist Church, is membership coordinator of the New York Ethical Society.

BEANS: See entry for Legumes.

Bear, Greg (20th Century)

Known in science-fiction circles for his short stories and novels, Bear wrote *The Forge of God* and the Nebula award-winning *Blood Music* and *Moving Mars*. When asked on the SciFi Channel's IRC server, The Dominion, what he thought of religion, Bear responded, "I'm fascinated by religion. Religion mixes storytelling with trying to understand our place in the world. The myths and religious background of the human race are a treasure trove of ideas, but as to whether I believe the dictates of any modern-day religion, the answer is flatly 'no.' "{CA}

BEAT GENERATION

The "beat generation" is a phrase used to describe writers in the 1950s who were essentially anarchistic and who rejected traditional social and artistic forms. The members looked for *beatific* illuminations such as those found in Zen Buddhism or other Eastern religions, and they used the rhythms of simple American speech and of be-bop and progressive jazz. Jack Kerouac, Chandler Broussard, Kenneth Rexroth, Allen Ginsberg, Lawrence Ferlinghetti, Gary Snyder, John Clellon Holmes, David Amram, and Gregory Corso are associated with the movement. The true nihilist of the group was William Burroughs. Some of the individuals were influenced by (Zen) Buddhism and other echoes of religious confessional, such as Red Indian and Mexican Peyote cults. In the 1960s, "beat" ideas and attitudes were practiced in a "beat" life style by people called "hippies." The second and third generation artists included Bob Dylan, the Beatles, Wolf Biermann, Andrei Voznesensky, and Yevgeny Aleksandrovich Yevtushenko. The hipster who defined "beat," a carnival term for someone fatigued and beaten down, was Herbert Huncke, whose last name appropriately rhymes with "junkie." A teenage runaway who used drugs as early as twelve and sold sex by the time he was sixteen, Huncke was a well-known hustler at New York's 42nd Street and Eighth Avenue Angle Bar. He introduced Burroughs to heroin, worked as a recruiter to find interviewees for sex researcher Alfred Kinsey, spent eleven years in prison, and wrote a variety of books. For Kerouac's *The Town and the City*, Huncke was the dominant character, Junkey. (See entries for David Amram, William Burroughs, John Cage, Allen Ginsberg, Herbert Huncke, and Royston Ellis.) {CE; OEL; *The Freedom to be Obscure* (1997)}

Beat, Jackie (20th Century)

Beat reveled in the fact that "her" drag show, "Jesus Christ, It's Your Birthday," was cited as being anti-Catholic by the 1998 Catholic League for Religious and Civil Rights. He had a small part in the Robert De Niro drag film, "Flawless."

BEATIFICATION: See entry for Pope

BEATLES, THE: See entry for Royston Ellis.

Beattie, Lucinda (20th Century)

Beattie is on the editorial advisory board of *Religious Humanism*, the quarterly published by the Fellowship of Religious Humanists.

Beattie, Paul H. (Died c. 1989)

Beattie was a Unitarian minister and President, Fellowship of Religious Humanism, when he signed Humanist Manifesto II. In 1980, he signed the Secular Humanist Declaration. At the Tenth International Humanist and Ethical Union (IHEU) World Congress held in Buffalo (1988), he addressed the group. Beattie has edited a Yellow Springs, Ohio, publication, *Religious Humanism*. {HM2; SHD}

Beauchamp, Philip: See entry for George Grote.

Beauchamps, George (20th Century)

Beauchamps, a teacher and educational administrator active in the formation of the Washington, D.C., Ethical Culture Society in the 1940s, was elected to the Ethical Fraternity of Leaders in 1947. A developer of a retirement center in Florida, Beauchamps has been active as Dean (counselor to Leaders) of the AEU Leaders Council. (See entry for Ethical Culture.) {EU, Howard B. Radest}

Beauregard, Claudius (1578—1664)

Beauregard (also Berigardus) was a French physician and philosopher. His *Circulus Pisanus* (1643) is considered an atheistic work. {BDF}

Beausobre, Louis de (1730—1783)

Beausobre was adopted by Frederick the Great out of esteem for his father, Isaac Beausobre, author of the *History of Manicheanism*. Louis wrote about skepticism of the wise (*Pyrrhonisme du Sage*, 1754), which the Parliament of France condemned to be burned. His anonymous *The Dreams of Epicurus* (1758) was an essay on happiness, reprinted with Holbach's *Social System* in 1795. {BDF; RAT}

BEAUTY

Although Aristotle, according to Diogenes Laërtius, believed that "Beauty is the gift of God," David Hume in *Of Tragedy* has written, "Beauty in things exists in the mind which contemplates them." Wolfgang Mieder'sCollection of *World Proverbs* (1986), all apparently devised by males, illustrates the significance of Hume's statement:

- He who marries a beauty marries trouble.
  —*African (Yoruba)*
- Beauty does not ensnare men; they ensnare themselves.
  —*Chinese*
- Beauty without virtue is like a rose without scent.
  —*Danish*
- Beauty is but dross if honesty be lost.
  —*Dutch*
- Beauty is but skin deep.
  —*English*
- One can neither put beauty into the pot, nor loveliness into the kettle.
  —*Estonian*
- Beauty and folly are often companions.
  —*French*
- Beauty is a good letter of introduction.
  —*German*
- Beauty will sit and weep; fortune will sit and eat.
  —*Indian (Tamil)*
- The beauty of a chaste woman makes bitter words.
  —*Irish*
- She who is born a beauty is born betrothed.
  —*Italian*
- Though she may be a beauty, it is but one layer of skin.
  —*Japanese*
- Genuine beauty appears from the morning; no eye fluids will spoil it.
  — *Libyan*
- The beauty of the man is in his intelligence, and the intelligence of the woman is in her beauty.
  —*Moroccan*
- Beauty will fade, but not goodness.
  —*Philippine*
- Beauty of the chaste is a virtue, that of a whore a quality.
  —*Russian*
- No one can live on beauty, but one can die for it.
  —*Swedish*
- It's good to behold beauty and to live with wisdom.
  —*Yiddish*

Contemporary freethinkers are aware that the Western world's concept of beauty is based upon Ancient Greek and Roman standards. They are particularly aware in the event their own physique nowhere nearly measures up, which aesthetes find unfortunate.

Aphrodite, the Greek goddess of beauty, was identified with Venus by the Romans. "Aphrodite" by Praxiteles is said to have been modeled by his lover, Phryne, a prostitute. The work is also said to have been the first monumental statue of the female nude. When authorities accused Phryne of immoral conduct, she stood before them, pulled her clothing down to her waist, and asked the judges "Is desire immoral? Are you immoral? What is immorality?" Transfixed, they ruled in her favor and, in the words of poet Patricia Storace, Phryne became "the only woman in antiquity to have won a lawsuit with her own eloquent breasts." (See entries for Aesthetics, Aphrodite, Doryphorus, Phallicism, and Phidias.) {Patricia Storace, *The New York Review of Books*, 3 October 1996}

Beauvoir, Simone de (1908—1986)

An existentialist, feminist author, freethinker, and consort of Sartre, Beauvoir taught philosophy in several colleges. The Vatican in 1956 prohibited reading of her *The Second Sex* (1949), a profound study of the status of women. Film critic David Denby, however, described the book in 1996 as "the single most important feminist text of the century." The Vatican also prohibited reading of her existentialistic novel, *The Mandarins* (1954).

Beauvoir's monumental treatment of the aged in several cultures is *The Coming of Age* (1970). Germaine Greer, in *The Change: Women, Aging and the Menopause* (1992), uses Beauvoir as an example of *anophobia*, the irrational fear and hatred of old women, citing her "fizzled out" mid-life affair with Claude Lanzmann.

In *The Second Sex*, according to biographer Margaret Crosland, Beauvoir displayed "an energetic anger, directed not only towards men, the jailers of women in man-made institutions, but also, as the book proceeds, at women themselves." But despite her anger, intelligence, and strength, Beauvoir lamentably allowed herself to be dominated by Sartre and other men, Crosland writes. In *Past Imperfect, French Intellectuals, 1944—1956,* Tony Judt faults Beauvoir as well as Sartre for having argued away the brutalities of Stalin. Either they were deluded or perverse, Judt states, for they refused to test their political thoughts against political realities. Beauvoir's love affair with novelist Nelson Algren is documented in her letters. On her death she was buried alongside her lifelong companion, Sartre, while wearing Algren's wedding ring. (For details of her love affair with Bianca Lamblin, a student she seduced and then introduced to Sartre, who seduced her also, see entry for Jean-Paul Sartre.) {Simone de Beauvoir, "Facts and Myths About Women," *Free* Inquiry, Winter 1998-1999; CE; EU, Hazel E. Barnes; ILP, *Index Additus*, 15 December 1961; Clancy Sigal, *The New York Times Book Review*, 27 December 1998; TYD}

Bebel, (Ferdinand) August (1840—1913)

A German Socialist leader, Bebel was a freethinker, an antimilitarist, and a founder of the German Social Democratic Party. In the Reichstag, Bebel went so far as to say that "the aim of our party is on the political plane the republican form of State; on the economic, Socialism; and on the plane which we term the religious, atheism. . . . Christianity is the enemy of liberty and of civilization. It has kept mankind in chains." According to McCabe, Bebel was zealously opposed to theology, and was, "like all the Socialist leaders of his time, an atheist and freely expressed it in his work on *Woman and Christianity*." {BDF; CE; JM; JMR; JMRH; RAT; RE; TYD}

Beccaria, Cesare Bonesana [Marchese di] (1738—1794)

An Italian criminologist, jurist, and economist, Beccaria wrote one of the most influential books of the eighteenth century, *Crimes and Punishments* (1764). His ideas, which were praised by Voltaire, affected penal methods for the better throughout the whole of Europe.

According to Robertson, "Even were he not known to be a deist, his strictly secular and rationalist method would have brought upon him priestly suspicion; and he had in fact to defend himself against pertinacious and unscrupulous attacks, though he had sought in his book to guard himself by occasionally 'veiling the truth in clouds.' "

Beccaria owed his intellectual awakening first to Montesquieu and above all to Helvetius—another testimony to the reformative virtue of all freethought." Other 18th-century Italian freethinkers Robertson names are as follows:

- **Alfieri**, one of the strongest anti-clericalists of his age;

• **Count Algarotti** (1712—1764), a distinguished aesthetician;

• **Bettinelli**, the correspondent of Voltaire and author of *The Resurrection of Italy* (1775);

• **Count Dandolo**, author of a French work on *The New Men* (1799);

• **Filangieri**, whose work on legislation won high praise from Franklin but was put on the *Index* by the papacy;

• **Ferdinando Galiani**, a wit among the French *philosophes*;

• **Antonio Genovesi** (1712—1769), "redeemer of the Italian Mind" and chief establisher of economic science for Italy;

• **Giannone**, author of the great anti-papal *History of the Kingdom of Naples* (1723), who died in Sardinia after having been confined there for twelve years.

McCabe, however, speculates as to whether or not Beccaria was an atheist. Italy was not a safe place for heretics. Beccaria had to publish his treatise abroad and anonymously—and he, as he said, "heard the noise of the chains rattled by superstition and fanaticism." {BDF; CE; JM; JMR; JMRH; RAT; RE}

Becher, Erich (Born 1882)

Becher was a German philosopher who taught at the Münster University. A monist in philosophy, or critical realist, he was a utilitarian in ethics. Becher regarded reality as psychic but rejected the idea of a separable soul. {RAT}

Beck, Joe (20th Century)

Beck heads the Humanist Counseling and Services Center and has been accepted as a secular humanist counselor at all the Catholic hospitals in the Buffalo, New York, area. E-mail: <jbeck@buffnet.net>. On the Web: <www.HumanismServices.com>.

Beck, Lewis W(hite) (20th Century)

In the 1950s, Beck wrote reviews for *The Humanist*, at which time he taught philosophy at the University of Rochester. He is author of *Early German Philosophy* (1969), *Actor and Spectator* (1975), and *Essays on Kant and Hume* (1978).

Becker, Karl (20th Century)

Becker's *Freigestige Bibliographie* lists freethought works in German. {FUS}

Becker, Myrna (20th Century)

Becker is a regional director in New York State of the Council for Secular Humanism.

Becker, Richard J. (20th Century)

An Albany, New York, humanist, Becker in 1996 participated in the international conference of ethical humanists in Mexico City.

His e-mail: <rbecker518@aol.com>.

Becker, Walter Frederick [Sir] (Born 1855)

A ship owner, Becker was known for his philanthropy. He founded, maintained, and was chairman of the Maternity and Rescue Home at Turin. During the War he founded, maintained, and directed a hospital at Turin for the British Expeditionary Force. Sir Walter was an agnostic. {RAT}

Beckers, Hubert (1806—1889)

Beckers was a German philosopher who followed Schelling's pantheism and wrote a number of works on Schelling and philosophy. {RAT}

BECKETT MEMORIAL LIBRARY

The Len Beckett Memorial library in New Zealand has the largest collection of freethought literature in the Southern Hemisphere. {*The New Zealand Rationalist & Humanist Newsletter*, July 1998}

Beckett, James M. (19th Century)

In 1845 in New York City, Beckett became recording secretary of the Infidel Society for the Promotion of Mental Liberty. The group had hoped to become a national freethought society. {FUS}

Beckett, Samuel (1906—1989)

One of the greatest modern writers in English, Beckett was an unbeliever. He was born on Good Friday to affluent, Protestant, Anglo-Irish Dubliners. His mother was moody and demanding, his father was a steady person, his older brother was likable, and as a youth he enjoyed tennis courts, a croquet lawn, maids, gardeners, stables, pets, and a happy childhood. In 1923 at the time of Irish independence, Beckett went to Trinity College to read French, graduated with first-class honors, and in 1928 went to the École Normale Supérieure in Paris as an English Assistant. The 1920s in Paris allowed him not only a change from the parochialism of his home but also an introduction to the post-war views on post-order, post-hope, post-belief, and pre-postmodernism. Absurdism was a popular topic of the time.

Lois Gordon in *The World of Samuel Beckett, 1906—1946* (1995) tells of the friendship of James Joyce and Beckett. They liked each other, took long walks, smoked cigars, drank, enjoyed such repartee as "What do you think of the next life?" "I don't think much of this one." It was a time when writing was fragmented, when language was said to be a distortion of experience, when artists painted blank canvases, and Cézanne became popular in the very museums which once had banned his work.

Nancy Cunard's Hours Press published Beckett's *Whorescope*, fewer than one hundred lines of arcane incoherence which Beckett described: "I wrote the first half before dinner . . . had a guzzle of salad and Chambertin at the Cochon de Lait, went back to the École and finished it about three in the morning. . . . That's how it was and them were the days." One of his sexual partners, Peggy Guggenheim, called him Oblomov. A friend, Walter Lowenfels, said Beckett, who had begun to drink heavily and refused to hold a job, told him,

> All I want to do is sit on my arse
> and fart and think of Dante.

After forty-two rejections, *Murphy*, his first novel, was published in 1938, and it eliminated the usual elements of plot, character, and setting. One reviewer described it as "verbal acrobatics . . . too allusive to be generally comprehensible," but its royalties allowed him to pay his debts. Also in 1938, Beckett, stabbed by a neighborhood pimp, almost died and was possibly saved by a young woman who came to his assistance. She, it transpired, was Suzanne Deschevaux-Dumesnil and became his companion, then his wife. The two joined the Resistance, and, although he was awarded the *Croix de Guerre* and the *Médaille de la Résistance*, he kept the honors quiet for over thirty years, feeling war was dumb as well as distracting to a writer.

Eugen Weber, author of *The Hollow Years: France in the 1930s* (1996), remarks about Beckett's war service, "Rejecting the humanism of grand principles and sentimentalism, Beckett was a moralist of impotence, rather like Camus—but, unlike Camus, of impotence asserted. Anti-idealists can have ideals, too." Beckett once heard Jung speak, Weber has written, but the people who entertained him most were the Marx Brothers, Charlie Chaplin, Laurel and Hardy, and Buster Keaton. Little wonder that in 1969, Beckett came up with his thirty-second play, *Breath*, described by Weber as "a pile of rubbish, a breath, and then a cry." Weber finds that the composer John Cage had much in common with Beckett, for Cage in a Beckett-like serious prank wrote *Imaginary Landscapes* for twelve randomly tuned radios, and his composition entitled *4'3"* is one in which the performer does not play.

According to the Irish poet John Montague, Beckett included "God bless" in his greetings, an "uncanny salutation, a familiar Irish phrase made strange by his worldwide reputation for godlessness." Beckett wrote principally in French and lived in Paris. Jim Herrick, in *New Humanist* (January, 1990), states that Beckett's "bleak vision (like that of Philip Larkin on a smaller scale represented the negative minimum of our beliefs—that we are alone in the universe except for one another, that there is no hope in the end, and that there is nothing of value except what we give it. From this minimum, however, he created works of such pathos and beauty that he almost contradicted himself."

He was awarded the Nobel Prize in 1969, after the success of his *Waiting for Godot* (1952, written in French, and 1956, translated by Beckett into English), in which he comes across as a philosopher. Martin Seymour-Smith notes, ". . . for there is as little more than philosophy in it as is possible under theatrical conditions. However, these conditions, like the ones created by fiction, imply an inescapable empiricism: paradoxically, the philosophy is filtered through the reality, if only of the illusion, and becomes a parody of itself. God is more Charl*ot* (Chaplin: real fun) than 'God,' who is conspicuously not there in any form." At the play's end, the joke seems to be on the audience, which has assumed Godot is "God." But God is not there in any form, and this is one of Beckett's purposes. "If Godot were God I would have called him that," Beckett said in a little known statement.

Murphy, one of Beckett's memorable characters, requested in his fictional will, "With regard to the disposal of these my body, mind, and soul, I desire that they be burnt and placed in a paper bag and brought to the Abbey Theatre, Lr Abbey Street, Dublin, and without pause in what the great and good Lord Chesterfield calls the necessary house, where their happiest hours have been spent, on the right as one goes down into the pit, and I desire that the chain be pulled upon them, if possible during the performance of a piece, the whole to be executed without ceremony or show of grief." Except that when his friend Cooper lugged the ashes but stopped off at a pub, a fight ensued and the bag of ashes scattered so that "by closing time the body, mind, and soul of Murphy were freely distributed over the floor of the saloon; and before another dayspring greyened the earth had been swept away with the sand, the beer, the butts, the glass, the matches, the spits, the vomit."

Unlike his works and life, Beckett's own funeral and burial were traditional. {CE; TRI; TYD; Eugene Weber, "The Anti-Hero as Hero," *The New Republic*, 6 May 1996}

Beckford, William (1759—1844)

Beckford, the son of the Lord Mayor of London, wrote *Vathek* (1786), an Oriental story written in French and erroneously said to have been written in three days. The work celebrates pederastic love. Melville, who cleared his character of many gossipy charges, stated that Beckford "leant towards Agnosticism." He believed in an "Eternal Power" and rejected all creeds.

In 1784 when his powerful uncle, Lord Loughborough, a chief justice, revealed Beckford's love for a cousin, William ("Kitty") Courtenay, Beckford for sixty years was forced to live as an outcast. Some of the boys he loved remained his friends, but he is said never to have adjusted to the ruin of his reputation. Beckford bought Gibbon's library and wrote about Italy, Spain, and Portugal. {GL; RAT}

Beckman, David (20th Century)

Beckman, while a member of the Doubters' Club at Amherst College in Massachusetts, was one of the founding members of Campus Freethought Alliance. {*International Humanist News*, December 1996}

Beckwith, Burnham P(utnam) (Born 1904)

Beckwith in 1984 wrote *The Decline of US Religious Faith, 1912 to 1984*. {*Free Inquiry*, Spring 1986}

BED

- Politics doesn't make strange bedfellows: marriage does.

—Groucho Marx

Bedborough, George (19th Century)

Bedborough, a secularist, was the first editor of *The Adult, The Journal of Sex* (1897). One of its contributors, Lucy Stewart, argued with consistency that freethinkers ought to support free love on the utilitarian grounds that it would maximize happiness, since with birth control there would be no need to worry about producing unwanted children.

In 1898, when he was arrested for selling Havelock Ellis's *Sexual Inversion*, a Free Press Defence Committee formed, members of which included Grant Allen, George Bernard Shaw, Edward Carpenter, Hyndman, Foote, Frank Podmore, W. M. Thompson, Truelove, Holyoake, Robertson, and Herbert Burrows. However, at his trial Bedborough capitulated and pleaded guilty. *The Adult*, which had been taken over by Henry Seymour, came to an end upon Bedborough's pleading guilty. {RSR}

Beddoes, Thomas (1760—1808)

A physician, Beddoes was reader in chemistry at Oxford (1788—1792) but resigned, under pressure, on account of his sympathies with the French Revolution and his attacks on the clergy. A deist and friend of Erasmus Darwin, Beddoes was an enthusiast for human progress. Said Southey, "From Beddoes I hoped for more good for the human race than any other individual." {RAT}

Bedingfield, Richard (1823—1876)

Bedingfield was a pantheistic writer. He wrote as "B.T.W.R." in *National Reformer* and in 1870 established *Freelight*. {BDF}

Beecher, John (20th Century)

Beecher, a Southern freethinker from a prominent New England family, wrote *Collected Poems, 1924—1974* (1974) and *Tomorrow is a Day* (1980). {*Freethought History* #14, 1995}

BEELZEBUB or Beelzebul

Beelzebub is the name in the New Testament for the chief of the devils, or Satan. The Old Testament mentions Beelzebub (Baal Zebub) once, as a "lord of flies" of the Philistine city of Ekron. In Milton's *Paradise Lost*, Beelzebub was a fallen angel ranking next to Satan. {ER}

Beem, Albert Kent (20th Century)

Beem, a freethinker, wrote *Inspirations of a Free Religious Movement* (1901) and *The Natural vs. the Supernatural in Religion* (1904?). {GS}

Beesley, Winfield (20th Century)

Beesley, a freethinker, wrote *A Brave New Look at Belief* (1973). {GS}

Beesly, Edward Spencer (1831—1915)

An English positivist, Beesly taught history in 1860 at University College in London. He was one of the translators of Comte's *System of Positive Polity*. {BDF; RAT}

Beeson, Jack (1921—)

An American composer in the department of music at Columbia University in New York City, Beeson responded to the present author as follows concerning humanism:

> Your inquiry and its additional material is welcome, for it justifies (to me) my long-standing aversion to the word humanism. I've always thought it had some of the disadvantages—perhaps only to those who have learned German, rather than having been born into that language—of *Geist* and such. I think it is striking that your respondents do not so much wrestle with the word itself as to seize upon an adjective—somewhat predictably, in most cases.

Beeson has been both a Guggenheim and Fulbright fellow. {WAS, 28 August 1992}

Beethoven, Ludwig van (1770—1827)

Beethoven "used Humanist themes such as his *Third Symphony* (the *Eroica*, 1804), celebrating the memory of a great man; his *Fifth Symphony* (1808), portraying the triumph of mankind over fate; and his *Ninth Symphony* (1824—1826), assertive of the brotherhood of man and attaining its climax in a stirring setting to music of the poet Schiller's 'Ode to Joy.' There is no doubt that Beethoven himself was a real democrat at a time when it was not easy to be one," according to Corliss Lamont.

When about forty, Beethoven became totally deaf, but he continued to compose until his death. Robertson points out that Beethoven had no formal religion but believed in three ancient, pantheistic formulas: "I am that which is"; "I am all that is, that was, that shall be"; and "He is alone by Himself, and to Him alone do all things owe their being." When his friend Moscheles at the end of his arrangement of *Fidelio* (1805) wrote, "Fine, with God's help," Beethoven added, "O man, help thyself." Comments Robertson, "His reception of the Catholic sacraments *in extremis* was not his act. He had left to mankind a purer and a more lasting gift than either the creeds or the philosophies of his age."

Sir George Macfarren, writing of Beethoven in the *Imperial Dictionary of Universal Biography*, speaks of him as a "free thinker," saying the remarkable mass in C "might scarcely have proceeded from an entirely orthodox thinker." Sir George Grove, in his *Dictionary of Music and Musicians*, says, "Formal religion he apparently had none" and "the Bible does not appear to have been one of his favorite books." McCabe flatly says that Beethoven, reared a Catholic, quit the Church, was an apostate from their creed, and adopted Goethe's pantheism. Agreeing, Nicolas Walter labels Beethoven a pantheist, not a Christian.

Beethoven was known to have been quite boorish, particularly because of his deafness. No girlfriends are known to have been attracted to him. Rather, his attention allegedly was focused on a young nephew named Karl, who not only refused to return the affection but may have attempted to blackmail Beethoven by threatening to publicize such advances.

After enduring four surgical operations and expecting a fifth, Beethoven did write to Moscheles of his "hard doom." Ten days before his death, he wrote his friend Moscheles that he calmly accepted his fate "and only constantly pray to God that his holy will may ordain that while thus condemned to suffer death in life, I may be shielded from want. The Almighty will give me strength to endure my lot, however severe and terrible, with resignation to his will."

As pointed out by Robertson, Beethoven's deistic phrasing was followed by an example of his final comfort, "the noble liberality of the [London] Philharmonic Society," which had promptly sent him £100 in his need. When Beethoven was dying, he yielded to the pressure of Catholic friends and let a priest administer his sacraments. But when the priest left the room, Beethoven said, in the Latin words of the ancient Roman theater, "Applaud, my friends, the comedy is over." An apologist said Beethoven meant the comedy of life was over, not the comedy of a priest administering sacraments, an argument McCabe found implausible.

Two versions exist concerning his final day. Biographer Robert H. Schauffler wrote that the day after Beethoven signed his will, he was given a bottle of wine as a present and remarked, "Pity, pity—too late," then lapsed into unconsciousness. A violent thunderstorm began that afternoon and, following a loud crack of thunder, Beethoven rose in his bed, wide-eyed, lifting his right hand in a clenched and defiant fist, then fell back, relinquishing his hold on life.

Denying this, Nicolas Slonimsky, author of *Music Since 1900* and *My First Hundred Years*—he lived to the age of 102—checked with the Vienna weather bureau. Their records, he reported, did confirm that an electric storm had raged while Beethoven was *in extremis*. However, Slonimsky added that "the story that he raised his clenched fist aloft as a gesture of defiance to an over-bearing Heaven must be relegated to fantasy; he was far too feeble either to clench his fist or to raise his arm." (Slonimsky also found that, contrary to myth, snow did not fall at Mozart's funeral, for it was a clear day according to the Austrian weather bureau.) {AA; Alexander Cockburn, *The Nation*, 29 January 1996; CE; CL; HNS2; JM; JMR; JMRH; TSV; TYD}

BEETLES

Insects of the order of Coleoptera are the largest of the insect orders. Over 330,000 described species exist, the secret of their diversity being that as they evolved they developed a taste for flowers. Or so states Dr. Brian D. Farrell, a curator at the Museum of Comparative Zoology at Harvard University. Noting that the evolution of new species adapting to unexplored habitats or new ways of life accounts for much of the diversity of life, he told *New York Times* reporter Carol Kaesuk Yoon (28 July 1998), "Here was this huge, underexploited resource, the flowering plants. Insects that were able to evolve to make the shift to eat them, enjoyed the fruits, so to speak."The reason there are so many species on earth is, he feels, quite simple: Diversity begets diversity. It is no coincidence that the flowering plants are themselves so diverse because the beetles and other insects attacking them might have provided pressure for the evolution of new better-defended plant species. More plants led to the spawning of more beetles.

At the base of the beetle family tree were leaf beetles, snout beetles, and long-horned beetles that still eat the primitive gymnospers that they ate 200 million years ago when dinosaurs ruled the earth.

"Swarming the world," Yoon wrote in her interview with Dr. Farrell, "is a dazzling array of shapes, colors and sizes from gargantuan Goliath beetles to jewel-like tortoise beetles to dearly family ladybugs, beetles, with more species than any other plan or animal group on earth, are the undeniable rules of the planet."

Asked by theologians what he had gleaned from biology about The Creator, J. B. S. Haldane, an atheist and rationalist, responded in a way they could understand: "He must have had an inordinate fondness for beetles."

Beevers, David (20th Century)

Beevers is a writer for the *Atheist Network Journal*, which is edited by Victor King.

BEFORE THE CHRISTIAN ERA: See entry for B.C.E.

Begbie, Elphinstone Waters [Major-General] (1842—1919)

Begbie became a Brigadier-General in 1895 and served in the Abyssinian Campaign, the Duffla Expedition, and the Third Burmese War. He was a supporter of the Rationalist Press Association. {RAT}

Beggs, Keith (20th Century)

Beggs, when an executive director of the American Humanist Association, signed Humanist Manifesto II. {HM2}

BEHEADINGS

Saudi Arabia, for Islamic religious infractions, beheaded an average of 20.2 individuals per month in 1995. The average number per month in 1996 was 1.5, according to *Playboy* (January 1997).

Behmer, E. H. (20th Century)

In the 1950s, Behmer was a correspondent (Sweden) for *The Humanist.*

Behn, Aphra (1640—1689)

Behn was said by Vita Sackville-West to be the first English novelist to have supported herself by writing. *The Rover* (1677) was humorous and bawdy. *Oroonoko* (1688), based on her experiences in Surinam, is said to have been the first English philosophical novel.

Although married several times and widowed early, Behn had a relationship with John Hoyle, a gay man who was the center of many scandals. She was a friend of Nell Gwyn, the King's mistress. Known as "the incomparable Astrea," the name she used when she was Charles II's spy in Antwerp, she wrote homoerotic verse and was a dramatist at a time when women were just beginning to act in the theatres.

In *The Golden Age* Behn wrote, "[T]he gods, by teaching us religion first, first set the world at odds." {BYD; CE; GL}

Behrendt, Walter Curt (1884—1945)

When he signed Humanist Manifesto II, Behrendt was Vice President of the European Parliament, West Germany. {HM2}

Beier, Immy (20th Century)

At a 1997 seminar of the European Humanist Professionals held in London, Beier described her work as a counselor for humanists in the military. Trauma is like a knife which cuts through you, she said, and it is necessary to counsel those who surround the victims as well. {*International Humanist News*, September 1997}

Beit, Alfred (1853—1906)

Beit was the son of a German Jew who practiced the Lutheran religion, but his sons rejected both creeds. A close associate of Cecil Rhodes, Beit made a large fortune and left £2,000,000 for charitable and educational purposes and the development of South Africa.

His brother, Sir **Otto Beit** (1865—1930), also a freethinker, carried out the benevolent plans and was also a Trustee of the Rhodes Trust. {RE}

Bekker, Balthasar (1634—1698)

A Dutch rationalist, Bekker obtained a doctorate of divinity but was then accused of Soccinianism. Fleeing to Amsterdam, he wrote *World Bewitched* (1691), a work in which witchcraft and the power of demons are denied. He was then deposed from his place in the Church. Bekker was said to have been ugly, even to have looked like the devil he did not believe in. {BDF; RAT}

BELGIAN HUMANISTS

Belgium has the following groups and journals:

• *Centre d'Action Laique*, ULB, Boulevard Du Triumphe, 1050 Brussels

• *De Vrijzinnige Lezer* (a monthly in Dutch), Lange Leemstraat 57, B 2000 Antwerpen

• *De Vrijzinnige Micro*, Lange Leemstraat 57, B 2000 Antwerpen

• *Espace de Libertés*, Campus de la Plaine, ULB-CP 236, Avenue Arnaud Fraiteur, 1050 Brussels <espace@cal.ulb.ac.be>.

• *Federation des Amis de la Morale Laique*, Rue du Meridien 17, 1030 Brussels

• *Het Vrije Woord*, Lange Leemstraat 57, 2018 Antwerp <human@glo.be>. Contact is Marianne Marchand.

• *Humanistisch Jongreren Service* (IHEU), Rogierstraat 134, 12110 Brussels, Belgium.

• *La Pensée et les Hommes,* Avenue Adolpfe Buyl 105, 1050 Brussels

• *Lique de l'Enseignement et de l'Education Permante* (IHEU), Blvd. M. Lemonnier 110, 1000 Brussels

• *Mores*, a bi-monthly in Dutch of Humanistisch Verbond Belgie, is at Lange Leemstraat 57, 2018 Antwerpen

• *UCOS Nieuwsbrief* is at <lawauter@vub.ac.be>.

• *Unie Vrijzinnige Verenigingen* (Union of Humanist Associations) is a full voting member in Brussels of the International Humanist and Ethical Union. It operates as an umbrella organization within the Flemish part of Belgium and pays particular attention to moral counselling, youth and educational matters, and the separation of church and state.

• University Centre for Development Cooperation, Pleinlaan 2, Gebouwy, 1050 Brussels

Belgian astronomer Jean Dommanget signed Humanist Manifesto 2000.

In 1997, a five-floor headquarters of the *Centre d'Action Laïque* (CAL) was opened. The inauguration of the building was attended by Charles Picqué, Ministre-Président of the government, and Hervé Hasquin, Minister for the Brussels Capital Region. The European Humanist Federation, which now has two offices in the building, was represented by its Secretary General, Claude Wachtelaer, and Treasurer Werner Schultz. The International Humanist and Ethical Union (IHEU) was represented by its President Rob Tielman and Babu Gogineni. Philippe Grollet, the president of the Centre, spoke about the high profile humanism has in Belgium.

CAL was founded on 29 March 1969. Its monthly magazine *Espace de Libertés* has a circulation of ten thousand. It also publishes a bi-monthly *Passarelles.* CAL's Vice President Georges Liénard represented the IHEU and the European Humanist Federation at a 1997 International Symposium on Bio-Ethics that had been organized by the Council of Europe. The Flemish-speaking equivalent of the CAL is the *Unie Vrijzinnige Verenigingen*, which coordinates the activities of about thirty Flemish-speaking humanist groups.

The non-believer community in Belgium is represented by *Counseil Central Laïque* (CLL), a ten-member committee responsible for providing moral counseling within the armed forces, at the Brussels airport, and for representing the secularist case to the federal authorities.

Humanistisch Verbond is a full member of the IHEU, its largest individual member organization with almost eighty branches in Flanders.

Laïque Humanistische Präsenz was formed in 1988 to work in the German-speaking parts of Belgium. Its work covers nine communes in the German-speaking parts of Belgium. On the Web: <http:www.ulb.ac.be/cal/>. For information on the Web about *Humanistisch Verbond-Vlaanderen*: <http://134.184.16.171/>.

BELGIAN UNITARIANS

Unitarians in Brussels can be contacted by telephoning (32) 2-260 0226. Ulrich Kroener is at <ulrich@www.eiba.be>.

BELIEF

"Belief, when it is not simply traditional, is a product of several factors: desire, evidence, and iteration," Bertrand Russell wrote in 1938. Lord Russell added,

> When either the desire or the evidence is nil, there will be no belief; when there is no outside assertion, belief will only arise in exceptional characters, such as founders of religions, scientific discov-

ers, and lunatics. To produce a mass belief, of the sort that is socially important, all three elements must exist in some degree; but if one element is increased while another is diminished, the resulting amount of belief may be unchanged.

More propaganda is necessary to cause acceptance of a belief for which there is little evidence than of one for which the evidence is strong, if both are equally satisfactory to desire; and so on.

Freethinkers are frequently asked if they "believe" in God. Why, they respond, are they never asked if they believe in clouds or electricity? "Beliefs," noted sci-fi author Robert Heinlein, "get in the way of learning."

Mark Twain, discussing belief, wrote that "Loyalty to petrified opinion never yet broke a chain or freed a human soul." Asked if he believed in infant baptism, retorted, "Hell, I've *seen* it!"

Similarly, Steve Allen says he does not *believe* 2 + 2 = 4. He *knows* it. To *believe*, he reasons, is to reveal that you do not *know*, that you simply *believe*. In such a case, you might *believe* almost anything. {Lee Eisler, *The Quotable Bertrand Russell*}

BELIEVERS

- The believer is happy; the doubter is wise.

—Hungarian Proverb

- The most costly of all follies is to believe passionately in the palpably not true. It is the chief occupation of mankind.

—H. L. Mencken

- Religious beliefs and behavior can themselves be psychopathological.

—David Berman

- If there were a verb meaning "to believe falsely," it would not have any significant first person, present indicative.

—Ludwig Wittgenstein

Belinski, Vissarion: See entry for V. G. Byelinsky

Bell, Alexander Graham (1847—1922)

Bell was the inventor of the telephone and devices directed to the needs of the deaf. Although he attended Presbyterian and Episcopalian services, in 1902 he wrote his wife that "I am a Unitarian Agnostic."

In a 1998 biography, *Alexander Graham Bell*, James Mackay regaled readers with tales about Bell's inventions. Jean-Louis Forain, who had one of the first telephones in Paris, invited Edgar Degas for dinner and when he jumped to answer the ringing device Degas was amused: "Ah. The telephone. Now I understand—it rings, you jump." Queen Victoria in England was given two phones made of ivory and trimmed in gold. Bell answered the phone by saying not "Hello" but "Ahoy!" and was said to have been a night owl, a man who loved solitude. His mother had been next to deaf at the age of thirteen, forced to listen through an ear trumpet. Her son dropped out of school at the age of fifteen but showed his genius by inventing a device which helped the deaf hear. He taught the deaf speech, lip-reading, and anything else that might enhance their lives.

"Mr. Watson–come here–I want to see you," he told an assistant on 10 March 1876 in the first successful telephone call. Few know that in 1882 he invented a "vacuum jacket," today known as the iron lung. He also helped perfect the gramophone, developed a hydrofoil boat, and ordinarily worked from noon until 4 a.m.

Critics object to his view of eugenics, for in an 1883 lecture he proposed, "Those who believe as I do that the production of a defective race of human beings would be a great calamity to the world will examine carefully the causes that lead to the intermarriages of the deaf with the object of applying a remedy."

Bell died of diabetes. On 4 August 1922 on the day of his funeral in Nova Scotia, all telephone service in the United States was stopped for one minute in his honor at exactly 6:25 p.m. {CE; *The New Yorker*, 18 May 1998; U; UU}

Bell, Burton C. (20th Century)

Bell is a recording artist, the lead singer of Fear Factory, a Death Metal band. Asked if he questioned religion, he answered, "Totally." Asked if he is a non-believer? "I'm agnostic, really. I have no belief. I believe in personal spirituality, but letting a group of people tell you how you should worship or what your spirituality is is wrong." {CA}

Bell, Daniel (1919—)

Bell, a Harvard sociologist and political philosopher, wrote *Marxian Socialism in the United States* (1996). When asked about the seven categories of humanism, he responded to the present author: "May I add one category to your seven with which you have begun? This would be the category, 'All Too Humanism.' "

{WAS, 12 April 1989}

Bell, Evans: See Thomas Evans Bell.

Bell, J. D. (20th Century)

Bell, interested in the relationship between Jews and rationalists, has written on the topic for *The American Rationalist*.

Bell, Joann (20th Century)

Bell, the Executive Director of the American Civil Liberties Union of Oklahoma, is a freethinker who has written for *Freethought Today*.

Bell, Paul T. (20th Century)

Bell is editor in England of *The Sceptic* and correspondent on bio-astronomy for Mensa's newsletter *Spacesignal*. He has written in *New Humanist* concerning philosophical considerations about whether humans are the most advanced, in intelligence and technology, species on this planet.

Bell, Thomas Evans (1825—1887)

Bell, a major in the Madras army, wrote *Task of To-Day* (1851) and became Deputy-Commissioner of Police at Madras, retiring in 1865. He once contemplated selling his commission to devote himself to freethought propaganda, but he was deterred by the advice of his friends. An agnostic and secularist, of Holyoake's school, Bell wrote, "The age of faith has passed away, and Christianity is now a mere abstraction." {BDF; GS; RAT; VI}

Bell, William S. (Born 1832)

Bell, a Pennsylvania-born Methodist minister who was denounced for mixing politics and religion, preached in 1873 in the Universalist Church of New Bedford, Massachusetts. But in 1874 during his final service, he renounced Christianity and became a freethought lecturer. Bell, who wrote the *Handbook of Freethought* (1890), wrote about the French Revolution and wrote strong anti-slavery works. {BDF; PUT}

Bell-Cox, James A. (20th Century)

Bell-Cox is President of Atheists and Agnostics of Wisconsin. On the Web: <mbr@execpc.com>.

Bellah, Robert Neelly (1927—)

Bellah, along with Frederick E. Greenspan, has written in *Uncivil Religion* (1986) about the interreligious hostility in America between Catholics and Protestants, Christians and Jews, new religions and old religions, and liberals and conservatives in the same denominations.

Bellant, Russ (1949—)

Bellant, a freelance researcher and writer in Detroit, Michigan, has written books describing the political right wing. In *Free Inquiry*

(Winter 1995-1996), he described a Christian men's movement, Promise Keepers, which has been backed by the Christian Right. Bellant is author of *Old Nazis, the New Right, and the Republican Party* (1991).

Bellman, Carl Michael (1740—1795)

Bellman, a Swedish poet, was an unbeliever. (See entry for Scandinavian Unbelievers.)

Belot, Gustave (Born 1859)

Belot was a French positivist philosopher, a Chevalier of the Legion of Honour, Officer of Public Instruction, and member of *the Conseil Supérieur de l'Instruction Publique.* He translated Mill's *Logic* (1897) and wrote various positivist works. {RAT}

Bellows, Henry Whitney (1814—1881)

The first minister of All Soul's Unitarian Church at Broadway near Prince Street in New York City, Bellows was appointed by President Lincoln to head the Sanitary Commission. His influence led to the formation of the Unitarian Association, composed of individual Unitarians, not churches as the National Conference of Unitarian Churches had been. {CE; U; U&U; UU}

BELTRANE: May 1st, Beltrane, is a Pagan holiday. See entry for Halloween.

Benaceraff, Baruj (1920-)

Benacerraf was born in Venezuela, became a naturalized United States of America citizen in 1943, and served in the American Army from 1946 to 1948. He received the Nobel Prize (physiology) in 1960 and currently works for the Dana-Farber Cancer Institute in Massachusetts. Benacerraf signed Humanist Manifesto 2000.

Benavente y Martínez, Jacinto (1866—1954)

A Spanish dramatist, Benavente y Martínez was awarded the 1922 Nobel Prize in Literature. *Los intereses creados* (1907, *Bonds of Interest)* led him to be called "creator of the modern Spanish theater." In 1932, after the anti-clerical revolution which he applauded, he produced a play, *Santa Russia* (*Holy Russia*), in the preface of which he praised the materialism and atheism of the Russians. He described himself as a materialist. Benavente y Martínez wrote social satires, psychological dramas, children's plays, and allegorical-morality plays, but he was at his best in satirizing the aristocratic and upper middle-class life. {CE; JM; RE}

Benbassat, Jacques (20th Century)

Benbassat is associated with Secular Humanists of Greenville, South Carolina. (See entry for South Carolina Humanists.) {FD}

Bencze, Marton (20th Century)

Bencze is Bishop of the Hungarian Unitarian Church. (See entry for Hungarian Unitarians.)

Bendana, David (20th Century)

Bendana, while a student at Florida International University, was one of the founders of Campus Freethought Alliance. {*International Humanist News*, December 1996}

Ben-David, Joseph (1920—)

Ben-David, who was born in Prague of Jewish parents, became a Unitarian when young. At the time of the Nazi invasion of Czechoslovakia, he emigrated to Palestine where like Martin Buber he worked for cordial relations between Arabs and Jews.

Upon moving to the United States, he became active in the New York Chapter of the American Humanist Association, becoming its president in the 1960s and leading it more toward a religious humanism. Its previous roots had been more directed toward a naturalistic, non-theistic humanism. As such, he developed many sensitivity and encounter groups that confronted problems such as intimacy, sexual deprivation, and a healthy sex life (which were frowned upon by some of the earlier members), increasing the membership dramatically. Ben-David conducted hundreds of meetings and involved dozens of individuals, as had Charles Francis Potter in the 1920s and 1930s.

In 1970 Ben-David married **Alyson Ben-David** in a wedding ceremony which Corliss Lamont conducted. The couple is active in the Fourth Universalist Society of New York City. {HNS2}

Bender, Dennis (20th Century)

Bender is associated with the Capital District Humanist Society (Council for Secular Humanism). (See entry for New York Atheists, Freethinkers, Humanists.) {FD}

Bender, Hedwig (Born 1854)

A German writer, Bender was a conspicuous worker in the German woman-movement. She wrote a number of philosophical and rationalist works. Bender was a monist or pantheist (in the sense of Spinoza). {RAT}

Bender, Robert (1945—)

Bender is an Australian humanist, atheist, and lecturer who was adopted into a Jewish family. After reading some of Bertrand Russell's writings in 1965, he became an atheist. The author of seventeen textbooks on business subjects, he is active with the Victoria humanists and delivers an annual lecture at the Atheist Society's series of Melbourne University. {SWW}

Bender, Wilhelm (Born 1845)

A German rationalist and professor of theology at Bonn, Bender created a sensation at the Luther centenary in 1883 by declaring that the work of the Reformation was incomplete and must be carried on by the rationalists. {BDF}

Bendz, Fredrik (1973—)

Bendz studied pharmacology at the Biomedical Centre in Uppsala, Sweden. He plays basketball, says he is 6' 8" tall (204 cm.), weighs 205-210 pounds (94 kg.), and has size 47-48 shoes (13 in the United States, 12 in the United Kingdom). A dedicated humanist activist, he is webmaster for the Swedish humanist association. As an indication of his personable character, he likes heavy metal music, such as that of Uriah Heep, Black Sabbath, and Whitesnake; his favorite author is Tolkien; the people he admires are his grandmother, Einstein (despite his Zionism), Bertrand Russell, Darwin, Julian Huxley (despite his advocating eugenics), Voltaire, David Coverdale (despite his Christianity), Ken Hensley, and Michael Jordan. Bendz is one of the most articulate ethical humanists of anyone his age in any nation. He has written

> In my teenage years I considered theists to be stupid. I believed that no intelligent man could believe in superstition, which I thought religion was. Later, I came to realize that, although it is admittedly irrational, theism satisfies certain needs in people. However, it leads man in the wrong direction. When I discovered secular humanism, I found the right direction for man to fulfill his needs without turning to the irrational and absurd theories of gods.
>
> My basic philosophy is closely related to that of Julian Huxley. Everything in the world is part of an evolutionary process, and reli-

gious needs can only be satisfied by evolving all religion. This must be done in the light of science, not faith, and the more religions evolve the closer they will come to atheism. The ultimate religion, however, is secular humanism, for it has the highest image of god (none) and does not claim absolute certainty. Humanism is but a catalyzer of the evolution of religion, not an endpoint in itself.

God is an old man in the sky who has a beard? No theist today honestly believes God to be a man sitting in the sky, running the machinery of the universe. But whatever image theists have of their God is anthropomorphic. Whatever qualities they give their God, they are more or less painting a picture of a man with a long beard. The greater a religion's idea of God is, the further it is from an old bearded man and the closer it is to atheism. If you remove all human characteristics from somebody's image of God, nothing remains. Nothing but atheism.

For more autobiographical details, in which Bendz lists why he hates war, injustice, religion, "and everything else that hurts people," see his webpage: <http://www.update.uu.se/~fbendz>.
E-mail: <fbendz@update.uu.se>.

Benedict, Ruth: See entry for Margaret Mead.

Beneke, Friedrich Edward (1798—1854)

Beneke was a German philosopher, a critical empiricist who was opposed to metaphysical speculation (like that of Hegel). He regarded soul (a complex of forces) and body as two aspects of one reality, and he held that we have no knowledge of the nature of "the unconditioned."

Beneke's *Lehrbuch der Psychologie* (1833) and other works had an influence on German psychology and pedagogy.

Benes, Eduard [President] (1884—1948)

Benes, the president of Czechoslovakia (1935—1938; 1946—1948), adopted the political and social philosophy of T. G. Masaryk. After the Communist coup of February 1948, he reluctantly endorsed the new regime but resigned in June on the ground of illness, refusing to sign the new constitution and dying shortly afterward. Benes was an active freethinker who contributed to *Volná Myslenka*, organ of the freethought movement. {TRI}

Benham, Agnes (c. 1850—1910?)

Benham was an early Australian secularist, a member of the Australasian Secular Association in the 1910s. {SWW}

Benjamin, Lemoyne (19th Century)

Benjamin, a freethinker, wrote *A Commentary on Matthew* (c. 1895). {GS}

Benn, Alfred William (1843—1915)

Benn's *History of English Rationalism in the Nineteenth Century* is a classic study of rationalism and freethought. An agnostic, Benn was an honorary associate of the British Rationalist Press Association and a member of the Society for the Promotion of Hellenic Studies. {FUK; RAT; RE}

Bennet, Margaret (20th Century)

Bennet is active with the Secular Humanists of Merrimack Valley. (See entry for New Hampshire Humanists.) {FD}

Bennett, Angeline (20th Century)

Bennett is author of *Thinking is Good for the Mind*, a collection of atheistic poetry.

Bennett, Arnold (1867—1931)

According to David Tribe, Bennett was an avowed freethinker. Bennett wrote realistic novels about the industrial Midlands. He was influenced by Zola's literary naturalism. Among his works were *The Old Wives' Tale* (1908) and *These Twain* (1916). With Edward Knoblock, he wrote the play, *Milestones* (1912), and he also wrote the successful *Great Adventure* (1913). {CE; TRI}

Bennett, DeRobigne Mortimer (1818—1882)

An American freethought publisher and author, Bennett lived in Cincinnati for a number of years in the 1850s, manufacturing proprietary medicines and becoming wealthy. He started as a Shaker but founded the atheistic *Truth Seeker* in 1873. Anthony Comstock had Bennett arrested for sending a pamphlet by Ezra H. Heywood, a birth-control work, "Cupid's Yokes," through the mails. A tract entitled "An Open Letter to Jesus Christ" was read in court to bias the jury. A petition bearing 200,000 names was presented to President Hayes asking Bennett's release, but was not acceded to.

Bennett was jailed in Albany Penitentiary. Upon his release, he was greeted by a large reception at Chickering Hall, then selected as U. S. delegate to the International Freethought Congress at Brussels. His admirers sent him on a voyage around the world, after which he wrote *A Truthseeker's Voyage Round the World* (1882?). {BDF; EU, Gordon Stein; FUK; FUS; GS; PUT; RAT; RSR}

Bennett, Eliza Jane (1894—1983)

"Dolly" Bennett was a rationalist, an atheist, and the honorary secretary-treasurer and literature secretary of the Rationalist Association of New South Wales in Australia. She was active in arranging for "outback" children to "see the sea."

Bennett, (Enoch) Arnold (1867—1931)

Bennett was a British novelist who "was clearly Humanist in his philosophy," according to Corliss Lamont. Influenced by Zola's literary naturalism, Bennett wrote about the grim, sometimes sordid, lives of shopkeepers and potters in the "Five Towns," an imaginary manufacturing district in northern England, an example of which is *The Old Wives' Tale* (1908).

He was an honorary associate of the Rationalist Press Association (RPA), which in 1899 had been founded by Charles A. Watts. His agnostic views are found in *The Human Machine*. {CL; JM; RAT; RE}

Bennett, Gary L. (20th Century)

Bennett, in "Preventing School Violence: Is Religion the Answer?" (*Free Inquiry*, Fall 1999), notes that religionists "with their Bronze Age myths have had almost two thousand years to eliminate evil from Western civilization—and they have failed miserably." An aerospace consultant, he wrote *The Star Sailors* (1980).

Bennett, Henry Scott (1877—1959)

An Australian, Bennett from 1946 to 1948 edited a Sydney publication, *Ingersoll News*. A rationalist, socialist, and atheist, he was the first notable Australian-born freethinker. One of the finest of public speakers, he discoursed on social issues such as birth control, sexual mores, venereal disease, and mental health. In 1936, Bennett became secretary of the Rationalist Association of New South Wales. He considered that the sole inspiration of the world is found in "the ascertainment of the facts of the universe, the facing of those facts, and the doing of justice according to those facts."

Upon his death, his ashes were scattered on the Northern Suburbs cemetery, and his library was bequeathed to the National University. {FUK; SWW}

Bennett, John (20th Century)

Bennett, a Life Member of the Foundation for Freedom From Religion, taught at the University of Montana, Western Washington University, and the University of Arkansas. He received a Lifetime

Achievement Award from the College English Association, of which he was a President. Bennett is the founder and director of the Myers Center for the Study of Human Rights. {*Freethought Today*, November 1997}

Bennett, Mary (19th Century)
Bennett edited the atheistic *Truth Seeker* from 1882 to 1883.

Bennett, Rosemary (20th Century)
Bennett is active in Britain with the Harrow Humanists.

Bennett, Ruth (20th Century)
Bennett addressed the Tenth International Humanist and Ethical Union (IHEU) World Congress held in Buffalo (1988).

Bennion, Francis (Alan) (Roscoe) (20th Century)
Bennion is author of *The Sex Code: Morals for Moderns* and writes for *New Humanist.* He has little regard for the Golden Rule, quoting George Bernard Shaw to the effect that the only Golden Rule is "that there are no golden rules." Instead, Bennion invites humanists to study moral philosophy in earnest and develop an ethics "that starts to mean something" (*New Humanist*, February 1994). A past chairman of the Professional Association of Teachers, he has noted the following:

- Haggadah, the Talmud writer, said: "I've learned much from my teachers, and from my colleagues more than from my teachers, and from my students more than from all."
- Ralph Waldo Emerson wrote, perhaps with more wit than judgment: "I pay the schoolmaster, but 'tis the schoolboys educate my son."
- Stravinsky said that he had learned throughout his life as a composer chiefly through his mistakes, and pursuits of false assumptions, not by his exposure to founds of wisdom and knowledge.
- Beverley Nichols, educated at Marlborogh and Balliol, began his autobiography with the words "I am entirely self-taught."

Bennis, Warren Gameliel (1925—)
Bennis, a consultant and author on organizational development, is a secular humanist. On the staff of the School of Business of the University of Southern California, Bennis is a trustee of Antioch College and an editor of *Journal of Humanist Psychology.*

Benson, Andrew D. (20th Century)
Benson is author of *The True Origins of Christianity and the Bible.* On the Web: <http://www.prudentialpublishing.com/>. {*Secular Nation*, July-September 1999}

Benson, Steve (20th Century)
The name of Benson calls to mind the late President of the Church of Jesus Christ of Latter-day Saints, Ezra Taft Benson, who was U.S. Secretary of Agriculture from 1953 to 1961. His grandson, Pulitzer-prize-winning cartoonist Steve Benson, caused a sensation by leaving that church in 1993.

The *Arizona Republic*, for which he is a political cartoonist, published Benson's reasons, including his disagreement with the church over doctrine, history, faith, and treatment of women. Because of his outspokenness, threats were made that he would be expelled from the church, and attempts were made to intimidate his family into silence. When Benson's teenage daughter, the great-grand-daughter of the then current Mormon president, told her Mormon-youth religion class "that just as the denial of the Mormon priesthood to black men had been racist, so the denial of the Mormon priesthood to women was sexist," she said she received no adequate answer. Benson's wife, Mary Ann, "was appalled at a Mormon patriarchal system that protected pedophiles and minimized the pain suffered by victims of sexual abuse." The oldest son said, "Dad, I'll tell you why there's religion in the world—to control people by scaring them into believing that if they don't obey, they're going to hell." "Does this mean now we're Christian?" their six-year-old daughter asked when they left the church. Benson has reported that he is relieved at having left the church with its "offensive notions of polygamy, racial superiority, blood sacrifice, polytheism, and Masonic-cult temple rituals." Abandoning the church, the family found, was exhilarating and freeing.

In 1999 Benson received an award for excellence in the media at the Freedom From Religion Foundation conference in San Antonio, Texas. A winner of the Pulitzer Prize in 1993, he is a nationally syndicated cartoonist. {CA; *Freethought Today*, June-July 1994 and August 1999}

Bentham, Jeremy (1748—1832)
Bentham is author of *An Introduction to the Principles of Morals and Legislation* (1789). His utilitarianism strongly influenced John Stuart Mill. Mill's and Bentham's work, according to Corliss Lamont, "was quite humanistic in its total effect . . . the philosophic counterpart of the profit-motive theory of Adam Smith and other exponents of laissez-faire economics."

According to G. W. Foote, "Bentham exercised a profound influence on the party of progress for nearly two generations. He was the father of Philosophical Radicalism, which did so much to free the minds and bodies of the English people, and which counted among its swordsmen historians like Grote, philosophers like Mill, wits like Sydney Smith, journalists like Fonblanque, and politicians like Roebuck. As a reformer in jurisprudence, politicians like Roebuck. As a reformer in jurisprudence he has no equal. His brain swarmed with progressive ideas and projects for the improvement and elevation of mankind; and his fortune, as well as his intellect, was ever at the service of advanced causes. His skepticism was rather suggested than paraded in his multitudinous writings, but it was plainly expressed in a few special volumes. 'Not Paul, but Jesus,' published under the pseudonym of Camaliel Smith is a slashing attack on the Great Apostle. 'The Church of England Catechism Explained' is a merciless criticism of that great instrument for producing mental and political slaves. But the most thorough-going of Bentham's works was a little volume written by Grote from the Master's notes—'The Influence of Natural Religion on the Temporal Happiness of Mankind'—in which theology is assailed as the historic and necessary enemy of human liberty, enlighten."

His *Deontology, or the Science of Morality* was prohibited by the Vatican to be read, as were other of his works from 1819 to 1835. However, in none of his published works does the distinguished jurist profess atheism. Just the same, Berman as well as A. Benn make the case that Bentham was an atheist. McCabe, similarly, wrote that Bentham was "a declared atheist and in unpublished manuscripts he contemptuously called Christianity 'Juggernaut.' In collaboration with the historian Grote he, under the pseudonym Philip Beauchamp, wrote an *Analysis of the Influence of Natural Religion on the Temporal Happiness of Mankind* (1822), in which all religion, natural or supernatural, is attacked."

Bentham argued for a tolerant attitude to homosexuals. He attributed prejudice against them as being irrational hatred and antipathy. Louis Crompton of the University of Nebraska wrote that Bentham identified what is now called homophobia and directed his efforts to analyzing it: "In Bentham's view, it was this negative bias that needed explanation, not the phenomenon of same-sex desire. He finds its origin in religious asceticism inspired by the superstitious fear of a vengeful deity and in the desire of men who lead profligate lives to gain a reputation for virtue by damning a sin they are not inclined to. He excoriates the contemporary press for intensifying popular prejudice by an unvaried tone of vituperation that made rational debate impossible. With respect to contemporary literature. Bentham takes to task Henry Fielding, Tobias Smollett, and certain French and Germany novelists for introducing homophobic episodes in their fiction." For Bentham, so long as homosexual acts had no bad consequences such as unwanted pregnancies, abortion, infanticide, and female prostitution, there were "beneficial effects of certain of these modes of enjoyment."

Bentham pre-planned his death, writing in "Auto-Icon, or Further Uses of the Dead to the Living" about the ultimate of utilitarianism: preserving "a population of illustrious Auto-Icons," or preserved bodies. Upon his death, he directed that his body should be dissected in front of friends. His head was mummified. The skeleton was reconstructed and a wax head replaced the original, whereupon he is still displayed in his own clothes in University College, London. There is the wide-brimmed straw hat with a black ribbon tied in a bow, the black coat, the vest, the brown leather trousers, the woven leather slippers, brown gloves, and a ruff-embellished shirt. His skull resides in a small box, decorated with the college crest. Atop the philosopher's body is a surrogate head consisting of a puffy wax image. Twice a year the philosopher's followers still remove him from the case and in the main refectory of University College enjoy a Bentham Society dinner with their leader at the head of the table. Tom Weil has written, "After Bentham's demise technicians found his head difficult to embalm as the object exuded an unfreezable, oil-like substance which made the flesh intractable. When one observer suggested that the freeze-proof liquid might well serve to oil chronometers used in cold areas, a wit noted that this might lead to the killing of philosophers for their oil," and the suggestion was not followed.

Fred Whitehead, visiting in 1995, described making "a pilgrimage to his (un)hallowed remains":

> There, in a dark corridor, was a large wooden cabinet, with a man dressed up in 18th-century clothes, almost as if he had just sat down for a little rest. That is, indeed, the moral remains of Bentham. I was told that the head is a wax substitute for the original, which is housed in a vault on the College premises. . . . [At] the 150th annual meeting of the College Committee in 1976, the minutes recorded him "Present but not voting."

Although he died in 1769, his will dating to 1769 had left his body for the purpose of science, "not out of affectation of singularity, but to the intent and with the desire that mankind may reap some small benefit in and by my decease, having hitherto had small opportunities to contribute thereto while living." Dr. Southwood Smith delivered a lecture over Bentham's remains, three days after his death, in the Webb Street School of Anatomy, in which he said,

> Some time before his death, when he truly believed he was near that hour, he said to one of his disciples, who was watching over him: "I now feel that I am dying; our care must be to minimize the pain. Do not let any of the servants come into my room and keep away the youth: it will be distressing to them, and they can be of no service. Yet I must not be alone: you will remain with me, and you only; and then we shall have reduced the pain to the least possible amount." Such were his last thoughts and feelings.

{BDF; CB; CE; CL; EU, Delos B. McKown; FO; *Freethought History* #18, 1996, contains photos of the head and of Jeremy; FUK; Louis Crompton, GL; HAB; ILP; JM; JMRH; PUT; RAT; RE; TRI; TYD; U; UU}

Bentley, Arthur F. (1870—1957)

Philosopher and author with John Dewey of *Knowing and the Known* (1949), Bentley wrote to the present author concerning humanism:

> I align myself with the more liberal elements of naturalistic humanism, and I regard John Dewey as continuing to be our leader in such inquiry. More loosely (though without further detail of personal examination) I find myself in broad sympathy with Professor Harry Overstreet's confession of faith as he sets it forth in his letter to you of August 1951, a copy of which you were kind enough to send me. Humanism covers a wide extension. I, in contrast, work in a limited range. Let us hope that this differentiation of effort will prove itself useful in our parallel investigations of the future.
>
> In the earlier stages of my work (say, fifty years ago), I characterized my inquiry as an attempt to fashion a tool. In slow stages I have watched this tool develop. In more recent years it has localized itself as cross-section of society (quiescent) and as group-pressure and pressure group (action) with the two types uniting as both material and method in transactional development. Progress has already been made with the examination of knowings-known in transactional framework and we may regard the book, *Knowing and the Known*, as the most advanced presentation now available in this direction. Some of the older forms of treatment are still being deemed worthy to fight over, but these lie outside my range and include subject-object, subjective-objective, individual-social, and psychological-sociological. These minor disturbances will before long, we hope, wear themselves out and cease to waste our time. . . .
>
> . . . To be transactional will involve the rejection of split postulation in cases where the split fails to be mentioned by the workers in the field but is simply presumed to be in charge behind the scene. Such cases include assumptions about subject and object, individual and social, which cases must be won on their merits or rejected on their de-merits, and not hidden in the bushes.
>
> Except for the extreme individualists scattered among the American Humanist Association membership, I am inclined to think that a reasonable degree of harmony can be established between the Humanist and his friends.

In 1954, Bentley was named Humanist of the Year by the American Humanist Association. Also that year, he wrote *Inquiry into Inquiries*. {HNS; HNS2; WAS, 17 November 1956}

Bentley, Richard (1662—1774)

The greatest of English classical scholars, Bentley exposed the 4th-century *Epistles of Phalaris* (1699), and the Vatican placed his work on its list of prohibited reading. {ILP}

Bentley, William (1759—1819)

Bentley, a Unitarian clergyman, wrote a valuable historical source which covered the years 1784—1819 and was entitled *Diary*. Thomas Jefferson had asked him to be chaplain of Congress and later asked him to be President of the University of Virginia, but Bentley declined, saying he preferred to remain as minister of the East Church in Salem, Massachusetts.

At a time when people were intolerant of Catholics, Bentley invited a priest to stay with him for a few days and found him a meeting place. His diary is cited because he includes details of life at that time. For example, he scoffed at sightings of a supposed 100-foot sea serpent off Marblehead; he described Abigail Adams and told what kind of clothing she wore; and he stated that it was the Quakers who had first introduced stoves to heat the religious meeting houses. {EG; CE; FUS}

Béranger, Jean Pierre de (1780—1857)

Béranger, a celebrated French lyrical poet, wrote a satire on the Bourbons that twice led to his imprisonment. However, he was elected to the Constituent Assembly in 1848. Among his selections are "*Le Roi d'Yvetot*," "*Ce n'est plus Lisette*," "*Le Grenier*," and "*Le Dieu des bonnes gens*." Wheeler states that like Burns, with whom he has been compared, "all his songs breathe the spirit of liberty, and several have been characterized as impious." A rationalist, Béranger claimed in a letter to Sainte-Beuve to have "saved from the wreck an indestructible belief." {BDF; CE; JMR; JMRH; RAT}

BERDACHE

Although anthropologists have popularized the term to represent a transvestite American Indian man who functioned in a feminine role, "*Berdache* was never used in any Native communities," Wesley Thomas, a Diné, said at the University of Washington. He stated that it derives from an Arabic word, *bardadj*, which was used to describe male slaves who served as (anally receptive) prostitutes. The roles varied within each Nation.

For example, We'wha (1849—1896) lived his life as a female member of the Zuni Nation and was accepted by his people as a *lhamana*. Thomas described himself as *n'dleeh*-like, which is Diné and also Navajo for "being in a constant state of change."

When with American Indians, Thomas identified himself as Two-Spirit, but when in Western society he called himself gay in order to be understood. Homophobia, according to F. Thomas Edwards, a Cree, "was taught to us as a component of Western education and religion. We were presented with an entirely new set of taboos, which did not correspond to our own models, and which focused on sexual behavior rather than the intricate roles Two-Spirit people played. As a result of this misrepresentation, our Nations no longer accepted us as they once had. Many of the Indians had to come to terms with their sexuality in urban settings, separate from our cultures. We had to 'come out' in the Western world. But the journey into the mainstream left many of us lonesome for our homes." (See entries for Homosexuality and We'wha.) {*Village Voice*, 2 July 1996}

BERBERS: See entry for the Berber singer Lounes Matoub, who was murdered in Algeria "for his freethinking and his defiant mountain music."

Berent, Irwin M. (20th Century)

Berent, with Rod Evans, wrote *Fundamentalism: Hazards and Heartbreaks* (1994), which investigates what has gone wrong with religious fundamentalism and why.

Berg, Knut (1922—)

A Norwegian, Berg wrote "Even in Hell You Find Humanists" in the *International Humanist* (December, 1989).

Bergegren, Hinke (1861—1936)

Bergegren, a Swedish journalist, was a non-theist. (See entry for Scandinavian Unbelievers.)

Bergel, Joseph (19th Century)

Bergel was a Jewish rationalist, the German author of *Heaven and Its Wonders* (1881) and *Mythology of the Ancient Hebrews* (1882). {BDF}

Berger, Allen (20th Century)

Berger, a cultural anthropologist, was cited by the Freedom from Religion Foundation as its "1993 Freethinker of the Year." Prof. Berger describes himself as "an unbelieving Jew teaching in a Catholic college," St. Joseph's in Rensselaer, Indiana.

He co-founded GIDEANS International (God Is Definitely Erroneous And Not Safe) as well as UNGOD (Unholy Nihilists for Godlessness Over Deism).

Berger, Moriz (19th Century)

In Trieste, 1883, Berger's *Materialism in Conflict with Spiritualism and Idealism* was published. {BDF}

Bergh, Henry (1811—1888)

Bergh, one of the founders in 1866 of the American Society for the Prevention of Cruelty to Animals, is a philanthropist who was a Unitarian. Long angry about the mistreatment of animals, Bergh obtained support for a Declaration of the Rights of Animals, and among those who signed were Unitarians Horace Greeley, George Bancroft, Peter Cooper, and William Cullen Bryant. In 1875, he was one of the founders of the equally unique group, the American Society for the Prevention of Cruelty to Children. {CE; EG}

Bergk, Johann Adam (1769—1834)

A German philosopher, Bergk wrote *True Religion*, "recommended to rationalists and destined for the Radical cure of supernaturalists, mystics, etc."

His son, **Theodor Bergk**, a German humanist born in 1812, wrote *History of Greek Literature* (1872). {BDF}

Bergman, G. Merle (20th Century)

Bergman, a freethinker, wrote *Realtheism: A Religion and Bible for the Humanist Age* (1987). {GS}

Bergman, (Ernst) Ingmar (1918—)

Bergman, a noted Swedish film writer and director, was recipient in the Netherlands of the 1965 Erasmus Award for his contribution to the arts. He has won numerous awards, including the 1970 Best Director Award of the National Society of Film Critics; the 1976 Goethe Prize; and the 1977 Gold Medal of the Swedish Academy. His "The Virgin Spring" won the 1960 Academy Award; "Cries and Whispers" won the 1972 Best Film Award of the National Society of Film Critics; and "Fanny and Alexander" won the 1984 Academy Award for Best Foreign Language Film Direction.

The son of a Lutheran pastor, he has shown in several of his works, particularly "The Seventh Seal" and "Winter Light," his dissatisfaction with the faith of his upbringing and his shift from belief to disbelief. In his 1987 autobiography, *The Magic Lantern*, Bergman wrote,

> I have struggled all my life with a tormented and joyless relationship with God. Faith and lack of faith, punishment, grace, and rejection, all were real to me, all were imperative. My prayers stank of anguish, entreaty, trust, loathing, and despair. God spoke, God said nothing. . . . No one is safe from religious ideas and confessional phenomena. . . . We can fall victim to them when we least expect it. It's like Mao's flu, or being struck by lightning. . . . The lost hours of that operation provided me with a calming message. You were born without purpose, you live without meaning, living is its own meaning. When you die, you are extinguished. From being you will be transformed to non-being. A god does not necessarily dwell among our capricious atoms.

{E}

Bergman, Gerald R. (20th Century)

Bergman, writing "God, Chance, or Human Factors?" in *The American Rationalist* (September-October 1995), stated that rationalists "must be cautious at arriving at unwarranted assumptions such as 'someone up there' wanted us to behave in certain ways, or wanted certain things to happen. Time, unforeseen occurrence, and chance befall us all, and one must clearly 'test all things and hold fast to what is true and good.' "

In "Religious Beliefs of Scientists: A Survey of the Research" (*Free Inquiry*, Summer 1996), he wrote, "The existing literature consistently concludes that very few eminent scientists today are devoutly religious, and most do not hold to any conventional theistic religious beliefs."

In "Religion and Medicine: the Case of Christian Science" (*The American Rationalist*, January-February 1999), Bergman concludes with Mark Twain's comment that whenever Christian Science *does* die out some other irrationality will, unfortunately, take its place.

Bergman, Jerry (20th Century)

For *The American Rationalist* (March-April 1997), Bergman wrote "The Final Test."

Berigardus, Claudius: See entry for Claudius Beauregard.

Berkeley, George (1685—1753)

Berkeley, an Anglo-Irish philosopher and clergyman, believed his body of writing completely disproved atheism: It is God who determines what is right and wrong: "Nothing is a [moral] law merely because it conduceth to the public good, but because it is decreed by the will of God, which alone can give the sanction of a law of nature to any precept; and there can be no solid morality without religion." As explained by Hartshorne, Berkeley believed that "ideas that are merely ours are under control of our wills, whereas what we perceive physically is forced upon us all according to a common system. The only force we know from the given is will. The only adequate will-cause of the orderly constraint we feel in perception is God. Thus all data are signs in a single vast language by which God communicates to us." With Locke, Berkeley held that theoretical atheism must of necessity lead to moral chaos. {CE; ER; FUK; HAB}

Berkeley, Humphrey (1926—)

Berkeley, a freethinker, was treasurer of the Howard League for Penal Reform in England. {TRI}

Berkenhout, John (1731—1791)

The son of a Dutch merchant who settled at Leeds, England, Berkenhout was a physician. His principal work is entitled *Biographia Literaria* (1777), a history of English literature. In the work he loses no opportunity to display his hostility to the theologians, and he is loud in his praises of Voltaire. {BDF; RAT}

Berkshire, August (20th Century)

Berkshire is an activist-atheist from Minneapolis, Minnesota For *Secular Nation* he wrote "Voucher Schemes and Fairness (January-March 1999) and "Creative Medical Uses for Placebos and Prayer" (April-June 1999).

Berlin, Isaiah [Sir] (1909—1997)

Berlin, a major philosopher and historian of ideas at Oxford University in England, shared with Plato the distinction of having been an intellectual who never wrote a major book.

Born in Riga, Latvia, he was the son of a timber merchant and landowner. His grandfather on his mother's side was a Hasidic rabbi of the Lubavitch tradition. His family moved to St. Petersburg, witnessing two Russian revolutions in 1917, then immigrated in 1921 to London, where it had business interests.

As a boy, Shaya (as he was known then) had some religious education but found the Talmud a "very, very boring book," adding, "I could never figure out why I should care why the bull gored the cow." He continued his religious education in London, where as a youth he had his bar mitzvah.

"I never had it in me to do a great masterpiece on some big subject," he said. But he wrote on a variety of subjects. He translated Turgenev and wrote *Karl Marx* (1939), *Historical Inevitability* (1954), *The Age of Enlightenment* (1956), *Four Essays on Literature* (1969), and *The Crooked Timber of Humanity* (1990). The latter work's title comes from Kant's "Out of the crooked timber of humanity no straight thing was ever made." What this meant to Berlin was that mankind must be wary of dogmatism, of utopianism, or of any system of thinking which pursues the ideal. Berlin argued not for utopianism but for pluralism, for the notion

> that there are many different ends that men may seek and still be fully rational, fully men, capable of understanding each other and sympathizing and deriving light from each other, as we derive it from reading Plato or the novels of medieval Japan—worlds, outlooks, very remote from your own.

His 1959 essay, "Two Concepts of Liberty," made a distinction between negative liberty (that which the individual must be allowed to enjoy without state interference) and positive liberty (that which the state permits by imposing regulations that, by necessity, limit some freedoms in the name of greater liberty for all. He argued, Marilyn Berger noted in *The New York Times* (7 November 1997), that both kinds of liberty were required for a just society.

Berlin once made a distinction between two types of mind: the hedgehog, which knows one big thing; and the fox, which knows lots of little ones. Thinkers who fixate on one big idea—Plato, Dante, Pascal, Proust, Dostoevsky, Marx, Hegel, or for that matter someone who would investigate a subject such as humanism for decades—are hedgehogs; whereas those who have many little ideas, such as Aristotle, Goethe, Pushkin, Balzac, Joyce, and Turgenev are foxes. Tolstoy, he felt, was a fox who wanted to be a hedgehog. Most of Berlin's friends, wrote Michael Ignatieff (*The New Yorker*, 28 September 1998), saw him

> as an arch-fox—quick-witted, darting from subject to subject, eluding pursuit. Yet he also longed to be a hedgehog—to know one thing, to feel one thing more truly than anyone else. He had reached what he recognized was a critical stage: either he would go on to develop a serious intellectual engagement of his own or he would decline into being what he feared most—a "chatterbox."

With Hegel, he held that "freedom consists in being at home." Everyone, he concluded, needed to belong to a group. He was convinced, as was German philosopher Johann Gottfried Herder, of man's basic need to be part of a particular human community with its own traditions, language, art, and imagination to shape his emotional and physical development. However, he noted, "I have no idea how one stops one group, one race, from hating another. The hatred between human groups has never been cured, except by time." In the 18th Century, he noted, one could believe that nations could live peacefully side by side. "Perhaps in the 18th century you could believe that," he added, noting that the excesses of nationalism made such a view unrealistic.

Berger, commenting about Berlin at the time of his death, said Berlin had been known for his view that the utopian notion of one big answer that is knowable and self-contained must always be fallacious because it does not take into account the cultural pluralism and conflicting values that are part of humanity's "crooked timber." Kant had written that "Out of the crooked timber of humanity no straight thing was ever made," a view which inspired the title of Berlin's 1990 work, *The Crooked Timber of Humanity*.

The 1997 publication of his *Sense of Reality: Studies in Ideas and Their History* underlined his deserved reputation for being a great essayist, conversationalist (Robert Darnton has compared him with Diderot), and rhetorician. The seventh and last volume in a series of his essays, the work rejected the common belief that utopians are simply rebels against social laws and historical development but, rather, are people who think they have discovered those very laws whereas none such actually exist. In the 19th century, he noted, thinkers

> believed that human society grew in a discoverable direction, governed by laws; that the borderline which divided science from utopia . . . was discoverable by reason and observation and could be plotted less or more precisely; that, in short, there was a clock, its movement followed discoverable rules and it could not be put back.

However, the utopians' faith that science can plot society's future has led to still further problems, he asserts. By placing their faith in the laws of social and historical development, utopians "place excessive faith in laws and methods derived from alien fields, mostly from the natural sciences." This, he cites, is evidence of a lack of the sense of reality. Critics generally hailed the octogenarian's work as evidencing his ability to make philosophy come alive.

Berlin was a fervent Zionist, "not because the Lord offered us the Holy Land as some people, religious Jews, believe," he said, adding,

> My reason for being a Zionist has nothing to do with preserving Jewish culture, Jewish values, wonderful things done by Jews. But the price is too high, the martyrdom too long. And if I were asked, "Do you want to preserve this culture at all costs?" I'm not sure that I would say yes, because you can't condemn people to permanent persecution. Of course assimilation might be a quite good thing, but it doesn't work. Never has worked, never will. There isn't a Jew in the world known to me who somewhere inside him does not have a tiny drop of uneasiness vis-à-vis *them*, the majority among whom they live. They may be very friendly, they may be entirely happy, but one has to behave particularly well, because if they don't behave well they won't like us

A serious opera buff and a sought-after conversationalist, he was a friend of Freud, Nehru, Stravinsky, Boris Pasternak, T. S. Eliot, W. H. Auden, Chaim Weizmann, Virginia Woolf, Edmund Wilson, Aldous Huxley, Bertrand Russell, and Felix Frankfurter.

Ignatieff has detailed Berlin's affection for a famous beauty, Akhmatova, who was twenty years older than he and twice married. When Patricia Douglas, a married woman with children, came to take care of him on an occasion when he was suffering from a bad cold, he surprised her in a raw display of feeling by pulling her into bed with him. Also, he loved Aline Halban, who was married at the time to an Oxford colleague, and also with children. When she left her husband, she and Berlin were married in 1956 at Hampstead Synagogue, a sign that he may have been closer to Judaism than some of his contemporaries suspected.

The posthumous publication of his last essay, "My Intellectual Path" (*The New York Review of Books*, 14 May 1998), discussed Oxford philosophy before the Second World War. He told of his first interest in philosophy and in the work of G. E. Moore and Bertrand Russell when an undergraduate at Oxford in the late 1920s and early 1930s. The "fashionable view" of verificationism

> was that the meaning of a proposition was the way in which it was verifiable—that if there was no way whatever of verifying what was being said, it was not a statement capable of truth or falsehood, not factual, and therefore either meaningless or a case of some other use of language, as seen in commands or expressions of desire, of in imaginative literature, or in other forms of expression which did not lay claim to empirical truth.

He never became "a true disciple," however, always believing

> that statements that could be true or false or plausible or dubious or interesting, while indeed they did relate to the world as empirically conceived (and I have never conceived of the world in any other way, from then to the present day), were nevertheless not necessarily capable of being verified by some simple knockdown criterion, as the Vienna School and their logical positivist followers asserted. From the beginning I felt that general propositions were not verifiable in that way. Statements whether in ordinary use or in the natural sciences (which were the ideal of the Vienna School), could be perfectly meaningful without being strictly verifiable. If I said "All swans are white," I would never know if I knew this about all the swans there were, or whether the number of swans might not be infinite; a black swan no doubt refuted this generalization, but its positive verification in the full sense seemed to me unattainable; nevertheless it would be absurd to say that it had no meaning.

His last essay also discusses monism (about which he always felt skeptical); Giambattista Vico (the first philosopher, a Catholic, to have conceived the idea of cultures); J. G. Herder (the father of cultural nationalism (whom he found not to be a relativist and who held that mankind "was not one but many"); romanticism (although Marx and others held that perfection is a goal, "I reject this huge metaphysical interpretation of human life in toto—I remain an empiricist, and know only what I am able to experience, or think I could experience, and do not begin to believe in supra-individual entities—nevertheless I own that it made some impact on me."); pluralism ("I came to the conclusion that there is a plurality of ideals, as there is a plurality of cultures and of temperaments," a view he held is not relativistic.); freedom; determinism ; and the pursuit of the ideal. The essay concludes,

> To go back to the Encyclopedists and the Marxists and all the other movements the purpose of which is the perfect life: it seems as if the doctrine that all kinds of monstrous cruelties must be permitted, because without these the ideal state of affairs cannot be attained—all the justifications of broken eggs for the sake of the ultimate omelette, all the brutalities, sacrifices, brainwashing, all those revolutions, everything that has made this century perhaps the most appalling of any since the days of old, at any rate in the West—all this is for nothing, for the perfect universe is not merely unattainable but inconceivable, and everything done to bring it about is founded on an enormous intellectual fallacy.

The essay takes on added significance because Berlin had written his views at the request of Ouyang Kang, professor of philosophy at Wuhan University in China, in order that they could be translated and included in a volume about contemporary Anglo-American philosophy, which hitherto had been largely unavailable in China.

A posthumous work, *The Roots of Romanticism* (1999), suggests that because they could not compete with the French in social, political, and philosophical matters, the Germans developed the Romantic movement, "the greatest transformation of Western consciousness, certainly in our time." To illustrate, he describes the thinking of Fichte, Goethe, Hamann, Herder, and Schiller.

Berlin was President of the British Academy from 1974 to 1978. He became a Humanist Laureate in the Council of Secular Humanism's International Academy of Humanism.

"I don't mind death," he said of his own death. "I'm not afraid of it. I'm afraid of dying for it could be painful. But I find death a nuisance. I object to it. I'd rather it didn't happen. . . . I'm terribly curious. I'd like to live forever." (An astute commentary about Berlin was written by Alan Ryan in *The New York Review of Books*, 17 December 1998) {CE; *The Economist*, 27 September 1997; FUS; Robert Darnton, *The New York Review of Books*, 26 June 1997; Marilyn Berger, *The New York Times*, 7 November 1997}

Berlioz, Louis Hector (1803—1869)

Berlioz, who obtained fame by his dramatic symphony of "Romeo and Juliet" (1839), was made chevalier of the Legion of

Honor. The nonliturgical oratorio *The Childhood of Christ* was completed in 1854. Berlioz's ideas of orchestration influenced many later composers. Although the *Catholic Encyclopaedia* claims Berlioz was a Catholic, McCabe states that Berlioz often admitted in his letters that he was an atheist. In G. K. Boult's *Life of Berlioz* (1903), a letter is included which was written shortly before the French composer died and in which he says, "I believe nothing." Earlier, in his *Memoirs*, Berlioz related how he scandalized Mendelssohn "by laughing at the Bible." He also scandalized others by his well-publicized love affairs. {BDF; CE; JM; RAT; RE; TRI; TYD}

Berman, David (20th Century)

Berman is the highly esteemed author of *A History of Atheism in Britain: From Hobbes to Russell* (1988) and *George Berkeley: Idealism and the Man* (1994). A professor at Dublin's Trinity College, he shows, according to Tim Madigan of *Free Inquiry*, "that atheism, while not openly avowed until late in the eighteenth century, was implicit in many of the writings of some of the seventeenth century's most influential thinkers. Even in the present day, it remains the view that dare not speak its name." Berman's research has been said to continue and sometimes correct that of J. M. Robertson. He has written book reviews for the British *New Humanist*. {FUK}

Berman, Eleanor (1934—)

In the 1950s, Berman was an associate editor of *The Humanist*. She is author of *Away for the Weekend* (1996). {HNS}

Berman, Milton (20th Century)

Berman wrote *John Fiske: The Evolution of a Popularizer*. {FUS}

Bernadin de Saint-Pierre, Jacques Henri (1737—1814)

Bernadin de Saint-Pierre, a French naturalist and author, was a friend of Rousseau, by whom he was strongly influenced. His chief work, *Études de la Nature* (1784), which sought to prove the existence of God from the wonders of nature, influenced the French romanticists. He succeeded Buffon as head of the Botanical Garden and was a professor under the Revolution. According to McCabe, "the atheists smiled at his 'natural religion,' but, like Rousseau, he did good work amongst sentimental folk." {CE; JM}

Bernal, Martin G(ardner) (1937—)

Bernal, a professor of government and a Chinese scholar at Cornell, is the British author of *Black Athena: The Afroasiatic Roots of Classical Civilization* (1987), a work that in 1996 has been refuted by numbers of scholars.

Bernal is interested in that which is not European or Greek, what usually is called "pre-Hellenic." Unlike other scholars, he finds the Greek culture represents "a mix of the native Balkan-Indo-European-speaking population with Egyptian and western Semitic populations. The linguistic and cultural mix was extraordinarily productive in cultural terms." Further, he finds that 80% of the non-European words in Greek are in fact Egyptian or Semitic. "Humanism," he believes, "is rooted in the late-Egyptian religious concept that human beings can become 'god.' The belief that humanity has divinity within itself is essentially Egyptian or African, and was transmitted to modern Europe through the hermetic texts. . . . Though you could say that the atheist tradition can only be traced back to Greek and Latin thinkers, humanism, in the centrality of the 'person,' is a very Egyptian idea."

The earliest example of monotheism, he writes in an interview with Norm R. Allen Jr., "is that of Akhenaton, the Egyptian pharaoh of the 14th century B.C.E. And the earliest trace of monotheism in Judaism is really from the 8th century B.C.E. . . . I very much doubt that we can go as far as Freud did in his book *Moses and Monotheism*, and say that Moses took monotheism from Akhenaton's reforms in Egypt, but there seems to be no doubt that Egyptian religion had both polytheistic and monotheistic trends, and that Judaism borrowed from it." As for their differences, "One thing that is characteristic of Egyptian religion and not Judaism is the emphasis on knowledge. In Judeo-Christian thought the emphasis is on faith. And the idea of knowledge—which again is humanistic in that human beings attempt to understand and manipulate spiritual and other systems—is very different from the position of subjugation of the worshiper who accepts with blind faith whatever happens. Also, organizationally, monasticism started in Egypt with a church hierarchy, rituals like the shaving of priests' heads and things like that. Egypt provided the model of Western religion and religious institutions and structures." Bernal, cautioning both Eurocentric and Afrocentric scholars, posits the need to be disinterested and unprejudiced when writing history.

Refuting Bernal's theories, Mary R. Lefkowitz has written *Not Out of Africa: How Afrocentrism Became an Excuse to Teach Myth as History* (1996). Also, she and Guy MacLean Rogers have edited *Black Athena Revisited* (1996), a thorough attack by nineteen scholars from Rome and Oxford as well as from Howard University and Harvard. For example, although Bernal insists that the ancient Egyptians were not only African but explicitly black, scholars from Howard University, Boston University, and the University of Michigan state that they were Mediterranean peoples, neither Sub-Saharan blacks, Nubians, nor Caucasian whites, that their craniofacial morphology has nothing whatsoever in common with Sub-Saharan Africans', and that attempts to force the Egyptians into a "black" or "white" category have no biological justification. "Substituting fiction for fact is," according to Howard University's Frank M. Snowden, "is a disservice to blacks."

Meanwhile, whereas some molecular biologists have concluded that all family trees lead back to a single African woman, who lived some 200,000 years ago, Dr. Alan Templeton, a geneticist at Washington University in St. Louis, believes otherwise. He as well as Pennsylvania State University's Mark Stoneking and the University of Michigan's Milford Wolpoff say it is possible that the evolution to modern humans occurred roughly simultaneously in many places. In short, according to *The New York Times* (19 May 1992), scholars continue to debate whether or not there was "an African Eve." (For a negative view of Bernal's view, see the entry for Afrocentrism. Also, see "Anxieties of Influence" by Jasper Griffin in *The New York Review of Books*, 20 June 1996) {AAH}

Bernard, Claude (1813—1878)

A French physiologist, Bernard wrote *La Science Experimentale*, which Paul Bert says introduced determinism in the domain of physiology. Upon his death, Bernard was buried at the expense of the French Republic. McCabe wrote of Bernard, "As he was educated by the Jesuits and the Church was allowed some share in his funeral ceremonies, Catholics always claim the great scientist as 'one of us.' It is ridiculous because in his published works he makes no secret of his agnosticism. He does this repeatedly in his chief work, *An Introduction to the Study of Experimental Medicine* (1865). He says that 'the best philosophical system is to have none at all,' that philosophy represents 'the eternal aspiration of human reason toward knowledge of the unknown,' and that it deals with 'questions that torment humanity and have never yet been solved.' In private his language was less stately. Sir Michael Foster quotes him saying that the Vespers [the Sunday evening service in Catholic churches] is 'the servant girls' opera.' " {BDF; JM; RAT; RE}

Bernard [Saint] (1090?—1153)

Bernard the ecclesiast, in his *Meditationes Piissimae*, opined that "Man is nothing more than . . . a sack of dung, the food of worms." He feared the philosophic treatment of theological problems, preferring an essentially mystical theology. Among his beliefs were that "a Christian glories in the death of a pagan, because thereby Christ himself is glorified," which must surely have inspired individuals as they endured the unbearable difficulties of traveling long distances during the Crusades in order to kill. {ER}

Bernard, Ethan (20th Century)

Bernard is treasurer of the Society for Logic and Reason at Oregon State University in Corvallis. E-mail: <bernarde@ucs.orst.edu>.

Bernard, Henry Meyners (Died 1907)

Bernard was a biologist who worked under Haeckel at Jena. He translated A. Lang's *Text-Book of Comparative Anatomy* (1891) and wrote several biological works. In *Some Neglected Factors of Evolution* (1911), he spoke of the "intellectual dreams" of the churches as "frightful nightmares to those who wake up and think rather than feel." {HNS2; RAT}

Bernard, Joe (20th Century)

Bernard is founder and director of Imagine a World of Wanted Children (IWC). He edits its periodical and another entitled *Quest and Controversy*. A regional director of the American Humanist Association, Bernard spoke in 1994 at the 14th annual HUMCON conference sponsored by the Alliance of Humanist, Atheist, and Ethical Culture Organizations of Los Angeles County. {FD}

Bernard, Victor (20th Century)

Victor Bernard is a local humanist activist in Pittsburgh, Pennsylvania. (See entry for Pennsylvania Humanists.) {FD; *Free Inquiry*, Summer 1991}

Berners-Lee, Tim (1956-)

Berners-Lee, a physicist who was born in London, is credited with creating the World Wide Web. Frustrated because he could not share research with colleagues around the world, he devised the system of electronic links to information that spread like a spider's web. Frustrated by what he thought was his poor memory, he devised a program that allowed him to jump, via links, from one bit of information another. What was new about his hypertext was that the links were direct, random, and also flexible.

His most revolutionary idea, Ms. E. J. Graff has explained (*World*, May-June 1999), was his 1989 proposal for a global hypertext project to be known as the World Wide Web, one that would let Internet users anywhere share their knowledge with all other users. No matter what software or operating system had been used to create it, Berners-Lee conceived of hypertext tools that would enable any user to view any document. These included URLs (universal resource locators), HTTPs (hypertext transfer protocols, the "addresses" that are typed into a Web browser's window to get the user to some destination), and HTMLs (hypertext markup language, which the Web browser reads to allow users to view a document).

"On Sundays Berners-Lee packs his family into the car and heads for a Unitarian-Universalist church," *Time* has reported. "As a teenager he rejected the Anglican teachings of his parents; he can't bring himself to worship a particular prophet, a particular book. But 'I do in fact believe that people's spiritual side is very important,' and that it's 'more than just biology.' He said he liked the minimalist Unitarian dogma theologically vague but believing in "the inherent dignity of people and in working together to achieve harmony and understanding."

He can accept the notion of divinity so long as it is couched abstractly as the "asymptote" of goodness that we strive toward and does not involve "characters with beards." He hopes the Web will move the world closer to the divine asymptote.

To a reporter he mentioned that a verse he had heard in church came to mind, but all that he could remember are fragments: "All souls may . . . to seek the truth in love." His voice trailed off and, in a single motion, he swiveled his chair to find the exact quotation "and made fluid contact with his IBM Thinkpad."

Berners-Lee is head of a W3 Consortium at MIT's Laboratory for Computer Science in Boston, and since his invention of the World Wide Web he reportedly has made very little money from the invention he has described: "You feel you're playing a part in the world brain, contributing to something very large and connected."

According to Ms. Graff, Berners-Lee "is a fundamentalist libertarian, believing that idea and information should move without hindrance. Thus when you find a hate site on the Web, 'it is right to be horrified,' he says. 'Being horrified and taking some action is part of the process.' Freedom of speech, in this view, can be countered only by more freedom of speech—whether on real-world or on cyberspace street corners."

In 1998 Berners-Lee received a $270,000 MacArthur Fellowship Award in recognition of his pioneering of work on "a revolutionary communications system requiring minimal technical understanding to locate and distribute information throughout the world at very low cost." {*Time*, 19 May 1997, International Edition; *USA Weekend*, 15-17 August 1997; *World*, May-June 1999}

Bernhardt, Sarah (1845—1923)

Bernhardt, generally called the greatest French actress of recent times, was asked by the composer of operas, Charles François Gounod, if she ever prayed. "No," she replied, according to A. Carel's *Histoire anecdotique des contemporains* (1885). "Never. I'm an atheist." To her disgust, Gounod (who "vacillated between mysticism and voluptuousness," according to one of his biographers) then fell to his knees and prayed for her.

In the winter of 1923, while preparing for a dress rehearsal, Bernhardt suddenly slipped into unconsciousness. "When do I go on?" she inquired, upon coming to. But she never again was able to act, becoming bedridden because of ill health. When she was able to walk, she soon collapsed again and, upon being informed that journalists were outside, said they could just wait: "All my life reporters have tormented me enough. I can tease them now a little by making them cool their heels." The following day, she died. {CE; JM; TYD}

Bernstein, Aaron (1812—1884)

Bernstein, a rationalist born of Jewish parents, translated *Song of Songs* (1834) but published it under the pseudonym of A. Rebenstein. {BDF; RAT}

Bernstein, Alvin (20th Century)

Bernstein, a retiree in California who formerly taught European history, has written about Voltaire and Pierre Bayle for *Truth Seeker*. For *Secular Nation* (October-December 1998), he wrote that extreme religionists are tampering with our notions of right and wrong, making right wrong and wrong right.

Bernstein, Eduard (1850—1932)

Bernstein was a German politician and socialist, a Deputy for Breslau in the Reichstag and a leader of the minority group. He rejected the theories of Karl Marx and followed the Kantian philosophy (but not theology). In his view, socialism would be the final result of liberalism, not revolution. Bernstein was an agnostic who opposed the Nazis. {CE; RAT}

Bernstein, Leonard (1918—1990)

An eminent American composer and conductor, Bernstein wrote "Mass" (1971), which he described as "a theater piece for singers, dancers, and players" and was performed at the opening of the John F. Kennedy Cultural Center in Washington, D.C. He argues melodramatically with God in his "Kaddish" symphony and mass and features his uncloseted bisexuality in the opera, "A Quiet Place." Bernstein is known for symphonic works, chamber music, choral music, and musicals such as "On the Town" (1944), "Candide" (1956) and "West Side Story"(1957). He also is known for his various love affairs, the homosexual ones of which are described in Charles Kaiser's *The Gay Metropolis 1940—1996* (1997).

In 1976, after having been married for twenty-five years to the Chilean actress Felicia Montealegre and brought up three children with her, he left his wife for a young man. "The darker the color, the better," one Broadway star reported.

Although nominally Jewish—David Denby has thoroughly outlined his musical connections with Judaism—Bernstein accepted a Humanist of the Year award from the American Humanist Association. The award was to have been given in 1990, the year of his death. {CE; David Denby, "The Trouble With Lenny," *The New Yorker*, 17 August 1998}

Berquin, Louis de (1489—1529)

Berquin was a French martyr whose great crime, according to his friend Erasmus, was openly professing hatred of the monks. Although his works were ordered to be burned. he was commanded to abjure his heresies, and he was sentenced to perpetual banishment, Berquin appealed to the Parliament. That appeal was rejected, and he was burned the same afternoon at the Place de la Grève. Wheeler says "he died with great constancy and resolution." {BDF}

Berré, Denise (20th Century)

Berré spoke at the 1992 IHEU Congress in the Netherlands, describing how an ethical education is provided in secondary schools in Belgium. From the age of six to eighteen, children follow a "philosophical" class chosen by their parents. Teachers of humanist courses are employed by the state, not by the humanist organizations.

Berry, Dale (20th Century)

Berry has reviewed books for *The American Rationalist* (January-February 1999).

Berry, Newton (20th Century)

Berry, with Madalyn Murray O'Hair, wrote *The Best of "Dial An Atheist"* (1982). {GS}

Berry, Paul (20th Century)

A teacher, environmentalist, and author, Berry wrote *Wake of Dreams: Reflections of Hawaii* (1993). He has identified population growth and government inertia as major problems. Berry teaches economics at Punahou, Hawaii.

Bers, Mel (20th Century)

Raised a nominal Jew "but not in any religious sense," Bers told fellow members of the Secular Humanist Community of Upstate New York, Western Massachusetts, and Southern Vermont, that he reacted against the "50-50" implications of being an agnostic, and he became a secular humanist. He added that he is grateful that his life has been free from the *sturm* and *drang* of religious angst. {*The Humanist Monthly*, September 1998}

Bert, Paul (1833—1886)

A French scientist and statesman, Bert held radical opinions and as Minister of Public Instruction organized French education on a secular basis. His strong anti-clerical views induced much opposition, particularly because of his *The Morality of the Jesuits* (1880). In 1886 he was made Governor-General of French Indo-China. His rationalism is seen in *Le Cléricalisme* (published 1900).

Foote, describing Bert, wrote the following:

> His father educated him in a detestation of priests, and his own nature led him to the pursuit of science. He took the degree of Doctor of Medicine in 1863, and three years later the degree of Doctor of Science. His political life began with the fall of the Empire. After the war of 1870–71 he entered the Chamber of Deputies, and devoted his great powers to the development of public education. Largely through his labors, the Chamber voted free, secular, and compulsory instruction for both sexes. He was idolized by the school-masters and school-mistresses in France. Being accused of a "blind hatred" of priests, he replied in the Chamber: "The conquests of education are made on the domain of religion; I am forced to meet on my road Catholic superstitions and Romish policy, or rather it is across their empire that my path seems to me naturally traced."
>
> Speaking at a mass meeting at the Cirque d'Hiver, in August, 1881, Gambetta himself being in the chair, Bert declared that "modern societies march towards morality in proportion as they leave religion behind." Afterwards he published his scathing *Morale des Jesuites*, over twenty thousand copies of which were sold in less than a year. The book was dedicated to Bishop Freppel in a vein of masterly irony. Bert also published a scientific work, the *Premiere Année d'Enseignement Scientifique*, which is almost universally used in the Frenell primary schools. During Léon Gambetta's short-lived government Bert held the post of Minister of Public Instruction. In 1886 he went out to Tonquin as Resident-General. Hard work and the pestilential climate laid him low and he succumbed to dysentery. When the news of his death reached the French Chamber, M. Freycinet thus announced the event from the tribune:
>
> I announce with the deepest sorrow the death of M. Paul Bert. He died literally on the field of honor, broken down by the fatigues and hardships which he so bravely endured in trying to carry out the glorious task which he had undertaken. The Chamber loses by his death one of its most eminent members, Science one of its most illustrious votaries, France one of her most loving and faithful children, and the Government a fellow-worker of inestimable value, in whom we placed the fullest confidence. Excuse me, gentlemen, if because my strength fails me I am unable to proceed.

Foote continued:

> The sitting was raised as a mark of respect, and the next day the Chamber voted a public funeral and a pension to Paul Bert's family. Bishop Freppel opposed the first vote on the ground that the deceased was an inveterate enemy of religion, but he was ignominiously beaten, the majority against him being 379 to 45. Despite this miserable protest, while Paul Bert's body was on its way to Europe the clerical party started a canard about his "conversion." Perhaps the story originated in the fact that he had daily visited the Hanoi Hospital, distributing books and medicines and speaking kind words to the nuns in attendance. It was openly stated and unctuously commented on in the religious journals, that the Resident-General had sent for a Catholic bishop on his death-bed and taken the sacrament; and as inventions of this kind are always circumstantial, it was said that the Papal Nuncio at Lisbon had received this intelligence. But on December 29 the Papal Nuncio telegraphed that his name had been improperly used; and two days later, when the French warship touched at the Suez Canal, Madame Bert telegraphed that the story was absolutely and entirely false.

{BDF; FO; RAT}

Bertani, Agostino (1812—1886)

An Italian patriot, Bertani was a physician who took part with Garibaldi and Mazzini in organizing the ambulance services. A declared freethinker, he was elected deputy to the Italian Parliament. {BDF; RAT}

Berthelot, Dolly Haik-Adams (20th Century)

Berthelot, a Unitarian, is author of *What Became of a World That Was Perfectly Square* (1994), a fable about diversity and change. She is a past president of the Pensacola, Florida, Unitarian Fellowship.

Berthelot, Pierre Eugéne Marcelin (1827—1907)

A French chemist and member of the French Academy, Berthelot was a founder of modern organic chemistry. He was the first to produce organic compounds synthetically (including the carbon compounds methyl alcohol, ethyl alcohol, benzene, and acetylene). Berthelot was an honorary associate of the Rationalist Press Association, which in 1899 was founded by Charles A. Watts. Two of his works are *Chimie organique fondée sur la synthèse* (1860) and *Leçons sur la thermochimie* (1897).

Berthelot, according to McCabe, "almost made a parade of his scorn of creeds and his atheism. He wrote several books on his views, and he sent for public reading at the International Congress of Freethinkers at Rome in 1904, which I attended, a letter in which he denounced the 'poisonous vapors of superstition' and hailed the coming of a 'reign of reason.' The message is published in Dr. L. B. Wilson's *Trip to Rome* (1904)." {CE; JM; RAT; RE}

Berthold, S. M. (20th Century)

Berthold, a freethinker, wrote *Thomas Paine: America's First Liberal* (1938). {FUS}

Berthollet, Claude Louis [Comte de] (1748—1822)

Berthollet was a French chemist whose contributions to chemistry include the analysis of ammonia and prussic acid and the discovery of the bleaching properties of chlorine. His greatest contribution was in his *Essai de statique chimique* (1803), in which he presented his speculations on chemical affinity and his discovery of the reversibility of reactions. Napoleon took him as one of his *savants* to Egypt, making him a Count and Senator for his scientific services. Berthollet, who is not claimed by Catholics, remained a skeptic. {CE; RAT; RE}

Berti, Antonio (1816—1879)

An Italian physician, Berti wrote many scientific works. A freethinker, he was a member of the Venice Municipal Council and of the Italian Senate. {BDF}

Berti, Domenico (1820—1897)

Berti was an Italian philosopher and statesman. A liberal theist or pantheist, he admired Giordano Bruno and throughout his career was a moderate progressive and anti-clerical. {RAT}

Bertillon, Alphonse (1853—1914)

Bertillon was a French criminologist whose work in 1879 culminated in the establishment of the Bertillon system of measurement, which was adopted in many countries. The English police adopted it in 1896. Bertillon, who shared his father's (Louis Adolphe Bertillon's) advanced views, wrote a number of works on anthropology and criminology. {RAT}

Bertillon, Louis Adolphe (1821—1883)

Bertillon, a French anthropologist and physician, did a statistical study of the French population in 1874. With A. Hovelacque and others, he edited the *Dictionary of the Anthropological Sciences*. In a letter to Bishop Dupanloup in 1868, he wrote, "You hope to die a Catholic. I hope to die a Freethinker." {BDF; RAT}

Berton, Pierre (1920—)

Berton is a Canadian journalist and author. He has been the managing editor of *Maclean's* in Toronto, a columnist in various journals, a panelist on "Front Page Challenge, CBC," and chancellor of Yukon College (1988—1993). He is the author of thirty-nine books, including *The Royal Family* (1953), *Adventures of a Columnist* (1960), *The Dionne Years* (1977), *The Invasion of Canada, 1812—1813* (1980), and *Farewell to the Twentieth Century* (1996). In 1992 he was named to the Canadian Newspaper Hall of Fame and in 1996 received the Responsibility in Journalism Award of the Committee for Investigation of the Paranormal.

In a 1994 interview on Canadian public television, Berton was asked his views on the Christmas season. He replied that he was an atheist and felt it was all nonsense. {CA; E}

Bertrand de Saint-Germain Guillaume Scipion (Born 1810)

Bertrand was a French physician who wrote *The Original Diversity of Human Races* (1847) and *Descartes as a Physiologist* (1869). He was a freethinker. {BDF}

BERTRAND RUSSELL SOCIETY

The Bertrand Russell Society (1806 Rollins Drive, Alexandria, Virginia 22307) publishes the quarterly *Russell Society News* and distributes a semi-annual copy of the journal of the Bertrand Russell archives at McMaster University in Canada. Its international membership includes numerous eminent thinkers.

Officers in 1999 were as follows: Kenneth Blackwell, Chairman; Alan Schwerin, President; Jan Loeb Eisler, Vice President; Peter Stone, Secretary; and Dennis Darland, Treasurer.

Directors are as follows: James Alouf; Stefan Andersson; Derek Araujo; Kenneth Blackwell; Kevin Brodie; Dennis Darland; Jan Loeb Eisler; Nicholas Griffin; Robert T. James; Justin Leiber; Gladys Leithauser; John R. Lenz; Timothy Madigan; Chandrakapala Padia; Ray Perkins; Stephen Reinhardt; David Rodier; Harry Ruja; Alan Schwerin; Warren Allen Smith; Tom Stanley; Peter Stone; Thom Weidlich; and Ruili Ye.

Honorary Members are: Sir Alfred Ayer; Noam Chomsky; Ken Coates; Peter Cranford; Elizabeth R. Eames; Paul Edwards; Antony Flew; Michael Foot; Paul Kurtz; Taslima Nasrin; David F. Pears; Willard Van Orman Quine; Conrad Russell; and Katharine Russell Tait.

Past awardees of the Bertrand Russell Society Award: Paul Arthur Schilpp (1980); Steve Allen (1981); Henry Kendall (1982); Joseph Rotblat (1983); Dora Black (1984); Robert Jay Lifton (1985); People For the American Way (1986); John Somerville (1987); Paul Kurtz (1988); Paul Edwards (1989); Planned Parenthood (1991); Sir Karl Popper (1992); Harry Ruja (1993); Zero Population Growth (1995); W. V. O. Quine (1996); Irving Copi (1998); Henry Morgentaler (1999). On the Web: <http://www.google.com/search?q=cache:1167503&dq=cache:www.users.drew.edu/~jlenz/brs.html>. (See entry for Lee Eisler.)

Berwick, George J. (Died 1872)

Berwick was a physician appointed surgeon to the East India Company in 1828. He wrote *Awas-i-hind, or A Voice from the Gangse, Being a Solution of the True Source of Christianity, By An Indian Officer* (1861).

He also wrote tracts under the signature of "Presbyter Anglicanus." Berwick was a freethinker. {BDF}

Besant, Annie (1847—1933)

An English freethinker who later became a Theosophist, Besant was a close associate of Charles Bradlaugh. Edward Royle has described her contribution to freethought and radicalism, calling her the greatest female orator of her day, and saying she can be credited for much of the success of the National Secular Society between 1874 and 1886 in England. George Bernard Shaw knew her well:

> Annie Besant, a player of genius, was a tragedian. Comedy was not her clue to life: she had a healthy sense of fun; but no truth came to her first as a joke. Injustice, waste, and the defeat of noble aspira-

tions did not revolt her by way of irony or paradox: they stirred her to direct and powerful indignation and to active resistance.

In 1878 when a petition in Chancery was presented to deprive her of her child on the ground of her atheistic and Malthusian views, Sir G. Jessell granted the petition. When Besant encountered the famed Russian occultist and theosophist, Madame Helena Petrovna Blavatsky, in 1889, she converted and within two years had become theosophy's main leader, spending the rest of her life in India, where she led the Congress Party (1917). Theosophy, a mystical view that insight into the nature of God and the world can be obtained through direct knowledge, is found in Oriental theologies and has included adherents such as Jakob Boehme, F. W. J. Schelling, and Emanuel Swedenborg.

Anne Taylor has written *Annie Besant: A Biography* (1992), which details her series of emotional (but apparently not physical) attachments to Charles Bradlaugh, Edward Aveling, J. M. Robertson, Bernard Shaw, William Stead, and Herbert Burrows. J. Gordon Melton has edited *The Origins of Theosophy: Annie Besant—The Atheist Years* (1990). From 1883 to 1888, Besant edited the weekly London publication, *Our Corner*.

Charles Leadbeater, who at the Australian Convention of Theosophists in 1922 was accused of everything from ventriloquism to pederasty, said "spirits" once informed him that in other ages Mrs. Besant acquired twelve husbands for whom she roasted rats and Julius Caesar married Jesus Christ, stories which gullible theosophists repeated as truths.

The theosophy part of Besant's career has little to do with secularism, but the Besant-Bradlaugh partnership between 1874 and 1886 was immensely important. Arthur Moss's verdict in 1915 was that in England Besant "was unquestionably the most learned, the most eloquent, and the most powerful lady advocate of Freethought that this country every produced."

She also, Paul Edwards wrote in *Reincarnation* (1996), was a foolish believer in reincarnation. (See entry for Birth Control.) {BDF; CE; EU, Edward Royle; FUK; FUS; PUT; RSR; SWW; TRI; WSS}

Best, Mary (20th Century)

Best, a freethinker, wrote *Thomas Paine, Prophet and Martyr of Democracy* (1927). {FUS}

Bestic, Allan (20th Century)

A freethinker, Bestic wrote *Praise the Lord and Pass the Contribution* (1971). {FUS}

Betham-Edwards, Matilda (1836—1919)

Betham-Edwards was a writer of novels and works on France, where she lived for forty years. In 1891 the French government made her an *Officier de Instruction Publique*. Betham-Edwards's obituary notice in the *Positivist Review* described her as "an uncompromising opponent of the Catholic Church . . . hardly more tolerant of the Anglican Church."

She was said to have been too "Voltairean" to join the positivists. {RAT}

Bethell, Richard [Baron Westbury] (1800—1873)

Bethell, a Lord Chancellor of Great Britain, after a career at the bar became Attorney General and in 1861 head of the House of Lords. He presided at one of the heresy trials and, in the words of a legal humorist, "took away from the orthodox members of the Church of England their last hope of eternal damnation." His verdict, in short, relieved clergymen of the need to believe in hell.

Jowett quoted Bethell as once having said about the Reformation, "You cut off the head of one beast, the Church of Rome, and immediately the head of another beast, the Church of England, makes its appearance." McCabe finds that although Bethell made no public declaration, it is not clear whether he was a non-Christian theist, an agnostic, or an atheist. {JM; RAT; RE}

BETHLEHEM: See entry for Christmas.

Bettinelli, Saverio (1718—1808)

An Italian ex-Jesuit, Bettinelli was a friend and admirer of Voltaire, sharing his deism. He had been rector of the Royal College at Parma (1751—1758) but, upon being suppressed, stepped down and remained nominally in the ranks of the clergy. {RAT}

Beverland, Hadrianus (1654—c. 1712)

A Dutch classical scholar and nephew of Isaac Vossius, Beverland wrote a treatise on Original Sin, *Peccatum Originale* (1672), which contended that the sin of Adam and Eve was their sexual inclination. The book caused a great outcry and was burned. Beverland was imprisoned and his name was struck from the roles of Leyden University. {BDF}

Bevan, Aneurin (1897—1960)

Bevan, a British politician, served as a Labour member in Parliament (1929—1960). A leader of the party's left wing (1951—1960), he was known for having administered the National Health Service. Bevan, an internationally noted politician, was an agnostic. {*New Humanist*, September 1996; TRI}

Bevington, L. S.: See entry for L. S. Guggenberger.

Beyer, Linda C. (20th Century)

Beyer is editor-in-chief of *World*, the journal of the Unitarian Universalist Association in Boston.

Beyerstein, Barry L. (1949—)

Beyerstein, a professor of psychology at Simon Fraser University in Vancouver, is on the executive council of the Committee for the Scientific Investigation of Claims of the Paranormal, which publishes *Skeptical Inquirer*. He has written for *Humanist in Canada* and signed Humanist Manifesto 2000.

Beyle, Marie Henri: See entry for Stendhal.

BEZ DOGMATU (Without Dogma)

A humanistic Polish quarterly, *Bez Dogmatu* is at Instytut Wydawniczy "Ksiazka I Prass," ul. Twarda 60, 00-818, Warszawa, Poland.

Bharati, Agehananda (Died 1989)

Bharati, an Austrian-turned-Hindu-turned Humanist, taught anthropology at Syracuse University in his final years. After Nazi Germany's fall, Leopald (his original name) traveled to India and joined with Ramakrishna Ashram, becoming in charge of editing the complete volumes of Vivekananda, the founder of the Ashram. He found "silly, ignorant aspects of the great Swamiji," according to Innaiah Narisetti, but retained them as the words of "a divine person." Because the Ashram Swamis could not tolerate Agehananda's agnostic, rationalistic attitude, he was expelled from the Ashram. Writing an autobiography, *The Ochre Robe*, he exposed Vivekananda as well as Ramakrishna Ashram, and the book was banned in India by the government of Prime Minister Nehru despite objections from radical humanists, rationalists, and atheists. Bharati also revealed how Vivekananda commercialized Yoga through his guide books. *Tantric Yoga* is also critical of Hindu aesthetics and sex practices in the name of religion.

When he was initiated into the Hindu fold as Sanyasi in Varanasi burial grounds, he was named Agehananda Bharati, then toured Indian holy places on foot and studied the scriptures in Sanskrit. In 1952 he met M. N. Roy in Dehradun, became interested in the scientific method and logical systems in regard to religion, and taught in the universities of Benares and Delhi for a short time. (See material by Innaiah Narisetti on the Web: <avana.net/~jshankar/index.htm>.)

Bhargava, Pushpa Mittra (20th Century)

A renowned scientist, Dr. Bhargava is the former and founding director of Centre for Cellular and Molecular Biology in Hyderabad. He has been a visiting professor in several European and American universities. Bhargava, who designed "The Method of Science" exhibition on display at Birla Science Museum, Hyderabad, is a former chairperson of the Indian Rationalist Association. Bhargava signed Humanist Manifesto 2000.

Bhattachariya, Debasis (1967—)

In Calcutta, Bhattachariya is a law clerk who is a leading protagonist in rationalist campaigns. A member of the Science and Rationalist's Association of India, he is a "guru buster" who helps expose gurus, swamis, yogis, and others claiming mystical powers.

Although Mother Teresa won the Nobel Peace Prize for her relief work in the slums of Calcutta, Bhattachariya has stated, "Mother Teresa has a clean image, and there is no doubt that she has helped the poor. But in the end, we believe that Mother Teresa is not at all any better than all the other godmen and godwomen, because she helps to place a more kindly mask on the overall exploitation in our society." (See entry for Prabhir Ghosh.) {*The New York Times*, 10 October 1995}

Bhatti, Indirius Dominic (20th Century)

Bhatti is director of the Unitarian Universalist Christians of Pakistan. (See entry for Unitarian Universalist Christians of Pakistan.)

Bhatty, Margaret (20th Century)

Bhatty is on the staff of the *American Atheist* and reports on religious events in India. A feminist journalist, she lives in Nagpur. One of her paperbacks is entitled, *An Atheist Reports from India* (1987).

BHEEM PATRIKA

Bheem Patrika is an Ambedkar journal published fortnightly by Bheem Patrika Publications in Hindi and English. It is at ES - 393A Abadpura, Jalandhar - 144 003, Punjab, India.

Bianchi, Angelo (1799—1862)

Also known as Aurelio Bianchi-Giovini, this Italian man of letters wrote *The Life of Father Paoli Sarpi* (1836), which was put on the *Index* and led to his being in constant strife with the Roman Church. For attacks on the clergy in *Il Republicano* at Lugano, Bianchi was forced to flee to Zurich, thence to Milan. His principal works are the *History of the Popes* (1850—1864) and *A Criticism of the Gospels* (1853). {BDF}

Biandrata, Giorgio (c. 1515—1591)

Seeking refuge in Poland because of his heretical religious opinions, the Italian physician Biandrata was accepted and in 1565 organized the Minor Reformed Church. It was Unitarian in outlook and gained the allegiance of a significant portion of the Polish nobility. He became a leader of the Socinian party but was assassinated in 1591. {BDF; EU, Paul H. Beattie}

BIBLE, THE

For non-believers, a person's bible is that which he prizes. For some, that could be the works of Robert G. Ingersoll. Or Shakespeare. Or Voltaire. Or *The Economist*.

For Jews, Christians, and Muslims, the Holy Bible is a library of 39 books of the Old Testament. For Catholics and Protestants, it includes the 27 books of the New Testament. The Apocrypha, consisting of 14 additional books, are considered by Protestants to be of dubious authenticity. Pseudepigraphon are any of various pseudonymous or anonymous Jewish religious writings, one being the *Psalms of Solomon*.

Byblos was an ancient Phoenician city from which papyrus was exported and on which books were written. To describe the product, the ancient Greeks used *biblia*, the plural of the Greek noun *biblion*. Latin readers mistook the word for the feminine singular. As a result, "bible" is a singular noun for what really is a library of 66 to 80 books.

Although some fundamentalists insist that God literally dictated the Bible, crossing each *t* and dotting each *i*, the collection of books has been variously translated and some translations differ widely from others. Some of the versions of the Old Testament, chronologically listed, are as follows:

- Septuagint (Greek), which was made in Alexandria from about the 3rd century B.C.E. to the 1st century of the Christian Era;
- the Old Latin; the Peshitta (Syriac);
- the Syro-Hexaplar (Syriac);
- four Coptic (Egyptian versions);
- the Latin Vulgate, made by Jerome toward the end of the 4th century.

Some of the versions of the New Testament are as follows:

- the Old Latin version, originated by the end of the 2nd century and probably in Africa;
- the Diatessaron, made by Tatian in about 160;
- the Old Syriac;
- the five Egyptian (Coptic) versions;
- the Armenian;
- the Latin Vulgate, made by Jerome after 380.

The Masoretic was made by scribes who compiled the Masorah, consisting of notes on the textual traditions of the Hebrew Old Testament and compiled during the first millennium of the Christian era. The notes are not critical, merely describing what is the correct form of the text, and the Masorah accumulated from about 500 to about 1100.

In the present century, a number of translations have been made of all the books of the Bible. A recent editing omits terms considered anti-feminist, and some groups demand that God not be defined or described as masculine. "The Bible says . . . ," although frequently expressed as a truism by believers, does not clearly state which of the widely different versions is "the absolutely true one."

Negative comments about the Bible are numerous:

- The Bible. That is what fools have written, what imbeciles command, what rogues teach, and young children are made to learn by heart.

—Voltaire

- I find some passages of the Bible of correct morality, and others of so much ignorance, untruth, charlatanism, and imposture.

—Thomas Jefferson
Letter to William Short, 13 April 1820

- It is odd that God learned Greek when he wanted to turn author, and that he did not learn it better.

—Friedrich Nietzsche

- It ain't those parts of the Bible that I can't understand that bother me, it's the parts that I do understand.

—Mark Twain

- When I think of all the harm the Bible has done, I despair of ever writing anything to equal it.

—Oscar Wilde

- So far as I can remember, there is not one word in the Gospels in praise of intelligence.

—Bertrand Russell

- Scriptures, n. The sacred books of our holy religion, as distinguished from the false and profane writings on which all other faiths are based.

—Ambrose Bierce

- The total absence of humor from the Bible is one of the most singular things in all literature.

—Alfred North Whitehad

- "The Good Book"—one of the most remarkable euphemisms evercoined.

—Ashley Montagu

- God, isn't God a shit!

——Randolph Churchill's comment when reading the Bible, as reported in Evelyn Waugh's *Diaries*.

- The inspiration of the Bible depends on the ignorance of the gentleman who reads it.

—Robert G. Ingersoll

- Y'say grammarians prescribe that books of the Bible should not be italiziced? Wait until the homophobes read that "Jesus is in John."

—Allen Windsor

(See entries for *Biblical rancy*; Charles Bufe, who has described its many contradictions; Farrell Till, editor of *Skeptical Review*; and for Kenneth E. Nahigian, who declares that the Septuagint version is a "sloppy" translation.) {ER; RE}

BIBLE CODE

A 1997 book by Michael Drosnin, *The Bible Code*, purports to show that messages concerning modern events, such as the assassination of Yitzhak Rabin and Clinton's election in 1992, were "encoded" in the Bible about 3,000 years ago. Using a computer program, Drosnin "uncovered" the alleged messages.

Hector Avalos, however, called the work "one of the most alarming examples of pseudo-science and pseudobiblical scholarship of 1997." Drosnin, in a statement Avalos reported for the

Committee for the Scientific Examination of Religion, is simply using a more sophisticated version of the game called Scrabble to resurrect the biblical numerology of yore. {*Secular Humanist Bulletin*, Fall 1997}

THE BIBLE FOR CHILDREN

Children's bibles became popular in the 16th and 17th centuries. However, as pointed out by Ruth B. Bottigheimer in *The Bible for Children, From the Age of Gutenberg to the Present* (1996), the record was occasionally falsified for children.

Noah's drunkenness, for example, disappeared from most German and British children's Bibles. Roman Catholic versions kept it in but added some face-saving excuses. A 1714 edition suggested that Noah became drunk because the Flood had prevented him from taking wine for a year.

As for the handling of Abraham's near murder of his son Isaac, Christianity's Oedipal story in reverse, Isaac's age of 37 was gradually infantilized over the years until he became the eight-year-old child familiar in pictures.

Jephthah's murder of his young daughter was covered in 1915 by emphasizing "the providence of God Almighty, His justice and mercy." Lot's peace offering of his virgin daughters to the Sodom mob was said in 1824 to be "perfectly consonant with the usage of those times and countries . . . doing evil that good might come." His later incest with those same daughters, if described at all, was attributed to their depravity and, in one version, the story became "Lot Loses His Chastity."

Bottigheimer gave so many other examples that most parents would likely hesitate to mention the Bible to their children, choosing instead junior versions of *Gulliver's Travels*, *Robinson Crusoe*, or even Bottigheimer's *Grimm's Bad Girls and Bold Boys*.

BIBLE STORIES, NOT FOR CHILDREN

Jonathan Kirsch's *The Harlot by the Side of the Road: Forbidden Tales of the Bible* (1997) lists the following stories in the Bible:

- Lot impregnates his daughters (*Genesis* 19:1-38)
- Hamor rapes Dinah with consequences (*Genesis* 34:1-31)
- Tamar, the harlot by the side of the road (*Genesis* 38:1-26)
- The bridegroom of blood: Zipporah circumcises (*Exodus* 4:24-26)
- Jephthah sacrifices his daughter (*Judges* 11:1-40)
- The traveler hacks up his concubines (*Judges* 19:1-30)
- Tamar is raped by her brother (*2 Samuel* 11:2-15; 12:9-25; 13:1-22)

{Wolf Roder, *FIG Leaves*, February 1999}

THE BIBLE SAYS

Quiz: According to the rubric, "the Bible says" which of the following?

- Satan (or the Devil) tempted Eve to eat of the forbidden fruit;
- God punished Adam and Eve by driving them out of Paradise;
- God destroyed the tower of Babel;
- God destroyed the city of Sodom because its inhabitants engaged in homosexual practices;
- the plagues were punishment for the evil that the Egyptians did to the Israelites;
- Balaam was a wicked person who cursed Israel.

According to James L. Kugel's *The Bible As It Was* (1997), all are false statements.

Kugel, the Star Professor of Hebrew Literature at Harvard University, provides information as to how the interpretation by early scholars on the Torah altered people's perceptions of biblical teachings. For example, he shows that Isaac did not ask (as the Bible reads, "Who are you, my son?" but rather "Who are you? My son?" In turn Jacob did not reply, "I am Esau, your first born," but rather, "I am. [But] Esau is your first born." Kugel laments the fact that over the past few centuries a Protestant captivity of the Bible and of biblical scholarship has ensued, and his work is meant to illustrate "the Bible As It Was Not."

Although nine of ten Americans are said to have a Bible, few are aware that all the following are false:

- The "forbidden fruit" of *Genesis* was an apple.
- Jesus was an only child.
- Mary Magdalene, one of Jesus's friends, was a harlot.
- Jonah spent three days in the belly of a whale.
- Jesus was born on December 25th.

{Phyllis Trible, "What God Meant to Say. . . ,"
The New York Times Book Review, 21 December 1997;
Kenneth C. Davis, *Don't Know Much About the Bible? (1998)*}

THE BIBLE, HUMOR IN

No humorous items appear in the entire Holy Bible. However, Terry Sanderson suggests the following:

Q: Which American state is mentioned in the Bible?
A: "And Noah looked from the Ark and saw . . ."
Q: What was the longest day in the Bible?
A: There was no eve the day Adam was created.
Q: Why did the Catholic Church in Tottenham purchase an adjoining pub with stripteasers, the Silver Lady?
A: To prepare Catholic children for the shock of what grown-ups look like without their clothes.

The *Playboy* edition of the Bible, Don Wigal of New York City has extrapolated (in *The Freethinker*, February 1997; *New York*, 25 August 1997}, should include the following erotic listing:

I	V
II	VII
III	VIII
IV	X

THE BIBLE, BLOOPERS: See entry for Michael Ledo.

THE BIBLE, TRANSLATIONS (GULLAH)

The Bible has been translated into many languages. Following is an example from one book that was released (1994) by the American Bible Society. The comparison with the King James Version is in Gullah, a historic African-English language spoken mainly in coastal South Carolina but which is closely related to the English-based Creole language spoken in the Caribbean. Gullah's grammatical structure comes from West Africa.

The Gospel According to Luke

2:10. And the angel said unto bring you good tidings of great joy, which shall be to all people.

2:11. For unto you is born this day in the city of David a Savior, which is Christ the Lord.

6:20. And he lifted up his eyes on his disciples, and said: Blessed be ye poor: for yours is the kingdom of God

24:6. He is not here, but is risen.

De Good Nyewes Bout Jedus Christ Wa Luke Write

2:10. Bot de angel tell um say, "Mus don't feah! A habe good nyews. Cause ob dis nyews, oona gwine rejaice tommuch."

2:11. Cause A come fa tell oona, "Right now, dis day, a Sabior done bon fa oona. He de Promise Chile, Christ, de Lawd. An e bon een David town!"

6:20. Jedus look at e ciple dem an tell um say, "Oona bless fa true, oona po people. Cause God esef da rule oba oona!"

24:6. "Jedus ain't yah. E done git op from mongst deded, an e da libe gin!"

BIBLICAL ERRANCY

Biblical Errancy (3158 Sherwood Park Drive, Springfield, Ohio 45505) is published monthly. The publication is thorough in its critical analysis of the Bible. Dennis McKinsey, its editor, is one of the major unbelievers with a scholarly understanding of the Bible and its many contradictions.

Jim Hill and Rand Cheadie's *The Bible Tells Me So: Uses and Abuses of Holy Scripture* (1966) notes the following contradictions along with numerous other examples:

> Drink no longer water, but use a little wine for thy stomach's sake and thine often infirmities.
> *I Timothy 5:23*
>
> Wine is a mocker, strong drink is raging: and whosoever is deceived thereby is not wise.
> *Proverbs 20:1*
>
> I will therefore that men pray everywhere, lifting up holy hands, without wrath and doubting.
> *1 Timothy* 2:8
>
> But thou, when thou prayest, enter into thy closet, and when thou has shut thy door, pray to thy Father which is in secret.
> *Matthew* 6:7
>
> The Lord is a man of war.
> *Exodus* 15:3
>
> Thou shalt not kill.
> *Exodus* 20:13

BIBLIOFANTASIAC

Bibliofantasiac is published by C. F. Kennedy (39 Claremore Ave., Scarborough, Ontario, Canada M1N 3S1. E-mail: <tangle@interlog.com>.

Bichat, Marie François Xavier (1771—1802)

A French anatomist and physiologist, Bichat wrote the *Physiology of Life and Death*. Wheeler has described him as "a martyr to his zeal for science." {BDF; RAT}

Bickersteth, Henry [Baron Langdale] (1783—1851)

Bickersteth, one of the many freethinking distinguished British jurists of the nineteenth century, refused the position both of Attorney General and Lord Chancellor but was Master of the Rolls.

Lord Langdale and his friend Bentham agreed about the subject of religion, except Bentham was more atheistic. According to one of his biographers, Hardy, Bickersteth was "destitute of religious feeling," but he seemed to have held some shade of intellectual theism. {JM; RAT; RE}

Biddle, John (1615—1661)

Biddle was the founder of English Unitarianism, although a Church of the Strangers, one with a Socinian influence, had been established in London as early as 1550. Biddle started as a master of the Gloucester Grammar School in England. He was dismissed for his denial of the Trinity. In 1647 he was imprisoned and his book burned by the hangman. In 1654 he was again imprisoned, then banished in 1655 to the Scilly Islands. After the Restoration when he returned to London, he again was arrested, and this time, in 1661, he died in prison. {BDF; CE; JMR; JMRH}

Bierbower, Austin (19th Century)

Bierbower, a freethinker, wrote *Principles of a System of Philosophy* (1870). {GS}

Bierce, Ambrose (1842—1914?)

The last of ten children, Bierce was the son of a father who liked books but did not like long-term employment. His mother was a pious matron. Tellingly, Bierce once started a series of tales, "The Parenticide Club," with "Having murdered my mother under circumstances of singular atrocity"' in another, he wrote, "Early one June morning in 1872 I murdered my father—an act which made a deep impression on me at the time."

Bierce volunteered in the Ninth Indiana Infantry Regiment, was promoted to brevet major for his courageous service in several bloody battles including Shiloh, Chickamauga, Stones River, Resaca, and Pickett's Mill, and wrote credible novels about war. In one short story, "Chickamauga," he included grisly details, and in "An Occurrence at Owl Creek Bridge," a spy as he is being hanged dreams of his beloved wife, the dream interrupted by the snapping of his neck. Ever the witty pessimist, who defined a year as "a period of 365 disappointments," Bierce did not spend his entire life in the gloomy fashion most assumed was his lot. He edited two issues of *The Lantern* for the exiled Empress Eugenie, wrote for Hearst newspapers, married a socialite, settled comfortably in Marin County, and raised three children.

The Devil's Dictionary (1911, originally in 1906 called *The Cynic's Word Book*) was addressed to "enlightened souls who prefer dry wines to sweet, sense to sentiment, wit to humor, and clean English to slang." Characteristic entries include the following:

> *Advice*, n. The smallest current coin.
> *Bore*, n. A person who talks when you wish him to listen.
> *Christian*, n. One who believes that the New Testament is a divinely inspired book admirably suited to the spiritual needs of his neighbor.
> *Clergyman*, n. A man who undertakes the management of your spiritual affairs as a method of bettering his temporal ones.
> *Edible*, adj. Good to eat, and wholesome to digest, as a worm to a toad, a toad to a snake, a snake to a pig, a pig to a man, and a man to a worm.
> *Faith*, n. Belief without evidence in what is told by one who speaks without knowledge, of things without parallel.
> *Garter*, n. An elastic band intended to keep a woman from coming out of her stockings and desolating the country.
> *Heathen*, n. A benighted creature who has the folly to worship something that he can see and feel.
> *Labor*, n. One of the processes by which A acquires property for B.
> *Marriage*, n. A community consisting of a master, a mistress, and two slaves, making in all, two.
> *Martyr*, n. One who moves along the path of least resistance to a desired death.
> *Mugwump*, n. In politics one afflicted with self-respect and addicted to the vice of independence. A term of contempt.
> *Pray*, verb. To ask that the laws of the universe be annulled in behalf of a single petitioner confessedly unworthy.
> *Prejudice*, n. A vagrant opinion without visible means of support.
> *Rack*, n. An argumentative implement formerly much used in persuading devotees of a false faith to embrace the living truth.
> *Scriptures*, n. The sacred books of our holy religion, as distinguished from the false and profane writings on which all other faiths are based.

A Unitarian, Bierce wrote, "If there is a God—a proposition that the wise are neither concerned to deny nor hot to affirm—nothing is more obvious than that for some purpose known only to himself he has ordered all the arrangements of this world utterly regardless of the temporal needs of man. This earth is about the worst that a malevolent ingenuity, an unquickened apathy, or an extreme incapacity could have devised."

Among his other sardonic observations, Bierce found that "Christians and camels receive their burdens kneeling." As for books: "The covers of this book are too far apart." The ideal epitaph: "Here lies 'So-and-so'-as usual." As for being cautious: "Don't believe without evidence. Treat things divine with marked respect—don't have anything to do with them. Do not trust humanity without collateral security."

Bierce was depicted in the movie, "The Old Gringo." In it, he dies but it is not clear where or how. Roy Morris Jr. in *Ambrose Bierce, Alone in Bad Company* (1996) speculates that Bierce may have killed himself while heading toward Mexico. He had once told his best friend and publisher, Walter Neale, that he intended to shoot himself at or near the Grand Canyon. Before Morris's work, Joe Nickell in *Ambrose Bierce is Missing* claimed similar information.

Others have said, without factual evidence, that Bierce was held captive and killed by a tribe of Brazilian Indians. What is known is that in 1913 Bierce set out to observe the Mexican revolution, to seek "the good, kind darkness," and, mysteriously, was never again seen. (See "The Enlightened Cynicism of Ambrose Bierce" by Glenn Odden, *Free Inquiry*, Fall 1996) {CE; JM; PA; RAT; David S. Reynolds, *The New York Times Book Review*, 18 February 1996; OCAL, OEL, TYD; U; UU}

Bieri, John G. (20th Century)

In the 1950s, Bieri, while in the department of biochemistry and nutrition at the University of Texas, Medical Branch, in Galveston, wrote book reviews for *The Humanist*.

Biersted, Sonia (20th Century)

Biersted, a humanist, wrote *A Humanistic View of Religion* (196—?). {GS}

BIGAMY

> • Bigamy, n. A mistake in taste for which the wisdom of the future will adjudge a punishment called trigamy.
>
> **—Ambrose Bierce**
> *The Devil's Dictionary*

In church law, bigamy is a word for the valid marriage after the death of the first spouse. But in criminal law, it involves contracting marriage while already married. Around the year 1655, the Frankish Diet, a Protestant body, legalized bigamy as a means of replenishing the population of Europe, which was badly decimated by the recent Thirty Years War.

In 1922 in a Sheffield, England, courtroom, accused bigamist Theresa Vaughn admitted under oath that in the past five years she had acquired sixty-one husbands in fifty cities throughout England, Germany, and South Africa, averaging a marriage a month.

Gays and lesbians, who almost universally cannot marry, smile at their legal inability to become bigamists or even polygamists. {ER; PA}

BIG BANG THEORY

Cosmologists Edwin Hubble and Milton Humason in the 1920s concluded that the universe not only is expanding but that the galaxies themselves are flying away from one another. This was said to be the result of a hypothetical "big bang" which had exploded between ten and twenty billion years ago, an explosion which is still continuing. Using a thirty-three-foot telescope atop Mauna Kea in Hawaii, astronomers in 1994 found a surprising abundance of deuterium in the distant, and therefore early, universe. The ratio of about two atoms of deuterium for every 10,000 hydrogen atoms is tentatively considered confirmation of the theory. But scientists are aware that many more observations and much more investigation will be needed to prove the theory, if indeed it is possible to prove.

Keeping up-to-date on the theory is a daily task. At the start of 1997, it was estimated that the end of the universe will happen 10,000 trillion trillion trillion trillion trillion trillion trillion trillion (10 to the hundredth power) years from now. The Sun is expected to die in about five billion years, reduced to an extinct remnant known as a white dwarf. Earth's oceans would boil away from the heat, and life would no longer be possible. The end of all star formation, the end of the stelliferous era, could come in 100 trillion years. Black holes will gobble up the white dwarfs. A black hole's final moment might be an explosive blast of radiation, followed by a dark era. Or, perhaps, the universe will collapse of its own weight. At the other end of the Big Bang, in short, may simply be the Big Sputter.

Meanwhile, the scientific community does not at all accept the creationist theory of the origin of the universe, one which cites the Old Testament book, *Genesis*. Instead, they continue their free inquiries into the subject and look forward to new findings in tomorrow's journals. [See entries for Cosmology, Murray Gell-Mann, and RNA. Also, the entry for Steven Weinberg gives a clear explanation of "before the big bang."}

Biggett, Adam (20th Century)

Biggett, a freethinker, wrote *Gems and Garbage* (1950?). {GS}

BIGOT

• The mind of the bigot is like the pupil of the eye: the more light you pour upon it, the more it will contract.

—Oliver Wendell Holmes

• Bigot, n. One who is obstinately and zealously attached to an opinion that you do not entertain.

—Ambrose Bierce
The Devil's Dictionary

BIHAR RATIONALIST SOCIETY

The Bihar Rationalist Society (a member of the International Humanist and Ethical Union) is at 216-A, S.K. Puri, Patna-800 001, Bihar, India. Its President is Dr. Ramendra of the philosophy department of Patna University, and its general secretary and treasurer is Dr. Kawaljeet. A non-party, non-profit, educational society, Bihar Buddhiwadi [Rationalist] Samaj [Society] was formed in 1985 to promote rationalism, humanism, atheism, and secularism. Bihar is a major Hindi-speaking state, the second most populous state of India after Uttar Pradesh. Its founding members in 1985 were Dr. Ramendra; an elder sister Kiran Nath Datt; brothers Shivendra and Manavendra; and two friends, Ramanand Mandal and Rahul Prasad. The Buddhiwadi Foundation, which publishes a Hindu quarterly, *Buddhiwadi*, promotes computer literacy and the scientific outlook.

On the Web: <http://www.myfreeoffice.com/buddhiwadi>. {*International Humanist News*, December 1997}

BIG BEN (The Bell in the Clock Tower of the Houses of Parliament in London): See entry for Benjamin Hall.

Bihldorff, Carl (1910—1990)

The Rev. Carl Bihldorff, of the Louisville, Kentucky, Unitarian Church, wrote in 1940 about Unitarianism's history:

> To begin with, so far as is known, the name *Unitarian* originated in Hungary. Rev. Charles Graves in his *History of Unitarianism* says that Peter Bod, the Transylvanian historian, relates that in 1557 the Diet of Thorda in Transylvania passed an edict granting universal freedom of worship. At about the same time the various religious bodies within the country formed a league of toleration pledging themselves not to persecute one another. The members of this league were popularly called "The United" or "Unitarians."
>
> So at first the title Unitarian had no theological or denominational significance. It simply indicated a fraternal relationship embracing all kinds of Christian believers. But these first "Unitarians" did not long remain united. Dissension arose over sharp differences of belief. Those who held that a belief in the Trinity is fundamental to Christian faith charged those more lax with being guilty of an "unpardonable sin."
>
> As a result the dogmatic Trinitarians withdrew from the "United" league of fraternity and tolerance. Those who remained loyal members of the league continued to be known as "Unitarians," but not because of any Unitarian beliefs. However, wrote Bod, "It was natural and unavoidable that the title should come at last to mark the distinguishing faith of those persons who remained loyal to the 'league' for those who place tolerance and fraternity above doctrines and dogmas are already on the threshold of Unitarianism."

At the time of his retirement in 1975, Bihldorff was minister of the First Parish Church (Unitarian) in Brookline, Massachusetts.

Bijleveld, J. (20th Century)

In 1952, Bijleveld was the organizing treasurer of the newly founded International Humanist and Ethical Union (IHEU). "Humanism," he has said, "is concerned with how we live—how we feel—not just how we think."

Bilbao, Francisco (1823—1865)

Bilbao was a Chilean whose sharp attacks against the Catholic Church are found in his *La sociabilidad chilena* (1844) and *Evangelio americano* (1864). Catholicism, he argued, denied the most fundamental principles of the republic: sovereignty of men and reason. As a result, the Chilean church accused him of blasphemy, and Bilbao was brought to trial. {EU}

BILL OF RIGHTS FOR UNBELIEVERS

In 1998 the Campus Freethought Alliance issued a "Bill of Rights for Unbelievers," stating unbelievers shall the right to . . .

I. Think freely and autonomously, express their views forthrightly, and debate or criticize any and all ideas without fear of censure, recrimination, or public ostracism.

II. Be free from discrimination and persecution in the workplace, business transactions, and public accommodations.

III. Exercise freedom of conscience in any situation where the same right would be extended to believers on religious grounds alone.

IV. Hold any public office, in accordance with the constitutional principle that there shall be no religious test for such office.

V. Abstain from religious oaths and pledges, including pledges of allegiance, oaths of office, and oaths administered in a court of law, until such time as these are secularized or replaced by non-discriminatory affirmations.

VI. Empower members of their community to perform legally

binding ceremonies, such as marriage.
VII. Raise and nurture their children in a secular environment, and not be disadvantaged in adoption or custody proceedings.
VIII. Conduct business and commerce on any day of their choosing, without interference from laws or regulations recognizing religious days of prayer, rest, or celebration.
IX. Enjoy freedom from taxation supporting the government employment of clergy, and access to secular counseling equivalent to that provided by chaplains.
X. Declare conscientious objection to serving in the armed forces under any circumstance in which the religious may do so.
XI. Live as citizens of a democracy free from religious language and imagery in currency, public schools and buildings, and government documents and business.

{*Free Inquiry*, Fall 1998}

Billaud-Varenne, Jean Nicolas (1756—1819)

A French conventionalist, Billaud-Varenne became advocate to Parliament about 1785, denounced the government and clergy in 1789, and proposed abolition of the monarchy in 1791. He withdrew from Robespierre after the feast of the Supreme Being, saying, "Thou beginnest to sicken me with thy Supreme Being." He was exiled in 1795 and died at St. Domingo in 1819. {BDF}

Billings, Josh [pseudonym of Henry Wheeler Shaw] (1818—1885)

Billings is the American humorist who wrote homespun philosophies in a rural dialect. He often is quoted by secularists for his "It's better to know nothing than to know what ain't so." His humor is best illustrated by the annual *Farmer's Allminax* (1869—1880). {CE}

Billings, M. E. (20th Century)

Billings, a freethinker, wrote *Crimes of Preachers in the United States and Canada (*1924?). {GS}

Binet, Alfred (1857—1911)

A famous French psychologist whose name is given to certain types of intelligence tests, Binet was director of the laboratory of physiological psychology at Paris University. In *L'âme et le corps* (1905), he rejected the belief in a soul separable from the body, but Binet was not a dogmatic materialist. {RAT; RE}

Binga, Timothy (20th Century)

Binga is director of the Center for Inquiry Libraries at the Amherst, New York, headquarters.

Binns, William (19th Century)

Binns, a freethinker, wrote *Christianity in Relation to Modern Thought* (1864). {GS}

BIOGRAPHICAL DICTIONARY OF ANCIENT, MEDIEVAL, AND MODERN FREETHINKERS

On the Web, Internet Infidels, Inc., a non-profit organization, has much material about the existence of a god, church/state separation, the possibility of life after death, mysticism, and the interface between science and religion. Joseph McCabe's *Biographical Dictionary of Ancient, Medieval, and Modern Freethinkers* is at <http://www.infidels.org/library/historical/joseph_mccabe/dictionary.html>.

Bion (3rd Century B.C.E.)

Bion of Borysthenes, near the mouth of the Dneiper, was a Scythian philosopher who flourished about 250 B.C.E. He was sold as a slave to a rhetorician, who afterwards gave him freedom and made him his heir. In Athens, Bion was a student of Theodorus the Atheist.

Two of his recorded sayings are "Only the votive tablets of the preserved are seen in the temples, not those of the drowned" and "it is useless to tear our hair when in grief since sorrow is not cured by baldness." {BDF}

BIOPHILIA

Humanist Laureate E. O. Wilson has defined biophilia as the ineffable and natural sense that human beings are intimately related to all species, animal and plant alike.

Biot, Jean Baptiste (1774—1862)

Biot was a French astronomer who was admitted to the Institut, the English Royal Society (1815), and the Legion of Honour (1814). Besides many technical works, he published a eulogy of Montaigne (*Éloge de Montaigne*) in 1812 and was a rationalist. {RAT}

Birch, William John (1811—1863)

Birch was an English freethinker, author of *An Inquiry into the Philosophy and Religion of Shakespeare* (1848) and *An Inquiry into the Philosophy and Religion of the Bible* (1856). {BDF; RAT; VI}

Bird, Henry (Born 1839)

Bird, of Barston in England, went to America in 1860 and located at Newark, New Jersey, where he became known as a horticulturist. After discarding Episcopalianism, he became a Congregationalist and then an atheist. Bird was president of the Newark Liberal League and once wrote

'Tis your prerogative and mine to doubt;
How do you know? is truth's own scout;
Facts fear no foes, the truth will out,
Though crushed will rise, and error rout.

{PUT}

BIRDS

Birds evolved from dinosaurs. However, this was not realized until the end of the 20th century when fossils of two turkey-sized animals were discovered beneath an ancient lake bed in the Liaoning Province in northeastern China. The Caudipteryx, "tail feather," had the most feathers, including a large tail fan. The Protarchaeopteryx featured feathers but no evidence of a wing. Archaeopteryx, the earliest known bird, has been dated at 140-million to 150-million years old. Protarchaeopteryx and Caudipteryx are dated at 120-million to 136-million years old.

There are approximately 8,600 species of birds, ranging from the ostrich (which can weigh 300 pounds and be 8 feet tall) to the bee hummingbird (which can weigh a tenth of an ounce and be less than 3 inches tall). An estimated eighty species of birds may have become extinct since the 17th century, according to some environmentalists.

Birk, Rainer (20th Century)

Birk, a physician from Danbury, Connecticut, is a member of Mensa and an activist upon behalf of the International Humanist and Ethical Union.

E-mail: <rbirko@aol.com>. On the Web: <http://members.aol.com/rbirko/>.

Birkhead, L. M. (1855—1954)

A Unitarian minister who was one of the first to suggest devise some kind of humanist document and then helped write Humanist Manifesto I, Birkhead was on the advisory board of Charles Francis Potter's First Humanist Society of New York.

In Kansas City, where for many years he was minister of the Unitarian Church there, he invited Sinclair Lewis to speak, at which time the well-known novelist gave "God" a few minutes to prove "His" existence by striking him dead. The assembled Unitarians were reportedly amused, but others in the city were quite upset with Lewis's depiction of them in his *Elmer Gantry* (1927).

When informed that Lewis just before his death had written the present editor that he was a naturalistic humanist but that some religionists were claiming he had had a deathbed conversion, Birkhead replied to the present author concerning Lewis's postcard, "I doubt that it will kill off the legends, but at least the truth will be available." Among the Little Blue Books which Birkhead wrote were "Is Elmer Gantry True?", "Religious Bunk Over the Radio," and "Can Man Know God?"

Birkhead was well-known as the national director of Friends of Democracy, an organization which exposed American fascists, also Christian fundamentalists such as Gerald L. K. Smith. (See entry for John Steinbeck.) {CL; EW; HM1; HNS; WAS, 24 April 1951}

BIRMINGHAM (England) HUMANIST GROUP

Information is available from Tova Jones by telephoning 0121 4544692.

Birney, William (19th Century)

Birney, a freethinker, wrote *Hell and Hades* (c. 1900). {GS}

Biro, John (20th Century)

Biro, of the University of Florida, is a committee member for The Hume Society, the group which is engaged in scholarly activity concerning David Hume.

Birren, Faber (1900—1988)

A leading expert on color texture, Birren was a naturalistic humanist who reviewed books for *The Humanist* in the 1950s. A resident of Fairfield County, Connecticut, and New York City, Birren worked as a color consultant and wrote *Color in Modern Packaging* (1935) and *The Story of Color* (1941). He not only chose colors for the interiors of skyscrapers but also for airplanes and automobiles. He was an active member of the Stamford, Connecticut, Unitarian Society.

BIRTH CONTROL: See entry for Sex Education.

Birx, H. James (1941—)

Birx, who chaired the Canisius College sociology-anthropology department from 1980 to 1995, was named "Distinguished Educator" in 1999 by that Buffalo, New York, institution.

He is author of the CHOICE award-winning *Theories of Evolution* (1984), *Human Evolution* (1988), and *Interpreting Evolution: Darwin and Teilhard de Chardin* (1991). Birx has written introductions for both Darwin's *The Voyage of the Beagle* and *The Descent of Man*, Nietzsche's *Thus Spake Zarathustra*, Haeckel's *The Riddle of the Universe*, Wallace's *Island Life*, and Sir Julian Huxley's *Evolutionary Humanism* (all for Prometheus Books), as well as over 350 articles and reviews.

Birx is on the editorial board of *Philo*, *Proteus*, *Free Inquiry*, *Bertrand Russell Society Quarterly*, *Razonamientos* in Spain, and *Common Sense* in Russia. In 1980, he signed the Secular Humanist Declaration. He is a Secular Humanist Mentor of the Council for Secular Humanism and an honorary associate of the New Zealand Association of Rationalists and Humanists.

Birx's *Who's Who in the World* entry contains the following:

> An understanding of and appreciation for the true place of our own species within this material universe requires taking both a cosmic perspective and the evolutionary framework seriously.

Birx has been a Visiting Scholar at Harvard University (1997-1998) as well as a Visiting Professor at both Moscow State University and St. Petersburg State University in Russia. He has also given invited lectures at Yale University, Princeton University, Johns Hopkins University, University of Kansas–Lawrence, University of Hawai'i-Manoa, Oxford University, Trinity College–Ireland, and the Humboldt of Berlin (among others).

Birx is a Visiting Research Scholar at the Center for Inquiry-International in Amherst, New York, and an elected member of the Executive Committee for the Afro-Asian Philosophy Association in Cairo, Egypt.

Of the various prominent secular humanists, Birx—a signer of Humanist Manifesto 2000—has been described as one of the foremost, not only for thoroughly knowing his subject matter (which includes anthropology, the history of science, and evolutionary thought) but also for being a genuinely outgoing individual who has encouraged numbers of individuals on several continents to search for truths rather than believing others' alleged truths.

E-mail: < birxh@canisius.edu>. On the Web: <http://www.canisius.edu/~birxh>. {SHD; WAS, numerous conversations}

BISEXUAL CONCERNS

The Unitarian Universalist Office of Bisexual, Gay, Lesbian, and Transgender Concerns is at 25 Beacon Street, Boston, Massachusetts 02108. On the Web: <obgletc@uua.org>.

BISEXUALITY

If the Hebrew God was originally "one," it might logically follow that God the Creator was, therefore, a bisexual entity. Few, however, accept such a thesis. The Ancient Greek Zeus, however, was definitely bisexual and his love for the most beautiful of mortals, Ganymede, was so intense that Zeus disguised himself as an eagle, seduced him, and carried him to Mount Olympus where Ganymede was the object of love—discreetly termed a cupbearer—among the other divinities. Zeus, as compensation to Ganymede's father for the loss of his son, gave him a team of beautiful, light-footed horses.

In *Vice Versa: Bisexuality and the Eroticism of Everyday Life* (1995), Marjorie Garber wittily defined bisexuality as "that upon the repression of which society depends for its laws, codes, boundaries, social organization—everything that defines 'civilization' as we know it." She examined bisexuality among bohemians of the past—in Harlem, in Greenwich Village, in Bloomsbury, and in Georgia O'Keeffe's New Mexico, Oscar Wilde, Virginia Woolf—and offers the following thesis:

> Why do we resist the idea that erotic life is all part of the same set of pleasures, that there is only one sexuality, of which the "sexualities" we have so effectively and efficiently defined are equally permissible and gratifying aspects? Because to do so would threaten the social structures on which "civilization" and "society" are built. And because much modern eroticism depends, in part, upon the sensation or perception of daring, of breaking a law or flaunting a taboo.

(See entries for Ganymede, Kallamachusa, and Rob Tielman.)

Bishop, George (20th Century)

Bishop, a freethinker, wrote *Faith Healers: God or Fraud?* (1967). A professor of political science at the University of Cincinnati, he lamented in "What Americans Really Believe" (*Free Inquiry*, Summer 1999) that "the persistence of the religious worldview in America may be due in significant measure . . . to the strength of the cultural fundamentalist movement in our society in recent years that has succeeded in getting its message and agenda into the public schools, the mass media, and other social institutions." Assisting, he noted, is "the low level of scientific literacy about human evolution in American society as compared to other developed nations." {GS}

Bishop, William (20th Century)

Bishop, while a student at the University of Florida, signed the Campus Freethought Alliance's 1998 "Bill of Rights for Unbelievers."

BISHOPSGATE FOUNDATION

In 1995 after traveling in England, Fred Whitehead wrote of his visit to the Bishopsgate Foundation:

> The ancient City of London, more or less one square mile, was surrounded by walls, with gates for entry; even though the walls are

now gone, there are traditional sections named for the gates—and one of these is Bishopsgate, where one of the most important and colorful collections of Freethought literature is housed.

The story of the Bishopsgate Foundation (formerly the Bishopsgate Institute) is splendidly told in a centenary history written by its librarian, Mr. David Webb. It begins thus: "The site of the Bishopsgate Institute straddles the Eastern fringe of the City of London—three quarters within the city, one quarter outside Tower Hamlets; the boundary line runs through the present Lending Library, marked by appropriate plaques set in the walls and floor." The actual gate itself was demolished in 1760, "as a mere traffic obstruction."

In the late 19th century, we learn, "a shining light in the gloom" was the Rector of St. Botolph's church, Rev. William Rogers, whose "advocacy of secular education . . . earned him the nickname of 'Hang Theology Rogers' . . . . He erected baths, wash houses and drinking fountains . . . established soup kitchens in the winter for the army of casual laborers attracted by railway work," and so on.

The origin of the Institute was in "small local charities which accrued to the church of St. Botolph, in the form of donations, wills and bequests, over a period of almost 400 years." On Rogers's initiative, these were consolidated, and during 1893-94, a building was erected "to comprise a large hall with seating accommodation for 500, a lending library with 50,000 volumes. . . and a reference library for 10,000 volumes."

There had been vocal opposition from some to the very notion of a "Free Library . . . that a number of louts may have a nice warm room in which to read the worst novels and the sporting news in the papers and neglect their natural work!" In spite of this, over time the library became not only heavily used, but developed as a major resource for the history of London.

For instance, the London Topographical Society has had its offices in the building since 12961, and their excellent historical maps are available by writing the Foundation. . . .

Important Freethought collections have found a home at the Bishopsgate: "The library of the National Secular Society was deposited on permanent loan in 1981, including the substantial (over 3000 items) and unique collection of materials on the life and career of Charles Bradlaugh, assembled by his daughter, Hypatia Bradlaugh Bonner; in 1982 the archives of the London Co-operative Society were deposited . . . in more recent years the library of the Freedom Society, the pioneer East End anarchist organisation has been acquired, as well as part of the cooperative collection of the ICA pioneer, Paul Derrick." Half of the personal library of George Jacob Holyoake, who coined the term "secular" is here; his correspondence is at the Cooperative Union in Manchester.

Also here is "the personal library of George Howell, who had been MP for Bethnal green North-east in the 1880s, and earlier secretary of the Reform League and the Plimsoll Committee."

But then Webb relates the most remarkable story of all: "The single most famous manuscript in the collection is the Minute Book of the First International Working Men's Association, 1866-69, whose history Howell at one time hoped to write. This first meeting of what later became the Communist International., is celebrated particularly from the inclusion of Karl Marx as one of the delegates, and the manuscript remains a key document in the history of International Communism."

{When in 1919 one of the governors, David Anidjar Romain, insisted on banning the Minute Book], through the intervention of no less than Winston Churchill, Ivan Maisky, then the Soviet ambassador to Britain, personally made a transcript of the Minute Book, and it was eventually published in Moscow in 1950. . . .

To sum up: The Bishopsgate is one of the best Freethought libraries in England, and certainly one of the best catalogued and most accessible.

The Bishopsgate Foundation is at 230 Bishopsgate, London EC2M 4QH, United Kingdom. {*Freethought History* }

Bismarck, Otto von (1815—1898)

Bismark, the German statesman, speaking in the Prussian upper house in 1886 said, "The Catholic priest, from the moment he becomes a priest, is a sworn officer of the Pope." {TYD}

Bissell, Malcolm H. (20th Century)

Bissell was professor emeritus at the University of Southern in California when he signed Humanist Manifesto II. In 1952, he was a director of the American Humanist Association. {HM2; HNS; HNS2}

Bissel, Shelton (20th Century)

Bissell, a freethinker, wrote *Unofficial Christians* (c. 1918). {GS}

Bithell, Richard (Born 1831)

An English agnostic who entered the services of the Rothschilds in 1865, Bithell wrote *Creed of a Modern Agnostic* (1833) and *Agnostic Problems* (1887). He was one of the leading members of the Rationalist Press Association. {BDF; RAT; RSR; TRI}

Bixler, J. S. (Born 1894)

Bixler wrote book reviews on ontology for *The Humanist* in the 1950s, when he was President of Colby College. He wrote *Religion in the Philosophy of William James* (1926).

Bizet, Georges (1838—1875)

Bizet, whose given name was Alexandre César Léopold Bizet, is the composer of the opera, *Carmen*. In 1886, Bizet wrote, "I should write better music if I believe a lot of things that aren't true," which is said by some to be a reference to France's Catholicism as well as to his personally being troubled by the dominant positivist philosophy of his day. "I have always read the ancient pagans with infinite pleasure," Bizet wrote in a work emphatically rejecting Christianity, "while in Christian writers I have found only system, egoism, intolerance, and a complete lack of artistic taste." Bizet's tomb is in the huge Père-Lachaise cemetery in eastern Paris, near the tombs of Molière, Chopin, Proust, and Oscar Wilde. His marker includes a bronze relief harp. {JM; RAT; RE; TRI; TYD}

Björk (20th Century)

A recording artist, Björk has gone on record as saying, "If I get into trouble, there's no God or Allah to sort me out. I have to do it myself." She added, "I do not believe in religion, but if I had to choose one, it would be Buddhism. It seems more livable, closer to men. I've been reading about reincarnation, and the Buddhists say we come back as animals and they refer to them as lesser beings. Well, animals aren't lesser beings, they're just like us. So I say fuck the Buddhists." {CA}

Bjorklund, Gustaf (20th Century)

Bjorklund, a freethinker, wrote *Death and Resurrection From the Viewpoint of the Cell-Theory* (1910). {GS}

Bjørkmann, Edwin August (Born 1866)

Bjørkmann, an American writer born in Sweden, edited the *Minnesota Post* (1892—1894) and worked on the *Minneapolis Times* (1894—1897). In New York he worked on the *Sun* and *Times* (1897—1905). In *Gleams* (1912) Bjørkmann wrote of "the diminishing core of mystery left for our emotions to feed on" and added that his god is "the future." {RAT}

Bjørnson, Bjørnstjerne (1832—1910)

A major figure in Norwegian literature, Bjørnson championed the rights of the oppressed and was a freethinker who succeeded Ibsen as director of the Ole Bull Theater in Bergen. He wrote the Norwegian national anthem, "*Ja, vi elsker dette landet*" ("Yes, we love this land forever"). Although his father was a Lutheran clergyman, Bjørnson was a Darwinian who rejected traditional religion.

In 1903, Bjørnson received the Nobel Prize in Literature. Norwegian humanists are particularly proud that he wrote his works in a country with such a strong Lutheran church. In 1882 Bjørnson published the first attack upon dogmatic Christianity published in Norway, a resumé of C. B. Waite's *History of the Christian Religion*. In *Beyond Our Power* (1883), he attacks the Christian belief in miracles, and in *Beyond Human Might* (1895) he says social change must originate in the schools.

Bjørnson was an honorary associate of the British Rationalist Press Association, which Charles A. Watts had founded in 1899. When Bjørnson died, the British literary weekly, *Athenaeum*, wrote that "European literature had sustained no such loss since Victor Hugo." (See entry for Scandinavian Unbelievers.) {BDF; CE; JM; JMR; JMRH; PUT; RE}

BLACK

Freethinkers and rationalists who are white are sometimes unaware of the semantic overtones of being *white*:

- white (e.g., when used with positive overtones):

upright; fair; free from spot or blemish; free from moral impurity; innocent; pure ("a white wedding"); unmarked; "a white lie" or "white magic" (not intended to cause harm); "one of the white days of his life" (fortunate); "a white Christmas" (beautifully snowy and white); "white fury" (passionate); "a white-beard" (an elderly man); "white-collar worker" (one who does not have to wear work or protective clothing); "a white elephant" (revered animal); "white knight" (one who rescues another); "white list" (approved items or individuals); "white man's burden" (the alleged duty of white peoples to manage the affairs of the less developed nonwhite peoples); whiteness (freedom from stain); white room (one that is clean); whitesmith (an ironworker who finishes or polishes the work); "a white tie dinner" (one that is formal); the Great White Way (the dynamic, theatrical section of Broadway in New York City); white blow (semen: used both by the literary and the cultured levels); the White Highlands (affluent suburbs which surround a multi-racial, deprived, inner city); "white bread" (American slang for someone who is virtuous or well bred, albeit dull and insipid); etc.

However, note how the Anglo-Saxon language treats *black*:

- black (examples, when used with negative overtones)

the color of night (scary); the color of melancholy (thought to have been caused by black bile), grief, loss; the color of death; the color worn by Lucifer, Nazi storm troopers, Italian Fascists, bad guys in old westerns, Darth Vader, the Wicked Witch of the West, motorcycle gangs, and Dracula; in *The Trial*, Joseph K is arrested by ominous men dressed in black; nuns, monks, priests wear black; black holes; blackmail; blackballing; the black market; black cats (bad luck); "black dogs" (frequent depressions, as described by Winston Churchill); "black with rage"; "black intrigue"; "a black mark given for a transgression"; "a black deed" (evil); "black magic" (connected with the Devil); "black Friday" (a disaster); blackball (to vote against); Black Death (the Plague of the 14th century); black eye (a bad reputation); black flag (a pirate's flag that bears a skull and crossbones); blackguard (servants or rude people or those who use bad language); blacklist (contains list of those boycotted); blackmail (extortion); Black Maria (a patrol wagon); Black Mass (a travesty of the Christian mass ascribed to worshipers of Satan); black (hashish from the Indian subcontinent or the Himalayas); black stuff (a drug user's euphemism for opium); black velvet (black women seen as sexual partners or sex objects); "black as a sweep's arse" (slang for very black); "black as the ace of spades" (slang for utterly black); "black as Toby's arse" (pitch-black; "black cat with its throat cut" (slang for female pudenda); "black peter" (in Australia, a solitary-detention cell); blackwash (to blacken someone's character); etc.

Blacks are understandably displeased with such semantic overtones of commonly used words, which they have been known to ascribe to "thin-lipped whitey crackers." (See entry for Noah, who punished his son Ham by giving him a black skin. Also, see *Partridge's Concise Dictionary of Slang and Unconventional English*, edited by Paul Beale.)

BLACK CAT ENTERPRISES

Black Cat Enterprises (POB 21201, Columbus, Ohio 43221) publishes Solstice notecards and "Women of Freethought" calendars. It is operated by Carole Gray. {FD}

BLACK DEATH

The Black Death in 1347-1349 killed millions in Asia and North Africa. As many as one in three European also were killed.

BLACK ELK: See entry for Dostoyevski's Epilepsy.

BLACK HOLES: See entry for Edwin Powell Hubble.

Black, Algernon D. (1900—1993)

A teacher and the leader emeritus of the New York Society for Ethical Culture, Black at the time of his death was the Society's foremost elder statesman. A graduate of Ethical Culture schools, Black became the Society leader in 1932 and the senior leader in 1942. When Felix Adler died in 1933, Black was among those who helped translate the movement into programs to meet the crises of the Depression. Under his direction, the Encampment for Citizenship began (1946), and various committees against discrimination in housing, racial discrimination, and violations of civil rights were formed. He broadcast the Society's weekly Sunday meetings over radio station WQXR, and his commentaries were broadcast on many other stations.

In 1966, Mayor John V. Lindsay appointed Black to lead a new Civilian Complaint Review Board for the city's Police Department. Black, son of Russian Jewish immigrant parents, agreed with Adler that what is needed is a religion based on ethics rather than creed and theology.

Like Adler, Wolfgang Saxon has written, Black "saw a pragmatic faith without God, a belief in the infinite worth of the individual, the centrality of ethical principles, and the urgency to redeem the democratic promise by improving the lot of the poor and fighting privilege." According to James F. Hornback, Black although a humanist declined to sign Humanist Manifesto II "out of loyalty to the larger inclusiveness of Ethical Culture." In addition to writing many addresses, Black wrote *Our Godless Age* (1943) and *The People and the Police: The Story of the Civilian Review Board* (1986). He was a contributing editor in 1933 to *The Standard.* (See entry for Ethical Culture.) {CL; EU, Howard B. Radest; PK}

Black, Bob (20th Century)

Black is author of *The Abolition of Work and Other Essays* (1986). An Albany, New York, freethinker who has written for *Freethought Perspective* (June 1999), he holds that religion "is deceitful, depraved, and absurd." As for "Oriental mysticism," it is "pushed by greedy gurus with lice in their ears."

Black, Hugo L. (1886—1971)

Supreme Court Justice Black, in commenting about why humanist Roy R. Torcaso should not be refused his commission as a notary public under a Maryland law requiring all public officers in the State to profess belief in God, observed as follows: "Among religions in this country which do not teach what would generally be considered a belief in the existence of God are Buddhism, Taoism, Ethical Culture, Secular Humanism and others."

However, secular humanists were quick to point out that theirs is a philosophic, not a religious, organization. In 1995, the Ninth Circuit Court of Appeals ruled in a case brought by John Peloza that secular humanism is not a religion. Peloza, a Capistrano, California, teacher, had sued his school district, charging that by requiring him to teach evolution in science class the district was violating the First Amendment, forcing him to teach the "religion" of evolution. The Court of Appeals dismissed his suit, calling parts of it "patently frivolous." The Court further ruled, "Peloza's complaint at most makes this claim: the school district's actions establish a state-supported religion of evolution, or more generally of 'secular humanism.' . . . We reject this claim because neither the Supreme Court, nor this circuit, has ever held that evolutionism or secular humanism are 'religions' for Establishment Clause purposes. Indeed, both the dictionary definition of religion and the clear weight of the case law are to the contrary."

Justice Black, in short, had made his remark as a *dicta*, or personal remark. This carries no legal weight. {CE; CL}

Black, Joshua (20th Century)

Black, a member of the Campus Freethought Alliance at Princeton University, signed the 1998 "Bill of Rights for Unbelievers."

Black, Miriam (20th Century)

Black, while a student at the University of Colorado at Boulder and a member of Campus Heretics, was one of the founders of the Campus Freethought Alliance. {*International Humanist News*, December 1996}

Blackham, H(arold) J(ohn) (1903—)

Blackham has been Chairman, Social Morality Council, Great Britain, and a former director of the British Humanist Association. Among his books are *Objections to Humanism* (1963), *Six Existentialistic Thinkers* (1990), and *The Future of Our Past: From Ancient Greece to Global Village* (1996). In 1977, he was elected an honorary associate of the British Rationalist Press Association. He is on the editorial board of *The Humanist*. In 1980, he signed the Secular Humanist Declaration. He has written that "Unitarianism in England is negligible intellectually. Of course, the *Hibbert* survives and holds a place, but that is because it is open to all comers in its fairly broad field. The Unitarians here are hostile to humanism. They are diminishing and count for little." Blackham, Jaap van Praag, and Julian Huxley were the key founders of the International Humanist and Ethical Union (IHEU), an organization which in 1974 granted him a Humanist Award "for his long and creative service to humanism in England and in the world." From 1944 to 1965, he had edited the Ethical Union's *Plain View*. In 1978, Blackham received the group's special award "for 25 years of devoted service to IHEU."

In the *New Humanist* (July 1993), he is interviewed by Jim Herrick and recalls his involvement with humanistic causes. At the age of ninety, his sharp mind recalled his early interest in religion, his meeting Stanton Coit, his teaching philosophy and current affairs, his becoming chairman of the Ethical Union, his being in the Auxiliary Fire Service during World War II, his involvement in the founding of the British Humanist Association, his involvement with the World Union of Freethinkers, his working with Julian Huxley, and the writing of his several books. Stalin, he stated, "was not a Marxist-Leninist in his heart. He paid lip-service to the creed, but was a Russian Czar, an imperialist who used the dictatorship of the proletariat to extend the dominion of the Russian State. The KGB was a continuation of the surveillance of the Czarist police-state. Asked if liberal humanism is dead, Blackham reacted by saying, "How can it be dead really? It may be outmoded, or not the vogue, but what is the implication of saying it's dead. Sartre said that liberalism was a betrayal to the Nazis of civilisation. To the liberal everything is worth entertaining, all is a level ground, everyone can exchange views. You have to make choices, you can't be liberal in the sense of entertaining all things. But liberal humanism can's possibly be dead. It is not merely, nor mainly an attitude: it is a commitment to which one gives priority."

In 1993, Blackham completed a history of Western Europe from a new, transforming perspective, part of which was published in *New Humanist*. The work is entitled *The Upshot of History*, and it focuses on three claims to universality, those of Hellas, Zion, and Romanitas. They have led, he states, to our awareness of One World with its evident disorders, which he names: "disproportion between the prosperity enjoyed by the few industrialised nations and the penury endured by thousands of millions in the so-called Third World; the aggravation of over-population; the ecological damage, entailing serious threats to the survival of many species, and even of life on the planet; the existence and availability without adequate controls of annihilating weapons that make international security a political priority." By recognizing such problems, he asserts, man has the chance to go beyond Hellas, Zion, and Romanitas. . . to universality.

Bernard Farr, reviewing *The Future of Our Past*, lists the following as the key points in Blackham's humanism:

- adequate self-awareness, in the light of science and history
- taking responsibility for shaping the future of the planet in specific ways through the application of escalating knowledge
- awareness of making these decisions in One World with attention to global tasks and obligations in the face of the global threats to health, wealth, and environment
- willingness to take responsibility for the consequences of these decisions together, globally
- acceptance of individual responsibilities for contributing to the collective task-and through this acceptance enacting one's personal identity
- the call to transcend previous limited understanding of the "universal" offered in the "Hellas," "Zion," and "Romanitas" visions.

Farr's major criticism is that Blackham thinks of "global" as the world shrunk to the image of the West, that the East is overlooked as has been the case for so long in the past. {CL; FUK; HM2; HNS; HNS2; *New Humanist*, November 1993 and June 1996; PK; SHD; TRI; WAS, 20 September 1955}

Blackmun, Harry Andrew [Supreme Court Justice] (1908—)

Blackmun, who as a Supreme Court Justice in the 1980s tended toward a liberal view in civil rights cases, wrote an article for *The Humanist*. He is not known, however, to have gone on record concerning his personal philosophic outlook. {CE; HNS2}

BLACKPOOL AND FYLDE (England) HUMANISTS

Information is available from Secretary D. Baxter by telephoning 01253 726 112

Blackwelder, Spencer (1920—1996)

Blackwelder, who worked in real estate businesses, was among the first of the U.S. Army personnel to occupy Japan after its surrender in World War II.

A freethinker who was active in humanist groups, Blackwelder had recently been honored by Atheists United with a dinner shortly before his death from septicemia, a form of cancer.

Blackwell, Alice Stone (1857—1950)

Blackwell, a Unitarian, was a reformer and suffragist. She was the daughter of Lucy Stone and Henry Brown Blackwell.

Blackwell, Antoinette Louisa Brown (1825—1921)

One of the pioneers in the women's rights movement in nineteenth-century America, Blackwell wrote *The Sexes Throughout*

Nature (1875). In 1908 she founded and became minister of the All Souls Unitarian Church in Elizabeth, New Jersey. Blackwell, the first woman ordained by one congregation, is said to have been an inspiration to Olympia Brown, the first woman minister ordained by a recognized denomination. In the 1920 political election, at the age of ninety-five, Blackwell finally was able legally to vote. {CE; EG; U; U&U}

Blackwell, Elizabeth (1821—1910)

Blackwell was the first female in the country to receive a medical degree (from Geneva Medical College, now Hobart). In 1857 she founded the New York Infirmary for Women and Children, and in 1875 she helped establish in England the London School of Medicine for Women. Blackwell was an Episcopalian and also a Unitarian. {CE; U}

Blackwell, Emily (1826-1910)

Blackwell, Elizabeth's sister, was a physician and a Unitarian.

Blackwell, Kenneth (20th Century)

Blackwell is the archivist emeritus of the Bertrand Russell Library. In 1997 he became secretary of the Bertrand Russell Society.

Blackwell, Milford (20th Century)

Blackwell in the 1970s was on the advisory board of the Humanist Society of Greater New York.

Blackwood, Dorothy (20th Century)

Blackwood is active in Blackpool and Fylde humanist affairs. With some other English tourists, she visited Cuba in 1994 and found that religion is not taught in schools. Writing in *The Freethinker* (June 1994), she argues that the thirty-eight year trade blockade against Cuba should be ended.

Blagosvyetlov, Grigorevich E. (1826—c. 1885)

Blagosvyetlov is an author who translated Mill's *Subjection of Women* into Russian. A native of the Caucasus, he edited a magazine, *Djelo* (*Cause*). {BDF; RAT}

Blair, David Graham (1939—)

Blair, who broke the Australian record for a 100-mile run in 1961, spent six years in Canada, where he was active in the Edmonton Humanist Group and the Kingston Unitarian Fellowship. As an academic at the University of Technology in Australia, he lectures on quantum mechanics and sonar research.

Blair is an active member of the Sydney Humanist School of Philosophy. {SWW}

Blair, Eric Arthur: See entry for Orwell, George.

Blake, James (19th Century)

Blake, a freethinker, wrote *The Bible Weighed in the Balance and Found Wanting* (1855). {GS}

Blake, Lillie Devereaux (1833—1913)

"I live to redress the wrongs of my sex," Blake wrote as a teenager in 1849. In 1873 she protested against Columbia University's exclusion of women, and in 1893 spoke to the International Congress of Women, which was held in connection with the World's Columbia Exposition. Appointed in 1895 to head a "Committee on Legislative Advice" by the National American Woman Suffrage Association (NAWSA), she fought in 1899 her removal by Susan B. Anthony as illegal. When Anthony retired, Blake was encouraged to run for the group's presidency but withdrew before the vote "for the sake of harmony." In 1910 she was placed in a sanitarium and died after breaking her hip in 1913. Gaylor has described Blake as "a Deist at most." {WWS}

Blaker, Kimberly (20th Century)

Blaker is president of the Southeast Michigan Chapter of the Freedom From Religion Foundation. She is founder and treasurer of Freethinkers for Humanity.

Blakemore, Colin (Brian) (1944—)

In 1986, Blakemore was elected as an honorary associate of the Rationalist Press Association. He has written *The Mind Machine* (1988) and *Vision* (1991). Blakemore, who works at the University Laboratory of Physiology, Oxford, signed Humanist Manifesto 2000.

BLAMESGIVING DAY

If Thanksgiving is a day to thank God for giving us what we have, it made sense to rationalist Gordon Stein to balance the holiday with Blamesgiving Day, a time to blame God for giving us what we have. {*American Rationalist*, January-February 1994}

Blampied, Henry A. (c. 1850—1920?)

"Harry" Blampied was a rationalist and freethinker. In 1913, he was secretary of the Victorian Rationalist Association in Australia. {SWW}

Blanc, (Jean Joseph Charles) Louis (1811—1882)

Blanc, a French socialist politician, journalist, and historian, wrote *Organisation du travail* (1840), which outlined his ideal of a new social order based on the principle "Let each produce according to his aptitudes . . . let each consume according to his need." The first stage in achieving his goal was to have a system of national workshops controlled by working men with the support of the state. As a member of the provisional government of 1848 he insisted on the establishment of these workshops, but his plan was sabotaged by other leaders of the government and he fled to England, remaining there until 1871. Blanc wrote a thirteen-volume *Histoire de la Révolution française* (1847-1862) which showed his admiration of Jacobinism. Upon his return to France, he became a member of the National Assembly in 1871 and later was a leader of the left in the chamber of deputies. Marx labeled Blanc's ideas "utopian socialism." Blanc was an atheist who often expressed his complete rejection of religion. {CE; JM; RAT}

Blanchard-Gaillard, M. A. (20th Century)

Blanchard-Gaillard heads *the Association Unitarienne Francophone* (AUF, Les Hautes-Sieyes, Route des Courbons, 04000, Digne, France).

Blandrata, Georgius: See entry for Ferenc David.

Blanqui, Louis Auguste (1805—1880)

A French politician and communist, Blanqui was the younger brother of Jerome Blanqui, the economist. In 1830 he was condemned to death, but his sentence was commuted to imprisonment for life and was subject to brutal treatment till the 1848 revolution set him at liberty. In 1865 he wrote articles on monotheism in *Le Candide*, and after the revolution of 1870 he demanded the suppression of worship. Again imprisoned, he was liberated and elected a member of the Commune. Arrested by Thiers, he was imprisoned again. Blanqui's motto was, "*Ni Dieu ni maître*" (Neither God nor master). {BDF; RAT; TRI}

Blanshard, Brand (1892—1987)

A professor emeritus of philosophy at Yale University when he signed Humanist Manifesto II, famed aestheticist Brand Blanshard was a Humanist Laureate in the Academy of Humanism. In 1980, he was a signer of the Secular Humanist Declaration. For *The Humanist* in the 1950s, Blanshard the expert on beauty reviewed Bertrand Russell's novel, *Nightmares of Eminent Persons.* He found that "all his characters, when they open their mouths, speak the language of that eminent philosopher, Lord Russell. A passionate young lover says to his love, 'I begin to think that perhaps we have lived, hitherto, with somewhat too limited preoccupations.' Such talk creaks. And Russell is always using his characters to score points. But then after all, what does one want of a philosopher? The points are generally sound ones, wittily put; and at times they go to the heart of the matter." Asked to comment upon humanism, Blanshard wrote to the present author:

> I have much sympathy with ancient humanism and classical humanism, though less with the other types. The main point to make about all these types, in my opinion, is that values do not depend on scientific or speculative beliefs; for any mature mind, they are self-validating. No one really believes that the pain of a broken leg is bad or the pleasure of Kreisler and his violin good because custom or the Deity or evolutionary advantage has so decreed; anyone who knows roughly what the two experiences are alike can rank them with confidence—a confidence that remains the same through the loss or acquisition of new connections in philosophy and theology.
>
> What we want in these days is a greater sensitiveness to values. Their metaphysical status is unimportant, but after all, *has* importance.

Blanshard's fullest statement as to his philosophic outlook is found in his *The Nature of Thought* (1939). In 1954, he wrote *On Philosophical Style* and in 1962 *Reason and Belief.* Often classified as an "idealist," he preferred the term "rationalist." A Fellow of the British Academy, Blanshard was a past president of the American Philosophical Association and, in addition, of the American Theological Society. Blanshard once wrote,

> If the nose of rationalism is once admitted under one's tent, a large and formidable camel is soon likely to follow the nose.

{CL; HNS; HM2; SHD}

Blanshard, Paul (1892—1980)

One of the best-known critics of organized religion in his day, Paul Blanshard (brother of Brand Blanshard) wrote *American Freedom and Catholic Power* (1950), *Communism, Democracy, and Catholic Power* (1951), *God and Man in Washington: The Church-State Battlefront in Congress, in the Supreme Court, in the Presidential Campaign* (1960); and *Religion and the Schools: The Great Controversy* (1963). Also, he was editor of *Classics of Free Thought* (1977), which includes essays concerning Bradlaugh, Burbank, Darrow, Darwin, Diderot, Draper, E. Haldeman-Julius, Holyoake, the Huxleys, Ingersoll, Jefferson, McCabe, Mencken, Paine, Russell, Shelley, Twain, Voltaire, and Wheless. In 1954, Ernest Nagel wrote about him in *Sovereign Reason.* Blanshard was a signer of Humanist Manifesto II. {FUS; HM2}

Blanshard, Rufus (20th Century)

An English instructor at the University of Connecticut in the 1950s, Blanshard wrote book reviews for *The Humanist.* The son of Paul Blanshard, he has written about Conrad Aiken as well as Spenser, Defoe, and Landor.

Blasche, Bernard Heinrich (1776—1832)

A German pantheist, Blasche was the son of a professor of theology and philosophy. Among his works are *Kritik des Modernen Geisterglaubens* (Criticism of Modern Ghost Belief), and *Philosophische Unsterblichkeitslhre* (*Teaching of Philosophical Immortality*). {BDF}

BLASPHEMY

The *Catechism of the Catholic Church* (1994) states that blasphemy "is directly opposed to the second commandment. It consists in uttering against God—inwardly or outwardly—words of hatred, reproach, or defiance; in speaking ill of God; in failing in respect toward him in one's speech; in misusing God's name." Blasphemy, states the catechism, "is in itself a grave sin."

Leonard W. Levy, in *Blasphemy, Verbal Offense Against the Sacred, From Moses to Salman Rushdie* (1993), demonstrates how "treason against God" can be interpreted as treason against the state and a violation of freedom of religion. Religious leaders, he details, have often engaged in "the very vituperation that they wish to deny others, and he discusses how Pericles, Euripides, Giordano Bruno, Anne Hutchinson, Roger Williams, William Penn, Thomas Paine, and Salman Rushdie all have been charged with blasphemy. Levy discusses the trial of Jesus, whom the Jews rejected as the Messiah and who was considered a rabble-rouser by the Romans. Although the records are lost, he finds that Jesus was a blasphemer according to Jewish law but was found guilty of political, not religious, offenses by the Romans.

The last-known American to serve time in prison for blasphemy was Charles C. Moore. An authoritative work by a rationalist on the subject is Nicolas Walter's *Blasphemy Ancient and Modern* (1990). An even more complete study is David Nash's *Blasphemy in Modern Britain: 1789 to the Present* (1999). Nash notes that a key clue to blasphemy case outcomes is the judge one receives. Had Lord North not been a convinced Catholic, G. W. Foote might not have spent a year in prison. If Judge Alan King-Hamilton had not been a homophobe, say gays, *Gay News* editor Denis Lemon might not have received a prison sentence, albeit suspended. {*New Humanist,* March 1999}

Blatch, Harriot Eaton Stanton (1856-1940)

The daughter of Elizabeth Cady Stanton, Blatch was a Unitarian suffragist like her mother.

Blatchford, Robert (1851—1943)

Blatchford wrote *God and My Neighbor, Essays of An Infidel* (1903). In the book, he spoofs the various Christian beliefs, saying no proof for anything is offered. Has anyone seen God? Why would he create twenty millions of suns, come to earth, be born of a woman, get crucified, die, stay in a tomb for three days, then come to life again in order to go back to Heaven? Not one-third of mankind believes such nonsense, and of those who do Blatchford suggests that not one in ten is "a true Christian and a true believer." {FUK; RAT; RSR; TRI}

Blathwayt, Linley [Lt. Colonel] (1839—1919)

Blathwayt served in the 79th Highlanders during the Indian Mutiny Campaign. He also served with the Expeditionary Force in China (1860—1862) and the Bhootan Expedition (1864—1865). He retired from the Bengal Staff Corps in 1880. Blathwayt was an agnostic and a member of the Rationalist Press

Blau, Joseph Leon (1909—1986)

Professor emeritus and formerly chairman of the department of religion at Columbia University, Blau wrote *Modern Varieties of Judaism* (1972) and edited works concerning religious freedom. A renowned student of Judaica, he signed Humanist Manifesto II and listed himself in *Who's Who* as "a long-time humanist." In 1980, he signed the Secular Humanist Declaration. {CL; FUS; HM2; SHD}

Blaustein, Albert P. (1921—1994)

In 1992, Blaustein received the 1992 Raymond B. Bragg Award for Distinguished Service to the Principles of Humanism in St. Louis. He had been counsel, consultant, and draftsman in preparing more than twenty constitutions, including those of the Russian Federation, Poland, Peru, Romania, Brazil, Bangladesh, Nepal, Fiji, Zimbabwe, Niger, and Liberia. In the 1970's, Blaustein tried, unsuccessfully, to persuade the leaders of the new majority-rule government of Zimbabwe to grant equal rights to women. But he acknowledged that for a constitution to work, it must reflect a country's culture and history. In a 1983 interview, he said, "We cannot put constitutions together like prefabricated henhouses." Although he praised the United States Constitution as one which had worked well, even in crises—Blaustein noted that "When Mr. Nixon left power, the only person with a gun was a policeman directing traffic"—he said, if asked to revise it, he would make the right to privacy and freedom of travel explicit provisions. Among his books is the twenty-two-volume *Constitutions of the Countries of the World* (1971), co-edited with G. H. Flang. Also, he co-authored *Desegregation and the Law* (1985). Blaustein was Professor of Law Emeritus of the Rutgers University School of Law until his retirement in 1992.

Bleibtreu, Carl (Born 1859)

Bleibtreu was a German poet and critic, a leading representative of naturalism in German letters. His dramatic works were published in three volumes (1889), and he wrote fifty further volumes. Like G. B. Shaw, Bleibtreu was scornful of materialism and Christianity. {RAT}

Blein, F.A.A. [Baron] (Born 1767)

Blein, a French baron, wrote *Essais Philosophiques* (1843). Blein was a freethinker. {BDF; RAT}

Bletzer, Russell (20th Century)

Bletzer, a freethinker, wrote *Is Humanism Obsolete?* (1976). {GS}

Blewitt, Neil (Deceased)

Blewitt was an active New Zealand rationalist and humanist. In Britain's *The Freethinker* (September 1993), he wrote "A Letter to the Lord," addressing God as "Dear Sir or Madam." Acknowledging that if Proteus, the son of a god, could transform himself into a dragon, a flood, a panther, a tree, and fire, God could similarly transform Himself into a ghost and His own son "as easily as you once transformed yourself into a disembodied voice, a cloud, and fire." But, Blewitt demands, "Who *did* create harmful bacteria and viruses?"

In "Poor Old Judas!" (*The Freethinker*, January 1996), Blewitt wittily speculated about such serious matters as (a) What if Noah's ark had capsized?; (b) What if, at the moment of Creation, God had said, "Dammit—I've forgotten the words!"; (c) "What if Mary had miscarried or given birth to twin girls?"; and (d) "What if the angel had been unable to move the stone from the entrance to Jesus's tomb?" The possibilities, he concluded, are legion. (See Neil Blewitt's "Face-to-face with the Son of Fred," *The Freethinker*, July 1997 and May 1999)

Blewitt, Ruth (20th Century)

Blewitt, writing in the *New Zealand Rationalist and Humanist* (August 1991), has described freethinker Robert Thressell.

Blignieres, Célestin de (19th Century)

A French positivist of the Polytechnic school, Blignieres wrote *The Positive Doctrine* (1867), a popular exposition of the positivist philosophy. {BDF}

Blind, Karl (1826—1907)

A German Republican, Blind in 1848 led the second republican revolution in the Black Forest, was made a prisoner, and was sentenced to eight years of imprisonment. He was liberated in 1849 when people broke open the prison. Banished from France, he went to Brussels, then to England. Blind was an atheist. {BDF; JM; RAT}

Blind, Mathilde (1841—1896)

Blind, the step-daughter of Karl Blind, took his name and shared his exile. In her autobiography she explained that she also shared his atheism. Her "character," reported Dr. R. Garnett, "was even more noble than her poetry." Blind was one of the founders of Newnham College for women. {JM; RAT}

Blishen, Edward (1920—1996)

Blishen, an educator, broadcaster, writer, and critic, wrote the preface to Margaret Knight's edition of *Humanist Anthology* (1994). In it, he stated that

> I am cheered in my perishing bones by David Hume, who said he could not well imagine what excuses he could make to Charon in order to obtain a little delay. And I am grateful for a perception I had at fourteen, that is now most serviceable in removing all possibility of obscene panic rooted in the religious view of things, and that was most trenchantly expressed by Charles Darwin, quoted here: "I can indeed hardly see how anyone ought to wish Christianity to be true: for if so the plain language of the text seems to show that the men who do not believe, and this would include my father, brother, and almost all my friends, will be everlastingly punished."

Blishen had written articles for *The Freethinker* over a period of three decades. He was an honorary associate of the National Secular Society and in 1995 became an Honorary Associate in the Rationalist Press Association. Blishen was once described by Nicholas Tucker, a fellow educationist, as "one of the freest thinkers. We are very fortunate to have him at our own particular time, a writer who is totally independent, individual, honest, and unfailingly skillful in all he ever does."

At a secular funeral conducted by his family, Nicholas Tucker described Blishen as a "humanist" who was "an advertisement for the human race, which is something all humanists should aspire to be." {*New Humanist*, December 1996}

BLISS

Dante the non-scientist wrote, "The love of God, unutterable and perfect, flows into a pure soul the way light rushes into a transparent object." Religionists point to the sensations of calm and transcendence during meditation, citing Angelus Silesius's mystical notion of the "pure nothing, concealed in now and here."

Such notions of the alleged bliss obtained from meditation have been noted by scientists. Eugene d'Aquili, professor of psychiatry at the Hospital of the University of Pennsylvania, and Andrew Newberg, a fellow at the hospital's nuclear medicine program, have scanned the brains of people before and during meditation. They have found that sensations of calm and transcendence during meditation are reflected in the increased activity in the brains' frontal lobes behind the forehead and decreased activity in the parietel lobes at the top rear of the head. "When somebody has religious experiences, this is what it's doing to them," Newberg has reported. His view is that the brain's amygdala, which translates sensory impressions into emotions, "generates a sense of religious awe attached to behaviorally 'marked' ritual gestures such as bows or signs of the cross." His study, reported in *Zygon* (Summer 1998), builds on research tying hallucinations, out-of-body sensations, and déjà vu to activity, or suppression of activity, in parts of the brain.

Bliss, William (20th Century)

"Illegal Religion in Our School," an article by Bliss, appeared in Joseph Lewis's freethought magazine, *Age of Reason* (May, 1968).

Blithell, Richard (19th Century)

Blithell, a freethinker, wrote *Agnostic Problems* (1887). {GS}

Bliven, Eliza Mowry (Born 1845)

Bliven was the daughter of a Universalist mother and a freethinking father. Early on, she noticed a similarity between the miracle stories and adjudged them just stories, whether Greek, Roman, or Judeo-Christian. In 1895 she married Samuel D. Bliven, an atheist, and at that time wrote, "I am a Materialist. I believe there is not Hell, Heaven, Devil, God, nor future life. We knew nothing before we were born, and we can know nothing after we are dead." She wrote for the Oregonian *Torch of Reason*, the Kansan *Freethought Ideal*, the Illinoian *Freethought Magazine*, the Californian *Humanitarian Review*, and the Kentucky *Blue Grass Blade*. Bliven was editor of *Materialism: 100 Proofs There is No God* (c. 1907), and in 1908 she wrote, "What Women Ought to Do Instead of Church Work." {*Freethought History*, #17, 1996; GS; WWS}

Blixen, Karen (Isak Dinesen) [Baroness] (1885—1962)

A Danish author, Blixen wrote primarily in English and became well-known for *Out of Africa* (1937), an autobiographical account of her life on a Kenya coffee plantation. In it, she described good and evil—God and Satan—which are like warring forces that force all creatures to accept their fate. She also wrote *Seven Gothic Tales* (1934), *Winter's Tales* (1942), and *Last Tales* (1957). A freethinker, she wrote under the name of Isak Dinesen. (See entry for Scandinavian Unbelievers.) {CE; EU, Faith Ingwersen}

Bloch, Ivan (1872—1912)

Block, a German sexologist and social reformer, was a monist (atheist). In a symposium honoring Haeckel's eightieth birthday, Block described Haeckel as "the St. George who has slain the dragon of the ills of modern man and has ruthlessly branded all the dualistic survivals of prescientific culture as obstacles to the mental and moral progress of humanity." {JM; RAT}

Blodgett, Delos Abiel (Born 1825)

Blodgett, who was born of New England parentage in New York State, left home at the age of twenty and became a raftsman and boatman working his way down the Allegheny, Ohio, and Mississippi rivers, finally landing in New Orleans. In western Michigan he formed a large logging operation and became engaged in farming, banking, and real estate. A Whig until the formation of the Republican party, he was always an agnostic in religion. {PUT}

Blois, Ralph S. (1926-)

Canadian-born, Blois claims to have become an atheist when fourteen. In his early twenties, concerned with the fractionalization of freethought, he started *Fact* (Freethought ACTion), which he published twice monthly for three years in Rockford, Illinois. Blois was national secretary for the American Rationalist Federation and secretary for the Illinois State chapter. Over the years he has written for freethought publications, edited *Rationalist News*, and won numerous awards in advertising. {*Freethought Today*, August 1999}

Blokesberg-Fireovid, Robert (20th Century)

Blokesberg-Fireovid is associated with the Northeast Atheist Association. (See entry for New York Atheists, Freethinkers, Humanists.) {FD}

Blontrock-Suys, Lydia (20th Century)

A licentiate in classical philology, Blontrock-Suys has trained college teachers in non-denominational moral education. She is Honorary President of the Belgian Humanist Union. In 1988, Blontrock addressed the Tenth International Humanist and Ethical Union (IHEU) World Congress held in Buffalo.

BLOOD

Without the fluid that circulates in the heart, arteries, capillaries, and veins of a vertebrate animal, the animal would not be able to carry nourishment and oxygen to, and bring away waste products from, all parts of the body. Not until 1937 was a blood bank established, a place where blood or plasma is stored for future use. Bernard Fantus, one of the signers of Humanist Manifesto I, established that bank.

As Douglas Starr in *Blood: An Epic History of Medicine and Commerce* (1998) has pointed out, blood has figured heavily in world events. The court physician—William Harvey (1578-1657)—was the first to demonstrate, and he did it without the aid of a microscope, how the heart works and how blood circulates from arteries through capillaries to veins, then returns to the heart. *Excitatio anatomica de motu cordis et sanguinis I animalibus* (On the Movement of the Heart and Blood in Animals) was published in 1628, but acceptance of his findings were slow in coming. It was even later that it was understood how blood carries oxygen and other nutrients around the body.

Bloodletting occurred from antiquity through the 18th century. Mika Waltari's *The Egyptian* (1945) described how around the year 1000 B.C.E. it was practiced. It also occurred in Arabic and Indian medicine and sometimes was prescribed for pneumonia, fevers, back pain, diseases of the liver and spleen, rheumatism, headaches, melancholia, hypertension, and apoplexy. A signer of the Declaration of Independence, Dr. Benjamin Rush, used his lancet in Philadelphia in 1793, convinced that he could help hundreds of sufferers of yellow fever. Many died but some lived—inasmuch as yellow fever is not always fatal, Rush took credit for curing those who lived. They might, however, have lived despite his efforts. In 1789, General George Washington, who had a strep throat, was bled to death by well-meaning Virginia physicians.

Some physicians not only took blood out, they put animal blood and other fluids in. Following Jean-Baptiste Denis's view that "Sadness, Envy, Anger, Melancholy, Disquiet . . . corrupt the whole substance of the blood," a calf's and lamb's blood was infused to make mad men sane. Although almost everyone died from receiving animal blood, the treatment remained popular for nearly two centuries.

In the late 1950s Louisiana and Arkansas made it a misdemeanor for physicians to transfuse a black person's blood to a white person unless the recipient granted permission, this despite scientific evidence that the blood of the two races is technically indistinguishable.

Alexis Carrel (1873-1944), who believed in faith healing and mysticism, became a major name in the world of successful blood transfusion. Ryoichi Naito, an advisor to the notorious Japanese Army Unit 731 that carried out atrocities in the occupied city of Harbin, Manchuria, later founded the financially successful Japan Blood Bank—when it later was named the Green Cross, at its peak it became worth $1.5 billion. Blood, Starr has detailed, had become big business.

Thousands of hemophiliacs infected in the 1980s died of AIDS because blood received during transfusions had not been screened. So did many others throughout the world until a more reliable HIV-screening test became available. Unfortunately, as Starr's research showed, blood bankers often inhumanistically take unnecessary risks, saving money by using inadequate screening, thereby protecting their hospitals, blood banks, and companies from expense and inconvenience. (See entry for Bernard Fantus.) {Helen Epstein, "Blood & Money," *The New York Review of Books*, 4 February 1999}

BLOOD RELATIVES

People who are related to another by birth rather than by marriage are called blood relatives. A first cousin, for example, is the child of one's aunt or uncle. Genealogy is the study of family lineage.

Primitive tribes often claimed descent from bears, wolves, and other animals. Ancient Greeks and Romans traced their ancestry to gods and heroes. The genealogies in the Bible probably originated in oral tradition.

In the Middle Ages status and the transference of possessions depended upon the tracing of family lines, a condition that continues in countries such as England to the present day. In the United States, however, pedigree has not been crucial in determining status or in transferring property.

During World War II, to avoid any suspicion of conspiracy, Franklin D. Rossevelt and Winston Churchill kept from the public that they were blood cousins, descended from Henry Howland, whose son John was a passenger on the *Mayflower*. (CE; Wynne James 3rd, *The New York Times Book Review*, 7 March 1999)

Bloom, Harold (1930—)

Calling himself "an unbelieving Jew of strong Gnostic tendencies," Bloom—like Jung and some contemporary existentialists—has been influenced by Gnosticism, a gloomy 3rd century outlook. Gnostics thought of the universe as an evil creator's prison into which, as described by L. S. Klepp, "some sparks of divinity have fallen, trapped in human bodies but able to be liberated by the knowledge of their origin in the hidden true God." Bloom's *J*, in which he speculates as to the gender—female?—of whoever wrote the Bible, and *The American Religion: The Emergence of the Post-Christian Nation* (1992), place him in the forefront of controversial contemporary writers about religion. He writes of Joseph Smith, Mary Baker Eddy, Charles Taze Russell, and Lucina Umphreville in a way that displeases both the pious as well as the heretics. He is fascinated by Pentecostals, New Agers, Christian Scientists, and Mormons, finding Joseph Smith a "religious genius" who, in Klepp's words, "burrowed so deeply into the Bible that he came out on the other side, arriving at a faith resembling archaic Judaism but offering everyone the possibility of becoming a self-made God Almighty." Klepp in a critique adds, "I only wish he had reeled in a few more, such as Cyrus Reed Teed, the hollow-earth prophet, or Thomas Lake Harris and his theory of erotically matched souls. They may not make a great contribution to the national welfare, but what would the national comedy be without them?" (*The Village Voice*, 28 July 1992)

In a controversial work, *The Western Canon, The Books and School of the Ages* (1994), Bloom—called by some a psychologist, not a literary critic—argues that Shakespeare is the touchstone for all writers who come before and after him, that literature is where titans meet and clash, and that the major titans number twenty-six, whom he divides into three historic ages:

- The Aristocratic Age: Shakespeare is named as having no precursor and as having left no one after him untouched: Dante; Chaucer; Cervantes; Montaigne; Molière; Milton; Samuel Johnson; Goethe
- The Democratic Age: Wordsworth; Austen; Whitman; Dickinson; Dickens; George Eliot; Tolstoy; Ibsen
- The Chaotic Age: Freud; Proust; Joyce; Woolf; Kafka; Borges; Neruda; Pessoa; Beckett

His book's appendixes then list several hundred specific works which he critiques as being major, stating, "I would think that, of all the books in this first list, once the reader is conversant with the Bible, Homer, Plato, the Athenian dramatists, and Virgil, the crucial work is the Koran [sic]. Whether for its aesthetic and spiritual power or the influence it will have upon all of our futures, ignorance of the Koran is foolish and increasingly dangerous."

In his first list, titled "The Theocratic Age," Bloom cites *Gilgamesh*, *The Egyptian Book of the Dead*, The Holy Bible (*Authorized King James Version*), The Apocrypha, and *Sayings of the Fathers (Pirke Aboth)*. These are followed by *The Mahabharata*, *The Bhagavad-Gita*, and *The Ramayana*. Works of the ancient Greeks he cites are by Homer, Hesiod, Archilochos, Sappho, Alkman, Pindar, Aeschylus, Sophocles, Euripides, Aristophanes, Herodotus, Thucydides, Heraclitus, Empedocles, Plato, and Aristotle. Then he lists Hellenistic Greeks such as Meander, Callimachus, Theocritus, Plutarch, Lucian, and "Aesop"; then Romans such as Plautus, Terence, Lucretius, Cicero, Horace, Persius, Catullus, Virgil, Lucian, Ovid, Juvenal, Martial, Seneca, Petronius, and Apuleius; then authors and works of the Middle Ages before Dante, such as Saint Augustine, the Koran [sic], Snorri Sturluson, Wofram von Eschenbach, Chrétien de Troyes, *Beowulf*, *The Poem of the Cid*, Christine de Pisan, Diego de San Pedro. Finally, he lists several hundred works by authors in "the Aristocratic Age" and "the Chaotic Age," including, among the 161 American authors writers listed in the present work (as being non-theists), the following:

> Conrad Aiken, Paul Bowles, Kay Boyle, Willa Cather, E. E. Cummings, Theodore Dreiser, F. Scott Fitzgerald, Langston Hughes, Robinson Jeffers, Tony Kushner, Sinclair Lewis, Vachel Lindsay, Norman Mailer, John P. Marquand, Edgar Lee Masters, Eugene O'Neill, John Steinbeck, May Swenson, Gore Vidal, Kurt Vonnegut Jr., William Carlos Williams, Edmund Wilson, and Richard Wright.

As expected, scholars raced to inquire why some writers were included and why others were excluded. For example, not included are Mary McCarthy, Henry Miller, and Allen Ginsberg. Bloom's response has been that he is not in the business of being politically correct, that he holds different standards of excellence from those who are complaining. His disparagers he describes as being ideologues of the "six branches of the School of Resentment: Feminists, Marxists, Lacanians, New Historicists, Deconstructionists, Semioticians." Yes, he admits, certain women or certain African American authors have not made the list, but in the world of art would one include lesser artists in any analogous canon? If so, he reasons, "When the School of Resentment becomes as dominant among art historians and critics as it is among literary academics, will Matisse go unattended while we all flock to view the daubings of the Guerrilla Girls?"

Robert M. Adams, author of works on Erasmus, Voltaire, and Sir Thomas More, mentions that in the 1930s he had known about Bloom's "Ivy League predecessors, Paul Elmer More and Irving Babbitt. Their basis program—making allowance for the different dialect of those distant days—was to reaffirm the classical (canonical) literary values." But although New Humanism created a considerable stir for a limited time in limited circles, "the New Humanism faded without a climactic battle into the Old New Humanism, then into the Late New Humanism, and finally into a formula which now arouses nothing more than an incurious 'Huh?' Adams concludes that Bloom "at his best is a rewarding and humane critic; one feels obliged to express gratitude for his many passing generosities before dismissing his Western canon with a gentle 'Thank you, but no, thank you.'"

In a 1994 interview with Adam Begley, Bloom told how he despises "resentniks" and the "rabblement of lemmings"—Marxist critics, feminists, New Historicists, anyone who might read a poem as a social document, mix politics with literature, or in any way dilute the primacy of the esthetic. Bloom particularly dislikes Derrida, Foucault, Lacan, the French theorists, and the deconstructionists. They in no way, he holds, measure up to the standards set by, for example, Shakespeare, Dante, Goethe, Emerson, Tolstoy, Wallace Stevens, or Hart Crane. As to why only one of John Updike's novels is included but nine of Philip Roth's selections are, Begley suggests that "Updike once referred to Bloom's criticism as 'torturous,' while Roth is the would-be canonizer's pal."

As for Shakespeare, Bloom argues that he was the author who invented something which had not existed before, "personality," inwardness, what it means to be human. In *Shakespeare: The Invention of the Human* (1998), he develops the view that no other author in English surpasses the bard's universal genius. George Wilkins, who might have had a hand in writing "Pericles," is described as a "lowlife hack." Thomas Kyd's *Spanish Tragedy* is rejected as "hideously written and silly." John Webster, George Chapman, Thomas Middleton, and Ben Jonson are all written off as second-raters, critical barbs which critic James Shapiro (*The New York Times Book Review*, 1 November 1998) found unfortunate.

According to Begley, Bloom asks "what it would mean for America to have a spiritual life that is not identified with or rooted in organized religion." The goal of Bloom's criticism appears to be to goad readers into living that life, which admittedly few will be capable of achieving. At Yale, where "the dominant orthodoxy was T. S. Eliot—inspired New Criticism, Bloom observed how he felt somewhat out of place because "I am very Jewish, and lower-class Jewish at that."

A 1996 work, *Omens of Millennium: The Gnosis of Angels, Dreams and Resurrection*, examines the two-millennia-old belief system that emphasizes knowledge of "the God within." The current fad of angel worship, he declares, is a "debased parody of Gnosticism."

In short, the eccentric, idiosyncratic Bloom is Jewish at times and an "unbelieving Jew" at other times. But he is neither a religious nor a secular humanist nor is he attracted to any one philosopher, although he cites many philosophers in his works. Further, Bloom is unacquainted with *Free Inquiry*, adding as he autographed one of his books for a male inquirer at a book-signing party, "No, my dear, I belong to no particular philosophic movement." (See Robert M. Adams, "Bloom's All-Time Greatest Hits," *The New York Review of Books*, 17 November 1994.)

Bloom, Marvin (20th Century)

Bloom, an associate professor of social welfare at the State University of New York, is a secular humanist.

Blossom, Laurel (20th Century)

Blossom, a Unitarian, wrote *The Papers Said* (1993), a collection of poetry.

Blount, Charles (1654—1693)

A deist, Blount with his father's (Henry's) help produced *Anima Mundi* (1679), which outlines his cautious unbelief. In *Great is Diana of the Ephesians* (1680), however, he attacks the principle of revelation and clericalism in general. The book was condemned to be burned, but probably because of the influence of the Blount family he avoided being prosecuted. Macaulay once described Blount as "an infidel, and the head of a small school of infidels who were troubled with a morbid desire to make converts." This, according to Robertson, was at a time when Macaulay was himself privately "infidel." Blount is said to have shot himself because he could not marry his deceased wife's sister. {BDF; FUK; HAB; JMR; JMRH;RAT; RE}

Blount, Henry [Sir] (1602—1682)

One of the founders of deistic rationalism in England, Blount was a prominent figure in public life and served on several Royal Commissions. In *The Oracles of Reason* (published 1693), there is a Latin poem by Sir Henry in which he professes pantheism (the world being God's body) and rejects personal immortality. His eldest son, Sir Thomas Pope Blount, was openly deistic. His second son, Charles, professed to be a Christian but was regarded as one of the chief leaders of the early deists. {RAT; RE}

Blount, Roy Jr. (20th Century)

In his novel, *Be Sweet, A Conditional Love Story* (1998), Georgia-born Blount relates having sung in Sunday school,

> Red and yellow, black and white,
> They are precious in His sight;
> Jesus loves the little children of the world.

all the while wondering "Why did they teach us that song if they didn't mean it?" Life, he relates, consists of freeing one's self from much of what is learned in childhood.

Blount, Thomas Pope [Sir] (1649—1697)

Blount, the eldest son of Sir Henry Blount, was Commissioner of Accounts in the House of Commons. His *Essays on Several Subjects* (1692), which have been compared favorably to the writing of Montaigne, was openly deistic. {RAT}

Blum, Carol (1934—)

Blum, a freethinker, wrote *Diderot, the Virtue of a Philosopher* (1974) and *Rousseau and the Republic of Virtue* (1986). {GS}

Blum, Howard (20th Century)

Blum is a mortgage broker and publisher of the newsletter, "The Howard Line." A freethinker, he is an area coordinator for The Concord Coalition, a nationwide non-partisan group of concerned citizens for America's future. He has written for *Truth Seeker*.

Blum, Mildred H. (20th Century)

Blum was a secretary of the American Ethical Union when she signed Humanist Manifesto II. {HM2}

Blum, Robert (1807—1848)

Blum was a German patriot and orator. He took an active part in progressive political and religious movements, publishing *The Christmas Tree* and other publications. In 1848 he became deputy to the Frankfort Parliament and head of the Republican Party. One of the promoters at the insurrection of Vienna, he showed bravery in the fights of the students with the troops. Blum was shot in Vienna in 1848. {BDF; RAT}

Blumberg, Albert E. (1906—1997)

Blumberg, an idealistic philosophy professor who was an oft-harassed Communist Party official, fought in the 1940s and 1950s for economic and social reforms. In 1940, he had been cited by Congress for contempt inasmuch as he refused to identify party members to the House Un-American Activities Committee. He became one of the first Communists convicted under a provision of the 1940 Smith Act equating party membership with conspiring to overthrow the Government. In 1977, and despite his Communist past, the son of Lithuanian immigrants won election as leader of Manhattan's 71st Assembly District.

While philosophy department chairman at Rutgers University, he was a respected member known for his having received a doctorate from the University of Vienna, where he had been attracted to the Vienna circle of logical positivists. Blumberg wrote an acclaimed textbook, *Logic: A First Course.*

A Rutgers colleague, Dr. Peter Klein, described Blumberg as a master synthesizer who would often astound his colleagues by tapping his gavel during a rancorous dead-end debate, declaring, "I think I hear a consensus," then articulating an inspired compromise. {*The New York Times*, 13 October 1997}

Blumenfeld, J. C. (19th Century)

Blumenfeld is credited with having written *The Existence of Christ Disproved* (1841) in a series of letters by "a German Jew." Wheeler suspects that the name is someone's pseudonym. {BDF}

Blumenfeld, Warren J. (20th Century)

Blumenfeld is editor of *Homophobia: How We All Pay the Price* and co-author of *Looking at Gay and Lesbian Life*. In memory of Charles O. Howard (1961—1984), a gay person who was killed by gay-bashers after leaving a meeting of Interweave at the Unitarian Universalist Church of Bangor, Maine, Blumenfeld wrote, "The Conversion of a Gay-Basher." In it, he describes Jim Baines, who was then fifteen years old and was one of the three responsible for pushing Howard into a river where he was drowned. Baines now speaks out against homophobia, telling school groups, "Gay-bashing is wrong. Harassment is wrong. People are people no matter what we think they are, no matter what they do, or no matter how different they seem to us. None of us really has the right to judge somebody else." {*The World*, July-August 1994}

Blumler, Jay (20th Century)

A rationalist, Blumler is an emeritus professor of the University of Leeds and a former lecturer in social and political theory at Ruskin College, Oxford.

Blyth, P. G. (20th Century)

Blyth, a freethinker, wrote *Christianity and Tradition* (1906). {GS}

Boak, Deborah A. (20th Century)

Boak is a contributor to *The Freethought Observer*, a Texas publication that commenced in 1994. She was a founder of the North Texas Church of Freethought.

Boas, George (1891—1980)

Boas, a professor of philosophy at Johns Hopkins University, wrote *The Inquiring Mind* (1959) and edited *Romanticism in America* (1940). When asked if a philosophy, such as naturalistic humanism, could "spur the literary imagination as have deism, transcendentalism, or Christianity," he responded to the present author:

> Darwinism was a kind of naturalism, whether humanistic or not, I don't know. It certainly spurred writers' imaginations.

Positivism of the Comtean and Machian types was behind a good deal of nineteenth-century impressionism—to the point where it might even be called the philosophy behind the aesthetics of that movement. And Comte himself called his religious doctrines "humanism."

I fail to see why any philosophical doctrine might not have its literary counterpoint. A writer has to ask himself certain questions about human nature and the nature of the world in which the human drama is acted, and the answer will be—or might be expected to be—the greatest influence in the formation of his writings. The influence on natural science on Zola, on George Eliot, on Theodore Dreiser, was obvious, but sometimes such an influence is transmitted on the writer though another writer. Thus the *contemptus mundi* theme in the Middle Ages sprang directly from certain Christian doctrines of man's place in the universe. Such an attitude could manifest itself in painting directly by a Christian painter, but it could also be shown in the paintings of someone who was imitating the Christian painter and who never heard of the *contemptus mundi* theme. Similarly a novelist today who had never read Karl Marx would probably be influenced by his doctrines and would see society under the aspect of the class-struggle regardless of his own social views.

Consequently, if a novelist or poet should be convinced of the truth of naturalistic humanism, he would see men as having only this terrestrial life, as creatures of history possibly tragic, possibly comic, as individuals, not as examples of a class, and so on. If he really believed in the doctrine, his presentation of human beings would be different from that of a Catholic, a Pagan of ancient times, a Buddhist, or a Protestant. Wouldn't Sartre's own novels be evidence that atheistic humanism can "spur" the literary imagination? I would think that the influence of the various derivatives of Freudian psychology would be a kind of humanism. At any rate this was a relatively new conception of human nature, a conception which didn't rest upon any special theistic postulates and which could even be reconciled with one form of Catholicism, that which springs from the Franciscan movement.

{WAS, 20 February 1951}

Bob, Murray L. (20th Century)

Bob is author of *A Contrarian's Dictionary: 2000 Damnable Definitions for the Year 2000* (1998).

Bobb, John (19th Century)

From 1834 to 1835, Bobb edited a St. Louis, Missouri, publication entitled *Western Examiner*.

Boccaccio, Giovanni (1313—1375)

Author of the *Decameron* (1348—1353), Boccaccio was the illegitimate son of a French woman by a Tuscan merchant. Emulating his friend Petrarch, he became a Greek scholar and worked to reintroduce Greek works. His great secular classic, the *Decameron,* is a collection of 100 witty and occasionally licentious tales set against the somber background of the Black Plague. The stories have levity, license, humor, anti-clericalism, incipient tolerance, and an exuberance in the joy of living.

Papal authorities found the work difficult to tolerate, but they did partly because of such stories as that of "the Jew who," states Robertson, "after seeing the utter corruption of the clergy at Rome, turned Christian on the score that only by divine support could such a system survive. No Protestant ever passed a more scathing aspersion of the whole body of the curia than is thus set in the forefront of the *Decameron.*" (See entry for Classical Humanism.) {CE; JMR; JMRH; PUT}

Bocage, Manoel Maria Barbosa (1765—1805)

Bocage was a Portuguese poet, regarded as the greatest Portuguese poet since Camoens. On account of an open letter to Voltaire (*Verdades Duras*), in which he denied the immortality of the soul, he was imprisoned by the Inquisition in 1797 and was later prosecuted for joining the Freemasons. {RAT}

BOCHICA

For Chibcha Indians, Bochica is the supreme creator and lawgiver. {LEE}

Bockelson, Jan [John of Leiden] (1509—1536)

A tailor by trade before joining the radical Dutch Anabaptist movement, Bockelson was taken into captivity and, like Christ on the cross, was ridiculed by his captors for not saving himself if he was really the Messiah. Illustrative of a false Messiah, he was sentenced to death in 1536, was shackled to a stake, scorched with heated pincers, and detongued. {LEE}

Bode, Boyd H. (1873—1953)

Bode, author of *How We Learn* (1940), was an active member of the American Humanist Association. {HNS}

Bode, Carl (1911—)

Bode, a writer and educator, wrote *Mencken* (1969). He is an Episcopalian. {FUS}

Bode, Fritz (20th Century)

Bode in Germany heads an umbrella organization of free world view organizations. (See entry for German Humanists.) {FD}

Bodichon, Barbara Leigh Smith (1827—1891)

Bodichon was a British Unitarian and feminist who founded Girton College and was George Eliot's model for Romola. G. J. Holyoake, a close friend whose views she shared, published several pamphlets of hers. {RE; RAT; TRI; WWS}

Bodin, Jean (1520—1596)

Bodin was a French political writer. He wrote a book on demonomania, in which he appears to have been a believer. But in his *Colloquium Heptaplomeron* he has some severe attacks on Christianity in colloquies of seven persons: A Catholic, a Lutheran, a Calvinist, a pagan, a Moslem, a Jew, and a deist. Bodin died of the plague at Laon, northeast of Paris. {BDF}

Boerne, Ludwig (1786—1837)

A German man of letters and a politician, Boerne in 1818 gave up the Jewish religion, nominally for Protestantism but like his friend Heine for freethought. He wrote many works in favor of political liberty and translated Lammenais's *Paroles d'un Croyant.* {BDF}

Boerner, Wilhelm (Born 1862)

Boerner was an Austrian ethicist and monist. He was secretary of the Vienna Ethical Society (1902—1913) and secretary of the *Vienna Volks-Bildung Verein* (League of Popular Education, 1906-1909). {RAT}

Boeykens, Lily (20th Century)

Boeykens, from Belgium, is on the editorial board of *International Humanist.* In 1986 she addressed the Ninth International Humanist and Ethical Union (IHEU) World Congress held in Oslo. She is President of the International Council of Women and a board member of the Humanist Association of Belgium. In 1988, she participated in the Vatican-Humanist Dialogue in Amsterdam. At the 1993 Congress of the European Humanists in Berlin, Boeykens spoke about women's rights. She received in 1998 an award from the European Humanist Professionals for her many contributions to the promotion of humanism, particularly on behalf of women's groups and at the United Nations. {*International Humanist News,* May 1998}

Boggis, John (17th Century)

Wheeler cites Boggis as an atheist and a disbeliever in the Bible. {BDF}

BOGOMIL HERETICS: See entry for bugger.

Bohanan, Jim (20th Century)

Bohanan, a national radio talk-show host heard on Mutual Radio Broadcast Network, is a non-theist. Listeners have been told that he has seen no evidence to make him think a god exists. {CA; E}

Boichot, Jean Baptiste (Born 1820)

Boichot in 1849 was chosen representative of the people, but after the coup d'état he fled to England, then returned to France in 1854 where he was arrested and imprisoned at Belle Isle. Boichot was one of the council of International Freethinkers. {BDF}

Boiko, Vera (20th Century)

At the 1993 Congress of the European Humanist Federation (EHF) in Berlin, Boiko spoke concerning the need for women to partake in government. A People's Deputy of Russia, she lamented that the mortality rate is now higher than the birth rate in her country, that infant mortality is high, and that mortality from abortions has increased. Religions try often to take children out of their families and school, but American private entrepreneurs have invaded their school system. At the Congress, she heard the historian and deputy director of the Gorbachov Fund state that, with the fall of the USSR, there may now be only eight per cent of atheists in Russia.

Boileau-Despréaux, Nicolas (1636—1711)

Boileau-Despréaux was a French literary critic and poet, the spokesman of classicism. His critical precepts, found in *L'art poétique* (1674), led him to become revered as a literary lawgiver. Later, however, he was detested by the romantics. His satires on the clerical world, *Le Lutrin*, on women, and on life in Paris, led many to name him one of the major writers of the golden age of French letters—of these, McCabe states, both Boileau-Despréaux and Molière were freethinkers.

Boileau-Despréaux was a zealous polemicist, notably in quarrels with Desmarets de Saint-Sorlin and Perrault. The King, against the fierce opposition of the clergy, made him Royal Historiographer and compelled the Academy to admit him. {CE; JM; RE; TYD}

Boindin, Nicolas (1676—1751)

A procureur, or public prosecutor, in the royal *Bureau des Finances*, Boindin was not accepted into the French Academy because he was accused of being an atheist. It is said that when he conversed with Marmontel and others at the Café Procope, they used a conversational code: Soul was called *Margot*; religion, *Javotte*; liberty, *Jeanneton*; and the deity, *Monsieur de l'Etre*. When a police inspector unexpectedly inquired of them who was this Monsieur de l'Etre who behaved so ill, he was told, "Monsieur, he is a police spy." Fittingly, Boindin was refused "Christian" interment. He was buried, at night, *sans pompe*, without any ceremony inasmuch as his corpse was refused "a Christian burial." {BDF; JMR; JMRH; RAT}

Boissier, Marie Louis Gaston (1823—1908)

Boissier, a French historian, wrote chiefly on ancient Rome. Although he rarely revealed his own sentiments, according to McCabe, Boissier "was rightly denounced by the clergy as much more in sympathy with paganism than Christianity." Boissier is denounced as a skeptic in the Abbé Delfour's *Religion des contemporains* (1895). {JM; RAT; RE}

Boissiere, Jean Baptiste Prudence (Born 1806)

Boissiere was a French writer who, under the name of Sièrebois, published *Autopsy of the Soul* and a work on the foundations of morality. {BDF}

Boissonade, J. A. (19th Century)

Boissonade wrote *The Bible Unveiled* (1871). {BDF}

Boito, Arrigo (1842—1918)

Boito, an Italian poet and musician, wrote "Mefistofele," a bold work that Wheeler cites as having freethought overtones. Boito fought with Garibaldi against the Papal troops and later infuriated the Italian clergy by the frivolity with which he treated religion in his opera. A major Italian composer, Boito was a Chevalier of the Legion of Honour and a Commendatore. {BDF; JM; RAT; RE; TRI}

Bojaxhiu, Agnes (Mother Teresa): See entry for Teresa.

Bojer, Johan (1872—1952)

Bojer, the famed Norwegian novelist, was, according to Llewellyn Jones, a naturalist. *The Power of a Lie* (1903) and *The Great Hunger* (1916) are cited as examples of his fiction containing humanistic philosophy. Of his philosophic outlook, he wrote the present author,

> I am proud to learn that it is felt my two novels, *The Great Hunger* and *The New Temple*, are worthy of being mentioned among the works of Thomas Mann and other masters.
>
> You are dealing with a very interesting subject, and I fully agree with your opinion that the two express my outlook on humanism.

{CE; RAT; WAS, 6 February 1951}

Boland, Bryce (20th Century)

Boland, who has been working on his master's project in computer science, is president of the Auckland University Atheists in New Zealand. With true sophomoric wit, Boland has described himself to his opponents as a "crypto anarchist" whose interests include Christian burning and eating babies. On the Web: <bbol1001@cs.auckland.ac.nz>.

Boles, Donald (20th Century)

Boles wrote *The Bible, Religion, and the Public Schools* (1961). {FUS}

Boley, J. Dearness (20th Century)

Boley, a freethinker, wrote *Economic Freedom of Women Via the "Producer's" Religion* (1918). {GS}

Bolin, Andreas Wilhelm (Born 1835)

Bolin was a Finnish philosopher who translated Shakespeare into Swedish (6 volumes, 1879—1887) and wrote on the philosophies of Hume, Spinoza, and Feuerbach, of whom he was a great admirer. According to McCabe, Bolin's advanced rationalism "often drew upon him the attention of the reactionary Russian authorities before the Revolution." {BDF; RAT}

Bolingbroke: See entry for St. John, Henry.

Bolívar, Ignacio (19th Century)

Bolívar was a Spanish professor of natural history at the University of Madrid. A freethinker, he was one of the introducers in Spain of Darwinian ideas. {BDF}

Bolívar, Simón (1783—1830)

Bolívar was the South American revolutionary who led independence wars in the present nations of Venezuela, Colombia, Panama, Ecuador, Peru, and Bolivia, liberating them from Spanish rule. At one time the most powerful man on the continent, he had a vision of a united South America. But his dictatorial methods were resented and separatist movements shook the union. In 1828, having declared himself dictator, he barely escaped assassination by jumping from a high window and hiding with the help of Manuela Saenz. Soon afterwards, Venezuela and Ecuador seceded from

Greater Colombia, and in 1830 Bolívar resigned as president of Greater Colombia. Disillusioned at his failures, he said, "We have ploughed the sea." Although bitterly hated by many at the time of his death, today he is revered as Latin America's greatest hero and as its liberator.

In Bolívar's early travels to the United States and Britain, he became an atheist and was excommunicated by the Catholic Church. At the end of his life he was poor and in poor health. According to McCabe, "the clericals intrigued with his personal critics, and he was driven abroad and took his own life." {CE; JM; RAT; RE}

Boll, Marcel (Born 1886)

In 1954, Boll was elected an honorary Associate of the Rationalist Press Association. He is author of *Histoire des Mathematiques* (1974, 12th edition).

Bolle, Paul F. (20th Century)

Bolle wrote *George Washington and Religion* (1963). {FUS}

Bollier, David (20th Century)

Bollier, a freethinker, wrote *Liberty and Justice for Some* (1982). {GS}

Bölsche, Wilhelm (1861—1939)

Bölsche was a German writer who edited Goethe, Humboldt, Novalis, and Heine. He wrote over forty other volumes. His chief original work is *Das Liebesleben in der Natur* (2 volumes, 1898 and 1900). His study of Haeckel reveals his interest in and understanding of monism. {RAT}

Bolton, Brian (20th Century)

A freethinker, Bolton wrote *Secular Humanism and Radical Fundamentalism* (1988). {GS}

Bolzano, Bernard (1787—1848)

Bolzano, a teacher in Bohemia, was a realist and a philosopher who rejected the supernatural, keeping only a kernel of the Bible's ethics. His motto, "To be happy and to make others happy is the duty of man," is in the words of Putnam "Freethought in a nutshell." {PUT; RAT}

BOMBAY

In India, Mumbai is the new name for Bombay.

Bonaparte, Jérôme [Prince] (1784—1860)

Prince Jérôme, the youngest brother of Napoléon, "cherished a systematic hostility to every religious creed in general and the Catholic religion in particular," according to P. de la Garce's *History of the Second Empire*. Jérôme married an American lady, Elizabeth Patterson, in 1803, but his brother declared the marriage invalid because as a minor Jérôme lacked the necessary consent. Jérôme was made King of Westphalia and, in later years, was the mentor of his uncle, Napoléon III, although according to McCabe "he failed to break his political alliance with the Church, and President of the Senate." Although Catholics boast that he received the sacraments before death, according to McCabe Bonaparte "was unconscious when they smeared him with the sacred oils." {JM; RAT; RE}

Bonaparte, Napoléon I (1769—1821): See entry for Napoléon I (Emperor).

Bonaparte, Napoléon Joseph Charles Paul [Prince] (1822—1891)

Commonly called Prince Napoléon, or, more familiarly *Plon-Plon*, Bonaparte was the son of Jérôme and Catherine of Württemberg. Bonaparte took to politics and fought with the anticlericals after 1848. With the fall of the Second Empire, Bonaparte lived for some time in England where he was friendly with Charles Bradlaugh, whose atheism he shared. According to McCabe, "The clergy smeared him with their holy oils when he was dying, but he was unconscious and had never changed his views. French historians think him the cleverest of the family after Napoléon." {CE; JM}

Bonavino: See entry for Ausonio Franchi, the Italian ex-priest.

Bond, (Thomas) Edward (1934—)

Bond is a playwright, the son of an East Anglian laborer. He wrote *The Pope's Wedding* (1962) and such other provocative works as *The Fool* (1975) and *Summer* (1982). His work indicts capitalism. He claims that violence occurs in "situations of injustice" and that it therefore flourishes as "a cheap consumer commodity" under capitalism. His views continue to arouse extreme responses from critics and audiences. In 1997, Bond was named an honorary Associate of the National Secular Society. {OEL}

Bondi, Christine (20th Century)

Bondi is a former chairperson of the British Humanist Association Education Committee. She writes for *New Humanist*.

Bondi, Hermann [Sir] (1919—)

A professor of mathematics who retired from his position as Master of Churchill College, Cambridge, Sir Hermann Bondi KCB, FRS, is President of the Rationalist Press Association and the British Humanist Association. He was elected an honorary associate of the Rationalist Press Association in 1967. Also, he is a Humanist Laureate in the Council for Secular Humanism's International Academy of Humanism and an honorary associate of the New Zealand Association of Rationalists and Humanists.

In "A Non-believer Looks at Physics" (*New Humanist*, December 1990), he discusses other physicists' ideas and compares their views with his own on the subject of the compatibility of religion and science. He writes,

> When people ask me whether I am an atheist, I say that I cannot answer this question without a definition of God. To disbelieve in a Supreme Being gives it just about as much shape and context as to believe in it. If people tell me, as some do, that God is nature, I certainly do not disbelieve in nature. If people tell me that God is love, I certainly do not disbelieve in love. Tell me who your God is and then, and only then, can I say whether I disbelieve. If it is a God who has revealed himself and you firmly believe in that revelation, then my disbelief sets in. It is as an anti-revelationist, rather than as an atheist, that I would wish to be known.

Science, Churchill and Me: The Autobiography of Hermann Bondi includes how at the age of eighteen he arranged his parents' escape from Hitler's Germany. Among offices held, Bondi is a Vice-President of the Gay and Lesbian Humanist Association (GALHA). He signed Humanist Manifesto II and is a Humanist Laureate. In 1948, together with Fred Hoyle and Thomas Gold, he advanced the cosmological theory of the steady-state universe, on the whole now replaced with the Big Bang theory. In 1986, he read a paper at the Ninth International Humanist and Ethical Union (IHEU) World Congress held in Oslo. In 1992, he was extensively interviewed by *Free Inquiry* (Spring 1992). Also in 1992, his 67th Conway Memorial Lecture, "Humanism: The Only Valid Foundation of Ethics" (South Place Ethical Society), was published. In it, he states that "the morality of every religion is bad" and can be no valid foundation for ethics.

The Times Higher Education Supplement (18 September 1987) quoted Bondi in a witty discussion with Bishop John Robinson as follows:

> "God," said Bondi to Robinson, "was recently applying for a grant from a scientific institution to study the origins of Creation. It was declined on three grounds: first that there was no visible evidence that He had done any work on the subject for a long time; second because no one had been able to replicate the experiment; and third because the only records of it had not been published in any recognized scientific journal."

In 1993, the former chief scientist of the British Defense Ministry wrote to *Nature* that inasmuch as the world's major religions contradict each other, "a huge number of believers must be wrong. The variety of religions is a calamitously divisive force in human affairs. The less this factor is brought in, the better for all. This is especially incumbent on those working in a universal and global enterprise as science is." Predictably, his observation resulted in an avalanche of reader responses.

In a 1995 address at a Spanish humanist congress, Bondi spoke on "Science, Morality, and Humanism." He explained what he felt is the essential difference between "us humanists" and adherents of the many varieties of religion. First, "we are all struck with awe and wonder when we contemplate the universe around us, whether we think of the depths of space in astronomy, or of the incredible complexity of even the simplest forms of life, or of the structure of mountains, or of ecology, or of the intricate web of human relationships."

Some, however, "feel that all this wondrous world must have a designer, an architect, but one with no particular interest in humans, let alone in individuals. This was for example the view of Albert Einstein." Then there "are some who, while broadly agreeing with this view, have the ill-defined feelings (or hope) that this superintelligence might have some concern for us. Some Quakers and some Unitarians take this attitude."

The place where humanists differ, however, is in not agreeing with the view "that there exists some special 'revelation,' a particular form of firm and certain knowledge . . . whether this revelation is in the Gospels or the Qur'an or the Hindu Vedas or the Torah or the thoughts of Buddha or of Mao, etc. Such a revelation is the basis of virtually every religion. In the name of such a 'superhuman' (I would like to call it anti-human), certainly the most horrendous and repulsive deeds have been performed which stain human history. Therefore I am above all an 'anti-revelationist.' "

The revelationists, he lamented, regard all other religions (which of course contradict theirs) as false. Thus, "a vast number of sincere believers must be wrong. Since each of the religions has adherents of the highest intelligence and integrity, the conclusion is inescapable that it is in the nature of the human mind to be likely to be in error on religious matters. Any believers who are unaware of this fact are extraordinarily arrogant and in fact deny the common humanity of those who hold a different revelation to be true." Bondi's hope, he told the Spanish humanists, is that humanists, although modest in size, will continue to help transform the climate of opinion and make our world more humane and less intolerant.

In 1996, speaking at the fourth World Atheist Conference in India, Bondi compared the positive attitude of atheists with the arrogance of religion: "Though we are a minority with a small voice," he said, "our power of reason and persuasion is great. . . . We must reason with the religious and bring our positive values even to those who are stubborn in their delusions. To be human means to be in co-operation with others. We must value our neighbours across all categories. Yet we must stand up for our non-belief—the positive work of the Atheist Centre is a splendid example." He called upon nonbelievers to assert their views openly and looked forward to the time when it will not be respectable to be religious. {CL; *The Free Mind*, February 1996; HM2; *International Humanist News*, June 1995}

Bonghi, Ruggero (1828—1895)

Bonghi was an Italian philosopher and statesman who, at the age of eighteen, translated from the Greek several chapters of Plotinus. The following year he translated *Philebos*. He became professor of philosophy at Milan, was deputy to the Italian Parliament, and as Minister of Public Instruction (1874—1876) improved the schools of Italy and resisted the clericals. {RAT}

Bonham, John M. (19th Century)

Bonham, a freethinker, wrote *Secularism: Its Progress and Its Morals* (1894). {GS}

Bonheur, Marie Rosalie (1822—1899)

Bonheur, an internationally distinguished French painter known for her work depicting animals, was a pupil of her father, Raymond Bonheur. Her work gained her wide popularity, particularly in England and America. Her most famous painting, "The Horse Fair" (1853—1855), is in New York City's Metropolitan Museum. Cornelius Vanderbilt paid a then-record sum of $55,000 for the painting. T. Stanton, in *Reminiscences of Rosa Bonheur* (1878—1882), states that her friends thought her an agnostic, although McCabe found that she seemed at times to have used pantheistic language.

Not so well known is that Bonheur secured a special authorization from the French government to allow her to wear men's clothing "for reasons of health" and to allow her to wander through farms and slaughterhouses to research and sketch animal anatomy. Ironically, on one of the few occasions when she dressed as a woman, she was arrested for female impersonation.

On another occasion, teased by a man for going out unchaperoned in society, Bonheur retorted, "Oh my dear sir, if you knew how little I care for your sex, you wouldn't get any ideas in your head. The fact is, in the way of males, I like only the bulls I paint." This was evident to Nathalie Micas, with whom she lived for over forty years. When Micas died, an American painter, Anna Klumpke, moved into the house and stayed with her for the next seven years, until Bonheur's death at the age of seventy-seven.

Bonheur was the first woman ever to be awarded France's *Officier de la Légion d'Honneur*. She told friends she found the canine race more humane than inhuman humans. When a village priest of Tréveneuc once came to watch her work and, short-sighted, leaned over her shoulder to see better, she started painting nude bathers of both sexes. To her amusement, the indignant cleric left quickly.

Upon her death of pulmonary congestion, Bonheur was buried, according to her wishes, in a vault that included both Micas and Klumpke. She agreed to have a religious funeral but said, "Though I make this concession as regards my body, there is no change in my philosophical (not religious) creed." {CE; JM; WWS}

Boni, Albert (1892—1981)

In the 1950s, Boni was on the advisory board of Charles Francis Potter's First Humanist Society of New York.

Boni, Filippo de (1820—1870)

An Italian man of letters, Boni was editor of a standard *Biography of Artists*. He also wrote on the Roman Church and Italy, his "Italian Unbelief in the Middle Ages" being published in the *Annuario Filosofico del Libero Pensiero* (1868). DeBoni was elected deputy to the Italian Parliament. {BDF; RAT}

Boniface VIII (Pope) (1235—1303)

Benedetto Caetano was elected head of Christendom in 1294. During his quarrel with Philip the Fair of France charges were sworn on oath against Pope Boniface that he neither believed in the Trinity nor in the life to come, that he said the Virgin Mary "was no more a virgin than my mother"; that he did not observe the fasts of the Church, and that he spoke of the cardinals, monks, and friars as hypocrites. It was in evidence that the Pope had said, "God may do the worst with me that he pleases in the future life; I believe as every educated man does, the vulgar believe otherwise. We have to speak as they do, but we must believe and think with the few."

The Pope, however, had become pope after the abdication of Celestine V. To avoid schism, Boniface had imprisoned Celestine for life. The struggles he had with Philip IV of France were basically political, and after Boniface's death Philip forced Pope Clement V to repudiate many of the acts of Boniface, leading to the alleged charges of Boniface's heresies. Dante in *Canto XIX* voiced the contemporary opinion in Italy, placing the Pope deep in hell. {BDF; RE}

Bonnell, Kenneth (20th Century)

Bonnell in 1993 became President of Atheists United, which publishes a monthly newsletter, *Atheists United* (Box 5329, Sherman Oaks, California 91413), of which he is editor. He also writes for *Secular Nation*.

Bonner, C(harles) Bradlaugh (1890—1966)

Bonner is a freethinker and humanist. He was the grandson of Charles Bradlaugh and was president of the World Union of Freethinkers (WUFT). {FUK; HNS; TRI}

Bonner, Elena (1922—)

The wife of Andrei Sakharov, Bonner was awarded the "Distinguished Human Rights Award" in Amsterdam at the International Humanist and Ethical Union's Congress in 1992. When she was fourteen, her father, a member of the Executive Committee of the Comintern, was arrested. Six months later, her mother was arrested as "a relative to a traitor of his country." Her father was later executed without trial, and her mother spent eight years in a labor camp, during which time she saw her mother but once but somehow smuggled messages in and out of the camps. Being a child of parents who were "enemies of the people," Bonner said she was kicked out of the Komsomol and treated as some kind of pariah. During World War II, she rehabilitated herself by working as a nurse but was injured in a bombardment, the result of which led her to become almost blind. Despite exile in Gorki, hunger strikes with her second husband (whose fatal heart attack in 1989 she blames on Gorbachov and his associates), she continues to fight for causes threatening human rights. "If minorities cannot have a certain autonomy," she declared, "there will be a terrible bloodbath."

In 1993, Bonner was elected a Humanist Laureate in the International Academy of Humanism by the Council for Secular Humanism. Her 1993 essay, "The Rebirth of Democracy in Russia," is included in *Challenges to the Enlightenment, Essays in Defense of Reason and Science* (1994).

Bonner, Hypatia Bradlaugh (1858—1933)

Bonner, daughter of Charles Bradlaugh, was an active freethinker. Her atheist father had named her after Hypatia of Alexandria, the pagan lecturer who was torn to pieces by a mob of Christians in 415. She lectured widely for the Rationalist Press Association and complained that in person the Unitarians "always seemed to treat freethinkers with an acrimony special to themselves and us, nor would they handle the *National Reformer* in their bookstores." Upon her death, Chapman Cohen, president of the National Secular Society, noted that she belonged to "that small army of brave people who made it their duty, without thought of themselves or hope or expectation of reward, to strive for unpopular causes." {FUK; RSR; WWS}

Bonness, Wilhelm (20th Century)

Bonness was President of the West German *Bund Freireligiöser Gemeinden* when he signed Humanist Manifesto II. In 1966 at the Fourth International Humanist and Ethical Union World Congress held in Paris, he addressed the group, as he also did at the 1968 Second European Conference held in Hannover. {HM2}

Bonnet, Charles (1720—1793)

Bonnet was a Swiss natural philosopher. From 1752 to 1768 he was a member of the Grand Conseil. Contemporaries describe him as an atheist, but he was a deist and had somewhat mystic ideas about a future life. {RAT}

Bonnet, R. M. (20th Century)

Bonnet, who heads the European Space Agency, is a signer of Humanist Manifesto 2000.

Bonnycastle, John (c. 1750—1821)

Bonnycastle, a professor of mathematics at the Royal Military Academy, was a freethinker. He wrote several works on elementary mathematics. {BDF; RAT}

Bonser, Edna Madison McDonald (1875-1949)

A Universalist, Bonser was the first woman minister in Illinois.

Bonser, T. O. (19th Century)

Bonser, a freethinker, wrote *The Right to Die* (1885). {GS}

Bonstetten, Karl Victor von (1745—1832)

A Swiss deist, Bonstetten knew Voltaire and Rousseau. He wrote *Researches on the Nature and Laws of the Imagination* (1807) and *Studies on Man* (1821). {BDF; RAT}

Bonwick, James (1817—1906)

Bonwick was an anthropologist whose adventurous career in Tasmania and Australia made him a leading authority of his time on the natives of those islands. *Egyptian Belief and Modern Thought* (1878) makes a discreet attempt to show that all the Christian doctrines were borrowed from the ancient Egyptian religion. A theist, he held with Max Müller that "there has been no entirely new religion since the beginning of the world." {RAT}

BOOK OF J: See entry for Pentateuch.

BOOK OF THE DEAD

The Egyptian *Book of the Dead* is the oldest funerary literature, its Pyramid Texts of the Old Kingdom referring to the period from 2600 to 2300 B.C.E. The texts consist of charms, spells, and formulas for use by the deceased in the afterworld. Upon meeting the god of the underworld, Osiris, to face judgment, the mummy was advised that a cunning spell, well said, could hide unpleasant facts from the mind of the judge. {CE; DGC}

Bookchin, Murray (1921—)

Bookchin is one of the pioneers of the ecology movement. For three decades he has written essays and books on environmental issues, on the culture of cities, and on social ecology. His style, described as Hegelian by Nicolas Walter, conjoins Hegel's dialectics with evolutionary theory, suggesting a nature philosophy that he describes as "dialectical naturalism." *The Philosophy of Social Ecology* (1990) is one of his recent books.

Brian Morris, in *New Humanist* (June, 1992), writes that Bookchin "argues for the need to integrate the social philosophy offered by anarchism, with its stress on freedom and mutualism, with an ecological *natural* philosophy." The social and the natural he feels must be grasped in a new unity. This means that we must decentralize, restore bioregional forms of food production, diversify our technology and scale them down to human needs, and establish face-to-face forms of democracy. This does not involve, Bookchin argues, either the renunciation or the mindless deprecation of technology as such. Nor does it imply the denigration of science and reason. Bookchin has always remained true to—and has sought to develop—what is best in the humanist and rationalist traditions. As he states, "humanism does not involve the claim of humanity's 'superiority' over nature, but rather, and more significantly, it invokes an appeal to human reason, care, and a social ethics of co-operation."

BOOKS, CENSORSHIP OF

Censors, particularly those associated with authoritarian governments and religions, have been eager over the centuries to ban books. The American Library Association has listed the following as among the eleven most hated books, for example, about homosexuality:

James Baldwin, *Another Country*
William S. Burroughs, *Naked Lunch*
E. M. Forster, *Maurice*
Allen Ginsberg, *Howl and Other Poems*; introduction by **William Carlos Williams**
Radclyffe Hall, *The Wall of Loneliness*
Lesléa Newman, *Gloria Goes to Gay Pride* and *Heather Has Two Mommies*
May Sarton, *The Education of Harriet Hatfield*
Gore Vidal, *The City and the Pillar*
Alice Walker, *The Color Purple*
Walt Whitman, *Leaves of Grass*
Michael Willhoite, *Daddy's Roommate*

Following is a sampling of other titles which have been censored and which represent major authors and works

Boccaccio, *Decameron*
Erskine Caldwell, *God's Little Acre*
Casanova, Memoires
John Cleland, *Fanny Hill*
Frank Harris, *My Life and Loves*
Ernest Hemingway, *The Sun Also Rises*
James Joyce, *Ulysses*
Kama Sutra
D. H. Lawrence, *Lady Chatterley's Lover*
Henry Miller, *Tropic of Cancer*
Boris Pasternak, *Doctor Zhivago*
J. D. Salinger, *Catcher in the Rye*

Hundreds of other authors and titles, however, are cited in American Library Association materials.

The *Index Prohibitorum* was regularly brought up-to-date until Pope Paul VI decreed that it be discontinued.

Secular humanists abhor censorship in any form, holding that the denial of anyone's freedom to express or receive ideas is undemocratic and works against securing justice and fairness in society.

Booms, Marinus (17th Century)

Booms, a Dutch Spinozist and shoemaker, wrote freethought material, leading to his banishment. {BDF}

Boone, Albert [Colonel] (20th Century)

Boone, a freethinker, wrote *Our Hypocritical National Motto: In God We Trust* (1963). {FUS; GS}

Boorstin, Daniel J(oseph) (1914—)

A former Librarian of Congress, Boorstin has stated, "I have observed that the world has suffered far less from ignorance than from pretensions to knowledge. No agnostic ever burned anyone at the stake or tortured a pagan, a heretic, or an unbeliever." After entering Harvard University at the age of fifteen, Boorstin was a Rhodes scholar for three years, wrote *The Lost World of Thomas Jefferson* in 1948, and was a professor for twenty-five years at the University of Chicago. In *The Image* (1962), he wrote, "God is the Celebrity-Author of the World's Best Seller. We have made God into the biggest celebrity of all, to contain our own emptiness." In addition to *The Americans: The Democratic Experience* (1973, for which he won a Pulitzer Prize), he wrote *The Discovers* (1983) about Western scientists, and *The Creators* (1992) about Western artists. Hilton Kramer, reviewing the latter book in *The New York Times*, wrote, "If the term 'secular humanist' had not lately been so distorted by partisan rhetoric and ideological battles, it would be a useful way of describing both the strengths and weaknesses of the outlook that Mr. Boorstin brings to every realm of human endeavor. One of his models, in this respect, appears to be Edward Gibbon, about whom he writes with such a strong sense of identification that his account of the author of *The Decline and Fall of the Roman Empire* reads at times like an idealized self-portrait." In *Parade* (25 July 1993), foreign correspondent Tad Szulc asked Boorstin what he believes to the greatest danger the U.S. faces.

Boorstin responded, "The menace to America today is in the emphasis on what separates us rather than on what brings us together—the separations of race, of religious dogma, of religious practice, of origins, of language. . . . I think the notion of a hyphenated American is un-American. I believe there are only *Americans*. Polish-Americans, Italian-Americans, or African-Americans are an emphasis that is not fertile." Boorstin said he believed in an "American Humanism," which he defined as the legacy of Jefferson, whom he considered the most robust defense against the turmoil of our time.

The Seekers (1998) surveys those philosophers and thinkers who have contributed to his continuing quest to understand his world, leading *Harper's* editor Michael Lind to describe Boorstin as "a secular, skeptical moderate Northeastern liberal of the New Deal rather than the New Left school." In his *Who's Who* entries, Boorstin lists himself as Jewish.

Boosler, Elayne (20th Century)

A comedienne, Boosler has included in her act, "The Vatican is against surrogate mothers. Good thing they didn't have that rule when Jesus was born." {TYD}

Boote, Henry Ernest (1865—1949)

Boote was a rationalist, journalist, writer, and editor. Upon his arrival in Australia from England in 1889, he became involved in labor and trade union politics and publications. Boote was active in 1916 in anti-conscription and defense of the Industrial Workers of the World campaigns. {SWW}

Booth, Henry (20th Century)

Booth, a Chicago judge and an Ethical Culturist, was instrumental in founding the Bureau of Justice, which grew into the Legal Aid Society. {EU, Howard B. Radest}

Booth, James (1796—1880)

A lawyer, James practiced in the Chancery Courts. In *Problems of the World and the Church Reconsidered*, published anonymously in 1871, Booth rejected Christianity but remained an a theist. He reasoned that "truth, justice, and self-respect, which owe nothing to the Church, will not suffer from the extinction of a system of dogma which has too long usurped their place." {RAT}

Boothe, Robert O. (20th Century)

When he signed Humanist Manifesto II, Boothe was professor emeritus at California Polytechnic. {HM2}

Boppe, Herman C. (19th Century)

Boppe was editor of *Freidenker* in Milwaukee, Wisconsin. {BDF}

Borchardt, Jerry Wayne (20th Century)

Borchardt, a freethinker, wrote *Fundamentalist Creationism* (1981). {GS}

Borde, Frédéric (Born 1841)

Borde, a freethinker, was editor in Paris of *La Philosophie de l'Avenir*. {BDF}

Borges, Jorge Luis (1899-1986)

An Argentinian fiction writer, poet, and critic, Borges was educated in Europe and became associated with *ultraísmo*. Like that movement's pioneer, Spanish poet and critic Guillermo De Torre, Borges wrote in an extreme form of expressionism in which man is not the center of the universe and is, in reality, no more than a speck in his universe. The *ultraíst* elevated image and metaphor above plot or story, above ornament or rhetoric. For Borges, who was to become an anti-realist, life became escapism, art but an indulgence. He also became, to many, the greatest 20th century author never to win the Nobel Prize for literature.

Although he wrote much poetry, he is known for his short stories such as *Historia universal de la infamia* (1935; A Universal History of Infamy), which is a landmark in Latin American literature and the first work of

"Magic Realism." That term (*magischer Realismus*) first described writing of some of the German artists of a new objectivity (*neue Sachlichkeit*) characterized by clear, cool, static, thinly-painted, sharp-focus images, frequently portraying the imaginary, the improbable, or the fantastic but in a realistic or rational manner. In Argentina, however, "fantastic literature" is the Latin American term, one that also fits the Colombian writer Gabriel Garcia Marquez.

Borges's stories might tell about real or fictitious criminals. *Labyrinths* (1953) brought him an international reputation and was translated into English in 1962. Often his stories deal with the cyclical nature of time, are labyrinthine in form, are metaphysical in their speculations, are dreamlike in their endlessly reflected facets of reality and arcane knowledge. As an editor of *Proa*, he examined the idealism of David Hume and Bishop Berkeley. His *Collection Fictions* (1998) contains all his short stories in English.

Borges, whose ancestors include Portuguese Jews and English Quakers, did not follow any established religion or philosophy. On the contrary, according to *Current Biography* (1970), "he is committed to metaphysical speculation." On the other hand, in "Of Heaven and Hell," a poem in which he speculates about Judgment Day, he concludes that on that final day Inferno for the rejected will be the equivalent of no longer being able to see a loved one's face . . .but for the elected, Paradise.

Critic J. M. Coetzee, professor of general literature at the University of Cape Town, has described Borges's outlook:

> Borges's gnosticism—his sense that the ultimate God is beyond good and evil, and infinitely remote from creation—is deeply felt. But the sense of dread that informs his work is metaphysical rather than religious in nature: at its base are vertiginous glimpses of the collapse of all structures of understanding including language itself, flashing intimations that the very self that speaks has no real existence.
>
> In the fiction that responds to this dread, the ethical and the aesthetic are tightly wound together: the light but remorseless tread of the logic of his parables, the lapidary concision of the language, the gradual tightening of paradox are stylistic traces of an ironic self-control that stares back into the abysses of thought without the Gothic hysteria of a Poe.

Noga Tarnopolsky ("Borges in the Afterlife," *The New York Times*, 22 August 1999) claims that Borges was "fascinated in life by the idea of his own immortality. Disagreeing, Rodolfo A. Windhausen (*The New York Times Magazine,* 19 September 1999) retorted that her claim

> is incompatible with the writer's repeated statements on the subject. As I heard from him many times when I interviewed him in Argentina and the United States between 1976 and 1983, Borges summarily dismissed the idea of his own immortality. He loved to declare himself "an agnostic at heart." In 1985, a year before his death, the Buenos Aires newspaper *La Nación* reproduced his remarks at a lecture: "To die for a cause?" Borges asked rhetorically. "Nowadays, that's a form of stupidity. I am not a believer, and that takes anxiety away from the notion of death." When somebody in the audience asked him if his fame wouldn't make him live forever, he snapped, "Don't be a pessimist!"

{J. M. Coetzee, *The New York Review of Books*, 22 October 1998; OCE; WWTCL}

Borgia, Cesare (Caesar) (1476-1507): See entry for his father, Pope Alexander VI.

Borgia, Lucrezia (1480-1519): See entry for Pope Alexander VI, her father.

Borgia, Rodrigo: See entry for Alexander VI (Rodrigo de Borja).

Borgsford, Helgi (20th Century)

A liberal minister, Borgsford was once a director of the American Humanist Association.

Borman, Carolyn (20th Century)

Borman is President of *The Jewish Humanist.*

Bormans, Alex (20th Century)

Bormans has written book reviews for *The New Zealand Rationalist and Humanist.*

Born, Ignaz von [Baron] (1742—1791)

Born was a Jesuit-trained scientist and a favorite of Austria's Empress Maria Theresa, under whose patronage he published works on mineralogy. Active as a Freemason, and Illuminati, according to Wheeler, he wrote "a stinging illustrated satire entitled *Monchalogia*, or the natural history of monks." {BDF; RAT}

BORN-AGAIN CHRISTIAN

Non-believers are frequently challenged by "born-agains," Christians who claim they formerly lived a life of sin but have now "found the Lord."

The editor of *Pique*, asked in 1992 whether he was a born-again, gave the typical secular-humanistic response: "No, I was born right the first time." Further, as observed by Herb Caen, "The trouble with born-again Christians is that they are an even bigger pain the second time around."

Bork, Robert Heron (1927—)

Bork, a lawyer, author, educator, and former federal judge, was nominated in 1987 for the position of Associate Justice of the United States Supreme Court, but the Senate refused to confirm him. In *Slouching Toward Gomorrah: Modern Liberalism and American Decline* (1996), Bork dismissed secular humanism as unworkable:

> Secular rationalism has been unable to produce a compelling self-justifying moral code. . . . And with this failure, the whole enterprise of secular humanism—the idea that man can define his humanity and shape the human future by reason and will alone—begins to lose its legitimacy.

Börne, Ludwig (1786—1837)

Börne was a German author, the son of a Jewish banker named Baruch. He was compelled by a law against the Jews to abandon his position in the civil service, so in 1818 he formally adopted Christianity and changed his name. In reality, Börne was a rationalist. {RAT}

Borovoy, Alan (20th Century)

Borovoy, general counsel for the Canadian Civil Liberties Association, spoke at the 1996 conference of the Humanist Association of Canada in Toronto. He wrote "Civil Liberties in Canada: Erosion from Within." (*Humanist in Canada*, Winter 1998-1999)

Borrow, George (1803—1881)

Borrow was an English writer and traveler, a nomad who lived in England and on the Continent, where he was a translator and agent for the British and Foreign Bible Society. That group appeared not to know that Borrow, although religious in his youth, had become a pantheist. He eventually rejected Christianity entirely and, while admitting a "great spirit," refused to call it God.

Among Borrow's best works are the autobiographical *Lavengro* (1851) and its sequel, *Romany Rye* (1857). Borrow learned the language of the gypsies, writing *The Zincali; or . . . the Gypsies of Spain* (1841). {CE; JM; RAT; RE; TRI}

Borsari, Ferdinand (19th Century)

Borsari, an Italian geographer, wrote works about the American aborigines. He was a zealous propagator of freethought. {BDF}

Bos, H. J. M. (20th Century)

Bos of the Netherlands addressed the International Humanist and Ethical Union's (IHEU's) International Peace Conference in Zutphen (1983). He is author of *Lectures in the History of Mathematics* (1993).

Bosanquet, Bernard (1848—1923)

A philosopher and a freethinker, Bosanquet was active with the London Ethical Society. He was a neo-Hegelian, or absolute idealist, and he rejected the idea of personal immortality. (RAT; TRI)

Bosc, Louis Augustin Guillaume (1759—1828)

A French naturalist, Bosc was a tutor and friend of Madame Roland, whose *Memoirs* he published. Bosc, a freethinker, wrote many works on natural history. {BDF; RAT}

Bosch, Clement A. (20th Century)

Bosch was a signer of Humanist Manifesto II. {HM2}

Bosch, Madeline L (20th Century)

Bosch was a signer of Humanist Manifesto II. {HM2}

Boston, Robert (20th Century)

Boston is author of *Why the Religious Right is Wrong About the Separation of Church and State* (1993) and *The Most Dangerous Man in America? Pat Robertson and the Rise of the Christian Coalition* (1995). An assistant director of communications for Americans United for Separation of Church and State, he laments the de facto Protestant establishment of religion in the 1800s; the extreme and dangerous Christian Reconstruction movement; and the religious right's stealthy methods in obtaining its goals.

A journalist, he blasts the zealots of the religious right for spreading misinformation about the constitutional principle of the separation of church and state. Without such a separation, he argues, the United States cannot remain a free nation. (See Boston's "10 Reasons Why the Religious Right is Not Pro-Family, *Free Inquiry*, Winter 1998-1999.)

Bostrom, Christopher Jacob (1797—1866)

Bostrom was a Swedish professor at Uppsala. Besides many philosophical works, he published a trenchant criticism of Christianity's creed concerning hell. Bostrom's system, which was influenced by Leibnitz, was spiritualist and pantheistic. He held that only the absolute, which is undefinable, has real being. {BDF; RAT}

Boswell, James (1740—1795): See entry for David Hume.

Boswell, John Eastburn (1947—1994)

Boswell, a Yale University historian, died of AIDS in 1994. In 1980, he wrote a controversial work, *Christianity, Social Tolerance, and Homosexuality: Gay People in Western Europe From the Beginning of the Christian Era to the Fourteenth Century*, in which one of his aims was, in his words, "to rebut the common idea that religious belief—Christian or other—has been the *cause* of intolerance in regard to gay people. From 1050 to 1150, he found, there was "an efflorescence of gay subculture, with a highly developed literature, its own argot and artistic conventions, its own low life, it elaborate responses to critics."

In 1994, he provoked much debate with *Same-Sex Unions in Premodern Europe*, which was based on the study of more than sixty manuscripts from the 8th to the 16th century. In the 12th Century, he wrote, the ceremony of same-sex union had become a "full office" which involved burning candles, placing the parties' hands on the Gospel, binding their hands or covering their heads with the priest's stole, saying the Lord's Prayer, receiving communion, kissing, and sometimes circling the altar." Unmistakably," he held, the ceremony was "a voluntary, emotional union of two persons," one that was "closely related" to heterosexual marriage, "no matter how much some readers may be discomforted by this."

Boswell was an A. Whitney Griswold Professor of History at Yale in 1990, at which time he began a two-year term as chairman of the history department.

Garry Trudeau's comic strip "Doonesbury" was withheld by several newspapers because it included a reference to Boswell's describing "gay marriages." "They were just like heterosexual ceremonies," Trudeau wrote, "except that straight weddings, being about property, were usually held outdoors. Gay rites, being about love, were held *inside* the church!" (See entry for Homosexuality.)

Boss, Judith (20th Century)

A teacher in the philosophy department at the University of Rhode Island, Boss is author of "Is Santa Corrupting Our Children's Morals?" in *Free Inquiry*. The article developed her point that parents should not lie to children. Instead, they should take the time to "play pretend" with them, teaching what a myth really is. Her viewpoint is similar to that of the Canadian psychiatrist Brock Chisholm, who, however, was not a theist. While heading the World Health Organization (WHO), Chisholm created an international stir by suggesting that children should not be told that Santa Claus is *real*. {*Free Inquiry*, Fall 1991; *Free Inquiry*, Spring 1992}

Bossuet, Jacques Bénigne (1627—1704)

During the French Revolution, Maréchal cited Bossuet as being the *opposite* of an atheist. Bossuet, the Bishop of Condom [sic] and the tutor of the dauphin (father of Louis XV), attacked quietists, Fénelon, Jesuits, and Protestants. {CE; EU, Aram Vartanian}

Bothwell, David (20th Century)

Bothwell in Britain is active with the Wessex Humanist Network.

Bottomley, William (1882—1966)

Bottomley was a Unitarian, social reformer, and pacifist in Australia, where he arrived in 1926 from England. In his *The Man the Church Has Hidden* (1934), he argued that "Jesus the Miracle worker never lived" and that "apart from this earth, man has at present no existence." Both views revealed that the Christian influence shrank in the Melbourne Unitarian Church during Bottomley's ministry, a time during which he lectured that war is a betrayal of man's idealism. By 1969 the liberal side of the Unitarian group had become a humanist center actively involved in secular issues, whereas the conservative minority met separately as a "Unitarian Fellowship." {SWW}

Botsford, William (Born 1843)

Botsford, a San Francisco physician, was born in New Brunswick. A pronounced freethinker, he was vice-president of the California Liberal Union and said he regretted that more physicians, who shared his views, were afraid to express them. {PUT}

BOTULF-BLADET

Botulf-bladet, a Swedish quarterly of *HEF-Västeras*, is at the address, Torsgatan 47, 1 tr., 113 37 Stockholm, Sweden. E-mail: <christiaan.vos@vasteras.mail.telia.com>.

Botwinick, Isaac (20th Century)

Botwinick is activities coordinator of the Society for Logic and Reason at Oregon State University, Corvallis. E-mail: <botwinii@ucs.orst.edu>.

Boucher, E. Martin (1809—1882)

A French writer, Boucher conducted the *Rationalist* of Geneva. He wrote *Search for the Truth* (published 1884), a work on revelation and rationalism. {BDF}

Boucher de Crèvecoeur de Perthes, Jacques (1788—1868)

Boucher was a French archaeologist, employed on diplomatic missions by Napoleon. He was the first to establish the antiquity of man and the Stone Age in *De la création* (5 volumes, 1839-1841) and other works. Verlière described him in *Guide du Libre Penseur* as an advanced deist. {RAT}

Bougainville, Louis Antoine de [Count] (1729—1811)

Bougainville, a French navigator, accompanied Montcalm to Canada as aide-de-camp. Later, he established a colony on the Falkland Islands but had to surrender it in 1766 to Spain. He made a voyage around the world (1767—1769) with other naturalists, visiting Tahiti and the New Hebrides. The largest of the Solomon Islands is named for him, and his name is also given to the strait in the New Hebrides as well as to the bougainvillaea vine.

In the American Revolution he fought Admiral Hood at Martinique. His *Description d'un voyage autour du monde* (1771-1772, 2 volumes) helped popularize Rousseau's theories on the morality of man in his natural state. This inspired Diderot to write his *Supplément au voyage de Bougainville* (1772), a defense of sexual freedom. According to McCabe, Bougainville was a deist. {CE; JM; RAT; RE}

Bouglé, Charles (20th Century)

A French sociologist, Bouglé taught the history of social economy at the Sorbonne. In 1900 he published *Pour la Démocratie Français*, in which he criticized the clericals and expressed a moderate rationalism. {RAT}

Bouillier, Francisque (1813—1899)

A French philosopher, Bouillier wrote several works on psychology and contributed to *La Liberté de Penser*. His principal work was a history of the Cartesian philosophy. {BDF; RAT}

Bouis, Casimir (Born 1848)

Bouis, a French journalist, edited *La Libre Pensée* and wrote *Calottes et Soutanes* (1870), a satire on the Jesuits. {BDF}

Boulainvilliers, Henri de (1658—1722)

Boulainvilliers, Comte de St. Saire, was a French historian and philosopher. In addition to a historical work about the ancient French parliaments, he wrote a defense of Spinozism. His *Life of Muhammad* was the first European work doing justice to Islam. {BDF; RAT}

Boulanger, Nicolas Antoine (1722—1759)

A French deist, Boulanger wrote dissertations on Elisha, Enoch, and St. Peter. After his death his works were published by D'Holbach, who rewrote them. *Christianity Unveiled*, attributed to him and said by Voltaire to have been by Damilavile, may have been written by D'Holbach. The work was burned by order of the French Parliament in 1770. {BDF; RAT}

Boulding, Kenneth E(wart) (1910—1993)

An economist with the League of Nations (1941—1942), Boulding taught economics at the University of Michigan and wrote *The Image* (1956). Although his parents were deeply religious Methodists, Boulding became a Quaker as a young man and remained a passionate if unconventional Christian throughout his life. In philosophy he was a naturalist.

Boulding was a founder of the peace research movement in the United States. He helped initiate such efforts as the *Journal of Conflict Resolution*, the International Peace Research Association, and the Consortium on Peace Research, Education, and Development. He wrote voluminously in the field of economics and taught at the University of Colorado in Boulder.

Boulez, Pierre (1925—)

An eminent composer and conductor, Boulez is a freethinker. He has been a guest conductor of the Cleveland Symphony Orchestra and musical director of the New York Philharmonic Orchestra. An author of musical criticism, he wrote *Penser la Musique d'Aujourd'hui*.

Joan Peyser's authorized biography, *Boulez*, reports her experience that "At the chapel door he [a priest associated with a school Boulez attended] asked me if what he had been told was true: that Boulez no longer believed in God. I said it was and he replied, 'Then I won't show you the chapel where he prayed twice a day between the ages of six and sixteen.' " {CA; E}

Boult, Adrian Cedric [Sir] (1899—1983)

Sir Adrian Boult, English conductor of the Royal Philharmonic, the London Philharmonic, and other symphonic orchestras, was a member of two or more Unitarian churches and actively promoted Unitarianism. In his diary, he wrote like a theist, once noting that "Making pictures and patterns of the notes is not enough—knowing the composer's mind is not enough. I must pull down the ultimate beauty and truth of the music as God's imagination for healing and peace of mankind, through myself, to people on earth." {CE; U; UU}

Boulton, David (20th Century)

Boulton, editor of *The Sea of Faith*, is author of a pamphlet, "The Faith of a Quaker Humanist."

Boulton, Mary Bancroft (1912-1998)

Boulton was a psychotherapist who helped bring transactional analysis to New York in the 1960s. Popularized in 1964 by Dr. Eric Byrne, a San Francisco therapist who published what became a best-seller, *Games People Play*, transactional analysis is sometimes practiced in group sessions. It focuses on helping people change self-destructive behavior in relations with others. The techniques explores the various social and personal roles people assume.

Boulton, who helped found the New York Transactional Analysis Seminar, lived in Waverly Place in Greenwich Village, retiring from practice in 1990 and struggling for years with Parkinson's disease until her death.

Bourdet, Eugene (Born 1818)

Dr. Bourdet was a French positivist, author of works on medicine, education, and the positivist philosophy. {BDF}

Bourdieu, Pierre (20th Century)

Bourdieu, who teaches at the *Collège de France* and is a leading French sociologist, is author of *La Domination masculine* (1998). *The Economist* (24 October 1998) describes Bourdieu's theories as including

> a somewhat Manichaean conviction that social relations rest on domination: some people dominate, others are dominant. Unlike Marx, he does not believe that alienation and exploitation are primarily matters of economics. Domination, rather, is rooted in ancestral structure, perhaps even in the collective subconsious.

Men, he holds, have always been dominators, but this is so because culture has so shaped them that they have to continually prove their maschismo.

Historian Jeannine Verdès Lerouz accuses him of "sociological terrorism" and *Esprit* editor Olivier Mongin with Joël Roman equate Bourdieu's "far-left populism" with the "far-right populism" of Jean-Marie Le Pen.

Bourgeois, Léon Victor Auguste (Born 1851)

A French statesman, Bourgeois headed the Paris police in 1887. He entered the French Chambre and was the first French delegate at the Hague Conference (1902—1903). A noted pacifist, Bourgeois was an agnostic and "emphatically anti-clerical." In 1920 he was elected President of the Senate. {RAT}

Bourget, Paul (Born 1852)

Bourget was a French littérateur who wrote novels, essays on psychology, and studies of M. Rénan. Bourget was a naturalist. {BDF}

Bourke-White, Margaret (1904—1971)

Bourke-White, an American photo-journalist, was one of the original staff photographers at *Fortune*, *Life*, and *Time* magazines. She was noted for her coverage of the invasion of Russia, the liberation of Italy, and the horrors she found and photographed in German concentration camps. She also had a series on the rural South during the depression, mining in South Africa (perspiration beaded on the men's bodies), Korean guerrilla warfare, and portraits of world leaders.

Her books include *Purple Heart Valley* (1944) and *Portrait of Myself* (1963).

Bourke-White's parents were Ethical Culturists who had been married by Felix Adler. Minnie, her mother, was "a most bitter enemy to all religion and did not believe that there is a Supreme Being and will not do the least thing pertaining to religion," her husband Max White once said. Bourke-White was also married to the writer Erskine Caldwell, with whom she wrote *You Have Seen Their Faces* (1937).

For fourteen years she suffered from Parkinson's disease. The writer Norman Cousins once found her on her back, unable to get up. "Look, I'm just like a turtle," she joked. (The present writer, invited for a soufflé one night, arrived at her home to find the cook—his student, Shigeko Sasamori, one of the Hiroshima Maidens—absent and Ms. Bourke-White in the kitchen unable to break an egg. Mrs. Norman Cousins arrived just in time to start the dinner, which the present author finished, while Ms. Bourke-White served such large martinis that neither could remember much about the dinner. She conversed about the various awards she had received and which adorned her Darien, Connecticut, house's walls, told of her being attracted almost more to cameras than to men, spoke openly about the joys of being sexually liberated, and expressed no interest in the various organized religions.) {CE; WAS, interview}

Bourne, J. G. (20th Century)

Bourne, a fellow of the Royal College of Anaesthetists, hypothesized in the British *Freethinker* (June 1993) that Jesus may merely have fainted on the cross, surviving the crucifixion. Dr. Bourne describes himself as "a Christian atheist."

Bourneville, Magloire Désiré (Born 1840)

A physician and a French deputy, Bourneville was a physician to the asylum at Bicêtre. On the death of Louis Blanc, Bourneville was elected deputy in his place. He wrote *Science and Miracle* (1875) and *Hysteria in History* (1876). Bourneville also wrote a discourse on Étienne Dolet at the erection of a statue to that martyr. {BDF}

Boutmy, Émile Gaston (1835—1906)

Boutmy, a French sociologist, was a member of the Institut and the Legion of Honour. In *Taine, Scherer, Laboulaye* (1901), Boutmy expressed his agreement with the rationalism of his friends Taine and Scherer. {RAT}

Boutroux, Étienne Émile Marie (1845—1919)

A French philosopher, Boutroux taught in various universities, including the Sorbonne. He was an officer of the Legion of Honour, a member of the Institut, and correspondent of the British Academy. In his *Science and Religion in Contemporary Philosophy* (English translation, 1909), Boutroux stated that he is "not a dogmatic Rationalist who imposes à priori given and immutable forms." He was a liberal theist who pleaded for a sort of Christianity "without rites and dogmas." Boutroux did not accept personal immortality. {RAT}

Boutteville, Marc Lucien (19th Century)

A French writer and professor at *Lycée Bonaparte*, Boutteville wrote translations of Lessing and a work on *Morality of the Church and Natural Morality* (1866). For that book, the clergy turned him out of a professorship he held at Sainte-Barbe. In 1870 Boutteville edited the posthumous works of Proudhon. {BDF}

Bouveresse, Jacques (20th Century)

Bouveresse, a professor at the *Collège de France*, has been described by Richard Rorty as being "one of the very few philosophers anywhere who are equally at home in the tradition of post-Niezschean philosophy, which includes Martin Heidegger and Jacques Derrida, and in the so-called 'analytic,' largely Anglophone, tradition, which runs from Bertrand Russell through Wittgenstein to Donald Davidson." Rorty adds, "To the consternation, and often disgust, of his French colleagues, he prefers the latter."

In *Wittgenstein Reads Freud: The Myth of the Unconscious* (1996), Bouveresse declared that he disagrees with Jacques Lacan, who he alleges has bamboozled most French intellectuals "into conflating psychoanalysis and philosophy, to the detriment of both." Rorty agreed, adding that "Most Anglophone philosophers, even those most sympathetic to Freud, take Lacan to have been more a kook than a genius, and Mr. Bouveresse agrees." Bouveresse thinks that Wittgenstein can aid in understanding Freud's pretensions but that "Wittgenstein's general treatment of the sciences tends to undermine rather than enhance the strict distinction he is trying to establish between the situation of psychoanalysis and that of a discipline like physics."

Bouveresse signed Humanist Manifesto 2000.

Bovar, Orix (1917—1977)

A quiet, charismatic figure who drifted from astrology to mysticism, Bovar by the mid-1970s had attracted several hundred followers in New York and California, appealing to showbusiness types such as Carol Burnett and Bernadette Peters. When he announced that he was Jesus Christ and began celebrating Christmas on August 29th, his birthday, he lost some members. Arrested for failing to report a death, Bovar told investigating police that he was trying to raise his disciple from the dead. Shortly before having to appear in court to respond to the charges, Bovar jumped from his 10th floor apartment. {LEE}

Bove, Paul A. (1949—)

Bove, a professor in the University of Pittsburgh's English department, when asked about categories of humanism, responded to the present author:

> Coming of age among the Jesuits in the 1960's humanism seemed an ideal lost sight of by our country, its ruling classes, and its institutions. "Humanism"—that is, respect for others, other classes, other peoples, other races, other genders—all this needed to be accomplished to fulfill the promise of the humanistic vision that arose in the Renaissance, prospered in the Enlightenment, and seemingly disappeared in the miasma of misdirected American liberalism. The failure of the youth movements of the sixties to change our society and culture has made many academics, writers, and intellectuals of my generation realize that our own humanistic impulses were too consistent with the values of the State and its use of violence to provide the grounds for a reasonable opposition.
>
> So we turned to "anti-humanistic" writers to see how our most cherished traditions were complicit in and helped lead us to the worst acts of our recent history. Ironically, I think many of us did this because our own commitment to the most desirable elements of humanism never failed. We simply needed to understand more about how complex the phenomenon and ideology of humanism has been in the genealogy of our culture and politics. One must follow the road indicated by the best of "humanism"—including its critique of androcentrism—until some other historical possibility can be brought about. Somewhere in some library is a longish book by me of this subject, dating from 1986.
>
> {WAS, 22 May 1989}

Bovio, Giovanni (Born 1838)

Bovio, a professor of political economy in the University of Naples and deputy to the Italian parliament, was an ardent freethinker. He opposed the power of the Vatican and reconciliation between church and state. One of his works, *The History of Law*, was presented to the International Congress of Freethinkers in 1887. Bovio delivered the address at the unveiling of a monument in Rome to Bruno. {BDF; RAT}

Bowden, J. (20th Century)

Bowden, a freethinker, wrote *Bible Absurdities* (1968) and *Creation or Evolution* (1973). An Australian, he has been active with the Rationalist Society of New South Wales. {GS}

Bowditch, Nathaniel (1773—1838)

A mathematician, astronomer, navigator, and author of *The New American Practical Navigator* (1802), Bowditch was a seagoing mathematician who corrected some 8000 errors in Moore's *Practical Navigator*. His work is continued today by the US Hydrographic Office. Unitarians have claimed that he was a Unitarian. However, according to Robert Elton Berry's *Yankee Stargazer, The Life of Nathaniel Bowditch* (1941). "Bowditch . . . sold his pew in the East Church [Salem]. . . . After he had moved to Chestnut Street, it was more convenient for him to attend the First Church." The minister of East Church, William Bentley, was a Unitarian but since there was no formal Unitarian organization at that time he did not call himself a Unitarian minister. When Bowditch once was asked about his Unitarian beliefs, he modestly responded, "Of what importance are my opinions to anyone? I do not wish to be made a show of." {CE; EG; U; UU}

Bowden, John (1888—1981)

Bowden was a rationalist and critic of religious orthodoxy. He wrote *The Bible Contradicts Itself, Bible Absurdities* (1968) as well as *Archaeology and the Bible* (1968). {SWW}

Bowen, Barbara (20th Century)

Bowen in Britain is active with the Guildford Humanist Group.

Bowen, Brent (20th Century)

Bowen, once the President of Free Inquirers of Northeastern Ohio (PO Box 2379, Akron, Ohio 44309), became Vice President (marketing) in 1998.

Bowen, Charles Synge Christopher [Baron] (1835—1894)

Bowen, a British judge, rarely spoke about religion, but the poems and letters published by his biographer, H. G. Cunningham, show that Bowen was an agnostic. Further, according to McCabe, Bowen urged his friends to keep away from "all moods and phases of theological discussion." In a poem, Bowen speaks of "the illimitable sigh, breathed upward to the throne of the dead skies." {JM; RAT; RE}

Bowen, Francis (1811—1890)

When he reviewed Emerson's *Nature* for the *Christian Examiner*, the leading Unitarian publication of that day, Bowen criticized the work for its vagueness, mysticism, and general philosophical wrongheadedness. A logician, he found Emerson's view filled with Platonic idealism and lacking from an empirical viewpoint. Bowen was editor of *North American Review,* was a staunch critic of Darwin and evolutionary philosophy in general, and was an opponent of the educational reforms introduced at Harvard in the late 1860s. A Unitarian and an empiricist, he was described "as having no superior [as a historian of modern philosophy] at Harvard." {U&U}

Bowen, Zonia (20th Century)

Bowen is secretary of the Humanist Council of Wales.

Bower, William Clayton (1878—1957)

"I am reluctant to accept any label. But if I were to identify my position with reference to the several categories of humanism, it would definitely lie in the direction of naturalistic humanism," Bower wrote the present author when he was a professor emeritus of the University of Chicago in 1956. He continued:

> In regard to man's relation to reality, I hold (1) that, given his native equipment at birth, man becomes what he is as a person as a result of his experience; (2) that man's experience arises out of his interaction with his objective world of nature, society, the cultural tradition, and the extension of his immediately known world to cosmic dimensions; (3) that man's ideas and values are derived from his experience and that they change as his experience changes; (4) thus, that man's experience is bi-polar; the active, outreaching live human being, on the one hand, with his needs, desires, and capacities for conscious, reflective, and purposive thinking, and the objective world, on the other hand, also dynamic and in process of continuous becoming.
>
> I suspect that my thinking concerning the nature of man and his relation to his world has been most influenced by William James, John Locke, John Dewey, A. N. Whitehead, and George H. Mead.
>
> {WAS, 19 March 1956}

Bowers, B. L. (20th Century)

Bowers, a freethinker, wrote *A Selection of Poems by "Veritas"* (1936). {GS}

Bowers, Claude G. (1879—1958)

Bowers, a historian, wrote in *Jefferson in Power* (1936), "History has shown that on no subject can human passions be aroused to such a murderous frenzy as on that of man's relation to his Maker." {TYD}

Bowery, Leigh (1961—1994)

Bowery was a performance artist who once described himself as being "an unusually big heifer carting around sixteen or seventeen stones" (over 225 pounds). An Australian, Bowery was a costume designer for the English choreographer Michael Clark. He enjoyed being an exhibitionist and liked to appear in fetishistic outfits that he had both designed and sewed. A homosexual, he was described by some as an example of schlock, drag, and camp, but, according to Lucian Freud, Bowery was a shy and gentle person whose exhibitionism was a form of self-defense. Freud, who chose him as a model after the two met in London in the early 1990s, was impressed by "his wonderfully buoyant bulk, . . . especially those extraordinary dancer's legs." Bowery is depicted in many of Freud's works, his nude and huge body boldly showing his personal pride. The last painting, "Leigh Under the Skylight" (1994), shows him standing on a dais, posed in an unorthodox fashion with legs crossed, as if such a huge hulk could actually be a ballet dancer.

At the 1993 Wigstock drag festival in New York City, Bowery wore a foam mask and appeared to be something of a John Bull à la sumo wrestler as he sang and danced. In a shocker which any of the Freuds would have enjoyed analyzing, Bowery suddenly stopped singing, dropped onto a table, and appeared to be going into labor. When he opened his legs, out slowly popped a thin, naked girl named Nicola Bateman, who had been concealed under his garments. She was covered with fake blood, and the two were tied by an umbilical cord. Spectators were both startled and thrilled by one of the most unusual performances Bowery had ever conceived. The scene was captured in a 1995 movie entitled "Wigstock: The Movie."

Soon after the December 1993 show at the Metropolitan Museum of Art, he announced that he was going to Papua New Guinea. However, he slipped into a hospital, where he died early on New Year's Eve of meningitis and pneumonia, compounded by AIDS. He had discovered he was HIV-positive in 1988 but had not informed most of his friends because he was terrified that they would feel sorry for him. Bowery, wrote Hilton Als in *New Yorker* (30 March 1998), had enthusiastically enjoyed anonymous sex throughout his life. At one time he had an unrequited love affair with a seventeen-year-old artist by the name of Trojan, a chap in whose new apartment the two became roommates after Trojan made himself eligible for the housing by having set fire to his previous flat. "Star Trek" wallpaper and blue vinyl chairs were in the living room, and the doorbell played sex sounds until discontinued—"Every time someone pressed the bell and I heard all the gasping and moaning," Bowery explained, "I just thought it was Trojan having an asthma attack, so I never bothered to answer the door." Trojan died in 1986 after having become involved with filmmaker John Maybury.

With Bowery at the end were Freud; Nicola Bateman, the thin assistant he had recently married; and Big Sue, Freud's large female model. "My lights are still on, you know," were among the last words of the person who friends said was a freethinker.

Big Sue, in an obituary, wrote, "He was wearing his favourite costume—nothing." She said he looked "truly fantastic, just like himself, but empty." He was buried naked, Freud having paid to have the body shipped back to Australia where it was buried next to his mother. As if the show never ended, undertakers when attempting to lower the casket into the ground found the casket was too big for the allotted space. (See entry for Lucian Freud.) {John Richardson, "Postscript," *New Yorker*, 16 January 1995; Hilton Als, "Life As A Look," *The New Yorker*, 30 March 1998}

Bowles, Ada C. (1836—1928)

Bowles, a Universalist, was a suffragist, an abolititonist, a temperance supporter, and a home economist.

Bowles, Paul (1910—1999)

Bowles, sometimes called "the only American existentialist," was born in New York City. The son of a dentist whose "mere presence meant misery," he remembered, Bowles after World War II moved to Morocco, where he wrote *Blue Mountain Ballads* (1979—words by Tennessee Williams); *Next to Nothing: Collected Poems 1926-1977*, and the novels *The Sheltering Sky* (1949) and *Up Above the*

World (1966). An enigmatic figure, he insisted that no Westerner can comprehend Moroccan culture. He tried to explain it, however, to such of his many Tangier house-guests as Gertrude Stein (who originally suggested he move there), Tennessee Williams, and Aaron Copland (who once shared a house with him in Tangier).

Asked about humanism, he responded in 1956:

> One of the most backbreaking tasks is that of categorizing oneself. How can I know what kind of humanist I am, or, indeed, whether I am a humanist at all? I can get only to the point of believing that any intellectual is a humanist insofar as he performs the task of existing consciously rather than automatically. Beyond that I have nothing much to say. It seems to me that each religion is a set of regional game rules. They can be got on without, but it is a good deal less fun. The difficulty for humanity now consists in taking its own rules seriously; self-disciple is so much harder than obedience.

In 1989, he again responded:

> I don't know the meaning of "humanism," or what purpose it is supposed to serve. If I were obliged to endorse one of the seven varieties, I should have to choose atheistic humanism, even though the term "atheist" suggests a person who has given thought to the subject and rejected the concept of the existence of a divine consciousness. This is by no means my case; I am simply indifferent. (The question of religious belief vs. disbelief is to me a remote phenomenon, and of correspondingly slight interest.) So let it be "atheistic humanism." The other categories you list seem to me next to meaningless.

Bowles, winner in 1950 of the American Academy and Institute of Arts and Letters Award for Literature, is the bisexual depicted in "Naked Lunch," a film based upon the novel by William Burroughs. Conrad Knickerbocker, in a *New York Times* review, wrote that *The Sheltering Sky* ranked "with the dozen or so most important American novels published since World War II. Bowles avoided the spotlight and the world in which, according to Mel Gussow, he thought "innocence is corrupted and delirium thrives."

"When I die, there's no telling where the moonlight will find my hair," he once wrote in a song. He died of a heart attack and his body was taken from Morocco to Mont Lake, New York. {*The New York Times*, 19 November 1999; WAS, correspondence 1956 and 1989}

Bowles, Jane Auer (1917—1973)

Paul Bowles's wife, a writer who limped, once described herself: "I'm Jewish, homosexual, alcoholic, a communist—*and I'm a cripple!*"

Buried at the cemetery of San Miguel in Málaga, the body had been unclaimed by her husband when a freeway was built through the area. Alia Benlloch, a Spanish student from Marbella, asked Bowles for permission to rebury his wife—a late convert to Catholicism—in Marbella, about sixteen miles away. His response was that he did not "believe in graves" and that he had terrible memories of Málaga where Jane had been confined in a convent hospital for years before her death. But, propped up in bed with a painful leg and with tears in his eyes, he agreed to the request to allow her to pay for the reburial. In 1996, however, Málaga officials refused to allow such an essential literary figure to be moved elsewhere. *The New Yorker* (27 January 1997) quoted Bowles's letter to a friend, "I feel rather sorry for the girl from Marbella. I don't see why she should be stopped for carrying out her project. . . . But it is extraordinary that so much interest should have been aroused at this late date. . . . It shows that the age of books is not yet over." {CE; WAS, 31 July 1956 and 19 April 1989; CL}

Bowman, Hugh S. (20th Century)

Bowman is the secretary of the Glasgow, Scotland, Humanist Society.

Bowman, Leroy (1888—1971)

Bowman, a professor emeritus of sociology at Brooklyn College, was a prominent and active humanist, a member of the New York Chapter of the American Humanist Association. He was a state vice-chairman of the Liberal Party. Bowman was author of *Youth and Delinquency* and *The American Funeral.*

Bowman, Meg (1929—)

Bowman, who is co-chairperson of the Feminist Caucus of the American Humanist Association, teaches at San Jose State University in California. She is author of *Dramatic Readings on Feminist Issues: The Role of Atheists in the Third Wave* (1987), and *Sexism Exorcised* (1984). In 1994 at the 14th annual HUMCON conference sponsored by the Alliance of Humanist, Atheist, and Ethical Culture Organizations of Los Angeles County, Bowman spoke on "Female Genital Mutilation and Other Theocratic Traditions." She attended in 1995 the international women's conference in Beijing. Bowman, who became an atheist when a teenager, has described herself as follows:

> U.S. citizen by birth, Norwegian ancestry by parentage, atheist by intellect, single by good fortune, sociologist and teacher by profession, internationalist by choice, feminist by inclination, Humanist and Unitarian Universalist by affiliation, deviant by nature, grandmother by accident, social activist by experience, and writer by inspiration.

{HNS2; WWS}

Bown, Brian (1953—)

Bown, a social studies teacher in suburban Atlanta, refused at the start of the 1994 school year to observe a new state law requiring a brief period of "quiet reflection." As a result, he was suspended with pay for having lectured through the state-mandated period of silence and for having left without telling the principal that he would not preside over such a period. Bown was aided by civil rights supporters who agreed with his statement that "the Legislature very clearly intended to make it a moment of prayer." However, his fight is typical of the struggle between those who want praying officially allowed in public schools and those who consider such a practice unconstitutional.

Bowring, John (1792—1872)

Sir John Bowring was a politician, linguist, and writer. He was a disciple of Jeremy Bentham, whose principles he maintained in the *Western Review*, of which he was editor (1825). A member of Parliament, he translated Goethe, Schiller, Heine, and the poems of many countries. {BDF}

Box, Howard (20th Century)

When Box signed Humanist Manifesto II, he was a leader in Brooklyn of the Ethical Culture Society, where he served from 1960 to 1976. He then moved to a Unitarian ministry in Oak Ridge, Tennessee. Box is President of Religious Humanists (USA). (See entry for Ethical Culture.) {EU, Howard B. Radest; HM2}

Boxer, Charles R. (20th Century)

Boxer, who was in charge of British Intelligence in the Far East, was imprisoned for two years in the 1940s by the Japanese. An atheist, Major Boxer was married to Emily Hahn. (See entry for Emily Hahn.)

BOY SCOUTS

Founded in 1908 in Great Britain by Sir Robert Baden-Powell and incorporated in 1910 in the United States, the Boy Scouts organization is for individuals over twelve years of age. A companion Girl Scouts organization exists. Although critics have complained that such organizations, including those in Nazi Germany, are militaristic and authoritarian, the United States group has also been criticized by freethinkers, secular humanists, and Unitarians because Scouts are required to believe in one's duty to God and devotion to country; otherwise, they are not allowed to be members—as a result, many have been forced to lie by swearing to follow all items in the Scout Oath in order to become a Scout.

When told in 1998 that Unitarian children could not be awarded its own "religious emblem" in the various Scout troops, the Unitarians objected both to the Scout's bias against homosexuals and to the use of the term "God." Scout officials retorted that Unitarian Universalist boys could still be part of the 4.6-million member group so long as they abided by the restrictive rules. Atheists' children are illegible unless they swear they believe in God. In 1999 the New Jersey Supreme Court ruled that the organization's expulsion in 1990 of James Dale, a gay twenty-eight-year-old Eagle Scout and assistant scoutmaster, violated the state's antidiscrimination law, rejecting the Scouts' arguments that it is a private organization protected by the First Amendment. The court also dismissed the group's contention that homosexuality is immoral.

Boyd Orr, John Boyd Orr [1st Baron] (1880—1971)

A Scottish biologist, Lord Boyd Orr in 1949 received the Nobel Peace Prize. The first director of the United Nations Food and Agriculture Organization (1945—1948), he had such pessimistic prognostications on the world food situation that he was called an apostle of gloom. But his services in improving the situation won him not only the Nobel but also a peerage. He was a rationalist, an honorary associate of the Rationalist Press Association, and the International Humanist and Ethical Union Congress President in 1957. In his 1966 autobiography, *As I Recall*, Boyd Orr wrote:

> The most important question today is whether man has attained the wisdom to adjust the old systems to suit the new powers of science and to realize that we are now one world in which all nations will ultimately share the same fate.

{CE; FUK; HNS2; TRI}

Boyd, B. F. (19th Century)

Boyd, a freethinker, wrote *Open Letter to the Clergy* (1888). {GS}

Boyd, Bruni (20th Century)

Boyd, when she signed Humanist Manifesto II, was Vice President of the American Ethical Union. {HM2}

Boyd, John Thomas (19th Century)

Boyd was a supporter of the Leicester prospectus to raise funds for the National Secular Society. A cotton warehouse manager, he owned six of the one thousand £5 shares which were issued.

Boyd, Thomas (20th Century)

Boyd wrote *Poor John Finch: Inventor of the Steamboat* (1935). {FUS}

Boydston, Jo Ann (1924—)

Boydston is Director Emeritus of the Center for John Dewey Studies. Also, she is a contributing editor for *Free Inquiry*. The Center was commenced in 1961 at Southern Illinois University at Carbondale in order to make a concordance of philosophical terms in the works of Dewey. It now has completed a critical thirty-seven volume edition entitled *The Collected Works of John Dewey, 1882—1953*.

The Council for Secular Humanism headquarters library in Buffalo, New York, houses the Jo Ann and Donald Boydston Library of American Philosophical Naturalism, a large collection of volumes concerning philosophic naturalism and containing material by or about John Dewey, George Santayana, Sidney Hook, and Ernest Nagel, among others. She signed Humanist Manifesto 2000.

Boyer, Andrew Jackson (Born 1839)

Boyer, from Roxbury, Pennsylvania, spent his early life as a Christian, then abandoned the orthodox hell, then the authenticity of the Bible, then the divinity of the mythical Christ, then "all the clouds of superstition." In Dayton, Ohio, he published *Woman's Advocate* from 1868 to 1871, and in Chicago he began publication of *Nineteenth Century*, a radical reform journal which was discontinued after the great fire. For two days after that fire, Boyer was the only one in possession of any type and issued the only daily or other newspaper in that city. Moving to Denver, he commenced the *Daily Times* and editorialized upon behalf of Horace Greeley for president. He then moved to Oakland, starting the *Tribune*. In Sacramento he started the *Daily Gazette* and in San Francisco the *Commercial Advocate*, the *Mission Mirror*, and the *American Patriot*. {PUT}

Boyer, Paul D. (20th Century)

Boyer, who signed Humanist Manifesto 2000, won the Nobel Prize in Chemistry in 1997. He called the manifesto "the finest statement of what is needed for the future of the human race that I have read.

Boyesen, Hjalmar Hjorth (1848—1895)

Boyesen, a Swedish-American writer, taught German at Cornell University and was professor at Columbia University in New York from 1880 to 1895. He wrote a number of literary works of a rationalist character. {RAT}

Boyle, Humphrey (19th Century)

Boyle was one of the men who left Leeds for the purpose of serving in Richard Carlile's shop when the right of free publication was attacked in 1821. He gave no name and was indicted and tried as "a man with name unknown" for publishing a blasphemous and seditious libel. To prove his case, he read portions of the Bible in court which he said were obscene. When sentenced to prison, he remarked, "I have a mind, my lord, that can bear such a sentence with fortitude." {BDF}

Boyle, Kay (1903—1992)

A novelist and teacher at San Francisco State College in California, Boyle wrote impressionistic stories such as *Wedding Day* (1930) and *The Smoking Mountain* (1951). In a novel, *Plagued by the Nightingale* (1931), an American girl and her French husband, who has a hereditary disease, must decide whether to have a child in order to receive his legacy. *Death of a Man* (1936) told of an American girl's renunciation of her love for a Nazi physician. *A Glad Day* (1938) and *American Citizen* (1944) are collections of poems.

Once an expatriate living in Paris, Boyle was long a member of the Institute of Arts and Letters of the American Academy. Asked about humanism in 1989, she responded:

> [I am] a mixture of two humanisms: Naturalistic Humanism and Ancient Humanism. Sorry not to be more explicit at the present time. [Dictated during her illness by her secretary, A. Doherty].

A year later, however, as a resident in a retirement community, she was converted to Catholicism, the religion of her husband, Baron Joseph Franckenstein. Her son, Ian, has explained to the present author that his father

> came from a long-tradition Austrian Catholic family, and Kay had a deep love and respect for his mother, who was a devout Catholic. My sister Faith and I were raised Catholic by my father. Kay always assumed a rather neutral position, allowing us to be brought up thus and never, to my knowledge, did she ever interfere or for that matter attend a Mass throughout those years we were growing up in Connecticut. She was truly, at the time, a non-believer, a naturalist, a humanist. . . . Mother once said to me: "Catholics look after and take care of each other." I knew what she really meant was the fraternity that existed that appealed to her, not the sacraments or the

'ritual' of being Catholic, or even the belief in a Supreme Being. Kay felt that becoming a Catholic would bring her peace of mind. So in December 1991 she was baptized by Father Gerry O'Rourke.

I feel it was an act that was more a "placebo" effect rather than a conscious dedication to and acceptance of a God, the Blessed Trinity, etc. She never read or studied any formal catechism or literature on Catholicism, before or after her conversion. . . . I believe that despite these developments late in her life, Kay died a naturalist who loved all people, and whose works reflected that throughout her long literary career. Kay always listened to her inner voice and acted upon that. She never lacked the courage to do so.

{CE; WAS, 10 February 1989}

Boyle, T. Coraghessan (20th Century)

Boyle, a novelist, wrote *Riven Rock*, *Descent of Man*, and *World's End.* Interviewed in *Book* (December 1998-January 1999), Boyle said

> I am an atheist and a nihilist. I think all my life I've been struggling to recover my faith or belief in something, but I can't. I wish I could, but I just can't. . . . This is a time when hip is the rule, irony is the rule, sarcasm is the rule, and science is the rule. And I know all the arguments. I know Kierkegaard says you have to make the leap of faith, even though it's absurd. I know that science is as much voodoo as God is because there is no foundation to it, and I know that the unanswered questions are unanswerable. And I would love to make the leap of faith, and believe in something. But I believe in nothing. And it causes me tremendous despair and heartbreak.

{CA}

BOYLE'S LAW

Robert Boyle (1627-1691) was the Anglo-Irish physicist and chemist whose precise definitions of chemical elements and reactions signaled the separation of chemistry from alchemy. His physical theory that supported an early form of the atomic theory of matter was called the corpuscular philosophy. Boyle's Law is the principle that at a constant temperature the volume of a confined ideal gas varies inversely with its pressure. {CE}

BOYS

"Nobody can misunderstand a boy like his own mother, said Norman Douglas.

Bozarth, G. Richard (20th Century)

Bozarth is a Texan freethinker and atheist who has written *The Means and End of Freethought, A Case Against Madalyn Murray O'Hair: Interrelated Essays on an Experience, All the Way Alone, The Terminally Ill Sea Scrolls*, and *No Time to Wallow in the Mire.*

Bozian, Richard C. (20th Century)

A physician and professor of medicine emeritus of the University of Cincinnati's College of Medicine, Bozian is active with the Cincinnati Free Inquiry Group.

Brabrook, Edward William [Sir] (1891—1904)

Brabrook was an anthropologist, President of the Anthropological Institute and of the Folk-Lore Society (1901—1902). An agnostic, Brabrook was an honorary associate of the Rationalist Press Association. {RAT; RE}

Brace, Charles Loring (1826—1890)

A Unitarian, Brace was a social reformer who founded (1853) the Children's Aid Society of New York. {CE}

Bradbury, Ray (Douglas) (1920—)

One of the better-known science fiction authors, Ray Bradbury wrote *The Martian Chronicles* (1950) and *Dandelion Wine* (1957). In 1953, he wrote *Fahrenheit 451*, a picture of a future totalitarian state in which people learn from state-operated television what they are allowed to know. The state allows no books, and individuals with any books are burned along with their libraries.

Bradbury, a Unitarian, writes about racial, religious, and cultural questions. In 1972, he wrote a volume of poetry, *When Elephants Last in the Dooryard Bloomed.* {CE; UU}

Braddock, Elizabeth (1899—)

Braddock was a secularist and Labour Member of Parliament. {TRI}

Braden, Charles S. (Born 1887)

In Vergilius Ferm's *Encyclopedia of Religion* (1945), Braden of Northwestern University defined "religious humanism" as follows:

> Although humanists have appeared in many periods of the world's history, by religious humanism is generally meant a relatively recent movement, born doubtless of the modern scientific age, which has discarded all dependence upon anything outside of man himself for the attainment of the good life. Man is "on his own" in the universe which is essentially indifferent to him. Whatever satisfaction he is to enjoy he must achieve by his ability to control the physical world about him or through his manipulation of social forces which can thus be made to serve him. He is entirely this-worldly in his outlook. Science is the key to his hope of a better world.
>
> John H. Dietrich, a Unitarian minister, is frequently called the "father" of religious humanism, and most of the leaders of the movement have been furnished by the Unitarian church. Indeed the humanist churches constitute for the most part the left wing of Unitarianism. The most representative statement of their position was the so-called Humanist Manifesto issued in May, 1933, which declares in part: Humanism asserts that the nature of the universe depicted by modern science makes unacceptable any supernatural or cosmic guarantees of human values. . . . Religion must formulate its hopes and plans in the light of the scientific spirit and method. . . . Religion consists of those actions, purposes and experiences which are humanly significant. Nothing human is alien to the religious. It includes labor, art, science, philosophy, friendship, recreation—all that is in its degree expressive of satisfying human living. The distinction between the sacred and the secular can no longer be maintained. The goal of humanism is a free and universal society in which people voluntarily and intelligently cooperate for the common good. Humanists demand a shared life in a shared world. While religious humanism is generally non-theistic, there are many who call themselves theistic humanists or religious humanists. They are at one with the radical wing in their insistence upon human values and their denial of the *complete* impotence of man to work out his own salvation. Man cannot, they hold, achieve salvation without most vigorous self-effort, but he is not left wholly alone, for God works with him. Furthermore their outlook is not wholly this-worldly although they do not stress the future life. That, they are content to trust to a good and wise God.
>
> Representative writings of religious humanism include: Curtis Reese, *Humanist Religion* (1931); A. E. Haydon, *The Quest of the Ages* (1929); Charles F. Potter, *Humanism—A New Religion* (1930); R. W. Sellars, *Religion Coming of Age* (1928); J. C. F. Auer, *Humanism States its Case* (1933).

Religious Humanism, a Yellow Springs, Ohio, publication which commenced in 1966 and has been edited by Paul H. Beattie, encourages "religious" humanism. Howard Box is President of Religious Humanists (USA). (See entries for Comte; G. B. Foster; Howard Box; positivism; and American Humanist Association.) {ER}

Bradford, Marion (20th Century)

Bradford in 1997 became part-time administrator for the London office of the International Humanist and Ethical Union (IHEU). {*International Humanist News*, December 1997}

Bradford, Rod (20th Century)

Bradford, who has completed a video called "The Truth Seekers" which traces the history of the *Truth Seeker*, is a freethinker.

Bradlaugh, Alice (1856—1888)

The daughter of Charles Bradlaugh, the sister of Hypatia [Bonner], and the brother of Charles Bradlaugh, Alice actively helped her father and taught French in the Hall of Science's school that had been started by Edward Aveling in the autumn of 1879. She wrote, "The Mind as a Bodily Function." {FUK; PUT; RE; RSR}

Bradlaugh, Charles (1833—1891)

An English freethinker, along with William Gladstone one of the best orators of his day, Bradlaugh was the first president of the National Secular Society (1866), working with Annie Besant. As a boy, according to Foote, Bradlaugh was "an eager and exemplary Sunday School scholar" of St. Peter's Church, Bethnal Green, and studied the Thirty-Nine Articles and the Gospels as a preparation for confirmation. Finding discrepancies he wrote to the incumbent, the Rev. J.G. Packer, for his "aid and explanation." The net result of these inquiries was that the youth was obliged to leave his father's home, and "from that day until his death his life was one long struggle against the bitterest animosity which religious bigotry could inspire." Bradlaugh soon afterwards attended the "infidel" meetings in Bonner's Fields, and later came into contact with the militant Freethinkers of the earlier decades of the nineteenth century, Richard Carlile, the brothers Holyoake and others. From this time until 1868, when he became a candidate for Parliament, he carried on a vigorous Freethought propaganda under the name of "Iconoclast." During this period, and for some time afterwards, he was also actively working for Republicanism. In his short *Autobiography* (1873) he refers to his lectures on "The Impeachment of the House of Brunswick." "I have sought," he says, "and not entirely without success," to organize "the Republican movement on a thoroughly legal basis."

A towering figure of English freethought and a pronounced atheist, Bradlaugh In 1860 established the *National Reformer*, an uncompromisingly atheistic journal, which at first had to contend against a host of difficulties, including a Government prosecution to compel him to find securities against the publication of matter of a blasphemous or seditious nature. His successful defence resulted in the repeal of the Security Laws. Bradlaugh's knowledge of the law was wide, but apart from this he showed remarkable penetration in perceiving the legal points involved in the charges brought against him. In 1876, when he and Mrs. Besant were prosecuted for publishing a Malthusian work, his accurate knowledge of the law again stood him in good stead. They were convicted, but the conviction was quashed on appeal. In 1866 Bradlaugh founded the National Secular Society and remained its President until 1890. The Society is still flourishing and keeps a strong current of popular Freethought in movement all over England.

Bradlaugh had major difficulties becoming a member of Parliament. In April 1880 he was elected at the general election, tried to affirm rather than swear the religious oath on the Bible, was refused, then announced he would take the oath instead. This was also refused. In May and June of 1880, he refused to withdraw and was imprisoned overnight in the Coock-Tower. In July 1880 he affirmed and took his seat, but this was declared illegal and the seat was declared vacant in March 1881. He then was re-elected in April 1881, tried to take the oath three times, and was forcibly prevented from entering Parliament to do so in August 1881. In February 1882, he tried to take the oath twice, administered the oath to himself, was forced to resign, was re-elected in March 1882. He then tried to take the oath in May and July 1883, administering the oath to himself in February 1884, at which time his seat was declared vacant. Re-elected in February 1884 and again in November 1885, he was finally allowed to take the oath and take his seat in January 1886. In 1888 he introduced an Affirmation Bill but, ironically, died before being able to take advantage of the legislation.

His creating the National Secular Society remains one of his major freethought contributions. Of atheism, Bradlaugh wrote, "The Atheist does not say 'There is no God,' but he says 'I know not what you mean by God'; the word 'God' is to me a sound conveying no clear or distinct affirmation. I do not deny God, because I cannot deny that of which I have no conception, and the conception of which, by its affirmer, is so imperfect that he is unable to define it to me." One of his provocative books was *Humanity's Gain from Unbelief* (1849). As noted by Berman, Bradlaugh unlike some of his predecessors, was willing to "take the war into the 'enemies' camp" and was quite thorough in his atheism." From 1854 to 1859, he edited *London Investigator* and in 1860 he became an editor of *National Reformer*. Two years before his death, Bradlaugh introduced a bill to repeal the Blasphemy Laws in England. Just before his death, the House of Commons passed a resolution expunging from its Journals the many bitter entries of former years. However, Bradlaugh was in a coma at the time and never learned of the belated gesture. Meanwhile, his attempt to abolish the Common Law offence of blasphemy failed and "still disfigures our democracy," editor Peter Brearer of *The Freethinker* has written.

Although G. J. Holyoake was no admirer, he said of Bradlaugh that "He was the greatest agitator, within the limits of the law, who appeared in my time among the working people." Although he attracted fierce loyalties and strong aversions, none denied his power, effectiveness, and what George Bernard Shaw described as his "passion and conviction." Josiah Wedgwood remembered a friend telling how Bradlaugh "described to us how the shadow of the Cross lay like a black curse across all history, and as he spoke of the horrors of Christianity great tears rolled down his face."

Although a considerable part of Bradlaugh's life was devoted to political work, it is probably as the "image-breaker," the protagonist of Freethought, that he will be longest remembered, according to Foote. In the mid-1850s, he was, in his words, "honored by the *British Banner*" with a leading article vigorously assailing him for his lectures against Christianity. This "assailing" never ceased during his life, and was by no means confined to his views and opinions. He wrote numerous pamphlets. The "Plea for Atheism" appeared in 1877. In the debate with the Rev. W.M. Westerby on "Has or is Man a Soul?" (1879), and elsewhere, he showed his complete rejection of belief in a future life.

Bradlaugh died on January 30, 1891. His daughter, Mrs. H. Bradlaugh Bonner, took minute precautions to procure "signed testimony from those who had been attending him," that during his last illness he had never uttered a word directly or indirectly bearing upon religion. The last words she heard him speak during the night of his death "were reminiscent of his voyage to India." Despite this testimony, Foote wrote, "The traditional Christian falsehoods on this subject are still circulated and the writer of this notice is constantly encountering them. As recently as 1932, Mrs. Bradlaugh Bonner found it necessary to refute the absurd story about her father's holding a watch and challenging God to kill him in sixty seconds. Such mendacities no longer yield the amusement of novelty to Freethinkers; rather, they are considered a tribute to Bradlaugh's greatness.

In 1994, more than a century after his death, Bradlaugh was again in the news. A Church of England clergyman had urged that a statue of Jesus should replace that of "the atheist MP" which stands in Abington Square, Northampton, the town which first elected him to Parliament in 1880. The suggestion was considered "crass and offensive," in the words of Barbara Smoker, and the town newspaper editorialized, tongue-in-cheek, that, yes, the statue might better be replaced by the Bishop of Durham.

The newspaper then reported Smoker's statement that "No one can deny that Charles Bradlaugh—an outstanding Radical Liberal of the 19th century—really existed . . . whereas Jesus is probably no more historic than Aladdin or Peter Pan."

In 1995, the town of Northampton officially named its park "Bradlaugh Fields," a place with hedgerows and ponds, and natural grassland areas. (See *Radicals, Secularists, and Republicans* by Edward Royle for a detailed description of Bradlaugh.) {BDF; CE; EU, Edward Royle; FO; *The Freethinker*, January 1998; FUK; HAB; HNS2; JM; JMR; JMRH; PUT; RAT; RE; RSR; TRI; TYD; VI; WSS}

Bradlaugh, Charles Jr. (1859—1869)

The son of Charles Bradlaugh, Charles Jr. was the youngest of his three children. He died of scarlet fever at a time when his father was experiencing marital as well as financial problems.

Bradlaugh, Susan Hooper (19th Century)

Bradlaugh, wife of Charles Bradlaugh, was the daughter of a London freethinker and married Charles in 1855. When he chose a public over a private life, she moved to Midhurst in Sussex. According to Royle, she was a chronic alcoholic. {RSR}

Bradlaugh-Bonner, Hypatia (1858—1935)

An English freethinker like her father, Charles Bradlaugh, Hypatia and her husband, Arthur Bonner, formed a publishing company that republished many of Bradlaugh's pamphlets. She also edited a freethought periodical called the *Reformer*. She wrote "Princess Vera" and other stories. {EU, Gordon Stein; PUT; RAT; RE}

BRADLAUGH HOUSE

The Humanist Centre was officially opened on 21 June 1994—the Summer Solstice as well as the International Humanist Day—at Bradlaugh House in London. The four national Humanist organizations—the British Humanist Association, the National Secular Society, the Rationalist Press Association, and the South Place Ethical Society—all moved their offices there, which is next door to Conway Hall in Bloomsbury, at 47 Theobald's Road, London WC1X 8SP.

Bradley, Francis Herbert (1846—1924)

Bradley, a British philosopher, wrote *Ethical Studies* (1876), *Principles of Logic* (1882), and *Appearance and Reality* (1892). In logic, Bradley attacked the psychological tendencies of empiricism by differentiating sharply between the mental act as a psychological event and its universal meaning; to him only the latter was the concern of logic. In metaphysics, Bradley held that many phenomena considered real, such as space and time, are only appearances. Reality, which he called the Absolute, is an all-inclusive whole that transcends thought. An agnostic, Bradley wrote, "There is but one reality" and it is "not the God of the Churches." It is "inscrutable." In *Essays on Truth and Reality*, Bradley defined God as "the Supreme Will for good which is experienced within finite minds," and he rejected any belief in immortality. {CE; JM; RAT; RE}

Bradley, Lydia Moss (1816—1908)

Bradley, an educator and a philanthropist, was a Universalist and a Unitarian. She founded Bradley University.

Braekstad, Hans Lien (1845—1915)

Braekstad, a Norwegian freethinker, has made English translations from Bjørnson, Asbjørnsen, and Anderson. An agnostic, he was an active director for many years of the Rationalist Press Association. {BDF; RAT}

Bradstreet, Anne (c. 1612—1672)

An early American poet, considered the first significant woman author in the American colonies, Bradstreet came with her father to Massachusetts in the Winthrop Puritan group in 1630.

A Nonconformist and the mother of eight children, she had descendants who include Unitarians William Ellery Channing, Wendell Phillips, and Oliver Wendell Holmes. {CE; OCE}

Braga, Teófilo [President] (Born 1843)

Braga was a positivist and one of the Portugal's Republican leaders. In addition to writing poetry, he is author of *A History of Portuguese Literature*, a ten-volume work in which he applied the positivist principles of Comte in his general history of the nation's literature. An anti-clericalist who was involved in the Revolution of 1810, he was chosen as first president of the new republic of Portugal (1910-1911) and served again briefly in 1915. His teaching had a positive effect upon Portuguese intellectual life. Braga published more than one hundred works on literature, science, and philosophy. Although he joined the positivists, as an atheist he took an active part in the International Freethought movement. {BDF; JM; RE; TRI}

Bragg, Billy (20th Century)

A recording artist, Bragg is known for his songs about love and politics. In profiles, he is referred to as an atheist. {CA}

Bragg, Raymond B. (1902—1979)

A Unitarian minister, Bragg helped draft Humanist Manifesto I when only thirty years old. A student of Dr. A. Eustace Haydon as well as Curtis Reese, he graduated from Meadville in 1928 and went on to a two-year ministry in Evanston, Illinois. Edwin H. Wilson in *The Genesis of a Humanist Manifesto* (1995) gives a rather complete picture of Bragg the man and the organizer, telling of Bragg's qualifications about following many of Charles Francis Potter's suggestions.

Although Roy Wood Sellars in his advanced years may have thought he had written more of the manifesto than he did, Dr. J. A. C. F. Auer of Harvard University in 1953 wrote in a letter,

> I think you are under a misapprehension when you say that the Manifesto was originally written by Professor Sellars. I think that the first draft was originally made by Curtis Reese and Raymond Bragg. I recollect this because a copy was sent to me immediately after it had been drawn up and it was not a carefully written statement. Indeed, in many points it did not resemble the present Manifesto.

Wilson, however, believes Sellars wrote the first draft, "probably—according to Raymond Bragg—using as background notes from a lecture on the nature of value which he gave about that time at the University of Chicago." The manifesto, Wilson concludes, was definitely "a collective achievement" by Reese, Haydon, Bragg, Sellars, and himself.

Bragg was President of the American Humanist Association, its second, from 1941 to 1943 and wrote book reviews for *The Humanist* in the 1950s. With John H. Dietrich, Bragg wrote the popular *Humanist Pulpit.* The All Souls Unitarian Church in Kansas City, Missouri, at which he had preached, is the scene of Bragg Symposiums in his honor. Bragg also signed Humanist Manifesto II.

In 1998, Ed Doerr edited *Timely and Timeless, the Wisdom of E. Burdette Backus*, including a foreword by Jack Mendelsohn. It is an anthology of pulpit and radio addresses. Doerr wrote, "Burdette Backus' writing, his work, and his life are among the finest expressions of the best in Humanism and Unitarian Universalism and illustrate the very considerable overlap between these two traditions." (See entry for the American Humanist Association.) {CL; ER; FUS; HM1; HM2; HNS; HNS2}

BRAHMA

- Brahma, n. He who created the Hindoos, who are preserved by Vishnu and destroyed by Siva—a rather neater division of labor than is found among the deities of some other nations. The Abracadabranese, for example, are created by Sin, maintained by Theft, and destroyed by Folly. The priests of Brahma, like those of the Abracadabranese, are holy and learned men who are never naughty.

—Ambrose Bierce
The Devil's Dictionary

Brahma is one of the Hindu trimurti: Brahma, Vishnu, and Shiva. Relatively unimportant, he has few temples in his honor in India. The neuter Brahman, of which he is the personalized form, plays a major role in philosophic Hinduism. {ER; DGC}

BRAHMAN, BRAHMIN

In the Upanishads, Brahman has come to stand for the ultimate world-ground of reality. He is "neti, neti," or "not this, not that," and is absolute, impersonal, and ultimately indescribable. All the gods—Brahma the creator, Vishnu, Shiva, Krishna, and the lesser deities—can be assimilated to Brahman as personal manifestations of a reality that is itself impersonal or super-personal. Emerson, upon showing an interest in Hindu thought, wrote a poem, "Brahma," which addresses the subject of a universal creative force, an all-inclusive power, something which he developed into a pantheistic symbol of nature, an Over-Soul. Fellow Bostonians of high social standing who are known for their cultivated intellect and taste have been termed Brahmins. Philosophic naturalists find all such mysticism as incapable of being tested and, therefore, philosophically meaningless. {ER}

Brahms, Johannes (1833—1897)

Brahms, the famed German composer, wrote music in almost every genre except opera. His lieder are worldwide favorites, as are his songs and chamber music. "Brahms and Schubert, my two favorite gay composers," wrote Larry Kramer.

Biographers dispute whether or not Brahms before his thirteenth birthday "played the piano at night in bars" in low-class dives and brothels surrounding the docks in his native Hamburg. Jan Swafford in *Johannes Brahms: A Biography* (1998) speculates:

> Johannes was surrounded by the stench of beer and unwashed sailors and bad food, the din of rough laughter and drunkenness and raving obscenity. . . . Between dances the women would sit the pre-pubescent teenager on their laps and pour beer into him, and pull down his pants and hand him around to be played with, to general hilarity. . . . There may have been worse from the sailors. Johannes was as fair and pretty as a girl.

Some, including Kurt Hoffmann in *Johannes Brahms und Hamburg* (1986), deny he played anywhere at all before he was fourteen. Some say he romanced Robert Schumann's widow, Clara. Others say Schumann did not attempt suicide because Brahms had sent him a "too-candid" letter lamenting his inability to accompany Clara on the piano because of her absence. Some say Schumann starved to death because of problems Brahms brought on—Schumann once confessed to his diary to homosexual fantasies—others that Schumann died of tertiary syphilis. Most agree that Brahms was difficult, lonely and independent, gruff and tender.

Less than a month after Schumann died, Brahms and Clara traveled with two of the children to Switzerland, after which he returned to Hamburg, never again to be part of the Schumann family. As to why the twenty-three-year-old Brahms did not marry a woman with seven children remains unknown. His attachment to Clara remained strong, and he was not known to have suffered any guilt for his frequenting prostitutes.

Although he is thought by many to have been a Protestant because of his "German Requiem," Brahms once said of that work that it should have been called a "Human Requiem." Brahms was less "religious" than Beethoven. This he reveals in letters to Herzogenberg, in which he wrote that he was a complete agnostic.

One critic described his "Four Serious Songs," written a year before he died, as being his "supreme utterance of noble thoughts." Observed McCabe,

> The words to the first, as a matter of fact, reject and almost ridicule the idea of personal immortality.

Although he wrote much religious music, Brahms remained unchurched. Paul Edwards has cited Brahms as being a non-theist. {CE; *Freethought History*, #21, 1997; JM; RAT; RE; Charles Rosen, "Aimez-Vous Brahms?" *The New York Review of Books*, 22 October 1998; TRI; TYD}

BRAIN: For the brain's ability to triumph over reality, see entry for Healing. In "Sleeper," Woody Allen objected to the reprogramming of his brain: "You can't touch my brain. It's my second favorite organ!"

Brain, Lord (1895—1966)

Brain, a freethinker, was president in England of the Family Planning Association. {TRI}

Bramall, Margaret (1916—)

Bramall in England was secretary of the National Council for the Unmarried Mother and Her Child. {TRI}

Brameld, Theodore (1904—1987)

When he signed Humanist Manifesto II, Brameld was a visiting professor at the City University of New York. Among his books are *Minority Problems in the Public Schools* (1945), *Patterns of Educational Philosophy* (1971), and *The Teacher as World Citizen* (1974). {HM2}

Bramwell, Doug (20th Century)

Bramwell is an English freethinker who has reviewed books for *The Freethinker* (August 1998).

Bramwell, George William Wilshire [Baron] (1808—1892)

Bramwell was an eminent British judge and Lord Justice of Appeal who, after his death, was found to have been an agnostic all along. His biographer, Fairfield, says that Bramwell belonged to "that band of enlightened and advanced Liberals who used to make joyous demonstrations of kid-gloved agnosticism at the annual British Association Meetings." The letters included in the Fairfield volume confirm this. {JM; RE}

Brancatisano, Fortunato (20th Century)

Brancatisano was an active member of the American Humanist Association. {HNS}

Branden, Nathaniel (20th Century)

Branden is a long-time associate of Ayn Rand. He shares his mentor's atheism and disdain for religion. In *The Disowned Self* and *Breaking Free*, he discussed the destructive effects of religious faith on self-esteem and psychological well-being. In *Full Context*, an Objectivist publication, Branden denied rumors that he had embraced "God, altruism, and flying saucers." {CA}

Branden, Victoria (20th Century)

A Canadian atheist, Branden in 1979 wrote *Mrs. Job, Flitterin' Judas,* and *Understanding Ghosts*. She has stated, "I started on a career of atheism at a young age when I was trying to teach the story of Noah's Ark in Sunday School, and one of my students burst into tears at the thought of God drowning all the poor little bunnies and pussycats."

Brandes, Edvard Cohen (Born 1847)

An eminent Danish freethinker, Brandes was the brother of Georg. An outspoken materialist, he attracted attention when, upon his election in 1871 to the Danish *Folkething* (the House of Representatives), he refused to take the customary oath. Although the government endeavored to unseat him, he was finally allowed to affirm, thus establishing a precedent for future cases. Meanwhile, he continued to declare that he believed in neither the Christian nor the Jewish God, according to Robertson.

As editor of a Copenhagen daily paper, he gave space to well-written freethought articles of the scientific and philosophical kind. He was imprisoned for having allowed some material to be published. {PUT; RAT}

Brandes, Georg Morris Cohen (1842—1927)

Brandes, a Danish literary critic, was influential in bringing European thought to a wide audience in Denmark, Iceland, and Scandinavia. He has been described as "the greatest critic since Taine." Because he was a "cultural" Jew and an atheist, in 1870 he was refused the chair in aesthetics at the University of Copenhagen. In 1902, however, he was granted that same chair. *Main Currents in Nineteenth-Century Literature* (6 volumes, 1872—1890) was an attack on provincialism and reaction. Brandes introduced feminism to Denmark. Also, he wrote *Jesus, A Myth* (1925). Brandes opposed romanticism and helped direct Scandinavian literature toward realism and a concern for social issues. When he spent some time in Berlin, coming under the influence of Nietzsche, he was attacked during the war for maintaining total neutrality. According to Robertson, Brandes was an active freethinker.

Brandes was an honorary associate of the British Rationalist Press Association, which in 1899 had been founded by Charles A. Watts. McCabe writes that both Brandes and his brother "were outspoken Agnostics." {BDF; CE; JM; JMR; PUT; RAT; RE; TRI}

Brandin, Louis Maurice (1874—1940)

Author of a *Hebrew-French Glossary of the XII Century* (1906), Brandin was a French philologist. A Laureate of the Institute (Prix Chavée), he rejected all creeds. {RAT}

Brando, Marlon (1924—)

On 16 May 1990, homicide detectives arrived at the Beverly Hills, California house of actor Marlon Brando. Paramedics had found the body of Dag Drollet. Christian Brando, Marlon's thirty-two-year-old son, had blurted out to the police that he had, in an accident, killed his pregnant half-sister Cheyenne's Tahitian boyfriend. Brando told a detective that Cheyenne, her mother, Tarita, and her boyfriend, Dag Drollet, had at his invitation been living in the house, that he had brought Cheyenne from Tahiti to Beverly Hills a week prior in order to see a psychiatrist, that he had not heard any shot, but that he found Christian holding a large handgun and his son had told him he had just shot and killed Dag. (In 1995, a heartbroken Cheyenne, age twenty-five, hanged herself at her mother's home in Tahiti. Called a troubled girl whose life was plagued by drugs and who was intrigued by mysticism, she upon previous occasions had tried to commit suicide, once trying to hang herself with a dog chain. Accusing her father of conspiring with her brother to kill Drollet, Cheyenne claimed on a television program that Brando had molested her as a child. Tahitian authorities were unable to question him, because Brando refused to return to the island.)

When called to testify at his son's trial, the more than 300-pound Marlon Brando strode to the witness stand. The clerk recited the oath, followed by "so help you God?" "No," the actor expostulated, "I will not swear on God. I will not swear on God, because I don't believe in the conceptional sense and in this nonsense. What I will swear on is my children and my grandchildren." The judge interceded quickly, "We have a different oath we can give him," and Brando then affirmed that what he was about to state was the whole truth and nothing but the truth.

In the courtroom was Jacques Drollet, the victim's Tahitian father, who heard Brando describe how, when Dag's body was brought out, "I asked some officers to unzip the bag, and I wanted to say good-bye and admire him properly. I kissed him, told him I loved him, and that is all." Christian was eventually sentenced to six years for voluntary manslaughter and an additional four years because a gun was used in the commission of the crime which, according to Peter Manso in *Brando: The Biography* (1994), meant the son would be eligible for parole in about four and a half years.

Brando, as was the case with his son, never finished tenth grade, and he is not known to have written his views concerning philosophy. Married several times and reportedly the father of nine children, he admitted to the judge upon winning custody of Christian's son, "I think, perhaps, I failed as a father."

Most regard Brando as the foremost practitioner of method acting, the sensation who in Tennessee Williams's *A Streetcar Named Desire* (1947) starred not only on Broadway but also in the film. His famous cry, "Stella!", which brought his character Stanley's wife back into his arms, is cited as having firmly established his reputation as a major actor. Sent to Tahiti to play Fletcher Christian, Brando earned his first big money although MGM was having financial problems at the time. According to Manso, "There was also talk that Brando had tried to add homosexual overtones to the role of Fletcher Christian. Brando's foppish portrayal annoyed Richard Harris, particularly during a scene in which Brando was supposed to slap Harris in the face. Brando merely flicked his wrist."

In Paris in 1976, Brando responded to contentions that "The Missouri Breaks" was pervaded with homosexuality: Brando replied, "Homosexuality is so much in fashion it no longer makes news. Like a large number of men, I, too, have had homosexual experiences and I am not ashamed." Gossip columnists hastened to add that Brando and Wally "Mr. Peepers" Cox had been a lifetime item, adding that Brando was basically bisexual with an interest in Tahitian women who would not "tie him down." However, biographer Peter Manso categorically denies the Cox gossip, although he adds about his subject, who was "deemed too 'pretty' " at the start of his career to wearing size fifty-two underwear now, "There's no doubt he's been bisexual." Manso delights in reporting that "people claimed" to have seen a photograph in which Brando was performing fellatio on an unidentified man, then adds "word had it" that the picture was some unexplained practical joke. Critics have complained that Manso asserts much but proves little.

After hitting the $1 million salary level with "The Fugitive Kind," Brando was to continue with such hits as "Last Tango in Paris" and The Godfather." At the 1973 Academy Awards ceremony, when Liv Ullmann and Roger Moore announced that Brando had won over nominees Michael Caine, Laurence Olivier, and Paul Winfield, an Apache Indian, Sacheen Littlefeather, approached and announced, "I'm representing Marlon Brando this evening, and he has asked me to tell you . . . that he very regretfully cannot accept this very generous award. And the reasons for this are the treatment of American Indians today by the film industry and on television in movie reruns."

For more than a decade beginning in the early 1960s, Brando committed himself to protesting social injustice. A 1994 autobiography, *Brando: Songs My Mother Taught Me*, ghostwritten with Robert Lindsey and revealing little which was new, did not mention his children or their problems but did include, "Whatever grains of optimism survive in me about the evolution of mankind are centered in the belief that genetic alteration, however fraught with danger, is the only possible solution."

Although Jill Neimark considers Brando an inhumanist because of the alleged bad treatment of his children, Brando is a freethinker in his philosophic outlook.

Brandon, James (18th Century)

Brandon was one of the "coterie of infidels." (See entry for North Carolina Freethinkers.)

Brandt, Reinhard (1937—)

Brandt, in Germany, is a corresponding member of The Hume Society, a group engaged in scholarly activity concerning David Hume. He wrote *David Hume in Deutschland* (1989).

Brandt, Willy [Chancellor] (1913—1992)

The German political leader Willy Brandt's original name was Herbert Ernst Karl Frahm. When Hitler came into power, Brandt fled to Norway, then to Sweden. In Germany after World War II, he became chancellor (1969—1974) with the support of the Free Democratic party and President of the Socialist International in 1976. The author of *North-South: A Program for Survival* (1980), Brandt was an unbeliever. {*New Humanist,* August 1997}

Brann, William Cowper (1855—1898)

Brann, who published the monthly *Iconoclast*, "the Only American Magazine That Ever Secured 100,000 Readers in a Single Year," let it be known what he thought about the proselytizing Baptists as well as the anti-Catholic and anti-Semitic American Protective Association. He also wrote vicious material about impoverished African Americans, and his muckraking got him into trouble with Baylor University. Ryan has written, "Brann had agnostic leanings but was never an atheist. He held to no particular line in politics and fought no crusades for such liberal reforms as women's suffrage. His primary value to American literature was as a pacesetter. His kind of brash, sprightly, freewheeling journalism was an inspiration to radical thinkers and writers in the century that dawned two years after his death."

"In 1893," Brann wrote in *Iconoclast*,

> I spent several days at El Paso in the company of two learned Hindu priests who had attended the World's Fair and were making a tour of this country, studying our institutions and occasionally giving lectures explanatory of their own religion. . . . The younger of the priests declared that Christian missionaries had been the curse of Asia. 'Wherever they go they are followed by dangerous disease, by drunkenness, violence, and lewdness. I do not say that they teach evil, but evil follows them. The Asiatics do not seem to grasp the good in your religion, but are quick to assimilate all the bad in your civilization, all the barbarism of your God.
>
> Strange that you have made such wonderful progress in all things else and have not been able to civilize your Deity. We will listen to your preachers, but they will not listen to us. We seek knowledge, that we may the better teach. For that we come from the Antipodes. We admire your Government, we stand worshipful before your science and your industry, but your religion causes us to laugh. It must have been made by children. Your ministers do not want to learn—they dare not. Their religious education is finished—bounded by one book, and it is simply a *chechil* for the cast—off garments of the world. Your Bible is the religious rubbish heap, upon which grow, I am told, 500 different kinds of weeds—each trying to crown the others off. . . . You are a great people, but your God seems to delight in ignorant worshippers rather than the praise of wisdom.

Speaking of the Baptists, Brann commented that "the only problem with the Baptists was that they don't hold 'em under long enough."

A photo of Brann and one of his articles from the Waco, Texas, *Iconoclast* are found in *Freethought on the American Frontier* (1992), which concludes that Brann was basically an atheist. In 1911, *Brann the Iconoclast: A Collection of the Writings of W. C. Brann* was published. {EU, William F. Ryan; *Freethought History #15*, 1995, and #18, 1996

Brannon, Carl (20th Century)

Brannon holds the facetious office of "Minister of Evil" of Oregon State University's Society for Logic and Reason in Corvallis. His e-mail: <brannonc@ucs.orst.edu>.

Branting, Karl Hjalmar (Born 1860)

A Swedish socialist, Branting was sentenced in 1888 to three months in prison for blasphemy in his paper, *Social Democraten.* Branting was a leader of the Swedish Social Democrats. {BDF; RAT}

Branwyn, Gareth (20th Century)

Branwyn is on the editorial board of *The Truth Seeker*, the freethinkers' publication in San Diego, California.

Bratteng, Steve (20th Century)

Bratteng is associated with the Austin, Texas, Humanists. (See entry for Texas Atheists, Freethinkers, Humanists.) {FD}

Bratton, Fred Gladstone (Born 1896)

Bratton wrote *The Legacy of the Liberal Spirit.* {FUS}

Brauer, Gerald C. (20th Century)

Brauer wrote *Protestantism in America, A Narrative History* (1953). {FUS}

Braun, Lily (1865—1916)

A German writer and reformer, Braun was a member of a German aristocratic (1865—1916) family who defied her relatives and became an active freethinker, feminist, and Socialist. Her aunt, Countess Clotilde von Hermann, disinherited her for her advanced ideas.

According to McCabe, Braun's contemptuous rejection of Christianity is often shown in her *Memoiren einer Sozialisten* (2 volumes, 1900). {JM; RAT}

Braun, Peter (20th Century)

Braun, while a student at the University of Wisconsin in Milwaukee, was one of the founding members of Campus Freethought Alliance. {*International Humanist News*, December 1996}

Braun, Wilhelm von (1813—1860)

Braun was a Swedish poet, a humorist who satirized many Bible stories. {BDF; RAT}

Braunlich, Edward (20th Century)

Braunlich, a Unitarian in Ontario, is author of *A Book of Braunlich: The Thoughts of a Unitarian Layman* (1993).

Bray, Charles (1811—1884)

A self-taught freethinker, Bray was the brother-in-law of Charles Hennell. Upon marrying, Bray said he took Volney's *Ruins of Empires* "to enliven the honeymoon." On one trip to Italy, Mary Ann Evans (George Eliot) accompanied the Brays and said he greatly influenced her philosophic outlook. His works on *The Philosophy of Necessity* (1841) and *Cerebral Psychology* (1875) are the keys to his thought. In the year of his death, Bray wrote that since he had no hope or expectation or belief even in the possibility of continued individuality after death, the opinions which served him so satisfactorily in life "will do to die by." {BDF; RAT}

Bray, Henry Truro (20th Century)

Bray, a freethinker, wrote *Essays on God and Man* (1916). {GS}

Bray, Rosemary L. (20th Century)

Bray, who grew up as an African American Catholic, became an atheist, then attended the Community Church of New York because it had been the church of her husband's childhood and a bastion of liberal religious and social activism. Influenced by Margaret Atwood's statement that if she ever decided to have a religious life, she would do it with the Unitarians; but "the only problem was that the music was terrible." Bray, now a ministerial intern at the Unitarian Church of Montclair, New Jersey, is author of the memoirs *Unafraid of the Dark* (1998). She describes herself as being an agnostic Unitarian. {*The New York Times Magazine*, 7 December 1997}

BRAZILIAN POSITIVISTS

The influence of Comte's positivism has been substantial in Brazil. The flag carries one of Comte's favorite slogans, "Order and Progress." Although Comte was anti-organized religion, he did not object to the establishment of a positivist version of the church in Brazil. Miguel Lemos and Raimundo Teixera Méndez led in founding the *Apostolado Positivista do Brasil*, which in all respects became a church, with temples, services, and dogma. Elsewhere in Brazil, however, in the so-called School of Recife, positivism remained non-religious and theoretical.

The *Centro Positivista do Parana* (Rua Comendador Araujo C493 CEP 80420, Curitiba, Parana, Brazil) is an associate member of the International Humanist and Ethical Union.

A Brazilian who signed is José Leite Lopes, professor emeritus of Centro Brasileiro de Pesquisas Físicas. {See the *Encyclopedia of Unbelief*, which cites such Brazilian positivists as Constant Botelho de Magalhaes (1836—1891), Luis Pereira Barreto (1840—1923), and Ruy Barbosa (1849—1923). Also, see entry for Pedro Mendoça.}

Brearey, Pam (20th Century)

A journalist, Brearey was married for twenty-eight years to Peter Brearey and supported his work for *The Freethinker*. She resides on the north Orkney island of Sanday.

Brearey, Peter (1939-1998)

Brearey, who was born in Dewsbury, Yorkshire, was largely self-educated. As a reporter, reviewer, and editor, he became a well-known Yorkshire journalist. Altogether, he contributed to more than three hundred publications. Surprisingly, he had run away from home when fourteen but had learned to speak Urdu.

In collaboration with his wife, Pam, he helped to establish National Health Service internal journals in Bradford, York, Wakefield, Pontefract, and Huddersfield. He was founding editor of *Healthview*, newspaper of the Yorkshire Regional Health Authority. He was an active member of the National Union of Journalists and a former chairman of its Wakefield branch. In addition, he was Vice-President of the National Secular Society.

In 1993, Brearey was appointed editor of *The Freethinker*, the journal founded by G. W. Foote in 1881. Under its editorship he expanded the publication considerably and encouraged the letters page as a forum for controversial ideas.

When he told Keith Porteous Wood how ironic it was that he had developed cancer of the lungs, not of the liver, Brearey explained he had smoked an ounce of tobacco daily but had given up drink eighteen years previously. His brand of humor was devastating, Wood observed, saying Brearey had added, "It looks like I won't be coming to your millennium party—I have been given a terminal diagnosis."

At his secular humanist funeral ceremony, former *Freethinker* editor Bill McIlroy said Peter was a staunch defender of reforms that enabled thousands to live happier and more honest lives. "He had the vision and patience of the true reformer. In his own way, he endeavoured to bring light into dark corners." After tributes at the Brearey's' home on the north Orkney island of Sanday, he was carried a short distance to an adjoining plot of ground where he was buried. {*The Freethinker*, May 1998}

BREASTFEEDING: See entry for Marian Leonard Tompson.

Breasted, James Henry (1865—1935)

Breasted, a noted American historian, left the Church and became professor of Egyptology at the Oriental Museum. He spent many years in research in Egypt, and his *Conquest of Civilization* (1926) became a standard work on ancient history. An agnostic, Breasted was an Honorary Associate of the Rationalist Press Association. {RE}

Brecht, Bertold (1898—1956)

Brecht was an avowed freethinker, according to David Tribe. The German dramatist and poet wrote *Man is Man* (1926), an expressionist work, and he developed his revolutionary "epic theater," designed to create—using bright lights, films, and mottoes displayed on cards—a politically conscious distance between the spectator and the stage. His *Threepenny Opera* (1928), with music by Kurt Weill, reflected Brecht's social views. During the Nazi period, Brecht went into exile in Denmark, then settled in the United States, moving in 1948 to East Berlin. There, he directed the state-supported Berliner Ensemble.

Brecht's attempt to codify his aesthetics, according to Michael Feingold, translator of six of his plays, began well before his conversion to Communism. Like his politics, his aesthetics was always under construction, changed with time, situation, atmosphere, and even impulse. His theory was only a theory, for he was not basically an intellectual and, as Feingold has written, "a theory to any artist is just a provisional guideline for finding a path through the work."

His conduct toward women was one long parade of offenses, yet many befriended and helped him. His secretaries may or may not have had their work plagiarized and their emotions abused, but if in truth he used any of their work he also transformed his borrowings from Kipling, Goethe, folk songs, even Salvation Army hymns. In a television exchange in the early 1960, Kenneth Tynan asked actor Richard Burton "What do you think of Brecht?" Burton replied, "Awful, pretentious, dull, pedestrian." Retorted Tynan, "To that I say illuminating, passionate, poetic, humanist." Brecht's diaries document his heterosexual exploits, but also he was interested in Arthur Rimbaud's and Paul Verlaine's relationship and wrote realistically about homosexuals. {CE; *The Economist*, 17 October 1998; Michael Feingold, *Village Voice*, 8 September 1998; GL; TRI; TYD}

Breen, Walter (20th Century)

Breen, a New York City humanist writing in *The Humanist Newsletter* (Summer 1953), discussed the political dilemma for humanists during the McCarthy era:

> Since the humanist's basic postulates commit him to a belief in individual freedom and hence in some sort of democracy, it is folly for him to imagine such a system apart from the above [democratic stand]. Instead of there being 150 million rulers in this country, there are a few thousand politicians of none too great abilities who have wheedled their supremacy out of the political ignorant millions. To retain supremacy in a wartime context, they must show authoritarian fangs. The only answer is for intellectually competent people to espouse humanistic notions, whether they *call* themselves humanists or no, and at the same time for people with these views to infiltrate the government, both in civil service and elective capacities.

In the same issue, naturalistic humanists Mark Starr and William Heard Kilpatrick took a similar stand. Starr specifically recommended joining Americans for Democratic Action and, in New York State, the Liberal Party.

Breitenbach, Wilhelm (Born 1857)

A German writer and publisher, Breitenbach was one of Haeckel's leading supporters, especially in his periodical, *Die Neue Weltanschauung*. He was president of the Humboldt Association for Scientific Philosophy and editor of the Humboldt library. {RAT}

Bremer, Frederika (1801-1865)

Bremer, a Swedish Unitarian, was a novelist, feminist, and pacifist.

Brennan, William J. [Supreme Court Justice] (1906–1997)

A U.S. Supreme Court Justice, Brennan in 1987 said on National Public Radio, "Religious conflicts can be the bloodiest and cruelest conflicts that turn people in fanatics." {TYD}

Brenneman, Richard J. (20th Century)

Brenneman, author of *Deadly Blessings* (1990), examines three controversial court cases involving faith healing. He delves into the minds of those who believe that faith can cure ills.

Brent, Jeani (20th Century)

Brent is President of Atheists and Other Freethinkers (PO Box 15182, Sacramento, California 95851), which publishes a monthly newsletter, *AOF News & Views*.

Brentano, Franz (1838—1917)

Ordained a Catholic priest in 1864, Brentano taught at Würzburg (1866—1873) and in 1874 became professor of philosophy at Vienna. In 1880 he retired in order to write and study. *Psychologie vom empirischen Standpunkte* (1874) tries establishing psychology as an independent science. Freud studied with Brentano, who also influenced Edmund Husserl and Alexius Meinong. Brentano resigned from teaching because of the declaration that the Pope was infallible. A few years later, he left the Church. In his philosophy, Brentano in the main followed Lao-tzu and adopted an eclectic spiritualist system. {CE; RAT}

Brereton, Irene (20th Century)

Brereton is an editor emeritus of *Humanist in Canada*.

Brereton, J. Lloyd (1901—1977)

Brereton, the founder and an editor of the *Humanist in Canada*, signed Humanist Manifesto II. In 1977, he received the Canadian Humanist of the Year Award. He has been termed the most influential figure in the early development of the Canadian humanist movement. {FUK; HM 2}

Bresson, Léopold (Born 1817)

A French positivist, Bresson was director of an Austrian railway company. He wrote *Idés Modernes* (1880). {BDF}

Breton, Andre (1896—1966)

A principal theorist of the surrealist movement, Breton has written, "Everything that is doddering, squint-eyed, infamous, sullying, and grotesque is contained for me in this single word: God." {CE; PA}

Breuk, Yvonne (20th Century)

In the Netherlands, Breuk is President of *Humanistisch Verbond*.

Brewer, Colin (20th Century)

"Like many people in Britain, I do not believe in either a deity or an afterlife, but when taking a full history from my patients, I always ask about the nature and strength of their religious beliefs," Brewer has written (*New Humanist*, June 1992). A psychiatrist and member of the Voluntary Euthanasia Society's Executive Committee, he also reviews books for *The Freethinker*. Brewer is alarmed at the numbers of cases of "deathbed proselytizing" which he has observed, pleading that "in the hour of death god save us from the god-squad." In 1980 he wrote *Can Social Work Survive?*

Brewer, Ebenezer Cobham (1810—1897)

Brewer was an English author who in 1884 compiled *A Dictionary of Miracles*. The preface, which disclaims the idea of attacking miracles, is merely a discreet preparation of the reader for a rejection of the Christian claims. {BDF; RAT}

Brewer, Gwen W. (20th Century)

An emeritus professor at California State University at Northridge, Brewer signed Humanist Manifesto 2000.

Brewer, Nancy (20th Century)

Humanist counselor Brewer signed Humanist Manifesto II. {HM2}

Brewington, Selena (20th Century)

While a student at the University of Oregon, Brewington was a founding member of Campus Freethought Alliance and President of Students for Freedom From Religion. {*Intl. Humanist News*, December 1996}

Brewster, Harold Leland (20th Century)

Brewster wrote his 1940 University of Southern California dissertation on "An Objective Study of the Oratory of Robert Green Ingersoll." {FUS}

Brewster, Henry (1851—1908)

Brewster was a writer who was born in France of an American father, one of the few English authors who could write in perfect French. His *L'âme paienne* (1902) was a manual of advanced ethical "paganism," in which he disdains all religion. {RAT}

Briand, Aristide (1862—1932)

A French statesman, Briand helped complete the secularization of France. He was Minister of Public Instruction and Cults (1906), President of the Council (1909), Minister of Justice and Cults (1914), and Premier (1915). Based upon one of his reports, the law of the separation of Church and State was instituted. An idealist and an agnostic, Briand was an eloquent opponent of the Church. {RAT; RE; TRI}

Briars, David (1946—)

Briars in 1993 edited *Freethinker's Directory* (Route 1, B-45, Craftsbury, Vermont 05826), a work with over 600 listings which in his words "is designed to help a-theists, freethinkers, non-goddists of all kinds to locate each other and to work together. Most of us have felt the debilitating isolation and self-doubt that comes from living in a world where religion and mob-thinking define the meaning of contentment, morality, and self-worth."

Included are such publications as *Free Inquiry, Monkey's Uncle, and Bureau of Public Secrets* as well as such organizations as the Czech Republic's Prometheus Society of Bratislava, Norway's *Det Norske Heningsamfunn* (Society of Norwegian Heathens), and India's Atheist Centre. {*Freethought History*, #8, 1993}

Brichto, Sidney (20th Century)

With Richard Harries, Brichto edited a symposium, *Two Cheers for Secularism* (1998). The thirteen essays are by "believers, half-believers and non-believers" of Christian, Jewish, and Muslim backgrounds.

According to Nicolas Walter, the religious contributions "are the most misleading (secularism inevitably seen as insufficient, and Nazism and Communism predictably seen as examples of secularism), and the Muslim ones are particularly disappointing, but some of the semi-religious ones are interesting and all the non-religious ones (by Frederic Raphael, Karen Armstrong, and John Mortimer) are stimulating." {*New Humanist*, October 1998}

Brick, Aaron (20thCentury)

Brick, a student at Johns Hopkins University, signed the Campus Freethought Alliance's "Bill of Rights for Unbelievers" in 1998.

Bridges, Dan (20th Century)

Bridges is co-president of Atheists of Colorado.

Bridges, Horace (1880—195-?)

Bridges from 1913 to 1945 was a leader of the Chicago Ethical Culture Society. He wrote *The God of Fundamentalism* (1925). A. Eustace Haydon once told another Ethical leader, James F. Hornback, that Bridges was outspoken against the Midwestern religious humanism of his day. Members and leaders, however, could be humanists then and did not need to consider humanism a religion. Bridges, groomed by Coit as a liberal empiricist, turned theological and social conservative as Leader under Adler. Bridges died an Episcopalian in the 1950s. {EU, Howard B. Rades; RAT}

Bridges, John Henry (1832—1906)

An English positivist, Bridges wrote *Religion and Progress*. He contributed to the *Fortnightly Review* and translated Comte's *General View of Positivism* (1865) and *System of Positive Polity* (1873). {BDF; FUK; RAT; TRI}

Bridie, James (1888—1951)

James Bridie is the pseudonym of Osborne Henry Mayor, a witty playwright who wrote such fanciful plays as "The Sleeping Clergyman" (1933) and "Storm in a Teacup" (1936). Bridie was an honorary associate of the British Rationalist Press Association.

Briefer, Charles (20th Century)

In 1972, Briefer was Executive Editor of *The New Awareness*, a magazine of the Humanist Society of Greater New York. He was an executive of Columbia Records.

Brier, Uri (20th Century)

Brier is active with the Humanists of Fairfield County. (See entry for Connecticut Atheists, Humanists.) {FD}

Brieux, Eugene (1858—1938)

Sometimes called "the French Bernard Shaw," Brieux was a member of the French Academy and an officer of the Legion of Honor. His play, "*La foi*" ("The Faith," literally, although the English translator calls it "False Gods") expresses his disdain of religion in the form of a study of priestcraft in ancient Egypt. {JM; RAT; RE}

Brigance, William Norwood (20th Century)

Brigance wrote *A History and Criticism of American Public Addresses* (1943), a critique which included Robert G. Ingersoll. {FUS}

Briggs, Arthur E. (20th Century)

An attorney, Briggs in 1942 became a leader in the newly founded Los Angeles Ethical Culture Society. {EU, Howard B. Radest; HNS}

Briggs, Austin Jr. (20th Century)

Briggs wrote *Novels of Harold Frederic* (1969). {FUS}

Bright, Charles (1832—1903)

An Australian, Bright was a freethinker, journalist, editor, and orator. He edited *Melbourne Punch* (1863) and contributed to Marcus Clarke's *Humbug*. He edited the weekly *Liberal* in Sydney from 1882 to 1884. From 1878 to 1890, Bright was a lecturer in Dunedin of the Freethought Association. Although a deistic freethinker who rejected orthodoxy, he was converted to spiritualism and became a full-time lecturer for the Victorian Association of Progressive Spiritualists. {FUK; SWW}

Brightman, Edgar Sheffield (1884—1953)

Writing in Vergilius Ferm's *Encyclopedia of Religion* (1945), professor of philosophy Brightman of Boston University defined the following terms:

> **agnosticism** (Greek *a-*, not, and *gignoskein*, to know) The belief that certain knowledge has not been attained, either in some particular field (usually the religious), or in any and all fields of supposed knowledge. Agnosticism often shades into skepticism, but the agnostic leaves open the possibility of future knowledge, while the skeptic (except for the methodological type) denies any such possibility. The term "agnostic" was first used by T. Huxley in 1869 (*OED*); he based it on *Acts* 17:23.
>
> **atheism** (Greek *a-*, not, and *theos*, god) 1) The denial that there is any god, no matter in what sense "god" be defined. 2) The denial that there exists a being corresponding to some particular definition of god; frequently, but unfortunately, used to denote the denial of God as personal (the denial of theism), or, more particularly, of a personal God as defined in particular (e.g., trinitarian, Catholic, or Calvinistic) creed.
>
> **skepticism** (Greek, *skeptein*, to reflect or consider) Antonym, dogmatism. 1) The view that no knowledge (or no certain knowledge) is possible; based on deceptiveness of the senses, fallacies in reasoning, incompleteness of evidence, etc. 2) The view that some particular type of knowledge is inherently impossible; e.g., metaphysical knowledge of things in themselves as distinguished from experience (Kant), or of the objects of religious belief such as God and immortality (cf. H. Spencer, "the Unknowable"). 3) The method of complete doubt at the outset of investigation; e.g., Descartes' methodological skepticism, and F. H. Bradley's view that skepticism means "to become aware of and to doubt all preconceptions."

(See entry for Atheistic Humanism.) {ER}

BRIGHTON AND HOVE (England) HUMANISTS

Information concerning the group is available from David Morris, 40 Cowper Street, Hove, England.

Brighton, Susie (20th Century)

In *The Sexual State of the Union*, pro-sex activist Brighton wrote, "I don't believe in their God or their Satan, and that kind of faith genuinely seems backward to me, a sign of ignorance and fear. I see their dedication and power, but the true believers might as well be worshipping a cheeseball as far as I'm concerned." {CA}

Bril, Jakob (1639—1700)

Bril was a Dutch mystical pantheist. His works were published during the 17th century in Amsterdam. {BDF}

Brinkman, Piet (20th Century)

Brinkman is Director of Humanist Media Support in The Netherlands. On the net: <support@human.nl>. (See entry for Dutch Humanist Movement—Websites.)

Brinton, Clarence Crane (1898—1968)

Brinton wrote *The Portable Age of Reason Reader* (1956) and *History of Western Morals* (1959). {FUS}

Brinton, Daniel Garrison (1837—1899)

Brinton was an army surgeon and a professor of ethnology, one of the pioneer ethnologists in America. He became President of the American Association for the Advancement of Science. In his *The Religious Sentiment* (1875), Brinton rejected the belief in immortality and "crumbling theologies" but remained a theist. {JM; RAT}

Briskman, Lawrence (20th Century)

Briskman is a lecturer in philosophy at the University of Edinburgh in Scotland.

Brismee, Desiré (1822—1888)

A Belgian printer, Brismee as editor of *Le Drapeau* underwent eighteen months in prison. An eloquent speaker and the principle founder of *Les Solidaires*, he was the life-long secretary of that society. Some of his orations were printed in *La Tribune du Peuple*. {BDF}

Brisson, Eugène Henri [Premier] (1835—1912)

Brisson, a French statesman, attained every position short of the Presidency of the Republic. He was twice President of the Chambre (1881—1885 and 1895—1898) and twice Premier (1885 and 1898). Brisson took an active part in secularizing the schools and destroying the power of the Church. {RAT; RE}

Brissot, Jacques Pierre de Warville (1754—1793)

An active French revolutionist, Brissot wrote against the legal authority of Rome. He is credited with *Philosophical Letters upon St. Paul and the Christian Religion* (1783), for which he was imprisoned in the Bastille the following year. To avoid a second imprisonment, he went to England and America, then returned to France at the outbreak of the Revolution. Brissot formed the Girondist party, protested against the execution of Louis XVI, and was executed with twenty-one of his colleagues in 1793. Wheeler called Brissot a lover of freedom in every form. {BDF}

Bristol, Augusta (1835—1910)

Bristol, an American educator and poet, represented American Freethinkers at a nineteenth-century International Conference in Brussels. Her chief work was *Science and its Relations to Human Character* (1878). {BDF; RAT}

Bristor, Michael (1984—)

When twelve, Bristor finally was awarded an Honor Roll certificate that had been denied him for three years by a Catholic teacher in a public elementary school in Minnesota. "Michael needs a little God in his life," she had said, and her school spent $40,000 of taxpayers' money unsuccessfully fighting the claim of the Bristor family. In 1996, Bristor was awarded a "mini-freethinker" plaque and award by the Freedom From Religion Foundation. {*Freethought Today*, August 1996}

BRISTOL (England) HUMANISTS

Information about the Bristol Humanists is available from Margaret Dearnaley, 0117 9502960, or from Hugh Thomas on 0117 9871751.

Bristor, Mary Lou (20th Century)

Bristor, an atheist in Hayward, Wisconsin, was confronted by an angry Christian who exclaimed, "I just can't understand, if you haven't any belief in God or an afterlife, why do you get out of bed in the morning?"

Replied Ms. Bristor, "That's easy. I have to pee."

BRITISH COLUMBIA HUMANISTS

The British Columbia Humanist Association in 1997 arranged a course on humanism at Eldercollege in Capilano College. The teachers were Theo Meijer, Dale Beyerstein, Ernest Poser, Glenn Hardie, and Pat Duffy Hutcheon. Address: PO Box 60516 Granville Park, Vancouver, British Columbia V6H 4B9.

E-mail: <theom@mindlink.bc.ca>. On the Web: <http://www.vcn.bc.ca/humanist>. {*Humanist In Canada*, Summer 1997}

BRITISH ETHICAL UNION: See entry for Ethical Culture Society.

BRITISH HUMANIST ASSOCIATION (BHA)

The Union of Ethical Societies, formed in 1896, became the Ethical Union in 1920 and the British Humanist Association in 1967. It is headquartered at Bradlaugh House, 47 Theobald's Road, London WC1X 8SP, United Kingdom. A Humanist umbrella organization, it absorbed the Ethical Union in 1967. A registered charity, the BHA has as its object the advancement of humanism. In 1995, Robert Ashby was appointed its Executive Director. (Telephone: 071 430 0908.)

BRITISH HUMANIST GROUPS: See entry for United Kingdom, Freethought and Humanist Groups.

BRITISH UNITARIANISM

One Britisher came up with the following definition: "Unitarians believe in one God, no devil, and twenty shillings in the pound." (See entry for General Assembly of Unitarian and Free Christian Churches.) {Internet}

Brittanicus, Scepticus (18th Century)

Someone calling himself Scepticus Brittanicus wrote *An Investigation of the Essence of the Deity*, choosing the pseudonym out of fear of being discovered. Scepticus never openly avows himself an atheist, but his work theologically is more extreme than deism.

He questions a deity which is "omnipotent, incomprehensible, immaterial, invisible, and immutable" as being "contradictory and inconsistent." Berman finds such a view of the mind surprisingly modern and naturalistic (but also Aristotelian): "for him 'the soul of man instead of being a distinct being from the body, is merely the body considered relatively to some of its functions.'" In Chapter VII he argues, predictably enough, that the moral effects of belief in the theological God have been bad. Although he does not explicitly commit himself to atheism, his specific remarks on atheism are sympathetic. . . . "An atheist," he says, "is a man, who destroyeth chimeras prejudicial to the human species." Scepticus is also critical of deism and the views of Thomas Paine. His atheistic criticism, reasons Berman, is a counterpart to that of Dr. Samuel Francis, who likely was another pseudonymous author who feared using his own name. {HAB}

Britten, Benjamin [Baron Britten of Aldeburgh] (1913—1976)

An eminent English composer, said by some to be the greatest since Purcell, Britten wrote "A Young Person's Guide to the Orchestra" (1945) and "War Requiem" (1962). His operas include "Peter Grimes" (1945), "The Turn of the Screw" (1954), and "Death in Venice" (1973). His "Billy Budd" was famously homoerotic, and Britten did not try to conceal his homosexuality. In 1976, he was named a life peer.

According to Tribe, Britten was a non-believer. Britten's gay lover for over forty years was the British tenor Peter Pears, for whom he wrote most of his solo vocal works and all of his major tenor roles. The two are buried side by side in Aldeburgh, England, which is the site of a music school the two founded in 1947. {AA; CE; TRI; TYD}

Britten, Emma H. (19th Century)

Britten, a freethinker, wrote *The Faiths: Facts and Frauds of Religious History* (1889). {GS}

Britton, John B. (1926—1994)

Boston-born, Britton received his medical degree in 1949 from the University of Virginia. After serving in the Army in Korea and teaching at the Medical College of Georgia in the 1950s, he settled in North Florida. A self-described atheist, he spent much of his early practice delivering babies. Reporter Sam Howe Verhovek said Britton turned to providing abortion services because he thought women should be allowed to exercise their legal right to abortion. "I won't be bluffed by fanatics," he said, although another physician—David Gunn—was killed nearby his clinic in 1993. Britton sometimes wore a bullet-proof vest, but on 29 July 1994 he and his bodyguard were shot to death and his wife injured by a former Presbyterian minister, Paul J. Hill, who was excommunicated by that group because of his strong views. Hill on national television prior to the shooting had repeatedly said that killing an abortionist would be biblically justified homicide. "Oh, Mommy, Mommy, don't kill me," Hill had a record of screaming as women entered the Pensacola, Florida, clinic. Although the police had warned Dr. Britton of death threats, Britton shrugged off the threats, saying, "Being shot by a madman has always been a risk."

Broad, C(harlie) D(unbar) (1887—1971)

Broad, an atheist, has been called by A. J. Ayer one of the two most important Cambridge philosophers of the century. The other was J. E. Mc Taggart. His works include *Perception, Physics and Reality* (1913); *Five Types of Ethical Theory* (1930); *Ethics and the History of Philosophy* (1952); and *Induction, Probability and Causation* (1968). Paul A. Schilpp's *The Philosophy of C. D. Broad* (1959) contains critical essays on some of Broad's views, along with Broad's replies. Described as being judicious and witty, he went about classifying all possible answers to some carefully clarified question, weighed the pros and cons of each, then made a tentative suggestion for the most plausible. In perception, he held, we are presented with sensa, whose occurrence is the effect of events in the brain in virtue of a peculiar kind of causation, that these sensa are not literally spatio-temporal parts of the perceived objects but provide literally true information about their spatio-temporal character and relations, and that physical objects must also have other characteristics which provide their qualitative filling. {T. L. S. Sprigge, OCP}

Broadhead, George (20th Century)

Broadhead, a freethinker, is editor of the English *Gay and Lesbian Humanist* (34 Spring Lane, Kenilworth, Warwickshire CV8 2HB). Also, he is Secretary of the Gay and Lesbian Humanist Association (GALHA) at the same address.

Broca, Pierre Paul (1824—1880)

Broca, a French anthropologist, founded the School of Anthropology and taught Gratiolet, Topinard, Hovelacque, and Dr. Carter Blake, who translated his treatise on *Hybridity*. Broca established *The Review of Anthropology*. In philosophy, he inclined to positivism. He became a Senator. {BDF; PUT; RAT; RE}

BROCK UNIVERSITY

Student humanists at Brock University. St. Catharines, Ontario, Canada are on the Worldwide Web: <http://www.secularhumanism.org/cfa/orgs.html>.

Brock, Thomas D. (20th Century)

In 1957, Brock, a freethinker, wrote *History of the People's Church, 1856–1956*, concerning a liberal church in Kalamazoo, Michigan. {GS}

Brockman, Chris (20th Century)

Brockman in *What About Gods?* (1978) flatly states in a book for children that although it may be difficult to assert non-belief, gods are simply mythical creatures invented by humans. In light of such a minority viewpoint, he encourages young people to "keep on thinking" in order to understand how organized religion has become what it is.

Brockway, Fenner (1888—1988)

A British socialist whose family were missionaries, Brockway rejected religion while a youth though never becoming an atheist. He called himself a "reverent agnostic," according to Nicolas Walter.

Brockway was a Shavian vitalist, a practicing ethical humanist who lectured at South Place Ethical Society, and he frequently contributed articles to *New Humanist*. {TRI}

Brockway, Robert W. (20th Century)

A professor emeritus at Brandon University in Manitoba, Canada, Brockway wrote "On the Eve of the New Century" for *Humanist in Canada* (Spring 1999). After surveying what has happened in the past century, he has become optimistic that imperialism and capitalism will have reached their apogee and the future will include a revival of the humanistic spirit of progressivism and reform.

Brodie, Benjamin Collins [Sir] (1817—1880)

Brodie was a chemist. At Oxford he had refused to subscribe to the Thirty-nine Articles, later explaining that "it is as hard for a dog to run with thirty-nine stones round its neck." Dr. Jowell once complained to Brodie that "you do not leave any place for religion at all." McCabe labels him as one who held "at the most a vague Theism." {RAT; RE}

Brodie, Janet Farrell (20th Century)

Brodie, in *Contraception and Abortion in 19th-Century America* (1994), shows how the first birth control information was published by freethought publishers in the United States and England. She cites Annie Besant, Charles Bradlaugh, Ezra Heywood, Abner Kneeland, Charles Knowlton, Robert Dale Owen, the *Boston Investigator*, and other such leaders. According to Fred Whitehead, the late Gordon Stein once told him that Brodie's work was the first dealing with the history of birth control that gave due credit to Freethinkers. {*Freethought History*, #24, 1997}

Brodsky, Joseph (1940—1996)

A Russian poet who has lived in the United States since 1972, Brodsky often writes about loss and exile. In 1987 he received the Nobel Prize in Literature. Asked about humanism and notified he was said to have been termed a believer, Brodsky responded to the present author, "I am for humanism without an adjective." {WAS, 3 February 1988}

Broga, Theophilo (Born 1843)

Broga was a professor in the University of Lisbon and an outspoken freethinker. He introduced evolutionary philosophy into his native country. He was a member of the International Freethought Federation and the International Federation of Peace and of Liberty. One of his works was *As Modernas Ideias de Litterature Portuguesa*. {PUT}

Brogden, John (20th Century)

A Unitarian minister in Spokane, Washington, Brogden was a naturalistic humanist who admired the work of Mead and Dewey. {HNS}

Brogdon, Kyoko (20th Century)

Brogdon was one of the original incorporators of Atheists of Florida.

Brokmeyer, Henry C. (c. 1826—1906)

According to Denton J. Snider, Brokmeyer along with William Torrey Harris sparked what has become known as the St. Louis Movement. The two were nonconformists who helped break up the last slave auction in St. Louis, on New Year's Day, 1861. A photo of Brokmeyer and the monument called *Naked Truth* appears in Whitehead and Muhrer's *Freethought on the American Frontier* (1992).

BROMLEY HUMANISTS

For information about the Bromley Humanists, telephone D. Elvin at 0181 777 1680.

Bronder, Dietrich (1921—)

When he signed Humanist Manifesto II, Bronder was with *Bund Freireligioser Gemeinden*, West Germany. In 1966 he addressed the Fourth International Humanist and Ethical Union World Congress held in Paris, as he did also in 1968 at the Second European Conference held in Hannover. {HM2}

Bronowski, Jacob (1908—1974)

A Polish-born British scientist who died in East Hampton, New York, Bronowski wrote about poets such as William Blake. His other works included *The Identity of Man* (1965) and *The Ascent of Man* (1973). He rejected "scientific" or secular humanism but admitted to being a lower-case "h" humanist, writing, "Humanism . . . is the expression of the human gift for undogmatic inquiry and for rational thought." Bronowski was an Honorary Associate of the Rationalist Press Association (1958—1974) and was active in the British Humanist Association, the Ethical Movement, and the International Humanist and Ethical Union.

When asked about Ivan Karamazov's statement in Dostoyevski's novel, "Without God, anything is permitted," Bronowski replied, "Science will create values, I believe, and discover virtues, when it looks into man; when it explores what makes him man and not an animal." His outlook is expressed in the following, from a television series called *The Ascent of Man* and spoken in Auschwitz:

> When people believe that they have absolute knowledge, with no test in reality, this is how they behave. This is what men do when they aspire to the knowledge of gods. . . . Science is a very human form of knowledge. We are always at the brink of the known, we always feel forward for what is to be hoped. Every judgment in science stands on the edge of error and is personal. Science is a tribute to what we can know although we are fallible. In the end the words were said by Oliver Cromwell: "I beseech you, in the bowels of Christ, think it possible you may be mistaken" . . . . We have to cure ourselves of the itch for absolute knowledge and power. We have to close the distance between the push-button order and the human act. We have to touch people.

Bronowski addressed the First International Congress on Humanism and Ethical Culture in Amsterdam (1952).

Brontë, Emily Jane (1818-1848)

Patrick Brontë (1777-1861, an Anglican clergyman of Irish birth, had three daughters who became well-known novelists: Charlotte (1816-1855—pseudonym Currer Bell), Emily (pseudonym Ellis Bell), and Anne (1820-1849—pseudonym Acton Bell). Branwell (1817-1848), his son, drank to excess and squandered his many talents.

Of the children, Emily was the heretic. Unlike Charlotte, she had no close friends, wrote few letters, and was closest to her sister Anne. They created an imaginary world of Gondal, which became the setting for many of Emily's poems. At a time when women found it easier to choose male-sounding pseudonyms in order to get published, the sisters turned out much material and their identity was not known even to their publishers.

Emily is best known for her *Wuthering Heights* (1846), a masterfully complex work which evokes place, poetic grandeur of vision, and a highly original handling of Gothic and Romantic elements inherited from lesser works. Although at the time she was not recognized for her genius of creativity, she also was unknown for the excellence of her poetry.

Some will claim that the daughter of the Anglican clergyman showed her devout religiosity in her poetry:

> O God within my breast,
> Almighty! Ever-present Deity!
> Life—that in me has rest,
> As I—undying Life—have power in Thee!

And

> No coward soul is mine,
> No trembler in the world's storm-troubled sphere:
> I see Heaven's glories shine,
> And faith shines equal, arming me from fear.

However, in *Emily Brontë, Heretic* (1994), Stevie Davies noted that when in 1845 Charlotte opened Emily's cache of poems she realized that "these were not common effusions, nor at all like the poetry women generally write." They were without sentimentality or pietism.

> She knew we lived our lives on a battlefield in which the chief law is universal strife; class faces class; tribe versus tribe; every man's and woman's hand against his or her neighbor. She had been mendaciously told that women had gender but no sexuality to speak of; natural selflessness; the power to spell her name but not to write out her identity. Emily would not vanish or beautify. She took no pleasure in veneer of face or the emollient dilution of terrible truth for the benefit of other people's feelings. You were told to be a nice woman, thoughtful of others, sweet and biddable. She was not nice, but proud, discourteous and misanthropic. She lived for herself and, owning her own soul, also owned up to what she was, including the anger and violence which she shared in common with the race. In retreating from the world she did not merely claim a refuge but a distance, from which to angle back at society her severe mirror with its permanent message to people who "knelt to God and worshipped crime"—the universal message no one wanted to hear.

At her brother Branwell's funeral—he died of tuberculosis—Emily caught a cold. Soon the same disease began to overcome her, wasting her talent as well as her body. She refused medical help, deriding homeopathy as "another form of quackery." She also refused help from her family, as if Charlotte's concern for her well being threatened her personhood and independence. "There is not room for Death," Emily wrote in "Last Lines." In *Wuthering Heights* she had said of Death, "I put it on the landing of the stairs, hoping it might be gone in the morrow."

> And if I pray
> The Only prayer that moves my lips for me
> Is leave the life that now I lead
> And give me liberty.

One day, just after telling Charlotte that at last because of the unbearable pain she was willing to see a physician, Emily died on the sofa in a dining room. Her faithful dog Keeper, who had been at her bedside during her illness, and her father led the funeral procession to the family vault, and Keeper lay outside her bedroom and howled for days. Anthony Bell Nicholls conducted a service, at which it was noted that Emily had so wasted away that her coffin was only sixteen inches wide. Two weeks later, Anne learned she, too, had tuberculosis.

As to whether Brontë died an Anglican, Tim J. Madigan has called her "more of a pantheist than anything else," citing the findings of Stevie Davies. {Rebecca Fraser, *The Brontës* (1988); Juliet Baker, *The Brontës* (1994)}

Brook, W. O. (19th Century)

Brook, a freethinker, wrote *Reason Versus Authority* (1871). {GS}

Brooke, Rupert (1887—1915)

Brooke, a British poet of great promise who was a victim of World War I, showed his freethinking, for example, in "Heaven," a work which satirizes the Christian myth. In other poems, he is doubtful about a future life. "The laugh dies with the lips," he says. Although he occasionally refers to God, he was clearly moving to agnosticism, writes McCabe. He was buried on the island of Skyros in the Aegean Sea. Someone chose a cairn of pink and white marble stones, with a cross at both ends of the grave. On the larger of the two crosses, someone arranged: "Here Lies the Servant of God Sub-Lieutenant in the English Navy Who Died for the Deliverance of Constantinople from the Turks." {JM; PA; RAT; RE}

Brooke, Stopford Augustus (1832—1916)

Brooke, at one time Chaplain-in-Ordinary to the Queen, seceded from the Church in 1880 and devoted himself to letters. He remained a theist and did not, as is sometimes said, become a Unitarian. {RAT}

BROOKLYN (NEW YORK) HUMANISTS

After the founding in Manhattan of New York Humanists, which became affiliated with the American Humanist Association in 1953, President Warren Allen Smith encouraged setting up clubs in Greenwich Village, Morningside Heights, and Brooklyn. In 1953 the first such meeting in Brooklyn was held November 13th at the home of Prof. and Mrs. H. Van R. Wilson.

In the 1990s and until her death, Carmel Kussman led the Brooklyn chapter of the American Humanist Association. {*The Humanist Newsletter*, November-December 1953}

BROOKLYN SOCIETY FOR ETHICAL CULTURE

The Brooklyn Society for Ethical Culture was organized by Henry Newman, a non-theistically oriented humanist. David Freudenthal, who was in charge of rationing of gasoline during World War II in Brooklyn, was its President. Other early activists in the group were Rose Walker, Janet Samuels, Selma Freudenthal. E-mail for Eric Freudenthal: <eric.freudenthal@NYU.edu>.

Brooks, David M. (20th Century)

Brooks, a freethinker, wrote *The Necessity of Atheism* (1933). {FUS; GS}

Brooks, Samuel Wood (1840—1915)

Brooks was a rationalist, newspaper proprietor, editor, and politician. He arrived in Australia from England in 1863 and as a Wesleyan minister joined an 1865 mission to Fiji. When his relations with a neighboring planter's wife were discovered, he resigned. In 1909 he became first Secretary of the Brisbane branch of the Rationalist Press Association. He later formed the Queensland Rationalist and Ethical Society. Although a rationalist, he was buried privately by a Methodist minister. {SWW}

Brooks, Van Wyck (1886—1963)

Author of *The Writer in America* and critic and Pulitzer Prize-winner for *The Flowering of New England* (1936), Brooks wrote the present author about humanism:

> I find myself in the closest possible agreement with the statement of "The Beliefs of Humanists" in a leaflet, "Concerning the American Humanist Association."

Five years later, he went on record:

> I would like to add the following quotation from Santayana's *The Genteel Tradition at Bay* as further defining my position: "Why is nature? Are not the higher sides just as natural?"

{CE; CL; HNS; WAS, 20 February 1951 and 13 April 1956}

Brooksbank, William (Born 1801)

A freethinker, Brooksbank wrote for publications such as the *Reasoner*, the *Pathfinder*, and the *National Reformer*. He was an intimate friend of James Watson. {BDF}

Brophy, Brigid Antonia (1929—1995)

A well-known novelist and writer, Brophy campaigned for various causes. Her *Hackenfeller's Ape* (1953) contained a Shavian and animal rights subtext. Most of her works are said to indicate her atheism, including two pamphlets, "Religious Education in state Schools" (Fabian Society, 1967) and "The Longford Threat to Freedom" (National Secular Society, 1972). In *The Adventures of God in His Search for the Black Girl: A Novel and Some Fables* (a Shavian title), God tries to show that his "fictitious" nature as a being is entirely one created by man. Her point is that when people take the fiction for the truth they fail to illustrate how the human race is "a species uniquely capable of imagination, rationality, and moral choice."

An activist, she battled to bring about a Public Lending Right so that writers might reap financial reward for library use. With Maureen Duffy, Ted Willis, and Francis King, she campaigned from within the Writers' Action Group until complete victory was achieved. She was a Vice President of the Gay and Lesbian Humanist Association (GALHA). Also, she was President of the National Anti-Vivisection Society and, since 1984, an honorary associate of the Rationalist Press Association.

A bisexual, Brophy often referred to marriage as "an immoral institution" but nonetheless married art historian Michael Levey in 1954. He became director of the National Gallery in 1973 and was knighted in 1981. Her literary agent, Giles Gordon, described her as a "deeply shy, courteous woman" who wrote delightful thank-you letters and kept to rigorous standards in her work. "Woe betide the 'editor' who tried to rewrite her fastidious, logical, exact prose, change a colon to a semi-colon (or vice-versa), or try to spell 'show' other than 'shew,' slavish Shavian that Brophy was." Their unconventional marriage resulted in much publicity and discussion in the British press and literary circles, particularly because she favored bisexuality and opposed monogamy and institutional heterosexuality.

Upon her death, Nicolas Walter commented in *The Guardian* (16 August 1995) that "Brigid Brophy was more than an opponent of religion. She was a committed and valued member of the freethought movement for more than thirty years, an active speaker and writer for the British Humanist Association and the National Secular Society, a helpful supporter of the Committee against Blasphemy Law and an Honorary Associate of the Rationalist Press Association, the author of eloquent pamphlets and articles on religious education and sexual education, marriage and censorship, and a good friend."

Her will included the following:

> I am a declared and indeed a proselytising atheist. I do not wish to impose on anyone who loves or esteems me so much as a veneer of civil hypocrisy. I scorn to allow my name to be made a pretext for a further exercise of the hypocrisy institutionalised in religious per-

> sons and organisations. For those reasons it is my considered and deeply earnest wish, in which I happily know my husband and daughter will concur, that my death should not be marked or my life commemorated by any religious ceremonial.

Brophy for many years supported the National Secular Society and the Rationalist Press Association. {GL; OEL; TRI}

Brosses, Charles de (1709—1777)

Brosses, a historian and president of the Dijon Parliament, was a deist and a contributor to Diderot's and d'Alembert's *Encyclopédie*. His published letters (*Lettres familieres*) illustrate the superficial religion and the barely concealed irreligion of his time. President Brosses gave a remarkable picture of Pope Benedict XIV, a liberal pope who begged him for the latest saucy stories about the dissolute French court and Cardinal as well as about the Rome of that time. {JM; RAT; RE}

BROTHEL

"The Anglo-Saxons and the Judeo-Christians were not fun-loving when it came to sex," laments a New York freethinker. The Old English word *breothan*, to decay, is the root for *brothel*, which now has the negative connotation of being a "house of prostitution," the latter word of which also has a negative connotation of "unworthiness."

Such was not always the case. In 1998, *Agence France-Presse* reported that a team of Greek archeologists recently unearthed a brothel that dates to the first century B.C.E., one believed to be the oldest home of the oldest profession found in Macedonia. The Salonika site had a large circular room which housed twenty-five latrines and an adjoining rectangular room that served as the brothel. Attached were two small swimming pools, one filled with hot and the other with cold water, and a dining room. Dr. Polyxeni Velini, a Greek archeologist, found various relics, including a red pitcher with a phallic spout and a glass vase decorated with Venus carrying a horn of plenty. After dining, Dr. Polyxeni said, the clients were entertained by women or young boys. {*The New York Times* 17 February 1998}

Brother Toby: See entry for Tolbert H. McCaroll.

BROTHERHOOD

• I want to be the white man's brother, but not his brother-in-law.

—The Rev. Martin Luther King

• Marilyn Monroe married a Protestant [James Dougherty], a Catholic [Joe DiMaggio], and a Jew [Arthur Miller], and divorced them all: that's what I call brotherhood.

—Harry Golden

Brothier, Léon (19th Century)

Brothier wrote a *Popular History of Philosophy* (1861) and contributed to the Swiss *Rationalist* of Geneva. {BDF}

Broun, Heywood Campbell (1888—1939)

An American newspaper columnist and critic who worked on the New York *Tribune* (1912—1921) and the New York *World* (1921—1928), Broun later wrote for the New York *World-Telegram* and the *Post*.

Known as a champion of underdogs, he criticized social injustice and backed the emerging labor unions. A founder of the American Newspaper Guild and its first president from 1933 until his death, he ran unsuccessfully for Congress as a Socialist. He once wrote,

> Precarious is the position of the New York newspaperman who ventures any criticism of the Catholic Church. There is not a single New York editor who does not live in mortal terror of the power of this group. . . . If the church can bluff its way into a preferred position, the fault likes not with the Catholics but with the editors.

Because of his candid criticism of organized religion, Broun along with H. L. Mencken was a precursor of today's secular humanists. {CE}

Broussais, François Joseph Victor (1771—1838)

Broussais was a French physician and philosopher. A disciple of Bichat, he did much to reform medical science by his *Examination of Received Medical Doctrines*. Despite his bold opinions, he was made Commander of the Legion of Honor. Broussais expressed his disbelief in any creator "without hope or fear of another life."

With respect to immortality, Broussais wrote, "I have no fears or hopes as to a future life, since I am unable to conceive it." His views on the God idea were equally negative: "I cannot," he said, "form any notion of such a power." {BDF; FO; RAT}

Broughman, Lord (20th Century)

Broughman, a freethinker, wrote *On the Origin of Evil* (1915).

Brout, Betty Lea (20th Century)

Brout is on the Board of Governors of The Humanist Institute. In addition to being an American Humanist Association counselor, she is a psychotherapist and a clinical social worker.

Brown, Anton (20th Century)

A freethinker, Brown wrote *Dignitarian Way* (1960). {GS}

Brown, Arthur (Born 1884)

A jurist, Brown taught in India at Cotton College and Calcutta University. He was a member of the Rationalist Press Association.

Brown, Charlotte (20th Century)

Brown, of Illinois Wesleyan University, is on the Executive Committee of The Hume Society, a group engaged in scholarly activity concerning David Hume.

Brown, Darlene (20th Century)

Brown is contributing editor on the staff of *Freethought Today*.

Brown, Diana M. (20th Century)

Brown, who lives in Switzerland, was a participant on a panel discussing human rights at the 1996 Humanist World Conference held in Mexico City. She lamented that in the world there are twice as many female than male illiterates and stated that sooner or later of necessity the population must decline. The alternative to population control, she said, would be to allow nature to take its course of pestilence, war, and famine. Brown is past chairman of the United Kingdom charity Population Concern and co-founder of the World Population Foundation in the Netherlands.

At the Centenary Conference in 1999 of the Rationalist Press Association in Birmingham, England, Brown spoke on "Population: Is There a Rational Solution?" She is the IHEU's representative to the UN at Geneva. Brown signed Humanist Manifesto 2000. E-mail: <dianabrown@hotmail.com>. {*International Humanist News*, December 1996; *Humanist in Canada*, Spring 1997}

Brown, Egbert Ethelred (1875—1956)

A noted African American, a Unitarian preacher, Brown established the Harlem Community Church, later named Harlem Unitarian Church, in New York at 175 West 137th Street, serving as its minister from 1920 to 1956. A Jamaican, he preached there from 1908 to 1920, but moved to New York when he was dismissed from a civil service job.

Although he received some support from John Haynes Holmes,

Brown was told by President Franklin Southworth of the Meadville Theological School that "as there was no Unitarian Church in America for colored people, and . . . as white Unitarians require a white minister he was unable to predict what my future would be at the conclusion of my training."

His Harlem church had many financial problems and met at the American West Indian Association Lodge Rooms, the YWCA, or the YMCA (where a plaque was installed in 1994 by the Fourth Universalist Society of New York). Brown is described in the Rev. Mark Morrison-Reed's *Black Pioneers in a White Denomination.* {U&U}

Brown, Ford Madox (1821—1893)

A painter who completed a large number of religious pictures, Brown "had no religion at all," according to McCabe. Brown's grandson and biographer, Ford Madox Ford, wrote, "In his early days he was a conventional member of the Church of England; in later years he was an absolute Agnostic with a great dislike of anything in the nature of priestcraft." {RAT; RE}

Brown, George Washington (19th Century)

Brown, a freethinker, wrote *Researches in Oriental History* (1889). {GS}

Brown, George William (Born 1820)

A physician born of Baptist parents, Brown when seventeen was expelled by the Baptists for repudiating the dogma of an endless hell. His editing in Kansas of the *Herald of Freedom* led to his office being destroyed by a pro-slavery mob, his type thrown into the river, and his being arrested but released without trial.

Brown contributed to the *Ironclad Age* and other American freethought papers. {*Freethought History* #27, 1998}

Brown, George William (Born 1820)

Born of Baptist parents, Brown at the age of seventeen was expelled from church for repudiating the dogma of an endless hell. He edited the *Herald of Freedom* in Kansas. In 1856 his office was destroyed by a pro-slavery mob, his type thrown into the river, and he along with others was arrested but later released without trial. His *Researches in Jewish History* included data concerning the rise and development of Zoroastrianism and the derivation of Christianity. {BDF; PUT}

Brown, H. S. (19th Century)

Brown, a freethinker, wrote *A Compendium of the Bible of the Religion of Science* (1885). {GS}

Brown, Harley (20th Century)

Brown, a member of the Alliance of Secular Humanist Societies, signed Humanist Manifesto 2000.

Brown, Hiram Chellis (20th Century)

Brown, a freethinker, wrote *Historic Bases of Religion* (1906). {GS}

Brown, Hugh Byron (19th Century)

A freethinker, Brown wrote *The "Safe" Side* (187—?). {GS}

Brown, Ivor (20th Century)

In *What I Believe* (1947), Brown wrote of his freethought and belief in Humanism.

Brown, J. Hullah (20th Century)

Brown, a freethinker, wrote *The Perfect Circle* (1943). {GS}

Brown, Jerry (20th Century)

Brown, a member of Atheists United, has written "22 Plain Truths of Atheism" for *Secular Nation* (September-October 1996).

Brown, John Armour (1839—1907)

Brown resigned his eldership in the United Presbyterian Church in Scotland, devoting his energies to manufacturing. He was a senior partner in Glasgow of the firm of Brown and Polson. A member of the Rationalist Press Association, Brown encouraged musical education. {RAT}

Brown, Joseph (19th Century)

In the 1890s, Brown of Newcastle, England, was secretary of that community's secular organization. {RSR}

Brown, Lester Russell (1934—)

A senior fellow, Overseas Development Council, when he signed Humanist Manifesto II, Brown now heads and was the founder of Worldwatch Institute. In 1991, he was named Humanist of the Year by the American Humanist Association.

Brown has written *World Without Borders* (1972) and *Increasing World Food Output* (1965). "Despite the end of the cold war," he has written, "the world is still spending close to $780 billion for military purposes, much of it designed to deal with threats long past." {HM2; HNS2}

Brown, Margaret (20th Century)

Brown, when she signed Humanist Manifest II, was an associate professor at State University of New York College at Oneonta. {HM 2}

Brown, Marjorie M. (1884-1987)

A Unitarian, Brown was an author who wrote *Lady in Boomtown.*

Brown, Marshall G. (1906—)

Marshall co-wrote, with Gordon Stein, *Freethought in the United States, A Descriptive Bibliography* (1978). {FUK; FUS}

Brown, Noel (20th Century)

Brown addressed the Tenth International Humanist and Ethical Union (IHEU) World Congress held in Buffalo (1988).

Brown, Olympia (1835—1926)

In 1863, Brown was the first woman in the United States to become a minister ordained by a denomination, the Universalist. The first, others say, was Lydia Jenkins (1860), who was licensed as a minister. By the late 1800s and early 1900s, Universalism had the largest proportion of women ministers of any denomination. While minister in Bridgeport, Connecticut, Brown was opposed by a small faction that did not want women in the pulpit, resulting in her resigning and moving to a parish in Racine, Wisconsin. {CE; EG; EU, Paul H. Beattie; U&U; U}

Brown, Pat (20th Century)

Brown, who lives in Berkeley, California, is a freethinker who writes for *Truth Seeker*. An activist, he opposes routine circumcision and massive television-watching.

Brown, Rita Mae (1944—)

A feminist author in New York City, one noted for her work on lesbian subjects, Brown has written for *Free Inquiry* (Summer 1987). She is author of *Rubyfruit Jungle* (1973), *Venus Envy* (1990), and *Riding Shotgun* (1996). Brown has been termed "the queen of Southern sexual farce."

In 1964 Brown was expelled by the University of Florida in Gainesville for her outspokenness about civil rights and the need for greater racial integration. Molly Bolt, the outspoken lesbian character in *Rubyfruit Jungle*, a semiautobiographical work in which she includes more of her views, never apologizes for her sexual orientation, and she refuses to be a conformist either for the heterosexual majority or the New York lesbian subculture. {GL}

Brown, Robert Delford (1930—)

Brown is a dadaist who bills himself as "founder, leader, prophet, president, and saint of the First National Church of the Exquisite Panic, Inc., at the Great Building Crack-Up." An artist, he purchased a building, had an architect "crack-up" the building by gutting it, then turned it into a combination studio and residence at 251 West 13th Street, New York, NY 10011. Passersby saw "St. Ben Turpin" in the window of the "Chapel of Pharblongence" and observed a "Map of Nevada" on a terrace floor. Brown explained that instead of people futilely trying to get to Heaven or to Nirvana, he guaranteed to get them to Nevada: he simply constructed a roadmap, using various art forms. In 1998 he sold the building, and the new owners removed all references to the "exquisite panic."

He has been exhibited at the Gallery of Modern Art in Washington (1965), the Kansas City Art Institute (1971), the Rhode Island School of Design (1978), and the Fondazione Mudima in Milan (1992). Brown is author of *Hanging* (1967), *Ulysses, An Altered Plagiarism* (1975), and *Teachings of the First National Church of the Exquisite Panic, Inc.* (1991). Brown's entry in *Who's Who*:

> I want the image to assume primary importance in all my work. Dazzling technique and established procedures are so often used not to enlighten but to obfuscate one's vacuity. The artist's responsibility is to tell the truth as he sees it, not to enhance his own self-importance as an expert, thereby perverting his responsibility as a moral force in society.

Brown has been a member of the Secular Humanist Society of New York. On the Web: <http://www.funkup.com>.

Brown, Roy (20th Century)

Brown is a member of the Alabama Freethought Association. For the *Alabama Freethinker* (July 1998), Brown wrote "Fundamentalism as a Destroyer of Cultures."

Brown, Roy W. (20th Century)

Brown, a Swiss who founded the World Population Foundation, wrote "The Day of Six Billion"—on 12 October 1999 that number of humans were estimated worldwide. Brown signed Humanist Manifesto 2000. {*International Humanist News*, December 1999}

Brown, Sterling Allen (1901—1989)

Brown is an African-American poet who has taught at Howard University and Lincoln University. His *Collected Poems of Sterling A. Brown* (1990) contains "Slim in Hell," which is reprinted in Whitehead and Muhrer's *Freethought on the American Frontier* (1992).

Brown, Titus L. (1823—1887)

Brown was a physician who studied in New York, then settled at Binghampton, New York. He contributed to *Boston Investigator* and in 1877 was elected President of the Freethinkers Association. In 1884, Brown wrote *The Contract.* {BDF; FUS; PUT; RAT}

Brown, Walston Hill (Born 1842)

A banker and contractor, Brown married Robert Ingersoll's daughter Eva and was, like her, an agnostic. He contracted work in railway construction and was a Fellow of the National Academy of Design. {RAT}

Brown, William Montgomery [Bishop] (1855—1937)

Brown, the ex-Bishop of Arkansas, a Communist, and in his last days Bishop in the Old Catholic Church, was threatened in 1924 with expulsion from the Episcopal Church. In 1926, he wrote *My Heresy*. He had read the work of Joseph McCabe and become a skeptic. McCabe helped him write works which he put out to the embarrassment of the bishops. "He was," McCabe said, "a man of mediocre intelligence and very high but simple character, and his wealth (inherited) attracted cranks who, he later admitted, fatally complicated my defence of him. He was deposed but a few years later was ordained—he did not tell me what it cost—bishop of the Old Catholic Church. He explained that he thought the Church could be made a great social power if its formulae were taken symbolically, but I suspect it was rather from a sort of loyalty to the memory of the pious rich lady who had had him educated for the Church and left him her fortune. He was, in fact, a dogmatic materialist, did not believe in the historicity of Christ, and admitted God only as a label for whatever goodness there is in the universe." {FUS; GS; JM; RAT; RE}

Brown-Séquard, Charles Edward (1817—1894)

Brown-Séquard was a physiologist who had been born in Mauritius. In 1852 he took part in the Republican and anti-clerical movement against Napoleon III and was compelled to flee to America. Returning to France, he edited the *Journal de Physiologie* (1858—1864), lectured at the London Royal College of Surgeons (1858), and delivered the Croonian Lecture (1861). {RAT}

Browne, George Buckston [Sir] (1850—1945)

Browne was a surgeon, an honorary gold medalist of the Royal College of Surgeons, Life President of the Harveian Medical Society, and Trustee of the Hunterian Collection. Sir Buckston was donor of Down House (Darwin's home) and of the Royal College of Surgeons Research Farm in Kent. {RE}

Browne, Lewis (1879—1949)

Browne wrote *Stranger Than Fiction: A Short History of the Jews* (1927).

Browne, Noel (1916—1997)

Browne was a noted Irish physician who, upon being elected to parliament in 1948, was made health minister on his first day. He built many hospitals, established a blood transfusion service, proposed free maternity and gynecological services, and believed that free medical care was a human right. In 1951 when Roman Catholic Church forces objected to "educating women in motherhood" and taxing the community to pay for it, perhaps even tolerating contraception, Browne resigned. Even in his childhood Catholic school, he had had a reputation for "anarchist tendencies," and in his twenties when he was close to death with tuberculosis he declined a priest's offer of last rites "as gently as I could." With his later experience in psychiatric medicine, he came to the view that the church had a repressive effect on the mind, particularly on sex. The church, as well as politicians, were accepting emigration as inevitable for solving Irish problems, and Browne disagreed vehemently. To the end of his life, he expressed strong views on politics—he had sat in the Dail as an independent—contraception, divorce, the influence of priests, the drain of emigration, poverty, and the IRA. {*The Economist*, 31 May 1997}

Browne, Stella (1880—1955)

Browne was vice-chairman of England's Abortion Law Reform Association. {TRI}

Browne, Thomas [Sir] (1605—1682)

A British physician and writer, Browne wrote a treatise, *Religio Medici* (1642), which was a mixture of faith and skepticism. In 1646, that work about the religion of a physicist was placed on the Roman *Index*. Although he disputed many popular superstitions, Browne partook of others. His *Hydriotaphia, or Urn-Burial,* treats cremation among the ancients, clearly showing his deism and skepticism about any future life. In it, he says that "a dialogue between two infants in the womb concerning the state of this world might handsomely illustrate our ignorance of the next"; "The religion of one seems madness unto another"; and "I perceive the wisest heads prove, at last, almost all skeptics." {BDF; JM; RAT; RE; TYD}

Browne, William George (1768—1813)

A traveler, Browne explored Africa (1792—1798) and made sarcastic observations on Christian Europe. In politics, Browne was a republican and in religion a freethinker. He set out in 1812 for a journey across Asia and was murdered in Persia in 1813. {RAT}

Brownell, Baker (1887—1965)

A professor of philosophy at Northwestern University and a contributor to *The Philosophy of Santayana*, Brownell in 1951 wrote of humanism to the present author:

> Humanism, I imagine, is a philosophy in which values are directional aspects of our behavior. Without going too far into this difficult problem, it can be said that values are characteristic of action and have no meaning apart from actions and their alternatives and problem situations. Values belong to men and men's behavior. They are not transcendent fixations in an order somehow different from our own, nor is their authority necessarily absolute or supernatural. Thus, humanism first of all is a philosophy in which values are limited, human-centered, dynamic, or directional in action. They are within behavior, not beyond it.
>
> But humanism may also involve a notion as to the nature of human life that has important implications. Human life is not merely a succession of events; it is a pattern of events, a form or drama of behavior, with its own kind of unity or completeness. This at least is our working assumption in the activity of living. This configurational aspect of life is the seat of values and the source of our significance. It is organic in form as over against the mechanical; it is an order or priority of actions that comprehends not only the past but the projection or creation of the future. It includes not only the specific action and the proximate events on either side of it that we call the causal antecedent and consequent after the manner of strict science, it includes also a larger, organic configuration that we call the human community. This is known imaginatively, sometimes religiously. The human being so far as he knows purpose or freedom is within the configuration of the community. The community may be described as a group in which men know one another well, or in other words, a group where they are related to one another as whole people not merely as functional fragments. Human values cannot survive except in groups, necessarily small, in which the members are related to one another rather fully, familiarly, face to face. As communities of men tend to be replaced by wide-ranging organizations in which functions become more specialized and men are related to one another more and more narrowly, fragmentally and anonymously, civilization dies, moral responsibility declines, and external authority replaces inner initiative. This in modern times is illustrated by industrial urbanism. It is the enemy of humanism and of human beings.
>
> As a philosophy humanism is based on the morals of self-reliance—where self here means the human configuration of community. But humanism is also a philosophy of risk; it has no final norm or standard. It remains to be seen whether men can do without one.

In 1956, he added:

> Humanism to me means primarily a threshold for values. Thus the authority for values in the world, whatever that may involve, is solely in the human situation. It is not absolute, supernatural, or otherwise transcendent to living human beings except as those finalities may be an interpretive or poetic aspect of human life. What the human being himself is I do not fully know. He has great interpretive potentialities, for we can find in him a vast diversity of being, but I am confident that he is within the natural order, not above it. Values are oriented in him not by virtue of a unique status or superiority in the universe that he may have but by virtue of the fact that we who evaluate happen to be human. Our capacity to make evaluations is thus unique in this particular sense, but there is no indication that our values somehow escape the human limit and situation into a realm of outer absolutes.
>
> I suppose I fit best in the category of naturalistic humanism. But I am doubtful about categorizing so fluid a notion as humanism. Its fluidity indeed is one of its most significant characteristics. In several ways I probably do not fit in any one of the categories.
>
> I think I have been influenced less by specific writers than by the general climate of life which they may have helped to establish or make articulate. In college my teachers Santayana, Royce, and James Houghton Woods, different as they are, influenced me, always on the background of Plato and Meister Eckehart. After college the thrust of scientific ideology, James and especially Dewey, and the movement of human projects and events were most influential. This diversity of sources, if they are the sources, may seem hopelessly aggregative or eclectic. Still there are, as a fact, a great many things in the world, nor is there any certainty that they are all systematized, except perhaps in human behavior.
>
> {WAS, 2 February 1951 and 12 May 1956}

Brownfield, Charles (20th Century)

When he signed Humanist Manifesto II, Brownfield was assistant professor at the Queensborough Community College of the City University of New York. {HM2}

Brownfield, Costantia (20th Century)

When she signed Humanist Manifesto II, Brownfield was a registered nurse. {HM2}

Browning, Robert (1812—1889)

To some, the English poet Browning shows a Christian optimism and confidence in spiritual values, as expressed in "Abt Volger," "Love Among the Pairs," and "Pippa Passes" (1841).

"I am no Christian," Browning once wrote. McCabe, however, found that Browning began to have doubts about his creed in mid-career, as shown in his *Christmas Eve* and *Easter Day*. Gradually, he shed all beliefs except God and immorality, as shown in *La Saisiaz* (1875). "Soul and God stand sure," Browning wrote, with the customary dogmatism of the incomplete skeptic. Joseph Warren Beach agreed, holding that Browning is best described as having been a religious liberal. {CE; ER; JM; RAT; RE; TYD}

Brownjohn, Alan Charles (1931—)

Brownjohn, an English poet, wrote *Travellers Alone* (1954), *The Railings* (1961), and *Collected Poems 1952—1983*. His work can be described as good-humored, ironic, urbane, and socially conscious. He attended the festive launch for Bradlaugh House in 1994. In 1994, Brownjohn became an Honorary Associate of the Rationalist Press Association.

His work, he has written, shows "that we inhabit a universe without a god and a life without supernatural perpetuation. We need to make the best of that, a better 'best' than is made of it by the religious, who have to spend so much time explaining away the fact that religion is so often the face of ignorance, intolerance, and atrocity. A positive *ir*religion is the assumption in my writing; not harped on, I hope, but an undercurrent in nine books of verse and two or three excursions into fiction."

Brownjohn, who was a teacher and lecturer for twenty-five years, is devoted to being a British citizen: "I realise that it is partly because we are so lucky in being one of the least religious nations on earth." {*New Humanist*, February 1996}

Brownson, Orestes August (1803—1876)

First a Presbyterian Calvinist, then an anti-Calvinist, then a Universalist, Brownson became a skeptic and eventually a Unitarian. A spokesman for the working class, he became friendly with George Ripley and the movement of Transcendentalism. Choosing to be a Unitarian minister, he embraced a revivified Christology and eventually converted to Catholicism. *The Works of Orestes A. Brownson* (Detroit, 1882—1887) total 20 volumes. {CE; U; U&U}

Bruce, Lenny (1925—1966)

A cynical, surreal, and intensely comic comedian, Bruce in *The Essential Lenny Bruce* (1967) is quoted as quipping

> Christ and Moses standing in the back of St. Pat's, looking around. Confused. Christ is, at the grandeur of the interior, the baroque interior, the rococo baroque interior. Because his route took him through Spanish Harlem, and he was wondering what the hell fifty Puerto Ricans were doing living in one room when that stained glass window is worth 10 G's [thousand dollars] a square foot.

He also is known for

> If anyone in the audience belives that God made your body, and your body is dirty, the fault lies with the manufacturer.

A 1964 television appearance by the "filthy-mouthed" Bruce on the "Steve Allen Show" was censored by the network. Upon Bruce's death, the Los Angeles Police Department allowed photographers one hour to shoot Bruce's body, face down and sprawled in a doorway of his dilapidated Hollywood Hills home. {TYD}

Bruce, Nigel (20th Century)

Bruce was the first convener of the Scottish Humanist Council, which publishes *Scottish Humanist*. He heads a David Hume Commemoration Committee, which has erected a statue of Hume in Edinburgh and also refurbished Hume's mausoleum. Hume, he laments, is better known in the United States of America than in Scotland. Calling Hume the central figure of the Scottish Enlightenment, Bruce notes his profound influence among European philosophers, including Adam Smith, Adam Ferguson, Diderot, D'Alembert, Immanuel Kant, and Bertrand Russell.

Bruce has been a member of the Humanist Society of Scotland for three decades and has written widely in *The Scotsman*. {*Free Inquiry*, Winter 1996-1997; *Humanism Scotland*, Autumn 1997}

Brudno, Ezra (20th Century)

Brudno wrote *Ghosts of Yesterday* (1935). {FUS}

Bruneau, Louis (20th Century)

Bruneau wrote *Uncommon Sense: A Series of Lectures by Uncle Louie to his Nephew Mot*. An employee of the Polaroid Corporation, he received a plaque inscribed "To the Savior of Polaroid" in recognition of his expertise concerning quality control. With the plaque came the billionth roll of Polaroid film that was suitable memorialized in bronze. A non-believer in any afterlife, Bruneau was an ardent humanist. {Humanist Association of Massachusetts newsletter, November-December 1997}

Brunner, John: See entry for Science Fiction Writers on Philosophy.

Bruno, Giordano (1548—1600)

Bruno was born at Nola, near Naples, ten years after the death of Copernicus, and ten years before the birth of Bacon. At the age of fifteen he became a novice in the monastery of San Domenico Maggiore, and after his year's novitiate expired he took the monastic vows.

Studying deeply, according to Foote, he became heretical, and an act of accusation was drawn up against the boy of sixteen. Eight years later he was threatened with another trial for heresy. A third process was more to be dreaded, and in his twenty-eighth year Bruno fled from his persecutors. He visited Rome, Noli, Venice, Turin and Padua. At Milan he made the acquaintance of Sir Philip Sidney. After teaching for some time in the university, he went to Chambery, but the ignorance and bigotry of its monks were too great for his patience. He next visited Geneva, but although John Calvin was dead, his dark spirit still remained, and only flight preserved Bruno from the fate of Servetus. Through Lyons he passed to Toulouse, where he was elected Public Lecturer to the University. In 1579 he went to Paris. The streets were still foul with the blood of the Bartholomew massacres, but Bruno declined a professorship at the Sorbonne, a condition of which was attending mass. Henry the Third made him Lecturer extraordinary to the University. However, Paris became too hot to hold him, Foote wrote, and Bruno went to London, where he lodged with the French Ambassador. His evenings were mostly spent with Sir Philip Sidney, Fulke Greville, Dyer, and Hervey. So great was his fame that he was invited to read at the University of Oxford, where he held a public debate with its orthodox professors on the Copernican astronomy. Leaving London in 1584, he returned to Paris, and there also he publicly disputed with the Sorbonne. His safety being once more threatened, he went to Marburg, and then to Wittenberg, where he taught for two years.

Bruno became the greatest philosopher of the Italian Renaissance. Regarded as an infidel and a heretic, he wrote many dialogues: *On the Cause, Principle, and Unity; On the Infinite, the Universe, and the Worlds; The Ash Wednesday; Supper; The Cabala of the Horse Pegasus; The Expulsion of the Triumphant Beast*; and *The Heroic Frenzies* (1584). After being unfrocked, he tried to convince the church about some of his controversial ideas, but he was then condemned both by the Venetian Holy Inquisition in 1592 and by the Roman Holy Inquisition in 1593. By challenging all dogmatism, including that of the Copernican cosmology, he concluded that absolute truth cannot be postulated nor can there be any limits to the progress of knowledge. The Vatican's *Index Librorum Prohibitorum* (1948) prohibits not just one but *all* his books, the entry reading . . .

> **Bruno**, Giordano.
> *Opera omnia*. Decr. S. Off. 8 febr 1600.

During the French Revolution, Maréchal considered Bruno one of the major atheists of all time. Robertson called Bruno "the typical martyr of modern freethought. He may be conceived as a blending of the pantheistic and naturalistic lore of ancient Greece, assimilated through the Florentine Platonists, with the spirit of modern science (itself a revival of the Greek) as it first takes firm form in Copernicus, whose doctrine Bruno early and ardently embraced."

H. James Birx has described Bruno as a pacesetter whose far-sighted opinion was that "the center of the eternal and infinite cosmos is everywhere and its circumference is nowhere." Bates College Professor Peter Bertocci, however, called Bruno an inconsistent rationalist but one who influenced Spinoza, Leibniz, Descartes, and Schelling.

As a Dominican, Bruno once made a pun on *domini canes*, or "hounds of the Lord," so his powerful antagonism to orthodox unreason got off to an early start, growing as he got older. The Inquisition charged that he believed the following: "that there is transmigration of souls; that magic is right and proper; that the Holy Spirit is the same thing as the soul of the world; that the world is eternal; that Moses, like the Egyptians, wrought miracles by magic; that the sacred writings are but a romance (*sogno*); that the devil will be saved; that only the Hebrews are descended from Adam, other men having descended from progenitors created by God before Adam; that Christ was not God, but was a notorious sorcerer (*insigne mago*), who, having deceived men, was deservedly hanged, not crucified; that the prophets and the apostles were bad men and sorcerers, and that many of them were hanged as such."

Found guilty of being "the obstinate heretic," Bruno was kept in a dungeon cell for seven years. On February 10th, 1600, he was led out to the Church of Santa Maria, and sentenced to be burned alive, or, as the Holy Church phrased it, to be punished "as mercifully as possible, and without effusion of blood." Haughtily raising his bead, he exclaimed: "You are more afraid to pronounce my sentence than I to receive it." He was allowed a week's grace for recantation, but without avail; and on the 17th of February, 1600, his tongue was gagged, he was stripped naked, bound to a pole, and killed by having a flaming torch touched to his body. To the last he was brave and defiant. He contemptuously pushed aside the crucifix they presented him to kiss; and, according to one of his enemies, Bruno had the nerve to die without a plaint or a groan. According to M. Bartholomews' biography, Bruno stood at the stake in solitary and awful grandeur. There was not a friendly face in the vast crowd around him. It was one man against the world. McCabe called Bruno "a Pantheist, dazed by a world in which he found Protestants as intolerant as Catholics and hampered in his speculations by the poverty of the science of his day. (For information on the Web about Bruno, e-mail Guido del Giudice <delgiud@tin.it>. {BDF; CE; CL; ER; EU, H. James Birx; FUS; HNS2; ILP; JM; JMRH; PUT; RAT; RE; TRI; TSV; TYD; U}

Brunsman, August (20th Century)

Brunsman, while a student in 1998 at Ohio State University, signed the Campus Freethought Alliance's "Bill of Rights for Unbelievers."

Bruun, Geoffrey (Born 1898)

A distinguished historian, Bruun wrote book reviews for *The Humanist* in the 1950s, including a critique of Erich Kahler's *Man the Measure*. Bruun was a close friend of Priscilla Robertson, who at that time was editor of *The Humanist*.

Bruys, Pierre de (Died 1126)

Bruys, a rebellious priest and founder of the Petrobrusian sect that doubted the doctrine of transubstantiation, wrote, "God is no more in the church than in the marketplace. . . . The priests lie in pretending that they make Christ's body and give it to the people for their salvation." {TYD}

Bruzzese, Vincent (1973—)

Bruzzese, while a graduate sociology student at Stony Brook University, was one of the founding members and is the president Society Against Religion, a national organization affiliated with the Atheist Alliance. On the Web: <nogod1@aol.com>. {*International Humanist News*, December 1996}

Bryan, John (Died 1918)

When Bryan, a freethinker and atheist, died in Cincinnati, Ohio, he left the State of Ohio five hundred acres of forest and meadowland near Yellow Springs, Ohio, to be used as a natural history preserve. His will specified that there should never be any church or religious exercises on the grounds. Three Ohio governors (Davis, Cox, Donahey) vetoed acts of the state legislature to accept the land with such a stipulation, but over the veto of Governor Donahey the Legislature passed a bill in 1923 and accepted the land. {Cincinnati, Ohio, *Fig Leaves*, May 1995}

Bryant, Louise (1885—1936)

Emma Goldman once wrote, "I do wish sometimes I were as shallow as a Louise Bryant; everything would be so simple." Bryant, a Greenwich Village radical and bohemian who had moved from Nevada and Portland, was a friend of Charles Erskine Scott Wood and one of his protégés, John Reed. She joined Reed in 1916, married him after leaving a Portland dentist, Paul Trullinger, became involved in New York City with the Provincetown Players, had affairs with Eugene O'Neill and others, hid Reed's manuscripts during the crackdown on Bolshevik sympathizers after World War I at their 1 Patchin Place address in New York City's Greenwich Village, and figured as one of the characters in Reed's *Ten Days That Shook the World*, later becoming known as a character in the movie "Reds."

Although only in Russia for four months, she wrote *Six Red Months in Russia* (1918), which critic Dorothy Gallagher and others have described as not being a serious work of reference.

Mary V. Dearborn's *Queen of Bohemia* (1996) describes Bryant's life as a freethinker and social climber, mentioning that when Bryant returned alone from Russia, ahead of Reed, she began an unsuccessful attempt to renew her affair with O'Neill. She was with Reed in Moscow when he died in 1920 of typhus. Marrying a rich and social William Bullitt, telling him she was twenty-nine although she was thirty-eight, Bryant then lived the life of a rich man's wife, complete with clothes, servants, houses. When she began an affair with Gwen Le Gallienne, a sculptor, the marriage ended in divorce.

After developing a rare and disfiguring Dercum's disease, she lost custody of her daughter as well as control of Jack Reed's papers.

At the age of fifty, Bryant died in a $2-a-night hotel. Those who knew her said that, although she made speaking tours on behalf of the Revolution and was a strong fighter for woman suffrage, Bryant was a martini-drinking and ether-sniffing individual who spoke and wrote with hyperbole.

Bryant, William Cullen (1794—1878)

Before he was twenty-one, Bryant had written such memorable poems as "The Yellow Violet," "To A Waterfowl," and a purely pagan poem in which there is no "Christian hope" nor "source of redemption" theme, "Thanatopsis." Putnam remarks that the latter poem "might have been written by some old Greek. It is natural and human." In 1826, Bryant became associate editor of the New York *Evening Post*, and from 1829 until his death he was part owner and editor in chief. A defender of human rights, an advocate of free trade and of the abolition of slavery, he also was the earliest American theorist of poetry. His editorial influence contributed to the setting up in New York City of Central Park, which he envisioned as a public place where city dwellers could relax in a natural setting. New York City named a major park, the one adjacent to the 42nd Street Library, after him.

Bryant was a member in New York City of the Unitarian Church of All Souls. {CE; CL; PUT; U; UU}

Bryson, Lyman (1888—1959)

Bryson was editor of *The People's Library* and *Science and Freedom* (1947). Of humanism, Bryson wrote to the present author,

> I suppose I could properly be called a humanist; at any rate, that name has often been applied to me by friendly critics, and I would be most sympathetic with "naturalistic humanism." However, I would be inclined to assimilate this with classical humanism, although the writings of some of the men cannot be taken to express my point of view. It seems to me quite wrong to suppose that classical humanism must be as anti-democratic as are the ideas of men like Babbitt and T. S. Eliot.

{WAS, 20 August 1954}

Buba: See entry for Jews and DNA.

Buber, Martin (1878—1965)

A Jewish philosopher, Buber was active in Zionist affairs. He was greatly influenced by the mysticism of the Hasidim and by the Christian existentialism of Kierkegaard. "The atheist staring from his attic window," he wrote as a backhanded compliment, "is often nearer to God than the believer caught up in his own false image of God."

In *God and the Philosophers*, Paul Edwards noted that late in Buber's career he propounded the theory of the "*Gottesfinsternis*," or the eclipse of God. Buber held that "God is not only a self-revealing but also a self-concealing God. Let us realize what it means to live in the age of such a concealment, such a divine silence." Evil is thus explained without abandoning belief in God. Such horrors as Auschwitz or Bosnia "do not show that there is no God—they merely show that at times God is silent." {CE}

Bucali, Leonardo (16th Century)

Bucali (also Busali) was a Calabrian abbot of Spanish descent. When he became a follower of Servetus, he fled to Turkey in order to have the safety denied him in Christendom. {BDF}

Buchan, John (1875—1940)

Buchan, an historian, wrote the often quoted definition, "An atheist is a man who has no invisible means of support." He also was known as Baron Tweedsmuir. {CE; PA}

Buchanan, George (1506—1582)

Buchanan, a Scottish historian and scholar, composed *Franciscanus et Fratres*, a satire on the monks which helped hasten the Scottish reformation.

The work, however, exposed him to the vengeance of the clergy. Not content with calling him an atheist, Archbishop Beaton had him arrested and confined in St. Andrew's Castle. Escaping to England, Buchanan said he found Henry VIII burning men of opposite opinions at the same stake for religion. Buchanan then went to Paris but was again subjected to persecution, was seized by the Inquisition, was immured for a year and a half in a monastery, and eventually returned to Scotland.

He wrote numerous poems, satires, and political writings, including a history of Scotland and *De Jure Regni, the Rights of Kings.* {BDF}

Buchanan, James [President] (1791—1868)

Buchanan, a Presbyterian and the only unmarried United States President, once stated, "I have seldom met an intelligent person whose views were not narrowed and distorted by religion."

Writer Carl Sterrazza Anthony has speculated about the fifteenth president of the United States's sexual orientation. He located letters to Alabama Senator William Rufus de Vane King, with whom Buchanan shared rooms in Washington, D.C., for a long time. Anthony implied the two were lovers, that a letter Buchanan once wrote to King read, "I am selfish enough to hope you will not be able to procure an associate who will cause you to feel no regret at our separation." {AA; TYD}

Buchanan, John (20th Century)

Buchanan wrote *Thomas Paine: American Revolutionary Author* (1976). {GS}

Buchanan, Robert (1813—1866)

A socialist, Buchanan wrote *Religion of the Past and Present* (1839) and the *Origin and Nature of Ghosts* (1840). Because in Scotland socialists were prosecuted for lecturing on Sunday, Buchanan was prosecuted and fined for refusing to take the oath of supremacy. After the decline of Owenism, Buchanan wrote for the *Northern Star* and edited the Glasgow *Sentinel.* {BDF; RAT}

Buchanan, Robert (1841—1901)

The son of Robert Buchanan, Buchanan was a poet and novelist. His *Idylls and Legends of Inverburn* (1865) and *London Poems* (1866) were two of his works. An improvident man, he died in want but was known for being anti-religious. {RAT}

Buchanan, Walter James [Sir] (Born 1861)

Buchanan, a physician, was Diplomate in State Medicine at Dublin University. He entered the Indian Medical Service in 1887, taking part in the Hazara and Lushai Expeditions. In 1892 he transferred to Bengal, becoming Superintendent of the Central Jails at Bhagalpur and Alipur. His *Manual of Jail Hygiene* (1900) and *Tours in Sikkim* (1917) were followed by his editing the *Indian Medical Gazette.* A lieutenant colonel in the Indian Medical Service, he was Inspector General of Prisons for Bengal. Sir Walter was a member of the Rationalist Press Association. {RAT}

Buchler, Justus (Born 1914)

Buchler, a philosopher who has written about Charles Peirce, George Santayana, and others, was chairman of the Columbia University department of philosophy from 1950 to 1956, then taught at the State University of New York at Stony Brook. He is author of *The Obiter Scripta of George Santayana* (1936), *The Philosophy of Peirce* (1940); *Chapters in Contemporary Civilization in the West* (2 volumes, 1946), *Concept of Method* (1985), and *Metaphysics of Natural Complexes* (1989). With others, he wrote *The Philosophy of Bertrand Russell* (1944), criticizing Russell's subjectivism. Buchler is one of the contributors to *American Philosophic Naturalism in the Twentieth Century* (1994).

Büchner, Alexander (Born 1827)

The brother of Friedrich Büchner, Büchner taught philosophy at Zürich and foreign literature at Caen University. He wrote works on Shakespeare, Chatterton, Heine, and *A History of English Poetry.* Büchner was a rationalist. {RAT}

Büchner, Friedrich Karl Christian Ludwig (1824—1899)

A German naturalist-empiricist philosopher, Büchner wrote *Force and Matter* (1855), which went through twenty-one editions and resulted in his being forced to resign as a teacher of medicine at the University of Tübingen. He believed that our only guide has to be experience, that however discomforting the truth is we must pursue that truth. In 1881, he founded the *Deutscher Freidenkerbund,* the German League of Freethinkers. Insisting that knowledge is relative, and protesting the transcendental philosophies which Kant had inspired in Germany, he railed against theological interpretations of man and the universe.

Brother of the famous dramatist Georg Büchner, he lived at a time when scientists such as Darwin, Lyell, Huxley, and Haeckel were making discoveries which confirmed his own views. The theory of evolution, he believed, would oust creation theories. He also held that belief in a natural world order would succeed belief in miracles, and that "monis"—the view that force and matter, mind and body are a unity—would replace dualistic theories.

McCabe notes that although Büchner did not call himself a materialist but said he was "a Monist (meaning, like Haeckel, that matter and energy are two different aspects of one reality), his book was called 'the Bible of Materialism,' and had an enormous circulation in Europe." McCabe adds that "like Haeckel, [Büchner] was a man of fine emotions and very high ideals. It is amusing to reflect that their theory that matter and energy are two aspects of the same thing, at which the philosophers scoffed everywhere, is the modern scientific doctrine. They were wrong in saying that this is not materialism, since both are essentially measurable and therefore material (as opposed to spiritual)." {BDF; CE; CL; EU, G. A. Wells; PUT; RAT; RE; RSR; TRI}

Büchner, Georg (1813—1837)

A German dramatist, student of medicine, and political agitator,

Büchner although dying in his twenties wrote the powerful drama, *Danton's Death* (1835), which was a pessimistic view of the French Revolution and revolutionary politics. His *Wozzeck* (1837) was a psychological study of an alienated character that Alban Berg adapted for his opera. His *Leonce and Lena* (1850) was a comedy. Büchner's plays, not staged until long after his death, were unorthodox in subject and style. Like his brothers Alexander and Friedrich, Georg was a non-theist. {CE}

Buchwald, Art (1925—)

In his syndicated newspaper column, Buchwald has humorously written that

> The new threat to this country, if you believe the Moral Majority and the television preachers, is not Communists or fellow travelers but secular humanists. The secular humanists are the ones who are brainwashing our children with books about evolution, sex, race relations, ERA, and naughty words. This means we have to get the books out of the schools and libraries. The book censors are starting to organize, the moral crusade has begun, and the hunt for secular humanists is on.

The problem, Buchwald continues, is that it is not easy to recognize a secular humanist. Not unless

> . . . he openly admits he thinks Darwin's theory of evolution makes sense. Secular humanists are not joiners. They don't have cells where they plot anti-American and anti-God propaganda. Most of them work alone, doing historical research, writing textbooks and novels, and explaining how babies are born. They pollute children's minds with how the world is rather than how the anti-humanists would like it to be. What makes them so dangerous is that secular humanists look just like you and me. Some of them could be your best friends without your knowing they are humanists. They could come into your house, play with your children, eat your food, and even watch football on television with you, and you'd never know that they have read *Catcher in the Rye, Brave New World, and Huckleberry Finn.*

A Pulitzer Prize winner in 1982, Buchwald indicates in his writing that he is not averse to the secular humanist outlook. {*Free Inquiry*, February 1981}

Buck, Florence (1860—1925)

During the 1893 World's Parliament of Religions, Buck was ordained a Unitarian minister. She was the first woman to receive an honorary Doctor of Divinity degree from Meadville (1920). Her writings include *Religious Education for Democracy* (1919) and *The Story of Jesus* (1917). In 1919, she assembled *The Beacon Hymnal.*

Buck, Pearl S. (1892—1973)

Buck, who won the Nobel Prize for Literature in 1938 and is known for *The Good Earth* (1931), once wrote, "I feel no need of any faith than my faith in human beings. Like Confucius of old, I am so absorbed in the wonder of earth and the life upon it that I cannot think of heaven or angels." In *What America Means to Me* (1947), she wrote, "It may be that religion is dead, and if it is, we had better know it and set ourselves to try to discover other sources of moral strength before it is too late." {TYD}

Buckland, Paul (20th Century)

Buckland, who is in the British Humanist Association, was guest speaker at the 1994 annual conference of Scottish Humanists.

Buckle, (Henry) Thomas (1821—1862)

Buckle may never have gone to a university, but before his death at the age of forty he had written a highly praised two-volume study called *History of Civilization in England.* Opposed to any kind of "great man" theory of the causes of historical development, he held that the leaders of countries are "creatures of the age, never its creators." Buckle read nineteen different languages and, although a friend of Charles Darwin and John Stuart Mill, was a theist, stated McCabe, who admired his having written in what we now call the materialistic conception of history. He was not, however, a Christian, although he said he believed in God and immortality. {BDF; FO; JM; JMRH; RAT; RE; TRI}

Buckley, Michael J. (20th Century)

Buckley, a Catholic priest, is author of *At the Origins of Modern Atheism* (1990).

Buckley, William F. Jr. (1925—)

Buckley, in *God and Man at Yale* (1951) charged Yale with drifting away from its Christian foundations in order to teach "relativism, pragmatism and utilitarianism," in the spirit of John Dewey. A syndicated columnist and host of television programs, he is the conservative author of *Spectrum of Catholic Attitudes* (1969).

"By the philosophical laws of certitude, you can't 'know' there is a God," he told *New York Press* (9-15 June 1999). "It's a matter of faith. I only go so far as to say that I would find it much more difficult to disbelieve than to believe."

Buckman, Robert (20th Century)

Buckman, an English-born Canadian who is a medical oncologist at Sunnybrook Hospital, was named Canada's Humanist of the Year in 1994. The host of TV-Ontario's "Vital Signs," he is author of five books, has starred in and co-written three television series, and is an associate professor at the University of Toronto. He signed Humanist Manifesto 2000.

Buckman included in "Twice Around the World and Still Stupid" the following, which reminded some of his hilarious appearance on the Monty Python show. "To me," said the President of the Humanist Association of Canada,

> . . . humanism is what you are left with if you strip away what doesn't make sense. I was always attracted by science, and the more I learned, the more I found that many established world-philosophies (particularly among some of the organized religions) didn't make any form of intuitive sense. Undoubtedly they bring great comfort to their believers, but I found that I was unable to sincerely believe in any divine architecture to the cosmos, or in any predetermined destiny for any race or creed or even for any individual.
>
> From my teenage years onwards, I basically came to think that we humans are a most peculiar species huddled together in a rather uneven and random way on a rather pleasant planet, and it's up to us to do our best. I have never felt that we can look for assistance elsewhere. What we see around us is what we've got. Now that might sound as if I am some sort of unemotional reductionist—a B. F. Skinner playing the role of doctor—but I know that I am not.
>
> Accepting a humanist view of our world does not mean that you don't feel love, anger, fright, tenderness—or even humour. A humanist basis simply allows you to spend less of your time twisting what you see and contorting it to fit somebody else's idea of what ought to be. Of course I could be wrong: but if I am I don't think I shall have done all that much damage on the way—on average, humanists don't.
>
> {*Humanist in Canada*, Summer 1999}

Buckminister, Joseph Stevens (1784—1812)

Buckminister, who entered Harvard at the age of thirteen, received an A.B. in 1800. His liberal message of rational religion influenced Unitarians to bring the German higher criticism of the Bible to America. He believed the Bible should be read in its historical context, subjected to the same scrupulous scholarly investigation given other texts from antiquity. {U&U}

Buckner, Ed (20th Century)

Buckner is vice president for External Communications in Georgia of the Atlanta Freethought Society. He also is a regional director of the Council for Secular Humanism.

Buckner, Edward M., and **Michael E. Buckner** (20th Century)

The Buckners wrote *Quotations That Support the Separation of State and Church* (1994), a work which has six sections: U. S. Constitution, Treaties, State Constitutions; Founding Fathers (and others of that era); Presidents and similar leaders; Supreme Court rulings; other famous Americans; and foreign sources. {*Freethought History* #9, 1994}

BUDDHA, BUDDHISM

Buddha is a title given to the founder of Buddhism, a life-denying religion which holds that suffering can be remedied through enlightenment. He is also called the Tathagata [he who has come thus], Bhagavat [the Lord], and Sugata [well-gone]. His name was Siddhartha Gautama.

Siddhartha corresponds to *the* Buddha as Jesus does to *the* Christ, although many erroneously fail to distinguish between their personal names and their titles. When seventy-four-year old Pope John Paul visited Sri Lanka in 1995, Buddhist leaders boycotted a meeting with him. They took exception to remarks in his best-selling book, *Crossing the Threshold of Faith*, in which he referred to "negative" aspects of Buddhism and called its goal of nirvana "a state of perfect indifference to the world." The Pope, in calling Buddhism atheistic, echoed the belief of some theologians that Buddhism's quest for the sense of ultimate detachment called nirvana, while it acknowledges and worships deities, is more a philosophy than a religion on divine salvation. In Buddhism, the Pope wrote, "we do not free ourselves from evil through the good which comes from God; we liberate ourselves only through detachment from the world, which is bad."

Although some contemporary Buddhists are naturalistic in their philosophical outlook, others are not. In 1996 when a new temple was constructed in New York City, Phra Maha, the resident monk, heard from parishioners they had seen ghosts that inhabited the building. Mrs. Rungson Vichitlakakran, for example, said her husband caught the faint image of a "big American man," who before vanishing said, "Hi." The temple's administrator, Prueksawatnont, suggested the ghosts may have been appeased by the spirit house which had been added in the back yard. Phra Maha, saying he had seen no ghosts, sagely added that someone who meditates will attain a degree of peace and not see ghosts.

American celebrities who have shown an interest in Buddhism include John Cage, Harrison Ford, Allen Ginsberg, Richard Gere, Chicago Bulls coach Phil Jackson, Patti Smith, Oliver Stone, and Uma Thurman. (See entries for Mansel Davies and for Siddhartha Gautama, his personal name.) {CE; ER; *New York Times*, 16 July 1996}

BUDDHA'S TOOTH

When the Buddha was cremated in India in 483 B.C.E., it is said that four of his teeth were plucked from the cremation pyre. One of the teeth remained—but later disappeared—in India. Two of the teeth were taken to Sri Lanka. One tooth is said to be in China. The worship of relics has a long tradition in Buddhism, as in other major religions. In 1994, when China lent Thailand a burnt finger bone which was said also to have been taken from the funeral pyre, live television recorded the event. Also in 1994, when the Chinese lent its Buddha's tooth for a celebration in Myanmar, hundreds of thousands of Burmese visited the tooth. It was encased in an ornate urn that was encrusted with jewels and was shaped like a small pagoda. It was carried around Yangon on a platform dragged by an elephant draped in traditional silk robes, with four other elephants which followed.

BUDDHISM AND SECULAR HUMANISM

Brian Nicol, Chair of the Mid-Warwickshire branch of Amnesty International and a member of the Coventry and Warwickshire Humanists, has compared Buddhism with secular humanism:

- Buddhism as a doctrine has quite a lot in common with Humanism.

1) It is non-theistic and rational in its approach.

2) In practical terms, its ethical structure is sympathetic, though Humanists do not go in for meditation as a helpful tool for improvement.

3) It accepts that people have to take responsibility for their own actions and suffer or benefit by the consequences.

- We [Humanists] differ mainly in the ultimate goal of Nirvana. Humanists see the rewards of good action to be solely on earth, and death is the end of consciousness. We do not believe in reincarnation. To believe in reincarnation is an act of faith. even Buddha offered no proof. Moreover, there is a school of Buddhist thought that plays down reincarnation (and by implication Nirvana?) as not being essential to Buddhism. Rather like the Christian "Sea of Faith" people who seek to reclassify much of the biblical ideology as mythology rather than fact. If this were to gain ground, Buddhism and Humanism would have even more in common.

{*Gay & Lesbian Humanist*, Summer 1998}

BUDDHISM, ISLAM, AND EPISCOPALIANISM

Diana Eck, a teacher of comparative religion at Harvard University, points out that in 1998 there are more Muslims than Episcopalians in the United States and more Buddhist temples in suburban backyards than is generally realized.

BUDDHIST CHURCHES OF AMERICA

Buddhist Churches of America, organized in 1899, is at 1710 Octavia Street, San Francisco, California 94109.

BUDDHISTS: For an estimate of the number of Buddhists in the world, see entry for Hell.

BUDDHIWADI

A rationalist quarterly in Hindi, *Buddhiwadi* is at 216 A, S. K. Puri, Patna 800 001, Bihar, India. E-mail is: <mnath@giascL01.vsnl.net.in>.

The Buddhiwadi Foundation, which promotes rationalism and humanism in India, publishes a Hindi quarterly, *Buddhiwadi* (The Rationalist) and Buddhiwadi Newsletter. It also runs an institute, Priya Academy, for promoting computer literacy and the scientific outlook. On the Web: <http://www.myfreeoffice.com/buddhiwadi>.

Buehrens, David B. (20th Century)

Buehrens, a long-time secular humanist, has spoken about history, evolution, and ethics to the Humanist Society of Metropolitan New York.

Buehrens, John Allan (1947—)

Buehrens in 1993 was elected the sixth president of the Unitarian Universalist Association. A Harvard graduate, he is son of a Slovak-American Roman Catholic mother and a father of Protestant background. In Dallas, Texas, he had been in charge of the tenth largest Unitarian Universalist congregation on the continent, and he was co-minister of New York City's Unitarian Church of All Souls. One of his stated goals has been to increase the membership of the Unitarians and Universalists to 250,000 by the year of 2001.

Buehrer, Edwin T. (20th Century)

Buehrer is a Unitarian minister who is a humanist. He wrote *The Art of Being* (1971). {HNS}

Buell, John (20th Century)

Buell, who co-authored *Sustainable Democracy: Individuality and the politics of the Environment* with Tom DeLuca, has written for *The Humanist* (USA).

Buen, Odon de (Born 1884)

Buen was a Spanish writer on *Las Dominicales*. A professor of natural history at the University of Barcelona, he wrote *From Christiania to Treggurt*, an account of a scientific expedition. He translated *Memoirs of Garibaldi*. In 1889, Buen was a delegate to the Paris Freethought Conference. {BDF}

Buen y Del Cos, Odon de (Born 1863)

A Spanish geographer, Buen y Del Cos made scientific expeditions in Africa and Europe and was in 1886 appointed naturalist on the scientific exploration of the *Blanca*. One of the most outspoken rationalists of Spain, he had numerous works listed on the *Index Prohibitorum*. {RAT}

Bufalini, Maurizio [Senator] (1787—1875)

An Italian physician, Bufalini published an essay on the Doctrine of Life in opposition to vitalism. As a result he was accused of materialism but became a professor at Florence as well as a member in 1860 of the Italian Senate. {BDF}

Bufe, Charles (20th Century)

Bufe is co-editor with J. R. Swanson of *The American Heretic's Dictionary*, and he edited *The Heretic's Handbook of Quotations* (1992). In the latter book are sections devoted to sex, politics, religion, atheism, Hell, and other subjects. Under Biblical contradictions, Bufe includes the following:

• I have seen God face to face, and my life is preserved.

—*Genesis* 32:30

No man hath seen God at any time.

—*John* 1:18

And I [God] will take away mine hand, and thou shalt see my back parts; but my face shall not be seen.

—*Exodus* 33:23

• Honor thy father and thy mother.

—*Exodus* 20:12

If any man come to me, and hate not his father and mother, and wife, and children, and brethren, and sisters, yea, and his own life also, he cannot be my disciple. [Jesus is being quoted.]

—*Luke* 14:26

• . . . resist not evil; but whosoever shall smite thee on thy right cheek, turn to him the other also.

—*Matthew* 5:39

. . . thou shalt give life for life, eye for eye, tooth for tooth, hand for hand, foot for foot, burning for burning, wound for wound, stripe for stripe.

—*Exodus* 21: 23-25

• Happy is the man that findeth wisdom, and the man that getteth understanding.

—*Proverbs* 3:13

For in much wisdom is much grief; and he that increaseth knowledge increaseth sorrow.

—*Ecclesiastes* 1:18

Buffett, Warren Edward (1930—)

Buffett, one of the world's richest men, is an entrepreneur who is chairman of the board of Berkshire Hathaway Inc., a corporation whose stock reached over $80,000 per share in 1996. Since 1968 he has been a life trustee of Iowa's Grinnell College. Asked in 1997 if he was a supernaturalist or a naturalist, a believer or a non-believer, Buffett responded to the present author, "Agnostic." However, his wife, the daughter of a Disciples of Christ minister, is a theist. Buffett became an agnostic when very young, avoids houses of worship, and tells people his concerns are entirely secular.

Roger Lowenstein, in *Buffett: The Making of an American Capitalist* (1995), found that the financier "did not subscribe to his family's religion. Even at a young age he was too mathematical, too logical, to make a leap of faith. He adopted his father's ethical underpinnings, but not his belief in an unseen divinity." "The nice thing about an agnostic," Buffet has said, "is you don't think anybody is wrong." {*The New York Times*, 9 May 1997; WAS, 13 February 1997}

Buffon, Georges Louis Leclerc [Comte de] (1707—1788)

Count Buffon, the keeper of the Jardin du Roi who made it a center of research during the Enlightenment, was a deist. His 44-volume *Histoire naturelle* (1749—1804) was a brilliant compendium of data on natural history. In that history, he included a "theory of the earth" which inspired Laplace's theory of evolution. The Catholic authorities compelled him to alter certain passages which they declared anti-scriptural.

Herault de Seychelles, in his *Voyage à Montgar*," said that Buffon told him, "I have named the Creator, but it is only necessary to take out the word and substitute the power of nature." He adds that Buffon, who became a member of the French Academy, rejected any belief in immortality. {BDF; CE; JM; JMR; JMRH; PUT; RAT; RE}

Bugge-Wicksell, Anna (Born 1862)

Bugge-Wicksell was speaker of the Norwegian Society for the Emancipation of Women from 1888 to 1889. In 1888 she attended the International Peace Conference in Switzerland. She was a freethinker. {PUT}

BUGGER

A "bugger" is a sodomite, one who engages in anal or oral copulation with a person of the opposite sex. The slang expression originated when the Bogomil ("lovers of God") heretics sent emissaries from their base in Bulgarian in the 11th and 12th centuries in order to contact heretics in Western Europe. These travelers were known as *Bulgarus* (late Latin) and *Bougre* (Middle French). The name was imported into Middle English along with a loathing of the heretics as well as their practices.

According to linguist Tony Thorne, "One offence which heretics of all persuasions were accused of was unnatural vice, hence the transformation of Bulgarians into buggers."

Although to some the word is but a mild pejorative, to others it is still a negative or "snarl word" referring to sodomy. To still others, it refers to the sexual act of choice.

Buggle, Franz (1933—)

Buggle's *Denn sie wissen nicht, was sie glauben* (1992) is, according to Fred Whitehead (*Freethought History*, #24, 1997), "an important contribution to German freethought, even though he largely ignores the freethought tradition." An atheist, Buggle is professor of psychology at the University of Freiburg im Breisgau. In his work he laments the fact that there are so few serious critics of Christianity in Germany today. He cites six: philosopher Hans Albert; writer Günther Anders; journalist Rudolf Augstein; philologist, critic, and historian Karlheinz Deschner; philosopher-theologian Joachim Kahl; and Ernst Topitsch.

Bugliosi, Vincent (20th Century)

Bugliosi is a legal commentator and the former Los Angeles prosecutor who convicted Charles Manson. *Helter Skelter* is an account of the murders and the trial.

In *Outrage: The Five Reasons Why O. J. Simpson Got Away With Murder*, he expresses his non-belief in a subsection entitled "God, Where Are You?" in which he writes:

• I'm an agnostic.
• In my own little mind, I, for one, can't be sure at all there's a God.
• I like Clarence Darrow's observation about the existence vis-à-vis non-existence of God: "I do not pretend to know what ignorant men are sure of."

{CA}

Buisseret, Albert (20th Century)

Senator Buisseret was elected an honorary associate of the Rationalist Press Association in 1952.

Buisson, Ferdinand Édouard (1841—1932)

A French educator and Nobel Peace Prize winner, Buisson produced the *Dictionnaire de pédagogie* (1882—1893) and was active in working for civil rights. A pacifist, he attended (1867) the first congress of the International Peace League. Buisson was an honorary associate of the Rationalist Press Association, which Charles A. Watts had founded in 1899. {CE; RAT; RE}

Buitendijk, Gosuinus van (18th Century)

Buitendijk (or Buytendyck) was a Dutch Spinozist who wrote an Apology at the beginning of the eighteenth century. He was banished in 1716. {BDF}

Buitenweg, Rob (20th Century)

A lecturer in philosophy of law at the University of Humanist Studies in Utrecht, Buitenweg at a 1998 conference of European Humanist Professionals discussed whether or not human rights are essentially humanist. If human rights are universal, he asked, would others have to accept humanism and, if so, would this not be a form of imperialism? Humanism, he continued, can be connected with human rights but can also be seen as a life stance, which all might not share. There is an ontological and ethical element to humanism: on the one hand how we interpret life and what we are, on the other how is life to be lived. According to Buitenweg, humanism tends to offer a public morality but must guard against neglecting the matter of realizing a fulfilled life. {*International Humanist News*, May 1998}

Bukowski, Charles (1920—1994)

A writer, Bukowski in *Life* (December 1988) wrote, "For those who believe in God, most of the big questions are answered. But for those of us who can't readily accept the God formula, the big answers don't remain stone-written. We adjust to new conditions and discoveries. We are pliable. Love need not be a command or faith a I am my own God. We are here to unlearn the teachings of the church, state, and our education system. We are here to drink beer. We are here to kill war. We are here to laugh at the odds and live our lives so well that Death will tremble to take us." {TYD}

Bulfinch, Charles (1763—1844)

Bulfinch, architect for the U.S. Capitol as well as the Massachusetts statehouse, was a Unitarian who owned pew 56 at King's Chapel in Boston, Massachusetts. His father, who had ordained James Freeman as minister of that church, was its warden. His grandfather Apthorp was once of the richest men in Boston and had given much of the money to build King's Chapel.

Bulfinch got the job as architect of the Capitol because Benjamin Henry Latrobe resigned from the job. Although Bulfinch thought the great dome should be lower, he made some changes, writing to his wife,

> The view is beautiful and am convinced that a great city must grow up, and in anticipation we think that we see it before us;—not exactly so in reality; the public buildings are distant two miles or so from each other, and a small village has grown around each. These are connected by spacious streets, lined with trees. The whole has an imposing air, especially while Congress is in session, from the number of carriages traversing the grand avenue.

{CE; EG; U; UU}

BULGARIAN HUMANISTS

At a 1995 Berlin conference arranged by the International Humanist and Ethical Union (IHEU), Iordan Zaprianov stated that as of 1995 no humanist group were meeting. In Bulgarian, he reported, the word "atheist" is synonymous with "communist." Nevertheless, a silent majority of non-believers exists, and he proposed creating a Bulgarian humanist group. (See entry for Bugger.)

Bullard, Beulah L. (20th Century)

When Bullard signed Humanist Manifesto II, she was a humanist counselor. {HM2}

Buller, Charles (1806—1848)

A politician, Buller supported the reform party, along with J. Mill, Grote, and Molesworth. Jowett quotes Buller as saying, "Destroy the Church of England, sir! Why, you must be mad. It is the one thing which stands between us and real religion." {RAT}

Bullert, Gary (20th Century)

Bullert wrote *The Politics of John Dewey* (1983).

Bullett, Gerald (Born 1893)

Bullett was a novelist, one who wrote in the *Rationalist Annual* (1938) and edited Montaigne's *Book of Good Faith* and Butler's *Fair Haven* for the Rationalist Press Association. "Rationalism," he held, "must be part of the mental make-up of every man who claims to think for himself." However, in his *Problems of Religion* (1938), he agrees rather with Bergson in preferring instinct or intuition to reason. {RE}

Bulloch, Jude [Father] (20th Century)

Cardinal Hume in 1996 received complaints that Father Bullock, of the St. John the Evangelist Church in Islington, north London, did not believe in God, Heaven, or Hell. Further, Bulloch preached that prayers are simply meditations, and he "dumped" the idea of the soul, questioned the Virgin Birth, and defended his views as "just a reinterpretation of the term God in non-supernatural terms." {*The Freethinker*, October 1996}

Bullock, Alan (1914—)

In *The Humanist Tradition in the West* (1985), Bullock wrote that although humanists in the eighteenth and nineteenth centuries may have underestimated the darker side of nature, such is no longer true: "Between the 1880s and the 1930s, a new version of humanism was beginning to emerge which had broken with the optimistic assumptions of the earlier phrase and accepted that its starting-point had to be recognition of the divided nature of man, of the irrational forces in individual human beings and in human society which such pioneers as Ibsen, Freud, and Max Weber had made explicit."

Bullock, Laurence Frederick (c. 1892—1976)

"Lawrie" Bullock was an English church-going Protestant who migrated to West Australia after the first World War. A member of Australia First, he was interned during World War II. In 1968, he and John Campbell revived the dormant Rationalist Association of South Australia, and when it became the Atheist Foundation of Australia (AFA) Bullock became its secretary-treasurer. In 1970 he became the first vice president of the Atheist Society of Australia. {SWW}

Bullock, Edna (1915—)

Bullock, widow of photographer Wynn Bullock, is a photographer whose work has been included in over one hundred individual and group shows in the United States and abroad. *Edna's Nudes* (1997), edited by her daughter Barbara Bullock-Wilson, contains many of the nude photographs for which she has become known. Bullock is a member in California of the Unitarian Universalist Church of the Monterey Peninsula. {*World*, September-October 1997}

Bullough, Bonnie (1927—1996)

Bullough, who had been a dean of nursing at the State University of New York at Buffalo, was a Humanist Laureate in the Council for Secular Humanism's International Academy of Humanism. Also, she was a Secular Humanist Mentor of the Council for Secular Humanism, was on that group's Faith-Healing Investigation Project, and was a contributing editor for *Free Inquiry*. In 1966 she became a Fulbright lecturer in Cairo. With her husband, Vern L. Bullough, she wrote *Women and Prostitution, A Social History* as well as *Sexual Attitudes: Myths and Realities* (1995). She spoke in Delphi, Greece, at the 1995 International Multidisciplinary Conference on Human Behaviour and the Meaning of Modern Humanism in. Also in 1995, she and her husband were given an Alfred C. Kinsey award for outstanding contributions to the scientific study of sexuality. With her husband, Bullough went to Berlin, Beijing, Amsterdam, Toronto, and elsewhere, proclaiming the virtues of humanism. In Ghana, she brought contraceptive information to women.

Gerald Larue, at a commemoration ceremony following her death, told of her somewhat unhappy childhood, of her having been born into a Mormon family and never having known her father.

Larue mentioned that she had written and co-authored more than 160 refereed articles as well as another fifty and over twenty chapters in a variety of books. Bullough, who suffered from interstitial lung disease, chose to spend her last hours playing a game of bridge and, just before dying, left her husband Vern with a list of jobs to do, including the final preparation of a book she was completing. This illustrated, Paul Kurtz wrote, that she "did not believe in the illusion of immortality. She thought that the best response to death is the reaffirmation of life." (See entry for Vern L. Bullough.) {*Free Inquiry*, Summer 1996; HNS2}

Bullough, Vern L. (1928—)

Once the dean of natural and social sciences, State University of New York at Buffalo, Bullough is a member of the secretariat of the Council for Secular Humanism's International Academy of Humanism and is on the board of directors of the Committee for Secular Humanism. Also, he is on the Council for Secular Humanism's Committee for the Scientific Examination of Religion and is a Secular Humanist Mentor.

In the 1950s, when he was an assistant professor of history at Youngstown University, he reviewed books for *The Humanist*. Bullough addressed the Tenth International Humanist and Ethical Union (IHEU) World Congress held in Buffalo (1988). In 1992 he was named Dean of the Institute for Inquiry, an organization which offers courses in humanism and skepticism and sponsors an annual summer session as well as periodic workshops. He also was presented with a Distinguished Humanist Service Award in Amsterdam at the 40th IHEU Congress "for his life-long commitment to humanism and his outstanding contributions to the fields of sexology, history, and the health care profession, where he has sought to apply the highest humanist values."

With his wife, Bonnie, Bullough wrote *Women and Prostitution*, "The Causes of Homosexuality: A Scientific Update" (*Free Inquiry*, Fall, 1993), and *Sexual Attitudes: Myths and Realities* (1995). "It is no longer possible to argue that either nature or nurture alone is the answer," they wrote concerning the causes. "It is clear that both are involved in producing sexual preference." The work describes prostitutes who became Christian saints, the U.S. Army saddle which was designed to prevent stimulation of the male penis, the Talmudic prohibitions against widows owning dogs lest they use them for sexual satisfaction, and the role menstruation played in Lizzie Borden's murder trial. The two also wrote *Sexual Attitudes, Myths and Realities* (1995).

Bullough's "Science, Humanism, and the New Enlightenment" is in *Challenges to the Enlightenment, In Defense of Reason and Science* (1994). He wrote *Science in the Bedroom: A History of Sex Research* (1994), an extensive review of the unsatisfactory history of studies of sexuality. Bullough also wrote an introduction to *Toward A New Enlightenment, The Philosophy of Paul Kurtz*. He is author, co-author, or editor of more than forty books. In 1996 Bullough spoke at the Humanist World Congress held in Mexico City. He is a member of the Secretariat of the International Academy of Humanism.

From 1994 to 1998, Bullough was co-president of the International Humanist and Ethical Union (IHEU), during which time he built up a positive reputation for his wit and sagacity. In 1995, he and his wife were given an Alfred C. Kinsey award for outstanding contributions to the scientific study of sexuality.

Bullough signed Humanist Manifesto 2000. His e-mail: <vbullough@csun.edu>. (See entry for Homosexuality.)

BULLSHIT: See entry for George Carlin.

BULLSHITUS EPISCOPALIS

Nicolas Walter, describing religionists' statements which change depending upon their audiences, says the practice is called *bullshitus episcopalis*. {*Freethinker*, June 1996}

Bulmash, Mark (20th Century)

Bulmash is treasurer in Michigan of *The Jewish Humanist*.

Bulsseret, A. [Senator] (20th Century)

Senator Bulsseret was an honorary associate of the Rationalist Press Association in 1995.

Bulwer-Lytton, Edward George Earle Lytton (1803—1873)

A friend of William Godwin, Bulwer-Lytton is known for his *Last Days of Pompeii* (1834). In *Devereaux* (1829), 1st Baron Lytton sympathetically depicted an atheist, greatly affecting the outlook at that time of a young George Eliot. {CE; EU, Vincent N. Paananen}

BUND FREIRELIGIOSER GEMEINDEN DEUTCH-LANDS

The German humanist organization, *Bund Freireligioser Gemeinden Deutchlands* (Ulmenweg 5, 63263 Neu-Isenburg, Germany), is a member group of the International Humanist and Ethical Union (IHEU). It publishes *Wege Ohne Dogma*. (See entry for German Humanism.) {HNS2}

BUND GEGEN ANPASSUNG

Bund Gegen Anpassung, a German atheist organization, publishes *Ketzerbreife* (heretical letters) at Post Fach 254, D-7800 Freiburg, Germany. {FD}

Bunde, Carl (1907—1996)

Bunde, a physician, decided when a youth that "religion is bunk!" He held that philosophy is a poor second to science as a source of understanding. An activist, he was one of the founding members of the Cincinnati, Ohio, Free Inquiry Group (FIG). Bunde, amused that people have difficulty in defining secular humanism, declared, "Just look up the two words in the dictionary. Humanism is concerned with the interests and aspirations of human beings. Secular means without religion. Just put them together. Secular humanism seeks to satisfy human needs and aspirations through use of human intelligence and the sciences. {*Fig Leaves*, August 1996}

Bunge, Mario Augusto (1919—)

Bunge is the Argentina-born Frothingham professor of foundations and philosophy of science at McGill University in Canada. A Humanist Laureate in the Council for Secular Humanism's International Academy of Humanism, he addressed the Tenth International Humanist and Ethical Union (IHEU) World Congress held in Buffalo (1988). In Madrid in 1995, he spoke on the subject, "*A Favour de la intolerancia.*" Bunge is author of more than 400 articles and 35 books on physics, metaphysics, semantics, epistemology, philosophy of science, and ethics. He wrote "Counter-Enlightenment in Contemporary Studies" in *Challenges To The Enlightenment, In Defense of Reason and Science* (1994), *Finding Philosophy in Social Science* (1996), and with Martin Mahner *Fundamentals of Biophilosophy* (1997).

In 1996 he spoke at the Humanist World Congress in Mexico City on how informatics is a double-edged weapon: involved are both formation and deformation. Humanists, he noted, welcome technical innovation but although it can empower some it moves others further from the center of society and, therefore, does not necessarily lead to an egalitarian society. One of our present concerns, he warned, is that of the excess of information: to know something, we must ignore much information. Computers, unfortunately, lack intuition, he observed, and the internet cannot replace libraries. Although husband and wife can communicate on the screen, they will not settle for the satisfaction of "virtual love." Just the same, we have every right to be enthusiastic about technology, Bunge stated, but technology needs to be used with intelligence and moderation. He signed Humanist Manifesto 2000. {HNS2; *International Humanist News*, December 1996; *New Humanist*, December 1996}

Bunge, Martin Ludwig Detloff (20th Century)

Bunge, a freethinker, wrote *Billy Sunday, the Last Prophet of a Dying Religion* (19—?). {GS}

Buñuel, Luis (1900—1983)

Buñuel, a Spanish director and anarchist who delighted in portraying social hypocrisy in his movies, is known for such godless films as "*L'Age d'or*" (1930), "*Los Olvidados*" (1949), and "Exterminating Angel" (1962). "Thank God, I'm still an atheist," he was known to have told friends. {*Paris Notes*, December 1998-January 1999; *Freethought Today*, February 1999}

Burbank, Luther (1849—1926)

An eminent plant breeder, creator of "the Burbank potato," Burbank was a Unitarian from time to time. That is, he said he went to a church because he liked hearing what the minister might say. He also liked to read E. Haldeman Julius's Little Blue Books, and Robert G. Ingersoll was one of his favorite authors. In his *Why I Am an Infidel* (1926), Burbank wrote the following:

> • Science, unlike theology, never leads to insanity. Science . . . has opened our eyes to the vastness of the universe and given us light, truth, and freedom from fear where once was darkness, ignorance, and superstition. There is no personal salvation, except through science.
>
> • Most people's religion is what they want to believe, not what they do believe.
>
> • Those who take refuge behind theological barbed wire fences quite often wish they could have more freedom of thought, but fear the change to the great ocean of scientific truth as they would a cold bath plunge.
>
> • Those who would legislate against the teaching of evolution should also legislate against gravity, electricity, and the unreasonable velocity of light, and also should introduce a clause to prevent the use of the telescope, the microscope, and the spectroscope or any other instrument . . . used for the discovery of truth.
>
> • What is the use of assuring Fundamentalists that science is compatible with religion. They retort at once, "Certainly not with our religion."
>
> • And to think of this great country in danger of being dominated by people ignorant enough to take a few ancient Babylonian legends as the canons of modern culture. Our scientific men are paying for their failure to speak out earlier. There is no use now talking evolution to these people. Their ears are stuffed with *Genesis*.

Edgar Waite, a reporter, interviewed Burbank 22 January 1926 for the San Francisco *Bulletin*, and the resultant headline was

I'M AN INFIDEL, DECLARES BURBANK,
CASTING DOUBT ON SOUL IMMORTALITY THEORY

The reporter had asked Burbank about Henry Ford's views in favor of reincarnation. Burbank had replied,

> A theory of personal resurrection or reincarnation of the individual is untenable when we pause to consider the magnitude of the idea. On the contrary, I must believe that rather than the survival of all, we must look for survival only in the spirit of the good we have done in passing through. This is as feasible and credible as Henry Ford's own practice of discarding the old models of his automobile. Once obsolete, an automobile is thrown to the scrap heap. Once here and gone, the human life has likewise served its purpose. If it has been a good life, it has been sufficient. There is no need for another. But as a scientist, I can not help feeling that all religions are on a tottering foundation. None is perfect or inspired. The idea that a good God would send people to a burning hell is utterly damnable to me. I don't want to have anything to do with such a God.

What particularly riled readers who were believers was his statement, "I am an infidel today. I do not believe what has been served to me to believe. I am a doubter, a questioner, a skeptic. When it can be proved to me that there is immortality, that there is resurrection beyond the gates of death, then will I believe. Until then, no." Thousands complained, and Dan Barker among others has cited Wilbur Hale as saying that in Burbank's zeal to respond with letters containing "logic, kindliness, and reason in order to convince and help the bigoted," Burbank "grew suddenly old attempting to make reasonable a people which had been unreasonable through twenty stiff-necked generations. . . . He died, not a martyr to truth, but a victim of the fatuity of blasting dogged falsehood."

One of the few men admitted to his house at Santa Rosa, in the few months before he died, was Joseph McCabe. "I found him advanced even beyond the vague Emersonian theism of his earlier years," McCabe reported. "He agreed to see me, he said, though he was tired and ill, because of his admiration of my work as a Rationalist. He had just raised a storm by a public declaration that he did not believe in a future life, and his biographer Wilbur Hall repeats this." At Burbank's memorial service, Judge Ben Lindsey addressed an estimated 10,000 people. Maynard Shipley has written, "Several Roman Catholic priests were seen in the audience, but several of them left the open-air services in Doyle Park, offended in their narrow dogmatism by Lindsey's ringing challenges." Part of Lindsey's speech included the following:

> One of the saddest spectacles of our times is the effort of hidebound theologians, still desperately trying to chain us to the past—in other forms that would still invoke the inquisitions, the fears, and the bigotries of the dark ages, and keep the world in chains. The chains of lies, hypocrisies, taboos, and the superstitions, fostered by the dying, but still the organized, relentless outworn theology of another age. They refuse to see that in their stupid lust for power they are endangering all that is good.

{CE; CL; *Freethought Today*, August 1993; FUS; JM; RAT; RE; TYD; U; UU}

Burch, Brian (20th Century)

Burch has reviewed books for *Humanist in Canada.*

Burchell, Iona (20th Century)

Burchell in *New Humanist* (December 1996) wrote of H. G. Wells's literary foresight and imagination.

Burckhardt, Jakob (1818—1897)

Burckhardt was a Swiss historian who wrote of humanism in *Die Cultur der Renaissance in Italien*) (Renaissance Civilization in Italy, 1860). In his posthumously published *Weltgeschichtliche Betrachtunger* (1905), he tells that he rejected all creeds and churches. {JM; RE}

Burdach, Karl Friedrich (1776—1847)

Burdach was a German physiologist whose work on physiology and anthropology popularized those sciences. The former was placed on the *Index Librorum Prohibitorum* for its "materialistic tendency." {BDF; RAT}

Burdett, Francis [Sir] (1770—1844)

Burdett, a British banker and reformer, was a wealthy man who, according to McCabe, "worked so devotedly for social and radical reforms that he was imprisoned in the Tower of London and the workers threatened to attack it and deliver him."

McCabe adds that it is "now the fashion to praise narrow-minded bigots like Shaftesbury, who had to barricade his windows against the workers, and ignore such an unselfish and effective worker as Burdett. He worked with Bentham and Place and was, like them, an atheist. Mrs. de Morgan says in her Reminiscences that Burdett was 'what in these days would be called an Agnostic.'" {JM; RAT; RE; TRI}

Burdon, William (1764—1818)

Burdon wrote *Materials for Thinking*, his principal work, which went through five editions in his lifetime. He also addressed *Three Letters to the Bishop of Llandaff* and wrote some objections to the annual subscription to the Sons of the Clergy. {BDF; RAT}

BUREAU OF PUBLIC SECRETS

The Bureau of Public Secrets (POB 1044, Berkeley, California), distributes "The War and the Spectacle" and looks for new approaches for survival of consciousness and approaches for effective activism. {FD}

Burgers, Thomas Francis [President] (1834—1881)

Burgers, President of the Transvaal (South Africa) Republic, was educated for the Church at Utrecht University, but he was suspended for heresy when he began to practice in the Transvaal. According to McCabe, Burgers "entered politics and won such high regard for his ability and integrity that, as the historian of South Africa, Theal says, the Boers, who are as a body bigoted, decided to overlook his heresies and made him their President. They were uncomfortable when it appeared, from a volume of stories he had written which was published after his death (*Toneelen uit ons Dorp)* [Tales from our Village], that he was an agnostic. {JM; RAT; RE}

Burgess, Anthony (1917—1993)

Burgess, a prolific British novelist, composer, librettist, essayist, semanticist, translator, and critic, is best known for his *A Clockwork Orange*, which depicted a somewhat bleak vision of a violence-ridden future. An admirer of Laurence Sterne, James Joyce, and Evelyn Waugh, he once wrote, "I was brought up a Catholic, became an agnostic, flirted with Islam, and now hold a position which may be termed Manichee. I believe the wrong God is temporarily ruling the world and that the true God has gone under. Thus I am a pessimist but believe the world has much solace to offer: love, food, music, the immense variety of race and language, literature, and the pleasure of artistic creation." Llewela Isherwood Jones, a distant relative of Christopher Isherwood whom he married in 1942, was assaulted during World War II in London, an attack which resulted in the loss of their expected child. Burgess once stated that the brutality depicted in *A Clockwork Orange* stemmed in part from the assault upon his wife. The novel is the story of a murderous, Beethoven-loving teenage gang leader in a complacent and conformist society in the near future. "In this welfare state," critic Herbert Mitgang has written of the novel which was made into a movie, "roving bands of delinquents fight, steal, and rape to assert their freedom against the conformity of a clockwork society. The novel is written in a dialect of the author's own invention. Its language, called *nadsat*, is a mixture of English and American slang, Russian, Gypsy talk, and odd bits of Jacobean prose."

Paul Theroux has written that he valued his friendship with Burgess because "I felt that I somewhat resembled him. We had both been raised Catholic, in the age of the Latin Mass, and, as the liturgy had become folksy and English-speaking, with show tunes played after the Consecration instead of the Agnus Dei, and all that hugging and hand-holding, he had lapsed and so had I. But the Church had done its work, and we both still regarded our souls as stained indelibly with sin."

In a 1991 *The Economist*, Burgess wrote, "I wish people would think of me as a musician who writes novels, instead of as a novelist who writes music on the side. Music is a purer art because it has no direct relationship to human events. It's totally outside the field of moral judgment. That's why I prize it." In the same article, he was quoted as fearing "the coming darkness," adding that he seesawed between feelings of self-indulgence and belief. "I don't think there's a heaven, but there's certainly a hell. Everything we've experienced on earth seems to point toward the permanence of pain." Among Burgess's sixty-five musical compositions are "The Blooms of Dublin," an operetta based on James Joyce's *Ulysses*, and "A Clockwork Orange 2004," a musical stage version of his novel.

Burgess, Thomas (19th Century)

Burgess, a freethinker, wrote *Tracts on the Divinity of Christ* (1820). {GS}

BURIAL PRACTICES

Practices concerning burial of the deceased vary widely. According to A. Eustace Haydon, signer of Humanist Manifestos I and II, man has always been a protestant against death. In *The Encyclopedia of Religion*, he illustrates by citing the following:

- Confucianism alone has accepted a "good death" as the normal term of a life fully lived.

- In the early world death seemed unaccountable. Primitive thinkers could not believe that sickness and death were intended to have a place in the human scene. They explained that it must have come as a result of a mistake or failure of one of the lower animals or the disobedience, or curiosity or carelessness of the first human pair. Usually the woman was blamed. Some stories attribute man's loss of immortality to the anger or enmity of a god. Whatever the theory regarding the origin of death, rarely was the death of the individual taken as natural. Some deaths were clearly the work of nature gods acting in storm or lightning or torrent. Death by violence might result from the superior magic of an enemy, the malignancy of an unhappy ghost, or a hostile spirit. Death by disease was commonly credited to sorcery. Masters of magical techniques, of powerful curses and spells, with or without the help of malicious spirits, were believed to be effective dealers in death.

- The many modes of treatment of the dying and the dead are the result of the accretion of ages and combine ideas drawn from earlier and later levels of culture. Some practices arose from a primitive fear of contact with the defilement and danger of death—carrying the dying out of the house, lifting him from the bed to die in contact with the earth or in a prepared grave; abandonment of the dying, destruction of the hut in which he died, or removal of the settlement from the death scene; preparation of the dead for burial by medicine men or professional corpse handlers immune to the death danger; and the universal rites of protection and purification. Some practices depend upon the idea of a separable soul—calling to the spirit to come back immediately after death, instructing the dead man regarding his changed condition and separation from his former habitat, safeguarding the living from the death demon or from the dead if he should become an angry and malignant ghost. When the dead man dwelt where his body was placed, he was fed there, consulted, advised as to happenings in the family. The later idea of a special abode for souls in a realm of the fathers a heaven or paradise gave rise to ceremonies to secure safe passage. Extreme unction in Christianity, recitation of the *Patet* and *Ashem—vohu* by the Parsis are such rites for the dying. In Tibet a lama draws the soul out of the body immediately after death and shows it the way to the Western Paradise. Teachers of the dead instruct the Moslem in his tomb how to reply to two examining angels. Because customs are retained after the ideas underlying them are outgrown, death and burial practices are often complex and confusing but the rites clearly combine three purpose—to protect the survivors from the dangerous contact with death, to initiate the dead man into his new status of separation from the living, and to give him safe conduct to his new abode.

• Immediately after the death most peoples wash the corpse, close the eyes and change the clothes. Sometimes the hair and nails are cut and the feet tied. Weeping is not universal. In some cases it is expected; there may even be hired mourners. In old Japan the relatives wept while friends caroused. Hinduism and Zoroastrianism forbade tears because they hurt the dead or made his passage to the afterlife difficult. It was bad form to weep for a Moslem saint or for an old man in China. Food for the dead was sometimes provided; more frequently the mourners ate a meal in the presence of the corpse setting aside a portion for him. In many lands friends watch the body while it is waiting for burial. This "wake" is often the occasion for feasting and eulogizing of the dead man. The watchers are supposed to protect his body and soul from demon assault. In Buddhist countries the priests recite the sacred texts in relays, day and night, during this period. Death also demands a change of garb and appearance for the mourners, usually a reversal of the ordinary mode. Black and white garments are most common. Moslem women wear blue. Sometimes all customary work must be stopped, care of the body neglected for a time, and no jewelry or adornments worn. It may be that this altered appearance, like the wreath or branch placed outside the death house, was once intended to give warning of the presence of the pollution of death.

• The funeral may follow within a few hours after death or may be delayed several months. Primitive precautions to guard against the return of the soul still linger in some lands, for example, taking the body out through a window or a hole broken in the wall, going to the grave and returning by circuitous routes, crossing water, turning the body around several times on the way. The funeral procession is often elaborate. In cultures thousands of years old it may combine primitive with more sophisticated usages or forms contributed by the successive religions that have shaped the lives of the people. The funeral may include images, animals, musicians or noisemakers to clear the path of evil influences, specially selected wailers, public recognition of the virtues of the dead man, provisions for his future well-being, carrying or recitation from a sacred book, rites to safeguard the mourners. Circumambulation [ceremonial walking around an object or person] of the corpse, of the church, of the grave, of the funeral pyre is practically universal.

• Many modes of disposal of the dead are used. Priestly preference may give one form dominance in an area but uniformity is rare. The monetary, moral, social, or ecclesiastical status of the dead man may decide the mode. Eating the corpse was an approved practice in some tribes. Exposure in trees, on platforms or on the ground was common. In ancient Iran the dead were given to the dogs and birds. The modern Parsis retain this practice by exposing the bodies to vultures on the towers of silence. In one form of disposal in Tibet the flesh is cut from the bones and fed to dogs and birds. The bones are then buried or crushed, mixed with meal, and given to the animals. A more careless variant of this form is throwing the body into water or jungle or desert places. There is a ceremonial mode of burial in water when the body is placed in canoe or ship, escorted to the deep and the vessel sunk or set on fire. Cave burial has been practiced since prehistoric times. Commonest of all forms in past ages and generally preferred in modern cultures are burial in the earth and cremation. The Egyptian theory of the afterlife required the preservation of the body which led to the construction of magnificent tombs for the aristocrats. In Tibet the bodies of grand lamas are embalmed and kept on display for worship as deities.

• Generally slaves and common people received less ceremonial treatment than priests, kings, and nobles. Children dying before initiation were disposed of with little ceremony. The unbaptized in Christian Europe were denied church burial and a place in holy ground. The unmarried, barren women, and women dying in childbirth who might become vengeful ghosts were often buried with rites to counteract the danger. Criminals, suicides, lepers, and those who met accidental death were in many lands refused burial rites, thrown away, or buried with protective ceremony.

• The body may be buried in a crouching or sitting posture, or lying extended on the side or back, with or without a coffin. The orientation of the face is fixed by tribal or religious tradition. The East is the favorite direction, but some peoples turn the dead toward the sunset, the South, the North, the old home of the clan, the birthplace of the dead man, or the holy city of his faith. In ancient times it was customary to put into the grave food and drink, tools, weapons, personal belongings, clothes, money, and mementos of his friends. In important man might take with him in death his wives, companions, servants, his favorite horse, and dogs. This waste of human life and property was overcome later by the substitution of effigies of persons and symbolic forms of material goods.

• A feast usually followed the funeral at the tomb, or at the home or both and was often repeated at stated times afterward until the dead man was settled in his new abode. Thereafter he shared in anniversary feasts or in the general ceremony in which all souls were fed. In some lands, however, the feeding of the dead was a fixed ritual of the family cult. The annual and anniversary feasts tended to become memorial occasions.

• Before taking up the regular routine of living, purification was necessary for all closely in contact with the dead. If the impurity remained, as some thought, from one to thirty days, the usual work, attire, or toilet could not be resumed during that time. Individuals and the home, sometimes the village, had to be cleansed of pollution. The individual was purified by passing through fire or smoke, touching fire or water, sprinkling with water or cow's urine, or by taking a bath. Fumigation or sprinkling with cleansing fluids made the death room safe again. There were also formal ceremonies to separate the dead from the living and restore the normal rhythm of life. The mourning period varies widely from a few days to three years.

(See entry for Funerals.) {ER}

BURIAL PRACTICES, CATHOLIC

Roman Catholics bring the body to the church, where "divine" services are held. Interment of the body is made in "consecrated" ground. The liturgical service expresses sorrow over the bereavement, a plea for God's mercy toward the "departed soul," and a buoyant confidence in the promised "resurrection." The service for baptized infants is entirely joyous, since they are assured of Heaven. Inasmuch as Catholic burial is a "privilege of union" with the Church, it is not granted to unbaptized persons, to baptized non-Catholics (unless either of these had expressed a desire to become Catholics), or to nominal Catholics who died as unrepentant public "sinners." {ER}

BURIAL PRACTICES, FREETHINKERS OR SECULAR HUMANISTS

The non-churched ordinarily have an entirely progressive attitude toward death.

First, they are aware that death is final, so they live their life knowing it is the only life they will live. By having children, they transmit their genes and experience immortality thereby. If they do not have children, they are aware that immortality may only be available if they, for example, have composed music, written a poem, created some work that will live on, or otherwise made the Earth a better place. If they have planned for death, American non-believers draw up a Last Will along with a Living Will (appointing someone to act in their behalf in the event they become incapable and are otherwise unable to make final decisions of a medical nature) as well as a Health Care Proxy. Some choose commercial funerary establishments and arrange for embalming, coffins, gravestones. Others donate their bodies to anatomy departments and direct that their cremains by disposed of by burial in a family plot or elsewhere. Some keep the cremains on the fireplace mantle or scatter them in pre-designated places. Some direct that their cremains be mixed in with the cremains of whoever was their "significant other" in lifetime. Some plan a memorial service at a future date, and it is not uncommon that food, fruit, desserts, wine, and other refreshments are served.

John Dewey's memorial was held in the Community Church (Unitarian) in New York City; at its conclusion, and following the singing of Dewey's favorite music (a Negro Gospel song), the minister, Donald Harrington, exited with one hand guiding Mrs. Dewey and the other carrying the cremains. Norman Cousins's memorial was held in the Ethical Culture Society in New York City, as was Isaac Asimov's and singer Michael Callen's. The Callen memorial featured many musical selections, including a hearty performance of some gay ballads by his group, The Flirtations. Fernando Vargas's memorial was held in the recording studio he had founded. After a favorite bartender had served his favorite drink (a Manhattan, up) along with accompanying tidbits, Vargas's friends related their memories of Vargas while in the background the music he had recorded for Liza Minnelli, her first demonstration record, one with Marvin Hamlisch accompanying on the piano, was played over the loudspeakers. Hairdresser Luke Stanton's friends followed his direction to hand out a printed program, in which he included the Council for Secular Humanism's "Affirmations of Humanism: A Statement of Principles," and the ceremony was filmed.

BURIAL PRACTICES, TIBETAN

"Sky burial" is one of three principal ways that Tibetans traditionally return their dead to the earth. Cremation and "water burial" are two of the ways, but wood for burning is expensive and not all localities have a river into which the corpses can be cut into small pieces for the fish to eat.

Sky burial involves a Buddhist monk's stripping flesh from bone, using a sledgehammer to crush each bone into fragments, then allowing as many as fifty vultures to perform the ecologically sound way to dispose of the dead. He works alone and is paid the equivalent of five dollars per body. Family members observe the rite from a distance, close but not so close they can actually witness it. "When the body dies, the spirit leaves, so there is no need to keep the body," a monk by the name of Garloji told *New York Times* reporter Seth Faison (3 July 1999). "The birds, they think they are just eating. Actually, they are removing the body and completing part of life's cycle."

Buridan, Jean (c. 1295—1356): See entry for Ass, Buridan's.

Burigny, Jean Lévesque de (1692—1795)

A French writer who became a member of the French Academy, Burigny wrote a treatise on the *Authority of the Pope*, a *History of Philosophy*, and a letter in answer to Bergier's *Proofs of Christianity*, published in Naigeon's *Recueil Philosophique*. {BDF; RAT}

Burkart, Bob (20th Century)

Burkart, an active member of the Free Inquiry Society of Central Florida, has spoken to the group about his friendship with the Robert Ingersoll family and told of Ingersoll's influence upon his life.

Burke, Kenneth (1897—1986)

Burke, a music and literary critic for *The Dial* and *The Nation*, wrote *The Philosophy of Literary Form* (1941), *A Grammar of Motives* (1945), and *A Rhetoric of Motives* (1950). He was a visiting professor of English at the University of Chicago (1949—1950). Believing that literature is a form of "symbolic action," Burke drew on data from the social sciences. Asked his view of humanism, he replied to the present author:

> To fill my needs, you will have to add another department, probably to be called "Linguistic Humanism." That is: Based on definition of man as the "typically symbol-using animal." Nearer to modern empiricism, perhaps, than to Aristotle's definition of man as "rational animal." Yet way over on the side of Aristotle, as compared with, say, the Watson views of behaviorist "conditioning." If we think of nature as purely physical (the sheerly material things and operations that are left when you hypothetically prescind "words," "meaning," "consciousness," and the like), then language could be said to "transcend" nature. But it is not a "supernatural" transcendence in the theological sense, since it can be analyzed on a purely empirical basis. Nor is it necessarily anti-theological, since the analysis of language can provide no grounds for denying its derivation from a "beyond" (in fact, the analysis might even seem to call for some such hypothesis, in a mildly skeptical sort of way).
>
> Perhaps the most complete statement of my position, from the standpoint of the present study, is my essay, "Linguistic Approach to Problems of Education," that is to appear in the 1955 Yearbook of the National Society for the Study of Education.
>
> {WAS, 25 September 1954}

Burkert, Walter (1931—)

Burkert, a German-born Greek language educator and historian, moved to Switzerland in 1969, where he is professor of Classics at the University of Zurich. Winner of the Ingersoll Prize in 1992, he has written *Lore and Science in Ancient Pythagoreanism* (1972), *Homo Necans* (1983), *Greek Religion* (1985), *Greek Mystery Cults* (1987), and *The Orientalizing Revolution* (1992). The work on Greek religion covered the period of 800 to 300 B.C.E. and was widely acclaimed.

In 1996, he wrote *Creation of the Sacred: Tracks of Biology in Early Religions*. Even in the Upper Paleolithic Period, Burkert found, religious practices existed, and, inasmuch as Neanderthal men had ceremonies for the dead, "religion" of a sort existed even then. As to why religion has lasted, he takes issue with those social anthropologists who study cultures as autonomous systems. Rather, he holds, "the idea of the supernatural emerges within the landscape of nature. . . . If reality appears dangerous or downright hostile to life, religion calls for something beyond experience to restore the balance." How it does this, by consoling individuals, he explains by giving examples from all parts of the world and not only from Paleolithic caves but also from ancient Greece.

Commenting upon Burkert's thesis, Norman Cohn, professor of history emeritus at the University of Sussex and a Fellow the British Academy, relates that Burkert finds rank at the very heart of religion, "a sense of dependence, subordination, and submission to unseen superiors. In ancient religions, gods were the powerful ones, the rulers over man and nature. They were called lord, king, and they expected human beings to honor them. On the other hand, just like human lords and kings, gods had obligations to their inferiors; notably, they were responsible for their protection and security." Burkert disagrees, as Freud maintained, that gods represent the permanent fixture, the father, insisting that the role of authority goes back to pre-human stages of evolution. "Monkeys and apes are acutely aware of hierarchy, and the attention of inferiors is always concentrated on those above them in the hierarchy," Cohn explains. Rank, in short, imposed order on chaos. If humans experienced catastrophes, as illustrated in the *Iliad* and the Old Testament, they needed explanations, tended to blame themselves, then felt impelled to make atonement in the hope of being forgiven.

Burkert holds that organisms, from plants to primates, make signs and react to signs, that "the human psyche excels in this ability to create sense" by developing the art of *divinatio*, or "divine activity." Religion, then, is a tradition going back to the beginnings of mankind, of attempting to communicate with unseen forces. By its organization, it helps people cope and contributes to a sense of coherence and stability in the world. Cohn, although he thought more attention could have been given to the ethical dimension of religion, found Burkert's arguments persuasive, adding that "meaninglessness is in the long run intolerable: if that is how the world is, people are impelled to pretend otherwise." {*The New York Review of Books*, 9 May 1996}

Burkhardt, Frederick Henry (20th Century)

Burkhardt, a humanist who during World War II was an instructor of philosophy at the University of Wisconsin, wrote, "Freedom of worship is one of the great democratic freedoms for which we are fighting. Presumably this ideal means that an individual is also free *not* to worship. At any rate, a considerable number of humanists, naturalists, agnostics, and others who reject supernaturalism assume that it is their democratic right to follow their view of the nature of things without external interference." {HNS}

Burmeister, Hermann (Born 1867)

A German naturalist, Burmeister was a physician at Halle. In 1848 he was elected to the National Assembly, and in 1850 he went to Brazil. His principal work is *The History of Creation* (1843). {BDF}

Burmeister, Johann Peter Theodor (19th Century)

Burmeister was a German rationalist and colleague of Ronge. He wrote under the name of J. P. Lyser. {BDF}

Burnet, Frank Macfarlane [Sir] (1899—1985)

An Australian rationalist, atheist, medical scientist, immunologist, and Nobel Prize winner (1960), Burnet conducted studies of viruses that infect bacterial cells which proved crucial in the advancement of genetic engineering. His *Endurance of Life* (1978) showed a profound commitment to humanitarian issues. At death, he had no need for religious consolation, writing, "In the end we die, and for most of us it is as if we never had been. To the individual, death is the same nothingness as existed before mind began to dawn in infancy."

On his tombstone is inscribed the words of Plato's tribute to Socrates: "A man who threw off ideas like sparks which caused a blaze that leapt across to the minds of others." {SWW}

Burnet, M. L. (1905—)

Burnet was a member of the American and also the British humanist associations. He edited the Ethical Union's *News and Notes*. {HNS; TRI}

Burnet, Pat (20th Century)

Burnet is associated with Humanists of Portland-Vancouver Metro Area. (See entry for Oregon Rationalists, Humanists.) {FD}

Burnet, Thomas (c. 1635—1715)

The master of the Charterhouse, Burnet after the Revolution was appointed chaplain and clerk of the closet to the king. In 1692 he published *Archaeologiae Philosophicae*, and the cry of heresy led to the loss of his position at court. In posthumous works, he rejected Christian teaching so extensively that he was probably a deist. {RAT}

Burnett, Greg (20th Century)

Burnet is a writer for *Atheist Network Journal*, which is edited by Victor King.

Burnett, James (1714—1799)

Burnett, Lord Monboddo, was a learned Scottish writer and judge. His work on the *Origin and Progress of Language* (1773—1792) studied man as one of the animals, which resulted in some derision at that time, particularly because he held that the orangutan was allied to the human species. He also collected facts about savage tribes in order to throw light on civilization. Burnett discussed philosophy with Hume, Adam Smith, Robertson, and Lord Kames. {BDF; RAT; RE}

Burnett, John (1729—1784)

Burnett was a philanthropist who spent large sums in charities. "He gave up attending public worship lest he should be committed to the creed of a Church," stated the *Dictionary of National Biography*. Burnett was a deist. {RAT}

Burnham, J. H. (19th Century)

Putnam cites Burnham as one of the ablest lecturers and writers in the freethought field. Once a Methodist, Burnham resigned and moved to Saginaw, Michigan, where he devoted himself to the pioneer work of Liberalism. {PUT}

Burnouf, Émile Louis (Born 1821)

Burnouf was a French writer who became professor of ancient literature to the faculty of Nancy. He translated selections from the *Novum Organum* of Bacon and the Bhagavad-Gita. His heresy is pronounced in his work on the *Science of Religions* (1878), in his *Contemporary Catholicism*, and *Life of Thought* (1866). {BDF; RAT}

Burnouf, Eugène (1801—1852)

Burnouf, a French Orientalist and cousin of Émile, opened up the Pali language to the Western world. He maintained that the treasures of Buddhism were essentially atheistic. Burnouf translated numerous Oriental works, which provided much original information about Zend, the Avesta, and Zoroastrians. He wrote *Introduction to the History of Indian Buddhism*. {BDF; RAT}

Burns, Cecil Delisle (20th Century)

Burns in 1918 was appointed a lecturer at South Place Ethical Society. In 1934, he wrote *A New Faith for a New Age*. {FUK}

Burns, Douglas (20th Century)

Burns wrote *Buddhism, Science, and Atheism* (1965). {FUS}

Burns, Gene (20th Century)

Burns, a radio-talk-show host in the Boston area, is a non-theist. {E}

Burns, Gene (20th Century)

Burns, a Bay Area radio talk show host, on several occasions has told his California listeners that he is an agnostic. {CA}

Burns, H. G. (20th Century)

Burns was a member in the 1940s of the Los Angeles Scientific Humanist Group. {HNS2}

Burns, John (1858—1943)

Burns, a statesman, in his youth fell under the influence of Paine and Robert Owen and joined the Secularists. He became a Labour leader and was president of the Local Government Board (1905—1914) and of the Board of Trade (1914), resigning as a protest against the declaration of war. Stead described him as an agnostic and "an austere moralist who neither drinks nor smokes nor bets nor swears." {RAT; RE}

Burns, Robert (1759—1796)

Burns, the Scottish poet and songwriter loved by many throughout the world, including Robert Ingersoll, showed in his letters that he was substantially a deist, shading into a Unitarian. His "A Prayer in the Prospect of Death" and "A Prayer Under the Pressure of Violent Anguish" are unevangelical. His freethought is evident from such productions as the "Holy Fair," "The Kirk's Alarm," and "Holy Willie's Prayer." His allusions to Jesus in letters to Mrs. Maclehose, who wanted him to confess, exclude orthodox belief. If he mentions God, it is of a benevolent creator. "Still I am a very sincere believer in the Bible; but I am drawn by the conviction of a man, not the halter of an ass," he wrote in a letter to Mrs. Dunlop. "Though I have no objection to what the Christian system tells us of another world, yet I own I am partial to those proofs and ideas of it which we have wrought out of our own heads and hearts," he added. He is known as a satirist and mitigator of the crudities and barbarities of Scottish Presbyterianism, and although many thought of him as an "infidel," states Robertson, he actually "was either a deist or a Unitarian—presumably the former." What was clear was that he mocked Calvinism, which "sends one to heaven and ten to hell." Maurice Lindsay, in *The Burns Encyclopedia* (1970), wrote that "The only fair conclusion to be reached from studying all Burns's references to religion is surely that his position lay somewhere between these two extremes: that he was, in fact, as C.E.M. Joad once described himself, 'a wistful agnostic.'" In his own words, Burns once wrote,

> God knows I'm no the thing I should be.
> Nor am I even the thing I could be.
> But, twenty times, I rather would be

An atheist clean,
Than under gospel colors hid be.
Just for a screen.

McCabe also cites these lines as showing he had advanced little beyond agnosticism:

O Thou Great Being! what thou art
Surpasses me to know.

In March 1788, Burns in a letter wrote the following: "An honest man has nothing to fear. If we lie down in the grave, the whole man a piece of broken machinery, to moulder with the clods of the valley—be it so! At least there is an end to the pain and care, woes and wants. If that part of us called mind does survive the apparent destruction of the man,—away with old wives' tales! Every age and every nation has a different set of stories; and, as the many are always weak, as a consequence they have often, perhaps always, been deceived. A man conscious of having acted an honest part among his fellow creatures, even granted that he may have been the sport at times of passions and instincts, goes to a great unknown Being who could have no other end in giving him existence but to make him happy; who gave him these passions and instincts and knows their force. It becomes a man to think for himself particularly in a case where all men are equally interested and where, indeed, all men are equally in the ark. Religious nonsense is the most non-sensical nonsense. Why has a religious turn of mind always a tendency to harden the heart? All my fears are for this world!" {BDF; CE; JM; JMR; JMRH; PUT; RAT; RE; U; UU}

Burns, Robert E. (20th Century)

An Australian humanist, Burns is author of *The Wrath of Allah* (1995). He exposes, according to Nicolas Walter, "the bad side of a religion which is little known to outsiders but is claimed to be good by outsiders as well as insiders. After a brief introduction, there are chapters on the Koran, Muhammad, the Hadith (traditional sayings by and about Muhammad), some of the most unpleasant Muslim individuals and actions from the 7th to the 20th century, the treatment of women, the good side of Islam, and so on."

Although finding the work one-sided to the point that "one almost feels sorry for the Muslims," Walter commends it for its useful information. {*New Humanist*, August 1995}

Burr, Aaron [Vice President] (1756—1836)

Burr, who served in the American Revolution, was a United States senator from New York (1791—1797) and was Thomas Jefferson's Vice President. Because of his and Alexander Hamilton's political hostility, for Hamilton had aided Jefferson and later contributed to Burr's defeat in his race to be Governor of New York, he challenged Hamilton to a duel. Hamilton was mortally wounded (1804) and became the first of two of the Founding Fathers to die in a duel (the other being Button Gwinnett [1735—1777], a signer of the Declaration of Independence from Georgia). The duel ended Burr's political career. In 1807, Burr was tried for treason but was found not guilty of plotting with General James Wilkinson to colonize the Southwest.

Biographers Herbert S. Parmet and Marie B. Hecht tell of Dr. P. J. Van Pelt's attempts to convert Burr to Christianity toward the end of his life. Burr, who had dealt with other well-meaning clergymen, would not be intimidated. But Van Pelt was insistent, staying with Burr through the night on what doctors agreed would probably be the end. In the morning, Van Pelt again asked Burr if he was ready to accept salvation. "On that subject I am coy," were Burr's final words, for he fell asleep and died that afternoon.

Burr is buried at the Princeton Cemetery in Princeton, New Jersey, the epitaph reading, "A Colonel in the Army of the Revolution. Vice-President of the United States, from 1801 to 1805." {CE; PA}

Burr, William Henry (Born 1819)

Burr is author of *Self-Contradictions of the Bible*, which was compiled in 1859 and is a freethought classic. He also is the anonymous author of *Revelations of Antichrist*, a learned book which exposed the obscurity of the origin of Christianity and seeks to show that the historical Jesus lived almost a century before the Christian era. One of the official corps of photographers for the House of Representatives in Washington, D.C., from 1865 to 1869, he voluntarily resigned to devote himself to literary pursuits. Although a spiritualist, Burr was "a thorough radical on religious questions," according to Putnam. {BDF; FUS; PUT}

Burrell, Sidney A. (20th Century)

Burrell wrote *The Role of Religion in Modern European History* (1966).

Burroughs, John (1827—1921)

Burroughs, the naturalist, was both a nature-lover and a non-supernaturalist in his outlook. His *Walt Whitman, Poet and Person* (1867) was the first to give adequate recognition to the genius of his poet friend, for he found Whitman's "genteel poverty appealing, his obscurity noble." Burroughs's interest in philosophy is shown in *Time and Change* (1912), *The Summit of the Years* (1913), *The Breath of Life* (1915), and *Accepting the Universe* (1922). A friend of John Muir, Edison, Ford, and other important men of his day, Burroughs wrote a biography entitled *My Boyhood* (1922). When he described automobiles as despoilers of nature, Henry Ford tempted him with a gift of a new Model T Ford, which led to photos of Burroughs touring the countryside by car and entertaining the Fords at his writing retreat, Slabsides, near the Hudson River. As pointed out by biographer Edward J. Renehan Jr., Burroughs was raised as the seventh of ten children by a devoutly religious mother and a boorish and bigoted but equally religious father, but Burroughs considered religion "hocus pocus." He observed, "The atmosphere of our time is fast becoming cleared of the fumes and deadly gases that arose during the carboniferous age of theology."

Among his comments on religion, found in his diary and in *The Light of Day* (1900), are the following:

- Science has done more for the development of Western civilization in 100 years than Christianity did in 1,800 years.
- The deeper our insight into the methods of nature . . . the more incredible the popular Christianity seems to us.
- When I look up at the starry heavens at night and reflect upon what is it that I really see there, I am constrained to say, "There is no God." . . . It is not the works of some God that I see there. . . . I see no lineaments of personality, no human traits, but an energy upon whose currents, solar systems are bubbles.
- The Christianity you believe in is a whining, simpering, sentimental religion.
- Joy in the universe, and keen curiosity about it all—that has been my religion.

McCabe, calling him an atheist, said Burroughs expressly rejected the belief in God and immortality and referred to "the God we have made for ourselves out of our dreams and fears and aspirations."

Burroughs was a member of the American Academy of Arts and Letters. (See entry for hocus pocus.) {CE; CL; JM; RAT; RE; TSV; TYD}

Burroughs, William S(eward) (1914—1997)

Burroughs, known internationally as a scatological writer and one with a dim view of humanity, was the grandson of the man behind the famed Burroughs adding machine. He attended private schools, earned a degree in English at Harvard, and like his wealthy grandfather was against any form of collectivism. His mother was daughter of a Methodist minister, and she called *Naked Lunch* "that wretched book." He originally had intended to call the work *Naked Lust*, but Allen Ginsberg misread his handwriting and the wrong title stuck.

Burroughs has been termed "arguably the most influential American prose writer" of the period from the mid-1950s to the mid-1990s, this because his style influenced Thomas Pynchon and other writers. Avant-garde painters, musicians, and filmmakers were influenced by his utilization of what previously had been impermissible ideas. Like others in the group called "the beat generation," Burroughs, using down-and-out "street" language and experience, wrote with an emphasis on an escape from the conventional, the puritanical, the "square." Instead, his interest was in the visionary, in the celebration of a human drive powered by drugs, sex, wheels, drink, conversation. "If you're dealing with a religious son-of-a-bitch," Burroughs once advised, "*get it in writing*. He's got the Lord telling him how to fuck you on the deal."

In *Junkie* (1953), he wrote in stomach-wrenching fashion of his drug addiction. *Naked Lunch* (1959) experimented with collage technique, a novel using "cut-up" collation and surrealistic descriptions of his fifteen-year addiction to drugs:

> I awoke from The Sickness at the age of forty-five, calm and sane, and in reasonably good health except for a weakened liver and the look of borrowed flesh common to all who survive The Sickness. . . . I have no precise memory of writing the notes which have now been published under the title *Naked Lunch*. The title was suggested by Jack Kerouac. I did not understand what the title meant until my recent recovery. The title means exactly what the words say: NAKED Lunch—a frozen moment when everyone sees what is on the end of every fork. The Sickness is drug addiction and I was an addict for fifteen years.

David Cronenberg's film in 1991, reported *The Economist* (9 August 1997), "disgusts even Trainspotting-hardened audiences with typewriters that metamorphose into talking bumholes and cockroaches that emerge from every sort of human emission and excretion." *Nova Express* (1964) and *The Wild Boys* (1971) describe his obsession with the underworld and homosexual fantasy.

My Education: A Book of Dreams (1995), finished when he was eighty, describes his life: "Survival is the name of the game. It's all a film run backward." That included a 1951 scene of pathos in Mexico, in which in real life he had said to Joan Vollmer, his common-law wife, "It's time for our William Tell act." She had giggled, put a shot glass on her head, and watched him fire his Star .380 automatic at her. He missed the shot glass, entering her brain through her forehead and blowing her head off. The Mexican authorities arrested him on the spot and sentenced him to thirteen days for "criminal imprudence." The shock is not only in his receiving such a sentence but also in his never revealing for sure if he knew what he was doing and in reading such of his statements as "anything in the past as far as I'm concerned is of no importance."

If killing his common-law wife bothered him for the rest of his life, he could at least point to having done the good deed of marrying Ilse Klapper, a German Jew running from the Nazis, and allowing her to emigrate to the United States. His son Billy, however, never accepted a father who lived with young boyfriends in Tangier, guys who tried to seduce him also. He died at the age of thirty-three from cirrhosis of the liver, having become a heavy user of drugs and alcohol.

Burroughs had undergone triple bypass surgery in 1991 and had quit smoking after the operation. He had, however, suffered from a leaky heart valve and eventually died of a heart attack. The last entry in his journal, written the day before he died: "Love? What is it? Most natural pain-killer. What there is. LOVE."

He was survived by his companion and manager, James Grauerholz, who was with him at the Lawrence, Kansas, hospital in which he had died.

Burroughs was said to have had no interest in organized religion, preferring Zen-like observations such as "It always makes me nervous to see a cat on a ledge. . . . Suppose a bird flew by?" However, in an interview reported by David Ulin in *Village Voice* (12 August 1997), Burroughs in the year before his death said he was frightened at the prospect of dying because "we don't know it. We can't." At the same time, he took a philosophical view of mortality. "I believe in God," he told Ulin, "and always have. I don't know how anyone could read my books and think otherwise. In the magical universe, nothing happens unless some power or something wills it to happen. It's as simple as that. It comes down to the Big Bang Theory. Somebody triggered the Big Bang." (See entry for Beat Generation.) {CE; GL; OEL}

Burrows, Herbert (1845—1922)

Burrows, who with J. A. Hobson and J. M. Robertson followed Moncure Conway as one of a panel of three lecturers at South Place Ethical Society, was an independent thinker. Edward Royle, in his research on Annie Besant, states that Burrows helped guide her toward theosophy. {EU, Edward Royle; FUK; TRI}

Burt, Thomas (1837—1922)

Burt was a statesman, the son of a miner and a person who had only two years of schooling before becoming Parliamentary Secretary to the Board of Trade (1892—1895). A friend and supporter of Bradlaugh, Burt at the funeral of H. Boyle in 1907 did not conceal his own skepticism about any future life: "We have but faith; we cannot know," he quoted Tennyson, adding, "and some of us have little enough faith." {RAT; RE}

Burton, John Hill (1809—1881)

Burton was a historian who, in conjunction with Sir J. Bowring, edited Bentham's works. In 1843 he published *Benthamiana*. Burton's chief work is a *History of Scotland*. He was a practical utilitarian who, in 1854, became secretary to the Prisons Board. {RAT}

Burton, Richard Francis [Sir] (1821—1890)

Burton was the son of Joseph Burton, a military man who refused to testify against Queen Caroline for her allegedly scandalous behavior in Italy and therefore left England, taking his family abroad. Young Burton, who grew up in France and Italy and missed out on an English public-school education, was recognizably a genius who at the age of fourteen could beat four opponents simultaneously. He had lost his virginity in Italy at the age of thirteen. While at Trinity College Oxford for five terms, he was sent down for attending a steeplechase against school regulations, whereupon he reacted by riding a tandem-driven dogcart through his college master's flower garden. For much of his remaining life he was accused of being a snob, but his hauteur was more often turned on superiors, not inferiors.

Joseph Epstein, commenting upon Mary S. Lovell's *A Rage to Live: A Biography of Richard and Isabel Burton* (*The New Yorker*, 23 November 1998), cited Burton's accomplishments:

> He knew some twenty-nine foreign languages and at least a dozen dialects, and at one point tried to learn the language of monkeys. He was the first non-Muslim to make a successful pilgrimage to Mecca posing as one of the faithful, and the first to penetrate the ancient kingdom of Harar, in Somalia. He was the first Westerner to discover Lake Tanganyika, in an attempt to find the source of the Nile. He served as a spy in peacetime India and as an officer in the Crimean War. He prospected for gold in Egypt, West Africa, and Brazil. He wrote what is thought to be the best book on sword fighting of the nineteenth century. He introduced the word "safari" into the English language and is said to have introduced Turkish delight [a candy consisting of jellylike cubes] to Europe. He was one of the earliest translators of the "Kama Sutra" and of the "Arabian Nights," and he also wrote poems in the manner of the classics of Arabic literature.

"Explorer, anthropologist, linguist, erotologist, universal genius—[he] could easily have turned up as a character in a Joseph Conrad novel," Epstein adds. While serving in India, bored with the way of life of the English in India, Burton regularly took Army examinations in Hindustani, Gujarati, and Persian, invariably finishing first among his competitors. Some called him "a white nigger," for he had several Indian mistresses who, likely, gave him a feeling for "the syntaxes of native Life" needed to help in translating the *Kama Sutra*. A master of disguise, he had himself circumcised in his early thirties in order to pass as a Muslim—during an 1853 pilgrimage to Medina and Mecca, he became the first European infidel to enter Mecca as "one of the people." His *Pilgrimage to El-Medinah and Meccah* became one of the best books on Arabia.

Lovell speculates that in Africa Burton contracted syphilis, perhaps a cause for his and his wife's having no children. When Isabel Arundell, daughter of an aristocratic Catholic family, met Burton in 1851, she was sure he was to be her life companion despite her parents' objections. A believer in magic and prophecy, she was told by a Gypsy whose named happened to be Burton that "[y]ou will be as we are, but far greater than we are. Your life is all wandering, change, and adventure. One soul in two bodies in life or death, never long apart." She was crazily superstitious, believing that Richard could call to her from afar, felt she was both psychic and clairvoyant, and reveled in dreams and omens.

A faithful and dutiful wife, Isabel was said to be fearless and idealistic, a defender of her husband against all negative criticism, one who guided his finances. She overlooked his heretical opinions, which included the view that African missionaries "did more harm than good" and that polygamy is not immoral. She was aware that he did research into male brothels in India. She gladly showed Bedouins that English women can be experts at riding horses, and she enjoyed in Damascus keeping a pet panther cub. When Burton translated the *Kama Sutra* and made an unexpurgated translation of *Arabian Nights* (16 volumes, 1885-1888), she was aware that gossips would wonder if he used their conjugal bed to test the Eastern configurations.

The freethinking Joseph McCabe met her in his clerical days and said she was a bigoted Catholic. Foote agreed, stating that according to her story, Burton had his own fits of Catholicism, outspoken agnosticism and Eastern mysticism, but consistently maintained that in religion "there were only two points, Agnosticism and Catholicism."

Four days before he died, Mrs. Burton alleged, he "wrote a declaration that he wished to die a Catholic, but a few weeks previously upset her by 'an unusual burst of agnostic talk at tea.'" She had the extreme unction of the Catholic Church administered to him, but everybody in the house and every member of Burton's staff except the maid was surprised at her sending for the priest. Burton was actually dead when these "last comforts" of the Church were administered—Lady Burton afterwards fully admitted this. Nevertheless "he had three Church services performed over him, and 1,100 masses said for the repose of his soul," according to Thomas Wright's *Life of Sir Richard Burton.*

Meanwhile, Mrs. Lynn Linton referred to Burton as a "frank agnostic," who "had systematically preached a doctrine so adverse" to Christianity. She alleged that his memory was dishonored by his wife's demeanor at the time of his death. Lady Burton was said to have resented this charge with considerable indignation, but her own statements in *The New Review* (November, 1892) confirm such. Also, "Sir Richard was a very good friend of mine," wrote Rev. H. R. Hawes, "and one whom I held in high esteem. Sir Richard once said, 'I know nothing about my soul, I get on very well without one. It is rather hard to inflict a soul on me in the decline of my life.' "

Burton's niece, Georgina M. Stisted, wrote of the scene,

> The shock of so fatal a terminus to his illness would have daunted most Romanists desirous of effecting a death-bed conversion. It did not daunt Isabel. No sooner did she perceive that her husband's life was in danger, than she sent messengers in every direction for a priest. Mercifully, even the first to arrive, a man of peasant extraction, who had been appointed to the parish, came too late to molest one then far beyond the reach of human folly and superstition.

Burton's *Selected Papers on Anthropology* contains further sarcastic references to Holy Week in Rome and its theatricals, to "the horde of harpies" that prey on visitors, the contrast between the richly decorated churches, and the crowd of beggars imploring alms "in God's name," and to the brisk trade in "holy things—images, crucifixes and rosaries, blessed by his Holiness."

Burton's niece Georgiana Stisted in *The True Life of Sir R. F. Burton* called him "a sturdy Deist" but said he believed only in "an unknowable and Impersonal God." This, said McCabe, made Burton a Spencerian Agnostic.

Isabel designed for him a stone mausoleum in the shape of a desert tent, considered by many to be a notable monstrosity of Victorian taste, complete with camel bells to tinkle in the wind. She later arranged to be interred in the mausoleum, placed lower than her husband. {BDF; CE; Joseph Epstein, *The New Yorker,* 23 November 1998; FO; JM; RAT; RE; TYD}

Burton, Robert (1577—1640)

"One religion is as true as another," Burton, an English clergyman wrote in *The Anatomy of Melancholy* (1621). {TYD}

Burtt, Edwin Arthur (1892—1983)

A philosopher, Burtt during the 1950s was on the advisory board of Charles Francis Potter's First Humanist Society of New York. He was a signer of Humanist Manifesto I and wrote for *The Humanist.* Writing of Jesus, Burtt mentions that Jesus's theory of the world is supernatural and "is squarely opposed to the scientific naturalism that a frank assessment of experience increasingly compels modern men to accept." Jesus, he finds, had "no appreciation of the value of intelligence as the most dependable human faculty for analyzing the perplexities into which men fall and for providing wise guidance in dealing with them. . . . Jesus took entirely for granted and without criticism the economic structure prevalent in his day, with its assumption of an absolute right on the part of employers to make such profits as they are able and to treat their workmen according to whatever whim may seize them. Those who work but an hour in the evening may be rightfully paid the same wage as those who have toiled through the long heat of the day, if the employer so will. In fact, God's relations with men are often compared with those of a haughty and capricious employer with his workmen; he is master of body and soul, and may properly do with them, in time and eternity, whatever it may please him to do. He is subject to no standard of right beyond his own arbitrary will. (*Mark* 12: 14-17; *Matthew* 20: 1-16.) Of course, Jesus believed that God is kindly disposed toward those men who turn to him in sincere repentance."

His considerable influence upon the early humanist movement has been described by Edwin H. Wilson in *The Genesis of a Humanist Manifesto* (1995). Bragg commented in 1933 about one draft,

> It seems to me that a natural reading of this statement would assume that it commits itself to a particular theory of naturalism, excluding all other naturalisms such as the Aristotelian, which would allow a certain metaphysical reality to teleological relations, irreducible to casual connections of the material and genetic types. It would assume that the humanism denies the reality and religious value of all entities transcending human experiences, whereas, if I have read my humanist friends correctly, all that they mean to insist upon as essential is that if such entities are accepted their meaning and value for us may be constructed in terms derived solely from human experience. It would assume that humanism denies the legitimacy of carrying over terms (such as God) from the older religious framework, whereas all that is needful to insist upon is that if these terms are carried over they must be fully and honestly reinterpreted in terms consistent with scientific truth and shareable human values.

Burtt, of Cornell University's Sage School of Philosophy, wrote *Types of Religious Philosophy* (1939). He placed religious humanism in a broad setting, comparing Bertrand Russell's humanism with that of Roy Wood Sellars's in *The Next Step in Religion.*

According to Wilson, Burtt contrasted Sellars's realistic humanism with pragmatic humanism. {CL; EW; FUS; HM1}

Butler, Adam (20th Century)

Butler is director of the Birmingham, Alabama, Freethought Society and is a member of the Executive Council of the Campus Freethought Alliance.

Butler, William (1929-)

Butler, the author of a book for juveniles, *The Butterfly Revolution* (1961), has a "dislike of the Bible and belief in atheism," according to *Banned Books* (1998).

A production and program director for Pacifica Radio stations, Butler has been a lecturer in literature at Bennington College and also at Kita-Kyushu University in Fukuoka, Japan. He wrote *The Bone House* (1972) and *A God Novel* (1969), the latter of which is about a young boy who takes a golden crown from a statue of the Virgin Mary. It is a story of the boy's "spiritual quest" in which an Indian mystic appears, suggests that mankind is part of a divine chaos, and leads the boy to feel a communion with all gods, including Poseidon. (See entry for Banned Books.)

Bury, J(ohn) B(agnell) (1861—1927)

Bury is cited by Robertson for his authoritative *A History of Freedom of Thought* (1913). That work contained the following:

> If the history of civilisation has any lesson to teach it is this: there is one supreme condition of mental and moral progress which it is completely within the power of man himself to secure, and that is perfect liberty of thought and discussion. The establishment of this liberty may be considered the most valuable achievement of modern civilisation and as a condition of social progress it should be deemed fundamental.

An Irish historian and writer about the Ancient Greeks and the East Roman Empire, Bury is himself an example of a person devoted to the freedom of thought and "championship of the law of liberty." McCabe writes that Bury never concealed his Agnostic opinions and was openly associated with the Rationalist Press Association. He did much service to freethinkers, wrote McCabe, for his history.

When McCabe wrote his *Biographical Dictionary of Modern Rationalists*, McCabe said Bury "was generous enough to write me that I was the only man who could have done it." Bury became an honorary associate of the Rationalist Press Association, and his rationalism is voiced in the preface to *The Idea of Progress* (1920). {CE; FUK; JM; JMR; RAT; RE; TRI}

Buschman, Harold (20th Century)

Buschman, who taught at the University of Kansas City, became editor of *The New Humanist* in 1929, having been with the journal from its start. A student of A. Eustace Haydon, he determined to publish young writers of promise, and he chose such writers as Edwin E. Aubrey, Theodore Brameld, Hadley S. Dimock, A. E. Haydon, Walter Horton, Frank H. Knight, Douglas Clyde MacIntosh, Wilhelm Pauk, Werner Petersman, Roy Wood Sellars, Matthew Spinka, and Henry Nelson Wieman, some of whom were theists.

In the 1950s, Buschman wrote book reviews for *The Humanist*. (See entry for American Humanist Association.) {EW}

Bush, Malcolm (20th Century)

Bush, vice-president of Voices for Illinois Children, wrote *Families in Distress: Public, Private, and Civil Responses* (1988). He has written that Jane Addams "was the original secular humanist, rejecting Christianity and socialism alike as formal beliefs though she took inspiration from both." {*Free Inquiry*, Fall, 1993}

Bushman, Charles Henry (20th Century)

As his 1963 M.A. thesis at Long Beach State College, California, Bushman wrote "The Ethos of Robert Green Ingersoll." {FUS}

Busiek, Kurt (20th Century)

A comic book writer, Busiek wrote *Astro City*, *Thunderbolts*, and *Ninjak*. Asked on the Internet about his religious views, he said,

> I'm an agnostic, to the extent that I think about it at all. I consider religions interesting, and the idea of a higher being or beings within the realm of possibility, but I haven't heard or seen anything yet that would make me a believer. However, I don't require my characters to share my approach to these things—as is doubtless pretty obvious. {CA}

Butler, Adam (1978—)

In Alabama, Butler established a freethought student club which was organized to counter high school bible clubs. In 1996 the recent graduate from high school was given a "Freethinker of the Year" award by the Freedom From Religion Foundation, Inc. He is one of the founding members of Campus Freethought Alliance. In 1998 he signed the Alliance's "Bill of Rights for Unbelievers." {*Freethought Today*, October 1996 and May 1998; *International Humanist News*, December 1996}

Butler, Grant (20th Century)

Butler, a minister of the Unitarian Church of the Larger Fellowship, reviewed books for *The Humanist* in the 1950s.

Butler, James (20th Century)

A freethinker, Butler wrote in the 1910s about the state of religious liberalism and conservatism. {GS}

Butler, M. B. (19th Century)

Butler, a freethinker, wrote *I Believe and I Think* in the 1800s. {GS}

Butler, Samuel (1612—1680)

Butler, an English poet, was a clerk to Sir Samuel Luke, one of Cromwell's generals, whom he satirized as Hudibras. Butler expressed the opinion, "Religion is the interest of churches / That sell in other worlds in this to purchase."

In *Hudibras* (1663), Butler wrote, "So 'ere the storm of war broke out, religion spawn'd a various rout/Of petulant capricious sects, the maggots of corrupted texts." {BDF; RAT; TYD}

Butler, Samuel (1835—1902)

Butler satirized English social and economic injustices in *Erewhon* (1872, "Nowhere" spelled backwards, a mock utopian novel). "Christ was crucified once," he has written, "and for a few hours. Think of the thousands he has been crucifying in a quiet way ever since."

His *Way of All Flesh* (1902) described the importance of shedding the religion in which one unthinkingly has been brought up. The novel included, " 'Tis better to have loved and lost than never to have lost at all," a paraphrase of Alfred Lord Tennyson's lament upon the death of his beloved friend, Arthur Hallam, " 'Tis better to have loved and lost, than never to have loved at all." In a spoof of Alexander Pope's remark that "An honest man's the noblest work of God," Butler wrote, "An honest God's the noblest work of man."

Butler's interest in homoerotic male friendships is found not only in the religious characters of Ernest Pontifex, Towneley, Pryor, and Overtson in *The Way of All Flesh* but also in his own close friends.

In 1861 Butler met Charles Paine Pauli in New Zealand and supported him financially for the next thirty years. Upon Pauli's death, Butler was shocked to learn that Pauli had been supported by two other men, had amassed a fortune, and had omitted any mention of Butler in his will. Another friend, the Swiss Hans Faesch, died young and Butler wrote an emotional poem about him as well as wore a lock of Faesch's hair in a pendant.

His *Shakespeare's Sonnets Reconsidered* (1899) argued that the playwright had a young male lover who betrayed him much as Pauli had betrayed Butler.

Although Butler's work was popular, he pleased few in philosophy because he was anti-Christian but also bitterly anti-Darwinian. Butler did not believe in a personal God, yet he maintained that there was mind and purpose in the universe. George Bernard Shaw was his one disciple, but the progress of evolutionary science since their time has made their criticisms "hopelessly outdated," McCabe observes.

After a prolonged illness, Butler died while being attended by his devoted manservant, Alfred Catie, and his companion-biographer, Henry Festing Jones. {BDF; CE; GL; JM; RAT; RE; TRI; TYD}

Butterfield, Rufus (Born 1817)

A Californian pioneer, Butterfield was raised a Methodist but discarded all orthodoxy when young. In 1849 Butterfield went to California, where he became a vice president of the California Liberal Union and an outspoken freethinker. {PUT}

BUTTERFLY EFFECT

All things are connected, say those who describe the "butterfly effect," that for example the flutter of a wing in the Amazon rain forest can allegedly set off a storm in California.

Butterworth, Edward J. (20th Century)

Freethinking researchers sometimes quote Butterworth's *The Identity of Anselm's Proslogion for the Existence of God with the Via Quarta of Thomas Aquinas* (1990).

Buttmann, Philipp Karl (1764—1829)

A German philologist, Buttmann was librarian of the Royal Library at Berlin. He wrote *Myth of the Deluge* (1819) and in 1828 a learned work on mythology. {BDF}

Butts, R. Freeman (1910—)

Butts in 1950 wrote *The American Tradition in Religion and Education*, which includes references to freethought. {FUS}

Buzot, François Léonard Nicolas (1760—1793)

Buzot was a French Girondin, a lover of Madame Roland. He died from starvation when hiding after the suppression of his party in 1793. {BDF}

Byelinsky, Vissarion Grigoryevitch (also Belinski) (1811—1848)

An eminent literary critic, arguably Russia's best, Byelinsky was an original thinker who contributed greatly to the Russian revolutionary movement. At Moscow when he joined Herzen and Bakunin, he was expelled for attacking serfdom (1832). In 1834 he began to write his *Literary Reveries*, still a highly respected work for its critiques.

Byelinski regretted that he could not write his true beliefs, which were not published until after 1917, because critical ideas that he espoused were forbidden at that time. However, to Gogol he wrote,

> A man like Voltaire who stamped out the fires of fanaticism and ignorance in Europe by ridicule is, of course, more the son of Christ, flesh of His flesh and bone of His bone, than all your priests, bishops, metropolitans, and patriarchs, Eastern or Western.

The letter later became a quasi-sacred text of the Russian left. For reading such material Dostoevski was arrested and, originally, sentenced to death.

As for the Russian people's being "the most religious in the world," he replied in 1847, "That is a lie. . . . They have too much healthy common sense." Byelinski, who is said to have adopted the pantheistic philosophy of Hegel and Schelling, was influenced to atheism by Feuerbach.

Byelinski died, a comparatively young man, of consumption. According to Alexei Gostev, since Byelinski's time literary criticism in Russia became a criticism of authorities and a substitution of open political discussion inasmuch as such discussions then were forbidden. When, after his death, the chief of the secret police, Baron Dubelt, read the above cited letter to Gogol, he responded, "It is a pity that he died. We would have left him to rot in jail." {BDF; CE; EU, Hugh McLean; RAT; WAS, conversations with Alexei Gosteve, 1998}

Bynner, Witter (1881—1968)

Bynner was a poet who wrote *Journey With Genius: Recollections and Reflections Concerning the D. H. Lawrences* (1951). With Arthur Davis Ficke (under the pseudonyms of Emanyek Morgan and Anne Knish), he wrote *Spectra* (a hilarious hoax in 1916 that parodied free verse).

On the subject of humanism, he wrote the present author:

> I am almost as hesitant about subscribing to the tenets of any humanistic group as I should be toward the tenets of any deist group. All in all, I am definitely on the side of the humanists in that I feel mankind and its troubles and attainments to be itself a process of deity-experiencing both the pains and the beauty of growth.
>
> I am certainly not persuaded that there is an all-wise, all-good, and all-powerful deity running the show. . . . Nursery games—or actually harmful indulgences—are what most adult religious doctrines and practices seem to me now. In Christianity especially—or what it has come to be–I can only feel the individual's shelving of responsibility and acceptance of a god's sacrifice to be even more sadistic and morbid than the succession of sacrifices in earlier religions. And to brand procreation of life as the original sin is certainly to blame not man but God as the original sinner, the first procreator; while certainly the doctrine of virgin birth is as morbid as anything in history.
>
> But I devote too much space to only one of the mythologies–in making my point that man should be rid of them all except as more or less interesting fiction. China's is the only great culture which has had resurrection. Immediate aspects of its return are deplorable; but I believe that, still strong behind them, the humanistic foundation of China's life survives, as recorded in the teachings of Confucius and still better in the sayings of Lao-tzu.
>
> By now it is clear that my stand is with and for "Naturalistic Humanism," except that I would not call it "born of the modern scientific age." Besides and after the two great Chinese I have named, I would list, as influential in forming my humanistic faith, Lucretius, Shakespeare, John Keats, George Meredith, Walt Whitman, and Bertrand Russell.

A. L. Rowse in his *Homosexuals in History* (1977) mentions that Hart Crane "did not care for the professionalism of accredited homosexual circles, rather deploring . . . a poet whom I recognize as an acquaintance of D. H. Lawrence," obviously a reference to Bynner.

Later, when Crane attempted to overcome his alcoholism and waterfront sexual escapades during which sailors would beat him up, Crane married the former wife of the alcoholic writer, Malcolm Cowley.

Bynner intuitively predicted the marriage would not work, that the two inevitably would drink and squabble, that Crane would never be able "to do any work in such a hurly-burly." As worded by Rowse, "On his way back to New York he dropped quietly into the sea, his work unfinished." What Bynner learned was that in 1932 Crane was aboard a ship and had, suddenly and without warning, jumped overboard, calling out, "Goodbye, everybody."

One of Bynner's poems was "The Reading of Books":

Till the final word may be farewell to evil and to good,
Make the Hubbard's cupboard your hermit-call,
God's beard your babyhood.
For the Bible is a Mother Goose,
when all is said and done:
So read them both and make good use of
what they tell you, son.

In the 1950s, Bynner wrote some book reviews for *The Humanist.* He also transmitted his "Credo," adding to the present author, "This Credo, mostly as it is, was set down in my twenties. In my seventies I find little reason to change it."

CREDO

Most formalized religions have been engendered in the assumption of a more or less personal God, the creator and control of life. But the latest religion is as baffled as was the earliest by the question, What and why was the Beginning of God? By assuming a God, we only place the mystery a remove away. We beg the question. Humanity, moreover, has equipped Godhead with perfection and omnipotence; and then it has accepted the basic impossibility that out of perfection and omnipotence can come the creation, in humanity at least, of imperfection, frailty, ignorance. We attempt to explain the paradox by attributing to the Godhead perfect motives beyond our comprehension; but the fact that we remain poor uncomprehending victims of witnesses of injustice and barbarity supposedly concocted in heaven for our good, the very fact that we suffer by not understanding, is an imperfection or an impotence which no such explaining can explain. So the religions impose still other paradoxes on our conception of the Godhead. They direct us, for instance, to pray to Him for defence and benefit, although such prayer infringes upon God's all-wisdom and contradicts the orthodox doctrine of our ignorance as to what is good for us. Truly faithful or logical acceptance of a perfect God would exact of human beings complete acquiescence and inaction. If Perfection stood all-powerful, what judgment or action by us would be necessary?

The western world has dramatized the difficulty by having us try to cast out imperfection as with the help of a Father. Even Christ kept, in his own personality, something of the old Hebrew authority of a father, which probably accounts in part for the Trinitarian doctrine. But Christianity has acknowledged more than it realizes of a deeper Christ when it calls its God the son of man, approaching therein an Oriental concept of the evolution of God through all life. When Jesus says that the Kingdom of God is within us, he would seem to mean that we are members not only of one another but of inherent perfection. His latest considerable group of interpreters have met the basic issue another way. Sensing the weakness of the ancient idea that evil can be co-existent with a perfect God, they have denied the existence of evil except as a human illusion. They try to bolster the perfection of God by foisting the mistake of imperfection upon us, although we are parts of God: a perfect whole with imperfect parts. They attribute "error" to the handiwork of a perfect Creator: their God, without need of making mistakes, yet errs through us. It is still the error of trying to believe in an already perfect God.

This historical conception of a personal God, of a force outside us, wholly powerful, was sure, moreover, to become for the human individual a conception of his own image given power over his fellows. It is this persistent conception which has caused and sanctioned wars and blind obedience, jealousies and woes. And of a part with the conception of fixed divine identity has been the conception of fixed human identities.

No life can be individual and separate in the sense that it can exclude other lives or can be life at all if it cease to grow and change. Only as it becomes consciously inclusive of other lives and included in them can I think that it becomes conscious of the spirit of life at large.

An individual's vanity, his wish to proceed in some later existence with the same separate personality he has had here, seems to me an obstacle of pain and untruth against the way of life. Are we strictly what we mean when we call ourselves individuals? Are we not many people inside ourselves? Do we not begin compact of many ancestors? Do we not add to these still other lives from lovers, friends, and books? If identity survive, does death conclude its bounds? Must one's separate soul continue at the age of ten, twenty, or sixty, according to the date of the body's death?Is the spirit to be moulded by the happening of death into an endless fixity?

Surely if we are to continue in consciousness, it can only be as we realize all life to be our final and very self. Experimenting, suffering, learning with God in His growth toward that perfection which is in His blood and ours, a man becomes mankind and mankind God. The meaning dawns in life, in hope, in thought, in deed. If evil come, or error, it is not as something which might be prevented by an existent omnipotence, it is not some discipline which omnipotence visits upon us in a cryptic tyranny of justice; it is as something in the growing experience of God. And by use of evil, as by use of good, it is God as well as ourselves who can lose or gain. You, no less than any man and no more, except by degree of realization, may be coexistent and coeternal with God.

Happiness consists in the consciousness and use of that existence. A hint of the sweetness of such faith, such possible consummation, is given your body through its dissolving union with the body of one whom you love. Even though the fruit of such union seem to be a furtherance of separateness, the desire of lover for lover is a desire to enclose and to be enclosed, an urge and ache for oneness. And with the separation of bodies by death may come still more strongly the realization of oneness, the penetration of peace through chance and change, the gradual integration. For

. . who shall be my enemy
When he is I and I am he?

Such rumination may, of course, be only one more happy guess; but, without the morbidity of most religions, it is a stimulus to responsible and helpful living, a human or divine faith like that of Mark Twain's child, found in her diary after her death, that there may be "a heaven or something better."

(See entry for Arthur Davis Ficke.)
{CE; CL; HNS; WAS, 11 April 1956}

Byrdall, Thomas (17th Century)

Byrdall wrote a freethought work, *A Glimpse of God* (1665). {GS}

Byrne, John (20th Century)

Byrne, a writer and comic book artist, is a non-theist. He made his views known in his column, "A Flame About This High," which appeared in his comic book, *Next Men.* {CA; E}

Byron, George Gordon Noel Byron [6th Baron] (1788—1824)

Byron had a clubfoot but swam the Bosphorus; was a baron but opposed industrialists and monopolies; was a poet but broke all the classical rules; and was philosophic but raised a storm of abuse for the skeptical attitude shown toward religion in his *Cain* (1821). Byron's clubfoot was worsened by the treatments of quack doctors, and his obese, somewhat hysterical mother habitually referred to him as her "little lame brat."

His father, Captain John ("Mad Jack") Byron drank himself to death by the time the boy was three and also managed to squander most of his wife's fortune. Further evidence of his colorful childhood: His mother once attempted to beat him to death with a pair of fire tongs, his nurse seduced him when he was nine, and he conquered his overweight by starvation diets and the consumption of laxatives. The 5' 7" Byron always walked with a limp, but he made great efforts to overcome his physical shortcomings by excelling in sports, including boxing, fencing, riding, cricket, and swimming. At Cambridge, he kept both a tame bear and a mistress whom he liked to dress as a boy.

When rumors circulated concerning an incestuous relationship between the poet and his half sister, Augusta Leigh, Byron did not deny anything, adding, "I could love anything on earth that appeared to wish it." However, he married Anne Isabella Milbanke, a highly educated mathematician who hoped she could tame "the wild lord." On their wedding night Byron told her, "It is enough for me that you are my wife for me to hate you!" When she became pregnant, he acted insanely, tormenting her by shooting off guns in her bedroom. Eventually, he acceded to her request for a separation. By this time he had become a recognized poet, known for having a coach designed after that of his hero, Napoleon, one which contained a bed, library, and complete dining and cooking facilities.

Lady Caroline Lamb once described Byron as being the most notorious of the Romantic poets because he was "mad–bad–and dangerous to know." Lord Byron's detestation of convention is epitomized in his epic-satire and acknowledged masterpiece, *Don Juan* (1819—1824). He also wrote *Childe Harold* (1812—1818) and *The Prisoner of Chillon* (1816). *Cain* (1821), which was anti-religious, was denounced from the pulpits, and was not allowed to be copyrighted (which allowed freethinkers to appropriate the work widely).

To the Rev. Francis Hodgson in 1811, Byron wrote, "I do not believe in any revealed religion. . . . I will have nothing to do with your immortality; we are miserable enough in this life, without the absurdity of speculating upon another. . . . The basis of your religion is injustice; the Son of God, the pure, the immaculate, the innocent, is sacrificed for the guilty." He added

> I am no Platonist, I am nothing at all; but I would sooner be a Paulician, Manichean, Spinozist, Gentile, Pyrrhonian, Zoroastrian, than one of the seventy-two villainous sects who are tearing each other to pieces for the love of the Lord and the hatred of each other.

When Lord Byron took his seat in parliament, he insisted upon doing so "without the oath." Like his father, Byron was not a member of the Church of England. Colin McCall, commenting upon Byron's outlook, has written that although Byron's most searching religious questioning has to do with evil, "this does not make him an atheist, like Shelley. Shelley, in fact, once mentioned that he had "not the smallest influence over Lord Byron" on the question of religion, adding "if I had I certainly would employ it to eradicate from his great mind the delusions of Christianity." As J. M. Robertson said, Byron was 'too wayward to hold a firm philosophy.' "

An estimated two hundred women, mostly of the lower class but including Caroline Lamb and his Italian mistress, Countess Teresa Guiccioli, attested to his virility (as did a large number of men, particularly nubile Mediterranean boys he hired as valets or pages; he is said to have consulted a doctor about a relaxation of his friend Nicolo Giraud's sphincter muscle, describing him as "the most beautiful being I have ever beheld"). A. L. Rowse in *Homosexuals in History* (1977) relates further tales of Byron's poetic inspirations, including the Ravenna gondolier who inspired, "Tita's heart yearns for you, and mayhap for your silver broadpieces." Byron's liaison with the seventeen-year-old stepsister of poet Shelley's wife, Mary, resulted in a daughter, Allegra. After settling in Venice, and spending five years with Countess Teresa Guiccioli, he became bored with his mistress and decided to go to Greece in order to fight for Greek liberation from the Turkish empire. He had long before identified himself with the cause of "liberalism," once using his hereditary seat in the House of Lords to deliver a celebrated attack on industrialists and monopolies.

As for religion's reliability, Byron wrote:

> Even gods must yield; religions take their turn,
> 'Twas Jove's, 'tis Mahomet's, and other creeds
> Will rise with other years, till man shall learn
> Vainly his incense soars, his victim bleeds–
> Poor child of doubt and death,
> whose hope is built on reeds.

Claude Rawson, a professor of English at Yale, has succinctly described the poet:

> Byron's life was lordly and rakish. In the family seat of Newstead Abbey, the young lord imitated the blasphemous and orgiastic practices of the Hell-Fire Club. He and his friends, wearing monkish dress, drank Burgundy from a human skull and, "after reveling on choice viands, and the finest wines of France," one of his guests wrote, proceeded with unmentionable "evening diversions" until the small hours. In addition to several renowned and high-profile heterosexual romances, as well as a string of humbler amours with maidservants and prostitutes, he had a series of homosexual attachments. Pedophilia, incest, masochism, cross-dressing (he danced in woman's dress with a Greek boy and liked his women to wear men's clothes) were part of his repertory. His most scandalous mistress, Lady Caroline Lamb, married to a future prime minister, liked to dress as a pageboy. He appears to have told her she reminded him of John Edleston, his most beloved homosexual lover, a Cambridge choirboy who had died of consumption.

Byron contracted a fatal illness, malarial fever, in Greece while helping Prince Alexander Mavrocordatos unify the divergent Greek forces. Thomas Moore's *Byron's Life and Letters* describes the final moments: "Exposure, which his declining health was unfitted to bear, brought on a fever, and the soldier-poet of freedom died without proper attendance, far from those he loved. He conversed a good deal at first with his friend Parry, who records that 'he spoke of death with great composure.' The day before he expired, when his friends and attendants wept round his bed at the thought of losing him, he looked at one of them steadily, and said, half smiling, '*Oh questa a una bella seena*!' (Oh this is a fine scene!) After a fit of delirium, he called his faithful servant Fletcher, who offered to bring pen and paper to take down his words. 'Oh no,' he replied, 'there is no time. Go to my sister–tell her–go to Lady Byron–you will see her, and say . . . .' Here his voice became indistinct. For nearly twenty minutes he muttered to himself, but only a word now and then could be distinguished. He then said, 'Now, I have told you all.' Fletcher replied that he had not understood a word. 'Not understand me?' exclaimed Byron, with a look of the utmost distress, 'what a pity!–then it is too late; all is over.' He tried to utter a few more words, but none were intelligible except 'my sister–my child.' After the doctors had given him a sleeping draught, he reiterated, 'Poor Greece!–poor town!–My poor servants! my hour is come!–I do not care for death–but why did I not go home?–There are things that make the world dear to me: for the rest I am content to die.' He spoke also of Greece, saying, 'I have given her my time, my means, my health–and now I give her my life! What could I do more?' About six o'clock in the evening he said, 'Now, I shall go to sleep.' He then fell into the slumber from which he never woke. At a quarter past six on the following day, he opened his eyes and immediately shut them again. The physicians felt his pulse–he was dead."

At the end, when bloodletting had further weakened him, Byron's face was so swollen that he was barely recognizable. Phyllis Grosskurth in *Byron* (1997) describes how part of his skull and his internal organs were removed for grisly souvenirs, and then his body was stitched back up.

Because of his allegedly scandalous personal life, Byron was not allowed burial in Westminster Abbey. For one thing, he was never forgiven for satirizing the parson whose "jokes were sermons, and his sermons jokes."

Byron was then buried in the family vault beneath Hucknall Paris Church at Hucknall Torckard, not far from Newstead. Byron's own views on the subject of death-beds had been expressed in a letter to Murray, dated June 7th, 1820. "A death-bed," he wrote, "is a matter of nerves and constitution, not of religion." He also remarked that "Men died calmly before the Christian era, and since, without Christianity."

Byron's vault was opened twice, the first time in 1852 when a velvet-draped coffin containing the body of his thirty-eight-year-old daughter Augusta Ada, by his wife Annabella, was lowered into it.

In 1938, the lid of his coffin was removed and the poet was seen again 114 years after his burial. The opening was motivated by the church vicar's desire "to clear up all doubts as to the poet's burial place and compile a record of the contents of the vault." First, the wooden lid of his lead casket was raised. Inside was another lid made of lead, and when this was raised, there was still a third lid, made of wood. When the final lid was pulled off, A. E. Houldsworth, the church warden, noted the following:

> . . . we were able to see Lord Byron's body which was in an excellent state of preservation. No decomposition had taken place and the head, torso, and limbs were quite solid. The only parts skeltonised were the forearms, hands, lower shins, ankles and feet, though his right foot was not seen in the coffin. [Houldsworth later wrote biographer Elizabeth Longford]: "His right foot was detached from his leg and lay at the bottom of the coffin."] The hair on his head, body, and limbs was intact, though grey. His sexual organ shewed quite abnormal development. There was a hole in his breast and at the back of his head, where his heart and brains had been removed. These are placed in a large urn near the coffin."

The following day, the coffin was closed, the vault sealed, and Byron was left alone.

However, Byron's heart and lungs, in another version of the story, are buried in Italy near Shelley's body (minus Shelley's heart—or liver—which Trelawny during the cremation had plucked out for return to Mary Shelley in London).

Little known until publicized in the mid-twentieth century was Byron's having fallen in love in Cephalonia during the last months of his life. He had helped a Greek widow, then had fallen in love with her fifteen-year-old son Lukas. Hiring him as a page, he bought Lukas a uniform and gave him a command of a troop of thirty soldiers. When Lukas contracted a fever, Byron doctored him and gave him his own bed. Lukas, however, irritated him by asking for money and luxuries, and one of Byron's last three poems, "On This Day I Complete My Thirty Sixth Year," speaks of his being in love with a person who does not return the affection "though it be my lot / To strongly–wrongly–vainly–love thee still."

Augusta Ada, who was born in 1815 of his ill-fated marriage to Annabella Milbanke, saw little of her father and was fifteen before she found that he was a famous poet. A mathematician like her mother, she almost bankrupted her husband by applying her mathematical techniques to racetrack betting. At the age of thirty-six, she died.

The other daughter, whose mother was Claire Clairmont who had followed Byron to Switzerland and Italy, was variously called Alba, Clara, and finally Allegra. Although never legitimized, she was supposed to have received a legacy from her father's estate. However, she died of a fever in the convent where he had installed her to "get a proper Catholic upbringing," just before her sixth birthday. (See entry for Shelley. Also, see Nancy H. Medved's and Irving Wallace's essays on Byron in *The People's Almanac,* essays which document much of the above; and Colin McCall's "Byron Raises Cain" in *The Freethinker* [March 1996) and "Byron: Enemy of English Cant," *The Freethinker,* May 1998]) {BDF; CE; CL; FO; ILP; PA; ILP; JM; RAT; Claude Rawson, *The New York Times Book Review,* 9 May 1999; RE; RSR; TYD}

Bytel, G. M. (20th Century)

Bytel, a former dancer, is a Dutch painter and designer. In 1996 she participated in the 1996 Humanist Conference in Mexico City.

CABALA

Cabala is a general name for Jewish mysticism and includes a type of occult theosophical formulation of the doctrines of Judaism. Every word, letter, number, and accent of the Scriptures is believed to contain mysteries. The principal written sources are *Sefer Yezira* (*Book of Creation*, translated in 1894 but possibly written in the 3rd century B.C.E.) and *Zohar* (partially translated in 1949), written by Moses de León in the 13th century but attributed to a 2nd-century scholar, Simon ben Yohai. When Jews were expelled from Spain in 1492, Isaac Luria developed cabala and found many adherents, including the pseudo-Messiah Sabbatai Zevi. In the 18th century, a movement founded by a reputed miracle healer, Baal-Shem-Tov and known as Hasidim, continues to influence present-day Hasidic Jews. One of the signers of Humanist Manifesto II, Joseph L. Blau, has written *The Christian Interpretation of the Cabala in the Renaissance* (1944). (See "Cabala" by Joseph L. Blau in the *Encyclopedia of Philosophy*, Vol. 2.) {CE}

Cabanis, George Paul Sylvester (Born 1859)

An artist and a poet, Cabanis wrote a humanist *Life of Christ* and other works. An admirer of Haeckel, Cabanis was a monist. {RAT}

Cabanis, Pierre Jean George (1757—1808)

Cabanis has been called "the father of the materialistic physiology." A friend of Mirabeau, whom he attended in his last illness, Cabanis also was an intimate of Turgot, Condorcet, Holbach, Diderot, and other distinguished freethinkers. His works are mostly medical, the chief being *Des Rapports du Physique et du Morale de l'Homme*. In that work Cabanis is accused of being a superficial dabbler who said that the brain secretes thought just as the liver secretes bile. As pointed out by McCabe, however, Cabannis said that "the brain is a special organ, specially designed to produce thought, just as the stomach and intestines are destined to effect digestion." When later he says that "the brain digests impressions and organically secretes thought," it is clearly a figurative way of stating the same scientific fact. Cabanis was a deist, not an atheist. He believed in the existence of an intelligent First Cause. {BDF; JM; RAT; RE}

Cabell, James Branch (1879—1958)

A Virginian author of short stories, novels, and poetry, Cabell was a freethinker with an urbane writing style as shown in his *The Soul of Melicent* (1913), revised as *Domnei* (1920). The work is the start of a series concerning the pseudo-erudite romances of Dom Manuel, set in a mythical medieval country called Poictesme. *Jurgen* (1919) concerns a poetical pawnbroker who makes a pact with the Devil to find his missing wife, and in his resultant pursuits he has erotic adventures, visits Hell where he marries a vampire, and is allowed (disguised as Pope John XX) to visit the Heaven of his grandmother, where he ascends God's throne before reverting to his previous dull married life with the wife he finally finds. The book was banned, bringing him a great amount of needed publicity, and he then turned out a large body of work. {CE; EU, William F. Ryan}

Cabet, Etienne (1788—1856)

A French Utopian socialist, Cabet was elected to the chamber of deputies in 1831. But, following his bitter attacks on the government, he exiled himself to Great Britain (1834—1839), where he developed a theory of communism influenced by Robert Owen. In his *Voyage en Icarie* (1840), Cabet depicted a society in which an elected government controlled all economic activity and supervised social affairs. A popular book, it led to the establishment of an Icarian community on the Red River in Texas. Other Icarian communities, dedicated to "Humanity" but none surviving after 1898, rose in Nauvoo, Illinois, and Corning, Iowa. Cabet died in St. Louis, Missouri. {CE}

Cable, Louis W. (20th Century)

Cable is a freethinker, author of "The Bloody Bible," in *Freethought Today* (June-July 1997). On the Web he has the Skeptics Corner, which features his writing: <http://www.inu.net/skeptic>.

Cable, Paul (20th Century)

Cable has written for *New Humanist* (September 1996) about "What's Wrong with Political Correctness?"

Cadogan, Peter (20th Century)

Cadogan in the 1970s was general secretary of the South Place Ethical in London. {FUK}

CADMUS: See entry for Egyptian Civilization.

Cadmus, Paul (1904—1999)

Cadmus, the controversial painter of "The Fleet's In!" and "The Seven Deadly Sins," became a distinguished member of the American Academy of Arts and Letters in 1974. In 1984, he was the subject for a video-recording, "Paul Cadmus, Enfant Terrible at 80." At the time, a *New York Times* reviewer noted,

> Recent interest in representational painting has fostered an appreciation of artists whose realist modes, long out of the stylistic and commercial mainstreams, are now receiving renewed attention. . . . For Mr. Cadmus, best known for his earlier, more accessible works, including the much reproduced New York street and restaurant scenes and Coney Island panoramas, also practices a dark, more personal, visionary magic realism in which black humor and distant allusions are endemic.

Cadmus and an early lover, Jared French, spent time on the island of Majorca, where he painted "Shore Leave" and "YMCA Locker Room." His circle included Christopher Isherwood, W. H. Auden, George Balanchine, George Platt Lynes, George Tooker, Lincoln Kirstein (the husband of his sister Fidelma), and E. M. Forster.

He was unsure about his ancestry: "I think my ancestors sailed from Jutland (Denmark) around 1710. My father's side may have been Dutch and, like Erasmus, Latinized the name. My mother, conceived in Spain, was born in New York. Her father was Basque, her mother Cuban. Maybe I was just a cad to begin with," he joked, "and the name was Latinized."

His parents, both artists, encouraged their son and their daughter, Fidelma, to study art, and Cadmus began with an interest in antiques. One day at the National Academy of Design in uptown Manhattan and knowing that older art students had nude models to work with, he peered through a peephole and saw a naked female. "I had never seen a stranger in the nude. It was a revelation," he told journalist Richard Goldstein. Naked men would follow. It was the start of his becoming the artist who painted the male body with more sensuality, Goldstein observed (*Village Voice*, 18 May 1999), than any American artist of the century:

> "The Fleet's In!" [is] the 1934 painting that made him an art star. In this knowing study of carousing sailors, there are not only buns and baskets on proud display but loose ladies admiring the briny trade and even a fey gentleman offering a cigarette to an eager gob. The navy was not amused. An outraged admiral had the painting removed before it could be shown at the Corcoran Gallery in Washington, D.C. A sequel, "Sailors and Floosies" (1938), featuring the angelic seaman in slumber, grasping his crotch, fared no better in San Francisco; "in the interest of national unity," it was taken off the wall.
>
> In "Shore Leave" (1933), a gay man is clearly propositioning a

willing sailor, but what one notices first is the ripe women in the foreground and a recumbent swab with his bulging crotch in full view. Sometimes the queers come out to play, as in "Fantasia on a Theme by Dr. S." (1946), which is set on Fire Island. But usually the artist's eye is drawn to what is often ignored in modern painting: a casually muscled male physique and an utterly open attitude. Looking at this pantheon of locker-room studs, seafood Sampsons, and young waifs lounging in the playground with baseball bats jammed between their legs, one sees a quality beyond the ideologically mandated worship of the working class. Call it longing.

"I was fascinated by the sailors, and I used to sit on a bench and watch them all the time," Cadmus recalls. In fact, Riverside Park around 96th Street was a prime cruising ground in the 1930s, largely because it was where the warships docked. "The uniforms were so tight and form-fitting that they were an inspiration. I was young enough to be propositioned by the sailors, who would offer to take me back to the boat, but I never went. They were too unattractive, or maybe I was too timid. I don't know."

"The male nude has been a specialty of my own oeuvre," Cadmus agreed, "when I am not being concerned with the foibles of people in daily life: men, women, and children. . . . We are made, we are told, 'in God's image,' and we assume that He was not clothed by Armani or Brooks Brothers or, if He is She, not attired by Balenciaga or Donna Karan."

In 1992, Lincoln Kirstein, the founding director of the New York City Ballet, wrote a definitive study, *Paul Cadmus*, which described his relationship with other artists and writers, including W. H. Auden. E. M. Forster, while posing for a portrait, was said to have passed the time reading aloud passages from *Maurice*. Kirstein described Cadmus's work as being "executed with the technical virtuosity and anatomical precision of the Renaissance masters that celebrate the beauty of the human body." Agreeing, Guy Davenport in an introduction for *The Drawings of Paul Cadmus* (1989) stated that "Not since Michelangelo has any artist done so many studies of the male nude." He included dozens of such examples.

Cadmus, who in 94 years completed over 120 paintings, delighted in such observations. "I do love Michelangelo's male forms," he has said, adding that "Michelangelo's women often look like males with grapefruits attached." "It seems that genitalia," Cadmus lamented about the public taste, "equal pornography." But not for him personally: "My penis is not the most important organ in my body. My eyes are."

In 1989, after a discussion about philosophy, he responded to the present author's request for his views about humanism:

> Your request should have a worthy answer but it would take me days to try to compose one (as I used to do when I first began writing to E. M. Forster). The subject is too complicated for this feeble old mind to go into deeply. The simple description of a humanist is *one who is interested in humans* (not as profound as the Oxford Universal Dictionary's definition, "a student of human affairs, or of human nature").
>
> I'm no student. I guess I somewhat fit in Naturalistic Humanism #7.

Later, in an interview at his Connecticut home, Cadmus discussed religion and his increased interest in the philosophy of naturalistic humanism. "I've always liked the story of the Albigensians," Cadmus mused, "who were besieged by the Pope at Beziers. His soldiers asked him: 'How do we know the heretics from the Christians?' The Pope replied, 'Burn them all. God will know his own.' " A devout Catholic until he was seventeen, he then "shed it all."

Cadmus is cited by Charles Kaiser in *The Gay Metropolis 1940—1996* (1997) as having painted key individuals and scenes of that period. Kaiser noted that Cadmus met Jon Andersson, 27, when he himself was 59 and "I never wanted to be with anyone else." That included the time he was invited to a long-ago party by Truman Capote. Capote's long-time companion Jack Dunphy told him he could not bring a male guest, that "Truman said he didn't want to ask 'a bunch of fags' to his party." This infuriated Andersson and was one of the few times the two did not appear together in public or private. At a book signing when Kaiser referred to Cadmus as the only artist to draw so many male nudes, the then ninety-two-year-old quipped, "Well, there was Michelangelo."

Kaiser quotes Cadmus as having been interviewed by Alfred Charles Kinsey: "He took homosexuality just as calmly as he did his work with wasps. He interviewed me about my sex life–how many orgasms, how big it was, measure it before and after." Kinsey even went to dinner at Cadmus's house following the interview.

Cadmus died five days before his 95th birthday, which he had joyously celebrated two weeks earlier with several hundred friends at the D. C. Moore Gallery in New York City. {"Men Without Women, Paul Cadmus as Curator," National Academy of Design, 1999; "The Great Impresario: Lincoln Kirstein," *The New Yorker*, 13 April 1998; WAS, 28 May 1989 and numerous conversations; Warren Allen Smith, "Paul Cadmus: Artist-Humanist," *Free Inquiry*, Summer 1996}

Cadogan, Peter (20th Century)

Cadigan, a secretary of the South Place Ethical Society in the 1970s, called his outlook "Apocalyptic Humanism."

Caesalpinus: See entry for Cesalpino, Andrea.

Caesar, (Caius) Julius (100?—44 B.C.E.)

According to Lamont, Caesar "avowed his unbelief in immortality and was contemptuous of the supernaturalist rituals and sacrifices that he carried out for the sake of political expedience." Robertson remarks that "the greatest and most intellectual man of action in the ancient world had no part in the faith which was supposed to have determined the success of the most powerful of all the ancient nations." Whereas the illiterate Marius carried about with him a Syrian prophetess, and Sulla carried a small figure of Apollo as an amulet, Caesar was a convinced freethinker who disbelieved in the popular doctrine of immortality. If he offered sacrifices to gods in whom he did not believe, he was simply following the habitual procedure of his age. Froude has written that Caesar's writings "contain nothing to indicate that he himself had any religious belief at all. He saw no evidence that the gods practically interfered in human affairs. . . . He held to the facts of this life and to his own convictions; and as he found no reason for supposing that there was a life beyond the grave he did not pretend to expect it." A memorable evaluation, penned by Alexander Pope: "Caesar, the world's great master and his own."

His detractors, however, call him a demagogue who forced his way to dictatorial power and destroyed the republic. As for his personal morality, legend has it that Caesar had an affair with the king of Bithynia. Also, Suetonius wrote

> Home we bring our old whoremonger;
> Romans lock your wives away.

{BDF; CE; CL; JMR; JMRH; TYD}

Cagadas, Roberto (20th Century)

Cagadas is a leader of the Unitarian Universalist Church of the Philippines, 065 Rovira Road, Bantayan, Dumaguete City 6200, Negros, Philippines.

Cage, John (1912—1992)

A controversial composer famous for his unorthodox musical theories and experimental compositions, Cage with a "prepared piano" used metal, rubber, wood, and other objects on a piano's strings, altering its sound. He held that all sound, including that which is nonmusical, is part of the "total soundspace." Cage's " 4' 33" " (1952) consists of 4 minutes and 33 seconds of silence along with random environmental sounds that happen to occur.

Upon arriving in New York City, he boarded with Peggy Guggenheim, enticed Virgil Thompson's coterie by his good looks and talent, divorced, slept with, among others, architect Philip Johnson, and fell in love with Merce Cunningham, with whom he shared the rest of his life.

Books he wrote include *Silence* (1961) and *A Year From Monday* (1968). According to two works reprinted in 1997, his *I-VI* and, with Joan Retallack, *Musicage: Cage Muses on Words Art and Music*, he became more folksy in the 1960s, now substituting jeans and a denim shirt for his 50s tie and jacket. He was accorded cultural superstardom by the 1980s and was generally regarded as one of the most important arts figures in the second half of the century. Cage's unorthodox punctuation is illustrated in a lecture on the word *imitation*:

> the greeks went r**I**ght up to the door of tre**M**ble too much for that actually
> **I**n
> **T**hese nucle**A**r
> insigh**T**
> po**I**nt five times ten
> h**O**w much more
> exter**N**al

Upon turning eighty, Cage was described by some as a musical anarchist and by others a musical liberator. Traditionalists regard him as the former, for he fails to use musical notation in the way others have used it for centuries. For example, a 1991 work utilizes "time brackets" sections lasting 75 seconds, during which the musicians are directed to play for the first 45 seconds, and they must finish between the 30th and 75th second–the timing is entirely up to the musician, which has led many to say that no two performances of the work can be the same and that this is "liberating."

Not a Eurocentrist, Cage (along with Allen Ginsberg) was drawn to Asian concepts in philosophy. His politics as he grew older became radically anarchist/leftist and by the 1970s he embraced aspects of Maoism.

When, two months before his death, he was asked by the present author for his views on humanism, the Iowa-educated musician, a practicing Buddhist, wrote,

> If there are only seven humanisms, as your letter indicates, I choose number seven, secular humanism. But if one were added that connected with zen and Tibetan Buddhism together with technology (Fuller, McLuhan, Nano Technology), I would choose that.

{CE; WAS, 3 June 1992}

CAHIERS RATIONALISTES

A French rationalist monthly, *Cahiers Rationalistes* is at 14 rue de l'Ecole-Polytechnique, 75005 Paris, France.

Cahill, Edward (20th Century)

Cahill, a freethinker, wrote *Freemasonry and the Anti-Christian Movement* (1939). {GS}

Cahuac, John (19th Century)

Cahuac, an English bookseller, revised an edition of Palmer's *Principles of Nature* (1819). For this he was prosecuted at the instance of a "Vice Society." The matter, however, was compromised, but he again was prosecuted in 1820 for selling the *Republican*. {BDF}

CAIN

The first non-humanist depicted in the Judeo-Christian Bible was Cain, who was Adam and Eve's eldest son. In a fit of jealousy, Cain killed his brother Abel and became a fugitive.

Some Mormons have believed that Cain's ancestors were punished by being stricken black, an unpopular view among African-American believers as well as non-believers. In the twentieth century it was rejected by most in the Church of Jesus Christ of Latter-day Saints. (See entry for Christian Identity.)

Cain, Stanley A. (1902—)

Author of *Vegetation of the Great Smoky Mountains* (1930), Cain is a naturalist and freethinker who has taught botany at the University of Michigan.

Caine, William Ralph Hall (Born 1869)

A writer and the brother of Sir Hall Caine, Caine was a journalist on the *Liverpool Mercury*. For several years he represented a department of the Manx Legislature in London, and he edited the *Court Circular*, the *Family Churchman*, and *Household Words*. Caine has been active in supporting the British Rationalist Press Association. {RAT}

Cairns, Fred I. (20th Century)

Cairns, a humanist, was a liberal minister. {HNS}

Caldecott, Ernest (20th Century)

A Unitarian minister, Caldecott signed Humanist Manifesto I. In 1944, for the Second Humanist Convention in Los Angeles, Caldecott wrote:

> Humanism is the conviction that, as far as we know, human intelligence, ethically exercised, and applied to the phenomena of the universe, can produce the best possible conditions and make available to mankind the finest development. This is different from supernaturalism, which posits not only the existence of an all-powerful Being, but one who intervenes in the affairs of men, and who aids man in achieving what otherwise would be impossible. Humanism is predicated on the assumption that it is the essential nature of the universe, which produced man, to provide the conditions in which he can best thrive. Even this statement tends to be teleological, for, when we observe that the universe "provides" something the implication can easily be that a "Provider" exists. Actually, we are employing the word "provide" in the same sense in which the physical scientist speaks of "nature's design," as though nature were conscious and directive. Humanists aver that we do not know the "ultimate" nature of the universe, nor even if there be such. We know nothing of origins or ends. Our knowledge is confined to existences. . . .
>
> The human being is less than a speck in the scale of the teeming centuries which amount to aeons of time. But since it is man who measures, and it is not known that anything exists more worthy of consideration (and also more needing it), we assert again that "the proper study of mankind is man." Supernaturalism impedes progress. This is not to suggest that all forms of orthodoxy, religious, political, economic, and social, are inimical to the race. On the contrary it happens that some persons, orthodox in this are liberal in that. A Roman Catholic, accepting on faith the things he believes for his soul's salvation, may still think for himself in politics, although he is less likely to do so than he who thinks out his own philosophy of living. What must be noted is that the irrationalism of supernaturalism leads astray. Consistent supernaturalism would necessarily be harmful. Its superstitions are enormous. It is blind unreasoning belief. Its exponents are rarely men of learning and never of vision. The obvious is the real to them. The miraculous is normal. . . .

> It is highly important that humanists associate with others of their kind for effectiveness, at the same time not falling into the errors of visionaries who expect a few persons to change the world over-night. The best we can reasonably hope for is to act as leaven. There we can be very helpful. That enough rational thinkers exist is probably self-evident. Up to now the emancipated seem to sense no need for group relationship. Thence the weakness of Unitarianism and Universalism. Were those who agree with the philosophy of either movement linked up with them, they would constitute a power greater than obtains anywhere on the planet. The spearhead of this force might well be humanism. The time for such joining of forces is here.

{FUS; HM1; HNS}

Calder, Ritchie [Lord] (1906—1982)

In the National Secular Society's centenary brochure, Calder wrote that when Bradlaugh agitated for birth control of the world's population, there were then 1,200,000,000 humans on Earth. He estimated there would be more than 6,000,000,000 by 1995. Explaining in his own views, Calder wrote *Future of a Troubled World* (1983). Secularists have consistently warned against the danger of over-populating our planet. {TRI}

Calderino, Domizio (1445—1478)

Calderino was a learned writer of the Renaissance who lived in Verona and in Rome. Bayle says Calderino, who edited and commented upon many of the Latin poets, was without religion. {BDF}

Calderon, Alfredo (Born 1852)

Calderon was a Spanish journalist, freethinker, and lawyer who, in addition to having written books on law, edited *La Justicia.* {BDF}

Calderon, Lauresmo (Born 1847)

Calderon y Arana, a propagator of Darwinian ideas in Spain, was a professor of chemistry in the University of Madrid. {BDF}

Calderon, Salvador (Born 1851)

A Spanish geologist and naturalist, Calderon y Arana was a professor at the University of Seville. He made scientific travels in Central America and wrote on geological subjects. His brother was Lauresmo Calderon. {BDF; RAT}

Calderone, Mary Steichen (1904—1998)

Calderone, the daughter of the photographer Edward Steichen, was named Humanist of the Year by the American Humanist Association in 1974. In 1953, she was medical director of the Planned Parenthood Federation of America. From 1954 to 1975, she was executive director of the Sex Information Educational Council of the United States, becoming its president in 1975. In 1980, she received the Margaret Sanger Award from the Planned Parenthood Federation. She enjoyed asking young audiences for a four-letter word ending in "k" that meant sexual intercourse. When they tittered, she answered "talk": "We never talk to each other as nonsexual people." Human sexuality, she explained, goes far beyond the sex act—it is multifaceted and must not be hidden in a shroud of secrecy nor lowered to the level of erotic expression.

"Sometimes," she wrote, "sex becomes a problem because of our inability to talk openly and objectively about it. . . . It is interesting to note that in the vocabulary of some cultures there is a rich supply of entirely acceptable words to describe the varieties of sexual love and parts of the body especially involved in it. . . . How much better if [we too] had an ample, pleasant array of language with which to talk to each other about sex!" Sex education, she insisted, should start in kindergarten, leading enemies such as the Christian Crusade, the John Birch Society, and Moral Majority to accuse her of being an "aging sexual libertine."

A nominal Quaker, she was plunged into depression upon the death from pneumonia of her eight-year-old daughter. Calderone wrote *Talking With Your Child About Sex* (1982) and *Family Book About Sexuality* (1987). Although she and Dr. Frank Calderone separated in 1979, the two never divorced. He died in 1987. {HNS2}

Caldicott, Helen Broinowski (1938—)

In 1982, Caldicott was named Humanist of the Year by the American Humanist Association. An Australian-born pediatrician, she wrote *Nuclear Madness: What Can You Do?* (1979) and has established anti-nuclear groups in several countries. She has written, "How stupid that we lack the imagination to settle conflicts, so we have to go and kill each other. And the people who get killed are not the men and women . . . who are having a problem with each other; the people who get killed are our kids–17 and 18 year olds, little boys. They are sent off as instruments by people who can't solve their conflicts . . . [who] don't take the time to work out how to get in the other person's frame of reference and understand them and make capitulations and concessions." Her 1996 work, *A Desperate Passion*, is an autobiography describing the friends and enemies she made in her anti-nuclear crusades. {HNS2}

Caldwell, Erskine (1903—1987)

Caldwell was a proletarian novelist who wrote *Tobacco Road* (1932) and *God's Little Acre* (1933), both of which librarians often hid on special shelves and required permission in order that they be checked out. With his photographer-wife Margaret Bourke-White, he collaborated on *You Have Seen Their Faces* (1942). Asked his view in 1951 concerning humanism, Caldwell replied to the present author,

> I prefer leaving critical comment of that nature left to others far better qualified.

Some critics have pointed to Caldwell's anti-Semitism. But in "Deep South," he exposes a fundamentalist Christianity which promises a "better world" that never comes. He includes details of the rituals of snake handling, of speaking in tongues (glossolalia), and bloodletting. With his father, he felt fundamentalism was a dangerous narcotic for poor Southern workers who had little hope or other entertainment. But what readers have liked has been his description of those very people: Jeeter Lester, a sharecropper in *Tobacco Road* who has fifteen children, who pawns off his own daughter for a turnip; a daughter, Pearl, who was married when only twelve years old; a near-catatonic mother; a grandmother so worthless she is left to die when run over by a car; a dumb son named Dude who marries Sister Bessie Rice, a widowed preacher, when promised he could blow the horn in her new car; and Jeeter's daughter with the hare-lip:

> Ellie May's upper lip had an opening a quarter of an inch wide that divided one side of her mouth into unequal parts; the slit came to an abrupt end almost under her left nostril. The upper gum was low, and because her gums were always fiery red, the opening in her lip made her look as if her mouth were bleeding profusely.

Caldwell's fame soared in 1946 when *God's Little Acre* was reissued, but after his marriage to Margaret Bourke-White ended—she left him often but once wrote him a cable, saying simply, "My pussy grows cold for you"—he was accused of writing inferior work and many magazines refused to publish his work. {WAS, 14 February 1951}

Caldwell, John Taylor (20th Century)

Caldwell is author of *Come Dungeons Dark*, a biography of Guy Aldred, an atheist and anarchist. His autobiography is *Severely Dealt With—Growing Up in Belfast and Glasgow.*

CALENDAR

The earliest calendars were naturally crude. The earth completes its orbit about the sun in 365 days 5 hours 48 minutes and 46 seconds, whereas the moon passes through its phases in about 29 1/2 days, amounting to more than 354 days 8 hours 48 minutes. The discrepancy between the years is inescapable, and a major problem in devising a calendar has been to harmonize the solar and lunar reckonings. (If God really exists, humanists jocularly explain, He is an exceedingly poor mathematician.)

The Egyptians worked out a formula for the solar year (12 months of 30 days each, five extra days a year, and an extra day every four years). The Ancient Jews dated their calendar from Creation, Ancient Greeks dated theirs from the first Olympic Games, and Islam from the flight from Mecca. The old Chinese calendar was devised to have six 60-day cycles, each cycle having 10-day periods and three such periods going to make up a month. It will be 4698, Year of the Dragon, in China when it is 2000 in Chicago. The Maya divided the year into eighteen 20-day periods, with a 5-day period at the end—they brilliantly began each month using a day 0, not day 1.

The Romans dated their calendar from the foundation of Rome by the legendary Romulus. *Ad Urbe Condita*–from the foundation of the city–was pegged at 753 B.C.E. When Rome emerged as a world power, superstition held that even numbers were unlucky, so the Roman calendar has months that were 29 or 31 days long, with the exception of February, which had 28. However, four months of 31 days, seven months of 29 days, and one month of 28 days added up to only 355 days. Therefore, they invented an extra month–Mercedonius–of 22 or 23 days, which was added every second year. Caesar, being advised by astronomers that the Roman calendar was far off, ordered a sweeping reform in 45: One year, made 445 days long by imperial decree, brought the calendar back in step with the seasons. Then the solar year (with the value of 365 days and 6 hours) was made the basis of the calendar. Every fourth year was made a 366-day year. Caesar also decreed that the year should begin with the first of January, not with the vernal equinox in late March. This calendar, the Julian, is still the calendar of the Eastern Orthodox churches. Unfortunately, the year is 11 1/2 minutes shorter than the figure written in Caesar's calendar, and after a number of centuries, even those few minutes add up. Meanwhile, from 20 B.C.E. to 20 C.E. is not 40 years: it is 39 inasmuch as there was no Year Zero.

Around 1600, when Rosalind in Shakespeare's *As You Like It* described the world as "almost 6,000 years old," she was somewhat echoing Archbishop Ussher, who in 1564 had authoritatively given the time of creation as having been 4,004 B. C. E.

Roger Bacon once sent a memorandum in the 1200s to Pope Clement IV that although Caesar could decree that the vernal equinox should not be used as the first day of the new year, the vernal equinox is still a fact of Nature. By the 16th century, time had displaced the vernal equinox to March 11th from March 21st. In 1582 Pope Gregory XIII rectified this error by suppressing 10 days in the year 1582 and ordained that thereafter the years ending in hundreds should not be leap years unless they were divisible by 400. The year 1600 was a leap year under both systems, but 1700, 1800, and 1900 were leaps years only in the unreformed calendar. The present generally accepted calendar is called the Gregorian. The reform was not accepted in England and the British colonies in America until 1752. The Gregorian was called the New Style (N.S.) and the Julian the Old Style (O.S). George Washington's birthday, therefore is 22 February 1732 (N.S.) and 11 February 1731 (O.S.). Thomas Jefferson's tombstone reads:

Born April 2, 1743 O.S. Died July 4, 1826.

A "fixed" 13-month "civil" cosmic calendar has been proposed for the first day of the 21st century, 31 December 2000. As described by William H. Becker (*Mensa Bulletin*, March 1995), the calendar's first regular weekday would be Monday, with all weeks starting on Monday and ending on Sunday. Becker's 13-month calendar re-names all the months and is astronomically sound. It has quarters of 91 days (13 weeks), and Leap Years are any year evenly divisible by four, except that years ending in "00" are Leap Years only if they are divisible by 400. The 28-day months are named as follows: Helio, Mercury, Venus, Terra, Luna, Ares, Jove, Kronos, Uranus, Neptune, Pluto, Galaxy, and Cosmos. For example, America's Fourth of July would be on Jove 15th. Christmas Day would be Cosmos 22nd. World Day would be the day just before Helio 1st, which is the day after Cosmos 28th. The first day of a year would be Monday, Helios the 1st. If one were born on a Thursday, all succeeding birthdays would always be on a Thursday. Such a calendar might appeal to many inasmuch as no month would be named after a Roman god, December which linguistically looks as if it is the tenth month would no longer be used, and astronomers would be expected to welcome the new terminology. Not addressed are the weekday names–Tiu, for example, is related to a Teutonic war god; Woden, or Odin, was the supreme Norse god; Thor was a Norse god of thunder; Friday is named after Frigga, a Norse goddess associated with sex; Saturn was a Roman god of agriculture.

On Mars, where mankind may one day settle, a year will have a length of 668 days, 23 hours, 52 minutes, and 32 seconds in Earth time, or 668.61561 sols (days). William H. Becker (*Mensa Bulletin*, May 1995) has extrapolated that a seven-sol week divided into 668.61561 gives a year of 95 7-day weeks, with 3.6151 sols short of a full Mars year, a shortage which could become a Mars Leap Year for any year ending in 66 or any year ending in 32 in an even-numbered century. This would keep the calendar in sync with the seasons. The Earth and Mars calendars could only be compared by multiplying the Earth year by .5316514. Ergo the Earth year 2001 would see the start of Mars year 1065 at its northern hemisphere winter solstice, if such a point were established as Mars New Year's Day. The Mars calendar might be 95 five-week months long and have 19 months.

What to call the months and days on Mars? Humanists like Arthur C. Clarke would likely come up with Ganymede or other such names which have no connection with Judeo-Christianity. (For other calendar ideas, see entries for Gilbert Romme [Republican], Auguste Comte [Positivist], and Stanley Stokes [Rational]; also see entry for Time.) {CE; David Ewing Duncan, *The Calendar*}

Calenzio, Eliseo (c. 1440—1503)

An Italian writer, Calenzio was preceptor to Prince Frederic, the son of Ferdinand, King of Naples. He wrote a number of satires, fables, and epigrams, some of which are directed against the Church. {BDF}

Calhoun, Charles (20th Century)

Calhoun edited the monthly *Progressive Forum* in Los Angeles from 1923 to 1930. {FUS}

Calhoun, John Caldwell [Vice President] (1782—1850)

Calhoun, the US Senator from South Carolina and Vice President under Andrew Jackson and John Quincy Adams, was a Unitarian who gave money to build the church in Washington. He was listed on its first membership roll. However, William C. Meigs wrote in a 1917 biography of Calhoun, "He was brought up a Presbyterian . . . but he himself never joined any faith. He attended the Episcopal Church in later years, and is said to have aided in founding a church of that sect, but neither the Episcopal creed nor the formulated one of any religion can have appealed to him with much force, and he equally contributed to the erection of the first Unitarian Church in Washington, and is said to have been among 'its warm friends and consistent adherents.'"

A 1950 biography by Margaret L. Coit wrote that Calhoun would not join a church:

> Even his friends had no idea where he stood. Some believed him a deist, others a Swedenborgian. Furthermore, he gave money to build the Unitarian Church in Washington and "on the first roll of this Washington parish" can be found his name. "Unitarianism is," he announced with his characteristic dogmatism, "the only true faith and will ultimately prevail over the world.

{CE; EG; UU}

CALIFORNIA ATHEISTS, FREETHINKERS, HUMANISTS

California has the following groups:

- Alliance of Humanist, Atheist, and Ethical Culture Organizations of Los Angeles County, 8491 Sunset Boulevard, Suite 240, West Hollywood, California 90069.
- American Association for the Advancement of Atheism (AAAA), 1863 Falconcer Court, Vista, California 92083–the group was founded in 1908 and incorporated in 1925. Kei Kanbit is a contact.
- American Atheists, Inc. Dave Kong is a contact in San Francisco. <dksf@atheists.org>
- Atheist Coalition (Atheist Alliance), POB 4786, San Diego,

California 92164. Howard Kreisner is the president. E-mail: <atheistcoalition@hotmail.com>.

• Atheists and Other Freethinkers (ASHS), PO Box 15182, Sacramento, California 95851-0182 (916) 920-7834. E-mail: <hkocol@hotmail.com>.

• Atheists of San Francisco Region (Atheist Alliance), PO Box 31523, San Francisco, CA 94131-1523; (415) 648-1201. Contacts are Ray Romano at <ray75511@aol.com> and <jack-massen@aol.com>.

• Atheists United (Atheist Alliance), POB 5329, Sherman Oaks, California 91423. Alexander Prairie was the president until 1993.

• Cedar Springs Library, 43378 Cedar Springs Road, Auberry, California 93602. Bill Young is a contact for the library, which is a non-profit foundation that maintains a library of freethought materials.

• Center for Inquiry West, 5519 Grosevnor Blvd., Los Angeles, CA 90066. <www.cfiwest.org>.

• College of the Siskiyous humanists are at <http://www.secularhumanism.org/cfa/orgs.html>.

• Ethical Culture Society of the Bay Area is at (415) 522-3758 and <sanfrancisco@aeu.org>.

• Ethical Culture Society of Los Angeles, POB 370425, Reseda, California 91337; E-mail: <losangeles@aeu.org>

• Ethical Culture Society of San Diego is at <sandiego@aeu.org>.

• Fellowship of Humanists, 411 West 28th Street, Oakland, California 94609. LeRue Grim is president of this organization which was founded in 1935 and is one of the oldest continuously existing humanist organizations.

• Freethinker's Society, POB 25863, West Los Angeles, California 90025 (310) 479-6318

• Freethinkers of Ventura County (FTVC), PO Box 346, Somis, California 93066; (805) 386-4232. Contact is Charlotte Poe. E-mail: <frthvc@aol.com>.

• Gay and Lesbian Atheists and Humanists of Los Angeles County (213) 667-0838

• Gay and Lesbian Freethought Forum, 1213 North Highland Ave., Hollywood, California (213) 666-3875

• Humanist Association of Los Angeles (AHA), 22316 Barbacoa Drive, Saugus, California 91350. Lisa-Jo Corbin-Singletary is the contact (213) 462-7649. On the Web: <http://www.hala.org/>.

• Humanist Association of San Diego, POB 86446, San Diego, California 92138. Philip Paulson is the contact, (619) 280-8595. E-mail: <pkp@ix.netcom.com>. On the Web: <http://www.godless.org/hasd/hasd.html>.

• Humanist Association of the Greater Sacramento Area (AHA), 142 Juniper Street, Vacaville, California 95688. Mildred McCallister is the president. On the Web: <http://www.cwo.com/~pkelley /index.html>.

• Humanist Center–Humanist Fellowship of San Diego (AHA), POB 87662, San Diego, California 92138. William Lindley is the contact. E-mail: < warren@bookwarren.com>.

• Humanist Club of Long Beach (AHA), 3316 Roxanne Avenue, Long Beach, California 90808. Peter Ballou is the contact.

• Humanist Community (AHA), 3032 Warm Springs Drive, San Jose, California 95127. Bill Jacobsen is the executive director.

• Humanist Community of San Francisco (AHA, ASHS), POB 31172, San Francisco, California 94131; (650) 342-0910; Jay Martin is the contact at <martinjg@flash.net>.

• Humanist Community of the Peninsula (AHA), 350 Ludeman Lane, Millbrae, CA 04030. Greydon Wellman is the contact. (415) 345-2765. E-mail: <athalsfj@aol.com>.

• *Humanist Community Serving Stanford University*, a monthly newsletter at PO Box 60069, Palo Alto, California 94306-0069. Bill Jacobsen, contact, PO Box 60069, Palo Alto, CA 94306; phone (415) 969-3630). On the Web: <www.humanists.org/>.

• Humanist Fellowship of the First Unitarian Society of San Francisco (AHA), 170 Oak Park Drive, San Francisco, California 94131.

• Humanist Society of Berkeley (AHA), 100 Arlene Lane, Walnut Creek, California 94595. Howard Gonsalves is the president.

• Humanists of Inland Communites, PO Box 1001, San Jacinto, CA 92581; Joe Bernard, President, (909) 658-2491.

• Humanists of Orange County, Peter O. Anderson, contact member, 20 Owen Court, Irvine, CA 92612-4042; Phone: (714) 854-4305.

• Humanists of Riverside County (AHA), 42010 Mayberry Avenue, Hemet, California 92344. Joe Bernard is the regional director of the Southern California region of the AHA.

• Humanists of the Desert Communities, contact member Phil Russo, PO Box 719, Palm Springs, cA 92263-0719.

• Humanists of the Pomona Valley (AHA), POB 376, Claremont, California 91711. Joe Gorman is the contact.

• Humanists of the San Joaquin Valley (AHA), contact Bill Young at (209) 855-2438, PO Box 515, Auberry, California 93602.

• Institute of Humanistic Science, A-35, 5175 Luigi Terrace, San Diego, California 92122. James W. Prescott in 1975 established the group as a division of the AHA "to provide a mechanism to support research and educational projects to develop a scientific basis for Humanistic ethics and moral values." Phone: (714) 645-6802. E-mail: <jwprescott@aol.com>.

• Los Alamitos High School Atheists are at <http://www.secularhumanism.org/cfa/orgs.html>.

• Rational Inquirers of Orange County (ASHS), 1931 East Meats #115, Orange, California 92865.

• San Diego State University Atheist Coalition: <http://www.secularhumanism.org/cfa/orgs.html>.

• Santa Barbara Humanist Society (ASHS), PO Box 118, Santa Barbara, CA 93102; (805) 687-8619

• Secular Humanists of Los Angeles (ASHS), POB 10517, Marino Del Ray, CA 90295. (310) 305-8135; E-mail: <cfi-west@worldnet.att.net>.

• Secular Humanists of the East Bay (ASHS), POB 830, Berkeley, California 94701. (510) 486-0553. Contacts: Eric Worrell, Jesse Cordell, and Sarita Cordell. E-mail: <eew@eew.com>.

• Secular Humanists of Los Angeles (SHOLA), PO Box 10517, Marina Del Rey, CA 90295 (310) 305-8135. E-mail: <cfi-west@worldnet.att.net>.

• Set Free!, 9766 Chapman Ave. (#192), Garden Grove, CA 92840. Contact: Mark Smith at <JCnot4me@aol.com>.

• Society for Humanistic Judaism of Los Angeles, 1261 Loma Vista, Beverly Hills, California 90210.

• South Bay Secular Humanists, POB 4396, Mountain View, California 94040. Jim Stauffer is a contact.

• University of California at Irvine's Campus Freethought Alliance group is found on the Web: <www.secularhumanism.org/cfa/orgs.html>.

• University of California at Santa Cruz on the Web: <www.secularhumanism.org/cfa/orgs.html>.

Calisher, Hortense (1911—)

Calisher, who has taught at various universities and is a member of the American Academy of Arts and Letters, is noted for stories she has written in which she interprets character. *False Entry* (1961), for example, is about a character known only by his pseudonym, Pierre Goodman, and his involvement in an Alabama trial, testifying against racists in the murder of a Negro. Asked about humanism, she responded to the present author as follows:

> Category? Writing, one hopes to ignore categories.
> (See *Herself: An Autobiographical Memoir.* "Category is the true crocodile.")
>
> Humanist? A fine word. Works best when it collates with its immediate text."

{WAS, 11 June 1992}

Call, Lon Ray (1894—1916)

Raised a Baptist, Call was influenced by Curtis Reese, one of the leaders of the Humanist movement, and became like Reese a Unitarian minister. As a minister-at-large, he founded thirteen Unitarian churches. {U&U}

Call, Wathen Mark Wilks (1817—1890)

Call, an English positivist, entered the ministry in 1843 but resigned his curacy about 1856 on account of his change of opinions, which is recounted in his preface to *Reverberations* (1876). Call contributed largely to the *Forthrightly* and *Westminster Review.* {BDF; RAT}

Callaghan, William J. (20th Century)

For his 1958 Columbia University Ph. D. dissertation, Callaghan wrote "Philosophy of Francis E. Abbott." {FUS}

Callahan, Tim (20th Century)

Callahan, in *Bible Prophecy: Failure or Fulfillment?* (1997), examined Old Testament claims of biblical prophecy. He included material concerning contemporary attempts to interpret prophecy in light of apocalyptic expectations.

Callas, Plutarco [President] (1877—1945)

Callas was a strong secular President of Mexico. The Spanish clergy tried in the 1920s to get the United States to annex Mexico in order to stop his influence. {TRI}

Callaway, Charles (1838—1915)

Callaway, a geologist, was educated for and entered the Nonconformist ministry, but he seceded on doctrinal grounds and became an outspoken agnostic. He supported the Cheltenham Ethical Society and was an honorary associate of the Rationalist Press Association. {RAT}

Callaway, Howard (20th Century)

Callaway is the student representative on the Board of Governors of The Humanist Institute.

Callen, Michael (1954—1993)

Callen, a writer and singer who embodied for a dozen years the possibility of long-term survival with AIDS, was an atheist. He was one of the authors of *How to Have Sex in an Epidemic: One Approach* (1983, with his companion Richard Dworkin along with Richard Berkowitz and Dr. Joseph A. Sonnabend). He became well-known for his solo album, "Purple Heart," and a quintet called the Flirtations. Dr. Jeffrey Laurence in the *New York Times Book Review* wrote in 1990 that Callen had managed in his book to "capture the spirit and eccentricities of men and women who, shouldering an extraordinary burden, simply will not break." Callen is credited with encouraging the use of the phrase "safe sex" and of obtaining acceptance of "person with AIDS" rather than "AIDS victim."

Callen was an honorary member of the Secular Humanist Society of New York's AIDS-support group (AASH), which held a joyous memorial in his honor when the prescribed shark cartilage and other treatments he had been taking were unable to keep him alive. At a memorial held in the Ethical Culture Society, the Flirtations sang, refreshments were served, and many individuals recounted Callen's happy as well as gay life.

Callet, Pierre Auguste (Born 1811)

Callet was a French politician and the editor of the *Gazette* until 1840. At the 1851 coup, he took refuge in Belgium, returned to France, was then imprisoned for writing against the Empire. In 1871 he was again elected representative for the department of the Loire. His chief freethought work is *L'Enfer* (1861), an attack upon the Christian doctrine of Hell. {BDF}

Calloway, Charles (20th Century)

A freethinker, Calloway wrote *Does Determinism Destroy Responsibility?* (1905). {GS}

Calverton, V. F. (1900—1940)

Calverton, a freethinker, wrote *The Making of Man* (1931) and The *Passing of the Gods* (1934). {FUS; GS}

Calverley, Charles Stuart (1831—1884)

A poet who translated Latin and Greek poetry, Calverley wrote verse in Latin, English, and Greek. In a biographical sketch, prefixed to his *Complete Works* (1901), his friend Sir W. J. Sendall stated, "To mere dogmatic teaching he was always and for ever impervious." {RAT}

CALVINISM

• Calvinism was the child of indigestion.

—Robert G. Ingersoll

• The sexual act can be barbaric, brutally selfish, and self-aggrandizing, or loving and revelatory. It can be infantile and ludicrous, or spiritually exalted and profound. It can be narcissistic, heedless, and exploitative, or devotional. In the course of one person's life, it can, at one time or another, be all these things. But the particular character of a consensual act is manifest only in the intimate connection of two minds. When it is exposed to an audience, it deconstructs as something inevitably prurient, automatically scandalous. This is especially true in America, where one of the abiding shames of the Calvinist mind is that only a Son of God can be conceived without animal intercourse.

—E. L. Doctorow
The New Yorker, 12 October 1998

Calvinism refers to the religious doctrines of John Calvin (1509-1564). During a sudden conversion in 1532, he was told by God that God is omnipotent; to do God's will is man's first duty; in Adam this was possible; in the Fall of Man this power was destroyed; humans are therefore rightfully damned; God in Christ redeems whomever He wills; that these elect whom he has so willed live by faith in union with Christ, etc. Freethinkers are quick to note that Calvin was even less humorous than most of his fellow theologians.

Calvo, Rafael (Born 1852)

Calvo was a Spanish actor and dramatic author. He was both a pronounced Republican and a freethinker. {BDF}

Cambacérès, Jean Jacques [Prince] (1753—1824)

Cambacérès was a French statesman, a distinguished lawyer who during the Revolution was President of the Convention and one of the Council of Five Hundred. Under Napoleon, he was one of the chief authors of the famous Code Civil, then the finest such in the world. He was made Prince, Duke of Parma, and Arch-Chancellor of the Empire. A deist, Cambacérès was banished by Louis XVIII when the royalty and church were restored. {JM; RAT}

Cameron, Dean Eikelberry (1962—)

Cameron, an actor, co-authored the screenplay of "Lost Weekend" (1984) and has written numerous other works. He has appeared in various television shows, on one of which when asked if he believed in God responded, "No god. Next caller." "I don't believe in god, satan, angels, an afterlife, a creator, or any of those dangerous myths," Cameron has written. "I trust in science, objective truth, wonder, and mankind." {CA}

Camisani, Gregorio (Born 1810)

Camisani, an Italian who translated the *Upas* of Captain R. H. Dyas and other works, was a freethinker who taught languages in Milan. {BDF}

Cammer, Michael (20th Century)

Cammer, an artist and academic, has written that he does not believe in any sort of spirituality and, in fact, disdains religion. On the faculty of Albert Einstein College of Medicine, he does not discuss religion at the job. Of humanism, he wrote to the present author:

> I find irreconcilable contradiction in how scientists can believe in any religion. Esthetics and knowledge have no need for pseudo-explanations or crutches for worry over non-acceptance of non-comprehension. Anyhow, my credentials as a humanist are that I'm pretty much a lefty or libertarian even though I'd like to make a buck. But I have been remiss; I have done no conspicuous protesting since the Gulf Massacre when I painted a huge NO WAR sign in my painting studio window overlooking the intersection of 125th Street and Broadway in New York City.
>
> {WAS, 23 November 1993}

CAMP QUEST

A summer camp for secular humanist children, Camp Quest, was inaugurated in 1996. Its address: Camp Quest, 6404 Pheasant Run, Loveland, Ohio 45140.

Campanella, Tommaso (1568—1639)

During the French Revolution, Maréchal cited Campanella as being only a "possible" atheist. The Italian Renaissance philosopher never left the church, but he had frequent troubles with the authorities. His *City of the Sun* (1602) is similar to Plato's *Republic* in that it designs a utopia, when a new era of earthly felicity should begin.

For non-believers his major importance is that he anticipated what came to be known as the scientific attitude of empiricism. As for his private views on religion, Campanella defended himself when first arrested and tried during the Inquisition. In Calabria in 1599, he was arrested on charges of heresy against the Spanish Government of Naples. Upon appeal to Rome, he was sentenced to perpetual imprisonment in the prison of the Holy Office. He was put to the torture seven times, his torments on one occasion extending over forty hours, but he refused to confess. He was dragged from one prison to another for twenty-seven years, during which he wrote some sonnets, a history of the Spanish monarchy, and several philosophical works. Released from prison by the intervention of Pope Urban VIII, Campanella fled to France, where he met Gassendi, and to Holland, where he met Descartes.

Julian Hibbert has remarked that Campanella's *Atheism Subdued* (1631, *Atheismus Triumphatus*) might better be entitled *Atheismus Triumphaus* (*Atheism Triumphant*), for the strongest arguments are on the heterodox side. {BDF; CE; EU, Aram Vartarian}

Campbell, Ada (c. 1855—1915?)

Campbell was an early Australian secularist and activist. Described as "a lady whose bold, outspoken, and fearless lectures have been the means of spreading Freedom of Thought," she lectured widely on freethought subjects. Although threatened in Wellington with prosecution for "charging on Sunday," the Judge of Queensland ruled in her favor: "Lectures do not come under the head of amusements and therefore cannot legally be interfered with by any Government." An 1886 *Otago Daily Times* wrote that Campbell was "undoubtedly a very clever woman, with a powerful pleasant voice, considerable oratorical ability, and a neat form of mimicry" which "occasionally descended to the verge of vulgarity." {SWW}

Campbell, Alexander (1796—1870)

Campbell was a socialist from Glasgow. Upon the death of Combe in 1827, he became a socialist missionary in England, taking an active part in the co-operative movement. He also agitated for an unstamped press, for which he was tried and imprisoned at Edinburgh, 1833—1834. About 1849 Campbell returned to Glasgow and wrote on the *Sentinel.* In 1868 he summed up the opinion of many Owenites: "I am heart-sick of theology, and consider it a great waste of time to discuss the old Book. . . . When I compare the past Freethought platform with the present, it seems to me that there was more real progress made in the past when Robert Owen was propounding the old social ideas." In 1867, Campbell was honorary president of the Eclectic Society. {BDF; FUK; RSR; VI}

Campbell, Archibald (19th Century)

In 1856, Campbell founded the Auckland Secular Society in New Zealand. {FUK}

Campbell, Bruce (20th Century)

Campbell, the executive director of the Canadian Centre for Policy Alternatives, wrote (with Maude Barlow) *Straight Through the Heart: How the Liberals Abandoned the Just Society*. He has written for *Humanist in Canada* (Summer 1996).

Campbell, Colin (20th Century)

In 1988, Campbell was elected as an honorary associate of the Rationalist Press Association. A reader in sociology and Head of Department at the University of York, he has gained an international reputation for his work on "the cultic milieu" and the occult as well as irreligion. His *Towards a Sociology of Irreligion* (1971) discussed the secularist, positivist, ethical, and rationalist movements in the United States and Britain, as well as the first account of the emergence of the humanist movement in the 1960s. He also wrote *The Myth of Social Actio*n.

Campbell has been on the board of the Rationalist Press Association, is a contributor to *New Humanist* and *Question*, and is a regular speaker on behalf of humanism. In Birmingham, England, at the Centenary Conference of the Rationalist Press Association in 1999, he spoke on "The Easternization of the West: The Threat to Rationalism in the New Millennium." {FUK}

Campbell, Frances (20th Century)

Campbell in Scotland is active with the Stirling Humanists.

Campbell, Ellen (20th Century)

Campbell is executive director of the Canadaian Unitarian Council (Suite 706, 188 Eglinton Avenue East, Toronto, Ontaro M4P 2X7, Canada). E-mail: <cuc@web.net>.

Campbell, Glen (20th Century)

Campbell was executive director of the Canadian Unitarian Council in Toronto.

Campbell, John Archibald (1906—1976)

Campbell was an Australian freethinker, activist, and quantity surveyor. Upon migrating from England, he became active in the Humanist Society of South Australia, being elected as its president in 1966. From 1967 to 1968, he was president of the Council of Australian Humanist Societies, and in 1969 with Laurie Bullock he re-established the Rationalist Association of South Australia, becoming its president and editor of the monthly *Rationalist.* When the organization changed its name to the Atheist Foundation of Australia, he was elected president and retained that office until his death. Campbell was noted as a prolific writer of hard-hitting articles and leaflets. {SWW}

Campbell, Joseph (1904—1987)

Campbell, a mythologist, folklorist, and educator, wrote *The Hero With A Thousand Faces,* which inspired a "Star Wars' series of motion pictures.

He is also known for having written *Myths to Live By*. Although purportedly anti-Semitic, no definitive study proves this. Asked his view about humanism, Campbell responded to the present author:

> I have never thought of myself as being a humanist, nor can I find in any of the seven categories you have defined a spot into which I fit or should like to fit–except, of course, the first [humanism, devotion to human interests; the study of the humanities], which is so broad as to include practically everybody in the world. My sympathies are rather with the Platonists and Stoics than with the line of thinkers suggested by your rota of "Ancient Humanism," and although I admire some of the writers named in the category of "Classical Humanism," I am not of their species; indeed, I think of Classical Humanism as a fossil in the field of contemporary thought–like, say, Judaism or Catholicism.
>
> From the movements described as theistic humanism, atheistic humanism, and communistic humanism, I should like to dissociate myself absolutely. The *contradictio in adjecto* involved in the term "theistic humanism" seems to me too silly for discussion; the negativism of atheistic humanism controverts both the idea of human decency that I share with the classical humanists and that sense of the supernatural wonder of being which is for me the richest gift and delight of human experience; while the association of a systematic liquidation of whole classes of humanity with the term "humanism," which is implied in the fraudulent rubric "communistic humanism,"I find monstrous. Finally, the position of "naturalistic humanism" I long ago abandoned, consciously and without regret, after having been trained to it in the hallowed morgue of Columbia University.
>
> The term "humanism," in short, remains associated in my mind with a tradition that has contributed to my education but denies my experience–a stilted tradition it seems to me, not open to the winds of mystery and rapture that are synonymous with the breath of life. For nature is to me supernatural in its mystery, and absolutely so. Moreover, I include in my view of nature both man and his civilizations: these I find justified and wonderful, not because they are potential of something, but in their actuality, right here and now. Hence I lack both the "nausea" of the Existentialists and that lean toward improvement which is characteristic of the naturalistic humanists. I do not believe, as Dr. Overstreet does [in a letter to the present author, one quoted herein], that "the goal of human development lies in the greatest possible fulfillment of human powers," or that man lives "to bring to fruition the powers with which nature endowed him." Some people live for such things and receive awards (as they should) for their services to the race; others live to enjoy with friends the rich wine of life in one or another of its manifestations, and I believe that I am of this sort–preferring the vintage of Lao-tze to that of Lin Yu-tang, James Joyce to that of Bertrand Russell, and Henry Thoreau to that of John Dewey and his thoughtful brood.
>
> The Occidental writers whom I regard as having most strongly influenced my development are Goethe, Schopenhauer, Nietzsche, Spengler, Leo Frobenius, Heinrich Zimmer, Carl G. Jung, Thomas Mann, and James Joyce. The Oriental list includes Ananda K. Coomaraswamy and D. T. Suzuki. But I should also mention–with emphasis–the sculptor Antoine Bourdelle, whose Paris studio in the winter of 1927–1928 was the scene of my timely rescue from the rising rocket of naturalistic humanism and establishment in the beatific vision of *les grandes lignes de la nature*. I hope that these brief paragraphs may be of use . . . [and I am led] to believe that I may be a humanist after all, though of a sort not yet numbered in your list.

Campbell, in *Myths to Live By* (1972), wrote, "What gods are there, what gods have there ever been, that were not from man's imagination." He also wrote, ". . . god is a metaphor for that which transcends all levels of intellectual thought. It's as simple as that." Theists as well as non-theists find much to like in Campbell's outlook. {TYD; WAS, 15 June 1956}

Campbell, Margaret Mollie (1930—)

Campbell, born to a fundamentalist Ana-Baptist mother who limited her education on religious grounds and forbade her becoming a nurse, later rejected all religion. Upon arriving in Australia in 1962, she joined the New South Humanist Society and became its secretary in 1986. {SWW}

Campbell, Patrick (1917—)

Campbell's "Joseph Lewis–Champion of Forethought" was published in Lewis's freethought journal, *Age of Reason* (May, 1963). The New Zealand Rationalist Association in 1964 published his *The Mythical Jesus*. {FUK; GS; TRI}

Campbell, Philip (20th Century)

Campbell is a specialist in astrophysics and atmospheric physics. Before becoming editor of *Nature* in 1995, he was founding editor of *Physics World* for the Institute of Physics. In Birmingham, England, at the Centenary Conference in 1999 of the Rationalist Press Association, Campbell spoke on "Irrationality in the Public Communication of Science."

Campbell, Steuart (20th Century)

Campbell, a rationalist, is author of *The Loch Ness Monster* (1991) and *The UFO Mystery Solved* (1994). He makes the case for an "Astronomical Mirage Hypothesis," that a celestial body (for example, a planet) that is just below the horizon is not, in fact, invisible, but is visible by means of atmospheric refraction which causes the light from it to be "bent." As a result, the celestial body presents itself as being above the horizon briefly and moving rapidly.

E-mail: <explicit@cix.co.uk>. On the Web: <http://www.users.zetnet.co.uk/stockton>.

Campbell, Theophilia Carlile (19th Century)

Campbell, a freethinker, wrote *The Battle of the Press as Told in the Story of Richard Carlile* (1899). {FUK; GS}

Campbell, Thomas (1777—1844)

A Scottish poet and reformer, Campbell was educated for the ministry but became a skeptic and turned to poetry. He played a part in the project to break the religious tyranny of Oxford and Cambridge Universities by founding the University of London as a purely secular institution. He rejected the idea of immortality, but McCabe states that Campbell "wavered between a pale theism and agnosticism." Dean Milman and Macaulay were among his pallbearers. Although in his poems Campbell resented "superstition's rod," he was buried in Westminster Abbey. {JM; RAT; RE}

Campbell, W. A. (20th Century)

A freethinker, Campbell wrote *Did the Jews Kill Jesus, and the Myth of the Resurrection* (1927) and *The Crucifixion and Resurrection of Jesus* (1933). {GS}

Campell, Steuart (20th Century)

In *The Rise and Fall of Jesus* (1996), Campell, who had a fundamentalist Christian youth, attempts to assess and interpret fact, especially historical fact, on the assumption of the non-divinity of Jesus. {Eric Stockton, *New Humanist*, December 1996}

Campion, William (19th Century)

A shoemaker by trade, Campion worked as a shopman in Carlile's and was tried for selling Paine's *Age of Reason*. After a spirited defense, he was found guilty and was sentenced to three years' imprisonment. In prison he edited, in conjunction with J. Clarke, R. Hassell, and T. R. Perre, the *Newgate Monthly Magazine*. {BDF}

CAMPUS FREETHOUGHT ALLIANCE (CFA)

In 1996, students from fifteen campuses launched an alliance for atheists, humanists, and skeptics. Represented were students from the following universities, and more were soon added:

Alabama U at Birmingham (Adam Butler)
Amherst College (David Beckman, Nathan Hartshorn: Doubters' Club)
Auckland United Atheists, New Zealand (Alex Clark)
Birmingham-Southern College (Bradley Davis)
British Columbia U (Michael Kraft of Humanists' Society)
Brock University, St Catherines, Ontario, Canada (Sara E. Moodie)
California U at Irvine (Doug Semier)
Chicago U (Scott Oser)
Christopher Newport U, Virginia (Christopher Green, Gautam Srikanth)
Colorado U at Boulder (Miriam Black of Campus Heretics)
Columbia U (Joel Finkelstein)
Florida International U (David Bendana)
Guelph U (Diana Carter)
Harvard (Derek Araujo)
Houston U (Joe Lynch)
Illinois U at Chicago (Michael S. Valle)
Kalamazoo College (Jason Pittman)
McGill U, Montreal, Quebec, Canada (Stephen Ban)
Marshall U (Deidre Conn; Chad Docterman)
Maryland at College Park (Alireza Aliabadi, Keith Augustine, Brianna Waters)
Massachusetts Institute of Technology (Sarah Carlson)
Minnesota U (Nicholas J. Rezmerski)
Missouri U at Kansas City (Anthony Walsh)
New Mexico State U (John F. Kennedy)
Ohio State University
Oregon U (Selena Brewington)
Pennsylvania State (Daniel Smith)
Puget Sound U at Tacoma, Washington (Nancy Richardson)
Queens U, Ontario, Canada (Jascha Jabes)
State University of NY at Albany (Carrie Fowler)
State University of NY at Buffalo (Etienne Rios)
Stony Brook U (Vincent Bruzzese)
Tel Aviv U, Israel (Amnon Eden)
Temple University, Philadelphia, Pennsylvania (Tim Law)
Tennessee U at Martin (Jason Tippitt)
Texas U at Austin (Michael Lowry)
University College, Los Angeles (Vagan Karayan)
University of Buffalo
Webster (John Muhrer)
Western Washington U (John Simons)
Wisconsin U (Peter Braun, Eric Shook)
Yale University

They issued "A Declaration of Necessity," calling attention to an increasing opposition to freethought and working toward the establishing on campuses skeptical, secular, and freethinking organizations.

In 1998 they issued a "Bill of Rights for Unbelievers."

Officers as of the summer of 1998 were as follows:

- Derek Carl Araujo, President (Harvard)—following his graduation in 1999, Amanda Chesworth became President:
- Daniel Farkas, Vice President (Yale)
- Deidre Conn, Secretary (Marshall)
- August Brunsman, Treasurer (Ohio State)
- David Schummer, Press Coordinator (SUNY Buffalo)
- Adam Butler (Alabama at Birmingham), Pearl Chan (Harvard); Chris Mooney (Yale); Bill Bishop (Florida); Paula Duckhorn (College of Lake Country)—Executive Council

The complete list of groups and officers is found on the Web: <http://www.secularhumanism.org/cfa/>.

(See entry for Bill of Rights for Unbelievers.)
{*International Humanist News*, December 1996}

Camus, Albert (1913—1960)

Camus, the novelist whose works illustrate contemporary humanism, was born and reared in Algeria. Partly of Alsatian, partly of Spanish, descent, he was raised as a member of the French white underclass. His father had been killed in France in October 1914, during which battle he became stone blind and suffered terrible wounds. His mother, left with two sons, worked as a domestic in an Algerian slum quarter, leading Camus to remark later, "I did not learn about liberty from Karl Marx. I learned it from being bone-poor." Tubercular from boyhood, he ran an amateur theatre company, "The Team," a troupe in which no one was a star. The members not only acted but also built sets, sold tickets, and did whatever other jobs were required. Camus looked upon theatre, wrote Olivier Todd in *Camus: Une Vie* (1996), as a social duty not as a vehicle for glamor. He also enjoyed journalism and, when he married (briefly) for the first time he had four typesetters as his witnesses. As an editorialist for *Combat*, he favored Algeria's liberation, which did not occur, however, until two years after his death. Camus had envisioned a federation in which Algeria and France would be equal partners, a dream which never transpired. Todd also detailed the surprising multiplicity of Camus's sexual relationships, describing his skill as a seducer and also the connection between his mood of guilt shown in *La Chute* and his second wife Francine's suicidal attempt of throwing herself out of a window.

In 1948, talking to some Dominican priests, Camus said, "I shall not, as far as I am concerned, try to pass myself off as a Christian in your presence. I share with you the same revulsion from evil. But I do not share your hope, and I continue to struggle against this universe in which children suffer and die."

In 1957, upon winning the Nobel Prize for Literature, he became the first African author–not Wole Soyinka of Nigeria, who won in 1986, or Naguib Mahfoux of Egypt, who won in 1988–to be honored. The Swedish Academy cited his "important literary production that with clear-sighted earnestness illuminated the problems of the human conscience in our times."

His three major works were *The Stranger* (1942), *The Plague* (1947), and *The Myth of Sisyphus* (1942). The first, with its famous opening lines ("Mother died today, or maybe it was yesterday."), showed humans as being outsiders trying to obtain self-awareness in a world they do not understand. It is the story of a thoughtless killer, one whose major wish upon the day of his execution was that he would be greeted by "an enormous crowd who would call out to him in hatred." How tragic, Camus is saying in the novel, that man is a stranger to his environment, a stranger to the humanism of which he is a natural part. *The Plague* is an allegorical account of the efforts by determined people in Oran, Algeria, to fight an epidemic, individuals who assert their humanity by rebelling against their circumstances. (In 1863, a plague had wiped out half the population of his birthplace, Mondavi.) Its character, the atheistic Dr. Rieux, struggles valiantly against the disease, in contrast with the laissez-faire attitude of Father Paneloux, who preaches that the plague has been sent as a punishment by God. The latter work develops his theory of the absurd. Camus wrote with a distinctly humanistic viewpoint: "In a universe suddenly divested of illusions and lights, man feels an alien, a stranger. His exile is without remedy since he is deprived of the memory of a lost home or the hope of a promised land. This divorce between a man and his life, the actor and his setting, is properly the feeling of absurdity."

Although, like Sartre, Camus wrote of "the absurd," he did so in a distinctly different and more constructively humanistic fashion. Sartre tended to think negatively concerning man's absurd and meaningless existence on earth, whereas Camus expressed no nausea at such absurdity, choosing instead to accentuate the positive concerning our existence. An admitted lover of the sun, a pagan, a person who adored life, Camus treated "absurdism" as intellectual. It might be absurd that war is normal or that the deadly bacillus is a fact of life, but humanity needs to love that which is inevitable in this imperfect life of ours. Such a tragic humanism, to Camus, was not to be confused with pessimism.

Martin Seymour-Smith describes how Camus blamed Christianity for the introduction of the notion of original sin, and although Camus recognized life's injustices he knew that man must be positively dedicated to life, must develop a moral responsibility, and must be anti-nihilist. Meursault, the anti-Christ of *L'Étranger,* hates Christ for his sacrifice–for that sacrifice involved pain. As Seymour-Smith points out in *Who's Who in Twentieth-Century Literature* (1976), Camus's "anti-Christianity is one of the most absolute of modern times. (He was courted by some Christians and has–naturally–been described as ultimately Christian)." In *Le Mythe de Sisyphe*, he portrays a man, Smith-Seymour states, not unlike that of the true Nietzsche, "who is doomed to perform an absurd task but who may nevertheless learn to be happy in it. This is a paradox: accept meaninglessness but then fight it with every weapon you have." Adds Seymour-Smith, "Had he lived he could well have gone on to become the world's foremost novelist."

"Violently attacked in the 1960s and 1970s, when theoretical debate ran rife," wrote Germaine Brée, "Camus has emerged in the 1980s as one of the precursors of a revolt against the constraints and evils of totalitarian systems. He has become a classic but a classic whose work has not lost its bite."

Camus was asked in 1960 to contribute to the present work his views concerning humanism, and his secretary responded that he would do so just as soon as he returned from a trip. But it was on that trip that his life ironically and absurdly ended, in a crazy burst of speed by a car he was not driving. Near that wreck was found a mud-stained briefcase containing 144 pages of almost indecipherable handwriting that made up the first draft of the early chapters of a novel based closely on his life. His wife, Francine, knowing her husband was on poor terms with Sartre and other Left Bank luminaries, decided against publication at that time. In 1952, Sartre had broken publicly with Camus over his essay, "The Rebel," in which Camus had denounced Soviet concentration camps. "One thing that Hegel and I have in common," Sartre wrote, "is that Camus has read neither of us."

But in 1994, a time Alan Riding has observed, when "leftist intellectuals no longer rule the roost in Paris," Camus' daughter Catherine published the work under the title *Le premier homme* (*The First Man*). It glorifies Algeria, his birthplace, the nation which he was unable to commit to independence for that would have meant, in his mind, the permanent loss of his childhood home. The work takes up the questions of morality, "how we should act" and how we should live if we do "not believe in God or in reason." Its main character, Jacques (who is a thinly disguised Camus), "was 16, then he was 20, and no one had spoken to him, and he had to learn by himself, to grow alone, in fortitude, in strength, find his own morality and truth, at last to be born as a man."

The work's release resulted in a reassessment of Camus's literary stature. Upon its publication, many in France, where *The Stranger* is required reading in many schools, held that Camus had finally triumphed over Sartre, for it was Sartre who tarnished his old friend's reputation and it was the "anti-humanists" who had contributed to the fashionable view that Camus had declined in status as a writer. The intellectual complaint was that Camus rejected violence and terror in all its forms, particularly in the Algeria he knew and loved. His denunciation of totalitarianism in the Soviet Union and his failure to commit himself to Algerian independence under Arab rule, observed *The New York Times* critic Michiko Kakutani, had "earned him the enmity of the left, while his literary endeavors–engagé, earnest and devoted to the consideration of moral issues–struck the fashionable new avatars of structuralism as old-fashioned, sentimental, and contemptibly humanistic."

Paul Edwards, in *God and the Philosophers*, noted that

> Camus never uses an argument like Sartre's appeal to free will. His certainty that there is no God seems to stem from his belief that the universe and more specifically human life is "absurd." By this he means that the universe is indifferent to the human demand for rationality and justice. Camus's view that human life is absurd and what we should infer from it is worked out in *The Myth of Sisyphus.* Sisyphus has been condemned by the gods to roll a rock to the top of a mountain. As soon as he reaches the top, the rock starts rolling down, and Sisyphus has to start all over again. This cycle is repeated forever. "If this myth is tragic," Camus wrote, "that is because its hero is conscious. Where would his torture be, indeed, if at every step the hope of succeeding upheld him?"

André Glucksmann and Bernard-Henry Lévy, the so-called "New Philosophers," scorned Camus for his "moralizing" obsession with responsibility. But now Glucksmann and Lévy have lost all favor, alleges Tony Judt of New York University: "They have been discredited by their casual resort to future History to justify present crimes, and by the ease with which they asserted that others must suffer for the sins of their own fathers. The lucidity and moral courage of Camus's stand shine through today in a way that was not possible in the polarized world of 1958 [when Camus had written]. 'As for me, I find it disgusting to beat the other man's breast, in the manner of our judge-penitents.'" Judt continues: "What Camus understood perhaps better and earlier than any of his (metropolitan) contemporaries was not Arab nationalism–though as early as 1945 he had predicted that the Arabs could not much longer be expected to tolerate the conditions under which they were governed–but the particular culture of Algeria's inhabitants, and the price that would be paid should anyone attempt to shatter it. The lost world of French Algeria is at the center of his last, unfinished novel, and it is a subject to which French readers are open now in a way that would have been unthinkable in 1960, when the manuscript was found in Camus's briefcase at the scene of his death." (See letter, below, from James T. Farrell.) {CE; EU, Germaine Brée; Jeannette Lowen, "The Search for Connection Between Two Worlds," *Free Inquiry*, Winter 1996-1997; TYD}

CANADIAN ATHEIST

The *Canadian Atheist* is at PO Box 41613, 923 12th St., New Westminster, British Columbia V3M 6L1.

CANADIAN FREETHINKERS

Canadian freethought dates to the Toronto Freethought Society in 1873 and in Montreal to *L'Institut Canadien* in the 1840s. (See Gordon Stein's *Freethought in the United Kingdom and the Commonwealth*, which contains a bibliography. Also see entry for William Dawson Le Sueur, A Canadian man of letters who has been called "the Sage of Ottawa.")

CANADIAN HUMANIST NEWS

A quarterly, *Canadian Humanist News* is at PO Box 3736, Postal Station C, Ottawa ON, K1Y 4J8, Canada. E-mail: <hac@magi.com".

CANADIAN HUMANISTS

British Columbia boasts the highest percentage of Canadians claiming no religion: 30% compared to the national average of 12%. In Greater Vancouver, 31% choose "none" when asked their religious affiliation. Mia Stainsby, writing in the *Vancouver Sun*, explains this as follows: "It's a gorgeous province with more tempting things to do than go to church or a temple on Sunday. We're said to be a more pleasure-loving province. The 'nones' group is top-heavy with young people, who also are attracted to B.C."

On the Web: <www.secularhumanism.org/cfa/orgs.html> and <magi.com/~hac>.

Brock University humanists are on the Web: <http://www.secularhumanism.org/cfa/orgs.html>.

The Canadian Humanist Association is on the Web: <http://infoweb.magi.com/~hac/hac.html>.

Canadian Humanist News has the E-mail of <hac@magi.com>.

Canadian Humanist Publications, Box 3769, Postal Station C, Ottawa, Ontario, Canada K1Y 4J8, is an associate member of the International Humanist and Ethical Union.

Canadians for Intellectual Freedom is an ad hoc group of humanists, atheists, and freethinkers, according to *Canadian Humanist News*, February 1998.

The Humanist Association of Canada (HAC), PO Box 3736, Station C, Ottawa, Ontario, Canada K1Y 4J8, is a full member of the International Humanist and Ethical Union.

The Humanist Association of Ottawa Newsletter is a monthly obtained from PO Box 8733, Postal Station T, Ottawa, Ontario, K1G 3J1.

Humanist Association of Toronto, Box 44512, 2376 Eglinton Ave. East, Toronto M1K 5K3. Phone: (416) 966-1316. E-mail: <mail@humanist.toronto.on.ca>. On the Web: <www.humanist.toronto.on.ca>.

Humanist in Canada, a quarterly, is at PO Box 3769, Postal Station C, Ottawa, Ontario, K1Y 4J8. E-mail: <jepiercy@cyberus.ca>.

The Humanists' Society at the University of British Columbia, of which Michael Kraft is President, is on the Web at: <www.ams.ubc.ca/Clubs/Social/humanist/>.

McGill University's Atheist, Agnostic, and Secular Humanist Society in Montreal, Quebec, is on the Web: <http://www.secularhumanism.org/cfa/orgs.html>.

University of Regina humanists are on the Web at: <http://www.secularhumanism.org/cfa/orgs.html>.

John McTaggart of Alberta has compared Canadian and Netherlands humanist movements. His thorough research concluded that the lack of success in Canada's humanist movement is attributable to (a) the absence of strong secular or irreligious themes in the development of Canadian society; (b) a greater degree of formal separation between church and state—a "naturalistic," rather than a "pluralistic" approach, which is characteristic of the Dutch model, and has ensured that humanists in the Netherlands have received state support for many of their projects; and (c) the abolitionist approach of the Canadian movement.

Svend Robinson, a member of the Canadian Parliament, has gone public as being both gay and a non-theist. (See entries for William Algie, J. Lloyd Brereton, British Columbia Humanists, John McTaggart, Henry Morgentaler, and Peter R. Smith.) {*Freethought Today*, November 1995}

CANADIAN UNITARIANS

The Canadian Unitarian Council (CUC) includes forty-four congregations from coast to coast, ranging in size from 500 members to small fellowships. An estimated five thousand adults and almost eight hundred children are members.

Unlike Unitarian movements in Transylvania, England, and the United States, the Canadian movement did not arise from indigenous roots. Its earliest members were immigrants who brought their religion with them. The first congregation was established in Montreal in 1842. New Ones were affiliated with British and American associations. The CUC was established in 1961.

According to the CUC, until fifty years ago most Canadian congregations were Christocentric in belief and practice, but now the majority is humanist. Like Unitarians everywhere Unitarians currently have moved toward a deeper spirituality drawing on the insights of ecology, feminism, and world religion.

In 1998 Ellen Campbell was Executive Director of the CUC, 188 Eglington Avenue East, Toronto, Ontario M4P 2X7 Canada. On the Web: <http://www.web.net/~cuc> and <http://www.uua.org/icuu/icuu-northamerica.html>. E-mail: <cuc@web.net>.

Canby, Henry Seidel (1878—1961)

Canby, a founder of *Saturday Review of Literature* and its editor until 1936, wrote *Thoreau: A Biography* (1939) and many books of literary and social criticism. Asked his views concerning humanism, Canby responded to the present author that it would take a week of work and ten or fifteen thousand words. But, he added,

> I wrote in the 20's several essays for the *Saturday Review* on humanism from the literary angle, and even spoke at the famous meeting at Carnegie Hall. My interests, however, were much more literary than philosophical, and in my busy life since I have not kept up in any scholarly fashion, though I have done quite a little reading.
> {WAS, 5 April 1949}

CANDOMBLÉ

The strongest of Brazil's syncretist religions, Candomblé mixes the nature-based beliefs some four million slaves brought from Africa with the Catholicism of the Portuguese colonists. Its pantheon of orixas—gods and goddesses of wind, oceans, still water, metals, and fire—correspond to Catholic saints and appear in masks and swaying skirts of raffia. At one time the rituals of animal sacrifice, possession, music, and dance were thought to be a form of devil worship. One individual, a priestess by the name of Cleusa Millet (1931-1998), is credited along with her mother of transforming Candomblé into a religion accepted in the highest levels of Brazilian society. {Diana Jean Schemo, *The New York Times*, 25 October 1998}.

Canestrini, Giovanni (Born 1835)

An Italian naturalist, Canestrini taught natural history at Geneva and is known for his popularization of the works of Darwin, which he translated into Italian. At Padua, where he taught zoology, anatomy, and comparative physiology, he published a *Memoir of Charles Darwin* (1882). {BDF; RAT}

Canfield, Russell (19th Century)

Canfield edited *Temple of Reason* in Philadelphia from 1835 to 1837.

Canney, Maurice Arthur (1872—1941)

Canney was a professor at Manchester University and a member of the editorial staff of the *Encyclopaedia Biblica* (1897—1903). From 1912 on, he edited the *Journal of the Manchester Egyptian and Oriental Society*. His chief works were *An Encyclopaedia of Religions* (1921) and *Givers of Life* (1923) {RE}

CANNIBALISM

- Cannibal, n. A gastronome of the old school who preserves the simple tastes and adheres to the natural diet of the pre-pork period.

—Ambrose Bierce
The Devil's Dictionary

- "Must have been someone he ate."

—Comedian Bob Hope
in "The Road to Zanzibar,"
upon hearing an African native burp

Cannibalism, which is associated with a superstitious belief that the eater will absorb the magical powers of whatever he eats, has involved eating penises, breasts, hearts, brains, and other human parts, but it also has included "eating the god" (as it was called in Mexico) or food and drink in which the god was believed to be incarnated. Aztecs, according to Frazer, made dough images of Huitzlipochtli that were blessed by the priests long before Catholics arrived in Mexico. Westermarck's *Origin and Development of the Moral Ideas* (1926) described cannibalism on four continents.

Preservèd Smith's work on theophagy emphasized the religious aspects of communion, the sacrament of figuratively eating the body and drinking the blood of God. Early Christians ate the dough image of a child at Easter, which may have given rise to the pagan charge of killing and eating children. The partaking of corn and wine at the Eleusinian mysteries may have influenced the Christian idea of a Eucharist. Rendel Harris in *Eucharistic Origins* (1927) suggests that the Christian rite was taken almost bodily from the cult of Isis and Osiris. *Cannibalism from Sacrifice to Survival* (1995) by Hans Askenasy, discussing "man's last taboo," states that most "appear to need a few taboos and for the time being cannibalism seems to serve that purpose admirably."

The Christian view about "transubstantiation," or the Eucharist or communion, is that the worshiper is eating the body of Christ, symbolized by bread, and drinking His blood, symbolized by wine. Catholic doctrine holds that these substances turn miraculously into the substance of Christ. Freethinkers often hold that most Christians do not fully understand transubstantiation, often avoiding services at which communion is served.

In *The Man-Eating Myth: Anthropology and Anthropophagy* (1979), William Arens differed from many of his fellow scientists. He claimed there has never been a human culture that has routinely eaten its dead or that killed and devoured its enemies. Exceptions were noted, but these involved incidents such as people starving after an accident or during famine.

Different viewpoints are easily found. The Caribs ate not for appetite but to render an enemy's spirit harmless, Caribbean journalist Larry Millman has written. First, they stuffed the body with herbs and spices, then trussed it on a pole, roasting it over a medium fire while women basted the body, lard being caught in calabash gourds. Reportedly, the French tasted the best, the Dutch were flavorless, the Spaniards tough and stringy. No related taste test was supplied for missionaries. (See entries for Communion, Preservèd Smith, and Theophagy. *Suddenly Last Summer* (1958) by Tennessee Williams brought up the subject.) {RE}

Cannizzaro, Stanislao (1826—1910)

An Italian chemist, Cannizzaro joined the Garibaldians and was elected to the Sicilian parliament. He was awarded the Gran Cordone. Besides chemical works, Cannizzaro wrote *L'Emancipazione della ragione* (1865) and other rationalist volumes.

Cannizzaro, Tommaso (1837—1916)

An Italian poet, Cannizzaro translated Omar Khayyam and the sonnets of Camoens. His *Tramonti* contains many rationalist poems, as in the ode on the death of Victor Hugo: "Inexorable enemies of truth,/Ye priests and kings and brothers of the dark." {RAT}

Cannon, Ida Maud (1877-1960)

Cannon, a Unitarian, was a social worker who became known as the founder of medical social work.

CANON

For theists, a canon is an ecclesiastical law or code of laws which a church council has established. Included in a canon are, for example, the books of the Bible which are officially accepted as Holy scripture. In addition, the canon is that part of the Mass which ends just before the Lord's Prayer. Also, a canon is a clergyman who belongs to the chapter or the staff of a cathedral or collegiate church.

For non-theists in the humanities, the canon is that body of Western thought and art that is considered to be at the core of our education. But who is to determine which works are to be included? Harold Bloom in *The Western Canon, The Books and School of the Ages* (1994) concentrated upon twenty-six major authors and included dozens of others he considered central to the canon. Shakespeare is ordinarily considered pre-eminent, and Bloom included Molière, Ibsen, and Beckett. But by not including Racine, Lope de Vega, Strindberg, Chekhov, Shaw, Brecht, or Pirandello, he was criticized heavily. Similarly, he included Tolstoy and Proust, but no Dostoyevsky, Gogol, Turgenev, Flaubert, Balzac, or Stendhal. In the humanities, no agreement is to be found as to what works are definitely part of the canon.

Cantab, A. (19th Century)

A freethinker, Cantab wrote *Jesus Versus Christianity* (1873). {GS}

Cantoni, Carlo (1840—1906)

An Italian philosopher, Cantoni edited the *Rivista Italiana di Filosofia* and wrote philosophical works of a Kantian complexion. A Senator, Cantoni was Rector of Pavia University. {RAT}

Cantor, Nathaniel (20th Century)

Cantor has been an active member of the American Humanist Association. {HNS}

Capaldi, Nicholas (1939—)

A professor of philosophy at Queens College of the City University of New York (CUNY), Capaldi is author of *The Art of Deception* (1987). {*Free Inquiry*, Fall, 1982}

Cape, Emily Palmer (Born 1865)

Cape was an American writer, the first woman student at Columbia College. She studied sociology under Prof. Lester Ward and, like him, was an agnostic. With Ward, she compiled *Glimpses of the Cosmos* (12 volumes, 1913). Both Ward and she were agnostics and ardent humanitarians. {RAT}

Capek, Maja V. (1888-1966)

A Czechoslovakian Unitarian minister, Capek helped create the Flower Communion and introduced it to Unitarians in America and Europe.

Capek, Norbert Fabian (1870—1942)

The founder of Unitarianism in Czechoslovakian, Capek first became interested in liberal religion at the 1910 Berlin Congress of the International Association of Religious Freedom, which he had attended at President Jan Masaryk's urging. The Liberal Fellowship, which led to the establishment of the Religious Society of Czechoslovakian Unitarians, was founded in 1923.

In his *The Absolute At Large* (1944), he included a typically humanistic observation: " 'You know,' Father Jost declared, 'the loftier the things in which a man believes, the more fiercely he despises those who do not believe in them. And yet the greatest of all beliefs would be belief in one's fellow men.' "

A fellow Unitarian, Richard Henry, has written that it is difficult to be sure about details of Capek's death:

> Norbert and his daughter, Zora, were arrested on March 28, 1941. They were imprisoned first in Pankrac prison in Prague, then sent to different prisons: Norbert to Ceske Budjovice, Zora to Dresden. Capek arrived in Dachau concentration camp on July 5, 1942, and was sent on a transport from Dachau to Hartheim Castle, near Linz, Austria, on October 12th that same year, where he was gassed. Nazi authorities gave the family the date of his death as November 3, 1942. (Bureaucratic convenience rather than truth determined dates given out for such matters by Nazi authorities.) That information was relayed by Karel Haspl, his son-in-law and successor, to Frederick M. Eliot, then President of the AUA, who repeated the (mis-) information in an editorial in the *Christian Register* in November 1942. Official records in the archive at Dachau confirm the date of the transport and list Norbert as one of the prisoners so transported.

{pdhenry@compuserve.com>; U; WAS, 21 April 1998}

CAPITAL DISTRICT HUMANIST SOCIETY

The Capital District Humanist Society is an organization of humanists in Upstate New York, Western Massachusetts, and Southern Vermont. E-mail: <cdhs@global2000.net>.

CAPITALISM

Capitalism is an economic system which involves a free market. Philosophers and non-believers are free to be capitalists, socialists, communists, libertarians, or supporters of other economic systems. Of concern to freethinkers is that the combined wealth of the world's richest 225 people at the end of the century was $1 trillion, whereas the combined annual income of the world's poorest 2.5 billion people was also $1 trillion.

However, Roman Catholics, according to their catechism, are advised that "any system that subordinates the basic rights of individuals and of groups to the collective organization of production is contrary to human dignity. Every practice that reduces persons to nothing more than a means of profit enslaves man, leads to idolizing money, and contributes to the spread of atheism. 'You cannot serve God and mammon.' The Church has rejected the totalitarian and atheistic ideologies associated in modern times with 'communism' or 'socialism.' She has likewise refused to accept, in the practice of 'capitalism,' individualism and the absolute primacy of the law of the marketplace over human labor. Regulating the economy solely by centralized planning perverts the basis of social bonds; regulating it solely by the law of the marketplace fails social justice, for there are many human needs which cannot be satisfied by the market. Reasonable regulation of the marketplace and economic initiatives, in keeping with a just hierarchy of values and a view to the common good, is to be commended."

According to one wag:

- Capitalism = exploitation of man by man.
- Socialism = the reverse.

Caplan, Arthur (20th Century)

Caplan, who is Director of the Center fot Bioethics and Trustee Professor of Bioethics at the University of Pennsylvania, is a leading bioethicist. He wrote *When Medicine Went Mad* (1992) as well as several hundred articles and reviews in professionaljournals. In "The Future of Engineering Humans" (*Free Inquiry*, Fall 1999), he explains that the major influences on his thinking have been Ernest Nagel, John Dewey, and Sydney Hook, adding, "I think of myself as a pragmatist, although I am not quite sure my pragmatism is the same as Dewey's. I am also influenced by biological thinking about evolution and genetics so that I am somewhat Aristotelian in outlook. And my real hero was Socrates, who I think knew what he did not know and pushed others hard to be sure what they thought they knew was really true."

Capone, Al(phonse) (or Alfonso Capone) (1899—1947)

Capone, the American gangster who contributed generously to the Catholic Church, was indicted in 1931 by a Federal grand jury for evasion of income tax payments. His business card indicated he was a used furniture dealer. In 1939, physically and mentally shattered by syphilis, about which he was so puritanical he had not asked for physicians to help, he was released. His Mt. Carmel Cemetery grave in Chicago, Illinois, has the epitaph, "My Jesus Mercy." (See entry for WASP. Digby Baltzell the sociologist considered Capone "one of the organizing geniuses of his generation.)

Capote, Truman (1924-1984)

- Truman Capote has made lying an art. A *minor* art.

—Gore Vidal

- Good career move.

—Gore Vidal
upon hearing about Capote's death

Born Truman Streckfus Persons, Capote achieved fame with his first novel, *Other Voices, Other Rooms* (1948). He also wrote *The Grass Harp* (1951), *Breakfast at Tiffany's* (1958), and *In Cold Blood* (1966), the latter of which was described as a "nonfiction novel" inasmuch as it told of actual events but in novelistic form. He became a member of the American Academy of Arts and Letters.

Cappon, Alexander (1900—)

Cappon wrote *The Scope of Shelley's Philosophical Thinking* (1935). He also worked on the staff of *The New Humanist* and later joined its editor, Harold Buschman, on the faculty of the University of Kansas City. There, Cappon edited the *University of Kansas City Review* and was a professor of English. {EW}

Captain Sensible: See entry for Sensible, Captain.

CAPYBARAS

Capybaras are large guinea-pig-like animals that live in Venezuela. According to zoologists, they are mammals. The Roman Catholic Church, however, classifies them, for culinary purposes, as fish. {*The Economist*, 7 November 1998}

Caracappa, Michael G. (20th Century)

Caracappa is a rationalist who writes for *The American Rationalist*. Reviewing L. Sprague de Camp's *The Ape-Man Within* (1995), Caracappa wrote,

> It is false to say white Americans enslaved blacks. It needs to be correctly restated: Certain white Americans before 1865 enslaved certain blacks who lived before 1865.

Carazo, Rodrigo [President] (1926—)

Carazo addressed the Tenth International Humanist and Ethical Union World Congress held in Buffalo (1988). He is President of the University of Peace, A Catholic, and an ex-President of Costa Rica.

Cardano, Girolamo (1501—1576)

Cardano, better known as **Jerome Cardan**, was an Italian mathematician and physician. He was excluded from the Milan College of Physicians because of his illegitimate birth, at which time he and his young wife were compelled to take refuge in the workhouse. Understandably, his first work was an exposure of the fallacies of that faculty. In 1563 he was arrested for heresy, was released, and was deprived of his professorship.

Despite some superstition, Cardano is said to have done much to forward science, especially by his work on algebra. Scaliger accused him of atheism. Pünjer says, "Cardanus deserves to be named along with Telesius as one of the principal founders of natural philosophy."

On September 20th, 1576, he is said to have starved himself in order to verify his own prediction of his death at that time. {BDF}

Cardaronella, Loretta (20th Century)

Cardaronella is active with the Secular Humanist Society of Las Vegas. (See entry for Nevada Humanists.) {FD}

Cardiff, Ira D. (20th Century)

Cardiff is a humanist who wrote *If Christ Came to New York* (1940?) and *What Great Men Think of Religion* (1945). {FUS; GS; HNS}

Carducci, Giosuè (1835—1907)

Winner of the 1906 Nobel Prize in Literature, Carducci ranks with the greatest of the modern Italian poets, including fellow unbeliever Leopardi. He was strongly anti-Catholic. Among his works are *Inno a Satana* [Hymn to Satan] (1865) and *Rime e ritme* (1898). In an 1857 poem he wrote, "*Il secoletto vil che cristianeggia* [This vile christianizing century]." In 1860 he became professor of Greek in Bologna University but was suspended for a time because of an address to Mazzini.

In 1865 he wrote a fiery "Hymn to Satan" and, according to McCabe, never abandoned his atheism in the days of his fame. In *Naturalismo Italiano*, Carelle quotes Carducci as saying, "I know neither truce of God nor peace with the Vatican or any priests. They are the real and unaltering enemies of Italy." In 1876, Carducci was elected as republican deputy to the Italian Parliament for Lugo di Romagna. {BDF; CE; JM; JMR; RAT}

Carey, Alexander Edward (1922—1987)

Carey was an Australian humanist, farmer, and psychologist. A lecturer in social and applied psychology at the University of New South Wales, Carey wrote and lectured extensively. He was active in opposing Australian involvement in the Vietnam War and, for some years, was vice-chairman of the Humanist Society of New South Wales.

Carey, Alice (Born 1820)

A Universalist, Carey was a storyteller and a poet. She was the first president of Sorosis, the early women's intellectual and feminist organization.

Carey, Richard (1952—1996)

Carey was an active member of the Humanist Association of Massachusetts.

Cargill, Oscar (1898—1971)

A professor of English at New York University and author of *Walt Whitman's Leaves of Grass* (1950), Cargill wrote the present author in 1954 about his views on humanism:

> I certainly would not apply the term "naturalistic humanism" to my own thinking. Whereas I think I would be satisfied with the phrase "scientific humanism," if I understand what Julian Huxley means by that term. I am afraid that I am a "do-gooder" and an experimentalist in the sense that John Dewey and William James were experimentalists.
>
> I object to the phrase "naturalistic humanism" because naturalism means to me determinism. So far as I can see, one's thinking is determined only by the heritage of one's time and one may make choices among the ideologies represented by that intellectual heritage. I objected very much years ago when a critic termed by thinking positivistic criticism.

{WAS, 17 August 1954}

Carley, Adam L. (20th Century)

Carley, who holds a number of patents and has been instrumental in the starting of several business, is a graduate of the Massachusetts Institute of Technology. In *Free Inquiry* (Fall 1994) he wrote, "What is 'Consciousness'?", concluding that when scientists eventually determine the answer the genetic blueprint of consciousness will be so all-encompassing it "might fit on your PC's hard disk." But consciousness-explaining, he holds, will not be accepted as comfortably as evolution was. "A breakthrough not in science but in education would be required for that." The article won the 1994 Selma Forkosch Award for the journal's best article that year.

Carlile, Eliza Sharples (c. 1805—1861)

The second (common-law) wife of Richard Carlile, Eliza Carlile was the first female freethought lecturer in England. When Charles Bradlaugh needed a place to stay, after being accused of atheism by his pastor, Eliza boarded him. She edited *Isis*, a London publication, in 1832. Carlile wrote *The Glossary of the Bible, Chiefly Designed for Children* (c. 1830). {BDF; EU, Joel H. Wiener; FUK; GS; VI}

Carlile, Jane (19th Century)

The first wife of Richard Carlile, Jane Carlile carried on his business during his imprisonment. In 1821, she was sentenced to two years' imprisonment. Of her three children, Richard, Alfred, and Thomas Paine, the last edited the *Regenerator*, a Chartist paper published in Manchester in 1839. {BDF; FUK}

Carlile, Mary-Anne (19th Century)

A freethinker, Carlile wrote *The Defence of Mary-Anne Carlile to the Vice Society's Indictment* (1821). {GS}

Carlile, Richard (1790—1843)

An English journalist, reformer, and freethinker born at Ashburton in Devonshire, Carlile spent an entire lifetime advocating freethought and republicanism. He also resisted the blasphemy laws. in order to secure freedom of the press spent over nine years and four months in jail, nearly one-third of his adult life. He had to pay fines amounting to many thousand pounds. Among his crimes were publishing the suppressed works of Thomas Paine, William Hone, and his own *Political Litany* (1817). He supported birth control, universal suffrage, and freedom to publish including material on phrenology and mesmerism. Although Robertson holds that "Carlile had always been a deist, and, now near his end [he lapsed] into a kind of theistic mysticism," Berman holds that Carlile was never a deist, that he was first an agnostic, later an atheist. McCabe agrees, stating that from 1821 onward Carlile was an aggressive atheist. In a letter Carlile flatly asserts, "I am an atheist" and "there is no God," signing the letter, "Your atheistical friend, Richard Carlile." "The fable of a god or gods visiting the earth did not originate with Christianity," he declared, further riling the religionists.

Carlile is considered to be the first atheistic leader who exerted a wide influence by means of the periodical, mass meetings, and the courtroom. Berman states that Charles Southwell took over the championship of atheism from Carlile, "who had moved away from atheism in the 1830s to a confused form of mystical theism." He was an editor of such publications as *The Republican* (1819—1826), *The Moralist* (1823), *Lion* (1828—1829), *Prompter* (1830—1831), and *Scourge* (1834—1835). Once, when his house was seized because he refused to pay church-rates, he put life-size figures of a devil and a bishop arm-in-arm in his shop window in the center of London. Eventually, he wore out his persecutors, who quit troubling him. The British *Dictionary of National Biography* wrote that he "did more than any other man for the freedom of the press."

Thirteen days before his death Carlile penned these words: "The enemy with whom I have to grapple is one with whom no peace can be made. Idolatry will not parley; superstition will not treat on covenant. They must be uprooted for public and individual safety." He was attended in his last illness by Dr. Thomas Lawrence, the author of the once famous "Lectures on Man."

Wishing to be useful in death as in life, Carlile devoted his body to dissection. The family complied with his wish, and the post-mortem examination was recorded in the *Lancet*. The burial took place at Rensal Green Cemetery, where a clergyman insisted on reading the Church Service over his remains. According to Foote, Carlile's eldest son Richard, who represented his sentiments as well as his name, "very properly protested against the proceedings as an outrage upon the principles of his father and the wishes of the family. Of course the remonstrance was disregarded, and Richard, his brothers, and their friends left the ground. . . . After their departure, the clergyman called the great hater of priests his "dear departed brother" and declared that the rank Materialist had died "in the sure and certain hope of a glorious resurrection." {BDF; EU, Joel H. Wiener; FO; FUK; HAB; JM; JMR; RAT; RE; RSR; VI; TRI; TYD}

Carlin, George Denis (1937—)

A comedian who has appeared on numerous major television shows, Carlin has also been in many movies. In 1972 he received a Grammy award for best FM/AM comedy recording. The author of *Sometimes A Little Brain Damage Can Help*, he is often critical of the devoutly religious in his humor. "Religion is just mind control," he has stated.

In a 1995 appearance on Tom Snyder's CBS talk program, Carlin defended his non-belief in a "man in the sky" who tells you "where you shouldn't put your hands." To *The New York Times*, he confirmed that although he attended Cardinal Hayes High School in the Bronx, "They gave me the tools to reject my faith. They taught me to question and think for myself and to believe in my instincts to such an extent that I just said, 'This is a wonderful fairy tale they have going here, but it's not for me.' "

In one of his acts, Carlin said

> One of the things humans did wrong was to believe in this guy God, to believe that there's really a man in the sky who cares about any of this, and who directs our feelings or thoughts or has a report card or a scorecard on our behavior. This is really a crippling belief. And what religions do is to use it to control people and scare them.

In *Brain Droppings* he further develops his freethinking:

> I've begun worshiping the sun for a number of reasons. First of all, unlike some other gods I could mention, I can see the sun. It's there for me every day. And the things it brings me are quite apparent all the time: heat, light, food, a lovely day. There's no mystery, no one asks for money, I don't have to dress up, and there's no boring pageantry. And interestingly enough, I have found that the prayers I offer to the sun and the prayers I formerly offered "God" are all answered at about the same 50-percent rate.

During a 1999 HBO special, "You Are All Diseased," Carlin in a live recording said,

> In the Bullshit Department, a businessman can't hold a candle to a clergyman. 'Cause I gotta tell you the truth, folks. When it comes to bullshit, big-time, major league bullshit, you have to stand in awe of the all-time champion of false promises and exaggerated claims, religion. No contest. No contest. Religion. Religion easily has the greatest bullshit story ever told.

In a 1999 interview with James A. Haught, Carlin told of his positive views about feeling connected with the universe, said of the Vatican that it "is up to its ass in political troublemaking and deal-making," called Opus Dei "another semisecret organization," and compared the Bible to "The Three Little Pigs," "Little Red Riding Hood," and "Humpty-Dumpty": "There is no Humpty-Dumpty and there is no God. None. Not one. No God. Never was."

Carlin became the first recipient of the Freedom From Religion Foundation's "The Emperor Has No Clothes Award." (See entry for Emperor Has No Clothes Award.) {CA}

Carlson, Anton J. (1875—1956)

Carlson was a scientist who signed Humanist Manifesto I. In 1953, he was named Humanist of the Year by the American Humanist Association. A professor of physiology at the University of Chicago, Carlson was known on the campus as "Ajax," the nickname given him because of his resemblance to the Greek hero who fought his battles without calling on the gods for aid. He denied the existence of a life after death, leaving the Lutheran ministry, and at the age of twenty-nine received fame by establishing that the heartbeat begins with the nerve and then reaches and sets off the heart muscle.

He commenced his University of Chicago classes at 7 a.m., and once flunked half of the senior class for failure to pass a surprise examination. One of the world's leading authorities on the physiology of hunger and on the properties of various foods, he proved the nutritive properties of oleomargarine at a time when oleo was illegally sold unless its coloring was separate from the oleo. This was required in order to distinguish it from creamery products. He also insisted that alcoholics be treated as sick persons rather than delinquents and treated them accordingly. He fought for vivisection, saying, "If man isn't worth more than a dog, then our efforts to improve man are in error."

Carlson was the 94th president of the American Association for the Advancement of Science, and he was an adviser to Herbert Hoover's U.S. Food Administration program after World War I. Medical history credits him with refuting the theory of Dr. Ivan Pavlov concerning the ebb and flow of gastric juices. Most of Carlson's research in this connection was done on himself, and he was able to prove to the satisfaction of many noted scientists that gastric juices do not flow according to the stimuli supposed by Pavlov to be responsible. His major books were *The Machinery of the Body* and *The Control of Hunger and Disease*.

In *Science and the Supernatural* (1945), Carlson wrote, "Science nurtures inquiry, the supernatural stifles it. . . . The supernatural has no support in science, is incompatible with science, [and] is frequently an active foe of science. It is unnecessary for the good life." {FUS; HM1; HNS; HNS2}

Carlson, Eric W. (20th Century)

When he reviewed books for *The Humanist* in the 1950s, Carlson was an English teacher at the University of Connecticut. He is author of *Emerson's Literary Criticism* (1995).

Carlson, John (20th Century)

Carlson is a production editor of the atheistic *Truth Seeker*.

Carlson, Sarah (20th Century)

Carlson, while a student at the Massachusetts Institute of Technology, was one of the founding members of Campus Freethought Alliance and of MIT's Atheists, Agnostics, and Humanists. {*International Humanist News*, December 1996}

Carlson, Shawn (20th Century)

Carlson, who heads the Society for Amateur Scientists, is on the Council for Secular Humanism's Faith-Healing Investigation Project.

Carlton, Henry (1785—1863)

Carlton was an American jurist, a judge of the Supreme Court in Louisiana. His *Liberty and Necessity* (1857) showed him to be a deist as well as determinist. Ueberweg called him the "Anthony Collins of America." {RAT}

Carlyle, John Aitken (1801—1879)

The brother of Thomas Carlyle, John Carlyle was a writer who translated Dante's *Inferno*. {RAT}

Carlyle, Thomas (1795—1881)

Carlyle, who intended originally to enter the ministry, left the University of Edinburgh because he developed strong religious doubts. In his reading of German literature, he became influenced by Goethe as well as the transcendental philosophers. *Sartor Resartus* (1833—1834) details a spiritual autobiography in which he saw the material world as mere clothing for the spiritual one. The God of his beliefs was an immanent and friendly ruler of an orderly universe. In his portraits of the great leaders of the French Revolution, he extended his view of the divinity of man. What he liked about Voltaire, he once wrote, is that he "gave the death-stab to superstition." At the age of fifteen, he had horrified his mother with the question, "Did God Almighty come down and make wheelbarrows in a shop?" A friend of Emerson, Carlyle conveyed to susceptible readers a non-Christian view of existence, according to Robertson. He also knew Henry James Sr., who summed up Carlyle as "the same old sausage, fizzing and sputtering in his own grease."

"It is not possible that educated, honest men can even profess much longer to belief in historical Christianity," he declared. His heresy clearly appears in *Life of John Sterling*. Although in *Sartor Resartus* he appears to follow the lines of Goethe's pantheism, Carlyle confided to the poet Allingham, who wrote in his diary that Carlyle told him, "I have for many years strictly avoided going to church or having anything to do with Mumbo Jumbo [a reference to the Christian God]. . . . We know nothing. All is, and must be, utterly incomprehensible." Once asked if he was a pantheist, Carlyle retorted, "No, never was; nor a *pot-theist*, either." In a biography, J. A. Froude wrote, "We have seen him confessing to Irving that he did not believe as his friend did in the Christian religion," that "the special miraculous occurrences of sacred history were not credible to him."

Froude shocked many by doing what Carlyle had asked him to do, write a truthful biography. As a result he included details of Carlyle's impotence and the unhappiness of the Carlyles' marriage, items that led to accusations that he had been a traitor to his friend.

According to biographers David A. Wilson and David W. MacArthur, in the last week of his 85th year, after several weeks of pain during which he could barely speak, Carlyle awoke from a sound sleep and to his niece said, "So this is Death–well. . . . " {BDF; CE; FUK; JM; JMR; JMRH; RAT; RE; RSR; TRI}

Carlysle, Brian (20th Century)
Carlysle is on the staff of the atheistic *Truth Seeker*.

Carmack, John (20th Century)
Carmack is the lead programmer for and software owner of such computer games as "Wolfenstein 3rd," "Doom," and "Quake." He has written that he has no belief in luck, fate, karma, or god(s), that the only casino game that interests him is Blackjack. {CA}

Carnap, Rudolf (1891—1970)
Carnap was a German-American philosopher, a logical positivist, and author of *The Logical System of Language* (1937). Asked about humanism, he replied to the present author,

> I should say that among the positions outlined I would choose naturalistic or scientific humanism as nearest to my position. (I would not like the label "religious humanism." Indeed, "atheistic humanism" would fit better, but this should, of course, not be interpreted in the sense of existentialism.) I find myself in agreement with the basic attitudes as explained in Corliss Lamont's book, disregarding minor differences in questions of epistemology and the like.

(See Norman M. Martin's entry for Carnap in the *Encyclopedia of Philosophy*, Vol. 2.) {CE; HNS; WAS, 13 August 1954}

Carneades (c. 213 —129 B.C.E.)
A teacher in Plato's Academy, Carneades worked out a theoretical formulation with Arcesilaus that showed nothing can be known by our senses or our reason. He therefore was one of the first of the academic skeptics. H. J. Blackham, in *New Humanist* (January 1990), explains that Carneades "redeemed epistemology by shifting the question from the objectivity of sense perception to using the subjectivity of perception, brought under control in different levels of permanent suspension of judgment, but in well-founded judgments of probability."

Bertrand Russell in his *History of Philosophy* (1945) relates how Carneades taught young Romans anxious to ape Greek manners and acquire Greek culture by expounding the views of Aristotle and Plato on justice. The next lecture, however, refuted all that he had said in his first, "not with a view to establishing opposite conclusions, but merely to show that every conclusion is unwarranted."

Charles Hartshorne described Carneades's skepticism by saying he thought logic must take account of free will and the probable indeterminateness of the future. Thus "x will occur" may be neither true nor false, since there may at present exist no cause to make it so. Really, "x will occur" and "x will not occur" are both false if the truth is that x may-or-may-not occur. Hartshorne, noting that none of the writings of Carneades survive, cites Levi ben Gerson as insisting that where there is no determinate reality, all determinate assertions are false. {BDF; CE; ER; EU, Richard H. Popkin; JMRH}

Carnegie, Andrew (1835—1919)
Carnegie, a famed philanthropist, was an agnostic, according to Moncure Conway. From youth he was a skeptic, as illustrated by his mother's telling him one sabbath, "You would have enjoyed the sermon today, Andrew. There wasn't a word of religion in it." Carnegie once said he was "a disciple of Confucius and Benjamin Franklin." He is credited with having given away $332,000,000. during his lifetime, a sum which included 2,811 free public libraries in the United States, England, and Scotland as well as 7,689 church organs in several countries, once saying this was "in the hope that the organ music will distract the congregation's attention from the rest of the service."

When asked for funds that missionaries to China could use, Carnegie refused, saying that "we do a grievous wrong to the Chinese by trying to force our religion upon them against their wishes."

As for any afterlife, he said, "I will give a million dollars for any convincing proof of a future life."

As for prayer, he declared, "I have not bothered Providence with my petitions for about forty years." As for God, "I don't believe in God. My God is patriotism. Teach a man to be a good citizen and you have solved the problem of life."

Although he never joined a church, he attended the Universalist church in New York City of which his wife was a member. Her minister, in fact, had married the two. {CE; EG; JM; RAT; RE; TYD}

Carneri, Bartholomâus von (1821—1909)
Carneri was a German writer who sat in the Austrian Parliament with the Liberals. He wrote *Morality and Darwinism* (1871) and *Der Mensch als Selbstweck* (Humanity as its Own Proper Object) (1877). He was one of the founders of the Monistic Association. {BDF; RAT}

Carnes, Paul (20th Century)
Carnes was a President of the American Unitarian Universalist Association from 1977 to 1979. {U}

Carney, Kevin G. (20th Century)
Carney is an atheist who wrote "Spirituality Without God." {*RFD*, Summer-Fall 1996}

Carolla, Adam (20th Century)
Carolla, co-host of a nightly syndicated radio and MTV talk show, "Love Line," regularly tells listeners that he is an atheist. "Nah, there's no bigger atheist than me," he has said. "Well, I take that back. I'm a cancer screening away from going agnostic and a biopsy away from full-fledged Christian." {CA}

Carnot, Lazare Hippolyte (1801—1888)
Carnot, a French statesman, edited a Saint-Simonian journal and was in the Parliament. At the Revolution of 1848 he became Minister of Public Instruction, and in 1876 he was a member of the Senate. Carnot was a Republican and was resolutely anti-clerical. {RAT}

Carnot, Lazare Nicolus Marguerite [Count] (1753—1823)
A French military engineer and statesman, Carnot served the Republic and then Napoleon, who raised him to the highest honors. Originally Catholic, Count Carnot became an atheist. Of his grandsons **Lazare Hippolyte** (1801—1888) was a distinguished and anti-clerical statesman. **Marie Carnot** was equally anti-clerical in politics and became President of the Republic.

Lazare's son, **Sadi Nicholas Leonard Carnot** (1796—1832) turned to science and was a leading figure in French physics. {JM; RAT; RE}

Carnot, Marie François Sadi [President] (1837—1894)
Carnot, the fourth President of the French Republic and eldest son of Lazare H. Carnot, originally sat on the Left in the Chambre.

In 1887 he was, by 616 out of 827 votes, elected President of the Republic. At the height of his popularity, the freethinking Carnot was assassinated by an Italian anarchist. {RAT}

Carnot, Sadi Nicolas Léonard (1796—1832)

Carnot was a French physicist, the son of L. N. M. Carnot. A freethinker, he wrote *Réflexions sur la puissance motrice du feu* (1824), containing what is known as "Carnot's Principle" and which laid the foundations of the science of thermodynamics. {RAT}

Caro, Elme (1826—1887)

A French philosopher, Caro rejected the belief in a personal God or personal immortality in his *Idée de Dieu* (1864). He was elected to the French Academy in 1875. Caro once wrote, "Science has conducted God to its frontiers, thanking him for his provisional services." {RAT}

Caroline of Ansbach [Queen Consort] (1683—1737)

Caroline, the queen consort of George II of England, was a German noble who married George when he was the Prince of Hanover. The mother of three sons and five daughters, she studied philosophy and after reading Leibnitz discarded Christianity. After George's accession in 1727, Caroline gave active support to Sir Robert Walpole, and her influence over the king lasted until her death.

Her house near London was frequented by many English Deists of the time. When she had to administer the Kingdom in her husband's absence, she refused to take the oath. She also refused the ministrations of the Church of England although she was pressed to do so by the Archbishop of Canterbury on her deathbed.

Lord Hervey in his *Memoirs* described her as "a Deist believing in a future life." McCabe declares it "is ludicrous of British writers to pretend that she was not a freethinker."

Lord Hervey spoke of "the irreligion of the Queen in desiring to have no clerical prayers by her death-bed," causing much court tattle; whereupon Walpole revealed *his* sympathy with the Queen's views by advising the Princess Emily in the presence of a dozen people, to "let the farce be played: the Archbishop will act it very well. . . . It will do the Queen no hurt, no more than any good; and it will satisfy all the wise and good fools, who will call us atheists if we don't pretend to be as great fools as they are." {JM; JMRH; RAT; RE; WWS}

Caron, Sandra M. (20th Century)

Caron was the third moderator of the Unitarian Universalist Association, presiding from 1977 to 1985.

Carpenter, Edward (1844—1929)

Carpenter, ordained as a minister in 1869, became a Fabian socialist, renouncing religion when he was thirty and quitting the Church. A friend of Walt Whitman, Carpenter wrote a long unrhymed poem about social reform entitled *Towards Democracy* (1863—1902). He also wrote *Homogenic Love and Its Place in a Free Society* (1894), *Love's Coming of Age* (1897), and *Intermediate Types Among Primitive Folk* (1914). These books proposed equality between the sexes, were gay-positive, and showed that in primitive societies homosexual behavior was often considered normal and sometimes even exalted.

His religious nonbelief is evident in *Myth, Magic, and Morals, A Study of Christian Origins* (1910). Carpenter's rationalism is shown in *My Days and Dreams* (1916). However, the English *Freethinker* states he was no secularist, that "his writings mingled elements of rural Utopianism with mysticism. But neither was he a conventional superstitionist. . . . Carpenter could be said to have been a courageous pioneer of both modern feminism and of Gay liberation, and his writings still may be read with profit and pleasure."

Carpenter's love of George Merrill inspired E. M. Forster's representation of the love of Maurice Hall and Scudder, the gamekeeper, in *Maurice*. {GL; RAT; RE; RSR; TRI}

Carpenter, Maria Weston (1806-1885)

Carpenter, a Unitarian, was a teacher, an abolitionist, and a juvenile justice reformer.

Carpenter, William Benjamin (1813—1885)

A naturalist, Carpenter held the medal of the Royal Society and the Lyell medal of the Geological Society. He was a corresponding member of the Institute of France. He was theistic (in a liberal sense) but was not a Unitarian. {RAT}

Carr, Herbert (Born 1857)

Carr was a philosophical writer and the President of the Aristotelian Society. A leading champion of Bergson, he was in agreement with his heterodox views concerning theism. {RAT}

Carr, Steve (20th Century)

Carr is a regional director in Missouri of the Council for Secular Humanism.

Carra, Jean Louis (1743—1793)

Carra, a French man of letters and Republican, wrote *History of Moldavia* and an *Essay on Aerial Navigation*. He espoused the revolution and was a member of the Jacobin club. His freethought sentiments are evident from his *System of Reason* (1773), his *Spirit of Morality and Philosophy* (1777), and *New Principles of Physic* (1782—1783). In the National Assembly, he voted for the death of Louis XVI but was guillotined with the Girondins. {BDF; RAT}

Carrel, Jean Baptiste Nicolas Armand (1800—1836)

Carrel was called by Saint Beueve "the Junius of the French press." Secretary to Thierry, he edited the works of P. I. Courier and established *The Nation* in conjunction with Thiers and Mignet. Carrel was known as the leading journalist of his time, and John Stuart Mill praised his work. Several of his journalistic articles led to duels and, in an encounter with Émile de Girardin, Carrel was fatally wounded. On his deathbed, he said, "*Point de prêtes, point d'église*. (No priests nor church)." {BDF; RAT}

Carrera, Asia (20th Century)

An actress in adult films, Carrera told Luke Ford, in a profile entitled "Bud & Hyapatia & Asia: Porn in the Family," that

> I've always been an atheist. Science explains everything. There is no meaning in life except to be the best at something. If only I could be the best at something, perhaps my parents would love me. . . . Religion is silly. When you're dead, you turn into a source for future flowers and plans. . . . I don't know what's on the other side of death and it scares me. Darkness and nothingness scare me. I'd rather face the miseries of my day-to-day life than turn into darkness.

{CA}

Carrier, Richard C. (20th Century)

Carrier, when a student at Columbia University in 1998, signed the Campus Freethought Alliance's Bill of Rights for Unbelievers.

Carrière, Moritz (1817—1895)

Carrière was a German philosopher who followed Hegel in his earlier writings, then professed a pantheism (which he called theism) similar to the ideas of Fichte. Finite minds are, he held, acts of a pantheistic divine will. {RAT}

Carrington, Athol Egbert (1895—1980)

Carrington, a New Zealander, was a rationalist, editor, and activist who stated that when he read Joseph McCabe's *The Existence of God* "the cobwebs of religion were swept from my mind." He visited Auckland in 1923 and heard Joseph McCabe, after which he became the first editor of the Auckland Rationalist Association's *Truth Seeker*. Carrington wrote under the pseudonym of A.E.C. and is considered to be in the forefront of New Zealand's rationalist leaders. {FUK; SWW}

Carrington, Dora (1893—1932)

Lytton Strachey spent the last sixteen years of his life in a *ménage à trois* with Carrington, a painter, and her husband, George Partridge. A 1995 movie, "Carrington," was directed by Christopher Hampton and detailed her escapades with others, mainly non-theists, of the Bloomsbury group. Carrington was barely educated, but her misspelled letters reveal a sensitivity and wit which held a profound appeal to the homosexual Strachey. He, in turn, supplied her with a refreshing interest in intellectual rather than in animalistic sexual matters. Neither was attracted to organized religion. Carrington, a graduate of the Slade School of Art, was a person lacking in confidence, yet many men fell in love with her because of her aura of milkmaid innocence. After overcoming her long period of virginity, she had many affairs but kept Strachey as her major love. After his death, she committed suicide when but thirty-eight.

Carroll, Damian (20th Century)

Carroll has never actively "converted" anyone to humanism, he wrote in *Humanist Monthly* (December 1998). "But I know lots of people whose religious views were affected because they saw I was able to be a happy, moral person without God's guidance," he added, according to the Scotia, New York, publication.

Carroll, Devin (20th Century)

Carroll is active with the Humanists of the San Joaquin Valley (AHA). He has helped develop non-theistic publications and activities for young people. (See entry for California Atheists, Humanists.) {FD; HNS2}

Carroll, William Joseph (1882—1975)

Carroll was an Australian rationalist, writer, and freethinker who used the nom de plume of "Ame Perdue." He wrote several satiric novels and poems, including *The New Rubaiyat* and *Man's Inhumanity to Man*. {SWW}

Carruth, Hayden (1921—)

Carruth is a poet who was editor of *Poetry* (1949—1950). He was recipient of the Vachel Lindsay prize (1954), the annual Brandeis University poetry award (1959), the Harriet Monroe prize of the University of Chicago (1960), the Carl Sandburg prize (1963), and numerous others, including a grant of $10,000 in 1967 from the National Foundation on Arts and Humanities. Among Carruth's many works are *The Crow and the Heart* (1959); *After the Stranger* (1965); *The Bloomingdale Papers* (1975); and *Paragraphs* (1975).

Asked in 1994 about humanism, Carruth responded to the present author,

> You may enroll me among the "non-theists," if you wish. My writing contains many explanations of my position though I have never written expressly on this topic. Perhaps the best explanation is in my essay, "The Nature of Art," *Ohio Review* (#49). The essay will be included in my forthcoming *Selected Essays and Reviews*.
>
> {WAS, 7 December 1994}

Carson, Joseph (Died 1995)

Carson was charter member of the Humanists of Iowa and served as its treasurer at one time.

Carson, Rachel (1907—1964)

A marine biologist, Carson wrote *Silent Spring* (1962) to show the dangers involved in the use of insecticides. A humanist, she also wrote *Under the Sea Wind* (1941), *The Sea Around Us* (1951), and *The Edge of the Sea* (1954). Her *Silent Spring* probably did more than any other single book or event to set off the new environmental movement which commenced in the United States in the 1960s. She called the chemicals used for insect and week control "elixirs of death," adding, "For the first time in the history of the world, every human being is now subjected to contact with dangerous chemicals, from the moment of conception until death." In graphic terms, she explained that "As few as 11 large earthworms can transfer a lethal dose of DDT to a robin. And 11 worms form a small part of day's rations to a bird that eats 10 to 12 earthworms in as many minutes." Her work was greeted with ridicule and denunciation by the chemical industry and parts of the food industry, and *Newsweek* accused her of raising "paranoid fears" akin to those of "such cultists as antifluoridation leaguers, organic-garden faddists, and other beyond-the-fringe groups." Complained a federal pest control member, "I thought she was a spinster. What's she so worried about genetics for?" Actually, Carson, who was fifty-five when the book was published, had been diagnosed as having the cancer that would later kill her.

Although called a spinster, a term she abhorred, she was not an unloving spinster. In Martha Freeman's *Always, Rachel: The Letters of Rachel Carson and Dorothy Freeman, 1952—1964*, one of Carson's letters to Freeman included the following:

> You must have sensed that I couldn't express myself adequately last night. What I wanted to do was hold you in my arms to be able to tell you just what your happiness means to me. Can you possibly know? Your voice came over so clearly that you seemed to be quite near–so near, dear, it made me ache to be with you.

Growing up on a farm in western Pennsylvania, she became an amateur naturalist and was fascinated by Darwinism, according to Paul Brooks's *The House of Life* (1972). Brooks tells the story that when her mother, the daughter of a Presbyterian minister, told her that God had created the world, she retorted, "Yes . . . and General Motors created the Oldsmobile, but *how* is the question." Carson often anthropomorphized nature, attributing human feelings to fish and animals. "I have spoken of a fish 'fearing' his enemies," she explained, "not because I suppose a fish experiences fear in the same way that we do, but because I think he *behaves as though he were frightened*."

Carson's sense of rectitude was remarkable, notes Daniel J. Kevles, who heads the Program in Science, Ethics, and Public Policy at the California Institute of Technology: "Because she was earning so much money from *The Sea Around Us*, she returned a fellowship to the Guggenheim Foundation. Her sensitivity to nature was informed by a Thoreau-like transcendentalism: letters from readers, she said, "suggest that they have found refreshment and release from tension in the contemplation of millions and billions of years–in the long vistas of geologic time in which men had no part–in the realization that, despite our own utter dependence on the earth, this same earth and sea have no need of us."

Toward the end of her life, Carson battled failing eyesight, angina, and the pain of cancer. Having been encouraged by Freeman to play the piano, Carson wrote in her last letter to Freeman,

> Not long ago I sat late in my study and played Beethoven and achieved a feeling of real peace and even happiness. Never forget, dear one, how deeply I have loved you all these years.

(Donald Fleming in *Perspectives in American History* (1972, No. VI) discusses transcendentalism in Carson's writings.)

Carson, Rhode B. (20th Century)

A freethinker, Carson wrote *Physician of No Value: The Repressed Story of Ecclesiastic Flummery* (1979). {GS}

Carter, Abram B. (20th Century)

Carter heads *The Savant of Virginia*, a publication for members who were in the now formally dissolved Society of Evangelical Agnostics and for a wide range of independent thinkers. (See entry for Virginia Freethinkers, Humanists.) {FD}

Carter, Diana (20th Century)

While a student at the University of Guelph, Carter was one of the founding members of Campus Freethought Alliance. {*International Humanist News*, December 1996}

Carter, Lee (20th Century)

A professor of communications in Los Angeles, Carter wrote *Lucifer's Handbook* (1977). {FUS}

Carter, Nicholas (20th Century)

Carter is author of *The Christ Myth* (1993).

CARTESIAN

• Cartesian, adj. Relating to Descartes, a famous philosopher, author of the celebrated dictum, *Cogito ergo sum*—whereby he was pleased to suppose he demonstrated the reality of human existence. The dictum might be improved, however, thus: *Cogito cogito ergo cogito sum*—I think that I think, therefore I think that I am; as close an approach to certainty as any philosopher has yet made.

—**Ambrose Bierce**
The Devil's Dictionary

Cartier-Bresson, Henri (1908—)

A French photojournalist, Cartier-Bresson became renowned for his countless memorable images of 20th century individuals and events. In 1944, after escaping from a German prison camp, he organized underground photography units. Cartier-Bresson was a founder of the Magnum photo agency, and he wrote *The Decisive Moment* (1952), *People of Moscow* (1955), *China in Transition* (1956), *The World of Henri Cartier-Bresson* (1968), *The Face of Asia* (1972), and *About Russia* (1974).

In an interview with Michel Nuridsany (*The New York Review of Books*, 2 March 1995), Cartier-Bresson spoke of having gone to a Cole Fénelon, a Catholic school that prepared one for the Lycée Condorcet. One day, he related,

> . . . the proctor there caught me reading a volume of Rimbaud or Mallarmé, right at the start of the school year, in the lower sixth. He said to me: "Let's have no disorder in your studies!" He used the informal *tu*–which usually meant you were about to get a good thrashing. But he went on: "You're going to read in my office." Well, that wasn't an offer he had to repeat: I did read there, for a year. It's why I never managed to graduate. But I read everything you could possibly read: Proust, the Russian novelists, *An Outline of Psychoanalysis*, Nietzsche, or course. And a book on Schopenhauer that led me to Romain Rolland and to Hinduism. That had a huge effect on me. I had never been a Christian believer. My mother once said: "Poor dear, if only you had a good Dominican confessor, you wouldn't be in such a fix!" But at the same time, she gave me *Jean Barois* [a novel by Roger Martin du Gard] to read, and the pre-Socratics. She was a left-wing Catholic. Myself, I'm a libertarian.

{CE}

Carus, Julius Viktor (1823—1903)

Carus was a German zoologist and freethinker. He was keeper of the anatomical museum at Oxford, and he translated Darwin's works and the philosophy of G. H. Lewes. {BDF; RAT}

Carus, Karl Gustav (1789—1869)

A German physiologist and pantheist, Carus taught comparative anatomy and wrote *Psyche*, a history of the development of what he called the human soul. Carus was a friend of Goethe, and he subscribed to the monistic or pantheistic philosophy. {BDF; RAT}

Carus, Paul (1852—1919)

A German-American who settled in Chicago, Carus was a philosopher. With funds supplied by his father-in-law, Carus attempted to propagate monism (on more philosophic lines than Haeckel's system) in America. He founded *The Monist* and *The Open Court*. In 1943, an edition was published of his *God: An Enquiry into the Nature of Man's Highest Ideal, and a Solution*. {GS; RE}

Caruso, Maire (20th Century)

Caruso is on the board of directors of Society Against Religion.

Carvalho e Melo, Sebastião José de: See entry for Pombal.

Carver, Charles (20th Century)

Carver wrote *Brann and the Iconoclast* (1957), a short biography of the freethinker. {*Freethought History #15*, 1995}

Carver, Raymond (1938—1988)

An American short story writer, Carver was inducted into the American Academy of Arts and Letters in 1988. Nick Sweet (*New Humanist*, June 1996) has discussed how Carver's stories develop the humanist theme of moving to maturity and independence. Carver was both a novelist and a poet. His works include *Will You Please Be Quiet, Please?* (1977), *What We Talk About When We Talk About Love* (1982), *Cathedral* (1984), and *Elephant* (1988).

Cary, Alice (1820—1871)

Cary, an Ohio poet, was prominent in Horace Greeley's circle. An abolitionist, she wrote hymns and poems, inspiring Whittier's "The Singer." Her sister, also a Unitarian, was Phoebe Cary. {U}

Cary, Joyce (1888—1957)

Cary, a British novelist who studied art in Edinburgh and Paris, took part in the Balkan War (1912—1913) and served with the Nigerian regiment in the Cameroons campaign, 1915—1916. His early novels about Africa described the relations between Africans and their British administrators. *The Horse's Mouth* (1944) was chiefly concerned with the life of Gulley Jimson, the artist. *Art and Reality* (1958) was a study in aesthetics. *The Captive and the Free* (1959) was an unfinished novel which had a religious theme.

Asked about humanism, Cary responded to the present author:

> I don't know what kind of a humanist I am.
>
> My position is roughly and very shortly: (1) The world is finally one unity: "nature" includes "human nature"; (2) In the unity we find altruistic as well as aesthetic values, good will, and also evil will; (3) Values obtain only in a personal free will. Therefore, you have to fit a person, and values, into your unity; (4) This means that the unity is ultimately personal and free *but* it contains a complex mass of evil; (5) Daily experience makes us know the battle between good and evil in which the good is often beaten; the dilemma is always charged with tragedy, in justice, every kind of cruelty; (6) Some of the evil is pure evil–wicked evil; some derives from chance–the unity is shot through with luck. It is always bedevilled by deterministic causation. The two often work together; i.e., a child is born to tubercular parents (luck) and inherits a physique (determinism) which is open to tuberculosis, and so he dies young; (7) Any answer proposed to this complex situation must account for (a) the freedom of the moral and immoral will; (8) the determination of the "material" world [an illegible word here is possibly "governed"] at the least by statistical laws which, I should say, are good evidence of a fixed consistency in spite of Planck's views as I understand them.

The only answer I can propose which is, of course, purely conceptual is that since the world is "so" and not "otherwise," it *must* have a permanent character. That is, a real and actual free will requires a consistent form in actuality. Such a dual existence is known to [illegible words] in our bodies. It is therefore not beyond imagination. It is, no doubt, something a good deal larger than our imagination and probably of a quite different order. Yet we know what we know.

{WAS, 28 February 1951}

Cary, Neal (20th Century)
Cary is the national outreach director of American Atheists as Volunteers. E-mail: <ncaryatheists.org>.

Cary, Phoebe (1824—1871)
Phoebe and Alice Cary were poets whose work was moralistic and idealistic. Both were Unitarians.

Casale, Jerry (20th Century)
A recording artist, Casale was a founding member of Devo and a co-writer of "Whip It." Asked by *Billboard* about the role of "devolution" in Devo's style, Casale answered, "Like the Bible, devolution is basically an extended joke. One man's doughnut is another man's death." {CA}

Casanova, Giovanni Jacques de Seingalt (1725—1798)
An Italian writer, Casanova entered the Church and received the minor orders. Abandoning the Church, he began a life of adventure, as shown in his *Memoirs* (12 volumes, 1828—1838). At various times he was secretary to a cardinal, an officer in the Venetian army, a violinist, a librarian, and a secret police-agent. Casanova translated the *Iliad* into Italian. {RAT}

Casas, Yoloxóchilt (20th Century)
Casas, a Mexican, spoke on health, sexuality, and medical information at the 1996 Humanist World Congress held in Mexico City.

Cash, W. J. (20th Century)
Cash's *The Mind of the South* (1941) is an overview which draws together history, sociology, and literature. {*Freethought History* #14, 1995}

Casimir-Périer, Jean Paul Pierre [President] (1847—1907)
Casimir-Périer served two terms (1890 and 1893) as President of the French Chambre, and in the heat of the conflict with the Church was elected President of the Republic (1894). He gave valuable evidence for the accused at the trial of Dreyfus, and throughout his political life cooperated in the secularization of France and the destruction of the power of the Church. {RAT; RE}

Casler, Lawrence (20th Century)
Casler is a professor emeritus in the Department of Psychology, at the State University of New York in Geneseo. An atheist, he has written *Is Marriage Necessary?* and has written for *American Atheist*.

Caspari, Otto (Born 1841)
A German philosopher, Caspari in his works attempted to reconcile philosophy with modern evolutionary science and, a monist himself, gave much valuable support to Haeckel. {RAT}

Cassara, Ernest (1925—)
Cassara is author of *Hosea Ballou: The Challenge to Orthodoxy*, a study of the nineteenth-century Universalist, and of *Universalism in America* (1971).

Cassels, W(alter) R(ichard) (1826—1907)
Cassels spent much of his early life in India, serving in the Legislative Council of Bombay from 1863 to 1865. Only after his *Supernatural Religion: An Inquiry into the Reality of Divine Revelation* went into a sixth printing did it occur to others that the popular work which was published anonymously was his. A nephew of Dr. Pusey, Cassels wrote under his own name *Eidolon and Other Poems* (1850) and *A Reply to Dr. Lightfoot's Essays* (1889). In a scholarly criticism of the Bible he confessed a belief in an impersonal God, but he later rejected this and professed agnosticism. {BDF; FUK; RAT; RE}

Casserly, J. V. Langmead (20th Century)
Casserly, a freethinker, wrote *The Retreat from Christianity in the Modern World* (1952). {GS}

Cassirer, Ernst (1874—1975)
Cassirer, a German neo-Kantian, is cited by some naturalistic humanists as having influenced them. However, he basically was an idealist, not a naturalist or a materialist. (See James Gutmann's letter, below.). {CE}

Casson, Herbert (20th Century)
Casson, a freethinker, wrote *The Crime of Credulity* (1901). {GS}

CASTE
In India, a caste is any of four classes, comprising numerous subclasses, which constitute Hindu society. One's social class is separated from that of others by distinctions of hereditary rank, profession, or wealth.
Castes in a colony of social insects such as ants include workers or soldiers who carry out a specific function. (See entry for Poopathi Manckham, who objects to the caste system. Also see the critique in the entry for V. R. Narla.)

Castelar y Ripoli, Emilio (1832—1899)
Castelar was a Spanish statesman and journalist who became known for his writing of a novel, *Ernesto* (1855). He was a professor of history and philosophy at the University of Madrid, was foreign minister, and then president (1873—1874) of Spain's first republic. He ruled as a dictator and was partially successful in restoring order to the war-torn country. "We have not the same republican traditions possessed by Italy and France," he wrote. "Our people, always at war, have always needed a chief, and this chief required not only the sword of the soldier to fight, but the scepter of the monarch to rule. Notwithstanding this ancient monarchical character, there are regions which have been saved from the monarchy, and which have preserved their democracy and their republic. There still exist in the north provinces possessed of an autonomy and an independence which give them points of resemblance to the Swiss cantons. The citizens give neither tribute nor blood to the kings. Their firesides are as sacred form the invasion of authority as those of the English or of the Americans. . . . Our Cortes of Castile succeeded frequently in expelling the ecclesiastical and aristocratic estates from their sessions. Our Cortes of Aragon attained such power that they named the government of their kings, and obtained fixed days for their sessions. Navarre was a species of republic more or less aristocratic, presided over by a king more or less respected. And the Castilian municipalities were in the Middle Ages true democratic republics."
Although a representative of Republican Spain, a noble orator, a literary exponent, he was more an idealist than a materialist, according to Putnam, who added that Castelar "studies history, we might say, of Hegel, which makes history a kind of divine romance." Although a nonorthodox Christian, Castelar was something of a theist. He favored a federative republic like that of America, not a centralized republic like that of France. But he was overthrown by a military coup d'état. After the restoration (1875) of Alfonso XII, Castelar became a member of the political opposition in the Cortes. {BDF; CE; PUT}

Castelli, David (Born 1836)
An Italian writer, Castelli held the chair of Hebrew in the Institute of Superior Studies at Florence and translated *Ecclesiastes* with notes. His rationalist works included *Talmudic Legends* (1869), *The Messiah According to the Hebrews* (1874), and *The History of the Israelites* (1887). His numerous works on Hebrew literature are rationalistic. {BDF; RAT}

Castellio, Sebastian [also: **Castalion, Châtillon**] (1515—1563)
A Swiss school rector whom John Calvin frowned upon because of his unauthorized Latin and French translations of the Bible, Castellio was horrified when Calvin had Michael Servetus murdered because of theological differences. So he wrote *Concerning Heretics*, in which (using a pseudonym, Martinus Bellius) he condemned Calvin as the murderer of Servetus. Stefan Zweig (1881-1942) has described in *The Right to Heresy: Castellio Against Calvin* (1951) how Calvin plotted the heretic Castellio's death, which was thwarted by Castellio's illness and death from "an overtaxed heart." {CE; JMRH; TSV}

Castiglione, Ruggero de Palma (20th Century)
Castiglione, an Italian, addressed the Fourth International Humanist and Ethical Union World Congress held in Paris (1966) and also at the Second European Conference held in Hannover (1968).

Castilhon, Jean Louis (1720—1793)

Castilhon, a French man of letters, edited the *Journal of Jurisprudence*. His freethought shows in his *Essay on Ancient and Modern Errors and Superstitions* (1767) and in his *History of Philosophical Opinions* (1769). {BDF}

Castillo Rojas, Marco (20th Century)

A lawyer and notary, Castillo is president of *Asociación Ético Humanista Costarricense* (ASEHUCO), the Costa Rican Association of Ethical and Secular Humanists. He was instrumental in the founding of *Asociación Iberoamericana Ético Humanista* (ASIBEHU), the Ibero-American Ethical Humanist Association of Spanish-speaking humanists in the Americas. Castillo, one of the leading human rights lawyers in Costa Rica, was a participant in the 1996 Humanist World Congress held in Mexico City. E-mail: <asibehu@sol.racsa.co.cr>.

Castle, Marie Alena (20th Century)

Castle is the activist President of Atheist Alliance, Inc., the Democratic Alliance of Autonomous Atheist Societies (Box 6261, Minneapolis, MN 55406).

She is co-chair of the Minnesota Atheists, and is one of the counsels for *Secular Nation*. In 1994 at the Toronto Conference of the Coalition for Secular Humanism, Atheism, and Freethought (CSHAFT), she spoke on "Dealing With the Religious Right." Castle has stated that humanists should not be on the defensive, that they have already won. She cites the Enlightenment, the founding of constitutional democracies around the world, the Bill of Rights, the New Deal, and the humanistic arts and sciences. "Our problem," she holds, "is not to establish humanism but to defend and preserve it." Declare victory, she advises, and move forward. It is the triumph of humanism which "has brought on the rise of an aggressive religious fascism," she insists, appealing to humanists, atheists, and secular organization to work together for the preservation of our victory. In 1996 in Vijayawada, India, she gave the valedictory address at the fourth World Atheist Conference, during which she particularly stressed the importance of political action. Her e-mail: <mac@mtn.org>. {*The Free Mind*, February 1996}

Castro, Fernando (1814—c. 1874)

A Spanish philosopher and historian, Castro had been a priest. But on his death-bed he confessed himself a freethinker and had a secular burial. {BDF}

Castro, Fidel (1926—)

Castro is the Cuban revolutionary and premier of Cuba who toppled Cuban dictator Fulgencio Batista y Zaldivar in 1959, installing his own Marxist-Leninist dictatorship. An atheist who has called his philosophic outlook "humanism," he has been a symbol of revolution and social change in Latin America and elsewhere. "Liberty with bread, without terror–that is, Humanism," he stated when first displacing the Batista government. His government, however, did not carry out that slogan. He campaigned for the socialistic nationalizing of industry, the confiscating of foreign-owned property, the collectivizing of agriculture, and improving of the average person's quality of life. However, this "humanism," according to most other professed humanists, led more than one million Cubans to flee the island because of his authoritarian and undemocratic rule. Those who fled, called *la escoria* (scum) or *gusanos* (worms), decry the *chivatos* (informers) who did not flee. Meanwhile, with the incredibly fast fall of other Marxist-Leninist governments in the 1990s, Castro remained a solitary symbol of his brand of humanism. His 1996 meeting with the Pope at the Vatican led him to say, "As a child, I never would have imagined that one day I would have lunch with cardinals and meet with a Pope." Little wonder, for he long ago went on record:

> When I was a young boy, my father taught me that to be a good Catholic, I had to confess at church if I ever had impure thoughts about a girl. That very evening I had to rush to confess my sin. And the next night, and the next. After a week, I decided religion wasn't for me.

As pointed out by Sidney Hook and other humanists, communistic humanism was destined to fail because it is not founded upon freedom, the significance of the individual, and political democracy. In mid-1994, Castro in a pragmatic decision invited some of the *gusanos* to return to their former country.

In 1998 he invited Pope John Paul to visit Cuba. Asked by reporters if this implied he was no longer an atheist, Castro said,

> I can say one thing. I respect those who believe and those who do not believe. If you say you do not believe, you offend those who believe. If you say you believe, you offend those who do not believe. In a way you become a preacher. I am not a preacher. I do believe in mankind and in the goodness and nobility of man. I believe the world should live in a way that is just and rational.

{CE; E; *The Economist*, 16 August 1997}

CASUISTRY

Casuistry involves specious or excessively subtle reasoning that is intended to mislead or to rationalize. For example, by interpreting the religious doctrine that "thou shalt not kill," a casuist might accuse physicians of unethically killing germs.

Catalano, John (20th Century)

Catalano is a freethinker who has written about Richard Dawkins for the Freethought Society of Greater Philadelphia.

CATASTROPHISM: See entry for uniformitarianism.

CATEGORICAL IMPERATIVE

In his *Critique of Pure Reason* (1781), Kant defined the ultimate moral obligation that applies a priori to everyone in all circumstances:

- Act according to that maxim which you could wish to be a universal law of nature upon which every one should act at all times;
- Always treat humanity in yourself and others as an end and never as merely a means;
- Act always as if you were a member of a merely possible kingdom of ends.

Following such commands, he believed, is a categorical imperative, a moral obligation that is unconditionally and universally binding.

McCabe, however, said that Kant "was a man of very isolated and eccentric life who had been reared in a strict puritanical environment, and he never attempted to study the moral consciousness of others, so that his ethical philosophy is rather an analysis of one highly sophisticated individual conscience. His critics said that as he had destroyed the foundations of the ordinary arguments for God and immortality in his *Critique of Pure Reason*, he felt compelled to appeal to 'practical reason.' Neither psychology nor the modern science of ethics countenances his idea." {CE; ER}

CATHARISM

The Cathari (also known as Albigenses) were a medieval, puritanical, and heretical movement called, by theologian Herman Hausheer of Lamoni, Iowa, "a repristination of Manichaeism and Gnostic christology, maintaining to be the only true church of a holy hierarchy and efficacious sacraments." Translated, this means that the group claimed to have had proof that Jesus did not die on the cross, that he married Mary Magdalen, that they settled in the Languedoc, and that their heirs founded the Merovingian dynasty that united Christian Europe under Charlemagne. (See Emmanuel Le Roy Ladurie's *Montaillou*, which by studying Inquisition notes describes the life of a medieval village.) {ER}

Cather, Willa (1867—1947)

Cather, a short story writer and novelist, is one of the great writers of the 20th century. She celebrated the strength of the frontier settlers in *O Pioneers* (1913) and *My Antonia* (1918). Her *Death Comes for the Archbishop* (1927) is considered one of her best works. She is known as a master of the craft of fiction, as evidenced not only by her fiction but also by her *On Writing* (1949).

While on the editorial staff of *McClure's Magazine* in 1907 and 1908, Cather wrote a scathing work, *The Life of Mary Baker G. Eddy and the History of Christian Science* (republished 1992), which brought her much negative criticism. Like Samuel Clemens, who had called Eddy "queen of frauds and hypocrites," Cather presents a negative view of Eddy's life and writings. However, a Canadian newspaperwoman named Georgine Milmine originally was credited as having been the author. In fact, to her death Cather denied having written the book, either unwilling to be known as a comic writer or, as critics claim, was tacitly acknowledging that Milmine was biased and had supplied her with material for its sensational and commercial value. Critic Michael Warner (*Voice*, 17 Aug 93) wrote concerning the Eddy biography: "The heroine comes off with as much pathos, hilarity, and will as any character in Cather's fiction. Each chapter shows Mrs. Eddy venturing into new realms of implausibility, a bombazine Cortez of the ridiculous. The suspense lies in wondering how much farther she can go, and she never fails to satisfy. This is the woman, after all, who had an adult-size cradle made to order so she could be rocked to sleep. She had her second husband (the exquisitely queer Mr. Eddy came third) cover a nearby bridge with sawdust to deaden the sound of neighbors' footsteps. At night, she sent him out to kill discordant frogs. By the time Eddy was forty, she had raised nervous illness to an art form—and that was before she became its theorist. Like her principal rival in hysterical science, Sigmund Freud, Mary Baker Eddy did not begin the major part of her career until the age of fifty. Perhaps Cather felt reluctant to take credit for such a splendid character, who was still alive when the biography was published."

Puritan critics accused Cather of being a lesbian, citing how from the ages of fourteen to eighteen she so strongly identified as a male that she dressed in men's clothing, got a crew cut, and called herself William Cather Jr. In 1895 in the Nebraska *Journal*, she condemned Oscar Wilde for his alleged homosexual acts. However, in 1895 she wrote a rhapsodic newspaper commentary on Sappho, whose lyre "responded only to a song of love." Her critics, particularly religionists sensitive about her attacks on Mary Baker G. Eddy, disclosed that Cather in 1905 had left her lover, Isabelle McClung in Pittsburgh, later burning all their correspondence, and had moved to Greenwich Village in New York City, where she lived the rest of her life, for almost forty years, with Edith Lewis, another Nebraskan. One of her biographers, Sharon O'Brien, said that Lewis phoned her not to use the word "lesbian" in writing of Cather. "When I told her this wasn't possible, she hung up," wrote O'Brien, who then added that "Cather herself invited me to tea at her Bank Street [New York City] apartment. 'I want you to know,' she said, pouring me a cup, 'that I am not gay.' 'What about the letters to Louise Pound?' I asked. As soon as I spoke, the dream abruptly ended. I could not tell if I had silenced or convinced her." O'Brien explained that while at Duke University, she had come across romantic love letters to Pound, her friend at the University of Nebraska, "in which Cather agreed that relationships like theirs were 'unnatural.' " O'Brien's work, *Lives of Notable Gay Men and Lesbians: Willa Cather* (1994), took fifteen years to research and argues that if Cather were alive today she would not at all mind being outed, that flouting convention when she thought she was right was part of her character.

Cather's other critics were surprised that her work was so popular, that readers were buying plots about mule-riding priests in nineteenth-century New Mexico and about non-shocking romance.

Clifton Fadiman as well as Lionel Trilling considered her as a person writing of the past and acting as if she was not of the present. Trilling observed that she lived in a world of Freudians but wrote in "defense of gentility." *The Catholic World* commended her for high standards, aware that she was a nominal Episcopalian, for not stooping to "crude realism, Freudism, inchoate prose, shallow philosophy." Her final years were spent tending a case of chronic tendinitis in her right hand. Awaking one day from an afternoon nap, she complained of a headache, then died of a cerebral hemorrhage. *The Nation* in an obituary described her as a minor novelist, one "remote from the talents and problems of the past two anxious decades." Only in the 1990s did "William" Cather's reputation increase, partly because of a new evaluation of her lesbianism and her feminism. (See entries for Christian Science and Louise Pound.) {Joan Acocella, "Cather and the Academy," *The New Yorker*, 27 November 1995; CE; GL}

Catherine II [Catherine The Great] (1729—1796)

Catherine the Great, Empress of Russia, was a German princess chosen by Czarina Elizabeth partly on the recommendation of Frederick II of Prussia, to be the wife of the future Czar Peter III. Accepting the Orthodox faith, she changed her original name, Sophie, to Catherine. Becoming "completely Russian" made her popular with important political elements who opposed her eccentric husband, whom many considered a drunken boor. When her husband ascended to the throne in 1762, a group of conspirators headed by her lover, Grigori Orlov, proclaimed Catherine the autocrat. Shortly afterward, Peter was murdered. Catherine then began great projects of reform, drawing upon the writings of Beccaria and Montesquieu to serve as guides. An enthusiastic patron of the arts, she wrote memoirs, comedies, and stories. She corresponded with the French encyclopedists, including Voltaire, Diderot, and d'Alembert. Although she had many lovers, only Orlov, Potemkin, and P. L. Zubov were said to have been influential in government affairs. She was succeeded by her son, Paul I.

McCabe notes that Catherine found it difficult being in a world where the Church was supreme and life was coarse and unrestricted. She particularly had little regard for the sex-part of the Christian code. (On Broadway in the 1940s, Mae West played the starring role in "Catherine the Great," which detailed her many sexual escapades. In one scene, she asks her homosexual hairdresser what he wants for Christmas. He responds what he really wants is one of her discarded lovers.) Because of her friendship with the French encyclopedists, who were largely responsible for her glorious contemporary reputation, she learned a humanitarianism which the Church ignored, and she began a great program of social reform in Russia (in education, sanitation, administration of justice). The French Revolution and execution of the King caused a reaction in her mind and character and all reform was suspended. But, according to McCabe, she remained a Deist. Robertson also called her a deist, "a satirist of bigots in her comedies," one who accomplished what Peter had planned, the secularization of Church property. Robertson lamented the fact that "her half-crazy son Paul II, whom she had given cause to hate her, undid her work wherever he could." {CE; JM; JMR; JMRH; RAT; RE; WWS}

Cathey, Bruce E. (20th Century)

A New York City bibliographer, Cathey is writing *Traditional Religious Issues: A Bibliographic Guide to Rationalist/Humanist/Secularist Perspectives*. Gordon Stein wrote the foreword before his death, and the work is scheduled for printing in 2000.

catholic

Freethinkers, agnostics, atheists, and members of the liberal religious groups are frequently known for their catholic, or universal, interests. Often aspiring to be Renaissance-like scholars, they encourage individuals to be catholic in their interests and to be experts in several areas. (See Bertrand Russell's entry for a critique, not of *catholic*, but of Catholic.)

CATHOLIC CATECHISM

In 1994, a *Catechism of the Catholic Church* was issued and became a runaway best-seller for its sixteen different publishers. *Catechism*, a word rooted in the Greek for "oral instruction," has meant a manual of religious doctrine since the late Middle Ages. Johannes Paulus II (John Paul, Bishop, Servant of the Servants of God for Everlasting Memory) wrote an introductory note, and in a separately bound introduction Joseph Cardinal Ratzinger, the Vatican official in charge of doctrine, wrote a note striking out against "those interests which portray the Catechism as inimical to progress." He singled out by name Hans Küng, the Swiss theologian known for his liberal Catholicism and complaint that the work is an assertion of power by the Church's "Roman party." Some Americans were critical of the Vatican's decision to continue using gender-insensitive words, for example using "Man" for "Humanity." Other Americans, although finding the 853-page work has its good points, are aware that many do not agree with the Church declarations in regard to contraception, divorce, and abortion. They note that the catechism persists with the medieval teaching that the only legitimate end of sex is procreation. In fact, contraception is said to be "intrinsically evil," and it is condemned more harshly than homicide, which is declared sometimes permissible. The catechism also condemns *in vitro* fertilization, even if the husband and wife supply their own sperm and egg, inasmuch as such "established the domination of technology." Further, it is "not possible" for women to be ordained.

Catholics generally accept the idea that some items of doctrine have to be accepted . . . on faith. For example: the divinity (and humanity) of Christ; his death and resurrection; the virginity of Mary; the power of prayer. However, many Catholics do not agree with Pope John Paul that the "ordinary magisterium"—all church teaching—requires absolute acceptance. In fact, that teaching has changed over the years. For example, at one time the Roman Catholic church banned artistic images of Christ, prohibited the payment of interest, allowed priests to marry; and expected inquisitors to torture. Pope Paul VI abolished the *Index Prohibitorum*. John Paul II retracted the church's 17th-century denunciation of Galileo. A 1907 encyclical condemning "modernism," The *Economist* has observed (29 April 1995), "is now regarded as an embarrassment at best." (See entry for the Rev. Richard P. McBrien, an outspoken liberal Roman Catholic theologian.)

CATHOLIC CRITIQUE OF HUMANIST MANIFESTO I: See entry for Humanist Manifestos.

CATHOLIC POPES: See entry for Pope. For a description of one pope's wild parties, see the entry for Alexander VI.

CATHOLIC RELATIVISM

The Roman Catholic Church rarely talks about heresy, but in 1997 the Vatican's doctrinal authorities found a seventy-two-year-old Sri Lankan priest, the Rev. Tissa Balasuriya, guilty of having "deviated from the integrity of the truth of the Catholic faith." As a result, he was excommunicated, formally cast out of the communion of the church.

Another case of excommunication in recent times was against Archbishop Marcel Lefebvre in 1988, after he flouted the reforms of the Second Vatican Council. Similarly, the Pope severely criticized and cracked down on the Swiss theologian Hans Küng, a professor at Tübingen

University in Germany; the Rev. Charles E. Curran, who taught at Catholic University in Washington, D.C.; and the school of liberation theologians from Latin America whose anti-establishment, populist views often overlapped with leftist social ideals in the 1970s and 1980s. However, Father Küng observed of the Sri Lankan's excommunication, "This is much tougher, perhaps because he is a third-world theologian. It is very serious for this man, and it is very unjust, but it is the consequence of the system. This is the system as it works, and as it will work as long as Catholicism doesn't get rid of a doctrine that says the Pope is always right." Observed a fellow member of Father Balasuriya's order, "I love my order; the fraternal bonds are very strong; but you have to respect the mission of the church. The Pope and the bishops have a responsibility for teaching by the Scriptures, for interpreting by tradition." The Sri Lankan had been accused of challenging such beliefs as original sin and the Immaculate Conception. {Celestine Bohlen, *The New York Times*, 7 January 1997}

CATHOLIC WOMEN

In *The Recovering Catholic: Personal Journeys of Women Who Left the Church* (1995), Joanne H. Meehl writes about women of many walks of life who have rejected the Roman Catholic faith. The denigration of females by the male clergy, abortion, contraception, and the role of women in the Church are discussed. Meehl speaks of the "Great Goddess" matriarchal culture, leading R. E. Wolke and others to wonder why she would wish to replace the illogic of one religion for another. {*The American Rationalist*, September-October 1995}

CATHOLICISM

"Catholicism," wrote lapsed Catholic Anthony Burgess in his memoirs, "is, in a paradox, a bigger thing than the faith. It is a kind of supranationality that makes one despise small patriotisms."

Freethinkers, although highly critical of Catholicism, generally refrain from trying to change the beliefs of its Catholic adherents. (See entry for Cross-Dressing.)

CATHOLICISM—INTRIGUE IN THE VATICAN: See entry for *Vatican, Gone With the Wind in the.*

CATHOLICS, FORMER

Sherry Bishop is author of *Immaculate Misconceptions: A Self-Help Book for Former Catholics* (Veranda Press, PO Box 626, Carlsborg, WA 98324). The book is based on her own experience as well as that of other former Catholics. The first part details how they were hurt by their childhood experiences in Catholic churches and schools. The second part offers suggestions for healing.

Catlin, George (20th Century)

Catlin was on the board of directors in England of Archibald Church's *The Realist: A Journal of Scientific Humanism* (1929—1930).

CATOPITHECUS

In 1992, an ancient and extinct animal known as Catopithecus was first reported to Dr. Elwyn Simons of Duke University. "This is the earliest animal known from the higher primates, the group that humans, apes, and monkey are in," Simons has declared. According to an analysis of skull, jaw, and teeth fossils found in what now is an Egyptian desert, this oldest ancestor of apes, monkey, and humans was a squirrel-size animal that lived 36,000,000 years ago. Simons said he had no doubt about his find because of the distinctive features of the Catopithecus fossils: shovel-shaped front upper teeth; a skull with a flattened face; forward-looking eye sockets, and a fused forehead bone. In lower primates, like lemurs, this forehead bone is separated.

If his interpretation is accepted, higher primates, like gorillas, chimpanzees, and humans all evolved from this tiny animal.

Meanwhile, Dr. Bert Covert of the University of Colorado at Boulder notes that specimens found in China and Algeria were older but were "extremely fragmentary" and that their species classification was uncertain. "Simons's material is between plausible and compelling" as the oldest higher primate fossil, Covert reported in a 1995 issue of *Science*, the journal of the American Association for the Advancement of Science. "The other material I would place between unlikely and plausible. We cannot resolve the issue right now."

Catt, Carrie Clinton Lane Chapman (1859-1947)

Catt, a suffragist and pacifist who favored many Unitarian causes, was founder of the League of Women Voters.

Cattaneo, Carlo (1801—1869)

Cattaneo was an Italian philosophical writer. He founded *Il Politecnico* and after flinging himself into the revolutionary movement was compelled to flee to Switzerland. The Swiss appointed him professor at Lugano, where he became known as the "Auguste Comte of Italy." After the defeat of the Austrians he was several times elected to Parliament, but, being a Republican as well as a rationalist, Cattaneo refused to enter the Camera. {RAT}

Cattell, Charles Cockbill (1830—1910)

Cattell was English leader of the Birmingham freethought and republicanism of the 1850s. He was an important figure in the national organization of freethought groups. In the 1870s he wrote *What Is A Freethinker?* and he wrote *The Dark Side of Christianity* (190—?). Originally a member of the Church of England, he left it and studied science and logic, then called himself a secularist. Secularism he regarded as atheistic but is not atheism. The pseudonym he used was Christopher Charles. {FUK; GS; PUT; RAT; RSR; VI}

Cattell, Christopher Charles (1830—1910)

Cattell wrote in English secular journals and was author of *Against Christianity* and *The Religion of This Life*. He worked in the co-operative and labor movements and the Sunday League. {BDF}

Catterall, Eric (Died 1977)

An Australian poet, Catterall wrote *The Verse and Worse of a Militant Rationalist*. Ron Marke in the work's introduction, wrote, "Eric contracted polio as a child. He had a violent father who said it's useless sending a cripple to school, so he was denied any education. The doctors declared he would never walk, but Eric knew better. He battled on his feet, crippled as he was, and at eleven years of age left home for the bush and nature. He acquired a horse, taught it to lay down so that he could get on it as he had no strength in his legs or feet. . . . He was a self-taught and learned man; most of his knowledge came from books and experience, and he was fairly conversant in a lot of subjects."

The following, quoted by *Freethought History* (#23, 1997), is from Catterall's "Priests Will Rule Forever":

We banned The Pill, I'll tell you why,
We profit when the babies die.
From Christening, from funeral lie . . .
We cash in when the parents cry. . . .

We say "OUR FLOCK" of sheep or geese!
Let's make it "SHEEP," for these we fleece.
Our two legged sheep . . . may they increase!
For then our graft will never cease.

It helps us that governments aid our schools.
Let us implant the Pope's own rules.
If government aid for our church cools
They'll lose the votes of all the fools.

So "TAX THE CHURCH" is branded "red"
And schools from rational thought have fled.
"Give us the child," as we have said,
"And we will rule until it's dead."

Catullus [Caius Valerius Catullus] (84?—54? B.C.E.)

Catullus's "love poems are among the most moving in all literature," wrote Lamont. "[He] was a sort of ancient Omar Khayyam in his general attitude of irrepressible pleasure-seeking in this vale of delight." "Suns may rise and set; we, when our short day has closed, must sleep on during one perpetual night," Catullus wrote.

Some of his poems were addressed to the faithless Lesbia, and other pieces include elegies, epigrams, and works that are obscenely derisive. "On the Death of Lesbia's Sparrow" is one of his better known works. {CE; CL; GL; TYD}

Cauffiel, Phyllis C. (20th Century)

Cauffiel is associated with the Humanists of Northwest Ohio (AHA). (See entry for Ohio Atheists, Humanists.) {FD}

Cauldwell, D. O. (20th Century)

Cauldwell, a freethinker, wrote *A Modern Analysis of Biblical Sex Scandals* (1947). {GS}

Caumont, Georges (c. 1845—1875)

Caumont, a French writer who suffered from consumption, wrote *Judgment of a Dying Man Upon Life* as well as a humorous and familiar work, *Conversations of a Sick Person with the Divinity*. He died at Madeira. {BDF}

CAUSALITY

Which came first, the chicken or the egg? Causation in philosophy deals with the relationship between two events or states of affairs such that the first brings about the second. Flip a switch, and the light comes on. But all events may not have an antecedent cause, and naturalists in philosophy are interested in the quantum theory, which implies that some events occur at random. Rationalists tend to search for a priori principles governing what kind of thing may or cannot cause some other kind of thing.

Hume argued that knowledge of causes must come from experience. John Stuart Mill was unable, however, to supply a satisfactory positive account of just what causal connection is. Bertrand Russell subsequently claimed that an advanced scientific understanding of the world needs no such notion. According to Flew, modern analyses regard the need for such a notion "as explicable through the subjunctive conditional 'If e1 had not occurred, e2 would not have occurred,' but little is clear about what makes such a remark true." {Antony Flew, *A Dictionary of Philosophy*).

Caute, David (20th Century)

Caute, a former literary editor of *The New Statesman* and Fellow of All Souls College, Oxford, is author of *Fatima's Scarf* (1998). Although his is a controversial work critical of Muslim theology, much like *Satanic Verses* by Salman Rushdie and *Shame!* by Taslima Nasrin, Caute is not an Islamic apostate. {*The Freethinker*, May 1998}

Cavafy, C. P. (1863—1933)

Cavafy was regarded by literary historian C. A. Trypanis as "the most original of all the modern Greek poets." A recluse whose work was never commercial during his lifetime, he lived in the Greek community of Alexandria and worked as a petty bureaucrat. Adept at investing in the stock exchange, he eventually retired from the Ministry of Irrigation.

His major themes were philosophy, history, and hedonism, and his work was critical of patriotism, heterosexuality, and Christianity. To E. M. Forster, Cavafy was poet at a "slight angle to the universe." To Lawrence Durrell, he was the likely character of the presiding poet in *The Alexandria Quartet*. W. H. Auden and Marguerite Yourcenar wrote about him, some of his work was translated by Stephen Spender and James Merrill, he inspired etchings by David Hockney (1966) and photographs of males nudes by Duane Michals (1978).

Peter Christensen of Marquette University described Cavafy as one who deliberately rejected Classical Greece in favor of a decadent Hellenism. Cavafy was also inspired by the last days of the Ptolemies, Cleopatra, and her lover Marc Antony. In *Anekdota Peza* (*Unpublished Prose*), he indicates a love for Alexander Mavroudis (Alex Madis), a minor poet and Parisian playwright. In "Bandaged Shoulder," in which he takes the bloody rag of a wounded soldier to his lips, he writes homoerotically as he implies that the blood confirms his love for the injured man.

His other work with sexual overtones, often describing one-night stands in seedy places and published two decades after his death, seldom describes a mutual love or a long-term relationship. A freethinker, Cavafy died of throat cancer. {GL}

Cavaignac, Éleonore Louis Godefroy (1801—1845)

A French journalist who struggled against the reactionary monarchy, Cavaignac was one of the founders of the *Société des Amis du Peuple* and the *Société des Droits de l'Homme*. He was imprisoned and exiled, but in 1841 Cavaignac returned to France. J. S. Mill called him "the intensest of atheists." {RAT}

Cavalcante, Guido (1230—1300)

A noble Italian poet and philosopher, Cavalcante was a friend of Dante and a leader of the Ghibbelin party. Bayle wrote that "it is said his speculation has as their aims to prove there is no God. Dante places his father in the hell of Epicureans, who denied the immortality of the soul." {BDF}

Cavallotti, Felice Carlo Emanuel (1842—1873)

Cavallotti was an Italian poet and journalist, a pronounced atheist. He was elected a member of the Italian parliament in 1873. {BDF; RAT}

Cave, Henry (17th Century)

Cave, an atheist, wrote *The Darkness of Atheisme Expelled by the Light of Nature* (1683). {GS}

Cave, Nick (20th Century)

A recording artist, Cave told a *Boston Globe* reporter (September 1998) that he "is an atheist but loves the Bible." Cave is a singer for such punk bands as Birthday Party and the Bad Seeds. {CA}

Cavendish, Henry (1731—1810)

Cavendish, one of the great British pioneers of the science of chemistry, was a recluse and most of his writings were published posthumously. His chief researches were on heat, in which he determined the specific heats for a number of substances, although his findings were not recognized until later. He wrote on the composition of air; on the nature and properties of a gas that he isolated and described as "inflammable air," now known as hydrogen; and on the composition of water, which he demonstrated to consist of oxygen and "inflammable air." He determined that the density of the earth led him to state it as 5.48 times that of water.

His biographer, G. Wilson, quotes his attitude on religion from a contemporary scientist: "As to Cavendish's religion, he was nothing at all." He never went to church. Cambridge University is the site of the Cavendish Physical Laboratory, named in his honor. {CE; JM; RAT; RE}

Cavett, Dick (1936-)

A Nebraska-born entertainer, television comedy writer, club performer, and television show host, Cavett is widely known by TV viewers. He wrote (with Christopher Porterfield) *Cavett* (1974) and *Eye on Cavett* (1983).

On one of his programs, he mentioned that he finds it impossible to maintain any religious faith:

> This is my religious problem: it would be wonderful to believe in the most fundamental way. It would make life easier, it would explain everything, it would give meaning where none is apparent, it would make tragedies bearable. If I went to a revival meeting, I have no doubt I could be one of the first to go down on my knees. It seems as if the only religion worth having is the simplest possible religion. But something about the fact that all it takes to make it so is deciding it *is* so puts me off. Knowing it could instantly make me much happier makes it somehow unworthy of having.

Of his grandfather, a fundamentalist Baptist minister, Cavett is quoted in *Cavett*, "I hope there is a God for Grandpa Richards's sake, but don't much care if there is one for mine." {CA}

Cavia, Mariano de (1855—1920)

Cavio was a Spanish journalist and critic. He edited the *Liberal* of Madrid. {BDF}

Cavour, Camillo di (1810—1861)

With Mazzini and Garibaldi, Cavour wrote *The Other Creators of the Kingdom of Italy*. Cavour was a freethinker. {TRI}

Cayce, Edgar (1877—1945)

Cayce, an American folk healer, was a believer in reincarnation and an inspiration for contemporary New Age spiritualists. His views were found ludicrous by Paul Edwards in *Reincarnation* (1996).

Cayla, Jean Mamert (1812—1877)

A French man of letters, Cayla edited the *Emancipator* of Toulouse, a city about which he wrote a history. Among his numerous anti-clerical brochures were *The Clerical Conspiracy* (1861); *The Devil, His Grandeur and Decay* (1864); *Hell Demolished* (1865); and *The History of the Mass* (1874). {BDF; RAT}

Cazeau, Charles J. (20th Century)

Cazeau, a geologist and pre-evolution spokesperson, writes for *Free Inquiry*. He is author of *Physical Geology* (1976) and *Science Trivia* (1986). {*Free Inquiry*, Summer 1982}

Cazelles, Émile Honoré (Born 1831)

Cazelles, the French translator of Bentham's *Influence of Natural Religion* (1875) also translated Mill's *Subjection of Women* and his *Autobiography* and *Essays on Religion*. {BDF; RAT}

Cecco Stabili d'Ascoli (1269?–1327)

Cecco is an example of one of the most daring heretics of the later Middle Ages. His given name was Francesco degli Stabili. A professor of philosophy and astrology at Bologna, he knew Dante and was one of his detractors. In fact, he has been described as "representing natural science, against the Christian science of Dante." Combining a strong anti-Christian feeling with the universal belief in astrology, Cecco had declared that Jesus lived *come un poltrone* (like a sluggard) with his disciples, and died on the cross, under the compulsion of his star. [Albertus Magnus and Pierre d'Ailli, Cardinal and Bishop of Cambrai, also cast the horoscope of Jesus.] Because of such heresy, including his having accused Dante of heresy, Cecco in 1327 was burned at the stake in Florence. {BDF; CE; JM; JMR; JMRH; RE}

Cée, Jean-Paul (Born 1839)

Cée, the founder and president of the *Comité d' Études Morales* (Committee on Moral Laws), was an officer in the French navy. He was in Rome during the pontificate of Pius IX, observed the splendor of Roman Catholic rites, and while in Dahomey witnessed human sacrifices. In Paris at the 1889 Universal Freethought Congress, he discussed his travels and recommended that freethinkers found a Committee on Moral Laws, which idea was accepted. Cée's position on socialism was nearer to the English concept of nationalism, not to the socialism of Marx, Liebknecht, or Bebel. {PUT}

CELEBRITY

- A celebrity is one who is known to many persons he is glad he doesn't know.

—H. L. Mencken

CELEBRITY ATHEIST LIST

Jim Lippard is webmaster for the "Celebrity Atheist List," one which keeps track of public statements by individuals that they are non-believers. On the Web: <www.primenet.com/~lippard/atheist.celebs/>.

CELIBACY

The *Catechism of the Catholic Church* (1994) states that "All the ordained ministers of the Latin Church, with the exception of permanent deacons, are normally chosen from among men of faith who live a celibate life and who intend to remain celibate 'for the sake of the kingdom of heaven.' Called to consecrate themselves with undivided heart to the Lord and to 'the affairs of the Lord,' they give themselves entirely to God and to men. Celibacy is a sign of this new life to the service of which the Church's minister is consecrated; accepted with a joyous heart celibacy radiantly proclaims the Reign of God." (See entry for Peter.)

Abstinence from sexual intercourse is, to freethinkers, the strangest of all aberrations. It is not practiced in any other part of the animal kingdom. (See entries for Chastity and Andrew Greeley.)

Celko, Jaroslav (20th Century)

Celko founded the Prometheus Society in Slovakia. Estimating in 1995 that 72% of adults declare themselves to have a religious belief, while only 18% say they are non-religious, Celko comments that "the efforts of religious organizations to ground all social activities in religion are finding substantial support not only with politicians, but also with certain and state officials." Atheism, which is connected with communism, is seen as the source of amorality, crime, and pornography. As a result, Celko believes that the development of humanism in Slovakia is uphill work. He signed Humanist Manifesto 2000. {*International Humanist News*, June 1995}

Cellarius, Martin (16th Century)

In 1527, Cellarius published *On the Works of God*. The earliest anti-Trinitarian book, it preceded by four years Michael Servetus's *On the Errors of the Trinity*. {BDF}

Celsus, Aurelius (c. 125—175)

Celsus was a pagan philosopher whose *True Discourse* was lost but which showed him to have been an aggressive antagonist of Christianity. Origen's *Contra Celsus* (*Against Celsus*), which refers to the lost book, is a rebuttal of the philosopher's outlook and attacks Celsus's objections to the Christian gospels. Why did Jesus not know that Judas Iscariot would betray him, Celsus argued. Had not the author of Mark said that Jesus had foreknowledge but that the prophecy had to be fulfilled? Had not the author of John had Jesus arrange the betrayal by giving the piece of bread to Judas? As quoted by Origen, Celsus gave a picture of a prophet-ridden Palestine, where many self-proclaimed prophets were claiming to be the god or the son of god or a divine spirit. Jesus, according to Celsus, was but one of these wandering healers and professed miracle workers. "Before accepting any belief one ought first to follow reason as a guide," Celsus wrote, "for credulity without enquiry is a sure way to deceive oneself." Fortunately, Origen, one of the most learned of the Fathers, considered Celsus the most formidable opponent of the Church, for had he not written about Celsus we would not know about him today inasmuch as the Church decreed that all his works had to be destroyed.

In 1987, R. Joseph Hoffmann translated and published Celsus's *On the True Doctrine: A Discourse Against the Christians*. {BDF; EH; RE}

CEMETERY

A cemetery is a graveyard, a place set aside to bury the dead. The original Greek *koimeterion*, referred to a "dormitory" or "sleeping place," however. Early Christian writers referred to the Roman catacombs and later to consecrated churchyards as cemeteries. Shakespeare, among others, complained that when some cemeteries could hold no more bodies, new bodies were buried in the same plots. Therefore,

Good friend, For Jesu's sake forbear
To dig the dust enclosed here.
Blest be the man that spares these stones;
Cursed be he that moves my bones.

Many contemporary secularists, finding that cemeteries have become commercialized along with an entire funeral industry, often avoid cemeteries altogether. They ask that their cremains be scattered rather than buried. By so doing, they avoid ending up in a "garden of honor," a "garden of memories," a "memorial park mausoleum," or a "burial cloister." No Stiffyville, no last home, no skeleton park, no bone orchard, no God's acre for them. (See entries for Jessica Mitford and for Death, A Freethinker's.)

CENSORSHIP

• Run, don't walk, to the first library you can find and read what they're trying to keep out of your eyes. Read what they're trying to keep out of your brains. Because that's exactly what you need to know.

—Stephen King,
novelist whose *Salem's Lot*, *Carrie*, and *Cujo* have been censored in schoolsand libraries despite his being a theist.
(See entry for Books, Censorship Of.)

• "What Every Girl Should Know"—Nothing, by order of the U.S. Post Office.

— In place of Margaret Sanger's newspaper column in *The Call*, the newspaper printed this notice.

CENSUS OF NON-THEISTS AND NON-BELIEVERS

A study in the 1990s showed that an estimated 66% of the world's population is non-Christian and 34% is Christian. (See entry for Hell.)

CENTAURS

The centaurs in Greek mythology were creatures half man and half horse. They had been fathered by Ixion (although some stories credit his son, Centaurus). These centaurs were uncouth and savage, except for Chiron, who became friends and a teacher of men. Their half-brothers, the Lapiths, engaged them in a battle which Ovid described, were depicted on the Parthenon, and sculpted by Michelangelo. (See entry for Tartarus.) {CE}

CENTER FOR INQUIRY—Amherst, New York

In 1995, a 20,000 square foot educational and administrative center for the Council for Secular Humanism, *Free Inquiry*, and *Skeptical Inquirer*, was dedicated in Amherst, New York. Entertainer Steve Allen, Nobel Laureate Herbert Hauptman, and Paul Kurtz were among the several hundred dignitaries who attended. Adjacent to Buffalo's Amherst campus, the building houses all of the Council for Secular Humanism's editorial, administrative, and warehouse operations. Its library complex, which has a 50,000-volume capacity, houses the largest freethought collection in the world.

CENTER FOR INQUIRY—Kansas City

The Center for Inquiry Midwest is at 6301 Rockhill Road (Suite #412), Kansas City, Missouri 64131. Prof. Verle Muhrer is Executive Director; Richard Tolbert is special projects director; Steve Carr is in charge of operations; Henry Wahwussuck is prison outreach coordinator.

CENTER FOR INQUIRY—Los Angeles

During 1996 donors gave or pledged almost $1.5 million to two capital fund drives benefiting construction of the Center for Inquiry—West, which will be built in the Los Angeles, California, area. Like the Center for Inquiry in Amherst, New York, it will house offices of the Council for Secular Humanism and the Committee for the Scientific Investigation of Claims of the Paranormal (CSICOP).

CENTER FOR INQUIRY—Moscow

The Center for Inquiry at Moscow State University was inaugurated in 1997 and was cosponsored by the newly formed Russian Humanist Society and the International Academy of Humanism. An estimated fifty scientists and philosophers spoke. Professor Valerii Kuvakin is president of the Society. In attendance from the United States were Jan Eisler of the St. Petersburg, Florida, Humanist Society, Timothy J. Madigan of *Free Inquiry*, and Dr. Paul Kurtz. {*Free Inquiry*, Winter 1997-1998}

CENTER FOR INQUIRY—Oxford: See Centre for Critical Enquiry.

CENTER FOR INQUIRY INSTITUTE

The Center for Inquiry Institute, Box 664, Amherst, New York 14226, offers courses in humanism and skepticism. It also sponsors an annual summer session and periodic workshops. The first Dean of the Council for Secular Humanism group was Vern Bullough. The current dean is Reid Johnson. Executive Director is Theodore Manekin. Special projects Director is Thomas Flynn. Chief Financial Officer is Barry Karr. Publications Coordinator is Lewis Vaughn.

The board of directors includes Vern Bullough, Thomas Casten, Kendrick Frazier, David Hehehan, Lawrence Jones, Joseph Levee, and Robert Worsfold.

CENTER FOR RATIONAL THOUGHT

The Center for Rational Thought is found on the Web: <http://www.teleport.com/~preacher>.

CENTER FOR THE SCIENTIFIC INVESTIGATION OF CLAIMS OF THE PARANORMAL (CSICOP)

Barry Karr is Executive Director of the Committee for the Scientific Investigation of Claims of the Paranormal (CSICOP), PO Box 703, Amherst, New York 14226. E-mail: <Skeptinq@aol.com>. Web: <www.csicop.org>.

CSICOP's executive council includes the following: James Alcock, Barry Beyerstein, Thomas Casten, Kendrick Frazier, Martin Gardner, Ray Hyman, Philip Klass, Joe Nickell, Lee Nisbet, Amardeo Sarma, and Eugenie C. Scott. Associate members are Lawrence D. Jones and Mario Mendez-Acosta.

CENTER OF THE UNIVERSE

The Earth used to be the theologian's center of the universe. Later, the Sun. Later our Galaxy. Hubble and other astronomers and cosmologists have shown that no center exists for the galaxies.

CENTRAL AMERICAN HUMANISTS

In 1989, the Costa Ricans founded their *Asociación Ético Humanista Costarricense* (ASEHUCO), an association of ethical humanists.

In 1994, with the financial assistance of the International Humanist and Ethical Union (IHEU) then in Utrecht, an association for all Spanish-speaking ethical humanists in the Americas was founded: *Asociación Iberoamericana Ético Humanista* (ASIBEHU). Instrumental in the group's being founded were Rob Tielman in the Netherlands, Dr. Paul Kurtz of the Council for Secular Humanism, and Warren Allen Smith. Its first president was Alexander Cox Alvarado of Costa Rica.

On the Web: <http://idt.net/~wasm/asibehu>.

CENTRAL LONDON HUMANISTS

For information, telephone Cherie Holt on 0171 916 3015 or Hilary Leighter on 01895 632096.

CENTRE D'ACTION LAIQUE

Centre d'Action Laique (IHEU), is a Belgian French-speaking humanist group at CP 236, Campus de la Plaine U.L.B., Boulevard du Triomphe, 1050 Brussels, Belgium Cp236, Campus de la Plaine. In 1997 its five-story headquarters building was inaugurated. (See entry for Belgian Humanists.)

CENTRE FOR CRITICAL STUDIES IN RELIGION, ETHICS, AND SOCIETY

In 1995 at a Methodist school, Westminster College, Oxford, England, the Centre for Critical Studies in Religion, Ethics, and Society was inaugurated. Present among others were Jim Herrick, Paul Kurtz, and Nicolas Walter. Dr. Kurtz, during the dialogue between humanism and religion, commented, "Humanism, I submit, because of its emphasis on the dignity, value, and happiness of each individual, its reliance on critical thinking and scientific technology to solve human problems, and its desire to build a genuine democratic world community, is the most appropriate philosophy for the age. . . . However, it is clear that if humanism is to gain ground in the future, it will need to forge dramatic new ideals that can heighten the imagination and inspire commitment and devotion to them. But the question remains: Can it do so without betraying its skeptical methodology?" The Centre was sponsored by the Council for Secular Humanism's International Academy of Humanism. R. J. Hoffmann, its director at Westminster College, Oxford University, has written that the centre is

> . . . for the study of the humanist tradition, which is here defined very broadly to include both secular/rationalistic shades of humanism as well as religious/liberal religion shades. I am myself a Unitarian (perceived by most of my colleagues on the "secular" side, I fear as being therefore a "soft" humanist), but I am also a senior editor of the journal *Free Inquiry* and an advocate of dialogue between the denominations of the movement. I have little defence for occupying this middle ground (Antony Flew once accused me of occupying a muddled ground) except that I feel comfortable doing so and because I came to humanism through Unitarianism and still need the consolation of its patron saints.
>
> {WAS, 24 October 1996}

CENTRO COSCIENZA

Centro Coscienza, an Italian humanist group, is at Corso Di Porta Nuova, 16-20121, Milan, Italy. {FD}

CENTRO POSITIVISTA DO PARANA

Centro Positivista do Parana is at Rua Comendador Araujo 531, 80420-000 Curitiba, Parana, Brazil. It is an associate member of the International Humanist and Ethical Union.

CEREMONIES

Barthez, a French physician and friend of D'Alembert, was once shown by the Archbishop of Sens a number of works relating to the rites of his see. Barthez is said wittily to have observed, "These are the Sens ceremonies, but can you show me the *sens* [sense] of ceremonies?" (See entry for Paul Barthez.)

Ceresole, Pierre (1879—1945)

Ceresole was the Swiss founder of Service Civil International. He was a pacifist, a conscientious objector, and the assistant secretary of the International Fellowship of Reconciliation. {TRI}

Cerniglia, Mimi (20th Century)

Cerniglia, a board member in several elective positions of the American Association of University Women in North Carolina, is treasurer and vice-president of Freethinkers, Inc.

CERTAINTY

• Convictions are more dangerous foes of truth than lies.

—**Friedrich Nietzsche**

• Doubt is not a pleasant mental state, but certainty is a ridiculous one.

—**Voltaire**

Cerutti, Joseph Antoine Joachim (1738—1792)

Cerutti was an Italian writer who joined the Jesuit Society and taught with distinction at Jesuit colleges. He then embraced the deistic opinions of philosophers he read. His *Bréviaire Philosophique* (to which he put the name of Frederic the Great) and his *Les jardins de Betz* (1792) reveal his skepticism. Cerutti accepted the Revolution, delivered a funeral oration in memory of Mirabeau, and was elected to the Legislative Assembly. {RAT}

Cervantes, Saavedra Miguel de (1547—1619)

Cervantes is a major Spanish novelist, dramatist, and poet. In his youth and in the service of a cardinal, he studied philosophy and literature in Italy. His left arm was permanently crippled in the naval battle of Lepanto (1571), and when captured by Barbary pirates in 1575 he was sold as a slave, eventually becoming the property of the viceroy of Algiers. Américo Castro, in *El Pensamiento de Cervantes*, avers that *Don Quixote de la Mancha* (Part 1, 1605; Part 2, 1615) is more than just a parody of chivalry, that it is a profound study of the cultural times and contains elements of the author's unbelief. Quixote [Quijote], the gentle old man who goes crazy over the ideals of chivalry, is the Spanish Everyman. He is the typical Spaniard who recognizes that the glory of Spain is in the past and, in the end, takes the expedient route of confessing his sins and leading the illusional life of being a good Catholic. The work also is his most anticlerical. In Cervantes's time, the Inquisitors had their hands full now that the Protestant Reformation had arrived.

Erasmistas, followers of Desiderius Erasmus of Rotterdam, were considered heretics, Lutherans, or some kind of crypto-Protestants, and Cervantes was aware of their influence. Actually, according to John Devlin, Cervantes was most unorthodox:

> Because of the Inquisition, writers had to disguise their message; basically Cervantes was heterodox. The author is constantly tampering with reality and posing the question as to what reality is. Thus, Cervantes is supposedly attacking the ultimate foundations of belief. For example, the knight fell upon the poor traveling barber and snatched his basin from his head. The Don was convinced that the basin was Mambrino's helmet. Quijote's companions discussed the matter at the inn and split the difference: from one point of view it was obviously a barber's basin; from another it was Mambrino's helmet.
>
> The scholastic "principle of contradiction" states:
>
> What is, is.
> What is not, is not.
> What is, is not what is not.
>
> Once this principle is abandoned, the floodgates for multiple skepticism are open. The foundations of society are undermined and the ordered Thomistic logic of the Catholic church and its teachings are exposed to grave doubt.

Cervantes, in *Novelas ejemplares* (1613), included twelve original tales of piracy, gypsies, and human passions, drawn from his own experience, and his work in general had a major influence upon development in Europe of the novel. Despite the anticlericalism in parts of his writings, his work never made the *Index Librorum Prohibitorum*. {CE; EU, John Devlin; JMRH}

Cervone, Ed (1945-)

Cervone, an artist whose representational works are highly erotic, is a non-believer. He never knew his father, a German naval officer who commanded a submarine sunk by the Allies during World War II. His Latvian mother, who had fled to Germany to escape the Russian army, married an American soldier, and Cervone was raised in the United States, renamed by his stepfather.

Two books containing his erotic drawings are *Ed Cervone* (Janssen Verlag, Berlin, 1995) and *Ed Cervone: Phantasies of Gay Sex* (Janssen Verlag, Berlin, 1996).

Cesalpino, Andrea (1519—1603)

An Italian botanist and physiologist, Cesalpino (also called Andreas Caesalpinus) was physician to Pope Clement VIII. Linnaeus considered him the first true systematist and admitted his obligations to his Cesalpino's *Plantis* (1583). In *Demonum Investigatio*, Cesalpino contended that "possession" by devils is amenable to medical treatment. His *Quaestinum Peripateticarum* (5 books, 1588) was condemned as teaching a pantheistic doctrine similar to that of Spinoza, and Bishop Parker denounced him. Cesalpino founded the botanical garden at the University of Pisa. {BDF; CE}

Cesareo, Giovanni Alfredo (Born 1861)

An Italian poet and critic, Cesareo taught Italian literature at the University of Palermo. His rationalism is seen in his sympathetic article on Renan in the *Nuovo Antologia* (1892). {RAT}

Cevallos Estarellas, Pablo (20th Century)

Cevallos, who teaches at the Catholic University of Santiago in Guayaquil, Ecuador, is a secular humanist with a special interest in logic and critical thinking. He is active with *the Asociación Iberoamericana Ético Humanista*, a group of Spanish-speaking ethical humanists in Central and South America.

In 1996 he spoke about humanism in Latin America at the Humanist World Congress held in Mexico City. In 1997, he was awarded a Fulbright scholarship to study at Montclair State University in New Jersey. E-mail: <cevallop@ucsg.edu.ec>.

Chadbourn, Catalina (20th Century)

In 1995, Chadbourn became President of the University of Minnesota Atheists and Humanists (UMAH).

Chadwick, John White (1840—1904)

Minister for forty years of the Second Unitarian Church in Brooklyn, New York, Chadwick was a prominent spokesman for the radical wing of late 19th-century American Unitarianism. He championed the theories of evolution, arguing that Darwin helped confirm a view of nature and humanity as part of an evolving cosmos unified by a God who was revealed in that evolutionary process.

His biographies of Theodore Parker (1900) and William Ellery Channing (1903) were highly praised, and his anti-supernaturalism was basic to his philosophic outlook. {U&U}

Chaeremon (1st Century C.E.)

An Alexandrian rationalist and one of Nero's tutors, Chaeremon explained the Egyptian religion as a mere allegorizing of the physical order of the universe. He regarded comets, however, as divine portents. {JMR; JMRH}

Chaho, J. Augustin (1811—1858)

A Basque man of letters, Chaho wrote *Philosophy of Comparative Religion* and a Basque dictionary. At Bayonne, he edited the *Ariel*, which in 1852 was suppressed and he was exiled. {BDF}

Chainey, George (19th Century)

Chainey edited the semi-monthly Boston publication, *Infidel Pulpit*, in 1881. He wrote *The Infidel Pulpit* (c. 1880) and *Relics of Barbarism* (1881). {GS}

Chait, Leonardo (20th Century)

Dr. Chait, who signed Humanist Manifesto 2000, and **Virginia Li**, his wife, formed a trust to help fund the Center for Inquiry–West in the Los Angeles area. They were among the first of the donors for the West Coast center for secular humanism.

Chakraberty, Chandra (20th Century)

Chakraberty, a rationalist in India, wrote *The Outline of Rationalism* (1938). {GS}

Challemel-Lacour, Paul Armand (1827—1896)

A French statesman, Challemel-Lacour taught French literature at Zurich, then returned to France in 1859 and joined the anti-clerical politicians, especially Gambetta. From 1880 to 1882 he was French Ambassador at London, where he was attacked by the Irish Catholics. He became President of the Senate in 1893. His *Pensées d'un Pessimiste* is rationalistic. {RAT}

Chaloner, Thomas (1595—1661)

A member of Parliament, Chaloner was a witness against Archbishop Laud and was one of the King Charles Judges. Wood has said that Chaloner "was as far from being a Puritan as the east is from the west" and that he "was of the natural religion." His *True and Exact Relation of the Finding of Moses His Tomb* (1657) was a satire directed against the Presbyterians. Upon the Restoration, Chaloner fled to the Low Countries and died in Zeeland. {BDF; RAT}

Chamberlain, Arthur Neville [Prime Minister] (1869—1940)

Chamberlain, the "man with the umbrella," was a British statesman who stated that Hitler, a rational person like himself, would not go to war, that he could be trusted despite his record. This resulted in the "appeasement" that culminated in the Munich Pact—had Chamberlain admitted that Hitler could be stopped by force, Chamberlain would have had to admit that his own policies had been wrong, thereby endangering his own political reputation.

He once described Spanish dictator Franco as "a gallant Christian gentleman." After the British debacle in Norway in 1940, Chamberlain was forced to resign as prime minister, leading non-appeasers to suggest he be rapped over the head with his often-photographed umbrella.

However, in 1993, a political biography of Winston Churchill has suggested that Britain should not have gone to war against Adolf Hitler. John Charmley in *Churchill: The End of Glory* suggests that Chamberlain and his supporters knew Britain lacked the power to defeat Hitler, that it was more expedient to be prudent realists and allow Germany to assume a dominant role in Europe, even though Hitler's methods were disapproved as being coarse. Otherwise, Britain would either lose to Germany or become a slave to American power while the Soviet Union replaced Germany as the dominant power in that area. But when Hitler invaded Poland in 1939, Chamberlain was forced, Gaddis Smith of Yale has said in reviewing the Charmley thesis, "to go to war rather than accept a *fait accompli*, as it had over Czechoslovakia at and after Munich in 1938-1939."

A biography by David Dilks in 1984 states that although Chamberlain was grounded in the austere tradition of Unitarianism, "He felt no close affinity with many established institutions. He drew no daily comfort or hope of salvation from religious faith. He would not attend church." {CE; EG; TRI; U; UU}

Chamberlain, Basil Hall (1850—1918)

Chamberlain, son of Vice-Admiral Chamberlain and brother of Houston Stewart Chamberlain, settled in Japan and became on authority who taught Japanese philology at the Tokyo Imperial University. He wrote a dictionary or cyclopedia entitled *Things Japanese* (1902) and *The Invention of a New Religion* (1912). Chamberlain, an agnostic, was an honorary associate of the British Rationalist Press Association. {GS; RAT; RE}

Chamberlain, Daniel Henry [Governor] (1835—1907)

Chamberlain was a Governor of South Carolina. He took part in the Civil War, then became Attorney General (1865—1872) and Governor (1874—1877). All assumed he was an orthodox believer in religion.

But upon his death, the *North American Review* published a document stating Chamberlain had been a "freethinker" all along, that he rejected "the idea of a presiding or controlling Deity," and that he was skeptical about a future life. {JM; RAT}

Chamberlain, Houston Stewart (1855—1927)

Chamberlain, a writer who was an enthusiastic Wagnerian and a student of science and philosophy, was a rationalist with some leaning to Hindu mysticism. He wrote *Immanuel Kant* (1921). Purportedly, however, his mysticism may have influenced Adolf Hitler. {RAT}

Chamberlain, Joseph (1836—1914)

Chamberlain, a Unitarian, headed the National Liberation Federation in England. "I have always had a grudge against religion for absorbing the passion in men's nature," he once stated. {TRI}

Chambers, Betty (20th Century)

Chambers was a four-term President of the American Humanist Association, serving from 1973 to 1979. She is assistant to the President of the American Humanist Association, is on the editorial board of *The Humanist*, is editor of *Free Mind*, and is active in the Puget Sound Humanist organization in Washington.

Chambers signed Humanist Manifesto II. (See entry for Washington Atheists, Humanists.) {FD; HNS2}

Chambers, Ephraim (c. 1680—1740)

Chambers originated the Cyclopaedia of Arts and Sciences, the first edition of which procured him admission to the Royal Society. A French translation gave rise to Diderot and D'Alembert's *Encyclopédie*. He also edited the *Literary Magazine*, making known his infidel opinions.

The encyclopedia was placed on the Roman *Index*, but Chambers was buried in the cloisters of Westminster Abbey. {BDF; RAT; RE}

Chambers, Jerry (20th Century)

Chambers was on the board of directors of the American Humanist Association in the 1950s.

Chambers, Robert (1802—1871)

A deist, Chambers rejected both the divine creation and religious fundamentalism's miracles. He did, however, believe in a First Cause. His *Vestiges of the Natural History of Creation* (1844) is said by Birx to be the most important work on organic evolution to appear between Lamarck and Charles Darwin. However, it contained errors of fact and interpretation, and the year Chambers died Darwin published his own more scientifically oriented *Descent of Man*.00 McCabe labels him a non-Christian theist. {CE; EU, H. James Birx; JMR; RAT; RE}

Chamfort, Sébastian Roch Nicolas de (1740—1794)

A French writer known for his maxims and epigrams, Chamfort was popular at court because of his acute observations on literature, morals, and politics, this despite his republican beliefs. He was admired by Jean Rostand. Albert Camus called him a "true classic" and "a moralist as profound as Mme. de Lafayette or Benjamin Constant, and he takes his place, in spite of or because of his impassioned blindness, among the great creators of a certain art in which the truth of life is at no point sacrificed to the artifices of language." W. S. Merwin, reviewing Claude Arnaud's biography, *Chamfort* (1992), states that the philosopher E. M. Cioran spoke of Chamfort with respect and that Cyril Connolly "adopted Chamfort as a kind of private cult figure. . . . [Connolly] got away with it partly because his readers (as he must have assumed) knew little about Chamfort." During the French Revolution, with its Reign of Terror, Chamfort the freethinker was denounced. Eventually, he committed suicide. {CE; JMR; JMRH}

Chamisso, Adelbert von (1781—1838)

A French poet and naturalist, Chamisso in 1815 sailed round the world in the *Rurik*, and on his return he became custodian of the Berlin Botanical Institute. Many of his poems are bitterly anti-clerical, and he was both a skeptic and a rationalist. {RAT}

Champion, Henry Hyde (1859—1928)

"Harry" Champion was a socialist propagandist who arrived in Australia from India in 1890, then returned to England in 1891. He was a friend of Annie Besant's daughter, Mabel Besant-Scott. In Australia in 1898 he married Elsie Belle, sister of woman emancipist and suffrage worker, Vida Goldstein. The Goldsteins converted to Christian Science, which presented a medical problem for Champion, said to have had a venereal disease. Champion's days for activism or campaigning for the secular cause diminished after his marriage. From 1906 to 1909, he was President of the Victorian Socialist Party. {SWW}

Champion, Rafe Alfred (1945—)

Champion, who grew up on a dairy farm in Tasmania, is an Australian humanist, liberal agnostic, biologist, technical editor, and writer. An admirer of the humanist philosophy of Karl Popper, Champion joined the New South Wales Humanists, establishing a working group on birth control and family planning. He is a joint author of *Discrimination and Intellectual Handicap*.

Champollion, Jean François (1790—1832)

Champollion was a French Eyptologist who read Arabic, Persian, and Sanskrit as well as ancient Egyptian. He is credited with learning the secret of the hieroglyphic inscriptions (1822). Although the Church still claims him, his biographer, Hartleben, reproduced a discussion of religion which Champollion wrote and concludes that he had quit the church because of his skepticism. {JM; RAT; RE}

Chan, Pearl (20th Century)

Chan, a Harvard University member of the Campus Freethought Alliance, was a 1998 signer of the Bill of Rights for Unbelievers.

Chance, Janet (1885—1953)

Chance, a freethinker, was head in England of the Abortion Law Reform Association. {TRI}

Chancellor, John (1927—1996)

An American reporter, news anchor, and commentator for NBC, Chancellor was "the wise man with ready wit," Jack Thomas wrote in the *Boston Globe*. In an interview the year before Chancellor died of cancer, Thomas asked if he feared death and was told, "not as much as I would have thought." Thomas then asked what he thought happens after death, to which Chancellor replied, "I've been an agnostic for as long as I can remember . . . so I don't know where we go. But if it turns out that the lights are just turned off and nothing happens, well, that's OK." {E}

Chand, Gopi (20th Century)

Chand was an eminent Telugu litterateur. Although he was a radical humanist much of his life, he converted to mysticism and became a disciple of Sri Aurobindo in his last days.

Chandler, D(avid) R(oss) (1938—)

Chandler is book review editor of *Religious Humanism*, the quarterly of the Fellowship of Religious Humanists. He is author of *Toward Universal Religion* (1996).

Chandler, John (20th Century)

Chandler, who teaches philosophy at the University of Adelaide, is active in the Humanist Society of South Australia.

Chandler, Michael (20th Century)

Chandler, a high school principal, received the 1997 Freethinker of the Year Award by the Freedom from Religion Foundation. A native of Alabama and a graduate of that state's university, he successfully challenged a 1993 law promoting prayer in public schools. Alabama's governor, however, counseled schools not to comply but did not appeal the ruling. "Extremists," Chandler has said, "use this majority rule argument—which is mob rule—to force religion down your throat. My civil rights are not up for majority vote." {*Freethought Today*, March 1998}

Chandrasekhar, Subrahmanyan (1910—1995)

Chandrasekhar was elected in 1968 as an honorary associate by the Rationalist Press Association. A theoretical astrophysicist, he was on the faculty of the University of Chicago. Among his books are *An Introduction to the Study of Stellar Structure* (1939) and *Ellipsoidal Figures of Equilibrium* (1969). From 1952 to 1971, he was managing editor of *The Astrophysical Journal.*

In 1994 Chandrasekhar was elected to the Royal Society and in 1983 was awarded the Nobel Prize. In a December 1995 obituary in *New Humanist,* Hermann Bondi noted that Chandrasekhar's uncle, Sir C. V. Raman, was also a Nobel Laureate. Bondi included details about a quarrel with Sir Arthur Stanley Eddington, in which Chandrasekhar showed that the ultimate fate of a star that has exhausted its nuclear fuel; it contracts and can reach equilibrium in a highly condensed state of future density only if its mass is less than the "Chandrasekhar limit"; more massive stars must go on contracting without limit, ending up as a "Black Hole." Eddington, however, argued against this, and Bondi speculates, "My suspicion is that he, a devout Quaker who firmly believed in an orderly universe, was unwilling to accept that something as singular (and to him obnoxious) as a Black Hole could form naturally. This is another instance where deep faith can make an otherwise friendly and reasonable person behave nastily and irrationally."

Changeux, Jean Pierre (1936—)

A professor at *Collège de France* and *Institut Pasteur,* Changeux is a Humanist Laureate in the Council for Secular Humanism's International Academy of Humanism. He is author of *L'Homme neuronal* (1983) and co-editor (with M. Konishi) of *The Neural and Molecular Basis of Learning: Report of the Dahlem Workshop on the Neural and Molecular Bases of Learning* (1987). In 1994, he wrote *Raison et plaisir*. He signed Humanist Manifesto 2000.

With Alain Connes, a distinguished mathematician, Changeux wrote *Conversations on Mind, Matter, and Mathematics* (1995). The conversation by Changeux, the celebrated neuroscientist and molecular biologist, with Connes pointed up differences of opinion on basic matters. Connes chides Changeux for not grasping some points about quantum physics, for example. But Changeux relates and questions to his vision of humans as being complex biological systems, the result of millions of years of evolutionary changes. He thinks of mathematics as a human construction, the result of having been shaped by the intricacies of neural wiring and cultural transmission.

Changeux, according to Philip Kitcher, the Presidential Professor of Philosophy at the University of California in San Diego, includes an overview of the fundamentals of neuroscience which "is a model of lucidity."

Channing, William Ellery (1780—1842)

A prominent writer and a major figure in liberal religion, Channing was instrumental in identifying the goals of contemporary Unitarianism. Of Channing, Lamont has written, "While the world-view of the Unitarians was certainly non-Humanist, they were on the whole liberals in theology and also backed most of the important social reforms of the nineteenth century. They gave emphasis, too, to the right of individual religious freedom and welcomed into the Unitarian fellowship even those who questioned the existence of a personal God."

It is generally held that Channing is the single most important figure in the history of American Unitarianism. {CE; CL; ER; FUS; U; U&U; UU}

Channing, William Henry (1810—1884)

The nephew of William Ellery Channing, William Henry Channing became a Unitarian minister and also collaborated with James Freeman Clarke and others on the Transcendentalist and Unitarian periodical, *Western Messenger*. Although he influenced the Brook Farm commune to embrace Charles Fourier's ideas, the commune collapsed after the fire of 1846. His emphasis on Unitarianism focused on the church's need to work for the progress of the human race as a whole, not simply emphasize the individual. {CE; U; U&U}

Chantrey, Francis Leggatt [Sir] (1781—1841)

An eminent British sculptor, Chantrey abandoned "all Christian and religious feelings," his biographer Holland states. Chantrey's large fortune was left to the Royal Academy to found the trust that is still known as the Chantrey Bequest. {JM; RAT; RE}

CHAOS

In Greek mythology, Chaos was the unfathomable space out of which all—including Gaea, the mother of all things—arose. Another version is that Eurynome rose out of Chaos, creating all things. The concept of chaos has come to refer to the confusion of matter, out of which the universe grew. In mathematics, physics, and other fields, according to James Gleick's *Chaos: Making A New Science* (1987), chaos has taken on a contemporary significance, as illustrated in the work of the physicist Mitchell Feigenbaum, the Polish-born mathematician and inventor of fractals Benoit Mandelbrot, and the mathematician James Yorke.

In current usage, between order and chaos lies complexity. Order, or stability, is a static, repeating state. {CE}

Chapin, Augusta Jane (1836—1905)

One of the first Universalist women to be ordained, Chapin was active in the temperance movement and a founding member of the Association for the Advancement of Women. She was a leading organizer of the 1893 World's Parliament of Religions and the first woman in America to be awarded an honorary Doctor of Divinity degree. {U; U&U}

Chapin, Edwin Hubbell (1814—1880)

Minister of the Universalist Church of the Divine Paternity in New York City, Chapin was said to be one of the greatest orators of his day. Religion, he preached in a pragmatic way, is "not merely a theory of existence" but a "working-power." {U; U&U}

Chapin, Lydia Maria (Born 1802)

A Unitarian, Chapin was a 19th century author. {U}

Chapin, Schyler Garrison (1923—)

Chapin has been director of the Masterworks Columbia Records Division of CBS (1959—1962), vice president of programming of Lincoln Center for the Performing Arts (1964—1965), the Acting General Manager of the New York Metropolitan Opera (1972—1973), and in 1994 became the Cultural Affairs Executive of the City of New York. Chapin, a member of All Souls Church in New York City, is author of an autobiography, *Musical Chairs* (1977), and *Leonard Bernstein, Notes from a Friend* (1992).

CHAPLAIN

Before the 20th century, a chaplain was a priest who served an institutional chapel or was appointed to the army or navy. The term may first have been applied to the priest-custodian of the cape (*cappella*) of St. Martin of Tours.

In the 20th century, chaplains are still assigned to the Armed Forces. In the Netherlands, for example, a special post of Humanist Chaplain exists in light of the large numbers of Dutch who are humanists. Harvard University has created the position of Humanist Chaplain, a person who works with agnostics, atheists, and other freethinkers on the faculty and in the student body.

In 1998 when Denis Cobell was named by Lewisham's mayor the "Mayor's chaplain—humanist officiant," a priest objected that such an appointment by the English mayor "sends out completely the wrong signals to people—especially if they are going to call him chaplain." Cobell quickly retorted that the title "Father" was hardly less confusing. (See entry for Harvard Chaplaincy.)

Chaplin, Charles Spencer [Sir] (1889—1977)

Sir Charlie Chaplin, who was knighted one year before his death, was the English film actor known internationally as the Little Tramp. With his baggy trousers, black derby, cane, and over-sized shoes, he entertained audiences in silent short movies, then silent features, and in 1940 movies with sound. With D. W. Griffith, Douglas Fairbanks, and Mary Pickford, he co-founded United Artists in 1919.

His features include "The Kid" (1920), "The Gold Rush" (1924), "City Lights" (1931), "The Great Dictator" (1940), and "Limelight" (1952). Oona O'Neill, daughter of playwright Eugene O'Neill, was his fourth wife. On political grounds, Chaplin was barred from returning to the United States, so he resided in Switzerland.

Born in London, Chaplin was the son of a music hall singer who left the boy's mother before the child was two and saw him rarely thereafter, dying in 1901. His mother when he was but a child was certified insane in 1903. Chaplin and a brother survived the workhouse and several poor-law schools, then entered showbusiness. Ironically, by 1916, Chaplin was earning more money than the President of the United States.

In *My Autobiography* (1964), Chaplin wrote,

> There is a fraternity of those who passionately want to know. I was one of them. But my motives were not so pure; I wanted to know, not for the love of knowledge but as a defence against the world's contempt for the ignorant. So when I had time I browsed around the second-hand bookshops. In Philadelphia, I inadvertently came upon an edition of Robert Ingersoll's *Essays and Lectures*. This was an exciting discovery; his atheism confirmed my own belief that the horrific cruelty of the Old Testament was degrading to the human spirit.

The pompous-sounding title of his autobiography reminded Wesleyan University professor Jeanine Basinger of Katharine Hepburn's *Me*. She terms Walter Kerr's *The Silent Clowns* as the best film book about Chaplin's works and Lita Grey Chaplin's *My Life With Chaplin* as the one written by an ex-wife with the longest list of complaints.

Joyce Milton's *Tramp* (1996) described Chaplin's movies between 1931 and 1940 as handmade products in an era of mass production. She tells of his Dickensian childhood and his view of Communists: "They presented themselves as the representatives of the oppressed classes, with whom he identified, and they also purported to have the one correct answer to every question." But he was not a party member and became disaffected with the group by the end of the 1920s. The Chaplin Milton portrayed is a petty individual, one who started lawsuits against his friends but one whose talent was in creating unique, hilarious movies. She depicted Chaplin as a great admirer of the Russian Revolution, quoting a 1942 remark of his that the American people were beginning

> to understand the Russian purges, and what a wonderful thing they were. Yes, in those purges the Communists did away with their Quislings and Lavals and if other nations had done the same there would not be the original Quislings and Lavals today.

Rarely, lamented Milton, had the Stalinists "received such a ringing endorsement."

The *Manual of a Perfect Atheist* quotes Chaplin:

> By simple common sense I don't believe in God, in none.

Colleen Moore, in her autobiography, *Silent Star*, described how in 1922 Chaplin invited her and the four owners of First National Pictures to his home. He had heard that Robert Leiber, its president, had purchased Papini's "Life of Christ," and Leiber nodded yes. Chaplin nodded also, saying, "I want to play the role of Jesus. Although everyone appeared to be stunned by his request, Chaplin followed with:

> I'm a logical choice. I look the part. I'm a Jew. And I'm a comedian. And I'm an atheist, so I'd be able to look at the character objectively. Who else could do that?

Although he did not choose Chaplin, Leiber said wistfully, "It would be the greatest religious picture ever made, but I'd be run out of Indianapolis." (See entry for Church of Jesus Christ of Latter-Day Saints, which for some reason post-baptized Chaplin. Also, see entry for the atheist, Pier Paolo Pasolini, who directed "the greatest religious picture ever made." The entry for George Orwell indicates the creator of Big Brother thought Chaplin was Jewish.) {CE; Tim Madigan, *Free Inquiry*, Spring 1991}; *The New York Times* 28 July 1996}

Chapman, Antony M. (20th Century)

Chapman is on the Board of Directors of the British Rationalist Press Association. He is associated with the Humanist Media Committee and is a director of the Rationalist Press Association.

Chapman, John (Born 1839)

Chapman was a freethinker who wrote for and was the proprietor of *Westminster Review*.

Chapman, Linda (20th Century)

Chapman is Member at Large of Arizona Secular Humanists.

Chapman, Stephen James (1954—)

Chapman, a columnist, was associate editor of *The New Republic* (1978—1981), and since 1981 he has been editorial writer and columnist for *The Chicago Tribune*. Chapman has gone on record as being a non-theist:

> What I no longer understand, looking back on my life as a Christian, is the capacity to believe in something so outlandish as the existence of an Almighty God—much less one who created us all one by one, cherishes our immortal souls, intervenes on behalf of those who call upon his name, and holds a place for his faithful in an everlasting paradise. None of us has ever seen this being; none of us has ever heard him, except in the silence of our heads; none of us can produce a piece of evidence as large as a mustard seed that what we think of as God is anything more than a thought. Our scientists can see stars that have been dead for a billion years; they can document microscopic bacteria that concluded their brief lives on earth eons ago. But of God we have no trace, except for the testimony of scribes writing of events neither they nor those around them every witnessed—and the faith of millions of people who have managed to convince themselves that he lives and reigns somewhere in the sky.

{CA; E}

Chappell, Arthur (20th Century)

Chappell, in a *Freethinker* (June 1994) article entitled "Humanism Keynote of Starship Space Quests," disagrees with any critics who hold that the program's creator, Gene Roddenberry, is guilty of militarism, racism, or fascism. Rather, he argues, "*Star Trek* is essentially a science fiction vision of mankind humanising a dangerous and exciting universe." And he notes that Roddenberry was a passionate humanist.

Once, he relates, Roddenberry was asked to put a padre in the regular cast in order to explain Christian values to aliens. The author wisely put his foot down: "How could you have a chaplain if you've got that many people of different and alien beliefs on your ship? With as many planets as we were visiting, every person on the ship would have to be a chaplain!"

Chappellsmith, Margaret (Born 1806)

Chappellsmith was a writer of political articles in the *Dispatch* and lectured on socialism and freethought. Moncure D. Conway mentioned that Chappellsmith was the first female lecturer of the English Communists established by Robert Owen and others, in

Broughton, a little village twenty miles north of the New Forest. Of this community, which Margaret Reynolds (her maiden name) joined, and where she became personally acquainted with many of the leading English freethinkers, Conway remarks as follows:

The English Communists, the first considerable body in England who ever professed Materialism, and the only party, perhaps, that never possessed it, made their first practical settlement in Hampshire, at a time when society was hard and cold, taxation heavy, the people ignorant, and workingmen homeless. Robert Owen—the first to bring a breath of courage upon those evil days with which the present generation opened—and his disciples set up a propagandism, and subscribed money to create that situation in which it should be impossible for men to be depraved or poor. Looking around on the besotted and criminal, Owen said, "Give me a tiger and I will educate it!"

> In that faith he called around him the most earnest men of his time, for the effort which represented more high sentiment and spiritual hope than any movement England has seen. . . . Harmony Hall (the name of the Community at Broughton) came to know discord, and after a few years of struggle came to an end, by a complication of disorders such as are too familiar in such experiments to require mention in detail.

When Harmony Hall, "the English Brook Farm," broke up, the Chappellsmiths moved to America. In 1850 she contributed to the *Boston Investigator*. {BDF; SAU; WWS}

Chaptal, Jean Antoine Claude [Count de Chanteloup] (1756–1832)

A French chemist and statesman who had been trained in medicine, Chaptal turned to chemistry and rendered great service to the Revolution and to Napoleon, who made him a count. Chaptal retired at the royalist-clerical reaction but was, in spite of his freethinking, recalled and sent to the Home of Peers by the King. His great-grandson, the Viscount Chaptal, says in his *Souvenirs sur Napoleon* that he "had no religion" but believed in "a sort of Providence." {JM; RAT; RE}

CHARACTER

• What you are thunders so that I cannot hear what you say to the contrary.

—Ralph Waldo Emerson

• Four characteristics seem to me jointly to form the basis of an ideal character: vitality, courage, sensitiveness, and intelligence. I do not suggest that this list is complete, but I think it carries us a good way. Moreover, I firmly believe that by proper physical, emotional, and intellectual care of the young, these qualities could all be made very common.

—Bertrand Russell
Education and the Good Life (1926)

Charbonnel, Victor (20th Century)

A writer who had been educated for the Catholic priesthood, Charbonnel left the priesthood and the Church in 1897. He then became a leader and propagandist of rationalism in France, founding *La Raison* in 1901 and becoming co-editor of *L'Action* in 1902. {RAT}

Charavay, Gabriel (19th Century)

In France, Charavay rejected religion and was a humanitarian and materialist.

CHARISMATIC RELIGION: See entry for Pentecostalism.

Charles, Andrew (20th Century)

Charles, writing in *Freethought Today* (June-July 1996), includes the following as "Freethought's Greatest Hits" in music:

• Baker, LaVern, "Saved"—a satirical testimony of a liar-cheater-hootchykoo dancer turned Salvation Army bass drum thumper

• Barker, Dan and Kristin Lems, "My Thoughts Are Free"—by the production assistant of *Freethought Today*, a performer who also wrote "Reason's Greetings! All Year 'Round"

• Berlin, Irving, "Pack Up Your Sins (And Go to the Devil in Hades)"—the tune tells why Hell is so much more fun than Heaven

• Burdon, Eric, "Sky Pilot"—an emotional critique of religion's complacency during wartime

• Charming Beggars, "Tales You Tell"—an excoriation of preachers

• Crawford, Anthony, "Fit In"—an expression of the plight of not being able to believe in God and wondering how he "fits in"

• Crosby, Stills & Nash, "Cathedral"—a surrealistic flight through Winchester Cathedral that lands firmly onto unbelief

• Dead Kennedys, "Frankenchrist"—a slam on televangelists

• Dyer-Bennet, Richard, "The Vicar of Bray"—about a vicar determined to keep his job no matter who is on the throne, or how much he has to compromise himself

• Gershwin, George and Ira Gershwin, "It Ain't Necessarily So"—those things you read in the Bible

• Harding, John Wesley, "The Devil In Me"—the British singer recounts his dirty deeds, then reveals his true identity: humanity

• Head, Murray and the Trinidad Singers, "Superstar"—a comment about Jesus

• Head, Murray, Ian Gillan and others, "Jesus Christ Superstar"—views the "son of God" in an earthly light

• Hills, Joe, "The Preacher and the Slave"—among the many recorded versions of Hill's "In the Sweet By and By" re-write are those of "Haywire" McClintock and poet Carl Sandburg

• Lehrer, Tom, "Vatican Rag"—he admitted poking fun at the ritual but not at the religion, then suggested that the most sacrilegious song is "Praise the Lord and Pass the Ammunition," which implies "that God approves of A killing B but not B killing A."

• Lennon, John, "God"—an unapologetic response to his once having been forced to apologize for saying the Beatles were "more popular than Jesus"

• Lennon, John, "Imagine"—a vision of a religionless, peaceful world

• Living Colour, "Cult of Personality"—the black musicians warn about personality cults

• M.C. 900-foot Jesus with D. J. Zero, "I'm Going Straight To Heaven"—a white freethought rapper mocks streetcorner preachers, even distorting his voice to make it sound like it's going through a bullhorn.

• Nine Inch Nails, "Terrible Lie"—God is cursed for making the world and the singer so lousy; then the singer pleads for a reason to believe

• Robbins, Marty, "I'll Go On Alone"—a country song about a wife's conversion to born-againism, leading the husband to go on alone

• The Temptations, "You Make Your Own Heaven and Hell Right Here on Earth"—an obscurity from their "Psychedelic Shack" album

• XTC, "Dear God"—an unabashedly atheistic anthem produced by Todd Rundgren

Many musical groups have members who are freethinkers. For example, the Headstones, a Toronto group that has performed in Canada, the United Kingdom, and the United States, has four

Unitarians: Tim White, bass; Trent Carr, guitar; Steve Carr, tour manager; and Beverly Carr, publicist.

A rock group, the Headstones, are on the Web at: <http://ww.headstones.com>.

Charles, Martin S. (20th Century)

In 1931, Charles edited *Godless World* in Oakland, California.

Charleton, Walter (17th Century)

Charleton, an atheist, wrote *The Darkness of Atheism Dispelled by the Light of Nature* (1652). {GS}

Charma, Antoine (1801—1869)

A French philosopher, Charma was denounced for his impiety by the Count de Montalembert in the Chamber of peers, which resulted in an unsuccessful attempt to unseat him as a professor of philosophy at Caen. Charma wrote many philosophical works, including an account of Didron's *Histoire de Dieu.* {BDF; RAT}

Charron, Pierre (1541—1603)

Charron's *La Sagesse* (1601) presented Montaigne's thoughts and quickly made the Vatican's list of prohibited books in 1605. His writing emphasized that nature, like mankind, has failings and inconsistencies, that both are reflections of the divine. Franck has written that "the scepticism of Charron inclines visibly to *sensualisme* and even to materialism." Jesuits denounced his work as "a brutal atheism." {BDF; CE; EU, Vivien Thweatt; ILP; RAT; RE}

Chartier, Émile Auguste (1868—1951)

Using the pseudonym, Alain, Chartier wrote of his belief in an ethic of agnosticism based on a realistic acceptance of the limitations of human understanding. His work, states Thweatt, contributed to a new secular humanism. Alain wrote for *La Nouvelle Revue Française.* {EU, Vivien Thweatt}

Charvaka (Ancient India)

Charvaka, or Lokayata, is a philosophic and materialist movement in India that rejects the ideas of karma and moksha (spiritual liberation). Its adherents are atheistic and do not believe in a future life: Only this world exists. No outstanding individual is representative of the group.

A. J. Mattill Jr., in "An Ancient Atheist" (*The American Rationalist,* January-February 1999), describes the materialistic view of Charvaka, that matter is eternal and consists of the four elements: earth, air, fire, and water. Naturalistically, not supernaturalistically, there is no heaven, hell, transmigration of souls, retribution, reward, punishment. The Supreme Being was the earthly ruler of a state, one expected to be the arbiter of right and wrong in society. Charvaka rejected the authority of the Vedas, advocated trying to achieve happiness here and now, and found all religion to be an aberration. Mattill concludes that some of us "may prefer Epicurus' description of the *summum bonum* to Charvaka's." However, the outlook protested the superstitions of its day, and modern rationalists are much indebted to the Charvaka manner of thinking. (See Dr. Dakshina Ranjan Sastri's *Charvaka Philosophy,* which was published in Calcutta in 1967.)

CHARVAKAM

A Telugu monthly, *Charvakam* is at B. Ramakrishna, Nidamarru, Mangalagiri 522 503, India.

Chase, Stuart (1888—1985)

An economist, the social scientist who probably coined the term "New Deal" used by Franklin Delano Roosevelt, Chase is author of *A New Deal* (1932); *A Tyranny of Words* (1938), which Sinclair Lewis referred to as the most important book of 1938; and *The Proper Study of Mankind* (1948). In 1951, he wrote the following about humanism:

> Your question baffles me a little, because, since I took up semantics, I'm pretty shy of hard and fast categories. I've been called a "scientific humanist," whatever that means, and of the categories you named in your letter, I'm sure I belong more with Julian Huxley and John Dewey—though I am not so sure about Thomas Mann and George Santayana. A handy book published by Simon & Schuster in 1939, edited by Clifton Fadiman and entitled *I Believe,* contains a summary of my point of view, together with the views of Thomas Mann, Franz Boas, Havelock Ellis, Julian Huxley, John Dewey, Albert Einstein, Lewis Mumford, Joseph Krutch, and many others.
>
> Using the operational definition of the physicists (see P. W. Bridgman, *The Logic of Modern Physics,* where the label comes out of what one does), I would seem to fall under 'Naturalistic (or Scientific) Humanism.' All my books deal with aspects of the scientific method applied to various phrases of human behavior. I have never been able to see how intuition, Authority, or common sense can save us in the long run, helpful as they may sometimes be in the short run. Only knowledge can save us, and knowledge depends on the scientific method—gathering the facts, evolving a theory to explain them, and applying standards of verification which other competent observers can repeat. The process is cumulative, and perhaps the major characteristic of the participant is the ability to say: 'I was wrong.'
>
> With the release of atomic energy, the fulcrum of the scientific method must now swing to problems of human behavior, especially ways and means for reaching agreement; for getting along with other races, religions, nations, classes, to the end of abolishing war, and using the new energy to establish world-wide standards of economic and emotional security. Finally, I believe that most of us use our minds far below capacity—like a power house operating at half load. Scientists are now in the process of discovering ways and means to improve the load factor. (See W. R. Ashby, *Design for a Brain*; J. Z. Young, *Doubt and Certainty in Science*; Sir George Thomson, *The Foreseeable Future*). Assuming the process successful, a whole new dimension opens for mankind: what now seems desirable may prove a blind alley; what now seems impossible becomes negotiable. I carry around a private picture which I call "The Man on the Cliff." He is that human being, outlined against the sky, which we might all be if the bonds of ignorance now holding us were loosened.

In 1954, Chase wrote again, stating that he considered himself "80% a Humanist." He asked *The Humanist* to consider reviewing his latest humanistic work, *Some Things Worth Knowing* (1958). *The Humanist Newsletter* (September-October 1953) quoted him as saying:

> I tend to be guided in conscious decisions by four criteria: (a) that I am a creature of this earth; (b) that I am a member of a human group; (c) that it is meaningless to judge other members of the group until the biological and psychological facts are in; and (d) that progress depends not on revealed authority, not on ethics and morals, which shift with the folkways, but on using the scientific attitude in social as well as in physical affairs.

{CE; WAS, 23 March 1951}

Chasman, Deborah (20th Century)

Chasman, a senior editor at Beacon Press, was a finalist for the 1995 Literary Market Place award for individual achievement in editorial trade publishing. She was recognized for attracting to Beacon such prominent authors as Doris Grumbach, Faye Moskowitz, Richard Mohr, and Cornel West. {*World,* May-June 1995}

Chastelet du Lomont, Gabrielle Emilie [Marchioness] (1706—1749)

Chastelet (or Châtelet) du Lomont came from a noble family and learned Latin, Italian, English, and Spanish before she was sixteen years of age. She published a work on physical philosophy called *Institutions de Physique* (1740) and translated Newton's *Principia*. Chastelet lived for thirteen years with Voltaire at Cirey between 1735 and 1747, and addressed to him her Deistic work, *Doubts on Revealed Religions* (1792). According to McCabe, it can be said of the marchioness, one of the most beautiful and accomplished women of her time, that "in this case the godly do not claim the brilliant lady." Her *Treatise on Happiness* was praised by Condorcet. {BDF; JM; WWS}

Chastellux, François Jean de [Count] [Marquis de] (1734—1788)

Count Chastellux was a soldier, traveler, and writer. Voltaire praised his *On Public Happiness* (1776). His article on "Happiness" in the *Encyclopédie* was suppressed by the censor because it did not mention God. {BDF; RAT}

CHASTITY

- Chastity: the most unnatural of the sexual perversions.

—Aldous Huxley
(also attributed to Anatole France.)

- We may eventually come to realize that chastity is no more a virtue than malnutrition.

—Alex Comfort
(See entry for Virgins.)

Chateaubriand, François René, Vicomte de (1768—1848)

The founder of romanticism in French literature, Chateaubriand was the most important French author of his time. *The Martyrs* celebrates Christianity's victory over paganism. Despite the accumulating evidence of geology and paleontology, Chateaubriand persisted, Robertson lamented, "with his grotesque theorem that God made the world out of nothing with all the marks of antiquity upon it—the oaks at the start bearing 'last year's nests'—(on the ground that) if the world were not at once young and old, the great, the serious, the moral would disappear from nature, for these sentiments by their essence attach to antique things." Robertson adds, "It is humiliating, but instructive to realize that only a century ago a 'Christian reaction' in a civilized country was inspired by such an order of ideas (as found in Chateaubriand's *Gémoe di Christianisme (The Genius of Christianity)* [1802]) and that in the nation of Laplace, with his theory in view, it was the fashion thus to prattle in the taste of the Dark Ages." {CE; JMR}

Châtelet, Gabrielle Émilie du (Marchioness): See entry for Chastelet.

Chatterton, Thomas (1752—1770)

Called "the marvelous boy poet," Chatterton wrote poems which he pretended were written by one Thomas Rowley in the fourteenth century and discovered by him in an old chest in Redcliffe Church. Several of his poems were deistic in content. In his letters he professed his rationalism. "I am no Christian," he wrote to his family shortly before his death. When he visited London in 1769 and had bitter experiences, he destroyed himself in a fit of despair. {BDF; RE}

Chattopadhyaya, Debiprasad (1918—1993)

Prof. Chattopadhyaya, a noted academician and philosopher of international repute, taught more than two decades in Calcutta, Bombay, and other colleges in India. His expertise in Indian philosophy and his emphasis on the study of the history of science and technology were guides to students and researchers trying to understand the complexities of development of knowledge in India. In 1987 he was elected National Fellow of the Indian Council of Philosophical Research. He was a member of the German Academy of Sciences and was the first Indian to be awarded the D. Sc. (*honoris causa*) from the Academy of Sciences, Moscow. Among his major publications were *Lokayata: A Study in Ancient Indian Materialism* (1959); *Indian Philosophy: A Popular Introduction* (1964); *Science and Society in Ancient India* (1977); *Indian Atheism* (1980), a Marxist analysis; and *Tagore and Indian Philosophical Heritage* (1984). {FUK}

Chaucer, Geoffrey (1340?—1400)

Although in *The Canterbury Tales* (1387, unfinished) the Parson is designed to be a model for the truly religious to follow, Chaucer delights in relating how religion works in practice. His Pardoner, for example, uses religion for personal gain. Yes, the lascivious friar is "full of dalliaunce and fair language" for "yonge wommen" and he depicts the essentially pagan Miller and Wife of Bath as colorful souls. Do not blame me, Chaucer is saying, if the doctor I describe loved gold so much, if a pilgrim was more Epicurean than Christian, and if animal bones were sold as saints' bones to gullible country parsons: I am just relating what happened. What with the religious restraints placed upon everyone at that time, how better could Chaucer editorialize concerning what he found wrong in society. His understanding of how people actually speak is exemplified by his use of such words as erse (arse, ass), fart, quent (cunt), shitten, and piss, which apparently were not frowned upon inasmuch as he was simply a reporter of the language. Those who made their living from religion were placed on the defensive, and Chaucer became a revered iconoclast to his supporters.

In his *Studies in Chaucer* (1892), Lownsbury calls Chaucer an advanced freethinker. Commenting on lines 1809 to 1825 of "The Knight's Tale," he asks: Can modern agnosticism point to a denial more emphatic than that made in the fourteenth century of the belief that there exists for us any assurance of the life beyond the grave?

Lownsbury says Chaucer grew more opposed to the Church as time went on and was "hostile to it in such a way that implies an utter disbelief in certain of its tenets." A retraction is appended to some editions of the Tales, but it is generally rejected as spurious, McCabe holds. {BDF; CE; EU, Victor N. Paananen; JM; RE}

Chaumette, Pierre Gaspard (1763—1794)

A French revolutionary destined to lose his head, Chaumette as a youth received botany lessons from Rousseau. He embraced the revolution with ardor and was among the first to assume the tricolor cockade. Nominated a member of the Commune in 1792, he took the name of Anaxagoras to show his little regard for his baptismal saints. He abolished the rod in schools, suppressed lotteries, instituted workshops for "fallen women," established the first lying-in-hospital, had books sent to the hospitals, separated the insane from the sick, founded the Conservatory of Music, opened the public libraries every day (instead of two hours per week, as in the *ancien régime*), replaced books of superstition by works of morality and reason, put a graduated tax on the rich to provide for the burial of the poor, and was the principal mover in the feasts of Reason and closing of the churches. Accused by Robespierre of conspiring with Cloots "to efface all idea of the Deity," Chaumette was guillotined. {BDF; RAT}

Chauncy, Charles (1705—1787)

A leader of the liberal or Arminian theological movement in New England, Chauncy was a Universalist who argued that punishments of hell were not eternal, that all humanity would be redeemed. His *The Mystery Hid from Ages and Generations* (London, 1784), is one of the earliest documents of American liberal theology. {CE; FUS; U&U}

Chaussard, Pierre Jean Baptiste (1766—1823)

Chaussard was a French man of letters who, after the Revolution, took the name of Publicola and published patriotic odes, *Esprit de Mirabeau*, and other works. He was preacher to the Theophilanthropists and became professor of *belles lettres* at Orleans. {BDF; RAT}

Cheam, Michael (20th Century)

Cheam is the secretary of the Humanist Society of Western Australia. His E-mail is <mcheam@WCOMPER1.telstra.com.au>. (See entry for Australian Humanists, Freethinkers.)

Cheetham, Henry H. (20th Century)

Cheetham wrote *Unitarianism and Universalism: An Illustrated History* (1962). {FUS}

Chekhov, Anton Pavlovich (1860—1904)

Chekhov was an eminent Russian short-story writer, dramatist, naturalist, and physician. The grandson of a serf, and the third of six children born of a grocer, he was whipped often by his father as well as by the choirmaster in church, where he was made to sing for hours while kneeling on freezing stones. When his father went bankrupt and the family departed Taganrog for Moscow in search of work, Chekhov was left to fend for himself. It was a time when many found a new church and dogma in the radical movement. As an indication of his outlook at the time, he advised a brother to refrain from force and deceit and to "work at it constantly, day and night. You must never stop reading, studying in depth, exercising your will. Every hour is precious." When thirty and called an "unprincipled" writer by the editor of a journal, Chekhov protested, "I have never toadied, nor lied, nor insulted. . . . I have never written a single line that I am ashamed of today."

Upon graduating from Moscow University in 1884, he wrote that he was able to divide his time between "medicine . . . my lawful wife, and literature . . . my mistress." His record of humanitarian work was impressive. He wrote about a prison colony on the Siberian island of Sakhalin, basing it on a medical-statistical survey of conditions there, bringing to the public's attention the horrors of the Russian penal system. To alleviate famine in his region in 1891—1892, he treated peasants in a clinic on his estate, helped build schools, endowed libraries, and purchased horses to be distributed to peasants for transporting grain. Not one to believe in universal salvation, he had no faith in the intelligentsia en masse, placing his hopes on individuals because "They're the ones who really matter." On a visit to Nice, he wrote in a letter, he was pleased at finding no "Marxists with their self-important faces."

His *Ivanov* in 1887 launched Chekhov as a dramatist, and he came to be lionized in artistic circles. His work depicted mortals subject to the depredations of time and chance, as shown in *Three Sisters* and *The Cherry Orchard*. In the latter work, acceptance of the loss of the orchard means new possibilities for Ranevskaya and her daughter. Richard Gilman, in *Chekhov's Plays: An Opening into Eternity* (1997), describes Chekhov's unhappiness about Stanislavsky's production of *The Cherry Orchard*: "With the exception of two or three parts nothing in it is mine. I am describing life, gray, ordinary life, and not this tedious whining. They make me either a crybaby or simply a bore." Although Stanislavsky complained that Chekhov came to rehearsals and "messed everything up for us," Gilman points out that Chekhov was masterful in telling us about the familiar, giving us a perspective on everyday experience which is different from the conventional assumptions, and offending cherished beliefs about ourselves and the world.

The best single source on Chekhov's thought, according to Aileen Kelly, a fellow of King's College, Cambridge, remains the selection of his letters translated by Michael Henry Heim and introduced and annotated by Simon Karlinsky in 1973. Of particular importance, Karlinsky points out, is Chekhov's asserting that his medical training in the empirical methods of the natural sciences had been the formative influence on his literary work. A writer, he held, should be faithful to the empirical reality of the world and of human behavior. Little wonder that he revered Tolstoy but was repelled by his didactic story "The Kreutzer Sonata," whose treatment of human sexuality exposed the great writer "as an ignorant man who has never at any point in his long life taken the trouble to read two or three books written by specialists." Writers, Chekhov lamented, had only a smattering of scientific method and were prone to the delusion that mankind was on the verge of resolving the ultimate mysteries of existence. Criticized once for having taken no clear position on the question of pessimism, he retorted,

> It is not the writer's job to solve such problems as God, pessimism, etc.; his job is merely to record who, under what conditions, said or thought what about God or pessimism.

This did not imply, Kelly added, a moral relativism. Chekhov wanted "to depict life truthfully and to show in passing how much this life deviates from a norm." But no one can define that norm: "We all know what a dishonest deed is, but what is honour?—we do not know." Therefore, one needs to be guided by the good that has withstood the test of time: liberation of the individual from oppression, prejudice, ignorance, or domination by his passions.

"It is obvious that nature is doing everything in her power to rid herself of all weaklings and organisms for which she has no use," he wrote, comparing the famine and cholera threatening his region at the beginning of the 1890s with an influenza epidemic then affecting horses in central Russia. Life's evanescence and unpredictability need to be accepted without resentment, for nature "gives a person equanimity. And you need equanimity in this world. Only people with equanimity can see things clearly, be fair, and work."

His outlook showed him to be an attentive reader of Darwin. Kelly wrote that Chekhov, like Darwin not one to be gloomy about the way things are,

> believed that the romantic yearning for a world modeled on religious or rational ideals of perfection had blinded mankind to the beauty and rich potential of the world they actually lived in. The history of Russian exploration in the Far East, which he read in preparation for his trip to Sakhalin, was "enough to make you want to edify man, but we have no use for it, we don't even know who those people were, and all we do is sit within our four walls and complain what a mess God has made of creating man."

"Alas! I shall never be a Tolstoyan!" Chekhov wrote to Suvorin. "In women what I like above all is beauty, and in the history of humanity, culture, which is expressed in rugs, carriages with springs, and keenness of thought." In short, Chekhov did not accept Tolstoy's ideal of moral perfection, which demanded the sacrifice of all the attachments and desires that distracted mankind from the pursuit of a narrowly defined good. His humanistic outlook included having a fascination for lives utterly different from his own. He dreamed of how it would feel to have "a wife, a nursery, a little house with garden paths," or to be a country gentleman, a university professor, a retired navy lieutenant, a traveler, or an explorer.

Chekhov earned enduring international acclaim for his stories and plays. In 1888, "The Steppe," a story in his third collection, won the Pushkin Prize. His plays became acclaimed when produced by the Moscow Art Theater.

In 1901 he married the actress Olga Knipper, the interpreter of many of his characters. Three years later, he died of tuberculosis, the symptoms of which he had had for almost a decade but chose to ignore. When Tolstoy arrived at his hospital bed to discuss death and immortality, Chekhov remained unpreoccupied by ultimate questions, choosing instead to inquire about becoming a military doctor in the Russian Far East.

His wife described his final moments in a scene that sounds Chekhovian. His doctor had ordered champagne to ease his breathing. Chekhov sat up, announced to the doctor in German, "*Ich sterbe.*"

> Then he picked up his glass, turned to me, smiled his wonderful smile and said, "It's been such a long time since I've had champagne." He drank it all to the last drop, lay quietly on his left side and was soon silent forever. The . . . stillness . . . was broken only by a huge nocturnal moth which kept crashing painfully into the light bulbs. . . . [Then] the cork flew out of the half-empty champagne bottle with a tremendous noise.

"His ideas on religion are not clear," wrote McCabe, "but he stood well outside the Church." For 20th century secular humanists, Chekhov is the person who wrote, inspiringly, that life "is given only once and one wants to live it boldly, with full consciousness and beauty." {CE; JM; Aileen Kelly, "Chekhov the Subversive," *The New York Review of Books*, 6 November 1997; RE; TRI; TYD}

Chemin-Dupontes, Jean Baptiste (Born 1761)

One of the founders of French Theophilanthropy, Chemin-Dupontes published many writings, the best known of which is *What Is Theophilanthropy?* The Society of Theophilanthropes which he formed had as an active member Thomas Paine. {BDF}

Cheney, Ednah Dow Littlehale (1824-1904)

Cheney, a suffragist, civil rights activist, and editor, was a Universalist, Unitarian, and member of the Free Religious Association.

Chénier, Marie André de (1762—1794)

Considered by many the greatest French poet in 18th century France, Chénier was active in the early stages of the French Revolution but was horrified by Jacobin excesses. A freethinker, he contributed denunciatory pamphlets to the *Journal de Paris*, an organ of moderate royalism. His *Élegies* (published posthumously, 1819) and *Bucoliques* were consummate examples of his work, as was *Iambes*, which had stirring political satires in verse. Robespierre had him arrested in March, 1794, and just three days before the end of the Terror Chénier was guillotined. His life inspired the opera *Andrea Chénier* (1896) by Umberto Giordano. Chênedolle said of Chénier's *Hermes*, a work in imitation of Lucretius, that Chénier "*était athée avec délices* (was a delightful atheist)." {BDF; CE; JMR; JMRH; RAT; RE}

Chénier, Marie Joseph de (1764—1811)

Chénier, brother of André, was a French poet whose first successful drama was "Charles IX" (1789). A Voltairean, he satirized in *Nouveaux Saints* (1801) those who returned to the old faith. {BDF; RAT}

Cherbuliez, Charles Victor (1829—1899)

A French novelist and freethinker, Cherbuliez wrote *Noirs et Rouges* (1881). He became an Officer of the Legion of Honour in 1892. He was admitted to the French Academy in 1881. {RAT}

Chernyshevsky, Niakolai Gavrilovich (1828—1889)

A Russian intellectual and the leading disciple of Visarion Belinsky inside Russia, Chernyshevsky advocated basic agrarian reform and emancipation of the serfs. He translated Mill's *Political Economy* and wrote on *Superstition and the Principles of Logic* (1859). A forerunner of the Russian revolutionary movement, he envisioned the village commune as a transition to socialism. In 1864 he was sentenced to the Siberian mines where, after heartrending cruelties, he became insane and died. {CE; BDF}

Cherbury, Lord: See entry for Edward Herbert.

Cherrington, Bet (1912-1998)

Cherrington was born in Lucknow, India, where her father was in the Indian Civil Service. An activist who took part in Liberal politics, she was a fighter for women's rights and abortion law reform. *Facing the World: An Anthology of Poems for Humanists* (1989) is an expression of her wide literary knowledge and her committed humanism. Jim Herrick conducted Cherrington's funeral ceremony.

Cherry, Matt (1967—)

Cherry has worked in senior positions for humanist organizations in three countries. Having gained in 1989 a B.A. honors in philosophy from University College London (known as "The Ungodly Hole on Gower Street" because of its freethinking tradition dating back to its founder Jeremy Bentham), he started working in 1990 for the British Humanist Association. He led the Young Humanists, organizing a successful week-long international young humanist conference in 1991. That same year he became director of development and public relations at the British Humanist Association, for which he became editor of *Humanist News*.

At the end of 1993 he joined the staff of the International Humanist and Ethical Union (IHEU) as Secretary for Development and Public Relations, the office of which at that time was in The Netherlands. In 1995, he moved to Amherst, New York, becoming Executive Director of the Council for Secular Humanism and the International Secretariat for Growth and Development of the IHEU.

Cherry was coordinator of the 1996 Humanist World Congress held in Mexico City. In 1999 he helped establish the Center for Inquiry branch in Los Angeles, California. Cherry signed Humanist Manifesto 2000. E-mail: <ficherry@aol.com>. On the Web: <http://www.secularhumanism.org/iheu/>. {*International Humanist News*, December 1996}

Cherubini, Mario Luigi Carlo Zenobio-Salvadore (1760—1842)

Cherubini, an Italian composer who started at the age of ten, wrote a mass at thirteen, and an opera at nineteen, was King's composer in London, then in France. He hailed the Revolution and composed hymns and anthems for its feasts as well as an opera, "Epicurus."

He also wrote an immense amount of religious music, making him a favorite in the Catholic Church. Yet Cherubini was a freethinker all the time. His Catholic biographer Bellasis quotes the evidence of his daughters that Cherubini was "not mystical but broad-minded in religion" and admits that there is no evidence that he received the sacraments of the Church before death. McCabe attests that Cherubini did not. {JM; RAT; RE}

Chesen, Eli S. (20th Century)

A freethinker, Chesen wrote *Religion May be Hazardous to Your Health* (1972). {FUS; GS}

Chesnutt, Vic (20th Century)

A singer and songwriter, Chesnutt mentions his atheism in his songs, sometimes characterizing himself as "a backsliding atheist." {CA; E}

Chesterton, G(ilbert) K(eith) (1874—1936)

Chesterton, the English author, conservative, and Catholic apologist, wrote the following barb concerning Middleton Murry's atheism:

> Murry, on finding *le Bon Dieu*
> Chose *difficile à croire*
> Illogically said "*Adieu*,"
> But God said "*Au Revoir*."

Chesterton also wrote, "From time to time, as we all know, a sect appears in our midst announcing that the world will very soon come to an end. Generally, by some slight confusion or miscalculation, it is the sect that comes to an end."

Chesworth, Amanda (1971-)

Chesworth is a Campus Freethought Alliance Coordinator for the Council for Secular Humanism. A Canadian by birth, she works with youth program in high schools and campuses. {*Secular Humanist Bulletin*, Spring 1999}

Chevalier, Bernadette (20th Century)

Chevalier wrote *L'Atheisme dans le Monde Moderne* (1969), a Swiss work utilizing a Catholic viewpoint. {GS}

Chevalier, Joseph Philippe (1806—1865)

A French chemist, Chevalier wrote *The Soul from the Standpoint of Reason and Science* (1861). {BDF}

Cheves, Charles (20th Century)

Although raised a Southern Baptist, Cheves is a Florida attorney who is a freethought activist.

Chidley, William James (c. 1860—1916)

Chidley was an Australian social and sex reformer. In *The Answer* he claimed that "our false coition makes villains of us all," that the best method of human copulation is for the inert penis to be first drawn by suction or presence of air into the erect and distended female vagina. Publishing the book resulted in his being convicted for selling an indecent publication, which he had done while walking the streets with only a short voile tunic. After repeated convictions, Chidley was committed to a lunatic asylum where he died of arteriosclerosis. {SWW}

Chies y Gomez, Ramon (1845—1893)

One of the foremost freethought champions in Spain, Chies y Gomez was educated at his father's direction without religion. He wrote for a Madrid journal, *La Discusion*, took part in the Revolution of 1865, and at the proclamation of the Republic in 1873 became civil governor of Valencia. In 1881 he founded *El Voto Nacional* and in 1883 *Las Dominicales del Libre Pensamiento*. When the police forcibly closed the International Freethought Congress at Madrid in 1892, Chies alluded to the incident at the republican convention, predicting the fall of a monarchy which, instead of being the servant of the people, was but the henchman of the church. Upon his death, the funeral started with a hearse which was followed by three hundred carriages and ten thousand persons. The municipal council attended in a body. {BDF; PUT; RAT}

Child, Lydia Maria Francis (1802—1880)

A Unitarian and novelist, Child wrote an antislavery tract, *An Appeal in Favor of That Class of Americans Called Africans* (1833) which influenced William Ellery Channing's *Slavery* (1835). She was an advocate of women's independence, a historian of religion, and an editor of *National Anti-Slavery Standard*. One of her major works was the two-volume *History of the Condition of Women in Various Ages and Nations* (1835). Originally baptized an orthodox Congregationalist, Child supported the Free Religious movement and for a time was a convert to Swedenborgianism. She usually attended Unitarian services, however, and among her friends were William Lloyd Garrison, Maria Weston Chapman, William Ellery Channing, Margaret Fuller, Theodore Parker, and Anne Whitney. She was highly eulogized upon her death from heart disease by Wendell Phillips, and John Greenleaf Whittier recited a memorial poem in her honor at the funeral.

"It is right noble to fight with wickedness and wrong," she wrote in *Over the River and Through the Woods* (1842); "the mistake is in supposing that spiritual evil can be overcome by physical means."

In a biography, Carolyn L. Karcher notes that as early as the 1830s Child was vindicating the rights of women, Indians and, particularly, African-American slaves. She was a "household name" during her lifetime, but her works and influence have been all but "erased from history." Karcher found Child's writings had an anti-Catholic, anti-French, and anti-Irish bias. {BDF; CE; JM; PUT; RAT; U&U; WWS}

Childe, (Vere) Gordon (1892—1967)

Childe, the son of an Australian clergyman, became a rationalist, political historian, and archaeologist. In *How Labour Governs* (1916) he concluded that the parliamentary system was a creation of the upper classes. From 1946 to 1956, he was professor of prehistoric European archeology at the University of London. {SWW; RE}

CHILDREN

• As the twig is bent, the tree inclines.

—Vergil

• Give me the children until they are seven, and anyone may have them afterward.

—St. Francis Xavier

• A baby is an inestimable blessing and bother.

—Mark Twain,
"Letter to Annie Webster," 1 September 1876

• The child is father of the man.

—William Wordsworth

• There was a little girl
Who had a little curl
Right in the middle of her forehead;
And when she was good
She was very, very good,
But when she was bad she was horrid.

—Henry Wadsworth Longfellow

• We've had bad luck with our kids—they've all grown up.

—Christopher Morley

• You can learn many things from children.
How much patience you have, for instance.

—Franklin P. Jones

• I abhor their [children's] company, because I can only regard children as defective adults, hate their physical ineptitude, find their jokes flat and monotonous.

—Evelyn Waugh
who shipped his children off to school
as soon as he could and avoided them
as much as possible during the holidays

• Your children are not your children. They are the sons and daughters of Life's longing for itself.

—Kahlil Gibran

• I've got two wonderful children—and two out of five isn't bad.

—Henny Youngman
American comic

• So, remain the benevolent despot, vary your errors, spank little, sit-on if necessary, scream infrequently, threaten rarely, groan often, question organized activities, support their interests, control television watching, and act silly on occasion while trying to ignore snotty words as you attempt to read their feelings. Trust them to imitate us—30 years on down the pike.

—Robert E. Kay, M.D.

Richard Dawkins considers the practice of giving children a religious appellation absurd. Calling a four-year-old a Muslim, a Sikh, or a Christian implies the child can have "developed theological opinions." In *The Independent* (19 December 1996), he said it would be laughable to "speak of a four-year-old monetarist Eurosceptic, a four-year-old dialectical materialism, or a four-year-old neo-Kantian [but] we accept 'Muslim child' or 'Christian child' without thinking." He continued, "If a child is the child of an atheist," does that make her an atheist child?" {Michiko Kakutani in a review of Auberon Waugh's *Will This Do?*, *The New York Times*, 23 June 1998}

CHILEAN FREETHOUGHT, HUMANISM: See entries for José Victorino Lastarria and Francisco Bilbao.

CHILTERN (England) HUMANISTS

Details about the group are available by telephoning 01296 623730. Antony Chapman is one of its contacts.

Chilton, Marcus (William) (1815—1855)

Chilton, a bricklayer who became a typesetter and then one of the editors of the British *Oracle of Reason*, wrote in the *Movement* and the *Reasoner*. He was an Owenite. {BDF; FUK; RAT; VI}

CHIMERA

• *Quaestio subtilissima, utrum chimera in vacuo bombinans possit comedere secundas intentiones.*
A most subtle question: whether a chimera bombinating in a vacuum can devour second intentions.

—François Rabelais (1494?-c. 1553)
Pantagruel, II: viii

• A memory of yesterday's pleasures, a fear of tomorrow's dangers, a straw under my knee, a noise in mine ear, a light in mine eye, an anything, a nothing, a fancy, a Chimera in my brain, troubles me in my prayer. So certainly is there nothing, nothing in spiritual things, perfect in this world.

—John Donne (1571?-1631)
XXI Sermons (1660)

• What the sage poets taught by th' heavenly Muse,
Storied of old in high immortal verse
Of dire chimeras and enchanted isles
And rifted rocks whose entrance leads to Hell,—
For such there be, but unbelief is blind.

—John Milton (1608-1674)
Comus (1634)

• What a chimera then is man! What a novelty! What a monster, what a chaos, what a contradiction, what a prodigy! Judge of all things, feeble worm of the earth, depository of truth, a sink of uncertainty and error, the glory and the shame of the universe.

—Blaise Pascal (1623-1662)
Pensées

• Know then thyself, presume not God to scan;
The proper study of mankind is man.
Placed on this isthmus of a middle state,
A being darkly wise and rudely great;
With too much knowledge for the Sceptic side,
With too much weakness for the Stoic's pride,
He hangs between, in doubt to act or rest;
In doubt to deem himself a God or Beast;
In doubt his mind or body to prefer;
Born but to die, and reas'ning but to err;
Alike in ignorance, his reason such,
Whether he thinks too little or too much;
Chaos of thought and passion, all confused;
Still be himself abused or disabused;
Created half to rise, and half to fall;
Great lord of all things, yet a prey to all;
Sole judge of truth, in endless error hurled;
The glory, jest, and riddle of the world.

—Alexander Pope (1688-1744),
Essay on Man. Epistle II

• These unhappy people were proposing schemes for persuading monarchs to choose favourites upon the score of their wisdom, capacity, and virtue. . . .of instructing princes to know their true interest by placing it on the same foundation with that of their people: of choosing for employment persons qualified to exercise them; with many other wild impossible chimeras, that never entered before into the heart of man to conceive, and confirmed in me the old observation, that there is nothing so extravagant and irrational which some philosophers have not maintained for truth.

—Jonathan Swift (1667-1745),
Voyage to Laputa in *Gulliver's Travels* (1726)

• How chimerical, the wildly fanciful and highly improbable plots fabricated by those believers who think there is a supernatural and an afterlife! Yet how chimerical that they have succeeded so surprisingly with their biblical tales whereas Chimera—the mythological fire-breathing she-monster composed of a lion, goat, and serpent—is relatively unknown either as a creature or a concept.

Chimeras now are references to the coming together of cells from two people that live in one person, such as during pregnancy, organ transplantation, and blood transfusion. How chimerical that during pregnancy the mother's body does not reject the fetus as a foreign tissue! How chimerical that your blood might today flow within my body, or mine within yours! How chimerical that my heart might one day beat within your breast, or yours within mine!

—Allen Windsor

CHIMPANZEES

The chimpanzee, not the Neanderthal man, is mankind's closest living relative. A 1997 study of Neanderthal DNA concluded that interbreeding of Neanderthals and humans was never possible. (See entry for Homo sapiens.)

CHINESE CURSE, THE

• May your life be interesting!

—Anonymous

CHINESE FENG SHUI: See entry for Superstition.

CHINESE FOLK RELIGIONS: For number of adherents, see entry for Hell.

CHINESE HUMANISTS

Although Finngeir Hiorth in "Whither Freethought?" (*New Humanist*, December 1998) asserts that "In ancient China atheism was no real option," Antony Flew notes that the observation although true is likely to be misleading. For, he wrote (*New Humanist*, March 1999), "it may suggest that atheism in ancient China, like apostasy in fully Islamic states today, was a capital offence. The truth is that the language of Imperial China contained no word for a supposedly omnipotent personal Creator. Atheism was thus not 'no real option' because it was suicidal, but because the Chinese had yet to learn what it is that atheists have as such to disbelieve."

Westerners know about two main streams of Chinese thought, the traditionalist and moralistic Confucianism (founded by Kongfu-zi, the Pinyin transliteration of Kung-fu Tzu); and the mystical and quietistic Daoism (Taoism), founded by Lao-zi (Lao Tzu) and Zhuang-zi (Chuang Tzu). According to Nicolas Walter (*New Humanist*, October 1998),

> Most thinkers belonged to one or other (or more) of these traditions, which differed between and among themselves but which generally shared assumptions about the twin essences (*yang* and *yin*), the divinity of heaven, the propitiation of fate and spirits, reverence for ancestors and the past, and the practical importance of magic and ritual.

Mo-zi (Mo Tzu) in the 5th Century B.C.E. advocated altruism and asceticism based on utilitarian and leading to pacifism. Yang Chu in the 4th Century B. C. E. advocated individualism and hedonism based on pessimism and leading to egoism. Also, there was Wang Chong, described by Joseph Needham as "one of the greatest men of his nation in any age." (See Joseph Needham, *Science and Civilisation in China—The History of Scientific Thought*, 1956).

Walter, surveying the various masters of early Chinese thought, concluded:

> Just as we may wish that Europe had followed the philosophers of Ionia and Athens and Alexandria rather than the theologians of Constantinople and Rome and Geneva, we may wish that China had followed Wang Chong rather than all the other hundred schools, and we should pay tribute to a precious spirit of enlightenment and reason in a dark and irrational age.

China, since becoming a Marxist state, has made it difficult for freethinking philosophers to travel and exchange views with Westerners. One of the few known humanists is Xiao Xuehui, a philosopher in Sichuan province. However, by rejecting the official Marxist doctrine that morality is determined by economics, she was imprisoned, released after nineteen months, then not allowed to teach. In 1995, the International Humanist and Ethical Union (IHEU) started an international campaign to protest Dr. Xiao's treatment and to press the Chinese authorities to honor her human rights.

At the Shang Xin-Jian Institute of Philosophy, the group which studies humanism is called Study Group of the History of Western Humanism (IHEU), Beijing Academy of Social Sciences, 25 Xi-San-Huan Bei Lu. Youzheng Li, of the Institute of Philosophy, CASS, Beijing, signed Humanist Manifesto 2000. In China, 2000 is the Year of the Dragon, 4698. (See entries for Xiao and Yong-shen.)

CHINESE PHILOSOPHY

See an extensive discussion of Chinese philosophy by Wing-tsit Chan in the *Encyclopedia of Philosophy*, Vol. 2. Most in the Western world admit and lament their ignorance concerning philosophy in the Eastern world. (Also, see entries for Tai-tsung and Xiao.)

Chisholm, Brock (1896—1971)

The first Director General of the United Nations World Health Organization wrote to the present author about humanism:

> While I have never considered the matter of a label for my particular set of attitudes, it appears that I might be listed as a naturalistic humanist, if such listing is desirable. Basically, my attitudes are founded on the fact, as I see it, that man is only just at the beginning of the development of his intellectual powers. For many centuries man has been presuming to provide answers for questions totally beyond his capacity. For instance, I believe that everything encompassed in the field known as 'theology' might advantageously be left for study by generations in the far distant future. At this state of human development our reliable knowledge is confined entirely to the field of nature. In the field of nature, there is still enough investigation, research, and understanding to do to occupy fully all the best brains of the human race for many generations into the future.
>
> I see no limit to the potential understanding of the human as long as he can resist the temptation to introduce magic and the "supernatural" into his system of beliefs. Tentative belief, based on acceptable evidence, and changeable with the introduction of new or more convincing evidence, is a very valuable instrument. "Faith," meaning a rigidly held certainty, if unchangeable with the introduction of new evidence, or only changeable at the expense of a feeling of guilt, I believe to be a serious barrier to man's continuing evolution. Any systematized faith, protected by ritual and dogma, and developing vested interests in real estate, salaries, prestige, and power, will tend to slow man's development of his highest powers.

In 1959 the American Humanist Association named Dr. Chisholm their Humanist of the Year. He addressed the Third International Humanist and Ethical Union World Congress held in Oslo in 1962. From its formation in 1968 until his death in 1971, Dr. Chisholm was the first honorary president of the Humanist Association of Canada.

Dr. Chisholm was a distinguished Canadian psychiatrist who once made the headlines because of his view that Santa Claus should be taught as a myth to youngsters rather than as a real individual whom they will come to learn does not really exist. Jove, for example, is taught as a myth, and other gods one day will be, also, he reasoned. {CL; HNS; HNS2; TRI; WAS, 24 June 1956}

Chitwood, Marci (20th Century)

Chitwood in 1998 became assistant editor of *Figleaves*, the newsletter of Cincinnati's Free Inquiry Group.

Choate, Lowell F. (20th Century)

Choate was editor of *Progressive World* (1947) and the *American Rationalist*. {FUS}

CHOCOLATE

Anthropologists from Cornell University and the University of California at Berkeley, California, have located evidence of a village in the Ulúa Valley in northwestern Honduras which was continuously occupied for 3,000 years, until about 1000 C.E. The valley was renowned in pre-Columbian America for the quality of its cocoa beans, and Montezuma at the time of the conquistadors was said to have drunk cups of chocolate beverage every day. By 1500 Spanish explorers had returned samples to Europe, in 1657 the drink netted luxury prices in a London shop and in 1765 chocolate was manufactured in Massachusetts.

Instead of wafers at communion, secularists choose wafers with chocolate at home. {CE; Henry Fountatin, *The New York Times*, 17 November 1998}

Choi, Jaihi (20th Century)

A Korean, Prof. Choi addressed the Fourth International Humanist and Ethical Union World Congress held in Paris (1966).

Chomsky, Avram Noam (1928—)

A noted American linguist, Chomsky addressed the Fifth International Humanist and Ethical Union World Congress held in Boston (1970). In 1995, Chomsky became an Honorary Associate of the Rationalist Press Association. Speaking at the opening plenary of the 1999 Socialist Scholars Conference in New York City, he cited Thomas Paine as an inspiration, then detailed why freedom without opportunity is a dubious gift—the United States aid to the poor is the most miserly in the world, he lamented, suggesting that the International Monetary Fund is not on the side of the world's poor despite its claims.

Chomsky has called the Bible "probably the most genocidal book ever written." Noting polls that show large percentages of Americans believing the Bible, he lamented that

> the figures are shocking. Three-quarters of the American population literally believe in religious miracles. The numbers who believe in the devil, in resurrection, in God doing this and that—it's astonishing. These numbers aren't duplicated anywhere else in the industrial world. You'd have to maybe go to mosques in Iran or do a poll among old ladies in Sicily to get numbers like this. Yet this is the American population.

Unlike the structural linguists, who study language by starting with minimal sounds, Chomsky posited a rudimentary or primitive sentence, from which many syntactic combinations evolved through a series of transformational rules. The Chomskyan generative grammar was a theory that focused almost exclusively on syntax, or the rules of sentence formation. A rival view, such as that advanced at the University of Chicago by James McCawley, was called generative semantics and held that the study of grammar must necessarily involve the study of logic and meaning as well.

Leibniz's *New Essays Concerning Human Understanding* (1704) defended "innate ideas" against Locke's attack, and Chomsky revived the concept of "innate ideas" in his *Cartesian Linguistics: A Chapter in the History of Rationalist Thought* (1966).

Chomsky presently teaches at the Massachusetts Institute of Technology, and his most recent theory of language is called the Minimalist Program. Imagine, he told reporter Margalit Fox of *The New York Times* (5 December 1998), that some divine superengineer, in a single efficient stroke, endowed humans with the power of language where formerly they had none. This simple idea, the Minimalist Program, is the cornerstone of his approach to the discipline he founded in 1957. Although previously he had taught that an inborn mental endowment allows human beings to acquire, use, and understand language, the Minimalist Program streamlines his previous views, dispensing with concepts like "deep structure" and "surface structure," both of which were more or less canonical in his earlier work. Some have spoken of Chomsky's introduction of his theory of language in 1957 in the same breath with Darwin's theory of evolution and Freud's theory of the unconscious so far as its importance in the history of ideas. {CA; CE; E; HNS2}

Chorley, Robert Samuel Theodore [Baron of Kendal] (Born 1895)

Lord Chorley was an honorary associate of the Rationalist Press Association when Bertrand Russell was its president. He was editor of *Arnould's Law of Marine Insurance* and President of the Haldane Society. He wrote *Charley and Giles' Shipping Law* (1987).

Chorowsky, Karl (20th Century)

Chorowsky, a Unitarian minister who found theists as well as humanists in his congregations, served in Brooklyn, New York, as well as in Westport, Connecticut.

Choukri, Mohammed (20th Century)

A Moroccan author, Choukri wrote *For Bread Alone* (translated into English by Paul Bowles), *The Tent*, and *Jean Genêt in Tangier*. An atheist, he was asked by Ludmilla Biebl in *Spitting Image #2* if he was unafraid of becoming a victim of the Islamic fundamentalists. "There is no point in being afraid," Choukri responded. "If it happens, it happens." {CA}

CHRIST

Christ is a word which came from the term *Christos*, meaning "anointed with oil" [the Greek translation of the Aramaic *Meshicha*; Hebrew, *Mashiakh*]. Even by the time of Paul of Taursus, Christ became more of a proper noun than a title. In the Christian religion, Jesus is the personal name of its founder, Christ his title—his last name, many do not realize, is not Christ. (See entries for Christmas and for Jesus. For an atheist's account, see "The Origin and Establishment of the Christ Myth," by John M. Davis, in *Secular Nation* (Fall 1995].) {ER}

Christesen, Clement (1911—)

"Clem" Christesen is an Australian rationalist, literary journalist, and editor. In 1940, he founded the *Meanjin Quarterly* and was its editor until 1975. Christesen was a one-time vice-president of the Council for Civil Liberties and a director of the Rationalist Association of Australia Ltd.

CHRISTIAN

• Christian, n. One who follows the teachings of Christ insofar as they are not inconsistent with a life of sin.

—**Ambrose Bierce**

• I don't know whether to laugh or cry. We give them a nice Jewish boy to worship, five books—no charge. And what do we get in return? Crusades, the Inquisition, pogroms, the Holocaust. And now they want us to join them in heaven? I'll take hell any day!

—Harriet Levenbaum Kean

CHRISTIAN ADHERENTS

Of the 5,772,000 humans in 1996, an estimated 66% are not Christians and a total of 34% are Christians, according to mid-1997 estimates. (See entry for Hell.)

CHRISTIAN ATHEISM

• Thomas J. Altizer (1927—) is an American theologian who is termed a Christian atheist. "Only by accepting and even willing the death of God in our experience can we be liberated from a transcendent beyond, an alien beyond which has been emptied and darkened by God's self-alienation in Christ."

• Paul Van Buren (1924—) in *The Secular Meaning of the Gospel* claims that it is no longer possible to speak of God acting in the world. Science and technology have made the old mythology invalid. A simple faith in the Old Man in the Sky is now clearly impossible, but so has been the more sophisticated belief of the theologians. Thus, Van Buren holds, we must do without God and hold on to Jesus of Nazarath. The Gospel is "the good news of a free man who has set other men free."

• William Hamilton (1924—) wrote *Radical Theology and the Death of God*. He, Altizer, and Van Buren are all listed as Christian atheists in Karen Armstrong's *A History of God*.

Freethinkers, rationalists, and secular humanists find all such ratiocination impossible to follow, comparing Christian atheism to the experience of playing a game of cricket using General Henry M. Robert's *Rules of Order*.

CHRISTIAN COALITION

The Christian Coalition (1801-L Sara Drive, Chesapeake, VA 23320) was founded in 1989 by Pat Robertson "to give Christians a voice in government. We represent a growing group of nearly 2,000,000 members and supporters who believe it's time for people of faith to have a voice in the conversation we call democracy." Or so its Online homepage reads at <http://www.cc.org>.

The Executive Director is Randy Tate. The group's Families 2000 Stragegy has the aim of "recruiting 100,000 volunteers to serve as liaisons between their churches and local Christian Coalition chapters—an effort to mobilize hundreds of thousands of pro-family activists by November 2000."

Key beliefs:

- Pro-life [code for: being against abortion]
- Pro-family [code for: being against homosexuality]
- Pro-religious freedom [code for: vote the nonbelievers out of office]

The two organizations that have been the most efficient in fighting this right-wing religious group are People For the American Way (2000 M Street NW, Suite 400, Washington, DC 20036 <www.pfaw.org>); and the Interfaith Alliance at <http://www.tialliance.org>, whose president is the Rev. J. Philip Wogaman and whose executive director is the Rev. Dr. C. Welton Gaddy.

Many benefit "from the fiction that religion has been banned from the public schools," George B. Pyle has editorialized in *The Salina Journal*, Salina, Kansas. "Some may be truly anti-religious. But the rumor is more likely to be spread by those who claim to follow a Christian faith. It can certainly boost Christian Coalition fund-raising." Pyle then reports that those who complain "that God has been banished from the public schools are very much mistaken. . . . There are as many prayers in the public schools as there are prayerful people. If our children are murdering each other, we must find something other than a lack of faith to blame." {*The New York Times*, 31 May 1999}

CHRISTIAN ETHICS

According to Bertrand Russell's *Education and the Modern World* (1932), "The fundamental defect of Christian ethics consists in the fact that it labels certain classes of acts 'sins' and others 'virtue' on the grounds that have nothing to do with their social consequences. An ethic not derived from superstition must decide first upon the kind of social effects which it desires to achieve and the kind which it desires to avoid. It must then decide, as far as our knowledge permits, what acts will promote the desired consequences; these acts it will praise, while those having a contrary tendency it will condemn."

Through such an emphasis laid upon sexual virtue, Russell wrote in *Marriage and Morals* (1959), "The Christian ethics inevitably . . . did a great deal to degrade the position of women. Since the moralists were men, woman appeared as the temptress; if they had been women, man would have had this role." Only in modern times, Russell suggests, have women regained the degree of freedom which they enjoyed in the Roman Empire. Constantine made Christianity the official religion of the Roman Empire, a move which led to women's freedom being curtailed under the pretense of protecting them from sin. Only during the French Revolution were the laws of property and inheritance altered in order that women could recover their rights of inheritance which had been lost over the time of a dozen centuries.

CHRISTIAN HUMANISM

Two Protestants, Karl Barth and Paul Tillich, referred to their outlooks at times as being that of Christian Humanism.

CHRISTIAN IDENTITY

Christian Identity is an example of a hate group which embarrasses not only most Christians but also most Americans. Mark Thomas, for example, runs a Pennsylvania neo-Nazi group known as Christian Identity near Seisholtzville, Pennsylvania. In 1994 at a Hitler Youth Festival several hundred "skinheads" and other white supremacists met. "It is the trademark of the Jew to make us feel dirty and unworthy," stated the monthly newsletter, *The Watchman*. In Idaho, a similar racist group—the Aryan Nation—is active. Both groups hold that the first chapter in the Bible claims that Jewish people are descended from Cain, who was a descendant of the devil snake and Eve. White people, they hold, are descendants of Abel, who was a descendant of Adam and Eve. They hold that there are two main races, Jews and white people, with everyone else being classified under "beasts of the field." God's chosen are not the Jews, in short: His chosen are whites of northern European extraction. Jews are Satan's children and blacks are subhuman.

Their culture, which glorifies violence, made its way to the United States from England in the early 1980s, according to the Southern Poverty Law Center in Alabama. However, William Potter Gale, a retired Army colonel, had founded the Posse Commitatus, an anti-government group active during the 1970s and early 1980s. One large group, in Elohim City (City of God), Oklahoma, was founded by ex-Mennonite Robert G. Millar, who claims he was divinely led to the site. Millar has said that "this people [the Germanic and Scandinavian peoples] represents 9% of the population of the world. They control 50% of the wealth of the world. So it's evident that the promises of God have come to pass." Similar groups exist in Germany and elsewhere in Europe. In 1994, sixty-four white supremacist and neo-Nazi groups were active in Pennsylvania alone. An estimated two thousand incidents against Jews occurred nationally in 1994, according to the Anti-Defamation League of B'nai B'rith.

In 1996, the Rev. Helen Young, a Montana Protestant minister, interviewed a group, the Freemen, which had threatened government officials and was being indicted for bank and mail fraud. They told her that as believers in Christian Identity they believed that God created white gentiles as a superior race, descended directly from Adam and Eve. Jews, they held, descended from a sexual union between Eve and Satan. Whites, therefore, are the true "Israelites," a lost tribe that had migrated to America, the new promised land but one now corrupted by Jewish influence. Although Christian Identity was condemned by the National Council of Churches, the group issued documents calling on those would be "free" to sever ties to government, by not paying taxes and shunning Social Security cards, marriage licenses, and building permits. Ms. Young listened for four hours, then called their beliefs disgusting. Journalist Gustav Niebuhr, writing in *The New York Times* (12 April 1996), described the group's twenty-page "edict," or manifesto, which describes two categories of citizens: "We the People," or white males, subject to "God's law," the Constitution, and its first ten amendments; and other racial groups, enfranchised only by "man's law," the 14th Amendment's guarantee of equal protection. "Free" white males have lost control of the country, said one of their leaders, Rodney Skurdal, and "We the People are now ruled by foreigners/aliens." In a message to others, the Christian Identity group proclaimed, "This is a religious war between the Freemen characters, i.e., American nationals, in their attempt to return to their one and only true Almighty God and His laws."

CHRISTIAN MARRIAGE

Roman Catholic bishops in the United States went on record in 1994 concerning marital roles: marriage must be characterized by "mutual submission" of a husband and wife to each other.

In 1998 Southern Baptists, the largest Protestant denomination and an increasingly conservative force among American religious organizations, amended its essential statement of beliefs to include a declaration that a woman should "submit herself graciously" to her husband's leadership and that a husband should "provide for, protect, and lead his family":

> The husband and wife are of equal worth before God. Both bear God's image but each in differing ways. The marriage relationship models the way God relates to His people. A husband is to love his wife as Christ loved the church. He has the God-given responsibility to provide for, to protect, and to lead his family. A wife is to submit graciously to the servant leadership of her husband even as the church willingly submits to the headship of Christ. She, being "in the image of God" as is her husband and thus equal to him, has the God-given responsibility to respect her husband and to serve as his "helper" in managing their household and nurturing the next generation.

The president of the Southern Baptist Theological Seminary in Louisville, Kentucky, R. Albert Mohler Jr., declared that submission of wives to their husbands is "not a modern idea" but "is clearly revealed in Scripture." He added that "the secular world may hear it as strange, but it is, we believe, God's pattern." To critics he said if they would read the Bible they would see that God in the fifth chapter of the *Letter to the Ephesians* "says" that just as Christ is head of the church so the husband is "head of the wife." Just "as Christ loved the church" so the husband, not the wife, was "to provide for, to protect, and to lead" their families, all the while recognizing that "husband and wife are of equal worth before God."

However, according to Baptist official Herb Hollinger, "I don't know anyone who would say, 'If you don't believe [wives must be submissive to their husbands] you can't be a member of our church.'" Jerry Falwell, a noted fundamentalist Christian, not a Southern Baptist, agreed with the Baptists' statement, adding that marriage also was not a sacred ceremony that could ever be enjoyed by homosexuals.

(Wags wondered if the Southern Baptist United States President, Bill Clinton, had discussed the ruling with his wife, a Methodist; or if the Southern Baptist wife of the Southern Baptist Vice President Al Gore was submissive or ungraciously non-capitulative, passive or active, masochistic or sadistic. Other wags wondered when Bible literalists such as Mohler and Falwell would show their faith by washing each other's feet during 7 p.m. telecasts.)

The Southern Baptists also have boycotted the Walt Disney Company, complaining that the entertainment giant condones homosexuality. In 1996 it voted to appoint a missionary specifically to evangelize Jews and went on record as opposing divorce, homosexual unions, and abortion.

Although the Southern Baptists are, like the Mormons, on the conservative end of Protestant thinking, the more liberal churches are the Friends and the Congregationalists. Their adherents have the more contemporary view that the Biblical references are statements of the early church, not of Jesus, ideas that had been written but then later interpreted to support patriarchal and sexist outlooks. {*The New York Times*, 10 June 1998}

CHRISTIAN MEGACHURCHES

Charles Trueheart in *The Atlantic Monthly* (August 1996) describes the "full-service" mostly Protestant churches which are winning millions of "customers" with pop-culture packaging. They may, he holds, be building a new form of community. Mariners Southcoast Church in Newport Beach, California, has an orchestra which plays upbeat soft rock with cappuccino carts dispensing "the secular sacrament" while numbers of seminars draw hundreds of individuals from throughout the area. Prince of Peace Church in suburban Minneapolis, Next Church in Dallas, Texas, Willow Creek Community Church in South Barrington, Illinois, and Wooddale Church in Eden Prairie, Minnesota, are examples of such megachurches which use contemporary music rather than pipe organs, old hymnals, and robed choirs to attract hundreds, sometimes thousands, of members. Willow Creek, for example, boasts 15,000 worshippers. Saddleback Valley Community Church in Mission Viejo, California, has a seventy-nine-acre campus, a 10,000-seat auditorium, 11,000 worshippers, and a building which cost more than $50 million. An estimated 400 megachurches were in business as of 1996.

CHRISTIAN NATION

Many Christians refer to the United States of America as "a Christian nation," this despite the clear statement to the contrary of President John Adams in 1797. Referring to the Treaty between the United States and Tripoli, Adams said "the Government of the United States of America is not in any sense founded on the Christian Religion."

Many individuals, however, still continue to argue that because ours is a Christian nation, for example, it follows that religion can be taught in the public schools, "In God We Trust" can appear on our currency and our courtroom walls, and other such extensions can be concocted. In 1995, as an "olive branch" to Jews, the executive director of the Christian Coalition, Ralph E. Reed Jr., said it was a "blatant wrong" for some on the religious right to talk of the United States as a "Christian nation." Such a phrase, he held, conjures up for Jews fearful historical memories of the Inquisition, of "barbarous acts" against Jews like pogroms, the establishment of ghettos and the Holocaust, and other such persecutions.

Disinterested viewers doubt that such a declaration will sway those who believe that God is deaf to Jews' prayers and that America is not necessarily a place where non-Christians should be welcome. [See entry for John Adams.]

CHRISTIAN NUDISM

"Father God, we present ourselves to you in humble gratitude," intoned the seventy-two-year-old preacher. Reporter Jennifer Lee of *The Wall Street Journal* (11 August 1997) described the scene as the Nottingham, New Hampshire, congregation rose to sign the opening hymn, "What a Friend We Have in Jesus."

Many Christian believe they will stand naked before God on Judgment Day. This group, Lee wrote, does not want to wait. The Rev. Harry Westcott stepped out from behind the pulpit "naked except for white sneakers and a black watch. The accompanist, his fingers skimming the keyboard of the Wurlitzer, is similarly undressed." Although worshipers have the option of wearing clothing and some wear their Sunday best, others wear "their birthday suits."

Christian nudist publications are proliferating, as is nudism generally, Lee reported. "If you believe that the human body is a creation of God in his own image, there is nothing shameful or harmful about being nude," the Rev. Westcott preached, citing *Isaiah* 20:2. Opponents cite parts of *Genesis*.

Meanwhile, freethinkers have seldom gone on record as opposing nudism. In fact, the editor of *Sunshine and Health* in the 1950s was an active members of the American Humanist Association. (See entry for Nudity.)

CHRISTIAN RECONSTRUCTION, DEBUNKING THE MOVEMENT

The radical wing of the Religious Right is a group called Christian Reconstruction. Its leaders would replace democracy with a government that enforces their version of biblical law. One of its key individuals is James Dobson, a child psychologist who launched Focus on the Family in 1977. Debunking of the Christian Reconstruction Movement can be found on the Web: <http://www.servecom/thibodep/cr/cr.htm>.

CHRISTIAN RIGHT

Skipp Porteous in *Freedom Writer* (May-June 1999) listed the following top ten Religious Right organizations:

- American Family Association—headed by the Rev. Donald Wildom, 61, of Mississippi
- Chalcedon—founded by the "father of Christian Reconstruction," the 82-year-old R. J. Rushdoony.
- Christian Coalition—Pat Robertson, the 69-year-old founder boasts of a large membership but is a paper tiger having trouble with the Internal Revenue Service
- Coalition On Revival—led by Jay Grimstead, 65, the group bent on creating a theocracy in America is "burned out."
- Concerned Women for America—founded by Beverly LaHaye, 69, now led by Carmen Pate and somewhat unproductive of any results.
- Oregon Citizens Alliance—headed by Lon Mabon, the group is now defunct.
- Focus on The Family—is the 800-pound gorilla of the Religious Right; founded by James Dobson, 64.
- Free Congress Foundation—founded and directed by Paul Weyrich, who has announced, "We have lost the culture war."
- NACE/CEE—the National Association of Christian Educators and Citizens for Excellence in Education was founded by Robert Simons, 74; had some success in electing conservative Christians to school board seats.
- Operation Rescue—once loud and boisterous, this antiabortion group founded by Randall Terry has lost most of its steam.
- Traditional Values Coalition—Run by the Rev. Lou Sheldon, 65, and his family, it is primarily an antigay organization.
- Christian Action Network—headed by Martin Mawyer, formerly of the Moral Majority, it is another primarily antigay organization.
- Eagle Forum—founded by Phyllis Schlafly, it almost single-handedly defeated the Equal Rights Amendment.
- Ruthrford Institute—a conservative Christian advocacy group was founded by John Whitehead, who made a break from his former Christian Reconstructionist views and now approaches issues from a more liberal viewpoint.
- Promise Keepers—once feared by some as the "third wave," it now is merely a ripple. Rallies planned for state capitals on 1 Jan 2000 have been canceled for fear of the Y2K bug.

CHRISTIAN SAINTS

Lavender Lists (1990) makes note of the following "noteworthy saints":

- St. Aelred of Rievaulx

  "of twelfth-century England, left writings expressing deep feelings for male spiritual friendship. To control his carnal impulse, Aelred fasted and took icy baths.

- St. John the Evangelist (the Apostle)

  "also known as the Beloved Disciple whom Jesus loved and who lay on Jesus' bosom at the Last Supper. Medieval sculptures of John asleep with his head in Christ's lap gave rise to mystical texts in which John is said to have enjoyed the milk of the Lord."

- St. Moses the Hungarian (11th Century)

  "was sold as a slave to a polish noblewoman who developed a yen for him, but he preferred to stay with his fellow Russian prisoners rather than marry her. Angered by his refusal, she finally had Moses whipped and his genitals cut off. He eventually entered a monastery, where he constantly warned the other monks to avoid women and sin. He was canonized by the Russian Orthodox Church."

- St. Sebastian

  "has been venerated by homosexuals since at least the second half of the nineteenth century, as well as by male artists looking for an excuse to draw a nude male body."

- St. Sergius and St. Bacchus

  "were said to have been lovers."

CHRISTIAN SCHOOLS, FUNDAMENTALIST

Fundamentalist schools have been established across America, allegedly because parents believe and want to follow *Deuteronomy* 6:7's injunction, "And thou shalt teach [God's commandments] diligently unto thy children". According to Christian Schools International, at least 3,200 member schools existed in 1998 with 600,000 pupils who had been taken out of public schools.

When is a Christian school a fundamentalist school? *The Economist* (6 June 1998) answers:

> There are no hard-and-fast rules; but an unequivocal belief in creationism is probably the most reliable indicator. So is a sense of ministering to the whole child. "We believe that every human has three parts: spirit, body and soul, and that we should minister to all three parts," says John Burges, the principal and only full-time teacher at Grace [Christian School, Mason, Texas].

The "Accelerated Christian Curriculum," which Grace uses, has a Christian slant:

> The history curriculum carries the notion of America's "manifest destiny" far beyond Monroe's dreams. Spain was defeated in North America because it was Catholic. George Washington was preserved by a miracle during the French-Indian war. All Muslims are "descendants of Isaac's half-brother Ishmael." Above all, "Americanism" is the divine template for the world.

Grace is pragmatic in some respects. In deer season the whole school goes hunting (physical education), butchers a deer (biology), then cooks it (home economics) into venison burgers for the school lunch. And everyone says grace first.

CHRISTIAN SCIENCE

Christian Science is a denomination founded by Mary Baker Glover Patterson Eddy. Widowed six months after her marriage to George W. Glover, and separating from dentist Daniel Patterson in 1866, she married Asa Gilbert Eddy in 1877. She gave birth to one child, also named George W. Glover. The church Mrs. Eddy founded is centrally organized and directed but, as pointed out by Gaius Glenn Atkins who once taught homiletics and sociology at Auburn Theological Seminary in North Marshfield, Massachusetts, it functions denominationally in local churches with their own buildings, leaders and "readers," stated times, and forms of worship. The "Mother Church" in Boston was in its origin a variant of American Protestantism, although it has since extended internationally. *Science and Health* was a book in which Mrs. Eddy explains the philosophy of Christian Science, which is pure idealism: "Nothing is real and eternal; nothing is spirit—but God and His ideal; evil has no reality." In short, Atkins writes, "Since God is good, He cannot have created nor be responsible for all the shadowed side of life. Man is 'God's spiritual idea' and belongs by right to an order in which there is neither sickness, sin, sorrow, or death. Such things are errors of his mortal mind. They have no reality for him save as he admits them. Deny them and they cease to exist. There are, therefore, two fundamentally opposed systems of belief, the true and the false. Man is entangled in a false system of belief whose sources Mrs. Eddy does not convincingly trace. He may escape that entanglement with all its consequences by affirming the other system and demonstrating his affirmation by faith, self-discipline, and practice." Adds Atkins, "One may say, therefore, that Christian Science is a philosophy, a semi-theology, a system of Biblicism and a psycho-therapy effectively organized, amply financed and aptly propagated. Its followers have an unusually strong group consciousness."

Two leading critics of Christian Science have been Mark Twain in *Christian Science* (1907) and Willa Cather in *The Life of Mary Baker G. Eddy and the History of Christian Science* (1908). *Village Voice* critic Michael Warner has written, "Eddy's own prose style is one of the wonders of the modern world. She took the English language to places it had never been before. Together with Artemus Ward and Erma Bombeck, she stands in the front rank of American humorists, writing in such masterful deadpan you can still hear a 19th-century pin dropping. She writes, for example, 'Obesity is an adipose belief of yourself as a substance.' (Sentences of this grandeur prompted Mark Twain, in a 1903 work called *The Literary Guillotine*, to pose as the judge of a lawsuit by Henry James against Mary Baker Eddy. James argues that Eddy has infringed on his ownership of 'the patent obscure sentence.' Judge Twain concludes that Eddy beat James to it.) As philosophy, Eddy's writing is a minor branch in the American pragmatist tradition, telling us that the world we encounter has already been shaped by our beliefs about it. But Eddy concludes that if reality is shaped by belief it must be delusional and malign, and thus she veers from pragmatism into the gothic. When you treat a patient with a fever, she instructs, 'the fever is to be argued down,' and your argument should go like this: 'Inflammation is not inflammation or redness and soreness of any part; this is your belief only and this belief is the red dragon the King of beasts which means this belief of inflammation is the leading lie out of which you get your fright that causes chills and heat.' In later life, Eddy gave herself over to these gothic tendencies. Her greatest creation in this vein is the theory of malicious animal magnetism (MAM). Eddy thought that several of her enemies—all former disciples—were poisoning her with MAM, and that she could tell which enemy was working on her at any given moment because each produced the effects of a different poison: when one was thinking about her, she felt strychnine; when another, arsenic. If nothing else, such fantasias show that Eddy shared with Cather a marked distaste for the merely commonplace. Eddy wrenched herself free of the ordinary, and this got Cather's attention. It also prompted in Cather the moral melancholy that would become the distinctive note of her mature style." (See entries for Samuel Clemens, Willa Cather, Caroline Fraser, and Martin Gardner.) {ER; RE; *Village Voice*, 17 August 1993}

CHRISTIAN WRITERS: See entry for theistic humanism.

CHRISTIANITY

- In reality we Christians are nothing more than a sect of Jews.

—G. C. Lichtenberg

- It is surely high time to recognize that Christianity is a busted flush: we can no longer view the Bible reverentially and uncritically as a God-given guide to faith and morals. Nor (if we use the same canons of critical scholarship that have been applied to Church history since the time of Gibbon) can we give credence to the claim of any Church to embody an authentic divine revelation or ongoing sacramental channel of grace.

—Daniel O'Hara,
a former Anglican curate (1968—1970)
and Rationalist Press Association Director

Christianity, which is professed by Eastern, Roman Catholic, and Protestant bodies, is a religion derived from Jesus—the Christ, the Messiah, the second person of the Trinity—as interpreted from a series of books called the Holy Bible. Over the centuries, Christianity has developed from its original roots in Judaism, despite sporadic persecution, being spread through the Roman Empire by missionaries, notably St. Paul, and it was recognized by Emperor Constantine in 313 as the official religion of Rome. The First Council of Nicaea in 325 condemned such heresies concerning the nature of Christ as Arianism (the belief that the Son of God was not the same as the Father but was an agent for creating the world), Nestorianism (a belief that divine and human persons remained separate in the incarnate Christ), and Monophysitism (a belief that Christ's nature remains divine and was never human although Jesus took on an earthly and human body). Some basic sources for understanding Christianity are as follows:

Michael Arnheim, *Is Christianity True?* (1984)
J. G. Davies, *The Early Christian Church* (1965)
Helen Ellerbe, *The Dark Side of Christian History* (1995)
Asher Finkel, *The Pharisees and the Teacher of Nazareth* (1964)
R. M. Grant, *Augustus to Constantine* (1970)
R. Joseph Hoffman, *The Origins of Christianity*
Philip Hughes, *History of the Church* (3 volumes, 1949)
K. S. Latourette, *History of the Expansion of Christianity* (1937—1945)
Jules Lebreton and Jacque Zeiller, *A History of the Early Church* (4 volumes, 1944—1946)
Hans Lietzmann, *The History of the Early Church* (4 volumes, 1961)

"Ever since the start of public opinion polling in the late 1930s," complain Roger Finke and Rodney Stark in *The Churching of America 1776—1990: Winners and Losers in Our Religious Economy* (1992), "surveys have always found that virtually *everyone* has a religion [in the United States]. I know of no national survey in which as many as ten percent answered 'none' when asked their religious affiliation. But the nation's churches cannot possibly seat ninety percent of the population. More careful investigation reveals that for many, their claim to a religious affiliation amounts to nothing more than a vague recollection of what their parents or grandparents have passed along as the family preference. . . . Can students who think they go to the Pisscaple Church have ever seen the word Episcopal? Or what of Presditurians?"

Some Christians claim the United States has always been a Christian nation. Stephanie Thomas in Virginia wrote *The Economist* (15 January 1994) that "Until *Engel v. Vitale* (1962) America, in both its public and private life, was an openly Christian nation. Until that decision struck down 'prayer in the public schools,' everyone acknowledged that although no particular denomination was entitled to be 'established,' the very fabric of America's culture as well as its government was grounded and founded on Christian principles. Indeed, both the words and deeds of Thomas Jefferson clearly indicate that this is what was intended. As Justice Joseph Story indicated, the institution of the church was to be isolated from the institution of the state." However, President Washington in 1797 confirmed and signed the Treaty between the United States and Tripoli in which appears the significant statement, '. . . the Government of the United States of America is not in any sense founded on the Christian Religion.' "

"Organized Christianity," wrote R. Gallienne, "has probably done more to retard the ideals that were its founder's than any other agency in the world." What Christianity has accomplished, most of its critics agree, is a remarkable ability to convince its adherents that their souls are stained indelibly with sin.

As to why Christianity incorporated the Old Testament instead of using just the New Testament, Irving Kristol in *Neoconservatism: The Autobiography of an Idea* (1995) has suggested

> They [the church fathers] needed the Old Testament for certain key statements that are not found in the New Testament, or at least are not found there in an emphatic way, such as that when God created the world, he saw that "it was good." That is an Old Testament doctrine. It became a Christian doctrine, and it is crucial to any orthodoxy, in contrast to gnosticism, which says that no one knows who created the world—a demiurge or whatever—but that the world is certainly bad.

(See entries for John Adams, Arianism, Civilization,
Thomas Jefferson, Monophysitism, and Nestorianism.)
{CE; ER; *Freethought History* #8, 1993}

CHRISTIANITY, FOUNDER OF

Ferdinand Christian Baur (1826—1860), the pioneering German Scripture scholar who headed what was known as the Tübingen School, tried to explain the evolution of Christianity in terms of a rigidly maintained Hegelian philosophy of history. In its earliest stage, he found, Christianity was a form of Judaism: Jesus was the Messiah of the Jews, not the founder of a world religion. In contradistinction to this view (*thesis*), Paul maintained that Jesus was the Messiah of the whole world, and Christianity was wholly distinct from Judaism and thus unrestricted by the Mosaic law (*antithesis*).

The British novelist A. N. Wilson, in *Paul: The Mind of the Apostle* (1997), holds that Paul is the one who created Christianity, not Jesus, and expected that his research would "change the way we think about Christianity." What disturbs many is Wilson's picture of Paul himself: once a wealthy tent maker who supplied the hated Roman forces; a former member of the Jerusalem temple guard who had not only persecuted Jesus's followers but probably even had a role in the death of Jesus himself. {ER; Peter Steinfels, *The New York Times*, 22 March 1997}

CHRISTIANS: For an estimate of the number of Christians in the world, see entry for Hell.

CHRISTIANS AND GAYS

In 1998 *Time* reported the following quotations in its issue entitled "The War Over Gays" (26 October 1998):

- God hates fags.

—Sign carried by the Rev. Fred Phelps of the
Westboro Baptist Church in Topeka, Kansas,
and his band of protesters at the 1998 funeral of
Matthew Shepard, a 21-year-old Wyoming gay man
beaten to death by two heterosexuals
who disliked homosexuals.

- We are standing with the G.O.P. [Republican Party] against the Sodomites.

—The Rev. O. N. Otwell,
one of several protesters wanting to ban a Republican
gay group from the Texas party's convention.

• You should try to show them a way to deal with [homosexuality] just like alcohol . . . or sex addiction . . . or kleptomaniacs.

—Trent Lott, the U. S. Senate majority (Republican) leader on television during june. He also suggested that gays are sinners and said he got his views "in the Bible."

• wage the war against the homosexual agenda.

—Gary Bauer's website for the Family Research Council calls homosexuality "destructive"

• the acceptance of homosexuality is the last step in the decline of Gentile civilization.

—Pat Robertson of the Christian Broadcasting Network, who also warned that hurricanes could hit Orlando, Florida, because of gay events there.

CHRISTIANS, HIDDEN

Christianity was banned in Japan in 1612, having been introduced by Francis Xavier in 1549. The government, concerned about dual loyalties the Christian converts might have, crucified, boiled, drowned, burned, or otherwise murdered those who disputed the banning. Many gave up, but those who did not became *kakure Kirishitan*, or hidden Christians. In 1873 when Christianity was again legalized, most of the 50,000 or so hidden Christians returned to conventional Christianity.

A few, however, re-created from memory in the 1820s their version of Biblical stories. As described in *The Economist* (11 January 1997), the young Holy One debated with Buddhist priests, "as twelve-year-old Jesus was said to have done with the Jewish elders. Two men, Ponsha and Piroto (i.e., Pontius Pilate), are told to kill all children of five and under, an echo of Herod's order. Mary gives birth in a stable, but the innkeeper who had spurned her then takes her in: in a wonderfully Japanese touch, he offers her a hot bath."

Little wonder, say freethinkers, that the initial Biblical stories written long after the facts were similarly stretched.

Christie, Dame Agatha (1891—1976)

Christie, the English detective storywriter who in 1971 was named Dame Commander, Order of the British Empire, may or may not have been a philosophic naturalist. In her story, "The Hound of Death" (1933), however, she wrote, "The things we call supernatural are not necessarily supernatural at all. An electric flashlight would be supernatural to a savage. The supernatural is only the natural of which the laws are not yet understood."

CHRISTMAS

Christians object to the shortening of Christmas to "Xmas" by commercial concerns and others. Non-believers, however, editorialize their feelings about the holiday by calling it "Xmess." The Rationalist Society of St. Louis, describing the event as "Christmyth," has published the following:

• December 25: Christmas was given this date because it was strongly identified with pagan rites, the winter solstice, and numerous feats already celebrated close to that date. In fact, Dec. 25 was so strongly identified with pagan rites that many felt it sacrilegious to observe Jesus's birth then. The ancient Roman calendars identified Dec. 25 as the Birthday of the Unconquered Sun, the Intermediary of the One and Only Supreme God, the Sovereign Master of Heaven. Emperor Aurelian consecrated a temple to this god on Dec. 25, 274 C.E. [Common Era], well before agreement was reached on the date of Christ's birth. The final selection of Dec. 25 as the date to celebrate Christmas may have been given a boost by Constantine who was a worshiper of the Unconquered Sun. There has been no unanimity in acceptance of this date; there have been movements by Christians to remove it from the ecclesiastical calendar. (See entry for Stanley Stokes.)

• Bethlehem: To fulfill his role as king of the Jews, Jesus had to be born in Bethlehem, as were Joseph and David. But it was reported that Jesus was a Nazarene. Some way was needed to explain why a man from Nazareth was born in Bethlehem. The story of the census allowed the writers of the Gospels to not only move their central character to the appropriate city of birth, but to also conveniently explain the circumstances surrounding his birth in a stable, which just happened to parallel the conditions under which similar saviors were born. There is no historical evidence that such a census was conducted in any year that could possibly have been that of Jesus's birth.

• We Three Kings: This notion was not unique to the Jesus story. The birth of Socrates (469 B.C.E.) and Krishna (1200 B.C.E.) were both also marked by the presentation of the gifts of gold, frankincense (a type of incense made from resins of a tree found in the Mideast), and myrrh (another type of incense made primarily from the tree gum resin of the myrrh tree; also used as an embalming compound and a drug). The arrival of Magi with gifts was a virtual cliché, also reported earlier in the myths of Osiris, Zoroaster, and Mithra. The Magi were actually a Persian priestly caste that arose to prominence under Zoroastrianism. Biblical accounts do not establish the number of Magi, so various traditions have arisen in depicting this aspects of the nativity scene. The notion that there were three is likely because three gifts were mentioned. The Magi are also occasionally identified as kings, although this is not contained in the Gospel accounts.

• Nativity Scene: The popular scene, including animals, has been traced back to St. Francis of Assisi. But the traditions tapped by St. Francis go back much further even than the supposed time of Jesus's birth. The stable could very well be an adaptation of the cave, which was the birthplace of numerous other savior gods which preceded him. However, stables are also frequently cited as origin points for gods. The astrological explanation is that the constellation Capricorn, the Goat, was directly under the earth at the time of the winter solstice. This constellation was also known as the Stable of Augeas, which was cleaned by Hercules. Similar tales have been traced back to at least 1700 B.C.E., the date of an Egyptian nativity scene from the Temple of Amen at Luxor. This depiction was intended to relate the birth of the first-born sons of the Pharaohs, but did so in a manner that would be instantly recognized by Christians.

• Mary: The Egyptian god Isis is said to have been the most important model for the character Mary, mother of Jesus. In Alexandria in the fourth century the Temple of Isis and the Church of St. Mary were next door neighbors, and pagans and Christians viewed the two as largely interchangeable. Isis was actually called Meri, and is said to have made occasional personal appearances before her more devout worshippers. Isis, also a virgin, was a gentle mother-goddess who was an intercessor on the behalf of mortals. Joseph had an Egyptian counterpart in the earth god, Seb. In the Egyptian tongue, "Jo" means god, so that if this is put together with the name Seb, we have approximated the name Joseph. Likewise, as Mary begat Jesus, Isis begat Horus. As Isis and Seb hid Horus from the serpent Herut, Mary and Joseph hid Jesus from Herod. The similarity of the names of the mythical Herut and the historical Herod was apparently too much for the authors to the Gospels to ignore. They had to work him into the story with the Massacre of the Innocents, totally unsubstantiated by any historical accounts, but easily explainable by examining parallel myths.

Wick Allison, former publisher of *National Review* and author of *That's in the Bible?*, figures that Jesus was born in 6 B.C.E. (Before the Christian Era). Dionysius Exiguus ("Denny the Runt") designated the first year after the birth as anno Domini (year of our Lord) 1, so Jesus would have been born in the year before that: not the year 0, but 1 B.C.E. Christian scholars complained that Dionysius erred, that Jesus had not been born in the *753rd* year of the old Roman calendar: Herod the Great, King of Judea, they argued, had died in the *750th* year after Rome was founded, so if Jesus was born in Herod's reign then Dionysius was at least three years off, maybe five. Allison uses other evidence—Luke may have confused Quirinius with Quintilius, writing that a census was taken "while Quirinius was governor of Syria," but it was Quintilius who was legate in Syria from 6 to 4 B.C.E. The man-hours spent in such mathematics has been staggering, everyone agrees.

Janis Ian, in *The Advocate* (12 December 1995), told of a gay male couple wishing to educate their son about Christmas. "If we start early, he'll have more time to get over it later on," remarks one of the two dads, whose forebears were Catholic priests. They invite Ian to help re-create the Last Supper for a Christmas dinner, but she points out that the Last Supper did not take place until late April. Going ahead, nevertheless, they invite twelve friends for a re-enactment of the meal. All goes well, particularly when Jason decides, after being told how the story ends, to play Judas and gets kissed by the person (a lesbian) playing Jesus. Mary, they decide, is not present because "they probably had her back in the kitchen." The youth is said to have enjoyed the religious re-enactment, except he had a quick tantrum upon finding that he would not at the end collect the thirty silver dollars.

Christmas has no relevance for freethinkers, who regard it as a time of inflated prices and sales of un-needed items. As observed by Jimmy Cannon, "Christmas is a holiday that persecutes the lonely, the frayed, and the rejected." (See entries for Thomas William Flynn, often dubbed "the anti-Claus"; Charles Follen; Humanist Holidays; and Rick Ganulin.)

CHRISTMAS CAROLS: "We Wish You a Merry Solstice," "Arrest Ye Merry Gentlemen," "Deck the Halls with Calls of Folly": these are new humanistic lyrics for old religious tunes. See entry for David J. Gornik.

CHRISTMAS TREE: See entries for Eliza and Charles Follen, who introduced the custom to America.

CHRIST'S PENIS

Penises in various societies have been revered, sometimes even been eaten by victorious warriors who believed they would then receive added sexual potency from such a diet. A *fascinum* in Latin was the image of an erect penis which people hung up in their rooms, wore around necks, or worshiped as an aid to warding off the evil eye.

Diane Ackerman, noting that the word *fascinate* refers to penises, is fascinated by the religious interest in the male organ. The penis of the crucified Jesus Christ, for example, has long been an object of adoration. "Hundreds of Renaissance churches," she writes, "claimed to have part of Christ's penis as a holy relic. His circumcised prepuce, the only mortal part of him left on earth when he ascended to heaven, was treasured as a miraculous fertility aid. Women prayed at Christ's foreskin for help in conceiving. Thirteen of those relics survive today. The best known, at the Abbey Church in Chartres, was said to be responsible for thousands of pregnancies."

Connecticut painter and photographer Anne Rowland, partly in response to the fundamentalist hysteria surrounding art work sponsored by the National Endowment for the Arts in the late 1980s, holds that "if we assign a gender to God, we must accept the deity as a sexual being, with all the ramifications that entails."

At the Gregg Kucera Gallery in Seattle, Washington, she exhibited in a 1991 show entitled "Dictu Sanctificare" not only "Jesus's Penis" (which was erect and circumcised, leading some "size queens" to comment about its smallness) but also "God's Penis" (which was flaccid and not circumcised, leading other wags to ask why He had not been mutilated).

She also exhibited "God's Beard," "Mary Magdalene's Hair," "Eve's Fig Leaf," "Jesus When He Was Just An Embryo," and other such works. Rowland is concerned about the politicization of religion in America and the censorious stance of the fundamentalist right. Fundamentalists have been infuriated by such a blasphemous cock-up. Others, however, noting that God's penis is flaccid whereas Jesus's is erect, compliment Rowland for giving an entirely original meaning to "religious member." (See entry for Circumcision.) {ACK}

CHRISTOPHER NEWPORT UNIVERSITY

Humanists at Christopher Newport University in Newport News, Virginia, are on the Web at: <www.secularhumanism.org/cfa/orgs.html>.

Christopher, James (1942—)

An editorial associate of *Free Inquiry*, Christopher founded an alternative to Alcoholics Anonymous (AA). Calling it the Secular Organization for Sobriety (SOS), he has organized a large number of groups which do not utilize the "higher power" concept of AA's 12-step plan. His program has received much favorable attention from a variety of counselors in medical and scientific circles in this and other nations. Christopher, who is a Secular Humanist Mentor of the Council for Democratic and Secular Humanism, is author of *SOS Sobriety, The Proven Alternative to 12-Step Programs* (1992). Christopher was a participant in 1996 at the Humanist World Congress held in Mexico City. (See entry for the Secular Organization for Sobriety.)

CHRONOLOGICAL ERAS: See entry for Eras.

Chubb, Percival (1860—1960)

An Englishman and charter member of the London Ethical Culture Society, Chubb became an Ethical Culture leader in New York, having been recruited and trained by Stanton Coit. From 1898 to 1904, he edited *Ethical Record*. From 1911 to 1933, he led the St. Louis society and was emeritus until his death. (See entry for Ethical Culture.) {EU, Howard B. Radest; HNS; RAT}

Chubb, Thomas (1679—1747)

An English deist, Chubb was one of the first to show rationalism among the common people. Gradually relinquishing supernatural religion, he came to consider that Jesus Christ was of the religion of Thomas Chubb. In his *A Farewell to His Readers* (1747), he appears to reject both revelation and special providence. {BDF; FUK; RAT}

Chugerman, Samuel (20th Century)

Chugerman wrote *Lester F. Ward: The American Aristotle* (1939). {FUS}

Chuman, Joseph (20th Century)

Chuman, a classics graduate of City College of New York who received his doctorate in religion at Columbia University, started Ethical Culture leadership training in 1967. He led briefly in Essex County, New Jersey, then settled as Leader in Bergen County. Chuman signed Humanist Manifesto II and has been on the editorial board of the *International Humanist*. He is on the Board of Governors of The Humanist Institute and is one of the members of the IHEU's Committee on Religious Extremism and Rational Inquiry.

In 1998 at the International Humanist and Ethical Union's congress in Mumbai, Chuman spoke about the resurgence of religion in North America, lamenting the fact that fundamentalists have become a powerful political force. E-mail: <jchuman@idt.net>. (See entry for Ethical Culture.) {EU, Howard B. Radest; HM2}

CHURCH AND STATE

President Thomas Jefferson's tombstone describes him not as a former President but as the father of the University of Virginia and the author of the Declaration and of the Virginia Statute for Religious Freedom. The latter was a law which he and James Madison struggled for nine years to get through the legislature. "The Virginia Statute," wrote Anthony Lewis in *The New York Times*, "not only rejected official support for a single, established church. It forbade neutral support for all denominations: which is what some Americans want government to do today. The statute's principles informed the religion clauses of the First Amendment, which was drafted by Madison."

Lewis, noting that in the 1800 campaign for President, Jefferson was attacked as an atheist, added, "In fact he believed in God despite his dislike of priesthoods and his rejection of biblical revelation, saying he "was a sect of one." He believed that diversity of creeds and separation of church from state would actually strengthen religion in America, a prediction which has proved true. In the absence of state involvement, religion has thrived.

On the Jefferson Memorial in Washington is carved his statement: "I have sworn upon the altar of God, eternal hostility against every form of tyranny over the mind of man," which he wrote about activities of the clergy. Lewis notes that Jefferson and John Adams, political opponents and longtime friends, both died on 4 July 1826, the 50th anniversary of the Declaration of Independence. Adams's last words were, "Jefferson still lives." (See entry for Protestants and Others United for the Separation of Church and State.)

CHURCH AND STATE (Ireland)

A quarterly, *Church and State* can be reached by contacting P. Maloney, Box 159, Cork, Ireland.

Church, Archibald (20th Century)

Church was editor of *The Realist, a Journal of Scientific Humanism* from 1929 to 1930. Lancelot Hogben was one of its contributors.

Church, Henry Tyrell (Died 1859)

Church was a lecturer and writer who edited Tallis's *Shakespeare*. He contributed to the *Investigator* when it was edited by Bradlaugh. {BDF}

Church, Mary Ann (19th Century)

Although not ordained, Church was listed in the *Universalist Register* (1838), making her the first woman in Canada to be officially recognized as a preacher.

CHURCH OF CHRIST

The Church of Christ, organized in 1830, is at PO Box 472, Independence, Missouri 64051.

CHURCH OF EUTHANASIA

The C of E (not to be confused with the Church of England) is led by the Rev. Chris Korda (PO Box 261, Somerville, MA 02143). In the tradition of the ancient May-Pole worshippers and heathen Free Spirits, the group is noted for its craziness. For example, it has One Commandment: "Thou Shall Not Procreate." The Four Pillars of the Church are Suicide, Abortion, Cannibalism, and Sodomy. In their efforts to restore "balance between Humans and the remaining species on Earth," they advocate "massive *voluntary* population reduction, which will require a leap in Human consciousness to a new *species awareness.*" Included among the 100,000 of bumper stickers the group has sold are the following:

- Save the Planet—Kill Yourself
- Eat People Not Animals
- Prevent AIDS—Aim for the Chin
- Thank You for Not Breeding
- Eat a Queer Fetus for Jesus
- God is Coming, Stick Out Your Tongue

The Church's on-line journal, *Snuff It*, is found at <http://www.envirolink.org/orgs/coe>. "Unfortunately," according to the Rev. Chris, "the group attracts Humanists like flies on crap, so the conversation tends to be dull to say the least. We occasionally try to liven things up a bit by posting sermons or articles from Snuff It. Feel free to lurk there, annoy the Humanists, and flame the idiots who post pro-life messages." {*Freethought History*, #23, 1997}

CHURCH OF GOD IN CHRIST

The Church of God in Christ, which has over 5,000,000 members, is at 939 Mason Street, Memphis, Tennessee 38126.

CHURCH OF JESUS CHRIST OF LATTER-DAY SAINTS

Commonly called Mormons, members of the Church of Jesus Christ of Latter-Day Saints believe that their founder, Joseph Smith, had golden tablets revealed to him by God. Those tablets, translated as the *Book of Mormon*, were dropped from the sky at Palmyra, New York. Mormons followed Smith westward, founding Salt Lake City in Utah in 1847, three years after a mob murdered Smith and his brother Hyrum in 1844. Under the leadership of Brigham Young, the Mormons weathered hardships and built a communal economy. Plural marriages within the group prevented Utah's admission to the Union until 1896, but in 1890 the church withdrew its sanction of polygamy. The church is led by a three-member First Presidency and by the Council of Twelve (the Apostles).

Mormons believe in baptizing those who died without hearing the Mormon message. As a result, they have established massive genealogical records which include an estimated 200,000,000 people who were baptized and added to the index. Included are Anne Frank, Joan of Arc, St. Francis of Assisi, Charlie Chaplin, W. C. Fields, and other non-Mormons. Because of intense pressure from Jewish groups, the Church of Jesus Christ of Latter Day Saints signed an agreement to remove from their Index all Jewish Holocaust victims, except those with descendants who are current Mormons and approve of their Jewish ancestors' inclusion.

A separatist group, the Reorganized Church of Jesus Christ of Latter-Day Saints, was organized in 1852 and has its headquarters in Independence, Missouri.

D. Michael Quinn, in *Same-Sex Dynamics Among Nineteenth-Century Americans: A Mormon Example* (1996), found that "most of Utah went apoplectic" at his assertions that several prominent Mormons might be gay. "When I wrote that [Mormon Church founder] Joseph Smith slept with men all his life," he told *The Advocate*, 3 March 1998), I meant *slept* with them." Quinn also alleged that the former director of the Mormon Tabernacle Choir never married and referred to his protégés as his "boy chums" and "the loves of [his] life." Quinn, who had been a full professor at Brigham Young University," resigned in 1988 and was excommunicated from the church in 1993. Quinn—himself a homosexual—laments the church's homophobia and its hyprocisy. (See entries for Steve Benson, grandchild of Ezra Taft Benson, a Mormon leader; for non-theists Charles Chaplin and W. C. Fields; and for Virgil Thomson.) {CE}

CHURCH OF POSITIVISM

In 1881 in Brazil the Church of Positivism was established. It emphasized the views of Auguste Comte, whose slogan "Order and Progress" appears on the Brazilian national flag.

CHURCH OF THE EXQUISITE PANIC: See entry for Robert Delford Brown.

CHURCH OF THE HOLY SPOOK

Shane McGowran is the Irish singer-author of a freethinking "Church of the Holy Spook."

CHURCH OF THE LARGER FELLOWSHIP

The Church of the Larger Fellowship, 25 Beacon Street, Boston, Massachusetts 02108, provides a ministry to Unitarian Universalists all over the world. For individuals who live nowhere near a Unitarian Universalist society, the organization keeps in touch by mail.

CHURCH ORGANISTS: See entry for Andrew DeMasi.

CHURCH UNIVERSAL AND TRIUMPHANT

The Church Universal and Triumphant, a Montana sect, was founded in 1957 by Elizabeth Clare Prophet and her husband Mark. The group has its roots in theosophy and has told the press that it establishes "direct mystical contact with divine principle through contemplation, revelation, and other techniques." Ms. Prophet claims to receive dictations from a host of spirits called Ascended Masters.

When the group in 1980 issued a warning of an imminent Soviet missile strike that could destroy the United States, several thousand followers sold belongings, left their families, and crammed into bomb shelters in mountains on the northern boundary of Yellowstone National Park. Enthusiasm waned when no attack occurred. Ms. Prophet, whom many followers call Mother, announced in 1997 that she and her fourth husband, Edward Francis, had divorced, which further disillusioned members, who had been told that "the marriage is divinely inspired." {*The New York Times*, 2 March 1997}

Churchill, Charles (1731—1764)

In *Gotham* (1763), Churchill, an English poet and satirist, wrote, "Faith is a necessary fraud at best." {TYD}

Churchill, R. C. (20th Century)

A freethinker, Churchill wrote *English Literature and the Agnostics* (1944) and *Art and Christianity* (1945). {GS}

Churchill, Randolph (1911-1968): For a comment by the son of Sir Winston Churchill, see entry for Bible.

Churchland, Patricia Smith (20th Century)

Churchland, a professor of philosophy at the University of California at San Diego, is a Humanist Laureate in the Council for Secular Humanism's International Academy of Humanism. She is the author of *Neurophilosophy and Alzheimer's Disease* (1992), *Neurophilosophy: Toward A Unified Science of the Mind-Brain* (1986), and *The Computational Brain* (1992).

In *Free Inquiry* (Fall 1995), she further developed contemporary notions of consciousness, neuroscience, and ethics. (See entries for Adam Carley, consciousness, and John R. Searle.) {CA; E}

Churchland, Paul (1942—)

Churchland, who teaches at the University of California in San Diego, is author of *The Engine of Reason, the Seat of the Soul: A Philosophical Journey into the Brain* (1995). For *The Journal of Philosophy* in 1981, he wrote, "Eliminative Materialism and Propositional Attitudes." He is married to Patricia Smith Churchland. {CA; E}

Chydenius, Anders (19th Century)

Chydenius was a noted non-theist in Finland. (See entry for Scandinavian Unbelievers.)

Chypere, John (20th Century)

A freethinker, Chypere wrote *A Psychoanalysis of Jesus Christ* (1986). {GS}

Ciardi, John (1916—1986)

A member of the Institute of Arts and Letters of the American Academy, Ciardi once proposed to *The Humanist* editor Priscilla Robertson that John Holmes be the magazine's poetry editor. She appointed Holmes soon thereafter. Ciardi had taught at Harvard and Rutgers, was poetry editor of *Saturday Review*, and translated

Dante's *Inferno*. His poetry is witty and includes vernacular diction. Three of Ciardi's works are *Homeward to America* (1940), *I Marry You* (1958), and *For Instance* (1979). A personable man, Ciardi had a special way with words. Asked what gentility is, he replied, "Gentility is what is left over from rich ancestors after the money is gone." He also once confided that of the various contemporary poets, he was one of the few who could afford a Cadillac. Ciardi was a signer of Humanist Manifesto II. {CE; HM2}

Ciccone, Madonna Louise Veronica: See entry for Madonna

Cicero, Marcus Tullius (106—43 B.C.E.)

According to Corliss Lamont, Cicero "showed an absolute disbelief in all the accepted practices of divination, but thought they should be fostered 'on account of popular opinion and of their great public utility.' "

During the French Revolution, Maréchal cited Cicero as being only a "possible" atheist. Robertson explains that Cicero devised a religious make-believe which paralleled the State. His outlook can be looked at as being historically, not theologically, appropriate for his day. He swears, for example, that "the Gods" exist, albeit it is their glory to do nothing. Yet, he held that "There are no miracles" and "What old woman is so stupid now as to tremble at those tales of hell which were once so firmly believed in?" In the last three years of his life, he reinforced his reputation as a major classical skeptic by writing *Concerning the Nature of the Gods* (44 B.C.E.), by which he made Greek philosophy accessible to Latin audiences, according to Gaskin. {CE; CL; EU,; JM; JMR; JMRH; TYD}

CIRCUMCISION

Male circumcision is an operation—a barbaric custom, according to many—which removes the foreskin covering the glans (so-called because of its acorn-like shape; acorn in Latin is *glans*) of the penis.

As a religious rite it was widespread throughout the Middle East before being introduced among the Hebrews, presumably by Abraham. Jews ordinarily perform the rite on the eighth day after the birth of the male child, and the practice is said to be a sign of the covenant between God and man. (Jewish comics have been known to say that although a *mohel*'s pay is lousy, at least the guy gets good tips. . . .)

According to the *Village Voice*, inflation has apparently resulted, and five hundred dollars has been charged in 1996 "for hacking a foreskin." *Acts* 15, however, states that Christians need not practice circumcision. Saint Catherine of Siena claimed that Jesus gave her his foreskin as a wedding ring, allowing her to become his bride "not with a ring of silver but with a ring of his holy flesh, for when he was circumcised just such a ring was taken from his holy body." She whipped herself three times a day, according to Ackerman: once for her own sins, once for the sins of living people, and once for the sins of the dead.

Although male circumcision is said to be performed as a sanitary measure, there are arguments both pro and con. Those who favor circumcision sometimes point out that penile carcinoma is almost unheard of in circumcised men; that circumcised boys are ten to twenty times less prone to urinary tract and bladder infections than their uncut peers; and that circumcision is associated with a 50-90% reduction in transmission of HIV (*Nature*, 1994). Kenyan microbiologist Maina Kahindo in 1999 described his study that found circumcised men were less likely to become HIV-infected.

Of 219,755 boys born in United States armed forces hospitals, a tenfold increase in the incidence of urinary tract infection was found among those who were uncircumcised. As for any pain involved, rabbis stated that a 30% lidocaine cream is applied thirty minutes before the procedure. Others, however, find it a brutal practice and blame organized religious groups for abusing children before they are able to object.

As times change, *mohalim* (the plural form for *mohel*, pronounced moyle) are presented with new problems. At a Bethesda, Maryland conference in 1998, they discussed how the *mohalim* could make the rite as meaningful as posssible to a gay or lesbian couple who have given birth to or adopted a baby: does the child of an interfaith couple need to be immersed in a *mikvah*, or ritual bath, or does the bris itself suffice? What should the mohel do when families ask for a postponement so that a grandparent can afford to attend from afar? Is a religious circumcision covered by insurance or managed care? And how do mohalim use the Internet to inform the public?

Are all Jews circumcised? Ronald Goldman, a Boston psychologist who founded The Circumcision Research Center in 1991, claims more than 200 Jewish-identified members are not. For example, Moshe Rothenberg is a Brooklyn, N.Y., social worker and high school guidance counselor who has held a bris-sans-circumcision meeting for more than a hundred local families, "a welcoming ceremony, a celebration of the newborn" that includes tree-planting, singing, dancing, or similar events. His son, 9-year-old Samuel is not circumcised. He cites scripture that he believes supports abjuring circumcision, but the majority of Jews counter that his interpretations are twistings and distortions.

Since the 1960s, some children in presumably frivolous lawsuits have demanded of parents that they replace their lost foreskins. Some studies indicate a reduction of such operations in the United States, although Jane E. Brody in *The New York Times* (25 May 94) estimates that 86% of newborn boys in this country are being circumcised. A number of Humanist leaders have said circumcision should be for medical reasons only. On the topic, Joseph Lewis wrote *In the Name of Humanity* (1956). In the 1990s, secular humanist groups have met to discuss circumcision, and Robert Gorham Davis in "The Unkindest Cut of All" (*Free Inquiry*, Fall, 1993) discussed the subject.

A 1997 study by National Health and Social Life researchers at the University of Chicago found that circumcision in the United States was most prevalent among white men and men from educated families (96% in Jewish families questioned but only 54% for Hispanic men). Circumcised men were found to be engaged in a wider range of sexual practices, like oral and anal sex and masturbation, but that routine circumcision did not, contrary to some past studies, lead to lower rates of sexually transmitted diseases. Since 1989, the American Academy of Pediatrics has been neutral on circumcision, leaving it up to parents and pediatricians.

"Which is better, to be or not to be circumcised?" Neither, according to current views, unless there is some specific medical reason. In England, circumcision levels dropped from 85% to near zero in the 1950s. In the 1990s, the United States was the only Western country (except for Israel) that still circumcised a majority (66% in 1995) of baby boys.

Pediatrics (March 1999), summarizing new information, reported that the American Academy of Pediatrics found no "medical indication" for circumcision, reversing its findings in 1989 that circumcision might bring "potential medical benefits." Although in the 1960's over 90% of American-born boys were circumcised before leaving the hospital, the figure has dropped to 60% today. The figure for Hispanic and Asian immigrants is closer to 36%.

Female circumcision, which involves the excision of the labia minora and clitoris (clitoridectomy), is common in Islam and in certain tribes of Africa, South America, and elsewhere. Africans who have worked to abolish the removal of all or part of a girl's external genitalia, usually to insure virginity or control sexuality, include New York human rights lawyer Seble Dawitt and Wellesley College filmmaker Salem Mekuria. Both oppose the practice and call for its eradication, but they argue that Africans must lead the fight, that "superior Western attitudes do not enhance dialogue or equal exchange of ideas. . . . Neither Alice Walker nor any of us here can speak for [African women]; but if we have the power and the resources, we can create the room for them to speak, and to speak with us as well." In 1993, Sudan, Kenya, Egypt, Ivory Coast, and Burkina Faso had taken legal or policy measures against genital mutilation. A leading secular humanist, Bangladesh's Taslima Nasrin, herself a physician, has written of her utter contempt for individuals who would genitally mutilate a child.

In 3001, according to Arthur C. Clarke's science-fiction novel, much will have changed:

> Circumcision made a lot of sense in primitive times but no longer. By the mid-twenty-first century so many malpractice suits had been filed that the American Medical Association had been forced to ban it. The practice, however, continued a century later, until "some

unknown genius coined a slogan—please excuse the vulgarity—"God designed us: circumcision is blasphemy."

{ACK; Sheila Anne Feeney, *NY Daily News*, 27 May 1997; *The Economist*, 27 Nov 1999}

Cirrincione, Gerald Angelo (20th Century)

Cirrincione, who is a talk show host on "Jazz and Conversation," and a cable interviewer on "Omniverse," is a freethinker who writes for *Truth Seeker*.

CIVIL RELIGION: See entry for Conor Cruise O'Brien.

CIVILIZATION

"Civilization" to many is a word with as many useless encrustments as "humanism." Some Europeans have joked that the symbol of American civilization is the tail fin on a Cadillac automobile. Lexicographers define civilization as "a relatively high level of cultural and technological development." *The Economist* in 1994 inquired why one group of men felt the need to kill another group, suggesting that what is involved is a conflict of specific interests, a clash of life-shaping ideas; and one group's belief that it is in blood and bone superior to the rest. The fundamental fear, that there will be a general war between Islam and the West, was followed by, "Not again, for heaven's sake." In short, the editors hoped that in the 20th century we would not return to the time of Pope Urban II, who in a sermon at Claremont in 1095 brought about the First Crusade against Islam. At the same time, *The Economist* noted the potential problems, the differences between the two groups concerning ideology, skin color, and conflicts of interest.

In 3001, according to the novel of the same name by Arthur C. Clarke, the character Ted Khan is described as being "still famous back on Earth for at least two of his sayings: 'Civilization and Religion are incompatible' and 'Faith is believing what you know isn't true.' "

Meanwhile, Samuel Huntington, a professor of Harvard University, holds that there currently are eight civilizations, or cultures, five of which (the Latin American, African, Slavic, Hindu, Japanese, Buddhist) are not potential problems. The three cultures he cites are (a) the West, the Euro-American culture that is the product of the Renaissance, the Reformation, and the Enlightenment, and is the begetter of modern capitalism and democracy; (b) Confucian, the body of ideas that has grown up around the Chinese language and the habits of public life that are said to belong to the Chinese region; and (c) Islam, which claims to be an idea based upon a transcendental certainty, that of the word of God, revealed syllable by syllable to Muhammad in a dusty corner of Arabia 1,400 years ago, and copied down by him into the Qur'an.

Brian Beedham of *The Economist* argues that the West and the 1.2 billion followers of Islam have every reason to cease their perpetual confrontation, that they should not overlook the Confucian. (See entry for K'ung Fu-tzu.)

Cjecka, Victor (20th Century)

Cjecka started editing *Vek Rozumu* in New York in 1910, later moving his monthly publication to Berwyn, Illinois.

Clafin, Adelaide Avery (19th Century)

Clafin was one of the early graduates, 1896, of Meadville/Lombard Theological School, and she was ordained as a Unitarian minister in 1897. {*World*, May-June 1995}

Clampett, W. Frederick (20th Century)

Clampett, a freethinker, wrote *Luther Burbank, "Our Beloved Infidel": His Religion of Humanity* (1926). {FUS}

Clanton, Gordon (1942—)

Clanton was an assistant professor at Trenton State College in New Jersey when he signed Humanist Manifesto II. {HM2}

Clapp, Theodore (Born 1792)

Clapp, a Unitarian, was a pioneer religious liberal in New Orleans, Louisiana. {U}

Claretie, Jules Armand Arsène (1840—1910)

A French writer, Claretie wrote biographies of celebrities, La libre parole [Free Speech] (1868), and Camille Desmoulins (1875).

The 1868 work was the result of having been refused by the minister of Public Instruction to lecture on one occasion, whereupon Claretie issued a vigorous defense of free thought and speech. Claretie, one of the leading French writers in the second half of the nineteenth century, was a member of the French Academy. {BDF; JM}

Claretie, Jules Arsène Arnaud (Born 1840)

Claretie was a French author who won distinction as a journalist and drama critic. His *La Libre Parole* (1868) was a rationalistic defense of free speech. Claretie was a Commander of the Legion of Honour and a member of the French Academy. {RAT}

Clarey, (Reynold) Arnold (1897—1972)

Clarey was an Australian rationalist, Unitarian, accountant, and politician. A Freemason, he opposed state aid to denominational schools. {SWW}

Clark, Alex (20th Century)

Clark, of the Auckland United Atheists in New Zealand, was one of the founding members of Campus Freethought Alliance. {*International Humanist News*, December 1996}

Clark, Brad N. (20th Century)

Clark, a correctional educator in California, is a member of Atheists and Other Freethinkers in Sacramento.

He wrote "How Religion Impedes Moral Development" in *Free Inquiry* (Summer 1994) and "Acts of God and Other Disasters." (*Secular Nation*, Fall 1994).

Clark, Dorine (20th Century)

"The Masochistic Myth" by Clark appeared in Joseph Lewis's freethought magazine, *Age of Reason* (January, 1966). For the same publication, she wrote "The Voice of the Truth" (January, 1967).

Clark, Harry Hayden (1901—1971)

Clark edited *Poems of Freneau* (1929). {FUS}

Clark, Jaden (20th Century)

Clark, a secular humanist who writes reviews for the *Gay & Lesbian Humanist*, wrote the film script for "Wavelengths." It is a short, stylish film about a quest for gay love in contemporary London.

Clark, Jonas Gilman (1815—1900)

Clark was an American philanthropist. The $2,000,000 he gave for the founding of Clark University was called "the largest sum ever given in New England up to that time by any individual for education." Clark was a rationalist and expressly stipulated that no religion was to be taught in it. However, its first president, Stanley Hall, pressed Clark to allow it. {RE}

Clark, Oscar (20th Century)

Clark, a New Zealander who is working for a doctorate in chemistry, is treasurer of Auckland University Atheists. With sophomoric wit, he has described his hobby as "inventing a cult Christian Killer (I, II & III) series of games."

Clark, Thomas Welbourne (20th Century)

Clark, associate director of the Institute for Naturalistic Philosophy in Cambridge, Massachusetts, has noted that humanism has been broadly naturalistic but that it now is at odds "with the postmodern denial of universal, perspective-neutral reason." He edited *The Novel in India* (1970). In "Humanism and Postmodernism, A Reconciliation" (*The Humanist*, Jan-Feb 1993),

Clark concluded that "Humanists will always want to argue naturalism against theism, evidence against faith, rationality against superstition, and the individual against the herd; but to find allies for the *real* fight, the pragmatic recommendation is to see where one's presumed opponents stand on *practical* issues. When and if agreement is reached about ends and means, many ideological differences can safely remain unresolved. The humanistic project will continue on in as many different guises and under as many different names as our tolerance for ideological diversity will permit."

In "Secularism and Sexuality" (*The Humanist,* May-June 1994), he makes the case for gay equality. In the scientific view, he notes, everything in nature, including sodomy, is literally and unavoidably natural. The harm of homosexual behavior or homosexual partnerships is simply and only a function of homophobia and heterosexism, he holds, and after homosexual marriage is adopted in keeping with the U. S. Constitution's protection, "many will wonder what all the fuss was about. How could anyone have supposed that being gay or lesbian was intrinsically immoral or deviant or sick? On what basis, precisely, did they think that homosexuals should be denied *any* right or privilege given to heterosexuals?" Says Clark, the central truth is that prejudice against homosexuals is "a religiously incited and secularly unfounded bigotry."

Clark's web site regarding naturalism is <http://www.naturalism.org>.

Clark, W. E. (20th Century)

Clark, a freethinker, wrote *Can Jesus Save?* (1910). {GS}

Clark, Warner (20th Century)

Clark has been an active member of the American Humanist Association. {HNS}

Clarke, Arthur C(harles) [Sir] [C.B.E.] (1917—)

Clarke, a preeminent writer of science fiction, a Commander of the British Empire who was knighted in 1997, emigrated in 1956 from England to Sri Lanka, where he became one of that island's major figures. He is Chancellor of the University of Moratuwa and of the International Space University in Sri Lanka.

In 1968, he wrote the memorable science fiction work, *2001.* The dean of the science fiction genre, he has become internationally famous partly because his work has been turned into realistic motion pictures, notably "2001," which have captured the imaginations of so many viewers. Science fiction, which sometimes resembles Utopian fiction, is a literary type whose writers have included Mary Shelley, Poe, Verne, Fitz-James O'Brien, and H. G. Wells. Samuel Clemens's *A Connecticut Yankee in King Arthur's Court* is exemplary of the genre. Aldous Huxley, Ray Bradbury, and Kurt Vonnegut Jr. have used it as an instrument of social criticism.

When a farm lad in Minehead, England, Clarke had a job as mail deliverer that required him to ride his bicycle on winter nights. He had already started a serious collection of science fiction magazines, and from his bicycle the teenager gazed into the night sky, sure that one day men would walk on the moon and leave their bootprints on the red sands of Mars. His certainty that the exploration of space was inevitable found few that were in agreement. Even in the RAF he was considered some kind of screwball, always talking about the British Interplanetary Society and taking it for granted that rocket-launched satellites could be made to remain stationary over the Earth. When the Nazi V-2 rockets began raining terror on British cities, his "crackpot views" suddenly became credible.

Beginning in the mid 1940s and with the subsequent travel into outer space, authors such as Clarke have extended science fiction into new realms, extrapolating about the future of space travel and anticipating the resultant problems and challenges which will face humankind.

Neil McAleer, in *Arthur C. Clarke, The Authorized Biography* (1992), reveals the following details about the author whose books have sold more than fifty million copies:

- During World War II, inductees into the RAF who had no religious affiliation were required to put "Church of England" on their dogtags. Clarke, who unhappily had gone to an Anglican Sunday school as a farm lad, refused. "I got the man who was handling the paperwork and made them change it to pantheist," he explained. From his youth, he has had a consistent aversion to organized religion, saying faith is no substitute for knowledge.

- In 1943 while in the RAF, he complained to C. S. Lewis that his novels attacked scientific humanism in general and scientists and astronauts in particular.

- Early in 1970, he told the *Playboy* interviewer, "I have a longstanding bias against religion that may be reflected in my comments," adding that he could not forgive religions for the wars and atrocities they have inspired. Many, said Clark, "confuse religion with a belief in God. Buddhists don't necessarily believe in a god or a supreme being at all; whereas one could easily believe in a supreme being and not have any religion." Clarke knew Buddhism well, having chosen in the 1970s to live in Sri Lanka.

- When a "20 / 20" ABC camera once captured the parade of the Buddha's tooth, the Perahera, Clarke observed to the reporter, "I'm anti-mysticism. I'm very anti the sort of lamebrains who accept anything fanciful, nonsensical like pyramid power, astrology, which is utter rubbish, much UFOlogy, flying saucers. There's so much garbage floating around and on the newsstands. This is one thing that does worry me about the present mental state of the West, not only the United States. At the same time, I'm sure there are many very strange things in the universe."

- When in the USSR it was revealed that *2010: Odyssey Two* takes place aboard Cosmonaut Leonov's spaceship, officials at first were delighted. But then they read the book's dedication:

  Dedicated, with respectful admirection,
  to two great Russians both depicted herein:
  General Alexei Leonov
  Cosmonaut, Hero of the Soviety Union, Artist
  and
  Academician Andrei Sakharov
  Scientist, Nobel Laureate, Humanist

  Sakharov had been banished to Gorky two years prior, and officials thereupon banned the book.

- His story, "The Nine Billion Names of God," describes two computer engineers hired by a sect of Tibetan monks to program and run a computer to help generate the nine billion names of God, which they have worked on for three centuries. They believe that once their goal is reached, God's purpose will end and mankind will have completed its reason for existence. Clarke's memorable endline: "Overhead, without any fuss, the stars were going out." When he read the story in 1997, the Dalai Lama wrote to Clarke, "Your short story titled 'The Nine Billion Names of God' was particularly amusing."

- His story, "The Star," has an opening line that describes the conflicting scientific and religious systems of belief: "It is three thousand light-years to the Vatican."

• To Pope Pius XII's statement that exploring space is simply to fulfill mankind's God-given potential, Clarke wrote, "Any path to knowledge is a path to God—or to Reality, whichever word one prefers to use."

• Father Lee Lubbers, a Jesuit priest and one of the dozens McAleer interviewed for the book, recalls that when he met the man who had first predicted telecommunications via satellite, Clarke stepped out from behind his desk, extended his right hand, "as though he were protesting dramatically that I was going to convert him before he could reach the other end of the room," all the while saying, "I am an atheist."

• In 1975, addressing the U.S. Congress, Clarke remarked, "It is true that we must cherish and conserve the treasures of this fragile Earth, which we have so shamefully wasted. . . . It may be that the old astrologers had the truth exactly reversed, when they believed that the stars controlled the destinies of men. The time may come when men control the destinies of stars."

Mark Nuttal, a reporter for the London *Times* interviewed Clarke (4 Aug 1992), asserting there had been a spate of books linking science and an ultimate creator with titles such as *The Mind of God.* And would he comment, please? To which Clarke responded, "I remain an aggressive agnostic."

Time, in a special Fall 1992 issue, "Beyond the Year 2000," published Clarke's "The Hammer of God," a story set in the third millennium about an asteroid that imperils the earth—it was only the second piece of fiction ever to be published by the magazine, the first having been a 1969 selection by Aleksandr Solzhenitsyn. The story was further evidence of Clarke's agnosticism and philosophic naturalism, and it pointed up the dangers of any increases in religious fundamentalist groups around the world.

A member and an active supporter of the Secular Humanist Society of New York, Clarke has long been on record as being a nonbeliever. "It may be that our role on this planet is not to worship God," he once wrote, "but to create him." A Humanist Laureate in the Council for Secular Humanism's International Academy of Humanism, Sir Arthur signed Humanist Manifesto 2000 .

Isaac Asimov, also an active supporter of the Secular Humanist Society of New York, was his friend and sparring partner. As for Clarke's ability to reconcile materialistic science with a kind of mystic imagination, Asimov wrote:

> Old Arthur C. Clarke of Sri Lanka
> Now sits in the sun sipping Sanka
> Enjoying his ease
> Excepting when he's
> Receiving pleased notes
> from his banker.

Clarke, the man who first put forward the concept of a communications satellite in 1945, also predicted then that the first flight around the moon would be in 1967— a year early—and that the first manned moon landing would be between 1970 and 1972—just six months off. His longer-term forecasts were not so accurate: that the first flight around Mars would be in 1980 and the first landing there would be in 1990. In 1966 he predicted that the actual colonization of other planets would take place by the year 2000. And he believes "there's a 99% chance of life all over the universe and a 90% chance of intelligent life being all over the place as well." By 2015, he has recently stated, a baby will have been born on Mars.

Clarke extrapolated further in a 1997 novel, *3001*. The character of Frank Poole, who had been killed by Hal the computer in *2001*, is accidentally discovered in a frozen state. He awakes in a rather dull utopia, in which organized religion, circumcision, meat-eating, madness, prisons, and poverty have all disappeared. Earth's ten billion humans became no longer habitable, so a remaining one billion now lived in a cartwheel, its rim in orbit, its spokes reaching down to the earth at the hub. Poole, after getting his bearings, leaves for the Jovian satellite Europa, finding one of the big black monoliths mentioned also in *2001*, *2010*, and *2061*, monoliths which imply a connection with the meaning of existence.

The visionary Clarke at one point cites Lucretius, who

> . . . hit it on the nail when he said that religion was the by-product of fear—a reaction to a mysterious and often hostile universe. For much of human prehistory, it may have been a necessary evil—but why was it so much more evil than necessary—and why did it survive when it was no longer necessary?

He also notes that

> . . . most of the other religions, with a few honorable exceptions, were just as bad as Christianity. . . . Even in your century, little boys were kept chained and whipped until they'd memorized whole volumes of pious gibberish, and robbed of their childhood and manhood to become monks. . . . Perhaps the most baffling aspect of the whole affair is how obvious madmen, century after century, would proclaim that they—and they alone!—had received messages from God. If all the messages had agreed, that would have settled the matter. But of course they were wildly discordant—which never prevented self-styled messiahs from gathering hundreds—sometimes millions—of adherents, who would fight to the death against equally deluded believers of a microscopically differing faith.

Lest that leave any doubt as to his outlook, Clarke informed the media that he considered the Pope as well as Mother Teresa two of the most dangerous people in the world, this because of their doctrinal stands on condom usage, the rights of women to become church leaders, sexuality, family planning, etc.

"Would you argue that anyone with strong religious beliefs was insane?" Poole asks Dr. Khan in *3001*. Khan replies, "In a strictly technical sense, yes—if they really were sincere, and not hypocrites. As I suspect ninety percent were." (See "God, Science, and Delusion," a chat about mankind, morality, and religion that Matt Cherry had with Sir Arthur, in *Free Inquiry*, Spring 1999.) {CA; CE; E; WAS, extensive correspondence}

Clarke, David (20th Century)

An experienced Unitarian minister with a doctorate, Clarke commenced in-service training with West Coast Ethical Culture Societies in the 1980s. (See entry for Ethical Culture.)

Clarke, James Freeman (1810—1888)

Clarke, a Unitarian and a theologian, edited the *Western Messenger* (1833—1840) and taught at Harvard Divinity School. He was a member of the Transcendental Club, along with Bronson Alcott and Ralph Waldo Emerson. Clarke was active in the anti-slavery, woman-suffrage, and other reform movements. He wrote *Ten Great Religions* (1872—1883) and *Non-Essentials in Religion* (1878). {CE; EG; U; U&U}

Clarke, John (19th Century)

A Methodist who then changed his opinion by studying the Bible, Clarke became one of Carlile's shopmen. In 1824 he was tried for selling a blasphemous libel of *The Republican* and after a spirited defence, in which he read many of the worst passages in the Bible, was sentenced to three years' imprisonment. While in prison he wrote *A Critical Review of the Life, Character, and Miracles of Jesus* (1825, 1839), a work showing with some bitterness much bold criticism and Biblical knowledge. {BDF}

Clarke, Malcolm Gordon (1910-1999)

Clarke, who was born in Lahore and who once fled South Africa because of its apartheid regime, taught mathematics in Zambia and became head of Science and Education at the University of Lusaka. An avowed atheist and a subscriber to *Freethinker*, he willed that he be cremated with no service. {*Freethinker*, July 1999}

Clarke, Marcus Andrew Hislop (1846—1881)

Clarke was an early Australian atheist, journalist, and author. He wrote for the Melbourne *Argus* and the *Victorian Review*. One of his noted articles in 1879 was "Civilisation Without Delusion," in which he described the new civil society that had abandoned belief in miracles and Christ's divinity; "where the fear of judgment and the hope of redemption had lost their force and there was no longer absolute certainty of any life other than this." When accused of being an atheist, he began a literary debate and was said to have scored a notable victory. {BDF; SWW; RAT; RE; TRI}

Clarke, Rebecca Sophia (1833-1906)

Clarke, a Unitarian, wrote children's books.

Clarkson, Frederick (20th Century)

Clarkson, a widely published journalist, author, and public speaker, co-authored with Skipp Porteous *Challenging The Christian Right: The Activists Handbook*. To successfully counter religious fundamentalism, he holds, "will likely depend on our ability to reclaim the legacy of Madison and Jefferson—as articulate, passionate, and credible advocates of pluralism, and as active and strategic practitioners of participatory democracy." {*Free Inquiry*, Fall 1996}

CLASSICAL HUMANISM

At the end of the Middle Ages, or from the 14th to 16th centuries, a revival of letters commonly known as the Renaissance occurred. During this period a genuine desire arose among some scholars to bring about an emancipation of thought and education from what they considered to be excessive domination on the part of the medieval Church over their thoughts and actions. Such was the beginning of classical humanism, an interest in *studia humanitatis, litterae humaniores*, and so-called polite learning.

Although some of the classical humanists were anti-clerical and critical of the Church, such an attitude was not a prerequisite. What was wanted was not an elimination of control but rather a broadening of outlook on the part of the Church toward the development of individual learning and research. In fact, classical humanists often were supernaturalists and members of the Church. At least two—Nicholas V and Leo X—were Popes. After Pope Martin V in 1417, the papacy increasingly warmed to humanistic ideas, and a Vatican Library document defines Renaissance humanism as a "belief not in the unique value of the individual but in the transcendent value of scholarship."

Whereas ancient humanism is, by definition, a thing of the past, classical humanism has persisted and is prevalent even today. Contemporary classical humanists, however, are not so concerned with theological criticism as were their historical namesakes, for most are educators interested in the problems of the humanities, as contrasted with the sciences. When, for instance, one sees titles such as "The Liberal Arts in Public Education," "Scholarship and Humanism," and "Humanism in Education," classical humanism is being discussed.

The two greatest classical humanists of the Renaissance period in Italy were Francesco Petrarca (Petrarch) and Giovanni Boccaccio. Both looked to the "humaner letter" for their mental salvation, and in so doing they dug up forgotten classics, helped restore the culture of the past, and assisted in recapturing some of the mighty spirit of early thinkers.

One of the most extensive lists of classical humanists is to be found in Paolo Giovio's *Elogia* (published in Antwerp, 1557). Giovio included Pietro Pompanazzi, who championed a purified Aristotelianism, as against neo-Platonism, and brought about a new interest in the classics—somewhat of a typical classical humanist, he believed in the soul and the possibility of miracles; Gemisthos Pletho, the scholar who encouraged the study of Plato and neo-Platonism and whose aim seems to have been the substitution of a neo-Platonic mysticism for Christianity; Pico della Mirandola; Giordano Bruno, who was steeped in Platonic and Pythagorean speculations and was later to influence such philosophers as Spinoza, Leibniz, Descartes, and Schelling; Campanella, whose humanism was manifest in his belief that man can truly know only himself, that like can be known only by like, and that therefore man cannot know anything of the universe except through the medium of sense-perception; Pietro Bembo; Bruni; Trapozuntius the Cretan; Cardinal Bessarion; Valla, whose *De Voluptate* was an imitation of Cicero's *Tusculans*; Beccadelli, sometimes called the poet of pornography; Enea Silvio dei Piccolomini; Platina; Michael Chrysoloras; Theodore Gaza; Johannes Argyropulos; Demetrius Chalcondylas; Musurus of Crete; Lascaris; Lorenzo de' Medici; Ermolao Barbaro; Politian; and Savanarola.

Other classical humanists: Luigi Marsiglio, leader of the Florentine club of humanists; Coluccio Salutati, Chancellor of State whose letters set the pace for style at that time; Cosimo de' Medici, founder of the Florentine Academy; Marsiglio Ficino; Estienne Dolet, champion of a Ciceronianism against Erasmus and, because he was burned in Paris for heresy, a martyr of the Renaissance; Adrien Turnebe, teacher who advanced Greek scholarship; Julius Caesar Scaliger, writer who attacked Erasmus; Robert Estienne, publisher with his brother, Henri Estienne, of numerous classical publications; Ludovico Vives and Telesio, who boldly criticized the strong entrenchments of Aristotelianism; and Giovanni Pico della Mirandola, who favored Platonism to such an extent that he was finally brought under the ban of the Church.

Well-known French classical humanists were Michel de Montaigne and Rabelais. Also, there were the following: Jean de Montreuil, a disciple of Petrarch; Nicholas de Clemanges, known for his Ciceronian eloquence; John Lascaris, who taught Greek at the University of Paris; Jerome Aleander, who added the study of Hebrew at the University of Paris; Guillaume Budé, sometimes called the best Greek scholar of his day in Europe; Lefevrew d'Etaples, who translated the Bible; and Guillaume Farel.

German classical humanists included Johann Reuchlin; Ulrich von Hutten; Philip Melanchton; and the following: Alexander Hegius, one of Erasmus's professors; Gregor von Heimburg, scholar of the Italian humanists though often repelled by them; Peter Luder, renowned student of his day; Mutianus Rufus, leader of the Erfurt group of humanists; Rudolf Agricola, leader of the Heidelberg group and of whom Erasmus said was "the first to bring us out of Italy a breath of higher culture"; Johann Eik, opponent of Luther at Ingolstadt; Urbanus Rhegius, zealous supporter of Luther; Wilibald Pirkheimer, leader of the Nuremberg group of humanists; Conrad Peutinger, an Augsburg humanist; Jacob Wimpfeling, a Strasbourg schoolmaster; and Sebastian Brant, satirist from Strasbourg.

Spanish humanists included Antonio Lebrixa and Cardinal Ximenes.

Scottish thinkers in the same tradition were George Buchanan and Andrew Melville.

A hotbed for classical humanism in England was the Oxford Group, from which came such supporters as the four "Oxford reformers," Thomas Linacre, William Grocyn, John Colet, and William Lyly. Generally considered to be the most important English humanist, however, was Sir Thomas More, a contemporary of the Dutch "humanist of humanists," Erasmus. Additional English classical humanists included the following: Sir Thomas Elyot; Sir Thomas Smith and Sir John Checke, who established Greek at Cambridge; William Baldwin; John Leland; John Bale, John Stow; William Camden; Thomas Wilson; Richard Hooker; John Fisher; William Tyndale; William Latimer; and Roger Ascham, sometimes called "the last humanist" because his style was allegedly so perfect that it was no longer necessary for the English to travel abroad for a humanistic model.

The chief Italian collectors of manuscripts were Guarino Veronese and Poggio Bracciolini, ardent bibliophiles, along with Angelo Ambrogini and Francesco Filelfo.

But of all the classical humanists, Erasmus is perhaps the most famous, and his influence upon the Oxford Group and English classical humanists was considerable.

Erasmus, More, and Colet all remained in the Church, although never hesitating to offer what they considered to be constructive criticism. More's *Utopia*, as well as Sir Francis Bacon's *New Atlantis* and Campanella's *City of the Sun*, advanced and furthered the principle that experiment and research with their resulting discoveries were to be used for human well-being, an idea which gave an added impetus to the natural sciences and the part they should play in assisting the improvement of material and social conditions of mankind. {CE; ER; Warren Allen Smith, "The Seven Humanisms."}

Claude-Constant (19th Century)

Claude-Constant was author of a freethinkers' catechism, published at Paris in 1875. {BDF}

Clausse, Arnold (20th Century)

At the Ninth International Humanist and Ethical Union (IHEU) World Congress held in Oslo (1986), Prof. Clausse from Belgium received a Humanist Award "for his contribution to the advance of humanist thought, especially in the fields of education and psychology." He wrote *L'epopee laique, ou la conquete des libertés* (1982).

Clausson, Nils (20th Century)

A teacher in Regina, Saskatchewan, Clausson wrote "In Search of the Gay Lifestyle" (*Humanist in Canada*, Spring 1999). It is illogical to talk about a heterosexual or a homosexual lifestyle, he reasoned.

Although people belong to a different culture, one would not for example say that Muslims with their different culture "have a different lifestyle." Or "being black in America, or native in Saskatchewan, or of French descent in Quebec is not a lifestyle. To use the word in that context is to trivialize the lives of blacks, natives, and Quebecois." Clausson finds redundant the phrase "chosen lifestyle," and he points out that one can go from multiple sexual partners to serial monogamy, thereby changing lifestyles. But a gay person in a city who moves to the country will not by so doing change his fundamental identity.

Clavel, Adolphe (Born 1815)

Clavel was a French positivist and physician. {BDF}

Clavel, F. T. B. (19th Century)

A French author of a *Picturesque History of Freemasonry* and also a *Picturesque History of Religions* (1844), Clavel had Christianity take a subordinate place in religious history. {BDF}

Clayton, Robert (1695—1758)

Clayton successively was Bishop of Killala, Cork, and Clogher. In 1756 he proposed in the Irish House of Lords the omission of the Nicene and Athanasian creeds from the liturgy.

A legal prosecution was instituted, but he died, Wheeler reports, from nervous agitation before the matter was decided. {BDF}

Cleanthes (c. 331—232 B.C.E.)

Cleanthes was the second head of the Stoic school, the philosopher who followed Zeno. His *Hymn to Zeus* is said to have blended free will and fate.

Cleave, John (19th Century)

Cleve was a bookseller, one of the pioneers of a cheap political press. He started the *London Satirist* and *Cleve's Penny Gazette of Variety* (1837—1844). In 1840, he was sentenced to four months' imprisonment for selling Haslam's *Letters to the Clergy*. {BDF}

Cleland, John (1709—1789)

Cleland wrote *Fanny Hill, or the Memoirs of a Woman of Pleasure* (1748—1749) which censor Anthony Comstock has called "the most obscene book ever written." What Comstock found was thirty acts of copulation and perversion but no four-letter word. Fanny was a fifteen-year-old lass whose acrobatic bedroom experiences netted Cleland twenty guineas but earned £10,000 for its printer. However, the bookseller, Drybutter, was punished in the pillory for having "altered the language of the book for the worse after it had been favorably noticed in the *Monthly Review.*" Lord Granville, when he presided over the Privy Council, got Cleland a pension of £100 per year so long as Cleland promised that he would write no more dirty books. Irving Wallace has written, "Cleland's *Fanny Hill* remained the major underground classic of erotic literature for over two centuries, until it was published openly by the New York firm of G. P. Putnam's Sons in 1963. Putnam's was taken to trial, won, lost an intermediate appeal, and in 1964 won again in New York's Court of Appeals, 4 votes to 3. Fanny Hill was free at last." For some reason, the 18th century work never made the Vatican's list of prohibited reading.

Although in his later life Cleland was accused of being a sodomite, such may have been a conjecture based on an interpretation that he was the first-person narrator, Fanny, of *Fanny Hill.* {GL; PA}

Clemenceau, Georges [Premier] (1841—1929)

Twice the premier of France (1906—1909; 1917—1920), Clemenceau was called "the Tiger." Trained as a physician, he was in conflict with Napoleon III because of a belief in republicanism, so he went (1865) to the United States as a journalist and teacher. When Napoleon III was overthrown (1870), Clemenceau returned to France and had a stormy life in politics, once being implicated in a Panama Canal scandal. A passionate defender of Alfred Dreyfus, he later led France during World War I and was a main antagonist of Woodrow Wilson at the Paris Peace Conference. The humanist historian Geoffrey Bruun wrote a definitive biography (1943), as did Wythe Williams (*The Tiger of France*).

E. M. Forster, however, said of the Tiger who "urged millions to die" that "[P]inch the book where you will, and it does not move. Not only are the characters 'dead' . . . being mere bundles of qualities, but the scenery, the social face of Paris, is also defunct."

"As a result of quarrels over heresies," Clemenceau wrote, "what massacres followed among Christians in the name of the common God of universal charity." Clemenceau was an honorary associate of the British Rationalist Press Association, which in 1899 had been founded by Charles A. Watts. Before dying, he asked for no burial procession, no official or religious ceremony, and a tomb without inscription and surrounded by a simple iron railing. {CE; Robert Craft, *The New York Review of Books*, 6 May 1999; BDF; JM; RAT; RE; TYD}

Clemens, Samuel [Mark Twain] (1835—1910)

"Both Mark Twain and his inventor, Samuel Clemens, continue to give trouble to those guardians of the national mythology to which Twain added so much in his day, often deliberately," Gore Vidal has written. He then cites an "academic critic," Guy Cardwell, who "tells us that Clemens was sexually infantile, burnt-out at fifty (if not before), and given to pederastic reveries about little girls, all the while exhibiting an unnatural interest in outhouse humor and other excremental vileness." Vidal adds, "It is hard to believe that at century's end, academics of this degraded sort are still doing business, as Twain would put it, at the same old stand." Referring to Cardwell's description that Clemens was "banal anal," Vidal comments, "as opposed to 'floral oral?' "

Vidal is one of many, including William Dean Howells, Bernard DeVoto, Van Wyck Brooks, and Lionel Trilling, who have praised the unique American writer generally considered to be one of its top humanists.

Mark Twain's *What Is Man?* (1906) and *Letters from Earth* (published posthumously in 1962) contain a savage attack on orthodox

Christianity. Generally conceded to be one of the foremost if not the foremost of American authors, Clemens is noted for his humor and philosophic gems:

- Man is the only animal that blushes. Or needs to.
- Adam was but human—this explains it all. He did not want the apple for the apple's sake; he wanted it only because it was forbidden.
- When angry, count a hundred; when very angry, swear.
- He (Satan) hasn't a single salaried helper; the Opposition employ a million.
- The first thing a missionary teaches a savage is indecency. He makes him put clothes on. He is as innocent and clean-minded up to that time as were our first parents before the Lord and not ashamed. He hid the knowledge of indecency from them; the missionary doesn't.
- Satan to newcomer, with discontent: "The trouble with you Chicago people is that you think you are the best people in Hell—whereas you are merely the most numerous."
- Martyrdom covers a multitude of sins.
- There is nothing more impressive than a miracle, except credulity that can take it at par.
- Clothes make the man? Nonsense! Clothes are not important. Why, I'd rather associate with Sarah Bernhardt, without a stitch on, than with General Grant in full uniform!
- In God We Trust. It is simple, direct, gracefully phrased. It always sound well—In God We Trust. I don't believe it would sound any better if it were true.
- It ain't those parts of the Bible that I can't understand that bother me—it's the parts that I do understand.

With Voltaire-like wit, he satirized hypocrisy and gullibility in *The Man That Corrupted Hadleyburg* (1900), which some considered cynical. He mercilessly attacked Mary Baker Eddy's new religion in *Christian Science* (1907), which some said was sacrilegious. His daughter, Clara, suppressed *Letters from Earth* for a long time after his death, believing Soviet Union intellectuals were using it to mock American values. In their *Freethought on the American Frontier*, Whitehead and Muhrer conclude that basically Clemens was a theist. The late critic Philip Foner wrote, in *Mark Twain: Social Critic*, a good analysis of the writer as an infidel: "It is true that, rather early in life, Twain began to doubt the truth of his religious teachings, and, as his faith in Christian dogma vanished, he rejected orthodox religion. Nonetheless, Twain was deeply interested in the relationship of institutionalized religion to man and society, particularly in reconciling Christian ethics and the social structure of his own day. Hence, while he indicted the influence of religion and the church when it served to fetter man and society, he also called for a religion and a church that would help man and society. A sincere, courageous, vital, realistic, dynamic religion for him meant one that would inspire people to create a better world. He urged all churches, as a major step toward this goal, to tear from Christianity all the camouflage of self-deception, hollow sham and hypocrisy, to strip it of the ornamentation of the ages and to return to the original, sound principles of Jesus Christ—the ethics of humanity. Although Clemens would not like to have been called a philosopher, he might agree to being described as the first philosopher ever to discuss the moral position of the God who created flies." Twain in his *The Book of Mormon* called the Mormon bible "an insipid mess of inspiration. It is chloroform in print." In *Following the Equator*, he observed, "There are those who scoff at the schoolboy, calling him frivolous and shallow. Yet it was the schoolboy who said 'Faith is believing what you know ain't so.'" In *Pudd'nhead Wilson's Calendar*, he wrote, "Let us endeavor so to live that when we come to die even the undertaker will be sorry."

Huckleberry Finn, generally said to be his best work, has also been termed *the* major United States novel. Its theme, man's inhumanity to man, has appealed to adolescents, as has his *Tom Sawyer*, with its humanistic and happy ending. Secular humanists are particularly interested in some of the lesser-known works that show his philosophic outlook: Extracts *From Adam's Diary* (1904); *Eve's Diary* (1906); and *Captain Stormfield's Visit to Heaven* (1909).

Clemens was one of the first seven chosen by secret ballot to be one of the original members of the American Academy of Arts and Letters. He did not, however, receive the most votes: William Dean Howells, whose works have not had the long life of Twain's, did. Clemens, however, received more than Henry James.

In 1908, responding to a person who asked if he would include Jesus among the 100 greatest men of history, Clemens said he would include Jesus as well as Satan. "These two gentlemen," he explained, "have had more influence than all others put together, and 99% of it was Satan's." He added that the devil is "worth very nearly a hundred times as much to the business as was the influence of the rest of Holy Family put together."

Clemens and wife Lizzie, daughter of Judge Jervis J. Langdon of Elmira, New York, had three daughters and one son. His personal misfortunes were many. His son died in infancy, and one daughter died in her teens. When his wife died, Clemens never remarried. Some critics have suggested that his personal troubles led him to become misanthropic. But even when he was in bankruptcy, he was a public hero, one who was greatly in demand as a speaker. Clemens enjoyed speaking out bitterly on public issues, for example denouncing imperialism and objecting to the European subjugation of the Congo. In the year before Clemens died, his daughter Jean drowned Christmas morning in the bathtub in her father's house in Redding, Connecticut. As a result, his daughter Clara, who was married to Ossip Gabrilowitsch, inherited his entire estate.

A known prankster, Clemens once arranged that his obituary be printed in New York newspapers, after which he had cabled from London that "the reports of my death are greatly exaggerated." When he died in Connecticut, he was too weak to speak and had written a note to his nurses, "Give me my glasses." On the bed when he died was Thomas Carlyle's *French Revolution*. (See entries for Christian Science, Mary Baker Eddy, and Alfred Kazin.) {BDF; CE; CL; EU, William F. Ryan; FUS; JM; RAT; RE; TRI; TSV; Gore Vidal, *The New York Review of Books*, 23 May 1996}

Clement, Ron (20th Century)

Clement has been active with the Humanist Community of Central Michigan. (See entry for Michigan Humanists.) {FD}

Clements, Tad S. (20th Century)

Author of *Science versus Religion* and *Science and Man: The Philosophy of Scientific Humanism* (1990), Clements is Emeritus Professor of Philosophy at State University of New York College at Brockport. He addressed the Tenth International Humanist and Ethical Union (IHEU) World Congress held in Buffalo (1988). Clements, co-editor of *Religion and Human Purpose* (1987), signed Humanist Manifesto 2000.

Clemetshaw, C. (Born 1864)

A French writer who used the name Cilwa, Clemetshaw was a delegate to the International Congress in 1887 and was editor of *Le Danton*. {BDF}

Clendening, Logan (20th Century)

According to Fred Whitehead's *Freethought History* (#1, 1992), Dr. Clendening was one of the most successful medical journalists in early 20th century America. A professor at the University of Kansas School of Medicine, he defined his outlook as being that of a freethinker.

CLERGY

- Clergyman, n. A man who undertakes the management of our spiritual affairs as a method of bettering his temporal ones.

—**Ambrose Bierce**
A Devil's Dictionary

- A clergyman is one who feels himself called upon to live without working at the expense of the rascals who work to live.

—**Voltaire**

- Of learned men, the clergy show the lowest development of professional ethics. Any pastor is free to cadge customers from the divines of rival sects, and to denounce the divines themselves as theological quacks.

—**H. L. Mencken**

Clericus, B. B. C. (20th Century)

Clericus, possibly an Englishman's pseudonym, wrote *Religion* (1942). {GS}

Cleveland, Patricia (20th Century)

Cleveland is director of the Lake Hypatia Freethought Hall, near Talladega, Alabama. Also, she is on the board of directors of the Freedom From Religion Foundation. {*Freethought Today*, May 1996}

Cleveland, Roger (1945-)

Cleveland, with his wife Patricia, is on the board of directors of the Freedom From Religion Foundation. A former paper-mill worker, he started the Alabama Freethought Association in 1989 to combat what he saw as the incursion of religion into state government. {*The New York Times Magazine*, 7 December 1997}

Cleyre, Voltairine de: See entry for De Cleyre.

Clifford, Dick (20th Century)

Clifford is President of the Humanist Society of South Australia. Also, he is that group's webmaster: <rmc@adelaide.on.net>.

Clifford, John (20th Century)

Clifford, who has Unitarian ties in Edinburgh and London, is on the Worldwide Web: <www.geocities.com/Heartland/Hills/2038>.

Clifford, Martin (c. 1600—1677)

An English rationalist, Clifford was Master of the Charterhouse (1671) and published anonymously a treatise of *Human Reason* (1674). In the *Nouvelle Biographie Générale*, Clifford is amusingly described as an "English theologian of the order des Chartreux," who, it is added, was "prior of his order." Robertson states that although Clifford makes no overt attacks on religion and points out that many modern wars have been on subjects of religion, he adds that reason alone, fairly used, will bring a man to the Christian faith, that he who denies this cannot be a Christian. {BDF; JMRH; RAT}

Clifford, William Kingdon (1845—1879)

"It is wrong, always, everywhere, and for everyone," Clifford wrote, "to believe anything upon insufficient evidence." An English mathematician-philosopher, the son of a bookseller, he formulated skepticism as an ethical imperative and was one of the first to appreciate the relevance of Darwin's evolutionary theory to human ethics.

When thirty-one, he delivered "The Ethics of Belief" (1876) to the Metaphysical Society, a group that met in London nine times a year to discuss philosophical ideas and religious beliefs. Members included William Gladstone, Thomas Henry Huxley, Archbishop Henry Manning, John Ruskin, and Alfred Lord Tennyson.

He wrote *Seeing and Thinking* (1879); *Lectures and Essays, Volumes I and II* (1879, edited by Leslie Stephen and Frederick Pollock, with an introduction by Pollock); *Mathematical Papers* (1882, edited by Robert Tucker); and. *The Common Sense of the Exact Sciences* (published in 1946, with a preface by Bertrand Russell). His attacks on Christianity were profound. Religion, "that awful plague which has destroyed two civilizations," had its priests, "at all times in all places the enemy of all men," he accused. With Thomas Henry Huxley, he was a member of the Metaphysical Society. Wheeler cites Clifford as "an outspoken Atheist, and he wrote of Christianity as a religion which wrecked one civilisation and very nearly wrecked another." Putnam says that Clifford, next to Darwin, Huxley, and Tyndall, is along with R. A. Proctor the ablest scientist to aid English freethought during the nineteenth century. Foote added that Clifford "utterly dismissed from his thoughts, as being unprofitable or worse, all speculations on a future or unseen world." Further, "as never man loved life more, so never man feared death less," which was similar to Spinoza's *Homo liber de nulla re minus quam de morte cogitat* (A free man thinks less of nothing than of death.). Clifford died of consumption, first giving exact directions as to the disposal of his works. His wife, **Lucy**, the daughter of John Lane and a close friend of Henry James, wrote *Mr. Keith's Crime* (1885) and shared her husband's rationalism. She has written in the Rationalist Press Association annual. "The Virtues of 'The Ethics of Belief'," by Timothy J. Madigan (*Free Inquiry*, Spring 1997), is discueed Clifford's outlook, pointing out that Clifford "wished to motivate all members of society to utilize their intellectual abilities to the highest degree and—aware of the growing doubts about traditional Christian beliefs that had helped to gird society up to that time—he felt a personal responsibility to use his own gifts to further the cause of rationalism." Madigan has edited *"The Ethics of Belief" and other Essays by W. K. Clifford* (1999), the most thorough Clifford study to date. {BDF; EU, Peter H. Hare; FUK; PUT; Tim Madigan, March 1997; RAT; RE; TRI}

Clinchy, Everett R. (20th Century)

A freethinker, Clinchy wrote *All in the Name of God* (1934). {GS}

Cline, Austin (20th Century)

Cline is a German Literature graduate student at Princeton University. He founded the Princeton Freethought Association. In Pennsylvania, he is a regional director of the Council for Secular Humanism.

Cline, Henry (1750—1827)

Cline, a surgeon and a skeptic who admired Horne Tooke, "thought there was a cause superior to man, but believed that nothing was known of the future," according to the *Dictionary of National Biography*. {RAT}

Clinton, William Jefferson (1946-): See entry for Roma.

Cliteur, Paul (20th Century)

Cliteur was once president in the Netherlands of *Humanistisch Verbond*. He is professor of philosophy at Technical University Delft. At the 1994 Toronto conference of the Coalition for Secular Humanism, Atheism, and Freethought (CSHAFT), he spoke on the subject of "Humanism and Ethics/Humanism and Postmodernism." Postmodernism, he holds, is a revolt against the Enlightenment, against the grand narrative of the Enlightenment. As a result, secular humanists need to be against postmodernists and, although many are atheists, would do well to refute their methodology. In 1995, in Madrid, he spoke on "A New Approach to Government Support of Morals." E-mail: <jfencpc@law.LeidenUniv.nl>. {"The Challenge of Postmodernism to Humanism," *New Humanist*, August 1995}

Clitomachus (Fl. 129 B.C.E.)

The fifth head of the New Academy, as contrasted with Plato's Old Academy, Clitomachus is remembered because Carneades left no written works but Clitomachus taught Carneades's philosophic skepticism in four hundred treatises. As described by Bertrand Russell in his *History of Philosophy* (1945), the two

> set themselves against the belief in divination, magic, and astrology, which was becoming more and more widespread. They also developed a constructive doctrine, concerning degrees of probability; although we can never be justified in feeling certainty, some things are more likely to be true than others. Probability should be our guide in practice, since it is reasonable to act on the most probable of possible hypotheses. This view is one with which most modern philosophers would agree. Unfortunately, the books setting it forth are lost, and it is difficult to reconstruct the doctrine from the hints that remain.
>
> {JMRH}

CLITORIS: See entry for Federico Andahazi, who described Mateo Colón as the first man to discover the female organ, at least within the world that he knew.

CLOCKWORK UNIVERSE

God, some say, created the universe, which like a clock needs Him to keep it wound up. Just as the clock's gears are governed by the laws of physics, so are the universe's. During the Enlightenment, scientists held that Newton's laws of motion and the law of universal gravitation explained the behavior of the solar system. Some young freethinkers, entirely ignorant of ratchet wheels, drums, winding squares, and springs, fail to comprehend the concept of a clockwork universe, pleading tongue-in-cheek that they have never experienced anything but digital. (See entry for Aristarchus of Samos.) {DCL}

Clodd, Edward (1840—1930)

Clodd was a banker and anthropologist who, from 1906 to 1913, was chairman of the Rationalist Press Association. He wrote *The Childhood of Religions* (1875); *The Story of Creation* (1888); and *Pioneers of Evolution* (1897). {FUK; RAT; RE; TRI}

CLONING

A clone is something that appears to be a copy of some original form. In a science lab, a clone can be reproduced or propagated asexually, such as in the cloning of a frog (or a plant variety), with the intent of using the result to fight diseases, infertility, and animal extinction.

Mary Shelley's *Frankenstein, or the Modern Prometheus* in 1818 tells of the Genevan medical student of natural philosophy who stitches together a body, bringing it to life. The creature is rational and articulate, one who enjoys Goethe, Plutarch, and *Paradise Lost* but is lonely and displeased with his unusual origin. When Dr. Frankenstein refuses to create a female counterpart, his creation murders his brother, his friend Clerval, and his bride Elizabeth. He is then pursued to the Arctic by the doctor, who dies in the pursuit after relating the story to Walton, an English explorer in the Arctic. In movie and other versions, the creature is driven mad and murders the good doctor himself. The work has been regarded as the first of science fiction stories, although it also is a version of the myth of the Noble Savage, in which a nature essentially good is corrupted by ill treatment.

Science fiction writers such as Ray Bradbury, Ursula K. LeGuin, and William Gibson continued the tradition, as did Philip K. Dick, author of "Do Androids Dream of Electric Sheep?" from which the cult film "Blade Runner" was made. Dick envisioned a world, journalist Brent Staples has written, "where in vitro fertilization and cloning are passé and have given way to the wholesale manufacture of synthetic human life."

In 1996 Ian Wilmut announced in Scotland that he and his colleagues at Roslin Institute had, indeed, scraped a few cells from the udder of a 6-year-old ewe, then fused them into a specially altered egg cell from another sheep, resulting in a lamb named Dolly, the first instance of cloning an adult mammal. The lamb was named Dolly after the well-endowed country music star, Dolly Parton. In 1998 Dolly became a mother the old-fashioned way.

Free Inquiry (Summer 1997) devoted an entire issue to the subject. Included was a declaration in defense of cloning and the integrity of scientific research that was signed by thirty-one members of the International Academy of Humanism.

A 1999 study, however, found genetic abnormalities in cloned animals. *Nature* (May 1999) found that the sheep named Dolly, the first animal that was a clone of an adult, may show a sign of aging, appearing, in effect, older than the original animal that was cloned. Although the initial findings are tentative, they indicated that Dolly's cells had slightly stunted telomeres, the tickertape-like appendages to chromosomes. Telomeres are like a virtual aging clock for cells grown in the laboratory, shortening with each cell division and marking off the number of divisions remaining before a cell dies. The telomeres in older animals tend to be shorter than they are in younger animals, according to Gina Kolata in an evaluation of the scientists' announcement. (See entry for Ian Wilmut.) (OEL; *The Economist*, Brent Staples, *The New York Times*, 1 Mar 1997; and Gina Kolata, *The New York Times*, 27 May 1999}

Clooney, George (1962-)

An actor, Clooney was in "E.R.," a television series, from 1984 to 1985 and from 1994 to 1999. He has been in numerous movies, including "Batman & Robin (1997).

Sharon Waxman, profiling him in the *Washington Post* (28 September 1997), quoted him: "I don't believe in Heaven and Hell. I don't know if I believe in God. All I know is that as an individual, I won't allow this life—the only thing I know to exist—to be wasted." {CA}

Cloots, Johann Baptist [Baron] (1755—1794)

Cloots (or Clootz) was a Prussian enthusiast, a nephew of Cornelius de Pauw. In 1780 under the pseudonym of Ali-gier-bet, an anagram of Bergier, he published *The Certainty of the Proofs of Mohammedanism*, a parody of the of *Certainty of the Proofs of Christianity*. With Paine, Priestley, Washington, and Klopstock, Cloots was made a French citizen, and in 1792 he was elected to the Convention by two departments. Cloots de-baptized himself, taking the name Anacharsis, becoming a prime mover in the Anti-Catholic Party and declaring that there is no other God but Nature. Incurring the enmity of Robespierre, he and Paine were arrested as foreigners.

Imprisoned for two and a half months at St. Lazare, Cloots was then brought to the scaffold with the Hébertostes, where he died calmly, first uttering materialist sentiments, saying "Let me lie under the green sward so that I may be reborn in vegetation." "Nature," he said, "is a good mother, who loves to see her children appear and reappear in different forms. All she includes is eternal, imperishable like herself. Now let me sleep!" He ended as one of a tumbril-load of victims, nineteen in all. {BDF; RAT}

Close, Converse (19th Century)

Close, a freethinker in Grattan, Michigan, was an invalid who contributed articles to the *Truth Seeker* and other liberal journals. For him, freethought "was a power in man's heart and brain to eventually make the real paradise of this world." {PUT}

CLOSET, CLOSETED

To be "closeted" carries the connotation of having motives that are secret. One can be a closeted atheist although a nominal Catholic, for example.

A "closet queen" in the 1940s and 1950s referred to a crypto-homosexual. "And are you a practicing homosexual?" accusers asked individuals seeking positions, for example, in top-secret government posts, implying that they would be denied such jobs because they would be easy to blackmail. "No," one exceptional out-of-the-closet homosexual reportedly responded, "I am an *accomplished* homosexual."

Bill Bonano's *Bound by Honor: A Mafioso's Story* (1999) described the author's understanding of why J. Edgar Hoover, who headed the Federal Bureau of Investigation, assigned only "about half a dozen" agents to "organized crime." Removing seven or eight photos from a manila envelope and showing them to gangster Joe Bonano, lawyer Roy Cohn said, "You know, [Hoover] still won't use the term Mafia." According to Bonano's son, "Most were five-by-seven shots, a couple were eight-by 10s. They were all pictures of Hoover in women's clothing. His face was daubed with lipstick and makeup and he wore a wig of ringlets. In several of the photos, he posed alone, smiling, even mugging for the camera. In a few others, he was sitting on the lap of an unidentified male, stroking his cheek in one, hugging him in another, holding a morsel of food before his mouth in yet another." Because Hoover knew the photographs existed, Bonanno alleges Hoover feared being blackmailed. The photos were said to have been taken by Lewis Rosenstiel "at a party on a houseboat in the Keys, 1948-1949."

During a period in which homosexuality was called a sickness by psychiatrists, and reinforced by religionists with appeals to sacred books, gay individuals chose then, and often still do choose, to be closeted.

Clough, Arthur Hugh (1819—1861)

An English poet, Clough was a skeptic and was somewhat cynical. He has been said to be closer in spirit to the 10th than to the 19th century. He wrote *Blasting the Rock of Ages* (published in 1925). His poetry, including "Say Not the Struggle Naught Availeth," "Dypsichus," and "Mari Magno," reveal not only his doubts about religion but also about himself.

On an 1852 trip to the United States, he gained the friendship of Emerson and Longfellow. Clough is the Thyrsis of Matthew Arnold's "Monody." Leslie Stephens has said of Clough, "He never became bitter against the Church of his childhood, but he came to regard its dogmas as imperfect and untenable." According to McCabe, Clough "wavered a little, as poets do, but in his final declaration on religion he is practically agnostic, not Unitarian, with a thin lingering shade of theism or pantheism." {BDF; CE; GS; JM; JMR; RAT; RE; TRI}

Clouston, Thomas [Sir] (1841—1915)

A physician and lecturer on mental diseases at Edinburgh University, Clouston was president of the Edinburgh Royal College of Physicians and editor of *The Journal of Medical Science*. He rejected belief in a separable mind and severely criticized what he called "religionists." {RAT; RE}

Clunas, John (20th Century)

Clunas in Scotland is active with the Aberdeen Humanist Group. He has had articles in *Humanism Scotland*.

COALITION FOR SECULAR HUMANISM, ATHEISM, AND FREE THOUGHT

The Coalition for Secular Humanism, Atheism, and Freethought, Box 32, Buffalo, NY, 14215, is a group which espouses secular humanism, freethought, rationalism, secularism, agnosticism, and atheism. It seeks joint action on secular humanist and freethought positions on issues of concern to people, including values, morality, and ethics. {FD}

Coate, Lowell H. (20th Century)

In Los Angeles, Coate and a group of Quaker humanists broke away from their denomination and in 1939, at a meeting of the First Universalist Church, established the Humanist Society of Friends. {HNS2}

Coate, Lowell L. (20th Century)

Coate was an editor of *The American Rationalist*. {EU, Eldon Scholl}

Coates, Collinson (1885—1981)

Coates, the son of a freethinker, became an apprenticed shoemaker in Liverpool, England, at the age of fourteen. Emigrating to Western Australia in 1912, he became active in the Australian Labor Party. In 1958 he co-founded the Western Australian Secularist Fellowship, which continued until about 1980. At the age of 95, Coates published an anti-war book, *Almost Too Late*.

Coates, J. B. (20th Century)

Coates, a freethinker, wrote *A Challenge to Christianity* (1958), which in an appendix contained "A Humanist Manifesto." {GS}

Coates, Jack (Born 1892)

Writing in *Literary Guide*, Coates spoke of the need to develop secular humanism in the Rationalist Press Association (RPA). Science without ethics could destroy the world, he held. Agreeing with Emmanuel Mournier's *Esprit* (1932) and with J. P. van Praag, the Dutch leader, Coates founded in 1945 the London Personalist movement. {TRI}

Cobb, Irvin S(hrewsbury) (1876—1944)

A noted humorist, columnist, and author, Cobb wrote over sixty books. Best known for his humorous stories of Kentucky local humor, he wrote an autobiography entitled *Exit Laughing* (1942). Upon his death, he left a "To Whom It May Concern" letter for Edwin J. Paxton Sr., publisher of the Paducah *Sun-Democrat*, which read in part as follows:

> In death I desire that no one shall look upon my face and once more I charge my family, as already and repeatedly I have done, that they shall put on none of the bogus habiliments of so-called mourning. Folds of black crepe never ministered to the memory of the departed; they only made the wearers unhappy and self-conscious.
>
> I ask that my body be wrapped in a plain sheet or cloth and placed in an inexpensive container and immediately cremated—without any special formality or ceremony. If anybody tries to insert me into one of those dismal numbers run up by the undertaker's dress-making department, I'll come back and ha-nt 'em. Nor do I crave to make my mortal exit in a tailcoat with white tie and artificial pearl studs. I'll be done with after dinner speaking forever, so why dispatch me hence in the regalia of the craft? When a man dies with his sins, let the sins die with the man. That's what I say and it sums up such speculations as I might ever have had touching on the future state, if any.
>
> When convenience suits, I ask that the plain canister—nothing fancy there, please—containing my ashes shall be taken to Paducah, and that at the proper planting season a hole shall be dug in our family lot or elsewhere at Oak Grove and a dogwood tree planted there and the ashes strewn in the hole to fertilize the tree roots. Should the tree live, that will be monument enough for me.
>
> But should my surviving relatives desire to mark the spot further, I make so bold as to suggest that they use either a slab of plain Kentucky limestone set flat in the kindly earth, or a rugged natural boulder of southern granite bearing a small bronze plate with my name on it and, if it seems pertinent, the year of my birth and the year of my death. Also on the bronze tablet or the stone slab, as the case may be, and provided it doesn't cost too much, I'd like to have inscribed certain lines, as I remember them, from the epitaph which Robert Louis Stevenson wrote for himself:
>
> These be the lines you 'grave for me;
> Here I lie where I long to be.
> Home is the hunter, home from the hill,
> And the sailor home from the sea.
>
> [Ed. note: To correct the record, Stevenson's lines were as follows:]
>
> *This be the verse you grave for me:*
> *Here he lies where he longed to be;*
> *Home is the sailor, home from sea,*
> *And the hunter home from the hill.*
>
> And, thank you, no flowers. Does anybody feel moved to send flowers, I'd prefer that they give the money they'd spend there to some local non-denominational charity.
>
> Above all I want no long faces and no show of grief at the burying ground. Kindly observe the final wishes of the undersigned and avoid reading the so-called Christian burial service which, in view of the language employed in it, I regard as one of the most cruel and paganish things inherited by our forbears from our remote pagan ancestors.

In deference to the faith of our dear mother, who was through her lifetime a loyal though never a bigoted communicant of that congregation, perhaps the current pastor of the First Presbyterian church would consent to read the Twenty-Third Psalm, which was her favorite passage in the Scriptures and is mine since it contains no charnel words, no morbid mouthings about corruption and decay and, being mercifully without creed or dogma, carries no threat of eternal hell fire for those parties we do not like, no direct promise of a heaven which, if one may judge by the people who are surest of going there, must be a powerfully dull place, populated to a considerable and uncomfortable degree by prigs, time-servers, and unpleasantly aggressive individuals. Hell may have a worse climate but undoubtedly the company is sprightlier.

As an aside I might add that my notion of an ideal religion would combine the dignity and the beauty of the Romanist ritual with certain other ingredients. The good taste and the ability of the Unitarians and Episcopalians—a trait not too common to some of the evangelical groups—to mind their own business. To these add the noble ethics and the splendid tolerance expressed in Reform Judaism; the study in independence and the good business principles of the Mormons; the gentle humility and ordered humanity of the Quakers, plus the militant zeal and unselfish devotion of those shock troops of the Lord—the Salvation Army. If, based on this combination, there was a determination to practice the sectless preachments and the teachings of Jesus Christ, who was the first true gentleman of recorded history and the greatest gentleman that ever lived, I might not have joined the fold but certainly I'd have stood on the sidelines and cheered for it.

By the way, have you ever noticed that in time of war not the most passionate partisan dares to ask the Prince of Peace to bless his bloody arms and forward his bloody deeds? He invokes the aid of the God of unjustified battles as created by the ancient Hebrews.

Well, I reckon that will be about all except that I extend, in passing, my affectionate and grateful regards to the gracious and generous folks who make up so overwhelmingly the dwellers in my home community and my native section. You've been mighty good to me and I appreciate it. Much obliged, you-all, and good-by and bless you and prosper you.

(signed) Irvin S. Cobb
New York, Dec., 1943

Cobb, John Storer (19th Century)

A freethinker, Cobb wrote *The Efficacy of Prayer* (1883). {GS}

Cobb, Leslie (20th Century)

Cobb was President of the Secular Society of New York, members of which in 1949 included Eva Ingersoll Wakefield and Sherman Wakefield.

Cobb, Sylvanus (1798—1866)

A Universalist minister, Cobb founded the *Christian Freeman and Family Visitor*, a publication which made him the most influential Universalist social reformer before the Civil War. {U&U}

Cobbe, Frances Power (1822—1908)

A British philanthropist and author of works on religious and social questions, Cobbe has been described by Underwood: "Her position, as I understand it, being that of the most liberal phase of Unitarianism; or, perhaps, more correctly, that of a Free Religionist; for Miss Cobbe, in spite of her advanced Liberalism, is the most reverent Theist." She met Theodore Parker when he was on his deathbed, and she found him calm, serene, not desirous of death but resigned to the inevitable. She was present at his burial in the Protestant cemetery at Florence, and she edited his life and letters. Moncure Conway observed that she weighed nearly three hundred and fifty pounds and had to walk on crutches, "which gives one a sad feeling that this enormous size is far from being the result of, or accompanied by, health." But he found her witty and charming, an excellent conversationalist. "Morality may exist in an Atheist without any religion," Cobbe once wrote, "and in a Theist with a religion quite unspiritual." {SAU}

Cobell, Denis (20th Century)

Cobell, who had been Vice President of Britain's National Secular Society, was elected President in 1997. He is publisher of *The Freethinker* and writes book reviews for *New Humanist*.

He also is chair of the Lewisham Humanist Group and was honored by being made the "Mayor's chaplain—humanist officiant." When a priest objected that such an appointment by the Mayor of Lewisham "sends out completely the wrong signals to people—especially if they are going to call him chaplain," Cobell retorted that the title "Father" was hardly less confusing. {*The Freethinker*, August 1998}.

Cobbett, William (1762—1835)

Cobbett wrote *Legacy to Parsons* (1835). He had been the person who brought Thomas Paine's bones to Britain in 1819—the bones, however, have since been lost. Cobbett was an anti-Malthusian. {FUK; GS, TRI}

COCAINE

Vin Mariani, a drink manufactured by a Corsican named Angelo Mariani, was an elixir invented in 1863 and awarded a gold medal by Pope Leo XIII. Around 1878 Pope Pius X also was on record as enjoying the drink. According to Richard Rudley's *Encyclopedia of Psychoactive Substances*, the drink consisted of wine laced with cocaine. {Colin McCall, *The Freethinker*, May 1998}

Cockburn, Alexander (20th Century)

Cockburn, a columnist for *The Nation*, has often gone on record as being a non-theist, a rationalist, and a profound skeptic. (See entry for Graham Greene.) {CA}

Cocteau, Jean (1889—1963)

Cocteau (the plural of cocktail, according to a jocular Manhattan dipsomaniac) was a French writer, visual artist, and filmmaker. He was ten when his father committed suicide. A school dropout, he made his Sorbonne the Paris cafes, galleries, theatres, and lovers. The actor Edouard de Max, who once played opposite Sarah Bernhardt, guided the decadent youth "through the Parisian scene (with the approval of Cocteau's mother)," according to the critic Charles Shively.

A leader in the 1920s of the avant-garde, he had as his first success a novel, *Les Enfants Terribles* (1929), which in 1950 he made into a film. Upon meeting Sergei Diaghilev and asking why he was noncommittal concerning his work, the Russian ballet impresario and art critic is said to have adjusted his monocle and replied, "Astonish me," inspiring Cocteau to write for the ballet. "Parade," which used Picasso's sets and costumes, Satie's satirical music, and Cocteau's wild scenario of acrobats, a juggler, and a girl riding a bicycle duly astonished the audiences, Parisian critics agreed.

At first attracted to de Max, Igor Stravinsky, and older men, Cocteau then turned to the very young: John Le Ray, whom he described as "young, handsome, good, brave, full of genius, unaffected, everything Death likes"; Raymond Rodriguet, a teenager whose death in 1923 left Cocteau devastated; Maurice Sachs, who stripped his apartment of his belongings; Jean Bourgoint, called by Glenway Wescott "one of God's fools"; Jean Desbordes, a Resistance fighter whose eyes were plucked out by the Nazis; and the actor Jean Marais who was the beast in the 1946 film "Beauty and the Beast" which Cocteau directed, to name but a few. When Marais was twenty-four, he met Cocteau and promptly fell in love with him, their relationship lasting until Cocteau's 1963 death. Marais died in 1998.

Smoking opium as an experiment to enhance his senses, Cocteau stopped because the drug put his sexuality to sleep. An anarchist, he disliked both the French government and the Nazi conquerors. "Religious, political, and literary judges, whether Roman Catholic, Communist, or academic, repelled him because of their pretensions to absolute knowledge," Shively found. He added that although, during his drug recovery, Cocteau turned briefly to Catholicism and received communion, he "fled the church after falling for a handsome monk."

On the day Edith Piaf died, 11 October 1963, Cocteau recorded a tribute to her that the French radio broadcast. Later that day, Cocteau himself died. {AA; CE; Charles Shively, *The Gay and Lesbian Literary Heritage* [1995]}.

CODESH: See entry for the Council for Secular Humanism. It was a coincidence that the acronym for Council of Democratic and Secular Humanism so closely resembled the Hebrew word for "holy." Also, "democratic" in the title was thought to be redundant, and the organization's title was shortened in 1995.

COFFEE

Coffee was once banned in the Christian world, accused of being the Devil's brew. In 1600, however, Pope Clement VIII developed a taste for the beverage (was instructed by God?) and lifted the prohibition.

Cogdell, G. D. (20th Century)

Cogdell wrote *What Price Parochiaid?* (1970).

COHABITATION

Cohabitation involves the living together of two individuals who are not married. The term applies mainly to heterosexuals inasmuch as same-sex individuals are almost universally not allowed to marry legally.

Although cohabitation was illegal in all American states until 1970, it is now considered to be routine. More than half of all first marriages are preceded by cohabitation, reported *The Economist* (6 February 1999), and a quarter of unmarried women aged between twenty-five and thirty-nine are cohabiting. According to Kathleen Kirnan of the London School of Economics, people who lived with one partner whom they then married were no more prone to divorce than those who married in "the old-fashioned way."

Some Quakers, as well as others, have been known to cohabit as a deliberate statement that the state has no right to make couples "marry" and pay for a license. Any such decision between a man and a woman, or the fact of their cohabitation without a civil or religious ceremony, is called a "common-law marriage" and is treated differently depending upon the district or state in which they live.

Cohen, Chapman (1868—1954)

Cohen, an English freethought advocate, was the first generation of freethought leaders not to have known Bradlaugh. He emerged as Foote's successor in the Edwardian years, and he was president of the National Secular Society from 1915 until 1949. Born of a Jewish family, he studied the history of freethought and by the age of eighteen had read works by Spinoza, Locke, Hume, Berkeley, and Plato. When he moved from Leicester to London in 1889 Cohen knew little about the National Secular Society, coming across the Secularists entirely by accident. Hearing a Christian Evidence Society lecturer in Victoria Park mimicking an old man with a speech impediment, Cohen intervened to rebuke the lecturer. The following week he himself opposed the Christian, and the secularists who were present invited the young stranger to join them. As was later remarked, the first freethought lecture he had ever heard was his own.

Cohen's first experience of journalism was editing John Grange's Bradford *Truth Seeker* while its editor was ill in 1896. The following year he became involved with the *Freethinker*, and following Wheeler's death in 1898 Cohen became Foote's loyal assistant. Cohen wrote the five-volume *Essays in Freethinking*, and in his *Bradlaugh and Ingersoll* (1933), he criticizes what Berman calls "the Spinozistic and metaphysical component of Bradlaugh's atheism, the thesis that existence or substance can be 'conceived in itself,' with 'no relation to any other thing.' This Cohen calls 'metaphysical moonshine' and 'unthinkable.' If existence is the sum of phenomena [as Bradlaugh holds], then whether we use the one term or the other [i.e., substance or the sum of phenomena] we are saying the same thing." Cohen has written, "The agnostic sees that there is a definite amount of mystery about the working of the universe, and he frankly admits that there may be some motivating force animating that universe in a way which our minds cannot appreciate. . . . The whole Agnostic position is against dogmatism in any shape or form." McCabe considered Cohen's *God and the Universe* to be among Cohen's chief works. "Morality Without God" was one of his more than sixty books and pamphlets. Cohen's *Theism and Atheism* (1921) also has been rated as one of his best. He also wrote *Almost an Autobiography: The Confessions of a Freethinker* (1940).

By the end of the war in 1945, Cohen was an old man who, having served the freethought movement for years, was loath to relinquish the leadership. At a stormy conference in 1948, however, he was urged to give up the presidency, which he did in 1949, and in 1951 he handed over the *Freethinker* to F. A. Ridley.

At his funeral, an officiant declared, ". . . the name of Chapman Cohen will be linked in the history of human liberation with those of Voltaire, Thomas Paine, Robert Ingersoll, Charles Bradlaugh, and the whole glorious army of freedom-loving pioneers." {EU, Victor E. Neuburg; FUK; HAB; RE; RSR; TRI}

Cohen, Edmund D(avid) (1943—)

A psychologist, attorney, and author of *The Mind of the Bible Believer*, Cohen has written for *Free Inquiry*. Christianity, he feels, is only a mind-game, a deadening mass-compulsion neurosis. Atheists, he feels, instead of criticizing Christianity for its jumbled facts and scrambled morality should expose its weaknesses now by detailing how it uses the psychology of indoctrination. Cohen, who was a born-again Christian but broke with Pat Robertson, has in a 1993 article described the rise to prominence of fundamentalist Christian psychiatric inpatient programs:

> The first of these was Palmdale (California) General Hospital, where both Jim and Tammy Bakker were treated in 1977. Three such programs, Minirth-Meier Clinics, Rapha, and New Life Treatment Centers, have grown rapidly into large, multi-state health care businesses. These have become major influences on the larger conservative church subculture through books and videotape teaching packages. It is common for the latest book in Thomas Nelson Publishers' Minirth-Meier Series, or the latest book by Robert S. McGee, founder of Rapha, or Stephen Arterburn, chairman and CEO of New Life Treatment Centers, to be a Christian bookstore bestseller.

Cohen's e-mail address: <edcohen@bellatlantic.net>. {*Free Inquiry*, Spring 1987 and Summer 1993}

Cohen, Hermann (Born 1842)

Cohen, a Jewish philosopher who was head of the Neo-Kantian Rationalist school in Germany, wrote about philosophy and literature. He professed a kind of idealistic theism. {RAT}

Cohen, Larry (1947-)

A film director, producer, and screenwriter, Cohen has been a television writer for "NYPD Blue." He created "Branded" (1965-1966); was film writer for numerous movies, including "Guilty as Sin" (1993); was director-producer-writer of "Bone" (1972); "Hell in Harlem" (1973); "The Private Files of J. Edgar Hoover" (1978); and was producer-writer of "Maniac Cop II" (1990).

His most irreverent horror movie was "Demon" (1976), in which a New York City cop investigates a bizarre series of homicides committed by murderers possessed by a demon from outer space. When confronted by police, each murderer claims that God told him to commit the crimes. For Cohen, this was part of a general critique of religion:

> I don't relate to anyone who is a professional religionist . . . who has the ego to tell us that they know God's will, and can tell us what God thinks and what God likes and what God is, and how God feels about integration, South Africa, and AIDS. Everybody's got a different idea what God thinks; the crazy guy on the corner knows about as much as the guy in St. Patrick's Cathedral—none of them know anything. . . . People say, "Reverend Moon—what a crook!" and I say, But what about the Pope?" It's all the same, anybody who starts telling you what God thinks should be locked up immediately.

{CA}

Cohen, Morris R(aphael) (1880—1947)

Cohen, wrote Corliss Lamont, is "one of the most important American philosophers since William James." His *The Faith of a Liberal* (1946) emphasized that dogmatism in any field is abhorrent. The book discussed a liberal thinker's views about Bertrand Russell, Einstein, Huxley, Spinoza, Dante, Heine, Justice Brandeis, Justice Holmes, Sacco and Vanzetti, and others. Cohen, who taught philosophy at City College of New York wrote of liberalism,

> Revolutionaries and reactionaries alike are irritated and perhaps inwardly humiliated by the humane temper of liberalism, which reveals by contrast the common inhumanity of both violent parties in the social struggle. Liberalism on the other hand regards life as an adventure in which we must take risks, in which there is no guarantee that the new will always be the good or the true, in which progress is a precarious achievement rather than an inevitability.

Felix Frankfurter, reviewing Cohen's *A Dreamer's Journey, the Autobiography of Morris Raphael Cohen* (1949), noted that Cohen "identified philosophy with 'natural curiosity or wonder about the nature of the world, things, life, knowledge, art, religion and morality as roads leading to a common concern with perennial problems,' turning that curiosity in upon himself and proving that the adventures of the mind can be as exciting as the deeds of soldiers and statesmen." Because it gave insight into the making of a significant mind as well as a deep glimpse into the makings of America, Frankfurter compared the book to Jacob Riis's *The Making of an American*, Booker T. Washington's *Own Story*, and Mary Antin's *The Promised Land.* {CE; CL; TYD}

Cohen, William Sebastian [Senator] (1940—)

Cohen, a Unitarian, was U. S. Senator from Maine (1979—1996) and is currently Secretary of Defense at The Pentagon.

He wrote *Of Sons and Seasons* (1978); *Roll Call* (1981); *Getting the Most Out of Washington* (1982); *A Baker's Nickel* (1986); *One-Eyed Kings* (1991, with Gary Hart); *The Double Man* (1985, with George Mitchell); *Men of Zeal* (1988, with Thomas B. Allen); and *Murder in the Senate* (1993).

On the Web: <www.bates.edu/~jwallace/reps/billcohen.html>.

Cohn, Norman (1916-)

Cohn's *The Pursuit of the Millennium* (1957) was a history of popular religions and social movements in Europe from the eleventh to the sixteenth century, one inspired by his Latin and medieval German and French studies at Oxford.

Norwegian *Humanist* editor Terje Emberland has described the Cohn work as "still the standard work on the subject," one written in a clear, classical style such as the following:

> The group of starving, blood-spattered flagellants, who in summer 1349 storm Frankfurt's gates and slaughter the town's Jews in a religious-ecstatic orgy of killing. "The Master from Hungary," a renegade monk who at Easter 1251 gathers a rag-tag army of several thousand paupers—shepherds, beggars, thieves, and prostitutes—who with raised pitchforks capture the villages of Picardy on the order of the Holy Virgin.

Emberland noted that Cohn's shedding light on the ancient collective fantasies helps us understand today's religious madness, such as the doomsday sects which are starting as the year 2000 approaches, and the collective suicide, assassinations, or mass murder experienced in the 1990s at Waco (Texas), Quebec, and Japan.

Cohn's view about the "Kingdom of God":

> I believe that both Jesus and the first Christians expected that those who gained salvation would inhabit a purified and regenerated world with purified and regenerated bodies, but that this teaching gradually became unacceptable to the Church and was interpreted spiritually.

One of the reasons that the myth of his resurrection spread, Cohn wrote, is that Jesus did not fulfill the Millanarian expectations. If Jesus had not fulfilled his task in his lifetime, followers reasoned, this must mean that his Messianic role had to happen after his death.

Cohn's *Warrant for Genocide*(1966) concerns "the basic myth of the Jew as God's demonic opponent." Despite the lessening of the power of religion in our time, the tradition of hating Jews lives on. Says Cohn, "Religiously substantiated anti-Semitism is preached today by people who otherwise do not believe one whit in Christianity."

Europe's Inner Demons (1976) noted the need for societies in crisis to seek scapegoats:

> According to this fantasy, in the centre of society there exists a secret community that constantly threatens the established order and which commits acts that are totally repulsive—quite simply inhuman—namely cannibalism, child sacrifice, and incest.

The book includes how heretics were persecuted in the Middle Ages and how witch hunts started in the fifteenth century:

> One might just as well believe that the first Christians sacrificed infants as believe that witches and heretics did so. . . . The fact that such accusations have nevertheless proved to be long-lived is due to the fact that they meet societal needs. To put it cynically, a society threatened by dissolution and crisis may be consolidated by constructing such an imaginary group [that] can also be slaughtered in righteous wrath.

Witch trials "were primarily a demonisation of fellow Christians," Cohn notes. Today witches are depicted as the heroic bearers of a peace-loving, female fertility religion, a view he rejects out of hand. The popularity of such a view is connected with a feminist myth that underpins their view of the historical battlefield in the eternal struggle between the sexes, Christianity representing the repressive patriarchy, the witches standing for the feminine, soft, ecological values.

Cohn, in the interview with Emberland, did not come across as an optimist on behalf of common sense. "Unfortunately," Cohn said, "it would seem that no human folly disappears forever. Collective fantasies—indeed, fanatical irrational belief—are still present in our to all intents and purposes so secularised and rational society, and the creation of demons and saviours takes place just as much now as in the middle Ages." {*New Humanist*, March 1998}

Cohn, Ruth C. (20th Century)

Cohn, a member in the 1970s of the advisory board of the New York Chapter of the American Humanist Association, was the founder-director of the Workshop Institute for Living-Learning. In 1972 she was named Psychologist of the Year by the American Academy of Psychotherapists.

Coit, Stanton (1857—1944)

A British Ethical Culture leader, Coit was a colleague of Felix Adler. He founded in 1886 the first settlement house in the United States (known today as the University Settlement). In 1887, he headed the South Place Ethical Society in London. Among his writings are *National Idealism and A State Church* (1907) and *The Spiritual Nature of Man* (1910) and *Congregations: South Place and Others.*

According to James F. Hornback, "Coit, a self-styled humanist, was always too empirical, liturgical, and willing to translate Christian words and symbols into humanism, for Adler's taste. Yet, he recruited and trained several of the second- and third-generation

Leaders for Adler's movement: Golding, Chubb, O'Dell, Hynd, and Collier."

McCabe wrote that where Coit uses "God" in his works, he means "the Good." Others objected that a humanist would do better to avoid such an ambiguous term. (See entries for Ethical Culture and for Freethought.) {CL; EU, Howard B. Radest; FUK; HNS2; RAT; RE; RSR; TRI; WSS}

COITUS

- If a Jew has a coitus with a Gentile woman, whether she be a child or three or an adult, whether married or unmarried, and even if he is a minor aged only nine years and one day—because he had willful coitus with her, she must be killed, as is the case with a beast, because through her a Jew got into trouble.

—Maimonides
"Prohibitions on Sexual Intercourse"
{Israel Shahak, *The Nation*, 6 July 1998}

Coke, Henry John (1827—1916)

Coke was a freethinker, the author of *Creeds of the Day* (1883), or collated opinions of reputable thinkers. The third son of the first Earl of Leicester, Coke served in the navy during the first China War, 1840—1842.

He published accounts of the siege of Vienna in 1848, at which he was present. And he was private secretary to Horsman, the Chief Secretary for Ireland, 1854—1858. {BDF; RAT}

Colby, Clara (1846—1916)

Although born in England, Colby moved to Wisconsin in 1849. In 1869 she was graduated by the University of Wisconsin, was the valedictorian, and was in that university's first class of women. After teaching Latin there, she moved to Nebraska and became known for her woman's suffrage efforts. She adopted two children, including a Sioux Indian baby girl, "Lost Bird," found by Clara's husband in the arms of her slaughtered mother after Wounded Knee.

Colby was the first woman designated as a war correspondent during the Spanish War. Although she belonged to the Congregational church, she introduced and defended resolutions denouncing patriarchal religious dogma, notably at the 1885 woman suffrage convention. Olympia Brown, who wrote a memorial of her, classified Clara's views as "New Thought," adding that she believed, "God and I are one, and I am the one." {WWS}

Colden, Cadwallader (1688—1776)

A colonial scholar and political leader of New York, Colden was born in Ireland of Scottish parents. During the administration of George Clinton (1686—1761), the colonial governor, Colden was an influential member of the governor's council. In his fifty-five years of active public life, he made himself one of the most learned men in the colonies.

Principles of Action in Matter (1751) critiqued Newton's principles. Colden was a botanist of the Linnaean system of classifying flora, and he contributed to the medical literature of the colonies. In *History of the Five Indian Nations* (1726), Colden described the Iroquois tribes. His works show a close connection to Enlightenment naturalism. (See entry for Colden written by Paul Kurtz in *The Encyclopedia of Philosophy*.) {CE}

Cole, Alfred S. (20th Century)

Cole, a member of the American Humanist Association, wrote with Charles R. Skinner a biography of John Murray, *Hell's Ramparts Fell* (1941). {HNS}

Cole, David (20th Century)

A liberal minister, Cole was a member of the American Humanist Association. {HNS}

Cole, Edward William (1832—1918)

Cole, of Cole's Book Arcade in Melbourne, is one of Australia's better known unbelievers. A freethinker and publicist, he was criticized for doubting the validity of miracles in a work, *The Real Place in History of Jesus and Paul.*

His book arcade was a meeting place for freethinkers for more than fifty years, known for providing "rich food for the imagination of those with honest doubts." {SWW}

Cole, George Douglas Howard (1889—1959)

Howard in 1958 became an honorary associate of the Rationalist Press Association (RPA). He was an economist, a socialist, and a labor historian. From 1939 to 1946, he was president of the Fabian Society.

Cole wrote *A Short History of the British Working Class Movement* (3 volumes, 1927) and *A History of Socialist Thought* (5 volumes, 1953—1960). With his wife, Margaret Isabel (Postgate) Cole, he wrote over thirty detective stories. In 1939 he took part in the International Congress of Freethinkers. (Entry for George Orwell indicates the creator of Big Brother thought Cole was a Communist sympathizer, a shallow person, and a diabetic.) {FUK; RE}

Cole, Margaret (Born 1893)

Cole, a freethinker, was active in the Fabian Society. She wrote *The Story of Fabian Socialism* (1971). {TRI}

Cole, Peter (Died 1587)

Cole was a tanner of Ipswich who was burned for blasphemy in the castle ditch, Norwich, in England. A Dr. Beamond preached to him before the mayor, sheriffs, and alderman, "but he would not recant," reported Hamont. {BDF}

Cole, Robert (20th Century)

A freethinker, Cole wrote *Religion or Superstition—Which?* (1939). {GS}

Cole, Stewart G. (Born 1892)

Cole, who wrote *The History of Fundamentalism* (1931 and 1971), was asked by the present author his views of humanism and responded,

> The idea of humanism is subject to a number of interpretations. Some are contradictory, others complementary. My own point of view includes selective elements from "naturalistic" humanism and "theistic" humanism.
>
> I believe that we understand the meaning of man as we observe him and his kind against the backgrounds of history—human, prehuman, and cosmological—which are functionally related and which imply a single stream of unfolding reality.
>
> I believe that we comprehend the significance of man as we attempt to identify our own persons [sic] with his high adventures in every aspect of living in the contemporary world. As far as we know, man is Nature's highest form of creative life. He has unmeasured impulses for achieving the good, full life of mankind. Thus we pay allegiance to the dignity of the human individual, to the inherent endeavors of human society to improve its lot, and to those forces of the cosmos, the democratic movement, the arts and the sciences, and of personal initiative which contribute to the enhancement of these values.
>
> Furthermore, it is my belief that these forces are spiritual in character. They are of the very nature of the dynamic universe itself. They inhere in cosmic-human reality, and invite personal loyalty to them. If individuals and societies disregard them in any particulars, they suffer human reverses; as they support them, they rise in the moral and spiritual scale. This universal process of social achievement versus human reverses suggests the field of modern man's religion.
>
> Its implications are traced in John Dewey's *A Common Faith* and in the anthology, *This Is My Faith* (Harper's 1956).
>
> {WAS, 13 August 1956}

Coleman, Kari (20th Century)

A veteran of film and television roles, Coleman is a skeptic who acknowledges her godlessness and her ability to fool people about psychic powers:

> I think I have finally found my answer to those people who tell me that skepticism takes the joy out of life, that you need God to experience morality, and that without him it's just a heartless existence. People [who thought I had psychic powers] were happy to talk.

They really just wanted to go over funny stories about a loved one they'd lost or just sit and remember them out loud with someone. When I took away the voodoo, the fact that we had "shared" didn't go away. There is all the joy you need in human interaction. I really made sure that after we were done I gave each person, for lack of a better way of saying this, a part of me. I felt I had taken away something fake and I needed to replace it with something real. Human contact, human caring, human interaction.

{CA}

Coleman, William Emmette (Born 1843)

Coleman, a Virginian, became a radical non-Christian Spiritualist at the age of sixteen. Raised in the midst of slavery, he saw the enormity of the institution and was in full sympathy with William Lloyd Garrison and other reformers. He also became an advocate of universal suffrage, prison reform, peace, temperance reforms, and total separation of church and state. Coleman dramatized *East Lynne*, which was shown on a New York stage, and he was a columnist for that city's *Clipper* and also its *Mercury*. Coleman wrote many tracts and was the Kansas representative in the Centennial Congress of Liberals at Philadelphia in 1876.

A charter member of the National Liberal League, he often spoke on Darwinism, spectrum analysis, and the parallelism between biologic and philologic evolution. Coleman was a strong critic of theosophy and "asserted that the so-called feats of magic claimed to be performed by Madam Blavatsky and the Indian adepts were sleight-of-hand tricks—mere jugglery." {PUT}

Colenso, John William (1814—1883)

Colenso was a master at Harrow who, after writing a famous *Treatise on Algebra* (1849), became first Bishop of Natal. His *The Pentateuch and Book of Joshua Critically Examined* (1862—1879) made a great stir and was condemned by both Houses of Convocation and its author declared deposed. In 1865, the Privy Council declared the deposition "null and void in law." Colenso pleaded the cause of the natives at the time of the Zulu War. {BDF; TRI}

Coleridge, John Duke [Sir] (1820—1894)

Coleridge, Lord Chief Justice of England, showed his liberality in mid-career by working for the suppression of religious tests at the universities. But, as is usual in such cases of men of his position, the full extent of his heresy was known only to intimate friends until he died. In a letter to a brother-judge and fellow-heretic, Lord Bramwell, Coleridge wrote, "Of ecclesiastical Christianity I believe probably as little as you do," adding that he thought that religion will last "longer than is good for the world." {JM; RAT; RE}

Coleridge, Samuel Taylor (1772—1834)

Coleridge, like fellow Unitarian minister Ralph Waldo Emerson, was a major transcendentalist of his day. His "Rime of the Ancient Mariner," "Christabel," and "Kubla Khan" continue to be popular with readers of all ages, some of whom recognize that "Christabel" deals with the subject of lesbianism. His *Biographia Literaria* (1817) is a major work, but some accuse him of having borrowed heavily from German idealist philosophers.

Ved Mehta relates the story (*New Yorker*, 11 November 1991) that the headmaster of his school was unhappy with young Coleridge "for having confessed that he was a non-believer and therefore didn't want to be a clergyman." As an adult, Coleridge wrote extensively on religion, philosophy, and literature as well as lectured on Shakespeare.

He was greatly influenced by William Godwin. His essay, "Religion," mentions the heresy of Socinianism, suggesting that a Socinian is "a man who has passed from orthodoxy to the loosest Arminianism, and thence to Arianism, and thence to direct Humanism." Nicolas Walter has pointed out that Coleridge's use of "Humanism" was one of the first times Unitarians utilized the term, that his reasoning helped lead American Unitarians to alter the word's meaning.

For Coleridge's arthritic condition, a physician in 1801 prescribed laudanum, a tincture of opium. Although not an opium addict by choice, Coleridge became addicted to the drug and wrote "Kubla Khan" while under its influence. At one point, in 1814, he took a pint of laudanum a day, diluting it with quince juice and flavoring it with cinnamon. Friends are said to have urged him to reduce the dose of the drug which friends and chemists surreptitiously supplied. As corroborated by Althea Hayter's *Opium and the Romantic Imagination* (1968), others at that time—Dickens, Scott, Bulwer Lytton, Mrs. Gaskell, Elizabeth Barrett Browning—took the drug that even babies were dosed with: Godfrey's Cordial or Mother Bailey's Quieting Syrup. Coleridge suffered massive bowel movements and eruptions from it, but laudanum gave him the physical relief that was so necessary, not to mention led him into poetic dreams, trances, reveries.

Martin Gardner points out that Coleridge erred in *The Ancient Mariner when* he wrote, "The Sun's rim dips, the stars rush out: At one stride comes the dark." This is followed by a "horned moon" climbing in the east, a crescent moon with "one bright star within its nether tip." A moon rising after sunset has to be full, not crescent shaped. Perhaps Coleridge intended the scene to be a supernatural omen, Gardner adds.

Richard Holmes has written that Coleridge was melancholic, constipated, a heavy drinker, and toward the end of his life looked twenty years older than he actually was. He left his wife and their three children to go to Malta in 1804, partly to escape his wife, staying for three disorganized decades with friends such as the John Morgans and the James Gillmans. His play, "Remorse" was too metaphysical for Lord Byron, who commented, "I wish he would explain his explanation."

Biographia Literaria was written in six weeks and was encouraged by John Morgan, who in defense of the charge that his friend had borrowed passages wholesale from Friedrich Schelling, said that they "form a kind of psychodrama within the heart of '*Biographia*.' " The work has been described by novelist Penelope Fitzgerald as his "personal philosophical journey from the materialism of Locke to the perception that faith in God is not only beyond reason but a continuation of it."

Robertson quotes Coleridge's objections to being called an atheist, writing, "Little do these men know what atheism is. Not one man in a thousand has either strength of mind or goodness of heart to be an atheist. I repeat it. Not one man in ten thousand has goodness of heart or strength of mind to be an atheist." But Robertson although agreeing that Coleridge, like Wordsworth, was not an orthodox Christian does find that Coleridge although a liberal in religion was attracted to mysticism.

Coleridge, in short, discarded much of organized religion but believed, as did other Unitarians of the day, in some greater force, or "God." This "God" he observed while watching a beetle on the surface of the water, casting "a cinque-spotted shadow fringed with prismatic colours on the sunny bottom of the brook," or while scouring the beauties so often overlooked in nature. (James Fenton's "A Lesson from Michelangelo," *The New York Review of Books*, 23 March 1995, relates William Wordsworth's disliking "Kubla Kahn," Dorothy Wordsworth's embarrassing Coleridge by calling her drinking vessel Kubla Can, and Byron's being most favorably impressed by the work.) {CE; Penelope Fitzgerald, *The New Yori Times Book review*, 11 April 1999; JMR; JMRH; PUT; TRI; TYD}

Colins, Jean Guillaume César Alexandre Hippolyte [Baron] (1783—1859)

Colins was a Belgian socialist, the founder of "collectivism." He wrote nineteen volumes on social science. Colins denied monotheism as well as pantheism, and he taught the natural immortality of the soul. A number of his disciples propagated his opinions in *Philosophie de l'Avenir*. {BDF; RAT}

COLLEGE FREETHINKERS: See entry for Campus Freethought Alliance.

COLLEGE OF CHARLESTON, SOUTH CAROLINA

Humanists at the College of Charleston are at <http://www.secularhumanism.org/cfa/orgs.html>.

COLLEGE OF LAKE COUNTY, ILLINOIS

Humanists at the College of Lake County are at <http://www.secularhumanism.org/cfa/orgs.html>.

COLLEGE OF THE SISKIYOUS, CALIFORNIA

Humanists at College of the Siskiyous are found at <http://www.secularhumanism.org/cfa/orgs.html>.

COLLEGES, MOST AND LEAST RELIGIOUS

A 1996 survey of 56,000 students at 310 of the top colleges in the United States revealed the following:

- Most "Religious":

Mormon Brigham Young; Grove City; Furman; Loyola Marymount; Stamford; Holy Cross; University of Dallas; Notre Dame; Baylor; and Calvin

- Least "Religious":

Reed; Bennington; Bard; College of the Atlantic; San Francisco Art Institute; Eugene Lang; Sarah Lawrence; Deep Springs; Hampshire; New College of the University of South Florida

{*Freethought Today*, December 1996}

Collet, Dobson (1812—1898)

Collett, a secular activist, was secretary of the Newspaper Stamp Abolition Committee (1849) in England. {VI}

Collet, Sophia Dobson (19th Century)

Sophia Collet, a sister of Dobson Collet, composed several hymns for the South Place chapel, of which she was a member. {VI}

Colette, Jules-Joseph (1829-1903)

Colette, father of the eminent French author, was a non-believer. His wife, **Adèle Eugénie Sidonie Landoy** (1835-1912), was the freethinking daughter of Adèle Chatenay and Henri-Marie Landoy, a quadroon whom she described as "the Gorilla." Her father was a manufacturer of chocolate, the slabs of which were laid out in the open at evening but by morning often had imprints of cat paws. She had first been married to Jules Robineau-Duclos, known to people in her village as "The Savage," an uncouth and heavy drinker. She baptized her children but did not accept the dogma, the Catholic ritual, or the Catholic holidays. An atheist and a Fourierist, she fostered free will in her children, sometimes being chastised by her husband for talking about the catechism with her daughter, then denying religion's worth.

Sidonie-Gabrielle Colette (1873-1954), who described herself as the daughter of a "quadroon," did not follow in her parents' non-religious ways, although she was anything but orthodox in her views. She became an outstanding French writer of the first half of the century. Called Gabri, she experimented with opium, was bisexual, and her novels concerned the pleasures and pains of love. Her first husband was Henri Gauthier-Villars (who was called Willy and who, despite rumors, never locked her in a room to force her to write); after their divorce in 1906 she married Henry de Jouvenel in 1912 and Maurice Goudeket in 1935. Moralists of all stripes complained, but she became the "sensation of *tout Paris*," a legendary figure in the capital city. Her novels included the "Claudine" series (1900-1903), *Chéri* (1920), and *Gigi* (1945). Surrounded by her cats, Colette died peacefully in her Palais-Royal apartment that overlooked Paris.

Captain Colette served under Napoleon III in the Battle of Melegnano, losing a leg. Just after it was removed, the Emperor asked about him. Pointing to his leg, the captain—his just amputated leg wrapped in a towel—responded, "Mother and child are doing well." Sartre, aware of his reputation in heterosexual matters, once called him "a local gay blade." When the Chevalier de la Légion-d'honneur died, the family draped over his coffin his Captain of the First Zouave's tunic—the wasp-waisted jacket of an officer in the Second Empire. {Claude Francis and Fernande Gontier, *Creating Colette*, 1999; Judith Furman, *Secrets of the Flesh* (1999)

Collette, Merrill (20th Century)

A journalist in Venezuela, Collette has written for *Free Inquiry* (Fall, 1988).

Collette, Robert D. (20th Century)

Collette is active with the Humanists of South Pinellas in Saint Petersburg, Florida. (See entry for Florida Atheists, Humanists.) {FD}

Collier, Curt (1961-)

Collier is leader of the Riverdale Yonkers Society for Ethical Culture in New York. He travels to New York once or twice a week to fulfill his duties, but he lives in Corpus Christi, Texas, where he works as an audiologist. "The Bible has been used as a weapon against people," he has said. "What humanists need to realize is that not all believers in the Bible believe in it in the same way. There is a difference between the way a Presbyterian looks at it as opposed to a Fundamentalist." He prefers the term "non-theist" to describe his outlook, adding, "An atheist is certain there is no God. For an agnostic, the jury is still out. I'm a non-theist. I really don't care whether people believe or don't believe in a god."

Collier at one time studied in Israel to become a rabbi. "I see humanism as coming out of a religious background. Humanism is not a break from the past. In Judaism, we have a group of people who put justice at the center of their religious belief, and that's the humanist message today."

Collier, John (1850—1934)

Collier, a British painter and the son of Lord Monkswell, married a daughter of Professor Huxley. When she died, he defiantly married her sister, accomplishing much in the way of reforming the law which forbade marrying a deceased wife's sister. Collier wrote *Religion of an Artist* (1926). An agnostic, Collier was contemptuous of all theology. He was overheard by McCabe as saying that few artists, in fact, have any religious feeling at all. "I've steered clear of God," he said. "He was an incredible sadist." Collier was an honorary associate of the Rationalist Press Association. {GS; JM; RAT; RE; TYD}

Collier, W. Edwin (20th Century)

In 1934, Collier became a Philadelphia leader of the Ethical Culture Society. James F. Hornbach has described Collier as being an "ethical mystic and transcendentalist" who had been recruited by Stanton Coit from the Church of England. (See entry for Ethical Culture.) {EU, Howard B. Radest}

Collin, Christen Christian (Born 1857)

A Norwegian writer, Collin taught European literature at Christiana and was a member of the historical-philosophical faculty of that university. He has co-operated with the Ethical movement. {RAT}

Collins, Anthony (1676—1729)

Collins, whom McCabe termed a deist but others have called a theist, was described by T. H. Huxley as a "Goliath of Freethinking." A friend of Locke, he developed Locke's principles. His books include *Essay Concerning the Use of Reason* (1707), *Discourse on Freethinking* (1713), and *Discourse on the Grounds and Reason of the Christian Religion* (1724). The 1713 book occasioned a great outcry, as it argued that all belief must be based on free inquiry, that the use of reason would involve the abandonment of supernatural revelation. Deism was made in a manner fashionable because of the controversial book, because of its style and sincere outspokenness.

Although termed by Bentley an atheist, Collins once wrote, "Ignorance is the foundation of Atheism, and Freethinking the cure of it." But he was attacked widely. Joseph Smith in *The Unreasonableness of Deism, or, the Certainty of a Divine Revelation* (1720) called deists in general "the Wicked and Unhappy men we have to deal with."

Collins often engaged in controversy with the clergy, wrote against priestcraft, and debated with Dr. Samuel Clarke "about necessity and the moral nature of man," stating the arguments against human freedom, observed A. C. Fraser, with "a logical force unsurpassed by any necessitarian."

With respect to Collins's controversy on "the soul," Huxley said, "I do not think anyone can read the letters which passed between Clarke and Collins without admitting that Collins, who writes with wonderful Power and closeness of reasoning, has by far the best of the argument, so far as the possible materiality of the soul goes; and that in this battle the Goliath of Freethinking overcame the champion of what was considered orthodoxy.

Berkeley, however, claimed that Collins had announced "that he was able to demonstrate the impossibility of God's existence," obviously the exaggeration of an opponent. According to the *Biographica Britannica*, "Notwithstanding all the reproaches cast upon Mr. Collins as an enemy to religion, impartiality obliges us to remark, what is said, and generally believed to be true, upon his death-bed he declared 'That, as be had always endeavored, to the best of his abilities to serve his God, his King, and his country, so he was persuaded he was going to the place which God had designed for those who love him': to which he added that 'The Catholic religion is to love God, and to love man'; and he advised such as were about him to have a constant regard to these principles."

Upon Collins's death, the Earl of Egmont, John Percival, wrote the following: "Of Collins Esq. deceased December 1729 . . . [he] is a Speculative Atheist and has been for many years, as he owned to Archibald Hutchinson Esq. who told it to Dr. Dodd M.D. and he to me." (See entries for Infidel and for Jonathan Swift.) {BDF; CE; EU, David Berman; FO; FUK; HAB; JM; JMR; RAT; RE}

Collins, Daniel S. (20th Century)

Collins was a leader of the Unitarian Fellowship of Jonesboro, Arkansas, when he signed Humanist Manifesto II. {HM2}

Collins, Erin (20th Century)

Collins is a publicity chairman for and activist member of the University of Minnesota Atheists and Humanists.

Collins, John (20th Century)

In 1953, Collins was president of the Greenwich Village Humanist Club in New York City. His group of college students met in the Rienzi Coffee House on 107 MacDougall Street, carried copies of *The Humanist*, and challenged any existentialists to a verbal duel. Items discussed at meetings, according to *The Humanist Newsletter*: "proselytizing the city's intelligentsia by publicizing the basic concepts of naturalistic humanism; setting up an 'ethical clearing house' committee whose members would be on guard to back up, in public statements, difficult or unpopular moral actions which individuals have taken and which are felt to be particularly humanistic; forming a committee to help orient foreign students who want to learn about the United States without beating treated as heathens who are expected to join whatever sect the guide happens to belong to; visiting sects or groups desirous of comparing, sharing, or modifying our . . . or their . . . views; and listing worthy organizations already in existence, such as the Eye Bank, the World Calendar Association, and the Prison Association of New York, whose goals are commendably humanistic."

Collins's interest in the investigation of cosmic and sub-atomic phenomena led him to complain about the view, "There is no causality or determinism in nature." His retort was that "this may be a valuable heuristic axiom when it comes to observing the path of an electron, but if it were applied literally to large scale phenomena, it would mean, among other things, that science is impossible. As Waldemar Kaempffert pointed out in the *Times* of July 1953, 'What is only a probability in the atom is as good as certainty in a rock.' The 'free will' controversy, it seems, is not going to be resolved by a cyclotron." (See entry for Greenwich Village Humanist Club.)

Collins, John Churton (1848—1908)

A British writer, Collins wrote studies of Voltaire and Bolingbroke. He had refused to take up a clerical career and, becoming a skeptic in his early years, had been disinherited. In a memoir by his son, prefixed to *The Life and Memoirs of J. C. Collins* (1912), a note explains that his father believed in God but not immortality or Christianity. He was, however, appreciative of the French deists. {JM; RAT; RE}

Collins, M. J. (20th Century)

In Uganda, Collins leads a humanist group known as the K. Executive Club. (See entry for Africa, Freethought and Humanism in.) {FD}

Collins, May (19th Century)

Collins is a freethinker who wrote *A Plea for the New Woman* (1896). {GS}

Collins, Nigel (20th Century)

Collins is active in Britain with the Cotswold and Cheltenham humanists. He also is a leader of the Humanist Funeral Network. In 1998 he became a director of the Rationalist Press Association.

Collins, William Whitehouse (1853—1923)

An Anglo-American freethought publisher and editor, Collins was a secularist both in Australia and in New Zealand. He wrote a rationalist burial service and a variety of freethought pamphlets. From Christchurch, New Zealand, he edited *Tribune* (1894—1895) and the monthly and bi-monthly *Examiner* (1907—1917). He also edited the Australian journals, *Freethinker & New South Wales Reformer* (1886) and *Freedom* (1889—1890). Collins founded in Sydney the Freethought Press, was a president of the Rationalist Association of New South Wales, and was an honorary associate of the Rationalist Press Association. Collins was the great grandson of Chartist John Collins. {EU; FUK; RSR; SWW}

Collis, David (20th Century)

A dealer of freethought books, Collis collected a large number of works which were purchased by the University of Wisconsin Library. {FUK}

Collyer, Robert (1823—1912)

"The blacksmith preacher," Collyer became a Unitarian minister who continued being a blacksmith during his early manhood, having worked fourteen-hour days in grinding poverty at the age of eight. He was associated with the First Unitarian and the Second Unitarian groups in Chicago. During the Civil War, he worked with the Sanitary Mission, giving first aid, comfort, and ministry to the wounded. With no medical background, however, he felt he was ill-suited to the job. He saw action in Washington, D.C., and Missouri. Collyer, after making several trips back to his native England, died of a stroke.

On the Web: <www.btinternet.com/~mike.dixon/collyer.htm>. Collyer's last pastorate was at the Church of the Messiah in New York. {CE; U}

Collymore, Errold D. (20th Century)

Collymore, an African American, is a prominent Unitarian.

Colman, Lucy N. (1817—1906)

An American reformer, Colman spent most of her life advocating the abolition of slavery, women's rights, and freethought. A radical in many ways, she opposed *white* as well as *black* slavery and devoted herself to *woman's* as well as *man's* rights. She accused the churches of being in complicity with slavery, and she even renounced the liberal Unitarians and Universalists. "Christianity demands entire subordination to its edicts. Until the majority of the people are emancipated from authority over their minds, we are not safe," she wrote in *Reminiscences* (1891). Colman was a contributor to *Truthseeker*, fighting against Anthony Comstock and his censorship, and *Boston Investigator*. {BDF; PUT; RAT; RE; TYD; WWS}

COLOMBIA, ATHEISTS IN: See entry for Antonio José Restrepo. Ruben Ardila, professor of psychology at Colombia's National University, signed Humanist Manifesto 2000.

Colón-Ríos, Etienne (20th Century)

Colón-Ríos is a Puerto Rican secular humanist. He is assistant to the secretary of *Asociación Iberoamericana Ético Humanista* (ASIBEHU).

COLORADO: See entry for Jefferson, Territory of.

COLORADO FREETHINKERS, HUMANISTS

Colorado has the following humanist groups:

• American Atheists, Inc., Margie Wait is in Lakewood. E-mail: <aachat@atheists.org>, and <irep@atheists.org> and <art@atheists.org>.

• American Humanist Chapter of the Mountain and Plains Region, A-512, 1780 South Bellaire Street, Denver, Colorado 80222. Lewis Dunlap is the contact.

• Atheists of Northern Colorado (ASHS; Atheist Alliance Inc.), PO Box 2555, Loveland, CO 80539-2555; (970) 577-0015. On the Web: <http://www.atheistalliance.org/anx/>.

Co-founders: Guy and Victoria McCoy <vgmccoy@juno.com>
President: Calvin Wichern <cwichern@aol.com>
Vice Presidnet: Jan Abbott <jan@tesser.com>
Secretary: Debra Mathewson: <mark_m@sprynet.com>

• Freethinkers of Colorado Springs, Colorado. (719) 535-0321.

• Humanist Association of Pikes Peak (AHA), POB 195, Colorado Springs, CO 80901. Sarah Primm and John Ramsay are contacts. (719) 635-2416.

• Humanists of Boulder, Colorado (AHA), 455 South 38th Street, Boulder, Colorado 80303. Darryl Mehring is the contact.

• Humanists of Colorado, 10124 E. Jewell Ave. (#8), Denver, Colorado 80231. Ken Roberts is President.

• Humanists of Denver, Colorado (AHA), 2230 East Columbia Place, Denver, CO 80210-6009; (303) 759-0875. Darwin K. Rolens, President; contact, Ken Roberts.

• Humanists of the Durango Region, Colorado, (303) 259-2216

• University of Colorado at Boulder's Campus Heretics are on the Web: <http://www.secularhumanism.org/cfa/orgs.html>.

• University of Colorado at Colorado Springs Freethinkers are on the Web: <http://www.secularhumanism.org/cfa/orgs.html>.

• Walk Away, 1700 Rutledge Court, Fort Collins, Colorado 80526. Jim Hoyne leads the local group in supporting recovering fundamentalists.

Colotes (3rd Century B.C.E.)

Colotes of Lampsacus was a hearer and disciple of Epicurus, with whom he was a favorite. He wrote a work in favor of his master's teachings. Colotes held it was unworthy of a philosopher to use fables. {BDF}

Colton, Helen (20th Century)

Colton wrote *The Gift of Touch*, which describes the importance of cuddling newborn babies to comforting elderly parents. In 1998 she was a presenter at the American Humanist Association's convention.

Columbus, Christopher [Cristóbal Colón in Spanish; Cristoforo Colombo in Italian] (1451—1506)

In a letter from Jamaica to Spain's King Ferdinand and Queen Isabella, Columbus mentioned that he had read Roger Bacon's *Opus Majus*, a work which suggests the possibility of reaching India by sailing westward. To his credit, Columbus proceeded with the westward voyage although few (including two friars, one a Franciscan, the other a Dominican) were supportive of the risky venture. Even members of his crew were mutinous, sabotaging the *Pinta*'s rudder. And when a meteorite fell near the superstitious seamen, it was interpreted as a bad omen, described by Columbus as follows: ". . . when the sea made up considerably without wind, [the crew] were astonished. I saw this as a sign from God. As with Moses when he led his people out of captivity, my people were humbled."

Long before this, Eratosthenes (275—194 B.C.E.) had calculated with great accuracy the circumference of the earth and the distance of the sun and moon. Posidonius (circa 135—50 B.C.E.) had suggested that India could be reached by sailing across the Atlantic—he erred, however, by estimating that India was 70,000 stadia across the Atlantic from Europe. In short, even in Columbus's time it was known that the world was "round," even if the point had not yet been proven.

Five hundred years later, Isaac Asimov has observed that anyone with adequate supplies to keep three ships sailing could not have *missed* landing somewhere in the Americas, from Argentina to Canada. The truly great feat, Asimov declared, was not solely that Columbus landed but that he had *not* landed . . . in Asia. What this meant, philosophically, was that Aristotle as well as earlier thinkers could now be doubted, and this helped pave the way for Copernicus and later scientists to give us the more accurate picture we now have of our universe. In short, America had been found . . . and Aristotle had been found lacking.

W. R. Anderson, President of the Leif Ericsson Society in Chicago, claims that the tax lists now in the Vatican show there were at least 1,000 families on the continent in the 12th century. In 1488, four years before the discovery by Columbus, these individuals requested the Pope to send a bishop and priest, "and he ordained and sent them a new apostle by the name of Mathias." In addition, Canadian scientists have excavated Basque as well as Norse traces in Iceland and Newfoundland, all of which preceded Columbus's landings.

Who *did* discover America? Not Columbus, not Leif Ericsson, not the Indians, according to Ronald Fritze in *Skeptic* (Vol. 2, No. 4, 1994). He explains, "The prehistoric hunters who were the ancestors of the Native Americans and crossed the Bering Landbridge some 15,000 years ago were the true discoverers of the Americas. Furthermore, Leif Ericsson and other Norse seafarers reached the Americas in the decades after 1000 CE (Common Era). The testimony of the Norse sagas has been confirmed by the discovery of a genuine Norse archaeological site at L'Anse aux Meadows on Newfoundland which may have even been Leif Ericsson's own camp."

Despite all the publicity, then, it possibly was the pagans—Asian as well as European—who beat the Christians to the continent named by the latter group. It is the latter group, however, which is being held responsible for its barbarous treatment, in the name of religion, of the descendants of the discoverers of the Americas: the native Americans, variously called Native Americans or American Indians. Historians at some point, and in keeping with new discoveries, will likely replace "Indian" and "American" with words more precise than these erroneous references to India and Amerigo Vespucci. Some of the Eskimo people of Canada, for example, understandably insist upon being called Inuits (the plural of *inuk*, or person), not American Indians.

"We are condemning the Spanish conquest," protested Candido Martinez in Honduras at an October 12th Columbus Day holiday in 1997. "These are 505 years that we are not celebrating because the truth is that for 505 years we have been executed, our ancestors were assassinated." Protestors pulled down a six-foot statue of Columbus, broke off its head and hands, and painted it red, symbolic of blood. Similar protests took place in 1997 in Chile and El Salvador. {CE; Reuters, 12 October 1997}

COMADRE

Freethinkers who dislike being termed a "godmother" have no objection to being called a comadre. Ordinarily, a comadre or compadre assists in the intellectual growth of a child (comhijo and comhija?). No legal obligation to provide financial assistance is involved, nor to adopt children if their situation becomes dire—relatives fulfill that role. (See entries for compadre, comhija, comhijo, and godparenting.)

Comazzi, Giovanni Battista [Count] (17th Century)
An Italian writer, Comazzi wrote *The Morals of Princes* (c. 1680), a commentary on the lives of the Roman Emperors, with heterodox reflections. {RAT}

Combe, Abram (1785-1827)
One of a noted Scottish family of seventeen, Combe after becoming acquainted with Robert Owen founded a community at Orbiston. He devoted nearly the whole of his large fortune to the scheme. Combe wrote *Metaphysical Sketches of the Old and New Systems* and other works advocating Owenism. {BDF}

Combe, Andrew (1797—1847)
A physician and brother of Abram Combe, Andrew aided his brother George in founding the Phrenological Society. He wrote popular works on the *Principles of Physiology*. {BDF; RAT}

Combe, George (1788—1858)
A phrenologist and educationalist, Combe after meeting Spurzheim published *Essays on Phrenology* (1819) and founded the *Phrenological Journal*. In 1828 he excited controversy with his *Constitution of Man*, which called for removing the chimeras of special providence and the efficacy of prayer. His last work, *The Relations Between Science and Religion* (1857) upheld a secular theism. George Eliot, with whom he spent a fortnight, was a friend. Combe is said to have done more than any man of his time, save Robert Owen, to further the cause of secular education. {BDF; RAT}

Combes, Emile (19th Century)
Combes was a leading supporter in the final achievement of France's separation of church and state in 1905. Commencing 10 April 1868 Flaubert, Taine, Renan, and others celebrated the event and toasted Combes. At the 1868 banquet "roast beef with Champeaux potatoes and a tarte Tatin were washed down with kir and regional wines by 200 committed anti-clerics" in a three-hour feast at the Mutualité Hall in Paris. {*Freethought History* #14, 1995}

Combes, Justin Louis Émile (1835—1921)
Combes was a French statesman who had studied for the priesthood but abandoned the Church before ordination. A physician, he also went into politics, becoming Minister of Public Instruction (1895—1896) and Minister of the Interior and Premier (1902—1905). He presided over the final stages of the separation of Church and State. Although many French rationalists complained of his leniency to the church, Catholics everywhere denounced him as their bitterest enemy. {RAT; RE}

Combes, Paul (Born 1856)
Combes, a French writer, wrote *Darwinism* (1883) and other works which popularized science. {BDF}

COMEDY: See entry for Tragedy.

COMET
A comet in the sky is a fearful sign that God or the gods are unhappy. Or so the view was held until astronomers explained that it is a celestial body consisting chiefly of ammonia, methane, carbon dioxide, and water. Whereas in ancient minds comets were blamed for fires, famines, pestilence, and wars, Comet Hale-Bopp in 1997, the brightest to pass inside Earth's orbit in more than four hundred years, was watched with awe and admiration by more people than ever before.
Aristotle used *kome*, or "hair of the head," to mean "luminous tail of a comet" and used *kometes*, "wearing long hair," to mean that which today is known as those rare balls of dirty ice that release gases and dust that glow in the sun's radiation, resulting in their extraordinary splendor. (See entry for Alan Hale, discoverer of Comet Hale-Bopp in 1995.)

Comey, Arthur C. (20th Century)
Comey was an active member of the American Humanist Association. {HNS}

Comfort, Alex (20th Century)
Comfort's *The Pattern of the Future* (1949) included his favorable views of scientific humanism.

COMHIJO, COMHIJA
When told in 1980 that freethinkers might one day replace *godfather* and *godmother* by *compadre* and *comadre*, Fernando Vargas of Costa Rica suggested *godchildren* could then be replaced by *comhijo* and *comhija*. He warned, however, that compadre also connotes a crony and a comadre can be a gossip. (See entries for compadre and comadre.)

Commager, Henry Steele (1902—1998)
Commager, an eminent historian, author with Samuel Eliot Morison of *The Growth of the American Republic* (1930), a standard college textbook for four decades, taught at Amherst (26 years), Columbia (18 years), and New York University (12 years). *The American Mind* (1951) explored the nation's cultural and philosophical forces. *The Empire of Reason* (1977) rejected historian Charles A. Beard's views, which he termed "sterile" economic determinism, and held that the principles of the Age of Enlightenment only envisioned by great European philosophers had actually been carried out by 18th and early 19th century Americans.
In 1951, asked about humanism, he replied to the present author:

> I know nothing about naturalistic humanism and have therefore nothing to write you.

Later, however, he accepted a pending Humanist of the Year award from the American Humanist Association.
An opponent of the war in Vietnam, he said "Having the United States in Vietnam is like having the Chinese invade the shores of Long Island!"
Critics complained that although he arguable was "the greatest anthologist American ever produced," he gave too little attention to Native Americans and African Americans.
Commager wrote *Theodore Parker: Yankee Crusader* (1936), a biography of the Unitarian reformer. "History is a story," Commager once wrote, and "if history forgets or neglects to tell a story, it will inevitable forfeit much of its appeal and much of its authority as well." {CE; FUS; WAS, 14 February 1951}

Commazzi, Gian-Battista (18th Century)
Count Commazzi wrote *Politica e Religione Trovate Insieme Nella Persona di Giesù Cristo* (1706—1707), in which he makes Jesus to be a political imposter. The work was rigorously confiscated at Rome and Vienna. {BDF}

COMMITTEE FOR THE SCIENTIFIC EXAMINATION OF RELIGION (CSER)
The Committee for the Scientific Examination of Religion (CSER), Box 703, Amherst, NY 14226, is headed by Hector Avalos. For the Council for Secular Humanism, it was organized to examine the claims of Eastern and Western religions and of well-established and newer sects and denominations in the light of scientific inquiry. It is interdisciplinary, including specialists in biblical scholarship, archaeology, linguistics, anthropology, the social sciences, and philosophy who represent differing secular and religious traditions.

COMMITTEE FOR THE SCIENTIFIC INVESTIGATION OF CLAIMS OF THE PARANORMAL (CSICOP)
The Committee for the Scientific Investigation of Claims of the Paranormal is an international organization that publishes *Skeptical Inquirer* (Box 703, Amherst, NY 14226-0702). Its leaders include

Paul Kurtz, chairman; Barry Karr, Executive Director and Public Relations Director; Joe Nickell, Senior Research Fellow; and Lee Nisbet, Special Projects Director.

CSICOP's executive council includes James E. Alcock, psychologist at York University in Toronto; Barry Beyerstein, biopsychololgist of Simon Fraser University in Vancouver, British Columbia, Canada; Kendrick Frazier, science writer and editor of *Skeptical Inquirer*; Martin Gardner, author and critic; Ray Hyman, psychologist at the University of Oregon; Philip J. Klass, aerospace writer and engineer; Paul Kurtz, chairman; Joe Nickell, senior research fellow; Lee Nisbet, philosopher at Medaille College; and Eugenie Scott, physical anthropologist and executive director of the National Center for Science Education.

In addition to its Amherst, New York, office, the Center for Inquiry has offices in Kansas City, Missouri; Los Angeles, California; and Moscow, Russia.

Dedicated to science and reason, *Skeptical Inquirer* encourages the critical investigation of paranormal and fringe-science claims from a responsible, scientific point of view and disseminates factual information about the results of such inquiries to the scientific community and the public. It also promotes science and scientific inquiry, critical thinking, science education, and the use of reason in examining important issues. On the Web: <www.csicop.org>.

COMMITTEE FOR THE STUDY OF KORANIC LITERATURE

The Committee for the Study of Koranic Literature was formed by the Council for Secular Humanism to examine the foundations, claims, and practices of Islam and its holy book, the Qur'an.

Chairman of the committee is Ibn Warraq (a pseudonym—the individual fears he will be attacked by religious fundamentalists).

COMMON MORAL DECENCIES

Paul Kurtz makes the point that, left to our own devices and free of early childhood conditioning, humans recognize what is moral and decent. Theological doctrines are not a desirable test of what is decent, in short.

Kurtz includes as examples: altruism; integrity; honesty; truthfulness; and responsibility. "Humanist ethics is amenable to critical, rational guidance," he wrote in "The Affirmations of Humanism: A Statement of Principles." "There are normative standards that we discover together. Moral principles are tested by their consequences."

Common, Thomas (20th Century)

In 1896 Common began the publication of Nietzsche's works in English. He became one of the leading English authorities on the German philosopher. In his *Scientific Christianity* (1904), Common rejected all religion. {RAT}

Commoner, Barry (1917—)

Commoner, a biologist and educator, represented the International Humanist and Ethical Union (IHEU) at a UN conference on environment in Stockholm (1972). In 1970, he had received the first Humanist award of that organization, for his contribution to the cause of ecology.

COMMUNALISM

Communalism is found in two forms. First, some groups advocate what often is religious communalism, or group ownership of the goods and property of their community of individuals. Several religious groups including the Shakers [officially known as the "United Society of Believers in Christ's Second Coming"] were communalists and their society was called, by some, a religious communistic settlement.

Also, some groups are more interested in their own minority or ethnic group than in society as a whole. To counter such groups, in Britain the Alliance Against Communalism and for Democracy in South Asia was founded after the demolition of the Babri Masjid in Ayodhya and the communal riots that followed in 1992.

Their aims are to oppose communal forces in South Asia and to rally together anti-communal forces in Britain; to expose what they hold are lies and myths propagated by the communalist forces and to obtain and disseminate reliable information about the communal situation in India; to combat in Britain the influence and ideology of all communalist forces; to work in solidarity with all secular and progressive forces; and to support the struggle for a genuine secular democracy in South Asia.

The anti-communalists have opposed the *fatwa* against Salman Rushdie, have opposed anti-secularist forces in India, and have opposed fundamentalists who for thousands of years have victimized the untouchable class. {*International Humanist News*, December 1993}

COMMUNION CHALICE: See the entries for Ganymede and for theophagy.

COMMUNISTIC HUMANISM

In the early years of the 20th century, a philosophic-political movement commenced for the express purpose of establishing a classless society in which all goods were to be socially owned. Karl Marx expressed the theories of the movement, and Vladimir Ilyich Lenin, who led the successful Communist revolution in Russia, modified those theories. The theory that property should be held in common was not new, for the Incas had an Ejido property-and-work system. The Ancient Greek concept of a world of communal bliss and harmony without the institution of private property was described in Plato's *Republic*. The Jewish Essenes and early Christian communities were communally oriented. Thomas More's *Utopia* proposed forms of communal property ownership in reaction to what the author felt was the selfishness and depredation of growing economic individualism. Thomas Münzer and the Anabaptists upheld communism in the Peasants' War. Robert Owen, Étienne Cabet, Charles Fourier, Pierre Joseph Proudhon, Friedrich Engels all modified earlier communistic concepts. Communistic settlements in the United States during the 19th century included the Amana Church Society in Iowa; the Harmony Society in Pennsylvania; Zoar, in Ohio; the Labadists in Maryland; the Oneida Community in New York; Brook Farm in Massachusetts; and settlements founded by the Shakers, Mormons, Mennonites, Dukhobors, and Jansenites. Some, such as the Amana Church Society were Christian; others, such as those inspired by Marx's *Communist Manifesto* (1848) and his *Das Kapital* (1867, 1885—1894) were atheistic.

In short, theists as well as atheists have been attracted to the communitarian philosophy. Where they have differed has been in their proposals for achieving such goals. Marx believed himself to be the messenger of a new social gospel, for the propagation of which he wrote all his books and pamphlets and became internationally famous not as a philosopher but as a political reformer. Numbers of intellectuals and others rallied to the cause of Marxism, hoping to carry out its theory of socialism including the labor theory of value, dialectical materialism, the class struggle, and dictatorship of the proletariat until a classless society could be achieved. To achieve such goals, Communist parties developed in many countries with the goal of establishing a single authoritarian party which could control state-owned means of production with the professed aim of establishing a stateless society. With the Russian Revolution of 1918, the Union of Socialist Soviet Republics (USSR) was formed to govern about one-seventh of the earth's land area. Leon Trotsky's former secretary, Raya Dunayevskaya, describes Karl Marx as having been a thoroughgoing philosophic naturalist, one who at first had called his outlook "a new humanism," by which he meant a *Marxist* humanism.

Asked what was wrong with communism, Bertrand Russell in *Power* (1938) responded,

> I think the most important thing that is wrong in communist doctrine is the belief in benevolent despotism, a belief which is really ancient and existed in all sorts of communities, but has always proved itself wrong, because when you take a benevolent man and make him a despot, his despotism survives but his benevolence rather faces away. The whole theory of communism is that you give an enormous amount of power to people who are adherents of a certain creed, and you hope that they will exercise that power benevolently. Whereas it seems to me that everybody—with very few exceptions—misuses power, and therefore the important thing is to spread power as evenly as you can, and not give immense power to some small clique.

Although the First, Second, and Third International or Comintern (1919) called for the uniting of all the workers of the world for the coming world revolution, which would be followed by the establishment of a dictatorship of the proletariat and state socialism, Joseph Stalin set up a "socialism in one country" plan, believing that the USSR should, alone, build a true Communist system which could serve as a model for other nations to follow. By the 1930s, when the party began purges, it became evident that in practice Communism, contrary to the hopes of theorists and intellectuals, had created in the USSR a giant totalitarian state that dominated every aspect of life and denied the ideal of individual liberty. In the 1990s, however, the USSR literally came to an end.

"Humanism" used in conjunction with Marxism or communism, however, has been rare, an exception being Cuba's Fidel Castro. An atheist, Castro hopes to carry out humanistic goals by improving the lot of the lower classes, uprooting the advantages previously enjoyed by the propertied classes, collectivizing agriculture, and expropriating all native and foreign industry. In the 1960s his prospects for succeeding were generally applauded, but by the 1990s and with the fall of the USSR his prospects have diminished tremendously. This is particularly evident in light of the fact that hundreds of thousands of Cubans have fled in fear from what they describe as being the non-humanistic, totalitarian nation Castro has chosen to mold. Castro has termed his philosophy "communistic humanism." Others have termed it "inhumanism-by-politburo."

By 1997, the very term "communistic humanism" had become rarely if ever utilized. (See entries for Raya Dunayesvskaya and Mihailo Markovic.) {CE}

COMMUNISTIC RELIGIOUS SETTLEMENTS

Large numbers of religious sectarian groups within the Hebrew-Christian tradition have from time to time attempted to organize their life on a collectivist basis. Duke University's Howard E. Jensen has detailed several such groups:

- early Hebrew-Christian Communities, in which complete communism in consumption goods first appeared among the Hebrews and included the largely celibate communities of the Essenes in the 2nd Century B.C.E.; also, revivals of Christian communism such as found in the Benedictines 6th- century monastic order and the 17th century Jesuits in Paraguay
- early Modern Sectarian Communities, such as those of the Waldenses, the Albigenses, the Cathari, the Apostolican Sect of Alanzo in Italy and France, the Beghards of France and Germany, the English Lollards of Norfolk, the Bruges Weaving Friars, the Dutch Fraternity of the Common Life, the Bohemian Taborites, the Moravian Brethren, and others;
- the Labadists in Maryland, disciples of Jean de Labadie (1610—1674), a former French Jesuit who preached the perfectibility of man, who settled in Elkton, Maryland, on a 3,750 acre tract;
- German Separatist Communities, all found in Pennsylvania and as exemplified by the disciples of Johann Kelpius (1673—1708), Johann Conrad Beissel (1690—1768), and George Rapp (1757—1847); and in Ohio with Joseph Michael Bimeler (1778—1853), as well as in Buffalo, New York, with Christian Metz (1794—1867) and Barbara Heinnemann;
- Bishop Hill Colony, a Scandinavian Lutheran group led by Eric Janson in Bishop Hill, Illinois;
- Shaker Communities, such as those of the "United Society of Believers in Christ's Second Coming" led by Mother Ann Lee (1736—1784) in New England states and New York, Ohio, Kentucky, Florida, Iowa, and Indiana;
- the Bruderhof or Huterite Communities, followers of Jacob Huter, an early 16th-Century Mennonite reformer; a contemporary Bruderhof group, one founded in Germany in 1920, is an offshoot of Anabaptists and is distantly related to the Amish. Its rituals include adult baptism. In 1996 its membership was estimated to include 2,100 U. S. members and 500 in England. The Bruderhof frowns on rock music, bans television, and most of its members refuse to vote. Members live in spartan dormitories, no salaries are paid, everything from clothing to boxes of cereal is distributed according to need, and people who join give their possessions to the community and are assigned tasks—either in the businesses or in the community. Their combined revenue was over $20 million in 1995, with profit of about $9 million, according to *The Wall Street Journal* (5 July 1996).
- the Doukhobors, a Russian communistic religious sect which settled in Canada in 1897;
- Mormon Communism, such as the United Order of Enoch which was established by the Mormon prophet, Joseph Smith, in Ohio and Missouri.

{ER}

COMMUNITARIANSM

Communitarianism involves small cooperatives or collectivist communities, combined with a campaign to restore basic moral values. Amitai Etzioni, a German who studied with Martin Buber, liked Buber's I-and-Thou philosophy and developed a concept in line with communitarianism. Etzioni designed a "communitarian platform," which recognizes that a child's first encounter with society's values is in the family. Then he or she goes to school, becomes a member of the neighborhood and finally a member of the community of communities, society itself. His approach, found in the *Communitarian Quarterly*, has been encouraged in the 1990s by such diverse figures as Vice President Al Gore, Bush cabinet member Jack Kemp, and former Unitarian Universalist Association President Bill Schulz.

Called a "darling of reconstructed Democrats," Etzioni recommends "public humiliation" of criminals. Requiring that certain kinds of convicts wear signs that identify them in public, he has stated without mentioning Hester Prynne of *The Scarlet Letter*, is "a surprisingly effective and low-cost way of . . . expressing the moral order of a community." (For negative critiques of communitarianism, see "The Politics of Restoration," *The Economist*, 24 Dec 1994; and "Communitarian Conceits," *The Economist*, 18 March 1995.) {Warren R. Ross, "Are You a Communitarian Without Knowing It?" *World*, September-October 1994}

COMMUNITY

Many freethinkers, particularly those on the World Wide Web, foresee a future Earth that is not a representative community but is participatory. It will not emphasize national boundaries but, rather, will aim toward humanistic participation by all peoples.

In light of mankind's past history, particularly its religiosity about killing those who are at all different, the change will not be an easy one. However, if and when humans are easily interconnected in cyberspace, optimists expect democracy and freedom will occur in a fashion undreamed of prior to the advent of computers.

COMPADRE

Freethinkers who dislike the term "godfather" often prefer being called compadre. Ordinarily, a comadre or compadre assists in a child's intellectual growth. No legal obligation to provide financial assistance is involved, nor to adopt children if their situation becomes dire—relatives fulfill that role. (See entries for comadre, comjiha, comhijo, and godparenting.)

Comparetti, Domenico (Born 1835)

An Italian philologist, Comparetti taught at the Institute of Superior Studies in Rome. In his many works on the classic writers, he evinces his pagan partialities. Comparetti edited *La Rivista di Filologia*. {BDF; RAT}

Compayré, Jules Gabriel (1843—1913)

Compayré was a French educationalist who taught at Pau, Poitiers, and Toulouse. From 1881 to 1889 he sat in the Chambre and in 1866 was admitted to the Higher Council of Public Instruction. A member of the *Institut*, Compayré was one of the leading French teachers and a thorough rationalist. "We rely no longer," he wrote, "on the religious sentiment, on belief in the supernatural. We appeal solely to reason and nature." {RAT}

COMPASSION IN DYING

Compassion in Dying is a unique American organization that has assisted a number of seriously ill people who have wanted to commit suicide. (See entry for Ralph Mero, a Unitarian minister who is its executive director.)

Compton, Arthur Holly (1892—1962)

An eminent American physicist, Compton helped develop the atomic bomb. He shared the 1927 Nobel Prize in physics for his discovery of "the Compton effect" (the increase in the wavelengths of X rays and gamma rays when they collide with and are scattered from loosely bound electrons in matter). Dr. Compton once wrote, "If we ascribe to God the beauties of the world, we must likewise hold him responsible for the most ugly crimes." {CE}

Compton-Burnett, Ivy [Dame] (1884-1969)

A British novelist of note, Compton-Burnett studied classics, became a prolific writer, and was made a Dame in 1967. In the upper-class Victorian or Edwardian society she described, the characters frequently belonged to large families and spanned several generations. Her plots included examples of domestic crime that ranged from adultery or incest or child abuse to murder and fraud.

Pastors and Masters (1925), *Brothers and Sisters* (1929), *A Family and a Fortune* (1939), *Manservant and Maidservant* (1947) are examples of work which A. N. Wilson has described: "In the age of the concentration camp, when, from 1935 or so to 1947, she wrote her very best novels, no writer did more to illumine the springs of human cruelty, suffering and bravery."

Wilson in *God's Funeral* 1999) points out that Compton-Burnett's novels uniformly made the point that religion had had its day. {OEL}

COMPUTERS: See entries for Tim Berners-Lee and Ted Nelson.

Comstock, Anthony (1844—1915)

Comstalk, a morals crusader born in New Canaan, Connecticut, advocated the suppression of obscene literature. He wrote a comprehensive New York state statute (1868) which forbade immoral works, and in 1873 he arranged for strict Federal postal legislation against obscene matter. His New York Society for the Suppression of Vice was credited with having destroyed 160 tons of literature and pictures. D. M. Bennett's *Anthony Comstock: His Career of Cruelty and Crime* (1878) cited Comstock as a ruthless persecutor, the "Roundsman of the Lord," in a class with Torquemada and Calvin. In fact, Comstock bragged that he had convicted enough people to fill a passenger train of sixty-one coaches, not counting the many who had been driven to suicide.

When Ida Craddock was hauled into court for having written *The Wedding Night*, a work about a maiden lady who imagined she was the chosen bride of Heaven's lustiest angel, Comstock described the work as "indescribable obscenity." Craddock left the court, went home, and turned on the gas. Comstock, although mocked as an old wheezer, justified her suicide by saying that he was "stationed in a swamp at the mouth of a sewer," that "in my heart I feel God approves" putting writers of obscenity—as well as publishers and tavernkeepers—out of business.

In 1905 he unsuccessfully tried to block a New York production of "Mrs. Warren's Profession," immediately making a hit of the play and establishing overnight the reputation of an "Irish smut dealer," author George Bernard Shaw. In 1913 he ordered the removal of a painting "September Morn," from a gallery on Manhattan's 46th Street, leading to publicity that made it one of the world's most famous paintings. In his vigilant career, Comstock sought prosecutions against James Joyce, D. H. Lawrence, Mae West, radio programs, and true-detective magazines.

In 1915 the Society for the Suppression of Vice, aware that Comstockery had become "the world's standing joke at the expense of the United States," in Shaw's words, named John Summer to assume Comstock's duties. Comstock died soon afterwards, and by 1950 the organization had ceased to exist. (See entries for D. M. Bennett and Elizabeth Slenker.) {CE; Jay Maeder, *New York Daily News*, 29 April 1999}

Comte, Auguste (1798—1857)

Positivism, which holds that theology and metaphysics are imperfect modes of knowledge, was Comte's far-reaching philosophic system. Positive knowledge, he held, is verifiable by the empirical sciences and concerns natural phenomena and their properties and relations. His viewpoint developed into a kind of "Catholicism minus Christianity." "The universe displays no proof of an all-directing mind" and "The heavens declare the glory of Kepler and Newton," he wrote. Brazil's flag has the Comtean motto, *Ordern e Progresso*, thereby being the sole national emblem which perpetuates a philosopher's words. In 1881 a Positivist Church formed in Brazil, and his thought also became popular in other parts of Latin America. Known as the originator of sociology, Comte felt man passes through three stages: the theological, in which he ascribes to the supernatural whatever he does not understand; the metaphysical, in which ideas are thought to be the key to natural phenomena; and the positive, in which phenomena are explained using a scientific method of reasoning. Religion he placed on a higher level than sociology, but for him humanity was the object of worship and no metaphysics was involved.

In 1825 Isidore Marie Auguste François Xavier Comte married, but the union proved unhappy. In the following year he lectured but broke down under an attack of brain fever, which occasioned his detention in an asylum. He speedily recovered and continued his writing and lecturing.

Comte once wrote, "I am not an atheist, because that is to take theology seriously." In 1864, the Vatican prohibited reading of his *Cours de philosophie positive* (1830—1842). His last work, *Subjective Synthesis* (1856) verges on the mystical. Comte invented "altruism," which he explained is the opposite of egoism. His concept of altruism has been elaborated upon by Spencer, Mill, and a number of admiring contemporary sociologists, of whom Ayn Rand is not one. Mill speaks of Comte as the superior of Descartes and Leibniz. Comte also coined the word "positivism," a philosophic system of thought that denies any validity to speculation or metaphysics. J. Cotter Morison said, "Comte belonged to that small class of rare minds, whose errors are often more valuable and stimulating than other men's truths." McCabe says that although Comte insisted on "positive" thought—hence the common name Positivism—and refused to be called an atheist, in fact Comte was just that.

Comte died of the painful disease of cancer in the stomach,. M. Littre, his greatest disciple and author of *Auguste Comte et la Philosophie Positive*, described his last days: "The fatal hour arrived, M. Comte, who had borne his malady with the greatest fortitude, met with no less firmness the approach of death. His bodily weakness became extreme, and he expired without pain, having around him some of his most cherished disciples." (For a description of the Positivist calendar—which had thirteen months of twenty-eight days each, plus a Festival of all the Dead and, on leap years, a Festival of Holy Women—see *The London Heretics, 1870—1914*, by Warren Sylvester Smith; also, see entry for Brazil's Church of Positivism.) {BDF; CE; CL; ER; EU, Christopher Kent; FUK; HNS2; ILP; JM; JMR; RAT; RE; TRI; WSS}

Comte, François Charles Louis (1782—1837)

Comte, the brother of Auguste Comte, was a French writer. He founded *Le Censeur* (1814) and incurred fines and imprisonment for his attacks on reaction. He retired to Switzerland, where he taught natural law at Lausanne. He returned to France and in 1811 entered the Chambre and the French Academy. An anti-clerical, Comte wrote *Traité de législation* (4 volumes, 1827—1835), for which he obtained the Academy's Monthyon Prize. {RAT}

Conant, Joseph A. (Born 1830)

Conant, according to Putnam, was a freethinker in Maine, a member of the Fort Fairfield Liberal League. His father was a Universalist, which appealed to his son until he read Ingersoll's lectures and found what he said was something better than even liberal Christianity. Conant, father of nine sons and two daughters, built a log hut, cleared away the native forest, threshed the grain by hand, and hauled it through the woods with horse and sled, then took a boat nine miles to the mill where it was ground. {PUT}

CONCERN

A humanistic monthly, *Concern* is at 4450 Fieldston Road, Bronx, New York 10471.

CONCORD SAGES

For a number of years, a group known as the Concord Sages met informally for philosophical discussion. Often they met at the home of Ralph Waldo Emerson in Concord, Massachusetts, and their interests included religion and economics as well as philosophy. They were inspired by the spirit of revolutionary Europe, German philosophy, Wordsworth, Coleridge, and Carlyle. *The Dial*, their literary organ, was edited by Margaret Fuller and later by Emerson. In "Nature" (1836), Emerson outlined his views of transcendentalism. Included among the Concord sages were Emerson, Henry David Thoreau, Nathaniel Hawthorne, Bronson Alcott, and the younger William Ellery Channing. (See entry for Transcendentalism.) {Carlos Baker, *Emerson Among the Eccentrics: A Group Portrait*; OCA; OCE}

Condillac, Étienne Bonnot de (1715—1780)

The French philosopher who developed sensationalism, Condillac held that all knowledge comes from the senses, that there are no innate ideas. He was a member of the Academy of Sciences (1769) and of the French Academy (1795). Attempting to simplify Locke's theory of knowledge, Condillac argued that all conscious experience is simply the result of passive sensations. Nevertheless, he retained the Cartesian dualism of soul and body, thus attempting to harmonize his deterministic psychology with his religious views. Robertson categorizes Condillac as an abbé whose *Essays on the Origin of Human Knowledge* (1746) was essentially rationalistic and anti-theological, adding that he was a materialist. McCabe states that Condillac was "a priest but was too virtuous for the French clergy and was too able and honest to keep the faith." {BDF; CE; JM; JMR; JMRH; PUT; RAT; RE}

CONCUBINES

Jewish law is said to permit married men and single men to maintain a *pilegash* (concubine), a concept which is said to have been in practice throughout Jewish history and advocated by the Godel Hador Rabbi Yaakov Emdin.

In 1996 Brooklyn, therefore, Shalom Bayis (Household Peace) operated a telephone hotline through which men could meet women willing to serve as kept mistresses. The organization insists concubines offer an alternative to divorce and are acceptable based on the Torah, the Five Books of Moses that form the basis for written Jewish law. The organization, however, has been denounced by Rabbi Fabian Schonfeld of Kew Gardens Hills in New York, calling it "nonsense, lies, and fabrications."

"I'm a father of six children. I'm married 28 years," stated one forty-nine-year-old caller. "You can reach me on my beeper. All right?" Another said, "It is very urgent. I have a long-term marriage, but my [wife] is not into sex, and I need something on the side." Most sought a clandestine relationship, not a live-in concubine. "Do I love my wife? I still don't know what love is, and we never talk about sex because that's how we were raised. I would say 60% of my married friends are miserable. I have spent thousands of dollars in counseling, and then I called Shalom Bayis and I really liked the message," a third person stated. However, Isaac Abraham, a Hasidic spokesman in Brooklyn, retorted that Shalom Bayis "isn't quoting from Jewish law. It is quoting from Heidi Fleiss [a prominent madam of a brothel]." After as many as 2,000 calls daily to the Bayis hotline were being made, the service ceased because of community criticism.

Concubinage is not limited to any one organized religion. It is found universally. {New York *Daily News*, 29 December 1996 and 7 January 1997}

CONDOM

The Bishop of Condom, Jacques Bénigne Bossuet (1627-1704)—tutor of the dauphin (father of Louis XV)—did *not* invent the flexible sheath used for contraceptive purposes. Condom is a town in France's southwestern region of Armagnac known particularly for its *liquer*, *foie gras*, the Three Musketeers . . . and nothing manufactured from rubber.

Condoms are devices which, dating back at least to the Egyptians 3,000 B.P. (Before the Present), were made of linen.

In the 1840s, according to Hoag Levins, with the advent of the vulcanization of rubber the first "safe and effective interface [became possible] between machinery and internal human organs." A 19th century act of Congress, the Anthony Comstock Law, prohibited contraceptives, including "immoral rubber articles," and was supported by leading religious leaders. The law, however, resulted in a condom undergound in which the objects were sold furtively in barbershops and shoeshine parlors. By World War II millions of condoms were issued to avoid the spread of venereal disease. The Reality female condom, made out of polyurethane, is currently in wide use.

It is common knowledge that most men and women prefer to have naked sex, that in moments of passion neither partner thinks about applying a condom. However, fear of getting a venereal disease or AIDS is a major inducement to use the preventive, consummately humanistic devices.

Condon, Charles M.(olony) (1953—)

Condon, the Attorney General of South Carolina, is noted for being "defender of God, the South, and the unborn." He once proposed an "electric sofa" rather than an electric chair to speed executions. He favors preserving the State Capitol's Confederate flag. He supported the Citadel's fight to bar female cadets. He holds that a viable fetus is a person under the state's child abuse laws, that therefore a woman who uses illegal drugs while she is pregnant can be charged with neglect, manslaughter, even murder. A Roman Catholic, Condon received national notoriety in the late 1990s for having refused to swear in a justice of the peace who was an atheist.

Condon, Richard J. (1919-1999)

Condon, the author of *Our Pagan Christmas* (1974), was once a Vice President of the National Secular Society. A prolific contributor to the *Freethinker*, he received a tribute in that publications October 1999 issue. Bill McIlroy officiated at the funeral, held at the South Essex Crematorium, for the lifelong atheist.

Condorcet, Marie Jean Antoine Caritat [Marquis de Nicolas] (1743—1794)

Condorcet's pious Picardy mother dedicated him to the Virgin Mary, keeping him in girls' clothes until he was eleven. A French philosopher, political leader, leader, and mathematician, Condorcet was a freethinker and encyclopedist at the time of the Revolution. His work, *Theory of Probability* (1785), was a valuable contribution to mathematics. According to Robertson, Condorcet wrote *Esquisse d'un tableau historique des progrés de l'esprit humain* (1795), "in which the most sanguine convictions of the rationalistic school are reformulated without a trace of bitterness or of despair."

Edward Goodell, in *The Noble Philosopher* (1994), describes the person entrusted with drafting a constitution for France following the French Revolution. He includes Condorcet's "Sketch for a Historical Picture of the Progress of the Human Mind," which develops the idea that the human race is progressing toward an ultimate state of perfection. In 1776 Condorcet published his atheistic *Letters of a Theologian*, and he wrote in favor of American independence and against Negro slavery.

Upon his election to the National Assembly, of which he became secretary, he moved that all orders of nobility were abolished. He voted against the death of the king, siding with the Gironde group. He also protested the butcheries of the pious Robespierre. This put him at risk, and he fled to the home of Madame Vernet, then left fearing this would bring her into trouble.

"He cared as little for his life," Foote quotes Morley as saying, "as Danton or St. Just cared for theirs. Instead of coming down among the men of the plain or the frogs of the Marsh, he withstood the Mountain to its face." While hiding from those who thirsted for his blood, and burdened with anxiety as to the fate of his wife and child, he wrote, without a single book to refer to, his novel and profound *Esquisse d'un Tableau Historique des Progres de l'Esprit Humain*.

Morley reported that "among the many wonders of an epoch of portents this feat of intellectual abstraction is not the least amazing." Despite the odious law that whoever gave refuge to a proscribed person should suffer death, Condorcet was offered shelter by a noble-hearted woman, who said, "If you are outside the law, we are not outside humanity." But he would not bring peril upon her house, and he went forth to his doom.

He died either of exhaustion or by poison self-administered. According to Putnam, however, although he hid he also got hungry and entered a tavern, calling for an omelette. Asked how many eggs in his omelette, he replied "a dozen." "What is your trade?" he was asked. "A carpenter." "Carpenters have not hands like these and do not ask for a dozen eggs in an omelette," they exclaimed, whereupon they demanded his papers. He had none, so the villagers seized him, bound him, and he was cast into a cold, damp prison cell. Arrested at Clamartsous-Meudon, he was conducted to prison at Bourg-la-Reine. Wounded in the foot, and exhausted with fatigue and privation, he was flung into a miserable cell. "On the morrow," Morley stated, "when the gaolers came to see him, they found him stretched upon the ground, dead and stark. So he perished—of hunger and weariness, say some; of poison ever carried by him in a ring, say others." The Abbe Morellet, in his narrative of the death of Condorcet, *Memoirs*, stated that the poison was a mixture of stramonium and opium, but he added that the surgeon described the death as due to apoplexy.

His wife, **Marie Louise Sophie de Condorcet** (1764—1822), married him in 1787. She shared her husband's ideas and at his death supported herself by painting and writing. She translated Adam Smith's *Theory of Moral Sentiments* and was a thorough rationalist. (See entries for Arthur O'Connor and E. O. Wilson.) {BDF; CE; FO; JM; JMR; JMRH; PUT; RAT; RE; TRI}

Cone, Orello (1835—1905)

A disciple of German biblical scholarship, Cone was one of the foremost biblical scholars to have taught at St. Lawrence University in Canton, New York. An author of several books, he also contributed frequently to the *Universalist Quarterly*. {U&U}

Conerly, Porter W. (20th Century)

Conerly, a freethinker, wrote *Genealogy of the Gods* (1957). {GS}

CONFESSION

• Nothing spoils a confession like repentance.

—Anatole France

CONFIRMABILITY PRINCIPLE: See entry for Verifiability, or Verification, Principle.

CONFIRMATIONS

Confirmation is involved when in a relation between propositions one supports or adds credence to another. Confirmation theory hopes to delimit what kind of proposition or theory is confirmable. In Carnap's kind of inductive logic, it is the relation between evidence and hypothesis. Popper, however, denies that experience ever confirms the hypotheses of a scientific theory. And others, including Feyerabend, advocate epistemological anarchy with no established criteria to separate rubbish from sensible theory. The Finnish logician, Jaakko Hintikka, has developed a system of confirmation theory which eliminates the difficulty about measuring the confirmation of laws, as distinct from the confirmation of predictions about individuals. All those named, however, have been critiqued negatively. No unanimity has been found.

Christians, however, arrange "confirmation" by "baptizing" or by "laying on of hands" or "unction" (or both), thus giving what is claimed "full initiation into Christian discipleship" with its gift of the Holy Spirit—so understood in the early and mediaeval Church on the basis of *Acts* 8:114-17, 19: 1-7.

In Iceland and Finland, to give but two examples, people are initiated at birth/confirmation into the Lutheran Church. Only a small percentage choose any other denomination. The church receives tax money, so everyone's income is skimmed for taxes, and employers are also skimmed regardless of whether their employees are members of the church—"I know," said humanist Paul Harrison of Turku, Finland, "because I managed a language school a few years ago and the tax office insisted on the tithe although the staff was all foreigners who didn't know Luther from a *lukather*."

However, in Sweden, according to Jone Johnson, "if you avow yourself an atheist and not a member of any church, you get a refund of a portion of your tax money (that which otherwise would go to the churches in proportion to declared membership, approximately). In Norway, your proportion of the money that the government gives to the established church can be diverted to the church of your choice—or, in the case of 50,000+ humanists, to their equivalent programs, such as for children's coming-of-age type programs." The Icelandic Humanist Association encourages parents to designate their newly born as humanists during the time of confirmation paperwork. {AF; OCP; Hope Knutsson and Paul Harrison to WAS, 9 May 1999}

CONFUCIANISM

Called Ju Chia (the School of the Learned) in Chinese, Confucianism advocated true manhood (jên) as the highest good, called the superior man (chün tzu) the ideal being, and sought the cultivation of life (hsiu shûn) as man's supreme duty. Not quite a religion, in the Western sense, it has served the purpose of a religion, offering hope to the oppressor and oppressed alike.

In his *Chinese Humanism* (1985), Universalist minister Kenneth Patton wrote of his appreciation for Confucianism, which he found had abolished human sacrifice, had been this-worldly, and had treated spiritual matters as being related to the highest ethical standards of character.

Dr. David Lawson, a Montreal-based writer and poet currently teaching in China, discusses in "Humanism in China" (*The Humanist*, May-June 1993) how the Eastern and Western humanisms interrelate. He takes up how the various political factions in China have reacted to Confucian thought. *The Analects of Confucius*, translated by Simon Leys of Sydney University in Australia in 1997, is one of the most readable versions. (See entries for Civilization and for K'ung Fu-tzu, with Bertrand Russell's critique.) {CE; ER; RE}

Confucius: See entry for Kongfu-zi, the Pinyin system of spelling Kung-fu Tzu. Confucius is a word invented by Christians acquainted with Latin but ignorant of Chinese. For an estimate of the number of Confucians worldwide, see entry for Hell.

CONGRESS OF SECULAR JEWISH ORGANIZATIONS

The Congress of Secular Organizations (CSJO, 19657 Villa Drive North Southfield, MI 48076; phone: 248-569-8127) had the following officers in 1998: Chair: Jeff Zolitor; Vice-Chair: Julie Gales; Executive Director: Roberta Feinstein; Treasurer: Joan Kurtz; Recording Secretary: Bess Katz; Teen/Young Adult Liaison: Karen Knecht; Executive Committee: Rhea Seagull, Renee Lipson, and Bennett Muraskin; Teen Representative: Jennifer Knecht; Young Adult Representative: Denora Knecht; NAF co-chair: Bobbie Varble; Past Co-Chairs: Lawrence Schofer, Ph.D., and Jack Rosenfeld; System Operator and Site Maintenance: Jeff Zolitor.

Congreve, Richard (1818—1899)

An English positivist, Congreve was a follower of Comte and influenced many to embrace positivism. He translated Comte's *Catechism of Positive Philosophy* (1858) and wrote many brochures. Congreve also conducted a small "Church of Humanity." {BDF; FUK; RAT; TRI}

Conklin, Edwin G. (20th Century)

Conklin has been a supporter of the American Humanist Association. {HNS}

Conn, Deidre C. (20th Century)

Conn, while at student at West Virginia's Marshall University, was one of the founders of and is an officer of Campus Freethought Alliance. In 1998 she signed the Alliance's "Bill of Rights for Unbelievers." She is a contributing editor of the *Secular Humanist Bulletin*, the Vice President of Rationalists United for Secular Humanism (RUSH), and a regional director in Kentucky of the Council for Secular Humanism. E-mail: <Conn3@marshall.edu>. {*International Humanist News*, December 1996}

CONNECTICUT ATHEISTS, HUMANISTS, SKEPTICS

Connecticut has the following groups:

• Connecticut Skeptical Society, PO Box 456, Cheshire, CT 06410-0456

• Freethinkers/Thomas Jefferson Society, Box 200, Southbury, Connecticut 06488. Dr. Robert Wolsch is the contact. (203) 262-6123

• Humanist Association of Central Connecticut (ASHS) (AHA), 27 Thornton Street, Hamden, CT 06517. (203) 281-6232. Dr. David Schafer is the contact at <djschaf@compuserve.com>.

• Humanist Friendship Center of Western Connecticut (AHA), 19 Homestead Avenue, Danbury, Connecticut 06810. Robert Wolsch is a contact.

• Humanists of Fairfield County (AHA), 17 Whipoorwill Lane, Westport, Connecticut 06840. Uri Brier is a contact.

• Hvmanist Book Clvb—the first of its kind, it was located in New Canaan, Connecticut; see entry for Humanist Book Club, now no longer in existence.

• Northeast Atheist Association (ASHS), Box 63, Simsbury, Connecticut 06070. (203) 596-0545. Publishes *The Northeast Atheist*. Contacts: Janos Palotai and John C. Parker. E-mails: <janict@aol.com> and <jparker04@snet.net> and <president@northeastatheist.org>.

• Yale College's Humanist Society is at <http://www.secularhumanism.org/cfa/orgs.html>.

Connolly, Cyril Vernon (1903-1974)

Connolly was a distinguished English editor and critic, one who played a significant role in the literary life of England from the 1930s until his death. He was a regular contributor to the *New Statesman*, was the literary editor of the *Observer* (1942-1943), and reviewed for the *Sunday Times*. With Sir Stephen Harold Spender, he founded *Horizon* and edited it from 1939 to 1950. He wrote only one novel, *The Rock Pool* (Paris, 1936; London 1947), allegedly because he was too much a perfectionist and found it difficult to live up to his high standards. He said that he was a "lazy, irresolute person, over-vain and over-modest, unsure in my judgments and unable to finish what I have begun."

His favorite themes included the hazardous lure of literary immortality, the dangers of early success, and the joy of eating well, drinking the best wines, and traveling widely.

"When we die we become what we have loved," he held, "and that, were I to be vaporised tomorrow, the bulk of me would soon be staring out at the world through those topaz panes at which I now dream my life away looking."

He liked Lucretius's views concerning death and died of arteriosclerosis, hypertension, and cardiac failure. According to Anthony Hobson, "like a poet, in the sense that Erasmus used the word himself, that is, a humanist whose life is based on the study of classical ethics and ancient literature." His tombstone quotes the *Aeneid*, "*Intus aquae dulces vivoque sedilia saxo* (Within are fresh waters and seats from the living stone).

"Those of us who were brought up as Christians and who have lost our faith have retained the Christian sense of sin without the saving belief in redemption. This poisons our thought and so paralyzes us in action," Connolly declared. In *The Unquiet Grave* (1945), he wrote, "Believing in Hell must distort every judgment on this life." In *Horizon* in his later years, he backtracked, observing that man was now "betrayed by science, bereft of religion, deserted by the pleasant imaginings of humanism against the blind fate of which he is now so expertly conscious."

According to a 1997 biography by Jeremy Lewis, Connolly suggested that an appropriate memorial service should be held at Sotheby's, complete with a "sung bibliography" and the chanting of a "wanted list." Connolly the gourmet laughed when it was suggested that he be buried clutching a bottle of Worcestershire sauce "in case the chef's British." (See Jeremy Lewis's *Cyril Connolly: A Life* (1999). {OEL; TYD}

Connor, Bernard (1666—1698)

A physician born in County Kerry of a Catholic family, Connor became court physician to John Sobieski, King of Poland. His *Evangelium Medici* (1697), in which he attempts to account for the Christian miracles on natural principles, led to his being accused of atheism. {BDF}

Conover, Bev (20th Century)

Conover is a contributing editor of *Atheist Nation* (PO Box 3217, Chicago, Illinois 60654).

Conrad, Jane Kathryn (1916—1996)

Conrad, a Coloradan non-believer who was raised a Jew, called herself a religious non-believer. Jehovah, she has written, was originally a pagan tribal deity of Jews even as Allah was an ancient tribal god of Arabia. Monotheism, she added, was borrowed from Egyptian and Persian cultures: "God is a word, a semantic expression of something you picture in your imagination. This being is usually a form of parental substitute. It returns you to the comfort of a mother's womb when you have no responsibility and all your needs were taken care of without personal effort. There comes a day when a school child realizes Mother Goose is a story, Santa Claus is Daddy, and the Tooth Fairy a parent. But some adults cannot reject their infantile Superman whom they named 'God' and for them 'God-belief' causes intellectual retardation."

Her 1978 book, *The Pillars of Religion* included favorable comments concerning Madalyn Murray O'Hair, but in 1983 she wrote *Mad Madalyn*, which she said is based on "personal knowledge of the O'Hair family; correspondence to and from and about her; radio programs; published articles; newsletters; information from former associates; and telephone calls from coast to coast." Her purpose, she stated, was "to make the public aware that they should not judge all Atheists by the image projected by Madalyn O'Hair."

Since 1978, Conklin edited *Humanist Quest for Truth*. Her *The Loose Mother Goose*, "illegitimately conceived" in 1981, includes the following:

• Mary, Mary, quite contrary
  How did your baby grow?
  With an invisible Pop
  Who in your bed did flop
  A Jesus seed to sow.

• Little Miss Muffet
  Sat on a tuffet
  Worrying if the rent she could pay
  When along came an electronic preacher
  Whose program had reached her
  And conned her pennies away.

• There was an old woman who lived in a slum
  She had many children because she was dumb
  She knew not of condoms or birth control pills
  And that is the source of her family's ills.

In 1993, during the Pope John Paul II's visit to her state of Colorado, Conrad suggested that the irreverent arrange a "pope tent" and set the buffet with Vatican vittles that would include popesicles, hot cross buns, angel food cupcakes, devil's food cake, deviled eggs, soul food, vaticanned ham, hot buttered popecorn, Royal Crown cola, flavored sparkling holy water, Ten Commandments cakes . . . plus five loaves and two fishes. In the sky overhead an airplane was to be sent with a banner, STOP THE POPEULATION EXPLOSION. She circulated her witty material in a publication, *The Now and Then Irreverent Review*.

Conrad of Marburg (Died 1233)

One of the most notorious early officers of the Inquisition, Conrad was a secular priest. In 1231, after Pope Gregory IX's promulgation of the centralized Inquisition, Conrad was put in charge of destroying heresy, particularly Waldensianism, in Germany. He was also charged with reforming monasteries and denouncing corrupt priests. So efficient was he in executing suspected heretics that he frightened the German clergy as well as the nobility, including Count Henry of Sayn. Soon after the count was accused of heresy in 1233, a council of bishops and priests were summoned to hear the charges. When the council declared Count Henry innocent, Conrad refused to accept the council's verdict. Along with a Franciscan monk, Conrad was mysteriously murdered five days later. {EH}

Conrad, Joseph (1857—1924)

Theodore Józef Konrad Korzeniowski, the Ukrainian-born English novelist known as Joseph Conrad, so mastered English that he rose to the front rank of British novelists. A master mariner, he retired from the merchant fleet in 1894, and his works, all written in English, include *The Nigger of the Narcissus* (1897), *Lord Jim* (1900), *Nostromo* (1904), *The Secret Agent* (1907), *Under Western Eyes* (1911), and *Chance* (1913). He also wrote the novellas *Youth* (1902), *Heart of Darkness* (1902), and *Typhoon* (1903).

His work portrayed the conflict between non-western cultures and modern civilization, and it remains popular not only among pre-college but also college students. In *Some Reminiscences* (1912), Conrad wrote, "The ethical view of the universe involves us in so many cruel and absurd contradictions that I have come to suspect that the aim of creation cannot be ethical at all," an avowal of his agnosticism.

> Sleep after toyle, port after stormie seas,
> Ease after warre, death after life, does greatly please.

Conrad was buried with the above epitaph at the St. Thomas Church Cemetery in Canterbury, England.

(David Denby evaluates contemporary criticism of *Heart of Darkness*, discussing how far Conrad should be judged negatively for writing within the confines of his own time, in "Jungle Fever," *The New Yorker*, 6 November 1995.)

{JM; PA; RAT; RE; TRI; TYD}

CONSCIENCE

The "conscience," in religious terminology, is thought of as an independent source of moral insight: as the sense or consciousness of the moral goodness or blameworthiness of one's own conduct, intentions, or character together with a feeling of obligation to do right or be good. Theologians, unable to derive conscience from a human source, call it a "divine endowment."

Intuitionists, however, call it an innate endowment. Some regard it as a direct perceptual capacity. Others stress its emotional quality, which involves feelings of approval or disapproval. Still others explain it as the direct and authoritative guidance of our moral life.

Meanwhile, Freudians speak of the id, ego, superego, and libido. The children who have been rewarded for following the arbitrary rules of society, or punished for not so doing, have a strong superego and are not expected to hurt others unless given sufficient reason. Otherwise, they are punished by conscientious parents.

Believers' children are taught behavior which is consistent with their religious precepts, and similarly they are not expected to hurt others. Children of believers who misbehave, however, may be guilty of "sinning" and are punished for having transgressed religious as well as societal rules.

Bertrand Russell in *What I Believe* (1925) wrote, "In the orthodox Christian conception, the good life is the virtuous life, and virtue consists in obedience to the will of God, and the will of God is revealed to each individual through the voice of conscience. Conscience is a most fallacious guide, since it consists of vague reminiscences of precepts heard in early youth, so that it is never wiser than its possessor's nurse or mother."

Others have gone on record:

- Conscience is a mother-in-law whose visit never ends.

—H. L. Mencken

- The inner voice which warns us that someone may be looking.

—H. L. Mencken

- Conscience and cowardice are really the same things. Conscience is the trade-name of the firm.

—Oscar Wilde

CONSCIOUSNESS

- We know nothing about the intrinsic quality of physical events except when these are mental events that we directly experience.

—Bertrand Russell

A, if not *the*, major unsolved mystery is what causes consciousness. We know about its vivid sensations, pressing thoughts, indomitable urges. But, asks philosophy professor Colin McGinn of Rutgers (*The New York Review of Books*, 10 June 1999), "How does consciousness fit into the scientific world-picture so laboriously constructed since the seventeenth century? How does it relate to the physical world of atoms, space, and fields of force? How is it that the organ known as the brain contrives to usher consciousness into existence?"

John R. Searle, McGinn explains, has three principal theses in *Mind, Language, and Society: Philosophy in the Real World* (1999):

(1) Consciousness consists of inner, qualitative, subjective states and processes, such as experiences of red, thoughts of skiing, feelings of pain;
(2) Consciousness cannot be reduced to the "third-person phenomen"' investigated by the neurosciences;
(3) Consciousness is nevertheless a "biological process," a higher-order natural feature of the organic brain.

Searle says there are also biological processes in at least three senses:

(1) They characteristically occur in organic systems, unlike computer programs;
(2) they must have resulted from the process of natural selection and not from intentional design, unlike CDs and bell-bottoms;
(3) they are genetically based rather than learned or acquired, unlike knowledge of history and typing skills.

McGinn, however, faults Searle for his not being entirely naturalistic, for his not ultimately resolving the problem, for his not being completely convincing as to why cells in a brain can allow one to imagine that London is a dingy city. How consciousness is explained by Paul M. and Patricia S. Churchland's *On the Contrary: Critical Essays, 1987-1997* (1999), is entirely unlike Searle's approach. McGinn says, "Searle takes our common-sense view of the mind seriously and resists attempts to reduce or eliminate it in favor of a materialistic metaphysics; Churchland regards the very idea that human beings have beliefs and desires as a false theory of how our brains work, soon to be replaced by a better theory that describes us according to neuroscience."

McGinn found both views intelligible, but mistaken. Consciousness "cannot just spring into existence from matter like a djinn from a lamp," he states. "There may be an explanatory theory of the psychophysical link somewhere in Plato's heaven; it is just that our minds are miles away from grasping what this theory looks like." (See entries for Adam L. Carley, Frances Crick, Patricia and Paul Churchland.)

CONSEIL CENTRAL LAÏQUE

Since 1972, the Belgian and Flemish humanist groups have coordinated their activities by means of a ten-member committee called the *Conseil Central Laïque* (CCL). Since 1981 it has been legally recognized as representing the non-believer community in

Belgium. As such, it is responsible for providing moral counseling within the armed forces, is found at the Brussels airport, and represents the secularist case to the federal authorities. (See entry for Belgian Humanists.)

CONSEQUENCES

• In nature there are neither rewards nor punishments—there are consequences.

—**Robert Ingersoll**

CONSERVATIVE

• Conservative, n. A statesman who is enamored by existing evils, as distinguished from the Liberal, who wishes to replace them with others.

—**Ambrose Bierce**
The Devil's Dictionary

Considine, Michael (1885—1959)

Considine was an Australian rationalist, union militant, and labor politician. In 1919 he was imprisoned for three weeks for having said, "Bugger the King. He is a bloody German bastard." Upon his death, the former Catholic was cremated after a rationalist service. {SWW}

CONSILIENCE

Edward O. Wilson's *Consilience: The Unity of Knowledge* (1998), according to Paul Kurtz, seeks to defend the sciences "against the forces that would undermine their integrity, to integrate knowledge across the disciplines and branches of knowledge, and to apply this knowledge for human betterment." Wilson praises the Enlightenment's goal "to demystify the world and free the mind from the impersonal forces that imprison it" and, claims Kurtz, offsets charges by the critics who include "a bevy of postmodernist deconstructionists, cultural relativists, ecofeminists, Afrocentrists, neo-Marxists, philosophic Feyerabendians, and Kuhnians and Latourian social constructionists." Explaining his view of the difference between coherence and consilience, Wilson argues that we must attempt consilience anew, given the great progress in recent decades in many of the sciences, and he offers his own generalized account of what this should include.

Richard Rorty is quoted in *The New York Times* (2 May 1998) as disagreeing with Wilson's thesis. Rather than thinking about human nature, "which strikes me as having very little interest," he said, rather than seeking to reduce human activities to biological tendencies, Wilson is more interested in the multiple ways in which humanity can be studied and described. Using the analogy of a computer Rorty suggested that Wilson gives too much importance to the hardware, while what we really care about is the software. Thus, consilience, he suggested, is limited and limiting. Wilson, however, holds that software—culture, behavior, and social organizations—is not added onto hardware; it grows out of it and is partly indistinguishable from it. We cannot separate our biology from our culture. Both Wilson and Rorty are members of the International Academy of Humanism. (For the distinction between coherence and consilience, see entry for E. O. Wilson.) {Paul Kurtz, *Skeptical Inquirer*, July-August 1998}

Constant de Rebecque, Henri Benjamin (1767—1830)

A French-Swiss political writer and novelist, Constant was a tribune under the first consul, Napoleon (1799—1801). But when Germaine de Staël was expelled (1802), he went with her to Switzerland and Germany, publishing pamphlets attacking Napoleon and urging constitutional government and civil liberties. When Napoleon returned from Elba, however, Constant accepted an office under him. His semi-autobiographical *Adolphe* (1816) is highly regarded for its style, and in 1951 an unfinished novel, *Cécile* was discovered and reviewed favorably. According to Robertson, Constant along with Flaubert, Zola, Daudet, Maupassant, and the DeGoncourts were all rationalists. Wheeler, however, states that Constant professed Protestantism, although at heart he was a skeptic and "a second Voltaire." Constant's son was executor to Auguste Comte. {BDF; CE; JMR; JMRH; RAT}

CONSTITUTION OF THE UNITED STATES OF AMERICA

The Constitution of the United States, a 1787 document embodying the fundamental principles upon which the American republic is conducted, was ratified in 1788. It established the system of Federal government that began to function in 1789. Of particular importance to rationalists and other freethinkers is the Constitution's First Amendment:

> Congress shall make no law respecting an establishment of religion, or prohibiting the free exercise thereof; or abridging the freedom of speech or of the press; or the right of the people peaceably to assemble, and to petition the government for a redress of grievances.

In 1995, some religious fundamentalists suggested that the following proposals for amendments to the Constitution should be discussed and put into action:

> In order to secure the unalienable right of the people to acknowledge God according to the rights of conscience, neither the United States nor any State shall deny benefits to or otherwise discriminate against any persons on account of their religious expression, belief, or identity; nor shall the exercise by the people of full and equal rights to freedom of speech, press, association or religion be construed as an establishment of religion because of its religious content.
>
> Neither the United States nor any state shall abridge the freedom of any person or group, including students in public schools, to engage in prayer or other religious expression in circumstances in which expression of a non religious character would be permitted; nor deny benefits to or otherwise discriminate against any person or group on account of the religious character of their speech, ideas, motivations or identity. Nothing in the Constitution shall be construed to forbid the United States or any State to give public or ceremonial accommodation to the religious heritage, beliefs, or traditions of its people. The exercise, by the people, of any freedoms under the First Amendment or under this Amendment shall not constitute an establishment of religion.

Such proposals, however, would entirely change the separation of church and state envisioned by the American Founding Fathers. They would, of course, lead to a theocracy. (See entry for First Amendment.) {Isaac Kramnick and R. Laurence Moore, *The Godless Constitution: The Case Against Religious Correctness* (1996)}

Conta, Basil (1845—1882)

A Romanian philosopher, Conta taught at the University of Jassy in Moldavia. In 1877 he published a theory of fatalism which, states Wheeler, "created some stir by its boldness of thought." {BDF; RAT}

Conti, Thomas Antonio (1941—)

An actor, writer, and director, Conti is the Scottish-born Tony Award winner for his 1979 appearance on Broadway in "Whose Life Is It Anyway." He has appeared in numerous films and on television. When *The Big Issue* inquired of him in 1996, were he to be given a time-machine, when would he take it, where would he go, and why, he replied, "Nazareth 35 A.D., to find Jesus the carpenter and tell him of the trouble he caused." {*The Freethinker*, April 1996}

CONVERSION, LOGICAL

For philosophers, conversion is a form of immediate inference in which the order of the terms is reversed. In logic, a proposition obtained by conversion is a converse, which is a theorem formed by interchanging the hypothesis and conclusion of a given theorem (e.g., "no P is S" is the – of "no S is P"). To convert is to transform a proposition by conversion.

CONVERSION, RELIGIOUS

A religious convert is one who has been converted from one religion to a different religion. Jews have become Christians (e.g., Jean-Marie Cardinal Lustiger was the son of Jewish parents); Christians, Muslims (e.g., Benjamin Chavis, former head of the National Association for the Advancement of Colored People, joined Louis Farrakhan's Nation of Islam in 1997); Muslims, Buddhists; Buddhists, Hindus; Hindus, Moslems; Moslems, Jews; etc. Many of the organized religious groups have missionaries, whose job it is to convert individuals from what is held to be a "wrong" viewpoint to that of a "right" viewpoint.

The United State Department in 1997 released a report on seventy-eight countries, detailing the discrimination, repression, and violence that befell those who practiced the "wrong faith." For example:

• Algeria: In July 1996, the Armed Islamic Group (GIA) after declaring its intention to eliminate Jews, Christians, and polytheists from Algeria, kidnapped and killed seven

Roman Catholic monks in central Algeria, and the Catholic Bishop of Oran was murdered at his home.
• Bosnia and Herzegovina: In July 1996 a Roman Catholic church, the last in the town in the Muslim-controlled town of Bugojno, was firebombed.
• Germany: Scientologists, including American citizens, were reportedly discriminated against and harassed.
• Indonesia: Atheism is banned, and rioters destroyed churches and a Buddhist temple on the East Java coast to protest the leniency of a sentence given to a Muslim by an Indonesian judge for slandering Islam.
• Iran: Non-Muslims may not proselytize Muslims, and Muslims who convert to another faith, such as the Baha'i, are considered apostates and may be subject to the death penalty.
• Singapore: The Government banned Jehovah's Witnesses in 1972 on the grounds that the group opposes military service.
• Sudan: Forced conversion to Islam of Christians, animists, and other non-Muslims takes place as part of Government policy. Reports abound that Christian children have been forced into re-education camps where they are given Arab names and raised as Muslims.

{AF; *The New York Times*, 27 July 1997}

Conway, John (20th Century)

Conway is a legend in computer science because in 1970 he was the first to create an artificial life simulation that he called the "Game of Life." Although a game, it does simulate the "birth" and "death" of organisms according to a set of simple rules.

In Charles Seife's 1994 article in *The Sciences*, Conway exults about the nature of discovery, finding that mathematics is not cold, that "the whole damn thing is sensual and exciting. I like what it looks like, and I get a hell of a lot more pleasure out of math than most people do out of art!"

He does, however, feel like an artist:

> I like beautiful things—they're there already; man doesn't have to create beauty. I don't believe in god, but I believe that nature is unbelievably subtle and clever. In physics, for instance, the real answer to a problem is usually so subtle and surprising that it wasn't even considered in the first place. That the speed of light is a constant—impossible! Nobody even thought about it. And quantum mechanics is even worse, but it's so beautiful, and it works!

{CA}

Conway, Moncure Daniel (1832—1907)

An Anglo-American social reformer, Conway was once a Methodist minister but changed his convictions through the influence of Emerson and Hicksite Quakers. For a time, he called himself a Unitarian. Conway disbelieved in Christ's divinity, debunked biblical miracles, and spoke of Eastern religions as being just as valid and valuable as Christianity.

He is best known for his ministry of London's South Place Ethical Society. It had originated as a universalist Baptist congregation in the late eighteenth century and had become a Unitarian chapel by the time of the ministry of W. J. Fox. Conway moved his group in the direction of religious humanism and gave it links with the American Ethical Culture movement. D'Entremont notes that Conway had a heterodox freethought approach which still is a tradition at South Place Chapel.

In 1860, he commenced editing the monthly *Dial* from Cincinnati, Ohio. His *Earthward Pilgrimage* (1870) was the artistic record of a gifted preacher's progress from Wesleyan Methodism, through Unitarianism, to a theism which was soon to pass into agnosticism and rationalism. In 1876 he wrote *Human Sacrifice in England* and, in 1894, *Centenary History of the South Place Society*. Conway's autobiography in 1904 is valuable for its sketch of leading nineteenth-century figures.

Conway died in Paris. "To the last," wrote J. M. Robertson, "I never found him despairing, never even apathetic." (See "Freethought Congregations: South Place and Others" in *The London Heretics* by Warren Sylvester Smith. For a criticism of Moncure's work on Thomas Paine, see the entry for John Keane. Also see entry for Katherine Conway Nicholson; Conway was her great uncle.) {BDF; CE; EU, John D'Entremont; FO; FUK; FUS; HNS2; JM; JMR; JMRH; RAT; RE; RSR; TRI; WSS}

Conway, William Martin (1856—1937)

An art expert and a traveler of international fame as a climber, Conway disdainfully defined religion as "man's description of his ideas about the great unknown, his projection upon the darkness of what he conceives that darkness to contain." {JM; RAT; RE}

Conybeare, Frederick Cornwallis (1856—1924)

Conybeare wrote *Myth, Magic, and Morals* (1910), an agnostic's study of Christian origins. He also wrote *Russian Dissenters* (1962) and *A Grammar of Septuagint Greek* (1980).

An Orientalist and a tutor of great erudition at Oxford University, he was a member of the Rationalist Press Association (RPA). In several learned works he criticizes Christianity and even more severely the myth theory of Jesus. {JM; RAT; RE}

Conyers, Lisa (20th Century): See entry for Crime.

Coogan, Michael D. (20th Century)

Coogan with Bruce M. Metzger edited *The Oxford Companion to the Bible* (1993). The work is written in a scholarly and not necessarily skeptical point of view.

Cook, Alfred W. (20th Century)

Cook is President of the North American Committee for Humanism. Also, he is the Secretary and Assistant Treasurer of The Humanist Institute.

Cook, E. V. (20th Century)

In Vancouver, Canada, Cook edited *The Rationalist* starting in 1914. {FUK}

Cook, Fred (20th Century)

Cook, an American, is a Vice-president of the International Humanist and Ethical Union. E-mail: <conachi@aol.com>.

Cook, J. H. (Born 1819)

Cook, originally from Connecticut, lived a childhood amid that state's blue laws and its Methodist revivals. Exceedingly poor, he had no shoes for the first ten years of his life and often subsisted upon a potato and salt to eat. At ten he went to the poor-house, where he was abused, then "bound out to an aristocrat who treated me like a slave. I took to my heels for liberty, and traveled one hundred and fifty miles, barefooted." Somehow, he became a driver on the canal, "like Garfield," and in 1830 was an Abolitionist "almost as early as Garrison." In 1840 he was a woman suffragist and dress reformer. In 1835, he wrote, "when I discovered that 'the brain is the organ of the mind,' theology, priestcraft, and all their fearful concomitants fled from me, and ever since I have been an Atheistic humanitarian, at great cost, however, with personal insult and often peril. . . . My doors and windows were twice smashed in at midnight, and I had to flee for my life. . . . I was a Spiritualist for over forty years, but science now compels me to be a Monist and a Secularist." Unfortunately, he spent his old age in poverty, in Kansas. {PUT}

Cook, Kenningale Robert (1845—1886)

"If God was omnipotent could he make what happened *not* have happened?" asked the young Cook to his puzzled mother and father, the Vicar of Stallbridge in England. Although intended for the Church, he declined to subscribe to the articles. In 1877, Cook became editor of the Dublin *University Magazine*, in which appeared some studies of the lineage of Christian doctrines and later published as *The Fathers of Jesus*. {BDF; RAT}

Cook, Maria (1779—1835)

Cook is generally considered to have been the first woman, in 1811, to have preached in Universalist pulpits. When she was jailed on a trumped-up vagrancy charge in Cooperstown, New York, by some anti-Universalist, she preached to the prisoners after frustrating the magistrate's attempts to get her to pay any respect to their authority. {U&U}

Cook, Ransom (19th Century)

Cook was president in the 1840s of the United Moral and Philosophical Society, which may have been headquartered in Buffalo, New York. {FUS}

Cook, William Glanville Lau (20th Century)

Cook, who went to Australia in 1938, edited the *Australian Rationalist* from 1969 to 1975. A rationalist, schoolteacher, secretary, editor, and raconteur, he had been born in Fiji, the son of a Methodist missionary. Although a trainee for the Methodist ministry, he failed the final oral examination by rejecting belief in eternal damnation. He then became a secondary school teacher, was active in the formation of the Left Book Club, and was active in the Rationalist Society of Australia. {FUK}

Cooke, William (19th Century)

With Joseph Barker, Cook wrote "The Authentic Report of the Theological Discussion Between the Rev. W. Cooke and Mr. Joseph Barker" (1845). {GS}

Cooke, William (1956—)

Cooke, a lecturer in the School of Art and Design, Manukau Institute of Technology, is on the editorial committee of the New Zealand *Rationalist and Humanist*. He is President of his country's Rationalists and Humanists Association. In 1997 he was working on a Ph. D. project, "The Best of Causes: A Critical History of the Rationalist Association." He is author of *Heathen in Godzone* (1998), a work which evaluates the rationalist movement in New Zealand and cites Joseph McCabe as having been an inspiration for starting the New Zealand Rationalist Association. Cooke signed Humanist Manifesto 2000.

Cookes, Walter David (1878—1976)

Cookes, a footwear manufacturer, joined the Rationalist Society of Australia in 1911 and was local secretary of the Perth District in 1914. During the 1930s, Cookes became involved with an Australia First movement, a small group of pro-fascist, pro-monarchist, pro-Australian nationalists, which led to the disruption of the rationalist organization. {SWW}

Cooley, P. J. (20th Century)

Cooley was a freethinker who wrote *Evolution* (1901). {GS}

Coon, Carl [Ambassador] (1927—)

Coon, once the United States Ambassador to Nepal (1981—1984), is an outspoken atheist. He describes his outlook as being that of progressive humanism. Asked about his outlook, he responded, "Yes, Carleton Coon was my father. Growing up listening to him sound off gave me a head start toward becoming a full-fledged humanist." Coon's "progressive humanism" is described in detail on the Web: <http://www.progressivehumanism.com/>. E-mail: <carlcoon@citizen.infi.net>.

Coon, Carleton Stevens (1904—1981)

Coon, an eminent American anthropologist, archaeologist, and educator, discovered in 1939 the remains of a Neanderthal man in Africa. He taught (1934—1948) at Harvard and in 1948 became professor of anthropology at the University of Pennsylvania and curator of ethnology at the University Museum there.

His *Origin of Races* (1962) argued that certain races had reached the *Homo sapiens* stage of evolution before others, which he found explained why different races achieved different levels of civilization.

Coon wrote *Races* (1951), *The Seven Caves* (1957), *The Story of Man* (2nd edition 1962), *The Living Races of Man* (1965), *The Hunting Peoples* (1971), and his autobiography, *Adventures and Discoveries* (1981). Coon was non-theistic in his writings.

Cooper, Anthony: See entry for Shaftesbury.

Cooper, James R. (19th Century)

Cooper, a Manchester radical publisher and bookseller, was a member in England of the Manchester Secular Society. {VI}

Cooper, John Charles (20th Century)

Cooper wrote *Religious Pied Pipers: A Critique of Radical Right-Wing Religions* (1981) and *Roots of the Radical Theology* (1988). {GS}

Cooper, John Gilbert (1784—1824)

Cooper, a poet and enthusiastic disciple of Lord Shaftesbury, published *Life of Socrates* (1749), for which he was coarsely attacked by Warburton. Cooper wrote some poems under the signature of Aristippus. {BDF; RAT}

Cooper, Peter (1791—1883)

A Unitarian, Cooper built in the U.S. one of the earliest locomotives, "Tom Thumb." Cooper made his money in glue, iron, and a forerunner of Jell-O. In addition to promoting New York City public schools, he founded the tuition-free Cooper Union (1859) as a free institution of higher learning, a pioneer evening engineering and art school (attended by Thomas Edison, Augustus Saint-Gaudens, Felix Frankfurter). In 1860, Lincoln made a speech in the Great Hall of Cooper Union that helped pave his way to the presidency. In 1876 Cooper was the Greenback Party candidate for US president. Of 234 nominees in the first election to the Hall of Fame for Great Americans in 1900, he was one of twenty-nine to be elected.

In *Political and Financial Opinions of Peter Cooper* (1877), Jaches describes Cooper as "so broad, sincere, and catholic in his religious principles that I believe he would be recognized by any minister of the Christian religion as a truly religious man." To this, however, McCabe responds, "It is the usual religious way of saying that a freethinker is a 'true Christian' if he is a fine man."

Once when asked to sum up his philosophy, Cooper responded, "I have endeavored to remember that the object of life is to do good." Upon his death at the age of ninety-two, an estimated 3,500 hundred Cooper Union students and more than 12,000 others assembled to pay their respects. Cooper left no money for any religious purpose, but he was a member in New York City of the Unitarian Church of All Souls. {BDF; CE; EG; JM; RE; U}

Cooper, Robert (1819—1868)

Cooper, with Charles Bradlaugh, edited *London Investigator* from 1854 to 1859. A secularist writer brought up in a freethought family, he became at age fourteen a teacher in the co-operative schools of Salford. At fifteen, he lectured, and by seventeen he became an acknowledged advocate of Owenism and secretary to Robert Owen. One of his lectures, on Original Sin, sold twelve thousand copies when he was eighteen.

His pamphlet, "Deathbed Repentance" (1852), is one of the earliest detailed exposures of the lies fabricated by Christians in regard to the last days of prominent freethinkers. The Bishop of Exeter in the House of Lords denounced his *Holy Scriptures Analysed* (1832), resulting in Cooper's losing a job he had held for ten years. In 1858 he remodeled his *Infidel Text-Book* into a work, *The Bible and Its Evidence*.

Shortly before his death, Cooper wrote, "At a moment when the hand of death is suspended over me, my theological opinions remain unchanged; months of deep and silent cogitation, under the pressure of long suffering, have confirmed rather than modified them. I calmly await, therefore, all risk attached to these convictions. Conscious that, if mistaken, I have always been sincere, I apprehend no disabilities for impressions I cannot resist." Cooper was not related to Thomas Cooper, to whose lectures on "God and a Future Life" he wrote a reply in 1856. {BDF; FO; FUK; PUT; RAT; RSR; VI}

Cooper, Steve (20th Century)

Cooper is a businessman and the author of *Liberty to Live* (1980) and *To Hell with God?* (1991). He is an honorary associate of the New Zealand Association of Rationalists and Humanists.

Cooper, Thomas (1759—1840)

A natural philosopher, Cooper became professor of medicine at Carlisle College and later taught chemistry and political economy in South Carolina College, of which he became President (1820—1834). This position he was forced to resign because of his religious views. In philosophy a materialist, in religion a freethinker, in politics a democrat, he urged his views in many pamphlets. {BDF; FUK; RAT}

Cooper, Walter (Born 1814)

An English Chartist and freethinker, Cooper brought Holyoake into touch with Christian Socialists. {VI}

Cooper, William (Born 1822)

Cooper was a secularist, a founder of the Rochdale Pioneers and a leading Rochdale Co-operator in England. {VI}

Coornhert, Dick Volkertszoon (1522—1590)

A Dutch humanist, poet, and writer, Coornhert became secretary of the city of Haarlem. He had a profound horror of intolerance and defended liberty against Beza and Calvin. The clergy vituperated him as a Judas and as instigated by Satan. The magistrates of Delft drove him out of their city. Coornhert translated Cicero's *De Officiis* and other works. Bayle said of Coornhert that he communed neither with Protestants nor Catholics. {BDF}

Coots, Max A. (20th Century)

Coots, parish assistant at New York City's Universalist Church of the Divine Paternity, preached a 1953 sermon, "The Little Gods of Humanism." These he described as man and nature, and Coots insisted they were false. The reaction of liberal Christians to humanism, he was quoted as saying in *The Humanist Newsletter* (Summer 1953), is one of fear and loathing, for humanism is a threat. Saying that once upon a time he was a humanist and an atheist, Coots added that instead of fleeing from Christianity's imperfections, liberals should stay within the church to reform and cleanse it. Humanism, he lamented, is beginning to have its own saints and saviors, and their writings are becoming "sacred." As examples, he gave Benjamin Franklin, George Santayana, and Charles Francis Potter.

"Humanists do not exist because they are perverse and want to shatter time-honored traditions," he reasoned. "They are simply disillusioned seekers." Universalists do believe that man is important, he said, but the ultimate theology of Universalism is theism and belief in something beyond man. "When the solar system ceases to exist in millions of years," he ejaculated, "then what will the humanists do?"

Told of the sermon, Charles Francis Potter wrote, "I'm sorry that Rev. Max Coots, preaching in my former pulpit, apparently is quite unaware of what is happening in his own denomination. The five most successful and respected Universalist ministers I know—one in the Far West, two in the Midwest, and two in New England—are out-and-out ardent Humanists and proud of it. And, as everyone knows, or should, 'the reaction of liberal Christians to humanism' is not by any means 'one of fear and loathing,' as Mr. Coots alleged, for the majority of Unitarian ministers and Ethical leaders in America are now counted among the humanists."

Cope, Edward Drinker (1840—1897)

Cope was a paleontologist, one of the most eminent of his time and a leading champion of Darwinism in America. His *Theology of Evolution* (1887) showed him to be a theist, but Cope did not believe in immortality. Cope's large collection of fossil mammals are at the American Museum of Natural History in New York. He believed that evolution arose from an organism's inner urge to attain a higher state of being. {CE; JM; RAT; RE}

COPERNICAN THEORY

The Copernican Theory is that the earth rotates daily on its axis and, along with the other planets in the solar system, revolves around the sun. *De Revolutionibus Orbius Coelestium* [On the Movement of Heavenly Bodies, c. 1530] was denounced by the Vatican in 1616 and only removed from the Vatican's *Index Prohibitorum* two centuries later, in 1822. Modern astronomy was built upon the book's findings. In 1999 Pope John Paul II, in Torun, Poland, Kopérnik's birthplace, indulged in apologetics, stating, "Although Copernicus himself saw his discovery as giving rise to even greater amazement at the Creator of the world and the power of human reason, many people took it as a means of setting reason against faith."

Meanwhile, it was Aristarchus 1800 or so years earlier than Kopérnik who had discovered the movements of the planets around the sun, not the Latinized Copernicus, who erred in thinking the sun was the majestic symbol of God. (See entry for Aristarchus of Samos.) {CE; CL; ER; *The New York Times*, 8 June 1999; TYD}

Copernicus, Nicholas: See entry for Nicholas Kopérnik.

COPT

Copts are Egyptians who are descended from people of ancient or pre-Islamic Egypt. Their Afro-Asiatic language is Coptic. The Coptic Church is a Christian church in Egypt, one that adheres to the Monophysite doctrine. Freethinkers usually are ignorant about theological inventions, but Monophysites hold that physically there is a unity of the divine and human in Christ, a third part of the Trinity. However, the flesh becomes transformed into divine nature, a distinction that confounds all but the most attentive freethinkers.

Corben, Herbert Charles (1914—)

Corben, a physicist and educator, is author of *Classical and Quantum Theories of Spinning Particles* (1968) and *The Struggle to Understand* (1992), in which he relates the pitfalls of superstitious explanations. His *Who's Who* listing includes the following: "Faith in the order of nature is a source of both certainty and wonder. The certainty is my foundation; the wonder is my religion. Together, they form the quest for truth that influences every area of my life. I am fascinated by the unsolved problems both of science and mankind, and I am dedicated to finding accurate solutions. In sharing knowledge through research and teaching, I believe that the certainty is reinforced, the wonder multiplied, and truth interpreted and carried forward."

Corbin-Singletary, Lisa-Jo (20th Century)

Corbin-Singletary is active in the Humanist Association of Los Angeles. (See entry for California Atheists, Humanists.) {FD}

Corcoran, John (1937—)

At the Tenth International Humanist and Ethical Union (IHEU) World Congress held in Buffalo (1988), Corcoran addressed the group. He was editor of *Ancient Logic and Its Modern Interpretations* (1974) and *Tarski's Logic, Semantics, Meta* (1983). Corcoran teaches philosophy at the State University of New York at Buffalo.

Corina, F. J. (20th Century)

In Bradford, England, Corina edited the English monthly, *Freethought News* from 1947 to 1950. He wrote *God and the Co-op: Will Religion Split the People's Movement?* (c. 1935). {FUK; GS}

Corl, Ed (20th Century)

Corl, a member of the Atheists of Florida, said on a Tampa, Florida, radio program that all of us *need* to question ideas. Children do not automatically think to question their parents about myths such as Santa Claus, but this is a part of maturing, one that applies equally to subjects considered sacred by some adults.

CORNELL UNIVERSITY HUMANISTS

Cornell University at Ithaca, New York, has a humanist group on the Web at <http://www.secularhumanism.org/cfa/orgs.html>.

Cornell, Ezra (1807-1874)

Cornell founded Cornell University in Ithaca, New York. A civic benefactor, noted in his day, he worked with Samuel Morse in promoting a new invention, the telegraph. Cornell was a Unitarian.

Corner, George Washington (1889—1981)

An anatomist and medical historian who identified the hormone progesterone, Dr. Corner was an educator and the author from 1927 on of such books as *Attaining Manhood: A Doctor Talks to Boys About Sex* and *Attaining Womanhood: A Doctor Talks to Girls About Sex.* At that time, very few books were available for adolescents, who were likely embarrassed to ask librarians or any other adults for such material.

Corner's books were among the first to break the strict Puritanism rampant in so many of the nation's libraries. Concerning humanism, Corner wrote the present author:

> I suppose that my views place me in the class of naturalistic humanism. I am not enough of a philosopher to offer comments that would be of further use.
>
> {WAS, 30 April 1956}

Cornette, Henry Arthur Marie (Born 1852)

Cornette was a Belgian professor of Flemish literature at Antwerp. He wrote for *L'Avenir* of Brussels and in *Revue Socialite.* Cornette also published separate works on *Freemasonry* (1878), *Pessimism and Socialism* (1880), and *Freethought Darwinism.* {BDF; RAT}

Cornish, Brenda (1922—)

Mrs. Keith Cornish was a Baptist Sunday School teacher before resigning her membership in 1970. She is a member of the South Australia Rationalist Association and a founding member, and treasurer since 1989, of the Atheist Foundation of Australia Inc. {SWW}

Cornish, Keith Stanton (1916—)

Reared a Baptist, Cornish was a youth worker and lay preacher but came to reject Christianity as being false and unethical. In 1970 he joined the South Australia Rationalist Association and then was elected Vice-President of the Atheist Foundation of Australia. Upon the death of John Campbell in 1976, Cornish became president and then editor of *The Australian Atheist.* {SWW}

Cornish, Louis Craig (1870—1950)

Cornish, who had been secretary to an Episcopal bishop, became a Unitarian minister and eventually president of the American Unitarian Association (1937—1937). During that period, the Depression made it difficult for him to carry out his duties. But he worked for international religious cooperation and led an investigation in the 1920s into the alleged persecution of Unitarians in Transylvania. {U&U}

CORNWALL (England) HUMANISTS

For information, write B. Mercer, "Amber," Short Cross Road, Mount Hawke, Truro TR 4 8EA; or telephone 01209 890690.

CORPSE WORSHIP: See entry for Charles Allen, who held that corpse worship, as distinguished from theophagy (the symbolic eating of God), necrophilia (the erotic interest in corpses), or necrophagia (the feeding on corpses), is "the protoplasm of religion."

Corson, E. O. (20th Century)

Corson in the 1950s edited the *Humanist World Digest*, which was published by the Humanist World Fellowship of California. The publication sought "to present Humanism as a religious philosophy which denies no particular faith, but which provides a path over which all people can travel toward a unity that rises above the barriers of the beliefs which divide them. In behalf of this common faith, we emphasize a constructive approach rather than opposition to traditional philosophies." He commenced the publication because "we are trying to fill a void the American Humanist Association has missed, that is, an objective approach through Humanism to man's problems of survival in a democratic world order. Dr. Packard's 'Answer in Greece,' Dr. Zeuch, and other writers who have given thought to that approach are some examples." {WAS, 28 September 1955}

Cortez, Carlos (20th Century)

Cortez, whose woodcuts were often depicted in publications of the Industrial Workers of the World (IWW), is often called the elder statesman of that anarchist group of "Wobblies." His father had been a member of the IWW, and his mother was a German socialist-pacifist. During World War II, Cortez served two years in the federal penitentiary at Sandstone, Minnesota, for refusing to fight "the bosses' war," and as a poet, artist, editor, and public speaker he is one of the union's best known figures. In one of his poems, "City of Angels," he writes ". . . A real Oakie town / Where white-robed salvationists / Fleece their flocks / In architectural monstrosities / Called Temples of Everlasting / Mystic Revelation." His work is included in *Crystal-Gazing in the Amber Fluid & Other Wobbly Poems* (1990). {*Freethought History #8, 1993*}

Corvin-Wiersbitski, Otto Julius Bernard von (1812—1886)

A Prussian Pole who traced his descent from the Roman Corvinii, Corvin-Wiersbitski wrote *History of the Dutch Revolution* (1841) and *History of Christian Fanaticism* (1845), which was suppressed in Austria. When he took part with the democrats in 1848, he was condemned to be shot on 15 September 1849, but the sentence was commuted and he spent six years of solitary confinement in prison. Moving to London and becoming a correspondent to the *Times*, he reported on the American Civil War and afterwards the Franco-Prussian War as a special correspondent. {BDF; RAT}

Cosic, Dobrica [President] (20th Century)

Cosic, a former President of Yugoslavia, is a signer of Humanist Manifesto 2000.

COSMOLOGY

Cosmology is a branch of metaphysics that deals with the nature of the universe. To an astronomer who is a naturalist, however, cosmology is a science that aims at a comprehensive theory of the creation, evolution, and present structure of the entire universe. Bertrand Russell has written extensively on the subject, as have contemporary astronomers attempting to fathom the "big bang theory" of the origin of the universe.

Religionists have used the "five ways" of Aquinas to prove that things "go back to infinity" and therefore to a "first cause." Cosmologists who are naturalists, however, do not accept that cosmological argument, stating that they have no evidence that there *has* to have been a beginning. The conservation of mass and energy theory holds that the quantity of mass and energy does not change and will continue to stay the same, so that although we may not know if humans will be alive one thousand years from now we do know that the quantity of mass and energy will not have increased or decreased then.

Timothy Ferris, in *The Whole Shebang* (1997), stated that science can tell us nothing about God: "In a creative universe God would betray no trace of his presence, since to do so would rob the creative forces of their independence. . . . All who genuinely seek to learn . . . are united in not having *a* faith but faith itself. . . . For God's hand may be a human hand, if you reach out in loving kindness, and God's voice your voice, if you speak the truth."

Lee Smolin, in *The Life of the Cosmos* (1997), advanced what some claim is not a verifiable scientific theory. Smolin avers that when a very large star collapses of its own dead weight, it forms a black hole, a kind of tear in the fabric of space-time. Out the other end of every black hole, he adds, pops a new universe with slightly different physical laws. If that universe, burgeoning from its own Big Bang, can also make stars massive enough to collapse into black holes, it will produce more offspring. Indeed, our own universe emerged, he speculates, through a black hole in some other universe.

George Johnson, writing of Smolin's hypothesis (*The New York Times*, 27 July 1997), interprets this as meaning that universes multiply like rabbits. The result is a universe of universes, dominated by the ones that are fittest—those best equipped to make the stars and black holes that allow them to reproduce. These are also the universes capable of supporting complex phenomena like life. Although Johnson found Smolin's theories of interest, he concluded that much more serious research needs to be completed "for some kind of laws of complexity." Scientist Dennis Overbye, however, has pointed out (*The New York Times*, 13 July 1997) that if physicist Smolin is right, science is on the verge of a new kind of synthesis that will explain not just the birth of the universe but also, for the first time, why life and beauty are inescapable parts of that universe.

At a Pritzker Symposium and Workshop on the Status of Inflationary Cosmology in 1999, Andrei Linde of Stanford University explained to cosmologists his theory of eternal inflation, in which countless universes are born every second. If an explosive event such as the Big Bang occurred, he reasoned, and it was followed by a brief phase of rapid cosmic expansion, then one can posit that this could happen an infinite number of times, and may well have. "So universes reproduce like rabbits," Alan Guth of the Massachusetts Institute of Technology observed. Linde continued that if parallel universes exist, each would have started with its own Big Bang, grown from a separate inflationary bubble, and probably acquired entirely different laws of physics. Ours may not be a typical universe and, instead of four dimensions of space-time in this universe, other universes could have as many as eleven dimensions, still others only three. Cosmologists at the conference included Rocky Kolb and Michael Turner of the University of Chicago; Sir Martin Reese of Cambridge University; P. James E. Peebles of Princeton University; and Stephen Hawking, who observed that the cosmic inflation theory "does a good job" supporting the Big Bang." John Noble Wilford, a science editor, noted that Allan Sandage's comment to the attendees that in broad outline their scenario of cosmic history was a lot like St. Augustine's 1,600 years ago met with laughter, but "the cosmologists were not appreciably humbled." Sandage, who was born in 1926 and converted to Christianity in 1980, has been attacked widely by new rival teams of cosmologists. Commenting upon such attacks, an aging Sandage sadly said, "It's a disaster for me. It's a psychological disaster. I mean, you just can't imagine. . . . If you permit it, the world will either break your heart or turn your heart to stone." (See entry for Steven Weinberg, with his explanation of the current views of cosmologists.) {CE; *The New York Times*, 9 February 1999 and 25 July 1999}

Costa, Margarita (20th Century)

In Argentina, Costa is a corresponding member of The Hume Society, a group engaged in scholarly activity concerning David Hume. She is author of *Filosofia y formacion humana* (1978).

COSTA RICAN HUMANISTS: See entry for *Asociación Ético Humanista Costarricense* (ASEHUCO). Also see entries for Costa Rican Presidents Jose Figueres Ferrer and Francisco Morazán.

Costikyan, Edward Nazar (1924—)

Costikyan, a lawyer, has been law secretary to Judge R. Medina of the U.S. District Court of New York (1949—1951) and in 1994 became special advisor to the Mayor of New York City on school decentralization and borough government.

He wrote *Behind Closed Doors, Politics in the Public Interest* (1966) and *How to Win Votes* (1980). Costikyan since 1976 has been on the board of editors of the *New York Law Journal*. He is a member of New York City's All Souls Unitarian Church.

Costley, William E. (20th Century)

Costley, a freethinker, wrote *The Pagan Foundations of the Christian Religion Exposed* (1922). {GS}

Cote, Charlotte (20th Century)

Cote wrote *Olympia Brown* (1989), a biography of the first woman to be ordained by a denomination. Brown was a Universalist.

Cotes, Peter (1912—)

Cotes in 1952 directed a play that opened in Nottingham before transferring to West End, a "little thriller" which had a mixed press. But more than forty years later the play, Agatha Christie's *The Mousetrap*, is still running. A freethinker, he contributes newspaper obituary notices of stage folk to *The Guardian* and is author of *Thinking Aloud: Fragments of Autobiography* (1993). {TRI}

Cotereau-Visla, Jean (Born 1898)

In the 1950s, Cotereau was a correspondent (France) for *The Humanist*. He is author of *Laicite, sagesse des peuples* (1965). In 1953, he edited *La Raison*, a bi-monthly in French which was the official organ of the French National Federation of Free Thinkers. In 1966, he became President of the World Union of Freethinkers. {TRI}

Cotes, Peter [Sydney Arthur Rembrandt Boulting] (1912-1998)

Cotes, a British theatrical producer and director, was supervising producer of Channel 7 in Melbourne (1961-1962). An actor, television as well as film director, and producer, he supervised 35 film and 65 theatre productions in Britain, New York, and Australia. To circumvent the Lord Chamberlain's rules about "obscene" language on the public stage, Cotes formed a theatre in Manchester and two in London, turning them into theatre clubs rather than public theatres.

His publications include "*No Star Nonsense* (1949); *The Little Fellow* (1951); *A Handbook for the Amateur Theatre* (1959); *Robey* (1972); and *Thinking Aloud: Fragments of Autobiography* (1993).

After marrying the Canadian actress and fellow freethinker **Joan Miller**, the two in "Pick-Up Girl" (1946) included such edgy topics as venereal disease, juvenile sex, child abuse, and four-letter words. His connection with freethought involved launching three plays by secular dramatist Ted (Lord) Willis: *Look in Any Window, The Young and the Guilty*, and *Women in a Dressing Gown*. Cotes contributed to *The Freethinker*, and Miller was a collaborator on *Freethought and Humanism in Shakespeare* (1964). {David Tribe, *Death of a Freethought Stalwart, The Freethinker*, November-December 1998}

Cothran, Andrew (20th Century)

In 1966 for his Ph. D. at the University of Maryland, Cothran wrote a dissertation on freethinker Emanuel Haldeman-Julius. {FUS}

COTSWOLD (England) HUMANISTS

For information, contact Philip Howell, 2 Cleevelands Close, Cheltenham GL50 4PZ; or telephone 01242 528743.

Cotta, Bernhard (1808—1879)

A German geologist, Cotta wrote *The Dendroliths* (1832). He wrote many geological treatises and did much to support the nebular hypothesis and the law of natural development without miraculous agency. Cotta also wrote on phrenology. {BDF}

Cotton, Henry John Stedman [Sir] (1845—1915)

Cotton was Home Secretary to the Indian Government (1896—1898) and Chief Commissioner of Assam (1898—1902). In those offices, and later as M. P. for Nottingham, he applied a rare idealism to the settlement of Indian problems. Sir Henry was a positivist of high character, according to McCabe. {RAT; RE}

Cotton, Ian (20th Century)

Cotton, in *The Hallelujah Revolution* (1996), describes the rise of the new charismatic religious groups sweeping Great Britain. The new Evangelical movement focuses on "miracles," the supernatural, and the transcendental.

Couchand, Paul Luis (20th Century)

Couchand, a freethinker, wrote *The Book of Revelation—A Key to Christian Origins* (1932). {GS}

Coughlin, David R. (20th Century)

A freethinker, Coughlin wrote *Review of the Bibles* (1916). {GS}

COUNCIL FOR SECULAR HUMANISM (CSH)

The Council for Secular Humanism is the organization which publishes *Free Inquiry* and which sponsors many organizations, including the following:

- African Americans for Humanism
- Alliance of Secular Humanist Societies
- Committee for the Scientific Examination of Religion
- Inquiry Media Productions
- Institute for Inquiry
- International Development Committee
- James Madison Memorial Committee
- Robert G. Ingersoll Memorial Committee
- Secular Organization for Sobriety (SOS)
- Secular Humanist Aid and Relief Effort (SHARE)
- Society of Humanist Philosophers

The Alliance of Secular Humanist Societies (ASHS) is a network of regional groups in several dozen United States and ten Canadian cities.

The International Academy of Humanism consists of eminent members from nations around the world. The Council's headquarters is at 3965 Rensch Road, Amherst, NY 14226.

In 1995, the Council for Secular Humanism's board of directors voted to change the corporation's name from the Council for Democratic and Secular Humanism (CODESH) to the Council for Secular Humanism. The board in 1999 consisted of the following: Paul Kurtz (Chairman); Vern Bullough; Jan Eisler; Jonathan Kurtz; Joseph Levee; Kenneth Marsalek; Jean Millholland; and Robert Worsfold. In 1999 Robert Price became the Executive Director.

On the Web: <http://www.secularhumanism.org>. (See entries for *Free Inquiry* and Secular Humanism.)

COUNCIL OF AUSTRALIAN HUMANIST ORGANIZATIONS

The Council of Australian Humanist Organizations, a member of the IHEU, is at 137 B Princess Street, Kew, Victoria 3101, Australia.

Countryman, Valery (20th Century)

Countryman, who in 1993 became editor of *Secular Subjects*, a publication of the St. Louis, Missouri, Rationalist Society, has written about Ethan Allen and other secular subjects for that newsletter. In Rochester, New York, she spoke in 1994 on "Female Freethinkers" at a 1994 Robert G. Ingersoll commemoration of Ingersoll's work on behalf of women's equality. On the Web: <www.SecularHumanism.org/library/aah/countryman_3_4.html>.

Coupland, Douglas Campbell (1961—)

Coupland, an author and a non-theist, is known for writing *Generation X: Tales for an Accelerated Culture* (1991); *Shampoo Planet* (1992); *Life After God* (1995); and *Microserfs* (1996). He writes for numerous periodicals, including *The New York Times*, *The New Republic*, and *Artforum*.

Most of what organized religion stands for, Coupland illustrates in his stories, is external to what makes humans humanistic. "I was raised in a totally secular environment," he told interviewer Alexander Laurence in 1994. "That germ of Judeo-Christian thinking wasn't there to begin with. You can't imagine it there. It simply wasn't there. You are presuming that I'm some lapsed Christian. I'm not. I'm working from zero." {CA; E}

Coupland, Georgina (20th Century)

Coupland in Britain is active in the Preston Humanist Group.

Courier, Paul Louis (1772—1825)

A French writer, Courier de Méréwrote many pamphlets which were directed against the clerical restoration, for which he was imprisoned, then was apparently assassinated. He had had a presentiment, according to Wheeler, that bigots would kill him. {BDF; RAT}

COURTLY LOVE

During the Middle Ages and entirely apart from religion, a set of attitudes known as courtly love developed. According to the ideal of courtly love, a knight or nobleman worshiped a lady of high birth. His love for her inspired him to do great things on the battlefield and elsewhere. There usually was no physical relationship or marriage and, in fact, the lady was usually married to another man. Such a humanistic concept led many to practice a form of human brotherhood that elevated the status of women. {DCL}

Courtney, Janet E. (19th Century)

Courtney's *Freethinkers of the Nineteenth Century* (1920) is considered a classic study of freethought.

Courtney, Leonard Henry [Baron] (1832—1918)

Courtney was a British statesman, a lawyer who entered politics and rose to first-rank positions. He published a *Diary of a Church-Goer*, in which he confessed that he has no religious beliefs beyond a liberal theism and that a large number of distinguished churchgoers like himself do not believe in Christianity. According to McCabe, Courtney was a non-Christian theist who rejected the idea of a future life. {JM; RAT; RE}

Courtney, William Leonard (1850—1928)

Courtney was a writer, the editor of the *Fortnightly Review* from 1894 onward. In a symposium, *Do We Believe?* (1905), he wrote that "a hard, definite, logical, and systematic religious faith is almost an impossibility in the England we know." His definition of God: "the sum of individual consciousness." {RAT; RE}

Cousens, M. Bonnie (20th Century)

Cousens is Executive Director of the Society for Humanistic Judaism.

Cousin, Victor (1792—1867)

Cousin was a philosopher, one of the leading French thinkers of the early nineteenth century. He translated and edited the works of Plato, Proclus, Descartes, and Abelard (27 volumes). In his own eighteen works he is eclectic and a pantheist as regards religion. {JM; RAT; RE}

Cousins, Norman (1915—1990)

A consummate opinion maker who received over fifty honorary university and college degrees, Cousins was an essayist who was best known as the editor of the *Saturday Review of Literature* and, later, of *Saturday Review*. The latter journal drew a connection between current events and the various types of literature, showing the influence of one upon the other.

The Good Inheritance: The Democratic Chance (1942) spoke of the potential for greatness that exists in America. *Modern Man is Obsolete* (1945) included his ideas about humanity in the atomic age. *Anatomy of an Illness* (1979) was based upon his experience with a life-threatening illness, telling about the healing ability of the human mind and the medical value of laughter.

Cousins occasionally attended Unitarian and Ethical Culture meetings. In the 1950s he arranged to bring a group of "Hiroshima Maidens," girls whose bodies were disfigured by the atom bomb's explosion in their city, to receive surgical and medical attention in United States hospitals. One, Shigeko Niimoto, lived at his New Canaan, Connecticut, home and became a part of his family.

Members of the Friends volunteered to house the other girls. Cousins's editorials, lectures, and books on Albert Schweitzer and other subjects show him to be one of his time's major independent thinkers. He was well-known internationally and had visited Schweitzer at his African hospital. For the Unitarians in Westport, Connecticut, Cousins donated the pulpit in memory of Schweitzer. Active on behalf of the World Federalists, Cousins once was sent by President Kennedy to negotiate the release of two Catholic priests with Soviet leader Nikita Khruschev, after which he visited the Pope to inform him of the project.

A memorial service for Cousins, held at the Manhattan Ethical Culture Society, included eulogies by Ved Mehta; Unitarian minister Homer Jack; Walter Hoffman of the World Federalists; McGeorge Bundy; Horace Sutton; and Yevgeny Yevtushenko, who said that the world contains clever pessimists who through ruse argue for military destruction and war. "But Norman Cousins was a clever optimist," Yevtushenko observed, lamenting that no one of his stature appeared able in the 1990s to speak for man and mankind quite the persuasive way Cousins was able to do.

At that memorial service, his brother Robert read a letter written for the occasion by Norman himself, in which the thoughtful humanist stated that he hoped people "would come away from this joyous event better than when they came in." (See entries for Albert Einstein and for Albert Schweitzer.) {FUS; WAS, extensive conversations}

Coveney, Joseph (19th Century)

An Irishman who came to the United States in 1826, Coveney was memorialized in 1874 by a monument at Michigan's Oak Ridge Cemetery. Made of red granite, the monument is etched with slogans such as "The more religion, the more lying. . . . The more priests, the more poverty. . . . All Christian denominations preach damnation to the others." According to *Free Inquiry* (Winter 1991-1992), the monument has been vandalized by individuals trying to erase the inscriptions, and its spire was toppled.

Coventry, Henry (c. 1710—1752)

Coventry wrote *Letters of Philemon to Hydaspus on False Religion* (1736). A deist, he was a native of Cambridgeshire in England. {BDF; RAT}

COVENTRY AND WARWICKSHIRE (England) HUMANISTS

For information, write Waverley Day Centre, 65 Waverley Road, Kenilworth; or telephone 01926 58450.

Coward, Noel (Pierce) [Sir] (1899-1973)

An actor from the age of twelve, Coward was an accomplished singer and became a major playwright. He wrote *The Vortex* (1924), *Hay Fever* (1925), *Private Lives* (1930), and *Blithe Spirit* (1941), all filled with satirical humor and witty dialogue. His two volumes of autobiography are *Presnt Indicative* (1937) and *Future Indefinite* (1954).

Some Brtish humanists claim he was a non-believer, pointing to many witty pokes at religion which are found in his various works. {*Gay and Lesbian Humanist*, Summer 1999}

Coward, William (1656—1725)

A physician, Coward wrote *Second Thoughts Concerning the Human Soul*, which excited indignation by denying natural immortality. The House of Commons (17 March 1704) ordered his work to be burned. {BDF; RAT}

Cowell, Henry (20th Century)

Cowell, an executive in 1915 of the English National Secular Society, was dismissed from jury duty because he affirmed instead of swore the oath. The prosecution then objected to him. The objection pointed up the fact that an affirmation was allowed only when grounds were given why the oath was not acceptable. The freethinker still had to make public confession of his unbelief before he could take advantage of the Bradlaugh Act, and this still exposed him to ridicule and prejudice. Meanwhile, the Christian who simply preferred to affirm, but had no objection to the oath, was also excluded. {RSR}

Cowell, Henry Dixon (1897-1965): See entry for Lou Harrison.

Cowen, Joseph (1829—1900)

Cowen was a politician and reformer. He smuggled revolutionary literature into Italy, Hungary, and France in the years of reaction, and he spent large sums in aiding the cause of reform and progress. As M.P. for Newcastle in England, he opposed a Bill to increase the number of bishoprics, saying that the country wanted no more "sleek and oily parsons." He called religious creeds "the ghosts of obsolete opinions" and was a cordial ally of Bradlaugh. {RAT; RE; VI}

Cowley, John Paul (1904—1985)

Cowley, a professor of literature in Cedar Falls at the University of Northern Iowa, co-sponsored the Humanist Club with Martin L. Grant. The school's 1948 yearbook, *Old Gold*, described it as a "deep thinkers club" with the following aims: "Believing their college training alone does not supply the integration of ideas so necessary in the development of a personal philosophy, the members meet weekly and discuss their own and others' individual philosophies. Subjects cover all fields, including ethics, aesthetics, determinism, planned economies, social action, and Unitarianism. Although larger campuses have clubs of similar purpose, this is the first of its name on any campus." Cowley was a Unitarian who did not mention that fact in class but who illustrated his outlook by interestingly and thoroughly discussing with his students deism, transcendentalism, Emerson, Thoreau, and authors associated with Brook Farm. His octogenarian widow, **Helen Cowley**, is still an active Unitarian.

Cowley, Malcolm (1898—1989)

Cowley was an editor of *New Republic* and author of popular editions of selected works by Hemingway, Faulkner, Hawthorne, Whitman, and F. Scott Fitzgerald. He wrote to the present author concerning humanism:

> I am a humanist, yes, but not a naturalistic humanist. Naturalistic humanism, so-called, implies an oversimplified notion of the nature of man. Communism makes the same mistake (which is not to confuse naturalistic humanists with communists, except on this one point).
>
> The mistake is to regard humankind as composed simply of the individual integers of the human race that we see or read about or have enumerated or find traces of in caves or rocks—a plus b plus c to the nth power equals the human race. Add the integers together and the result is less than the human race, because each human society is also an integer, and because individual human beings are all of the incomplete and unable to subsist by themselves without the support of the society to which they belong. The society is something invisible, yet real and measurable in many of its effects.
>
> In order to represent this invisible reality, men invented religions, which are essentially based on the dual nature of man—as individual and as part dependent on the whole. Rituals and ceremonials are therefore an essential part of human society, because they are designed to render visible and tangible this relationship that we sense but cannot see. Any state belief will therefore become a religion—and unless it faces the problem squarely it will become an impoverished and ultimately dangerous religion (as communism has become in Russia).
>
> What I am saying is not to question the application of the scientific method to human society. It is simply to suggest that the sci-

entific method has so far, and in most cases, been asking the wrong questions.

As for naturalistic humanism, as represented by *The Humanist*, I sympathize deeply with most of its aims and wish strongly to endorse its campaign for civil liberties and for secular education. It is going at these matters in exactly the right way, by organizing groups and giving them a feeling of cohesiveness (i.e., by becoming a sort of church). On the philosophical side it doesn't go far enough.

In *Exile's Return* (1934) and *A Second Flowering* (1973), Cowley wrote of the "lost generation" of authors. {CE; WAS, 21 March 1951}

Cox Alvarado, Alexander (1964—)

Cox, a university statistician in San José, Costa Rica, is the first president of the *Asociación Iberoamericana Ético Humanista* (ASIBEHU), an Ibero-American Ethical Humanist Association for Spanish-speaking secular humanists in Central and South America, including the Caribbean. Cox participated in the 1996 Humanist World Congress in Mexico City and the 1998 Humanist World Congress in India. At both, he spoke of the Latino humanists' aim to keep church and state separate, to have the right to choose an abortion, and to back rights of gays and lesbians. His E-mail addresses: <acox@conare.ac.cr> and <asibehu@sol.racsa.co.cr>. On the Web: <http://idt.net/~wasm/asibehu>.

Cox, Donald W. (1921—)

Cox, who is president of the Hemlock Society of Delaware Valley, is author of *Hemlock's Cup: The Struggle for "Death With Dignity* (1993) and *Doomsday Asteroid* (1996).

Cox, Eva (20th Century)

Cox was named the 1997 Australian Humanist of the Year. A lecturer at the University of Technology in Sydney, she is author of *Leading Women: Tactics for Making a Difference* (1996). She commented as to how women in a position of power can contribute to a more caring and people-centered style of leadership. {*Australian Humanist,* May 1997}

Cox, George William (the Right Rev.) [Sir] (Born 1827)

Although he entered the Church, Cox devoted himself to history and mythology, writing *Mythology of the Aryan Nations* (1870). In 1886 he became Bishop of Bloemfontein. Cox is credited with the authorship of the *English Life of Jesus*, published under the name of Thomas Scott. At the Church Congress of 1888 he read an heretical paper on Biblical Eschatology. {BDF; FUK}

Cox, James A. (20th Century)

Cox, vice president of Atheist Alliance, Inc., is a contributor to *Free Inquiry.* and to *The Freethought Observer*, a Texas publication which commenced in 1994. Editor in Chief of Midwest Book Review, he reviews current freethought and atheist books for *Secular Nation* and is webmaster for the Atheist Alliance. E-mail: <mwbookrevw@aol.com>. On the Web: <http://www.execpc.com/~mbr/bookwatch>.

Coyer, Dennis (20th Century)

An atheist and an activist, Coyer is found on the Web: <http://www.execpc.com/~dcoy/humanist>.

COYOTE

For Crow Indians, Coyote is the God of Creation. {LEE}

Coyteux, Fernand (Born 1800)

A French writer, Coyteux wrote a materialistic system of philosophy and studies of physiology. {BDF}

Cozzens, James Gould (1903—1978)

A Pulitzer Prize-winning novelist for *Guard of Honor* (1948), Cozzens when asked by the present author about humanism responded:

> I suspect you've confused me with Norman Cousins—something both Mr. Cousins and I are used to. I imagine he would be, but I am not at all interested in semantical studies. Still, if it could be of some indirect use, I don't mind commenting: (1) Humanism, I'm afraid, connotes for me exactly the kind of vaporing exhibited in the examples of the reply you sent; (2) Like Herr Mann, I trust I fall in none of the categories; but, in my case, for the more ignoble reason that I'm not a proud sympathizer with the secret of man but simply a writer; (3) Many writers, not excluding several you name as having commented, strongly influenced me, by sounding like such asses when they neglect their business and shoot their faces off, against what I gather is humanism; (4) When what a writer thinks cannot be told from his regular line of writing, or when he feels he has to supplement that with explanatory pronouncements, he's probably unable to think at all; and I'm sure no present or future persons of judgment, whether literary historians or lay readers, will have the faintest interest he says he thinks he thinks.
>
> {WAS, 19 April 1956}

Crabbe, George (1754—1832)

An English poet, Crabbe in *The Borough* (1810) wrote, "See yonder preacher to his people pass / Borne up and swelled by tabernacle-gas." {TYD}

Craddock, Ida (Died 1902)

Craddock believed so strongly in the purification of the marriage relation which, being something of a mystic, she regarded as a communion with God. Her work was censored by Anthony Comstock and she was sentenced to three months at the work house on Blackwell's Island, where inmates called her a "ministering angel."

Upon being released, she continued her writings. Comstock arrested her again. After bail, she cut the veins of her wrists and turned on the gas in her room, leaving a letter:

> I maintain my right to die as I have lived, a free woman,
> not cowed into silence by any other human being.

Wrote Macdonald in *Fifty Years of Freethought*,

> Personally Mrs. Craddock was a surprisingly lovely woman.
> She and Comstock were the Beauty and the Beast.

{WWS}

Craggs, R. S. (20th Century)

Craggs, an Ontario humanist, possesses a first Canadian edition of Thomas Paine's *Age of Reason*. The work was published in Toronto in 1887 because Canadian law prohibited its importation.

Craig, Edward Thomas (Born 1804)

A social reformer, Craig was editor in 1831 of the *Lancashire Co-operator*. He contributed largely to radical and co-operative literature. At the age of eighty-four, Craig wrote *The Science of Prolonging Life*. {BDF}

Crain, Esther (20th Century)

Crain is an editorial assistant for *World*, the journal of the Unitarian Universalist Association in Boston.

Cramer, C. H. (20th Century)

A freethinker, Cramer wrote *Royal Bob* (1952), a well-received biography of Robert Green Ingersoll. {FUS}

Cramer, Johan Nicolai (Born 1812)

Cramer was a Swedish writer who was ordained a priest in 1842 and who then resigned in 1858. In religion he denied revelation and insisted on the separation of church and state. His *Separation from the Church* was a freethinker's annotations on the reading of the Bible. {BDF; RAT}

Cranbrook, James (Born c. 1817)

Reverend Cranbrook, born of strict Calvinistic parents, gradually emancipated himself from dogmas, became a teacher, and for sixteen years was minister of an Independent Church at Liscard, Cheshire, England. In 1866 he published *Credibilia*, an inquiry into the grounds of Christian faith. Cranbrook's *Religious Education of Children* was posthumously published in 1908. {BDF; GS}

Cranch, Christopher Pearse (1832—1892)

A transcendentalist, Cranch worked on *Western Messenger* and *The Dial*, was educated at the Cambridge Divinity School, became a Unitarian minister, left as a minister in 1842, then became a landscape artist. His mildly satirical caricatures of transcendentalism became popular, especially his drawings of Emerson as a "transparent eyeball" and a pumpkin, based on passages from Emerson's *Nature*. He shows his freethought sentiments in *Satan: A Libretto* (1874). {RAT; U&U}

Crane, Caroline Julia Bartlett (1858—1935)

Inspired by the Iowa Sisterhood, Crane became a Unitarian minister who encouraged church use for such activities as a kindergarten, a gymnasium, and courses in domestic science and industrial arts for women. She also was active in the new field of urban sanitation and the establishment of standards for meat processing.

Crane, (Harold) Hart (1899—1932)

Crane, the Ohio-born poet, published only two books in his lifetime but was recognized as an outstanding poet of his era. *White Buildings* (1926) contains mystical perceptions, and *The Bridge* (1930) is a long, mystical work. He used symbols such as Columbus, Pocahontas (the "mythological nature-symbol chosen to represent the physical body of the continent, or the soul," he explained), Rip Van Winkle, Poe, Whitman (whose influence was major), the subway, and the Brooklyn Bridge (which symbolizes man's anonymous creative power unifying past and present).

An alcoholic and a homosexual, Crane was constantly plagued by money problems and guilt feelings, avoiding religionists who considered his homosexuality sinful. Friends who tried to help him found he was a severe trial. His attraction to virile sailors was well known during his Greenwich Village days, and he once explained, "Let my lusts be my ruin, then, since all else is a fake and a mockery." In short, he wanted to be humiliated. He resided in 1931 in Mexico with Katherine Anne Porter, when both were Guggenheim Fellows, and she once wrote to him

> You must either learn to stand on your own feet as a responsible adult, or expect to be treated as a fool. Your emotional hysteria is not impressive, except possibly to those little hangers-on of literature who feel your tantrums are a mark of genius. To me they do not add the least value to your poetry, and take away my last shadow of a wish to ever see you again.

In plain language to the first Guggenheim Fellow to raise hell and get jailed, she continued to advise that he must stay sober and get to work. This was followed by a letter from Henry Allen Moe, of the Guggenheim Foundation:

> There's no use in getting mad at this letter; protests have been made in several governmental channels and I cannot ignore them, which I have no desire to do anyway. So I put my cards on the table and tell you that you are making yourself liable to deportation; and, if that happens, your support form the Foundation must cease. . . . So that's that, and that's flat. The Fourth of July is coming: and that will make a grand occasion for you to go on a *final* bust or quit making a nuisance and a fool of yourself and the Foundation. Take your choice and go to it.

According to his correspondence, he admitted he could not remember what he did when he was drunk. Miss Porter, however, is described by Crane biographer John Unterecker as saying

> His voice at these times was intolerable: a steady, harsh inhuman bellow which stunned the ears and shocked the nerves and caused the heart to contract. In this voice and with words so foul there is no question of repeating them, he cursed separately and by name the moon, and its light: the heliotrope, the heaven-tree, the sweet-by-night, the star jessamine, and their perfumes. He cursed the air we breathed together, the pool of water with its two small ducks huddled at the edge, and the vines on the wall and the house. But those were not the things he hated. He did not even hate us, for we were nothing to him. He hated and feared himself.

Crane's work was noted for showing his haunted alienation. Other writers marveled at his ability to complete such complex poetry with rich imagery, verbal ingenuity, and meticulous craftsmanship. As he was returning from Mexico, and after having destroyed a David Siqueiros painting with a razor, he unexpectedly went to the side of the ship, called "Goodbye, everybody," jumped overboard, and drowned.

Tennessee Williams was so affected by such a loss of genius that in his will he asked that his body be placed in a sack and dumped overboard in the same area that Crane had drowned. Other writers lamented that, had Crane lived at the time of the Stonewall riots, he would have recognized that his sexual orientation was not a preference, not something to have compounded his major guilt feelings.

Peggy Cowley, who expected to marry him, had been told by him, "I'm not going to make it, dear. I'm utterly disgraced." Crane's mother, who had been the smothering type, continued to cling after his death. She vainly sought a publisher for his "Posthumous Works," claiming her son was dictating new poems to her from beyond the grave. {AA; CE; James Fenton, *The New York Review of Books*, 23 October 1997; OEL}

Crane, Stephen (1871—1900)

Sometimes termed the first modern American writer, Crane is known for introducing realism into American fiction. The fourteenth and last child of an itinerant New Jersey family, he was the son of a Methodist minister who died when Crane was eight. By the age of seven Crane had written some poetry and by fourteen had written a story. His maternal godfather, Jesse T. Peck, a Methodist bishop, was the president of Syracuse University, where Crane attended for one semester but confessed he disliked "the cut-and-dried curriculum." He dropped out of a ministerial seminary and, an orphan by the age of twenty, he moved into the old Art Students' League building in New York, encouraged as a writer by Hamlin Garland and William Dean Howells to write about Bowery flophouses for the newspaper syndicate Bachellor-Johnson. That he did, but he lived on cheap food, dressed miserably, had matted hair, and smelled of cigarettes and garlic.

By the age of twenty-four, he had written *Maggie: A Girl of the Street* under the pseudonym Johnston Smith, published it privately with money borrowed from his brother, and was dismayed that it was not a commercial success. However, he then wrote a runaway best seller, *The Red Badge of Courage* (1895), despite having no personal experience of war.

In 1896 he was sent by a newspaper syndicate to cover a nationalist uprising in Cuba, but the ship sank after leaving Jacksonville, Florida. After rowing thirty hours he and the ship's broken-armed captain made it back to Florida, an experience that inspired "The Open Boat" (1898). H. G. Wells described the story as "an imperishable gem." Crane then shipped off to write about the Greek-Turkish war over Crete, finding the noise of battle "the most beautiful sound of my experience, barring no symphony."

Cora, an English lover who had been the madam of the Hotel de Dream, lived with him in England as his common-law wife, but after nine months he left to write about the Spanish-American War. When he found he had tuberculosis, he returned and with Cora moved into a 14th-century Sussex estate called Brede Place. The run-down place had bats and no electricity or plumbing, but guests included Joseph Conrad and H. G. Wells. Cora nursed him when he had a series of lung hemorrhages and an abscess in the rectum area and, searching for a cure, rushed him to Baden-Baden, where he received morphine to help control the pain but died soon after arrival and before his thirtieth birthday.

Although not at all active in his parents' Methodism, he did have a belief in a finite God. However, he wrote the following poem:

A God in Wrath

A god in wrath
Was beating a man;
He cuffed him loudly
With thunderous blows
That rang and rolled over the earth.
All the people came running.
The man screamed and struggled,
And bit madly at the feet of the god.
The people cried:
"Ah, what a wicked man!"
And
"Ah, what a redoubtable god!"

{Linda H. Davis, *Badge of Courage*, 1998; OCAL, OEL}

Crane, Walter (1845—1915)

Crane was an artist who received the Grand Cross of the Crown of Italy (1903) and the Albert Gold Medal (1904). He collaborated with William Morris. In *An Artist's Reminiscences* (1907), Crane said that early in life he cleared his mind of "superstitious shadows and theological bogies" and "decided for Freethought." {RAT; RE}

Cranston, Alan (1914-)

A former Senator from California (1969-1993), Cranston was Executive Secretary of the Council for American-Italian Affairs 1945-1946; President of the California Democratic Council (1953-1957), and President of the United World Federalists (1949-1952). He served in the United States Armed Forces from 1944 to 1945.

Cranston, long a fighter for democratic causes, signed Humanist Manifesto 2000.

Crapsey, Algernon Sidney (1847—1927)

With M. M. Mangasarian, Crapsey wrote *Did Jesus Really Live?* (1908). {GS}

Craven, M. B. (19th Century)

Craven, an American, wrote a critical work on the Bible entitled *Triumph of Criticism* (1869). {BDF}

CRAWLEY, WEST SUSSEX (England) HUMANISTS

For information about the Crawley Humanists in West Sussex, England, write Charles Stewart, 50 Boswell Road, Tilgate, Crawley RH 10 5AZ; or telephone 01293 511270.

Cream, Shannon (20th Century)

Cream, a California atheist, has written in *Freethought Today* (March 1996) of his difficulties in fighting religion in public schools. He, in fact, had to remove his son from a school that was trying to inculcate Christianity. "As atheists and freethinkers," he wrote,

> we must resolve to speak up. We must become as involved and active as those that oppose us. If our atheism is to be ethical it demands a commitment from us to identify ourselves; to do so with pride, confidence, and assuredness. It demands that we learn to roar.

CREATION: See entry for Genesis.

CREATIONISM (Soteriology)

Creationism is the literal belief that the creation of the world and all its creatures took place in six calendar days, as described in *Genesis*. Peter A. Bertocci, who taught at Bates College in Lewistown, Maine, has defined creationism as a theory that "God is the immediate creator of every new-born human soul at the moment of conception. The soul is not the product of physical or parental generation or of divine emanation."

Bill Hicks, a Texan comedian, in telling British audiences about one of the absurdities of American culture, has observed, "Ever notice how people who believe in creationism look really un-evolved? Their eyes real close together. Eyebrow ridges. Big, furry hands and feet. 'I believe God created me in one day.' " To which Hicks tacks on, "Looks like he rushed it."

William Silvert of Halifax, Nova Scotia, has reasoned that if in Kansas—where creationism must be taught—the evolutionists win the minds of young Kansans, we all win; if the creationists come out on top, it proves that evolution can proceed backward as well as forward.

Derek C. Araujo, a Harvard student, asked E. O. Wilson why in 1997 no one contests such theories as multiple theories, electromagnetic theory, quantum theory, and cell theory but the theory of evolution sparks controversy. Wilson responded:

> To put in a kind of parable, the reason is that the jet flights we take do not depend upon the acceptance of Darwinism. Richard Dawkins said recently about postmodernists, who are also relatively unfriendly to the idea of the natural sciences as a source of objective truth, "I've never met a postmodernist at 30,000 feet." Here may be the core truth about the obstinacy of creation thought: Through confidence in one's immortality, and through the deep satisfaction and benefits that come from tribal affiliation with a group that has clearly defined sets of ideas and dogmas, you receive considerable psychological and economic benefits, and there occur very few losses. On the other hand, understanding the world as materially based and logical, evolutionary self-assembly does not confer such advantages. It is demonstrably true, but it does not give you the same social benefits. It gives in the long term a deeper psychological advantage. And it is certainly a better grasp of the world, and I think increasingly it's going to be important for global stabilization through development of ethical codes and mutual understanding across cultures. But for day to day living and satisfaction, religious beliefs are far more potent, even as they create considerable disagreement and strife among the different sects.
>
> Another view that's been often discussed with reference to this problem is that the human brain appears to have been programmed by evolution to be easily indoctrinated. There's an advantage to fitting in quickly with a tribal group, and to go along, to cooperate, and to engage in some amount of self-sacrifice for the group. This gives, over thousands of generations, an advantage in survival and personal reproduction.

(See the entry for Soteriology, which in the 1990s is the less commonly used term. Also see entries for Cretinism, Eye, and the National Center for Science Education.)

{Derek C. Araujo, Campus Freethought Association Newsletter #1, 17 March 1997; DCL; *New Yorker* 10 Jan 2000}

Creed, Carmen (20th Century)

Creed, writing about "The Visible Atheists" at the University of South Florida (*Secular Nation*, July-September 1998), noted that a group from Atheists of Florida has operated a table since 1994 at a flea market there, sandwiched in between food and clothing vendors and Scientologist, Muslim, and Christian religious booths.

Creede, N. C. (Born 1843)

Creede served as a United States scout on the plains of Nebraska, Wyoming, Colorado, and Dakota for seven years. He was in a number of battles with the Sioux and other hostile tribes. A successful prospector and miner, he was a freethinker and a liberal all his life.

He had no patience to listen to anything that is superstitious or orthodox, did not believe in life after death, and said there is no God to worship and no devil to fear.

Creel, H. C. (20th Century)

Creel was one of the early religious humanists. When *The New Humanist* first appeared in April 1928 as "a Bulletin of the Humanist Fellowship," he as president of the fellowship wrote the following:

> Humanism, to be worthy of its ideals, neither can be a neo-ecclesiasticism nor a neo-scholasticism. We are interested, primarily, in building a society in which every human being shall have the greatest possible opportunity for the best possible life. Insofar as we are Humanists, every secondary interest must be judged by the prime criterion.

{EW}

Creeley, Robert (1926—)

Creeley, a member of the American Academy of Arts and Letters, is an author, poet, and editor. Asked by the present author about humanism and belief, he has written,

> I don't finally believe in any fixed identity for "God" or whatever else one might call such a content. I think people, myself included, believe in belief, so to speak, need that communal sharing of a premise. Thus "God" provides and is provided. But the determining means and content, in the context of physical world otherwise, is, for me, literally *people*, literally *human*. Fixed foci of that potential, premises that become locked without revision, dogmatic presumptions that will not be considered anew, are all destructive in my own sense of things. I recall William Carlos Williams's quotation of Hans Morgenthau in a late poem: "Hitherto men have been unable to realize their wishes. Now that they can realize them, they must either change them or perish. . . ."
>
> I believe that very deeply. I despair in a world that cannot change its mind or recognize its own confusion. I had been thinking of all this in a poem recently published (*Conjunctions: 21*):
>
> CREDO
>
> *Creo que si* . . . . I believe
> *it will rain*
> *tomorrow*. . . . I believe
> *the son of a bitch*
>
> is going into the river. . . .
> I believe *All men are*
> *created equal*—By your
> leave a leafy
>
> shelter over the exposed
> person—*I'm a*
> *believer* creature
> of habit but without
> *out there* a void of
> pattern older
> *older* the broken
> pieces no longer

salvageable bits
but incommensurate
chips yet must
get it back together.

In God we
trust emptiness privilege
will not not *perish*
perish *from this earth—*

In particular echo
of inside pushes
at edges all these years
collapse in slow motion.
As it gets now impossible
to say, it's your hand
I hold to, still
your hand.

The will to believe,
the will to be good,
the will to want
a way out.

Humanness, like
you, man. Us - pun
for once beyond reflective
mirror of brightening prospect?

I believe what it was
was a hope it could be
somehow what it was
and would so continue.
A plan to walk out on,
fair enough. *Jump!* said the pirate.
Believe me if all
those endearing young charms . . .

Here, as opposed to there,
Even in confusions there seems
still a comfort,
still a faith.

I'd as lief
not leave, not
go away, not
not believe.

I believe in belief . . .
All said, whatever I can think of
comes from there,
goes there.

As it gets now impossible
to say, it's your hand
I hold to, still
your hand.

The poem has the usual "difficulties" of poetry, perhaps, but it's nonetheless what I'd think to say.

Creeley is a novelist (*The Island*, 1963), a storyteller (*The Gold Diggers*, 1954; 1965), an editor (*Selected Writings of Charles Olson*, 1967), and writer of numerous works of poetry, a 1971 volume of which was entitled *1234567890.*

The critic Martin Seymour-Smith has written that Creeley writes "in short, imageless lines, broken, unmusical, rigorously pragmatic, faithful to their moment alone." Smith adds that Creeley has been greatly influenced by William Carlos Williams, Charles Olson, and John Dewey. Black Mountain College, where he taught as did Olson, Paul Goodman, and Allen Ginsberg, was greatly influenced by Dewey, who was a visitor there. Creeley edited *The Black Mountain Review* (1954—1957), describing the efforts of the college founded by J. A. Rice to provide a heuristic type of creative education.

In 1994 his *Echoes* was published. Creeley currently is the Samuel P. Capen Professor of Poetry and Humanities at the State University of New York in Buffalo.

In a painting by R. B. Kitaj, "The Ohio Gang" (1964), Creeley is depicted as a bearded man with a squint. {WAS, 15 January 1994}

Crees, Adrian (20th Century)

Crees, an Australian rationalist, is author of *Anatomy of Religion*. Its preface includes the sentence, "I have set out to make a case against religion," and he proceeds to evaluate Christianity, Hinduism, Buddhism, Islam, primitive religion, sects, cults, missions, and the psychologists and psychiatrists who seem to be overlooking the sickness of religion.

CREMATION

- Surprise me!

Fernando Vargas
asked by Warren Allen Smith, executor of his estate,
if he preferred cremation or having the body-in-the-casket
transported from New York for burial in Costa Rica

Some religious groups do not allow cremation, although freethinkers and secular humanists leave the decision entirely up to the individual or the executor of the person's estate. An entire cremation and urn in New York City is available for under $500., whereas the charge by funeral parlors for services and caskets may cost in the thousands of dollars. One American undertaker has offered a coffin fitted with a mobile telephone, air conditioning, a light, and a computer toy, all in case the corpse revives.

According to the *Catechism of the Catholic Church* (1994), "The Church permits cremation, provided that it does not demonstrate a denial of faith in the resurrection of the body."

The Economist (15 April 1995) has reported that the Chinese government estimates that cremation saves 6,700 hectares (about 16,556 acres) of farmland, 3 million cubic metres of timber, and 10 billion yuan ($1.2 billion) a year. The Chinese ban what used to be the tradition of burning paper money as an offering to the dead. People who burn money or buy wreaths "do so to show off," according to the Chinese *People's Daily*. (See entry for Memorial Societies.) {*The Economist*, 4 January 1997.}

Cremer, William Randal [Sir] (1838—1908)

Cremer was a reformer, a British working man who entered politics and worked so zealously for peace and other humanitarian ideals that he won a Nobel Prize. According to his biographer, Howard Evans, Cremer rejected Christianity but remained "religious." {JM; RAT; RE}

Cremonini, Cesare (1550—1631)

An Italian philosopher, Cremonini taught philosophy at Padua from 1591 to 1631. A follower of Aristotle, he excited suspicion by his want of religion and his teaching the mortality of the soul. Both the Jesuits and the Inquisition ordered him to refute some of his views, which he refused.

Bayle states the Cremonini did not believe the soul is immortal, and Larousse stated that Cremonini was not a Christian. {BDF}

Crescas, Hasdai (14th Century)

Crescas, a Spanish Jew, wrote *The Refutation of the Christian Principles,* which in 1992 was translated into English for the first time by Daniel J. Lasker. His purpose was to encourage his fellow Jews not to convert to Christianity. Crescas believed in Old Testament theism, but he rejected New Testament Christianity. His work is of historical interest in that he used his belief in Judaism to "prove" the falsity of Christianity.

Crescini, Vincenzo (Born 1857)

An Italian philologist, Crescini taught at Genoa and Padua universities. A Cavalliere of the Crown of Italy, was a positivist of the Ardigò school. {RAT}

CRETINISM

When a computer's spellchecker is working, *cretinism* might be a suggested correction for *creationism*. When the spellchecker is *not* working, such an error still implies a degree of wisdom. However, "cretin" is a word from the Vulgar Latin *christianus*, meaning poor fellow, one whom God allowed to be born with a deficiency of thyroid hormone and therefore is dwarf-like, has dystrophy of the bones, and is mentally retarded.

Apologists have struggled to explain God's actions. Physicians, meanwhile, have no difficulty supplying lucid explanations for dystrophy.

Crèvecoeur, J. Hector St. John (1735—1813)

An American author and agriculturist, Crèvecoeur introduced the culture of the American potato into Normandy and of alfalfa into the United States. In *Letters From an American Farmer* (1782), he wrote, "Persecution, religious pride, the love of contradiction, are the food of what the world commonly calls religion." {TYD}

Crichton, (John) Michael (1942-)

An author, film director, and a physician, Crichton received a 1996 Emmy Best Dramatic Series Award for "E," a popular television show about emergency room personnel. He was co-screenwriter of "Jurassic Park" (1993) and "Twister" (1996). As Jeffrey Hudson, he wrote *A Case of Need* (1968), and as John Lange *Odds On* (1966). *The Andromeda Strain* (1969) brought him much notoriety, and interviewers marvel that a writer is also an expert on medicine. In his 1993 autobiography, *Travels*, Crichton tells of his fascination with Buddhism when, as he was told, it was a religion that doesn't believe in God. "I found it interesting," he observed, "that I liked this religion, because for many years I had been vociferously atheistic and anti-religion." {CA}

Crick, Bernard (Rowland) (1919—)

A professor of politics, University of London, Crick was elected as an honorary associate of the British Rationalist Press Association in 1976 and is a Humanist Laureate in the Council for Secular Humanism's International Academy of Humanism. The 1973 Voltaire Lectures include his *Crime*, Rape and *Gin* (1975). In 1980, he signed the Secular Humanist Declaration. A bee-keeper and theatre critic, he has edited *Machiavelli: The Discourses* (1971) and *Political Thoughts and Polemics* (1989). "My mother was a thrice yearly Christian: Christmas, Easter, and Armistice Day," he has written, adding that, "I still like the language and liturgies of the Church of England. . . . But the absurdity of it began to dawn after the closing words of the Bishop of Croydon's last confirmation class: 'Remember boys, when the Archbishop's hands descend on your head you are one with God the Father, God the Son, God the Holy Ghost—and no hair oil." Like Koestler, he stated, "I am a 'pious atheist.' Our ever-ready anti-God does sometimes seem a little old-fashioned. We get nowhere if we blame the revival of militant religious fundamentalism on religion. It is how we behave to each other that matters more than what we believe. Is this heresy or humanism?"

In 1994 an essay by Crick, "A Humanist Perspective for Britain," was included in *Challenges to the Enlightenment, Essays in Defense of Reason and Science*. In *The Astonishing Hypothesis: The Scientific Search for the Soul* (1994), Crick makes the case that it is difficult if not impossible to argue any longer that a conscious mind can survive the organic death of the brain. Crick, the literary editor of *The Political Quarterly*, signed Humanist Manifesto 2000. (See entry for Arthur Koestler.) {SHD}

Crick, Francis Harry Compton [O. M.] (1916—)

A Nobel Prize Laureate in medicine (jointly) in 1962, Dr. Crick has been the J. W. Kieckhefer Distinguished Professor at the Salk Institute since 1977. He signed Humanist Manifesto II and is a Humanist Laureate in the Council for Secular Humanism's International Academy of Humanism. In 1980, he signed the Secular Humanist Declaration. Crick was elected as an honorary associate of the Rationalist Press Association in 1962, and he is an Honorary Associate of the National Secular Society. He wrote *Of Molecules and Men* (1967) and co-wrote with J. D. Watson *The Double Helix* (1968). With Dr. Watson, Dr. Crick discovered the structure of D(eoxyribo) N(ucleic) A(cid) in 1953.

His *Astonishing Hypothesis: The Scientific Search for the Soul* (1993) is an outspoken attack on religious concepts of the soul. For Crick, our minds are nothing more than the behavior of neurons. "You are nothing but a pack of neurons," he declares. As he puts it, a single nerve cell is actually a dumb thing, but dumb in "subtle ways." What he finds astonishing is that from these dumb units emerge the powers of the human mind. Viewed as a machine, the brain "handles an immense amount of information all at once, in one perceptual moment. Much of the content of this rich body of coherent information is constantly changing, yet the machine manages to keep various running records of what it has just been doing." No man-made machine is capable of such, and Crick laments that both religion and philosophy have failed to understand human consciousness. (See entry for Friedrich Miescher regarding DNA. Also, see the interview of Crick by Thomas W. Flynn and Timothy J. Madigan in *Free Inquiry*, Fall 1994). {CA; CE; E; HM2; SHD}

CRIME

Lisa Conyers and Philip D. Harvey, in "Religion and Crime: Do They Go Together? (*Free Inquiry*, Summer 1996), found that, "Surprisingly, recent research suggests that a religious person is more likely to commit a crime than a non-religious person. One can even argue that the more religious the society, the more likely it is to have high crime rates." They cite numerous studies, including work by Bertrand Russell, also noting that religion does not deter war. Conyers is a writer and researcher based in Mount Vernon, Washington. Harvey is a writer on a wide variety of public policy issues from Washington, D.C. They cited the World Rank Research Team's *Where We Stand*, which found that "91% of the population in the United States believes in God. That compares with 48% in the United Kingdom and 47% in Japan. . . . The percent of people who believe in their religious leaders is 43% in the United States. It is only 6% in Japan and 3% in the United Kingdom and Germany. The portion believing in Hell is 76% in the United States. Compare that with 53% in Japan, 38% in Australia, 35% in the United Kingdom, and 16% in Germany."

CRIMES AGAINST NATURE

Religionists refer to homosexual acts as crimes against nature, oblivious to the fact that homosexuality is found in species throughout nature.

Freethinkers hold the view that two major crimes against nature are celibacy—which is a perversion of nature—and all environmentally unsound practices—which destroy or pollute the Earth's natural environment.

Crisp, Quentin (1908—1999)

A gay critic and author of *The Naked Servant*, Crisp told a gathering of Unitarian Universalists in New York City that he was not attracted to any of the organized religions. He was, in general, a rationalist about theology, morals, and ethics. On a trip to Northern Ireland, he bravely informed his audience that he was an atheist, "Yes, but is it the God of the Protestants or the God of the Catholics in whom you don't believe?" a person called out. As for religion, he has said, "Well, it *has* done terrifying things. Religious ideas are inflammatory in a way that I find difficult to understand. There are very few wars over the theory of relativity. Very few heated arguments, for that matter."

Asked several years later in 1998 if he is an atheist, he responded,

> If God is the universe—which encloses the universe, or if God is the cell inside the cell, or if God is the cause behind the cause—that I

> can believe—I can not believe in a God susceptible to prayer—that's a lot of rubbish. This is nonsense. I would never teach a child to pray. I would tell them your fate is sealed.

And is death final?

> Well, I hope so. Eternal life is something I wouldn't wish on my worst enemy.

What would have been a better life for you? What would be different?

> I would be different. I would be a woman. Now I am only manly in that I have no emotion, otherwise I'm feminine. If I had been a woman, I would have been acceptable.

The Naked Servant, a shocker when first published in 1968, described his having received a government stipend while working at illustrating books and modeling nude in art schools. The work not only revealed that he had taken money for sex but also described his unique style of clothing. By 1968, he has noted, "The symbols which I had adopted forty years earlier to express my sexual type had become the uniform of all young people." Reviewing "The Godfather" in *Christopher Street* (Issue #153), Crisp advised moviegoers: "This picture stops just short of being blasphemous, but viewers should be warned that it denounces Catholicism at least as vigorously as it attacks the Mafia. In one early scene, we are shown a Vatican official offering Mr. Pacino the control of a vast conglomerate enterprise in exchange for sufficient money to cover its own ill-advised investments. The narrative also manages to drag in Pope John Paul I who, in real life, died so suspiciously soon after his enthronement and who was rumored to have been poisoned with lethal cups of tea."

In 1993, octogenarian Crisp played the role of Queen Elizabeth I in a Sally Potter movie, "Orlando," based on the novel by Virginia Woolf. Movie critic George Brown remarked, "Although Crisp looks more like Victoria than Elizabeth I, he's every inch a devouring queen." His effeminancy was such that he never attempted to hide his sexual orientation. Asked at the American Embassy in Grosvenor Square if he was a practicing homosexual, Crisp responded, "I didn't practice. I was already perfect." Crisp, who termed computers "demon machines," found absurd any idea that a god would be susceptible to prayer, and he does not believe in a hereafter, telling *Advocate* columnist Lance Loud (10 August 1993),

> I'm ready, I've made my will, my hands are folded, my eyelids lowered. And I don't expect to be back. Not like Shirley MacLaine, who never seems to express fatigue when it comes to reincarnation. Doesn't she *ever* think, "No! Not any more!' "

As for funerals, Crisp told *New York*'s Patricia Falvo, they "are rather horrid. All that standing in the pouring rain in the churchyard while people say how wonderful you were. They can just put me in a plastic bag and shovel me into a Dumpster. I don't care."

Crisp died just before opening his one-man show, "An Evening With Quentin Crisp," in London. His last great exit, he would have regretted, was not onstage. {E; GL; *The New York Times*, 22 November 1999; WAS, numerous discussions, 1995—1997}

Critias (c. 460—403 B.C.E.)

Critias, an Athenian political leader and writer, was an aristocrat who studied philosophy with Socrates. He wrote poems and tragedies but is best remembered as one of the Thirty Tyrants imposed on Athens by the Spartans. He became known for his rapacity and bloodthirstiness. When Thrasybulus led his forces against the Thirty, Critias was killed in battle.

As for his outlook, Critias declared, "It was man who first made men believe in gods." {"The Archive," *Journal of the Leslie-Lohman Gay Art Foundation, Spring 1998;* CE; TYD}

CRITICISM

> • Before you criticize a man, walk a mile in his shoes. That way, when you do, you'll be a mile away and have his shoes.
>
> —Anonymous

Those in the majority usually hold that criticism involves adverse judgments. Those in the minority think of criticism as the art of evaluating, of making discriminating judgments about creative works, of investigating origins of documents (including the so-called sacred bibles).

Crittenden, Henry William (1881—1970?)

Crittenden was an Australian rationalist, maverick, agitator, and noted public lecturer in the early days of Australia's rationalist movement. He was associated with the formation of the Rationalist Association of South Australia in 1919. Crittenden wrote *Behind the Black Curtain,* which he sub-titled "a book of unholy revelations." {SWW}

CROATIAN FREETHINKERS: See entry for Radovan Vukadinovic, who signed Humanist Manifesto 2000.

Croce, Benedetto (1866—1952)

Croce's philosophic outlook, related to idealism, was that reality consists of spirit that is monistic in manifestation. A staunch opponent of Fascism, he was a leader of Italy's Liberal Party. In 1934, the Vatican prohibited the reading of all of his works. His views on idealism have many negative critics among naturalistic and secular humanists, who find valuable his views on aesthetics. One philosopher and his chief English follower, Wildson Carr, said Croce's philosophy is neo-Hegelian but "the religious activity has no place in it. To him religion is mythology." {CE; HNS2; ILP; JM; RAT}

Croffut, William Augustus (1835—1915)

Croffut wrote *The Vanderbilts and the Story of Their Fortune* (c. 1886), *Religion in Our Colonies* (c. 1898) and *Was Jesus Christ a Myth?* (c. 1900). {GS}

Croly, David (1829—1889)

Croly, an American positivist, was a journalist on the *New York Herald* and editor of the *New York World* until 1872. He wrote a *Primer of Positivism* (1876). {BDF; RAT}

Cromie, Peter (20th Century)

Cromie was on the board of directors of the American Humanist Association in the 1950s.

Crommelin, Peter (20th Century)

A freethinker, Crommelin wrote in England for *The Freethinker.*

Crompton, Arnold (20th Century)

Crompton is author of *Unitarianism on the Pacific Coast: The First Sixty Years* (1957) and *Memoirs of a Freethinker* (1964). {GS}

Crompton, Henry (1836—1904)

A lawyer, Crompton was an active positivist after 1859, succeeding Congreve in London in 1899. His chief work is *Letters on Social and Political Subjects* (1870). {RAT}

Cromwell, Arthur G. (20th Century)

Cromwell wrote *Why I Do Not Believe in God* (1956). {GS}

Cromwell, David (20th Century)

Cromwell works in remote sensing oceanography. For *New Humanist* (March 1998), he has written about physicists' concerns with Theories of Everything (TOEs), the search for a theory which binds together our understanding of all the forces in the universe. Einstein, he noted, searched for a TOE for almost three decades, then commented, "We have to admire in humility the beautiful harmony of the structure of this world as far as we can grasp it. That is all."

Cronenberg, David (1943—)

The Canadian-born Cronenberg has been praised for directing such films as "Stereo" (1969); "Crimes of the Future" (1970; "They Came From Within" (1976): "Rabid" (1977); "The Brood" (1979); "Fast Company" (1979); "Scanners" (1981); "Videodrome" (1983), "The Dead Zone" (1983); "The Fly" (1986); and "Dead Ringers" (1988). In *Esquire* (February 1992), he described himself as not just an atheist but a total nonbeliever."

"My parents were both atheists," he told an interviewer in *Film Threat* (February 1997), "so it was never a big issue, and if I wanted to become an Orthodox Jew, it was never, 'You must not do that.' And I certainly went through all those things as a kid wondering about the existence of God or not, but at a very early age, I decided we made it up because we were afraid and it was one way to make things palatable." {CA; E}

Cronin, Helena (20th Century)

Cronin, a senior research associate in the Zoology Department at Oxford University, wrote *The Ant and the Peacock*. In Birmingham, England, at the centenary conference of the Rationalist Press Association in 1999, she spoke on "Natural Born Co-operators: Darwinism for Policy-makers."

CRONUS: See entry for God.

Crook, Margaret Brackenbury (1886—1972)

The first female minister to have sole charge of a large church in England, Crook wrote *Women and Religion* (1964), which is said to be probably the first book of feminist theology and biblical criticism published in the latter half of the 20th century.

Crosbie-Goold, Nathaniel (1921—)

"Nat" Crosbie-Goold is an Australian humanist, rationalist, and dentist. He has been active with the Rationalist Society and was honorary secretary of the Rationalist Association of Australia Ltd. {SWW}

Crosby, F. W. (19th Century)

A freethinker, Crosby wrote *Real and Ideal Christianity* (c. 1898). {GS}

CROSS: The Christian cross is a sex symbol, according to B. Z. Goldberg. See the entry for Sex Symbols.

Cross, Carolyn (20th Century)

Cross in 1972 was on the advisory board of the Humanist society of Greater New York.

Cross, David (20th Century)

A comedian, Cross on the televised "Politically Incorrect" said, "I was born Jewish, but I am an atheist. I don't believe in God." In January 1999 he told viewers on his website, "Again, thanks for watching and although there is no God, have an enjoyable holiday gift time. Yours in Christ, David." {CA}

Cross, Mary Ann: See entry for George Eliot.

Cross, William (19th Century)

Cross, a freethinker, wrote *Random Thoughts on Religion and the Bible*. He also wrote *The Devil, A Myth* (1872). {GS}

CROSS-DRESSING, TRANSVESTISM

To cross-dress is to wear clothing characteristic of the opposite sex. Cross-dressing is found even in preliterate and peasant groups in mainland Asia and Africa, according to *The Encyclopedia of Religion* (1995).

Agathon (c. 450—400 B.C.E.), the tragic poet, greeted literary friends dressed like a woman in long robe, saffron-colored tunic and cape, with a bust-bodice, a hair net, and tight-fitting buskins. Boy prostitutes who did the same in public, however, were regarded as shameful and an Athenian proverb said of them that it was "easier to hide five elephants in one's armpit" than to hide one of these boys.

Jonathan Ned Katz, in *Gay American History* (1976) details female as well as male cross-dressing. The practice was common among American Indians, who allowed a person, usually a male, to assume the sexual identity and was granted the social status of the opposite sex. "Manlike women" often had the reputation of having supernatural powers, and they made prophecies. Further, they were not treated negatively but, on the contrary and both in the Americas and in Asia, were valued for their being so different.

When a priest puts on his robes for the Sacrifice, he is likely unaware that he is partaking in institutionalized cross-dressing. "The flowing gown," wrote B. Z. Goldberg in *The Sacred Fire* (1958), "the stole he wears around his neck, and the vestment, are all suggestive of similar symbolism in ancient pagan faiths, in which the priests attired themselves appropriately for the worship of their goddesses. The vestment, itself a symbol, bears upon it still others; there is the cross both in back and in front, and from beneath the crosses extend the golden rays of the sun in themselves suggestive of the great life-giving force in nature," the cross itself a sexual symbol.

In General Custer's Seventh Cavalry, a corporal by the name of Nash was accompanied by his wife, who was a laundress. Upon Mrs. Nash's death in 1878, when garrison ladies went to lay her out, they found that "Mrs." Nash was actually a man, Don Rickey Jr. The finding so scandalized the corporal that he committed suicide with his revolver. Katz details many other instances of transvestism, dressing in the manner usually associated with the opposite sex, including examples in Polynesia.

The theatre and the cinema provide many examples of cross-dressing: Holly Woodlawn (a Puerto Rican man performing as a woman); Rollerarena (the Greenwich Villager on rollerskates who dresses in flowing chiffon gown with gaudy sunglasses and a magic wand in one white-gloved hand); Pope Paul II (nicknamed "Maria Pietissima" by his predecessor, Pius I); Charles Pierce (well-known showbusiness "drag queen"); Gertrude Stein (who often was mistaken as to her gender); St. Joan of Arc (who preferred men's clothing); Charles Ludlam (actor / director / playwright / star of the Ridiculous Theatre); Ethyl Eichelberge (prominent "drag queen"); Divine (rotund man in several movies, in one of which he attacks and gulps down all the food in a refrigerator); Dottie of Bloolips (prominent "drag queen"); Marlene Dietrich (an eminently beautiful male whether in sailor's uniform or tuxedo); John Lithgow (who was the football player turned transsexual in "The World According to Garp"); Billy Tipton (the American jazz pianist and saxophonist, married and father of three adopted children, who was found in 1989 to be a woman); Barbra Streisand (who dressed as a yeshiva boy in "Yentl"); Julie Andrews (who dressed as a man in "Victor/Victoria" and was photographed with New York City Mayor Rudy Giuliani, dressed as a woman, in 1997); Julia Roberts (with fake mustache and a baseball cap in "Sleeping With the Enemy"); Robin Williams (who as Mrs. Doubtfire became a cinematically classic figure); and Jack Lemmon, Milton Berle, and any number of other Hollywood stars. Examples of female cross-dressing are found in Julie Wheelwright's *Amazons and Military Maids*, and include enlistees on both the Union and Confederate sides during the American Civil War. In a British republican magazine, *Republic*, editor Edgar Wilson has described cross-dressing in the House of Lords. Even in the mid-1990s when the Bishop of Chester attempted to enter the Upper House in civilian clothes, he was turned away and told to put on his skirt. One of the arguments for keeping the monarchy and the House of Lords, some argue, is that the royalty enjoy dressing differently from the common people.

New York's Francis Cardinal Spellman looked so "spiffy" in his clerical dress that many gays called him "Franny." "The closest I can get by with that," gays have been known to add, "is during Halloween, when all us girls can come out without fear of being bashed by the religious zealots!" And on one occasion as Cardinal Spellman turned to the side during a St. Patrick's Cathedral mass, a voice with an African timbre peeled out, "Girl, twirl that skirt!" (See entry for Rosa Bonheur.)

Crossman, Richard (1907-1974): See entry for George Orwell.

Crothers, Samuel McChord (1857—1927)

Starting as a Presbyterian, Crothers achieved national prominence as a lecturer and essayist. A Unitarian minister, he is best known as author of *Gentle Reader* (1903), in which he expressed the view that reading simply for pleasure, rather than for the express purpose of becoming intelligent, is most comforting. {U&U}

Crousse, David Goodman (19th Century)

Crousse was a French pantheistic philosophy and author of *Principles, or First Philosophy* (1829) and *Thoughts* (1845). {BDF}

Crowded House (20th Century)

Crowded House, a group of American recording artists, has gone on record as being non-theistic. {E}

Crowe, Deloris (20th Century)

A retired English and social studies teacher, Crowe wrote "An Atheist, Oh Dear!" for *Freethought Today* (August 1998).

Crowe, W. S. (19th Century?)

Crowe wrote *The Solemn and the Serious—A Difference.* {GS}

Crowl, F. M. (20th Century)

Crowl was author of *Thoughts and Inspirations* (1906). {GS}

Croy, Homer (20th Century)

Croy in 1927 wrote about Charles Smith in *World's Work.* {GS}

Crozier, John Beattie (Born 1849)

Crozier was an English writer of Scottish border parentage. He favored a Constitution of the World and wrote *The Religion of the Future* (1880) and *Civilisation and Progress* (1885). {BDF; RAT}

CRUCIFICTION

• Some scientists question whether the nailing of an individual's hands to a cross would allow the weight of the body to be held. Despite the omnipresent pictures of Jesus's being so nailed by the Romans, a question arises as to whether the body's weight would be too much to be held in place, that the Romans might have used a different approach than the one sculptors and artists have depicted so often.

• The Easter parish magazine for Highclere, Caux Easton and Ashmansworth, Berkshire, England, contained the following declaration by the Rev. Timothy F. Horsington: "I believe in the reality of our Lord's Crucifiction, the Empty Tomb, and His Risen Presence with us each day as passionately as I did when I offered for the Ministry 32 years ago."

{*The Freethinker*, May 1994}

CRUCIFIX

Bavarians for years have required that a crucifix be hung in each of the state's 40,000 classrooms. When in 1995 the Constitutional Court ruled 5-3 that the practice be banned. "How would a practicing Christian in a class with something like 80 percent Muslims feel if the majority suddenly decided to hang a verse from the Koran on the wall?" Judge Johann Friedrich Henschel asked. Disagreeing, Friedrich Cardinal Wetter of Munich said parents alone should have the power to decide. The decision was on a case brought by Ernst Seler, a Bavarian artist, composer, and follower of the philosopher Rudolf Steiner, who did not want to send his three children to schools where the "image of a bleeding, half-naked male corpse" was displayed. In 1996, a Rhode Island exorcist who pushed a crucifix into his mother's mouth to rid her of evil spirits was charged with "assault with a dangerous weapon."

CRUCIFIXION

Crucifixion, a mode of execution adopted by Rome from Carthage, was a torture that racked every part of the body and protracted the pain over many hours or days. Saint Augustine had the following interpretation of the crucifixion of Jesus:

> Like a bridegroom Christ went forth from his chamber, he went out with a presage of the nuptials. . . . He came to the marriage bed of the cross, and there, in mounting it, consummated his marriage, . . . He lovingly gave himself up to the torment in place of his bride, and he joined himself to the woman for ever.

Wrote Ackerman, "At its most soulful and mystical, religious love sounds much like erotic love." (See " 'Sblood" in entry for Hamlet and "gadzooks" in entry for God- ; alsosee entry for Kersey Graves.) {ACK}

Crucius, Thomas Theodor (17th Century)

Crucius wrote *The Origine of Atheism in the Popish and Protestant Churches* (1684).

Crumb, George (1929—)

Crumb, a composer who teaches at the University of Pennsylvania, responded (4 July 1992) to the present author as follows concerning his seven categories of humanism:

> I feel that humanism pure and simple (your first category) most nearly describes my own mode of thinking.

CRUSADES

Between the 11th and 13th centuries, European Christians undertook "holy wars" with papal sanction for the purpose of recovering the "Holy Land" from the Muslims. Pope Urban II at the Council of Clermont (1095) encouraged these religious battles, and the Crusaders were called such because they were given crosses to carry. The bloodshed which followed was not entirely for the glory of insuring that one religion would become dominant over another religion, however. Nobles soon found that land and loot were available, and Italian cities found new trade possibilities with the Near East.

• The First Crusade (1095—1099) resulted in the conquest of Jerusalem, which later fell.
• The Second Crusade (1147—1149) was a dismal failure.
• The Third Crusade (1189—1192), led by Holy Roman Emperor Frederick I, Philip II of France, and Richard I of England, failed to recapture Jerusalem.
• The Fourth Crusade (1202—1204) resulted in a side trip to Constantinople, which was seized.
• The Children's Crusade (1212) may have removed unruly children from the streets (homeless children, often because their parents had been killed in other crusades), but it also ended with thousands of them being sold as slaves or pathetically dying of disease and hunger.
• The Fifth Crusade (1217—1221) failed in its attempt to conquer Egypt.
• The Sixth Crusade (1228—1229) was short-lived when a truce was arranged with the Muslims by Holy Roman Emperor Frederick II.
• Three other crusades in the 13th century were unsuccessful, and in 1291 Akko (Acre), the last Christian stronghold, fell.

Steven Runciman, a British scholar and diplomat, in *A History of the Crusades*, wrote, "Unlike Christianity, which preached a peace it never achieved, Islam unashamedly came with a sword." Bernard Lewis, in *The Middle East: A Brief History of the Last 2,000 Years* (1996), differs from the prevailing academic view in his assessment of the Crusades. Although Europeans have made much of the crusades, these holy wars were in his estimation entirely trivial. (See entry for Herbert J. Muller.) {CE}

Cruse, Howard (1944-)

Cruse, creator of the syndicated cartoon "Wendel," has written about his outlook:

> Exiting from Christianity came at about age fourteen for me. The final crisis was prompted by reading Mark Twain's *The Mysterious Stranger*. That was my first full-scale realization that art can change lives. I don't subscribe to the belief systems of any organized religion I've encountered; don't believe there are any Higher Powers who worry about whether I masturbate or not; definitely don't believe in the concept of cosmically-ordained sin or post-life punishment; and will be quite surprised if my individual consciousness survives death, though I allow myself fantasies of playing around in the "tunnel of light" for a few minutes before disbanding my psychic molecules to go where they will.
>
> I think they call people like me agnostics, since I make no pretenses to certainty about any of this. But agnostic is such a dry, unpoetic term. The very idea of agnostic cartoons sounds like a real yawner!
>
> {WAS, 19 April 1999}

CRYING

• Q. What do you do when a woman cries?
A. I usually cry with her.

—Frank Sinatra, Singer, a nominal Catholic

• I cried all the way to the bank.

—Wlaziu Liberace, singer,
after hearing some hostile criticism of his work

CSER: See entry for the Committee for the Scientific Examination of Religion.

Cserski, Johannes (Died 1894)

Cserski began his career as a Catholic priest in Prussia. In 1844 he and some friends left the church and established Free Religious communities. The following year, a mob of Christian peasants, directed by fanatical priests, made an attack upon him, and the hussars had to be called in to subdue the demonstration and escort Cserski into Posen. He then traveled from city to city, lecturing and speaking. For many years he lived in poverty at Schneidemuhl, a wreck of his former self. According to Putnam, Cserski was a freethinker for over fifty years. {PUT}

CSH

The Council for Secular Humanism, no longer called CODESH, is at 3965 Rensch Road, Amherst, NY 14226. In 1999 Robert Price became the Executive Director. On the Web: <www.secularhumanism.org>.

CSHAFT

CSHAFT is an abbreviation of the Coalition for Secular Humanism, Atheism, and Freethought. The group in 1994 had its conference in Toronto, Ontario, Canada.

CSICOP

CSICOP is an abbreviation for the Committee for the Scientific Investigation of Claims of the Paranormal. The group of skeptics publishes a quarterly journal, *Skeptical Inquirer* (Box 703, Buffalo, NY 14226).

Csikszentmihalyi, Mihaly (20th Century)

A research psychologist, Csikszentmihalyi has written about finding meaning in daily existence. His *Flow: The Psychology of Everyday Experience* (1991) and *Finding Flow: The Psychology of Engagement with Everyday Life* (1997) explain that by flow he refers to how people find happiness"

> People who seem to feel most positive about their lives possess a set of common characteristics," he has said, "such as knowing clearly what they have to do, getting feedback on what they are doing, and being able to match their abilities with the opportunities for action so that skills and challenges are in balance. When those characteristics are present, people begin to concentrate very highly. As a result they forget the problems of everyday life, and they seem to step into a kind of alternative reality. That consolidation of characteristics is what I call the "flow experience."

The author (whose name is pronounced *chick-sent-me-high-ee,* a Hungarian name that means "of St. Michael of Csik," a Transylvanian province) is professor of education and psychology at the University of Chicago. {Tim Madigan, "An Interview with Mihaly Csikszentmihalyi," *Free Inquiry*, Summer 1998}

Csongvay, Attila (1941—1993)

Csongvay was born in a small village near Szentgerice, Romania, where his father had served for over thirty years as a Unitarian minister. At a time when many Unitarian ministers were in Romanian prisons, he chose to study theology despite much harassment his family endured during the long Ceausecu regime. In 1991 when he preached at the Fairfax Unitarian Church in Oakton, Virginia, he arranged for a partner-church relationship between their congregation and his church. (*World*, May/June 1994)

CUBAN FREETHINKERS, HUMANISTS: See entries for Félix Varela and José Luz y Caballero.

Cuffeler, Abraham Johann (17th Century)

A Dutch philosopher and doctor of law, Cuffeler was one of the first partisans of Spinoza. He wrote *Specimen Artis Ratiocinandi* (1684), a work on logic which did not name him as author but contained his portrait. {BDF}

Culhane, Claire (1919—1996)

Culhane was an advocate of prisoners' rights in Canada. She opposed the Vietnam War and Canada's role in it, fasting on Parliament Hill. Just prior to her death in 1996, she accepted being the Humanist Association of Canada's 1996 Humanist of the Year. {*Humanist in Canada*, Summer 1996}

Cullen, Countee (1903—1946)

Cullen, the African American poet of the Harlem Renaissance, wrote an epic poem about lynching, "The Black Christ" (1929). The 900-line piece exemplified Cullen's brilliant poetic layering of racial and gay themes. Alden Reimonenq, of St. Mary's College of California, has noted that Jim, its main character, can be viewed "not only as the persecuted black who is falsely accused of rape, but also as the victim of heterosexism." Jim is associated with Lycidas, Patroclus, and Jonathan, "all characters who have had long-standing associations with gay readings of their respective texts," leading Reimonenq to declare that Cullen's poetry "in the context of the gay closet in which it was written is the cornerstone on which to rebuild Cullen's reputation as a gay poet laureate and as the inaugurator of a black gay male poetic tradition."

Although married early in life to W. E. B. DuBois's daughter Yolande and to Ida Roberson only six years before his death, Cullen had "a steady string of male lovers in the United States and France." {GL}

CULT

- A cult is a religion with no political power.

—Thomas Wolfe

Freethinkers generally consider all organized religions to be exclusive groups of persons sharing an esoteric interest, and the sects which they have generated are cults dedicated to the pursuit of doctrines to which they are devoted and which they preach.

A cult might inculcate the view that there is a supernatural, that Something That Arose From Nothing is a Super God, that there is life after death, that one can communicate with the supernatural through prayer, that one can live after death, et cetera.

CULTURE SECULAR SOCIETY

The Culture Secular Society is at Rada Krajowa, UL. Koszykowa 24, 00-553 Warsaw, Poland. It is an associate member of the International Humanist and Ethical Union.

CULTURES: See entry for Civilization.

Cummins, Maria (1826-1866)

Cummins was a Unitarian and an author whose works were not widely known.

Cummins, Robert (1897—1982)

Acting as the general superintendent of the Universalist Church of America (1938—1953), Cummins failed to gain admission of his church into the Federal Council of Churches. That Council's view was that Universalists were "insufficiently Christian." {U&U}

Cummings, Edward Estlin (1894—1962)

An American poet with unorthodox punctuation, one influenced by Ezra Pound and Gertrude Stein, Cummings once wrote, "Not for philosophy does this rose give a damn." He is the author of *The Enormous Room* (1922), an autobiographical narrative describing his work with the American ambulance corps in France during World War I and his imprisonment by the French for about six months in a concentration camp. Despite the filthy surroundings and inhumane treatment by officials and jailers, Cummings maintained his sense of humor, exalting a person's human values in the face of what he considered to be sheer ignorance. At one time, Cummings was the associate minister of the South Congregational Church (Unitarian) in Boston.

James D. Hart has described Cummings's work as showing "his transcendental faith in a world where the self-reliant, joyful, loving individual is beautifully alive but in which mass man, or the man who lives by mind alone, without heart and soul, is dead. The true individual Cummings praised, often reverently and with freshness of spirit and idiom, but the 'unman' was satirized as Cummings presented witty, bitter parodies of and attacks on the patriotic or cultural platitudes and shibboleths of the 'unworld.' This poetry was marked by experimentalism in word coining, the shifting of grammar, the blending of established stanzaic forms and free verse, flamboyant punning, typographic distortion, unusual punctuation, and idiosyncratic division of words, all of which became integral to the ideas and rhythms of his relatively brief lyrics."

After being asked several times by the present author as to his philosophic outlook, he wrote:

> since you insist:I rather imagine that
> "the approach to philosophy" of any
> artist worth his salt is neither "naturalistic"
> nor "supernaturalistic"; but aesthetic.

Years after the poet Marianne Moore gave The Dial Award to Cummings, she thanked him for a book: "Blasphemous, inexorable, disrespectful, sinful author though you are—you received a cordial welcome at my door today." (Capital letters, however, *did* apply when Cummings wrote his name. When the composer David Diamond caught one editor who typed the name "e. e. cummings," Diamond expostulated, "E. E. Cummings would come from Patchin Place with a whip had he known you lowercased his name! His daughter is furious if anyone does today. All his books, as was his signature, are in capital letters. Only his poetry does the Mallarmer (sic) letters, small type (Mr Jacobs)." *Columbia Encyclopedia* is one such sourcebook which mistakenly has not capitalized his name.] (See entry for Robert Frost.) {CE; *The Selected Letters of Marianne Moore*, 1957; U; UU; WAS, 1960}

Cummings, F. D. (19th Century)

Cummings, a freethinker, wrote *Religion and the Bible* (1894). {GS}

Cummings, G. Duncan (20th Century)

A freethinker, Cummings wrote *When You Go To Heaven* (1921). {GS}

Cumont, Franz Valery Marie (1868—1947)

Cumont was a Belgian archaeologist who studied Mithraism, a subject which had hitherto been much neglected. He wrote *Mysteries of Mithra* (1903), which described Christianity's greatest rival. Cumont's rationalism—as professor at the University of Ghent he had to be discreet—is better seen in his *Afterlife in Roman Paganism* (1922). His works on ancient Rome did much to correct libels of the pagans. {RAT; RE}

Cunard, Nancy (1896-1965): See entry for George Orwell.

Cunningham, Norma (20th Century)

Cunningham is vice-president Central of the Executive Council of the Freedom For Religion Foundation.

Cunningham, William (20th Century)

Cunningham, a freethinker, wrote *What Atheism Means to Me* (1926). {GS}

CUNT

According to Inga Muscio's *Cunt: A Declaration of Independence* (1999), cunt "was once a term of respect that evolved from Chinese, Egyptian, Indian, Irish, and Latin titles reserved for priestesses and derived from the names of goddesses."

Ackerman holds that the Hindu goddess Kali, personifying the life-giving vulva, or cunt, energy of the world, was called *Cunti* or *Kunda. Kunta* was the Old Norse word for the female genitals, and prehistoric German was *kunton.* However, she argues, there is a hidden prejudice about the baseness of women when we use *cock* and *cunt.* "A man's pleasure," she reasons, "is his penis, and a woman's pleasure organ is her clitoris, not her vagina. Even if we're talking about procreation, it's not accurate: a man's penis delivers sperm and can impregnate, and a woman's womb contains eggs, which can become fertile. Equating the man's penis with the woman's vagina says, in effect, that the natural order of things is for a man to have pleasure during sex, and for a woman to have a sleeve for man's pleasure. In classical Latin *vagina* means 'sheath for a sword.' Aeneas, for example, put his sword into his *vagina.* It perpetuates the notion that women aren't supposed to enjoy sex, that they're bucking the natural and social order if they do." The British media consistently has banned the word *cunt*, an illustration as to the perpetuation of the notion. {ACK}

Cuper, Frans (17th Century)

Cuper was a Dutch author who, under the pretense of refuting Spinoza, sustained his arguments by feeble opposition. The work, *Arcana Atheismi Revelato* (1676), was denounced as written in bad faith. Cuper, however, maintained that the existence of God could not be proved by the light of reason. {BDF}

CUPID

• Cupid, n. The so-called god of love. This bastard creation of a barbarous fancy was no doubt inflicted upon mythology for the sins of its deities. Of all unbeautiful and inappropriate conceptions this is the most reasonless and offensive. The notion of symbolizing sexual love by a semisexless babe, and comparing the pains of passion to the wounds of an arrow—of introducing this pudgy homunculus into art grossly to materialize the subtle spirit and suggestion of the work—this is eminently worthy of the age that, giving it birth, laid it on the doorstep of posterity.

—Ambrose Bierce
The Devil's Dictionary

CURAÇAO HUMANISTS

In Curaçao, the Netherlands Antilles, the humanist group is known as Association "Humanist Conscience," Vesuviusstraat 2, Willemstad, Curaçao. {FD}

Curie, Marie (Manya) [Sklodowska] (1867—1934)

A codiscoverer of radium, Marie Curie was the daughter of a Polish freethinker but was reared by a Catholic mother. She abandoned the Church before she was twenty, and her marriage with Pierre Curie was a purely civil ceremony because, she says in her memoir of him, "Pierre belonged to no religion and I did not practice any." The two were co-winners in 1903 of the Nobel Prize in Physics, and when in 1911 she won the Nobel Prize in Chemistry she became the first person to have won two such prizes. Some in the Swedish Academy allegedly tried to persuade her not to accept the second Nobel Prize that they had just awarded her, but she accepted it just the same.

Einstein described her thusly:

> Madame Curie is very intelligent, but has the soul of a herring [*Häringseele* in the German original], meaning that she is lacking in all feelings of joy and sorrow. Almost the only way in which she expresses her feeling is to rail at things she doesn't like. And she has a daughter [Irène] who is even worse—like a Grenadier [an infantryman]. The daughter is also very gifted.

But, as pointed out in Susan Quinn's *Marie Curie: A Life*, what Einstein did not know was that a few years before Einstein met her, Mme. Curie, then a widow, had a love affair with Paul Langevin, a French physicist who was married and had four children. The tabloid press printed the story, and at least five duels were provoked by the scandal, one of which involved Langevin himself.

When she died on the Fourth of July, 1934, Einstein remarked that she was, "of all celebrated beings, the only one whom fame has not corrupted."

Her funeral, arranged by her two daughters, Irène and Eve, was purely secular. Eve wrote a biography of her mother, relating that all members of the gifted family were freethinkers. Their two daughters were Irène (Mme. Joliot) and Eve. *Mme. Curie* (1937), by her younger daughter, repeated that all the members of the family were rationalists. The elder daughter was awarded the Nobel Prize for Physics jointly with Fréderic Joliot-Curie, her husband, in 1935.

In 1995, Marie Curie and her husband Pierre were enshrined in France's Pantheon, the 70th and 71st people who are buried there. Sophie Bertholet is also buried there alongside her husband, the renowned chemist Marcellin Bertholet, but Marie Curie, according to President Mitterand, is "the first lady in our history honored for her own merits." {CE; CL; JM; RE; TRI}

Curie, Pierre (1859—1906)

A codiscoverer of radium, Pierre Curie was an atheist. The feminist agitation following his death led to such glorification of his wife that the fact that he had had an equal share in the research was generally pushed out of sight. He had been, however, a professor at Paris University. He remained a skeptic all his life and had a civil funeral. {CE; CL; RE; TRI}

Curran, Pete (19th Century)

Curran gave an 1893 lecture in London's Hall of Science on "The Relation of Freethought to Socialism." In the late 1880s and 1890s, socialist ideas infiltrated many secularist societies in England. {RSR}

Currie, Justin (20th Century)

Currie is lead singer, songwriter, and bass player for the Scottish pop-rock band Del Amitri. In *Village View* (9-15 October 1992), Currie explained that he is "fiercely atheist," that "I wasn't raised in a religious family, so I've never really had to reject anything. There is, however, a lot to be said for Christian morality. There are some strong altruistic ideals that run through Christianity; but believing in something you can't see, touch, feel, or hear in any way . . . the whole idea of blind faith, following orders—that's where fascism comes from." {CA}

Currier, Nathaniel (1813—1888)

Currier, a lithographer of prints typically picturing race horses, trains, and steamships, was a member of the Unitarian Church of All Souls in New York City. {U; UU}

Curros, Enriquez (19th Century)

Curros, a Spanish poet, was prosecuted by the Bishop of Santiago, of Galicia, for his collection of poems entitled *Airs of My Country*. However, Curros was acquitted by a jury. {BDF}

Curry, Glenn (1951-)

Curry, who is president of Freethought Society of Wisconsin, has been involved in various church-state actions, including fighting local public institutions (such as city libraries that close on religious holidays), religion-biased intrusions in public schools (such as allowing Christian but not pagan sayings), and proselytizing of students by teachers. A single father of four, Curry runs T.E.A.M. Work, his technology-based company that specializes in computer networking and internet consulting. E-mail: <glenn@teamworkweb.com>. {WASM, 24 February 1999}

Curry, John (1950—1994)

Curry was an Olympic and World Champion ice skater, winner of a gold medal in 1976. At his request and upon his death from an AIDS-related illness, Curry was cremated and given a non-religious, humanist funeral at which David Turner of the British Humanist Association officiated. {*The Freethinker*, May 1994}

Curry, Rob (20th Century)

Curry is secretary of Humanist Association: St. Petersburg, Florida. E-mail: <rob.curry@usa.net>.

Curtin, John Joseph (1885—1945)

Curtin was a rationalist and a prime minister in Australia. Although he did not publicly proclaim his unbelief, he was influenced and inspired by rationalists Tom Mann and Frank Anstey. Active in the anti-conscription campaign, Curtin was convicted and fined for remarks about revolution. The Scullin Ministry did not offer a portfolio to Curtin, allegedly because Scullin was a devout Catholic and disliked Curtin's having left the faith. When Scullin retired in 1935, Curtin was then elected leader of the Labor Party. Shortly before he died, he was visited by Scullin who said, "I know you don't believe much in God, Jack, but don't you think it's time you made peace with your Maker?" Replied Curtin, "I've seen it through like this so far, and I am not going to change now." {SWW}

Curtis, S. E. (Died 1847)

An English freethinker, Curtis wrote *Theology Displayed* (1842) and is credited with *The Protestant's Progress to Infidelity*. {BDF}

Curtis, Thomas (19th Century)

A San Francisco poet, Curtis was materialistic and scientific but saw the real beauty of life does not need to be expressed in terms of "God" or of "immortality." Life is glorious as it actually is, he held. Curtis also felt no need to believe in angels or an afterlife, and he spent his life in Philadelphia and San Francisco speaking out as a reformer. {PUT}

Cusack, Nora (20th Century)

Cusack, a volunteer Secretary of the Freedom From Religion Foundation, has said she comes from a family of Unitarian freethinkers and that she values "the importance of First Amendment issues, including the separation of church and state." {*Freethought Today*, January-February 1999}

Cusanus, Nicholas (15th Century)

Cusanus, a profound thinker, was a non-theist, according to William Edelen, a contributor to *Truthseeker* (#1, 1995).

Cushing, Max Pearson (Born 1896)

Cushing wrote *A Study of Eighteenth-Century Radicalism in France* and *Baron D'Holbach* (1914). {GS}

Cushman, Charlotte (Saunders) (1816—1876)

Cushman was a Boston-born actress who started as an opera singer, then became famous for her ability to play both male and female parts in legitimate drama. Known for her Shakespearean roles, Cushman also gained a reputation for playing the part of Meg Merrilies in an operatic dramatization of *Guy Mannering*. As a Unitarian youngster, Charlotte had sung in the choir at the Unitarian church which the family attended, one in which Ralph Waldo Emerson was minister. As an actress, she performed throughout the United States and in England. For a time, she lived in England as well as in Italy. {CE; EG; U}

Cutner, Herbert (Born 1881)

Cutner is author of *A Short History of Sex Worship* (1940), *Jesus: God, Man, or Myth* (1950), and *G. W. Foote: His Life and Times* (1955). In *Freethinker* (1952), he wrote, "I cannot say that I am particularly enamoured of this word *Humanism* which now appears to be co-opted by anybody and everybody." {FUK}

Cuypers, K. (20th Century)

Cuypers, a Belgian, was on the first Board of Directors in 1952 of the International Humanist and Ethical Union (1952). At the 1962 Congress of the IHEU, held in Oslo (1962), at the Congress held in Paris (1966), at the Second European Conference (1968) held in Hannover, at the Sixth World Congress held in Amsterdam (1974), and at the Seventh World Congress held in London (1978), he addressed the group.

CYBERNETICS AND CYBERSPACE

Cybernetics, a theoretical study made popular in the 1940s by Harvard's Norbert Wiener, involves the comparative study of control and communcation in humans and machines. With the advent of computers, modems, the World Wide Web, and online facilities, cyberspace became a distinct revolutionary aspect of life by the end of the 20th century.

"Humanism and the Infomedia Revolution" by Paul Kurtz appeared in *Free Inquiry* (Winter 1996-1997) as well as *New Humanist* (December 1996). Individuals anywhere in the world were now able to use the search facilities to find, for example, information about atheism, agnosticism, freethought, secular humanism, and philosophy in general. Sitting in his underwear in Manhattan, a netizen could consult the cataloguing system of university libraries around the world in order to find bibliographical details. Individuals anywhere else in the world could, by finding the Manhattan scholar's home page, see photographs of the individual as well as could e-mail electronic letters to the person. Universities and industries took advantage of the new revolutionary facility, arranging for conferences as to how technology was changing the rest of culture.

In the present work, cyberspatial addresses are shown within the symbols < and >:

Council for Secular Humanism
<http://www.secularhumanism.org>
International Humanist and Ethical Union
<http://www.secularhumanism/org/iheu/>
Association of Iberoamerican Ethical Humanists
<http://idt.net/~wasm/asibehu >

CYNICISM

• Cynicism is an unpleasant way of saying the truth.

— **Lillian Hellman**

• The power of accurate observation is commonly called cynicism by those who have not got it.

—**George Bernard Shaw**

• Cynic, n. A blackguard whose faulty vision sees things as they are, not as they ought to be. Hence the custom among the Scythians of plucking out a cynic's eyes to improve his vision.

Ambrose Bierce
The Devil's Dictionary

• A cynic is not merely one who reads bitter lessons from the past. He is one who is prematurely disappointed in the future.

—Sidney Harris

• A cynic is a man who, when he smells flowers, looks around for a coffin.

—**H. L. Mencken**

CYNICISM, IN PRAISE OF

Tim Madigan's "In Praise of Cynicism" cites Antisthenes as the founder of Cynicism and Diogenes of Sinope as the most noted of the Cynics. "The basic message of the Cynics," wrote Madigan, "was that one should live according to nature. Civilization is artificial, and the more one gets caught up in its clutches, the less one is true to oneself." Happiness, the Cynics felt, *is* achievable during one's lifetime. Contemporary humanism, Madigan holds, would do well to familiarize itself with the Cynics:

> Today's world is still in the grips of Platonic idealism. A healthy dose of old-fashioned Cynicism wouldn't do it any harm. And for those who find this life an interesting one, and would prefer to postpone any possible visit to an afterlife for as long as they can, it is good to remember that Diogenes, for all his cheekiness, is reported to have lived to the ripe old age of ninety. Cynicism, it seems, can be good for one's health.

As for Diogenes, he lived in a wine barrel, tried to eat his meat raw, advocated public masturbation, and reportedly urinated on individuals he disliked. Another cynic, Hipparchia, "travelled around with her husband, had intercourse publicly, and went out to dinners," according to one of her biographers. Other cynics were Menippus, Varro, and Lucian. Origen, by pointing to the example of Diogenes's life, did so to defend the poverty of Jesus, and other church fathers cited him in their defenses of monasticism. St. Augustine found nothing good to say about him, but Erasmus valued Diogenes as highly as he did Socrates. {R. Brancht Branham and Marie-Odile Goulet-Cazé, *The Cynics*, 1997; *Free Inquiry*, Fall 1991}

Cyprianus, Thasius Caecilius [Saint Cyprian] (c. 200—258)

St. Cyprian was father of the Church, bishop of Carthage (c. 248), and was perhaps a disciple of Tertullian. In his middle age, he converted and became the most powerful bishop in Africa. He championed Pope St. Cornelius against the attacks of Novatian, helping avert a schism. During the persecution of Christians by the Roman emperor Decius, many apostatized. Cyprian called for strictness but ultimate forgiveness for the truly contrite, and he argued for the authority of the bishop as ground for the church's unity. When he fell into a dispute with Pope Stephen I on the validity of baptism, Cyprian believed persons so baptized had to be rebaptized upon entering the church.

The question was settled in favor of the Roman teaching, and Cyprian was martyred in the persecution of Valerian. As such, he was the first Christian priest to suffer death in Africa, having been condemned for inciting and ordering his fanatical followers to desecrate, vandalize, and destroy the pagan altars, temples, and statues. He was held responsible for cutting the noses, ears, arms, legs, and heads of many pagan statues that one currently sees in European museums. His biographer, Pontius, wrote that Cyprian was "the officer of Christ . . . who commanded the idols to be destroyed." Just before he was beheaded on 14 September 258, Cyprian said, "God be thanked." As pointed out by Bolder Landry (*Truth Seeker*, #1, 1995), the savaged statues we now can observe "are evidence of the hatred of the 'saintly man.' " {CE}

Cyrano de Bergerac, Savinien (1619—1655)

A French freethinker and novelist later romanticized by Edmond Rostand's 1897 verse drama, Cyrano according to countryman Lachèvre "was the initiator of the rationalistic philosophical spirit, having as its object the destruction of Christianity." His work attacked priest, pope, the supernatural, and immortality. His *Chanticler* was a biting satire of the clergy, for he depicted them as the birds and beasts of the night. When his tragedy "Agrippine" was performed, La Monnoye relates that from the pit came shouts of "Oh, the wretch! The Atheist! How he mocks at holy things!" Cyrano's posthumously published *Voyages to the Moon and Sun* (1656) had him, like Copernicus, looking at the earth as it moved around the sun, and he found ours to be only one of an infinite number of worlds in a universe that is infinite. Busson said Cyrano "took the most irreligious stand for his time." Observes Robertson, "At times Cyrano writes like a deist; but in so many other passages does he hold the language of a convinced materialist, and of a scoffer at that, that he can hardly be taken seriously on the former head. In short, he was one of the first of the hardy freethinkers who, under the tolerant rule of Richelieu and Mazarin, gave clear voice to the newer spirit. Under any other government, he would have been in danger of his life: as it was, he was menaced with prosecutions; his *Agrippine* (1654) was forbidden; the first edition of his *Pédant joué* (1654) was confiscated; during his last illness there was an attempt to seize his manuscripts; and down till the time of the Revolution the editions of his works were eagerly bought up and destroyed by zealots." Cyrano knew personally Campanella, Gassendi, Lamothe Le Vayer, Linière, and Rohault. {BDF; CE; JMR; JMRH; *Free Inquiry*, Fall 1991; RE}

CZECH-AMERICAN FREETHINKERS AND RATIONALISTS

For Czech American freethinkers, see *Freethought in the United States* (1978) by Gordon Stein. A Freethinker orphanage was once built in the Nusle district of Prague with the support of American freethinkers. The last chairman of the Union of Citizens Without Religion from 1946—1952 was the Czech-American Emanuel Voska, according to Josef Haubelt at Svotsovická 10/2834, 14100 Prague 4—Sporilov II, Czech Republic.

CZECH REPUBLIC FREETHINKERS, HUMANISTS

A major Czech humanistic group is the Prometheus Society (IHEU), Palkovicova 14, 821 08 in Bratislava.

Postmark Praha (Orego, Box 30, 251 01 Ricany, Czechia) is edited by Ken Biggs.

At a 1995 Berlin conference arranged by the International Humanist and Ethical Union, Josef Haubelt said the churches in the Czech Republic are influential beyond their numerical support. Although 56% of the population is non-denominational, Catholics run a crusade to increase their influence in culture, education, and health matters. According to Haubelt, the freethought movement before the First World War fought for the national interest. The first Czech Republic was partly freethinking. Churches claimed "retrieval" of buildings, but also freethinkers aimed at retaining their name and restoring their property. A major interest of the Czech humanists is campaigning for human rights.

CZECH REPUBLIC UNITARIANS

Dr. Norbert Capek was introduced to Unitarianism when he was in the United States and, following World War I, he returned to Prague and with the help of American friends started a free Unitarian church which grew in size and popularity. A writer, lecturer, composer of Unitarian hymns, Capek also is known as the one who created the Flower Communion in 1923, a service that is carried out in Unitarian churches around the world. The Unitarian "flaming chalice" is an emblem of Czech origin. In 1942, Capek died as a martyr in a Nazi concentration camp.

Capek was instrumental in 1922 of the founding of a Religious Liberal Fellowship and in 1930 of the founding of the Czech Unitarian Association. In the 1930s Prague had one of the largest Unitarian congregations in the world.

In 1997, a delegation of American Unitarian Universalists led by the Rev. John Buehrens met with the Czech Republic's deputy minister of culture to ask him to rescind his government's recognition of the Prague Unitarian congregation led by the Rev. Vladimir Strejcek. The Czech Republic officials, however, concluded that the dispute was internal and refused to repudiate Strejcek despite the appeals by the UUA and the International Council of Unitarians and Universalists (ICUU). The exiled Prague congregation president is Ivana Kocmanova.

Under the leadership of Miloslav Starosta Sternova (18,158 00, Praha 5, Czech Republic), an estimated six hundred members were members in 1996 of congregations in Prague, Brno, Pilsen, and Litvinov. Contact: Miloslav Starosta. The chairperson of the Czech Unitarian Association is Miroslav Starosta, Sternova 18,158 00 Praha 5, Czech Republic. {*World*, September-October 1997}

Czerski, Johannes (Born 1813)

Czerski was a German reformer. At first a Catholic priest, he broke with the church in 1844 and associated himself with Ronge, married, and was excommunicated. Czerski wrote several works against Roman Catholicism. {BDF}

Cziepl, Scott (20th Century)

Cziepl is on the board of directors of Society Against Religion.

Cziko, Gary (20th Century)

An educational psychologist, Cziko is author of *Without Miracles: Universal Selection Theory and the Second Darwinian Revolution* (1995). According to H. James Birx, an expert on Darwin and evolution, Cziko "rejects outright miracles, innatism, teleology, and natural theology," and his book is "a strictly Darwinian presentation that balances the current attack on evolution."

Czolbe, Heinrich (1819—1873)

A German materialist, Czolbe published *New Exposition of Sensationalism* (1855), in which everything is resolved into matter and motion. Lange says Czolbe's life "was marked by a deep and genuine morality." {BDF; RAT}

Daar, Judy (20th Century)

Daar, a paralegal, is active in the Secular Humanists of the East Bay in California. She co-authored with Dan Dugan an article, "Are Rudolf Steiner's Waldorf Schools 'Non-Sectarian'?" for *Free Inquiry* (Spring 1994).

Dabholkar, Narendra (20th Century)

Dr. Dabholkar of Satara, the eighteenth-century capital of the independent state of Maharashtr in India, founded an anti-superstition movement called Andha Shraddha Nirmoolan Samiti (ANIS), which is related to the international group of skeptics, CSICOP, the Committee for the Scientific Investigation of Claims of the Paranormal. (See entry for Govind N. Deodhekar.)

DADA

As a counterforce to philosophers' seriousness and people's general desire to find meaning, some European artists and writers from 1916 to 1923 flouted conventional aesthetic and cultural values, calling themselves dadaists. Dada, a French word for hobbyhorse and an English word of baby-talk origin, inspired creative people to produce works such as "Nude Descending Staircase" that were marked by nonsense, travesty, and incongruity. (See entries for avant-garde and Robert Delford Brown.)

DAEDALUS: See entry for David E. H. Jones.

Dagnall, Leslie J. (20th Century)

In 1972, Dagnall was President of the Board of Directors of the Humanist Society of Greater New York.

Dagne, Robert Addison (20th Century)

Dagne wrote *Is the Bible the Infallible Word of God?* (19–?) {GS}

Dahl, Arnold (20th Century)

Dahl is on the board of directors of the Freedom from Religion Foundation.

Dahl, Frances (1914-1999)

Dahl, a feminist married to Arnold Dahl was on the board of directors of the Freedom from Religion Foundation. An obstetrical nurse, she died of cancer at the age of eighty-four.

Dahlitz, Ray (1926—)

Dahlitz is editor of *The Humanist Rationalist Bibliography* and author of *The Development of the Rationalist Movement in Australia.* He is a member of the Melbourne University Freethought Society, the Rationalist Society of Australia, the Humanist Society of Victoria, the Rationalist Association of New South Wales, and the Australian Skeptics. He also heads the Council of Australian Humanist Societies (CAHS).

Dahlitz has written for *The New Zealand Rationalist and Humanist.* In 1994, he edited *Secular Who's Who, A Biographical Directory of Freethinkers, Secularists, Rationalists, Humanists, and Others Involved in Australia's Secular Movement From 1850 Onwards.* E-mail: <rayday@vic.bigpond.net.au>.

DAISY CHAIN, COSMIC: See entry for Allen Ginsberg.

Dakron, Ron (20th Century)

A poet and novelist, Dakron in a 1997 interview with Philip Collins told about the rage that in part inspired his first book, *Infra.* It was not a personal rage, he explained, "not anger at any person or class or belief system, more a rage against existence—against that quality of existence which seems to batter and defeat us. I wasn't enraged all day or anything; actually, I got involved in this tender affair during the creation of *Infra*; but I was pretty ticked off about humans versus the cosmos. And me on the losing side. It seemed, and still does, like we're getting a bum rap." When asked from whom, he replied, "Well, since I'm an atheist, I don't think from anyone in particular. But spirit is where you find it. And at twenty-eight I was finding it in honing some kind of weapon from language. *Infra* is my broadsword attack on language—a lot of poetic grunting and smashing." {CA}

Dalai Lama [Tenzin Gyatso] (1935—)

Tibet's supreme temporal and religious head, the Dalai Lama, won the Nobel Peace Prize in 1989. Although a Buddhist and said to be a non-theist, he has followers whose worship includes seeking Nirvana, reciting prayers, intoning hymns, and using various shamanistic elements. To become the grand lama, he was considered to have been born at the exact moment either Dalai or Panchen died. In 1959 he gave up cooperating with the Chinese and fled into exile, traveling widely and pleading the Tibetan cause.

In 1997, shown Arthur C. Clarke's "The Nine Billion Names of God," the Dalai Lama responded, "Your short story titled 'The Nine Billion Names of God' was particularly amusing." Apparently, the Dalai Lama was unaware of Clarke's purpose in showing him the story.

Christopher Hitchens, columnist in *The Nation* (27 July-3 August 1998), collected some facts about "The Divine One":

- After donating 45 million rupees, or about 170 million yen, to the Dalai Lama, Shoko Asahara was rewarded by several high-level meetings with the Dalai Lama. Asahara was leader of the Supreme Truth" cult in Japan and spreader of sarin nerve gas on the Tokyo subway.

- Supporters of the Dorge Shugden deity—a "Dharma protector" and an ancient object of worship and propitiation in Tibet—have been threatened with violence and ostracism and even death following the Dalai Lama's abrupt prohibition of this once-venerated godhead. A Swiss television documentary graphically intercuts footage of his Holiness, denying all knowledge of menace and intimidation, with scenes of his followers enthusiastically flaunting "Wanted" posters and other paraphernalia of excommunication and persecution.

- While he denies being a Buddhist "pope," the Dalai Lama is never happier than when brooding in a celibate manner on the sex lives of people he has never met. "Sexual misconduct for men and women consists of oral and anal sex," he has repeatedly said in promoting his book on these matteers. "Using one's hand, that is sexual misconduct." But, as ever with religious stipulations, there is a nutty escape clause. "To have sexual relations with a prostitute paid by you and not a third person does not constitute improper behavior."

{CE; Dalai Lama letter to Arthur C. Clarke, 27 February 1997; E}

Dale, Antonius van (1638—1708)

Van Dale, a Dutch writer, wrote *The Origin and Progress of Idolatry and Superstition* and another work, translated into English by Aphra Behn, under the title of *The History of Oracles and the Cheats of Pagan Priests.* He applied the historical method to his subject and showed that the belief in demons was as old and as extensive as the human race. {BDF}

Dale, Riepe (20th Century)

Dale wrote *The Naturalistic Tradition in Indian Thought* (1961). The work discusses the early Ajivikas and Carvakas views of the naturalistic elements of Jainism, Hinayana Buddhism, Samkhya, and Vaisesika.

Daleiden, Joseph L. (20th Century)

Daleiden's *The Final Superstition: A Critical Evaluation of the Judeo-Christian Legacy* (1994) is a dialogue with God. God is asked about various organized religions, which allows Daleiden to highlight the weaknesses of theism. When the subject of the existence of God arises, the format of a dialog weakens, for it becomes illogical to question the existence of an entity that is capable of responding.

The work, however, takes up the arguments against theism and religion in a novel way. God, represented as "G" in the dialogue, is shown willing to take up arguments that have been used to defend deism. Daleiden, a former Roman Catholic who never deliberately missed Mass until the age of twenty-six, has been a director of corporate planning for Amertech.

The author of *Science and Morality—Normal Behavior in the 21st Century*, Daleiden at the 1999 convention of Humanists of Florida spoke on the subject of "Raising Children Without Religion."

d'Alembert, Jean le Rond: See entry for Alembert.

Dali, Salvador (1904-1989)

A Catalan who became a leading surrealist artist, Dali is best known for his "Persistence of Memory" (1931). He has been portrayed by Ian Gibson in *The Shameful Life of Salvador Dali* (1998) as paranoia personified. A timid child fascinated with buttocks and fearful of locusts, Dali confided in his *Unspeakable Confessions*

> For a long time I experienced the misery of believing I was impotent. . . . Naked, and comparing myself to my schoolfriends, I discovered that my penis was small, pitiful and soft. I can recall a pornographic novel whose Don Juan machine-gunned female genitals with ferocious glee, saying that he enjoyed hearing women creak like watermelons. I convinced myself that I would never be able to make a woman creak like a watermelon.

Gibson holds that Dali had an unconsummated love affair with the poet Federico Garcia Lorca, the greatest friend of his youth, but masturbation was his only sexual activity throughout life, despite his love for poet Paul Éluard's wife Gala (born Helena Diakanoff Devulina in Kazan). Gala, according to John Richardson (*Vogue*, December 1998) was "one of the nastiest wives a major modern artist ever saddled himself with" and

> With her White Russian terror of Communism, Gala also managed to subvert the liberal ideology that Dali had shared with the fellow geniuses of his student days, Lorca and Buñuel. Disdaining the Marxism of the other Surrealists, the former atheist [Dali] and anarchist went over to totalitarianism and its by-product anti-Semitism. Far from showing any sympathy for the proletariat, Dali reportedly announced, apropos of his surreal penchant for the macabre, that he preferred train accidents in which the third-class passengers suffered most. He hailed the swastika as "the fusion of Left and Right, the resolution of antagonistic movements." On another occasion he described Hitler, childishly, as a nurse, and also talked with relish of biting "into the doting and triumphal sweetness of the plump, atavistic, tender, militarist and territorial back of [this] nurse."

Dali unconditionally supported Franco's fascistic regime in Spain and was a Roman Catholic.

Dalin, Olof Von (1708—1763)

Dalin, a Swedish poet, was a non-theist. (See entry for Scandinavian Unbelievers.)

Dall, Caroline Wells Healey (1822-1912)

Dall, a Unitarian, was a reformer and advocate of women's rights. {U}

Dalton, Gloster (19th Century)

Dalton was a charter member of the Independent Christian Church of Gloucester, Massachusetts, the first Universalist congregation in North America.

He was the first African American Universalist, according to David Johnson, minister of First Parish in Brookline, Massachusetts.

Dalvi, G. R. (20th Century)

At the Third International Humanist and Ethical Union World Congress held in Oslo (1962), Dalvi from India addressed the group.

Daly, Mary (20th Century)

Daly wrote *The Church and the Second Sex* (1968). Selections from her work are included in *A World Religions Reader* under Secular Humanism.

Damilaville, Étienne Noël (1721—1768)

A French writer, Damilaville was a friend of Voltaire, Diderot, d'Alembert, Grimm, and d'Holbach. He contributed to the *Encyclopédie* and in 1767 published an atheistic attack on the theologians, entitled *Theological Honesty*.

Voltaire called Damilaville "one of our most learned writers." Larousse says "he was an ardent enemy of Christianity." McCabe suggests that some of the encyclopedic entries were actually written by abler individuals who borrowed Damilaville's name. {BDF; JMRH; RAT}

Damiron, Jean Philibert (1794—1862)

Damiron was a French philosopher, a pupil of Cousin, from whom he adopted his eclectic system. In 1833 he was made a chevalier of the Legion of Honour and in 1836 a member of the Institut. He wrote harshly of the materialists, professing a philosophic theism and relegating Christianity to "children and weaklings." {RAT}

Dana, Charles Anderson (1819—1897)

Dana was associated as a young man with the Brook Farm, but he left in order to be managing editor under Horace Greeley of the New York *Tribune* (1849—1862). A liberal, he was dismissed at the outbreak of the Civil War because of his chauvinistic outlook, after which he became assistant secretary of war (1864), then part owner of the New York *Sun* (1867), which he edited in a lively manner. With George Ripley, Dana edited the *American Cyclopaedia* (1858—1864). {FUS}

DANCE

Christian religionists and theologians are, arguably, not much interested in dance, but those secularists for whom philosophy is of basic importance are devoted to dance in all its forms. Contemporary Bible Belt Christians have been known to frown upon dancing, a social activity which can involve bodily touching. Dance enthusiasts, however, relish the activity.

Primitive dances are the basis for many of the folk dances of contemporary times. War dances, dances devoted to the seeking of success in battle or thankfulness for victories, are international in character. Native American medicine men have been associated with dances of exorcism, of invocation, of asking for help in farming or hunting or the fertility of men and animals. Dances of courtship and of ecstasy have been popular in Africa, in Ancient Greece (where the choral dance honored Dionysus), in India, in Japan, in China, everywhere throughout the world.

The ballet first appeared in Italian courts in the 16th century and became popular in France during the reign of Louis XIV. Other forms included the minuet (France), the Morris Dance (England), the mazurka (Poland), the czardas (Hungary), the bolero (Spain), the tarantella (Italy), the galop (Germany) the polka (Bohemia) the highland fling (Scotland), the jig (Ireland), and American dance versions called the Virginia reel, the clog dance, the cakewalk, the two-step, the turkey trot, the Charleston, the Lindy Hop, the boogie woogie, the jitterbug, the twist, the frug, and numbers of others. Lincoln Kirstein's *Book of the Dance* (1942) and *The International Encyclopedia of Dance* (1998) make clear the attraction of this humanistic form of rhythmic activity. {CE}

Dandolo, Vincenzo (1758—1819)

Count Dandolo was an Italian chemist, author of *Principles of Physical Chemistry. The New Men* (1799) shows his antagonism to religion, and he wrote other works on vine, timber, and silk culture. {BDF; RAT}

DANDRUFF

> • History does not record anywhere at any time a religion that has any rational basis. Religion is a crutch for people not strong enough to stand up to the unknown without help. But, like dandruff, most people do have a religion and spend time and money on it to derive considerable pleasure fiddling with it.
>
> **—Robert A. Heinlein**
> as expressed by a character in
> *Time Enough for Love*

Daniel, Stephen Hartley (1950—)

Daniel wrote *John Toland* (1984) and *Myth and Modern Philosophy* (1990). {FUK}

Danielsson, Tage (1928—1985)

Danielsson, a popular Swedish actor, debater, and producer, is an atheist who has written "Second Thoughts," a poem in his *Tankar från roten* (Thoughts From the Root) with overtones of *1 Corinthians* 13: 1-13 which includes the following:

> I believe in doubt.
> Doubt is the basis of all knowledge,
> the engine of all change.

Doubt is, to be doubtlessly sure,
the prerequisite of faith.
He who believes without first doubting
is an exulting blockhead and a tinkling cymbal.
And he who believes without at the same
time doubting is hardly less of an exulting blockhead
and hardly less of a tinkling
cymbal.
Faith can remove mountains
but doubt can put them back in
place again. . . .
And now abides
faith, hope, doubt, these three;
but the greatest of these is doubt.
Or maybe it was love.
Now, damn it, I am uncertain again!

The book, written because he thought the Social Democratic government did not listen to the Swedish people, was a humorous collection of satirical poems and anecdotes. {Translation by Fredrik Bendz and Warren Allen Smith, 23 May 1997}

DANISH HUMANISTS

In Denmark, the Danish Humanist Debate (IHEU) is at Bjaelkevangen 2c, 2800 Lyngby, Denmark. (See entries for A. B. Drachmann, author of *Atheism in Pagan Antiquity* and Scandinavian Unbelievers.) {FD}

DANISH UNITARIANS

In 1900, influenced by Norwegian and British Unitarians, Danes built a church which centered its outlook around the teachings of Jesus, God the Father, the Golden Rule, and "love thy neighbor." Its aim was to bring religious, philosophical, and scientific views together. Individuals were responsible for their own way of life and religious views, and all have the freedom to disassociate from dogmatic exterior authority in favor of reliance on an inner authority.

In 1998 one fellowship of thirty-five families and seventy "supporters" is at Dag Hammarskjolds Alle 30, 2100 Kobenhaven, O, Denmark. Lene Lund Shoemaker is a contact. On the Web: <www.uua.org/icuu/icuu-europe.html>.

DANISH-AMERICAN FREETHOUGHT: For a discussion of Danish-American freethinkers, see *Freethought in the United States* by Gordon Stein.

Dankert, Piet (20th Century)

President of the European Parliament, Dankert presided over the International Humanist and Ethical Union's (IHEU's) International Peace Conference at Zutphen (1983) in the Netherlands. He is author of *Europe Without Frontiers* (1989).

D'Annunzio, Gabriele [Prince] (1863—1938)

An Italian poet, novelist, dramatist, and soldier, D'Annunzio started as a gossip columnist for Roman society, then became a writer who, Garry Wills has said, had a "largely unhealthy influence on Italian culture and politics." This is because his novels and plays combined a nostalgic decadence with the technological optimism of the Futurists.

Saddled with debts, he moved to Paris, becoming a literary lion and collaborating with Claude Debussy on a play with music, *The Martyrdom of Saint Sebastian.* The saint's role was taken by D'Annunzio's lover, the dancer Ida Rubenstein, who rated the Church's denunciations for her transvestism. The Church, for which he always expressed a profound contempt, put all his work on the *Index.* The Pope expressly warned Catholics not to read anything by him. In one of his works, the Prince describes himself (in the guise of one of his characters) as "a princely artist of magnificent sensuality." D'Annunzio, states McCabe, led the Neo-Pagan movement in Italy and was an atheist.

At the outbreak of World War I, he returned to Italy and was instrumental in persuading Italy to join the Allies, arguing that it was a way of advancing Italian imperialism. John Woodhouse's *Gabriele D'Annunzio: Defiant Archangel* (1998) describes D'Annunzio's winning many Italian medals in the war, but his sea raid on an Austrian base on the Dalmatian coast sank no ships—none were in the Bay of Buccari when his three little torpedo boats infiltrated those waters by night. What the poet did was to leave satirical messages that bobbed in bottles, then wrote of the battle as if it had been an epic encounter. He flew over Austrian lines dropping bombs as well as pamphlets at the enemy and lost sight in one eye when his pilot crash-landed. Claiming that Achilles had shouted *Eia alala*! to his chariot horses, D'Annunzio convinced the Italian army to adopt the ancient cry as their own. Woodhouse relates many instances of his subject's bravado, including once photographing as the city of Versailles' slogan of defiance an obscene expression from the World War trenches, *Me ne frego* ("I jack off on it").

At first, D'Annunzio was a Socialist and scorned Mussolini's alliance with the Papacy, but he was reconciled politically—Mussolini gave him his title—and his life in his later years was marred, states McCabe, "by unhappy political adventures and the loss of his literary brilliance." He spent his final years at an abandoned villa on Lake Garda, turning the place into a shrine to his activities and works. Much of Fascism's street theater, wrote Wills,

> was taken from the secular liturgies D'Annunzio had invented in his parliamentary campaigns, his war ceremonies, and his reign at Fiume. . . . Mussolini did not want any interference in or criticism of what he was doing with D'Annunzio's tactics, so he immobilized the poet by wedging him into his shrine with pillows stuffed all around him. He showered him with honors, commissioned a grand edition of all his works, subvented Il Vittoriale with funds and mementos from the World War.

{JM; *The New York Review of Books*, 4 March 1999; RE; TRI}

Dante Alighieri (1265—1321)

Dante, the Italian poet whose description of Hell in *The Divine Comedy* (begun about 1300) is often treated as gospel by believers, supported Holy Roman Emperor Henry VII and was opposed to the temporal power of Pope Boniface VIII. He died, ironically, a few hours after writing the final lines of *Paradiso*, the third section of *The Divine Comedy.*

Dante's *Inferno* described Hell as containing nine circles: Limbus, Upper Hell with four circles, and Lower Hell with four circles.

- **Limbus**—humans who arrived here suffered by neverbeing able to attain Heaven.
  Circle #1— Limbo housed spirits who were not sinful; e.g., Christians who lacked baptism; and pagans if they "did not duly worship God."
- **Upper Hell**— for individuals guilty of sins less offensive to God
  Circle #2—The Lust Circle: here were placed carnal sinners.
  Circle #3—The Violence Circle: here was housed those with sins of gluttony and incontinence.
  Circle #4—The Avarice and prodigality Circle: here were misers, spendthrifts, abusers of worldly goods, people who were prodigal.
  Circle #5—The Anger Circle: here were the sullen and wrathful
- **Lower Hell**— for individuals guilty of sins very offensive to God: in this area, called the "City of Dis," are those whose sins were not due to incontinence or desire or temper but to permanent evil, bestiality, despoiling
  Circle #6—The Heresy Circle: here were Epicureans and other materialistic freethinkers **(presumably rationalists, secular humanists, agnostics, etc.)** who denied the immortality of the soul and regarded a comfortable life as the highest good.
  Circle #7—The Violence Circle: for sodomites, usurers, suicides, people who are violent against nature.
  Circle #8—The Deceit Circle: here are ten concentric circles which include deceivers, panderers, seducers, flatterers, falsifiers, soothsayers, barrators, hypocrites, evil counselors, creators of strife, counterfeiters, murderers (who are buried head downwards in a hole), thieves, those guilty of simony (using their ecclesiastic office for personal gain), and schismatics (including Mahomet/Muhammad).
  Circle #9—The Treachery Circle: for individuals guilty of the fraud of treachery; it is called the Giudecca (so named from Judas Iscariot), and sinners are wholly and forever imprisoned in ice.

{CE; Dante, *The Inferno*; PA}

Danto, Arthur C(oleman) (1924—)

The Johnsonian Professor of Philosophy at Columbia University, Danto in 1983 was President of the American

Philosophic Association. In 1965, he wrote *Nietzsche as Philosopher*, one of the authoritative biographies recognized by other philosophers. In 1980, he signed the Secular Humanist Declaration. Danto wrote *Mark Tanney: Visions and Revisions* (1992) and *Beyond the Brillo Box: The Visual Arts in Post-Historical Perspective* (1993). In *Columbia* (Spring 1993), he describes how in 1948 he entered the Columbia University graduate program in philosophy as a probation student, not having had any previous undergraduate courses in philosophy. In fact, he "had no great interest in philosophy and certainly no intention of becoming a philosopher. Rather, philosophy seemed a good way for me to draw the benefits of what remained to me from the GI Bill, enabling me to be in New York while I pursued my real ambition, which was to become an artist." He did, in fact, become an artist and also he became the art editor of *Nation*. In the *Encyclopedia of Philosophy*, Danto wrote the entry for "Naturalism." His special expertise, according to Robert Sharpe of the University of Wales in Lampeter, is aesthetics, "where he is largely responsible for bringing the idea of the 'art world' into prominence." Danto is the recipient of the prestigious Frank Jewett Mather Award for Art Journalism, given by the College Art Association.

In 1994, Danto wrote *Embodied Meanings: Critical Essays and Aesthetic Meditations*, showing not only his openmindedness about art and artists but also his broad understanding of the international world of art. Evaluating the photographic achievement of the controversial artist, Robert Mapplethorpe, Danto in 1995 wrote *Playing With the Edge*. In 1997 his *After the End of Art* is a discussion of contemporary art and the pale of history. Based on his Mellon Lectures, the work of art criticism tells how art has changed, how there no longer is any special way it has to "look," how art in essence is whatever artists make. It does not, he states controversially, have to have an explicit social or political message. {HM2; OCP; SHD}

Danton, Georges Jacques (1759—1794)

A French revolutionist, Danton was one of the chief organizers of the Republic once Louis XVI could no longer be king. Carlyle called him the Tital of the Revolution and certainly its greatest figure after Mirabeau. In the alarm caused by the invasion, he urged a bold and resolute policy. Danton was a member of the Convention and of the Committee of Public Safety. At the crisis of the struggle with Robespierre, who charged him with atheism, Danton declined to strike the first blow and disdained to flee. With all his faults, said Carlyle, "he was a Man; fiery-real, from the great fire-bosom of Nature herself." Some of his phrases were like pyramids, standing sublime above the drifting sand of human speech. It was he who advised "daring, and still daring, and ever daring." It was he who cried, "The coalesced kings of Europe threaten us, and as our gage of battle we fling before them the head of a king." It was he who exclaimed, in a rapture of patriotism, "Let my name be blighted, so that France be free."

"They dare not" arrest him, he said; but he was soon a prisoner in the Luxembourg. "What is your name and abode?" they asked him at the tribunal. "My name is Danton," he answered, "a name tolerably known in the Revolution: my abode will soon be Annihilation; but I shall live in the Pantheon of History." Replying to his infamous indictment, his magnificent voice "reverberated with the roar of a lion in the toils." The President rang his bell, enjoining calmness, said Carlyle, in a vehement manner, "What is it to thee how I defend myself?" cried Danton; "the right of dooming me is thine always. The voice of a man speaking for his honor and life may well drown the jingling of thy bell!"

Foote describes how, on the way to the guillotine, Danton bore himself proudly. Poor Camille Desmoulins struggled and writhed in the cart, which was surrounded by a howling mob. "Calm, my friend," said Danton, "heed not that vile *canaille*." Herault de Sechelles, whose turn it was to die first, tried to embrace his friend, but the executioners prevented him. "Fools," said Danton, "you cannot prevent our heads from meeting in the basket." At the foot of the scaffold the thought of home flashed through his mind. "O my wife," he exclaimed, "my well-beloved, I shall never see thee more then." But recovering himself, he said, "Danton, no, weakness!" Looking the executioner in the face, he cried with his great voice, "You will show my head to the crowd; it is worth showing; you don't see the like in these days." The next minute that head, the one that might have guided France best, wrote Foote, was severed from his body by the knife of the guillotine. "What a man this Danton was! With his Herculean form, his huge black head, his mighty voice, his passionate nature, his fiery courage, his poignant wit, his geniality, and his freedom from cant, he was a splendid and unique figure." An atheist, Foote continued, "he perished in trying to arrest bloodshed. Robespierre, the Deist, continued the bloodshed till it drowned him. The two men were as diverse in nature as in creed, and Danton killed by Robespierre, as Courtois said, was Pyrrhus killed by a woman!" {BDF; FO; JM; JMRH}

Dantone, Gerry (20th Century)

Dantone helped found the Long Island, New York, chapter of the Council for Secular Humanism. A commercial real estate broker, he has degrees in chemical engineering from Polytechnic Institute of New York and in finance from St. John's University. Dantone has a record label, Infidels Records, and his band called "UniversalDice.com" wrote, recorded, and performed a humanistic rock opera on CD called "My Name is Thomas."

The rock opera is about the loss of faith by a man of the cloth. E-mail: <infidelsre@aol.com>. (See entry for Freethought Music.)

Danz, John (20th Century

Danz once was a director of the American Humanist Association. He generously supported the San Francisco Humanist Society in the 1940s and wanted, according to Edwin H. Wilson, "a sharp break between organized humanism and the Unitarian movement." Ethnically Hebrew, Danz suggested the building of "humanist temples." {EW}

DAOISM

The religion built around the Chinese philosopher Lao-zi (Lao-Tzu), a contemporary of Kongfu-zi (Kung-fu Tzu) uses language which is mystical. McCabe has written, however, that many experts hold that both were atheists, that "the fact that (Lao-Tzu) spoke of Heaven (the word chosen by some translators) is not decisive. Some Chinese scholars hold that he meant only what the Stoics called the Law of Nature. The religion, Daoism (Taoism), which he is commonly said to have founded, has as little relation to his teaching as the Roman Catholic system has to the teaching of Jesus." Lao-zi, if he existed, lived in the 6th century B.C.E. {CE; JM; *New Humanist*, October 1998; RE}

Dapper, Olfert (Died 1690)

A Dutch physician who occupied himself with history and geography, Dapper had no religion and was suspected of atheism. He traveled through Syria, Babylonia, and other distant places in 1650. A translator of Herodotus (1664), Dapper also wrote a *History of the City of Amsterdam* (1663). {BDF}

Darabi, Homa (Suicide 1994)

Darabi, an Iranian physician, "ended her life as an act of protest against the way the Islamic Republic was treating Iranian women, especially educated ones," said her sister Parvin. She had been politically active since her student days. In 1960, she was briefly imprisoned for protesting against the Shah's regime. In 1963, she married a classmate and, after graduating from the University of Tehran Medical School, practiced in a rural village.

In 1979 Khomeini decreed that all women must wear the Islamic dress (hijab) at work. Dr. Darabi refused, and for a long time her unique status protected her. In 1990, however, the government transferred her to Iman Hussein Hospital, the director of which, one of Dr. Darabi's former students, was a strict fundamentalist who insisted that she wear the full Islamic hijab. This she declined to do, saying it was too difficult to examine a patient swathed in so much material. As a result, she was discharged, sued in court, and lost after four years. Darabi's end as a martyr is described by Martha Shelley's *Rage Against the Veil: Self-Immolation in Tajrish Square, Tehran* (1994).

Darabi, Parvin (20th Century)
Darabi was a signer of Humanist Manifesto 2000.

Darget, Etienne (Died 1778)
Darget was a French freethinker, the private secretary to Frederick the Great (1745—1752). {BDF}

Darlington, C(yril) D(ean) (1903—)
Darlington wrote *Story of the Rationalist Press Association* (1949). Differing with most humanists, he opposed miscegenation. A biologist and botanist, Darlington wrote *Conflict of Science and Society* (1948); *Facts of Life* (1953); and *Darwin's Place in History* (1958). {FUK; GS}

Darmesteter, James (1849—1894)
Darmesteter, a French orientalist, taught the Iranian languages at the *Collège de France* and translated the Zend Avesta for *The Sacred Books of the East* (1880—1883). Darmesteter rejected the Jewish faith in his youth, and "he never, in the heaven of his thought, replaced the Jewish God on his overturned throne," wrote Gaston Paris in *Penseurs et Poètes* (1896). Darmesteter taught a vague theism, rejecting the idea of a future life. {RAT}

Darnton, Robert (20th Century)
Darnton is author of *The Corpus of Clandestine Literature in France, 1769—1789* (1995) and *The Forbidden Best-Sellers of Pre-Revolutionary France* (1995). In the former, he includes a checklist of 720 forbidden books, the first thirty-five of which he arranged in order of popularity:

1. Mercier, *The Year 2400*
2. Mairobert (authorship is uncertain), *Anecdotes of the Countess du Barry*
3. D'Holbach, *System of Nature*
4. Mercier, *Tableau of Paris*
5. Raynal, *History of the Two Indies*
6. Mairobert and Moufle d'Angerville, *Historical Journal. . . by K. de Maupeou*
7. Du Laurens, *Arentino*
8. Anonymous, *Philosophical Letter*
9. Coquereau, *Memoirs of the Abbé Terray*
10. Voltaire, *The Maid of Orleans*
11. Voltaire, *Questions About the Encyclopaedia*
12. Anonymous, *Memoirs of Louis XV*
13. Mairobert, *The English Observer*
14. Lambert (?), Translation of *Memoirs of a Woman of Pleasure* (i.e., Cleland's "Fanny Hill")
15. D'Argens (?), *Thérèse the Philosopher*
16. Anonymous, *Collection of Merry Songs*
17. Linguet, *Philosophical Essay on Monasticism*
18. D'Holbach, *Critical History of Jesus Christ*
19. Bérage (?), Translation of *The Secretest Mysteries of Freemasonry*
20. Linguet, *Petition to the Royal Council*
21. Franco (?), *The Errant Whore*
22. D'Holbach, *Christianity Unveiled*
23. Rousseau, *Works*
24. Bretonne, *The Peasant Perverted*
25. Milot, *A School for Girls*
26. D'Holbach, *Good Sense*
27. Linguet, *Letter to the Count de Vergennes*
28. Helvétius, *On Man*
29. D'Holbach, *Social System*
30. Languinais, *The Accomplished Monarch*
31. Voltaire, *Portable Philosophical Dictionary*
32. D'Angerville, *The Private Life of Louis XV*
33. Anonymous, *The Merry Lyre*
34. Morlière, *Ecclesiastical Laurels*
35. Latouche (?), *History of Dom B., Carthusian Porter*

The books were all banned by the authorities and, Darnton reports, were often printed by *the Société typographique de Neuchâtel* in Switzerland, then shipped down the Rhône or Rhine or across the Jura mountains.

Darrow, Clarence (1857—1938)
Darrow, the famed Scopes Trial lawyer, said:

> I don't believe in God, because I don't believe in Mother Goose. . . . I do not consider it an insult, but rather a compliment to be called an agnostic. I do not pretend to know where many ignorant men are sure—that is all that agnosticism means.

Although called a "most religious man" and "one of the few true Christians" by some, others termed him an atheist and an antichrist. However, he clearly had stated,

> I am an agnostic because no man living can form any picture of it (God). You may believe in the force but not in the object.

Darrow was highly influenced by Schopenhauer and, according to Burr, held that the "mistaken belief that men deliberately choose to be sinners and criminals has provided the excuse for inflicting pain and punishing them, and for imagining a God who will torture them in hell forever."

Darrow used his philosophy to replace hatred with compassion, and he fought against capital punishment. In the trial of the so-called "Nietzschean" murderers Loeb and Leopold, he was successful in their not being given the death sentence. To McCabe, he said that he never sought to enable such criminals to escape punishment but only the death sentence, to which he morally objected.

Not About Nightingales (1938) by Tennessee Williams commences:

> This play is dedicated to the memory of Clarence Darrow, The Great Defender, whose mental frontiers were the four corners of the sky.

The work described a prison atrocity in which convicts on a hunger strike in a Pennsylvania prison were roasted to death in a steam-heated cell. Williams was aware of the Loeb and Leopold executions and their nationally famous lawyer. In the "monkey trial," in which biology teacher John T. Scopes was charged with teaching Darwinian views, Darrow eloquently spoke out against religion. His works include *Resist Not Evil* (1904), *Crime, Its Cause and Treatment* (1925), and *The Story of My Life* (1932). His law partner at one time was Edgar Lee Masters. Darrow was an honorary associate of the British Rationalist Press Association, which Charles A. Watts founded in 1899. {CE; EU, John R. Burr; FUS; HNS2; JM; PA; TRI; TSV; TYD; U}

Darusmont, Frances (1795—1852)
A feminist and daughter of a Scottish freethinker, Darusmont adopted her father's views and while in her teens wrote a defense of the Epicurean philosophy. A lecturer on freethought, she was described by the *Dictionary of National Biography*, "Few have made greater sacrifices for conviction's sake or exhibited a more courageous independence." {JM; FUS; RAT}

Darwell, Stephen (20th Century)
Darwell, of the University of Michigan, is on the Executive Committee of The Hume Society, a group engaged in scholarly activity concerning David Hume.

Darwin, Charles Robert (1809—1882)

One of the greatest rationalists of all time, Darwin established the theory of organic evolution known as Darwinism. He also is one of the most misunderstood authors. His father, a 350-pound jolly gentleman, once said of his son that he "cared for nothing but shooting, dogs, and rat-catching," and his school records show that as a child Darwin was lazy and a poor student. While studying theology at Cambridge University, he changed his field of interest to something more interesting: beetles. Later, and not divulging his heart palpitations, Darwin was accepted as an unpaid naturalist on H.M.S. *Beagle*, which was bound for South America and from which he recorded data over a five-year period (1831—1836) that resulted in the formulating of his concept of evolution. His views were defended by Huxley in England, Haeckel in Germany, Vladimir Kovalevski in Russia, and Asa Gray in America. Although accused of believing that man descended from apes, Darwin held, as defined by Webster, "that natural selection favors the survival of some variations over others, that new species have arisen and may continue to arise by these processes, and that widely divergent groups of plants and animals have arisen from the same ancestors." *The Descent of Man* (1871) supplemented and elaborated upon the structure of his theory of what he termed *The Origin of Species.* (For an earlier theorist about evolution, see entry for Anaximandros.)

Darwin married his first cousin, Emma Wedgwood, who was descended as he was from the pottery patriarch Josiah Wedgwood. After his five years exploring South America and being seasick during many of his travels, Darwin lived sixteen miles from London at Down House in Kent, where in a wheeled armchair in his study there he wrote *Origin of Species*. The place also was something of a refuge from London's dirt and violence, an ideal place for the semi-invalid he became. As to what his physical problem was, physicians even today are unsure. He may have suffered from a blood parasite, or maybe some strong psychosomatic component was his problem.

Concerning religion, Darwin wrote, "The mystery of the beginning of all things is insoluble by us, and I for one must be content to remain an Agnostic." Unitarians have claimed him as one of their group, but upon his death it was Francis Galton, his cousin, who helped arrange Darwin's burial in Westminster Abbey. The Canon of St. Paul's, with some "discomfort and misgiving," allowed the burial, mainly because of pressure from Huxley, the Canon of Westminster, the Dean of Westminster, the president of the Royal Society, journalists, scientists, and any number of preachers who at this point, according to Adrian Desmond and James Moore in *Darwin*, vied with each other for the honor of praising the "agnostic in the abbey." They also state that it was Lyell's newly published *Principles of Geology* that convinced Darwin of evolutionary naturalism and led him slowly but inexorably away from Christianity.

Darwin, according to a Herman Hausheer, a theologian of the 1940s, "proposed to reconcile evolution with traditional ethics through the concept of adaptation. He never could bring himself to regard natural selection as a means in the hands of Providence. First a theist and later an agnostic, Darwin rejected religion when he assumed that religion depended upon a definite scientific view. Those who see in Darwinism the final destruction of religion fail to realize that religion does not rest upon a hypothesis concerning the origin of living beings any more than that it rests upon an Aristotelian-Ptolemaic cosmology. Organized religion undermines its own existence by affiliating itself with and demanding of its members a blind subscription to any scientific system. Living religion has no biology and cosmology. It does not rest upon unexplainable natural events, but upon the experience of the heart." Numerous other apologists continue to try to explain the profound challenge Darwin's concepts brought to theism.

Darwin's *Autobiography* (published 1887) describes his change from having a naive acceptance of Christianity to becoming a reluctant agnostic to the point in which he "gradually came to disbelieve Christianity" and wondered why everyone else had not, also. He adds, "I have steadily endeavored to keep my mind free, so as to give up any hypothesis however much beloved (and I cannot resist forming one on every subject), as soon as facts are shown to be opposed to it."

To a German student in 1879, Darwin wrote, "Science has nothing to do with Christ, except in so far as the habit of scientific research makes a man cautious in admitting evidence. For myself I do not believe that there ever has been any revelation." In his *Life and Letters*, he relates that between 1836 and 1842 he had come to see "that the Old Testament was no more to be trusted than the sacred books of the Hindoos." He rejected design and said, "I for one must be content to remain an agnostic." The essence of Darwin's philosophy was that organized complexity has arisen from primeval simplicity, entirely without the help of any designer or pre-existing cause. Others can deny this, and do, but the theory of natural selection remains the major theory for explaining fully the wonders of nature.

We humans are a bundle of design compromises, *The Economist* (29 July 1995) wrote in appreciation of Darwin's views, "engaged in an endless arms race between parasites and their host. Our bodies—evolved in the African savannah—are poorly adapted to the modern world. We are tyrannised by the side-effects of genes selected for benefits we have yet to discover." The continued evolution of his theories, as evidenced by numbers of current books on the subject, show Darwinism is a unifying theory that is being used to look at old problems in new ways. Physicians, for example, should be cautious about routinely treating symptoms; they should know that using aspirin will bring down the fever in chickenpox and comfort the sufferer, but that will seriously prolong the infection. Looking at human beings and their illnesses as the products of a long evolutionary history is in itself a salutary exercise. Darwin, the failed doctor, is wisely being consulted by contemporary doctors, among others, who understand the significance of his ideas.

Chided by individuals who misunderstood his theory, Darwin fought back: "For my part, I would as soon be descended from a baboon as from a savage who mistreats his enemies, treats his wives like slaves, and is haunted by the grossest superstitions."

"For myself," he wrote, "I do not believe in any revelation. As for a future life, every man must judge for himself between conflicting vague probabilities." He professed himself an agnostic, regarding the problem of the universe as beyond our solution. Robert Lewins, M.D., knew Darwin personally, and had discussed this question with him. Darwin was much less reticent to Lewins than he had shown himself in a letter to Haeckel. In answer to a direct question "as to the bearing of his researches on the existence of an anima, or soul in man, he distinctly stated that, in his opinion, a vital or spiritual principle, apart from inherent somatic (bodily) energy, had no more locus standing in the human than in the other races of the animal kingdom."

In reviewing Matt Ridley's *The Origins of Virtue: Human Instincts and the Evolution of Cooperation* (1998), Frank J. Sulloway in *The New York Review of Books*, 9 April 1998) commented about ongoing controversies over the Darwinian perspectives which Ridley's work brings up:

> In this often heated debate, it does not really help for adversaries to argue about whether human behavior is genetically or culturally determined (it is both); about whether human consciousness invalidates the effects of natural selection (consciousness is natural selection's most remarkable product, not its antithesis); about whether Darwinian theory robs us of our free will (it clearly does not); or about whether Darwinians can be usefully divided into narrow-minded "ultras," who attribute everything to natural selection, and open-minded "pluralists" (they cannot be so divided). Critical empiricism, not debating skills on either side, will ultimately resolve these controversies. As Charles Darwin taught us more than a century ago, openness to diverse lines of evidence and a dogged dedication to hypothesis testing are the enduring Darwinian virtues.

In *The Darwin Legend* (1995), James Moore wrote that the reports of Darwin's deathbed conversion, although often repeated, are without substance. Francis Darwin told T. H. Huxley in 1887 that any such allegations were "false and without any kind of foundation," calling such stories "a work of imagination." He affirmed that his father died an agnostic. Of his sons, Sir Francis became a leading botanist, Sir George Howard a distinguished astronomer at Cambridge, and two others became successful engineers. All, stated McCabe, were agnostics.

His eldest son, Francis, wrote the following concerning his father's death: "No special change occurred during the beginning of April, but on Saturday 15th he was seized with giddiness while sitting at dinner in the evening, and fainted in an attempt to reach his sofa. On the 17th he was again better, and in my temporary absence recorded for me the progress of an experiment in which I was engaged. During the night of April 18th, about a quarter to twelve, he had a severe attack and passed into a faint, from which he was brought back to consciousness with great difficulty. He seemed to recognize the approach of death, and said, 'I am not the least afraid to die.' All the next morning he suffered from terrible nausea and faintness, and hardly rallied before the end came."

Darwin is buried in Westminster Abbey, London. The gravestone is a floor slab with name and vital dates. As recently as 1916, Sir Francis had to refute a lying story about his father's agonizing deathbed, and the story cropped up again, with embellishments, in *The Churchman's Magazine* (1925). (See entry for Erasmus Darwin. A recent work on Darwinism is Daniel C. Dennett's *Darwin's Dangerous Idea: Evolution and the Meaning of Life* [1995], in which Darwinism is favorably seen as a corrosive acid that is capable of dissolving many of our earlier beliefs in sociology and philosophy—see entry for Daniel C. Dennett. A major biography, reviewed in *The New York Review of Books* [4 April 1996] by Stephen Jay Gould, is Janet Browne's *Charles Darwin: Voyaging* [1996]. Also, see the entry for H. James Birx, one of the leading Darwin scholars.) {BDF; CE; Stephen Jay Gould, *Rocks of Ages*; HNS2; JM; JMRH; PUT; RAT; TRI; TYD}

Darwin, Erasmus (1731—1802)

The paternal grandfather of Charles Darwin wrote *Zoonomia: or the Laws of Organic Life* (1794), for which he was accused of atheism. He was, however, a philosophic naturalist, physician, and deist. He had a theory about the origin of all life which anticipated the current "primeval soul" hypothesis of many current scientists, including the Russian biochemist, A. I. Oparin. The Vatican prohibited the reading of his works in 1817. In 1879, Ernest Krause in a biography said of Darwin, "He was the first who proposed and consistently carried out a well-rounded theory with regard to the development of the living world—a merit which shines forth more brilliantly when we compare it with the vacillating and confused attempts of Buffon, Linnaeus, and Goethe. It is the idea of a power working from within the organisms to improve their natural position." This is an idea which, developed by Lamarck, was modified by his grandson into the doctrine of natural selection. The idea of "the descent of man" from a simian species had been broached before him by Buffon and Helvétius in France, and Lords Kames and Monboddo in Scotland. According to A. Benn, Darwin, rather than a deist, was an atheist along with Bentham, Godwin, and Charles Fox. But Darwin did believe in "the Great Architect" of the cosmos, a "Great First Cause" which breathed life into the primal filament, giving it the potentiality to evolve. Even the Unitarians were too orthodox for him, and, in fact, he described Unitarianism as a feather-bed to catch a falling Christian.

Often unnoticed is the first sentence of Percy Bysshe Shelley's preface to Mary Shelley's *Frankenstein*. As Stephen Jay Gould and others have pointed out, "he had, in order to justify Dr. Frankenstein's experiment, alluded to Erasmus Darwin's atheistical view on the possibility of quickening matter by electricity."

Darwin's death was singularly peaceful. "At about seven o'clock," said his grandson, "he was seized with a violent shivering ill, and went into the kitchen to warm himself. He retired to his study, lay on the sofa, became faint and cold, and was moved into an armchair, where, without pain or emotion of any kind, he expired a little before nine o'clock." To a friend a few years prior, he had written, "When I think of dying it is always without pain or fear." {BDF; CE; EU, H. James Birx; FO; HAB; JM; JMR; JMRH; RAT; RSR; TRI; TYD}

Darwin, Francis [Sir] (1848—1925)

Darwin, the third son of Charles Darwin, taught botany at Cambridge and was President of the British Association in 1908. Besides the biography of his father, Darwin wrote many papers on botany and in 1919 sent a cordial greeting to the Rationalist Press Association dinner. {RAT}

Darwin, George Howard [Sir] (1845—1912)

Darwin, the second son of Charles Darwin, taught astronomy at Cambridge. He wrote the accepted theory of the moon's origin. {RAT}

Darwin, Leonard [Major] (Born 1850)

Darwin, the youngest son of Charles Darwin, was in the Staff Intelligence Department of the War Office from 1885 to 1890. He was President of the Royal Geographical Society, Chairman of the Eugenics Education Society, and Treasurer of the National Committee for Combating Venereal Diseases. {RAT}

DARWINIAN MEDICINE

Randolph M. Nesse and George C. Williams, in *Why We Get Sick* (1995), argue that the human body is adapted to life as hunters and gatherers in the Paleolithic communities of 100,000 years ago. Although our way of life has changed since then, they state, our genetics have not. In the Stone Age, humans enjoyed finding the rare sweet and fat foods; today, we find it difficult to suppress that ancient reflex. Their "Darwinian medicine" treats the symptoms differently. Although a physician might try to bring down a fever or counter an allergic reaction, the Darwinian approach is that the fever is a defense mechanism for putting bacteria at a disadvantage, that suppressing it may prolong the disease although admittedly bringing comfort to a sufferer. Deans of medicine point out that the concepts of Darwinian medicine cannot be tested rigorously. As critiqued by journalist Nicholas Wade, "Physicians seek immediate causes (what infectious agent is making this patient sick?), whereas evolutionists seek ultimate causes (what genetic adaptation has made humans vulnerable to this disease?)." {Nicholas Wade, "Ask Dr. Darwin," *The New York Times Magazine*, 19 Feb 1995}

Dasgupta, Santanu (20th Century)

Originally from India, Dasgupta lives and works in Sweden. He is a scientist at BMC, the Biomedical Center which is Scandinavia's largest such. Like his fellow Bengali Taslima Nasrin, Dasgupta is a non-theist. {WAS, 1997 interview}

Datta, Amlan (20th Century)

A leading Indian radical humanist, Datta is the former Vice-Chancellor of Tagore's Vishwa Bharati University, Tagore's university. Datta gave the keynote address, "The Finer Spirit of Humanism," at the 1998 World Humanist Congress in Mumbai. Datta signed Humanist Manifesto 2000. {*International Humanist News*, December 1998}

Datta, Kiran Nath (20 Century)

Datta is a trustee of the Buddhiwadi Foundation. (See entry for Buddhiwadi Foundation.)

Daubermesnil, François Antoine (Died 1802)

A French conventionalist who was elected deputy of Tarn in 1792, Daubermesnil became a minister of the Council of Five Hundred. He was one of the founders of Theophilanthropy. {BDF}

Daudet, Alphonse (1840—1897)

The author of *Letters from My Mill* (1869) a collection of inspiring short stories, Daudet was rationalistic and humanistic in his outlook, according to Lamont. McCabe said that although Daudet, who was less outspoken about religion but hardly less hated by the clergy, was an atheist. Daudet's son, Léon, was editor for the Roman Catholic paper, *Action française.*

The Vatican in 1927 and 1932 prohibited the reading of Leon's *Les Bacchantes* and *Le Voyage de Shakespeare* (1896). Alphonse Daudet died of a venereal disease. {BDF; CE; CL; ILP; JM; JMR; RAT; TRI}

Daunou, Pierre Claude François (1761—1840)

Daunou was a French politician and historian. His father entered him in the congregation of the Fathers of the Oratory, which he left at the time of the Revolution. The department of Calais elected him with Carnot and Thomas Paine to the Convention. After the Revolution, Daunon became librarian at the Pantheon. A friend of Garat, Cabanis, Chenier, Destutt Tracy, Ginguen, and Benjamin Constant, he was noted for his benevolence.

One of Daunou's works was *Historical Essay on the Temporal Power of the Popes* (1810). {BDF; RAT}

DAVENPORT BROTHERS

Joe Nickell, in "The Davenport Brothers: Religious Practitioners, Entertainers, or Frauds?" (*Skeptical Inquirer*, July-August 1999), describes two Buffalo newsboys—thirteen-year-old William Henry Harrison Davenport (1841-1877) and his brother Ira Erastus (1839-1911) Davenport—whose spiritualism and trickery netted a fortune of at least $600,000. Although many believed them, Ira confessed to Harry Houdini (1874-1926) that "Ira Davenport positively disclaimed Spiritualistic power in his talk with me, saying repeatedly that he and his brother never claimed to be mediums or pretended their work to be Spiritualistic."

Davenport, Allen (1773—1877)

A social reformer, Davenport contributed to Carlile's *Republican* and wrote an account of the life and works of Thomas Spence, the reformer. Davenport published a volume of verse, *The Muses' Wreath* (1827). {BDF}

Davenport, John (1789—1877)

Davenport was a deist and a teacher. He wrote *An Apology for Mohammed and the Koran* (1869) as well as *Curiositates Eroticoe Physiologae*, or tabooed subjects freely treated. Davenport died in poverty. {BDF}

David: See entry for Allen Windsor.

David of Dinant (c. 1160—1206)

David, a scholar accused of promoting pantheistic materialism, was probably born in Belgium. A teacher of philosophy at the University of Paris, he identified Aristotle's "primary matter" with God and divided reality into three categories: matter (bodies), intellect (souls), and spirit (eternal substance).

The Church, however, found such views heretical: God was not embodied in all things but, rather, was a separate creator of all. As a result, David's work was condemned and his books were burned. Further, it was decreed that anyone who possessed David's writings after 25 December 1210 was a heretic. {EH; BDF}

David, Francis (1510—1579)

Appointed the court preacher to King John Sigismund of Transylvania, David (also known as Ferencz David) is reported to have said,

> There is no greater piece of folly than to try to exercise power over conscience and soul, both of which are subject only to their Creator.

David was successively a Roman Catholic, a Lutheran, and an anti-trinitarian, preaching in 1566 against the doctrine of the Trinity. He went further than Socinus and declared there was "as much foundation for praying to the Virgin Mary and other dead saints as to Jesus Christ." In consequence, he was accused of blasphemy. At the Diet of Torda in 1568, he spoke in favor of tolerance for *all* religious groups. Under his influence, King John Sigismund proclaimed complete religious toleration in Transylvania—King John is cited as being the first Unitarian king in world history.

In 1579, after being condemned as a heretic, David died in a prison in Deva. (See entry for Hungarian Unitarians.) {BDF; EU, Paul H. Beattie; U}

David, Ferenc Francis (1840—1897)

The first Unitarian minister in Hungary, David refused to worship Christ as God. As a result, he and his followers were persecuted, and he died in jail. He had converted to Unitarianism before 1567, inspired by the Italian physician, Georgius Blanciatta, and later he advocated that Christ need not be worshiped at all. David's followers were known as "*Nonadorantes*," or individuals who did not accept adoration of the Christ. {UU}

David, Jacques Louis (1748—1825)

A French painter, one of the leading painters of his time, David had been painter to the king but, joining the Jacobin Club, became a member of the Convention and voted for the king's death. On the restoration, David was banished along with other freethinkers, and his family was not allowed to bring his body back to France for burial. One of his most famous paintings is "The Murder of Marat" (1793). {BDF; JM; RAT}

Davidoff, Denise (20th Century)

Davidoff is the fifth moderator of the Unitarian Universalist Association. She began presiding in 1993 and is noted for her quest for religious equality and separation of church and state.

Davids, Caroline Augusta Rhys (20th Century)

Davids, the daughter of the Reverend J. Foley, Vicar of Wadhurst, was an orientalist. She married Professor Rhys Davids in 1894, and both were rationalists. A Pali scholar, she translated Pali poetry and was an authority on the philosophic aspect of Buddhism. She wrote *Buddhist Psychological Ethics* (1900), *Psalms of the Early Buddhists* (1909—1913), and *Buddhism* (1912). {RAT}

Davids, Thomas William Rhys (1843—1922)

An Orientalist, Davids was a professor of Pali and Buddhist literature at London. He was respected as one of the highest authorities on ancient Hindu religion, insisting in his works that the Buddha was an atheist. In an 1879 public lecture ("Is Life Worth Living?"), Davids rejected Christianity and the idea of immortality. McCabe termed him "probably an atheist."

Davidson, Donald (1930—)

Davidson has been described as being one of the most important of contemporary secular philosophers.

A professor at the University of California in Berkeley, he wrote Essays on Actions and Events (1980) and co-authored (with Patrick Suppes and Sidney Siegal) Decision Making: An Experimental Approach (1957).

A major concern of his is the number of interconnected themes in the philosophy of language, the philosophy of action, and the philosophy of mind. {AF}

Davidson, Edward H. (20th Century)

Davidson, with William J. Scheick, wrote *Paine, Scripture and Authority: The Age of Reason as Religious and Political Idea* (1994). The book, according to Gordon Stein, claims "that *The Age of Reason* was not written so much to express Paine's views on religion as it was to tell his views on the political system that was dependent upon religion for its survival." {*The American Rationalist*, July-August 1994}

Davidson, John (1857—1909)

A poet, Davidson despised academic philosophy but wrote many philosophical works. In *The Testament of John Davidson* (1908), he expounds a rationalist and partly Nietzschean creed. In *God and Mammon* (1907), he states, "I would have all men come out of Christendom into the universe." {RAT}

Davidson, Samuel (19th Century)

Davidson, who had a doctorate in divinity, wrote a critical work, *The Canon of the Bible: Its Formation, History, and Fluctuations*, in 1875.

Davidson, Thomas (Died 1826)

A bookseller and publisher, Davidson was prosecuted by the Vice Society in 1820 for selling the *Republican* and a publication of his own, the *Deist's Magazine*. Fined £300, Davidson was also sentenced to two years in the Oakham Gaol. {BDF}

Davidson, Thomas (1840—1900)

A philosophical writer, Davidson emigrated from Scotland to America. A close student of Catholic philosophy, he was invited by the Pope to cooperate in publishing the works of Thomas Aquinas. Davidson was, however, "agnostic as to the ultimate principle of things" and rejected all creeds. He worked with the American Ethical Societies and founded a New Fellowship at London, out of which the Fabian Society evolved. {RAT}

Davie, William (18th Century)

Davie, a co-founder of the University of North Carolina at Chapel Hill which opened in 1795, was accused of bringing Continental ideas of dancing and polite society as well as religious skepticism to the campus. (See entry for North Carolina Freethinkers.)

Davies, A(rthur) Powell (1902—1957)

As the Unitarian minister of All Souls Church in Washington, D.C., Davies was an eloquent speaker, sometimes described as "the greatest preacher of the twentieth century."

Justice William O. Douglas summarized Davies's outlook:

> America . . . must take the leadership in a world which has become a single, vast, reluctant community.

Davies had a part in founding Americans for Democratic Action, and he opposed the witch-hunting of the Joseph McCarthy era. Under his leadership, restaurants in the area of Washington, D.C., were desegregated. He favored the establishment of the Atomic Energy Commission, which put nuclear matters out of military and into civilian hands.

"There is no God in the sky," he preached. "God is in the heart that loves the sky's blueness." When a parishioner told him her son had, thanks to God, survived a catastrophe, Davies was shocked and replied, "What sort of God is that, playing favorites in this fantastic fashion!"

As for hell, he wrote, "The hell that we must try to avoid is the one that will rain down upon us from the skies if we are not wise enough to win the struggle for freedom, justice, and brotherhood." {U; U&U}

Davies, Blodwen (20th Century)

Davies was a member of the American Humanist Association. He wrote *A Study of Amber* (1973), about the Mennonites and their religion. {HNS}

Davies, C. Maurice (20th Century)

Davies, a freethinker, wrote *Unorthodox Religion* (1969). {GS}

Davies, Charles Maurice (1828—1910)

Davies, a writer, was ordained priest of the Church of England in 1852. He joined the staff of the *Daily Telegraph* (1870—1875) and published a series of articles on the religious life of London. In 1882 he left the church, and Cecil Rhodes employed him to investigate the sources of Gibbon's *Decline*. {RAT}

Davies, J. (19th Century)

An English freethinker, Davies wrote *A Short Sketch of the Scripturian's Creed* (1822). {GS}

Davies, Jean (20 Century)

Davies is the former President of World Federation of Voluntary Euthanasia Societies, former Chair of the British Voluntary Euthanasia Society, and a current European Community member of Voluntary Euthanasia Societies, United Kingdom.

Commending the Dutch experience, Davies has said,

> It is no wonder that the vast majority of Dutch citizens are pleased to have this possibility of choosing not to have a lingering death, even though the numbers who need this help to a good death are small. Medical advances continually enable us to live longer, which is wonderful as long as we are reasonably sound in mind and body. But we all know how miserable the closing stages of life can be; the right to choose to curtail that suffering seems likely to be increasingly asserted, and achieved, worldwide.
>
> {*International Humanist*, October 1998}

Davies, John C. (18th Century)

An English Jacobin, Davies in 1797 published a list of contradictions of the Bible under the title of *The Scripturian's Creed.* He was prosecuted and imprisoned. {BDF}

Davies, Joseph E. (1876-1958): See entry for George Orwell, who considered the American ambassador to the USSR "very stupid."

Davies, Ken (20th Century)

Davies is active in England with the Cardiff Humanists.

Davies, Mansel (1913—1995)

Davies, an emeritus professor of chemistry and author of a Thinker's Library volume on the development of science as well as books on molecular science, wrote in *New Humanist* (May 1994) that scientists eliminate absolute status from their conclusions, whereas the largely Greek-based Christian thought is dogmatic. An alternative and coherent outlook, he suggests, is offered by Theravada Buddhism, which can claim that (a) its over-riding concern is for the truth, which must be empirically sustainable; (b) the supernatural cannot, by its very nature, be found in this world; (c) the whole of our world is one and no distinctions are acceptable on the basis of sex, race, or beliefs, provided no harm is done to other individuals; and (d) there are no absolutes." A member of the

Rationalist Press Association since 1934, he wrote for *New Humanist* about Buddhism—in 1990, he wrote *A Scientist Looks at Buddhism*—and about Joseph Needham's history of Chinese science. A conscientious objector, he participated in the Pugwash talks, believing as he did in international collaboration. Davies was a committed supporter of the Welsh people and Welsh language.

Davies, Owen Thomas (1820—1893)

Davies, who was born in South Wales, landed at New Orleans, Louisiana, in 1850 and went into the coal mining business. His invention, which lessens the dangers of mining, is still used. Davies was a freethinker. {PUT}

Davies, Paul (20th Century)

A mathematical physicist, Davies won the 1995 Templeton Prize for Progress in Religion, a prize of one million dollars. The prize's previous winners have been Mother Teresa, the Rev. Billy Graham, Lord Jakobovits [a former chief rabbi of Britain and the Commonwealth), and Michael Novak, a neo-conservative Roman Catholic scholar. Davies, an Australian and professor of natural philosophy at the University of Adelaide, has written over twenty books, among them *The Mind of God* (1992), which discusses the nature of human consciousness, order in nature, and ideas about the universe's origin. "The more we discover about the world," Davies has said, "the more we find there's a purpose or design behind it all." However, he has described himself as not being a conventionally religious person, instead describing himself "as Einstein described himself," one who holds a deep reverence for nature and is convinced that the universe has a design or purpose." Many Einstein scholars object to that description.

Davies, Peter Maxwell [Sir] (1934—)

Davies, an eminent English composer and conductor, has written extensively for ballet, orchestra, ensemble, piano, and solo instruments. He became President of the Composer's Guild of Great Britain in 1986. Critic K. Robert Schwarz has described one of Davies' works, begun in the early 1960s but not performed until 1987: "Take the orgiastic sexuality, formalist complexity, and delirious excess of a Peter Greenaway film, cross it with the caustic political commentary of a Bertolt Brecht play, and you will have a point of reference from which to approach 'Resurrection.'" The ninety-minute work, performed on a compact disk by the BBC Philharmonic under his direction, has, Schwarz wrote, "little in the way of conventional narrative. A nameless family mouths 'traditional' values but practices only hypocrisy. The son, the opera's hero, is a dummy who never once sings; he is a nonconformist who must be made to fit into a puritanical society. Three surgeons devise an elaborate series of operations to remedy his supposed defects. The first dissects his brain, seeking to rectify his moral and intellectual faults; the second examines his heart, correcting his emotional and religious failings, and the third adjusts his 'sexual proclivities' by removing his testicles. But the surgery goes awry, and the patient is resurrected as the Antichrist, announcing the impending apocalypse. . . . The libretto is witty, often ingenious and viciously anticlerical. (A minister sings: 'For we can make the Book mean just anything we please,' And use it as a weapon to bring you to your knees./ With the promise of salvation shining on your steadfast face, / By the word of God, this Book, we can keep you in your place.'). The composer helpfully describes in clinical detail the transformation he has in mind during the metamorphosis of the patient into the Antichrist: 'Despite the lack of testes, which the Surgeons removed, the Patient's penis slowly becomes erect—a huge submachine gun, directed over the audience.' Mr. Davies," continues Schwarz, "is nearly as scandalous musically. 'Resurrection' is a triumph of post-modern eclecticism, filled with gleefully colliding historical styles that are never deployed haphazardly. A chamber orchestra, vocal soloists and a rock band are called on to perform music that ranges from angular atonality to parodies of Bachian chorales, from Edwardian ballads to 1960's rock. As in his maniacal 'Eight Songs for a Mad King,' of 1969, Mr. Davies somehow manages to turn these diverse idioms to the service of compelling theater, and even to give the impression of structural coherence."

Sir Peter, it is evident, enjoyed protesting against the sexual conformity demanded in a Thatcherite England and a Reaganite America. A recurring theme of "Resurrection," Schwarz notes," is the homophobia spouted by the hypocritical political and religious establishments. In one particularly memorable scene, three of society's supposed moral guardians—a Policeman, a Judge, and a Bishop—have an unscheduled meeting in a stall of a public lavatory." {K. Robert Schwarz, "A Portrait of the Antichrist as a Young Composer?" *The New York Times*, 14 January 1996}

Davies, Philip (20 Century)

Davies, who for several decades had developed in England a reputation for his Biblical scholarship, came out as a "born-again atheist" on a 1999 BBC1 religious magazine program, "Heaven and Earth."

Davies, Robertson (1913—1995)

"Fanaticism is . . . overcompensation for doubt," wrote the Canadian playwright and novelist in *Manticore*. (See entry for Ghosts.)

Davies, Stevie (20th Century)

Davies is an award-winning novelist and biographer who lives in Cheshire, Great Britain. She is author of *Emily Brontë, Heretic.*

Davies, Tony (20th Century)

Davies is author of *Humanism* (1997). Nicolas Walter, reviewing the book in *New Humanist* (March 1997), found the work of interest but lacking in scope. Finngeir Hiorth similarly found the work failed to include material about Paul Kurtz, Corliss Lamont, J. P. van Praag, or M. N. Roy. {*The American Rationalist*, September-October 1997}

Davies, William H. (1871—1940)

Davies was a noted Welsh "tramp" who wrote *Autobiography of the Super-Tramp* (1917) after spending years with American hobos. The work received George Bernard Shaw's attention and praise. Davies was a freethinker. {RI}

Da Vinci: See entry for Leonardo.

Davis, Arthur M. (20 Century)

Davis, writing "Good People—Bad People" in *Secular Nation* (October-December 1998), wonders why Moses walked down from Mt. Sinai with two stone tablets, on which was a commandment: "Thou shalt not kill," then orders his army to butcher thousands of men, women, and male children (*Numbers* 31:14,17-18).

Davis, Ben (20th Century)

Davis writes the "Gospel according to Benny Joe" in *Strange Angel* (1991). As described by Walter Hoops, the book "brings out the hypocrisy of fundamentalists while giving us a touching account of growing up Pentecostal." As to why Pentecostals meet in shabby buildings instead of building churches, the sensible answer is that if the Saviour returns per schedule what is the need for such luxury? "The author," writes Hoops, "who had his eye fixed on a preaching career turned out to be gay and consequently had a 'born again' experience he did not expect. He dedicates the book to all the ducks who refuse to live as chickens."

Davis, Bradley (20th Century)

Davis, while a student at Birmingham-Southern College, was one of the founders of Campus Freethought Alliance. {*International Humanist News*, December 1996}

Davis, Charles (20th Century)

Davis, with Carolynne Simms, is author of *Why I Left the Roman Catholic Church*. Davis is a British theologian.

Davis, Elmer (1890—1958)

A newspaper man, radio commentator, and author of *But We Were Born Free* (1954), about an attack by Senator Joseph McCarthy, Elmer Davis wrote concerning humanism:

> I am afraid I have never attempted to define my philosophic position, even to myself. Naturalistic humanism seems, from your definitions, to be about the nearest of those you mention; but I am skeptical about the ability of mankind to attain the good life at any time soon. This due to something that might be called original sin or original stupidity—whatever it is, there is plenty wrong with the human race.
>
> {CE; WAS, 19 July 1954}

Davis, John M. (20th Century)

Davis is author of a two-part article on "The Origin and Establishment of the Christ Myth" in *Secular Nation* (Fall 1995 and Winter 1995). "The Jesus myth," he explains in a scholarly work, "may have begun as an Essenic legend, a faction of Mithraism, or a hybrid created by the Roman conquerors of Palestine. When all the elements of older myth are stripped away, very little remains of Jesus Christ."

Davis, R. C. W. (20th Century)

Davis, a retired teacher from Los Angeles inner-city schools, is a freethinker who has written in *Truth Seeker* of the joy of sex at the age of seventy. "The more intensely one invests love, affection, excitement, and respect," he has written from his home in Mexico, "the more richly they are rewarded in those post-September years, the doldrum years of life—if you allow them to be so." He advises, "And of course, Mr. McNoodle, if you can't rise to the occasion this time around, that doesn't mean you're hors de combat for the night," for as he explains, "five fingers can constitute an effective cavity," oral sex has its special virtues, and there's always *mañana*.

Davis, Robert (20th Century)

The Iowa-born Davis, a past president of the Bertrand Russell Society, is a non-theist and a Russell scholar.

Davis, Robert Gorham (1908—1998)

An activist and humanist, Davis was a professor of English and Comparative Literature at Columbia University. In 1957 he became a visiting professor and stayed for nearly twenty years, retiring in 1976. In 1973 he won the Distinguished Teacher Award at the Columbia School of General Studies, at which time it was noted that he had helped reorganize the University Senate to give students a voice in the governance of the university.

Like many other intellectuals of his time, Davis was interested in left-wing politics and joined the Communist Party, leaving after becoming disillusioned with Communism following the Hitler-Stalin pact of 1939.

Davis wrote influential studies of John Dos Passos, C. P. Snow, and James T. Farrell. A reviewer of fiction for *Partisan* Review, *Commentary, The American Scholar,* and *The New York Times Book Review,* he taught creative writing at Harvard and at Columbia taught a course in comparative religion called "Metaphor, Symbol and Myth." He was a contributor to *Freethought Today* and, in a letter to *The New York Times* (5 July 1992) commented that

> The God who "revealed Himself" in the Scriptures knew no more of the world and its future than those He presumably addressed. Jesus warned that the final days of tribulation were near: "Truly, I say to you, this generation will not pass away till all these things take place." But they did not take place, and have not yet. On no clear evidence theologians and philosophers declare God to be omniscient and omnicompetent. Plainly if there were such a God who really wished to reveal Himself to mankind, He could do so in a way that left no doubt.

Commenting upon an Op-Ed tribute by Arthur Schlesinger Jr. to Reinhold Niebuhr, Davis wrote,

> As theologians now acknowledge, original sin is an illusion, too, based on the folk tale of Adam and Eve, and some impossible genetics. St. Augustine, one of its originators, conceived it largely in sexual terms. As a direct result of Adam's sin men's lusts, he declared, became separated from their wills. These effects, along with weakened will and intelligence, were transmitted through 'corrupted semen' to all Adam's descendants.

Such a transmission of original sin through propagation, he noted, was reformulated at the Council of Trent and repeated as late as 1950 in an encyclical of Pius XII, which "leaves the doctrine of evolution an open question" but still declares in conclusion, "Original sin is the result of a sin committed, in actual historical fact, by an individual named Adam, and it is a quality native to all of us, only because it has been handed down by descent from him."

Despite what Schlesinger says of Niebuhr's debt to Augustine and Calvin, Davis commented in a *Times* letter (23 June 1992),

> we can certainly rule out original sin as Augustine invented it, a Lamarckist well before Lamarck. As for Calvin and freedom, it was under Calvin, theocratic ruler of Geneve, that Servetus was, for unorthodox writings on the Trinity, burned alive.

In his *New York Times* obituary, Davis was praised by Schlesinger for his "honorable and honest" character . {*Free Inquiry*, Fall 1990}

Davis, Singleton Waters (20th Century)

In Los Angeles, Davis edited *Humanitarian Review* (1903—1911). In 1907 he wrote *A Future Life?* {FUS}

Davis, William B. (20 Century)

Davis is an actor who has been seen on the television series "X-Files" and is called "Cancer Man," because of his chainsmoking of cigarettes. In *Rolling Stone* (15 May 1997), he told interviewer Anthony Bozza that he did not believe in UFOs, that "I think we live in a very barren universe. Our task is essentially existential. If we're going to have any meaning in this universe, we have to make it for ourselves. It's not going to come from outside." {CA}

D'Avoine, C. L. (20th Century)

In Bombay, D'Avoine edited the Indian journal, *Reason*, from 1931 to 1946. {FUK}

Dawkins, (Clinton) Richard (1941—)

Dawkins's father, who worked in the British colonial service in Nyasaland, now Malawi, moved to Kenya at the outbreak of the Second World War. Richard, his son the zoologist, was born in Nairobi. While an undergraduate, he was taught at Oxford University by Niko Tinbergen, the Dutch-born animal behaviorist (and, later, Nobel Prize winner). His doctorate developed a mathematical model of decision-making in animals.

His works include *The Selfish Gene* (1976), in which he described his theory of the self-replicating "meme," as a way of understanding the transmission of human culture and ideas. His *The Blind Watchmaker: Why the Evidence of Evolution Reveals a Universe Without Design* (1986) became a best-selling study of Darwinian design. Ian Parker has appropriately called Dawkins "Britain's village atheist," as is illustrated by his "case against God" which is entitled, "Lions 10, Christians Nil" (*New Humanist,* June 1992) and which concludes,

> Science offers us an explanation of how complexity (the difficult) arose out of simplicity (the easy). The hypothesis of God offers no

> worthwhile explanation for anything, for it simply postulates what we are trying to explain. It postulates the difficult to explain, and leaves it at that. We cannot prove that there is no God, but we can safely conclude that He is very, very improbable indeed.

A leading evolutionary theorist, Dawkins is author of *Viruses of the Mind, The 1992 Voltaire Lecture* (British Humanist Association), which in friendly user fashion describes how computer viruses wreak havoc and how, analogously, children's minds have long been "shaped by evolution to soak up the culture of her people," leading to beliefs in the absurdities of religion. He describes in a "medical textbook" a viral infection:

> 1. The patient typically finds himself impelled by some deep, inner conviction that something is true, or right, or virtuous: a conviction that doesn't seem to owe anything to evidence or reason, but which, nevertheless he feels as totally compelling and convincing. We doctors refer to such a belief as "faith."

Matt Cherry, reviewing the Dawkins book, wrote in *New Humanist* (March, 1993):

> Viruses are distinguished from other self-replicators, because they are harmful to their hosts (one reason why some consider the human species to be a virus on the planet Earth). Therefore, Dawkins's charge that religion is a virus of the mind rests on the argument that religion would not be accepted if judged by the criteria best adapted to selecting true beliefs and beneficial behaviour. The arguments that religion is false and harmful are familiar and accepted by most rationalists, and rejected by religionists. *Viruses of the Mind* is therefore unlikely to change the mind of any religious believers familiar with rationalist arguments.

In 1993, Dawkins wrote for *Free Inquiry* (Summer, 1993) about computer viruses as being a model for an informational epidemiology: "It is no wonder that child brains are gullible, open to almost any suggestion, vulnerable to subversion, easy prey to Moonies, scientologists, and nuns. Like immune-deficient patients, children are wide open to mental infections that adults might brush off without effort." He is not pessimistic about the future, however, adding, "Many children emerge unscathed from the worst that nuns and mullahs can throw at them. Anthony Kenny's [who was exalted by the "laying on of hands" to celebrate Mass when he was ordained as a Roman Catholic priest] own story has a happy ending. He eventually renounced his orders because he could no longer tolerate the obvious contradictions within Catholic belief, and he is now a highly respected scholar. But one cannot help remarking that it must be a powerful infection indeed that took a man of his wisdom and intelligence—now president of the British Academy, no less—three decades to fight off. Am I unduly alarmist to fear for the soul of my six-year-old innocent?" The article, an abridged version of *Dennett and His Critics: Demystifying Mind* (1993), is included in *Challenges to the Enlightenment, Essays in Defense of Reason and Science* (1994).

In 1994 in "The Vision Thing" on English Channel Four, Dawkins made powerful arguments for a philosophy devoid of supernaturalism and for an enthusiastic celebration of life without the baggage which religion embraces.

"If all the achievements of scientists were wiped out tomorrow," Dawkins has said, "there would be no doctors but witch doctors, no transport faster than a horse, no computers, no printed books, no agriculture beyond subsistence peasant farming. If all the achievements of theologians were wiped out tomorrow, would anyone notice the smallest difference?"

In 1995, Dawkins wrote a book that offered a novel answer to the basic philosophic question, What is the purpose of life? In *River Out of Time: A Darwinian View of Life* (1995), he paints a new picture of Samuel Butler's response, that a chicken is an egg's way of making another egg.

From his viewpoint as an evolutionary biologist, Dawkins posits that the central purpose of evolution is the survival of DNA, not of the beings that are the DNA's temporary expression. Life perhaps began when the first molecule of RNA, DNA's elder cousin, got itself more or less accurately replicated in some natural stew of chemicals on the primitive earth. The first living cells, the first plants and animals, emerged merely because they were better mechanisms for repeating that first ancient accident of replication." In short, the purpose of life is for DNA to endure, not for humans to bow to one of the various supernatural divinities. According to Dawkins, DNA is not just a human's way of making another human: "The universe we observe has precisely the properties we should expect if there is, at bottom, no design, no purpose, no evil and no good, nothing but blind, pitiless indifference."

Parker has said that Dawkins is considered by man both arrogant and aggressive, a person who scraps eloquently and energetically with bishops, charlatans, and astrologers (declaring that all the latter should be jailed). "I'm a friendly enough sort of chap," Dawkins told Parker. "I'm not a hostile person to meet. But I think it's important to realize that when two opposite points of view are expressed with equal intensity, the truth does not necessarily lie exactly halfway between them. It is possible for one side to be simply wrong."

In 1989, Dawkins was elected an honorary associate of the Rationalist Press Association. Also, he is a Humanist Laureate in the Council for Secular Humanism's International Academy of Humanism as well as an Honorary Associate of the National Secular Society. In 1996, Dawkins was named Humanist of the Year by the American Humanist Association. He is an honorary associate of the New Zealand Association of Rationalists and Humanists. Dawkins signed Humanist Manifesto 2000.

For the international secular humanist quarterly, *Free Inquiry*, he is a senior editor. In its pages (Spring 1998), he wrote about "The Emptiness of Theology" that

> Science has eradicated smallpox, can immunize against most previously deadly viruses, can kill most previously deadly bacteria. Theology has done nothing but talk of pestilence as the wages of sin. . . . What has theology ever said that is of the smallest use to anybody? When has theology ever said anything that is demonstrably true and is not obvious? . . . The achievements of theologians don't do anything, don't affect anything, don't mean anything. What makes anyone think that "theology" is a subject at all?

His *Climbing Mount Improbable* (1996), according to Roy Silson,

> minimises technical language while providing clear and critical explanations of the concepts, subtle mechanisms, and interactions now associated with natural selection. . . . Apart from its subject, which ought to be part of the education of all caring humans, it exemplifies a model of careful rational thought which others would do well to copy.

"There is no reason for believing that any sort of gods exist and quite good reason for believing that they do not exist and never have," Dawkins wrote in "The Improbability of God." In the same article, he wrote that the Argument from Design "has been destroyed as a reason for believing in a God."

Unweaving the Rainbow: Science, Delusion, and the Appetite for Wonder (1998) reveals Dawkins's dismay that most people have muddle-headed views about reality, that they are therefore attracted to superstition, fantasies, and all kinds of pseudoscience. However, organisms have always been indifferent to any putative greater good, he again states, and "natural selection is never aware of the long-term future. It is not aware of anything. Improvements come about not through foresight but by genes coming to outnumber their rivals in gene pools. . . . There is no foresight."

On the Web: <www.cs.wisc.edu/~krisna/dawkins.html>.

(See Dawkins's "Science and Sensibility, Where We Stand at the End of Millennium," *Free Inquiry*, Spring 1999.) {CA; E; *Free Inquiry*, Winter 1993 and Winter 1996-1997; HNS2; "The Improbability of God," *Free Inquiry*, Summer 1998;*New Humanist*, November 1994; Nicholas Wade, "Double Helixes, Chickens and Eggs," *The New York Times Magazine*, 29 January 1995; Jan Parker, "Richard Dawkins's Evolution," *The New Yorker*, 9 September 1996}

Dawn, A(lexander) F(elix) (1900-1997)

Dawn was a humanist activist, a member of the Ethical movement and the Rationalist Press Association from around 1922. **Donna Dawn**, his wife, is also a humanist activist. {*New Humanist*, March 1998}

Dawson, B. (19th Century)

In Spennymoor, England, in 1879, Dawson raised the tricolor flag from his summer house and announced he was ready to receive National Secular Society members. He exemplifies how the initiative for starting freethought groups often rests with a single individual. {RSR}

Dawson, Joseph Martin (20th Century)

Dawson, a freethinker, wrote *Separate Church and State Now* (1948), *Baptists and the American Public* (1956), and *The American Way in Church, State, and Society* (1979). {GS}

Dawson, Oswald (19th Century)

Dawson was secretary in 1893 of a Leeds, England, Legitimation League. With Wordsworth Donisthorpe and J. Grevz Fisher, the League and official secularism were close in their goals: to secure legal rights for illegitimate children. But when Dawson began to advocate free love, even such lovers of liberty as Frederick Millar and J. H. Levy were alienated. In 1895 the League admitted that its purpose was to register cohabitation without marriage, and by 1897 free love was openly advocated in the *Adult*. At this point the *Freethinker* parted company, and Arthur and Hypatia Bonner refused to include the League in their *Directory of Reform Societies*.

For secularists of this period, sexual irregularities were something to be avoided: they were reformers, not revolutionaries, in morals as in politics. {RSR}

Day, Dorothy (1897-1980)

Day, a nonbeliever-turned-Catholic, started as a young beauty who was known for drinking and intellectualizing with the radicals in a Greenwich Village bar called the Hell Hole. She became a paramour of Eugene O'Neill, who modeled a character in his "Moon for the Misbegotten" after her. *The New York Times* described her *The Eleventh Virgin* (1923) as "one more adolescent novel." An anarchist and pacifist, she detailed her bohemianism and radical ways in a memoir, *The Long Loneliness*. Day did not become a Catholic until she was thirty.

"Entertaining Angels," a 1996 movie about her, implies that she embraced Catholicism not from an understanding of its theology but, rather, from her romantic disappointment. Her lover, Lionel Moise, is shown dropping her off at an abortionist's before skipping town; and her common-law husband, Forster Batterham—an English atheist—is shown refusing to marry her after she gave birth to their daughter in 1927.

She called the infant Tamar, Hebrew for "little palm tree." "I did not want my child to flounder as I had often floundered," she explained upon deciding to have the infant baptized a Catholic. Although terrified that any of her radical friends would catch her in prayer, she nevertheless attended catechism classes and, upon meeting an itinerant French intellectual—Peter Maurin, who urged her to live "little, simple, and poor" à la St. Francis of Assisi—adopted Catholicism and started publishing. *The Catholic Worker*, which cost her $57 to found in 1933, sold for one penny. Its circulation grew from 2,500 to 200,000 by the time the U. S. entered World War II.

Day's left-wing religious movement was devoted to humanistic causes, feeding and housing the poor. Her precepts were elementary: Feed the hungry; give drink to the thirsty; clothe the naked; shelter the homeless; care for the sick; visit prisoners; comfort the afflicted; and afflict the comfortable. Leading thinkers—Jacques Maritain, John LaFarge, Hilaire Belloc, Thomas Merton, Cesar Chavez, Daniel and Philip Berrigan—found her an inspiration. Abbie Hoffman, the flower-child of Vietnam war resistance, called her "the first hippie." A priest called her "a trumpet calling for all of us to find Christ in the breadlines."

Day visited Fidel Castro in Cuba, fasted in St. Peter's Square for peace, and worked with the poor mainly at St. Joseph House on Manhattan's East 1 Street. The newspaper she founded has not raised its cost—it still costs one penny. (See entry for Greenwich Village Humanist Club.) {Brian Kates, New York *Daily News*, 12 April 1999}

Day, Helen Hamilton Gardener (Born 1858)

Day was an American writer and rationalist. Her *Men, Women, and Gods* and *Facts and Fictions of Life* (1895) indicate her freethinking. {RAT}

Daytre, Carol (20th Century)

Daytre in 1972 was Vice President of the Humanist Society of Greater New York.

De Angulo, Jaime (20th Century)

De Angulo wrote *The "Trial" of Ferrer* (1920). {GS}

De Cordova, June E. (20th Century)

De Cordova, for a 1942 M.A. thesis at the University of Michigan, wrote a study of Robert G. Ingersoll's speeches. {FUS}

DEAD SEA SCROLLS: See entry for Essenes.

DEAD WHITE EUROPEAN AUTHORS, DEAD WHITE MALES

Collegiates have long been required to read those writers who constitute the so-called "core of Western literature," writers who are, therefore, the "proper object of serious literary study." The University of Chicago had its Great Books, promoted in 1946 by the University of Chicago's Chancellor Robert Maynard Hutchins and listing those books considered most worthy of a student's attention. Clifton Fadiman had his *Lifetime Reading Plan* (1959), inspired in part by his visit to a New Canaan, Connecticut, high school and being a participant in the oral examination being given to that school's honors English class. Harold Bloom in the 1990s has his *Western Canon*. Bloom's canon includes *the* fewer than fifty or so true heavyweights (all covered by Cliff's Notes, a series of "cram books" which survey authors and their works in the event the collegiate believes there is insufficient time to read the originals). Also, it includes another eight hundred fifty authors.

The **DWEA**s (sometimes called **DWM**s, although the authors are not always males), or "dead white European authors" included in most such lists are these: Shakespeare, Dante, Chaucer, Cervantes, Montaigne, Molière, Milton, Johnson, Goethe, Wordsworth, Austen, Whitman, Dickinson, Dickens, George Eliot, Tolstoy, Ibsen, Freud, Proust, Joyce, Woolf, Kafka, Borge, Neruda, Pessoa, and Beckett. In addition are the ancient Greeks, Aeschylus, Sophocles, and so forth.

However, critic McGrath complains that Bloom includes Kenneth Koch but not Sylvia Plath; Tony Kushner but not John Guare; Nora Neale Hurston but not Alice Walker. McGrath adds, "*Especially* not Alice Walker, who in the text gets slammed more than once as an example of the kind of writer overvalued by the 'academic lemmings,' as Bloom calls them. Almost all of Roth makes the cut but only one novel by Updike (*The Witches of Eastwick*). Just two books by Nabokov but four by Walter Abish. O'Hara but not Thurber. J. P. Marquand but not V. S. Pritchett. And so on and so on. It's hard to tell whether the choices are the product of fine discrimination or simply the result of an hour or so of shelf-gazing." At issue is whether schools are properly preparing students by emphasizing mainly the DWEAs or DWMs.

Where, complain the critics, are the African authors, the Asian, and the others representative of the entire human race, not just those who are English-speaking. (See entry for Harold Bloom.)

DEADLINES

- Because I was too fucking busy and vice versa!

—Dorothy Parker
when asked why she had not
gotten a story in on deadline

Dean, Paul (1789—1860)

An associate of the aged John Murray of the First Universalist Church in Boston, Dean assumed the pastorate of this most influential of the denomination's churches when Murray died. But he disagreed with Hosea Ballou, who rejected all future punishment and insisted on a limited but real suffering for sinners after death, eventually leaving the Universalists and becoming a Unitarian unhappy that his "Restorationist" movement in opposition to Ballou had failed. {U&U}

Dear, Russell (20th Century)

Dear writes for the *New Zealand Rationalist and Humanist.* He has noted that although some religionists fear the "theory" of evolution, they might better fear the Quantum Theory and the Theory of Relativity. Meanwhile, they write letters to editors happily proclaiming that the Flat Earth Society still exists.

DEATH

- I believe that when I die, I shall rot, and nothing of my ego will survive. I am not young, and I love life. But I should scorn to shiver with terror at the thought of annihilation. Happiness is nonetheless true happiness because it must come to an end, nor do thought and love lose their value because they are not everlasting.

That sentiment, from Bertrand Russell's *What I Believe* (1925), is common among philosophic naturalists. Supernaturalists may wish for immortality and survival in some future existence. Most non-believers, however, side with Clarence Darrow's "The Myth of Immortality," which recognizes the hopelessness of finding any evidence that the individual will persist beyond the grave. The purpose of life is to *live*, not to invent fanciful metaphysical schemes about a hereafter. "When we fully understand the brevity of life," Darrow wrote, "its fleeting joys and unavoidable pains; when we accept the fact that all men and women are approaching an inevitable doom: the consciousness of it should make us more kindly and considerate of each other. This feeling should make men and women use their best efforts to help their fellow travelers on the road, to make the path brighter and easier as we journey on. It should bring a closer kinship, a better understanding, and a deeper sympathy for the wayfarers who must live a common life and die a common death."

Robert Ingersoll wrote that he liked K'ung Fu-tse's response when asked about the possibility of a hereafter: "How should I know anything about another world when I know so little of this?" Ingersoll, no believer in Heaven or Hell or Immortality or Soul, wrote, "The only thing that makes life endurable in this world is human love, and yet, according to Christianity, that is the very thing that we are not to have in the other world. We are to be so taken up with Jesus and angels that we shall care nothing about our brothers and sisters that have been damned. We shall be so carried away with the music of the harp that we shall not even hear the wail of father or mother. Such a religion is a disgrace to human nature."

Disposing of the dead varies depending upon tribal customs. Eating parts of a corpse (necrophagia) has been an approved practice in some tribes. In ancient Iran the dead were given to the dogs and birds. Medieval Chinese emperors were buried with their horses, soldiers, and food to speed them on their way. Parsis expose the bodies to vultures on "the towers of silence." In Tibet the flesh might be cut from the bones and fed to dogs and birds, whereupon the bones are buried. The body might be thrown into water or jungle or desert places. The Bishnoi of India, a caste of farmers, cover their dead in salt and place them in an unmarked trench. The most common forms in modern cultures are burial in the earth and cremation. Organized religion has developed varied rituals which range from the simple to the complex.

A corpse has three possible fates in India, according to Jonathan Parry's essay, "The End of the Body": "It is eaten as carrion and turns to excrement; it is buried and turns to maggots; or it is burnt and turns to ash." Of these, cremation is not only a more ecology-conscious method but is also a sacrificial offering. Deformed, disfigured, or lame individuals are not deemed worthy of cremation and usually end up in the cleansing stream of the Ganges. Parry tells of a corrupt official in Bihar, one who in life was a bad individual, whose corpse despite being smeared with flammable resins refused to burn, implying that water can cleanse but that fire must not be contaminated by badness.

Non-believers often arrange cremations, which are followed some time afterward by memorial services that recall humorous and serious moments in the life of the deceased. It is not uncommon to find, at such memorials, that laughter mixes with plentiful food and drink, music, and perhaps movies showing highlights of their friend's life.

In France the majority of Catholics are buried, cremation's fire being too closely associated with Hell. In some American states, bodies can be buried legally in the backyard. In Mexico the Cipreses del Bosque graveyard contains bodies buried standing up, rather than lying down. In pre-Islamic times, Egyptian dead faced east to the rising sun.

Burial plots sometimes cost considerably more than others do. It is generally agreed that the cemetery with the most cachet is that of Père Lachaise—its opening in 1804 was marked by Abélard's and Héloïse's reburial together. They were eventually joined by Chopin, Oscar Wilde, Modigliani, and Jim Morrison. At the Montmartre cemetery are buried Belioz, Degas, and Nijinsky.

Some cemetery caretakers have problems when the living protest that the dead have been buried near a former enemy. Frank Lloyd Wright's third wife's friends, unhappy that he was buried with his second wife, dug the body up, cremated it, and reburied his cremains with hers.

The biggest French graveyard contains 130,000 unidentified soldiers in the ossuary at Douaumont, near Verdun. Electric crematoriums are providing less expensive funerals for many in India. Three thousand Chinese, approving of Deng Xiaoping's ashes being scattered at sea in 1997, had been "sent off" the same way within two years.

Elisabeth Kübler-Ross summarizes the five stages of dying: denial, anger, bargaining, depression, and acceptance.

Other observations on death:

- It's not that I'm afraid to die. I just don't want to be there when it happens. . . . . When I'm dead, I'm dead. I'll worry about it then.

  —**Woody Allen**

- Sleep is lovely, death is better still, not to have been born is of course the miracle.

  —Heinrich Heine

- Those who welcome death have only tried it from the ears up.

  —Wilson Mizner

- I did not attend his funeral, but I wrote a nice letter saying I approved of it.

  —**Mark Twain**

- Die, my dear Doctor? That's the last thing I shall do!

  —Lord Palmerston

- If you don't go to other people's funerals, they won't go to yours.

  —Anonymous

- Grave, n. A place in which the dead are laid to await the coming of the medical student.

  —**Ambrose Bierce**
  The Devil's Dictionary

(See entries for A. Alvarez, Burial Practices, Cremation, Memorial Societies, and Jessica Mitford. For an account of the *only* individual who ever outwitted death, see the entry for Sisyphus.)

{CE; *The Economist*, 14 November 1998; ER}

DEATH AND TOMBSTONES

- Here lies an Atheist
  All dressed up
  And no place to go

  —found in a Thurmont, Maryland, cemetery

- Here lies Ezekial Aikle
  Age 102
  The Good Die Young

  —found in an East Dalhousie Cemetery, Nova Scotia

- Here lies Ann Mann
  Who lived an old maid
  But died an old Mann
  Dec. 8, 1767

  —tombstone in a London, England, cemetery

- Anna Wallace
  The children of Israel wanted bread
  And the Lord sent them manna.
  Old clerk Wallace wanted a wife,
  And the Devil sent him Anna.
  —tombstone for Anna Wallace, Ribbesford, England
- Sir John Strange
  Here lies an honest lawyer,
  And that is Strange.
  —on an English tombstone
- Under the sod and under the trees
  Lies the body of Jonathan Pease.
  He is not here, there's only the pod:
  Pease shelled out and went to God.
  —from an 1880s tomb, Nantucket, Massachusetts
- Harry Edsel Smith
  Born 1903 – Died 1942
  Looked up the elevator shaft to see
  If the car was on the way down. It was.
  —on Smith's tombstone in Albany, New York
  {Cloudsmith on the Internet}

DEATH WITH DIGNITY NET

The Death With Dignity Net is on the Web: <http://www.islandnet.com/~deathnet>.

DEATH, A FREETHINKER'S

When he learned he had Kaposi's sarcoma, Fernando Vargas accepted the fact that he had a limited time to live. A freethinker with a sense of humor about his once having been a Catholic altar boy, Vargas objected to expressions such as "*ravaged* by cancer," "an AIDS *victim*," and "the *battle* against AIDS." He once had had hepatitus, he often had had colds, and he reasoned that the cancer named after Austrian dermatologist Moritz Kaposi (1837-1902) was just another physiological problem to confront his body.

When first hospitalized, the electrical engineer—who as a sound engineer had recorded Liza Minnelli's first demonstration record in a studio he co-owned—read astronomy books and magazines, always with the aim of keeping current. When one day a priest visited his room and in some kind of spiritual act touched the forehead of the sleeping patient who shared the room, Vargas gruffly ordered him out and complained for the rest of the day about having been upset by "a shaman in black." The priest's visit, he complained, was worse than his having to suffer such "excruciatingly intensive internal pains."

"Dying is a natural act," Vargas said. "It is so unnatural to think of it as a 'battle' or something that will be followed by a wishful continuation of life." His primary physician reported he had never before seen such inspiring behavior by a person who lived only six months after being diagnosed with cancer. (See entry for Fernando Vargas.)

DEATHBED VISIONS

- No Hindu is on record as having met either the Virgin Mary or Jesus Christ.
  —Paul Edwards

DEBAPTISM

Barbara Smoker has devised a "de-baptism certificate," one whereby former members of religious groups can "come forward" and have their past baptisms canceled. {*The Freethinker*, October 1998}

DEBATE: See entry for Elenchus, the method Socrates used to refute the thinking of others.

DEBAUCHEE

- Debauchee, n. One who has so earnestly pursued pleasure that he has had the misfortune to overtake it.
  —**Ambrose Bierce**
  The Devil's Dictionary

De Beauvoir, Simone: See entry for Beauvoir.

De Benneville, George (1703—1793)

An itinerant preacher of Universalism, de Benneville was the son of French Huguenot parents who escaped religious persecution by fleeing to England. When he preached his Universalism in France, he was arrested and condemned to death by guillotine. When De Benneville received a reprieve he moved to Germany, Holland, and Philadelphia, where in 1741 he was among the first, if not the first, of Universalist ministers in the country. {FUS; U; U&U}

De Bergerac: See entry for Cyrano.

de Boer, Madzy Rood (20th Century)

At the Eighth International Humanist and Ethical Union (IHEU) World Congress in Hannover (1982), Prof. de Boer of the Netherlands addressed the group.

De Bona, Maurice Jr. (20th Century)

De Bona, an atheist, wrote *God Rejected: A Summary of Atheistic Thought* (1976) and *Atheist Reality of the Brain* (1995). {GS}

De Bosis, Adolfo (20th Century)

De Bosis is an Italian poet. With D'Annunzio, he founded *Il Convito* and is a Cavalliere of the Crown of Italy. His agnosticism is expressed in *Amori ac Silentio* (1914). He scouts the Christian message and urges us to turn away from "the double mystery of the where and whence." {RAT}

De Buen, Oden (19th Century)

De Buen was a professor at the University of Barcelona, Spain, and one of the active freethinkers of his time. He edited *La Republica* and *El Radical* as well as contributed to *Las Dominicales del Libre Pensamiento*. He was at the International Freethought Congress held in Paris, 1889, and spoke out for peace movements. {PUT}

De Camp, L(yon) Sprague (1907—)

De Camp is author of technical and science fiction titles. A skeptic of UFO sightings, he has written for *Free Inquiry*. In addition to his "Conan" series, he was technical advisor to the film "Conan the Barbarian." His numerous works include verse, fiction, television scripts, and non-fiction. {*Free Inquiry*, Spring 1982; FUS}

De Cleyre, Voltairine (1866—1912)

An American freethinker and anarchist, De Cleyre was named by her father, an admirer of Voltaire. When twenty-one, she was seduced, then abandoned, by a former preacher from Scotland who was lecturing on socialism.

She married a freethinker, James B. Elliott, a Thomas Paine aficionado like herself. Reichert has written of her friendship with Emma Goldman and her personal life. Goldman is said to have asked to be buried alongside Voltairine's grave, which was said to have been an indication of her major contributions to American anarchism; however, gay historians Jonathan Katz, Adrien Saks, and Lynne Yamaguchi Fletcher, believe the request was more an emotional one.

In 1886, De Cleyre edited a Midwestern publication, *Progressive Age*. Although she could have earned large sums of money for speaking and writing, De Cleyre lived and worked in slums all her life.

In "The Gods and the People," she wrote,

What have you done, O Skies,
That the millions should kneel to you?
Why should they lift wet eyes,
Grateful with human dew?

Where the swamps of humanity sicken,
Read the answer in dumb, white scars.
You, Skies, gave the sore and the stricken
The light of your far-off stars.

(See article by Gordon Stein in *The American Rationalist* (Mar-Apr 1995.)
{EU, William O. Reichert; WWS}

DECLINE OF HUMAN CREATIVITY

Some individuals' creativity appears to increase exponentially the older they get. Of the exceptions, individuals who reach a peak, then decline to their own and others' dismay, Edmund Clerihew Bentley noted

> There is a great deal to be said
> For being dead.

{Timothy Garton Ash, *The New York Review of Books, 22 October 1998*}

De Coninck, Lucien (20th Century)

When De Coninck signed Humanist Manifesto II, he was a professor at the University of Gand (Ghent), Belgium. In 1966 in Paris, De Coninck addressed the Fourth International Humanist and Ethical Union World Congress. {HM2}

De Coster, Charles (1827—1879)

A Belgian writer, De Coster was the son of a high official of the Papal Embassy at Brussels. After teaching literature at Ixelles Military Academy, he wrote *Légende de Thyl Ulenspiegel* (1868), a story of Flemish life in the days of the Inquisition. {RAT}

De Croo, Herman (20th Century)

A Belgian, De Croo addressed the Eleventh International Humanist and Ethical Union (IHEU) World Congress held in Brussels (1990).

De Dominicis, Saverio (Born 1845)

De Dominicis was an Italian educationist. He was one of the first Italians to adopt Darwinism, which he defended against the clergy. De Deominicis is a positivist. {RAT}

De Duve, Christian René (1917—)

A Belgian chemist, biologist, and educator, de Duve has been a member of the editorial board of *Subcellular Biochemistry* (1971—1987), *Preparatory Biochemistry* (1971—1980), and *Molecular Cellular Biochemistry* (1973—1980). A holder of numerous international honors, in 1974 he was awarded the 1974 Nobel Prize for his investigation of the structure of cells.

In his textbook, *A Guided Tour of the Living Cell*, de Duve wrote: "If you equate the probability of the birth of a bacterial cell to that of the chance assembly of its component atoms, even eternity will not suffice to produce one for you. So you might as well accept, as do most scientists, that the process was completed in no more than one billion years and that it took place entirely on the surface of our planet." What was difficult, he added, was getting the simplest chemicals to the first specialized cells, after which "it took no more than 150,000 generations for an ape to develop into the inventor of calculus." According to science writer Malcolm W. Browne, when de Duve was asked whether "some guiding hand" was needed for the process, he responded,

> The answer of modern molecular biology to this much-debated question is categorical: chance, and chance alone, did it all, from primeval soup to man, with only natural selection to sift its effects. This affirmation now rests on overwhelming factual evidence.

But the succession of chances that created life did not operate in a vacuum, he said. "It operated in a universe governed by orderly laws and made of matter endowed with specific properties. These laws and properties are the constraints that shape evolutionary roulette and restrict the numbers that can turn up. Among these numbers are life and all its wonders, including the conscious mind." In a follow-up of that *New York Times* article (4 July 1995), De Duve wrote the present author as follows:

> I subscribe without reservation to the principle of free inquiry, untrammeled by any dogma, preconceived idea, or ideological bias. My recent efforts have focused on the origin of life, which I try to explain entirely in terms of the laws of physics and chemistry. I see the emergency of life as a highly deterministic process that was bound to occur under the conditions that prevailed on Earth four billion years ago and would likewise occur anywhere and any time similar conditions prevailed, a cosmic imperative.
>
> However, I believe it is wrong to identify free inquiry with atheism, which rests on faith no less than does religious belief. This point has been lucidly made by the Hungarian-Swedish virologist and cancer specialist George Klein, who, protesting not to be an agnostic but an atheist, writes (p. 203) in *The Atheist and the Holy City* (MIT Press 1990): "I am, indeed, an atheist. My attitude is based on faith. . . . The absence of a creator, the nonexistence of God is my childhood faith, my adult belief, unshakable and holy."
>
> I do not share my friend's faith but rather keep an open mind, faced with—and awed by—the mystery that surrounds the origin of the universe of which we are a part. My own reading of the scientific facts presently available on the nature, origin, and evolution of life has led me to reject the concept of a meaningless universe, advocated by Jacques Monod, Steven Weinberg, and other scientists: If the universe is not meaningless, what is its meaning? For me, this meaning is to be found in the structure of the universe, which happens to be such as to produce thought by way of life and mind. Thought, in turn, is a faculty whereby the universe can reflect upon itself, discover its own structure, and apprehend such immanent entities as truth, beauty, goodness, and love. Such is the meaning of the universe, as I see it.
>
> Not all scientists may agree with my reading of the facts. But this does not entitle them to claim scientific legitimacy for their own reading, often misleadingly presented to the lay public as ineluctably enforced by scientific knowledge. I have tremendous faith in modern science and have devoted my life to it. But I feel that science should not be arrogant.

De Duve added that his *Guided Tour of the Living Cell*, published more than ten years ago, does not deal with the origin of life, that [m]ore to the point would have been his *Blueprint for a Cell* (1991) and, especially, his latest book, *Vital Dust, Life as a Cosmic Imperative* (1995), out of which are excerpted the passages quoted in [the above] letter. {H. James Birx, *Free Inquiry*, Winter 1996-1997; WAS, 12 July 1995}

De Felice, Francesco (Born 1821)

An Italian writer, De Felice took part in the revolution of 1843, and when Garibaldi landed in Sicily was appointed president of the provisional council of war. A freethinker, he wrote on the reformation of elementary schools. {BDF}

DeFord, Miriam: See entry for Miriam deFord.

De Greef, Guillaume Joseph (Born 1842)

De Greef was an advocate at the Brussels Court of Appeal. He wrote *Introduction to Sociology* (1886). He also wrote for *La Liberté* (1867—1873) and *Le Societé Nouvelle.* {BDF}

De Gruson, Eugene Henry (1932—)

De Gruson, curator of the Haldeman-Julius Collection at Pittsburg State University at Pittsburg, Kansas, is author of *E. Haldeman-Julius: Freethinker*, a work that imitates Haldeman-Julius's Blue Book size. A librarian and educator, he wrote *Kansas Authors of Best Sellers* (1970), *Goat's House: Poems* (1986); and *James Tate: A Descriptive Bibliography* (1989).

De Grytnäs, Per (17th Century)

De Grytnäs was a noted Swedish unbeliever. In 1619 he was hanged as a renegade for denying "pure evangelical doctrine." (See entry for Scandinavian Unbelievers.)

De Gubernatis, Angelo [Count] (1840—1913)

De Gubernatis was an Italian Orientalist and writer. He studied Sanskrit under Bopp and Weber at Berlin. He wrote *Zoological Mythology* and compiled and in large part wrote a *Universal History of Literature* (18 volumes, 1882—1885). In addition, Sig. de Gubernatis edited *La Revista Europea* and the *Revue Internationale*. The count was a member of the American Philosophical Society. In his *Dictionnaire International* (1891, 2 volumes), he writes, "Our ideal temple is far vaster than enclosed by any Church . . . and it does more for the luminous peace and happiness of the world." {BDF; JM; RAT}

De Harven, Emile Jean Alexandre (Born 1837)

De Harven was the anonymous author of a work on *The Soul: Its Origin and Destiny* (1879). {BDF}

De Kay, Sam Hoffman (20th Century)

In 1977, De Kay's Ph. D. dissertation at Columbia University was on Frances Ellingwood Abbot. {FUS}

De la Casas, Bartolom: See entry for Hernan Rodriguez.

Debidour, Élie Louis Marie Marc Antoine (Born 1847)

A French historian, Debidour was dean of the faculty of Letters, Nancy (1886—1890). He was an Officer of the Legion of Honour and a member of the French Academy. His *L'Église Catholique et l'État sous la troisième République* (2 volumes, 1906) is a rationalist chronicle of the relations of church and state. {RAT}

Debierre, Charles (19th Century)

Debierre was a French writer, the author of *Man Before History* (1888). {BDF}

Debrovner, Charles H. (20th Century)

Debrovner, a physician, is President of the Board of Governors of The Humanist Institute in New York City.

Debussy, Claude (1862—1918)

Debussy, an eminent French composer, a giant among musicians, was an exponent of musical impressionism. He used a whole-tone scale, unusual relationships of harmony, dissonance, and other non-traditional musical ideas. His tone poem, "Prelude to the Afternoon of a Faun" (1894), was inspired by a Mallarmé poem. His orchestral works include "Nocturne" (1899) and "La Mer" (1905). His best-known piano work is "Clair de lune; Estampes" (1903).

According to McCabe and Lamont, Debussy rejected the supernaturalist creeds and insisted upon a purely secular funeral. {CE; CL; JM; RAT; TRI; TYD}

Decker, Clarence Raymond (20th Century)

Decker, who helped Harold Buschman edit *The New Humanist* in the 1930s, joined him on the faculty of the University of Kansas City. An administrator, he subsequently became president of Farleigh Dickinson University in New Jersey. He wrote *Victorian Conscience* (1977). {EW}

DECLARATION OF HUMAN RIGHTS: See Universal Declaration of Human Rights, a major humanistic document.

DECONSTRUCTION

Merriam-Webster's dictionary did not add the word *deconstruction* until 1993, citing its meaning as "a method of literary criticism that assumes language refers only to itself rather than to an extratextual reality, that asserts multiple conflicting interpretations of a text, and that bases such interpretations of the philosophical, political, or social implications of the use of language in the text rather than on the author's intention."

A method of textual analysis, the 1960's brainchild of Jacques Derrida, deconstruction (his coinage) has been applied to literary theory, linguistics, and philosophy. Derrida, who taught philosophy at the Sorbonne and was influenced by Martin Heidegger, emphasized the "indeterminacy" of texts as well as their "unreliability." He exposed the metaphysical assumptions involved in positive, systematic discussions of knowledge, and his criticism of academic structuralism led to what is called "post-structuralism." Derrida, according to *Columbia Encyclopedia*, holds that "all texts are based on hierarchical dualisms, where one element is regarded as essentially true; all systems of thought have an assumed center, or Archimedean point, upon which they are based. In a deconstructionist reading, this unconscious and unarticulated point is revealed, and in this revelation the binary structure upon which the text rests is imploded. Thus what appears stable and logical is revealed to be illogical and paradoxical. To a deconstructionist, meaning includes what is left out of the text or ignored or silenced by it."

Interdisciplinary scholarship in the 1980s and 1990s is regarded as an outgrowth of deconstruction and a partial acceptance of its aims. Basically, deconstruction is a philosophy that challenges the view that language can represent reality. Derrida's late 1960s antitheory theory has led to much scholarly wordplay.

Typically, J. Douglas Kneale of the University of Western Ontario has written, the deconstructionist looks for binary oppositions in a text: (a) he studies how the oppositions are hierarchically structured; (b) he then temporarily postulates the text to say the opposite; and (c) he then reasserts the opposition, declaring a nonhierarchical relationship of "difference."

The foremost American proponent of literary deconstruction, according to critic Michiko Kakutani, has been Yale University professor Paul de Man. Deconstruction, states Kakutani, "purveys a stylishly nihilistic view of the world, which insists that all meaning is relative, that all truth is elusive, and therefore futile. Such critical approaches irreparably divorce intellectual discourse from morality and ethics, and posit an ahistorical world in which actions have no consequences and language has no real meaning. Together with society's current eagerness to blur the lines between fact and fantasy, reality and appearance, deconstructionists and like-minded thinkers foster a climate in which idealogues and propagandists, like the Holocaust deniers, can try to assail those two pillars of human civilization: memory and truth." As for de Man's wartime writing for a pro-Nazi publication during World War II, Derrida characterized those writings as the work that "a very young man wrote for a newspaper, almost a half century ago, for less than two years, in very singular private and political circumstances many of which remain unclear to us." Derrida has offered deconstructive readings of de Man's pro-Nazi articles, which according to Kakutani, "purported to show that the texts subverted their own declared intentions, a tactic not dissimilar to those employed by Holocaust deniers, who routinely take factual evidence of the Holocaust and deconstruct it to support their own assertions."

Admitting the subject is difficult, journalist Mitchell Stephens has tried to explain: "To deconstruct a 'text' (a term defined broadly enough to include the Declaration of Independence and a Van Gogh painting) means to pick it apart, in search of ways in which it fails to make the points it seems to be trying to make. Why would someone want to 'read' (defined broadly) like that? In order to experience the impossibility of anyone writing or saying (or painting) something that is perfectly clear, the impossibility of constructing a theory or method of inquiry that will answer all questions or the impossibility of fully comprehending weight matters, like death. Deconstruction, in other words, guards against the belief—a belief that has led to much violence—that the world is simple and can be known with certainty. It confronts us with the limits of what it is *possible* for human thought to accomplish." Although at one time it was feared by some that deconstruction would destroy the academy by questioning Western values, Kneale says those fears have proved to be unfounded. He holds that "[a]fter nearly three decades of productive theory and practice, deconstruction remains one of the most significant developments in twentieth-century critical thought." Stephens, meanwhile, concludes that "[m]any otherwise unmalicious people have in fact been guilty of wishing for deconstruction's demise—if only to relieve themselves of the burden of trying to understand it."

"Unquestionably, the work of the Yale critics and, subsequently, that of a younger generation of critical readers has helped to legitimate and popularize deconstruction as a form of literary criticism," Kneale has written, "but their efforts have done more than promote a fashionable style of thought and writing. Deconstruction has forced critics to reexamine their philosophical assumptions and to rethink their own language. . . . Deconstruction remains one of the most significant developments in twentieth-century critical thought."

Differing and referring to a 1983 *New Criterion* article entitled "Destroying Literary Studies," the noted literary scholar René Wellek warned that deconstruction and other exercises in "extreme skepticism and even nihilism" threatened to undermine "all literary study, interrupt tradition, dismantle an edifice built by the efforts of generations of scholars and students."

That so many in America have become intrigued by Derrida's works, according to Mark Lilla, "attests to the strength of Americans' self-confidence and their awesome capacity to think well of anyone and any idea. Not for nothing do the French still call us *les grands enfants*." (See entries for Harold Bloom, Post-Modernism, Post-Modernist Criticism of Humanism, and Post-Structuralism.) {CE; Mark Lilla, "The Politics of Jacques Derrida, *The New York Review of Books*, 25 June 1998}

Dedijer, Vladimir (20th Century)

Dedijer is author of *The Yugoslav Auschwitz and the Vatican: The Croatian Massacre of the Serbs During World War II* (1992). He referred to his outlook as being that of humanism.

DEDUCTION

In logic, deduction is the process of reasoning that moves from the general to the specific. If, for example, all humans have two legs, and John is a human, one can deduce that John has two legs. (Teratologists, however, point out that some special people are born with more than two legs.)

The opposite is induction, or moving from the specific to the general. When we bite into an onion, we generalize from past experience that the onion will taste a certain unique way that is different from all other tastes. Hume held that it is not *necessary* that whatever looks like an onion will taste the way we have generalized it will taste. (For a discussion of induction, see "Scepticism and the Problem of Induction" by Paul Edwards, in *A Modern Introduction to Philosophy* [1973].) {DCL}

DEDUCTIVE-NOMOLOGICAL THEORY: See entry for Carl G. Hempel.

Dee, Jeff (20th Century)

Dee, of the Atheist Community of Austin, wrote "The Glorification of Ignorance" in *Secular Nation* (April-June 1999).

Dee, Michael J. (20th Century)

"There are no more metaphysics among the educated Japanese," wrote Dee in *Conclusions* (1917). "Why should there be among us?" {TYD}

Dees, Morris (20th Century)

In 1994, the American Humanist Association named Dees, a crusader for racial justice, a 1994 Humanist Distinguished Service Awardee. He wrote *Hate on Trial* (1993) and *The Gathering Storm* (1996).

Deffand, Marie Anne de Vichy-Chamrond du [Marchioness] (1697—1780)

One of the most famous French women of the 18th century, Deffand in her salon entertained the leading freethinkers of France and England. While a girl in convent school, she had become a skeptic and it was a tradition that she routed the celebrated court preacher who was brought to reason with her.

A witty marchioness, when a cardinal told her that it was disputed whether St. Denis carried his head twenty or thirty yards after it had been cut off, she replied, "Ah, my lord, it is only the first yard that *really* matters." McCabe states that some considered her the purest writer of French after her friend Voltaire. {JM; RAT}

Defoe, Daniel (1660?—1731)

Author of the first true novel in English, *Robinson Crusoe* (1719—1722), Defoe was educated in a Dissenters' academy, a school for Protestants who were not Anglicans, and almost became a Presbyterian minister, choosing instead to go into business, where he went bankrupt by 1692. Crusoe not only rescues his man Friday from the cannibals but also learns how to overcome life's difficulties, all the while preserving his human integrity. *Moll Flanders* (1722) is a realistic story of a London prostitute and thief. *Journal of the Plague Year* (1722) is equally realistic and, in many ways, timely. The Vatican prohibited the reading of his *History (Political) of the Devil*. Defoe was nearly sixty years old before he started to write novels, and he is noted for being a freethinking individual who was self-reliant, industrious, and filled with a feeling of moral responsibility. "Whores and priests will never want excuse," he declared in *The True-Born Englishman* (1701), in which he also included, "Of all the plagues with which mankind are cursed/Ecclesiastic tyranny's the worst."

In his 1722 account of a plague, Defoe stated by way of anticipation: "N.B.—The Author of this Journal lies buried in that very Ground [Bunhill Fields], being at his own desire, his sister having been buried there three or four years before." However, Defoe did not die until 1731. His choice of Bunhill Fields points up the fact that burials outside churches had come into practice, because Londoners during the time of Pepys and Wren began complaining about "body-stuffed sanctuaries." Bunhill, named for the Bone Hill where in the sixteenth century more than a thousand cartloads of bones from charnel houses had been dumped, was known as the Dissenters' burial ground, a place according to Tom Weil "where free thinkers could escape the fee-grabbing clergy and their costly consecrated terrain in favor of less expensive, secular real estate."

A 1998 biography by Richard West, *Daniel Defoe: The Life and Strange, Surprising Adventures*, tells of his becoming a political commentator and satirist, a merchant—he traded in woolen goods and wines—and a speculator in marine insurance. By 1692 he had gone bankrupt because of £17,000 in debts. Defoe described his plight in a couplet:

> No Man has tasted differing Fortunes more,
> And Thirteen Times I have been Rich and Poor.

{CB; CE; ILP; TYD}

deFord, Miriam Allen (1888—1975)

DeFord was a published writer from the time she was twelve, a freethinker since she was thirteen, and a feminist all her life. A writer of mystery and science fiction stories, true-crime accounts, biographies, poems, and other works, she won the 1961 Edgar Award of the Mystery Writers of America. A member of the editorial board of *The Humanist*, she was an honorary secretary of the Rationalist Press Association.

The author of *Who Was When: A Dictionary of Contemporaries* (1940), deFord was married to the scientist, Maynard Shipley. She wrote the present author concerning humanism:

> Since the Latin language has been one of the chief interests of my life, I suppose I might call myself a lexicographical Humanist; or, without being an Existentialist, with my convinced views on religion I might well be called an atheistic Humanist. But all in all, taking your definitions at face value, naturalistic Humanism perhaps comes closest to my beliefs. As Maynard Shipley said, "It is quite enough if one devote oneself to the welfare of humanity." No other devotion is needed. I am inclined to look on the word Humanism

as just another in the series of terms by which we try to describe a philosophy oriented toward man instead of toward a supernatural system—one with Rationalism, Free Thought, Secularism, Agnosticism, Atheism, and all the rest.

I consider religion—any religion—to be the greatest curse of humanity, and I confess I am not altogether comfortable with some of the mildly religious-minded people included in the American Humanist Association, even though in general I am in accord with their principles. My ethical views and ideals are completely naturalistic. I come nearer, perhaps, to Lucretius than to any philosopher since, and if any writer has influenced me, it is he. I cannot, however, say that either writers or speakers have done more than reinforce the view I first worked out for myself at the precocious age of thirteen! As for the other Humanisms, that is one of my chief objections to the word—that it connotes so many disparate and contradictory things. Semantically, it is too fuzzy a word for exact definition.

In 1973, deFord signed Humanist Manifesto II. In 1975 she was recognized with the Humanist Pioneer Award of the American Humanist Association. {FUS; HM2; HNS; PK; WAS, 16 March 1956}

Degler, Carl N. (20th Century)

Degler is a freethinker and historian. His *The Other South: Southern Dissenters in the Nineteenth Century* (1974) contains information about Southern abolitionism and the Readjusters in Virginia. He also wrote *In Search of Human Nature* (1991). {*Freethought History #14*, 1995}

DEICIDE

Deicide, which J. G. Frazer discussed in *The Golden Bough* (1890), refers to the killing, either real or symbolic, of a god. For example, a 1993 multi-media production about the life of Jesus was postponed at New York City's Radio City Music Hall because the live show entitled "Jesus Was His Name" included some lines to which the American Jewish Committee and the Anti-Defamation League of B'nai B'rith objected. To resolve the problem, a statement was read at each performance of the thirty-two-city American tour, one that stressed that "most Christian denominations" reject the view that the Jews killed Jesus Christ. The inference was that some Christians *do* believe that it was the Jews, not the Romans, who killed their Christ. (See entry for Anti-Semitism.) {CE}

Deicide (20 Century)

Members of Deicide, a deathmetal rock band, in a 1996 interview told *Rock Out Censorship* that they were atheists with satanic views. Not explained was why atheists should have any connection with Satan, a theistic invention. {CA}

Deininger, Whitaker T. (20th Century)

Deininger, chairman in the 1950s of the University of Dubuque's philosophy and religion department in Iowa, wrote reviews for *The Humanist*.

DEISM

Deism was a rationalistic movement that started in the seventeenth and continued into the eighteenth century. Its adherents, who were mainly opposed to revealed religion in general and Christianity in particular, held that nature's existence is obvious and that no further proof, such as that found in the Bible, is needed of a Creator or Supreme Architect of the Universe. Organized religion was scorned for encouraging superstition, and biblical revelation was considered spurious. Both the Old and New Testament were attacked as being a collection of inauthentic, not revealed, writings. Voltaire, one of the most famous, argued that belief in miracles is, logically, blasphemous, implying as it does that God has somehow bungled His creation and needs to make repairs. The deists emphasized morality, and they denied that the Creator, once his creation was finished, interfered further with the natural laws of the universe. Petitionary prayers could not be expected to be answered, for the Creator has gone and cannot hear them. Using the analogy of the watchmaker, He had created the world, He was now elsewhere, and man's interest now needs to be in the thoughtful utilization of His creation, not in the Creator who presumably will remain unknown. Basically, deism was a system of thought which advocated natural religion. The light of nature—*lumen naturae*, or reason—was man's only reliance.

Deist authors and their works included Thomas Morgan (*The Moral Philosopher*, 1737); Thomas Chubb (*Discourse Concerning Reason*, 1731; *True Gospel of Jesus Christ*, 1739; and *Posthumous Works*, 1748); John Toland (*Christianity Not Mysterious*, 1696); and Matthew Tindal (*Christianity as Old as the Creation, or the Gospel A Republication of the Religion of Nature* (1730). Tindal, whose work sometimes is called "the deist's bible," was not so restrained in his criticism of Christianity as was Lord Herbert of Cherbury (1583—1648), who is called "the father of deism." Lord Herbert simply commended natural religion for its reasonableness.

In addition to Voltaire, the ranks of the deists included Jean-Jacques Rousseau, Benjamin Franklin, Thomas Jefferson, and George Washington. The Founding Fathers of the United States were particularly attracted to deism, for they could no longer accept the Church of England nor the King of England as God's representative on Earth. Nor did they desire the formation of a national church, choosing instead to write a Constitution that guaranteed religious freedom for believers and non-believers alike. Ethan Allen's *Reason the Only Oracle of Man* (1784) and Thomas Paine's *The Age of Reason* (1794—1795) were deistic works. Many of the deists were Freemasons, and the Masonic ritual is in keeping with deistic thought.

Deism differs from theism, although Samuel Johnson's *Dictionary* in 1827 defined the two words as synonymous. Both posit God, although deists are more apt to use a term such as Supreme Architect of the Universe. Deism indicates a philosophical, as opposed to a dogmatic, belief in God, and deists emphasized natural theology as contrasted with revealed. Eighteenth-century deism appealed to the liberalism of Unitarianism and Universalism, two churches which were protesting Calvinism and were attempting to reconcile religious belief with scientific thought. But by the first decade of the nineteenth century, deism had lost much of its influence among major writers, who were becoming interested in a new philosophic and literary movement: transcendentalism. However, even in the 20th century, some still choose to label themselves as deists and publish *Think!* (Box 47016, St. Petersburg, Florida 33743).

Deism, according to J. C. A. Gaskin's *Varieties of Unbelief from Epicurus to Sartre* (1989), is "[b]elief in a god who ordered the universe and masterminds its general laws but has no concern with such particular effects as individual men and women and has made no special revelation of its (his or her) nature or purposes to the human race." Gaskin differentiates deism from attenuated deism, the "[a]cknowledgment of the possibility of some inconceivably remote and unknowable creator-god who is neither concerned with nor of concern to the human race, nor thinkably like a human person."

The case for deism as made by E. O. Wilson (*The Atlantic Monthly*, March 1998) includes the following:

> Deistic belief, by persisting in attenuated form to this day, has given scientists a license to search for God. More precisely, it has prompted a small number to make a partial sketch of Him (Her? It? Them?), derived from their professional meditations.
>
> Few scientists and philosophers, however, let alone religious thinkers, take scientific theology very seriously. A more coherent and interesting approach, possibly within the reach of theoretical physics, is to try to answer the following question: Is a universe of discrete material particles possible only with one specific set of natural laws and parameter values? In other words, does the human imagination, which can conceive of other laws and values, thereby exceed possible existence? Any act of Creation may be only a subset of the universes we can imagine. On this point Einstein is said to have remarked to his assistant Ernst Straus, in a moment of neo-deistic reflection, "What really interests me is whether God had any choice in the creation of the world." That line of reasoning can be extended rather mystically to formulate the "anthropic principle," which asserts that the laws of nature, in *our* universe at least, had to be set a certain precise way so as to allow the creation of beings able to ask about the laws of nature. Did Someone decide to do it that way?

Wilson then adds:

> The fatal flaw in deism is thus not rational at all but emotional. Pure reason is unappealing because it is bloodless. Ceremonies

stripped of sacred mystery lose their emotional force, because celebrants need to defer to a higher power in order to consummate their instinct for tribal loyalty. In times of danger and tragedy especially, unreasoning ceremony is everything. Rationalism provides no substitute for surrender to an infallible and benevolent being, or for the leap of faith called transcendence. Most people, one imagines, would very much like science to prove the existence of God but not to take the measure of his capacity.

(See the entry for World Union of Deists. Also see the article by Ernest Campbell Mossner for deism in the *Encyclopedia of Religion*, Vol. 2. Also see the entries for Clockwork Universe, for Pierre Viret, and for Ethan Allen. For deism (1624—1760) in the United Kingdom, see Gordon Stein's *Freethought in the United Kingdom and the Commonwealth*. In his *Freethought in the United States*, Gordon Stein also refers to Canadian deism.) {CE; ER; DCL}

DEISTS, WORLD UNION OF

The World Union of Deists, Box 47026, St. Petersburg, Florida 33743) publishes information concerning Thomas Paineand other deists.

D'Holbach, Paul Henry Thiry: See Holbach, Paul Henri Thiry.

Dekker, Eduard Douwes [Multatuli] (1820—1887)

An eminent Dutch novelist, known by the pseudonym Multatuli, served in Java, where he became an advocate of reform in colonial administration. His *Max Havelaar* (1860), partly autobiographical, is a satirical account of the vain efforts of an enlightened official to counter exploitation of the native population under colonial rule. D. H. Lawrence admired the work, writing an introduction to Siebenhaar's translation in 1927. Dekker had desired to free the Javanese from the oppression of their princes, but the government would not help him and he resigned and returned to Holland in 1856. The next four years he spent, in poverty, vainly seeking justice for the Javanese.

Writing under the pen name of Multatuli, he made a masterly indictment in *Max Havelaar* of the Dutch rule in India. *The Freethinker* (March 1994) contains Dekker's "Seeker's Lament," a poem which describes his farewell to religious faith. His *Ideën (7 volumes, 1862—1879)* is full of the boldest heresy. Wheeler called Dekker "the greatest Dutch writer and freethinker of [the nineteenth] century." Dekker's corpse was burned in the crematory at Gotha.

Tim Madigan and Tom Flynn, of the Council for Secular Humanism, were photographed at the Multatuli statue in Amsterdam in a Winter 1992 issue of *The Secular Humanist Bulletin*. "His trenchant criticisms of religious smugness got him into trouble," Madigan observed, "but he also helped expose the immorality of the basic premises of colonialism. And while he may not have gotten the recognition he deserved during his lifetime, it is good to know that his works are being kept alive by contemporary Dutch humanists. He is so well-known in the Netherlands today that a brand of coffee was named after him." {BDF; JMRH; PUT; RAT}

DeKoning, Lucien (20th Century)

DeKoning, active in the International Humanist and Ethical Union (IHEU), has consistently attacked organized religion.

DeKruif, Paul: See the entry for Theism.

Delacroix, Eugène (1798—1863)

Delacroix has been described by Corliss Lamont as a French painter who "participated actively in the secular and democratic tendencies of the age." An admirer of fellow atheist Diderot and France's foremost painter of the romantic movement, Delacroix opposed the neoclassical school of Jacques-Louis David (1748—1825), who for a generation had been the virtual art dictator of France. Among the Delacroix masterpieces in the Louvre are "The Bark of Dante," "Women of Algiers," and "Tiger Attacking a Horse." The Copenhagen Museum exhibits his portrait of George Sand.

Delacroix, whose full name was Ferdinand Victor Eugène Delacroix, abhorred cemeteries, thinking of them as places of oblivion. He described a cemetery in Dieppe as "less forbidding than that frightful Père-Lachaise, less silly, less limited, less bourgeois. Forgotten graves overgrown with grass, clumps of rosebushes and clematis perfuming the air in this sojourn of death; perfect solitude, moreover, ultimate conformity with the object of the place and with the necessary purpose of what is there, which is to say silence and forgetfulness." But later he chose to join the Parisian elite, directing in his will that

> My tomb will be in the cemetery of Père-Lachaise, on the heights, in a place somewhat removed. There will be neither emblem, bust, nor statue.

{CB; CE; CL; JM; RAT}

Delage, Marie Yves (Born 1854)

Delage, a French zoologist who achieved an international eminence, was an Officer of the Academy and of Public Instruction, Chevalier of the Legion of Honour, Laureate of the Institut, and President of the Zoological Society of France (1900). He edited the *Année Beiologique* and had a reputation for being an enemy of all obscurantism. As for the theories of the soul of spiritual philosophers like Plato and Augustine, Delage dryly added, "We find an analogous idea among many savages." {RAT}

Delambre, Jean Baptiste Joseph (1749—1822)

Delambre, an eminent French astronomer and mathematician during the Revolution is known for his historical works, including a six-volume *Histoire de l'astronomie* (1817—1827). A student under Lalande, he became, like his master, an atheist.

Along with P. F. A. Méchain, he measured for the French government an arc of the meridian between Barcelona and Dunkirk. His astronomical computations, especially a table of the motions of Uranus, led to his discovering four formulas in spherical trigonometry, and these are known as Delambre's analogies.

He died, after a long and painful illness. In announcing his death, a pious journal (*L'Ami de la Religion et du Rio*) wrote:

> It appears that this savant had the misfortune to be an unbeliever. We Wish we could announce that sickness had brought him back to the faith; but we have been unable to obtain any information to that effect. Like Lalande, the dying astronomer was faithful to the convictions of his life.

Delambre was buried at Père la Chaise, Cuvier pronouncing a discourse over his grave. {BDF; CE; FO; JM; JMR; JMRH; RAT}

Deland, Margaret(ta) Wade Campbell (1857—1945)

Deland's *John Ward, Preacher* (1888) contained the unusual plot of a minister who is torn between his own strict Calvinism and his wife's liberalism. Deland also wrote *The Rising Tide* (1916), about the Suffrage Movement. *If This Be* (1935) and *Golden Yesterdays* (1941) are autobiographical. {FUS}

Delaney, Joe (20th Century)

In 1995, Delaney became vice president of the University of Minnesota Atheists and Humanists (UMAH).

De la Ramée, Marie Louise: See entry for Ramée, Marie Louise de la.

Delavigne, Jean François Casimir (1793—1843)

Delavigne was a French poet. His drama, *Les Vépres Siciliennes*, was directed against the royalist-clerical reaction. Delavigne exulted in the 1830 Revolution, composing a hymn, "La Parisienne," which for a time rivaled the "Marseillaise." With Béranger, he shared the inspiration of the people against clericalism. {RAT}

DELAWARE HUMANISTS

Roy Torcaso of the Mid Atlantic Region (AHA), 3708 Brightview Street, Wheaton, Maryland 20902, is coordinator for the District of Columbia, Delaware, Maryland, and Virginia.

Delbanco, Andrew (20th Century)

Delbanco, a humanities professor at Columbia University, is author of *The Death of Satan: How Americans Have Lost the Sense of Evil* (1995). Satan is dead, Delbanco notes, having been replaced in the 1800s, a Me Century, by pride, which became "not just a legitimate emotion but America's uncontested god." The new demon included scapegoating by the likes of a crusader "who construes evil as a malignant, external thing—a thing alien to himself—[which] is by far the worst kind of barbarian.

Delbanco, wrote critic Tad Friend in *New York* (8 November 1995), "declares that scapegoating—a habit of demonization he now sees in open anti-Semitism, in victimology on college campuses, and in the predatory Dark Woman of films like "Fatal Attraction"—is a failure of moral imagination. . . . The struggle of the twentieth century was to keep this proficient hater from seizing the world." Friend continues, stating that Delbanco's "touchstone of sanity is Saint Augustine, the monist who declared evil not an external enemy but simply the absence of God. Satan is thus not a horned seducer but an internal deficit, a blindness.

Delbanco traces the Augustinian line from Jonathan Edwards through Emerson and Lincoln, John Dewey and Reinhold Niebuhr, and more recently Norman Mailer and Thomas Pynchon. All chime variations of Delbanco's gloss on [Jonathan] Edwards: 'God, in arranging what seem the accidents of our lives, bears no responsibility for what we become. This is our burden, and ours alone.' " Friend then comments, "Mailer and Pynchon's insistence on moral responsibility is notably secular, but Delbanco resists that wrinkle: 'Without reverence for something [transcendent],' he believes, we'll be powerless against the next Stalin. Delbanco thus exemplifies the modern dilemma he describes: He is an atheist nostalgic for the clarity of theodicy, for the outworn language of sin. It's not entirely clear why, given Delbanco's own ambivalence about the puritanical 'opening mood of American civilization,' which he characterizes as a 'peculiarly calm self-loathing—a hatred of the self continuous with an unresentful love of God." {TYD}

Delboeuf, Joseph Remi Léopold (1831—1896)

A Belgian writer, Delboeuf taught at the University of Lièwge. In his *Prolegomena to Geometry*, he suggests that even mathematical axioms may have an empirical origin. Baldwin classified him as being a positivist. {BDF; RAT}

Delbos, Étienne Marie Justin Victor (1862—1916)

Delbos was a French philosopher who taught, successively, at Limoges, Toulouse, and Paris. He was a rationalist of the spiritual school and a great admirer of Spinoza. {RAT}

Delbos, Léon (Born 1849)

Delbos, whose father was Spanish, his mother Scottish, spoke many languages, including Arabic and Sanskrit. In addition to many education works, he wrote *L'Athée,* an atheistic and freethought romance. In 1885 he wrote *The Faith in Jesus not a New Faith*. Also, he contributed to the *Agnostic Annual* and called himself an agnostic. {BDF; RAT}

Delcassé, Théophile (Born 1852)

A French statesman, Delcassé during 1913—1914 was Ambassador at Petrogad. He was a Chevalier of the Legion of Honour and held the highest orders of Russia, Denmark, Belgium, Japan, and China. A rationalist, Delcassé supported the Government's action against the Church. {RAT}

Delepierre, Joseph Octave (1802—1879)

A Belgian bibliophile, Delepierre was secretary of Legation to England for thirty-five years. His daughter married N. Truebner, who published his *L'Enfer* (Hell, 1876). {BDF}

Delescluze, Louis Charles (1809—1871)

A French journalist and revolutionary, Delescluze was arrested in 1834 for sedition. In 1835, implicated in a plot, he took refuge in Belgium. In 1848 Delescluze issued *La Revolution Démocratique et Sociale,* after which he was imprisoned, then banished to England. In 1868 he published *Réveil,* for which he again was fined and sentenced to prison for ten years. In 1859 he was amnestied, then imprisoned. Delescluze became head of the Commune Committee of Public Safety and died at the barricade. {BDF}

Deleu, P. (20th Century)

Deleu, a Belgian physiologist, addressed the International Humanist and Ethical Union's (IHEU's) International Peace Conference in Zutphen (1983).

Deleyre, Alexandre (1726—1797)

A French writer, Deleyre at an early age entered the order of Jesuits, then changed his faith and became the friend of Rousseau and Diderot. He contributed to the *Encyclopédie*. Deleyre embraced the Revolution with ardor, was made deputy to the Convention, and in 1795 was made member of the Institute. {BDF; RAT}

Delgado, José (20th Century)

A Humanist Laureate in the Council for Secular Humanism's International Academy of Humanism, Dr. Delgado is Chairperson of the Department of Neuropsychiatry at the University of Madrid. At the Tenth International Humanist and Ethical Union (IHEU) World Congress held in Buffalo (1988), Delgado addressed the group.

In Madrid in 1995, he spoke on the subject, "*Bases neuronales del humanismo.*" His "Neurobiological Bases of Beliefs" is included in *Challenges to the Enlightenment, Essays in Defense of Reason and Science* (1994). In 1995, he attended the first International Multidisciplinary Conference on Human Behaviour and the Meaning of Modern Humanism in Delphi, Greece. Also in 1995, Delgado wrote *In Search of God.*

Delgado signed Humanist Manifesto 2000.

Delibert, Joseph (Died 1999)

Delibert was a past president and honorary trustee of the New York Society for Ethical Culture.

Delius, Frederick (1862—1934)

An English composer of German parentage, Delius was influenced by Grieg. He is known for combining romanticism and impressionism in music that is characterized by free structure and rich chromatic harmony. One of Delius's works is *On Hearing the First Cuckoo in Spring* (1912), and he also wrote operas, including *A Village Romeo and Juliet* (1907). *A Mass of Life* is set to Nietzsche's text *Also Sprach Zarathustra* and is for two choirs and a double size orchestra. The work celebrates the joys of being alive, of dancing and drinking, of climbing moutains, and looking at girls' ankles.

Terry Sanderson has described Delius's atheism (*The Freethinker*, August 1996 and May 1997). He relates the time when Eric Fenby visited Delius and was told,

> Eric, I've been thinking, the sooner you get rid of all this Christian humbug the better. The whole traditional conception of life is false. Throw those great Christian blinkers away and look around you, stand on your own two feet and be a man. . . . Sex plays a tremendous part in life. It's terrible to think we come into this world through some despicable act. Don't believe all the tommyrot the

priests tell you; learn and prove everything by your own experience. {TRI; TYD}

Dell, Floyd (1887-1969)

Dell edited the monthly New York journal, *Arbitrator*. Known along with Max Eastman as one of the nation's prominent intellectual leftists, he was known in New York City's Greenwich Village as a socialist, a Freudian, a radical, and a bohemian. Dell wrote eleven novels, a number of reviews and essays, at least a dozen plays, and several works of nonfiction. An editor of *The Masses*, he described the magazine as one which "stood for fun, truth, beauty, realism, freedom, peace, feminism, revolution."

Dell, John Henry (1832—1888)

An artist and poet, Dell contributed to *Progress*, wrote *Nature Pictures* (1871), and *The Dawning Grey* (1885), a volume of verse imbued with the spirit of democracy and freethought. {BDF}

Dell-Bryan, Luree (20th Century)

Dell-Bryan and Jeff Lowder are responsible for the secular web site of the Internet Infidels: <http://infidels.org>.

Delon, Michel (20th Century)

Delon, writing in the Parisian *Les Cahiers Rationalistes*, cites the Belgian cultural historian Roland Mortier as also being a rationalist.

DELTA

"Delta," according to David Sterrett (*The Freethinker*, June 1996), is a noun from the Greek letter D, "the dark triangle," or pudendum. "The reason for the River Nile exit point to the sea being called the Nile Delta should be obvious, especially as in the spring it is richly red and the spring inundation is responsible for the abundant fertility and revival of the land. Thus one can see the logic behind the fertility rites of the Egyptian Religious System."

Deluc, Adolphe (Born 1811)

Deluc, a professor of chemistry at Brussels, collaborated on *La Libre Recherche*. {BDF}

De Luca, Anthony J. (20th Century)

De Luca, a freethinker, wrote *Freud and the Future Religious Experience* (1976). {GS}

Delvaux (18th Century)

Delvaux, a professor at the University of North Carolina, allegedly was a skeptical French ex-monk. (See entry for North Carolina Freethinkers.)

de Man, Paul (1919—1983)

At Yale University, de Man was described as "the deconstructionist guru." Deconstructionists, in approaching any text, dismantle it—they note, for example, its unchic, élitist, anti-feminist presuppositions. With such criticism, they expose what is considered to be the text's inherent contradictions. David Lehman's *Signs of the Times: Deconstruction and the Fall of Paul de Man* (1992) pokes fun at the movement. To illustrate, he attempts to obtain an explanation of "clitoral hermeneutics" from a deconstructionist attending a conference of the Modern Language Association, knowing deconstructionists always view words as shifting in meanings and that no one interpretation of words is any more correct than any other. Prof. de Man himself has been deconstructed by Lehman, who points out that the native Belgian wrote nearly 200 articles for Nazi-controlled newspapers before teaching at Bard College from 1949 to 1951. Lehman also details now Artine Artinian, who was depicted as Aristide in Mary McCarthy's *The Groves of Academe*, was betrayed by deMan, how deMan married Patricia Kelley although he was still married with three children to Anne de Man, and how one of those children described his father as a Felix Krull, a reference to Thomas Mann's "confidence man."

Alan Ryan, commenting upon the posthumous publication of *Aesthetic Ideology* (1996), observed that "Like other famous—or moderately famous—figures whose youthful misdeeds come to light only at their death, Paul de Man is now almost impossible to see clearly."

A number of deconstructionists have been highly critical of secular humanism. (See entries for Deconstruction and Postmodernist criticism of humanism.)

DeMasi, Andrew (1947—1993)

DeMasi, a professional harpsichordist, was a Jesuit-trained father. The Jesuits had taught him to think so logically, he said, that he had left Roman Catholicism for Nestorianism (a heretical group which followed Nestorius in the 5th century), then joined one of Madalyn Murray O'Hair's atheistic groups which gave him little or no support, and then joined AASH (an agnostic, atheist, secular humanist group for people who were HIV-positive).

"Rev. DeMasi, Andrew," as he was listed in the telephone book, described in *American Gay & Lesbian Atheists* (July 1993) his treatment by ministers of the Trinity Lower East Side Lutheran Church, East 9th Street in Manhattan, New York. They had dubbed him an "AIDS Victim" and told him in 1993 that his job as church organist was no longer available. "I was the leper among the clean, a sinful faggot among the divine," he said, whereupon he filed a grievance with the New York Human Resources Commission but correctly guessed that his case would take longer than he had to live.

Additionally, DeMasi lamented not having received help from his union, the American Guild of Organists, "although the crushing fact is that the vast majority of those on the board are gay themselves, knowing that a large number of us are employed in churches as entertainers for the divine." On his last day as organist, a dozen of his supporters from the Agnostics, Atheists, and Secular Humanists (AASH) group seated themselves at the Lutheran service where he played the first prelude, then sat silently as circulars were handed out to explain his predicament, ask for an apology, and plead for payment for past services. The minister, however, with the Lutheran bishop's wife in attendance, continued the service a cappella, and DeMasi was replaced as the organist. DeMasi suffered greatly during his several hospital stays but gently died of Kaposi's sarcoma in the arms of his companion, Colin Kenney. Members of Agnostics, Atheists, and Secular Humanists (AASH) in New York City held a secular memorial in his honor.

De Maupassant, Guy: See entry for Maupassant.

Demlinger, Floyd O. (20th Century)

Demlinger wrote *Free Minds Venturing* (1969). {FUS}

DEMOCRACY

In Ancient Athens, between 35,000 and 40,000 male citizens participated in "democracy." Joyce Carol Oates, however, has observed another side of the coin: "Excluded by reason of sex were approximately as many Athenian women, and the city-state contained an unknown number of slaves, male and female, who were (of course) excluded from citizenship."

Secular humanists and atheists cannot subsist in a non-democratic environment. Democracy implies that two sides of an argument can persuade each other or come to a compromise, which is impossible in, for example, an Islamic fundamentalist society. (See entry for Egalitarianism.)

Democritus (c. 460— 370 B.C.E.)

Often described as "the so-called laughing philosopher," Democritus was the father of the atomic theory and a materialist. A wealthy atheistic philosopher, Democritus traveled to Egypt and over a great part of Asia. He may have been acquainted with Leucippus. The philosophy in the sixty works were ascribed to him emphasized consistent mechanistic postulates which required no supernatural intervention, differing from the abstractions of his predecessors, Anaxagoras (who emphasized mind) and Empedocles (who emphasized harmony and discord). He thought everything was composed of atoms, tiny particles which cannot be seen but which have the same matter in different size, shape, and weight, matter that is underived, indivisible, indestructible. A hedonist, he taught that the true end of life is happiness achieved in inner tranquillity. A skeptic, he observed that "truth is sunk in an abyss." He is said to have laughed at life in general, which Montaigne says is better than to imitate Heraclitus and weep, because mankind is not so unhappy as it is vain. A. T. Cole, in *Democritus and the Sources of Greek Anthropology* (1967), wrote about the forerunner of current secular thinking. Santayana's *Reason in Science* states, "A thorough materialist, one born to the faith and not plunged into it by an unexpected christening in cold water, will be, like the superb Democritus, a laughing philosopher." {CE; CL}

Demonax (2nd Century)

A cynical philosopher, Demonax rejected all religion. Lucian wrote an account about Demonax and his views. {BDF}

De Montalvo, Soledad (20th Century)

"I was suddenly inspired to describe the Judeo-Christian god as a penis which has been endowed with cosmic significance," De Montalvo has written. In *Women, Food, and Sex in History* (1988), she starts the four-volume work which surveys the world's history. "Sluts in Huts" describes how women got men out of the Stone Age. Later chapters tell which kings and others died of venereal diseases, how children were used sexually, and how the male penis was worshiped. Madalyn O'Hair wrote the foreword.

Demora, Gianbattista (19th Century)

Demora was director of the *Libero Pensatore* of Milan, and he wrote some dramatic works. {BDF}

De Morgan, Augustus (1806—1871)

De Morgan, a mathematician, refused to graduate at Cambridge on account of the theological tests. Calling himself an "unattached Christian," he remained a theist and declined to join the Unitarians. Although he had a sympathetic interest in spiritualism, he has been wrongly cited as a spiritualist, according to McCabe. {RAT}

Demosthenes (384—322 B.C.E.)

"We believe whatever we want to believe," wrote the Athenian orator and statesman, Demosthenes. {TYD}

Deng Xiaoping [Communist Party Chairman] (1904—1997)

Deng (whose old-style name was Teng Hsiao-ping), when a student in Paris, met a fellow student, Zhou Enlai, and adopted the name Xiaoping (little peace). During the 1966-1969 cultural revolution, he was branded a "capitalist roader," he was twice purged from power (1967, 1976), and he was sent for "re-education" to a tractor factory. He was twice "rehabilitated" (1973, 1977), first by Zhou Enlai, and after Zhou's death and being forced into hiding, he was finally reinstated and became the controlling force in China. In 1981 he was named at the Communist Party Congress to lead the newly created Central Advisory Commission. In 1993, his youngest daughter, Deng Rong (whom he calls Mao Mao, or Little Kitten) published a biography of her father, relating that in 1930 his first wife, Zhang Xiyuan, died in childbirth, and that his second, Jin Weiyan, a factory worker, divorced Mr. Deng in 1933, when he was deemed politically incorrect and under severe criticism. The third, Zhuo Lin, appears in photos to be about 4 feet 10 inches, and her husband is around 5 feet tall. The book, rather than being negative, is reportedly a work which places her non-theistic father in China's revolutionary history. An atheist, Deng found that his reputation became tarnished in 1989 when he sanctioned the army's massacre of more than two thousand unarmed pro-democracy demonstrators in Beijing's Tiananmen Square.

Denham, Hector (1842—1913)

Denham was a Belgian sociologist who worked with the positivists in his earlier years, collaborating with Littré in his *Philosophie Positive.* In later years, he was an aggressive agnostic and socialist. "Positive science," he wrote, "arrays itself against religion, destroying the myths and fables which confine humanity in ignorance and delusion."

De Niro, Robert (1945-)

In a 1998 interview with James Lipton, dean of the Actors Studio, actor De Niro was asked what he would say when he arrives at the pearly gates. His response to God: "You've got a lot of explaining to do."

Denis, Hector (Born 1842)

Denis was a Belgian advocate and professor of political economy and philosophy at Brussels University. He wrote on social questions and contributed to *La Liberté, la Philosophie Positive*. Denis was a member of the Council of the International Federation of Freethinkers. {BDF}

Dennett, Daniel Clement (1942—)

A philosopher, author, and professor at Tufts University, Dennett in 1995 wrote *Darwin's Dangerous Idea: Evolution and the Meanings of Life* (1995). He has written about artificial intelligence, supporting the view that mind stuff is explained by brain stuff, that we are in no need of explanations involving spiritual nonsense. He defends the idea that simple organisms are well described as automata and that, as Darwin's theory states, we all are descended from such simple mechanisms. Our bodies, our actions, and all the ethical and intellectual issues which we face can be accounted for by evolution. In fact, he explicitly identifies this view with the secular humanists. In an interview (*Free Inquiry*, Fall 1995), Dennett discussed in more detail his vision of the future of artificial intelligence. A director of the Center for Cognitive Studies at Tufts University, he once helped develop a humanoid robot named Cog.

John R. Searle, in a profound discussion of Dennett's views, concludes that consciousness remains a mystery. But he feels that Dennett, along with Francis Crick, Gerald Edman, and Roger Penrose, "in their quite different ways, are at least on the right track. They are all trying to explain how the physical matter in our head *could* cause subjective states of sentience or awareness."

John Maynard Smith, professor of biology at the University of Sussex, highly approves Dennett's understanding of Darwinism. If we comprehend Darwin's dangerous idea, however, we are forced "to reject or modify much of our current intellectual baggage—for example, the ideas of Stephen Jay Gould, Noam Chomsky, Jerry Fodor, John Searle, E. O. Wilson, and Roger Penrose." Smith continues, quoting Darwin, "He who understands baboon would do more toward metaphysics than Locke." Central to Dennett's thesis is "that evolution by natural selection is an algorithmic process." Before Darwin, philosophers and biologists held that the complex adaptations of living things implied some intelligent designer. Darwin's dangerous idea, however, is "that adaptations can arise by natural selection, without need of intelligence: that is, they can be the products of an algorithmic process." Dennett repeatedly uses the analogy of "cranes" and "skyhooks," devices for lifting things. A crane, explains Smith, "is a structure or process which is itself the product of the natural selection of replicating entities, but which, once it has arisen, makes it possible for still more complex structures to evolve." Before sex, there was no way in which different replicators could unite to form a new individual. "Once sex did arise," however, "it greatly accelerated the evolutionary process. Sex is, in Dennett's terminology, a crane. Sex did not arise because it would accelerate evolution in the future: natural selection does not have foresight. Indeed, there is still controversy among evolutionary biologists about how and why sex did originate, although," Smith adds, "I think that a plausible account is now possible."

Dennett's view of evolution, Smith continues, "is one of cranes building cranes building cranes, each new crane arising by an essentially mindless process of selection. I fully agree with this view." Skyhooks, however, "are a stark contrast. They are mysterious lifting devices, whose origin cannot be explained. It is Dennett's thesis that we must eschew skyhooks and make do with cranes." Smith's *The Major Transitions in Evolution* (1995) is an account of this succession of cranes, starting with the origin of the first replicators and the genetic code, and ending (so far) with the origin of human language. The problem is to explain how each new crane arose by a process of selection, without miracles, or "skyhooks."

Dennett and Smith agree that the world is free of skyhooks but that we can live happily in such a world. In Smith's words, "No matter how mindless the processes of evolution may be, they have, in fact, produced a world of astonishing beauty, which we can enjoy, and ought to protect.

In 1996, Dennett's *Kinds of Minds, Toward an Understanding of Consciousness* continues developing his view that the brain evolved like all other organs and explaining that consciousness has a material basis, like any other mental ability. He is a contributing editor on *Philo* and a signer of Humanist Manifesto 2000. {CA; E; "The Mystery of Consciousness," *The New York Review of Books*, 2 and 16 November 1995; John Maynard Smith, "Genes, Memes, & Minds," *The New York Review of Books*, 30 November 1995}

DENOMINATIONS, RELIGIOUS: See entry for Hell.

Denslow, Van Buren (19th Century)

Denslow, an American, was author of essays on *Modern Thinkers* (1880), to which Colonel Ingersoll wrote an introduction. He wrote on the value of irreligion in *Truthseeker* and other journals. {BDF; PUT}

DENTISTRY

"Dentists are humanistic?" a person unacquainted with paradox might ask. But how else explain that the Etruscans in the 7th century B.C.E. made crowns and bridges if not because of their desire to alleviate human pain. The Phoenicians, Egyptians, Greeks, and Romans developed dentistry, which then became an almost lost art during the Middle Ages. A Spanish Moor, Abulcasis, was one of the few who knew about dental surgery in the 10th century.

Sir Peter Ustinov, in a serious moment, related that in the 12th century dentists came to work with a drummer to drown the patient's cries. James Wynbrandt in *Toothsome Tales and Oral Oddities from Babylon to Braces* (1998) confirmed this, adding that in the past it was commonly believed that toothworms caused decay. Pliny the Elder, before being fatally overcome by Vesuvius's volcanic fumes, advised eating a mouse twice a month to prevent toothache. Pierre Fauchard, one of the founders of modern dentistry, recommended that tooth-drawers and barber-surgeons use urine as a mouthwash.

Today, however, many humanistic dentists are said to have chosen their field because "I don't want to hurt people." {CE; WAS, Ustinov interview}

Denton, William F. (1823—1883)

An English-born poet, geologist, and lecturer, Denton emigrated to the United States and published *Poems for Reformers* (1856) as well as lectured on freethought and temperance topics. In 1872 he published *Radical Discourses on Religious Subjects* and in 1879 *Radical Rhymes*. In Australasia, Denton died of a fever while conducting scientific explorations in New Guinea. {BDF; FUK; PUT; RAT}

D'Entremont, John (20th Century)

D'Entremont wrote *Moncure Conway, 1832—1907* (1978). {FUK; GS}

Deodhekar, Govind Naratab (Dev) (1919—1997)

Deokhekar, formerly a left-wing activist in India, moved to the United Kingdom in 1951 and played an active role in the British humanist movement for over three decades. He was from Bombay and had worked in Maharashtra, India, to combat superstition. In *New Humanist* (October 1992), he described the variety of superstitions he had found in India. These included the following: magicians, or godmen (who allegedly trace lost relatives or promise to cure AIDS); lucky stones (which are worn to ward off the evil effect of one planet or another); possession of spirits (which really are mental disturbances but some exorcists have been successfully prosecuted for fooling people that they can rid the spirits); ghosts (which have scared entire communities into leaving their village for one day); bhanamati (in which stones fall on roofs or things move around a house, always traceable, however, to human hands; animal sacrifices (in return for expected favors, and an estimated 500,000 goats are sacrificed, along with chickens and even buffaloes); masochistic rituals (in which mini-spears are inserted under the bare skin of the back); devdasis (whereby girls who develop a strand of tangled hair, or dreadlocks, are dedicated to some Deity and serve the carnal needs of visitors); and astrology (which is especially liked by upper and middle-class Hindus). ANIS, which is something like PSICOP in the United States, is an organization devoted to exposing god-men and their tricks in front of large audiences in James Randi style.

In 1992, Deodhekar retired as chairman of G. W. Foote & Co., publishers of *The Freethinker*, and as treasurer of the National Secular Society but remained a director. After his death in Muscat Oman from a heart attack, a memorial meeting was held at Conway Hall, at which many spoke: Bill McIlroy; Jim Herrick; Daniel O'Hara; David J. Williams; Peter Brearey; Keith Porteous Wood; Terry Sanderson; Nicolas Walter; and Denis Cobell. Deodhekar was praised as a freethought stalwart on two continents. {*New Humanist*, March 1997}

Deogratias, Ssekitooleko (20th Century)

Deogratias heads the Uganda Humanist Association (UHASSO), which is at PO Box 4427, Kampala, Uganda.

De Paepe, César (1842—1890)

Dr. Paepe, a Belgian socialist, became a printer with Désiré Brismée, the founder of Les Solidaires, a rationalist society. Proudhon confided to him the correction of his works. One of the foremost members of the International, De Paepe attended all its congresses as well as those of the International Federation of Freethinkers. His funeral was the occasion of a great public demonstration, in which university professors, lawyers, doctors, municipal officers, freethought societies, Freemason lodges, and labor unions participated. Over two hundred wreaths were sent from freethought societies in Paris, Madrid, Rome, Berlin, Lyons, Amsterdam, and Marseilles. {BDF; PUT; RAT}

De Pasquale, Rob (20th Century)

A New Yorker, De Pasquale is a freethinker who has little interest in organized religion. An eloquent humanist activist, he reads widely and profoundly.

De Posada, Joachim (20th Century)

De Posada is a member of the Ibero-American Commission, a group of leaders in Spanish-speaking countries. He is a management consultant who has been known to successfully impersonate a "psychic," in order to encourage people to think critically.

De Potter, Agathon Louis (Born 1827)

A Belgian economist, De Potter wrote many works on social science. He was a collaborator on *La Ragione (Reason)* and *La Philosophie de l'Avenir*. {BDF; RAT}

De Potter, Louis Antoine Joseph (1786—1859)

De Potter, Agathon's father, was a Belgian politician and writer. He lived ten years in Rome, writing *Spirit of the Church* (6 volumes), which were put on the *Index*. A strong upholder of secular education in Belgium, he was arrested more than once for his radicalism, being imprisoned for eighteen months in 1828. In 1830 he became a member of the provisional government, afterwards lived in exile in Paris, then wrote an anti-clerical *History of Christianity* (8 volumes, 1836—1837). De Potter also compiled a *Rational Catechism* (1854) and *a Rational Dictionary* (1859). {BDF; RAT}

Depasse, Hector (Born 1843)

A French writer, Depasse edited *La République Francaise* and was a member of the Paris Municipal Council. In *Clericalism* (1877), he urged the separation of church and state. Depasse wrote many little books on *Contemporary Celebrities*, among them Gambetta, Bert, and Ranc. {BDF}

Depestre, René (20th Century)

A Haitian socialist who wrote about *Négritude*, Depestre referred to his outlook as being that of humanism.

Deraismes, Maria (1835—1894)

A French writer and lecturer, Deraismes wrote comedies. *Aux Femmes Riches* (1865) was an appeal on behalf of her gender. The Masonic Lodge of Le Pecq, near Paris, invited her to become a member, and she was duly installed under the Grand Orient of France. She not only was the first female Freemason but also was president of the Paris Anti-clerical Congress of 1881. Her journal was entitled *Le Républicain de Seine et Oise*. Deraismes was an active rationalist and president of various Freethought societies. With V. Schoelcher, she presided at the Anti-Clerical Congress at Paris in 1881. {BDF; RAT; WWS}

D'Ercole, Pasquale (19th Century)

An Italian professor of philosophy in the University of Turin, D'Ercole wrote a work on "Christian Theism," in which he held that the principles of philosophic theism are undemonstrated and at variance both with reality and with themselves. {BDF; RAT}

De Renesse, Camille [Count] (20th Century)

A freethinker, De Renesse wrote *Jesus Christ: His Apostles and Disciples in the Twentieth Century* (1904). {GS}

De Rosa, Peter: See entry for Peter de Rosa.

DER FRIEDENKER

A humanistic quarterly in German, *Der Freidenker* is at Postfach 54, 1153 Wien, Austria.

DeRosier, John (20th Century)

DeRosier, a political cartoonist, spoke in 1996 on "I Was A Child of God: From Mormon To Freethinker," at a Lake Hypatia freethinkers' convention in Alabama. {*Freethought Today*, May 1996}

Derozio, Henry Louis Vivian (1809-1831): See entry for V. R. Narla.

Derrida, Jacques (1930—   )

Derrida, who taught philosophy at the Sorbonne, has written of the "deconstruction" of Western rationalist thought, analyzing the thought of Husserl, Hegel, and other major philosophers. His theories are found in *Writing and Difference* (1967) and *On Grammatology* (1967).

In his work, he challenges the primacy of the spoken language, which can so easily be altered by the written language, concluding that writing by its ability to alter speech and thought written language creates rather than merely transmits meaning. Derrida was deeply influenced by the work of the philosopher Martin Heidegger.

When it was revealed that Heidegger was a dues-paying member of the Nazi Party from 1933 to 1945, Derrida, using deconstruction, tried to mitigate his intellectual mentor's actions. If Heidegger had broken his postwar silence over revelations about the Nazi death camps, Derrida reasoned, other intellectuals "would then be more likely to feel dismissed from the duty" of re-examining his thought.

Critics hold that Derrida's deconstruction purveys a stylishly nihilistic view of the world. Supporters cite him as "perhaps the world's most famous philosopher—if not the only famous philosopher." "If no one understands what you are saying, why do you expect anyone to listen?" he was asked in 1998. He responded frostily, "Why don't you ask a physicist or a mathematician about difficulty? Deconstruction requires work. If deconstruction is so obscure, why are the audiences in my lectures in the thousands? They feel they understand enough to understand more." (See entry for Deconstruction and its somewhat illogical appeal to Americans, who "think well of anyone and any idea.") {CE; *The New York Times*, 30 May 1998}

Dershowitz, Alan Morton (1938-   )

One of the civil liberties lawyers involved in absolving the noted athlete, O. J. Simpson, of the charge that he had murdered his wife and another person, Dershowitz is a member of the Harvard Law School. A passionate supporter of Jewish causes, he makes clear in *Vanishing American Jew* (1997) that his attachment to Judaism is primarily cultural, not spiritual. He refers to his "borderline agnosticism" and states, "God is not central to my particular brand of Jewishness. Even if a voice came down from wherever secular voices come down from and proved conclusively that God did not exist. Being Jewish, to me, transcends theology or deity."

Further on the subject, he wrote, "I consider myself a committed Jew, but I do not believe that being a Jew requires belief in the supernatural," to which he added that disbelievers must not accept second-class status in a nation whose traditions and laws forbid tests of faith as a condition of citizenship or office holding. {CA; *Free Inquiry*, Summer 1999}

DERVISH

A Moslem dervish, like a Catholic monk, is a member of any of various ascetic orders. Some of those orders perform whirling dances during which chanting becomes like an ecstatic devotion. In their "communing with the infinite" through ecstatic dance, the dervishes strike some freethinkers as engaging in exercises of mystical eroticism, exhibiting a kind of wild-man spirituality.

Jalaluddin Rumi, who conceived the dance as part of a lifelong quest for religious rapture, was born in Central Asia in 1207. He was the son of a Muslim mystic who had fled to Konya, Turkey, before the advance of Genghis Khan's horde. A believer, he used religious terminology in the extensive poetry he wrote, but he scorned the rituals and dogma of established faiths, believing that truth is to be found in each human heart. He proclaimed himself "not Christian or Jew or Muslim, not Hindu, Buddhist, Sufi, or Zen. The door is open to everybody. There are hundreds of ways to kneel and kiss the ground." Rumi, known in Turkey as Mevlana, or "our master," has irritated many political authorities because of his esoteric and pantheistic teachings, along with his belief that "worldly power means nothing." {Stephen Kinzer, *The New York Time*, 29 December 1998}

Desa, Guiseppe (Died 1767)

Desa was the son of a poor carpenter, was said to have been born in a stable, and became St. Joseph of Copertino, also known as the "Flying Monk" because of his levitations during ecstatic states. At school he was called "open mouth" because of his tendency to sit motionless with mouth agape, staring at the heavens. One hundred years after his death, the Church made him a saint. {LEE}

De Sade: See entry for Sade.

De Sanctis, Francesco (1818—1883)

De Sanctis, an Italian literary critic, was twice a Minister of Public Instruction. He became a leading literary critic and was strongly disliked by the positivists as well as the clericals. De Sanctis was a philosophic theist, or pantheist, influenced by Hegel, and far removed from Christian orthodoxy. {RAT}

Desbarreaux, Jacques Vallée (1602—1673)

A French poet and skeptic, Desbarreaux was great-nephew of Geoffrey Vallée, who was burned for being a non-believer in 1574. Many stories are told of his impiety. One concerns his feasting on eggs and bacon. When suddenly it thundered, Desbarreaux threw the plate out the window, derisively adding, "What an amount of noise over an omelette!" Some say he recanted and wrote a poem beginning, "Great God, how just are thy chastisements." But Voltaire assigns this poet to the Abbé Leveau. {BDF}

Descartes, René (1596—1650)

No scientist today will defend dualism, a concept associated with Descartes—the French scientist and philosopher. Dualism holds that consciousness has some kind of a different source from the material we have inside our heads. In the words of A. J. Ayer, "Descartes has few contemporary disciples. Not many philosophers of whatever persuasion believe that we are spiritual substances."

However, Descartes has interested religionists and philosophers for four centuries with his views including mind and matter's being different substances. "If you would be a real seeker after truth, it is necessary that at least once in your life you doubt, as far as possible, all things," Descartes wrote. Because he was charged with being an atheist and threatened with execution by the church, he failed to finish many works which he had started.

Generally described as the founder of modern philosophy, and originator of "I think, therefore I am," he considered himself a convinced Catholic. Church officials, however, thought he was too critical.

Unlike contemporary naturalists, he was a dualist, like Plato. Descartes' *Discourse on Method* (1637) is his most widely read book. All his philosophic works were prohibited by the Vatican in 1663. In 1720, the Vatican added his *Meditationes de prima philosophia* (1641), and Descartes was forced to flee his country *"parce qu'il y fait trop chaud pour lui."* He burned his *Traite du Monde* (*Treatise on the World*) lest he should incur the fate of Galileo. During the French Revolution, Maréchal cited Descartes as being only a "possible" atheist, one who denied final causes. Robertson offers a possible explanation, that Descartes "all through his life anxiously sought to propitiate the Church; and his scientific as well as his philosophic work was hampered in consequence."

Stephen Gaukroger, in *Descartes: An Intellectual Biography* (1996), develops the thesis that the Church's 1633 condemnation of Galileo split Descartes's thinking in two ways: first, he looked outward when young, with the hope that he could explain how the world functioned, why, for example, rainbows are multi-colored, why meteors fly, why blood moves through the veins; but second, he looked inward when older, trying to ascertain certainty and what it is that constitutes selfhood. Gaukroger discusses why Descartes, the pioneer of modern philosophy and science, did not imitate Galileo and challenge the Church. Why, he speculates, did Descartes not speak out against ecclesiastical doctrine while living in a safe Dutch Protestant environment? Gaukroger makes the point that atheism in 1625 had a negative connotation, that atheists of that day might be accused of holding that God's existence cannot be demonstrated through reason; that some atheists subscribed to determinism; and that God's omnipotence by being tied in with the finite world necessarily had to be limited. "Not one among these atheists, and certainly not Descartes," noted Harvard's Peter Galison, "pressed for a materialist and godless world." Galison is favorably impressed by Gaukroger's thesis, finding that "it is a never-ending source of astonishment that Descartes can still be so absolutely strange and so absolutely familiar. There is the Descartes who argued that magnetism be best understood as tiny screws whirling through space, or who insisted that the lowly pineal gland was the seat of the mind, or who posited a universe of whirlpools set in motion by an unknowable God; and there is the Descartes whose notions of certainty, of mind against matter, and of human subjectivity are as familiar as the face in the mirror."

Paul Edwards, in *Immortality* (1992), confirms that Descartes believed in God as well as in *human* survival after death. (See entry for E. O. Wilson.) {CE; CL; ER; EU, Richard H. Popkin and Aram Vartarian; Paul Galison, "Mr. Cogito," *The New Republic*, 13 May 1996; ILP; JMR; JMRH; PA; PUT}

Deschamps, Léger Marie (1716—1774)

Deschamps, known also as Dom Deschamps, was a French philosopher who had entered the Order of Benedictines, then lost his faith by reading an abridgment of the Old Testament. He became a correspondent of Voltaire, Rousseau, d'Alembert, Helvetius, and other philosophers. *"Ce prête athée,"* as he was called by Franck, was the author of a treatise entitled *La Vérité, ou le Vrai Système,* in which he appears to have anticipated all the leading ideas of Hegel. God, he says, as separated from existing things, is pure nothingness. An analysis of his work, which remained in manuscript for three-quarters of a century, was published by Professor Beaussire (1855). {BDF; RAT}

Deschanel, Emile Auguste Étienne Martin (Born 1819)

Deschanel was a French senator who wrote in *Revue Independante*, *Revue des Deux Mondes*, and *Liberté de Penser*. For writing against clericalism in the last journal, Deschanel, a professor of modern literature at the College of France, was deprived of his chair. He then moved to Belgium, never recanting his outlook. {BDF; RAT}

Deschanel, Paul Eugène Louis [President] (Born 1856)

The son of Emile Deschanel and the President of France from 1898 to 1902, Deschanel published speeches and dates that indicate he shared his father's anti-clericalism. {RAT}

Dechert, Alan (20 Century)

Deschert, an activist supporter of the International Humanist and Ethical Union, favors a "year zero campaign" in light of the Y2K [Year 2000] problem [of some computer programs not being able to handle the four-digit figure]. If we were to reset the calendar, he has jocularly argued on behalf of the Global Era Calendar project, "that'll give us more time to figure out what to do with the year 10,000."

E-mail: <adechert@aol.com>. On the Web: <http://members.go2zero.com>.

Deschner, Karlheinz (20th Century)

Deschner, a writer and church critic from Germany, was given a Humanist Award in 1993 at the European Humanist Congress held in Berlin. He reported that his *History of the Criminality of Christianity* (1993) has sold widely in Mexico and Spain. {E}

Des Essarts, Jules (Born 1849)

A Belgian freethinker, Des Essarts became a printer, edited the *Journal de Charleroi*, and made a name for his vigorous attacks on kingdom and church. In 1893, after one of his proposals, a Temple of Science was erected in Charleroi, which became the seat of a grand freethought demonstration in which over one hundred and twenty-eight societies were represented. The Catholic clergy were enraged, he happily reported. {PUT}

Deshmukh, Gopal Rao (1823—1892)

Deshmukh was the pioneer of rationalism in Maharashira, India. Born of an aristocratic family, he served the government in various capacities and brought periodicals and books, attacking the oppressive customs and propagating rational ideas. Sardar Gopalrao Deshmukh, called "Lokahitawadi," was the first Maharashtrian to analyze the Hindu society from an economic point of view.

His unbiased attitude toward the British led him to blast the myth of their divine origin. He insisted that Indians should not patronize British goods, and he stressed purchasing indigenous items. Many attacked him for his spiritual praise of the Britishers.

Deshumbert, Marius (Born 1856)

Deshumbert was a French ethicist, the founder and secretary of the *Comité International Pour la Pratique de la Morale fondé sur les lois de la Nature.* He wrote concerning French grammar and on his naturalist theory of morals. {RAT}

Deslandes, André François Bourreau (1690—1757)

Deslandes became a member of the Berlin Academy and wrote numerous works, mostly under the veil of anonymity, the principal being *A Critical History of Philosophy* (3 volumes, 1737). His *Pygmalion*, a philosophical romance, was condemned by the Dijon parliament in 1742. *Dying Merrily* (1732) and *On the Certainty of Human Knowledge* (1741) were both directed against religion. {BDF; RAT}

Des Maizeaux, Pierre (1673—1745)

Des Maizeaux edited the works of Bayle, Saint Evremond, and Toland, whose lives he wrote as well as those of Hales and Chillingworth. Anthony Collins was his friend, and at his death left him his manuscripts. These he transferred to Collins's widow and they were burned. Repenting, he returned the money. Des Maizeaux was secretary of the Royal Society of London. In writing Walpole, Des Maizeaux railed at "the blind zeal and stupidity cleaving to superstition." {BDF; FUK}

Desmond, Adrian J. (1947—)

Desmond has completed biographies of Darwin (1991) and Thomas Henry Huxley (1994). The latter work ends in 1870, when Huxley had twenty more years to live. He also wrote *Politics of Evolution* (1989) and *Huxley, the Devil's Disciple* (1994). In *Huxley: Evolution's High Priest* (1997), Desmond shows how Huxley demolished his Christian opponents, demonstrated with his big toe how to make "spirit raps," and scorned "the religious observance of Positivism." At the same time Huxley abhorred the "Bradlaugh atheists." Desmond terms Huxley "the world's greatest scientific synthesiser." {Gordon Stein, *The American Rationalist*, September-October 1995; Colin McCall, *The Freethinker*, July 1997}

Desmoulins, Lucie Simplice Camille Benôit (1760—1794)

A French revolutionary writer, Desmoulins was a fellow student of Robespierre at Paris and became an advocate and an enthusiastic reformer. In July 1989 he incited the people to the siege of the Bastille, and thus began the Revolution. He edited *La Vieux Cordelier* and *Révolutions de France et de Brabant*, in which he stated that Mohammedanism is as credible as Christianity.

Desmoulins was a deist to some, an atheist to others, and he preferred paganism to Christianity. Both creeds were more or less unreasonable, he said, but folly for folly he preferred Hercules slaying the Erymanthean boar to Jesus of Nazareth drowning two thousand pigs. Carlyle called Desmoulins a man of genius, "a fellow of infinite shrewdness, wit—nay, humor."

During the Terror, when the court asked his age, Desmoulins said, "Thirty-three—same as the sans-culotte Jesus." (*Culotte* refers to breeches; *sans* means *without.*) Desmoulins was executed with Danton in 1794, and his amiable wife, **Lucille Desmoulins**, also an atheist, shared his fate a few days later. {BDF; JM; RAT}

Desnoiresterres, Gustave le Brisoys (1817—1892)

Desnoiresterres was a Frenchman of letters, author of *Epicurines et Lettres, XVII et XVIII Siècles* (1881) and *Voltaire et la Société au XVIII Siècle*, an important book in eight volumes. {BDF}

DeSola, Ralph (20th Century)

DeSola was editor of the atheistic *Truth Seeker* from 1988 to 1989. In 1983, he wrote *Great Americans Examine Religion from A to Z.* {GS}

Des Périers, Jean Bonaventure (c. 1510—c. 1544)

Des Périers was a French poet and skeptic who was brought up in a convent, only to detest the vices of the monks. He may have known Rabelais, whom he mentions as "Francoys Insigne." The protégé of Marguerite of Valois, he defended Clement Marot when he was persecuted for making a French version of the Psalms. Des Perioers wrote the *Cymbalum mundi* (1537), a satire upon religion, published under the name of Thomas de Clenier à Pierre Tryocan and suppressed by the printer because of its anti-Christian content. The work consisted of skeptical dialogues in the manner of Lucian, and it led Protestants to accuse him of atheism and *libertinage.* Frenchmen are said to have considered his name a "hissing and a byword," although later French scholars considered des Périers in a class with Rabelais and Marot. Des Périers fled and, perhaps by suicide, died in order to escape persecution. {BDF; CE; FUK; JMR}

Desraimes, Maria (Born 1835)

Desraimes was a French writer and lecturer. She made her name first as a writer of comedies. Upon behalf of her gender, she wrote Aux Femmes Riches (1865). She became the first female Freemason when invited by the Masonic Lodge of Le Pecq, near Paris, and she was installed under the Grand Orient of France. Desraimes presided over the Paris Anti-Clerical Congress of 1881 and wrote an extensive journal, Le Républicain de Seine et Oise. {BDF; RSR}

Dessaix, Joseph Marie [Count] (1764—1834)

Dessaix was a French general under Napoleon. In 1803 he was made Commander of the Legion of Honour, and in 1809 Count. At the restoration, he was imprisoned and was never reconciled with the royalist clericals. In 1830 he commanded the National Guard. {RAT}

De Sterio, Marius Dées (20th Century)

De Sterio is the International Humanist and Ethical Union's (IHEU's) representative at the Council of Europe. He is President of the NGO Human Rights grouping.

E-mail: <alexandre.dees-de-sterioci.educ.lu>.

DESTINY

Destiny, n. A tyrant's authority for crime and a fool's excuse for failure.

—**Ambrose Bierce**
The Devil's Dictionary

Destriveaux, Pierre Joseph (1780—1853)

A Belgian lawyer and politician, Destriveaux wrote several works on public rights. He was a freethinker who in 1835 had been deposed by the Catholic ministry. {BDF; RAT}

Destutt de Tracy, Antoine Louis Claude [Comte] (1754—1836)

A French philosopher and psychologist, Destutt de Tracy, although active in the Napoleonic government, was important for his leadership of the ideologists, disciples of Condillac. The ideologists contributed to such later psychological developments as the James-Lange theory of emotions. Using Condillac's reduction of consciousness to the reception and combination of sensations, Destutt de Tracy developed a philosophy of education for post-Revolutionary France. In a letter to Adams, Jefferson described Destutt as "the greatest intellectual writer of the age." A freethinker, he wrote the four-volume *Elémens d'idéologie* (1800—1815). Destutt, a member of the French Academy (1808), is said until his dying day to have read Voltaire enthusiastically. {BDF; CE; JM; JMR; JMRH; RAT}

Des Vignes, Pietro (13th Century)

Des Vignes was secretary to Frederick II (1245—1249. Mazzuchelli attributes to him the treatise *De Tribus Impostoribus.* {BDF}

DET NORSKE HEDNINGSAMFUNN

The Society of Norwegian Heathens, known as Det Norske Hedningsamfunn, is at St. Edmundsvei 39 C, 0280 Oslo, Norway. Its journal is *Oss Hedninger Imellom* (Among Us Heathens). (See entry for Norwegian Humanists.) {FD}

DETERMINISM

• Free will and determinism are like a game of cards: the hand that is dealt you is determinism; the way you play your hand is free will.

—**Norman Cousins**

Determinism, a view opposed to libertarianism (or belief in freedom of the will), is a philosophical thesis that conditions control the course of events. An extreme form of determinism is the belief in predestination, the doctrine that God in consequence of His foreknowledge of all events infallibly guides those who are destined for salvation. (Early Presbyterian ministers who tried to convert nonbelievers heard complaints such as, "God does not want me to join or contribute money to you for He would already have guided me to do so" or "You say man cannot save himself solely by relying on his own powers? That I can be redeemed only by the initiative of a gracious merciful God? That I am some kind of pawn?")

Determinism also is opposed to the Principle of Emergence, which states that truly novel and unpredictable events may occur out of the composite of forces in a situation. It is often understood as ruling out Free Will. (In the *Encyclopedia of Philosophy*, Vol. 2, are thorough discussions of ethical determinism, logical determinism, theological determinism, physical determinism, and psychological determinism.) {CE; DCL}

Detrosier, Rowland (1796—1834)

Detrosier was a social reformer and lecturer, the illegitimate son of a Manchester man named Morris and a Frenchwoman named Detrosier. Self-educated, he gave Sunday scientific lecturers and published several discourses in favor of secular education. He founded the first Mechanics' Institutes (Manchester and Salford) and the Banksian Society of Manchester. Also, he became secretary to the National Political Union. A deist, Detrosier presided over a theistic chapel at Stockport. Like Bentham, who became his friend, Detrosier bequeathed his body for scientific purposes. (See entry for Gwyn A. Williams.) {BDF; RAT; VI}

Deubler, Konrad (1814—1884)

The son of poor Upper Austrian parents, Deubler became the friend of Feuerbach and Strauss and was known as "the peasant philosopher." Haeckel, in a letter to him, wrote, "If Diogenes, when he went around with his lantern, could have seen you, he would have blown it out." In 1854 Deubler was indicted for blasphemy, serving two years' hard labor and imprisonment. In 1870 he was made Burgomaster by his fellow-townsmen in Goisern, near Ischl, which office he resigned. In his will he bequeathed the interest of three thousand gulden for the support of poor children in the school he had erected. {BDF; PUT; RAT}

Deurhoff, Willem (1650—1717)

Deurhoff was a Dutch writer who, although educated for the church, gave himself to philosophy and translated the works of Descartes. Accused of being a follower of Spinoza, Deurhoff was forced to leave his country, taking refuge in Brabant. {BDF; RAT}

Deutsch, Emmanuel Oscar Menahem (1829—1873)

Deutsch was a German-Jewish orientalist. He was one of the first European scholars of his time in Hebrew, Greek, and Latin. He wrote essays on the Talmud (1867) and on Islam (1869) in the *Quarterly Review*. An agnostic, he wrote a series of scathing articles in the *Times* on the Vatican Council (1869). {RAT}

DEUTSCER FREIDENKER-VERBAND

A German group which publishes *Diesseits* is *Deuthcer Freidenker-Verband*, Hobrechtstrasse 8, W-1000 Berlin 44, Germany. Another publication, *Freidenker*, is published by a group based in Dortmund at Postfach 75, 0-1040, Berlin, Germany. (See entry for German Humanists.) {FD}

Dev, Sanjiv (20th Century)

Dr. Dev, a rationalist in India, is a landscape painter, author, and philosopher of aesthetics.

Devi, Prativa (20th Century)

Devi actively supports atheism in India. With Umesh Patri, Devi wrote "Progress of Atheism in India" (*Secular Nation*, Fall 1994).

DEVIL

- I spell God with 2 o's and the devil without the d."

—Anonymous Unitarian Minister prior to 1850

Non-believers find ludicrous the concept of supernatural devils or the Devil, who in later Jewish and early Christian usage is identified with Satan. A theological concept, it rests on the assumption that there is a source of all evil and that the source is bent upon enslaving mankind. Shirley Jackson Case, once a teacher at the University of Chicago's Divinity School, has written, "As the responsibility for evil in recent times has been saddled more definitely upon man himself, modern theological thought has become somewhat dubious about the actual personality of the Devil." Some apologists, however, write lengthy treatises as to why God in His omnipotence, omniscience, and omnipresence would allow a Devil to confront mankind, being always close at hand to tempt and destroy the faithful whenever he might catch them off their guard. Other apologists, however, are quick to emphasize the theological importance of Satan in Christianity, although in pre-exilic Jewish thought the figure of Satan was entirely unknown and the mention of Satan three times in the Old Testament is post-exilic, showing evidence of having been borrowed from the Zoroastrians' power of evil known as Ahriman.

Elaine Pagels, in *The Gnostic Gospels* (1979), developed the revolutionary viewpoint that early Christianity was not at all a unified movement and faith. Now a professor of religion at Princeton, she shattered many previous views, even winning from Harold Bloom the view that her work displayed "devoted and sound scholarship." Her *The Origin of Satan* (1995) develops the view that the Devil in the sacred Judeo-Christian literature and the rise of demonization was a terrifying component of Christianity. Angels are found in the Hebrew Bible, but demons are not. The Essenes and the followers of Jesus had the concept of Satan, or Belial or Beelzebub, and the four Gospel writers show a typology of God and Satan, Us and Them. According to David Remmick, "Although the Gospels tell a story of the moral genius of Jesus—his lessons of charity, redemption, and love—they also tell a parallel story in which the enemies of Jesus threaten tribal unity on earth and are, moreover, incarnations of Satan. This second story, in which the Gospel writers create a psychology of cosmic war," stated Remmick, "has influenced the course—the tragic course—of Western history." For example, the *Gospel of Mark* deviates from Jewish tradition and describes (3:23-27) the ministry of Jesus in constant battle with the "kingdom" of Satan, leading to what Pagels describes as the creation of such a powerful Satan in the orthodox Christian cosmology that it became not only a foundation for anti-Semitism but also a pattern of viewing the world. "Such visions have been incorporated into Christian tradition and have served, among other things, to confirm for Christians their own identification with God and to demonize their opponents—first other Jews, then pagans, and later dissident Christians called heretics." The viewpoint has been used by fundamentalists, from Pat Robertson to the ayatollahs, Remmick remarked.

Pagels, after securing permission to the Gnostic *samizdat* [suppressed literature which has clandestinely been published], learned that in the Gospel of Philip, the birth of Jesus derives from the unity of the Father of All, a masculine divinity, and the Holy Spirit, a distinctly feminine presence. According to Remmick, Pagels finds that the text mocks the orthodox notion of Mary's conception of Jesus independent of Joseph: "They do not know what they are saying." The early-Christian movement, she states, showed great openness toward women—Jesus himself flouted Jewish tradition by talking freely with women—and, as confirmed by Remmick, "the Gnostics generally affirm that tradition in their texts." Tertullian, an enemy of Gnostics, was outraged at the idea of women flocking to heretic sects, writing, "These heretical women—how audacious they are. They have no modesty; they are bold enough to teach, to engage in argument, to enact exorcisms, to undertake cures, and, it may be, even to baptize!" By the year 200, Christian feminism was stopped by Paul's *First Epistle to Timothy*: "Let a woman learn in silence with all submissiveness. I permit no woman to teach or to have authority over men; she is to keep silent." Pagels added, "Nearly 2,000 years later, in 1977, Pope Paul VXi, Bishop of Rome, declared that a woman cannot be a priest 'because our Lord was a man!' "

Pagels has concluded, "When I read the Gospels now and I come across the figure of Satan, instead of gliding over it as part of the story, I see it as raising a sort of warning flag, and I think, Ah, what is this writer doing now? What is the clue? What group of people are we speaking about and who is saying this? I become really interested in the structure of who is being demonized and who is doing the demonizing. . . . There was a time, for instance, when very few people who didn't suffer from it were aware of racism as an idea. Now this question is a part of our culture. It's not undone, but most people find it impossible to be unaware of racism. The same is true of sexism or homophobia. So that, too, is what the work on Satan and demonization is about. It's about being aware." (See "The Devil Problem," *The New Yorker*, 3 April 1995.) {ER}

DEVON (England) HUMANISTS

For information, write C. Mountain, "Little Gables," Burgmanns Hill, Lympstone, Exmouth EX8 5HN; or telephone 01395 265529.

Devore, Anita (20th Century)

Devore was the first president of HUMCON and spoke in 1994 at their 14th annual conference of the Alliance of Humanist, Atheist, and Ethical Culture Organizations of Los Angeles County, California.

De Voto, Bernard Augustine (1897—1955)

De Voto, an American writer and editor, wrote "The Easy Chair" for *Harper's Magazine* (1936—1938) and was editor of the *Saturday Review of Literature*. In addition to writing many books on history and literature, he was the official editor of the Mark Twain manuscripts and wrote *Mark Twain's America* (1932).

Asked about humanism, De Voto responded to the present author, "I'm too ignorant to have a philosophy. The only person on your list I've ever read is T. S. Eliot. At a guess, I would be instinctively against all positions you name. The words which name them are so hideous that the thinking must be hideous, too." {CE; WAS, 25 July 1954}

De Vries, Peter (1910—1993)

A writer and editor, De Vries was for a time an editor of *Poetry* and later was on the staff of *The New Yorker*, where he was known for his humorous, sophisticated work about Connecticut. He was a member of the American Academy of Arts and Letters.

In his *Blood of the Lamb* (1961), he wrote the following:

> "You don't believe in God," I said to Stein.
> "God is a word banging around in the human nervous system. He exists about as much as Santa Claus."
> "Santa Claus has had a tremendous influence, exist or not."
> "For children."
> "Lots of saints have died for God with a courage that's hardly childish"
> "That's part of the horror. It's all a fantasy. It's all for nothing."

and later,

> "You ought to be ashamed," a woman in an Easter bonnet told Stein. "Your race gave us our religion. . . . From ancient polytheism, the belief in lots of gods," the woman continued a little more eruditely, "the Hebrew nation led us on to the idea that there is only one."
> "Which is just a step from the truth," said Stein.

(TYD)

DE VRIJE GEDACHTE

The official journal of Dutch Free Thinkers is *De Vrije Gedachte*, POB 1087, 3000 BB Rotterdam, The Netherlands. E-mail: <DVG@netcetera.netcetera.nl>.

DE VRIJZINNIGE LEZER

A Belgian monthly in Dutch, *De Vrijzinnige Lezer* is at Lange Leemstraat 57, B 2018 Antwerpen, Belgium.

DE VRIJZINNIGE MICRO

De Vrijzinnige Micro is at Lange Leemstraat 57, B 2018, Antwerpen, Belgium.

Devuyst, Luc (20th Century)

Devuyst, a Belgian, is on the editorial board of *International Humanist.* He addressed the International Humanist and Ethical Union's (IHEU's) Second Moral Education Conference held in Brussels (1985).

De Waal, Frans (20th Century)

Why would a secular humanist behave ethically without some divine power to direct and enforce such actions? In *Good Natured: The Origins of Right and Wrong in Humans and Other Animals* (1996), de Waal holds that we inherited our capacity and need for ethics from our simian ancestors.

Wolf Roder, reviewing the book, found that de Waal faces a heavy burden of proof inasmuch as animals cannot be interviewed as to their ethical or selfish motives; however, using a wealth of data on chimpanzees, pygmy marmosets, gorillas, bonobos, baboons, and Japanese macaques, de Waal "goes a long way towards proving his case." (*Fig Leaves*, August 1996; *Free Inquiry*, Winter 1996-1997)

Dewey, John (1859—1952)

Dewey, philosophic instrumentalist, psychologist, educator at Columbia University, and author of *The Quest for Certainty, Freedom and Culture* (1929), is one of the intellectual giants of the twentieth century. In *The Revival of Pragmatism* (1998), Richard Rorty is cited as calling Dewey one of the three most important philosophers of the century, along with Heidegger and Wittgenstein.

When in 1950 Humanist Clubs were being established at universities, Dewey wrote,

> I am much interested in learning of the plans for the formation of a Humanist Group among Harvard and Columbia students. The drift away from religious institutions founded on supernaturalism is marked among the intellectually-minded well-informed persons in every country. Even among those who remain nominally connected with institutions professing doctrines of a supernatural sort, there is a growing spirit of indifference to the kind of devotion to ideals which once marked these institutions. The enduring element in religion is genuine and ardent devotion to the cause of promoting the knowledge and practice of the highest moral aims of which man is possible.
>
> It is my firm belief that the Humanist Movement is based upon acknowledgment of the importance of beliefs and movements ardently concerned with this aim. It is particularly important that university men and women, who should influence popular sentiment and ideas in the future, realize the increasing inability of doctrines and institutions that in the past have been the carriers of inspiring ideals to meet the demands of the modern world, and should be active in furtherance of a substitute that possesses the required vitality.

Along with his statement, Dewey also sent a $1 check to Warren Allen Smith for membership in the Humanist Club at Columbia University, which later became a chapter of the American Humanist Association. Also in the 1950s, Dewey was on the advisory board of Charles Francis Potter's First Humanist Society of New York.

In *The Influence of Darwinism in Philosophy* (1910), Dewey states that he was not interested in "an intelligence that shaped things once for all but the intelligence which things are even now shaping." McCabe, however, holds that Dewey made a mistake in using any theistic references whatsoever. "In recent years," McCabe wrote,

> [Dewey] has advised a new sort of theistic formula: not that God is an objective reality but the relation of man to the ideal. He seems to have fallen into the common fallacy of philosophic moralists that most men need a God, but most men will not even understand what he means by God.

James Gouinlock makes the point that Dewey had no use for what he called militant atheism, of which Bertrand Russell's *A Free Man's Worship* is typical. Dewey insisted that a valid philosophy had to be evaluative, that one should be neither blind to the goods of nature and life nor adopt a position of wholesale acceptance. To Dewey, this is the religious quality of life.

He was the sole philosopher to sign Humanist Manifesto I. In fact, according to Edwin H. Wilson, Dewey signed the draft without change or comment. Dewey later explained in a letter to Corliss Lamont why he had signed the work:

> There is a great difference between different kinds of "Humanism" as you know; there is that of Paul Elmer More for example. I signed the humanist manifesto precisely because of the point to which you [Corliss Lamont] seem to object, namely because it had a religious context, and my signature was a sign of sympathy on that score, and not a commitment to every clause in it.
>
> "Humanism" as a technical philosophic term is associated with [F.C.S.] Schiller and while I have great regard for his writings, it seems to me that he gave Humanism an unduly subjectivistic turn—he was so interested in bringing out the elements of human desire and purpose neglected in traditional philosophy that he tends it seems to me to a virtual isolation of man from the rest of nature. I have come to think of my own position as cultural or humanistic Naturalism—Naturalism, properly interpreted seems to me a more adequate term than Humanism. Of course I have always limited my use of "instrumentalism" to my theory of thinking and knowledge; the word pragmatism I have used very little, and then with reserves.

Dewey was a member of and financial contributor to the American Humanist Association. Also, he was an honorary associate of the Rationalist Press Association, which in 1899 had been founded by Charles A. Watts. Although attacked by religionists on the right and by some on the left who felt he did not understand the nature of evil, Dewey's naturalistic approach to religious experience is considered by many today to be precisely that which is of paramount importance if mankind hopes to resolve the problems which organized religion presents. His approach was neither that of the melancholy atheist nor that of the otherworldly supernaturalist.

Some of his works are *Education: The School and Society* (1899); *How We Think* (1910); *Democracy and Education* (1916); *Reconstruction in Philosophy* (1920); *A Common Faith* (1934); *Logic* (1938); *Experience and Education* (1938); and, with Arthur Bentley, *Knowing and the Known* (1949). These writings show his rejection of authoritarian teaching methods, for he held education in a democracy is a tool to enable different people with different cultures to integrate their lives and vocations in progressive, constructive, democratic ways. For Dewey, truth was not an absolute. To solve problems, individuals searched for truths, not Truth, and these truths changed as their problems changed. His philosophic instrumentalism had no need for transcendental or eternal reality, and his educational philosophy known as "progressive education" made him the foremost educator of his day. His view of a "renascent liberalism" included a three-step strategy: first, it must develop historical perspective; second, it must reconstruct traditional liberal values; and third, it must inform, guide, and actively reconstruct social institutions and their practices.

Richard Shusterman of Temple University has called Dewey "probably the greatest of American pragmatist philosophers and certainly the most influential for cultural criticism and aesthetics." He adds that "Pragmatism has recently been revived in literary theory through the writings of Stanley Fish and Richard Rorty. But neither of them pays attention to Dewey's aesthetics, and indeed they present theories that are un-Deweyan in their disembodied 'textualism' and elitist professionalism. Though some of Dewey's aesthetic ideas and judgments may be dated, his work still represents the best point of departure for progressive pragmatist literary theory and aesthetics."

For Richard Rorty, Dewey was a philosophic giant, an anti-Communist social democrat who thought of pragmatism as a tool to expand human freedom. Like Sidney Hook, Dewey witnessed what Alan Ryan has described as "the high tide of American liberalism," and Rorty thinks of both as "hard to match among present-day American philosophers—or, for that matter, American intellectuals. Both men resemble such heroic nineteenth-century figures as John Stuart Mill in the sheer quantity of work they managed to get done, in the range of their curiosity, and in their ability to switch back and forth between abstract philosophy and concrete social issues with no sense of strain, and no diminution in intensity."

John E. Smith of Hamden, Connecticut, is of the opinion that Ryan made a mistake in reviewing Rorty's book about Dewey, thinking that Dewey urged his philosophical readers to turn away from "the problems of philosophy" to "the problems of men." Not so, Smith claimed (*The New York Times Book Review*, 14 June 1998), adding, "Dewey's advice was to turn away from 'the problems of philosophers,' by which he meant the puzzles (such as, How do I know that my neighbor has a mind?) that are so dear to professional philosophers, and deal instead with "questions which actually arise in the vicissitudes of life." Otherwise, to oppose "the problems of philosophy" to "the problems of men" would have been counter to Dewey's entire outlook.

Roberta Dewey was some forty-five years younger than her husband and upon his death late at 11 P.M. had telephoned Donald Szantho Harrington, minister of the Community (Unitarian) Church in New York City. Although Dewey was not a member of the church, he had once told his wife that if he died she should call Harrington, that he would know what to do. Upon arriving before midnight, Harrington recalled in an article for *Religious Humanism* (Summer 1994), he found that Mrs. Dewey fainted right after opening the door. The two adopted children, Belgian war orphans John and Adrienne, sensibly found some ammonia to revive her, after which it was decided that cremation should be the following morning at Fresh Pond Crematory in Queens. Dewey's body was covered with a sheet and blanket, the children were put to bed, and Harrington left by 2 A.M. The following morning, Harrington and Mrs. Dewey watched the coffin go into the tort for cremation. Although David Dubinsky and William Heard Kilpatrick volunteered to speak at a memorial, Mrs. Dewey did not want a long, drawn-out affair, saying Dewey hated those things, and she suggested that Max Otto of the University of Wisconsin in Madison should be the speaker.

At Dewey's memorial service, held 4 June 1952, Harrington spoke of Dewey's influence on American world life and thought, of his ability as a teacher to get others to speak, and of his personal memories of having driven Dewey from Chicago to Madison and back. "I thought I would get a lot of wisdom. Instead, he . . . kept me talking. All I can remember his saying was 'Possibly,' and 'You may be right!'" Harrington then read passages from the Bible, which surprised many in the audience, along with Matthew Arnold's "Rugby Chapel," George Eliot's "The Choir Invisible," and Samuel Taylor Coleridge's "Ode on Dejection." George Kykhuizen recalls in *The Life and Mind of John Dewey* (1973) that Harrington referred to Dewey as "one of the intellectual and moral giants" of all time, declaring that "when the full impact of his revolutionary thought reaches the heart of our society, some generations hence, scarcely a single social institution will remain as it is today."

Norman Thomas was present, as was William Heard Kilpatrick, both with their distinctively white hair. Of the several speakers, Max Otto was the one with the most amusing recollection. He had stopped Dr. Dewey on the campus one day and had asked him a question pertaining to philosophy. Dewey had looked down, cogitated, looked up, had looked around, and he had not said anything for minutes and minutes . . . and yet more minutes . . . and more. Just as Dr. Otto was about to interrupt, thinking maybe Dewey was suffering some illness, there ensued a long, complex response which was uttered slowly and distinctively, one so complete Otto could scarcely believe it had not been written down beforehand. A good question deserves a good answer, Dewey was showing. But, said Otto to much laughter, "I was very, *very* careful after that whenever I questioned Dr. Dewey about anything." Otto also said that Dewey's philosophy was like that of a mountain climber who climbs in order to see farther, and who, once he has climbed one mountain, presses on to a higher one simply to see farther yet. It was the continual quest for new vision and new vistas that marked the greatness of Dewey's mind. And what is man's purpose if he climbs all the mountains and there are no more to see, Dewey was once asked. Then, he responded, there would be no purpose in living.

A soloist sang "Swing Low, Sweet Chariot" and "The Balm of Gilead," the latter said to have been a favorite of Dewey's. At the end, Harrington took Mrs. Dewey with one hand and carried what appeared to be a water pitcher with the other, and the two led the audience out of the room. It was only then that some realized the cremains had been present throughout the service, that atop the altar had been a bronze urn, not a water pitcher.

Although Columbia University had wanted the ashes, Dewey's Alma Mater, the University of Vermont, received them as well as, later, Roberta Dewey's ashes.

Harrington recalled that at the ceremony he had met for the first time Dewey's four children from his first marriage (one of whom was adopted), that they seemed upset and angry that they had not been consulted and involved in the funeral arrangements. Harrington, however, had left all the announcements and notifications to Roberta for completion, and, although it now was too late, Harrington became aware that the children had not approved of their father's remarriage and were critical of their having adopted the two young children.

Currently, The John Dewey Society for the Study of Education and Culture publishes *Education and Culture: The Journal of the John Dewey Society* (1600 Maple Street, Carrollton, Georgia 30118). The journal, published twice a year by the John Dewey Society and the University of Iowa, is edited by Peter S. Hlebowitsh.

Alan Ryan, in *John Dewey and the High Tide of American Liberalism* (1995), argues that the thought of John Dewey is more relevant today than ever before, that a revival of his ideas is needed. Richard Wightman Fox of Boston University has commended Ryan for his description of Dewey's teacher-centered viewpoint, one which helped talented instructors to bring children to new levels of understanding by enlisting their innate interest in solving real problems, not only practical problems but intellectual and artistic ones. (See entries American Humanist Association, James Grasso, Alan Ryan, and Leon Trotsky.) {CE; CL; EU, James Gouinlock; EW; *Free Inquiry*, Winter 1994, devoted an entire issue to Dewey; FUS; HM1; HNS; HNS2; Richard Rorty, "Remembering John Dewey and Sidney Hook," *Free Inquiry*, Winter 1995-1996; TRI; TYD; WAS, 11 September 1950}

Dewey, Orville (Born 1794)

Dewey, a Unitarian minister, was a well-known orator of his day. {U}

Dewing, Frances R. (20th Century)

Dewing, according to the Morains' *Humanism as the Next Step*, is a person who utilizes the scientific method rather than depending on "truth by authority." {HNS2}

DeWitt, Dale (20th Century)

A minister of Community (Unitarian) Church in New York, DeWitt was once a director of the American Humanist Association. {HNS}

De Worms, Henry (1840—1903)

De Worms, the first Baron Pirbright, was a politician and the first Jew to be admitted to the Privy Council. In 1895, he was raised to the peerage. In 1886, he severed his connection with Judaism and married against the laws of the synagogue. De Worms wrote *The Earth and Its Mechanism* (1862). {RAT}

DeWolf, Mary Louise (1931-)

DeWolf, a second generation Floridian, is a Unitarian Universalist ministerial candidate. After careers as an educator and Unitarian Universalist Association field staff person, she is a graduate student in religious studies at the University of South Florida. DeWolf is a frequent Sunday speaker in Florida UU congregations. {WAS, 4 May 99}

Dexter, Caroline (1819—1894)

Dexter was an early Australian freethinker and radical feminist. A friend of the novelist George Sand, she moved to Australia and set up a school which taught elocution, literature, writing, and conversation. After a failed marriage, she settled in Melbourne, becoming a champion of women's rights. She stunned the local community by opening an Institute of Hygiene, advocating dress reform for women, divided skirts, and the abolition of corsets. Upon marrying a prosperous solicitor, William Lynch, she continued her freethought writing and became a patron of the arts. {SWW}

De Young, Mary (20th Century)

A freethinker, De Young wrote *Call to Reason* (1977). {GS}

Dharmalingam, A. M. (20th Century)

A freethinker in India, Dharmalingam wrote *Freethought in the Ancient World* (1977) and *Agrarian Structure and Population* (1991). {FUK; GS}

DHIMMIS: For information about non-Muslims in Muslim countries, see entry for Bat Yóer.

d'Holbach, Paul Henri Thiry: See entry for Holbach, Paul Henry Thiry de.

Diagoras (c. 415 B.C.E.)

According to Robertson, Diagoras of Melos was a poet who declared that the non-punishment of a certain act of iniquity proved that there are no gods. Diagoras had been a student of Democritus, who is said to have freed him from slavery. Allegedly, he became an atheist after being the victim of an unpunished perjury. He was accused of impiety, because he threw a wooden image of a god into a fire, remarking that the deity should perform another miracle and save itself.

As a result, he had to flee from Athens to Corinth. He was charged with divulging the Eleusinian and other mysteries, with making firewood of an image of Heracles in order to prepare a dish of lentils, and of telling the god to perform his thirteenth labor by cooking the preparation. As a result, a silver talent was offered to anyone who would kill him, or two talents if he could be captured alive. Somehow, he escaped and died in Corinth. {BDF; HAB; JMR; JMRH; TYD}

DIALOGUE

A quarterly newsletter in English, *Dialogue* is published by the American Ethical Union, 2 West 64th Street, New York, NY 10023.

Diamond, David (1915—)

Diamond, an American composer of note, studied with Roger Sessions and Nadia Boulanger. His work in the 1930s has been described as being neoclassical, after which he developed a romantic twelve-tone technique which he has used in a variety of styles. Composer of nine symphonies and various other works, he is best-known for "Rounds" (1944). Asked in 1992 what humanism connoted, Diamond replied to the present author,

> To believe in Man's possibility of self-improvement and the elimination of all superstitious mumbo-jumbo.

In 1995, Diamond elaborated further:

> Heine and his agnosticism has been interesting me all over again. The Sammons biography was fine but Ernst Pawel's (what a loss!) splendid Heine's *Last Paris Days* deals with this wonderfully. I think Heine liked the poetic splendour of Biblical times, as Flaubert did. But Heine, being Jewish, was more attuned to the rituals and ethics.
>
> Strange what [Arthur] Miller said [in a statement about secular humanism, quoted in his entry in the present work]. I know what he means, but the Wonder and Cruelty of the Universe makes me turn to Jeshua ben David of Nazareth when I am fed up with Man's viciousness and cruelty and greed. Yaweh, Jehovah, or Adonai, stopped talking directly to his human creation ever since Moses invented him, language and all.
>
> The new religious Right has me angry—it's the same crap fifty years later, and on and on. The majority of irrational humans are dumb-dums, non-thinking simpletons. But Cummings [in his entry, quoted in the present work] said it all much better.

In a *Who's Who* entry, Diamond wrote, "To have felt out of step in one's first years confirms one's invalidism in these last years: a sad story at best, with just a glimmer of hope before the next catastrophe." (See entry for E. E. Cummings.) {WAS, 16 June 1992 and 18 September 1995}

Diamond, John (20th Century; Deceased)

Diamond was one of the original incorporators of Atheists of Florida, Inc.

Diamond, Sara (20th Century)

Diamond, who writes on civil liberties subjects for *The Humanist*, is author of *Spiritual Warfare: The Politics of the Christian Right* (1989, is a columnist for *Z*, and has a doctorate in sociology.

DIANA: See entry for Great Mother Goddess. The virgin goddess of hunting and childbirth, like the Greek Artemis, Diana is traditionally associated with the moon and is revered by some of the more masculine lesbians.

Dias, E. (20th Century)

In 1908, Dias from São Paolo edited the Brazilian freethought journal, *Lanterna*, which was in Portuguese.

Diaz, Porfirio [President] (1830—1915)

Diaz, the President of the Republic of Mexico, was educated for the priesthood but quit the church, took to law and politics, and became the most famous leader of the anti-clericals. Because of his efforts, Mexico became a much safer place for freethinkers and other non-believers, and he drastically checked the corrupt Church in Mexico. In addition, the number of public schools rose from two to six thousand. {JM; PUT}

Dibble, R. T. (20th Century)

A freethinker, Dibble wrote "The Devil's Advocate" in *American Mercury* (1924). {GS}

Di Cagno Politi, Niccola Annibale (Born 1857)

An Italian positivist, Di Cagno Politi studied at Naples under Angiulli, wrote about the culture of his time, and contributed articles on positivism to the *Revista Europea*. {BDF}

Dick, Kenneth C. (20th Century)

Dick, a freethinker, wrote *Man, Father of the Gods* (1971). {GS}

Dickens, Charles (1812—1870)

Dickens was an amateur theatrical manager, a novelist, and the father of ten. His childhood, about which he would write, included working for a time in a blacking warehouse (a humiliation he is said never to have forgotten). He started out as a court stenographer and a parliamentary reporter, then wrote humorous sketches and became famous for his *Posthumous Papers of the Pickwick Club* (1836—1837).

In 1836, he married Catherine Hogarth, but after she gave birth to their ten children, the two separated in 1858 in what has been described as an unhappy marriage. Dickens painted rich portraits of all aspects of society in his work, and he dramatized abuses such as bad education, imprisonment for debt, and legal delays. His memorable characters include Ebenezer Scrooge, Uriah Heap, and Mr. Micawber, and among his noted works are *A Christmas Carol* (1843), *David Copperfield* (1850), and *A Tale of Two Cities* (1859). Dickens once wrote, "Missionaries are perfect nuisances and leave every place worse than they found it." He attended Unitarian services in London at the Little Portland Street chapel, where he was a close friend of the Reverend Edward Tagart.

Bleak House, which was published in monthly parts (1852—1853), marked a decline in his reputation for many of his contemporaries, but the work has been considered one of the high points of his achievement by George Bernard Shaw, G. K. Chesterton, Joseph Conrad, and Lionel Trilling. Dickens, perhaps desperate for a title, originally had intended to call the work *Tom-All-Alone's Factory That Got into Chancery and Never Got Out.*

In 1998 previously downplayed details about his private life appeared in magazines, including *Vanity Fair* (April 1998). Louise Brooks, a Paramount movie star legend known for epitomizing the Jazz Age and the sexual freedom of the 1920s, was described as having made a rough count of the men she had had sex with. She estimated a modest ten a year from the ages of seventeen to sixty, or 430. She divulged details that shocked many, including a statement that Dickens also was sex-driven and had a passion for young girls. Berkley Books editor-in-chief Tom Dardis quoted Brooks without otherwise documenting where she gained her information:

> In 1836 when Dickens married Kate Hogarth (20) he brought sister Mary (16), whom he really loved, to live with them. When Mary died in 1837 he nearly lost his mind. Upon reading *The Old Curiosity Shop* 1840—1841, old lady Hogarth [Kate and Mary's mother] made him laugh when she said he didn't fool her—he was Quilp and Mary was little Nell. (Nabokov used this allusion [Quilty] in *Lolita*.)

Dickens, at the end of his life, suffered from increased paralysis of the left side. With difficulty he could move about. It was a time when the main joy of living was for him to give public readings. He was still saddened by his children's unhappiness, by his unamicable separation from his wife, and by the continued social injustices he had written about for so long. On June 8th, according to biographer Edgar Johnson, Dickens was sitting with his sister-in-law, Georgina Hogarth, whereupon he suddenly announced that he had to go to London at once. Rising, he began to topple over while she attempted to hold him up. Unable to carry his weight, she let Dickens down slowly. "On the ground" were his last words as he slipped into a coma and died the following day. He is buried in the Poets' Corner, London's Westminster Abbey. The gravestone is a black marble floor slab with name and vital dates. {CB; CE; EG; OEL; PA; TYD; U; UU}

Dickinson, Emily (1830—1886)

Dickinson shares with Whitman the honor of being the major U.S. poet. Both had an unorthodox outlook concerning religion. Neither was a Bible-thumper nor church-joiner. Both were highly literate readers whose friends were often transcendentalists. Neither married. In her lifetime, Dickinson published fewer than a dozen poems, but today she is revered as a consummate writer. For the last twenty-five years of her life, Dickinson chose to live reclusively in The Homestead built by her grandfather, the founder of Amherst College. There, behind a stand of enormous hemlocks on Amherst's Main Street, she withdrew, often dressed in white, perhaps savoring an exhaustion brought on by her previous and emotional contact with others. Once when she brought a cousin to her bedroom, she locked the door, waved the key, and exclaimed, "Now *this* is freedom!" For it was here she could dream, here she could contemplate, and here she could write. Upon her death, her sister Lavinia found some two thousand poems in a camphor-wood chest in the bedroom.

One who might have made a difference was the critic Thomas Wentworth Higginson, who seemed not to have recognized her poetic genius. However, Dickinson disliked the fact that he corrected her poems. A married man, he is believed by some not to have had the sexual attraction for her which she possibly had for him. (One explanation: Higginson once wrote of William Henry Hurlbert, "I never loved but one male friend with a passion," having found him "like some fascinating girl" and modeling the hero of his *Malbone* (1869) after him. Complained Mrs. Higginson, the letters the two exchanged were "more like those between man and woman than between two men.")

One biographer allegedly reconstructed two love affairs that Dickinson had with women, a century after they occurred. When both were sixteen, Dickinson met Susan Gilbert. In letters to Susan, who became her future sister-in-law, Dickinson had included such lines as "Be my own again, and kiss me as you used to" and "The expectation once more to see your face again makes me feel hot and feverish, and my heart beats so fast." An 1858 birthday greeting to Susan, who have moved next door with her husband Austin, Emily's brother, begins:

> One Sister have I in our house—
> And one, a hedge away.
> There's only one recorded,
> But both belong to me.

Martha Dickinson Bianchi, Susan's daughter and Emily's niece, deleted many of such lines, which had first been published in 1924. However, Camille Paglia, for one, discounts any such gossip about a lesbian affair.

Mabel L. Todd, along with Higginson, a Unitarian, edited the body of Dickinson's work, bringing her much posthumous fame. Thomas Johnson in 1955 compiled a scholarly collection of her entire body of work. An even more impressive collection, containing 1,789 of her poems and edited by R. W. Franklin, is *The Poems of Emily Dickinson: Variorum Edition* (1999). Franklin respects her eccentric writing practices, including her erratic spelling, capitalization, and punctuation. Higginson may have found her style unconventional, but Dickinson had deliberately chosen unconventionality. When Higginson told her that her work resembled Whitman's in its unorthodox presentation, she responded, "I never read his Book—but was told that he was disgraceful."

What her letters and poems show is her inability to accept the orthodox religious faith of her day, although she longed for its spiritual comfort. "Home," she declared, "is the definition of God."

Immortality, she called "the flood subject" and she never gave up her belief in it.

For her, "The Bible is an antique Volume—/Written by faded men." Basically, she was something of a Unitarian, something of a transcendentalist, something of a religious humanist, something of a religious theist, and something of a humanistic aesthete:

> "Faith" is a fine invention, when gentlemen can *see*
> But microscopes are prudent, in an emergency.
>
> Some keep the Sabbath going to church;
> I keep it staying at home,
> With a bobolink for a chorister,
> And an orchard for a dome. . . .
>
> Elysium is as far as to
> The very nearest room,
> If in that room a friend await
> Felicity or doom. . . .
>
> I never spoke with God,
> Nor visited in heaven;
> Yet certain am I of the spot
> As if the chart were given. . . .
>
> My life closed twice before its close;
> It remains to see
> If Immortality unveil
> A third event to me. . . .
>
> Because I could not stop for Death,
> He kindly stopped for me;
> The carriage held but just ourselves
> And Immortality. . . .

Her epitaph

CALLED BACK

is ambiguous and may not have been chosen by her. She is buried in West Amherst, Massachusetts.

(See entry for Alffred Kazin, who wrote that Dickinson found Whitman's views about God "disgraceful."
{CE; GL; *The New York Review of Books*, 8 April 1999; OEL; TYD}

Dickinson, Goldsworthy Lowes (20th Century)

Dickinson was an economist who, in the *Hibbert Journal* (1908), wrote, "I do not think that a religion which ought properly to be called Christian can adequately represent the attitude of an intelligent and candid modern man." He held to a shadowy theism but was skeptical about personal immortality. {RAT}

Dickstein, Morris (20 Century)

Dickstein edited *The Revival of Pragmatism, New Essays on Social Thought* (1999). Essays are by Richard Rorty, Hilary Putnam, Judge Richard Posner, Stanley Fish, Richard Poirier, and Ross Posnock.

Dictos, Perry (20th Century)

Dictos has been President of Humanists of the San Joaquin Valley in California. He is author of *An Honest Look at the Bible: Everything You Wanted to Know About the Bible But You Were Afraid to Ask* (1997).

DIDDLING: See entry for pickpocketry, which tells the freethinkers' view that we do not choose *between* good and evil but, rather, *among* several options.

Dide, Auguste [Senator] (Born 1839)

Dide was a French writer and politician. A graduate in theology, he was criticized for the contents of his thesis and, after editing the *Protestant Libéral* for six years, joined the Independent Church and ended as a pure humanist. "We must believe not in metaphysical divinities," he wrote, "but in ourselves." A Senator, Dide was a member of the Legion of Honour and one of the founders of the *Société d'Histoire de la Révolution.* {RAT}

Diderot, Denis (1713—1784)

A French atheist and Encyclopedist, Diderot was a materialist philosopher. When readers passed by A, B, and C in the new encyclopedia, they found "Dieu," or God. "*Mon Dieu*, they exclaimed, "you cannot put an entry for ***Dieu*** in an encyclopedia! The very idea is blasphemous!" But Diderot did, and other corresponding entries were included which shocked the populace and theologians of that time. The *Encyclopédie ou dictionnaire raisonné des sciences, des arts et des métiers par une société de gens de lettres, mis en ordre et publié par M. Diderot et M. D'Alembert* (1745—1772) easily made the Vatican's list of prohibited reading in 1759. Diderot believed that God is an utterly useless idea in science and philosophy and the cause of endless dissension and inhumanity, notes Lester G. Crocker, who edited Diderot's *Selected Writings*.

In 1746 Diderot published *Philosophic Thoughts*, which was condemned to be burned but did much to advance freedom of opinion. In 1749 his *Letters on the Blind* resulted in his imprisonment at Vincennes because of its materialistic atheism. Rousseau, who called him "a transcendent genius," visited Diderot in prison, where he remained for three years. During the French Revolution, Maréchal considered Diderot one of the most important atheists of all time, finding that his work was a resounding blow against the church's reactionary ideas.

Diderot also was a novelist, satirist, and playwright, producing *The Father of the Family* (1758), the first "bourgeois drama." John Morley gave an interesting description of Diderot's personal appearance: "His conversational powers were great and showed the fertility of his genius." "When I recall Diderot," wrote Maister, "the immense variety of his ideas, the amazing multiplicity of his knowledge, the rapid flight, the warmth, the impetuous tumult of his imagination, all the charm and all the disorder of his conversation, I venture to liken his character to Nature herself, exactly as he used to conceive her—rich, fertile, abounding in germs of every sort, gentle and fierce, simple and majestic, worthy and sublime, but without any dominating principle, without a master and without a God."

Among Diderot's witty observations are the following:

- The Christian religion: the most absurd in its dogmas, the most unintelligible, the most insipid, the most gloomy, the most Gothic, the most puerile.
- The Christian religion teaches us to imitate a God that is cruel, insidious, jealous, and implacable in his wrath.
- Fanaticism is just one step away from barbarism.
- Skepticism is the first step toward truth.
- I have eyes and a heart and I like to look at a pretty woman, like to feel the curve of her breast under my hand, press her lips to mine, drink bliss from her eyes and die of ecstasy in her arms. Sometimes a gay party with my friends, even if it becomes a little rowdy, is not displeasing to me. But I must confess that I find it infinitely sweeter to . . . tell her whom I love something tender and true which brings her arms about my neck.

P. N. Furbank's critical biography, *Diderot*, shows that when Diderot could find no experts who dared write for his encyclopedia, he wrote the articles himself. And when a spy reported to the police some of the material he was working on, it was the king who saved him. According to Voltaire, who got the story from one of the king's servants, Louis had inquired how gunpowder worked, both in killing human enemies and in killing partridges. "Alas, it is the same with everything in the world," replied Mme. de Pompadour. "I don't know what the rouge I use is made of, and I should be hard put to it if someone asked me how my silk stockings are made." At this point, a duke informed Louis it was a shame he had had the encyclopedia confiscated, for it contained the answers. When the king sent footmen to find the volumes, according to Voltaire's story, Mme. de Pompadour learned the difference between French and Spanish rouge as well as how a stocking-machine worked. Meanwhile, the king learned how gunpowder worked and read all about the rights of the crown. Thereupon, the "dangerous work" was pronounced an "excellent book" and Diderot was protected. Rationalist that he was, Diderot "joined the party of humanity," illustrating that a philosopher not only lives by reason but also can be virtuous, decent, and regard civil society as his "divinity." Comte called Diderot "the greatest thinker of the eighteenth century."

Checkered as Diderot's life had been, his closing years were full of peace and comfort. Superstition was mortally wounded, the Church was terrified, and it was clear that the change the philosophers had worked for was at hand. As Morley observed, "the press literally teemed with pamphlets, treatises, poems, histories, all shouting from the house-tops open destruction to beliefs which fifty years before were actively protected against so much as a whisper in the closet. Every form of literary art was seized and turned into an instrument in the remorseless attack on *L'Infame*."

In the spring of 1784 Diderot was attacked by what be felt was his last illness. Dropsy set in, and in a few months the end came. A fortnight before his death he was removed from the upper floor in the Rue Taranne, which he had occupied for thirty years, to palatial rooms provided for him by the Czarina in the Rue de Richelieu. Growing weaker every day he was still alert in mind. He did all he could to cheer the people around him, and amused himself and them by arranging his pictures and his books. In the evening, to the last, he found strength to converse on science and philosophy to the friends who were eager as ever for the last gleanings of his prolific intellect.

On the evening of 30 July 1784, he sat down to table, and at the end of the meal took an apricot. His wife, with kind solicitude, remonstrated. "*Mais quel diable de nial veux-tu que cela me fasse?* (How the deuce can that hurt me?)," he said, and ate the apricot. Then he rested his elbow on the table, trifling with some sweetmeats. His wife asked him a question and, on receiving no answer, looked up and saw he was dead. He had died as the Greek poets say that men died in the golden age—they passed away as if mastered by Sleep. In the last conversation that his daughter heard him carry on, his last words were the pregnant aphorism that "the first step towards philosophy is incredulity." Incredibly, Diderot's son-in-law arranged for special dispensation to have Diderot buried in consecrated ground at Saint-Roch. (See entry for Ephraim Chambers, originator of the *Cyclopaedia of Arts and Sciences* [1728].) {BDF; FO; FUS; JM; JMRH; PUT; RAT; TYD}

Dieffenbach, Albert Charles (1876—1963)

Dieffenbach was a Unitarian minister who signed Humanist Manifesto I. His considerable efforts in helping formulate and editing the manifesto have been described by Edwin H. Wilson in *The Genesis of a Humanist Manifesto* (1995). A former editor of *The Christian Register* (Unitarian), Dieffenbach reviewed Charles Francis Potter's *The Faiths Men Live By* for *The Humanist*. From 1944 to 1949, he was minister of the Church of the Larger Fellowship, a correspondence group for Unitarians who did not live near other Unitarians. From 1944 to 1949, he was editor of the Wayside Pulpit. Dieffenbach wrote *Religious Liberty, the Great American Illusion* (1927). {FUS; HM1; HNS}

Diercks, Gustav (Born 1852)

Diercks was the German author of *History of the Development of Human Spirit* (1881—1882). He also wrote on Arabian culture in Spain (1887) and was a member of the German Freethinkers' Union. {BDF; RAT}

Dierenfield, Richard (20th Century)

Dierenfield wrote *Religion in the American Public Schools* (1962). {FUS}

DIESSEITS - ZEITSCHRIFT FUR AUFKLARUNG UND HUMANISMUS

A humanistic quarterly in German, *Diesseits-Zeitschrift fur Aufklarung und Humanismus* is at Hobrechtstrasse 8, D-12045, Berlin, Germany. E-mail: <hvdberlin@aol.com>.

Dietrich, Con (1918—1997)

Dietrich was a distinguished physicist, a committed humanist, and an early member of Ealing Humanist Association. He wrote *Uncertainty, Calibration, and Probability: the Statistics of Scientific and Industrial Measurement* (1973).

Dietrich, John Hassler (1878—1976)

A minister of the First Unitarian Church in Minneapolis, Dietrich also was on the advisory board of Charles Francis Potter's First Humanist Society of New York. He was a signer of Humanist Manifesto I. Also, he was the first Unitarian minister to refer to his way in religion as "humanistic," echoing elements of the Greek enlightenment and of the Renaissance. His friend, Curtis Reese, was another Unitarian clergyman to adopt the label "humanist." Dietrich liked Paine's "religion of humanity" and the ideas of thinkers as diverse as Ludwig Feuerbach, George Eliot, Auguste Comte, and Robert G. Ingersoll.

As an explanation of his outlook, he wrote, "Humanism simply ignores the idea of God, failing to see any evidence of intelligent purpose in the universe, which surely is the minimum basis of Theism. The attitude taken is one of open-mindedness and inquiry, not of denials. . . . Old religions assume that there is a personal God at the center and source of things, from whom all power and blessings flow. Religion consists in bringing oneself into right relation with this personality. . . . In contrast to this, the Humanist says that it is useless to try to determine just what is the ultimate center and source of all power and blessing. . . . The all-important thing is that we strive to bring ourselves into better relation with that portion of reality with which we come into actual contact. . . . If human life is to have meaning, we must give it that meaning. . . . The world is so saturated with the theism and supernaturalism of the Christian church that any other form of religious aspiration is regarded as impossible, if not unthinkable. . . . We perceive an apparently endless process of constant, related change, which we call evolution—not in the narrow sense that man has sprung from lower animals, but in the broad sense of a changing, developing mode of existence."

He also wrote, "Whereas the Christian church connects the power for goodness with one name in the world's history, humanism recognizes that goodness springs from many sources, so that its formula of worship would base itself, not upon the name of Jesus or Buddha [Siddhartha] or Mohammed alone, but would express reverence for the divergent forces of the universal good."

To a Western Unitarian Conference in Des Moines, he pointed out: "What you are calling the religion of democracy, I am calling humanism." Edwin H. Wilson has said that some of the Unitarian clergy who defended the rights of humanists, such as Dietrich and Reese, were "evolutionary theists," declaring that evolution was

God's way of creation. In contrast, Dietrich and Reese were frankly non-theists, unwilling to use such terminology.

In 1956, he elaborated upon changes in his views to the present author:

> I was one of the original, if not the original minister, to preach the interpretation of religion which I called Humanism and for twenty-five years I proclaimed this doctrine to large audiences in a Unitarian Church, but I no longer call myself a Humanist except in the sense you attribute to the lexicographer, "a term denoting devotion to humanity and human interests." I sometimes called my Humanist Religious Humanism and sometimes Naturalistic Humanism. In any case it was the Humanism now represented by the American Humanist Association and its various members, and I think is quite accurately defined by your definition of Naturalistic Humanism. But of late years, due to much reading and mature thought, my philosophy and religion have undergone a complete revision. I now think it a philosophy too narrow in its conception of the great cosmic scheme, about which we know so little, and concerning which we should be less dogmatic and arrogant. It in no wise reflects the humility which becomes the real seeker after truth. I see now how my utter reliance upon science and reason and my contempt for any intuitive insights and intangible values which are the very essence of art and religion was a great mistake. I think the Humanism of that period served a good purpose as a protest movement against orthodox dogmatism, but its day has passed.
>
> What I am trying to say is that the positive side of Naturalistic Humanism was and is fine—its insistence upon the enrichment of human life in its every form; but its negative side, cutting itself off from all cosmic relationship and denying or ignoring every influence outside of humanity was and is very short-sighted. In other words, it should not have drawn such a hard and fast line between Humanism and Theism, making them contradictory. That was all right so far as orthodox theology and supernaturalism are concerned, but there is a type of theism—a kind of naturalistic theism—which does not stand in direct opposition to a real Humanism, and I have come to accept that type of theism. Do not ask me to define it, for I still agree with Robert Herrick, when he said
>
> God is above the sphere of our esteem
> And is best known, not defining him.
>
> Perhaps I am a theistic humanist, but not in the sense you define it, or a humanistic theist. I like to think of myself as both a theist and a humanist.

More than two hundred of Dietrich's lectures have been published, and he wrote for the *Humanist Pulpit* (7 volumes, 1926-1933). (See entries for Charles S. Braden, Brian Eslinger, and Dorothy S. Grant.) {CL; EU, Paul H. Beattie; EW; FUS; HM1; HNS2; U; U&U; WAS, 17 August 1956}

Dietrich, Margaret (20th Century)

Dietrich, using the pseudonym Carleton Winston, wrote a biography of John Hassler Dietrich, *Circle of Earth* (1942). {FUS}

Dietrich, Marlene (1901-1992)

"If there is a supreme being, he's crazy," famed movie actress Dietrich once told a *Rave* reporter (November 1986). Her dissatisfaction with the explanations of theologians was in keeping with her independence of spirit. Her only child, Maria Riva, shocked not a few with a 1993 biography which listed her mother's lovers, one of whom—a lesbian identified as "the rhinoceros"—admittedly raped Riva.

The other of her mother's lovers included a who's who of notables: newscaster Edward R. Murrow; generals James M. Gavin and George S. Patton; actor Jean Gabin; novelist Erich Maria Remarque. There also were others: Edith Piaf, John Gilbert, Gary Cooper, Maurice Chevalier, Yul Brynner, José Iturbi, Hans Jaray, Brian Aherne, Adlai Stevenson, Michael Wilding, Mercedes de Acosta, Frank Sinatra. Also, there was her husband—Rudolf Sieber—to whom she is said to have shown or sent all the letters she received from her various lovers.

Molly Haskell has written of Maria's biography, *Marlene Dietrich* (1993), "Ms. Riva endorses Kenneth Tynan's axiom that Dietrich 'has sex without gender,' but I would say she is both genders, and she existed at a moment in time in a censored medium—romantic rather than sexual, glorying in a language of innuendo rather than clinical categories—when it was possible (in the von Sternberg-Dietrich masterpiece 'Morocco') to kiss a woman on the lips and run off after a man in the desert sand, to be love object and love subject simultaneously. She makes us wonder, safely, without having to lose sleep over it, what is a man and what is a woman, after all, if so much of one can exist harmoniously in the other?"

In her autobiography, she wrote of her having deserted Germany, become an American citizen, and joined the United States army as an entertainer. She toured widely and was honored by France with the Legion d'Honneur and the U.S. with a Congressional Medal. Of her battle-front experiences and how they led her to renounce her Calvinist faith, Dietrich wrote,

> Back in my early childhood I learned that God doesn't fight on any army's side. So there was little point in praying. Nonetheless, before every battle prayers were read, all kinds of incantations were recited, staged by all sorts of preachers. We attended these ceremonies and I saw how the soldiers stood in place, as though they couldn't believe their ears. I couldn't believe it either, but I counted for nothing. . . . Since then, I have given up belief in God, in a "light" that leads us, or anything of that sort. Goethe said, "If God created this world, he should review his plan."

Although most who know about Dietrich know and love only her films, her daughter Maria wasted no time following her mother's death in detailing the last moments: At the age of ninety-one, Dietrich had spent much of the last decade of her life in bed, using a casserole instead of rising to go to the bathroom, and subsisting on pills and alcohol. As critic Gabriele Annan has pointed out, Maria is an "Electra from Beverly Hills" who, like Euripides's Electra, is "almost a monomaniac from hate and brooding over her wrongs," one who "doesn't actually help anyone to kill Dietrich, but she disembowels and flays her after her death. She tears off her specially engineered corset to reveal the ugly breasts and—in later years—'the crepe-flesh of her hanging thighs.' "

Dietrich, who chose to live in France rather than Germany, spent most of World War II in the United States, entertained Allied troops, and refused offers from the Nazi Government to make movies. Despite the ambiguous relationship Dietrich had with her native Germany, she asked to be buried in her native Berlin, where her grave has been occasionally covered with excrement and vandalized with epithets. Her simple gravestone bears a cryptic inscription in German that proclaims, "Here I stand on the marker of my days." {TYD}

Dietrick, Ellen Battelle (19th Century)

Dietrick served on Elizabeth Cady Stanton's *Woman's Bible* committee, was a vice-president of the Kentucky Equal Rights Association in 1888, and in 1890 became president of the Boston Suffrage League. Her freethought is shown in "Cardinal Gibbon's Ignorance" (*Liberty*, 20 April 1895). {WWS}

Dietz, Robert S. (1914—)

Dietz, a member of the Foundation for Freedom from Religion, is a marine geologist who is active as one of the sponsors for the National Center for Science Education and who enjoys having "locked horns with the resurgent creationist movement and especially to the claim of 'scientific' creationism. The integrity of science must be defended from the onslaught of pseudo-science." he has written. "I find it particularly galling for religion to attempt to trade on the prestige of science." With John C. Holden, Dietz wrote *Creation / Evolution Satiricon* (1987).

Dietzgen, Joseph (1828—1888)

A German philosophical writer, Dietzgen was an exponent of materialism, especially in its application to Marxism. He advocated what he called a "dialectical monism," or materialism. The universe is one eternally evolving material reality. Thought is a function of the brain, and there is no basis for religion. He wrote *Das Wesen der menschlichen Kopfarbeit* (1869) and *Zur Philosophie des Sozialismus* (published 1923). {RAT}

Digby, Forster (20th Century)

Digby, professor of philosophy at New England College in New Hampshire, is author of "Abortion Is the Issue From Hell" (*Free Inquiry*, Summer 1996).

DIGITAL

In the world of computer science, the digital system distinguishes between only two values: 1 or 0, on or off. Data is encoded as a string of 1's and 0's.

A digital clock shows noon as 12:00 whereas an analog clock shows the big and little hands together, up at the top on the twelve. Cameras or video cameras which are digital use the digital format. A digital piano is one which is electric and can be made to sound like musical instruments other than the audio piano, for example a Medieval church organ or a celeste.

Dijkstra, Jaap (20th Century)

Dijkstra is director of the Dutch Humanist Institute for Development Cooperation (HIVOS), which is a Third World aid agency supported by the Government. HIVOS is like a religious aid organization, but it operates on an entirely humanistic line. He spoke at the 1992 IHEU Congress in the Netherlands.

Dilke, Ashton Wentworth (1850—1883)

Dilke, who was educated at Cambridge, traveled to Russia and Central Asia, then published a translation of Turgenev's *Virgin Soil.* He purchased and edited the *Weekly Dispatch*. Although he returned as a Member of Parliament for Newcastle in 1880, he resigned owing to ill health, in favor of John Morley, and died at Algiers. {BDF; RAT}

Dilke, Charles Wentworth [Sir] (1843—1911)

Dilke succeeded his father as baronet and owner of the *Athenaeum* and *Notes and Queries.* In 1874 he published an anticlerical novel, *The Fall of Prince Florestan*. A friend of Gambetta and the French rationalists, whose views he shared, Dilke led the Radicals in the House of Commons. {RAT}

Dillard, Annie (1945—)

Dillard, an author who won the Pulitzer prize for general non-fiction in 1974, has written for *Harper's* and for various newspapers. A member of the Thoreau Society, she has written poetry such as *Tickets for a Prayer Wheel* (1974) and *Mornings Like This* (1995). Her nonfiction books include *Holy the Firm* (1978), *The Writing Life* (1989), and *For the Time Being* (1999). In the latter work, she poses the old question as to why, if God exists, wickedness is permitted. She also notes that of eighty billion galaxies, each harbors at least one hundred billion suns andthat every 110 hours a million more humans arrive on the planet than die into the planet.

Dillard has written a memoir, *An American Childhood* (1987) and a novel, *The Living* (1992). In *Pilgrim at Tinker Creek* (1974), she included the following:

> I read about an Eskimo hunter who asked the local missionary priest, "If I did not know about God and sin, would I go to hell?"
> "No," said the priest, "not if you did not know."
> "Then why," asked the Eskimo earnestly, "did you tell me?"

In *An American Childhood* (1987), Dillard declares, "By dipping us children in the Bible so often, they hoped, I think, to give our lives a serious tint, and to provide us with quaintly magnificent snatches of prayer to produce as charms while, say, being mugged for our cash or jewels."

Dillard is a writer-in-residence at Wesleyan University, where she also teaches. In 1999 she was inducted into the American Academy of Arts and Letters. Some critics have noted that, as to why she thinks God permits suffering, she leans on Augustine and Aquinas. Asked specifically if any religious or philosophic label fits into her outlook, Dillard touched all bases:

> I haven't the foggiest idea. Is there such a thing as a freethinking Catholic? Of course I'm also an existentialist and to some extent a Unitarian, ditto Hasid, though the Hasids would deny it. Strongly! Also, I'm a neo-Platonist. And, of course, a fervent admirer of the sciences.

{TYD; WAS 10 March 1999}

Dille, R. (20th Century)

Dille was on the first Board of Directors in 1952 of the International Humanist and Ethical Union.

Diller, Phyllis (1917-)

An actress and an author, Diller in 1965 received the Best TV Comedienne Award from the *TV Radio Mirror*. She accompanied Bob Hope and his group to South Vietnam, Christmas 1966; appeared in numbers of plays and movies, wrote several books, and was a producer-writer of the "Phyllis Diller Shows" (1963-1964).

In David Kristof's and Todd Nickerson's *Predictions for the Next Millennium*, Diller is quoted as predicting the following for the year 3000:

> The constants all through the centuries will be the same: wine, women and song. Other than that, life will be very different technologically. In the year 3000 the universe will be expanding as it will forever, infinitely. We will probe outer space but never find life as evolutionized as ours. We were not created by a deity. We created the deity in *our* image. Life began on this planet when the first amoeba split. Mankind will still be seeking God, not accepting that God is a spirit; can't see it, touch it, only feel it. It's called *Love.*

{CA}

Dilloway, A. James (20th Century)

A representative of the International Humanist and Ethical Union (IHEU) at the United Nations, Dilloway has helped build the group's status as a Non-Governmental Organization (NGO) within the UN, both in Geneva and in New York City. In 1978 at the Seventh IHEU World Congress held in London, Dilloway addressed the group. He finds humankind's ten most pressing concerns as being the following:

- rapid population growth and urbanism
- the absence of overall global overseeing
- environmental decay
- authoritarian religious intolerance
- health standards, both physical and public
- systemic economic-financial defects and extreme poverty
- natural disasters
- arms exporting
- crime, terrorism, and the drug trade
- human rights dereliction and the treatment of women

{*New Humanist*, Dec 1995}

Dimick, Howard T. (20th Century)

Dimick, with other freethinkers, wrote *The Truth About American Evangelists* (1928). {GS}

Dimock, Marshall E. (20th Century)

Dimock in 1961 was the first moderator of the Unitarian Universalist Association.

Dinesen, Isak: See entry for Karen Blixen.

DINOSAURS

Fossils show that dinosaurs had "fingers" which corresponded to the first three digits of a human's hand. The two outer digits were found in older fossils. Scientists in 1997 were still disputing whether or not birds descended from dinosaurs. The wings of birds, according to *New York Times* science reporter John Noble Wilford (24 October 1997), "developed from the forelimbs of their reptilian ancestors and still bear skeletal traces of former fingers, which also had been reduced to three from five. The question is, Which three digits remain in bird wings? The answer could be a clue to whether dinosaurs or some earlier reptiles were direct ancestors of today's ducks and geese, pelicans, and cardinals." But the identity of the three major digits in bird wings remains an issue that has puzzled scientists for at least one hundred and fifty years. Until the end of the 20 century, no evidence existed that birds evolved from dinosaurs, not until fossils of two turkey-sized, feathered animals—protarchaeopteryx and caudipteryx—were discovered beneath an ancient lake bed in the Liaoning Province in northeastern China.

Dinter, Gustav Friedrich (1760—1831)

Dinter was a German educationalist. *Bible for Schoolmasters* was his best-known work, and it sought to give rational notes for teachers. Its explanations of "Jew books" excited much controversy. {BDF; RAT}

Dio Chrysostom (c. 50—117)

A Greek Sophist and orator, Dio lived in Rome at the time of Emperor Domitian, who subsequently banished him. Returning to Rome in the favor of emperors Nerva and Trajan, he leaned toward the philosophy of the Cynics and Stoics. With Plutarch, he shared in the revival of Greek literature of the first century. Some eighty orations on various subjects have been saved, some of which roundly denounce slavery more than a thousand years before any Christian leader did. According to McCabe, "He was not a Stoic, as is often said, but an atheist of the Epicurean-Stoic school which most Roman moralists followed. {CE; JM}

Diodorus Siculus (Died after 21 B.C.E.)

A Sicilian historian who in Greek wrote a world history in forty books, Diodorus Siculus is regarded by other historians as uncritical, repetitive, and unreliable. His work is valuable, however, as a source for the lost works of earlier authors, from whom he borrowed freely. One of his statements was that "It is to the interest of states to be deceived in religion." {TYD}

Diogenes (412—323 B.C.E.?)

When Diogenes pleaded with Antisthenes to teach him, the older man took a disliking to him and tried to beat him with his stick. But Diogenes refused to move, saying he wanted the wisdom which Antisthenes had to give. He wanted to do as his jailed father had done, deface the coinage because stamps were false and the men stamped upon them were, as Bertrand Russell described, "base metal with lying superscription." Diogenes believed virtue could be found in living the simple life, so he discarded eating utensils, drank from his hands, and lived like a dog—"cynic" means "canine." Like fakirs, he begged. Unlike most, he considered animals as well as humans his brotherhood. Worldly goods were of no account to him, for virtue and moral freedom came when one learned to free himself from desire. Prometheus, he proclaimed, was justly punished, for he erred by bringing man the arts and what has led to modernity. His home, for example, consisted of a tub-like burial pitcher. When Alexander the Great inquired what he could do for him, Diogenes retorted, "Only step out of my sunlight."

His refusal to accept ordinary conventions led to many stories about his eccentricities. For example, to show contempt for his generation and times, he carried a lantern during daylight hours, explaining he was looking "for an honest man."

He was known to embrace statues during the winter. Upon cracking a louse on a temple's altar rail, he said, "Thus does Diogenes sacrifice to all the gods at once." When chastized for masturbating in public, he replied, "Would that hunger could be alleviated by rubbing one's belly."

Passing by a tree from which female prisoners had been hanged, he observed, "Would that all trees bore such sweet fruit."

He lived in a wine barrel, tried to eat his meat raw, advocated public masturbation, and reportedly urinated on individuals he disliked.

Like the academic skeptics, he held that nothing can be known solely by our senses or our reason, and his views led to people's illustrating how easy it is to do without material wealth, how happy one can be eating simple food, how warm one can keep without expensive clothing, how silly it is to love one's native country, how futile to cry when friends or even one's own children die. Diogenes held that nothing is produced from nothing or reduced to nothing, that the earth is round and received its shape from whirling, and he made no distinction between mind and matter.

As Russell in his *History of Western Philosophy* remarks, one wonders who appreciated such views; "Was it the rich, who wished to think the sufferings of the poor imaginary? Or was it the new poor, who were trying to despise the successful businessman? Or was it sycophants who persuaded themselves that the charity they accepted was unimportant?. . . Popular Cynicism did not teach abstinence from the good things of this world, but only a certain indifference to them. In the case of a borrower, this might take the form of minimizing the obligation to the lender. One can easily understand," adds Russell, "how the word 'cynic' has acquired its present meaning." {CE; EU; TYD}

DIONYSUS

Dionysus (Bacchus), in Greek and Roman mythology, was the god of wine and of an orgiastic religion which celebrated the power and fertility of nature. Those who revered Dionysus were called Dionysians. In art a dionysian spirit is instinctual, irrational, and a festival observance held in seasonal cycles in honor of Dionysus was called Dionysia.

Theologians once mistook Dionysius the Areopagite for Dionysus. Dionysius (430?—367 B.C.E.) was a tyrant of Syracuse, known for fighting the Carthaginians in Sicily. His son Dionysius (395?—343?) succeeded him and was exiled in 343 for his despotic rule. Dionysius of Halicarnassus (1st century B.C.E.) was a Greek historian whose history of Rome is a source for early Roman history. Dionysius Exiguus (500?—560?) was a Scythian monk responsible for introducing the method of reckoning the Christian era from the birth of Christ. Termed "Little Dennis" or "Dennis the Runt," he began his system, not with a Year Zero but with a Year One. At that time Western arithmetic had not yet developed the concept of zero.

In the philosophy of Nietzsche, individuals who were dionysian displayed creative-intuitive power as opposed to critical-rational power. (See entry for Bacchus.) {CE; Stephen Jay Gould, *USA Weekend*, 19-21 September 1997}

Diop, Cheikh Anta (1923—1986)

Born of a Muslim peasant family in western Senegal, Diop attended Koranic schools. His doctoral thesis has been summarized by Sertima: "That Egypt was the node and center of a vast web linking the strands of Africa's main cultures and languages; that the light that crystallized at the center of this early world had been energized by the cultural electricity streaming from the heartland of Africa; that the creators of classical Egyptian civilization, therefore, were not the brown Mediterranean Caucasoids invented by Sergi, nor the equally mythical Hamites, nor Asiatic nomads and invaders, but indigenous, black-skinned, woolly-haired Africans; that Greece, mother of the best in European civilization, was once a child suckled at the breast of Egypt even as Egypt had been suckled at the breast of Ethiopia, which itself evolved from the complex interior womb of the African motherland." His thesis was labeled "unfounded" by the jury of the University of Paris, and it took Diop ten years and two more doctoral dissertations before he was granted his degree. Diop translated a major portion of Einstein's relativity theory into Wolof, the language of his people. In 1976 he became President of the World Black Researchers Association. A nominal Muslim, one who was highly critical of Islam, Diop according to Norm Allen "believed that Islam encouraged African Muslims to deny their historical roots. He bemoaned the fact that some Africans—especially chiefs—would rewrite history in a shameless attempt to trace their roots back to the prophet Mahomet." Although he is included in Allen's *African American Humanism*, Diop's philosophic or religious ideas are not specifically outlined. The direction of his thought, however, is scientific and naturalistic.

Mary Lefkowitz, a professor of classics at Wellesley College and author of *Women in Greek Myth*, is concerned that "Afrocentrists" overlook historical facts. For example, some state

- that Greek civilization dates from only 1000 B.C.
  (In fact, Greek-speaking peoples occupied the Greek mainland for at least half a millennium before that.)
- that Socrates was a figment of Plato's imagination.
  (In fact, the great philosopher is mentioned by several other contemporary writ ers, such as the comic poet Aristophanes and the historian Xenophon.)
- that Plato "studied for 11 years in Egypt."
  (It is very unlikely that he even went there.)
- that "Plato learned from Egyptian sages in Masonic Grand Lodges an Egyptian 'mystery' system."
  (In reality, there was no such system, and a literature about Greco-Egyptian philosophy did not come into existence until 500 years after Plato's death.).

Academics, Lefkowitz holds, must "come out of the closets of their specializations and complain, not only about biased interpretation but about deliberate misrepresentation and manipulation of facts, whether in their own subject areas or in someone else's. Unless they do, generations of students will come to believe that Aristotle put his own name and titles to nonexistent Egyptian treatises that he stole from a library that had not yet been built in a country that he never visited! Subjects like history and philosophy will be replaced by indoctrination, and each of us will believe the brand of 'truth' that best serves his or her own selfish purposes." (See entry for Mary Lefkowitz.)

Dippel, Johann K. (1672—1734)

Dippel was a German alchemist and physician. His *Papismus vopulans Protestantium* (1698) drew the wrath of the theologians of Geissen, and Dippel fled for his life. In 1705 he published his satires against the Protestant Church, *Hirt und eine Heerde*, under the name of Christianus Democritos. Dippel denied the inspiration of the Bible. {BDF; RAT}

DISBELIEF

• A thing that nobody believes cannot be proved too often.

—George Bernard Shaw

Disch, Thomas M. (20th Century)

Disch is author of *The Priest* (1995), in which the Rev. Patrick Bryce is a hard-drinking hypocrite who likes to perform oral sex on pubescent boys. Two of his colleagues are ex-lovers. His parishioners are guilty of a number of crimes ranging from multiple murder to anti-Semitism to siring illegitimate twins (one of whom, it transpires, is Father Pat). Disch subtitles the work *A Gothic Romance* and in mid-novel has the priest swap bodies with Silvanus de Roquefort, Bishop of Rodez and Montpellier-le-Vieux, whose expertise included delivering fire-and-brimstone homilies as well as performing amateur mastectomies on female heretics. One of the gay priests remarks about why the church continues its dogma about homosexuality: "In a way, that may be its problem—that it's in the nature of the church that it *can't* change. What's changed is the world around us."

DISCRIMINATION

In matters of differentiating quality, a gourmet carefully chooses what is eaten (savoring each bite) whereas a gourmand does not (cleaning up the plate even if it does not taste good). Such is generally considered an example of a gourmet's positive discrimination.

In matters of categorical rather than individual choosing, however, the person who prejudges discriminates by speaking or acting against an entire group because of its religion, race, or some other category. As an example, some discriminate against all short human beings, holding that anyone who is only five foot four inches tall is not really equal to those individuals who are taller. Shorter people, however, accuse tall people of eating more food, wearing larger garments, requiring higher ceilings, and needing more fuel to move about, therefore using up more of the planet's resources. Some individuals discriminate against "thin-lipped" people, whereas others discriminate against the "big-lipped." Some blonds claim to have more fun than brunets, whereas brunets are known to claim that the opposite is the case. Some adherents of religions are disgraced if someone in their family marries outside the religion. Other individuals or groups who are inhumanistically discriminated against include gays, lesbians, the left-handed, the red-haired, the green-eyed, the fat, females, and exceptional people (who are called derisive names, such as "freaks").

The Council for Secular Humanism includes in its statement of principles that its members attempt

> . . . to transcend divisive parochial loyalties based on race, religion, gender, nationality, creed, class, sexual orientation, or ethnicity, and strive to work together for the common good of humanity.

DISHONESTY

• I looked within the soul of the boy sitting next to me.

—Woody Allen
as a standup comedian in the 1960s,
explaining why he was expelled from college
for cheating on a philosophy examination

Disraeli, Benjamin [1st Earl of Beaconsfield] (1804—1881)

Disraeli, the British statesman and author, was born of Jewish parents but was baptized a Christian in 1817. As pointed out by Northwestern University English professor Lawrence Lipkind, although Disraeli was the most distinguished English Jew in history, Queen Victoria's favorite, technically he was not a Jew "for before his bar mitzvah he was baptized instead; without this conversion he could never have served in Parliament, according to law. His enemies portrayed him as a crypto-Jew, a sort of belated *marrano*. But in fact he was proud of the Sephardic ancestry epitomized by his name; and he was anything but secretive about it." "Man is made to adore and obey," he wrote in *Coningsby* (1844), "but if you will not command him, if you give him nothing to worship, he will fashion his own divinities." {TYD}

DISTRICT OF COLUMBIA HUMANISTS

• The American Humanist Associations coordinator for the District of Columbia, Delaware, Maryland, and Virginia is Roy Torcaso of the Mid Atlantic Region (AHA), 3708 Brightview Street, Wheaton, Maryland 20902.

• The American Humanist Association's contact member for the National Capital Area is Karen Stewart, 2130 P St Northwest (#1005), Washington, DC 20037; (301) 656-5621.

• The Maryland-DC Chapter has as its contact Mary Porter at (202) 546-7430.

• The Washington Area Secular Humanists are at Box 15319, Washington, DC 20003. On the Web: <http://www.wam.umd.edu/~kaugust/asatext/ wash.html>. Telephone (202) 298-0921. E-mail: <wash@poboxes.com>. Contact: Bahram Azad.

• The Washington Ethical Action Office, 6214 Crathie Lane, Bethesda, MD 10816 (301) 229-3759 welcomes cooperation concerning legislative action in Washington.

DITHEISM

Ditheism is a theological invention referring to a belief in or a theory about the existence of two gods or of two original principles. For example, one god could be good, the other evil, as in Manichaeism.

DIVINE

• Divination, n. The art of nosing out the occult. Divination is of as many kinds as there are fruit-bearing varieties of the flowering dunce and the early fool.

—Ambrose Bierce
The Devil's Dictionary

Devinen, divinen came from the Middle English, Middle French, and Latin. *Devinus* was a soothsayer. In French, *deviner* means "to guess." A divine, or minister of the gospel, is one skilled in guessing, or discovering by making known through divination. Divinity is the quality or state of being divine. God is said to be Divine. A forked rod believed to indicate the presence of water or minerals is called a divining rod. The Divine Right of Kings was a view, as expounded by James I and later Stuart adherents, that the king possesses a personal right to rule by virtue of his birth and the divine authority inherent in his person and not in his office.

One of the most colorful divines was Father Divine who, in the 1930s became a "lion" in Harlem. A cult leader primarily of fellow blacks, he allegedly healed people, performed miracles, and explained his possession of large sums of money by saying, "I have money without limit, because my money comes from God." His followers greeted him with the salutation "Peace," and he claimed millions of adherents. They surrounded him with signs: "Father Divine is God," "Father Divine is the Messiah," and "Father Divine is the King of Kings and Lord of Lords." Allegedly, he was George Baker Jr., born around 1880 of Gullah slave parents near Savannah, Georgia, a state in which he once was sentenced to the chain gang and later was tried for insanity because of his messianic claims and disorders incident thereto. He opened his first New York church in 1915 and moved to Harlem in 1933, where he converted hotels into "kingdoms" for his followers, provided an employment service, and distributed low-cost meals to the poor. "He has the world in a jug and the stopper in his hand," his followers chanted. Father Divine preached self-reliance and abstinence, encouraged them to shun sex, marriage, alcohol, tobacco, and profanity, and insisted that they refuse all public assistance. The 21-year-old white woman who had been an angel since childhood and who married the octagenarian in 1946 reportedly said she did not realize that marriage would require having sex with God. In disgust at all the lawsuits being brought against him, particularly by Faithful Mary—his most emphatic public champion, who for years ran the Harlem kitchens—Father Divine said he was going to leave his body and depart the earth for 1,900 years. Actually, he departed to Philadelphia. Through the 1950s and early 1960s, his church ignored the civil rights movement altogether. Upon his death at the age of 85, or perhaps 100, thousands of pilgrims gathered to watch the 5' 2" God arise out of his white coffin from the dead, but he failed to do so. His body is enshrined on the grounds of a mansion outside Philadelphia where Mother Divine—née Edna Rose Ritchings, who was seventy-three in 1998—lives and oversees church business.

As can be divined, contemporary secular humanists and freethinkers find meaningless the supernaturalistic overtones of the concept of divinity. {ER}

DIVISION OF HUMANIST COUNSELLING

The Division of Humanist Counselling (AHA) is at 7 Harwood Drive, Box 146, Amherst, New York 14226.

DIVORCE

Among the oldest divorce regulations to be found are those in the Assyrian code of Hammurabi, about 2300 to 2500 B.C.E. These provided that a man might divorce his wife at will without stating a reason. The Veddas of Ceylon did not permit divorce. A Zuni wife who no longer wished to keep her husband was allowed to place his personal belongings at the entrance of the house, at which time he was required to return to his parent's home. In the United States the first divorce was granted in Massachusetts in 1639.

The marriage custom sanctified by the Christian religion is the monogamous marriage involving a union between one man and one woman who agree to be dedicated to a total communion of life between the two partners and meant to persist for the entire duration of their joint lives. The implication is that if they do not stay together, they have failed. If they quit their job, however, and move on to something better, have they failed? This is not accepted as being analogous.

The struggle between Church and State over the control of marriage laws, and consequently divorce, has been won mostly by the Church. Many individuals, however, touted divorce without much effect on the status quo; for example, Plato, Aristotle, Pericles, Francis Bacon, Lord Nelson, Robert Burns, Lord Byron, and Benjamin Franklin. Henry VIII obtained a most difficult and highly publicized divorce when he succeeded in ridding himself of his first wife, Catherine of Aragon, in order to marry Anne Boleyn.

In some Arab countries, divorce for men is easy. All an Arab need do to divorce his wife is say three times, "I divorce thee."

The Romans set divorce-and-remarriage records only recently broken. Julius Caesar, called the "Queen of Bithynia" in his youth because of his homosexual activities, was married three times. Caligula had four wives; moreover, he committed incest with his sister, then forced her into marriage with his lover, Marcus Lapidus. Mark Antony divorced his pregnant wife, Octavia, by mail in order to marry Cleopatra. Other Roman serial monogamists: Augustus (3 wives), his daughter Julia (3 husbands), Claudius I (4 wives), Nero (3 wives). Charlemagne, emperor of the Holy Roman Empire, was married four times and repudiated his first wife a year after their wedding. Thomas F. "Tommy" Manville, who died in 1967, set the record for millionaire divorces—thirteen of them. His marriage to the seventh wife lasted only 7 1/2 hours.

None of the various groups of non-believers has taken a specific stand concerning the merits or shortcomings of divorce, which is the dissolution of the marriage contract (which ordinarily contains the words "until death do us part"). No statistics have been compiled as to whether non-believers divorce less, or more, often than believers. Members of the Society of Friends (Quakers) are known to dislike civil marriages, preferring "common law" cohabitation even though such is not recognized by the state. In the 1970s, the divorce rate in the United States was estimated to be around 50% and is believed to remain at that level. In China, the 1990 rate was 12%. By 1994, because of social changes and a receding interference in people's personal lives by the government, the figure increased to over 24%.

A number of eminent freethinkers have been married many times. Some argue that people of the same sex should be allowed to marry as well as divorce. And some have described monogamy as unnecessary monotony. Most agree that it is beneficial for the state to solemnize a marriage as well as provide the necessary conditions for any legal dissolution, spelling out property rights and rights of a separated couple's children.

Changes in the United States divorce laws during the last century have replaced the old concept that viewed husband and wife as one legal personality, that of the husband, and replacing it with allowing married women to own property, enter into contracts, bring legal suits, and otherwise act independently of their husbands.

A humanistic approach to dividing property and valuables has been devised by Steven Brams, a professor of politics at New York University, and Alan Taylor, a professor of mathematics at Union College. In *The Win-Win Solution: Guaranteeing Fair Shares to Everybody* (1999), they spell out a method that could also be used to settle disputes involving corporate mergers or peace negotiations in the Middle East. As described by Larissa MacFarquhar (*The New Yorker*, 16 August 1999):

> Each party gets a hundred points to divide among the goods in question. Suppose Brittany and Brandon own a house, a dog, tools, and a truck. Brittany never much liked the dog, or the home theatre Brandon installed in the house, but she loves the tools and her sense of self is all bound up in the truck. She values the truck at fifty, the tools at twenty-five, the house at twenty, and the dog at five. Brandon never learned to use the tools and always felt a little self-conscious driving the truck, but he considers the dog to be a close friend and hates the thought of moving the home theatre to a strange place. He values the dog at fifty, the house at forty, and the truck and the tools at five apiece. Each person is initially given the items he or she values most: Brittany gets the truck and the tools; Brandon gets the house and the dog. But that gives Brittany seventy-five points and Brandon ninety. In order to even things out, the house is sold, and Brandon gets three-quarters of the price (worth thirty points to him, leaving him with a total of eighty), while Brittany gets one-quarter (worth five points to her, leaving her also with eighty).

The Brams-Taylor method is not perfect and guarantees only that a sincere participant will receive at least fifty per cent "of the pie as he or she values it." Comments MacFarquhar, after noting that sparring partners might rank preferences dishonestly in order to deprive the other person with what the individual wants, comments, "Perhaps, though, the algorithm's inventors are wrong not to take spite seriously. They don't seem to believe that, for some, making a former loved one miserable may be genuinely more rewarding than the ownership of a household appliance." (See entry for Marriage, Forms of.) {CE}

Dix, Dorothea Lynde (1802—1887)

Dix was an American educator and reformer who campaigned to improve the treatment of prisoners, the mentally retarded, and the mentally ill. This was because she once had volunteered to conduct Sunday services for women inmates at an East Cambridge jail, and she was puzzled as to why so many of those who were confined were mentally ill, not criminals. When she inquired of the jailer why insane people had no heat in their part of the jail, she was told, "Lunatics don't feel cold like other people."

Dix, of whom it is said that 123 hospitals were built because of her work and influence, was a Unitarian who attended William Ellery Channing's church and tutored his children. {CE; EG; U}

Dixie, Florence Caroline (Douglas) [Lady] (1857—1905)

Dixie, a freethinker, wrote *Toward Freedom: An Appeal to Thoughtfulness and Women* (1904?) In 1879 she was correspondent of the *Morning Post* in the Zulu War. {GS; RAT}

Dixon, Charles and **M. J. Dixon** (20th Century)

The Dixons have been active in the American Humanist Association chapter of the Mid-South. (See entry for Arkansas Humanists.)

Dixit, Dharmalingam (20th Century)

An Indian freethinker, Dixit wrote *A Critique on Major Religions* (1980). {GS}

Djilas, Milovan [Vice-President] (1911—1995)

An author and the former vice-president of Yugoslavia, Djilas (pronounced GEE-lahss) was born in a poor Serb village in Montenegro, the son of an out-of-work army officer and an illiterate peasant woman.

When he went to Belgrade, he soon joined with Communist students in the struggle against the royalist dictatorship and its secret police. Although originally Tito's friend and a successful politician, he was jailed in 1956 upon publication of his *The New Class*, a critique of the Communist oligarchy which had to be published in non-Communist countries. He was released in 1961, re-jailed in 1962, and freed in 1966. Other of his works include *Conversations with Stalin* (1962), *Memoir of a Revolutionary* (1973), and *Tito* (1980).

Interviewed 26 December 1993 by *New York Times* reporter David Binder, Djilas told how imprisonment affects politically minded inmates: "It often hardens their will to power. Stalin was sent to prison five times, Hitler for five years." He went on to Yugoslav leaders who had spent time in prison: Tito: Franjo Tudgjman, the President of Croatia; Alija Izetbegovic, the President of Bosnia and Herzegovina, and others. "They wanted power," said Mr. Djilas. "I didn't want power. But prison transformed me, too. It transformed me from an ideologist into a humanist."

A revolutionary, soldier, political leader, and writer, Djilas in his own description, "traveled the entire road of Communism," from

Partisan guerrilla fighter against Nazi occupiers of Yugoslavia and ardent believer in Stalinism, through disillusionment and revulsion at the "all-powerful exploiters and masters" in had brought to power—Stalin first among them.

Djilas, whose *The New Class* (written in 1955 and 1956) was a devastating early critique of communism, correctly predicted that Mikhail Gorbachev's reforms would result eventually in the fall of Soviet communism. Although at first he had been a dogmatic Marxist, after breaking with Tito he became an anti-Marxist liberal. Upon writing the book, he and his wife Stefica took the finished manuscript abroad and survived on his foreign royalties. "He was the first dissident since Trotsky to challenge the Party-controlled state from the very summit of Communist power, the historian Michael Ignatieff has observed, "the first to apply Marxist categories to the sociology of his own autocracy; the first to risk political death by publishing abroad." To the end of his life, according to *The Economist*, Djilas—the best-known dissident in Communist Yugoslavia—kept a rifle on his desk.

In 1996, according to reporter Chris Hedges, "The books of Milovan Djilas, searing critiques of Communism that made the writer one of the best-known dissident intellectuals of the century, are nearly impossible to find in the city where he lived and wrote." In addition to being ignored in anthologies and biographies of Serbian writers, he is referred to as the one who oversaw the murder of Serbian Chetnik irregulars. "Morally, of course, he won," Miladin Zivotic who founded a dissident group, the Belgrade Circle with Djilas. "He is the greatest figure in our political history, but in the current climate he has no influence. Many of his books are not even translated."

At his death, he was buried in his native Montenegro. The death of communism was now an old story, and Djilas was remembered as one who openly insisted that a person cannot be both a Communist and a free man.

Djilas was a Humanist Laureate in the Council for Secular Humanism's International Academy of Humanism and a signer in 1980 of the Secular Humanist Declaration. {CE; *The New York Review of Books*, 4 March 1999; *The New York Times*, 19 January 1997}

DNA

D[eoxyribo]N[ucleic]A[cid] is a nucleic acid that carries the genetic information in the cell. It is capable of self-replication and synthesis of RNA.

Testing a person's DNA can lead to proving guilt of a murder as well as innocence of that murder, in the event someone else's DNA is found on the murdered person.

According to the Associated Press (27 May 1998), the blood on a "weeping blood" Virgin Mary plaque attracting thousands of pilgrims since 1996 turned out to have DNA matching the blood of its owner, Margarita Holguin Cazares of Dodge City, Kansas. Immediately, some claimed the identical DNA could be part of the miracle. (See entry for RNA) {*Freethought Today*, March 1999}

"DO SCIENTISTS BELIEVE IN GOD?"

In May 1998 at the annual Hay Literary Festival in Hay-on-Wye in Wales, two of the world's leading scientists were present. Richard Dawkins was asked, "Are you still as godless as you were?" and "Is the human race still evolving?" Observed biographer Brenda Maddox, "Dawkins's eyes rolled to the heaven he doesn't believe in, as for the zillionth time he heard the familiar questions. The answer to both was "Yes."

Maddox continued: "Stephen Hawking, the author of *A Brief History of Time*, got the same treatment. Did he recognize the importance of the spiritual side of people? The audience clearly expected that a man in Hawking's predicament might need the consolations of religion. He doesn't. Slumped like a folded bat in his motorized wheelchair, he croaked out his reply on his voice synthesizer: 'When the physical universe is fully explained by a Theory of Everything, we will not need "nonphysical entities." I hate mysticism. I like things crystal clear.' " {*The New York Times Book Review*, 5 July 1998}

Doan, Frank Carlton (20th Century)

Doan was a Unitarian minister who wrote *Religion and the Modern Mind* (1909), in which work he defended "humanism" and "modernism." {HNS2}

Doane, T. W. (19th Century)

Doane wrote *Bible Myths and Their Parallels in Other Religions* (1882), a comparison of the Old and New Testament myths and miracles with those of heathen nations of antiquity.

Dobell, Bertram (1842—1914)

A poet and publisher, Dobell wrote a life of James Thomson and published much of his prose and verse. Dobell's rationalism finds expression in *Rosemary and Pansies* (1904) and *A Century of Sonnets* (1910). {RAT}

Döbereiner, Johann Wolfgang (1780—1849)

A German chemist, Döbereiner taught at Jena. His works record a number of original discoveries, and he greatly advanced the science of his day. Goethe mentions him in his letters, and Döbereiner shared his philosophy. {BDF; RAT}

Dobrin, Arthur (1943—)

Dobrin, a history major from City College, came into Ethical leadership training after having served in the Peace Corps in Kenya (1965—1967). He is Leader of the Ethical Humanist Society of Long Island. The author of *Spelling God With Two O's* (1993) and *Ethical People and How They Get to Be That Way*, Dobrin was a participant in the 1996 Humanist World Congress held in Mexico City as well as in the 1999 convention of Humanists of Florida. (See entry for Ethical Culture.) {EU, Howard B. Radest}

Dobrolyubov, Nikolai Aleksandrovich (1836—1861)

A Russian author whose father was a priest, Dobrolyubov became a radical journalist. The freethinker's works were edited in four volumes by Chernuishevsky. *New Code of Practical Wisdom* expresses his rationalism. {RAT}

Dobson, Charles Emil (Died 1999)

Dobson was an active member of the Montreal Humanist Fellowship from the 1960s onward. When he retired to Sidney, British Columbia, he became a member of the Victoria Humanists. Dobson was a defender of world peace through law.

His wife Yvonne Dobson is an active member of the Victoria Humanists.

Docterman, Chad (20th Century)

Docterman, a student at Marshall University, Huntington, West Virginia, was one of the founders of Campus Freethought Alliance. At Marshall, he is president of Rationalists United for Secular Humanism, which he founded. {*International Humanist News*, December 1996}

DOCUMENTA Q

In 1996 the Beglian firm Peeters published *Documenta Q*, supposedly a first-century work composed mostly of the alleged sayings of Jesus. (See entry for Q.)

Dodd, Carl W. (20th Century)

Dodd, a freethinker, wrote *Dodd's Revelations* (1968). {GS}

Dodd, Stuart C. (1900—1975)

A pollster who outguessed other forecasters on President Truman's election, Dodd wrote *Techniques for World Polls* and taught at the University of Washington in Seattle. He is a secular humanist. He is author of *Social Relations in the Near East* (1975).

Dodel-Port, Arnold (1843—1908)

A Swiss scientist, Dodel-Port published *The New History of Creation* in 1875, then issued his world-famous *Botanical Atlas* in 1878. He also wrote *Biological Fragments* (1885) and *The Life and*

Letters of Konrad Deubler (1885), a work concerning "the peasant philosopher." Prof. Dodel-Port was an honorary member of the London Royal Society and vice-president of the German Freethinkers' Union. {BDF; RAT}

Dodwell, Henry (c. 1700—1784)

Dodwell, the eldest son of the theologian of that name, published a pamphlet entitled "Christianity Not Founded On Argument," which in a tone of grave irony contends that Christianity can only be accepted by faith. Dodwell was a deist. {BDF; RAT}

Dodworth, James (Died 1876)

Dodworth, a Sheffield, England, palette knife manufacturer, was a leading secularist. He was chairman of the National Reformer Company (1860—1862). {VI}

Doerr, Edd (20th Century)

Doerr, a signer of Humanist Manifesto II, was elected in 1995 as President of the American Humanist Association (AHA). For *The Humanist*, he writes on matters concerning church and state and is on the editorial board.

Doerr was executive director of Americans for Religious Liberty, has been an editor of *The American Rationalist*, and is on the editorial board not only of *The Humanist* but also of *The Truth Seeker*, a magazine for freethinkers.

From 1970—1982 he served as editor of *Church and State*. One of his ten books is *Religious Liberty in Crisis* (1988). Doerr addressed the Tenth International Humanist and Ethical Union (IHEU) World Congress held in Buffalo (1988). Since 1981, he has been editor of *Voice of Reason*. In *Catholic Schools: The Facts* (1993). In *The Case Against School Vouchers* (1996), he wrote against educational voucher plans, saying Catholic schools are sectarian institutions with discriminatory hiring and admissions policies.

Speaking in a fluent Spanish, Doerr participated in the 1996 Humanist World Congress in Mexico City. E-mail: <arlinc@erols.com>. {EU, Eldon Scholl; HM2; HNS2}

Dogberry, Obediah (19th Century)

Dogberry likely is someone's pseudonym, but from 1832 to 1834 he edited a publication from Rochester, New York, called *Liberal Advocate*. {FUS}

DOGMATISM

• The death of dogma is the birth of morality.

—Immanuel Kant

Dogmatism is a positiveness in one's assertion of opinion, particularly when that viewpoint or system of ideas is based upon insufficiently examined premises. A religious tenet which is accepted as dogma results in an individual's arrogantly expressing the view as if it is fact, for by definition dogma is a set of teachings laid down by the group and becomes a part of the essential beliefs of the group.

In *Fact and Fiction* (1969), Bertrand Russell comments that

> It is the nature of the human animal to believe not only things for which there is evidence, but also very many things for which there is no evidence whatever. And it is the things for which there is no evidence that are believed with passion. Nobody feels any passion about the multiplication table or about the existence of Cape Horn, because these matters are not doubtful. But in matters of theology or political theory, where a rational man will hold that at best there is a slight balance of probability on one side or the other, people argue with passion and support their opinions by physical slavery imposed by armies and mental slavery imposed by schools. So accustomed do people become to feeling certain where they ought to feel doubtful that they become incapable of acting on a probability.

Russell laments that those who have always lived in a dogmatic atmosphere will stay still in hopeless bewilderment, convinced that it is those who disagree who are wrong. {DCL}

Doherty, Earl (20th Century)

Doherty, a member of the Humanist Association of Ottawa, has written "The Jesus Puzzle." He has been an editor of *Humanist in Canada*. {*Humanist in Canada*, Summer 1996 and Spring 1997}

Dokulis, Milos (20th Century)

Dokulis is a Czech humanist who writes concerning perspectives for a humanist strategy in his nation's post-communist state, according to *International Humanist News* (December 1993).

Dolan, Chester (20th Century)

Dolan is past president of the New York Society for General Semantics. Also, he is a former senior technical writer for Union Carbide Corp. and former instructor of English for the extension division of City College of New York. He is author of *Holy Daze* (1992). In *Blind Faith: Confronting Contemporary Religion* (1995), he recounts the hate and insecurity that religion poses to the human community. The world, he urges, would be a far better place if we could exorcise our presumptuous gods, reject the religion of the mystics, live a life free of superstition, and realize that our destiny rests with us. "For Dolan," wrote Tony Akkermans in *The Freethinker*, "the religion of non-religionists is a call for nonconformity, for reason and for true love of one's fellow man. Any sermon or religious precept that has nothing to offer in the way of social welfare or peace for mankind deals with mysticism, not religion. The only religion that will serve mankind operates in nursing homes, prisons, mental institutions, and in the streets of ghettos, not in magnificent cathedrals. It demands study and reflection, not worship. It is a total and unrestricted development of ethics, not pageantry." {*The Freethinker*, January 1996}

Dolci, Danilo (1924—)

Dolci is a secular freethinker whose work on behalf of cremation has helped break down superstition on that subject, particularly in arguing against the idea that one's body and soul go on into a hereafter. {TRI}

Dolet, Étienne (1509—1546)

Dolet's name is inseparably connected with the Revival of Learning. His first taste of persecution was in 1533, when he was thrown into prison for denouncing in a Latin oration the burning alive of Jean de Cartuce at Toulouse. During the remaining thirteen years of his life he was five times imprisoned, and nearly half his days were spent in confinement. Dolet was acquainted with Rabelais, Des Periers, and other advanced men of his time. In 1538 he wrote *Commentarii linguae Latinae*, which had greatly influenced the French Renaissance. But when he published Protestant books of devotion and French translations of the Bible, he was indicted in 1542 as a heretic. He had been in prison a number of times and had numerous enemies, had even killed a man, had been pardoned, and had been forced to flee several cities. In 1546, however, Catholic France found Dolet guilty of heresy and atheism.

Sentence of death for blasphemy was pronounced on Dolet in the Chambre Ardents at Paris on August 2, 1546. He was condemned to be hanged, and then burned with his books on the Place Maubert. His widow and children were beggared by the confiscation of his goods to the king. It was also ordered that he should be put to the torture before his execution, and questioned about his companions; and "if the said Dolet shall cause any scandal or utter any blasphemy, his tongue shall be cut out, and he shall be burnt alive."

The next day he met his doom. He was hanged first, and then (for they were not very particular), probably while he still breathed, the faggots were lighted, and Dolet and his books were consumed in the flames. It is said that instead of a prayer he uttered a pun in Latin: *Non dolet ipse Dolet, sed pia turba doiet* ("Dolet himself does not grieve, but the pious crowd grieves)" Yet the confessor who attended him at the stake invented the falsehood that the martyr had acknowledged his errors. "I do not believe a word of it," wrote Erasmus. "It is the usual story which these people invent after the death of their victims." Dolet's real sentiments are expressed in the cantique, full of resignation and courage, which he composed in prison when death was imminent. A rough translation by R. C. Christie is, "A good heart, sustained with patience, never bends under evil, bewails or moans, but is always victor. Courage, my soul, and show such a heart; let your confidence be seen in trial; every noble heart, every constant warrior, maintains his fortitude even unto death."

Robertson, describing the scene, wrote, "The utter wickedness of the whole process at least serves to relieve by neighbourhood the darkness of the stains cast on Protestantism by the crimes of Calvin." But his death was "but a drop in the sea of blood then being shed in France by the Church," for mobs accompanied by the papal vice-legate of Avignon headed in 1545 for the land of Vaudois, "where three towns were destroyed, 3,000 persons massacred, 256 executed, six or seven hundred more sent to the galleys, and many children sold as slaves." Robertson added, "Thus was the faith vindicated and safeguarded." McCabe calls Dolet more a Protestant than an atheist. {BDF; CE; FO; JM; JMR; JMRH}

Dollison, John (20 Century)

Dollison in 1994 wrote *Pope-Pourri, Little Known Facts You May Not Remember from Sunday School, Including Why the Pope Wears a Pointy Hat, the Strange Fate of the Spring Nun, What the Baltimore Catechism Says, and Why St. Lucy Carries Her Eyeballs On a Platter.*

Bill Cooke, in a *New Zealand Rationalist and Humanist* (Winter 1998) review, noted, "Here are the stories of the naughty popes, the lunatic saints, the extravagant mortifications undergone to avoid thoughts about sex, the pagan origins of many Catholic doctrines and words, and the real story behind County Dracula." He found Dollison's work "an intelligent, rational dig at the Catholic Church, which also manages to be entertaining and amusing."

Doloff, Steven (20 Century)

Doloff, a professor of English and Humanities at Pratt Institute in New York City, wrote an article for African Americans for Humanism's *Examiner*, "How Many Prejudices Does It Take to Screw in a Lightbulb?"

Dominicis, Saverio Fausto de (Born 1846)

Dominicis was an Italian positivist philosopher who taught at Bari. He wrote *Education and Darwinism.* {BDF}

Dominiczak, Andrzej (20th Century)

Dominiczak, of the Federation of Polish Humanist Associations, spoke at a Berlin conference in 1995 which was organized by the Secretariat for Central and Eastern Europe of the IHEU and handled by the Humanistischer Verband Deutschland. He described the two campaigns which Polish humanists are undertaking: first, their support of democracy; and second, their insistence upon the need for ethical teaching. He also was a participant in the 1996 Polish Humanist Conference on European Integration held in Utrecht. {*International Humanist News*, December 1995; "Open Letter to the Polish Intelligentsia," *International Humanist News*, November 1996}

Dommanget, Jean (20th Century)

In 1995 Dommanget, of the Belgian Royal Observatory, was elected a Humanist Laureate in the Council for Secular Humanism's International Academy of Humanism. Dommanget signed Humanist Manifesto 2000.

Domville, William Henry (19th Century)

Domville, a freethinker, wrote *The Rights and Duties of Parents in Regards to Their Children's Religious Education and Beliefs* (1876). {GS}

DONATION OF CONSTANTINE: See entry for Hoaxes, Religious.

Don, Warwick (20 Century)

A retired senior lecture in zoology at the University of Otago, Don is a skeptic, humanist, and critic of creationism. He is an honorary associate of the New Zealand Association of Rationalists and Humanists.

Donisthorpe, Wordsworth (19th Century)

Donisthorpe in 1893 formed the Legitimation League, which was closely associated with the *Adult*. When the League in 1897 openly advocated free love, it lost its support from the secularists of the period. The *Freethinker* parted company, and Arthur and Hypatia Bonner refused to include the Legitimation League in their *Directory of Reform Societies.* (See entry for Oswald Dawson) {RSR}

Donius, Augustinus (16th Century)

Donius was a materialist who wrote *De Natura Dominis* (1581), a two-volume work referred to by Francis Bacon. In his book, Donius makes reference to the power of the spirit as being related to motion. {BDF}

Donkin, Horatio Bryan [Sir] (Born 1845)

Donkin, a physician, was a member of the Rationalist Press Association and a keen opponent of all obscurantism. He was a Commissioner of Prisons, sat on the Royal Commission for the Control of the Feeble-Minded, and in 1910 delivered the Harveian Oration on "The Inheritance of Mental Characters." {RAT}

Donne, John (1572—1631)

Donne, who was related on his mother's side to Sir Thomas More, was born into a devout Catholic family, his uncle being the leader of the Jesuit mission in England. After his father died when Donne was four, his mother married a Catholic physician, Dr. John Syminges, and Donne was educated at home by Catholic tutors. In 1615 James I urged him to enter the church, which he did, and James made him a chaplain-in-ordinary and forced Cambridge to grant him a doctorate of divinity. In the church Donne became a pluralist. His *Pseudo-Martyr* was an attack on Catholics who had died for their faith, and he encouraged surviving Catholics to take the oath of allegiance to James. In 1611 his *Ignatius His Conclave* was a scurrilous attack on the Jesuits. His wife died in 1617 at the age of thirty-three, after giving birth to their twelfth child.

Richard Rambuss of Tulane University has studied the following sonnet

> Batter My Heart
>
> Batter my heart, three-personed God; for, you
> As yet but knock, breathe, shine, and seek to mend;
> That I may rise, and stand o'erthrow me, and bend
> Your force, to break, blow, burn, and make me new.
> I, like an usurped town, to another due,
> Labour to admit you, but oh, to no end,
> Reason your viceroy in me, me should defend,
> But is captived, and proves weak or untrue,
> Yet dearly I love you, and would be loved fain,
> But am betrothed unto your enemy,
> Divorce me, untie, or break that knot again,
> Take me to you, imprison me, for I
> Except you enthral me, never shall be free,
> Nor ever chaste, except you ravish me.

and concludes,

> Expressing sheer impatience with divine measures to date, Donne metaphorically aligns the extremity of his longing for redemption and spiritual satisfaction with the desire to be taken and ravished by God in what amounts to a kind of trinitarian gang-bang. It isn't enough for him to be ravished, raped by Jesus alone, that is; Donne aggressively demands that the whole Godhead be enlisted in the task: "Batter my heart, *three-personed God.*"

Rambuss is impressed that, despite the frequency of sex with his wife, Donne desires yet more. {Richard Rambuss, "Pleasure and Devotion," in *Queering the Renaissance* (1994)}

Donohoe, Amanda (20 Century)

An actor, Donohoe has been cast as a bisexual lawyer on the television drama "L.A. Law," and in a horror film, "Lair of the White Worm," she played a reincarnated pagan priestess who belonged to a snake-worshipping cult that was stamped out by the early Christians. In one scene her character was required to spit venom on a crucifix. Asked by *Interview* about the scene, Donohoe responded, "I'm an atheist, so it was actually a joy. Spitting on Christ was a great deal of fun. I can't embrace a male god who has persecuted female sexuality throughout the ages. And that persecution still goes on today all over the world. {CA}

Doolittle, Hilda (H. D.) (1886-1961)

Doolittle spent her childhood in a Moravian community. Her mother was a leader of the semi-mystical Moravian church and traced her German-Polish family back to the Unitas Fratrum, a Bohemian brotherhood that left Germany in the 1840s and founded Bethlehem, Pennsylvania, where Doolittle was born. Her father, Charles Leander Doolittle, was a professor of astronomy at Lehigh University. When her father obtained a position at the University of Pennsylvania, the Doolittles attended the Quaker meeting house in Philadelphia.

While a student at Bryn Mawr, Doolittle became engaged to the upstart poet Ezra Pound (he suggested that if she found her name "quaint" she should change it to H. D.), whom she had first met in 1901, but she withdrew because of her parents' disapproval.

According to Jennifer S. Wilson in *The Gay and Lesbian Literary Heritage* (1995), Doolittle's first lesbian lover was Frances Josepha Gregg. After their meeting in 1910 what ensued "was a painful romantic triangle between Hilda, Frances, and Ezra, the emotional intensity of which H. D. never fully left behind. In its aftermath, H. D. sailed for Europe with Gregg and Gregg's mother where she soon began in earnest her literary career."

Pound introduced her to the literary avant-garde as "H. D., Imagiste," for her style was sparse, concrete, precise, and direct in its imagery. She met (and Wilson speculates possibly had an affair with) Brigit Patmore, who in 1912 introduced her to her future husband, Richard Aldington. Their relationship ended after six years and included adultery as well as the stillbirth of their child in 1915. In 1919 she gave birth (the father was a musicologist, Cecil Gray) to a daughter, Frances Perdita.

H. D. also befriended Annie Winifred Ellerman (who called herself Bryher), and the two commenced a lifelong love and partnership, Bryher marrying twice for appearances and H. D. having intermittent affairs. Although her poetry explored an often-tormented heterosexual life, she chose not to be "out" to the public because that would have been uncomfortable and risky. As a result, H. D. and Bryher introduced themselves as "cousins."

When Aldington enlisted into the army, H.D. took over his position as literary editor of the *Egoist*, remaining until 1917, being replaced by T. S. Eliot.

Her work, from *Sea Garden* (1916) to *Hymen* (1921) to *Helen in Egypt* (1961), showed not only a deep involvement with classical mythology and Hellenism but also a spare use of natural imagery, an experiment with *vers libre*, and mysticism. *Bid Me to Live* (1960) was a *roman-à-clef*, a stream-of-consciousness novel about her Bloomsbury years.

In the late 1920s, when Bryher married one of H. D.'s lovers, Kenneth Macpherson, giving him financial backing, H. D. became connected with German film directors G. W. Pabst and Fritz Lang. In Macpherson's "Borderline," she acted opposite actor-singer Paul Robeson "and momentarily fell in love with him," Alika Barnstone found.

Barnstone, in an introduction to *Trilogy* (1998), three works of H. D.'s poetry from the 1940s, notes that in her work about Freud H. D. had asked, "Do I wish myself, in the deepest unconscious or subconscious layers of my being, to be the founder of a new religion?" H. D., she notes, may not establish a new religion but "she certainly 'makes it new' while creating an eclectic scripture that derives from Egyptian, Greek, and biblical traditions." She synthesizes the Judeo-Christian tradition (including Gnosticism) with the Egyptian and Greek pagan traditions and "brings together the old and the new, the scientific and pragmatic, and the esoteric and mystical."

H. D. lived with Bryher in London during the war. When Pound supported fascism and favored Mussolini, she cut all relations, declining his request after some correspondence to see her in Kusnacht.

Tribute to Freud (1965) described her analysis by seventy-seven-year-old Freud in 1933. She owed much to Freud, whose reading of the unconscious she felt "would save mankind." He was like another Jesus to her, Jesus being only one of many prophets and visionaries. However, "there was an argument implicit in our very bones," and "I was a student, working under the direction of the greatest mind of this and perhaps many succeeding generations. But the Professor was not always right." Bryher helped her rescue and finance Jewish emigration to Switzerland, and when the Nazis invaded Austria, they helped members of the Vienna Psychoanalytical Society emigrate to London. Freud lived in a small apartment on Sloane Street where H. D. visited him. Upon his death in Hamstead in 1939, she was outspokenly touched by the loss.

In 1946 she moved to Lausanne, recovering from depression and electric shock treatment. In 1953 she suffered an abdominal occlusion, was honored by Yale when she returned in 1956, and in 1960 received the Gold Medal Award from the American Academy of Arts and Letters, their highest honor. On this occasion the present writer spoke to her about the state of poetry, and she was very appreciative of the many volumes of "exciting" work by new poets which New Directions Books was sending her. Asked if she knew anything about "religious humanism" or the kind of humanism found in the work of William Carlos Williams, a Unitarian, H. D. said,

> No, not really. Jesus *was* just a man, of course. The ancient Greeks have always been an inspiration, but I have not delved into philosophy that much. It's bad enough fighting off the label of "imagist."

H. D. had a stroke in 1961 and is buried on Nisky Hill in Bethlehem, Pennsylvania. (See entries for John Hus and Moravian Church.) {GL; OEL; conversation with WAS mid-May 1960}

DOOMSDAY: See entry for Norman Cohn.

Doray de Longrais, Jean Paul (1736—1800)

A French man of letters, Doray de Longrais wrote a freethought romance, *Faustin, or the Philosophical Age*. {BDF}

Dority, Barbara (20th Century)

Dority, Joseph McCabe, and George Smith have been called three of the better known writers of freethought works. For *The Humanist*, she writes a regular column, "Civil Liberties Watch." Dority is president of Humanists of Washington, executive director of the Washington Coalition Against Censorship, and co-chairperson of the Northwest Feminist Anti-Censorship Task Force. {HNS2}

Dormand, John [Baron Dormand of Easington] (1919—)

In 1989, Dormand was elected an honorary associate of the Rationalist Press Association. Lord Dormand, who studied government at Harvard, entered the House of Commons in 1970 and the House of Lords in 1987, after having been chairman of the Labour Party. Because of his complete inability to accept the non-rational basis of religion, he has stated, he became an atheist. He disliked the mumbo-jumbo of religious services and the dressing-up of priests and bishops. In his view, there is need for a much wider expression of the rationalist and humanist viewpoints, particularly in broadcasting.

Dorsey, J. M. (19th Century)

Dorsey wrote *The True History of Moses* (1855), an attack on the Bible. {BDF}

Doryphorus

Doryphorus of Polyclitus was said to have had one of the most beautiful human bodies ever conceived, the kind which contemporary iron pumpers dream about. He is said to have been chosen by Nero to be his husband. (See entry for Alexander Pope.)

Dos Passos, John Roderigo (1896—1970)

Dos Passos was an American novelist whose first success, *Three Soldiers* (1921), was followed by another, *Manhattan Transfer* (1925). In a trilogy, *U.S.A.* (1937), he developed a kaleidoscopic technique to portray life, one which combined narration, stream of consciousness, biographies, and quotations from newspapers and magazines. His early left-wing views gave way to a conservatism evident in his less power later novels, such as his second trilogy, *District of Columbia* (1952).

In 1949 on the subject of humanism, Dos Passos wrote the present author,

> Lord, I'm afraid I don't know how to answer. I've spent my life trying to escape these classifications and am entirely ignorant of the philosophical vocabulary. What kind of humanists were Erasmus and Rabelais and Montaigne and Sir Thomas More? They lived in a period of violent ideological warfare that bears some relation to our own unhappy age. I don't pretend to have attained that lofty eminence, but some such attitude as theirs is the attitude I think a man of letters should strive for.

In 1951, he added,

> I don't see that classical humanism was incompatible with science. The scientific approach grew out of it. Frankly, it's rank nonsense to attribute anti-scientific views to Erasmus, etc., which may be alleged by some—there's evidently more confusion in the use of this term. When I speak of humanism I use the word in the standard historical sense as applying to the general Renaissance, scholarly outlook. I can't see that that was anti-scientific. The general "platonic" attitude could, I imagine, be spoken of as anti-scientific, in distinction with the Aristotelian, but the Aristotelian was also a priori.

In 1956, he elaborated on his earlier views:

> A definition of humanism is certainly in order, but I find it hard to find any single phrase sharp enough to give outline to a bedraggled word. Having spent my whole life trying to avoid classifications of this sort, I'm certainly not going to submit to one of the seven cat-

egories at this late date. I can find no valid objection to be included [as being in agreement with] the categories of ancient humanism and classical humanism. The names of the classical philosophers set all my sympathetic strings to humming. They taught us how to examine our world. Theistic humanism doesn't seem quite as limiting as atheistic humanism. Communistic humanism would seem to me to mean exactly the opposite of any of the various conceivable brands. Naturalistic humanism would seem to have as many varied meanings as a political platform; who will remember them after election? This leaves us exactly where we started. Humanism, though the word is as banal as a coin worn smooth of date and inscription, still connotes something. To me it connotes a frame of mind I would call vaguely good. It suggests freedom rather than slavery, fertility rather than sterility. the development of varied individualities in men rather than regimentation, the stimulation of charity and fellow feeling rather than of envy, hatred, and malice. Let's have more of it.

Dos Passos wanted and received a Protestant burial service, complete with church language, which was held in Baltimore at Trinity Church. {WAS, 1 April 1949, 15 February 1951, 27 October 1956}

Dos Santos, Emanuel (19th Century)

In Trinidad, Dos Santos in the 1890s edited a freethought publication, *Progress*. {FUK}

Dosamantes, Jesus Ceballos (19th Century)

Dosamantes was a Mexican philosopher, author of works on *Absolute Perfection* (1888) and *Modern Pharisees and Sadducees* (1889), the latter about mystics and materialists. {BDF}

Dostoyevsky, Fëodor (Mikhailovich) (1821—1881)

Dostoyevsky wrote about atheism but was a believer, stating that atheism sprang from our hatred of the world as it is. "To recognize that there's no God without recognizing at the same time that you yourself have become God makes no sense," he wrote. In 1849, he was arrested for membership in a secret political group, was exiled to Siberia where he was allowed to read only the Bible, and served for four years at hard labor. As a prisoner, he was forced to take part in a ceremony just prior to being executed, and at the last minute a pre-arranged reprieve was tendered, while he was standing in front of a scaffold. The incident so traumatized him that he is said to have been transformed from a youthful liberal into a fervently religious and orthodox believer.

Notes from the Underground (1864) was an existentialistic work which was followed by many literary successes, a major one of which was *Prestuplenie i Nakazanie (Crime and Punishment)* (1866). That consummate portrait of sin, remorse, and redemption was followed by *The Idiot* (1868), about a failed Christ figure. In 1872, he wrote *The Devils*, a portrayal of modern Nihilism in which he defines its ultimate consequences: "Starting from unlimited freedom, I arrive at unlimited despotism," leading Soviet critics to attack it decades later and resulting in its being made unavailable to Soviet readers. Another of his major works, and likely his most important, was *The Brothers Karamazov* (1880), in which he plumbs the depths and complexities of the human "soul."

As for Smerdyakov's dictum in *The Brothers Karamazov*, "If God doesn't exist, all things are permissible," Adolf Grünbaum and others have denied that theism is logically necessary as one of the premises of a systematic moral code. "Indeed," writes Grünbaum, "Smerdyakov's epigram boomerangs: Since atheism and theism are alike ethically barren, neither doctrine itself imposes any concrete moral prohibitions on human conduct."

Biographers Aimée Dostoyevsky and David Magarshack report that for spiritual guidance Dostoyevsky would open the Bible to the New Testament and, by random choice, would read whatever lines he came upon. When on January 25, 1881, he had a sudden hemorrhage and the physician was rushed to his bedside, Dostoyevsky asked his wife to open the Bible and read whatever she first saw. "And Jesus answering said unto himHold me not back for thus it becometh us to fulfill all righteousness." Apparently, Dostoyevsky felt this was a spiritual sign, and he said, "Did you hear? Hold me not back. My hour has come. I must die." Whereupon he bade farewell to his children and to his wife, slowly lost consciousness, and died that evening. From any vantage point, Dostoyevsky stands out as one of *the* towering figures of world literature. (See entry for V. Belinski.) {CE; CL; ER; EU, Hugh McLean; *Free Inquiry*, Fall 1992; PA; TDY}

DOSTOYEVSKY'S EPILEPSY

Physicians today talk about a left-temporal-lobe seizure called "Dostoyevsky's epilepsy," a rare condition. Freud thought Dostoyevsky was a hysterical epileptic, a condition which he believed was psychogenic in origin. Thom Jones noted that such an epileptic, in the split second before a fit, experiences an "ecstatic well-being unlike anything an ordinary mortal could hope to imagine. . . . Dostoyevsky was nervous and depressed, a tormented hypochondriac, a compulsive writer obsessed with religious and philosophic themes. He was hyperloquacious, raving, etc. & etc. His gambling addiction is well known. By most accounts he was a sick soul."

Jones, who writes that he personally has had such a seizure, added, "It is thought that St. Paul had a temporal-lobe fit on the road to Damascus. Paul warns us in *First Corinthians* that God will confound the intellectuals. It is known that Muhammad composed the Qur'an after attacks of epilepsy. Black Elk [A Sioux holy man and Christian] experienced fits before his grand 'buffalo' vision. Joan of Arc is thought to have been a left-temporal-lobe epileptic. Each of these in a terrible flash of brain lightning was able to pierce the murky veil of illusion which is spread over all things. Just so did the scales fall from my eyes. It is called the 'sacred disease.' "

Jones added, "Even Dostoyevsky, the fervent Christian, makes an almost airtight case against the possibility of the existence of God in the Grand Inquisitor digression in *The Brothers Karamazov*. It is probably the greatest passage in all of world literature, and it tilts you to the court of the atheist. This is what happens when you approach Him with the intellect." {*The New Yorker*, December 2, 1991; Eve LaPlante, *Seized* (1993)}

Douai, Adolf (19th Century)

A freethinker, Douai wrote *Autobiography*, which was translated by Richard H. Douai Boerker. {*Freethought History* #15, 1995}

DOUBT

Doubt involves withholding assent from a proposition as well as from its contradictory. It is common to doubt without having any reasonable reason, but to doubt because of rational reasons or facts is more in the spirit of free inquiry. Whereas the former may doubt that a mystical force does *not* run the universe, the latter may doubt that such a force can ever be verified.

DOUBTERS

- The believer is happy; the doubter is wise.

—Hungarian Proverb

- Men become civilized, not in proportion to their willingness to believe, but in proportion to their readiness to doubt.

—H. L. Mencken

- To believe is very dull. To doubt is intensely engrossing. To be on the alert is to live. To be lulled into security is to die.

—Oscar Wilde

- To knock a thing down, especially if it is cocked at an arrogant angle, is a deep delight of the blood.

—George Santayana

Doughty, LeGarde S. (20th Century)

Doughty, a writer of science fiction, is a naturalistic humanist who wrote *The Music Is Gone*. {HNS}

Douglas, George (c. 1830—1910?)

In 1886, Douglas was the original president of the Australasian Freethought Union. {SWW}

Douglas, John Sholto [Sir] (1844—1900)

Douglas, the eighth Marquis of Queensberry, sat as elected representative peer for Scotland from 1872 to 1880, having succeeded to the marquisate in 1858. He was a strong supporter of Bradlaugh and of secularism, and in 1880 the Scottish peers refused on account of his opinions to re-elect him as one of their representatives in the House of Lords. In 1882 he protested publicly in the theatre against what he regarded as a caricature of a freethinker in Tennyson's *Promise of May*. His own book, *The Spirit of the Matterhorn* (1881), was written in blank verse. "I particularly request," he ordered, "that no Christian mummeries or tomfooleries be performed at my grave, but that I be buried as an agnostic." {RAT; RE; TYD}

Douglas, Marjory Stoneman (1890-1998)

Douglas wrote *The Everglades: River of Grass* (1947), which helped change the way Americans look at wetlands and which led to the restoration of South Florida's fragile wetlands. Without her advocacy and efforts, the wetlands would have been drained.

She grew up in a religious household yet proclaimed herself an agnostic. For a short time, she was married to a ne'er-do-well who went to prison for passing bad checks. He introduced her to sex, and, she told Stephen W. Byers of *Outdoor Life*, she "enjoyed it while it lasted," then denied herself the pleasure for the rest of her life. During World War I she served in Europe with the American Red Cross. In 1916 she joined Mrs. William Jennings Bryan to argue for the women's suffrage amendment before Florida state legislators but found that "talking to them was like talking to graven images. They never paid attention to us at all."

Before her death she stipulated that there be no religious ceremony and said she did not believe in an immortal soul. {*The New York Times Magazine*, 3 January 1999}

Douglas, Norman (1868—1952)

"Pagan to the core" and "an unashamed connoisseur of pleasure" were epithets associated with Douglas, an Austrian-born son of a Scottish father and a Scottish-German mother. A member of the British Foreign Office (1893—1901), he purchased property on Capri, where he wrote eight books on subjects ranging from child labor abolition to travel to the fictional island of Nepenthe. In *South Wind* (1917), he describes Thomas Heard, Bishop of Bambopo, and his reaction to the islanders' unorthodox views on moral and sexual questions. In what David Leon Higdon has described as "a series of Rabelaisian conversation pieces," Douglas made "murder palatable to a bishop." D. H. Lawrence depicted Douglas as James Argyle in *Aaron's Rod* (1922). Although married to his cousin and the father of two sons, Douglas and his companion Guiseppe Orioli lived variously in Paris, St. Malo, Menton, Florence, Lisbon, London, and Capri. {GL}

Douglas, Stephen Arnold [Judge] (1813—1861)

Douglas was a statesman, a lawyer, the Secretary of State for Illinois, and Judge of the United States Supreme Court. He also was an unsuccessful candidate for the presidency, known particularly for being the "Little Giant" who was pitted against Abraham Lincoln in the Lincoln-Douglas debates, during which Lincoln first gained a national reputation. According to his obituary, Douglas "never identified himself with any Church." McCabe states that Douglas was a theist and an advocate of religious liberty. {JM; RAT}

Douglass, Frederick (1817—1895)

An American abolitionist and freethinker, Douglass escaped from slavery in 1838. In 1847 when English friends purchased his freedom he established *North Star*, a Rochester, NY, publication which advocated abolitionism through political activism. According to Howard-Pitney, author of *The Afro-American Jeremiah: Appeals for Justice in America*, Douglas "moved from a God-centered, humanly passive religion toward a human-centered creed stressing the efficacy of human will, good works, faith in human progress, and the perfectibility of humankind. By the 1850s, Douglass was a thorough-going religious liberal, or humanist. His liberal Protestantism coexisted comfortably with Enlightenment ideals of natural law and reason. Douglass's humanistic worldview was anchored in both Christian theology and natural rights philosophy, and his experience with religion helped form and support his humanistic faith." Robertson describes Douglass's views as being as heterodox as Lincoln's, adding that he knows this from personal information.

"I can see no reason," he wrote in 1845, "but the most deceitful one, for calling the religion of this land Christianity. I look upon it as the climax of all misnomers, the boldest of all frauds, and the grossest of all libels."

In a Fourth of July lecture, he said, "I would say, welcome infidelity! welcome atheism! welcome anything . . . in preference to the gospel as preached [by those who] connect the very name of religion into an engine of tyranny and barbarous cruelty." [AAH, David Howard-Pitney; CE; JMR; TYD}

Douthit, Jasper Lewis (1834—1927)

Douthit was a frontier circuit-riding preacher and church builder, a pattern of career and life usually found among the evangelical Protestant denominations. He was early attracted to Unitarianism by its creedal freedom and the antislavery reputation of James Freeman Clarke as well as of Theodore Parker. He preached a Christ-centered brand of Unitarianism and his differences with other Unitarians became so pronounced he founded a periodical, *Our Best Words* to compete with Jenkin Lloyd Jones's *Unity*. Today, he might better be known as a Protestant and a Congregationalist. The churches he commenced in Illinois were in the Shelbyville area. {U&U}

Dove, C. Clayton (20th Century)

Dove, a freethinker, wrote *The Miracles of St. Martin* (1924). {GS}

Dover, Cedric (20th Century)

A freethinker, Dover wrote *The Kingdom of Earth* (1931). {GS}

Dowden, Edward (1843—1913)

Dowden was an Irishman who rose to the first rank in the academic literary world in England. His *Life of Shelley* (1886, 2 volumes) contains candid appreciations of great skeptics, and Dowden was an agnostic. In his *Studies in Literature* (1878), Dowden rejects Christian doctrines, is skeptical about a future life, and recognizes a God only as "an inscrutable power." {JM; RAT}

Dowling, Alan: See the entry for Theism.

Dowman, Constance (20th Century)

Dowman was a devoted secretary and a director of the Rationalist Press Association. She worked full-time for forty-two years.

Downie, Colin (20th Century)

Downie is President of the Humanist Association of Canada.

Downey, Margaret (1950—)

Downey is president of the Freethought Society of Greater Philadelphia, which in 1994 successfully secured an official resolution in that city to designate June 8th as Thomas Paine Day. In 1996, the third such day was observed. Also in 1994, she appeared in a commemoration of Robert G. Ingersoll's work on behalf of women's equality, "Elizabeth Cady Stanton Meets Susan B. Anthony," playing the role of Anthony, at a Rochester, New York, meeting of the Ingersoll Memorial Committee. Downey is director of the Anti-Discrimination Support Network and edits the Freethought Society's newsletter, *The Greater Philadelphia Story* (PO Box 242, Pocopson, Pennsylvania 19366).

In 1996 at the 2nd Annual Atheist Alliance Convention, held in Minneapolis, she spoke on the subject "An Atheist Activist and Proud of It." At the 3rd such annual event, she spoke on "It's Not Easy Being Green." Downey is on the Board of Directors of the American Humanist Association, of The Humanist Institute, and of the Freedom From Religion Foundation. In addition, she is a contributing editor of the *Secular Humanist Bulletin* and a regional director of the Council for Secular Humanism. Her e-mail: <downey1@cris.com>.

Doyle, Arthur Conan [Sir] (1859—1930)

The English author and creator of Sherlock Holmes, Doyle, appeared not to believe in Biblical miracles: "It isn't true that the laws of nature have been capriciously disturbed; that snakes have talked; that women have been turned into salt; that rods have brought water out of rocks." Similarly, a freethinking sentiment was expressed when he wrote, "Dogmas of every kind put assertion in the place of reason and give rise to more contention, bitterness, and want of charity than any other influence in human affairs."

At first buried on the Windlesham estate in Crowborough, Sussex, England, the Doyle's remains later were removed to the Village Cemetery, Minstead, Hampshire, England. {PA; TYD}

Doyle, Doris (20th Century)

Doyle is an editorial associate for *Free Inquiry*, an editor at Prometheus Books, and the managing editor of *Skeptical Inquirer*.

Doyno, Victor (20th Century)

Doyno, a professor of English at the University of Buffalo, edited *Mark Twain, American Skeptic* (1995), in which he argues that, although Clemens was not a systematic philosopher, he was a skeptic for most of his life.

Draco (or Dracon) (Flourished 621 B.C.E.)

Draco, an Athenian chief magistrate and law codifier, prescribed death for the most trivial of offenses, believing that murder must be punished by the state and not by vendetta. Aristotle and Plutarch described Draco as explaining the lack of gradations in his punishments. Try as he could, Draco said he could not think of any more severe measure. Such extremism, now called Draconian, was approved by the American Puritans, as evidenced by Connecticut's severe blue laws which called for Draconian measures to punish, for example, children who talked back to their parents.

Athenians presumably loved Draco. In 590 B.C.E., there was a testimonial in his honor at the theater of Athena. As Draco entered the open-air arena, the partisan crowd rose, cheered, and threw their hats and cloaks clothing upon him—which custom today is analogous to throwing confetti or ticker-tape today. Unfortunately for him, the volume of garments was so great that Draco was smothered to death. {PA}

Drachmann, A. B. (20th Century)

Drachmann, a professor of classical philology in the University of Copenhagen, *Atheism in Pagan Antiquity* (1922), a work which is considered a classic in its subject area.

DRACULA: See entry for Bram Stoker.

Draghicesco, Dimitrie (20th Century)

A Rumanian humanist, Draghicesco defines "God" as "the more or less complete omnipotence, omniscience, and benevolence to which man as a race can approximate in the long run." {CL}

Dragut, Eugene-Alexandru (20th Century)

Dragut is the vice-president of the Humanist Movement of Romania. He is active in the Humanist Party of Romania, a political group not interested in governing at the present time but working to become a factor of social equilibrium, able to influence political decisions.

Drake, Durant (20th Century)

A philosopher, Drake defines "God" as "the universal self in each of us, our good will and idealism and intelligence which binds us together and drives us on by inner compulsion toward that ideal life for which in our better moments we strive." {CL}

Drake, W. Gordon (20th Century)

Drake wrote *In the Cool of the Day* (1956). {GS}

Drange, Theodore M. (20th Century)

Drange, a professor of philosophy at West Virginia University, wrote "Biblical Contradictions Regarding Salvation" (*Free Inquiry*, Summer 1994), in which he finds that "the entire foundation of soteriology, or the doctrine of salvation, is undermined by the given biblical contradictions, for there is no other basis for that doctrine than the Bible."

Drange, a supporter of Internet Infidels, is a contributing editor on *Philo*, for which he wrote "Nonbelief vs. Lack of Evidence: Two Atheological Arguments" (Spring-Summer 1998); and "Incompatible-Properties Arguments: A Survey" (Fall-Winter 1998).

His *Nonbelief and Evil* (1998) contains two arguments for the nonexistence of God. "Why does God permit evil?" theologians ask. The question he poses, however, is "Does the evil in the world provide good reason to deny the existence of God?" He then discusses the Argument from Evil and also the Argument from Nonbelief, concluding that the latter is an important issue in the philosophy of religion.

Draparnaud, Jacques Philippe Raymond (1772—1805)

Draparnaud, a French physician, taught natural history at Montpelier. His discourses on life and vital functions show his skepticism, as does his *Philosophy of the Sciences and Christianity* (1801). {BDF; RAT}

Draper, George O. (20th Century)

Draper was a freethinker who wrote *Searching for the Truth* (1902). {GS}

Draper, John William (1811—1882)

An English-American scientist, historian, and philosopher, Draper emigrated to America, teaching chemistry and natural history at New York University. He is said to be the first in New York to use Daguerre's process, and the picture which he took of his sister in 1840 is the oldest surviving photographic portrait. A chemist and physiologist, he wrote a rationalistic classic, History of the Conflict Between Religion and Science (1874), which aroused great controversy. He also wrote History of the Intellectual Development of Europe. McCabe called him an anti-Christian but a theist.

"There is no limit to understanding the world in natural rather than supernatural terms," he declared. "The history of science is not a mere record of isolated discoveries; it is a narrative of the conflict of two contending powers, the expansive force of the human intellect on one side, and the compression arising from traditionary faith and human interest on the other." {BDF, CE; Stephen Jay Gould, *Rocks of Ages*; JM; RSR; TYD}

Draper, Peter (20th Century)

When he signed Humanist Manifesto II, Dr. Draper was on the staff of Guy's Hospital Medical School in London. In 1978 he addressed the Seventh International Humanist and Ethical Union (IHEU) World Congress held in London. Draper is editor of *Health Through Public Policy* (1991).

DRAVIDIAN ASSOCIATION

The Dravidian Association is at 50 EVK, Sampath Road, Madras 7, India. The Dravidar Kazhagarn, or "Self-Respect Movement," was founded by Periyar. It is militantly anti-religious and strongly opposed to the Brahmin caste. The group is strong in the south of India.

Drayton, Michael (20th Century)

Drayton is chairperson of Interweave, which publishes *Interweave World*, journal of Unitarian Universalists for Lesbian, Gay, Bisexual, and Transgender Concerns.

DREAMERS

• A dreamer is one who can only find his way by moonlight, and his punishment is that he sees the dawn before the rest of the world.

—Oscar Wilde

Dreier, Frederik (1827—1853)

Dreier, a Dane, wrote *Spiritual Belief and Freethinking*. (See entry for Scandinavian Unbelievers.)

Driesch, Hans Adolf Eduard (Born 1867)

A German philosopher, Driesch is a neo-vitalist who rejects the idea of "soul" but speaks of God as an "Absolute Reality" of unknown features. He wrote *The Problem of Individually* (1914). {RAT}

Dreikurs, Rudolf (1897—1972)

In 1952, Dr. Dreikurs, whose interests included psychiatry, marriage, and parenthood, was Vice President of the American Humanist Association. In 1953, he was on the first Board of Directors of the International Humanist and Ethical Union (IHEU). {HNS; HNS2}

Dreiser, Theodore (1871—1945)

When *Sister Carrie* (1900) was published, readers were shocked by Dreiser's descriptions of the characters' irreligion and illicit sexual behavior, this despite the fact that his publisher had already expunged 40,000 words from the original manuscript. *An American Tragedy* (1925) similarly describes false piety, questions matters of free will, and shows greedy capitalists perverting Christian ideals. As described by William F. Ryan, "Dreiser's attitudes metamorphosed within American socialism, and he joined the Communist party late in life. But there is no evidence that he was an atheist. He scorned

Catholicism and the Protestant churches, claiming in his autobiographical writings—among them, *Dawn* (1931)—that those orthodox churches had perverted Christianity with political concerns and the pursuit of material wealth. Dreiser called for a 'pure religion and undefiled,' one grounded in good works and human compassion." His atheism and hostility to organized religion is evident in his statements, "All forms of dogmatic religion should go. The world did without them in the past and can do so again" and "Assure a man that he has a soul and then frighten him with old wives' tales as to what is to become of him afterwards, and you have hooked a fish, a mental slave." {CE; CL; EU, William F. Ryan; JM; TRI; TYD}

Dresden, Edmond (Died 1903)

Dresden (or Dresdon) was a British philanthropist about whom not much is known. However, at his death he left his entire fortune, apart from bequests to servants, of almost two million dollars to hospitals and the National Lifeboat Institution. He directed that this inscription should be cut on his tombstone: "Here lie the remains of Edmond Dresden, who believed in no religion but that of being charitable to his fellow man and woman, both in word and deed." {JM}

Drews, Arthur (Born 1865)

Drews was a German freethinker who wrote *The Christ Myth* (1910; 1998) and *The Witnesses to the Historicity of Jesus* (1912), in which he denies the historicity of Christ. In his work, Drews expounds a pantheistic monism. {GS; RAT}

Dreyfus, Ferdinand Camille (19th Century)

Dreyfus is author of *Evolution of Worlds and Societies* (1888). {BDF}

Drohan, Francis Burke (20th Century)

Drohan, a freethinker, wrote *Jesus Who? The Greatest Mystery Never Told* (1985). {GS}

DROIT DU SEIGNEUR

The "right" of a lord to deflower, on her marriage night, any bride of any of his vassals came to be known as *droit du seigneur*. An inhumanistic custom, it is cited by Wole Soyinka as being similar to *gbese le*, the placing by a Yoruban monarch of his royal slipper, symbolically, on any woman who catches his fancy, after which she is assigned to his harem. {*The New York Times*, 18 April 1999}

Droysen, Johann Gustav (1806—1882)

Droysen, a German historian, edited Frederick the Great's correspondence and wrote other important works, some in conjunction with his friend Max Duncker. {BDF}

Drucker, Catherine (20th Century)

Drucker in *New Humanist* (May 1995) wrote about how Lee Kuan Yew has fought against free speech in Singapore. As Campaigns Coordinator of Article 19, she examined the process he used and concluded that an independent judiciary cannot exist in the absence of free institutions, including a free press.

DRUGS: See entry for Australian and New Zealand Humanists.

DRUIDS

• Druids, n. Priests and ministers of an ancient Celtic religion which did not disdain to employ the humble allurement of human sacrifice. Very little is now known about the Druids and their faith. Pliny says their religion, originating in Britain, spread eastward as far as Persia. Caesar says those who desired to study its mysteries went to Britain. Caesar himself went to Britain, but does not appear to have obtained any high preferment in the Druidical Church, although his talent for human sacrifice was considerable. Druids performed their religious rites in groves, and knew nothing of church mortgages and the season-ticket system of pew rents. They were, in short, heathens and—as they were once complacently catalogued by a distinguished prelate of the Church of England—Dissenters.

—**Ambrose Bierce**
The Devil's Dictionary

Drummond, William [Sir] (c. 1770—1828)

Drummond entered Parliament as a member for St. Mawes, Cornwall, in 1795. In 1796 he became envoy to the court of Naples, and in 1801 was the ambassador to Constantinople. His principal work is *Origines* (4 volumes, 1824—1829), or remarks on the origin of several empires, states, and cities. His *Oedipus Judaicus* (1811) boldly questions many legends of the Old Testament, to which it gave an astronomical significance. {BDF; RAT}

Druskowitz, Helene (Born 1858)

Druskowitz, who was awarded the doctorate of philosophy at Dresden, wrote a life of Shelley in 1884 and a book on freewill and the new doctrines in 1883. {BDF; RAT}

Druten, Van (20 Century)

Druten told a 1998 Minneapolis symposium on "The Role of Religion in Public Life" that from his humanistic viewpoint religion is a "spurious aid to morality" and that violence often has its roots in religion. {*Secular Nation*, July-September 1998}

Druyan, Ann (20th Century)

Druyan, third wife of the late Carl Sagan, is a novelist and the secretary of the Federation of American Scientists. At Sagan's memorial service, she told of his and her exuberance at their having included an interstellar message along with the music of Bach, Beethoven, and others in two NASA Voyager spacecraft now beyond the outer solar system. At a speed of 40,000 miles per hour, the recordings are traveling in space and have a projected "shelf life" of a billion years, she stated.

Commenting about Sagan's movie, "Contact," which opened after his death, Druyan, who co-wrote the picture, said,

> This is really painful. But also, in a way, when you love somebody with all of your heart and they die, part of you is walking around thinking, "I want the whole world to remember this person and feel what I feel." . . . Because I don't believe in an actual afterlife, it means a lot to me that Carl's ideas and what we stood for are given a kind of dramatic expression in this movie.

Druyan in 1997 was named "Freethought Heroine" by the Freedom From Religion Foundation, which cited her having been vocal in protecting her late husband's memory from the slur of "deathbed conversion" stories since he died of pneumonia. {"Sagan's Movie's One in a Billion," *New York Post*, 9 July 1997}

Dryden, John (Born 1850)

Dryden, who was a director of the Rationalist Press Association from its inception, was a merchant. He was London correspondent of the New York *Truthseeker*. {RAT}

Drysdale, C. V. (1874—1961)

Drysdale, a freethinker and son of Charles R. Drysdale, chaired in 1881 the first Medical Congress on family planning. {TRI}

Drysdale, Charles Robert (1829—1907)

Drysdale founded the Neo-Malthusian league, which Margaret Sanger credited with having inspired her in her birth control efforts. His uncle, George R. Drysdale, was the courageous publisher cited by Margaret Sanger as having edited, revised, and widely circulated Charles Knowlton's *Fruits of Philosophy*. Drysdale wrote *Predicaments of Love* (republished in 1991). {RAT; RSR}

Drysdale, George (1825—1904)

In his *Elements of Social Science* (1854, originally titled *Physical, Sexual and Natural Religion*), Drysdale in a chapter on the "Evils of Abstinence" argued that young people of both sexes would be helped to better health and happiness by "moderate indulgence in sexual intercourse." He held that "complete sexual abstinence is in every case an evil, and more especially so in the years immediately after puberty." In 1861 secularists quarreled vigorously over such views. George and Charles R. Drysdale were brothers. {RSR; TRI}

D'Souza, Frances (20th Century)

D'Souza spoke to humanists in 1995 at Conway Hall concerning Article 19 of the Universal Declaration of Human Rights, which states that "Everyone has the right to freedom of opinion and expression; this right includes freedom to hold opinions without interference and to seek, receive, and impart information and ideas through any media and regardless of frontiers." What, she mused, happens if we can establish that speech can lead to violence. "What," she illustrated, "will result, if I stand on a table and say 'Let's kill Salman Rushdie'?" Freedom of expression, she reasoned, is especially important because, without it, it is impossible to secure other human rights. To maintain an independent press is the only way to preserve democracy. "We need," she stated, "to be extremely vigilant of all our sources of free speech. We should support plurality, diversity, and a multiplicity of outlets." D'Souza is author of *The Refugee Dilemma* (1980). {*New Humanist*, May 1995}

DUALISM

Dualism, in philosophy and theology, is any system that explains phenomena by two opposing principles. In philosophy, the dualism may be of mind and matter, or mind and body. In theology, the two principles may be of good and evil. No serious contemporary scientist will defend dualism, the concept identified with Descartes that somehow there is a different source of our consciousness than the matter which we have in our heads.

A philosopher at the University of Santa Cruz, California, David Chalmers, has made a recent attempt to revive dualism. In *The Conscious Mind: In Search of a Fundamental Theory* (1996), Chalmers rejects materialism of all kinds. He attacks Francis Crick and Christopher Koch for their suggestion that consciousness is linked with patches of brain electro-activity in the 35-75 hertz range. Chalmers claims they are only guessing about the brain's workings. *The Economist* (20 July 1996), however, found his various arguments interesting but unconvincing. (See entry for Descartes, and see the *Encyclopedia of Philosophy*.) {DCL}

Dubcek, Alexander A. (1921—1992)

Dubcek, when speaker of the Czechoslovakian Parliament, was awarded the 1990 International Humanism Prize by the International Humanist and Ethical Union (IHEU). He said that that group's aims, "which [have] in mind the values of the very greatest for mankind," were in line "on the whole with my feelings and convictions. Humanity and morality! The values that have always been standing in front of the values mankind strives for. Values which give shape to human characters and give life a human dimension. . . . In the combination of these values, I see a symbol of the endeavours of the whole of mankind without barriers or frontiers." A Slovakian, he had as one of the national minority been active after World War II in the Communist underground. Becoming head of the Slovakian Communist Party's central committee, then its first secretary, Dubcek relaxed censorship and worked toward a gradual democratization of Czech political life. His bold attempt in 1968 to give his country "socialism with a human face" was crushed when Soviet-led Warsaw Pact troops invaded. He was arrested and taken to Moscow, following which he served briefly as ambassador to Turkey (1969-1970), then maliciously demoted to a job as a forester in the region of Slovakia, then fell into official disgrace. At the time of his death, he was the leader of Slovakia's Social Democrats. A Kremlin press aide in 1988 allegedly joked that the difference between Dubcek and Mikhail Gorbachev was twenty years, for Dubcek had decried the moral rot and profligate incompetence of Brezhnev's empire at a time when few others dared. His autobiography, *Hope Dies Last* (1993), published posthumously, contains an afterword by its editor and translator, Jiri Hochman: "He tried to see the good side of everything. . . . He always assumed that everyone had good intentions. He was often let down, but that never changed his basic nature." {CE; *Free Inquiry*, Winter 1990-1991}

Duberman, Martin (1930—)

A historian who has taught at Harvard, Yale, Princeton, and Lehman College, Duberman founded in 1991 the Center for Lesbian and Gay Studies of the City of New York University's Graduate School. Among his many works are *Charles Francis Adams* (1961), *In White America* (1963), *James Russell Lowell* (1967), *Visions of Kerouac* (1977), and *About Time: Exploring the Gay Past* (1986). A non-believer, Duberman has inspired a number of gays and lesbians during a period in which homosexuality was coming, in their description, "out of the closet." He wrote *Stonewall* (1996), one of the better volumes describing the 1969 riots on behalf of human rights by homosexuals in New York City's Greenwich Village. {WAS, 5 December 1996}

Dubko, Elena (20th Century)

Dubko, a philosophy lecturer at Moscow University, is Vice-President of Ethical Dialogues. That group aims to unite ethicists, sociologists, enthusiasts, and humanists. She spoke at a 1995 Berlin conference arranged by the International Humanist and Ethical Union (IHEU), at which time she was somewhat pessimistic about the political situation and the state of humanism in Russia. {See Elana Dubko, "Ethical Dialogues in Moscow," *New Humanist*, December 1995.}

Duboc, Julius (Born 1829)

Duboc was a German writer and journalist. He translated the *History of the English Press* and wrote in 1875 an atheistic work, *Das Lieben Ohne Gott* (Life Without God), with the motto from Feuerbach, "No religion is my religion, no philosophy my philosophy." {BDF; RAT}

Dubois, Paul François (1795—1874)

Dubois was a French educationist who accepted the philosophy of Cousin, his teacher, and taught, successively, at Falaise, Limoges, Besaçon, and Paris. In 1824 he took up Saint-Simonianism and was imprisoned for his bold utterances. The Revolution of 1830 freed him, and he was appointed General Inspector of Public Instruction. In 1831 he entered the Chambre and in 1840 succeeded M. Cousin as Director of the Normal School. {RAT}

Dubois, Pierre (19th Century)

A French skeptic, Dubois in 1835 published *The True Catechism of Believers*, a work ordered by the Court of Assizes to be suppressed and for which the author was condemned to six months' imprisonment and a fine of one thousand francs. He also wrote *The Believer Undeceived*, a work on the evident proofs of the falsity and absurdity of Christianity that was put on the *Index* in 1836. In 1979, Dubois's *Bidochet le petit ogre* was republished. {BDF}

Du Bois, W(illiam) E(dward) B(urghardt) (1868—1963)

DuBois, the American civil rights leader and author, ranks with Frederick Douglas and Martin Luther King Jr. as being among the greatest champions of African American rights and liberty. He cofounded (1909) the National Negro Committee which became (1910) the National Association for the Advancement of Colored People. In addition he edited the NAACP magazine, *The Crisis*, until 1932. In 1961, he joined the Communist party, moving to Ghana, where he directed production of a multivolume *Encyclopedia Africana* and adopted Ghanian citizenship.

When seventeen and in a missionary college where religious orthodoxy was stressed, Du Bois found he was quite capable of meeting the orthodoxy

> with argument, which I did. My "morals" were sound, even a bit puritanic, but when a hide-bound old deacon inveighed against dancing I rebelled. By the time of graduation I was still a "believer" in orthodox religion, but had strong questions which were encouraged at Harvard. In Germany I became a Freethinker.

According to Howard-Pitney, Du Bois's "basic philosophical and ethical position was internally consistent, even though he combined a scientific intellect with an idealistic, poetic soul. On the one hand, he was an empiricist-materialist who turned reflexively to naturalistic understandings and explanations of human behavior. He was thus attracted to 'scientific socialism' and the Marxist idea that history is determined by economic forces. Du Bois was not religious in any traditional sense; indeed he was something of an anticleric. At the same time, he believed in a creative force directing the universe and in the immortality of the soul, and there was an undeniably spiritual dimension to Du Bois' imagination and expression. . . . 'Love is God and Work is His prophet,' he declared. 'We make the world better by the gift of our service and our selves. So in some mystic way does God bring realization [of a better world] through sacrifice." Howard-Pitney states that Du Bois relied heavily upon biblical language, finding religious symbols and nomenclature "deeply expressive of his own highest hopes and longings." Although he recognized the black church's role, according to Howard-Pitney, Du Bois "was a humanist and a rationalist, not a theist or a supernaturalist. Antirational dogma repelled him, and he ceased participating in organized worship as a young adult."

Among his witty observations are the following:

- The kind of sermon which is preached in most colored churches is not today attractive to even fairly intelligent men.

- The theology of the average colored church is basing itself far too much upon "hell and damnation." . . . We are still trained to believe a good deal that is simply childish in theology. . . . Our present method of periodic revival [involves] the hiring of professional and loud-mouthed evangelists and reducing people to a state of frenzy or unconsciousness.

- Half the Christian churches of New York are trying to ruin the free public schools in order to replace them by religious dogma.

{AAH, David Howard-Pitney; CE; TYD}

Dubois-Reymond, Emil (1819—1896)

A German physiologist of French and Swiss descent, Dubois-Reymond demonstrated that electrical changes accompany muscle action. An atheist, according to Paul Edwards, Dubois-Reymond argued against the existence of God on the ground that no cosmic brain can be discovered that would serve as the physiological foundation of a divine mind. He wrote, "Before he can allow a psychical principle to the universe, [the student of nature] will demand to be shown somewhere within it, embedded in neurine and fed with warm arterial blood under proper pressure, a convolution of ganglionic globules and nerve-tubes proportioned in size to the faculties of such a mind." Logical positivists used Dubois-Reymond's views in their discussions as to whether or not God operates without a body. {BDF; CE; EU, Paul Edwards; RAT}

Dubuisson, Gabriel (20th Century)

In Montreal, Canada, Dubuisson has been editing a French publication, *Raison*, since 1979.

Dubuisson, Paul (19th Century)

Dubuisson, a French positivist, wrote *Grand Types of Humanity*. {BDF; FUK}

Dubuisson, Paul Ulrich (1746—1794)

Dubuisson was a French dramatist and revolutionary, a close friend of Cloots, with whom he suffered on the scaffold, 24 March 1794. {BDF; RAT}

Du Cann, C. G. L. (20th Century)

Du Cann, a freethinker, wrote *How the Churches Betray Their Christ* (c. 1920?) and *Will You Rise from the Dead? (1940s?).* {GS}

Ducasse, C. J. (1881—1969)

Ducasse, according to "Survival as Transmigration" in Paul Edwards's *Immortality*; believed in reincarnation but did not believe in God. He was a former head of the Association for Symbolic Logic (1936—1938), which he had helped found. Edwards humorously and thoroughly attacks Ducasse's views in *Reincarnation: A Critical Examination*. {PE}

Duckhorn, Paul J. (20th Century)

Duckhorn is an activist member of the Campus Freethought Alliance. She is a student at the Lake Villa Community College near Chicago, Illinois. In 1998 she signed the Alliance's "Bill of Rights for Unbelievers."

Duclaux, Agnes Mary Frances (Born 1857)

Duclaux was a writer who translated Euripides. At Paris her salon was thronged with scholars and literary men. She wrote the life of Renan. In 1888 she married J. Darmesteter and, upon his death, married the Director of the Pasteur Institute, Duclaux. {RAT}

Duclos, Charles Pinot (1704—1772)

Duclos was a witty French writer who was admitted into the French Academy in 1747 and became its secretary in 1755. A friend of Diderot and d'Alembert, he wrote *Considerations sur les Moeurs*. {BDF; RAT}

Ducos, Jean François (1765—1793)

Ducos was a French Girondist. Elected to the Legislative Assembly, he demanded on 26 October 1791 the complete separation of the state from religion. He shared the fate of the Girondins, crying with his last breath, "Vive la Republique!" {BDF; RAT}

Ducros, Louis (1921—)

Ducros is author of *Les Encyclopedistes* (1967). He also wrote works on Diderot, d'Alembert, Rousseau, Heine, and Schopenhauer.

Du Deffand, Marie (1697—1780)

A *Marchioness*, Du Deffand was a witty literary French woman. Chamfort related that when young and in a convent she preached irreligion to her young comrades. The abbess called in Massillon, to whom the little skeptic gave her reasons. He departed, saying, "She is charming." For half a century, her house in Paris was the resort of eminent authors and statesmen. For years she corresponded with Horace Walpole, D'Alembert, and Voltaire.

One anecdote is that to the Cardinal de Polignac, who spoke of the miracle of St. Denis walking when beheaded, she said, "*Il n'y a que le premier pas qui coûte.*" And to the curé of Saint Sulpice, who came to her death-bed, she said, "*Ni questions, ni raisons, ni sermons.*" {BDF}

Dudgeon, William (Flourished 1775)

Dudgeon was a Berwickshire deist, whose works were published privately in Edinburgh in 1765. In 1994, Dudgeon's *The Philosophical Marks* was republished. {BDF; RAT}

Dudley, Christopher [Senator] (19th Century)

Dudley, an avowed deist, served seven times as State Senator for Onslow County. (See entry for North Carolina Freethinkers.)

Dudley, Dean (20th Century)

A freethinker, Dudley wrote *History of the First Council of Nice* (1901). {GS}

DUELLING: See entry for Christopher Marlowe.

Dufay, Henri (19th Century)

Dufay is the author of *La Legende du Christ* (1880). {BDF}

Duffy, David Evan (1941—)

Duffy is a humanist activist who arrived in Australia in 1952 from London. He has been the convenor of the Sydney Humanist Society's "Open Forum" and served as President of the Humanist Society of New South Wales during the period of 1988 to 1991. {SWW}

Duffy, Maureen Patricia (20th Century)

Duffy is President of the Gay and Lesbian Humanist Association (GALHA) (34 Spring Lane, Kenilworth, Warwickshire CV8 2HB, England). She has published plays, poetry, and non-fiction (including a life of Afra Behn, *The Passionate Shepherdess*, 1977). She is best known, however, for her novels: *That's Who It Was*; *The Paradox Players* (1967), *Wounds* (1969), *Capital* (1975), and *Londoners*(1983), the latter a sardonic view of the writer's lot. Homosexuality appears in many of her works, including *Restitution* (1999), about three individuals in London and Berlin who are searching for something in their past. {*Gay and Lesbian Humanist*, Summer 1999; OCE}

Dugan, Dan (20th Century)

Dugan, an inventor and audio engineer in San Francisco, co-authored with Judy Daar an article, "Are Rudolf Steiner's Waldorf Schools 'Non-Sectarian'?" in *Free Inquiry* (Spring 1994).

Dugdale, Henrietta (1826—1918)

Dugdale was an early Australian secularist, freethinker, suffragist, and dress reformer. She blamed religion for most of society's gross abuses, saying, "Christianity was another despotism formed by man to humble women." She recommended castration for persistent rapists, and she was an outspoken opponent of male dominance. A vegetarian who grew and cooked most of her own food, she designed her own "rational" costume with a divided skirt. A member of the Eclectic Association and the Australasian Secular Association, she helped form the Victorian Women's Suffrage Society, some of whose members complained about her iconoclastic secularism. {SWW}

Duhamel, Georges (1884—1966)

Duhumel, Goncourt Prize winner, member of the French Academy, founder of the Utopian Group (1906—1908), and a critic of unchecked industrialization in *America: The Menace*, wrote the present author concerning humanism:

> *Je réponds sans retard à votre lettre, reçue hier soir et qui a dû me rejoindre ici. Félix Tallemand n'exprime en rien ma position morale personnelle, vous pouvez vous en douter. C'est un affreux bonhomme qui ne croit qu'à une chose, à son intérêt temporal. Si, parvenu au seuil de la mort, il lance un cri d'angoisse, c'est parce que la maladie éveille en lui le sentiment qu'il y a peut-être dans le monde autre chose que des affaires à traiter, c'est parce que la maladie fait naître en lui, pour la première fois, le remords.*
>
> *Je ne suit ni naturaliste, ni unanimiste, ni purement déterministe. Médecin d'origine, je me suis composé, à force de vivre parmi des savants remarquables, une philosophie biologique faite évolutionnisme, de mutationnisme et d'une sort de finalisme, c'est-à-dire de la reconnaissance dans certains phénomenes d'un ordre préétabli (Lucien Cuenot. Invention et Finalité en Biologie. Flammarion, editeur).*
>
> *Depuis ma seizième année, j'ai quitté, au point de vue métaphysique, la foi religieuse dans laquelle j'avais été élevé. J'ai longtemps dit que j'étais un agnostique désespéré. Je dis maintenant que je suit an agnostique chrétien. Cela signifie que j'observe de mon mieux la morale chrétienne. Quant à la métaphysique chrétienne il ne dépend pas de moi de l'accepter sans ce que l'on appelle la grâce. Je suis en bonne intelligence avec les agnostiques purs et avec les croyants.*
>
> *Eventuellement, vous trouveriez tout cela expliqué dans les cinq volumes de mémoires que j'ai publiés au Mercure de France sous le titre général de* Lumieres de l'Abîme, Biographie de mes fantômes. Le temps de la recherche. La Pesée des âmes. Les espoirs et les épreuves. *Les deux premiers de ces volumes ont paru en anglais, chez Dent, sous le titre:* Light on My Days.

Duhamel, in the above letter, calls himself a physician who is neither just a naturalist nor purely a determinist. He states that when he was sixteen years old he was a "hopeless agnostic" but that now he is a Christian agnostic on good terms with agnostics as well as with believers. Félix Tallemand does not at all express his personal moral position, and he hopes to make all this clear in the five volumes of a memoir he published under the general title of *Lumieres de l'Abîme*, which in English is called *Light on My Days*. (See entry for Charles Mayer, who, although Duhamel stated he was a Christian agnostic, describes Duhamel as being a naturalistic humanist who is unacquainted with that phrase.) {WAS, 14 August 1954}

Duhecquet, H. M.: See entry for H. D. Robinson.

Duhig, James Vincent (1889—1963)

Duhig, who had been brought up and educated as a Catholic by his Irish parents, was the nephew of, and was sometimes confused with, the Australian Roman Catholic Bishop in Brisbane, James Duhig.

As an outspoken critic of all hypocrisy, Duhig delighted in baiting his distinguished relative, announcing that religious belief frustrated honest thinking. Duhig was a medical practitioner in Australia. {TRI}

Dühring, Eugen Karl (Born 1833)

Dühring was a German writer who, though blind, wrote many works on science. He wrote a *Critical History of Philosophy* (1869—1878) and *Science Revolutionized* (1878). In 1879, his death was maliciously reported. {BDF}

Dujardin, Édouard (1861—1949)

Dujardin, a freethinker, wrote *The Source of the Christian Religion, A Critical History of Ancient Judaism* (1910). {GS; RAT}

DUKE UNIVERSITY HUMANISTS

The humanist group at Duke University in North Carolina os pm tje Web: <http://www.secularhumanism.org/cfa/orgs.html>.

Duke, Barry (20th Century)

Duke in 1996 was elected the treasurer of the National Secular Society. He was one of the seven original subscribers in 1978 to the National Secular Society Limited's Articles of Association. Duke's partner, Brian Parry, died in 1996 and received a secular humanist funeral conducted by Denis Cobell.

In 1998 upon the death of Peter Brearey, he became acting editor of *The Freethinker*. E-mail: <iduke@compuserve.com>.

Dulaure, Jacques Antoine (1755—1835)

A French archeologist and historian, Dulaure in 1788—1790 published six volumes of a description of France. Elected to the

Convention in 1792, he voted for the death of the King. Proscribed as a Girondist, Dulaure then fled to Switzerland.

He was one of the Council of Five Hundred, 1796—1798. Although he wrote a learned *Treatise on Superstitions*, he is best known for his *History of Paris* and *Short History of Different Worships* (1825), in which he deals with ancient fetishism and phallic worship. {BDF; RAT}

Dulaurens, Henri Joseph (1719—1797)

A French satirist, Dulaurens was brought up in a convent, became a priest, then published a satire against the Jesuits, who forced him to flee for his life to Holland, where he lived in poverty. He edited *L'Evangile de la Raison*, a collection of anti-Christian tracts by Voltaire and others and wrote *L'Anti-papisme révelé* (1797). Dulaurens was caustic, cynical, and vivacious. {BDF; RAT}

Dulk, Albert Freidrich Benno (1819—1884)

Dulk was a German poet who became a physician but was expelled for aiding in the Revolution of 1848. He traveled in Italy and Egypt. In 1865 he published *Jesus der Christ*, embodying rationalism in prose and verse. {BDF; RAT}

Duller, Eduard (1809—1853)

Duller, a poet and historian born in Vienna, wrote *History of the Jesuits* (1840) and *The Men of the People* (1847—1850). {BDF}

Dulley, David (20th Century)

An English Unitarian, Dulley is author of *Conversations With Mona* (1993), in which he examines important religious, societal, and economic questions with a humanistic eye in imagined debates with his tortoiseshell cat, Mona.

Du Marsais, César Chesneau (19th Century)

A French grammarian and philosopher, Dumarsais wrote against the pretensions of Rome and contributed to the *Encyclopédie*. He is credited with *An Analysis of the Christian Religion* and with *Essai sur les Préjugés* by Mr. D. M., although the latter may have been written by Holbach with notes by Naigeon.

Du Marsais edited Mirabaud's anonymous work on *The World and Its Antiquity* and *The Soul and Its Immortality* (1751). {BDF}

Dumas, Alexandre fils (1824—1895)

The chief creator of the 19th century comedy of manners, Dumas wrote *La Dame aux camélias (Camille*, 1848*)*, which became a sensation. Verdi adapted it. Dumas was the bastard son of a father, Dumas *père*, who died a Catholic.

Dumas *fils* may or may not have been a philosophic naturalist, but he earned the enmity of the Vatican, which included in its *Index of Prohibited Books* all his novels as well as, in 1880, *La question du divorce*.

He thought there should be a revolt against romantic morality, he exposed excesses of the wealthy, he smiled at bourgeois Puritanism, and he propounded psychological as well as social questions.

"If God were suddenly condemned to live the life which He has inflicted on men," Dumas once wrote, "He would kill Himself."

Dumas's Parisian tomb relates that "death interests me much more than life, for life belongs to time while death forms part of eternity." McCabe called Dumas a deist who was inclined to mysticism. {CB; CE; ILP; JM; RAT; TRI; TYD}

Du Maurier, George Louis Palmella Busson (1834—1896)

Du Maurier, an English novelist and artist, was a noted illustrator for *Punch*. He wrote such novels as *Peter Ibbetson* (1892) and *Trilby* (1894). The former was largely based on his early childhood in Paris and turned on two supernaturally related dreams. Du Maurier was the freethinking grandfather of Daphne Du Maurier (1907-1989), the author of *Rebecca*. {RAT; TRI}

Dumont, Léon (1837—1877)

A French writer and Darwinist, Dumont wrote on *Haeckel and the Theory of Evolution* (1873). Dumont wrote in *La Revue Philosophique*. {BDF; RAT}

Dumont, Pierre Étienne Louis (1759—1829)

Dumont was a Swiss writer who, as a Protestant minister, was held to be a brilliant preacher. But his faith decayed, and he came to England as tutor to Lord Shelburne's children. In 1814 upon returning to Switzerland, Dumont rejected his clerical status and, as member of the Grand Council, worked for prison reform on Bentham's principles. {RAT}

Dunant, Jean-Henri (1828—1910)

A Swiss philanthropist who founded the International Red Cross, Dunant shared with Frédéric Passy the first Nobel Peace Prize (1901). A humanitarian, Dunant was a freethinker. {CE; TRI}

Dunayevskaya, Raya (1910—1987)

Dunayevskaya, the noted Marxist scholar and former secretary to Leon Trotsky, wrote specifically that "Marxism is Humanism" in *The Humanist Alternative* (1973). She held that despite a hundred-year burial of Marx's Humanist essays, Marx's Humanism has made history, revolutionary history. No other philosophic writing can compare with it. In our era, it was the Hungarian revolution of 1956 that brought Marx's Humanism onto the historic stage. By unfurling the Humanist banner and laying down their lives in the struggle for freedom *from* communism, the Hungarian freedom fighters gave new life to Marx's original definition of his unique world view as a new Humanism or thoroughgoing naturalism, as against "communism [which] is not itself the goal of human development—the form of human society." Similarly, the battle of the Czechs for "socialism with a human face" was Marxist Humanism at its best.

Her viewpoint was not that of James T. Farrell, Sidney Hook, and many other humanists who may have shared with Marx a disbelief in supernaturalism but did not share his political or collectivist outlook. {PK}

Dunbar, Anthony P. (20th Century)

A freethinker, Dunbar wrote *Against the Grain: Southern Radicals and Prophets 1929—1959*, in which he tells about Southern ministers who formed a loose-knit but militant wing of the "Social Gospel" movement. {*Freethought History #14*, 1995}

Duncan, Colin (1915—1989)

Duncan was an Australian humanist, engineer, and lobbyist. A committed activist in the humanist movement for more than twenty years, he worked with the Gun Control Lobby and the Voluntary Euthanasia Society of Victoria, of which he was president in 1983. His efforts contributed to the passing of favorable "Dying With Dignity" legislation. On his death, the eulogy was delivered by Nigel Sinnott. {SWW}

Duncan, David (Born 1839)

An educationist, Duncan from 1867 to 1870 was Herbert Spencer's private secretary. He compiled the four volumes of the *Description Sociology.* In 1870 he was appointed professor of logic and moral philosophy at the Presidency College in Madras, and in 1899 he became Vice-Chancellor of Madras University.

His *Life and Letters of Herbert Spencer* (1908) shows his adherence to the rationalist philosophy. {RAT}

Duncan, Isadora (1878-1927)

Duncan, a noted dancer, first created works based on Greek classical art. Inspired by ancient Greek drama, she pioneered an expressive movement that differentiated itself from other such movements, often dancing barefoot to music that had not been expressly written for dance. She wore a Greek tunic and flowing scarves, gaining fame in Berlin, Paris, Moscow, and London.

Her various biographers cite Duncan's freethinking and describe her dramatic death: in Nice, her scarf was caught in the wheel of an open car in which she was motoring, and she was choked to death. {CE}

Duncker, Maximilian Wolfgang (1811—1886)

Duncker was a German historian, author of *History of Antiquity* (1852—1857). He abolished the old distinction of sacred and profane history and freely criticized Jewish records. Duncker took an active part in the events of 1848 and 1850, and he was appointed Director-General of the State Archives. {BDF; RAT}

Dunham, Barrows (1905—1995)

A professor of philosophy at Temple University, Dr. Dunham in his *Giant in Chains* (1953) negatively criticizes for an entire chapter the present author's seven categories of humanism. Mainly he objects both to "labeling" and to the terminology.

In 1956, he wrote concerning humanism:

> All the great shibboleths of middle-class philosophy are there: "eclectic," "modern scientific age," "faith," "human personality," "freedom and significance of the individual." These terms have two sets of opposites. If you take "systematic" instead of "eclectic," "medieval religious age" instead of "faith," "human soul" instead of "human personality," and "subordination" instead of "freedom and significance of the individual," you have the characteristic concepts of feudal ideology which the middle class overthrew during the seventeenth and eighteenth centuries. Now, if you take as a second list "systematic," "age of human control over both physical nature and society," "science," "human organism," and "fulfillment of man's needs by co-operative social life," you get the characteristic socialist concepts which, it appears, are in turn to replace middle-class philosophy. There is a nice dialectic in these relations, for the last set of concepts has obviously drawn upon the other two and has succeeded in unifying the material thus gathered.
>
> But the concepts expressive of Naturalistic Humanism, couched as they are in terms so honorific as to be commonplaces of advertising and public relations, show a resolute wish to be neither feudal nor socialist. The last part of Mr. Smith's definition rejects "Communistic Naturalism" not only because of immediate political pressures but because the two theories represent different historical epochs and antagonistic social systems. . . . As may be imagined, Mr. Smith got no candidates for that.

At the time the book came out, Dunham was dismissed by Temple University for being a "left-winger," a suspected Marxist.

In 1956, not long after Senator Joseph McCarthy's anti-Communist witch-hunts had become commonplace, Dunham added to his thoughts concerning humanism:

> There is a theory and practice of the right relation between theory and practice. This discipline develops the larger generalizations about our place in nature; it refines our ways of choosing and of doing; it seeks to make us, or at any rate our descendants, secure in life and abundant in talent. Such a discipline is at once humanistic and philosophical. Its theme is salvation: human salvation, that is to say, not the salvation of apes or angels. For the first of these do not philosophize, and the second do not exist.
>
> For myself, I think philosophy assures us that the universe is a process of change, all of it knowable and some of it controllable. Part of the knowable and controllable is the happy place man can make for himself in nature. He will do it, I fancy, economically by social ownership of the land and the means of production, politically by the universal extension of personal liberties and of participation in public affairs. It may even be that government, which is violence made licit, will one day shrink to mere administration.
>
> I leave to others the labelling of these notions, asking only that I be spared the timid classifications, and at the same time that I be not exposed unfairly to comment by the police.

(See entry for Albert C. Barnes.)
{CE; *Freethought History* #20, 1996; WAS, 9 October 1956}

Dunlap, Andrew (19th Century)

A freethinker, Dunlap wrote "A Speech Delivered Before the Municipal Court of the City of Boston in Defence of Abner Kneeland on an Indictment for Blasphemy" (1834). {GS}

Dunlap, Lewis H. (20th Century)

Dunlap, who operates a humanist bookstore, is on the Board of Directors of the American Humanist Association and chairs their Chapter Assembly. At their 1993 Philadelphia annual conference, he was named a Humanist Pioneer. (See entry for Colorado Humanists.) {FD}

Dunn, Ellis (20th Century)

Dunn in 1996 succeeded Don Baham as President of the Humanists of the Portland-Vancouver Metro Area (HPVMA) in Oregon.

Dunn, Ian (1944-1998)

Once described as "the best known Scottish gay person," Dunn was active in Scottish politics and was a long-standing member of GALHA, the Gay and Lesbian Humanist Association. An early pioneer of gay activism, he was one of the founders of *Gay News* in the 1970s and also the International Lesbian and Gay Association (ILGA).

Dunn, John Thomas (1919—1986)

Dunn was an Australian rationalist, humanist, and engineer. In the 1950s he was a committee member of the Rationalist Society of Australia, and he was president of the Humanist Society of Victoria in 1969 and again in 1980. Dunn was a protagonist for cooperation or amalgamation of rationalists and humanists in Australia. {FUK; SWW}

Dunn, Russell (20 Century)

Dunn, in "The Kite That Brought Down Religion" (*Humanist Monthly*, Scotia, New York), credited Benjamin Franklin with showing how a lightning rod is more than just a practical device for sparing tall buildings from a strike. When churches installed the rods, despite their concern that this would be tantamount to admitting a lack of faith in God's divine judgment, science came out victorious.

Duns Scotus: See entry for Aureol.

Dupont de Nemours, Pierre Samuel (1739—1817)

A French economist, Dupont de Nemours became President of the Constituent Assembly. He was a Theophilantrophist to some, but in *Philosophie de l'univers* (1796) he avowed that he was a deist. {BDF; JM; RAT}

Dupuis, Charles François (1742—1809)

Origine de tous les Cultes by Dupuis was scientifically rational and is said to have been popular among the more intelligent of French freethinking proletariats. Robertson holds that Renan's *Vie de Jesus* is comparable. During the Reign of Terror, Dupuis saved many lives at his own risk. Afterwards, he was one of the Council of Five Hundred and president of the legislative body. His *Origine* traced solar worship in various faiths, including Christianity, and it was described as "a monument of the erudition of unbelief." McCabe described Dupuis' views as holding that religious myths can be traced to astronomical truths. {BDF; JM; JMR; JMRH; RAT}

Duran de Huerta, Martha (20th Century)

Duran, at the 1996 Humanist World Conference in Mexico City, spoke about the Zapatistas, a group of Indians out of favor with the Mexican government. When surrounded, and when they cannot even send messages by Satellite (the name of a mule they use), they transmit by internet, she jocularly reported in her comments about how modernity is to be found even in an indigenous society. But she lamented that women less than eighteen years of age are serving in the army and looked forward to cessation of the battles. Zapatistas, she holds, are humanists in that they put the will of the community above vested interests.

Durang, Christopher (1949—)

Durang is a dramatist who wrote the humorous "Sister Mary Ignatius Explains It All For You."

For *Free Inquiry* (Spring 1996), he wrote a humorous article, "The Lost Encyclical Against Penicillin," in which the Pope utters a long dictum which bans anti-biotics, explaining that "God created bacteria and viruses for the purpose of infecting organisms sometimes seriously, sometimes less seriously—and we must never presume to interfere with the right order of God's creation."

God created syphilis, the Pope continues, "to infect sexually immoral people, and cause them suffering and eventual death. In no way should a man-made anti-biotic interfere with this God-given process. Also, the fear of syphilis is a natural encouragement toward marital fidelity, which could not otherwise hold its own in a free market." He continues his tongue-in-cheek reasoning, "It is especially sinful to use anti-biotics to block the natural path of syphilis as intended by God."

Durang is author of *Baby With the Bath Water* (1984) and *Marriage of Bittle and Boo* (1987). In an off-Broadway production of "Laughing Wild," he appeared as the Infant of Prague. He sang and tried to dance with Julie Andrews in the Sondheim revue "Putting It Together." "Betty's Summer Vacation," a 1999 work that was an exercise in absurdism, led *Village Voice* (23 March 1999) critic Michael Feingold to observe,

> Guaranteed to offend almost everyone with some aspect of its bright-cheeked, amoral bluntness, the play gives no quarter even to what seems to be Durang's own wistful desire, expressed through Betty, for some guiding principle that can govern human relations in a world where everything is trafficked in so openly that all modes of decency have broken down. . . . [The play shows] we've gone from the Freudian into the Sadeian Age.

Durant, Ariel (1898—1981)

The freethinking wife of philosopher Will Durant, Ariel Durant wrote volumes seven to eleven of the eleven-volume *Story of Civilization*. {CE}

Durant, James 4th (20th Century)

When he signed Humanist Manifesto II, Durant was a professor at Polk Community College in Winter Haven, Florida. {HM2}

Durant, Will(iam) (James) (1885—1981)

An eminent philosopher who wrote *The Story of Philosophy* (1926) and numerous other volumes, Durant in the 1950s was on the advisory board of Charles Francis Potter's First Humanist Society of New York. His comprehensive *Story of Civilization* (1933—1975), written partly with his wife Ariel, has led some to refer to Durant as being a contemporary Renaissance humanist.

Invited to speak on "The Origins of Religion" at a New York assembly of the Francisco Ferrer Association, Durant told the group that sex is a sub-current in religion and "the phallus had in many places and forms been worshiped as a symbol of divine power." The New Jersey bishop immediately excommunicated Durant and when the press reported the incident Durant's mother collapses in shock and his father ordered him to move out of their home.

Of religion, he (with Ariel) wrote the following:

> • Does history support a belief in God? If by God we mean not the creative vitality of nature but a supreme being intelligent and benevolent, the answer must be a reluctant negative.
>
> • Is Christianity dying? Is the religion that gave morals, courage, and art to Western civilization suffering slow decay through the spread of knowledge, the widening of astronomic, geographical, and historical horizons, the realization of evil in history and the soul, the decline of faith in an afterlife and of trust in the benevolent guidance of the world? If this is so, it is the basic event of modern times, for the soul of a civilization is its religion, and it dies with its faith.
>
> • *Sapere aude*—"to dare to know"—became the motto of this *éclairissement*, or enlightenment, this Age of Reason triumphant and fulfilled. . . . Man could at last liberate himself from medieval dogmas and Oriental myths; he could shrug off that bewildering, terrifying theology, and stand up free, free to doubt, to inquire, to think, to gather knowledge and spread it, free to build a new religion around the altar of reason and the service of mankind.

{CE; FUS}

Duranty, Walter (1884-1957): See entry for George Orwell.

During, Zoë (20 Century)

During is president of the Auckland branch of ALRANZ, a trustee of the Pacific Foundation of Health, and a longtime campainger on moral, social, and health issues. During is an honorary associate of the New Zealand Association of Rationalists and Humanists.

Durkheim, Émile (1858—1917)

A French sociologist, Durkheim taught philosophy at, in succession, Sens, Saint Quentin, and Troyes. He held that the collective mind of society was the source of religion and morality and that the common values developed in society, particularly in primitive societies, are the cohesive bonds of social order. The creeds, which he rejects, will eventually die, he held. Durkheim wrote *The Rules of Sociological Method* (1895), *Le Suicide* (1897), and *The Elementary Forms of Religious Life* (1912). {CE; RAT}

Duruy, Jean Victor (1730—1796)

Duroy was a French historian who in 1863 became Minister of Education, rousing the wrath of the clergy by his reforms, particularly in improving the education of girls. He was compelled to resign in 1869, then entered the Senate. In 1875 he was admitted to the Institut. He wrote *Histoire des Romains* (2 volumes, 1843—1844), *Histoire des Romains jusqu'à la mort de Théodore* (7 volumes, 1876—1885), and *Histoire des Grecs* (2 volumes, 1886—1888). {RAT}

Dushman, Saul (20th Century)

Dushman, a scientist, was a member of the American Humanist Association. {HNS}

DUTCH ATHEISM

D. Noordenbos wrote *Het Atheisme in Nederland in De Negentiende Eeuw* (1931).

DUTCH FREETHINKERS, HUMANISTS

Dutch refers to people in the Netherlands, a word connoting lands that are below sea level. The country is also called by the name of one of the its provinces, Holland. Dutch freethought and humanist groups and publications include the following:

• *De Vrije Gedachte*, POB 1087, 3000 BB Rotterdam, The Netherlands, is the official journal of Dutch Free Thinkers. On the Web: <dvg@netcetera.netcetera.nl>.
• *De Vrije Gedachte* (Free Thought), PO Box 1087, 3000 BB Rotterdam, The Netherlands
• Dutch Humanist Home Front (Dutch "Humanist Homes for Soldiers), G. Reinoldweg 5A, 8084 JH, 't Harde, The Netherlands
• Dutch Humanist Study Centre, PO Box 797, 3500 AT Utrecht, Netherlands
• *Ego*, a monthly humanist magazine for soldiers, is at Oranje Nassaulaan 71, 1708 BC Zeist, The Netherlands
• *European Humanist Professionals*, a yearly in English, is at P.O. Box 797, 3500 AT Utrecht, The Netherlands; tel: +31-30-1390189; fax: +31-30-2390170; <hsn@uvh.nl>.
• *Het Humanistisch Archief*, Dutch Humanist Archives and Documentation Centre, Van Asch van Wijckskade 28, 3512 VS Utrecht, The Netherlands; tel: +31-30-2390164; fax: +31-30-2390170; <humarc@uvh.nl>.
• *HIVOS Magazine*, a Dutch quarterly of Humanist Development Cooperation, is at Raamweg 16, 2596 HL Den Haag, The Netherlands
• *HOM-Nieuwabrief*, a Dutch quarterly, Humanist Human Rights, is at PO Box 114, 3500 AC Utrecht, The Netherlands
• *Humanist*, a Dutch monthly of the Humanistisch Verbond Nederland, is at Postbus 75490, 1070 AL Amsterdam, The Netherlands <hv@euronet.nl>.
• Human Broadcasting Foundation (HOS), Borneolaan 17, Postbus 135, 1200 AC Hilversum, The Netherlands
• Humanist Committee on Human Rights (HOM), PO Box 114, 3500 AC Utrecht, The Netherlands.
• Humanist Foundation for Housing the Aged (HSHB), Postbus 70510, 1007 KM Amsterdam, The Netherlands
• Humanist Institute for Cooperation with Developing Countries (HIVOS), Raamweg 16, 2596 HL Den Haag, The Netherlands. <http://www.dds.nl/~hivos/>
• *Humanistisch Verbond Nederland* (IHEU) has moved to Postbus 75490, 1070 AL Amsterdam, The Netherlands
• Humanistas Organisation for Social Work, Postbox 71, 1000 AB Amsterdam, The Netherlands
• *Humus*, a magazine of Humanistisch Verbond for Activists in the Organization, is at PO Box 114, 3500 AC Utrecht, The Netherlands
• International Association for Intercultural Education, c/o APBO 'Pieter Batelaan,' Sumatralaan 37, 1217 GP Hilversum, The Netherlands
• *JH-Nieuwsbrief* has moved to Postbus 75490, 1070 AL Amsterdam, The Netherlands
• *Kader Kringloop Krant, a magazine of Humanitas for its activists,* is at Postbus 71, 1000 AB, The Netherlands
• *Praktische Humanistiek*, a Dutch quarterly for humanist counselors, is at Postbus 470, 3500 AL Utrecht, The Netherlands <swp@pi.net>.
• *Rekenschap*, a cultural/scientific quarterly magazine in Dutch and English, is at Postbus 75490, 1070 AL Amsterdam, The Netherlands <hv@euronet.nl>.
• *Socrates*, a foundation for professorships in humanist studies, is at Nieuwegracht 69A, 3512 LG Utrecht, The Netherlands
• University for Humanist Studies (UvH), PO Box 797, 3500 AT Utrecht, The Netherlands
• *Van Mens tot Mens*, a monthly of Humanitas, is at Postbus 71, 1000 AB Amsterdam, The Netherlands <info@lb.humanitas.nl>.
• *WisselKrant*, a Dutch quarterly, is at Postbus 75490, 1070-AL Amsterdam, The Netherlands <hv@euronet.nl>.

Commenting upon the progress made by the Dutch Humanist Association, Tony Akkermans has written that the group now has considerable status. "The prime minister and half the cabinet attended its 40th anniversary celebrations. There are Humanist counsellors in prisons, hospitals, and the armed forces. Voluntary euthanasia is widely available. There is no unnecessary censorship. Schoolgirl pregnancies are the lowest in Europe. Sixty percent of the population now say that they have no religion. All this momentous change in just four decades!"

DUTCH HUMANIST HOME FRONT (Humanist Homes for Soldiers)

The Dutch Humanist Home Front is at G. Reinoldweg 5A, 8084 JH, 't Harde, Netherlands.

DUTCH HUMANIST INSTITUTE FOR DEVELOPMENT COOPERATION (HIVOS): See entry for Jaap Dijkstra. On the Web: <http://wwwdds.nl/~hivos/>.

DUTCH HUMANIST LEAGUE: See entry for *Humanistisch Verbond*.

DUTCH HUMANIST MOVEMENT, WEBSITES

Websites of the Dutch Humanist Movement include the following:

• Humanist E-Zine, Dutch and international news and articles about the humanist movement: <www.human.nl/index.htm>
• The Column, written by Yvonne Breuk, President of *Humanistisch Verbond*, about the 24-hour economy: <http://www.human.nl/Actualiteiten/Column/index.htm>
• Media, with information about radio, television, new media, and printed media: <www.human.nl/Actualiteiten/Media/index.htm>
• Organisations, with Dutch and international links: <www.human.nl/organisaties/index.htm>
• Calendar: summary of activities, meetings, workshops, exhibitions, etc.: <www.human.nl/Agenda/1998/index.htm>

{Piet Brinkman, the Internet, 5 Aug 1998}

DUTCH HUMANIST STUDY CENTRE

The Dutch Humanist Study Centre is at PO Box 797, 3500 AT Utrecht, Netherlands.

DUTCH PHILOSOPHY: See *Encyclopedia of Philosophy*, Vol. 2.

DUTCH SCIENTIFIC HUMANITARIAN COMMITTEE

The Scientific Humanitarian Committee was founded in The Hague in 1911 by the liberal Dutch lawyer and nobleman Jacob Schorer. He was convinced that it is not necessary to prove the biological origins of homosexuality and held that homosexuals like other humans have the right to give meaning and shape to their own lives so long as they do not damage the right to self-determination of others. His humanistic approach was attacked by the churches and by the Nazis. {Rob A. Tielman, *Free Inquiry*, Fall 1997}

DUTCH UNITARIANS

Unitarians in The Netherlands can be contacted by telephoning (31) 71-14-09 88.

Dutrieux, Pierre Joseph (1848—1889)

Dutrieux was a Belgian physician who, traveling to Cairo, was named with the courtesy title of bey. He was a freethinker.

Dutton, Denis (20 Century)

Dutton, a senior lecturer in the philosophy of art at the School of Fine Arts, Canterbury University, is an honorary associate of the New Zealand Association of Rationalists and Humanists.

Dutton, Thomas (1767—1815)

A theatre critic, Dutton published a *Vindication of the Age of Reason by Thomas Paine* (1795). He edited the *Dramatic Censor* (1800) and the *Monthly Theatrical Reporter* (1815). {BDF}

Duvernet, Théophile Imarigeon (c. 1730—1796)

A French writer, Duvernet was tutor to the Comte de Saint-Simon, then abbé and head of the Collège de Clermont. He was sent to the Bastille in 1781 for his *Disputes de M. Guillaume*, but he continued writing deistic works despite the jailing. In 1786 he published a eulogistic *Vie de Voltaire*, and other strongly worded rationalist writings followed. {RAT}

Dworkin, Andrea (20th Century)

An opinionated left-of-center activist, Dworkin has been called a Nazi both by Rush Limbaugh and *The Nation*. When asked by journalist Norah Vincent about her political views, she admitted to being "basically a Jacobin" and definitely not a communist. "But I do believe that it's one thing to talk about the redistribution of wealth. It's quite another thing to talk about the redistribution of power. That's more what interests me."

Asked if she believed in God, Dworkin responded, "Sometimes. . . .I really don't. I'm really an agnostic. I really don't know. . . . On the other hand, in my daily life, I constantly believe that God is chasing me. I feel we know each other very well. I had a very strong [Jewish] religious upbringing and I know I still use a lot of what I learned in it. I'm agnostic, but I have a mental engagement with, at least, my idea of God." She continued,

> When I was a kid I used to be really fascinated with Catholicism. It had my attention because I thought that confession was this totally brilliant thing. I think, I'm not the only one to have observed that, in a way, Freud made confession Jewish. However, very early on I began to think about abortion, and I began to see the Catholic Church as an enemy. And that's pretty much how I see it now, although that's not the only reason.
>
> For people who aren't raised Christian, Christianity is very bewildering [b]ecause you have these people who eat the body of their lord and drink his blood and they think other people are crazy.
>
> {*New York Press* 4-10 February 1998}

Dyas, Richard H. (19th Century)

An Army captain, Dyas wrote *The Upas* (1877). A freethinker, he resided for a long time in Italy and translated several of the works of C. Voysey. {BDF}

DYSLEXIA

Dyslexia is a learning disorder, one in which letters in a word are mistakenly inverted: e.g.,

> Workers of the world, untie!
> Fido is my god's name.
> I don't believe in Almighty Dog.

Dyson, A. E. (20th Century)

In 1958 Dyson, then an agnostic, and the Rev. Andrew Hallidie Smith established the Homosexual Law Reform Society in England. Dyson is author of *Yeats, Eliot, and R. S. Thomas* (1981) and *Liberty in Britain 1934—1994, a Diamond Jubilee History of the National Council for Civil Liberties* (1994). He cites the prominent role of eminent freethinkers such as the NCCL's first President, E. M. Forster. {GS}

Dziamka, Kaz (20th Century)

Dziamka, in *Freethought Today* (January-February 1996), described being raised a Polish Catholic who, moving to the United States, became a freethinker. Among other courses at Technical Vocational Institute (TVI), where he was an instructor in the Arts and Sciences Department, he taught "The American Humanist Tradition: Why Our Gods Have Failed." "If human beings don't solve their problems, then nobody—no god or gods—will," he declared. When his contract was not renewed, however, the course did not continue being taught.

Dziamka's doctoral thesis at the University of New Mexico was "Utopia and Freedom in American Culture." In 1996 upon the death of Gordon Stein, Dziamka became editor of *The American Rationalist*, and in 1999 he was named a Humanist Pioneer by the American Humanist Association. **Barbara Dziamka**, his wife, is also a non-theist.

On the Web: <freethought.org/org/ar/> and <http://www.infidels.org/org/ffrf/fttoday/june_july96/dziamka.html>. {*Freethought Today*, June-July 1996}

Dzielska, Maria (20th Century)

Dzielska's *Hypatia of Alexandria* (1996) tells of the rivalry between Cyril (later St. Cyril, the bishop of Alexandria, Egypt) and Orestes, the recently arrived civil authority. Siding with the Christian Orestes, Hypatia was termed a "witch" devoted to the occult and she was killed by an Alexandrian mob of *parabolans*, strong-arm enforcers for the church. {Gordon Stein, "Hypatia as a Freethought Heroine," *Free Inquiry* Fall 1996}

Dziemidok, Bohdan (20th Century)

Dziemidok, a professor at the Institute of Philosophy and Sociology at the University of Gdansk, Poland, is the humanist author of *Contemporary American Philosophy of Art*. In *Free Inquiry* (Winter 1992-1993), he wrote on "John Dewey's Contribution to the Theory of Valuation." Dziemidok is author of *On the Aesthetics of Roman Ingarden* (1989) and *The Comical* (1993).

EALING (England) HUMANISTS: For information telephone Derek Hill at 0181 422 4956 or Charles Rudd at 0181 904 6599.

Earl of Rochester: See entry for John Wilmot.

Earl, Michael Scott (20th Century)

Earl, who spent two years as a missionary for the Church of Jesus Christ of Latter Day Saints, once labored full-time in pursuit of converts to Mormonism. He abstained from music, dating, television, radio, physical contact with family members, even foregoing his favorite soft drinks. Now a freethinker, he is active in the Free Inquiry Society of Central Florida. In a five-part taped series, "Bible Stories Your Parents Never Taught You" (1999), Earl attacks the widely-held presumption that the Holy Bible is a good book.

Earles, Beverley M. (20th Century)

A humanist who was an activist in New Zealand, Earles is on the editorial board of *The Humanist* and is vice-president of the American Humanist Association. In 1989 she received a Ph. D. in religious studies at the University of Wellington in New Zealand for a study, "The Faith Dimension of Humanism," which was one of the first to research organized humanism. In 1992, she was a teacher of English on the faculty of Kansas State University. Earles is not only an activist in humanism but also in feminism, and she laments the fact that the contributions of humanist women have not been more widely recognized.

Her "Outstanding Humanist Women—Dora Russell in Particular" was featured in the Spring 1994 *Feminist Caucus Newsletter*. In 1999, now a faculty member in New York City of the Humanist Institute, she was named by the American Humanist Association as a Humanist Pioneer. {*Free Inquiry*, Winter 1987-1988; HNS2}

EARTH

• I don't know if there are men on the moon, but if there are, they must be using this earth as their lunatic asylum.

—**George Bernard Shaw** (1856-1950)

• Man makes a great fuss about this planet which is only a ball-bearing in the hub of the universe.

—Christopher Morley (1890-1957)

Earth is the fifth largest planet of the solar system, the only one known to support life. It has one natural satellite, the moon. Its change of seasons is caused by the tilt (23.5°) of Earth's equator to the plane of the orbit. It speeds like a top and like a merry-go-round horse on a carousel that is itself riding on a larger carousel, and the entire amusement park is moving through space. It sits in a cosmic shooting gallery, one that includes speeding blocks of ice and rock, one chunk of which sixty-five million years ago collided with it and the resultant tumult killed off the dinosaurs.

Earth rotates on its axis at about 1,037.5 miles an hour at the equator. The speed of a trip around the Sun is about 66,700 miles an hour. Meanwhile, the solar system is in a more-or-less circular orbit around the center of the galaxy at an average velocity of about 220 kilometers a second, about 492,126 miles an hour, according to *Facts on File Dictionary of Astronomy*, and the galaxy is moving at about 19.4 kilometers a second, or about 43,396 miles an hour, toward a point in the constellation Hercules called the solar apex. It is estimated to be at least 4.55 billion years old.

Earth's origin remains a controversial subject. Philosophers speculate that there will come a time, long before the sun dies, when the Earth's inner fires will die down, and elements vital to life will cease being recycled into the environment by volcanic eruption and tectonic uplift.

The Anglo-Irish Bishop James Ussher's 17th century research of the Holy Bible concluded that Earth had been created at 9 a.m. (some say noon and threaten to become schismatics) on October 23rd, 4004 B.C.E.

Therefore, on 23 October 1996 a 6000th birthday party for Earth was held by secular humanists at the Buffalo, New York, Center for Inquiry. The party, complete with cake, was attended by Tim Madigan (dressed as Noah), biology professor Clyde Herreid (dressed as Darwin), and anthropologist H. James Birx (dressed as himself). A jocular press conference followed the appropriate libations, toasts, and thanks to God. (See entries for Eratosthenes, Flat Earth Theory, and Bishop James Ussher.) {CE; ER}

EARTH DAY

Earth Day, which is celebrated at the Vernal or Spring Equinox, is an important observance for freethinkers. (See entry for Humanist Holidays.)

Earwaker, Epenetus (19th Century)

The appropriately named Earwaker was a lecturing assistant to the humanitarian deist, Joachim Kaspary, at outdoor London meetings of the National Secular Society in the 1880s. {RSR}

EASTER

Easter as a strictly religious holiday has no relevance for freethinkers. The day is named after a spring goddess, Eastre. Pagan practices included the exchange of gifts, such as Easter-eggs, and by generous hospitality to friends and the poor.

Christians, starting at the end of the second century, celebrate the feast of the resurrection of Christ on an Easter Sunday, a date variously prescribed but set by the Council of Nicaea in 325 as the first Sunday following upon the spring equinox. Today, the event is generally held on the first Sunday following the first full moon after the spring equinox.

Indicative of the confusion of pagans' and religionists' observances at that time of the year, Ken Alley in *Once Upon a Pew* describes a church bulletin's editing which ended, "This being Easter Sunday, we will ask Mrs. Johnson to come forward and lay an egg on the altar." (See entries for John Shelby Spong and for Humanist Holidays.) {ER}

Easterbrook, Gregg (20th Century)

Although a believer, Easterbrook in *Beside Still Waters: Searching for Meaning in an Age of Doubt* (1998) thinks God is not omniscient and not omnipotent. If it were otherwise, he holds, God would not be the morally imperfect being He is. Easterbrook is yet another contemporary novelist who hopes to be remembered for postulating a bizarre interpretation of theology that might appeal to those who otherwise would remain potential doubters.

Easterman, Daniel (20th Century)

Easterman is a novelist and an honorary fellow in the Centre for Middle East and Islamic Studies in the University of Durham. A writer for the English *New Humanist*, Easterman is author of *The Judas Testament* (1994) and *The Final Judgment* (1996).

EASTERN ORTHODOX CHURCHES

The Eastern Orthodox churches derive from the church of the Byzantine Empire that adheres to the Byzantine rite and acknowledges the honorary primacy of the patriarch of Constantinople. Includes are the Greek Orthodox Archdiocese of North and South America and the Orthodox Church in America. As with other churches, all are dependent upon financial contributions if they are to continue their colorful as well as aromatic services.

Eastman, Eleanor (20th Century)

Easterman at the Fourth Annual Atheist Alliance convention in St. Louis was given a Lifetime Achievement Award. {*Secular Nation*, July-September 1998}

Eastman, Max (1833—1969)

Eastman, the editor of radical periodicals until 1923, was for many years a Communist and a leader of American liberal thought. He later rejected Communism and wrote several books attacking it. Eastman's most popular work was *Enjoyment of Laughter* (1936), and among his autobiographical works was *Love and Revolution* (1965).

In 1949, he wrote the present author concerning humanism,

> I never think of myself, and never have, as being any kind of an 'ist" or subscribing to any "ism." Even in regard to Socialism, I maintained this attitude to the extent possible in my editorials in the old *Masses* and *The Liberator*.

{CE; WAS, 24 April 1949}

Eaton, Cyrus (Stephen) (1883—1979)

Eaton, a Nova Scotia-born industrialist and banker who became a naturalized citizen of the United States, wrote several books, among them *Third Term Tradition* (1940) and *The Engineer as Philosopher* (1961). A Fellow of the American Academy of Arts and Sciences and a member of the American Council of Learned Societies, the American Academy of Political and Social Sciences, and the Royal Norwegian Academy of Sciences. Eaton started in business by holding a business position with John D. Rockefeller Sr. He later organized Canada Gas & Electric Corporation, organized Republic Steel Corporation in 1930, and was a director of Inland Steel, Youngstown Sheet & Tube, Cleveland Trust Co., Sherwin-Williams Co., Baltimore and Ohio Railroad Co., and numerous other corporations.

Eaton was famous for having been the initiator of the Pugwash Intellectual Life Conferences starting in 1956, accused by many as being politically "left-wing." In the 1950s and 1960s he advocated the then unpopular view that there should be increased diplomacy between the United States and the Soviet Union. He was recipient in 1960 of the Lenin Peace Prize. According to Edwin H. Wilson, Eaton "was an early supporter of humanism. He and [A. Eustace] Haydon were lifelong friends." {EW; HNS2}

Eaton, Clement (Born 1898)

Eaton's *The Freedom-of-Thought Struggle in the Old South* (1964) contains much information on freethinkers famous and obscure. He also wrote *Jefferson Davis* (1977). {*Freethought History #14*, 1995}

Eaton, Daniel Isaac (1752—1814)

A bookseller in England, Eaton in 1792 was prosecuted for publishing Paine's *Rights of Man*, but the prosecution fell through. Afterwards, he published *Politics for the People* and *Political Dictionary* (1796), for which he again was prosecuted. To escape punishment, he fled to America. Upon returning to England, he was seized along with his property. Books to the value of £2,800 were burned, and he was imprisoned for fifteen months.

He called his shop "The Ratiocinatory," and he translated the rationalist works of Fréret and Helvétius. In 1811, he issued the first and second parts of Paine's *Age of Reason*, and in 1812 he was tried before Lord Ellenbourgh on a charge of blasphemy for issuing the third and last part. This time he was sentenced to eighteen months' imprisonment and to stand in the pillory.

The sentence evoked Shelley's spirited *Letter to Lord Ellenbourgh*. Shortly before his death, Eaton again was prosecuted for publishing George Houston's *Ecce Homo*. {BDF; FUK; PUT; RAT}

Eaton, David (Died 1992)

Eaton, an African American who became senior minister at All Souls Unitarian Church in Washington, D.C., favored such social action causes as assistance to local minority youth and alleviating world famine. His church in 1985 welcomed a refugee fleeing from Central America, and his sermons were anti-racist and pro-reconciliation.

Ebacher, Tom (20th Century)

Ebacher, an atheist in Kensington, Minnesota, has written about the value of humanitarianism for *Secular Nation* (April-June 1998) and about "First Cause" (April-June 1999).

Eberhard, Johann August (1739—1809)

An influential German deist, Eberhard was driven out of the Church for the heresy of having written his *New Apology of Sokrates; or the Final Salvation of the Heathen* (1722). In effect, it placed the Greek philosopher on a level with Jesus, which trinitarians claimed was blasphemy, although Lessing reportedly enjoyed the work. Frederick the Great liked Eberhard's direction of thought, making him a Professor of Philosophy at Halle, where he later opposed the idealism of both Kant and Fichte. Eberhard wrote a *History of Philosophy* (1788). {BDF; JMR; JMRH; RAT}

Eberty, Gustav (1806—1887)

Eberty was a German freethinker, the author of several controversial works. {BDF}

Ebury, Eva (1906—1997)

Ebury was a chiropodist who, with her husband **Len Ebury**, held morning and afternoon outdoor meetings in Hampstead for the North London Branch of the National Secular Society. He was the speaker, she the seller of *The Freethinker*. Terry Mullins conducted her secular service at St. Marylebone Crematorium. {*The Freethinker*, February 1997}

Eby, Kermit (20th Century)

A sociologist at the University of Chicago, Eby wrote book reviews for *The Humanist* in the 1950s.

Echegary, José (1833—1916)

A Spanish dramatist, mathematician, physicist, economist, and politician, Echegary from 1874 to 1905 wrote sixty-eight plays, becoming the leading playwright of his day. He shared the 1904 Nobel Prize in Literature with Frédric Mistral. He was a professor of mathematics who became Minister of Education, then of Finance, in the Liberal Government (1867—1874). With the return to power of the clerical-royalists he took up letters, expressed his rationalism, and was popular for thirty years. {CE; RE}

Echtermeyer, Ernst Theodor (1805—1844)

Echtermeyer was a German critic who, with A. Ruge, founded the *Hallische Jahrbücher*, which contained many free thought articles. He taught at Halle and Dresden, where he died. {BDF; RAT}

Eckermann, Johann Peter (1792—1854)

Eckermann, a German scholar and author, was Körner's secretary and Goethe's assistant. He taught English and German at the University of Jena and later was librarian at Weimar, where the Grand Duke made him a Councillor. Eckermann's *Conversations With Goethe* (1836—1848, 2 volumes) provide excellent biographical evidence. In 1838 Eckermann was appointed Councillor and Librarian to the Grand Duke of Weimar. He shared Goethe's liberal pantheism. {RAT; RE}

Eckerson, Judith (20th Century)

Eckerson is Consulting Leader with the Northern Virginia Ethical Society. Her e-mail: <eckerson@erols.com>.

Eckhoff, Erik (20th Century)

Eckhoff and his wife, **Dagfinn Eckhoff**, founded the Pagan Society in Norway. (See entry for Scandinavian Unbelievers.)

Eckler, Peter (19th Century)

In New York, Eckler edited the semi-monthly publication, *Age of Reason*, from 1848 to 1851. {FUS; PUT}

Eco, Umberto (1929—)

Eco is an Italian novelist, essayist, semiologist, and scholar. From 1954 to 1959, he was employed by Italian television and from 1963 to 1964 was a lecturer in aesthetics at the University of Turin. In his first novel, *The Name of the Rose* (1980; translated in 1983), he told of the struggle between church and state as mirrored in recent Italian history. The work combines detective fiction, medieval philosophy, and moral reflection, encapsulating his semiotic theory and how signs are produced and interpreted in the world. The subject is also dealt with in *Theory of Semiotics* (1976).

Speaking to critic Herbert Mitgang about his work, Eco stated, "We are always approaching the time of anti-Christ. In the nuclear age, we are never far from the Dark Ages." Speaking to *Time* about his *Foucault's Pendulum* (1988; translated 1989), Eco remarked, "This was a book conceived to irritate the reader. I knew it would provoke ambiguous, nonhomogeneous responses because it was a book conceived to point up some contestation." Other of his works are *Filosofi in liberta* (1958), *The Role of the Reader* (1979), and *The Limits of Interpretation* (1991), the latter being a profound interpretative study of interpretation itself.

"I think," Eco has written, "that the duty of a scholar is not only to do scientific research but also to communicate with people through various media about the most important issues of social life from the point of view of his own discipline."

In "The Birth of Ethics" (*Index on Censorship*, 19 March 1997), Eco wrote,

> I am of the firm belief that even those who do not have faith in a personal and providential divinity can still experience forms of religious feeling and hence a sense of the sacred, of limits, questioning and expectation; of a communion with something that surpasses us. What you ask is, what there is that is binding, compelling, and irrevocable in this form of ethics.

He has written *How to Travel With a Salmon, and Other Essays* (1994), humorous pieces from an Italian newspaper column, "Diario Minimo." The work includes "How to Be a TV Host" and "How to Go Through Customs," along with other selections that include the paradoxical. In 1995 he wrote *The Island of the Day Before* and *Six Walks in the Fictional Woods*. In the latter, which is a study of the interaction of the reader and what he reads, he uses the metaphor of words: the path one finds; exploring; identifying a tree; camping; living in a tree house. "The Model Reader, he holds, "is a sort of ideal type whom the text not only foresees as a collaborator but also tries to create."

In 1995, Eco became a Humanist Laureate in the Council for Secular Humanism's International Humanist Academy. In 1999 he was inducted as an honorary member into the American Academy of Arts and Letters. (See entry for Legumes.) {CE; *Contemporary Authors*, Vols. 77-80, 1979}

ECONOMICS

• An economist is someone who doesn't know what he's talking about—and makes you feel it's your fault.

—Pasi Kuoppamäki of the Bank of Finland
at <www.etla.fi/pkm/JokEc>

Economics is a social science that deals with the production, distribution, and consumption of goods and services. It also is concerned with the theory and management of economics or economic systems. How humans allocate scarce resources in order to produce various commodities and how those commodities are distributed has been studied from the days of the ancient Greeks. Plato in his *Republic* described a model society on the basis of a careful division of labor. Aristotle attributed great importance to economic security as the basis for a healthy society and found the middle-sized landowner the ideal citizen.

Other leading economists from various nations:

> Cicero, Vergil, Varro, Hume, Adam Smith, David Ricardo, Malthus, John Stuart Mill, Friedrich List, Henry C. Carey, C. H. Saint-Simon, Robert Owen, Charles Fourier, Louis Blanc, Wilhelm Roscher, Bruno Hildebrand, Karl Knies, Karl Marx, William Stanley Jevons, Leon Walras, Karl Menger, John Bates Clark, Alfred Marshall, Knut Wicksell, John Maynard Keynes, Gunnar Myrdal, Sir Arthur Lewis, Joseph Schumpeter, and Arthur Pigou.

{CE}

ECUADOR FREETHINKERS, HUMANISTS

Two presidents of Ecuador, Vicente Rocafuerte (1783—1847) and Eloy Alfaro (1864—1912), implemented anticlerical reforms, particularly in the field of education.

A leading contemporary Ecuadorian secular humanist is Pablo Cevallos, a teacher of logic in Guayaquil at the Catholic University. His e-mail: cevallop@ucsg.edu.ec>. (See entries for Pablo Cevallos and Juan Montalvo.)

ECUMENISM

Ecumenism, the promoting of worldwide unity or cooperation, is a movement to promote better understanding among different religious groups, for often extreme violence has resulted when adherents have insisted that non-adherents were enemies who were preaching false views. Those involved in the ecumenical movement do not hope to change others' views. They hope to limit violence which has been caused by religionists in the name of religion.

To the surprise of many, *La Civilta Cattolica*, a Jesuit journal, included the statement,

> God may have spoken through books as diverse as the Muslim Koran, the Hindu Vedas and Bhagavad-Gita, and the sacred texts of China's Taoism and Japan's Shintoism.

Whether this passed the attention of the Vatican censors is not clear. {*Awake*, 22 August 996; DCL}

Edamaruku, Joseph (1934—)

At the Indian Rationalist Association's international conference held in New Delhi in 1995, Edamaruku gave a history of the association. He and his wife, **Soley Edamaruku**, have been rationalist pioneers in the Indian state of Kerala. {FUK; GS}

Edamaruku, Sanal (1955—)

Edamaruku has written widely expressing his concern about the conflicts between Hindus and Muslims in India. He is of the opinion that any solution needs to involve an insistence upon keeping India a secular state as well as liberalizing and modernizing its society.

He has written sixteen works, including two novels and several hundreds of articles, on various aspects of rationalism, humanism, secularism, and ethical politics. His magic shows have helped expose the Babas and the Guru-politics nexus of India. With the numerous volunteers he has trained, he undertakes "walks on fire" to disprove Babas claims. Edamaruku appears regularly in the media and is an active symbol of the ongoing fight for scientific temper in India.

A second generation rationalist, he is the son of Joseph Edamaruku and Soley Edamaruku, who were pioneers of the rationalist movement in Kerala, the southern state of India.

He joined the rationalist movement as a student activist in 1970 and was the convenor of the Rationalist Student Movement. Moving to Delhi in 1977, he became active in the rationalist movement. At his insistence, a 1980 All-India Conference for rationalists was organized at Mumbai (Bombay) for the purpose of rewriting the constitution of the Indian Rationalist Association. In 1983, he was elected as the youngest General Secretary of the Association. In 1981 he started Indian Atheist Publishers, which has published numerous rationalist books including several translations of western freethought classics and contemporary books.

The Indian Rationalist Association joined the International Humanist and Ethical Union (IHEU) in 1992 upon his initiative. Edamaruku has been a Board member of IHEU since then and has addressed gatherings and conferences in Europe and America.

In 1995 at New Delhi, the First International Rationalist Rationalist Conference was hosted by Edamaruku and the Indian Rationalist Association. An International Alliance Against Fundamentalism, of which Edamaruku was Founder President, was inaugurated during this conference. In 1996, his novel, *Sanmarganishtante Ikkilikal* (The Ticklings of the Moralist), was published.

In Birmingham, England, at the centenary conference of the Rationalist Press Association in 1999, he spoke on "Rationalism in the Third World in the 21st Century." Edamaruku signed Humanist Manifesto 2000. {WAS, November 1998}

Eddy, Richard (1828—1906)

Eddy has been called the leading 19th century historian of Universalism. In 1876 he was elected president of the Universalist Historical Society, and he edited the *Universalist Quarterly*. {FUS; U&U}

Edel, Abraham (Born 1908)

Edel has been professor of philosophy at City College of New York, City University of New York, and the University of Pennsylvania. Among his books are *The Theory and Practice of Philosophy* (1946), *Science and the Structure of Ethics* (1961), and *Anthropology and Ethics* (1959). Edel was one of the contributors to *American Philosophic Naturalism in the Twentieth Century* (1994). {CL}

Eddington, Arthur Stanley [Sir] (1882—1944)

Eddington, an English physicist and astronomy, made major contributions to the study of stars, their evolution, motion, and internal constitution.He was a pioneer in understanding the theory of relativity, which he expounded in *Mathematical Theory of Relativity* (1923) and *The Internal Constitution of the Stars* (1926). Eddington did not believe in the God of the theologians, but he was a member of the Society of Friends. He held that he did not believe in the existence of a material universe—an attitude which is as deadly to Christology as to Materialism—and held that electrons and stars are just ideas in the mind of God.

Because his work is marred by entirely false statements about the earlier state of science in regard to the nature of atoms, physicists reject and criticize his views on indeterminism or the breakdown of the law of causality. In his Swarthmore Lectures to Quakers in 1929, McCabe reported, Eddington "explains that he regards proof of the existence of God as superfluous: that you know it as you know the existence of a friend." (See the entry for Subrahmanyan Chandrasekhar, who differed with Eddington on some important astronomical matters. Also see entry for Susan Stebbing, whose criticism of Eddington has been called a model of clarity.) {CE; RE}

Eddy, Mary Baker (1821—1910)

Eddy in 1866 founded the Christian Science movement, a variant of American Protestantism, and in 1908 founded its daily newspaper, *Christian Science Monitor*. A three-volume biography by Robert Peel is the one approved by Christian Science authorities, but Samuel Clemens and Willa Cather have written entirely negative views of Eddy. Martin Gardner, in *The Healing Revelations of Mary Baker Eddy*, claims that Eddy "copies shamelessly, often word for word," from John Ruskin, Thomas Carlyle, and others, particularly Phineas Parkhurst Quimby, the man from whom Gardner maintains Eddy took the central idea of Christian Science. She is buried at Mount Auburn Cemetery in Cambridge, Massachusetts, a circle of eight Corinthian columns on an elevated base marking her tomb.

Unlike other denominations, the Church of Christ, Scientist (which claims to have 2,400 different churches), declines to publish membership figures. (See entries for Willa Cather, Christian Science, Samuel Clemens, Martin Gardner.) {Caroline Fraser, "Mrs. Eddy Builds Her Empire," *The New York Review of Books*, 11 July 1996}

Edel, Joseph Leon (1907—1997)

Edel [pronounced ay-DELL], Pulitzer Prize winner in 1963 for his five-volume biography of Henry James, also wrote *Bloomsbury: A House of Lions*. Asked about the various categories of humanism, he wrote the present author,

> These are all such long definitions and what is needed is brevity, for there lies clarity. I therefore offer:
>
> > The feeling for, and study of, all that pertains to the human order as distinct from the Divine.
>
> I think of this as necessary because of the gross distortions of definition that have occurred in recent years especially under the conservative tutelage. I don't see the need for "secular" if you accept my definition. It defines itself.

Edel between 1957 and 1959 was president of the American Center of PEN, and in 1969 and 1970 he was president of the Authors Guild. In 1972 he was elected a member of the American Academy-Institute of Arts and Letters. {CE; WAS, 14 February 1989}

Edelen, William (20th Century)

Edelen, a newspaper columnist and editor of *The Edelen Letter*, is a freethinker who writes for *Truth Seeker*. He flew for twelve years as a U.S. Marine Corps pilot, flying both fighter planes and transports in World War II and Korea. After receiving his Master of Theology degree from McCormick Theological Seminary (at the University of Chicago), he served as a Presbyterian minister, then took up anthropology at the University of Colorado.

Edelen is a long-time promoter of religious literacy, pointing out such facts that resurrected gods before Jesus included Attis and Mithra. A collection of his articles, *Toward the Mystery*, examines the chains which bind so many theists' minds.

Edell, Dean (20th Century)

Edell, a radio medical talk-show host, has gone on record as being a non-theist. During his nationally syndicated radio talk shows, usually in response to topics such as near death experiences or anti-abortion protests by the religious right, Edell responds that he has no belief in religion or in an afterlife. {CA; E}

Edelman, Gerald M(aurice) (1919—)

A 1972 Nobel Prize winner in medicine-physiology, Edelman heads the Department of Neuroscience at The Scripps Research Institute in La Jolla, California, where he is researching cell adhesion molecules which control the embryonic development process of cell differentiation.

In *Bright Air, Brilliant Fire* (1992), he looks forward to a second Enlightenment in which the major scientific underpinning will be neuroscience, not physics. "The problem then," he states, "will be not the existence of souls, for it is clear that each individual person is like no other and is not a machine. The problem will be to accept that individual minds are mortal." {*Secular Nation*, Fall 1994}

Edelman, Marian Wright (20th Century)

Edelman, the first black woman to be admitted to the Mississippi Bar, served as a staff attorney and activist for the National Association for the Advancement of Colored People from 1963 to 1968.

She served as director of the Harvard University Center for Law and Education from 1971 to 1973. In 1984, she was named the Humanist Distinguished Service Awardee by the American Humanist Association.

Edelmann, Johann Christian (1698—1767)

Called by Robertson one of the most energetic freethinkers of his age, Edelmann wrote *Unschuldige Wahrheiten* (Innocent Truths), "in which he takes up a pronouncedly rationalist and latitudinarian position, but without rejecting 'revelation.'" Later influence by the deists led Edelmann to withdraw from the Pietist camp, "attacking his former associates for the fanaticism into which their thought was degenerating." His *Moses mit aufgedecktem Angesichte* (Moses with Unveiled Face) (1740) was "an attack at once on the doctrine of inspiration and on that of the Mosaic authorship of the Pentateuch," containing the argument that no religion is of importance. His works, including *Christ and Belial* (1741) were burned in various German cities.

Robertson wrote that

> Edelmann's teaching was essentially Spinozist and pantheistic, with a leaning to the doctrine of metempsychosis. As a pantheist he of course entirely rejected the divinity of Jesus, pronouncing inspiration the appanage [the rightful endowment] of all; and the gospels were by him dismissed as late fabrications, from which the true teachings of the founder could not be learned; though, like nearly all the freethinkers of that age, he estimated Jesus highly.

Mirabeau praised him, and Guizot called him a "*fameux esprit fort.*" {BDF; JMR; JMRH; RAT}

EDEN

Eden, the Biblical site of the mythical Adam and Eve, is a Judeo-Christian concept which hinders students seeking facts about the origin of life.

Eden, Amnon (20th Century)

Eden, while a student at Tel Aviv University in Israel, was one of the founding members of Campus Freethought Alliance. {*International Humanist News*, December 1996}

EDINBURGH (Scotland) HUMANISTS: For information, write 2 Saville Terrace, Edinburgh EH9 3AD; or telephone 0131 667 8389.

Edis, Taner (20th Century)

Edis, who is at Iowa State University in Ames, is a supporter of Internet Infidels.

Edison, Thomas Alva (1847—1931)

Despite deafness and only three months of formal schooling, Edison was one of the most productive inventors of all time. "Genius," he held, "is 99% perspiration and 1% inspiration." While still in his teens, he said he "ate his way" steadily through fifteen feet of books on the shelves of the Detroit Public Library, this after having read when ten years of age Gibbon's *Decline and Fall* and Hume's *History of England*.

"What does God mean to me?" Edison once wrote. "Not a damned thing! Religion is all bunk." He also wrote, "All Bibles are man-made" and "When a man is dead, he is *dead*," and "I have never seen the slightest scientific proof of the religious theories of heaven and hell, of future life for individuals, or of a personal God." In 1910, he told *The New York Times* in an interview, "I cannot believe in the immortality of the soul. . . . No, all this talk of an existence for us, as individuals, beyond the grave is wrong. It is born of our tenacity of life—our desire to go on living—our dread of coming to an end as individuals. I do not dread it, though. Personally, I cannot see any use of a future life."

Edison invented the carbon microphone (1877), the record player (1878), the incandescent lamp (1879), and the kinetoscope (1889). In 1996, however, the French proposed commemorating the 100th anniversary of the invention of cinema by Auguste and Louis Lumière, by which they hoped to dramatize that they, not Edison with George Eastman, invented the cinema. Edison's kinetoscopic camera, they hold, was no more than the precursor of television; to view it, one had to peep into a box.

As to whether "his 1,093 patents are all to be credited to his undisputed genius or to the work of many assistants," Martin Gardner also has had doubts. In "Thomas Edison, Paranormalist" (*Skeptical Inquirer*, July-August 1996), Gardner chooses not to discuss the world's most famous, most prolific inventor's foibles: "his temper tantrums, his lust for money, his efforts to purloin ideas, his boasts about war weapons that never existed, or his disastrous relations with his two wives and his children."

What Gardner does focus on is Edison's changing religious opinions, his lifelong interest in psychic phenomena, and his gullibility. As a youth he admired Thomas Paine but, Gardner notes, unlike the deist Paine Edison did not believe in God, the soul, or an afterlife. At the time a pantheist, Edison liked to call nature the "Supreme Intelligence," indifferent and merciless toward humanity. But in 1920, Gardner avers, Edison came to believe in an afterlife and actually worked on an electrical device for communicating with the dead, a change which befriended him to Christian leaders.

Edison's second wife, eighteen years his junior, was a devout Methodist who thought evolution a plot of Satan. In 1926 Edison was quoted as referring to God as both a "Great Power" and a "Creator." And he praised Christianity as the wisest and most beautiful of world religions.

Matthew Josephson in his biography, however, said that when Edison's wife entertained six Methodist bishops and a theological debate ensued, Edison said, "I'm not going to listen to any more of this nonsense!" and stormed out. Allegedly, the Edisons agreed from that point on not to discuss religion and lived happily until his death at age eighty-four.

Also according to Gardner, Edison in his old age was bamboozled by a magician, Berthold Reese (1841—1926). Houdini the magician had been impressed by Reese's skill but had, during a séance with him, "caught him cold-blooded. He was startled when it was over, as he knew that I had bowled him over. So much so that he claimed I was the only one that had ever detected him." Of Edison's faith in Reese, Houdini wrote Conan Doyle, "That he fooled Edison does not surprise me. He would have surprised me if he did not fool Edison. Edison is certainly not a criterion, when it comes to judging a shrewd adept in the art of pellet-reading [a pellet being a billet rolled into a ball]." When an article in the *New York Graphic* unveiled some of Reese's techniques, Edison was so furious he wrote the editor that he had watched Reese several times, that on each occasion he had written something on a piece of paper when Reese was not near or when he was in another room, and that in no case was one of the papers handled by Reese. "Yet he recited correctly the contents of each paper." An account of Reese's methods by Ted Annemann in *The Jinx* (1936, Summer Issue) included a photograph of Reese, his hand holding a cigar that he habitually smoked during his performances because it made it easier to palm a folded billet.

Gardner reports a number of Edison's failed predictions, that the talking motion picture would not supplant the regular silent motion picture; that the possibilities of the aeroplane in 1895 had been exhausted "and we must turn elsewhere"; that the radio craze would die out; that more electricity would be sold for electric vehicles; that only direct current should be used; etc.

Gardner, however, is one of the few to have viewed Edison in such a light. As for that device to communicate with departed souls, Haught among others holds that Edison "played games with his detractors," citing Edison's statement, "It will give them a better opportunity to express themselves than Ouija boards or tilting tables." As for the minister's inquiry about the need for installing lightning rods on the church spire, Edison had replied, "By all means, as Providence is apt to be absent-minded."

Two years before he died, Edison had a conversation with the well-known atheist, Joseph Lewis, saying, "The great trouble is that the preachers get the children from six to seven years of age, and then it is almost impossible to do anything with them. Incurably religious—that is the best way to describe the mental condition of so many people. Incurably religious." Similarly, biographers Matthew Josephson and Wyn Wachhorst pointed out that Edison was incurably *irreligious*, that he rejected three fundamental tenets of Christianity: Christ's divinity, a personal God, and immortality.

In 1948, D. D. Runes edited Edison's *Diary and Sundry Observations*. According to his biographer, Ronald W. Clark, Edison on 18 October 1931, at the age of eighty-four, died after having been in a coma for five days. Just before he lapsed into the coma, he looked out the bedroom window and across the valley by his home. "It is very beautiful over there" were his last words. {CE; FUS; JM; RAT; RE; TSV; TYD}

Edman, Irwin (1896—1954)

Chairman of the philosophy department at Columbia University, Edman was a naturalist in philosophy, along with Ernest Nagel. He was graduated by Columbia University in 1917, began lecturing in philosophy there in 1918, and headed the department in 1945. Edman combined pragmatism with his interest in esthetics, as shown in *Philosopher's Holiday* (1938). A foremost American writer on the philosophy of George Santayana, he wrote his political views in *Fountainheads of Freedom* (1941). Edman is noted for being a spokesman in the liberal tradition of William James and of John Dewey.

A strong believer in education and the importance of fighting evil, he remarked, "When we give up the battle, the devil must smile as he watches us relax—under the guidance of theologians," a wry reference to his contempt for those theologians. In his *Candle in the Dark* (1939), Edman wrote, "Men in the nineteenth century were sad that they could no longer believe in God; they are more deeply saddened now by the fact that they can no longer believe in man."

In *Four Ways of Philosophy* (1937), Edman notes that the naturalist admits some religious impulse in man, but "the supernaturalist insists that this impulse which nature generates cannot be satisfied by nature save as seen in a supernatural context. To which the naturalist retorts that nature generates some impulses, possibly, which cannot be satisfied, as a man may be hungry without proving thereby that food is in his neighborhood or his reach." {CL; HNS; TYD}

Edson, Charles Leroy (1881—1975)

In his autobiography, *The Great American Ass* (1926), Edson tells of his freethinking outlook. His *Whale Meat: A Shocking Portrayal of Our Tribal Belief In Free Food from the North Pole* (1924) speaks of God as a tribal artifact. His photo and excerpts from some of his writing are in Whitehead and Muhrer's *Freethought on the American Frontier.*

Edson, Katharine Philips (1870-1933)

Edson, a Unitarian, was a suffragist, reformer, and labor arbitrator.

EDUCATION

- Education is the transmission of civilization.

—Ariel and Will Durant

- There is one kind of co-education that everybody believes in—the co-education of teachers and students.

—John Dewey

- You must unlearn what you have learned.

—Yoda, the Jedi master
in George Lucas's *Star Wars*

"We are committed," the Council for Secular Humanism states in its "Affirmations of Humanism," "to the application of reason and science to the understanding of the universe and to the solving of human problems. We deplore efforts to denigrate human intelligence, to seek to explain the world in supernatural terms, and to look outside nature for salvation. We believe that scientific discovery and technology can contribute to the betterment of human life."

Some critics of secular humanism associate it with John Dewey, complaining about his relativistic outlook. "Religious people," Jim Herrick has noted, "are now commonly attacking the 'relativism' of secular teaching. Secularists believe in relativism in the sense that we must take account of a situation in order to decide on the moral behaviour, but they are not 'relativists' in that they believe in the possibility of universally shared principles of behaviour." (See entry for Morality.)

EDUCATIONAL HERETICS PRESS

Educational Heretics Press at 113 Arundel Drive, Bramcote Hills, Nottingham, NG9 3FQ, England, is publisher of works such as *The Freethinker's Guide to the Educational Universe* (1994) by Roland Meighan.

Edward, Marshall (20th Century)

Marshall, in *Columbian Magazine* (1911), wrote "Thomas A. Edison on Immortality." {GS}

Edwards, Brian (20th Century)

Edwards is a broadcaster, raconteur, author of *The Public Eye* (1971), and editor of *Right Out: Labour Victory '72* (1973). He is an honorary associate of the New Zealand Association of Rationalists and Humanists.

Edwards, Chilperic (20th Century)

Edwards, a freethinker, wrote *The Oldest Law in the World* (1906). {GS}

Edwards, Don (1915—)

A Unitarian, Edwards served as national chairman of Americans for Democratic Action starting in 1965. A California congressman, in 1996 he was given the American Humanist Association's distinguished service award.

Edwards, Ian (1929—)

Edwards is an Australian humanist and medical general practitioner. He has been chairman of the Humanist Society of New South Wales, and he co-authored *Sex for Modern Teenagers* (1969) and *A Humanist View* (1969). {SWW}

Edwards, James J. (20th Century)

Edwards is author of *A Skeptic's Look at the Bible.*

Edwards, John (20th Century)

Edwards, an American, participated in 1980 at the 2nd World Atheist Conference in India.

Edwards, John Passmore (1823—1911)

Edwards was a British philanthropist, a poor boy who had educated himself and made a large fortune in journalism. "His papers set a standard of truth and idealism," states McCabe, "that is hardly known any longer, and his money was lavishly distributed amongst educational and philanthropic institutions (70 of which bear his name)." Edwards was influenced by Emerson and, in his *A Few Footprints* (1906), says he is an agnostic. McCabe, who knew him, agreed that Edwards was "a Spencerian Agnostic" and took a helpful interest in the early stages of the Rationalist Press Association. {JM; JMRH; RAT; RE}

Edwards, Paul (1923—)

Edwards is an American philosopher "who is mixed one part analytic philosopher to one part philosophe," according to Professor Michael Wreen of Marquette University in the *Oxford Companion to Philosophy* (1995). He is then described as being editor-in-chief of the *Encyclopedia of Philosophy* (8 volumes, 1967), "a massive Enlightenment work with a notable analytic sensibility" which "focuses on such traditional philosophical issues as God, free will, immortality, induction, and the nature of value-judgements." The Right Honorable Lord Quinton of Trinity College, Oxford, has called the encyclopedia "superior in every way to all its predecessors" and "there has been nothing since to compare with it."

A professor of philosophy who has taught at Brooklyn College, New York University, and the New School University, Edwards wrote the introduction to Bertrand Russell's *Why I Am Not A Christian* (1957). He also wrote *The Logic of Moral Discourse* (1955), *Buber and Buberism* (1970), *Heidegger on Death* (1979), and *Voltaire* (1989), *Immortality* (1992), *Reincarnation: A Critical Examination* (1996), and numerous scholarly articles.

In *Immortality* (1992), Edwards writes of "Karmic Tribulations" and "The Dependence of Consciousness on the Brain," providing thirty-four essays by a variety of thinkers on the subjects of survival and immortality.

- Those believing in *human* survival he lists as

  Aquinas, Descartes, Geach, MacKay,
  Priestley, and Tertullian.

- Those believing in some form of God without believing in survival, he states, are

  Mill and Voltaire.

- Those who believe in survival without believing in God are

  Ducasse and McTaggart.

- And of the many who reject both belief in God and in survival are Ayer, Flew, and Hume.

Long a leader of and inspiration for humanists, Edwards is an honorary member of the Secular Humanist Society of New York. In 1983, he was elected an honorary associate of the Rationalist Press Association. In addition to writing the foreword to *The Encyclopedia of Unbelief* (1985), he signed Manifesto II and is a Humanist Laureate in the Council for Secular Humanism's International Academy of Humanism. In addition, Edwards is a contributing editor to *Free Inquiry* and to *Philo*.

David Berman, reviewing Edwards's *Immortality* in the British *New Humanist*, was generally favorable and mentioned that the book has an "occasional joke. Thus in his discussion of dualism he mentions the (supposed) comment of one behaviourist to another: 'You are fine—how am I?'" But he denies that Hume was a "frankly irreligious" philosopher. Berman, however, is intrigued by the Edwards view that "there is probably no consensus against dualism among contemporary philosophers."

Students smile upon relating that when Edwards lectures and mentions a name or a work he suspects they have not read, he exhorts them with "Barbarians, you are barbarians, barbarians! You *must* read *everything* ever written by [e.g., Hume] before tomorrow's class!" On the following day, it is likely that someone in a back row *will* be questioned about yesterday's assigned author, whether or not the student is auditing the course or taking it for credit. The front rows of his classes are usually filled to capacity.

Students soon learn, also, not to inquire about Sidney Hook, who was once his department chairman and in whose room he once shared space. "I was so happy," Edwards might retort, his face filled with glee, "that when he died his photo and obituary did *not* make page one of *The New York Times*!" Although the two shared many philosophic beliefs, Edwards is quick to go on record as to his heartfelt feelings: that a pretty girl should not be overlooked, or that public interest in Ayn Rand and R. D. Laing is fading in the 1990s, or that Nietzsche was not a true misogynist.

In his 1995 Prometheus Lecture, a three-part series covering Nietzsche, Freud, and Wilhelm Reich given at New York's New School for Social Research, Edwards stated that "the elimination of error is almost as important as the discovery of truth." To everyone's surprise, over three hundred attended the lectures, including some who had been in his classes thirty years prior. "Yes," Edwards emphasized, "I have the anti-religious bug. Freud had it, too, but not Reich. Lucretius had it. So did Nietzsche, Hume, and Bertrand Russell."

Edwards stated that he does not object to others having their religious beliefs—the Australian aborigines very likely need such—but he holds that any educated individual today who has heard about logical positivism or read the works of contemporary philosophers and persists in mysticism or supernaturalism is not one of his kind. Further, he does not apologize for pointing out their weaknesses.

He cited as a major goal his attempt to separate a philosopher's bad from his or her good concepts. To avoid weighing the bad and the good is to indulge in shoddy research and will confuse future researchers who, if lazy, will regrettably repeat those falsities and others will then repeat them, also. As examples, he noted the false "facts" that Hume was a deist and that Wittgenstein died a Catholic.

Confirming the individualistic as well as honest approach which Edwards brings to philosophy, Wreen has written that "[a] deep respect for science and common sense mark Edwards's writings, and he is well known for his use of humour as a lethal weapon against philosophers whom he regards as pompous purveyors of platitudes, especially Heidegger and Tillich."

In 1996, Edwards wrote a devastating study entitled *Reincarnation, A Critical Examination*. As to why a rationalist would write about such a patently absurd topic, Edwards's response is that there is widespread belief in them. Dr. Elisabeth Kübler-Ross, in fact, has never heard an argument for life after death that she does not endorse, he laments. Whereas some make decisions based on reincarnationist beliefs, he adds, others make money on retailing reports of astral adventures. Edwards is at his most devastating in discussing the "interregnum," where souls await their next body, and the absurdities of "astral clothing." "The book," wrote Kenneth Blackwell, "is salutary in revealing the persistence of nonsense and the persisting need for education, logic, and good sense."

Edwards signed Humanist Manifesto 2000. A commendably concise summary of Edwards's viewpoint is "God and the Philosophers," which he wrote as an entry for the *Oxford Companion of Philosophy*. A forthcoming book with that title is in the works. (See entries for Freud, Hume, Nietzsche, Wilhelm Reich, and Bertrand Russell.). {CA; Kenneth Blackwell, Russell: The Journal of the Bertrand Russell *Archives, Winter 1998-1999; E*; HM2; HNS2; OCP}

Edwards, Robyn (20th Century)

Edwards is a humanist activist in Western Australia. E-mail: <robyned@ozemail.com.au>

Edwards, Samuel (20th Century)

Edwards wrote *Rebel! A Biography of Thomas Paine* (1974). {FUK; GS}

Edwards, Sandy (20th Century)

Edwards is an active member of Humanist Society of Scotland. E-mail: <ase1@st-andrews.ac.uk>.

Edwards, Thomas (18th Century)

A freethinker, Edwards wrote *A Discourse on the Limits and Importance of Free Enquiry in Matters of Religion* (1792). {GS}

Edwien, Andreas (1921—)

Edwien, a Norwegian, wrote *Is Christianity a Danger to World Peace?* (1977) and *Jesus in Conflict with Human Rights* (1979). (See entry for Scandinavian Unbelievers.)

Edwords, Frederick E. (1948—)

In addition to being Executive Director of the American Humanist Association since 1980, Edwords in 1994 became managing editor of *The Humanist* following Rick Szykowny's resignation. As such, he is one of the major leaders of humanistic thought. As such, however, he also receives blame for the decline of the humanistic journal.

Edwords is credited with launching a journal, *Creation/Evolution*, which was devoted exclusively to answering the religious right's creationist arguments. He has spoken at international humanist conferences in Costa Rica and Mumbai, emphasizing that humanists must address the new technologies.

Because the American Humanist Association held the copyrights to Humanist Manifestos I and II and did not approve of the Council for Secular Humanism's naming the next manifesto III, Edwords did not sign the newly named Humanist Manifesto 2000. E-mail: <edwords@juno.com>. On the Web: <http://www.humanists.net/> and <http://www.infidels.org/org/aha/>. (See entry for New York Atheists, Freethinkers, Humanists.) {CL; FD; HNS2}

Edwords, Mary (20th Century)

Edwords is an American activist and humanist. Her e-mail: <75332.3305@compuserve.com>.

Eenens, Ferdinand (1811—1883)

Eenens was a Belgian writer who wrote *La Vérité* (1859), a work on the Christian faith and *Le Paradis Terrestre* (1860), an examination of the legend of Eden.

He used such pen names as Le Père Nicaise, Nicodème, and Timon III. {BDF}

Eeramani, K. (20th Century)

In Madras, India, Eeramani since 1973 has been editing *Modern Rationalist.* {FUK}

Effen, Justus van (1684—1735)

Effen was a Dutch writer. While secretary of the Dutch Embassy at London, he conceived the idea of a weekly like the *Spectator* and founded *Le Misanthrope*, later *Le Journal Littéraire*, and finally (1731—1735) *De Hollandsche Spectator*. In 1722 he translated into Dutch Mandeville's deistic *Free Thoughts on Religion.* {RAT}

Efremov, Yuri Nikolaevich (20th Century)

Efremov, who is department head of Sternberg Astronomical Institute at Moscow State University, signed Humanist Manifesto 2000.

EGALITARIANISM

Egalitarianism is a belief in human equality, particularly with respect to social, political, and economic rights. That is not to say that all humans are or could be the same, which is profoundly illogical. The rights inherent in egalitariarianism make diversity not only possible but also desirable.

Some Christians may look forward to a Heaven in which all are equal in the eyes of God. Freethinkers enjoy their diversity in the here and now. They can flourish, however, only if they can live where their rights are respected *not* to believe in the supernatural.

Egan, Greg (20th Century)

A science fiction writer from Australia, Egan in an interview in *Eidolon 11* (January 1993) said

> I was raised as a Christian, and I still retain a lot of the values of Christianity. The trouble with basing values on religions, though, is that the premises of most of them are pure wishful thinking; you either have to refuse to scrutinise those premises—take them on faith, declare that they "transcend logic"—or reject them. As Paul Davies has said, most Christian theologians have retreated from all the things that their religion supposedly asserts; they take a much more "modern" view than the average believer does. But by the time you've "modernised" something like Christianity—starting off with "*Genesis* was all just poetry" and ending up with "Well, of course there's no such thing as a personal God"—there's not much point pretending that there's anything religious left. You might as well come clean and admit that you're an atheist with certain values, which are historical, cultural, biological, and personal in origin, and have nothing to do with anything called God.
>
> [Asked what inspires him to write], most of my "inspiration" is very transparent. *The Cutie* was triggered by reading that childless adults in the United States were buying themselves Cabbage Patch dolls—and that one couple had even had an exorcism performed on theirs. I'm still not sure if that was apocryphal or not. *The Moral Virologist* was a fairly direct response to religious fundamentalists blathering on about AIDS being God's instrument. I thought someone should point out that, even on their own terms, this was a blasphemous obscenity. I suppose that story was also guided by the example of "creation science"; believing in doctrine is bad enough, but if you start trying to reason from it, you churn out an ever-growing list of absurdities which you also have to believe.
>
> {CA}

Egner, Russell Forrest (20th Century)

A freethinker, Egner wrote *In Search of Truth* (1951). {GS}

EGO

A Dutch humanist monthly for soldiers, *Ego* is at Oranje Nassaulaan 71, 3708 GC Zeist, The Netherlands.

EGOISM

In ethics, egoism is opposed to altruism. Spinoza held that egoism is a necessary corollary of the supreme instinct of self-preservation, for "no one ever neglects anything which he judges to be good, except with the hope of gaining a greater good." Egoists hold that the ends and motives of human conduct are the good of the individual. Altruists, however, hold that the criterion of morality is the welfare of others. For Nietzsche, all altruistic sentiment is cowardice. Herbert Spencer held that the conflict between the two can be traced to the conflict of the individual with his family, his group, his race, and people like him. The two could be reconciled, he thought, through social discipline. {CE}

THE EGOIST: See entry for *Freewoman.*

EGOTIST

- Egotist, n. A person of low taste, more interested in himself than in me.

—**Ambrose Bierce**
The Devil's Dictionary

Egren, Michael (20th Century)

Egren is Vice President in Michigan of *The Jewish Humanist.*

EGYPTIAN CIVILIZATION

The peoples of Egypt and the Near East were said to have made their appearance, according to Jasper Griffin of Oxford University, in myths

> in connection respectively with the Greek heroine Io (who went to Egypt in the form of a cow) and with the hero Cadmus, sprung from the same family but living in Phoenicia. Cadmus came back to his birthplace, Greece, bringing with him the alphabet, and became the founder of the city of Thebes, the great-granddaughters of Io, the fifty Danaids (daughters of Danaus, another eponym, this time of the Danaans, an old name for the Hellenes), returned to Greece in flight from their hated suitors, their cousins, the fifty sons of Aegyptus.

When forced to marry them, all but one of the Danaids cut their bridegrooms' throats on their wedding night. Such a myth has led many human males to universal feelings of alarm, Griffin has written,

> . . . at the thought of marrying, and being helpless in the presence of, a woman—about whom, when you came down to it, you really knew very little.
>
> {Jasper Griffin, "Anxieties of Influence," *The New York Review of Books*, 20 June 1996}

EGYPTIAN FREETHINKERS AND HUMANISTS

- *Averroës Today* (published in English and Arabic twice per year), PO Box 5101, Heliopolis West, Cairo, 11711—is of interest to freethinkers. Mourad Wahba, its president, signed Humanist Manifesto 2000.
- Afro-Asian Philosophy Association (is an Associate Member of the International Humanist and Ethical Union in London)—the group has held conferences in Cairo on "Enlightenment and Human Rights" and "Terrorism and Teaching Philosophy."

EGYPTIAN RELIGION

Much confusion surrounds the study of ancient Egyptian religion, and current research finds contradictory myths and beliefs riddled with inconsistencies. What is clear, however, is that five centuries before the introduction of monotheism by the Hebrews, five centuries before the first prophet appeared in Judea, Ikhnaten had imposed monotheism. However, according to McCabe, "the people, instead of perceiving it to be a higher truth, gladly joined with the priests in getting it suppressed and polytheism restored." (See J. H. Breasted's *Development of Religion in Ancient Egypt* (1912) and Siegfried Morenz's *Egyptian Religion* [1973].) {CE; RE}

EHF: See entry for European Humanist Federation.

Ehrenfeld, Sylvain (20th Century)

Ehrenfeld is one of the IHEU's representatives to the United Nations.

Ehrenreich, Barbara (1941—)

Ehrenreich is an atheist, socialist, and feminist who writings have been published in *Time, The Nation, Ms., Mother Jones, Esquire, Vogue, New Republic,* and *The New York Times Magazine.* With Deirdre English, she wrote *Witches, Midwives, and Nurses: A History of Women Healers* (1972), which exposed male dominance of female health care. She also wrote *The Hearts of Men: American Dreams and the Flight from Commitment* (1983); *Fear of Falling: The Inner Life of the Middle Class* (1989); and *The Worst Years of Our Lives: Irreverent Notes from a Decade of Greed* (1990). In the latter work, she mentions that her great-grandmother, Mamie O'Laughlin, once called for a Catholic priest to administer last rites for her dying father. When he sent word he would not perform the ceremony unless Mamie gave him $25 in advance, she was so outraged by the priest's greed that she eventually became an atheist. As for her descendants, Ehrenreich added, "Furthermore, whether out of filial devotion or natural intelligence, most of us have continued to avoid organized religion, secret societies, astrology, and New Age adventures in spiritualism."

In 1998 she was the American Humanist Association's Humanist of the Year. The Freedom From Religion Foundation named her "Freethought Heroine 1999" at their annual national convention held in San Antonio, Texas. {CA; E; *Free Inquiry*, Spring 1998; WWS}

Ehrenreich, Gerald A. (20th Century)

When he signed Humanist Manifesto II, Ehrenreich was an associate professor at the University of Kansas School of Medicine. {HM2}

Ehrenreich, Barbara (20th Century)

In *Blood Rites: Origins and History of the Passions of War* (1997), Ehrenreich takes up the theme of war and what is the central rite of so many ancient religions, blood sacrifice. "I was preoccupied with ritual blood sacrifice as a kind of antecedent to war or socially sanctioned violence in which people have traditionally invested very powerful feelings and ideas of religious significance," she stated in a *Free Inquiry* interview (Winter 1997-1998).

Humanism is in Ehrenreich's family tradition. The story goes that it began with her great-great-grandmother in the 1800s in Montana. She rejected religion after she could not afford the fee a Catholic priest demanded to attend to her dying father. "I think that, like the Japanese and the Germans in the 1930s and 40s, we are equally wrapped up in nationalism as our unofficial—and un-examined—religion," she has lamented. {*Free Inquiry*, Spring 1998}

Ehrlich, Anne (20th Century)

A senior research associate in biology at Stanford, Ehrlich served as a consultant to the White House Council on Environmental Quality's Global 2000 Report. In 1985 she received the American Humanist Association's Distinguished Service Award. "Over 60% of the earth's land surface is being used in some degree or another by human beings," she has written. "Most of what remains is desert, mountaintops, or arctic areas. . . . But we are only one of somewhere between five and thirty million species of organisms that exist on this planet. It is obvious that we consume much more than our share of earth's biological productivity. So . . . whatever your cause, it is a lost cause without population control."

Ehrlich, Paul (1932—)

Ehrlich, an educator and biologist, wrote *How To Know Butterflies* (11961), *Process of Evolution* (1963), *Population Bomb* (1968), *Global Ecology: Readings Toward a Rational Strategy for Man* (1971), *Race Bomb* (1977), *The Population Explosion* (1990), and a variety of other works which warn about overpopulation in the poorest countries and overconsumption in the richest countries.

Ehrlich has described creationists as "a group of morons"; he puts down "flacks of the pesticide industry" because "they have no shame"; he shrugs off most scientists who, unlike himself, do "dull ignorant work that is of no significance to humanity"; and he has described any economists who assert that there are no known physical limits to growth as being "totally imbecilic."

A controversial and outspoken scientist, he does not believe birth control can work, calling it "nonsensical." He would, in fact, favor the forcible sterilization of Indian men who have more than three children.

Like the naturalistic humanists of the 1950s who, Cassandra-like, warned about the danger of the human population explosion, Ehrlich has appeared on television to predict that, with the globe's population heading toward ten billion by the middle of the 21st century, Western countries can be expected to gobble up the resources needed by the impoverished throngs of Asia, Africa, and Latin America. In 1990 Ehrlich became a MacArthur Prize fellow.

Eichorn, Johann Gottfried (1752—1827)

Eichorn was a German Orientalist and rationalist. He was professor of Oriental Literature and afterwards professor of theology at Gottingen. In *A Commentary on the Apocalypse*, he tends to uproot belief in the Bible as a divine revelation. Eichorn is said to have lectured every day for fifty-two years. {BDF; RAT}

Eichorn, Nat (20th Century)

Eichorn is active with the American Humanist Association chapter in Tucson. (See entry for Arizona Atheists, Humanists.)

Eichtal, Gustav d' (1804—1886)

Eichtal was a French writer, born of a Jewish family. He became a follower of Saint Simon and was one of the founders of the *Société d'Ethnologie.* Eichtal published *Les Evangiles* (1863), a critical analysis of the gospels. After his death, his son published his *Mélanges de Critique Biblique* (Miscellanies of Biblical Criticism), in which he studied the name and character of "Jahveh." {BDF}

Einstein, Albert (1879—1955)

An internationally eminent theoretical physicist, who formulated the relativity theory, Einstein is a symbol of genius in the 20th century. As a boy, he lived in Munich and Milan, studying at a cantonal school in Switzerland, graduating from Zürich's Federal Institute of Technology, and later becoming a Swiss citizen. In 1910 he became full professor at the German University in Prague, then returned to Zürich, resuming his German citizenship. In 1921 he won the Nobel Prize in physics, notably for his work on the photoelectric effect. He taught at the Institute for Advanced Study in Princeton, New Jersey, from 1933 to 1940. His property, however, was confiscated in 1934 by the Nazi government and he was deprived of his German citizenship. In 1940 he became an American citizen, although McCabe reports that the Catholic hierarchy denounced him as an atheist when he was invited to America.

In addition to being known for his relativity theory, he is known for his contributions to the development of the quantum theory and for the unified field theory. He alerted Pres. Franklin D. Roosevelt to the possible use of atomic energy in bombs, but Einstein remained a pacifist throughout his life. His formulation of a general theory of relativity that included gravitation as a determiner of the curvature of a space-time continuum revolutionized almost all fields of study. Hume and Mach, he once stated, were the philosophers who impressed him the most favorably. The "general" theory suggested that space itself is not just a stage for the material world to act on, but is an active participant in the play. For example, space gets bent out of shape by any matter that is hanging about in it. His "special" theory of relativity showed that an object can be two different sizes for two different people, and that they can perceive the time between two events to have different durations.

Norman Cousins told the story that when he took his young daughter to see the distinguished Princeton professor, she had ingenuously informed Einstein that he was the smartest man in the world and she marveled at all the little objects that graced his desk. He described several of them to her.

"And why do you have this rock?" he was asked, for it appeared to be a rock like all other rocks anywhere. "To remind myself," he responded, "that it is something I do not thoroughly understand." (For something else Einstein did not understand, see the entry for Marie Curie.)

In their *Private Lives of Albert Einstein,* biographers Roger Highfield and Paul Carter cite Einstein's acquaintance with Marie Curie but state he had little regard for women's intellectual potential in the sciences. "I'm not much with people," he stated, "and I'm not a family man. I want my peace. I want to know how God created the world." So he came up with the relativity principle (a person's speed in a car can be relative to the ground, the moon, the farthest galaxy) and the absolute value of the speed of light. He also came up with the equation, E = mc2, which changed physics as well as nuclear fission and the history of mankind. Little wonder that when Franz Kafka was in the same room with Einstein in 1911 or 1912, Kafka—although one of the most creative thinkers of the time—sat "tongue-tied in a corner."

Einstein was on the board of advisors of Charles Francis Potter's First Humanist Society of New York and was an honorary associate of the Rationalist Press Association, of which Bertrand Russell was then president. Einstein once wrote, "I do not believe in immortality of the individual, and I consider ethics to be an exclusive human concern with no superhuman authority behind it. . . . Teachers of religion must have the stature to give up the doctrine of a personal God, that is, give up that source of fear and hope which in the past placed such vast power in the hands of priests." His final will left his manuscripts and royalties to Hebrew University.

Raised as he was by non-religious parents, Einstein was not involved in religious activities, but he did identify with his Jewish heritage and became an outspoken Zionist. In *Living Philosophies* (1930), Einstein wrote, "I cannot imagine a God who rewards and punishes the objects of his creation, whose purposes are modeled after our own—a God, in short, who is but a reflection of human frailty. Neither can I believe that the individual survives the death of his body, although feeble souls harbor such thoughts through fear or ridiculous egotism. It is enough for me to contemplate the mystery of conscious life perpetuating itself through all eternity, to reflect upon the marvelous structure of the universe which we can dimly perceive, and to try humbly to comprehend even an infinitesimal part of the intelligence manifested in nature."

Eight years later, in 1938, he revised those sentiments:

> Things [have grown] even worse than a pessimist of the deepest dye would have dared prophesy. In Europe to the east of the Rhine free exercise of the intellect exists no longer, the population is terrorized by gangsters who have seized power, and youth is poisoned by systematic lies. The pseudo-success of political adventurers has dazzled the rest of the world; it becomes apparent everywhere that this generation lacks the strength and force which enabled previous generations to win, in painful struggle and at great sacrifice, the political and individual freedom of man. Awareness of this state of affairs overshadows every hour of my present existence, while ten years ago it did not yet occupy my thoughts. It is this that I feel so strongly in re-reading the words written in the past. And yet I know that, all in all, man changes but little, even though prevailing notions make him appear in a very different light at different times, and even though current trends like the present bring him unimaginable sorrow. Nothing of all that will remain but a few pitiful pages in the history books, briefly picturing to the youth of future generations the follies of its ancestors.

He disagreed with Kant that particular concepts of time and space are necessary premises for thought, concepts that are innate in the human mind. Rather, he held, all concepts including physical ones are "free inventions of the human intellect" which can be modified in the event they do not compare with one's experiences. Our intuition about the physical world, he held, is based on sensory experiences and can be fundamentally in error.

In 1950, Einstein wrote *Essays in Humanism.* The Helen Dukas (who was his secretary) and Banesh Hoffman editing of *Albert Einstein: The Human Side* (1979) quotes him as writing in German to a Colorado banker in 1927: "My religiosity consists in a humble admiration of the infinitely superior spirit that reveals itself in the little that we, with our weak and transitory understanding, can comprehend of reality. Morality is of the highest importance—but for us, not for God." Also, he stated in a letter,

> It was, of course, a lie what you read about my religious convictions, a lie which is being systematically repeated. I do not believe in a personal God, and I have never denied this but have expressed it clearly. If something is in me which can be called religious, then it is the unbounded admiration for the structure of the world so far as our science can reveal it.

In 1941, Einstein delivered a paper on "Science and Religion" at the Jewish Theological Seminary in New York, pointing out, "Nobody, certainly, will deny that the idea of the existence of an omnipotent, just, and omnibeneficent personal God is able to accord men solace, help, and guidance; also by virtue of its simplicity the concept is accessible to the most undeveloped mind." Students of Einstein's thought have remarked that if Einstein had a God, it was the God of Spinoza, not the God of the organized religions. But they are amused that, as Abraham Pais's "Subtle Is the Lord" (1982) reports, "Of Bergson's philosophy he [Einstein] used to say, 'God forgive him.'" However, Einstein did once write,

> It was, of course, a lie which you read about my religious convictions, a lie which is being systematically repeated. I do not believe in a personal god and I have never denied this but have expressed it clearly.

McCabe noted that "Catholic prelates in the United States denounced him, with their usual crudeness, to the public as an atheist, and he replied that he believes in a 'great Power,' the source of order and beauty." McCabe adds, "Agnostic is the accurate description of his opinion, but Einstein has never made any serious study of religious issues." When Einstein declared that "God does not play dice with the universe," speaking about quantum explanations of what goes on within atoms, many clergymen jumped to the erroneous conclusion that Einstein was a believer. But Einstein's "cosmic religion" was his way of expressing an awe of our universe, an entity too profound to be adequately understood. Catholic Bishop

Fulton J. Sheen, disagreeing, quipped, "Who ever wanted to die for the Milky Way!"

Haught quoted *The Private Albert Einstein* (1992) by Peter Bucky, a young confidant of the genius:

> Einstein told me many times that he did not believe in a single God. He said he could not imagine how God could manifest himself in a human countenance. Rather, he believed that there was a cosmic force that could develop things that mortal men could not even begin to understand. . . .
>
> I recall his telling me that, during his earlier years, when he would apply for various positions and come to a column asking for details about his religion, he would mark down "dissident," thus demonstrating his disinterest in any one faith. . . . During an interview with Professor William Hermanns, Einstein once said that he could never accept any conceptualization of God that was based on fear, either fear of life or fear of death, or one that required a blind belief, totally removed from logic. Nor did he envision God in any personal sense. In that respect, he said that if he were to talk about a personal God, he would consider himself to be a liar.

In 1994, astronomers using the Hubble Space Telescope confirmed Einstein's theory about black holes. *The Ultimate Einstein*, a CD-ROM, attempts to explain the scientist's various theories and makes possible a study of Einstein's skepticism. It shows how at one time he considered nationalism as "ugly," for he lived through the horrors of World War I, but he came to hold that nationalism can help create human dignity. The work shows how he rejected conservatively defined religion, tells of his advocacy of the values of the Enlightenment, and speaks of his love of classical literature. He took pride in knowing about Jewish culture but when asked later in life if he cared to succeed a Jewish scientist (Chaim Weizmann) as president of Israel, he declined.

"What really interests me," Einstein once remarked, "is whether God had any choice in the creation of the world." Such a comment, said Dennis Overbye, deputy science editor of *The Times*, was not a reference to a "white-bearded man sitting up in Heaven toting up sins and dispensing favors to prayerful supplicants." Rather it was Einstein's way of asking (a) could the universe be any other way than it appears to be? or (b) if not, how much room remains in that universe for things like chance and miracles? Overbye reasons that "A God with no choice, of course, might seem to be a cold comfort or even no God at all, at least in the traditional sense." To Einstein, then, God

> was a code word for the mystery and grandeur of the universe, the wellspring of awe, a reminder that there was something at the core of existence that all his equations could only graze, as he said once, "something we cannot penetrate."

He accepted the fact, Overbye added, that the most incomprehensible thing about the universe is that it is comprehensible, that humans will never know the answer to some questions, but that science is nothing if not the search for reasons, "for the smoking gene in our coiled cells, the atom of consciousness, the quantum butterfly flapping its wings at the heart of the world."

Einstein had a child shortly before his marriage in 1902 with a Swiss student, Mileva Maric, a marriage that ended in divorce and involved trying to put their illegitimate daughter up for adoption and sending their mentally disturbed son, Eduard, to a Swiss psychiatric home, where he was not visited by his father—Eduard died wretchedly. Michelle Zackheim's *Einstein's Daughter: The Search for Lieserl* (1999) claims—Jeremy Bernstein thinks Zackheim has no real evidence, calling most of the study "a wild goose chase"—that the daughter was born severely retarded, possibly with Down syndrome, and died at twenty-one months after a bout with scarlet fever. The daughter was never adopted and, instead, was left with her parents in the Vojovodina region of Serbia. The Einsteins had two other sons—Albert Jr. and Eduard.

In 1919 Einstein married his second cousin, Elsa Einstein, a widow who had two daughters, and upon her death in 1936 he spent his last two decades unmarried. He died of an abdominal aneurysm. His will reveals that Helena Dukas, his "secretary-housekeeper," received more than his own relatives, that she was to receive from a special trust "all of my manuscripts, copyrights, publication rights, royalties and royalty agreements, and all other literary property and rights, of any and every kind or nature whatsoever." Upon her death, his stepdaughter Margot Einstein was to receive such moneys, and upon her death the property was to be delivered to the Hebrew University in Israel. His violin was willed to his grandson, Bernhard Caesar Einstein. Although the will contained no provisions for his funeral or burial, Einstein's vital organs, including his brain, were removed for scientific study. He then was cremated. Einstein's last book was entitled *Essays in Humanism* (1950).

(Einstein, whose parents were Hebrews, was not a Jew; the present work distinguishes between a Hebrew and a Jew, referring to the former as a descendant from one of a group of northern Semitic peoples including the Israelites, and to the latter as a person regardless of his mother's religion who—like Sammy Davis, an African American—chooses the Jewish religion and its basic theology. See the John Holmes entry concerning a comment about a poem by Einstein, and see the entry for Edwin Powell Hubble.) {Jeremy Bernstein, in *The New York Times Book Review*, 19 Dec 99, claims Zackheim's book is erroneous in claiming Einstein had syphilis—Zackheim countered that he had written, "I merely posed the medically sound possibility that *if* he had syphilis, as his friend and physician Janos Pleasch posited, it *could* have had an impact on the health of his first- and third-born children"; CE; CL; HNS2; JM; RE; *The Economist*, 8 November 1997; TRI; TYD}

Einstein, Morris (19th Century)

A freethinker, Einstein wrote *Origin and Development of Religious Ideas and Beliefs, as Manifested in History and Seen by Reason* (1871). {GS}

Eisenstadt, Barbara Lynn (20th Century)

An American secular humanist, Eisenstadt in 1996 attended the international conference of ethical humanists in Mexico City. Her e-mail: <blefilm@aol.com>.

Eisler, Jan Loeb (20th Century)

Eisler, who was married to Lee Eisler, has been on the board of directors of the American Humanist Association. A life member of the AHA, she is vice-president of the statewide chapter, Humanists of Florida, and a board member of Humanists of the Suncoast as well as Humanists of St. Petersburg. She is treasurer of both Liberals United and the Tampa Bay chapter of Americans United for the Separation of Church and State. In addition, she is acting treasurer of the Bill of Rights Network, vice president of the Bertrand Russell Society, and editor of a humanistic newsletter, *Family Matters* (Box 664, Amherst, NY 14226). In her professional life, she is a registered nurse. She has taught advanced cardiac and trauma life support. In her early years, as an activist she participated in Freedom Marches and bears the scars inflicted during one of those marches. Eisler was a participant at the 3rd Annual Atheist Alliance Conference and is a life member of the Hemlock Society, the Bertrand Russell Society, and Atheists of Florida. In addition, she is a member of the Freedom From Religion Foundation and a regional director of the Council for Secular Humanism. In 1997 she journeyed to Russia to help inaugurate a Center for Inquiry at Moscow State University. Eisler, who in 1999 was elected Vice President of the IHEU, signed Humanist Manifesto 2000. Eisler's e-mail: <hasp@gte.net>.

Eisler, Lee (1909—1998)

A founding member of the Bertrand Russell Society, and a key individual responsible for that group's international success in continuing to further research concerning Russell as well as publicize Russell's timeless views, Eisler edited the society's definitive newsletter for decades. A secular humanist, Eisler was an active member of the New York society.

In 1971, he wrote *Morals Without Mystery*. One of his most useful works is *The Quotable Bertrand Russell* (1993), which presents the British philosopher's thinking on a number of topics of continuing interest. Eisler pored over Russell's books along with numerous articles and countless newspaper and magazine stories, outlining the material around questions. For example, he asks, "What is the basic problem in Africa?" or "How can a child be taught to love its parents?" or "What's wrong with St. Paul's views on marriage and sex?" Eisler then lists Russell's written answers, giving the reader the satisfying experience of feeling that Russell is present and is answering questions that it would take a person ages to find if forced to read all eighty-nine books that Russell wrote during his ninety-eight years. Eisler, a retired New York writer of advertising, lived in Florida at the time of his death. {WAS, numerous conversations}

Eisler, Riane (20th Century)

Eisler wrote *The Chalice and the Blade*, which studies how societies became patriarchal. {HNS2}

Eisler, Rudolph (1873—1926)

An Austrian philosopher, Eisler was secretary of the Vienna Sociological Society and editor of the Philosophico-Sociological Library. His dictionaries of philosophers and philosophy are of great value to scholars, and Eisler's own monistic views are given in his *Leib und Seele* (1906). {RAT; RE}

EL BOLETIN-ÉTICO-HUMANISTA: See entry for *Asociación Iberoamericana Ético Humanista* (ASIBEHU), the Spanish-speaking association of ethical humanists with headquarters in Costa Rica.

Elbert, J. C. (20th Century)

Elbert is treasurer of the University of Minnesota Atheists and Humanists.

"Elborch, Conrad von" (Born 1865)

Elborch was the pseudonym of a Dutch writer who, when Wheeler published *Biographical Dictionary of Freethinkers*, did not want his name revealed because of his position. The individual also wrote as Fra Diavolo, Denis Bontemps, and J. Van den Ende. Elborch translated a rare Latin treatise, *De Tribus Impostoribus*, about three Impostors—Jesus, Moses, and Mohammed—with an important bibliographic and historical introduction. {BDF}

Elders, Fons (1936—)

Fons, professor of the University for Humanist Studies in Utrecht, discussed the meaning of humanism and the nature of its cultural context at the 1993 Congress of the European Humanist Federation in Berlin. In a debate with Paul Kurtz, Fons cited the heterogeneous traditions of humanism a pagan Graeco-Roman tradition; an Alexandrian tradition with hermetic gnosis and ramifications in Arab humanism; catharism; kaballah; Renaissance humanism; Chasidism (a mystic movement spread among Polish Jews in the second half of the 18th century); Freemasonry. He also named Christian humanism, an Enlightenment humanism, and a post-modern humanism.

The humanism he prefers resembles Mondrian's "Boogie-Woogie" painting: the interplay between vertical and horizontal colors—a dynamic between the visible and invisible dimension of human existence. For him, humanist spirituality is the source of inspiration for the arts and for lifestyles, for the erotic and nature-oriented values, and for an open attitude to non-Western cultures. Elders added,

> I would like to contribute to a revival of the pagan and gnostic humanist traditions, not in opposition to the Enlightenment values, but to liberate the classic and romantic values of the Enlightenment from their mutual stalemate; to liberate Western culture and Western humanism from their superiority complex. Along these lines we have a chance to develop a humanism worthwhile to the new generations on the different continents and in the various cultures, while slowing restoring our disequilibrium with Gaia.

At a 1995 conference in India, Elders said that humanism had been enriched by the culture of India. Alexander the Great had two teachers, the Greek Aristotle and an Indian guru. Arab humanism from the 8th to the 12th century was essential to the development of the Renaissance, he explained. Socrates and the Buddha were comparable in their empirical observation, questioning, and observation on suffering. Humanism, he added, is a multi-cultural phenomenon that should be broad and inclusive so that a liberal Muslim or a Christian in sympathy with a human position should be allowed to participate.

He is said to be proud of having been the first actor to appear frontally nude on Dutch television.

Elders is one of the members of the IHEU's Committee on Religious Extremism and Rational Inquiry. He was a participant at the 1996 Humanist World Congress held in Mexico City on the idea of "Tolerance as a Core Value of Secularism." In 1997 Elders wrote *Humanism Toward the Third Millennium*. E-mail: <eldersf@xs4all.nl>. {*International Humanist News*, December 1996; *New Humanist*, February 1996 and December 1996}

Eldridge, Paul (20th Century)

Eldridge, a freethinker, wrote *Michel de Montaigne: Skeptic and Atheist* (1950). {GS}

ELECTRONIC MINISTRIES

Electronic preachers took in roughly $3.5 billion in 1996, according to Ole Anthony, director in Texas of Trinity Foundation, an independent evangelical watchdog group. He is outraged that out of a donor pool of about five million people, 55% are elderly women and roughly one-third belong to society's poorest and neediest." According to him, "the church should be ashamed of allowing these businesses to prey on the elderly, the poor, and the desperate and do it in the name of God." {*The Economist*, 31 May 1997}

ELEPHANT: See entry for Animal.

ELENCHUS

Elenchus is a Greek word that signifies asking questions with a view to determining the cogency or credibility of what a person has said. The procedure was central to Socrates's method of examining the ideas of others, as shown in Plato's early dialogues such as the *Protagoras*. By showing the speaker's confusions, inconsistencies, or other flaws, Socrates was often able to refute the individual's views, resulting in his winning no friends. {OCP}

Elesin, Milan (20th Century)

An atheist in Yugoslavia, Elesin is webmaster for an atheistic group. On the Web: <http://SOLAIR.EUnet.yu/~milane/mses-book.html>.

Elfenbein, Hiram (20th Century)

A freethinker, Elfenbein wrote *Organized Religion: The Greatest Game of Make- Believe* (1968). {GS}

Elfman, Danny (20th Century)

A film score composer and recording artist, Elfman was formerly with the disbanded Oingo Boingo and is best known for his orchestral scores for movies such as "Batman," "Men in Black" and "Mission Impossible." He wrote the opening theme for "The Simpsons," a television series.

"I don't believe in life after death," he told Joshua A. Fruhlinger, adding,

> I kind of hope that there's a Hell. I hope that there's a Heaven and that I'm qualified for Hell. 'Cause that's where I would definitely want to go. You know, if there is a Heaven and a Hell, I hope that involves the Russian plan. I've always loved the Russian version of Hell, where all the writers and the interesting people are gonna spend their time gathering. It's just like this big house in like the middle of somewhere. If there is a Christian version of Heaven, I know I don't want to go there. Awful bad. Jews don't have Heaven and Hell. It's not really part of that way of thinking. If there is any kind of Hell, I would like to think it's along the lines as presented in *Master Margarita*, a Russian novel, and that nails it for me.

{CA}

Eliade, Mircea (Died 1986)

Eliade was a Romanian Unitarian who, after being on the staff of the Sorbonne, became chairman of the Department of History of Religions at the University of Chicago. He was one of the pioneers in the systematic study of the history of religions, showing that the myths and symbols of many early roots of all religions are similar. He wrote *The History of Religious Ideas*, *The Myth of the Eternal Return*, and *The Sacred and the Profane.* Also, he edited the sixteen-volume *Encyclopedia of Religion.*

Eliot, Charles William (1834—1926)

President of Harvard from 1869 to 1909, Eliot edited the *Harvard Classics* (1909—1910). Henry James wrote a biography of the Unitarian Eliot, and Eliot wrote a biography of his son Charles (1859—1897), who planned the park system of Greater Boston. "Thoughtful people," he once wrote, "have dismissed the anthropomorphic idea of God as monarch, king, or Lord of Hosts, with all the imperial and feudal-system ideas of God which have so long prevailed not only among the masses of mankind, but among the intellectual leaders of the race. No ideas about God have changed so much, however, as the ideas about him as creator. . . . No thinking person now accepts as anything but primitive myth or fanciful poetry the story of the Garden of Eden." According to McCabe, Eliot turned from Unitarianism at an early date to the vague pantheism of Emerson. Eliot's *The Happy Life* (1896) states that some religion is necessary but that orthodox religion is impossible. {CE; HNS2; JM; RAT; RE; U; UU}

Eliot, Charlotte Champe Stearns (1843-1929)

A Unitarian, Eliot was the mother of T. S. Eliot, the poet. Her father-in-law was William Greenleaf Eliot, the Unitarian minister and founder of Washington University in St. Louis.

Eliot, Frederick May (1889—1958)

While Frederick May Eliot was President of the American Unitarian Association, its membership grew 75%. He is one of the better-known Unitarian ministers of the first part of the twentieth century. Although some thought he was a humanist, he preached on behalf of a nondogmatic theism, based on an understanding of the word *God* as symbolic of the deepest human needs and strivings. {U; U&U; UU}

Eliot, George (Marian Mary Ann Evans) (1819—1880)

Taking a masculine pseudonym in a time when women had problems in succeeding as writers, Evans wrote *Scenes of Clerical Life* (1858), *Adam Bede* (1859) and *Silas Marner* (1861). In the former, Eliot shows in three tales the hopelessness and helplessness of most private lives. In Chapter 17 of *Adam Bede* she reveals goals for humanity not unlike those of present-day secular humanists. She also demonstrated the demands of a secular morality that for her replaced, and in most respects duplicated, the demands of Christianity's revealed system of morality. Early on in life, she was favorably impressed by the sympathetic treatment of the atheist in Edward Bulwer-Lytton's *Devereaux* (1829), and her philosophic outlook became that of a rationalist. At the age of twenty-two, she refused to accompany her father to church, which has been interpreted both as a sign of her individuality and also of her refusal to be dominated by a male. Evans was encouraged by the brother-in-law, Charles Hennell, of her friend, Charles Bray. Hennell wrote *An Inquiry Concerning the Origin of Christianity* (1838).

"Human affection," she wrote, "is the only power for salvation on this earth." For Evans, Christian dogmas were "dishonorable to God" and pernicious to human happiness. She further showed her freethinking outlook by translating Strauss's famous *Life of Jesus* and Feuerbach's *Essence of Christianity*, the latter being the work of a profound atheist. Foote tells that in a conversation Eliot had with a Mr. Myers, they talked of God, immortality, and duty: she gravely remarked, "How inconceivable the first, how unbelievable the second, and how peremptory and absolute the third."

Germaine Greer, in *The Change: Women, Aging and the Menopause* (1992), cites George Eliot as a woman who, without benefit of plastic surgery, found romance in mid-life and beyond. Eliot once wrote, "If Christianity turned the clock of general progress back a thousand years, it turned back the clock two thousand years for women."

As for her physical appearance, Moncure Conway said she was "a finely-shaped woman, and quite large, though not in the sense in which Hawthorne describes English female largeness. She is by no means corpulent, nor are there any suggestions of steaks and sirloins about her, but she is of large skeleton. She is not meager, either, but has the look of being made out of fine clay. She is blonde, with very light auburn hair; clear, serene, smiling eyes; beautiful teeth. She has also gracious and easy manners, with an undefinable air of unworldliness—of having been made for large and fine societies, but never entered them. In a word, she is a woman who, though not handsome, would personally satisfy her most ardent admirers." Underwood, however, mentions that Eliot was "nervously sensitive as to her lack of beauty and will not on that account consent to sit for any kind of picture."

"The pseudonym of George Eliot," wrote Underwood, "under which she first appeared as a novelist, and the careful assumption of masculinity throughout the pages of *Adam Bede*, while it puzzled and led astray the public as to her identity, did not long deceive as to her sex. The woman's tender heart and keen sense of injustice made palpable the true woman's nature all through her book. Theodore Parker, writing to Frances Power Cobbe in 1859, remarks: 'I am reading *Adam Bede*, a quite extraordinary book. But I wonder that any one should have doubted that a woman wrote it. Strange is it that we tell the universal part of our history in all that we write!'"

When Eliot met George Henry Lewes, who wrote a biography of Goethe, he was married and unable to obtain a divorce, having given his name to his wife's child by another man. He encouraged her to write fiction and for twenty-five years was the person she considered her "true" husband–although not legally married to him, she even took his surname, adding Eliot because it "was a good mouth-filling, easily pronounced word." Not even her publisher was told of the pseudonym, and one of the few who guessed that George Eliot might be a woman was Charles Dickens. The only work she published under her real name was her translation of Feuerbach's *Essence of Christianity* (1854).

When Lewes died of cancer, and only eight months before her own death, Eliot married for the first time. Her husband, John Cross, was twenty years younger. On their honeymoon in Venice, Cross is said to have jumped out of the hotel window, landing in the Grand Canal. He was not injured. Neither ever explained the incident. Gossips, however, spread the rumor that his sixty-year-old wife made too many sexual demands on her husband. As readers of her *Middlemarch* will remember, however, gossip and rumor may be quite powerful forces but are not always to be trusted.

A 1994 television version of Eliot's *Middlemarch*, her penultimate novel, received excellent reviews both in Europe and in America. One of the few negative reviews came from Nicolas Walter, who regretted that as a convinced freethinker Eliot never gave freethought a proper place in any of her books. Louis Menand, writes in a lengthy critique in *The New York Review of Books* (12 May 1944), "Nietzsche thought that what George Eliot wanted was Christian morality without the Christianity. 'They have got rid of the Christian God,' he says of the English in *Twilight of the Idols*, with Eliot in mind, 'and now feel obliged to cling all the more firmly to Christian morality.' He was being contemptuous, of course (and he probably hadn't read any of Eliot's novels); but many other commentators have assumed that Eliot did write her books in order to articulate a post-Christian moral and social philosophy, and they have devoted themselves to the business of deciphering it. It's this idea of Eliot as, in some systematic sense, a moralist that is responsible for the assumption that modern readers (and modern viewers) will find her preachy and dull." Nicolas Walter, commenting upon Rosemary Ashton's *George Eliot: A Life* (1996), termed Eliot "a thorough rationalist." Although she treated religion sympathetically and understood when people turned to the "forms and ceremonies" for comfort, Colin McCall observed, "she preferred "to *do without opium*."

"My childhood," she wrote, "was full of deep sorrows—colic, whooping-cough, dread of ghosts, hell, Satan, and a Deity in the sky who was angry when I ate too much plum-cake." In death, she would no longer have sorrow or, as pointed out in her humanistic poem, "Oh, may I join the choir invisible." She is buried at Highgate in the northern part of London, not far from the grave of Karl Marx and next to the graves of George Jacob Holyoake, Charles Watts, and George Lewes—for a time, Eliot lived with the freethinking Lewes. Eliot's biography, written by her second husband, states that "her long illness in the autumn had left her no power to rally. She passed away about ten o'clock at night on the 22nd of December, 1880. She died, as she would herself have chosen to die, without protracted pain, and with every faculty brightly vigorous. . . . Her body lies in the next grave to that of George Henry Lewes at Highgate Cemetery; her spirit, the product of her life has, in her own words, joined 'the choir invisible, whose music is the gladness of the world.'" Eliot's grave is marked by a simple grey stone obelisk. {CB; CL; CE; EU, Victor N. Paanamen; FO; FUK; JM; JMRH; PUT; RAT; SAU; TRI; TSV; WWS}

Eliot, Maude Howe (1854-1948)

Eliot, the daughter of Julia Ward Howe, was an author, a social reformer, and a Unitarian.

Eliot, Samuel Atkins (1862—1950)

Eliot, the son of Harvard President Charles William Eliot, was elected secretary of the American Unitarian Association in 1898. During his presidency, Unitarians, who emphasized liberal values, became a noted national organization. There is an Eliot Chapel in Kirkwood, Missouri. {FUS; U&U}

Eliot, Thomas Lamb (1841—1936)

After building a strong Unitarian church in Oregon, one of the principal centers of the Pacific Northwest Unitarians, Eliot was a leader in founding Reed College in 1911. {U&U}

Eliot, T(homas) S(tearns) (1888—1965)

Eliot, an American-English poet and critic, was assistant editor of the *Egoist* (1917—1919). His *Prufrock and Other Observations* (1917) and *The Wasteland* (1922) received critical acclaim, expressing as they did the anguish and barrenness of modern life and the isolation of the individual, particularly as reflected in the failure of love.

In 1910 and 1911 in Paris, while he studied at the Sorbonne, Eliot is said to have had a homosexual relationship with Jean Verdenal (1889—1915), who died in battle, after which in 1917 Eliot hurriedly married his first wife, Vivien. In 1927, Eliot espoused Anglo-Catholicism, turning from spiritual desolation to hope for human salvation, accepting religious faith as a solution to the human dilemma. In 1948, he won the Nobel Prize in Literature.

"It's clear that T. S. Eliot was by nature dour," a Harvard psychologist, Dr. Jerome Kagan, has said. The observation was also made in the 1940s by H. Willard Reninger who, at a conference meeting where Eliot had just entered, wryly reported that the room temperature dropped ten degrees. Reninger, however, was an Eliot fan up until the time Eliot moved from his earlier naturalism to an Anglican supernaturalism.

Ezra Pound, as editor of Eliot's *The Waste Land* (1922), recommended cutting the poem "Saint Narcissus," which Gregory Woods of the Nottingham Trent University in England has described as "that peculiar fusion of pagan and Christian imagery that now appears at the end of the *Complete Poems*. Woods noted that Hart Crane, among others, assumed that Eliot was homosexual. Eliot's love for Verdenal is said to be "one of the central facts" of the work, with the so-called Hyacinth girl of the poem's opening section being the poet's sentimental memory of "a friend coming across the Luxembourg Gardens in the late afternoon, waving a branch of lilac." The figure, like Verdenal, dies in a trench, which Eliot describes as, "He who was living is now dead."

Anthony Julius, in *T. S. Eliot, Anti-Semitism, and Literary Form* (1996), depicted Eliot as an anti-Semite whose anti-Semitism is integral to his poetry. "Anti-Semitism," Julius wrote, "did not disfigure Eliot's work, it animated it. It was, on occasion, both his refuge and his inspiration, and his exploitation of its literary potential was virtuous." An example, which manages to insult both Jews (many of whom lived in a North London suburb, Golders Green) and blacks:

> Bolo's big black bastard queen
> Was *so* obscene
> She shocked the folk of Golder's Green.

In an essay collection, *After Strange Gods* (1934), Eliot wrote that "reasons of race and religion combine to make any large numbers of free-thinking Jews undesirable." In later editions he withdrew the statement. (See entries for Alfred Kazin and for Neo-Classical Humanism, which Eliot supported. Also see entry for his Unitarian mother, Charlotte Champe Stearns Eliot.) {CE; James Wood, "After Strange Gods," *The New Republic*, 29 July 1996; GL}

Eliot, William Greenleaf (1811—1887)

Eliot, an early exponent of New England Unitarianism in the Midwest, founded and guided Washington University in St. Louis. He was a major spokesman for a conservative and Christologically-oriented Unitarianism in the West, in opposition to the more radical religion that characterized the Western Unitarian Conference later in the century. {U&U}

Elizabeth I (Queen) (1533—1603)

McCabe says that although many think it a paradox or a strain of evidence to claim monarchs of Christian lands as freethinkers, he feels the Queen of England from 1558 to 1603 was a freethinker, as was Caroline and a number of others. "She studied seriously in youth," he wrote of Queen Elizabeth I, "but she had to make her way cautiously in 'an age that was so brave and beautiful and blackguardly' (as Lynd calls it) because the rival Christians were religious cut-throats. She was, moreover, vigorous and masculine to a degree of coarseness. I am convinced that she belonged to what is now called 'the Third Sex.'"

Green in his standard *Short History of the English People* (Ch. viii, 83), says that "no (other) woman who ever lived was so totally destitute of the sentiment of religion." Professor Pollard says in his authoritative *Political History of England* (VI, p. 180) that "it can hardly be doubted that she was skeptical or indifferent." "She was a humane ruler," concludes McCabe, "until Catholic plots forced her to change her policy." But, he adds, "Her persecution of Catholics was not religious in motive. She held to a policy of toleration until the Catholics began to plot against her. The suggestion of some that her 'virginity' implies religious belief is frivolous and is excluded by the boisterous vulgarity of her character. An application to her case of our modern knowledge of the glands might solve that problem." {JM; JMRH; RE}

Elkin, E. H. (20th Century)

Elkin, from the United Kingdom, was on the first Board of Directors of the International Humanist and Ethical Union (IHEU).

Ellerbe, Helen (20th Century)

Ellerbe's *The Dark Side of Christian History* (1995) discussed the origins of Christianity, how out of persecution it became the state religion of the Roman Empire, and how it commenced persecuting others. The author, in passing, stated that her book "is in no way intended to diminish the beautiful work that countless Christian men and women have done to truly help others."

Ellerbee, Linda (1944—)

Ellerbee, a broadcast journalist, has been a newscaster, a disc jockey, a program director, a reporter, a co-anchor, and commentator. For NBC-TV, she was a reporter for the "Today Show" and co-anchor for "Weekend NBC News." She has written *And So It Goes: Adventures in Television* (1986) and *Move On: Adventures in the Real World* (1991). According to Atheist Celebrities on the internet, Ellerbee is a non-believer. {E}

Ellero, Pietro (1833—1914)

Ellero was an Italian jurisconsult, a counselor of the High Court of Rome and a professor of criminal law in the University of Bologna. His *Scritti Minori, Scritti Politici*, and *La Question Sociale* were all placed on the Vatican's *Index*. {BDF}

Elliot, Hugh Samuel Roger (Born 1881)

A scientific writer, Elliot translated Lamarck's *Philosophie Zoologique* (1914), edited the *Letters of J. S. Mill* (1910), and wrote *Modern Science and the Illusions of Professor Bergson* (1912). Elliot rejected agnosticism as inadequate and urged the adoption of "scientific materialism." {RAT}

Elliotson, John (1791—1868)

A physician at St. Thomas's Hospital in 1822, Elliotson made many contributions to medical science. By new prescriptions of quinine and creosote, he excited some hostility in the profession. He was the first in England to advocate the use of the stethoscope. He also was one of the first physicians to discard knee-breeches and silk stockings and to wear a beard. In 1831 he was chosen professor at University College but, becoming an advocate of curative mesmerism, resigned his appointments in 1838. He was founder and President of the London Phrenological Society, edited *Zoist* (13 volumes), translated Blumenbach's *Physiology*, and defended materialism. Thackeray dedicated *Pendennis* to him, and Elliotson also received a tribute of praise from Dickens. {BDF; RAT}

Elliott, Ebenezer (1781—1849)

Elliott was a radical poet whose anniversary was often celebrated by English freethinkers. {GS}

Elliott, Elizabeth (20th Century)

Elliott has been a major benefactor in the acquisition of Freethought Hall, the Freedom From Foundation's national office in Madison, Wisconsin. The hall's library is named in her honor.

Elliott, John Lovejoy (1868—1942)

In 1895, Elliott founded New York's Hudson Guild. He was instrumental in the founding of the National Association for the Advancement of Colored People (NAACP). Elliott served with Norman Thomas, Roger Baldwin, and John Haynes Holmes in the Civil Liberties Union (1917), which later became the American Civil Liberties Union (ACLU). With Eleanor Roosevelt's help, he started the Good Neighbor Committee, to give economic assistance to refugees coming from Europe. Elliott, in short, was a freethinker and a doer. James F. Hornbach has described Elliott as being "a warm farm boy from the civil-libertarian Illinois Lovejoys and Ingersoll-supporting Elliotts." (See entry for Ethical Culture.) {EU, Howard B. Radest}

Elliott, Maud Howe (1854—1948)

Elliott, the daughter of Julia Ward Howe, attended Unitarian services.

Elliott, Sarah Barnwell (1848—1928)

Elliott, a Georgia-born novelist, wrote *Felmers*, a novel depicting the conflict between rationalism and Christianity, an unusual theme in 1879. Her *Jerry* (1891) described the Tennessee mountain people with whom she lived most of her life.

Ellis, Albert (1913—)

Ellis, a noted clinical psychologist who founded and is the executive director of the Institute of Advanced Study in Rational-Emotive Therapy, signed Humanist Manifesto II. He is a contributing editor to *Free Inquiry*. In 1966, he wrote *Sex Without Guilt*. In 1989 with Raymond J. Yeager, he co-authored *Why Some Therapies Don't Work, the Dangers of Transpersonal Psychology*. In addition he has written more than fifty books for professional and popular audiences. "If devout religiosity, therefore, is often masochism," he has written, "it is even more often dependency. For humans to be true believers and to also be strong and independent is well nigh impossible. Religiosity and self-sufficiency are contradictory terms. . . . According to orthodox religious *shalts* and *shalt nots*, you become not only a *wrong-doer*, but an arrant *sinner* when you commit ethical and religious misdeeds; and, as a sinner, you become worthless, undeserving of any human happiness, and deserving of being forever damned (excommunicated) on earth and perhaps roasted eternally in hell." "The more sinful and guilty a person tends to feel," he wrote in his role as a psychotherapist, "the less chance there is that he will be a happy, healthy, law-abiding citizen. . . . He will become a compulsive wrongdoer." In *Case Against Religiosity*, Ellis declares that "devout theists often ignore, deny, and hallucinate about reality; and the more devout they are—as the long history of religion shows—the more delusionary and hallucinatory they seem to be." In 1971, he was named Humanist of the Year by the American Humanist Association. In 1980, he signed the Secular Humanist Declaration. Dr. Ellis, who is on the editorial board of *The Humanist*, is an honorary member of the Secular Humanist Society of New York. (See "Why I Am a Secular Humanist, An Interview with Albert Ellis," *Free Inquiry*, Summer 1997). {cA; E; HM2; HNS2; SHD; TYD; WAS, conversations}

Ellis, Alfred Burdon (1852—1894)

A writer, Ellis entered the army and served in the Ashanti and Zulu wars. In 1878 he became District Commissioner at Quettah, and in 1892 he was made a colonel. His long stay in West Africa allowed him to make a thorough study of native life and languages, and his works on the religions of the Gold and slave coasts are of historical importance. {RAT}

Ellis, Bret Easton (20th Century)

Ellis wrote *Less than Zero* (1980) and *American Psycho*, the latter a controversial novel that led Robert Love of *Rolling Stone* (4 April 1991) to ask him if he believed in God. Ellis responded, "No, I don't believe in God. That's such a strange thing to admit in an interview." {CA}

Ellis, Brian David (1929—)

Ellis, an Australian rationalist and philosopher, has taught at La Trobe University since 1966. A member of the Rationalist Society of Australia, he wrote *Rational Belief Systems* (1979) and *Truth and Objectivity* (1990). {SWW}

Ellis, Charles (20th Century)

Ellis wrote *"Christian" and "Mormon" Doctrines of God* (1902). {GS}

Ellis, Donald Geoffrey de Vere (1926—1990)

Ellis was an Australian rationalist, humanist, and public servant. He was a member of the Rationalist Association of Southern Australia before the name changed to Atheist Foundation of Australia in 1970. He was a joint founder in 1962 of the Humanist Society of South Australia. Ellis also was president of Keep Our State Schools Secular (KOSSS), the Skeptics, and co-founder of the South Australia Voluntary Euthanasia Society. {SWW}

Ellis, H(enry) Havelock (1859—1929)

Sometimes called "the Darwin of sex," Ellis was an English freethinker and psychologist who espoused open marriage. In "Impressions and Comments," he wrote,

> Had there been a Lunatic Asylum in the suburbs of Jerusalem, Jesus Christ would infallibly have been shut up in it at the outset of his public career. That interview with Satan on a pinnacle of the Temple would alone have damned him, and everything that happened after could have confirmed the diagnosis. The whole religious complexion of the modern world is due to the absence from Jerusalem of a Lunatic Asylum.

When at the age of thirty-two the bisexual and (then) impotent Ellis married novelist and manic-depressive Edith Lees, both were virgins. They maintained separate living quarters for six months a year, kept their finances separate, and agreed to have sex outside the marriage. In her six-month "vacation," his wife took up with a lesbian. . . . In 1898, a British bookseller was arrested for selling Ellis's *Sexual Inversion* (1897), inasmuch as sex was considered a forbidden subject in publishing then. In 1928 his *Studies in the Psychology of Sex* (1897—1928) was so controversial that in the U.S. only doctors could purchase it. However, many of his views are commonplace today: The male reaches a peak of sexual activity at a lower age than the female; masturbation is common as well as harmless; women have multiple orgasms; older people are sexually responsive; before adolescence, children are sexually aware and act as sexual beings; women become frigid mostly because they are repressed when young and because men don't know how to make love effectively.

When he was sixty, Françoise Cyon brought Havelock out of his impotency, but he could not afford to have her move in with him. Fortunately, Margaret Sanger offered her a salary as Ellis's secretary, leading to two decades of their relative bliss. Sanger had been a sex partner, as had poet H. D. (Hilda Doolittle), who was intrigued that Ellis enjoyed watching her urinate.

Ellis helped reform the prevalent repressive attitudes toward sex in his day, foreshadowing the women's liberation movement. He coined the terms "narcissistic" and "autoerotic" and asked the kinds of questions that in the eighteenth century had been asked by Diderot and Voltaire. "There is a very intimate connection between hypnotic phenomena and religion," he wrote in *Impressions and Comments* (1914). His agnosticism is shown in *Affirmations* (1897) and *My Life* (published 1940). {CE; HNS2; JM; PA; RAT; TRI; TYD}

Ellis, J. Spencer (Born 1838)

Spencer, whose father was a Congregational minister and whose mother was a pious Christian lady, found freethought through his elder brother, **J. Harris Ellis**. Harris was a friend of G. J. Holyoake, Robert Cooper, and other freethought leaders. Spencer secured a job on the London *Times* for thirteen years, then moved in 1876 to Toronto where he became printer of *Secular Thought*. At an 1891 freethought convention in Canada, Ellis was made its editor. He lectured on freethought in principal Canadian cities. {FUK; PUT}

Ellis, Royston (1941—)

A British-born poet, novelist, and travel author, Ellis left England in 1962, dropped out of school, performed poetry with rock groups such as Cliff Richard and the Shadows (whose first biography he wrote), then with The Beatles before they became famous. He appeared on television and stage with a guitarist called Jimmy Page, who eventually led Led Zeppelin. In the 1960's he lived first in the Canary Islands (the setting of his first novel, *The Flesh Merchants*). From 1966 to 1980, he lived in Dominica, Windward Islands (setting of his million-copy bestsellers such as the historical novel, *The Bondmaster*, which he wrote as Richard Tresillian). Since 1980 he has lived in Sri Lanka and covered the Indian Ocean by writing guide books. *India By Rail* (1993), an insider's view, tells how 7,000 trains operate throughout India. He also has written *The Story of Tea* as well as travel books and articles about Mauritius, Sri Lanka, and the Maldives.

Steve Turner, in *Cliff Richard, The Biography* (1993), describes how as a sixteen-year-old Ellis left school and toured with the Beatles—Ellis suggested the spelling (not Beetles, which they had chosen), convincing them they were part of the Beats, the individuals who were unfairly being beaten down because they were unconventional. At performances, the Beatles provided the music and Ellis provided the rocketry (poetry read to rock 'n' roll). He showed John Lennon and Paul McCartney how to break down a Benzedrine nose inhaler and sniff the strips inside to produce a mild high. This was, Lennon later recounted, their first experience with drugs. The Beatles immortalized him in the song "Paperback Writer."

Only eighteen years old, Royston wrote *Driftin' With Cliff*, in which he described life on the road with Britain's top pop singer, Cliff Richard. Turner described Royston as

> . . . Britain's first teenage pundit, an Allen Ginsberg of suburban London. The fact that he wore a beard and had worked as an office boy, duster salesman, gardener, milk-bottle washer, building labourer, and farm hand by the age of eighteen helped confirm the image. . . . His first volume of poems, *Jiving to Gyp*, was dedicated [to Cliff Richard], and he was soon asked by television programmes to explain what teenagers were all about. He ended up with his own series, "Living For Kicks," in which he explored the controversial issues of the day such as pep pills and sex before marriage.

Ellis. a cogent musical commentator—his 1961 paperback *The Big Beat Scene* still stands up as an appraisal of early British rock 'n' roll—met the fledgling Beatles (in May 1960). "The first time we ever heard about gayness was when a poet named Royston Ellis arrived in Liverpool with his book *Jiving With Gyp*," McCartney has recalled. "He was a Beat poet. Well, well! Phew! You didn't meet them in Liverpool. And it was all 'Break me in easy, break me in easy . . . .' It was all shagging sailors, I think. We had a laugh with that line."

"One in every four men is homosexual," Ellis told McCartney, according to Barry Miles's *Paul McCartney* (1998):

> So we looked at the group! One in every four! It literally meant one of us is gay. Oh, fucking hell, it's not me, is it? We had a lot of soul-searching to do over that little one.

The "one" was their manager, Brian Epstein, who in 1962 signed a management contract with them for twenty-five per cent of their gross receipts, after a certain threshold was reached and after he got them a recording contract.

McCartney's biographer adds the following:

> "Polythene Pam" was another of John's songs written in India and originally destined for the White Album. It was inspired by Stephanie, a girlfriend of the Beat poet Royston Ellis, whom the Beatles backed at Liverpool University in 1960. On 8 August 1963, the Beatles played at the Auditorium in Guernsey, the Channel Islands. Royston Ellis was working as a ferryboat engineer on the island and invited John to come back to his flat. John told *Playboy*: "I had a girl and he had one he wanted me to meet. He said she dressed up in polythene, which she did. She didn't wear jackboots and kilts, I just sort of elaborated. Perverted sex in a polythene bag. Just looking for something to write about." Royston Ellis told Steve Turner: "We all dressed up in them and wore them in bed. John stayed the night with us in the same bed." Paul remembered meeting Royston in Guernsey: "John, being Royston's friend, went out to dinner with him and got pissed and stuff and they ended up back at his apartment with a girl who dressed herself in polythene for John's amusements, so it was a little kinky scene. She became Polythene Pam. She was a real character." John: "When I recorded it I used a thick Liverpool accent because it was supposed to be about a mythical Liverpool scrubber dressed up in her jackboots and kilt."

Under the pseudonym Richad Tressillian, Ellis became a best-selling author of The Bondmaster series—over a million copies were sold of the paperbacks with a historical background and a description of the lives and loves of 19th century West Indian whites and the workers on their estates. Under the same pseudonym he wrote a best-selling series, Fleshtraders, again about 19th century miscegenation and adventures but this time set in Mauritius. In Dominica, in addition to being the real estate developer for the Marquis of Brisol and a Reuters correspondent, he edited *The Educator*, a journal favorable to the Premier, Edward LeBlanc.

In 1983, some of his poetry was included in *The Penguin Book of Homosexual Verse*, poems from his "Cherry Boy." He has written extensively about railroads in Sri Lanka and is known for his definitive guide to railroads in Southeast Asia and for his travel guidebook about Mauritius.

A Man for All Islands (1998) is a biography of Maumoon Abdul Gayroom, President of the Maldives. With photographer Gemunu Amarasinghe, he wrote *A Maldives Celebration*. An autobiographical work, *Toni the Maldive Lady: My Story* (1999), written with Ellis's help, is by and about a British lady who considers all Maldivians her family and sends books to libraries in the islands.

Asked in 1991 about humanism, Ellis wrote,

> Since the age of 14, I have not known exactly what I am, nor do I care, having decided at the age of 14 that it was not god who created man but man who created god. My first book, *Jiving to Gyp* (gyp means hell) published when I was 18, contained raunchy atheistic poems.

Ellis lectures on *Queen Elizabeth II* trips from Bombay to Singapore, he writes extensively, and he is a Life Fellow of the Royal Commonwealth Society. A photo and article, "England's Ginsberg," was featured in *Gay and Lesbian Humanist* (Autumn 1999).

(Cliff Richard, parenthetically, became a born-again Christian.)
{WAS, 11 September 1991 and numerous conversations}

Ellis, Sallie (Born 1835)

Ellis, a Unitarian, began what she called the Post Office Mission. {U}

Ellis, Thomas (19th Century)

In the 1870s, Ellis was an active leader in England of Manchester's Lancashire Secular Union. {RSR}

Ellis, Warren (20th Century)

A British comics writer, Ellis has credits that range from mainstream works such as Marvel's *Excalibur* to more adult-oriented fare such as *Transmetropolitan*, the latter work featuring a character inspired by Gonzo journalist Hunter S. Thompson. As for why Marvel decided to abort a project entitled "Last Gasp," which he had been writing, Ellis explained, "Something bad was going to happen [in the story]. It grew out of my atheism, my hate, and, curiously, my little-seen optimism." {CE}

Ellis, William (1794—1872)

A nonconformist missionary sent to Polynesia in 1816, Ellis in his *Tour Through Hawaii or Owhyhee* (1827) includes the following glimpse of a society Robertson suggests Lucretius would have liked: "We asked [the natives] who was their God. They said they had no God; formerly they had had many: but now they had cast them all away. We asked them if they had done well in abolishing them. They said 'Yes,' for tabu had occasioned much labour and inconvenience, and drained off the best of their property. We asked them if it was a good thing to have no God. . . . They said perhaps it was; for they had nothing to provide for the great sacrifices, and were under no fear of punishment for breaking tabu; that now one fire cooked their food, and men and women ate together the same kind of provisions." {CE; JMR; JMRH; RAT}

Ellis, William (1800—1881)

Ellis was a philanthropist who began work as a clerk at the age of fourteen and rose to the position of chief manager of the Indemnity Marine Insurance Company. Inspired by the works of J. S. Mill, whose "idealist agnosticism" he shared, Ellis founded nine Birkbeck Schools in England at his own expense and wrote textbooks for them. At one time, he gave lessons to the royal children at Buckingham Palace. Ellis was a friend of Holyoake and helped in a wide range of social reforms. {RAT; RE}

Ellis-Hagler, Elizabeth (20th Century)

Ellis-Hagler is vice president of the Unitarian Universalist Service Committee.

Ellison, Harlan Jay (1934)

"The two most common elements in the universe," Ellison wrote in an entry for *Who's Who in America*, "are hydrogen and stupidity." The author's 5" entry in that work lists books (64 are noted), numbers of scripts for television, films, short stories, mysteries, computer games, and science fiction works. Ellison was scenarist for "I, Robot" (1978), and his various works have been credited as inspiration for The Terminator. Ellison, who is highly regarded by other science fiction authors, has gone on record as being a non-theist. "I am so far beyond atheism," Ellison the essayist wrote, "there isn't a word in the English language dictionary to describe me." {CA; E}

Ellison, Ralph Waldo (1914-1994)

Ellison's semi-autobiographical account of a young black intellectual's search for identity was *Invisible Man* (1952). The work won him the National Book Award, the Presidential Medal of Freedom, a seat in the American Academy of Arts and Letters, and a position as the Albert Schweitzer Professor of Humanities at New York University that netted him one of the largest salaries received by any English teacher at the time.

On the one hand, *Invisible Man* has been seen by some as showing a character that is *only* seen as an incarnation of his race, a person battered about by both blacks and whites who impose their visions of racial identity on him, a person whom people physically but not humanistically see. One critic, Edward Rothstein (*The New York Times*, 16 May 1999), sees Ellison as portraying and defending American ideals, as seeking some way "to reveal the nature of America's racial trauma without being either political or prescriptive," not as an "Uncle Tom" or careerist who produced "obsequious bleatings of white appeasement."

His second novel was to have been the story of a "little boy of indefinite race who looks white and who, through a series of circumstances, comes to the reared by [a] Negro minister," a person who eventually grew up to become a virulently racist United States senator. In 1967, however, a fire at his summer house burned the 360 pages he had finished—he had no duplicate copy. Ellison understandably was devastated.

Juneteenth, a 2,000-page manuscript that Ellison left at the time of his death, was edited by his literary executor, John Callahan. A *New Yorker* excerpt (12 April 1999) tells how the novel's narrative "alternates between the old minister's lyrical recounting of the events of the past and the senator's feverish, dreamlike reminiscences. . . . [T]he senator remembers his life in the late nineteen-twenties, the period between his black childhood and his white adulthood, during which he travelled through the Southwest, posing as a professional filmmaker, and had a brief but intense affair with an Oklahoma girl." Below, a dreamlike scene in which the former minister is on a picnic date with "a teasing brown," a light-skinned girl:

> A bee danced by as on a thread. I felt a suspension of time. Standing still, my eyes in the tree of blossoms, I let it move through me. Eden, I thought, Eden is a lie that never was. And Adam? His name was Snake. And Eve's? An aphrodisiac best served with raw fresh oysters on the half shell with a good white wine. The spirit's there. . . . She arose she rose she rose up from the waves.

Ellison did not go clearly on record as to his belief or non-belief in any organized religion.

Ellsworth, Will (20th Century)

Ellsworth wrote "Coping With Hate in America" in *HSH News*, newsletter of Houstonians for Secular Humanism (December 1998). Less than five percent of those found guilty of hate crimes, according to his research, were members of organized hate groups.

Elo, Pekka (20th Century)

Elo edits the quarterly magazine, *Humanisti* (Vallikatu B.A.I., SF 02600 Espoa, Finland) of the Humanist Union of Finland, where he is Director of Ethical Education. He spoke about ethical education in schools at the 1995 conference of humanists and atheists in India. E-mail: <pekka.elo@oph.fi>. {*New Humanist*, February 1996}

Elphinstone, Mountstuart [The Honourable] (1779—1859)

Elphinstone, a statesman, served in Nagpur, Poona, Bombay, and elsewhere. He was one of England's more enlightened and conscientious administrators in India or, as described in the *Dictionary of National Biography*, "It is remarkable that a man so *sceptical*, retiring, unselfish, and modest should be one of the chief founders of the Anglo-Indian Empire." Elphinstone, a deist, wrote *History of the Hindu and Muhammadan Periods*. {RAT}

Éluard, Paul (1895—1952)

A poet and leading exponent of surrealism, Éluard was a member of the French resistance in World War II. A humanist, he wrote *Mourir de na pas mourir* (To die of not dying, 1924) and, with André Bréton, *L'Immaculée Conception,* 1930). {CE}

Elvin, Diana (20th Century)

Elvin has encouraged the formation of small humanist groups throughout England. "You don't need many people for a house group," she has written. "Get any two or three Humanists together and they'll start a discussion." {*The Freethinker*, June 1996}

Elvin, Lionel (1905—)

Elvin in 1965 became president of the Humanist Teachers Association. In 1986, he was elected an honorary associate of the British Rationalist Press Association. He has directed the University of London's Institute of Education.

"I was brought up in a Bible-Christian home," Elvin wrote in *New Humanist* (November 1994), adding the following:

> But there was discussion, especially about the Sunday sermons, and discussion leads to questions. (Perhaps that was what Santayana had in mind when he said that Protestantism was half-way between Catholicism and Atheism.) My first serious question came when I was in elementary school during the First World War. A visiting parson had led the school in prayer and had called out, 'God, damn the Germans!' The God I had been told about in my pacifist home had said, 'Love your enemies.' Both could not be right. Which was?
>
> A few years later I decided to read about religion systematically. The result was that by the time I went up to Cambridge I had given up all religious belief. After ten years as a Fellow of my college and five as Principal of Ruskin College, I became Director of the Educational Department of UNESCO. That deepened my feeling that you could find good people (and ones that were not so good) pretty well irrespective of their avowed beliefs or disbeliefs, for my colleagues were of every kind. It also made it clearer than ever to me that to hold that one god (your own) was the one true one and the others false was less reasonable than to see all supposed gods as mythical expressions of man's subjective hopes and fears.
>
> I came back to England to be a Professor and then Director of the London University Institute of Education, and I took a vigorous part in the debate about religion in the publicly maintained schools. Many seriously committed Christians (who are in a minority in this country now) are fighting a desperate rearguard action to keep a hold on the minds of the young through the schools. They will fail. We have too many religions now. And few even nominally religious parents will tell their young that they will go to Mr. Patten's Hell if they do not behave properly. Neither they nor their children believe there is a Hell now.
>
> But many of this large middle group have a feeling that in some vague way religious education may help their children to be morally good. (A study of the history of religions and their wars and oppressions ought to lead them to doubt that.) How believing that one person is three persons and vice-versa, or that an ordinary wafer and a drop of wine can become the actual body of someone long since dead, can help you to lead a better life is not exactly clear. Nevertheless, this is where our fight lies. If we can show people that morality does not depend on holding beliefs that cannot be rationally defended we shall do much to free coming generations from religions that, although they may have tolerant adherents, have in their institutional and popular forms led to terrible fanaticism and cruelty.

Elvin signed Humanist Manifesto 2000. {TRI}

ELYSIUM

• Elysium, n. An imaginary delightful country which the ancients foolishly believed to be inhabited by the spirits of the good. This ridiculous and mischievous fable was swept off the face of the earth by the early Christians—may their souls be happy in Heaven!

—Ambrose Bierce
The Devil's Dictionary

E-MAIL

Electronic mailing over the Intertnet, known as E-mail and available only toward the end of the century, has been widely used by international freethinkers. For example, listed below are some humanist magazines and their e-mail addresses:

AAH Examiner (United States of America)
cfiflynn@aol.com

American Atheist Newsletter
aanews@atheists.org

American Atheist
fzindler@atheists.org

American Rationalist rsslbarb@aol.com

Ateo (Italy) uaarpd@tin.it

Atheist Coalition (USA) lekkerspikkels@msn.com

Botulf-bladet (Sweden) christiaan.vos@vasteras.mail.telia.com

Canadian Humanist News hac@magi.com

De Vrije Gedachte (The Netherlands) DVG@netcetera.netcetera.nl

Diesseits (Germany) hvdberlin@aol.com

Espace de Libertés (Belgium) espace@cal.ulb.ac.be

Europe et Laicité (France) eurolaic@club-internet.fr

Family Matters (USA) familynews@secularhumanism.org

Family of Humanists (USA) lloydk@teleport.com

Focus (USA) rca001@aol.com

Free Inquiry (USA) freeinquiry@secularhumanism.org

Free Mind (USA) humanism@juno.com

Freethinker (United Kingdom) jim.rpa@humanism.org.uk

Frettabref Sidmenntar (Iceland) hopeful@islandia.is

Fri Tanke (Sweden) gunnar.staldal@stockholm.mail.telia.com

Fritänkeren (Norway) fritanke@human.no

Gay and Lesbian Humanist (United Kingdom) galha@bigfoot.com

Greater Philadelphia Story (USA) downey1@cris.com

Het Vrije Woord (Belgium) human@glo.be

HIVOS Magazine (The Netherlands) hivos@hivos.nl

Humanism Scotland ahenness@aol.com

Humanist (USA) *thehumanist@juno.com*

Humanist (The Netherlands) hv@euronet.nl

Humanist (Norway) humanist@human.no

Humanist Association of Canada Newsletter cb787@freenet.carleton.ca

Humanist in Canada jepiercy@cyberus.ca

Humanist Outlook (India) pnarain@ignca.ernet.in

Humanist Viewpoints (Australia) jtendys@triode.net.au

Humanisten (Sweden) mikael.goransson@migor.se

Humanisti (Finland) pekka.elo@oph.fi

Humanity (United Kingdom) robert@humanism.org.uk

Humanus (Norway) skaara@human.no

International Humanist News jim.rpa@humanism.org.uk

Kristall (Germany) ortrun.e.lenz@t-online.de

Les Idées en Mouvement (France) info-lligue@ligue.cie.fr

Libero Pensiero (Italy) roberto.laferla@agora.stm.it

Modern Rationalist(India) periyar@giasmd01.vsnl.net.in

New Humanist (United Kingdom) jim.rpa@humanism.org.uk

New Zealand Humanist iain-middleton@clear.net.nz

New Zealand Rationalist and Humanist bill@freethought.org.nz

Philo (USA) fivaughn@aol.com

Praktische Humanistick (The Netherlands) swp@pi.net

Radical Humanist (India) mrcssc@bom2.vsnl.net.in

Reasonings (USA) mbr@execpc.com

Rekenschap (The Netherlands) hv@euronet.nl

Revista Peruana de Filosofia Aplicada (Peru) rpfa@geocities.com

Secular Humanist Bulletin (USA) shb-editor@secularhumanism.org

Secular Nation (USA) mac@mtn.org

Secularist (India) freedom@bom3.vsnl.net.in

Skeptical Inquirer (USA) skeptinq@aol.com

SOS International News Letter (USA) sosla@loop.com

South Australian Humanist Post rmc@adelaide.on.net

Stargazer, Starwalker, Sunrise Journal (USA) lloydk@teleport.com

UCOS Nieuwsbrief (Belgium) lawauter@vub.ac.be

Van Menss tot Mens (The Netherlands) info@lb.humanitas.nl

Vapaa-ajattelija (Finland) val@val.pp.fi

Victorian Humanist (Australia) leeman@connexus.apana.org.au

WisselKrant (The Netherlands) hv@euronet.nl

EMANATIONISM

Emanationism, as illustrated in the work of Plotinus, is opposed both to evolutionism and creationism. Through emanation, the Godhead was thought to have originated the world by a series of hierarchically descending radiations through intermediate stages to matter. The idea has been obliterated by evolutionism in contemporary times. {See *Encyclopedia of Philosophy*, Vol. 2.}

EMBALMING

• Embalm, v.t. To cheat vegetation by locking up the gases upon which it feeds. By embalming their dead and thereby deranging the natural balance between animal and vegetable life, the Egyptians made their once fertile and populous country barren and incapable of supporting more than a meagre crew. The modern metallic burial casket is a step in the same direction, and many a dead man who ought now to be ornamenting his neighbor's lawn as a tree, or enriching his table as a bunch of radishes, is doomed to a long inutility. We shall get him after awhile if we are spared, but in the meantime the violet and rose are languishing for a nibble at his *glutoeus maximus*.

—Ambrose Bierce
The Devil's Dictionary

The American funeral industry, according to Jessica Mitford, justified the necessity of embalming dead bodies to guard public health. However,

Dr. Jesse Carr, the chief of pathology at San Francisco General Hospital and professor of pathology at the University of California Medical School explained to her "that in cases of communicable disease, a dead body presents considerably less hazard than a live one. 'There are several advantages to being dead,' he said cheerfully. 'You don't excrete, inhale, exhale, or perspire.' " Mitford also quoted a Canadian health minister who stated unequivocally, "Embalming serves no useful purpose in preventing the transmission of communicable diseases." There was also no law to enforce it. As a result of her book, the Federal Trade Commission Consumer Protection Bureau attempted to regulate the funeral industry. Lobbyists intervened to thwart their efforts, but one ruling stuck, that it is "a deceptive act or practice for a funeral provider" in any way to imply that embalming is legally required. (See entry for Jessica Mitford) {A. Alvarez, *The New York Review of Books*, 24 September 1998}

Emberland, Terje (20th Century)

Emberland is the editor of the Norwegian *Humanist.*

Emerling, Michael (20th Century)

Emerling, a freethinker, wrote *Theistic Objections: An Autopsy* (1972). {GS}

Emerson, Alfred E. (Born 1896)

An entomologist, zoologist at the University of Chicago, and an editor of *Ecology*, Emerson wrote the present author concerning humanism:

> Of the various aspects of 'Humanism' defined in the mimeographed sheets recently sent me, I find myself in essential accord with NATURALISTIC HUMANISM but I have reservations about the others and would be opposed to some such as COMMUNISTIC HUMANISM. I hope the modern Humanist groups are not trying to reconcile everything ever called Humanistic.
>
> Not only would I subscribe to a philosophy based upon Naturalism as contrasted to Supernaturalism, but I would also emphasize the creative and self-correcting aspects of scientific knowledge applied to all fields of human enquiry. We certainly do not yet have all the answers and I see no possibility of absolute knowledge through modern science or any other method of gaining knowledge.
>
> I thus see a never-ending increase in knowledge and understanding, but I see no end to this pursuit. Although I see no end, I do see trends and progress, as you may detect in the article in *The Scientific Monthly* (February 1954) entitled, "Dynamic Homeostasis: A Unifying Principle in Organic, Social, and Ethical Evolution."
>
> {WAS, 12 May 1956}

Emerson, Gloria (20th Century)

"Father, forgive. They know not what they do."

Emerson reacted this way in the 1960s upon learning in Vietnam as a *New York Times* reporter that fellow Americans had started bombing Hanoi. Shocked, she ran through the streets in the middle of the night. Then, she recalled, I ran through the streets in the middle of the night and "I wrote on the wall in Magic Marker, 'Father, forgive. They know not what they do.' And I don't even believe in God." {Hendrik Hertzberg, "The Sixties," *The New Yorker*, 9 Aug 1999}

Emerson, Goldwin (20th Century)

Emerson, a retired professor of education at the University of Western Ontario, wrote "God and the Mosquito," in which he shows that the religionists' "argument by design" has the benefit of simplicity but "is overly simplistic and generates more questions than it answers." {*Humanist in Canada*, Winter 1998-1999}

Emerson, Mary Moody (1774-1863)

A Unitarian, Emerson was a writer whose unpublished works foreshadowed the ideas of her nephew, Ralph Waldo Emerson.

Emerson, Ralph Waldo (1803—1882)

Emerson, the third of six sons (two sisters died in early childhood), was greatly influenced in his youth by his father's sister, Mary Moody Emerson, who was 4' 3" tall and slept in a coffin-shaped bed. She was, he felt, "the best writer in Massachusetts," and his manuscript of her letters and his recording of their conversations totaled 870 pages.

Although his father was nonreligious, a Unitarian minister, his aunt was a "deistic pietist" whose motto was "Always do what you are afraid to do." She came to disapprove of her nephew's ideas, but from her he learned to think for himself. His mother, widowed when Emerson was eight, ran a boardinghouse to keep her five children out of poverty. Waldo, as he was called, did not seem destined for greatness, and at Harvard he graduated thirtieth in a class of fifty-nine. He suffered from eye trouble and had early symptoms of tuberculosis.

As pointed out by Carlos Baker, an Episcopalian, in *Emerson Among the Eccentrics* (1996), the kindly, self-controlled man with unusual friends had a hellish youth. His father died when Emerson was eight. His young wife, Ellen, died after their eighteen months of marriage; his brothers had traces of madness and died young. He proposed by letter to his second wife, Lydia Jackson, later confessing he knew he could never have written the kind of romantic love letter she wanted. Baker's book, about the thinkers and hangers-on who surrounded Emerson, is consummate in its details.

A careful journal-keeper, he included whose work he read (his transcendentalism was inspired by Coleridge, Wordsworth, and Carlyle), quotations he liked, and arguments he worked out. He looked into the mystical writings of Pythagoras, Plotinus, Schelling, Schleiermacher, Swedenborg, and Böhme, and he read from Chinese, Indian, and Persian religious literature. By writing his comments into the journal, which amounted to some 263 volumes of observations, anecdotes, epiphanies, and dreams that totaled more than 3,000,000 words, he was aided in remembering ideas and constructing new essays.

In his journal are described the personal losses which so affected him—his wife Ellen died in 1831; his brother Charles died in 1836, and two of his other siblings died in childhood, one having been retarded from birth; his son Waldo died in 1842. His second marriage, to Lydia Jackson in 1835, resulted in her calling him Mr. Emerson. Robert D. Richardson Jr.'s *Emerson: The Mind on Fire* (1995) implies that Lydia treated him coolly but loved him greatly. The journals also describe his closeness to Margaret Fuller and to Caroline Sturgis, leading Richardson to speculate, without specifics, that "in the early 1840s Emerson was living emotionally, though not physically, in what would now be called an open marriage."

A Unitarian minister (1829 to 1832) and a leading transcendentalist along with Coleridge, Emerson believed in humankind's need to think independently. At the Second Church of Boston, he left because of some differences with his congregation—he demanded that he *not* be required to administer "the silly Lord's Supper." Following is an excerpt from one of his final sermons, delivered on 9 September 1832:

> The Lord's Supper
>
> Having recently given particular attention to this subject, I was led to the conclusion that Jesus did not intend to establish an institution for perpetual observance when he ate the Passover with his disciples; and, further, to the opinion, that it is not expedient to celebrate it as we do. I shall now endeavor to state distinctly my reasons for these two opinions.

I. The authority of the rite

What did [the expression "this do in remembrance of me"] really signify? . . . . I see natural feeling and beauty in the use of such language from Jesus, a friend to his friends; I can readily imagine that he was willing and desirous, when his disciples met, his memory should hallow their intercourse; but I cannot bring myself to believe that in the use of such an expression he looked beyond the living generation, beyond the abolition of the festival he was celebrating, and the scattering of the nation, and meant to impose a memorial feast upon the whole world. . . . But still it may be asked, why did Jesus make expressions so extraordinary and emphatic as these — "This is my body which is broken for you. Take; eat. This is my blood which is shed for you. Drink it." I reply they are not extraordinary expressions from him. They were familiar in his mouth. He always taught by parables and symbols. It was the national way of teaching and was largely used by him. Remember the readiness which he always showed to spiritualize every occurrence. He stooped and wrote on the sand. He admonished his disciples respecting the leaven of the Pharisees. He instructed the woman of Samaria respecting living water. He permitted himself to be anointed, declaring that it was for his interment. He washed the feet of his disciples. These are admitted to be symbolical actions and expressions. Here, in like manner, he calls the bread his body, and bids the disciples eat. . . . But it is said: "Admit that the rite was not designed to be perpetual. What harm doth it? Here it stands, generally accepted, under some form, by the Christian world, the undoubted occasion of much good; is it not better it should remain?"

II. This is the question of expediency

1. If the view which I have taken of the history of the institution be correct, then the claim of authority should be dropped in administering it. . . .

2. It has seemed to me that the use of this ordinance tends to produce confusion in our views of the relation of the soul to God. It is the old objection to the doctrine of the Trinity, —that the true worship was transferred from God to Christ, or that such confusion was introduced into the soul, that an undivided worship was given nowhere. Is not that the effect of the Lord's Supper? I appeal now to the convictions of communicants—and ask such persons whether they have not been occasionally conscious of a painful confusion of thought between the worship due to God and the commemoration due to Christ. For, the service does not stand upon the basis of a voluntary act, but is imposed by authority. . . . I am so much a Unitarian as this: that I believe the human mind cannot admit but one God, and that every effort to pay religious homage to more than one being, goes to take away all right ideas. I appeal, brethren, to your individual experience. . . .

3. Passing other objections, I come to this, that the "use of the elements," however suitable to the people and the modes of thought in the East, where it originated, is foreign and unsuited to affect us. Whatever long usage and strong association may have done in some individuals to deaden this repulsion, I apprehend that their use is rather tolerated than loved by any of us. We are not accustomed to express our thoughts or emotions by symbolical actions. Most men find the bread and wine no aid to devotion and to some, it is a painful impediment. To eat bread is one thing; to love the precepts of Christ and resolve to obey them is quite another. . . . The statement of this objection leads me to say that I think this difficulty, wherever it is felt, to be entitled to the greatest weight. It is alone a sufficient objection to the ordinance. It is my own objection. This mode of commemorating Christ is not suitable to me. That is reason enough why I should abandon it. If I believed that it was enjoined by Jesus on his disciples, and that he even contemplated making permanent this mode of commemoration, every way agreeable to an eastern mind, and yet, on trial, it was disagreeable to my own feelings, I should not adopt it. I should choose other ways which, as more effectual upon me, he would approve more. For I choose that my remembrances of him should be pleasing, affecting, religious. I will love him as a glorified friend, after the free way of friendship, and not pay him a stiff sign of respect, as men do to those whom they fear. . . .

4. Fourthly, the importance ascribed to this particular ordinance is not consistent with the spirit of Christianity. The general object and effect of this ordinance is unexceptionable. It has been, and is, I doubt not, the occasion of indefinite good; but an importance is given by Christians to it which never can belong to any form. My friends, the apostle well assures us that "the kingdom of God is not meat and drink, but righteousness and peace and joy, in the Holy Ghost." I am not so foolish as to declaim against forms. Forms are as essential as bodies; but to exalt particular forms, to adhere to one form a moment after it is outgrown, is unreasonable, and it is alien to the spirit of Christ. . . . What I revere and obey in [Christianity] is its reality, its boundless charity, its deep interior life, the rest it gives to my mind, the echo it returns to my thoughts, the perfect accord it makes with my reason through all its representation of God and His Providence; and the persuasion and courage that come out thence to lead me upward and onward. Freedom is the essence of this faith. It has for its object simply to make men good and wise. Its institutions, then, should be as flexible as the wants of men. That form out of which the life and suitableness have departed, should be as worthless in its eyes as the dead leaves that are falling around us. . . . [T]hat for which Jesus gave himself to be crucified; the end that animated the thousand martyrs and heroes who have followed his steps, was to redeem us from a formal religion, and teach us to seek our well-being in the formation of the soul. The whole world was full of idols and ordinances. The Jewish was a religion of forms. The Pagan was a religion of forms; it was all body—it had no life—and the Almighty God was pleased to qualify and send forth a man to teach men that they must serve him with the heart; that only that life was religious which was thoroughly good; that sacrifice was smoke, and forms were shadows. This man lived and died true to this purpose; and now, with his blessed word and life before us, Christians must contend that it is a matter of vital importance—really a duty, to commemorate him by a certain form, whether that form be agreeable to their understandings or not. Is not this to make vain the gift of God? Is not this to turn back the hand on the dial? Is not this to make men—to make ourselves—forget that not forms, but duties; not names, but righteousness and love are enjoined; and that in the eye of God there is no other measure of the value of any one form than the measure of its use? . . . Influenced by these considerations, I have proposed to the brethren of the Church to drop the use of the elements and the claim of authority in the administration of this ordinance, and have suggested a mode in which a meeting for the same purpose might be held free of objection. My brethren have considered my views with patience and candor, and have recommended unanimously an adherence to the present form. I have, therefore, been compelled to consider whether it becomes me to administer it. I am clearly of opinion I ought not. This discourse has already been so far extended, that I can only say that the reason of my determination is shortly this: —It is my desire, in the office of a Christian minister, to do nothing which I cannot do with my whole heart. Having said this, I have said all. I have no hostility to this institution; I am only stating my want of sympathy with it. Neither should I ever have obtruded this opinion upon other people, had I not been called by my office to administer it. . . . As it is the prevailing opinion and feeling in our religious community, that it is an indispensable part of the pastoral office to administer this ordinance, I am about to resign into your hands that office which you have confided to me. It has many duties for which I am feebly qualified. It has some which it will always be my delight to discharge, according to my ability, wherever I exist. And whilst the recollection of its claims oppresses me with a sense of my unworthiness, I am consoled by the hope that no time and no change can deprive me of the satisfaction of pursuing and exercising its highest functions.

McCabe is critical of Emerson but says the fact that Emerson refused to continue as a Unitarian minister "definitely puts him in the class of freethinkers." He added that Emerson "believed in an Over-Soul or World-Soul (as others put it) and might be described as a Pantheist. He did not like the label Transcendentalist or any other label and did not care to pin himself to any definite religious formulae. Although his dogmatic intuitionist ethic is not suitable for our time and it led to a good deal of ethical narrowness, he was a fine force in American life in the last century."

A leader among liberal Unitarians, Emerson wrote a poem about "The Oversoul," a term which for him replaced the Judeo-Christian God and was something of a Platonic ultimate, that "Form of the Good" to which all else is connected. His delivering of "The Divinity School Address" in 1838 was a major event in religious liberalism, for he said, "God resides not in formal religion but in Nature, not in rites, but in persons. A more secret, sweet, and overpowering beauty appears to man when his heart and mind open." Harvard officials interpreted this as meaning he had rejected Christianity, and they were indignant. He was not invited back to Harvard until 1866, when he finally was granted an LL.D. degree.

The New England intelligentsia helped him with the Transcendental Club, its publication called *The Dial*, and the Brook Farm experiment. He became a spokesman for the transcendentalists, as did in varying degrees Henry David Thoreau, Margaret Fuller, Hawthorne, Lowell, Longfellow, Bryant, Whittier, Melville, and Whitman.

Among Emerson's humanistic gems are the following:

- I am the doubter and the doubt,
  And I the hymn the Brahmin sings.
- I like a church; I like a cowl;
  I love a prophet of the soul;
  And on my heart monastic aisles
  Fall like sweet strains, or pensive smiles;
  Yet not for all his faith can see
  Would I that cowlèd churchman be.
- If eyes were made for seeing,
  Then Beauty is its own excuse for being.
- Things are in the saddle, And ride mankind.
- The reward of a thing well done, is to have done it.
- Whoso would be a man must be a nonconformist.
- Go put your creed into your deed, nor speak with double tongue.
- A foolish consistency is the hobgoblin of little minds, adored by little statesmen and philosophers and divines. With consisten cy a great soul has simply nothing to do.
- I like the silent church before the service begins, better than any preaching.
- When Nature has work to be done, she creates a genius to do it.
- Speak what you think now in hard words, and tomorrow speak what tomorrow you think in hard words again, though it con tradict everything you have said today.
- Other world? There is no other world!
  Here or nowhere is the whole fact.
- We should not forgive the clergy for taking,
  on every issue, the immoral side.
- The cure for theology is mother-wit.
- As men's prayers are a disease of the will,
  so are their creeds a disease of the intellect.
- I knew a witty physician who . . . used to affirm that if there was disease in the liver, the man became a Calvinist, and if that organ was sound, he became a Unitarian.
- Things are in the saddle, And ride mankind.
- The reward of a thing well done, is to have done it.
- Whoso would be a man must be a nonconformist.
- Things are in the saddle, And ride mankind.
- The reward of a thing well done, is to have done it.
- Whoso would be a man must be a nonconformist.

Nietzsche was favorably influenced by Emerson. Erwin Schrödinger as well as Arthur Koestler found favor with Emerson's view that after death we "lie in the lap of immense intelligence," that being the Absolute Mind, a "great reservoir of consciousness" according to Paul Edwards in *Immortality*. Matthew Arnold pronounced Emerson's essays "the most important work done in prose" in the nineteenth century. Not so praiseworthy were Hawthorne, Melville ("I do not oscillate in Emerson's rainbow"), T. S. Eliot, and Yvor Winters. But, Harold Bloom wrote, "The mind of Emerson is the mind of America, for worse and for glory, and the central concern of that mind was the American religion, which most memorably was named 'self-reliance.' "

When elected to the Hall of Fame for Great Americans (which was built on the Bronx campus of New York University), Emerson received 87 of the 97 possible votes, bettered only by Washington, Lincoln, Webster, Franklin, Grant, John Marshall, and Jefferson. Three decades prior, Emerson had been fooled into believing that a recently found 10' 4 1/2" 2900-pound Cardiff, New York, giant was a fossil.

Emerson is buried on a rising ground called Authors' Ridge at Sleepy Hollow Cemetery in Concord, Massachusetts. The site is marked by a large granite boulder gravestone. Nearby are the remains of Henry David Thoreau and Louisa May Alcott. Emerson is flanked by **Lidian Emerson**, his wife, by their son Waldo, who died at age five, and their daughter Ellen. Ellen's epitaph reads that although "of a fine mind, she cared more for persons than for books." (See reference to his vice-presidency of the Free Religious Association in the entry for Ethical Culture. Also see entry for William Furness.) {CE; CL; ER; EU, William F. Ryan; FUK; FUS; HNS2; JM; JMR; JMRH; PUT; RAT; RE; TRI; TSV; TYD; U}

Emerson, William (1701—1782)

Carlyle liked the English mathematician Emerson, recalling that he told Mrs. Gilchrist, "Emerson was a Freethinker who looked on his neighbor, the person, as a humbug. He seems to have defended himself in silence the best way he could against the noisy clamor and unreal stuff going on around him." Emerson compiled a list of Bible contradictions. Although the *Encyclopaedia Britannica* has stated that there is no foundation for the statement of Carlyle and others that Emerson was a skeptic, the Rev. W. Bowe candidly admits in his *Some Account of the Life of W. Emerson* (1793) that Emerson rejected Christianity. {BDF; RAT; RE}

Emery, Linda (20th Century)

Emery, a fundamentalist turned humanist, is an instructor in English at Boise State University in Idaho.

Emlyn, Thomas (Died 1741)

Emlyn in 1703 was imprisoned at Dublin, Ireland, for his anti-trinitarian beliefs. {U}

Emmett, Robert (1778—1803)

Emmett was an Irish revolutionist who was expelled from Dublin University for his sympathy with the National Cause in 1798. McCabe, calling him an Irish patriot, remarked that "there was much more freethinking in Ireland much more freedom to think 150 years ago than there is today, and the priests carefully conceal the opinions of patriots like Emmett, O'Brien, O'Connor, etc., whom they hold up to youth today. Emmet went to France and there imbibed republicanism and deism, and on his return he organized a revolution."

In 1802 he was found guilty of insurrection and was sentenced to be executed. Emmett made a memorable speech before receiving sentence, and on the scaffold he refused the services of a priest, saying he was "an infidel by conviction." The cause of his capture was his having returned to Ireland in order to see once more his sweetheart, the daughter of Curran. {BDF; JM; RAT; RE}

EMPATHY

"Don't . . . touch . . . me!" exclaimed a teacher whose artificial leg had come off and a student had offered to help him up. The still-angry Vietnam veteran, in short, wanted no pity.

To show empathy (*einfühlung* in German) is to identify with and understand another's feelings—empathetic humanists, for example, would aim to put themselves in others' shoes before taking certain actions. One humanist made a sincere friendship with a paraplegic by arranging eye-level contact (e.g., sitting on a street curb) on almost all occasions. Being seated at a table with a dwarf allows both to have eye-level contact and to avoid "looking down" on a person. Unsighted individuals often demand not to be led, preferring to follow. At the time of someone's death, the immediate family often wants total privacy, not unsolicited visits.

Although commercial Hallmark sympathy cards are preferred by those who could be accused of valuing sympathy over empathy, those who do not feel in a superior position say they seldom sympathize with "the poor suckers who are not as fortunate as I am." To be empathetic, one sees things through the eyes of the person who is being addressed. Troubled people often become more troubled when sympathized with. Those who differ retort that sympathy involves a mutual understanding of affection, not a feeling of superiority, that saying "I am sorry" when sincerely felt is simply a harmless expression of their compassion.

Empedocles (c. 495— 435 B.C.E.)

The first to state a principle that is now central to physics, Empedocles taught that everything is composed of four underived and indestructible roots: fire, water, earth, and air. The atmosphere, not a mere void, actually has a corporeal substance. "In the absence of the void or empty space he explained motion as the interpenetration of particles, under the alternating action of two forces, harmony and discord," explains the *Columbia Encyclopedia*. He explicitly denied anthropomorphic deity: "None of the gods has formed the world, nor has any man; it has always been." Further, states Robertson, he threw out "a certain glimmer of the Darwinian conception—perhaps more clearly attained by Anaximandros—that adaptations prevail in nature just because the adaptations fit organisms to survive, and the non-adapted perish." {CE; JMR; JMRH; TYD}

EMPEROR HAS NO CLOTHES AWARD

"The Emperior Has No Clothes Award" is given by the Freedom From Religion Foundation to prominent Americans who call public attention to the shortcomings of religion. It is a gold-colored statuette of the royal figure of folktale notoriety. Just as the cautious subjects of that tale's emperor did not wish to call attention to his being naked, not dressed in the most wondrously beautiful cloth that only the very wise could see, "so people echo religious inanities because it is the thing to do," the Foundation holds. The first award went to comedian George Carlin.

EMPEROR WORSHIP

The kings of Egypt, Babylonia, and Persia were said to have been semi-divine beings. "The ideal king of the Jews," wrote Shirley Jackson Case of the University of Chicago's Divinity School, "was to be an individual especially anointed by God and thus a superman." Among the Greeks, heroes were half-divine and became fully divine after dying on earth. Alexander the Great, for example, was considered an incarnate deity. Julius Caesar was voted divine honors, called apotheosis, by the Roman senate upon his decease. Caligula and Domitian demanded that incense be burned before Caesar's image. According to Case, Jews, "being recognized as an established social group that refused to take this oath," were excused, but Christians lacked this social prestige and for two centuries were subject to intermittent persecution for their refusal to say "Caesar is lord." {ER}

EMPIRICISM

Empiricism is a philosophical doctrine that all knowledge is derived from experience. Such a position is opposed to rationalism, denying as it does the existence of innate ideas. Empiricists hold that all ideas are derived from experience, that knowledge of the physical world can be nothing more than a generalization from particular instances, that it can never reach more than a high degree of probability. John Stuart Mill was the first to treat the subject, and among its other leading advocates have been John Locke, George Berkeley, and David Hume. James K. Feibleman in *Foundations of* Empiricism (1965) and Fraser Crowley in *A Critique of British Empiricism* (1968) write about the epistemological doctrine. Stuart Brown, editor of *British Empiricism and the Enlightenment* (1996), begins with Herbert of Cherbury and the Cambridge Platonists and with Newton and the early English Enlightenment. Locke is cited as being a key figure. {CE; ER; RE}

Empson, William (1906—)

Empson, the English critic and poet, wrote a classic of modern literary criticism, *Seven Types of Ambiguity* (1930). An atheist, he wrote *Milton's God* (1961). {*Free Inquiry*, Fall 1992}

ENCYCLICAL

Humanists or freethinkers ordinarily issue "memos" or even "manifestos" for general or wide circulation. In the Roman Catholic Church, however, a papal letter addressed to the bishops or to the hierarchy of a particular country is called an encyclical. Encyclicals by religionists ordinarily lay down policy on religious, moral, or political issues. {DCL}

ENCYCLOPEDIA

An encyclopedia—a word taken from the Greek, meaning a circle of knowledge—was originally meant to compile knowledge but, equally important, to give it shape. A Roman 6th century encyclopedia was divided into Divine and Human categories. A 9th century Arabic encyclopedia set priorities by beginning with discussions of power and war and ending with entries on food and women. During the 17th century, alphabetical encyclopedias began to thrive, as did cross-referencing and detailed indexing.

ENCYCLOPÉDIE, ENCYCLOPEDISTS

The *Encyclopédie; ou, Dictionnaire raisonné des sciences, des arts, et des les métiers* was the work of the French Encyclopedists, or philosophes. Originally, it was to have been a translation of the Chambers *Cyclopedia* under the editorship of Abbé Gua de Malves, but the project was abandoned because of disagreements. The publisher, Le Breton, then agreed to let Denis Diderot and Jean le Rond d'Alembert edit an entirely new work, and they were aided by Quesnay, Montesquieu, Voltaire, J. J. Rousseau, Turgot, and others. A first volume was produced in 1751, and its rational, secular emphasis infuriated the Jesuits, who attacked the work as irreligious. In 1759 Alembert resigned as editor, but Diderot with the help of the chevalier de Jaucourt brought the clandestine printing of the work to completion in 1772. Of its twenty-eight volumes, eleven were devoted to plates illustrating the industrial arts. In the shop, a printer deleted some articles which contained overly liberal opinions, but the work represented a successful championing of the skepticism and rationalism of the Enlightenment. In 1780, a five-volume supplement and a two-volume index were added. The encyclopedia stressed scientific determinism, attacked legal, juridical, and clerical abuses, and was a factor in the intellectual preparation for the French Revolution. Upon seeing the collection, and it is available for example in the 42nd Street Public Library in New York City, the viewer is amazed at the quality of workmanship, the scope, and particularly the large size of the books. {CE}

ENDANGERED SPECIES

Freethinkers everywhere are concerned about the fact that so many species are being lost for a variety of ecological reasons. In the United States alone, 717 endangered species of animals have been listed in 1999 by private as well as government sources. These range from the Alabama beach mouse and the American alligator to the Wyoming toad and the yellow-shouldered blackbird. "The fewer any species, the less likely we will ever eventually be able to make significant, large-scale, balanced, complete and thorough ecological repair/remedy," wrote Drew Kovaly and Jeff Walther in *Green Light* (September 1999), journal of the International Naturist Church.

ENDOWMENTS

Males (as well as females) are intrigued by the story of Adamastor, whose penis was so monstrously huge that he and the nymph Thetis were unable to have sex. Gore Vidal's "Live From Golgotha" (1982) described the Bishop of Ephesus, the heterosexual Timothy who was said to have had "the largest dick in our part of Asia Minor," and was represented as having been an acolyte and "love toy" of St. Paul.

Spy, an irreverent magazine quite interested in all kinds of endowments, pulled a blasphemous prank in which it "measured the power of the Almighty Dollar against America's most Bible-thumpin', cross-bearin' academic institutions" (September-October 1996):

> Posing as R. Stephen Atkinson, the financial advisor to a born-again billionaire named Mildred Goldstein, the slick journal contacted Christian colleges, offering cash from the fictional Goldstein, who was described as an ailing octogenarian widow with no living relatives who wanted to leave $20,000,000. to the first school that could accommodate her dying wish: "Incorporate Goldstein into the name of their Christian school." Schools and their suggested possible solutions:
>
> - Southwest Baptist University
>   The Goldstein College of Christian Education
> - College of the Holy Cross, Worcester, MA
>   The Goldstein Institute for Jesuit Studies
> - Catholic University
>   change the sports team's name from the Cardinals to the Goldsteins
> - Seton Hall's Immaculate Conception School
>   Goldstein Seminary and School of Theology
> - Southern Methodist U's Perkins Chapel
>   Goldstein Chapel
>
> The various schools were only temporarily duped. The endowments were never realized. Seton Hall, in fact, decided that the offered endowment was too small to buy the "kind of connection" that it would take to rename the school.

"It proves," quipped a Manhattan wag, "that it takes a large endowment to make the right kind of connection."

Engels, Friedrich (1820—1895)

Corliss Lamont listed Engels as a materialist with a humanistic outlook. A German socialist, Engels with Karl Marx founded "scientific socialism," collaborating with him to write the Communist Manifesto (1848).

When Marx died in 1883, Engels edited his writings, including the second and third volumes of *Das Kapital* (1883—1894), which established the materialist interpretation of history. Belfort Bax, a British atheist and socialist who knew him, called Engels a "devout atheist."

Secular humanists such as Sidney Hook and Paul Kurtz have objected to the Marxist approach, which is not founded upon freedom, the significance of the individual, and political democracy. {CE; CL; JM; RAT; RE; TRI}

Engle, Marvin (20th Century)

Engle is president of the North Palm Beach, Florida, chapter of the Council for Secular Humanism. He also is a regional director of that Council.

Engledue, William Collins (1813—1859)

Engledue was President of the Royal Medical Society of Edinburgh. He was a contributor to the *Zoist* and published an exposition of materialism under the title of *Cerebral Physiology* (1842). {BDF}

Englefield, F. R. H. (Died 1975)

Englefield, who wrote *The Critique of Pure Verbiage* (published 1990), is a philosopher whose work gives more illumination than many traditional works, according to A.R.B. Ferguson in *New Humanist* (November 1993). Englefield also wrote *Language: Its Origin and Its Relation to Thought* (1977) and *The Mind at Work and Play* (published 1985).

English, George Bethune (1787—1828)

An American writer and linguist, English wrote *Grounds of Christianity Examined* (1813), which excited some controversy. English had a gift of language, passing for a Turk with a Turkish ambassador, and surprising a delegation of Cherokees by disputing with them in their own tongue. English wrote a reply to his critics, *Five Smooth Stones Out of the Brook*, and two letters to Channing on his sermons against infidelity. {BDF; FUS; RAT}

ENGLISH HUMANISM

Voltaire admired England for its combining freedom of speech, religious tolerance, the rational thinking of John Locke and Isaac Newton, and political moderation. For him, the essence of British freedom was the stock exchange:

> a place more venerable than many courts of justice, where the representatives of all nations meet for the benefit of mankind. There the Jew, the Mohametan, and the Christian transact together as tho' they all profess'd the same religion, and give the name of Infidel to none but bankrupts.

Voltaire's view that England was tolerant in matters of religion is not true, wrote Neal Ascherson in *The New York Review of Books* (20 May 1999). What Voltaire had required, he said, was "a mythical neighbor country whose virtues would show up the vices and shortcomings of France," adding "he also insisted that the English political system of limited monarchy and bourgeois liberties could be exported—even across the Channel. Skeptics objected that coconuts that ripened in India did not ripen in Rome."

Ian Buruma's *Anglomania: A European Love Affair* (1999) states that the very qualities that Voltaire rejected were ones embraced by Goethe and the German writers of the late 18th and early 19th century. Shakespeare was adopted as virtually a German poet, a great Saxon bard unshackled by the Aristotelian rules of classical theater, writing with extraordinary power about the human conditions. In Buruma's words, Shakespeare was "the Nordic genius Germans had been waiting for." Yes, but Ascherson adds that Shakespeare also was a *Volksgenosse* in Nazi Germany, where his works were declared to be "German classics" in September 1939. In 1940 as the Nazi armies prepared for the invasion of Shakespeare's land, *Macbeth* and *Hamlet* with their lonely Nordic heroes arming for battle against fate were the plays they liked best.

Buruma, whose great-grandparents were Continental European Jews, found that many think of Britain as the land of freedom and tolerance, of Magna Carta, parliamentary democracy and refuge to political dissidents from Voltaire to Salman Rushdie. To others, it is a place of genteel tradition, stable institutions, aristocratic privilege, capitalism, and empire.

English humanism dates at least to the mid-18th century. The Humanistic Religious Association of London's 1 September 1853 Constitution included the following:

> In forming ourselves into a progressive religious body, we have adopted the name "Humanistic Religious Association" to convey the idea that Religion is a principle inherent in man and is a means of developing his being towards greater perfection.
>
> We have emancipated ourselves from the ancient compulsory dogmas, myths, and ceremonies borrowed of old from Asia and still pervading the ruling churches of our age.

In "Humanism in the Eighteenth Century" (*The Humanist*, 1951), James V. Grasso described the objectives of the Association, which included spreading the knowledge of the time and to foster the cultivation of the sciences, philosophy, and the arts.

An up-to-date listing of local humanist groups in England, Wales, Scotland, Northern Ireland, and the Irish Republic is found bi-monthly in *Humanist News*, the newsletter of the British Humanist Association (47 Theobald's Road, London WC1X 8SP, England). {EW; Alexander Stille, *The New York Times Book Review*, 2 May 1999}

ENGLISH HUMANISTS: See a listing in the entry for United Kingdom, Freethought and Humanist Groups.

ENGLISH LANGUAGE

It is difficult to explain the following to anyone learning the English language:

- A fire engine has no fire and is not on fire.
- Eggplant contains no egg, hamburger no ham, pineapple no pines or apples.
- Quicksand does not work quickly, and a guinea pig is neither from Guinea nor is it a pig.
- Writers write . . . but fingers do not fing, grocers do not groce, and hammers do not ham.
- Teachers have taught, but preachers have not praught; vegetarians eat vegetables but humanitarians do not eat humans.
- The plural of tooth is teeth, but the plural of booth is not beeth; of goose is geese, but of moose is not meese.
- In English one recites at a play and plays at a recital; ships by truck and sends cargo by ship; has a nose that runs and feet that smell; parks on driveways and drives on parkways.
- A wise man and a wise guy are opposites.
- A house burns up as it burns down; to fill a form out, we fill it in; an alarm clock goes off by going on.

Fortunately, muse freethinkers, such a dynamic language is relative, not absolute, and was invented by humans, not gods.

ENGLISH UNITARIANS

Jeffrey J. Teagle heads the General Assembly of Unitarian and Free Christian Churches (1-6 Essex Street, Strand, London, WC2R 3HV, England).

According to John Clifford,

> England has approximately 170 congregations ranging in size from three or four to one hundred fifty. A broad swath from Liverpool through Manchester to Sheffield would take in the majority of our English congregations and members. There is another concentration in the Southeast, centred on London. The majority of these Unitarians would describe themselves as liberal Christians, and the worship patterns tend to be very similar to what one would find in most non-conformist (i.e., non-Anglican/Episcopalian) chapels, although the content would normally be noticeably different. Most of these congregations would have a strong denominational and/or district identity although there are a few that are fiercely independent. Some of the latter are strong congregations in a liberal Christian ould. There are a very few congregations of clear humanist, universalist, or theist practice, but most would be more accurately described as amalgamations. The role of the minister, particularly in worship, would be the strongest single influence in this, but we have democratic structure and our Management Committees also play a role in determining public profile.
>
> Many English and Welsh congregations trace their origins to the Act of Uniformity of 1662 (called the "Great Ejection" by dissenters) when liberals were forced out of the State Church and they formed independent local congregations (frequently called Presbyterian, although no consistent system of higher courts was set up).
>
> Other of our congregations in England and Wales trace their roots to the General Baptist congregations of the mid-18th Century. They believed in General Salvation, i.e. universalism, and adult baptism.
>
> A few of the Universalist congregations founded in mid-18th century became Unitarian in the early 19th century as Priestley and his followers were making that name a focus for various dissenting groups.
>
> In the Manchester area there was a group of dissenting Methodist congregations that became Unitarian during the 19th century.
>
> Some of our congregations were actually founded as Unitarian congregations either as spin-offs from an existing congregation or as the result of internal missionary work. At one point there were also several "domestic mission," i.e., community service centres in deprived urban areas, but only one of these remains and it is a congregation more than a domestic mission.
>
> We British Unitarians have a denominational name given to us by history that we seem to lack the will to change. It is, The General Assembly of Unitarian and Free Christian Churches, usually abbreviated by us to "GA." So when we talk about ourselves collectively we frequently do not even use the word Unitarian. Also, inasmuch as North American usage permeates our society, many of us are starting to refer to our Annual Meetings as our GA. Very confusing, but be aware that when a British Unitarian says GA s/he may not be talking about our annual gathering but about the denomination as a whole. Or s/he may be talking about the central secretariat based at Essex Hall in London, which I serve.

{WAS, e-mail from John Clifford)

ENLIGHTENMENT

"Enlightenment" is a term for the rationalist, liberal, humanitarian, and scientific trend of 18th century Western thought. The period is also known as the Age of Reason.

Its achievements include the 17th-century empiricism of Francis Bacon and Locke as well as by Descartes, Spinoza, and others. Other representatives of the Enlightenment are such thinkers as Voltaire, J. J. Rousseau, Montesquieu, Adam Smith, Swift, Hume, Kant, G. E. Lessing, Beccaria, Thomas Paine, Thomas Jefferson, and Benjamin Franklin. The social and political ideals they presented were enforced by "enlightened despots" such as Holy Roman Emperor Joseph II, Catherine II of Russia, and Frederick II of Prussia. Diderot's *Encyclopédie* and the U. S. Constitution are representative documents of the Age of Reason.

Not all individuals consider the Enlightenment mankind's finest intellectual achievement. On the contrary, they argue that it has become a catastrophic error. Johann Gottfried Herder's *Another Philosophy of History* (1774) challenged the universalist, optimistic character of Enlightenment thought.

Theodor Adorno and Max Horkheimer, in *Dialectic of the Enlightenment* (1972), asked, according to *The Economist* (16 March 1996), "why mankind, far from advancing to an ever closer harmony, had sunk into an abyss of hitherto unimaginable barbarism; why science, far from serving its Enlightenment purpose of enlarging human understanding, had only served the cause of human cruelty. Their answer was that the Enlightenment had been doomed all along to serve totalitarian goals." (For some dangerous illusions about the Enlightenment, see the entry for Gertrude Himmelfarb. The most influential works of modern counter-Enlightenment are by writers such as Alasdair MacIntyre, Michael Sandel, Roberto Unger, and Christopher Lasch in America. In England, John Gray. *Satori* is the Japanese word for the state of enlightenment sought in Zen Buddhism.) {CE}

Ennis, Garth (20th Century)

Ennis, a comic book artist and writer of *Preacher* and *Hellblazer*, has gone on record in *Wizard: The Guide to Comics #62* (October 1996) as being a non-theist:

> I'm an atheist, really. But everyone seems to think I'm some terrible lapsed Catholic who suffered the worst of a Catholic upbringing and had the crap kicked out of him by nuns and monks. In actual fact, I'm not Catholic, and I never had any kind of direct religious upbringing at all, although I was exposed to the inevitable religious influence that growing up in Ireland will give you.

{CA; E}

Ennius, Quintus (239—169? B.C.E.)

A Latin poet regarded by the Romans as the father of Latin poetry, Ennius aspired to being Rome's Homer. He introduced the Latin qualitative hexameter and the elegiac couplet, smoothed the current roughness of Latin diction, and gave a definitive artistic base to Latin poetry. As a teacher of Greek and belles lettres, for he was of Greek descent, he translated Euhemerus. Cicero says of him that he "followed" as well as translated Euhemerus, and his favorite Greek dramatists were freethinking Euripides and Epicharmus, both of whose works he translated. Ennius attacked the popular superstitions, particularly soothsaying and divination, which appealed to Henry David Thoreau as well as to other of his contemporaries. {CE; JMR; JMRH}

Eno, Brian (1948—)

Eno (his full name is Brian Peter George St. John de la Salle Eno) is a composer, musician, and producer. He co-founded the rock group, Roxy Music, and has been a solo musician since 1973. He produced "Evening Star" with Robert Fripp; "My Life in the Bush of Ghosts" with David Byrne; and "The Joshua Tree (U2). As a video artist he was in "Mistaken Memories of Mediaeval Manhattan" (1981).

When his music was described as being "godless," he responded,

> Well, I'm an atheist, and the concept of god for me is all part of what I call the last illusion. The last illusion is someone knows what is going on. That's the last illusion. =Nearly everyone has that illusion somewhere, and it manifests not only in the terms of the idea that there is a god but that knows what's going on but that the planets know what's going on. Astrology is part of the last illusion. The obsession with health is part of the last illusion, the idea that there's that if only we could spend time on it and sit down and stop being unreasonable with each other we'd all find that there was a structure and a solution underlying plan to it all, for most people the short answer to that is God.

{CA; E}

Ensor, George (1769—1843)

Ensor was an Irish writer whom Bentham described as clever but impracticable. A deist and freethinker, he wrote severe criticisms of the Bible. Ensor's works included *The Independent Man* (1806), *A Review of the Miracles, Prophecies and Mysteries of the Old and New Testaments* (1816), and *Natural Theology Examined* (1836). {BDF; FUS; JM; RAT}

Eon de Beaumont, Charles d' [Chevalier/Chevalière] (1728—1810)

A Catholic, a spy in the service of Louis XV, a captain of Dragoons, a female impersonator (as Lia de Beaumont): d'Eon was all of these. He became lady-in-waiting and even read to Czarina Elizabeth as she relaxed in her bath. His mission was to prevent the signing of a military treaty between Russia and England (one promising Russian support if France attacked England's sovereign state of Hanover). The Empress, according to Carol Orsag, heeded "Lia's" advice and refused to sign the treaty.

Since the age of four, d'Eon had been dressed in feminine attire by his mother, who had preferred having given birth to a girl. Although successful as a female agent, Charles also distinguished himself in the French Army during the Seven Years War, as a captain in the Dragoons, and as an unofficial ambassador to England. When twenty-six, he was made a chevalier in the Order of Saint-Louis.

Louis XV charged d'Eon to prepare the way for a French invasion of England, a fact unknown in 1763 to France's full-time ambassador, the Comte de Guerchy. When the ambassador ordered d'Eon to give up the title of minister plenipotentiary, d'Eon did the unheard of: he refused, apparently considering that his rapid advancement made him invulnerable. Threatening blackmail, he published some highly confidential documents. This made him a hero to the English and resulted in Louis XV's intervention upon his behalf. But some time in 1770 d'Eon dropped a hint that he was a woman.

Gary Kates, in *Monsieur d'Eon Is A Woman: A Tale of Political Intrigue and Sexual Masquerade* (1995), researched two dozen biographies and much anecdotal trivia known in France as *petite histoire* but was unable to determine why. What is known is that d'Eon did not deny it and some—the pamphleteer Charles Théveneau de Morande—even claimed to have fondled d'Eon's vagina. Kates, a history professor at Trinity University in Texas, suggests that d'Eon was neither a transvestite nor a transsexual, that his decision to live as a woman (whom he considered "spiritually" superior to men) was an intellectual one.

For almost a century in England, France, and throughout Europe, debates raged over Charles's "true" sex, with over $2,000,000 wagered on the "she-man." Some bribed servants and resorted to window climbing in order to win their bets, but all attempts at carrying him off and displaying his sexual parts publicly were unsuccessful.

Princeton's Robert Darnton has written that d'Eon's manuscripts, according to Kates, "showed him to have believed in an idiosyncratic variety of Augustinian Catholicism built on the hatred of men (especially Jews, owing to their emphasis on circumcision), a vision of a gender-free Garden of Eden (Adam seems to have been the first hermaphrodite), and moral insights" which Kates considered "exceptionally rich and original," such as: "God created [woman and man], the one for doing good, the other for doing bad. So long as a man is a man, the earth is his; so long as a woman is a woman, virtue is hers." Although d'Eon had contact with freethinkers like Voltaire and Paine, he continued his commitment to the Catholic Church, was an arch royalist, was an early enthusiast for the French Revolution, a war hero, a blackmailer, an ascetic, an exhibitionist and athlete, a student of Saint Paul, a student of Horace, a woman, a man—in short, a bundle of contradictions.

In 1810, after remaining in London through the French Revolution and most of Napoleon's rule, still dressed as a woman, d'Eon died, poor and obscure. His housemate, the widow of a British naval officer, dressed the body for burial. She and one physician declared that he was definitely a male with a male sexual apparatus that was inspected, sketched, and cast in plaster by experts. Other medical experts, knowing that the newspapers could not get enough of the story, claimed he was a hermaphrodite. All agreed d'Eon had been a master spy. {PA}

EPAINESS: See entries for Edward Everett and for Oratory.

Ephron, Nora (20th Century)

A writer and director of such movies as "Michael" and "Steeplechase," Ephron has declared that she is not a believer in God "in a formal sense." She directed "Sleepless in Seattle," which was nominated in 1993 for an Academy Award as being the best original screenplay. {New York *Daily News*, 19 January 1997}

Epicharmus (Died c. 450 B.C.E.)

A Sicilian Greek comic poet, Epicharmus, by writing about other than personal satire and mythological burlesque, was the first to write a coherent artistic comedy. According to Robertson, his treatment of the deities on stage was "in a spirit of such audacious burlesque as must be held to imply unbelief." Epicharmus was translated by the Roman poet Ennius. {CE}

Epictetus (c. 50—138)

Epictetus, a Phrygian Stoic philosopher, wrote nothing, but his disciple Arrian set down his teachings in the *Discourses* and the *Encheiridion.* McCabe, saying shorthand was known at that time, theorizes that Arrian quoted Epictetus directly. He adds that Epictetus "belonged to the small religious wing of the Stoic movement and his extravagances of virtue illustrate again the danger of introducing any mysticism into ethics. The absurd suggestion that he borrowed from Christ is refuted by the dates. His chief interest is to remind us that all the moral sentiment attributed to Jesus in the gospels were familiar in the first century."

The brotherhood of man is a key feature in his Stoic outlook, for Epictetus believed mankind on earth is a collection of prisoners in an earthly body. Inasmuch as Epictetus was lame much of his life, and possibly had been a slave, he was somewhat meek, not being negative about government or religion. As described by Bertrand Russell, Marcus Aurelius wrote that Epictetus "used to say, 'Thou art a little soul bearing about a corpse,' that Zeus could not make the body free, but he gave us a portion of his divinity. God is the father of men, and we are all brothers. We should not say, 'I am an Athenian' or 'I am a Roman,' but 'I am a citizen of the universe.' If you were a kinsman of Caesar, you would feel safe; how much more should you feel safe in being a kinsman of God? If we understand that virtue is the only true good, we shall see that no real evil can befall us." As for any afterlife, "Where are you going? It cannot be to a place of suffering; there is no Hell." He had also written, "I was not, and was conceived; I loved, and did a little work; I am not, and grieve not," which W. K. Clifford chose as his epitaph.

In 1992, James R. Stockdale, the Vice Presidential candidate who ran with Ross Perot, surprised some potential voters by declaring he was a devotee of Epictetus's philosophy. {CE; ER; JM; JMRH; RE; TYD}

EPICUREANISM

J. C. A. Gaskin, in *Varieties of Unbelief from Epicurus to Sartre* (1989), defined Epicureanism as a "complete (and the original) humanistic-materialistic philosophy whose particular stance with regard to gods is to acknowledge that inactive, uncreating gods exist *as part of* the material universe. However, these inactive gods have no care for us nor we any duty to or dependence on them."

Epicurus (341—270 B.C.E.)

Epicurus "taught that there are no deities who intervened in human affairs and that mortal man has no existence after death," Corliss Lamont wrote. Angelo Juffras points out that Epicurus did not deny there were gods; he denied that any such gods control events, particularly astronomical occurrences. Nor, as found in *Aphorisms*, could gods affect human affairs:

> Either God wants to abolish evil, and cannot; or he can, but does not want to. . . . If he wants to, but cannot, he is impotent. If he can, but does not want to, he is wicked. . . . If, as they say, God can abolish evil, and God really wants to do it, why is there evil in the world?

His emphasis upon denying an afterlife helped remove human anxiety about any fear of divine judgment and eternal punishment, thereby denying the very basis of the popular Greek religion of that day but not offending the prejudices of the Athenians. The Romans Lucretius and Diogenes were among his many followers, and his influence lasted 700 years in the form of a creedal following. During the French Revolution, Maréchal cited Epicurus as being one of the greatest atheists of all time.

Epicurus taught in a community of thinkers which he called the Garden, one which included some women and at least one slave. (A Buffalo wag agrees that no garden should be without these.) Bertrand Russell describes Epicurus's distaste for Nausiphanes, apparently a follower of Democritus and whom he described derisively as The Mollusc. Also, Epicurus failed to acknowledge the extent of his indebtedness to Democritus, as well as to Leucippus. In fact, "he asserted that there was no such philosopher—meaning, no doubt, not that there was no such man, but that the man [Leucippus] was not a philosopher." Although 300 of Epicurus's works were lost, Russell holds that Lucretius hews closest to Epicurus's viewpoints.

Pleasure and tranquillity, Epicurus felt, were good. "The beginning and the root of all good is the pleasure of the stomach; even wisdom and culture must be referred to this. The pleasure of the mind is the contemplation of pleasures of the body. By contemplating pleasure rather than pain, we can achieve virtue through prudence in the pursuit of such pleasure. Rather than active (dynamic) pleasures, we should pursue passive (static) ones. The former consist in the attainment of a desired end accompanied by pain; the latter consist in a state of equilibrium, which results as Bertrand Russell has described it as "the kind of state of affairs that would be desired if it were absent."

Passive pleasure does not depend upon pain as a stimulus to desire. It is as if it is more pleasant to be in the state of just having eaten moderately rather than in the state of having a voracious desire to eat. Therefore, it is the absence of pain, rather than the presence of pleasure, which really is the wise man's goal. As for social pleasures, the safest is friendship. Or, as Russell describes the Epicurean outlook, "Eat little, for fear of indigestion; drink little, for fear of next morning; eschew politics and love and all violently passionate activities; do not give hostages to fortune by marrying and having children; in your mental life, teach yourself to contemplate pleasures rather than pains.

Physical pain is certainly a great evil, but if severe, it is brief, and if prolonged, it can be endured by means of mental discipline and the habit of thinking of happy things in spite of it. Above all, live so as to avoid fear." Russell's view is quite different from Epictetus's summary of Epicurus: "This is the life of which you pronounced yourself worthy: eating, drinking, copulation, evacuation, and snoring."

Epicurus of Samos held that two of the greatest sources of fear were religion and the dread of death, which were connected, since religion encouraged the view that the dead are unhappy. He therefore sought a metaphysic which would prove that the gods do not interfere in human affairs, and that the soul perishes with the body." In his own words, Epicurus stated, "the supreme purpose of philosophy should be to introduce tranquillity and happiness into human life." Augustine, however, called his views "a philosophy of swine."

Dante's *Inferno* estimates that more than a thousand followers of Epicurus, "who make the soul die with the body," are in Hell. Among them, he specifies Emperor Frederick II, the Guelph Cavalcante Cavalcanti, Ottavio Cardinal Ubaldini (who died in 1273), the Ghibelline noble Farinita (Manente degli Uberti, chief of the Florentine Ghibellines, who was a wise and valiant leader who died in 1264. In 1283 Salmone da Lucca, an Inquisitor, condemned him, his wife, his sons, and his grandsons as heretics. His bones were then thrown away, his property confiscated, and his goods were sold).

When Epicurus died, his school—the Garden—memorialized him with a monthly feast. (See entries for Ancient Humanism; for his mistress, Leontium; and for Philodemus) {BDF; CE; CL; ER; EU, Angelo Juffras and Aram Vartanian; HNS2; JM; JMR; JMRH; RE; TYD}

EPIDEMICS

McCabe has edifying information concerning the epidemics in history and their relation to religion. The Castle of Sant' Angelo (Holy Angel) at Rome, for example, "is an historic memorial of the tragedy of the substitution of the individualist and other-worldly ethic of Christianity for the social ethic of the Romans. The building is really the tomb of the Emperor Hadrian, who had presided over the empire of an estimated 100,000,000 people at the greatest height that civilization had reached in 3,500 years of history. Five centuries later the tomb, now converted into a Christian monument, rose above a city that had sunk from 1,000,000 to 40,000 people and from a brilliant height to squalor, poverty, and dense ignorance. The statue of an angel, commemorating the supposed miraculous arrest of a plague by angels in the days of Gregory I, is a symbol of the appalling social retrogression. The cultivated region around Rome had become a poisonous swamp, and the pious Pope, who was eager to destroy what was left of Roman culture, used the very worst measures (crowded churches, processions, etc.) to combat the infection that crept into the city. The normal death-rate in Europe had become so high that populations which now treble in a century took four centuries to double—England rose from two to four millions between 1066 (*Domesday Book*) and 1500—and ghastly epidemics swept periodically over the Continent. In tenth-century France (when Arab medical and sanitary science was at its height) there were forty-eight famines and epidemics in seventy-three years.

The Black Death (1348—1251), which was probably bubonic plague, is estimated to have had 25,000,000 victims, besides the horrible sufferings of millions who recovered, or about two-thirds of the population of Europe. The "mummy pills" which many took as a preventive were made from the bodies of people who had died of the plague. Epidemic hysteria (the Flagellants, the Dancing Mania, etc.) added, when pestilence ceased, to the horrors." McCabe cites as the best sources Hecker's *Epidemics of the Middle Ages* (1844) and G. G. Coulton's *The Black Death* (1929).

Since the time AIDS (Acquired Immune Deficiency Syndrome) was identified in 1981, the Roman Catholic Church has specifically insisted that the use of condoms during sexual relations or the distribution of clean needles to addicts is not preferable to abstinence. Human sexuality is for the purpose of conjugal love of man and woman, fecundity is a gift and an end of marriage, every baptized person is called to lead a chaste life with Christ as the model of chastity, believers are instructed by the Catholic Church.

Meanwhile, it has been predicted that AIDS, the 20th-Century's plague, will be worse and more widespread than were all the previous epidemics to date. {RE}

EPIPHENOMENALISM

Epiphenomenalism consists of a group of doctrines about mental-physical causal relations. These are defined in *The Oxford Companion to Philosophy* and, as Paul Edwards has observed, T. H. Huxley was a pioneer proponent of the idea. The theory implies that human beings do not survive the death of their bodies in any form whatsoever. {PE; OCP}

EPISCOPAL CHURCH OF AMERICA

The Episcopal Church, organized in 1789, is at 815 Second Avenue, New York, NY 10017. It calls itself "in communion with the see of Canterbury: in England. On the Web: <http://www.ecysa.angelican.org..

EPISTEMOLOGY

Epistemology is a study or a theory of the nature and grounds of knowledge, focusing on the limits and validity of knowledge. In short, "How do we know what we know?" John Dewey is one of many naturalists who have written on the subject.

Logical positivists, by positing the verification principle, tried to define the testable scope of epistemology. One can "know," for example, from the readings on a Fahrenheit thermometer the relative temperature of a room. One cannot "know," however, "the origin of nothing as compared with something". . . nor if karma and fate are valid concepts . . . nor if the Christian God has the same seven bodily openings as humans. (See entry for Richard Dawkins.) {For a thorough study of the subject, see the *Encyclopedia of Philosophy*, Vol. 3.}

E PITAPHOS: See entries for Edward Everett and for Oratory.

E PLURIBUS UNUM: The Latinate *e pluribus unum*, "one out of many," is found on the Great Seal of the United States. Religionists often mistakenly translate the phrase as "One nation, under God."

Epstein, Harriet (20th Century)

Epstein writes "First Person" for *The Humanist*. She is a freelance writer and lecturer in the New York City area.

"EQUAL UNDER GOD"

In 1997 President Bill Clinton of the United States of America at a "town hall" meeting in Akron, Ohio, said

> We live in a country that is the longest-lasting democracy in human history, founded on the elementary proposition that we are created equal by God. That's what the Constitution says. And we have never lived that way perfectly, but the whole history of America is in large measure the story of our attempt to give a more perfect meaning to the thing we started with—the Constitution and the Bill of Rights.

However, as pointed out by Pauline Maier, a professor of American history at the Massachusetts Institute of Technology, the "elementary proposition that we are created equal by God" is *not* in the Constitution:

> "[T]he thing we started with," and keep trying to "give a more perfect meaning to," is not the Constitution and the Bill of Rights but the assertion of human equality in the Declaration of Independence. To be fair, Bill Clinton is not the only American who gets our basic documents all mixed up. Still, a man sworn to "preserve, protect and defend the Constitution" should have a better idea of just what the document does and does not say. A champion of affirmative action should also have a better grasp on the connection between that effort to achieve racial equality and "the thing we started with."
>
> {*The New York Times*, 7 December 1997}

EQUALITY: See entry for Egalitarianism.

ERAS

A period of time which is reckoned from a specific date that serves as a basis of its chronological system is called an era. Following are examples of chronological eras in 1999:

Era	Year	Began in 1999
Byzantine	7508	14 Sep
Jewish	5760	10 Sep at sunset
Roman	2752	14 Jan
Babylonian	2748	24 Apr
Japanese	2659	1 Jan
Grecian	2311	14 Sep or 14 Oct
Christian	1998	1 Jan
Diocletian	1716	12 Sep
Indian (Saka)	1921	22 Mar
Islamic/Muslim	1420	16 Apr at sunset

{*World Almanac and Book of Facts*, 1998}

Erasmus (or Desiderius Erasmus) (1469—1536)

Erasmus, the Dutch scholar and Renaissance humanist, revolted against the other-worldliness of medieval Christianity but never rejected its supernaturalism. He frequently cited Greek and Roman philosophers and authors, leading Constandse to refer to Erasmus as a pagan rather than a Christian.

Erasmus valued the human conscience and felt that good and evil has existed for all nations and all times. His emphasis was upon making peace among all people, and he rarely used ecclesiastical dogmas as his starting point.

His influence was widespread, and it was said that Pope Paul had once considered making him a cardinal. But in Spain, his followers, called *erasmistas*, came to be considered heretics or some kind of crypto-Protestants.

McCabe cites Erasmus as a great freethinker of his time, adding that he was probably the bastard son of a Dutch priest and his niece. Although we may not know the full extent of his skepticism, McCabe wrote, "he did use his very wide influence to scourge the Roman Church and at times the whole Christian world." He despised both Rome and Lutheranism, but had "no inclination to die for the truth," he said.

McCabe adds that Erasmus "loved comfort (usually at the expense of a friend or patron) and had rather a cynical and Rabelaisian outlook upon life; though this and his discretion about the truth will not surprise any who know the age and the state of the Church. The Catholics burned his fine edition of the Greek New Testament, yet tolerated the grossest license, and the Reformers were sour against the Humanist culture which Erasmus loved. While he did much to ensure the success of the Reformation—he has been described as 'the man who laid the egg that Luther hatched'—Luther detested him."

After joining the monastery in 1488, Erasmus is said to have become enamored of Servatius Rogerus, who may have accepted, then spurned, his attentions. The platonic friendship with William Blount, Fourth Lord Mountjoy, was his most enduring friendship. (For a listing of the classical humanists, see the entry under Classical Humanism. Forest Tyler Stevens of Johns Hopkins University has an entire chapter on Erasmus's alleged homosexuality in *Queering the Renaissance* (1994), edited by Jonathan Goldberg. He analyzes the "love" letters between Erasmus and young Servatius Rogerus. See entry for Preservèd Smith.) {CE; CL, ER; EU, Anton L. Constandse; HNS2; JM; JMRH; RE}

Eratosthenes (c. 275—195 B.C.E.)

A Greek scholar and astronomer who was the head of the library in Alexandria, Eratosthenes was a versatile writer of poetry as well as works on theater, geography, astronomy, mathematics, tilt of the earth, as well as the earth's size and its distance from the sun and the moon. He calculated the circumference of the round earth to be 24,000 miles (less than 1,000 miles off the true value) and the distance to the sun to be 92,000,000 miles, a stunningly close estimation. In short, this ancient Greek freethinking philosopher knew the world was round.

It was not until 1577—1580 that Sir Francis Drake's sailors became the first Englishmen to circumnavigate the world, proving Eratosthenes's theory. The scholar's jest concerning the gods is evident in his poem dedicated to Pan:

> His pierced shepherd-pipe,
> His hairy mantle, his club,
> Daphnis the lover of women now dedicates to his dear Pan.
>
> O Pan, receive these gifts of Daphnis;
> For like him you love music, like him you are luckless in love.

{CE}

Erdmann, Johann Eduard (1805—1892)

A German philosopher, Erdmann in 1829 entered the Lutheran ministry but abandoned it in 1832. He taught philosophy at Halle University, where his work on the history of philosophy showed him to be a Hegelian. Erdmann thought that soul and body are aspects of one reality. {RAT}

Erdmann, Marie (20th Century)

When Erdmann signed Humanist Manifesto II, she was an elementary school teacher. {HM2}

Erdmann, Robert L. (20th Century)

When he signed Humanist Manifesto II, Erdmann was associated with the International Business Machines company. {HM2}

Erdo, Janos (20th Century)

Bishop Erdo heads the Unitarian Church in Romania. (See entry for Romanian Unitarians.)

Erickson, George A. (20th Century)

Erickson, from Minnesota, is on the board of directors of the American Humanist Association. He is Vice President of Humanists of Minneapolis-St. Paul.

Erickson, Gerald M. (1927—)

Erickson, professor of classics and Near Eastern studies at the University of Minnesota, is faculty advisor for a student group named University of Minnesota Atheists and Unbelievers. He holds that religion and morality are not necessarily related, that all too often they are at odds with each other. {*Secular Nation,* November-December 1996}

Erickson, James G. (1925—)

Erickson, a freethinker, wrote *Book of Freeman Cartoons* with Harry Fowler in 1940. The cartoons he drew for E. Haldeman-Julius's newspaper, *The American Freeman,* were widely known. An atheist, he served in the infantry during World War II and in his first letter-to-the-editor mentioned that he was an atheist and had been in a foxhole. The FBI compiled a total of 358 pages on Erickson, because he "has the power to influence people by his ability to cartoon and he, therefore . . . would be dangerous to the United States if we should become engaged in a war with Russia." His response, upon finding the file made available under the Freedom of Information Act, was that he wondered in a nuclear war if he would have had time. Erickson has been an admirer of Madalyn Murray's American Atheists. {*Freethought History* #17, 1996; GS}

Erickson, Jason (20th Century)

In 1996, Erickson, a student of geology, became co-president of the University of Minnesota Atheists and Humanists. Although confirmed in the Christian faith at the age of fourteen, he became an atheist at the age of fifteen. Erickson was one of the founding members of Campus Freethought Alliance. {*Freethought Today,* April 1997; *International Humanist News,* December 1996}

Erickson, Kai T. (20th Century)

Erickson is author of *Wayward Puritans: A Study in the Sociology of Deviance* (1960).

Erickson, Stephanie (20th Century)

In 1996, Erickson, a geology student, became co-president of the University of Minnesota Atheists and Humanists. {*Freethought Today,* April 1997}

Ericson, Edward L. (20th Century)

Ericson is a former president of the American Ethical Union and a leader of the Washington, D.C. (1959—1971) and New York Ethical Culture societies. A Unitarian and signer of Humanist Manifesto II, he is on the editorial board of *The Humanist,* is a contributing editor of *Religious Humanism,* and was one of the principal founders of Americans for Religious Liberty. He addressed the 1966 Fourth International Humanist and Ethical Union World Congress held in Paris. In the 1980s, Ericson became a "free lance" writer and a lecturer. He is author of *The Humanist Way* (1988) and *American Dream Revisited* (1993). (See entry for Ethical Culture.) {CL; HM2; HNS2; PK}

Ericsson, John (1803—1889)

An American inventor, Ericsson after serving for some years as engineer in the Swedish Army moved to England, where he perfected the invention of the steam-propeller for ships. The conservatism of British shipbuilders drove him to America, where he won an international reputation as an engineer and inventor. He constructed the monitors which played an important part in the Civil War. Ingersoll, who was intimately acquainted with Ericsson, described him as "one of the profoundest Agnostics I ever met." {JM; RAT; RE}

Erigena, John Scotus (615—677)

Erigena was an Irish philosopher in a time when the Irish were known as "Scots" in Europe. He took the name Erigena, which means "born in Erin" and was one of the most brilliant of the Irish scholars who, in the short period when some culture still survived in Ireland—the Anglo-Saxon invasions had ruined it in England—migrated to France. Several times he was condemned by the Church, and the work of his that survives (*De Divisione Naturae*) is, according to McCabe, vaguely pantheistic. He is said to have held against the boorish bishops that "reason precedes faith." Disagreeing with McCabe, Dermot Moran in a 1989 study argued that God is the source of all things. {JM; JMRH; RE}

Erion, Gerald J. (20th Century)

Erion is Associate Dean of the Center for Inquiry Institute (CFII), which is an educational group that provides a Certificate of Proficiency to students of humanism. The group's address is PO Box 703, Amherst, NY 14226. E-mail: CFIinstit@aol.com.

Ernst, Max (1891—1976)

Ernst, the German painter who was a member of the Dada movement and a founder of surrealism, scandalized believers with a 1926 painting, "The Blessed Virgin Chastising the Child Jesus Before Three Witnesses: A.B. [André Breton], P. E. [Paul Eluard], and the artist." Depicted is a big-breasted Mary about to slap a young, perhaps five-year-old, blond Jesus.

Viewers were sure to question how an all-perfect God in the form of His Son could possibly have done anything wrong that would have demanded his mother's punishment. At any rate, the tyke's buttocks are appropriately blushing and his apparently detachable halo has fallen onto the floor. The painting hangs in the Museum Ludwig, Cologne, Germany. {CE}

EROS

In Greek religion, Eros was symbolic of love in all its manifestations: physical passion at its strongest; tender, romantic love; playful, sportive love. The god of love, Eros was represented as a winged youth armed with bow and arrows. Some legends described Eros as one of the oldest of the gods, born from Chaos and personifying creative power and harmony. Most described him as the son of Aphrodite and Ares. Poets ascribed to Eros that which all in love have experienced: the frenzies and agonies of love. To some, Eros was also the god of fertility. In Roman myth, where he was called Amor or Cupid, he was represented as a naked, winged child, the son and companion of Venus. Legend also has it that he fell in love with Psyche, sweeping her off to an isolated castle but forbidding her to look at him inasmuch as he was a god. As lovers will do, she disobeyed, he abandoned her, and she ceaselessly searched for him until at last the two were reunited and she became immortal. {CE}

Ernesti, Johann August (1707-1781)

Ernesti was a German critic, a professor of classical literature at Wittenberg and Leipzig. A philologist, Ernesti insisted that the Bible must be interpreted just as any other book must be. {BDF}

ERRANCY LIST

The Skeptical Review has as its e-mail address <errancy@infidels.org>.

Erwin, Greg (1947—1999)

Erwin was president of the Humanist Association of Ottawa, a member-at-large of *The Humanist in Canada*, and a contributing editor of the *Secular Humanist Bulletin*. He published, edited, and distributed *Lucifer's Echo*, a monthly electronic magazine of atheism, humanist, and freethought that was distributed over the Internet. Erwin also was a supporter of Internet Infidels.

Born in the United States, Erwin moved to Canada in 1968 and became a Canadian citizen. He was behind the campaign for all humanists who were formerly members of churches to have those churches remove their name from their membership records, and he provided information to anyone who asked how to get excommunicated. At the 1994 Toronto conference of the Coalition for Secular Humanism, Atheism, and Freethought (CSHAFT), Erwin was elected president.

In a memoriam, Trevor Banks wrote

> Greg had recently retired very early after twenty-six years in the public service, latterly with the National Parole Board. He had obtained a degree in Modern Languages at Carleton University. Soon after his arrival in Canada, at a retreat in the Laurentians, he met his beloved wife and devoted friend Paddy, with whom he had the good fortune to spend the next twenty-nine years of his life. . . . He served as President of HAO and, later, as 1st Vice President of HAC. Humanism could not have wished for a better ambassador. He was always willing and eager to devote his time and immense talents to spreading the philosophy of humanism to the world through interviews on the radio and TV and on the internet. His online periodical, "The Nullifidian," was a masterpiece of rational humanistic dialogue and polemic.
>
> (*UU News*, 31 Jan 1999)

Erwin, Milo (19th Century)

Fred Whitehead in *Freethought History* (#3, 1992) quotes a statement by Erwin in *The History of Williamson County, Illinois* (1976):

> I met some old men who told me that in an early day, when they neither had gospel nor meetings, that the people were peaceable, friendly, and happy; and as soon as preachers came into the country they got up "isms," "sects," and "systems," which ended in jars and feuds among the people, and that they have never seen any peace since.

Esau, Reed (1965—)

Esau, a software engineer in Minnesota, founded the Celebrity Atheists, Agnostics, and Other Non-Theists on the internet in 1995 in response to a statement made by a nationally syndicated late-night radio talk-show host. The host had attempted to marginalize those who are skeptical of religious ideas as being members of an ideological class—radical left-wing Marxists. Esau found, however, that

> my experience said otherwise, so I launched this clever bit of counter-propaganda on the World Wide Web. The list is a collaboration of sorts, relying on its thousands of readers for submissions and updates. I play the role of editor, collecting and organizing information for publication. The list has but a single purpose in mind: to defuse the misconception that we are of a single mind. In a non-partisan manner, it attempts to show, by quoting those with whom most of us are familiar (celebrities), that you can find non-theists across the political and ideological spectrum.

Esau is amused that the talk-show host is no longer on the air. A motorcyclist, Esau relaxes by racing around the Canadian and American byways. {WAS, 25 March 1997}

Escherny, François Louis d' (1733—1815)

The Swiss author of *Lacunes de la Philosophie* (1783) and *Equality* (1795), Escherny became the associate of Helvetius, Diderot, and Rousseau, whom he much admired. His work displays his freethought. Escherny accepted the French Revolution in its sober beginnings but was later repelled by the Terror. {BDF; RAT; RE}

ESKIMO: See entry for Inuit.

Eslinger, Brian (20th Century)

Eslinger, minister of the Unitarian Universalist Fellowship of Ames, Iowa, has a humanistic outlook that emphasizes acting ethically. Discussing a meeting with two daughters as they recounted stories of their ninety-year-old father who was dying, he heard of the father's active life of service to others, which he described as being one humanist perspective. Religious humanism, he added,

> has always had many [viewpoints]. For instance, early in the century, as humanism was forming in Unitarianism, a group represented by Francis Ellingwood Abbott believed, in Abbott's words, that "science is destined to be the world's Messiah" and had, in fact, replaced God. On the other hand, the Rev. John Dietrich, while embracing reason, did not sweep all knowledge into science. "I consider [the meaning of our finer emotions] as important as the message of reason," he said. In the place of a narrow focus on science, Dietrich emphasized all experience.
>
> I myself focus on how our experiences affect our actions, how we act ethically. A universal of humanism is the optimistic belief that human beings can perform saving acts, that indeed only we can. Where can we find encouragement to struggle and celebrate in this world? I do not rely on supernatural forces. My inspiration comes to me through my own senses, though I realize the senses are shaped and influenced by heredity, society, and history. In this complicated relationship reason plays a crucial role. As imperfect beings we understand that our views are not the final word on anything, but through reason we can understand how limited our perspectives are and learn from the perspectives of other people.
>
> My time with the grieving family [of the ninety-year-old father] deepened my feeling that a quiet life, lived with purpose, can

affect many lives around it. Was the women's father a humanist? I don't know, but he taught me about being human.
{*World*, November-December 1997}

Esolen, Anthony M. (20th Century)

Esolen, who teaches English at Providence College in Rhode Island, translated and edited Lucretius's *On the Nature of Things* (1995).

ESOTERIC

• Esoteric, adj. Very particularly abstruse and consummately occult. The ancient philosophies were of two kinds: *exoteric*, those that the philosophers themselves could partly understand, and *esoteric*, those that nobody could understand. It is the latter that have most profoundly affected modern thought and found greatest acceptance in our time.

—**Ambrose Bierce**
The Devil's Dictionary

ESPACE DE LIBERTÉS

A humanistic monthly in French, *Espace de Libertés* is in Belgium at Campus de la Plaine ULB-CP 236, Avanue Arnaud Fraiteur, 1050 Brussels. <espace@cal.ulb.ac.be>.

Espenschied, Judith (20th Century)

The first Ethical Culture Leader up to 1999 to give birth after entering leadership, Espenschied was an active young parent in Washington, a graduate student of philosophy, and one who became president of the National Leaders Council. (See entry for Ethical Culture.)

ESPERANTO

In Esperanto, the artificial international language invented by a Polish oculist, Ludwig Lazar Zamenhof, "humanism" is **homaranismo.**

Espinas, Alfred (Born 1844)

A French philosopher who with Ribot translated Spencer's *Principles of Psychology*, Espinas wrote studies on *Experimental Philosophy in Italy* and on *Animal Societies* (1877). Espinas is a Chevalier of the Legion of Honour and a member of the *Institut*. {BDF; RAT}

Espronceda, José de (1810—1842)

So obnoxious was Espronceda when he was fifteen years old that he was imprisoned, then banished. In London and Paris, the young radical came under the influence of Byron and Hugo, then fought with the people in the Paris Revolution of 1830. When the Spanish king died, Espronceda returned to Madrid but was again banished for too free expression of his opinions. Among his works are lyrical poems; an unfinished epic, *El Pelayo*; and a poem about the Devil-World, *El Diablo-Mundo*, which shows the influence of Faust and Don Juan. His God, he said, was Liberty and

I unheedingly follow my path,
At the mercy of winds and of waves.
Wrapt thus within the arms of Fate,
What care I if lost or saved.

{BDF; JM; RAT; RE}

Esquiros, Henri Alphonse (1812—1876)

Esquiros was a French poet. In his *Évangile du Peuple* (1840, for which he suffered eight months' imprisonment, he rationalizes the life of Jesus. Esquiros was elected anti-clerical member of the Legislative Assembly in 1848 but was compelled to flee in 1851. A devoted rationalist, he became a member of the Provisional Government in 1870, the National Assembly in 1871, and the Senate in 1875. {RAT}

ESSENCE: See *Encyclopedia of Philosophy*, Vol. 3.

ESSENES

The Essenes were members of a Jewish sect that was born of the ferment of ideas in the few centuries before the time of Jesus, when, according to McCabe, "the imperialist-military movements led to a very wide mingling of cultures." Josephus mentioned them in his *Jewish War*, and some have speculated that Josephus might have been an Essene. What Josephus tells of their doctrines and practices "has a singular resemblance to the manner of life which the Jesus of the Gospels recommends," McCabe notes, implying that many so-called Christian ideas were not original. For example, the Essenes lived in monasteries. They went about Judaea in pairs, healing the sick and exhorting men to virtue. They were vowed to celibacy and poverty, carried no money or change of garments, and had to avoid oaths. Their preaching laid great stress on peace and justice.

DeQuincey contended that the early Christians *were* Essenes, and the fact that, while they must have been a prominent feature of the religious life of Judaea, they are never mentioned in the Gospels raises a suspicion that the Christians of the second generation tried to suppress knowledge of them. Inasmuch as the Essenian sect goes back to at least 100 B.C.E., the implication is that the philosophy of love preached by Jesus was not the Word of God but, rather, the view of the Essenes. Further, there is evidence of Persian and Hellenistic influences in the sect's thought.

In 1997, Stephen J. Pfann, director in Jerusalem of the Center for the Study of Early Christianity, told a conference of several hundred scholars that the bitter contests over the scrolls had been resolved, that the caves in which the scrolls had been found had now passed from Jordanian to Israeli control, and that it was now possible to concentrate upon interpretations of the desert sect and its impact on both Judaism and Christianity.

According to Pfann, in about 30 B.C.E. the Maskil, the leader of a strict and ascetic Jewish sect known as the Essenes, wrote some notes to instruct a two-year novitiate before he could be accepted as a full-fledged Sons of Light and allowed to enter the community. Ordinarily, written notes were not made lest they fall into the "profane" hands of the Sons of Darkness. Pfann reported that "The Essenes held sacred sessions every night to study sacred texts and find their meanings. They believed they were called into the wilderness to discern divine revelation in the Torah. So the early stages of their discussion was recorded in code until a final version was prepared by the Maskil. He was the visionary. He floated between heaven and earth. He sought revelation in nature, in the movement of the sun, moon, and stars."

Freethinkers' interest in the scrolls is focused on the findings by John Allegro. He has charged that the Catholic Church deliberately suppressed parts of the Essene texts. As of 1995, the Dead Sea Scrolls had not been fully made public and, again, the implication was that powerful vested interests are adamant in wishing to keep them secret lest it become obvious that Jesus was simply another Essene, nothing more.

A 1998 work, Hershel Shanks's *The Mystery and Meaning of the Dead Sea Scrolls*, disagrees with Edmund Wilson's earlier assessment, that the most important of the scrolls foreshadowed Christian doctrine. Wilson found that the Qumran sect was "more than Bethlehem or Nazareth, the cradle of Christianity." Shanks disagrees, holding that "Jesus is not in the scrolls," that the scrolls are Jewish, not Christian, documents, and that their value lies in revealing that "we had not previously known about the situation of Judaism at the dawn of Christianity." According to Shanks, the Scrolls show there were several Judaisms when Christianity was born. One was Christianity, the other Rabbinic Judaism. Richard Bernstein, writing in *The New York Times* (1 April 1998), found the Shanks view "arresting, even shocking to some. We can be thankful to Mr. Shanks for illuminating the documents that produced it, even as we wish he had given us fuller explanations of the scholarly and theological debates that the discovery of the scrolls has always entailed." (See entry for Edmund Wilson, author of *The Scrolls from the Dead Sea* [1955].) {CE; *The New York Times*, 27 July 1997; RE}

Essex, R. S. (20th Century)

Essex, a freethinker, co-wrote with Sidney Dark *The War Against God* (1937). {GS}

ESTABLISHED CHURCH

If a government supports a church as a national institution, that church is the established church.

In England, the Church of England is the established church, although efforts have been made to "disestablish" the church, with opponents of the idea known as anti-disestablishmentarians.

The Presbyterian Church is the established church in Scotland, the Lutheran in Scandinavian countries.

Esteve, Pierre (c. 1700—1748)

A French writer, Esteve wrote a *History of Astronomy* and an anonymous work on the *Origin of the Universe Explained from a Principle of Matter* (1748). {BDF}

Estienne, Henri (1528—1598)

Estienne was a French printer who, at the age of eighteen, assisted his father in collating thc manuscripts of Dionysius and Halicarnassus. In 1557 he established a printing office of his own, issuing many Greek authors. His *Apologie pour Herodote* is designed as a satire on Christian legends and directed against priests and priestcraft. As a result, he was driven from place to place. Sir Philip Sidney highly esteemed him and "kindly entertained him in his travaile." Garasse classes him with atheists. {BDF}

Estrella, Hugo (1964—)

For the *International Humanist News* (December 1997, October 1998, and December 1998), Estrella has described the struggle of freethinkers in Argentina. In addition to being Executive Director of *Sociedad Humanista-Ética Argentina*, he is Executive Director of Y/S Pugwash Argentina. Estrella signed Humanist Manifesto 2000. E-mail: <humanistarg@usa.net>.

ETERNAL LIFE

Alexander Nehamas, a Princeton professor in the humanities and philosophy, has written of "eternal life" that

> The idea that there is such a thing as an eternal life and that it is in most ways more important than this life—though it has produced a number of great goods—I think has generally caused immensely greater misery than it has helped the world.
>
> First of all, it has completely devalued, for many of those who believe in it, their present life. Second, it has made many of those people who believe in it live in constant fear and guilt for what's going to happen to them afterward. And it has prevented them from doing anything to get rid of that fear and guilt by acting right because, if anything, they will get their just deserts [six] later on.
>
> Faith in the eternal life, which means faith in an absolute justification if you are on the right side, has caused some of the worst treatment of human beings by other human beings.
>
> {*The New York Times*, 31 October 1997}

ETERNITY

• If by eternity is understood not endless temporal duration but timelessness, then he lives eternally who lives in the present.

—**Ludwig Wittgenstein**

(See *Encyclopedia of Philosophy*, Vol. 3.)

ETHICAL CULTURE

Felix Adler (1851—1933) inaugurated the Ethical Culture movement in New York City in 1876. Although trained to succeed his father as rabbi of Temple Emanuel in New York, Adler revolted against the theology and ceremonialism of the Hebrew religion. With a few sympathizers who left the synagogue with him, he founded a society pledged "to assert the supreme importance of the ethical factor in all relations of life, personal, social, national and international, apart from any theological or metaphysical consideration."

The society holds its own religious services, but members may have other religious affiliations. Societies were formed in Chicago (1882) by William M. Salter; in Philadelphia (1885) by S. Burns Weston; in St. Louis (1866) by Walter L. Sheldon; in Brooklyn (1906) by Leslie Sprague; and in Westchester County (1927) by David S. Muzzey. In New York, the Ethical Culture Schools introduced the systematic teaching of ethics in all the grades.

On Adler's death in 1933, the senior leadership of the New York society passed to his colleague for forty years, Dr. John L. Elliott. Other leaders have included Horace J. Bridges in Chicago; W. Edwin Collier in Philadelphia; J. Hutton Hynd in St. Louis; and Henry Neumann in Brooklyn. Two outstanding books concerning the movement are David S. Muzzey's Ethics as a Religion (1951) and Howard B. Radest's *Toward Common Ground* (1969).

James F. Hornback, whose Columbia University doctoral dissertation was about Ethical Society founders, wrote the following in 1986 to the present author about Adler and the Ethical Societies:

> The Society for Ethical Culture in the City of New York, as it was soon incorporated, began in May 1876 with a meeting of the largely personal following of twenty-five-year-old **Dr. Felix Adler**, whose inaugural (or trial) sermon in his father's Temple Emanu-El (German, Reform) in New York had ended long expectations of his being a rabbi. Why? His "Judaism of the Future" would be open to all people, and he had neglected to mention any "special mission" for "the Jewish people," or even their God. The gentlemen of the Board were shocked and quickly agreed with him on severance. Adler disclaimed atheism, or even agnosticism, but had a deep Kantian sense of the independence and the supremacy of ethics in human life *and* in the cosmos—"the Ought," as he put it for teaching children, "in all its awful majesty."
>
> The railroad-banking tycoon **Joseph Seligman** endowed a lectureship for Adler at the new and liberal Cornell University, where President Andrew D. White (later author of the classic *History of the Warfare of Science and Theology in Christendom*) defended his wide-ranging lectures on "Oriental Language and Literature" from Christian and orthodox critics. When his contract was not renewed in 1876, Adler went back to his friends in New York City, with whom he had met on weekends, to start his Society.
>
> A fringe member of the Emerson circle, Adler also joined the Free Religious Association (FRA) and its annual intellectual conferences in Boston, founded in 1867 and lasting into the twentieth century. He became president in 1879, with **Ralph Waldo Emerson** as vice-president, succeeding the more aloof intellectual **Octavius B. Frothingham**, Unitarian, of New York. But he declined a second term, declaring that the Free Religious Association concentrated too much on what Kant (and Aristotle) had called "the starry heavens above," and not enough on "the Moral Law within."
>
> Adler's activism (schools, charities, visiting nurses, child labor, etc.) attracted other young men of the Free Religious Association: **William M. Salter** from Iowa, Knox College and Harvard Divinity School, who chose to stay with Adler and lead an Ethical Society in Chicago (1882—1883) rather than go to the new "Ethical Basis" Unitarian Society in Minneapolis; **S. Burns Weston**, victim of a Unitarian "heresy" trial for not preaching the "Unitarian Christianity" specified in the bequest supporting his church in Leicester, Massachusetts; and **Walter L. Sheldon**, a New Englander whom Weston met in school at Berlin, suffering from scientific and philosophic destruction of his Fundamentalism. Weston went as Adler's founding Leader in Philadelphia (1885), and Sheldon, after much fuming over Adler's anti-scientific attitudes, to be first leader in St. Louis (1886). Stanton Coit, a self-recruited Emersonian from Ohio, teaching English at Amherst, understudied with Adler but found a movement of his own with the leading ethical philosophers (Sidgwick, Muirhead, Bosanquet, Caird, Stephen, etc.) in the London (1886) and the conversion in name only of the South Place

Religious Society (1793) into Ethical Society (1888). Coit, a self-styled humanist, was always too empirical, liturgical, and willing to translate Christian words and symbols into humanism, for Adler's taste.

Yet Coit recruited and trained several of the second- and third-generation (quarter-century) Leaders for Adler's movement: Golding, Chubb (self-trained, a charter member of the London Society and the Fabians), and O'Dell (a humanist never really accepted by Adler as a Leader); and then Hynd (humanist, St. Louis) and Collier (ethical mystic and transcendentalist, Philadelphia). Under Coit's daughter Virginia (Lady Flemming)) and those previously mentioned, the British Ethical Union has gone much more unambiguously humanistic since his death in 1944.

Adler's departure from Judaism drew emotional criticism from Jewish loyalists for many years, and still does, although it was without bitterness or denial of valuable heritage on his part. He gave two reasons. First, however noble or ethical at its best, Judaism is "a racial religion." (The concept of "race" was to yield to "ethnic" or "ethnocentric" with Huxley and Hadden in the 1930s, and to "racist" as a negative attitude with Ashley Montagu and others, later on.) Second, Judaism's "unitary concept" of God was less true to reality for Adler than an ideal or transcendental "community of spirits" or "Spiritual Universe." He affirmed a "Host of Gods" rather than "the God of Hosts." He opposed Zionism until death in 1933.

Disappointed and often taunted over vastly disproportionate numbers of Jews in his societies and schools ("seldom exceeds 100%," quipped Rabbi Stephen Wise's son, James W., in his Adler chapter in *Jews Are Like That*), Adler steadfastly refused to make his movement explicitly Jewish, or to sanction a parallel movement for gentiles. (Even today, one hears from the uninformed or the malicious, who have often said so to me, that Ethical Societies are more appropriate for Jews, and the Unitarians or even the Humanists for "Christians.") In Starting or in recognizing new societies, Adler was to take great care in finding sponsoring committees of prominence and varied background, and giving them professional Leaders who shared his universalism in this matter.

In St. Louis in 1883, Adler sternly disavowed a distinguished group of German freethinkers, both Jewish and gentile, who were followers of Ex-Senator Carl Schurz and his *Westliche Post*. They had long called their own activities *Ethische Kultur*. On hearing of Adler's movement, they invited him "to give his episcopal benediction." Instead, he spoke at great length on his own views, monopolizing a large audience, according to a young reporter, Adolphe de Castro, who was later U.S. Consul in Madrid. By 1886, Adler and Weston had found Sheldon as a Leader, and formed a sponsoring committee chaired by attorney Charles Nagel (later President Taft's Secretary of Commerce and Labor), whose wife was Louis Brandeis's sister. Freethinkers were conspicuously absent, as were the noted St. Louis Hegelians (W. T. Harris, Louis Soldan, Denton Snyder, etc.). But the society began with a cross-section of religious and ethnic backgrounds, which it has maintained despite an over-representation of Jewish background (15 to 18% according to a 1986 questionnaire) and under-representation of blacks (1 to 2%).

Adler's second generation of Leaders (roughly 1900—1925) remained loyal to a generally idealist-transcendentalist philosophy: **John Lovejoy Elliott**, a warm farm boy from the civil-libertarian Illinois Lovejoys and Ingersoll-supporting Elliotts (in New York, 1894—1942); **David S. Muzzey**, Yankee seminarian turned American historian at Columbia and Barnard (part-time, New York, 1895—1965); Alfred W. Martin, Jewish-Christian-Unitarian theist who left his Free Church in Seattle to write and teach comparative religions (New York, 1907—1931); **Anna Garlin Spencer**, minister, Free Religious Society, Providence, Rhode Island, 1889—1904 (New York, 1904—1913), then moved on in feminist protest to teaching, with expressed sympathy of Weston and Chubb); **Percival Chubb**, charter member, London, and first secretary, Fabians, to United States as writer, lecturer, and teacher of English and drama (soon in Ethical Culture High Schools), editor *Ethical Record* (1898—1904), later Leader (St. Louis, 1911—1933, emeritus till death, 1960); **Horace J. Bridges**, British laborer (printing) groomed by Coit as liberal empiricist, turned theological and social conservative as Leader under Adler, died Episcopalian in the 1950s (Leader, Chicago, 1913—1945); **George O'Dell**, British empiricist and humanist, trustee and then president of National Union of Clerks and Administrative Workers (1906—1913), assistant to Coit in the British Ethical Union (1903—1913), then executive secretary of American Ethical Union and editor of *The Standard* (1913—1947); **Henry Golding**, British businessman and Ethical layman, career change late, till early death (New York, 1923—1931); and **Henry Neumann**, college teacher of English and education, youngest of second generation and professed bearer of Adler's philosophy into third and fourth, when he died a tolerant humanist (Brooklyn, 1911—1966). Many Humanists will remember the kindly octogenarian.

The small but distinguished third generation (1925—1950 and after) veered sharply toward humanism, excepting **W. Edwin Collier**, a Coit recruit from the Church of England who remains in active retirement (Ethical-Unitarian) a transcendental mystic (Philadelphia, 1934—1952). **Algernon D. Black**, a graduate of Ethical Culture Schools and Harvard, joined Adler's staff in 1923, was made a Leader in 1932, headed ethics teaching in the schools for many years, led actively in the larger community for more than fifty years, and is now emeritus. Though a humanist, he declined to sign Manifesto II out of loyalty to the larger inclusiveness of Ethical Culture. (So did **Horace L. Friess**, Adler's son-in-law and literary-biographical executor, who taught humanist philosophy and comparative religions for many years at Columbia, and served as a part-time Leader and trainer of Leaders in New York from 1952 until death in 1975). **Joseph L. Blau**, a renowned student of Judaica and teacher of American philosophy and religion (retired as department head) at Columbia, did sign Humanist Manifesto II and listed himself in *Who's Who* as "a long-time humanist," with an explicit credo. The late **Jerome Nathanson**, a journalist and student of philosophy, did John Dewey's authorized interpretation, with few direct quotations or phrases, for Scribner's (*John Dewey: The Reconstruction of the Democratic Life*, 1951), worked often in cooperative Ethical-Humanist projects (including church and state and the Conferences on Science and Democracy in 1943, 1944, and 1945), used "religious" terminology with explicit misgivings, and signed Manifesto II shortly before his final illness (Leader, New York 1940—1975). **J. Hutton Hynd**, the Scottish Congregationalist who became a humanist with Coit, was forthright in his rejection of traditional religions (favorite address, "The Fundamentalists Are Right"), though willing (as I am) to make use of their incidental institutional wisdom, beauty and "trappings." While in St. Louis (1933—1950), he continued the Sheldon and Chubb heritage of sound institutionalism, though with far less social consciousness. He returned to semi-retirement in the British movement, and died in 1970.

V. T. Thayer, made a member of the AEU Leaders Council—then called the Fraternity of Leaders—as Adler's trusted though Dewey-ite Director of Ethical Culture Schools, 1928—1947, was one of the signers of the first Humanist Manifesto in 1933. So was **Frank Swift**, a young British-Canadian Unitarian in training for Ethical leadership in St. Louis, New York, and Boston, who died that December as a good Samaritan on icy roads. The news of their signing was mercifully kept from Dr. Adler in his final illness. Incidentally, I have always shared Dr. Thayer's reluctance to call Humanism, or even Ethical Culture, "religious" for the alleged advantages in public acceptance or law. He believed, as I do, in complete equality of "rights" for "religious" and "non-religious" institutions and individuals, rather than fudging meanings. And he warned of the Fundamentalist backlash against our double standard.

The fourth generation of Ethical Leaders was forthrightly humanistic. The late **Henry B. Herman**, an Ethical Culture and Wisconsin graduate and experienced social worker, started Leadership training in New York in 1942 with **J. F. Hornback** and **William D. Hammond** (long a Unitarian minister, now retired). Herman led in New York and briefly in Westchester County (1946—1965) before moving to the Wisconsin Student Union, where he died young in 1971. Hornback led in Westchester (1947—1951) and in St. Louis until going emeritus in 1984. **Sheldon Ackley**, fired from teaching philosophy at Gettysburg College, for atheism, was recruited by **Joseph Blau** as the highly successful first Leader of the Long Island Society (1950—1959). He returned to university administration and teaching, coming back after early retirement to be an explicitly "Secular Humanist" Leader in New York in 1982. **Matthew Ies Spetter**, a Dutch humanist, journalist, and Holocaust survivor, taught in the schools, then led in Brooklyn (1953—1955) and in Riverdale-Yonkers since 1955. **Walter Lawton**, a Baptist minister turned businessman and society president, has led in Northern Westchester, Queens, Chicago, and Westchester (1958—); **Barbara Raines**, a teacher of science long active in Philadelphia, moved west and became Leader of the West Coast Council for Ethical Culture in 1960, where she specialized in humanistic psychology, and then returned briefly to leadership in Northern Westchester in 1970; **Douglas Frazier**, a veteran Unitarian- Universalist minister, led in Los Angeles (1958—1964) and Bergen County, New Jersey (1964—1968); and **Harold J. Quigley**, a Presbyterian dismissed for heresy, in Cleveland, Los Angeles, and Chicago (1962—1981).

Younger men who joined the fourth generation were the humanistic Unitarians: **Edward L. Ericson** in Washington (1959—1971) and New York until going "free lance" as a writer and lecturer in 1984; **Khoren Arisian** in Boston (1966—1968) and New York (1968—1979), and now at the traditionally humanistic Minneapolis Unitarian Society; and **Howard Box** in Brooklyn (1960—1976) until his return to the Unitarians in Oak Ridge. Their contemporary, **Howard Radest**, came from a New York high school and Columbia College into Leadership training and military service, after which he became Leader in Bergen in 1956, executive director of the AEU in 1964, and after a few years of teaching philosophy at Ramapo College, New Jersey, director of Ethical Culture Schools in 1979. Radest is also Dean of the Leadership-Training Institute of the North American Committee for Humanism (NACH) and one of the "Troika" of co-chairmen of the IHEU, which includes **Bert Schwarz** of Holland and **Mihaelo Markovic** of Yugoslavia.

Older men who joined the fourth generation as Leaders were **A. Eustace Haydon** in Chicago (1945—1955) and **Lester Mondale** in Philadelphia (1952—1959), both signers of Humanist Manifestos I and II; and **George Beauchamp**, a teacher and educational administrator active in formation of the Washington Society during World War II, who was elected to the Fraternity of Leaders in 1947. Haydon, the Canadian Baptist turned Unitarian and Humanist, succeeded the liberal Professor Foster (his teacher) in history of religions at the University of Chicago Divinity School (1929—1945). To him, religion was "the shared quest for the good life"—a ridiculously broad definition, to my mind, but one which was no doubt broadening and humanizing to several generations of clergy and teachers. His selection by the remnants of the Chicago Society to succeed their contemptuously anti-humanistic, anti-socialist Leader, **Horace Bridges**, assured the depletion of their once great resources, as the wealthy Dr. Bridges insisted on a pension. Dr. Haydon gave his eloquent basic address many times in the decade following his second retirement (1955—1965), and in Los Angeles his last decade (1965—1975). Mondale, the youngest signer of Manifesto I and spokesman for humanism in Unitarianism and Ethical Culture for many years, is still active as a speaker, conference-goer, and *Humanist* magazine columnist from his longtime Ozark Mountain retreat. Beauchamp, in semi-retirement since 1957 as developer of a retirement center in Florida, is still active as Dean (counselor to Leaders) of the AEU Leaders Council.

A transitional figure between the fourth and fifth generation (1975 to 1986), **M. Michael Grupp** belongs more with the fifth in philosophy and style, as he emphatically refused to sign Humanist Manifesto II because hr regarded it as too rationalistic and non-religious for Ethical Culture. He has been a Leader since 1965 in Southern Connecticut, Queens, Westchester, and Brooklyn—a frequent youth worker and ethics teacher. Other veteran fifth-generation Leaders are **Joseph Chuman**, a classics graduate at City College, now completing a doctorate in religion at Columbia, who started leadership training in 1967, led briefly in Essex County, New Jersey, and then settled as Leader in Bergen; **Arthur Dobrin**, a history major from City College, who came into Ethical leadership training after Peace Corps service in Kenya (1965—1967), has led in Long Island since 1968 through community service and poetic flair, and is now a doctoral candidate in social work at Adelphi; **Donald Montagna**, now a business trainee and member in New York who worked briefly with Dobrin, then took his skills in organizational development and psychology into leadership of the Washington Society in 1972; **Michael Franch**, a student and teacher of history, entered leadership in Baltimore in 1975, edited *ethical society* initially for the AEU (as a more Ethical movement-centered, religious, and economical publication than *The Humanist*, co-sponsored with the AHA from 1969 until 1977), and then completed his doctorate with free-lance employment in 1984; and **Judith Espenschied**, long a leadership prospect as an active young parent in Washington, a graduate student of philosophy, finally entering leadership in Philadelphia in 1982, bearing another child soon after (the only Ethical Leader ever to do so), and now President of the National Leaders Council. Only Chuman of this fifth generation signed Humanist Manifesto II in 1973, although Franch and Espenschied with their more naturalistic philosophies (less psychological or existential) might well have done so.

Also joining Ethical Leadership after intensive training in the 1980s are three young mothers: **Lois Kellerman** of New York and **Susan Bagot** of Washington, "certified" in 1983 as Leaders in Queens and a new society in Northern Virginia, respectively; and **Judith Toth**, for several years executive secretary and an organizational trainer in Washington, for leadership in Baltimore in 1985, part time, in her third training year. **David Clarke**, an experienced Unitarian minister with a doctorate, is doing his in-service training with West Coast societies.

Also fifth generation through late entry into Ethical Leadership are **John Hoad** from Barbados and Cambridge Divinity School, twenty-five years a Methodist minister and seminary president in the West Indies, who came from Princeton Seminary studies (and has now completed his Ph. D.) during Jeff Hornback's doctoral leave (1980—1981) and stayed on, overlapping, to succeed him; **Gerald Larue**, longtime Humanist and recent AHA Board member, professor emeritus of religion at UCLA and still teaching and counseling there part time, was introduced officially as Leader in Los Angeles at the AEU Assembly of 1982; and **Jean Kotkin** an Ethical member, school parent, and longtime volunteer in New York, succeeded Howard Radest in the AEU office, at first cut back in policy and finance to "administrative secretary," then rising rapidly through style and titles again to "executive director," and now, since her successful application for leadership status several years ago, to the new title of Leader for National Development. An ardent "religious" humanist with strong sympathies toward the psychological humanism of the fifth generation, she did nevertheless sign Humanist Manifesto II and administers the Humanist Institute for NACH. John Hoad, similarly oriented now, might not have signed in 1973. And Jerry Larue, though not on early printed lists of signers, might have signed eventually.

Thus, the AEU, which began as an Adler-dominated federation of the first four American societies in 1886, was largely a voluntary organization for correspondence, platform-exchange, annual or semi-annual conventions, and official approval of Leaders. The International Ethical Union (IEU), started in Eisenach in 1896, included Ethical societies in Great Britain, Germany, Austria, Switzerland, France, Italy, and Tokyo up to World War I. The IEU sponsored important Moral Educational Congresses, with published proceedings, and one Inter-National Races Congress in London in 1911. Moral Education Congresses resumed after the war, every four years from 1922 in Geneva, Rome, Paris, and Krakow, and plans were aborted for the next one in Berlin. But there was little else in the IEU between the wars, and Ethical societies faded out in all but Great Britain and Vienna. Hence the need for revival, with the strange new Humanists, after World War II.

After Adler, the AEU remained loose and poorly financed. George O'Dell, who succeeded Weston as its secretary and publisher, eked out a living doing pastoral work for New York and pulpits for Unitarians. He was retired (back to England) in 1947, and succeeded by a series of far more highly paid editors, executive secretaries, and staff specialists, supported by a per capita assessment formula for the societies starting at $10 and now with a ceiling about four times that. After Henry Neumann volunteered to edit the failing *Standard* (then *Ethical Outlook*), the AEU stabilized under Radest's capable administration, with an ecumenical co-sponsorship of *The Humanist* instead. Even as Adler had cut loose his finely conceived *International Journal of Ethics* (1890—1914) on the mistaken grounds that "it does not count for the movement" (too many naturalists, pragmatists, utilitarians, etc.), so did the younger Leaders and smaller societies, with or without Leaders, vote the AEU out of *The Humanist* under Paul Kurtz at the St. Louis Assembly of 1977. They did not heed, or did not care, that Kurtz was his own man in editorial policy and management, and not a servant of the AHA, which was soon to break with him, too, and switch to Lloyd Morain. (Although often disagreeing with Paul Kurtz on his conservative politics and radicalism on lifestyles, I consider him a good and challenging editor—as I do Morain. The break for AHA was more personal than philosophic.)

In 1926, *The Fiftieth Anniversary of the Ethical Movement 1876—1926* was published and contains historical information about the group's origins.

Membership in the twenty Ethical Culture congregations peaked in the 1960s at about 5,800 and, according to the *Kansas City Star* (7 August 1993), had diminished to 3,050 members in the 1990s, "more than half . . . in New Jersey and New York."

Ethical Culture is found on the Web: <http://www.aeu.org/society.html>. (For a continuation of Dr. Hornback's historical sketch of the relationship between the Ethical Culture groups and the American Humanist Association, see entry for American Humanist Association. Also see entry for South Place Ethical Society.) {CE; ER; PUT; RE; WAS, 1986}

ETHICAL CULTURE SOCIETIES

- California
  - Ethical Culture Society of the Bay Area (415) 522-3758; <sanfrancisco@aeu.org>
  - Ethical Culture Society of Los Angeles, PO Box 370425, Reseda, CA 91337 <losangeles@aeu.org>.
  - Ethical Culture Society of San Diego <sandiego@aeu.org>
- District of Columbia
  - Washington Ethical Society, 7750 16th St. NW, Washington, DC 20012 (202) 882-6650; <wes@aeu.org>
- Illinois
  - Ethical Humanist Society of Greater Chicago, 7574 North Lincoln Ave., Skokie, IL 60077; (847) 677-3354; chicago@aeu.org>
- Iowa
  - Iowa Ethical Union <iowa@aeu.org>
- Maryland
  - Baltimore Ethical Society, 1323 North Calvert St., Baltimore, MD 21202 (410) 581-2322; <baltimore@aeu.org>
- Massachusetts
  - Ethical Society of Boston, PO Box 38-1934, Cambridge, MA 02238 (617) 739-9050
- Missouri
  - Ethical Society of St. Louis, 9001 Clayton Road, St. Louis, MO 63117 (314) 991-0955
- New Jersey
  - Ethical Culture Society of Bergen County, 687 Larch Ave., Teaneck, NJ 07666; (201) 836-5187
  - Ethical Culture Society of Essex County, 516 Prospect St., Maplewood, NJ 07040 (201) 763-1905
  - Princeton Ethical Humanist Fellowship, PO Box 3286, Princeton, NJ 08543; (609) 924-6492; <princeton@aeu.org>
- New York
  - Brooklyn Society for Ethical Culture, 53 Prospect Park W., Brooklyn, NY 11215 (718) 768-2972
  - Ethical Culture Society of Queens, 207-03 3rd Ave., Bayside, NY 11361 (718) 631-2807
  - Ethical Culture Society of Suffolk, PO Box 134, Commack, NY 11725 (516) 499-0726
  - Ethical Culture Society of Westchester, 7 Saxon Wood Road, White Plains, NY 10605 (914) 948-1120
  - Ethical Humanist Society of Long Island, 38 Old Country Road, Garden City, NY 11530 (516) 741-7304
  - Ethical Society of Northern Westchester, 108 Pinesbridge Road, Ossining, NY 10562 (914) 941-3544
  - New York Society of Ethical Culture, 2 West 64th St., New York, NY 10023 (212) 874-5210
  - Riverdale-Yonkers Society for Ethical Culture, 4450 Fieldston Road, Bronx, NY 10471 (718) 548-4445
- North Carolina
  - North Carolina Society for Ethical Culture, PO Box 3132, Chapel Hill, NC 27515

- Pennsylvania
  Philadelphia Ethical Society, 1906 S. Rittenhouse Square, Philadelphia, PA 19103 (215) 735-3456
- Texas
  Ethical Culture Fellowship of Austin, PO Box 160492, Austin, TX 78716 (512) 306-1111
- Virginia
  Northern Virginia Ethical Society, PO Box 984, Vienna, VA 22183 (703) 437-3161 <noves@aeu.org>

ETHICAL DIALOGS

A Russian freethought group is Ethical Dialogs, c/o Ethics Department, Faculty of Philosophy, Moscow State University, 119899 Moscow B-234, Russian Republic.

ETHICAL HUMANISM: See entry for Secular Humanism.

ETHICAL NATURALISM: To determine whether an "ought" can be deduced from an "is," see *Encyclopedia of Philosophy*, Vol. 3.

ETHICAL RECORD

Ethical Record is published by South Place Ethical Society at Bradlaugh House, 47 Theobald's Road, London, WC1X 8SP, United Kingdom. It reports on lectures, with brief letters, notices, and similar items.

ETHICAL RELATIVISM

In ethics, ethical relativism is the belief that nothing is objectively right or wrong. The definition of right or wrong depends on the prevailing view of a particular individual, culture, or historical period. Although in the Trobriand Islands it was once ethical in the evenings for young women to climb through the open windows of eligible bachelors, such a practice is frowned upon in London and elsewhere. In Morocco and Greenwich Village, New York City, males who are friends can hold hands in public, a practice that could result in violence in America's Bible Belt or in other parts of the world. {DCL}

ETHICAL UNION

The Union of Ethical Societies, which was formed in 1896, became the Ethical Union in 1920. In 1967, the organization became the British Humanist Association. {Nicolas Walter, *New Humanist*, February 1996}

ETHICS

Ethics is a philosophic discipline that deals not only with what is good and bad but also with moral duty and obligations. Naturalists who have written on the subject include William Kingdon Clifford, "The Ethics of Belief" and "The Ethics of Religion" (1880); G. E. Moore, Principia Ethica (1903); Bertrand Russell, Marriage and Morals (1929) and The Conquest of Happiness (1930); and P. H. Nowell-Smith, Ethics (1954). Also, humanistic philosophers A. J. Ayer, Albert Schweitzer, and Bernard Williams have written extensively on the subject. The oldest continuing organization to have focused on humanistic ethics is South Place Ethical Society, founded 14 February 1793. The group meets in Conway Hall and serves as the potential focus of the British Humanist movement. Bertrand Russell's views on ethics (*Power*, 1938) included the following:

- The fundamental defect of Christian ethics consists in the fact that it labels certain classes of acts "sins" and others "virtue" on grounds that have nothing to do with their social consequences. An ethic not derived from superstition must decide first upon the kind of social effects which it desires to achieve and the kind which it desires to avoid. It must then decide, as far as our knowledge permits, what acts will promote the desired consequences; these acts it will praise, while those having a contrary tendency it will condemn. (*Education and the Modern World*, 1932)

- It's very difficult to separate ethics altogether from politics. Ethics, it seems to me, arise in this way: a man is inclined to do something that benefits him and harms his neighbors. If it harms a good many of his neighbors, they will combine together and say, "Look here, we don't like this sort of thing, and we'll see to it that it doesn't benefit the man," and that leads to the criminal law, which is perfectly rational. {*Bertrand Russell Speaks His Mind*, 1969}

- The power conferred by military conquest often ceases, after a longer or shorter period of time, to be merely military. All the provinces conquered by the Romans, except Judea, soon became loyal subjects of the Empire, and ceased to feel any desire for independence. In Asia and Africa the Christian countries conquered by the Mohammedans submitted with little reluctance to their new rulers. Wales gradually acquiesced in English rule, though Ireland did not. After the Albigensian heretics had been overcome by military force, their descendants submitted inwardly as well as outwardly to the authority of the Church. The Norman Conquest produced, in England, a royal family which, after a time, was thought to possess a Divine Right to the throne. Military conquest is stable only when it is followed by psychological conquest, but the cases in which this has occurred are very numerous.

(See the entry for ethics in the *Encyclopedia of Philosophy*, Vol. 3.) {CE; ER; JMRH; RE}

ETHNIC CLEANSING

Ethnic cleansing "is a euphemism for religious genocide," wrote Victor Boldt. "Ethnic Albanians," for example are Kosovo Muslims and should be so described by the media. {*Humanist in Canada*, Winter 1999-2000}

ETHNOGRAPHY, ETHNOLOGY

Anthropololgists who specialize in scientifically describing specific human cultures are ethnographists. Those who compare human cultures—their language, religion, technology—are ethnologists. Ethnology deals with the origin, distribution, and characteristics of the races of mankind.

ETISK-FORBUND: See entry for Norwegian Humanists.

Ettel, Konrad (Born 1847)

Ettel was an Austrian freethinker. He wrote many poems and dramas. His freethinker's catechism, *Grundzuge der Naturlichen Weltanschauung* (1886) reached a fourth edition. {BDF}

Etu, Samuel (20th Century)

Etu, a Nigerian educator, is active in the Lagos humanist group and in his library has a complete set of the published writings of Robert G. Ingersoll. {HNS2}

Etzioni, Amitai: See entry for Communitarianism.

EUCHARIST

- Eucharist, n. A sacred feast of the religious sect of Theophagi.

—**Ambrose Bierce**
The Devil's Dictionary

For believers, the Eucharist is an act of worship which was instituted at the Last Supper and in which bread and wine are consecrated and consumed.

Freethinkers sometimes confuse the Eucharist with a player of euchre, the thirty-two-card game in which, after being dealt five cards, one is required to take at least three tricks in order to make a trump and win. The player is then said to have euchred his opponent. Euchring someone involves deceiving them. (See entries for Hocus Pocus and for Theophagy.) {DCL}

Eucken, Rudolf Christoph (1846—1926)

Eucken was a German philosopher who won the 1908 Nobel Prize in Literature. His philosophy, activism, stressed personal ethical effort rather than intellectual idealism and was praised by humanists. Eucken, however, preferred the word *activism*. He wrote *The Truth of Religion* (1901) and *Knowledge and Life* (1913). {CE}

Eudes, Emile François Désiré (1844—1888)

Eudes was a French Communist, a chemist who was condemned with Régnard to three months' imprisonment for writing in *La Libre Pensée*. Joining the ranks of the Commune, Eudes became a general. When the Versailles troops entered Paris, he escaped to Switzerland. On his return, he wrote with Blanqui. {BDF}

Eudo de Stella (12th Century)

With a smutty mouth, a hermit from Brittany called Eudo (of the Star) preached that he was a second Christ. One enraged chronicler wrote that "although Eudo was uneducated and scarcely knew the letters of the alphabet, he discoursed and preached from Holy Writ with a filthy mouth. Although not in holy orders, with impious boldness he disgracefully celebrated Mass, to the error and the destruction of the corrupted people." It was a time of harsh winters and bad harvests, and those with no resources who joined his wandering band allegedly stole whatever the group needed. They also attacked churches and monasteries, rationalizing that they were not preaching the truth anyway.

In 1148 the Archbishop of Rouen sent soldiers who captured and imprisoned Eudo. He died while on a diet of bread and water, and his leading disciples were executed by burning. {EH}

EUGENICS: See entry for Francis Galton.

Eugenius IV (1382—1447)

Pope Eugenius IV (1431 to 1447) in a 1442 decree (quoted in derision by Joseph McCabe) wrote, "We decree and order that from now on, and for all time, Christians shall not eat or drink with Jews, nor admit them to feasts, nor cohabit with them, nor bathe with them. Christians shall not allow Jews to hold civil honor over Christians, or to exercise public offices in the state."

Euhemerus (fl c. 300 B.C.E.)

A contemporary of Epicurus, Zeno, and Pyrrho, Euhemerus of Tegea, according to W. K. C. Guthrie, was an atheist. {CE; EU; JMR}

EULOGY

• Eulogy, n. Praise of a person who has either the advantages of wealth and power, or the consideration to be dead.

—**Ambrose Bierce**
The Devil's Dictionary

EUNUCHS, FEMALE

Shobha Nehru—a eunuch who became a figure in Hissar, India, politics—was born of an upper-class Hindu family, was raised as a girl, but was born a eunuch.

Because eunuchs are shut out by Hinduism's strict caste system, she adopted Islam but took the last name of India's first prime minister, Jawaharial Nehru. In Jonathan Karp's front-page account of her story (*The Wall Street Journal*, 24 September 1998), eunuchs in India are described as being

> a subculture of sexual outcasts who rank lower in India than the untouchables. They are notorious for crashing weddings, singing raunchy songs and dancing until paid to leave. . . . ." I used to entertain people by dancing," says Ms. Nehru, whose husky voice contrasts with her attire, a delicately draped sari in the colors of the Indian flag—saffron, white and green. "Now I entertain them by doing good, humanitarian deeds."

As a politician in the southern city of Bangalore and then in the State of Haryana, Nehru performs only when invited and bestows blessings rather than curses. In one squatter colony, she has successfully helped lobby for water supply and better roads, winning a 1995 election and working to improve civic amenities and reduce crime as well as police abuse. She would like to run for Parliament. Another eunuch ran unsuccessfully in 1996 under the slogan, "You don't need genitals for politics. You need brains."

According to Karp, born eunuchs are the élite among India's *hijras*, an Urdu word for "impotent ones." Considering themselves neither men nor women, *hijras* generally adopt feminine names and dress. They may have been born

> with deformed genitalia; a small fraction are hermaphrodites, and others are homosexual cross-dressers. Some males undergo castration to be accepted in the community. Eunuchs deny longstanding allegations that they kidnap and castrate boys to keep their secret society alive, though over the years there have been a number of documented cases of adolescent boys being forcibly mutilated sexually.

Ancient sacred Hindu texts contain references to "the third sex" and descriptions of impotent men who danced and cast spells. The Hindu epic *Ramayana* tells of the god-king Ram who was banished to the forest where he urged all men and women followers to go home. Being neither, the eunuchs waited fourteen years for his return and were blessed for their devotion. Scholars have said, however, that the episode does not appear in the most widely accepted Ramayana texts.

Estimates vary as to how many *hijras* India has, somewhere between 50,000 and 1.2 million. Karp has stated that they are more commonly ridiculed or reviled than revered today and often are consigned to a life of begging. In Bombay they are known to ask commuters for money or be flashed. "Many Indians believe eunuchs have occult powers," Karp found, "so they pay."

EUNUCHS, MALE

God in his mercy, according to the Bible, does not allow eunuchs or those who have had their "stones crushed" (i.e., their testicles smashed) to enter the Kingdom of Heaven.

A male eunuch is a castrated human male, one who can get an erection but who cannot ejaculate a bodily fluid. Eunuchs were used as harem chamberlains in Asia, and they have been employed as servants in wealthy or royal households, as during the court of Constantinople under the Byzantine emperors, from whom the Ottoman sultans adopted the practice. Narses, a Byzantine general, is one of the most famous early eunuchs; Carlo Broschi Farinelli is one of the better known of recent times. Moslems were not noted for using eunuchs, although the sale of young males to be eunuchs was once an important element in African trade.

Shakespeare, who used eunuchs in *Antony and Cleopatra* and *Twelfth Night*, knew of the Vatican's castrati. The Shakespearean acting companies used castrati to play women's roles and who, as explained by Steven Orgel in *Impersonations: a The Performance of Gender in Shakespeare's England* (1997), enabled the introduction of overt sexuality, simultaneously hetero-sexual and homosexual, into the world of ecclesiastical celibacy.

The Papal choir used *castrati* until the beginning of the 19th century. Inasmuch as the Church did not permit females to sing in the churches, it was necessary to "manufacture" male sopranos. Pope Leo XIII finally issued orders to "get rid of them." Meanwhile, Leo XIII found the scandal in theatre-life (not churches) in various parts of Italy (not Rome) and indignantly suppressed it. According to McCabe, "It was one of the most notorious facts in Roman ecclesiastical life and was found in many other Italian churches, until the Pope's secular authority over Rome was ended in 1870."

The custom of using eunuchs in choirs spread from Constantinople, and in the 18th century the male heroes' roles were sung by *castrati*. Bishop Liutprand of the tenth century tells in his *Antapodosis* that Christians—he means Christians in monasteries—used to collect Christian boys, castrate and rear them, and sell them as harem-eunuchs to the Moslems. As late as the 17th century, Jews were castrated and the mutilation publicly exhibited in Rome, for intercourse with Christian prostitutes.

In 1996, ninety-four-year-old San Yaoting, allegedly the Chinese emperor's last eunuch, died in Beijing. As a young boy, he was emasculated in a crude operation arranged by his family, who hoped for money. He then became the emperor's eunuch, a person trusted to enter the inner courtyards of the palace where the women of the imperial family and harem lived. The operation to remove what was called his "three precious" was performed using only hot chili sauce as a local anesthetic.

In 1997, a bizarre cult known as The Heaven's Gate and led by Marshall Herff Applewhite, the sixty-six-year-old son of a Presbyterian minister, believed that the Hale-Bopp Comet was, actually, related to Biblical predictions. Its thirty-nine members committed suicide together, believing the "Higher Source" was about to recycle the Earth and the only hope for survival was to pass through death at the right time and be beamed up by an intergalactic UFO piloted by the late Ms. Bonnie Nettles for a journey back "home." One-third of the men had been castrated, in keeping with *Matthew* 19:12 and St. Paul's invitation for his detractors to " . . . I would that they go and castrate themselves" (*Galatians* 5:12). Like traditional Christian monks and nuns, the cult's members were supposed to be completely celibate.

Freethinkers find the subject of castration by religionists intriguing but inhumanistic. {CE; *The Economist*, 4 January 1997; *The New York Times*, 20 December 1996; RE}

EUPRAXOPHY

A coinage by Paul Kurtz, eupraxophy means "good practice and wisdom." It is a description of secular humanism's being an ethical, philosophical, and scientific outlook, one which emphasizes a nonreligious way of life and cosmic outlook.

Nicolas Walter as early as 1989 was negatively critical of the coinage, asking if humanism is *a* or *an* eupraxophy and observing that the word sounds peculiar. "I wonder," he wrote, "whether anyone who seriously proposes the adoption by humanists of such a term as *eupraxophy* is thinking of them as human; and whether, if we seriously offered it to the wider public, we would be thinking of them as human. . . . I find it hard enough explaining what I mean by humanism and why I work for the humanist movement without wanting to make a complete fool of myself."

In Kansas City, Missouri, Verle Muhrer has defended use of the term, and the secular humanist building there is called The Eupraxophy Center.

Euripides (c. 480—405 B.C.E.)

Euripides—who wrote, "He was a wise man who originated the idea of God—was "closest . . . of the great Greek writers," wrote Lamont, "to being a complete Humanist."

Illustrating that the gods do not determine your fate, so why waste your time with superstition, Euripides the playwright wrote: "Vain, vain were prayer and incense-swell and bull's blood on the altars." Robertson, commenting upon how such a view challenged a current view on the gods, stated that "If Euripides has nowhere ventured on such a terrific paradox, as the *Prometheus*, he has in a score of passages revealed a strain of skepticism which, inasmuch as he too uses all the forms of Hellenic faith, deepens our doubt as to the beliefs of Aeschylus."

Melanippe by Euripides begins with an audacious first line that evoked a great uproar: "Zeus, whoever Zeus be, for I know not, save by report." He further depicts the gods as sometimes lawless and his characters impeach them as such or declare there can be no truth in the "miserable tales of poet" which so represent them.

As regards his constructive opinions, Robertson wrote, "We have from him many expressions of the pantheism which had by his time permeated the thought of perhaps most of the educated Greeks." A skeptic of the aggressive type, Euripides has been described as "Euripides the Rationalist" because of his systematic assault on the religion of his day. Of his eighty works, only eighteen are extant, and these include *Medea* (431 B.C.E.), *Electra* (413 B.C.E), and *Orestes* (408 B.C.E). His *The Bacchae* is a tragedy but one which has both a cross-dresser and two old men who are out cruising for hot dates.

In 1995 Greek archeologists reported they had located the island cave on Salamis near Athens where Euripides probably wrote some of his ancient masterpieces. {CE; CL; JM; JMR; JMRH; *The New York Times*, 13 January 1997; RE; TYD}

EUROPE

Europe is the sixth largest continent. As a word, Clive James has pointed out,

> Europe goes back a long way: Assyrian inscriptions speak of the difference between *asu* (where the sun rises; i.e., Asia) and *ereb* (where it sets). As a place, Europe is old even by the standards of dynastic China and Pharonic Egypt. As an idea, though, Europe is comparatively new: the word European didn't turn up in the language of diplomacy until the nineteenth century, and to *think* of Europe as one place had always taken some kind of supervening vision. Whatever unity existed within it came not through a unifying idea but through the exercise of power, and did not last.
>
> {*The New Yorker*, 28 April 1997}

EUROPE ET LAICITÉ

A humanistic quarterly in French, *Europe et Laicité* is at 11 rue des Huguenots, 94420 Le Plessis-Trevise, France. <eurolaic@club-internet.fr>.

EUROPEAN HUMANIST FEDERATION (*Fédération Humaniste Européene*)

The European Humanist Federation (EHF) was formed in 1991 to present the humanist outlook and to defend the rights of unbelievers in Europe before the Council of Europe and the European Parliament. In Berlin in 1993, the EHF had its initial congress. Member organizations at the outstart were Belgium, Britain, Denmark, Finland, France, Germany, Hungary, Italy, Luxembourg, Netherlands, Northern Ireland, Norway, Poland, Romania, Russia, Scotland, Slovakia, Sweden, and the former Yugoslavia. The Executive Committee in 1995 consisted of Steinar Nilsen (Norway) as President, Ann-Marie Franchi (France) and Rob Tielman (the Netherlands) as Vice-Presidents, Claude Wachtelaer (Belgium) as Secretary, and Klaus Sühl (Germany) as Treasurer General. In 1998 the Secretary General was Claude Wachtelaer and Nilsen remained as President. {*International Humanist News*, April 1996 and October 1998}

EUROPEAN HUMANIST PROFESSIONALS

In 1994, the former International Association of Humanist educators, counselors, ceremony officiants, and staff members of humanist organizations was renamed the European Humanist Professionals. The group in 1995 met in Oslo. Its annual publication is obtained from Postbus 797, 3500 AT Utrecht, The Netherlands. Tel: +31-30-1290189; fax: +31-2390170; <hsn@uvh.nl>.

EUROPEAN UNITARIANS

Gevene Hertz if president of the European Unitarian Universalists (EUU, Frydenlundsvej 49, DK-2950 Vedbeck, Denmark).

EUU was founded in 1982 and includes seven fellowships of about two hundred adults and one hundred children with many members at large. The fellowships are led by religious education coordinators. Many members are Americans living permanently or temporarily in Europe. On the Web:
<http://www.nordita.dk/~hertz/euu.html>.

Eusebius (4th Century?)

Gilbert Murray's *Four Stages of Greek Religion* contains the following "Pagan's Prayer":

> May I be no man's enemy, and may I be the friend of that which is eternal and abides. May I never quarrel with those nearest to me; and if I do, may I be reconciled quickly. May I never devise evil against any man. May I love, seek, and attain only that which is good. May I wish for all men's happiness and envy none. May I never rejoice in the ill-fortune of one who has wronged me. When I have done or said what is wrong, may I never wait for the rebuke of others, but always rebuke myself until I make amends. May I win no victory that harms either me or my opponent. May I reconcile friends who are wroth with one another. May I, to the extent of my power, give all needful help to my friends and to all who are in want.
>
> May I never fail a friend in danger. When visiting those in grief, may I be able by gentle and healing words to soften their pain. May I respect myself. May I always keep tame that which rages within me. May I accustom myself to be gentle, and never be angry with people because of circumstances. May I never discuss who is wicked and what wicked things he has done, but know good men and follow in their footsteps.

Murray cites Eusebius as being possibly a 4th-century Greek. Eusebius of Caesarea (c. 263—339?) was a Greek apologist and church historian, bishop of Palestine (314?—339) who played a part in the controversy over Arianism. Similarly Eusebius of Nicomedia (died 342) was a Christian churchman and theologian, leader of the heresy of Arianism and bishop of Nicomedia (330—339) as well as patriarch of Constantinople (339—342). The former objected to parts of the Nicean Creed and later did not support it. The latter signed the Nicene formulary but was exiled by Constantine, later becoming his advisor and an Arian. {CE}

EUTHANASIA

Euthanasia involves permitting a hopelessly sick or injured human, or animal, to be put to death as painlessly as possible. The *Catechism of the Catholic Church* (1994), however, states that "sick or handicapped persons should be helped to lead lives as normal as possible. Whatever its motives and means, direct euthanasia consists in putting an end to the lives of handicapped, sick, or dying persons. It is morally unacceptable." It was not morally unacceptable to Sigmund Freud, who in 1939 ended his pain-filled life with morphine. Nor in the 1950s to the humanist minister Charles Frances Potter, who was president of the New York Euthanasia Society.

The legality of euthanasia has been and continues to be tested in diverse places around the world. Derek Humphrey, founder of the Hemlock Society (USA) and author of *Final Exit* (1992), assisted his own wife, Jean, to die. Dr. Jack Kevorkian, a retired pathologist, challenged the State of Michigan to legalize euthanasia by assisting individuals there to die by the use of his home-made "suicide machine," and successfully completed several dozen euthanasias before being jailed. His confinement, to many, has made him a martyr.

Physicians, it is generally agreed, have for centuries eased patients out of their final days of physical misery, but always with the threat of litigation and possible punishment—Freud's own physician provided him with morphine. The Netherlands reportedly has the most liberal legal system for allowing euthanasia. In 1994, 1424 cases (roughly 2.1% of annual deaths) were reported there. Meanwhile, as they sometimes point out, viewers of horse racing on television have seen horses mercifully shot after breaking their legs in an accident, and they also have seen human beings kept alive for years in a state of vegetation.

Bertrand Russell, in *Unpopular Essays* (1959), wrote as follows:

> The whole conception of "Sin" is one which I find very puzzling, doubtless owing to my sinful nature. If "Sin" consisted in causing needless suffering, I could understand, but on the contrary, sin often consists in avoiding needless suffering. Some years ago, in the English House of Lords, a bill was introduced to legalize euthanasia in cases of painful and incurable disease. The patient's consent was to be necessary, as well as several medical certificates.
>
> To me, in my simplicity, it would seem natural to require the patient's consent, but the late Archbishop of Canterbury, the English official expert on Sin, explained the erroneousness of such a view. The patient's consent turned euthanasia into suicide, and suicide is sin. Their Lordships listened to the voice of authority and rejected the bill.

(See entries for Australian and New Zealand Humanists, Jean Davies, Sigmund Freud and Karl-Henrik Nygaard.)

EUTHANASIA IN THE NETHERLANDS

"Active euthanasia has been practiced in The Netherlands for more than twenty years," according to Pieter V. Admiraal, considered by many to be the world's leading spokesperson for the right to physician-assisted suicide. "Today the total number is estimated as 3,500 to 4,000 cases a year." {*Free Inquiry*, Winter 1996-1997}

Eutyches (c. 378—452)

Eutyches headed a monastery near Constantinople (modern Istanbul). When he originated the Monophysite heresy, holding that Christ had one nature that mingled human and divine elements, that after the incarnation He possessed only the divine nature, Eutyches was declared a heretic. An anti-Nestorian, he was subject of a general council ordered by Flavian, the Patriarch of Constantinople. The council met in Ephesus in 449 and by sheer physical violence annulled the excommunication of Eutyches (leading Pope Leo to call it the Robber Synod). In turn this led to the Council of Chalcedon (451), which ruled that Jesus Christ possessed two natures in one person, thereby condemning both Eutyches as well as Nestorius while approving Cyril of Alexandria. This led the Egyptian church, along with the Ethiopian, to adopt Monophysitism, as did the patriarchates of Jerusalem and Antioch.

Eventually, Eutyches was again deposed and exiled. Monophysitism exacerbated the growing division between the eastern and western branches of Christianity, and despite Justinian I's attempts to unite the groups, an enduring split followed between the Eastern Orthodox and the Roman Catholic churches. The Arab conquests of Syria, Palestine, and Egypt made the schism permanent. {CE; EH; ER}

EVANGELICAL LUTHERAN CHURCH IN AMERICA

The Evangelical Lutheran Church in America, organized in 1870, is at 8765 West Higgins Road, Chicago, Illinois 60631. It represents over 5,100,000 members.

EVANGELISM

- Evangelist, n. A bearer of good tidings, particularly (in a religious sense) such as assure us of our own salvation and the damnation of our neighbors.

—**Ambrose Bierce**
The Devil's Dictionary

Evangelism refers to zealous preaching, as through missionary work. Matthew, Mark, Luke, and John were evangelists, as are Protestant preachers or missionaries who travel in order to disseminate what they hold is the gospel truth. An "Evangelical" believes in the sole authority and inerrancy of the Bible, holding that salvation can be obtained only through regeneration and in a spiritually transformed personal life. {DCL}

Evans, David Egan (1974-)

Evans was born and raised in Utah. While being raised as a Mormon, he found that his parallel interests of science and Mormon theology led him to recognize the inherent contradictions. During his two-year mission for The Church of Jesus Christ of Latter-day Saints, his skepticism turned to humanism. Upon his return of a completed mission, he joined the American Humanist Association, later becoming a board member of the Humanist of Utah. A computer technical specialist for Packard Bell NEC, he is a student working toward a Bachelor's Degree in physics, his minors being philosophy and chaos theory. E-mail: <dave@intelligentinquiry.com>. On the Web: <http://intelligentinquiry.com/>.

Evans, Don (20th Century)

Evans is Secretary of the Washington Area Secular humanists in the nation's capital.

Evans, Elizabeth Edson (19th Century)

Evans, a freethinker, wrote *The Christ Myth* (1900). {GS}

Evans, Gareth John (1944—)

Evans is an Australian humanist, atheist, lawyer, and politician. He has been a Senator in Victoria since 1978 and a leader of the government in the Senate since 1993. In 1990 he received Humanist of the Year Award.

A commitment to humanism and a generally non-religious view of the world stems from his 1958 experiences of Billy Graham's first crusade in Australia—at the age of fourteen, Evans became a committed and comprehensive skeptic, then an agnostic, now an atheist.

Reading Bertrand Russell's *Why I Am Not A Christian*, he reports, was a major influence on his thought. {SWW}

Evans, George Henry (1803—1855)

Evans emigrated from England to New York while a child. He set up as a printer, publishing the *Correspondent*, the first American freethought paper. He also published the *Working Man's Advocate, Man*, *Young America*, and the *Radical*. He editorialized upon behalf of delivery of mail on Sundays, the limitation of the right to hold lands, the abolition of slavery, and other reforms.

His brother became one of the chief elders of the Shakers. Evans died in Granville, New Jersey. {BDF; FUS; RAT; RE}

Evans, John (19th Century)

A freethinker, Evans wrote *History of All Christian Sects* (1875). {GS}

Evans, Mary Anne: See entry for George Eliot.

Evans, Richard M. (1933-1998)

Evans taught educational psychology at the University of Houston, Morningside College, and the U. S. Naval Academy. A colonel, he was commander of the Marine Corps Communications Electronics School. One of the founders of the Free Inquiry Society of Central Florida, he named its newsletter *Veritas*. Upon retiring, he had become public relations director for the area's symphony orchestra before his death from cancer.

Evans, Rod (20th Century)

Evans, with Irwin M. Berent, wrote *Fundamentalism: Hazards and Heartbreaks* (1994), which investigates what has gone wrong with religious fundamentalism and why.

Evans, T. (19th Century)

In the 1880s, Evans in what was considered a rare event wrote for *Secular Review* in Welsh about a freethought group which had started in Rhybydd. {RSR}

Evans, William (1816—1887)

Evans, of Swansea, became a follower of Robert Owen. He established *The Potter's Examiner and Workman's Advocate* (1843) and wrote in the co-operative journals under the anagram of Millway Vanes. {BDF}

Evansgardner, JoAnn (20th Century)

Evansgardner, from Pennsylvania, is on the board of the Freedom From Religion Foundation.

Evanson, Edward (1731—1805)

Evanson was a theological critic who had been a vicar but entertained so many doubts about the Trinity that he began expressing heretical opinions. In 1771 he was prosecuted, but because of some irregularity in the proceedings escaped any consequences.

In 1773 he addressed a letter to the Bishop of Lichfield, trying to show that either Christianity was false or else the orthodox churches were, and in the following year he resigned. His *The Dissonance of the Four Generally-Received Evangelists* (1792) rejected all the gospels, except Luke, as inauthentic. The work resulted in a controversy with Dr. Priestley and, as described by Wheeler, "a considerable share of obliquy and persecution from the orthodox." {BDF}

Evatt, Elizabeth Andreas [Justice] (1933—)

The Honourable Justice Evatt is an Australian reformer and barrister. As president of the Law Reform Commission, she said, "Australia should be prepared to examine its dominant cultures, religions, and practices in the light of human rights standards, as well as evaluating the religions and practices of minorities. We should apply the same critical eye to Judaeo-Christian as to Islamic practices. Just as polygamy may be thought to be incompatible with standards of equality, so may be many Christian practices."

Evatt has held a number of prominent appointments including, in 1989, being chairperson of the United Nations Committee on the Elimination of Discrimination Against Women. She has edited two books: *A Guide to Family Law* and *Do It Yourself Divorce.* {SWW}

EVE

The Judeo-Christian Eve is unflatteringly depicted as the mother of two sons: one a killer, one the killed. (See a discussion of "The African Eve" under the entry for Martin G. Bernal. For the oldest naturalistic humanist, see entry for Lucy.)

Evêmeros: See entry for Euhemerus.

Everett, Charles Carroll (1829—1900)

A librarian and instructor in modern languages, Everett taught at Harvard's Divinity School about non-Christian religions. He was a Unitarian who believed that Christianity was the "absolute" religion because of the university of its application, its intuitive nature, and its grounding in the person of Jesus. He defined religion in *Theism and the Christian Faith* (1909) as "the Feeling toward a Spiritual Presence manifesting itself in Truth, Goodness and Beauty, especially as illustrated in the life and teaching of Jesus and as experienced in every soul that is open to its influence." {U&U}

Everett, Edward (1794—1865)

Everett was a Unitarian minister who became Governor of Massachusetts, President of Harvard, a U.S. Senator, and a Secretary of State. But he is remembered as being the one who orated for two hours preceding Lincoln's delivery of the 272-word "Gettysburg Address." Garry Wills in *Lincoln At Gettysburg, The Words That Remade America* (1992), relates how Everett had been Emerson's teacher at Harvard and was a transcendentalist. Trained in Germany in the classics and a professor of Greek at Harvard, Everett was a practitioner of elaborate classical oratory.

But it was Lincoln (whom Wills calls "a Transcendentalist without the fuzziness") who had the classical ***epitaphios***, with its two essential sections: ***epainesis***, or praise for the fallen; and ***parainesis***, or advice for the living. Like Pericles, he and Everett in their "Dedicatory Remarks" and "Oration," respectively, gave a tribute to fallen warriors which is remembered and which established a model for future American funeral orations. Lincoln was never a student of Everett, but as described by Wills "the two speakers drew on a shared philosophical tradition both men honored." In Boston, Everett had been pastor of the Brattle Street Church. {CE; EG; U; UU}

Everett, Millard S(penser). (Born 1897)

When he wrote reviews for *The Humanist*, Everett was in the philosophy department at Oklahoma Agricultural and Mechanical College.

Everett, Walter Goodnow (20th Century)

Everett wrote *Moral Values* (1918). {GS}

Evershed, Mary (19th Century)

A freethinker, Evershed wrote "Two Letters Addressed to the Bishop of Ripon, On Secularism, the Holy Scriptures, and the Geophysical Position of the Garden of Eden" (1876?). {GS}

EVIL

Evil, the antithesis of good, is a concept which leads to the philosophical problem, Why does evil exist in the world? Traditional Christian belief ascribes evil to the misdeeds of men, to whom God has granted "free will." Dualism, an explanation found in Zoroastrianism and Manichaeism, holds that two opposing principles exist in the universe. The biblical Job is a literary treatment of the problem, as is Archibald MacLeish's *J.B.* Many contemporaries reason that if there were an all-powerful God, He could have prevented evil. If God were truly and perfectly good, He would have prevented evil. The fact that evil exists in incompatible, therefore, with the traditional God.

Perhaps we all want to have a touch of evil in us, Jean Cocteau dramatized. In *Beauty and the Beast*, the movie version of which starred Greta Garbo, the monster metamorpohosizes into a handsome prince and Garbo states, "Give me back my beast!"

The British biologist Lyall Watson, writing in *Dark Nature: A Natural History of Evil* (1996), defines evil as a violation of the ecological order. The word *evil* comes from *ubiloz*, an Old Teutonic word with a root meaning "up" or "over." Aristotle thought of moderation as a "golden mean," but Watson refers to the "Goldilocks Effect, nature's way of getting things 'just right.'" Although living objects have "an innate predisposition towards equilibrium," he states, an amoral and persistent competition of genes to stay alive helps upset that equilibrium.

He cites such examples as the spotted hyena that bears twins and "within minutes of birth one of the cubs attacks its twin, sometimes savaging a brother or sister that has not yet even emerged from its amniotic sac" in order to fight for a parent's nurture. (See John Updike's "Elusive Evil, An Idea Whose Time Keeps Coming," *The New Yorker*, 22 July 1996)

Numbers of humanists have expressed themselves on the subject—almost all major creative humanists have included evil characters in their operas, paintings, short stories, dramas, novels, plays, etc. However, the average individual finds the entire concept nebulous and concentrates, instead, upon laws that delineate that which is good and punish that which society considers bad.

As a result, what is "evil" or bad in one setting might be considered "good" or legal in another, depending upon legislation enacted by individuals in the various communities.

Bertrand Russell in *Selected Papers of Bertrand Russell* (1927) divided evil into three classes:

- evils due to a physical nature: death, pain, and the difficulty of making the soil yield a subsistence;
- evils springing from defects in the character or aptitudes of the sufferer: ignorance, lack of will, and violent passions;
- evils that depend upon the power of one individual or group over

another: these comprise not only obvious tyranny, but all interference with free development, whether by force or by excessive mental influence such as may occur in education.

(See entries for Lawrence Ferlinghetti and Iago; and discussion of evil in the *Encyclopedia of Philosophy*, Vol. 3. Also, see entry for pickpocketry, which tells the freethinkers' view about diddling: that we do not choose *between* good and evil but, rather, *among* several options.) {RE}

Evison, Joseph (19th Century)

Evison, whose nickname was "Ivo," edited the weekly *Rationalist* in Auckland, New Zealand, from 1885 to 1886. {FUK}

EVOLUTION

"Under the restraining influence of the Church," notes the *Columbia Encyclopedia*, "no evolutionary theories developed during some fifteen centuries of the Christian era to challenge the belief in special creation and the literal interpretation of the first part of *Genesis*; however, much data was accumulated that was to be utilized by later theorists." The work cites secular humanist James H. Birx's *Theories of Evolution* (1984) as a major explanation of "acquired characteristics," "natural selection," and the theories of A. R. Wallace, Charles Robert Darwin, and others.

Creationists and Christian fundamentalists do not accept the Darwinian theory of evolution. Pope John Paul in 1996 decreed, however, that the theory of evolution was "more than just a hypothesis," after which Cardinal John O'Connor of New York suggested it is possible that the first life on Earth was a "lower animal," that Adam and eve were "some other form" than man and woman.

Darwin's original theory as modified, however, is generally accepted by scientists and has been enhanced with evidence from biochemistry and molecular biology, all the while utilizing his basic study of comparative anatomy, embryology, geographical distribution, and paleontology.

The origins of humanity are believed to lie in Africa. Over a million years ago, people of a species known as *Homo erectus* moved into Asia, then fragmented with one group—Neanderthal man—spreading into Europe. A second migration 100,000 years ago saw a new human species—*Homo sapiens*—move from Africa, at which time these newcomers replaced their older relatives and modern humanity came into its own. Or so the neat story goes, according to *The Economist* (26 February 1994). However, such a view is changing. In 1891 *Homo erectus* fossils were found in Java and have been dated at being between 700,000 and 1,000,000 years old. According to Carl Swisher and Garniss Curtis of the University of California at Berkeley, those Javan fossils are much older, perhaps 1,800,000 or even 1,900,000 years old and making them contemporary with bones from East Africa.

If their findings are accepted, the African and Asian populations of *Homo erectus* may actually be separate species. In such a case, they hold, *Homo erectus* migrated into Africa, rather than out of it. Few evolutionists doubt, states *The Economist*, "that the ultimate origins of human beings lie in Africa. *Australopithecus*, the only begetter of all things hominid, is found nowhere else." Not yet, yes, reply Chinese scientists who are diligently searching for such a specimen.

In 1999 when Kansas legislated that creationism *had* to be taught in schools in addition to the theory of evolution, William Silverton of Halifax, Nova Scotia, wittily observed that no one can lose: "if the evolutionists win the battle for the minds of young Kansans, then of course we all win; if the creationists come out on top, it proves that . . . evolution can proceed backward as well as forward."

"Lucy," the skeleton of one of the oldest human forebears which was found in 1974, has been determined by geologists to be 3.2 million years old, plus or minus 10,000 years. Named for the song "Lucy in the Sky With Diamonds," she rests in a wooden box in a safe in Addis Ababa, Ethiopia. (See entries for Evil, Genesis, and Richard Hawkins. *Cretinism or Evilution*, a newsletter published by E. T. Babinski [109 Burwood Drive, Simpsonville, SC 29681], pokes fun at creationism and critics of evolutionism.) {CE; JMRH; Michael Ruse, editor, *Philosophy of Biology*; PUT; RE}

EVOLUTION AND FAITH

Pope Pius XII cautioned in a 1950 encyclical, "Humani Generis," that although the faithful might regard evolutionary theory as just that—a "serious hypothesis"—they must not proclaim it as "certain doctrine."

Pope John Paul II in a solemn statement delivered in 1996 to the Pontifical Academy of Sciences, declared that "fresh knowledge" produced by scientific research now led to the "recognition of the theory of evolution as more than just a hypothesis." As in the past all creation stemmed from the hand of God, the Pope noted, even if the human body proved to have its origins in "living material that pre-exists it," but Roman Catholics must believe that "the spiritual soul is immediately created by God."

Inasmuch as teaching in Catholic schools and universities in most countries was already generally accepted as a standard part of the curriculum, the Pope's declaration had little effect. A headline in the conservative daily *Il Giornale* blared out, THE POPE SAYS WE MAY DESCEND FROM MONKEYS.

Ewart, Gavin Buchanan (1916—1995)

Ewart in 1994 became an Honorary Associate of the Rationalist Press Association. In *New Humanist* (August 1995), he wrote:

> I was born in London in February 1916, of Scottish descent. My father was a surgeon at St. George's Hospital in the days when it was still at Hyde Park Corner. I was educated at Wellington College and Christ's College, Cambridge. I did classics at school and university—though I switched to English for my last two years at Cambridge. Reading Lucretius, with his denunciations of conventional religion, may have affected me (also, perhaps, Thomas Hardy). My father, if not an atheist, was certainly an agnostic of an anti-Presbyterian kind. My grandfather **James Cossar Ewart** was a Darwinian Professor of Natural History at the University of Edinburgh. In order not to offend the Sabbath sensibilities of Penicuik, I remember being forbidden to play with a ball on Sunday. My upbringing, therefore, except outwardly (in Scotland) and for conformist reasons, was not a pious one.
>
> From the age of 16 I interested myself in poetry; and in 1933, when I was seventeen, my first 'adult' poem was published by Geoffrey Grigson in *New Verse*, heavily influenced by the poetry of T. S. Eliot and Ezra Pound. I came later under the influence of W. H. Auden, whom I still consider the greatest English-language poet of this century. My first book was published in 1939 and since then, apart from the period of the War when I wrote very little, I have continued writing poems very steadily. There are two major collections—*The Collected Ewart 1939—1980* and *Collected Poems 1980—1990*. The latest book is *85 Poems*. All are published by Hutchinson. I also edited, in 1978, *The Penguin Book of Light Verse*. The work of which I am most proud is the Michael Braude Award for Light Verse that I was given in 1991 by the American Academy.

Ewart also wrote *Londoners* (1964) and *Other People's Clerihews* (1983), a clerihew being an epigrammatic verse-form invented by Edmund Clerihew Bentley and consisting of two rhymed couplets, usually dealing with the character of a well-known person; e.g.,

> Sir James Jeans
> Always says what he means;
> He is really perfectly serious
> About the Universe being Mysterious.

In a foreword to Bet Cherrington's compilation, *Facing the World: An Anthology of Poetry for Humanism* (1989), Ewart observed: "The rationalist and the atheist must be stoical. There is no afterlife, and justice may never be done. Bernard Shaw once wrote that all great truths begin as blasphemies. It's certainly true of this one, as the persecution of unbelievers throughout the centuries adequately proves. If we want justice on the earth, in this life, we must get it ourselves." {OEL}

Ewerbeck, August Hermann (19th Century)

Ewerbeck was born in Dantzic but, after the events of 1848, lived at Paris. He translated into German Cabot's *Voyage en Icarie* and several works by Feuerbach. In *What Is In the Bible?* he translated from Daumer, Ghillany, Luetzelberger, and B. Bauer. {BDF}

EXCELLENCE

• Be not elated at any excellence that is not your own. If the horse in his elation were to say, "I am beautiful," it could be endured; but when you say in your elation, "I have a beautiful horse," rest assured that you are elated at something good that belongs to a horse.

—Epictetus

EXCEPTIONAL PEOPLE

Not all human beings resemble the classic beauty exemplified by Ancient Greek statuary. In the animal (and insect) world, those who differ greatly are the subject of teratology, the study of "exceptional people" or malformations or so-called "monstrosities."

Dwarfs, for example, have a defective cartilage or bone growth that usually is genetically transferred. Midgets' bodies are proportionately correct miniatures caused by a malfunction of the pituitary gland, which often can be corrected with hormonal treatments. Numbers of midgets (munchkins) were hired to perform in the M-G-M Studios film, "The Wizard of Oz," which starred Judy Garland. Children often love dwarfs and midgets.

Frederick Drimmer's *Very Special People, the Struggles, Loves, and Triumphs of Human Oddities* (1973) and Leslie Fiedler's *Freaks* (1993) describe other "exceptional people," which is the descriptive phrase used by many empathetic freethinkers. (See entry for Teratology.) {Todd S. Purdum, *The New York Times*, 3 November 1997}

EXCOMMUNICATION

Excommunication is thought by believers to be the gravest of all ecclesiastical censures. It involves formal expulsion from a religious body. Spinoza was excommunicated by the Jews. The Holy Roman Emperor, Frederick I, was twice excommunicated, first by Pope Innocent III and then by Innocent IV. The Vatican lists excommunicates as either *vitandi* (those whom the Holy See has expressly excommunicated by name as persons to be specially shunned in religious matters and so far as possible in secular matters) or *tolerati* (the other excommunicates). Muslims have been known to be far more severe upon finding any of their adherents accused of grave offenses. Some Protestant groups have placed all responsibility for final disciplinary action in the assembly church body, whereas others delegated the responsibility to a church council or committee—most, however, have abandoned the practice. Anyone who dies excommunicate is not publicly prayed for, and excommunicates are invited to repent and return in order to be readmitted.

Greg Erwin, the Canadian who is president of the Coalition of Secular Humanists, Atheists, and Freethinkers (CSHAFT), urges former members of churches to *remain* excommunicates, not seek repentance and return to the church. If their names have not been removed from the membership records, he urges individuals to insist that they *be* removed. (See entry for Greg Erwin.) {CE; ER; RE}

EXISTENCE: Do centaurs, dragons, and Pegasus exist? Do qualities, relations, numbers, and abstract objects exist? A cogent explanation is found in "Existence" in the *Encyclopedia of Philosophy*, Vol. 3.

EXISTENTIALISM

Pascal, St. Augustine, Socrates, Karl Jaspers, Miguel de Unamuno, and even the novelist Norman Mailer have been associated with the philosophical system called existentialism. So have theologians Karl Barth, Martin Buber, Rudolf Bultmann, Søren Kierkegaard, and Paul Tillich. Chiefly a 20th century movement in philosophy, existentialism centers on individual humans, who are trying to live out their lives in an unfathomable universe, one in which they with free will they must try to determine without certainty what is right or wrong or good or bad. The self-declared existentialist among the major thinkers is Jean-Paul Sartre, whose summary description, "existence precedes essence," means that the essence or idea of God and the gods came fairly recently, that matter existed long before humans invented such deities. Sartre believed that there is no fixed human nature, that mankind is totally free, that mankind with such a dread responsibility is understandably anguished. Naturalistic and secular humanists have been negatively critical about some aspects of existentialism, explaining that, although existence precedes essence, the negativism of Sartre need not necessarily follow. A. J. Ayer in *Rationalist Annual* (1948) accused Sartre of systematically misusing, in his ontology, the verb "to be." Ayer and other atheists much preferred a positive humanism, such as that of Camus. On the subject, Delmore Schwartz has quipped, "Existentialism means that no one else can take a bath for you."

The First Existentialist Congregation (Unitarian Universalist) of Atlanta, Georgia, was voted in 1995 the "Most Welcoming Spiritual Organization" by readers of the gay/lesbian/bisexual weekly *Southern Voice*. The congregation is the only Unitarian Universalist group that cites existentialism in its title. (See a detailed discussion of existentialism in the *Encyclopedia of Philosophy, Vol. 3.*)

EXORCISM

Exorcism is a novel theological invention by which practitioners, or exorcists, expel an evil spirit, usually using some kind of incantation.

In Paris the Notre Dame Cathedral's exorcist is the Rev. Claude Nicolas, who holds that "there are a lot of things brewing that disturb people. There are all sorts of sects and black cults. Some people believe there is a spell on them. Some openly talk about the Devil. Of course," he added, "the evil spirit often disguises a serious mental problem." Taking more of a Medieval approach, the Vatican claims that the demand for exorcism has steadily grown. As a result, it has encouraged bishops to appoint more exorcists. The Devil, the Church teaches, is real and evil spirits exist.

The official exorcist for the Archdiocese of New York is the Rev. James LeBar, a "soldier of the Cross" who performed ten exorcisms in 1998. "Maybe only 10% of the people who contact us requires [sic] an exorcism," he told a *Daily News* religion reporter (6 Feb 99), "and that's after the required psychiatric and medical examinations."

Meanwhile, since the 1970s, charismatic Christians have been sweeping through the ranks of mainstream Protestant and Catholic churches, telling their followers they were possessed by the demons of nicotine, alcohol, abortion, homosexuality, and more. {*The New York Times*, 15 June 1998}

EXTRATERRESTRIAL LIFE

Freethinker Tom Paine, after befriending scientists Benjamin Martin and James Ferguson, became convinced that through science one can find his own way without the aid (or hindrance) of kings and priests. The three were intrigued by globes of the earth and, in Paine's words, "the natural bent of my mind was to science. As soon as I was able, I purchased a pair of globes." This led him to argue that "there is room for millions of worlds as large or larger than ours, and each of them millions of miles apart from each other. . . . The inhabitants of each of the worlds of which our system is composed enjoy the same opportunities of knowledge as we do." In short, Paine was one of the first in Colonial America who held such an advanced view.

In the 1950s, Julian Huxley, among others, extrapolated that some forms of life exist in other parts of the universe, adding that it would be presumptuous for those of us on Earth to assume that we are the only forms of life throughout the various galaxies.

Paul Davis, in *Are We Alone? Philosophical Implications of the Discovery of Extraterrestrial Life* (1995), is one of many others who hold that life exists in extraterrestrial places. He supports a program called SETI, the search for extraterrestrial intelligence, which beams radio telescopes at thousands of star systems in the hope that signals will be received from "out there."

Were a signal received, he reasoned, the discovery would be even more profound than the Copernican and Darwinian revolutions. "If human intelligence is just an evolutionary accident, as orthodox Darwinists claim," he writes, "then there is no reason to expect that life on other planets will ever develop intelligence as far as we have." But if we ever do detect some alien intelligence, "it would suggest that there is a progressive evolutionary trend outside the mechanism of natural selection."

It would also suggest that we are not alone in the vastness of space, that "[t]he certain existence of alien beings would give us cause to believe that we, in our humble way, are part of a larger, majestic process of cosmic self-knowledge." Particularly important, such a discovery would undermine the religionists' faith in *Genesis* and organized religion itself, not that theological apologists would soon be put out of business.

In 1996 a 13,000-year-old meteorite fragment from Mars , ALH84001, was found in the Allan Hills in Antarctica by a group of American researchers led by David McKay of the Johnson Space Center in Houston, Texas. It initially appeared to have traces of alien life forms, whereupon several theological apologists were quick to point out that God had sent all the fallen angels to Mars, which explained how life had gotten there.

The scientific community recalled that an 1864 meteorite known as the Orgueil impact at first was thought to contain, in the words of Bartholomew Nagy, "organized elements."

Later, and although Dr. Nagy never himself claimed he had found traces of life, the elements turned out to be particles of furnace ash and grains of ragweed. As of mid-1996, scientists generally held that the only way to be sure of life on the Red Planet is to go to Mars and return with some samples of rock. (See entry for Milky Way.) {Timothy Ferris, "A Message From Mars," *The New Yorker*, 19 August 1996}

EYE

Creationists argue that the eye could not have developed through evolution, that only God could have created such an organ. However, according to Richard Dawkins in *New Statesman and Society* (16 June 1995), Swedish scientists have used a computer program to demonstrate that a single light-sensitive cell could develop into a fish eye in 400,000 years. {*Skeptical Inquirer*, November-December 1995}

Eysenck, H(ans) J(urgen) (1916—)

A professor of psychology at the London University Institute of Psychiatry, Eysenck is chief editor of *Behaviour Research and Therapy*. Among his books are *The Biological Basis of Personality* (1967), *Sense and Nonsense in Psychology* (1957), and *Description and Measurement of Personality* (1968). Eysenck was active in the British humanist movement. {HM2; PK; TRI}

Ezekiel, Moses Jacob (1844-1917)

Ezekiel was an American sculptor who served in the Confederate Army (1864-1865), afterwareds studying sculpture in Berlin and Italy. He greeted the Freethought Congress of 1904. {RAT}

Faber, Roger J. (1931-)

Faber, a freethinker, wrote *Clockwork Garden: On the Mechanistic Reduction of Living Things* (1986). {GS}

Fabre d'Eglantine, Philippe François Nazaire (1755-1794)

A French revolutionist and playwright, Fabre d'Eglantine was chosen as a deputy to the National Convention. He voted for the death of Louis XVI and proposed the substitution of the republican for the Christian calendar. With his friend, Danton, Fabre d'Eglantine was executed in 1794. {BDF}

Fabre, Ferdinand (1830-1898)

Fabre was a French novelist who abandoned his early studies for the priesthood. His novel, *Les Courbezon* (1861), was crowned by the Academy. His *L'abbé Tigrane* (1873) won for him a high position. In 1883 he became librarian of the Bibliothèque Mazarin. In his many stories of clerical life, Fabre is tender to his old Church, but he remained outside it. {RAT}

Fabre, Jean Henri (1823—1915)

Fabre, a French entomologist, was the son of a priest. His books on insect life, although in some respects corrected by later scientific work, had a high international reputation. Although religious writers quote him as one of their "great Catholic scientists," D. G. Legros in a biography expressly says that Fabre was "free from all superstition and quite indifferent to dogmas and miracles." Although Fabre refused even to read Darwin's *Origin—the* Athenaeum wrongly said in its obituary notice that he was an early adherent of Darwinism—he was, states McCabe, "merely a stubborn Vitalist, like Butler. He was a Theist, but, as his chief biographer, D. G. Legros, says, he was 'free from all superstition and quite indifferent to dogmas and miracles.' " {JM; RAT; RE}

Fabricatore, Bruto (1824-1869)

Fabricatore was an Italian writer whose father Antonio had the honor of having a political work placed on the *Index* in 1821. Fabricatore took part in the anti-papal Freethought Council of 1869 and has written works on Dante and others. {BDF; RAT}

Fagan, Brock (20th Century)

Fagan, a professor of English at the University of Northern Iowa in the 1940s, was an iconoclast, a unitarian, an Emersonian, a pessimist, and a particular favorite of students because of his outspoken views about the weaknesses of human institutions. He fearlessly taught about atheism, deism, transcendentalism, and the literary, philosophic humanism favored by Midwestern Unitarianism. Some Iowans knew him only as the person who wrote iconoclastic as well as acerbic letters to the editor so often on so many topics.

Fagan, John (19th Century)

In 1862 Fagan began to work on behalf of London's National Secular Society, and from 1870 he devoted his evenings and Sundays to walking round freethought and republican meetings selling the *National Reformer* and freethought publications. {RSR}

Faggi, Adolfo (Born 1868)

Faggi was an Italian philosopher. He wrote works on psychology and philosophy, his *La Religione e il suo Avvenire* (1892) being both rationalistic and positivistic. {RAT}

Faguet, Auguste Émile (1847-1916)

Faguet taught literature at the Sorbonne. A leading literary and dramatic critic, he was a Chevalier of the Legion of Honour and a member of the French Academy. In *Voltaire* (1895), he deprecates active hostility to Christianity. The work is a type of "non-aggressive agnosticism." {RAT}

Fahnestock, Leroy W. (20th Century)

Fahnestock's "The Problem of Man" appeared in Joseph Lewis's freethought publication, *Age of Reason* (January, 1964). He was a generous contributor to Joseph Lewis and his Freethinkers of America.

Fahringer, Catherine (1922-)

Fahringer founded the Freethought Forum. An atheist, she hesitates when people assume she is like Madalyn Murray O'Hair, saying, "There *are* other atheists out there. They are beautiful people. Madalyn's not, unfortunately." Fahringer, from Texas, is on the board of directors of the Freedom From Religion Foundation. {WWS}

Fahs, Sophia Lyon (1876-1978)

Fahs, who was born in China where her parents were Presbyterian missionaries, was the principal figure in the remaking of Unitarian religious educational materials during the 1930s. Not until she was eighty-two was she ordained into the Unitarian ministry. She recognized the often overlooked importance of early childhood education, and she worked to provide suitable materials to be used with Unitarian youth. A posthumous work of hers is *Old Tales for a New Day* (1981). {GS; U; U&U}

Fairfield, Roy P(hilip) (1918-)

Fairfield is a former professor of political science at Antioch University in Ohio. Also, he is a director of the Union for Experimental Colleges. Fairfield edited *Humanistic Frontiers in American Education* (1971). In 1980, he signed the Secular Humanist Declaration. In addition, he is a Secular Humanist Mentor of the Council for Secular Humanism and a contributing editor of *Free Inquiry*. He was a key person giving editorial guidance in the writing of Humanist Manifesto II and signed Humanist Manifesto 2000. {HM2; HNS2; PK; SHD}

FAIRNESS AND ACCURACY IN REPORTING

Fairness and Accuracy in Reporting is found on the Web: <http://www.org/fair/>.

FAIRY

When one religion triumphs over another, states Paul G. Morrison, who was curator of the rare book room at the University of Chicago libraries, "the gods of the vanquished faith may be identified with those of the victorious one, or rejected as demons. The Celtic religion evaded both prongs of this fork, and by shrinkage of the old gods made fairies, brownies, or 'little people' of them. Thus they are still here, still helpful, although sometimes mischievous, and always shrink from holy water and the sign of the cross."

No professional philosopher is known to have verified through testing that such exist, except as a meaningless postulation. However, a Greenwich Village wag alleges that a large numbers of fairies have been seen in the rest rooms of churches, libraries . . . and even skirting about in offices of the most prestigious philosophy departments. {ER}

FAITH

Faith (*fiducia*) refers in religion to a trusting and confident belief, without any proof, in God. One can have implicit faith that God exists and that He will reward those who seek to know Him. The clergy during the Middle Ages were required to have explicit faith in what was termed "the intelligent acceptance of the doctrines of the Church, and involving therefore a clear apprehension of the details of those doctrines." Faith (*fides*) is a reference to our perceptual awareness of our material environment; for example, when driving we have faith that the approaching car will stay on its side of the road, at least until we see otherwise.

Lord Russell in *Bertrand Russell on God and Religion* has been quoted on the subject:

> We may define "faith" as a firm belief in something for which there is no evidence. We do not speak of faith that two and two are four or that the earth is round. We only speak of faith when we wish to substitute emotion [feelings] for evidence. The substitution of emotion for evidence is apt to lead to strife, since different groups substitute different emotions. Christians have faith in the resurrection, Communists have faith in Marx's theory of value. Neither faith can be defended rationally, and each is therefore defended by propaganda and, if necessary, by war.

Quips on the subject include the following:

- "Faith" is a fine invention
  When Gentlemen can *see*—
  But *Microscopes* are prudent
  In an Emergency.

  —**Walt Whitman**

- Faith, n. Belief without evidence in what is told by one who speaks without knowledge, of things without parallel.

  —**Ambrose Bierce**
  The Devil's Dictionary

- A casual stroll through the lunatic asylum shows that faith does not prove anything.

  —**Friedrich Wilhelm Nietzsche**

- Though I do not believe that a plan will spring up where no seed has been, I have great faith in a seed. Convince me that you have a seed there, and I am prepared to expect wonders.

  —**Henry David Thoreau**

- Faith may be defined briefly as an illogical belief in the occurrence of the improbable.

  —**H. L. Mencken**

- Faith is when you believe something that nobody in his right mind would believe.

  —Archie Bunker,
  a character in the 1970 sitcom "All in the Family"

- Faith without reason is madness.

  —**Lloyd Dettering**

- It takes a lot more faith to live this life without faith than with it.

  —Peter De Vries

- Faith is believing what you know isn't true.

  Ted Kahn, in *3001* by
  —**Arthur C. Clark**

{See *Encyclopedia of Philosophy*, Vol. 3, for a detailed discussion; ER}

FAITH ATHEISM (Faitheism)

Faith Atheism is a recent Internet coinage. According to its proponents the "faitheists" agree on the following:

- No God or gods exist.
- Neither humans nor the universe was created by a "higher" power.
- There is no immortal soul nor is there an afterlife.

Calling themselves religious, the faitheists differ from the standard variety of atheists, who do not regard atheism as a religion. Instead, faitheists realize that it is impossible to prove that no god or gods exist, just as theists cannot prove that a god does exist. The faitheists, however, have faith that no god exists.

{*The Freethinker*, November-December 1998}

FAITH IN GOD

A 1916 survey of 1000 randomly selected scientists by James Leuba, an atheist, indicated that of the 600 who responded 50% said they believed in personal immortality but only 40% believed in God. A 1997 study by Edward J. Larson of the University of Georgia found that the depth of religious faith among scientists had not changed much. The new study found that 40% of the biologists, physicists, and mathematicians who responded to the same questions said they believed in God, the kind who answers prayers. Meanwhile, 93% of the general American public continues to believe in God, according to national polls. (See entry for James Leuba.)

Falck, Hans S. (20th Century)

When he signed Humanist Manifesto II, Falck was distinguished professor of the Menninger Foundation. He wrote *Social Work: The Membership Perspective* (1988). {HM2}

Falconi, Carlo (20th Century)

Falconi wrote *The Popes in the Twentieth Century: From Pius X to John XXIII* (1967).

FALLACIES

Fallacies in philosophy can be categorized as follows:

- **formal**, involving the calculus of propositions; e.g., using p and q, non-p, non-q;
- **informal**, involving ambiguities and vagueness; e.g., does "Men are unwise" mean all, or some?;
- **errors in non-deductive reasoning** and in observation; e.g., the illusion that the land is rolling when one goes ashore after having become used to the rolling of a ship;
- **errors in discourse**; e.g., inconsistency; *petitio principii*; *a priori* fallacies; *ignoratio elenchi*; is "I haven't got no money" proof of an educated individual's having enough to buy a dinner, or proof of an uneducated individual's inability to buy a dinner?;
- **errors of interrogation**; e.g., "Have you topped reading your horoscope?", which, if answered yes, means you once did; and, if answered no, that you still read your horoscope; although in fact you have never wasted your time on such;
- **errors in explanation and definition**; e.g., in which the definitions lead to circular arguments; and
- **philosophic fallacies**; e.g., arguing "is" from "ought."

(See a discussion by J. L. Mackie in the *Encyclopedia of Philosophy*, Vol. 3.)

Fallières, Clément Armand [President] (Born 1841)

Fallières was the eighth President of the French Republic. In 1876 when he entered the Chambre, he was a supporter of Gambetta's anti-clerical campaign. In 1890 he was Minister of Justice and Cults, during which time he severely checked the clergy. Fallières was a rationalist. {RAT}

FALSIFIABLE

That which is falsifiable can be shown to be false:

- The only state capitol building in Iowa is in Des Moines.

That which is unfalsifiable cannot be shown to be false:

- God told me to do it.

FAME

- There is only one thing in the world worse than being talked about, and that is *not* being talked about.

  —Oscar Wilde

FALSIFICATION: See entry for Karl Popper.

FAMILY

The family is an "obsolete and exploitative institution," according to Tom Flynn:

> (1) Like priestcraft, matrimony, and monarchy, the family is just the sort of pre-Enlightenment institution that secular humanists and other progressives have historically striven to undermine. At humanism's core lies enmity toward all things medieval, authoritarian, and obscurantist. As medieval holdovers go, the family may be short on obscurantism, but it's drenched in authoritarianism. It's second only to matrimony in transmitting the idea of women as brood animals. In perpetuating the idea of children as property, it has no peer. The family must go.

(2) In our overpopulated world, the family lends luster to the idea that everyone should find a partner of the opposite sex and pump out babies. Recent trends toward fewer births per family (in the industrial world, at least) are laudable. But why not a society where forming a family and reproducing are simply viewed as two options among many–options *jointly* exercised by, perhaps, only a third of the reproductive-age population? That would really give us a handle on population control! The family must go!

Finally, (3) the family stands in the way of another implicit humanist goal: decoupling sex from reproduction and reproduction from parenting. The birth control explosion of the 60s emancipated much sex from reproduction. Yet even today, few can imagine anyone but themselves raising their kids, as though conception and childbirth imply anything about one's capacity to prepare a child for today's complex world.

{Tom Flynn, "What's Wrong With the Family," *Secular Humanist Bulletin*, Summer 1997}

FAMILY MATTERS

Family Matters, a quarterly of the Council for Secular Humanism, is a newsletter of the Secular Family Network. t is at P. O. Box 664, Amherst, NY 14226-0664. The editor is Jan Loeb Eisler.

E-mail: <familynews@secularhumanism.org>.

FAMILY OF HUMANISTS

Family of Humanists (PO Box 4153, Salem, Oregon 97302) publishes magazines for youth: *Sunrise Journal* (to age 8); *Stargazer* (ages 8 to 11); *Starwalker* (ages 12 and up). Also, an adult newsletter is available from <LloydK@Teleport.com>.

FAMILY VALUES

In the 1990s, many used "family values" as a code word meaning "anti-homosexuality." Politicians who pointed to any breakdown in the family social structure argued for a return to Biblical standards. The Bible's message, they stated, is not only one of charity but also one in which individuals have a duty to themselves and to their family to take responsibility where they can.

Ferdinand Mount, in his *The Subversive Family*, found just the opposite. The Christ's message, he said, was

• I am come to set a man at variance against his father, and the daughter against her mother, and the daughter-in-law against her mother-in-law. And a man's foes shall be they of his own household.

and

• If any man come to me, and hate not his father, and mother, and wife, and children, and brethren, and sisters, yea, and his own life also, he cannot be my disciple.

{London Sunday Times, 3 November 1996}

FANATICISM

• A fanatic is a man who does what he thinks the Lord would do if only He knew the facts of the case.

—Finley Peter Dunne

• A man is a fanatic if he thinks one matter is so overwhelmingly important that it outweighs anything else at all. To take an example, I suppose all decent people dislike cruelty to dogs; but if you thought that cruelty to dogs was so atrocious that no other cruelty should be objected to in comparison, then you would be a fanatic." And he added that fanaticism is important "because a very great part of the evils that the world is suffering is due to fanaticism.

—Bertrand Russell

Bertrand Russell Speaks His Mind (1969)

(Also, see Bertrand Russell's comments in the entry for Islam.)

Fang Fuy Ruan (20th Century)

Fang Fuy Ruan from China addressed the Tenth International Humanist and Ethical Union World Congress held in Buffalo (1988). Fang is author of *Sex In China* (1991).

Fanon, Frantz Omar (1925—1961)

Fanon was born in Martinique, educated in France, and became an Algerian psychiatrist and editor of the Algerian National Front's newspaper. In *Black Skin, White Masks* (1952), he called for an anti-colonial revolution led not by the proletariat but by the peasants of the Third World. Fanon looked forward to a new breed of humanistic man, modern yet proud of his nonwhite heritage, which would emerge from such a struggle. {CE}

Fantus, Bernard (1874—1940)

Born in Budapest, Fantus came to the United States in 1889 and became a professor of pharmacology at the University of Illinois and editor for twenty-two years of *The Yearbook of Therapeutics*. In 1937 Fantus established the world's first blood bank. He was a signer of Humanist Manifesto I and the posthumous recipient in 1976 of the American Humanist Association's Humanist Pioneer Award. Fantus in 1935 wrote,

> Rest treatment should merely be a preliminary to the more important portion of therapy: the refitting of the individual for work and life. . . . Vocational rehabilitation, actual training for a trade, is a need of the chronically sick and permanently disabled . . . and [is] the single most important problem of medical statesmanship today.
>
> {FUS; HM1}

Farber, Ellen (20th Century)

Farber is Executive Director of the Humanist Society of Metropolitan New York.

Farber, Marvin (1901—1980)

Farber was the long-time chairman of the Department of Philosophy at the State University of New York at Buffalo. A naturalist in philosophy, he developed a theory of evolution that had terrestrial and cosmological aspects. "Concerning evolution," anthropologist H. James Birx has written,

> perhaps no other single theory in the annals of natural science so clearly points out that the human animal with its mental activity and resultant sociocultural environs is but a recently recent (geologically speaking) product of universal history. . . . Like Ludwig Feuerbach, whom he greatly admired, Farber saw all religions as being essentially grounded in the psychosocial wants, needs, and desires of our very vulnerable species within the processes of nature itself." Birx believes that Farber represents a scientific naturalist and rational humanist viewpoint that is "ontologically grounded in an uncompromising and unapologetic materialism.

Farber was influenced by Ralph Barton Perry's *General Theory of Value* (1926), Alfred North Whitehead's *Symbolism: Its Meaning and Effect* (1927), and Clarence Irving Lewis's *Mind and the World-Order* (1929), as well as by his teacher Edmund Husserl. Farber is author of *The Foundation of Phenomenology* (1943), in which he criticizes Husserl's subjectivist philosophy; *Naturalism and Subjectivism* (1959), a major work which clarifies the crucial distinction between ontology and epistemology; and *Basic Issues of Philosophy: Experience, Reality, and Human Values* (1968). He was a contributor to *American Philosophic Naturalism in the Twentieth Century* (1994).

Farber, Sala (20th Century)

Farber is Executive Director in New York City of the Corliss Lamont Chapter of the American Humanist Association.

Fard, Wallace D.: See entry for Nation of Islam.

Fargus, Frederick John (1847—1885)

A novelist who wrote under the name of Hugh Conway, Fargus achieved fame with his *Called Back* (1883), which sold nearly half a million copies. His poem, "The Unknowable," rejected Christianity and accepted only "the unknown God." In a letter to Mrs. Lynn Linton he congratulated her on having made "a great step towards the destruction of illogical creeds," and said of his friends that "with scarcely one exception those intellectually worth their salt are Agnostics." {RAT}

Farkas, Daniel (20th Century)

Farkas, while a student at Yale University in 1998, signed the Campus Freethought Alliance's "Bill of Rights for Unbelievers."

Farmer, Fannie Merritt (1857—1915)

An eminent cooking expert, the director of the Boston Cooking School, Fannie Farmer is known for having written major books on the art of cooking. Her publisher, Little, Brown, found that they had sold more copies of her cookbook than they did of *Little Women.*

One of her secrets was to insist upon using exact measurements, "a level 1/4 cup of butter," for example, not "a piece of butter the size of a walnut." Farmer came from a close family, and she and her three younger sisters are said to have attended the Unitarian church on Sundays. {CE; EG; U; UU}

Farmer, Frances (1914—1970)

John M. Davis has written about Farmer, a 1930's film star, about whom a movie, "Frances" (1982), was made starring Jessica Lange. The sixteen-year-old Frances wins a $100 first prize in a national student writing contest, but it turns out that her essay was entitled "God Dies," and parents are horrified at such a youth who is a hellbound atheist.

Farmer, when charged with drunk driving, had a series of mental problems, was confined to an insane asylum, tried to escape, was given a transorbital prefrontal lobotomy, and the result was that her prior sarcasm and resistance to authority disappeared.

In 1958, she appeared on a TV program saying "faith in God" had helped her to be cured, but she began to drink heavily and died of cancer in 1970. Davis holds that Farmer was deprived of due process of law by faulty decisions made by psychiatrists, and he claims her mother was entirely wrong in blaming Communists for having driven her daughter crazy. {*Secular Nation*, Summer 1995}

Farmer, James (1920—1999)

Farmer, Director of the Public Policy Training Institute, was a noted African American who signed Humanist Manifesto II. He was on the editorial board of *The Humanist.* In 1966, he wrote *Freedom When?* and, in 1985, *Lay Bare the Heart.* Founder and first director of the Congress of Racial Equality, Farmer led the first organized civil-rights sit-in in U. S. history at an all-white Chicago restaurant.

In 1976, the American Humanist Association named him a Humanist Pioneer. {HM2}

Farn, J. C. (19th Century)

Farn wrote *Pictures of Controversy* (185—?). {GS}

Farner, Henry George (20th Century)

Farner, a freethinker, wrote *Heresy in Art* (1918). {GS}

Farquhar, John (1751—1826)

Farquhar, the son of poor parents, settled in India, then returned to England a millionaire. He offered the city of Aberdeen £100,000 to found a college in which no religion should be taught. With pain, the pious city fathers refused. Farquhar openly rejected Christianity and thought Brahmanism superior to it. {RAT; RE}

Farr, Bernard C. (20th Century)

Farr is the former head of the School of Theology at Westminster College, Oxford, and also was director of research and academic programmes. He is a member of the planning group for a Humanist Studies Advanced Certificate Diploma to be offered by Westminster College. Farr wrote *An Education of Modern Spiritualities* (1996).

Farrah, Frederick (19th Century)

Farrah was a radical publisher and bookseller in London. He continued the work of the Fleet Street House. {FUK; VI}

Farrar, Ed (20th Century)

Farrar signed Humanist Manifesto II. {HM2}

Farrar, Eliza (1791-1870)

A Quaker and a Unitarian, Farrar was an abolitionist and a writer of children's books.

Farrell, C. P. (19th Century)

Farrell, who was Robert G. Ingersoll's brother-in-law, was Ingersoll's "authorized" publisher from the beginning. {FUS}

Farrell, James T(homas) (1904—1979)

When Farrell, the Chicago author, wrote *Studs Lonigan* trilogy (1932—1935), Catholics were incensed by his literary naturalism and descriptions of the Church. They would have been even more irritated had they known Farrell married Nora Kaye when she was fourteen or so. This he told Gore Vidal but never listed her as his wife in *Who's Who.* The marriage was annulled, and later Kaye became ballet master Antony Tudor's principal interpreter.

Farrell became one of the best and best-known novelists of his decade. When asked by the present author about humanism he wrote,

> I am struck by the names you list as among the supporters of naturalistic humanism: John Dewey, Thomas Mann, Lewis Mumford [Ed. note: Mumford was later removed when in his correspondence he agreed that he was a "holistic," not a naturalistic or scientific or secular, humanist]. There is much in Mann and Mumford which decidedly runs counter to Dewey's views. I wonder if you have stated the position of naturalistic humanism too broadly and generally for it to be meaningful? My contribution to the *Partisan Review* symposium on religion, published last summer (15 March 1951), indicates my views. I was a Catholic until I was twenty-one. I don't have any violent feelings about it, and if people want to believe, it is their business. As for Mumford, he is just mixed up and obscurantic.
>
> I fear you are too concerned with a category here. What is the precise content of public conduct of some of those whom you mention? Mann is a naturalistic humanist or isn't he? But he accepts honors from the East German puppet government of the Russian slave masters. Corliss Lamont for years has defended the crimes of Stalin. The consequences of action and the conduct of men must be the measure here, in the Deweyean sense. In his *History of Materialism*, Lange (the nineteenth-century German scholar) remarked that, in his view, the influence and ideas of Plato, Aristotle, and Socrates marked a regression in thought. Then, he remarked to the effect that men went on having insight, and they thought that their insights were necessarily derivable from these 'regressive' thinkers. He added that when the great progressive thought of an epoch wears thin and goes down, men go on having insights, and then, they believe that their insights, the truths they discover, are necessarily linked with regressive ideas. There is a point here. People think their beliefs and their formal ideas necessarily give them the clue to truth and insight. It isn't always the case. Insights and conduct are often in contradiction with beliefs and with ideas, formally held.

In 1958, Farrell added,

> Camus is a humanist—a fine and honest spirit, more so this than a thinker.

Farrell's experiences as a baseball enthusiast and a pupil of Catholic schools served as the basis of *Young Lonigan* (1932), which cartoonist-writer Jules Feiffer and many others claim was their first memory of reading a "forbidden book." In that novel, Farrell describes the young William Lonigan, nicknamed Studs, who plays baseball and basketball, smokes secretly, fights, Jew-baits, shoplifts, and experiments with sex. The various characters include Father Gilhooley, gang members, a middle-aged homosexual, and one gang member who deserts the gang when his girlfriend refuses him simply because he is a Jew. Farrell, a master of literary naturalism, describes with sociological thoroughness what a squalid urban environment does to its inhabitants.

Tommy Gallegher's Crusade (1939) tells of a boy's joining a priest's anti-Semitic campaign. *Silence of History* (1963) describes Eddie Ryan, who loses his faith in Catholicism. The Catholic hierarchy was expectedly "underwhelmed" by Farrell's fiction. In addition to many novels, Farrell wrote *A Note on Literary Criticism* (1936), describing his Marxist views, *Literature and Morality* (1947), and *My Baseball Diary* (1957).

In *The Humanist*, Farrell reviewed MacLeish's *J.B.* He was not nearly so favorable as John Ciardi in his *Saturday Review of Literature* critique. Farrell complained that Ciardi exaggerated by claiming that the book represents "the birth of a classic." Farrell found MacLeish's humanism was posed in terms of despair, and he preferred the humanistic outlook of Bertrand Russell's "A Free Man's Worship."

{CE; HNS; WAS, 15 August 1951 and 21 March 1958}

Farrell, Sophia (20th Century)

Farrell is an active member of Rabbi Sherwin T. Wine's Birmingham Temple.

Farrington, Benjamin (20th Century)

Farrington was an English rationalist, an author who wrote for *Rationalist Annual.*

Farrington, Matthew (19th Century)

Farrington was active in the antislavery cause, finding himself in danger several times from New York City proslavery mobs. Upon moving to Bremer County, Iowa, where he taught in the public schools, Farrington became president of the Liberal League of Northern Iowa and also of the Iowa State League in the latter part of the 1890's. {PUT}

Fass, Donald J. (20th Century)

In 1972, Fass was named vice-president of the New York Chapter of the American Humanist Association.

Fast, Howard (1914—)

Fast, a novelist who wrote *Citizen Tom Paine* (1943) and *Spartacus* (1952), won the Stalin Peace Prize in 1953 but later returned the money he received. A member of the Communist Party, Fast served a prison term (1950) for refusing to cooperate with the House Committee on Un-American Activities. In *The Naked God* (1957, he describes his political experiences.

Asked about humanism in 1951 after his term in prison, Fast responded to the present author:

> I find myself somewhat bewildered by the various categories of humanism. It would seem to me that humanism is an expression of action rather than fancy thinking. The only kind of humanism I know is that kind which has a regard for the dignity and the lives of human beings. I don't know what you would call it nor do I think it is important to give it a label. But I do know that in terms of such humanism, very few people are humanists.
>
> By no stretch of the imagination can any humanism I might conceive of fit into the political expression which has turned Korea into a graveyard and turned the Korean cities into piles of ashes and rubble. This may be the expression of what Mr. [Sidney] Hook likes to refer to as democracy as against his hatred for bolshevism. You see, I don't even consider Mr. Hook a candidate for the school of humanity.

{CE; WAS, 15 February 1951}

FATE

Que sera, sera! What will be, will be. Fate is a belief which implies an inevitable and usually an adverse outcome. Epictetus and the Stoics held that the will of God is inescapable whether one wishes it or not. John Stuart Mill wrote, "A Fatalist believes, or half believes (for nobody is a consistent Fatalist), not only that whatever is about to happen will be the infallible result of the causes which produce it (which is the true Necessitarian doctrine), but, moreover, that there is no use in struggling against it; that it will happen however we may strive to prevent it." Muslims hold that whatever happens—a famine, a drought, an accident—it is the will of Allah. Meanwhile, Louisa May Alcott wrote, "Resolve to take fate by the throat and shake a living out of her."

Naturalists, who are more interested in mathematical probabilities and human capabilities, are not fatalists.

Father Anthony: See entry for Joseph McCabe.

Father Divine (George Baker): See the entry for Divine.

FATWA

As an indication of its importance, the word *fatwa* was not in the 1992 *American Heritage Dictionary* or the 1993 *Merriam Webster's Collegiate Dictionary*, but it is frequently used in the media to refer to a Muslim edict. A *fatwa* is a Hindu and Muslim legal term, meaning a formal legal opinion, hence a judicial sentence, given by a canon lawyer. "The earth is flat. Whoever claims it is round is an atheist deserving of punishment": In 1993, Sheik Abdel-Aziz Ibn Baaz, the supreme religious authority of Saudi Arabia, a blind theologian, issued that *fatwa*.

Another Muslim fundamentalist theologian, Sheikh Omar Abdel Rahman of Egypt, issued a *fatwa* authorizing five Islamic militants to assassinate Egypt's President Anwar el-Sadat in October 1981. The sheik later was on trial in New York City for plotting to blow up the Lincoln and Holland tunnels and other landmarks.

In 1989 the Ayatollah Rudollah Khomeini of Iran called for the death of Salman Rushdie, whose *The Satanic Verses* he regarded as a sacrilegious ridiculing of the Prophet Mohammed. In Bangladesh, Muslim religious fundamentalists issued a fatwa against Taslima Nasrin, forcing her to seek refuge in Sweden. Except in the Muslim world, Rushdie and Nasrin are considered among the most courageous people of their time.

Although secularist opponents of Islamic rule have mocked the fatwas, their harsh or contradictory nature has done lasting damage to the image of Islam, according to journalist Youssef M. Ibrahim in Paris. He cited the group of young Egyptian fundamentalists who ambushed and stabbed Naguib Mahfouz, the Egyptian Nobel laureate for literature. They claimed that his *Children of Gebelawi* (1959) had scoffed at religion and insulted the Prophet Mohammed.

Fatwas are often issued on such questions as whether one should fast during an airline flight and on whether charitable donations from belly dancers are accepted as good works by God. (See entries for Taslima Nasrin and Salman Rushdie. Also, see Ibn Warraq's *Why I Am Not A Muslim.*) {ER}

Fauche, Hippolyte (1797—1869)

Fauche was a French Orientalist who translated the *Mahabbrata*, the *Ramayana*, and the plays of Kalidasa. He was a freethinker who wrote for *La Liberté de Penser*. {BDF}

Faulkenberry, Alfred (20th Century)

Faulkenberry, when ordered along with other jurors to pray in an Alabama courtroom, refused and walked out. The practice received considerable media attention, and a lawsuit by the Alabama Freethought Association was started in 1997 against the presiding judge. He and his wife, Carol Faulkenberry, have written for *AAH Examiner*, the newsletter of African Americans for Humanism. {*Freethought Today*, April 1997}

Faulkenberry, Carol (20th Century)

Faulkenberry, a freethought activist and wife of Al Faulkenberry, is author of "The Steeple on the Kmart" in *Freethought Today* (June-July 1998). She also wrote a humorous "An Uppity Old Atheist Woman's Dictionary" (1999).

Faulkner, Charles W. (20th Century)

An African American psychiatrist and a syndicated columnist based in Washington, D.C., Faulkner has written critically of religion and has called for the need of critical thinking. During the Iran-Contra trial calling Colonel Oliver North, which had a jury of twelve African American men and women, both attorneys began their arguments with an unusual emotional appeal to the jury: They quoted words from the Bible. This, Faulkner states, is because most assume that black jurors are "brainwashed" by religion. Even if North was guilty, could a religiously inspired jurist find a guilty man innocent simply because he or she believed deeply in religion? The tactic, Faulkner wrote in a column on "The Misuse of Religion" (6

November 1989), actually works sometimes. "What goes around, comes around" implies that God will punish evil-doers, but Faulkner retorts that if you want someone punished you had better do it yourself. And to readers who complain that he is "against" religion, he replies that his major problem with religion "is that it has not found a way to confront the realities that we face daily, such as drug sales, drug murders and drug rehabilitation, AIDS, homosexuality, and the right of people to believe or disbelieve in religion and still be respected as 'right thinking' individuals." A minister, by utilizing cadence, including occasional intonation or chants, can provide an atmosphere which "drains the body of stress, relaxes the mind, and heightens one's suggestibility to such a degree that the individual often becomes much like a human robot that responds almost automatically." In his *Dollars and Sense* 7, no. 2 (June-July 1981), Faulkner discusses the psychological effects of religion on the masses and finds "the society in which the black church exists is perhaps more ruthless and inconsiderate than we had reason to expect . . . . The way to treat this age-old addiction is not to tear the victim away from the beloved church but to entice, if at all possible, the heartless society that controls, restricts, and manipulates the influence of the black church and its influence on the masses."

Interviewed by Norm Allen Jr., Faulkner explains the appeal of African American religious leaders such as Louis Farrakhan and Al Sharpton: "The likelihood of blacks ever getting themselves out of the turmoil that they're currently in becomes stronger with the use of militancy." Asked about the resolution passed by the Association of Black Psychologists which states that white religious images such as those representing Jesus, Mary, and the angels have had a very negative effect on the collective self-esteem of black children, Faulkner replies, "Oh, I agree with the resolution totally . . . . I think that blacks are outcasts in religion just as much as they are historically. But I think that the most important point is that millions of blacks are very close to the church, but still pray to a white leader." And can humanism be made attractive to African Americans? He replies: "I think that humanism has to be in a position to produce a practical program that has practical, easy-to-evaluate results. If you look at astrology, for instance, many black people hold very strongly to astrology because they need a crutch. What kind of inspiration can humanism provide? Humanism has to provide some means whereby blacks can feel that if they accept it, they will become more successful and happier."

Faulkner signed Humanist Manifesto 2000. {AAH}

Faulkner, Peter (1933—)

Faulkner, author of *Humanism in the English Novel* (1976), lists his politics as Socialist and his religion as Humanist. He is the reader in the School of English and American studies at Exeter University in England, he has written for *New Humanist*, and has been editor of the *Journal of the William Morris Society*. {"The Socialist Humanism of William Morris," *New Humanist*, September 1996}

Faulkner, William (1897—1962)

Faulkner, a major American novelist, was an outright freethinker, according to David Tribe. Faulkner in 1949 received the Nobel Prize in literature and is known for *The Sound and the Fury* (1929), *The Hamlet* (1940), *A Fable* (1954, winner of a Pulitzer Prize), and *The Reivers* (1962, winner of a Pulitzer prize). *As I Lay Dying* (1930) is cited by the American Library Association as a book that book-banners target.

The family name originally had been Falkner, and he was the great-grandson of William C. Falkner, the prototype of the Colonel Sartoris who was described in his novels centered on "Jefferson" in the mythical Yoknapatawpha County. In accepting the Nobel Prize, Faulkner made a brief statement about his belief "that man will not merely endure: he will prevail . . . because he has a soul, a spirit capable of compassion and sacrifice and endurance" and "the writer's duty is to write about these things." His use of "soul" and "spirit" had no theological overtones, and he was disinterested about religious matters.

In 1994, Meta Wilde died. Her 1976 best seller, *A Loving Gentleman: The Love Story of William Faulkner and Meta Carpenter Wilde*, details an eighteen-year romantic affair which they had had and which started while she was working as a script supervisor on the 1936 film, "The Road to Glory," for which Faulkner was a co-writer. {TRI; TYD}

Faupel, A. D. (20th Century)

Faupel was a Unitarian minister who withdrew his following from the Oakland, California, group, calling the new schismatic group the Fellowship of Humanists. It became the first and oldest affiliate of the American Humanist Association. {EW}

Faure, François Felix [President] (1841—1899)

Faure was the sixth President of the French Republic. The son of a worker who made a fortune in business and rose to high positions in politics as an anti-clerical liberal, Faure while President from 1895 to 1899 was responsible for the drastic laws against the Church that were passed in those years. He died of apoplexy. {JM; RAT; RE}

Faure, Sébastian (1858—1942)

In his *Twelve Proofs of the Nonexistence of God*, Faure wrote,

> For centuries kings, rulers, churches, leaders have been treating the people like a vile, miserable herd to be fleeced and butchered. And for centuries the disinherited–thanks to the deceitful marriage of Heaven and the terrible, frightful vision of Hell–have been docile and have stood misery and slavery. It is time that this odious sacrilege, this abominable fraud came to an end! The heaven of which they have incessantly spoken to you, the heaven with which they try to lessen your misery, deaden your pain, and suffocate the protest which, in spite of everything, comes from your heart, is unreal and deserted. Only your hell is populated and exists. . . .

{FUS; RAT}

Faust, Johann or Faustus (16th Century)

According to legend, Faust was a learned German doctor who performed magical feats and who died under mysterious circumstances. He had allegedly sold his soul to the devil (personified by Mephistopheles in many literary versions) in exchange for youth, knowledge, and magic power. Christopher Marlowe's play *Dr. Faustus* (c. 1588) was one of many variations on the legend, as were Goethe's *Faust* (1808—1833) and Thomas Mann's *Doktor Faustus* (1947). Klinger, Chamisso, Grabbe, Lenau, Berlioz, Gounod, Schumann, Liszt, Boito, Spohr, and Busoni are just a few of the many creative artists who have been inspired by the legend. {CE}

Faust, M. (20th Century)

Faust, a freelance writer who reviews films for books such as *Video Movie Guide* and *The Complete Guide to Videocassette Movies*, writes "Film Reviews" for *The Humanist*.

Fausto, Sebastiano Da Longiano (16th Century)

Fausto at the beginning of the sixteenth century is said to have projected a work, *The Temple of Truth*, with the intention of overturning all religions. He translated the *Meditations of Antoninus* and wrote observations on Cicero (1566). {BDF}

Fawcett, Edgar (1847—1904)

Fawcett was a poet, an admirer of Ingersoll. "He called himself an Agnostic Christian," states McCabe, "mixing skepticism on fundamentals with an ill-informed moral admiration of Christianity in his *Songs of Doubt and Dreams, Agnosticism and Other Essays* (1889." Fawcett had no belief in God, but he had a moral admiration of the Christian ethics. {FUS; JM; RAT; RE}

Fawcett, Henry (1833—1884)

A British economist and statesman, Fawcett although he became blind at the age of thirty-five was professor of economics at Cambridge and held high political offices. A monument to him was erected in Westminster Abbey by public subscription.

In Leslie Stephen's biography, Fawcett is said to have regarded theological controversy as "miserable squabbles." McCabe says the Right Honorable Henry Fawcett, who in 1880 became Postmaster General, shared the agnosticism of J. S. Mill. A monument was raised by public subscription and erected in Westminster Abbey. {JM; RAT; RE}

Fawkener, Everard [Sir] (1684—1758)

Fawkener was the London silk-merchant at whose house Voltaire lived when he was in England. He was knighted and appointed ambassador to Constantinople in 1735. Voltaire, in one of his letters, describes Fawkener "smiling with his human philosophy at the superstitious follies of believers." {RAT; RE}

Faymonville, Philip R. (20th Century)

Faymonville has been a member of the American Humanist Association. {HNS}

Fearn, Blanche (1911—1995)

An ardent freethinker, Fearn was a member of the Executive Council of the Freedom From Religion Foundation, Inc. At the age of fourteen, she protested bible-reading in the public school she attended. Like her French convent-educated mother, she rejected religion when young. Her memorial service was held at Ormond Beach's Unitarian Society.

Fears, Herbert (20th Century)

Fears is Past President of the British Columbia Humanist Association in Canada. In a critique of humanistic Judaism's leaders unwillingness to join humanist alliances, Fears wrote (*Humanist in Canada*, Spring 1998), "It would seem that the secular Jews who adopt the humanist nomenclature are, by their isolationism, merely subscribing to the conceit of the 'chosen ones' held by their religious counterparts. Not exactly a productive way of achieving common goals considering how few we secularists are, methinks."

Fechner, Gustav Theodor (1801—1887)

Fechner's *Elements of Psychophysics* (1860) "admitted no difference between body and soul." In religion he was mystical and is often regarded as a liberal Christian. The orthodox disowned him. {RAT; TRI}

FÉDÉRATION DES AMIS DE LA MORALE LAIQUE

In Belgium, *Fédération des Amis de la Morale Laique* (IHEU), is at Du Meridien 17, 1030 Brussels, Belgium. {FD}

FÉDÉRATION HUMANISTE EUROPÉENE: See entry for European Humanist Federation.

Feeney, Gayle (20th Century)

Feeney heads the Australian and New Zealand Unitarian Association (ANZUA, 25 Burneway Street, Sunshine, Victoria 3020, Australia).

Feer, Henry Léon (Born 1830)

Feer was a French Orientalist known chiefly for his Buddhistic studies (1871—1875). {BDF}

FEET WASHING

Because Jesus was said to have washed the feet of his disciples before the Last Supper, his example continues to be followed by dignitaries in the Catholic church as well as by members in rituals of such Protestant groups as the Dunkers [Dunkards], the Mennonites, and the River Brethren.

Non-believers are impressed negatively by the symbolism, although one New York philosophy department chairman is known to have enjoyed other kinds of foot fetishism. (See entry for Mennonites.) {ER}

Feherty, David (20th Century)

A professional golfer, Feherty has gone on record as being a non-theist: "If God wanted people to believe in him," he reasoned, "why'd he invent logic then?" {E}

Fehr, Howard F. (1901—1981)

The mathematician who edited New Thinking in School Mathematics and helped introduce the "New Math." Fehr while at Teachers College, Columbia University, wrote to the present author about humanism:

> Fundamentally, I am not a student of philosophy except in so far as it affects my work in education. My whole basic philosophy of life, of course, is conditioned by the training and thinking I have done within the field of mathematical science. As such, I am in very great agreement with [Julian] Huxley's point of view. I agree with the naturalistic humanism approach to the solution of the problems of man. In fact, the definition [of naturalistic humanism] as found in Ferm's *Encyclopedia of Religion* [describes] the most promising way under present knowledge that man can hope to achieve good life.
>
> {WAS, 29 July 1954}

Feiffer, Jules (1929-)

A freethinker whose satirical cartoons in New York's *Village Voice* began bringing him fame in 1956, Feiffer is one whose humanism shows in his concern about the breakdown of communication: between the state and the citizen, between black and white, between man and woman. He wrote "Little Murders" (1965), a play that involves black humor; *Harry: the Rat With Women* (1963), a novel; and the screenplay for "Carnal Knowledge" (1971).

"Christ died for our sins," he has written. "Dare we make his martyrdom meaningless by not committing them?" {CE}

Feigl, Herbert (1902—)

When he signed Humanist Manifesto II, Feigl was professor emeritus of philosophy at the University of Minnesota. In 1966 Feigl addressed the Fourth International Humanist and Ethical Union World Congress held in Paris. In 1980, he signed the Secular Humanist Declaration. Feigl wrote *Inquiries and Provocations* (1981). {HM2; HNS; SHD}

Feinstein, Michael (1956—)

A sophisticated singer-pianist, Feinstein has more than thirteen recordings on the market. He was a 1992 Grammy nominee and has performed at the White House during the past three administrations, mainly music from the1930s to 1950s and including Ira Gershwin, Irving Berlin, and Cole Porter tunes. Asked about religion, Feinstein has said he identifies with none whatsoever. "I was born Jewish," he told *Advocate* reporter Jeffrey Newman, "but I haven't observed Judaism since I was twelve."

Feldman, Ruth (20th Century)

Feldman is an editor of *Humanistic Judaism*.

Feldmann, Annette B. (20th Century)

Feldmann, an atheist, headed the Shelley Society in New York City and is a member of the Percy Bysshe Shelley Society in London.

Fellens, Jean Baptiste (Born 1794)

Fellens, a professor of History in France, was author of a work on pantheism (1873). {BDF}

Fellini, Federico (1920—1993)

Fellini, an Italian film director, is described in *Columbia Encyclopedia* as having written screenplays for such neorealistic films as Rossellini's "Open City" and "Paisan" and who, in 1950, "quickly abandoned neorealism in favor of professional actors and scripted tales of almost fable-like simplicity expressing a humanistic outlook." "La Strada" (1956) and "La Dolce Vita" (1960) received international acclaim. His films then "became a celebration of life, with swirls of color, international casts of distinctive faces, and camera gymnastics substituting for traditional drama." Other of his major films are "8 1/2) (1963) and "Satyricon" (1969).

"Like many people," he has declared, "I have no religion, and I am just sitting in a small boat drifting with the tide. I live in the doubts of my duty. . . . I think there is dignity in this, just to go on working. . . . Today we stand naked, defenseless, and more alone than at any time in history. We are waiting for something, perhaps another miracle, perhaps the Martians. Who knows?" {CE; TYD}

Fellinton, David (20th Century)

Fellinton is Vice President of Rationalists United for Secular Humanism.

Fellowes, Robert (1771—1847)

Fellowes gave up his religious views in favor of deism, as evidenced in his *The Religion of the Universe* (1836). He was proprietor of the *Examiner* and a great supporter of the London University. {BDF; RAT}

Fellows, John (18th Century)

Fellows, a freethinker and a freethought publisher, was a personal friend of Thomas Paine. {FUS}

Fellows, Otis (1908—1993)

Fellows taught in the humanities department at Columbia University. A noted scholar, he co-edited with Norman Torrey *The Age of Enlightenment* (1942, revised 1971), which is a leading anthology of 18th-century French literature. At Columbia, Dr. Fellows taught French and Romance philology, later becoming chairman of the Italian department. An authority on Denis Diderot, he founded Diderot Studies, a periodical published in Geneva which he edited. His best-known work is *Diderot* (1977), a biography and appreciation. In addition, he wrote *From Voltaire to "La Nouvelle Critique": Problems and Personalities* (1970) and a 1953 collection of Georges Simeon's detective stories.

Fellows, Will (20th Century)

Fellows, a Unitarian, wrote *Farm Boys: Lives of Gay Men from the Rural Midwest* (1996), stories of fifty gay men who grew up on Midwestern farms.

FELLOWSHIP OF RELIGIOUS HUMANISTS

The Fellowship of Religious Humanists is at PO Box 597396, Chicago, Illinois 60659.

Felmet, Joe (20th Century)

When he signed Humanist Manifesto II, Felmet was a humanist counselor. {HM2}

Fels, Joseph (1854—1914)

Fels, a philanthropist, began life as a poor boy but made a fortune in the soap business. He used his money and energy to promote reform. According to Mary Fels in a biography, Fels was a non-Christian theist. {JM; RAT; RE}

Felton, Cornelius C. [University President] (19th Century)

Felton, a Unitarian, was a classical scholar who was once President of Harvard University. {U}

FEMALE RIGHTS: See entry for Robbi Robson, who represented the International Humanist and Ethical Union (IHEU) in 1995 at the UN's Fourth World Conference in Beijing, China.

FEMALE SEXUALITY

• A woman experiences "three delights in intercourse": one from the motion of her own sperm, a second from the motion of the male sperm, and a third from the motion or rubbing that takes place in coitus.

—From *Canon of Medical Knowledge*, a compendium by **Avicenna**, the Arab physician and philosopher, c. 1030 (translated into Latin in the 12th century)

• Woman is defective and misbegotten, for the active force in the male seed tends to the production of a perfect likeness in the masculine sex; while the production of woman comes from a defect in the active force . . . or influence.

—St. Thomas Aquinas, 13th Century)

• *Obimeè*! The devil knows how to do so much between husband and wife. He makes them touch and kiss not only the honest parts but the dishonest ones as well. Even just to think about it, I am overwhelmed by horror, fright, and bewilderment. . . . You call this holy matrimony?

—From *Rules of Married Life*, Brother Cherubino da Siena, 15th century

• Many women die without having experienced the extreme of pleasure. . . . The motive force which in them calls out for pleasure is so delicate and the source of it so distant, that we need not be surprised if pleasure does not come at all or gets lost upon the way.

—From "On Women," **Denis Diderot**, 1772

• No human hand is capable of communicating to the tissues such rapid, steady and prolonged vibrations, and certain kneading and percussion movements, as the vibrator.

—From "Principles of Electro-medicine, Electro-surgery and Radiology" by Anthony Matijaca, who prescribed vibratory sessions to relieve "female troubles." 1917

• We have long understood that the development of female sexuality is complicated by the fact that the girl has a task of giving up what was originally her leading genital zone, the clitoris, in favor of a new genital zone, the vagina.

—From *Female Sexuality*, **Sigmund Freud**, 1931

• Some of the psychoanalysts and some other clinicians insist that only vaginal stimulation and a "vaginal organism" can provide a psychologically satisfactory culmination to the activity of a "sexually mature" female. It is difficult, however, in the light of our present understanding of the anatomy and physiology of sexual response, to understand what can be meant by a "vaginal organism."

—From *Sexual Behavior in the Human Female*, **Alfred C. Kinsey** et al., 1953

• Men make their own orgasms during sex: women should be able to as well.

—From *The Hite Report on Female Sexuality*, by Shere Hite, 1976

• For the purposes of this deposition, a person engages in "sexual relations" when the person knowingly engages in or causes contact with the genitalia, anus, groin, breast, inner thigh, or buttocks of any person with an intent to arouse or gratify the sexual desire of any person.

—From the definition of sexual relations that U. S District Judge Susan Webber Wright allowed in the deposition of President William Jefferson Clinton in the Paul Corbin Jones lawsuit, 1998 ("The Truth About Sex at Any Given Moment," by Camille Sweeney, *The New York Times Magazine, 16 May 1999)*

FEMALES

• After a woman gets too old to be attractive to men, she turns to God.

—**Honoré de Balzac**

• A woman will flirt with anybody in the world as long as other people are looking on.

—Oscar Wilde

• Women are like elephants to me—I like to look at 'em, but I wouldn't want to own one.

—**W. C. Fields**

• Nature has given woman so much power that the law cannot afford to give her more.

—**Samuel Johnson**

• Women who insist upon having the same options as men would do well to consider the option of being the strong, silent type.

—**Fran Lebowitz**

• What passes for woman's intuition is often nothing more than man's transparency.

—George Jean Nathan

• Women should be obscene and not heard.

—Groucho Marx

• A woman without a man is like a fish without a bicycle.

—Gloria Steinem

• [I love them] because women are beautiful and they have two ovaries and they have breasts and no prostate.

—Bill Cosby

• Women are beautiful and wonderful creatures. I enjoy their company. I am not a dirty old man. I am a very sexy senior citizen. They can drive men proverbially up the wall, across the ceiling, and down the other side, and we love them.

—A British seventy-six-year-old Tory peer, in 1998

"Man" in Old English or Anglo-Saxon was universal and referred to all humans equally. *Waepman* was the word for a male human, *wifman* for the female human. Although some contemporary feminists object to the use of "man" to include women as well as men, the objection is not to its historical origins, which were gender-free. The newly coined pronoun "(s)he" is considered by many to be redundant. With some chariness, women who lead a group choose to be called a "chair," but it is believed more prefer "chairwoman," or "chairperson," or to continue using "chairman."

Natalie Angier's *Woman, An Intimate Geography* (1999) points out that woman are seldom credited for being stronger, more sexual, more aggressive, and more adaptive. She notes that a woman's X chromosome is six times larger than the Y and has a "vastly higher gene richness." The woman's egg is the largest cell in the body, the only spherical one, "a geometer's dream," "the true sun, the light of life."

Freud erred, Angier notes, with his theory that clitoral orgasm is "infantile" and vaginal orgasm "mature," whereas in fact the clitoris has no greater end than to serve women's pleasure, and that is end enough. A man's penis is for urinating and ejaculating, but the clitoris is a special organ that is capable of repeated stimulation and multiple orgasm. How inhumane, she reasons, that clitoridectomy is practiced annually on some two million women, mainly in Africa. "Genital cutting is an extreme abuse of human rights. Like slavery and apartheid, it is unacceptable," she cries.

As for abortion, does the uterus belong to the woman who houses one, or, in the case of pregnant women, does it belong to the fetus, or the fetus's representatives in the form of church and state? Or to doctors who, Ms. Angier says, overindulge the urge to cut by performing more Caesarean sections and hysterectomies than are warranted? Angier, in no uncertain terms, insists that each woman must be the mistress of her own corporeal house—let the church and state butt out! {Marilyn Yalom, *The New York Times*, 8 April 1999}

FEMALES AND THE JUDEO-CHRISTIAN BIBLE

In 1895, Elizabeth Cady Stanton wrote the following:

> The Bible teaches that woman brought sin and death into the world, that she precipitated the fall of the race, that she was arraigned before the judgement seat of Heaven, tried, condemned, and sentenced. Marriage for her was to be a condition of bondage, maternity a period of suffering and anguish, and in silence and subjection, she was to play the role of a dependent on man's bounty for all her material wants. . . . Here is the Bible position of woman briefly summed up.

Helen H. Gardener noted the following references concerning women in the Judeo-Christian Bible:

> • The Bible teaches that a father may sell his daughter for a slave (*Exodus* XXI: 7), that he may murder her and still be a good father and a holy man (*Judges*, XIX: 24). It teaches that man may have any number of wives; that he may sell them, give them away, or change them around, and still be a righteous man. It teaches almost every infamy under the heavens for woman, and it does not recognize her as a self-directing free being. It classes her as property, just as it does a sheep; and it forbids her to think, talk, act, or exist except under conditions and limits defined by some priest.
>
> • Wives, submit yourselves unto your husbands as unto the Lord.
>
> • For the husband is head of the wife, even as Christ is the head of the church.
>
> • Let the woman learn in silence with all subjection.
>
> • But I would have you know that the head of every man is Christ, and the head of the woman is man.
>
> • Neither was the man created for the woman, but the woman for the man.

{John Updike, *The New Yorker*, 14 September 1998; PUT}

FEMALES AS CATHOLIC PRIESTS

In 1998 a recently excommunicated Catholic cleric, the Rev. Pat Buckley, defied the Vatican by ordaining sixty-seven-year-old Frances Meigh as a priest in his ministry. "It is not the body that is being ordained, but the soul. Gender is irrelevant," Buckley told his congregation. But the Church, the official faith of four of Ireland's more than five million citizens, retorted that Buckley had no authority to ordain anyone.

Meigh, who paints religious icons and lives as a hermit, said she would now be known as the "very Rev. Mother Frances." Married and the mother of three children before getting her marriage annulled by Church authorities, she was one of many controversial remarried divorcees in Buckley's former ministry in Northern Ireland.

Elsewhere around the world, women are not allowed to become Catholic priests. {Associated Press, 16 September 1998}

FEMALES WHO PASSED AS MEN

In *Suits Me* (1998) Diane Wood Middlebrook lists women who have passed as men: Billy Tipton, born Dorothy Lucille Tipton, a musician whose five wives allegedly were unaware Billy was a female; Charlotte Clarke, an 18th-century cross-dressing actress; Jack Bee Garland, a turn-of-the-century adventurer who feigned muteness, worked as a newspaper correspondent, and wandered the streets of San Francisco giving money to the hungry and homeless; James Miranda Stuart Barry, a 19th-century physician credited with performing the first Caesarean section in Britain; and Catalina de Erauso, a 17th-century conquistador granted a pension by Philip IV of Spain. {Holly Brubach, *The New York Times*, 28 June 1998}

FEMALES, DEGRADATION OF

Christian ethics emphasized sexual virtue, which did much to degrade the position of women, according to Bertrand Russell. (See his critique in the *Quotable Bertrand Russell*. Also see entries for Christian Ethics, Marriage, and Cecilie Rushton.) (Edward Royle's *Radicals, Secularists, and Republicans* has a discussion of "Women, Sex, and Birth Control in Britain, 1866—1915.")

FEMALES, GENITAL MAIMING OF

More than ninety percent of Egyptian girls undergo surgical practices that are erroneously called "female circumcision." The essentially African practice, which predates Islam in Egypt, is intended either to control or prevent sexual intercourse or rob it of pleasure. Aziza Hussein, the wife of a former Ambassador to the United States, spoke at the 1994 International

Conference on Population and Development held in Cairo, and she added that the practice must absolutely be discontinued in the name of humanity. Even in educated families, she said, one-third of the girls are mutilated, and the Coptic Christians also are guilty of genital maiming. Using an anatomically correct wooden model of female buttocks and genitals, Mrs. Hussein demonstrated to members of the conference what genital mutilation is and what irreversible damage it inflicts on little girls wherever the practice is allowed.

The Centers for Disease Control and Prevention reported in 1996 that more than 150,000 women and girls of African origin or ancestry in the United States may be at risk of having the genital rite performed or have already been cut. The rite is common in twenty-eight countries that span Africa's midsection, although it varies widely in its prevalence and severity. One twenty-eight-year-old mother, Halima Ali Haqui Sheeky, whose eleven-year-old daughter attends a Texas school, explained to reporters while her seventeen-month old daughter was curled up in her lap, "We were taught that this was a way of insuring a girl's good behavior. It prevents them from running wild. Women should be meek, simple and quiet, not aggressive and outgoing. This is something we just accept."

The practice is not required by the Qur'an, John Hartung has pointed out. He adds that the vast majority of Muslims do not clitoridectomize or infibulate women: "Millions of Christians, mostly in Ethiopia, perform clitoridectomy as a religious duty, and some, mostly in the Sudan, add infibulation. Even some Jews perform clitoridectomy, notably Ethiopian Jews, most of whom now reside in Israel, where the practice continues. It is practiced in the Mideast, Indonesia, Malaysia, India, and Pakistan and was until recently among the Christian Skoptsy in Russia." (See the entry for Genital Maiming, for in 1997 Egypt's High Court ruled that genital cutting of girls is no longer allowed.) {*The New York Times*, 28 December 1996 and 3 January 1997}

FEMALES, INDIAN: See entry for Gauri Bazaz Malik.

FEMALES, MUSLIM

The Prophet specified the exact size of the stick with which a man may beat his wife. It should be no thicker than one man's thumb.

FEMALE PHILOSOPHERS

Although males have historically predominated in philosophy, following are some examples of works by or about female philosophers of note:

- Kennedy, Ellen, and Susan Mendus, eds., *Women in Western Political Philosophy: Kant to Nietzsche* (1987)
- Le Doeuff, Michèle, *Hipparchia's Choice: An Essay Concerning Women, Philosophy, etc.* (1991)
- Okin, Susan Moller, *Women in Western Political Thought* (1981)
- Waithe, Mary Ellen, ed., *A History of Women Philosophers*, 4 volumes (1984)
- Warnock, M., *Women Philosophers* (1996)

Specific names include the following: Hypatia, recipient of a lynching incited by St. Cyril; Queen Christina, who was implicated in the death of Descartes by asking him to rise in the Swedish winter dawn to give her lessons; Anne Conway; Susan Haack; Harriet Taylor; Catherine Cockburn; Susan Stebbing; Suzanne Langer; Hannah Arendt; Iris Murdoch; Mary Midgely; and Simone de Beauvoir. (See entry for Philosophers, Female.)

FEMINISM

- One is not born, but rather becomes, a woman.

Simone deBeauvoir

- She freed us from then corset. Women don't pass out today. . . . We can breathe. She put the A-frame dress on us, showed our legs, removed the focus from the waist, bobbed our hair, and we were off and running.

—Jane Fonda
on an ABC telecast
telling how fashion designer Coco Chanel
had influenced women

Man has colonized nature, women, and the Third World, complained Vandana Shiva in *Staying Alive*. She accused Europeans and North Americans of being dependent on the colonies of powerless peoples everywhere, within or beyond their borders (blacks, women, and the jobless) to preserve a high standard of living. Science, she argued, was advanced by men (white men) to reduce nature to usable and rejectable parts. She and Maria Mies in *Ecofeminism* (1995) develop the thesis that feminism is interconnected with the fact that neither communism nor capitalism has spread the world's wealth with justice nor have women been fairly treated throughout the world. Feminism, which an increasing number of authors have taken up as a movement around which to rally, is a belief in the social, political, and economic equality of the sexes.

Ms. Gloria Steinem, the sexagenarian who in a 1995 *New York Times* interview with Molly O'Neill was described as "America's best-loved feminist," has described herself as a congenital optimist. Although she discerned an anti-feminist mood in the 1994 election results, resented the number of terrorist acts at abortion clinics, and was disappointed at the dissent among some women who call themselves feminists, she predicted that feminism will not be dampened by temporary setbacks. In *Revolution Within: A Book of Self-Esteem* (1993), she described her background and told of starting *Ms.*, a magazine that served as a vehicle for the feminist movement. In 1995, she told her interviewer, social change comes in fits and starts. "The first wave was about women gaining a legal identity, and it took 150 years. The second wave of feminism is about social equality. We've come a long way, but it's only been twenty-five years. You don't change consciousness without backlash." She described how William F. Buckley Jr., Arianna Huffington, Elizabeth Fox-Genovese, and Helen Alvarez argued on a television program, "Firing Line," in favor of the resolution "The women's movement has been disastrous."

But Betty Friedan, Karen Burstein, Camille Paglia, and Kathryn Kolbert refuted such allegations that the women's movement had precipitated the breakdown of the American family. "Twenty years ago, feminism was blamed for the beef boycott," Steinem said. "Now divorce. Feminism isn't responsible for divorce; marriage is responsible for divorce. Women used to say, 'I am *not* a feminist, but.... Now, they say, 'I *am* a femini. . . but. . . .' Feminism is acceptable. We just have to get that sentiment to the polls. The main task now is getting people out to vote.... What's important is that we have progressed enough that being a feminist is no longer seen as some fringe activity. It is mainstream enough for anti-feminists like Camille Paglia to need to say that they are feminists."

In some parts of the world, the feminist cause is either unknown or non-existent. The Council for Secular Humanism, in its "Affirmations," is pro-feminist. Betty Friedan is a member of its Academy of Humanism. (See entries for Margaret Fuller, Devil, Camille Paglia, and Cecilie Rushton.)

FEMINIST CAUCUS OF THE AMERICAN HUMANIST ASSOCIATION

The American Humanist Association's Feminist Caucus (PO Box 429, Madison, Wisconsin 53701) was founded in 1977 by co-chairpersons Gina Allen, Meg Bowman, and Annie Laurie Gaylor. (See entry for Women.)

FENG SHUI: See entry for Supernaturalism.

Fénelon, François de Salignac de la Mothe (1651-1715)

During the French Revolution Maréchal cited Fénelon, the French theologian, as being the opposite of an atheist. He was banished for his mystical instruction in faith, and his quietism brought a long quarrel with his former patron Bossuet, also cited by Maréchal as the opposite of an atheist. Pope Innocent XII condemned the writings of Fénelon. {CE; ER; EU, Aram Vartarian}

Fenichell, Stephen (1956—)

Fenichell has been an American Humanist Association treasurer. {CL}

Fenn, Wallace O. (20th Century)

Fenn has been a member of the American Humanist Association. {HNS}

Fenn, William Wallace (1862—1932)

Dean of Harvard's Divinity School, Fenn played a key role in moving the Western Unitarian Conference out of the control of Jenkin Lloyd Jones and, eventually, in securing the healing of the split between the American Unitarian Association and the western radicals. {U&U}

Fenton, Don (20th Century)

Fenton is on the staff of *Secular Nation*, the international Atheist Alliance magazine that commenced in 1994.

Fenton, James (1949—)

Fenton, who is called the poet Auden's heir, is professor of poetry at the University of Oxford. Highly respected in Britain, Fenton like Auden was elected Oxford University's official poet. Highly original both in his work and life, Fenton has, in the words of Ian Parker,

> lived with a pet monkey in Phnom Penh, farmed prawns in the Philippines, eaten a bowl of live ants–that sort of thing. Almost by accident, he has made a fortune from a musical, 'Les Misérables.' Perhaps most famously, he was the foreign correspondent who rode on the first North Vietnamese tank to reach the Presidential Palace during the fall of Saigon in 1975.

Fenton, who was born in Lincoln, in the north of England, is one of four children of a vicar, now Honorary Canon Emeritus of Christ Church, Oxford. In "God, A Poem" (1983), Fenton described the disappointment inherent in belief:

> ". . . . I didn't exist at Creation,
> I didn't exist at the Flood,
> And I won't be around for Salvation
> To sort out the sheep from the cud–
>
> "Or whatever the phrase is. The fact is
> In soteriological terms
> I'm a crude existential malpractice
> And you are a diet of worms.
>
> "You're a nasty surprise in a sandwich.
> You're a drawing-pin caught in my sock.
> You're the limpest of shakes from a hand
> Which I'd have thought would be firm as a rock,
>
> "You're a serious mistake in a nightie,
> You're a grave disappointment all round—
> That's all that you are," says th' Almighty,
> "And that's all that you'll be underground."
>
> (Ian Parker, "Auden's Heir"
> {*The New Yorker*, 25 July 1994)

Fenzi, Sebastiano (Born 1822)

An Italian writer, Fenzi in 1849 founded the *Revista Britannica*. He wrote for *L'Italiano* and also wrote a credo which is a non-credo. {BDF}

Ferencz, József (1908—1994)

Ferencz's grandfather, of the same name, was a bishop of the Transylvanian Unitarian church, and in 1971 Ferencz was elected bishop of the Unitarian Church of Hungary. He led the church for seventeen years and was chief editor from 1971 to 1989 of *Unitárius Élet*.

Fergus, James (Born 1812)

A Scot, Fergus was the son of a Presbyterian but, upon reaching Canada, spent three years in a Quaker settlement and learned the trade of a millwright. He then transacted business throughout the Midwestern United States, moving to and laying out the town of Little Falls, Minnesota, in 1854.

Fergus helped build dams and bridges across the Mississippi, drove cattle, acted as the first recorder of Alder Gulch at Virginia City, was for many years a citizen of Lewis and Clark country and moved eventually to Montana. Fergus was a freethinker. {PUT}

Ferguson, Andrew R.B. (20th Century)

Ferguson is a member of the British Rationalist Association. He has written book reviews for *New Humanist*. In "A Foundation for *Critique of Pure Verbiage*," a work by F. R. H. Englefield, Ferguson calls the book an important one for understanding the nature and function of language. Unlike most religious and philosophical writing, which allegedly goes "round in circles," the Englefield work is a "readable exposition of how and why such verbiage has continued to hold a respected place in academic and popular thought since the time of classical Greece. {*New Humanist*, February 1996}

Ferguson, Anne (20 Century)

Ferguson writes a column, "Adam's Rib," in the *New Zealand Rationalist and Humanist*.

Ferguson, Martha and **Philip** (20th Century)

The Fergusons are editors of Cincinnati's Free Inquiry Group newsletter, *FIG Leaves*.

Ferguson, O. Andrews (20th Century)

Ferguson is a coordinator for the American Humanist Association in the states of Alabama, Georgia, Mississippi, North Carolina, South Carolina, and Tennessee. (See entry for North Carolina Humanists.) {FD}

Feringa, Frederik (Born 1840)

A Dutch writer, Feringa contributed to *De Dageraad* (The Daybreak) over the signature of Muricatus. He wrote *Democratie en Wetenschap* (Democracy and Science, 1871) and *De Vrye Gedachte* (Freethought). {BDF}

Ferlinghetti, Lawrence (1913—)

An American author and publisher, Ferlinghetti helped found the City Lights Bookshop, which was a center for writers of the Beat Generation. He encouraged Allen Ginsberg, among other authors. His *A Coney Island of the Mind* (1958) contains the sentence, "I am waiting for them to prove that God is really American."

Asked if he has ever been an active or inactive member of some religious group, Ferlinghetti responded in the negative. He added he does not believe in an afterlife and cited his "Big Fat Hairy Vision of Evil" in *Starting from San Francisco* (1956), part of which is as follows:

> Evil evil evil evil
> World is evil
> Life is evil
> All is evil
> if i ride the horse of hate
> with its evil hooded eye
> turning world to evil. . . .
>
> Evil evil evil evil evil evil evil
> even if three naked monkeys
> see no hear no speak no evil
> Ebony Buddha With Three Eyes
> is evil to evil eyes
> Bronze Image Dancing Krishna is evil
> Tibetan Conquerer of Death
> draped in human skin
> is evil
> Singing Bodhisattva
> is evil
> in evil eyes. . . .
>
> Horse will catch me in the living end
> He'll lie down on top of me
> in my horsehair grave. . . .

Horse will lick my horsy face
with his gluepot tongue
Horse will puke on me
Poop his baked potatoes out on me
in death's insanity
and i will eat this naked lunch
that turns me into him
in the death of that god
which is consciousness itself
Ah but i will not look out
before that date
three Horse's fur windows
and vomit landscapes!

{CE; TYD; WAS, 23 Apr 97 and 29 Oct 97}

Fernández Flores, Rafael (20th Century)

A Mexican, Fernández spoke about science and superstition at the 1996 Humanist World Congress held in Mexico City.

Fernau, Rudolf (19th Century)

A German, Fernau wrote *Christianity and Practical Life* (1868), *Zoologica Humoristica* (1882), and *Religion as Ghost and God Worship*. {BDF}

Feroe, Sandra (20th Century)

Feroe is co-chairperson of Atheists of Colorado. She has written for *Secular Nation* (October-December 1998).

Feron, Emile (Born 1841)

A Belgian advocate, Feron was Councillor of the International Freethought Federation. {BDF}

Ferrari, Guiseppe (1811—1876)

Ferrari was an Italian philosopher, a disciple of Romagnosi, a study of whose philosophical writings he published in 1835. Upon being attacked by the Catholic party, he was exiled and moved to Paris, where he became a collaborator with Proudhon and a contributor to the *Revue de Deux Mondes*. In 1842 he became a professor of philosophy at Strasbourg, an appointment soon canceled on account of his opinions. In 1859 he was elected to the Italian Parliament, where he remained one of the most radical members until his death at Rome. {BDF; RAT}

Ferrer, Francisco (1859—1909)

Ferrer founded his "Modern School," a purely secular one, at Barcelona in 1901. "No priest and no religion, no prayers, and no devotions inspired by any creed of supernaturalistic affinities, found shelter under its auspices," Foote has reported. Such roused the bitter antagonism of the clergy, who stirred up the authorities against him. He was imprisoned and his property confiscated. But new schools were established in many localities. In 1906, a bomb explosion at Madrid furnished the pretext for serious charges against Ferrer. Three years later another pretext was furnished by a civil disturbance in Barcelona. He was falsely charged with complicity in the rising and condemned to be shot, a sentence that was carried out on 12 October 1909. Pope Pius X sent a gold-handled sword engraved with his felicitations to the military prosecutor who had obtained Ferrer's death. Ferrer's *The Origin and Ideals of the Modern School* (1913) was posthumously published. (See William Heaford's article on Ferrer in *Freethinker*, 14 May and 7 June 1931.) {FO; GS; TYD}

Ferrer y Guardia, Francisco (1859—1909)

A famous freethinker and teacher, Ferrer was convicted on false evidence as a revolutionary by the Spanish monarchy and executed in 1909. Ferrer called "belief" an "ancient error" and was an early exponent of progressive education. In his "Modern School" (1902) there were to be no rewards or punishment, and no competition. Music and current affairs were emphasized. The schools were to be free of any religious indoctrination, he wrote in his *Origin and Ideals of the Modern School* (published in 1913). At one time, there were more than forty branches of the Modern School in Barcelona and more than 120 schools which followed his methods. His belief in science and in the female potential riled Church officials. In 1906 when King Alfonso XIII was almost assassinated Ferrer, held in prison without trial for eleven months, was arrested as a suspect. Acquitted, for an anarchist had thrown the bomb, Ferrer organized the International League of Rational Education. But Bishop Casanas continued fighting "the partisans of the godless school," and Ferrer's trial was said to have been a mockery of justice. Pope Pius X inscribed a gift sword to the "Procureur" of the Military Tribunal for his part in ridding Spain of the antichrist. As described by McCabe, Ferrer "incurred the mortal hatred of the clergy. Inasmuch as he was also a philosophic Anarchist of the gentle Tolstoi school, the government willingly obliged the bishops and, after a gross travesty of a trial, had him shot. He was a man of high character and ideals." Ferrer y Guardia left behind, on the walls of his dungeon, "Let no more gods or exploiters be served; let us learn rather to love each other." {CE; CL; EU, Kit Mouat; JM; RAT; RE}

Ferrero, Guglielmo (1871—1942)

Ferraro, an Italian man of letters and historian, collaborated with his father-in-law, Cesare Lombroso, in writing *La donna delinquente* (1893), a criminological study of female offenders. He was an outspoken critic of fascism and, exiled by Benito Mussolini, became professor of history at the University of Geneva, Switzerland, in 1930. He wrote *The Greatness and Decline of Rome* (1902—1907, 5 volumes). In 1908 he was Lowell lecturer in America. When invited to contribute to a symposium on the future life, Ferrero wrote that he did not believe in it. Ferrero was a positivist, not in a religious sense; in fact, McCabe labels Ferrer an agnostic. {JM; RAT; RE}

Ferri, Enrico (Born 1856)

Ferri, once a professor of criminal law at the University of Siena, became a member of the Italian Parliament. He wrote a large work on the non-existence of free will. With Professor Lombroso, he was a leader of an Italian school of criminal law reform. Asked by McCabe if all Italian Socialists had given up the Catholic faith, Ferri wrote back, "Yes, and they reject every religion under the sun." {BDF; JM; RAT; RE}

Ferri, Luigi (1826—1895)

An Italian philosopher, Ferri wrote *History of Philosophy in Italy* (1868) and *The Psychology of Pomponazzi*. He was a corresponding member of the French *Institut*, member of the Academia dei Lincei and of the Council of Higher Education, and Chevalier of the Order of Merit. {BDF}

Ferrick, Thomas (20th Century)

When he signed Humanist Manifesto II, Ferrick was a leader of the Ethical Society of Boston. He is Harvard University's Humanist Chaplain and has stated that the chaplaincy "celebrates humanity in its earthly and evolutionary context. Its main appeal is to the skeptical inquirer and the idealistic student of an agnostic or atheist inclination." Ferrick is on the Board of Directors of the American Humanist Association. E-mail: <thomas_ferrick@harvard.edu>. (See entries for Chaplain, John Loeb, and Massachusetts Humanists.) {FD; HM2; HNS2}

Ferrière, Emile (Born 1830)

Ferrière was a French author of *Literature and Philosophy* (1865), *Darwinism* (1872), and *The Apostles* (1879, a work which challenged early Christian morality. Another work that showed his freethinking was *Paganism of the Hebrews Until the Babylonian Captivity* (1884). {BDF}

Ferris, Timothy (1944—)

A journalist who is emeritus professor at the University of California at Berkeley, Ferris has made his name writing about scientific matters. *The Red Limit: The Search for the Edge of the Universe* (1983) and *Coming of Age in the Milky Way* (1988) were followed by *The Whole Shebang: A State-of-the Universe(s) Report* (1977). In the latter work, Ferris writes that the big-bang theory is not a temporary theoretical fashion, likely to be changed when further astronomical findings are reported. Rather, it is almost certain to endure as part of any future theory of the universe. Such a conclusion, he adds, "may seem curious to readers of the many newspaper and magazine articles that have appeared during the past decade proclaiming that this or that observational finding has put the big-bang theory in jeopardy."

"There is more to the world than this world, and more to this world than we know," Ferris notes. After a conference of theologians and cosmologists, however, a telecast of the event showed

> . . . several religious people sitting around, and they turned to each other with smug smiles and said, "Well it just goes to show that the man of science laboriously climbs the mountain and gets to the top and finds that the man of religion has been there all the time."
>
> Well, that's crap! . . . What I find repugnant is the easy assumption in some quarters of religion that one or another scientific finding has simply confirmed what they already knew.
>
> {Before the Big Bang," *The New York Review of Books,* 12 June 1997}

Ferucci, Franco (20th Century)

Ferruci, an Italian born professor of literature at Rutgers University, is author of *The Life of God.* (See entry for God Himself.)

Ferry, Jules François Camille (1832—1892)

Ferry, a French statesman, became Minister of Public Instruction and was responsible for secularizing the schools. He also was a Premier and the President of the Senate. A thorough agnostic, as shown in his *Discours et Opinions* (1903), he was a noted leader of the anti-clericals. {JM; RAT; RE}

Ferry, Luc (20th Century)

Ferry, a professor of philosophy at the Sorbonne and the University of Caen, was elected a Humanist Laureate in 1993 by the Council for Secular Humanism's International Academy of Humanism. He is described as being in the forefront of the younger French intellectuals and philosophers.

Ferry wrote *Political Philosophy* (1991), the first part of a projected four-volume work on rights. He rejects a simple return to the ancient philosophers, arguing that the ideals of equality and human rights that have been developed in modern times need also to be included. Kant and Fichte, he holds, have much to teach us about rights, which are germane only if we accept the contemporary idea of human rights that they need to be shared by all humans simply by virtue of the fact we all *are* humans. He also wrote *The System of Philosophies of History* (1992), *From the Rights of Man to the Republican Idea* (1992), *Homo Aestheticus* (1993), *The New Ecological Order* (1995), and *Why We Are Not Nietzscheans* (1997).

With Alain Renaut, Ferry wrote *French Philosophy of the Sixties: An Essay on Antihumanism* (1990). The discursive work tells about the 1968 student uprisig in France, then discusses French Nietzscheanism (Foucault), Heideggerianism (Derrida), Marxism (Bourdieu), and Freudianism (Lacan). Ferry and Renaut argue against "anti-humanism" and argue for a faith in our sovereignty over ourselves. In so doing, they are negative about the dominant French philosophical currents since 1968 and align themselves more with Kant, Fichte, the Marburg and Frankfurt schools, Habermas, Raymond Aron, and Karl Popper. Bernard-Henri Lévy's *Adventures on the Freedom Road: The French Intellectual in the 20th Century* (1995) is negatively critical of the work. Ferry and Renault also wrote *Heidegger et les modernes* (1988; *Heidegger and Modernity,* 1990), in which they claim that Heidegger, when he is a humanist, is a critic of National Socialism. Clearly, Ferry is a "non-metaphysical" humanist.

FERTILITY RITES

An important pagan myth was the search of the earth goddess for her lost or dead child or lover—Isis and Osiris; Ishtar and Tammuz; Demeter and Persephone. Such a myth symbolized the birth, the death, and the reappearance of vegetation, when acted out in a sacred drama, and it was the fertility rite par excellence, according to the *Columbia Encyclopedia.* Other rites involved magic, such as kindling of fires (symbolizing the sun) and scattering the reproductive organs of animals on the fields, displays of phallic symbols, and ritual prostitution. At one time in India, it was believed that a fertile marriage would result if virgins were first deflowered by means of the lingam, a stone phallus symbolizing the god Shiva. Sacrifices of both humans and animals were believed to release the powers embodied within them and so make the fields or forests productive where the sacrifices had taken place. Many ancient fertility rites have persisted in modified forms into modern times. The Maypole dance which young children so love, for example, derives from spring rituals glorifying the phallus. Religious fundamentalists, in a Pat Robertson-approved ceremony termed "See You At the Pole," gather at flagpoles and pray, apparently unaware that they are duplicating an ancient pagan ritual of phallic worship as performed by druids and other pagans in northern Europe before being stopped by Christian leaders. {CE}

Fessenden, Larry (20 Century)

A film director, Fessenden was asked by Peter Graham about his independent film "Habit" (1995), which Graham called "a horror movie that has a romantic and nostalgic tone," then commented that that sounded religious. Fessenden responded,

> Yes and no. I'm a wretched atheist and existentialist. I don't believe in God at all. I think there's nothing. On the other hand, I'm probably more religious than the average Joe, because I feel that there's something to be revered. The wind and the trees, the mystery. *Habit* is about that other thing, the mystery. Sam wants to believe in this other power, that this woman he's dating is a vampire, that she's the undead. He buys into something that is ludicrous and romantic. He has this great yearning and there's no way for him to show that.
>
> {CA}

FETISH

A fetish is an inanimate natural or man-made object believed to have magical power, either from a will of its own or from a god that has transformed the object into an instrument of its desires. A fetish with great power is often declared *taboo.* Stones, feathers, shells, carvings in wood can be fetishes, and fetishism can include using objects as substitutes for male genitalia. Preachers have been known to use a choir robe as a fetish. Women have been known to use the Christian cross. Unless fetishism is coupled with other psychological disturbances, it is not considered a serious disorder. (See entry for Animism.) {CE}

Feuerbach, Friedrich Heinrich (1806—1880)

The son of a famous German jurist, Feuerbach at first studied philology, then chose to preach what his brother Ludwig taught. He wrote *Theanthropos* (1838), a series of aphorisms, and *Religion of the Future* (1843—1847). Like his brother Ludwig, Friedrich was a freethinker. {BDF; JM; RAT; RE; PUT}

Feuerbach, Ludwig Andreas (1804—1872)

Author of *The Essence of Christianity* (1841, translated by George Eliot in 1854), Feuerbach was a leading German atheist, materialist, "sensuousist," and naturalist. A disbeliever in personal immortality and suspicious of idealism, he was a leading skeptic. In 1828 he became a lecturer in the University of Erlangen, but soon had to retire owing to the offence caused by his "Thoughts on Death and Immortality," in which he attacked the belief in an immortal "soul." As early as 1839, Feuerbach held that Christianity had in fact long vanished not only from the reason but also from the life of mankind, that it was nothing more than a fixed idea. God, he held, is merely man's projection of man's [inner nature. Riepe relates Feuerbach's intellectual strengths and weaknesses, showing how he influenced the 19th-century Protestant thought as well as the outlooks of Richard Wagner, Marx, Engels, Friedrich Nietzsche, Karl Barthe, Marbin Buber, Martin Heidegger, Sidney Hook, and Sartre. When Marx read Feuerbach, he concluded that "philosophers have only interpreted the world; the point is to change it." Buber, the Jewish philosopher credited Feuerbach with having "introduced that discovery of the *Thou* which has been called 'the Copernican Revolution' of modern thought." Hook described Feuerbach's psychology of religion as "still the most comprehensive and persuasive hypothesis for the study of comparative religion." Among his observations:

- God has not created man, but man created God.
- It is as clear as the sun and as evident as the day that there is no God and that there can be none.
- Christianity has in fact long vanished, not only from the reason but also from the life of mankind, and it is nothing more than a fixed idea.
- Whenever morality is based on theology, whenever right is made dependent on divine authority, the most immoral, unjust, infamous things can be justified and established.

According to H. James Birx, Feuerbach represents a significant philosophical break from such early German idealists as Leibniz, Kant, and Hegel, providing "a starting point for a naturalist humanism. He embraced the scientific-rational attitude, acknowledged the value of both the natural and social sciences, and incorporated the theory of biological evolution into his own conceptual framework of man within nature. In essence, Feuerbach saw humanity within sociocultural development and our species as a product of organic history."

Although a Christian of the evangelical type–Brewin Grant–claimed that he "died in despair," Feuerbach's friend Carl Scholl, who delivered an address at his grave, visited him every morning during his last illness. Scholl said that Feuerbach was suffering from bronchitis and endured severe pain with great fortitude. He died 13 September 1872 "in a slumber so peaceful that those present scarcely noticed that he was dead." (For Mao's view on Feuerbach, see the entry for Marxism.) {BDF; CE; CL; ER; EU, Dale Riepe; FO; Van A. Harvey, "The Re-Discovery of Ludwig Feuerbach," *Free Inquiry*, Winter 1996-1997; FUS; HNS2; JM; JMR; PUT; RAT; RE; Carl Scholl, *Dem Andenken Ludwig Feuerbach* (1872); TRI; TYD}

Feyerabend, Paul (1924—1994)

Reviewing Feyerabend's autobiography, *Killing Time* (1995), Richard Rorty wrote, "Paul Feyerabend, who died in 1994 at the age of 70, was the Norman Mailer of philosophy. Like Mailer, he was a soldier in World War II (but on the wrong side). Feyerabend, too, was brilliant, brave, adventurous, original and quirky. Both liked to shock: Mailer used to say that we face a choice between cancer and homosexuality, Feyerabend once tried to put modern medicine and voodoo on an epistemological par. And there are other resemblances. Feyerabend was an exuberant political radical, but nobody could pin down his political views. He was a celebrated womanizer (even though, as this autobiography reveals, he never experienced sexual intercourse, having been rendered impotent at twenty-one by a bullet that pierced his spinal cord and left him on crutches, and in almost constant pain, for the rest of his life). His life was disorganized, and he sometimes treated his wives, lovers and colleagues very badly indeed. Feyerabend remains a hero to a sizable minority of philosophers, but the majority think of him as having had too little self-discipline to fulfill his early promise."

That sizable minority liked the ex-Nazi officer's views because he sided more with Frege and Husserl who wanted philosophy, in Rorty's words, "to be an autonomous, ahistorical discipline that discerns ineluctable formal structures of reality, experience or language" rather than with Heidegger and Dewey, who felt that cutting philosophy loose from history would produce "only sterile scholasticism."

"Some philosophers of science, in particular Paul Feyerabend," wrote Paul Kurtz in *Towards a New Enlightenment*, "deny that there are *any* objective methods [of science] at all. There is no method, he says, it all depends on cultural or social conditions of the time. This position, I submit, is absurd. It reduces science to utter subjectivism. My retort is that there is a real world out there, and that some methods are more effective than others. In any case, science is a cooperative, intersubjective venture, testing its hypotheses by evidence, experiment, and consistency, and we cannot say that 'anything goes' and that one theory is as good as any other, and/or that the paradigms that are fashionable are those that win out." (See entry for Consilience.) {Richard Rorty, "Untruth and Consequences," *The New Republic*, 31 July 1995}

Feynman, Richard P. (1918—1988)

In *What Do You Care What Other People Think?* (1988), the Nobel Prize-winning American physicist Feynman who once worked on the Manhattan Project wrote,

> In those days, in Far Rockaway, there was a youth center for Jewish kids at the temple. . . . Somebody nominated me for president of the youth center. The elders began getting nervous, because I was an avowed atheist by that time. . . . I thought nature itself was so interesting that I didn't want it distorted (by miracle stories). And so I gradually came to disbelieve the whole religion.

Genius, The Life and Science of Richard Feynman (1992) is the title of a biography by James Gleick. Feynman shared the Nobel Prize with Julian Schwinger and Shinichiro Tomonaga. They developed QED (Quantum Electrodynamics) into a theory that encompassed all electromagnetic properties of electrons. In so doing, it covered all of physics and physical chemistry except gravitation and nuclear structure. In 1943 he worked at Los Alamos, working on the atomic bomb until it was tested two years later. He is credited with identifying the cause of the *Challenger* space shuttle tragedy. Gleick reports that at the graveside of his father, Feynman read no prayers, that he was a vehement atheist.

The Meaning of It All: Thoughts of a Citizen Scientist (1998), written by Michelle Feynman and Carl Feynman, told of his view that "Science makes an impact on many ideas associated with religion, but I do not believe it affects moral conduct and ethical values." He also held that "the metaphysical aspects of religion have nothing to do with the ethical values, that the moral values seem somehow to be outside the scientific realm." The work gives his materialistic, nontheistic view of the cosmos.

Freeman Dyson has called Freynman "the most original mind of his generation." He also was a bongo player with a sense of humor. When he was dying of cancer, for example, *The Los Angeles Times* offered him an advance copy of the obituary to obtain any suggestions for changes. "No thanks," the confident atheist replied, because to do so "ahead of time" would take "the element of surprise out of it." Gleick also quotes what Feynman, in anticipation of death, thought:

> You see, one thing is, I can live with doubt and uncertainty and not knowing. I think it's much more interesting to live not knowing than to have answers, which might be wrong.
>
> {*Free Inquiry*, Spring 1998}

Fichte, Johann Gottlieb (1762—1814)

Fichte, the famed German philosopher, held to a dialectical idealism which attempted to unify the theoretical and practical aspects of cognition that had been set apart by Kant. Kant's noumenal realm was rejected, "making the active indivisible ego the source of the structure of experience. This led to his postulation of a moral will of the universe, a God or absolute ego from which all eventually derives and which therefore unites all knowing," states the *Columbia Encyclopedia*.

Fichte's *Kritik aller Offenbarung* (Critique of all Revelation, 1792) led to charges that he was attempting to throw over Christianity and set up the worship of reason. This led to his wife's being insulted in the streets of Jena, his house being riotously attacked in the night, and his moving, although the High Consistory of Weimar acquitted him of all charges. His *Wissenschaftslehre* ("Doctrine of Knowledge" [1794–1795]) brought him into conflict with the Kantians, and when accused of atheism he retorted the charge on the utilitarian theists, then resigned his Jena position.

According to Robertson, after attacks from religionists as well as from philosophers, Fichte "remained a philosophic Ishmael, warring and warred upon all around. He was thus left to figure for posterity as a religionist 'for his own hand,' who rejected all current religion while angrily dismissing current unbelief as 'freethinking chatter.' If his philosophy be estimated by its logical content as distinguished from its conflicting verbalisms, it is fundamentally as atheistic as that of Spinoza." McCabe calls Fichte an idealist pantheist, not an atheist. {BDF; CE; ER; EU; HNS2; JM; JMR; JMRH; RAT; RE}

Ficino, Marsilio (1433-1499)

An Italian philosopher, Ficino was a notable reviver of Platonism during the Renaissance. (See entry for Paul Kristeller.)

Ficke, Arthur Davison (1883—1945)

An Iowa-born poet, Ficke conspired with another humanistic author, Witter Bynner, by writing *Spectra*, a literary hoax that satirized modernism in poetry. His *Mr. Faust* has a New Yorker working with Satan to overcome disillusionment, ending with a spiritual peace that is humanistic.

His most philosophic work is *Tumultuous Shore* (1942). In "An Ungodly Man," Ficke writes ironically about an artist:

> His paintings were treasured,
> But he was disliked because
> He cursed the church, he drank much gin,
> He followed wenches by the score;
> He was a man of utter sin.
> Our matrons turned him from the door.
>
> He died at last, of too much gin. . . .
> We are a Christian folk; and we
> Treasure, forgiving of his sin,
> His pictures for posterity.

In "Prayer for a Lady," he ends by addressing "God":

> This prayer I offer unto Thee
> Aware of its futility.
> Full well I know Thou canst do naught,
> Being but a figment of my thought.

Ficke's "In This Hour," describes his humanism:

> I pray you, in this hour's confusion go
> Not back again into the old belief
> That all man's life is brutish, harsh, and brief,
> And that what has been, always will be so.
> Earth has seen many a great hope's overthrow
> And many a noble dream go down in grief;
> Yet still persists the parable of the leaf
> That spring unfolds above the endless snow.
>
> Be not too sure that evil in this hour
> Has strength to make as nothing all our gain
> And leave us naked to the whirlwind's wrath.
> Through earlier, darker days than these, some power
> Of man, mere man, endured its night of pain,
> Then strode one footstep higher up the path.
>
> {CL; *The Humanist Newsletter*, September-October, 1953}

FIDEISM

Around 1885, the term "fideism" came to mean a reliance on faith, not reason, in the pursuit of religious truth. Thus, according to this view, Christianity, Islam, or any other religion rests on premises that are accepted by faith. John Hick, who taught theology at the University of Birmingham, is an example of a fideist, one who held that belief in God includes believing that God created goodness as well as evil. But belief in God, he held, is not incompatible with the fact that evil is found in the world. Hick argued against the seeming incompatibility of believing that, if God is perfectly loving, He must wish to abolish evil; that if He is all-powerful, He must be able to abolish evil. Even if the arguments for the existence of God were not valid, Hick held, faith in God "stands ultimately upon the ground of religious experience and is not a product of philosophical reasoning."

Fideism, in short, holds that everything that can be known about God or divine things is known only or primarily by faith, never by reason alone. Bertrand Russell noted that, as a new theology, fideism "cannot be refuted since it does not profess to prove its points." Ernest Nagel similarly found that fideism "is impregnable to rational criticism."

J. C. A. Gaskin, in *Varieties of Unbelief from Epicurus to Sartre* (1989), defined fideism as "[t]he position that the teachings of Christianity or of Islam or whatever are justified because all knowledge rests on premises accepted by faith." {ER}

Fieger, Geoffrey (20 Century)

Fieger, the lawyer and champion of Dr. Jack Kevorkian—the advocate and practitioner of assisted suicide—ran for Governor of Michigan in 1998.

In early 1996 Fieger compared the Orthodox rabbis to Nazis when they issued a statement condemning assisted suicide as a violation of Jewish teaching. "They're closer to Nazis than they think they are. Orthodox Jews are not different than the right-wing Christian nuts. If you're a religious nut, you're a religious nut," he told *The Detroit News*.

He described Michigan Governor John Engler, a Republican, as "the product of miscegenation between barnyard animals and human beings" and said of the Governor's children that "unless they have corkscrew tails, those kids are not his."

He has called Adam Cardinal Maida, the Roman Catholic Archbishop of Detroit, a "nut" and described the Pope by saying he would prefer taking advice from "Joe the wino." As for Jesus: "[J]ust some goofball that got nailed to the cross."

A freethinker who is not a member of any religious group but has said he is ready to "keep all my options open," explains on his Web page that "I have no difficulty with the unfettered practice of religious beliefs" but do not want them incorporated into law. (See entry for Jack Kevorkian.)

Field, Frank (19th Century)

Field, of Oldham, was an active leader of the Lancashire Secular Union in England in the 1870s. {RSR}

Fielding, Henry (1707—1754)

Fielding is the English dramatist whose novel, *Tom Jones* (1749), made him a major name in literature. The title character was presented as Fielding's concept of the ideal man, one in whom goodness and charity are combined with common sense. "No man has ever sat down calmly unbiased to reason out his religion," Fielding wrote, "and not ended by rejecting it." {TYD}

Fielding, William John (1886-1972?)

An internationally known author, Fielding was an executive secretary of Tiffany & Co., the New York jewelers. Later he became secretary-treasurer of the Louis Comfort Tiffany Foundation, an art institute the purpose of which is to aid young artists.

Fielding wrote thirty Little Blue Books, which sold more than six million copies at the height of their popularity in the 1920s and through the 1940s. He also wrote ten books on psychology, sexology, anthropology, and related subjects, the best known of which, *Sex and the Love-Life* (1927, sold more than one million copies. The Library of Congress requested that the book be translated into braille for the benefit of the blind.

As a president of the Thomas Paine Foundation, he helped popularize the ideas and works of Paine. In 1964 he participated in the dedication of a monument to Paine in the latter's birthplace, Thetford, England. His "Thomas Paine Returns to Thetford" appeared in Joseph Lewis's *Age of Reason* (January 1965).

Fielding also wrote *Shackles of the Supernatural* (1938; 1969); *Strange Customs of Courtship and Marriage* (1942); and *All the Lives I Have Lived* (1972).

From Girard, Kansas, Fielding had edited *Know Thyself* from 1923 to 1924; wrote articles for the New York Socialist daily, *Call*, from 1911 through 1923; was editor of a Socialist Party weekly, the Newark, New Jersey, *Leader* from 1915 to 1920; had articles in the atheists' *Truthseeker* in 1923 and in the 1940s; wrote for the Freethinkers of America's *Age of Reason* in the 1950s and 1960; wrote for the London *Freethinker* in the 1950s and 1960s; wrote for *American Rationalist* in the 1960s and 1970s; and wrote for the United Secularists of America's *Progressive World* in the 1960s and 1970s.

An outspoken advocate of birth control, he worked with Margaret Sanger. Fielding died in Rockville Center, New York. {FUS}

"Fielding-Hall," (Harold Fielding Patrick Hall) (1859—1917)

A writer on Burma, Fielding-Hall in his *Soul of a People* (1898) rendered considerable service to Rationalism by showing–and it was widely read and discussed–that an Asiatic Buddhist people, the Burmese, was superior in general character to any in Europe or America. His own creed, given in *The World-Soul* (1913), is Emersonian in that he accepted only an Unknown Power or World-Spirit, rejecting both Christianity and immortality. {RAT; RE}

Fields, Annie Adams (1834-1915)

Fields was a Unitarian, an author, a literary hostess, and a charity worker. Upon the death of her husband James Fields, the editor of *Atlantic*, she lived with Sarah Orne Jewitt.

Fields, Emmett F. (1928—)

Fields is author of *Atheism—An Affirmative View* (1981) and *Is the Bible the Word of God?* (1986?). In an interview with Fred Whitehead, Fields described his collection of freethought literature. Raised to believe Christianity, he found it necessary later to [fight] my way this hole that I had been put in by indoctrination. I thought I must be the only person in the world that ever had these ideas. All of the free thought information that was written and not available, I couldn't find, I knew nothing about it. I had a heck of a struggle and then I started finding people who thought the way I came to think and telling me about these books, and I started looking for them." Fields currently has three to four thousand freethought works. A CD-ROM entitled "Bank of Wisdom" (PO Box 926, Louisville, Kentucky 40201) includes out-of-print freethought materials. {*Freethought History* #14, 1995; GS}

Fields, James T. (19th Century)

Fields, a Unitarian, was a well-known publisher in the 1800s. He was editor of the *Atlantic*. {U}

Fields, Joseph (20 Century)

Fields, a retired bus driver in New York City, told BBC Radio in a 1998 interview how as an African American he had felt great relief when as a young man he had ridded himself of the Christianity he had been raised to believe in. A member of the American Humanist Association, Fields in 1998 attended the International Humanist and Ethical Union conference in Mumbai, India.

Fields, W. C. (William Claude) (1879—1946)

Fields, famed comedian, film star, juggler, and atheist, said, "Prayers never bring anything. . . . They may bring solace to the sap, the bigot, the ignorant, the aboriginal, and the lazy–but to the enlightened it is the same as asking Santa Claus to bring you something for Xmas." Fields had a popular and ongoing feud on radio with ventriloquist Edgar Bergen's dummy, Charlie McCarthy, who once joked, "Pink elephants take aspirin to get rid of W. C. Fields." Viewers noticed his big nose, first for its acne, eczema, and, later, its condition caused by drinking too much liquor. Viewers also laughed at his screen persona, which showed him to have a bedeviled wife. He also was pictured as disliking small children, saying, "I like children. If they're properly cooked." And "Uncle will give you some nice razor blades to play with," lines by his Elmer Prettywillie to a baby in "It's the Old Army Game." And "Children should neither be seen nor heard from–ever again." In actuality, Fields doted on his grandchildren and once planned to open an orphanage.

Among other of his various quips are the following:

- I always keep a supply of stimulant handy in case I see a snake, which I also keep handy.
- What contemptible scoundrel stole the cork from my lunch?
- My illness is due to my doctor's insistence that I drink milk, a whitish fluid they force down helpless babies.
- The cost of living has gone up another dollar a quart.
- Once, during Prohibition, I was forced to live for days on nothing but food and water.
- Will Hays [a censor of movies] is my shepherd, I shall not want; he maketh me to lie down in clean postures.
- Anybody who hates dogs and loves whiskey can't be all bad.

A cantankerous man whom fellow boozer John Barrymore thought would make a great Lady Macbeth, Fields remained to the end the "definite personality" he told an interviewer in 1935 he wanted to be. When he recognized that "the Man in the Bright Nightgown" had come for him in 1946, as his last act Fields put his finger to his lips, looked around the room at those who were there, and winked.

Undertakers in Philadelphia practice the world's most difficult profession, he once quipped, because morticians there cannot always tell if they are burying a live or a deceased person. Although his epitaph is widely believed to state I WOULD RATHER BE LIVING IN PHILADELPHIA, the bronze plaque on a marble niche front at Forest Lawn in California lists only his name and the vital dates. {CB; CE; Simon Louvish, *Man in the Flying Trapeze, the Life and Times of W. C. Fields* (1997); PA}

Fierstein, Harvey (1954—)

Fierstein is author of the Broadway play, "Torch Song Trilogy," which consists of three separate plays ("The International Stud," "Fugue in a Nursery, and "Widows and Children First!"). It was unusual in that he wrote it to get attention as an actor, not a playwright. Fierstein, whose hoarse voice is related to a childhood accident, won two Tony Awards for his author-star performance as Arnold Beckoff in an off-beat "traditional family values" plot. Playgoers who saw "Torch Song Trilogy" laughed wildly at the bunny shoes designed for him by designer Mardi Philips and in which he campily tramped around, fully aware that a bunny is also the object of sexual desire. Following is a sample of Fierstein's wit:

- Gay liberation should not be a license to be a perpetual adolescent. If you deny yourself commitment then what can you do with your life?
- . . . when I grew up we had no positive images if we were gay. I was totally lost—I was just this fat faggot living out in Brooklyn. All I knew about gays was that they always got beaten up in some Philip Marlowe movie.
- I wish that homosexuals were born with a little horn in the middle of their forehead so we couldn't hide so easily. At least if you can't hide, you have to stand up and fight.

Fierstein was the librettist and Jerry Herman was composer and lyricist of the Broadway production of "La Cage aux Folles" (1983). On "Uncensored," a Public Broadcasting System program, Fierstein said he was both a cultural Jew and an atheist. {AA; CA; E; GL}

Figueras y Moracas, Estanilas (1810—1879)

A Spanish statesman and orator, Figueras y Moracas was elected in 1851 to the Cortes, was exiled in 1866, then returned in 1868. He fought the candidature of the Duc de Montpensiéer and became President of the Spanish Republic in 1873. Figueras y Moracas died poor and, according to his wish, was buried without religious ceremony. {BDF; RAT}

Figueres Ferrer, José [President] (1906—1990)

Figueres was the Costa Rican president who abolished the army, setting an unusual precedent that his successors have left unchanged. "What other nations in history, including the Vatican, have ever taken such profound action?" declared freethinker Fernando Vargas, a fellow Costa Rican.

Despite bitter opposition, Figueres instituted a sweeping program of welfare legislation, public works, and educational reform. Although Figueres was a freethinker, his son (who in 1994 became the country's president) is not. {CE}

Figuiera, Guillem (Born c. 1190)

Figuiera was a Provençal troubadour and precursor of the Renaissance. His poems were directed against the priests and the Court of Rome. {BDF}

Filagieri: See entry for Beccaria.

Filangieri, Gaetano (1752—1788)

Filangieri was an Italian writer on legislation, his principal work being *La Scienza della Legislazione* (1780). In the fifth volume he deals with pre-Christian religions, and the work was put on the Catholic *Index* of prohibited reading. {BDF; RAT; RE}

Filipe, Nuno (20 Century)

A Portuguese writer who uses the pseudonym "Atheos," Filipe is critical of what he calls "the lie that is Christianism":

> *No Cristianismo, só o facto de se duvidar de* deus é considerado pecado. Não é o cepticismo a atitude a seguir por um homem sensato? E se o cristianismo está correcto, porque tenta afastar o homem do *fruto proibido*? Porque tenta afastar o conhecimento do homem?
>
> [In Christianism, just the fact of doubt about *god* is considered a sin. Isn't scepticism the attitude of a wise man? If Christianism is right, why does it try to put away man from the *forbidden fruit*? Why does it try to put away knowledge from man?]
>
> {CA}

Filler, Louis (1912—)

When he reviewed books for *The Humanist*, Filler was on the faculty at Antioch College. He wrote *Voice of Democracy: David Graham Phillips* (1978).

Fillible, Kent (20th Century)

Fillible is a local humanist activist in Shreveport, Louisiana. {*Free Inquiry*, Spring 1991}

Fillmore, Millard [President] (1800—1874)

Fillmore, the 13th United States President, was born in a log cabin. Once a lieutenant in the Anti-Masonic party, he joined the Whig Party and was reelected three times to the House of Representatives. Becoming Vice President on the Whig ticket with Zachary Taylor, he succeeded to the Presidency when Taylor in 1850 died of cholera. Upon learning of Taylor's death, he wrote to the cabinet, "I have no language to express the emotions of my heart. The shock is so sudden and unexpected that I am overwhelmed." In the 1856 election, Fillmore ran on the Know-Nothing Ticket.

Although opposed to slavery, Fillmore felt it best if the nation be held together. In supporting bills that the antislavery people opposed, he said, "I well know that by so doing, I must lose the friendship of many men. The man who can look upon a crisis without being willing to offer himself upon the altar of his country is not fit for public trust."

During his administration a treaty was approved with the help of Commodore Perry which opened trade with Japan. On the lighter side, the Fillmores were responsible for starting the first library in the White House and replacing a fireplace with a cook stove for kitchen use, according to Gillis. (Gillis also credits the Fillmores with installing the first bathtub there, but actually this story was a hoax perpetuated by H. L. Mencken.) Daniel Webster was his Secretary of State, but because of a division of the slavery issue he was not renominated by the Whig convention in 1852.

Fillmore opposed Lincoln's election and supported the Fugitive Slave Law, which required the return of escaped slaves to the South. He was a charter member of the First Unitarian Church of Buffalo, holding pew #70. {CE; EG; U; UU}

Filter (20 Century)

Filter is a group of contemporary recording artists who are known for the song, "Hey Man, Nice Shot!" During a February 1996 chat session on Prodigy, the band was asked how God had influenced their mind and responded, "We respect people's spirituality. Just don't come up to my fucking face and tell me about God, because for thousands of years organized religion has done nothing more than fuck up science and, in general, any kind of scholastics." Another band member added, "I don't believe in some old man with a beard telling me I can't have sex with my girlfriend because I'm not married and I'm condemned to Hell for the rest of eternity." {CA}

Finch, A. Ellen (19th Century)

A freethinker, Finch wrote *The English Free-Thinkers of the Eighteenth Century* (1879). {GS}

Finch, John (19th Century)

Finch was chairman of the Rational Society Congress of 1844. {VI}

Finch, Robert (20th Century)

Finch is President of Humanists of Houston (HOH), Texas. In 1995, HOH was host of the Southwest Regional Humanist and Freethought Conference.

Findlay, Christopher (20th Century)

Findlay, a rationalist, has written for England's *New Humanist*. Reviewing Antony Grey's *Speaking of Sex* (1994), Findlay finds that Grey "makes no prescription for an ideal sexual vocabulary; he concludes that 'the language of the market place and of the streets will carry on, as it always has, being the most compelling form of sexual discourse.'"

Findlay continues, "In a brief discussion of the language of the tabloids, [Grey] actually welcomes their 'enthusiastic employment of vulgar language' as 'making sexual discussion less solemn'–he welcomes their use of the 'jolly notion of "bonking," which is indeed a new word uncorrupted by being used as a term of abuse (like 'f***ing' [Ed. note: fucking] or 'c**t' [Ed. note: cunt]), which Grey rightly decries."

Findlay notes that a common way to avoid the shock many feel at hearing some words is to use innuendo, as is done in pop songs. "It enables us to share intimate mental images without the embarrassment of explicit terms, and," Findlay adds, "is perhaps the most widely used of all forms of sexual discourse."

Findley, George (19th Century)

Findley, a second-hand book seller, was a member of the Leicester, England, freethought group. He led a group of positivists. The Leicester group in 1885 played cricket on a Sunday, openly challenging Sabbatarian prejudices. The police took their names and addresses. The following week, the team was attacked by a mob which tore up the wickets and threw the ball in the river.

The ball, one of the secularists observed, "was rescued by a sensible dog." {RSR}

Fine, Stacie (20th Century)

Fine is Community Development Director of the Society for Humanistic Judaism.

Finey, S. J. (20th Century)

Finey, a freethinker, wrote *The Bible, Is It of Divine Origin, and Influence?* (1859). {GS}

Finger, Ben Jr. (20th Century)

Finger's poetry was included in *The Humanist Newsletter* (Summer 1953):

Faith in Man

When strife and rank injustice mar the earth,
How can a thinking man ignore their clutch?
How can I even trust in my own worth,
Knowing that I have fallen short so much?
Peace is removed by many a weary mile,
And faith is deeply challenged by such greeds
As make it seem a sacrilege to smile.

And yet, recall the pageant of great deeds.
Think about all the heroes who have grown
To heights of character. . . . When thus we scan
Man's arc of life, we certainly have known
Enough of good to give us faith in man!

Fingerman, Bob (20 Century)

Fingerman, a writer and comic artist, has created a wide variety of atheistic protagonists in his comic books. "I thank both my parents for their atheism," he has written, "That was a great way to be brought up." {CA}

FINGERPRINTING: See entry for Francis Galton.

Fink, George A. (20th Century)

An Iowan, Fink once was a director of the American Humanist Association. {HNS}

Fink, Margaret (1933—)

Fink is an Australian atheist, art teacher, and film maker. She produced "The Removalists" (1974) and "My Brilliant Career" (1978), both feature films. In *Who's Who of Australian Women*, Fink describes herself as "an art teacher, an anarchist, and an atheist." {SWW}

Finke, Heinrich (Born 1855)

Finke was a German historian, an Archivist of Schleswig (1882—1887), teacher of history at Münster University (1887—1897), and professor of history at Freiburg University in 1898. In 1906 he was made Privy Councillor. Finke was a frequent lecturer for the German monists and was a strong supporter of Haeckel. {RAT}

Finkelstein, Joel (20th Century)

Finkelstein, while a student at Columbia University, was one of the founding members of Campus Freethought Alliance. {*International Humanist News*, December 1996}

Finlay, Thomas (19th Century)

Finlay, a freethinker, wrote "Defence, Prepared for Delivery by Thomas Finlay, Charged Before the High Court of Justiciary, City of Edinborough, 24 July, 1843, with Vending Blasphemy" (1843). {FUK; GS}

FINNISH FREETHINKERS, HUMANISTS

"Since over 90% of Finnish people are initiated at birth/confirmation into either the Lutheran Church or (a very minor percentage) the Eastern Orthodox denominations," explained humanist Paul Harrison about how the state pays money to churches, "your income is already skimmed for taxes as a matter of course. Employers are also skimmed regardless of whether their employees are members of the church or not (I know, for I managed a language school here a few years ago. The tax office still insisted on the tithe, although the staff was practically all foreigners and didn't know Luther from a *lukather*)." In Turku, Harrison's e-mail is <intereng@netti.fi>.

Finnish groups and journals include the following:

• Humanist Union of Finland (IHEU), PO Box 793, 00101 Helsinki 10

• *Humanisti*, a quarterly, PL 793, 00101 Helsinki; <pekka.elo@oph.fi>.

• *Life and Education in Finland* is at Museokatu 18 A 2, 00100 Helsinki

• Union of Freethinkers of Finland is at Siltasaarenkatu 15 C 65, 00530 Helsinki

• *Vapaa Ajattelija* (Free Thinker), Siltassarenkatu 15 C-65, 00530 Helsinki; <val@val.pp.fi>.

A concise description of the history of the Finnish Humanist Union has been written by its chairman, Gunn Väyrynen, in *International Humanist News* (October 1995). Finland was for many centuries the eastern part of the Swedish kingdom. After the war of 1808—1809, Sweden lost this part to the Russian Empire. Finland did not become independent until 1917.

Until the end of 1922, every Finnish citizen had to belong to some Christian congregation. One of the first to insist upon and legally obtain a civil, rather than a religious, marriage was Rolf Lagerborg, a friend of sociologist and well-known humanist Edvaard Westermarck (1862—1939).

The Finnish Humanist Association formed in 1968 and publishes a quarterly, *Humanisti*, edited by Pekka Elo. In the 1980s, the chairman was Jussi Pikkusaari. An estimated five hundred are members of the Humanist Union of Finland.

The Kalevala, Finland's national epic, was translated into English by Eino Friberg, a Finnish-born Unitarian Universalist minister who lived primarily in the United States. (See entries for Eino Friberg and Scandinavian Unbelievers; also see Gunn Väyrynen, "The Humanist Movement in Finland," *International Humanist News*, October 1995)

FINNISH-AMERICAN FREETHINKERS: Finnish-American freethinkers are discussed by Gordon Stein in his *Freethought in the United States.*

Fiorentino, Francesco 1834—1884)

Fiorentino taught philosophy at Spoletto in 1860, in Bologna in 1862, and in Naples in 1871. He was elected deputy to Parliament in 1870. A disciple of Felice Tocco, Fiorentino paid special attention to the early Italian freethinkers, writing upon *The Pantheism of Giordano Bruno* (1861). He also wrote on Pompanazzi, Telesio, Strauss, and Spinoza. In the *Nuova Antolgia*, he wrote on Vanini, Caesalpinus, Campanella, and Bruno. Fiorentino was a friend of Bertrando Spaventa, succeeding to his chair at Naples in 1883. {BDF; RAT}

Firbank, (Arthur Annesley) Ronald (1886—1926)

Firbank, the son of Thomas Firbank, a Member of Parliament, and Lady Firbank, converted to Catholicism in 1907. In "Odette d'Antrevernes," he described a pious girl who prays for a vision of the Virgin Mary but, instead, encounters a destitute prostitute. When he visited Rome in order to take holy orders, Firbank found that the "Church of Rome wouldn't have me, and so I mock her." What followed, Corinne E. Blackmer of Southern Connecticut State University has described, were fictional characters "of homosexual choirboys, lesbian nuns, cross-dressing priests, salacious bishops, flagellants, and self-canonized saints."

Santal (1921) describes a young Islamic boy's religious aspirations. *The Flower Beneath the Foot* (1924), includes a character, Laura de Nazianzi, who becomes a saint by renouncing heterosexual romance and joining "the lesbian Convent of the Flaming Hood." *Concerning the Eccentricities of Cardinal Pirelli* (1926) has a cardinal baptizing a police puppy named Crack and ends when the naked cardinal ("elementary now as Adam himself") drops dead while pursuing a choirboy named Chicklet around his church.

Readers, Blackmer noted, found in *Vainglory* a description of Monsignor Parr as "something between a butterfly and a misanthrope, [who] was temperamental, when not otherwise . . . employed."

Firbank died probably of acute alcoholism, was accidentally buried in a Protestant cemetery, then subsequently was reinterred in a Catholic cemetery. {GL}

Fireman, Peter (20th Century)

A freethinker, Fireman wrote *Christianity, A Tale and A Moral* (1931). {GS}

Firkins, Oscar W. (1864—1932)

Firkins, an English professor at the University of Minnesota, wrote "The Two Humanisms: A Discrimination" in *The New Humanist* (March-April 1931). Saying the "two cults" of literary and philosophic humanists "co-exist quite without coherence; almost without collision," he concluded, "Each has an intuition as a basis. The faith in reason as savior is, after all, a faith; the future, its chosen witness, holds its tongue. {EW}

FIRST AMENDMENT

The United States Constitution's First Amendment prohibits government-established religion and guarantees freedom of worship, of speech, of the press, of assembly, and to petition the government.

In the 1990s, the Ninth Circuit Court of Appeals, ruling against a science teacher who stated that his school district violated the First Amendment of the United States Constitution by forcing him to teach the "religion" of evolution, stated that secular humanism is *not* a religion. Secular humanists have always claimed the same, that theirs is a philosophic movement. On the Web: <http://www.fac.org>. (See entries for Hugo L. Black and Constitution of the United States.)

FIRST CAUSE

The argument for God's existence, according to St. Thomas Aquinas's "Five Ways," is that of a "First Efficient Cause, to which everyone gives the name of God." The concept involves a belief that everything has been caused by something other than itself. An infinite series of such causes cannot be, so the argument goes. Whatever it was that was the initial cause is, therefore, God.

However, naturalists in philosophy argue that no such cause has been or can be located, that even if there were there is no evidence that it had divine attributes or absolute goodness. (See entries for Genesis and God. Also, see Antony Flew's *A Dictionary of Philosophy*,) {AF; OCP}

FIRST HUMANIST SOCIETY OF NEW YORK

In 1929, Charles Francis Potter, a Unitarian minister who had served as Clarence Darrow's biblical expert at the Scopes "Monkey" Trial, founded the First Humanist Society of New York. (See entry for Charles Francis Potter.) {HNS2}

FIRST INTERNATIONAL CONGRESS ON HUMANISM AND ETHICAL CULTURE

The First International Congress on Humanism and Ethical Culture, was sponsored in the early 1950s by Dutch, Austrian, British, and American Humanist and Ethical societies. {HNS2}

FIRST NATIONAL CHURCH OF THE EXQUISITE PANIC: See the entry for Robert Delford Brown.

Firth, Raymond William [Sir] (1901—)

A professor emeritus of anthropology, University of London (1944—1968), Firth was elected an honorary associate in 1943 of the Rationalist Press Association. He also is a Humanist Laureate in the Council for Secular Humanism's International Academy of Humanism. Among his works are *Art and Life in New* Guinea (1936), *Symbols, Public and Private* (1973), and *Human Types* (1975). He edited *Man and Culture: An Evaluation of the Work of Malinowski* (1957). Firth signed Humanist Manifesto II and Humanist Manifesto 2000.

In *New Humanist* (March, 1993), Sir Professor Raymond Firth wrote:

> I was born in New Zealand, in 1901. My liberal-minded parents brought me up as a Christian, undogmatically, in the Methodist Church, in which I remained until I came to England in 1924. But by then my religious faith had slipped away, by an intellectual route of scepticism. Though only some anthropologists are humanists, my own anthropological studies confirmed my review of religion as a human art, not requiring any assumptions of an ultimate reality such as God or Mind, independent of the human world. In its many varieties, religion has been associated with some of the finest aesthetic creations in music, painting, literature. It has also been a cover for some of the most bitter, cruel and violent conduct of people against one another. In both these respects it conforms to an interpretation in terms of essentially human characteristics.
>
> For me, two primary assumptions are the value of knowledge and the value of human personality. Neither assumption needs any divine authority to back it. Morality, like religion, is a human social construct, and it is man's existence in society which gives meaning and value to belief and conduct.

I am well aware that such positions face intellectual challenges of a philosophical order. But I take my stand on probabilities. We can argue about the nature of reality, and the impossibility of proof of negative assertions such as There is no God. But I argue that a central part of any assumptions about reality lies in the existence of human individuals. These are linked in extremely complex, powerful organisations, with elaborate figurative, symbolic justification. Sensitive and intricate to a high degree, they generate immense intellectual invention and fantasy. Hence the probability of any further superhuman forces or entities being responsible for human affairs, including religion, seems extremely low. Assertions about revelation, and relations with transcendental beings or powers can be clearly seen as imaginative invention, often corresponding to vested interest of a social, economic or political order.

(See Firth's "An Anthropological Interpretation of Religion," *Free Inquiry*, Fall 1996.) {CE; HM2; SHD}

Fischart, Johann (c. 1545—1614)

Fischart was a German satirist called Mentzer. His satires in prose and verse were written in a Rabelaisian style and are often directed against the church. {BDF}

Fischer, Edmond H(enri) (1920—)

Dr. Fischer, winner of the Nobel Prize in Physiology and Medicine in 1992, was born in Shanghai, studied in Europe, and is a biochemist at the University of Washington, Seattle, Washington. Asked about humanism, he responded to the present author:

> I don't know in which category you want to include me, but I am definitely a non-theist. I do not believe in a Supreme Being and I do not believe in the existence of any God.

{WAS, 1 December 1994}

Fischer, Ernest G. (20th Century)

Fischer wrote *Marxists and Utopias in Texas* (1980). {*Freethought History #15*, 1995}

Fischer, Ernst Kuno (1824—1907)

Fischer was a German philosophy whose rationalist sentiments of the first volume of his *History of Modern Philosophy* (1853) brought about his retirement. He taught at Jena and Heidelberg. Fischer wrote sympathetically on Bruno and Goethe and expounded a modified Hegelian system. {RAT}

Fischer, J. C. (Died 1888)

Fischer was a German materialist, the author of a work on the freedom of the will in 1858 and a criticism of Hartmann's *Philosophy of the Unconscious* in 1872. {BDF}

Fischer, Johann Georg (1816—1897)

A German poet, Fischer wrote dramas which celebrate the defeat of the Papacy in the Middle Ages. In 1882 Fischer received the Order of Personal Nobility. {RAT}

Fischer, Kuno (Born 1824)

Fischer in 1856 was appointed professor of philosophy at Jena, Germany. His chief works are *History of Modern Philosophy* (1852—1732); *Life and Character of Spinoza; Francis Bacon* (1856), and *Lessing* (1881). {BDF}

FISH SYMBOL: See entry for Ichthus.

Fisher, Carrie Francis (1956—)

Fisher, the daughter of well-known entertainers Eddie Fisher and Debbie Reynolds and the former wife of composer-performer Paul Simon, has appeared in numerous movies. *The Portable Curmudgeon Redux* (1992) quotes her as saying,

> I love the idea of God, but it's not stylistically in keeping with the way I function. I would describe myself as an enthusiastic agnostic who would be happy to be shown that there is a God. I can see that people who believe in God are happier. My brother is. My dad is, too. But I *doubt.*

{CA; E}

Fisher, David (20 Century)

Fisher is an activist with the Humanist Society of Queensland in Australia. E-mail: <humanist@petrie.starway.net.au>.

Fisher, Dorothy Canfield (1879—1958)

A famed novelist who served on the editorial board of the Book-of-the-Month Club, Fischer was a humanist. She wrote *The Montessori Mother* (1913) and *The Biography of An Outlook On Life* (1953). {CE; HNS}

Fisher, Ebenezer (1815—1879)

Fisher, who headed the Universalists' new theological school at St. Lawrence University in Canton, New York, confronted the school's poor financial situation and was successful in keeping it from the brink of extinction in its early years. Fisher was an ordained Universalist minister. {U&U}

Fisher, H(erbert) A(lbert) L(aurens) (Born 1865)

Fisher wrote a critical work, *Our New Religion: An Examination of Christian Science* (1930).

Fisher, J. Greevz (19th Century)

Fisher was vice-president in 1893 of the Legitimation League, a group which at first had the support of secularists until it openly advocated free love. (See entries for Wordsworth Donisthorpe, the League's president, and Oswald Dawson, its secretary.) {RSR}

Fisher, Joseph L. (20th Century)

Fisher was the second moderator of the Unitarian Universalist Association, serving from 1961 to 1977.

Fisher, Julie (20 Century)

Fisher, of the Texas Hill Country Freethinkers in Pipe Creek, Texas, wrote "Being Honestly Atheist" in *Secular Nation* (April-June 1999).

Fisher, Raymond (20th Century)

Fisher wrote his 1968 Ph. D. thesis at the University of Illinois on Robert G. Ingersoll's rhetorical principles. {FUS}

Fisher, Vardis (1895—1968)

During the Depression years of the 1930s, Fisher was hailed as one of the most promising authors of the American West. He was author of thirty-six published books, was published in French, German, Italian, Spanish, and Danish, and wrote on the evolution of man and religion. Tim Woodward's biography, *Tiger on the Road*, cites Fisher's view that most people would rather meet a tiger on the road than face the truth about themselves.

Among his "Testament of Man" books are *Darkness and the Deep* (1943), about the evolution of the ancestors of man; *Intimations of Eve* (1946), about prehistorical matriarchy and moon worship; *Jesus Came Again* (1956), which rejects the divinity of Jesus; *A Goat for Azazel* (1956), about the pagan origins of Christianity; *Peace Like A River* (1957), about female subjugation and extreme Christian asceticism; *My Holy Satan* (1958), about the horrors of the Inquisition); and *Orphans of Gethsemane* (1960), a semi-autobiographical work about our male-dominated, Judeo-Christian, Western society, its values, and its wars.

Upon his death, the Mormons attempted to claim Vardis as one of their own, which so infuriated his widow, **Opal Fisher**, that she issued press releases confirming her husband's and her own atheism. She was a member of American Atheists and a regular contributor to its journal until her death in 1995. {Richard M. Andrews, Internet memo, 10 May 1997}

Fiske, John (1842—1901)

Fiske was an American author, a lecturer on philosophy at Harvard (1872—1879) and its librarian (1872—1879). He wrote *Myths and Mythmakers* (1872); *Outlines of Cosmic Philosophy* (2 vols., 1874); *Darwinism and Other Essays* (1879); *Excursions of an Evolutionist* (1883); and *The Idea of God as Affected by Modern Knowledge* (1885). An enthusiastic follower of Spencerian evolution, Fiske tried to reconcile orthodox religious beliefs. Religious writers quote him as an orthodox Christian, but J. S. Clark in *Life and Letters of J. Fiske* (1917, 2 volumes) shows that Fiske accepted only an "unknowable" god and immortality (as an act of faith) and rejected Christianity. According to Patrick Romanell, Fiske was clearly a naturalist in the same tradition as John Dewey and Morris R. Cohen.

"Is it honest for me to go and sit there on communion day and drink the wine and eat the bread while feeling it all to be mummery?" Fiske wrote in an 1860 letter to his mother. He also wrote, "[Christianity's past is] the history of fraud, superstition, misery, and bloodshed, until these last two centuries, when its power has dwindled almost to nothing. . . . One and all, the orthodox creeds are crumbling into ruins everywhere. We now witness the constructive work on a foundation that will endure through the ages. That foundation is the god of science–revealed to us in terms that will harmonize with our intelligence." {BDF; CE; JM; RAT; RE; Patrick Romanell, *Free Inquiry*, Winter 1995-1996; TYD}

Fitch, John (1743—1798)

Fitch, originally a Methodist, founded the Universal Society in Philadelphia. He left his church because his fellow Trenton, New Jersey, Methodists censured him for working on Sundays in order to supply American troops during the Revolutionary War. {FUS}

FitzGerald, Edward (1809—1883)

The translator of the *Rubaiyat of Omar Khayyam* (1859), Fitzgerald actually paraphrased rather than translated the 11th-century poet. Omar Khayyam humanistically counseled living life to the fullest while one can. Fitzgerald also wrote *Euphranor* (1851), which was a Platonic dialogue, and *Polonius* (1852), which was a collection of aphorisms. A recluse and a skeptic, Fitzgerald was attracted to Persian skepticism and also translated Calderon. {BDF; CE; CL; JM; RAT; RE; TRI; TSV; TYD}

Fitzgerald, F(rancis) Scott (Key) (1896—1940)

The literary spokesman of the "jazz age," the decade of the 1920s, F. Scott Fitzgerald was a colorful novelist whose marriage to Zelda was known for its madcap life style. As a young man working at an advertising agency, he lived at 200 Claremont Avenue at Tiemann Place in New York City, where for an Iowa laundry he coined the slogan, "We keep you clean in Muscatine." By his early twenties, he had written *This Side of Paradise* (1920) and *The Beautiful and the Damned* (1922). His masterpiece was *The Great Gatsby* (1925), a devastating portrait of the so-called American Dream, one that measures love and success in materialistic terms only. Fitzgerald originally had entitled the book *The High-Bouncing Lover*. *Tender Is the Night* (1934) had as its theme the spiritual malaise of American life, which he had experienced even before writing his final novel, *The Last Tycoon* (published in 1941), about a Hollywood studio mogul. The work was unfinished, for Fitzgerald died at the age of forty-four of a heart attack while working as a scriptwriter in Hollywood.

In *The Great Gatsby*, Fitzgerald describes a sign in front of an oculist's shop: "The eyes of Doctor T. J. Eckleburg are blue and gigantic–their retinas are one yard high." Some have insisted that he was symbolizing God by using the eyes with the yard-high retinas. Others feel he was illustrating what can trigger a response from a person's superego. Still others note that retinas cannot be seen, that Fitzgerald meant pupils or irises.

Although raised a Midwestern, genteel, Roman Catholic youth in St. Paul, Minnesota, Scott as an adult became known as a spoiled rich boy who lived with reckless and stupid extravagance, one who was unable to hold his liquor. He and his Alabama belle, Zelda, were married in 1920 at St. Patrick's Cathedral in New York despite her family's concern about their Episcopalian daughter's marrying a non-Protestant.

Their zany life together has been documented by biographers Jeffrey Meyers, Andrew Turnbull, and Arthur Mizener, among others. Any number of documented drunken scenes revealed his dissipation and flamboyant lifestyle: He once tipsily told airline passengers that his Hollywood mistress, Sheilah Graham, was "a great lay"; while he was a houseguest of Sara and Gerald Murphy, he threw their gold-flecked Venetian wineglasses over the garden wall; when the Murphys objected, he threw a can of garbage onto their patio while they were dining; when he was in France and an old lady tendered a tray of candies and nuts, he kicked the tray from her hands; with lipstick he wrote on the expensive dress of his friend John Peale Bishop's wife; he got into a number of fistfights, usually losing; etc. Zelda, as a reminder of their friendship, once removed her black panties and tossed them to New York literary and drama critic Alexander Woollcott.

The curious enjoyed dishing the dirt about Fitzgerald, and in 1924 when Zelda had an affair with a French aviator she reported that, in comparison, Fitzgerald was "inadequate." Ernest Hemingway, one of his many drinking buddies, included a passage in *A Moveable Feast* about the size of Fitzgerald's penis and gossips whispered that although Fitzgerald had a scorn for "fairies" he himself may have had homosexual experiences. To Zelda he once wrote, "The nearest I ever came to leaving you was when you told me you thought I was a fairy in the Rue Palatine," for she had accused him of having a relationship with Hemingway. Of Hemingway, Fitzgerald had once written, "I really loved him, but of course it wore out like a love affair. The fairies have spoiled all that," implying that their friendship had stopped because of such gossip. Graham, according to Meyers, knew about the relative sizes of penises, however, and "she found the tubercular, drug-addicted and often alcoholic Fitzgerald a creditable performer–'very satisfactory . . . in terms of giving physical pleasure.' After lovemaking, they would lie happily in each other's arms for a long time." The homosexual gossip continued, however, despite his describing homosexuals unscientifically as "Nature's attempt to get rid of soft boys by sterilizing them."

Critic Sally Eckhoff, reviewing two of Matthew J. Bruccoli's books, *Fitzgerald and Hemingway: A Dangerous Friendship* (1994) and *F. Scott Fitzgerald: A Life in Letters* (1994), notes, "From all the evidence now available, we can safely believe Hemingway's assertion that Mrs. Fitzgerald had told her husband that his dick was too small. During a drunken lunch at Michaud's, the distraught Scott spilled the beans to Ernest [Hemingway]—both repaired to the *hommes* room to size up the problem.

" 'Forget what Zelda said,' I told him. 'Zelda is crazy,' " Hemingway wrote in his chapter called "A Matter of Measurements." (According to Edmund Wilson, Hemingway tried to dilute Scott's anguish about his penis by claiming 'it only seemed to him small because he looked at it from above. You have to look at in a mirror.' Fitzgerald didn't buy it.) Hemingway complained to Max Perkins that 'almost every bloody fool thing I have ever seen or known him to do has been directly or indirectly Zelda inspired,' but added, 'I would not have Scott imagine I believed this for the world.' " Hemingway knew that Zelda sneered about *The Sun Also Rises*, saying it was about "bullfighting, bullslinging, and bullshit."

In his last letter to his daughter "Scottie" (Frances Scott), written the month he died, Fitzgerald wrote, "But be sweet to your mother at Xmas despite her early Chaldean rune-worship which she will undoubtedly inflict on you at Xmas," a reference to her having become a fanatic Christian. Fitzgerald, however, expressed no interest in organized religion and, as was evident to his friends, was a non-believer and no longer a Catholic.

His handwritten will speaks of "the uncertainty of life *and the certainty of death*" [emphasis added]. The will is surprising in that it mentions Zelda's insanity, giving her all of his household and kitchen furniture "in the event she shall regain her sanity." In previous letters to Scottie he had written, "I decided to marry your mother after all, even though I knew she was spoiled and meant no good to me. I was sorry immediately I had married her."

Zelda outlived him eight years, dying in 1948 at the age of forty-seven, a hopeless schizophrenic, in a sanitorium fire. Her last years were spent clutching a Bible and writing about the apocalypse. Scott's estate and literary-property interests passed to their only child, Frances Scott Fitzgerald. {CE}

Fitzhugh, Louise (20 Century)

According to the American Library Association's *Banned Books* (1998), Fitzhugh's "The Long Secret" "pokes fun at religion."

Fitzhugh, Percy (19th Century)

Fitzhugh was a freethinker who wrote *The Religion of Bloodshed* (c. 1895). {GS}

Fitzjohn, George S. (20th Century)

A freethinker, Fitzjohn wrote *War in Heaven* (19–?). {GS}

Fitzpatrick, Brian Charles (1905—1965)

Fitzpatrick was an atheist, rationalist, civil libertarian, journalist, historian, and adviser to governments. Son of a Catholic father and a Presbyterian mother, neither of whom practiced their faiths after marriage, Fitzpatrick was active in founding the Australian Council for Civil Liberties. He opposed state grants to religious schools and was identified with many secular causes. {SWW}

FitzRoy, John Somerset [5th Baron]: See entry for Lord Raglan

Flach, Vera (20th Century)

Flach wrote *A Yankee German in Texas* (1973). {*Freethought History #15*, 1995}

FLAGELLATION

Flagellation, which involves self-punishment by means of whipping, was considered a way to do penance for one's sins, particularly in thirteenth-century Catholic Europe. The flagellants marched in processions through cities, sometimes dressed in black with hoods which covered their heads. But their self-whippings sometimes became extreme and ecclesiastics began to express their disapproval. In 1349, Pope Clement VI forbade the flagellants' displays of whipping, hymn singing, and praying. In the United States, the Third Order of Franciscans continued the practice in New Mexico, and in Colorado it was continued by La Fraternidad Piadosa de Nuestro Padre Jesús Nazareno. Freudians have described flagellation as being sexually oriented.

Secular humanists, unless they are seriously into masochism, ordinarily avoid being flagellated. (See entry for Gherardo Segarelli.) {EH; ER; RE}

FLAMING CHALICE: See entry for Czech Republic Unitarians.

Flammarion, Nicolas Camille (1842—1925)

"Spiritualists deceive the public," states McCabe, "by alleging that Flammarion adopted their creed. He never did. He thought many of the phenomena were genuine while exposing a great deal of fraud, but that they were due to 'unknown forces'—which is the title of his book on the subject—not to spirits." McCabe quotes Flammarion, a French astronomer, as writing, "The supernatural does not exist," and labels him a theist, but anti-Christian.

However, Flammarion wrote, "Men have had the vanity to pretend that the whole creation was made for them, while in reality the whole creation does not suspect their existence." And his *Dreams of an Astronomer* includes the following:

> Man has conceived a God in his own likeness. It is in the name of this pretended God that monarchs and pontiffs have in all the ages, and under cover of all religions, bound humanity in a slavery from which it has not yet freed itself. . . . It is in the names of the gods of Olympus that the Greeks condemned Socrates to drink the hemlock; it is in the name of Jehovah that the high-priests and Pharisees crucified Jesus. It is in the name of Jesus, himself become God, that fanaticism ignominiously condemned to the stake men like Giordano Bruno, Vanini, Étienne Dolet, John Huss, Savanarola, and numerous other heroic victims; that the Inquisition ordered Galileo to belie his conscience; that thousands and thousands of unfortunates accused of witchcraft were burnt alive in popular ceremonies; it was with the express benediction of Pope Gregory XIII that the butchery of St. Bartholomew drenched Paris in blood.

{JM; RAT; RE; TYD}

Flanner, Janet (1892-1978): See entry for George Orwell, who considered the *New Yorker* author, once a "red baiter," a dishonest careerist.

FLAT EARTH THEORY

"The earth is flat. Whoever claims it is round is an atheist deserving of punishment." That is the religious edict, or fatwa, which was issued in 1993 by Sheik Abdel-Aziz Ibn Baaz, the supreme religious authority of Saudi Arabia. The sheik is a blind theologian or, to distinguish him from other theologians, a sightless theologian. On the Web: <http://flatearth.tdolby.com/>.

Aristotle and Thomas Aquinas both believed the earth is spherical. (See entry for *Fatwa.*)

FLATLAND

Flatland (POB 2420, Fort Bragg, California 95437) is a journal of Situationists. Its editor is Jim Martin. {FD}

FLATWOODS FREE PRESS

Flatwoods Free Press, which has published A. J. Mattill's *Seven Mighty Blows of Traditional Belief*, is at Route 2, Box 49, Gordo, Alabama 35466.

Flaubert, Gustave (1821—1880)

Flaubert took five years to write his masterpiece, *Madame Bovary* (1867), about a romantic young woman married to a dull provincial doctor. The book resulted in his being prosecuted on moral grounds. Prior to this, when in 1846 his friend Alfred Le Poittevin married (but who once had written him, "We are something like one single man, and we live of the same life"), Flaubert was enraged and wrote, "I experienced, when he married, a very deep stab of jealousy." Also, after having a homosexual experience in Egypt, Flaubert wrote to Bouilhet, "You ask me whether I consummated that piece of work in the baths. Yes, I did. It was with a big young guy covered with smallpox marks who wore an enormous white turban." In a letter to a friend about visiting the Turkish baths, Flaubert confided, "One admits one's sodomy, though sometimes you do a bit of denying, and then everybody teases you and you end up confessing."

In her correspondence with Flaubert, George Sand advised him to get married, and he complained to the Princesse Mathile that her "perpetual pious optimism . . . sometimes sets my teeth on edge." Their unlikely friendship has been described by Barbara Bray in *Flaubert-Sand: The Correspondence* (1993), leading critic Julian Barnes to observe, "George Sand continues to trip–how could she not?—like an aesthetic Florence Nightingale. She is his old, devoted friend, still and always; yet in literary matters she is no replacement for his lost 'left testicle,' the poet Louis Bouilhet, who had died in 1869. Increasingly she comes across as something between an agony aunt and Little Mary Sunshine."

In *Salammbo* (1863), he writes about ancient Carthage. *L'Éducation sentimentale* (1870) was a revision of an earlier novel. *The Temptation of St. Anthony* (1874) was written three times. *Three Tales* (1877) contains his short story, "A Simple Heart." All of his output shows him to have been a slow writer, one intent on finding *le mot juste*, the exact word.

Quite the worldly author, Flaubert was a master of the realistic novel, one who did not spend all his time simply moving his quill. He also did not approve the guilt-clad morals of his time, quipping, "A man has missed something if he has never woken up in an anonymous bed beside a face he'll never see again, and if he has never left a brothel at dawn feeling like jumping off a bridge into the river out of sheer physical disgust with life."

In *Madame Bovary*, the pharmacist is given these lines:

> I have a religion, my religion, and I even have more than all the others with their mummeries and their juggling. . . . I believe in the Supreme Being, in a Creator, whatever he may be. I care little who has placed us here below to fulfill our duties as citizens and parents; but I don't need to go to church to kiss silver plates, and fatten, out of my pocket, a lot of good-for-nothings who live better than we do. For one can know him as well in a wood, in a field, or even contemplating the ethereal heavens like the ancients. My God is the God of Socrates, of Franklin, of Voltaire, and of Beranger! I support the *Profession du Foi du Vicaire Savoyard* and the immortal principles of '89. And I can't admit of an old boy God who takes walks in his garden with a cane in his hand, who lodges his friends in the belly of whales, dies uttering a cry, and rises again after three days; things absurd in themselves, and completely opposed, moreover, to all physical laws, which proves to us, by the way, that priests have always wallowed in squalid ignorance, and tried to drag whole nations down after them.

Commenting upon letters with George Sand which are in *Flaubert-Sand: The Correspondence* (1993), *The Economist* (5 June 1993) observed,

> They had their differences. Flaubert was a vehemently reactionary anti-Christian, arguing always against the need to assist or promote the weak and meek. Sand (who was seventeen years Flaubert's senior) was a true daughter of the French revolution; Flaubert, examining it with his head rather than his heart, saw dismal proof of human stupidity, the failing he excoriated in *Bouvard et Pécuchet*. He was appalled by modern life; Sand, although older, embraced it wholeheartedly.

New Yorker (26 July 1993) added that she had been called "a latrine" by Baudelaire but praised as "France's Byron" by Chateaubriand for her much publicized liaisons with Frédéric Chopin and Alfred de Musset. Meanwhile, there were Flaubert's pathological ties to his mother, or his inclination to seek out (for either sexual or platonic bonds) viragoesque older women, such as Eulalie Foucaud, Elisa Schlésinger, Louise Pradier, Louise Colet, and Sand. He and Sand also had views on sexual abstinence, on the nature of the literary vocation, and on the afterlife. Flaubert once wrote, "Artists (who are priests) risk nothing by being chaste, on the contrary!" On reincarnation: "I was boatman on the Nile, procurer in Rome at the time of the Punic wars, then Greek rhetorician in Suburra. . . . I was pirate and monk, mountebank and coachman–perhaps Emperor of the East. . . . Many things would be explained if we could know our *real* genealogy." To which Sand starkly replies, "I think I was once a plant or a stone."

Neither J. M. Robertson nor Jacqueline Marchand cite Flaubert as clearly being a freethinker, although his works have appealed to freethinkers. Skeptics like his view that "It is necessary to sleep upon the pillow of doubt." McCabe particularly liked *The Temptation of St. Anthony*, which he states "sufficiently shows what he thought of the Church." (See entries for Adamastor, George Sand, and Felix Pouchet.) {ACK; BDF; JM; JMR; JMRH; RE; TRI; TYD}

Flaws, Gordon G. (19th Century)

Flaws was a freethinker who wrote *Sketch of the Life and Character of Saladin* (1880s?). {FUK; GS}

Fleck, Gustav Peter (1909—1995)

Fleck, a Netherlands-born banker and former securities firm executive, became an ordained Unitarian Universalist minister in 1984. He was founder of the Amsterdam Overseas Corporation, which evolved into the current Rothschild's, Inc. Outside the Rothschild family, Fleck was the only person to serve as a partner and director in both the French and English Rothschild houses. He wrote *The Mask of Religion* (1980), *The Blessings of Imperfection* (1987), and *Come As You Are* (1993). Fleck was an associate minister of the First Parish, Brewster, Massachusetts, and also served several Unitarian fellowships.

Fleck, Roger L. (1919-1999)

Although he was baptized by a Presbyterian minister who was an officer in the local Ku Klux Klan and also was born with cerebal palsy, Fleck became a freethinker in his teens and served during World War II. He worked thirty years for Continental Airlines, helped desegregate a camp for crippled children run by the Lions Club, and was on the board of directors of Big Brothers and Sisters in Houston, Texas. Fleck was a life member of Freedom From Religion Foundation. {*Freethought Today*, March 1999}

Fleishman, Norman (20th Century)

When he signed Humanist Manifesto II, Fleishman was Executive Vice President of Planned Parenthood World Population in Los Angeles, California. {HM2}

Fleming, Caleb (18th Century)

A freethinker, Fleming wrote *Three Letters Concerning Systematic Taste* (1755). {GS}

Fleming, Donald (20th Century)

Fleming wrote *John W. Draper* (1950). {FUS}

Fleming, John William (1863—1950)

"I will not go on bended knee before any man, nor kiss the ring of any Pope," exclaimed "Chummy" Fleming, who arrived in Australia from England in 1884. The bootmaker, agitator, and anarchist attended Australian Freethought Association conferences and, while working in Ballarat, was the local secretary. One of those who instituted the first Victorian May Day meetings, he carried a flag inscribed ANARCHY. Upon his death, his cremated ashes were scattered around the Yarra Bank forum, where he had spoken almost every Sunday for more than fifty years. {SWW}

FLEMISH HUMANISTS: See entry for Belgian Humanists.

Flemming, Anna (19th Century)

Flemming was minister of the Universalist Church of Avon, Illinois, in the 1880s.

Flemming, Virginia (1904—1992)

Flemming addressed the First International Congress on Humanism and Ethical Culture held in Amsterdam (1952). Lady Flemming was the daughter of Stanton Coit, the British Ethical Culture leader, and helped transform his Ethical Church into the Ethical Union and then into the British Humanist Association. {HNS}

Fletcher, Joseph Francis III (1905—1992)

A theologian who once was an ordained Episcopal priest, Fletcher became a pioneer of medical ethics, teaching at the University of Virginia. He wrote eleven books and more than 350 articles. In 1954, he published *Morals and Medicine* which, according to his *The New York Times* obituary, argued "the case for active euthanasia, for telling the truth to dying patients, for artificial insemination and for sterilization of those judged unfit for parenthood." Sen. Joseph R. McCarthy once dubbed him "the Red Churchman," for he was twice beaten unconscious while lecturing in the South for the Southern Tenant Farmers' Union. Added *The Times*, "In the late 1960's, he renounced belief in God and publicly espoused humanism, although he maintained many of his ties to religious groups and members of the clergy."

In 1974, Fletcher was the American Humanist Association Humanist of the Year. In 1986 he was elected an honorary associate of the British Rationalist Press Association. He served on the Council for Secular Humanism's Committee for the Scientific Examination of Religion, signed Humanist Manifesto II, and is a Humanist Laureate in the Council for Secular Humanism's International Academy of Humanism. {HM2; HNS2; SHD}

Fletcher, Laadan (1920—)

Fletcher, raised a Christian fundamentalist in England, renounced religion when twenty-five. He migrated to West Australia in 1968, lecturing at the University of West Australia. He has been an officer in the Humanist Society and a long-term member of the West Australia Voluntary Euthanasia Society. {SWW}

Fletcher, Ronald (1921—1992)

In 1986, Fletcher, the well-known sociologist, was elected an honorary associate of the Rationalist Press Association. He is author of the pamphlet, "A Definition of Humanism." Fletcher was critical of the Catholic teaching on sex which he described as "a tissue of illogicality, an overstrained and unconvincing attempt to make medieval mumbo jumbo fit the knowledge and problems of the modern world . . . an infallible guide to muddle and misery." {TRI}

Flew, Antony (Garradi Newton) (1923—)

Flew, in the *New Humanist* (July 1993), has written: "My father, like his father before him, was a Methodist minister. So at age thirteen I was sent to the excellent boarding school founded by John Wesley for the education of the sons of his itinerant preachers. But Kingswood's religion was no longer premised, as was that of its founder, upon the belief that the unredeemed are destined for eternal torture. So what, to the distress of all concerned, I rejected in my middle teens as manifestly incompatible with innumerable familiar facts was belief in the existence of a God both omnipotent and good. It was only later, and with particular reference to Islam, that I came to appreciate the appropriateness of the characteristically Hobbist observation that ' . . . in the attributes which we give to God we are not to consider the signification of pious intention, to do him the greatest honour we are able.' For although every surah (chapter) of the Qur'an begins 'In the Name of God, the Merciful, the Compassionate' it proceeds to present Allah as a sort of cosmic Saddam Hussein, forever torturing all those who fail to believe, worship, and obey. I joined the RPA in the early fifties, contributing to the old *Literary Guide* fairly regularly. My first book, entitled with the brash confidence of youth *A New Approach to Psychical Research*, was published by C. A. Watts in 1953. Most of its successors have been similarly concerned to promote rationality. David Hume, the subject of two, was treated as the first major thinker of the modern period whose philosophy was through and through secular, this-worldly and human-centred. The titles of others indicate the same concern: *Thinking about Thinking*; *A Rational Animal: Philosophical Essays on the Nature of Man*; *Darwinian Evolution*; *The Logic of Mortality*; and *Thinking about Social Thinking* (1995). My final fling–the first set of Prometheus Lectures plus other essays in atheist humanism–is due out from Prometheus in the fall." That volume is entitled *Atheistic Humanism* (1993), in which he supports the pragmatic implications of scientific naturalism.

A professor emeritus of philosophy at Reading University in England, Flew is a member of the Secretariat of the Council for Secular Humanism's International Academy of Humanism. In 1976, he was elected an honorary associate of the British Rationalist Press Association, and he is an honorary associate of the New Zealand Association of Rationalists and Humanists. He signed Humanist Manifesto II. *The Presumption of Atheism* (1976) a collection of his philosophical essays, has been reissued as *God, Freedom and Immortality*. Flew is a contributing editor of *Philo*.

David Berman in *New Humanist* (October, 1988) has remarked in a review of *Logic of Mortality* (1984), "Of course, Flew's style and standpoint will come as no surprise. For (with the exception of A. J. Ayer) he is surely the best-known living philosophical unbeliever in the English-speaking world." Flew, who also does not believe in any survival after death, is a contributing editor of *Free Inquiry*.

In *Immortality*, Paul Edwards writes of him:

> Flew in many places makes it clear that he is not a radical materialist, admitting that mental processes are irreducible to bodily phenomena. At the same time he insists that human beings are "creatures of flesh and blood" and these creatures of flesh and blood are the subjects of sensations, feelings, and thoughts.

In 1987, with Gary Habermas, Flew wrote *Did Jesus Rise From the Dead? The Resurrection Debate*. In 1994 his essay, "The Terrors of Islam," was published in *Challenges to the Enlightenment, Essays in Defense of Reason and Science*. In it, he suggests that Islam and its weaknesses need to be studied much as Christianity has been, and inasmuch as Islam is intolerant of all such critical dissent it will be up to rationalists and humanists to do the job. As for the supernatural, Flew has declared, "Stuff is all there is; while everything which is not stuff is nonsense."

In Birmingham, England, at the centenary conference of the Rationalist Press Association in 1999, his lecture was entitled "Against the New Irrationalism." (See entries for Paul Edwards, Colin McCall, and Michael Martin.) {CA; E; HM2; HNS2; TRI; TYD}

Flexner, Abraham (1866—1959)

The director of The Institute for Advanced Study at Princeton, Flexner was a naturalistic humanist. On his ninetieth birthday, *The New York Times* in 1956 interviewed the "intellectual giant who did more than any other man to give this nation a sound system of medical education," finding he did not want a birthday party because it would interrupt all the work he had to do. His philosophy, he said, is, "You gain happiness by helping others." {CE}

Flis, Andrej (20th Century)

Flis, a professor of sociology at the University of Cracow in Poland, holds that the Roman Catholic Church is increasingly alienating itself from European culture. He is author of "The Polish Church as an Enemy of the Open Society." {*Free Inquiry*, Winter 1996-1997; *New Humanist*, September 1996}

FLOOD, THE

Genesis recounts the story of a massive deluge, a story believed to be a variant of the Babylonian legend but refined and adapted to fit the theological and moral ideas of Israel. In the biblical version, Yahweh both willed the flood and gave advance warning to Noah. (In Iran, the high god instructed Yima to build a walled enclosure to save the good people. In India the flood was not the result of a divine decree but one of the series of cosmic cataclysms which periodically destroy the world. In one version, Vishnu took the form of a great fish to save Manu, who had befriended him.)

Such a flood, said to have occurred in 4004 B.C.E., involved forty feet of sea level rise every hour for the 960-hour period in *Genesis*. A problem for religious fundamentalists who accept such a tale is that Earth contains no sediment deposits in ponds, lakes, oceans, and caves of the same age, 4004 B.C.E. Also, all the glaciers are not of the same age. Then, too, there is a glaring omission of micro-organisms in the *Genesis* tale, and the ever-increasing fountain of illogic overflows.

The appeal of the flood story is also found in tales told by other early religions, including those of the American Indians. (See entry for Genesis.) {*Skeptical Inquirer*, September-October 1995}

Floquet, Charles Thomas (1828—1896)

A French statesman who edited the *Temps* and the *Siécle*, Floquet was one of the most ardent supporters in the National Assembly of the anti-clericalists. He was one of the chief opponents of Boulangism and fought a duel with Boulanger himself.

Floquet was one of the workers of the Gambetta group who prepared the way for the disestablishment of the Church in France. {RAT}

Flor, Bjorn (20th Century)

A Norwegian humanist, Flor in 1996 participated in the international conference of humanists in Mexico City. <bjorn.flor@nrk.no>.

Florence, Lella (1887—1966)

Florence was a freethinker who fought in England for reform of abortion laws. {GS}

Florence, Sargant (1890—)

Florence, a sociologist, was a leader of freethinkers. {GS}

FLORIDA ATHEISTS, HUMANISTS

Florida has the following atheist and humanist groups:

- Atheists of Florida (ASHS), PO Box 3893, Ft. Pierce, Florida 34948; (305) 936-0210. Web: <www.execpc.com/~aai/florida>. E-mail: <athalflc@aol.com>.
- Atheists of Florida, Tampa Bay Chapter (Atheist Alliance), POB 130753, Tampa, Florida 33681.

• Atheists of Florida, Palm Beach Chapter, 374 Golfview Road, North Palm Beach, Florida 33408; e-mail: <schisler@earthlink.net>.

• Atheists of Florida, St. Augustine Chapter, PO Box 860132, St. Augustine, Florida 32086 (904) 808-1884.

• First Coast Freethought Society, PO Box 558, Ponte Vedra Beach, Florida 32004; (904) 285-1205. Earl Coggins is the Contact. E-mail: <bbperry2@worldnet.att.net>.

• Florida International University Humanists: <www.secularhumanism.org/cfa/orgs.html>

• Florida State University humanists are at <www.secularhumanism.org/cfa/orgs.html>.

• Free Inquiry Society of Central Florida (ASHS), PO Box 4365, Winter Park, Florida 32793-4365; (407) 262-1915. Cathy Giordano is the contact, *Veritas* the newsletter. E-mail: <fisofcf@aol.com>. On theWeb: <reasonworks.com/cff/veritas.htm>.

• Freethinker Society of Sarasota Bay, 5230 Lake Village Drive, Sarasota, FL 34235 (941) 379-5137

• Humanist Society of Gainesville, 1708 N.W. 10th Ave., Gainesville, Florida 32605; (352) 336-6343.

• Humanist Association: St. Petersburg, PO Box 8099, Madeira Beach, Florida 33738 (727) 391-7571. On the Web: <http://home1.get.net/HASP/>. Jan Eisler's E-mail: <hasp@gte.net>.

• Humanist Association of West Central Florida, PO Box 6675, Lakeland, FL 33807; (941) 701-7407; Ken Schmidt is the contact:. E-mail: <kas007@earthlink.net> and <jayoung@mindspring.com>. On the Web: <http://www.cris.com/~eugenio/hawcf.htm>.

• Humanist Society of Gainesville (AHA), 1708 N.W. 10th Avenue, Gainesville, Florida 32605; (352) 336-6343. Hugo Borresen and Abby Goldsmith, contacts. On the Web: <http://www.afn.org/~afn59918>.

• Humanist Society of Greater Fort Walton Beach (AHA), 308 Pontevedra Drive, Niceville, Florida 32578. Kenneth Gibbs is a contact.

• Humanist Society of South Pinellas (AHA), POB 3641, Saint Petersburg, Florida 33731. Robert D. Collete is its contact.

• Humanists of Broward County, Alan MacDonald, President, 9548 NW 38 Court, Fort Lauderdale, FL 3351-5945 (954) 749-3938

• Humanists of Florida, Sol Klotz, President, 3206 Middlesex Road, Orlando, Florida 32803 (407) 896-3955 <http://www.applicom.com/humanist/>.

• Humanists of Fort Myers, Bill D'Albora, contact, 11220 Caravel Circle SW 301, Fort Myers, FL 33908; phone: (941) 454-0136

• Humanists of Greater Fort Walton Beach, William H. White, contact, 338 Okaloosa Road NE, Fort Walton Beach, FL 32548; phone: (904) 243-5247.

• Humanists of Indian River: The Ed Wilson Memorial Chapter, Joe Allison, President, 255A Ocean View Lane, Indiatlantic, Florida 32903 (407) 777-6933

• Humanists of Northeast Florida, Mimi Cerniglia, PO Box 1143, Ormand Beach, Florida 32175 (904) 676-2954

• Humanists of the Nature Coast, 6134 W. Pinedale Circle, Crystal River, FL 34429. Jackie Evans and Scott Forbes, contacts; phone: (352) 563-2857. E-mail: <sco@citrus.infi.net>.

• Humanists of the Palm Beaches (ASHS), Marvin Engle has been its President, 860 Lakeside Drive, North Palm Beach, Florida 33408.

• Humanists of Polk County, Kenneth A. Schmidt, president, P.O. Box 6675, Lakeland, FL 33807; phone: (904) 701-7401. E-mail: <pts2000@earthlink.net>

• Humanists of Tallahasee (AHA), POB 7038, Tallahassee, Florida 32314.

• Humanists of Volusia/Flagler County, 356 Seminole Drive, Ormond Beach, Florida 32174; (904) 676-2954. E-mail: <mimi-jc@aol.com>.

• Humanists of the Gold Coast (AHA), #606, 500 Ocean Boulevard, Boca Raton, Florida 33432. Dr. Albert Maizels is its president. (407) 338-9622

• Humanists of the Sun Coast (AHA), Hal East, Secretary-Treasurer, 317 Highland Ave N, Clearwater, Florida 34615 (813) 446-0312

• Humanists of the Treasure Coast, The Phillip Appleman Chapter is presided over by Bill Green, 835 18th St (#504), Vero Beach, Florida 33960 (561) 569-7314

• Rollins College freethinkers and humanists: <www.secularhumanism.org/cfa/orgs.html>.

• Secular Humanists of South Florida (ASHS), 4341 NW 16th St. (#208), Fort Lauderdale, Florida 33313; (954) 717-0477. E-mail: <humanist@web2000.net>. On the Web: <www.seflin.org/human/human2.htm>.

• Thomas Jefferson Societies (USA), Suite 601, 6020 Shore Boulevard South, Gulf Port, Florida 33707. Its contact is Sydney Goetz, and the group was formed to combat the forming of bible clubs in schools.

• University of Florida's Campus Freethought Alliance (CFA) chapter can be e-mailed care of Bill Bishop: <afn55009@afn.org>.

• University of Florida Humanistic Atheist Students Association is on the Web: <www.secularhumanism.org/cfa/orgs.html>.

• University of South Florida's Campus Freethought Alliance (CFA) can be telephoned: George Giannakoulias (727) 443-1751.

FLORIDA INTERNATIONAL UNIVERSITY

Florida International University humanists are at <www.secularhumanism.org/cfa/orgs.html>.

FLORIDA STATE UNIVERSITY

Florida State University humanists are at <http://www.secularhumanism.org/cfa/orgs.html>.

Flourens, Gustave (1821—1880)

Flourens was a French writer. His drastic rationalism was shown in articles in *La Pensée Nouvelle* and in his *Science de l'homme* (1865), leading the clergy to secure his dismissal and resulting in his going to Crete. There he took part in the insurrection and sat in the National Assembly. Returning to France in 1868, Flourens was imprisoned for his utterances and was shot, fighting for the Commune. {RAT}

Flourens, Marie Jean Pierre (1794—1867)

A French scientist, Flourens published a work on the nervous system of vertebrates and was then admitted into the Academy of Sciences. He became perpetual secretary in 1833. One of his popular works was *Human Longevity and the Quantity of Life on the Globe*. His son, Gustave (1838-1871), succeeded his father as professor of natural history at the *Collège de France*. Also an atheist and anti-clerical, he was deposed from his chair for writing *Science de l'homme* (1865). After taking up radical politics, Gustave was shot for fighting for the Commune. {BDF; RAT; RE}

FLOWER COMMUNION: See entry for Maja V. Capek.

Flower, Benjamin (18th Century)

For libeling Bishop Watson in 1799, Flower was imprisoned. An independent freethinker, he published *Political Register* (1807—1811). Eliza Flower was his eldest daughter.

Flower, Benjamin Orange (Born 1858)

An American writer, Flower founded and edited the *Arena* (Boston), then the *Coming Age* (1896—1904), finally combining the two as the *Arena* (1904—1909). He edited the *Twentieth-Century Magazine* (1909-—1911) and wrote widely, including a life of Whittier. {RAT}

Flower, Eliza (1803—1846)

Flower, a musical composer, devoted herself to providing music for South Place Chapel after it seceded from the Unitarian connection under W. J. Fox. She composed sixty-three of the hymns found in their book. Flower shared Fox's theism and she and her sisters are described in Harriet Martineau's *Five Years of Youth and Deerbrook*.

Sarah Flower, a sister, also was a freethought activist and was lyricist for her sister's music. {*Freethought History #9*, 1994; RE}

Floyd, William (Edward Gregory) (20th Century)

An atheist and author of many works on freethought, Floyd during the 1950s was on the advisory board of Charles Francis Potter's First Humanist Society of New York.

An outspoken atheist, Floyd was the openly atheistic signer of Humanist Manifesto I and author of *Christianity Cross-Examined* (1941). {FUS; HM1}

Flügel, J(ohn) C(arl) (1884—1955)

Flügel was a Freudian psychologist who joined the Promethan Society in the 1930s. In 1976 his *The Psychology of Clothers* was published. {TRI}

Flynn, Thomas William (1955—)

A senior editor of *Free Inquiry* and founding co-editor of the *Secular Humanist Bulletin*, Flynn co-founded Catholics Anonymous with Thomas Franczyk. He heads Inquiry Media Productions, and in addition to writing on atheism and humanism is a producer of many solid humanistic works. He is a Secular Humanist Mentor, has been a member of the board of directors of the Council for Secular Humanism, and currently serves as secretary. He also is director of the Center for Inquiry-International. In 1993, he designed the museum at the Robert Green Ingersoll Birthplace in Dresden, New York, which is open to the public each summer.

In *The Trouble With Christmas* (1993), Flynn takes a positive stand against non-believers' celebrating Christmas, declaring the pagan solstice should be disregarded altogether.

In Toronto in 1994, he spoke at the conference of the Coalition for Secular Humanism, Atheism, and Freethought (CSHAFT). In 1996, he spoke about the dangers of anti-scientific thought at the Humanist World Congress held in Mexico City. Flynn is a signer of .

In January 2000, Prometheus Books is scheduled to publish Flynn's first novel, *Galactic Rapture*, a science-fiction black comedy about a small-time religious con man on a backwater planet, a person who gets mistaken for the next incarnation of Christ.

Flynt, Larry (20th Century)

Flynt is the controversial publisher of *Hustler*, which many term a pornographic journal. In 1978 he was shot by Joseph Paul Franklin, who was upset that the magazine had depicted a white woman and a black man. Milos Forman produced a film, "The People vs. Larry Flynt," which was about Flynt's colorful life and how the shooting resulted in his being permanently disabled, confined to a wheelchair.

On a "Larry King Live" show (10 January 1996), he was asked if the reason he thought Jerry Falwell is a hypocrite is because he didn't believe in God, Flynt replied, "I am not saying he don't believe in God. I am just saying *I* don't believe in God. That puts me at odds with him." In a 1984 "satire" ad in which Flynt had depicted Falwell, he was sued for $1,000,000 but won the case and did not have to pay.

Frank Rich, a *New York Times* critic, wrote that Flynt, unlike so many others who claimed to have been embarrassed that reporters were writing that President Bill Clinton had had sex in the White House, admitted that he personally was a self-proclaimed seller of smut: "Mr. Flynt's candor is downright refreshing. . . . In the land of the pious hypocrite, the honest pornographer is king."

The First Amendment to the Constitution, Flynt insists, is the cornerstone of American independence: "Rights and civil liberties cannot be taken for granted, and that has become my cause. It's a perfect cause for an iconoclast because the things you have to fight for are often unpopular."

"If I can leave any kind of legacy," Flynt has written,

> I'd like to have expanded the parameters of free speech. If something isn't worth going to jail over, it's not worth very much. I did more than five months in a federal prison because I called a judge a "fucking asshole." But you know what? That wasn't a low point in my life. For me, it was a high point. . . .I know I'm rebellious, iconoclastic, and independent. Fundamentally, however, I say what I mean and I mean what I say, and that's more than I can say for a lot of others. Besides, I don't think life is fun unless you live it on the edge.

{CA; E; *P.O.V.*, April 1999}

Fo, Dario (1926—)

Fo, the son of a railway stationmaster and part-time actor, is an iconoclastic Italian playwright-performer. He was awarded the Nobel Prize in Literature in 1997. The Swedish Academy likened him to the "jesters of the Middle Ages" who relied on wit, irreverence, and even slapstick humor to mock authority while "upholding the dignity of the downtrodden."

The Vatican immediately condemned the award, *L'Osservatore Romano* writing that "Giving the prize to someone who is also the author of questionable works is beyond all imagination." The church had been a frequent target of Fo's satire.

The Wall Street Journal described Po as an anti-American and an ignoble prize winner. "No normal theater fan," wrote Stephen Schwartz on the editorial page, "would go to see 'We Can't Pay, We Won't Pay'–which glorifies the looting of a supermarket."

The United States State Department twice granted Fo and his wife, actress Franca Rame, waivers to enter the country, although he was refused in the 1980s under longstanding laws denying visas to people who took part in antigovernment activities or belonged to the Communist Party, which Fo did. His "Accidental Death of an Anarchist" in 1970 was hit play in Italy and Britain. "Mister Buffero," a television program, was deemed in 1977 by the Vatican to be the "most blasphemous show in the history of television."

"The Pope and the Witch," staged in 1992 in San Francisco, features a news conference at which the Pope, who has turned pro-abortion and pro-drug legalization, confuses a children's gathering in St. Peter's Square with an abortion rights rally.

Instead of delivering a formal lecture before the Swedish Academy, the seventy-one-year-old satirist distributed twenty-five pages of caricatures and doodles, lampooning critics who had derided the academy for bestowing its illustrious Nobel Prize for Literature on "a trouble-making iconoclast." He mocked the "sublime poets and thinkers" who he said had been tumbled from their Parnassian heights by his winning. "In reaction to this typhoon, insults are hurled at the Swedish Academy. You've overdone it this time: the Nobel Prize to a comedian-playwright-actor! Who's ever heard of such a thing?" He then thanked the academy for giving him and his wife and collaborator, Franca Rame, inspiration to "continue doing what we set out to do from the start: to attack, with laughter and reason, in song and in mime, every form of oppression and injustice." {CA; *The Wall Street Journal*, 13 October 1997}

FOCUS

A humanistic monthly, *Focus* is published at 687 Larch Avenue, Teaneck, New Jersey 07666-2301; E-mail: <rca001@aol.com>.

Foerster, Norman (1887—1972)

Foerster, a "neo-humanist," edited a well-known textbook, *American Poetry and Prose* (1970), and he wrote *American Criticism* (1962) and *Humanism and America* (1967). In 1949, asked about humanism, Foerster responded to the present author:

> Whatever changes there have been in my conception of humanism are stated in my books. I have said nothing about Existentialism and have nothing to say now, because I know far too little about it. "Naturalistic humanism" (Sellars, Haydon, et al.) seems to me a contradiction in terms. One might as well speak of a carnivorous vegetarianism. I assume you have seen Professor Mercier's recent book.

In 1956, he added,

> My conception of humanism is, in essentials, that of Irving Babbitt. Babbitt's object was not to offer something new and provincially modern, but simply to revive the 'truths of the inner life' as they appear in the humanist tradition since Aristotle and Confucius and are sanctioned by the religious tradition since Jesus and Buddha [sic].
>
> Abjuring all forms of authority, he reaffirmed, on the basis of immediate experience, the fundamental doctrines and the way of life that have characterized the "wisdom of the ages." Humanism, in this approach, is dualistic, sharply opposed to the monistic naturalism upon which modern thought, art, and life so largely rest.
>
> What is central in the humanist outlook, so conceived, seems to me perennially sound and fruitful. But in matters of spirit and method, and in application to specific domains of modern civilization–political, economic, social, artistic–there is room for wide differences.
>
> One of the goods of humanism is diversity. I have indicated my position more fully in the concluding chapter of *American Criticism.*

{WAS, 24 March 1949 and 3 August 1956}

Foerster, Wilhelm (Born 1832)

Foerster was a German astronomer, a director in 1865 of the Berlin Observatory. He educated his children without religion and headed the German Ethical Movement. A Privy Councillor, Foerster was almost the only German professor to oppose the War. {RAT}

Follen, Charles (1746—1840)

A German reformer, Follen was an Abolitionist teacher and a Unitarian minister. He was Harvard's first professor of German literature. He introduced German to the Harvard curriculum and, also, introduced the Christmas tree to New England. Some of his lectures are found in his *Works* (1841—1842), edited by his wife, Eliza Lee Cabot Follen (1787—1860). Also, Follen wrote *Hymns for Children* (1825) and *Poems* (1839). {U}

Follen, Eliza Lee Cabot (1787-1860)

Follen, a children's author and abolitionist, introduced the Christmas tree custom to America. She and her husband, Charles, were both Unitarians.

FOLLY

- Human folly goes up and down, but it always exists, and its depths have never been plumbed.

—Samuel Cummings (1927-1998),
an American-born Englishman called the
international king of the arms trade,
a person who sold guns to dictators in
Central America favored by the United States,
to Fidel Castro to fight the Batista regime,
to Taiwan, and to various African groups
trying to overthrow their national governments.

Fonblanque, Albany William (1793—1872)

Fonblanque was an English journalist, the son of an eminent lawyer. In 1820 he was on the staff of the *Times* and contributed to the *Westminster Review. In* 1830 he became editor of the *Examiner*, retaining his post until 1847. His caustic wit and literary attainments did much to forward advanced liberal views. Some of Fonblanque's editorials were published under the title of *England Under Seven Administrations.* {BDF; RAT}

Fonda, Jane (1937-)

Fonda, the daughter of actor Henry Fonda, appeared in Broadway and in films in the early 1960s. While married to director Roger Vadim (1965-1973), she made "La Ronde" (1964) and "Barbarella" (1968). She married Tom Hayden in 1973.

Fonda won Academy Awards for "Coming Home" (1978) and "Klute" (1970). She was in "Cat Ballou" (1965), "Barefoot in the Park" (1967), "They Shoot Horses Don't They?" (1969), "The China Syndrome" (1979), "On Golden Pond" (1981), "Agnes of God" (1965), "The Morning After" (1986), "Old Gringo" (1989), and "Stanley and Iris" (1990).

Politically active in anti-nuclear and feminist peace movements, she incurred the wrath of many for visiting North Vietnam in 1971, earning the derisive title of "Hanoi Jane." Later she received the thanks of many for her strong anti-war stand at a time when her views were decidedly unpopular. A 1985 Roper Poll listed as her the fourth most admired woman in America.

Fonda, who married fellow freethinker Ted Turner in 1991, is author of various weight-loss and workout books.

Foner, Philip S(heldon) (1910—)

Foner, a freethinker, wrote *Mark Twain, Social Critic* (1958). {FUK; GS}

Fontane, Theodor (1819—1898)

Fontane was a German poet and novelist. A non-Christian theist, he wrote *Gedichte* (1851). {RAT; RE}

Fontanier, Jean (17th Century)

Fontanier was a French writer accused of blasphemies in a book entitled *Le Tresor Inestimable.* Wheeler has the opinion that Garasse, with little reason, called Fontanier an atheist. However, Fontanier met the fate of blasphemers and was burned at the Place de Grève in 1621. {BDF}

Fontenelle, Bernard Le Bovier De (1657—1757)

A nephew of Corneille, Fontenelle was called by Voltaire the most universal genius of the reign of Louis XIV. Educated at the Jesuit's College, he went to Paris in 1674, wrote some plays and *Dialogues of the Dead* (1683). In 1687, his *History of Oracles* was attacked by the Jesuit Baltus as impugning the Church Fathers. In 1699, Fontenelle was made secretary to the Academy of Sciences, a post he held forty-two years. L'Abbé Ladvocat, commenting on Fontenelle's books, said, "as these books contain many things contrary to religion, it is to be hoped they are not his." He referred to *Doubts on the Physical System of Occasional Causes*, *Resurrection of the Body*, *The Infinite*, and a *Treatise on Liberty*. Fontenelle nearly reached the age of one hundred and, a short time before he died when asked if he felt any pain, replied, "I only feel a difficulty of existing." {BDF; RAT}

FOOD

One of the best parts about not dying is that one can continue eating. Non-believers are religiously sensuous about carbohydrates, fats, minerals, proteins, and vitamins. Philosophic naturalists and atheists are rumored to eat chocolate *religiously*.

They marvel, however, at Catholics who at one time were ordered *not* to eat meat on Fridays; Jews who *never* eat pork chops or bacon; Muslims who *never* eat ham or drink a vodka martini; Rastafarians who proscribe eating meat, dairy, salt, or white sugar; Mormons who must not drink Coca Cola; or Santerians who, fulfilling revelations by *iyaloshas* (priestesses), feed the *orishas* sacrificial animals instead of eating them.

FOOL

- Fool me once, shame on you. Fool me twice, shame on me.

—Anonymous
but frequently quoted by freethinkers after
learning that Santa Claus is not a person and that
Jesus could not possibly have risen from the dead.

Foot Washing: See entry for Feet Washing.

Foot, Dingle (Mackintosh) [Sir] (1905—)

Lord Foot, a barrister and politician, became a Liberal Member of Parliament (United Kingdom) for Dundee, 1931—1945. In 1945, he was a member of the British Delegation to the San Francisco Conference. He was Solicitor-General from 1964 to 1967 and chairman of the Society of Labour Lawyers from 1960 to 1964. In 1995, Lord Foot, a non-believer, was named an Honorary Associate of the Rationalist Press Association. {*New Humanist*, September 1996}

Foot, Michael [Right Honorable] (1913—)

A British journalist, lawyer, and politician, the Right Honorable Michael Foot in 1992 was made an Honorary Associate of the Rationalist Press Association. He also is an Honorary Associate of the National Secular Society. In 1952 he became editor of the *Tribune* in London. He has been a Labour Member of the United Kingdom Parliament for a division of Monmouthshire and for the Devonport division of Plymouth. The Rt. Hon. Foot's works include *Armistice 1918—1939* (1940); *The Trial of Mussolini* (1943); *Parliament in Danger* (1959); *The Politics of Paradise* (1988); and books on Aneurin Bevan and Harold Wilson. He wrote an introduction to a new edition of Bertrand Russell's *Autobiography* (1998).

At the opening of Bradlaugh House in 1994, Foot cut a ribbon, which officially opened the premises. Barbara Smoker jovially introduced him as "a man of letters who used to have some connection, I believe, with politics." {TRI}

FOOTBALL

Most forms of football are derived from many ancient games, especially *harpaston* and *harpastrum*.

In 1998 a consignment of World Cup footballs had to be withdrawn from sale in Rotherham, South Yorkshire. Produced in India, they were overprinted with the national flags of participating nations, including that of Saudi Arabia. Inasmuch as the Saudi flags bears the words "There is no God but Allah and Muhammad is his prophet," Muslims objected that to kick a ball bearing such "holy" words from the Qur'an would be "a gross insult." {*The Freethinker*, June 1998}

Foote, Edward Bliss (1829—1909)

Foote was born in Ohio and was taught as a twelve-year-old Presbyterian to regard Paine, Hume, and Voltaire as frightfully vicious men. He became the editor of the first paper published in New Britain, Connecticut, and while visiting in Boston heard the Unitarian minister, Theodore Parker. He also heard the liberal Unitarian minister, O. B. Frothingham, and contributed money to D. M. Bennett's *The Truth Seeker*. Foote, a physician, opposed the first Comstock bill in 1872, and in 1876 Foote was fined $3,500 for having sent through the mails an innocent pamphlet treating on physiological subjects and advocating the right of married people to regulate the size of the family through the use of contraceptives. When in 1873 Susan B. Anthony was fined $100 for daring to cast a vote in Rochester, Foote sent his check for $25 to assist in paying the unjust fine. Foote was a member of the Federation of Freethought, the Secular Union, the Manhattan Liberal Club, the Institute of Heredity, and the Constitutional Liberty League. {PUT; TRI}

Foote, Edward Bond (1854—1912)

Foote, son of Edward Bliss Foote, was sent by his parents, then Unitarians, to a school which taught much orthodox theology. But he became a physician and shed his religion under the instruction of O. B. Frothingham. A member of the Liberal Club in New York City, he gave a lecture on "The Blue Glass Craze" on the same platform with Walt Whitman and others of that radical 8th Street circle. In 1888 he was made president of the club. Of himself, Foote once wrote, "As a hygienist I favor (and almost practice) vegetarianism, avoid tobacco, and apply prohibition of alcoholics to myself. I am one of the neo-malthusian cranks who would limit population, and my pet hobby is eugenics, or the right of every child to be well born, or not at all. So I also advocate woman suffrage, and the sexual emancipation of women, less bondage in marriage, far greater freedom in divorce, and believe that every child born should be as legitimate in law as in nature. . . . As to religion, I am Agnostic, subscribe to the articles of the Secularists, and find myself pretty closely in accord with the Positivism of Mr. T. B. Wakeman. . . . Lastly, I look forward to cremation, and anticipate nothing further." {PUT}

Foote, George William (1850—1915)

An English freethinker and publisher, Foote was a president of the National Secular Society (NSS) in 1890. In Plymouth when Foote was four, his father who was a custom officer died, and Foote was brought up an Anglican. But at the age of fifteen, he became a Unitarian under the liberalizing influence of the Rev. J. K. Applebee. In 1868 he went to London, where he joined the Young Men's Secular Association and was soon working energetically for Freethought and Republicanism. Both as a speaker and as a writer he early showed a power of thought and expression which, combined with utter fearlessness, was to make him later so great an asset to the Freethought cause. During the decade 1870—1880 Foote contributed to the *Secular Chronicle* and the *National Reformer*; founded, in conjunction with G.J. Holyoake, the *Secularist*; edited the *Liberal*; and wrote a number of pamphlets, including "Heroes and Martyrs of Freethought" and "God, the Soul and A Future State: a Reply to Thomas Cooper." In 1881 he established the *Freethinker*, a journal that was destined to become a powerful factor in spreading Freethought throughout England. From 1883 to 1887 be edited *Progress*, which contained many articles of literary merit.

During his presidency of the NSS, financial problems predominated and in 1902 he personally became bankrupt. A radical and an individualist, he was a social Darwinian. In his *Flowers of Freethought* (1893), he wrote, "The mental serf is a bodily serf too, and spiritual fetters are the agencies of political thralldom. The man who worships a tyrant in heaven naturally submits his neck to the yoke of tyrants on earth. He who bows his intellect to a priest will yield his manhood to a king." He also wrote, "We cannot fathom the Infinite–it is enough for us to love and serve humanity."

A.D. McLaren, in an updating of Foote's *Infidel Death-Beds*, described some of Foote's problems: "Though the prosecutions of Foote for 'blasphemous libels' published in the *Freethinker*, constitute an important chapter in the story of his life, it is impossible here to enter into details concerning them. He was served with his first summons in July, 1882, and at the Court of Queen's Bench was compelled to find securities for £600. The next trial arose out of the illustrations in the Christmas number of the same year and had more serious consequences. For this offence he was, in March, 1883, sentenced by Judge North, a Roman Catholic, to twelve months' imprisonment "as an ordinary criminal subject to the same discipline as burglars. Replied Foote, 'I thank you, my lord. Your sentence is worthy of your creed.' Nearly two months later Foote was tried again on the first indictment, before Lord Chief Justice Coleridge, and defended himself in a speech which is now one of the classics in the literature of its kind. For a detailed account of these prosecutions the reader is referred to Foote's 'Prisoner for Blasphemy,' and the 'Defence of Free Speech."

"Apart from his thirty-five years' work on the *Freethinker*," McLaren continued, "during the whole of this period Foote was in various other ways–writing books and pamphlets, lecturing and debating–serving the cause to which he had early decided to devote his life. In 1882 appeared 'The God the Christians Swear By,' during Charles Bradlaugh's parliamentary struggle, 'Blasphemy No Crime,' and 'Death's Test,' afterwards enlarged into *Infidel Deathbeds*. The last, like 'A Lie in Five Chapters?' (1892), in which he ran to earth the story of a 'converted Atheist,' which the Rev. Hugh Price Hughes had started, was more than an exposure of "lying for the glory of God." Foote discerned as clearly as any man ever did the influence of superstitious beliefs on personality, and the fatal ease with which they are made to serve the purposes of the professional soul-saver. 'The Bible Handbook,' in which W.P. Ball collaborated, appeared in 1885, and 'Crimes of Christianity' in 1887. In producing the latter, which is a veritable store-house of historical facts for the Freethought propagandist, he had the assistance of his life-long friend, J. M. Wheeler. 'Rome or Atheism' (1892) shows that power of going straight to the point which characterized all Foote's work. It also shows exactly where he himself stood. The Newman brothers are made the text for a keen analysis of the Roman Catholic's "certitude" and the Protestant's "right to private judgment"; the disintegration of Protestantism is seen to be inevitable; and the field will be left to the two great protagonists who already "march steadily forward to their Armageddon." His views on death and a future life are concisely expressed in "The Gospel of Secularism," contributed to *Religious Systems of the World.* The *Secularist*, he says, will give no assent to any proposition of whose truth he is not assured, and 'declines to traffic in supernatural hopes and fears.' "

Foote's literary and artistic tastes were catholic. He liked the works of Titian, Angelico, and Turner; Beethoven, Wagner, and Chopin; Shakespeare, Byron, Shelley, and Browning. His favorite novelist was his friend George Meredith, but he also liked Richardson, Fielding, Thackeray, and George Eliot. Among the poets he thought highly of were George Herbert, Cowper, Morris, and Swinburne. In theology, he possessed works by St. Basil, St. Augustine, Thomas à Kempis, Erasmus and, his favorite, Hooker.

F. J. Gould remembers Foote's "Victorian regularity in his frock-coat, black tie, and restraint of gesture." Foote was five feet ten inches, of average build, had a beard, and his hair turned to gray in his early fifties. Henry Salt recalled of Foote that "It was always an intellectual treat to hear him speak." Aldred in his autobiography wrote of Foote, "I saw him as a would-be priest, even when they styled themselves Freethinkers and Atheists. . . . Foote in particular, and Cohen as his lieutenant, had to be not only the priests but the popes of the Freethought movement," similar comments of which previously had been alleged about Bradlaugh and Holyoake.

Chapman Cohen, upon Foote's death, wrote as follows: "To me it will always be some consolation that he died as he would have wished–in harness. . . . When I saw him on the Friday (two days) before his death he said, 'I have had another setback, but I am a curious fellow and may get all right again.' But he looked the fact of death in the face with the same courage and determination that he faced Judge North many years ago. A few hours before he died he said calmly to those around him, 'I am And when the end came his head dropped back on the pillow, and with a quiet sigh, as of one falling to sleep, he passed away." {BDF; EU, Edward Royle; FO; FUK; JM; JMR; PUT; RAT; RE; RSR; TRI; TYD; WSS}

Foote, Henry Wilder (20th Century)
Foote wrote *The Religion of Thomas Jefferson* (1960). {FUS}

Forberg, Friedrich Karl (1770—1848)

A German philosopher, Forberg became attached to Fichte's philosophy. An article he wrote with Fichte, "The Ground of Our Faith in Divine Providence," brought on them a charge of atheism, and their journal was confiscated by the Electorate of Saxony. Religion, Forberg held, consists in devotion to morality, and he wrote *An Apology for Alleged Atheism* (1799). {BDF; RAT}

Forbes, Milton L. (20th Century)

Forbes is author of *The Messiah* (1989) and *Out of the Mists of Time: Who Wrote the Bible and Why* (1992).

FORBIDDEN BOOKS: See a listing of such works in pre-Revolutionary France, which are included in the entry for Robert Darnton. Also see *Index Librorum Prohibitorum*

Ford, Arthur L. (20th Century)

Ford, a humanist, wrote *Joel Barlow* (1971 and *The Poetry of Henry David Thoreau* (1970). {GS}

Ford, Gerald N. (20th Century)

Ford, a chartered accountant, is Treasurer of the Humanist Association of Canada (HAC).

Forder, Robert (1844—1901)

Forder was the son of a Norfolk agricultural laborer who was himself sent out to work in the fields when he was eight. At the age of sixteen he went to London and, after being rejected by the army because he was "too puny," he worked as a laborer in the boiler-shop of a firm of marine engineers at Deptford. Attending open-air radical and freethought meetings, he became a freethinker and a republican, then a Reform League organizer. In 1877 he became general secretary of the National Secular Society. During the imprisonment of Foote, Ramsey, and Kemp in 1883, Forder undertook charge of the publishing business. {BDF; FUK; RSR}

FORECASTLE

A forecastle is the section of the upper deck of a ship located at the bow forward of the foremast.

It is also called the fo'c's'le, the only word in English with three apostrophes: a delight for grammarians who argue with absolutists that such a construction is impossible.

Forel, Auguste (1848—1931)

A Swiss physiologist who taught psychiatry and was director of the asylum at Zurich, Forel wrote on a variety of subjects. His work, *Ants* (1904), was awarded the Academy Prize. He wrote on the anatomy of the brain, insanity, prison reform, and social morality. His chief rationalist work is *Vie et mort* (1908). Forel, the leading scientific man of modern Switzerland, described himself as an Agnostic. {RAT; RE}

Ford, Charles Henri (1913—)

Ford, a photographer, is widely known as having been Pavel Tchelitchew's lover for twenty years. He is the brother of actress Ruth Ford, whom he once memorably photographed in a flimsy, flowery dress with her young arms wrapped around a barber pole. The photo also contains three children dressed for winter and peering unexplicably into a shop window. Ford's portraits in the 1930s were distinctive, as were his 1950 photos in Italy, including one of the photographer James Van Der Zee and the surrealist poet André Breton. A poet and a novelist (*The Young and the Evil* was co-authored with Parker Tyler in 1933), Ford was once editor of the now defunct surrealist magazine, *View*. His friends besides Tyler included Gertrude Stein, George Platt-Lynes, Jean Cocteau, Andy Warhol, and Pier Paolo Passolini, among others.

Discussing his view of organized religion, Ford has stated that he is not interested in such matters. He did, however, express an interest in Buddhism. {WAS, conversations, 1997}

Ford, Henry (1863—1947)

The famed maker of horseless carriages was allegedly an atheist and, allegedly, a pro-Nazi. As the apostle of mass production, Ford manufactured 15,000,000 Model T Fords starting in 1908. Some anti-Semitic articles in Ford's *Dearborn Independent* brought him legal problems, and he was involved in numerous other lawsuits and controversies with bankers, financiers, union leaders, and others. Throughout his life, he never allowed outside investments in any of the Ford holdings.

Ford contributed to a monthly paper, *The Humanist*, which was published at Humanity House by the British Humane Association in the 1920s. It was politically right-wing and, despite its title, was not associated with the rationalist, freethought, or secular humanist organizations.

In 1925 Ford publicized his views in favor of reincarnation, leading his friend Luther Burbank to challenge them in a headline-capturing story in the San Francisco *Bulletin* of 22 January 1926: I'M AN INFIDEL, DECLARES BURBANK, CASTING DOUBT ON SOUL IMMORTALITY THEORY. If Ford were an atheist, as alleged, he apparently is one of the few atheists on record who believed in "reincarnation of the soul." (See entries for Luther Burbank and Paul Edwards, the latter of whom ridiculed Ford's ideas about reincarnation.) {CE}

FOREPLAY

Born-again freethinkers often object that although they have been relatively successful in discarding most of the religious baggage they were saddled with in youth, they have found it difficult to overcome the feelings of guilt about sex that were instilled by the religion of their parents' choice.

Particularly harmful, many have said and written, is the lack of sex education that they received either from their family or their schools. Foreplay, the intimate sexual stimulation that precedes intercourse, is either entirely overlooked by men or, according to women, is that which involves a half-hour of begging.

Few freethinkers appear to agree, at least in printed materials, as to the ages at which sex education should start and by whom it should be taught. Few, however, disagree that sensuousness is humanistically delightful.

Forest, Lester (20th Century)

In the 1960s, Forest was a vice president of the American Humanist Association.

Forester, C. S. (1899—1966)

Forester, the English writer of the Hornblower novels and *The African Queen* (1935), wrote the present author concerning humanism:

> I'm an ignorant person, and completely incapable of commenting on naturalistic humanism. Maybe I have a blind spot, a kind of tone-deafness with regard to philosophy.
>
> {WAS, 20 February 1951}

Forester, Marilyn (20th Century)

Forester is Secretary of the Board of Directors of the Atheist Network, a Houston, Texas, group which formed in 1991.

FORGIVENESS, CHRISTIAN

- I sent for the wench to clean my room, and when I came in I kissed her and felt her, for which God forgive me

—William Byrd
The Secret Diary
Of William Byrd of Westover, 1709-1712

Forkosch, Morris (20th Century) and **Selma Forkosch** (20th Century)

The Forkosches established an endowment for giving annual awards for the best humanist article and the best humanist book. In 1997 Jim Herrick was a recipient for his article, "When Humanists Embrace the Arts." The 1997 book award was given to New Zealand philosopher Kurt Baier for *Problems of Life and Death: A Humanist Perspective*.

Forlong, James George Roche (Born 1824)

Major General Forlong, who was educated as an engineer, joined the Indian Army in 1842. He fought in the South Mahrata campaign of 1845—1846 and in the second Burmese war. On Burma's annexation, he became head of the survey, roads, and canal branches. In 1858 and 1859 he traveled extensively through Egypt, Palestine, Turkey, Greece, Italy, and Spain, returned to India and Upper Bengal, and from 1872 to 1876 was secretary and chief engineer to the Government of Oudh. In his youth an evangelical preacher, he became a student of Eastern religions, archaeology, and languages, and wrote *Rivers of Life*, in which he set forth the evolution of all religions from their radical objective basis to their present spiritual developments. Himself a freethinker, Forlong illustrated in a chart with streams of color the movements of thought from 10,000 B.C.E. to the present time. {BDF; RAT; RE}

Forman, James (1928—)

Forman, an African American, wrote *The Making of Black Revolutionaries* (1985), in which according to Norm Allen Jr. he discusses his atheism and his contempt for "religious crap." In 1994 Forman received the Council for Secular Humanism's African American Humanist of the Year award in Orlando, Florida. {CA; E}

FORNICATION

The act of copulating, considered by some as one of mankind's most important pleasures but by others a disgusting and obscene act, is ordinarily referred to as fornication in "proper" company. In ultra-proper company and with a French tonality, "*le fucking*" is used, apparently to soften the dreaded Anglo-Saxon sound.

One of the founders of the Secular Humanist Society of New York has suggested, non-facetiously, that lovers might well be rated on a Kinsey-like one-to-seven scale, that a one be granted to those who egocentrically consider copulation as something only for their own satisfaction or as something that is dirty, but that a seven be given those who make an art of the act for however many parties are pleasurably involved. "Where," he speculated, "might Alcibiades, Jefferson, Shelley, Florence Nightingale, Whitman, Emily Dickinson, Einstein, Bertrand Russell, and Mae West have ranked?"

Technically, fornication is consensual sexual intercourse between two persons not married to each other, at least in Christian countries. Specifically, according to the *Catechism of the Catholic Church* (1994), "Fornication is carnal union between an unmarried man and an unmarried woman. It is gravely contrary to the dignity of persons and of human sexuality which is naturally ordered to the good of spouses and the generation and education of children. Moreover, it is a grave scandal when there is corruption of the young." The negative treatment of the entire subject of sex by Christian theologians has resulted in the sex act's being taught as something that is "committed," or bad. Pope John Paul II in a 1993 encyclical, *Veritatis Splendor*, refers to pre-marital sex, masturbation, homosexuality, and artificial insemination as "intrinsically evil. If acts are intrinsically evil, a good intention or particular circumstance can diminish their evil, but they cannot remove it. They remain 'irremediably' evil acts per se and in themselves are not capable of being ordered to God and to the good of the person." In short, one is not supposed to *enjoy* sex.

Roget's *Thesaurus*, under "sexy," adds: "SEE IMPURITY." "Fuck you!" is usually expressed as an intensive phrase, as is "Get to fuck out of here," both vulgarisms not expressed in "polite" society. The wry expletive, "Well, fuck me!", usually is followed, according to slang expert Eric Partridge, with the equally wry "Later" or "No thanks." Similarly negative connotations surround expressions such as "You're a fuck up, you fucker, so fuck off!" In short, in the Western World most references to copulation and fornication are negative in intent, allegedly a sign of organized religions' successes in degrading the pleasures of sex. It is rare to hear "fuck" used in a positive sense, certainly not when uttered by a man who talks of a woman as being "a good fuck." Teachers of grammar have been known to become embarrassed by saying that the sentence, "I smell good," involves use of the copulative verb *smell* (as in a reference to one's cologne). Instead, they call it a linking verb. ("I smell well" refers to a sensitive, unclogged nose.)

Bertrand Russell in *Marriage and Morals* (1959) discusses how an enjoyable act, such as having sex, was turned into a sin and what this led to:

> Catholicism has always had a certain degree of toleration for what is held to be sin.
>
> The Church has recognized that ordinary human nature could not be expected to live up to its precepts, and has been prepared to give absolution for fornication provided the sinner acknowledge his fault and did penance. This practical toleration was a method of increasing the power of the clergy, since they alone could pronounce absolution, and but for absolution fornication would entail eternal damnation.
>
> The outlook of Protestantism has been somewhat different, in theory less severe, but in practice, in some ways more so. Luther was much impressed by the text, "It is better to marry than to burn," and was also in love with a nun. He inferred that in spite of vows of celibacy, he and the nun had a right to marry, since otherwise, given the strength of his passions, he would have been led into mortal sin. Protestantism accordingly abandoned the praise of celibacy, which had been characteristic of the Catholic Church, and wherever it was vigorous it also abandoned the doctrine that marriage is a sacrament, and tolerated divorce in certain circumstances. But Protestants were more shocked than Catholics by fornication, and altogether more rigid in their moral condemnations.
>
> The Catholic Church expected a certain amount of sin, and arranged methods for dealing with it; the Protestants, on the contrary, abandoned the Catholic practice of confession and absolution, and left the sinner in a much more hopeless position than he occupies in the Catholic Church. One sees this attitude in both its aspects in modern America, where divorce is exceedingly easy, but adultery is condemned with far more severity than in most Catholic countries.

Two leading secular humanists, Bonnie and Vern Bullough, wrote widely on the subject. Their general overview is similar to that of the average person on the street, that—like sleep and food—sex provides one of life's intrinsic joys, that–whether one is bisexual, homosexual, or heterosexual–sex when not under (or over) practiced is a pleasant necessity and helps one maintain mental and physical well-being. The opposite of one who feels that sex is evil, an act for which "guilt feelings" need to follow, is the individual who has a healthy and positive view concerning sex, who regards fornication as an art to be developed. Meanwhile, those who fuck, shit, and piss are admonished by The Puritanical Powers That Be to fornicate, excrete, and urinate. For the healthy person, fornication is one of life's major pleasures, a major humanistic right. (See entry for Swearing.)

Fornos, Werner (20th Century)

President of the Population Institute since 1982, Fornos in 1991 was named Humanist of the Year by the American Humanist Association. He wrote *Gaining People, Losing Ground* (1987). {HNS2}

Forrest, W. M. (20th Century)

Forrest, a non-theist and freethinker, wrote *Do Fundamentalists Play Fair?* (1926). {GS}

Forrester, George (20th Century)

Forrester wrote *The Faith of an Agnostic, or First Essays in Rationalism* (1902). {GS}

Forster, E(dward) M(organ) (1879—1970)

A leading British novelist of the twentieth century, Forster highlighted the difficulty of forming human relationships in his best-known work, *A Passage to India* (1924). In 1968, he received the British Order of Merit. *Maurice* (1914) was published after his death, and it was revolutionary in that he treated homosexuality as an inherent trait rather than simply a manner of behaving.

Upon his mother's death, he wrote, "Surely she will give up being dead now." He also wrote, "I want to love a strong young man of the lower classes and be loved by him, and even hurt by him." As for his democratic outlook, "Love and loyalty to an individual can run counter to the claims of the State. When they do–down with the State, say I, which means that the State would down me."

Jim Herrick (*New Humanist*, May, 1990) spoke of Forster's humanism upon an occasion when Forster's cousin, Philip Whichelo, donated a portrait of Forster to the Gay and Lesbian Humanist Association. He cited Forster's description of humanism in his essay on Gide and George: "The humanist has four leading characteristics–curiosity, a free mind, belief in good taste, and belief in the human race."

In *Two Cheers for Democracy* (1951), Forster wrote,

> I do not believe in belief. But this is an age of faith, in which one is surrounded by so many militant creeds that, in self defense, one has to formulate a creed of one's own. Tolerance, good temper, and sympathy are no longer enough in a world which is rent by religious and racial persecution, in a world where ignorance rules, and science, which ought to have ruled, plays the subservient pimp. Tolerance, good temper, and sympathy–well, they are what matter really, and if the human race is not to collapse, they must come to the front before long. But for the moment they don't seem enough; their action is no stronger than a flower battered beneath a military jack-boot. They want stiffening, even if the process coarsens them.
>
> Faith to my mind is a stiffening process, a sort of mental starch, which ought to be applied as sparingly as possible.

Forster once wrote, "Two cheers for democracy; one because it admits variety, and two because it permits criticism. Two cheers are quite enough; there is no occasion to give three. Only Love, the Beloved Republic, deserves that.... I cannot believe that Christianity will ever cope with the present world-wide mess, and I think that such influence as it retains in modern society is due to its financial backing rather than to its spiritual appeal."

During World War I, while working in Egypt for the International Red Cross, Forster had a passionate liaison with a young tram conductor, Mohammed el Adl, whose premature death in 1922 greatly affected him. In 1930 he started a long-lasting relationship with a police constable, Bob Buckingham, one that continued even when Buckingham married in 1932 and lasted until Forster's death in the Buckinghams' home in 1970.

In addition to stating his views in "What I Believe," Forster wrote "An Alternative in Humanism" and "How I Lost My Faith," which were included in a Rationalist Press Association booklet. During his retirement in Cambridge, Forster was President of the Cambridge Humanist Society. Although he was not an active member, Forster knew of and worked with the British Humanist Association. (See entry for Edward Carpenter.) {CE; CL; *Gay and Lesbian Humanist*, Summer 1999; GL; TYD}

Forsyth, David (20th Century)

Forsyth, a freethinker, wrote *Psychology and Religion, A Study By A Medical Psychologist* (1935). {GS}

Fortlage, Karl (1806—1881)

Fortlage was a German psychologist, a professor of psychology at Berlin and then of philosophy at Jena. At first a follower of Hegel, he abandoned his system and attempted to blend the "transcendental Pantheism" of Fichte with empirical psychology. Fortlage rejected theism in his *Darstellung und Kritik der Beweise des Dasein Gottes* (1840). {RAT; RE}

Foscolo, Nicolo Ugo (1778—1827)

Fosco, an Italian poet, was an enthusiastic follower of Alfieri. In 1797 Fosco published a deistic tragedy, *Tieste*, for which he was called before the Venetian Inquisition. He greeted the French Revolution and Bonaparte, serving in the French Army. In 1809 he became professor of rhetoric at Pavia University, but the return of the Austrians drove him to Switzerland. In 1816 he settled in London. Foscolo's works were published in eleven volumes (1850—1859). {RAT}

Fosse, Bob (1927-1987)

Fosse, the dancer-choreographer-director, was not known to be a believer in the supernatural or in an afterlife. He won ten Ton awards for his stage work and his movies included "Sweet Charity," "Cabaret," and "All That Jazz."

At the opening of a revival of "Sweet Charity," Fosse was enroute to the theatre when he had a massive heart attack. As he would have wanted, the show went on. In his will he left $25,000 for sixty-six friends to "have dinner on me. They all have at one time or other during my life been very kind to me. I thank them." The humanist-like dinner was held in Central Park's Tavern on the Green in New York, and attending were such guests as novelist E. L. Doctorow, Liza Minnelli, Buddy Hackett, Dustin Hoffman, and Roy Scheider.

Foster, Abigail Kelley (1810—1887)

Foster was an American abolitionist and advocate of women's rights. After teaching in several Quaker schools, she began a crusade against slavery, becoming one of the first female lecturers before sexually mixed audiences. Her fellow churchgoers refused to take up the slavery issue, holding that each follower must follow his or her own divinely inspired directives. Foster, however, believed in passive resistance. When she refused to speak out within the church, the men at one point rose and carried her out. When they re-entered, she did also, and the women were so shocked by her actions that she was beaten as she was being carried out again. {CE; Carole Gray, "Nineteenth-Century Women of Freethought," *Free Inquiry*, Spring 1995}.

Foster, Alfred William (1886—1962)

Foster was an Australian rationalist, socialist, and pacifist who became Mr. Justice Foster, Deputy President of the Conciliation and Arbitration Commission. The Catholic *Advocate*, when a witness claimed he had told a boy there is "no hell, sonny," wanted him deported to Mexico or Russia, where he could "rail at religion without restraint." After all, they reasoned, the boy's mind might never recover from such a shock. However, the boy's mother, a Mrs. Ryan who said the *Advocate* had wrongly assumed by their name that they were Catholic, sided with Foster, ending the incident.

When the Rationalist Association was incorporated as a registered company in 1925, Foster became the first chairman, holding the position until 1935. In 1940 he became an Honorary Associate of the Rationalist Press Association of England. Sir John Barry spoke at Foster's secular ceremony, telling of Foster's courage, wisdom, and compassion through which he had achieved "the only immortality he would have desired." {SWW}

Foster, George Borman (1858—1918)

Foster was an ordained Baptist minister who taught philosophy at McMaster University in Canada and then at the University of Chicago starting in 1895. His *Finality of the Christian Religion* (1906) and *The Function of Religion in Man's Struggle for Existence* (1909) gave him the reputation of being a great teacher and a champion of freedom in religious thinking. Because of his concern with the problem of the objective validity of religious faith, and especially with the problem of the ontological reference of the God-idea, he started to move from a theistic supernaturalism to a humanistic naturalism.

However, his critics say, he confused many because he continued *emotionally* to use the God-idea which *intellectually* he thought had no ontological validity. As a result, states philosopher Hjalmar Johnson of Augustana Theological Seminary, Foster's thought has exercised a great influence upon the rise and development of "religious humanism" in America.

Foster, (Alicia Christian) Jodie (1962—)

Foster, after her graduation from Yale University, made her acting debut in the television show, "Mayberry, RFD" (1969). In addition to numerous other television shows, she has been in such movies as "Tom Sawyer" (1973); "Kansas City Bomber" (1972); "Alice Doesn't Live Here Any More" (1975); "Taxi Driver" (1976) (for which she was an Academy Award nomination); "Foxes" (1980); "Carny" (1980); "Stealing Home" (1988); and "The Accused" (1988). In 1991, she won an Oscar, as did Anthony Hopkins, for "Silence of the Lambs."

In 1997 she starred in "Contact," the movie based upon Carl Sagan's 1985 novel of the same name in which she played a radio astronomer dedicated to searching for clues to life beyond Earth. "Like Ellie in the movie," film critic Betsy Pickle of the *Knoxville News-Sentinel* reported, "Foster doesn't believe in a supreme spiritual being." Although saying she respects religious belief and has studied it, "As far as in my own life, I only have questions. Just as the character says in the movie, as a scientist, I'd have to say that there is no evidence. . . ." In fact, she added, she had never believed in God nor practiced a religion:

> It's only as I got older that I really got interested in it. I didn't have any religious background. My mother had a lot of religious background; my brothers and sisters did. But for some reason, I was the last in the family, and it was the '60s, and it just didn't trickle down.
>
> The only church I'd ever been into, I think, the only service that I've ever attended, was the cathedral of the Vatican–because you went to Rome, and you want to go in. And I think I've been to Notre Dame a few times because it's really pretty.

{CA; *The Freethinker*, November 1997}

Foster, Robert G. (20th Century)

Director of the Menninger Foundation's marriage counseling service and training program, Foster was a naturalistic humanist.

Foster, Stephen Symonds (1809—1881)

Foster, a freethinker, wrote *The Brotherhood of Thieves* (1886). He was husband of the American abolitionist, Abigail Kelley Foster. (He is not the gay composer, Stephen Foster (1826-1864), who wrote "O Susannah," "De Camptown Races," and "The Old Folks At Home." {GS}

Foucault, Michel (1926—1984)

Called by critic Alan Ryan the most famous intellectual figure in the world when he died, Foucault followed Jean-Paul Sartre in gaining the attention of those who were interested in philosophic-literary ideas. In *The Order of Things* (1966), Foucault pronounced "the death of Man," describing the individual as but a "rift in the order of things." His target was Marxists, and he held that the intellectual "spoke the truth to those who had yet to see it, in the name of those who were forbidden to speak the truth: he was conscience, consciousness, and eloquence." He also declared that biology did not exist in the eighteenth century because "life itself did not exist."

In *The Passion of Michel Foucault*, James Miller tells that Foucault's fellow students thought he was half mad, that he had attempted suicide when young, that he was under psychiatric care more than once. Miller emphasizes the Nietzschean strain in Foucault's life and work, adding that Foucault became an excellent director of studies at Uppsala's Maison Française, where he gave a post in the department to his lover, Daniel Defert. Defert was the one who inspired Foucault to look "more intellectual" by shaving his head.

Foucault later headed the philosophy section at a new university in Vincennes, leaving after enjoying anarchic battles with the riot police, for a position at the *Collège de France.* His *Discipline and Punish* (1975) helped him become a cult figure in the United States. In *Madness and Civilization* (1965; translated in 1970), Foucault detailed how within social practices are morally disturbing power relations. In *History of Sexuality* (1984), he discussed the self's relationship to itself, calling it "ethics." Foucault died of AIDS, having likely contracted the disease in San Francisco bathhouses. Although called an anti-humanist, Foucault is not generally accused of being pro-theist or pro-supernaturalist. He once referred to himself as being "neither a Hellenist nor a Latinist." (For references to Foucault's homosexuality, see *Queering the Renaissance* (1994), edited by Jonathan Goldberg.) {CE; GL}

Fouda, Farag (Died 1992)

Fouda, a distinguished secular thinker in Egypt, was assassinated in 1992 by Moslem extremists, according to Salman Rushdie in "The Struggle for the Soul of Islam" in *The New York Times* (11 July 1993). According to Rushdie, "We should understand that secularism is now the fanatics' most important target."

Fouillée, Alfred Jules Émile (1838—1912)

Fouillée was a French philosopher who was crowned by the Academy of Moral Sciences for two works on the philosophy of Plato and Socrates. His Sorbonne thesis, *Liberty and Determinism*, was attacked by Catholics. He was author of *History of Philosophy* (1875) and was considered, with Taine, Ribot, and Renan, the principal representative of French philosophy of his time. His system was known as that of *idèes-forces*. In his attempt to reconcile idealism and naturalism, Fouillée held that ideas are themselves forces. {BDF; CE; RAT; RE}

Foulkes, Paul (1923—)

During a National Secular Society lecture, Foulkes, a philosopher, outlined five criteria he recommended for the organization: no party lines, no absolutes, no censorship, no sacred books, and no sacred names.

FOUNDING FATHERS

The "founding fathers" were members in 1787 of the convention that drafted the United States Constitution. Although religious fundamentalists erroneously state they were Christians, in reality they were highly literate individuals whose views on liberal democracy were shaped largely by the works of Montesquieu and other French Enlightenment philosophers, as well as their English counterparts John Locke and Thomas Hobbes. (See entries for Montesquieu, Locke, and Hobbes.)

Fourier, François Marie Charles (1772—1837)

A major French social philosopher, Fourier developed what can be described as a socialistic utopia. His *Théorie des quatre mouvements* (1808) developed the idea that man could create a world in which social harmony could exist. To do this, an economic group composed of 1,630 people and called a "phalanx" would live in a phalanstery, or community building, and work would be divided among people according to their natural inclinations.

One of his disciples, Victor Prosper Considérant, according to critic Julie Martin, had a strong impact on Colette's mother, Sido. Considérant thought "that the free expression of every passion—homosexuality, polygamy, unfettered sexual drives—would create social harmony and bring about a new social order." He tried to establish Fourierism in Texas, and others interested in his ideas were Albert Brisbane and Horace Greeley. The Transcendentalists' Brook Farm for a time was Fourierist, although the most successful of the communities was the North American Phalanx at Red Bank, New Jersey. Fourier himself was an independent, a non-Christian, one who was not an anti-clerical atheist and one who believed in the transmigration of souls. He further believed in a divine Providence and claimed to have discovered the "plan of God" for man, but like Owen he had an unbounded and heterodox faith in human goodness and perfectibility. {BDF; CE; JMR; Julie Martin, *The New York Times Book Review*, 14 February 1999; RAT; RE; TRI}

Fourier, Jean Baptiste Joseph [Baron] (1768—1830)

Fourier, an eminent French mathematician and physicist, was known for his researches on heat and on numerical equations. He originated Fourier's theorem on vibratory motion. Fourier accompanied Napoleon to Egypt. Although hated by the clergy because of his scientific triumphs and persecuted under the restored royalty, he was not prevented from being admitted to the French Academy as well as the British Royal Society and other learnèd bodies. {JM; RAT; RE}

FOURIERISM

Fourierism was an early 19th-century system for social reform as advocated by Charles Fourier. He proposed that small self-sustaining communal groups be organized for society's good. (See entry for François Marie Charles Fourier.)

Fowler, Carrie (20th Century)

Fowler, while a student at the State University of New York at Albany, was one of the founding members of Campus Freethought Alliance. {*International Humanist News*, December 1996}

Fowler, Jeanne (20th Century)

Fowler is the Atheist Coalition representative to the Atheist Alliance, having succeeded Howard Kreisner in 1996. {*Freethought Observer*, November-December 1996}

Fowler, Jeaneanne (20th Century)

Fowler, a research fellow at the University of Wales College in Newport, wrote *Humanism: Beliefs and Practices* (1999), in which she describes the system of belief based without reference to the supernatural.

In a review, Nicolas Walter (*The Freethinker*, November 1999), noted the work's "fulsome forewords by Hermann Bondi and Paul Kurtz, leading figures in two of the largest humanist organisations in the English-speaking world" and its attention more to "centralist humanism" than to the more militant forms of freethought "as represented by the National Secular Society and the Rationalist Press Association." Walter found, however, that the work "deserves our gratitude for trying so hard to explain what we are up to." More favorable views have been expressed by officials of the British and American humanist groups. Fowler has written a book on Hinduism and reportedly is writing one on Taoism.

Fowles, John (1926-)

Fowles is an English novelist whose works combine psychological probings—chiefly of sex and love—with an interest in the social and philosophical context of human behavior. *The Collector* (1963) was about a shy man who, in a hapless search for love, kidnaps a girl and keeps her captive. *The French Lieutenant's Woman* (1969) parodied early novelistic devices and described the social mores of Victorian England. He also wrote *The Magus* (1966); *The Ebony Tower* (1974); *Daniel Martin* (1977); *Mantissa* (1982), and *A Maggot*(1985). Fowles was nominated for the 1999 Nobel Prize in Literature but lost to Günter Grass.

In a review of *Wormholes* (1998), *The New York Times Book Review* commented that "Religion is one of several subjects (environmentalism is another) for which Fowles retires elegance in favor of the bludgeon. 'Being an atheist,' he tells us, 'is a matter not of moral choice, but of human obligation.' " {CA}

Fox, Avril (1917—)

In 1965, the British Humanist Association helped to form TRACK. Fox and some independent secularists formed COSMO, both of which groups advocate radio and television freedom. {GS}

Fox, Charles James (1749—1806)

Fox, an orator and British statesman, upon being dismissed by George III as lord of the treasury, attacked the government's policy in North America. During the War of Independence, he defiantly wore the colors of the Americans in the House of Commons. A bitter opponent of William Pitt, he favored the French Revolution and opposed British intervention in the French Revolutionary Wars, greeting the fall of the Bastille as "one of the greatest and best events in history."

Fox also argued for the political rights of Roman Catholics as well as dissenters, and he is remembered as a great champion of liberty and an enemy of slavery. According to A. Benn, Fox was an atheist at a time when only Godwin and Bentham dared to admit such. Lord Holland, his nephew, confirmed that Fox was "no believer in religion" and, although he allowed his wife to have prayers when he was dying, he took no notice and said that he "did not like to pretend any sentiments he did not entertain." {CE; HAB; JM; RAT; RE}

Fox, Elizabeth Vassale [Lady Holland] (1770—1845)

Fox, the wife of the third Baron Holland, was described by Greville in *Memoris* as "a social light which illuminated and adorned England, and even Europe, for half a century." An atheist like her famous uncle, she was known, Greville adds, "to be wholly destitute of religious opinions." {JM; RE}

Fox, George (1835—1914)

Fox, a rationalist and parliamentarian, has been described in Australia as "the father of organized Rationalism in Queensland." The Queensland Rationalist and Ethical Society had almost one hundred members at the time of his death. {SWW}

Fox, George M. (20th Century)

Fox, a freethinker, wrote *The Vanishing Gods* (1984). {GS}

Fox, George T. (20th Century)

A freethinker, Fox wrote *Priestly Celibacy Exposed* (c. 1910). {GS}

Fox, Henry [First Baron Holland] (1705—1774)

Fox, the father of C. J. Fox, was an English statesman, for many years the leader of the House of Commons. Lord Chesterfield said he "had no fixed principles either of religion or morality," implying he detested Fox. The Chalmers *Dictionary* states that Fox "was an excellent husband and he possessed in abundance the milk of human kindness." {JM; RAT; RE}

Fox, Henry Richard Vassale [Third Baron Holland] (1773—1840)

A distinguished politician, Fox fought for Liberal reforms and warmly defended the Greek and Spanish rebels against feudalism. Holland House was the chief center in London of heresy as well as of beauty and wit, notes McCabe, who quotes the Rev. Sydney Smith on Fox: "There never existed in any human being a better heart, or one more purified from the bad passions, more abounding in charity and compassion, and which seemed to be so created as a refuge to the helpless and oppressed." {JM; RE}

Fox, Jane (20th Century)

In 1994, Fox was named editor-designate of *Scottish Humanist* (11A Strathkinness High Road, St. Andrews, Fife KY16 9UA, Scotland), succeeding Eric Stockton and commencing in 1995. {*Freethought History*, #24, 1997}

Fox, Nancy L. (20th Century)

An Oregon secular humanist, Fox was daughter of a missionary in China. In "True Religion and the 'Mishkids'" (*Free Inquiry*, Fall 1998), she told how in order to rid herself of her father's influence she "flew the coop." When in his nineties her father, "blind to the void in our relationship" that his religionism had caused, pleaded for her to visit him at his nursing home, she replied, "Not now, Father, too busy. Some other time." She added, "I'm not proud of that response. And never again did I see that stranger. Soon after, he died. His ensuing epitaphs? Rave reviews nationwide." Many freethinkers have experienced similar situations in which they have grown out of the religion "into which they were born."

Fox, Ray (20th Century)

Fox in Britain is active with the Wiltshire Humanists.

Fox, Robin Lane (1946—)

Fox is a teacher of ancient history at the University of Oxford. He wrote *Pagans and Christians* (1987). In *The Unauthorized Version, Truth and Fiction in the Bible* (1992), he shows that the Bible is replete with falsification and error, can therefore not be the "word of God," but is an important collection containing human comments about existence. In the book's preface, Fox explains, "I write as an atheist, but there are Christian and Jewish scholars whose versions [of the bible] would be far more radical than mine. They will find this historian's view conservative, even old-fashioned, but there are times when atheists are loyal friends of the truth." {CA}

Fox, William Johnson (1786—1864)

The South Place Ethical Society originated as a universalist Baptist congregation in the late eighteenth century. It had become a Unitarian chapel by the time of Fox's ministry (1817—1853). Moncure Conway followed Fox, ministering to the Society from 1864 to 1885 and moving it in the direction of religious humanism. Originally, Fox had been a Congregationalist, then became a Unitarian. One of his first published sermons was on behalf of toleration for deists at the time of the Carlile prosecutions in 1819. He advanced from the acceptance of miracles to their complete rejection. A prominent worker for radicalism, he contributed to the *Westminster Review*, *Weekly Dispatch*, and *Daily News*. His works, which include spirited *Letters to the Working Classes*, and a philosophical statement of *Religious Ideas*, were published in twelve volumes (1865—1868). {BDF; *Freethought History* #18, 1996; FUK; RAT; RE; VI; TRI}

Fragell, Levi (1939-)

A leading Norwegian humanist, Fragell after receiving his M.A. in comparative religion worked in education, journalism, and public relations. When seventeen, however, he had started his professional life as a preacher in a Pentecostal church.

Fragell was President of the Norwegian Humanist Association (1976-1981), its Secretary General (1982-1991), and Editor from 1976 to 1997 of its *Human-Etikk* (later *The Humanist*). The Association, which was founded in 1956, has since 1976 increased its membership to 60,000 from 1,700 paying members.

After serving as Vice-President of the International Humanist and Ethical Union (IHEU), he became President in 1998. Fragell is contributing editor to *Free Inquiry* and is on the editorial board of *International Humanist.* He has taken part in all IHEU congresses since the one in London in 1978.

In 1996, he and sixteen Norwegian humanists attended the fourth World Atheist Conference in Vijayawada, India. He also attended the 1996 Humanist World Congress held in Mexico City, participating on a panel which discussed philosophic humanism in the cyber-age. In 1997, following the meeting of IHEU board of directors meeting, he spoke at the annual humanist lunch in London and also was featured speaker on the occasion of Humanist Days in Finland. Fragell signed Humanist Manifesto 2000.

His e-mail addresses:
<fragell@human.no> and <lfragell@online.no>. {*Free Inquiry*, Winter 1990-91; HNS2; *International Humanist News*, December 1996}

FRANCE

Although two-thirds of the French describe themselves as Catholic, an estimated one in ten goes to mass regularly, according to *The Economist* (30 March 1996). The *cinq à sept*, when businessmen and businesswomen slip out of the office for a secret visit to their loves, is believed to be common, the magazine's findings continued. An estimated 89% of French men and 84% of French women claim to be happy with their sex lives. Other polls show that 72% of men and 86% of women claim always to have been faithful to their spouses. Also, that 93% of the French say they "have confidence" in the family and 89% hope it will remain. However, an estimated 2,200,000 couples live together out of wedlock, seven times as many as twenty years ago in a 1960 study. Only a few (7%) of the French regard "living in sin" as morally wrong. More than one in three of all French babies are now born out of wedlock, one of the highest rates in Europe (after Iceland, Sweden, Denmark, and Norway). Further, outside traditionalist Catholic circles illegitimacy no longer carries a stigma. Although two out of every five marriages in France end in divorce, cohabiting couples have been found to be more than five times as likely to separate as married ones. (See entries for French Humanists and Intellectuals.)

France, (Jacques) Anatole (1844—1924)

Anatole France's *Penguin Island* (1908) has a nearsighted priest baptizing a large group, regretfully finding they are penguins—the trouble his act causes to the alarmed authorities in an animal-less Heaven makes this allegorical and satirical novel diabolically provocative. Although he received the Nobel Prize in Literature, all his works were prohibited by the Vatican in 1922. An atheist, France never accepted the historicity of Jesus. In fact, he once wrote favorably about Pontius Pilate. Philosophically, according to William F. Ryan, he stood somewhere between Epicurean thinking and contemporary existentialism "and was, in fact, among the first to pronounce the human condition and the state of the universe *absurd*." In contrast to St. John Chrysostom, who said, "Virginity stands as far above marriage as the heavens above the earth." France held that of all the sexual aberrations, chastity is the strangest. "If fifty million people say a foolish thing, it is still a foolish thing," France once observed.

In a letter to the International Congress of Freethinkers at Paris in 1905, France wrote, "The thoughts of the gods are not more unchangeable than those of the men who interpret them. They advance–but they always lag behind the thoughts of men. . . . The Christian God was once a Jew. Now he is an anti-Semite." {CE; CL; EU, William F. Ryan; ILP; JM; RAT; RE; TRI; TYD}

Franceschini, Mark (Died 1992)

Franceschini was the partner-in-life of atheist activist Don Sanders, with whom he popularized the American Gay and Lesbian Atheists association and edited its publication. In 1995, when Sanders also died of AIDS, cremains of both were mixed and interred in an undisclosed place to insure that Franceschini's Roman Catholic parents would be unable to remove the remains for a religious ceremony by the same church from which he sought excommunication because of his distaste for its doctrines.

Franch, Michael (20th Century)

Franch, a student and teacher of history, entered Ethical Culture leadership in Baltimore in 1975, edited *ethical society* initially for the AEU (as a more Ethical movement-centered, religious, and economical publication than *The Humanist*; the publication was co-sponsored with the AHA from 1969 to 1977). He has since completed his doctorate with free-lance employment in 1984. (See entry for Ethical Culture.) {EU, Howard B. Radest}

Franchere, Hoyt G. (20th Century)

With T. F. O'Donnell, Franchere wrote *Harold Frederic* (1961). {FUS}

Franchi, Anne-Marie (20th Century)

Franchi, from France, is on the editorial board of *International Humanist*. At the Tenth International Humanist and Ethical Union (IHEU) World Congress held in Buffalo (1988), and Franchi spoke at the Eleventh held in Brussels. She is a Vice-President of the European Humanist Federation.

"Franchi, Ausonio" (Born 1821)

Franchi was the pen name of Francesco Cristoforo Bonavino, an Italian ex-priest. Ordained in 1844, he became skeptical because of the practice of the confessional and quit the job for philosophy, having ceased in 1849 to believe in church dogmas. His principle work is *The Philosophy of the Italian Schools* (1852).

From 1854 to 1857, he established *La Razione* (Raison) and *Il Libero Pensiero* at Turin as well as became an active organizer of anticlerical societies. In 1866 he published a criticism of positivism and, in 1868, became professor of philosophy in the Academy of Milan. {BDF}

Francis, Convers (1795—1863)

A Unitarian minister in Watertown, Massachusetts, Francis encouraged the young Theodore Parker but disagreed with Parker's later advocacy of absolute religion. Francis supported Emerson and joined the Transcendental Club, gaining the trust of both the moderate Unitarians and the younger transcendentalists who began to go beyond the Unitarian theological synthesis in the later 1830s. {U&U}

Francis, Samuel (18th Century)

A physician, Dr. Francis was an 18th century atheist who argued his atheism eloquently. Berman speculates that Francis might have been a pseudonym, for virtually nothing is known about the man. But if it was not, Samuel Francis, M.D., "must have been a daring man to sign his name to such a radical work as *Watson Refuted* (1796)," which was a strong attack against a Bishop Watson, "even granting that he never explicitly professes himself an atheist." {BDF; FUK; HAB}

Francis, William Boyd (20th Century)

An Alaskan actor, Boyd enjoys appearing in the person of Robert Ingersoll at occasions such as the 22nd annual National Convention of American Atheists in 1992. He dresses the part and plays the role, citing the actual words of the famed agnostic.

Franck, Adolph (1809—1893)

A French philosopher, Franck was a member of the Institut and was professor of law and also classical languages at the Collège de France. A rationalist and a Jew, Franck edited the *Dictionnaire des sciences philosophiques* (6 volumes, 1843—1849). {RAT}

Franckenstein, Ian (20th Century): See entry for Kay Boyle.

Francoeur, Robert (20th Century)

Francoeur is on the editorial board of San Diego's freethinker magazine, *The Truth Seeker*. He is author of *Utopian Motherhood* (1970).

François de Neufchateau, Nicolas Louis (1750—1828)

Count François de Neufchateau was a French statesman, poet, and academician. In his youth he became secretary to Voltaire, who regarded him as his successor. He favored the Revolution and was elected to the Legislative Assembly in 1791, becoming President of the Senate from 1814 to 1816. As a member of the Directory in 1797, he circulated d'Holbach's *Contagion Sacrée.* {BDF; RAT; RE}

Franczyk, Thomas (20th Century)

A founding co-editor of the *Secular Humanist Bulletin*, Franczyk is also co-founder of Catholics Anonymous. In addition, he is a Secular Humanist Mentor of the Council for Secular Humanism and an editorial associate of *Free Inquiry*.

Frank, Henry (20th Century)

Frank, a freethinker, wrote *The Doom of Dogma and the Dawn of Truth* (1901). {GS; FUS}

Frank, Jerome D(avid) (1909—)

Prof. Frank of the United States presided over the Fifth International Humanist and Ethical Union World Congress held in Boston (1970). He is author of *Sanity and Survival in the Nuclear Age* (1982).

Frank, Philipp (1884—1966)

Frank has been a member of the American Humanist Association. He was author of *Science and the Modern Mind* (1958). {HNS}

Frank, Waldo (1889—1967)

Frank was a radical critic of United States society, one who was active in left-wing causes from the 1930s to the 1960s. He wrote *Our America* (1919) and *South American Journey* (1943).

Asked about humanism, he responded to the present author,

> I have a somewhat negative attitude toward the contemporary use and usefulness of the term Humanism. It meant something indeed in the Renaissance and after, when men who were Christians, by faith or by culture only, began to modulate their values from the domain of the Supernal to the domain of man. Humanism was a perfect instrument for differentiating the philosophies of such men as Descartes and Spinoza and Leibnitz, the arts of such men as Rabelais and Shakespeare, from the otherworldly tonalities of the Scholastics, the transcendental mystics, and the Byzantine or pre-Raphaelite painters.
>
> "But today? The very fact that Catholics, atheists, Platonists, Marxists, Pragmatists, et al., can all claim to be humanists reveals, it seems to me, the vulnerability of the term. There is much in the naturalist humanism of Spinoza, in the theological humanism of Aquinas, in the mathematical humanism of Kepler and Bruno, which appeals to me–and which has nourished me. But there has been a pendulum swing since the modulation from the transcendental to the human. What is needed now is a *definition* of the human in terms beyond what the word humanism connotes in most of its modern uses. This definition will entail new knowledge of the cosmic and new methods for achieving this knowledge and making it viable. I doubt if the leaders in this search will have much use for the term Humanism. It belongs to history, rather than to contemporary methodology.
>
> {WAS, 14 August 1956}

Franke, Egon (20th Century)

Franke is a Member of Parliament and Minister for German Affairs (Germany). He presided over the Eighth International Humanist and Ethical Union (IHEU) World Congress held in Hannover (1982).

Frankel, Charles (1917—1979)

Frankel, who was a professor of philosophy at Columbia University, wrote of history and value theory. Like John Dewey, his emphasis was on practical philosophy, not metaphysical speculation. His works include *The Faith of Reason* (1948), *The Case for Modern Man* (1956), and *Pleasures of Philosophy* (1972). Frankel's outlook was entirely naturalistic, and he reviewed books for *The Humanist*.

In 1988 the Charles Frankel Prize in the Humanities was established and is given to five Americans "who have made contributions to cultural life by bringing the humanities to a wider audience." Nominations are solicited by the endowment and narrowed to a list of finalists by the National Council on the Humanities, an advisory board to the agency. The chairman of the endowment was Sheldon Hackney who, in 1996, chose as recipients novelist Rita Dove; historian Doris Kearns; political philosopher Daniel Kemmis; scholar of Hispanic literature Arturo Madrid; and television journalist Bill Moyers. {CL}

Frankel, Jeff (20th Century)

Frankel is active with the Decatur, Illinois, *Independent Atheist.* (See entry for Illinois Atheists, Freethinkers, Humanists.) {FD}

Frankland, Edward [Sir] (1825—1899)

"An exceptionally brilliant and accomplished man of science," according to the *Dictionary of National Biography*, Frankland received several gold medals for his discoveries in chemistry. He was a member of the French, Berlin, Bavarian, Petrograd, Bohemian, and Swedish Academies of Science. In his autobiography, *Sketches from the Life of E. Frankland*, Frankland explains that he discarded Christianity and was a complete agnostic. {JM; RAT; RE}

Franklin, Benjamin (1706—1790)

Deist Franklin irked the theists with his common sense philosophy devoid of supernaturalism and religiosity. "Lighthouses are more helpful than churches," Franklin declared. Joyfully pursuing French women while being the United States minister to France, he set a pace that Lafayette and Thomas Jefferson found difficult to match. William Franklin, the last royal governor of New Jersey, was his illegitimate son.

To President Ezra Stiles of Yale University, Franklin in a 1790 letter just before his death wrote,

> Here is my creed. I believe in one God, Creator of the Universe. That he governs it by his Providence. That he ought to be worshiped. That the most acceptable service we render to him is doing good to his other children. That the soul of man is immortal, and will be treated with justice in another life. . . .
>
> As to Jesus of Nazareth, my opinion of whom you particularly desire, I think his system of morals and his religion, as he left them to us, the best the world ever saw or is like to see; but I apprehend it has received various corrupting changes, and I have, with most of the present Dissenters in England, some doubts as to his divinity; though it is a question I do not dogmatize upon, having never studied it, and think it needless to busy myself with it now, when I expect soon an opportunity of knowing the truth with less trouble. . . . I have ever let others enjoy their religious sentiments, without reflecting on them for those who appeared to me unsupportable and even absurd.

In 1728, he had written his views in *Articles of Belief and Acts of Religion*. Franklin, who quit the Presbyterian Church and was a deist, according to McCabe, was a member of and financial contributor to the First Unitarian Church in London.

Many consider his *Autobiography* (1771—1778), which covers only his early years, one of the finest examples of the genre in any language. His proposal for a one-chamber Congress was not accepted—the sole example of unicameralism in the United States is Nebraska.

Turgot summed up Franklin's services: *Eripuit coelo fulmen, sceptrumque tyrannis.* [He wrested the thunderbolt from heaven and the sceptre from kings.] A different view was held by theologians: Franklin by developing the lightning rod denied to deity an avenue of punishment for the wicked.

A different view was also held by his political enemies, who knew of his early devotion to England and the king, his being twenty-six years older than Washington and almost fifty older than Madison and Hamilton, his aristocratic notions (he proposed at the Constitutional Convention that all members of the executive branch in the new federal government serve without pay), and his willingly spending over one-third of his lifetime outside his country.

At the age of eighty-four, Franklin was in great pain and left the world willingly and peacefully. His daughter was with him and said she hoped he would get better and live many more years. "I hope not," he retorted, escaping pain only by the use of opium. Later that day, April 17, 1790, he was advised to move on his bed in order to breathe more easily.

His last words were, "A dying man can do nothing easy." (See entry for Native Americans–Ethnic Cleansing.) {BDF; CE; CL; EU, A. Owen Aldridge; FUK; FUS; HNS2; JM; RAT; RE; TRI; TYD; U; UU}

Franklin, Charlotte (20th Century)

Franklin, a rationalist, wrote "Religion and the Younger Woman" in *New Humanist* (November 1989) and a review, "Sisters in Arms: Catholic Nuns through Two Millenia," in *New Humanist* (November 1997).

Franklin, Robert D. (20th Century)

A humanist who was director of the Toledo Public Library, Franklin is a former President of the United World Federalists of Toledo.

Fransham, John (1730—1810)

A native of Norwich, Fransham became a teacher of mathematics, renounced the Christian religion, professed paganism, and wrote several treatises in favor of disbelief. {BDF; RAT}

Frantz, Mary and **John** (20th Century)

The Frantzes are Wisconsin physicians and philanthropists whose contributions have funded the Skepticism and Paranormal Library at the Center for Inquiry." {Mary Frantz, "The Ultimate Gift," *Free Inquiry*, Fall 1996}

Fraser, Caroline (20th Century)

Fraser, author of *God's Perfect Child* (1999), wrote a book exposing Mary Baker Eddy and the Church of Christ, Scientist. Attacked by Eddy followers, Fraser remarked in *The New York Times* (12 September 1999):

> Thousands of people believe all manner of things, testifying to abduction by space aliens and seeing Jesus in oil stains and tortillas; however sincere the believers and however large their numbers, their belief is not evidence of accuracy. Moreover, the preventable deaths of Christian Science children are facts, not "tales," and they lie at the heart of the moral failure of Christian Science.
>
> Dostoyevsky once posed the question: "Imagine that you are creating a fabric of human destiny with the object of making men happy in the end, giving them peace and rest at last, but that it was essential and inevitable to torture to death only one tiny creature…and to found that edifice on its unavenged tears, would you consent to be the architect on those conditions?" Mary Baker Eddy and her followers did consent, and the children of Christian Scientists have been paying the price ever since.

Frauenstädt, Christian Martin Julius (1813—1879)

A philosopher and disciple of Schopenhauer, Frauenstädt was made his literary executor by Schopenhauer. Also a pessimist, Frauenstädt wrote *Letters on Natural Religion* (1858) and *Letters on the Philosophy of Schopenhauer.* {BDF; RAT}

Frazer, Felix J. (20th Century)

In the 1950s, Frazer was an editorial associate on *Humanist World Digest, A Quarterly of Liberal Religion.*

Frazer, James George [Sir] (1854—1941)

Frazer's *Golden Bough* (1890) and *Totemism and Exogamy* (1910) supplied so many anthropological examples of religious practices in various parts of the world that what previously had been thought to be peculiarities of the sacred Christian cult now were seen to be variations of world practices. As a result, the problem was no longer whether Christianity was a supernatural revelation–it was to determine if the central narrative was historical in any degree whatsoever. Among other facts he provided were that in China, "if the God does not give rain they will threaten and beat him; sometimes they publicly depose him from the rank of deity."

Anthropologists have been quick to point out that many primitive peoples were sometimes unafraid of their gods, that sometimes they beat their fetishes to secure attention or they punched them in the face to illustrate their dissatisfaction. Frazer's comparative studies of magic, folklore, and religion showed similarities between primitive and Christian cultures. McCabe notes that Frazer once scolded him for describing him as a Rationalist, but that in the second edition of his *Golden Bough* Frazer acknowledged that his work "strikes at the foundations of beliefs in which the hopes and aspirations of humanity through long ages have sought a refuge."

According to McCabe, the Dean of the Chapel of Trinity College said after Frazer's death, "He was not an atheist. I would say perhaps that he held his judgment in suspense." In other words, adds McCabe, he was an agnostic, but the Dean gave him a religious funeral. {CE; JM; JMR; RAT; RE; TRI}

Frazier, Douglas (20th Century)

When he signed Humanist Manifesto II, Frazier was a leader of the American Ethical Union. A veteran Unitarian-Universalist minister, he was a Leader of the Los Angeles Ethical Culture Society (1958—1964) and that of Bergen County, New Jersey (1964—1968). (See entry for Ethical Culture.) {HM 2}

Frazier, Kendrick (20th Century)

Frazier, editor of *Skeptical Inquirer*, is a leader of the Committee for the Scientific Investigation of Claims of the Paranormal. In 1995, he received the Humanist Pioneer Award by the American Humanist Association. He wrote *The Hundredth Monkey and Other Paradigms of the Paranormal* (1991).

Frederic [Empress]: See entry for Maud Mary Alice.

Frederic, Harold (1856—1898)

Frederic, who at age nineteen was a reporter on the *Utica Observer* and at age twenty-two became its editor, later became the London correspondent of *The New York Times.* A novelist, he wrote *The Copperhead* (1893), describing the intolerant attacks upon Abner Beach, a New York farmer who opposed Abolition at a time when that movement was sweeping the North during the Civil War.

His most popular novel was *The Damnation of Theron Ware* (1896), which described a Methodist minister's "fall" and which has been praised highly a century later by fellow novelist Joyce Carol Oates. {FUS}

Frederick, J. George (20th Century)

Frederick wrote *Humanism as a Way of Life* (1930). {GS}

Frederick, Scott (20th Century)

Frederick, a freethinker, wrote *Religious Intolerance and Secularist Opposition in America* (1975). {GS}

Frederick II [Holy Roman Emperor] (1194—1250)

Called by Wheeler "the greatest man of the thirteenth century and founder of the Renaissance," Frederick II was elected to the throne in 1210. He promoted learning, science, and art, founded the Universities of Vienna and Naples, had the works of Aristotle and Averroës translated, and was the patron of many of the able men of his time.

For his resistance to the tyranny of the Church, he was twice excommunicated (by Pope Innocent III and Innocent IV). In 1228, he expelled Pope Gregory IX from Rome. Wheeler wrote that "for some heretical words in his letter, in which he associates the names of Christ, Moses, and Mohammed, he was reported author of the famous work *De Tribus Impostoribus*. He addressed a series of philosophical questions to Ibn Sabin, a Moslem doctor. He is said to have called the Eucharist *truffaista*, and is credited also with the saying, "Ignorance is the mother of devotion." In 1225 Frederick married Yolande and claimed the crown of Jerusalem. At Jaffa he made a treaty by which Jerusalem, Nazareth, and Bethlehem were surrendered to the Christians, with the Mosque of Omar being left to the Muslims. In 1229 he crowned himself King of Jerusalem. In 1245, after excommunicating Frederick and declaring him deposed, Innocent IV himself fled to Lyons. Meanwhile, the election in 1246 of an anti-king to Conrad IV, Frederick's youngest son, plunged Germany into civil war. Although the war in Italy turned in Frederick's favor in 1250, in December the king died of dysentery. With Frederick II's rule the great days of the German empire ended and the rise of states in Italy had begun. Frederick II is often described as having been one of the most arresting figures of the Middle Ages. (See entry for Epicurus.) {BDF; CE; FO; JM; RE}

Frederick II [The Great] (1712—1786)

The first modern freethinking king, Frederick the Great of Prussia was despised by his tyrannical father, Frederick William I, who also was unhappy with his son's interest in French art, literature, and a Prussian lieutenant, Hans von Katte. When the somewhat effeminate Frederick and Hans tried to escape to England, the two were arrested and imprisoned. The king then forced his son to watch as the twenty-five-year-old Katte was beheaded. Afterwards, the king arranged his son's marriage to Elizabeth of Brunswick-Bevern, but they separated soon afterwards and Frederick continued to show no interest in women. Moving to Rheinsberg, he wrote *Anti-Machiavel*, an idealistic refutation of Machiavelli. Also, he struck up a long correspondence with Voltaire.

According to A. L. Rowse in *Homosexuals in History* (1977), Frederick "didn't care what anybody said or thought about him. He was a cynic on this score about others as about himself; he had told Voltaire: 'We've got here a cardinal and several bishops, some of whom make love before and others behind–good fellows who persecute nobody.' On observing a soldier he recognized, fettered in irons: 'Why is that excellent soldier in irons?' 'For bestiality with his horse.' To the officer in charge: 'Fool–don't put him in irons: Put him in the infantry.' "

Upon his father's death and as soon as he became king, Frederick made Katte's father a field-marshal. To the disinterested, Frederick became known as an outstanding leader, one who abolished torture and increased religious tolerance, saying "every man must get to heaven his own way." According to Robertson, Frederick was the great deist king of the deist age, although he disapproved of his morals and states that as a ruler he did not act up to the ideals of the school of Voltaire. Called an "enlightened despot," according to the *Columbia Encyclopedia*, "he instituted important legal and penal reforms, set up trade monopolies to create new industries, forwarded education, and accomplished internal improvements such as drainage projects, roads, and canals. Though he improved the lot of his own serfs, the nobility had more control over their peasants after his reign than before. He was tolerant in religious matters, personally professing atheism to his intimates. Cold and curt, he relaxed only during his famous midnight suppers at Sans Souci, his residence at Potsdam. There he was surrounded by a group of educated men, mostly French, that included, at times, Voltaire (who broke with him in 1753 but who later resumed his friendship from a safe distance), d'Alembert, La Mettrie, and Maupertuis. . . . He failed to appreciate such men as Lessing and Goethe, who were among his most ardent admirers."

Upon Voltaire's death, Frederick pronounced his eulogium before the Berlin Academy, denouncing "the imbecile priests," and declaring that "the best destiny they can look for is that they and their vile artifices will remain forever buried in the darkness of oblivion, while the fame of Voltaire will increase from age to age, and transmit his name to immortality."

"That he was a Deist, the protector of Voltaire and other Deists," wrote McCabe, "even a Jesuit has never questioned." In Dante's *Inferno*, Frederick II and more than a thousand followers of Epicurus are in Hell. To avoid just such a happenstance, one of Frederick's subjects, solicitous about his immortal soul, sent him a letter full of pious advice. "Let this," he said, "be answered civilly; the intention of the writer good." Shortly afterwards, according to Carlyle, "For the most part he was unconscious, never more than half conscious. As the wall clock above his head struck eleven, he asked: "What o'clock?" "Eleven," answered they. "At four," murmured he, "I will arise." One of his dogs sat on its stool near him; about midnight he noticed it shivering for cold: "Throw a quilt over it," said or beckoned he; that, I think, was his last completely conscious utterance. Afterwards, in a severe choking fit, getting at last rid of the phlegm, he said, "We are on the hill, we shall go better now." {BDF; CE; EU; FO; JM; JMR; JMRH; RE; TYD}

Fredin, Nils Edvard (Born 1857)

Fredin, a Swedish writer, published translations of modern poets and Col. Ingersoll's writing. The Swedish Academy in 1880 awarded him first prize for an original poem. {BDF}

Fredkin, Ed (20th Century)

Fredkin is a computer scientist, a college dropout who at the age of thirty-four became a full professor at the Massachusetts Institute of Technology. Robert Wright's *Three Scientists and Their Gods* (1988) mentions Fredkin's outlook: "I guess what I'm saying is: I don't have any religious belief. I don't believe there is a God. I don't believe in Christianity or Judaism or anything like that, okay? I'm not an atheist. . . . . I'm not an agnostic. . . . I'm just in a simple state. I don't know what there is or might be." {CA}

Fredson, Patrick (20th Century)

Fredson has debunked the idea of miracles for *The American Rationalist* (March-April, 1995). He often writes for the journal.

FREE INQUIRY

Free Inquiry (Box 664, Amherst, NY 14226-0664) is a journal of secular humanism published quarterly by the Council for Secular Humanism at its headquarters located at 1310 Sweet Home Road in Amherst. Chairman of the editorial board is Timothy J. Madigan, who served as its editor for years.

Paul Kurtz is editor-in-chief; Lewis Vaughn is editor; Andrea Szalanski is managing editor; Matt Cherry is deputy editor; senior editors are Vern L. Bullough, Richard Dawkins, Thomas W. Flynn, Martin Gardner, James A. Haught, Gerald A. Larue, and Taslima Nasrin; associate editors are Molleen Matsumura, Wendy McElroy, and Norm R. Allen Jr.; frontlines editor is Chris Mooney; contributing editors are Jo Ann Boydston, Paul Edwards, Albert Ellis, Roy P. Fairfield, Charles Faulkner, Antony Flew, Levi Fragell, Adolf Grünbaum, Marvin Kohl, Thelma Lavine, Joe Nickell, Lee Nisbet, J.J.C. Smart, Svetozar Stojanovic, Thomas Szasz, and Richard Taylor; book review editor is Timothy Binga; editorial associates are Lois Porter and Warren Allen Smith; cartoonist is Don Addis.

The journal is the leading publication of secular humanism in the United States. E-mail: <freeinquiry@secularhumanism.org>. On the Web: <http://www.secularhumanism.org>. (See entry for Secular Humanism. For a critique of the magazine, see entry for Literature and Secular Humanism.)

FREE INQUIRY NETWORK

The Free Inquiry Network is at Box 2668, Glen Ellyn, Illinois 60138. On the Web: <http://www.freeinquirynetwork.com>.

FREE MIND

Free Mind (235 Coffman Union, 300 Washington Ave SE, Minneapolis, Minnesota 55455) is the newsletter and forum of the University of Minnesota Atheists and Humanists. On the Web: <http://www.umn.edu/nihome/m207humanist/>.

FREE MIND

Free Mind (7 Harwood Drive, PO Box 146, Amherst, NY 14226) is the membership newsletter of the American Humanist Association. E-mail: <humanism@juno.com>.

FREE MIND

A monthly, *Free Mind* is at 4116 Candlewood Drive S.E., Lacey, Washington 98503-4422.

FREE RELIGIOUS ASSOCIATION

The Free Religious Association (FRA) was formed in 1867 by "splendid gadflies and dissenters within the denomination" of Unitarianism. According to David Robertson, they were "not very influential as church builders or organizers. Their importance was in the intellectual stimulus that they provided to the denomination. Although in an immediate sense they had few followers, they were an advance guard, generally ahead of the religious thinking of mainstream Unitarianism and thus fighting an often frustrating battle. But the direction of their thinking–away from supernaturalism toward science, away from theism toward Humanism, and away from ecclesiasticism toward social reform–charted important directions in denominational development in the twentieth century."

Henry W. Bellows, Cyrus Bartol, Ralph Waldo Emerson, Octavius Brooks Frothingham, and Bronson Alcott were among the early leaders. Emerson was vice-president in 1879, succeeding Frothingham. But Emerson declined a second term, declaring that the FRA concentrated too much on what Kant (and Aristotle) had called "the starry heavens above," and not enough on "the Moral Law within." An extensive chapter on the subject is found in David Robertson's *The Unitarians and the Universalists* (1985). According to Edwin H. Wilson, "The Free Religious Association never went beyond what it called *humanistic theism*, and, because of the intense individualism of its members and gathering of dissents, its exciting meetings—usually front-page newsworthy—soon ended." (See entry for Ethical Culture.) {EW; HNS2; U&U}

FREE WILL

- Free will and determinism are like a game of cards. The hand that is dealt you is determinism. The way you play your hand is free will.

—**Norman Cousins**

Philosophers hold that free will is the belief that human beings are the authors of their own actions. Individuals holding such a view reject the idea that human actions are determined by external conditions of fate, such as divine will. In short, humans will have little luck in convincing the traffic policeman that they had been ordered by Hermes or Zeus to travel in excess of the speed limit. Such an excuse would likely not result in "Godspeed," which refers to success, as in "God prosper you."

Free will just might, according to Robert Wright, be an illusion. In *The Moral Animal: Why We Are the Way We Are* (1994), Wright argues that morality was "designed" by evolution and allows us to maximize our genetic legacy by increasing our chances of staying alive and having lots of babies. We fool ourselves about our goodness, he holds, by acting credibly as if our motivations are not what they are, thereby deceiving others into complying with our wishes. (See entry for predestination.)

Freebury, Julia Anne (1923—)

Freebury is an atheist, feminist, and civil libertarian activist. Migrating in 1950 to Australia from England, she became active from 1968 to 1970 with the Abortion Law Repeal Association, working to help women get abortions and celebrating when a court case, "the Judge Levine ruling," absolved several physicians of abortion charges. As a result, the law in New South Wales was less restrictive than the rewritten laws in Britain or South Australia and enabled abortions to be performed without the threat of the doctor being charged and found guilty by a jury. {SWW}

Freedman, Noel (20th Century)

Freedman, a professor of Old Testament at the University of Michigan, is a member of the Council for Secular Humanism's Biblical Criticism Research Project.

FREEDOM FROM RELIGION FOUNDATION

The Freedom From Religion Foundation (FFRF) publishes *Freethought Today* (Box 750, Madison, Wisconsin 53701), the only freethought newspaper in the United States. The foundation was founded in 1978. With 3,500 members nationwide, it is the largest organization of unbelievers in the United States.

The editor is Annie Laurie Gaylor. Its major spokesperson is Dan Barker, the fundamentalist-minister-turned-freethought-activist who is a nationally known speaker for the Foundation. The newspaper gives wide coverage of national freethought groups and meetings, its numerous photographs illustrating numbers of ordinary, nice-looking individuals, not at all stereotypical of what believers imagine non-believers to look like. <http://www.infidels.org/org/ffrf>.

FREEDOM OF RELIGION

William Sierichs Jr. (*The American Rationalist*, January-February 1996) has explained what "freedom of religion" is:

> What is freedom of religion if it is not most specifically freedom *from* religion?
>
> Freedom of religion means that the Christian is free from having to participate in the religion of the Muslim; the Muslim is free from the religion of the Hindu; the Hindu is free form the religion of the Jew; the Jew is free from the religion of the animist; and so forth.
>
> Even within religions, freedom of religion means freedom from religion. The Episcopalian is free from the particular religious beliefs and practices of the Lutheran, who is free from the religious beliefs and practices of the Baptist, who is free from the Roman Catholic, who is free from the Presbyterian, who is free from the Methodist, who is free from the Church of Christ, and so forth. Similarly, Sunni and Shiite in America are free from each other; and Orthodox, Conservative, and Reform Jews can ignore each other....

FREEDOM WRITER

Freedom Writer (PO Box 589, Great Barrington, Massachusetts 01230) is a First Amendment newsletter edited by Skipp Porteous.

Freeman, Anthony (20th Century)

Freeman, "the Bishop's Adviser for Continuing Ministerial

Education in the Diocese of Chichester," is a Church of England priest who, upon writing *God n Us* (1993), was "sacked" by his Bishop, the arch-conservative Dr. Eric Kemp. Freeman preached his last sermon in July 1994. In his book, Freeman described his "conversion experience" from a fairly traditional liberal Anglo-Catholicism, according to critic Daniel O'Hara, to a radical rejection of all forms of supernaturalism and an admission that religion is entirely a human invention. O'Hara reasons that if Freeman had waited until he became Bishop before coming out as a crypto-atheist, he might have more likely kept his job as a priest in the Church of England. Freeman's book is "in the forefront of a radical re-interpretation of Christianity in humanistic, this-worldly terms," writes O'Hara. "He is quite frank about there being no God, no life after death, no ultimate reference point outside human judgement on ethical questions."

Jim Herrick, however, claims Freeman has made only the first step in liberating himself of his Christian experience, adding he should take the next step, that of leaving the concept of God altogether: "You have crossed most of the water, tread the last stepping-stone, and [should] join us for a completely liberating experience." {*New Humanist*, November 1993}

Freeman, Arthur (20th Century)

For the English *New Humanist*, Freeman reviewed John Carroll's *Humanism: The Wreck of Western Culture*, finding it exceedingly hostile to the Enlightenment and to contemporary humanism. "We are left wondering what sort of person the author is and what readers will get from his book," Freeman concludes. In *New Humanist* (December 1995), he reviewed *The Cambridge Dictionary of Philosophy* and also *The Oxford Companion to Philosophy*. Neither book, he found, has satisfactory entries on humanism, positivism, atheism, or agnosticism, and neither discusses secularism or ethicism.

Freeman, James (1759—1835)

Freeman was the first avowedly Unitarian minister in the United States. The American Revolution had cut Episcopalians off from their ecclesiastical leaders in England, particularly George III, and the minister of Boston's King's Chapel, a loyalist, was forced to flee. In the absence of any other qualified clergyman, Freeman was appointed. But he had difficulty with the doctrine of the Trinity and, contemplating resigning, recommended instead that his church modify such a tenet. This they were not about to do, nor could they accept him simply because he said he subscribed to the Scriptures. However, the congregation in 1787 split away, voting him in as their minister. Therefore, the First Episcopal church in New England now became the first Unitarian Church in the New World. Enemies called Freeman a "liberal" or an "Arminian," but he chose the word "Unitarian" to describe his views, partly because of his friendship with William Hazlitt. Freeman wrote *Sermons on Particular Occasions* (1812) and *Eighteen Sermons and a Charge* (1829). {FUS; U; U&U}

Freeman, M. A. (19th Century)

Mrs. Freeman was the daughter of a freethinker, her father being known as "a Thomas Paine Infidel." Her maternal grandmother, whose maiden name was Elizabeth Ann Harris, was cousin to John Quincy Adams. Freeman was chairman of the finance committee of the American Secular Union in Chicago. Active with the Chicago Secular Union, she published the *Chicago Liberal* in 1891. {PUT; WWS}

FREEMASONRY

The Ancient Free and Accepted Masons, a fraternal order with almost three million members in the United States and six million worldwide, has been described as the largest secret society in the world. It started among the cathedral-building guilds of 16th-century Europe, and its member masons showed their secularism by decorating the religious with gargoyles, flora and fauna, and some scenes which bordered on the grotesque. In recent times, Its membership has dropped, for example from 350,000 in the 1950s to fewer than 100,000 today in New York State. *Anderson's Constitutions* (1723), the bylaws of the oldest extant lodge, the Grand Lodge of England, cite religious toleration, loyalty to local government, and political compromise as being basic to the Masonic ideal.

The first Grand Lodge in the Americas was one in Philadelphia (1730), of which Benjamin Franklin was a member. John Hancock, Paul Revere, George Washington, Andrew Jackson, Theodore Roosevelt, Voltaire, Giuseppe Mazzini, Giuseppe Garibaldi, Franz Joseph Haydn, Wolfgang Amadeus Mozart, Johann von Goethe, William Hogarth, Johann von Schiller, Rudyard Kipling, Wolfgang Amadeus Mozart, George Pike, Franklin Delano Roosevelt, Harry Truman, Douglas MacArthur, Irving Berlin, and a number of world leaders have been members. Some of the British Masons are the current patron, Prince Michael of Kent; the occasional celebrity like Arthur Conan Doyle or Peter Sellers; and various past Princes of Wales. The current Prince, Charles, turned down an invitation to join, and his father, Prince Philip, is a member but never participates.

In 1738, Pope Clement XII issued a bull which expressed the Catholic Church's disapproval of Masonry. Totalitarian states–most recently, Nazis and fascists in Italy, Austria, and Germany as well as right-wing politicians in the former Soviet Union and Communist China–have consistently opposed the lodge's existence. Fundamentalist Christians are anti-Masonry, declaring that the Masonic symbols–the square and compass–are satanic devices.

By 1764, the Empress of Austria, Maria Theresa, suppressed the Masonic order, after Pope Clement XIII issued a bull *In Eminenti*, threatening Masons with excommunication. According to the late Dr. William B. Ober, "The stated position of the Roman Catholic Church is that it holds that the beliefs and observances of Freemasonry constitute it a deistic or pagan religion and that the Masonic oath and secrecy imposed are canonically unlawful."

Masonry rested on a deistic outlook. Rather than being theists, who hold that God created the universe and continues to interfere in the universe by such methods as miracles and special revelations, Masons were deistic in their elaborate symbolic rites and ceremonies. A Great Architect of the Universe, one of the terms preferred to using "God," had created the universe, but that architect does not interfere in the universe. Further, petitionary prayers to the Creator, who has moved on to other places, are unnecessary and futile. Although few philosophers in the 20th century are deists, inasmuch as more specialized philosophic choices are available, deism made a profound impact particularly during the 18th century.

In 1877, the Grand Orient of France cut out references to the "Grand Architect" and required no belief in God or immortality.

Masonry is found in some Catholic countries, for a Mason can be of any or no organized religion so long as he professes belief in the Supreme Architect of the Universe, however the individual defines the term. The Catholic Church, however, objects to Freemasonry because it is a secret fraternity which practices a "natural religion," one which lumps the Gospel with other religions and other philosophies. The two views, Masons hold, are not incompatible. A 1985 report to the Catholic Bishops Conference quotes the oath taken by Master Masons, or Third Degree Masons as follows: "The swearer binds himself to upholding his duties under no less penalty than that of having my body severed in two, my bowels taken from thence and burned to ashes, the ashes scattered to the four winds of heaven. . . . "

The first of her gender to become a Mason was Maria Deraismes, a freethinker who was invited by the Masonic Lodge of Le Pecq, near Paris, in the latter half of the nineteenth century. The **Order of the Eastern Star**, which is limited to Master Masons and their female relatives, is a subsidiary lodge. Two organizations for girls are **Job's Daughters** and **Rainbow Girls**. The organization for boys is **DeMolay**, named after Jacques DeMolay (who some allege was gay). The civil and philanthropic efforts of the Masons are well-known, and the **Shriners**–famous for their antics at parades–are noted for their contributions to hospitals.

In a 1991 best-selling book, *The New World Order*, religionist Pat Robertson linked Jews and Freemasons. He suggested they are co-conspirators in a "grand design" to eliminate private property, national governments, and traditional Judeo-Christian theism. Specifically, he wrote about "the world designs of a well-known but secret fraternal order," reviving the discredited Christian right arguments of the 1920s and 1930s which were made by William Dudley Pelley and Gerald B. Winrod. William L. Fox, archivist of the Scottish Rite of Freemasonry, Southern District, has accused them of believing "that Jewish capitalists and radicals, assisted by remnants of the Bavarian Illuminati, who had in their minds infiltrated European Freemasonry, were cooperating to destroy Christian civilization." Fox denies all such charges, saying that the purpose of Freemasonry "is to provide opportunity for men of diverse backgrounds to gather in neutral territory for fellowship and charitable undertakings."

Fred Whitehead, in *Freethought History* (#24, 1997), has a scholarly article, "The Freemasonry Connection," about Freethought and Freemasonry. He highlights the importance of Dutch publishers in issuing Deist and dissenting books during Freemasonry's early period, points out that Jefferson was not a Freemason but partook of the general culture of Enlightenment that prevailed in the early Republic, and notes that both the Freemasons and the Freethinkers presently suffer from declining memberships. (See entries for Freethinkers and for Edward Cahill. Also see entry for Maria Desraimes, the first female Freemason.) {CE; ER; RE}

FREEMASONRY—SECRETS OF

For more than 350 years, Masons have tried to conceal their secret rituals. Each who becomes a member takes an oath stating that if he (females are not allowed to join) reveals secrets of Freemasonry, he will have his throat cut, his tongue torn from his mouth, and his bowels burned to ashes.

However, secrets of Freemasonry have become published. For example, Warren Hoge in *The New York Times* (29 March 1998) revealed the following:

> To become a Freemason, for instance, a man must present himself outside the closed door of a lodge in shirtsleeves with the left breast bared, a blindfold across his eyes, a hangman's noose draped around his neck, a shoe on one foot, a slipper on the other and one trouser leg rolled up. Upon entry, he is confronted with a dagger pointed at his bare nipple and the chanting of men in blue goatskin aprons with wands in their hands and ornamental chains draped across their chests.
>
> Even the notorious secret handshake is no longer unknown to outsiders, referred to as "profanes" in Freemason-speak. It is accomplished by pressing a thumb on the space between the knuckles, with the exact position depending upon one's level—apprentice, fellow of the craft or master Mason—and then gripping.

FREETHINKER

The Freethinker is a secular humanist monthly that was founded by G. W. Foote in 1881. It is edited by Peter Brearey (24 Alder Avenue, Silcoates Park, Wakefield, WF2 OTZ) and published by G. W. Foote & Co. (Bradlaugh House, 47 Theobald's Road, London WC1X 8SP).

On the Web, the editor can be reached at <editor@freethinker.co.uk>. On the Web: <http://www.freethinker.co.uk>.

FREETHINKER YOUTH CAMP

The Freethinker Youth Camp is a joint effort of the Changeology Learning Centre and the Colorado Springs Freethinkers. It is designed to provide a summer experience for freethinking youth. On the Web: <http://www.evolvefish.com/camp>.

FREETHINKERS, FREETHOUGHT

Independently of authority, a freethinker forms opinions on the basis of reason. Freethinkers reject supernatural authority as well as ecclesiastical tradition, for it is felt that bowing to authority leads people to essentially identical conclusions concerning morality and religion. Anthony Collins made the term known in his *Discourse of Freethinking Occasioned by the Rise and Growth of a Sect Called Freethinkers* (1713), and in England the freethinkers although not breaking completely with Christianity were vitally interested in deism. In France, however, Voltaire entirely renounced Christianity, and the Encyclopedists similarly rejected organized religions. Freethought has influenced the philosophies both of the Freemasons and, in France, the Culte de l'Être. Organizations which have furthered freethinking including the American Rationalist Association, the American Secular Union, the Freethinkers of America, and the Freedom from Religion Foundation (FFRF). The present work quotes heavily on the subject from John MacKinnon Robertson's *Short History of Freethought, Ancient and Modern* (1914) and Gordon Stein's editing of *The Encyclopedia of Unbelief* (1985).

For Lord Russell, "To be worthy of the name, [a freethinker] must be free of two things, the force of tradition and the tyranny of his own passions. No one is completely free from either. What makes a freethinker is not his beliefs but the way in which he holds them. If he holds them because his elders told him they were true when he was young, or if he holds them because if he did not he would be unhappy, his thought is not free; but if he holds them because, after careful thought, he finds a balance of evidence in their favor, then his thought is free, however odd his conclusions may seem. Freedom from the tyranny of passion is as essential as freedom from the influence of tradition. The jealous husband who suspects his wife of infidelity on inadequate grounds, and the complacent optimist, who refuses to suspect her when the evidence is overwhelming, are alike permitting passion to enslave their thought; in neither of them is thought free." On the Web: <http://freethought.com>. (See entries for Libertinage and John Toland.) {CE; Lee Eisler, *The Quotable Bertrand Russell*; RE}

FREE-THINKERS' DAY

Harvard University's Humanist chaplaincy in 1993 submitted Free-thinkers' Day, October 12th, as a proposed "holy" day which students could observe. In 1994, "Freethought Week," from October 8th to 15th, was declared in proclamations by the governors of Missouri and Texas, partly because of pressures from David Schreiber and Catherine Fahringer of the Freedom from Religion Foundation. Cities which proclaimed the freethought week included Philadelphia, Madison, Baltimore, St. Louis, Cincinnati, and Portland. (See entry for Humanist Holidays.)

FREETHINKER'S DIRECTORY

"Freethinker's Directory" is a directory which lists freethought groups, listed by locality, name, and type of organization. David Briars edits the publication at RD 1, B-45, Craftsbury, Vermont 05826. {FD}

FREETHINKING ACTIVIST NONBELIEVING NEW YORKERS (FANNY)

In 1998 Dennis Middlebrooks and Warren Allen Smith founded Freethinking Activist Nonbelieving New Yorkers, a liaison to humanistic groups in the New York City area, one that catered to the interests of fellow agnostics, atheists, secularists, humanists, philosophic naturalists, or freethinkers.

Agreeing to be honorary members were painter Paul Cadmus; novelist Sir Arthur C. Clarke; clinical psychologist Albert Ellis; "M*A*S*H" originator Ring Lardner Jr.; Bangladeshi gynecologist-poet Taslima Nasrin; lexicographer Allen Walker Read; novelist Kurt Vonnegut Jr., and sculptor Anita Weschler.

Chairpersons in addition to the two founding members were Victor Acevedo, Dana DiTullio, Darren Schmidt, Herbert A. Tonne, Eric Walther, and Irving Yablon. Membership was closed except to those "doers" who had completed an individual activist project and had been approved by the founder-directors.

Projects carried out by the group were varied: placing an "In Memoriam" in *The New York Times* on the centenary of the death of Robert G. Ingersoll, and toasting him at a plaque in his honor at the

Hotel Gramercy in New York; introducing Taslima Nasrin to India's Dr. Innaiah Narisetti, Ecuador's Pablo Cevallos, and Russia's Dr. and Mrs. Valerii Kuvakin; arranging contacts with journalists for Ibn Warraq, author of *Why I Am Not A Muslim*; commencing a Taslima Nasrin homepage and informing four hundred international journalists and human rights officials of her week-by-week struggle to escape from Bangladesh; entertaining Argentine humanist leader Hugo Estrella; showing 23-year-old University of Moscow graduate student Alexei Gostev where John Dewey taught at Columbia University and lived at 1158 Fifth Avenue; publicizing and moderating lectures by Dr. Paul Edwards; covering Dana DiTullio's research about Siloism for interested groups; toasting Irving Yablon, who joined a Missouri atheist group that picketed the Pope's visit in 1999; helping arrange the BBC recorded interview of Joseph Fields and Warren Allen Smith regarding African American humanists; working with the BBC to record comments by Smith for their "World Service" radio program in regard to human rights and humanism; celebrating the birth or death dates of eminent freethinkers at Tom Paine's "Marie's Crisis" bar; writing humanistic comments for various letters-to-the-editor columns; and compiling a list of alternatives to the 12-step Higher Power AA groups in the area. On the Web: <http://idt.net/~wasm/fanny.html>.

FREETHOUGHT

On the Internet, an international link is available to archives, criticism, debates, events, lists, literature, magazines, newsgroups, organizations, people, satire, and statistics. Its address: <http://www.infidels.org>.

The Freethought Web contains an extensive directory of World Wide Web sites on freethought. Matt Cherry has described being online as "feeling like a kid in a candy shop with no adults anywhere." Included are links to major philosophers, to creationism, to intellectual history, to the various religions, to skepticism, to Bertrand Russell, etc.

On the Web: <www.kaiwan.com/~lucknow/horus/intel.html>.

FREETHOUGHT EXCHANGE

The Freethought Exchange (Gnostic Press, PO Box 202447, Arlington, Texas 76006) is a bi-monthly newsletter of news and views about the community of unbelief. Contributions of up to two pages of material are printed free, and longer selections are charged $5 and up per page.

FREETHOUGHT FORUM

Freethought Forum, a monthly of the Humanist Fellowship of San Diego, is at PO Box 87662, San Diego, California 92128-7662.

FREETHOUGHT HISTORY

Freethought History (Box 5224, Kansas City, Kansas 66119) is a scholarly monthly, generally conceded the most authoritative of its kind, published by Fred Whitehead. Whitehead, a history professor, wrote *Freethought on the American Frontier*.

FREETHOUGHT MUSIC

"Modern rock" and "alternative rock" as well as "rap" music often contain freethought ideas. Sarah McLachlan on the album *A Testimonial Dinner–the Songs of XTC* sings a song, "Dear God," which is atheistic.

On Gerry Dantone's Infidels Records label, Dantone's band called UniversalDice.com has recorded and performed one of his humanistic rock operas entitled, "My Name is Thomas," which is available on the World Wide Web.

Other examples of those who have sung freethought and atheistic works are Tori Amos; Emerson, Lake & Palmer; Genesis; Metallica; Ministry; Monty Python; Nine Inch Nails; The Residents; and Rudy Schwartz. (See entries for Andrew Charles, Gerry Dantone, and Residents.) {*Fig Leaves*, April 1996}

FREETHOUGHT OBSERVER

The Freethought Observer (PO Box 202447, Arlington, Texas 76006) became a bi-monthly in 1994 and was edited by Tim Gorski.

In 1996 *The Freethought Observer* became a section within *Secular Nation*, which in 1997 discontinued including it.

FREETHOUGHT PERSPECTIVE

Freethought Perspective is published by Leland W. Ruble, 833 Orchard Street, Toledo, Ohio 43609. The associate editor is Dr. Dorothy B. Thompson.

FREETHOUGHT TODAY

Freethought Today (PO Box 750, Madison, Wisconsin 53701) is published ten times a year and is edited by Annie Laurie Gaylor. In addition to top-notch coverage of violations of church-state separation, the publication has included a compilation by Denise McLaughlin of "Black Collar Crimes," cases from coast to coast in which officials of various religious bodies are cited in news articles for rape, abuse, sexual molestation, pornography, and various types of sexual misconduct. On the Web: <http://www.infidels.org>.

FREEWOMAN

Freewoman, which began on 23 November 1911, initially was "A Weekly Feminist Review." From 12 May 1912 on, however, it was "A Weekly Humanist Review" that conveyed the combination of feminist and masculinist views. Although it ceased in 1912, it was revived as the *New Freewoman* in 1913, "An Individualist Review," and on 1 January 1914 it became *The Egoist*. {*New Humanist*, December 1998}

Frege, Gottlob (1848—1925)

Frege, one of the founders of symbolic logic, wrote a two-volume work, *The Basic Laws of Arithmetic* (1893—1903), demonstrating that mathematics is derived solely from deductive logic, that it is not synthetic as Kant had posited. However, Bertrand Russell and others pointed out some serious contradictions in his work, and Frege wrote few other original works. Michael Dummett, in *Origins of Analytical Philosophy* (1993), holds that Frege was the most important contributor to the science of logic since Aristotle, adding that German-speaking philosophers have contributed more to analytical philosophy than have English- or French-speaking writers. {CE}

FREIDENKER

A humanistic German monthly, *Freidenker* is at Shonalcher Str. 2, 70597 Stuttgart, Germany.

FREIDENKER VEREINIGUNG DER SCHWEIZ

A Swiss member of the IHEU is *Freidenker Vereinigung Der Schweiz,* PO Box CH-3001, Bern, Switzerland. It publishes the monthly *Frei Denker*. {FD}

FREIDENKERBUND OESTERREICHS: See the entry for the Austrian, Martin Panosch.

FREIE HUMANISTEN NIEDERSACHSEN

Freie Humanisten Niedersachsen, a full member of the International Humanist and Ethical Union, is at Otto-Brenner-Str. 22, D-30159 Hannover, Germany.

FREIGEISTIGE AKTION

In Germany, Freigeistige Aktion(IHEU), Fasanenweg 8, 31535 Neustadt 1, Germany, publishes a quarterly, *Kristall*. {FD}

Freiligrath, Ferdinand (1810—1876)

Freiligrath was a German poet who, when he professed his faith in *Mein Glaudbenbekenutniss*, was forced to flee his country. Returning in 1848, he joined Karl Marx on the *Neue Rheinische Zeitung*. Again prosecuted, he fled to London where he was honored as one of the best poets of the time. {BDF; RAT}

FRIENDS GENERAL CONFERENCE

The Friends General Conference, organized in 1900, is at 1216 Arch St. (1-B), Philadelphia, Pennsylvania 19107. Over 2,400 houses of worship serve their members, who often are called Quakers.

FRIENDS OF RELIGIOUS HUMANISM (FRH)

Friends of Religious Humanism (7 Harwood Drive, PO Box 1188, Amherst, NY 14226-7188) is an organization founded in 1962 by Edwin H. Wilson, Lester Mondale, and others as the "Fellowship of Religious Humanists." Its purpose is to advance humanism within the Unitarian Universalist denomination and to promote religious humanism in general. Mira Poudrier, the group's office manager, oversees the publication of a semi-annual journal, *Religious Humanism*. The organization's stated purpose is as follows:

> To promote and encourage the religious, ethical and philosophical thought and life of our members and society. To this end, (we) shall arrange lectures, encourage writing, publish periodicals and other literature, hold discussion groups, seminars and conferences, endeavoring to provide both inspirational materials and scholarly studies which apply the scientific spirit and methods to the materials of ethics and religion.

Following are statements by some of FRH's supporters:

> Like most persons of this persuasion, I regard myself as a Religious Humanist not because of having been converted to a creed; a faith; not because of my having signed a membership card in a crusading fraternity of believers. The term Religious Humanism is more descriptive of a state of mind, of an attitude with respect to philosophy, religion, ethics, than it is a label for another "ism."
>
> —Lester Mondale
> *Religious Humanism: A Testimonial*

> I have been enthusiastic about our Religious-Humanist Fellowship because it presages an enlargement of humanism, a creatively different emphasis in humanism . . . life's dimensions and puzzles, for their happy resolution, demand rationality, but not bellicosity, required is an imaginative psychology as well as an analytical logic, an inward look as well as an extraversion...to hold eternity in an hour and to see the world in a grain of sand are valid human endeavors...it is an honest and valid emotional appeal to still undefined values of tomorrow as they stand in tension with the values which have egregiously failed our today. For motivational insight maybe we need a Prometheus. Or in remembering another mythmaker, maybe we need to see things as a little child.
>
> —Robert Hoagland
> *A New Dimension of Humanism*

> Humanism is a celebration and a promise; it celebrates the integrity of human reason, responsibility and compassion, and it promises a satisfying lifestyle that can be counted on. No more deprecation of the human condition; rather, an opportunity to remain true to ourselves by having both feet in this world and responding to the challenges of existence with excitement and pragmatic service to others. Humanism is religion come of age; at long last we humans can live dignified lives, finite creatures though we may be. At long last, men, women and children can find ultimate fulfillment through bringing out the best in humanity for the sake of humanity.
>
> —Beverley Earles

> YES: Humanism can be religious; indeed, the most meaningful and liveable kind of humanism is itself a religious way of understanding and living life. It offers a view of [people] and [their] place in the universe that is a religious philosophy...overarching and undergirding it all, there can be a haunting sense of wonder which never leaves one for whom life itself is a mystery and miracle. Where did we come from, why are we here, where are we going with all the effort, frustration, the grief, the joy? To be caught up in this sense of wider relatedness, to sense our being connected in live ways with all the world and everyone in it, is the heart dimension of religion, whatever its name.
>
> —Peter Samson
> *Can Humanism Be Religious?*

Freireligiöse Rundschau

Freireligiöse Rundschau, a quarterly in German of Freireligiösen Landesgemeinde Würtemberg, is at Oberer Kirchhaldenweg 59, 70195 Stuttgart, Germany.

Freke, William (17th Century)

About 1663, Freke (or Freeke) wrote *A Brief But Clear Confutation of the Trinity*, which upon being brought to the attention of the House of Lords was ordered to be burned by the common hangman. Freke was prosecuted by the Attorney General and fined £500. {BDF}

Fremlin, John (1913—1995)

Fremlin, a member in England of the Birmingham Humanist Group, was Professor of Applied Radioactivity at the University of Birmingham. A nuclear physicist, he wrote *Be Fruitful and Multiply* and *Power Production: What Are the Risks?* The former title was ironic, for the work rejected the Biblical injunction and demonstrated the necessity of popular limitation, world-wide. {*The Freethinker*, June 1995}

FRENCH ACADEMY

L'Académie français is France's learnèd society, one of the five societies of the *Institut de France*. The Academy received its royal letters patent in 1635, and its membership of forty ("the forty immortals") were formed to govern French literary effort, grammar, orthography, and rhetoric. Cardinal Richelieu, the chief minister of Louis XIII, was its founder, and following his death the patronate went (1643) to Pierre Séguier, the chancellor. On his death (1672), King Louis XIV assumed the position of *protecteur*, which ever after remained a prerogative of the head of the French state. In 1793 the suppression of the academies ended the French Academy, but it reappeared in the second class of Napoleon's *Institut* (1803). The French Academy has been conservative in its recording forms (for it does not legislate) concerning orthography and has discouraged the use of "foreign" words and spellings.

Although many of France's greatest writers have been members of the Academy, the most prominent of those who did not attain membership are Molière, Marquis de La Rochefoucauld, Duc de Saint-Simon, Jean Jacques Rousseau, Honoré de Balzac, Gustave Flaubert, Stendhal, Émile Zola, and Marcel Proust. Not coincidentally, most of these writers were anti-clerical. {CE}

FRENCH HUMANISTS

In 1995, French tax authorities reported that 50,000 taxpayers, the highest number ever, had declared income from their work as stargazers, healers, mediums, and similar occupations. By comparison, the country had fewer than 30,000 Roman Catholic priests and some 6,000 psychiatrists. The state-run Minitel on-line system which is found with computers in millions of French homes offers clients to choose, under the heading "astrology," over four hundred listings for tarot card readings, horoscopes, and other astral advice. A 1986 poll found that 25% of the French believed the devil existed. In 1995 that figure had jumped to 34%.

To offset such, several humanist groups have existed in France, the nation where teenagers are taught logic and philosophy in school. From 1993 to date, the following groups and publications were active:

• *Cahiers Rationalistes* (a monthly), 14 rue de l"Ecole-Polytechnique, 75005 Paris

• *Centre d'Anatole France*—an exclusively atheistic group with no religious connections, it is militantly anti-Catholic and anti-clerical.

• *Centre Laïque de l'Europe*—founded over 13 years ago, the group of socialists and radicals is interested in laicite, or influence by lay people, especially in relation to recent developments on the church-state separation.

• *Cercle Condorcet*—the group, now four years old, meets monthly in Paris and reflects on issues similar to the concerns of the *Ligue d'enseignement,* or *League of Educators.*

• *Cercle Diderot*—the group is named after the 18th-century philosopher and eminent encyclopedist and is dedicated to keeping his legacy alive.

• *Cercle Ernest Renan*—the group is devoted to Biblical study and studies religious dogma from a skeptical angle.

• *Europe et Laicité,* a quarterly, 11 rue des Huguenots, 94420 Le Plessis-Trevise <eurolaic@club-internet.fr>.

• Knights of La Barre—the group, named after an 18th-century Chevalier who was executed for blasphemy, supports anti-clericalism and is critical of Catholicism.

• *La Libre Pensée*—founded before the 1870 commune de Paris by radicals, marxists, anarchists, and anti-clericalists, the group is working to insure that the EEC gives equal rights to non-believers, not just to the believers who are in the majority. Its address is 10-12, Rue Des Fosses St. Jacques, 75005 Paris

• *La Raison,* 10-12 rue des Fosses-Saint Jacques, 75005 Paris

• *Les Idées en Mouvement,* 3 rue Recamier 75341 Paris, Cedex 07 <info-ligue@saturne.cie.fr>.

• *Raison Présente,* a quarterly, 14 rue de l'Ecole-Polytechnique, 75005 Paris

• *Union Rationaliste*—founded in 1930 by academics at the time of the growth of fascism, the group sees itself as part of the struggle against all forms of dogmatism.

• Signers of are R. M. Bonnet of the European Space Agency; Jacques Bouveresse, professor of philosophy, Collège de France; Jean-Pierre Changeux, professor of neurobiology, Collège de France; Gérard Fussman, professor at Collége de France; Jacques Le Goff, specialist in French Middle Age Civilization and Literature, ENESS; Jean-Claude Pecker, astronomer, Collège de France; and Evry Schatzman, astronomer, former President of the French Physics Association.

(See entries for France and Intellectuals.)

FRENCH PHILOSOPHY: See the *Encyclopedia of Philosophy,* Vol. 3. (A first-rate discussion of post-World War II philosophy is Tony Judt's *Past Imperfect: French Intellectuals, 1944—1956.*)

FRENCH PROTESTANTS

> • Protestants have been in the vanguard of most of the great liberalising ideas and reforms in French history: the declaration of human rights, the abolition of slavery, the market economy, the devolution of power from the centre, the spread of state education, the separation of church and state, advocacy of contraception and divorce.
>
> {*The Economist,* 18 April 1998}

FRENCH UNITARIANS

A. Blanchard-Gaillard heads the Association Unitarienne Francophone, which has a Christian theology similar to that of Transylvanian Unitarianism.

Three small groups in France (Paris, Nancy, Digne) and one Swiss group in Geneva publish *Unitarian Approaches.* M. Blanchard-Gaillard is at Les Hautes-Sieyes, Route des Courbons, 04000, Digne, France).

Unitarians in Paris can be contacted by telephoning (33) 1-42 77 96 77.

French, Alice (1850—1934)

French was the oldest of six children whose family had been founders of the Davenport, Iowa, Unitarian Church. One of the first regionalist authors to write realistically about Iowa and Arkansas, she wrote a number of works including *A Slave to Duty and Other Women* (1906). According to an editor and critic, Susan Koppelman, French had a lifelong partnership with Jane Allen Crawford. The two divided their year between Davenport and their plantation in Arkansas. "French's subtle, almost sly portrayals of ties between women who love each other," stated Koppelman, "are now being appreciated." {GL}

French, Charles (20th Century)

French is active with Friends Free of Theism in Richfield, Minnesota. He is on the board of the Freedom From Religion Foundation. (See entry for Minnesota Atheists, Humanists.) {FD}

French, Marilyn (1929—)

French addressed the Ninth International Humanist and Ethical Union (IHEU) World Congress held in Oslo (1986). She is author of *The Women's Room* (1977), *The Bleeding Heart* (1980), *Her Mother's Daughter* (1987), *War Against Women* (1992), and *A Season in Hell* (1998).

Asked about humanism, French responded to the present author:

> My parents were raised Catholic but had left the church by the time I was born. My mother, an agnostic, suggested I might be interested in religion and sent me to the Catholic Church for religious instruction shortly before my ninth birthday. I was extremely devout for a year but could not get answers to any of my questions, and when a priest scolded me for questioning I left the church. I was thirteen. I called myself a deist for a few years, having read Tom Paine. But I have been an atheist since I was eighteen, and at present am a well-informed but implacable foe of organized religion.
>
> {WAS, 19 December 1994}

French, Roderick (20th Century)

French's 1971 Ph. D. dissertation at George Washington University was on "The Trials of Abner Kneeland—A Study in the Rejection of Democratic Secular Humanism." {FUS}

Freneau, Philip (1752—1832)

The first professional journalist, Freneau was a propagandist as well as a satirist for the American Revolution and for Jeffersonian democracy. He edited papers, including the partisan *National Gazette* (Philadelphia, 1791—1793) for Jefferson. In addition, he was the earliest important American lyric poet, the author of such works as "The Wild Honeysuckle" and "Belief and Unbelief." In the latter 1815 poem, he wrote,

> Humbly Recommended to the Serious
> Consideration of Creed Makers
>
> What some believe, and would enforce
> Without reluctance or remorse,
> Perhaps another may decry,
> Or call a fraud, or deem a lie.
>
> Must he for that be doomed to bleed,
> And fall a martyr to some creed,
> By hypocrites or tyrants framed,
> By reason damned, by truth disclaimed? . . .

They who extort belief from man
Should, in the out-set of their plan,
Exhibit, like the mid-day sun
An evidence denied by none.

From this great point, o'erlooked or missed,
Still unbelievers will exist;
And just their plea; for how absurd
For evidence, to take your word!!

Not to believe, I therefore hold
The right of man, all uncontrolled
By all the powers of human wit,
What kings have done, or sages writ;

Not criminal in any view,
Nor–man!–to be avenged by you,
Till evidence of strongest kind
Constrains assent, and clears the mind.

{CE; FUS}

Frère-Orban, Hubert Joseph Walther (1812—1896)

Frère-Orban was a Belgian statesman who started as a lawyer in Liège and led the Liberals. In the Chambre in 1847, he became Minister of Public Works, then Minister of Finance (1848—1852). In 1857 he brought down the Catholic Ministry and was again Minister of Finance (to 1870). He was Premier 1868—1870 and 1878—1884, during which time he drastically checked the clericals. {RAT}

Fréret, Nicolas (1688—1749)

Fréret was a French historical critic, a pupil of Rollin. He became a member of the Academy of Inscriptions in 1714. For a discourse on the "Origin of the Franks," he was incarcerated for four months in the Bastille, where he read Bayle so often he could repeat much from memory. Fréret was an unbeliever and the alleged author of the atheistic *Letters from Thrasybulus to Leucippe*, although the author might actually have been the Baron d'Holbach. {BDF; FUK; GS; RAT}

FRÉTTABRÉF SIDMENNTAR

An Icelandic quarterly, *Fréttabréf Sidmenntar* is published by the Icelandic Ethical Association, Aesufell 4 APT 2F, 111 Reykjavik, Iceland. <hopeful@islandia.is>.

Freud, Lucian (1922—)

Freud, the painter, is the son of an architect who was the youngest of Sigmund Freud's three sons. He is the husband of sculptor Jacob Epstein's daughter, Kitty, and is known to many as having once been a long and close friend of the painter Francis Bacon. In his youth he is said to have set fire to Cedric Morris's art school. He is also said to share his grandfather's interest in zoology, one of his early drawings being that of a dead monkey which shocked viewers long before his contemporary paintings of nude fat people appeared. Calling psychoanalysis "unsuited to the life span," Freud claims to be fairly ignorant of his grandfather, who died when Lucian was sixteen. He told John Richardson that he liked his grandfather's "humor and generosity and his fondness for conspiracy," which Richardson explained "is a trait that Lucian seems to have inherited, though not to the extent of convening a secret committee, as Sigmund Freud permitted Ernest Jones to do in 1912, with the sole purpose of shielding him and his controversial work from prying outsiders." These days, Richardson adds, Lucian Freud might do with such a shield in light of how prurient critics like to pry into his paintings "that depict the women in his life–friends, his daughters, mistresses–without any clothes on."

As for painting his daughters in the buff, Freud has explained, "What could be more natural? I paint only people who are close to me. And who closer than my children. If I had thought it odd to paint them, I would never have done so. For me, painting people naked, regardless of whether they are lovers, children, or friends, is never an erotic situation. The sitter and I are involved in making a painting, not love. These are things that people who are not painters fail to understand. Besides, there is something about a person being naked before me that invokes consideration–you could even call it chivalry–on my part: in the case of my children, a father's consideration as well as a painter's."

One of the nudes he has painted is Leigh Bowery (1961—1994), a homosexual (who died of AIDS), a performance artist from Australia. Freud says he is drawn to homosexual models "because I respect their courage," and his 1993 great back view of Bowery in New York City's Metropolitan Museum of Art shows that the artist has been influenced by German art such as Dürer's "Adam and Eve." Freud's "And the Bridegroom" depicts both the mountainously huge Bowery and the toothpick-like Nicola as they lie naked on a bed. In an analysis, Richardson comments that the two are turning away from one another, "ambivalently in what could be taken–or more likely mistaken–for postcoital repose." Viewing the 1993 Freud exhibition, Bowery wore a dress. "I've copied Lucian in thousands of ways," he told reporter Margalit Fox. "Whatever he makes for dinner, I make for dinner. I copy the clothes he wears and the phrases he uses." In return, Freud copies Bowery, sometimes using New York transvestite slang, the model told a reporter before picking up his skirt and gliding out of the museum. "So it's slightly a two-way street."

Freud, who is not a believer in the various organized religions, has works at the Tate Gallery in London, the National Gallery in Melbourne, the Museum of Modern Art and Metropolitan Museum of Art in New York, and elsewhere around the world. (See entry for Leigh Bowery.)

Freud, Sigmund (1856—1939)

The eminent founder of psychoanalysis, Freud early on rejected the use of hypnosis, developing a technique called free association that allowed emotionally charged material which the individual had repressed in his unconscious to emerge to conscious recognition. His application of psychoanalytic theory to cultural problems has been wide, in areas such as anthropology, education, art, and literature. One little-known fact is that Freud's first research was a study of the gonads of an eel. He is author of *The Interpretation of Dreams* (1900); *The Psychopathology of Everyday Life* (1904); *The Id and the Ego* (1923); and *Totem and Tabu* (1918).

When the American poet Hilda Doolittle, better known simply as H.D., visited Freud in 1933, she found "the death-head swastika chalked on the pavement leading to the professor's door." Inside his Viennese office, she found he had a large collection of archaeological artifacts on his desk "like a high altar." Picking a tiny Athena from the collection, he offered it to her, saying, "*This* is my favorite. She is perfect…only she has lost her spear." The significance of handing the bisexual H.D. a figurine of the bisexual Athena was filled with sexual implications, which he may or may not initially have intended, according to her *Tribute to Freud* (1956). But the story illustrates his intense interest in the Ancient Greeks which, combined with his knowledge of Judaism, led to his controversial work on monotheism and Moses.

Moses and Monotheism (1938) implies that Moses was not a foundling Jew. Rather, he was a high-born Egyptian, a member of Akhenaten's intellectual elite. Moses obtained his monotheistic concepts from the Egyptian religion of Aton, choosing the Hebrews, a poor group of alien people who had settled in a border province, as his people, making Egyptians out of them in order that they could profit by his country's culture. In addition to monotheism, he gave them two other Egyptian "gifts": the practice of circumcision, and the Aton cult's ethical code. In short, Moses obtained his idea of one god from a human, not from a supernatural source, a viewpoint which immediately drew negative criticism from most leaders of the organized religions and others with vested financial interests. "Religion," Freud wrote, "is an attempt to get control over the sensory world in which we are placed by means of the wish world which we have developed inside."

By the age of forty-two, Freud, the author of *Three Contributions to the Sexual Theory* (1905) and who had married a cousin and had had six children, said, "Sexual excitation is of no more use to a person like me." At the age of fifty-six, he said that "at the bottom of his heart" he had found sexual intercourse" degrading," according to *People's Almanac #2*, because he was unable to discuss sex with his children.

Freud's work, Monsignor Fulton J. Sheen said in a 1947 sermon, is based on "materialism, hedonism, infantilism, and eroticism." Sheen's attack called attention to the religionists' concern that psychiatry and psychology were providing alternative, nonspiritual explanations for religious experiences. Freud was accused of treating religion as a comforting illusion, something which a mature person or society would outgrow. (Ironically, as pointed out by Peter Steinfels in *The New York Times* (3 Jan 1993), the president of the American Psychiatric Association, is a Catholic. That group's president-elect as well as the president and the president-elect, and secretary general of the World Psychiatric Association, are Catholics, also.)

"Neither in my private life nor in my writings," Freud wrote in a letter to Charles Singer, "have I ever made a secret of being an out-and-out unbeliever." However, he also wrote, "When a man is freed of religion, he has a better chance to live a normal and wholesome life." And "Religions originate in the child's and young mankind's fears and need for help. It cannot be otherwise." He also wrote, "The Catholic Church so far has been the implacable enemy of all freedom of thought" and, to colleague Ludwig Binswanger in 1927, "The Nazis? I am not afraid of them. Help me rather to combat my true enemy...Religion, the Roman Catholic Church." Freud was an honorary associate of the Rationalist Press Association (RPA), of which Bertrand Russell later was president.

On the subject of religion Freud wrote

> In my *Future of an Illusion* I was concerned much less with the deepest sources of the religious feeling than with what the common man understands by his religion—with the system of doctrines and promises which on the one hand explains to him the riddles of this world with enviable completeness, and, on the other, assures him that a careful Providence will watch over his life and will compensate him in a future existence for any frustrations he suffers here. The common man cannot imagine this Providence otherwise than in the figure of an enormously exalted father. Only such a being can understand the needs of the children of men and be softened by their prayers and placated by the signs of their remorse.
>
> The whole thing is so patently infantile, so foreign to reality, that to anyone with a friendly attitude to humanity it is painful to think that the great majority of mortals will never be able to rise above this view of life.
>
> It is still more humiliating to discover how large a number of people living today, who cannot but see that this religion is not tenable, nevertheless try to defend it piece by piece in a series of pitiful rearguard actions.
>
> One would like to mix among the ranks of the believers in order to meet these philosophers, who think they can rescue the God of religion by replacing him by an impersonal, shadowy and abstract principle, and to address them with the warning words: "Thou shalt not take the name of the Lord thy God in vain!" And if some of the great men of the past acted in the same way, no appeal can be made to their example: we know why they were obliged to.

George J. Stack has written of Freud's attitude toward religion: "*The Future of an Illusion* (1927) is a terse, sharp critique of religion. It emphasizes the psychogenic origin of belief in God (who is characterized as a projection of the child's vision of a powerful, stern father), the obsessive-compulsive nature of ritual and prayer, the illusory nature of religion as based upon 'omnipotence of thought,' and infantile feelings of dependence. In sum, Freud argued that religion is a 'universal neurosis' that must be outgrown if men would attain independence of mind and maturity." In that book, Freud had written, "Religion is comparable to a childhood neurosis." Gaskin, who states that although Freud had been brought up to observe Jewish religious customs, he "seems never to have had any serious *belief* in God or in gods. But he has much to say about religion in a number of his published works. His frequently repeated contentions are that 'the psychical origin of religious ideas . . . are illusions, fulfillments of the oldest, strongest, and most urgent wishes of mankind'; and that 'the primal father figure was the original image of God.'" Gaskin adds that Freud "argues in close detail, and with evidence, that human beings, being the sort of creatures they are, *need* to believe in gods," that religion is based upon wish fulfillment.

Freud's views were controversial in his own time and continue to be so. Simon LeVay, whose *The Sexual Brain* (1993) develops the view that the brain's hypothalamus produces what is called male- and female-typical sex drive and who found the nucleus of the hypothalamus smaller–sometimes absent–in gay as compared to straight men, has said when asked if he views Freud as a savior or a scourge, "A scourge, absolutely. He started the idea that homosexuality was a state of arrested development caused by defective parenting. He himself was not homophobic. He wrote some things that were very gay-friendly, particularly toward the end of his life. Nevertheless there's an incredible amount of unnecessary guilt and blame that has to be laid at his doorstep. What happened with homosexuality is exactly what happened twenty years ago with schizophrenia, with everyone blaming parents for making their kids schizophrenic. I can't imagine what it does to a parents."

Freud was not homophobic. In fact, unexpurgated correspondence with the young Wilhelm Fliess, a psychologist, reveal that Freud definitely had a "crush" on him. Fliess was not that interested in returning the love, however, but from him Freud developed ideas concerning bisexuality and from him he adopted terms such as "latency period" and "sublimation." For a time, also, Freud was attracted to Jung, an attraction that wore off and eventually led to a break when Freud was in his fifties, whereupon Freud exulted that he was finally rid of that Jung and his pious gang. Jung, it transpired, was anti-Semitic, an occultist, and pro-Nazi, until the Nazis were defeated, after which he tempered his views. Freud also disapproved of Jung's having made a pass at a patient, Ms. Spielrein, who had insufficient money to pay his fee, after which she became his own patient.

Although critics of psychoanalysis are many, supporters of Freud point out that no other thinker has made creativity and imagination more democratically available. "Creativity," Jonathan Lear has written, "is no longer the exclusive preserve of the divinely inspired, or the few great poets. From a psychoanalytic point of view, everyone is poetic; everyone dreams in metaphor and generates symbolic meaning in the process of living. Even in their prose, people have unwittingly been speaking poetry all along."

Paul Edwards has perceptively noted that little evidence exists that any of Freud's patients, including Gustave Mahler and Bruno Walter, were ever cured. Just the same, and although it is partly true that Freudianism has currently diminished somewhat in importance, Edwards holds that it is imperative to retain such of Freud's truly great contributions as the concepts of repression (the unconscious exclusion from the conscious mind of painful impulses or fears or desire), transference (the process by which emotions and desires originally associated with a person are unconsciously shifted to another person, often an analyst), and parapraxis (the slip of the tongue which reveals a subconscious motive). Edwards is not at all positive about Freud's having been attracted to Lamarckism, to parts of Freud's dream theory, to his view that paranoia is caused by repressed homosexual feelings whereas many homosexuals are not at all repressed or paranoiac, and to his inexcusably having fabricated some data in order to support certain theories.

Freud's final days have been described in Peter Gay's *Freud: A Life For Our Time* (1988). Cancer had eaten away much of his jaw, the cancer gave off such a putrid smell that even his dog avoided him, Freud lost weight, and he began to be less alert mentally. Losing such a great quality of life and knowing that his intolerable pain could not be relieved by medicine, he arranged with his physician, Dr. Max Schur, to inject morphine and allow him to lapse into a coma. The father of psychiatry clearly was a believer in euthanasia. The funeral address was delivered by Ernest Jones, the surviving member of Freud's close associates. Jones praised Freud's unwavering love of truth and his hatred of deception. "As never man loved life more, so never man feared death less."

The cremains were buried in a Grecian urn, which he had admired and owned, at Golder's Green Cemetery in London, England. (See entries for Ernest Jones and for Adolf Grünbaum, the latter of whom holds that Freud's ideas about repression can be accepted only when tested against data obtained from control groups, but "no such data have become available during the past century." *Unauthorized Freud: Doubters Confront a Legend* by Frederick C. Crews is meant "to expose [Freud's] system of psychological propositions to the same kind of scrutiny one would apply to any other aspiring science." Also see entry for Hilda Doolittle, who helped Freud escape from the Nazis to London.) {CE; CL; ER; EU, George J. Stack; HNS2; JM; *News & Views, Humanists of North* (New) *Jersey*, June 1998; PA; RE; TRI; TYD}

Freud, Vera (20th Century)

Freud is a permanent representative of the International Humanist and Ethical Union at UNESCO and is the official representative in Europe for Child Haven International. She participated in the 1996 Humanist World Congress held in Mexico City. In a 1999 talk to the Unitarian Fellowship of Ottawa, she discussed women, traditions, and progressive action. {*Humanist in Canada*, Autumn 1999}

Frey, Stephen H. (20th Century)

An atheist who wrote many letters to Pennsylvania newspaper editors, Frey was attacked by many Christian readers. His experiences were described in *Freethought Today* (June-July 1996}. He has written for *Freethought Perspective* (April 1999 and June 1999).

Frey, William (1839—1888)

Frey was the adopted name of a Russian positivist and philanthropist. Disgusted with the oppression and degradation of his country, he went to New York in 1866 and established co-operative communities and also Russian colonies in Kansas and Oregon. In 1881 he went to London in order to influence his countrymen. A year before his death, he revisited Russia. {BDF}

Freycinet, Charles Louis de Sanices de (1828—1923)

A French statesman, Freycinet was a President of the Senate, Minister of Public Works, twice Minister of War, twice Foreign Minister, and three times Premier. He was a member of the French Academy and author of a number of economic and mathematical works. {RAT; RE}

Freytag, Gustav (1816—1895)

Freytag was a German novelist. From 1848 to 1870 he was joint editor of *Die Grenzboten*. His chief novels are *Soll und Haben* (3 volumes, 1855) and *Die Verlorene Handschrift* (1864). His rationalism is expressed in his letters and essays. {RAT}

FRI TANKE

A Norwegian humanist publication, *Fri Tanke* is at Boks 6744, St. Olavs pl, 0130 Oslo, Norway.

Friberg, Eino (20 Century)

The Finnish-born Friberg has lived primarily in the United States and is a retired Unitarian Universalist minister. In the mid-1970s he began translation into English of the *Kalevala*, Finland's national epic. The work, published in 1988 with memorable artwork, is said to follow the Hiawatha-type meter of the original poetry. However, the reverse is the case: Longfellow copied the work's meter for his poem.

George C. Schoolfield of Yale, noting the excellence of Friberg's translation, wrote that whereas W. F. Kirby in 1907 had translated II.143-148 of Runo Two (Väinäimöinen's scornful reply to the little man of the sea) as Väinäimöinen, old man and steadfast,

Answered in the words which follow:
"You have hardly been created,
Neither made, nor so unproportioned,
As to fell this mighty oaktree,
Overthrow the tree stupendous."

Friberg, in comparison, wrote in the 1988 translation with a directness at once simple and effective:

But old Väinäimöinen answered:
"Maybe you were never made,
Neither made nor intended,
To become the Big-Oak breaker,
Destroyer of the dreadful tree.

Friedan, Betty Naomi (1921—)

Friedan, founder in 1966 of the National Organization for Women (NOW), is a leading social reformer and feminist. *The Feminine Mystique* (1963. 1984) attacked the popular notion that women could find fulfillment only through childbearing and housewifery. In 1969, she denounced lesbians as a "lavender menace," for which comment she apologized in 1977 at their Houston conference. She has also written *Women's Lib* (1972), *It Changed My Life* (1985), *Second Stage* (1991), *The Fountain of Age* (1993), and *The Second Stage* (1998). In 1975, Friedan was named Humanist of the Year by the American Humanist Association. She signed Humanist Manifesto II, having been influenced greatly by Abraham Maslow.

A biography by Judith Hennessee, *Betty Friedan, Her Life* (1999), suggests that Friedan's abrasiveness has always been part of her problem. Her marriage was an unhappy one, complete with physical fights in which she was punched or pushed down. She is seen by some as the victim of sexism, anti-Semitism, and taunts about her sterotypically big nose. Others, however, have been inspired by her exhorting women to free themselves of their own crippling ideas of themselves. Judith Shulevitz, a senior editor at *Slate* in a review of the Hennessee work (*The New York Times*, 9 May 1999), mentions that today Friedan is "mostly written off as obsolete—too bourgeois for left-wing feminists, too feminists for the family-values right and too kooky for everyone else."

When nominated as one of Council for Secular Humanism's

Laureates in the International Academy of Humanism, she accepted, saying that unfortunately feminism, liberalism, emancipation, and humanism are still dirty words in many parts of the U.S. In 1988, Friedan addressed the Tenth International Humanist and Ethical Union (IHEU) World Congress held in Buffalo. Friedan is on the editorial board of *The Humanist.* {CE; HM2}

Friedkin, William (1939-)

Friedkin directed such films as "The Exorcist" (1973); "The Boys in the Band" (1970); and "The French Connection" (1971, Academy Award winner). In *Sight and Sound* (July 1998) he was referred to as an "agnostic Jew." {CA}

Friedman, Kinky (20th Century)

Friedman, a musician and author, has gone on record as being a non-theist. {E}

Friedrich, Carl J(achim) (1901—1984)

A Harvard University professor, Friedrich wrote reviews for *The Humanist* in the 1950s. He is author of *New Image of the Common Man* (1950). Asked about humanism, he responded to the present author:

> I wish I could clearly choose one of the seven categories, but are they really on a level? Do we not all use at times the word *humanism* in the general connotation the lexicographer gives it, do we not carry with it the lessons of ancient humanism, do we not all start from classical humanism? I would exclude from myself atheistic and communistic humanism, but I suspect that I am something of a combination of a theistic and a naturalistic humanist. But in contrast to the description of theistic humanism, I believe in man's capability of working out a good part of his personal development (salvation seems to me a pre-judicial term, involving a *petitio principii*) apart from a supernaturalistic philosophy, but I do at the same time believe that he will be greatly aided in this struggle by the possession of a faith in supernatural powers, and more especially a faith in God. You seem to imply that only the naturalistic humanist acknowledges that he might be wrong; I think that this is equally true of others. Indeed, Thomas Aquinas' famous dictum: *Ignoramus, ignorabimus* shows that intellectual humility is one of the main virtues of the true Christian.
>
> But what I miss most in your categorical scheme is the recognition of humanism outside the tradition of Greece, Rome, and the Judeo-Christian religious faith, except for very recent phenomena. But what of the humanism in China, in India, and so on? It seems to me that our great problem today is the recognition of a *pan-humanism* which while fully recognizing the support it may receive from various religious faiths would stress the common core of all human beings in their striving for the higher forms of self. May I add one further thought which seems to me crucial for humanism today, and which is inadequately recognized by many, especially those whom you call classical neo-humanists. There has been in the past and there is in some humanist circles at present a strong tendency to think of humanism as an elitist doctrine for the few. It was so with the Stoics, with the Humanists of the sixteenth century, and with the Confucians. It is also true of the followers of Babbitt, T. S. Eliot, and Ortega y Gasset. It is my conviction that humanism today must be non-elitist. To put it affirmatively, humanism must be based upon a belief in the common man. This belief represents very serious difficulties but they must be faced. We do not longer accept the easy-going rationalism of the eighteenth century as expressed in Thomas Paine's *Common Sense*. And yet, humanism, pan-humanism calls for the recognition that man's communal capacity is not the possession of an intellectual or cultural elite. The kind of belief I am talking about you can find in Dostoyevsky, more especially in *The Brothers Karamazov*. But you can also find it in Abraham Lincoln's political philosophy and in Gandhi's best thought.
>
> You ask which writers most influenced me. This is hard to say. Kant, Thomas Aquinas, and Aristotle certainly are very important. But the common man himself, my country neighbors here and abroad, has taught me most.
>
> {WAS, 4 September 1956}

FRIENDS, SOCIETY OF: See the entry for Quakers.

FRIENDSHIP

- Friendship goes dancing round the world proclaiming to us all to awake the praises of a happy life.

—**Epicurus**

- Be thou familiar, but by no means vulgar;
  Those friends thou hast, and their adoption tried,
  Grapple them to thy soul with hoops of steel.

—William Shakespeare

- Friendship is the finest balm for the pangs of despised love.

—Jane Austen

- I have lost friends, some by death . . . others by sheer inability to cross the street.

Virginia Woolf

FRIENDSHIP LIBERAL LEAGUE OF PHILADELPHIA: See entry for K. M. Whitten.

Fries, Jacob Friedrich (1773—1843)

Fries, brought up as a Moravian, became a deist and a German philosopher of the neo-Kantian rationalistic school. He wrote a *System of Metaphysics* (1824) and a *Manual of the Philosophy of Religion and Philosophical Aesthetics* (1832). In his *History of Philosophy*, Fries criticized Kant's proofs of God and immortality. {BDF; RAT}

Friess, Horace L(eland) (1900—1975)

The son-in-law of Felix Adler, Friess was a chairman of the Department of Religion at Columbia; an editor of *The Review of Religion*; and a board member of the American Ethical Union. He became a leader of the New York Ethical Culture Society in 1942. With H. W. Schneider, he wrote *Religion in Various Cultures* (1932). In 1952 Friess addressed the First International Congress on Humanism and Ethical Culture in Amsterdam. From 1952 until his death, he served as a part time Leader and trainer of Leaders in New York. He was Felix Adler's literary-biographical executor. (See entry for Ethical Culture.) {EU, Howard B. Radest; HNS; PK}

FRITANKEREN

Fritänkeren (Freethinker), a Swedish quarterly, is at Torsgatan 47, 1 tr., 113 37 Stockholm, Sweden. E-mail: <gunnar.staldal@stockholm.mail.telia.com>.

Fritchman, Stephen Hole (1902—1981)

A controversial Unitarian minister because of his political engagements, Fritchman edited the *Christian Register* but lost the job because he moved the magazine from a denominational periodical to a more broadly political one. At odds with Frederick May Eliot, Fritchman left the editorship and became minister of the First Unitarian Church in Los Angeles from 1947 to 1969. *Heretic: A Partisan Autobiography* (1977) contains his views concerning liberal religion and his reactions to being called a "pinko" [a pro-Marxist]. *For the Sake of Clarity* (1992) is a collection of his addresses. {U&U}

Fritsche, Mike (20th Century)

Fritsche is editor of *The Free Mind*, newsletter of the University of Minnesota Atheists and Humanists. He also is that group's Vice President.

Froebel, Friedrich (1782—1852)

Froebel, the son of a poor Lutheran pastor, ranks with Pestalozzi as one of the major educators. He founded the kindergarten system.

Froebel's theories on education are based on a belief in "the divine unity of nature," so that spiritual training became a fundamental principle.

He stressed the importance of pleasant surroundings, self-activity, and physical training in the development of the child. However, the clergy bitterly opposed his work, and the Prussian government obliged by closing his schools on the ground that Froebel would not have Christian lessons in them.

McCabe cites Pastor Schmeidler as stating that Froebel was not a Christian but had vague pantheistic views. {CE; JM; RAT; RE; TRI}

Frohman, Daniel (20th Century)

Frohman was on the advisory board of Charles Francis Potter's First Humanist Society of New York.

Frolov, Ivan Petrovich (20th Century)

Humanism is the most appropriate philosophy for the future, Frolov states in *Man, Science, Humanism* (1990). A Russian who was editor of *Pravda*, he writes about Marxism from a philosophical viewpoint. Frolov is editor of *The Dictionary of Philosophy* (1985).

Fromkin, David (20th Century)

In *The Way of the World: From the Dawn of Civilizations to the Eve of the Twenty-first Century* (1998), Fromkin avoids including the moral seriousness most historians traditionally utilize. Instead, he takes the position that the meaning of human history is natural, not divine. Humans are therefore obligated to accept that, as our population increases but our cultures become fewer, history is universal, not otherwise.

A professor of international relations, Fromkin lists eight stages in universal history:

- the emergence of the hominid line, apes with brains, in prehistoric Africa;
- the discovery of agriculture and the creation of the first cities—settlements whose residents were not all farmers;
- the sudden rise of universalizing religious and moral systems all over civilized Eurasia in the sixth century B. C. E.;
- the birth of the idea of world civilization with the empires of ancient Eurasia;
- the rise of rationalism and empirical science;
- the irreversible encounter, after the 15th century, between human societies in Eurasia and Africa and those in the Americas;
- the industrial modernization that began in the 18th century; and
- the steady movement toward democratic government centered in the 19th century and the unsteady movement toward decolo nization and world law in the 20th.

{William R. Everdell, *The New York Times Book Review*, 17 January 1998}

Fromm, Erich (1900—1980)

An eminent social philosopher and psychoanalyst, author of *The Sane Society* and *Escape From Freedom* (1941), Fromm at Eva Ingersoll Wakefield's and the present author's invitation addressed a Humanist Society of New York meeting in the 1950s and told those assembled that he basically was a naturalistic humanist. Although Fromm started as a disciple of Freud, he came to believe an individual is the result of his body and his culture, that it is easy for those who are the products of an industrial society to become estranged from themselves. Such views were considered controversial when he taught at Columbia University. In 1966 Fromm was named Humanist of the Year by the American Humanist Association.

In his *Man for Himself* (1947), Fromm wrote, "If faith cannot be reconciled with rational thinking, it has to be eliminated as an anachronistic remnant of earlier stages of culture and replaced by science dealing with facts and theories which are intelligible and can be validated." {CE; CL; HNS; HNS2; TYD}

Frommer, Arthur (20th Century)

Frommer edited *The Bible and the Public Schools* (1963). {GS}

Frost, Robert (1874—1963)

Frost, a four-time Pulitzer Prize winner for the excellence of his poetry, has been a biographer's delight, filled with unique complexities.He had an ancestor who, upon being intimate with an American Indian girl, was banished from Kittery, Maine, and was not allowed to return until he married an English wife. Frost had a father who was an atheist and a mother who was a mystical Swedenborgian mother. His own philosophical outlook ranged between his parents' extremes:

> I turned to speak to God
> About the world's despair
> But to make bad matters worse
> I found God wasn't there.

His parents had met as fellow schoolteachers. His Scottish mother was born Isabelle Moodie in Leith, near Edinburgh. Her father had been a sea captain who drowned soon after she was born. Her mother was "a hussy who ran away from the arduous duties of motherhood," so the eleven-year-old Isabelle was sent to Ohio. Here, she published poetry with Swedenborgian overtones and attempted to support her family by being a schoolteacher, at which biographers have said she failed. Frost later described her as "a queer woman" with "incipient insanity."

The famous poet's homelife was anything but pleasant. His only sibling, Jeanie, was eventually sent to a mental institution, where she wrote her brother, "I am very peculiar and did not start right. If I ever was well and natural it was before I can remember." His wife, Elinor, bore many children: the oldest, Elliott, died of typhoid fever when three—although the mother thought the death was because of "God's judgment," Robert blamed himself for not having obtained the best medical care; a daughter, Elinor Bettina, died soon after she was born; son Carol killed himself with a deer rifle when thirty-eight; Marjorie died of a postpartum infection; Irma had an unhappy marriage and was eventually committed to an insane asylum. Frost's wife, two years before Carol's suicide, died of a heart attack—after her death Robert wrote to a friend, "God damn me when he gets around to it." Alone, the poet asked his daughter Lesley to let him live with her, and according to biographer Lawrance Thompson

> She said she had seen him cause so much injury to the lives of his own children—particularly to Irma, Carol, and Marjorie—that she would not permit him to move into her home, where he might also injure the lives of her two daughters. Her rage increased as she went on to insist, through her tears, that she could not forgive him for his having ruined her mother's life. It was his fault, she said, that her mother was dead, for it was his own selfishness which had forced her mother to climb those stairs to the upper quarters, repeatedly. . . . Then she hurt him most by concluding that he was the kind of artist who never should have married, or at least never should have had a family.

Encyclopedist Sherman Wakefield, the husband of Robert Ingersoll's granddaughter, Eva Ingersoll Wakefield, wrote the present writer, "I note with interest that you had a conversation with Robert Frost recently and don't quite get the combination of Unitarianism and Swedenborgianism. He must be awfully confused, religiously. I wrote July 18th and got no answer from him" (27 December 1954). The reference was to a dinner at Frost's publisher's home in New Canaan, Connecticut. After two pre-dinner cocktails with the salty, grandfatherly poet, the present writer remarked that some say he sounds as if he might be a Unitarian in the following sentiment:

> Some say the world will end in fire,
> Some say in ice.
> From what I've tasted of desire
> I hold with those who favor fire.
> But if it had to perish twice,
> I think I know enough of hate
> To say that for destruction ice
> Is also great

And would suffice.

and

Forgive, O Lord, my little jokes on Thee
And I'll forgive Thy great big one on me.

His reply to the question was that his mother was a Swedenborgian. "Yes, but *you*, Mr. Frost?"

Again, he replied that his mother's Swedenborgianism was an important part of her life. It became evident that although Frost deliberately had chosen to be a member of no organized religion, he found his mother's devotion "beautiful" and he was not about to question her theism.

At this point, the publisher's teenage son interrupted, revealing that the present writer liked E. E. Cummings's poetry better than his. Frost smiled at such adolescent ingenuousness, then revealed that at *Poetry*, a major magazine for established as well as new poets, Cummings truly was the only individualistic poet who was writing at that time. Frost was then told about an Iowa professor's analysis of the symbolism of "Birches." He listened intently to the academic discussion of what Frost purportedly had used as symbols in the work, then resolutely replied, perhaps fired by the several cocktails,

The next time you see that prof, tell 'im "Up your ass!"

Frost proceeded to mention his friendship with Iowa poet James Hearst, with whom he said he shared a "religious love of nature." Frost said that he had made a major mistake when first he had bought a 30-acre farm in Derry, New Hampshire–he had purchased it rather quickly, whereas any other farmer, particularly Hearst, knows that you take plenty of time checking land out before you purchase it. As a result, his neighbors never quite accepted him as a farmer.

Although a final attempt was made to bring up the subject of his outlook on religion, mentioning terms like theism, agnosticism, atheism, and naturalistic humanism, Frost remained noncommittal. "You feel that if you respond, you will upset the many believers who are your supporters?" I finally said. Like many other authors of his time period, he pleaded that his work contains all such answers.

A work which does provide something of an answer is *Masque of Mercy*. In it, Frost has a character, Brother's Keeper, who in his attempt to understand Jesus takes the unitarian approach through Palestine rather than the Christian approach through Rome, remarking that Paul has almost theologized Christ out of Christianity.

Beneath Frost's Wordsworthian and Emersonian woodland philosophy, however, was a troubled and combative spirit. Not so well known was that after the death of his wife Elinor in 1938, Frost took Kathleen Morrison not only as his secretary but as his lover, this despite her still being married to novelist and Harvard professor Theodore Morrison. Jeffrey Meyers, in *Robert Frost: A Biography* (1996), reveals that a previous biographer, Lawrance Thompson, was also a lover of Kathleen Morrison and agreed with her, against Frost's wishes, that his biography would not mention her affair with the poet. Meyers also relates that Hart Crane wrote a letter telling of his admiration for Frost's daughter Lesley, to which Frost commented, "Fortunately for Lesley, the homosexual, suicidal Crane was not really interested in women." Another member of Morrison's harem, for Frost was not alone, was Bernard De Voto, who writer who became editor of *The Saturday Review of Literature*.

Frost's influence upon others was monumental. B. F. Skinner credited Frost with advising him to become a writer instead of continuing his college work. Numbers of others credited him with inspiring them in their creative endeavors. His public readings were so numerous Allen Ginsberg called them "relentless" and said, "He created an audience for poetry readings. . . . He was the first voyager, a kind of pioneer, the original entrepreneur of poetry." At one such reading, John Updike recalled, the author of *A Masque of Reason* (1945) that had been panned by left-wing critics turned to Archibald MacLeish in the audience and, in an obvious reference to his Broadway success "J.B.," which spoke of "Our labor . . . is to learn through suffering to love," retorted, "People think everything is solved by love. Maybe just as many things are solved by hate." Updike noticed that MacLeish "smiled, slightly, through the assault; he knew his man, and perhaps had heard it all before." But it illustrated, Updike added, Frost's admission one time that "There's a vigorous devil in me."

Although he once had studied philosophy with George Santayana, Frost was not wholly convinced by the Harvard teacher's considering religion an expression of symbolic, not literal, truth. Doubt, he agreed, is a part of faith. But, as pointed out by Jay Parini in *Robert Frost, a Life* (1999), Frost's "many doubts never added up to a denial of basic things of the spirit, since spirit was a vital part of his dualism, along with matter."

On Frost's eighty-fifth birthday, Lionel Trilling described "Fire and Ice" (1923) and "Bereft" (1928) as having been written by a "poet of terror," noting his gloomy and malicious side. But in 1961, on President John F. Kennedy's Inauguration Day, Frost made a memorable and happy appearance on the platform to read a poem written especially for the occasion:

Summoning artists to participate
In the august occasions of the state
Seems something artists ought to celebrate . . .
A golden age of poetry and power
Of which this noonday's the beginning hour. . . .

In the blinding winter sunlight, however, Frost was unable to read his text in the glare and the wind. Giving up, he recited a poem that he knew by heart.

It was on that day that, stunning the freezing crowd by removing his overcoat, Kennedy at the last minute changed

Ask not what your country will do for you,
but what you will do for your country.

to

Ask not what your country can do for you,
but what you can do for your country.

When Frost entered a hospital for the final time, he told a reporter, "I don't take life very seriously. It's hard to get into this world and hard to get out of it. And what's in between doesn't make much sense. If that sounds pessimistic, let it stand." Actually, it sounded entirely unlike something his mother would have said. Rather, it was the sentiment of his father, the Harvard Phi Beta Kappa non-theist.

Frost died unexpectedly during an operation for appendicitis. Friends recalled that he once spoke about an epitaph, remaking "I would have written of me on my stone: I had a lover's quarrel with the world." (See the entry for James Hearst.) {CE; PA; John Updike, "Poet on the Fault Line," *The New Yorker*, 15 March 1999; WAS interview 1954}

Frost, William Prescott Jr. (Died 1885)

The father of the poet Robert Frost was, as described by John Updike (*The New Yorker*, 15 March 1999), "the only child of a New Hampshire farm family, a Harvard Phi Beta Kappa, a San Francisco journalist with political ambitions, a drinker, a professing atheist, a gun lover, a sometimes abusive husband and parent." When he died, he left his wife Belle and family with eight dollars.

Frothingham, Octavius Brooks (1822—1895)

A leader of the radical wing of late 19th-century Unitarianism and a founder of the Free Religious Association, Frothingham was the son of a Boston Unitarian minister, Nathaniel Langdon Frothingham. He favored Transcendentalist theology rather than a conservative version of Unitarianism, and befriended Theodore Parker during his ministry in Salem, Massachusetts. His *Religion of Humanity* (1873) is considered a central statement of modernist thinking in theology, and in his *Transcendentalism in New England* (1876) he made important contributions to the early historiography of the Transcendentalist movement. Among Frothingham's parishioners was sculptor Augustus Saint-Gaudens. (See entry for Felix Adler and for Free Religious Association.) {BDF; CE; FUS; RAT; U; U&U; CE}

Froude, James Anthony (1818—1894)

Froude was son of an Archdeacon of Totnes. He became a rationalist and abandoned his clerical life, explaining the change in *Nemesis of Faith* (1848). The editor of *Fraser's Magazine* for many years, he wrote *Life of Carlyle* (1882), which provoked much controversy because, states McCabe, of its "giving away the early impotence of Carlyle." His translation of Lucian's most characteristic *Dialogue of the Gods*, Wheeler wrote, "is done with too much verve to allow of the supposition that the translator is not in sympathy with his author." {BDF; JM; RAT; RE}

Fruchtman, Jack Jr. (20th Century)

Fruchtman wrote *Thomas Paine: Apostle of Freedom* (1994), a biography that updates previous works. However, according to John Keane, Fruchtman mistakenly depicted Paine as "something of a country bumpkin" who was "clearly out of his element in these [intellectual] circles." (See entry for John Keane.)

Fry, Elizabeth (1780—1845)

A noted prison reformer in England, Fry was a Unitarian. {U}

Fry, John (17th Century)

Fry was a colonel in the Parliamentary army. In 1648 he was called to the House of Commons, where he voted that Charles I be put on trial and sat in judgment when sentence was passed. His *The Accuser Shamed* (1649) was ordered to be burned for speaking against "that chaffie and absurd opinion of three persons in the Godhead." Fry was then charged with blasphemy. {BDF; RAT}

Fryer, Peter (1927—)

Fryer, a freethinker, wrote *Mrs. Grundy* (1963). {TRI}

FUCK

Considered an obscene word, *fuck* first appeared in "Flen Flyys," a poem written before 1500. The work satirized Carmelite friars of Cambridge, England, with its title taken from the first words of the poem, "Flen, flyys, and freris" [fleas, flies, and friars]. One of its lines, "*Non sunt in coeli, quia gxddbov xxkxzt pg ifmk*," when decoded (according to *The American Heritage Dictionary of the English Language*, 1992), becomes "fvccant vvivys of heli," or, fully decoded, "They are not in heaven because they fuck wives of Ely [a town near Cambridge]."

Inasmuch as the word has become so common and so over-used, even in print, some freethinkers have recommended *futter* as a replacement in order to bring back the overtones previously communicated. Carl Muller, in "Giving the middle finger to the Bulgarian" (*The Island*, Colombo, Sri Lanka, 20 February 1999), wrote:

> [W]e have the old English word "futter," which in the worst sense means to "roger," which the Scots admit to after they have done to a girl what comes naturally. "Futter" used to be in fashion for a long time and it is a pity that the word fell into disuse. The Roman poet Martial frequently used the word "*futuere*" (from which "futter" came) and this in turn was derived from "*fundo*," meaning to pour out, ejaculate, discharge semen. Funny, we abandoned the seemingly innocuous "futter" for a four-letter word with more resonance. The point is, "futter" belonged to polite conversation while the word in use today is certainly not. We still have to painfully insert asterisks when forced to convey the word although I don't, but then, that is part of my—shall we say—charm.

Fukuzawa, Yukichi (1834—1901)

According to Robertson, "The late Yukichi Fukuzawa, who did more than any other man to prepare the Japanese mind for the great transformation effected in his time, was spontaneously a freethinker from his childhood; and through a long life of devoted teaching he trained thousands to a naturalist way of thought." He adds that in 1894 there were no fewer than 71,831 Buddhist temples and 190,803 Shinto temples and shrines in Japan, that it is a difficult task in Japan to rid the average individual of a great amount of commonly held superstitions. Fukuzawa wrote *An Outline of a Theory of Civilization* (1973). {JMR}

Fulghum, Robert (1937—)

A part time minister, author, and lecturer, Fulghum wrote *All I Really Need to Know I Learned in Kindergarten* (1958), *It Was On Fire When I Lay Down On It* ((1989), *Uh Oh* (1991), and *Maybe (Maybe Not)* (1994). A Unitarian, he made a forty-city book tour for charity in 1994, raising a million dollars for such diverse groups as the American Civil Liberties Union, the Interlochen Center for the Arts, Amnesty International, and the Children's National Medical Center. He was a graduate of Starr King School for the Ministry, the Berkeley, California seminary for Unitarian Universalists. He served Unitarian churches in Washington State for more than twenty years. {*World*, May/June 1995}

Fulks, Clay (20th Century)

Fulks, a freethinker, wrote *Christianity, A Continuing Calamity* (1950). {GS}

Fuller, Margaret: See entry for Sarah Margaret Fuller.

Fuller, (Richard) Buckminister (1895—1983)

An architect and engineer, Fuller developed "energetic" geometry (1917), the "4-D" house (1928), a self-contained, dustless unit which could be transported by air; the streamlined Dymaxion auto (1933); and the Dymaxion house (1944—1945). His geodesic domes have been used widely for military and industrial purposes. A controversial thinker, Fuller in 1969 was named Humanist of the Year by the American Humanist Association.

"Sometimes," Fuller declared, "I think we're alone. Sometimes I think we're not. In either case, the thought is quite staggering."

Fuller greatly enjoyed lecturing, but his sense of time was such that upon at least one occasion, in New Canaan, Connecticut, half his audience left after one hour and fifteen minutes. Then. half of those who remained left after another half-hour. Although a master of ceremonies walked on stage and discreetly suggested he had only five more minutes, Fuller continued speaking until the lights were turned off by the one of only three people who remained–the one who had keys to lock the auditorium. {CE; HNS2; TYD}

Fuller, (Sarah) Margaret (Ossoli) (1810—1850)

An important personage in literary circles, Fuller was an ardent feminist who in her *Woman in the Nineteenth Century* (1845) treated the subject in its economic, intellectual, political, and sexual aspects. A leader of transcendentalism, she edited its journal, the *Dial*, and was a friend of Emerson (who later edited the *Dial*), Thoreau, Hawthorne, and others in that philosophic movement. She did not favor the movement's Brook Farm utopian experiment, and she has beer described as Emerson's token woman in the Transcendental Club.

Fuller's father was a Jeffersonian liberal who, elected to Congress for four terms, opposed the extradition of fugitive slaves. He also opposed the Missouri Compromise, which admitted a slave state, and he was against the Seminole War. Margaret was his eldest child, and before she was nine she studied Greek, French, and Italian as well as read Vergil, Cicero, Horace, Livy, and Tacitus. Thomas Wentworth Higginson, the Unitarian minister who encourage Emily Dickinson and her, once observed that the Massachusetts Fullers were energetic to the point of being "without a particle of tact." Her Fuller grandfather had been a minister who lost his pulpit because, in the words of critic Millicent Bell, "he was suspected of insufficient zeal for the Revolution" and who later refused to vote for the ratification of the new Federal constitution "because it implicitly sanctioned slavery."

Fuller's influence on other authors was major. She has been identified as Zenobia in Hawthorne's *Blithedale Romance*. Lowell caricatured her as Miranda in his *Fable for Critics*. Hawthorne's Hester

Prynne in *The Scarlet Letter* echoed Fuller's argument for women's progressive liberation. A stimulating talker, she once conducted conversation classes for society women on social and literary topics.

Horace Greeley made her the first literary critic of the New York *Tribune*. For the *Tribune* she wrote about Italy's Revolution of 1848—1849, having married the Marchese Ossoli, a follower of Mazzini, and moving with her husband to Rome and taking part in the struggle. (The two may not actually have married, for she was evasive about the subject to her friends.)

Millicent Bell states that Fuller tended to see herself as having masculine and feminine traits–"masculinity being a label for her logical powers, her love of knowledge, her assertiveness, her longing for active life. She also had a feminine side, she felt, a side that was poetic and emotional and responsive to nature as well as caretaking–and this she identified with her mother who exemplified the Victorian Angel in the House and loved gardening and babies.

Her *Woman in the Nineteenth Century* theorized that all men have some measure of the womanly and that all women have some measure of the manly. Her biographer, Mason Wade, as well Jonathan Katz in *Gay American History,* states that although Fuller was bisexual in writings which survived her, these were severely bowdlerized after her death by Emerson, W. H. Channing, and J. F. Clark, allegedly to "protect her reputation." Contemporaries knew of her being attached to the intelligent wives of several Harvard professors as well as to an older English girl who was the object of a sentimental crush, and to the future abolitionist writer Lydia Maria Child.

Fuller was a Unitarian who, unlike the deists, thought that God is immanent in man and nature, that individual intuition is the highest source of knowledge, and that individualism, self-reliance, and rejection of traditional authority are keys to humankind's happiness. Her reputation in the 1960s and 1970s has undergone a major revival, and she is coming to be understood as a pioneering feminist, an important literary critic, and a central figure in the Transcendentalist movement. Her place in literary history is presently being reassessed and her life and writing is being recognized as "a vindication of women's right to think." Contemporary critics are agreeing with the landmark *History of Woman Suffrage* (1881): "Margaret Fuller possessed more influence upon the thought of America than any woman previous to her time." She is credited with having formulated the issues that were central for the 1848 Seneca Falls convention on women's rights. Without equality, she insisted, marriage was a union between parent and adopted child or master and slave. Bell adds, "She repudiated the idea that women's freedom of occupation would break up the home, and pointed out that the hard labor of working-class women proved that women were not too delicate to assume the burdens of men while an upper-class woman was likely to have already escaped into the frivolous pursuit of 'animation for her existence.'" Women could do anything: "Let them be sea-captains if you will." Often quoted is her general statement, "I accept the Universe!"

At Brook Farm, she experienced communitarian ideals, but she came to see the Utopian commune as embodying an economic and social critique of the larger society. Bell notes that Fuller "moved from the belief in private solutions to the acceptance of the need for political change. Channing, a follower of Fourier, had become a more important influence on her than Emerson. . . . In the year of *The Communist Manifesto*, which she may not have read, she saw some form of socialism as 'the inevitable sequence to the tendencies of the era.' Unlike many of America's intellectuals–Emerson, Hawthorne, Melville included–who had recoiled from the English Chartists and the Paris revolutionaries of 1848, she was drawn to the radical ideas of the European rebellions. The Jeffersonian democracy in which she had always believed no longer seemed an ultimate human aim." She began to disparage America for maintaining slavery and for the war with Mexico, saying America had become "stupid with the lust for gain . . . shamed by an unjust war." Many hold that Emerson, fearful of the commotion she would cause upon returning, urged Fuller to delay her return home. It was her political views, as well as the gossip of Rome that had preceded her, which would surely have embarrassed her writer friends. Elizabeth Barrett Browning, describing Fuller's last months in Italy, said Fuller had become "one of the out & out *Reds*."

Fuller and the marquis had to flee from Italy because of their strong rebellion against the Papacy. Unfortunately, she was drowned with her husband and infant son when their ship wrecked an estimated four hundred yards off the Fire Island, New York, shoreline. Only the baby's body was recovered.

Thoreau traveled to the scene the next day, found Ossoli's coat, and wrote in his journal: "I have in my pocket a button which I ripped off the coat of the Marquis of Ossoli, on the seashore, the other day. Held up, it intercepts the light,–an actual button,–and yet all the life it is connected with is less substantial to me, and interests me less, than my faintest dream. Our thoughts are the epochs in our lives; all else is but a journal of the winds that blew while we were here."

Never recovered was her manuscript of the history of the Italian revolution. {BDF; CE; EG; FUS; JM; TSV; RAT; RE; TYD; U; WWS}

Fulpius, M. (19th Century)
In Switzerland, Fulpius edited *Rationaliste* in the 1860s.

FUNDAGELICALS: See entry for Delos B. McKown.

FUNDAMENTALISM

• Fundamentalism is an ideology that diverts people from the path of natural development of consciousness and undermines their personal rights.

—**Taslima Nasrin**

"Fundamentalist" has its root in the "fundament," "foundation," "of the buttocks," "backside," etc.

In Christian theology, fundamentalism is a conservative 19th- and 20th-century movement. Fundamentalists believe that the statements in the Bible are literally true, which puts them at odds with the theory of evolution. In the 1920s and to date, the Evangelical movement has opposed liberalism and secularism. Fundamentalists throughout the Christian or Muslim world are noted for their rigid adherence to fundamental or basic principles, principles for which they are willing to die if necessary.

Marlene Winell wrote *Leaving the Fold: A Guide for Former Fundamentalists and Others Leaving Their Religion* (1993), and Edward T. Babinski wrote *Leaving the Fold: Testimonies of Former Fundamentalists* (1995).

Herb Caen, in *San Francisco Chronicle* (20 July 1981), wrote a secular critique of fundamentalism: "The trouble with born-again Christians is that they are an even bigger pain the second time around." (See entry for *Walk Away*, a newsletter for ex-fundamentalists. See entry for fatwa, a device used by Muslim fundamentalists.) {DCL; TYD}

FUNDAMENTALIST CHRISTIAN: PAT ROBERTSON

• Charismatic TV preacher, international businessman, presidential candidate in 1988, founder of Regent university, would-be Third World evangelist and entrepreneur, self-styled political boss, [Pat] Robertson is on a mission from God. He wants a godly nation, which sounds to his enemies like a fundamentalist Christian state, one that might apply the Word to all facets of American life (much as the Afghan Taliban and Iranian mullahs are applying their Word). Robertson denies working toward a theocracy. He isn't likely to start flogging women for showing their faces, or lopping off the hands of thieves, and he most certainly wouldn't ban television (as the Taliban did). He wants a country where abortion is outlawed, where the Bible is back in schools, where "children are cared for by two married, heterosexual parents." He wants a popular culture that is strictly PG, that, he says, "glorifies not what is seamy and sordid and violent but what is good, beautiful and noble." He wants to combat the "white witchcraft, black magic and satanic worship" he sees behind astrology, UFOs, Zen and New Age religions, and he wants to encourage a strictly patriarchal view of marriage: "Christ is the head of the household, and the husband is the head of the wife." He wants to save the world, but first and mostly he wants to save America.

—Mark Bowden,
"The Holy Terror," *Playboy*, February 1999

FUNDAMENTALISTS ANONYMOUS

Fundamentalists Anonymous, Box 20324 Greeley Square Station, New York, NY 10001, publishes a newsletter. {FD}

FUNERALS

• Funeral, n. A pageant whereby we attest our respect for the dead by enriching the undertaker, and strengthen our grief by an expenditure that deepens our groans and doubles our tears.

—Ambrose Bierce
The Devil's Dictionary

"Funerals," Quentin Crisp holds, "are rather horrid. All that standing in the pouring rain in the churchyard while people say how wonderful you were. They can just put me in a plastic bag and shovel me into a Dumpster. I don't care."

Jessica Mitford would have died laughing. Her *The American Way of Death* (1963) made fun of the funeral industry with its "morticians" and "caskets" and "floral tributes" instead of funeral directors and coffins and flowers. Not long after her death, the following advertisement appeared in New York's *Daily News* (8 August 1996):

UNITY FUNERAL CHAPELS, INC.

> . . . Our basic goals have been to improve the service of our chapels. Since the 1980's, we have invested half a million dollars in renovations (almost always using African-American contractors) which has resulted in state-of-the-art chapels. In fact, our chapels are such a class act because of the exquisite outer and inner quality of our edifices. Unity Funeral Chapels have wall-to-wall carpeting, modern air conditioned, cushioned chairs, private family and reposing rooms, sensitive-to-your-needs courteous, efficient, highly skilled funeral directors, price quotes by phone, a unique pre-arrangement program, the latest model customized powder-blue Cadillac hearses owned by Unity Funeral Chapels, and the latest model Cadillac limousines rented from Black-owned agencies. Overall, Unity employs twenty-two individuals from the African-American community. Unity also contributes to community educational and recreational programs.
>
> Let's bury the rumors now: Unity Funeral Chapels Inc. is a totally African-American-owned and operated enterprise, and God willing, we intend to remain so. . . .

Mitford, late in life, had been asked what sort of funeral she wanted. An elaborate one, she responded gravely, that had "six black horses with plumes and one of those marvelous jobs of embalming that take 20 years off."

She added that she wanted "streets to be blocked off, dignitaries to declaim sobbingly over the flower-smothered bier, proclamations to be issued–that sort of thing." Unity Funeral Chapels, Inc., had she known, could expertly have served her final needs. (See entry for Burial Practices.)

Fürbringer, Max (Born 1846)

Fürbringer was a German anatomist who taught at Heidelberg, Amsterdam, and Jena. A Privy Councillor, he was a leading anatomist in Germany. Fürbringer acknowledged himself a monist and eulogized Haeckel as "a hero of science" and "prophet" of truth. {RAT}

Furnemont, Léon (Born 1861)

A Belgian advocate, Furnemont founded the Circle of Progressive Students. He represented Young Belgium at the funeral of Victor Hugo. A Councillor of the International Federation of Freethinkers, he was director of a monthly journal, *La Raison*, in 1889. {BDF}

Furness, Frank (Born 1839)

Furness, a skilled 19th century architect, was a Unitarian. {U}

Furness, Kenneth (20th Century)

When Furness signed Humanist Manifesto II, he was executive secretary of the British Humanist Association. {CL; HM2}

Furness, William Henry (1802—1896)

After the Philadelphia Unitarian Church was founded in 1796 by Joseph Priestley, it continued without a minister until Furness became the minister, and he served for fifty years. Furness rejected, in his *Remarks on the Four Gospels* (1836), the use of the biblical miracles as a basis for Christian faith, which allied him with the Transcendentalists on the miracles question. Furness thought the miracles occurred but were natural events, that religious faith does not require confirmation of supernatural events. His Hegelian-influenced *Christianity a Spirit* (1859) shows his interest in German philosophy. Furness preached the funeral sermon of his lifelong friend Emerson in 1882. {U&U}

Furniss, James J. (19th Century)

Furniss, a freethinker, wrote *The Anonymous Hypothesis of Creation* (1877). {GS}

Furnivall, Frederick James (1825—1910)

Furnivall was a writer who, although not a Christian, devoted himself to educational work with the Christian Socialists. He helped to found the Working Man's College (1854) and was active in the Sunday League and other progressive organizations. Furnivall founded the Early English Text Society and the Chaucer, Wyclif, Shelley, and Browning Societies.

He was an agnostic and an honorary associate of the Rational Press Association. {RAT; RE}

Fussman, Gérard (20th Century)

Fussman, a professor at the Collège de France in Paris, signed Humanist Manifesto 2000.

Futrell, Mynga (20th Century)

With Paul Geisert, Futrell wrote *Different Drummers, Nonconforming Thinkers in History* (1999).

FUTURE

> Future, n. That period of time in which our affairs prosper, our friends are true, and our happiness is assured.

—Ambrose Bierce
The Devil's Dictionary

Mankind enjoys speculating about what the future will bring. Utopias and dystopias are described in detail by writers of fiction and science fiction.

Although it is impossible to foresee what is by definition obscure, John Maddox has made an attempt in his *What Remains to be Discovered: Mapping the Secrets of the Universe, the Origins of Life and the Future of the Human Race* (1998). He offers the big questions: How did the universe begin? How does the universe work? Did galaxies or stars come first? When and how did life commence? When and how did sexual reproduction commence? What are consciousness, memory, imagination?

Einstein's "general relativity (gravitational) theory" and the theory of quantum mechanics are, he holds, "perhaps the two outstanding intellectual achievements of this century." He adds, "As a direct consequence of the structure of D. N. A., both the internal working of the cell and the mechanism of inheritance in plants and animals (including the development of embryos from fertilized eggs), has become susceptible to laboratory investigation."

But the more we know, the more contradictions are apparent. Out of these contradictions must come future discoveries. Maddox's book contains summaries of our present knowledge, but in 3001 his look into the future will likely amuse whoever is able to locate his, as well as Sir Arthur C. Clarke's fictional *3001*, extrapolations. {Christopher Lehmann-Haupt, "The Century Ahead for Science," *The New York Times*, 16 November 1998}

Fuykschot, Cornelia (20th Century)

Fuykschot is a humanist living in Gananoque, Ontario. Writing in *Humanist in Canada* (Spring 1999), she told of successfully complaining to the Canadian Radio and Telecommunications Commission (CRTC) about daytime religious programs that were getting on her nerves.

Gaarder, Jostein (1952—)

A Norwegian, Gaarder is author of "a novel about the history of philosophy" called *Sophie's World* (1995), one which in 1996 had sold nine million copies in thirty-six languages by offering philosophy without tears. The work begins 2,600 years ago and ends in the late 1800s. Jim Herrick found the work has "a humanist outlook" and "is difficult to put down." Herrick found that in the first lesson we learn that "[t]he aim of the early Greek philosophers was to find *natural*, rather than supernatural, explanations for natural processes." The concluding instruction covers Darwin, Freud, and the "Big Bang." A clear understanding of rationalism is in place: while considering early Greek philosophy, it is indicated that "a rationalist is someone who believes that human reason is the primary source of our knowledge of the world." Descartes's rationalism is also recounted: "The more self-evident a thing is to one's reason, the more certain is that it exists." The work was written to intrigue and enlighten youngsters who like their fiction embedded in philosophy, Herrick added, and for adults who like their philosophy laced with fiction.

Gabarro, Bartolomé (Born 1846)

A Spanish writer, Gabarro founded in Barcelona an anti-clerical League of Freethinkers pledged to live without priests. When some two hundred anti-clerical groups in over a hundred lay schools formed, the Church became concerned. When Dr. Gabarro denounced the assassins of a freethinker, he was pursued for libel, sentenced to four years in prison, and forced to fly to Cerbere on the frontier, where he published an anti-clerical journal, *La Tronada.* Gabarro has written many brochures and an important work on Pius IX. {BDF}

Gabelli, Aristide (Born 1830)

An Italian writer, Gabelli wrote *The Religious Question in Italy* (1864) and *Man and the Moral Sciences* (1869), in which he rejects all metaphysics and supernaturalism. {BDF}

Gabriel, Ralph H. (1890—1987)

Gabriel, a historian at Yale University (1915—1958), wrote *The Course of American Democratic Thought* (1956) and *Religion and Learning at Yale* (1958). Asked about his views concerning humanism, Gabriel responded to the present author:

> I read your categories of humanism with interest. They seem to me to be excellent and will be useful to me. As for myself, I do not know exactly where I fit. I do not know the realities of the cosmos. I only know that man with his hopes and aspirations, his capacity to sacrifice for an ideal is part of it. He uses the abilities with which he is endowed not only to maintain life but to find some meaning for it. His efforts to discover meaning ends in mystery. His attempt through the use of reason to add to his knowledge of the cosmos has brought a vast increase in that knowledge beyond the frontiers of which, however, lies mystery. To push out this frontier, to penetrate the mystery is his greatest challenge. I find that contemplation of the mystery brings that humility which is one of the virtues taught by religion.
>
> For me the aspirations (part of the cosmos) of men suggest an essence or being greater than man, worship of whom gives added strength for dealing with the vicissitudes of life.
>
> {WAS, 10 July 1956}

Gabriel, Toni (20th Century)

In the 1970s, Gabriel was a humanist counselor associated with the Humanist Society of Greater New York.

Gabrielle, A. G. (19th Century)

Gabrielle, a freethinker, wrote *Life and Immortality of Man* (1898). {GS}

Gaddis, William (1922-1998)

Gaddis was an innovative author of complex novels. He attended Harvard College (1941-1945) until he and a friend were asked to leave because of an altercation with the police. He became a fact checker for *New Yorker* (1945-1947), a Guggenheim fellow (1981), a MacArthur Prize fellow (1982), a Rockefeller grantee (1976), and a member of the American Academy of Arts and Letters.

His four published novels—*The Recognitions* (1955), a Faust-like work about a clergyman's son who becomes a painter, an examination of spiritual bankruptcy; *J. R.* (1975), a harsh depiction of greed, hypocrisy, and banality in the business world; *Carpenter's Gothic* (1985), a depiction of American society's moral chaos, an attack on religious charlatanism; and *A Frolic of His Own* (1993), about a motorist who arranges his own car accident, then experiences the absurdities of the legal world—"stand tall and totemic in the field of modernist literature," wrote critic Mel Gussow. He was compared to James Joyce and Thomas Pynchon for the 1955 work. Other critics compared him to Malcolm Lowry and Herman Melville, Cynthia Ozick calling him "an American original."

Because of some harsh criticism about his first novel from Granville Hicks and others—one wrote, "What this sprawling, squalling, overwritten book needs above all is to have its mouth washed out with lye soap"—he published nothing for two decades, earning a living by writing for the Pfizer pharmaceutical company. Although one of the least read of important American writers, he developed a wide underground reputation for writing demanding, perceptive, and inventive novels. "Like most American novelists, Willie didn't have any grounding in belief of any kind," the critic Frederick Karl said. "He was alone, no religious revival, no reaching for spiritual salvation. Irony became his fall-back position, his world view. He found everything artificial and deceptive and conspiratorial—counterfeit. That was his great theme." As Gaddis once remarked, "Stupidity—and I don't mean ignorance—is a central issue of our time."

In a characteristic aside, he wrote in *The Recognitions*, "The Irish mathematician Sir William Rowan Hamilton calculates that Jesus in assumption, being drawn up through space at a moderate rate, would not yet have reached the nearest of the fixed stars." "I think he thought God was a terrible joke," his literary agent Candida Donadio remarked. Following Gaddis's death in 1998, the cognoscenti awaited the posthumous publication of *Agape Agape*. {Philip Gourevitch, *The New Yorker*, 28 December 1998; "In Memoriam," *The American Rationalist*, March-April 1999}

Gadow, Hans Friedrich (1855—1940)

A zoologist, Gadow was educated under Haeckel at Jena and studied at several other German universities. Migrating to England, he became Strickland Curator and Lecturer on Zoology at Cambridge. In the symposium honoring Prof. Haeckel (*Was Wir Ernst Haeckel Verdanken* (1914), Gadow describes himself as an Agnostic. {RAT; RE}

Gaede, Erwin A. (1917—)

When Gaede signed Humanist Manifesto II, he was a minister of the Unitarian Church in Ann Arbor, Michigan. He wrote *Politics and Ethics* (1983). {HM2}

Gagarin, Yuri (1934—1968)

Gagarin, the atheist and Soviet astronaut, amused large numbers when, speaking from space in 1961, he reported, "I don't see any god up here." {TYD}

Gage, Matilda Joslyn (1826—1898)

A suffrage leader and author of *Woman, Church and State* (1893), Gage collaborated with fellow freethinkers Elizabeth Cady Stanton and Susan B. Anthony in their *History of Woman Suffrage* (1881—1886). Gage, an atheist, was President of the National Women's Suffrage Association. "The careful student of history will discover that Christianity has been of very little value in advancing civilization," she wrote, "but has done a great deal toward retarding it." With Anthony and Stanton, she considered the Church the great obstacle to woman's progress. (See entry for Gerda Lerner.) {BDF; CE; EU, Gordon Stein; JM; Lois K. Porter, "Matilda Joslyn Gage," *Free Inquiry*, Winter 1993; PUT; RAT; RE; TYD; WWS}

Gagern, Carlos von (1826—1885)

Gagern was educated in Berlin, and he became acquainted with Humboldt when traveling to Paris in 1847. In Spain he studied Basque life in the Pyrenees; served in the Prussian army; and became a friend of Wislicenus and the free-religious movement. In 1852 he went to Mexico. In the French-Mexican expedition he was taken prisoner, later becoming the military attaché for Mexico at Berlin. His freethought appears in his memoirs, *Dead and Living* (1884) and in *Sword and Trowel* (1888). {BDF}

Gagern, Heinrich, Freiherr von (1799—1880)

Gagern, a Hessian parliamentary leader and leading advocate of German unity, became president of the Frankfurt Parliament in 1848. In his *Critik des Völkerrechts, mit practischer Anwendung auf unsre Zeit* (Critique of International Law, with Practical Application to Our Time, 1840), Gagern made reference to humanism and the idea of humanity as distinct from that of classical humanism. {CE}

GAIA: See entry for Fons Elders.

GAIA HYPOTHESIS

James Lovelock, a British atmospheric chemist and Lynn Margulis, an American microbiologist, developed the Gaia Hypothesis. It involves the view that our planet's surface functions like a giant organism, one interconnected whole. Named after the Greek earth goddess, it has attracted pagans and mystics as well as atmospheric chemists, ecologists, oceanographers, microbiologists, and geologists. Gaia: The Society for Research and Education in Earth System Science is an organization that encourages interdisciplinary research into the Gaia hypothesis.

Tyler Volk, an associate professor of biology at New York University and a member of Gaia's board of directors, is author of *Gaia's Body: Toward a Physiology of Earth* (1998). Interviewed by *The New York Times* reporter Jill Neimark (11 August 1998), he explained that

> Gaia started with a stupendous metaphor and a unique scientific insight, and I think Lovelock has a special charisma. In a simple sentence, traditional Gaia theory postulates something called "comfortable conditions for life," and asserts that the Gaian system maintains those conditions. It looks at the constancy of temperature, climate, gasses, the ocean environment.
>
> The million-dollar questions that Lovelock first asked [a quarter of a century ago] was, Why is atmospheric oxygen constant at 21 percent, the level needed to maintain complex life? But I think there's been too much emphasis on the ill-defined idea of comfort and on environmental stability. I think the key is almost the opposite: the flow and flux of life, of the chemical processes of organisms over the entire planet. The sheer, raw power of life. . . . If you want to worship mystery, studying the global metabolism is a great way to go.

Gaidoz, Henri (1842—1932)

Gaidoz was a French philologist. He was a professor of Celtic at *the École Pratique des Hautes Études* in 1876. He founded the *Revue Celtique* (1870) and the folklore magazine *Mélusine* (1877). His works indicate his rationalist outlook. {RAT}

Gaillot, Jacques (1935—)

Gaillot, a leftist Bishop of Evreux in Normandy, France, was dismissed in 1995 by the Vatican, although thousands of supporters celebrated Mass at the Cathedral of Notre Dame on his final day. "This is the most beautiful day that I have had as Bishop since my arrival in 1982," he said. The Church had been trying for years to rein him in and made him sign a statement pledging loyalty to established church doctrine. He had criticized church-run schools and contradicted the church's doctrine by opposing the use of nuclear weapons for any purpose, even to deter war. He also flouted church doctrine condemning the use of contraceptives. To a gay magazine, he said in 1989 that failing to advise people who were at risk of contracting AIDS to protect themselves with condoms was tantamount to violating the biblical commandment against murder. The Vatican removed him, giving him the meaningless title of Bishop of Partenia, an inactive diocese in Mauritania. "When I think of what happened to me," Gaillot observed, "I think of the Spanish Inquisition. But the church is my family. After this, I will find some way, perhaps in a monastery, to continue my work, to reflect, to continue to work with the outcasts of life—prisoners, victims of AIDS, the homeless."

Gaines, Steven S. (20th Century)

Gaines, a freethinker, is author of *Marjoe* (1973) and *Heroes and Villains* (1995).

Gaines, William M. (Born 1922; Deceased)

Gaines was founder and long-time publisher of *Mad*. Tim Madigan has said that Gaines "may well have been one of the most influential freethinkers of all time—his magazine has always been in the forefront of giving the raspberry to dogmatism wherever it appears. He should take his rightful place in the pantheon of humanist heroes, although I'm sure his first act would be to slip a whoopy cushion under Voltaire's seat." An atheist, Gaines had as his motto, "Don't take anything too seriously," and that included satire itself. {Maria Reidelbach, *Completely Mad: A History of the Comic Book and Magazine*; *Secular Humanist Bulletin*, Winter 1995}

Gaitán, J. Z. (20th Century)

Gaitán, from Mexico, addressed the Fourth International Humanist and Ethical Union World Congress held in Paris (1966).

Gaitskell, Hugh Todd Naylor (1906—1963)

Gaitskell was a British statesman who in 1945 entered Parliament as a Labour member and from 1950 to 1951 was chancellor of the exchequer. A moderate, he succeeded Clement Attlee as party leader in 1955. Gaitskell, according to Nicholas Walter, was not a believer. {*New Humanist*, September 1996}

Gajewski, Karen Ann (20th Century)

Gajewski is associate editor and production manager in Amherst, New York, of *The Humanist*. {HNS2}

Galanskov, Yuri (Died 1972)

A Russian poet, Galanskov in 1961 edited *Phoenix.*, which was not a political publication. He wrote a "Chelovecheski Manifest," or Humanist Manifesto, for his journal, was sent to a psychiatric hospital, and died in a Soviet labor camp.

Galanter, Vera (20th Century)

Galanter is a representative of the International Humanist and Ethical Union at the United Nations in New York.

GALAXIES

A galaxy is a large aggregation of gas, dust, and typically billions of stars. Held together by the gravitational attraction between its parts, it rotates and thereby is prevented from collapsing on itself. An estimated hundred billion galaxies exist, including our own: the Milky Way.

People in the early part of the 20th century became aware that the Milky Way was not "out there," but, rather that the Earth is a part of the Milky Way Galaxy along with over 100 billion stars including the sun. By the end of the century they had evidence from the Hubble Space Telescope that the faintest and most distant objects ever sighted—galaxies of stars more than twelve billion light years away—had been detected. A sighting penetrated for the first time to within about one billion light years of the very beginning of the universe, showing that even then there were galxies with huge families of stars.

In 1997, astronomers found "Red Arc in CL1358+62," a galaxy some 13 billion light-years from the Earth. In 1998, 0140+326RDI and dubbed RD1 was sighted at the Keek Observatory in Hawaii—the tiny galaxy on the other side of the universe was the most distant object ever before seen from Earth. It was identified the prior year by Dutch researchers from the University of Groningen and an American team from the Lick Observatory in California. If the universe is about 13 billion years old, RD1's light is believed to take about 12.2 billion years to reach Earth. It is almost 90 million light-years father away from Earth than the previous record-holder and is made of the earliest generation of stars to appear in the universe. GRS 1915+105 is a celestial object, a "black hole" around and into which a disc of gas swirls. It was the first object in the Milky Way galaxy that was found to show "superluminal motion," for it shoots out a pair of gaseous jets at close to the speed of light. GRS 1915+105 recently has been shown to drag space with it as it spins. To observe black holes, astronomers utilize the Rossi x-ray Timing Explorer (RXTE), a satellite owned by America's space agency, NASA.

Astronomers estimate how old the universe is by dividing the distance to a galaxy by its speed of recession, concluding with the "Hubble time," which is how long the galaxy must have taken to get that far away from earth since the Big Bang, when everything was in one place. That simple calculation, however, does not give the age of the universe directly, because the expansion was faster in the past than it is now. The dating is corrected by assuming that if the universe has exactly the critical density—the usual assumption up to now—then the age of the universe works out to two-thirds of the Hubble time. At the start of 1998 many astronomers were speaking of the likelihood that the currently expanded universe will never collapse again in a catastrophic reversal of its birth event, the Big Bang, nor ever come to a virtual standstill. Instead, the likelihood is that the cosmos will continue to grow bigger and bigger, colder, darker, and emptier. Forever.

In 1998 at a San Diego, California, meeting of the American Astronomical Society, it was announced that two radio telescopes—the Dwingeloo in the Netherlands and the Parkes in Australia—have detected, respectively, forty and one hundred three *new* galaxies previously obscured by the Milky Way.

In 1999 at the end of the century, philosophers marveled about the discovery that astronomers for the first time have identified a solar system with planets that revolve around a star other than the Sun. Now, unlike at the beginning of the century, as noted by Richard Panek, we are well aware that we are "but the blink-of-an-eye inhabitants of one of several specks of dust circling an ordinary star at the edge of an average galaxy among 125 billion others in the universe!" (A bawdy Manhattan wag is said to have been overheard arguing with a religious ideologue and complaining as well as purposely mispronouncing, "It's a pity you guys know more about Uriah than you do about Uranus!" See entries for Extraterrestrial Life, and for Milky Way.) {CE; *The Economist*, 17 January 1998; *The New York Times*, 31 July 1997, 13 March 1998, and 17 April 1999}

Gale, Richard (20th Century)

Gale is professor of philosophy and a fellow of the Center for Philosophy of Science at the University of Pittsburgh. He is a contributing editor on *Philo*, for which he wrote *R. M. Adams's Theodicy of Grace"* (Spring-Summer 1998).

Gale, Zona (1874—1939)

Gale's "Miss Lulu Bett" won a Pulitzer Prize in 1921. It was an ironic, feminist look at small-town life. Although in religion Gale may have gone through a mystical phase, her biographer August Derleth wrote that she agreed with her father's view, "The spirit of man is God; that is the only God there is." Her life's theme was a belief that "Life is something more than that which we believe it to be." {WWS}

Galbraith, John Kenneth (1908—)

Galbraith, a Canadian-born economist, was an adviser to Pres. John F. Kennedy. A Keynsian, he believed government should fight its unemployment problems by spending and should use more of its wealth to improve public services. He wrote *The Affluent Society* (1959), *The Age of Uncertainty* (1977), and *Economics in Perspective* (1987). In 1985 the American Humanist Association made Galbraith Humanist of the Year. {CE; HNS2}

Galdós, Benito Pérez: See entry for Pérez Galdós, Benito.

Gales, Joseph (1786—1860)

Gales, a deist, was a leading newspaperman in North Carolina. He owned *The Raleigh Register* and had a controlling interest in *The National Intelligencer*. (See entry for North Carolina Freethinkers.)

GALHA: See entry for Gay and Lesbian Humanist Association.

Galiani, Ferdinando: See entry for Beccaria.

Galifret, Yves (20th Century)

A professor emeritus of neurophysiology at the University Pierre and Marie Curie, Dr. Galifret is executive director, *l'Union Rationaliste*, and a Humanist Laureate in the Council for Secular Humanism's International Academy of Humanism. His essay, "Religious Dogmatism and Materialist Reductionism versus Humanism," is in *Challenges to the Enlightenment, Essays in defense of Reason and Science* (1994). He signed Humanist Manifesto 2000. {SHD}

Galileo Galilei (1564—1642)

Most have forgotten that Galileo invented the thermometer as well as the telescope. He also discovered the stellar composition of the Milky Way, but he is chiefly remembered as being an astronomer, physicist, and mathematician whose observations contradicted Aristotle's teachings. Julian Kane, a professor of geology at Hofstra University, has written that Galileo "disproved the Ptolemaic theory, sanctioned for centuries by the Church, which held the Earth to be the central and principal object in the universe, about which all celestial objects orbited. By default, the Copernican theory of planets (including Earth) orbiting the Sun was the only credible one remaining. The Church's belated removal [in 1992] of its 1633 condemnation of Galileo comes 376 years, 7 months, and 26 days after the 1616 decree that attempted to intimidate and restrict the great scientist." However, Kane adds, "Copernicus did not discover the movements of the planets about the Sun. His observations, published in 1543, confirmed the heliocentric theory first promulgated 1.800 years earlier, about 270 B. C. E., by the Greek astronomer Aristarchus of Samos, who attributed the annual reappearance of the constellations in the same celestial position to the Earth orbiting the Sun. This, and periodic reappearances of Mercury, Venus, Mars, Jupiter, and Saturn, in the same respective celestial places, persuaded him to proclaim that all planets orbit the Sun."

The Church brought Galileo before the Inquisition, charging him—not with having fathered three children born of a liaison with Marina Gamba of Venice, whom he never married—as follows:

> Whereas you, Galileo, son of the late Vincenzio Galilei, of Florence, aged 70 years, were denounced in 1615, to this Holy Office, for holding as true a false doctrine taught by many, namely, that the sun is immovable in the center of the world, and that the earth moves, and also with a diurnal motion; also, for having pupils whom you instructed in the same opinions; also, for maintaining a correspondence on the same with some German mathematicians; also for publishing certain letters on the sunspots, in which you developed the same doctrine as true; also for answering the objections which were continually produced from the Holy Scriptures, . . . this Holy Tribunal being desirous of providing against the disorder and mischief which were thence proceeding and increasing to the detriment of the Holy Faith by the desire his Holiness and of the Most Eminent Lords Cardinals of this supreme and universal inquisition, the two propositions of the stability of the sun, and the motion of the earth, were qualified by the Theological Qualifiers as follows:

> 1. This proposition that the sun is in the center of the world and immovable from its place is absurd, philosophically false, and formally heretical; because it is expressly contrary to the Holy Scriptures.
>
> 2. The proposition that the earth is not the center of the world, nor immovable, but that it moves, and also with a diurnal action, is also absurd, philosophically false, and, theologically considered, at least erroneous in faith.
>
> And, in order that so pernicious a doctrine might be altogether rooted out, not insinuate itself further to the heavy detriment of the Catholic truth, a decree emanated from the Holy Congregation of the Index prohibiting the books which treated this doctrine, declaring it false, and altogether contrary to the Holy and Divine Scripture. . . . We order you during the next three years to recite, once a week, the seven penitential psalms, reserving to Ourselves the power of moderating, commuting, or taking off, the whole or part of the said punishment or penance.
>
> 22nd, June 1633

Newton was inspired by Galileo's findings, which inspired Newton's laws of motion. Many critics feel that Galileo should not have given in to the Inquisition. After his books were banned, he became blind in 1638. The Pope denied him permission to see doctors in Florence, and Galileo died a believing Catholic while still under house arrest. An account of how the Jesuits applied every jot and tittle of the Trent declarations to favor Aristotle over Galileo is found in Pietro Redondi's *Galileo: Heretic*.

Robertson terms Galileo "an orthodox Catholic," saying the worst part of his sentence was having all his works, published and unpublished, placed on the *Index Expurgatorius* and "the gag thus laid on all utterance of rational scientific thought in Italy—an evil of incalculable influence." (See Joseph McCabe's *Rationalist Encyclopedia*, which contains examples of how historians have incorrectly dealt with the life and findings of Galileo; he focuses on the untruthful Catholic versions.) {CE; CL; ER; HNS2; JMR; JMRH; PUT; RE; TDY}

Gall, Franz Joseph (1758—1828)

Gall was the founder of phrenology. A physician in Vienna, he devoted much time to the study of the brain and lectured on craniology there. With Dr. Spurzheim, he taught their system of phrenology in various cities of Europe. Contemporary neurology and anthropology have refuted the theory, calling it a form of quackery. Apart from phrenology, Gall contributed materially to knowledge of the brain and nerves, and his works are on the *Index Prohibitorum*. He refused religious ministration at death. {BDF; RAT}

Gallagher, Liam (20th Century)

The lead singer of Oasis, a British band, Gallagher emulates John Lennon and shares some of his iconoclastic views about religion. "We are bigger than Jesus," he said of Oasis. "Oasis is bigger than God," said his brother Noel, also in the band.

As reported by Paul Lester's *Oasis: The Illustrated Story*, Gallagher believes:

> I live for now, not for what happens after I die. If I die and there's something afterwards, I'm going to hell, not heaven. I mean, the devil's got all the good gear. What's God got? The Inspiral Carpets and nuns. Fuck that.

{CA}

Gallatin, Albert (1761—1849)

A statesman educated in Europe, where he adopted deism, Gallatin made a fortune in the United States and entered politics. He served as Secretary of the Treasury under President Jefferson and was Minister to France. A leader of the Republican (Jeffersonian) minority, Gallatin was active in advocating financial reform and in opposing war with France. He attacked all war, slavery, and other evils. Gallatin was one of the founders of New York University, saying America should have "a foundation free from the influence of the clergy." When the clergy "wormed their way in," McCabe noted, Gallatin walked out in disgust. His son James confirmed in his diary that his father was a follower of Voltaire. {CE; JM; RAT; RE; TYD}

Gallaway, B. P. (20th Century)

Gallaway edited *Texas the Dark Corner of the Confederacy: Contemporary Accounts of the Lone Star State in the Civil War* (1994). {*Freethought History #15*, 1995}

Galletti, Baldassare (Died 1887)

Galletti, a pantheist of Palermo, translated into Italian Feuerbach's *Death and Immortality* and selections from Morin. {BDF}

Gallichan, Walter (Born 1861)

Gallichan, who used the pen-name of "Geoffrey Mortimer," was a frequent contributor to rationalist periodicals. In 1891 he wrote *Tales from the Western Moors*, a work of fiction. His rationalist views are found in *The Religion of Kindness* (1916). {RAT}

Gallie, Roger (20th Century)

Gallie, of the University of Nottingham, was a director of the 1996 Hume Conference of The Hume Society, a group engaged in scholarly activity concerning David Hume.

Gallihan, Walter M. (20th Century)

Gallihan, a freethinker, wrote *The Religion of Kindness* (c. 1916). {GS}

Galpin, Thomas (20th Century)

Finding Jesus at a Bench (191—?) is a freethought work written by Galpin. {GS}

Galsworthy, John (1867—1933)

Galsworthy is a British novelist who once asserted that "Humanism is the creed of those who believe that, in the circle of enwrapping mystery, men's fates are in their own hands—a faith that for modern man is becoming the only possible faith." Known for his *The Forsyte Sage* (1922), Galsworthy dealt with three generations of a complacent upper-middle-class family from the 1880s to the 1920s. When he won the Nobel Prize, he gave away the money and maintained charities that remained secret until after his death. When the Society of Authors demanded that he be buried in Westminster Abbey, the clergy refused to admit the remains of so wicked a man. Shortly before his death, however, Galsworthy had strongly attacked any kind of church burial and said, "Scatter my ashes." His agnosticism is best seen in *Moods, Songs, and Doggerels* (1911), but he evidences a vague and wavering theism in "A Dream," in which poem he states, "My faith but shadows that required of men." Although some assumed he had been knighted, Galsworthy always refused the "honor." {CE; CL; HNS; JM; RAT; RE; TYD}

Galt, Tom (20th Century)

A naturalistic humanist, Galt wrote *The Story of Peace and War*, *Seven Days from Sunday* (1956), and *The World Has A Familiar Face* (1981). He has reviewed books for *The Humanist*.

Galton, Francis [Sir] (1822—1911)

A grandson of Erasmus Darwin and son of a rich Quaker, Galton traveled to Africa in 1850 and wrote a popular *Art of Travel*, distinguishing himself by many writings bearing on heredity. In his *Inquiries into Human Faculty and Development* (1883), Galton gives statistical refutation of the theory of prayer. Galton was secretary of the British Association from 1863 to 1868, president of the Geographical Section in 1862 and 1872, and president of the Anthropological Section in 1877 and 1885. Also, he was president of the Anthropological Institute. Sir Francis is credited for coining the word *eugenics*. The system he established for classifying fingerprints is still in use today. In a letter to his friend Darwin, Galton wrote, "Your book drove away the constraint of my old superstition as if it had been a nightmare." His biographer, Karl Pearson, described Galton as one who had ceased being "an orthodox Christian in the customary sense" as early as 1846. {BDF; CE; JM; JMRH; RAT; RE}

Galtung, Johan (20th Century)

A professor of sociology at the University of Oslo, Dr. Galtung is a Humanist Laureate in the Council for Secular Humanism's International Academy of Humanism. He is author of *Limits to Growth and Class Politics* (1980) and "Poor Countries vs. Rich: Whom Will NIEO Benefit?" (1987). In 1980 he was presented with *Social Science—For What? A Festschrift for Johan Galtung*. At the Ninth International Humanist and Ethical Union (IHEU) World Congress held in Oslo (1986), Galtung presided. In 1998 Galtung was President of the International Humanist and Ethical Union's 14th World Congress in Mumbai, at which he spoke on "Towards Year 2000: On the Basis of the Humanist World View." {*Humanist in Canada*, Autumn 1999; *International Humanist News*, December 1998}

GAMAB

Gamab is one of many African gods, the Supreme God living in the heavens. {LEE}

Gambetta, Léon Michel (1838—1882)

A French republican leader, Gambetta opposed Napoleon's Second Empire and was prominent in the provisional government following the empire's fall in 1870. In 1871 he helped create the Third Republic, pursuing as premier a moderate policy between the radicals and the monarchists. He appealed to the radicals with his cry, *"Le cléricalisme—voilà l'ennemi"* (Clericalism—that's the enemy). A professed disciple of Voltaire, Gambetta admired Comte and was an open opponent of clericalism. Writer Frederic Harrison has said that Gambetta "systematically and formally repudiated any kind of acceptance of theology." During his lifetime he never entered a Church, even when attending a marriage or a funeral, but stopped short at the door, and let who would go inside and listen to the mummery of the priest. In his own expressive words, he declined to be "rocked asleep by the myths of childish religions." He professed himself an admirer and a disciple of Voltaire. Every member of his ministry was a Freethinker, and one of them, the eminent scientist Paul Bert, was a militant atheist. Speaking at a public meeting not long before his death, Gambetta called Comte the greatest thinker of this century, saying that it was Comte who proposed to "reorganize society, without God and without king, by the systematic cultus of humanity."

Upon his death, *Pays*, a journal edited by Paul de Cassagnac, reported that Gambetta "dies, poisoned by his own blood. He set himself up against God. He has fallen. It is fearful. But it is just." Two years prior to his death, M. Feuillet des Conches, formerly Vicar of Notre Dame des Victoires and then honorary Chamberlain to the Pope, told the *London Times* that Gambetta had brought a brace of wax tapers to offer in memory of his mother, had knelt before the Virgin, dipped his fingers in holy water, and made the sign of the cross. "Either the priest mistook some portly dark man for Gambetta," Foote wrote, "or he was guilty of a pious fraud."

While lying on his death-bed Gambetta listened to Rabelais, Molière, and other of his favorite but not very pious authors, read aloud by a young student who adored him. Almost his last words, as recorded in *The Times* were, "Well, I have suffered so much, it will be a deliverance." The words are calm, collected, and truthful, Foote notes. There is no rant and no quailing. It is the natural language of a strong man confronting Death after long agony. Shortly afterwards, he breathed his last. No priest administered "the consolations of religion," and he expressly ordered that he should be buried without religious rites.

Gambetta's public and secular funeral was one of the largest gatherings ever before witnessed in Paris. {BDF; CE; FO; JM; RAT; RE}

GAMBIA, ATHEISM IN

In Gambia, there has been a Gora Society for atheists and freethinkers. (See *Freethought In the United Kingdom and the Commonwealth* by Gordon Stein.)

Gambini, William (20th Century)

Gambini, an artist who during the 1940s and 1950s studied with the abstract expressionists in Greenwich Village, New York City, completed an acrylic painting of Thomas Paine, whom he admired for his freethought.

Gambon, Ferdinand Charles (1820—1887)

Gambon, a French communist, became an advocate and founded the *Journal des Ecoles* in 1839. The Empire drove him into exile, but he returned when an amnesty was declared in 1859. In 1869 he refused to pay taxes. As an elected deputy at Paris in 1871 he was one of the last defenders of the Commune. Imprisoned, he was released in 1881. Gambon favored the abolishment of a standing army. {BDF; RAT}

GAMMA-RAY ASTRONOMY

Gammay-ray astronomers are interested in finding the origin and nature of periodic gammay-ray emissions from extraterrestrial sources. An extension of X-ray astronomy to the extreme shortwave end of the spectrum, the study is interested in events such as supernovae and black holes.

In 1999 for the first time, astronomers saw brilliant, visible light and a burst of gamma rays coming almost simultaneously from the same point in the sky. The gamma-ray burst appeared to have been made brighter, or "lensed," by a galaxy lying between Earth and the distant burst. {CE}

Gandhi, Indira (1917—1984)

"There exists no politician in India daring enough to attempt to explain to the masses that cows can be eaten," declared Indian Prime Minister Gandhi. She was the daughter of Jawaharlal Nehru. In 1984 she was assassinated by Sikh members of her body guard unit following an attack on the Golden Temple in Amritsar, the Sikhs' holiest shrine. {CE; TYD}

Gandhi, (Mahatma) Mohandas Karamchand (1869—1948)

The Mahatma (great-souled) preached Muslim and Christian ethics along with the Hindu, and he was a proponent of *satyagraha* (passive resistance). Gandhi has appealed to many religious humanists—he was technically a secularist, not a humanist—and, for example, members of New York's Community Church (Unitarian) at 40 East 35th Street erected a statue of him which can be seen at the southwest corner of Union Square in Manhattan.

In 1893, unsuccessful as a lawyer in India, Gandhi traveled to South Africa, where he was successful and led the Indian community. Renouncing material wealth, he dressed in a loincloth and shawl, symbolic of his Hindu abstemiousness and abandonment (1905) of Western clothing. His threatened "fasts unto death" successfully achieved political concessions, and his highly publicized doctrine of non-violence and truth-force were echoes of Thoreau's essay, "Civil Disobedience" (1849). They would later influence pacifists as well as civil rights officials and Martin Luther King Jr. During World War II, Gandhi was loyal to the British Government, but when India did not receive self-government after the Amritsar Rebellion and the Rowlatt Enactments, Gandhi declared 6 April 1919 a day of National Humiliation. He exhorted Indians to be passively resistant. In 1921 he had become the recognized leader of the Indian National Congress, which had as its goal complete national independence.

A devout Hindu, he accepted Jesus's Sermon on the Mount and parts of the Bhaghavad Gita as guides for his non-violence. "The most heinous and the most cruel crimes of which history has record," he wrote in *Young India* (1927), "have been committed under the cover of religion or equally noble motives." His use of a hunger strike and a fast unto death as spiritual instruments forced the British to institute a program of gradual power sharing, but only after Gandhi was interned in 1942.

In 1946, he publicly confessed that he had been taking naked girls to bed with him for many years—to test his mastery of celibacy. (His father had died while in the act of intercourse.) In 1947, British India was divided into two states; Gandhi argued against forming the independent state of Pakistan. However, in the year of Gandhi's death a conflict between India and Pakistan commenced, and more than one million died in the battles between Hindus and Moslems (1947—1948, 1965, 1971). Critics such as the playwright Ajit Dalvi have written of Gandhi's troubled relationship with his eldest son, Haribal, who, according to *The Economist* (29 August 1998), "boozed, whored and converted to Islam." Their grandson's biography of Gandhi's wife, Kasturba, told that Gandhi's sudden vow of chastity at the age of thirty-seven exemplified sacrifices he had heaped upon her throughout her life. Yogesh Chadha's 1997 biography cited Gandhi confessing,

> I have a strain of cruelty in me . . . such that people force themselves to do things, even to attempt impossible things, in order to please me.

He once threatened to evict his wife for having failed to clean an untouchable's chamber pot, and he disowned Harilal for marrying without his permission. The various critics have focused not only on his heroism in breaking the British Empire with hunger strikes and a spinning wheel but also upon his cruelty.

Unlike those believers who seek immortality in mausoleums, Hindus seek oblivion in cremation. A simple marker at Rajghat in New Delhi indicates where Gandhi was cremated after his assassination by a Hindu fanatic who had been angered by Gandhi's solicitude for the Moslems. Some of his ashes were given to friends, some were taken to Allahabad, some were placed in the State Bank of India in Cuttack, and forty-nine years after he was killed his ashes in 1997 were handed over to his great grandson, Tushar Arun Gandhi, who immersed them into the mother river (the Ganga Ma). Meanwhile, still other of Gandhi's ashes are found at the Self-Realization Fellowship Lake Shrine in Pacific Palisades, California. {CB; CE; ER; FUK; PA; TYD}

Gandhi, Radha (20th Century)

Mrs. Gandhi has been on the Executive Committee of the Andhra Pradesh Chapter of the Indian Radical Humanist Association, Jubilee Hills, Hyderabad.

GANESH

Ganesh is the elephant-headed god of learning in Hinduism. In 1995, thousands of people in India rushed to Hindu temples after reports that statues of gods were miraculously drinking milk. Bringing milk in earthen and steel pots, tumblers, and jugs, people converged on temples that had reproductions of Ganesh. In a spoon, scientists offered milk mixed with colored pigments to a statue in a temple in New Delhi, according to the Associated Press, and although the milk disappeared from the spoon. Although the milk disappeared from the spoon, it soon coated the statue. This the scientists attributed to surface tension, saying molecules of milk were pulled from the spoon by the texture of the statues. In Jamshedpur, in the north, police had to use bamboo canes to control a crowd of five hundred that tried to storm a temple. "The gods have come down to earth to solve our problems," a business executive was quoted as observing, further evidence that Indian folklore is replete with tales of miracles which an estimated nine hundred million people believe in. (See Warren Allen Smith, "Debunking Mysticism in India," *Skeptical Inquirer*, May-June 1996) {*The New York Times*, 22 September 1995}

Ganeval, Louis (Born 1815)

A French professor in Egypt, Ganeval wrote a work on Egypt and *Jesus devant l'histoire n'a jamais vécu*. The first part, published in 1874, was prohibited in France, but the second part was published at Geneva in 1879. {BDF}

Gannett, Ezra Stiles (1801—1871)

Gannett, a colleague of William Ellery Channing at Boston's Federal Street Church, was a key member of a group of young liberal ministers who formed the American Unitarian Association in 1825, a step Channing had not supported. Gannett's five main beliefs were in "filial reverence for God, brotherly love for man, a grateful faith in Christ, receiving him as the revelation of divine and the model of human character; the reality of the spiritual world and regeneration, consisting in such a change of the temper and way of life as may be brought by one's own will and effort." Such views put him at odds with the transcendentalists, and Gannett explicitly rejected Theodore Parker's intuitionist views. By contemporary standards, Gannett was but a borderline non-believer. {U; U&U}

Gannett, William Channing (1840—1923)

Gannett followed his father, Ezra Stiles Gannett, into the Unitarian ministry, but he supported a noncreedal and anti-supernaturalist religion, agreeing with the Free Religious Association. He helped Jenkin Lloyd Jones edit *Unity* and became one of the staunchest defenders of western radicalism. His major work for the organization was his lyrical and persuasive description of the mind of liberal religion, *The Things Most Commonly Believed To-day Among Us* (1887). Gannett once wrote, "Jesus is not the only wonder-born child of the Bible, though no one else is born so wondrously as he. Recall the cradle-miracles of Isaac, Samson, Samuel, and John the Baptist. . . . The first few pages of the 'Light of Asia' tell of another Virgin Mother—the mother of Buddha. . . . In the old Persian religion, Zoroaster, its founder, and Sociash, the expected Savior, are both described as virgin-born. In China the people glorify their emperors by tracing back their family to such a miracle. In Greece and Rome, heroes like Hercules and Romulus, philosophers like Pythagoras and Plato, great conquerors like Alexander and Caesar, were here and there accounted for by miracles of birth." {U; U&U}

Ganulin, Rick (20th Century)

Ganulin, a lawyer who does not mind being called an infidel and a heretic, spoke to the Freedom From Religion Foundation meeting in Madison in 1998.

Saying he was "half-Sephardic Jew and half-Ashkenazi Jew," Ganulin added that "I have a major problem with the idea of a chosen people and a promised land." In 1998 he filed a challenge to the statute known as 5 U.S. Code, Section 6103 Subpart A, which lists Christmas Day as a federal holiday.

> It's peculiar as can be that Christians celebrate the birth of Jesus Christ on December 25. Christians generally—anyone I've ever asked—are not even aware that Jesus Christ is the nickname for the person who lived, perhaps, at some point, and as far as anyone knows, would have been called Joshua Ben Joseph. It's generally accepted the December 25 is not the birthdate. So that having a celebration on December 25 which is not the birthdate of a person whose name is not Jesus Christ celebrating most likely by eating ham—which is something that person would never have eaten—is peculiar. But peculiar or not, Christmas is Christian.

GANYMEDE

The Hebrews' God appears *not* to have gone on record as having been bisexual, but the Greeks' Zeus *was* enamored of the naked and lovely Trojan boy, Ganymede. Zeus, in fact, carried the chap away and made him "cupbearer to the gods," a legend which implies Zeus's bisexuality.

Richard Rambuss, in *Queering the Renaissance* (1994), suggests that Thomas Traherne (1637—1674), the chaplain to Sir Orlando Bridgeman and lord keeper of the Great Seal was, like Zeus, enamored of a lovely boy: Jesus. In a poem entitled "Love," Traherne is rapt at the prospect of Christ selecting him as

> His Ganymede! His life! His joy!
> Or he comes down to me, or takes me up
> That I might be His boy
> And fill, and taste, and give, and drink the cup.

By Traherne's time, comments Rambuss, "the rapture of Ganymede had long since been widely spiritualized as a Christian allegory of the devout soul's ascent to God. Indeed, as Leonard Barkan notes, Claude Mignault, the commentator on Alciati, goes so far as to align Jupiter's love for Ganymede and Christ's invitation to 'Suffer little children to come unto me.' Moreover, Alan Bradford suggests that the figure of Ganymede as cupbearer to the gods would have also appealed to Traherne in terms of his own vocation as bearer of the Communion chalice." In short, Traherne made it clear he wanted to see himself as Christ's boy-bride. (See entries for Greek Religion, Kallimachos, and Allen Windsor.)

Garadzga, Viktor Ivanovich (20th Century)

At the Tenth International Humanist and Ethical Union (IHEU) World Congress held in Buffalo (1988), Garadja from the USSR addressed the group. A work of his on religion and science is *Nauka i teologia* (1972). Garadzga was president of the Soviet Institute for Atheism.

Garafalo, Janeane (1965—)

Garafalo, an actress and comedian, in an interview in *Showbiz* (August 1995) said she no longer believed in God. "He just seems very man-made to me. There are so many theories, and no everyone can be right. It's human nature to need a religious crutch, and I don't begrudge anyone that. I just don't need one." She has played a role in *The Truth About Cats and Dogs*, and on the David Letterman telecast Garafalo joked that in light of her atheism some higher power must be responsible for making her see the same reruns over and over. As for her religious belief, she added, "the glass is half empty as far as I'm concerned." {E}

Garatttini, Silvio (20th Century)

Garattini, director of *Instituto Richerche Farmacologiche Mario Negri* in Italy, signed Humanist Manifesto 2000.

Garbarino, James (20th Century)

Garbarino, a Unitarian, is author of *Let's Talk About Living in a World with Violence* (1993), a workbook for children ages seven to eleven.

Garber, Bob (20th Century)

Garber is editor of *News and Views*, the publication of the Humanists of North Jersey in Glen Rock, New Jersey. (See entry for New Jersey Freethinkers, Humanists.) {FD}

Garbo, Greta (1905—1990))

Although rumored to have been an unbeliever, partly because her ability to portray sexual passion was associated in some people's minds as being sacrilegious and that therefore she *must* be "irreligious," Garbo—born Greta Gustaffson in Sweden—does not qualify. According to *Loving Garbo, the Story of Greta Garbo, Cecil Beaton, and Mercedes de Acosta* (1994) by Hugo Vickers, GG (as she called herself) had an affair with, among others, the homosexual Cecil Beaton, an English scenery and costume designer who once attended a party in pink chiffon and a bustle. And she may have had an affair with Leopold Stokowski. George Brent, Fifi D'Orsay, and Marie Dressler. One of Garbo's lesbian lovers, Mercedes de Acosta, was known also for having had affairs with Marlene Dietrich, Isadora Duncan, and Eva Le Gallienne. But Garbo never married, nor did she ever again speak to de Acosta after her 1960 memoir about their affair. Garbo, in fact, became known for her inaccessibility, saying offscreen, "Why don't they leave me alone?' and 'I want to be left alone,' and memorializing William A. Drake's line in the 1932 script of "Grand Hotel," "I want to be alone." Vickers comments that, to console each other because of Garbo's inaccessibility, Beaton and de Acosta resorted to exchanging news about their previous love. The tragic heroine of "Annie Christie" (1930), "Anna Karenina" (1935), and "Camille" (1936) was famed on the movie screen for being the lover with "one of the most beautiful faces of the 20th century," but she detested the film industry and the studio system. Beaton found her dull and he tired of her "saying no to everything including Life." Relationships meant little to her, he observed, and she was little interested in intellectual matters.

In 1995, biographer Barry Paris made the case in *Garbo* that de Acosta was one of the great loves of Garbo's life. "I would see her above me, her face and body outlined against the sky, looking like some radiant, elemental, glorious god and goddess melted into one," de Acosta was quoted as saying. In the 1930s the two took a vacation in the Sierra Nevadas where they swam in the nude and cooked their own food. Garbo's other love was said to be Lilyan Tashman, a "slinky blond" and former Ziegfeld girl who was bulimic and who eventually died of a brain tumor. Paris alleges that Garbo as a pre-teen had several affairs with girlfriends and "possibly also with her sister, Alva." Paris also states that various sources insist that Garbo had several abortions performed by a doctor on retainer at MGM, her company. He includes such other trivia as that Garbo did *not* have big feet, that her size 7AA was ideal for a 5' 7" woman; she never said, "I want to be alone," but, rather, "I want to be *left* alone"; that when a made-for-TV movie touted its leading lady as "the new Greta Garbo," she growled, "There is only one Garbo!"; and while on Fire Island when a parade of gay men passed by, she said, "Should be called 'Royal Island.' It's filled with kveens!"

Garbo, according to Barry Paris, cooked with peanut oil, loved fresh vegetables, but disliked buying flowers because "What's the point? They'd only die." Known for her tart rejoinders, she replied to an individual offering a dinner invitation, "How do I know I'll be hungry on Wednesday?" Begged by fans for her photo, she replied, "Why do they want my picture? I'm not their relative." When Adrian, her couturier, suddenly resigned from MGM, she told him, "I'm very sorry you're leaving. But you know, I never really liked most of the clothes you made me wear." Her "Whatever you suggest, it's no" was illustrative of her frequent imperiousness. Paris wrote that "the metabolism that photographed as listless sensuality was really closer to fatigue. What looked like a migraine on Joan Crawford was, on Garbo, 'an intense form of sexual yearning. Few could believe the simple truth—that the connection between Garbo's erotic screen essence and her private sexuality was nonexistent."

Her interests, particularly during her legendary seclusion from 1941 until her death, were going to bed early, exercising, being massaged, eating organically grown vegetables, collecting a cache of dynel-haired toy trolls, and pursuing homeopathic cures. She was cremated and her ashes were interred at a secret spot few know about. In 1999 her cremains were buried at her birthplace outside Stockholm. As for her alleged non-belief, no, she was interested in theosophy.

Garborg, Arne (1851—1924)

Garborg, founder of *Fedraheim* (1877), a Norwegian weekly, encouraged reforms in religion and politics as well as in social, linguistic, and agrarian matters. He favored use of Landsmall, a rural dialect based on Old Norse, as a literary language, and he translated the *Odyssey* into that dialect. In his *The Hill of Innocent* (1895), he showed how human faith can defeat the powers of darkness. The tragic disintegration of two morally bankrupt and guilt-ridden men was depicted in his novels, *Tired Men* (1891) and *Peace* (1892). He is considered in Norway a major writer of the naturalistic school and a clever controversialist. {BDF; *Free Inquiry*, Winter 1990-91}

Garcia, J. M. Leon (Born 1865)

A foremost Venezuelan freethinker, Garcia against his will be placed in the Episcopal school in Caracas by his parents, who hoped he would become a priest. However, he did not, choosing to join the Liberal party and becoming editor of the freethought journals, *Eco Publico* and *El Libre Examen*, in which he conducted warfare against the clergy and church. Garcia is one of the founders of the Venezuelan Freethought Societies. Although knowing he was a pronounced materialist, officials appointed Garcia to head public instruction in the territory of Yuruari in 1892. {PUT}

García Lorca, Federico (1898—1936)

Internationally recognized as one of Spain's most prominent lyric poets and dramatists, García Lorca who was murdered by Spanish fascist forces has become a legendary tragic hero.

Lorca's sexual rejection by painter Salvador Dalí and his friendship with filmmaker Luis Buñuel have been well documented by various authors, including a stormy relationship with Emilio Aladrén Peroja, a young sculptor, which led to his "mysterious emotional crisis" that inspired him to move to New York City in 1927. His "Ode to Walt Whitman and an unfinished *The Destruction of Sodom* revealed his contradictions concerning homosexuality. In Spain, according to Francisco Soto of New York's College of Staten Island, "Lorca was forced to censure and speak only indirectly of homosexual desire. Even after his death, his homosexuality remained severely closeted in Spain" and continued to be overlooked by many Spanish critics. Soto added, "Although many reasons have been cited for Lorca's assassination (among them, his liberalism, his rebellion against traditional values, his communist leanings), it is evident that his homosexuality was not absent from the motives of those fascists loyal to Francisco Franco, *el caudillo*, who tortured and killed him. Spain's traditional inquisitorial Catholicism refused to permit the expression of a sexuality at variance with the dominant Christian morality. This intolerant environment well explains Lorca's fears and deliberate concealment of his homosexuality both in his personal life and in his work." Lorca, who was not a member of any organized religion, had a freethinkers' outlook and was nontheistic. {GL}

Garcia-Vao, Antonio Rodriguez (1862—1886)

A Spanish poet and lawyer, Garcia-Vao wrote for *Los Dominicales del Libre Pensiamento*. His *Echoes of a Free Mind, Love and the Monks* was a satire, a study of Greco-Roman philosophy. A promising freethinker, Garcia-Vao was stabbed in the back at Madrid a week before Christmas, 1886. {BDF}

Garde, Jehan de la (16th Century)

Garde, a bookseller, was burned together with four little blasphemous books at Paris in 1537. {BDF}

Gardener, Helen Hamilton (1853—1925)

In 1885 Gardener wrote *Men, Women and Gods* (1885) securing a preface by Robert G. Ingersoll. Three of her novels were translated into German. She was a freethought lecturer, a quite uncommon calling in her time. With humor and a knowledge of science, Gardener refuted a current view that women's inferiority is because of their small brain size. Gardener, an outspoken agnostic, was dubbed "Ingersoll done in soprano" by the *New York Sun* and "the pretty infidel" by the *Chicago Times*. (See entry for Woman and the Bible.) {EU, Gordon Stein; FUS; *Freethought History #9*, 1994; PUT; RAT; RE; WWS}

Gardner, Gerald (20th Century)

Gardner, a Pennsylvanian, is on the board of the Freedom From Religion Foundation.

Gardner, Martin (1914—)

Gardner, a science commentator, is co-chair of the Council for Secular Humanism's Center for Inquiry Capital Fund Drive. His second edition of *Fads and Fallacies in the Name of Science* (1957) continues to be cited by various sources. He is the author of *On the Wild Side*, a collection of provocative essays from his *Skeptical Inquirer* column. In 1991, he wrote *The New Age, Notes of a Fringe Watcher*. In 1993, *The Healing Revelations of Mary Baker Eddy* shows how Eddy "copies shamelessly, often word for word," not only from John Ruskin, Thomas Carlyle, and others, but also from Phineas Parkhurst Quimby. Gardner maintains Quimby was the one from whom Eddy took the central idea of Christian Science. *The Flight of Peter Fromm* (1994) is a novel about a young Pentecostal who loses his faith while a student at the University of Chicago Divinity School. It details the mental journey many in the freethought movement have to make as a minority group. In 1996, he wrote *Weird Water* and *Fuzzy Logic, More Notes of a Fringe Watcher*, in which he stated his findings about modern cosmology, the superstring theory, the theology of astronomers, and archeological nonsense.

Gardner has been called a "deist" in *Free Inquiry*, for in *The Night Is Large: Collected Essays, 1938—1995* (1996) he states that he believes in God while simultaneously admitting that atheists have the better arguments. In *The Whys of a Philosophical Scrivener*, he explains in an entire chapter why he is not an atheist. In short, he states that he is a "philosophical theist," adding, "I believe because it consoles me." (See entry for Urantia Book.) {*Free Inquiry*, Fall 1992}

Garibaldi, Guiseppe (1807—1882)

Garibaldi, the famed Italian patriot and soldier, fought in a variety of countries—Italy, Uruguay (where he met Anita Ribeiro da Silva, marrying her in 1842), Sardinia, Sicily—and for a time worked in New York for an Italian soap and candlemaker on Staten Island. Taken prisoner by Victor Emanuel's troops, he wrote his *Rule of the Monk*, a work exhibiting his love of liberty and hatred of the priesthood. He hoped to free Rome from the Papal government. He called the church "the Holy Shop," and his quarrels with Mazzini (who was a theist) were largely over religion. In the preface to his *Memoirie Autobiografiche*, he wrote, "The priest is the personification of falsehood, the liar is a thief, and the thief an assassin."

His English biographer, Theodore Bent, reported that in his old age Garibaldi grew more and more skeptical. "One of his laconic letters of 1880," Bent wrote, "illustrates this. It was as follows: 'Dear friends,—Man has created God, not God man. Yours ever, Garibaldi.'"

A member of the Masonic Lodge, Garibaldi called himself a socialist. However, both Marx and the anarchist Mikhail Bakunin disagreed, calling him a naturalist. Although he was elected to the Italian parliament in 1874, it was as a great revolutionary hero for the Western world as a whole that he is mainly remembered. Garibaldi's body was cremated and, although he had his sarcophagus built at Caprera, his family yielded to the wish of the government, and Garibaldi was buried at Rome. {CE; BDF; FO; JM; PUT; RAT; RE; TYD}

GARIFUNA

The Garifuna, who are descended from Carib-Arawak Indians and runaway West African slaves, lived in the Caribbean island of St. Vincent during the 1600s but were later deported by the British to Honduras. Over the centuries, there has been little mixing with those of European descent, and the Garifuna continue to speak an African-based language. They constitute less than five percent of the Honduran population. *Hudutu*—a soup of mashed plantains, fish, and conch meat—is a traditional meal, accompanied by beer and *gifiti*, a strong aromatic liqueur. "The Island Caribs were said to believe that after death the spirits might become mischievous, annoying, and even bringing harm to the living," Gonzalez has noted. "To avoid this, the Caribs made spirit offerings of food and drink. Shamans (*buwiyes*) consulted the spirits from time to time on behalf of afflicted people, and the spirits were also helpful to the society at large in predicting the outcome of battles, counteracting sorcery, and exacting revenge on enemies. The spirits might speak through the *buwiyes* or through dolls or puppets made of bones of the dead wrapped in cotton, called *rioches*. Sometimes, too, they would enter into the bodies of women and speak through them."

Such beliefs, their Christian conquerors found, were difficult to replace. In Crotona Park, New York, Garifunans comprise more than half of the immigrant population from Honduras. Traditional Garifuna music does not use Western instruments, and in the Bay Islands off the Honduras coast no electricity was available up until only recently. Some Garifunans, who are named after their leader, Garifuna, have been converted by missionarying Christians. {Nancie L. Gonzalez, *Sojourners of the Caribbean, Ethnogenesis and Ethnohistory of the Garifuna*, 1988}

GARLIC

Hippocrates prescribed garlic for an infected lung. The ancient Egyptians swore oaths on the herb, much as some contemporaries do on the Bible. And Chinese sacrificial lambs were seasoned with garlic. By the first half of the present millennium foods—and cultures—lacking in garlic were generally considered backward.

By the 1700s, especially in Britain and America, the smell of this member of the lily family (which includes chives, leeks, and onions) had become synonymous with promiscuous, poor, and superstitious peasant cultures, according to food critic Molly O'Neill.

Not that one could smell a Catholic, a wag might quip, but if the person came from the Mediterranean rather than Northern Europe, there was a mathematical probability that the individual was a Catholic of Roman or some other persuasion.During the Elizabethan era, cleanliness was equated with godliness, and strong scents were said to be associated with lustiness and the Devil himself. "Measure for Measure" has Lucio denouncing the Duke as a man who "would eat mutton on Fridays" and "would mouth with a beggar, though she smelt of brown bread and garlic."

First Lady Eleanor Roosevelt religiously chewed raw garlic to improve her memory. Contemporary freethinkers, also, have been known to be generous in their use of *Allitum sativurm*. {*The New York Times Magazine*, 18 April 1999}

Garner, Richard (20th Century)

Garner in *Beyond Morality* (1994) claims that a compassionate amoralism combined with non-duplicity and clarity about the use and limits of language is more likely to produce a decent world than any secular or religious moral system.

Garnett, Edward William (1868—1937)

Garnett, the son of Richard Garnett, was a writer. He wrote the novel, *The Paradox Club*, three plays, and other works. His rationalism is seen in his completion of his father's *Life of W. J. Fox* (1910). {RAT}

Garnett, Lucy Mary Jane (Died 1934)

Garnett, a writer, was the daughter of Thomas Garnett. Her works on Greece and Turkey show she discusses the Turks without Christian bias, and she is equally impartial in her *Greek Folk-Poesy* (1885). {RAT}

Garnett, Richard (1835—1906)

Although Garnett could read Greek, German, and Italian at the age of thirteen, he refused to go to Oxford or Cambridge. Instead, he entered the service of the British Museum, becoming superintendent of the reading room. From 1895 to 1897, he was President of the Bibliographical Society. Garnett's rationalism is found in *Twilight of the Gods* (1888) and *Life of W. J. Fox* (1910).

His notice in the *Dictionary of National Biography* states that he "cherished a genuine and somewhat mystical sense of religion which combined hostility to priestcraft and dogma with a modified belief in astrology." {RAT; RE}

Garramone, Michael (20th Century)

Garramone is an editor of the newsletter of the Secular Humanist Community of Upstate New York, Western Massachusetts, and Southern Vermont at PO Box 2148, Scotia, New York 12302. A native Albanian raised as a nominal Catholic, he studied at two seminaries, first an Eastern Orthodox tradition and then one that is Russian Orthodox, but discovered ultimately that he is an atheist.

Garrett, Ruby D. (20th Century)

Col. Garrett of Kansas City was a director of the American Humanist Association in 1952. {HNS}

Garrido, Fernando (1821—1883)

Garrido was a Spanish writer, author of *Memoirs of a Sceptic* (1843). He also wrote a work on *Contemporary Spain* (1862), *The Jesuits*, and a *History of Political and Religious Persecutions*, the latter rendered into English in conjunction with C. B. Cayley. {BDF}

Garrimone, Michael (20th Century)

Garrimone is an associate editor of the Capital District Humanist Society, PO Box 2148, Scotia, New York 12302.

Garrison, H. D. (19th Century)

Dr. Garrison of Chicago, Illinois, wrote a freethought pamphlet, "The Absence of Design in Nature" (1876). {BDF}

Garrison, James H. (20th Century)

Garrison wrote *Unorthodox Facts* (1940). {FUS}

Garrison, William Lloyd (1805—1879)

The American abolitionist's humanistic credo was, "My country is the world, my countrymen are mankind." Garrison founded the *Liberator* in 1831, helped organize (1833) the American Anti-Slavery Society, and opposed the Civil War until Lincoln issued the Emancipation Proclamation in 1862. An outspoken man, Garrison was the most famous of abolitionist leaders. But, as McCabe points out, the clergy have seen to it that Americans do not know Garrison rejected Christianity and was, at the most, a deist if not an atheist. He never went to church and was reviled by the Unitarian clergy as well as the others. "All Christendom professes to receive the Bible as the word of God, and what does it avail?" he wrote. The biography his children wrote says their father "quite freed himself from the trammels of orthodoxy." Upon falling ill in May 1879, he remarked, "I feel as if the machinery were giving way." His children remained constantly by his bedside, and he was intermittently delirious but sometimes expressive. When his physician asked if he wanted anything, Garrison said, "To finish it up!" That evening he fell into a twenty-four hour coma and died. {CE; CL; JM; PUT; RAT; RE; TYD}

Garth, Samuel [Sir] (1672—1719)

Garth was an English poet, wit, and physician. He helped to establish dispensaries and criticized them negatively in a poem, "The Dispensary." Sir Samuel was made physician to King George I. Reimmann's *Historia Universalis Atheismi* (1725) lists Garth as an atheist. {BDF; RAT; RE}

Garth, Jon: See entry for Madalyn Murray O'Hair.

Gaskell, Elizabeth Cleghorn (1810—1865)

Generally known as Mrs. Gaskell, she was the daughter of Unitarian minister William Stevenson and wife of Unitarian minister William Gaskell of the Cross Street Chapel in Manchester, England. She wrote *Mary Barton* (1848), *Cranford* (1853), and the *Life of Charlotte Brontë* (1857). In *Elizabeth Gaskell: A Habit of Stories* (1993), biographer Jenny Uglow states that Mrs. Gaskell is said to have known almost everyone of note in England and is quoted as being a lover of good food: She imagined that heaven must consist largely of "eating strawberries and cream forever." When *Ruth* (1853), the story of a "fallen woman" was condemned by reviewers and withdrawn from libraries, Gaskell wrote to a friend that she felt like St. Sebastian tied to a tree and shot through with arrows. The work, however, showed the relevance of Unitarianism as both a religious and a social force.

Contemporary critics, who complain that Ruth did not have to die and be punished, find *Wives and Daughters* (1866) her best work. It describes the joys and sorrows common to middle-class village life. Gaskell was strongly influenced by the rationalists and by the scientific thought of Enlightenment figures such as Hobbes, Locke, Newton, Priestley, and Bentham. She wrote that Unitarians of her day "refused to accept the notion of original sin or the doctrine of atonement: Jesus was revered as a teacher and example, not a vehicle of grace." {CE; U; UU}

Gaskin, Ida (20th Century)

Gaskin, a Shakespearean scholar and educator, is an honorary associate of the New Zealand Association of Rationalists and Humanists.

Gaskin, J(ohn) C(harles) A(dams) (20th Century)

Gaskin's *Varieties of Unbelief: From Epicurus to Sartre* (1989) is an anthology of atheistic works and includes Percy Bysshe Shelley's *A Refutation of Deism* (1814) and David Hume's "Of the Immortality of the Soul" and "Of Suicide." Gaskin is thorough in covering not only major non-believers but also in quoting directly from their works. He includes the following: Ayer; Cicero; Collins; d'Holbach; Epicurus; Feuerbach; Freud; Gibbon; Hobbes; Hume; Lenin; Lucretius; Marx; Nietzsche; Paine; Palmer; Russell; Sartre; Schopenhauer; Sextus Empiricus; Shelley; and Voltaire. His editing of *The Epicurean Philosophers* (1995) contains translations of the main surviving writings by Epicurus and his followers.

Gaskin is a corresponding member from Ireland of The Hume Society, a group engaged in scholarly activity concerning David Hume.

Gasking, Douglas Aidan Trist (1911—)

Gasking is an Australian freethinker, secularist, and philosopher. Son of an Anglican minister in Saskatchewan, Gasking was appointed in 1966 to teach philosophy in Melbourne. He developed a critical theory of knowledge in general and in particular was an antagonist of any alleged "special way of knowing." Gasking is a contributor to *The Australian Rationalist* and has spoken against religion to such organizations at the Melbourne University Freethought Society. {SWW}

Gasper, Louis (20th Century)

While minister of the Olivet Baptist Church in Cleveland, the Reverend William Gasper in the 1950s wrote the present author concerning humanism:

> I am no trinitarian. Of course not. I'm definitely emancipated from polytheistic notions and I can't even identify what one means by God. I realize that I am lonely in my area because of my views. However, I'm hoping this won't be for too long. I'm planning on teaching at the college or university level and am working on a Ph. D. in American Culture. I have been having difficulty with this plan, for it is difficult to secure a position with denominational schools, most of which want certain religious statements. Where this is not direct it is requested covertly and quite subtly. There is no help from the gods or others for those who do not follow the party line, as the saying goes nowadays. My only best hit perhaps is a state college.
>
> Incidentally, I made overtones to the Unitarians for ministerial fellowship. Evidently, Johnson [not further identified] does not want intruders and wishes to establish himself as a hierarch. The result is that he does not have the decency to present my application to a committee for examination. He must be reverting to some primitive aspect of religious control. [*The Humanist* editor] Ed Wilson told me I could expect something like that. I have been thinking about writing to the Universalists.
>
> Maybe I will with one final thrust before I bid adieu to all conventional religious groups, should that move fail to accomplish anything of a positive nature. How do I hold myself in a Baptist church? *Service* is the answer. My sermons are historico-comparative. They draw their own inferences, which are very seldom done by the average. Congregations hear but do not usually comprehend.

In 1927, Sinclair Lewis had written *Elmer Gantry* about a similar minister, a work which Gasper must have known about, and it is unknown whether Gasper remained a Baptist. Numerous other ministers expressed similar doubts about continuing to preach about God, but few have gone on record. {WAS, 1955}

Gassendi, Pierre (1592—1655)

A French priest who opposed Aristotle's authoritarianism, Gassendi was a skeptic sometimes called the father of modern materialism. In light of scientific findings of the day, he revived the atomic theory of Democritus and Epicurus, trying to reconcile atomism and Epicurean ethics with Catholicism. His pupil, Cyrano de Bergerac, agreed with much of his philosophic teaching but rejected his religious outlook. During the French Revolution, Maréchal cited Gassendi as one who seems to be an atheist only from the standpoint of the strictest religious orthodoxy. He remained, however, a supernaturalist but one who revived interest in the materialism of Epicurus and Lucretius. {CE; ER; EU, Aram Vartanian; JMR; JMRH}

Gaster, Theodor (1906—)

Professor emeritus of religion at Columbia University, and professor of religion at the University of Florida, Gaster is on the Council for Secular Humanism's Committee for the Scientific Examination of Religion.

Gastineau, Benjamin (19th Century)

Gastineau, a freethinker, wrote *Voltaire in Exile* (c. 1875). {GS}

Gaston, H. (19th Century)

Gaston was the French author of a brochure with the 1882 title, "*Dieu, voila, l'ennemi*" (God, the Enemy). {BDF}

Gatchell, Joseph (17th Century)

Gatchell, whose Universalism included the view that Divine mercy could not be satisfied with partial salvation or everlasting punishment, declared, "All men should be saved." As a consequence, Christians pierced his tongue with a red-hot iron.

Gates, William Henry (1955—)

Gates, the founder and chief executive officer of the Microsoft software company, is reportedly one of the world's richest men. In a 1995 interview on Public Broadcasting Service's David Frost program, Gates stated, "I don't know if there's a god or not. . . . I don't [believe in the Sermon on the Mount]. I'm not somebody who goes to church on a regular basis. The specific elements of Christianity are not something I'm a huge believer in. There's a lot of merit in the moral aspects of religion. I think it can have a very, very positive impact. [But] in terms of doing things I take a fairly scientific approach to why things happen and how they happen. I don't know if there's a god or not, but I think religious principles are quite valid."

His wife, Melinda, is Catholic and wants to raise their child, Jennifer, as a Catholic. "But she offered me a deal," Gates told a *Time* reporter. "If I start going to church—my family was Congregationalist—then Jennifer could be raised in whatever religion I choose."

Although tempted, because he said he would prefer that she have a religion that "has less theology and all" than Catholicism, he has not taken up the offer. "Just in terms of allocation of time resources, religion is not very efficient," he told the reporter. "There's a lot more I could be doing on a Sunday morning." {CA; E; *Time*, 13 January 1997}

Gaustad, Edwin Scott (20th Century)

A freethinker, Gaustad in *Dissent in American Religion* (1973) discusses "Heretics: Sinners Against Society." He is author of *Revival Revolution and Religion in Early Virginia* (1994). {FUS}

Gautama, Siddhartha [The Buddha] (c. 566—483 B. C. E)

Siddhartha, the Buddha and the son of a king (Suddhodana), was born in Lumbini in what is now the Kingdom of Nepal. He lacked belief in the Hindu scriptures (the Vedas), which he did not consider divine revelations. According to Lang, he rejected the authority of the priestly class (the Brahmans), the intermediaries between the Indian people and their gods. He believed in immediate experiences and reasoning powers, not revelation, in the search to understand the universe. He taught the middle path, how to avoid the extremes of severe asceticism and sensual indulgence. He believed that enlightenment (perfect enlightenment is the goal of Buddhism) is available to all, that meditation and education are the keys. He denounced the materialists for maintaining that events in the universe are chance occurrences, or determined by fate, independently of the karmic results of meritorious and demeritorious acts. He denied belief in a creator God and an external soul, so for all practical purposes he was an atheist. Little wonder that Bertrand Russell, asked what religion he would choose if he were *forced* to choose, is said to have mentioned Buddhism. Although there is a mystical element in the Buddha's outlook, Lang concludes, "Consequently, given the usual definition of atheism as the rejection of belief in a personal creator God, Buddhism is atheistic."

Similarly, Robertson, quoting Max Muller's *Selected Essays*, writes, "It cannot be denied that if we call the old Gods of the Veda—Indra and Agni and Yama—Gods, Buddha was an atheist. He does not believe in the divinity of these deities. What is noteworthy is that he does not by any means deny their bare existence. . . . The founder of Buddhism treats the old Gods as superhuman beings." Robertson adds, "Thus it is permissible to say both that Buddhism recognizes Gods and that it is practically atheistic." For example, Gautama did write, "If God permits such misery to exist He cannot be good, and if He is powerless to prevent it, He cannot be God."

"[Gautama] is chiefly interesting to us," wrote McCabe, "from the fact that, though the religion which now goes by the name of Buddhism is a crass and to a great extent corrupt mass of superstitions, he was an atheist. It is admitted that he was educated in the Sankhya philosophy, which was atheistic. Brahmanism had become so abstract a religion, while the mass of the people clung to the grossest myths, that there was a wide spread of atheism at that time. Gautama decided to devote his life to a purely humanist and very simple preaching of ideals of conduct among the people." McCabe cites Prof. T. Rhys Davids of Cornell as saying that Gautama "denied the existence of any soul" (cosmic or human). The *Encyclopaedia of Religion*, however, entrusts its article on Buddha to one of the clerical writers who held that Buddha *must* have believed in God. "These sophists," argues McCabe, "first argue that atheism is inconsistent with high ideals and then that any man whose ideals they cannot deny must have been a theist. The real authorities agree that Buddha was an atheist."

When Siddhartha died in 483 B. C. E., it is said that four of his teeth and a burnt finger bone were plucked from the cremation pyre. One of the teeth and the finger bone are in China, two of the teeth are in Sri Lanka, and the fourth tooth disappeared in India. Myanmar's largest and most revered religious shrine, the golden Shwedagon Pagoda in Yangon, is said to encase eight hairs of the Buddha. The worship of relics has a long tradition in Buddhism, just as it does in other major religions.

"Buddha" is a descriptive title, like President or Christ or Mahatma—if one can attain "perfect enlightenment," that person becomes a Buddha. To the unenlightened of the Western world, however, the Buddha is simply an icon on an ash tray for hoi polloi, a topless fatty with a navel, one upon whom cigarettes and cigars are extinguished.

The following have all gone on record as being Buddhists, although it is not clear whether they can be termed atheists or theists: Laurie Anderson, composer; Roberto Baggio, Italian soccer star; Leonard Cohen, poet and musician; Peter Coyote, actor; Harrison Ford, actor; Richard Gere, actor; Allen Ginsberg, poet; Oliver Stone, film director, producer; and Tina Turner, vocalist. (See entry for Allen Ginsberg.) {BDF; CE; CL; ER; EU, Karen Christina Lang; JM; JMR; JMRH}

Gautier, Théophile (1811—1872)

A French poet and writer of prose, Gautier wrote no definite work against priestcraft or superstition, but the whole tendency of his writings is pagan and, according to McCabe, shows his disdain for religion. His romanticism is not Christian, states Wheeler, and he made merry with "sacred themes" as well as conventional morality. Baudelaire called him an impeccable master of French literature, and Balzac said that of the two men who could write French, one was Gautier. Gautier was a leading exponent of art for art's sake, the view that formal, aesthetic beauty is the sole purpose of a work of art. His daughter, Judith, was the first woman to become a member of the Goncourt Academy. The French Academy, however, closed its doors against him on the ground that his *Mademoiselle de Maupin* was immoral. {BDF; CE; JM; JMRH; RAT; RE}

Gauvin, Marshall Jerome (1881—1978)

A Canadian freethinker and author of *Where Is Hell?* (1926), Gauvin once headed the Winnipeg Rationalist Society and later the New York-based National Liberal League. He was an editor of the atheist publication, *Truth Seeker*, until 1977, at which time he was ninety-six. According to McKillop, "It should be noted that Gauvin disagreed profoundly with the editorial direction of the magazine in the 1960s, when it set forward violent anti-Black and anti-Semitic views." One of his most valuable assets, Gauvin stated, was a collection of the writings of Robert G. Ingersoll. Gauvin wrote a foreword for *The Biography of Satan*, by Kersey Graves. {EU, A. Brian McKillop; FUK; FUS}

Gawn, Joan (20th Century)

A former president of the Humanist Association of Canada, Gawn lives in Chilliwack, British Canada. Once an elementary school teacher, she wrote "Raising Children Humanistically" for *Humanist in Canada* (Summer 1998).

GAY

• "When anyone asks if I'm gay," said Arthur C. Clarke on New Year's Eve in 1997, "I answer, 'No, just slightly cheerful.' "

In the 14th century, to be "gay" was to be "merry." In the 18th and in 19th centuries, the word was a euphemism for those who were sexually available or living an immoral life—invariably, it was applied to prostitutes. Later in the 19th, gay was used by some in Europe to connote "inversion," or love of the same sex. But in various 20th century countercultures as well as in the Armed Forces, it became an innocent-sounding term used by homosexuals among themselves. The theatrical milieu used the word widely in the mid 1960s and when homosexuals in the late 1960s began to assert themselves openly, "gay" supplanted the various alternative words and was expressed without any discriminatory overtones. In the 1990s, a number of gays started using the derisive term "queer" to describe themselves as well as to taunt homophobes.

Gay and lesbian criticism is one of the most recent of the critical and theoretical discourses to emerge from the "liberation" movements (New Left, anti-Vietnam War, counter-culture, black, and feminist) of the 1960s and early 1970s, notes Richard Dellamora of Trent University. His discussion and that of San Diego State University's Bonnie Zimmerman concerning gay theory and criticism is found in *The Johns Hopkins Guide to Literary Theory & Criticism* (1994). "As the 1990s progress," Zimmerman observes, "we find particularly rich and fruitful debates ongoing among lesbian critics and theorists over the nature of self, community, gender, and sexuality."

Many gays and lesbians, uncomfortable with what they perceive to be their church's homophobia, have left the various organized religions or started their own "religious fellowships." For example, there are Axios Eastern and Orthodox Christians; the Congregation Beth Simchat Torah, which is a member of the World Congress of Gay and Lesbian Jewish Organizations; Dignity (Catholics); Integrity (Episcopalians); and the Metropolitan Community Church (various Christian denominations). The Metropolitan Community Church was founded in 1968 by the Rev. Troy D. Perry, a Pentecostal minister who lost his church after acknowledging that he was gay. Los Angeles-based, it has an estimated 42,000 members in the United States and abroad. The largest gay church, the Cathedral of Hope in Dallas, Texas, has over 1,400 congregants.

Qwer Quarterly, North America's Lesbian and Gay Secular Humanist Newsletter, appeared briefly in 1993, then ceased publication. Its editor was Richard Seymour and included among its contributing editors were leading secular humanists such as Bonnie and Vern Bullough, Gerald Larue, and Rob Tielman. The Council for Secular Humanism, which publishes *Free Inquiry*, specifically affirms as one of its statement of principles, "We attempt to transcend divisive parochial loyalties based on race, religion, gender, nationality, creed, class, sexual orientation, or ethnicity, and strive to work together for the common good of humanity."

The Council for Secular Humanism promotes the *Gay and Lesbian Humanist* (PTT, 34 Spring Lane, Kenilworth, Warwickshire CV8 2HB, United Kingdom), which has been published quarterly in London by the Pink Triangle Trust since 1981. George Broadhead is its editor. (See entry for Homosexuality.) {Arthur C. Clarke to WAS, 4 Jan 1998}

GAY AND LESBIAN ATHEISTS AND HUMANISTS NEWSLETTER

A monthly, *Gay and Lesbian Atheists and Humanists Newsletter*, is published at 1718 M. St. NW, Box 157, Washington, DC 20036. E-mail: <klemO@ibm.net>.

GAY AND LESBIAN HUMANIST ASSOCIATION (England) (GALHA)

The Gay and Lesbian Humanist Association (34 Spring Lane, Kenilworth, Warwickshire, CV8 2HB, United Kingdom) was founded in 1979 to promote a rational approach to homosexuality and gay, lesbian, and bisexual rights as human rights. Its associated charity, The Pink Triangle Trust (PTT), publishes a quarterly magazine, *Gay & Lesbian Humanist* The group arranges meetings and provides affirmation ceremonies for gay and lesbian couples. GALHA is an associate member of the International Humanist and Ethical Union.

Officers are novelist Maureen Duffy, President; and Vice-Presidents are Tony Banks, M.P.; Professor Sir Hermann Bondi; Brigid Brophy; Dr. James Hemming; Sir Michael Levey; jazz singer George Melly; Claire Rayner; Dr. H. Stopes-Roe; Barbara Smoker; Prof. Rob Tielman; and Angela Willans. Honorary officers include Mike Savage, Chairperson; George Broadhead, who is Secretary and is the editor of *Gay and Lesbian Humanist* (Telephone-fax: 01926-858450); Peter Danning, Treasurer; and Keith Porteous Wood, Honorary Auditor.

GALHA is a full member of the Lesbian, Gay, and Bisexual Consortium, an umbrella group which has been set up with funding from the Home Office Voluntary and Community Unit.

The Pink Triangle is at <http://visitweb.com/ptt>. Katharine Lubar, the women's contact, is at <KatLubar@compuserve.com>; George Braodchead, <roysaich@humanists.freeserve.co.uk>; and Brett Humphreys, <brett@compuserve.com>. The Equality Alliance is at <http://equality-alliance.diversity.org.uk>.

GALHA can be reached by e-mail: <GALHA@bigfoot.com>. GALHA's website: <http://visitweb.com/galha>.

E-mail: Katherine Lubar is at <KatLubar@compuserve.com>; George Broadhead, <roysaich@humanists.freeserve.co.uk>; and Brett Humphreys, <brett@compuserve.com>. The Equality Alliance is at <http://equality-alliance.diversity.org.uk>.

GAY AND LESBIAN HUMANIST ASSOCIATION (New York)
The Gay and Lesbian Humanist Association (GALHA) in New York is headed by Allen Windsor. E-mail: <wasm@idt.net>.

GAY AND LESBIAN MUSLIMS: See entry for Homosexuals, Muslim.

GAY AND LESBIAN UNITARIANS
Gay and lesbian Unitarians are on the Web: <qrd.tcp.com/qrd/www/orgs/uua/uu-interweave.html>.

GAY PARTNERSHIPS
At the Europride event in Stockholm in 1998, Rolf Solheim from Norway's Human-Etisk Forbund joined Bill Schiller and Peter Froberg in a gay partnership ceremony. Schiller is co-ordinator of the international gay and lesbian cultural workers network. Froberg is a rock singer. "There may be occasions in the life of a couple when it must be made certain who is the primary person in your life, who can make decisions on your behalf if necessary," Solheim said, making it clear that his lover is his next of kin. Following the ceremony, guests—including a *Newsweek* photographer and the Swedish Minister of Culture—took part in a joyous Norwegian folkdance. {*International Humanist News* October 1998}

Gay, Ebenezer (1696—1787)
Gay, an early exponent of Arminianism, was a close associate of Charles Chauncy and an opposer of the Great Awakening. He believed in "supernatural" rationalism," a theology which insisted that the revealed religion of the Bible and the natural religion of rational speculation and scientific observation are in no sense incompatible. His work, including *National Religion, as Distinguish'd from Revealed* (1759), helped lay the groundwork for the liberalism of William Ellery Channing and his associates. {FUS; U; U&U}

Gay, Peter (1923—)
Gay, a history educator and author, wrote *Voltaire's Politics: The Poet As Realist* (1959), *The Party of Humanity, Essays in the French Enlightenment* (1964), *A Godless Jew: Freud, Atheism, and the Making of Psychoanalysis* (1987), and *Reading Freud: Explorations and Entertainments* (1990). *My German Question: Growing Up in Nazi Berlin* (1998) tells of his being not quite ten when Hitler came to power and sixteen when the family fled Germany. "There are three ways of becoming a Jew: by birth, by conversion, by decree," he wrote. But both his family and he were outspokenly atheists, awed by the Nazi decrees that considered Jews a race. Paul Edwards held that Gay's research is weak, that he "lies" by omitting balanced views, and that some of his translations of Voltaire are weak. "The elimination of error," Edwards emphasized, "is almost as important as the discovery of truth." Gay, he feels, is guilty of not sufficiently giving truthful accounts by willfully omitting certain facts. {FUK; FUS}

Gaylor, Anne Nicol (1926—)
A second-generation freethinker, Gaylor founded with her daughter Annie Laurie and a friend, John Sontarck, the Freedom From Religion Foundation at Madison, Wisconsin, in 1978. The group's president, she is active in various feminist causes and a contributing editor of *Freethought Today*. Her awards include Zero Population Growth Recognition Award (1983); Humanist Heroine Award, AHA, Feminist Caucus (1985); Commitment to Women Award, Women's Political Caucus (Wisconsin, 1989); Feminist of the Year Award, National Organization for Women (Wisconsin,1994); and Citation by the Wisconsin State Senate (1994). She is author of *Abortion Is A Blessing* (1976) and *Lead Us Not Into Penn Station* (1983), a collection of essays. Gaylor is on the board of directors of the Freedom From Religion Foundation. {EU, Gordon Stein; HNS2; WAS, 22 Mar 1998; WWS}

Gaylor, Annie Laurie (20th Century)
Daughter of Anne Nicol Gaylor and wife of Dan Barker, Gaylor is a freethought activist who edits *Freethought Today* for the Freedom From Religion Foundation in Wisconsin. She is author of *Woe to the Women: The Bible Tells Me So* (1981). For the American Humanist Association, she is co-chairperson of the Feminist Caucus. In 1994, she spoke in Rochester, New York, on "Female Freethinkers" at a Robert G. Ingersoll commemoration of Ingersoll's work on behalf of women's equality. On the Web: <www.infidels.org/org/ffrf/fttoday/algbio.html>.

Gaylor, Paul (20th Century)
Gaylor is a staff photographer for *Freethought Today*. He is on the board of directors of the Freedom From Religion Foundation.

Gay-Lussac, Joseph Louis (1778—1850)
A renowned French chemist and physicist, Gay-Lussac was a professor at the Sorbonne; made advances in industrial chemistry; improved the methods of analyzing gas mixtures; studied prussic acid and iodine; isolated cynagen. In addition, and in order to test the variation of the earth's magnetic field and the composition of the atmosphere at varying altitudes, he ascended in a balloon to a height of 7,016 meters (23,000 feet) in 1804. The Gay-Lussac Law, formulated around 1808, states that the volumes of gases that interact to give a gaseous product are in the ratio of small numbers to each other, and that each bears a similar relation to the volume of the product. After the Revolution of 1830, he entered the Chambre as an anti-clerical and became its President. Although he worked politically with the anti-clericals, the restored royalty made him a Peer of France. Gay-Lussac was closely associated with Arago and von Humboldt and shared their atheism. {JM; RAT}

Gazan, Jack (Died 1996)
Gazan was president of the Toronto Humanist Association in 1970—1971. He was one of the founders of the Humanist Association of Canada and its second president in 1971—1974. {*Humanist in Canada,* Summer 1996}

Gazeley, F. (20th Century)
Gazeley, of Bradford, Yorkshire, England, was a lecturer in the early 1900s of the British Secular League. {RSR}

Geddes, Patrick [Sir] (1854—1932)
Geddes, a Scottish biologist, had a wide range of social as well as scientific interests. He taught at University College, London, at Aberdeen, at St. Andrews, at Bombay, and at the Edinburgh School of Medicine. An honorary associate of the Rationalist Press Association, he was a practical idealist. {RE}

Geduld, Harry M(aurice) (1931—)
When he signed Humanist Manifesto II, Geduld was a professor at Indiana University. He established that school's first film study course and is the author of numerous works on film. He edited *The New York Times Film Encyclopedia* (1984). {HM2}

Gee, Maurice (20th Century)
Gee is a novelist, a four-time winner of the New Zealand Book Award and a two-time winner of the Wattie Award. He is author of *The Big Season* (1962), *In My Father's Den* (1972), *Going West* (1992), and *Loving Ways* (1996). Gee is an honorary associate of the New Zealand Association of Rationalists and Humanists.

Geeraerts, G. (20th Century)
At the International Humanist and Ethical Union's (IHEU's) International Peace Conference at Zutphen (1983), Dr. Geeraerts of Belgium addressed the group.

Gehrman, Mary Beth (20th Century)

The former managing editor of *Free Inquiry*, Gehrman is one of the editors of *On the Barricades, Religion and Free Inquiry in Conflict.*

Geiger, George Raymond (1903-1998)

Geiger was John Dewey Professor of Philosophy at Antioch College in Ohio, a position for which he had been recommended by Dr. Dewey himself. He continued teaching until 1969. Geiger was founding editor of the *Antioch Review*, a treasurer of the American Philosophical Association, and in the 1950s an associate editor of *The Humanist.*

Geiger wrote *The Philosophy of Henry George, The Theory of the Land Question, Toward an Objective Ethics, John Dewey in Perspective*, and *Science, Folklore and Philosophy.* After the death in 1981 of his wife, Louise, his companion was Joan Leon King. {HNS}

Geijer, E(ik) G(ustaf) (1785—1847)

A historian, Geijer is called by Robertson "the first recognizable champion of freethought in Sweden." His history of Sweden "is one of the best European performances of his generation." In 1820 upon publishing *Thorild*, he was prosecuted for his attack upon the dogmas of the Trinity and redemption, but he was acquitted by a jury, an acquittal which stayed religious prosecutions in Sweden for at least sixty years. A deist, Geijer was opposed to Unitarian Christianity. {BDF; JMR; RAT; RE}

Geijerstam, Gustaf (Born 1858)

Geijerstam was a Swedish novelist, one of the freethinking group called *Young Sweden.* {BDF}

Geiser, S. W. (20th Century)

Geiser wrote "Dr. Ernest Kapp, Early Geographer in Texas," in *Field and Laboratory* (January 1946). {*Freethought History #15*, 1995}

Geisert, Paul (20th Century)

Geisert is Vice President of Atheists and Other Freethinkers in Sacramento, California. With Mynga Futrell, he wrote *Different Drummers, Nonconforming Thinkers in History* (1999).

GEISHA: See entry for Mizuage.

Geismar, Martin von (19th Century)

Geismar was editor of a library of German rationalists of the eighteenth century in five parts, including some of the works of Bahrdt, Eberhardt, Knoblauch. {BDF}

Geismar, Maxwell (1909—1979)

A "radical" literary critic, editor of *Portable Thomas Wolfe* (1944) and author of *Writers in Crisis* (1942) and *Walt Whitman Reader* (1955), Geismar wrote the present author concerning humanism,

> I think that Thomas Mann was right in saying [to the present book's author] that writers do not and cannot belong to any one "school," philosophically, politically, and else wise, though they may move from one group to another at different times in their development and draw ideas and feelings from all groups; for the essence of a writer is both high individuality and communal roots.
>
> In terms of your listing, I think I would be closest to Classical Humanism and Naturalistic Humanism as a background for my own values. But what I think is really and perhaps desperately needed today is a new synthesis, and a new nourishing of the humanistic tradition; and some way of giving it a new mode of psycho-biological force and depth; of imbuing these ancient and tried human values with a new life spirit. That is what I am looking for in my own work, at least; while I have little patience with the recent movement to a new religious orientation—of "sin" or of social prestige, or both together.
>
> I am not particularly interested in Atheism or Communism within this framework of Humanism; but Atheists often have been great humanists, in fact, in what I know of American literature.
>
> {WAS, 7 May 1956}

Geldart, E. M. (19th Century)

Geldart, a freethinker, wrote *The Living God* (c. 1870).

Gell-Mann, Murray (1929—)

Gell-Mann, who received a Nobel Laureate in physics (1969), teaches at the California Institute of Technology. A theoretical physicist, he is a member of the science and grants committee of the Leakey Foundation. Also, he is a Humanist Laureate in the Council for Secular Humanism's International Academy of Humanism. Before winning the Nobel prize, Dr. Gell-Mann co-authored with Yaval Ne'eman *The Eightfold Way* (1964), which explains their scheme for classifying interacting particles. He has also written *The Quark and the Jaguar, Adventures in the Simple and the Complex* (1994). Stephen W. Hawking said it "is about how the wonderful diversity of the universe can arise out of a set of fairly simple basic laws. It is written by an expert in both the fundamental laws and the complex structure that they can produce." Of the book, Carl Sagan added, "It is always a pleasure to see a first-class mind grappling with the greatest mysteries, and at the same time resolutely resisting mysticism."

In 1994, science reporter William J. Broad of *The New York Times* (26 April 1994), wrote a front-page news article about Gell-Mann entitled TOP QUARK, LAST PIECE IN PUZZLE OF MATTER, APPEARS TO BE IN PLACE. The journalist described how an international team of 439 scientists working at the Fermi National Accelerator Laboratory had announced that the quest, begun by philosophers in ancient Greece to understand the nature of matter, may have ended in Batavia, Illinois, with the discovery of evidence for the top quark, the last of twelve subatomic building blocks which now are believed to constitute all of the material world.

Dr. Gell-Mann took the word quark from a line in James Joyce's *Finnegans Wake*: "Three quarks for Muster Mark." Gell-Mann predicted that quarks in normal matter came in groups of three: two up quarks and one down quark in protons; and two down quarks and one up quark in neutrons. The ideas were radical and strongly resisted, Broad explained, "partly because the fractional charges of his quarks seemed implausible. But his theories explained much, and were soon partly confirmed by particle discoveries." Although the discovery will not make any difference in everyday life, it is a high intellectual achievement. The Standard Model, which is central to understanding the nature of time, matter, and the universe, has now allegedly been validated. (For a review of *The Quark and the Jaguar* by Warren Allen Smith, see *Free Inquiry*, Summer 1996) {CE}

Gellion-Danglar, Eugène (Born 1829)

Gellion-Danglar was a French writer, a professor of languages at Cairo who became sous préfect of Compiègne in 1871. He wrote *History of the Revolution* (1830) and *A Study of the Semites* (1882). {BDF}

Gellner, Ernest André (1925—1995)

In 1979, Gellner was elected an honorary associate of the Rationalist Press Association. A social anthropologist, intellectual, and philosopher, he wrote *Words and Things* (1959), an attack on linguistic philosophy; *The Devil in Modern Philosophy* (1974); *Muslim Society* (1981); *The Psychoanalytic Movement* (1985), a sally against a closed self-perpetuating orthodoxy; and a study of rationalism, *Reason and Culture* (1992), in which he considers whether reason itself is another kind of superstition. For thirty-five years, Gellner 0taught at the London School of Economics. {*New Humanist*, June 1996}

Gemistus Pletho, Georgios (c. 1355—1452)

Wheeler lists Gemistus as a non-believer, citing Gennadius, the patriarch of Constantinople, who roundly accused him of paganism. However, Gemistus represented the Orthodox Eastern Church at the Council of Florence in 1439, led Cosimo de' Medici to found the Florentine Academy, and inspired the study of Plato that characterized the Italian Renaissance. In his *Laws* he advocated a polytheism similar to that of the ancient Greeks, rejecting Aristotle's criticisms of Plato. {BDF; CE}

Genard, François (Born c.1722)

Genard was a French satirist, writer of an irreligious work called *A Parallel of the Portraits of the Age, with the Pictures of the Holy Scriptures*. For this, he was placed in the Bastille, where, Wheeler believes, he died. {BDF}

GENDER

Gender refers to the grammatical categories: masculine, feminine, neuter. In recent years it has come to refer to sex-based categories (i.e., gender gap; the politics of gender). Rather than saying *policeman* or *stewardess*, those who distinguish between gender and sex refer to *police officer* and *flight attendant*. Similarly, a physician might evaluate the effectiveness of a medication as depending upon the sex (not the gender) of the patient. Generic man can foster ambiguity, such as in "Man, like other mammals, breast feeds his young." In practice, variation in usage is high, with sex and gender often being used interchangeably. To avoid gender bias, some women use their initials before their surname. Meanwhile, one is not always sure, because of the spelling of their names, of Terry's, Evelyn's, or Jean-Marie's gender or sex.

GENDER DYSPHORIA: See entry for N. L. Stones, a transsexual.

Gendre, Barbe (1842—1884)

A Russian writer in French, Gendre read the works of Büchner, Buckle, and Darwin, becoming a freethinker. Some of her writing was published in *La Justice* and the *Nouvelle Revue*. {BDF; RAT}

Gendre, Isaac (19th Century)

Gendre, a Swiss freethinker, upon his death received the following notice in the London *Echo* (29 July 1881):

> A second case of death-bed conversion of an eminent Liberal to Roman Catholicism, suggested probably by that of the great French philologist Littre, has passed the round of the Swiss papers. A few days ago the veteran leader of the Freiburg Liberals, M. Isaac Gendre, died. The Ami *du Peuple*, the organ of the Freiburg Ultramontanes, immediately set afloat the sensational news that when M. Gendre found that his last hour was approaching, he sent his brother to fetch a priest, in order that the last sacraments might be administered to him, and the evil which he had done during his life by his persistent Liberalism might be atoned by his repentance at the eleventh hour. This brother, M. Alexandre Gendre, now writes to the paper stating that there is not one word of truth in this story. What possible benefit can any Church derive from the invention of such tales? Doubtless there is a credulous residuum which believes that there must be "some truth" in anything which has once appeared in print.

{FO}

GENEALOGY: See entry for Blood Relatives. In *The Devil's Dictionary*, Ambrose Bierce defined genealogy as "an account of one's descent from an ancestor who did not particularly care to trace his own."

Gener, Pompeyo (1848—1920)

Gener was a Spanish philosopher, a member of the Society of Anthropology and author of *Death and the Devil* (1880). The work was dedicated to Renan. {BDF}

GENERAL ASSEMBLY OF UNITARIAN AND FREE CHRISTIAN CHURCHES

In England, Jeffrey J. Teagle heads the General Assembly of Unitarian and Free Christian Churches (1-6 Essex Street, Strand, London, WC2R 3HV, England).

GENERAL SEMANTICS: See entries for Alfred Korzybski and for Semantics.

GENESIS

> • It is easier to suppose that the universe has existed for all eternity than to conceive a being beyond its limits capable of creating it.
>
> **—Percy Bysshe Shelley**

> • Nonbelievers recognize that they cannot prove the nonexistence of God. They simply argue that a universe without a creator is the most economical premise consistent with all the data. An uncaused, undesigned emergence of the universe from nothing violates no principle of physics. The total energy of the universe appears to be zero, so no miracle of energy created "from nothing" was required to produce it. Similarly, no miracle was needed for the appearance of order. Order can and does occur spontaneously in physical systems.
>
> **—Victor J. Stenger**

The truly prosaic myths about the genesis of life are (a) that life arrived, according to Hesiod, when Aphrodite rose from the foam of the sea where Uranus's genitals had fallen after he had been mutilated by Kronus, that she (a/k/a Venus) was inseminated by many including Hermes, for whom she bore Hermaphroditus, and the shepherd Anchises, by whom she bore Aeneas; (b) that One Thing, breathless, breathed by its own nature; (c) that Ahura Mazda came out of nowhere and made the good earth and instructed man to till it; and that (d) the God who chose the Hebrews as his chosen people created a male Adam out of lifeless dust, then, as an afterthought, a subservient Eve to provide a second actor for a soap opera-like plot.

"In the beginning," *Genesis* erroneously does *not* state, "was thermophile." But therein lies the far more exciting and scientific explanation. No ancient ever dreamed of organisms which live in hot springs at the bottom of the oceans, creatures which use iron-containing chemicals as an energy source. "What inventive mind of the Mediterranean world," asks Oberlin College's Professor of Physics Daniel F. Styler, "could have imagined creatures as remarkable and diverse as zebras and amoebas?"

A thermophile called *Methanococcus jannaschi*, and which consists of organisms that grow at a high temperature, was first analyzed in 1996 by the Institute for Genomic Research in Rockville, Maryland. Dr. Craig Venter of the lab announced that *Methanococcus* is the third living organism to have its genome (all of its DNA) fully sequenced.

At issue is the revelation that life is divided into three parts:

- eukaryotes—e.g., animals, plants, fungi, single-celled creatures, slime moulds
- prokaryotes—cellular organisms such as a bacterium or a blue-green algae sans a distinct nucleus
- archea—thermophiles, the third living organism, one which can tolerate heat as much as 94° C. The thermophile recovered in 1996 by the deep sea vessel *Alvin* from a volcanic vent on the Pacific floor contained genes unlike anything ever before seen in biology.

Commenting on the find, *The Economist* (24 August 1996) wrote, "The most obvious explanation for why all life on earth might be descended from thermophiles is that the first living creatures were thermophilic. The early earth, after all, was quite a volcanic place, and the chemicals vomited from hot springs offer lots of possible ways in which creatures that do not use photosynthesis (the process that some bacteria and all plants use to generate energy from sunlight) can still make a living. This could imply that the split between the archea and the bacteria happened early in the history of life."

Representing a third kingdom of life, alongside the Prokarya and Eukarya, Archaea makes it clear that Aphrodite was not simply born of foamy seas or Adam simply made from lifeless dust. The universal ancestor has not yet, it becomes clear, been located.

A team of researchers at the State University of New York at Stony Brook found that while fossil evidence points to a great explosion of animal species beginning about 565,000,000 years ago, new genetic evidence suggests that their precursors may have emerged and evolved over a much longer period, perhaps a billion to 1.2 billion years. The earliest evidence for life, single-cell organisms resembling bacteria, is 3.6 billion years old. Earth is estimated to be about 4.6 billion years old.

But still not explained is how complexity developed. Richard Dawkins in *Climbing Mount Improbable* stated that "nobody knows how it happened," that "there are arguments to the contrary," that we "speculate" when we talk about the origins of life.

Some Chinese have denied the "out of Africa" thesis that human life spread after first commencing in Africa. Wu Xinzhi, of the Institute of Vertebrate Palaeontology and Palaeo-Anthropology in Shanghai, holds that people have been looking hard on that continent and that eventually a Chinse "Lucy"—the equivalent of a famous skeleton of the African hominid who lived 3,500,000 years ago—will be found. For many, the Han are a "pure" race not descended from Africans.

In the April 1997 issue of *Science*, German scientists announced their theory: that life on earth began around a volcano, perhaps at the deep-sea vents where molten lava boils through the ocean floor. Some 3.5- or 3.6-billion years ago, according to Dr. Claudia Huber of the Technical University of Munich, and Dr. Günter Wächtershäuser, a chemist, some kind of natural chemical reactions preceded the emergence of the first living cells. Or, in the words of Nicholas Wade in *The New York Times*,

> The recipe for creating life on a newborn planet consists of mostly lethal ingredients and would read something like this: Drop a handful of fool's gold (the mineral iron pyrites) and a sprinkle of nickel into water, stir in a strong whiff of rotten eggs (caused by the gas hydrogen sulfide) and carbon monoxide, heat mixture near the crackle and hiss of a volcano, and let simmer for an eon.

Dr. Christian de Duve observed that the theory is "an extremely interesting finding which fits with the idea that life may have originated in a volcanic setting." The new theory differs from that advanced by Dr. Stanley L. Miller, of the University of California at San Diego. He held that the locale for the origin of life was tidal pools and lightning strikes rather than in deep vents or other geothermal sources. In 1953, Miller had taken some water to represent the ocean, the gases methane, ammonia, and hydrogen to represent the early earth's atmosphere and sent electric sparks through the mixture to simulate lightning strikes. In several days, he found that many organic chemicals typical of living cells, including ammo acids, had formed within the concoction. His findings led to the view that it was only a matter of time for chemists to figure out how the building blocks might have combined naturally into the complex molecules of life.

Wächtershäuser credited the late philosopher Karl Popper for encouraging him in his studies. De Duve has noted that Wächtershäuser "disagrees with Stanley Miller and vice versa" but that their theories likely contained important elements of truth. "Life may have originated in a hot, deep sea environment rich in sulfur," he added. Observed Wade, "If so, such a dark hellish cradle would be a considerable elaboration on the 'warm little pond' in which Darwin, in an often-quoted letter, suggested that life began." (For the genesis of man, see entry for Evolution. Also, see entries for Flood and for RNA. For how old the universe is, see entry for Universe.) {CE; *The Economist*, 10 July 1999; Nicholas Wade, "Double Helixes, Chickens and Eggs," *The New York Times Magazine*, 29 January 1995; Daniel F. Styler, *The New York Times*, 28 August 1996; *The New York Times*, 25 October 1996; Nicholas Wade, *The New York Times*, 11 April 1997}

GENESIS, THE MYTH

Rafael A. Mirabal, from Caguas, Puerto Rico, wrote to the editor of *Time* (25 November 1996):

> Why do intelligent people still spend their time discussing fairy tales written by ignorant men about 2,000 years ago? *Genesis'* main lesson is to emphasize man's dismal failure in trying to create God in man's own image. The book's only relevance today is to the Jewish people, whose culture produced *Genesis*.
>
> Apart from its value as literature, *Genesis* has no meaning for the rest of us. As long as we keep giving this mythology a divine image, it will be impossible for modern man to transcend the dark ages we still carry in our minds.

Genestet, Petrus Augustus de (1829—1861)

Genestet was a Dutch poet and agnostic. He studied theology and for a time was a Protestant minister. *Leckedichtjes* (1860), his volume of poems and epigrams, show his rationalism. {BDF; RAT}

Genet, Jean (1910—1986)

A controversial French dramatist noted for his autobiographical narratives about homosexuality and crime, Genet wrote *Our Lady of the Flowers* (1943), *The Balcony* (1956), *The Blacks* (1958), and *The Screens* (1961), all examples of the theater of the absurd.

Amy Farmer, editor of *Voices/Writing*, has commented that "In the case of the Panthers [in *The Blacks*], Genet admitted his erotic attraction to black men; likewise, he was aware of the libidinal charge that hedged his fascination with the young soldiers of the PLO. However, erotic attraction leads to the clearer articulation of what Genet's work had always promised to do: establish a new ethic. Rather than ostracize and eroticize these new attractions, Genet attempts to use them as an incitement to dialogue and self-scrutiny. despite its focus on the male bonds of the military, *Prisoner of Love* also led to Genet's most sustained medication on women."

It would have been ironically absurd of Genet to have chosen belief over non-belief. He was a freethinker who, occupied with alleyway sexual escapades and prison-shower gang bangs, failed to go on record. {GL}

Genin, François (1803—1856)

Genin was a French philologist who, becoming one of the editors of the *National*, wrote spirited articles against the Jesuits. He published *The Jesuits and the Universities*. In 1845, the French Academy awarded a prize to his *Lexicon of the Language of Molière*. Genin edited Diderot and is known for his researches into the origin of the French language and literature. {BDF; RAT}

GENITAL MAIMING

"Circumcision made a lot of sense in primitive times," states Prof. Anderson in Arthur C. Clarke's *3001*. In the year of 3001, circumcision was no longer practiced because, as Anderson explains, "[S]ome unknown genius coined a slogan—please excuse the vulgarity—'God designed us: circumcision is blasphemy.' . . . By mid-21st century there had been so many malpractice suits that the American Medical Association had been forced to ban it." Clarke's plot wryly noted that anyone who had been "cut" in 3001 would be considered an anachronism.

Egypt's highest court in December 1997 issued a significant ruling: "Circumcision of girls is not an individual right under Sharia. There is nothing in the Koran that authorizes it." Violations, for anyone removing a girl's clitoris, to strip females of their sexual feelings, now carries a three-year jail sentence. Women's rights groups hailed the decision, saying that Islamic scholarship and Islamic jurisprudence look to Egypt for direction and the result would be far-reaching. Sheik Badri, commenting negatively, said the high court had made a mistake and the judge "would have to answer to God" for overturning a practice that had been condoned for fourteen centuries. Islamic conservatives maintain there is nothing wrong with the genital cutting. In extreme cases, some women's mutilated vaginas are stitched shut, then unstitched before and restitched after intercourse with their husbands, an attempt to make them appear to be permanently virgins. (See entries for Circumcision and for Women, Genital Maiming of.) {*The New York Times*, 29 December 1997}

GENIUS

As to whether philosophic geniuses understand each other, Bertrand Russell in *Understanding History* (1957) made some points: "A great deal of nonsense has been written about Aristotle and Alexander, because, as both were great men, and Aristotle was Alexander's tutor, it is supposed that the tutor must have greatly influenced the pupil. Hegel goes so far as to say that Alexander's career shows the value of philosophy, since his practical wisdom may be attributed to his teacher. In fact there is not the faintest evidence that Aristotle had any effect at all on Alexander, who hated his father, and was rebellious against everyone whom his father set in authority over him. There are certain letters professing to be from Alexander to Aristotle, but they are generally considered spurious. In fact the two men ignored each other. While Alexander was conquering the East, Aristotle continued to write treatises on politics which never mentioned what was taking place, but discussed minutely the constitutions of various cities which were no longer important. It is a mistake to suppose that great men who are contemporaries are likely to be quick to recognize each other's greatness; the opposite happens much more frequently."

GENOCIDE

Genocide, which is the ultimate crime against humankind, is the deliberate and systematic destruction by a government of a national, racial, political, religious, or cultural group. Although the term was coined recently, in 1944, genocide has been committed many times throughout history and the world. In the early American period, settlers were unmerciful in trying to completely kill off all Indians. In the Ottoman Turkey of 1894—1896 and again in 1915—1916, Armenians were massacred. In Nazi Germany in the 1930s and 1940s, an attempt to destroy European Jewry was made along with the killing of homosexuals and Gypsies. Although in Cambodia more than one million were killed or died from enforced hardships by 1978, that nation's prime minister, Pol Pot, has been accused of having had as his objective the extermination of all opponents, not just the Khmer people. A United Nations convention, which concluded in 1949, established the principles of the individual accountability of government officials who carried out the extermination policies, defined the crime of genocide, and provided for prosecution by national or international courts.

GENOME: See entries for Genesis, Richard Johnson Goss, and Human or Chimp.

Genovesi, Antonio: See entry for Beccaria.

Gensonné, Armand (1758—1793)

Gensonné was a French lawyer, one of the leaders of the Girondists. He was elected to the Legislative Assembly in 1791 and to the Convention in 1792. In the struggle with the Jacobins, Gensonné was an active champion of his party. With his colleagues, he was executed 31 October 1793. {BDF}

GENTILE

Gentile is a rendering in English of a Late Latin word (*gentilis*) used in the Septuagint to mean "non-Jew," "foreigner," or "heathen." *Acts* 11:20 relates how non-Jews (as distinguished from Jewish proselytes) were first admitted to the Church at Antioch. Paul became known as "apostle to the Gentiles" and before the writing of the *Epistle to the Romans* Gentile Christianity had come greatly to outnumber Jewish Christianity. Mormons also refer to non-Mormons as Gentiles. Freethinkers have little or no reason to use the word. {ER}

Gentilis, Giovanni Valentino (c. 1520—1566)

An Italian heretic, Gentilis fled Naples to Geneva to avoid persecution but, at the instigation of Calvin, was thrown into prison. Fearing the same fate as meted to Servetus, Gentilis recanted, wandered to Poland, joined Alciati and Biandrata, and was banished there for his innovations. Upon Calvin's death, he went to Switzerland, where he was arrested for heresy and was beheaded. *Ladvocat* reported that Gentilis "died very impiously, saying he thought himself honored in being martyred for the glory of the Father, whereas the apostles and other martyrs only died for the glory of the Son." {BDF}

Geoffrin, Marie Therèse (1699—1777)

A French lady distinguished as a patroness of learning and the fine arts, Geoffrin was a friend of Alembert, Voltaire, Marmontel, Montesquieu, Diderot, and the encyclopedists. She was noted for her benevolence, for the *Dictionnaire Encyclopédie* was made possible largely through her liberality. {BDF; JMRH; RAT; RE; WWS}

Geoffroy Saint-Hilaire, Étienne (1772—1844)

Geoffroy Saint-Hilaire was a French zoologist, a member (1798–1801) of Napoleon's scientific staff in Egypt and a professor at the Museum of Natural History (1793—1840). In his *Philosophie anatomique* (1818—1822, 2 volumes), he outlined his theory that all animals conform to a single plan of structure. At the age of seventeen, Geoffroy Saint-Hilaire was made a canon of the Church, but he became a deist and turned to science. As he rose to the supreme rank in zoology, he helped prepare the way for the acceptance of evolution, especially by opposing the reactionary Christian zoologist Baron Cuvier. Geoffroy Saint-Hilaire remained a Deist with "a fanaticism of humanity as his religion," according to his biographer, illustrated by the fact that during the Revolution of 1830 he saved the life of the Archbishop of Paris. {CE; JM; RAT; RE}

Geoffroy Saint-Hilaire, Isidore (1805—1861)

Geoffroy Saint-Hilaire, the son of Étienne Geoffroy Saint-Hilaire, was professor of zoology at Bordeaux, then at the Paris Museum (1841), and finally at the Medical Faculty (1850). He wrote a biography of his father, edited his father's notes on the French expedition to Egypt, and issued the works of Buffon. The founding of the Paris Acclimatisation Society was chiefly due to him. {RAT}

George III (King) (1738—1820)

George III, King of Great Britain at the time of the American Revolution, was expert at arranging taxation without representation. When his faithful subjects became not so faithful, they also lost their faith in his being God's representative on Earth. Nor did they turn the job over to the Pope in the Vatican. Instead, they arranged for the separation of the various religions and the new secular state, setting a revolutionary model for others. George, the Church of England's leader, suffered greatly because of his former subjects' defamatory, humiliating, and derogatory insults. The appropriately named blueblood of all bluebloods also suffered from porphyria, a hereditary disease. George's urine came out blue, his scalp became blistered, to which sucking leeches were applied, and his being administered quinine, camphor, calomel and other emetics and purges led him to awake sounding like a maniac and howling like a dog.

Christopher Hibbert's *George III: A Personal History* (1998) tells how the king built four libraries at Buckingham Palace that favorably impressed a visiting Dr. Johnson. He liked farce, laughed uncontrollably at slapstick, and enjoyed dressing up. Although a staunch Church of Englander, he tolerated Methodists and Quakers but not Catholics. When anti-Catholic paranoia during the Gordon riots occurred, with rumors that Jesuits were plotting to overthrow him and Benedictines were poisoning the city's flour, George reufsed to relax the laws against the Catholics.

George, Leonard (20th Century)

George is author of *Crimes of Perception: An Encyclopedia of Heresies and Heretics* (1995). In other times, George would have had his hands cut off and his book burned for writing such a volume. He details six hundred entries as to what have been considered heresies. George is a psychologist and lecturer who lives in Vancouver, British Columbia.

George, Lyman Fairbanks (20th Century)

George, a freethinker, wrote *The Naked Truth of Jesusism from Oriental Manuscripts* (1914). {GS}

GEORGIA FREETHINKERS, HUMANISTS

Georgia has the following groups:

• American Humanist Association, Mid-Atlantic Region (AHA), A-140, 1 College Row, Brevard, North Carolina 28712. O. Andrews Ferguson is the contact.

• Atlanta Freethought Society (FFRF)(ASHS), POB 813392, Smyrna, Georgia 30081 (707) 641-2903. On the Web: <http://www.concentric.net/~theafs>. E-mail: <theafs@cris.com>.

• Georgia Institute of Technology freethinkers are at <www.secularhumanism.org/cfa/orgs.html>.

• Humanists of Georgia (AHA), POB 2385, Stone Mountain, Georgia 30086. Tom Malone, once its director, has been succeeded by Wanda Randall.

GEORGIA INSTITUTE OF TECHNOLOGY

The Georgia Institute of Technology campus freethought society is at <http://www.secularhumanism.org/cfa/orgs.html>.

Gerard, Ralph W. (20th Century)

Author of *Food for Life* (1965), Gerard is a humanist who at the University of Michigan was a professor of neurophysiology in the Mental Health Institute.

Gerber, Elisabeth M. (20th Century)

A professional musician and former orchestral assistant to the BBC Symphony Orchestra in London, Gerber co-edits the Mid-West Freethinker newsletter.

Gerber, John (20th Century)

A freethinker, Gerber wrote *The Psycho-Neurosis Called Christianity* (1969). {GS}

Gerber, Rona M. (20th Century)

Gerber reviewed *Women Without Superstition* for *The Freethinker* August 1997), finding it "clearly demonstrates the close connection between the institutions of religion and the oppression of the powerless slaves, women, lower-class workers, and children."

Gerdes, Jürgen (20th Century)

Gerdes, of *Freie Huministen Niedersachsen*, has fought with that German humanist organization against the inclusion of a mention of God in the new constitution of the German Federal Republic. "The law—especially the constitution of a modern democracy," Gerges has argued, "has to be absolutely free of any references to God. Otherwise a continuously growing part of the society will be discriminated against by a religious majority. As a humanist I can't accept the attempts of the political establishment, to work as an instrument of the churches." Gerdes's E-mail: <gerdes-hannover@t-online.de> (*International Humanist News*, March 1994)

Gerhard, H. (1829—1886)

Gerhard was a Dutch socialist who wrote for *De Dageraad* and was a correspondent of the *Internationale*. {BDF}

Gerhard, A. H. (Born 1858)

Son of the foregoing, Gerhard was a headmaster of a public school and one of the editors of *De Dageraad*. {BDF}

Gerling, Fr. Wilhelm (19th Century)

Gerling was the German author of *Letter of a Materialist to an Idealist* (1888), to which Fran Hedwig Henrich Wilhelmi contributed a preface. {BDF}

GERMAN-AMERICAN FREETHOUGHT: See *Freethought in the United States* by Gordon Stein, which covers the subject of German-American freethinkers.

GERMAN CRITICS OF RELIGION: See entry for Franz Buggle.

GERMAN FREETHOUGHT

In 1981, Joachim Kahl (of Marburg) and Erich Wernig (of Köln), wrote a study of freethought in Germany, *Freidenker, Geschichte und Gegenuart*.

North-German Freethinkers are on the Web: <http://www.geocities.com/CapitolHill/Lobby/7083>.

GERMAN FREETHOUGHT AND HUMANISM

Der Spiegel in 1997 reported that the number of theists had dropped to 45%, down from 50% in 1993. During the same period, the number of avowed atheists rose from 20% to 28%. Only one-fourth of Germans said they believed in Jesus Christ. The decline matched the trend in other West European nations. {*The Secular Humanist Bulletin*, Winter 1997—1998}

German organizations and journals that are members of the International Humanist and Ethical Union are as follows:

• Bund Freireligiöser Gemeinden Deutschlands, Wörthstrasse 6a, 67059 Ludwigshafen

• *Diesseits - Zeitschrift fur Aufklarung undHumanismus*, a quarterly, is at Hobrechtstrasse 8, D-12045 Berlin <hvdberlin@aol.com>.

• Freie Humanisten Nidersachsen, Otto-Brenner-Str. 22, D-30159, Hannover; e-mail: <Gerdes-Hannover@t-online.de>

• *Friedenker*, a monthly, Shonalcher Str. 2, 70597 Stuttgart

• Freigeistige Aktion Fasanweg 8, 31535 Neustadt 1

• *Freireligiöse Rundschau*, Oberer Kirchhaldenweg 59, 70195 Stuttgart, Germany

• *Humanismus Heute, Zeitschrift für Kultur und Weltanschauung*, an academic quarterly of Humanistischer Verband Deutschlands, is at Hobrechtstrasse 8, D - 12043 Berlin, Germany

• Humaniste Aktion is on the web: <http://home.t-online.de/home/humanist.aktion/>.

• Humanisticher Verband Deutschlands, Hobrechtstrasse 8, D-12043 Berlin; <hvdberlin@aol.com>

• Internationaler Bund der Konfessionslosen und Atheisten , Chausseestrasse 8, D-10115 Berlin

• *Kristall Zeitschrift fur Geistesfreiheit und Humanismus*, a quarterly, is at Schillerstrasse 50, D-63263 Neu-Isenburg <ortrun.e.lenz@t-online.de>.

• *Miz*, Wurzberger Strasse 18a, 63739 Aschaffenburg

• *Wegeohne Dogma*, Freireligiose Verlagsbuchandlung, L 10. 4-6, 68161 Mannheim

For information about Freireligiöse Landesgemeinde Pfalz: <http://members.aol.com/FLGPfalz/index.htm>. An umbrella organization of free world view organizations is Dachverband Freier Weltanshauungsgemeinschaften. It is operated by Fritz Bode, Langenstucken 12, 2819 Morsum, Germany.

GERMAN UNITARIANS

The Unitarian Fellowship in Germany was an outgrowth of a liberal Protestant movement in the 1870s and was established in 1950 as a lay-led movement which tends toward scientific and philosophical humanism. Its members maintain the liberty of their individual beliefs but agree on a number of basic ideas about religion, life, man, and community. There are thirty-three communities and a cooperative but independent youth fellowship (Bund Deutsch Unitarischer Jugend), all organized according to democratic principles.

A Unitarian conference center is at Klingberg, near Hamburg, and its contact is Gunde Hartman, Schulberg 5, D-89435 Finningen, Germany.

In Frankfort/Main, Wolfgang Jantz is a contact at Deutscherrnufer 12, 60594 Frankfort/Main.

Unitarians in Heidelberg can be contacted by telephoning (49) 621-58-1718; in Kaiserlautern, (49) 6395-8595); in Munich, (49) 821-47-2486 or (49) 89-28-2326; and in Wiesbaden, (49) 612-87-2109.

German, Charles W. (20th Century)

German, in his *Letters, Lectures, Addresses* (1909), wrote, "Whatever may be true of men's creed, nothing is clearer than the fact that the personality and the sovereignty of God are not a large factor in the practical life and thought of our age." {TYD}

GERMANIC LANGUAGE

• In the German language the fish is a he, the scales are she, and the fishwife it.

—**Mark Twain**

GERMANIC PHILOSOPHY: See *Encyclopedia of Philosophy*, Vol. 3.

GERMANIC RELIGION

Like most ancient religions, the Germanic religion was polytheistic and had twelve main gods. Included were Woden (or Odin, the chief god for whom Wednesday is named); Tiw (or Tyr, for whom Tuesday is named); Thor (or Donar, for whom Thursday is named); Balder; Freyl; Freyja; and Frigga (Odin's wife, queen of the heavens, a deity of love and the household, and for whom Friday is named). All dwelled is Asgard, each in his or her own palace. Woden's Valhalla was the site of many banquets attended by the Valkyries and dedicated to the dead heroes, who lay dead by day but feasted with the others by night. Unlike gods of other peoples, the Norse gods were not immortal and despite eating the apples of Idun became extinct. It was prophesied that Loki, who led the forces of evil and darkness, would attack Asgard, ending the gods' existences and resulting in Earth's being destroyed by fire. Out of its ashes, however, came a mixture of the glacial waters of Nifheim (land of ice and mist) and the warm winds of Muspellsheim (land of fire). A new generation would rise because of the two first creatures—the giant Ymir, who would father a race of giants; and the cow Audhumia, who would give birth to the first god, Buri. His son, Borr, would father Odin, Vili, and Ve. They together destroy Ymir, fashioning heaven and earth from his body. From two trees were fashioned the first humans: Ashr (Ask) and Embia. The gods' temples were attended by priests who divined the future, accepted presents for the gods, and guarded sacred groves. Near a root of the great ash tree Yggdrasill dwelled Norns, or Fate. Fate was one of the most important concepts of Germanic religion, and humans and gods were subject to it. {CE}

Germond, J.B.L. (19th Century)

Germond was editor or Marèchal's *Dictionnaire des Athées* (1833). {BDF}

Germond, Jack (20th Century)

Germond, a journalist, columnist, and commentator, has gone on record on the telecast, "The McLaughlin Group," as being a non-theist. {CA; E}

Geroult de Pival (Died c. 1772)

Geroult was a French librarian at Rouen and probably the author of *Doutes sur la Religion* (1767). {BDF}

Gerrand, James Hamilton (1919—)

Gerrand is an Australian humanist and aviation engineer. He has been editor of *The Australian Humanist* and was secretary of the Humanist Society of Victoria, the Council of Australian Humanist Societies, and the Rationalist Society of Australia. {SWW}

Gershwin, George (1898—1937) and **Gershwin, Ira** (1896-1983)

The Gershwin brothers were composer and lyricist of some of the best-known and most important American original and popular musical works. George, who did not go on record, may or may not have been interested in organized religion. Ira, however, was so unhappy when George died of an inoperable brain tumor at the age of only thirty-eight that he suffered a guilt complex, saying, according to Michael Feinstein, he would gladly have died in George's place if he could have, "and for the rest of his life he never believed in God."

The two are noted for "The Back Bay Polka," which teases the puritanism of Beantown:

Don't speak the naked truth—
What's naked is uncouth;
It may go in Duluth—
But not in Boston. . . .
Somewhere the fairer sex
Has curves that are convex,
And girls don't all wear specs—
But not in Boston.

Their opera, *Porgy and Bess*, had the humorous number "It Ain't Necessarily So":

. . . The things that you're liable
To read in the Bible,
It ain't necessarily so. . . .
Methus'lah lived nine hundred years.
Methus'lah lived nine hundred years.
But who call dat livin'
When no gal'll give in
To no man what's nine hundred years?

Alan Jay Lerner described Ira as the only man he knew who was "cute." Harry Warren said Ira never had had a bad word for anyone. Louis Calhern told a door-to-door encyclopedia salesman he needed no such work because he knew Ira.

In 1937, while playing the piano with the Los Angeles Philharmonic, George lost consciousness, skipped a few bars, then continued as if nothing had happened. Later he said he had had the sensation of smelling burning rubber. Two months later, he had the same experience. Orchestra leader Mitch Miller confirmed Gershwin had told him the same story three years prior. Although Gershwin underwent many tests, refusing to submit to a spinal tap, the tests were inconclusive. Some described him as being a hypochondriac.

On July 9th after playing the piano, he fell into a stuporous sleep that deepened into a coma. Neurosurgeons removed a brain tumor, but he died several hours later without regaining consciousness. A biopsy revealed that the tumor was a fulminating growth, one which probably would have recurred even had he survived the initial operation. {PA; *The New York Times*, 1 December 1996}

Gerson, Simon W. (1909—)

Gerson, a freethinker, was executive editor of the *Daily Worker*, a major left-of-center publication which included a strong emphasis upon civil liberties and was anti-capitalistic. He wrote *Pete: the Story of Peter Cacchione, New York's First Communist Councilman* (1976). Although retired as editor of *People's World*, he contributes to the *People's Weekly World*.

Gerstein, Joseph (20th Century)

Gerstein is president of the Humanist Association of Massachusetts and is co-editor of its newsletter (Box 1125, Cambridge, Massachusetts 02238). In 1996, speaking in Vijayawada, India, at the fourth World Atheist Conference, Gerstein suggested that non-theists should not use the word "God" but, instead, should speak of gods or god ideas.

On "spirituality," he explained, we should celebrate art, music, communal experience, and beauty. Equally important, he urged making atheist ethics explicit, adding, "We must not be mere debating societies." {FD; HNS2}

Gestefeld, Ursula Newell (1845—1921)

Gestefeld, a freethinker, wrote *A Modern Catechism* (1892). {GS}

Geyer, Denton L. (20th Century)

Geyer, a professor of philosophy at the University of Missouri, was a naturalistic humanist who has reviewed books for *The Humanist.*

GHANIAN HUMANISTS

Hope N. Tawiah leads the Ghanian humanists at the Rational Centre (IHEU), POB 558 Art Centre, Accra, Ghana.

Ghillany, Friedrich Wilhelm (1807—1876)

Ghillany was a German critic who in 1835 became professor of history at Nurenberg. His principal work is on *Human Sacrifices Among the Ancient Jews* (1842). He also wrote about pagan and Christian authors of the first four centuries. Under the pseudonym of Richard von der Alm, he wrote *Theological Letters* (1862), *Jesus of Nazareth* (1868), and a collection of opinions of heathen and Jewish writers of the first four centuries upon Jesus and Christianity. {BDF; RAT}

Ghisleri, Arcangelo (1855—1938)

Ghisleri, an Italian geographer, adopted rationalism in his nineteenth year. He founded the *Rivista Republicana* (1878) and edited *Cuore e Critica* and *La Geografia per Tutti*. He said, "The battle of Freethought must also be waged against all who, though they do not believe in God or priest, maintain religion and priests because they are good policemen." {RAT}

Ghosh, Prabhir (1945—)

Ghosh, president of the Indian Science and Rationalists' Association, has led a group which since 1949 has busily exposed fraudulent "godmen." Journalist John F. Burns found Ghosh and India's "guru busters" are mostly atheists but include activists raised as Hindus, Muslims, and Christians. Rationalists are said to number 86,000 members in 300 branches across India.

In 1995, when millions of Indians stayed away from work to try to see milk-drinking idols, Ghosh set out to show, reported Burns, "that any liquid, including milk, can be made to rise from a spoon through the porous ceramics used for the idols through capillary attraction." In 1994, however, he and several companions ended up with cuts, bruises, and fractures after a fracas at the annual meeting in Calcutta of India's main astrological society. He then had dared the astrologers to write on a piece of paper when Prime Minister Rao, the sitarist Ravi Shankar, and other prominent Indians would die. "They say, 'It's possible to forecast anything,' " Ghosh said. "So I said, 'Fine, let's forecast something that will interest every Indian.' " Bouncers were summoned, and Mr. Ghosh ended up in a hospital.

For Ghosh, battling the belief in the supernatural has been a life-long battle. His skepticism, according to Burns, began when he was a teenager living in a town outside Calcutta. Cutting classes at school, he went about bearding holy men who demonstrated their mystical powers on the street by walking on hot coals and by other tricks Mr. Ghosh said were taken from the repertory of country-fair magicians. "I saw how people were being fooled," he said, "and I saw how this fraudulent spiritualism was being used to exploit the poor."

By his personal record, Ghosh has exposed 150 gurus and swamis as frauds, effectively putting them out of business. In 1993, when Balak Brahmachari, a prominent guru died and was laid out, the disciples claimed he had not died but, instead, had gone into a deep trance. After fifty-five days, police were summoned to carry the badly decomposed body away for cremation, setting off street battles in which scores were hurt.

However, *Indian Skeptic* editor B. Premanand has claimed that the Indian Science and Rationalist Association was started in the 1980s, not in 1949, by Prabir Ghosh. He claims they do not have 86,000 members and 300 centers in India. And he states that Ghosh has now been expelled by his own members. (See entries for Debasis Bhattachariya and for Indian Humanists, Rationalists.) {CA; E; *The New York Times*, 10 October 1995}

Ghosh, S. (20th Century)

In the 1950s when he was Secretary of the Indian Rationalist Association, Ghosh was a correspondent (India) for *The Humanist*. Ghosh had been a founding member of the Indian Rationalist Association. {FUK}

GHOSTS

Ghosts come in three varieties, the first two of which are "believed" in by individuals who have an incomplete understanding of science, the same types of individuals who believe that Heaven is "up" and Hell is "down":

- apparitions—are spiritualistic manifestations of a person or object in which a form not actually present is seen with such intensity that observers believe in its reality; individuals using polished stones, hypnotic suggestion, incantations, and crystal gazing claim these are evidence of the presence of supernatural spirits.
- poltergeists [German: knocking ghost]—are certain phenomena, such as rapping, movement of furniture, and breaking of crockery, for which there is no apparent scientific explanation; individuals who perform séances claim these are evidence of the presence of supernatural spirits.

The third variety is found in literary works; e.g., Shakespeare's *Hamlet* or Henry James's *Turn of the Screw*:

- figurative ghosts—writers sometimes include ghosts in their works with the intention of casting a spell or creating a mysterious mood; the Canadian author, Robertson Davies, when asked if he believed in supernatural emanations, said, "I believe in them the way Shakespeare believed in them. They're a way of exemplifying something which you know to be true but which is very hard to give substance to. Why does Hamlet see his father's ghost? It's in order that he may recognize what he knows in the depths of his own mind. It doesn't really mean that people are floating around in nighties looking for somebody to scare."

(See entry for Holy Ghost.) {CE; *The New York Times Book Review*, 5 February 1995}

Giammanco, Roberto (1926—)

Giammanco is editor of *La Nuova Ragione*, the journal of Italy's Giordano Bruno Freethought Association. He has written for *Free Inquiry*. Three of Giammanco's books are *Dialogo Sulla Societa Americana* (1964), *Black Power* (1967), and *La Piu Lunga Frontiera dell'Islam* (1983). {*Free Inquiry*, Summer 1991}

Giannone, Pietro (1676—1748)

Giannone was an Italian historian who attacked paper power in his *History of the Kingdom of Naples*. Excommunicated, he fled to Vienna, then to Venice. Seized by night and cast before sunrise on the papal shore, he somehow escaped to Geneva. When enticed to Savoy, he was arrested by order of the King of Sardinia and confined in prison until his death. Giannone's deistic attacks upon the Papacy were his downfall, but he inspired many by his twenty years of historical work. {BDF; RAT; RE}

Gibbon, Edward (1737—1794)

A young convert to Catholicism, Gibbon then formally reconverted to Protestantism. But in writing *The History of the Decline and Fall of the Roman Empire* (6 volumes, 1776—1788), he became a skeptic and offended the pious by his including historical criticism of Christianity in his mammoth work. Macaulay, for example, thought Gibbon "most unfair" to religion. Less than five feet tall in height and bulbously fat, he was a figure of ridicule, even while serving as a member of Parliament. He opposed the American Revolution but looked with some favor upon the later French Revolution, which he found to be more radical. "Religion," he wrote concerning why babies are "born" into a church, "is a mere question of geography." In 1783, the Vatican prohibited his work from being read.

Gibbon wrote in *History of the Decline and Fall of the Roman Empire*, "A state of scepticism and suspense may amuse a few inquisitive minds. But the practice of superstition is so congenial to the multitude that, if they are forcibly awakened, they still regret the loss of their pleasing vision. . . . So urgent on the vulgar is the necessity of believing, that the fall of any system of mythology will most probably be succeeded by the introduction of some other mode of superstition." Robertson emphasizes Gibbon's beginning a new era of historical writing, "not merely by its sociological treatment of the rise of Christianity, but by its absolutely anti-theological handling of all things." Gibbon was recognized internationally for the scope and quality of his work, and, adds Robertson, "the sheer solidity of [his] work has sustained it against a hundred years of hostile comments." Not all appreciated Gibbon. Samuel Coleridge once observed, "Gibbon's style is detestable, but it is not the worst thing about him."

His views on Christianity are indicated in a famous fifteenth chapter, called by Foote a masterpiece of grave and temperate irony. When Gibbon wrote that "it was not in this world that the primitive Christians were desirous of making themselves either agreeable or useful," every sensible reader understood his meaning, Foote added.

In 1994, two versions of the Gibbon history were issued, the first with an introduction by Hugh Trevor-Roper, the second edited by David Womersley. The former includes Oliphant Smeaton's editorial footnotes in addition to Gibbon's own. The latter leaves Gibbon's text but includes the "Vindication" in which Gibbon trounced critics of his treatment of Christianity.

Lord Russell also believed Gibbon is a major historian because of his historic exposure of the crimes and futility of Christianity. In his *Understanding History* (1957), Russell wrote: "His chief virtue is that, although his portraits of individuals are often disappointing, his sense of the march of great events is sure and unerring. No one has ever presented the pageant of history better than he has done. To treat in one book the whole period from the second century to the fifteenth was a colossal undertaking, but he never lost sight of the unity of his theme, or of the proportions to be presented among its several parts. This required a grasp of a great whole which is beyond the power of most men, and which, for all his shortcomings, puts Gibbon in the first rank among historians."

A similar view was expressed by Robert D. Kaplan, who wrote of the three volumes that "they constitute a general theory of history, a controversial interpretation of the birth of Christianity, an extended essay on military elites and the fickleness of public opinion, and an unequaled geographical and cultural primer on Europe, the Middle East, and Asia."

Gibbon, whom McCabe labeled a deist "on the way to agnosticism," died of dropsy, in London. After being tapped in November, he removed to the house of his devoted friend, Lord Sheffield. The last volumes of the *Decline and Fall* had been published in May of 1788, and a week before he expired in 1794 he returned to his lodgings in St. James Street, London. Lord Sheffield described his final moments:

> During the evening he complained much of his stomach, and of a feeling of nausea. Soon after nine he took his opium draught and went to bed. About ten he complained of much pain, and desired that warm napkins might be applied to his stomach. He almost incessantly expressed a sense of pain till about four o'clock in the morning, when he said he found his stomach much easier.
>
> About seven the servant asked whether he should send for Mr. Farquhar (the doctor). He answered, no, that he was as well as the day before. At about half-past eight be got out of bed and said he was "plus adroit" than he had been for three months past and got into bed again without assistance, better than usual. About nine he said he would rise. The servant, however, persuaded him to remain in bed till Mr. Parquhar, who was expected at eleven, should come. Till about that hour be spoke with great facility. Mr. Farquhar came at the time appointed, and he was then visibly dying.
>
> When the valet-de-chambre returned, after attending Mr. Farquhar out of the room, Mr. Gibbon said, "*Pourquoi est-ce que vous me quittez*?" (Why do you leave me?) This was about half-past eleven. At twelve o'clock he drank some brandy and water from a teapot, and desired his favourite servant to stay with him. These were the last words he pronounced articulately. To the last he preserved his senses; and when he could no longer speak, his servant having asked a question, he made a sign to show that he understood him.
>
> He was quite tranquil, and did not stir, his eyes half shut. About a quarter before one he ceased to breathe.
>
> (The valet-de-chambre observed that he did not, at any time, evince the least sign of alarm or apprehension of death: *Last Days of Gibbon*, in Milman's edition of Gibbon, Vol. I., Introduction.)

(See entry for John XII, a pope whom Gibbon described as an adulterer.) {BDF; CE; FO; FUK; ILP; JMR; JMRH; Robert D. Kaplan, *The Atlantic Monthly*, March 1997; PUT; RAT; RE; TRI; TYD}

Gibbon, J. M. (1875—1952)

Gibbon's *Atheism and Faith* (1904) was a provocative book in its time. The author was a dedicated atheist.

Gibbs, Kenneth (20th Century)

Gibbs is active with the Humanist Society of Greater Fort Walton beach in Niceville, Florida. (See entry for Florida Atheists, Humanists.) {FD}

Gibran, Khalil [Jubran Khalil Jubran] (1883-1931)

Gibran, a Lebanese poet, novelist, and painter, wrote *The Prophet* 1923) and *Jesus, the Son of Man* (1928). His work expresses his deeply religious and mystical nature. Some feel that the platonic love shown in his correspondence with fellow Lebanese author May Ziadeh is evidence of his using her as his "beard" and her using him as her "skirt," a reference to their homosexuality.

Gibson, Ellen Elvira (1821—1901)

Gibson, an American, was a public school teacher whose study of the Bible brought her to the freethought platform. At the outbreak of the American Civil War, she organized Ladies' Soldiers' Aid societies and was elected chaplain to the 1st Wisconsin Volunteer Artillery. President Lincoln endorsed the appointment, which was questioned. In fact, the Secretary of War refused to muster her in because she was a woman. By an act of Congress in 1869, she received pay for her services as chaplain. While in her line of duty, she contracted malaria and was almost totally disabled from its effects. Gibson wrote anonymously *Godly Women of the Bible* (c. 1875) and has contributed to the *Truthseeker*, *Boston Investigator*, and *Ironclad Age*, under her own signature and that of "Lilian." Of the Bible, she wrote

> Away with its false teachings, fables, pagan mythology, and abuse of woman, and assist her to free herself from these shackles and to overcome these vile aspersions descending down from the dark ages and settling like a pall over her existence and the existence of the race.

{BDF; PUT; WWS}

Gibson, Roland (1902—)

When Gibson signed Humanist Manifesto II, he was President of the Art Foundation of Potsdam, New York. He wrote *Japanese Abstract Art* (1964). {HM2}

Gilson, Étienne (1884-1978)

A French historian of medieval philosophy, Gilson along with Jacques Maritain is a Thomist.

Gicca, Francisco (20th Century)

In Argentina, Gicca edited *Progresso* from 1908 to 1912.

Giddings, Franklin Henry (1855—1931)

Giddings was a leading American sociologist, a professor at Columbia University, a president of the American Sociological Society, and author of many works including *The Scientific Study of Human Society* (1924). His explanation of social phenomena was based on the principle of "consciousness of kind"—his theory that each person has an innate sense of belonging to particular social groups. Giddings's freethought is best seen in his *Pagan Poems* (1914). {CE; JM; RAT; RE}

Gide, André (1869—1951)

Winner of the Nobel Prize for Literature in 1947, Gide, a French Protestant, raised many eyebrows with his works. *The Immoralist* (1902), which revels in hedonism and describes bisexuality, portrays a young person contravening ordinary moral standards. His *If It Die* (1924) was an autobiographical account of some of his own homosexual experiences, for the Protestant in him could not resist confessing. When he visited Algeria and stayed there for three years, Gide found no Protestant obfuscations about same-sex love, falling for "a voluptuous native boy, Athman," according to A. L. Rowse in *Homosexuals in History*. Then at the age of forty-three and although married, he had a sexual relationship with sixteen-year-old Marc Allégret, who later became a well-known film producer.

Critics have noted that by expressing adolescents' unrest, his works had a large and favorable following among adolescents. Gide's work showed humans seeking out their own natures, even though they might conflict with the majority's view of ethics. He used myth in the satirical story, *Prometheus Misbound* (1899), and he helped bring about a reform of French colonial practices in Africa in his *Travels in the Congo* (1927). In 1950, the last volume of his *Journal*, which he commenced in 1889, was published. Among other things, it described his long-standing (although non-sexual) friendship with Oscar Wilde. The work contained more than a million words, described his search for God and his moral crises.

Ann Sheridan's *André, A Life in the Present* (1999) explains how Gide's travels to North Africa distanced him from the stiff upbringing he had had. In the Kasbah, he met men who did not shield themselves from sensuality. Although Oscar Wilde and Lord Alfred Douglas paid young Arab boys in order merely to watch them, Gide is said to have found the sexual union something close to being sacred, not in the religious sense but in the sense that without hope of Heaven one can be transported by the sexual act into a world of joy and reverence.

Although he refused a nomination to the French Academy, he accepted in 1947 an honorary doctorate from Oxford University. The Vatican prohibited all his works in 1952, after his death and after his having won the Nobel Prize for Literature. (See Anthony Lane's "The Man in the Mirror," which describes Gide's "unmatched hedonism," *The New Yorker*, 9 August 1999.) {CE; GL; ILP, additus, 15 December 1961; TRI}

GIDEON

Gideon, or Jerubaal, was a 12th-century Israelite warrior of the tribe of Mannasseh. A judge of Israel, he opposed the Baal cult and defeated the Midianites, which led to a generation of peace for Israel. Many American hotels have copies of a Gideon Bible which have been contributed by an international laymen's association, The Gideons. That group was organized in 1899 by John H. Nicholson, Samuel E. Hill, and William J. Knights of the Janesville, Wisconsin, YMCA, with the evangelical intent of putting Bibles not only in hotel rooms but also in hospitals and penitentiaries.

Wisconsin freethinkers, however, supply an adhesive label to be placed inside the Gideon bibles. It cites *Judges*, chapters 6-9, to indicate that Gideon was not a person of exemplary character, adding the following:

- Gideon slaughtered thousands in battle by plotting with the "Lord" to use treachery.
- Gideon murdered thousands more for worshipping "false gods."
- Gideon plundered the bodies of his victims (to fashion a jeweled priestly vestment).
- Gideon fathered an offspring who killed sixty-nine of his stepbrothers.

"Millions of people have been hoodwinked by what their clergy and leaders have told them of the Bible," the label distributed by *Freethought Today* explains. "Make up your own mind about the Bible—read it for yourself." (See entry for Emily Hahn, whose father said of the Gideon Bible, "Read it and laugh.")

Gielgud, John [Sir] (1904—)

A consummate actor who has excelled in plays by Pinter, Wilde, and Shakespeare (notably *Hamlet*), Gielgud starred in the telecast, "Brideshead Revisited," and appeared in movies like "Arthur," which earned him an Oscar. United States officials once denied him an entrance visa, citing his 1953 arrest on gay sex charges in London, at which time he was fined a small sum for "importuning."

Gielgud lives in Buckinghamshire with his companion Martin Hensler in a 17th-century house which once belonged to Sir Arthur Bryant, the historian. Asked by interviewer David Frost in 1992 if he had ever wanted to be a father, the eighty-eight-year-old replied, "I never wanted to have children. I'd be terrified they'd inherit all my worst qualities." Asked what he was like as a child, the son of a stockbroker replied, "Very conceited, very effeminate, much too fond of my voice." And asked if he believed in God or a hereafter, Sir John graciously replied, "No, I'm afraid not." {CA; CE; E}

Gienke, Martin A. (20th Century)

While an undergraduate in San Diego, California, Gienke became a Unitarian. After serving in the United States Air Force in England for three years, he married a Cambridge girl and became active in the Cambridge Unitarian congregation, where he has served as a Council member. Also, in the 1980s he was chairman of the Publicity Committee for the General Assembly. E-mail: <mag2@cam.ac.uk>.

Gier, Audra and **Delta Gier** (20th Century)

The Giers are active with the Kansas City Mid-Continent Humanists (AHA). (See entry for Missouri Humanists.) {FD}

Giessenburg, Rudolf Charles d'Ablaing van (Born 1826)

One of the most notable of Dutch freethinkers, Giessenburg was an unbeliever in youth. With Junghuhn and Günst, he started *De Dageraad* and from 1856 to 1868 was one of the contributors, usually under his name, "Rudolf Charles." A man of great erudition, Giessenburg wrote *Het verbond der vrije gedachte* (The Alliance of Freethought); *de Tydgenoot op het gebied der Rede* (The Contemporary in the Reign of Reason); *De Regtbank des Onderzoeks* (The Tribunal of Inquiry); *Curiosities van allerlei aard* (Curiosities of Various Kinds). {BDF; RSR}

Gieve, Edouard C. (20th Century)

Gieve, a freethinker, wrote *What Christianity Has Done For This World* (19—?). {GS}

Gifford, Adam [Lord] (1820—1887)

Gifford, founder of the Gifford Lectures, was a Scottish judge made a lord for his distinction in law. He left $400,000 to the Scottish universities to promote lectures "for the study of natural theology." The plan fell through, as all such foundations by freethinkers do, states McCabe, because the clergy influenced changes which Gifford had not envisioned. Not only was Gifford no Christian but also he was no theist—he enthusiastically followed Emerson in ethics and Spinoza in philosophy. "We are," he wrote, "parts of the Infinite—literally, strictly, scientifically." The Gifford Lectures, in short, were arranged by a pantheist. {JM; RAT; RE}

Gifford, William (20th Century)

A freethinker, Gifford wrote *The Seekers: Why Christian Orthodoxy is Obsolete* (1954). {GS}

Gift, Mary (20th Century)

Gift, a freethinker, edited *Truth is a Shattered Mirror* (1946). {GS}

Gil, Gilberto (1942—)

A noted Brazilian-born musician and songwriter, Gil served for a time on the city council of Salvador, his hometown in the Afro-Brazilian state of Bahia. He spoke out against racism and social injustice while championing the environment. When he resigned that office, he blamed his "lack of talent in politics. I'm a humanist, and politics is not humanist."

"During the dictatorship," Gil has observed, "there was a lack of other means for political expression, so music became one of the most important ones. That's not the situation now [in 1994], but music is still an important tool because it deals with ideas and feelings and visions—everything that matters for life." {New York *Daily News*, 29 June 1994}

Gilbert, Amos (19th Century)

Gilbert wrote *Memoir of Francis Wright* (1855). {FUS}

Gilbert, Claude (1652—1720)

Gilbert was a French advocate who, in 1700, had a book printed which contained neither the name of the author or the printer. Entitled *Histoire de Calejava, ou de l'isle des hommes raisonables, avec le paralelle de leur Morale et du Christianisme*, the volume was suppressed because of its attack on Judaism and Christianity. Only one copy escaped destruction, and that was purchased in 1784 by the Duc de La Vallière for 120 livres. The 329-page book was in the form a dialogue. {BDF}

Gilbert, John Mark (1964—)

"I think that humankind would be better off without the concept of God," Gilbert holds. A Minnesota software engineer, he is an amateur astronomer, a philosophical materialist, a humanist, a liberal libertarian, an internationalist, and an atheist.

Gilbert has supplied much internet research concerning noted "dead non-theists." E-mail: <mark.gilbert@pobox.com>.

Gilbert, Richard S. (1936—)

When he signed Humanist Manifesto II, Gilbert was minister of the First Unitarian Church in Rochester, New York. He is a contributing editor of *Religious Humanism.* {HM2}

Gilbert de la Porée (1075—1154)

Gilbert was a philosopher, one of the brilliant scholars who during the eleventh century dared to try throwing off the shackles of dogma. He was closely associated with Abélard and shared his conviction that reason has its rights against faith. Although Abélard's bitter enemy, Bernard of Clairvaux, attacked him, Gilbert escaped condemnation for his heresies. {RE}

Gildon, Charles (1665—1724)

An associate of the most prominent freethinkers of the 1690s, and himself a radical freethinker, Gildon wrote *The Deist's Manual* (1705). A Roman Catholic, he befriended Charles Blount and upon reading Charles Leslie's *Short and easie method with the deists* (1698) became a militant Christian. He was not overly certain of any divine creation, writing, ". . . since our Correspondence with China, we have found they have Records & Histories of four or six thousand years date before our Creation of the World; and who knows but some other Nations may be (!) found out hereafter, that may go further." Berman finds that although Gildon appears to suppress atheism, his "bare theistic avowals were belied by weighty argumentation that pointed to atheism." {HAB}

Giles, John Allen (1808—1884)

Giles was headmaster of the City of London School, which post he left for the Church. The author of over one hundred fifty volumes of education works, Rev. Giles privately was a confirmed freethinker, intimate with Birch, Scott, and others. His heresy shows both in *Hebrew Records* (1850) and *Christian Records* (1854). {BDF}

Giles, Philip Randall (1917—)

Giles, who had been minister of various New England Universalist churches, helped in the merger of the Universalists and the Unitarians, which had its origins in the 19th century but which Giles and others made possible. An administrator, he became vice-president for field relations of the Unitarian Universalist Association from 1961 to 1963. Giles was the last Universalist general superintendent, and his last parish was the Universalist in Provincetown, Massachusetts. {U&U}

GILGAMESH

Gilgamesh is the hero of a work of some 3,000 lines, written on 12 tablets c. 2000 B.C.E. It was discovered among the ruins at Nineveh.

The story tells about Gilgamesh, whose ancestor Ut-napishtim had been the only survivor, along with his wife, of a great flood and had told him about a plant that gave eternal life. But when the plant was left unguarded, a serpent carried it off to Gilgamesh's embarrassment. When Enkidu, his companion (described in *The Columbia Anthology of Gay Literature* [1998]), dies, Gilgamesh tries to find from his friend's ghost what the afterlife is like and learns that it is not very pleasant.

Freethinkers note that the tablets pre-date the Jewish Old Testament, with its references to a flood, an afterlife, and a serpent as well as the love of David for Jonathan described in the first and second books of *Samuel* (c. 1012-872 B.C.E.). {CE}

Gill, Charles (Born 1824)

Dublin-born Gill published anonymously a work, *The Evolution of Christianity* (1883), which was quoted by Mr. Foote in his defenses before Judge North and Lord Coleridge. Gill also wrote a pamphlet on the blasphemy laws and edited, with an introduction, Archbishop Laurence's *Book of Enoch* (1883). {BDF}

Gilligan, Frank (20th Century)

A freethinker, Gilligan wrote *Free Thought and Humor* (1900s). {GS}

Gilliland, M.S. (Born 1853)

Miss Gilliland wrote *The Future of Morality* (1888) from the agnostic standpoint. {BDF}

Gilling, Bridget Sabina (1922—)

Gilling is an Australian humanist who migrated from England. During World War II, she served in the Voluntary Aid Department and married an Australian serviceman.

Gilling is an executive member of the Council for Civil Liberties, the Australian Consumer Association, the Penal Reform Council, and the Humanist Society of New South Wales. {SWW}

Gilman, Charlotte Perkins Stetson (1860—1935)

A Unitarian, Gilman wrote one of the first books on feminist theology, *His Religion and Hers: A Study of the Faith of Our Fathers and the Work of Our Mothers* (1923). She was admired by H. G. Wells, George Bernard Shaw, Theodore Dreiser, Zona Gale, and, in 1924, was called by Rebecca West "the greatest woman in the world today." Although she appeared to be a loose Deist, Gaylor has written, making reference to a "God" as a "naturally possessed power," Gilman rejected the unprovable afterlife, faith, obedience, sin, belief, "past-worship," rites, ceremonies, and holy books."

A firm believer in euthanasia, she took her own life, using chloroform, when pain from inoperable breast cancer became unbearable.

Gilmartin, Aaron S. (20th Century)

When he signed Humanist Manifesto II, Gilmartin was minister of the Mount Diablo Unitarian Church in Walnut Creek, California. He had also been minister in Seattle of the University Unitarian Church. {HM2}

Ginger, Ray (20th Century)

Ginger, a freethinker, wrote *Six Days or Forever?* (1958), the story of the Tennessee trial of John Thomas Scopes. He also wrote *The Bending Cross* (1992). {GS}

Gingold, Hermione (1898—1987)

Gingold was unique in showbusiness. "I believe in trying everything once—except country dancing and incest," the eccentric comedian once stated. "My father, James Gingold, was a stockbroker, and my mother also had a lot of time on her hands." When Gingold's marriage to Michael Joseph broke up, she said, "He asked me whether I wanted the children and I said no, he was welcome to them, but I'd like my cat." Other such comments are found in her *How To Grow Old Disgracefully* (1989).

Gingold was the British answer to Mae West, both mistresses of the double entendre. She hated dirty jokes and smutty material and, as late as 1969, refused to say the word *lavatory* on stage. Performing in South Africa in 1970 in "Fallen Angels," she found "Johannesburg and all it stood for" deeply repugnant. Of a play she wrote, she explained, "My play was taken from the original Russian—and I had trouble getting it away from him." Rarely without a lover, when eighty-one she was in love with a man of twenty-six and their relationship lasted longer than either of her marriages. "After I turned eighty-five," she remarked regretfully, "I found sex wasn't as important to me as it had been when I was eighty."

Although her father became a Buddhist, her parents never tried to influence her or her sister to choose a particular religion. "The more I see of life, the less I feel I know about it, so I'm still trying to make up my mind which religion I should choose. You could say I'm open to offers."

In her late eighties she thought of planning her funeral and recording her own eulogy as a way of avoiding sanctimonious remarks by a clergyman: "This is the last time I'll be talking to you; I do hope you all have a jolly funeral and champagne will shortly be served." Gingold died of pneumonia complicated by heart disease. {Sarah Lawson, "Wit and Irreligion," *New Humanist*, November 1989}

Gingrich, Candace (20th Century)

Gingrich, a lesbian and gay rights activist, is a non-theist. She has stated,

> I would have to be considered an agnostic at best. In my own life, I haven't found a need for organized religion. With all the hostile messages coming at me, including from the emissaries of various faiths, it's more urgent to believe in myself. Ultimately, we all have a responsibility to remind ourselves of our ability to be compassionate, respectful, and generous.

Her half-brother, Republican leader Newt Gingrich, has ingenuously expressed displeasure with the "life style" she has "chosen." (*Secular Nation*, January 1999)

Ginguene, Pierre Louis (1748—1816)

Ginguene was a French historian who, with Parny, was educated by Jesuits. He embraced the Revolution, wrote on Rousseau and Rabelais, and collaborated with Chamfort in the *Historic Picture of the French Revolution*. Thrown into prison during the Terror, he escaped on the fall of Robespierre and became Director of Public Instruction. Ginguene's principal work was a *Literary History of Italy*. {BDF; RAT}

Ginsberg, Allen (1926—1997)

Known as the "poet of the Beat Generation," Ginsberg—whether sober or, as referred to by *The Economist*, as sometimes "chemically enhanced"—memorably attacked American values in *Howl* (1956). The work, dedicated to Solomon, has had over 50 printings and led to his being tried on obscenity charges. It contained, for example, images of people who "walked all night with their shoes full of blood on the snowbank docks waiting for a door in the East River to open to a room full of steam-heat and opium." He also wrote *Kaddish and Other Poems* (1961) and *Mind Breaths* (1978).

Ginsberg grew up in Paterson, New Jersey, and became the protégé of William Carlos Williams, who lived nearby and was a major influence. Known for his outrageousness, he played finger cymbals at the Albert Hall in London. He called Ché Guevara "cute" and was expelled from Cuba. He sang duets with Bob Dylan. He chanted "Hare Krishna" on conservative William F. Buckley's television program.

Once at a poetry lecture attended by John Lennon and his wife Yoko, Ginsberg said, "Poetry is best read naked," then removed his clothes and hung a hotel notice, "Do Not Disturb," on his penis. The Lennons left in disgust.

Well-known as a homosexual, he was described by Saul Bellow, "Under all this self-revealing candor is purity of heart. And the only authentic living representative of American Transcendentalism is that fat-breasted, bald, bearded homosexual in smeared goggles, innocent in his uncleanness."

Ginsberg once pointed out that he slept with Neal Cassady, who slept with Gavin Arthur (the grandson of President Chester Arthur), who slept with Edward Carpenter, who slept with Walt Whitman, a "cosmic daisy chain" with poetic overtones and a circle ending. Ginsberg once tweaked Fidel Castro's beard for Cuba's harshness to homosexuals. Another of Ginsberg's lovers was Jack Kerouac.

In 1994 his *Holy Soul Jelly Roll: Songs and Poems (1948—1993)*, a set of four compact disks, was issued. Ginsberg reads from his various works, including "Kaddish (for Naomi Ginsberg 1894—1956)," which is about the insanity and death of his mother, who had been a left-wing Russian emigrant. His voice connotes a deep sorrow as he hymns his mother's death for more than an hour, including an ambiguous observation, "I know where you've gone—it's *good*." In his "Capital Air," he writes a protest against respectability, puritanism, politeness:

> I don't like Communist censorship of my books
> I don't like Marxists complaining about my looks
> I don't like Castro insulting members of my sex
> Leftists insisting we got the mystic fix
>
> I don't like Capitalists selling me gasoline Coke
> Multinationals burning Amazon trees to smoke
> Big corporation takeover media mind
> I don't like the top bananas that're robbing
> Guatemala banks blind.

Asked to comment specifically about humanism, Ginsberg wrote the present author,

> "Buddhist Humanism" might describe the union of Prajna (Wisdom of Emptiness) to Upaya (Skillful Means), characteristic of Dharma.

His reference was to Dharma, which, in addition to referring to Buddhist teaching as being the highest truth, denotes a quality or a condition of being or any existing thing or phenomenon.

In the previous two centuries, Kant, Coleridge, and Emerson, also intrigued by Asian concepts in religion and philosophy, included them in their transcendentalistic outlook. But in the present century, Ginsberg was one of the few Americans who drew upon such concepts.

Ginsberg died of liver cancer, and two Buddhist services were held in New York City's Chelsea district at the Shambhala Meditation Center, one in English, one in Tibetan. A practicing Buddhist, he studied at the Center. Sitting in a lotus position, many mourners sat on pillows. Philip Glass, Amiri Baraka, and Kurt Vonnegut Jr. were among those at one of the four-hour services. "There is no birth and no cessation," mourners chanted as gongs were struck, bells chimed, and incense burned. After his stepmother, Edith Ginsberg, said, "We'll all miss him desperately. So be it. Peace," "Kaddish," about his mother's death, was read. Ginsberg's cremains were divided into three parts to be kept at a Buddhist center in Colorado; at the Jewel Heart Buddhist Center in Ann Arbor, Michigan; and in the family plot at the B'nai Israel Cemetery in Newark.

As for the Buddhist view on reincarnation, Ginsberg never quite accepted it, according to his personal assistant, Bob Rosenthal. But Rosenthal added that should Ginsberg not return as one of the enlightened, he would at least "find a copulating couple and climb aboard." Aghast at that comment, Orlovsky hoped that in such a case Ginsberg would not attach himself to a pair of copulating crack addicts on Avenue D. (See the entry for John Cage.) {CE; GL; *The New York Times*, 13 April 1992; WAS, 3 June 1992}

Ginzburg, Vitalii L. (20th Century)

Ginzburg, chairperson of the Department of Physics and Astrophysics at Moscow University, signed Humanist Manifesto 2000. He is an advisor to the Russian Academy of Sciences. An atheist, Ginzburg believes "in the rational approach to interpreting facts and phenomena (even those that cannot be explained at first), to living life, to critically examining scientific data, and the materialistic viewpoint." He adds

> Modern humanism, in my view, is not possible without an active anticlerical position, materialism, and a scientific approach. I also have a commitment to moral and ethical principles, which have been developed by humanity during its long history. The church pretends to be the monopolistic interpreter of those principles, but that is not justified. The religious use them to confirm their dogmas and myths. . . .
>
> Religion and true science are not compatible. Religion, in essence, is not different from astrology or any other false science. The church is not a savior to society. It leads the "lost souls," using its own expression, away from reality. The church does not heal people but paralyzes their will; it does not inspire, but produces people with an impoverished spirit. For a normal, healthy person in a normal society, religion is like chains.
>
> {"The Failure of Faith in Russia," *Free Inquiry*, Winter 1998-1999}

Gioja, Melchiorre (1767—1829)

Gioja was an Italian political economist who advocated republicanism and was appointed head of a bureau of statistics. For his *La Scienza del Povero Diavolo* he was expelled from Italy in 1809. Gioja also wrote *Merit and Rewards* and *The Philosophy of Statistics*. {BDF; RAT}

Giono, Jean (1895—1970)

Giono, during the period between the two wars, wrote in praise of nature. He is said to have exemplified a new secular humanism that illustrated the simplicity of the pagan ideal. {CE; EU, Vivien Thweatt}

Giordano, Catherine April (20th Century)

Giordano, a secular humanist activist in New York City, upon moving to Florida was instrumental in the founding of the Free Inquiry Society of Central Florida (PO Box 196481, Longwood, Florida 32791). She edits the group's newsletter, *Veritas*.

E-mail: <fisocf@aol.com>.

Giotto (1267—1336)

Giotto, the Italian painter whose real name was Ambrogio Bordone, was one of the great pioneers of Italian painting in the Renaissance period. His work appears to depict the lives of St. Francis of Assisi and his early followers with sympathetic tenderness. But Vasari revealed that while Giotto painted these he relieved his feelings in a poem in which he drastically condemned the friars and their ideals. Vasari's passage is omitted from the English translation and all English biographies of Giotto, but there is a summary of the poem in Sir A. Crowe and G. Cavalcaselle's *New History of Painting* (1912). {RE}

Girard, Kansas

Girard, Kansas, was the town in which the Haldeman-Julius "Little Blue Books" were published. (See entry for Emanuel Haldeman-Julius.)

Girard, Ralph W. (20th Century)

Girard has been a member of the American Humanist Association. {HNS}

Girard, Stephen (1750—1831)

Girard, a French-born philanthropist, settled in Philadelphia as a shipowner and helped finance the U.S. in the War of 1812—in fact, he lent the government five million dollars. He called his vessels after the names of the philosophers Helvetius, Montesquieu, Voltaire, and Rousseau. A freethinker, he bequeathed $6,000,000 to found Girard College for fatherless boys. By a provision of his will, no ecclesiastic or minister of any sect whatever was to hold any connection with the college, or even be admitted to the premises as a visitor; however, the institution officers were required to instruct the pupils in secular morality and allow them to adopt their own religious opinions. His will, according to Wheeler, "has been most shamefully perverted." In a lawsuit which went all the way to the Supreme Court (Vidal v. Girard's Executors), the Court ruled the will did not actually aid infidelity or attack Christianity. Had it done either, the Court stated the will would have been invalid. Commenting, McCabe has stated that a favorite argument of the clergy is that freethinkers never found charitable institutions, so the clergy finds ways to change the original intent of the philanthropist. McCabe estimates that the estate of Girard—whom he cites as being a deist—was worth an estimated $40,000,000 in the mid-1940s. {BDF; CE; FUS; JM; PUT; RAT; RE}

Giraudoux, Jean (1882—1944)

Giraudoux is the French novelist whose drama, *The Madwoman of Chaillot* (1945), is a satirical work about materialism. He also completed several imaginative reinterpretations of Greek myths.

In *Judith* (1931), he wrote, "In times of death and famine, reason is on the side of the priests—who have their own kind of logic which cries for miracles and, on occasion, invents them." {TYD}

Girsh, Faye (20th Century)

Girsh, a Unitarian Universalist, became in 1997 the executive director of the Hemlock Society USA, a national right-to-die group. She is President of the San Diego Psych-Law Society and Psychologists in Addictive Behavior. A Harvard graduate, she spoke in 1999 at the American Atheists Inc. conference in St. Louis, Missouri.

Girshman, Karl and **Girshman, Rita** (20th Century)

The Girshmans spoke at the 1994 convention of the Freedom from Religion Conference in Madison, Wisconsin. They recounted how a Christian ministry operates in over seventy national parks, monuments, and forests, utilizing the services of over 350 student ministers, to which the Girshmans objected not only to the National Park Concessions at Big Bend but also to the National Park Service. Their complaint was that one morning while camping and lying in the nude after just having showered, a student minister used a pass key to enter and leave a printed invitation to come worship "our Lord and Savior" on Sundays and "Come as you are!" Suing, they won in a U.S. District Court, which agreed in 1995 that a Christian Ministry group is not allowed to use the symbol of the National Park Service on its stationery and that the Federal organization must post a disclaimer on park bulletin boards that it does not endorse any group or message and that "religious affiliation cannot be considered in hiring."

Gisborne, Maria (1770—1836)

Gisborne, a friend through Godwin of Shelley, was an atheist, according to Shelley's poetical "Letters to Maria Gisborne." {RAT; RE}

Gismo, Josiah (1818—1883)

Gismo founded the Leicester Secular Society. He was a mechanical engineer who came under the influence of the idealistic rationalism which Owen inaugurated and Holyoake sustained. In 1881 a hall was erected for the society, and Gismo lectured and debated there, giving it financial assistance. {FUK; RAT; RSR; TRI; VI}

Gismo, Sidney Ansell (Born 1860)

Gismo, the third son of Josiah Gismo, was also a mechanical engineer. He became president of the Secular Society and is an Honorary Associate of the Rationalist Press Association. {FUK; RAT; RSR; TRI; VI}

Gissing, George Robert (1857—1903)

Gissing, a novelist, developed rationalist opinions during a course of study at Jena, and he was for some years tutor to the sons of Frederic Harrison. An agnostic and a skeptic as regards immortality, he wrote that he felt there was "some purpose" in life but he could not accept "any of the solutions ever proposed." In *New Grub Street* (1891), Gissing depicts the dilemma of the poverty-stricken artist in an alien world. His friend, H. G. Wells, noted that Gissing was twice married, unhappily, to proletarian girls and that Gissing "felt that to make love to any woman he could regard as a social equal would be too elaborate . . . so he flung himself at a social inferior whom he expected to be eager and grateful." {CE; RE; RAT}

Gittos, M. (20th Century)

Gittos, a freethinker in Auckland, wrote *Is Progress Possible?* (1943). {GS}

Givishvili, Givi (20th Century)

Givishvili, a professor at the Institute of Terrestrial Magnetism, Ionosphere, and Radiowave Propagation, signed Humanist Manifesto 2000.

Gizycki, Georg von (1851—1895)

A German ethicist, Gizycki taught at Berlin University and was one of the leaders of the Berlin Ethical Society. He wrote studies of Hume and Shaftesbury and was joint editor of *The International Journal of Ethics*. Gizycki rejected all theology. {RAT}

Gjellerup, Karl (1857—1919)

A Danish poet and Nobel Prize winner, Gjellerup in his youth was devoted to the work of Herbert Spencer, then fell under the influence of Schopenhauer. McCabe states that his later work contained a rather grim idealism. Gjellerup's work shows the influence of Buddhism and Indian thought. {RE}

Gladstone, Herbert (20th Century)

Gladstone, who was born in New York City's Harlem, served in the U. S. Army during World War II, after which he was elected to the third highest office in the New Jersey State Assembly. He was appointed to the state's Civil Rights Commission, becoming its director. He is an active member now and member of the Executive Committee of the Humanists of the Palm Beaches in Florida, where he has retired.

Glanzman, Marge (20th Century)

Glanzman is active with the Humanists of North Carolina. (See entry for North Carolina Humanists.) {FD}

Glasgow, Ellen (1873—1945)

Glasgow, who won a Pulitzer in 1941 for *In This Our Life*, wrote many novels of note. In an essay quoted in *New Humanist*, she wrote,

> As a very small child, I was a believing animal. I believed in fairies; I believed in witches; I believed in white and gray and black magic; I believed in Santa Claus and in Original Sin; I believed in souls—not only in the souls of men and women and children and animals, but in the souls, too, of trees and plants, and of winds and clouds. I believed that, by some miraculous performances, all this countless multitude of souls would be taken care of, through a Sabbath day without ending, in an infinite Heaven. But in one thing, I cannot recall that I ever believed; and that was in the kind of God who had once savored the smoke of burnt offerings, and to whose ghost, in churches everywhere, good people were still chanting hymns of immelodious praise. From the paternal stock, I had inherited the single-minded Scottish creed of generations. On the distaff side I derived my free and easy faith from the gentler piety of the Episcopal Church. . . .
>
> I was only ten, I remember, when I told myself with a kind of cheerful desperation, "If I am damned, I am damned, and there is nothing to be done about it." What ever happened to the larger unredeemed part of creation, I would stand, with my mother, on the side of the heathen, and on the side, too, of our lesser brethren, the animals; for none of these disinherited tribes, I was assured, could expect so much as a crust or crumb of divine grace in the exclusive plan of salvation. Then gradually, as I grew up, these questions dissolved and evaporated, and at least ceased to disturb me. . . . I believe that there are many evils, but that the only sin is inhumanity; and I believe, too, that benign laughter is the best tonic for life. If life is sad, it is also a laughing matter, and it has its moments of rapture.

Glasser, Annabelle (20th Century)

When she signed Humanist Manifesto II, Glasser was a director of the American Ethical Union. She has been President of the American Ethical Union. {HM2}

Glazer, Gabriel (20th Century)

An Israeli who has been active with Secular Humanist Judaism, Glazer participated in a panel on secularism in the Middle East at the 1996 Humanist World Congress held in Mexico City. Also, he was a participant in the IHEU's 1999 conference in Mumbai. An Israeli barrister and solicitor, he is the IHEU's chairperson of the Committee on Religious Extremism and Rational Inquiry. His e-mail: <glazer@netvision.net.il>.

Gledhill, Lee (20th Century)

Gledhill is a British member of GALHA, the gay and lesbian humanist association. {*Gay and Lesbian Humanist*, Winter 1998}

Glennie, John Stuart Stuart (19th Century)

An English barrister, Glennie wrote *In the Morningland* (1873), or the law of the origin and transformation of Christianity. Scott published one of its chapters in *Christ and Osiris*. With H. T. Buckle, Glennie also wrote *Pilgrim Memories* (1875). {BDF; RAT}

Glicksberg, Charles I. (Born 1901)

When he reviewed books for *The Humanist* in the 1950s, Glicksberg was on the staff of Brooklyn College. {HNS}

Glimmer, James P. (1860—1941)

In Scotland, J. P. Glimmer of Glasgow was a leading freethought figure. He joined the Eclectic Society in 1879 and became active in local affairs as well as with the National Secular Society. One of the main critics of G. W. Foote in the 1890s, Glimmer then associated himself with the Freethought Federation. {FUK; RSR; TRI}

Glisson, Francis (1597—1677)

Glisson was an English anatomist and physician. For forty years he was appointed Regius Professor of Physics at Cambridge University. He discovered what is called Glisson's capsule in the liver, and he was the first to attribute irritability to muscular fibre. Dr. Glisson was eulogized by Harvey, and Boerhaave called him "the most accurate of all anatomists that ever lived." {BDF; RAT}

GLOSSOLALIA: See entry for Speaking in Tongues.

Glossop, Ronald J. (1933—)

Glossop, a Unitarian and a professor at Southern Illinois University, is author of *World Federation? A Critical Analysis of Federal World Government* (1993).

Glouberman, Mark (20th Century)

Glouberman, in Israel, is a corresponding member of The Hume Society, a group engaged in scholarly activity concerning David Hume.

GNOSTICISM

• Gnostics, n. A sect of philosophers who tried to engineer a fusion between the early Christians and the Platonists. The former would not go into the caucus and the combination failed, greatly to the chagrin of the fusionmanagers.

—Ambrose Bierce
The Devil's Dictionary

Gnosticism was a dualistic religious and philosophical movement of the late Hellenistic and early Christian eras. An occult group, it posed a threat to Christianity in the 2nd century, for Gnosticism taught a popular view that the spirit was held captive by evil archons. However, through the use of secret formulas, that spirit could be freed at death and restored to the heavenly abode. Had Gnosticism triumphed, Christianity would have become just another Greco-Roman mystery cult, according to Conrad Moehlman of the Colgate-Rochester Divinity School in Rochester, New York. Gnosticism eventually merged with Manichaeism, and in Iran and Iraq the Mandaeans represent the only Gnostic sect extant.

Harold Bloom, in *Omens of Millennium* (1996), holds that Gnosticism was not a creation of the real, hidden God. Rather, it was created by a rebellious Demiurge, a "bungler." It follows, Gnostics hold, that mankind predates the Fall, a divine spark of the real God exists in everyone's deepest self, and mankind has "the God within." (See entry for Devil.) {CE}

Gobineau, Joseph Arthur [Count] (1816—1882)

A French Orientalist, Gobineau was a leading authority on Persian history. He had the reputation of being the chief early proponent of the theory of Nordic supremacy, of being anti-democratic and anti-Semitic. McCabe states the allegation is an exaggeration but does not document his reasons. The count was a deist. His Catholic friends tried in vain to convert him in his last days and, failing to change his mind, administered the sacrament to him while he was unconscious. {CE; JM; RAT; RE}

Goblet, René (1828—1905)

Goblet, a French statesman said to have had a major influence later on Adolf Hitler, worked with the anti-clerical Liberals of the Third Empire. In 1871, he was appointed General Procurator to the Court of Appeal at Amiens. Later, entering the Chambre, he became Minister of the Interior, Minister of Education, Premier, and Minister of Foreign Affairs. As Minister of Education, he excluded the clergy from the schools, and as leader of the Radical-Socialists he supported every measure against the Church. {RAT; RE}

Goblet D'Aviella, Eugene [Count] (1846—1925)

Goblet d'Aviella was a Belgian anthropologist and a professor at Brussels University, where he taught the history of religions. He was so well known as a freethinker, however, that when he was invited to deliver the Hibbert Lectures at Oxford, the authorities of Balliol College refused the use of a room for the purpose (1891). {JM; RAT; RE}

GOD

God is a class name, like "angel" or "demon." When capitalized to show what believers call "respect," it is a title, like President, Christ, Mahatma, Buddha, Pfc. (private first class). Many mistake the word to be the sole name of the divinity of three monotheistic religions. They assume, as if they are on a first-name basis, that it is God, Bill, Jesus, Mohandras, Siddhartha, and Pfc. Luis Fantauzzi they are talking to or about.

But God's name is not *God.*

The ancient Hebrews considered YHWH, one of the various names for the divinity, as taboo and not to be uttered. They substituted Adonai, "my Lord," in order to avoid the ineffable, or that which should not be uttered. Elohim was the most common name for God in the Old Testament. As explained by Rolland Emerson Wolfe of Tufts College, "Elohim is a plural form which usually should be translated 'gods' (in contrast with individual deities such as Yahweh, Dagon, Bel, etc.) in documents written before the exile. During this period the singular form became so obsolete that, when monotheism came, elohim was retained in the plural but understood in the singular sense of 'God.' Usually, Hebrew writers speak of gods (elohim) and Yahweh (their god) before the exile but God (elohim) thereafter." God's name also appears, though rarely, as Shaddai.

Sub-standard slang expressions concerning God are numerous, with few speakers recognizing the origin of "gosh" or "golly" (euphemisms for God) and "gee" and "jeepers" (euphemisms for Jesus). Nor are they aware of the anatomic vulgarity "oddballs," or of the colorful epithet "bloody," an irreverent description of the dripping, crucified, and dying second person of the Trinity (as utilized by a mad and cursing Hamlet: "'Sblood, do you think that I am easier to be played on than a pipe?"). Similarly, "zounds" is a reference to Jesus's (His) wounds upon being crucified.

Jehovah (Yahweh, Jahve) was the personal name of Israel's god, but some hold that it is based on a mistake inasmuch as scholars believe the form Yahweh is not scripturally reliable. R. B. Y. Scott of the United Theological College in Montreal, Canada, notes that when for the first time vowels were inserted in the Hebrew Bible in the 7th century, the vowels of the word "aDoNaY" were written with the consonants YHWH, a tetragrammaton, in order to emphasize reverence. (Tetragrammaton refers to a four letter word such as the not-to-be-uttered name of God, YHWH, which is to be spoken only with the vowels of Adonai or Elohim. It is noteworthy that most Hebrew words have only three consonants.) "The form 'Jehovah' is a transliteration of the resulting hybrid, and first came into use in the 14th century through the failure of Christian scholars to recognize the origin and purpose of the vocalization; it has now by usage acquired by independent standing in English," Scott states.

Non-believers ordinarily capitalize God when referring to the major divinity of Judaism, Christianity, and Islam. They would also make such observations as the following:

- God, if the original Original, by definition would have been hermaphroditic and would not, as is the case with hermaphroditic snails, be addressed as "He."
- Typical of weak religious reasoning is the statement by Samuel S. Cohon, of the Hebrew Union College in Cincinnati, that "the worship of Yahweh as Israel's covenant God and Savior, the revelation of His will to the prophets and its embodiment in the various codes that comprise the Torah, and His demand of moral conduct from His worshipers are permanent elements of Judaism, which run unbroken from the days of Sinai to the present."
- Another illogical concoction by theologians is the concept of the Trinity, a dogma accepted by all Catholic and Eastern Orthodox Christians and by the principal Protestant churches that, as explained by Charles W. Lowry Jr. of the Virginia Theological Seminary in Alexandria, "God is one in being (or substance), power, and majesty, but subsists eternally in three co-equal, perfect persons or hypostates, to which are appropriate respectively the individual names Father, Son or Word (Logos), and Holy Spirit."
- Paul E. Johnson, of the Boston School of Theology, points out a conflict between the various religionists: that it is sacrilegious, according to some, not to believe that the proper name for God is Allah (or Al-lah) and that "There is no God but Allah."

The idea of a woman incarnating the Holy Spirit occurred around 1270 when an Italian prophetess, Gugliemites Gugliema, was considered by her followers as that incarnation—she also was said by some to have been the prototype of the Female Pope (also the High Priestess) card in the Tarot deck. In the early 1300s, Prous Beneta, a Beguine in Provence, was similarly thought to such an incarnation. The English-born founder of the American sect of celibate utopians called Shakers, "Mother" Ann Lee, taught that God had incarnated her just as He had incarnated the man, Jesus. Another woman, Jemima Wilkinson (1752—1819), was regarded as Christ returned, which she did not deny.

Theologians generally concede that the existence of God is unverifiable and must be accepted on faith. Immanuel Kant thought he had destroyed the ontological argument for God, that God *must* exist because God represents the highest concept and *must* have existence as one attribute. Kant argued that existence has no part of the content of an idea, which concept existentialists have emphasized and which they have used as an argument to support atheism. In essence, non-believers generally avoid the word except when referring to the God theologians preach about. They recognize that a Lutheran believes in God and that a Catholic and a Jew believe, also. But, in practice, non-believers are apt to relegate the concept to a collection of terms such as the following: male gods such as Uranus, his son Cronus, and his son Zeus; or the goddesses such as Uranus's mother and wife, Gaea (who was also mother and wife of Pontus, god of the sea); Cronus's wife and sister Rhea (who also was mother of Zeus); and Zeus's wife and sister, Hera. Of these, it is Cronus who fathered the great gods—Zeus, Poseidon, Demeter, Hera, Hades, and Hestia. His father, Uranus, had fathered Titans, Cyclops, and Hundred-handed Ones. But Cronus, dethroning his father, castrated him, whereupon Uranus's blood fell onto Earth, producing the vengeful Furies. And from Uranus's discarded flesh and the sea Aphrodite arose. What distinguishes the Hebrew's God from a Greek god is the latter's interest, shown in the Greek classics, in sex, marriage, pleasure, and humor. The various names, then, are descriptive terms of myths, traditional stories that involve supernatural elements and have occurred in a timeless past. "And where did the Milky Way come from?" the Greek child might ask. "When Hera was breast-feeding," would come the answer, "her baby bit her teat, she cried out, and as she pushed him away the milk spilled out onto the sky." The Greek myths are of value, like the myth of Santa Claus. Unless taken literally.

Philosophers who use the term "God" to describe any unifying concept (for example, cosmic energy, number, mind, world soul) are sure to confuse adherents to the major religions, who oppose the use of original Original, or Goodness. Carl Sagan, for example, has stated that if by "God" one simply means the set of physical laws that are found in the universe, "then clearly there is such a God. This God is emotionally unsatisfying. It does not make much sense to pray to the law of gravity."

Bertrand Russell has written much on the subject, for example in *What I Believe* (1925):

> God and immortality, the central dogmas of the Christian religion, find no support in science. It cannot be said that either doctrine is essential to religion, since neither is found in Buddhism. . . . I do not pretend to be able to prove that there is no God. I equally cannot prove that Satan is a fiction. The Christian God may exist; so may the gods of Olympus, or of ancient Egypt, or of Babylon. But no one of these hypotheses is more probable than any other: they lie outside the region of even probable knowledge, and therefore there is no reason to consider any of them.

On a recording, "Speaking Personally," Russell said, "The whole attitude of the Christian toward God is based on Oriental tyrannies, monarchies. It's the attitude one took toward the King. And it's an attitude which a modern man should consider abject and contemptible." In a 1950 Australian radio program, he further elaborated upon his not believing in God: "It is to the possible achievements of Man that our ultimate loyalty is due, and in that thought the brief troubles of our unquiet epoch become endurable. Much wisdom remains to be learned, and if it is only to be learned through adversity, we must endeavor to endure adversity with what fortitude we can command. But if we can acquire wisdom soon enough, adversity may not be necessary, and the future of Man may be happier than any part of his past."

God and god

The present work treats God as a proper noun, like *Calcutta*; e.g., "Some intelligent people worship God." The plural of God is gods; e.g., "Some intelligent people worship gods"—gods is an example of a common noun, like doppelgänger. Although the common practice is to write "the God of Christianity," the common noun for a deity is god, not God; ergo, writing "the god of Christianity" is entirely logical.

Of the gods, Woden and Jehovah and other such names are examples of proper nouns and are capitalized. If an indefinite article precedes God, it is a common noun and not capitalized; e.g.,

- gad, a minced pronunciation of God as found in an exclamation such as "Egad!" or "Gadzooks," which possibly is a reference to "God's hooks," the nails used in the alleged crucifixion of Jesus.
- godalmighty, as an interjection expresses surprise or dismay
- god-a-mercy, an expression of mercy or thanks
- godawful (slang), a stressing of *awful* in its colloquial sense
- god-botherer (slang), a parson; also, god-pesterer (slang), a bishop
- god box (slang), the remote control device for TV
- godcept (obsolete), gossip
- goddam, goddamn (slang since 1640), used to express displeasure
- god in the box (slang), a radio set
- goddery, an assemblage of gods
- godfather (slang), the leader of an organized crime family
- godfearing refers to having a reverent feeling toward God; being devout
- godforsaken or godforsaken refers to a forlorn or dismal area
- godfright (obsolete), god-fearing, devout, pious
- godful (obsolete), full of God, pious
- the godhead refers to God existing in three persons (God, Jesus, Holy Ghost)
- godhood refers to divinity, or the quality or state of being a god
- goddize, to make into a god or deify
- godify, to make into a god or deify
- godless refers to not acknowledging a god or gods
- godlet, a petty god or deity
- godlike, resembling God in some quality
- godliness, the quality of being godly
- godling is one of the lesser or minor gods; a godkin
- god love her (slang), Mother
- godly (slang) means "cool"; godly, of or pertaining to God
- godman, one who is both God and man, which is said of Jesus
- godoxious, a combination of godawful and obnoxious; repellent
- god rep (slang), the college chaplain
- god-slot (slang), a religious program on radio or television
- god squad, the, the forces of organized religion, especially in evangelical form; the phrase has been applied scornfully to the Salvation Army, doorstep zealots, and university Christian Unions alike
- God's Acre is capitalized if it refers to a specific churchyard's area
- god's balls (slang), usually shortened to oddballs
- godsbodikins, an irreverent reference to the deity's body
- godsend is something desirable that has come unexpectedly
- godship, used jocularly to refer to a god's position or personali ty, as in "your godship"
- godspeed, as in "I wish you godspeed," refers to success or good fortune. The reference is to *speden*, to prosper, and *sped*, Old English for success.

GOD AND THE PHILOSOPHERS: See a definitive article by Paul Edwards, "God and the Philosophers," in *The Oxford Companion to Philosophy*.

"GOD BLESS YOU": See entry for Superstition.

GOD (HIMSELF)

God, after emerging from primal chaos, created the cosmos and the life which would populate it. Then after a period of time He realized that His creation was terribly flawed. Worse, He found that He no longer could control what He had created. If corrections of the flaws were to be realized, those correction would of necessity have to come from the created, not the creator.

"Amid all that rotation of boulders in the void, I saw the small, derisory grain in the cosmic forest as the shelter of my only possible hope. Earth! . . . Earth was the flower of hope to which the cosmos had given birth," He lamented.

Whereupon, He wrote a God's-eye history of what He saw. And it came to pass that He encountered Moses, Parmenides, Heraclitus, Gautama (the one Eastern intruder among all the other Westerners), Jesus, Augustine, Isidore of Seville, Francis of Assisi, Thomas Aquinas, Dante, Columbus, Galileo, Shakespeare, Caravaggio, Mozart, Rousseau, Hölderlin, Melville, Freud, and Einstein. And He called his history *The Life of God (As Told By Himself)*.

Or so the Italian novelist and Rutgers University professor of literature Franco Ferrucci imagined in a 1996 work. Jack Miles, who wrote *God: A Biography*, observed that "Though mentioning neither Hegel nor Darwin, Mr. Ferrucci, in effect, fuses their visions but writes his own ending. For him, the ascending arrow is now in descent. Earth, in all its majesty, is beyond repair. God will miss it—'It won't be easy to abandon such beauty'—but He can do nothing about it." The work, he concludes, is a charming expression of Ferrucci's "boundless hopes for, and poignant disappointment in, his own human kind." {*The New York Times Book Review*, 14 July 1996}

GOD, ACCORDING TO JOHN DEWEY: See entry for Pragmatism.

GOD, DEFINED

> And God said unto them, "And whom do you say I am?
> And they replied, "You are the eschatological manifestation of the ground of our being, the ontological foundation of the context of our very selfhood revealed."
> And God said unto them, "What?"
>
> {Quoted on the Web}

GOD, GOODNESS AND MERCY OF

Anyone who is teary-eyed about the goodness and mercy of God, said a Manhattan Unitarian Universalist, should work for awhile in a hospital on a children's ward.

GOD, MESSAGES FROM

In Huddersfield, England, Shaista Javed, a 14-year-old Muslim, sliced a tomato in half and found a "miracle message" from God written inside. On one side of the tomato she read, "There is only one God." On the other, "Muhammed is the messenger." To the *Daily Mail*, she revealed the revelation, adding, "God made me buy that tomato. The Reuter news agency reported that a local storeowner said demand for tomatoes had soared.

GOD, NATURE OF

Rather than attribute cause and effect to a supernatural or supreme deity, secularists focus on the nature of man and the nature of the universe. (See entry for God.)

GOD, ON TELEVISION

Norman Lloyd, the director of "Steambath," a PBS Hollywood Television Theatre, portrayed God as a Puerto Rican locker-room attendant.

GOD, PHALLUS OF: See entry for John Allegro.

GOD, QUIPS ABOUT:

- Not even God is wise enough.

—Nigerian proverb

- Belief in a cruel God makes a cruel man.

—Thomas Paine

- God is the immemorial refuge of the incompetent, the helpless, the miserable. They find not only sanctuary in His arms, but also a kind of superiority, soothing to their macerated egos; He will set them above their betters.

—H. L. Mencken

- If God created us in his image we have more than reciprocated.

—Voltaire

- Beware of the man whose God is in the skies.

—George Bernard Shaw

- God, that dumping ground of our dreams.

—Jean Rostand

- God is all-powerful, and God is all-loving—and the world is what it is! How are you going to explain that?

—Lord Salisbury

- For me, the single word "God" suggests everything that is slippery, shady, squalid, foul, and grotesque.

—André Breton

- God is the Celebrity-Author of the World's Best-Seller. We have made God into the biggest celebrity of all, to contain our own emptiness.

—Daniel Boorstin

- I do not believe in God. I believe in cashmere.

—Fran Lebowitz

- The impotence of God is infinite.

—Anatole France

- Every man thinks God is on his side. The rich and powerful know he is.
—Jean Anouilh

- God: the Old One.
—Albert Einstein

- Whom the mad would destroy, first they make gods.
—Bernard Levin

- Some people think God is a Christian. Some people think God is a Moslem. Or a Jew. Or a Catholic. Or a Baptist. If you think about it, they can't all be right.
—Dan Barker

- Some people say it is not nice to question God. They think that believing the myth is more important than finding out what is really true.
—Dan Barker

- We can explain phenomenon without any need to refer to gods or God.
—Paul Edwards

(See the entry for Great Mother Goddess. Also, see *Encyclopedia of Philosophy*, Vol. 3.)
{CE; EH; ER; JMRH; RE}

God, Ubiquitous Perpetuity (20th Century)

According to the *New Haven Register* (15 February 1996), a San Rafael, California, man by the name of God was jailed on the latest of eighteen indecent exposure convictions. Mr. God had changed his name years ago (from Enrique Silberg) so that his "flashed" victims could receive "some type of awareness of God."

Pundits noted that upon his death, the former Mr. Silberg would be memorialized with headlines such as "GOD DIES."

GOD, WRATH OF

Judith Hayes, writing in *Freethought Today* (April 1995), provided a partial list of wrathful killing by God, as purported by the Old Testament:

- The entire population of the earth at the time of Noah, except for eight survivors (*Genesis* 7:23)
- Everyone in Sodom and Gomorrah (*Genesis* 19: 24, 25)
- Amalek and his people (*Exodus.* 17:8-16)
- 3,000 Israelites (*Exodus* 32: 27,28)
- 14,700 Jews (*Numbers* 16:44-49)
- The people of Og: "So they smote him, and his sons, and all his people, until there was none left him alive: and they possessed his land." (*Numbers* 21: 33-35)
- 24,000 people (*Numbers* 25: 4-9)
- All Midianite males (*Numbers* 31: 6-12)
- The Ammonites (*Deuteronomy* 2: 19-21)
- The Horims (*Deuteronomy* 2:22)
- The Amorites: ". . . utterly destroyed the men and the women and the little ones." (*Deuteronomy* 2:33-35)
- The Hittites, Girgashites, Amorites, Canaanites, Perizzites, Hivites, and Jebusites: ". . . thou shalt smite them, and utterly destroy them." (*Deuteronomy* 7:1-5)
- Everyone in Jericho but one family (*Joshua* 6:20, 21)
- 12,000 people of Ai (*Joshua* 8:19-29)
- All the people of Makkedah, Libnah, Gezer, Eglon, Hebron (*Joshua* 8 and 10)
- All the inhabitants of the land of Goshen: ". . . until they had destroyed them, neither left they any to breathe." (*Joshua* 11:14)
- The inhabitants of Hormah, Gaza, Askelon, Ekron (*Judges* 1:17-19)
- 10,000 Moabites, 10,000 Perizzites and Canaanites, 600 Philistines, 120,000 Midianites, 1,000 Philistines, 25,100 Benjaminites, and all the hosts of Sisera (*Judges* 1, 3, 4, 8, 15, and 20)
- 50,070 people of Bethshemesh (*1 Samuel* 6:19)
- All the Amalekites: "Slay man and woman, infant and suckling. . . . " (*1 Samuel* 15: 3, 7)
- 200 Philistines, to obtain their foreskins, in order to buy a bridge (*1 Samuel* 18:27)
- 22,000 Syrians, 70,000 people, 40,000 Syrians, and the Ammonites of Rabbah, tortured to death by the great King David (*2 Samuel* 8, 10, 12, 14)
- Every man in Edom (*1 Kings* 11:15)
- All the prophets of Baal (*1 Kings* 18:40)
- 100,000 Syrians (*1 Kings* 20: 28, 29)
- Moabite captains, and "fifties" (*2 Kings*, 1:9-14)
- 42 children and 185,000 Assyrians (*2 Kings* 2 and 19)
- 500,000 men of Israel, 20,000 Edomites, and 120,000 Judeans (*2 Chronicles* 13, 25, 28)
- 75,000 people (*Esther* 9: 15,16)

Godard, Jean-Luc (1930—)

Godard, according to Atheist Celebrities on the internet, is a non-believer. A motion picture director, he has directed such movies as *Opération Béton* (1954); *Breathless* (1959) which won the Jean Vigo Prize and is noted for its elliptical editing; *Weekend* (1968), with its analysis of social ideas; *Every Man For Himself* (1980); and written as well as directed *Passion (*1982) and *King Lear* (1988). His highly personal films are marked by a free-wheeling approach to content and style.

In *La Chinoise*, a voiceover engages in the following: "Woman: 'God, why have you forsaken me.' Man: "Because I don't exist.' "

Godard's *Hail Mary* caused riots by believers and smiles to non-believers. {CE; E}

Goddard, George J. (20th Century)

Goddard is a freethinker who wrote *Billy Sunday's Goat: More Harm Than Good in Revival* (1917). {GS}

Godden, G. M. (20th Century)

Godden, a freethinker, wrote *Militant Atheism* (1933). {GS}

GODDESSES

Dr. Marija Gimbutas (1921—1994), a native of Vilnius, Lithuania, received her doctorate in archeology from Tubingen University in Germany, then taught at Harvard and the University of California. An archeologist with a feminist view, she wrote three books which challenged traditional views of prehistoric societies: *Goddesses and Gods of Old Europe* (1974); *The Language of the Goddess* (1989); and *The Civilization of the Goddess* (1991).

Dr. Gimbutas's controversial thesis was that peace existed during the Stone Age, for goddesses were worshiped in a female-centered society. The two sexes, she held, lived together in harmony until about 6,000 years ago when a European culture of patriarchal invaders replaced the life-giving goddesses with war-like gods. Mythologist Joseph Campbell found her thesis had some merit, but others denied what they claimed is without any possible proof. Journalist Richard D. Lyons quotes University of Wisconsin historian Gerda Lerner, "that although Dr. Gimbutas's theory could never be proved, it could 'challenge, inspire, and fascinate' simply by providing an imaginative alternative to male-centered explanations." (See entry for Great Mother Goddess.)

Godfrey, W. S. (Born 1855)

Godfrey was a writer, a devout "Plymouth Brother" until 1888, when he changed the shade of his theology and entered Spurgeon's Pastors' College. From 1890 to 1895 he served as a Baptist minister, and in the latter year he abandoned Christianity. Thereafter, he occasionally lectured at South Place Chapel. His agnosticism is expounded in *Theism Found Wanting*. {RAT}

Godfrey, Walter Scott (20th Century)

Godfrey, a freethinker, wrote *Still Found Wanting, or the Critic Criticized* (1921). {GS}

Godin, Dave (20th Century)

Godin has written "Up Front" in England for *The Freethinker*. He writes on a variety of topics, including an obituary (February 1996) for the atheist actress Butterfly McQueen .

Godin, Noel (20th Century)

A Belgian prankster, Godin is known as *L'Entarteur* (the Pie Man) because, in his words,

> I'm part of a gang of bad hellions that has declared a pie war on all the unpleasant celebrities in every kind of domain. We began by targeting "empty" celebrities from the artistic world who appeared to think that they were the cat's meow. Then we attacked the French TV news business, and soon we began to pie political figures as well. . . . In November 1969 we pied Marguerite Duras, whose work represented for us the "empty" novel. . . . [We pied] Bill Gates because in a way he is the master of the world. Bill Gates was at the top of our list of victims because he could have been a utopian but he prefers being the lackey of the establishment. The attack against him is symbolic; it's against hierarchical power itself. Our war cry was explicit: "Let's pie! Let's pie the polluting lolly!"

Those involved in the *gloupinesques* (pie pranks) do not throw the pies—they put the pies point-blank in the face of the victim. At least four pies touched Gates's face, to the amazement of photographers who captured the scene for evening telecasts as well as newspaper front pages.

If the Microsoft billionaire were to return to Belgium, Godin was asked, would he and his cohorts pie him again?

> We shall see. But we declare war on all the governments of the world: on Tony Blair, on Bill Clinton, on the Pope. When the Pope

last came to Belgium, if we'd had a traitor sponsoring us, we'd have pied him. We had a strategy. For us, the Pope is a dangerous serial killer because he is against birth control. On our pie list, you will also find Demi Moore; and Tom Cruise and John Travolta, who are both members of Scientology.

{*Harper's*, May 1998}

Godkin, Edwin Lawrence (1831—1902)

Godkin, a journalist, was the son of a Presbyterian clergyman. In college, he rejected his early beliefs, became a journalist, and founded and edited *The Nation*. McCabe labels Godkin "a non-Christian theist." {JM; RAT; RE}

GODMEN AND GODWOMEN

Indian rationalists describe ministers of gods as "godmen" or "god-women" and, in counteracting their influence, call themselves "guru busters." (See entries for Prabhir Ghosh and Debasis Bhattachariya.)

GODPARENTING

Freethinkers who wish to have a special relationship to someone—becoming a protector, benefactor, friend, etc.—but who dislike terms such as "godfather" or "godmother" are sometimes known as **compadre**, co-father, or **comadre**, co-mother. (See entries for comadre and compadre.)

GODS: See entry for Ganesh, the elephant-headed god of learning.

GOD'S ARMY

The Army of God is a shadowy group which in 1997 took credit for two Atlanta bombings, one at an abortion clinic, one at a gay nightclub. It might have planted the nail-studded bomb that killed a woman and hurt one hundred at the 1996 Olympics. The purpose of God's Army, or "AoG" and the Army of God, is apparently to carry out the members' views as to what the Bible teaches. {*Secular Humanist Bulletin*, Fall 1997}

GOD'S PLAN

Theists, when asked why a particularly deserving person should have died so young or in such an unfortunate manner, frequently respond, "It's God's plan."

"What better proof that God is mad!" freethinkers have been known to retort.

Godwin, George (20th Century)

A freethinker, Godwin wrote *Priest or Physician: A Study of Faith Healing* (1942). {GS}

Godwin, Mary: See entry for Mary Wollstonecraft.

Godwin, William (1756—1836)

Godwin, the son of a dissenting minister, was an English philosopher, a skeptic, and "an anarchist." He greatly influenced Shelley, who married his daughter, Mary, author of *Frankenstein* (1818). (A doctor himself, Godwin must have mused at what he had wrought.) With the dramatist Holcroft, he developed an atheism which showed in his various works, including the posthumous *Essays Never Before Published*. In that work, he urges the abolition of all government, names the Christian God as the worst possible governor, one who destroys all that is good in human beings. His influence extended to Coleridge, who convinced him at one time to adopt a pantheistic worship of nature, and to Robert Southey and William Wordsworth.

Godwin's *Enquiry Concerning Political Justice* (1793) recorded the view that men are ultimately guided by reason and therefore, being rational creatures, could live in harmony without laws and institutions. His novels, *Adventures of Caleb Williams* (1794), *St. Leon* (1799), and *Fleetwood* (1805) contain similar humanistic views.

Godwin's last years, during which he tended to become more conservative and was a vague pantheist, were spent in poverty. A few days before his death, he wrote as follows to his daughter, Mrs. Shelley: "I leave behind me a manuscript, in a considerable state of forwardness for the press, entitled, 'The Genius of Christianity Unveiled: in a Series of Essays.' I am most unwilling that this, the concluding work of a long life, and written, as I believe, in the full maturity of my understanding, should be consigned to oblivion. It has been the main object of my life, since I attained to years of discretion, to do my part to free the human mind from slavery. I adjure you therefore, or whomsoever else into whose hands these papers may fall, not to allow them to be consigned to oblivion." Mrs. Shelley appears to have disregarded this solemn adjuration, for the work was not published until 1873.

Godwin is buried in a family plot with Mary Shelley, her son, and her husband Percy's heart, or possibly liver, at St. Peter's Church in Bournemouth, England. The tombstone reads, "William Godwin, Author of Political Justice, Born Mar 3, 1756 Died Apr 7, 1839 Age 50." (See entries for Mary Shelley and for Percy Bysshe Shelley.) {BDF; CE; EU, Peter H. Hare; FO; HAB; JM; JMR; JMRH; RAT; RE}

Goebbels, Paul Joseph (1897—1945)

The Baltimore *Sun* (28 July 1944) carried the following item: "The thanks of the German people, through the lips of Goebbels 'to the Almighty because he has taken the Führer into his gracious protection,' and their request through the same channel that 'he should continue to protect the Führer' is but a normal expression of the official German attitude. The belief often expressed in Allied countries that the Germans do not rely on Providence is mistaken. German soldiers still wear on their belt buckles the motto, 'God With Us.' " {CE}

Goeringer, Conrad (20th Century)

Goeringer, a contributing editor and senior researcher for *American Atheist Magazine*, has noted that "we're becoming a nation of constipated prudes when it comes to just about anything which might offend the sensibilities of different groups, many of them religious." He is American Atheists' director of online services and supervises the production of *AANews*. In 1999 he spoke at that group's "Opposing Theocracy" conference in St. Louis, Missouri, using slide presentations as he discussed Vatican politics, the murder of Roberto Calvi, and the involvement of the Holy See's bank with financial scandals.

Goethe, Johann Wolfgang von (1749—1832)

Goethe is said by Lamont to have had "a vague pantheistic belief." His *Faust* (1808) "is sometimes called *The Divine Comedy* of modern Humanism." No writer of his time begins to reach the heights of *Faust*. Goethe once recorded in a notebook that early in his seventh year (1 November 1758) the great Lisbon earthquake filled his mind with religious doubts. Goethe was influenced by Rousseau, Spinoza, and Schiller. With Schiller, he led the emancipation of Germany, according to McCabe and, especially in their *Xenien* (a collection of caustic epigrams, including many of religion), founded a freethought literature in Germany.

He called the "fairy-tale of Christ" unacceptable, and Chancellor von Müller remarked that, at times at least, Goethe doubted everything and believed in nothing. The crucifix, Goethe held, is "the most repugnant thing under the sun." In letters to Lavater, according to Robertson, Goethe "wrote quite explicitly that a voice from heaven would not make him believe in a virgin birth and a resurrection, such tales being for him rather blasphemies against the great God and his revelation in Nature." "We are pantheists when we study nature," wrote Goethe, "polytheists when we poetize, monotheists in our morality." Goethe also had been influenced by deism, for he was a member of the Masonic Lodge. He affirmed that he was unchristian, not anti-Christian, that he revered Jesus, as he did the Sun. But such views irked believing Christians, who called him "the great Pagan." Not one to be disturbed by criticism that his mind was in a state of verbalizing confusion, he boasted, "After all, I never thought about thinking." Robertson notes, "the permanently interesting teaching of his *Faust* is precisely that which artistically utters the doubt through which he passed to a pantheistic Naturalism."

Writing to Lavater in 1772, Goethe said, "You look upon the gospel as it stands as the divinest truth: but even a voice from heaven would not convince me that water burns and fire quenches, that a woman conceives without a man, and that a dead man can rise again. To you, nothing is more beautiful than the Gospel; to me, a thousand written pages of ancient and modern inspired men are equally beautiful."

Goethe's hostility to everything fundamental in Christian theology was unyielding, according to Foote, and continued from about his seventeenth year to the end of his long life. Heine, in his *De l'Allemagne*, notices Goethe's "vigorous heathen nature" and his "militant antipathy to Christianity." On the Continent hardly anyone would impugn the accuracy of this statement, Foote noted. As a young man Goethe's antagonism to the historic faith caused a marked estrangement between him and some of his friends. In 1788, after his return from his prolonged stay in Italy, he openly declared himself a pagan whose ideals and world-view accorded largely with those of Lucretius. Some of his letters to Lavater, Jacobi, Schiller and Zelter, contain unsparing criticism of Christianity and the claims made for it.

Goethe's "truly Julian hatred of Christianity" became less intense with advancing years, Foote wrote; but throughout life he rejected its cardinal doctrines on intellectual grounds and regarded some of them as serious hindrances to the growth of personality. Christianity's attitude to Nature, the doctrine of total depravity, the cult of sorrow, and its extremely unfavorable influence on art, and the orthodox scheme of salvation generally—all these elements of the faith strongly repelled Goethe.

Edward Carpenter, in *The Intermediate Sex*, implied that Goethe was bisexual. He cited *Wilhelm Meister*, the *Diwan* lyrics, and an essay on Winckelmann. Edgar Lee Masters in his biography of Whitman also suggests that Goethe along with Whitman, Shakespeare, Marlowe, and Michelangelo were "Uranians." In Goethe's case, no hard evidence is available and, as other writers have said, had he written about the pain of giving birth to a baby one would never have speculated that he had done that. Similarly, Kurt R. Eissler's psychological studies reinforced a scholarly school of thought ascribing latent homosexuality or bisexuality to him.

Karl Hugo Pruys, however, after a ten-year examination of 2,500 letters by Goethe and his contemporaries wrote *The Caresses of the Tiger: An Erotic Goethe Biography* (1997). He held that Goethe was not just a repressed homosexual or bisexual but was actively gay. Goethe's letters to the philosopher Friedrich Heinrich Jacobi suggested that the two men had a physical, homosexual relationship. He adds that Goethe had no known heterosexual relationship until his tryst in Rome with Christiane Vulpius, when he was thirty-nine. Pruys, referring to the poem "To the Moon," in which Goethe wrote about the joy of holding a friend to one's bosom and enjoying him.

In his later years Goethe avowed to Eckermann, a kind of German Boswell who in "Conversations with Goethe" included notes on the poet and his Weimar circle of friends, that the name which he would prefer to all others was *Befreier* ("liberator"). According to Foote, eleven days before his death, writing to Eckermann, Goethe said that Biblical questions can be viewed from two standpoints: either as a study in religious origins; or from the standpoint of the Church, which, feeble and transitory as it is, will continue as long as there are weak human beings in existence to need her good offices. In his letters to Zelter, the musician, one of the dearest of all his friends—Goethe's last letters, written after he had entered his eighties—are numerous passages showing his repugnance to Christianity's low estimate of human nature. His last letter to Zelter, a long one dated 11 March 1832 does not contain a word directly bearing on religion, but near the end there is the following remark: "It is strange that the English, the French, and now the Germans, too, like to express themselves incomprehensibly, just as others like to listen to what is incomprehensible." Again and again Goethe detested obscurantism, of that verbiage which expressed nothing real, the kind for which religionists are noted.

As to whether or not he believed in immortality, Goethe wrote as follows:

- This occupation with ideas of immortality is for people of rank, and especially for ladies who have nothing to do. But a man of real worth who has something to do here, and must toil and struggle to produce day by day, leaves the future world to itself, and is active and useful in this.
- The sensible man leaves the future world out of consideration.

Up to his eighty-second birthday, Goethe was in good health. Catching a cold on March 15, 1832, he lived only another week, with his friends and family present at the end. "Light! Light! More light!" he cried out in his sleep at one point. An hour later, he said to his daughter, Ottilie, "Come my little one, and give me your little hand." Then, writing figures and letters on the air with a forefinger, according to biographers Emil Ludwig and George H. Lewes, he succumbed. Eckermann, who saw the body prepared for burial, described it: "a perfect man lay in great beauty before me."

On 2 November 1970, seven people, including the former rector of Jena University and a director of the Museum of Early History in Weimar, exhumed Goethe's corpse, dragged it off to a nearby museum, and worked on its preservation for three weeks, after which the remains were returned to their crypt in the city of Weimar. The operation had begun as an attempt to repair a broken lock on the sarcophagus, but when the advanced state of decomposition of Goethe's remains was discovered, a more elaborate project was devised. According to a report not released until reported by the Frankfurter *Allegemeine Zeitung* (18 March 1999), the poet's skeleton was 5 feet 5 1/2 inches long, giving him a probable living height of 5 feet 6 1/2 inches, about average for his time. His high forehead, pointed chin, and sharp nose were strikingly similar to the portrait of him painted at the time of his death by Friedrich Preller. At the time of the exhumation, the plan was to preserve Goethe's remains in a glass coffin, like Lenin's, but that idea was dropped. Apart from the maceration and bone-reinforcement completed by the scientists, an intricate operation was undertaken to strengthen the laurel wreath that was found attached to Goethe's skull. The laurel wreath's leaves were washed and disinfected in alcohol before being treated in a solution to protect them against the mold. The wreath was then reattached to Goethe's skull. As for what was in the cranium, according to Roger Cohen (*The New York Times*, 19 March 1999), the scientists found only "a dustlike mass." {Alan Cowell, *The New York Times*, 21 September 1997; BDF; CE; FO; *Freethinker*, 31 January and 7 February 1932; HNS2; JM; JMRH; RAT; RE; TYD}

Goetz, Sidney M. (20th Century)

Goetz is on the Board of Directors of the American Humanist Association and was a former president of Humanists of Florida. He is the founder of the Thomas Jefferson Societies and an American Civil Liberties Union attorney. He spoke on the subject "Separation of Church and State—Why We Should Preserve It" at the 1999 convention of Humanists of Florida. {FD}

Goffin, Nicolas (Died 1884)

Goffin was founder of *the Societé de la Libre of Liége* and was president of *La Libre Pensée of Brussels*. He was one of the General Council of the International Federation of Freethinkers. {BDF}

Gogineni, Rajaji Ramanadha Babu (1968—)

Babu, as most people call Mr. Gogineni, was once was the youngest certified French language teacher in Hyderabad, India. He served as Joint Secretary of the Indian Radical Humanist Association until his 1996 appointment as Executive Director of the International Humanist and Ethical Union. As such, he is one of the best-known humanists in international circles.

At the time of moving to London, Babu was founder General Secretary of the South Asia Humanist Network; Trustee of the Indian Renaissance Institute; a secretary of the Indian Radical Humanist Association; and General Secretary of the Rationalist Association of India.

He has contributed articles to the French and English language press in India and Europe and co-edited two books, *Rationalist Essays* published in Chirala and *The Humanist Way*. Babu has participated in international humanist conferences at Brussels in 1990, in Amsterdam in 1992, in Mexico City in 1996, and in Mumbai in 1999. He became editor in 1999 of the *International Humanist News* as well as the husband of Sahana, an award-winning presenter on Telugu Satellite Channel Gemini TV.

In Birmingham, England, at the centenary conference of the Rationalist Press Association in 1999, Babu, who thinks one's outlook would do well to include humor, jocularly entitled his lecture, "Humanism and Ketchup." He is a signer of Humanist Manifesto 2000. His e-mail: <babu@iheu.org>. {*International Humanist News*, December 1996}

Gogol, Nikolai Vasilyevich (1809—1852)

Gogol was one of the most eminent of all Russian writers. His *Dead Souls* (1842) is a picaresque novel about a rogue who buys the names of dead people in order to profit by mortgaging them. The work was a call to reform society and free the serfs. But, outraged at that reaction, the politically conservative Gogol published *Selected Passages from Correspondence with Friends* (1846) in which he openly spoke his political mind. According to the University of California's Simon Karlinsky, Gogol believed that "Slavery was justified in the Bible and must not be abolished; social stratification had been decreed by God; and any reform or political change is an offense against Christianity."

When in 1852 Gogol, a strong believer in Christianity, confessed his homosexuality to Father Matthew Konstantinovsky, the bigoted and sinister priest prescribed abstinence from sleep and food in order to cleanse Gogol's "inner filth." In obeying, Gogol renounced literature and food, burned most of the second part of *Dead Souls*, and died of starvation a month later with the help of his doctors, "who in order to help him, bled him profusely and subjected him to treatments that were physical tortures." {GL}

Goguel, Maurice (1880—1955)

Goguel, a freethinker, wrote *Jesus the Nazarene—Myth or History* (1926). {GS}

Gohdes, Clarence (20th Century)

Gohdes wrote *Periodicals of American Transcendentalism* (1931). {GS}

Goicoechea, David (20th Century)

A professor of philosophy at Brock University in St. Catharines, Ontario, Canada, Goicoechea is one of the editors of *The Question of Humanism, Challenges and Possibilities* (1990). At the 1994 Toronto conference of the Coalition for Secular Humanism, Atheism, and Freethought (CSHAFT), Goicoechea spoke on "Humanism, Postmodernism, and Feminism." In essence, he is opposed to secular humanism and is a post-modern Catholic.

Goldberg, Henry (20th Century)

Goldberg, a freethinker, wrote *Christianity: Its Foundation and Its Final Death* (1908). {GS}

Goldberg, Isaac (1887—1938)

A freethinker, Goldberg wrote *Dictatorship Over the Intellect* (1935). {FUK; GS}

Goldberg, Stuart C. (20th Century)

Goldberg, formerly an Assistant United States Attorney, wrote *God on Trial 2000* (1999). The work denies the arguments of those who try to inject religion into our political life. He specifically indicts God for crimes against Job.

Goldberg, Whoopi (1955—)

Goldberg, an actress, in 1987 was honored with the Hans Christian Andersen Award for outstanding achievement by a dyslectic. She has starred in numerous movies, including "The Color Purple" (1985), and received an Oscar Award for "Ghost" in 1990 as best supporting actress, the second African American woman to win the honor. She also has appeared on the Broadway stage and in numerous telecasts, hosting her own talk show from 1992 to 1993. In 1999 she was the key participant on the telecast "Hollywood Squares."

Her original name was Caryn Johnson and, according to Celebrity Atheists online, Goldberg is a non-theist. However, some skeptics question this because of her frequent reference to "spiritual" subjects. Other skeptics await her own view in writing. {E}

Goldblum, Rebecca (20th Century)

When she signed Humanist Manifesto II, Goldblum was a director of the American Ethical Union. {HM2}

Goldhawke, J. H. (19th Century)

Goldhawke in *Solar Allegories* (1853) writes that the greater number of personages mentioned in the Old and New Testaments are allegorical beings. {BDF}

GOLDEN RULE

The advice to "Do unto others as you would have them do unto you" is undesirable, not golden, according to William Harwood:

> Suppose, for example, that a person earning minimum wage wants one of this planet's billionaires to give him a million dollars. The impossible rule would have him give the billionaire a million dollars, as clearly he is incapable of doing. Similarly, he might want the United Nations to appoint him President of Earth. Again, the universe is beyond his capacity. And what of the man who fantasizes about a supermodel ripping off his clothing and mating with him with callous indifference to his own desires or feelings? The golden rule says that he should do the same to her. In most jurisdictions that would be called rape.

Harwood finds preferable Zoroaster's admonition that one should not do to another whatever is hateful to himself, which is similar to the same advice given by Gautama, the Hindu *Mahabharata*, the Pharisee-authored *Tobit*, and the rabbi Hillel. {*The American Rationalist*, January-February 1999"

Goldie, George Dashwood Taubman [Sir] (1846—1925)

The founder of Nigeria, Goldie refused to have that country named Golderia. "The work's everything, the man's nothing," he reasoned. At one time he was president of the Royal Geographical Society and was in the Privy Council. In her memoir, *Sir George Goldie* (1934), **Lady Goldie** stated that her husband was an agnostic, had "left England to escape from the sound of the Church bells." Goldie had a great disdain of Christian doctrines and used to say that Christians had "always been hypocrites." Lady Goldie added that she was in complete agreement. {RAT; RE}

Goldin, Hyman Elias (Born 1881)

Goldin, a freethinker and secular humanist, wrote *The Case of the Nazarene Reopened* (1948). Before his retirement, he was a professor at Boston University. {GS}

Golding, Harry L. (20th Century)

Golding, when he reviewed books for *The Humanist*, was on the chemistry faculty at DePauw University.

Golding, Henry (20th Century)

From 1923 to 1931, British businessman and Ethical layman became a Leader of the Ethical Society in New York, 1923 to 1931. {EU, Howard B. Radest}

Golding, William [Sir] (1911—1993)

Golding is the English novelist who wrote *Lord of the Flies* (1954), a book which describes the struggle between good and evil and depicts youngsters who, marooned on a deserted island by a plane crash during a global atomic war, regress into blood-curdling tribal savagery.

Reminiscing about World War II, Golding once said that it had been a turning point for him: "I began to see what people were capable of doing. Anyone who moved through those years without understanding that man produces evil as a bee produces honey, must have been blind or wrong in the head." At another time he said, "Look out, the evil is in us all."

Martin Gardner has pointed out two science blunders in Golding's *Lord of the Flies*. In the book's second chapter, Ralph starts a fire by using the spectacles of the myopic Piggy; however, nearsighted (myopic) persons wear lenses that are concave, and only convex lenses can focus sunlight on a small spot. Second, in the fifth chapter Golding writes that the sun has just set, stars have appeared, and a "sliver of moon" is rising above the horizon—a moon rising after sunset, however, has to be full, not crescent-shaped.

After writing *The Spire* (1964) and *The Rites of Passage* (1980), Golding in 1983 was awarded the Nobel Prize for literature. Richard Monte, writing about Golding's reaction against rationalism, terms Golding "a pessimist and his work as a statement against rationality."

If *Sea Trilogy* is counted as one, Monte notes that in nine of Golding's novels "the fallen nature of humanity and hubris predominate. . . . His message is a powerful reminder of the task which faces humanity as it struggles to find ways of living humanely and rationally in a godless universe, where irrational forces and desires are a permanent threat to civilisation." (*New Humanist*, February, 1994).

"I am not a theologian or a philosopher. I am a story teller," Sir William said of his works, adding that he was not entirely a pessimist: "I think good will overcome evil in the end. I don't know quite how, but I have that simple faith."

As for death, he remarked, "I'd rather there wasn't an afterlife, really. I'd much rather not be me for thousands of years. Me? Hah!"

Goldman, Edwin Franko (1878—1956)

Once a pupil of Dvorak, Goldman composed over one hundred marches and in 1918 inaugurated a series of public outdoor concerts. His son, Richard, succeeded him as leader of the Goldman Band which was well-known for its free performances in New York City's Central Park. In the 1950s, Goldman was on the advisory board of Charles Francis Potter's First Humanist Society of New York. {CE}

Goldman, Emma (1869—1940)

An advocate of birth control, an anarchist, and a freethinker, Goldman believed that each generation needs to discard "the burdens of the past, which hold us all in a net." A major unbeliever, she was as unbelieving of Christianity as she became of the Russian Revolution, after having been deported from the United States to Russia after having obstructed the draft. "Religion is a superstition that originated in man's inability to solve natural phenomena," she wrote. "The Church is an organized institution that has always been a stumbling block to progress."

Goldman insisted upon the libertarian principle that "liberty is the mother of order, not its daughter," that this constitutes the highest wisdom yet developed. As such, she condemned the Bolshevik state as she had condemned the soulless church for its "cold, inhuman authoritarianism," writes Reichert. Gay historians Jonathan Katz, Adrien Saks, and Lynne Yamnaguchi Fletcher imply that letters from Almeda Sperry to Goldman were of a lesbian nature. {CE; EU, William O. Reichert; TYD; WWS}

Goldman, Solomon (1893—1953)

A religious humanist, Rabbi Goldman has been a member of the American Humanist Association. He wrote *The Ten Commandments* (1956). His refusal to sign Humanist Manifesto I has been described in Edwin H. Wilson's *The Genesis of a Humanist Manifesto* (1995). {HNS}

Goldsmith, Abbie (20th Century)

Goldsmith, the Board Secretary of Humanists of Florida, spoke on the subject "Abortion, Welfare Reform, and Sexual Orientation Issues" at the 1999 convention of Humanists of Florida.

Goldsmith, James [Sir] (1933—1997)

"Sir James Goldsmith is a protean figure: high-flying financial buccaneer, crusading politician, famously unconventional family man, who shares homes in London, Paris, Burgundy, Spain, and Mexico with his aristocratic wife, Annabel, his ex-wife and former secretary, Ginette, and his mistress, Laure Boulay de la Meurthe." So starts Sally Bedell Smith's article, "Billionaire with a Cause" in *Vanity Fair* (May 1997).

Goldsmith's mother was French Catholic, his father Jewish. The mother, although educated by nuns, had not made Catholicism a factor in his upbringing. "English and French," his brother Teddy has said of the brothers. "You are both, but you are neither. Catholic and Jewish. You are both but neither. You are a professional foreigner. We don't really belong, but we can look from the outside. We see what others don't see."

Sir James's father, Frank, had been born in Frankfurt into the prosperous German Goldschmidt family, which was distantly related to the Rothschilds. Faced with anti-Semitism, his family had moved to England, where the name changed to Goldsmith and Frank Goldsmith defeated George Bernard Shaw for a seat on the London County Council, later being elected to Parliament as a Conservative in 1909. A Jew whose family had been freethinkers for generations, he raised his children not as part of an established church.

Goldsmith, Oliver (1730?—1774)

Goldsmith's philosophic poem, *The Traveler* (1764), brought him early fame, and as one of Samuel Johnson's circle he became well-known. *The Good-Natured Man* (1768) and *She Stoops To Conquer* (1773) added to his reputation, particularly being liked because of their humor and warm humanity. *The Vicar of Wakefield* is his best-known novel. In 1823 the Vatican added to its list of prohibited books his *An Abridged History of England from the Invasion of Julius Caesar to the Death of George II.* His appetite for food and fine clothing nearly matched his inability to pay for either, according to his biographers (S. Gwynn, John Foster, and Ralph M. Wardle). When he was dying of a kidney ailment, Goldsmith had his pulse taken by the attending physician. "Your pulse is in greater disorder than it should be from the state of fever which you have. Is your mind at ease?" asked Dr. Turton. "No," the famed critic responded briefly in his last words, "it is not." {CE; ILP}

Goldsmith, William (20th Century)

Goldsmith, a freethinker, wrote *Evolution and Christianity* (1924). {GS}

Goldstein, Al (1935—)

Screw's editor, Goldstein, is a frank and confrontational sex-industry mogul. The son of a New York *Daily Mirror* worker, he started his weekly magazine in 1968 and, he has said, "It was the first newspaper to have a gay column. We accepted sex ads, we used four-letter words, we've never been euphemist—and that's my pride in the paper." He has been arrested at least nineteen times on charges of obscenity, observing, "I march to my own drummer, and my drummer talks about the one absolute, which is freedom. None of us can be sure what is right, so let's have all voices be heard." In short, he does not defend pornography per se, but does defend its right to exist.

His first sexual experience occurred, he has stated, when he was sixteen. His mother had told his uncle to take him to a prostitute. Goldstein has been married four times and once ran unsuccessfully for Sheriff of Broward County in Florida.

In one journal, he is quoted, "I always read Stuart Mill to [my son,

Jordan]. I brainwashed him like they do in Catholic school, but instead of reading him the Bible I read from the humanists and the liberals. The real liberals—not the phony New York liberals."

In another journal, however, he is quoted, "I actually see myself as a thoughtful cerebral intellectual. . . . I am very conscious of being a Jew named Goldstein. And I am very proud that my son, who went to Georgetown, a Jesuit college; [of its] 781 students—he finished first. He won the two-year Oxford scholarship. He's there now, and he's accepted for Harvard. So there's a Jewish word, *kvell*—"to be proud." I am so *haimish* and so bourgeois, and so proud of my son." This shows, Goldstein insisted, that he exemplifies family values. His will specifies that the son may *not* inherit the father's pornographic business.

In short, on the one hand Goldstein comes across as a nontheist, on the other, a cultural Jew. {CA; E; *Paper*, January 1997; *New York*, 10 February 1997; *Spy*, September-October 1997}

Goldstuecker, Theodor (1821—1872)

Goldstuecker, a Sanskrit scholar who was "of Jewish birth" but a freethinker by conviction, was a democrat in politics. Upon moving to England he helped Prof. Wilson prepare his *Sanskrit-English Dictionary*. Goldstuecker contributed important articles on Indian literature to the *Westminster Review*, the *Reader*, the *Athenaeum*, and *Chambers' Encyclopedia*. {BDF; RAT}

Goldziher, Ignacz (1850—1921)

Goldziher was a Hungarian Orientalist who taught Semitic Philology in Budapest. He wrote *Mythology Among the Hebrews* and other works on Semitic theology and literature. {BDF; RAT}

Goleman, Daniel (20th Century)

Goleman wrote *Emotional Intelligence* (1995), telling about the neurology of emotion and dealing with how poor emotional control interferes with the management of our lives. Love relationships break up because of poor communication and because partners do not know how to avoid damaging others' emotions.

"For Humanists this is an important issue," he wrote, "and is one where religious conservatives are squarely on the other side. As conservative Catholic Dale O'Leary says: Fear of the Lord, not self esteem, is the beginning of wisdom. . . . Schools exist to educate children, not to please them. Schools should be run on the principle that children, lacking education and experience, do not know what they need." {*Newsletter of the Humanist Association of Massachusetts*, May-June 1996}

Golly, Ed (20th Century)

Golly, a Floridian, is assistant secretary of Atheists of Florida. Upon his return from a humanist convention, when his airplane crashed, he wrote "On a Wing and No Prayer" for *Free Inquiry*, explaining why his not having died in the crash had nothing to do with the supernatural. E-mail: <athalfle@aol.com>.

Gomberg, Louis R. (20th Century)

A humanist counselor who signed Humanist Manifesto II, Gomberg is on the editorial board of *The Humanist*. In 1979, he was President of the American Humanist Association. {HM2}

Gomes, Peter (20th Century)

Gomes, minister of Harvard's Memorial Church, wrote *Fighting for the Bible*, a book that made him one of the most highly paid openly gay authors in the United States. At the inaugurations of both Presidents Reagan and Bush, he delivered benedictions.

Gomme, George Lawrence [Sir] (1853—1916)

A folklorist, Gomme was one of the chief authorities on the subject and founded the Folklore Society. He was knighted in 1911 and in 1916 became president of the Anthropological Section of the British Association. Gomme was a rationalist. {RAT; RE}

Gompers, Sophia Julian (1833?—1920)

Gompers, the wife of the American labor leader—Samuel Gompers, 1850-1924—who helped found the American Federation of Labor in 1886, was a member of Charles Francis Potter's New York Humanist Society. {*Humanist Newsletter*, November-December 1953}

Gomperz, Heinrich (1873—1942)

An Austrian philosopher, Gomperz taught philosophy at Berne University in 1900 and at Vienna University in 1905. In his philosophical works, he expounds an idealistic monism, similar to that of Avenarius. {RAT}

Gomperz, Theodor (1832—1912)

Gomperz was an Austrian philosopher. His *Greek Thinkers* (1901—1912) gave him a European reputation and was candid in dealing with the skepticism of the Greek philosophers. Gomperz was a friend of J. S. Mill and edited the German translation of Mill's works. {JMRH; RE}

Goncourt, Edmond Louis Antoine Huot de (1822—1896)
Goncourt, Jules Alfred Huot (1830—1870)

The Goncourt brothers, so closely associated in art and literature that everyone termed them *les deux Goncourts*, were art critics and historians of art, unsuccessful dramatists, promoters of Japanese art, and, in collaboration, authors of well-known novels of the naturalist school such as *Soeur Philomène* (1861) and *Mme. Gervaisais* (1869). Their *Journals des Goncourt* (9 volumes, 1887—1896) described Parisian society over a period of forty years. After Jules's death Edmond provided for the founding of the Goncourt Academy (which was officially recognized in 1903). It awards the annual Goncourt Prize for fiction.

According to Robertson, both were rationalists; McCabe calls both atheists. In a collection of epigrams (*Idées et sensations*) the two Goncourts define religion as "part of a woman's sex"; supernatural religion as "wine without grapes"; and life as "the unfruct of an aggregation of molecules." {CE; JM; JMR; RAT; RE}

Gonsalves, Howard (20th Century)

Gonsalves is president of the Humanist Society of Berkeley (AHA). (See entry for California Atheists, Humanists.) {FD}

Gooch, G(eorge) P(eabody) (1873—1968)

Gooch, in a foreword to John A. Hobson's *Rationalism and Humanism*, wrote, "Rationalism . . . is an attitude rather than a creed—a refusal to accept beliefs, conventions, and institutions merely because we find them in possession of the field. The progress of mankind is mainly due to the eager, inquiring, critical, inventive spirit, ceaselessly feeling its way towards a richer and more intelligent life." Gooch was one of the first English writers on German 18th-century history. His *History and Historians in the Nineteenth Century* (1913, 1946) has been termed one of the most valuable books of modern historiography. From 1906 to 1910, Gooch was a Liberal member of Parliament. {CE}

GOOD

For many secularists, "God" is simply a mis-spelling of Good. Good for others can be defined as the opposite of bad; and conforming "to the moral order of the universe" can be the majority's idea of goodness. For example: "He was a good man" uttered at his funeral; "This is a good painting" uttered by an auctioneer; and "Heroin is good stuff" uttered by an addict—all imply differing shades of morality. Similarly, Jeremy Bentham, John Dewey, and G. E. Moore have differing views as to what constitutes good and goodness. (Their differences are detailed in the *Encyclopedia of Philosophy*, Vol. 3.)

"Whereas the Christian church connects the power for goodness with one name in the world's history," John H. Dietrich wrote, "humanism recognizes that goodness springs from many sources, so that its formula of worship would base itself, not upon the name of Jesus or Buddha [Siddhartha] or Mohammed alone, but would express reverence for the divergent forces of the universal good."

Bertrand Russell, in *What I Believe* (1925), wrote, "The good life is one inspired by love and guided by knowledge." Upon this, he elaborated: "To live the good life in the fullest sense a man must have a good education, friends, love, children (if he desires them), a sufficient income to keep him from want and grave anxiety, good health, and work which is not uninteresting. All these things, in varying degree, depend upon the community, and are helped or hindered by political events. The good life must be lived in a good society and is not fully possible otherwise."

For the Tarahumara Indians in northern Mexico, good and evil are unimportant concepts. Instead, their world is one in which there is only that which is useful. Romayne Wheeler, a concert pianist who lives with them, reported that when he extolled the fiery sunset that raged across the western sky, the Tarahumara told him there was nothing beautiful about it because it meant there would be no rain. {Anthony DePalma, "Creel Journal," *The New York Times*, 19 December 1995}

GOOD FRIDAY

Good Friday has no relevance for freethinkers, except that Iowa farmers consider it a good time to plant potatoes The Friday before Easter Sunday is commemorated as the Crucifixion of Jesus. (See entry for Humanist Holidays.)

GOOD LIFE

"The good life is one inspired by love and guided by knowledge," wrote Bertrand Russell. The sentiment has become the motto of the Bertrand Russell Society. (See entry for Industrialism, which includes his indictment.)

Goodell, N. D. (19th Century)

Goodell was a pioneer freethinker of Sacramento, California, a "Forty-niner" who took three months to travel over the vast plains in order to search for gold. An architect, he erected many buildings in the Sacramento area. Goodell was early drawn into the Universalist church, and he became a radical freethinker. He was vice-president of the California Liberal Union. {PUT}

Goodheart, Lawrence B. (1945—)

Goodheart is author of *Abolitionist, Actuary, Atheist: Elizur Wright and the Reform Impulse* (1990).

Goodman, Barbara [Dame] (20th Century)

Goodman, an Auckland City Councillor and convenor of the Campaign for Tolerance in 1985-1986, is an honorary associate of the New Zealand Association of Rationalists and Humanists.

Goodman, Saul (20th Century)

Goodman is author of *The Faith of Secular Jews*. A Yiddishist, he holds that Jewish secularism is a lineal descendant of the Haskala (Jewish Enlightenment) and that it is viable for committed Jewish humanists.

Goodsell, Willystine: See entry for Ancient Humanism.

Goodwin, Joan W. (20th Century)

A Unitarian, Goodwin wrote *The Remarkable Mrs. Ripley: The Life of Sarah Alden Bradford Ripley* (1998). The work includes details about the transcendental movement.

Gopal, Kamal G. (20th Century)

Gopal is a National Council member of the Indian Rationalist Association and is managing editor of *Modern Freethinker*.

Gora (Goparaju Rama-chandra Rao) (1902—1975)

Editor of *The Atheist* and founder and head of the Atheist Center in Vijayawada, India, Gora developed a social, political, and economic program there. He fought not only superstition but also the system of castes. He has written, "Faith is an expression of the slave mentality" and "The essence of atheism is freedom of man. . . . Its objective is equality, its method sincerity, its instrument political action, its motor moral freedom." He is included by Jose M. F. Santana in the Swedish *Uskonnottomien Kalenteri* (The Non-Believer's Calendar, 1983). According to Deodhekar, "The reforms Gora fought for, such as the abolition of the caste system, with its inhumane system of untouchability, were also championed by theists such as Gandhi. But Gora's challenge was more fundamental. The root cause of social ills for Gora was the belief in God, which implied subordination of man to the divine will or *karma* or fate. He fearlessly and persistently demanded the uprooting of this unfounded belief, thus restoring self-confidence and free will to men and women."

In 1990, on its Golden Jubilee, the Atheist Centre was visited by a number of foreign dignitaries—from England there were Barbara Smoker, President of the National Secular Society; Dr. Harry Stopes-Roe, former Chairman of the British Humanist Association; Eric Stockton, Editor of the Scottish Humanist; and Jim Herrick. The celebration was presided over by Prof. Sir Hermann Bondi, President of the Rationalist Press Association. Said Bondi, "The Atheist Centre is an example which humanists throughout the world can quote from morn to night to demonstrate that our attitude can produce beneficial results. It's the best known example in the world of what unbelief can do for mankind." (*New Humanist*, May, 1990). Gora was a founding member of the Indian Rationalist Association. (See entries for Ramendra and for G. Vijayam.) {EU, Govind N. Deodhekar; FUK; HNS2; PK}

Gora, Saraswati (1912—)

Gora, with her husband, founded the Atheist Centre in Vijayawada, India. At a November 1992 conference on social progress and women, she and her husband were described as "champions of human equality and human liberation" who "worked vigorously for the development of women as equal partners in progress."

At the 1996 Fourth World Atheist Conference, she stated that "Human welfare is of paramount importance for us. Atheism is universal, transcending all boundaries. It is human centered. It aims for all round development of the personality. Human freedom and human dignity must be achieved. . . . Atheism is not an armchair philosophy or mere criticism of god or religion. It is a way of life to increase the moral freedom of the individual. Atheism is comprehensive in its approach and outlook." In 1997 in Bombay, she was awarded the Jankidevi Award for her work in behalf of socio-economic change in rural India. In 1998 she was awarded by the Telugu University of Hyderabad the Kaviraju Tripuraneni Ramaswami Chowdary Award for the promotion of rationalism. {*The Atheist*, February 1997; *New Humanist*, February 1996}

Gorani, Guiseppe [Count] (1740—1819)

Gorani, an Italian count, was an intimate and freethinking friend of Beccaria, d'Holbach, and Diderot. He wrote a treatise on *Despotism* (1770), defended the French Revolution, and was made a French citizen. He died, however, in Switzerland. {BDF; RAT; RE}

Göransson, Mikael (1942—)

In 1995, Göransson was elected President of Sweden's Human-Etiska Forbundet. He worked during his presidency to arrange a course for officiants of civil funerals. Swedish humanists have worked with Norwegian humanists for freedom of thought and religion in school. Göransson, who owns a company named MIGÖR!AB, explains that "Gör!" means "do," that he tries to bring theory and practice together in such a way that people "learn by doing." E-mail: <mikael.goransson@migor.se>. {*International Humanist News*, April 1996}

Gorbachev, Mikhail S. [President of the USSR] (1931—)

When President of the Soviet Union, Gorbachev was asked by Peter Jennings of ABC News (6 Sep 91) about his personal religious beliefs, to which he responded, "I am an atheist. But I (and I've never concealed this) I respect the feelings and the religious beliefs of each citizen, of each person. This is a question of personal sovereignty, and we have done a good deal so as to, in a legislative sense, guarantee each person the right to call himself what he wants, to allow each person to select his own religion. And I wanted—but I did feel it necessary to add that I personally am an atheist." (*The NY Times*, 7 September 1991) (In the same interview, Boris Yeltsin said personally he is superstitious and sometimes goes to church services "because during the service there's a kind of internal feeling of moral cleansing, as it were.")

According to Svetozar Stojanovic, a Yugoslavian professor who is in the International Academy of Humanism, Gorbachev inadvertently became the great liquidator of communism. "He didn't want nor did he plan it. . . . He tried only to reform communism but at the decisive moments he didn't want to try to save it by force." Stojanovic terms Gorbachev, whose mother was Christian, a Marxist humanist.

Inasmuch as Gorbachev once wrote a foreword for a Siloist publication, secular humanists muse as to whether he knew about Siloism or whether he approved of that group's interest in "green" and "humanism." The concensus within the secular humanist organization is that he did not.

In *Free Inquiry* (Winter 1997—1998), Gorbachev wrote about humanism:

> I believe strongly that the humanistic worldview of regarding humanity as one's main reference point, main goal, and highest value is inherent in human nature. On the other hand, we have to admit that human nature is not one-dimensional. Coupled with the good, the humane, is the opposite. We have all come across ideas and acts that are very remote from humanism. It is conditions and social relations in which humans find themselves that are partly responsible for that. But in spite of that, we could say that antihumanism contradicts the essence of *Homo sapiens*. . . .
>
> The experience of *perestroika* was multifacted, and here I would like to single out two aspects. One is that humanistic reforms are possible even in a society that is affected, even deeply, by totalitarianism. Such reforms are recognized and supported by society and people. If we consistently abide by humanistic principles, if we do not deviate from the moral approach, we can achieve very much. And *perestroika* achieved very much indeed—above all, the liquidation of totalitarianism and the establishment of democratic principles in our country. Naturally, it was impossible to achieve everything we expected and strived for.
>
> The second aspect of the *perestroika* experience is that the authentic humanistic, democratic transformation of society is not a simple task. One collides with the forces of the past. Moreover, Russian society does not have a tradition favoring such a transformation. Then there are the complexities of the reform itself. All this holds true especially for our own experiment, and in a country that had lived many years under an antihumanistic regime. But I believe that establishing authentic humanistic values even in democratic societies is not an easy task—the deficit of humanism is felt everywhere. . . .Humanism cannot be reduced to ideas and declarations of values. Above all else humanism means activism. In the name of humanity. This is my conviction.

Some question if Gorbachev has changed his thinking. At the end of a November 1996 interview on CSPAN's "Booknotes," he said, "I don't know how many years God will be giving me [or] what his plans are." Others say he was simply "speaking down" to hoi polloi.

Raisa Gorbachev (1932-1999), his wife who died of leukemia, like her husband was a freethinker. The daughter of a railway engineer, she attended the University of Moscow and met her husband while studying philosophy. Her doctoral disseration was entitled The Emergence of New Characteristics in the Daily Life of Collective Farm Peasantry." Until her husband became General Secretary of the Communist Party, she taught philosophy at Moscow University. {CA; E; *Free Inquiry*, Summer 1996}

Gordin, Harry Mann (20th Century)

Gordin, a freethinker, wrote *Science, Truth, Religion, and Ethics as Foundations of a Rational Philosophy of Life* (1924). {GS}

Gordon, A. R. Jr. (20th Century)

Gordon, who describes himself as an "atheistic humanist," is an oceanographer. A retired Air Force colonel, he has written freethought materials in *Freethought Today*.

Gordon, Adam Lindsay (1833—1870)

Gordon was an Australian poet. In 1865 he was elected to the Legislative Assembly of South Australia. His rationalism is shown in works such as *Sea Spray and Smoke* and *Bush Ballads*. {RAT; RE}

Gordon, Alexander (1692?—1754?)

The Vatican in 1733 prohibited the reading of Gordon's *The Lives of Pope Alexander VI and His Son Caesar Borgia, Comprehending the Wars in the Reigns of Charles VIII and Lewis XII, Kings of France, and the Chief Transactions and Revolutions in Italy, from 1492 to 1506, with an Appendix of Original Pieces*. A secretary of the Society of Antiquarians of the Egyptian Society, he once undertook to solve the mysteries of hieroglyphics and to illustrate "all the Egyptian mummies in England." Because of his business failures, he moved to South Carolina in 1741 as secretary to the newly appointed governor of the province, James Glenn. {ILP}

Gordon, Ann (20th Century)

A freethinker, Gordon in 1995 at Rutgers University had as a project the editing of the papers of Elizabeth Cady Stanton and Susan B. Anthony. *Freethought History #9*, 1994}

Gordon, Eleanor Elizabeth (1852—1942)

A close friend and associate of Mary Safford, the leader of the "Iowa Band" of "Iowa Sisterhood," Gordon was committed to liberal religious values and to the cause of fuller women's rights. She was an assistant minister of the Unitarian Church, Sioux City, Iowa (1885—1889), and minister from 1889 to 1896. Also, she was a minister in Iowa City, Burlington, and Des Moines as well as in Fargo, North Dakota, and Orlando, Florida. {U&U}

Gordon, Gene (20th Century)

Gordon is author of "Cyrano de Bergerac: The Man Who Thumbed His Nose at God," in *Free Inquiry* (Fall, 1991).

Gordon, Harold N. (20th Century)

When he signed Humanist Manifesto II, Gordon was a vice president of the American Ethical Union. {HM2}

Gordon, Henry (20th Century)

Gordon, a columnist for *The Toronto Sun*, has entertained many humanist events with his professional magic acts.

Gordon, Jesse (Died 1993)

Gordon was a leader of the Humanist Society of Metropolitan New York, a chapter of the American Humanist Association, from 1974 to 1993. He also had been on the editorial board of *The Humanist*. {FD}

Gordon, Rusty (20th Century)

Gordon is treasurer and membership chairperson of Humanists of the Palm Beaches in Florida.

Gordon, Sol (1923—)

When he signed Humanist Manifesto II, Gordon was a professor at Syracuse University. He now is professor emeritus of child and family studies there. With his wife, Judith, he has written *You Would If You Loved Me* (1978), *Did the Sun Shine Before You Were Born?: A Sex Education Primer* (1992), and Girls *Are Girls and Boys Are Boys: So What's the Difference?* (1991). The books encourage six-year-olds to teenagers to understand sexual differences and relate his findings that "young people who are knowledgeable about their sexuality are more likely to delay their first sexual experience. Knowledge isn't harmful; [yet] virtually all opposition in this country to sex education is based upon the supposition that knowledge is harmful."

In 1990, Gordon received the American Humanist Association's Humanist Distinguished Service Award. {HM2; HNS2}

Gordon, Thomas (c. 1684—1750)

A Scottish deist and political reformer, Gordon wrote a series of papers against the clergy in London, which D'Holbach translated into French. Walpole made him First Commissioner of the Wine Licenses. He translated Tacitus, Sallust, and Cicero. He was amanuensis to Trenchard, with whom he published *Cato's Letters* and a periodical entitled *The Independent Whig*, which he continued some years after Trenchard's death. Gordon married Trenchard's widow. {BDF; RAT; RE}

Gordon, William (Bill) (1925—)

Gordon, a sailor during World War II, survived an attack from the Japanese while on an aircraft carrier during which four hundred were killed. When he observed people thanking God for being saved, he told fellow Ohio atheists, his reaction was "God damn you God for killing them." Gordon is a radio personality who is active with the Free Inquirers of Northeastern Ohio. {*FINO Newsletter*, August 1997}

Gore, Albert Jr. (1948-)

Gore, the Vice President of the United States commencing in 1993, is a Baptist who believes in Heaven and in God.

Gore, Thomas Pryor [Senator] (1870—1949)

Gore, who was Gore Vidal's grandfather, was blind from ten years old. First the Populist Party's ablest and best known stump speech-maker, he then became a Democrat. A friend of Clarence Darrow, Gore backed the Indians against the oil interests in Oklahoma, where he was senator.

His grandson has written, "The odds are very much against losing an eye in an accident, but to lose two eyes in two separate accidents is positively Lloydsian." Vidal spent much of his youth reading to his grandfather, who, as shown in *Palimpsest* (1995), was a major influence in his life.

The Senator, such an outstanding speaker that he was known as the "Blind Orator," was once asked by a group of Baptist ministers to become a minister, for which he would receive an excellent salary and a fine house. When he declined, saying he did not believe in God, the ministers shot back, "Come now, Mr. Gore, that's not the proposition we made you."

Gorham, Charles Turner (20th Century)

Gorham is a freethinker and rationalist who wrote, in addition to over a dozen books and pamphlets, *The Gospel of Rationalism* (1949). {FUK; FUS; RAT}

Gornik, David J. (20th Century)

Comedy is a soothing way to get beyond the initial sting of attacking core values, Gornik (Box WWH, 36335 Reading Avenue, Willoughby, Ohio 44094) believes. Therefore he has written lyrics that espouse the compelling virtues of humanism and has put them to the tune of classic Christmas carols.

Samples:

- We Wish You a Merry Solstice
- Arrest Ye Merry Gentlemen
- Deck the Halls with Calls of Folly
- Away with the Deranger
- Come All Ye Mournful

{*Free Inquiry*, Spring 1999}

Gorky, Maxim (pseudonym of **Alexei Maximovitch Peshkov**) (1868—1936)

A Russian novelist, Gorky "showed distinct Humanist leanings" in his work, according to Corliss Lamont. Maxim (or Maksim) Gorky was a pseudonym of **Maximovich Pyeshov Aleksey**. Gorky once wrote, "This 'search for God' business must be forbidden for a time—it is a perfectly useless occupation." The father of Soviet literature, he founded the literary doctrine of socialist realism, now completely passé. It has never been established which anti-Soviet group, if any, assassinated him by poisoning his food. Lenin used to lecture Gorky, "All worship of a divinity is necrolatry [worship of the dead]. . . . Any religious idea, any idea of any god at all, even any flirting with a divinity is the most inexpressible . . . [and] dangerous foulness, the most hideous 'infection.' "

Ironically, Gorky became known as a foggy God-builder." Robertson, however, calls him "an absolute Naturalist," and McCabe says Gorky was contemptuous of all religion. In *Culture and the People* (1939), Gorki wrote, "Paradise is one of the crass fictions invented by high-priests and fathers of the Church, a fiction whose purpose it is to requite the hellish torments of people on earth with the soap-bubble of a hope of peace in another place." Many have speculated that Gorky was murdered, that while he was under medical treatment he was killed by a group known as "The Bloc of Rightists and Trotskyites." {CE; CL; EU, Jerry G. Pankhurst, Rolf H. W. Theen, Hugh McLean; JM; JMR; PA; RAT; RE; TRI; TYD}

Gorlaeus, David (17th Century)

Gorlaeus was a Dutch philosopher accused of being an atheist on account of his speculations in a work published after his death, *Exercitations Philosophicae* (1620). {BDF}

Gorman, Joe (20th Century)

Gorman is active with the Humanists of the Pomona Valley (AHA). (See entry for California Atheists, Humanists.) {FD}

Goron, Sol (20th Century)

Goron, who signed Humanist Manifesto 2000, is an emeritus professor of Syracuse University, Tel Aviv, Israel.

Gorski, Tim (20th Century)

Gorski, who also writes under the name of Timotheus, is editor of *The Freethought Observer* (Box 202447, Arlington, Texas 76006), which commenced in 1994. A physician, he was one of the founders of the North Texas Church of Freethought. "Secular humanists do not deny that religious beliefs play a role in people's lives," he has written. "Yet it was the insight of the Founding Fathers, who represented all points on the religious spectrum, that the government of a civil society ought to be neutral and aloof on religious matters, as the First Amendment mandates." Gorski's "Alternative Medicine Looks a Lot Like Religion" in *Secular Nation* (April-June 1998) points out homeopathy's and acupuncture's limitations. He is President of the Dallas/Fort Worth Area Council Against Health Fraud, Pastoral Director of the North Texas Church of Freethought, a supporter of Internet Infidels, a director of the Atheist Alliance Board, and a representative of the Metroplex Atheists. {*The New York Times*, 9 March 1996}

Gortner, Marjoe (1944—)

When four years old in 1949, Gortner performed his first marriage, having been ordained as a minister in the Church of the Old Time Faith. In the 1970s, however, he visited the American Atheist Center in Austin, Texas, reporting that he had abandoned all religious ideas. Steven Gaines wrote a book about Gortner's life, *Marjoe* (1973, which was turned into an Academy Award Winning documentary film.

Gorton, Ron (20th Century)

In Britain, Gorton is active with the Reigate and Dorking Humanist Group.

Gorton, Samuel (1592—1677)

Gorton, a pioneer of Christian Universalism, was driven out of Massachusetts because of his political and religious "radicalism."

Goss, C. W. F. (20th Century)

Goss wrote *A Descriptive Bibliography of the Writings of George Jacob Holyoake* (1908). {FUK; FUS}

Goss, Richard Johnson (1925—1996)

Goss, emeritus professor of biology at Brown University, in *Freethought Today* (October, 1992) wrote about a study in which 293 patients were divided into two groups, 192 of whom were to be the object of prayers seeking divine intercession on their behalf and the other 201 were not specifically to be prayed for. The study, "Positive therapeutic effects of intercessory prayer in a coronary care unit population" (*Southern Medical Journal* 81:826-829), concluded that intercessory prayers to the Judeo-Christian God *did* exert a positive effect on the recovery of cardiac patients. Finding the study quite unscientific, Goss retorted, "If my doctor prays for my recovery, I would consider a malpractice suit." He also questioned "what kind of benevolent God would ignore the plight of innocent controls." As for the human soul, Goss noted that clergymen, even those who accept evolution, cannot seem to explain how primates without souls became people "when a pair of ape parents begat a human baby."

An embryologist, Goss has devoted his professional career to the study of the regeneration of animal appendages and the regulation of organ and tissue growth. He wrote *The Physiology of Growth* (1978), *Deer Antlers: Regeneration, Function, and Evolution* (1983), and *Regulation of Organ and Tissue Growth* (1972). In "God and the Patent Office" (*Free Inquiry*, Fall 1995), Goss complained that "Representatives of all major religious denominations have now officially staked their claim to the human genome, the sum total of all genes that define what we are." He argued that it is highly debatable whether or not human genes should ever be patentable.

Gotesky, Rubin (Born 1905)

A teacher in the department of philosophy at the University of Georgia, Gotesky was an associate editor in the 1950s of *The Humanist*. {HNS}

Gott, J. W. (1866—1923)

Gott, who was imprisoned for blasphemy no less than four times between 1911 and 1922, founded the monthly *Truthseeker* in 1894. A businessman in the clothing trade, he was treasurer of the British Secular League in 1903. George William Foote was concerned that Gott would bring disrepute to the freethought movement because of his egotism, but others thought he carried on a commendable attack upon Christianity. {EU, Victor E. Neuburg; FUK; RSR}

Gottesman, Rick (20th Century)

Gottesman is a newsletter editor for the Capital District Humanist Society in Scotia, PO Box 2148, New York 12302.

Gottheil, Elias (19th Century)

A London freethinker, Gottheil was secretary of the East London Secular Society. He also was editor of the *Secularist* (1856). {VI}

Gottlieb, Sheldon Fred (1932—)

"I am Jewish—a humanistic skeptic if not outright atheist, but still a Jew," declared Gottlieb, professor of biological sciences at the University of South Alabama in Mobile. He added, "I respect—and selectively practice—many aspects of Jewish ritual, not because of their deistic mandates, but because of their great humanistic and ethical values." Like others into "humanistic Judaism," Gottlieb finds Judaism is in harmony with the finest humanist traditions, that it emphasizes deeds, not faith. For him, "Judaism is unlike other religiously based belief systems in that Jews may relinquish the deistic aspects of the religion and still consider themselves to be culturally and ethnically Jewish. Also, rational rejection must be distinguished from self-hate or anti-Semitic renunciation of the deistic aspects of Judaism." His *Who's Who* listing is "Do not permit nonsense, ignorance, mythology, superstition, irrationality, fear, and hate to spread." A fearless defender of Darwin in the Bible Belt, Gottlieb has organized conferences dealing with the implications of evolution. {*Free Inquiry*, Fall 1993}

Gottschalk, Charles (20th Century)

Gottschalk was President of the Humanist Quest of Milwaukee, Wisconsin, being succeeded in 1996 by Wendell J. Harris. {*Freethought Observer*, November-December 1996}

Goud, J. D. (20th Century)

Dr. Goud, a professor of zoology, is an active member of the Andhra Pradesh Rationalists Association in India.

Goueffic, Louise (20th Century)

In Toronto, Ontario, Canada, Goueffic since 1983 has edited *Atheism in Canada*.

Gould, Frederick James (1855—1938)

Gould was a British Ethical Culture leader. He has edited the *Leicester Reasoner*, and he wrote *The Agnostic Island* (1891) and *Life-Story of A Humanist* (1923). After serving as an Ethical Culture leader, he moved from London to run the Leicester Secular Society. Gould claimed to be an agnostic, atheist, ethicist, freethinker, Marxist, positivist, and secularist. His *Pioneer of Johnson's Court* (1929) is a history of the Rationalist Press Association from 1899 on. {CL; FUK; HNS; HNS2; RE; RSR}

Gould, Lawrence (20th Century)

Gould was on the advisory board of Charles Francis Potter's First Humanist Society of New York.

Gould, Morton (1913—1995)

Gould, a composer of numerous works including "Cowboy Rhapsody," "Lincoln Legend," and "American Salute," headed the American Society of Composers, Authors, & Publishers (ASCAP) from 1986 to 1994. Asked by the present author for his views of humanism, Gould responded:

> I think I fit in No. 1 (the lexicographic term, a devotion to human interests, and a study of the humanities) in the sense of a concern for human beings and the human condition, not necessarily always with love, but hopefully always with compassion.

{Bernard Holland, *The New York Times*, 22 February 1996; WAS, 4 June 1992}

Gould, Stephen Jay (1941—)

A Harvard paleontologist, Dr. Gould is a Humanist Laureate in the Council for Secular Humanism's International Academy of Humanism. His work on evolution is found in *Ever Since Darwin* (1977); *Hen's Teeth and Horses' Toes* (1982); *Full House: The Spread of*

Excellence from Plato to Darwin (1996); and *Dinosaur in a Haystack, Reflections in Natural History* (1996). In 1972, with Niles Eldredge, Gould proposed an evolutionary theory, of "punctured equilibrium," described by the *Columbia Encyclopedia* as "stating that many species may evolve relatively quickly, rather than through a continuous slow accretion of tiny species variations, then persist virtually unchanged for perhaps millions of years. The 'missing links' in evolutionary development sought since the time of Charles Darwin may thus not exist, the two hold. Elaboration of these concepts has led to extensive scientific debate." *Eight Little Piggies, Reflections in Natural History* (1992) is his sixth in a series of essay collections drawn from "a 208 monthly essay streak" in *Natural History*.

To *Life* (December 1988), Gould explained his outlook:

> We are here because one odd group of fishes had a peculiar fin anatomy that could transform into legs for terrestrial creatures; because the earth never froze entirely during an ice age; because a small and tenuous species, arising in Africa a quarter of a million years ago, has managed, so far, to survive by hook and by crook. We may yearn for a "higher" answer—but none exists.

In a 1993 speech at Columbia University, Gould contended that evolution is really like a big lottery. Natural history, he held, is not inspired by any survival of the fittest, as so many Darwinians hold, but by the survival of the luckiest. He debunks the view that the ascent of humans began with single cell organisms, then moved through slimy fish and reptiles and from hunched hairy beasts to *homo sapiens* in some progressive and orderly fashion. Rather, he says, evolution is a risky, messy business in which mass extinction can wipe out a highly species and spare other species. "You can be the most beautiful fish that ever swam," he says. "You can be perfectly equipped to survive. Then, one day the pond you live in dries up, and that's it, you die, no matter how fit you are." As proof, in *Wonderful Life*, he cites an inland sea that covered Western Canada some 570 million years ago in the rocks of what has been called the Burgess Shale. In that sea were creatures which have no existing relatives today, none that fit into existing classes, none whatsoever. "Why did some of the Burgess Shale species perish, while others lived to pass on their lineage to today's life forms?" He answers, "Nothing about many of the forms that didn't make it suggests that they were not fit for survival. In fact, many of those that died off were beautiful, elegant, highly successful life forms, challenging the long-held notion that from early life forms, such as those found in the Burgess Shale, we could tell which species would emerge later on." Therefore, he concludes, evolution is random, not progressive. Survival is just the luck of the draw.

In *Questioning the Millennium: A Rationalist's Guide to a Precisely Arbitrary Countdown* (1998), the title tell it all. He tells how the concept of the millennium sifted from some future thousand-year period of righteousness to a specific period in time based on an arbitrary calendar by a sixth-century monk Dionysius Exiguus. He even tells how "millennial" has two n's but "millenarian" has only one. And he delights in telling that the earth completes its circuit in just over eleven minutes less than 365 days and a quarter, resulting in the calendar's needing to make up for the mathematical difference. "What hath God wrought?" he asks, sarcastically.

Rocks of Ages: Science and Religion in the Fullness of Life (1999) makes the point that science and religion do not need to be in conflict. However, "many crucial problems in our complex lives find better resolution under the opposite strategy of principles and respectful separation." Using the Principle of NOMA (Non-Overlapping Magisteria), he shows that creationism is "a distinctively American violationof NOMA," that it is "political and specific, not religious at all."

E. O. Wilson and Richard Dawkins have rejected his NOMA thesis. So has Peter B. Denison, who summarized Gould's thesis as being simply "that there should be no controversy between science and religion." But "Gould wants to give religion authority over values and morals. Certainly secular philosophers also have much to say on those issues. . . . Gould would be almost right if we can truly separate true religion from superstition and the supernatural. Humanist religions like Ethical Culture can live quite happily with science, no matter how materialistic it is. But even then, when Humanists consider ethical problems they should be willing to use scientific methods of thinking." At an Arkansas creationism trial, Gould and six other expert witnesses showed, he said, that "'creation science' is nothing but a smoke screen, a meaningless and oxymoronic phrase invented as sheep's clothing for the old wolf of Genesis literalism, already identified in the Epperson case as a partisan theological doctrine, not a scientific concept at all—and clearly in violation of First Amendment guarantees."

Gould has been described as a respected scholar in his field, tropical snails, and one of the most entertaining contemporary writers of popular science. (CA; See "Evolution: The Pleasures of Pluralism," *The New York Review of Books*, 27 June 1997, which delineates his differences with Daniel Dennett. Also see the entry for paleontology, in which a basic Gould theory is questioned.) {CE; E; "Non-Overlapping Magisteria," *Skeptical Inquirer*, July-August 1999; Peter Denison, *Newsletter of the Humanist Association of Massachusetts*, January 2000}

Gould, Theresa (20th Century)

When she signed Humanist Manifesto II, Gould was a secretary with the American Ethical Union. {HM2}

Goulder, Michael (20th Century)

Selections from Goulder's writing are included in *A World Religions Reader* under Secular Humanism.

Gourmont, Rémy de (1858—1915)

A French critic, novelist, and leading critical apologist for the symbolists, de Gourmont wrote, "God is not all that exists; he is all that does not exist." He also declared, "Religions revolve madly around sexual questions." An atheist, he wrote in *Promenades philosophiques* that "while religion was always a paganism to the crowd, paganism was almost always the religion of superior minds." Among his works are *Les Chevaux de Diomède* (*The Horses of Diomedes*) (1923); *Le Problème du style* (1902), a linguistic study; and *Promenades littéraires* (1904—1928, 7 volumes), a critical collection. {CE; JM; RAT; RE; TYD}

GOUT

• Gout, n. A physician's name for the rheumatism of a rich patient.

—**Ambrose Bierce**
The Devil's Dictionary

Skeletal remains from the second millennium B.C.E. have been found indicating that gout was present at that early age. The condition, a painful swelling of the joints, particularly of the feet and hands, was mentioned by Plato, Seneca, Ovid, and Hippocrates. Lucian in the second century wrote two mock-tragedies, *Tragopodagra* and *Swift-of-Foot*, about the condition. Caused by a build-up of uric acid crystals in small blood-vessels and joints, it is avoided by eating sensibly, avoiding rich food, and drinking lots of water. Sufferers have included Helvétius, Gibbon, Benjamin Franklin. Wits with a knowledge of the drinking habits—port, madeira, benedictine—of the members of religious orders often associate them with the condition. {Roy Porter and C. S. Rousseau, *Gout: The Patrician Malady* [1998]}

Gouvea, Antonio (1505—1565)

Gouvea, or Govea, was a Portuguese jurist and poet. Calvin classed him with Dolet, Rabelais, and Des Periers as an atheist and a mocker. Govea wrote in Latin. {BDF}

GOVERNMENT

The late Samuel Edward Finer (1915—1993), an eminent British historian, wrote *The History of Government from the Earliest Times* (1997). *The Economist* (18 October 1997) reviewed the three-volume set of 1,776 pages, finding it "simply the best." In the work, states *The Economist*, Finer includes the ancient states of Sumer, Egypt, Persia, and Assyria; the classical states of Greece and Rome; the Byzantine and Caliphate empires of the near east; the Han, Tang, and Ming regimes of China; Tokugawa Japan; and the emergence of the "modern" states of Europe and North America.

Finer found that since 3200 B. C. E., an infinite variety of governmental forms have appeared. Four important forms he detailed:

- the "nobility polity," in which a group of aristocratic families dominate the state to the exclusion of both the monarch (if one exists) and the common people. Such polities, he found, are inherently unstable inasmuch as the aristocratic families usually fight among themselves with one of them coming out on top; however, there was the pure nobility polity in Poland in the late 17th and 18th centuries; and local landowners (pseudo-nobles) were the dominant power in much of 19th-Century Latin America.

- the "church polity," in which an organized priesthood comes to exercise state power; e.g., the old papal states under the bishop of Rome and Tibet under the lamas between 1642 and 1949. Because there is no Islamic priesthood in this sense, he argued that true church polities cannot emerge in the Islamic world.

- the "palace regime," which is the dominant form of polity during most of recorded history and is often admixed with clerical and noble elements. The supreme decision-making power rests with one individual, the monarch (king, prince, emperor, tyrant, dictator) even though the individual opts to delegate. Examples: Ancient Egypt; the Mesopotamian kingdoms; the Persian, Roman, Byzantine, Islamic, and Chinese empires; the absolutist monarchies of 18th-Century Europe.

- the "forum polity," which may not be democratic, as in much of post-revolutionary France, the form of a plebiscitary dictatorship. Forum regimes have in common the fact that authority to govern is conferred on the rulers from below, and what the people have given, the people may take away. Accountability is the dominant principle, persuasion rather than force its dominant method. Finer found Athens astonishingly well-run by the standards of its day, and Athenian democracy, having endured for 188 years, was overthrown only by external power.

- the "nobility polity," in which a group of aristocratic families dominate the state to the exclusion of both the monarch (if one exists) and the common people. Such polities, he found, are inherently unstable inasmuch as the aristocratic families usually fight among themselves with one of them coming out on top; however, there was the pure nobility polity in Poland in the late 17th and 18th centuries; and local landowners (pseudo-nobles) were the dominant power in much of 19th-Century Latin America.

According to Finer, the Chinese invented bureaucracy. The Jews invented limited monarchy (because only God was accorded supreme power). The Romans invented checks and balances; and medieval Europe invented parliaments and the idea of representation.

Govett, Frank (19th Century)

Govett wrote *Pains of Life* (1889), a pessimistic reply to Sir J. Lubbock's *Pleasures of Life*. Govett entirely rejects the consolations of religion. {BDF}

Govindan (20th Century)

Govindan is a leading radical humanist in India. He is well-known as a Malayalee litterateur and is the recipient of the Sahitya Academy Award.

GOY

Goy is a term used especially by Jews to speak disparagingly about non-Jews:

- . . . sure that any Jew is . . . superior to any goy.

—Charles Angoff

- . . . time enough for you to eat pork and be a goy.

—Charles Angoff

- . . . our children won't fall into the hands of the *goyim*.

—Isaac Metzker

The plural of goy (or goi) is goyim (or goys). The Yiddish word comes from the Hebrew *goy*, meaning people or nation.

GOYIM: See entry for goy.

Gozdzik, Michael (20th Century)

Gozdzik is a Polish Unitarian minister. (See entry for Polish Unitarians.)

GRACE

Grace is a theological invention involving the favor, love, and protection of God. According to the New Testament, God's grace that leads to salvation is a gift. Children, particularly at summer camps, offer their understanding of grace to the kitchen staff:

Rub-a-dub-dub,
Thanks for the grub.

Humanists refer to the Graces of Greek and Roman mythology, three sister goddesses (Aglaia, Euphrosyne, and Thalia), who dispense charm and beauty. Ambrose Bierce, in *The Devil's Dictionary*, jokingly defined them as "three beautiful goddesses, Aglaia, Thalia, and Euphrosyne, who attended upon Venus, serving without salary. They were at no expense for board and clothing, for they ate nothing to speak of and dressed according to the weather, wearing whatever breeze happened to be blowing. {DCL}

Grady, Charles Wesley (20th Century)

When he signed Humanist Manifesto II, Grady was a minister of the Unitarian Universalist Church in Arlington, Maine. {HM2}

Graff, E. J. (20th Century)

The author of *What Is Marriage For?* (1999), Graff describes same-sex marriages from the time of Old Testament Hebrews through medieval Catholic theologians to 19th century Utopians. She has called upon churches to recognize committed partners, to make it clear that if a couple wants to get married the congregation would be delighted to marry them, and to get involved in the local marriage politics, whatever they are. She and her partner, Madeline, had their ceremony and exchanged rings at a friend's house.

"Essentially," she told *World* (March-April 1999) when asked if opening up marriage to gay and lesbian couples will lead to the acceptance of polygamy, "same-sex marriage can only happen in a society that considers men and women to be not the same but equal. Polygamy, on the other hand, thrives only in societies where men are in charge and consider their wives part of their property. So philosophically, polygamy and same-sex marriage are completely opposed. One is feminist and one is patriarchal in the root sense of the word."

Graffin, Greg (20th Century)

Graffin, a vocalist in the group called Bad Religion, is a non-theist who believes neither in God nor Hell, as shown by his works:

In "Do What You Want" on the album *Suffer*;

I don't know if the billions will survive,
But I'll believe in God when 1 and 1 are 5.

In "God Song" on *Against the Grain*:

Religion is just synthetic frippery
Unnecessary in our expanding global culture efficiency.

In "Don't Pray On Me":

I don't know what stopped Jesus Christ
From turning every hungry stone into bread
And I don't remember hearing how Moses reacted
When the innocent first-born sons lay dead.
Well, I guess God was a lot more demonstrative
Back when he flamboyantly parted the sea.
Now everybody's praying.
Don't pray on me.

{CA;E}

Graham, Allen D. (19th Century)

A freethinker, Graham wrote *On Faith* (1872) and Cruelty and Christianity" (1874). {GS}

Graham, Jewel (20th Century)

Graham, a social welfare educator and a Unitarian, became President of the World YWCA.

Graham, Lloyd (20th Century)

Graham wrote *Deceptions and Myths of the Bible* (1975), a work that discusses misconceptions concerning derivations of biblical characters and events.

Graham, William (1839—1911)

Graham was an economist who became a professor of jurisprudence at Queen's College, Belfast. His *Creed of Science* (1881), a Spencerian work, admits an unknown Power but rejects immortality as "a doctrine begot of men's presumption." {RAT}

GRAMMAR

- Grammar, n. A system of pitfalls thoughtfully prepared for the feet of the self-made man, along the path by which he advances to distinction.

—Ambrose Bierce
The Devil's Dictionary

Grams, Phyllis Belle Stevenson (1915—1996)

Grams was an intrepid freethinker and activist in Wisconsin. A teacher, she was an early member of the Freedom From Religion Foundation and served on its Board of Directors. A tribute to Grams was published by *Freethought Today* (June-July 1996}.

Grange, John (19th Century)

Grange, in the 1890s, was active with J. W. Gott in reviving a Bradford, England, secular group. He wrote *Secularism* (c. 1910). {FUK; RSR}

Grant Duff, Mountstuart Elphinstone [Sir] (1881—1886)

The Right Honourable Grant Duff was M.P. for Elgin Burghs (1857—1881), Under-Secretary for India (1868—1874), and Governor of Madras. In 1901 he was admitted to the Privy Council. Grant Duff was an admirer of Renan and agreed with him that it is "impossible to control the human intellect by creeds or (1829—1906) articles of any sort or kind." He was a theist.

Grant, David (20th Century)

Grant, a freethinker, wrote *A Worker Looks at Jesus* (1938). {GS}

Grant, Dorothy Sweet (1905—)

For half her lifetime, Grant, a nonagenarian, has been active in Unitarian Universalist activities. She was one of four who organized the Cedar Falls, Iowa, Unitarian Fellowship in 1950, serving in several offices of that Black Hawk County organization and being its Director of Religious Education for nine years. During the 1950s, she organized seventeen new Fellowships and became the chairperson for the ninety-seven other Fellowships in the Midwest district. In 1985 and in 1986, she was named the Prairie Star District's "Unsung Unitarian Universalist."

Grant has written a number of works: *Symbols and Golden Rules* (1960); *Universalism in Iowa: 1830—1963, Symbols and Golden Rules of World Religions*, a manual for religious education directors (1960); *Record of the Unitarian Universalist Society of Black Hawk County 1962—1980*; *Excerpts from the Histories of Churches, Fellowships, Societies in the Prairie Star Unitarian Universalist District* (1987); *Thumb Nail Histories of Churches, Fellowships, Societies in the Prairie Star Unitarian Universalist District* (1987); *A Religious Journey* (1992); *A Lay-Woman's Unitarian World.* (1992); and *The Supper Club* (1993). In 1994 when she was eighty-nine, she wrote *The Unitarian Universalist Society of Black Hawk County*, a 131-year history (1863—1994) of the group and which includes a descriptive inventory of its acquisitions.

A Lay-Woman's Unitarian World. (1992) is autobiographical, telling of her father—a streetcar conductor in Minneapolis who was half-Swedish and half-Yankee and not into churchgoing—and her mother, a Norwegian immigrant. Although as a youth she had been a Presbyterian, Grant and her mother became interested in the views of Dr. John Dietrich, who spoke at the Shubert Theater in Minneapolis, and she enjoyed the lectures in such "sacrilegious" surroundings, the silent meditation rather than a vocal prayer, the absence of collecting money during the service, and the fact that printed leaflets of previous sermons were *sold* in the lobby, all characteristics of a different kind of religion and one which she joined and never left. At a Halloween dance in a young adult meeting of the Plymouth Congregational Church, she met Martin Grant, a botany grad student at the University of Minnesota. His father was a Congregational minister in Indiana. By Valentine's day the two were engaged, attended Unitarian services, and on one occasion listened to a Unitarian-sponsored lecture by Margaret Sanger "on the taboo subject of birth control." The work tells how with John Cowley, another professor at the University of Northern Iowa where both taught, a Humanist Club was formed at which the most active student was Warren Allen Smith and at which spoke the Rev. Kenneth Patton from Boston, the Rev. Edwin Wilson from Antioch, Ohio, and the Rev. Grant Butler from Des Moines. That club was to become the Cedar Falls Unitarian Fellowship.

For thirty-seven years of their marriage, she was secretary and assistant for Martin L. Grant. The first year of their marriage was spent in Tahiti, where she was initiated into doing botanical work for Martin. When they were in Hawaii (1934), she continued working for him, in the Bishop Museum. Later, when he worked for the government in Colombia during the war, she continued doing secretarial and botanical work. When they lived in Iran for two years while Martin taught at Pahlavi University, she went on all the field trips as log-keeper and assistant in the drying process of the ten thousand plants they collected. In Shiraz, she mounted one complete set of two thousand plants to give to Pahlavi, then made a similar set for the University of Northern Iowa.

After thirty-seven years of marriage, she divorced Martin, charging cruelty. At the age of sixty-two, needing to earn her own living, she became a classroom teacher at Head Start and, after a semester at the University of Nebraska, was made the Supervisor of Education for the Head Start program in Black Hawk and Buchanan counties, in charge of fifty adults and three hundred children. After four years, she did Early Childhood Education research for the next four years. Part-time for fifteen years, she worked for the Museum of the University of Northern Iowa. At the age of seventy, she resigned from Home Start and, at 80, retired from the Museum.

Grant in 1996 finished *My Norwegian Heritage*, a story principally about her mother who was born in Norway. Martin and Dorothy had three children—Gordon, Barbara Jean, and Lois—all of whom earned doctorates in astronomy, nursing, and anthropology, respectively.

Although the Grants were both humanists, once playing host when Edwin H. Wilson visited the University of Northern Iowa campus, friends have suggested that Martin was the theoretical, Dorothy the applied humanist. (See entry for Martin L. Grant.)

Grant, Gregory O. (20th Century)

When he signed the Humanist Manifesto II, Grant was a captain in the United States Air Force. {HM2}

Grant, Kerr [Sir] (1878—1967)

Grant, who was secretary of the Victoria Rationalist Association of Victoria about 1906, was an Australian who taught physics at the University of Adelaide. He co-invented the Steele-Grant micro-balance, which was sensitive to one-millionth of a milligram. Although brought up a Presbyterian, Grant described himself as a "tolerant agnostic with a strong sense of humour." {RAT; SWW}

Grant, Martin L. (1907—1968)

Grant was the son of an Indiana Congregationalist minister. While a professor of biology at the University of Northern Iowa in Cedar Falls, Grant in 1948 co-sponsored with John Cowley, a professor of literature, a Humanist Club. The school's 1948 yearbook, *Old Gold*, described it as a "deep thinkers club" with the following aims:

> Believing their college training alone does not supply the integration of ideas so necessary in the development of a personal philosophy, the members meet weekly and discuss their own and others' individual philosophies. Subjects cover all fields, including ethics, aesthetics, determinism, planned economies, social action, and Unitarianism. Although larger campuses have clubs of similar purpose, this is the first of its name on any campus.

In 1930—1931 he had a fellowship to collect the native plants of Tahiti, after which he was expected to write *Flora of Tahiti* for his University of Minnesota doctorate. The work was never finished. After his death, however, others completed the work.

His wife, Dorothy, accompanied him to Tahiti for the first year of his marriage. In 1934, the two went to Hawaii, where they did botanical research in the Herbarium of the Bishop Museum. In 1936, he earned his Ph. D. and became a professor at the University of Northern Iowa. For many summers he taught plant taxonomy at the Iowa Lakeside Laboratory, Lake Okoboji, Iowa. In 1944 and 1945, he was sent by the government to Colombia to locate *Cinchona officinalis*, the bark of which was collected by natives and sent to the United States to be made into Quinine for treating the military who contracted malaria in the various war zones.

Although a work, *Flora of Colombia*, was contemplated, it was never finished. From 1963 to 1965, the Grants lived in Shiraz, Iran, where Martin taught at the new Pahlavi University. The duo collected over ten thousand plants. The importance of Grant's botanical journals has been described by Dorothy S. Grant, F. Raymond Fosberg, and H. M. Smith's "Partial flora of the Society Islands: Ericaceae to Apocynaceae" in *Smithsonian Contributions to Botany* 17:i–vii, 1-85 (1974).

After thirty-seven years of marriage, the Grants were divorced. He then married a twenty-five year-old but, a month after the divorce, fell, broke his arm, and multiple myaloma (cancer of the bone) was discovered. He died a year later. (See entry for Dorothy S. Grant and for Warren Allen Smith.)

Grant, Robert (19th Century)

Grant, who at Edinburgh had instructed Charles Darwin about marine biology, was an outspoken atheist. Inasmuch as Darwin was wary about speaking out about religious issues, Darwin dropped Grant as a close friend, according to Adrian Desmond and James Moore in *Darwin* (1992).

Grant, Robert (20th Century)

Grant is one of the IHEU's representatives to the United Nations. A humanist counselor, he is author of *American Ethics*.

Grant, Ulysses S(impson) [President] (1822—1885)

Appointed by President Lincoln the commander in chief of the Union forces, Grant wore out the Confederates by sheer attrition, receiving Robert E. Lee's surrender at Appomattox in 1865. In 1868, Grant was elected the nation's 18th President.

Once expelled by West Point for his alcoholism, Grant, a Methodist, in an 1875 speech declared, "Keep the church and the state forever separated." His defending public schools against Roman Catholic schools was widely publicized, as was his statement, "I suggest the taxation of all property equally, whether church or corporation." Religionists fought back, pointing to Grant's notorious 1862 order expelling all Jews from his military department—he accused them of speculating in cotton.

"No political party can, or ought to, exist when one of its cornerstones is opposition to freedom of thought," Grant wrote in his *Memoirs* (Vol. 1, p. 213). "If a sect sets up its laws as binding above the state laws, whenever the two come in conflict, this claim must be resisted and suppressed at any cost."

Despite being fatally ill from cancer of the throat, Grant wrote the two-volume *Personal Memoirs* (1885-1886), which are ranked as being among the great military narratives of history. John Keegan, a British military historian, wrote, "If there is a single contemporary document which explains 'why the North won the Civil War,' that abiding conundrum of American historical inquiry, it is the *Personal Memoirs of U. S. Grant*." Mark Twain, smarting at how publishers had exploited him in the past, persuaded Grant not to accept 10% royalties from any publisher but, instead, to allow his new firm to publish the work in return for seventy percent of the net proceeds by subscription. Grant earned $450,000 for his family.

Hamlin Garland, his biographer, wrote that Grant "subscribed to no creed." The Rev. M. J. Cramer, however, said that Grant "believed the fundamental doctrines of the Christian religion," which McCabe retorts is like saying that a good freethinker has to be "a good Christian in the true sense." General Hallock, commenting upon Grant's sobriety, said it was remarkable for "a man who is not a religious man."

At the end of his life when unconscious, Grant was baptized, and when he unexpectedly recovered he exclaimed that he was surprised at what they had done to him. With his wife's remains, Grant lies in New York City in a tomb that was constructed in 1897 and made a national memorial in 1959. {CE; FUS; JM; RE; TYD}

Grassl, Gary C. (20th Century)

Grassl has an article, "Christian Profundity," in *The American Rationalist* (January-February 1993). The doctrine of the Trinity, he elucidates, holds that

> God the Father (the First Person of the Holy Trinity) begot God the Son (the Second person of the Trinity.
>
> God the Father and God the Son together brought forth God the Holy Spirit (the Third Person of the Trinity). God the Holy Spirit and the Blessed Virgin Mary begot God the son (Jesus Christ).
>
> Therefore, God the Father is the father and grandfather of God the Son, the father of God the Holy Spirit, and the father-in-law of the Blessed Virgin.
>
> God the Son (Jesus) is the son and grandson of God the Father, the father, son, and brother of God the Holy Spirit as well as the son, father-in-law and brother-in-law of the Blessed Virgin.
>
> God the Holy Spirit is the son of God the Father, the son, father and brother of God the Son (Jesus) and the husband of the Blessed Virgin.
>
> The Blessed Virgin is the wife of God the Holy Spirit, the daughter-in-law of God the Father, and the mother, daughter-in-law and sister-in-law of God the Son (Jesus).

Grassl then wryly observes,

> If Jesus is His father's father, does that mean He is His own grandfather?

If so, Grassl concludes,

> Glory be to the Father, and to the Son, and to the Holy Spirit. As it was in the beginning, is now, and ever shall be. Wisdom without end. Amen.

Grassl has offered the following poetry as "acceptable irreligious satire":

Pagan Bestiality

There once was a god known as Zeus,
who used many a ruse to seduce.
But when he was swain to sweet Leda,
he dove as a *swan* straight upon her,
besmirching her virginal honor.

Immaculate Conception

There still is a God known as Ghost,
all manner of shapes he can boast.
But when he fecundates Madonna,
he flies as a *dove* right upon her,
untainting her virginal honor.

Grasso, James V. (20th Century)

Grasso was an editorial assistant of *The Humanist* who wrote "Humanism in the Eighteenth Century" (July-August 1951). He set up a Humanist Club at Harvard University in 1950, at the time one was founded at Columbia University. John Dewey hailed the establishment of the two groups and was informed that the first such club had been founded in 1948 at the University of Northern Iowa in Cedar Falls. Grasso was executive director and a member of the board of directors of the American Humanist Association's Humanist Fellowship of Boston. (See entries for John Dewey, English Humanism, and Warren Allen Smith.)

Gratiolet, Louis-Pierre (1815—1865)

Gratiolet was a French naturalist noted for his research on the comparative anatomy of the brain. {BDF}

Grattan, C. Hartley (1900—1980)

Hartley, an economist and social analyst, wrote *The Critique of Humanism* (1930), *The Three Jameses: A Family of Minds* (1932, 1962), and *The Quest of Knowledge* (1955). Asked by the present author about humanism he responded:

> I am flattered that you should have concluded that I am an expert on the subject of humanism, but I must resign the post forthwith. I cannot qualify for the high honor. As you remark, everybody is a humanist today, unless he is a bitter Communist, for even the Communists of softer hearts claim to be humanist on occasion. I suppose I should claim the title, too, if pressed to do so, but I do not find it necessary to hold systematic views on the subject. Maybe humanism is to most people simply a synonym of good will. In fact, I think that is the case. Most of us manage to live with bits and pieces of philosophy strewn around our lives, but feel no strong urge to formulate a system or even fit our thinking into other people's systems. By and large
>
> I suppose my own thinking has been most strongly influenced, as far as philosophy goes, by John Dewey and William James. I really don't know, though, for I have not, in recent years, inspected the fragments of philosophy that clutter my mind. This is a rather sorry confession and it causes me to resolve to repair my deficiencies in this line. But as of this moment I'm afraid you'll have to demote me to the class of the hopelessly un-philosophical.
>
> {WAS, 1 April 1949}

GRAVE

• Grave, n. A place in which the dead are laid to await the coming of the medical student.

—Ambrose Bierce
The Devil's Dictionary

Graves, Charles (20th Century)

A Unitarian minister, Graves wrote

> The one real purpose of real religion, Unitarians believe, is not to prepare people for another life, but to inspire them to live this life as it ought to be lived. . . . Foreign missions have never commanded a general interest on the part of Unitarians. Their dislike of the proselytizing spirit, their intense love of liberty for others as well as themselves, and the absence of sectarian feeling have combined to make them, as a body, indifferent to the propagation of their faith in other countries. . . .
>
> No churches were organized by the representative of the American Unitarian Association. Those which have come into existence (India, Brazil, Switzerland, Japan, Holland, Norway, Denmark, South Africa, Australia, New Zealand, etc.) have been wholly at the initiative of the natives themselves. . . .
>
> There is no official census of Unitarian membership. This is due to the fact that usually Unitarian ministers have no great interest in church membership and also to the fact that the basis of membership is very different from what it is in other bodies. . . .
>
> The idea that immersion or sprinkling or signing with the cross with water upon adults or babes can effect any spiritual regeneration or in any way change the relation between human beings and deity is rejected. . . .
>
> An ancient ritual is a poor medium through which to convey modern ideas.

Graves is the author of *Proto-Religions in Central Asia* (1994). {UU}

Graves, Kersey (1813—1883)

Graves wrote *The Biography of Satan, or a Historical Exposition of the Devil and His Fiery Dominions*. The book was published in 1924 as a reprint of an 1873 edition published for the Truthseeker Company. Graves also wrote *The World's Sixteen Crucified Saviors* (1900), listing the following (which Gerald Larue, the humanist scholar, states is **not** historically accurate):

Krishna (of India), crucified 1200 B. C. E.
Crite (of Chaldea), crucified 1200 B. C. E.
Attis (of Phrygia), crucified 1170 B. C. E.
Thammuz (of Syria), crucified 1160 B. C. E.
Esus (of the Celtic Druids), crucified 834 B. C. E.
Bali (of Orissa), crucified 725 B. C. E.
Indra (of Tibet), crucified 725 B. C. E.
Iao (of Neoak) crucified 622 B. C. E.
Sakia (a Hindu God), crucified 600 B. C. E.
Alcestis (of Euripedes) crucified 600 B. C. E.
Mithra (of Persia), crucified 600 B. C. E.
Quexalcoatl (of Mexico), crucified 587 B. C. E.
Aeschylus (Prometheus), crucified 547 B. C. E.
Wittoba (of the Telingonese), crucified 522 B.C.E.
Quirinus (of Rome), crucified 506 B. C. E.
Jesus the Christ, crucified in 28 or 32 C. E.

In *The Bible of Bibles: Twenty-Seven "Divine Revelations,"* Graves describes twenty-seven bibles along with 2000 alleged biblical errors. Wheeler describes his research as being "of some vogue, but little value." {BDF; FUS}

Graves, Philip E. (20th Century)

Graves, a member of the Economics Department at the University of Colorado in Boulder, favors a voucher system as an alternative approach to curing the weaknesses of the present public schools. An atheist, he feels the primary beneficiaries will be inner-city poor who are currently "the most harmed" by the American public school system. {*Free Inquiry*, Summer 1999}

Graves, Robert (1895—1985)

Graves, an English poet, novelist, Renaissance figure, critic, and son of an Irish bishop, is best known for his poetry and for novels on Roman history. For a time, he taught literature in Egypt. He spent the Second World War in England, then went to Majorca, settling there permanently. A prodigious writer, Graves wrote an autobiography, *Goodbye To All That* (1929), which described his unhappy schooldays, the horrors of the trenches during the First World War, and the breakdown of his first marriage. At first a homosexual and friend of Siegfried Sassoon, Graves married a feminist artist, Nancy Nicholson, then left her and her thyroid condition, and moved on to Laura Riding, daughter of one of the founders of the American Socialist Party. When Graves introduced Riding to his mother and told her she was "a Jewess," he did so to taunt his mother, who, however, according to a Graves nephew, was not disapproving. When the two moved to Deyá, Majorca, in 1930, villagers assumed she was an eccentric spinster accompanied by her manservant, so commanding was she.

According to Miranda Seymour's *Robert Graves, Life on the Edge* (1995), Laura could do no wrong, not even when she refused for years to have sex. At one point, she talked Graves into helping her win the husband of one of their married selves; but when the attempt failed, she had hysterics and jumped from a third-floor window, saying, "Goodbye, chaps." He jumped to reach her, but from a window not so high. Riding, who broke her pelvis in three places and suffered a bent spinal cord and four broken vertebrae, claimed Graves ran after her down a fire escape. But Miranda Seymour, in *Robert Graves: Life on the Edge*, disbelieves Riding's story, finding there was no such fire escape. The incident only increased his matriarchal subservience, and to help pay the medical bills he wrote the war memoir, *Goodbye to All That*, finishing the first draft in two months. His works include *I, Claudius* and *Claudius the God* (both 1934); *The White Goddess*, a 1948 work which argued that true poets derive their gifts from the primitive, matriarchal Moon Goddess; *The Greek Myths* (1955), and *The Hebrew Myths* (1963, with R. Patai). Graves always denied that he had invented the White Goddess, claiming in *5 Pens In Hand* (1958) he had studied ancient beliefs and "the effects of such beliefs on worshippers."

Asked by the present author in 1951 about the several categories of humanism, Graves wrote:

> You give me credit for reading a number of philosophical books which I have never read and would not think of reading. I am a poet, and also a historian, and regard philosophy as a threat to my integrity in both fields. Humanism conveys nothing to me, unless a system of thinking based on the so-called humanities of mediaeval education; and these were based on Aristotle and forensic rhetoric, so what? "That bird's dead," as they say; and a neo-bird won't fly. If you want to know my views on the practical question of what is to be the future of religion in the West, see an article which appeared in *Tomorrow* about a year ago. It is an extra chapter for my *White Goddess*. My views on Socrates and the philosophical revolution he started will appear in the Spring number of the *Hudson Review* among other *White Goddess* addenda.
>
> Sorry to seem intransigent, but I really have found philosophy so blind an alley and there are so many poems to be written and historical problems to solve—I have just finished a book on the principles of textual distortion in the Gospels, and until this problem is settled and Jesus' sayings properly established, what the hell is the point of talking about Christianity?—that I lose my patience with the philosophs.

Critic Denis Donoghue in *The New York Review of Books* (4 April 1996) supplies another side of his life: "It is true that Graves's worldly muses were not loyal to him and left him one after another. Riding consorted with Geoffrey Phibbs and Norman Cameron before turning to Jackson. The next Muse, Judith Bledsoe, distributed her favors among several men. Margot Callas left Graves for Alastair Reid and later for Mike Nichols. Cindy Lee left him for Howard Hart. Juli Simon preferred Robert Page to Graves. But Graves, for his part, treated Nancy badly and Beryl worse. Beryl survived by giving much of her attention to animals and plants. When Riding stopped sleeping with Graves—because, she said, 'bodies have had their day'—he got Elfriede Faust pregnant, and colluded with both women to have the pregnancy terminated, Laura standing at the foot of Elfriede's bed the while to witness the operation."

In 1972, he began to lose his short-term memory. He told Edwin Newman that male homosexuality was "partly due to heredity, partly to environment, but largely because men now drink too much milk." Also in his later years he was instructed in Sufism by Idries Shah, then developed a sister for the White Goddess, a Goddess of Wisdom—"call her the Black Goddess"—who represents "miraculous certitude in love" and ordains "that the poet who seeks her must pass uncomplaining through all the passionate ordeals to which the White Goddess may subject him."

Those around him recognized toward the end of his life that he mixed sense with nonsense. By 1980 it was obvious to them that his physical and mental health had greatly failed. At the end, an old, old Graves spent much time sleeping and, on 7 December 1985, died. (See entry for Alastair Reid.) {WAS, 1 March 1951}

GRAVITY

With his discovery of gravity, Newton taught that understanding the cosmos is not confined to the divine. Alan Lightman, a senior lecturer in physics at the Massachusetts Institute of Technology, explained the significance:

> [F]or centuries Western culture was ingrained with the notion that some areas of knowledge are inaccessible, or forbidden, to human possession. In this view, humankind is entitled to comprehend only what God deigns to reveal. Zeus chained Prometheus to a rock for giving fire, the secret of the gods and the wellspring of advanced civilization, to mortal man. St. Thomas Aquinas (1225-74) distinguished between scientific knowledge, discoverable by the human mind, and divine knowledge, "higher than man's knowledge." Divine knowledge could "not be sought by man through his reason, nevertheless, once . . . revealed by God [it] must be accepted by faith." When Dante asks the divine Beatrice about the mysteries of the moon, she replies that "the opinion of mortals errs where the key of sense does not unlock." When Adam, in Milton's "Paradise Lost" (1667), questions the angel Raphael about celestial mechanics, Raphael offers some vague hints and then says that "the rest from Man or Angel the great Architect did wisely to conceal, and not divulge His secrets to be scann'd by them who ought rather admire."
>
> . . . However, a number of developments over the 16th and 17th centuries did succeed in introducing a new belief: that the entirety of the universe, at least its physical parts, was knowable and discoverable by human beings. This new belief, a belief in the unfettered entitlement to knowledge, was the most important intellectual development along the lengthy time line of the past millennium.
>
> Perhaps the most glorious culmination of the new thinking was Isaac Newton's "Principia" (1687). This monumental treatise established fundamental ideas like inertia and force, articulated general laws of motion of bodies under general forces, and proposed a specific law for the force of gravity.
>
> {Alan Lightman, "In God's Place," *The New York Times Magazine*, 19 Sep 1999}

Gray, Asa (1810—1888)

An American naturalist, Gray was the first to introduce Darwinism in America. He wrote an *Examination of Darwin's Treatise* (1861) and was professor of natural history at Harvard University. Gray succeeded Agassiz as Governor of the Smithsonian Institute. {BDF}

Gray, Benjamin Kirkman (1862—1910)

Gray, an economist, was a Congregationalist minister who, in 1894, transferred to the Unitarian ministry. Three years later, he left the Unitarians and devoted himself to social work and economics. Gray was a Socialist and a "mystic and freethinker." {RAT}

Gray, Carole (20th Century)

Gray operates Black Cat Enterprises (POB 21201, Columbus, Ohio 43221), which publishes Solstice notecards and "Women of Freethought" calendars. In *The Humanist* (Jan-Feb 1996), she wrote, "Atheism and Activism: The Life and Work of Eliza Mowry Bliven." {FD}

Gray, Douglas (20th Century)

Gray has reviewed books for *The American Rationalist* (January-February 1999). Richard Rorty, whom he calls an heir to the American pragmatist legacy of William James and Sidney Hook, is said in his *Achieving Our Country: Leftist Thought in Twentieth-Century America* to detect in postmodernist detachment "something very like religious fervor" and an interest in Derrida and Lacan to "satisfy the urges that theology used to satisfy."

Gray, Mora (20th Century)

Gray is Vice-President of Humanists of the Palm Beaches in Florida.

Gray, Ronald (20th Century)

Gray is a Life Fellow of Emmanuel College, Cambridge, and the author of books on Goethe, Kafka, Brecht, Ibsen, and others. In "Is There Antisemitism in the Gospels?" (*New Humanist*, March 1999), he describes anti-Semitism in Europe, discusses Jesus as a Jew, and generally concludes that "there are passages in the Gospels which can be and have been used to justify and encourage hatred and persecution of the Jews," that "the Bible and the Jesus it presents—not necessarily Jesus as he really was—are to be regarded as fallible products of history."

Gray, Spalding (1941—)

Gray, an actor, writer, and performance artist, starred in a monologue later made into a movie, "Monster in a Box" (1992), in which he states that he once believed in God and an afterlife but no longer does. He has acted in "The Killing Fields" (1984); "Swimming to Cambodia" (1987); and "Straight Talk" (1982). {E}

Gréard, Octave Vallery Clément (1828—1904)

Gréard was a French educationist. Catholics forced Jules Simon to dismiss him from his position as Inspector-General although he had been credited for creating "the new [secular] education in the primary schools of the Republic." Gréard was an atheist. {RAT}

GREAT ATTRACTOR

Astronomers in the 1990s found evidence for the existence of the Great Attractor, so called because it is a huge region of matter that is drawing in the Milky Way galaxy with its gravitational pull. According to Dr. Renée Kraan-Korteweg, an astronomer at the Observatory of Paris-Meudon outside Paris, she and her colleagues in 1996 sighted a massive galaxy cluster that appears to be at the Great Attractor's core. That cluster appears to be about three hundred million light-years away, in the direction of the constellation Norma. It perhaps contains ten percent of the Great Attractor's mass.

Freethinkers and other non-theists, rather than concentrating upon theological divinations such as "the ontological argument," are particularly interested in realistic findings which astronomers continue to make and which lead to new theories about the nature of the universe. (See entry for astronomy.)

GREAT BRITAIN UNITARIANS

The General Assembly of Unitarian and Free Christian Churches includes 183 member congregations in Scotland, England, Ireland, and Wales. Membership in 1998 included about 6,700 adults and 800 children.

There are 137 ministers and 7 lay pastors, of whom over fifty are retired. Some serve congregations of the non-subscribing Presbyterian Church of Ireland, a sister movement of the General Assembly which has congregations predominantly in Northern Ireland.

Unitarians are found in Great Britain as far back as the 15th century. The first Unitarian place of worship was Essex Church in London on the site of the present headquarters (Essex Hall, 1-6 Essex Street, London, WC2R 3HY). The inaugural service took place there in 1774. The British and Foreign Unitarian Association was founded in 1825. The General Assembly, its successor, was established in 1928.

According to the Assembly, Unitarians recognize that each person has the right and responsibility to think for himself or herself on religious matters. Understanding is gleaned from diverse sources—science, the arts, the exercise of human reason and reflection upon personal experience, as well as from scriptures of the world faith traditions. British Unitarians stress the value of congregational life, both as a support in one's personal spiritual journey and as a beacon of liberal religious values and social action in the local community. Many find the focus of their faith in the liberal Christian tradition whereas others adopt the religious humanist, theist, or other standpoints.

On the Web: <http://www.unitarian.org.uk>.

GREAT MOTHER GODDESS

In the ancient Middle Eastern religions, the great symbol of the earth's fertility was Great Mother Goddess. Creatively, she was the mother of all things, the periodic renewer of life. Adonis, Attis, and Osiris have variously been considered her son, lover, or both, and her death and resurrection are symbolized by earth's regenerative powers. The Great Mother Goddess was also worshiped in Greece, Rome, and Western Asia. In Phrygia and Lydia, she was known as Cybele. Among the Babylonians and Assyrians she was identified as Ishtar. In Syria and Palestine she appeared as Astarte. Egyptians called her Isis. In Greece she was variously worshiped as Gaea, Hera, Rhea, Aphrodite, and Demeter. In Rome she was identified as Maia, Ops, Tellus, and Ceres.

In Turkey, feminists find evidence of Diana of Ephesus, whose cult spread as far as Marseilles and who persists to the present day. A statue of her at the Naples Museum shows her as having a generous supply of fecundity symbols, and scholars noting that the multiple (over one dozen) breasts do not have nipples speculate as to whether they are meant to be bulls' testicles.

"Many attributes of the Virgin Mary," states the *Columbia Encyclopedia*, "make her the Christian equivalent of the Great Mother, particularly in her great beneficence, in her double image as mother and virgin, and in her son, who is God and who dies and is resurrected." {CE}

GREATER MANCHESTER HUMANIST NEWSLETTER

A quarterly, *Greater Manchester Humanist Newsletter* is at 64 Arbory Ave., Manchester M40 5HJ, United Kingdom.

GREATER PHILADELPHIA STORY

A bi-monthly of the Freethought Society of Greater Philadelphia's chapter of the Freedom From Religion Foundation, *Greater Philadelphia Story* is at Box 242, Pocopson, Pennsylvania 19366-0242. E-mail: <downey1@cris.com>.

Grebstein, Sheldon Norman (20th Century)

Grebstein wrote *Sinclair Lewis* (1962). {GS}

Greco, Karyl (20th Century)

Greco is on the Executive Board of the Humanist Society of Metropolitan New York. She is a humanist activist and practitioner of Rational Emotive Therapy.

GREEK ACADEMY

I. G. Kidd, in the *Encyclopedia of Philosophy*, Vol. 3, describes the public park and academy, equipped with a gymnasium and lecture facilities, which was a mile northwest of the Dipylon Gate of Ancient Athens. The Academy figured heavily in Ancient Greek thought and went through three phases: the **Old Academy** of Plato, Speusippus, and Xenocrates lasted from about 387 B. C. E. to 250 B. C. E. the **Middle Academy** of Arcesilaus and Carneades lasted until about 150 B. C. E.; and the **New Academy** of Philo of Larisa, which lasted until about 110 B. C. E. Emperor Justinian closed it in 529 of the Christian Era. {CE}

GREEK AND ROMAN GODS

Ancient Greek parents told their children that originally Gaea (the Earth) and Uranus (the heaven) had six sons and six daughters called Titans and Titanesses: Cronus, Iapetus, Hyperion, Oceanus, Coeus, Creus, Theia, Rhea, Mnemosyne, Phoebe, Tethys, and Themis. Uranus feared that his children might dethrone him and (as Freud later postulated) it so happened the Cronus with the help of his mother, Gaea, did castrate his father, thereby taking away his power. (Endogmatists, who believe in marriage within a specific group as required by custom or law, point to Cronus's having married his sister Rhea.)

Uranus's blood, falling on Earth, gave birth to the three Furies, goddesses of revenge. In turn, Cronus, fearing he, too, would be overthrown by one of his children, ate them, except that Rhea had replaced one—Zeus—

with a stone, and Zeus tricked his father into disgorging the children, then overthrew him, thereby becoming god of all the gods. Zeus with the help of the Olympians in defeating Cronus then punished his Titans: Atlas was consigned to holding the sky on his shoulders (which children were told is why the sky does not fall); Hecate, no longer the benevolent goddess, now became associated with ghosts and witchcraft; Helios became the sun god who rose in the morning and in his golden chariot crossed the sky; Prometheus, who according to one story created man out of clay and water, stole fire from the gods, and displeased the gods by giving fire plus hope to mankind, was spared punishment inasmuch as he had sided with Zeus; in other, Prometheus was chained to a mountain peak in the Caucasus, where an eagle preyed on his liver; and Selene, Helios's sister, became the moon goddess. So the parents of children with questions about revenge, castration, sex, and power had gods with which they could supply answers.

How to explain life's admixture of goodness and evil? The Titans divided the universe into lots: the sea went to Poseidon (who carried a Trident and could cause earthquakes); the heavens and earth went to Zeus (who sired Ares and Hebe with his sister Hera); and the underworld fell to Hades (also called Pluto, god not only of the dead but also of fertility on earth).

Zeus, quite the lover, fathered many gods. Among his male loves was Ganymede. Among his female loves were Callisto, Demeter, Dione, Eurynome, Leto, Maia, Mnemosyne, and Themis. Also, there were Danaë, Europa, Io, Leda, Semele, and Thetis. Among his offspring were Amphitryon, Athena (who sprung from his head), Dardanus, and Hercules. He ruled from his throne on Mt. Olympus, upheld morality, represented law and order, and punished evil. He was the one who sent thunderbolts, and he was possessor of aegis, a weapon used to terrify enemies and protect friends. Athena's aegis was a breastplate, covered with goatskin, bordered with snakes, depicting in the middle the head of the Gorgon Medusa.

People, children were told, are judged not only by their fellows but also by the gods. Tantalus and Sisyphus, for example, are symbolic of wickedness. When people die, a coin is put in their mouth and they are buried with a honeycake. Their spirit travels from earth to a westerly place, Hades, which contains the rivers named for their characteristics: Acheron (woeful); Cocytos (wailing); Lethe (forgetfulness); Phlegethon (fiery); and Styx (hateful). Charon meets the newly dead, transports them across the Styx and pockets the coins from their mouths while Cerberus, the dog with many heads and a tail of snakes, accepts the honeycake and insures that no unauthorized spirits can enter as well as no spirits can leave. It is here that Pluto and Persephone, the rulers of Hades, watch as the judges of the dead—Aeacus, Minos, and Rhadamanthus—consign the heroic and virtuous to the Elysian Fields or, if they are wicked, to Tartarus. Tantalus, who had divulged some of the gods' secrets and murdered his son Pelops was sent to Tartarus. His punishment included being hanged from the bough of a fruit tree; when he reached for a fruit, wind blew it away; when he bent to drink, the water receded. Sisyphus, whose cunning was such that he claimed to outwit Death, was consigned to pushing a heavy rock up a steep hill, toiling vainly (and inspiring Albert Camus's *The Myth of Sisyphus*).

The Romans, renaming the Greek gods, called Hades Orcus, Dis, and Avernus. The Roman religion was essentially animistic, and human destiny was thought to be controlled by *numina*, forces or spirits which existed in natural objects. Some of the gods were Vesta, guardian spirit of the hearth and fire; Lares and Penates, guardians of the house; Janus, guardian of the door who honored Terminus, protector of property boundaries. Offerings were made to the Lemures, to placate the spirits of the dead, and to the Manes, deities of the underworld. The supreme triad of gods during the earliest period of Roman state religion were Jupiter, Mars, and Quirinus. Later gods included Dionysus and Apollo. When the religious fervor diminished and state ceremonies no longer satisfied the populace, religious feeling degenerated. People then turned toward religious mysteries and the Middle Eastern cults: the Great Mother, Osiris, Sol, and Mithra. The new cults promised personal salvation and a blessed afterlife, and this led to Christianity's taking root at a time when people were tired of the old impersonal and controlled Roman worship. (Also, see entries for God and Great Mother Goddess.) {CE; ER}

GREEK CIVILIZATION

The "Hellenes" presumed that they were the descendants of a man called Hellen, just as the Dorians were of Doros, the Ionians of Ion. As to Hellen's parents, they were Deucalion and Pyrrha, a couple said to have survived "the Flood."

The classical antecedents of Western civilization have long served to justify the study of ancient Greece and Rome. However, particularly in the latter quarter of the twentieth-century Western scholars have pointed out that the Chinese did something on their own in philosophy and science, the Assyrians excelled in astronomy, and the Indians developed a unique architecture. (See entries for Afrocentrism and for Martin G. Bernal.)

GREEK HUMANISTS

The Delphi Society aims to contribute to great issues such as the prevention of global catastrophe, the creation of an environment supportive of peace and progress, and the prevention of a sixth mass extinction of life on the planet. The group belongs to the International Humanist and Ethical Union.

Dennis V. Razis, of the Delphi Society, signed Humanist Manifesto 2000.

GREEK ORTHODOX CHURCH: See entry for Eastern Orthodox Churches.

Greeley, Andrew Moran (1928—)

Greeley is author of *Religion: A Secular Theory* (1982), *The Catholic Myth: The Behavior and Beliefs of American Catholics* (1990), and *Religion as Poetry* (1995). A noted scholar in the sociology of religion, he was ordained a priest of the Roman Catholic Church in 1954.

Greeley, Dana McLean (1908—1986)

In 1961 Greeley became the first president of the newly formed Unitarian Universalist Association (UUA), the result of the merger of the American Unitarian Association (AUA) with the Universalist Church of America (UCA), a post he held until 1969. An early admirer of Theodore Parker and John Haynes Holmes, he also headed the Unitarian Service Committee before his election. Although he disliked seeing the end of the AUA, Greeley saw the merger with the Universalists as a necessary step in the progress of liberal religion. After his service as head of the UUA, Greeley returned to the parish ministry in Concord, Massachusetts. He has written *25 Beacon Street and Other Recollections*.

When he met Pope John in 1962 and told him he was the UUA president, Pope John told him,

> The Unitarians are the people who made a religion of all our heresies.

{U; U&U}

Greeley, Horace (1811—1872)

After founding the *New-Yorker* in 1834 (not be confused with *The New Yorker*, which began in 1925), Greeley combined it with other publications to form the *New-York Weekly Tribune*. As its editor and owner, he advised adventurers to "go West." A regular attendant at the Universalist church on Broadway and Orchard Street in New York City, he fought for black suffrage and amnesty for all Southerners following the Civil War. "There is no doctrine of Christianity," he wrote, "but what has been anticipated by the Vedas." Editor Greeley signed the bail bond which released Jefferson Davis from prison. Running for president in 1872 on the Liberal Republic Party ticket, he was soundly defeated by the incumbent President, U.S. Grant. {CE; TYD; U; UU}

Greeley, Roger E. (20th Century)

Greeley, a long-time Unitarian minister in Kalamazoo, Michigan, has appeared widely as an impersonator of Robert G. Ingersoll, dressing in clothing of the time, and quoting word-for-word what Ingersoll said on almost any subject which might be brought up. He has written *The Best of Humanism* (1987), *The Best of Robert Ingersoll* (1982), and *Thomas Jefferson's Freethought Legacy* (1995).

Greeley is Associate Dean of the Humanist Institute, a Secular Humanist Mentor of the Council for Secular Humanism, and a member of *The Truth Seeker*'s editorial board. {FUS; HNS2}

Greeley, W. Bradford (20th Century)

A Unitarian minister, Greeley welcomes non-believers and is author of *The Faith of a Religious Atheist.*

GREEN LIGHT

Green Light is the newsletter of the International Naturalist Church. {See entry for International Naturalist Church.}

Green, Benny (1927-1998)

Green, the son of David Green, a Jewish tailor and jazz saxophonist, was voted "the most promising new jazz musician" by a *Melody Maker* poll in 1953. He wrote what Barbara Smoker called "a shelf of books"—among them, literary biographies of P. G. Wodehouse and Bernard Shaw—and wrote the lyrics for several musicals, including *Boots with Strawberry Jam*) based on Shaw's early life), *Bashville* and *Valentine's Day* (based on two of Shaw's plays), and *Oh Mr. Porter* (about Cole Porter).

He edited the four-volume *Wisden Anthology*, was jazz critic of *The Observer* from 1958 to 1977, was a regular book reviewer for *The Spectator* from 1970 to 1980, and was film critic for *Punch* from 1972.

Married to actress Toni Kanal and the father of four children, he actively participated in the Shaw Society and was an Honorary Associate of the National Secular Society.

Long before he died of cancer at the age of seventy-one, he wrote an obituary for a newspaper:

> Benny Green, who died yesterday in his 99th year, was always adamant that he would live to be 100. However, arithmetic was never his strong suit. In the course of a life devoted to self-indulgence broken by idleness, he published more than 50 books. He practised no religion, which may explain why he finally died laughing.

At his funeral at Golders Green Crematorium, a jazz band played. As he had wished, his family scattered Green's ashes the following day in Regents Park. {Barbara Smoker, *The Freethinker*, July 1998}

Green, Christopher (20th Century)

Green, while a student at Christopher Newport University in Virginia, was one of the founding members of Campus Freethought Alliance. {*International Humanist News*, December 1996}

Green, Daniel (1907—)

Green has been an executive director of the American Red Cross in New York. He also worked for the New York Children's Aid Society and the Graham Home for Children. In his 80s, he published *Late Start* (1989) and *On Second Thought* (1993), both written after his eighty-second birthday. One poem, "Faith," starts, "Best friends deplore my lack of faith/ in god, the essence of their firm beliefs," ending, "No god, if he were god, would be/ so merciless. Man's sins, if any,/ are remnants of his brute beginnings./ Civility to be learned and earned/ by his will alone./ Heaven's help's a myth." Green is a retiree in Sarasota, Florida. {*Freethought History #12*, 1994}

Green, Henry L. (1828—1903)

In Chicago, Green edited *Free Thought Magazine* (1894—1903) in Buffalo, New York. In 1880, he compiled a listing of freethought works. Green was chairman of the executive committee of the National Liberal League and secretary of New York State Freethinkers' Association. {BDF}

Green, John Richard (1837—1883)

Green, a British historian, became irreligious at Oxford, was converted and ordained, then rejected Christianity and the belief in immortality. His heresies are confined to his letters, in which he sets out to "fling to the owls and the bats those old and effete theologies of the world's childhood." McCabe calls Green's *Short History of the English People* a classic. {JM; JMRH; RAT; RE}

Green, Joseph Frederic (Born 1855)

Green was a positivist who had been a minister of the Church of England from 1880 to 1886. Quitting the Church, he became secretary of the International Arbitration and Peace Association and a member of the Positivist Church and English Positivist Committee. {RAT}

Green, M. W. (20th Century)

A New Zealand freethinker, Green with C. Bright wrote *The Divine Origin of Christianity* (1879?). {GS}

Green, Ronald (20th Century)

When he signed Humanist Manifesto II, Green was an assistant professor at New York University. {HM2}

Green, Ruth Hurmence (1915—1981)

Green was a board member of the Freedom From Religion Foundation. A Missouri grandmother, she wrote *The Born Again Skeptic's Guide to the Bible* (1979; revised 1999) and *The Book of Ruth* (1980). "For his companions in eternity," she said, God "prefers *not* the accomplished, the brilliant, the stimulating, *not* the outstanding achievers who may not conform, but the docile, the gullible, the child-like, the nondescript nonentities with nothing to recommend their selection but blind belief." If these are the meek who will inherit the Earth, she reasoned, "Is it not your omnipotent, omniscient god who bestows such qualities? Where is the free will which would give justice to his reward and retribution?" When she was diagnosed with throat cancer, which made her life intolerable, she told few and, although she carried on normally as long as she could, she eventually took her own life by swallowing painkillers. {WWS}

Greenaway, Kate (1846—1901)

Greenaway was a painter whose work was praised by Ruskin. In her letters, she described herself as "religious in my own way," but she was agnostic about any belief in a future life and was not a theist. She thought it "strange beyond anything I can think to be able to believe in any of the known religions." {RAT; RE; TYD}

Greene, Betty (20th Century)

According to the American Library Association's *Banned Books* (1998), Greene has a book, *I Know You, Al*, which does not uphold the principles of the United States which were "established on the moral principles of the Bible." Her brand of freethought was not cited. (See entry for Banned Books.)

Greene, Brian (20th Century)

Greene is the Columbia University physicist who is noted for his radical research involving the string, or superstring, theory. In 1998-1999 he and several colleagues received a grant from the National Science Foundation to restructure high-level courses in the Columbia math department, with the hope of broadening their application to physics. (See entry for String Theory.)

Greene, (Henry) Graham (1904—1991)

Graham, a famed English novelist and playwright, joined the Catholic Church in 1927. His *Brighton Rock* (1938) contains a Catholic message, introducing as it does the concept of "the appalling strangeness of the mercy of God." He wrote about personal, religion, and political dilemmas as well as visited Haiti, Cuba, Mexico, Africa, and elsewhere in order to understand what matters in life. Haitians, for example, were angry at Greene's depiction in *The Comedians* (1966) of their dictator François (Papa Doc) Duvalier rule. In one scene the hotel-owner narrator speaks to a Haitian Communist, during which Greene contrasts the dedicated Communist with the faithless "comedians" of the world. The two speak of the corpse of a Haitian victim:

> "So he's gone," I said.
> "He died."
> "A natural death?"
> "Violent deaths are natural deaths here. He died of his environment."

Biographers Norman Sherry and Michael Sheldon in 1995 painted a picture of the author's mysterious life. He may, or may not, have been a liar, a whoremaster, a masochist, a quasi-pedophile, a racist, a snob, an anti-Semite, a spy, an adulterer. They write of his pleasure in receiving pain—cigarette burns, for example—during lovemaking, and they note his written records of befriending prostitutes in his various underworld explorations.

Greene once called Mexicans "hideous," described a victim during the Blitz as a "large fat foreign Jew" (which was later edited to a "large fat foreigner'), and openly betrayed not just Vivien, his wife and mother of his two children, but also Dorothy Glover, his mistress for nearly a decade: he took on as mistress Catherine Walston, twelve years his junior and a rich American. Meanwhile, he took tea with Ho Chi Minh, was friendly with Kim Philby, the spy, and took comfort in Charles Péguy's maxim that "The sinner is at the very heart of Christianity."

Was Greene the great Catholic mystery writer? According to Alexander Cockburn [*Nation*, 19 April 1991), Greene and Cockburn's father spoke with John Cornwell on the subject of Greene's beliefs. Do you believe in Satan, Greene was asked. "No, I don't think so." Do you believe in Hell? "I don't believe in Hell." Do you contemplate God in a pure, disembodied way? "I'm afraid I don't," replied Greene. Cockburn then quotes from his father's description of Greene's conversion to Catholicism, tape-recorded by Greene's biographer Norman Sherry in 1977. The elder Cockburn says that Graham quite early on "said to me that he had fallen madly in love with this girl, but she wouldn't go to bed with him unless he married her." So marry her, he was advised. "The trouble is that she won't marry me unless I become a Catholic." So, become a Catholic. "You of all people, a noted atheist!" responded Greene to his friend. "Go right ahead," said Cockburn, "take instruction or whatever balderdash they want you to go through, if you need this for your fuck, go ahead and do it." And Greene did, leading Cockburn later to observe, "So then I felt perhaps I'd done the wrong thing."

Meanwhile, the plot of *Heart of the Matter* (1948) had almost gotten Greene excommunicated because of his treatment of the subject of suicide—its epigraph was from Péguy: *Le Pécheur est au coeur même de chrétienté* . . ." ("The sinner is at the very heart of Christianity"). *End of the Affair* (1951) is told by an agnostic in love with a religious woman. And his complex and tortured relationship with the church is exemplified by words he penned on the endpapers of Frei Betto's *Fidel and Religion:* "I am for Doubt and against Dogma. A doubting catholic [sic] can work easily with a doubting communist." As for his personal life, Greene wrote some titillating descriptions of his affair with Catherine Walston, who was half-English by birth but American by nationality and upbringing. In one letter he wrote of wanting to lie in bed with her, reading Saint John of the Cross. In another, he told her he wanted to bugger her. In another, he wrote, "My dear, the important cigarette burn has completely gone. It must be renewed," a sadomasochistic reference. Catholics, denying his weaknesses and downplaying his anti-Semitism, insistently claim him as one of their own. {CE; OEL}

Greene, John Gardner (20th Century)

Greene has been a member of the American Humanist Association. {HNS}

Greene, Robert (1558—1592)

Greene was something of a feckless drunkard, a writer who abandoned his wife and children to throw himself on the mercies of tavern hostesses and courtesans. He wrote pamphlets and plays as a last resort when his credit failed, turning out excellent work for "Hee inherited more vertues than vices." Greene is known for his connections with Shakespeare, whom he attacked as an "upstart Crow, beautified with our feathers." Shakespeare, however, liked Greene's *Pandosto*, using it as his source for *The Winter's Tale*. C. S. Lewis has cited the following as evidence of Greene's "genuinely didactic verse, verse utterly unadorned and dependent for interest almost exclusively on its intellectual content":

> Oh wearisome Condition of Humanity!
> Borne under one Law, to another bound.
> Vainely begot, and yet forbidden vanity,
> Created sicke, commanded to be sound.

David Tribe cites Greene as being an avowed atheist, one who died of a surfeit of Rhenish wine and pickled herrings, although it may also have been plague, of which there was a severe outbreak in 1592. {OEL; TRI}

Greenhill, James A. (Born 1828)

Greenhill, a Scot, was brought up a Presbyterian. In 1851 he moved to New York, then Chicago, then to Clinton, Iowa in 1873. When he read Ingersoll's *Mistakes of Moses*, Greenhill decided he was no longer a Christian and, after reading Paine, concluded that he was a freethinker. Greenhill's occupation was that of a carpenter. {PUT}

Greening, Thomas C. (1930—)

When he signed Humanist Manifesto II, Greening was editor of the *Journal of Humanistic Psychology*. He is author of *Frank and Ernest Career Advice* (1990). {HM2}

Greenly, Edward (1861—1951)

A British geologist, Greenly wrote *The Geology of Anglesey* (2 volumes); *The Earth: Its Nature and History; A Hand Through Time* (a biography of Annie Greenly); and, with Howel Williams, *Methods in Geological Surveying*. In 1927 he wrote *The Historical Reality of Jesus*, in which he downplays the importance of Jesus, suggesting that a Joshua-cult had been in existence before the dawn of the Christian era and that "when alluded to in Greek-written documents the name would appear as 'Jesus.' " He was a member of the Rationalist Press Association. {RAT}

Greenough, John James (20th Century)

Greenough, a freethinker, wrote *The Origin of Supernatural Conception and Development of Religions from Prehistoric Times* (1906). {GS}

Greenspan, Louis (20th Century)

Greenspan is one of the members of the IHEU's Committee on Religious Extremism and Rational Inquiry.

Greenwald, Harold (1910—1999)

An author, lecturer, and psychoanalyst who became known as an expert on the psychology of prostitutes, Greenwald was active in the San Diego Humanist Fellowship.

He wrote a best-selling book, *The Call Girl: A Social and Analytic Study* (1958), and a Hollywood movie, "Girl of the Night." As a psychoanalyst, he interviewed sixteen prostitutes, six of whom were in analysis with him and ten who were interviewed by three of the women in analysis. He humanized the women, explaining why they had chosen their line of work, often because they had felt little love from either parent.

Other of his books were *Great Cases in Psychoanalysis* (1969); *Emotional Maturity in Love and Marriage* (1971) with Lucy Freeman; *The Sex-Life Letters* (1972) with his wife, Ruth Greenwald; *Active Psychotherapy* (1974); *Direct Decision Therapy* (1974); and *The Happy Person* (1984).

Greenwald, after graduating from Columbia University in 1956, gained quick prominence in psychoanalytic circles as a leading student of the Freud disciple Theodore Reik. He taught at Hofstra University in 1968 and 1969 and in Norway at the University of Bergen. In 1975 he became a Distinguished Professor at United

States International University in San Diego, and he served as president of the Academy of Psychologists in Marital and Family Therapy as well as president of the division of Humanistic Psychology of the American Psychological Association.

"What he founded was the opposite of psychoanalysis, which is what he started in," fellow secular humanist Albert Ellis said of Greenwald. "He said you make a decision to upset yourself; you don't get upset because of something that happened in your childhood." In short, Greenwald developed direct decision therapy, an offshoot of rational emotive behavior therapy. Instead of long sessions of quiet listening, he showed individuals that they are free to change decisions throughout life. In his view, decisions are the key to understanding personality and dysfunctional patterns. Even happiness, he argued, could be made as a decision. {Nick Ravo, *The New York Times*, 2 April 1999}

Greenwald, Ruth (1916—1994)

Greenwald was born in Minsk, Belarus, and obtained her doctorate at the age of sixty-four. At first a dancer, she became a psychotherapist. The wife of Harold Greenwald, she was an active member of the Humanist Fellowship of San Diego.

Greenway, Peter (20th Century)

Greenway, an atheist, is author and director of a movie, "The Baby of Mâcon," which in 1993 was described by critic Philip Ward "as the most direct attack on anti-humanist values in recent years." The film exposes the manipulation of humanity by totalitarian systems such as the Roman Catholic Church and, remarks Ward, "If the Roman Catholic church issued *fatwas*, the Pope would certainly have to single this movie out for its blasphemies, its subversive intent, and its brilliant use of Christian imagery mocked and derided in a way that Brueghel and Bosch would have recognised." Greenway, however, holds that an atheist cannot in the nature of his beliefs be guilty of blasphemy.

GREENWICH VILLAGE HUMANIST CLUB

In 1953, John Collins and Warren Allen Smith founded the Greenwich Village Humanist Club in New York City. Appealing to intelligentsia who were anti-existentialistic, they caroused with Dorothy Day followers in the White Horse Tavern and with New York University, Columbia, and other students at the Rienzi on MacDougall Street.

Priority items which the club discussed in 1953: (a) proselytizing the city's intelligentsia by publicizing the basic concepts of naturalistic humanism; (b) setting up an "ethical clearing house" committee whose members would be on guard to back up, in public statements, difficult or unpopular moral actions which individuals have taken and which are felt to be particularly humanistic; (c) forming a committee to help orient foreign students who want to learn about the U. S. "without being treated as heathens who are expected to join whatever sect the guide happens to belong to"; (d) visiting sects or groups desirous of comparing, sharing, or modifying our . . . or their . . . views; (e) listing worthy organizations already in existence, such as the Eye Bank, the World Calendar Association, or the Prison Association of New York, whose goals are commendable humanistic.

"Carry a *Humanist* magazine in your hand, and don't dress up," members were advised in order that they could recognize each other in some of the "dingy dives" they dared to demonstrate.

At the White Horse Tavern, some Dorothy Day Catholics once angrily shouted to a formally dressed Smith, "Go back, ya bum, to the East Side!" But Collins with an Irish brogue was able to convince those who were throwing the insults that these particular humanists were on the same, not on the opposite, side so far as social action was concerned. (See entry for John Collins.)

Greenwood, George [Sir] (1850—1928)

A politician, Greenwood entered Parliament in 1906 and was knighted in 1916. Under the pen-name of George Forest, he wrote *Faith of an Agnostic* (1903). Greenwood was a member of the Rationalist Press Association. {RAT; RE; TRI}

Greg, William Rathbone (1809—1881)

Greg was one of the founders of the Manchester Statistical Society. In 1840 he wrote on "Efforts for the Extinction of the African Slave Trade," followed in 1850 by his *Creed of Christendom*. Wheeler said of Greg, "His works exhibit a careful yet bold thinker and close reasoner."

His son, **Percy Greg**, edited *The Reasoner* during Holyoake's illness (1879). {BDF; VI; RAT}

Gregorovius, Ferdinand (1821—1891)

Gregorovius was a German historian. McCabe cites his *History of the City of Rome in the Middle Ages* as a work that "has never been superseded and is a mine of amusing information about the series of 'Holinesses.' It was translated into many languages and it is a symptom of the progress made fifty years ago that the critic of the Popes was enrolled as an honorary citizen of Rome. He was a non-Christian theist."

In Baroness von Suttner's album, Gregorovius wrote, "Priests place themselves between man and the Deity only as shadows." {JM; JMRH; RAT; RE}

Gregory, Richard Armand [Sir] (1864—1952)

Sir Richard Gregory, a naturalistic humanist, wrote *Gods and Men, A Testimony of Science and Religion* (1949). He was an astronomer, editor of *Nature* from 1919 to 1939, and President of the British Association (1940). In *Religion in Science and Civilization* (1940), Gregory accepted the word "God" in an impersonal sense. Sir Richard was an honorary associate of the Rationalist Press Association. {HNS; RE}

Gregory, William Henry [Sir] (1817—1892)

Gregory was M. P. for Dublin (1842—1847) and for Galway (1857—1871), but this did not prevent him from expressing his rationalist views and strongly advocating the Sunday opening of museums, and other reforms. From 1871 to 1877 Gregory was Governor of Ceylon, some of whose citizens called him "our God." He was known for being "eminently latitudinarian and indifferent to dogmatic religion." {RAT; RE}

Gregg, William (20th Century)

Gregg is a freethinker living in Elizabeth City, North Carolina.

Grenier, Pierre Jules (1838—1873)

Grenier was a French positivist, an author of a medical examination of the doctrine of free will (1868), which drew out a letter from Mgr. Dupanloup, Bishop of Orleans, who implored him to repudiate his impious doctrines. Grenier also wrote *Aphorisms on the First Principles of Sociology* (1873). {BDF}

Grethenbach, Constantine (20th Century)

Grethenbach, a freethinker, wrote *A Secular View of the Bible* (1902). {GS}

Greville, Charles Cavendish Fulke (1794—1865)

In Greville's *Memoirs* is a detailed diary of a politician and man of public affairs who for many years was clerk to the Privy Council. From 1820 to 1860 Greville told of his life in the inner circles of politics and power, and because he was trusted both by the Whigs and Tories he included lively portraits which, for example, include tales about people's unbelief.

He was, according to Sir H. Taylor, "avowedly Epicurean." {RAT; RE}

Grévy, François Paul Jules [President] (1813—1891)

Grévy became President of the French Republic. A Paris lawyer and freethinker, he had taken part on the anti-clerical side in the Revolution of 1848. After the *coup d'état* of Napoleon, he abandoned politics and became President of the Advocates. From 1879 to 1885, the period of the final collapse of Catholic Power, Grévy became the Republic's President. {RAT; RE; TRI}

Grey, Albert Henry George [Earl] (1851—1917)

Grey was a British statesman, at one time the Administrator of Rhodesia and later the Governor of Canada. Grey wrote that "the four men who opened the eyes of mankind most widely to the truths of human brotherhood" were Christ, Mazzini (a non-Christian theist), Robert Owen (an atheist), and Holyoake (an agnostic). Three out of four, McCabe implies, is not bad. {JM; RAT; RE}

Grey, Antony (1927—)

Grey, a rationalist, is author of *Quest for Justice: Towards Homosexual Emancipation* and *Speaking of Sex* (1992). He was one of the first active campaigners in England who supported the Wolfenden Report. In 1962, Grey became Secretary of the Homosexual Law Reform Society and the Albany Trust. In the 1960s and 1970s he was on the executive committee of the National Council for Civil Liberties in England. Grey, a leading English figure in the 1960s campaign to decriminalize male homosexuality, is a frequent contributor to *New Humanist.*

His *Speaking Out: Sex, Law, Politics and Society, 1954-95* (1997) was issued on the 30th anniversary of the passing of the Sexual Offences Act of 1967. "Coming out about one's orientation . . . must now be regarded as a positive duty," he wrote, "and those who remain in the closet should be left in no doubt that their self-serving hypocrisy is letting every other gay person down."

Upon being presented with the Gay and Lesbian Humanist Association's 1998 Pink Paper Lifetime Achievement Award, Grey remarked that he was gratified by the award, not just for himself but because it recognized the courage and dedication of the staff and volunteers who worked with him at the Homosexual Law Reform Society and the Albany Trust. However, he expressed disappointment that thirty years on from the 1967 law reform "we are still so far from achieving the equality of esteem and full social acceptance that is our due in the modern world." {*Gay & Lesbian Humanist*, Spring, 1998 and Winter 1998; *New Humanist*, August 1997; TRI}

Grieg, Edvard Hagerup (1843—1907)

Grieg was a composer who developed a strong nationalistic style that has come to be known as "the voice of Norway." Founder of the Norwegian Academy of Music, Grieg—aided by his wife, the singer Nina Hagerup Grieg who interpreted his songs—became a leading composer in his day. His "Concerto in A Minor for Piano and Orchestra" received excellent reviews, and in its first performance he was the solo pianist. Grieg is particularly known for his "Peer Gynt" (1876).

His interest in Unitarianism is described by David Monrad-Johansen in a 1945 biography in which Grieg is quoted: "During a visit to England in 1888 I was very much impressed by Unitarian opinions (trust in God alone—belief in a three-in-one God and in a son co-equal with Him is barred) and in the nineteen years that have passed since then I have stood by this conclusion." Upon his death, his wife gave in his honor an organ to the Copenhagen Unitarian Church. Not so well known, according to Marin Greif, was Grieg's interest in the "dazzlingly good-looking Australian composer and pianist Percy Grainger," whose good looks also dazzled Vachel Lindsay. {CE; EG; U}

Grierson, R. C. (19th Century)

Grierson, a freethinker, wrote *A Superhuman View of Mankind.* {GS}

Grieve, C. M. (1892—1978)

Grieve wrote under the pseudonym of Hugh MacDiarmid. He was a poet, a critic, and founder in 1928 of the National Party of Scotland. Expelled by the National Party in 1933, he joined the Communists and was expelled by them in 1938. In his *Stony Limits* (1934), Grieve offered a subtle statement of the MacDiarmidian metaphysic: "I will have nothing interposed / Between my sensitiveness and the barren but beautiful reality." His later work comprises a series of long, linguistically dense, poems amounting to a modern epic of the Celtic consciousness. According to David Tribe, Grieve was an avowed freethinker. {OEL; TRI}

Griffin, F. R. (Died 1983)

Griffin wrote *Humanist Attitudes* (1976) and was a founder and leading member of the Tyneside Humanists in England.

Griffin, Lepel Henry [Sir] (1838—1908)

Griffin entered the Indian Civil Service and became in time Superintendent of the Kapurthala State, Chief Secretary of the Punjab, and agent to the Governor-General of Central India. Upon returning to England in 1889, he became Chairman of the Imperial Bank of Persia. An agnostic, Griffin occasionally used theistic language in a loose sense. For example, in his section on "Sikhism and the Sikhs," in *Great Religions of the World* (1901), he says that Brahmanism "provided conceptions of the Deity as noble and exalted as those to be found in any religions of the West," and he recommended "that state of suspension of judgment which is somewhat inadequately designed Agnosticism." {RAT; RE}

Griffith Jones, George C. (19th Century)

A freethinker, Griffith Jones wrote *By Bread Alone* (1887). {FUK; GS}

Griffin, Nicholas (20th Century)

Griffin, a philosophy professor at McMaster University in Canada, is author of *The Selected Letters of Bertrand Russell* (1993) and *Russell's Idealist Apprenticeship* (1992). Griffin is one of the youngest surviving genuine correspondents of a man who, as a boy, knew people born in the 18th century, and in the 1960s he elicited thoughtful replies on the Vietnam War from Russell. He is on the board of directors of the Bertrand Russell Society. At the 1994 Toronto conference of the Council for Democratic and Secular Humanism (CSHAF), Griffin pointed out that Russell recognized the need for a plurality of "goods" for different people. The problem of providing a good life is a social as well as a person one, he added, because without food, shelter, and peace, it is not possible to lead the good life.

Griffith, William E. (20th Century)

Griffith wrote *Religion, the Courts, and the Public Schools* (1960). {GS}

Griffiths, Donald Islay (1901—1979)

Griffiths was an Australian rationalist, humanist, and builder. Born in Scotland, he lived in Fiji where his grandfather had been one of the earliest white settlers and had founded the *Fiji Times.* The

American mother of Mr. Griffiths was the first editor of the *Australian Women's Weekly.* Griffith was president of the Rationalist Society of Queensland for more than fifteen years and attended the 1965 Council for Australian Humanist Societies as a rationalist delegate. {SWW}

Grigg, Bill (20th Century)

Grigg, a freethinker in Elizabeth City, North Carolina, has written for *Freethought Perspective* (June 1999).

Griggs, Edward Howard (20th Century)

Griggs was one of the first to use *humanism* in a contemporary sense such as used by religious humanists. He wrote *Humanism: Studies in Personal and Social Development* (1899). His outlook combined elements of Christianity and classicism.

Grigoroff, Isabella (20th Century)

An Ottawa-based writer and communications consultant, Grigoroff wrote "Stephen Lewis on the Rise and Fall of Social Justice" (*Humanist in Canada*, Summer 1998). Lewis was Canada's former Ambassador to the United Nations and laments the significant decline in social justice over the past few years in Canada and the world.

Griggs, Henry (20th Century)

Griggs, a freethinker, wrote *The Book of Truth* (1914). {GS}

Griggs, William Clark (1932—)

Griggs wrote *Parson Henry Renfro: Free Thinking on the Texas Frontier* (1994). {*Freethought History #15,* 1995}

Grillparzer, Franz (1791—1872)

Grillparzer was an Austrian dramatist. His first tragedy, *Die Ahnfrau*, was presented at Vienna in 1817. In 1847 he was admitted to the Austrian Upper House. A great admirer of Kant and Goethe, Grillparzer was a theist. {RAT}

Grim, LeRue (20th Century)

When he signed Humanist Manifesto II, Grim was a secretary of the American Humanist Association. He is president of Fellowship of Humanity, which was founded in 1935 and is one of the oldest continuously existing humanist organizations. {FD; HM2}

Grimké, Sarah Moore (1792—1873)

A Quaker, Grimké was a leading American abolitionist and advocate of woman's rights. Although the daughter of an aristocratic slaveholding family, she wrote *An Epistle to the Clergy of the Southern States* (1830), in which she urged abolition of slavery. She and her sister, Angelina, were the first women who dared to speak in public for the black slave and then for woman's rights. (See entry for Gerda Lerner.) {CE}

Grimm, Friedrich Melchior von (1723—1807)

Baron Grimm was a German philosophic writer in French, best known for his literary correspondence with Diderot which was published in seventeen volumes (1812—1813). Grimm was an acquaintance of D'Holbach and with Rousseau, although Rousseau later found the two had become enemies. After the Revolution, Grimm was appointed by Catherine of Russia her minister at Hamburg. {BDF; RAT; RE}

Grimmond, Jo (20th Century)

A member of the British Parliament, Grimond addressed the Fifth International Humanist and Ethical Union World Congress held in Boston (1970).

Grin, S. Spencer (1928—)

When he signed Humanist Manifesto II, Grin was publisher of *Saturday Review/World.* He co-authored *World Education, Emerging Concepts* (1978). {HM2}

Gringore, Pierre (c. 1475—1544)

Gringore was a French poet and dramatist who satirized the pope and clergy, as well as the early reformers. {BDF}

Grisebach, Eduard (1845—1906)

Grisebach was a German writer who became consul at Bucharest, Petersburg, Milan, and Haiti. He wrote many poems, the best known of which was "The New Tannhaüser" (1875). He also translated *Kin Ku Ki Kuan,* Chinese novels. Grisebach was a follower of Schopenhauer, whose bibliography he compiled (1888). {RAT}

Griswold, N. F. (Born 1824)

Griswold was raised in New York and Connecticut. He learned the tinner's trade. A Universalist, he came across Colonel Ingersoll's work, then heard Ingersoll lecture in New Haven, and invited him to speak in Meriden. However, the Universalists refused the church for such a meeting, so Griswold left the group and became a freethinker. For him, the church was a prop of the rich man and the leech of the poor man. {PUT}

Groen van Prinsterer, Guillaume (20th Century)

A freethinker, Groen van Prinsterer wrote *Unbelief in Religion and Politics* (1975). {GS}

Groening, Matthew (1954-)

Groening, writer and cartoonist of "Life in Hell," wrote *Love is Hell* (1985), *Work is Hell* (1986), *School is Hell* (1987), *With Love from Hell* (1989), and numerous works about "The Simpsons," a program that is well known to television viewers.

When asked by David Wallis (*The New York Times Magazine*, 27 December 1998) how he responds to critics who consider Bart Simpson "a dreadful role model for children," he replied, "If you don't want your kids to be like Bart Simpson, don't act like Homer Simpson."

When told that he poked a lot of fun at organized religion and asked what is the most comical story in the Bible, Groening responded,

> I was very disturbed when Jesus found a demon in a guy and He put the demon into a herd of pigs, then sent them off a cliff. What did the pigs do? I could never figure that out. It just seemed very un-Christian. Technically, I'm an agnostic, but I definitely believe in hell—especially after watching the fall TV schedule.
>
> {*CA; Freethought Today,* February 1999}

Groethe, David (20th Century)

Groethe is vice-president Rockies of the Executive Council of the Freedom For Religion Foundation.

Groethe, Mary (20th Century)

Groethe, a South Dakotan, is on the board of directors of the Freedom From Religion Foundation.

Grof, Stanislaw (20th Century)

Grof, a believer in reincarnation, is cited by Paul Edwards as being, along with Elizabeth Kübler-Ross, one of the most credulous persons who ever lived.

Groh, Israel W. (19th Century)

Groh, a freethinker, wrote *How Can We Be Saved?* (1890?). {GS}

Grollet, Philippe (20th Century)

Grollet is President of *Centre d'Action Laïque*, which inaugurated a five-floor headquarters in Belgium in 1997. The headquarters is at the campus of the *Université Libre de Brussels.*

Groome, Francis Hindes (1851—1902)

Groome was a writer, the son of the Archdeacon of Suffolk. He married a woman of Gypsy blood and became one of the highest authorities on the Gypsies. In his appreciation of Fitzgerald (*Two Suffolk Friends*, 1895), Groome endorses his skepticism. {RAT}

Groos, Karl (1861—1937)

Groos was a German psychologist who taught at Giessen and at Basle University. Groos followed the pantheistic philosophy of Schelling. {RAT; RE}

Groppali, Alessandro (Born 1874)

Groppali was an Italian sociologist, a member of the Italian Positivist School. He called Ardigò "our greatest thinker and agreed with him in regard to religion. {RAT}

Gross, Dick (1954—)

Gross wrote "Altruism and Atheism" in the *New Humanist* (February 1995). He explains that goodness is not the preserve of the religious and that humanists need to build on this knowledge.

Gross, Paul R. (20th Century)

"Downsizing Darwin," by Harvard University's Gross, makes the point that the anti-Darwinist crusaders are not just asking that creationism be co-taught along with evolution but are working to insure that science be defeated wherever it conflicts with religion. {*Humanist Monthly*, Capital District Humanist Society, Scotia, New York, November 1998}

Grot, Nikolai Yakolevich (1852—1899)

Grot, a Russian psychologist, wrote numerous works on psychology and philosophy. He was strongly opposed to mysticism and metaphysics early on but later accepted metaphysics and natural religion, finally returning to empirical psychology and monistic pantheism. {RAT}

Grote, George (1794—1871)

Allegedly the author of *The Analysis of the influence of natural religion on the temporal happiness of mankind* (1822), Grote is believed by Berman to have been the writer who used the pseudonym Philip Beauchamp. However, John Stuart Mill who saw the work in manuscript thought it was "understood to have been partly compiled from manuscripts of Mr. [Jeremy] Bentham." The work is a masterpiece of atheism. Grote, who was descended from a Dutch family, was the historian of Greece. His *History of Greece* (11 volumes) took from 1846 to 1856, and this was followed by *Plato and the Other Companions of Socrates*. In 1833, he was elected as Radical M.P. for the City of London and retained his seat until 1841. In Parliament, he was chiefly known for his advocacy of the ballot. Grote's review of J. S. Mill's *Examination of Sir William Hamilton's Philosophy* (1861) shows that he retained his freethought until the end of his life.

"The great historian," wrote the Rev. Peter Anton, author of *Masters of History*, "passed away tranquilly and without pain, and thus was brought to a close a career singularly devoted, conscientious, and laborious, a life rich in virtue and honour and the esteem of the wise and the good." Mrs. Grote also wrote of the end: "Early in the month of June, a marked change supervened, and at the end of three weeks his honourable, virtuous, and laborious course was closed by a tranquil and painless death." Grote, although an atheist as was his wife Harriet, was buried in Westminster Abbey. Remarked Foote, "Three centuries ago Grote might have been burnt to death; but the custodians of Westminster Abbey are now anxious to enrich their precincts with celebrities, and the atheist historian is interred there with freethinkers like Ephraim Chambers, Sir Charles Lyell, and Charles Darwin." {BDF; FUK; HAB; JM; RAT; RE}

Grote, Harriet (1792—1878)

Mrs. George Grote shared her husband's opinions and wrote his life story. {BDF; RAT}

Grotius, Hugo (Huigh de Groot) (1583—1645)

Grotius, a distinguished Dutch jurist and humanist, is credited with having written the first definitive text on international law. He contended that natural law prescribes rules of conduct for nations, not just for private individuals. Drawing from the Bible as well as classical history, he maintained that it is criminal to wage war except for certain causes. A leading student of theology and biblical criticism, he observed, "He who reads ecclesiastical history reads nothing but the roguery and folly of bishops and churchmen." {CE; TYD}

GROUNDSWELL

Groundswell (PO Box 174, Prospect Park, Pennsylvania 19076) is a monthly edited by Ben Price and Tom Mulliam. It has poetry, cartoons, articles on politics, the economy, and subjects that explore the exploitation of conservative ideology and its effective campaign to obstruct personal and individual freedoms.

Gruber, E. L. (20th Century)

In the February 1958 issue of *The Rationalist Reporter*, Vol. I, #2 of a monthly bulletin of the New York Chapter of the Rationalist Press Association, Gruber wrote an editorial attacking the "visitors" who had almost succeeded in breaking up the group's previous meeting. The bulletin announced that the 28 February 1958 lecture would be held at the Henry George School with Prof. Paul Edwards of New York University speaking on "Clarence Darrow, American Heretic."

The bulletin's masthead noted that Bertrand Russell was then president of the Rationalist Press Association. Gruber was the group's local secretary.

Grudin, Robert (20th Century)

Grudin, professor of English at the University of Oregon, is author of *On Dialogue: An Essay in Free Thought* and *Time and the Art of Living*. In 1995 he founded the Endowment for Civic Humanism, which supports civic service programs in schools and research in civic humanism at universities.

Gruen, Karl (1817—1887)

A German author, Gruen was a friend to Proudhon and translated his *Philosophy of Misery*. In 1849 Gruen was arrested and condemned to exile, whereupon he moved to Brussels until 1962, then became a professor at Frankfort and later at Colmar. Gruen established a radical journal, the *Mannheim Evening News*, and he wrote biographical studies of Schiller (1844) and Feuerbach (1871). {BDF}

Gruet, Jacques (Died 1547)

Gruet was accused of being a heretic, but in actuality the charges against him were political, according to Robertson. He was tortured, but he refused to incriminate anyone else.

Charged with having written against John Calvin, Gruet finally pleaded guilty to the charges and prayed for a speedy death. That came when by order of Calvin "on July 26, 1547, his half-dead body was beheaded on the scaffold, the torso being tied and the feet nailed thereto."

Observed Robertson, "Such were the judicial methods and mercies of a reformed Christianity, guided by a chief reformer." Wheeler called Gruet a Swiss freethinker, adding that after his execution Gruet's papers were burned by the common hangman. {BDF; JMR; JMRH}

Grün, Karl (1817—1887)

Grün was a German author who wrote about Goethe, Schiller, and Feuerbach. He also wrote cultural histories of the sixteenth and seventeenth centuries. {RAT}

Grünbaum, Adolf (1923—)

Grünbaum is the Andrew Mellon Professor of Philosophy and Chairman of the Center for Philosophy of Science at the University of Pittsburgh. A Humanist Laureate in the Council for Secular Humanism's International Academy of Humanism, he is a contributing editor for *Free Inquiry* and *Philo* and a signer of Humanist Manifesto 2000. He has written, "The supposition that the godless lead meaningless lives is just an ideological phantasm."

In *Foundations of Psychoanalysis, A Philosophical Critique (*1984), Grünbaum "argues that Freud rests his case for the theory of repression on the superior therapeutic effectiveness of psychoanalysis in treating neuroses, and that such evidence is not available," writes Thomas Nagel in *The New York Review of Books* (12 May 1994). "His reading of Freud, and of the evidence, clinical and extraclinical, has been extensively criticized, notably by David Sachs, 'In Fairness to Freud,' *Philosophical Review*, Vol. 98, No. 3 (July 1989), and by various commentators in *Behavioral and Brain Sciences*, Vol. 9 (June 1986). More recently he has published *Validation in The Clinical Theory of Psychoanalysis* (1993), a further discussion of these issues, which include both new material and versions of previously published essays, some predating *The Foundations of Psychoanalysis.*" Nagel, a professor of law and philosophy at New York University, contrasts the views concerning Freud which are held by Grünbaum, Richard Wollheim, and Paul Robinson.

Paul Robinson, in *Freud and His Critics* (1993), lists three main anti-Freudians: Jeffrey Masson, who blames Freud's phallic-centered psychology for adding to the sufferings of women and children; Frank Sulloway, a philosopher of science; and Grünbaum, whom he considers the most influential. According to a review of the Robinson book in *The Economist* (28 Aug 1993), Grünbaum launches a three-pronged attack:

> His first target was the philosophers known as the hermeneutists, some of whom tried to transfer psychoanalysis from the sciences to the humanities by claiming that it was acausal. Mr. Grünbaum is understandably keen to demolish this line of intellectual retreat. It would render redundant his scientific critique of psychoanalysis. Mr. Grünbaum's second target is Karl Popper's claim that psychoanalysis is a pseudo-science because it is a catch-all that can explain every state of affairs. If this is true, it is immune to contradictory evidence and from being tested by Mr. Popper's rigorous method of falsifiability. It can only pass the less rigorous inductive test of reasoning from observable data.
>
> However, Mr. Grünbaum maintains that there are many propositions in psychoanalysis that can be falsified—e.g., Freud's theory of paranoia that sees it as a defence against active homosexuality. Mr. Grünbaum suggests that an epidemiological study carried out among active homosexuals in San Francisco could verify or falsify this theory. Mr. Grünbaum's third target is Freud himself. He attacks the methodology used to support Freudian claims for the efficacy of psychoanalysis—i.e., evidence from the couch. This does not measure up to his inductive method of scientific testing because it is too susceptible to charges of placebo effect—i.e., suggestibility on the part of the analyst. But Mr. Grünbaum over-emphasizes cure in psychoanalysis. It is more of a journey into the self. Freud himself was not much concerned with the notion of cure. In his main case histories, only the "Rat-Man" can be seen as a therapeutic success.

However, Grünbaum is said to be an admirer of Freud and sees himself as a constructive critic of psychoanalysis, not someone "out to get psychoanalysis." *The Economist*'s reviewer added that Robinson finds "the density of Mr. Grünbaum's prose serves to make it impenetrable to the lay reader."

Grünbaum's essay, "In Defense of Secular Humanism," is included in *Challenges to the Enlightenment, In Defense of Reason and Science* (1994). His essay, "Theological Misinterpretations of Current Physical Cosmology," appeared in the initial copy of *Philo* (Spring-Summer 1998). "My Exodus to Secular Humanism" (*Free Inquiry*, Fall 1999) tells how his reading of Schopenhauer's essays "soon disposed me toward atheism." By the age of thirteen, he explained, he had become a full-fledged atheist and would have declined to go through with the Bar-Mitzvah except that he did not want to embarrass his parents. He added,

> I have remained a lifelong atheist for two reasons: I do not know of any cogent argument for the existence of God, and I think there is telling evidence against it. As to the first reason, I find no merit at all, for example, in recent attempts to invoke the Big Bang cosmogony as a basis for divine creation.

(See entry for Fëodor Dostoyevsky.)

Grupp, Mel Michael (20th Century)

Grupp has been a Leader since 1965 of the Ethical Culture Societies in Southern Connecticut, Queens, Westchester, and Brooklyn. He has been a frequent youth worker and teacher of ethics. Emphatically refusing to sign Humanist Manifesto II, he explained that he regarded it as too rationalistic and non-religious for Ethical Culture. (See entry for Ethical Culture.) {EU, Howard B. Radest}

Grycz-Smilowski, Karol (Died 1959)

Grycz-Smilowski was a Polish pastor who re-activated Unitarianism in the first three decades of the century. (See entry for Polish Unitarians.)

Gruyer, Louis August Jean François-Philippe (1778—1866)

Gruyer, a Belgian philosopher, wrote an *Essay of Physical Philosophy* (1828), *Tabletès Philosophiques* (1842), and *Principles of Physical Philosophy* (1845). He held the atomic doctrine, that matter is eternal. {BDF; RAT}

Guadet, Marguerite Elie (1758—1794)

Guadet, an advocate, threw himself enthusiastically into the Revolution. He was elected Deputy for the Gironde. His vehement attacks on the Jacobins contributed to the destruction of his party, after which he took refuge. However, he was arrested and beheaded at Bordeaux. {BDF}

Gubrud, Lewis M. (20th Century)

When he signed Humanist Manifesto II, Gubrud was executive director of the Mediator Fellowship in Providence, Rhode Island. {HM2}

Guccione, Robert Charles Joseph Edward Sabatini (1930—)

A publisher, Guccione has published several magazines and founded *Penthouse*, a controversial publication with sex-oriented materials. He has been a cartoonist and greeting card design and produced a number of films, including "Caligula" (1979). Television shows he has produced include "Omni: Visions of Tomorrow," and "The New Frontier."

Peter Occhiogrosso's *Once A Catholic* quotes Guccione as saying, "I am not an atheist; I am probably an agnostic." However, he has insisted on sending his children to parochial schools and, on one occasion, encouraged one of his ex-wives to convert to Catholicism. {CA; E}

Guedeville, Nicolas (1654—1720)

A French writer, Gueudeville at first was a Benedictine monk and a distinguished preacher, but the boldness of his opinions drew on him the punishment of his superiors. He escaped to Holland and publicly abjured Catholicism. He wrote the *Dialogue of the Baron de la Hontan with an American Savage* (1704), a dialogue which is a bitter criticism of Christian usages. Guedeville translated Erasmus's *Praise of Folly* (1713), More's *Utopia*, and *C. Agrippa on the Uncertainty and Vanity of Sciences* (1726). {BDF}

GUELPH UNIVERSITY HUMANISTS

The Humanist Club of the University of Guelph is at <www.secularhumanism.org/cfa/orgs.html>.

Guépin, Ange (1805—1873)

Guépin was a French physician who taught at Nantes. He formed the first scientific and philosophical congress, which was held in Nantes in 1833. In 1854 he published his *Philosophy of the Nineteenth Century*. After the fall of the Empire, Guépin became Préfet of La Loire Inférieure but resigned because of ill health. Guépin was buried without any religious ceremony. {BDF; RAT}

Guéroult, Adolphe (1810—1872)

Guéroult early in life became a follower of Saint Simon. He wrote to the *Journal des Debats* and founded *l'Opinion National*. Guéroult was elected to the legislature in 1863, at which time he advocated the separation of church and state. {BDF; RAT}

Guerra-Junqueiro Abilio (Born 1850)

A Portuguese poet, Guerra Junqueiro wrote *The Death of Don Juan* and *The Death of Jehovah*, the latter an assault upon the Catholic faith from the standpoint of pantheism. {BDF; RAT}

Guerrero, Praxedis (1882—1910)

A Mexican anarchist and revolutionary, Guerrero was a leading member of the *Partido Liberal Mexicano*. During the revolution, he was killed. "Religion," he wrote in *Regeneración* (1910), "is the tool of tyrants in both home and presidential palace; its mission is to break people's spirits. . . . By whatever name, it is the most terrible enemy of woman. Pretending consolation, it destroys her consciousness. In the name of a sterile love, it snatches away real love, source of life, and human happiness. . . . It is the right arm of domestic and national despots; its mission is to domesticate; through the caress or whip, cage or noose, it's all employed toward one end: to tame. First the woman, because the woman is the mother and teacher of the child, and the child will be the man."

Guerrini, Olindo (1845—1916)

Guerrini was an Italian poet who sometimes wrote under the name of Lorenzo Stecchetti. In the preface to *Nova Polemica*, he declares, "*Primo di tutto dice, non credo in Dio* (First of all I say do not believe in God)." {BDF; RE}

Guedeville, Nicolas (1654—1720)

Guedeville was a French writer who, distinguishing himself as a Benedictine monk, preached so boldly that he drew the punishment of his superiors. He escaped to Holland and publicly abjured Catholicism. Guedeville translated Erasmus's *Praise of Folly* (1713), More's *Utopia* (1715), and C. Agrippa on the *Uncertainty and Vanity of Sciences* (1726). {BDF; RAT}

Guesde, Jules Basile (Born 1845)

Guesde was a French politician who established the first French Socialist organ, *L'Égalité*. Because of his advanced opinions while working in the Foreign Office, he was compelled to fly to Switzerland. Guesde was a strong rationalist and humanitarian. {RAT}

Guggenberger, Louisa Sarah Bovington (1845—1897)

A Quaker poet, Guggenberger was a Darwinian whose work Darwin appreciated although he confessed he seldom read poetry. Guggenberger submitted articles to *The Nineteenth Century*, *Mind*, and other publications. {BDF; RAT; RE}

Guichard, Victor (1803—1884)

Guichard was the Mayor of Sens and was elected deputy for the Yonne department. Exiled in 1852, he was again elected in 1871. Guichard's principal work is *La Liberté de Penser, fin du Pouvoir Spirituel* (1806). {BDF}

Guignebert, Charles (1867—1939)

Guignebert, a professor of history at the Sorbonne, was a leading authority on the Greek-Roman world about the beginning of the Christian Era. He wrote *Jesus* (1935) and *The Jewish World in the Time of Jesus* (1939). Guignebert was an honorary associate of the Rationalist Press Association. {RE}

Guild, E. E. (Born 1811)

Guild, born in Connecticut, became a Christian minister in 1835. But after numerous debates he turned Universalist. In 1844 he published *The Universalist Book of Reference*, followed by *Pro and Con*, in which he gives the arguments for an against Christianity. {BDF}

Guild, Polly and **Ted Guild** (20th Century)

The Guilds are program directors of the International Council of Unitarians and Universalists. They can be reached at 4 Kendal Common, Weston, Massachusetts 02193.

GUILLOTINE

- Guillotine, n. A machine which makes a Frenchman shrug his shoulders with good reason.

—Ambrose Bierce
The Devil's Dictionary

GUILT

- You know how Catholics are—passion in the dark and guilt the next morning.

—David Hare,
"The Blue Room," a Broadway play
(For a discussion of moral and legal or quasi-legal guilt, see the *Encyclopedia of Philosophy*, Volume 3.)

Guimet, Etienne Emile (Born 1836)

Guimet was a French traveler, musician, anthropologist, and philanthropist. The son of the inventor of ultramarine, whose business he continued, Guimet visited most parts of the world and collected objects illustrating religions. In Lyons, his fine museum which cost several million francs was presented to France, then was moved to Paris where he acted as curator. In 1880 he published *Annales du Musée Guimet*, in which original articles appeared on oriental religions. He attended the International Congress of Freethinkers at Paris in 1889. {BDF; RAT}

Guirlando, Giulio (Died 1562)

An Italian heretic, Guirlando was put to death at Venice for antitrinitarian heresy. {BDF}

Gulbrandsen, Natalie W. (20th Century)

Gulbrandsen was the fourth moderator of the Unitarian Universalist Association, serving from 1981 to 1993.

Gull, William Withey [Sir] (1816—1890)

Gull, a physician to the Queen, was Fullerian Professor of Physiology at the Royal Institution (1847—1849) and physician and lecturer at Guy's from 1856 onwards. A friend of James Hinton, he shared his pantheistic views. {RAT; RE}

GULLAH

Gullah is a historic African-English language spoken mainly in coastal South Carolina. (For a translation of *De Good Nyews Bout Jedus Christ Wa Luke rite* [*The Gospel According to Luke*], see entry for Bible.)

Gumplowicz, Ludwig (1838—1909)

A German jurist, Gumplowicz became a professor of public law at Gratz University. He regarded religion as a natural psychological-sociological phenomenon, and ethics as a code imposed on the individual by the group. {RAT}

Gunasekara, Victor (20th Century)

Gunasekara is the Australian secretary of the Humanist Society of Queensland. E-mail: <slsoc@uq.net.au>.

Gundling, Nicolaus Hieronymus (1671—1729)

Gundling was a German scholar and a deistic philosopher. He wrote *History of the Philosophy of Morals* (1706) and *The Way to Truth* (1713). One of the first German eclectics, he took much from Hobbes and Locke, with whom he derived all ideas from experience. {BDF; RAT}

Gunn, John (20th Century)

Gunn, a freethinker, wrote *Haldeman-Julius, the Man and His Work* (1924). {GS}

Gunnarson, Staffan (20th Century)

Gunnarson, who is active in Sweden's *Human Etiska Forbundet*, has written for the *International Humanist News*, questioning the wisdom of the International Humanist and Ethical Union's Declaration of Human Values. That declaration states that some things can "enable us to understand *without* reasoning, which he feels lets the doors fling widely open to religious claims on understanding without explanation, thus leading to an uncontrolled subjectivist chaos." He holds that humanists must remain rationalists who use scientific methods, that there are better ways to explain insight and creativity. {*International Humanist News*, October 1993 and December 1997}

Gunning, William D. (Died 1888)

Gunning was an American professor who had studied under Agassiz. He wrote *Life History of Our Planet* (1876) and contributed to *The Open Court*. {BDF}

Gunst, Frans Christiaan (1823—1886)

Gunst was a Dutch writer and publisher. With Junghuhn, he started *De Dageraad*, the organ of the Dutch freethinkers, which he edited from 1855 to 1867. For many years he was president of the Independent Lodge of Freemasons, and he wrote on *Adon Hiram, the Oldest Legend of the Freemasons*. Other of his works described the martyrs of the Spanish Inquisition, and he made comparisons of pagan and Jesuit morals. {BDF; RAT}

Gurbarg, Josephine R. (20th Century)

When he signed Humanist Manifesto II, Gurbarg was secretary of the Humanist Society of Greater Philadelphia. {HM2}

Gurbarg, Samuel J. (20th Century)

Gurbarg signed Humanist Manifesto II. {HM2}

Gurney, Edmund (1847—1888)

Gurney, a n English writer, assisted in founding the Society of Psychical Research (1882) and, with Myers and Podmore, published *Phantoms of the Living* (1886). In his *Tertium Quid* (2 volumes, 1887), while rejecting a personal God and expressing only a hope of a future life, he pleaded for an intermediate attitude between orthodoxy and positivism. {RAT}

Gurney, Joseph (Died 1894)

Gurney, a draper turned accountant, was secretary of the Northampton Freehold Land Society. He was a leader of Northampton secularists in the 1850s and 1860s. {RSR; RE; VI}

Gurney, Rod (20th Century)

Gurney, University of California at Los Angeles psychiatrist, was host in 1994 of the 14th annual HUMCON conference sponsored by the Alliance of Humanist, Atheist, and Ethical Culture Organizations of Los Angeles County. He is author of *The Human Agenda*.

GURU

A guru in Hinduism and Buddhism is a teacher or spiritual leader. He gives initiation into spiritual practice and instructs disciples, often maintaining a close relationship with them. Freethinkers and humanists on a diet might refer to someone as being the Guru of Lean, but the word is used only in a jocular way only.

Gustafson, Jodi (20th Century)

Gustafson is a Vice President of the University of Minnesota Atheists and Humanists.

Gustavus III of Sweden: See entry for Emanuel Swedenborg.

Gustofson, Walter (20th Century)

A member of the Department of English at Upsala College, East Orange, New Jersey, Gustofson wrote the present author concerning humanism:

> I would certainly call Pär Lagerkvist a humanist. He is not easy to place, and is therefore challenging and provocative. He is always evolving, never has his mind completely made up. In general, I suppose he is fundamentally a scientific naturalist, sceptical, empirical, especially in his periods of expressionism and despair. But other factors enter in, particularly artistic considerations; he may be an artist as much as a philosopher.
>
> He clings to humanistic ideals such as democracy, love, the nobility of the common man, little children, and so on. He hopes in the possible evolution of a superior type of religion. Christ, though possibly not a God, was a fine influence. Immortality, though it cannot be proved, can be the subject of longing. There are many facets to this work—life as set forth in his work is a fusion, a kind of fugue of many opposites, all necessary and important in the pattern.

Gustofson's own personal philosophy was not stated. {WAS, 25 August 1954}

Gutenburg, Larry (Died 1995)

Gutenburg, who was the president in New York City of People With Aids (PWA) in 1990 and remained a board member, was an atheist who helped found AASH (Agnostics, Atheists, and Secular Humanists Who Are Infected / Affected with AIDS / HIV Illness) in 1992. A political as well as a gay activist, Gutenburg co-founded in 1980 the Gay People's Radio Group at WBAI-FM in New York City and from 1983 to 1994 co-hosted "The Gay Show" at that station. He was a popular organizer who arranged interviews with manufacturers of drugs and helped arrange the lowering of drug costs to individuals whose immunization systems are assaulted by HIV. During his long illness, Gutenburg's parents and brothers were supportive and had, he wrote, "an open door policy towards me. AIDS has not interfered in my relations with my family," a situation of which he was proud. Gutenburg for a time worked on *The Body Positive*, a magazine about HIV/AIDS.

The end of his life was similar to that of other fellow AASH members, and just as he had visited them they visited him. When Gutenburg died, his friend Randy Wicker, owner of a Greenwich Village lamp shop, placed the cremains in the store's window, as had been pre-planned by the two jokesters, "so he could watch the boys go by."

Gutenberg's *Mazarin Bible* (c. 1455): See entry for incunabulist. For the individual who actually invented the printing press, see entry for Printing.

Gutmann, James (1897—1988)

A philosopher at Columbia University and author with Corliss Lamont of *Dialogue on George Santayana* (1959), Gutmann when asked about humanism by the present author wrote:

> Let me begin by paraphrasing the classical *Nihil humanum mihi alienum puto* and rendering it—No humanistic philosophy is alien to me. However, though dubious as to the value of pigeon-

holing ideas and of much labeling in philosophy, I feel sure that of the categories which you list, "naturalistic humanist" fits me best. Without wishing to be fussy I should prefer "humanistic naturalis"' to "naturalistic humanism" both because Nature includes Human Nature and because it is the setting in which men discover the pluriverse or creatively conceive it as a universe. This view of humanism, in its essentials, is, I believe, shared by all naturalistically inclined thinkers from the ancients to our day and even appeals to certain supernaturalists. Among the ancients, pre-Socratic philosophy, Socrates, Plato, and Aristotle, all seem to make most sense when interpreted in these terms.

This tradition of interpretation I first learned from F. J. E. Woodbridge forty years ago when he was expounding it along with George Santayana and John Dewey. Irwin Edman learned much from these men and carried on these teachings as have my other Columbia University colleagues, each in his own way and without constituting a "school of thought," since we would rather be a school of thinking and value variety and diversity of viewpoints as becomes the humanistic tradition.

Besides the ancients—including Hellenistic philosophers—I think I have learned most from the works of Spinoza, Schelling, and Nietzsche among the classics and, among contemporaries, from Felix Adler, John Dewey, and Ernst Cassirer. Most of them could appropriately be called both scientific and religious teachers and the values implied in both adjectives are precious to me. Though such use of the term "religious" may seem inadmissible (especially in the minds of those who identify religion with supernaturalism and theological or even ecclesiastical concerns), I believe that humanism can make room for a non-dogmatic, naturalistic, and ethical mysticism which will discover ever-increasing possibilities in human nature and its achievements.

Gutmann is editor of *Spinoza's Ethics* (1968) and author of *The Philosophy of Brand Blanshard* (1978). {WAS, 16 August 1956}

Guttierrez Galindo, Blanca (20th Century)

Guttierrez, a Mexican, spoke on "Art in Mexico, an Ethical Perspective," at the 1996 Humanist World Congress held in Mexico City.

Guttmacher, Alan F. (1894—1974)

When he signed Humanist Manifesto II, Guttmacher was president of Planned Parenthood Federation of America. {HM2}

Guyau, Jean Marie (1854—1888)

Guyau, a French author, is cited by Corliss Lamont as being a naturalistic humanist in his outlook. Guyau had been crowned at the age of nineteen by the Institute of France for a monograph on utilitarian morality. His principal works are *La Morale d'Epicure* (The Morality of Epicurus) and *Morale Anglaise Contemporaine* (Contemporary English Ethics). He wrote about the irreligion of the future and was an atheist and follower of M. Fouillée, his stepfather. All of Guyau's works were original and showed that his chief doctrine is the expansion of life. Nicolas Walter, lamenting that Guyau is almost unknown in the English-speaking world, has said that, like W. K. Clifford, Guyau died young of tuberculosis. "He had very original ideas about the 'irreligion of the future' and 'a morality without sanction or obligation.' " {BDF; CL; RAT; RE}

Guyau, M. (1854—1888)

Gauyau, a freethinker, wrote *A Sketch of Morality Independent of Obligation or Sanction* (1898). {GS}

Guynemer, A.M.A. de (19th Century)

Guynemer was the French author in 1852 of a dictionary of astronomy as well as an anonymous unbelievers' dictionary in 1869. {BDF}

Guyot, Yves (1843—1928)

An eminent French economist and statesman, Guyot was a member of the American Academy of Political and Social Science and also the English Royal Statistical Society. He was president of several French societies and, at one time, was Minister of Public Works. Early in life, when he edited a freethought paper, Guyot was an outspoken atheist and wrote several works criticizing religion. {JM; RAT; RE}

GWUP

GWUP is the acronym for Germany's Society for the Scientific Examination of Para-Science. (See entry for Armadeo Sarma.)

Gwynne, George (Died 1873)

Gwynne was a freethought writer in the *Reasoner* and *National Reformer*. He wrote under the pen name of Aliquis and was a patron of secularism. {BDF; VI}

Gyllenborg, Gustaf Fredrik (1731—1808)

Count Gyllenborg was a Swedish poet, one of the first members of the Academy of Stockholm and Chancellor of Upsala University. He published satires, fables, and odes that were named *The Passage of the Belt*. Gyllenborg's opinions were deistic, rationalist, and satiric. {BDF; RAT; RE}

GYPSIES: See entry for Roma.

Haas, Harry Forest (20th Century)

Haas was a freethinker who wrote *How to Psychoanalyze the Bible* (1939). {GS}

Haase, Hella S. (20th Century)

Haase is a novelist whose *Threshold of Fire* (1997) tells about 5th century Rome. Emperor Honorius is the ruler in 414, the religion of the Christ is the official religion, and paganism is supposed to be done away and its temples torn down. Enter Prefect Hadrian, a fanatical convert who is chosen to judge the trials of non-Christians, and the plot develops. {Reviewed by V. S. Petheram, *The Freethinker*, September 1997}

HABEAS CORPUS

- Habeas corpus, n. A writ by which a man may be taken out of jail when confined for the wrong crime.

—**Ambrose Bierce**
The Devil's Dictionary

Habermas, Jürgen (1929—)

A German philosopher, Habermas is known for being a proponent of critical theory, a social theory with Marxist roots which in the 1930s was developed by the Frankfurt School. He criticized industrial societies for doing whatever is necessary to attain given ends, an emphasis which he argued prevented them from appreciating the importance of communication action and coming to agreement with others. At the University of Frankfurt, he constructed a theory of "discourse ethics" according to which moral judgments would have validity if agreed to by agents in an ideal speech situation. His works include *Knowledge and Human Interests* (1968), *Theory of Communicative Action* (1981), *Moral Consciousness and Communicative Action* (1983), and *Between Facts and Norms: Contributions to a Discourse Theory of Law and Democracy* (1996). Habermas is a member of the Council for Secular Humanism's International Academy of Humanism. {CE}

HAC

HAC is an abbreviation of the Humanist Association of Canada. On the Web: <http://infoweb.magi.com/~godfree>.

Hachette, Jean Nicolas Pierre (1769—1834)

Hachette, a French mathematician, was prevented from taking a seat in the Academy of Sciences until 1831. However, he was one of the most noted of European mathematicians. {RAT}

Hachtroudi, Fariba (20th Century)

Hachtroudi, an Iranian who was forced to live in France because of his nontheistic outlook, spoke about intolerance at the 1996 Humanist World Congress held in Mexico City. Since the "savior" Khomeini took power in 1979, he noted, there had been a systematic dehumanization in Iran, where the law is founded in Providence and has been waiting 1,400 years to be put into practice. He lamented that the "sacred terror" has led to a vast flight to foreign countries, that prostitutes are burned alive, addicts are hanged, thieves have their limbs removed, and systematic torture is found in prisons. Half a million have died and another half a million are disabled. Suicide has increased fivefold. The greatest danger, he added, is that the world may come to accept the Islamic state of Iran and end the international fight for human identity. Khomeini died in 1989. {*International Humanist News*, December 1996; *New Humanist*, December 1996}

Hachtroudi, Mohsen (1906—1976)

Hachtroudi was an Iranian scientist, poet, and philosopher who had taught at Princeton and Teheran. "Ignorance is the source of all evil. Knowledge is a path to emancipation, but tolerance remains the essential tool for ultimate freedom," he wrote. "Dogmatism, even allegedly scientific, can lead to the worst catastrophes, as has already been the case. The Association for the Mohsen Machtroudi Foundation (17 rue Henry Monnier, 75009 Paris, France) is a not-for-profit, non-political association created to perpetuate his work.

Hacker, Jeremiah (19th Century)

In Portland, Maine, Hacker edited the monthly *Pleasure Boat* (1844—1860). He persuaded the state to "give every landless man in Maine, who would settle on it, one hundred and sixty acres of land for fifty cents an acre, and this to be paid in labor—making roads, etc." He also lectured "against priestcraft" and never charged for such. According to Putnam, Hacker was, in 1894, "probably the oldest Freethought lecturer in the world." {PUT}

Haddad, Ibrahim (20th Century)

From 1931 to 1933, Haddad edited the Arabic unbelievers' publication, *al-Duhur*, in Beirut, Lebanon. {EU}

Haddon, Alfred Cort (1855—1940)

Haddon was an ethnologist who taught at the Dublin Royal College of Science and later at Cambridge. He was President of the Royal Anthropological Institute and of the Ethnological Section of the British Association (1902—1903). Until his death, he was a member and supporter of the Rational Press Association, of which he was an honorary associate. {RAT; RE}

HADES

- Hades, n. The lower world; the residence of departed spirits; the place where the dead live.

—**Ambrose Bierce**
The Devil's Dictionary

Hadith

Males who are non-theists, but who are interested in comparison shopping, are likely unaware that according to the *Hadith*, which is the Islamic tradition of the sayings and the practices of the Prophet,

> Every man who enters Paradise shall be given seventy-two *houris* [and] no matter at what age he had died, when he enters Paradise, he will not age any further.

A *houri* is a voluptuous and alluring virgin in the Koranic paradise. As for not aging any further, others interpret Muhamad's promising that in Paradise all will remain in their twenties.

Hadith, as a discipline, consists of two branches. One is concerned with the validation of the individual traditions going back to the Prophet. The other contains the content (*matn*) as a source of religious authority. The *Hadith* is considered second in importance only to the Qur'an. Depending upon whether one is a Sunni or a Shiite, differing interpretations prevail. For an explanation see W. A. Graham, *Divine Word and Prophetic Word in Early Islam* (1977) and G. H. A. Juynboll, *Muslim Tradition* (1981).

Hadleigh, Boze (20th Century)

Hadleigh, an author who is a freethinker, wrote *Sing Out! Gays and Lesbians in the Music World*; *Hollywood Gays*; and *Hollywood Lesbians*.

Hadley, J. Harold (1912—1994)

When he signed Humanist Manifesto II, Hadley was minister of the Unitarian Universalist Church in Point Washington, New York. He was a consulting editor of *Religious Humanism*. Hadley spoke often of his Quaker origins. During his ministry from 1959 to 1977, he was an advocate of housing for the elderly and led his congregation to build a complex, which was named Hadley House in his honor. {HM2}

Hadrian (76—138)

Hadrian, the Roman Emperor whose full name was Publius Aelius Hadrianus, was learned in Greek and accomplished in poetry and music. He patronized artists and is known as one of Rome's better emperors. He instituted welfare payments for poor children, reduced taxes, codified the laws, and enacted legislation against the mistreatment of slaves. For six years he and Antinous, a Greek youth of great beauty, were inseparable. When Antinous drowned himself in 130 on a trip to Egypt, Hadrian was grief-stricken. (Their love has been written about by a member of the French Academy, the lesbian M. Yourcenar, and also by Anthony R. Birley in *Hadrian* (1998).

McCabe calls Hadrian an Epicurean atheist. Meanwhile, McCabe is one of the few who denies the legend of Hadrian's sodomy with Antinous. {JM; RE}

Haeckel, Ernst Heinrich Philipp August (1834—1919)

An early exponent of Darwinism in Germany, some of whose ideas have been proven erroneous, Haeckel wrote *The Riddle of the Universe* (1899), a comprehensive view of the soul, world, and God. A pantheist, not an atheist, he had a monistic view that there is no personal creator, no moral system in the world, and no Providence, writes Becker, who adds,

> The idea of God was sustainable to Haeckel only if one sees God as representing the ultimate cause. The theory of the origin of species and of spontaneous generation explain the origin and development of life and man. The soul is a summary of the functions of the brain, which will be extinguished by death. It is absurd to believe in personal immortality. Power and substance, energy and material are the attributes of substance.

Haeckel urged his fellow Germans to accept their evolutionary destiny, based upon his interpretation of Darwin, as a "master race" and urged them to "out compete" what he felt were "inferior" peoples. In the "Great Chain of Being" view, Africans were at the bottom whereas Europeans were the highest products of evolution. That view became a part of Hitler's *Mein Kampf*, to the dismay of many liberals who at first had liked the concept.

In 1906, Haeckel formed the Deutscher Monistendbund which, aided by the fact that if one opted out of religion in Germany, allowed one to escape taxes. It and Freigeistige Aktion gained more than one million members.

Haeckel was an honorary associate of the Rationalist Press Association (RPA). His name appeared as an Honorary Associate in the RPA's initial appeal for £1,000., and the RPA published his *Riddle of the Universe*. (See entry for Ivan Bloch.) {BDF; CE; CL; EU, Karl Becker; FUK; HNS2; JM; JMR; RAT; RE}

Hagen, Benjamin Olive (1791— 1877)

Hagen, a Quaker, embraced the views of Robert Owen and was a chief upholder, along with Mrs. Hagen, of Owen's views in the town of Derby, England. {BDF; VI}

Hagen, Dale (20th Century)

Hagen, an American ethical humanist, participated in the 1996 conference of humanists in Mexico City. His e-mail: <dhagen2801@aol.com>.

Hagtvet, Bernt (20th Century)

Hagtvet, of the University of Oslo's Department of Political Science, is a Norwegian signer of Humanist Manifesto 2000.

Hägerstiön, Axel (20th Century)

Hägerstiön is author of a general critique of religion, *Philosophy and Religion* (1964).

Hahn, Emily (1905—1997)

A mining engineer, a research physicist, a worker with the Red Cross in the Belgian Congo, Hahn was an early feminist, the author of more than 200 articles for *The New Yorker*. as well as fifty-four books, including *Hongkong Holiday* (1946), *England to Me* (1949), *Love Conquers Nothing* (1952), (1946), and *Once Upon a Pedestal* (1974).

In 1924 she traveled across the country in a Model T Ford, and *The New Yorker* published some of her experiences. In 1930, she wrote *Seductio ad Absurdum: The Principles and Practices of Seduction—A Beginner's Handbook*, a work containing her radical ideas about romance. In 1930, inspired by Charles A. Lindbergh's solo flight across the Atlantic, she went alone to Africa where she worked in a hospital and lived with a tribe of Pygmies.

In 1935, as *The New Yorker*'s correspondent in China, she met Mao Zedong and Chou En-lai, becoming a confidante of the Soong sisters (one of whom married Sun Yat-sen and the other Chiang Kai-shek), writing *The Soong Sisters* in 1941. While in China, Hahn had an affair with Sinmay Zau, spent time in opium dens, and became addicted to the drug. "I was young and I thought it was romantic to smoke opium. I was quite determined. It took me a year or so to become addicted, but I kept at it." Later, a hypnotist cured her of the habit.

In Hong Kong, she met the married Major **Charles R. Boxer**, a British intelligence officer, with whom she had a daughter [Carola Boxer Vecchi], proudly proclaiming the event at a time when illegitimacy was quite frowned upon. When the major was imprisoned by the Japanese, she brought food to him in the prison and avoided repatriation by saying she was Eurasian.

Eventually interned, she was sent back to the United States on the *Gripsholm* in 1943. In 1945, she and the major married and had a second child, Amanda.

In 1992, of humanism she wrote to the present author:

> I am no philosopher, but I seem to be on the side of most writers in opting for secular humanism, despite an uneasy feeling that I am not quite sure about humanism in general. Humans are not my favorite species, but I'm stuck with them.

As a follow-up, in an interview, Hahn told the present author that her father had been an atheist and an admirer of Robert G. Ingersoll.

> Daddy took Ingersoll's agnosticism hard. He really took it hard. He read to us out of the Bible to show us how silly the book was. In our village church in England, for I live there much of the time, my husband and I took our older daughter who was very religious and wanted to go to some Christmas or holiday service. And the vicar said, "Hello, Major Boxer, we don't see much of you." And my husband said, "No, you don't. My wife is an agnostic, and I am an atheist. We came for the child."

Laughing, she noted that only a small percentage of the English attend church any more. "Might this be an argument for disestablishmentarianism?" she was asked. "Yes," she retorted, "*they* should 'dis' a lot of stuff!"

Hahn, who became a member of the prestigious American Academy of Arts and Letters, is best known for her collection of stories, *Times and Places* (1970) In it was a story, "I Say This," about the plight of a Congolese woman she once met. Told she might be able to improve her lot, the woman had replied with the Kingwana word denoting skepticism, "*Wapi*," or "Sez you!"

Some day in the future, Hahn had tried to convince the woman, females in Africa will be much better off and they should work toward that goal. "Someday, you will have power to decide for yourself about everything," Hahn had advised.

The woman had listened intently, her eyes looking downward. She then looked up. "Lady," she ejaculated, "*Wapi*!" {WAS, 12 June 1992; WAS, 1996; *Free Inquiry*, Winter 1995-1996}

Haile Selassie: See entry for Ra.

Hailstork, Adolphus (1941—)

An African American who was raised an Episcopalian, Hailstork became a Unitarian and is a composer who teaches at Norfolk (Virginia) State University. David Lockington, associate conductor of the Baltimore Symphony, has said of a recent Hailsork composition he was preparing to perform that it is a "drawing together of African traditions with his very strong Eurocentric musical training. There's a wonderful blend going on." Hailstork agreed, saying, "From the European thing I get harmony, orchestration, structure; from the African American side of me, some harmony—the split thirds, blues scales, melody, and *rhythm*! If multiculturalism is the thing, a lot of it meets in me." {David Reich, "Crossover Composer," *World*, November-December 1994}

Hainisch, Marianne (1839—1936)

In 1894, Hainisch founded the ethical community in Austria with Friedrich Jodl. {TRI}

HAIR

Hair has been given a special significance in many religions. As described in Frazer's *Golden Bough*, for example, primitive peoples had certain hair styles for festivals, mournings, weddings, leaders, or medicine men. There were special styles for those in disgrace. According to Maynard L. Cassady, who was chairman of the Department of Religion at the University of Rochester in New York, Greek youths offered hair at initiation rites. Vedic students were instructed as how to wear their hair. Hindu ascetics and hermits set high store by hair arrangement (or disarrangement). In biblical times, long hair meant strength and integrity: The Biblical Samson's hair was said to be a source of his power. Israelites extolled long hair in contrast to the clipped heads of their enemies. A shaved head meant humiliation, punishment, or penance. Semites generally forbade shaving. In later times, Hebrew men cut their hair but regarded a woman's long hair as her glory. Christian monastic orders practiced use of the tonsure in a ceremony that involved cutting the subject's hair.

In 1486, the *Malleus Maleficarum* identified the hair of witches which was so laden with mystical powers that it was imperative witches should be shorn of their locks, as well as hanged by the thumbs, splashed on the head with alcohol, and set on fire. *Deuteronomy* allows warriors who become infatuated with their captives to marry, but first they must shave the women's heads and abstain from sexual relations for a month, a practice followed in succeeding centuries by soldiers who were "true" believers. When Joan of Arc cut her locks short, she shocked 15th century leaders, and many artists dared not paint the nineteen-year-old rebel with anything but a flowing mane of hair. As noted by Wake Forest University scholar Utrike Wiethaus, "Men felt very comfortable when they cut off women's hair," for this illustrated the male power to desexualize, ostracize, punish, or strip women of their identity. "But," added Ms. Withaus, "when women did it themselves—like Joan of Arc—the men just freaked out."

Some major as well as many minor rationalists, according to one Greenwich Village wag, are known to have been longhairs and/or hairsplitters. {ER}

Haire, Norman (1892—1952)

Haire, whose pseudonym was Wykeham Terriss, was an Australian sex reformer, gynecologist, rationalist, and freethinker. Son of Polish parents and the last of eleven children, he became a captain in 1919 and went to London, where he met Havelock Ellis and an associate of Magnus Hirschfeld, head of the Institute for Sexual Reform in Berlin. When Haire's *Hymen, or the Future of Marriage*, was published, the *Sunday Chronicle* in Australia asked that it be suppressed, whereupon the first printing sold out in three following days and Haire, although fined one hundred guineas, became famous. He then wrote under a pseudonym, publishing sex education articles in a mass circulation magazine, *Woman*, as a part of a war effort campaign to reduce venereal disease. His writing about frigidity brought the largest correspondence the magazine had ever received, but when an article on male masturbation was submitted the magazine's new editor balked. Still, the magazine's weekly circulation doubled, so in spite of loud complaints from Roman Catholic deputations, Haire's salary was trebled. In England, Haire participated in the founding of the World League for Sexual Reforms. {SWW; TRI}

HAITIAN HUMANISTS

Although no organized Haitian humanist groups have been formed, two contemporary authors—both socialists—have referred to their humanism: René Depestre and Jacques Roumain.

Hakeem, Helen (20th Century)

Hakeem is assistant secretary of the Executive Council of the Freedom From Religion Foundation.

Hakeem, Michael (20th Century)

Hakeem is a contributing editor of *Freethought Today*, which is published by the Freedom From Religion Foundation. He is chairman of that group's Executive Council.

Haldane, J(ohn) B(urdon) S(anderson) (1892—1964)

Son of John Scott Haldane, a British scientist who founded the *Journal of Hygiene* and made important contributions to mine safety, Haldane is known for his work as a geneticist. With John S. Huxley, he wrote *Animal Biology* (1927). His philosophic outlook is found in *Science and Life: Essays of a Rationalist* (1968). One of his more provocative books was *Fact and Faith* (1934), which shows his rationalistic outlook concerning religion. A Marxist who had disagreements with the Communist Party toward the end of his career, Haldane spent the last few years of his life in India, where he became a citizen. Haldane held that science was a source of social good through its application by the social administration, and to the end, which was a decade after Stalin's death, he took pride in being termed "a respectable Communist." "Capitalism," he had written in 1938, "did not arise because capitalists stole the land or the workmen's tools, but because it was more efficient than feudalism. It will perish because it is not merely less efficient than socialism, but actually self-destructive." Haldane was an honorary associate of the Rationalist Press Association (RPA).

"My practice as a scientist is atheistic," he has written. "That is to say, when I set up an experiment I assume that no god, angel, or devil is going to interfere with its course; and this assumption has been justified by such success as I have achieved in my professional career. I should therefore be intellectually dishonest if I were not also atheistic in the affairs of the world. And I should be a coward if I did not state my theoretical views in public."

One of his ancestors, Robert Haldane (1764—1843), once said he would "rather have devils than missionaries," and others in his family had believed in the Haldane tradition that the foundation of the state is seen as education, not administrators. Asked once what traits of God were evidenced by life on earth, Haldane thought of the 300,000-odd beetle species and facetiously remarked, "He must have had an inordinate fondness for beetles." {CE; FUK; RE; TYD}

Haldane, John Scott (1864—1936)

A physiologist sometimes mistakenly confused with John Burdon Haldane, Haldane was anti-materialistic and in a broad sense an advocate of vitalism but, according to McCabe, was "otherwise a Rationalist." {RE; TRI}

Haldar, Sukumas (20th Century)

A freethinker in India, Haldar wrote *The Lure of the Cross, An Inquiry into the Claims of Christianity* (1924). {GS}

Haldeman, Joe William (1943—)

Haldeman, a non-theist, wrote *Planet of Judgment* (1977); *All My Sins Remembered* (1977); *The Hemingway Hoax* (1990); and *Worlds Enough and Time* (1993). He was editor of *Cosmic Laughter* (1974). The treasurer of the Science Fiction Writers of America from 1970 to 1973, Haldeman became its president from 1992 to 1994.

During the Vietnam war era, he was turned down as a conscientious objector by his draft board because he was an atheist and had no minister to give him a letter. "All I did was point out that I was willing to spend six years in the Peace Corps, digging ditches in Africa, rather than go kill people," he said, concluding with a smile, "I wound up carrying a gun in Vietnam." {CA; E}

Haldeman-Julius, Alice (20th Century)

Haldeman-Julius in 1940 edited the *International Freethought Annual.*

Haldeman-Julius, Emanuel (1889—1951)

Haldeman-Julius's Little Blue Books were inexpensive, had a light-blue cover stock, and were eclectic in subject matter: sex, religion, anarchy, liberalism, Unitarianism, freethought—you name the subject matter hard to find in libraries of that time, and E. Haldeman-Julius printed it. In effect, he served as educator for the masses. Characterizing the average Christian minister, to the delight of his *American Freeman* readers, he might include the latest purported news from the Bible Belt: "Bishop Beerbelch pronounced today that he believes a religion without a Hell isn't worth a damn!" With his down-to-earth prose, he invited closet socialists or village atheists to mail in their orders, which his Girard, Kansas, company was quick to supply. In the *Encyclopedia of Unbelief* Ryan has a thorough description of the man and his activities, mentioning how he employed the talents of such diverse individuals as Bertrand Russell, Joseph McCabe, Leo Markun, Vance Randolph, T. Swann Harding, and C. Harley Grattan. In his "Meaning of Atheism," he wrote, "After all, the principal objection which a thinking man has to religion is that religion is not true—and is not even sane. . . . Throughout the greater part of its history, religion has been a form of 'holy' terrorism. . . . Wherever there is devout belief—there is also the inseparable feeling of fear. . . . Religion interferes with life and, being false, it necessarily interferes very much to the detriment of the sound human interests of life."

During World War II, Haldeman-Julius published McCabe's allegation that the Vatican was linked with the Axis powers, this being just one of over twenty books and pamphlets which he authored.

A 1948 exposé of the FBI allegedly stoked the wrath of J. Edgar Hoover. Haldeman-Julius in 1951 was found guilty of federal income-tax evasion and, while awaiting an appeal, mysteriously drowned in his Girard, Kansas, swimming pool. {EU, William F. Ryan; FUK}

Hale, Alan (20th Century)

Hale was the co-discoverer in 1995 of Comet Hale-Bopp, which should become an internationally spectacular celestial object during the spring of 1997. He is director of the Southwest Institute for Space Research, an independent research and educational organization based in Cloudcroft, New Mexico. He has written, "The idea that we on the Earth hold some type of privileged position within the universe, or that one particular group of individuals on this planet holds a supernaturally ordained privileged position over its other inhabitants, is recognized for the absurdity that it must be. In the long run, he holds,

> if we can convince our fellow human beings that the sights we see in the heavens—even something as wondrous as Comet Hale-Bopp will hopefully turn out to be—are purely natural phenomena, and that there is no need to invoke any supernatural or mystical elements as an explanation, then we will have taken a significant step toward preparing our society to deal responsibly with the technological and ethical issues with which it will be confronted during the twenty-first century.

What is particularly desirable at this time is a more enlightened and scientifically literate public. "The time is ripe for such an effort," he has written, "and I urge all freethinkers and rationalists who are reading this to work together with me toward bringing this to pass." Hale is a supporter of Internet Infidels. {CA; "The Unlimited Cosmos—A Personal Odyssey" by Alan Hale, *Free Inquiry*, Summer 1996}

Hale, Constance R. (20th Century)

Hale is a freethinker who writes for *Truth Seeker.*

Hale, Edward Everett (1822—1909)

A Unitarian minister, once chaplain of the U.S. Senate, Hale published anonymously in *Atlantic Monthly* "The Man Without a Country," a short novel which brought him much publicity and is still being read. He originated the Lend-a-Hand clubs, was related to the patriot Nathan Hale, and once taught at Boston Latin School.

Van Wyck Brooks said that, when a chaplain, Hale was asked, "Do you pray for the Senators, Dr. Hale?" "No," Hale responded, "I look at the Senators and pray for the country."

He was minister of Boston's South Congregational Church (Unitarian). {CE; U; U&U; UU}

Hale, M. (20th Century)

Hale, a freethinker, wrote "Atheism and Anarchy" (1924). {GS}

Halévy, Jacques François Fromentel Elie (1799—1862)

Halévy, a French composer, was a professor at the Paris Conservatoire, Commander of the Legion of Honor, and member of the French Academy. A friend of Renan, he shared his liberal theism. **Leon** (1802—1883), his brother, was a Hellenist who had several works crowned by the Academy. Both deserted the Jewish faith for freethought.

Léon's two sons, novelist **Ludovic** (1834—1908) and Orientalist **Joseph** (Born 1827), were both rationalists, also. {JM; RAT; RE}

Haley, Alex (1921—1992)

Haley was an African American who made millions of dollars on a1976 work, *Roots*, which allegedly traced his family back to its African origins.

The work, however, was plagiarized from Harold Courlander's *The African* and, according to Margaret Walker, from her own *Jubilee*. After becoming a literary star, Haley was sued by Courlander and settled after a five-week trial for $650,000. The presiding judge, Robert Ward, ruled that "Alex Haley perpetrated a hoax on the public," but he has added, "I encouraged a settlement because I believed that Alex Haley was a significant figure in the black community. I believe that Haley was a symbol. I believe that it would not serve any purpose to smash the symbol."

In other words, commented black columnist Stanley Crouch about the judge's "prototypical Caucasian paternalism," "If those darkies are happy with their African heritage hoax, let them have it. They're children anyway. The truth would overwhelm them, poor things." Proof of the statement is evident in a 1998 statue unveiled by Haley in Morningside Park, Knoxville, Tennessee. Large crowds come by to honor the Tennessean. {*Daily News*, New York, 12 April 1998}

Halifax, Charles Montagu, (George Savile) [1st Earl Of] (1661—1715)

An English statesman, once lord of the treasury, Halifax co-authored with Prior a parody of John Dryden's *The Hind and the Panther*, calling it *The Town and the Country Mouse* (1687). Britain's national debt can be traced to Halifax's proposing a system of government borrowing which established such a debt. In 1694, the Bank of England was founded using his and William Paterson's plan, and Halifax was appointed chancellor of the exchequer. In 1695 he designated Isaac Newton as warden of the mint. Although his contemporaries often called him a deist, even an atheist, Robertson states that his writings show Halifax was either an atheist or a Unitarian. {BDF; CE; JMR}

Hall, Benjamin [Baron] (1802—1867)

A member of the House of Lords in England, Hall is known to have stood up and attacked the Church of England for "great abuses in the management of ecclesiastical property." He insisted on the right of the Welsh to have church services in their own language and, a Unitarian, he was an early proponent of the separation of church and state. But it was during his position of Commissioner of Works that he achieved the most fame: By settling a dispute between the clockmaker and the architect at the time the clock was being constructed at the Houses of Parliament, Hall was memorialized because the clock then became known as Big Ben.

Hall, Covington (1871—1951)

Hall's work, *Dreams and Dynamite: Selected Poems*, was published in 1985. He has been called by Fred Whitehead "in the heritage of hard-core radical and working class Freethinkers and deserves to be better known today." A "son of the South," he was born of a Bourbon family in Louisiana. In 1904 he was chosen Adjutant General of the Sons of Confederate Veterans. {*Freethought History*, #16, 1995}

Hall, David (20th Century)

Hall, a scholar, in "Is the Universe a Duck or a Rabbit?", examined the thought of two theologians—John Hick and Fritjof Schuon—who, from different perspectives, both look at the possibility of transcendence. Their ideas in the humanist debate with religion of naturalism vs. transcendentalism, he found, ultimately beg the question of whether any concept of God is tenable. {*New Humanist*, September 1996}

Hall, Edward T(witchell) (1914—)

Hall, an anthropologist who did field work in Micronesia, is author of *Handbook for Proxemic Research* (1975), *The Fourth Dimension in Architecture* (1975) and *Beyond Culture* (1976). His *Who's Who* entry states, "The most difficult task in the world is to know one's self. But knowing others can aid in the performance of that task." Asked by the present author about humanism, he responded,

> I am a non-theist. I look at life with continuing and deep wonder, am a spiritual person, but I reject all organized or gnostic religions. Zen is as close as I can get. There is no way my insignificant mentality can pretend to understand how it all came about or how it works. I know my own life has been a succession of small and large miracles. How and why? No one person or persons are responsible if anything is. It is the reality that unfolds daily before my very eyes. It's *all* there for anyone who will take the trouble to look.
>
> {WAS, 20 November 1994}

Hall, Elizabeth (20th Century)

According to the American Library Association's *Banned Books* (1998), Hall is the author of *Possible Impossibilities*, a work which allegedly "would lead children to believe ideas contrary to the teachings of the Bible." (See entry for Banned Books.)

Hall, Frank A. (20th Century)

When he signed Humanist Manifesto II, Hall was minister of the Murray Universalist Church in Attleboro, Massachusetts. He later became minister of the Unitarian Church in Westport, Connecticut. In 1974, Hall wrote *An Evaluation of the Massachusetts Furlough Experience*, concerning prisons and prisoners.

Religious Humanism contains a play/pulpit drama in which "Man" talks to "God" and "Satan." The essence of the play suggested that God and Satan are aspects of our human psyche, that "truth" seems so "basic" it needs no explanation. An anthropomorphic god is, to paraphrase Paul's famous comment, "thinking like a child," Hall has observed, adding, "I choose not to use the G-word, but neither do I dismiss it as merely childish. When asked if I am a theist I respond with the appropriate question, 'What do you mean?' 'Humanist' often (if not usually) means 'humanistic' or 'humanitarian' to most folks, so we're all 'humanists.' " {HM2; WAS, 7 March 1995; *World*, May-June 1995}

Hall, Frank Oliver (1860—1941)

A leading spokesman for Universalism in the early part of the twentieth century, Hall was a pacifist who was active in the Church Peace Union, an organization funded by Andrew Carnegie, whose purpose was to explore avenues toward international peace through the leadership of the churches. He forcefully articulated the key tenet of Universalism, attacking the "hideous and sickening conception of God which makes him the creator of a little heaven for a select few and a big hell for the vast majority of the human race." He defined God as "the name we give to the creative energy," which is in line with modern speculative naturalism. The object of life, he affirmed in his *Common People* (1901), is development, and the purpose of the universe "is the production of the highest possible type of manhood and womanhood." {U&U}

Hall, G(ranville) Stanley (1844—1924)

Hall, an American psychologist and educator, wrote *Jesus, the Christ, in the Light of Psychology* (1923). "No priestcraft can longer make man content with misery here in the hope of compensation hereafter," he wrote in *Senescence* (1922). {GS; TYD}

Hall, Henry (19th Century)

In 1892, Hall wrote *Ethan Allen* . {FUS}

Hall, John Carey (Born 1844)

Hall was a positivist. Entering the consular service in Japan in 1868, he became Acting Vice-Consul at Yedo (1869) and was Consul-General at Yokohama (1902—1914). Hall has written on China and Japan and was one of the founders of the China Society. A member of the Positivist Church and the Rationalist Press Association, he contributed occasionally to the *Positivist Review*. {RAT}

Hall, Lucia K. B. (20th Century)

Hall is a biochemist, artist, and editor of the *San Diego Humanist*, published by the Humanist Association of San Diego. Her e-mail: <nhall@godless.org>.

Hall, Martin (20th Century)

In the 1960s, Hall was a director of the American Humanist Association.

Hall, Norman (20th Century)

Hall is the southwest liaison officer for the National Ocean Data Center in La Jolla, California. He is past president of the Humanist Association of San Diego (ASHS). His e-mail: <nhall@godless.org>. (See entry for California Atheists, Humanists.) {FD}

Hall, Robert (20th Century)

Hall, a freethinker, is professor of philosophy and sociology at the College of Steubenville in Ohio.

Hall, Sharlot (1870—1943)

Hall, who was born in frontier Kansas, was given her first name, an Indian name, by her uncle. Her family attended lectures by freethinker Samuel Putnam in 1895 and, although only twenty-four and he was fifty-six, she fell in love and wrote freethought poetry. His death in 1896 made headlines because the fully dressed bodies of Putnam and a young woman lecturer, Mary L. Collins, were found on the floor of a hotel room, asphyxiated by a gas leakage. Seeing the lot of her mother and most women, Hall vowed never to marry, once remarking, "The egotism of the average man is so great that he thinks he is a glorious sight—even with a wad of tobacco in his cheek and the spit drooling off his chin." {WWS}

Hall, Stuart (20th Century)

Hall in the 1950s edited with Edward Thompson *New Reasoner* and *Universities and Left Review*, both journals of socialistic humanism.

Hall, T. L. (20th Century)

Hall is active with the Humanists of South East Michigan. (See entry for Michigan Humanists.) {FD}

Halley, Edmund (1656—1742)

Halley, the eminent English astronomer, was the first to predict the return of a comet and the first to point out the use of a transit of Venus in determining the parallax of the sun. In 1667 he went to St. Helena to observe the southern skies, cataloguing 341 stars of the Southern Hemisphere. He financed the publication of his friend Isaac Newton's *Principia* and in 1720 was made the royal astronomer. Halley also discovered the proper motions of the stars and the acceleration of the moon's mean motion. Known in his lifetime as "the Infidel Mathematician," Halley was further memorialized in Chalmers's *Biographical Dictionary* as follows: "It must be deeply regretted that he cannot be numbered with those illustrious characters who thought it not beneath them to be Christians. . . . That he was an infidel in religious matters seems as generally allowed as it appears unaccountable." {BDF; JM; JMRH; RAT; RE}

Hallidie, Andrew Smith (1836—1900)

Hallidie, a Unitarian, invented the cable car. Also he founded the San Francisco Public Library and Art Society. {UU}

HALLOWEEN

Halloween, or Hallowe'en, is related to the Druid Feast of Samhain, at which time priests offered animal sacrifices and built bonfires (bone fires) on hilltops. Samhain—the word in Irish Gaelic for November is pronounced SOW-in—came to earth that night to collect the spirits of all who had died during the year. It is celebrated on November Eve and marks both the beginning of winter and Celtic New Year, one of the two holiest days in the pagan calendar (the other being May 1, or Beltane), when the veil between the worlds is thinnest, and the beloved dead can (and allegedly do) return to be with us.

By celebrating the season of darkness, demons and witches were let loose upon the earth to play tricks upon mortals. There were two ways to escape: fool them by dressing as one of them and escape their notice, or pacify them with sweet foods. "So much for the origin of trick or treat," a *New York Times* editorialist has observed.

But Patricia Kennealy Morris, a self-proclaimed witch, holds that Samhain (pronounced sah-win) is a joyful and solemn festival which has nothing whatever to do with the Devil or the demonic. "As Pagans," she has written, "we acknowledge neither the Christian God nor the Christian Adversary; our deities predate both. The Horned Lord who for us rules the winter half of the year is no devil but the male principle of the universe personified, represented (not surprisingly for a totemic hunting people like the Celts) as a man with the antlers of a stag. No Devil, no evil witches, no sacrifices: All those things were later Christian inventions, intended to turn the folk away from the ancient benign practices—and unfortunately succeeding all too well, as we see."

As for the jack-o'-lanterns, in Ireland lived a notoriously stingy drunkard named Jack who was said to have tricked the Devil into climbing an apple tree, where he was trapped. Jack made the price of freedom a promise from the Devil never to take his soul. Eventually Jack died and was rejected from heaven because of the meanness and his fondness for drink. When he tried Hell, he was rejected because of the Devil's old promise. But the Devil did give Jack a coal from the fire to light his journey from the netherworld. Jack placed the coal in a turnip he had been eating and began wandering the earth, homeless, waving his "jack-o'-lantern."

In times past, Irish children carved faces in Halloween lanterns made from potatoes and turnips. Upon reaching America, they discovered the natural superiority of the pumpkin as a receptacle for satanic fire. When the pumpkin, *Curcurbita pepo*, was first cultivated, it was for its seeds, which were a prized snack among the 6th-millennium B.C.E. cave dwellers of the Tamaulipas Mountains in Mexico. Then it was mixed with cornmeal for bread, filled with milk and made into custard, and baked in hot ashes. In the 1840s, it began to be used to create the grinning orange faces.

"Now on Halloween," concluded a *New York Times* editorialist, "the last great pagan holiday, the New World pumpkin grins through a night still redolent of Old World magic. It is impossible to imagine such effective ghoulish grimaces coming from a turnip." (See entries for vampire, witches, and zombies.) {"Consider the Pumpkin," *The New York Times*, 31 October 1994}

Halstead, Beverly (1933—1991)

A prominent paleontologist, Halstead wrote occasionally for the British *New Humanist*. He received considerable notoriety in 1987 at a meeting of the British Association for the Advancement of Science. With a partner, Dr. Helen Haste, he physically demonstrated the difficulty that dinosaurs would have had in managing sexual intercourse. At the time of his death, he was President of the Geologists' Association and of the geology section of the British Association. In a June 1988 article in *New Humanist*, he described the evening he "went for a final pee and to my incredulity and shock I emptied a full bladder of good thick deep red blood. No pain, just a vivid crimson stream." Cancer! To become empathetic to the feelings of those who learn for the first time they have cancer, his "On the Biology and Philosophy of Cancer" is a practical reference. His outlook utilized the humanistic tradition, of understanding through metaphor and rhetoric, which is in diametric opposition to the Cartesian tradition.

HAM

Ham, who was the Biblical Noah's son after whom the Hamitic languages were named, was black. Medieval Christianity as well as Islam forbade the enslavement of their own adherents, but some Christians saw blacks as descendants of Ham and, therefore, eternally cursed. Slavery of non-believers was not frowned upon and, in fact, the practice was thought a possible way to scare them into becoming believers. {*The Economist*, 31 December 1999}

Hamad, Alaa (20th Century)

Hamad, an Egyptian writer, was dismissed in 1994 from his job as an employee for thirty-five years of Egypt's tax authority following an allegation that he had written an immoral book. The novel was *Al-Firash* (*The Bed*), and it followed a previous work, *A Distance in a Man's Mind* (1991), which was critical of religion and resulted in his being sentenced to eight years in prison.

Haman

Haman, according to the Jewish Talmud, was a notorious anti-Semite. The Persian king Ahasuerus reportedly granted power to Haman, who became known for his anti-Semitism.

Hamerling, Robert (1830—1889)

A German poet, Hamerling translated Leopardis's poems. A freethinker, he wrote poems such as "Ahasuerus in Rome" (1866) and "The King of Sion." Hamerling also wrote a tragedy, *Danton and Robespierre.* {BDF; RAT}

Hamerstrom, Frances (1908-1998)

An internationally known field biologist, Hamerstrom was a conservationist and wildlife biologist. For fifty years she and her husband, **Frederick Hamerstrom**, lived in a Wisconsin house that had no running water, had not been painted since the Civil War, and had no heat aside from a few cast-iron wood-burning stoves. The two studied prairie chickens, helping to save the endangered species. He was a nephew by marriage to Clarence Darrow.

She wrote several books, including *An Eagle to the Sky* (1970) about nursing an eagle back to health, and *My Double Life* (1994), her autobiography. In 1986 she addressed the national convention of the Freedom From Religion Foundation on the subject of religion and animals. "No chewing gum, and no church," she said were the only two rules when their children were growing up.

A crack wing-shot with a Parker 20-gauge shotgun, she allocated her time applying the humanistic "Hamerstrom Rule of Thirds:

- spend a third of your time for the worthless red tape that your boss requires;
- spend a third of your time doing what is wanted of you; and
- spend a third of your time doing exactly what you please.

(*The New York Times*, 7 September 1998)

Hamerton, Philip Gilbert (1834—1894)

Hamerton, an artist and writer, refused to go to Oxford because he would not sign their Thirty-nine Articles. An etcher, novelist, and writer on art, Hamerton was joint founder of the *Portfolio* (1869).

In his posthumously published autobiography (1897), Hamerton avows his rationalism, though he thought that "true liberation" from theology would come by acquiring knowledge rather than by controversy. {RAT}

Hamilton, Ernest William [Lord] (1888—1939)

Hamilton, the son of the Duke of Abercorn, had a career in the Army followed by seven years in Parliament. He then wrote several novels and books on religion. Although a theist, Hamilton rejected all Church doctrines and the idea of a future life. "Church dogmas are doomed," he wrote in *Involution* (1912). {RAT; RE}

Hamilton, Alexander (1755-1804)

Hamilton, whose imprint on the United States is overlooked by those, some say, who overly emphasize George Washington, Thomas Jefferson, and John Adams as the major Founding Fathers, was a theist, not a deist.

Also, he was one of the most colorful people of his time: having been born on the West Indian island of Nevis it is possible he had some African ancestors in his past; his published letters to John Laurens to "put on the toga" and come with him to Washington imply a possible love for the American Revolutionary soldier—"Adieu: I embrace you tenderly. . . . My friendship for you will burn with that pure flame which has kindled you your virtues. . . . I love you," perhaps flowery language popular at the time rather than statements to be taken literally; having an adulterous affair with Maria Reynolds, which was the first great sex scandal in American politics; a person whose influence made Jefferson the President and Aaron Burr the Vice President, later being the one who thwarted Burr in becoming Governor of New York State; and after calling Burr a "dangerous man" and being challenged to a duel, lost his life in a Weehawken Heights, New Jersey, fight, dying at a physician's house on Jane Street (after crossing the Hudson River to Manhattan.

Hamiltonians complain that Jefferson owned slaves and thought they were naturally inferior whereas Hamilton thought they deserved citizenship and should serve in the Revolutionary War. Hamilton supporters add that Jefferson's ideal America was based on states' rights, agrarian capitalism, and isolationism whereas Hamilton envisioned the nation we have become, a centralized industrial superpower with civil rights enforced by the Federal Government. Detractors claim he seriously considered proposing an American monarchy not unlike that of England's.

Hamilton, whose image appears on the U.S. $10 bill is, appropriately, buried at the western end of New York City's Wall Street. {CE; Jonathan Ned Katz, *Gay American History*; Michael Lind, *The New York Times*, 3 and 8 July 1998}

HAMLET

- Are the commentators on Hamlet really made, or only pretending to be?

—Oscar Wilde

- Hamlet has been played by 5,000 actors—no wonder he is crazy.

—H. L. Mencken

- "Who," asked the priest after a Connecticut service, "comes anywhere near being as inspirational a figure as Jesus?"

"Hamlet," quickly replied a New Canaanite. "Because he was credibly human, fell in love, was witty with a sense of humor, accepted who his real father was and was a faithful son, didn't spout Christianity, was intellectual, loved the dramatic, was a Montaigne-like skeptic, was devoted to justice, exemplified. . . ."

"Enough!" replied the priest, whose favorite literary character was Hamlet also and who thought it better not to develop the case against the Prince of Denmark, a child of the Renaissance, a noble human being struggling against a corrupt world, a disillusioned idealist, the mouthpiece of his creator's thought, a person who had the consistency, or inconsistency, of life itself.

In a millennium issue of *The New York Times Magazine* (18 April 1999), editors asked numbers of individuals their answer to the question of what was the best—ideas, stories, inventions, etc.—responses which have been put into a "Times Capsule" that will not be opened until the year 3000.

"What was the greatest poem of the millennium?" they asked.

"*Hamlet*," responded Helen Hennessy Vendler, poetry critic and a professor in Harvard University's English Department. A member of the American Philosophical Society, she called the work "as lyric as it is dramatic" and "a celebration of skepticism."

Her evaluation made it clear she considers *Hamlet* a philosophic work and, although she did not use the specific words, it is one entirely in keeping with the philosophy of naturalistic humanism:

> Hamlet believes only in death—not in the Christian afterlife that was part of the ideology of his century. For him, the single question is, To be or not to be. Mortality is one uneasiness in him, murder the other, and it scarcely matters in the end whether mortality comes by murder, since what vexes Hamlet is mortality itself. Even the flesh of a king "may go to a progress through the guts of a beggar"; ultimately everything human comes to death, to the sun-kissing carrion and the omnivorous worm. . . .
>
> Hamlet—even after seeing the ghost—speaks merely of bad dreams that may come in the sleep of death. The remnants of belief have been scotched by his mordant university learning. In its repudiation of Christian consolation, "Hamlet" marks the philosophical turning point of our Western millennium: the moment in which that reflective skepticism so repellant to [Czeslaw] Milosz (who nonetheless shares it) becomes intellectually dominant. In the wake of the collapse of religious authority comes social revolution: "The toe of the peasant comes so near the heel of the courtier he galls his kibe. . . ."
>
> "Hamlet" is, then, our pre-eminent post-Christian poem, refusing both the redemptive linear plot of Christianity—by which God brings good out of evil—and the stable political hierarchy implicit in the Christian belief that regal authority is derived from God. Like most lyric poems, "Hamlet" exhibits a recursive structure: the deathblow repeats itself in the fortune of each main character; the morbid dumb show and the "mousetrap" play replicate the main murder plot; and the open graves of the innocent Yorick and Ophelia serve as gaping symbols of the tragedy's continual undersong of grief. Emily Dickinson once wrote, "He has found his Future who has found Shakespeare." It is our own future predicament that we find in this great dramatic poem, as we hear Hamlet's lyric obbligato musing over the gravediggers' stage.

HAMLET'S GHOST: See entry for Ghosts.

Hamlin, Hannibal [Vice President] (1809—1891)

Hamlin, the statesman who was Vice President under President Lincoln, was a Unitarian. {CE; U; UU}

Hammer, Armand (1898—1990)

Hammer, who expanded the Occidental Petroleum Corporation into a multibillion-dollar business, was known as an atheist as well as one of the world's richest men. A promoter of peace and economic ties with the Union of Socialist Soviet Republics, he was treated throughout the world as if a diplomat dedicated to ending the Cold War between the USSR and the United States.

Nearly one hundred million dollars of Occidental's funds went to the Armand Hammer Museum of Art and Cultural Center in Los Angeles. Danielle Mitterand, wife of the President of France, was present at the center's opening ceremony and was pledged three hundred thousand dollars to the Mitterands' private foundation.

Hammer also pledged well over one million dollars to the Salk Institute, and to the National Symphony Orchestra he pledged two hundred and fifty thousand dollars for playing "Happy Birthday" to him at his ninetieth birthday party. Others scheduled to benefit from his generosity were his art consultant, Martha Kaufman, and his physician, Rosamaria Durazo.

When he died, however, a different picture of Hammer came into view. It had been his Frances's, his wife's, money that had been used to start him in his successful business ventures. When Frances had become suspicious of the relationship between her husband and his art consultant, Kaufman had changed her identity to Hilary Gibson and had continued to be his mistress. So had the physician been his mistress. In addition, Hammer had had a number of illegitimate children with other ladies.

Meanwhile, he was serving as a conduit for dubious Russian artworks and was trafficking in fake Imperial Fabergé eggs that he authenticated as genuine with an official Fabergé stamp. Also, he allegedly was involved in bribery schemes said to have helped him land lucrative oil drilling and mineral concessions in Venezuela and Libya. To the Communist International in New York, he is said to have secretly distributed the equivalent of $600,000 in 1996 currency.

Jacob Jay Epstein, in a thorough investigation, has found that Hammer when he went to Russia in the 1920s had said he was an atheist. When later he went to Saudi Arabia and Libya in search of oil in the 1960s, he listed himself as Unitarian. But in his final days, he met with Rabbi Daniel Lapin of the Pacific Jewish Center and arranged a bar-mitzvah ceremony for December 11th, the first night of Hanukkah.

The day before, however, he succumbed of cerebral arteriosclerosis, and the various groups and individuals who had expected to inherit fortunes were to learn that he had left only around forty million dollars, much of which would be used to pay personal debts, legal bills, estate taxes, and the claims made in the suit by his wife Frances's estate.

It then became evident that when the final hammer pounded home, the sound was that of an entire life of deception. Had he lived but one more day, he would have officially become a Jew. {Edward Jay Epstein, *The New Yorker*, (23 Sep 1996)}

Hammerton, John Alexander [Sir] (1871—1949)

Hammerton, after a long experience in journalism including writing for *Punch*, the Harmsworth serial publications (*History of the World*, 1907—1909; *The World's Great Books*, 1909—1910, etc.), and other large-scale works of reference. Although he was knighted and received much fame, described in his autobiographical *Books and Myself*, he achieved a special feat. Attributed to him is the most popular of all twentieth century gestures: the "V" sign. He had sighted a "V" for victory sign apparently blazed by a Hawker Hurricane in the sky over the village of Firle in Sussex in the late 1940s.

When he wrote about it in *War Illustrated*, the sign replaced the customary "thumbs up" and was adopted throughout beleaguered Europe as a symbol of defiance to Nazism.

Sir John was an honorary associate of the Rationalist Press Association. {RE}

Hammon, William (18th Century)

Hammon reportedly wrote the first atheistic work in England, *Answer to Dr. Priestley's letters to a philosophical unbeliever* (1782). However, his name might be a pseudonym used by Dr. Matthew Turner. (See entry for Matthew Turner.) {FUK}

Hammond, William (20th Century)

A liberal minister, Hammond was once a director of the American Humanist Association. {HNS}

Hamond (Hamont), Matthew (Died 1579)

Hamond was an English heretic, by trade a ploughwright. He was burned at Norwich in 1579 for holding "that the New Testament and the Gospel of Christ were pure folly, a human invention, a mere fable." Previously, Hamond had been set in a pillory and both his ears had been cut off. {BDF}

Hamount, Matthew (16th Century)

Hamount was a doubter who was burned at the stake in Norwich, England, in 1529. Priests had accused him of saying that the Bible "is but foolishness, a mere fable; that Christ is not God or the savior of the world, but a mere man." {TYD}

HAMPSTEAD (England) HUMANIST SOCIETY

For information about the Hampstead Humanist Society, write N. I. Barnes, 10 Stevenson House, Boundary Road, London NW8 0HP.

Hampton, Henry (1940-1998)

Hampton was a producer whose television documentary, "Eyes on the Prize," according to the *Boston Globe*, "set the standard for nonfiction accounts of the civil rights movement." He was the founder of Blackside, Inc., served as a member of the Advisory Board of Beacon Press, and worked for the Unitarian Universalist Association from 1963 to 1968. During that time he called for clerical leaders to participate in the Selma-to-Montgomery civil rights march of 1965.

At the time of his death, Hampton was working on several projects, including *I'll Make Me a World: A Century of African-American Arts, Artists and Communities*, to be released in 1999, and The African-American Religious Experience.

Hamsun, Knut (1859—1952)

Knut Petersen, Norway's novelist best known by his chosen name of Hamsun, was an admirer of the Scandinavian rationalists Ibsen, Björnson, and Brandes. He worked in America as a tram-driver and barber before returning to Norway to become its leading writer. Although broadly classed as a pantheist, he held "no particular philosophy," stated biographer C. D. Marcus.

Hamsun wrote *Hunger* (1890). In a style now called literary naturalism, the work was greeted as one of the first "modern" novels, one that used a reflective, inner voice long before Proust or Joyce. The work was so influential that Isaac B. Singer in *Knut Hamsun, Artist of Skepticism* stated that "the whole modern school of fiction in the twentieth century stems from Hamsun."

He also wrote *Mysteries* (1892), *Pan* (1894), and *The Growth of the Soil* (1917). The latter work set simple agrarian values against those of the new industrial society and was awarded the 1920 Nobel Prize in Literature. Although Norwegians are somewhat and deservedly proud of him, they have written widely about being ill at ease concerning his flagrant Nazi sympathies. During World War II Hamsun supported the collaborationist government of Norway's pro-German and fascist leader Vidkund Quisling. In 1920 Hamsun sent his Nobel medal to German propagandist Herman Goering, and upon Hitler's death he openly mourned. In 1946 Hamsun was declared by psychiatrists to be permanently mentally disabled and was fined $80,000 for economic collaboration with the enemy.

In recent years Hamsun's reputation has improved. Admittedly a cynic who despised suffragettes and shared August Strindberg's misogynist views, Hamsun had an intense love of nature, an interest in the unconscious, and a humanistic concern for the material condition of the individual and its effect on one's spirit. Biographer Robert Ferguson in *Enigma: the Life of Knut Hamsun* (1988) describes him as having been a man of generosity and integrity. He was, say his defenders, very old and perhaps senile when he fell in with Norway's Nazis. One of his literary admirers is America's writer in Yiddish Bashevis Singer.

Levi Fragell, however, thinks Hamsun "did not criticize religion and, at the end of his life, expressed pro-Christian views." {CE; *The Economist*, 17 January 1998; OEL; RE}

Hanaford, Phebe Ann (Coffin) (1829—1921)

One of the first Universalist woman to be ordained (1868) to the ministry in New England, Hanaford had previously been a writer of fiction, poetry, children's books, and a life of Lincoln. Her religious background had been Quaker, she had adopted the Baptist faith of her husband, but encouraged by Olympia Brown she converted to Universalism. One of her last projects was a compilation of biographies of American women, *Women of the Century* (1877). {CE; U&U}

Hancock, John (1737—1793)

Hancock, whose name appears first (and largest) on the Declaration of Independence, was a member of the Masonic Lodge, the rituals of which have heavy overtones of deism and which are antithetical to theism. He was governor of Massachusetts (1780—1785 and 1787—1793). {CE}

Handy, Rollo (20th Century)

Handy, a former professor of philosophy at the State University of New York at Buffalo, is an authority on 19th German materialism.

Hankins, Frank H. (1877—1970)

Hankins signed Humanist Manifesto I. A social scientist who taught at Smith College, he was editor of *American Sociological Review* from 1936 to 1937. He wrote *Studies in the Social Sciences* (1908), *The Racial Basis of Civilization* (1926), and was an editor for *Webster's New International Dictionary*. In 1960, he was named a Humanist Pioneer by the American Humanist Association. Hankins, writing about his outlook, said

> Sociological and historical researchers have shown that the essential core of religion is devotion to those social values which bind men together in cooperative effort for group preservation and mutual welfare; and that these values are discovered through human experiences. Among those discovered in recent times are devotion to truth as exemplified in the scientific mentality, the dignity of individual man, and the ideals of democracy. Humanism thus becomes the next logical step in religious evolution; it is the heir and creative fulfillment of the Renaissance, the Reformation, and the democratic revolutions.

{EW; HM1; HNS; HNS2}

Hanlon, James O. (20th Century)

Hanlon was a New Zealand freethinker who wrote *Searchlight of the Bible, A Discussion Between a Christian and an Atheist* (1943). {FUK; GS}

Hanna, Emily (20th Century)

Hanna, while a student at the Massachusetts Institute of Technology in 1998, signed the Campus Freethought Alliance's "Bill of Rights for Unbelievers."

Hanna, Kathleen (20th Century)

Hanna is a recording artist who was a member of the 1990s punk band Bikini Kill but now is a soloist. She and the band were allied with the Riot Grrrl feminist movement and at one time said, "I don't believe in God, but I believe God invented four-tracks," a jocular reference to recording studio terminology. {CA}

Hanna, Peter (20th Century)

Hanna heads the New South Wales Rationalist Association in Australia. E-mail: <rational@mail.mpx.com.au>.

Hannay, Alistair (20th Century)

A freethinker, Hannay is professor of philosophy at the University of Trondheim, Norway. {SHD}

Hannay, James B. (20th Century)

Hannay wrote the two-volume *Sex Symbolism in Religion* (1922).

Hannotin, Émile (1812—1886)

Hannotin was a French deist, the editor of the *Journal de la Meuse*. He wrote *Philosophical Theology* (1846) and an "Essay on Man," in which he seeks to explain life by sensibility. {BDF; RAT}

Hanotaux, Gabriel Albert Auguste (1853—1944)

A French historian and statesman, Hanotaux was Minister of Foreign Affairs (1894—1896 and 1896—1898). An officer of the Legion of Honor, he wrote of his agnosticism in the introduction to Despagnet's *La République et le Vatican* (1906). Hanotaux was a member of the Academy. {RE}

Hansberry, Lorraine (1930—1965)

A prominent African-American playwright, Hansberry wrote *A Raisin in the Sun* (1959), the first play on Broadway by a black woman. She also wrote *To Be Young, Gifted, and Black* (1969). Her antipathy toward religious nonsense, shown in *Hansberry's Drama: Commitment Amid Complexity* (1991), is similar to that of other secular humanists. A lesbian, she connected homophobia and antifeminism, according to the University of Michigan's Dorothy H. Lee, "calling for analyses of ethical questions implicit in the social and moral inequities produced by patriarchal culture." In "The Sign in Sidney Brustein's Window" (1964), she boldly addressed the artistic and sexual issues of a white homosexual artist. Immune to orthodoxy, whether it came from whites or blacks, Hansberry confronted then-Attorney General Robert Kennedy about racism as easily as she addressed issues of sexism and homophobia in the black community. {*The Advocate*, 19 August 1997; CE; GL}

Hansen, Harold (20th Century)

When he signed Humanist Manifesto II, Hansen was President of the Space Coast Chapter, American Humanist Association. {HM2}

Hansen, Peter (1936—)

Hansen is Vice President of the New Zealand Association of Rationalists and Humanists. From 1992 to 1995, he was secretary of the Humanist Society. Hansen has had over five hundred letters and articles printed in newspapers and journals in New Zealand and Australia.

Hanson, Richard Davies [Sir] (1805—1876)

Sir Richard was Chief Justice of South Australia. He wrote *On Law in Nature* (1865), *The Jews of History* (1869), and *St. Paul* (1875). Hanson was a freethinker. {BDF; JM; RAT; RE}

Hanson, Robert J. (20th Century)

A freethinker, Hanson wrote *Errors of the Bible* (1978). {GS}

Hansson, Sven O. (20th Century)

Hanssen is the secretary of *Vetenskap och Folkbildning* (Swedish Skeptics), Box 185, 101 23 Stockholm, Sweden.

HANUKKAH

Hanukkah is an eight-day Jewish Feast of Lights which commemorates the victory of the Jewish warrior Judah the Maccabee over the Syrian king Antiochus Epiphanes twenty-two centuries ago. The Talmud relates that there was enough oil to light the menorah, the candelabrum, for only one day. Yet it burned for eight, until fresh oil could be found. There being no organized skeptics' society at the time, disinterested individuals to determine factually the quantity of oil, believers had faith that a miracle had occurred.

HAPPINESS

Happiness for some may be sadness, or "not one's cup of tea," for others. Lord Russell, in *Bertrand Russell Speaks His Mind* (1969), listed four important features of happiness: "The first is health; the second, sufficient means to keep you from want; third, happy personal relations; and fourth, successful work. . . . Anything you're good at contributes to happiness." As to what does not bring happiness, he added, "One thing is worry; and that's one respect in which I've become much happier as I've grown older. I worry much less and I found a very useful plan in regard to worry, which is to think, 'Now what is the very worst thing that could happen?' . . . And then think, 'Well, after all, it wouldn't be so very bad a hundred years hence; it probably wouldn't matter."

Schopenhauer thought of happiness as a negative factor, the brief cessation of pain and misery, which are the constant. Others have had these ideas:

> • Happiness, n. An agreeable sensation arising from contemplating the misery of another.
>
> —**Ambrose Bierce**
>
> • Do not feel envious of the happiness of those who live in a fool's paradise, for only a fool will think that it is happiness.
>
> —**Bertrand Russell**
>
> • The only really happy folk are married women and single men.
>
> —**H. L. Mencken**
>
> • Happiness is not something you experience. It's something you remember.
>
> —Oscar Levant
>
> • Every man is thoroughly happy twice in his life: just after he has met his first love . . . and just after he has left his last one.
>
> —**H. L. Mencken**

(The relative merits of happiness are discussed by Richard B. Brandt in the *Encyclopedia of Philosophy*, Vol. 3. See entry for Stephen King concerning Albert Camus's view that happiness is inevitable.)

HAPPY HUMAN

A humanistic symbol called the Happy Human was created by Denis Barrington and used by the British Humanist Association and other groups. (See entry for Denis Barrington.)

HARASS

To harass was, originally, to set a dog onto a person, a most inhumane act. The connotation came to mean persistent irritating or tormenting, illustrated by threats from the landlord to pay the rent, from demands by delinquents that merchants give them merchandise, and in the 1990s by females complaining about inhumanistic treatment they received while in the military forces. In the latter example, one pundit suggests that at issue is not one word but two.

Harburg, E. Y. (1896—1981)

Lyricist, librettist, and author, Harburg wrote "Earl Carroll's Sketchbook" (1929), "Ziegfeld Follies" (1934), and "Bloomer Girl" (1944). He was co-librettist of "Finian's Rainbow" (1947), and he wrote lyrics for such films as "Wizard of Oz" (1937) and "Kismet" (1944). For "Over the Rainbow," he received an Oscar by the Academy of Motion Picture Arts and Sciences. Although Jewish, Harburg once wrote:

> Poems are made by fools like me,
> But only God can make a tree,
> And only God who makes the tree
> Also makes the fools like me.
> But only fools like me, you see,
> Can make a god, who makes a tree.

{PA}

Hardaker, William (19th Century)

Hardaker, a freethinker, edited *Old Thoughts for New Thinkers* (c. 1883). {GS}

Hardebeck, John W. (20th Century)

In the 1960s, Hardebeck was a vice president of the American Humanist Association.

Hardee, R. A. (19th Century)

Hardee, a Floridian industrial pioneer, was a captain in the Confederate Army. He helped organize the Liberals of Florida, and he was outspoken concerning his own freethought. {PUT}

Hardie, Glenn M. (20th Century)

Hardie is author of "Charles Bradlaugh—Freethinker" in *Humanist in Canada* (Summer, 1991). He is past president and long-time secretary of the British Columbia Humanist Association. In 1999, he and his wife, **Lorraine Hardie**, were presented with the first ever Distinguished Service Awards by the British Columbia Humanist Association.

Hardin, Garrett James (1915—)

The author of *The Tragedy of the Commons*, an eminent ecologist, Hardin received the 1989 Humanist Distinguished Service Award from the American Humanist Association. In 1988, he wrote *Promethean Ethics, Living With Death, Competition, and Triage*. {*Free Inquiry*, Summer, 1982; HNS2}

Hardin, Louis [Moondog] (1916-1999)

"He was the most famous street person of his time, a hero to a generation," according to *The New York Times* obituary. "The gaunt, blind musician known as Moondog, who was celebrated among New Yorkers for two decades as a mysterious and extravagantly garbed street performer," wrote Glenn Collins, "went on to win acclaim in Europe as an avant-garde composer, conducting orchestras before royalty."

No matter the weather, Moondog could often be seen from the late 1940s to the early 1970s standing in mid-Manhattan around 54th Street and the Avenue of the Americas. He dressed in a homemade robe, sandals, a flowing cape, and a horned Viking helmet, the tangible expression of what he referred to as his "Nordic philosophy." At his side he clutched a long spear of his own manufacture. Hardin had recorded jazz-accented compositions, usually for small wind and percussion ensembles. One, "All Is Loneliness," became a hit when recorded by Janis Joplin. He also wrote soundtrack music for "Drive, He Said," a 1972 movie with Jack Nicholson.

Hardin was celebrated by Beat Generation poets and late-1960s flower children. According to Collins, he wrote Bohemian broadsides against government regimentation, against the world monetary system, and against organized religion. {Glenn Collins, *The New York Times*, 12 September 1999; WAS, conversations}

Harding, T(homas) Swann (20th Century)

Harding was a freethinker who wrote "Why I Am a Skeptic" (1929) and *The Popular Practice of Fraud* (1935). {GS}

Harding, (President) Warren G. (1865—1923)

In a 1922 address, President Harding stated, "In the experiences of a year of the presidency, there has come to me no other such unwelcome impression as the manifest religious intolerance which exists among many of our citizens. I hold it to be a menace to the very liberties we boast and cherish." (TYD)

Hardman, Martha J. (20th Century)

At a 1994 conference of the American Humanist Association's Board, of which she is a member, Hardman spoke on "A Stroll Through the Sexist Structure of English." The meeting was held at Stanford University in California. Her E-mail address: <afn11122@freenet.ufl.edu>.

Hardwicke, Edward (19th Century)

For twelve years Hardwicke was Surgeon Superintendent of the Government Emigration Service. He was an agnostic of the school of Herbert Spencer, and he contributed to freethought and scientific periodicals. {BDF}

Hardwicke, Herbert Junius (Born 1850)

Hardwicke, brother of Edward, was the principal agent in establishing the Sheffield Public Hospital for Skin Diseases. He published *The Popular Faith* (1884) and *Evolution and Creation* (1887). He has contributed to the *Agnostic Annual*. {BDF}

Hardwicke, William W. (19th Century)

Under the pseudonym of M. D. Alatheia, Hardwicke wrote the *Rationalist Manual* (1897). {GS; RAT}

Hardy, Alister Clavering [Sir] (Born 1896)

Hardy, a Unitarian, was a marine biologist and researcher in religious experience. He wrote *The Open Sea* (195—). {U}

Hardy, Thomas (1752—1832)

Hardy was unsuccessfully tried for high treason for having organized the London Corresponding Society. That group, inspired by the French Revolution and Thomas Paine, demanded mankind suffrage, equal electoral districts, annual parliaments, and payment of Members of Parliament. {TRI}

Hardy, Thomas (1840—1928)

A pessimistic humanist deeply influenced by Schopenhauer, a non-theist (according to Robert Graves), and a determinist, Hardy looked upon man as a puppet of fate and the cosmos as "a viewless, voiceless Turner of the Wheel." Without Christian supernaturalism, in short, some still retain an outlook of defeatism regarding man's hopes and man's progress on earth. Hardy's novels show how indifferent nature joins with the narrow views of 19th-century humanity to bring human lives to disaster in a godless universe. His "Oxen" is a poetic statement of the loss which one realizes when he gives up the psychological comfort and social cohesiveness that had been possible in the Christian era, but the small hope Hardy offers is that in a rural setting man might possibly be able to live meaningfully, that if the native returns to his roots he will be shaped positively by the seasons and the local traditions; but Hardy's pessimism persists, realizing that those traditions are vanishing.

Hardy's *Tess of the D'Urbervilles* (1891) and *Jude the Obscure* (1896) are set against a forbidding Dorset landscape (called Wessex in the novels) whose physical harshness echoes that of an indifferent, if not malevolent, universe. In the former, he has a reference to the kinds of hell-fire preachers who left messages of doom and damnation painted on walls and gateposts in rural Britain. Some considered the latter book immoral, because it dealt with sexual relations at a time when novelists avoided such. The Return of the Native (1878) describes the inability of people to adapt to other parts of the world, and it introduces the element of chance—if an important note is slipped under the door, but slides under the rug and is not seen, an entire plot can turn on the accident. For Hardy, people's lives are ruled not only by nature and fate but also by Victorian social convention, which is in keeping with his reference to "a being who had rejected with indifference the attitude of sex for the loftier quality of abstract humanism."

According to Jim Herrick, editor of New Humanist, Hardy, "was an impassioned if bleak novelist who had a slight connection with the Rationalist Press Association." Martin Seymour-Smith's Hardy (1994) suggests that Hardy was attracted "to a form of gnosticism, associated with the Manichaean belief in the power of the principle of evil in the world. His reply to the well-meaning Rev. A. B. Grosart in February 1888 asking his view on the possibility of reconciling awareness of 'the horrors of human and animal life' emphasised by Darwinism with the belief in 'the absoluteness and non-limitation of God' is deadly" and is as follows:

> Mr Hardy regrets that he is unable to suggest any hypothesis which would reconcile the existence of such evils as Dr. Grosart describes with the idea of omnipotent goodness. Perhaps Dr. Grosart might be helped to a provisional view of the universe by the recently published Life of Darwin and the works of Herbert Spencer and other agnostics.

To the critic Peter Faulkner, that letter suggests a Hardy well on the way to humanism. Already, Hardy was the friend of rationalists Leslie Stephen and Edward Clodd. However, in 1899 Hardy turned down the invitation of the Rationalist Press Association that he should become an Honorary Associate, arguing that he preferred to remain detached, that belonging to a philosophic association could be mis-read as propagandizing whereas his intent was "to be simply artistic & delineative. While thanking you for the proposal I will therefore decline associationship for the present."

Faulkner notes that in 1920 Hardy was invited to have himself included in Joseph McCabe's *A Biographical Dictionary of Modern Rationalists*. Again, Hardy declined, on the grounds that he was "an irrationalist rather than a rationalist, on account of his inconsistencies . . . he thinks he could show that no man is a rationalist, and that human actions are not ruled by reason in the last resort." In short, Hardy wanted to avoid categorization. He regularly went to church but was not a Christian. "I dream of an alliance between religions freed from dogmas," he said. In the "Apology" to *Late Lyrics and Earlier*, he flirted with categorizations, stating that he believed in an "evolutionary meliorism," a kind of Stoicism. In *Christmas* (1924), he wrote

> "Peace on earth!" was said. We sing it
> And pay a million priests to bring it.
> After two thousand years of mass
> We've got as far as poison gas.

Faulkner differs from others by declaring that "Hardy, then, despite his antipathy to aspects of Christian dogma and his sceptical view of the Nature of God, was no humanist. Seymour-Smith's summing up is justified by all the evidence that he gives: 'He was an uneasy man whose emotionally religious heart was divided from his agnostic head. . . . Tom's intellect stood bravely aloof from inventing, yet could not help yearning for, a "proof" of the existence of a universe that was ultimately benign.' "

Critic Karl E. Meyer has pointed out a reason Hardy was known as such a brooding figure:

> He not only destroyed the "diabolical diaries" of his first wife, Emma, but also dictated his memoirs to his second wife, Florence. She published them as her own life of the novelist after his death in 1928, enabling Hardy to design his own posthumous pedestal. (Three years after Florence's demise, the bibliographer Richard Purdy finally revealed the truth in a 1940 lecture.)

Hardy was the first novelist buried at London's Westminster Abbey since Charles Dickens. His heart, however, which a surgeon had removed and stored in a cookie can, was buried in Dorset at a Stinsford churchyard. {CB; CE; CL; EU, Victor N. Paananen; Peter Faulkner, *New Humanist*, May 1994; Robert Graves, speaking at John Masefield's memorial, is in Corliss Lamont, *Remembering John Masefield*.; Karl E. Meyer, *The New York Times*, 7 February 1998;TRI; TYD}

Hare, Peter H. (20th Century)

Hare is professor of philosophy at the State University of New York at Buffalo, an authority on atheism and the problem of evil, and a contributing editor on *Philo*. At the opening of the Jo Ann and Don Boydston Library of Philosophical Naturalism in 1995, Hare read a paper describing the illustrious American naturalist tradition in philosophy. He signed Humanist Manifesto 2000. Hare edited *Naturalism and Rationality* (1986) and *Doing Philosophy Historically* (1988). (See entries for naturalism and Richard Rorty.)

Hargreaves, W.J.R. (19th Century)

In Toronto in the 1870s, Hargreaves started the *Freethought Journal*. The first freethought in Toronto was formed in 1873, and a Freethought Association formed in 1877 to campaign for the taxation of ecclesiastical property, secular education, the abolition of the judicial oath, and "a free Sunday." {RSR}

Häring, Bernard (1913-1998)

A Roman Catholic scholar, Häring influenced the sweeping modernization of Vatican II by emphasizing a moral theology of Christian love rather than the cataloguing of sins. For centuries, moral theology—the study of the morality of human actions—had concentrated on sin: the causes, characteristics, degrees, and consequences of the gamut of wrongdoing. Beginning with *The Law of Christ* (1954), he pioneered a much broader approach that became the standard in Catholic seminaries and universities. When Pope Paul VI issued "*Humanae Vitae*," the declaration forbidding Catholics to use birth control, Father Häring was one of the most prominent dissenters. Although investigated by church officials, he was not charged with any offenses. {*The New York Times*, 11 July 1998}

Harkins, Albert (20th Century)

Harkins was a liberal minister who supported the American Humanist Association.

Harkness, Gustavus (20th Century)

Harkness was freethinker who wrote, "The Hebrew Pentateuch Analyzed" (1935). {GS}

Harkness, Robert (20th Century)

With H. S. Bennett, the Australian freethinker Harkness wrote "Christianity Versus Rationalism, a Debate." (1922). {GS}

Harlow, Ralph Volney (1884—1956)
Harlow wrote *Samuel Adams* (1923) and *Gerrit Smith: Philanthropist and Reformer* (1939). {FUS}

Harlowe, Marie (20th Century)
Harlow was a freethinker who wrote *Pagan Holidays in Christianity* (1903). {GS}

Harman, Moses (1830—1910)
A Midwesterner who was born in Virginia, Harman changed from being a Methodist minister to becoming a Universalist. His beliefs in freethought, populism, and socialism are included in his journal, *Lucifer*, a free love journal edited with his wife Lillian in Valley Falls, Kansas. A selection from the work, along with his photo, is included in Whitehead and Muhrer's *Freethought on the American Frontier* (1992). Harman also wrote *The Persecution and the Appreciation* (c. 1910). {EU, William F. Ryan; FUS; GS; PUT}

Harman, Lillian (Born 1870)
In *Lucifer, the Light-Bearer* (28 June 1899), Harman laments the race prejudice and antagonism which she found "so cruelly manifested in the South. And it South. And it must be admitted that only in a lesser degree is the feeling cherished by many in the North. A man or woman in whose veins flows even an infinitesimal proportion of negro blood is 'only a nigger'; and as such is cursed for being 'low' and 'ignorant,' or, if in spite of disadvantages, he or she has acquired education and refinement this fact is resented. The negro is thought to be fit only to be the slave, the servant, of the white man. He is an upstart, an interloper, he 'doesn't know his place,' if he aspires to equality of opportunity with his white brother. 'Knock him down, and kick him for falling,' is a slang expression sometimes heard. And this seems to be the settled policy of the white man (as a race) in dealing with his dark-hued half brethren."

On the contrary, Harman insists, no race is a superior race. "For I agree with a dear Methodist aunt who used to say to me in explanation of the fact that her affection for me was unchanged by our difference of opinion religiously and socially, 'There's room in the world for all of us, if we don't stick our elbows out!' "

Gaylor described Harman as being a freethinker. {WWS}

Harmensen, Jacob: See entry for Jacobus Arminius, the name by which he is better known.

Harnack, Adolf (1851—1931)
Harnack wrote a critical work, *The Expansion of Christianity in the First Three Centuries* (1904).

Harnack, Bill (20th Century)
Harnack is cited by the Morains as being one helpful in maintaining the quality and accuracy of humanist publications. {HNS2}

Harnett, James Richard (20th Century)
Harnett wrote his 1958 Ph. D. dissertation on the Ethical Culture movement. {FUS}

Harney, George Julian (1817—1897)
Harney was a staunch rationalist and an ultra-radical Chartist, the editor of several liberal publication. {RAT; VI}

Harnsberger, Caroline Thomas (20th Century)
Harnsberger wrote *Mark Twain's Views of Religion* (1961) and *Mark Twain's Clara* (1982). {FUS}

Haro, Julio (1955—1992)
"Julio Haro died at the age of 37. He was a gay man in a macho country, an atheist in a land of Catholics, a rebel raised in a family of conformists, a reggae-roller in mariachi territory," wrote Rubén Martínez concerning the star of El Personal, a major Mexican musical group in Guadalajara. Before becoming the darling of many Mexican intellectuals and a performer admired by many Mexican youths, Haro designed furniture, did graphic designing (for a restaurant called Bananas, the owners of which were horrified by his phallic fruits), taught history classes at a Catholic high school, and was eventually fired for trying to organize a teacher's union. When El Personal played in Mexico City, Haro became famous for his performances, although at the time he was seriously sick with an AIDS-connected disease. While thousand of his fans raved about the song, "La Tapatía," right-wing Catholic groups were spray-painting "*Homosexuales = SIDA.*" Gay rights activists responded by rewriting it, "*Homosexuales = VIDA.*" Despite his family's Catholicism, they nursed him in his final days and were disappointed that he "made no final deed with God" when the end came. He died in his brother's arms, there was no funeral, just a quick cremation. {Rubén Martínez, "To Live and Die in Guadalajara," *The Village Voice*, 27 June 1995}

Harper, Frances Ellen Watkins (1825—1911)
An African American Unitarian spokeswoman, Harper wrote an epic poem, *Moses: A Story of the Nile* (1869), using biblical imagery to demonstrate contemporary issues of slavery and reconstruction. Her purpose was to show why it is important for Americans to put their faith into practice. *Iola Leroy* is considered the first published novel by an African American. Harper taught in college, helped the Underground Railroad shelter freed slaves, and spoke out on abolition and women's suffrage. In a 1992 commemoration of her efforts by Unitarians in Philadelphia, it was pointed out that in her time some succumbed to the period's extreme stereotypes and refused to believe Harper was African American and female, claiming she was actually a man or a white woman in disguise. The 1992 event included erecting a headstone at what had been her unmarked grave.

Harper, Robert A. (20th Century)
A contributing editor to *The Humanist* in the 1950s, Harper was from Michigan.

Harriot, Thomas (1560—1621)
Harriot was an English mathematician who accompanied Raleigh to Virginia and published an account of the expedition. Harriot was a deist. {BDF}

Harrington, Donald Szantho (1914—)
Harrington has been a Unitarian minister in Hobart, Indiana, Chicago, and Beverly Hills, California. He then became minister of Community (Unitarian) Church in New York City. A conservative in religion, he headed New York's Liberal Party beginning in 1966. He is married to Vilma Szantho, who had been a minister in Hungary and who once was told by Albert Schweitzer that he was a Unitarian. A past president of United World Federalists, Harrington is author of *Religion in an Age of Science* (1965).

Asked by the present author about humanism, Harrington "hit all bases":

> My humanism is both naturalistic and theistic. I think of myself as a humanist because I recognize the subjective limitations under which all men live. I cannot say, 'In the beginning, God.' I can only say, 'In the beginning, a man thinking comes to believe that God was at the beginning.' My thought concerning life's origin, purpose, and meaning will always be colored by my human powers and limitations. I am a humanist because I rejoice in the power and the glory of human existence. I enjoy the human enterprise in all its mystery, its struggle with inner and outer darknesses., its emerging understanding of itself and its universe, its ongoing efforts for self and social improvement. I am a humanist because my patriotism reaches beyond my own home or country to embrace mankind.

I am a naturalist because I believe the universe is one, not two. It is a *uni*-verse—one unified order of being, structured according to a harmony of laws and principles which the human mind, if dimly, can begin to perceive and describe. This is one, natural universe we inhabit, and we come to understanding of it through the natural powers we have evolved of observation, reasoning, and intuition. We men are an integral part of its ongoing, natural processes, not separate and apart. We are not strangers here, but at home, both in time and eternity.

I am a theist because I believe that this natural, universal process, of which our human lives are an integral part, has some ultimate meaning and purpose. This I cannot now discern clearly, though I may find clues which seem to indicate a growing integration, an evolving cooperative relationship of all life processes, an increasing harmony of part with part. Yet, though I cannot prove that life has meaning, I believe it has. I have only two alternatives when I cannot prove a thing. I can say, Life has meaning. Or I can say, Life has no meaning. To say and believe that life has no meaning seems to be destructive of human and other values. To say and believe that life has meaning seems to enhance and encourage human and other values. Furthermore, such order as the universe displays, when seen in human experience, implies an integral intelligence. I choose to believe that there is intelligence, meaning, and purpose in this Larger Universal Life of which we are a part. Thus, I believe in God.

(See entry for John Dewey, at whose memorial service Harrington officiated.) {WAS, 26 July 1956}

Harrington, George (20th Century)

With others, Harrington wrote "The Truth About American Preachers" (1928). {GS}

Harrington, (Edward) Michael (1928—1989)

Harrington, an author, edited *Catholic Worker* (1951—1952) and *New Age* (19061—1962). He was a member of the national executive committee of the Socialist Party from 1960 to 1972 and was its national chairman from 1968 to 1972. In 1973 he became chairman of the Democratic Socialist Organizing Committee. He wrote *The Other America* (1963), *Toward a Democratic Left* (1968), and *Fragments of the Century* (1974). In *The Politics at God's Funeral* (1983), he declared, "I left the Catholic Church almost thirty years ago. It is relevant to my present attitudes that even though I rejected the Church . . . I clearly remain a 'cultural Catholic,' much as an atheist Jew is culturally Jewish. . . . To complicate matters further, I consider myself to be—in Max Weber's phrase—'religiously musical' even though I do not believe in God. . . . I am, then, what Georg Simmel called a 'religious nature without religion,' a pious man of deep faith, but not in the supernatural." {TYD}

Harriot, Thomas (1560—1621)

Harriot was a mathematician, a tutor to Sir Walter Raleigh. He accompanied Sir R. Grenville's expedition to Virginia in 1581. Harriot made many discoveries, and, according to McCabe, "was little behind Galileo in the use of the telescope." A deist, Harriot "cast off the Old Testament." {RAT}

Harris, Ben (20th Century)

Harris wrote *Human Gods* (1938). {FUS}

Harris, Beverly (20th Century)

Harris, who was a plaintiff in an Idaho lawsuit challenging commencement prayers in schools, received the 1995 Freethinker of the Year award at the annual Freedom From Religion Foundation convention. As a high school student who with her mother filed a lawsuit challenging commencement prayers, she and her family were publicly ostracized, their lives threatened, their cats were killed, her younger brothers were beat up, and their car tires were slashed. "Even knowing everything that I know now," she later observed, "I would do it all over again."

Harris, Frank (1856—1931)

Harris, a freethinker, was editor of *Contemporary Review*. {GS}

Harris, John (17th Century)

Harris, an early freethinker, wrote "A Refutation of the Objections Against and the Attributes of God in General" (1698). {GS}

Harris, Larry Wayne (20th Century)

Harris, author of a self-published work titled *Bacteriological Warfare: A Major Threat to North America*, is a follower of Christian Identity, the religious view that holds that Jews are the "children of Satan" and minorities are "mud people" who are not really human. In 1995 he pleaded guilty to mail fraud when Federal authorities charged he falsely stated that a laboratory had authorized him to purchase freeze-dried bubonic plague bacteria, which had been sent to his home. In 1997 he urged followers of the Third Continental Congress in Grandview, Kansas, to prepare for biological warfare and obtain antidotes to anthrax. In 1998 he was arrested and charged with the actual making of anthrax.

Harris, Leonard (20th Century)

Harris, a professor of philosophy at Purdue University, West Lafayette, Indiana, is an Advisory Board Member of African Americans for Humanism.

Harris, Michael (20th Century)

Harris, author of *Unholy Orders: Tragedy at Mount Cashel* (1990), is a leading Canadian journalist. His book describes the pattern of physical and sexual abuse at a religious orphanage, and he covers the decades through the administrations of several priests, brothers, and bishops in which adults both in and out of the church took sexual advantage of children. When several brothers were exposed for having committed sexual and physical abuse at Mount Cashel Orphanage, the police investigation was aborted and the social service inquiry was stifled. For years the church remained a law unto itself. Harris's book was the basis for a movie, "The Boys of St. Vincent" (1990), which received wide notoriety.

Harris, Richard (20th Century)

With Sidney Brichto, Harris edited a symposium, *Two Cheers for Secularism* (1998). The thirteen essays are by "believers, half-believers and non-believers" of Christian, Jewish, and Muslim backgrounds. According to Nicolas Walter, the religious contributions "are the most misleading (secularism inevitably seen as insufficient, and Nazism and Communism predictably seen as examples of secularism), and the Muslim ones are particularly disappointing, but some of the semi-religious ones are interesting and all the non-religious ones (by Frederic Raphael, Karen Armstrong, and John Mortimer) are stimulating." {*New Humanist*, October 1998}

Harris, Wendell J. (20th Century)

Harris in 1996 became President of the Humanist Quest of Milwaukee in Wisconsin. {*Freethought Observer*, November-December 1996}

Harrison, Alex (19th Century)

Harrison, a freethinker, wrote *Problems of Christianity and Skepticism* (1892). {FUK; GS}

Harrison, Austin (1873—1928)

Harrison, son of Frederic Harrison, was an editor of the *English Review*. A rationalist, he preferred Nietzsche to Comte. {RAT; RE}

Harrison, Frederic (1831—1928)

Harrison was an English positivist and member of the Metaphysical Society. He wrote *The Meaning of History* and *The Choice of Books*, and he translated the second volume of Comte's *Positive Polity*. A stylist and a man of letters, Harrison was one of the founders of the positivist school. His views on religion, from the positivist standpoint, are found in his *Creed of a Layman* (1905) and *The Positive Evolution of Religion* (1912). {BDF; FUK; RAT; RE}

Harrison, G. T. (20th Century)

Harrison wrote *Mormonism: Now and Then* (1961).

Harrison, Harry (20th Century)

Harrison, a writer of science fiction, has gone on record as being a non-theist. In his short story, "The Streets of Ashkelon," in *Two*

Tales and Eight Tomorrows, he relates how the only human living on a planet—one inhabited by curious, evolving, quite intelligent amphibians—teaches them science and logic. Then a ship lands and a spoiler missionary arrives to convert them all to Christianity. Harrison has complained that it is difficult to get atheistic stories published. {E}

Harrison, Hubert A. (1882—1927)

A noted African American intellect in his time, Harrison wrote for *The Call*, *The Truth Seeker*, *The Modern Quarterly*, *The Nation*, *The New Republic*, and other publications. An adjunct professor of comparative religion at the Modern School (later located at Stelton, New Jersey), he found much in Marx, Buckle, Spencer, Nietzsche, Schopenhauer, Lenin, Bertrand Russell, Dewey, and others to support his own ideas. As founder of the Liberty League and its newspaper, *The Voice*, Harrison soon learned that his views on religion and birth control were opposed by Catholics and Protestants alike. He greatly influenced Marcus Garvey as well as the Messenger Group headed by A. Philip Randolph and Chandler Owen. J. A. Rogers reports that once H. L. Mencken asked to meet Harrison, after which Harrison "was the center of the most serious discussion of the evening; for Theodore Dreiser, Heywood Broun, Ludwig Lewisohn, Charles Hansen Towne came over for the pleasure of talking with the distinguished Negro." Harrison, one of the intellectuals of the Harlem Renaissance, was editor of *The Masses* for four years and a member of the controversial International Workers of the World (the "Wobblies"). If he had to go to a Heaven that operated under the Jim Crow system, Harrison reasoned, he would prefer to go to the place ruled over by the only spiritual creature ever depicted as non-white: Satan. {J. A. Rogers, AAH}

Harrison, Jane Ellen (1850—1928)

Harrison was a lecturer on archaeology at Cambridge University and wrote important works on Greek religion, especially *Prolegomena to the Study of Greek Religion* (1912). Her rationalist attitude is expressed in her 1919 Conway Memorial Lecture: "The old orthodoxy is dead and may well be buried." She admitted an Immanent God who is "nothing but the mystery of the whole of things." Harrison was an honorary associate of the Rationalist Press Association. {RE}

Harrison, John F. C. (20th Century)

Harrison wrote *Quest for the New Moral World: Robert Owen and the Owenites in Britain and America* (1969). {GS}

Harrison, Charles Yale (1898—1954)

Harrison wrote *Clarence Darrow* (1931) and *Generals Die in Bed* (1954), the latter work about World War I. {FUS}

Harrison, Lilian (20th Century)

Harrison, an Australian humanist interested in Esperanto, is involved in Australian humanist activities.

Harrison, Lou (1917—)

A composer and member of the American Academy of Arts and Letters, Harrison was a student of Henry Cowell and Arnold Schoenberg. Also, he was music critic of the *New York Herald Tribune*. Harrison has taught at San Jose State University in California and at the East-West Center of the University of Hawaii.

On the subject of humanism he wrote to the present author:

> I have been called a "card carrying humanist" for a number of years and in ways possible to me have tried to aid the movement. As to my position in the sequence which is presented, the seven categories, I am unsure. However, I am personally certain, like my father before me, that "when you're dead you're dead," and simply turned off—all systems down. I have studied at some length and intensity what remains of Epicurus (and even given a short lecture on his ideas to a local humanist group) as well as Lucretius.
>
> I have also seriously studied congenial forms of Buddhism, and especially the presentation of basic material in A. J. Bahm's remarkable book, *The Philosophy of the Buddha*. Both Epicurus' Ataraxia and the Buddhist Nirvana seem to me to be conditions of equanimity in which one is fully "with it" all the time and can no longer be "shook up." Such a personal condition would be enormously difficult to achieve and I'm not sure that I'd want to, or could. Socially I am continually shocked by our human cruelty—it seems to have no limits and indeed seems a fundamental part of our kind, alas.
>
> I am enormously opposed to organized religion and feel that the Christians and Muslims are responsible for uncountable human and other beings' miseries. I continuously read in such science journals as I am able as a layman to understand. With the poet Lawrence Ferlinghetti I am for the dismantling of the Industrial Revolution, which I believe to be humankind's worst and probably last mistake. As humans we have lots of dirty habits, but I think that the filthiest of all is politics. I grew up in the "liberal thirties' and have lived in dismay during these last two administrations. Surely goodwill and overt love could be enlisted to temper the human suicidal drift. Anyway, I keep contributing as I'm able, and with the determination to do so as honestly and sharply as possible.

In 1992, Harrison's openly gay *Joys and Perplexities, Selected Poems of Lou Harrison* was published. In 1997, Harrison was named the American Humanist Association's Humanist Arts Awardee. He and William Colvig, a contractor and member of an electricians' union, have lived together in Aptos, California, since 1967.

In a biography, *Lou Harrison: Composing a World* (1998) by Leta E. Miller and Fredric Liebermann, Harrison's visits to composer Henry Cowell are described. Cowell, who went to jail for four years on a morals charge of homosexuality, was visited regularly by Harrison, who ferried musical scores back and forth. {HNS2; WAS, 11 Sep 1992}

Harrison, Paul W. (20th Century)

An activist Unitarian, Harrison lives in Finland. His e-mail: <inter.orfex@pp.weppi.fi>.

Harrison, Stanley R. (20th Century)

Harrison wrote a biography of Edgar Fawcett (1972). {FUS}

Harrison, Tony (20th Century)

Harrison, an English poet and dramatist, became an Honorary Associate of the Rationalist Press Association in 1995. He is author of *The Shadow of Hiroshima and Other Film/Poems* (1995), which includes the television poem he produced for the fiftieth anniversary of the Hiroshima atom bomb.

Hart, James H. (20th Century)

James in 1933 wrote "A Religious Mood" in *The New Humanist.*

Hart, William (19th Century)

A freethinker, Hart wrote *The Candle From Under the Bushel, or 1306 Questions to the Clergy and for the Consideration of Others* (1889). {GS}

Harte, (Frances) Bret (1836—1902)

The son of a Catholic professor and an adventurer at the age of nineteen, Harte went to California where he taught, clerked, and prospected for gold. His "The Luck of Roaring Camp," published in *The Overland Monthly*, which he had helped establish, brought him much success because of its stories of Western local color. His humorous dialect poem, "Plain Language from Truthful James" (also called "The Heathen Chinee"), helped establish him as a well-known author. He wrote "Outcasts of Poker Flat" and other stories, returning to the East in 1871, becoming the U.S. consul in Germany and Scotland from 1878 to 1885.

A Unitarian, he once was a correspondent for their *Register*, reporting about a traveling evangelist's visit in California, "We have been spared the cholera, but we have had Mr. Earle badly." He attended the church where his friend Starr King preached, and he also attended in New York where O. B. Frothingham preached. According to his biographer, Pemberton, Harte "was content to worship God through his works. . . . [He] never voiced a creed." As to any god, Harte once declared, "The creator who could put a cancer in a believer's stomach is above being interfered with by prayers." {CE; JM; RAT; RE; TYD; U; UU}

Hartikainen, Errikki (20th Century)

Hartikainen was secretary general of the Union of Freethinkers' Associations of Finland. (See entry for Scandinavian Unbelievers.)

Hartin, Deborah (20th Century)

Hartin in 1972 was on the advisory board of the Humanist Society of Greater New York. A transsexual who in 1970 had undergone male-to-female surgery, she fought for the rights of those who had sex change operations.

Hartland, Edwin Sidney (1848—1927)

Hartland, an anthropologist, wrote about comparative religion in *Legend of Perseus* (1894—1896, 3 vols.). The President in 1899 of the Folk-Lore Society, Hartland was an agnostic and an honorary associate of the Rationalist Press Association. {RAT}

Hartley, Nina (20th Century)

An actress in adult films, Hartley according to a profile written by Luke Ford entitled "Porn Jews," said

> I believe strongly in the heritage of Jews as educators. I feel very proud of the fact that if it weren't for the Jews, half the world would still be illiterate. I would like to know about Jewish religion as history, but as an atheist I see no reason to practice any religion . . . because it is organized superstiation . . . the opiate of the masses. . . . No, I don't believe in God. I was raised with no religion but a lot of morals. I definitely think that sex is natural and healthy, and that people have the absolute right to pursue their sexual preferences with other consenting adults without government or church intervention.

{CA}

Hartman, Franz (19th Century)

A freethinker, Hartman wrote *The Life of Jehoshua, the Prophet of Nazareth* (1889). {GS}

Hartman, Gunde (20th Century)

Hartman heads a Unitarian conference center at Klingberg near Hamburg. (See entry for German Unitarians.)

Hartmann, Jacob (19th Century)

Hartman was a freethinker who wrote *The Creation of God* (1893). {GS}

Hartmann, Karl Robert Eduard von (1842—1906)

Hartmann was a German pantheist, a pessimist in philosophy. He published *Philosophy of the Unconscious* (1869), *Self-Dissolution of Christianity and the Religion of the Future* (1875), and *The Crisis of Christianity in Modern Theology* (1870). Hartmann emphatically rejected belief in a personal God and immortality. {BDF; RAT; RE}

Hartmann, Klaus (1925—)

Hartmann is German Vice-President of the World Union of Freethinkers.

Hartogh Heys Van Zouteveen, Herman (Born 1841)

Hartogh, who in 1866 received a gold medal from the king of Holland for a treatise on the synthesis of organic bodies, was for some time professor of chemistry and natural history at The Hague. He lived at Delft, where he was made city councilor. He translated into Dutch Darwin's *Descent of Man* and *Expressions of the Emotions*, adding his own annotations. Although named a member of the Assen city council, he could not take his seat in 1873 because he refused the oath. Dr. Hartogh was director of the Provincial Archaeological Museum at Assen and a member of the Dutch Literary Society. For a long time, he was a member of the Dutch Freethinkers' Society. {BDF; RAT}

Hartshorn, Nathan (20th Century)

Hartshorn, while a member of the Doubters' Club at Amherst College in Massachusetts, was one of the founding members of Campus Freethought Alliance. {*International Humanist News*, December 1996}

Hartshorne, Charles (1897)

An instructor in philosophy and then research fellow at Harvard, Hartshorne later taught philosophy at the University of Chicago, Emory University, and the University of Texas. Those who knew him well knew of his intense interest in birdsong, for he was an ornithologist.

Said to be one of the most influential students in our day of Alfred North Whitehead and a leader of the school of process philosophy, he also was a force in the rising philosophical stature of Charles Sanders Peirce. Hartshorne's idea of "God" flows from two basic premises of process philosophy as most systematically elaborated by Whitehead: a conception of the universe in terms of becoming rather than being, and an insistence on the social nature of every aspect of reality. In process philosophy, God is a participant in cosmic evolution. As Hartshorne rendered his idea of God, it is one of religious value as well as philosophical consistency, one summarized by philosopher Peter H. Hare as "a temporal society of experiential occasions."

His *Beyond Humanism: Essays in the New Philosophy of Nature* (1937) envisioned a new philosophic movement, one that would progress and be a "genuine integration (for the first time) of all the modern motifs" of humanism, one for which a specific name, not humanism, would eventually arise. He also wrote *The Divine Relativity: A Social Conception of God* (1948) and *Omnipotence and Other Theological Mistakes* (1984).

Asked by the present author in 1946 to comment on the word "panentheism," Hartshorne wrote:

> It's too bad that I can't recall where it was that I learned the word panentheism. I didn't coin it, and for a good while after I first heard it I was accustomed to think it a rather foolish thing. But the more I thought about the problem of theism and pantheism the more I came to think a third term was needed, and "all *in* God" does seem to suggest that God is more than a mere totality of ordinary things, which would be compatible with "all *is* God." So I began using it.
>
> Since then I read somewhere about a use of the word going back a good while and wondered if that wasn't the earliest, but now I forget the reference. V. Ferm has a definition in the *Dictionary of Philosophy*, but it is less definite than I think one needs to be. And he doesn't go into the history of the thing at all.

(In Hartshorne's 1946 metaphysics class at the University of Chicago, the present author was nonplused by the elaborateness of Professor Hartshorne's professing. At the nearby Unitarian society that he attended,

Hartshorne was invited to speak to students interested in humanism, naturalism, or John Dewey, which he declined to do. Meanwhile, it was difficult to bring up anything but metaphysics in class. On the final day, when he asked the class to extrapolate as to the possible benefit metaphysics would be in our future, several students were exuberant and particularly praised his explanation of the difference between pantheism and panentheism. When it came the present writer's turn, I simply replied, "None." He laughed in the friendliest fashion, along with the class, knowing previously of my interest in naturalism. What I had not revealed to him, however, was my ignorance in being unable to follow his line of reasoning. Somehow I felt this was a personal deficiency upon my part and concluded that philosophy was not to be a part of my future, whereupon I switched my major from philosophy to literature, not even knowing at that time that there was a school of logical positivists who, like me, denied the validity of metaphysical assertions. Pantheism, however, has remained an interest, for which Hartshorne gets all the credit, although it still remains something of a mystery how any person as superior in intelligence as Dr. Hartshorne could possibly have chosen to spend his entire lifetime developing such metaphysical minutiae, i.e., panentheism, with such apparent relish. He likely viewed those with a converse view in similar fashion.)

(Marcus Borg of Oregon State University claims he is a panentheist, one who believes that everything is *in* God, that he is not a pantheist who believes that everything *is* God. Borg is an Episcopalian. As for Hartshorne's inability to recall where he learned the word "pantheism," see the entry for Karl Krause, who used the word in the 1830s.) {ER; OCP; U&U; WAS, 29 December 1946}

Hartt, Julian (20th Century)

With J. A. C. F. Auer, Hartt published *Humanism versus Theism* (1941). The two preferred a term other than "humanism" but held that some descriptive word for their forward-looking Unitarian views would eventually be found.

Hartung, John (20th Century)

Hartung, in "Love Thy Neighbor" (*Skeptic*, Vol. 3, No. 4, 1995), describes how the world's major religions espouse a moral code which includes injunctions against murder, theft, and lying. However, he holds that the rules codified by the Ten Commandments were intended to apply only within a cooperating group for the purpose of enabling that group to compete successfully against other groups. Also, this in-group morality has functioned, both historically and by express intent, to create adverse circumstances between groups by actively promoting murder, theft, and lying as tools of competition. A non-believer, Hartung has riled many by stating that contemporary efforts to present Judeo-Christian in-group morality as universal morality defy the plain meaning of the texts upon which Judaism and Christianity are based. Accordingly, he holds, this effort is ultimately hopeless. (See entry for Women, Genital Maiming Of.)

HARVARD CHAPLAINCY

Harvard University was one of the first universities to install a humanist chaplain. The chaplaincy was created to celebrate "humanity in its earthly and evolutionary context. Its main appeal is to the skeptical inquirer and to the idealistic student of an agnostic or atheist inclination. It is for those who prize the scientific, aesthetic, ethical, and democratic achievements of human beings, past and present. A Humanist rejoices in differences and variety, is comfortable with ambiguity, and values deed before creed." Thomas Ferrick, a signer of Humanist Manifesto II, is the current humanist chaplain. The chaplaincy also supports the Free Thought Society, which was founded by Harvard-Radcliffe undergraduates. (See entry for John Loeb.)

HARVARD DIVINITY SCHOOL

The Harvard Divinity School, which has a long-standing history with the Unitarian movement, is at 45 Francis Avenue, Cambridge, Massachusetts 02138. On the Web: <http://divweb.harvard.edu>.

HARVARD SECULAR SOCIETY

The Harvard Secular Society is on the Web: <http://www.secularhumanism.org/cfa/orgs.html>.

HARVARD UNIVERSITY

Harvard College, the oldest in the United States, was founded for men in 1636 and in 1638 was named for John Harvard, its first benefactor. Intended as a training ground for Puritan ministers, it expanded greatly and became much more generalized.

In 1819 the Harvard Corporation specifically recognized a "Faculty of Theology," and by 1826 fund-raising efforts were underway to build Divinity Hall. Congregationalists were much concerned that Unitarians would become influential in the school, and their fears were justified. During the ensuing controversy between the two groups, conservatives vs. liberals, William Ellery Channing was instrumental in leading the latter group. Congregationalists were soon to feel more at home at Yale. A Unitarian, Charles W. Eliot, was President of Harvard from 1869 to 1908, during which time the elective system was introduced and graduate education was developed.

Innumerable freethinkers, rationalists, and secular humanists have been faculty members not only of the university but also of the Divinity School. In 1996, however, Ronald F. Thiemann, the Divinity School's dean, wrote *Religion in Public Life*, in which he starts with the writings of John Rawls, then builds on thinkers such as Michael Sandel, Michael Walzer, Charles Taylor, and Jean Bethke Eishtain to propose what *Commonweal* editor has called "a revised liberalism that will allow religious views and voices equal legitimacy in public debate. . . . Strict separation of church and state, he points out, was a notion that came into common constitutional usage only in a 1947 Supreme Court opinion. Today it is used by many, on the bench and off, to say not only that state support for religion is unconstitutional but that religion itself has no legitimate place in public institutions." That a dean of the Divinity School would express such a stand is a sign of the immense change that has occurred at Harvard. {CE; *The New York Times Book Review*, 14 July 1996}

Harvey, John (19th Century)

A freethinker, Harvey wrote "One Shaft More" (1885). {GS}

Harvey, Van (1926—)

A professor emeritus of religion at Stanford, Harvey is on the Council for Secular Humanism's Committee for the Scientific Examination of Religion. He is author of "The Re-Discovery of Ludwig Feuerbach." Harvey is an authority on Ludwig Feuerbach. (*Free Inquiry*, Winter 1996-1997).

Harwood, Philip (1809—1887)

Harwood, a journalist, decided against Presbyterianism and chose Unitarianism, but his rejection of the miraculous stirred the Unitarians, so he became assistant to Fox at South Place Chapel in 1841. Harwood was an editor of various English journals, including *Saturday Review* (1868—1883). {RAT}

Harwood, William R. (20th Century)

Harwood has researched Yahweh and Jesus, tracing the beginning of the "god" concept through the Judaism of the first century to the monotheistic beginnings of Christianity and its emergence as a three-god creed in 325 of the Christian Era. In *Mythology's Last Gods*, Harwood contends that every teaching attributed to Jesus can be traced to a pre-Christian source. The chapter concerning St. Paul's fanciful misinterpretation of Jesus for his own ends, is entitled, "The Making of a God." Some critics, who hold that Jesus never existed, disagree with Harwood's view that Abraham is the first historical personality in the Bible. "If other scholars are doubtful about the historicity of later figures such as Moses, Joseph, David, and Solomon, not to mention Jesus," writes New Zealander rationalist Bill Cooke, "it is highly unlikely that Abraham is any more historically based. Harwood reviews books for *The American Rationalist*. {*Humanist in Canada*, Spring 1997}

Hasanat, Abul (20th Century)

When he signed Humanist Manifesto II, Hasanat was secretary of the Bangladesh Humanist Society. An East Pakistani (now called

Bangladesh), Hasanot addressed the Fourth International Humanist and Ethical Union Congress held in Paris (1966). {HM2}

Haseler, Stephen (1942—)

Haseler is professor of government at the London Guildhall University. He is chairman of Republic, a pressure group campaigning for the abolition of the hereditary principle in the selection of a Head of State and the Second Chamber.

A believer in disestablishmentarianism, Haseler is author of *The End of the House of Windsor* (1993), and he believes the humanist movement needs to take a leading part in the highlighting of the age-old connections and the need for their reform. {*The Freethinker*, May 1994}

HASIDIC JEWS: See entry for Cabala.

Haskins, Casey (20th Century)

With David I. Seiple, Haskins edited *Dewey Reconfigured: Essays on Deweyan Pragmatism* (1999). He is Associate Professor of Philosophy at Purchase College, State University of New York.

Haskins, Ethelbert (20th Century)

When he signed Humanist Manifesto II, Haskins was a director of the American Humanist Association. He currently is its treasurer. The Morains credit him as having "opened new understanding of how the crises in Afro-American leadership could be constructively resolved." {HM2; HNS2}

Haslam, Charles Junius (1811—1902)

Henry Hetherington in 1840 was tried for blasphemous libel for having published Haslam's *Letters to the Clergy of All Denominations Showing the Errors, Absurdities, and Irregularities of Their Doctrines* (c. 1850). This was an anti-Christian penny weekly that exposed scriptural contradictions and called for a Christianity devoid of common prayer, ritual, immortality, and superstition. {EU, John W. Wiener; FUK; RAT; VI}

Haslam, Fred (1833—1898)

Haslam from 1851 until his death worked on behalf of the goals of London's National Secular Society. In 1866 he helped break down Hyde Park railings, and he was a member of the International as well as a freethinker. A mattress-maker by trade, Haslam was badly paid as a result of female labor in his trade, and he took to lecturing to supplement his income. {RSR}

Hasquin, Hervé (1942—)

A Belgian, Hasquin addressed the International Humanist and Ethical Union's (IHEU's) Second Moral Education Conference held in Brussels (1985). He edited *Études sur le XVIII siecle* (1974).

Hassell, Richard (Died 1826)

Hassell was one of Carlile's shipmen. He was sentenced to two years of imprisonment in Newgate for selling Paine's *Age of Reason*. {BDF}

Hasson, Isaac (1915—)

In 1976, Hasson founded the Israel Secular Humanist Association, which produces a Hebrew periodical, *Breira Humanistit* and an English version, *Israel Humanist Alternative*. An atheist, Hasson in 1985 was a founding member of Israel's Secular Service Association.

Haste, Helen (20th Century)

Haste is professor of psychology at the University of Bath. She has stated, "The assumption of a Christian culture, nowadays being ratified, it seems, by Government thinking, is that the foundation of morality is religion: if you are not religious you cannot be moral. That is a very dangerous logic."

In Birmingham, England, at the centenary conference of the Rationalist Press Association in 1999, she entitled her lecture, "Are We Irrationally Frightened of the Irrational?" (*New Humanist*, May 1989).

Hastie, Jack (20th Century)

Hastie has written that nearly all prayer "contains metaphysical statements referring to phenomena which can never be confronted by observable facts and therefore either verified or falsified." As a result, freethinkers question the use of such words as "bless," "sin," "Satan," "merciful," "holy," or expressions such as "Lord Jesus, may my roots go down deep in you" or "God is the world's horizon." {*The Freethinker*, November-December 1998}

Hastings, George Tracy (Born 1875)

Hastings, a freethinker, wrote *Love, Evolution, and Religion* (1924). {GS}

HATE: For an example of one who unapologectically preaches hate, see entry for Khallid Abdul Muhammad.

HATRED

- Hatred, n. A sentiment appropriate to the occasion of another's superiority.

—**Ambrose Bierce**
The Devil's Dictionary

- One million Arabs are not worth a Jewish fingernail.

—Rabbi Yaacov Perrin in a funeral eulogy for Dr. Baruch Goldstein

Hattem, Pontiaam van (1641—1706)

A Dutch writer, Hattem was a follower of Spinoza, was inclined to pantheistic mysticism, and had several followers.

Haubelt, Josef (20th Century)

Haubelt in 1995 spoke at a Berlin conference arranged by the International Humanist and Ethical Union (IHEU). He stated that 56% of the population of the Czech Republic is non-denominational, and he reported that Czech humanists are diligent in their campaign for human rights. He wrote *Mikulas Kopernik* (1974). (See entry for Czechoslovakian Humanists.)

Haught, James A. (20th Century)

An associate editor of the *Charleston Gazette* and a senior editor of *Free Inquiry*, Haught in 1989 won the Hugh L. Hefner First Amendment Award for his articles in defense of the separation of church and state. In *Holy Horrors, an Illustrated History of Religious Murder and Madness* (1990), he gives examples of religious persecution during the Crusades; the Spanish Inquisition; witch hunts; human sacrifice of the Aztec civilization; the Holocaust; the mass suicide of Jonestown, etc. He believes his book is the first to survey "the phenomenon of religious homicide in its entirety." *Holy Hatred: Religious Conflicts of the '90s* (1995) demonstrates how religion often divides people and breeds hostility. Haught writes that religion—supposedly a source of kindness and brotherhood—has become one of the chief causes of hatred and war. As a result, he holds that "more voices [are] beginning to assert that religion can be a detriment to humanity. He also wrote *The Art of Lovemaking* (1992) and *Holy Hatred: Religious Conflicts of the '90s* (1997).

Haught's 1996 work, *2000 Years of Disbelief*, is a collection of individuals' statements concerning their disbelief. Haught signed Humanist Manifesto 2000. {CA; E; *Freethought Today*, June-July 1996}

Hauptli, Bruce W. (20th Century)

Hauptli is chairperson and associate professor of philosophy,

Department of Philosophy and Religion, Florida International University. His *The Reasonableness of Reason: Explaining Rationality Naturalistically* (1998) makes the point that naturalized epistemology can explain the reasonableness of a rationalist commitment.

Hauptman, Herbert Aaron (1917—)

Hauptman was co-recipient of the Nobel Prize in chemistry (1985). He is a professor of biophysical science at the State University of New York at Buffalo. Upon receiving the Humanist Laureate award, according to presenter Paul Kurtz, Hauptman gave "a very gloomy analysis of the critical issues confronting us in the next century, such as the abuse of power by strong nation states, racism and religious bigotry, the arms race, inequalities between the rich and the poor, and the violation of human rights." A member of the Council for Secular Humanism's International Academy of Humanism, he is author with Jerome Karle of *Solution of the Phase Problem* (1953), and he wrote *Crystal Structure Determination* (1972). Hauptman addressed the Tenth International Humanist and Ethical Union (IHEU) World Congress held in Buffalo (1988), he spoke at the 1995 dedication of the Center for Inquiry in Amherst, New York, and he signed Humanist Manifesto 2000. Hauptman's hobbies include hiking, swimming, and stained glass art.

Hauptmann, Gerhart (1862—1946)

A German dramatist, novelist, and poet, Hauptmann in his play "Before Dawn," showed the influence of the theories of Zola and Ibsen, inaugurating the naturalistic movement in German theater. In 1912 he won the Nobel Prize in Literature. McCabe finds he was somewhat mystic in his later years "but remained at the most a pantheist." {JM; RAT; RE}

Hauréau, Jean Barthelemy (1812—1896)

Hauréau was a French historian. At the age of twenty he wrote *The Mountain*, which showed his sympathy with the Revolution. In turn a journalist and a librarian, he wrote *Manual of the Clergy* (1844), which resulted in attacks by the clericals, and an erudite work, *Critical Examination of the Scholastic Philosophy* (1850). {BDF}

Hauser, Richard (1911—)

Hauser founded the Institute for Group and Social Development, which became the English Centre for Group Studies. {TRI}

Haüy, Valentine (1745—1822)

Haüy was a French philanthropist, one of the founders of theophilantropy. He helped enable the blind to read and founded the institute for the young blind in 1784. In 1807 Haüy went to Russia, staying until 1817 and devoting himself to the blind and to telegraphy. {BDF; RAT}

Havel, Václav (1936—)

Havel is a dramatist who has been President of the former country of Czechoslovakia, then President of the Czech Republic. He has stated that he is not "a proper Christian or Catholic" and he sees no point in worshipping God. But he is "conscious of a 'horizon,' an 'intimate-universal' partner of mine—who is sometimes my conscience, sometimes my hope, sometimes my freedom and sometimes the mystery of the world." He adds, "the salvation of this human world lies nowhere else than in the human heart, in the human power to reflect, in human responsibility." In his *Letters to Olga*, he mentions "my general faith in the meaning of things, in my hope."

Inspired by Heidegger and overlooking his having been a Nazi, Havel speaks of the universe as a living being. He laments that mankind sees the universe differently, sees it as something subservient. He talks about a Being, something spiritual which encompasses all of existence. Man unfortunately has lost sight of Being, relying on technology and rationalist ways of thinking. Therefore, man needs to return to an authentic sense of self, freed from false identities that are imposed by rationalism and technology. Havel has also talked about Gaia and about the Anthropic Cosmological Principle, which allegedly offers a proof of God's existence. In one of his Presidential addresses, he stated,

> Soul, individual spirituality, firsthand personal insight into things, the courage to be oneself and go the way one's conscience points, humility in the face of the mysterious order of Being, confidence in its natural direction and, above all, trust in one's own subjectivity as the principal link with the subjectivity of the world—these, in my view are the qualities that politicians of the future should cultivate.

Journalist Paul Berman, quoting the above, added that "conventional political people roll their eyes when Havel goes on in this particular vein. Yet to dismiss Havel's trippier ideas as 'fluff' (that is the word one of Havel's advisers used in a private conversation with me) would be a big mistake, I think." Berman quoted Czech philosopher Jan Patocka as noting that Havel has been the "main force" that keeps Czech democracy going, the "glue" that holds it together.

In 1993, speaking at a George Washington University graduation exercise in Washington, D.C., Havel sounded very much like a secular humanist:

> It seems to me that the challenge offered by the post-Communist world is merely the current form of a broader and more profound challenge to discover a new type of self-understanding for man, and a new type of politics that should flow from that understanding. As we all know, today's planetary civilization is in serious danger. We are rationally capable of describing, in vivid detail, all the dangers that threaten the world: the deepening gulf between the rich and the poor parts of the world, the population explosion, the potential for dramatic confrontations between different racial and cultural groups, the arming of whom no one seems able to stop, the nuclear threat, the plundering of natural resources, the destruction of the natural variety of species, the creation of holes in the ozone layer, and the unstoppable global warming. What is unsettling is that the more we know about such dangers, the less able we seem to deal with them.

He then stated, without explaining what metaphysics is,

> I see only one way out of this crisis: man must come to a new understanding of himself, of his limitations and his place in the world. He should grasp his responsibility in a new way, and reestablish a relationship with the things that transcend him. We must rehabilitate our sense of ourselves as active human subjects, and liberate ourselves from the captivity of a purely national perception of the world. Through this 'subjecthood' and the individual conscience that goes with it, we must discover a new relationship to our neighbors, and to the universe and its metaphysical order, which is the source of the moral order.

In 1994 at Independence Hall in Philadelphia, Havel said, "The modern age has ended." He added that not just the collapse of Communism or of Moscow's colonial empire has happened but also the era of rationalism that began with the Enlightenment. He explained that the end of the era of rationalism has been catastrophic, that although rationalism had welded together a global civilization, now people, "behind its back as it were, cling to the ancient certainties of their tribe." Therefore, "cultural conflicts are increasing and are understandably more dangerous today than at any other time in history. . . . By day, we work with statistics; in the evening, we consult astrologers." Havel cited two examples of post-modern science, the anthropic cosmological principle (first stated by the English physicist Brandon Carter in 1974) and the Gaia hypothesis (which was proposed in 1972 by the Englishman, James Lovelock)—each, he said, implies that life on earth is part of a larger purpose . . . that we are an integral part of higher, mysterious entities against whom it is not advisable to blaspheme." Self-transcendence is "the only real alternative to extinction"; man can realize liberty only if he "does not forget the One who endowed him with it." Of this, journalist Nicholas Wade has commented,

> A view of the world built on the anthropic principle and the Gaia hypothesis would not be "post-modern" science but rather a throwback to the numerology and astrology from which the era of rationalism has still not fully rescued us. Havel's diagnosis of our end-of-century discontents may be right. But transcendence is not the only solution. And to subvert rationalism into mysticism would be a cure more pernicious than the disease.

Although once mistakenly thought to have an outlook quite similar to that of American and European secular humanists—Nicolas Walter has called him an unbeliever—Havel has specifically mentioned that just as Heidegger once talked about the need for a god, "I really think that this civilization is in crisis and only a god can save it." In a 15 May 1996 address given in Aachen concerning the future of Europe concluded, "Europe will only be able to bear the cross of this world, and thus follow the example of Him in whom it has believed for two thousand years, and in whose name it has committed so much evil, if it first pauses and reflects upon itself, when—in the best sense of the word—it lives up to the potential inherent in the twilight to which it owes its name," a reference to the fact that the Akkadian word for Europe, *erebu*, means sunset or twilight whereas the word for Asia, *asu*, means sunrise.

Among those who are negative about Havel are Mario Bunge, who has termed Havel's thinking "obscurantism." Timothy J. Madigan, in analyzing Havel's philosophy, has concluded that it "is appropriate that the literary school that most influenced Havel was the Theater of the Absurd." (See entry for Michael Novak.) {Paul Berman, *The New York Times Magazine*, 11 May 1997; Mario Bunge, *Free Inquiry*, Winter 1998-1999; Václav Havel, "The Hope for Europe," *The New York Review of Books*, 20 June 1996; Timothy J. Madigan, *Free Inquiry*, Fall 1998; Nicholas Wade, *The New York Times Magazine*, 14 August 1994}

HAVERING & DISTRICT (England) HUMANIST SOCIETY

For information, write HOPWA House, Inskip Drive, Hornchurch; or telephone J. Condon at 01708 473597 or J. Baker at 01708 458925.

Havet, Ernest August Eugène (1813—1889)

Havet was a French scholar and critic, a professor of Greek literature at the Normal School. In 1855 he was made professor of Latin eloquence at the *Collège de France*. Havet's 1863 article on Renan's *Vie de Jesus* in the *Revue des Deux Mondes* drew much attention, and his four-volume work, *Christianity and Its Origins* (1872—1884) was a collection of rational criticism. Havet was a member of the Legion of Honour and of the Academy of Political and Social Science. {BDF; RAT; RE}

Haviland, E. Cyril (20th Century)

In Sydney, Australia, Haviland edited the monthly *Freethought* (1880—1881). {FUK}

Havlicek, Karel (1821—1855)

Havlicek wrote under the literary name of Havel Borovsky. In his *National News* and the *Slovan*, he waged a bitter journalistic war upon despotism and hierarchy. Twice he was tried for alleged high treason, and twice he was acquitted. One winter evening, however, Havlicek was kidnapped by the police, dragged away from his family, and imprisoned at Brixen, Tyrol. While in prison he wrote a satire in verse, "The Baptism of St. Vladimir," in which he ridiculed the belief in a personal god, efficacy of prayer, and the rights of despots. Havlicek was allowed to die in prison. {PUT; RAT}

HAWAII HUMANISTS, ATHEISTS, AND FREETHINKERS

Hawaii has the following groups:

- American Atheists, Inc., 733 Bishop St. (Suite 170-729), Honolulu, Hawaii 96813; E-mail:. <mkahle@atheists.org>.
- Hawaii Rationalists (ASHS), 508 Pepekeo Pl., Honolulu, Hawaii 96825; telephone (808) 395-5581
- Humanists of Hawaii, 1515 Nuuanu Queen Tower #48, Honolulu, HI 96717. (808) 524-3872 E-mail: <langton@pixie.net>.

Hawke, David Freeman (20th Century)

Hawke is author of an extensive Thomas Paine bibliography (1974). However, John Keane in *Tom Paine: A Political Life* (1995) has been negatively critical of the work's "sniping . . . to the point where readers are left wondering why Hawke ever bothered to write a biography of Paine." (See entry for John Keane.) {FUK; FUS}

Hawke, Robert (Bob) James Lee (1929—)

Hawke, who was Australia's Prime Minister from March 1983 to December 1991, was asked by a seven-year-old boy on a television show, "The Day Tonight," if he believed in God, Hawke replied, "Until I get some evidence one way or the other which is compelling to me, I'm going to have to remain an agnostic." {CA; E; Robert Pullan, *Bob Hawke: A Portrait* (1980)}

Hawkes, Jacquetta: See entry for Theism.

Hawkesworth, John (c. 1715—1773)

Hawkesworth was an English essayist and novelist. In 1761 he edited Swift's works with a life of that author. He then compiled an account of the voyages of Byron, Wallis, Carteret, and Cook for the government, for which he received £6,000; however, the work was censured as incidentally attacking the doctrine of Providence. Hawkesworth also wrote a popular novel, *Almoran and Hamet*. {BDF}

Hawking, Stephen (1942—)

Hawking's *A Brief History of Time: From the Big Bang to Black Holes* (1988) led many to exaggerate that he represented "the second coming of Einstein." His work in cosmology and physics places him as one of the most brilliant minds of his time, and his work on the physics of black holes is particularly original, although it is experimentally unverifiable. Suffering from amyotrophic lateral sclerosis (Lou Gehrig's disease), the noted theoretical physicist is confined to a wheelchair. (At one point, however, Hawking had a difficult divorce, after which he married his nurse, with whom he had been having an affair.) Unable to speak except by means of a special computer that synthesizes his voice when he presses buttons, he is a consummate example of a human who has succeeded despite egregious physical problems.

When Shirley MacLaine accidentally met him in a restaurant, the actress (who claims she remembers past existences before her present life) recognized him and, during a chat, asked whether or not he believed in God. Hawking reportedly smiled, touched the right buttons, and the machine oracularly ejaculated, "No!" Similarly, when his *A Brief History of Time* was published and a reporter asked if he believed in God, given the "mind of God" reference near the end of the book, Hawking responded, "I do not believe in a personal God."

Specifically, his not being religious is traceable to what matters most to him: "Why does the universe go to all the bother of existing?" This, according to Michael White and John Gribbin in their biography, makes him less an atheist but simply a person who "finds the idea of faith something he cannot absorb into his view of the Universe." Married and the father of two sons and one daughter, Hawking co-authored with G. F. B. Ellis *The Large Scale Structure of Space-Time* (1973). His collection of essays, published in 1993, is *Black Holes and Baby Universes*. Hawking is a member of the American Philosophical Society.

It is ironic, film critic Stanley Kauffmann has pointed out, that Hawking is something of a science-fiction creature, a person with a nearly disembodied brain. He is in the forefront of science at the same time that he is alive only because other scientists have laid the groundwork. Sophisticated devices with computer technology have made his existence possible, for without them he would be a mute prisoner within a useless body. {CA; E}

Hawkings, Gordon Joseph (1919—)

Hawkings is a humanist, a criminologist, and an author. Raised in England by his grandparents as an Anglican, he read Bertrand Russell and became a freethinker. He was Governor of the United Kingdom Prison Services but migrated to Australia in 1961, taking an appointment as senior lecturer in criminal law at Sydney University. With Norval Morris, Hawkings wrote *The Honest Politician's Guide to Crime Control* (1970) and "Humanism and the Crime Problem" in *A Humanist View* (1969). {SWW}

Hawkins, Dexter Arnold (1825—1886)

Hawkins was an American educationist who lectured on educational reform and was chiefly instrumental in securing a National Bureau of Education. His rationalism is found in *Roman Catholic Church in New York City* (1880). {RAT}

Hawkins, Ronnie (20th Century)

Hawkins, a professor of philosophy at the University of Central Florida, spoke on the subject, "Today's Ethics and Morality: How I Came By Them," at the 1999 convention of Humanists of Florida.

Hawley, Henry (Died 1765)

Hawley was a Scottish major-general who, by the terms of his will, prohibited Christian burial. {BDF}

Hawley, John S. (20th Century)

A freethinker, Hawley wrote *Tradition Versus Truth* (1903). {GS}

Hawthorne, Julian (1846—1934)

An American novelist, the son of Nathaniel Hawthorne, Hawthorne wrote about thirty novels, *A History of the United States* (1899), and several literary works. His father, he said, had a pew in the Unitarian Church at Liverpool, where the father was for a time stationed, and sent him to occupy it on Sundays (but never attended himself). However, Julian said he "never learned to repeat a creed, far less to comprehend its significance." According to McCabe in 1920, Hawthorne was a theist. In 1938 the memoirs of Julian Hawthorne were published. {RAT}

Hawthorne, Nathaniel (1804—1864)

One of the greatest of American authors, Hawthorne (whose sea captain father spelled his name Hathorne) came from a prominent Puritan family, his mother being a widow with solitary ways and a gloomy outlook. His *Twice-Told Tales* (1837) won him some recognition, but he found it necessary to work in a Boston customhouse in order to make a living. For a time he lived at Brook Farm, the transcendentalists' experiment in utopianism, but found the communal life not to his taste. *Blithedale Romance* (1852) is based on his experience at the farm. He married Sophia Peabody, a friend and follower of Emerson, Thoreau, and Margaret Fuller, taking a job as surveyor of the port of Salem (1846—1849), where he began writing his masterpiece: *The Scarlet Letter* (1850), the first U.S. psychological novel. Salem has never quite recovered from its record of having hanged nineteen in the 1690s, also crushing one to death. Although not one of the alleged witches was burned, some writers mistakenly have stated that they were.

The Salem that Hawthorne exposed had a fictional villain, the Puritan minister Arthur Dimmesdale, and a heroine, Hester Prynne, the adulteress required to wear a scarlet "A" but who triumphed over her "sin" because she confessed it openly whereas the minister had not. What Hawthorne excelled in was showing that era's sex hatred, its repression, its prurience, its relentless pressure to deny reality, its using a child as a pawn in adult power struggles. It has been said that *The Scarlet Letter* dates the decline of Puritan importance in the U.S., that it speeded the time when a *Playboy* or a *Playgirl* could be published, inasmuch as it depicted the effects adultery had on a girl in colonial America.

While living at Lennox, Massachusetts, Hawthorne befriended his neighbor, Herman Melville, becoming his closest emotional attraction, to Mrs. Hawthorne's dismay. Melville's elegy, "Monody," after Hawthorne's death included the following:

> To have known him, to have loved him
> After loneness long;
> And then to be estranged in life;
> And neither in the wrong;
> And now for death to set his seal—
> Ease me, a little ease, my song!

Mrs. Hawthorne was reportedly pleased when Franklin Pierce, her husband's college friend and now President, appointed him consul at Liverpool (1853—1857), rejoicing that they now would be living a convenient distance from Melville. (In letters discovered in 1983 in a barn in Gansevoort, New York, Ms. Robertson-Lorant noted Mrs. Hawthorne's description of her husband, "He hates to be touched more than anyone I ever knew.")

In 1864, while on a trip to the White Mountains with Pierce, Hawthorne suddenly died in Pierce's arms (which some wags have said was the inspiration for Melville's "Monody"; Gore Vidal implies it may not have been the first time Hawthorne had been in that proximity).

Recent biographers continue to mention Melville's opinion, confirmed by Hawthorne's son Julian, that he was convinced "Hawthorne had all his life concealed some great secret, which would, were it known, explain all the mysteries of his career." Biographer Philip Young claims that the secret was incest between Hawthorne and his sister Elizabeth. Another theory, mentioned by John Updike (*The New Yorker*, 28 Sep 1992), is that Hawthorne, a young man whose "androgynous beauty" often excited admiration, "was sexually molested by his uncle Robert Manning, with whom he shared, for a time, a bed in the overflowing Manning household." Eighteen years later, Hawthorne declined to attend Manning's funeral, and the villainous Judge Pyncheon in his *House of the Seven Gables* was a horticulturist, Manning's occupation. Whatever the secret, if indeed he had one, Hawthorne's tales of human loneliness, frustration, hypocrisy, eccentricity, and frailty made him a celebrated writer who remains a model for contemporaries. A work such as *The Scarlet Letter*, Updike notes, is of the quality of a classic and can be expected "to hold its secrets in living solution and to be, like life itself, ultimately indecipherable."

Robertson admired Hawthorne's lack of faith, "whatever his psychological sympathy with the Puritan past, wrought inevitably by his art for the loosening of its intellectual hold." His son Julian in *Hawthorne and His Circle* tells that when his father was in Liverpool he had a pew at the Unitarian Chapel there, that he used to send Julian to fill it, never going himself. Julian says he "never learned to repeat a creed, far less to comprehend its significance," to which some Unitarians showed amazement, saying Unitarianism is creedless. Hawthorne had been married in a Unitarian church, and his funeral was held in a Unitarian church. (See entries for Alfred Kazin and Herman Melville.) {CE; CL; FUS; JM; JMR; RAT; RE; U; UU}

Hawthorne, Sophia Peabody (1809-1871)

The sister of Elizabeth Parker Peabody and the wife of Nathaniel Hawthorne, Sophia Hawthorne was an author, writer, and Unitarian.

Hawton, Hector (Born 1901)

The editor of *Question* in Great Britain, Hawton is a well-known humanist. He works include *Why Be Moral?* (1947), *Men Without Gods* (1948), *The Humanist Revolution* (1963), and *Controversy: The Humanist / Christian Encounter* (1971). He signed Humanist Manifesto II. In 1957, Hawton was editor of *The Humanist*, in which British journal he once wrote that Gilbert Murray preferred "freethinker" to either "humanist" or "rationalist." In 1968 in Hannover, Hawton addressed the Second European Conference of the International Humanist and Ethical Union (IHEU). {FUK; HM2}

Hayden, William George [Governor-General] (1933-)

Hayden was Governor-General of Australia (1989-1996). In 1996 he was named Australian Humanist of the Year. The Australian *Humanist* (February 1996) stated that the award "is made because he has shown that an avowed atheist who describes himself as a secular humanist can occupy the position of Governor-General with mounting approval."

Hayden, in accepting, said, "To be a humanist, one has to exercise free will, to reason, to be rational, to avoid being the slave of some defunct ideology or the disciple of received wisdom. . . . [However], [b]eing an atheist—as I am—is not a necessary pre-condition for being a humanist." {CA}

Hayden, Charles Trumbull (19th Century)

Hayden was one of the foremost Arizonan merchants and businessmen of his time. He built mills, cultivated lands, established trade, irrigated the land, and was a defender of the rights of the people. He believed in the schoolhouse, not the church; the spade and pick-ax, not the cross. He believed in a paradise in this world now, not in some dream later. Hayden was an early American freethinker. {RE}

Hayden, Louis (20th Century)

In 1958, Hayden was chairman of a newly formed New York Chapter of the Rationalist Press Association. The group met at the Henry George School.

Hayden, William (20th Century)

In 1996 in Brisbane, the Honourable Bill Hayden A.C. was presented with the Australian Humanist of the Year Award. It was made in recognition of his caring for human values and rights as Minister of Social Security, his understanding of development issues as Minister of Foreign Affairs, his humanist attitude to euthanasia and to the rights of adoption of same-sex partners, and to his being an outspoken Governor-General. {E}

Haydn, Franz Joseph (1732—1809)

Haydn, a great master of classical music, was an Austrian freethinker who joined the Masonic Lodge. That organization was reviled for its being non-theistic, for being deistic. Its deistic rituals held that the Grand Architect of the Universe created the universe but did not interfere by causing miracles or special revelations. Beethoven studied under Haydn, and Mozart was one of his close friends. Two of his great oratorios, written in his old age, were "The Creation" (1798) and "The Seasons" (1801).

Austria was at war with France at the time, but Haydn's burial in the Hundsthrum churchyard was a quiet event. The local prison chief, Johann Peter, was an amateur phrenologist and chose, under cover of war, to study the head of such an illustrious man as Haydn. So two days after the interment, a small group of bribed officials assisted four workmen in exhuming the body, cutting off the head, then reburying the remains. After stripping the head of all flesh, Peter cheerfully pronounced that Haydn had "the bumps of music fully developed." Inasmuch as it was dangerous to return the skull, Peter kept it in a silk-lined box, eventually giving it to Joseph Rosenbaum, secretary to Haydn's patron, Prince Esterhazy. Frau Rosenbaum had a glass and ebony display case made for the relic. When the Prince, unaware of what had happened, decided to rebury Haydn in his private church at Eisenstadt eight years later, the robbery was discovered. Meanwhile, Rosenbaum's wife refused to give up the relic but, in a ruse, another skull was produced. Upon its being examined, however, the skull was found to be that of a man in his twenties, and Haydn had died in his seventies. Eventually, Peter's wife gave it to her doctor who gave it to the Austrian Institute of Pathology and Anatomy in 1832.

Haydn's actual skull was not reunited with his body until the summer of 1954 when, amid church music and flashbulbs and after Prince Paul Esterhazy promised to build a magnificent tomb if the head were returned, Haydn's head was finally joined to the rest of his body. {CE; PA}

Haydon, A. Eustace (1880—1975)

A Canadian-born ex-Baptist professor of religion who wrote frequently for *The Humanist*, Dr. Haydon signed Humanist Manifesto I as well as II. He was a Canadian Baptist turned Unitarian and humanist, and he succeeded his teacher, the liberal Professor George Burman Foster, in history of religions at the University of Chicago Divinity School (1929—1945). He had also followed Foster in the pulpit of the Unitarian Church in Madison, Wisconsin. In 1945 and following an anti-humanistic, anti-socialistic Leader Horace Bridges, Haydon became Leader of the Chicago Ethical Culture Society (1955—1965) and the Los Angeles Ethical Culture Society (1965—1975). In addition, he served as an officer of the American Humanist Association.

He has written, "More important than faith in God is devotion to the human ideals of which he has become the symbol. Too long the strong gods have been made to bear the burden. Wistfully man has watched for the day of divine action to dawn and ever heal the hurt of disappointment by more passionate faith. Hopes hung in the heavens are of no avail. What the gods have been expected to do, and have failed to do through the ages, man must find the courage and intelligence to do for himself. More needful than faith in God is faith that man can give love, justice, peace, and all his beloved moral values embodiment in human relations. Denial of this faith is the only real atheism. Without it, belief in all the galaxies of gods is mere futility. With it, and the practice that flows from it, man need not mourn the passing of the gods."

Edwin H. Wilson, in *The Genesis of a Humanist Manifesto* (1995), describes the considerable efforts that Haydon made in helping edit the first manifesto. (See entries for Ethical Culture and for burial practices, a subject upon which Haydon was an expert.) {CL; EU, Howard B. Radest; EW; FUS; HM1; HM2; HNS; HNS2}

Hayes, Judith (20th Century)

Hayes is the granddaughter and great-granddaughter of Lutheran ministers. But after spending two years reading the Bible, she says, she "realized that the Bible was little more than a convoluted collection of primitive, barbaric, and bewildering myths, a lousy read." In *Freethought Today* (May 1994), she wrote:

> If you thank God for the food on your table, you are saying that he put it there. A necessary component of this premise, the other side of the coin, is that if there is no food on your table, God is responsible for that, too. The power to give necessarily includes the power to withhold. When you thank someone for a gift it is because you understand that he or she had the choice of not giving it to you, but chose to do so anyway. Thanking God for your food, then, is the same as saying thank you for not withholding food. You are offering thanks for not being allowed to starve.

In 1996, she wrote *In God We Trust: But Which One?* Although she had written for *Freethought Today*, the journal of the Freedom From Religion Foundation, she severed her relationship in 1996, complaining she was unhappy with the production quality of the book. In 1997, calling herself "a happy heretic," she became a senior writer for *The American Rationalist*. Her homepage is at <http://www.thehappyheretic.com>. {*Freethought Observer*, November-December 1996}

Hayes, Kay (20th Century)

Hayes is Secretary-Treasurer of the Spokane, Washington, Freedom from Religion Foundation chapter of PAINE (People Actively Into Nontheisic Ethics). She has written for *Freethought Today*.

Hayes, Lester H. (20th Century)

When he signed Humanist Manifesto II, Hayes was public relations director of the American Income Life Insurance Company. {HM2}

Hayflick, Leonard (20th Century)

The author of *How and Why We Age* (1994), Hayflick is pleased that humans live so long. The perfect solution to a "successful" old age, he writes, is a "successful death, [one] where you have lived to what we think is a maximum life span—let's say about one hundred—with full retention of your cognitive and physical abilities, and then drop dead at the stroke of midnight." Hayflick disapproves of those who indulge in what he calls "grannyology" and advises, instead, acquainting ourselves with "the fundamental biology of aging." Most, he regrets, prefer books on grannyology. "You know," he writes, "if there was a God, my book would be on the best-seller list, too. But it ain't going to be. There's no God." {*New York*, 16 January 1995}

Hayhurst, Christine (20th Century)

In England, Hayhurst heads the International Association of Liberal Religious Women. The group, which is associated with the

Unitarian and Universalists, encourages the sharing of ideas and the search for spiritual identity in an international, interfaith community.

Hayman, Ronald (1932—)

Hayman is author of a highly rated biography, *Nietzsche as Philosopher* (1965). In addition to writing about Sartre, Proust, and Tennessee Williams, he wrote *Thomas Mann* (1995).

Haynes, Edmund Sidney Pollock (Born 1877)

Haynes, a lawyer and writer, married one of Huxley's granddaughters. He wrote in defense of liberty and for the reform of the divorce law. Haynes's rationalism is found particularly in his *Belief in Personal Immortality* (1913). An agnostic, Haynes was a life member of the Rationalist Press Association. {RAT; RE}

Hays, Mary Rose (20th Century)

Hayes is the business director of the Committee for the Scientific Investigation of Claims of the Paranormal, which publishes *Skeptical Inquirer*.

Hayward, Abraham (1801—1884)

Hayward was a lawyer, an editor of *Law Magazine* (1828—1844). He offended English rationalists in 1873 by an unpleasant letter on J. S. Mill in the *Times*. However, Hayward remained an agnostic. "No clergyman invaded his peace" at the time of his death, and his last words were, "We know nothing. There is something great." {RAT}

Hayward, F. H. (Born 1872)

Hayward in 1915 wrote *Paganism*. With E. M. White, he wrote a work about the English Ethical Culture leader Frederick J. Gould, *The Last Years of a Great Educationist* (1942). He also wrote *Educational Ideas of Pestalozzi and Frobel* (1979). {FUK; GS}

Hayward, Henry John (20th Century)

Hayward, a freethinker, wrote *The Gods Are Going* (194—?) {GS}

Hayward, J. K. (20th Century)

A freethinker, Hawyard wrote *A Rebuttal of Spiritism et al.* (1903). {GS}

Haywood, William Dudley (1869—1928)

An outspoken atheist, Haywood was a labor leader who in Colorado led the Cripple Creek strike in 1904. He once was defended by Clarence Darrow and found not guilty of assassinating a former governor of Idaho. The socialists forced him out of their party because of his militancy. As a founder of the International Workers of the World (IWW), he preached mass action and class struggle. Arrested at the start of World War I on charges of sedition, he jumped bail and fled to Russia, where he lived for the rest of his life.

Hazlitt, Henry (1894—1993)

Hazlitt was an economist whom H. L. Mencken in 1933 asked to succeed him as editor of the *American Mercury*, an iconoclastic journal founded by Mencken and George Nathan. From 1934 to 1956 Hazlitt wrote about economics for *The New York Times*, later writing for *Newsweek*. In 1949 he was asked his views about humanism and responded to the present author:

> I don't know exactly where I would fit into the categories unless I knew very clearly the criteria on which they were based. My guess is that my views would fall somewhere between classical humanism and naturalistic humanism. What I can say definitely is that they would not fall into the categories of theistic or atheistic humanism. If you must stick me in somewhere for the sake of schematic neatness, I suggest that I would probably fit with the least discomfort into the category of naturalistic humanism.

Hazlitt wrote *Anatomy of Criticism* (1933) and *Economics in One Lesson* (1946, 1988). He did not believe wage levels could be raised by union bargaining or legislating minimum wage laws. He also rejected Karl Marx's and John Maynard Keynes's interventionist strategies, emphasizing his basic and consistent belief in the free market system. {WAS, 28 March 1949}

Hazlitt, William (1737-1820)

A contemporary of Adam Smith, Hazlitt first joined the Presbyterian ministry but ultimately became unitarian in his outlook. He served several Unitarian churches: Wisbeach in 1764; Marshfield, Gloucestershire, in 1766; Maidstone 1770-1, during which time he met Dr. Benjamin Franklin; and Bandon, Cork, in 1780. For fifteen months, during which time his son William Jr. was born, Hazlitt preached in the Philadelphia area.

In 1784 he went to Boston upon hearing that the Brattle Street Church was open. Here he convinced lay members of the congregation that they could ordain him to the ministry without the authority of either a bishop or a council of ministers. His son, writing some years later, noted, "It was while we resided at Weymouth that my father assisted in preparing a liturgy for [James Freeman's] church which had been Episcopal and furnished him with a form of prayer used by Mr. [Theophilus] Lindsey in Essex Street Chapel, which they adapted to suit the Translantic Church."

Freeman wrote, "Before Mr. Hazlitt came to Boston, the Trinitarian doxology was almost universally used. That honest good man prevailed upon several respectable ministers to omit it. Since his departure, the number of those who repeat only scriptural doxologies has greatly increased." Freeman, who became the first minister of King's Chapel, was not joined by others. Jeremy Belknap found Hazlittle's company "disgusting," and John Eliot called him "the most conceited man I ever met with." Two years later William Bentley wrote of Hazlitt, "While at Boston he attached himself to the ingenuous Mr. freeman now Reader at King's Chapel and led that worthy man to some hasty measures in revising the Liturgy which may prove fatal to his establishment in that Society." Had Hazlitt not done so, Carl Scovel and Charles C. Forman speculate in *Journey Toward Independence: King's Chapel's Transition to Unitarianism* (1993), "King's Chapel might never have found models for liturgical reform and independent ordination."

Upon his retirement Hazlitt moved in England to Crediton, where he died.

Hazlitt, William (1778—1830)

Hazlitt, the essayist and English critic, aimed originally to be a minister. Instead, he became a master of the miscellaneous essay, writing on a variety of topics with his profound understanding. He befriended Coleridge, Lamb, Godwin, and Holcroft. In 1812 he gave a course of lectures on philosophy at the Russell Institution.

Among his writings are *Characters of Shakespeare's Plays* (1817) and *Dramatic Literature of the Age of Elizabeth* (1820), both of which inspired many to have a renewed interest in Shakespeare. His *Political Essays* (1819) declared, "The garb of religion is the best cloak for power." Thackeray described him as "one of the keenest and brightest critics that ever lived." As a child and son of a dissenting minister, Hazlitt listened to his father, a Unitarian, but objected to the rationalistic philosophy in his sermons and of the bible that used to kindle his father's "lack-lustre eyes." From 1793 to 1795 he attended the Unitarian New College. Hazlitt died impoverished, an unbeliever in any future life. {CE; JM; JMR; RAT; RE; TDY; U; UU}

Headingly, Adolphe S. (19th Century)

Headingly wrote *a Biography of Charles Bradlaugh* (1880). {GS}

Headlam, Stewart D. (20th Century)

Headlam, a freethinker, wrote *Charles Bradlaugh, An Appreciation* (1907). {GS}

Heaford, William (Born 1855)

In London during the early 1900s, Heaford was a lecturer for the British Secular League. {FUK; RAT; RSR}

Heald, Mark M. (20th Century)

When he reviewed books for *The Humanist* in the 1950s, Heald was on the faculty of Rutgers University.

Heales, Peter (20th Century)

Heales, who writes in England for *New Humanist*, is a tutor with Birbeck College Centre for Extramural Studies and the Workers Education Association. Also, he is secretary of the Sutton Humanist Group.

Healey, Denis Winston (20th Century)

Healey, a former Member of Parliament for Leeds East in England, was described by reporter Frances Welch of the *Sunday Telegraph*: "Avowedly atheist, Healey is not prepared to concede that human conscience points to the existence of God. Nor does he feel that God has anything to do with the spiritual uplift he gains from art. 'I think that the only worthwhile politician has a vocation, as a nun has a vocation. But I don't see that vocation coming from God because I don't believe in a personal God. I can cry over a Beethoven quartet and I'm deeply moved spiritually when I look at a painting by Mantegna or read poetry by Thomas Traherne. But you can't be convinced that it is God's influence if you don't believe in God,' Healey said. Asked if had ever felt the need to believe, Healey replied, 'People turn to God in the same way they turn to chauvinism if they're unhappy.' So he was too happy for religion? 'I dare say I am,' he grinned, escorting me to the door."

Healey, Robert M. (20th Century)

Healey wrote the acclaimed *Jefferson on Religion in Public Education* (1962). {FUS}

HEALING

People with limited education are highly impressed by individuals who claim they can heal others. Finding a healer who can "cure" their ailment is a goal made all the more important if extreme pain is involved. Healers appear to "cure" with some kind of supernatural intervention. Any reports from sufferers who are "terminal" cases but who have been "healed" receive wide publicity, and healers try to outdo other healers with their claims.

The shaman or obeah woman who can concoct a liniment, the religionist who uses "the laying on of hands" or other theological device, the peddler who sells snake oil: all have wide support from individuals who verify they "were healed," sometimes of cancer or many other ailments . . . almost anything excepting loss of limb.

"Laying on of hands" is what a "qualified" person does to "bless" by placing hands on another's head. The rite has been used as an exorcism before baptism, "to impart the Holy Spirit" to the newly baptised or "to transmit a special grace at ordination." The Prince of the Sanhedrin, named in the Gospels as one of the judges in the Jewish state until its destruction in 70 C.E., conferred authority upon a new member in this way. "In Egypt and Babylonia, the king and princes received authority for their offices by contact with the hands of the images of the gods," explained A. Eustace Haydon, who added, "A variant appears in the ancient Hebrew ceremony in which the priest annually transferred the sins of the people to the scapegoat. Underlying all such rites is the primitive idea of a mysterious potency which may be communicated by contagion."

Contemporary physicians and scientists are aware of the brain's triumph over reality. The "placebo effect" has been shown to lead to mechanisms that can turn belief into an agent of biological change. Patients, for example, are given a placebo (Latin for "I shall please"), a sham treatment. They think they are receiving some drug but actually are not. Sugar pills in various shapes, when administered, often resulted in surprising results. "If you expect to get better, you will," Dr. Irving Kirsch, a psychiatrist at the Univeresity of Connecticut has observed as have numerous others.

For example, a 1998 study of a baldness remedy found that 86% of men taking it either maintained or showed an increase in the amount of hair on their heads. But so did 42% of the men taking a placebo. Similarly, Venezuelan children who were asthmatic were given a sniff of vanilla along with a squirt of medicine from a bronchodilator twice a day. The vanilla odor alone increased their lung function 33% as much as did the bronchodilator alone. A Tulane University study by Dr. Eileen Palanace used a placebo to restore sexual arousal in women who said they were nonorgasmic. Hooked up to a biofeedback machine which they are told measures their vaginal blood flow, an index of arousal, they are shown sexual stimuli that would arouse most women. But experimenters who sent false feedback signals that their vaginal blood flow had increased, almost immediately became genuinely aroused.

"I was healed!" claim believers at religious meetings. "Of course you were," freethinkers observe. Or, as Dr. Howard Fields, a neuroscientist at the University of California at San Francisco has said, "We are misled by dualism or the idea that mind and body are separate." He recognizes that a thought is a set of neurons firing which, through complex brain wiring, can activate emotional centers, pain pathways, memories, the autonomic nervous system and other parts of the nervous system involved in producing physical sensations. {See Sandra Blakeslee, "Pladebos Prove So Powerful Even Experts Are Surprised," *The New York Times*, 13 October 1998; ER}

HEALING BY PRAYER: See entry for James Randi.

Heaney, Seamus Justin (1939—)

Heaney, the author of *Death of a Naturalist* and other poetry, is a member of the Irish Academy of Letters. He has been called "the best-known Irish poet since Yeats." Asked by *The Independent on Sunday* if he believed in life after death, he replied, "No. I believe in the atheist position, or Wordsworthian one—it's not in the Elysian fields but on this earth that we find our happiness, in the inner theatre or the theatre of relationships, in society or the home." In 1993, when he was asked in person if he is an atheist, Heaney replied testily to the present author that he is a "rock Catholic" and did not remember having made any such statement to any British journal.

Heape, Walter (Born 1855)

Heape, a zoologist, was Superintendent of the Marine Biological Association (1886—1888). In *Sex Antagonism* (1913), Heape compared the Christian belief in the miraculous conception of Christ to a belief of the Queensland blacks in spirit-conception—both "know the truth; it is only superstition which compels them to deny it." {RAT}

Heard, Gerald (20th Century)

Heard was a scientific humanist who wrote for *The Realist* (1929-1920) and was on its board of directors. {HNS2}

Hearn, Lafcadio (Yakumo Koizumi) (1850—1904)

Born in the Ionian Islands of Irish-Greek parentage, Hearn was educated first as a Roman Catholic. He studied in Ireland, England, and France before moving to the United States in 1869. Hearn's first work to gain notice was "Fantastics," a series of unusual sketches that appeared in a New Orleans newspaper. *One of Cleopatra's Nights* (1882) was his translation of some of Gautier's stories. In 1890, Hearn went to Japan as a journalist, adopted Buddhism, wrote what are considered his best works, married a Japanese woman, and taught in Japanese universities. In 1895, as Yakumo Koizumi, he became a Japanese citizen. Included among his best works are *Japanese Fairy Tales* (1902) and *Japan: An Attempt at* Interpretation (1904). Handicapped by partial blindness, Hearn was accused by the editor of the *Kobe Times*, as having been a priceless asset to the ruling caste and a myopic observer who was exploited by officials. In his outlook, Hearn was a Unitarian, but he adopted Buddhism and wrote that it was superior to Christianity. As his friend, Robert Young, mentioned, however, Hearn was short-sighted and not a good observer. {CE; JM; RAT; RE; U; UU}

HEARSE

- Hearse, n. Death's baby-carriage.

—Ambrose Bierce
The Devil's Dictionary

Hearst, James (1900—1983)

Hearst, an Iowa farmer-poet, was a religious or democratic humanist who was uncomfortable with all organized religions. Following are samples of the work of a man who, following a diving accident into shallow water, was confined to a wheelchair for most of his life. First, from "Belief":

> . . . We should stand often against the sun—
> And what of the work if it isn't done?
> For we are two neighbors who like to share
> A friendly word in the open air.
>
> And we should talk swiftly against the time
> When crops and men and women and rhyme
> Shall be as quiet as to us as stone—
> The time of forever we spend alone.

In "The Grail," he is naturalistic:

> What greater praise canst thou have
> Than that we seek the grail,
> Not in the heavens, Lord, among the stars' cold radiance,
> But in the furrow, the plowed field, the meadow,
> The places where it blooms for man in his short life.

In "The Reason for Stars," Hearst continues,

> I never wonder a lot about stars.
> I'm much too busy with things of this earth
> That show when a season of labor is done
> Just what the labor's been worth.
>
> Stars are all right to admire like flowers,
> I like to see pretty things when I'm done
> Working in the fields, but what do I care
> Whether a star is stone?
>
> There's plenty to learn in the ways of a seed.
> What do you get if you study the sky?
> It's greater for holding one fruit in my hand
> Than a heaven of stars in my eye.

Similarly, he philosophizes in "Cows Bawl on Sunday":

> The image of God
> in a warm mackinaw and rubber boots
> daily fights his way into the steaming barnyard
> into a multitude of hungry, angry, playful and determined animals
> through a cloud of raging sound
> to bring order out of chaos.
> Six times a week and rests not on the seventh—
> and there fails his divinity.

Critiquing Hearst's *Country Men* (1943), Dr. H. Willard Reninger of the University of Northern Iowa (UNI) wrote concerning the "Robert Frost of the Midwest,"

> He is suspicious of metaphysical systems and expects no final answers in this world. One would never catch Jim Hearst trying to crack the nut of the universe—he would work harder trying to understand a friend. Consequently he thinks and writes from no thesis. Fine meshes are suspect; he shakes no self-righteous sieve. His mind is eminently receptive, a listening mind with 'schools and creeds in abeyance.' Not argumentative, he is a man of peace, practicing a quiet self-reliance, but compromising at times because of his reluctance to offend a guest. Unlike his father, he is no swinging fighter for his ideals, winning, instead, through a personal appeal to one's humanity. . . . Jim Hearst believes that there may be no order in nature except the order imposed upon it by man. From nature man can learn isolated facts and lessons, but the totality he must forge for himself. Man is therefore obliged to impose an order on nature, on his own life, and on everything he makes. This order is necessary to give his life meaning, and above all man is in search of the meaning of existence: he must somehow wrench point and direction from his environment—a reason for being.

Asked about humanism, Robert Frost's respected friend responded to the present author:

> I don't know where I fit. I can go along with "democratic humanism" because it is vaguely reassuring. If it will help, I'm a backslid Congregationalist with firm leanings away from denominationalism. As my friend August Bang said, "Denominations are God's little kindergartens." Mostly I start with the individual as the hitching post for meanings and beliefs. There must be a point of reference somewhere and I like to start with a person. Then he can choose the ground he wants to stand on. There is nothing on this earth more important than people. People think the abstractions, make up the legends and myths, form and reform societies, contain the unconscious, the id, the super-ego—in spite of what some poets, scientists, and other generalizers would have you think.
>
> Maybe I'll change my mind later on, but it will be only a slight shift. Can you make anything out of this? I am more at home in the hayfield right now than in the various aspects of humanism.
>
> {WAS, 12 June 1949}

Heath, A. E. (20th Century)

Heath, when president of the Rationalist Press Association, wrote in 1956 of his dislike of the term "humanism" to describe a philosophic outlook. He made the case for rationalism.

Heath, Karl (20th Century)

Heath, in the British *Freethinker* (July 1993), wrote an essay, "Christianity is Evil." He penned an unfavorable review of Lee Eisler's *Quotable Bertrand Russell* in the same journal (January 1994), saying the book is too expensive at £14.50, that one would be better off to buy the 800-page *History of Western Philosophy* for only 50 pence.

HEATHEN

- Heathen, n. A benighted creature who has the folly to worship something that he can see and feel. According to Professor Howison, of the California State University, Hebrews are heathens.

—Ambrose Bierce
The Devil's Dictionary

Heathen, which originally denoted someone who was not Jewish and hence was not entitled to share in the promises of salvation and blessings in which the Jews believed, has come to mean anyone who does not acknowledge the God of the Bible, particularly those who are "irreligious" and "uncivilized." For example, secular humanists, Hindus, Buddhists, and philosophic naturalists are termed heathens by the Christians. {ER}

Heatherly, Marian (20th Century)

Heatherly is copy editor and permissions editor for *The Humanist*. Her column is "Worth Noting."

HEAVEN

Revelation XXI states that Heaven measures 12,000 furlongs in length, breadth, and also height. Robert L. "Believe It Or Not" Ripley in 1925 figured that that comes to

496,793,088,000,000,000,000 cubic feet.

Or about 1500 miles long in each dimension, give or take a few cubes. If 10 cubic feet for each human is allowed (it being assumed that non-humans are to be excluded), Heaven can hold

49,679,308,800,000,000,000 beings.

However, Ripley then figured that, assuming 25 years as a generation, and that roughly 77 generations of humans have existed simply since the time of Jesus, the number in the human family will have reached

302,231,454,657,293,676,543 humans

which is more than all humans who have ever lived.

(Mathematicians note that Ripley's calculations may not have taken into account that one's relatives increase in number but never overlap those being counted by others. And he assumes humanity's pool increases exponentially as one goes back in time, although the reverse is the case.)

At any rate, believe it or not, the good news in 1925 was that if almost all somehow made it to Heaven, they would be able to meet their father and mother and other family members (but not those relatives, of course, that were sinners or forgot us in their will).

However, as for those bad folks, the sinners, who are not allowed into Heaven, Hosea Ballou (1771—1852) taught that Hell could not—logically or ethically—exist, that all men at death will be saved by the love of God. If God is the ultimate of good, how could He reasonably reject *any* human being! Ripley had no comment on this, except that like Ballou he also included the entire human family.

Ripley's bad news, believe it or not, was that your parents would have met theirs, and theirs would have met theirs, theirs theirs, and so forth. It also would mean that because of the space limitations everyone would of necessity be stacked on each other's heads to a height of 113,236 miles, according to Ripley's figures. That's if they *stand*, not lie down. So to say hello to your dear oldest grandfather, who may be down toward the 113,000 miles bottom of the heap, assuming new arrivals are at the top of the heap, you will need to take about 39 years to descend, even if you are careful not to step on someone's ear as you do.

Extrapolating further, Ripley figured that if we met one relative a minute, and took off no time for sleeping, it would take 575,000,000,000,000,000 years to meet the entire human family, not counting any human beings who would be born after 1925.

In 1925, then, did Ripley believe in Heaven? Apparently not, and his 1929 book was popularly received, to the distress of the religious establishment. But philosophic naturalists and non-believers are distressed that religionists preach such an idea. Who is to blame, they ask, when a six-year-old Miami girl, having been told by her mother who was dying of AIDS that she was going to a wonderful place called heaven, sees her mother die, then calmly steps in front of a freight train in order to see her mother. Experts, instead of blaming the heaven-preachers, argue as to whether or not a very young child can commit suicide. Can such a youngster possibly grasp the finality of death? Remarked a child-adolescent psychiatrist at the University of Miami when the deliberate act took place in June, 1993, "I don't think we can ever know for sure what was on her mind." Meanwhile, the girl's adult cousin said the girl knew exactly what she was doing: "She said she'd seen an angel, and she was going to Heaven to be with the angel. So she just stood there with her eyes closed, and the train hit her." Believe it or not!

Others who have commented upon Heaven include the following:

- In heaven all the interesting people are missing.

  —Friedrich Wilhelm Nietzsche

- If I have any beliefs about immortality, it is that certain dogs I have known will go to heaven, and very, very few persons.

  —James Thurber

- Heaven, as conventionally conceived, is a place so inane, so dull, so useless, so miserable, that nobody has ever ventured to describe a whole day in heaven, though plenty of people have described a day at the seaside.

  —George Bernard Shaw

- Men have feverishly conceived a heaven only to find it insipid, and a hell to find it ridiculous.

  —George Santayana

- Only that person is wise who finds everything in life but also finds nothing in death but death. To the intelligent person, life is its own end; for that very reason, it is preparation for nothing.

  —Ludwig Feuerbach

- Heaven, n. A place where the wicked cease from troubling you with talk of their personal affairs, and the good listen with attention while you expound your own.

  —Ambrose Bierce
  The Devil's Dictionary

- He: What do you suppose comes after life?
  She: Just sort of a great merging with everything.
  He: Oh, I hope not! I'm a very bad merger!

  —Noel Coward, *Private Lives*

(See entry for Edwin Powell Hubble.) {CE; ER}

HEAVEN OR PARADISE?

Males doing comparison shopping might note the differences between the Christians' Heaven and the Muslims' Paradise. According to the *Hadith*, which is the Islamic tradition of the sayings and the practices of the Prophet:

> Every man who enters Paradise shall be given seventy-two *houris,* [and] no matter at what age he had died, when he enters Paradise, he will not age any further.

Some have interpreted Muhamad's views differently, saying in Paradise all will be in their twenties, that a frail centenarian would surely not have to spend eternity at that age.

Antony Flew has suggested that "any man who fears that even as an everlasting thirty-year-old he would not be able to do justice to the attractions of this eschatological brothel may be encouraged to learn that 'A man in Paradise shall be given virility equal to that of one hundred men.' " (See entries for Agung and for Heaven, Muslim.) {*New Humanist*, October 1998}

HEAVEN, A DEAD CERTAINTY

A 1997 poll by *U.S. News & World Reports* found that 67% of Americans are certain that Heaven exists. Further, 87% think they are likely to go there. Just 18%, however, thought all their friends would join them in Paradise. {Reuters, 23 March 1997}

HEAVEN, MUSLIM

In Muhammad the Prophet's day, belief in an afterlife was virtually nonexistent. To him, however, the Qur'an was "revealed," and the book contained eloquent descriptions of the dread day when resurrected bodies are joined with their souls and brought before the throne of God's judgment. First, a trumpet is blown; resurrection occurs; there is an ingathering of all persons for the judgment; an actual reckoning (*hisab*) is made; then comes a crossing of the Sirat bridge, the possibility of intercession (*shafaah*), and preparation is made for the final consignment either to the fires of hell (*al-nar*) or the garden of bliss (*al-jannat*).

Hell is a place where the tortures of the fire are fearful, the flames crackle and roar, fierce boiling waters are all around, the wind is scorching, and black smoke is everywhere. People sigh, they wail, their scorched skin is exchanged for new skin so they can experience the pain again and again, they drink foul liquids, boiling water is poured over their heads, and if they try to escape they are dragged back by iron hooks.

Heaven, however, is a Paradise. Here is found peace, contentment, gentle speech, pleasant shade from dark green foliage, fruits, cool drink, and the meat and wine one desires. In Heaven, one can recline on couches and be waited upon by manservants. Males have *huris*, young virgins said to have eyes like guarded pearls.

Some contemporary Muslims are in disagreement as to whether the descriptions are meant to be literal or figurative. "Literal" is the view of the majority, particularly those with little education. (See entry for Heaven or Paradise.) {Also see Ibn Warraq's *Why I Am Not A Muslim* [1995] and the *Oxford Encyclopedia of the Modern Islamic World* [1995]}.

HEAVENLY PLAIN: See entry for Shinto.

Hebbel, Friedrich (1813—1863)

Hebbel was a German tragedian and poet. His masterpiece, *Die Nibelungen* (1862), depicts the conflict of the pagan and Christian view of life. Hebbel was a pantheist. {RAT}

Hébert, Jacques René (1757—1794)

Hébert was a French revolutionist. He published the notorious *Père Duchêsne* and with Chaumette instituted the *Feasts of Reason.* He was denounced by Saint Just and guillotined. His widow, who had been a nun, was executed a few days later. {BDF}

Hébert, Marcel (20th Century)

Hébert, a French philosopher, wrote *Évolution de la foi catholique* (1905), in which he studied the Church from the outside, without hostility. He concluded that it will last, "but without any effective authority on all that thinks, acts, and advances in Humanity." Hébert believed that man has a sense of "the Divine," but he remained agnostic as regards personal immortality. {RAT}

HEBREWS: For history, see entry for Jews. For religion, see entry for Judaism. Not all Hebrews became Jews. Not all Jews are Hebrews. Many throughout history have chosen pagan Greek over religious Hebrew.

Hecataeus (c. 500 B.C.E.)

Hecataeus of Miletus, a predecessor of Herodotus, was among the earliest of un-believers, according to Angelo Juffras. Like Herodotus, Hecataeus traveled far, was called *historikos* (widely traveled), a teller of stories, an active inquirer. This led him to observe that "the beliefs of the Greeks are laughable," although it is not certain just what beliefs he had in mind. Bertrand Russell notes that Heraclitus had negative views of Hecataeus. Heraclitus, however, liked Teutamus, who believed that "most men are bad." Hecataeus, as one of the first individuals devoted to "inquiry"—*histoire* originally meant not "history," in the contemporary sense, but telling stories about one's inquiries—laid the foundation for *sophistés*, inquirers who had become wise men because of their traveling and story-telling, or sophists. {EU, Angelo Juffras}

Hecht, Anthony (1923—)

Hecht, an American poet who is a member of the American Academy of Arts and Letters, responded in 1989 to the present author concerning humanism:

> I feel much as Lionel Trilling did [in the quote you mailed], ill-at-ease with the term "humanism" though perhaps our reasons for discomfort are not the same. I'd be curious to find out if any of your respondents claim to enlist under the heading of "ancient humanist." As for me, I'm afraid that as currently used (without your fine distinctions) the term seems to mean little more than that the person to whom it applies is "a nice guy," and more particularly one who is nice by instinct and not by policy or doctrine. This essentially antinomian meaning is one of the things that makes me as hesitant and suspicious as I am. The word carries about as much weight these days as the word "socialism" in the phrase "National Socialism."
>
> In terms of plain usefulness, I still like to employ it as you did in your third definition, the one of "Classical Humanism," applied, as you indicate, to the likes of More, Erasmus, Montaigne, Petrarch, Boccaccio, Bacon, Colet, Vives, and so on. I wish I could claim to be able to enroll myself under such a heading, but apart from my ignorance, I would also have to be a great deal older than I am.

In 1992, he had further observations:

> Your categories intrigue me, not least of all because they are by no means exhaustive. None of them, for example, would embrace what Terence and Cicero meant in saying, "I am a man: nothing human is alien to me." I think this is clearly distinct from the second category of "collective philosophies" such as you enumerate. It furthermore occurs to me to wonder just how useful a term "humanism" can be if, as I shrewdly suspect, there are hardly any people who would categorically deny an affiliation to one or another of its varieties. If not too impatient to consider the question, even Hitler, I imagine, would declare himself a "humanist" (just as he regarded himself as a Socialist) on the grounds that he was generously concerned with the welfare of at least *some* fellow humans.
>
> I may say that I have no faith whatever in the "self-improvability of human personality" which you offer as a description of "secular humanism." This does not mean that I don't believe that individuals can improve themselves in important ways; they obviously do so simply by maturing, and most adults are more thoughtful and considerate of others than small children are. But in the main, I do not for a minute believe that the human race has become more humane or less given to barbarous inhumanity than obtained in any former period however "barbarous" or refined in its brutality. From my point of view, the most useful definition is the one you characterize as "classical humanism." It describes a particular era, and a latitudinous kind of culture that belonged to a certain period, and that is now past. There is nothing wrong nor especially pedantic about seeing humanism as something in the past. Up until recently the word "modern" was defined as "bearing upon the present," and concerned with whatever is "current." But now, it appears, we live in a "post-modern" world, and no one will ever be modern again.
>
> {WAS, 30 January 1989 and 5 June 1992}

Hecht, Ben (1893—1964)

Hecht was a New York-born journalist, novelist, playwright, and screenwriter of over sixty films, including Academy Award-winning "Underworld" (1927) and "The Scoundrel" (1935). His parents, who had come from Southern Russia, moved to Chicago, where at the age of ten he gave a violin concert. Later, he was an acrobat with a small circus in Wisconsin. In Chicago he became associated with that city's "literary renaissance" following World War I, working with Sherwood Anderson, Maxwell Bodenheim, and Pascal Covici. He liked the French symbolists (Gautier, Verlaine, Baudelaire), disliked Rousseau (a great big thumping fool") and Picasso ("an imposter of the arts"), and thought J. K. Huysmans was "the rajah of writing, his brain the splendid macaw of all literature."

Gargoyles (1922) was one of many of his works which received negative reviews. The *Greensboro (North Carolina) Daily News* called the book "a rambling, incoherent, formless string of incidents, unworthy of the name of story, bristling with innumerable pewter imitations of the steely satire of Masters, Mencken, Sinclair Lewis, and Maxwell Anderson." But Burton Rascoe in the *New York Tribune* described his *A Thousand and One Afternoons in Chicago* (1922, illustrated by George Grosz) glowingly:

> There is no newspaper writer in America who can touch him in imagination and literary treatment of police court happenings, hospital cases, street curb incidents—all the multitudinous events of city life. He is a poet; he is a wit; he is clever; he has feeling; and he has a sense of drama.

Similarly, James T. Farrell, although noting Hecht's love of the grotesque and mordant, liked his journalistic collection of stories about the city's back streets. Stanley Walker called his stories "something of a Bible, the perfect example of how 'human interest' stories should be handled."

A Jew in Love (1931) left readers wondering where art leaves off and obscenity begins. *Fantazius Mallare, A Mysterious Oath* (1922) left no doubt, for the book was sequestered by the government as "obscene literature," leaving Hecht a more unrelenting foe of censors than ever.

A $6,000 per week writer in Hollywood by 1937, Hecht was called "the Ishmael of the inquisitors." He was said to have been the only director who could chew gum and smoke a cigar at the same time and, also, the only one who could finish a picture ahead of schedule.

Hecht was an outspoken Anglophobe, because of England's stand on Israel. However, he gave Noel Coward his first starring movie role, in "The Scoundrel." Although listed in *Who's Who of American Jewry 1938—1939*, Hecht had rather strong non-theistic sentiments in *Fantazius Mallare's* dedication:

> This dark and wayward book is affectionately dedicated to my enemies...to the moral ones who have relentlessly chased God out of their bedrooms; to the moral ones who cringe before Nature, who flatten themselves upon prayer rugs, who shut their eyes, stuff their ears, bind, gag, and truss themselves and offer their mutilations to the idiot God they have invented (the Devil take them, I grow bored with laughing at them)...to the religious ones who wage bloody and tireless wars upon all who do not share their fear of life (Ah, what is God but a despairing refutation of Man?)...to the social ones who regard belching as the sin against the Holy Ghost, who enamel themselves with banalities, who repudiate contemptuously the existence of their bowels (Ah, these theologians of etiquette, these unctuous circumlocutors, a pock upon them)...to those and to many other abominations whom I apologize to for omitting, this inhospitable book, celebrating the dark mirth of Fantazius Mallare, is dedicated in the hope that their righteous eyes may never kindle with secret lusts nor their pious lips water erotically from its readings—in short in the hope that they may never encounter the ornamental phrases I have written and the ritualistic lines Wallace Smith has drawn in the pages that follow.

Of *Fantazius Mallare*, the novel of decadence in the tradition of *Against Nature* by Huysmans, Arthur C. Clarke remembers, "The awesome picture on page 75 was once the basis of a *Time* cover, about Toynbee. But it's the dungeon scene on page 106 that turned me on when first I saw it forty years ago." {TYD; WAS, 25 April 1997}

Hedberg, Erika (1976-)

Hedberg, while still a philosophy undergraduate, lectured at the Center for Inquiry Mid-West and became a volunteer in the Kansas City Eupraxophy Center and the Campus Freethought Alliance. In 1999 she became the Council for Secular Humanism's Coordinator for the Alliance of Secular Humanist Societies (ASHS).

Hedenius, Ingemar (1908—)

Hedenius, a Swedish professor of philosophy at Uppsala University, is a non-theist. (See entry for Scandinavian Unbelievers.)

Hedge, Frederic Henry (1805—1890)

The editor of *Christian Examiner* (1857—1861) and a Harvard professor of ecclesiastical history and German literature, Hedge was one of the principal supporters of the "new views" that came to be known in the 1830s as Transcendentalism. The Transcendental Club which met in the middle 1830s in the Boston area, in fact, was referred to as "Hedge's Club." He differed with Emerson and others, however, on the issue of the importance of the church in religious life. Emerson thought most institutions, including the church, were at best a necessary evil. Hedge argued that such institutions provide a necessary historical continuity that does not supersede religious intuition but supplements it in importance. With Henry W. Bellows, James Freeman Clarke, and the "Broad Church" group, he opposed the radicals of the Free Religious Association. {CE; FUS; U; U&U}

Hedin, Sven Adolph (Born 1834)

Hedin was a Swedish member of the "Andra Kammaren," or House of Commons. He edited the *Aftonbladet* (1874—1876) and wrote many radical works. {BDF}

HEDONISM

Hedonism is a outlook in which pleasure is the highest good. Aristippus and the early Cyrenaics believed pleasure is achieved by the complete gratification of all one's sensual desires. Epicurus, however, equated pleasure with the absence of pain. Utilitarianism, a form of 19th-century British hedonism, has been described as "the greatest happiness for the greatest number." As pointed out by Prof. Gilbert Murray, the Greek word *hedone* means "sweetness" rather than sensual pleasure. In that sense hedonism might be applied to the system of Epicurus or of Aristippus. {CE; DCL; ER; RE}

Heffron, Paul (20th Century)

Formerly a minister in the United Church of Christ, Heffron is an atheist-humanist who lives in Shoreview, Minnesota. {*Secular Nation*, October-December 1998}

Hefner, Hugh M. (1926—)

Hefner is the American publisher and businessman who launched *Playboy* in 1953, infuriating orthodox religionists because of the magazine's photographs of nude females and advice concerning hedonism. A strong defender of the First Amendment, Hefner takes some credit for advancing the sexual revolution that started in the 1950s and continued widely at least until the onset of the Age of AIDS. When Billy Graham preached to 44,300 people that AIDS may be "a judgment of God" for sin, Hefner commented, "I'm old enough to remember the Monkey Trial in the '20s and then reading about it as a schoolboy in the '30s. I was fascinated with the controversy surrounding evolution. To me, from a very early age, it was like superstition and bigotry on one hand and truth and beauty on the other. To be revisiting that crazy notion and others—like AIDS as some sort of retribution—is so preposterous! Society as it stands today certainly isn't worthy of entry into a new millennium. We may be technologically and scientifically advanced, but socially we are no more than superstitious savages."

Hefner's *Playboy Philosophy* (1962—1965) contains twenty-two sections. Asked by journalist Jeff Yarbrough if he believed in the concept of God, Hefner replied, "I don't. Whatever this awe-inspiring existence is all about, the answer does not lie in a book. The closest that I'm able to come to the concept of God is nature. The greatest religious experiences I've had are walking this property and walking through the redwood forest and feeling a sense of awe, of smallness." {*The Advocate*, 8 March 1994}

Hegel, G(eorg) W(ilhelm) F(riedrich) (1770—1831)

Although an untypical non-believer, Hegel in his *Phenomenology of the Mind* (1807) presented "one of the most influential sources of contemporary atheism." His universe centered around "absolute idealism," or world-soul, and he influenced Kierkegaard and Sartre. His idealism influenced Josiah Royce, William Ernest Hocking, Emerson, and Christian Scientists. John Dewey, however, broke away from Hegelian idealism early on. If there is any individual for Protestantism analogous to what Thomas Aquinas is for Roman Catholicism, a case could be made for Hegel.

In *Invitation to Learning* (1941), Bertrand Russell is negatively critical of Hegel's *Philosophy of History*: "[It] is a very important book indeed, judged by the effects it has had, and a totally unimportant book judged by any truth it may contain. [One effect is that it influenced Marx, who, of course, had an enormous effect.] [It is] important, partly because it presented a pattern in history—a scheme, a system—according to which historical events were supposed to have developed, which of course people like. It is a simple formula and they think 'now we understand it all'; if it is false, they do not notice it. I do not object to a man writing universal history, if he has the time; but I do object to the notion that there is a simple scheme or thread running through it all. . . . I think the course of history is subject to laws and is probably for a sufficiently wise person deterministic; but nobody is wise enough. It is far too complicated and nobody can work it out; and the person who says he has done so is a charlatan."

McCabe has half-hearted praise for Hegel: "His stress on spirit did much harm in European thought for a century and he was stuffily reactionary in politics. But though he professed (morally) to be a Christian, he scorned theology and did not believe in a personal God or immortality. When Heine mentioned the argument for God from the starry heavens, he [Hegel] retorted that the stars are leprosy on the sky, and when he was reminded of Kant's moral argument for a future life he said, 'So you expect a tip for nursing your sick mother and for not poisoning your brother.' "

Hegel had students of philosophy begin with Spinozism. He also is said to have remarked that of all his many disciples only one understood him, and he understood him falsely. Hegel was professor at Jena, Heidelberg, and Berlin, in which last city he died and was buried beside Johann Fichte. (For Mao's comments about Hegel, see the entry for Marxism. See Andrew Ferguson's "Popper, Englefield and Philosophy, *New Humanist*, November 1994, in which Ferguson states that "Popper is as effective as Englefield in showing that most of what Hegel wrote is meaningless rubbish [except in so far as it serves as a rationale for the state exercising absolute power].") {BDF; CE; CL; ER; EU, Volker Dürr; Lee Eisler, *The Quotable Bertrand Russell*; PA; RAT; RE; TRI; TYD}

Heidegger, Martin (1889—1976)

"Many people who learn that Heidegger lied over and over again about his Nazism, and that he did his best to ignore the murder of the European Jews, conclude that his writings can be neglected," wrote Richard Rorty. Despite his being a resentful, ungenerous, disloyal, and deceitful man, Heidegger deserves our attention, adds Rorty, because "he somehow managed to write books that are as powerful and as original as Spinoza's or Hegel's. Hans-Georg Gadamer, Jean-Paul Sartre, Emmanuel Levinas, Hannah Arendt, Michel Foucault, Jacques Derrida, and Jürgen Habermas all cut their teeth on those books. You cannot read most of the important philosophers of recent times without taking Heidegger's thought into account."

Heidegger, one of the founders of 20th-century existentialism (although he rejected the title), was a student of Husserl, succeeding him as a professor of philosophy at Freiburg, Germany. In his *Being and Time* (1927), Heidegger dealt with the concepts of "care," "mood," and the individual's relationship to death. He related the authenticity of being as well as the anguish of modern society to the individual's confrontation with his own temporality. In his confrontation with the world, Heidegger taught that man finds ties binding him to objects, companions, and life as well as finds his essential possibilities and his relationship to death. Strongly influenced by Kierkegaard, Dilthey, and Nietzsche, he in turn influenced the work of Sartre. Although Heidegger joined the Nazi party in Germany, he later said he had not been active in the party nor a believer in its philosophy or cultural policy. He did not, however, leave the party and once orated that "the Führer himself and he alone is the German reality, present and future, and its law." Somehow, he felt that the National Socialist revolution of the early 1930s, by using pre-Socratic philosophers' thoughts and the poetry of Friedrich Hölderlin, could be given a proper direction. Even after the Nazis showed no interest in his view of the direction Germany should take, he continued to support them, despite his denial. Further, he helped in the banning of prominent Jews—including his own teacher and patron, Edmund Husserl—from Germany University faculties. Also, he blocked the promotion of a former student by writing a confidential memo which accused him of having become "closely tied to the Jew Fränkel, formerly employed at Göttingen, and now dismissed from this university."

Scholars have become intrigued, as shown by Elzbieta Ettinger's *Hannah Arendt—Martin Heidegger* (1995), at how the Jewish Arendt had a four-year sexual relationship with Heidegger in 1924 when she was a student, and how he was able to sustain her emotional involvement until her death over five decades after they had met. If it was passion which led the married Catholic thirty-five-year-old Professor Heidegger to initiate the affair with a student, the fact that it was he, not she, who broke off the relationship is interesting inasmuch as he followed up with a self-centered and manipulative desire to keep in touch. Arendt believed his problem was his wife, Elfride. By the early 1930s, Arendt was aware that Heidegger was a Nazi. In 1933, as rector of the University of Freiburg, he was known to have blocked the promotions of Karl Jaspers, Eduard Baumgarten, and Max Mueller, all suspected of being anti-Nazi. When Jaspers's wife, a Jew, had cried at newspaper reports of anti-Semitism, Heidegger told Jaspers that "it makes one feel better to cry sometimes." Although some describe Heidegger as being an atheist, Heidegger studied Catholic theology thoroughly, and his search for Being is close to a kind of belief in God.

Bernhard Welte, a Catholic priest and Professor of Christian Philosophy of Religion at the University of Freiburg, delivered Heidegger's funeral speech. Heidegger's thought, he remarked, "has shaken the world and the century." He added that Heidegger's path was that of "perhaps the greatest seeker of this century." Richard Rorty, in his *Philosophy and the Mirror of Nature*, cites Heidegger—along with Hegel, Marx, Frege, Freud, and Wittgenstein—in a list of "individual men of genius who think of something new" and called him "one of the three most important philosophers of our century" (the others being Dewey and Wittgenstein). Disagreeing, Paul Edwards in "Heidegger's Quest for Being" (*Journal of Philosophy* 64:437—470) states that what is more likely is "that Heidegger will continue to fascinate those hungry for mysticism of the anaemic and purely verbal variety, the 'glossogonous metaphysics' of which his philosophy is such an outstanding example. The odds are that people afflicted in this way will exist for a long time; and if this is so, Heidegger will indeed be read and admired in future centuries. More sober and rational persons will continue to regard the whole Heidegger phenomenon as a grotesque aberration of the human mind." Edwards was amused that in a programmatic essay Sartre counted Heidegger as an atheist. "He did indeed reject Christian and Jewish theism," Edwards wrote in *God and the Philosophers*, "but he believed in an ultimate reality called 'Being,' which has striking similarities to the traditional deity. Being is in everything and is the source of everything. It is always referred to as 'the Holy' and as something 'transcendent' that cannot be adequately described in language taken from ordinary experience. It can be reached by various mystical techniques, especially one that Heidegger calls *Gelassenheit* and that has been facetiously described as a form of 'creative waiting.' It should be noted that Heidegger felt an affinity with medieval mystics, whom he frequently quoted with approval, and that he was unequivocally opposed to any form of naturalism." (See entry for Joseph Warren Beach.) {CE; ER; HNS2; Richard Rorty, *The New York Times Book Review*, 3 May 1998; TYD}

Heidelberger, Michael (1888—1992)

Heidelberger, a member of the New York Society for Ethical Culture, was a distinguished chemist who wrote textbooks and in 1950 was on the faculty of philosophy at the University of Uppsala in Sweden. The Belgian government once honored him for his immunochemical work in helping to cure African sleeping sickness. Heidelberger was one of the first students of the Ethical Culture schools in New York, having been enrolled from 1900 to 1905.

Heideman, Robert (20th Century)

Heideman, founder the president of Aquatic System International, was the vice-president of Freethinkers, Inc., and class honorman in the U. S. Navy's Aviation Ordinance School. The Center for Inquiry's librarian's office is named for Heideman.

Heidenstam, Verner von (1859—1923)

Known as "Sweden's Laureate," for he won a Nobel Prize, Heidenstam as a youth turned from the study of art to poetry. His first volume (*Pilgrimage*) was inspired by his extensive travels and contained heavy criticism of the clergy and their doctrines and professed agnosticism. "Superstition and faith are the same," he wrote. "Man's God is the priesthood's money chest." {RE}

Heikel, Viktor (19th Century)

With Mathilda Asp, Heikel founded in 1887 the first nonbelievers' organization in Finland. (See entry for Scandinavian Unbelievers.

Heilbroner, Robert Louis (1919—)

An author and economist, Heilbroner has gone on record as being a non-theist. His works include *Future as History* (1960), *Between Capitalism and Socialism* (1970), *Inquiry into the Human* Prospect (1974), *The Essential Adam Smith* (1986), and *Teachings from the Worldly Philosophy* (1996). A Guggenheim fellow, Heilbroner taught in New York at the New School for Social Research. {CA; E}

Heine, Heinrich (1797—1856)

One of the greatest of German lyric poets, Heine was born of Jewish parents. *Deutschland* (1844) is a work in which Heine, being a German of Jewish parents, satirizes German anti-Semitism. Of some 3,000 lyrics Schumann, Schubert, and others have put to music, his best-known song is "Die Lorelei."

Although claimed by some as being a religious man, having converted to Christianity as a youth, the conversion was a matter of convenience, meant to qualify him for a university appointment (in law) that he never received anyway. Nevertheless, he is known for his naturalism and, some say, his deism. In the 1850s he had written, "Christianity is useless for the healthy. . . . For the sick it is a very good religion." Also: "Alas, I had neither time nor mood to say there what I wanted—namely, that I die as a Poet, who needs neither religion nor philosophy, and has nothing to do with either. The Poet understands very well the symbolic idiom of Religion, and the abstract jargon of Philosophy; but neither the religious gentry nor those of philosophy will ever understand the poet."

"[A] slimy and greasy Jew—fit only to eat sausages made of toads," Carlyle called him. Neither was he liked by the Nazis, who burned his books and banished his works from the anthologies, preserving "Die Lorelei" under "author unknown." As for the separation of church and state, he declared, "I consider it a degradation and a stain on my honor to submit to baptism in order to qualify myself for state employment in Prussia."

Writers about Heine have argued both that Heine was either too Jewish, or not Jewish enough. They cite his "*Gedächtnisfeier*" ("Commemoration Service"):

Not a mass will be sung for me,
Not a *Kaddish* will be said,
None will say or sing a service
On the day that I lie dead. . . .

He continues that when his wife visits his grave, she should not be too sad and that his chubby child "must not walk home all the way;/ You'll see coaches standing ready/ At the barrier gate that day."

In 1995, Ernst Pawel's *The Poet Dying: Heinrich Heine's Last Years in Paris* states that Heine "never hid the fact that he was born a Jew; he was unashamedly attached to Jewish history and tradition, and he wrote a number of poems and an unfinished novel, *The Rabbi of Bacherach*, which incorporated and sometimes celebrated that history and that tradition. For most of his life, however, he was a passionate Deist, and he tended to make little of his Jewishness, as well as of his youthful conversion to Christianity. That conversion was clearly a matter of convenience, meant to qualify him for a university appointment (in law) that he never received anyway. He scorned Felix Mendelssohn for his more sincere Christian conviction: 'if I had the luck of being a grandson of Moses Mendelssohn,' he explained, 'I would surely not use my talent to set the pissing of the Lamb to music.' "

Heine died at the age of fifty-eight, having suffered since youth from syphilis. Some contemporary physicians, however, have diagnosed his case differently. They hold that his progressive paralysis of the spine could have been caused by either a congenital neuropathy or by amyotrophic lateral sclerosis (Lou Gehrig's disease). His last few years were lived as an invalid, morphine being administered to him through sores deliberately kept open on his back in order that the drug could be administered. He found it difficult to speak, and he often held one of his eyelids propped open in order to read or write.

About 1848 he became paralyzed and lost his eyesight, but he employed himself in literary composition with the aid of an amanuensis, writing poetry during his sleepless nights and prose during the day. His final illness, spent as a skeleton on his "mattress grave," was painful. He weighed but seventy pounds and, according to Pawel, was "nearly sightless, heavily sedated, often unable to speak beyond a whisper." Heine's biographers Lewis Browne and Eliza Butler say he maintained his sense of humor until the end. Asked if he was really incurable, he would reply, "Oh no, I'll die some day." And when someone suggested discreetly that his illness had been caused by excessive work, he would answer, "Well, it was *excess* at any rate." At the end of Heine's life, he was treated by "leeches, enemas, and cauterization of the spine . . . opium rubbed into sores deliberately kept open," according to Pawel.

As for his alleged deathbed conversion, Robertson has written, "[Heine's] characteristic profession of reconciling himself on his deathbed with the deity he imaged as 'the Aristophanes of heaven' serves so scantily to console the orthodox lovers of his matchless song. His criticism of Kant and Fichte is a sufficient clue to his serious convictions; and that 'God is all that there is' is the sufficient expression of his pantheism." Of the alleged conversion, McCabe states that Heine "was in fact an atheist and so remained until he was bed-ridden with spine-disease, when he rediscovered God. 'Put it down to morphia and poultice,' he told his friends. He scorned both Judaism and Christianity and never believed in a future life."

Others have claimed that basically Heine was a pantheist. In his last moments, always in pain, he jested that he would report God to the Society for the Prevention of Cruelty to Animals. When his wife sat beside him, praying for his soul, Heine replied in an unpantheistic way, and possibly for his wife's benefit, "*Dieu me pardonnera; c'est son metier*" (God will forgive me—that's His job).

Nicolas Walter described Heine as being "a perpetual outsider—a poor man among the rich, an intellectual among philistines, an internationalist among nationalists, a liberal among conservatives, an individualist among liberals, a German among the French, a Jew among Germans, a Christian among Jews, an infidel among Christians, a theist among infidels, always a free thinker in the widest sense."

When Heine's will was opened, it was found that he had left his entire estate to his wife, provided she would marry again. His reason for the condition was stated with Teutonic bluntness: "Because then there will be at least one man to regret my death." {BDF; CE; *The Freethinker*, December 1997; JM; JMR; JMRH; PA; PUT; RAT; RE; TYD}

Heine, Johan (20th Century)

Heine spoke in 1997 at a seminar of the European Humanist Professionals in London. He talked about military experiences after UN peace-keeping tasks and described having given psychological support for relief soldiers in Zaire.

Heinerman, John (20th Century)

With Anson Shupe, freethinker Heinerman wrote *The Mormon Corporate Empire* (1985).

Heinlein, Robert A. (1907—1988)

Heinlein was a noted science fiction author of the film "Destination Moon" and the novel, *Stranger in a Strange Land* (1961). In *Time Enough for Love*, he wrote, "History does not record anywhere at any time a religion that has any rational basis. Religion is a crutch for people. . . ." Of his youth he wrote,

> The faith in which I was brought up assured me that I was better than other people; I was *saved*, they were *damned*. . . . Our hymns were loaded with arrogance—self-congratulation on how cozy we were with the Almighty and what a high opinion he had of us, what hell everybody else would catch come Judgment Day."

In 1952, he wrote to his publisher:

> The idea that we could lose our freedom by succumbing to a wave of religious hysteria: I am sorry to say that I consider it possible. I hope that it is not probable. There's a deep latent strain of religious fanaticism in this, our culture. It is rooted in history and has broken out many times in the past—it is with us now. There has been a sharp rise in strongly evangelical sects in this country in recent years, several of which hold beliefs theocratic in the extreme. It is a truism that almost any religion, sect, or cult will legislate its creed into law if it acquires the political power to do so and will follow it by suppressing opposition and subverting education to seize early the minds of the young.

As for the supernatural, Heinlein wrote, "Men rarely (if ever) managed to dream up a god superior to themselves. Most gods have the manners and morals of a spoiled child."

A character in *Time Enough for Love* says,

> History does not record anywhere at any time a religion that has any rational basis. Religion is a crutch for people not strong enough to stand up to the unknown without help. But, like dandruff, most people do have a religion and spend time and money on it to derive considerable pleasure fiddling with it.

In 1956, he was asked about humanism and responded to the present author:

> I have made little formal study of philosophy and that little was mostly a long time ago. I am not expert in this field; I am engineer-turned-novelist. Humanism to me that which you defined in your letter as "Naturalistic Humanism." I am aware of the other meanings to this multi-valued word, but the other meanings strike me as having either historical interest only, or special or even mistaken connotations. This opinion probably reflects the fact that "Naturalistic Humanism" as defined in your letter most nearly reflects my own personal philosophy, of the seven categories you list.
>
> I seek no quarrel with any religionist; certainly I cannot assert that any creed is mistaken. Yet, if we stipulate without proof the existence of Deity, it seems to me inherently unlikely that one of His attributes would be that He would demand "worship" from his creatures and still less likely that He would expect of them faith or dogmatic belief without evidence. I think it still less likely that He would send messengers with Divine revelations armed with no better credentials than loud voices, legerdemain, and a conviction of righteousness. Moreover, I have not even any certainty about the beliefs, values, and hopes listed in the cited definition of naturalistic humanism. It *may* be that the human race, through its own efforts, can go on to greater heights, fuller understanding, and a more satisfactory life for all of us and our descendants. It would be pleasant to think so. But I do not find such a belief necessary to continue optimistic striving.
>
> We have our hands, we have our brains, we have the challenge all around us, and we have within (from whatever source) the will to strive. That is enough; there is no need to assert "belief" in that which we do not, as yet, know. The goals defined for naturalistic humanism are things which you and I and a large percentage of humans want and are willing to try hard to achieve—hands and brains and the materials at hand. Even if, in the long run, the goals should prove impossible, unreal, or beyond our human capacity, I see no alternative other than suicide in some form or other, personal or racial—and I have no taste for that. I think I have been most influenced in my views by T. H. Huxley, Eric T. Bell, Alfred Korzybski, parts of H. G. Wells's writings, and Socrates (*The Apologia*).

Upon his death, Heinlein's body was cremated.

{TYD; WAS, 31 August 1956}

Heinrich, Rolf (1946—)

Heinrich is editor of *Miz*, a publication for an international league of churchless individuals and atheists. He wrote *Verheissung des Kreuzes* (1982). (See entry for *Internationaler Bund Der Konfessionslosen Und Atheisten*.) {FD}

Heinzen, Karl Peter (1809—1880)

Heinzen was a German-American poet, an orator, and a politician. In 1845 he published at Darmstadt a work on the *Prussian Bureaucracy*, for which he was prosecuted and had to seek shelter in Switzerland. At Zurich he edited the *German Tribune* and the *Democrat*. In 1848 he participated in the attempted German Revolution, again fleeing, this time to New York. He established the *Pioneer* (then called *Freidenker*), first in Louisville, then in Cincinnati, New York, and Boston. Among his many works are *Letters on Atheism* (1856), *The Heroes of German Communism*, *The True Character of Humboldt* (1869), *The Rights of Women*, and *What is Humanity?* (1877). {BDF; RAT}

Heldberg, Jim (20th Century)

Heldberg works with American Atheists Inc. to encourage groups to affiliate. On the Web: <http://www.atheists.org/>.

HELL

• Hell is a place where the police are German . . . the motorists, French . . . the cooks, English.

—Bertrand Russell

The ancient Jews referred to the Sheol or Tophet, where departed souls exist ina gloomy surroundings in which, though not tormented, they wander around without joy.

The New Testament mentions Gehenna or Gehinom, which is named after the Valley of Hinnom, a place of punishment (a burial area outside the walls of ancient Jerusalem, as well as a site condemned by Biblical prophets as one where vile and wicked rites were practiced in ancient times. For Christians, Hell is an eternal abode, a place where souls are damned by the judgment of God and are never for eternity allowed to see God. Many believe the Christians borrowed the concept from Persia's Mithraism. Hell is a fiery place, one described in detail not in the Holy Bible but in Dante Alighieri's imaginative 14th-century work, *The Divine Comedy.*

Annie Dillard, in *Pilgrim at Tinker Creek* (1974), includes the following diabolical dialogue:

> I read about an Eskimo hunter who asked the local missionary priest, "If I did not know about God and sin, would I go to hell?"
>
> "No," said the priest, "not if you did not know."
>
> "Then why," asked the Eskimo earnestly, "did you tell me?"

If the television and other evangelists are correct, and everyone will go to Hell unless he or she believes in the Lord Jesus Christ, has been "washed in the Blood of the Lamb," been baptized, and is either free of, or has been pardoned for, sins, the following would not have been eligible as of mid-1994. It is not clear whether Jews and Muslims are eligible. However, they are listed below.

ADHERENTS OF NON-CHRISTIAN RELIGIONS AS OF MID-1998

Source: *1999 Encyclopaedia Britannica Book of the Year*
(Based on the UN's World Population Prospects)

Religion	Adherents in World
Muslims	1,164,622,000
83% Sunnites; 16% Shiites; 1% other	
Non-Religious and Atheists *	909,658,000
The category includes "persons professing no religion, non-believers, agnostics, freethinkers, dereligionized secularists indifferent to all religion." Also, "persons professing atheism, skepticism, disbelief, or irreligion, including antireligious (opposed to all religion)"	
Hindus	761,689,000
70% Vaishnavites; 25% Shaivites; 2% Neo-Hindus and reform Hindus	
Chinese Folk Religionists	379,162,000
Followers of traditional Chinese religion (local deities, ancestor veneration, Confucian ethics, Taoism; universism; divination; some Buddhist elements)	
Buddhist	353,794,000
56% Mayayana; 38% Theravada; (Hinayana), 6% Tantrayana	
Ethnic Religionists	248,565,000
New Religionists	100,144,000
Followers of Asian 20th Century New Religions, New Religious movements, radical new crisis religions, and non-Christian syncretistic mass religions, all founded since 1800 and most since 1945.	
Sikhs	22,322,000
Jews	14,111,000
Estimates vary widely. *The American Jewish Year Book* has different estimates	
Spiritists	11,785,000
Bahai's	7,666,000
Confucians	6,241,000
Non-Chinese followers of Confucius, mostly Koreans in Korea	
Jains	3,922,000
Shintoists	2,789,000
Other Religionists	1,313,000
Including 70 minor world religions, spiritist religions, Mandeans (38,000), New Age religions, quasi religions, pseudoreligions, parareligions, religious or mystic systems, religious and semireligious brotherhoods of numerous varieties, 274,000 Zoroastrians	
Total Non-Christians (67 %)	3,986,801,000
Total Christians (33 %)	1,943,038,000
Total Humans (100%)	5,929,839,000**

* Unitarians-Universalists and Ethical Culture Society and secular humanists are presumably included in the "Non-" category.

** A figure of 2 billion is the optimal or desired number of humans that Earth can comfortably support as its total population, or 3 billion at the very top, according to Zero Population Growth and similar population research groups. In September 1999, the world's population was estimated to have reached 6,000,000,000.

The Universal Almanac (1996) estimated somewhat different figures:

Region	Nonreligious	Atheist	%
East Asia	618,900,000	123,400,000	73.0
Former USSR	83,100,000	60,600,000	14.1
Europe	49,400,000	17,400,000	6.6
South Asia	18,400,000	5,100,000	2.3
North America	19,000,000	1,000,000	2.0
Latin America	12,900,000	2,400,000	1.5
Oceania	2,900,000	500,000	.3
Africa	1,300,000	100,000	.1
	805,900,000	210,500,000	

Up-to-date numbers from the above sources can be obtained at the ends of years, but skeptics doubt the accuracy of any such studies. When, for example, do churches *subtract* all those who die, move, or ask that their membership be discontinued?

Meanwhile, Christians bent on "saving" the world have at least two-thirds of the human population as conversion prospects. The painter Paul Cadmus, a secular humanist, believes that although there is no Hell there should be . . . "for individuals who tell other individuals that they should go to Hell." (See entries for Edwin Powell Hubble and for Dante, whose nine circles of Hell are found in his *The Inferno*.)

HELL ACCORDING TO *LA CIVILTA CATTOLICA*

God does not inflict pain "through angels or demons as is illustrated in many paintings or is read in the Divine Comedy," according to a Jesuit magazine in Rome, *La Civilta Cattolica* (July 1999). It "is not a 'place' but a 'state,' a person's 'state of being,' in which a person suffers from the deprivation of God." Hell's new makeover was supported by Pope John Paul II, who soon thereafter told visiting pilgrims that "more than a physical place, hell is the state of those who freely and definitely separate themselves from God, the source of all life and joy." In other words, the Pope said, it is not a loving God who sends people to hell, but individuals who consign themselves to hell through unrepentant sin. That hell is real is true, the Pope appeared to be saying, but his interpretation differs greatly from that of philosophic naturalists. For the Pope, both hell and Hell are still real. Meanwhile, the Rev. R. Albert Mohler Jr., president of Southern Baptist Theological Seminary in Louisville, Kentucky, disagreed with the Pope's stand, insisting that Hell is "a very real place of very real torment." In the Middle Ages, Jewish descriptions of hell included all sorts of terrible torments like boiling rivers.

For naturalists, "Hell" is one helluva theological invention. {Gustav Niebuhr, *The New York Times*, 18 September 1999}

HELL, BAPTIST

Hell, for most Southern Baptists, is the place of punishment described in the Bible: outer darkness, fire, torment, isolation.

HELL, BUDDHIST

The Buddhist Hell, according to some of the varied Buddhist leaders, consists of eight hot and cold places, each hell associated with a particular type of suffering. The tortures that are described develop compassion for the beings there and also create an incentive not to engage in the nonvirtuous behavior described.

HELL, ENDOTHERMIC OR EXOTHERMIC?

A Yale professor, according to America Online chatterers, gave his graduate students a take-home exam with but one question: "Is Hell exothermic (gives off heat) or endothermic (absorbs heat)?" Most students cited Boyle's law: gas cools when it expands and heats when it is compressed. One, however, wrote the following four-pointer:

> First, we need to know how the mass of Hell is changing in time. So we need to know the rate at which souls are moving into Hell as well as the rate they are leaving. One can extrapolate that, inasmuch as a soul cannot leave, no souls are leaving.
>
> Second, as to how many are entering Hell, religions that preach about Hell all state that if you're not one of theirs *you* will go to Hell. Inasmuch as there are more than one of these religions and inasmuch as most humans do not belong to more than one religion, it can be projected that all people will end up in Hell.
>
> Third, birth and death rates being what they are, the number of souls in Hell will increase exponentially. Further, inasmuch as Boyle's Law states that, in order for the temperature and pressure in Hell to stay the same, the volume of Hell has to expand as souls are added, therefore two possibilities are evident: one, if Hell is expanding at a slower rate than the rate at which souls enter Hell, then the temperature and pressure in Hell will increase until all Hell breaks loose; and two, if Hell is expanding at a rate faster than the increase of souls in Hell, then the temperature and pressure will drop until Hell freezes over.
>
> Now, therefore, if we accept the postulate given me by Miss Theresa Banyan during my freshman year that "It will be a cold night in Hell before I sleep with you," and in light of the fact that I still have not succeeded with her, then the second possibility cannot be true; ergo, Hell is exothermic.

HELL, JEWISH

The nature of hell is a mystery that Jews leave alone. The assumption, many Jewish theologians hold, is that God is caring and would not be a part of any sadistic punishment.

HELL, MUSLIM

The Muslim Hell is described as a fire having seven levels, the lowest of which crackles and roars with fierce boiling water, scorching wind, and wailing, wretched souls. (See entry for Heaven, Muslim.)

HELL, NON-THEISTIC

Hell is due north from the Norwegian city of Trondheim. It is a green and pleasant land where the only hot coals are those used for the traditional saunas. In 1997 there were six members of the Norwegian Humanist League. In short, Hell contains only six humanists.

HELL, ROAD TO

- The road to Hell is paved with good assumptions.

—Anonymous

HELL, ROMAN CATHOLIC

Hell, according to Roman Catholic theology, is a condition of self-chosen, permanent alienation from God, who bestows all "blessings."

HELLEN

The early Greeks supposed they were descended from a man called Hellen. (See entry for Greek Civilization.)

Heller, Adelle (20th Century) and **Heller, Reuben** (Died 1995)

Mr. and Mrs. Heller addressed the 14th annual HUMCON conference in 1994 which was sponsored by the Alliance of Humanist, Atheist, and Ethical Culture Organizations of Los Angeles, California. He was vice-president of Humanists of Los Angeles, co-founder of the sponsoring Alliance of Freethought Organizations, a past-president of the Los Angeles chapter of the Society for Humanistic Judaism., and a director of the American Humanist Association. (See entry for California Atheists, Humanists.)

Heller, Joseph (1923—1999)

A novelist who served as a bombardier in the air force during the Second World War, Heller wrote *Catch-22* (1961). Although it had taken him eight years to write, the work brought him instant fame. *Good as Gold* (1970) is a comic satire about Jewish New York and Washington politics. "Good God," states a character in *Catch-22*, "how much reverence can you have for a Supreme Being who finds it necessary to include such phenomena as phlegm and tooth decay in his divine system of creation?" {TYD}

Hellman, Lillian (1905—1984)

A New York dramatist, Hellman is author of *Little Foxes* (1939) and *An Unfinished Woman* (1969). She stirred the theatre in 1934 with *The Children's Hour*, in which a child maliciously accuses two of her teachers of lesbianism. It was based on a British case in 1810 in which the mother of a schoolgirl accuses Marianne Woods and Jane Pirie of "improper and criminal conduct" with each other. One negative criticism was that Hellman might lead some to commit suicide, but she insisted that the play was sound as written.

Toys in the Attic (1960) treated the theme of miscegenation. With Richard Wilbur, she collaborated on an adaptation of *Candide* (1957) for the Bernstein musical, based upon Voltaire's work, and she considered herself a freethinker like Voltaire.

As for evil, Hellman in *Watch on the Rhine* (1941) wrote, "Fashions in sin change." "She rightly saw that Zionism was the antithesis of communism, to whose cruelties," Martin Peretz has written, "she was loyal till the end, and she couldn't forgive Zionists their heresy."

She fought actively with Peretz, who had been chairman of The Jerusalem Foundation, screaming during a telephone conversation, "Fascism . . . Dashiell Hammett . . . Un-American Activities . . . immoral . . . disgusting" etc. "Yes," Peretz offered, "I did socialize with Roy Cohn. But at least I never socialized with Stalin." At this, she hung up and the two never again talked.

She was, off and on, companion to Dashiell Hammett (1894—1961), the crime novelist and author of *The Maltese Falcon* (1930), who died in 1960. Her will made a $2,500. bequest to Temple Israel of New York City to cover the perpetual care of her parents' cemetery plot in Hastings-on-Hudson, New York. Hellman, however, directed the executors of her more than $4,000,000 estate to purchase a cemetery plot and "suitable tombstone" in the Chilmark section of Martha's Vineyard. Among the famous who attended the funeral were John Hersey, Carl Bernstein, Jules Feiffer, William Styron, Mike Wallace, Ruth Gordon, and Norman Mailer. (In *Ex-Friends* [1999], Norman Podhoretz calls Hellman a Jewish anti-Semite.) {CE; Martin Peretz, *The New Republic*, 29 July 1996; TYD}

HELLO

Hello is used both to answer someone on the telephone as well as to express surprise. *Hola* is also found as a greeting both in Old French and in contemporary Spanish.

However, the commissioners of Kleberg County (Texas) voted unanimously in 1997 that residents should not use the word because a local man, Leonoso Canales, 56, a flea market operator, saw "Hell" in "Hello" and insisted, instead, that people greet each other with "heaven-o." (A wag observed that it may not be mere coincidence that there is an "anal" in "Canales.")

Hellwald, Friedrich von (1842—1892)

Hellwald was a German geographer and freethinker who, in addition to many works on various countries, wrote *Culture History* (1875). {BDF}

Helmholtz, Hermann Ludwig Ferdinand von (1821—1894)

For his discoveries in acoustics, optics, and electricity, Helmholtz became distinguished. He was of the foremost rank among natural philosophers of his day in Europe. Among his many works were *The Conservation of Force* (1847) and *Popular Scientific Lectures* (1865—1876). Helmholtz rejected the design hypothesis and was an outspoken German agnostic. {BDF; JM; RAT; RE}

Helms, Randel (20th Century)

A professor of English at Arizona State University, Helms is on the Council for Secular Humanism's Biblical Criticism Research Project. One of his works, *Gospel Fictions* (1988), develops the idea that the four Gospels of the New Testament are fictional narratives, composed as the culmination of an extensive literary and oral tradition—idealistic writings produced to serve a theological vision.

At the Tenth International Humanist and Ethical Union (IHEU) World Congress held in Buffalo (1988), Helms addressed the group. He is author of *Tolkien's World* (1974) and *Gospel Fictions* (1988).

Helvétius, Claude Adrien (1715—1771)

The French philosopher Helvétius, one of the Encyclopedists, utilized the materialist philosophy "as a powerful weapon against religious superstition and the reactionary Catholic Church," according to Corliss Lamont. Like Locke, Helvétius believed all are born with minds like blank tablets, and he maintained that we also are born with equal ability and that distinctions develop from the totality of educational influences. Jeremy Bentham as well as James Mill acknowledged being influenced by him, and he once was an honored guest of Frederick the Great. Helvétius had come from a line of celebrated physicians, and his large fortune was dispensed liberally in works of benevolence.

"A man who believes that he eats his God we do not call mad," Helvétius commented about communion; "a man who says he is Jesus Christ, we call mad." His *De L'Esprit* (1758, *On the Mind*) at first passed censorship but, upon finding its true character, the work was condemned by Pope Clement XIII and was burned by the order of Parliament in 1759 for the hardihood of his materialistic opinions. The indictment was that it was a collection "into one cover of everything that impiety could imagine, calculated to engender hatred against Christianity and Catholicism." Further, the censor was cashiered and Helvétius was dismissed from an honorary post in the Queen's household. Mme. De Deffand said, "He told everyone's secret." Condorcet explained in an essay why the book was so controversial:

> It is fanaticism that puts arms into the hands of Christian princes; it orders Catholics to massacre heretics; it brings out upon the earth again those tortures that were invented by such monsters as Phalaris, as Busiris, as Nero; in Spain it piles and lights up the fires of the Inquisition, while the pious Spaniards leave their ports and sail across distant seas, to plant the Cross and spread desolation in America. Turn your eyes to north or south, to east or west; on every side you see the consecrated knife of Religion raised against the breasts of women, of children, of old men, and the earth all smoking with the blood of victims immolated to false gods or the Supreme Being, and [presenting] one vast, sickening horrible charnel-house of intolerance.

On Man, published posthumously, was both atheistic and materialistic. As for Helvétius's last days, Condorcet wrote, "He felt his strength failing. An attack of gout, which flew to the head and chest, deprived him at first of consciousness and soon of life." Following his death his wife, Anne Catherine DeLingville Helvétius, retired to Auteuil, where her house was the rendezvous of Condillac, Turgot, d'Holbach, Morellet, Cabanis, Destutt de Tracy, and others. This reunion of freethinkers became known as the *Société de Auteuil*. Mme. Helvétius died in 1800. {BDF; CE; CL; FUS; JM; JMR; JMRH; RAT; RE; TYD}

Helvie, Clara Cook (1876—1969)

A Unitarian minister for over twenty years, Helvie compiled two historical manuscripts on women in the ministries of both the Unitarian and Universalist denominations: "Unitarian Women Minister" (1928) and "Necrology of Women Serving in the Universalist Ministry" (1950), both of which were never published but are a part of the Unitarian Universalist Association Archives and Harvard Divinity School historical documents. {*World*, May-June 1995; U; U&U}

Hemingway, Ernest (1898—1961)

Hemingway wrote in an essentially Humanist fashion without reliance on God or the supernatural, Corliss Lamont noted. Certainly his *For Whom the Bell Tolls* (1940) argues for human brotherhood. Readers empathized with his writing about courage, the fear of death, and the need to cultivate a stoicism which could help one handle ever-present despair. He is not known, however, ever to have gone on record concerning theism or non-theism.

When his particularly weak *Across the River and Into the Trees* (1950) resulted in a front-page *New York Times Book Review* article by John O'Hara, author of "Guys and Dolls," with a hyperbole to the effect that Hemingway is the greatest author in the English language since Shakespeare, intellectuals smiled, knowing perhaps secondarily that "Papa" was a poor speller. When his *Old Man and the Sea* (1952) followed and Papa Hemingway was asked by restaurateur Toots Shor how on earth he got a Nobel Prize (1954) for a simple fish story like that, Hemingway skipped any explanations of symbolism or levels of meaning. He simply explained that the old Cuban was really himself, the "fish" was really *Across the River and Into the Trees*, the sharks were the critics who had turned his work into shreds, and the faithful little boy was John O'Hara.

Although treated at the Mayo Clinic for mental illness, Hemingway apparently decided during a state of acute depression to kill himself, for which there were precedents in his family, rather than to seek help from physicians. His brother, sister, and father had taken their own lives, and in 1996 his granddaughter actress Margaux Hemingway died from taking an overdose of a sedative.

During the 1940s, he was incontestably one of the best-regarded novelists in the nation, but following his death he has been criticized negatively for his glorifying the killing of animals, his difficulty in relating to women as well as his condescending depiction of them, and his use of toughness to conceal his own limitations.

A 1954 unfinished work, edited by his 70-year-old middle son, Patrick, was published in 1998. Entitled *True at First Light*, it implies Papa Hemingway may have had a mysterious tribal bride or two. One, a Kenyan called Debba from the Wakamba tribe, was "very beautiful and quite young and more than perfectly developed." Whether she was actual or fictional is debatable, for Hemingway's mischievous streak and love of practical jokes included a boast that he had made love to the spy Mata Hari. She, however, was executed by the French the year before he arrived in Italy in 1918.

Hemingway's estate was worth over $5.8 million in 1990 dollars. He died owing the government about $50,000. His remains were buried at Ketchum Cemetery in Ketchum, Idaho. The gravestone is a large flat slab with name and vital dates only. (For allusions to his sexual proclivities, see entry for F. Scott Fitzgerald. John Lahr, in "My Mother the Ziegfeld Girl" (*The New Yorker*, 13 May 1996), describes how Hemingway once made a pass at his mother. Ann Douglas, in *Mongrel Manhattan in the 1920s* (1995) called Hemingway's mother "smothering," saying when he refused to apologize for leaving the house after midnight for a picnic, Grace Hemingway banished him from the household, promising that "when you have changed your ideas and aims in life, you will find your mother waiting to welcome you, whether it be in this world or the next." Also, see *Hemingway's Genders* (1994) by Nancy R. Comley and Robert Scholes, who go deeply into the subject of homosexuality.) {CE; CL; GL; PA}

Hemingway, Russell (20th Century)

A freethinker, Hemingway wrote, "Bible Numerology Proves Its Falsity" (1978). {GS}

HEMLOCK SOCIETY, USA

The Hemlock Society, USA, POB 11830, Eugene, Oregon 97440, publishes a quarterly journal and advises about patients' rights, living wills, and aid in dying. The group is non-sectarian and takes no stand on theological matters. (See entry for Faye Girsh.)

Hemming, James (1909—)

A British psychologist, Hemming was elected in 1979 as an honorary associate of the Rationalist Press Association. He is a signer of Humanist Manifesto II. He wrote *Individual Morality* (1969) and *Instead of God* (1986). He has been a President of the British Humanist Association and a Vice President of the Gay and Lesbian Humanist Association (GALHA). A member of the Labour Party, Dr. Hemming was disenchanted with the educational system, having firsthand knowledge inasmuch as he has taught in it. He addressed the 1978 Seventh International Humanist and Ethical Union (IHEU) World Congress held in London.

Writing in *New Humanist* (November 1993), Hemming asserted that "it is no longer just a *possibility* that life is widespread in the Cosmos; it is now a high *probability*. When probability becomes certainty, as it may at any time now, it will profoundly affect human thinking." As early as the 4th century B.C.E., he added, "the Epicurean philosopher, Metrodorus, neatly summed up the situation: 'to consider the Earth the only populated world in infinite space is as absurd as to assert that, in an entire field sown with millet, only one grain will grow.' " For Hemming, when such news does arrive, "It will offer the sort of stimulating new vision for which the young are desperate. Sex and drugs are not the answer to their quandary. Working together to raise the quality of life on Earth within the context of a living Cosmos could well be."

In an interview in *New Humanist* (September 1999), Hemming said he was uncertain when he became a humanist.

> I was the son of a clergyman and I gradually realised that I just could not follow what was expected of me. I didn't fall out with my father; we were very good friends; we reached an agreement to differ. At first I thought I was quite alone in my humanism, but eventually I

> discovered the British Humanist Association and joined them. This was a great release to me, because I now realised that I was a member of a community and not just staggering along on my own.

Hemming then discussed his having written *The Betrayal of Youth,* created educational material for Africa, been a witness for the *Lady Chatterley* trial, and become an activist in the Commonwealth Party during the Second World War. {HM2}

Hempel, Carl G. (1905—1997)

Hempel, known for his rigorous empirical approach to scientific logic, taught at City College of New York, Queens College in Flushing, Yale University, and the University of Pittsburgh. He taught at Princeton University from 1955 to 1973. The last surviving member of the Vienna Circle, he loathed the irrational and mystical thinking of late-19th-century Europe. With other similarly-minded philosophers, he advocated what was called "logical positivism," which argued that whatever could not be verified by experience was meaningless. Born in Oranienburg, Germany, he studied mathematics, physics, and philosophy at the Universities of Göttingen, Heidelberg, Vienna, and Berlin, working under Hans Reichenbach and receiving a doctorate from the latter in 1934 for work on probability. After fleeing Nazism to Belgium, he moved on to the United States in 1938. According to his former student, Adolf Grünbaum, Hempel's writings were so influential that for decades almost any rival theory of scientific explanation took his work as a point of departure.

In 1948 he produced his deductive-nomological theory, which holds that scientific conclusions are best deduced using logic and a larger law, or *nomos* in Greek. He built a precise mathematical foundation for explaining statistical, or probabilistic, answers. If a patient asks doctor about the chance of a cure, the doctor's explanation might, for example, be given as a probability—that in a given percentage of cases there is a cure. "That is an informal statement," he added. "It needed a systematic form." He then developed a model that served many philosophers as a master model.

He also dealt with how scientists gain confidence in a hypothesis in the first place. He developed models of the philosophy of confirmation in which a hypothesis is confirmed not only by findings but also by being in accord with larger principles, like historical or functional explanations. These models shaped all subsequent work on scientific explanation, observed Ford Burkhart in a *New York Times* obituary (23 November 1997).

Hempel wrote *Studies in the Logic of Confirmation* (1945); *Studies in the Logic of Explanation* (1948), and *Aspects of Scientific Explanation and Other Essays in the Philosophy of Science* (1965).

Hempel, Max (20th Century)

Hempel wrote a history of German freethought in the United States, *Was Sind die Freie Gemeinden?* (1902). {FUS}

Hemstreet, William (20th Century)

A freethinker, Hemstreet wrote *The Wayfarer's Plaint* (191—?). {GS}

Henault (Hesnault) Jean (Died 1682)

Henault was a French Epicurean poet, son of a Paris baker and a pupil of Gassendi. Bayle says Henault professed atheism and had composed three different systems of the mortality of the soul. His most famous sonnet is on "The Abortion." {BDF}

Henderson, Dillard W. (20th Century)

Henderson wrote "Studies Show the Inefficacy of Prayer" in *Freethought Today* (March 1996). He is a board member of the Freedom from Religion Foundation and lives in Michigan.

Henderson, Laurence Joseph (Born 1878)

Henderson, an American biochemist, wrote *The Fitness of the Environment* (1913), *The Order of Nature* (1917), and other scientific papers. In these works he rejects emphatically the idea of design in nature and all natural theology based on it, though he contends for a certain kind of teleology. He thinks Darwin's advance from theology to theism, and from theism to agnosticism, the normal growth, adding, "We shall never find the explanation of the riddle, for it concerns the origin of things." {RAT}

Henin de Cuvillers, Etienne Felix (1755—1841)

Baron Henin de Cuvillers was a French general and writer who served as a diplomat in England, Venice, and Constantinople. Wounded at Arcola in 1796, he was made Chevalier of the Legion of Honor in 1811. His principle work was on the subject of magnetism, and he suggested that the miracles of Jesus were not supernatural but were wrought by means of magnetism learned in Egypt. In other writings, particularly in reflections on the crimes committed in the name of religion, he showed himself the enemy of fanaticism and intolerance. {BDF; RAT}

Henley, William Ernest (1849—1903)

Crippled by tuberculosis of the bone, Henley nevertheless led an active and vigorous life as an editor. He introduced to readers such young writers as Kipling, Wells, and Yeats. Often quoted by secularists is his poem, "Invictus":

> Out of the night that covers me,
> Black as the Pit from pole to pole,
> I thank whatever gods may be
> For my unconquerable soul.
> In the fell clutch of circumstance,
> I have not winced nor cried aloud:
> Under the bludgeonings of chance
> My head is bloody, but unbowed. . . .
>
> It matters not how strait the gate,
> How charged with punishments the scroll,
> I am the master of my fate;
> I am the captain of my soul.

McCabe states that Henley wavered between atheism and theism. Philosophy, Henley held, was like chalk in one's mouth. {JM; RAT; RE}

Henne Am Rhyn, Otto (Born 1828)

A Swiss historian, Henne Am Rhyn was an editor at Leipzig and the State Archivist. A leading Swiss Freemason, he wrote various volumes on social and ethics, all rationalistic. In his autobiography he stated that he "cast off all the fetters of the creeds" at the university, although in his later work he is theistic. {RAT}

Hennell, Charles Christian (1809—1850)

A Unitarian, Hennell wrote an *Inquiry Concerning the Origin of Christianity* (1838) which Strauss thought was so important that he translated it into German. In a preface to his second edition (1841), Hennell spoke very plainly of "the large and probably increasing amount of unbelief in all classes around us," and made the then remarkably courageous declarations that in his experience "neither deism, pantheism, nor even atheism indicates modes of thought incompatible with uprightness and benevolence," and that "the real or affected horror which it is still a prevailing custom to exhibit towards their names would be better reserved for those of the selfish, the cruel, the bigot, and other tormentors of mankind." Hennell's writing is said to have influenced George Sand into becoming a freethinker. (See entry for Mary Hennell.) {BDF; JMR; RAT}

Hennell, Mary (1802—1843)

Hennell, the sister of C. C. Hennell, abandoned Unitarianism. Her "Outline of the Various Social Systems and Communities Which Have Been Founded on the Principle of Co-operation," which was published as an appendix to Bray's *Philosophy of Necessity* (1841). {RAT}

Hennell, Sara S. (19th Century)

Hennell wrote *Christianity and Infidelity* (1857) and *Thoughts in Aid of Faith* (1860). {GS}

Hennequin, Émile (1858—1888)

A French critic, Hennequin was on the staff of *Le Temps*. His *Critique Scientifique*, published a few weeks before his death, gave promise of great distinction. Hennequin was a thorough rationalist. {RAT}

Henning, Max (20th Century)

In Frankfurt, Germany, Henning edited *Freie Wort* in 1914.

HENOTHEISM

Henotheism is the worship of one god without denying the existence of other gods. The word dates to 1860.

Henricksen, Bruce (1941—)

A professor of English at Loyola University in New Orleans, Henricksen commented as follows to the present author's query about the various humanisms:

> Your inquiry seems to invite respondents to find the category of humanism each finds most congenial and then to explain why.
>
> If I were forced to a self-definition only employing your seven types of humanism, I would opt for a kind of *bricolage* made up of types 5 through 7—atheistic, marxist (but certainly not Stalinist), and naturalistic.
>
> The problem, however, is that the word "humanism" regardless of any attendant adjective, has become a code word for the repressive aspects of a Euro-centric and gender biased tradition that is now called into question. It is this questioning that Michel Foucault announces at the conclusion of *The Order of Things*, when he declares the end of the age of "man."
>
> Since I am persuaded by Foucault of the necessity for a radical critique of traditional forms of knowledge, I would decline to label myself as a "humanist." There is something in a name.

(See entry for Postmodernism.) {WAS, 24 April 1989}

Henriot, Emile (1889—1961)

Henriot is a distinguished French writer, author of *In Quest of a New Ethics*. Charles Mayer has termed Henriot a naturalistic humanist. (See entry for Mayer.)

HENRY VIII: See entry for Anglican Communion.

Henry, George (1827—1892)

A famous traveler, Henry was an agnostic. (See entry for his daughter, Mary Henrietta Kingsley.)

Henry, Josephine K. (1846—1928)

A freethinker, Henry wrote "Musings in Life's Evening" (c. 1920). A Kentucky women's rights advocate, she sent thousands of documents to Congress at her own expense and had over two hundred articles published in various newspapers. At the time when the last person to go to prison for blasphemy in the United States, Charles C. Moore, was released, Henry delivered the address of welcome. Before the Kentucky Constitutional Convention, Henry attempted to convince the writers to include women's rights in the new Constitution. In her correspondence with Elizabeth Cady Stanton, Henry was told that Stanton agreed with her in her atheism. {*Free Inquiry*, Spring 1995; GS; WWS}

Henry, William (20th Century)

Henry was co-author of "A Bible Guide for Truth Seekers" (19—?). {GS}

Henshaw, Donald E. (20th Century)

When he signed Humanist Manifesto II, Henshaw was a humanist counselor. {HM2}

Henschell, Darrel (20th Century)

Although raised a Jehovah's Witness and taught that his family was fortunate to be members of a religion of only .03% of the world's several billions that possessed "the Truth," Henschell soon found that many of the church's claims were conveniently unfalsifiable. It could not be demonstrated, for example, that Jesus returned invisibly in the year 1914. Also, Henschell found in *Matthew* 1:16

> And Jacob begat Joseph the husband of Mary, of whom was born Jesus, who is called Christ.

but in *Luke* 3:23

> And Jesus himself began to be about thirty years of age, being the son of Joseph, which was the son of Heli.

Henschell's further doubts concerning the Bible's contradictions led to his writing *The Perfect Mirror? The Question of Bible Perfection* (1996, PO Box 61274, Pasadena, CA 91116). Included are chapters on Christian doctrine, the Old and New Testaments, prophecy, and the doctrine of biblical inerrancy.

Hentoff, Nathan Irving (1925—)

Hentoff, a writer and columnist since 1957 for *The Village Voice*, wrote *The Collected Essays of A. J. Muste* (1966), *Black Anti-Semitism and Jewish Racism* (1970), *Blues for Charles Darwin* (1982), and numerous articles in various journals. He has written that he is "a Jewish atheist," apparently suggesting that his interest is cultural Judaism but that his outlook is non-supernaturalistic. He also describes himself as a "civil libertarian, left-wing, pro-lifer." {CA; E}

Hentz, Robert R. (20th Century)

Hentz is a retired scientist, formerly on the faculties of North Carolina State and Notre Dame. Among his several freethought poems, Hentz wrote "A Failure of Faith?":

> The preacher believed the Bible
> In its dictum on snakes
> Absolutely reliable.
> He held firm to his faith
> In refusing to take
> The serum for a bite
> By a rattlesnake.
> On the preacher's demise,
> The faithful concluded
> That he was deluded
> Not in his scriptural notion
> But in his strength of devotion.

{*Freethought History #9*, 1994}

Henwood, Doug (20th Century)

Henwood, an editor and economics journalist, is a contributing editor for *The Nation*, publisher of the *Left Business Observer*, and author of *Wall Street*. Not wanting to say he is an atheist, he explained, "I have no idea whether there's a god or not, and I don't think humans could ever know. I know that the people who think God has revealed itself to them are full of shit, though. On second thought, 'full of shit' is pointlessly hostile. Let me change that to 'I know that the people think that a god has revealed itself to them are hallucinating, tough.' " {CA}

Hepburn, Katharine (1907—)

"I'm an atheist, and that's it," Hepburn told a reporter for *Ladies' Home Journal*. The Academy Award actress, whose name was often mentioned with Spencer Tracy's, added, "I believe there's nothing we can know except that we should be kind to each other and do what we can for other people." A biography by Barbara Leaming, *Katharine Hepburn* (1995), reports that when thirteen Hepburn discovered the body of her fifteen-year-old brother, Tom, who had slowly strangled himself with a noose. "The Hepburns—candid about sex and all things controversial—tended resolutely to avoid speaking of their most troubling thoughts and emotions," Leaming explains in her thorough research of the platonic connection which Hepburn had with the married, abusive, and alcoholic Spencer

Tracy, who was said to have had a penchant for prostitutes and a history of venereal infection. Although Ms. Selden West, who in 1995 was writing "the authorized biography of Spencer Tracy" and who denied ever finding any evidence or medical records to indicate any such infection, Leaming defended her research, writing that "Orson Welles and others told me about Tracy's obsession that his visits to brothels and the venereal infections he contracted there had caused his son's deafness. Letters of those who knew Tracy testify to his often frantic state of mind. Katharine Hepburn, in a Sept. 7, 1944, letter to Philip Barry's wife, describes him as a wreck who fears he is about to go mad." Meanwhile, Leaming insists that Hepburn and John Ford "fell in love" and that his grandfather "was obsessed by Kate and found with her a degree of happiness and a peace of mind that he had never known before." Ford's grandson, Dan, claims that Leaming "greatly exaggerated the degree and the intensity of the Ford-Hepburn relationship."

In her eighty-eighth year, Hepburn had experienced having twenty biographers delve into her life and had continued to be a presence since her starring role in "Morning Glory" in 1933. {CA; CE; E; TYD}

Hepburn, Ronald W. (20th Century)

A freethinker, Hepburn wrote *Christianity and Paradox* (1958). His *Objections to Humanism* (1963) mentioned his unease at hearing theological language that was being used by Dewey as well as Huxley. For the *Encyclopedia of Philosophy*, he wrote "Agnosticism."

Heraclitus (c. 535—c. 475 B.C.E.)

A Greek philosopher of Ephesus, Heraclitus held that permanence is an illusion of the senses, that there is no permanent reality except that of change. He resented immoral religion, saying Homer and Archilochos deserved flogging. He also was critical about the absurdity of prayer, pietism, and the phallic worship of Dionysos. He taught that everything carries its opposite, heat and cold, day and night, evil and good, and all this exists only in the relation of contrast. For him, fire was something in which opposites are solved. No one, he held, has a personal soul, but all men share a soul in a universal soul—fire. If, then, being and non-being are part of every whole, what is real is the transitional state of becoming. Many of his followers were attracted to this kind of mysticism, Robertson writes, but his negative wisdom is said to have been substantially ignored.

Bertrand Russell finds Heraclitus largely hostile to the Bacchic religion of that time, "but not with the hostility of a scientific rationalist. He has his own religion, and in part interprets current theology to fit his doctrine, in part rejects it with considerable scorn." Russell cites these extant sayings of Heraclitus concerning the theology of his day:

- The Lord who is the oracle at Delphi neither utters nor hides his meaning, but shows it by a sign.
- And the Sibyl, with raving lips uttering things mirthless, unbedizened, and unper fumed, reaches over a thousand years with her voice, thanks to the god in her.
- To God all things are fair and good and right, but men hold some things wrong and some right.
- God is day and night, winter and summer, war and peace, surfeit and hunger; but he takes various shapes, just as fire, when it is mingled with spices, is named according to the savour of each.
- Religion is a disease, but it is a noble disease.
- Souls smell in Hades.
- Greater deaths win greater portions. (Those who die then become gods.)
- The way of man has no wisdom, but that of God has. . . . Man is called a baby by God, even as a child by a man. . . . The wisest man is an ape compared to God, just as the most beautiful ape is ugly compared to man.

Benn, an anti-materialist historian of philosophy, quotes Heraclitus as saying, "This universe, the same for all, was not made by any God or any man but was and is and ever shall be an ever-living fire." Known as "the Weeping Philosopher," Heraclitus as an idealist deplored and lamented the imperfections of men. {CE; ER; JM; JMR; JMRH; RE}

Hérault de Sechelles, Marie Jean (1760—1794)

Hérault was a French revolutionist, born of a noble family. Brought up as a friend of Buffon and Mirabeau, he gained distinction as a lawyer and orator before the Revolution. In 1792 he was made President of the Convention. Hérault edited the document known as the *Constitution of 1793* and was president and chief speaker at the national festival.

Drawing the enmity of Robespierre, Hérault was executed with Danton and Camille Desmoulins in 1794). {BDF; RAT}

Herbert, Auberon Edward William Molyneux (1838—1906)

A reformer and the son of the Earl of Carnarvon, Herbert left military service to study law, then lectured on history and jurisprudence at St. John's College (Oxford). Later, he entered politics. Herbert was a Spencerian agnostic as shown in *Nineteenth Century* (Aug-Sep 1901), and he was a supporter of Bradlaugh. {RAT; RE}

Herbert, Edward [1st Baron] (1583—1648)

Herbert, a First Baron of Cherbury, was interested in comparative religion. The Lord of Cherbury in Shropshire, Herbert during the civil wars espoused the side of Parliament. Although called "the father of English deism," Herbert despite his *De Veritate* (1624) was not widely read by 18th-century deists. Descartes read and criticized the work, which asserted the sufficiency of natural religion apart from revelation, and Locke differed with its rationalism. Robertson describes Herbert as being "in the full stream of the current freethought of England and France in the first quarter of the seventeenth century." McCabe termed him, because of his articles in *Nineteenth Century* (1901), "a Spencerian Agnostic and a supporter of Bradlaugh." {BDF; EU, E. Graham Waring; FUK; JM; JMR; JMRH; RAT; RE}

Herbert, Frank (20th Century)

According to the American Library Association's *Banned Books* (1998), Herbert is author of *Soul Catcher*, a work which allegedly "is a mockery of Christianity, and very much anti-God." (See entry for Banned Books.)

Herder, Dale (20th Century)

At Michigan State University, Herder wrote his 1975 Ph. D. dissertation on Haldeman-Julius Little Blue Books. {FUS}

Heredia, José Maria de (1842—1905)

Heredia, a Cuban-born French poet, wrote *Parnasse Contemporain* and *Les Trophées* (1893). A member of the French Academy, he was an admirer of fellow rationalist poets Chénier, Hugo, and Leconte de Lisle. {RAT}

HEREDITY

"Death," according to one Manhattan wag, "is genetically hereditary."

HERESY

- Heresy is a cradle, orthodoxy a coffin.

—Robert G. Ingersoll

Heresy is a belief or a teaching which is considered unacceptable by a religious group. Nontheists who use Christian swear words—e.g., Christ Almighty!—jocularly call such irrational utterances heretical.

George H. Shriver, editor of *Dictionary of Heresy Trials in American Christianity* (1997), includes the witchcraft trials in Salem, the many trials of Episcopalian James A. Pike, and the trial of Anne Hutchinson. In various case studies, the work indicates that heresy is a necessary part of all theology. (See entry for Tissa Balasuriya.) {DCL}

HERETIC, THE

The Heretic, a newsletter of the University of Minnesota Atheists and Humanists, commenced in 1994. Its editor, and the president of the University of Minnesota Atheists and Humanists (UMAH), was formerly Eric Snyder.

HERETICS

Heretics, nonconformists who either are baptized members of the Roman Catholic Church who have disavowed a revealed truth or are dissenters from any other established church, are described in detail by Charles S. Clifton's *Encyclopedia of Heresies and Heretics* (1992). His extensive listing starts with Cerdo and Simon Magus in the 1st century and continues to Michael Servetus and Giordano Bruno in the 16th century. The last in England to be burned for heresy was Edward Wightman, in 1612. (See entry for Catharism.) {BDF}

Herford, Robert Travers (20th Century)

Herford was president of the British and Foreign Unitarian Association from 1883 to 1914. At the turn of the century, and after writing about Judaism at the time of Jesus, he had a positive perspective about Pharisaism and often called himself a "Jewnitarian."

HERMAPHRODITES

• Hermaphrodite: A person possessing the organs of both sexes, as a man with both a penis and a brain.

—Carol Falkenberry
Atlanta Freethought Society

To believers, hermaphrodites are not God's mistakes; they simply prove how He works in mysterious ways. Some early biblical scholars believed that Adam—a hermaphrodite like his father—later divided into two people after falling from grace. In recognition, the Talmud lists regulations for individuals of mixed sex. Just the same, to religious fundamentalists the subject is not one to be discussed on Easter Sunday when dining with Grandmother.

The opposite was true. In ancient Greece, where Plato taught that originally there were three sexes—male, female, and hermaphrodite—but that over a period of time the third sex was lost. Meanwhile, in Greek mythology the tale was told of how Hermes and Aphrodite parented **Hermaphroditus**, who, at the age of fifteen, became half male and half female when, after falling in love with a nymph, their two bodies fused.

In *Myths of Gender: Biological Theories About Women and Men* (1993) by Anne Fausto-Sterling, a geneticist and professor of medical science, in some actual cases, "the testis and the ovary grow separately but bilaterally; in others, they grow together within the same organ, forming an ovo-testis. Not infrequently, at least one of the gonads functions well, producing either sperm cells or eggs, as well as functional levels of the sex hormones: androgens or estrogens." Also, there are pseudo-hermaphrodites who possess two gonads of the same kind along with the usual male (XY) or female (XX) chromosomal makeup.

But, explains Fausto-Sterling, "their external genitalia and secondary sex characteristics do not match their chromosomes." Some developed a phallus between 1.5 and 2.8 inches long, but they urinated through a urethra that opened into or near the vagina.

Although historically hermaphrodites have been forced to choose some established gender role and stick with it, some have refused to do so. Fausto-Sterling cites a Scottish hermaphrodite living as a woman in the 1600s and who was buried alive after impregnating his/her master's daughter.

Fausto-Sterling is of the opinion that the medical world should not intervene, that intersexuals should be allowed to develop naturally, unimpeded. She cites cases to allay parents' worries about rearing children who are intersexuals, showing that they adjusted to their status depending upon whether or not those around them accepted that intersexuality is not a disease to be corrected, as is taught by some.

Limpets, *The Economist* (16 March 1996) has pointed out, "start as males and then, when they have grown sufficiently large to produce eggs, become female. Some fish do it the other way round: if a female wrasse becomes big and tough enough to take over her group, she also becomes one of the boys. And snails have the best of both worlds. They are able to make both sperm and eggs in a single body, and thus inseminate others at the same time as they are, themselves, being inseminated." (See entry for Adam.)

HERMENEUTICS

Hermeneutics, in theology, is applied to the study of the general principles whereby the meaning of the Scriptures is to be ascertained. It requires a knowledge of the original languages of the Bible, and interpreters' qualifications are critiqued. In literature, hermeneutics refers to the art of interpretation of literature. (See entry for Adolf Grünbaum, who is a leading anti-hermeneuticist.)

Herndon, William H. (1818—1891)

Herndon was a friend, law partner, and biographer of Abraham Lincoln. His *Herndon's Lincoln: The True Story of a Great Life* (1889) focused on Lincoln's personal life and led to distortions, particularly in the case of the Ann Rutledge romance, according to D. H. Donald's *Lincoln's Herndon* (1948). Of Lincoln, Herndon wrote,

• Mr. Lincoln was an infidel, sometimes bordering on atheism.

• He never mentioned the name of Jesus, except to scorn and detest the idea of a miraculous conception.

• He did write a little work on infidelity in 1835—6, and never recanted. He was an out-and-out- infidel and about that there is no mistake.

• In 1834, while still living in New Salem and before he became a lawyer, he was surrounded by a class of people exceedingly liberal in matters of religion. Volney's *Ruins* and Paine's *Age of Reason* passed from hand to hand, and furnished food for the evening's discussion in the tavern and village store. Lincoln read both these books and thus assimilated them into his own being. He prepared an extended essay—called by many a book—in which he made an argument against Christianity, striving to prove that the Bible was not inspired, and therefore not God's revelation, and that Jesus Christ was not the Son of God. The manuscript containing these audacious and comprehensive propositions he intended to have published or given a wide circulation in some other way. He carried it to the store, where it was read and freely discussed. His friend and employer, Samuel Hill, was among the listeners and, seriously questioning the propriety of a promising young man like Lincoln fathering such unpopular notions, he snatched the manuscript from his hands and thrust it into the stove. The book went up in flames, and Lincoln's political future was secure. But his infidelity and his skeptical views were not diminished.

{CE; TYD}

HERO

In Greek mythology, Hero was a priestess of Aphrodite in Sestos. Leander, her lover, swam the Helleslpoint nightly from Abydos to see her. When a storm blew out the candle that was guiding him, and he drowned, Hero in despair threw herself into the sea.

Linguists, who "heroically" point to the fact that Hero was female, argue that it is not logical for those demanding "political correctness" of a word to underline gender, as in *human* or *mankind* or *history*. {CE}

Herodotus (484?—425? B.C.E.)

"The father of history," Herodotus is the Greek who first completed a secular narrative of history, "history" being a word derived from the Greek word for "inquiry." Henry Cary, in *The History* (1992), has translated the ancient writer's encyclopedic interests and curiosity about the customs and workings of early humankind.

Bertrand Russell, in *Understanding History* (1957), believed Herodotus is deserving of reading by contemporaries: "In the first place, he is full of amusing stories. Almost at the beginning of the book, there is the story of the vain king, Candaules, who regretted that no one but himself knew fully the beauty of his Queen, for which he wished to be envied. So he hid his Prime Minister Gyges behind a curtain, where he could see the Queen going naked to the bath. But she saw his feet sticking out and complained that he had offered her a mortal indignity. Then and there she made him a speech, 'Only two courses are open to you to expiate your offense,' she said, 'either you must die or you must kill the King and marry me.' Gyges had no difficulty in making his choice, and became the founder of the dynasty that ended with Croesus. . . . To anyone who enjoys anthropology Herodotus is interesting from his description of various barbarian customs as they existed in his day. Sometimes he is merely repeating travelers' tales, but very often he is confirmed by modern research. His survey of the nations and races known to him is leisurely and ample, and affords an admirable introduction to the ancient world for a previously ignorant reader. . . . The main theme of his history is the conflict of Europe and Asia, culminating, for his time, in the defeats of the Persians at Marathon and Salamis." Herodotus, says Lord Russell, implies that eventually Japan will be defeated and China and India will succeed to it as champions of Asia. "All these vast secular movements come within the framework suggested by Herodotus," said Russell in 1943. {CE; ER; Lee Eisler, *The Quotable Bertrand Russell*}

Heroma-Meilink, D. (20th Century)

At the Second European Conference of the International Humanist and Ethical Union (IHEU) held in Hannover (1968), Heroma-Meilink addressed the group.

Herpyllis: See entry for Aristotle, for whom Herpyllis was mistress.

Herreid, Clyde (20th Century)

Herreid, professor of biology at the State University of New York, is a skeptic and also a magician. Visiting the New Zealand rationalists, he spoke of the evolution-creation controversy in the United States, saying "the creationists tried to get equal time in schools for their misnamed 'creation science' nonsense that was tried first in Louisiana, then in Arkansas, both attempts of which failed. According to the *New Zealand Rationalist and Humanist* (April 1994), Herreid spurred his listeners to insure that no such controversy erupt within their school systems.

A noted Darwin impersonator, Herreid appeared as Darwin at the Center for Inquiry's facetious 6,000th Birthday of the Earth party, 22 October 1996. {RAT}

Herrick, C. Judson (1868—1960)

Herrick, an editor of *Journal of Comparative Neurology*, wrote his views about humanism to the present author:

> Humanism means to me, as a biologist, the search for those vital values that make for more efficient, productive, and satisfying living for all people. This statement is intentionally very general, because every domain of human experience and endeavor is significant for the enrichment of life. The artificial barriers which traditionally separate these domains must be broken down. This calls for a type of cooperation which is rare and a tolerance for ideologies which we may not share that is still more difficult to achieve. We look to science, philosophy, economics, art, religion, and every other field of human experience for reinforcement and guidance, and we aim to bring them together in a united effort for human betterment with all available resources.
>
> My personal conception of modern Humanism does not exactly fit any of the seven categories of your list. I am a scientific humanist, but life embraces more than science as conventionally defined. I cannot accept some of the restrictions insisted upon by most of the naturalistic humanists. A naturalist may (or may not) be a theist, if these terms are properly defined. I object to the dogmatic rejection, expressed by many humanists, of the legitimacy of any hypotheses regarding the supernatural. I grant that there is no scientific evidence for the supernatural. Obviously there cannot be, for natural science by definition deals only with the natural. Now, what is nature? We cannot talk rationally about the supernatural without first defining the natural. All science is a human construction, based on human experience. It cannot go further than the range of possible experience. This sets a logical and an operational limit to nature and to natural science as envisaged scientifically and practically. We may, accordingly, accept the definition given by Santayana in 1905, "Nature is the sum total of things potentially observable, some observed actually, others interpolated hypothetically." We cannot now say what are the limits of the observable, but assuredly there are such limits for any finite mind. It is, then, arrogant for any naturalist to dogmatize about what may, or may not, exist beyond those limits. The implications of this doctrine are far-reaching. Some of them are mentioned in the Epilogue of my book entitled *The Evolution of Human Nature* (University of Texas Press, Autumn 1956) and more fully elaborated in a short article which may at some later time see the light.
>
> This conception of a liberalized naturalistic humanism I got from my older brother, the late C. L. Herrick, as I have explained in his biography (Trans. Am. Philosophical Soc., *45 (1): 1-85,* 1955). Later influence came from many sources, notably William James, George Santayana, John Dewey, Roy Wood Sellars, and G. E. Coghill.

In 1956, Herrick was named Humanist of the Year by the American Humanist Association. His *New York Times* obituary described him as an internationally prominent neurologist, a leader in his field. He was quoted as writing, "A thought is a manufactured process as truly as a pair of shoes or a magnetic field. The conclusion that thinking is a mechanistic process, a natural function of physical organs, breaks down the last barrier which formerly blocked the path to scientific study of human nature—all of it, not merely the parts that we share with beasts." {HNS; HNS2; WAS, 29 July 1956}

Herrick, Jim (20th Century)

Herrick, an atheist and the author of works on the history of humanism, has written *Vision and Realism, a Hundred Years of the Freethinker* (1982); *Against The Faith* (1985), essays on deists, skeptics, and atheists; and *A Humanist Anthology* (1995). Herrick was on the editorial board of *International Humanist* and from 1993 to 1998 was editor of its successor, *International Humanist News*, which is the journal of the International Humanist and Ethical Union (IHEU). In addition, he is a former editor of *The Free Thinker* (1977—1981) and vice president of the National Secular Society. Herrick also is editor of *New Humanist*, the journal of the Rationalist Press Association, of which he is a member of the Board of Directors.

"Bible-smashing is tedious to people who have smashed their Bibles," Herrick quotes George Bernard Shaw in a lucid article, "*The Freethinker* Yesterday and Today" (*Freethinker*, June 1994). But ever since George William Foote's first issue of the journal in 1881, Herrick notes that it has remained imperative to continue attacking the evangelicals' "spread of pernicious myths and unnecessary hardship for children and parents." Unfortunately, he adds, early freethinkers if they were to look at the current situation "would be surprised that religion has proved so persistent in the face of so many intellectual arguments against it. This shows that it is not rational thought that keeps the churches alive but emotion, habit, and the desire for power."

In 1996, speaking at the fourth World Atheist Conference held in Vijayawada, India, Herrick noted that no one has ever been injured by the truth. Self-deception is what actually injures humankind. "We must nurture the positive side of our atheistic existence," he said, adding that

> Extremist religion and fundamentalism, whether from the Christian Moral Right or from Islam, is growing in the world. We must on no account demonise the Muslims. I have met tolerant and civilised Muslims, the Sufi tradition of art and mysticism is fine, and many artistic endeavours are superb. We must keep in dialogue and encourage the liberals.

In India, Herrick attended the Rationalist Conference held in 1996, at which fire-walking demonstrations were held to debunk the godmen who claim they have supernatural powers. He spoke on "Freedom of Speech as a Universal Human Right." Also in 1996, he participated in the Humanist World Congress in Mexico City. Here, he received a distinguished service award for his four years' editorship of *International Humanist News*. In 1998 he spoke at the IHEU's congress in Mumbai.

Herrick, one of the most recognized humanists around the world, resigned as the IHEU's newsletter editor but remains active in international rationalist and humanist affairs. He signed Humanist Manifesto 2000 but lamented that "it has a far too rosy view of human nature," "too much is left to the market economy," and "the potential for human conflict is underestimated. . . . Nevertheless, perhaps irrationally, humanists of goodwill cannot allow these reservations to dampen the power of human effort and human hope." E-mail: <jim.rpa@humanism.org.uk>. {*The Free Mind*, February 1996; FUK; *New Humanist*, February 1996; SHD}

Herriot, Édouard [President] (1872—1957)

A French statesman, Herriot was president of the French National Assembly. Known as a moderate leftist, anticlerical, and antimilitarist, he was leader of the Radical Socialist (Radical) Party, the dominant party in France from 1899 to 1940. In the avant-garde, he was an ardent advocate of a European confederation, as outlined in his *The United States of Europe* (translated 1930). When Bertrand Russell was its president, Herriot was an honorary associate of the British Rationalist Press Association. At his national funeral in 1957, a throng estimated at 300,000 persons assembled in the huge Place Bellecourt where Premier Guy Mollet described Herriot as "a great humanist, a fighter for social reform and educational opportunities, and a man who demonstrated perfectly that 'the good and useful life is that in which action and thought are mutually sustaining.' " (See letter in entry for Charles Mayer, who describes Herriot as being a naturalistic humanist.) {CE; CL; HNS; RE}

Hershaft, Alex (20th Century)

When he signed Humanist Manifesto II, Hershaft was a principal scientist at Booz Allen Applied Research. {HM2}

Hershey, John H. (20th Century)

In the 1950s, Hershey was a correspondent (Latin America) for *The Humanist*. {HNS}

Hertell, Thomas (19th Century)

Hertell was a judge of the Marine Court of New York and for some years was a legislator in New York. He wrote several small works criticizing Christian theology and exerted his influence in favor of state secularization. In 1895 he became president of the Infidel Society for the Promotion of Mental Liberty, a group which attempted to form a national freethought society. {BDF; FUS}

Hertwig, Oscar (1849—1922)

A German anatomist, Hertwig was director of the Berlin Institute of Anatomy and Biology and was a professor of general anatomy and embryology at the University. He was a member of the Royal Academy of Science, Privy Councillor, and joint editor of the *Archiv für mikroskopische Anatomie und Entwickelungsgeschichte*. Hertwig was an admirer of and student of Haeckel. {RAT}

Hertwig, Richard (1850—1937)

Hertwig, the brother of Oscar Hertwig, was a zoologist who taught at Königsberg, Bonn, and Munich. He was a Privy Councillor and the author of many works on zoology. He was an admirer of and student of Haeckel. {RAT}

Hertz, Gevene (20th Century)

Hertz is president of the European Unitarian Universalists (EUU, Frydenlundsvej 49, 2950 Vedbaek, Denmark). Also, she is Vice-President of the International Council of Unitarian Universalists (ICUU). "I consider myself more or less an atheist," Hertz has written, "in that I do not really believe in any sort of God who has or had any real effect on the world. On the other hand, I find myself thanking God each day when I go out and see the beauty around me, or think about the ways in which I am 'blessed' (fortunate?). I like to do it because I feel a need to express gratitude, but I don't 'really' believe anyone is listening." Her e-mail: <ghertz@nordita.dk>.

Hertzler, Arthur Emanuel (1870—1946)

Dr. Hertzler, called the legendary "Horse and Buggy" doctor by Fred Whitehead in *Freethought History*, was a freethinker. His work, *The Grounds of an Old Surgeon's Faith, a Scientific Inquiry into the Causes of War*, was republished in 1944.

Hertzogenberg, Heinrich von (1843—1900)

An Austrian composer and professor of composition at the Berlin Royal High School of Music, Hertzogenberg was an intimate friend of Brahms. Their correspondence shows that both were atheists. Although brought up as a Catholic, he became, according to McCabe, "as Rationalistic as Brahms," saying, "I believe nothing" and "He who has no faith must have emotions." {JM; RAT; RE}

Hervey, John [Baron] (1696—1743)

Hervey, a deist and intimate friend of Queen Caroline, wrote *Memoirs of the Reign of George the Second*, in which he says he "adopted all the anti-Christian opinions of the time" and had "a peculiar antipathy to the Church and churchmen." The work by the Baron of Ickworth describes the intrigue and politics of the court of George II. (See entry for Alexander Pope.) {CE; JM; RAT; RE}

Hervieu, Paul Ernest (1857—1915)

Hervieu was a French dramatist and novelist. His literary career opened in 1882 with *Diogène le chien*, and he became known also for his dramatic works and other writing. Hervieu was a Commander of the Legion of Honour and Honorary President of the *Société des Gens de Lettres*. {RAT}

Herwegh, Georg (1817—1875)

Herwegh was a German radical and a poet. Intended for the Church, he left that business for literature and found his *Gedichte eines Lebendigen* (Poems of a Living Man) aroused attention by their boldness. In 1848, he raised troops for the purpose of invading Baden. Failing, he took refuge in Switzerland and Paris. Herwegh died at Baden-Baden. {BDF}

Herzberg, Emanuel (19th Century)

A freethinker, Herzberg wrote *Gorilla Catechism* (1869). {GS}

Herzen, Alexandr Ivanovich (1812—1870)

Herzen was an eminent Russian writer and revolutionary leader. Although said to have been the son of Prince Jakoslav, Alexei Gostev has pointed out that Herzen was the illegitimate son of Ivan Alexandrovitch Yakovlev. Herzen's mother, a German, lived in his father's house but the two were not married, possibly because she was a strong Lutheran believer who did not want to join the Orthodox Church. Cross-confessional alliances were forbidden in pre-revolutionary Russia.

In 1834 Herzen (from the German *das herz*, or heart) was sent as a civil servant to the provinces because he had belonged to a socialist political circle. Upon returning in 1840 to Moscow he met and influenced Byelinsky with his revolutionary ideas, then was banished in 1847, never to return to Russia. In Paris he supported the Revolution of 1848, and in Switzerland he issued a periodical, *Kolokol* (The Bell). In 1857, he set up in London the first free Russian press abroad, one which published works that were prohibited in Russia and which passed into that country in large numbers.

Who Is to Blame? (1847) was a popular novel about a liberal hero who becomes disillusioned with Russian society. In 1848 after having been a leading Westernizer, Herzen modified his views toward the Slavophile faith in Russia's communal institutions, although he agreed that peasant communes would be the forerunners of a socialist society rather than as strongholds of tradition. *From the Other Shore* (1855) contained a critique of the European revolutions of the period. *My Past and Thoughts* (1855—1868) is a masterpiece of Russian literature. He was at odds with Karl Marx because of his belief that freedom must be for all, including those who do not agree with the author. When he read Feuerbach's *Essence of Christianity*, he wrote, "After reading the first few pages I jumped for joy. Down with the masquerade attire, away with double-talk and allegory. . . . We do not need to clothe reality in myths."

He concluded there is no God, that man is alone in the universe, and that man's purpose is to develop values and meanings of his own. "All religions," he declared, "have based morality on obedience, that is to say, on voluntary slavery. That is why they have always been more pernicious than any political organization. For the latter makes use of violence, the former—of the corruption of the will."

In 1875 his works which often expressed his atheism were published as a ten-volume set. *Selected Philosophical Works* (translated 1956) confirms his outlook as a freethinker, one who, in the words of Aileen M. Kelly, had an overriding "faith in the self-sufficing value of contingent existence." (WAS, interview with Alexei Gostev, 1998) {BDF; CE; Eileen M. Kelley, *Toward Another Shore: Russian Thinkers Between Necessity and Chance* [1998]; EU, Hugh McLean; RAT; RE; TYD}

Herzog, Arthur III (1927—)

Herzog, once an editor for Fawcett Publications, wrote *The War-Peace Establishment* (1965), *The Church Trap* (1968), and *The Rise, Fall, and Exile of the King of White Collar-Crime* (1987). In 1968 he was national public relations director of the Eugene McCarthy Presidential Campaign. Herzog in his *Who's Who* entry states,

> I do not believe that money and success should figure as strongly as it does in our estimate of what is a good life. Since it often does, though, I would point to perseverance as a major element of success. Another, mostly overlooked, is a lack of dogmatism and a belief in skepticism and personal happiness as ends in themselves.

{FUS}

Hestand, Alex (20th Century)

When he signed Humanist Manifesto II, Hestand was an author and a columnist. {HM2}

Hester, Paul (20th Century)

A recording artist, once a member of the now disbanded New Zealand-Australian band Crowded House, was asked on MTV Europe (30 September 1993) if he believed in God. "No!" he responded. "My father used to try to get me to go to Sunday school, but I wouldn't. {CA}

Heston, Watson (19th Century)

In 1890 *The Truth Seeker* printed Heston's *The Freethinkers' Pictorial Text-Book, Showing the Absurdity and Untruthfulness of the Church's Claim to be a Divine and Beneficent Institution and Revealing the Abuses of a Union of Church and State*. He included a series on Uncle Sam and the Priest, the Church Robbing the People, Sabbath Laws, the Church and Thomas Paine, Woman and the Church, Missionaries, Bible Doctrines and Their Results, Heaven, Hell, Persecutions of the Church, etc. The work, which is filled with cartoons of atheistic and freethought material, was reprinted in 1993 by H. H. Waldo (Box 350, Rockton, Illinois 61072).

HET HUMANISTISCH ARCHIEF

The Dutch Humanist Archives and Documentation Centre is at Van Asch van Wijckskade 28, 3512 VS Utrecht, The Netherlands; tel: +31-30-2390164; fax: +31-30-2390170; <humarc@uvh.nl>.

HET VRIJE WOORD

Het Vrije Woord is published monthly at Lange Leemstr 57, 2018 Antwerp, Belgium. E-mail: <human@glo.be>.

HETAIRAI

The women who came to ancient Athens and were known as Hetairai were not, as is often said, courtesans. They were "pals" or companions. Among the most famous was Aspasia, the unwedded wife of Pericles. (See entry for Aspasia.)

HETEROSEXUALITY

"Happiness? It's whenever I think about or am near my wife."

Directing one's sexual desire toward a person of the opposite sex is a universal characteristic, the subject of poetry, fiction, films, paintings, sculpture, music, and universal conversation.

However, in Ancient Greece, heterosexuality as it is now understood was unknown, or so argues Jonathan Ned Katz. They knew about procreation, of course. They knew about sex between women and men. They knew about sex between men and men as well as about sex between women and women. But they did not consider these things "opposites." Further, one form of sex was not considered to be a lesser type than another, Katz states in *The Invention of Heterosexuality* (1995). It was not considered unusual for a person to have same—as well as different—sex desires. He cites the French philosopher Michel Foucault, who wrote, "The Greeks did not see love for one's own sex and for the other sex as opposites, as two exclusive choices, two radically different types of behavior. The dividing lines did not follow that kind of boundary."

In New England from 1607 to 1740, in order to insure enough people to harvest the crops, an entirely different reasoning was used to encourage procreation. Same-sex experiences were penalized, as was masturbation. Churches preached against "sodomites" and "sapphists," and the death penalty for sodomy was established in all the colonies. Katz develops the argument that, like the Scottish tartan, heterosexuality (a word which Webster documents as first being used in 1892) is a recent concept. Karl Maria Kertbeny is credited with formulating the hetero/homo split, a usage which Krafft-Ebbing in *Psychopathia Sexualis* (1899) cited. Katz argues that attraction to or relationships with people of the other sex do not make one "heterosexual." Rather, sexuality is conceived as being on a continuum, that sexual desire and activity are better served without such strictly defining and limiting labels.

Contemporary heterosexuals, particularly religious fundamentalists, are entirely in disagreement with Katz's historical study. Their complaint is that he is not discussing the Judeo-Christian aspects of sex practices nor even that he approves of such.

One of the most memorable descriptions of the life a flagrant heterosexual enjoyed is found in Giacomo Casanova's (1725—1798) 12-volume *Mémoires*. He not only describes an extraordinary succession of sexual encounters but also provides a portrait of the manners of his time.

The Kinsey and other reports, as well as most people's understanding by conversing with friends, indicate that most people did not "choose" to be heterosexual, that they have been so since birth, and that they are content with such a status. There is little agreement, however, as to whether one's heterosexuality must involve, in a lifetime, one partner only.

"You marry a girl *not* because you want to live with her," observed a Manhattan wag concerning heterosexuality. "You marry a girl because you cannot live *without* her!" (See entry for Marriage.)

Hetherington, Henry (1792—1849)

An English radical reformer and one of the heroes of "the free press," Hetherington in the 1820s was attracted to freethought. A working-class organizer, he founded the Metropolitan Political Union in 1830, which was the germ both of trade unionism and of the Chartist movement. In 1830 the Government obtained three convictions against him for publishing the *Poor Man's Guardian*, and he was lodged for six months in Clerkenwell gaol. At the end of 1832 he was again imprisoned there for six months, his treatment being most cruel. An opening, called a window, but without a pane of glass, let in the rain and snow by day and night. In 1840 he was tried for blasphemous libel for publishing Charles Haslam's *Letters to the Clergy of All Denominations.* Hetherington, refusing to pay the fine which was levied, spent four months in Queen's Bench Prison. According to Hetherington, good deeds alone are what counts. He fought against the "taxes upon knowledge" by issuing unstamped *The Poor Man's Guardian* (1831—1835), a weekly newspaper for the people, established, contrary to "law," to try the power of "might" against "right." His persistency, however, had much to do in removing the taxes. From 1842 to 1843 in Glasgow he edited *Free-Thinkers' Information for the People.*

His will affirmed his atheism and condemned Christian theology as the "greatest obstacle to human improvement and happiness":

> As life is uncertain, it behooves every one to make preparations for death; I deem it therefore a duty incumbent on me, ere I quit this life, to express in writing, for the satisfaction and guidance of esteemed friends, my feelings and opinions in reference to our common principles. I adopt this course that no mistake or misapprehension may arise through the false reports of those who officiously and obtrusively obtain access to the death-beds of avowed infidels to priestcraft and superstition; and who, by their annoying importunities, labour to extort from an opponent, whose intellect is already worn out and subdued by protracted physical suffering, some trifling admission, that they may blazon it forth to the world as a Death-bed Confession, and a triumph of Christianity over infidelity.
>
> In the first place, then, I calmly and deliberately declare that I do not believe in the popular notion of the existence of an Almighty, All-Wise and Benevolent God—possessing intelligence, and conscious of his own operations; because these attributes involve such a mass of absurdities and contradictions, so much cruelty and injustice on his part to the poor and destitute portion of his creatures—that, in my opinion, no rational reflecting mind can, after disinterested investigation, give credence to the existence of such a Being.
>
> 2nd. I believe death to be an eternal sleep—that I shall never live again in this world, or another, with a consciousness that I am the same identical person that once lived, performed the duties, and exercised the functions of a human being.
>
> 3rd. I consider priestcraft and superstition the greatest obstacle to human improvement and happiness. During my life I have, to the best of my ability, sincerely and strenuously exposed and opposed them, and die with a firm conviction that Truth, Justice, and Liberty will never be permanently established on earth till every vestige of priestcraft and superstition shall be utterly destroyed.
>
> 4th. I have ever considered that the only religion useful to man consists exclusively of the practice of morality, and in the mutual interchange of kind actions. In such a religion there is no room for priests—and when I see them interfering at our births, marriages and deaths, pretending to conduct us safely through this state of being to another and happier world, any disinterested person of the least shrewdness and discernment must perceive that their sole aim is to stultify the minds of the people by their incomprehensible doctrines, that they may the more effectually fleece the poor deluded sheep who listen to their empty babblings and mystifications.
>
> 5th. As I have lived so I die, a determined opponent to their nefarious and plundering system. I wish my friends, therefore, to deposit my remains in unconsecrated ground, and trust they will allow no priest, or clergyman of any denomination, to interfere in any way whatever at my funeral. My earnest desire is, that no relation or friend shall wear black or any kind of mourning, as I consider it contrary to our rational principles to indicate respect for a departed friend by complying with a hypocritical custom.
>
> 6th. I wish those who respect me, and who have laboured in our common cause, to attend my remains to their last resting place, not so much in consideration of the individual, as to do honour to our just, benevolent and rational principles. I hope all true Rationalists will leave pompous displays to the tools of priestcraft and superstition.

Hetherington wrote this Testament nearly two years before his death, but he signed it with a firm hand three days before he breathed his last, in the presence of Thomas Cooper, who left it at the Reasoner office for "the inspection of the curious or sceptical." Thomas Cooper became a Christian, but he could not repudiate what he printed at the time, or destroy his "personal testimony," as he called it, to the consistency with which Hetherington died in the principles of Freethought. (See Gordon Stein , "Henry Hetherington," in *American Rationalist* (July-August, 1990.) {BDF; EU, Joel H. Wiener; FUK; RAT; RE; VI; TRI}

Hetherly, Marian (20th Century)

Hetherly writes "Worth Noting" for and is an editor of *The Humanist.*

HETUVADI

A rationalist, Oriya monthly, *Hetuvadi* is at 779, Pocket-5, Mayur Vihar-1, New Delhi 110 091, India.

HETUVADI

A rationalist, Telugu monthly, *Hetuvadi* is at 4-13-6, Ithanagar, Tenali, Andhra Pradesh, 522201, India.

Hetzer, Ludwig (16th Century)

Hetzer was an anti-trinitarian martyr. While an Anabaptist minister at Zurich, he openly denied the doctrine of the Trinity. As a result, he was condemned to death by the magistrates of Constance on a charge of blasphemy. The sentence was carried out 4 February 1529. {BDF}

Heusden, C. J. van (19th Century)

Van Heusden was a Dutch writer in *De Dageraad.* He wrote several works, one being *Thoughts on a Coming More Universal Doctrine.* {BDF}

Hewetson, Richard (20th Century)

A Californian, Hewetson is an honorary member of the Minnesota Atheists and a member of Atheists of San Francisco Region. In a *Secular Nation* (Fall 1994) article, he described how the San Francisco atheists built a secular book section in the San Francisco Public Library. Hewetson is on the board of directors of the Freedom From Religion Foundation.

Hewett, Pauline (20th Century)

Hewett in Britain is active with the Muswell Hill Humanist Group.

Hewitt, Cecil Rolph (1901—1994)

Hewitt, who wrote under the pen-name of C. H. Rolph, was a chief inspector of the City of London Police. Upon the death of his second wife, Jenifer Wayne, a BBC radio writer and producer, Hewitt "firmly continued to refuse to say the Creed," observed his friend, Peter Cotes. In one of his last books, *Further Particulars,* Hewitt wrote that although he might like to be a Christian, "I can't bring myself to make the leap from a vague sense of the numinous to Christian belief."

Hewlett, Philip (20th Century)

Hewlett's history of Canada's liberal religious movement is found in *Unitarianism in Canada* (1967) and *Unitarians in Canada* (1978).

Hewson, Arthur B. (20th Century)

After the American Rationalist Federation formed in 1955, Hewson in 1956 started *The American Rationalist,* a publication independent of the Federation. He is author of *Affirmative Rationalism* (1964). {EU, Eldon Scholl; FUS}

Heyse, Paul Johann Ludwig von (1830—1914)

The first German to win the Nobel Prize in Literature (1910), Heyse wrote *The Fury* (1855) and *Andrea Delfin* (1859). Robertson lists him as being a rationalist. In *Kinder der Welt* (1873), Heyse truculently criticized the churches. {BDF; JMR; RAT; RE}

Heywood, Abel (19th Century)

Heywood, a radical freethinker and an alderman, was active in the 1860s with the English Manchester Secular Union. {FUK; RSR}

Heywood, Ezra H. (1829—1893)

Heywood was something of an eccentric reformer, and many Liberals did not agree with him. Although he had a college education and was intended for the ministry, he devoted his life to the antislavery crusade, opposition to the Civil War, and other causes. He published *The Word*, which opposed rent, interest, taxes, tariffs, profits, war, marriage, and all monopolies. After being imprisoned for two years in a Charleston jail for his controversial stands, Heywood was released, then contracted a cold during his conduct of a labor reform convention in New York, Heywood died three days later in Massachusetts. {PUT; TRI}

Hibbard, W. D. (19th Century)

A freethinker, Hibbard wrote *Rays of Reason, or Religion Refuted* (1887). {GS}

Hibbert. Robert (1770-1849)

Hibbert, a philanthropist whose family made money from sugar plantations in Jamaica, was a Unitarian. He wished the trust to be known as "The Anti-Trinitarian Fund," but on the advice of lawyer Edwin Field eventually settled for a non-dogmatic title in deference to the political and religious climate of the day.

The Trust's foundation document, while not using the word Unitarian, was Unitarian in ethos. Although today's Trust includes a liberal Anglican on its Board, membership has been solidly Unitarian.

The History of the Trust, by Alan Ruston, is obtainable from the Trust office at 14 Gordon Square, London WC1HOAG, according to Trust Secretary Jim McClelland. It aided the *Hibbert Journal* 1920-1970). {WAS, e-mail from Jim McClelland, 5 September 1998}

Hibbert, Julian (1800—1834)

A British freethinker, Hibbert belonged to many "radical" organizations, was a generous benefactor to freethought causes, and worked with Richard Carlile and Robert Taylor to popularize anti-Christian works. Learning that a distinguished political prisoner had received a gift of £1,000, Hibbert remarked that a freethinking prisoner should not want equal friends, so he gave Carlile a check for the same amount. Hibbert spent nearly £1,000 in fitting up Carlile's shop in Fleet Street. He also commenced a *Dictionary of Anti-Superstitionists* and *Chronological Tables of British Freethinkers*. Carlile described him as "the most actively virtuous human being that I have ever known." Upon his death, Hibbert left £500 each to James Watson and to Henry Hetherington. {BDF; EU, Joel H. Wiener; FUK; RAT; RE}

Hibschman, Harry (20th Century)

Hibschman was a freethinker who wrote "Religion's Blight of American Divorce Laws" (1929) and "Should Church Property Be Taxed?" (1930). {GS}

Hickey, Thomas (1869—1926)

Hickey was a fiery radical who led a New York Knights of Labor strike for the nine-hour day. In 1904, he started a newspaper called *The Rebel* in Halletsville, Texas, and some of its special issues reached 100,000. He attacked the Texas prison system for its use of the bull-whip to discipline inmates, he published letters which blacklisted militant labor organizers from railroad employment, and he spoke eloquently against religion. The *International Socialist Review* said in 1910 that he was "a baby blizzard behind a shaggy beard and ponderous moustache. He seldom uses cuss words, but in debate he looks like he is filled with Irish wit and Irish fight." Not only did he attack the Catholic hierarchy for its damnation of socialism, but also he exposed various anti-Jesuit forgeries. {*Freethought History #15*, 1995}

Hickman, Larry A. (20th Century)

Hickman is professor of philosophy at Southern Illinois University in Carbondale. He is general editor of *The Correspondence of John Dewey* and director of the Center for Dewey Studies. Hickman points out that Dewey "realized that dogmatic religious and metaphysical views tend to break communication and isolate human beings from one another. In [Dewey's] view, technology offers the best hope for common action because it is the most basic and therefore the most common human project."

Hickman, a humanist, is author of *John Dewey's Pragmatic Technology* (1990).

Hicks, Elias (1748—1830)

Leader of the "Hicksite" Quakers who were non-trinitarian, Hicks was a friend of Walt Whitman's father, who introduced his son to Mr. Hicks's humanistic outlook. Because of his unitarianism, he was held responsible for the split in the American Society into Orthodox and "Hicksite" Friends in 1827.

According to Corliss Lamont, the liberal or Hicksite wing of Friends (Quakers) "has made the closest approach to Humanism" of the various Protestant groups. Hicks is credited with ridding the Friends of slavery and encouraging them to boycott products of slave labor. {CE; CL; ER}

Hicks, Granville (1901—1982)

Hicks was author of *The Great Tradition* (1933) and became a leading Communist critic and editor of *The New Masses*. He wrote a biography of *John Reed* (1936) and in his *I Like America* (1938) he explained the contemporary scene from the rationale of his political, communistic viewpoint. *The First to Awaken* (1940) was written with Richard M. Bennett and describes a New Hampshire man who wakes a century after being anesthetized in 1940 to find a revolutionary, humanistic, social, and industrial utopia. *Where We Came Out* (1954) describes the appeal of, and his disillusionment with, communism. In 1958, he became a frequent contributor to *Saturday Review*. Hicks wrote to the present author concerning his view of humanism:

> I do consider myself a naturalistic humanist. In spite of all the talk there has been about orthodoxy, I feel that naturalistic humanism is constantly gaining ground. I also feel that it has gained a great deal in flexibility and richness.
>
> {CE; WAS, 9 February 1951}

Hicks, L. E. (19th Century)

An American geologist, Hicks wrote *A Critique of Design Arguments* (1883). {BDF}

Hicks, Robert (20th Century)

Hicks is Vice-President of the Humanist Association of Toronto (HAT).

HICKSITE QUAKERS: See entry for Elias Hicks.

Hidalgo Tuñon, Alberto: See entry for Alberto Hidalgo Tuñon.

Higgins, Godfrey (1771—1833)

Higgins was an English archaeologist whose first work was entitled *Horae Sabbaticae* (1813), a manual on the Sunday Question. In 1829 he published *An Apology for the Life and Character of Mohammed* and *Celtic Druids*, which occasioned some stir on account of the exposure of priestcraft. Upon his death a two-volume work, *Anacalypsis*, was published, an attempt to draw aside the veil of the Saitic Isis, which he felt was an inquiry into the origin of languages, nations, and religions. Higgins was a deist. {BDF; FUK; RAT; RE}

Higgins, Richard (Dick) (1938-1998)

Higgins was an innovator in the 1960's avant-garde movement. A writer, poet, artist, composer, and publisher, he was a seminal figure in Happenings and the concrete poetry movement. He co-founded the anti-authoritarian Fluxus movement.

Higgins invented the term "intermedia" and listed forty-seven pages on his curriculum vitae—headings included visual art, movies and videotapes, music and sound art. *Foew&ombwhnw* was a 1969 book of essays, an acronym for "freaked out electronic wizard and other marvelous bartenders who have no wings." It combined the traditional and the iconoclastic and, like a prayer book, was bound in leather with a ribbon bookmark.

The founder of Something Else Press, he published (1964-1975) books and pamphlets by avant-garde writers such as Gertrude Stein, Richard Hulsenbeck, Merce Cunningham, John Cage, Emmett Williams, Claes Oldenburg, Luigi Russolo, and the 17th-century poet George Herbert.

With Allan Kaprow and others he planned and performed in the first Happenings. With George Macunius he established the loosely knit group known as Fluxus, which accepted *any* activity as art and played fast and loose with definitions. One of his compositions, "Dangerous Music No. 17" (1963), consisted of his wife—the poet Alison Knowles—shaving his head. "Dangerous Music No. 2" involved screaming as loudly as possible for as long as possible.

Higgins was a freethinker, entirely uninvolved with any organized religion. His interest was in anything *new*. {Roberta Smith, *The New York Times*, 31 October 1998}

Higginson, Edward Jr. (19th Century)

A freethinker, Higginson wrote, "Blasphemy, What It Is and On Whom Chargeable." (1830). {GS}

Higginson, Thomas Wentworth (1823—1911)

Higginson, known today as Emily Dickinson's friend and poetry critic, was a commander of the First South Carolina Volunteers (freedmen), a regiment of Negro troops. He championed the rights of Negroes at a time when the cause was unpopular. Previously, he had been the Unitarian minister of the First Religious Society (Unitarian) in Newburyport, Massachusetts, and of the First Church in Worcester, Massachusetts. An abolitionist political activist, he wrote *Army Life in a Black Regiment* (1870), hailed by some as an overlooked masterpiece. In Boston, he led a raid on the Court House to try to free fugitive slave Anthony Burns and was wounded in his attempt. He aided the Free Soil fight in Kansas and was a supporter of John Brown. He contributed to *Atlantic Monthly*, *Nation*, and *Harper's Bazaar*. He also became a spokesman for the rights of women, feeling that this was "the next great question" facing the country after the liberation of the slaves. Meanwhile, he was a prodigious writer and critic. His books include *Malbone* (1869), a novel; sketches, including *Oldport Days* (1873) and *Old Cambridge* (1899); the lives of Whittier (1902) and Longfellow (1902) for the "Men of Letters" series; biographies of Margaret Fuller (1884) and of his ancestor, Francis Higginson (1891); and an autobiographical account, *Cheerful Yesterday* (1898). Emily Dickinson is said to have been entranced by Higginson, who was the first to encourage her, although he tended to "correct" her poems. Later, he edited two volumes with Mabel L. Todd of Dickinson's verse (1890—1891). In Edward J. Renehan Jr.'s *The Secret Six* (1995), Higginson is described as the toughest-minded of a group of men who conspired with John Brown. The others included Theodore Parker, Samuel Gridley Howe, Julia Ward Howe, and Gerrit Smith. {CE; FUS; JMR; RAT; U; U&U}

HIGH SCHOOL HUMANISTS, FREETHINKERS

Numbers of secondary schools have humanist clubs or discussion groups. Those which are affiliated with the Campus Freethought Association are found on the Web at <www.secularhumanism.org/cfa/orgs.html>.

HIGHER POWER

A power is the rate at which work is done, expressed as the amount of work per unit time and commony measured in units such as the watt and horsepower. In physics, therefore, with more wattage or horsepower one obtains higher power.

Rabbi Sherwin T. Wine, founder of the Society for Humanistic Judaism, has observed that "One of the signs of personal strength is that we take blame for what we do wrong. The other sign is that we take credit for what we do right. We do not alienate our power by assigning it to someone else. . . . Strong people are comfortable in recognizing their own power . . . nor do they call their power 'a higher power.' " (See entries for Jim Christopher, Rational Recovery Self-Help Network, Secular Organization for Sobriety, and James Taylor.)

Highsmith, Patricia (1921—1995)

Once called "the most important crime novelist at present in practice," Highsmith was a successful writer. Critic Kathleen Gregory Klein has noted that Highsmith created a new fictional form, introducing the cult-figure serial killer Tom Ripley as a new type of criminal superhero. Of this, Sally R. Munt of Nottinghman Trent University in England wrote, "Lesbian and gay readers, themselves positioned in an uneasy relation to the law and its regulation of permissible behavior, find in Ripley the antithesis to state-sanctioned Christian virtue. He pushes transgression to the limit." {GL}

Higinbotham, George (1826—1892)

Higinbotham was an unorthodox Anglican, editor, independent legislator, lawyer, and judge. As Chairman of the Education Commission, he proposed in 1866 the withdrawal of public funds from church schools and establishment of state-controlled non-sectarian schools. On becoming Chief Judge in 1886, he continued support of responsible government, later refusing public honors because they originated in Britain. Higinbotham deplored the church's refusal to accept the findings of science, which led to its inability to nourish an educated laity's spiritual needs. {SWW}

Hikmet, Nazim (1902—1963)

Hikmet was a Turkish poet who started writing when he was eleven. While trekking across Anatolia in his late teens, he met several Turkish Communists and, impressed by their idealism, joined the party, which in 1922 was banned in Turkey. In 1938, an atheist and Communist, he was sentenced to twenty-eight years in prison on charges of inciting a military revolt, although the major evidence against him was that cadets were reading his books. When his health worsened, leftists including Jean-Paul Sartre, Pablo Neruda, Yevgeny Yevtushenko, and Pablo Picasso organized campaigns for his release. Set free in 1950, he fled to the Soviet Union where he lived for the rest of his life and where he wrote poems in homage to Lenin, Stalin, and the Chinese revolution.

The poet Denise Levertov has described his 17,000-line masterpiece *Human Landscapes* as

> a flashing-past of pictures, a cinematographic semi-autobiographical fiction that will capture the attention of the least scholarly, least spe-

cialist of readers. At the same time, it is a work to engage and hold the attention of poets and sophisticated habitual readers of modern poetry, for thigh it is long it is terse, condensed, charged: the work of a supremely confident, energetic, passionate, and powerfully imaginative poet.

Although in 1997 some of his friends wanted to return Hikmet's body from Moscow to Turkey, including Turkey's PEN (Poets, Essayists, and Novelists) President, Sukran Kurdakul, himself a dedicated secularist, the Islamic-based Welfare Party which controlled both the Culture Ministry and Istanbul's City Hall, would not allow it. {Stephen Kinzer, *The New York Times*, 27 February 1997}

Hill, Christopher (1912—)

In 1986, Hill was elected as an honorary associate of the Rationalist Press Association. He is author of many books, including *God's Englishman* (1970), *Antichrist in Seventeenth-Century England* (1971), and *John Bunyan and His Church* (1988).

Hill, Earl P. (20th Century)

A freethinker, Hill wrote "Godmanity" (1908). {GS}

Hill, George Birkbeck Norman (1835—1903)

A writer, Hill was a friend of Swinburne, Morris, and Rossetti, sharing their views. He edited Boswell (6 volumes, 1887), some of Johnson's works, and the letters of Hume and Rossetti. In one of his letters, he wrote, "Priestcraft in every form I hate, and dogma I laugh at." He thought Christianity "a very noble poem, but of such stuff as dreams are made of." {RAT}

Hill, George N. (19th Century)

Hill, a Bostonian, was one of the founders of the Ingersoll Secular Society. He originated the freethought calendar with T. B. Wakeman, and he was the first American to subscribe to the Bruno monument erected in Rome. {PUT}

Hill, Joe (1879—1915)

A freethinker and Swedish-American union organizer, Hill is the legendary hero of radical labor whose "Casey Jones" and "The Union Scab" songs are still popular, as is his "Preacher and the Slave," which is sung to the Christian tune "In the Sweet Bye and Bye":

Long-haired preachers come out every night,
Try to tell you what's wrong and what's right;
But when asked 'bout something to eat,
They will tell you with voices so sweet:

You will eat, by and bye,
In the glorious land above the sky;
Work and pray, live on hay,
You'll get pie in the sky when you die—that's a lie.

Hill, on an allegedly trumped-up murder charge, was executed by firing-squad in 1915. (CE; TYD)

Hill, John (20th Century)

A member of Freedom From Religion Foundation, Hill is a program manager for a Community Action Agency and a freethought activist with the Inland Northwest Freethought Society in Washington State.

Hill, Norman (20th Century)

A human rights activist in New York City, Hill has been influential in furthering the legacy of A. Philip Randolph. He wrote *The Railway Traveling Post Office of Great Britain and Ireland (1838—1975)* (1977). Hill is an Advisory Board Member of African Americans for Humanism. {AAH}

Hill, Sam (1940—)

Hill is a rationalist who wrote *Poems, Original and Collected* (1953).

Hillar, Marian (20th Century)

A physician who teaches biology at Texas Southern University in Houston, Hillar was a participant in the 1996 Humanist World Congress in Mexico City.

Hillary, Edmund Percival [Sir] (1919-)

Hillary, the famed mountaineer and explorer who was born in Auckland, New Zealand, was a member of John Hunt's Everest expedition. With Tenzing Norgay, he reached the summit of Mt. Everest in 1953, for which he was knighted. In 1958 he and a New Zealand expeditionary party reached the South Pole. His autobiography is *Nothing Venture, Nothing Win* (1975).

In a 1991 interview, he said, "I have no particular religious beliefs at all, but I am interested in all religions. In Tibetan Buddhism, one of the strongest features is that they believe that everyone must choose their own path in life. They don't try to convert you to their particular form of religion, but it's up to you to choose your own path. I like that very much indeed. I think that's a great approach to philosophy." {CA}

Hillebrand, Karl (1829—1884)

Hillebrand's father, Joseph, succeeded Hegel as professor at Heidelberg. Karl was involved in the revolutionary movement in Germany, being imprisoned in the fortress of Rastadt, from which he escaped to France. He taught at Strasbourg and Paris, where he became secretary to Heine. On the poet's death he removed to Bordeaux, becoming a naturalized Frenchman, then a professor of letters at Douay. During the Franco-Prussian war he was correspondent to the *Times* and was taken for a Prussian spy. In 1871 he settled at Florence, where he translated the poems of Carducci. Hillebrand was a contributor to the *Fortnightly Review*, *Revue des deux Mondes*, and *North American Review*. His best known work is on France and the French in the second half of the nineteenth century. {BDF; RAT}

Hiller, Aaron (1920—)

A freethinker, Hiller wrote *Diamonds in a Dunghill* (1982). He has acted on television, given sermons to Unitarian congregations, and written about religious liberty for a variety of journals. {*Freethought Today*, May 1996; GS}

Hillman, Harold (20th Century)

Hillman is the director of the Unity Laboratory of Applied Neurobiology, and the reader in physiology at the University of Surrey. He also is medical adviser to the Institute of Biological Psychiatry in Bangor, Wales. In *New Humanist* (July 1993), he argues that new scientific views may be suppressed by a scientific orthodoxy, and he considers ways in which dissident views might be more fairly dealt with. In *The Freethinker* (August 1994), he examines each word of the Lord's Prayer, suggesting the following as a text for our time:

God, who resides in Heaven, you are worthy of great respect. Your rule will be accepted on Earth, as it is Heaven. Give us food today, and forgive our sins, as we have forgiven those who have sinned against us [or, cancel our debts, as we have canceled debts owed to us]. Do not lead us into temptation, but deliver us from evil, because you have the power, the honour, and the glory for ever. This is true.

However, he continues, note what the prayer states:

(a) "Our father" can be read neither literally nor symbolically,

because both meanings are incompatible with the uniqueness of Jesus Christ as the son of God;
(b) Outside Earth, God's rule prevails, and sentient and conscious beings there obey it.
(c) God is not omnipotent yet, because his will is not being done on earth at present; or he is combating his own will;
(d) He creates sin, temptation, the human tendency to indebtedness and evil (or the evil one), as well as the human choice to do evil, so he is not all good. He also determines how far human beings succumb to these evils, while knowing beforehand how much they will. He also decides what punishments he inflicts on them for doing what he has permitted them to do or made them do, and he knows beforehand what they intend.

Hillman concludes that the Lord's Prayer, the most important affirmation of Christianity, contains affirmations contradictory to the basic tenets of Christianity. Others prefer a total rejection of Judeo-Christian concepts rather than a piece-meal reworking of the humanistic ideas within Judeo-Christianity.

Hilton, Randall (20th Century)

A liberal minister, Hilton was once a director of the American Humanist Association. {HNS}

Hilty, Palmer A. (20th Century)

When he signed Humanist Manifesto II, Hilty was an administrative secretary, Fellowship of Religious Humanists. {HM2}

Himmelfarb, Gertrude (20th Century)

The Enlightenment bequeathed many splendid achievements to mankind, wrote Himmelfarb (*The Wall Street Journal*, 5 May 1999), a professor emeritus of history at the City University of New York. But science and technology can be morally equivocal, she noted.

The Enlightenment, in light of this century's Holocaust, also bequeathed us some dangerous illusions:

> In our post-Enlightenment world, we have had to relearn what ancient philosophy and religion had taught us and what recent history has brought home to us: that material progress can have an inverse relationship to moral progress, that the most benign social policies can have unintended and unfortunate effects, that national passions can be exacerbated in an ostensibly global world and religious passions in a supposedly secular one, and that our most cherished principles (liberty, equality, fraternity, even peace) can be perverted and degraded—that, in short, progress in all spheres, not only in science and technology, is unpredictable and undependable.
>
> This may be the lesson of the millennium. Progress, yes, but a modest, cautious, amelioratory progress, chastened by the experiences of history and guided by a sense of human limits as well as possibilities.

Hinchman, Aaron (19th Century)

In 1843, Hinchman from Goshen, Ohio, edited *Self-Examiner*. {FUS}

Hinckle, William A. (20th Century)

Hinckle was a freethinker who wrote *The Evolution of Religion* (1910). {GS}

Hinds, Samuel (19th Century)

A freethinker, Hinds wrote, "A Reply to the Question 'Shall I Seek Ordination in the Church of England?' " (1871). {GS}

HINDU SKEPTIC

Aditya Mishra is a computer scientist who calls himself "the Hindu $kepti¢." "Aditya," a Vedic deity, is from Sanskrit and is a synonym for the Sun. He was the son of Adita, who was one of the two Vedic sister goddesses or matriarchs. The other is Diti, the progenitor of several children collectively known as Daityas. In this sense Aditya may have been the first born Aryan. Mishra, who has postgraduate degrees from Lucknow University in India and the University of Pennsylvania, had parents who arranged his marriage "to my wife Sushma when we were in teens and we are happy for that. We have made our home in south Florida and have a daughter who is a librarian."

On the Web: <http://www.smart1.net/aditya/>. E-mail: <a018967t@bc.seflin.org>.

HINDUISM

Hindus who believe in the transmigration of souls hold that karma (a force generated by a person's actions, held also in Buddhism) perpetuates transmigration and its ethical consequences in order to determine one's destiny in one's next existence. Through their karma individuals reap the rewards of good as well as bad actions in a series of lifetimes. Their Shiva, also called Mahadeva, is a "horned god" celebrated by the Indus Valley civilization, which combined Shiva worship with phallic worship. Shiva, like the fierce Vedic god Rudra, was a god of destruction as well as cosmic dissolution. Shiva's consort was Kali, which in Hindi means "the black one," and she is a goddess associated with disease, death, and destruction. Worshiped by some as the Divine Mother, particularly among the lower castes in Bengal, she is described as having skulls on her head, a bloody sword in one of her arms. Some of her devotees are Thugs, or Phansigars (stranglers), formerly a religious sect of murderers and robbers in India. Presumably, Kali was the contented spouse of Shiva, god of phallic worship. Putting a wealthy, unsuspecting traveler to death was a virtue, not a crime to be punished in the hereafter. The British, when they took over India, thought it expedient to put the Thugs and Phansigars out of business altogether, reportedly succeeding.

In 1994, the Hindu government reported that a total of 20,537 brides were killed between 1990—1993. "Dowry deaths" rose to 5,582 in 1993 from 4,836 in 1990. If the families of young Hindu brides cannot meet the illegal post-marriage dowry demands, they are doused in cooking kerosene and burned to death "accidentally," critics complain. (See entries for Agung and Gandhi. Also see a detailed discussion in the *Encyclopedia of Philosophy*, Vol. 4. For an estimate of the number of Hindus worldwide, see the entry for Hell.) {CE; ER; RE}

Hines, John (20th Century)

Hines in Britain is active with the Hastings and Rother Humanist Group.

Hines, Terence (20th Century)

Hines is author of *Pseudo-Science and the Paranormal: A Critical Examination of the Evidence* (1988).

Hins, Eugène (Born 1839)

Hins was a Belgian writer. As general secretary of the International, he edited *L'Internationale*, in which he laid stress on anti-religious teaching. Hins wrote *La Russie de devoilée au moyen de sa littérature populaire* (1883). "You waste your time and trouble in attacking clericalism," he wrote; "attack its root—religion." {BDF; RAT}

Hinton, James (1822—1875)

Hinton, a philosopher, was a surgeon by profession and a specialist in ear diseases. *The Mystery of Pain* (1866) developed a broad and rather mystic pantheism, but Hinton rejected the idea of a personal God. {RAT; RE}

Hinton, Richard W. (20th Century)

Hinton wrote *Arsenal for Skeptics* (1934). The author Rupert Hughes described it as providing "a great number of reasons for the enormous doubt which the churches bewail."

Hiorth, Finngeir (1928—)

Hiorth, born in Indonesia of Norwegian parents who served as missionaries for the Salvation Army, had a religious upbringing but ceased to believe in any god at the age of nineteen. He studied linguistics and philosophy in Norway, France, Germany, and The Netherlands, obtaining in 1962 his Ph. D. in Germany in theoretical linguistics.

He is author of *Zur formalen Charakterisierung des Satzes* (1962); *Timor: Past and Present* (1985); *Philosophers in Indonesia* (1983); *Verdslige livssyn* (Secular Views of Life, 1993); *Innføring i humanisme* (Introduction to Humanism, 1994); *Innføring i marxisme* (Introduction to Marxism, 1994); *Secularism in Sweden* (1995); *Opplysningstidens filosofi* (The Philosophy of Enlightenment, 1995); *Introduction to Atheism* (1995); *Introduction to Humanism* (1996); *Metafysikk og materialisme* (Metaphysics and Materialism, 1997);

and *Atheism in India* (1998). Hiorth also has published books on the German philosopher Leibniz (1966), on the Scottish philosopher David Hume (1973), on the American linguist Noam Chomsky (1974), and on the concept of power (1975).

From 1963 until his retirement in 1993 he was a lecturer, later a senior lecturer, in philosophy at the University of Oslo. He is a member of the World Union of Freethinkers (WUF) and of the International Humanist and Ethical Union (IHEU). In addition, he is a member of freethought organizations in Great Britain, India, Norway, and Sweden. He is an honorary associate of the New Zealand Association of Rationalists and Humanists.

Hiorth spoke at the Congress of the World Union of Freethinkers in Belgium, 1989. The word "freethinker," he found, has been adopted in French, German, Dutch, Spanish, Finnish, the Scandinavian languages, and other languages. Most early freethinkers were deists. By the 18th century, a few advocated atheism, a tendency which became more pronounced in the 19th century. Only since the 1960s has "secular humanism" been in current use. His survey of freethought, atheism, and naturalistic humanism is published in *New Humanist* (October, 1990).

Hiorth, who describes himself as "a convinced atheist and materialist," has noted that many atheists call themselves freethinkers, humanists, rationalists, or agnostics because "these names have their advantages, but also their weaknesses." *New Humanist* (October, 1990) published his "Freethought and Secular Humanism." In 1992 at the International Humanist and Ethical Union (IHEU) congress in Amsterdam, he addressed the group on the subject of the Indian philosopher, M. N. Roy, and his radical humanism.

Hippel, Theodor Gottlieb von (1741—1796)

Hippel was a German who wrote humorous poetry. He studied theology but resigned it for law, then became in 1780 burgomaster of Königsberg. His works, states Wheeler, "betray his advanced opinions." {BDF; RAT}

Hippo (5th Century B.C.E.)

Hippo, according to Robertson, is "the first specifically named atheist of Greek antiquity," so named by Plutarch. The dubious tradition runs that his tomb bore the epitaph: "This is the grave of Hippo, whom destiny, in destroying him, has made the equal of the immortal Gods."

Hippo had speculated as to physical origins in the manner of Thales, making water generate fire, and that in turn produced the world, but this is uncertain. What is known is that Kratinos wrote a comedy, *The Panoptai* (the "all-seer," or "all eyes"), in which the chorus is made to represent the disciples of Hippo and to wear a mask covered with eyes. {CE; JMR}

Hippocrates (c. 460—c. 370 B.C.E.)

Hippocrates, the Greek physician recognized as the father of medicine, was an early empiricist. He wrote no books, but according to Plato he taught that to treat any one physical problem the entire body needed to be taken into account. Materials called the Hippocratic Writings described the treatment and cure of physical problems. The Hippocratic Oath is probably of Pythagorean origin, but it has no supernatural overtones and prescribes that the physician is here "not to harm but to help." {CE}

Hippolyte, Lazare (1801—1888)

Hippolyte, the grandson of Count Lazare Carnot, was a distinguished anti-clerical French statesman. (See entry for Lazare Carnot.)

Hird, Dennis (1850—1920)

Hird took orders in the Church of England, but they decided against accepting him because of his novel, *A Christian with Two Wives* (1896) and for his Socialist views. From 1899 to 1909 he was principal of Ruskin College, Oxford, and he helped to found the Central Labour College at London, of which he was its first principal. An agnostic, Hird was a member of the Rationalist Press Association. {RAT; RE}

Hires, Harrison (1876—1955)

Hires has been a member of the American Humanist Association. In 1943, he wrote *For My Children*, essays of a freethinker. {HNS}

Hirn, Yrgö (Born 1870)

Hirn was a Finnish aesthetic writer. Works translated into English include *The Origins of Art* and *The Sacred Shrine*. The latter work is a study from the outside of Catholic art and poetry. Hirn has described himself as an agnostic who regarded Catholic doctrines merely as "strayings of the human mind." {RAT}

Hirsch, William (20th Century)

Hirsch wrote *Religion and Civilization, the Conclusions of a Psychiatrist* (1912). {FUS}

Hirschfeld, Magnus (20th Century)

Hirschfeld was the founder of the German Scientific Humanitarian Committee (1897—1933) in Berlin. A sexologist, he was a humanist, a secular Jew, and a socialist. "Through Science to Justice" (*Per Scientiam Ad Justitiam*) was his motto, and he was convinced that scientific progress would diminish prejudices against, among other things, homosexuality. His Committee was the first homosexual rights organization worldwide. (See entry for Norman Haire.)

{Rob A. Tielman, *Free Inquiry*, Fall 1997}

Hirshman, John Hans (1921—)

Hirshman is an Australian humanist and health services consultant. He has been City Medical Officer in Sydney, an executive member of the New South Wales Council for Civil Liberties, and a founder-member of the Humanist Society of New South Wales. In 1992, Hirshman was named Humanist of the Year. In *Humanist Viewpoints*, he was described as having "translated his humanist beliefs into practical action for humanity. We must take inspiration from his example and never overlook the connection between the words 'humanist,' 'humane,' and 'humanity.' In line with his life of practical action, John Hirshman has said, 'There are no theoretical humanists.' " {SWW}

Hirth, Georg (1841—1916)

Hirth, a German journalist and writer about art, edited the Leipzig *Deutsche Turnzeitung* (1863—1866). In 1868 he founded the *Annalen des deutsches Reichs*. Hirth was one of the founders of the Monist League. {RAT}

HISTORY

• History is the record of the many dead that are still alive; and of the reasons why so many who expected to live on are dead.

The above definition of history is by Prof. James Henry Leuba, a psychologist who once was a professor at Bryn Mawr. Voltaire, however, defined history as a trick played by the living upon the dead. (See entries for Heraclitus, Herodotus, and for James Henry Leuba. For a study of how religious history has been falsified, see Joseph McCabe's *Rationalist Encyclopedia*.)

HISTORY, REVISIONIST

Americans, invoking the country's 18th century founders' writings to support modern views, can easily become guilty of painting the past in rosy pink. Or so Michael Schudson argues in *The Good Citizen: A History of American Civil Life* (1998). For example, he points out that the much touted New England town meetings were, in fact, open only to property-owning men and, often, only to church members. Instead of being exemplary of pure democracy, the town meetings were controlled by the chosen few, often the richest and the church leaders. Little wonder, then, that attendance by the citizenry ranged from only 20% to 60% of eligible voters. Furthermore, and although "We the people" was at that time a remarkable outlook, "the people" eligible to vote did not include slaves, women, and the poor. In his study of how history has been revised by some, Schudson concluded, "We can gain inspiration from the past, but we cannot import it." Similarly, the columnist Christopher Hitchens has alleged that some revisionists of history have been anything but historians: Communists once airbrushed people out of history.

HISTORY, UNIVERSAL

Some historians write for a nonprofessional audience. Sir Walter Raleigh whiled away prison time writing "an universall Historie" but finished only one volume. Hegel's entire philosophy is something of a universal history, as is the fifty-page reply to it, Marx and Engels's *Communist Manifesto*. Toynbee's twelve-volume *Study of History* (1934-1961), William H. McNeill's *Rise of the West*, and Oswald Spengler's *Decline of the West* (1918) are further examples. René Sédillot wrote *History of the World in 300 Pages* in the 1940s.

David Fromkin, author of *A Peace to End All Peace* (1989) is about the diplomatic origins of the modern Middle East. Similarly, *The Way of the World* (1998) is a brief history of what has happened since the Big Bang. Fromkin has cited H. G. Wells's *Outline of History* (1920) as his main model. {William R. Everdell, *The New York Times Book Review*, 17 January 1999}

Hitchens, Christopher (20th Century)

A non-theist and author of "Minority Report" in *The Nation* (1 August 1994), the controversial journalist Hitchen wrote,

> Bertrand Russell was right, in my far-from-humble opinion, to conclude that all religions are rubbish in the same way. At any given period it might be true that Shi'a Islam, for example, or Roman Catholicism or Calvinism acted in a fashion more repulsive and intolerant than the 'mainstream' faiths. But these peaks of atrocity and stupidity have a way of flattening out over time, as if to give every confession its own chance at bat.

The Missionary Position: Mother Teresa in Theory and Practice (1995) finds Agnes Gouxha Bojaxhiu an evil and selfish old woman who has consorted with white-collar criminals and despots. She is, Hitchens avers, less interested in aiding the poor of Calcutta and elsewhere than in using them, wretched people with insufficient care and forced to confront their mortality, as a way to enhance and missionary her Roman Catholic beliefs. She once said to Malcolm Muggeridge that "the poorest of the poor are the means of expressing our love for God." In 1985, visiting Guatemala and walking where fresh-killed Indians were all about, she said when asked about those deaths, "Everything was peaceful in the parts of the country I visited. I do not get involved in that sort of politics." In 1988 she told Navin Chawla, "Leprosy is not a punishment, it can be a very beautiful gift of God if we make good use of it. Through it we can learn to love the unloved." One apostate, Susan Shields, told Hitchens, "In the homes for the dying, Mother taught the sisters how to secretly baptize those who were dying. Sisters were to ask each person in danger of death if he wanted a 'ticket to haven.' An affirmative reply was to mean consent to baptism. The sister was then to pretend that she was just cooling the patient's head with a wet cloth, while in fact she was baptizing him, saying quietly the necessary words. Secrecy was important so that it would not come to be known that Mother Teresa's sisters were baptizing Hindus and Moslems." When she left Haiti, having been presented with the *Légion d'Honneur*, she told Baby Doc's First Lady, Michèle Duvalier, "Madame President, the country vibrates with your life's work." Hitchens pulled out all the stops, and Murray Kempton, reviewing the work, extrapolated tongue-in-cheek that when Hitchens gets to Heaven and the Recording Angel opens his book, he will cry out with holy glee, "Christopher Hitchens? Bully for you."

When Hitchens signed a 1999 affidavit claiming that his friend Sidney Blumenthal once told him that Monica Lewinsky was "a stalker," he became the scourge of the literary left. Lewinsky was the White House intern who was brought to her knees by President Bill Clinton, who himself was almost brought to his knees for having lied about their sexual escapades. Blumenthal had sworn he never said she was "a stalker," leading Alexander Cockburn to call Hitchens "a Judas" by Alexander Cockburn, Victor Navasky to term him "an informer" by Victor Navasky, and many others to refer to him as Chris the Snitch. In *No One Left To Lie To* (1999), Hitchens lashes out at his opponents and, in a political tirade, claimed that "Clintonism poisons everything it touches." (CA; Matt Cherry interviewed Hitchens further about Mother Teresa in *Free Inquiry*, Fall 1996) {*E; he New York Review of Books*, 11 July 1996; TYD}

Hitchings, Catherine (20th Century)

Hitchings is author of *Universalist and Unitarian Women Ministers*, which details the biographies of more than 150 deceased Universalist and Unitarian ministers.

Hitchman, William (1819—1888)

Hitchman was an English physician who established *Freelight* and wrote a pamphlet, "Fifty Years of Freethought" (1882). {BDF}

Hitler, Adolf (1889—1945)

As pointed out in Michiko Kakutani's review of Ron Rosenbaum's *Explaining Hitler* (1998),

> [B]y the time Hitler came to power in 1933, racial anti-Semitism had already made Germany "pregnant with murder"; the scholar Hyam Maccoby contends that Christianity (with its pernicious anti-Semitic stereotypes) had by World War II created a craving for vengeance against Jews; and Richard Breitman, editor of *Holocaust and Genocide Studies*, argues that the traumas sustained by Germany in the early years of the century (a humiliating defeat in World War I, then starvation, inflation and a crushing depression) forged a desperation and rage that Hitler was able to channel against the Jews.
>
> At the same time, hard-core Freudians and psycho-historians intent on trying to map Hitler's psyche have come up with an assortment of explanations that effectively let Hitler off the hook, using what Mr. Rosenbaum calls "the Menendez defense" to depict him, astonishingly enough, as a victim. The famous psychoanalyst Alice Miller portrays Hitler as a victim of an abusive father; Erich Fromm, as the victim of an overbearing mother. Other thinkers have attributed Hitler's pathology to a "primal-scene trauma," to a missing testicle, to a sexual secret that "isolated him from the normal love of human beings," to a physical illness and to a self-hatred (stemming from his suspicion that his grandmother had a Jewish lover and that he himself was "tainted" by Jewish blood).

In *Hitler 1889-1936: Hubris* (1998), Ian Kershaw wrote that—although Hitler had an abusive father and a doting mother—there is no serious foundation to the rumors of hidden Jewish ancestry, deformity of the genitals, the incompetence or greed of a Jewish doctor at his mother's deathbed, or many of the other whispers about his background. But, as pointed out by Christopher Hitchens, "*Mein Kampf* was published as an initially unsuccessful vote-getter in 1925, and at that time social democracy was very strong and popular, and the German Jews were still quite secure. To describe either as the work of Satan was to show what you really thought. ['There is no making pacts with Jews,' he tells us he decided back in 1918 when he had recovered from his nervous collapse. 'There can only be the hard either-or. I. However, resolved to become a politician.']."

Although some mistakenly assume that the consummate symbol of evil in the 20th century was a non-believer, Hitler is an embarrassment to fellow Catholics for such of his statements in *Mein Kampf* (1940) as, "Therefore, I am convinced that I am acting as the agent of our Creator. By fighting off the Jews, I am doing the Lord's Work." At a Nazi Christmas celebration in 1926, he had said, "Christ was the greatest early fighter in the battle against the world enemy, the Jews. . . . The work that Christ started but could not finish, I—Adolf Hitler—will conclude." When he narrowly escaped assassination in Munich in November 1939, Hitler exclaimed, "Now I am completely content. The fact that I left the Burgerbraukeller earlier than usual is a corroboration of Providence's intention to let me reach my goal." To celebrate, Cardinal Michael Faulhaber sent a telegram instructing that a Te Deum be sung in the Munich cathedral "to thank Divine Providence in the name of the archdiocese for the Fuhrer's fortunate escape." This was followed by the Pope's personal congratulations. John Toland, a biographer, has written of Hitler's religion, "Still a member in good standing of the Church of Rome despite detestation of its hierarchy, he carried within him its teaching that the Jew was the killer of God. The extermination, therefore, could be done without a twinge of conscience since he was merely acting as the avenging hand of god—so long as it was done impersonally, without cruelty, Himmler was pleased to murder with mercy. He ordered technical experts to devise gas chambers which would eliminate masses of Jews efficiently and 'humanely,' then sent them east to stay in ghettos until the killing centers in Poland were completed. As late as 1941, Hitler told Gerhard Engel, one of his generals, "I am now as before a Catholic and will always remain so." In fact, he mandated that schoolchildren recite a prayer at the beginning of each school day. In *Albert Speer*, Gitta Sereny prints a letter Speer wrote to his daughter, Hilde, from Spandau prison on 9 January 1953, one in which he made it clear that Hitler "forbade his chosen circle, Hess, Goebbels, Göring etc. to leave their churches." Meanwhile, the princes of his church never requested his excommunication. McCabe labels Hitler a theist, for Hitler repeatedly cited God in public speeches and said he was a Christian.

A survey of *Mein Kampf* will surprise Jews who may not have noticed some of Hitler's choices of words and phrases, such as the following: thirty pieces of silver; God's grace; Lucifer; God's will; God's creation; "I sank down upon my knees and thanked Heaven"; God's image; devil shuns holy water; [and] sin against the will of eternal providence. Meanwhile, some secular humanists might be surprised to learn that some of Hitler's supporters called the Nazi philosophy a "New Humanism." In *La Fiction du politique* (1987), Philippe Lacoue-Labarthe referred to Nazism as "a humanism."

Hitler apparently did not receive any last rites of the Church. On 30 April 1945, he was told by his private pilot, Hans Baur, that a plane was available and was capable of flying as far as Argentina, Japan, Greenland, Manchuria (or Jerusalem, where admirers were supposedly ready to spirit him to a hideout in the Sahara. Hitler declined the offer. Instead, he dictated his final testament to Traudl Junge: "During these last three decades, all my thoughts and actions, and my entire life, have been moved solely by the love and fidelity I feel for my people. This has given me the strength to make the most difficult of decisions, the like of which no mortal has ever made before." At 3:30, a shot rang out. Artur Axmann, a Hitler youth leader, entered and found Hitler as well as Eva Braun, whom he had married two days prior. "I saw Eva Braun next to Hitler on the sofa," Axmann declared in 1995. "His upper body was leaning slightly to the side, with the head slumping down. His forehead and face were very white, and a trickle of blood was flowing down. I saw Eva Braun next to Hitler on the sofa. Her eyes were closed. There was no movement. She had poisoned herself and appeared to be sleeping." According to Axmann, two aides took the bodies outside, doused them with gasoline and burned them, continuing until they had used about fifty gallons. A Soviet general, Leonid Siomonchuk, confirmed to German interviewers that he was present when Hitler's dentist examined the corpse and declared that it was Hitler's. Hitler's remains were secretly stored in the East German town of Magdeburg, according to journalist Stephen Kinzer (*The New York Times*, 4 May 1995). A part of what may be Hitler's skull, with bullet hole, was removed before the cremation and shipped to Moscow, where Alzha Borkovich, a Russian archivist, displayed it in 1995 before German television cameras. {CE; Christopher Hitchens, *Vanity Fair*, February 1999; Michiko Kakutani, *The New York Times*, 30 June 1998; RE; TRI}

HITLER'S POPE

"Pope Pius XII helped Adolf Hitler destroy German Catholic political opposition, betrayed the Jews of Europe, and sealed a deeply cynical pact with a 20ty-century devil," wrote John Cornwell in *Hitler's Pope: The Secret History of Pius XII* (1999). Allowed to see Vatican materials that had been gathered years ago to support the process for Eugenio Pacelli's canonization, Cornwell was nonplussed upon finding that Pacelli was anti-Jewish, that he had implicitly denied and trivialized the Holocaust, and that after the way "he had retrospectively taken undue credit for speaking out boldly against the Nazis' persecution of the Jews." His contempt of Judaism was based on his belief that the Jews were behind the Bolshevik plot to destroy Christendom, referred to "their Jewish cult," once campaigned to remove black French troops from the Rhineland because he was convinced they were raping women and abusing children, and helped lead German Catholics in the millions to join the Nazi Party, believing that it had the support of the Pope.

Hitschmanova, Lotta (20th Century—deceased)

Dr. Hitschmanova for thirty-five years directed the Unitarian Service Committee, which was founded in 1945 to do something tangible in the field of service to less fortunate parts of the world.

Hittell, John S. (19th Century)

Hittell was an American freethinker, the author of the *Evidences Against Christianity* (1857), *A Plea for Pantheism, A Brief History of Culture* (1875), and *St. Peter's Catechism* (1883). {BDF}

HIV: See entry for Human Immunodeficiency Virus.

HIVOS

A Dutch quarterly of Humanist Development Institute for Development Cooperation, *Hivos* is at Raamweg 16, 2596 HL Den Haag, The Netherlands.

On the Web: <http://www.dds.NL/~hivos/>. E-mail: <hivos@hivos.NL>.) (See entry for Dutch Humanist Institute for Development Cooperation.}

Hoad, John (20th Century)

Hoad, for twenty-five years a Methodist minister and seminary president in Barbados, came to Ethical Leadership from the West Indies and the Cambridge Divinity School. He completed his Ph. D. at the Princeton Seminary and succeeded James F. Hornback as Leader of the St. Louis Ethical Culture Society.

Hoadley, George (1836—1902)

An American jurist, Hoadley was elected judge of the superior court of Cincinnati. He afterwards resigned his place and established a law firm. Hoadley was one of the counsel that successfully opposed compulsory Bible reading in the public schools. {BDF; RAT}.

Hoagland, Edward (Morley) (1932—)

A teacher of literature at Bennington College in Vermont and a member of the American Academy of Arts and Letters, Hoagland responded to a query by the present author concerning humanism:

> I'm a pantheist but of course include humankind in the family of nature, for better or worse. Am particularly relieved at the ending of the Cold War because in foreseeable wars we will only be killing ourselves, not that whole wider world.

Hoagland has studied with Thornton Wilder, John Ciardi, Alfred Kazin, John Berryman, and Archibald MacLeish. He is author of *Cat Man* (1954), *Red Wolves and Black Bears* (1976), and *City Tales* (1986). In a *New York Times Magazine* article (27 November 1994), Hoagland wrote,

> Reincarnation or a heavenly life is the ultimate comfort offered by every religion I am familiar with, and I don't want to be *me* for more than another 20 years anyway. Neither eternal oblivion nor me, but something else. Maybe moss. One could do worse. Moss, if left alone, seems to live about as long as people do; then it goes back to mulligatawny soup again.
>
> {WAS, 30 June 1992}

Hoagland, Hudson (1899—1982)

The president emeritus of Worcester Federation for Experimental Biology, Hoagland signed Humanist Manifesto II. In 1965, he was named Humanist of the Year by the American Humanist Association. A physiologist, he was president of the American Academy of Arts and Sciences from 1961 to 1964. {HM2; HNS2}

Hoagland, Robert S. (1906—1993)

Hoagland, who had once studied with Paul Tillich and Martin Buber, began his Unitarian ministry in Jamestown, New York, later serving in Exeter, New Hampshire; Ft. Wayne, Indiana; Chicago; Schenectady, New York; Tacoma, Washington; and Park Forest, Illinois. From 1972 to 1977, he edited the *Religious Humanist*. Hoagland was a signer of Humanist Manifesto II. {HM2}

HOAXES

Examples of hoaxes include the pseudo-fossils of Piltdown man which were planted by Charles Dawson; the pseudo-Celtic epic *Ossian* written by James Macpherson; and the pseudo-scientific article, "Transgressing the Boundaries–Toward a Transformative Hermeneutics of Quantum Gravity," in *Social Text* (Spring-Summer 1996) by Alan D. Sokal. The latter article consisted of a prank played by a New York University mathematical physicist which, tongue in cheek, drew various philosophical and cultural morals that the author said the editors accepted because "(a) it sounded good and (b) it flattered the editors' ideological preconceptions." Sokal's targets were the "postmoderns" in the humanities who, according to the University of Texas's Steven Weinberg, "like to surf through avant-garde fields like quantum mechanics or chaos theory to dress up their own arguments about the fragmentary and random nature of experiences." Sokal, after admitting to the hoax, explained that his goal was not so much to defend science as to defend the left from postmodernists, social constructivists, and other trendy leftists. (For information about Alan Sokal, see entry for Physics. Also, see entry for Hoaxes, Religious.) {*The New York Review of Books*, 8 August 1996}

HOAXES, PARANORMAL

The Committee for the Scientific Investigation of Claims of the Paranormal has cited the following top ten paranormal hoaxes:

- Roswell incident—a "flying disc" that crashed in Roswell, New Mexico, in 1947 was claimed to have been covered up by a Presidential order and that the craft's aliens, including details of an "alien autopsy" featuring a rubbery humanoid, were stored at secret installations. The disc was a government spy balloon, however. {*Skeptical Inquirer*, Winter 1990 and Nov-Dec 1995}

- spiritualism—modern spiritualism began in 1848 when two girls said they had received messages from a ghost who responded to their questions by knocking a certain number of times. Four decades later, however, the sisters revealed to a theater audience how they had secretly produced the rapping sounds. {*Skeptical Inquirer*, Winter 1983-1984 and Fall 1985}

• psychic phone networks—psychic ability has never been validated by scientific means, yet phone psychics have appeared to be clairvoyant and have produced a billion-dollar industry's pioneer network. Psychic Friends, one such company, filed for bankruptcy in the 1990s, an event that two thousand psychics employed by the network failed to foresee. {*Skeptical Inquirer,* Sep-Oct 1995}

• Shroud of Turin—the purported Holy Shroud of Jesus, bearing the imprints of an apparently crucified man, was shown by forensic tests to have been painted in tempera and a radio carbon testing yielded a date between 1260 and 1390. {*Skeptical Inquirer*, Spring 1982 and Spring 1989}

• Cottingley fairies—Two English schoolgirls in 1917 fooled many by taking close-up photos of winged fairies dancing in Cottingley Glen. Their hoax fooled the creator of Sherlock Holmes, Sir Arthur Conan Doyle. {*Skeptical Inquirer*, Summer 1982}

• crop circles—since the late 1970s mysterious swirled patterns appeared in southern English grain fields, which some said were caused by extraterrestrials. In 1991, however, two men demonstrated how they had made the first circles, which others copied and elaborated. {*Skeptical Inquirer*, Winter, 1992}

• Amityville horror—a couple in Amityville, New York, claimed they were driven out by spooky events in a house where in 1974 a man murdered his parents and siblings. The murderer's lawyer, however, confessed how, for money, he and the couple had "created this horror story over many bottles of wine." {*Skeptical Inquirer*, Winter, 1979-1980)

• Piltdown "missing link"—In December 1912 the long-sought-after "missing link" between man and his prehistoric ancestors was reportedly recovered near Piltdown Common in England. The bones were enshrined in the British Museum. But in 1953 the find was revealed to be a combination of ordinary human cranial pieces and the jawbone of an orangutan. {*Skeptical Inquirer*, Spring, 1980)

• psychic surgery—a phony healing procedure in which a practitioner appears to reach into a patient's body, without benefit of scalpel or anesthesia, to remove "tumors" and other diseased tissue was reported in brazil and the Philippines. However, psychic surgery is produced by sleight of hand with animal tissue and blood being used to give a realistic appearance. {*Skeptical Inquirer*, Spring, 1980)

• King Tut's curse—the tomb of the "boy king" Tutankhamen, discovered in 1922, had a curse written over the entrance. In 1980, however, the tomb's former security officer admitted the story of the curse had been circulated to frighten away thieves. {*Skeptical Inquirer*, Summer 1982). {Joe Nickell, *Skeptical Inquirer*, July-August 1998}.

HOAXES, RELIGIOUS

Nostradamus's "predictions" have fooled many, as revealed by James Randi in *The Mask of Nostradamus* (1990). Religious hoaxes, such as the Shroud of Turin, the Secret Instructions of the Jesuits, the Protocols of the Elders of Zion, the Donation of Constantine, Maria Monk, and Pope Joan, are detailed in Gordon Stein's *Encyclopedia of Hoaxes* (1993). Others would add the *Mormon Bible* and the "healings" of Father Divine and the Jehovah's Witness belief in the Millennium.

Some anti-religionists claim that Judaism pulled the greatest-ever hoax on mankind, by so successfully "selling" the idea of "faith," "moral fervor," "sin," and "eternal life with God in Heaven." Then, marketing it. (See Walter McCrone's *Judgment Day for the Shroud of Turin*, 1999)

Hobbes, Thomas (1588—1679)

In the spring of 1588, all England was alarmed at the news that the mighty Spanish Armada had set sail for the purpose of deposing Queen Elizabeth, bringing the country under a foreign yoke, and re-establishing the power of the papacy. In sheer fright, the wife of the vicar of Westport, now part of Malmesbury, gave premature birth to her second son on Good Friday, the 5th of April. This seven months' child used to say, in later life, that his mother brought forth himself and a twin brother Fear. Thomas Hobbes was delicate and nervous all his days, according to Foote. Yet, he was to reach the age of ninety-one.

This parson's son was destined to be hated by the clergy for his heresy. The Great Fire of 1666, following the Great Plague of the previous year, excited popular superstition, and to appease the wrath of God, a new Bill was introduced in Parliament against atheism and profaneness. The Committee to which the Bill was entrusted were empowered to "receive information touching" heretical books, and Hobbes's *Leviathan* was mentioned "in particular." The old philosopher, then verging on eighty, was naturally alarmed. Bold as he was in thought, his inherited physical timidity shrank from the prospect of the prison, the scaffold, or the stake. He made a show of conformity, and, according to Bishop Kennet, who according to Foote is not an irreproachable witness, Hobbes partook of the sacrament. It was said by some, however, that he acted thus in compliance with the wishes of the Devonshire family, who were his protectors, and whose private chapel he attended. A noticeable fact was that he always went out before the sermon, and when asked his reason, he answered that "they could teach him nothing but what he knew." He spoke of the chaplain, Dr. Jasper Mayne, as "a very silly fellow."

Disliked by the clergy, and especially by the bishops; owing his liberty and perhaps his life to powerful patrons; fearing that some fanatic might take the parsons' hints and play the part of an assassin; Hobbes is said to have kept a lighted candle in his bedroom. However, Foote notes, that is not mentioned in Professor Croom Robertson's exhaustive 1886 biography, and if true it was not for superstitious reasons but for his safety in the event he became sick at night.

Samuel Pepys, in his *Diary*, complained that in 1668 he paid three times the original price for *Leviathan*, simply because it is "a book the Bishops will not let be printed again." (In various scriptural accounts, Yahweh defeated a sea monster which was called *liwyathan*.) The work was well received in France and Germany, bringing Hobbes many admirers who continued to correspond with him for the remainder of his life. In his own country, the book's reputation received notoriety because of its author's alleged atheism.

Hobbes is described by Rudolph in the *Encyclopedia of Unbelief*: "The philosopher of Malmesbury was hated and feared by contemporaries for his heterodox views. His philosophical system is thoroughly materialistic and determinist, but the scandal he created was the carrying over of these same principles into theology. . . . Religion, according to Hobbes, is a distinctively human phenomenon, a habitual disposition to fear invisible powers. Hobbes attributes the disposition to fear of ghosts, ignorance of second causes, devotion toward what men fear, and taking casual events to be significant prophecies." Certainly, his materialism upset churchmen in France, where he visited. He thought the life of each person "nasty, brutish, and short" and built a philosophy around his mechanistic view that life is simply the motions of the organism, that man is a selfishly individualistic animal, that fear of violent death causes men to create government. *Leviathan* (1651) develops Hobbes's political philosophy. His works, prohibited from being read by the Vatican in 1649 and again in 1701 and 1703, are masterpieces of atheistic materialism and Epicureanism. Hobbes is known for his witty aphorism, that superstition is religion out of fashion, and religion superstition in fashion.

During the French Revolution, Maréchal cited Hobbes as being one of the greatest atheists of all time. Robertson describes him as "the most important thinker of his age, after Descartes, and hardly less influential. . . . Hobbes is in fact the anti-Presbyterian or anti-Puritan philosopher; and to discredit anarchic religion in the eyes of the majority he is obliged to speak as a judicial Churchman. Yet nothing is more certain than that he was no orthodox Christian. . . . Reviving as he did the ancient rationalistic doctrine of the eternity of the world, he gave a clear footing for atheism as against the Judaeo-Christian view." Berman, however, points out that in Hobbes's time atheism and irreligion were viewed with the greatest fear and horror, that no rational person could actually be an atheist. As a result, Berman believes Hobbes chose to remain "a covert atheist." At one point, a committee of Parliament in 1666 decided to investigate Hobbes, citing his "atheism" as a possible provocation of divine wrath leading to the outbreak of the plague in London.

When Hobbes submitted to King Charles his *Behemoth* (1668), a history of the period between 1640 and 1660, the king advised against its publication and the book was not published until three years after Hobbes's death. Gaskin cites Hobbes's friend John Aubrey as saying, "There was a report that some of the bishops made a motion to have the good old gentleman burned for a heretic." But, adds Gaskin, "Hobbes lived on, befriended by the rich and powerful, to die of natural causes in his ninety-second year." (He had played tennis until he was seventy-five.)

Foote wrote that Hobbes did not appear to have troubled himself about death. Bishop Kennel related that "the winter before he died he made a warm great-coat, which he said must last him three years, and then he would have such another." Even so late as August, 1676, four months before his decease, he was "writing somewhat" for his publisher to "print in English." About the middle of October he had an attack of stranguary, and "Wood and Kennet both have it that, on hearing the trouble was past cure, he exclaimed, 'I shall be glad then to find a hole to creep out of the world at.' . . . This story was picked up thirty years after Hobbes's death, and is probably apocryphal. If the philosopher said anything of the kind, he doubtless meant that, being very old, and without wife, child, or relative to care for him, he would be glad to find a shelter for his last moments, and to expire in comfort and peace."

At the end of November his right side was paralyzed, and he lost his speech. He "lingered in a somnolent state" for several days, said Robertson, and "then his life quietly went out."

McCabe says of Hobbes, "It is clear that he was at the most a Deist, and his psychology must have made him skeptical about a future life." Tim Madigan, however, considers Hobbes an atheist. (See an inclusive article by R. S. Peters in the *Encyclopedia of Philosophy*, Vol. 4.) {BDF; CE; CL; ER; EU, Ross Rudolph and Aram Vartanian; FO; FUK; HAB; JM; JMR; JMRH; Noel Malcolm, ed., *The Correspondence of Thomas Hobbes*; RAT; RE; TYD}

Hobhouse, Arthur [Baron] (1819—1904)

Hobhouse was a British judge widely respected for his character and idealism. He believed only in "a great ruling power of the universe" and, according to McCabe, "shortly before he died wrote a clergyman that the more he reflected 'the more my mind is led away from your objects and fixed upon others.' " {JM; RAT; RE}

Hobhouse, Leonard Trelawne (1864—1929)

Hobhouse, the son of Archdeacon Hobhouse, was a leading British sociologist. His *Mind in Evolution* (1901) and *Morals in Evolution* (1906, 2 volumes) received critical acclaim, but his rationalist views are found in *Development and Purpose* (1913). Hobhouse defined God as "that of which the highest known embodiment is the distinctive spirit of humanity." {RE}

Hobsbawm, Eric John Ernest (1917—)

Hobsbawm, a historian, became an Honorary Associate of the Rationalist Press Association in 1995. An emeritus professor of economics and social history at the University of London, he wrote *Labour's Turning Point* (1948), *The Jazz Scene* (1958), *The Age of Empire* (1987), and *Echoes of the Marseillaise* (1990).

Hobson, Fred C. (1943—)

Hobson, a freethinker, wrote *Serpent in Eden: H. L. Mencken and the South* (1974). {*Freethought History #14*, 1995}

Hobson, John A. (20th Century)

Hobson, in *Rationalism and Humanism* (1933), called upon British Rationalists to move on to Humanism as "the next step." A leading social scientist and ethicist, he, along with Herbert Burrows and J. M. Robertson, constituted a panel of lecturers following Moncure Conway's departure from the South Place Ethical Society. In 1957, the British Rationalists did change the name of their monthly journal to *The Humanist*. {CL; FUK; HNS; RAT; RE; TRI}

Hobson, Joshua (1810—1876)

Hobson, who was imprisoned as an infidel, published *Voice of the West Riding* (1833). {VI}

Hochart, Polydore (19th Century)

Hochart was a French historian who studied the alleged evidence in Roman writers in favor of Christ and early Christianity. In 1885 he published *Études au sujet de la persécution des chrétiens sous Néron* and *Études sur la vie de Sénèque*. {RAT}

Hochhuth, Rolf (1931—)

A German dramatist, Hochhuth wrote a provocative first drama, *The Deputy* (1963), which accuses Pope Pius XII and the Roman Catholic clergy of tolerating Nazi crimes against the Jews. He was a member of the German Evangelical Church. {CE}

HOCUS POCUS

Hoc est enim corpus meum (This is my body) is the essential formula used in the sacrament of the eucharist. States the Rev. John P. Mahoney of Providence College in Rhode Island, "The term *hocus-pocus* has an origin arising from English Protestantism as an attack on Catholic doctrine." Implied, states Mahoney, is that the Catholic doctrine of transubstantiation, abominated by Low-Church Anglicans, was absurd nonsense.

Hodges, John (20th Century)

Hodges wrote "Ethics: An Evolutionary Imperative" for *Secular Nation* (October-December 1998). One is good not because of promises of some afterlife but, "Considering that all of us are uncertain as to our time of death, if you want your personal story to end in victory, you will choose your actions at all times to be compatible with your desired legacy."

Hodgin, E. S. (20th Century)

Hodgin wrote *Confessions of an Agnostic Clergyman* (1948). {GS; HNS}

Hodgson, Brian Houghton (1800—1894)

An Orientalist, Hodgson spent years in the Indian Civil Service, serving at one time as Assistant Resident of Nepal. Burnouf called him "the founder of our Buddhistic studies." When he was asked about his religious views, Hodgson, an agnostic, said that "I do not care to talk about the unknowable." {RAT; RE}

Hodgson, Shadworth Hollway (1832—1912)

Hodgson was a philosopher who was president of the Aristotelian Society from 1880 to 1894. He wrote *Time and Space* (1865) and *The Metaphysic of Experience* (1898). He is seen to be an advanced rationalist in his *Philosophy of Reflection* (1878, 2 volumes), saying that "the notion of a soul as an immaterial substance is exploded" and that God is only "the spirit of the Whole." {RAT; RE}

Hodgson, William (1745—1851)

Hodgson was an English Jacobin, the translator of d'Holbach's *System of Nature* (1795). In 1794 Hodgson was confined in Newgate for two years for having drunk to the success of the French Republic. A physician, he spent his time in prison writing *The Commonwealth of Reason*. {BDF; RAT}

Hoekzema, Hans F. (20th Century)

Hoekzema is a member in The Netherlands of the board of Hivos.

Hoelderlin, J. C. F: See entry for Hölderlin, Johann Christian Friedrich.

Hoertdoerfer, Pat (20th Century)

Hoertdoerfer, a member of the Board of Governors of The Humanist Institute, is an Ethical Culture leader and a Unitarian Universalist minister in Massachusetts.

Höffding, Harold (1843—1921)

A professor of philosophy at the University of Copenhagen, Höffding wrote about Mill and Spencer. German editions have been published of his works *Grandlage der humanen Ethik* (Basis of Human Ethics), *Psychologie im Umries* (Outlines of Psychology, 1887), and *Ethik* (1888). In his numerous works, Höffding expounded a spiritual monism. He excluded a personal God and was agnostic as to personal immortality. The essential religious principle, he held, is "the conservation of values," moral and aesthetic, and "our greatest model is the Greek way of life." {BDF; RAT; RE}

Hoffer, Eric (1902—1983)

Hoffer, an author, was a longshoreman who called himself "a tourist in life" and who wrote *The Ordeal of Change* (1963), *Temper of Our Time* (1967), and *Reflections on the Human Condition* (1972). In *The True Believer* (1951), Hoffer wrote, "Self-righteousness is a loud din raised to drown the voice of guilt within us." A freethinker, he also declared, "It was the craving to be a one and only people which impelled the ancient Hebrews to invent a one and only God whose one and only people they were to be." {CE; TYD}

Hoffman, Amy (20th Century)

Hoffman is a Unitarian who is executive editor of the denomination's journal, *World*. She wrote *Hospital Time* (1997), a work selected for the "Books for the Teen Age 1998" exhibit at the New York Public Library. The book is a memoir about taking care of friends with AIDS.

"My book contains very edgy material—sex, death, and religious skepticism," she has written. "I'm serious when I say that I only wish my public library had handed me such books when I was an adolescent. I think it's a measure of the achievement of the lesbian, gay, bisexual, and transgender movement that libraries are now showcasing and even rewarding books like mine, which used to be hidden in obscure collections. It also reminds us of how vigilant we must be in resisting censorious hate groups that would ban our books, which often hold life affirming information for teenagers and the rest of us." {*World*, May-June 1998}

Hoffman, Irwin D. (Born 1901)

Hoffman, an artist, was on the advisory board of Charles Francis Potter's First Humanist Society of New York. He wrote *An Artist's Life* (1981).

Hoffmann, R. Joseph (20th Century)

An Oxford don, once in the humanities department at California State University in Sacramento, Hoffman chairs the Council for Secular Humanism's Biblical Criticism Research Project. With Gerald A. Larue, he edited *Biblical v. Secular Ethics, The Conflict*. They also edited *Jesus in History and Myth* (1986). Hoffman, a Unitarian and senior research fellow and tutor in church history at Westminster College, Oxford, is a senior editor on *Free Inquiry*. In 1987 he translated Celsus's *On the True Doctrine: A Discourse Against the Christians*. Celsus was an early critic of Christian scriptures and the Christians destroyed most of his works. His *The Origins of Christianity* has been cited by Gordon Stein as one of the best recent works on the subject. He edited *The Secret Gospels: A Harmony of Apocryphal Jesus Traditions* (1996).

In a foreword to the first issue of *The Journal for Critical Study of Religion, Ethics, and Society* (1996), according to Jim Herrick, "Hoffmann suggests that there have been many humanisms with nothing in common. There is the Old Guard Humanism of existentialism or pragmatism, of rationalists and empiricists, of ethicists and secularists. American humanism grew out of ethical culture, Unitarianism, frontier skepticism, and Boston Brahmanism. But humanism has become quaint and between 1950 and 1980 in decline, partly due to its persistence in fighting battles with religion which have already been won, although there had been a boost with the revival of fundamentalism as a clear-cut opponent. 'Liberal theology has effectively supplanted humanism as the church's most effective critic.' "

His e-mail is <hoffmann@patrol.i-way.co.uk>. (See the entry for Centre for Critical Studies.) {*New Humanist*, June 1996 and December 1996}

Hofstadter, Douglas (20th Century)

A professor at Indiana University, Hofstadter wrote *Godel, Escher, Bach* and *Le Ton Beau De Marot: In Praise of the Music of Language*. He has described himself as aa "non-religious person." {CA}

Hogarth, William (1697—1764)

Hogarth, an English painter, engraver, and art theorist, received his initial acclaim as a painter with a series of six morality pictures, including *The Harlot's Progress*, which he first painted, then engraved. Other of his works were *The Rake's Progress (1735), Marriage à la Mode* (1745), and *Analysis of Beauty* (1753). *The Shrimp Girl* and *Captain Coram* (1740) are considered masterpieces of British painting. Quite the satirist, Hogarth in *Gin Lane* and *Four Stages of Cruelty* depicted the cruelty, stupidity, and bombast he observed around him and on all levels of society. Hogarth was a Freemason as well as a deist.

Hogben, Lancelot (1895-1975)

Hogben, a physiologist, was professor of zoology at Capetown (1927—1930), professor of social biology at London University, and professor of zoology at Birmingham University. He was awarded the Gold Medal of the Royal Society of Edinburgh. In *What I Believe* (1938) he mentioned his own outlook as being that of humanism. Also, in 1938, he took part in the International Freethought Congress. *Dangerous Thoughts* (1939) included Hogben's essay, "The Creed of a Scientific Humanist." {RE; TRI}

Hogg, Thomas Jefferson (1782—1862)

Shelley's biographer and friend, Hogg was dismissed in 1811 from Oxford for defending Shelley's atheism. The biography was considered more about Hogg than Shelley, leading Mary Shelley to withdraw certain materials from Hogg's use. A successful lawyer, Hogg wrote *Shelley at Oxford* (published in 1904). Shelley may have written his *The Necessity of Atheism* in collaboration with Hogg, according to C. E. Pulos's *The Deep Truth*. However, Berman holds that Hogg was, as explained by Shelley, not the "original corruptor of my principles," that he was only an aide in helping him develop his viewpoints. {CE; HAB; RAT}

Hoggart, Richard (1918—)

Hoggart is a scholar and writer. From 1976-1984 he was warden of Goldsmith's College in London. *The Uses of Literacy* (1957) demonstrated his interest in literature, education, and the means of communication. A cultural critic, Hoggart became an Honorary Associate of the Rationalist Press Association in 1995. {OEL}

Hoggart, Simon (1946—)

With Mike Hutchinson, Hoggart wrote *Bizarre Beliefs* (1995). A journalist, he writes with a skeptical eye about pseudo-science and the paranormal.

Hoijer, Benjamin Carl Henrik (1787—1812)

Hoijer was a Swedish philosopher, a student at Upsala University in 1783 and a teacher of philosophy there in 1798. His promotion was hindered by his liberal opinions. By his personal influence and published treatises, according to Wheeler, he contributed much to Swedish emancipation. In 1808 he became professor of philosophy at Uppsala. {BDF}

d'Holbach, Paul Henri Thiry (1723—1789)

"If we go back to the beginning of things," said the 18th century encyclopedist, "we shall find that ignorance and fear created the gods; that imagination, rapture, and deception embellished or distorted them; that custom spares them; and that tyranny favors them in order to profit from the blindness of men." The Vatican prohibited all of Baron d'Holbach's works to be read, which is not surprising inasmuch as d'Holbach imitated the tactic of Voltaire and produced a small library of anti-Christian treatises under a variety of pseudonyms. His principal work, *System of Nature* (1770), came out under the name of Mirabaud, an actual person who was then dead. Described as a "thundering engine of revolt and destruction," it was the first published atheistic treatise of a systematic kind, according to Robertson, if Robinet is excepted. Berman quotes d'Holbach's letter to Diderot in 1765 that, although "the Christian religion is nearly extinct in England [and] the deists are innumerable; there are almost no atheists; those who are conceal it. An atheist and a scoundrel are almost synonymous terms for them." He also wrote,

- The atheist is a man who destroys the chimeras which afflict the human race, and so leads men back to nature, to experience and to reason.
- Ignorance of natural causes created the gods, and priestly impostures made them terrible.
- All religions are ancient monuments to superstitions, ignorance, ferocity; and modern religions are only ancient follies rejuvenated.
- If the ignorance of nature gave birth to the gods, knowledge of nature is destined to destroy them.
- The Christian burns the Jew at what is called an auto-da-fe because he clings to the faith of his fathers; the Roman Catholic condemns the Protestant to the flames, and makes a conscience of massacring him in cold blood.
- Sometimes the various sects of Christians league together against the incredulous Turk, and for a moment suspend their own bloody disputes that they may chastise the enemies of the True Faith.

Gordon Stein, in *Freethought History* (#3, 1992), points out that Anna Knoop's translation *Superstition in all Ages by Jean Meslier . . . Translated from the French* actually is not by Meslier but by Baron d'Holbach. The baron, publishing his highly anti-religious works in French, from Amsterdam, but with a false London imprint, published his works either anonymously or under the name of a recently-dead man. What Knoop mistook in an 1802 edition as a work by Meslier actually was *Le Bon Sens* (*Good Sense*) by d'Holbach. {CE; CL; ER; EU, Jeroom Vercrysse, translated by Gordon Stein; FUK; HAB; ILP; JM; JMR; JMRH; RAT; RE; TRI; TYD}

Holberg, Ludwig von [Baron] (1684—1754)

Holberg, "the Molière of Denmark," taught metaphysics and rhetoric at Copenhagen University. His comedies won a comparison with Molière's, while his satirical poems led many to compare him to Voltaire. His anti-clerical deism is particularly seen in his satire, *Nicolai Klimii Iter Subterraneum* (1741). {RAT; RE}

Holbrook, Stewart Hall (1893—1964)

Holbrook wrote *Ethan Allen* (1944). {FUS}

Holcroft, Thomas (1745—1809)

Holcroft was, successively, a groom, shoemaker, schoolmaster, actor, and author. His successful comedies were "Duplicity" (1781) and "The Road to Ruin" (1792). He translated the *Posthumous Works of Frederick the Great* (1789). For his active sympathy with the French Republicans, he was indicted for high treason, along with Hardy and Thomas Tooke, but was discharged without a trial. {BDF; RAT; RE}

HOLDEEN INDIA PROGRAM

The Holdeen India Program, 2562 36th Street NW, Washington, DC 20007, distributes trust income designated for use in India for social justice, maternity, child welfare, education, and migration expenses. Katharine Streedhar is its director.

Hölderlin, Johann Christian Friedrich (1770—1843)

Hölderlin was a German poet who withdrew from clerical training and devoted himself to letters and philosophy, adopting pantheistic views. He published *Hyperion* (1797—1799), a romance, and *Empedokles* (1800), a pantheistic drama. His mind failed soon afterwards, and for nearly forty years he remained childlike and powerless. Hölderlin is said to have played a large role in shaping Heidegger's philosophy. {BDF; RAT}

Holdridge, Herbert C. [General] (20th Century)

A retired Brigadier General of the United States Army, Holdridge widely circulated a 1955 letter to "defenders of the Constitution" concerning the Vatican's hostility "toward the freedoms expressed in the Constitution, specifically citing the Syllabus of Errors of Pius IX and the Encyclicals of Leo XIII. He called upon citizens to write all their elected officials to insure that "Catholic Action" groups not succeed in subverting U.S. laws, mentioning that within our borders "30 million potential traitors to our Constitution" live.

"Philosophically," he wrote, "I rejected orthodox Christianity as a child. Although I have not made a thorough study of the Humanist philosophy, I do respect its willingness to work here and now for human decency in every-day life. After all, Jesus of Nazareth is said to have stated, 'By their fruits shall ye know them.' It is obvious that our entire outlook on religions is undergoing a significant change, Billy Graham [a televangelist] notwithstanding." {WAS, 8 August 1955}

Holland, Clifford (1926—)

Holland, who was born in England but who moved to Canada and has taught philosophy, wrote *William Dawson Le Sueur* (1840-

1917) in 1993 about a Canadian man of letters. In 1995, he spoke in Costa Rica at the founding of the inter-American association of philosophers, *Asociación Iberomericana Ético Humanista*. Holland is a lecturer emeritus with George Brown College in Toronto. (See entry for LeSueur.)

Holland, Frederic May (1836—1908)
Holland, an American author, was ordained in 1863 as a Unitarian minister in Rockford, Illinois. Upon becoming broader in his views, he resigned, then wrote for the *Truthseeker* and *Freethinkers' Magazine*. His principal work is *The Rise of Intellectual Liberty* (1885) and *Atheists and Agnostics* (1885). {BDF; PUT; RAT}

Holland, J. G. (1819—1881)
An American editor and writer, Holland in *Everyday Topics* (1876) wrote, "It is a matter of surprise that men whose Christian honesty, purity, and self-devotedness are conceded on every hand, are often men with whom we do not like to associate." {TYD}

Hollander, Bernard (Born 1864)
Hollander, a physician, devoted his attention particularly to abnormal mental phenomena. He became an exponent of psychotherapy, founded the Ethnological Society, and edited the *Ethnological Journal*. His rationalist views are found in *Positive Philosophy of the Mind* (1891). {RAT}

Hollerorth, Hugo (20th Century)
Hollerorth wrote *Relating to Our World* (1974) and edited *Stone House Conversations* (1979), concerning Unitarian Universalist religious education.

Hollick, Frederick (1813—1900)
A socialist, Hollick became one of the socialist lecturers under Robert Owen. He held a public discussion with J. Brindley at Liverpool in 1840 on "What is Christianity?" On the failure of Owenism, he went to America, where as a physician he wrote works popularizing medical science. {BDF; RAT; VI}

Holley, Sallie (1818—1893)
Holley, a Unitarian, was an abolitionist and an educator.

Hollis, John (1757—1824)
An English skeptic, Hollis wrote *Sober and Serious Reasons for Skepticism* (1796), *An Apology for Disbelief in Revealed Religion* (1799), and *Free Thoughts* (1812). According to Wheeler, Hollis "came from an opulent dissenting family and was distinguished by his love of truth, his zeal in the cause of freedom, and by his beneficence." {BDF; RAT}

Hollis, Thomas (1720—1774)
Hollis, a wealthy and liberal man who refused to enter Parliament on account of its corrupt procedure, edited various works of Sidney, Locke, and Neville. Hollis did not attend church and "gave his name to no religious society that could be discovered." He was a deist and a Fellow of the Royal Society. {RAT}

Holloway, W. E. (20th Century)
Holloway, a freethinker, wrote "The Mystical Mood" in *The New Humanist*, May-June 1933) and *Rubaiyat of Today* (1938). {GS}

Hollows, Frederick Cossom (1929—1993)
"Fred" Hollows was a humanist, an anarcho-syndicalist, and an ophthalmologist. Born in New Zealand, he intended entering the church but found that "sex, alcohol, and secular goodness are pretty keen instruments and they surgically removed my Christianity, leaving no scars." Hollows, an ophthalmologist, pioneered identification and treatment of blinding eye diseases among Australian Aboriginal people. He also developed a three-year model prevention program to train local technicians to perform eye surgery in Eritrea, Nepal, and Vietnam.

In 1990, he won the Australian of the Year Award and, in 1991, was named the Humanist of the Year. "I am a humanist," he once wrote. "I don't believe in any higher power than the best expressions of the human spirit, and those are to be found in personal and social relationships. Evaluating my life in those terms, I've had some mixed results. I've hurt some people and disappointed others, but I hope that on balance I've given more than I've taken." {SWW}

Holly, William H. (20th Century)
A naturalistic humanist, Judge Holly served with the United States District Court in Chicago. A law partner of Clarence Darrow, Holly when a judge joined the American Humanist Association. {HNS}

Holmdahl, John (20th Century)
Holmdahl is on the editorial board of *The Truth Seeker*.

Holmes, Edmund Gore Alexander (Born 1850)
Holmes, a poet and educationist, wrote *A Confession of Faith* ("by an Unorthodox Believer," 1895). He rejects Christian doctrines but retains theism and the belief in immortality, saying, "I do not believe in the supernatural." {RAT}

Holmes, Frank (20th Century)
Holmes is in the Edinburgh, Scotland, Humanist Group and writes for *The Scottish Humanist* as well as *The Freethinker*.

Holmes, Harry (20th Century)
Holmes, a former diplomat and lifelong humanist, questions in "Humanism in the Next Century (*New Humanist*, September 1999), the nature of the path we are taking into the future. His concern is that the high early promise of humankind may now be wasting tragically away.

Holmes, James (19th Century)
Holmes was a lecturer for the National Secular Society in the Midlands of England during the 1880s. {RSR}

Holmes, Jesse (1864—1942)
A philosopher at Swarthmore College until 1941, Holmes defined "God" as "the unifying element within that moves men to unity in a brotherly world." He was a chairman of history for Friends' Sunday schools. {CL}

Holmes, John (19th Century): See entry for John Rogers.

Holmes, John (Albert) (1904—1962)
When Priscilla Robertson asked John Ciardi for a recommendation of someone to be poetry editor of *The Humanist*, Ciardi named his teacher, Holmes, who accepted the position (1957). A distinguished poet, Holmes was also Anne Sexton's teacher.

Among the first poems Holmes published was one the present writer located in German by Albert Einstein, a work which praised one of Einstein's teachers and contained a passing use of the word "God," which was not used in any theological sense. Holmes remarked that if anyone else had written such doggerel he would not have included it, but "it is always comforting to hear a student who states that a teacher has helped change his life." Holmes's *Selected Poems* was published posthumously in 1965. {U}

Holmes, John Haynes (1879–1964)
A leader of liberals in the social application of liberal theology,

Holmes believed with Francis Greenwood Peabody as to the necessity of religions facing the "social question." During World War I, he was a staunch pacifist. Holmes preached a form of economic socialism from his pulpit at New York's Church of the Messiah, and socialist leader Norman Thomas often attended. He worked with liberal reformist institutions such as the National Association for the Advancement of Colored People (NAACP) and the American Civil Liberties Union (ACLU). In 1919, he led the Church of the Messiah to become the Community Church (Unitarian), hoping to use the church as a proving ground for nonsectarian religion.

Holmes was one of the first Americans to recognize the significance of Mohandas Gandhi and his nonviolent movement, becoming Gandhi's chief American disciple and publicist. He wrote "Ten Reasons for Believing in Immortality" (1929), arguing that nothing in the universe is ever lost, all energy is conserved, therefore "spiritual energy" is immortal; but in dualism spiritual energy does not exist, and Holmes separated himself in his thinking from that of many of the other liberal Unitarians. Many hold that Holmes was so unorthodox a minister that even the Unitarians were too conservative for him.

Charles Francis Potter, for example, was not surprised that Holmes had refused to sign Humanist Manifesto I: "He has reverted to theism since he was over and saw Gandhi, whose simple faith in God made a great impression on Holmes. The latter has a very theistic order of service. He is also very pessimistic about the future of liberal religion, but that is partly due to his physical condition and partly to his sad experience with his apartment-hotel proposition." The latter was a reference to his having to live next door to his mid-Manhattan church in a commercial hotel.

When Holmes was accused by the House Un-American Activities Committee of being "under the control of the Communist Party," humanists Eva Ingersoll Wakefield and Warren Allen Smith wrote the committee, demanding that it apologize to Dr. Holmes.

In his Community Church (Unitarian), John Dewey's memorial service was held at a time when Donald Harrington was minister. In addition to his several books about religion, Holmes wrote an autobiography, *I Speak for Myself* (1959). He championed birth control, was a pacifist, and was a leader in the movement to abolish capital punishment. {CE; EW; U; U&U}

Holmes, Oliver Wendell Jr. (1841—1935)

Holmes was a lawyer, novelist, and member of the U.S. Supreme Court known as the "great dissenter" because of his frequent minority opinions, Holmes thought law could be understood only as a response to the needs of the society it regulated, that it is useless to consider law merely a body of rules developed logically by legal theorists. The son of one of the most famous American authors, and a person raised in the Boston Brahmin culture defined by men like his father but a person who had none of the sometimes expressed Brahmin anti-Semitism, he grew up reading Emerson's essays right off the press and late in life commented on T. S. Eliot, Proust, and Hemingway.

Holmes's masterpiece, *The Common Law* (1881), was the result of his having been armed with skeptical and secular inclinations, critic Thomas C. Grey has written. "Holmes set about mastering the technical details of the law, with the ultimate goal of reformulating its theoretical underpinnings. His project was to replace the prevailing theologically tinged or formalistic legal theories with a modern jurisprudence that draws its inspiration from Darwin and its methods from German historical scholarship and English utilitarianism. He labored for fifteen years, practicing law by day and studying and writing at night, first to master the law's substance, and then to reimagine it as at once a social instrument and a product of society's habits, desires, and ideals." The work, generally thought the most important work of American legal scholarship, commenced

> The life of the law has not been logic: it has been experience. The felt necessities of the time, the prevalent moral and political theories, intuitions of public policy, avowed or unconscious, even the prejudices which judges share with their fellow-men, have had a good deal more to do than the syllogism in determining the rules by which men should be governed. . . . In order to know what [the law] is, we must know what it has been, and what it tends to become.

Holmes was presiding officer of the Unitarian Festival (24 May 1859) and was active in publicizing Unitarianism. {CE; TYD; U; UU}

Holmes, Oliver Wendell Sr. (1809—1894)

A physician and author, Holmes was dean of the Harvard medical school (1847—1853) and Parkman professor of anatomy and physiology at Harvard. One of his important medical lectures opposed the practices of homeopathy.

He is known for "Old Ironsides" (1830), a protest against the scrapping of the fighting ship *Constitution*, and for *The Autocrat of the Breakfast Table* (1858), witty glimpses of life in a boardinghouse.

His novel, *Elsie Venner* (1861), had as its intention to "test the doctrine of 'original sin' and human responsibility." Elsie, a New England girl whose snakelike nature is traced to a prenatal snakebite her mother received, is a heroine said by some scholars to be inspired by Margaret Fuller.

Holmes's freethought is found in his *Mechanism in Thought and Morals* (1871). Dr. Holmes was a Unitarian who, according to McCabe, had no belief in a future life. {CE; JM; JMR; RAT; TYD; U; UU}

Holmes, Olivia (20th Century)

After being an interim minister of the Central Unitarian Church of Paramus, New Jersey, in 1999 Holmes became the Unitarian Universalist Association's Director of International Relations.

Holmes Robert L. (20th Century)

Holmes, a professor of philosophy at the University of Rochester, addressed the Tenth International Humanist and Ethical Union (IHEU) World Congress held in Buffalo (1988). He wrote *On War and Morality* (1989) and edited *Nonviolence in Theory and Practice* (1990).

Holmes, Samuel Allen (18th Century)

Holmes, a professor at the University of North Carolina at Chapel Hill, held a profession hated by faculty members who were Puritanical Protestants: his profession was that of a strolling actor. Holmes held that honesty and integrity were "deceptions and injurious pretenses" and his nihilistic outlook helped incite a riot on campus in 1799. (See entry for North Carolina Freethinkers.)

Holmes, Thomas: See entry for Jessica Mitford.

Holmes, Thomas Rice Edward (Born 1885)

Holmes, the brother of E. G. A. Holmes, was an educationist and a member of the Rationalist Press Association.

Holmes, William T. (20th Century)

Holmes, a freethinker and libertarian, has written "That is Law and What is Its Purpose? for *Truth Seeker* #123:1.

Holmes, William Vamplew (19th Century)

Holmes was one of Carlile's shopmen, who came from Leeds to

uphold the right of free publication. He was sentenced to two years in prison for selling blasphemous and seditious libels in *An Address to the Reformers of Great Britain.* While in prison he was told that "if hard labor was not expressed in [your] sentence, it was implied." On his release, Holmes went to Sheffield and commenced the open sale of all the prohibited publications. {BDF}

HOLOCAUST

"The Holocaust" is the name given to the period of persecution and extermination of European Jews by Nazi Germany. Ordinarily, the Nazi persecution of gypsies and homosexuals as well as members of other religious minorities is treated secondarily by all but a few historians. An estimated 20,000 Romas (Gypsies) were killed at the Auschwitz death camp in Poland because of a 1 August 1944 order issued by Heinrich Miller, the chief of the SS as well as the Gestapo.

In 1994 at a German Bishops' Conference with the Polish Bishops' Conference, a German lay theologian suggested that Roman Catholics should acknowledge that they share historical responsibility and guilt for the Holocaust. Hans Herman Henrix of the Catholic Theological Institute in Aachen spoke of "manifold guilt" of Catholics for a failure to resist the rise of the Nazis in Germany and the annihilation of Jews during World War II. The Vatican immediately issued a statement emphasizing that Henrix's draft was "in no way a projected document of the Holy See."

The Holocaust has both religious and secular implications, explains the *Columbia Encyclopedia*. The secular materials [on the subject] attempt to explain how it happened and what the reactions of the victims were. The religious materials focus on the problem of whether one can still speak in traditional Jewish terms of a God, active in history, who rewards the righteous and who maintains a unique relationship with the Jewish people. (The present author has no doubts about the explicit crimes toward humanity which occurred during the Holocaust—when Chief Clerk to the Adjutant General, Hq. Oise, in Reims, France, I viewed secret movies shot at several of the Holocaust sites even before the prisoners were liberated. Later in New York City, I taught two survivors of the concentration camp at Belsen, both with the identification numbers tattooed on their arms.)

Holst, Nils Olaf (Born 1846)

Holst, a Swedish geologist, was chairman of the Swedish Society for Religious Liberty. {BDF}

Holt, Bonnie (20th Century)

Holt, a Unitarian, wrote *Trouping America* (1992), about her parents, Floy Mann and Fred Byers, who toured the Midwest as vaudeville performers around the turn of the century.

Holub, Miroslav (1923—1998)

Holub, a leading Czech poet, was a distinguished scientist. In "They Asked the Gods," he questioned the need for religion. But interviewed in 1994 by Ra Page, Holub explained: "I didn't leave religion, but that was for political reasons. As medical students we were advised to leave the church, and as a protest I never left the Protestant church. For me, the question is not a general one, but an individual one. Deep in the dark gardens inside we can't escape religion. The question is what kind of religion: is Buddhism any more appropriate for a European soul?" (See entry for Poets.) {Ra Page, *New Humanist*, October 1998}

Holwell, John Zephaniah (1711—1798)

Holwell is noted for being one of the survivors of the Black Hole of Calcutta. A surgeon, he went to India, defended a fort at Calcutta against Surajah Dowlah, and was imprisoned with 145 others in the "Black Hole," about which he published *A Narrative*. Holwell succeeded Clive as governor of Bengal. When he returned to England, Holwell published a dissertation directed against belief in a special providence, and he advocated the application of church endowments to the exigencies of the state. {BDF; RAT}

HOLY GHOST, HOLY SPIRIT

The doctrine of the Trinity was the theological invention of Cappadocian Fathers (or Holy Spirit), whose work in the 4th century held that God is to be believed in and worshipped as both one and three. God is the Father. God is the Son. And God is the Holy Ghost (or Spirit). At a council held in Constantinople in 381, the doctrine was approved, adhering to Hebraic monotheism but also emphasizing the importance of Christ Jesus, "the Lord" and "only begotten Son" of God. In 381, the Council of Constantinople elaborated upon an earlier Nicene Creed. To that creed's statement of belief in the Father, the Son, "and in the Holy Ghost" was added "the Lord and Giver of Life; who proceedeth from the Father; who with the Father and the Son together is worshipped and glorified; who spake by the prophets." The New Testament, which was written over a somewhat earlier period, makes no mention of a doctrine of the Trinity. Thus, Jesus appears ignorant of it.

The Old Testament, however, mentions *ruah* (breath), a reference to the mysterious power noticed also in primitive religion that men sometimes become different from themselves. They become mad or have high enthusiasm, allegedly because *ruah* has been "breathed in" (*in + spirare*) to a person, who then becomes its instrument. *Ruah* was offered as an explanation for Samson's strength, for Saul's insanity, for Bezaleel's genius. Later, as explained by Ernest Findlay Scott of New York City's Union Theological Seminary, it became evident "with the frenzy in which a prophet uttered divine oracles; from the physical state of the prophet, it was transferred to his exalted mood, and hence to all divine impulse and knowledge and action." One day, it was anticipated, God would "pour out his Spirit on all flesh" (*Joel*, 2:28) and not just to his chosen prophets, leading to the day of Pentecost and the coming of the Spirit. Scott adds, "In the Synoptic teaching of Jesus himself the conception of the Spirit has little or no place."

In the 6th and 7th centuries, various councils in Constantinople fine-tuned the concept of the doctrine. The complexities have been described by Matthew Spinka of the Hartford Theological Seminary in Connecticut: "The Council of 680 convened by Emperor Constantine IV Poganatus (668—685), dealt with the mooted question of Monotheletism (one-will theory) which, by asserting that the two natures in Jesus Christ possessed only one common will of energy, practically conceded the substance of the Monophysite doctrine that He possessed only one nature—the divine. Even Pope Honorius of Rome had adopted this heresy. The Council of 680 condemned the one-will theory, and specifically anathematized Pope Honorius. Thus it completed the doctrinal formula regarding the two natures in Jesus Christ which had been centuries in evolving: It asserted that there were two natures, two wills, in one person in Jesus Christ."

Voltaire was amused by the subject and described the Holy Ghost's origin: "How unfortunately ambiguous is this Holy Ghost, this *agion pneuma* of which the *christicoles* have made a third god! The word meant only breath. You shall find in the gospel attributed to *John* (20:22): 'When he said this, he breathed on them, and saith unto them, Receive ye the Holy Ghost.' Take note that this was an ancient ceremony of magicians, to breathe into the mouth of those whom they desired to bewitch. There, then, is the origin of the third god of these maniacs."

Non-believers find the doctrine ludicrous, often citing it as one of the reasons they rejected organized religion. As expressed in doggerel:

> There once was a God known as Ghost.
> All manner of shapes he could boast.
> But when it was time for Madonna,
> He came as a fowl straight upon her,
> But stained not her Virginal Honor.

Or, in the vulgate, the Trinity: Daddy-O, J.C., and Spook. (See entry for *Bullshitus Episcopalis*.) {CE; ER}

HOLY QUARTET

Several million Catholics around the world had by 1997 signed petitions asking the Vatican to give Mary a bigger role in Catholicism. Although any papal elevation of Mary would anger other Christians who do not worship Mary, such a move would result in a Holy Quartet: God the Father, God the Son, God the Holy Spirit, and Mary (playing the multiple roles of daughter of the Father, mother of the Son, and spouse of the Holy Spirit). {"Cardinal O'Connor Backs 'Holy Quartet,' " New York *Daily News*, 20 August 1997}

HOLY SEE

In the Roman Catholic Church, the official name for the jurisdiction of the Pope is the Holy See. *See* means "seat" in Latin. {DCL}

HOLY WATER

The holy water into which Catholics dip is water from which the priest has driven out devils by conjuration and the addition of a little salt. It is a ceremony that goes back to at least the fifth century.

Freethinkers who "lace" their water with whiskey call the drink "holy water" but consider it heretical to add salt. {RE}

HOLY WRIT

Figuratively, a "holy writ" is any text that is presumed to speak with unquestioned authority. The term, however, ordinarily is used as a synonym of the Bible.

Holyoake, Austin (1827—1874)

An English secularist publisher, the younger brother of George Jacob Holyoake, Holyoake printed and published Bradlaugh's *National Reformer*. Secular societies, he believed, should be established as meeting places in various respectable communities. His mental emancipation came, he wrote, from hearing the lectures of Robert Owen and his disciples. He took part in the agitation for the abolition of the newspaper stamp—assisting when risk and danger had to be met—and he helped his brother in the production of *Reasoner* and other publications. Holyoake started Austin & Co. in 1864 and founded Fleet House in 1855. Wheeler notes that Holyoake "took pride in the character of Freethought, and was ever zealous in promoting its welfare. His amiable spirit endeared him to all who knew him."

Holyoake died of consumption and, according to Foote, he was conscious almost to the last, his major regret being that he could no longer fight the battle of freedom nor protect the youth of his little son and daughter. Two days before his death, Holyoake dictated his last thoughts on religion, which were written down by his devoted wife and printed in the *National Reformer* (19 April 1874). Following is a sample:

> Christians constantly tell Freethinkers that their principles of

> "negation," as they term them, may do very well for health; but when the hour of sickness and approaching death arrives they utterly break down, and the hope of a "blessed immortality" can alone give consolation. In my own case I have been anxious to test the truth of this assertion, and have therefore deferred till the latest moment I think it prudent to dictate these few lines. To desire eternal bliss is no proof that we shall ever attain it; and it has long seemed to me absurd to believe in that which we wish for, however ardently. I regard all forms of Christianity as founded in silliness. It is the expectation held out of bliss through all eternity, in return for the profession of faith in Christ and him crucified, that induces the erection of temples of worship in all Christian lands. Remove the extravagant promise, and you will hear very little of the Christian religion.
>
> As I have stated before, my mind being free from any doubts on these bewildering matters of speculation, I have experienced for twenty years the most perfect mental repose; and now I find that the near approach of death, the "grim King of Terrors," gives me not the slightest alarm. I have suffered, and am suffering, most intensely both by night and day; but this has not produced the least symptom of change of opinion. No amount of bodily torture can alter a mental conviction. Those who, under pain, say they see the error of their previous belief, had never thought out the subject for themselves.

Holyoake composed a "Secular Burial Service," which for a time continued to be in use by some freethinkers. {BDF; EU, Lee E. Grugel; FUK; RAT; RSR; VI, TRI; WSS}

Holyoake, George Joseph (1817—1906)

The oldest English leader of freethought and the founder of Secularism, Holyoake was an active social reformer. In 1842, he was charged with blasphemy and was sentenced to six months of imprisonment in Gloucester, after which he was a hero to radicals who opposed the laws that disallowed public statements against Christianity. According to Grugel, Holyoake defined secularism "as being a series of rational postulates about the world upon which all social and ethical action could rest." When Charles Southwell was sentenced to a year's imprisonment, Holyoake took on in the 1840s the editorship of *The Oracle of Reason*. At that time, he explained, "I had not become [an atheist till after the imprisonment of Mr. Southwell, which led me to inquire into the grounds of religious opinion more closely than I had before done, and it ended in my entire disbelief." In one of his speeches, Holyoake said, in answer to a question, that he would put the Deity on half-pay, after which he was tried and sentenced by Mr. Justice Erskine to six months in jail. After being jailed, he wrote *The History of the Last Trial by Jury for Atheism in England* (1851), in which he stated, "In early youth I was religious, and as I grew up I attended missionary meetings, and my few pence were given to that cause," a reference to his having been a Sunday School teacher while a teenager.

Berman makes the point that Southwell and Holyoake "claimed only to disbelieve in God, because there was no sufficient reason for belief. They did not, as they put it, directly deny there is a God." He edited *Movement* (1843 to 1845), *Reasoner* (1846 to 1872), *Counselor* (1861), *Secularist* (1876 to 1877), and *Present Day* (1883 to 1886). With Charles Watts, G. W. Foote, and W. S. Ross, he edited *Secular Review*.

Holyoake first used the word "secularist" in 1851, and he presided over the first Secular Conference at Manchester in 1852. Wheeler notes that Holyoake "did much to remove the taxes upon knowledge and has devoted much attention to Co-operation, having written a history of the movement and contributed to most of its journals." Although he was supplanted by Bradlaugh as the major secularist leader, Holyoake remained a favorite of the young. Harry Snell remarked that the young loved him "for the dangers he had passed, while seasoned reformers regarded him with the affection due to a revered colleague and teacher. . . . I remember the genial and gentle old man with great respect and some gratitude."

He died peacefully at Brighton in the presence of his wife and daughter. They reported that during his last few weeks of life he had taken a keen interest in the general election then pending. {BDF; EU, Lee E. Grugel; FO; FUK; HAB; JM; RAT; RSR; VI; TRI; TYD; WSS}

Holyoake, W. H. (Born 1818)

A Leicester bookseller, Holyoake was a leader of the English secularists in Leicester. {VI}

HOM

A Dutch quarterly of Humanist Human Rights, *Hom-Nieuwsbrief* is at PO Box 114, 3500 AC Utrecht, The Netherlands.

HOMARIANISMO

In Esperanto, the word for "humanism" is *homarianismo.*

Home, Henry [Lord Kames] (1696—1782)

Home was a Scottish judge who published *Remarkable Decisions of the Court of Session* (1728). He published *Essays on the Principles of Morality and Natural Religion* (1751) and *Sketches of the History of Man*, the latter a deistic book. McCabe calls him one of the early freethinkers who did not suffer their brilliant success in life to reduce them to silence about religion. The Scottish Church had seriously denounced his work. {BDF; JM; RAT; RE}

HOMEOPATHY

> • Homeopathy, n. A school of medicine midway between Allopathy and Christian Science. To the last both the others are distinctly inferior, for Christian Science will cure imaginary diseases, and they can not.
>
> —**Ambrose Bierce**
> *The Devil's Dictionary*

Homer (Flourished 850 B.C.E.?)

The traditional Greek epic poet, Homer is often referred to as the Poet of Paganism. The shade of Achilles, as told in his *Odyssey*, informed Ulysses. "Better to be the hireling of a stranger, and serve a man of mean estate whose living is but small, than to be ruler over all these dead and gone." In short, the hereafter was not something they looked forward to. Robertson does not designate him as a freethinker, however, pointing out that his special genius was giving permanent artistic definiteness of form to the Greek gods.

"The ancient world," translator Peter Green has written, "turned to Homer for instruction in everything from social decorum to moral excellence, from religious duties to the proper conduct of a battle. (This last, as Jonathan Shay demonstrated in *Achilles in Vietnam*, was not quite so foolish a trust as some have supposed.) Homeric epic was described by a later, more doctrinal age, somewhat patronizingly, as 'the Bible of the Greeks,' the best they could come up with, presumably, in the absence of the Nicene Creed and the Thirty-Nine Articles."

But not even Homer's name is certain. *Homeros*, which means "hostage," implies he might have been a prisoner of war. Half a dozen cities have competed as Homer's birthplace. Pindar opted for Smyrna, Semonides for Chios, others assumed he came from Ionia. Of the various translations of *The Odyssey*, Green prefers Robert Fagles's *Homer: The Odyssey.* {CE; CL; Peter Green, *The New Republic*, 24 February 1997; HNS2; JMR; JMRH}

HOMICIDE

> • Homicide, n. The slaying of one human being by another. There are four kinds of homicide: felonious, excusable, justifiable, and praiseworthy, but it makes no great difference to the person slain whether he fell by one kind or another—the classification is for advantage of the lawyers.
>
> —**Ambrose Bierce**
> *The Devil's Dictionary*

HOMINISM

Wilhelm Windelband, a German philosopher, suggested in *Introduction to Philosophy* (1914) that to avoid confusion between the meaning of pragmatism and humanism *hominism* might well be used for the latter word.

HOMO ATHEISTUS, HOMO IGNORAMUS, HOMO HALLUCINATUS, HOMO RELIGIONUS: See entry for Auckland University Atheists.

HOMO MUTILANS

• I think it would be greatly to our advantage if, instead of calling ourselves Homo sapiens, we called ourselves Homo mutilans, the mutilating species, the species that mutilates both mind and body, often in the name of reason, religion, tradition, custom, morality, and law. Were we to adopt such a name for our species, it might focus our attention upon what is wrong with us and where we might begin setting ourselves right.

—**Ashley Montagu**
The Humanist, July-August 1995

HOMO SAPIENS

Homo sapiens shared the planet with *Homo heidelbergensis* and *Homo erectus*—a species which originated in Africa an estimated 1.2-million years ago. For a time, students of prehistory thought *Homo neanderthalis* (the original caveman, a skeleton of which was found in the Neander valley in Germany in 1856, three years before Darwin's studies) might have had a place in the evolution of modern humanity, that interbreeding had been possible. In 1997, however, a study of Neanderthal DNA suggested that interbreeding had not taken place. The study, by Dr. Svante Paabo of the University of Munich in Germany, further indicated that the Neanderthals split off much earlier from the hominid line than modern humans did. Mankind's closest living relatives, studies have shown, are the chimpanzees, not the Neanderthals.

Homo sapiens, the modern species of human beings, is the only extant species of the primate family Hominidae. As to how hominids formed, one view is that the young species evolved in one place, Africa, and that it then expanded elsewhere around the world, replacing related species. Another theory is that there were multiple origins for the human species at different places. The Chinese, for example, believe the Han are a "pure" race not descended from Africans.

Any populations which may have originated in Africa and moved elsewhere then evolved into modern humans separately but not in total genetic isolation. "In this theory," science writer John Noble Wilford has written, "lies an explanation for human biological diversity as reflected in what are known as the different races." Wilford added that scientists of equal accomplishment take opposite sides, "while others hope some new discovery will resolve the issue." [See entry for Population, Human.] {*The Economist*, 12 July 1997; *The New York Times Book Review*, 2 February 1997}

HOMOEROTICISM

• [Michelangelo] thought the height of beauty was the young male body. . . . [Caravaggio's] Greek gods have the look of rent boys. We know for certain that [Da Vinci] never had a woman. Boys, yes.

—Robert Hilferty
an interview with Sister Wendy Beckett
in *Out* (March 1998)

• Eroticism is in the eye of the beholder. I see no reason to take on a judgment when you're simply describing a fact. Everybody knows about Leonardo da Vinci. That was the way God made him.

—Sister Wendy Beckett, 67-year-old
Catholic nun who has a televised series,
"Sister Wendy's Story of Painting"

• But these are facts the Church normally denies or condemns. Even your analysis of the *Mona Lisa* is insightfully outrageous. You're the only critic in the history of art who has dared to explain that inscrutable smile in terms of the artist's homosexuality. You say that Mona smiles because she knows that in spite of his brilliant portrait making he can never really know her intimately—meaning sexually.

—Robert Hilferty,
continuing the interview

• He's just painting away, unaware of what he is telling us about himself as well as about her. No one has ever said it, and I do think that it explains the smile. Isn't that just my good luck to have seen it as opposed to something extraordinary. . . . I [hesitate to] publicly deny what is at the moment the Church's teaching. I would not spell it out. But it is clear to those who can read between the lines.

—Sister Wendy Beckett,
continuing the interview

HOMOSEXUAL

Merriam-Webster Inc., the oldest and largest dictionary publisher in the United States, made plans in 1998 to remove offensive slurs and synonyms for "homosexual" in its on-line as well as printed thesauruses. Offending words: faggot; fruit; invert; limp-wristed; nancy; pederast; swish; uranist. The company previously had not included entries for ethnic or racial minorities like Jews, blacks, or people of Hispanic descent because many of the synonyms were negative.

On the other hand, some academics hold, it is important to date usages and include such words as "offensive slang" in dictionaries. Phrases change meanings, for example, a "gay deceiver" actually a reference to "falsies" or foam-plastic bust-forms used by heterosexual women. Similarly, "gay" and "queer," which formerly were considered to have negative overtones, were commonly used by same-sexers toward the end of the 20th century.

HOMOSEXUAL MARRIAGE

Denmark, Norway, and Sweden grant legal recognition to gay marriages. In 1996, Iceland became the fourth European country to allow such marriages. Although some United States critics have objected, particularly on religious grounds, complaining that "the flames of self-centered morality are licking at the very foundation of our society, the family unit," others such as Michael Kavey of Chappaqua, NY, have declared that "the real threats to the family unit are the high rates of illegitimacy, domestic violence, and divorce. Allowing consenting, committed couples to formalize their relationships under the law serves to strengthen the American family, not tear it apart."

In 1998 at a Canterbury, England conference of the world's Anglican bishops, those present voted overwhelmingly to endorse a resolution declaring homosexual activity to be "incompatible with Scripture" and advising against the ordination of homosexuals. The once-a-decade gathering at the Lambeth Conference voted 526 to 70, representing a victory for an international group of conservative bishops, particularly those from Africa and Asia. The resolution was nonbinding upon leaders who represent a reported 73 million Anglicans in 160 nations. (See entry for Marriage.) {*The New York Times*, 18 July 1996}

HOMOSEXUAL RIGHTS IN SOUTH AFRICA

South Africa, which has the most recent written constitution of major nations, includes the following:

• (3) The state may not unfairly discriminate directly or indirectly against anyone on one or more grounds, including race, gender, sex, pregnancy, marital status, ethnic or social origin, colour, sexual orientation, age, disability, religion, conscience, belief, culture, language, and birth.

• (4) No person may unfairly discriminate directly or indirectly against anyone on one or more grounds in terms of subsection (3). National legislation must be enacted to prevent or prohibit unfair discrimination.

• (5). Discrimination on one or more of the grounds listed in subsection (3) is unfair unless it is established that the discrimination is fair.

HOMOSEXUALITY

The United States consists of a combination of diverse communities which, on the one hand, prize their freedom to believe and do what they choose and, on the other hand, have historically been more affected by religious observance and curbed by religious restraints than have most other Western countries. To display one's sexual orientation may be a Constitutional and democratic right, but to do so often results in puritans' objections and feelings of guilt. For left-handed individuals to complain that they are discriminated against by tool makers or for women or members of ethnic minorities to object that they are discriminated against is allowable. For male or female prostitutes to ply their trade may be frowned upon by American religionists more so than by Latin American or European religionists, resulting in a double standard whereby some regularly use the prostitutes but decry what the prostitutes do. And for homosexuals even to admit that they are not celibate, let alone to hold hands on the street, can bring down the wrath of the religiously orthodox, who among others hold that homosexuality is a "preference" which is "treatable," not, as still others claim, a biological phenomenon related to one's genetic background and, like eye color, a profound and unchangeable part of themselves.

"The fear that 16-year-olds will be corrupted by older homosexuals is not necessarily valid," remarked *The Economist's* reviewer of *Sexual Behavior in Britain*. "Most psychiatrists believe a boy's sexual preference is fixed before 16." Gays note that in 1994 some psychiatrists may have erroneously felt that one "chooses" to be gay. In 1999, however, it would be difficult to find a psychiatrist—even in Britain—who would not have used the word "orientation" instead of "preference." "Queen Victoria, legend has it, refused to accept that women did that sort of thing," the reviewer added (*The Economist*, 29 Jan 1994).

In the search for sexual identity, with biologists and geneticists still attempting to find what determines a person's gender, other animals which are homosexual appear not to be affected by their status. In some non-Eurocentric societies, homosexuals are considered "special gifts of nature."

Elsewhere, as observed by journalist Chandler Burr, conservatives disapprove of the search for gay genes and the origins of sexual orientation, fearing homosexuality is not chosen and therefore needs to be tolerated. Liberals, on the other hand, worry that the search will lead "to eugenics and other medical misuses, and they distrust attempts to establish civil rights based on biology rather than on principle." Burr adds, "Conservatives misunderstand what this research does. Liberals' fears are misplaced."

At the root of much of the problem is the Judeo-Christian Bible. Early Christian leaders condemned homosexuality, and by the Middle Ages homosexuals were often tried and executed as heretics. Bishop Epiphanius linked homosexuality with the form of Christianity called Gnosticism and accused many of the Gnostics of heresy, warning against any sexual practices such as homosexuality that did not produce children. During the Middle Ages, in his attempt to break the power of soldier-monks known as Knights Templar, the French King Philip IV accused the monks of having secret homosexual rituals, tortured them to extract confessions of sacrilegious practices, and confiscated their considerable wealth.

Such a religious interpretation of the Bible has been more successful in giving Americans "guilt feelings" about their sexual practices than it has Europeans, Africans, or Asians (a generalization which is widely felt but difficult to prove). In the Mediterranean regions where Christianity arose, homosexuality was a fact of life.

An extensive listing of readings about homosexuality in literature is found in *The Columbia Anthology of Gay Literature, Readings from Western Antiquity to the Present Day* (1998). The earliest text, the *Epic of Gilgamesh* (3rd millennium B.C.E.), describes the friendship of Gilgamesh for Enkidu. The friendship of David and Jonathan, in the first and second books of *Samuel* (c. 1012-872 B.C.E.) came much later, as did the friendship tales in the *Iliad* (8th century B.C.E.) about Zeus and Ganymede, Achilles and Patroclus, Harmodius and Aristogeiton, Orestes and Pylades, and many others.

According to Chapter 19 of *Genesis*, the cities of Sodom and Gomorrah were destroyed with fire and brimstone around 1900 B.C.E. Centuries later, Philo of Alexandria and some religious writers interpreted this to have been an angry God's punishment for the inhabitants of the two cities. Such an interpretation hinges on an unlikely translation of the ambiguous Hebrew word meaning "to know," in only a few cases of which does its biblical use connote sexual activity, states Reay Tannahil in *Sex in History* (1982). Christians who cite the call in *Leviticus* for the death penalty for homosexuals do not, however, demand capital punishment for the sin of cursing one's parents (*Leviticus* 20:9) or for adultery (*Leviticus* 20:10).

Plato in his *Symposium* wrote that humanity first consisted of three sexes—its members were joined in pairs: two men, two women, or a man and a woman. To diminish their power and to teach them to fear the gods, Zeus cut each pair apart. As a result, he wrote, humans are said to spend their lives searching for their other half in order to enjoy the fullness of love.

In 594 B.C.E., Solon declared the death penalty for any adult who mingled in school yards with boys below the age of puberty, although poets of the time wrote homoerotically that "boys in the flower of their youth are loved," and there was no legal problem at that time for adults to have relationships with post-pubescent youths.

Around 580 B.C.E., Sappho in Lesbos wrote to her own students the earliest known lesbian writings, and around 393 to 387 B.C.E. Plato wrote *The Symposium*, *Phaedrus*, and other works celebrating homosexual love. In 371 B.C.E., a Sacred Band of Thebes formed in Greece, a military unit consisting of some 150 male couples and believed to be effective inasmuch as lovers would die together, not shame one another. Alexander the Great (356—323 B.C.E.), whose love for Bagoas is the basis for Mary Renault's *The Persian Boy*, is but one of numerous homosexuals whose personal life is discreetly overlooked by most. Hadrian (76—138 C.E.), who had a Greek lover, is another, his same-sex love described by Marguerite Yourcenar's masterpiece, *Memoirs of Hadrian* (1951).

Sixty or so years after the birth of Jesus, Saint Paul wrote in *Romans* 1:26-27 and *1 Corinthians* 6-9 statements that appear to support homophobia, although scholar John Boswell infers that the real intent of the writer was otherwise.

In 533, Byzantine Emperor Justinian I decreed that homosexuality and blasphemy are equally to blame for famines, earthquakes, and pestilences, and he ordered castration for offenders.

About 650, a manual used by priests, the Cummean Penitential, provided guidelines for homosexual sin. "Simple kissing" by two males under the age of twenty called for six special fasts. Kissing "with emission or embrace" called for ten special fasts. Mutual masturbation by men over twenty made the offenders liable to twenty days penance; for anal intercourse, the period jumped to seven years.

In 1073, all known copies of Sappho's lesbian poems were burned by ecclesiastical authorities in Constantinople and Rome. In 1210—15, the Council of Paris declared sodomy to be a capital offense. In 1252, St. Thomas Aquinas declared that God created the sex organs specifically and exclusively for reproduction, calling homosexual acts "unnatural" and heretical and inspiring intolerance of homosexuality throughout the Catholic world. About 1260, the legal school of Orleans ordered that women found guilty of lesbian acts must have their clitoris removed for the first offense, mutilated for a second offense, and that they be burned at the stake for a third. In 1450—1453, Pope Nicholas empowered the Spanish Inquisition to investigate and punish homosexuality.

In 1513, Balboa while exploring present-day Panama reported that "the most abominable and unnatural lechery is practiced by the King's brother and many other younger men in women's apparel," and Balboa threw forty of the offenders to his dogs. Other explorers reported that the Mayan people of Mexico were "great sodomites," and one wrote back that everyone in the New World seemed to practice sodomy.

In 1918, Earl Lind's *Autobiography of an Androgyne* was published, although he had begun writing it in 1899 at the age of 25. He considered himself to be an *androgyne*, an *invert*, and a *fairie*, by which words he meant he was psychologically a female with male genitalia. *Urnings*, he said, "love an adolescent as a normal man loves a woman, and desires active *paedicatio* [anal penetration] or else mutual *onanism* [masturbation]." *Fairies* are distinct from urnings, he wrote, for they "love the adolescent as a woman loves a man, and desire *fellatio* [oral sucking of the penis] or occasionally play the part of the *pathic* [bottom] in *paedicatio*." (In contemporary usage, fairies would be "bottoms," urnings "tops," and sodomites "trade.")

In 1967, Ronald Reagan, who was later to become the President of the United States, called homosexuality "a tragic illness."

In 1995, Robert Mugabe, the President of Zimbabwe, said that homosexuals have "no rights at all" and are "worse than dogs and pigs."

The Allyson Almanac (1989) cites numerous historical events involving homosexuality, ending with accounts of the 1980s in which hundreds of thousands of marchers in Washington, DC, demanded civil rights for homosexuals. The book lists where some religious organizations stood on the subject in the 1980s:

> • The Roman Catholic Church consistently has condemned all homosexual activity as inherently sinful. In 1986 the Vatican's Congregation for the Doctrine of the Faith issued a letter in which homosexuality was referred to as "behavior to which no one has any conceivable right." In 1994, Pope John Paul II preached that the

notion of gay or lesbian marriage is "a serious threat to the future of the family and society" and said such unions could not be "recognized and ratified as a marriage in society." He made the statement two weeks after the European Parliament in Strasbourg offered support for the idea of homosexuals' marrying and adopting children. Specifically, the *Catechism of the Catholic Church* (1994) notes that "tradition has always declared that homosexual acts are intrinsically disordered. They are contrary to the natural law. They close the sexual act to the gift of life. They do not proceed from a genuine affective and sexual complementarity. Under no circumstances can they be approved." However, the catechism continues, "The number of men and women who have deep-seated homosexual tendencies is not negligible. They do not choose their homosexual condition; for most of them it is a trial. They must be accepted with respect, compassion, and sensitivity. Every sign of unjust discrimination in their regard should be avoided. These persons are called to fulfill God's will in their lives and, if they are Christians, to unite to the sacrifice of the Lord's Cross the difficulties they may encounter from their condition."

Finally, "Homosexual persons are called to chastity. By the virtues of self-mastery that teach them inner freedom, at times by the support of disinterested friendship, by prayer and sacramental grace, they can and should gradually and resolutely approach Christian perfection." In short, past tradition appears to have been one thing, but now that it is 1994 homosexuals are told they did not "choose" their "condition," they can expect to encounter difficulties from non-homosexuals, and they are advised to be chaste. (See entry for Andrew Sullivan, the gay editor of *The New Republic,* who is a Catholic.)

• The Protestant Episcopal Church was the first denomination to ordain a woman who was openly lesbian.

• The Presbyterian Church in 1976 voted that it would be "injudicious if not improper" to ordain homosexuals to the ministry. At the same time, the Assembly reaffirmed a previous resolution which stated that the "practice of homosexuality is a sin."

• The United Methodist Church in 1975 unanimously approved a statement that declared that the bishops did not "advocate or support ordination for practicing homosexuals."

• The United Church of Christ in 1972 was the first to ordain an openly gay person to the ministry. In 1975, it affirmed the civil liberties of gay and bisexual persons, stating that the church "must bear a measure of responsibility for the suffering visited upon same-gender-oriented persons."

• The Southern Baptist Church in 1987 condemned homosexuality as "a manifestation of a depraved nature" and "a perversion of divine standards," being one of the most conservative among the mainline denominations.

• Judaism's Orthodox and Conservative synagogues generally take a dim view of the practice of homosexuality. In 1979, a Reform group, the Union of American Hebrew Congregations, upheld the human rights of homosexuals.

• The Unitarian Universalist Association has gone further than most other denominations to defend the rights of gay men and lesbians. A series of resolutions from 1970 on has upheld the rights of gay men and lesbians, and the group has an Office of Gay Concerns. Homosexuals as well as lesbians are often found as Unitarian ministers across the United States, as was the case in other denominations at the end of the century.

In the 1990s, gay groups among almost every denomination—Methodists, Mormons, Baptists, Catholics, Friends, United Church of Christ, Unitarian Universalists, etc.—have formed and have worked both outside and inside the national church organizations. A Universal Fellowship of Metropolitan Community Churches (5300 Santa Monica Boulevard #304, Los Angeles, California 90029), an ecumenical religious denomination which is predominantly gay and lesbian, is found throughout the United States.

Wainwright Churchill's *Homosexual Behaviour Among Males: A Cross-Cultural and Cross-Species Investigation* (1967) found that homosexual conduct has been observed by scientists among monkeys, dogs, bulls, rats, porcupines, guinea pigs, goats, horses, donkeys, elephants, hyenas, bats, mice, lions, rabbits, cats, raccoons, baboons, porpoises, and apes. Churchill added that "homosexuality among the apes is highly significant since man is in the same order of animal life."

Gay American History (1976), a documentary by Jonathan Katz, contains an extensive bibliography of books on the subject. Included is the fact that in 1776 Jefferson and other leading citizens began a thorough-going revision of Virginia law, stripping it of all former monarchical and aristocratic aspects and bringing it into conformity with republican principles. In 1777, Katz reports, "Thomas Jefferson was among those liberals who suggested that 'Rape, Sodomy, Bestiality . . . be punished by Castration,' rather than, as earlier, by death. As finally written, bill number 64, authored by Jefferson himself and 'Reported by the Committee of Advisors, 18 June 1779' adds polygamy to the list."

A. L. Rowse's *Homosexuals in History* (1977) describes how sexual ambivalence since ancient times has been one of man's major concerns and pleasures, and his research is echoed in many other volumes which describe homosexuality throughout the human as well as the animal world. Rowse names dozens and dozens for whom same-sex love was predominant.

Writing about Shakespeare's Hamlet, playwright Terrence McNally observed, "The greatest gay character ever written is Hamlet. . . . Reconsider his misogynic treatment of both his mother and his alleged girlfriend, reexamine his relationship with his best friend, Horatio, and check out his over-the-top enthusiasm for the theater and actors. If it takes one to know one, Hamlet is one. Trust me on this."

Both sadism and masochism occur in homosexuality. For example, Proust illustrated his own "peculiarity" in confiding to André Gide that he sometimes needed intense sensations to achieve orgasm, such as watching warring rats. Biographer Ronald Hayman further describes Proust's compulsion, "the lifelong habit of trying to buy good will. Even when making love or when having love made to him, he couldn't believe he was lovable." Ackerman writes that although Marcel Proust claimed *Remembrance* was not autobiographical, "most scholars believe it is, and that the narrator's entanglements with Albertine echo Proust's doings with his lover, Alfred Agostinelli." Instead of buying Alfred a Rolls-Royce, Proust bought him one of the first airplanes "and Alfred died in it, spinning into the Mediterranean where he drowned, which gave him the dubious honor of being one of the first people to die in an airplane crash." As Ackerman observes, Proust would probably have agreed with Baudelaire's definition of love as "an oasis of horror in a desert of boredom." Meanwhile, Proust played love voluptuously in his mind, caressing the memories with his pen.

A Gay American Indian Anthology (1988) by Maurice Kenny describe the American Indians' Berdache tradition, which placed effeminate men on a high social level among the Sioux, the Cheyenne, the Ponca, and other tribes. For example, "To the Cheyenne we were no curiosity. We were friends or wives of brave warriors who hunted for our cooking pots and who protected our *tipis* [teepees] from Pawnee. We went to the mountain for our puberty vision. No horse or lance or thunderbird crossed the dreaming eye which would have sent us into war or the hunter's lonely woods. To some song floated on mountain air. To others, colors and design appeared on clouds. To a few, words fell from eagle wings. And they took to the medicine tent, and in their holiness made power for the people of the Cheyenne Nation. There was space for us in the village. The Crow and Ponca offered deerskin when the decision to avoid the warpath was made. And we were accepted into the fur robes of a young warrior, and lay by his flesh and knew his mouth and warm groin, or we married (a second wife) to the chief. And if we fulfilled our duties, he smiled and gave us his grandchildren to care for." (See entry for Berdache, which is an Arabic, not an Indian, word.)

The Greek goddess Aphrodite was said by Hesiod to have risen from the foam of the sea where Uranus's genitals fell after Kronus mutilated the Greek god of the sky, the mythological father of the Titans. The story in 1867 inspired Karl Heinrich Ulrichs (1825—1895), a lawyer and early gay rights advocate, to call himself an *Urning* to the surprise of a convention of German jurists. Homosexuals have offensively been called *homos*, *pansies*, *fruits*, *fairies*, *fag[got]s*, *swishes*, *lesbos*, and *dykes*. Some have been called *intersexes*, *androgynes*, *epicenes*, *perverts*, and *gays*. Gore Vidal, who prefers *same-sex sex* to *homosexuality*, thinks *gay* is "a ridiculous word to use as a common identification for Frederick the Great, Franklin Pangborn, and Eleanor Roosevelt." (At Franklin Roosevelt's inaugural, Mrs. Roosevelt wore a ring given her by her close friend, Lorena Hickock.) Many contemporary homosexuals call themselves *queer* rather than or in addition to what they consider the passé word *gay*. *Queer* once was used to designate pickpockets and con men, for "queer as Dick's hatband" commonly was understood to mean "out of order." Later, as noted in Grose's *Classical Dictionary of the Vulgar Tongue* (1811), the word meant "wrong, improper." Many gays and queers in the 1990s show little or no interest in organized religions, which they document as being a major cause for their centuries of being considered immoral. They are apt to express, particularly in their numerous books and magazines, more interest in the Ancient Greeks, pointing to Athena's proud bisexuality and to Zeus's escapades with the male Ganymede. (See entry for a gay secular humanist publication, *Qwer*.)

Those, however, who are attracted to Christianity sometimes speculate that Jesus and at least some of his all-male "disciples" bonded not only religiously but also sexually. Monotheism, they note, originally meant the "oneness" of God, implying God's bisexuality. (See entry for Kallimachos.)

In 1986, when Canada Customs discovered that *The Joy of Gay Sex* discussed as well as depicted anal sex, a bookstore challenged the refusal and won the case. Judge Bruce Hawkins, of the trial-level court for civil cases in Ontario, observed, "To write about homosexual practices without dealing with anal intercourse would be equivalent to writing a history of music and omitting Mozart." Canada Customs then amended the guidelines, although many United States books continue to be refused entry.

The late John Boswell, called "a devout Catholic" by *The New Yorker*, contended in *Sex Unions in Premodern Europe* (1994) that the Catholic Church blessed homosexual marriages as recently as the 1700s and even used a kind of liturgy, complete with prayers, to perform them:

> Send down, most kind Lord, the grace of Thy Holy Spirit upon these Thy servants, whom Thou hast found worthy to be united not by nature but by faith and a holy spirit. Grant unto them Thy grace to love each other in joy without injury or hatred all the days of their lives.

Doug Stumpf, once Boswell's editor at Villard, mentions that most of the ceremonies were in Greek, language of the early Catholic Church, but that the following is from an elaborate fourteenth-century version originally in Serbian-Slavonic. It is one of eighty versions of the same-sex marriage ceremony in manuscripts dating from the eighth through the sixteenth centuries:

> Lord God almighty, who didst fashion humankind after thine image and likeness and give unto them eternal and everlasting life, who didst choose thy holy disciples and glorious apostles Peter and Paul, and Philip and Bartholomew, to be united not in the bond of birth, but in faithfulness and love, let these love each other without envy and without temptation all the days of their lives. It hath pleased Thee that thy holy martyrs Serge and Bacchus were united not in the bond of birth, but in spiritual faith and love. Grant also that these two servants of thine, N. and N., love teach other without jealousy or temptation. Let them abide all the days of their lives under the Holy Spirit and the prayers of our most pure Queen, the Mother of God, and all thy saints who have pleased Thee through the ages. For thine is the power and thine the kingdom, thine the strength and the glory, Father and Son.

Boswell implied that Jesus and John had some kind of same-sex relationship, that same-sex marriages occurred in sanctified churches, and that, as shown in the above excerpts, the unions invoked the names of God, disciples, and apostles. Apologists countered that perhaps the ritual was a form of "fraternal adoption" or something like a commemoration of "an undying spiritual bonding." In the fourteenth century, the same-sex ceremony began to be banned for the Church and society were "gripped by a rabid and obsessive negative preoccupation with homosexuality as the most horrible of sins," stated Boswell, who claimed same-sex unions are still being performed quietly in some parts of Eastern Europe. Cartoonist Gray Trudeau publicized the finding, having one of his comic strip's characters report that some Yale professor had written a book saying that "for 1000 years the church sanctioned rituals for homosexual marriages." Boswell is accustomed to controversy. In 1980, he wrote *Christianity, Social Tolerance, and Homosexuality*, maintaining that Christianity was not originally or inherently hostile to homosexuality. His work, he insists, can help people "incorporate [same-sex love] into a Christian life-style." A male couple in Washington, D.C., did choose one of his ceremonies for their wedding, wrote Bruce Holsinger in *The Nation*, but a priest in Hartford who used the rituals to perform a number of gay and lesbian marriages was immediately excommunicated.

Episcopal Bishop John S. Spong in his *Rescuing the Bible from Fundamentalism* (1991) wrote that St. Paul was a "self-loathing and repressed gay male." Spong also championed the ordination of women in the Episcopal Church and, in the 1980s, called on priests in his diocese to "bless" homosexual unions.

Bonnie and Vern Bullough have written "The Causes of Homosexuality: A Scientific Update" (*Free Inquiry*, Fall, 1993), in which after extensive and up-to-date research they conclude as follows: "Although the research on homosexuality is in a rapidly changing state, there is evidence accumulating to suggest that sexual preference [changed to "orientation"] is the product of a complex interaction between three factors: (1) a genetic predisposition; (2) physiological factors; and (3) the socialization process. It is no longer possible to argue that either nature or nurture alone is in the answer; it is clear that both are involved in producing sexual preference. Given the power of these influences and the small amount of control exercised by the individual, punitive political policies seem out of place. It seems just as silly to discriminate against someone for his sexual preference as it does for his race or age."

Linguistically, *homo* is the Greek for *same*, not Latin for *man*, and the word *homophobia* is Greek, not a mixture of Latin and Greek. *Homophobia* therefore means "hatred of homosexuals" although it appears to mean "hatred of one's own kind." Or so some linguists point out.

Simon LeVay of the Institute of Gay and Lesbian Education and Dean H. Hammer of the National Institutes of Health present evidence for a biological influence in male homosexuality in *Scientific American* (May 1994). However, in the same issue William Byne of the Albert Einstein College of Medicine argues that current data lack substance, that even if genetic and neuroanatomical traits turn out to be correlated with sexual orientation, causation is far from proved.

In its "Affirmations of Humanism: A Statement of Principles and Values," the Council for Secular Humanism specifies the stand of secular humanists:

> • We attempt to transcend divisive parochial loyalties based on race, religion, gender, nationalist, creed, class, sexual orientation, or ethnicity, and strive to work together for the common good of humanity.

Meanwhile, the majority's opinion in the United States against homosexuality—which usually is based on Biblical doctrine—stood fast at the end of the 20th century. Political leaders joined with religious leaders and millions of their supporters in justifying their widely held view that the social fabric demands no "giving in" to homosexual demands for the same equality accorded to women and ethnic groups such as African Americans. Protection under the law is already available for homosexuals, insist the majority. As for a possible ruling by the court in Hawaii that would recognize marriages between two people of the same sex, Congress was quick in 1996 to pass legislation barring such and allowing individual states to ignore same-sex unions which might be made legal in Hawaii or elsewhere. During the debate, Representative Barr, a Republican from Georgia, insisted that "America will not be the first country in the world that throws the concept of marriage out the window and for the very first time in the history of civilization says that homosexual marriages are as important as, and rise to the level of the legal and moral equivalency of, heterosexual marriage." Instead, he spoke for the majority by saying that "the flames of hedonism, the flames of narcissism, the flames of self-centered morality are licking at the very foundation of our society, the family unit." (See entries for Heterosexuality, Hostility, Immorality, N. L. Stones [a transsexual], and for the Gay and Lesbian Humanist Association. Hawaii in 1999 voted against adopting such legislation.) {AA; ACK; Terrence McNally, *Los Angeles Times*, 9 December 1996}

HOMOSEXUALITY IN LITERATURE: See *The Columbia Anthology of Gay Literature, Readings from Western Antiquity to the Present Day* (1998). The earliest examples are of the friendship of Gilgamesh and Enkidu (3rd Millennium B.C.E.) and *1 and 2 Samuel* (c. 1012-872 B.C.E.)

HOMOSEXUALITY IN ZIMBABWE AND ELSEWHERE

Zimbabwean President Robert Mugabe in 1995, at an international book fair group, said that the Gays and Lesbians of Zimbabwe (GALZ) group was excluded. When Nobel laureate Nadine Gordimer of South Africa and others objected, Mugabe responded that homosexuals have "no rights at all," that they are "worse than dogs and pigs," and that they should be hounded out of the country. "Let the Americans keep their sodomy, bestiality, stupid and foolish ways to themselves!" he ejaculated. Not long afterwards, in 1998, the Rev. Canaan Banana, Zimbabwe's president from 1980 to 1987, was found guilty of sodomy with young bodyguards, gardeners, and cooks. The charges grew out of a 1995 murder trial of a police inspector, Jefta Dube, who killed a colleague who had called him "Banana's wife."

Homosexuality is not given special moral or psychological significance in many cultures. In 1951, a survey of 190 different societies around the world reported that in 70% of those studied homosexual practices are considered acceptable behavior. The practices are found throughout the animal kingdom. {CE}

HOMOSEXUALITY, WHAT THE BIBLE SAYS

What the Bible "really" says about homosexuality, a study by Daniel Helminiak, is on the Web: <www.ezin.net/personal/steven/homo.htm>.

HOMOSEXUALS AND GOD

The Web site of the Rev. Fred Phelps, pastor of the Westboro Baptist Church in Topeka, Kansas, is <http://www.godhatesfags.com>.

HOMOSEXUALS, MUSLIM

Male and female homosexuals who are Muslim experience the same fears and doubts as those who are raised Christians.

Al-Fatiha Foundation (405 Park Avenue, Suite 1500, New York, NY 10022) is an international organization dedicated to lesbian, gay, bisexual, transgender, and questioning (LGBTQ) Muslims. In 1999 it arranged a first North American conference, "Creating a Community," in the hope that it would become the beginning of a movement to create a community and an identity. "My mother would commit suicide if she found out I was gay," a male said at the conference. "My father knows I'm gay but insists that I marry," another male said. "Please help me find a gay male in the States who will marry me and get me out of this country," a lesbian pleaded in an e-mail message.

Following is a typical non-academic discussion of the problems homosexual Muslim face, an attempt to assess the Qur'an and those who interpret its sacred text:

Re: Homosexuality and same-sex acts in Islam:

• There is a general consensus amongst the scholars of Islam (both past and present) that homosexuality is a deviation of man's true (heterosexual) nature. Thus the act of homosexuality is sinful and perverted and is viewed with contempt in most Muslim societies and Islamic countries.

• There are approximately seven verses in the Qur'an (the holy text of the Muslims) that supposedly refer to homosexuality and same-sex acts. The majority of these verses refer to the nation of Lot (the biblical nation of Sodom and Gomorrah). The following are examples of a few verses:

> We also sent Lut (Lot): he said to his people: "Do ye commit lewdness such as no people in creation ever committed before you? For ye practice your lusts on men in preference to women: ye are indeed a people transgressing beyond bounds." *Surah VII (Araf)*, Verses 80-81
>
> Of all creatures in the world, will ye approach males. And leave those whom Allah (God) has created for you to be your mates? Nay, ye are people transgressing all limits? *Surah XXVI (Shu'araa)*, Verses 165-166)
>
> If two men among you are guilty of lewdness, punish them both. If they repent and amend, leave them alone: for Allah (God) is Oft-Returning, Most Merciful. *Surah IV (Nisaa),* Verse 16

• There are approximately four hadith (sayings attributed to the Prophet Muhammad) in reference to homosexuality, same-sex acts, and cross-dressing. A few include the following:

> When a man mounts another man, the throne of God shakes – Prophet Muhammad (peace be upon him)
>
> Kill the one that is doing it and also the one that it is being done to. (in reference to intercourse) – Prophet Muhammad (peace be upon him)
>
> Cursed are those men who wear women's clothing and those women who wear men's clothing. – Prophet Muhammad (peace be upon him)

• During the time of the Prophet Muhammad (d. 632 AD) there was not one single case of a reported punishment or execution for homosexuality or same-sex acts. The first execution to ever have been carried out was during the time of the third Caliph, Omar, who ordered a homosexual man to be burned alive. Scholars at the time differed in opinion on this form of punishment, arguing that no human should be burned (according to the traditions of the Prophet Muhammad), thus it was decided that homosexuals should be thrown off of the highest building and then stoned to death.

• Islamic schools of thought and jurisprudence differ on the issue of homosexuality. Sex between males was treated differently by the various legal schools, on the basis of differing interpretation of the traditional literature. All the legal schools regard sex between males as unlawful, but they differ over the severity of the punishment. The Hanafite school (predominant in South Asia and East Asia today) maintains that it (same-gender sex) does not merit any physical punishment. The Hanbalites, on the other hand (predominant in the Arab world) believe that sex between males must be punished severely. The Sha'fi school of thought (also predominant in the Arab world) argues that punishment for sodomy can only be carried out if there are four adult male witnesses who actually see the penetration, "as though the key is going into the key whole."

• According to the Ahmadi Muslim Jama'at (a small sect within Islam), homosexual behavior is a symptom of the decadence of society. In an essay entitled "Homosexuality & Islam," the Ahmadi sect states (regarding the decadence of society), "As this process continues, people find and invent even more bizarre and perverted means to satisfy natural urges, and trends like child and adult pornography, bisexuality, homosexuality and bestiality appear." They go on to say that homosexuality "is utterly contrary to every natural law of human and animal life, and counter to the morals, purposes and institutions of a procreative society."

• The Ismaili sect of Islam (also known as the Agha Khani movement), with a population of approximately 2 million people, believes Islam to be a continuously evolving faith that must be reinterpreted to adapt to modern-day society and culture. Their spiritual leader, the Prince Agha Khan, who is thought to be a direct descendent of the Prophet Muhammad, has been open to dialogue and communication with progressive movements within Islam. Although he has not officially made any gay-affirming statements, it is believed that he will soon make a declaration regarding this issue.

• In 1988, scholars from Al-Azhar University, the oldest and most prominent Islamic school in the world, located in Cairo, Egypt, passed a fatwa (decree) that sex reassignment surgeries were permissible in Islam. The Grand Mufti of the University stated, "It is permissible to perform the operation in order to reveal what was hidden of male or female organs. Indeed, it is obligatory to do so on the grounds that it must be considered a treatment. . . . It is, however, not permissible to do it at the mere wish to change sex from woman to man, or vice versa." This fatwa has set a precedent for the Muslim transgender movement for acceptance within the bounds of the Islamic faith.

• There have been many executions and arrests of gay, lesbian, bisexual, and transgender Muslims. These stories range from executions in Afghanistan, deportations of transvestites and cross-dressers in Saudi Arabia, to the present-day corruption and sodomy trial of ex-Prime Minister Anwar in Malaysia. It is also estimated that since the 1979 Islamic Revolution in Iran, the government has executed more than 4,000 homosexuals.

• Although Islam has been declared as the official religion in most Arab countries (except for Lebanon), European law heavily influences their constitutions. For example, in Algeria, a country heavily influenced by French law(s), sodomy may be punished with imprisonment from two months to two years and a fine (500-2,000 Algerian dinars). Saudi Arabia, on the other hand, where shariah (Islamic law) was always enforced, liwat (sodomy) is to be treated like fornication, and must be punished in the same way. If muhsan (sane) and free, one must be stoned to death, while a free bachelor must be whipped 100 lashes and banished for one year. However a non-Muslim who sodomizes a Muslim must always be stoned to death. Sodomy is proved either by the culprit confessing four times or by the testimony of four trustworthy Muslim men.

• Since the occupation of Afghanistan, in 1992, by the extreme conservative army of the Taliban, there have been approximately 10 public executions in the country. The men, all accused of committing sodomy had a wall toppled on top of them. According to Taliban law, if the accused survive the execution after 30 minutes, they are innocent and are then taken to a hospital to be treated for their injuries.

• Islamic extremists tried to beat up a gay man and threatened to kill him at a London conference on "Islamaphobia," designed to promote understanding and tolerance of Muslim values, and attended by Muslim, Jewish, and Christian leaders. The conference, held in London, England, claimed that "Islam is wrongly and unjustly portrayed as barbaric, irrational, primitive, sexist, violent and aggressive." During the question and answer session, an OutRage! Activist and a former Muslim of Pakistani descent, asked the panel of speakers how negative attitudes towards Muslims among gay people could be overcome, given that Islam advocates the burning alive of homosexuals. Most of the conference (then) turned on him. He was surrounded by over a hundred Muslims who screamed abuse and threatened to kill him. None of the Muslim, Christian or Jewish leaders on the platform (panel) intervened to calm the situation or condemn the violence. One Muslim cleric shouted that he had no need to ask what Muslims thought of homosexuals: all he had to do was look at the audience's reaction. The man was quoted as saying, "Muslims want tolerance for themselves but not for lesbians and gays. They condemn Islamaphobia, while zealously promoting hatred and violence against homosexuals."

• Imam Siraj Wahaj, an African-American convert to Islam, and a prominent cleric and scholar of Islam in the United States was quoted as saying the following in 1992, in reference to the supposed opening of a gay mosque in Toronto: "I would burn down the masjid (mosque) myself, if I could."

• The Islamic Society of North America's Dr. Muzammil Siddiqi, answering a question posed on homosexuality, says, "Homosexuality is a moral disorder. It is a moral disease, a sin and corruption. . . . NO person is born homosexual, just like no one is born a thief, a liar or a murderer. People acquire these evil habits due to a lack of proper guidance and education." Attempting to explain why homosexuality is a sin, he says, "There are many reasons why it is forbidden in Islam. Homosexuality is dangerous for the health of the individuals and for the society. It is a main cause of one of the most harmful and fatal diseases. It is disgraceful for both men and women. It degrades a person. Islam teaches that men should be men and women should be women. Homosexuality deprives a man of his manhood and a woman of her womanhood. It is the most unnatural way of life. Homosexuality leads to the destruction of family life."

• Although mainstream Islam officially condemns homosexuality there is a growing movement of progressive-minded Muslims, especially in the Western world, who see Islam as an evolving religion that must adapt to modern-day society. It is within this movement that Al-Fatiha Foundation hopes to work in order to enlighten the world that Islam is a religion of tolerance and not of hate, and that Allah (God) loves His creation, no matter what their sexual orientation may be.

Some Muslims are outspoken concerning women's having to cover their bodies or men's being condemned for what they wear. Following is a typical response sent anonymously by one female on the Internet:

> Salaam all my brothers and sisters!
>
> I am curious, for those of us who support upholding the Hadith as part of the Deen. Can you explain to me how this makes us closer to God? How does my wearing a veil and hijab bring me closer to God? If we are going to use physical objects to make us closer to God, why don't we all just worship rocks and trees? How does barring me from the masjid because of my period bring me or anyone else closer to God? The Prophet (God bless him) wore a full beard and a mustache, and even this is incorporated in the hadith. So how does a beard and a mustache bring a man closer to God? I wonder about this because it seems that in our adoration of our Prophet (saw), we may have forgotten the ultimate goal of our religion—the contemplation of the Vision of The Beloved. Please do not count me among those who deny the respect and reverence that is due to Mohammed (saw), because he holds a special place in my heart and I admire him immensely. But I realize that Mohammed (upon whom be Allah's peace and mercy) was a man living in the 7th century. I can follow the religion that God sent him with. I can adore the Prophet (saw) and strive to incorporate aspects of his noble character into my own personality. But I cannot BE Mohammed (saw). I cannot be a Middle Eastern man living in the 7th century. The essential qualities of Mohammed's character can survive in modern times without bending the rules of the religion, however the practices which are attributed to him (stoning homosexuals, misogyny, comparing women to donkeys and suggesting that their periods make us impure) cannot. The Quran was sent down for ALL times. Why do we seek further additions to the Deen?
>
> Allah does not care what we look like, and all of our personalities are diverse. What exactly is "trying to look or behave like men" supposed to mean? Is there anyone that believes this crap— that because a man dresses in a skirt he is deserving of wrath from God? or a woman wearing shorter hair and trousers? LIES ALL LIES. May the angels rip out the tongue of whoever attributed this blatant LIE to our prophet (saw). I seek refuge in Allah, The Watchful, The Loving, against the accursed shaytan.

(See entries for Muslim Gays and for Muslim Women.)

HOMOSEXUALS, OTHER

The pansexual Bonobo, a rare breed of chimpanzees which is said most to resemble humans, engage in homosexual conduct.

Niankhkhnum and Khnumhotep (2400 B.C.E.?) reportedly shared life and death together. Their story is described on the World Wide Web: <http://www.sirius.com/~reeder/niankh.html>.

King Akhenaten (ruled 1379—1362 B.C.E.) followed Egyptian custom by marrying his mother and four other women, but he also had an intimate relationship with a man named Smenkhkare. The two males were assassinated by polytheistic (fundamentalist) priests who were unhappy that the king had introduced monotheism into the culture.

The Judeo-Christian Bible tells how Jonathan loved David so much the two made a covenant together. When Jonathan died, David lamented, "Thy love to me was wonderful passing the love of women."

When cited, heterosexuals usually are not listed as being such inasmuch as they constitute the majority and have never been considered freaks for having sex in the various manners and fashions in which they engage. {Jerry Sloan, *Freedom Writer Magazine*, July-August 1997}

Honderich, Ted (1933—)

In 1988 Prof. Honderich was elected an honorary associate of the Rationalist Press Association. Also, he is an Honorary Associate of the National Secular Society. A Canadian by birth, he once was literary editor of the *Toronto Star*. After studying with A. J. Ayer at University College, London, he became a British citizen. Honderich is author of *A Theory of Determinism: The Mind, Neuroscience and Life-Inquiries in Political Philosophy* and *Hierarchic Democracy and the Necessity of Mass Civil Disobedience*. He has edited *Philosophy As It Is* and *Philosophy Through Its Past*.

A lecturer at Yale and City University of New York, as well as British universities, he now is successor to A. J. Ayer as the Grote Professor of the Philosophy of Mind and Logic at University College, London. Honderich is a contributing editor of *Philo*. He signed Humanist Manifesto 2000.

HONDURAS FREETHINKERS, HUMANISTS: See entry for Francisco Morazán.

Honegger, Barbara (20th Century)

Honegger is on the editorial board of *The Truth Seeker*. She is author of *The Military Draft* (1982).

Honig, Herb (20th Century)

Honig in 1995 was vice president of the Humanists of North Jersey in Glen Rock, New Jersey.

HONOR

For Christians, honor emanates from God, the final moral Judge who is "the reader of all hearts." The "code of honor" refers to the inner consciousness of worth and delicate sense of rights and obligations felt by such a person. Dating to the 15th century, an Albanian code of honor (also called the Code of Lekë and named after the strict rules of behavior laid down by tribal leader Lekë Dukagjini) includes among its tenets: "An offense to honor is not paid for with property, but by the spilling of blood. . . . The person dishonored has every right to avenge his honor. . . . A man is dishonored if someone reneges on his pledged word. . . . An offense to honor is never forgiven." Journalist John Connolly has commented that the Code of Lekë "makes the Mafioso Code of Omerta look like it was written by Miss Manners. For those who do not take their directions from some authoritarian group, Shakespeare's observation in *King Richard II* is appropriate: "Mine honour is my life; both grow in one; / Take honour from me, and my life is done." {ER}

Hooge, Ord (20th Century)

A Canadian atheist, Hooge is found on the Web at <http://users.uniserve.com/~tfrisen/welcome.html>.

Hoogeveen, Elly (20th Century)

A humanistic counselor in the Netherlands, Hoogeveen described to the 1992 International Humanist and Ethical Cunion (IHEU) Congress how counselors are trained at the world's first humanist university, in Utrecht. She stated that a counselor's fundamental conviction is that every human being must give his or her own life meaning and make his or her own choices. The counselor, then, represents no belief in the traditional sense and counsels without judgment, without a message, and without a preconceived aim. What the counselor does is to work for the well-being of the client, helping people decide how to find their own way in life.

Hook, Sidney (1902—1989)

A philosopher at New York University, Dr. Hook was associated at the time of his death with the Hoover Institution on War, Revolution and Peace. He wrote *The Meaning of Marx* (1934), *From Hegel to Marx* (1936), *Heresy, Yes, Conspiracy, No* (1953), and a large number of books on American life. He was a Humanist Laureate in the Council for Secular Humanism's International Academy of Humanism.

On the subject of humanism, he wrote to the present author:

> Of the types of humanism you have described, I am a naturalistic humanist. However, I would modify the description as follows:
>
> NATURALISTIC HUMANISM—
> to the philosopher, a set of beliefs born of the modern scientific age and centered upon a faith in the supreme value and self-improvability of human personality; differs from theistic humanism by its rejection of any form of supernaturalism; from atheistic humanism by its avoidance of small-town, village exhibitionism, *épater les bourgeois*; and from communistic humanism by its opposition to any beliefs not founded upon freedom, the significance of the individual, and political democracy.
>
> My views are developed at greater length in my books *Pragmatism*

and the Tragic Sense of Life, The Quest for Being, and *The Place of Religion in a Free Society,* for example. Not all who call themselves naturalistic humanists really are, e.g., Corliss Lamont, a long time passionate apologist for Stalin's despotism, defender of the Moscow Trial Fabrications, and who has remained unrepentant even after the Kremlin admitted Stalin's infamies.

Hook's disagreements with Lamont were political, not philosophic, and his views on anti-Communism were instrumental in guiding others to work against Soviet policies. Being a critic of Soviet Communism became something of a monomania for Hook, leading Arthur Schlesinger Jr. to observe that Hook "[let] anti-communism consume his life to the point that, like Aaron's rod, it swallowed up nearly everything else."

Antony Flew in the *Encyclopedia of Unbelief* calls Hook "an almost exact contemporary of Ernest Nagel" and notes that both were distinguished former pupils and lifelong admirers of John Dewey.

Of philosophers in the twentieth century who are major figures in the movement of secular humanism, Sidney Hook is one of the first whom most would list. The scope and impact of his thought have been described in *Sidney Hook and the Contemporary World* (1968), edited by Paul Kurtz. In 1995, Edward S. Shapiro edited *The Letters of Sidney Hook: Democracy, Communism, and the Cold War,* making it clear that Hook was never a member of the Communist Party.

For Christopher Phelps in *Young Sidney Hook, Marxist and Pragmatist* (1997), Hook in his early days combined Karl Marx and John Dewey, "Americanizing Marxism." Theodore Draper found some weaknesses in Phelps's research, that, for example, the Communist Party had been sympathetic to Trotsky; according to Draper, the Communist Party always considered any sympathy with the Trotskyists to be counterrevolutionary.

For Richard Rorty, Hook and Dewey were philosophic giants. Both men "loathed the Communists' willingness to use 'anti-fascism' as an excuse for turning a blind eye toward the crimes of the bloodsoaked tyrant who then ruled Soviet Russia. Although both men distrusted Franklin Delano Roosevelt because he seemed to them not to go far enough, not to be sufficiently radical and experimental, they had no doubt that the alliance between the labor unions and the Democratic Party had helped to turn the country in the right direction."

Hook died just a few months too soon to witness what he had long hoped for, the collapse of the Soviet Union. (See entries for Howard Fast, Corliss Lamont, and Christopher Phelps. A detailed interview about humanism, Marxism, and related matters is found in *Free Inquiry* (Summer, 1988).) {CE; CL; EU, Antony Flew; HM2; HNS; HNS2; PK; Richard Rorty, "Remembering John Dewey and Sidney Hook, *Free Inquiry,* Winter 1995-1996; SHD; TYD; WAS, 20 March 1989}

Hooker, Herman (19th Century)

Hooker wrote *The Philosophy of Unbelief in Morals and Religion* (1844). {GS}

Hooker, Joseph Dalton [Sir] (1817—1911)

Hooker was an English naturalist who became renowned as a botanist. He was the first eminent man of science to proclaim his adoption of Darwinism. An intimate friend of Darwin, he helped in preparing the botanical material of his works. Hooker's distinction was such that he had nineteen gold medals and was a member of more than a hundred learned societies in different countries.

In Leonard Huxley's biography, it is clear that Hooker was an agnostic: "I distrust all theologians," he held, saying that the ultimate power of the universe is "inscrutable," that theism and atheism are just where they were in the days of Job, and the Jesus was simply an Essene monk.

Hooker directed Kew Gardens from 1865 to 1885. {JM; RAT; RE}

Hooper, Charles E. (20th Century)

Hooper was the Rationalist Press Association's first secretary. He wrote for *Ethical World, Literary Guide,* and *Agnostic Annual.*

Hooper, Ellen Sturgis (1812-1848)

Hooper, a Unitarian and a transcendentalist poet, was the sister of Caroline Sturgis Tappan.

Hooper, Smitty (20th Century)

Hooper is president of Humanists of Florida. (See entry for Florida Atheists, Humanists.) {FD}

Hoops, Walter (1902—1999)

Hoops was a senior writer for *The American Rationalist.* In 1991 he received a distinguished service award from the Council for Secular Humanism. In Germany in the 1920s, Hoops was secretary of a local Freethought organization. He has recalled that during a squabble between the Social Democrats and the Communists, the reactionary elements sang a ditty,

> *Und willst Du nicht mein Bruder sein,*
> (If you don't want to be my brother,)
> *So schlag ich Dir den Schaedel ein.*
> (I'll cut your head wide open.)

Hoops is author of *Our Rationalist Heritage* (c. 1965). In 1998 he was given a Lifetime Achievement Award at the Fourth Annual Atheist Alliance convention held in St. Louis. (See a tribute to Hoops in *The American Rationalist* (July-August 1999.) {EU, Eldon Scholl; FUS; *Secular Nation,* July-September 1998}

Hoover, Mel (20th Century)

Hoover, an African American, is a Unitarian minister. He is director of the UUA Faith in Action Department and is staff liaison to the Journey Toward Wholeness Transformation Committee. That group helps direct the Unitarian Unviersalist Association's antiracism efforts. {*World,* July-August 1998}

HOPE

- Abandon hope, all ye who enter here.

—The inscription at the entrance to Hell,
as described by Dante in *The Divine Comedy*

- He that lives upon hope will die fasting.

—Benjamin Franklin,
Preface to *Poor Richard's Almanac*

- Hope is the thing with feathers.

—Emily Dickinson

- Extreme hopes are born of extreme misery.

—Bertrand Russell
"The Future of Mankind," in *Unpopular Essays*

- From too much love of living,
From hope and fear set free,
We thank with brief thanksgiving
Whatever gods may be
That no man lives forever
That dead men rise up never; /
That even the weariest river
Winds somewhere safe to sea.

—Algernon Charles Swinburne

- Let us hope, for as yet there is no tax on hope.

—Bertrand Russell

Hope, Thomas (1770—1831)

Hope was a novelist and an antiquarian. He wrote the anonymous *Anatasius*, memories of a Greek, and *The Origin and Prospects of Man* (1831). {BDF; RAT}

HOPI

A group of Pueblo, formerly called Moki or Moqui, Hopi speak the Hopi language, are found mainly in northeast Arizona, and number around fifteen thousand.

According to their 900-year-old religious tradition, the Great Spirit Maasau'u, Guardian of the Earth, assigned them the duty of preserving the natural balance of the world and entrusted them with a series of ominous prophecies warning of specific threats and providing guidance on how to avoid them. Thomas Banyacya (1910-1999) in 1992 was allowed to speak at the General Assembly hall of the United Nations, where he sprinkled cornmeal on the podium, then delivered his message stressing the need for world leaders to listen to those still living in harmony with nature. "Hopi" means "peaceful," and they reject fighting in wars, particularly for another nation. {Robert McG. Thomas Jr., *The New York Times*, 15 February 1999}

Hopkins, Khristine (20th Century)

Hopkins is author of *Survivors: Experiences of Childhood Sexual Abuse and Healing* (1994). A Unitarian and a photographer, she collected photos of survivors which do not depict abuse but, rather, portray women as they confront their experience of abuse.

Hopkins, L. Thomas (20th Century)

A naturalistic humanist who taught at Columbia University, Hopkins wrote *The Emerging Self* (1954).

Hopkins, Mark (1801—1887)

Hopkins, the eminent editor and educator, is said to have had a general outlook similar to that of some Unitarians. A 1935 biography by J. H. Denison says of Hopkins that "He puts his finger on the weak point of Unitarianism, in that Christ was presented merely as an example. . . . [It] made of Unitarianism a rather cold ethical system in place of a religion of passionate devotion," leading him to be a "mediator between the old thought and the new."

Frederick Rudolph's *Mark Hopkins and The Log* (1956) states that "At [Amos] Lawrence's request Hopkins preached, as was hardly his custom, in the Unitarian Church in Boston which Lawrence attended." {CE; EG; U}

Hopper, Leon (20th Century)

Hopper, a Unitarian minister, heads the Partner Church Council (12902 SE 48th Place, Bellevue, Washington 98006). The council supports Unitarians in Eastern Europe by deepening solidarity and increasing mutual aid between and among partner churches and related institutions. (See *World*, July-August 1995.)

Hopwood, Freeman (20th Century)

Hopwood was a founder in 1925, along with Charles Smith and Woolsey Teller, of the American Association for the Advancement of Atheism. {FUS}

Horace (Quintus Horatius Flaccus) (65—8 B.C.E.)

Horace "had no faith in personal survival after death. His *Satires* (35 B.C.E.) and *Ars Poetica, Epistle to the Pisos* (c. 13 B.C.E.) are said to have influenced not only writers of his own age but also many English poets.

Horace's father had probably been sold into slavery in 88 B.C.E. when Venusia was captured and he was taken prisoner. Later given his freedom, he succeeded financially to the point that he could send his son Horace to Athens in order to study philosophy. Soldiering at the battle of Philippi in 42 B.C.E., Horace escaped but ingloriously left his shield behind, finding upon returning home that his father's house and farm were gone and he was without resources. However, he worked at a post in the treasury and not long afterwards became noted as a writer of *sermones*, satirical conversations.

In his descriptions of the joys of country life, Horace wrote epodes which described, for example, witches preparing to immolate a young man in order to use his organs for love charms; or praises for Octavian (soon to be granted the title of Augustus); or works with political themes; or his most famous, an ode which spoke of the warmth of wine that should accompany one's youthful and complex love affairs—he included some with the opposite as well as with one's own sex.

A close friend of Augustus, he once turned down the position of being letter writer for the dictatorial ruler of the Roman Empire, yet remained on his good terms.

Upon his death, Horace achieved a stature he had not had during his lifetime. Quintilian evaluated him as the only one of the lyric poets worth reading. Byron, and many others who had to struggle with what Quintilian described as "the variety of his figures of speech and the felicitous audacity of his choice of words," was negatively critical, writing, "Then farewell, Horace, whom I hated so/Not for thy faults, but mine. . . ." In short, Byron was summarizing the difficulties experienced by students in the 17th and 18th centuries who were required to read Horace's work with thoroughness.

Robertson points out that "Horace with his *credat Judaeus Apella*, and his frank rejection of the fear of the *Deos tristes*, was no believer. However, he was not one to cross the Emperor and was ready to lend himself to the official policy of religion."

Most readers are entirely unaware that Horace lived and died a bachelor or that he was short and fat and complained of premature baldness. Brad Walton of Carleton University has written about Horace's bisexuality, finding that he had numerous love affairs with persons of both sexes.

Horace lives on today because his work was not destroyed over the years, as was the work of many of his compatriots including Gallus and Varius. His influence upon the present has been surveyed by D. S. Carne-Ross and Kenneth Haynes in their *Horace in English* (1998). Today, few critics would deny that Horace inspiringly lifted Latin literature to the level of Greek. {CE; CL; GL; JMR; JMRH; Bernard Knox, "Horace, Our Contemporary," *The New York Review of Books*, 11 June 1998}

Horder, Thomas Jeeves [Lord] (1871—1955)

Horder, a consulting physician to the Cancer Hospital, Fulham, and other hospitals, was prominent in the promotion of public welfare. He was a president of the Harveian Society, the Medical Society of London, and the Eugenics Society. Horder also was an honorary associate of the Rationalist Press Association. {RE; TRI}

Horn, Kristian (1903—1981)

A biologist and professor at the University of Oslo, Horn founded Norway's humanist organization, *Human-Etikk Forbund*, with 250 of the nation's most prominent academicians, lawyers, and psychiatrists. He has been succeeded by Levi Fragell. (See entry for Scandinavian Unbelievers.) {*Free Inquiry*, Winter, 1990-1991}

Hornback, James F(ranklin) (1919—)

Hornback from 1947 to 1951 led the Westchester Ethical Culture Society, then from 1951 to 1984 led the Ethical Society of St. Louis, which is the fourth oldest (1886) and the second largest of the nation's Ethical societies.

A charter member of the American Humanist Association (1941), and a signer of Humanist Manifesto II, Hornback was President of the American Ethical Union from 1982 to 1983 and a board member of the International Humanist and Ethical Union (IHEU) from 1962 to 1966.

He attended IHEU Congresses in Amsterdam, London, Oslo, Paris, Boston, Hannover, and Buffalo. Hornback is the great-grandson of "Old Jim Hornback," Mark Twain's model of a benevolent country gentleman in *Huckleberry Finn* (Chapter 13). (See entries for American Humanist Association and for Ethical Culture.) {CL; EU, Howard B. Radest; HM2; HNS; HNS2}

Hornblower, John (19th Century)

Hornblower, a friend of G. J. Holyoake and who married his sister Caroline Holyoake, printed *Reasoner* until 1847. {VI}

Horneffer, Ernst (Born 1871)

A German writer, Horneffer studied Nietzsche together with his brother August. They edited Nietzsche's literary remains (1895), and Ernst delivered Nietzsche's funeral oration. Horneffer was a monist, the author of several rationalist works. He promoted Sunday lectures and the secular moral instruction of the young. {RAT}

Hornibrook, Ettie Rout (1877—1936)

Jane Tolerton in *A Life of Ettie Rout* (1993) describes the Australian-born and New Zealand-educated "guardian angel of the ANZACs" who was awarded the *Reconnaissance Française* for her work with the ANZACs and of her troops in France during and after World War I. Because of her writing about birth control, sexual equality inside marriage, a measure of free love, easier divorce, child care for single mothers, abortion when contraception failed, and eugenics, Ettie Rout was called "the wickedest woman in Britain" by one English Bishop. Among her titles were *Safe Marriage* (1922—banned in New Zealand); *The Morality of Birth Control* (1925), *Sexual Health and Birth Control* (1925), and *Sex and Exercise* (1925). With her friend H. G. Wells, she mobilized the court defense of Margaret Sanger's *Family Limitation* in 1923. Hornibrook criticized the "superstition" of Marie Stopes and, later, the policies of the American sex reform movement. Critic David Tribe has written, "Jane Tolerton [a distant relative by marriage] admires and yet reproaches her subject as a Humanist who loved all humanity but seemed unable to love, or be loved by, any one human being." Having contracted malaria in Egypt, Mrs. Fred Hornibrook took quinine but in the Cook Islands committed suicide by taking an overdose. {*The Freethinker*, December 1993; SWW}

Hornibrook, Fred A. (1877—1965)

Hornibrook, an Irishman who went to New Zealand in 1900 and later became prominent in the UK National Secular Society and *Freethinker*, married Ettie Rout in 1920. His *The Culture of the Abdomen* (1924) brought him critical fame. For the *New Zealand Rationalist and Humanist* he wrote the "London Calling" section.

Horniman, B. J. (20th Century)

Horniman was one of the early members of the Indian Rationalist Association. A journalist, he helped the group develop its earliest library of rationalist materials.

Horowitz, Alan S. (1910—1996)

Horowitz, a medical doctor, spent his last fifteen years confined to his bed in Dayton, Ohio. Interested in the subject of euthanasia, he had some reservations as to whether its legality might result in abuses. He favored obtaining a second opinion from a physician chosen by an independent panel.

Horowitz, Dan (20th Century)

Horowitz is a Florida freethinker, an editor, and a writer for *Truth Seeker*.

Horowitz, David (20th Century)

Horowitz, a writer and conservative activist, published *Ramparts*, a left-wing magazine, in the 1960s. Later he founded the Center for the Study of Popular Culture, a right-wing think tank. His autobiography is *Radical Son: A Generational Odyssey*, in which he wrote, "Socialism was a secular faith: I had been a believer, and I had been burned. I did not feel an opening in my soul for renewed risk. I had affection for the Old Testament God and was invariably moved during the service by the connection I felt, through the ancient prayers, to ancestors who lived millennia ago. But to God's actual existence, I remained stubbornly agnostic. If I believed in anything, it was the mystery itself." {CA}

Horowitz, Irving Louis (1929—)

When Horowitz signed Humanist Manifesto II, he was editor of *Society*. The publisher of Transactions Press, Horowitz is a professor of sociology at Rutgers University in New Jersey. {HM2}

Horsley, Victor Alexander Haden [Sir] (1857—1916)

An eminent British surgeon, Horsley was an active humanitarian. Paget in his biography tells of Dr. Horsley's agnosticism, adding, "If he had cared to be labeled, he would have written the label himself, Agnostic. . . . Popular theology and sham were utterly distasteful to him." {JM; RAT; RE}

Horwood, Martin (20th Century)

Horwood, director of development of the British Humanist Association, on the occasion of the BHA's 25th anniversary, was interviewed on a large variety of topics in the June 1988 *New Humanist*.

Hosh, John A. (20th Century)

Hosh has reviewed books, such as L. Sprague de Camp's *The Ape-Man Within* (1995) for *Humanist in Canada* (Spring, 1997).

Hosken, Fran (1919—)

Hosken, the founder, editor, and publisher of *Women's International Network News*, is an architect and planner. She is author of *The Function of Cities*, the *International Directory of Women's Development Organizations*, and *The Hosken Report: Genital/Sexual Mutilation of Females*. In 1987 she was honored by the Feminist Caucus of the American Humanist Association with the Humanist Heroine Award.

"Women around the world are uniting on their own issues and demanding to be heard on their own rights," she has written. Times are changing . . . in the greatest of social revolutions: the revolution for women's rights—women, who are still the largest and most oppressed majority in literally all societies." {HNS2}

Hosking, Marion Rosslyn (1926—)

Hosking is an Australian atheist, humanist, and community activist. She joined the Humanist Society of New South Wales in 1964, was a committee member from 1970 to 1975 and secretary until 1980, also edited their *Viewpoints* from 1972 to 1975. She has written articles on marijuana, domestic violence, and prostitution. Hosking describes the Humanist Society as a "catalyst for atheism to be involved in social issues."

Hoskins, Warren S. (20th Century)

When he signed Humanist Manifesto II, Hoskins was a humanist counselor. {HM2}

Hosmer, Frederick Lucian (1840—1929)

Hosmer, a Unitarian, was both a minister and a writer of hymns. He wrote *The Way of Life* (1877). {U}

Hosmer, Harriet (1830—1908)

Hosmer, daughter of Hiram Hosmer, a physician, and a member of a prominent Unitarian family, developed an interest in art after being taken to Rome by her father. A friend of Fanny Kemble and Elizabeth Browning, Hosmer became a sculptor who competed, but lost the competition, to create a monument for the grave of Abraham Lincoln. She did, however, create the monument for the grave of Edward Everett. When she studied and worked in Italy, Henry James described her as one of "that strange sisterhood of American lady sculptors who at one time settled upon the seven hills [of Rome] in a white marmorean flock." Among her visitors were Nathaniel and Sophia Hawthorne, and Hosmer may have been one of the artists depicted in Hawthorne's *The Marble Faun*. A Hosmer statue of Thomas Hart Benton stands in Lafayette Park, St. Louis, Missouri. {Jane Backstrom, "A Marmorean Flock," *The World*, January-February 1994; EG}

Hosmer, J. E. (19th Century)

Hosmer in 1896 founded the *Torch of Reason* in Silverton, Oregon, then moved it to Kansas City.

Hospers, John (1918—)

When he reviewed books for *The Humanist*, Hospers was in the department of philosophy at Brooklyn College. He later became director of the School of Philosophy at the University of Southern California. Hospers wrote *Meaning and Truth in the Arts* (1946), *Human Conduct* (1961), *Libertarianism* (1971), *Understanding the Arts* (1982, and numerous articles in the field of aesthetics. Hospers, a major supporter of Ayn Rand, edited *The Monist*.

Hossain, Ranjana (20th Century)

Hossain, Executive Director of the Assembly of Freethinkers in Dhaka, Bangladesh, participated in a panel on human rights at the 1996 Humanist World Congress in Mexico City. His E-mail address: <randhaka@usia.gov>.

Hostetler, John Andrew (1918—)

Hostetler is author of *Amish Society* (1963) and, in 1996, *Hutterites in North America*.

HOSTILITY

• The hostility to homosexuals has far more in common with anti-Semitism than it does with racism. Homosexuals, like Jews, are not, in the psychology of group hatred, despised because they are deemed to be weak or inferior, but precisely because they are neither. Jews and homosexuals appear in the hater's mind as small, cliquish, and very powerful groups, antipathetic to majority values, harboring secret contempt for the rest of society and sustaining a ghetto code of furtiveness and disguise. Even the details resonate. The old libel against Jews—that they would drink the blood of Christian children—has an echo today in the bigot's insistence that he has nothing against homosexuals per se, but doesn't want them allowed near his kids. The loathing for each group is closely linked to fear—and the fear is fanned, in many ways, by the distortion of a particular strain in Christian theology.

—Andrew Sullivan, a Catholic and senior editor at *The New Republic*

Hostos (y Bonilla), Eugenio Maria de (1839—1903)

Born in Puerto Rico, Hostos publicized the cause of Cuban independence. He taught in Chile, promoted education in Venezuela and the Dominican Republic, and was active in the movement for Puerto Rican independence (1898—1900). Virtues such as social tolerance and respect for others are central to his moral philosophy. In his *Moral Social* (Santo Domingo, 1888), he saw no necessary dichotomy between the concepts of individual good and social good. Rejecting the notion that man's intuitive or animal nature is inherently evil and in need of suppression by reason and will, Hostos held that man's rational, social, and individual aspects are indissolubly linked. His optimism, love of freedom, and respect and tolerance for opposing belief systems and diverse cultures were indicative of his abiding humanism. {CE}

Houdini, Harry (Erich Weiss) (1874—1926) Houdini was able to escape from bonds of every sort—handcuffs, straitjackets, locks, sealed chests under water, and organized religion. He also exposed fraudulent spiritualistic mediums and their phenomena, leaving to the Library of Congress his extensive library of magic.

Born Erich Weiss in Hungary, he adopted in New York the stage name Houdini, after Robert Houdin, a Frenchman often touted as the father of modern stage magic. Possibly because of his teen-aged rope-ties, he got his first job in a New York City necktie factory, then worked in vaudeville along with George the Turtle Boy, Myrtle Corbett the four-legged woman, and the original Siamese twins. With his wife, Bess, he perfected a famed "Metamorphosis" miracle in which, tied inside a sack with his hands bound behind his back, he was locked into a wooden trunk. Bess stood atop the trunk, hidden by a screen. But at the count of three when the screen was removed, Harry was standing on the trunk, the trunk was unlocked, and now inside the sack Bess was found, her hands bound behind her back. In 1900, he toured Europe, creating sensations by going to police stations (including Scotland Yard), challenging the police to lock him up, and escaping. Returning to New York after becoming Europe's best-known vaudeville attraction, Houdini even taught his fox terrier, Bobby, to escape from dogsized handcuffs and straitjackets. At the Hippodrome in 1918, he put a 10,000 pound elephant and Jennie her trainer into a wooden cabinet. Then, upon the firing of a pistol, both elephant and trainer had disappeared. "How on earth did he do it!" the crowds exclaimed.

A freethinker (although not an outspoken one) whose father had been a rabbi, Houdini wrote *The Unmasking of Robert-Houdin* (1908), *Miracle Mongers and Their Methods* (1920), and *A Magician Among the Spirits* (1924). *The Life and Many Deaths of Harry Houdini* (1993) by Ruth Brandon examines some of the magician's motivations and tells of his pettiness in trying to destroy all imagined and real rivals.

Contrary to popular belief, he had not died in one of his acts. Rather, while lecturing on spiritualistic tricks and his physical prowess, Houdini was given a hard blow to the appendix by a McGill University student named Whitehead and died as the result of complications resulting from an operation on his appendix. Whitehead had come to Houdini's dressing room to return a book and, after asking Houdini his opinion of biblical miracles, found that the magician declined to comment. Whitehead then asked Houdini if it was true he was in such good condition that he could withstand the hardest blows to the abdomen. Although he had fractured an ankle in the Water Torture Cell and was backstage resting his leg and posing for a portrait when Whitehead appeared, he stalled, then agreed to letting the student punch him a few times. The blows were shockingly low and to the right of the navel. To date, no one has been able to find any place where Houdini had bragged that he was that fit, nor is it clear why the student challenged him in such a way. Some skeptics even doubt the medical connection between a punch to the stomach and a ruptured appendix.

Just before he died, the infection in his bloodstream having caused irreversible damage, he held his wife's hand and told her that if he could possibly speak to her from the spirit world he would use the words "Rosabelle" and "Believe." He died on Halloween and, naturally, has not been heard from since.

His will included a bequest of $1,000 to the Society of American Magicians. It also has a codicil in which he canceled "the codicil giving my Spiritualistic library to the American Society of Psychic Research, the entire collection is to go with my Magical Library to the Congressional Library in Washington. The reason I object giving my Spiritualistic library to the American Society of Psychical Research is because I object to a dishonorable person like J. Malcolm Bird being connected with any reputable organization." Apparently Houdini thought he might come back from the dead, or perhaps he just enjoyed such publicity. His will directed that his body "be embalmed and buried in the same manner in which my beloved mother was buried upon her death, and that my grave be constructed in a vault in the same manner as my beloved mother's last resting place was constructed for her burial; and I also direct that I shall be buried in the grave immediately alongside of that of my dear departed mother."

Freud, who outlived Houdini by over a dozen years, is not known to have commented upon Houdini's burial wish, which included having his head cradled on a small bag of letters from his beloved mother. The coffin was made of bronze, not of wood such as used in Jewish burials.

On Halloween evenings, some members of the Society of American Magicians continue to re-enact the wand-breaking ceremony at his gravesite in the Machpelah Cemetery on Cypress Hills Street in Glendale, Queens. That ceremony had been a part of his funeral service in 1926. In 1994, to keep vandals away, the tradition—which had turned into a Jewish kaddish—was stopped by cemetery officials. However, no one today believes Houdini will ever get out of his coffin, as he had done in 1925 after being submerged in a metal box for an hour and a half at the Hotel Shelton swimming pool, 527 Lexington Avenue, New York City. {CE; *New Republic*, 17 February 1997; Anthony W. Robins, "Touring Houdini's New York, *The New York Times*, 28 October 1994; Teller, *The New York Times Book Review*, 15 December 1996}

Houf, Horace T. (20th Century)

Houf, a humanist who taught philosophy at Ohio University, wrote, "For men to retain the *ardor* of the historic religions and to direct this toward social welfare rather than toward the supernatural is the great desideratum."

Houghton (Arthur Leslie Noel Douglas Houghton) [Lord of Sowerby] (1898—1996)

A Parliamentarian and humanist, Douglas Houghton was active in the House of Lords and was a leading member of the Parliamentary Humanist Group. Son of a Methodist mother and a rationalist father, he attended Sunday school and learned early on that rituals "were the mumbo jumbo and symbolic gestures which kept religion going when faith had gone." Upon becoming Baron Houghton of Sowerby in 1974, he announced, "I am free as a bird to pursue the issues that I care about." Those issues included reform of the constitution, population and development, the House of Lords Industry Study Group, and teachers' pay, on which he chaired the 1974 inquiry. His interests also included animal rights.

In 1986 he was elected an honorary associate of the Rationalist Press Association, and although a Lord he "dared" to be an Honorary Associate of the National Secular Society. His wife, **Vera Houghton**, was also a rationalist. In his insistence that religious education is the duty of the churches, not the state, he remarked to the House of Lords, "I am mystified about the approach of so many Members of the Committee to this subject. Surely what we want is not a transient belief in some mystical concept of god from children who cannot comprehend it and who leave school with no more sense of what their behaviour or accountability to parent and society should be than they knew before."

Upon his death, Madeleine Simms wrote (*The Guardian*, 6 May 1996):

> The greatest of Douglas Houghton's many achievements in the minds of many of us will be the impetus he gave to the passing of the 1967 Abortion Act, the most important measure affecting the health and welfare of women since the passing of the National Health Service legislation. He was actively associated with this cause from the time he entered Parliament in 1949, and in 1962 he was one of only 29 parliamentary supporters of Joseph Reves, who unsuccessfully introduced the first Bill on this subject to much abuse from the religious fundamentalist lobby. In 1960 he gave active support to Kenneth Robinson, who tried to introduce a similar Bill which was also talked out by a group of Roman Catholic MPs. During this time, his wife Vera was Chairman of the Abortion Law Reform Association, and together they made a remarkable and tireless team which earned the admiration of Lord Silkin and Sir David Steel and all who were subsequently associated with this then unfashionable cause. Lord Houghton's life and work on behalf of women over half a century shows how very much more important it is to have feminists in Parliament, rather than just women.

{*The Freethinker*, June 1996; *New Humanist*, June 1996; TRI}

Hourani, George (1913—1984)

Hourani, a secular humanist, was professor of philosophy at the State University of New York at Buffalo. He wrote *Ethical Value* (1956), *Averroës on the Harmony of Religion and Philosophy* (1961), and edited *Essays in Islamic Philosophy and Science* (1975). {SHD}

HOURIS

> • Houri, n. A comely female inhabiting the Mohammedan Paradise to make things cheery for the good Mussulman, whose belief in her existence marks a noble discontent with his earthly spouse, whom he denies a soul. By the good lady the Houris are said to be held in deficient esteem.
>
> **—Ambrose Bierce**
> *The Devil's Dictionary*

Hoursi are voluptuous and alluring virgins in the Islamic paradise. Antony Flew has suggested that "any man who fears that even as an everlasting thirty-year-old he would not be able to do justice to the attractions of this eschatological brothel may be encouraged to learn that 'A man in Paradise shall be given virility equal to that of one hundred men.' "

Housman, A(lfred) E(dward) (1859—1936)

Corliss Lamont stated that Housman, like Hardy, was "disposed to a sombre and disillusioned Humanism." Housman wrote *A Shropshire Lad* and other verse. Housman's most characteristic theme is the passing of youth and the inevitability of death. Three of his works are "To an Athlete Dying Young," "When I Was One-and-twenty," and "With Rue My Heart Is Laden." Secular humanists like to quote "The Final Word" from his *Shropshire Lad*:

> Now—for a breath I tarry
> Nor yet disperse apart—
> Take my hand quick and tell me
> What you have in your heart.
>
> Speak now, and I will answer:
> How shall I help you, say;
> Ere to the wind's twelve quarters
> I take my endless way.

Housman's humor included

> When I was born into a world of sin
> Praise be to God it was raining gin.

and

> It is a fearful thing to be The Pope.
> That cross will not be laid on me, I hope.

Leigh W. Rutledge's *Fireside Companion* claims that on his deathbed Housman, when he was told a dirty joke by his physician, had replied, "Yes, that's a good one, and tomorrow I shall be telling it again on the Golden Floor."

When a memorial window was unveiled in an Abbey chapel by his pupil Enoch Powell, Alan Bostridge sang lyrics from "A Shropshire Lad" and Alan Bennett gave the address. John Ezard (*The Guardian*, 18 September 1996), wrote that the Abbey chaplain, the Rev. Jonathan Goodall, "had problems in finding anything suitably Christian to say about the author." Ezard added that Housman was "one of the bitterest God-haters to wield a pen." {CE; CL; GL; *Freethinker*, November 1996; TRI; TYD}

Housman, Laurence (1865—1959)

Housman wrote *Gods and Their Makers* (1897) and *The Religious Advance Toward Rationalism* (1929). It is a vague theism or pantheism, not based upon philosophy, and it contains an ethical admiration of Christianity not based upon history. McCabe labels A. E. Housman's brother only a "mild" rationalist. {RE; TRI}

Houston, George (19th Century)

After being imprisoned for two years in England for having translated d'Holbach's *Ecce Homo*, Houston fled to New York, where he edited the *Minerva*, reprinted his book, and started a freethought journal, *The Correspondent*. Wheeler cites that publication as "the first weekly Freethought journal published in America." However, it lasted only eighteen months (1827—1829). {BDF; FUS; JMR}

Houten, Samuel van (1837-1930)

A Dutch freethinker, Houten in 1869 was chosen a member of parliament. He wrote many works on political economy, and he wrote *Das Causalitatyesatz* (The Law of Causality). His rationalism is expressed in *Bijdragen tot den strijt over God, eigendom, en familie* (1878). {BDF; RAT}

Houtin, Albert (20th Century)

A freethinker, Houtin wrote *A Short History of Christianity* (1926). A rationalist, he was a librarian in Paris. {GS; RAT}

Hovelacque, Abel (Born 1843)

Hovelacque was a French scientist who wrote for Broca's *Revue d'Anthropologie*. With Letourneau, Thulié, and Asseline, Hovelacque founded the *Bibliothèque des sciences contemporains* and published therein *La Linguistique*. With G. Hervé he made a study of the *Negroes of Africa*. Hovelacque published choice extracts from the works of Voltaire, Diderot, and Rousseau, a grammar of the Zend language, and a work on the *Avesta Zoroaster and Mazdaism*. {BDF; RAT}

Howard, Bernard (20th Century)

Howard, professor emeritus in biochemistry at Lincoln University, is secretary of the New Zealand Skeptics. He is an honorary associate of the New Zealand Association of Rationalists and Humanists.

Howdon, John (19th Century)

Howden wrote *A Rational Investigation of the Principles of Natural Philosophy, Physical and Moral* (1840), in which he attacks belief in the Bible. {BDF}

Howe, Charles A. (1922—)

Howe's *The Larger Faith* (1993) is a brief history of the Universalist movement. He edited "Not Hell, But Hope," The John Murray Distinguished Lectures, 1987—1991, which are transcripts of lectures on important Universalists.

Howe, Daniel Walker (1937—)

Howe, a historian and educator, wrote *The Unitarian Conscience* (1987), a study of moral philosophy taught at Harvard and how it influenced Unitarians from 1805 to 1861. He also wrote *Victorian America* (1976) and *The Political Culture of the American Whigs* (1979). Howe is an Episcopalian.

Howe, Edgar Watson (1853—1937)

An American editor, Howe edited the *Globe* and the *Atchison Daily Globe*. He has written, "Religion is like an oil well—a promise of great happiness and prosperity *in the future*. But our problems are not in the future; they are of today." {RAT}

Howe, Irving (1920—1993)

A leading American literary and social critic, Howe was a Trotskyist who wrote for publications such as *The Partisan Review, The New Republic*, and *The New York Review of Books*. His works include *William Faulkner: A Critical Study* (1952), *Socialism and America* (1985), and an autobiography, *A Margin of Hope* (1982). He was known as one of the second generation of "New York intellectuals": with Saul Bellow, Leslie Fiedler, Elizabeth Hardwick, Richard Chase, William Barrett, Daniel Bell, Hannah Arendt, Isaac Rosefeld. The first generation had included Lionel Trilling, Diana Trilling, Philip Rahv, Alfred Kazin, Delmore Schwartz, William Phillips, Clement Greenberg, Harold Rosenberg, Dwight Macdonald, Mary McCarthy, F. W. Dupee, Paul Goodman, and Lionel Abel. In the 1950s a third generation, which had been influenced by Howe and the others, included Susan Sontag, Stephen Marcus, Norman Podhoretz, and Hilton Kramer. Howe in 1954 co-edited *A Treasury of Yiddish Stories*, works which emphasized human affirmation rather than religion.

York University's S. A. Longstaff has written about Howe's interest in modernism:

> Literary modernism had a way of cavalierly dismissing both liberal values and the world of daily existence that made several New York writers especially uneasy in their former allegiance. Modernism stood indicted, then, both because of the illiberalism of its pioneers (W. B. Yeats, Ezra Pound, Eliot, etc. al.) and because of the glib nihilism and apocalypticism of its post-1945 epigones. But its cardinal liability, Trilling, Bell, Howe, and even Sontag (*On Photograph*) all suggested in their different ways, was the divorce it posited between mind and external reality. This "disruption of *mimesis*" not only marginalized and depoliticized literature, it ruled out the notion of shared historical experience. With the ascendancy, in the 1980s, of semiotics, deconstruction, and other forms of textually centered rejections of high art and the authorial self, these warnings about the eclipse of narrative mimesis and the "cultural criticism" logical to it resonated widely among academic traditionalists. Indeed, the very careers of Howe, Bell, Trilling, Kazin, Dwight Macdonald, and other New York intellectuals took on a kind of emblematic significance in the 1980s.

Howe, asked about humanism, responded to the present author,

> I do not think I really know what the word *humanism* means any more. I doubt that it means anything but some vague aspirations to undefined goals. I am a socialist and believe that until we have a humane society all talk about humanism will help us very little. If I had the time at present, I would try to discover what humanism or any of its branches that you note are supposed to refer to; but since I don't have the time and since I am bored with all the vague talk about "moral values" and "human values," never specified or instances, I must regretfully ask to be excused from the symposium.

In religion, however, Howe clearly was a doubter as shown in his various works. {CE; JHG; WAS, 23 February 1951}

Howe, Julia Ward (1819—1910)

Author of the words to "The Battle Hymn of the Republic,"

Howe lectured and supported education and business opportunities for women. She edited the Boston *Commonwealth*, an abolitionist paper, and wrote about Negro emancipation and the need for a world peace organization. Howe, the first female to be elected to the American Academy of Arts and Letters, was "not so much a woman as a national institution," Malcolm Cowley explained later. Asked once what the ideal aim of life is, she had replied, "To learn, to teach, to serve, to enjoy."

A Unitarian, Howe gave many sermons before Unitarian audiences, and she was president of the Woman Preachers' Convention. She was the mother of Laura E. Richards and the wife of Samuel Gridley Howe, founder of the Perkins School for the Blind. Even when she was in her nineties, Howe "read Greek and Italian that she might not fall into intellectual laziness." {CE; EG; U; U&U; UU}

Howe, Norma (20th Century)

The author of books for young adults, Howe has written *God, the Universe, and Hot Fudge Sundaes* (1984), a work which book-banners cite as pushing "several items of the humanist agenda: death education, anti-God, pro-evolution, anti-Bible, anti-Christian, and logic over faith."

In "Peer Pressure and Children's Religious Belief" (*Free Inquiry*, Summer 1994), Howe writes that secular humanist parents "should have no qualms about allowing their children to join their friends as they worship so long as they have prepared the youngsters beforehand in several ways, the most important of which is equipping them with that indispensable tool—the skill of critical thinking."

Howe, Samuel Gridley (1801—1876)

Howe, an American reformer and philanthropist, was organizer of the New England Asylum for the Blind (later to be called the Perkins Institution), which he headed for forty-four years and which achieved much success in improving the education of the handicapped. Howe supported Dorothea Dix in her work for the insane and approved Horace Mann's educational reforms. A Unitarian as was his wife, Julia Ward Howe, he opposed slavery. {CE; EG; U}

Howell, Constance (19th Century)

Howell wrote *A Biography of Jesus Christ, Written for Young Freethinkers* (188—?). {GS}

Howell, Philip (20th Century)

Howell in Britain is active with the Norwich Humanist Group.

Howells, William Dean (1837—1920)

Novelist, critic, and editor, Howells championed literary realism. For fifteen years he was associated with the *Atlantic Monthly*, and from 1900 to 1920 he was noted for his column, "Easy Chair," in *Harper's Magazine*. He wrote a utopian work, *A Traveler from Altruria* (1894), but the novels for which he gained the most recognition were *A Modern Instance* (1882) and *The Rise of Silas Lapham* (1885). His *A Foregone Conclusion* (1875) depicted the agnosticism of a character called Ippolito in a time when fiction ordinarily avoided such a subject. His *Leatherwood God* (1916) features a frontier evangelist who considers himself a god.

A theistic Unitarian who had been brought up a Swedenborgian, Howells was one of the most highly regarded authors of his time. To his agnostic friend Parton, Howells said that there came into his life a new light "by which I saw all things that somehow did not tell for human brotherhood dwarfish and ugly." He was one of the original members of the American Academy, receiving more votes on the first secret ballot than Mark Twain and Henry James. {CE; JM; RAT; RE; TRI; U}

Howgate, Michael E. (20th Century)

Howgate, founder of London Student Skeptics, spoke at the 1994 annual dinner of the National Secular Society. A former Catholic, he became an unbeliever at the age of seventeen and an atheist at the age of nineteen. He has written for *The Freethinker* and is the founder-member of the Association for the Protection of Evolution (APE). Howgate is a director of the National Secular Society.

Howitt, William (1792—1879)

Howitt, a freethinker, wrote *History of Priestcraft in All Ages and Nations* (1855). {GS}

Howland, Arthur (20th Century)

Howland wrote *Joseph Lewis, Enemy of God* (1932). {FUS}

Howlett, Duncan (1906—)

Howlett is minister emeritus of All Souls Unitarian Church in Washington, DC. He served also in New Bedford and Boston, Massachusetts. From 1962—1965, he was chairman of the District of Columbia advisory committee to the U.S. Commission on Civil Rights, and he served on other District of Columbia commissions, including in 1962—1965 the Crime Commission. He was on the campaign staff in 1968 for Hubert Humphrey. Howlett is author of *Man Against the Church* (1954); *The Essenes and Christianity* (1957); *The Fourth American Faith* (1964); *The Critical Way in Religion* (1980); and *The Fatal Flaw: At the Heart of Liberal Religion* (1995). In the latter work, he notes that religious liberals have never achieved their goal, and he holds that this is because they come to a point at which they cease asking questions. Then, reaching out for new concepts, they return to the old dogmatic pattern of belief by faith. Howlett suggests that the failure of liberals to eliminate this contradiction from the new thought structure they sought to build has ultimately destroyed the movement, and he calls for a new struggle by religious liberals. In 1994 Howlett received the Award for Distinguished Service to the Cause of Liberal Religion by the Unitarian-Universalists. {FUS}

Hoyle, Fred [Sir] (1915—)

Hoyle, the distinguished mathematician and astronomer, was elected an honorary associate of the Rationalist Press Association in 1950. In 1948 with Hermann Bondi and Thomas Gold, he propounded the "steady state" theory of the universe. His work includes *Frontiers of Astronomy* (1955) and a science fiction novel, *The Black Cloud* (1957).

A 1994 autobiography, *Home Is Where the Wind Blows—Chapters of a Cosmologist's Life*, tells of his boyhood in Yorkshire and his scientific work concerning the origins of the nuclei of atoms. Hoyle led the Institute of Theoretical Astronomy in Cambridge, but in 1972 after problems with the administration he resigned.

In some parts of his autobiography, Hoyle states that the universe may well be the result of some intelligent design and that he regrets that such a view is not acceptable in a scientific journal. But he also appears to suggest that the universe might just as well *not* so be designed.

"Religion," he declared in *The Nature of the Universe* (1950), "is but a desperate attempt to find an escape from the truly dreadful situation in which we find ourselves. Here we are in this wholly fantastic universe with scarcely a clue as to whether our existence has any real significance. No wonder then that many people feel the need for some belief that gives them a sense of security, and no wonder that they become very angry with people like me who say that this is illusory." {CE; TYD}

Hoyne, James (20th Century)

Hoyne works with Walk Away, a group which supports recovering fundamentalists. (See entry for Colorado Humanists.) {FD}

Hruska, Roman Lee [Senator] (20th Century)

Hruska, who was the U. S. Senator from Nebraska, was a Unitarian.

Hsiung, Shih I. (1902—1996?)

In 1943, Hsiung was elected an honorary associate of the Rationalist Press Association. He has translated George Bernard Shaw, Barrie, Hardy, and Benjamin Franklin into Chinese. Also, he has written many books in English, including *Chinese Proverbs* (1952) and *Lady on the Roof* (1959).

Hsün-tzu (298—238 B.C.E.)

Said to be the most noted of the atheistic Chinese scholars, Hsün-tzu was against superstitious practices such as giving attention to magic and prayers as well as believing in omens and good luck. McInnis in the *Encyclopedia of Unbelief* surveys his views, as well as those of K'ung Fu-Tzu, Wang Chong, and other Chinese unbelievers. {EU, Donald MacInnis}

HTTP: See entry for Ted Nelson.

Hu Shih (1891—1962)

Hu Shih was ambassador to the United States (1938—1942) and chancellor of Peking University (1946—1948). A Chinese philosopher in Republican China, he observed, "In a sense, philosophers *are* kings. Kings reign only a short time, but philosophers sometimes rule the mind and the destiny of mankind for ages." Hu was influenced by the writings of Julian Huxley and John Dewey.

Hubbard, Alice (1874—1915)

Hubbard, an American writer, was married to Elbert Hubbard. Among her books is *An American Bible* (1911), in which she says of her husband:

> Content to live in one world at a time, he has the genuine faith which does not peep into the Unknown, but lives to the full to-day, assured that the power which cares for us here will not desert us there.

The Hubbards went down on the *Lusitania* when it was sunk 7 May 1915 off the Irish coast by a German submarine. {RAT; WWS}

Hubbard, Elbert (1856—1915)

A popular American author and publisher, Hubbard edited *Philistine*, a magazine which encouraged rugged individualism. Hubbard penned many barbs about organized religion, including the following:

- The clergy take theirs now—you get yours after you are dead.
- Who are those who will eventually be damned? Oh, the others, the others, the others.
- Heaven: The Coney Island of the Christian imagination.
- God: The John Doe of philosophy and religion.
- Miracle: An event described by those to whom it was told by men who did not see it.
- Christianity supplies a Hell for the people who disagree with you, and a Heaven for your friends.
- A good man in an exclusive heaven would be in hell.
- Theology is an attempt to explain a subject by men who do not understand it. The intent is not to tell the truth but to satisfy the questioner.
- A mystic is a person who is puzzled before the obvious, but who understands the nonexistent.
- Theology is Classified Superstition.
- Theology is voodooism; in matters of importance it is in the class with alchemy, astrology, palmistry, augury, and allopath medicine.

Hubbard wrote *The Philosophy of Elbert Hubbard* (1916). He and his wife were drowned on the *Lusitania*, which was sunk in 1915 by a German submarine in the Irish Sea. {CE; FUS; TYD}

Hubbard, L. Ron (1911—1986)

Hubbard wrote *Dianetics: The Modern Science of Mental Health* (1950), a work which led to the establishment of a sect called the Church of Scientology. Freethinkers generally consider the group a cult fueled by charging large amounts of money for its services and marvel that seemingly intelligent individuals join up. Or, as observed by critic John Leonard, Hubbard was just another second-rate sci-fi novelist who made a bundle when he started a religion. {*The Nation*, 15-22 June 1998}

Hubbell, C. Lee (20th Century)

Hubbell, an associate editor of *The American Rationalist*, signs his work "Rev. C. Lee Hubbell." His coinage for god beliefs is "godianity." *American Rationalist* (September-October 1990) published his "Scientists' Think-Tanks on God." {EU, Eldon Scholl}

Hubble, Edwin Powell (1889—1953)

An American astronomer born in Marshfield, Missouri, Hubble was the first to offer observational evidence to support the theory of the expanding universe, presenting his findings in what is now known as Hubble's Law. Not only is the universe bigger than anyone had thought but also it is getting bigger all the time, he showed. With Milton Humason, Hubble classified the different types of galaxies including irregular galaxies, three types of spirals and barred spirals, and elliptical galaxies. This he accomplished at a time when Heaven was believed by religionists to be "up" and Hell "down."

Astronomers in 1994, using the Hubble Space Telescope named after him, announced that they had found conclusive evidence for the existence of an extraordinarily powerful black hole in the center of the giant elliptical galaxy M87, which is 50,000,000 light-years away in the constellation Virgo. "This attractive force of collapses matter," reported John Noble Wilford in *The New York Times* (26 May 1994), "weighs as much as three billion Suns but is concentrated in a space no larger than the solar system. The discovery appeared to lay to rest any remaining skepticism about black holes, predicted by Einstein as part of his general theory of relativity. Over the last three decades, they were the ultimate goal of astrophysics, objects searched for with zeal but seemingly forever out of reach. While scientists theorized and searched, the concept became so widely intriguing and expressive that it crossed into popular culture. The very term black hole has entered everyday language as an all-purpose metaphor."

The Hubble telescope's findings indicate that the universe is from eight to twelve billion years old, leading scientists to speculate whether the Big Bang occurred eight or sixteen billion or even thirty-two billion years ago. Most now hold that the Earth is 4,500,000,000+ years old. Tomorrow's newspaper, complete with new astronomical findings, often revises such figures. (Gale E. Christianson's *Edwin Hubble, Mariner of the Nebulae* (1995) is a biography which describes Hubble as a cosmic egoist.) {CE}

Hubenák, Ladislav (20th Century)

Hubenák is a Slovakian humanist who is prominent in the Prometheus Society. (See entry for Slovak Humanists.)

Huber, Marie (1694—1753)

Huber was a Swiss deist born of Protestant parents. In her *System of* (1731), she opposed the dogma of eternal punishment. {BDF; RAT}

Huber, Mark W. (20th Century)

When he signed Humanist Manifesto II, Huber was a director of the American Ethical Union. {HM2}

Hudson, J. William (20th Century)

Hudson, a freethinker, wrote *The Old Faiths Perish* (1939). {GS}

Hudson, William Henry (1694—1753)

Hudson was private secretary to Herbert Spencer (1885 to 1889), a librarian at Cornell University (1890-1892), and professor of English literature at Leland Stanford University (1892—1901). He wrote, besides other works, *An Introduction to the Study of Herbert Spencer* (1894), *Studies in Interpretation* (1896), and *Rousseau and Naturalism in Life and Thought* (1903). Hudson shared Spencer's agnosticism. {RAT}

Hueffer, Francis (1845—1889)

A music critic, Hueffer was a Wagnerite and an editor of *New Quarterly Magazine*. A friend of W. M. Rossetti, Hueffer was equally rationalistic. {RAT}

Hueffer, Ford Madox (Born 1873)

Hueffer, son of Francis Hueffer and grandson of Ford Madox Brown, wrote a number of novels, poems, and literary works. In *Life of Madox Brown* (1896), he sympathetically records his grandfather's rationalism. {RAT}

Huerta, Victoriana [General] (1854—1916)

Huerta, a Mexican Indian soldier and at one time Provisional President of Mexico, was a thorough skeptic and anti-clerical. {JM; RAT}

Huet, Coenraad Busken (1826—1887)

A Dutch writer, Huet became minister of the Walloon Church at Haarlem but, through his freethinking, left the church in 1863 and became editor of various newspapers, afterwards living in Paris. Huet wrote *Letters on the Bible* (1857). {BDF; FUK; RAT}

Huett, Richard (20th Century)

Huett, a former editor-in-chief of the Dell Publishing Company, has written about the weaknesses of "creation science" in *Free Inquiry* (Winter, 1993).

Hugh, Frank C. (20th Century)

Hugh, a freethinker, wrote *Hell and Amen, the Voice of the Bad Lands* (1940). {GS}

Hugh, Lynn Harold: See the entry for Theism.

Hughes, Clovis (Born 1850)

Hughes was a French socialist, poet, and deputy. As a youth he had desired to become a priest, notes Wheeler, "but under the influence of Hugo left the black business." In 1871 he became head of the Communist movement at Marseilles, where he was sentenced to three years in prison. In 1881 he was elected deputy. {BDF}

Hughes, Frank (20th Century)

Hughes is author of a satire, *Letters and Essays of the Pope* (1953).

Hughes, Howard (20th Century)

Hughes, a professor who lectures at Manchester's Metropolitan University, represented the Gay and Lesbian Humanist Association at a 1999 meeting of England's Lesbian, Gay, and Bisexual Consortium.

Hughes, John (20th Century)

Hughes, a humanist activist in Sheffield, England, wrote "Who Has the Last Laugh When It Comes to religion" (*The Freethinker*, November-December 1998). The Old Testament, he found, is devoid of humor, God or Jehovah or Allah are entirely humorless, and humanists would do well to stay away from holy scripture because "it's no laughing matter."

Hughes, Langston (1902—1967)

A major figure in the Harlem Renaissance, Hughes was the son of a white father and a black mother, a mix of French, Indian, and African blood. He was discovered as a poet by Vachel Lindsay in 1925. During his career, which Arnold Rampersad has thoroughly detailed in a two-volume biography, *The Life of Langston Hughes* (Vol. 1, 1986; Vol. 2, 1988), Hughes traveled from one problem to the next, always with insufficient money, always finding that being an African American brought him problems, always being confronted with criticism for what he said and wrote, even being investigated by the Federal Bureau of Investigation.

Asked to go on record concerning humanism, Hughes informed his protégé, Gilbert Price, that he hesitated to respond (just as both avoided answering if they had enjoyed sharing a single bed while the two were on tour in Puerto Rico; they had, confided Price, to avoid having to pay for a double room, money always being a problem). Price, who had starred in his "Jericho-Jim Crow," was a baritone who enjoyed singing "At The Fcct of Jesus," with lyrics by Hughes. The song had been inspired, Hughes explained, by his childhood background.

Price, himself a Catholic, was unconvinced that Hughes was a trinitarian. So he asked Hughes to go on record for a friend, his personal agent whom Hughes knew, the present author, who was writing about the subject. But Senator McCarthy in 1950 had been looking for atheistic communists in the State Department, Price was told, and one had to be careful about going on record.

Hughes had written favorably about his travels to the USSR in the 1930s. He was attacked for a poem such as "Goodbye Christ," which includes

> Christ Jesus Lord God Jehova
> Beat it on away from here now
> Make way for a new guy with no religion at all—
> A real guy named
> Marx Communist Lenin Peasant Stalin Worker ME—
> I said, ME!

Years later, he apologized, saying the work was an error of immaturity. Also, Hughes did not have the resources, the support, or even the inclination that would be needed to fight the McCarthy Un-American Activities Committee.

Because of Price's request, Hughes in 1951 with understandable caution agreed only to write the following for the present author—privately, he told Price he was not a believer but admired Price's being one.

> Since I never was much of a student of philosophy (perhaps one should say in the academic sense), I am not quite sure what the difference is between the various humanisms you mention.
>
> My only suggestion would be that perhaps you might be able to garner something from my autobiography, *The Big Sea* (Alfred A. Knopf, Inc.), in which I tell how I write and how I feel about many things. Or see my poems.

In that 1940 book, Hughes has a story, "Salvation," which starts, "I was saved from sin when I was going on thirteen. But not really saved." He then describes how at a big religious revival at his Auntie Reed's church it came time "to bring the young lambs to the fold."

He had been forewarned that when you are saved you see a light and something happens to you inside and Jesus comes into your life. He and his friend Wesley endured the experience of waiting and finally Wesley whispered, 'God damn! I'm tired o' sitting here. Let's get up and be saved.' " So he got up and was saved. Langston, however, just sat because he saw no light and he could not see Jesus. Finally, he succumbed, and joyous singing filled the room while the new young lambs were blessed in the name of God.

The twelve-year-old cried that night, not because the Holy Ghost had come into his life, as his family was saying—he cried because he had lied, that he had not seen Jesus, that he didn't believe there was a Jesus any more since he didn't come to help.

Hughes wrote of illegitimacy, pimps, number-runners, alcohol, marijuana, and white folks.

> Pull at the rope!
> O, pull it high!
> Let the white folks live
> And the black boy die.
>
> Pull it, boys,
> With a bloody cry.
> Let the black boy spin
> While the white folks die.
>
> *The white folks die?*
> *What do you mean—*
> *The white folks die?*
>
> That black boy's
> Still body Says
> NOT I.

. . . and the Red Cross, which in 1943, had segregated blood donations . . .

> The Angel of Mercy's
> Got her wings in the mud,
> And all because of
> Negro blood.

. . . and hypocrisy . . .

> Detectives from the vice squad
> with weary sadistic eyes
> spotting fairies.
> *Degenerates*
> some folks say.
>
> But God, Nature,
> or somebody
> made them that way.
>
> Police lady or Lesbian
> over there?
> *Where?*

. . . and racism. . .

> My old mule,
> He's got a grin on his face.
> He's been a mule so long
> He's forgot about his race.
>
> I'm like that old mule—
> Black—and don't give a damn!
> You got to take me
> Like I am.

As for a will, Hughes decided that "one might as well have a little fun at one's own finalization," so the poet who believed in no afterlife, that after death one is nowhere, wrote a legal document asking that there be no public display of his body, that there be a swift cremation, and that the memorial service must consist "entirely of music," with no speaking whatsoever. Songs he suggested were "Precious Lord, Take My Hand" by Thomas Dorsey; "Nothing But a Plain Black Boy," by Oscar Brown Jr.; "St. Louis Blues," by W. C. Handy (to be played by a jazz group but without a singer); "Caravan" by Duke Ellington or "Blue Sands" by Buddy Collette; and finally "Do Nothing Till You Hear from Me" by Duke Ellington. His ashes were to go to the James Weldon Johnson Collection at Yale University.

Ironically, at the Benta Funeral Home, 630 St. Nicholas Avenue at 141st Street in Harlem, the body was on display the same day the American Academy met in New York City. Langston's arms were folded, "you know, laughing at us, I'm sure, cracking up," musician Randy Weston remembers. Lena Horne, Ralph Bunche, and many other notables were present. Gilbert Price, performing in Canada, sent his friend the humanist as his emissary. Arna Bontemps spoke a few solemn words and read a few of Hughes's poems about death. Weston's trio ended with "Do Nothing Till You Hear from Me." The ashes stayed in Harlem, at the Schomburg Center.

A bachelor, Hughes in a will left some money for his stepbrother's family. To the surprise of most, except those who knew Hughes had lived a lifetime of being sexually closeted (he once resisted the advances of Alain Locke and Countee Cullen, who tried to bring him out), he also willed money to Sunday Osuya, a young Nigerian black policeman he had met on a trip to Lagos. {AAH; CE; Helen Vendler, "The Unweary Blues," *The New Republic*, 6 March 1995; TYD; WAS, 21 February 1951}

Hughes, Rupert (1872—1956)

The Missouri-born novelist of the philosophic work, *Stately Timber* (1939), Hughes was the uncle of industrialist Howard Hughes. In the late 1920s, he created a stir because in a biography of George Washington he urged "that the cherry tree and other unfounded fables be dropped and the true grandeur of Washington's character and achievements be emphasized." Asked his views about humanism, Hughes wrote to the present author:

> I am certainly not theistic. I am perhaps atheistic humanistic. I think you'd better omit me as unclassifiable. . . .

A few days later, he added to his response:

> I am a "humanist" as opposed to a "divinist," may I say. I am an atheist. As for existentialism, I have read reams about it without getting any forwarder in mental grasp of just what it is supposed to be. I have read several of Sartre's works in French and enjoyed them as strong and ingenious fiction, with no clear notion of their philosophic meaning. As to "existence preceding essence," I am as much at a loss as the debater who was asked to define the word "is." I'd rather change the subject. My attitude toward man is neither optimistic nor pessimistic. I am a very cheerful person because I always expect the worst and never quite get it. I believe in writing for the happiness of humanity, or at least its physical and other comforts; but I have no hopes of Utopia, perpetual peace, one world, the millennium—or any radical change in human nature or its response to "improvements."

Hughes also wrote *We Live But Once* (1927); *Why I Quit Going to Church* (1934); *City of Angels* (1941), about Los Angeles; and *The Giant Wakes* (1950), about Samuel Gompers. {FUS; WAS, 11 February 1951 and 19 February 1951}

Hughes, Stephanie (20th Century)

Hughes, an atheist and second-generation freethinker, has written for *Freethought Today* (September 1996). As a pro-choice feminist, she favors allowing homosexual marriages.

Hugo, Victor Marie [Vicomte] (1802—1885)

Hugo, whose fame is attributable as much to his political courage as to his literary output, wrote fiction, dramatic works, and poetry that has inspired devotees of romanticism for ages. Leopold, his father, met Sophie, his mother, while being a revolutionary officer during the republican army's travels through western France. Victor, the third of their four children, was born two years before Napoleon's coronation. He rarely saw his father, who as General Count Leopold Hugo governed Central Spain during the Peninsular War. During that war his troops nailed their enemies' decapitated heads for all to see. Meanwhile, his mother was the lover of Victor de Lahorie, a fugitive military officer wanted by Napoleon's secret police for his having conspired against the emperor. As described in Graham Robb's biography, *Victor Hugo* (1998), Hugo's father said his son had been conceived on a mountainside in southeast France. Hugo became a patron saint of human freedom despite his unorthodox childhood. Or, in Robb's words, "The seemingly accidental wisdom of his mature work owes much to that endless patience with insoluble riddles which Hugo describes as the principal advantage of a miserable childhood." Robb goes into detail about Hugo's vast sexual energies for, in addition to his wife and Juliette, Hugo also paired up with actresses, maids, the barber's wife, his son's mistress, and others who could be seduced by the greatest master of the rhymed couplet.

Jean Cocteau in noting his colossal ego once quipped that "Victor Hugo was a madman who thought he was Victor Hugo," but Zola scholar Frederick Brown and others think that misses the point, "that fame may have been what girded Hugo against madness. Eugene, his brother, ended up in a lunatic asylum." Hugo is said to have enjoyed séances and reveled in the recognition that life is filled with paradoxes. Not surprisingly, some of the hierarchs of the Catholic Church thought him to be insane.

The sufferings of mankind, presented with compassion and literary skill, are depicted in *Notre-Dame de Paris* (1831) and *Les Misérables* (1862). Hugo eventually was elected to the French national assembly and the senate, and he is buried in the Panthéon.

In unfinished stories such as "*La Fin de Satan*" and "*Dieu*," he expressed his outlook about the nature of the Universe. Critic Paul Berman (in *The New Yorker*, 26 January 1998) found that one such "sappy" poem, "Magnitudo Parvi" about stars and huts and the universe, makes Hugo look "like a man orating in front of a mirror. You find yourself wondering if, for all his talent, he wasn't essentially a fake."

Whether or not Hugo was a philosophic naturalist or a strict non-believer, two of his books were named in the Vatican's list of prohibited reading in 1834 and 1864, respectively. According to McCabe, Renan met Hugo shortly before his death and was told by Hugo that Christianity would soon disappear and men would believe only in "God, the soul, and responsibility." McCabe has commented, "Like most poets and literary men, Hugo had more confidence than depth in his opinions about religion, and expressed them with an emphasis that scientific men usually avoid."

At one time Foote called Hugo a "fervent Theist, reverencing the prophet of Nazareth as a man, and holding that the 'divine tear' of Jesus and 'the human smile' of Voltaire 'compose the sweetness of the present civilization." He added that Hugo became a freethinker, free "from the trammels of creeds, and he hated priestcraft, like despotism, with a perfect hatred. In one of his striking later poems, '*Religion et les Religions*,' he derides and denounces the tenets and pretensions of Christianity. The Devil, he says to the clergy, is only the monkey of superstition; your Hell is an outrage on Humanity and a blasphemy against God; and when you tell me that your deity made you in his own image, I reply that he must be very ugly." Hugo's great oration on Voltaire, in 1878, roused the ire of the Bishop of Orleans, who reprimanded him in a public letter. The freethinking poet sent a crushing reply:

> France had to pass an ordeal. France was free. A man traitorously seized her in the night, threw her down and garroted her. If a people could be killed, that man had slain France. He made her dead enough for him to reign over her. He began his reign, since it was a reign, with perjury, lying in wait, and massacre. He continued it by oppression, by tyranny, by despotism, by an unspeakable parody of religion and justice. He was monstrous and little. The *Te Deum, Magnificat, Gloria tibi*, were sung for him. Who sang them? Ask yourself. The law delivered the people up to him. The Church delivered God up to him. Under that man sank down right, honour, country; he had beneath his feet oath, equity, probity, the glory of the flag, the dignity of men, the liberty of citizens. That man's prosperity disconcerted the human conscience. It lasted nineteen years. During that time you were in a palace. I was in exile. I pity you, sir.

Concerning this, Foote remarked, "Despite this terrible rebuff to Bishop Dupanlocup, another priest, Cardinal Guibert, Archbishop of Paris, had the temerity and bad taste to obtrude himself when Victor Hugo lay dying in 1885. Being born on February 26, 1802, the poet was in his eighty-fourth year, and expiring naturally of old age. Had the rites of the Church been performed on him in such circumstances, it would have been an insufferable farce. Yet the Archbishop wrote to Madame Lockroy, offering to bring personally 'the succor and consolation so much needed in these cruel ordeals.' " Monsieur Lockroy at once replied, according to the *London Times* (23 May 1885) as follows:

> Madame Lockroy, who cannot leave the bedside of her father-inlaw, begs me to thank you for the sentiments which you have expressed with so much eloquence and kindness. As regards M. Victor Hugo, he has again said within the last few days, that he had no wish during his illness to be attended by a priest of any persuasion. We should be wanting in our duty if we did not respect his resolution.

Hugo's death-chamber was thus unprofaned by the presence of a priest. He expired in peace, surrounded by the beings he loved.

His lack of consistency about religion has been commented upon by Colin McCall, who has written that Hugo dabbled in Spiritualism, suspected some supernatural hanky-panky, and held some belief in an unknowable God and a future life. Yet he was anti-Catholic and his revolutionary humanism included being opposed to the death penalty.

Juliette Drouet, his long-suffering mistress for over half a century, had complained that he used her toothbrush, wore filthy underwear, had deplorable personal hygiene, and once gave her fleas. She died in his arms two years before his own death. Suffering from pneumonia and certain that he was about to die, Hugo told Paul Meurice, a close friend, "Death will be very welcome," whereupon just before slipping into a coma he said softly, "I see black light." According to the *Times* correspondent in Paris, "Almost his last words, addressed to his grand-daughter, were, 'Adieu, Jeanne, adieu!'

And his last movement of consciousness was to clasp his grandson's hand."

There was great mourning at his death. Biographers Samuel Edwards and Joanna Richardson report he never came out of the coma. In order for a national funeral to be held, religionists arranged for the Pantheon to be secularized: the cross had to be removed. "All Paris"—two million or so, more than the city's entire population—attended his funeral. True to the simplicity of his life he ordered that his body should lie in a common coffin, and his pauper's hearse contrasted vividly with the splendid procession. {BDF; CE; FO; ILP; JM; Colin McCall, *The Freethinker*, April, 1998; RAT; RE; Graham Robb, *Victor Hugo: A Biography* (1998); TRI; TYD}

Huidekoper, Harm Jan (1776—1854)

After immigrating from the Netherlands in 1796, Huidekoper helped establish a Unitarian church at Meadville, Pennsylvania. Although an opponent of Transcendentalism, he assisted his son-in-law James Freeman Clarke both materially and by writing for the *Western Messenger*, the important early Unitarian and Transcendentalist publication.

In 1844, he took a lead in the establishment of Meadville Theological School, an institution that was needed to bolster Unitarianism's western presence. {U&U}

Hull, Daniel (20th Century)

Hull, a freethinker, wrote *Errors as to the Man Jesus of Nazareth* (1914). {GS}

Hull, Moses (1835—1907)

With W. F. Parker, Hull wrote *Which: Spiritualism or Christianity?* (1873). {GS}

Hultin, Ida C. (1858—1938)

Hultin was Unitarian minister who, in 1893, spoke at the Parliament of the World's Religions.

HUMAN BEINGS: See entries for Homo Sapiens and Population, Human.

HUMAN BROADCASTING FOUNDATION

A specialist member of the IHEU is the Human Broadcasting Foundation (Humanistische Omroep), Borneolaan 17, Postbus 135, 1200 AC Hilversum, Netherlands. On the web: <http://www.human.nl>.

HUMAN-ETIKK

The Norwegian *Human-Etikk*, which Levi Fragell edited from 1976 until 1997, was re-named *Humanist.*

HUMAN ETISK FORBUND I NORGE

A full member of the IHEU is *Human Etisk Forbund i Norge*, St. Olav's Plass 27, 0130 Oslo, Norway. Its mailing address is Postboks 6744, 0130 Oslo, Norway.

HUMAN ETISKA FORBUNDET I SVERIG

An associate member of the IHEU is *Human-Etiska Forbundet i Sverige*, Box 108, 69401 Hallsberg, Sweden. Its chairperson has been Mrs. Ebron Stranneby. The group publishes *Human-Etik*. (See entry for Swedish Secularism.) {FD}

HUMAN-ETISK

A Swedish bi-monthly, *Human-Etisk* is at Box 108, S-649 23 Hallsberg, Sweden.

HUMAN HORIZONS TV AND RADIO PRODUCTIONS

Human Horizons Television and Radio Productions is at 88 Islington High Street, London N1 8EW, United Kingdom. Its producer-director is Chris Templeton.

HUMAN IMMUNO-DEFICIENCY VIRUS

Human immunodeficiency virus (HIV), which was detected before 1981, has since led to an estimated fourteen million deaths. The HIV viruses, as do all retroviruses, invade cells as a fragment of RNA. HIV remains dormant and passively replicates in the invaded cells, resulting eventually in a compromise of the immune system and the syndrome known as AIDS (Acquired Immune Deficiency Syndrome). Many poorly educated people as well as religious leaders and their followers believe that God, by definition an omnipotent being, purposely has sent HIV to punish unbelievers and sinners. The virus, however, kills individuals without regard to gender, race, sexual orientation, political affiliation, and religious or non-religious affiliation.

Richard Preston in *The Hot Zone* (1995) claims that the Kinshasa Highway, which traverses sub-Saharan Africa, was not only a major transportation event but also allowed HIV to be swept out of central Africa, where it may have commenced, and made it possible to be distributed throughout the world. (See entry for AIDS and for the Plague.) {CE}

HUMAN NEPAL

HUMAN, the Humanist Association of Nepal, became an Associate Member of the International Humanist and Ethical Union in 1998.

HUMAN OR CHIMP

A United States human genome project has aimed to decode the three billion units of human DNA by 2003 or sooner. Most human genes are known to have an ancestry that includes the earliest animals, genes that are shared in common with other species.

Genoplex, a Denver company exploring chimp genes for medical reasons, thinks that chimpanzees, which are closely related to humans, will then be found to have only a few hundred genes different from humans, accounting for cognitive differences. At issue will be the ethical problem if it is proposed that these genes are inserted into chimpanzees.

The National Institutes of Health, the Energy Department, and the Wellcome Trust of London are vying with the Celera Corporation of Rockville, Maryland, to produce a count of the estimated 100,000 human genes. The hope is that by understanding human genomes, scientists will be able to improve the various medicines that can treat problems of the human organism. {Nicholas Wade, *The New York Times*, 20 October 1998 and 16 March 1999}

HUMAN POPULATION

Toward the end of the Twentieth Century, two major views were held about human origins. One held that modern humans evolved in sub-Saharan Africa and, in a later split, a small band then emigrated to populate the rest of the world. The other view was that only a handful of minor genes underlies superficial characteristics like hair and skin color,

In March 1999, the National Academy of Sciences reported the first fixed DNA difference between African and non-African populations, one that did not alter the fact that racial groups differ little at the genetic level. Rutgers University scientists Eugene E. Harris and Jody Hey hold that the first human population split was probably in Africa and that the modernity typical of people today developed later. In their sequencing of a 4,200-unit-long segment of DNA from the pyruvate gene in 16 Africans, 19 non-Africans, and 2 male chimpanzees, they concluded that the ancestral hominid sequence is 1.86 million years old. That is near the time that an archaic human species known as Homo habilis existed and confirms the idea that much of the genetic variation in living populations is extremely old. Although they do not say where the split took place, the Rutgers scientists estimate the effective size of the ancestral human population at a mere 18,000 hunter-gathers. Predictably, other scientists have questioned the statistics-based research. (See the entry for Population Explosion. For the number of non-Christians, see entry for Hell.) {Nicholas Wade, *The New York Times*, 16 March 1999}

HUMAN RIGHTS

Like race and citizenship, religion was not far behind in the exclusionist philosophy of rights, formulating codes to protect the rights of the faithful but denying the same to others—the Cross against the Crescent,

Buddhist versus Hindu, the believer against the infidel. Or simply religion versus secularism. Ground into powder beneath the hooves of the contending behemoths of religion, ideology, and race, each social unit ponders, at least periodically, how he or she differs from cattle or sheep, from the horses that pull the carriages of majesty, even when such choices are the mere expressions of the collective will. In order alone, ornamentation, social organization, technology, bonding, and even productive structures were all that defined the human species, then what significant properties marked out Homo sapiens as distinct from the rest of the living species?

Polarizations within various micro-worlds—us versus the inferior them—have long been armed with industrious rationalizations. Christian and Islamic theologians throughout history have quarried their scriptures for passages that stress the incontestable primacy of an unseen and unknowable Supreme Deity who has conferred authority on them. And to what end? Largely to divide the world into us and the rest. {Wole Soyinka, *The New York Times Magazine*, 18 April 1999}

HUMAN RIGHTS AND DEVELOPMENT REVIEW

A Bangladeshi annual publication in English, *Human Rights and Development Review* is at 68 Dhaka University Market, Sonargon Road, Kantagon, Dhaka-1000, Bangladesh.

HUMAN SACRIFICE

As proof to the gods that they were superior to mere humans, humans were often sacrificed throughout history. The Aztecs, for example, considered themselves "People of the Sun," the chosen people of the war god Huitzilopochtli. To insure that the sun would not disappear, they nourished the sun with human blood and hearts. Individuals captured during warfare were sacrificed on the steps of Aztec temples.

But other groups and other organized religions, worldwide, have slit the throats of those with different religious views, have sacrificed those who would not change their religions, have killed to save crops from drought or too much rain or to stop epidemics or to secure victory or to get favorable winds or to heal the sick or to propitiate the ghosts of departed ancestors, and have thanked their god or gods by the consummate prize, the ceremonial killing of a human being in order to appease divine anger. At times, the rite included a theophobic communing with a god by eating his human embodiment.

Freethinkers generally hold that human sacrifices were usually for the purpose of propitiating the gods who controlled weather and agriculture. People's fear of drought, food, locusts, and violent storms, in essence, was the root of all religion. {CE; DCG; ER}

HUMAN VALUES NETWORK

The Human Values Network is an online page "designed to make possible the sharing of visual information on all issues which affect Humankind." Beth Lamont is a key person at the site, which is sponsored by Half-Moon Foundation, PO Box 1080, Ossining, NY 10562. On the Web: <http://www.humanvalues.net/>.

HUMANA: See entry for Tvind, a cult.

HUMANISM

Humanism is not a basic technical term in philosophy, but it has been applied to various quasi-philosophical literary, political, and ethical movements. Admittedly, Humanism, whether capitalized or uncapitalized, is something of an eight-lettered semanticist's nightmare. Lexicographers think of it as a term denoting devotion to humanity. Historiographers associate it with ancient Hellenism. College freshmen sometimes study it as being related to the Matthew Arnoldian concept of culture. Fundamentalist seminarians are told that it represents a dangerous threat to supernaturalism. Existentialists describe their belief in man by it. And the intelligentsia associate it with the secular humanists, or related groups such as scientific humanists, religious humanists, naturalistic humanists, humanistic naturalists, and so forth.

In the 16th century, a ***humanist*** was one who studied Latin. A humanist was a Latinist. A ***humanitian*** was a scholar of the classics. Ben Jonson, for instance, explaining that he had read a great deal of history, wrote in *Cynthia's Revels* (1601), "I am a little humanitian." By 1617, *humanist* had extended its meaning to include a student of human affairs or human nature, and as humanitian came into disuse humanism came to mean one interested in either the study of the humanities or in human affairs. By the 19th century, it was commonly used to describe one devoted to human interests, as exemplified by Thomas Hardy's reference to "a being who had rejected with indifference the attitude of sex for the loftier quality of abstract humanism."

Contemporary linguists consider it fortunate that words cannot have their meanings fixed, either by literary dictators or authoritative dictionary publishers. That several definitions for *humanism* exist is a healthy sign indicating that the language is ever-changing and in a constant state of flux.

The most common connotation of humanism is that of devotion to human interests or ideals, to humanity, to human nature, and to human disposition. Such a meaning is universal, whether one is speaking of *el humanismo* (Spanish), *l'humanisme* (French), *Humanismus* (German), *humanisten* (Dutch), *l'umanismo* (Italian), *humanizmus* (Hungarian), or the equivalent in other tongues. Applied humanism is sometimes called ***humanitarianism***, although the word in the past has referred to those who deny the divinity of Christ but profess his human-ness. When Comte's "Religion of Humanity" was popular, positivists were sometimes called humanitarians.

So popular is the noun that following are some of the qualifying adjectives which have been applied to it:

> academic; aesthetic; agnostic; American; ancient; atheistic; Calvinistic; Catholic; Chinese; Christian; Christocentric; classical; communistic; Comtian; Congregational; decadent; deistic; democratic; dialectical; dualistic; dynamic; Einsteinian; empirical; Episcopalian; Epicurean; ethical; evangelical; evolutionary; existentialistic; free-thinking; fundamental; heathenistic; Hegelian; Hellenistic; heretical; humanistic; humanitarian; iconoclastic; idealistic; individualistic; instrumentalistic; integral; Jewish; liberal; literary; Marxian; materialistic; mechanistic; Methodist; modernistic; monistic; moral; mystical; naturalistic; neo-; neo-Platonic; new; nihilistic; optimistic; organic; oriental; orthodox; paganistic; pantheistic; Periclean; pessimistic; philosophical; planetary; poetical; political; positivistic; pragmatic; primitivistic; pseudo-; psychological; rationalistic; realistic; relativistic; religious; Renaissance; romantic; scientific; secular; skeptical; socialistic; sociological; speculative; Spinozist; spiritual; Stoic; supernaturalistic; theistic; theological; traditional; trinitarian; tragic; true; twentieth-century; Unitarian; Universalist; unorthodox; utilitarian. . . .

Contemporaries sometimes associate humanitarianism with the practice of philanthropy or altruism, with preaching the idea of universal brotherhood, and with indicting cruel conduct on the part of some toward fellow human beings. The nurse who applies a bandage, the stranger who guides the blind, the anonymous donor to a charity: these, too, are today's humanists and humanitarians.

In 1991, the International Humanist and Ethical Union (IHEU), meeting in Prague and aware of the need for a definition of humanism, adopted the following "Minimum Statement" after much debate:

> Humanism is a democratic, non-theistic, and ethical life-stance which affirms that human beings have the right and responsibility to give meaning and shape to their own lives. It rejects supernatural views of reality.

Inasmuch as it is a "minimum" statement, the one hundred or so member organizations are at liberty to add to it so long as they do not contradict or undermine the basic tenets. (See entries for life stance and teratology.) {CE; ER; *New Humanist*, February 1996}

HUMANISM AND SOLIDARITY

An associate member of the IHEU is Humanism and Solidarity, BP 15849, Kinshasa, Zaire.

HUMANISM IN ENGLAND: See entry for English Humanism.

HUMANISM SCOTLAND

Jane Fox edits *Humanism Scotland*, the official organ of the Humanist Society of Scotland at 11A Strathkinness High Road, St. Andrews KY16 9UA, United Kingdom. E-mail: <ase1@st.andrews.ac.uk> and <ahenness@aol.com>.

HUMANISM TODAY

Humanism Today is published annually at Box 191, 5901-J Wyoming NE, Albuquerque, New Mexico 87109.

HUMANISM, NATURALISTIC (or SCIENTIFIC)

Naturalistic (or scientific) humanism, to the philosophically-minded, is an eclectic set of beliefs born of the modern scientific age and centered upon a faith in, or an assumption of, the supreme value and self-improvability of human personality.

Sidney Hook, however, offered a suggested revision of such a definition:

> NATURALISTIC HUMANISM—
> to the philosopher, a set of beliefs born of the modern scientific age and centered upon a faith in the supreme value and self- improvability of human personality; differs from theistic humanism by its rejection of any form of supernaturalism; from atheistic humanism by its avoidance of small-town, village exhibitionism, *épater les bourgeois*; and from communistic humanism by its opposition to any beliefs not founded upon freedom, the significance of the individual, and political democracy.

The term was made popular in the 1950s by Corliss Lamont, with whom Hook differed in many respects—for example politically—which explains the last part of Hook's wording. Both Lamont and Hook, however, were non-theists. Julian Huxley and other humanist leaders used the analogous "scientific humanism," emphasizing that it is scientific in its outlook and is integrally related to the humanities.

"Secular" humanism has become the more common term in the 1990s to describe the same general outlook, which also makes the point of not being "religious." Critics have complained that the Paul Kurtz version of secular humanism under-emphasizes the importance of the humanities. The "Potpourri" columnist for *Free Inquiry*, for example, complained that a major weakness of secular humanism has been its leaders' emphasis upon the academically abstruse writings of its university-employed, professor-type philosophers. For secular humanism to succeed as a movement, he complained, it must have the input as well as the output of critics, satirists, poets, playwrights, and journalists as well as painters, sculptors, musicians: all who represent the humanities.

At the end of the century, many have gone on record as preferring "naturalistic humanism" or "humanistic naturalism" to the various other labels, explaining that they clearly connote a philosophic outlook that is both non-supernaturalistic and one that is integrally related to the humanities. (See entries for Humanism, Humanistic Naturalism, and Naturalistic Humanism Movement.)

HUMANISM, PER CURTIS REESE

Curtis Reese, the Unitarian minister who headed the American Humanist Association from 1949 to 1950, was one of the first of his denomination to write about Unitarian humanism. The following is from his introduction to *Humanist Sermons* (1927):

> **Humanism is not Materialism**. Materialism is the doctrine that "the happenings of nature are to be explained in terms of the locomotion of material." It is properly contrasted with Animism. It is mechanistic, not spiritistic. It belongs to the pre-electron period. While the mechanistic hypothesis of Materialism has served a useful purpose in scientific experimentation, it is now regarded by competent physicists as an inadequate hypothesis; and in the realm of psychology and sociology Materialism breaks down utterly. Humanism holds the organic, not the mechanistic or materialistic, view of life.
>
> **Humanism is not Positivism**. Positivism as a religion is an artificial system which substitutes the "worship of Humanity" (past, present, and future) for the "worship of God"—"the immortality of influence" for the "immortality of the soul," etc. Humanism, on the other hand, holds that the "Humanity" of Positivism is an abstraction having no concrete counterpart in objective reality, and that most "influence" far from being immortal is highly transitory. To Humanism "worship" means the reverential attitude towards all that is wonderful in persons and throughout all of life; a wistful, hopeful, expectant attitude of mind; not abject homage to either "Humanity" or "God." As to immortality, the Humanist shifts the emphasis from longevity to quality. But Humanism encourages research in the realm of the spirit. In his "Studies in Humanism," Schiller devotes a chapter to the most sympathetic yet critical discussion of "Psychic Research."
>
> **Humanism is not Rationalism**. Historically, the rationalist belongs in the group with the intellectualist, idealist, absolutist, not with the realist, pragmatist, behaviorist, humanist. "Reason" is Rationalism's God, just as "Humanity" is Positivism's God. Humanism finds neither absolute "Reason" nor "reason" as a faculty of the mind. But it finds intelligence as a function of organisms in various stages of development. To Humanism, dependence on the "Reason" is as fallacious as dependence on the "Bible" or the "Pope." Humanism's dependence is on intelligence enriched by the experience of the years; but it knows that intelligence is not an infallible source of either knowledge or wise conduct. Rationalism is dogmatic; Humanism is experimental.
>
> **Humanism is not Atheism**. Atheism is properly used as a denial of God. It is not properly used as a denial of a personal transcendent God. It is not properly used to describe monistic and immanent views of God. If and when the humanists deny the existence of a personal transcendent God, they are not Atheists any more than was Spinoza or Emerson. But, as a matter of fact, the Humanist attitude towards the idea of God is not that of denial at all; it is that of inquiry. The Humanist is questful; but if the quest be found fruitless he will still have his basic religion intact, viz., the human effort to live an abundant life.
>
> While the foregoing theories as such are not to be identified with Humanism as such, it should nevertheless be clearly understood that a Humanist might hold more or less tentatively any one of these theories, just as he might so hold any one of many theological theories. In its basic nature Humanism short circuits cosmological theories and lays supreme emphasis upon certain human attitudes which may or may not be enhanced by cosmologies.

HUMANISM, PROGRESSIVE

Progressive humanism, a new approach to the humanist philosophy, is expounded by Carl Coon, son of the eminent anthropologist Carleton Coon. On the Web: <www.progressivehumanism.com/>.

HUMANISM, RELIGIOUS

• Huxley defined Positivism as "Catholicism without Christianity." Humanism is rather like Protestantism without Christianity.

—**Joseph McCabe**
"Freethought and Atheism"

Humanist Manifesto I in 1933 brought to public attention for the first time, Edwin H. Wilson has noted, "a movement deeply rooted in the cultural life of the United States of America. This movement has been variously called religious humanism, naturalistic humanism, scientific humanism, and ethical humanism according to the varying backgrounds and emphases of its proponents." Wilson generally used the term "religious humanism," as did the signers of the manifesto. Although at the start those who termed themselves such were in the majority, the door was always open to unchurched freethinkers and rationalists. "Some writers," Wilson found, "have dealt with humanism as a religion, but in its inclusive sense it is also a philosophy and an ethical way of life."

Some of the early key figures in the Midwest were the Rev. Mary Safford and the Rev. Curtis Reese of the Des Moines Unitarian Church as well as the Rev. John Dietrich of the Minneapolis Unitarians.

Freethinkers and secular humanists generally dislike the adjective "religious" and agree with Supreme Court decisions that the movement is *not* a religion. "There is ample evidence," Thomas W. Flynn holds, "that mixing humanism and religion benefits neither humanism nor religion." "If," Paul Kurtz has reasoned, "we are to consider humanism 'religious' because of its devotion to a set of ideals, then why is not any and everything that a person is devoted to 'religious'; and may his or her set of beliefs be labeled as a 'religion'?" If so, it would follow, libertarianism, environmentalism, feminism, or vegetarianism will be considered a religion.

Large numbers of Unitarians and others, however, prefer to call themselves religious humanists, do not hesitate to use terms such as "spiritual," and—unlike the secular humanists—sometimes mingle with and cooperate with pagan humanists, mystical humanists, Christian Unitarians, and Unitarian theists. (See entries for Charles S. Braden and for *Religious Humanism*. For a definition of religious humanism, see the entry for Charles S. Braden. Also, see entry for Howard Box, President of Religious Humanists (USA). Mason Olds, in "What Is Religious Humanism?" [*Free Inquiry*, Fall 1996], wrote, "In traditional Western religions, it is believed that in order to be religious one must believe in God and in personal immortality. However, the advocates of religious humanism maintain that one can be religious without giving intellectual assent to either of these beliefs. He added, "When religious humanists pursue the living of the good life in the world, this is the ideal that motivates them, and thus it takes on a religious quality in Dewey's sense.") {EW}

HUMANISMS

In 1949 the present author, working with his sponsor Lionel Trilling at Columbia University on a graduate thesis, listed seven kinds of humanism after researching how libraries categorized their entries:

• 1 **humanism**—to the lexicographer, a term denoting devotion to human interests as well as one referring to the study of the humanities;

• 2 **ancient humanism**—to the historiographer, a term pertaining to the collective philosophies of such as Aristotle, Democritus, Epicurus, Lucretius, Pericles, Protagoras, and Socrates;

• 3 **classical humanism**—to the educator, a term referring to the ancient humanist views brought back into vogue during the Renaissance by such as Bacon, Boccaccio, Erasmus, Montaigne, More, and Petrarch;

• 4 **theistic humanism**—to the seminarian, a term including both Christian existentialists and those modern theologians who insist upon human values, upon man's capability of working out his salvation with his God, all within the framework of a supernaturalistic philosophy;

• 5 **atheistic humanism**—to the Continental critic, a term describing the philosophy of French playwright and novelist Jean-Paul Sartre and others;

• 6 **communistic humanism**—to political scientists, a term signifying the philosophic beliefs of some Marxists—for example, Cuba's Fidel Castro; Raya Dunayevskaya, former secretary to Leon Trotsky, averred that Karl Marx was a thoroughgoing naturalist who at first had called his outlook "a new humanism."

• 7 **naturalistic (or scientific) humanism**—to philosophers, an eclectic set of beliefs born of the modern scientific age and centered upon a faith in, or an assumption of, the supreme value and self-improvability of human personality

In the 1970s to 1990s, the seventh category frequently was called **secular humanism** and emphasized naturalism (as contrasted with supernaturalism) and this-worldliness (as contrasted with other-worldliness). A few preferred the term humanistic naturalism.

Nicolas Walter, having studied Warren Allen Smith's list of "seven humanisms," observed during a 1996 religion-humanist dialogue at the Centre for Critical Studies in Religion, Ethics, and Society in Westminster College, Oxford, that indeed there are many humanisms:

•1 the naturalistic philosophies of ancient Greece and Rome
•2 the "more human letters" ("*literaehumaniores*") of the Middle Ages
•3 the revived study of ancient Greece and Rome during the Renaissance (scholars of Greek and Latin first being called "humanists" at the end of the 15th century)
•4 liberal education in the arts, literature, history, "the humanities" (first called "humanism" by Niethammer at the beginning of the early 19th century
•5 the Unitarian and Universalist versions of Christianity and the Deist and Theist variations on it
•6 the programme of the Philosophes and Encyclopédistes during the Enlightenment
•7 the Utilitarianism of Bentham and Mill
•8 the Religion of Humanity of Comte and the Positivists
•9 the Scientific Socialism or Dialectical Materialism of Marx and Engels
•10 the antitheism of Shelley or Swinburne
•11 the rude Secularism of Holyoake and Bradlaugh
•12 the polite scepticism of Matthew Arnold and John Morley
•13 the Transcendentalism of Emerson and Thoreau
•14 the evolutionary naturalism of Darwin and Dawkins
•15 the Agnosticism of T. H. Huxley and W. K. Clifford
•16 the Pragmatism of Peirce and William James
•17 the Humanism of Schiller and the Hominism of Windelband
•18 the Instrumentalism of Dewey and Lippmann
•19 the Ethicism of Felix Adler and Stanton Coit
•20 the aestheticism of Wilde or Santayana
•21 the literary criticism of Irving Babbitt or F. R. Leavis
•22 the Scientific Humanism of H. G. Wells and Julian Huxley
•23 the Logical Positivism of Ayer and Ryle
•24 the critical rationalism of Russell and Popper
•25 the progressive Catholicism of Maritain or Schweitzer
•26 the atheistic Existentialism of Heidegger or Sartre
•27 the literary liberalism of E. M. Forster and Angus Wilson
•28 the syncretic sentimentalism of Kenneth Kaunda
•29 the vulgar humanism or humanitarianism of world politics, expressed by the Universal Declaration of Human Rights and all the other international conventions
•30 the neologistic nostrums of Harry Stopes-Roe and Paul Kurtz

Walter added that all the above are valid versions of humanism, that the International Academy of Humanism or the International Humanist and Ethical Union have no power to impose any "minimum statements." Neither, he did not add, had allegedly ever attempted to do so. As to his personal outlook,

> My own humanism is a pretty minimal one. It involves neither religion nor ritual; I am not a religious or ritualistic animal. It is entirely sane; my right-brain is fully occupied with art, music, and literature (as described by Jim Herrick), and humour. It is not a "life-stance" or "eupraxophy"; I have no more need for secular than for sacred nonsense. It avoids such terms as "spirit" and "worship," however, defined; I have no need for alien vocabulary. It perceives nothing as ultimately important; as A. J. Balfour said, nothing matters very much, and most things don't matter at all. I agree with Freud that religion is a neurosis (but so is psychoanalysis). I agree with the Marquis de Sade that nature is hostile to us. I agree with Matthias Claudius that "man is not at home in the world." I agree with Max Stirner that there is no such thing as "Man," only me and others like me. We should exorcise all the spectres which have haunted us, from God to Humanity itself.
>
> I am atheist about God, and agnostic about most other things in the same category. Questions about the value of existence or the meaning of life have no value or meaning. There are no categorical imperatives or fundamental principles. The ultimate reality is that there is no ultimate reality. The golden rule is that there are no golden rules. Here I may not share much common ground with some other humanists, but I can speak for many others.

(See Walter's *Humanism: What's in the Word* (1997), which was received just as the present work was being finished.)

{*New Humanist*, June 1996}

HUMANISMUS HEUTE

Humanismus Heute, Zeitschrift für Kultur und Weltanschauung, is an academic quarterly of Humanistischer Verband Deutschlands at Hobrechtstrasse 8, D - 12043 Berlin, Germany.

HUMANIST (Australia): See *Humanist Viewpoints*.

HUMANIST (Britain)

The Humanist in Britain was published from 1924 to 1927 and was basically about humanitarianism, not philosophic humanism. It was published by the British Humane Association, which Louis Campbell-Johnston founded. (See entry for *New Humanist*, edited by Jim Herrick.)

HUMANIST (Canada): See *Humanist in Canada*.

HUMANIST (Finland): See *Humanisti*.

HUMANIST (India): See entries for *Humanist Outlook* and *Radical Humanist*.

HUMANIST (Internationa): See *International Humanist News*.

HUMANIST (The Netherlands)

A Dutch monthly magazine of *Humanistisch Verbond Nederland*, *Humanist* is at Postbus 75490, 1070 AL Amsterdam, The Netherlands. E-mail: >hv@euronet.nl>.

HUMANIST (New Zealand): See *New Zealand Humanist*.

HUMANIST (Norway)

Humanist, Organ for Human-Etisk Forbund, is a Norwegian magazine (POB 6744, St. Olavs Plass, 0130 Oslo, Norway).

E-mail: <humanist@human.no>.

HUMANIST (Sweden): See *Humanisten*.

HUMANIST (United States)

According to the bi-monthly magazine's masthead, *The Humanist* (7 Harwood Drive, PO Box 1188, Amherst, New York 14226) "presents a nontheistic, secular, and naturalistic approach to philosophy, science, and broad areas of personal and social concern. It focuses on humanistic ideas, developments, and revolutions. In pursuit of free and open dialogue, *The Humanist* airs opinions that may not necessarily reflect those of the editors or the publisher, the American Humanist Association." Except for its original and long-time editor Edwin H. Wilson, the journal has had a history of troubles between its editors and the AHA Board of Directors.

Following is an historical list of editors of *The Humanist* and its predecessors (dated by issues of each periodical):

New Humanist
- From 1928, published by the Humanist Fellowship
- From 1930, published by Harold Buschman and Edwin H. Wilson
- From 1935, published by the Humanist Press Assn.
  - –Apr 1928 to Oct 1928: Stanley Stewart Newman
  - –Nov 1928 to May 1929: Herrlee G. Creel
  - –Dec 1929 to Dec 1934: Harold Buschman
  - –Feb 1935 to Autumn 1936: Raymond B. Bragg
  - (No publication appeared in 1937)

Humanist Bulletin
- Published by the Humanist Press Assn.
  - –Feb 1938 to Jan 1942: Edwin H. Wilson

The Humanist
- Published by the American Humanist Assn
  - –Spring 1942 to Mar-Apr 1956: Edwin H. Wilson
  - –May-June 1956 to Mar-Apr 1959: Priscilla Robertson
  - –June 1959 to May-June 1963: Gerald Wendt
  - –Jul-Aug 1963 to Nov-Dec 1964: Edwin H. Wilson
  - –Jan-Feb 1965 to Jul-Aug 1967: Tolbert McCaroll
  - –Sep-Dec 1967 to Nov-Dec 1978: Paul Kurtz
  - –Mar-Apr to Sep-Oct 1978: Lloyd L. Morain, acting editor during Paul Kurtz's sabbatical
  - –Jan-Feb 1979 to Jul-Aug 1990: Lloyd L. Morain
  - –Sep-Oct 1990 to Nov-Dec 1991: David Alexander
  - –Jan-Feb 1992 to Nov-Dec 1992: Rick Szykowny
  - –Jan-Feb 1993 to Sep-Oct 1993: Don Page
  - –Nov-Dec 1993 to Sep-Oct 1994: Gerry O'Sullivan and Rick Szykowny
  - Nov-Dec 1994 to date (2000): Fred Edwords

During the editorship of Paul Kurtz, *The Humanist* became the jointly sponsored publication of the American Humanist Association and the American Ethical Union. When the latter withdrew as co-publisher in 1978, a new charter was drafted and Lloyd Morain was elected editor.

Although the journal once was attacked by some as being a "house organ," in recent years it has been criticized by some for not being sufficiently so.

E-mail: <humanism@juno.com>. On the Web: <http://www.humanist.net>. (See entry for the American Humanist Association.)

HUMANIST ASSOCIATION OF CANADA

The Humanist Association of Canada, after twenty-seven years of existence, opened an Ottawa office in 1995. Dr. Henry Morgentaler, one of the association's three foundings members and its current honorary President, cut the ribbon. It is located at 2660 Southvale in Ottawa and publishes a quarterly newsletter. The mail address is POB 3736, Station C, Ottawa, Ontario, K1Y 4J8, Canada.

E-mail: <cb787@freenet.carleton.ca>. On the Web: <http://infoweb.magi.com/~godfree>.

HUMANIST ASSOCIATION OF FINLAND

The Humanist Association of Finland (IHEU), is at Box 793, 00101 Helsinki 10, Finland. {FD}

HUMANIST ASSOCIATION OF OTTAWA NEWSLETTER

A monthly, the *Humanist Association of Ottawa Newsletter* is at PO Box 8733, Postal Station T, Ottawa, Ontario, K1G 3J1, Canada.

HUMANIST ASSOCIATION OF SAN DIEGO

The Humanist Association of San Diego, California, can be e-mailed to <ix.netcom.com>.

HUMANIST ASSOCIATION: ST. PETERSBURG (HASP)

Jan Loeb Eisler heads the Humanist Association: St. Petersburg (13336 Gulft Boulevard #304, Madeira Beach, Florida 33708). Members are from surrounding cities such as Tampa, Clearwater Beach, and Bradentown. E-mail: <hasp@gte.net>.

HUMANIST ASSOCIATIONS

"Why don't the various humanist associations merge?"

To a June Capital District Humanist Society in Scotia, New York, Matt Cherry responded that there are several humanist associations: the American Humanist Association, the Council for Secular Humanism, the American Ethical Union, the Fellowship of Religious Humanists, the Freedom From Religion Foundation, the American Atheists, and a number of others. "Each group has its own, unique style of doing humanism," Cherry responded. "Thus each attracts a slightly different membership and subscribership, and each carries out a somewhat different mission. For example, the Council spends a little more time critiquing religious claims than does AHA, and the AHA spends a little more time applying humanism to the major social issues of our time." He added that the AHA has a more progressive socio-political tradition whereas the Council has one that is more supportive of free-market economics.

In the Netherlands, however, the various humanist groups function under an all-encompasing umbrella group.

HUMANIST BOOK CLUB: See entry for Hvmanist Book Clvb.

HUMANIST CEREMONIES

Britain's Jane Wynne Willson has been a key figure in the development of secular celebrations in the United Kingdom. Many non-religious people—although by no means all—feel the need for celebrations or ceremonies at important moments in their lives: rites of passage such as birth, graduation, marriage, and death. (See entry for Jonathan Kurtz Jr., whose Welcoming Celebration when he was ten weeks old was held in the Center for Inquiry in Amherst, New York.)

HUMANIST CLUB: For the first humanist club on a college campus, see entries for John Cowley, Martin L. Grant, and Warren Allen Smith.

HUMANIST COMMITTEE ON HUMAN RIGHTS

The Humanist Committee on Human Rights is at PO Box 114, 3500 AC Utrecht, Netherlands. On the Web: <hom@euronet.nl>.

HUMANIST COMMUNITY

Humanist Community is a monthly at Stanford University, South Bay Area, PO Box 60069, Palo Alto, California 94306.

HUMANIST COMMUNITY NEWS

A monthly, the *Humanist Community News* is at 3032 Warm Springs Drive, San Jose, California 95127-1875. E-mail: <dharris@best.com>

HUMANIST COMMUNITY AT STANFORD UNIVERSITY

The Humanist Community at Stanford University, an associate member of the International Humanist and Ethical Union, is at PO Box 60069, Palo Alto, California 94306-0069.

HUMANIST COMMUNITY OF THE PENINSULA

The Humanist Community of the Peninsula can be e-mailed: <athalsfj@aol.com>.

HUMANIST COUNCIL

In Britain, the Humanist Council was formed in 1950. The council, which had been suggested by Hector Hawton, coordinated the rationalist, ethical, secular, and positivist organizations.

HUMANIST ETHICAL EDUCATION ORGANISATION (HVO)

A specialist member of the International Humanist and Ethical Union, The Humanist Ethical Education Organisation (Pedagogisch Studiecentrum HumanistischVormingsonderwijs), is at Plompetorengracht 21 3512 CB, Utrecht, Netherlands. Tel +31-30-2341700; fax +31-2310794; E-mail: <psc@hvo.nl>.

HUMANIST FELLOWSHIPS

In April 1928 the Humanist Fellowship was a Chicago group, which with A. Eustace Haydon's encouragement, published *The New Humanist*. In 1947 it became incorporated and affiliated with the American Humanist Association. In 1954, its officers were as follows: Harold R. Rafton, President; Theodore L. Southack Jr., Vice President; Doris E. Sargent, Secretary; Greta B. Schirmer, Treasurer; Lisa T. Arey, Assistant Treasurer; James V. Grasso, Executive Director; Llewellyn Jones, Program Director; and Counsellor, Alfred E. Smith. Directors were Lisa T. Arey, James V. Grasso, William F. Lennon Jr., Tom O'Connor, Harold R. Rafton, Doris E. Sargent, Greta B. Schirmer, Hannah L. Siegel, and Theodore L. Southack Jr.

The Humanist Fellowship of San Diego, California, can be e-mailed: <warren@cyberheads.com>. {EW}

HUMANIST FRIENDSHIP CENTER

In Nigeria, the Humanist Friendship Center is at Omuoma Onicha, Ezinihitte Mbaise, Imo, Nigeria. Its president is Charles Ufomadu. {FD}

HUMANIST HANDBOOK

"Humanist Handbook" is a pamphlet published by the Ulster Humanist Association (25 Riverside Drive, Lisburn, BT 27 4HE £2.). Included in its explanations as to what humanism is are explanations of the twelve myths of Christmas and a discussion of gay and lesbian rights, abortion and women's rights, and humanist ceremonies.

HUMANIST HOLIDAYS (England)

Humanist Holidays (HH) was formed in 1965 to organize holidays together for humanists at the festive times of year and in the summer. The group is headed by Gillian Bailey, 18 Priors Road, Cheltenham GL 52 5AA.

HUMANIST HOLIDAYS (United States)

The Humanist chaplaincy of Harvard University has submitted a list of holidays worthy of celebration by humanistic students: **Freethinkers Day**, October 12; **United Nations Declaration of Human Rights Day**, December 15th; and **Earth Day**, the Vernal Equinox, March 20th. Paul Kurtz has written that it would be appropriate to add the following: the **Fourth of July**; **Bastille Day**; **May Day**; **Arbor Day**; **Labor Day**; and **New Year's Eve**. He believes the following are archaic and might well be abandoned: Good Friday; All Saints Day; Easter; Passover; Christmas; and Ramadan. **Nonbelievers' Day** is observed on October 8th, during the national freethought week of October 8th to 14th. Inspiration for setting the date was that Governor William Phips of Massachusetts on 12 October 1694 had issued an edict that spectral evidence would no longer be admissible in the courts. **World Humanist Day** is celebrated internationally on June 21st. (See entry for Halloween, the pagan holiday.)

HUMANIST HORIZONS

In 1996 the British Humanist Association relinquished its 50% holding of Humanist Horizons, a company formed to produce radio and television material, and it is now wholly owned by the Rationalist Press Association. The company's interest in Manuel Salazar, an exhibition of whose paintings was held and filmed in Conway Hall, may have contributed to the climate in which he was released from death row in Illinois. The company has produced "Mirad," a play about the Bosnian war, for broadcast by the BBC World Service. {"The Ad de Bont Interview," *New Humanist*, August 1997}

HUMANIST HUMOR

Mike Reiss, who co-conceived and produced The Simpsons television episode "The Springfield Files" (The Simpsons Meet the X-Files), is but one of many humanists whose humor marks their work. In "God Is Dead, After Weather and Sports" (*Skeptical Inquirer*, July-August 1999), he hypothesizes the following:

• Late in the millennium, when astrophysicists perfected the Grand Unified Field Theory, finding the last scraps of "missing matter" in the universe, they accidentally proved that God does not exist.
• The jig was up for religious leaders all over the world. A long suppressed introduction to the King James Bible was released: "This is a booke of instructional tayles for children and the weak of minde, and not to be taken too seriously." Israeli archaeologists confessed that words in the Dead Sea Scrolls such as "steam engine" and "toothpaste" proved them to have been a forgery. Chinese scholars admitted to having covered up the fact that the chubby smiling Buddha began life as a corporate logo for pickled eel in the third century. Jews, now able to eat pork without guilt, found it didn't taste nearly as good that way. Poor Hindus, eating the sacred cows, went from being hungry to being hypertense.
• Holidays passed into obscurity. Easter: in. Lent: out. Hanukkah, in. Yom Kippur, replaced with Hanukkah II. Ramadan was shortened from 28 days to 28 seconds.
• Houses of worship lost their tax-exempt status and were forced to shut down. Mosques became banks. Cathedrals were converted into multiplexes. Small churches became a chain of coffee shops called "St. Arbucks," successful until in 2004 they all went bankrupt.
• In 2008 the Catholic Church had a massive going out of business sale. "The Last Supper" now graces the lobby of Mitsubishi International in Osaka. The Sistine Chapel ceiling was moved intact to Trump's Vaticasino in Atlantic City. The Pope became just another celebrity, famous for being famous. He married Linda Evans.
• One thing did not happen in the post-God world: there was not a moral collapse
• On 18 July 2036, however, geologists taking deep core samples discovered there really was a Hell, to which we all are destined.

George Carlin is a leading humorist, whose secular humanist jibes about religion are profound. His 1999 Home Box Office show, "You Are All Diseased," is entirely blasphemous. "When it comes to bullshit—big-time, major-league bullshit—you have to stand in awe of the all-time champion of false promises and exaggerated claims: religion. . . . Religion has actually convinced people that there's an invisible man, living in the sky, who watches everything you do," he jokes, a man who "has a special list of ten things he does not want you to do—and if you do any of these ten things, he has a special place full of fire and smoke and burning and torture and anguish where he will send you to live and suffer and burn and choke and scream and cry forever and ever till the end of time. But He loves you." (See entries for George Carlin, Language and Communication and Marketing of Organized Religion; and for Russell, Bertrand—Humor of.) {*Free Inquiry*, Summer 1999}

HUMANIST IN CANADA

Humanist in Canada is a quarterly from POB 3769, Station C, Ottawa K1Y 4J8, Canada <jepiercy@cyberus.ca>.

HUMANIST INSTITUTE

The Humanist Institute is headquartered in the Ethical Culture Society building at 2 West 64th Street, New York, NY 10023. It is a post-graduate training program that, up to 1997, had graduated fifty-eight humanist leaders and has twenty-eight students in two classes. On the Web: <www.humanism.net/institute>.

HUMANIST INSTITUTE FOR COOPERATION WITH DEVELOPING COUNTRIES

A specialist member of the IHEU is the Humanist Institute for Cooperation with Developing Countries (HIVOS), Raamweg 16, 2596 HL Den Haag, Netherlands.

On the Web: <http://www.dds.nl/~hivos/>.

HUMANIST INTER-GROUP CONFLICTS

"I am well acquainted with the petty squabbles of the various religious sects with their intra- and inter-group conflicts," Herbert Tonne wrote in the Humanists of North Jersey newsletter (May 1998).

"But, it seems to me, we go them even better. In any case, we pride ourselves on our scientific approach and superior logic. I am quite ashamed of our sloppy organizational situation and inability and unwillingness to solve the problems." He referred to the inability of various humanist organizations—chapters of the American Humanist Association (AHA), chapters of the Council for Secular Humanism (CSH), the North American Committee for Humanism (NACH), and Freedom From Religion Foundation groups—to either unite or at least cooperate more willingly.

HUMANIST LIVING

Humanist Living, a quarterly of the American Humanist Association, is at 7 Harwood Drive, Amherst, New York 14226.

HUMANIST MANIFESTO I

Raymond B. Bragg, the associate editor of *The New Humanist*, initiated the project that resulted in the 1933 publication by a group of thirty-four liberal humanists which became known as Humanist Manifesto I. It defined the philosophical and religious principles that seemed to them fundamental. Signers included philosopher John Dewey, atheist William Floyd, historian Harry Elmer Barnes, and many leaders of Unitarian and Universalist societies including Edwin H. Wilson. Wilson's posthumously published *The Genesis of a Humanist Manifesto* (1995) is the most complete record of how the first manifesto was inspired, which individuals specifically contributed to its wordings, who declined to sign the work, and what Wilson, a nonagenarian at the time, remembered about the personalities of all those involved.

In 1995, Edwin H. Wilson's *The Genesis of a Humanist Manifesto* was posthumously published. In addition to describing how the manifesto came about and including all the individuals involved, he included critiques of those who did not sign, some invited, some not:

• William Amberson, editor of the *Journal of Social Psychology*, never responded.
• Paul Blanshard for a reason Wilson cannot explain either was not invited or did not sign.
• Harold Buschman who said he did not sign because of his "fear of creeds."
• Alfred Cole, a Unitarian minister, declined but later signed Humanist Manifesto II.

- Walton E. Cole, who had been minister of the Third Unitarian Church of Chicago decided against signing.
- Clarence Darrow, whose wife said her husband would not enter a church, did not respond; but his law partner, William H. Holly, later joined the American Humanist Association.
- George C. Davis, an official of the American Unitarian Association, declined.
- Irwin Edman was invited but never made a humanist commitment organizationally, although he was part of the humanistic influence stemming from Columbia University.
- C. Hartley Grattan, known for his broadside against the literary humanists, did not respond.
- Edward Howard Griggs, a Unitarian minister, whose *The New Humanism: Studies in Personal and Social Development* (1899) put him more in the category of a literary humanist along the lines of Irving Babbitt and Paul Elmer More.
- James H. Hart, minister of the Madison, Wisconsin, Unitarian Church, had some criticisms which included his feeling that a need for spirituality within a nonsupernatural framework can be incorporated with naturalistic humanism.
- E. Stanton Hodgin, a Unitarian minister, did not like labels; however, his *Confessions of an Agnostic Clergyman* (1948) old that he had been on the naturalistic and humanistic side of theological issues but was basically an agnostic.
- Rupert Holloway, later Unitarian minister in Madison, Wisconsin, was overlooked and never asked.
- John Haynes Holmes, minister of New York's Community Church, who wrote, "I have never at any time seen any necessary contradiction between humanism on the one hand and theism on the other," and who maintained a faith in immortality, God, and Puritanism.
- Robert J. Hutcheon, a professor at the Meadville Theological School and a Unitarian, in his *Frankness in Religion* (1929) spoke of his aim "to save for humanity the essential spiritual values which religious faith, and especially the Christian form, which it creates."
- Horace Kallen told Wilson that Dewey had once asked him to sign, but he explained that he told Dewey he had stronger objections to the first than the second manifesto.
- Cassius J. Keyser, a Columbia University mathematician, who stated he was in hearty accord with much of the manifesto but was unable to sign.
- Frank H. Knight, a University of Chicago economist, declined to sign, complaining about language concerning "a radical change in methods, controls, and motives" of "an acquisitive and profit-motivated society."
- Corliss Lamont, asked in 1972 why he had not signed, replied, "I have no idea. I wish I had," an obvious reference to a break-down in communication.
- Judge Ben Lindsay, known for his views favoring "companion-ate marriage," was invited but failed to respond.
- Walter Lippmann, whose 1929 *Preface to Morals* dealt with the "acids of modernity," was invited but did not sign.
- Everett Dean Martin, a Unitarian minister, was invited but was unresponsive and, in fact, mysteriously disappeared.
- Dr. Arthur E. Morgan, who was once the moderator of the American Unitarian Association but became a Friend, declined and never joined the American Humanist Association.
- Max C. Otto, although he declined to sign, did not waver in his humanism and was the author of important humanistic works. In his 1949 work, *Science and the Moral Law*, Otto had written, "All Humanisms have one thing in common.It is the ideal of realizing man's completest development. From here on they diverge."
- Dr. Harry Overstreet was asked but his wife, Bonaro, was not, apparently an oversight. Both belonged to the American Humanist Association.
- James Harvey Robinson was invited but did not respond.
- F. C. S. Schiller, who caustically noted that the manifesto had 50% more articles than the Ten Commandments and one more even than President Wilson's Fourteen Points.
- Harlow Shapley, the Harvard astronomer, who said he subscribed "almost in toto. But I wonder if we are ready for a religion of intelligence; and if so is it spontaneous enough, when nurtured by a deliberate manifesto?"
- Vincent Silliman, writer of humanistically oriented liberal service material, appears to have been overlooked and never asked.
- Thomas Vernor Smith, who never formally labeled himself a humanist, may not have approved because of its lack of "God language." Later, he was elected to the U. S. Congress as a Representative.
- Hugh S. Tigner, a Unitarian with humanist views, found the first five or six affirmations repugnant; Tigner wrote the group that he was tired of signing such documents; and regarded Humanism "as Mr. Hoover did Prohibition, as a 'noble experiment.' "
- Frank Waring, another Unitarian and humanist, was overlooked and was never asked.

The Roman Catholic perspective, by radio commentator the Reverend Michael J. Ahern, who broadcast regularly on the "Catholic Truth Hour," was as follows:

> With the Manifesto of the Religious Humanists, a Catholic finds himself in some agreement. He would agree that any religion must recognize its obligations to a better social order; should work for a greater social justice for all men; cooperate for the common good of human life and human happiness; use its best endeavors to cultivate all the arts, all the sciences, all the culture and all the emoluments of civilization; in a word, bring to pass on earth, the greatest sum of genuine human happiness in a genuine human brotherhood. But the Catholic cannot agree that this implies that this universal goal can be attained by purely naturalistic or materialistic means.

(See entry for Edwin H. Wilson. Also see, "The Lingering Humanist Manifesto I" by Lester Mondale, *Free Inquiry*, Fall 1996. The entry for Humanistic Naturalism explains why some secularists, including John Dewey, prefer that phrase to Naturalistic Humanism or Secular Humanism.) {EW}

HUMANIST MANIFESTO II

In 1973, Humanist Manifesto II, which further outlined humanist aims "as we approach the twenty-first century," was signed by several hundred individuals including Isaac Asimov, Sir Alfred Ayer, Paul Edwards, Antony Flew, Betty Friedan, Sidney Hook, Sir Julian Huxley, Paul Kurtz, Jacques Monod, Gunnar Myrdal, A. Philip Randolph, Andrei Sakharov, B. F. Skinner, and Edwin H. Wilson. The two documents contained recommendations for the future of humankind in the areas of religion and ethics. They also delineated humanist views on the meaning of life, civil liberties and democracy, the right to suicide, abortion, and divorce, euthanasia, sexual freedom, worldwide ecological and economic planning, and the building of world community. (See entries for Humanist Manifesto I and for Humanist Manifesto III.)

HUMANIST MANIFESTO III? HUMANIST MANIFESTO 2000?

In 1996, members of the Humanist Association of Massachusetts discussed a possible updated Humanist Manifesto III. The previous two manifestos were out of date, they suggested, citing the fall of communism, the prominence of the women's movement, the emergence of the gay movement, the re-appearance of internecine tribal-religious warfare, the penetration of outer space, the resurgence of religious fundamentalism, the evolution of the one-parent family, the "taming" of nuclear energy, the depletion of the fishing stocks, the denudation of the rain forest, the wonder of genetics with all its ethical dilemmas, and the internet and its new communities.

The Humanist (March-April 1998) announced an American Humanist Association (AHA) project of creating a third manifesto.

On the 25th anniversary of the second manifesto, *The Humanist* (September-October 1998) had a symposium about the need for such an updated manifesto. The symposium included varying views by Khoren Arisian, Bette Chambers, Albert Ellis, Thomas Ferrick, Paul Kurtz, Lester Mondale, Mary and Lloyd Morain, Henry Morgentaler, James W. Prescott, Howard B. Radest, and Herbert A. Tonne. At some point, Dr. Kurtz—who had declined to chair that symposium about Humanist Manifesto III—and the Council for Secular Humanism, which he headed, decided to come up with a manifesto that would follow the previous manifesto.

In mid-1999 a draft of "Humanist Manifest III: A Call for a New Planetary Humanism" was distributed for comments and signatures. The draft was made by Paul Kurtz, Roy W. Brown, Diana Brown, Joseph Edward Barnhart, Vern L. Bullough, James Haught, Valerii Kuvakin, Jean-Claude Pecker, Svetozar Stojanovic, Norm Allen, Matthew Cherry, Thomas W. Flynn, Ranjit Sandhu, and Lewis Vaughn.

The manifesto urged all members of the human family to

- embrace science and technology as tools to help solve the great social problems of the century;
- leave behind the magical thinking and mythmaking that are substitutes for reliable knowledge and impede human progress;
- recognize that moral principles should serve humanity and should not be based on inherited prescientific concepts that do not apply to a global, transformed future.

It set forth a new Planetary Bill of Rights and Responsibilities, recognizing that people everywhere have duties not only to their own society but to all citizens of Earth. It recommended that we "strive to end povery and malnutrition and provide adequate health care and shelter for everyone on the planet." In addition, the document called for a new planetary system of government that would include

- the formation of a World Parliament—a stronger and more effective version of the United Nations whose representatives would be elected on the basis of global population rather than national identity;
- a new transnational system of taxation, including a tax on the gross national product of all nations, to assist the underdeveloped areas to stabilize population growth and assist economic development;
- procedures for the regulation of multinational corporations and state monopolies;
- a more powerful World Court with real teeth to enforce its rulings;
- an end to the veto in the United Nations Security Council.

Once the draft was approved toward the end of 1999, copies were circulated and signators were contacted. The finished document, with final editing by Paul Kurtz, was entitled Humanist Manifesto 2000.

As to why the document was not called Humanist Manifesto III, an explanation was printed in the Council for Secular Humanism's *Free Inquiry* (Fall, 1999). The reasoning, in small print, was that the AHA held the copyrights to the first two manifestos, the implication being that the AHA would sue if the Council for Secular Humanism were to entitle the document as if it were the third of a continuing series.

Signators of Humanist Manifesto 2000, all of whom are listed herein, were named in the fall 1999 issue of *Free Inquiry* as follows:

Abelev, Garry I.
Adams, Phillip
Admiraal, Pieter V.
Allen, Steve
Allen, Norm Allen Jr.
Araujo, Derek
Ardila, Ruben
Arisian, Khoren
Azm, Sadik al
Babic, Jovan
Barnhart, Joseph E.
Baulieu, Etienne
Benaceraff, Baruj
Bhargava, Pushpa Mittra
Birx. H. James
Blakemore, Colin
Bonnet, R. M.
Bouveresse, Jacques
Boydston, Jo Ann
Boyer, Paul D.
Brown, Diana
Brown, Roy
Buckman, Robert
Bullough, Vern L.
Changeux, Jean-Pierre
Cherry, Matt
Clarke, Arthur C.
Cooke, Bill
Cosic, Dobrica
Cranston, Alan
Crick, Bernard
Datta, Amlan
Dawkins, Richard
Delgado, José
Dennett, Daniel C.
Dommanget, Jean
Edamaruku, Samal
Edwards, Paul
Efremov, Yuri Nikolaevich
Eisler, Jan Loeb
Elvin, Lionel
Estrella, Hugo Daniel
Faulkner, Charles W.
Firth, Raymond
Flynn, Thomas
Fragell, Levi
Fussman, Gérard
Ginzburg, Vitali
Gogineni, Babu
Hagtvet, Bernt
Hare, Peter
Haught, James
Hauptman, Herbert A.
Herrick, Jim
Honderich, Ted
Johnson, Reid

Klein, George
Kostelanetz, Richard
Kroto, Harold W.
Kurtz, Paul
Kuvakin, Valerii
Larue, Gerald A.
Lavine, Thelma Z.
Leakey, Richard
LeGoff, Jacques
Lehn, Jean-Marie
Li, Youzheng
Lopes, Leite José
MacCready, Paul
Madigan, Timothy J.
Martin, Michael
Matsumura, Molleen
Millholland, Jean C.
Molina, Mario
Mondale, R. Lester
Morgentaler, Henry
Murad, Ferid
Narasimhaiah, H.
Narisetti, Innaiah
Nasrin, Taslima
Nickell, Joe
Parikh, Indumati
Passmore, John Arthur
Pecker, Jean-Claude
Pedersen, Tove Beate
Pinn, Anthony B.
Radest, Howard
Rao, Avula Sambasiva
Ray, Sibnarayan
Razin, Alexander V.
Razis, Dennis V.
Rood, Max
Saginian, Armen A.
Saramago, José
Schafer, David
Schatzman, Evry
Schick, Theodore Jr.
Shaikh, Anwar
Skou, Jens C.
Smart, J.J.C.
Smith, Warren Allen
Stanosz, Barbara
Stenger, Victor J.
Stojanovic, Svetozar
Stopes-Roe, Harry
Subedi, Ganga Prasad
Tapp, Robert B.
Tarkunde, V. M.
Tarter, Jill
Taylor, Richard
Teimourian, Hazhir
Terzian, Yervant
Tielman, Rob A. P.
Tiger, Lionel
Tuñon, Alberto Hidalgo
Vaughn, Lewis
Venkatadri, Ravipudi
Vukadinovic, Radovan
Wahba, Mourad
Warraq, Ibn
Wilson, Edward O.
Wolpert, Lewis
Wynne Willson, Jane
Zayed, Martin

However, as AHA officials were quick to point out, "our" manifesto was issued by the AHA, not the IAH. Kurtz's having a manifesto copyrighted by the International Academy of Humanism (IAH) bordered upon being "unethical," in their view. Fred Edwords, in a *Humanist* (November-December 1999) review of Humanist Manifesto 2000, complained that

> the IAH cover letter sent this past June to sought-after signers, along with the confidential draft document, may have proved misleading. It referred to Humanist Manifesto II as "our previous Manifesto," as if it had been issued by the IAH instead of the AHA.

First, Edwords went on record that the AHA would eventually publish a Humanist Manifesto III. He also wrote that he had refused to sign the "2000" manifesto, saying that although he was given the chance he had found it "gorged to repletion with an ungodly excess of good ideas," it "runs far too long," and instead of being a manifesto and despite its many prominent signers it is "a learned essay so impractically wordy it needs a table of contents."

Thus, at the end of the century it was obvious to observers that the two major humanist organizations—the American Humanist Association (AHA) and the Council for Secular Humanism (CSH)—were not about to cooperate nor, as predicted by some, merge.

HUMANIST MOVEMENT, A CULT?

Bob von Holdt in "Mysterious Cult Misuses Humanist Label" (*Free Inquiry*, Summer 1990) described a "party" or sect which was set up in Argentina and is known as The Humanist Movement. It has a hierarchical and authoritarian structure that recognizes no democratic decision-making. It uses simple slogans like "for peace" and "against unemployment," concentrating upon young people who are "brainwashed" by means of exhaustive indoctrination and are then encouraged to recruit new youngsters.

"The Movement" follows the teachings of a somewhat mysterious Argentine named Mario Rodriguez Cobo, known by the nickname "Silo," whose ideology is referred to as siloism. It claims to have 10,000 to 20,000 hard-core "true believers" in over 50 countries, although siloists are said to greatly inflate their figures. Its activities appeared in the late 1980s as being primarily focused around San Francisco and New York City. To spread its messages, The Movement uses words such as "green" and "humanist" to appeal to larger numbers.

Von Holdt stated that one enters The Movement as a "group delegate." He or she then recruits ten other new members and becomes a "team delegate," with the ten recruits becoming his or her "base council." The next steps up the pyramid are general delegate, coordinator, and, finally, general coordinator. A 1984 document shows the siloist strategy as trying to promote the appearance of autonomy while maintaining tight internal control. Those who ask too many questions or "who try to hold things back" are invited "to retire so as to prevent our process from being delayed," according to one of The Movement's internal documents.

"Humanist Action's Humanism traces its roots to the first Western Humanists in the Renaissance. For us Humanism basically means that human beings come first. Not the State, not the Church, not the Corporations, not the great-god profit, but humans. This is common with other forms of Humanism. In addition we want to bring these ideas into actual practice, into our political reality," states a 1989 siloist publication in San Francisco.

The Movement's ideology also includes the concepts of "Synthetic Man" (all races and cultures on earth will naturally intermix, and evils such as racism, classism, and so forth will be eliminated because even the secondary psychic and sexual differences of humans will be reduced in humanity's evolutionary step upwards) and "Generational Dialectics" (basically a siloist rewrite of history as a continuous series of struggles of the young vs. the old, explaining why siloist organizing puts such a heavy emphasis on recruiting youth).

The global Green Movement has objected to The Movement's use of "green." Unlike the siloists, legitimate Green groups do not send people to other countries on "missions" to launch new organizations; they do not send funding to other countries; and they do not interfere in the internal politics of other countries. In short, the global Green Movement is as uneasy with The Movement's use of "green" as secular humanists are with The Movement's use of "humanist."

HUMANIST MOVIES

Humanism, Nicolas Walter has pointed out, "may be expressed in many ways, emotional and ethical and aesthetic as well as intellectual and ideological and philosophical." One of the most powerful media for humanist ideas has been the cinema. Responding to a *Guardian* question, the British Humanist Association suggested the following as being top humanistic films: "Singin' in the Rain," "Ginger and Fred," "Tampopo," "Life of Brian," "Truly Madly Deeply," "Casablanca," "Letter to Brezhnev," "My Left Foot," "The Snapper," and "Sense and Sensibility."

Walter's personal choices range far wider: "All Quiet on the Western Front" (United States, 1930); "Kameradschaft" (Germany-France, 1931); "La Grande Illusion" (France, 1937); "The Grapes of Wrath" (United States, 1940); "A Matter of Life and Death" (Britain, 1946); "Living" (Japan, 1952); "La Strada" (Italy, 1954); "The Unknown Soldier" (Finland, 1955); "Pather Panchali" (India, 1955); "Stars" (Germany-Bulgaria, 1959); "War and Peace" (Russia, 1967); and "Johnny Got His Gun" (United States, 1971). {New Humanist, *June 1996*}

HUMANIST MUSIC: See entries for Andrew Charles, Gerry Dantone, Residents, and Freethought Music..

HUMANIST NEWS

Humanist News is a bi-monthly publication of the British Humanist Association, Bradlaugh House, 47 Theobald's Road, London WC1X 8SP, United Kingdom.

HUMANIST NEWSLETTER, A BULLETIN OF NATURALISTIC HUMANISM

In 1953, Warren Allen Smith founded and edited *The Humanist Newsletter, A Bulletin of Naturalistic Humanism*, which became the newsletter of New York City's American Humanist Association chapter, which he also founded. Five thousand copies of issue #1 were distributed, but the subscription list settled at several hundred. Charles Francis Potter was contributing editor and wrote the following description of "the ideal humanist":

> The ideal humanist is a well-rounded person, intellectually informed, keenly intelligent, intuitively developed, and emotionally sensitive. He is well-balanced, appreciative of beauty in poetry, music, and art; that is, responsive to sound and harmony, form and color, and to the infinite inspirations of nature—sunsets and stars, mountain-tops and flowers—but, most of all, appreciative of the marvelous depths and heights, and infinite possibilities of human personality.

Subscribers included John Dewey, William Heard Kilpatrick, Mark Starr, Walter Breen, Horace Kallen, Eva Ingersoll Wakefield, Sherman Wakefield, Sidney Hook, Corliss Lamont, Homer Jack, James T. Farrell, Max Lerner, Erich Fromm, Joseph Wood Krutch, Paul Edwards, Rudolf Dreikurs, George Axtelle, and Harry A. Overstreet. The $2. per year subscription included membership in the Humanist Book Club, also founded by Smith and which supplied humanistic books at a discount. The publication ceased in December 1953, but the AHA chapter continued.

Its Action Committee in 1953, headed by Eva Ingersoll Wakefield, the granddaughter of Robert Green Ingersoll, wired Pres. Dwight Eisenhower, "We applaud and congratulate you on your letter to the American Library Association. All men will be the losers of the Cold War if it costs them the right of free inquiry." Sherman Adams, Assistant to the President, wired back, "Please accept the President's thanks for the message of June twenty-eighth which you sent him on behalf of the members of your Committee. Your kind words of approval and commendation are appreciated."

The committee also sent a letter to the President objecting to his appointment of Gov. James F. Byrnes of South Carolina as one of the U.S. delegates to the eighth U.N. General Assembly: "Naming such an individual, one who has consistently avowed racial inequality and segregation policies, is a shot-in-the-arm for Malanism and a travesty upon the ideals of American democracy." This time, Mr. Adams did not respond. (See entry for Columbia University librarian C. C. Williamson, who was angry that so few in New York were supporting the newsletter. "Let these N.Y. bitches wake up after the hierarchy and McCarthy have taken over. Don't you know that New Yorkers are the most conservative of animals; take a look at N. Y. Unitarians if you think local liberals are ready for humanism," he wrote.)

HUMANIST NORWAY

Humanist Norway's e-mail address is as follows: <humanist@human.no>.

HUMANIST ORGANISATION FOR SOCIAL WORK (HUMANITAS)

The Humanist Organisation for Social Work (Humanitas), a specialist member of the International Humanist and Ethical Union, is at Postbox 71, 1000 AB Amsterdam, Netherlands.

HUMANIST OUTLOOK

Humanist Outlook is an Indian quarterly published in English at POB 448, New Delhi 110 001, India. <pnarain@ignca.ernet.in>.

HUMANIST PARTY

The Humanist Party, also known as a feature of "siloism," is an organization which promotes its own style of humanism. Marcus Wende, in a booklet called "*Siloismus - Tarn -und Unterorganisationen einter Psychogruppe*," has written the following criticism:

> • The so-called Humanist Party also uses a variety of other names and was founded by the Argentinean Mario Luis Rodriguez Cobos. He uses the name Silo, which comes from Shiloh in *Genesis* 49:10 and is interpreted to mean "the ruler."
>
> • This group is concerned exclusively with achieving power and influence for a small leadership-circle. Their ultimate aim is to erect a totalitarian world-state. To achieve their purposes they exploit idealistically-minded young people and progressive organizations. When this movement or its subsidiary groups join other organizations, they soon appear as parasites, exploiting the reputation and the connections of the organizations joined. They show numerous characteristics of a destructive cult, as defined by Steven Hassan for example, control of the behavior of the minds and emotions of members. Their religious background is strongly gnostic.

Secular humanist and rationalist groups are concerned that some individuals and groups confuse siloism with secular humanism and rationalism. The group is accused of misusing the name "humanism" as a cover for its religious and political purpose of "saving the world." (See entry for Humanist Movement.) {*International Humanist News*, September 1997}

HUMANIST PRESS ASSOCIATION

The Humanist Press Association was successor to the Humanist

Fellowship and became the first organized national association of humanism in the United States.

According to Edwin H. Wilson, it was inspired by the Rationalist Press Association. Later, on the suggestion of Curtis W. Reese, it was reorganized as the American Humanist Association. {EW}

HUMANIST PROFESSIONAL

Humanist Professional is published at 4076 Hampshire Avenue N., Crystal, Minnesota 55427.

HUMANIST REVIEW

Humanist Review is published by the Israel Secular Humanist Society at POB 17141, Tel Aviv 61171, Israel. {FD}

HUMANIST SIG, MENSA

HUMSIG, a Humanist SIG (special interest group within Mensa, sometimes labeled "the high-IQ society), is run by Larry Reyka, POB 14123, Columbus, Ohio 43214.

HUMANIST SOCIETY OF FRIENDS

The Humanist Society of Friends (IHEU) is at PO Box 220, Hyde Park, Vermont 05655. On the Web: <http://humanist.net/hsof/>.

Larry Reyka, a chaplain of the Humanist Society of Friends and a member of the American Humanist Association, has described the group:

> In July of 1939, a group of Quakers, after reading the 1933 Humanist Manifesto and being greatly moved by it, made the big decision to leave the Quaker movement and become part of the new Humanist movement. In its tenets, they saw the promise of a genuine marriage between science and ethics that would put into action a new kind of religion and forge a new understanding of the word "religion".
>
> Humanism was to them a concept echoing the admonition voiced by Sir Morley of England, who said: "The next great task of Science is the building of a new religion," and which affirmed the thoughts of Sir Julian Huxley in his book Evolution in Action, where he wrote of "Evolutionary Humanism" as "perhaps capable of becoming the germ of a new religion . . . justified by facts."
>
> It was therefore with the goal in mind that this small band of former Quakers were responsible in 1939 for incorporating under the state laws of California the "Humanist Society of Friends" as a religious, educational, charitable nonprofit organization authorized to issue charters anywhere in the world, and to train and ordain its own ministry, who upon ordination were then accorded the same rights and privileges granted by law to the priests, ministers, and rabbis of traditional theistic religions.
>
> Today, the Humanist Society of Friends works as a subsidiary of the American Humanist Association to certify qualified members to serve in this special capacity, having assumed the duties of the American Humanist Association's former Division of Humanist Counseling.
>
> In communities all over, individuals certified to our unique ministry stand ready to provide ceremonial observances of the significant occasions of life.

HUMANIST SOCIETY OF GREATER NEW YORK

Under the executive directorship of Joseph Ben-David, the New York Chapter of the American Humanist Association flourished in the 1970s. (See entry for New York Chapter, American Humanist Association.)

HUMANIST SOCIETY OF NEW ZEALAND

The Humanist Society of New Zealand (IHEU) is at POB 3372, Wellington, New Zealand. {FD}

HUMANIST SOCIETY OF SCOTLAND

For information about the Scottish Humanist Society (IHEU), write Secretary George Rodger, 17 Howburn Place, Aberdeen AB11 6XT, Scotland; or the convener, Robin Wood, at 37 Inchmurrin Drive, Kilmarnock, Ayrshire KA3 2JD, telephone 01563 526710.

HUMANIST SOCIETY OF SCOTLAND, EDINBURGH GROUP

For information about Edinburgh Humanist Society, write 2 Saville Terrace, Edinburgh #H9 3AD or telephone 0131 667 8389.

HUMANIST SOCIETY OF SCOTLAND, GLASGOW GROUP

For information about the Glasgow Humanist Society, write Hugh H. Bowman, 25 Riverside Park, Glasgow G44 3PG; telephone 0141 633 3748.

HUMANIST UNION OF FINLAND

An associate member of the IHEU is the Humanist Union of Finland, PO Box 793, 00101 Helsinki 10, Finland.

HUMANIST VIEWPOINTS

A monthly, *Humanist Viewpoints* is published by Humanist House, 10 Shepherd Street, Chippendale, N.S.W. 2-0-9. Australia. The past editor, John Tendy, has been succeeded by Affie Adagio. E-mail: <affiea@hotmail.com>.

HUMANIST WORLD FELLOWSHIP

The Humanist World Fellowship before 1952 published *Humanist World*, which then was called *Humanist World Digest, A Quarterly of Liberal Religion.* The publication originally started in 1928 as *Welcome News*. E. O. Corson was editor and editorial associates included Felix J. Frazer, Phillip B. Oliver, Victor Yarros, and William E. Zeuch. The aims of the Berkeley, California, fellowship were as follows:

> 1. Full endorsement of the Universal Declaration of Human Rights approved by the General Assembly of the United Nations at the Plenary meeting December 10, 1948, and world-wide implementation and fulfillment of those rights at the earliest possible moment.
>
> 2. The use of science to serve society, creatively, constructively, and altruistically in the preservation of life, the production of abundance of goods and services, and the promotion of health and happiness.
>
> 3. The establishment and furthering of scientific integral education in all schools and colleges so as to emancipate all peoples from the thralldom of ignorance, superstition, prejudices and myths which impede individual development and forestall social progress.
>
> 4. The widest promotion of the creative arts so as to release all potential, artistic abilities and raise the general level of artistic appreciation.
>
> 5. The increase of social, recreational, and travel activities in order to broaden the outlook and improve the intercultural understanding among all peoples.
>
> 6. A quickened conservation of the world's natural resources, including human resources, so as to arrest their wasteful exhaustion and wanton destruction and thus insure their longest preservation and widest beneficial use for man's survival on this planet.
>
> 7. The inauguration of a world-wide economy of abundance through national economic planning and international economic cooperation so as to provide a shared plenty for all peoples.
>
> 8. The advancement of the good life on the basis of a morality determined by historical human experience and contemporary scientific research.
>
> 9. The development of a coordinated private, cooperative, and public medical program which will provide preventive as well as curative medicine and include adequate public health education and personal health counseling.

10. The expansion of United Nations functions (a) to include international police power with sufficient armed forces to prevent war and (b) international economic controls capable of preventing world-wide monopolies and/or cartels.

HUMANIST YOUTH

Humanist youth groups are found on the Web: <http://www.secularhumanism.org/cfa/orgs.html>.

HUMANIST, TIDSSKRIFT FOR LIVSSYNDEBATT

Humanist, Tidsskrift for Livssyndebatt, a Norwegian bi-monthly of *Human-Etisk Forbund i Norge*, is at PO Box 6744, St. Olavs Plass, 0130 Oslo, Norway.

HUMANISTE AKTION

Humaniste Aktion, a German humanist group of which Rudolf Kuhr is a contact, is on the Web: <http://home.t-online.de/home/humanist.aktion/>.

HUMANISTEN

A bi-monthly published in English, *Humanisten* is at Box 5048, S-402 21 Göteborg, Sweden <mikael.goransson@migor.se>.

HUMANISTI

A quarterly in Finnish of the Humanist Union of Finland, *Humanisti* is at PL 793, 00101 Helsinki, Finland. <pekka.elo@freenet.hut.fi>.

HUMANISTIC JUDAISM

Humanistic Judaism is a journal "for those who understand and appreciate the Jewish past and present in ways consistent with the best insights of modern thought, . . . for secular Jews who seek to celebrate Jewish holidays in a meaningful way, . . . for Jews who value their Jewish identity and seek an alternative to conventional Judaism, . . . that gives voice to the secular humanistic viewpoint on the critical issues of today." The tri-quarterly journal's address is 28611 West Twelve Mile Road, Farmington Hills, Michigan 48334. (For a negative critique, see entry for Society for Humanistic Judaism.)

HUMANISTIC MUSIC: See entry for Freethought Music.

HUMANISTIC NATURALISM

Although "naturalistic humanism" is the phrase which has been used by Corliss Lamont and many secular humanists, agnostics, and freethinkers, "humanistic naturalism" is the phrase which others prefer. For example, as found in the present work, the following responded to their choice of terms when asked:

Kenneth Lee Patton (Unitarian Universalist Leader, author of *Hello Man*)

[I am a Naturalistic Humanist in my outlook] . . . although I would prefer to call it Humanistic Naturalism, for I believe naturalism is the larger and more definitive term for the position I hold, and humanism only modifies it.

John Dewey (philosopher and educator; signer of Humanist Manifesto I)

"Humanism" as a technical philosophic term is associated with [F.C.S.] Schiller and while I have great regard for his writings, it seems to me that he gave Humanism an unduly subjectivistic turn—he was so interested in bringing out the elements of human desire and purpose neglected in traditional philosophy that he tends it seems to me to a virtual isolation of man from the rest of nature. I have come to think of my own position as cultural or humanistic Naturalism—Naturalism, properly interpreted seems to me a more adequate term than Humanism. Of course I have always limited my use of "instrumentalism" to my theory of thinking and knowledge; the word pragmatism I have used very little, and then with reserves.

Gutmann, James (philosopher and author with Corliss Lamont of *Dialogue on George Santayana)*

Let me begin by paraphrasing the classical *Nihil humanum mihi alienum puto* and rendering it—No humanistic philosophy is alien to me. However, though dubious as to the value of pigeon-holing ideas and of much labeling in philosophy, I feel sure that of the categories which you list, 'naturalistic humanist' fits me best. Without wishing to be fussy I should prefer "humanistic naturalism" to "naturalistic humanism" both because Nature includes Human Nature and because it is the setting in which men discover the pluriverse or creatively conceive it as a universe. This view of humanism, in its essentials, is, I believe, shared by all naturalistically inclined thinkers from the ancients to our day and even appeals to certain supernaturalists. Among the ancients, pre-Socratic philosophy, Socrates, Plato, and Aristotle, all seem to make most sense when interpreted in these terms.

This tradition of interpretation I first learned from F. J. E. Woodbridge forty years ago when he was expounding it along with George Santayana and John Dewey. Irwin Edman learned much from these men and carried on these teachings as have my other Columbia University colleagues, each in his own way and without constituting a "school of thought," since we would rather be a school of thinking and value variety and diversity of viewpoints as becomes the humanistic tradition.

If similarly forced to choose a label for his philosophic outlook and based upon findings of the present research, the present author would respond "humanistic naturalism" for the following reasons: (a) my basic outlook is naturalistic, not supernaturalistic; (b) the scientific method of reasoning is paramount in my search for truths; and (c) the humanities supply my inspiration for the good life. (See entries for Kenneth L. Patton, John Dewey, James Gutmann, and Warren Allen Smith.)

HUMANISTIC RELIGIOUS ASSOCIATION

The Humanistic Religious Association was formed in 1853. {See entry for English Humanism.}

HUMANISTIC SCIENCE INSTITUTE

Humanistic Science Institute can be e-mailed: <jwprescott@aol.com>.

HUMANISTISCH JONGREREN SERVICE

In Belgium, a humanist group is *Humanistisch Jongreren Service* (IHEU) at Rogierstraat 134, 12110 Brussels, Belgium.

HUMANISTISCH STICHTING HUISVESTING BEJAARDEN

A Dutch humanist group is *Humanistisch Stichting Huisvesting Bejaarden* (IHEU), at Postbus 70510, 1007 KM Amsterdam, Netherlands. It concerns itself with housing of the elderly.

HUMANISTISCH STUDIECENTRUM NEDERLAND

A Dutch humanist group in which all Dutch humanist groups work together is *Humanistisch Studiecentrum Nederland* (IHEU) at Postbus 797, 3500 AT, Utrecht, Netherlands.

HUMANISTISCH THUISFRONT

A Dutch group involved with obtaining humanist houses for the military is *Humanistisch Thuisfront* (IHEU), at Willemskade 19a, 8011 AD Zwolle, Netherlands.

HUMANISTISCH VERBOND

In 1946 the *Humanistisch Verbond* (Postbus 75490, 1070 AL Amsterdam, The Netherlands) was formed with the objective of "deepening the spiritual life of the non-denominational section of the Dutch population and participating in the spiritual reconstruction of our country. In 1996, the group celebrated its golden jubilee in Amsterdam. E-mail: <hv@euronet.nl>. {*International Humanist News*, April 1996}

HUMANISTISCH VERBOND BELGIE

A full member of the IHEU is *Humanistisch Verbond Belgie* at Lange Leemstraat 57, B-2018 Antwerpen, Belgium. It has about eighty branches in Flanders.

HUMANISTICHER VERBAND DEUTSCHLANDS

The *Humanisticher Verband Deutschlands*, a full member of the International Humanist and Ethical Union, is at Hobrechstrasse 8, 12043, Berlin, Germany. E-mail: <hvdberlin@aol.com>.

HUMANISTS OF THE PALM BEACHES (HOPB)

Marvin Engle heads Humanists of the Palm Beaches and in 1996 was named Florida Humanist of the Year. The group is affiliated jointly with the American Humanist Association (AHA) and the Alliance of Secular Humanist Societies (ASHS).

HUMANISTS, ETHICAL

Ethical humanism is a term used in Latin America. *Asociación Ético Humanista Costarricense* (ASEHUCO) commenced in 1989 and its president is Marco Castillo Rojas. The group can be contacted on the Web: <http://idt.net/~wasm/asibehu>.

Asociación Mexicana Ética Racionalista (AMER) published in 1995 the first issue of a quarterly, *Razonamientos*. On its editorial board are humanists from Argentina, Canada, Colombia, Mexico, the Netherlands, Peru, Spain, and the United States of America. E-mail: <mendezm@spin.com.mx>.

Asociación Ibero-Americana Ético Humanista (Apartado 1057, 2050 San Pedro, Costa Rica), which commenced in 1994 in San José, Costa Rica, is an association of Spanish-speaking ethical humanists in South, Central, and North America. The association was made possible by a generous grant from the International Humanist and Ethical Union (IHEU) and by the efforts of Rob Tielman, Matt Cherry, Paul Kurtz, Tim Madigan, and Warren Allen Smith. ASIBEHU's first president was Alexander Cox Alvarado. Its webmaster and executive director is Ricardo Otárola.

Sociedad Humanista-Ética Argentina is located in Córdoba, Argentina. Its executive director is Hugo Daniel Estrella. E-mail: <humanistarg@usa.net>.

On the World Wide Web: <http://idt.net/~wasm/asibehu>

HUMANISTS, LAUGHING

"Many naturalistic Humanists (when conversing with one another, one should add) dare to pinpoint their views more specifically by adding a qualifying adjective which places them apart from their brothers in the humanist movement and satisfies them that, semantically speaking, the fuller term communicates their 'exact' view on life," wrote Warren Allen Smith in *Humanist World Digest* (August 1955). He continued, "Witness, for instance, the 'scientific' naturalistic Humanists. These are the boys who have declined B.A. for B.S., who are today the world's leading experts in the breeding of angels (*Pterophyllum scalare*) or in Banjoewangi's musical mores. Their counterparts are the 'academic' naturalistic humanists, who know that Euripides did not believe in immortality nor Elmer Gantry in morality."

He cites as an example Lin Yutang who, as early as 1937, wrote how he studied philosophy . . . the incorrect way: "I do not read philosophy, but only read life at first hand." His teachers, therefore, were not Lucretius nor Pericles, but included a Soochow boatwoman with her profuse use of expletives, a cook's wife, a squirrel in Central Park, all news in boxes, and any writer who does not kill our sense of curiosity in life or who has not killed it in himself." (See entries for Lin Yutang and for Carl Jonas.)

HUMANITARIANISM

In theology, humanitarianism is a doctrine holding that Jesus was human only, not divine. In philosophy and in general usage, humanitarianism refers to being devoted to the promotion of human welfare and the advancement of social reforms.

If a vegetarian is one who eats vegetables, asks a Manhattan wag, is it in our best interests to tell uneducated people that we are humanitarians?

HUMANITAS

Humanitas (IHEU), at Postbus 71, 1000 AB Amsterdam, Netherlands, is an organization for social work. E-mail: <info@lb.humanitas.nl>. {FD}

HUMANITIES

The humanities are those subjects in the liberal arts which are concerned with human thought and culture: philosophy, literature, music, art, history, languages, architecture. Not included, for example, are chemistry and physics, subjects which are among those concerned with natural processes. In 1966 in the United States, the humanities accounted for 20.7 percent of all bachelor's and 13.8 percent of all doctoral degrees; in 1993, those percentages had dropped to 12.7 percent and 9.1 percent respectively, according to Alvin Kernan's *What's Happened to the Humanities?* (1997).

An intellectual concern is that schools and the media have been downplaying the humanities, emphasizing culture wars and debates over deconstruction, multiculturalism, and gender studies.

HUMANITY

In 1924 the *Positivist Review* changed its name to *Humanity*.

Humanity, the current United Kingdom publication of the British Humanist Association, is at 47 Theobald's Road, London, WC1X 8SP.

E-mail: <supy@supycro.demon.co.uk> and <robert@humanism.org.uk>.

HUMANKIND: See entry for Mankind, the word that was used more often toward the end of the century.

HUMAN-NEPAL

Human-Nepal is a Nepalese humanist organization.

HUMANS, DECLINE IN CREATIVITY: See entry for Decline of Human Creativity.

HUMANUS

Humanus, a bi-monthly in Norwegian, is at St. Olavs gate 27, 0166, Oslo, Norway. E-mail: <skaara@human.no>.

Humbles, Gladman C. (20th Century)

Humbles, an African humanist and the first black firefighter in Paducah, Kentucky, has written of his "personal path" to humanism in *AAH Examiner* (Fall 1993).

Humboldt, Friedrich Heinrich Alexander von (1769—1859)

Humboldt was a German naturalist who studied under Heyne and Blumenbach and who became director-general of mines. In 1799 he explored South America and Mexico, returning in 1804 with a rich collection of animals, plants, and minerals. Becoming a resident of Paris, Humboldt was friends with Lalande, Delambre, Arago, and other distinguished scientists. At the age of seventy-four he composed *Cosmos*. To Varnhagen von Ense he wrote in 1841: "Bruno Bauer has found me pre-adamatically converted. Many years ago I wrote, '*Toutes les réligions positive offrent trois parties distinctes: un traité de moeurs partout le même et très pur, un rêve géologique, et un mythe ou petit roman historique; le dernier élêment obtient le plus d'importance.'* " Later, he says that Strauss disposes of "the Christian myths." McCabe calls Baron Humboldt a vague pantheist, adding that his brother, Baron Karl Wilhelm (1767-1835), the founder of Berlin University, was a deist. {BDF; JM; RAT; RE}

Humboldt, Karl Wilhelm von (1767—1835)

Humboldt was a Prussian statesman and philosopher. When he went to Paris in 1789, he hailed the revolution with enthusiasm and, in 1792, published *Ideas on the Organisation of the State*. He became a friend of Schiller and Goethe, and in 1809 was made Minister of Public Instruction. Humboldt advocated a liberal constitution but, finding the King averse, retired at the end of 1819. Three things, Humboldt said, he could not understand: orthodox piety, romantic love, and music. Like his brother, Humboldt was a pantheist. {BDF; RAT; RE}

Hume, David (1711—1776)

A noted Scot, arguably one of the most important philosophers who ever lived, Hume wrote against the possibility of miracles: "A miracle is a violation of the laws of nature." Maréchal cited Hume, the first prominent European to be outspokenly non-theistic, as being one of the greatest atheists of all time. In the *Encyclopedia of Unbelief*, Antony Flew calls Hume the first major thinker of the modern period whose work was thoroughly secular, this-worldly, and man-centered. Hume once gave refuge to Jean Jacques Rousseau, although later they had a falling out. Hume is known for pressing the analysis of John Locke and George Berkeley to the logical extreme of skepticism. He could see no more reason for hypothesizing a substantial soul or mind than for accepting a substantial material world. He was a nominalist, one who rejected any rational or natural theology.

An Enquiry Concerning Human Understanding (1748) has a section X, "Of Miracles," in which Hume did not claim to show that miracles have never occurred. Rather, states William Grey of the department of philosophy, the University of New England, in Armidale, Australia, Hume addressed "the epistemological issue of what it is rational to believe, rather than the metaphysical question of what is and is not possible in our sort of world." One of his epistemological maxims was "A wise man proportions his belief to the evidence." And in a statement which echoed Ockham and has been called Hume's Razor, Hume wrote, "No testimony is sufficient to establish a miracle unless that testimony be of such a kind that its falsehood would be more miraculous than the fact which it endeavours to establish."

Robertson evaluates Hume's work as follows:

> Hume, knowing that strict skepticism is practically null in life, counted on leaving the ground cleared for experiential rationalism. And he did, insofar as he was read. His essay, *Of Miracles* (with the rest of the *Inquiries* of 1748-1751, which recast his early *Treatise of Human Nature* (1739), posits a principle valid against all supernaturalism whatever; while his *Natural History of Religion* (1757), though affirming deism, rejected the theory of a primordial monotheism, and laid the basis of the science of Comparative Hierology. Finally, his posthumous *Dialogues Concerning Natural Religion* (1779) admits, though indirectly, the untenability of deism, and falls back decisively upon the atheistic or agnostic position. Like Descartes, he lacked the heroic fibre; but like him he recast philosophy for modern Europe; and its subsequent course is but a development of or a reaction against his work.

Paul Edwards, however, concluded in "God and the Philosophers" (*Free Inquiry*, Fall 1998), "Hume has sometimes been called a deist, but in fact he was what we would now call an agnostic." Edwards pointed out that the works of Hume and Kant "had a significant impact on Christian and Jewish philosophy, resulting in the widespread adoption of a position known as 'fideism'—belief in God (or other religious propositions) on the basis of faith alone."

Although Hume's *Treatise on Human Nature* received little interest when published, friendly or hostile, his *Natural History of Religion* was furiously attacked by Warburton in an anonymous tract. Warburton, who had been chaplain to George II and was dean of Bristol, was a learned anti-deist. a warm friend of Alexander Pope and executor of Pope's estate.

Fortune was not so kind to Hume as fame. At the age of forty, his frugal habits had enabled him to save no more than £1,000. He reckoned his income at £50 a year, but his wants were few and his spirit was cheerful. In 1775 his health began to fail. Knowing that his disorder (hemorrhage of the bowels) would prove fatal, ten days before his death Hume amended his will, making arrangements for his nephew to publish his *Dialogues Concerning Natural Religion*. This was because his friend and fellow Scot, Adam Smith, was reluctant to have his own name associated with the work. In a five-page letter to the publisher, "The Life of David Hume, Esq; Written by Himself" (1777), Smith wrote, "Poor David Hume is dying very fast, but with great cheerfulness and good humour and with more real resignation to the necessary course of things, than any Whining Christian ever dyed with pretended resignation to the will of God." The publisher omitted the reference to "Whining Christians." Smith also toned down a remark Hume had once made, that perhaps Charon could be talked into delaying his passage to the other word in order to give him more time to rid the world of Christianity. "Good Charon, I have been endeavouring to open the eyes of people; have a little patience only till I have the pleasure of seeing the churches shut up, and the Clergy sent about their business; but Charon would reply, O you loitering rogue; that wont happen these 200 years; do you fancy I will give you a lease for so long a time? Get into the boat this instant." What Smith published, however, was "Have a little patience, good Charon: I have been endeavouring to open the eyes of the Public. If I live a few years longer, I may have the satisfaction of seeing the downfall of some of the prevailing systems of superstition."

Richard Taylor, emeritus professor of philosophy in Rochester, has contested the idea that Hume was a humanist. "He does not attack faith," Taylor wrote in *Free Inquiry* (Spring 1998). "Indeed, the final conclusion of [*Dialogues Concerning Natural Religion*] is that Cleanthes, the defender of religious faith, is the one who came closest to the truth. Hume's ethical writings were similarly antirationalistic. Morality, he convincingly claimed, rests not on reason, but on sentiment or feeling." Paul Kurtz, responding, wrote, "Hume belongs to the pantheon of humanist heroes because he surely was a precurser of contemporary secular humanism. He did not believe that we had any evidence for miraculous intervention, or in the immortality of the soul; he sought to relate the principles of ethics, not to divine deliverance, but to human experience. Thus his critique of theology is the most devastating that we have in modern philosophy."

Although there were some clerical libels about Hume's last hours, Hume rejected the concept of immortality to his dying day, at which time Adam Smith offered the encomium of Hume: "as approaching as nearly to the idea of a perfectly wise and virtuous man, as perhaps the nature of human frailty will permit." In a similar vein, D. G. C. MacNabb wrote of Hume, "The manner in which he faced his death from cancer was a paradigm of cheerful philosophic acceptance of annihilation, in the ancient Epicurean tradition."

Smith, one of Hume's most intimate friends, described how Hume had gone to London in April, 1776, and soon after his return he "gave up all hope of recovery, but submitted with the utmost cheerfulness, and the most perfect complacency and resignation." His cheerfulness was so great that many people could not believe he was dying. "Mr. Hume's magnanimity and firmness were such," said Adam Smith, that his most affectionate friends knew that they hazarded nothing in talking and writing to him as a dying man, and that, so far from being hurt by this frankness, he was rather pleased and flattered by it." His chief thought in relation to the possible prolongation of his life, which his friends hoped although he told them their hopes were groundless, was that he would have "the satisfaction of seeing the downfall of some of the prevailing systems of superstition." On August 8, Adam Smith went to Kircaldy, leaving Hume in a very weak state but still very cheerful. On August 28, he received the following letter from Dr. Black, the physician, announcing the philosopher's death:

> Edinburgh,
> Monday, August 26, 1776
>
> Dear Sir, — Yesterday about four o'clock, afternoon, Mr. Hume expired. The near approach of his death became evident in the night between Thursday and Friday, when his disease became excessive, and soon weakened him so much, that be could no longer rise out of his bed. He continued to the last perfectly sensible and free from much pain and feelings of distress. He never dropped the smallest expression of impatience; but when he had occasion to speak to the people about him, always did it with affection and tenderness. I thought it improper to write to bring you over, especially as I heard that he had dictated a letter to you, desiring you not to come. When he became weak it cost him an effort to speak, and he died in such a happy composure of mind that nothing could exceed it.

When Hume died, Benjamin Franklin proclaimed the date as a portent of the attraction of non-theism which would follow. Hume was buried a few days later on the eastern slope of Calton Hill, Edinburgh, his body being "attended by a great concourse of people, who seem to have anticipated for it the fate appropriate to wizards and necromancers."

"Thus," says Adam Smith in a 1776 letter to William Strahan, "died our most excellent and never to be forgotten friend. Upon the whole, I have always considered him, both in his lifetime and since his death as approaching as nearly to the idea of a perfectly wise and virtuous man as perhaps the nature of human frailty will permit."

Boswell and others were offended by accounts of Hume's "pagan" death and once wrote that "Were it not for his infidel writings, every body would love him. He is a plain, obliging, kind-hearted man." But when Boswell visited Hume seven weeks before his death, Hume told him that religion had a bad effect on morality: "He then said flatly that the morality of every religion was bad . . . [and] that when he heard a man was religious, he concluded he was a rascal, though he had known some instances of very good men being religious." Boswell was shocked by Hume's persistent infidelity and view that morality depends not on traditional religion but on an innate moral sense. Hoping for a deathbed conversion, Boswell visited the dying Hume and wrote in his diary,

> He then said flatly that the morality of every religion was bad, and, I really thought, was not jocular when he said that when he heard a man was religious, he concluded that he was a rascal. . . . Speaking of his singular notion that men of religion were generally bad men, he said: "One of the men of the greatest honor that I ever knew is my Lord Marischal, who is a downright atheist. I remember I once hinted something as if I believed in the being of a God, and he would not speak to me for a week."

Samuel Johnson thought it impossible to believe that Hume was actually dying a non-believer and informed Boswell, "He lies, Sir." Meanwhile, according to Boswell, Johnson, who never attacked Hume in print, wrote in his journal that "Hume and other infidels...destroyed our principles and put nothing firm in their place."

Knowing he was disliked by Johnson and others for his provocative views, Hume had written that, after all, such English critics were "relapsing into the deepest Stupidity, Christianity, and ignorance." When, finally, he would die a model and tranquil death, Hume felt, by his deportment he would further support the views he had so eloquently espoused. Any number of contemporary philosophers would agree, including Paul Edwards. In his *Immortality* (1992), Edwards, citing Hume as one who rejected not only God but also any belief in survival after death, is but one of many who publicly have stated that Hume is among the great philosophers of all time.

A twelve-foot-high statue in honor of Hume is on High Street in the center of Edinburgh, near Hume's home. Alexander Stoddard, the sculptor, rather than sculpting Hume in period dress chose to clothe him as a "universal man" who spoke beyond his time. The toga-clad Hume is seated, and in his hand he holds a blank tablet (*tabula rasa*). (David Fate Norton and Mary J. Norton have catalogued Hume's extensive collection of books, using "The David Hume Library" as the title of their National Library of Scotland work. Based on his 1854 edition, *The Philosophical Works of David Hume* was published as a four-volume work in 1996.) {BDF; CE; CL; ER; EU, Anthony Flew and Aram Vartanian; FO; FUK; FUS; HAB; JM; JMR; JMRH; D. G. C. MacNabb, *Encyclopedia of Philosophy*, Vol. 4; PA; PUT; RAT; RE; TRI; TSV; TYD}

HUME SOCIETY

The Hume Society is a group of more than four hundred individuals worldwide who engage in scholarly activity concerning David Hume and share the fruits of their efforts at annual conferences, through correspondence, the *Bulletin of the Hume Society*, and *Hume Studies*. Their address is The Hume Society, care of the Department of Philosophy, Occidental College, Los Angeles, California 90041.

On the Web: <http://www.hi.is/~mike/hume.html>.

HUMOR

• Nowhere in the Holy Bible does Jesus smile. The Ancient Greek gods, however, were known for their joviality and revelry. What does that say about Jesus-lovers?

—Anonymous

• Give a man a fish, and you'll feed him for a day. Give him a religion, and he'll starve to death while praying for a fish.

—Anonymous

• There is no better role to play among the great than that of jester.

—Denis Diderot,
Le Neveu de Rameau

• Wit makes its own welcome and levels all distinct-ions.

—Ralph Waldo Emerson,
"The Comic"

• Impropriety is the soul of wit.

—Somerset Maugham,
The Moon and Sixpence

• Wit is the epitaph of an emotion.

—Friedrich Nietzsche,
Miscellaneous Maxims and Opinions

• The quality of wit inspires more admiration than confidence.

—George Santayana,
The Sense of Beauty

• The way of joking is to tell the truth.

—George Bernard Shaw,
John Bull's Other Island

• The secret source of humor is not joy but sorrow. There is no humor in heaven.

—Mark Twain,
Pudd'n head Wilson

• Everything is funny as long as it happens to some-body else.

—Will Rogers,
The Illiterate Digest

• It's hard to be funny when you have to be clean.

—Mae West,
The Wit and Wisdom of Mae West

• "Don't pay any attention to that," the secular humanist parents told their young daughter who had learned about the Holy Trinity at school. "There's only one god, and we don't believe in him!"

—Anonymous on the Internet

• If only God would give me some clear sign! Like making a large deposit in my name at a Swiss bank.

—Woody Allen

• I'd hate to tell you what they call my son in Harlem.

Jocasta, to a Greek chorus in
"Mighty Aphrodite"
—Woody Allen

(See entries for Humanist Humor; and for Language and Communication and Marketing of Organized Religion.)

Humphrey, John Peter (1905-1995)

A Canadian academic and humanitarian, Humphrey authored the first draft of the Universal Declaration of Human Rights. In 1946 he became Director of the United Nations Division of Human Rights, presiding for twenty years over dozens of human rights commissions and the implementation of their resolutions. In Canada he founded the Canadian Human Rights Foundation and the Canadian branch of Amnesty Internation. Also, he was the Vice President and only Canadian ever to serve on the International Commission of Jurists.

Although for years René Cassin was regarded as the author of the Declaration and even received a Nobel Peace Prize in 1968, researchers later unearthed papers at the McGill University Library—where Humphrey was dean of law prior to his joining the UN—showing that he had written the original draft of the ideas. In 1946 Eleanor Roosevelt gave Humphrey the assignment to draft an international bill of rights, and his was the original draft of forty-eight articles. {Earl Doherty, "John Peter Humphrey, Unsung Canadian Hero," in *Humanist in Canada*, Wineter 1998-1999}

Humphrey, Nicholas (20th Century)

Humphrey is the first research fellow in parapsychology at England's Cambridge University who, in 1996, is a professor of psychology at the New School for Social Research in New York City. An activist, materialist, and anti-dualist, he has forthrightly declared, "After a hundred years of experiments into the paranormal, they have come up with nothing convincing. I want to show not only that these things don't happen, but that they are logically impossible, that the paranormal is all in the mind." According to *Skeptical Inquirer* (Winter 1993), he added, "Roman Catholicism without the paranormal would be nothing; it needs its miracles. But then who needs Catholicism? Praying has no paranormal benefits—statistically, it is not going to help. The most important work to be done in this area is to expose the fallacies. This is not a game. A lot of people are putting around misleading ideas, and others are being conned financially and intellectually."

Humphrey is a distinguished theoretical psychologist, a leading authority on the evolution of the brain. He is author of *A History of the Mind* (1992) and *Soul Searching* (1995), in which he gives an academic account of human nature and supernatural belief. Ub *Leaps of Faith: Science, Miracles, and the Search for Supernatural Consolation* (1996), Humphrey shows his impatience with educated people, including several Nobel Prize-winning scientists, who cling to the belief that the paranormal is real. {CA; E}

Humphreys, Brett (20th Century)

Humphreys is assistant editor in England of the *Gay and Lesbian Humanist.* (See entry for Gay & Lesbian Humanist Association [England].)

Humphry, Derek (1930—)

Humphry, founder of the Hemlock Society (USA), is author of *Final Exit* (1992), a manual about euthanasia for those who are persuaded that suicide is appropriate under certain circumstances. Humphry had assisted his own wife Jean's death, receiving much unfavorable publicity for having done so—*Let Me Die Before I Wake* (1981) details her final hours. In *Lawful Exit: The Limits of Freedom for Help in Dying* (1993), he includes ethical guidelines for the prevention of abuse, drawing heavily from the Dutch experience concerning euthanasia. In fact, he reprints in full the guidelines set up by the Parliament in the Netherlands. Also, he has written for *Free Inquiry.*

Humphry, who supports Dr. Jack Kevorkian, a retired pathologist who has assisted individuals to die by the use of his home-made "suicide machine," has said, "If people are revolted by what I'm saying and doing, then we must change the law. I'd be only too willing to stop." However, advising or encouraging another commit suicide is a felony, and the laws are intended to prohibit one-on-one, hands-on intervention. As a result, he laments, and until the laws are changed, individuals are forced to devise their own means, which is "a sad commentary on our society." These means include the following:

• cyanide (but it causes a violent death);
• kitchen chemicals (which might land the would-be suicide in the hospital on a stomach pump);
• automobile exhaust (which is a slow death);
• hanging (which is cruel for those left behind);
• lethal doses of morphine (which work slowly and frighten friends or relatives);
• tying a plastic bag around the head and fastening it with a rubber band;
• obtaining barbiturates with a prescription (which should be washed down with alcohol after a light snack, he advises).

Of the methods, Humphry in 1993 quoted three medical examiners in major cities who told him privately that "if they should ever need suicide to escape terminal suffering, the plastic bag would be their choice. . . . When a terminally ill person uses this technique, cooperating family members or friends remove the bag once breathing ceases and before the medical examiner arrives. Ergo, the death certificate lists the underlying illness." Until the euthanasia laws are changed, he laments, "such self-deliverance from suffering will go on. The desperate will use anything."

In *Tripod* (30 October 1995), Humphry was asked by Anthony Qaiyum which religious groups were his biggest opponents, and he responded that the Roman Catholic Church is "a dedicated opponent." Asked if he personally was a religious person, Humphry responded, "No, I'm an atheist." On the Web: <http://www.finalexit.org/dhumphry/>. {CA; E; *Free Inquiry*, Winter, 1988-1989}

HUMUS

Humus, which was a humanist magazine in Dutch of Humanistisch Verbond for activists in the organization, is no longer published. It had been in Utrecht.

Huncke, Herbert (1915—1996)

Huncke's name appropriate rhymes with junkie, and he was the hipster who defined "beat." A drug user as early as twelve, a street hustler by the time he was sixteen, a petty as well as unrepentant thief all his life, and a perennial drug addict, Huncke inspired numbers of writers in the 1940s and later. He introduced William S. Burroughs to heroin, told Jack Kerouac about the term "beat," a carnival word that describes people who are fatigued and beaten down, and guided Allen Ginsberg and John Clellon Holmes around New York City's Times Square with its hustlers, bars, and sex establishments. Huncke became the character Ancke in Holmes's *Go* (1952) and was the title character (Herbert) in Burroughs's *Junkie* (1962). In Jack Kerouac's *The Town and the City* (1950) and appeared in many Ginsberg poems, including *Howl!* (1956), which referred to "Huncke's bloody feet."

Asked in the 1960s about religion, Huncke, who had spent eleven years in prison, smiled and pointed to a nice-looking youngster up ahead, saying, "Now, *there's* my walking god!"

A Columbia University-centered literary group, including Ginsberg and Kerouac, found Huncke a colorful character. He knew Alfred Kinsey, who had hired him to recruit others for his sex research studies. Sometimes locking himself in subway men's rooms, the only place he could work in peace, he scribbled away in his notebooks. He wrote what he called "automatic prose": *Huncke's Journal* (1965), *Elsie John and Joey Martinez* (1979), *The Evening Sun Turned Crimson* (1980), and *Guilty of Everything* (1990). His longtime companion, Louis Cartwright, was killed in 1994, and when it became difficult to pay the rent at Manhattan's Chelsea Hotel it is said that Jerry Garcia of the Grateful Dead helped. At the age of eighty-one, Huncke died of congestive heart failure. Jeremiah Newton was a key individual in helping arrange the non-theistic memorial. {Robert McG. Thomas Jr., *The New York Times*, 9 August 1996}

Huneker, James Gibbons (1860—1921)

A critic, Huneker besides many works on music wrote *Iconoclasts* (1905) and *Visionaries*, both of which McCabe says are studies of heretics in which Huneker does not conceal his own skeptical opinions. {JM; RAT; RE}

Hung Sin-tsuan (19th Century)

After repeatedly failing the national civil service examinations in Kwantung Province, China, Hugo came across a Christian pamphlet, "Good Words for Exhorting the Age." Believing he understood the meaning of the hallucinations he had suffered during his break-down six years prior, he proclaimed himself a messiah, one sent by Heaven to drive out the Tatars and restore in his own person the succession to China. With a disciple, Feng Yun-shan, Hung engineered the Tai Ping Rebellion (1850—1865), a revolt against the ruling Ching (or Manchu) dynasty. The extreme poverty, crowded conditions, widespread xenophobia, and general discontent under the alien Manchus attracted legions of follows. His armies captured hundreds of cities, most notably Nanking in 1853. Hung swallowed poison in 1864, six years before the fall of Nanking to Manchu forces. His rebellion is estimated to have cost hundreds of thousands of lives. {LEE}

HUNGARIAN HUMANISTS

The Hungarian Humanist Association (IHEU) is at Szemere Street 10, 1054 Budapest, Hungary. According to Peter Tibor Nagy, who spoke in Berlin at an IHEU conference in 1995, an estimated three hundred humanists are in the Hungarian association. Largely intellectuals, they lobby political parties, speak at trade unions, and try to gain influence in the press and in educational circles.

Their journal, *Alight*, includes material concerning human rights, religious education, and denominational schools.

Vilagossoag is published at Szenese Street 10, H-1054 Budapest.

HUNGARIAN PHILOSOPHY: See the entry in the *Encyclopedia of Philosophy*, Vol. 4.

HUNGARIAN UNITARIANS

Hungary in 1998 had twelve congregations and twenty-one fellowships with a membership of around 25,000.

In 1568 Francis David was a key figure in the Unitarian movement. From that time until 1920 Transylvania belonged to Hungary. In the 16th century more than a hundred congregations existed in the territory of present Hungary. After the Roman Catholic Counter-reformation, Unitarians could only be found in Transylvania. They came back to Budapest and the present-day Hungary after the revolution in 1848-1849.

The First Budapest Church was founded in 1876. At the end of the last century and the beginning of the present century, several more Unitarian churches were founded and consider themselves to be liberal Christian bodies.

Bishop of the Hungarian Unitarians is the Rev. Marton Bencze. Deputy Bishop is the Rev. Ilona St. Ivanyi Orbok, the Unitarian Church in Budapest, H-1055 Budapest, Nagy Ignac utca 4, Hungary. On the Web: <http://www.uua.org/icuu/icuu-europe.html>. (See entry for Francis David.)

Hunsberger. Bruce (20th Century)

Hunsberger is professor of psychology at Wilfrid Laurier University in Waterloo, Canada. He co-authored *Amazing Conversions: Why Some Turn to Faith and Others Abandon Religion* (1997). In *Free Inquiry* (Summer 1999), he wrote about new findings that offer compelling clues that there are social-psychological causes of faith.

Hunt, Harriot (1805—1875)

Hunt, a Universalist, practiced medicine for fourteen years at a time when women physicians were frowned upon. When she applied to Harvard Medical School, she was refused. In 1850 she applied again, stating she had been practicing medicine for fourteen years, and this time she was reluctantly accepted though told she should not expect to receive a medical degree. "No woman of true delicacy would be willing in the presence of men to listen to the discussion of subjects that necessarily come under the consideration of the student of medicine," some Harvard medical students protested.

Ironically, when the college term began, Hunt was ill and had to cancel her studies. Eventually, eighteen years after she began treating patients, she received an honorary M.D. degree from the Female Medical College in Philadelphia. {EG}

Hunt, James (1833—1869)

Hunt was a physiologist, the founder and first president of the Anthropological Society. He wrote the *Negro's Place in Nature*, a work on stammering and other matters. {BDF; RAT}

Hunt, James Henry Leigh (1784—1859)

Hunt was a poet, essayist, and critic, one who was educated with Lamb and Coleridge at Christ's Hospital in London.

With his brother John, he edited the *Sunday News* (1805), then the *Examiner* (1808). They were condemned to pay a fine of £500 each and to be imprisoned for two years, this because the journal had called the prince regent an "Adonis of fifty."

During the imprisonment, Hunt procured the friendship of

Shelley and Byron, with whom, after editing the *Indicator*, was associated his editing the *Liberal*. In his *Religion of the Heart* (1853), Hunt repudiates orthodoxy. {BDF; RAT; RE}

Hunt, John Gabriel (1952—)

Hunt is author of *The Dissenters: American Voices of Opposition* (1993), a discussion of the struggles against slavery, against war, for women's rights, for social and economic justice, and in support of civil liberties. He also wrote *The Essential Winston Churchill* (1955).

Hunt, Morton (20th Century)

Hunt, author of *The Story of Psychology* (1994) and *The New Know-Nothings: The Political Foes of the Scientific Study of Human Nature* (1998), finds nothing transcendental, nonmaterial, or "spiritual" about the mind (which some refer to as the soul). Rather, he observes psychology as a naturalistic subject which investigates nerve transmission, the neuropsychological mechanism, and other psychological studies which explain much of what the ancients had attributed to the soul. Hunt, a secular humanist, wrote "The Biological Roots of Religion: Is Faith in Our Genes" (*Free Inquiry*, Summer 1999).

Hunt, Stephen (19th Century)

Hunt furthered the cause of freethought in Ohio, often siding with unpopular causes. {PUT}

Hunt, Thornton Leigh (1810—1873)

Hunt, a freethinker, was the son of Leigh Hunt and was acting editor of the *Daily Telegraph* (1855—1872). {RAT}

Hunt, W. F. (19th Century)

Hunt, a merchant, made a protest against the oath as early as 1875 in a London Chancery Court. Sir George Jessel permitted him to "swear by his word." Previously, Hunt had deserted Spurgeon's chapel for secularism, and he was a member of the Rationalist Press Association. {RAT}

Hunter, Edith Fisher (1919—)

Hunter is author of *Sophia Lyon Fahs: A Biography* concerning the life of the prominent Unitarian.

Hunter, H. Bruce (20th Century)

Hunter is associated with the American Humanist Association's Human Concerns Center in Dallas, Texas. (See entry for Texas Atheists, Freethinkers, Humanists.) {FD}

Hunter, Michael (20th Century)

Hunter is co-editor with David Wootton of *Atheism From the Reformation to the Enlightenment* (1992). The period covered, from about 1500 to 1780, had previously not been covered in as great detail.

Hunter, Thomas Alexander [Sir] (Born 1876)

A philosopher, Hunter was born in London, was educated in New Zealand, and in 1909 became professor of philosophy and psychology at New Zealand University. He was Vice-Chancellor of the University and President of the Australasian Association of Psychologists and Philosophers.

Sir Thomas was an Honorary Associate of the Rationalist Press Association and President of the New Zealand Rationalist Association. {RE}

Hunter, William Alexander (1844—1898)

A professor of Roman law at London University College (1869—1878) and of jurisprudence (1878—1882), Hunter strongly supported Bradlaugh in the House, and he gave his advanced rationalist views in a lecture delivered for the London Sunday Lecture Society, *The Past and Present of the Heresy Laws* (1878). {RAT}

Hurd, Lyse (20th Century)

Hurd is a Camp Quest counselor and a group home therapist who focuses on abused and neglected children. She has written for *Family Matters*, the newsletter of the Secular Family Network, and in 1995 she became a Board Member of the Cincinnati Free Inquiry Group.

Hurt, Walter (19th Century)

Hurt, who edited a Cincinnati freethought newspaper, *The Gatling Gun*, was jailed on the charge of circulating obscene literature. {Cincinnati, Ohio, *Fig Leaves*, May 1995}

Hurst, John F. (1834—1903)

Hurst's *History of Rationalism* (1865) is a classic study, one that includes literature of Unitarianism and Universalism. It ranks with W. E. H. Lecky's *History of the Rise and Influence of the Spirit of Rationalism in Europe* and J. B. Bury's *History of Freedom of Thought*. Hurst also wrote *Literature of Theology* (republished, 1977).

Hurston, Zora Neale (1891—1960)

An African American anthropologist, ethnologist, and a novelist during the Harlem Renaissance of the 1920s, Hurston wrote *Their Eyes Were Watching God* (1937) and *Dust Tracks on a Road* (1942). She had been born to a family of sharecroppers in Notasulga, Alabama, in 1891, about ten years before any date she ever admitted to. When at Columbia University she studied with Franz Boas, she called him "Papa Franz," after which he teased her by saying she was his daughter, "just one of my missteps." Hurston influenced many other African American female authors, including Alice Walker, and during her life she published more books than any other black American woman. In "Religion," which is a part of *Dust Tracks on a Road*, she humorously describes meetings of the Missionary Baptist Church into which she was born, then tells how doubt led her away from organized religion to the point that "I am one with the infinite and need no other assurance." {AAH}

Hus, Jan (John Huss) (1369?—1415)

Hus, the martyred Czech religious reformer also known as John Huss, studied theology at the University of Prague, was then ordained a priest, and preached in the Czech language at the Bethlehem Chapel. Hus after translating John Wyclif's *Triologus* into Czech attacked the abuses of the church until a point that other priests became hostile toward him. In 1410 he was excommunicated and fled to a castle near Tabor where he wrote his chief works, including *De ecclesia*. By denying the infallibility of an immoral pope, he earned the reputation of being one of the main forerunners of the Protestant Reformation. Upon being captured, he was imprisoned, then tried as a heretic, then burned at the stake, his martyrdom setting off the Husite Wars (1419—1434). As a result, he became a national hero. His followers, known as Hussites, were unable to flourish and were to find that Bohemia which had been overwhelmingly Protestant in the mid-16th century became Catholic by both force and persuasion. The Hussite movement, whose members were sometimes called Adamites, is noted for having attacked feudalism and the Roman Catholic Church, the two main bulwarks of medieval society. (See entries for Hilda Doolittle and Moravian Church.) {CE; U}

Husbands, Munroe (1909-1984)

After World War II Unitarianism experienced an enormous surge of Unitarian fellowships. The success of these lay-led religious societies, not merely churches without ministers, is credited to Husbands, a director of fellowships for the American Unitarian Association (AUA).

He traveled extensively to organize the groups, which usually had "developed an antipathy toward the entire religious vocabulary: worship, God, prayer, invocation, benediction." Never a minister, he described his work in "Fellowship Can Accomplish Anything It Will." {*Christian Register*, April 1957; U&U}

Hutcheon, Pat Duffy (20th Century)

Hutcheon is a sociologist and former professor of education. A humanist with an interest in the evolution of scientific humanist thought, she has written *A Sociology of Canadian Education* and *Leaving the Cave: Evolutionary Naturalism in Social Scientific Thought* (1996). At the 1994 Toronto Conference of the Coalition for Secular Humanism, Atheism, and Freethought (CSHAFT), Hutcheon spoke on "Humanism and Spirituality."

She also has written "Harriet Martineau, the Woman Who Thought Like a Man," "The Epicurean Humanism of Omar Khayyam," "Was the Buddha the First Humanist?", and "Renaissance Humanism and Its Unitarian Offshoot." On the Web: <http://www.humanists.net>. {*Humanist in Canada*, Summer 1996, 1997, and 1998. In that journal's winter 1998 issue she wrote of "The Monistic Naturalism of Ernst Haeckel."}

Hutcheon, Robert J. (20th Century)

Hutcheon wrote *Frankness in Religion* (1929) and *Humanism in Religion Examined* (1931). (See entry for Humanist Manifestos.)

Hutcheson, Francis (1694—1746)

Hutcheson was a philosopher who, instead of preaching in Ireland where he was born, abandoned the idea and opened a school. The success of his *Inquiry into the Original of our Ideas of Beauty and Virtue* (1725) and his *Essay on the Nature and Conduct of the Passions* (1728) brought him offers of preferment, which he refused, as "his theology differed little from the optimistic Deism of his day," according to the *Dictionary of National Biography*. He was a utilitarian and approached closely to the "greatest happiness" principle. {RAT}

Hutchinson, James M. (1922-1998)

When he signed Humanist Manifesto II, Hutchinson was minister emeritus of the First Unitarian Church in Cincinnati, Ohio. He served congregations in Windsor, Vermont; Trenton, New Jersey; Flushing, Lake Mohegan, Huntington, and North Suffolk in New York; Atlanta, Georgia; Salem and Sherborn, Massachusetts; Golden, Colorado; Memphis, Tennessee; and Toronto, Ontario. He was a contributing editor of *Religious Humanism*. {HM2}

Hutchinson, Mike (20th Century)

With Simon Hoggart, Hutchinson wrote *Bizarre Beliefs* (1995). The British representative of the Committee for the Scientific Investigation of Claims of the Paranormal, Hutchinson writes with a skeptical eye about pseudo-science and the paranormal.

Hutchinson, William R. (20th Century)

Hutchinson wrote *The Transcendental Ministers* (1959). {GS}

Hutchison, Harold J. (20th Century)

When he signed Humanist Manifesto II, Hutchison was a humanist counselor. {HM2}

Hutten, Ulrich von (1488—1523)

Ulrich was a German poet and reformer, born of a noble family. He was sent to Fulda to become a monk but fled in 1504 to Erfut, where he studied *humaniora*. After some wild adventures in Wittenberg, Vienna, Pavia, and Bologna, he became a common soldier in Maximilian's army, hoping to free his country from sacerdotalism. Most of Hutten's writings are satires against the Pope, monks, and clergy. Persecution drove him to Switzerland, but the Council of Zurich drove him out, and he died on the isle of Ufnau, Lake Zürich. {BDF}

Hutton, Ian (1950—)

Hutton, a poet and writer of children's stories, was editor of the atheistic *Truth Seeker*, succeeding James Prescott, who was editor from 1989 to 1990. In 1993, Hutton was succeeded by William B. Lindley.

Hutton, James (1726—1797)

Hutton's *Investigation of the Principles of Knowledge* (1794) reveals the author's freethinking, and his *Theory of the World* (1795) was denounced as atheistic. Dr. Hutton, a Scot, has been termed "the first great British geologist" by the *Dictionary of National Biography*. Others have called him "the father of geology." His *Theory of the Earth* (2 volumes) is a basic book. Chambers said of Hutton that his works "abound in sceptical boldness and philosophical infidelity." In 1794 when he published a deistic work in three volumes, the study reportedly caused a sensation. {BDF; JM; JMR; JMRH; RAT; RE}

Huxley, Aldous (1894—1963)

Although the most mystical of the Huxley family, the author of *Brave New World* (1932) did declare the following humanistic views:

- Facts do not cease to exist because they are ignored.
- If we must play the theological game, let us never forget that it is a game. Religion, it seems to me, can survive only as a consciously accepted system of make-believe.
- History reveals the Church and the State as a pair of indispensable Molochs. They protect their worshiping subjects, only to enslave and destroy them.
- Jerusalem is . . . the slaughterhouse of the religions. . . . {One is touched by} the hopelessness of the inhabitants of Jerusalem, for whom the holiest of cities is a prison of chronic despair punctuated by occasional panic when the hand grenades start flying.
- I'm all for sticking pins into episcopal behinds.
- Mr. Mercaptan went on to preach a brilliant sermon on that melancholy sexual perversion known as continence.

In 1946 Huxley wrote a foreword to a postwar edition of the novel. He regretted having failed to predict nuclear fission and wished he had offered an alternative other than a primitive religion, "half fertility cult and half Penitente ferocity." His "third" way would have embraced Henry George economics, Prince Kropotkin politics, and a humane technology that sought "the unitive knowledge of the immanent Tao or Logos, the transcendent Godhead or Brahman." {HNS2; TYD}

Huxley, Francis (20th Century)

When Julian Huxley was asked in the 1950s to review a book by Vercors for *The Humanist*, he recommended his son, Francis, as an appropriate naturalist and humanist. Francis Huxley is author of *The Invisibles* (1966), concerning voodoo (Vaudou) gods in Haiti.

Huxley, Julian Sorrell [Sir] (1887—1975)

Biologist and scientific humanist, grandson of Thomas Henry Huxley, Sir Julian Huxley was the first head of UNESCO and a key founder along with Jaap van Praag and H. J. Blackham of the International Humanist and Ethical Union (IHEU). In 1956, he responded to the present author regarding his views of humanism:

> My views on what humanism is can be found in my presidential address to the International Humanist and Ethical Union, which was published in *The Standard* (journal of the American Ethical Union) of October-November 1952.

In that address, he had said,

> As I see it the world is undoubtedly in need of a new religion, and that religion must be founded on humanist principles. When I say religion, I do not mean merely a theology involving belief in a supernatural god or gods; nor do I mean merely a system of ethics, however exalted; nor only scientific knowledge, however extensive;

nor just a practical social morality, however admirable or efficient. I mean an organized system of ideas and emotions which relate man to his destiny, beyond and above the practical affairs of every day, transcending the present and the existing systems of law and social structure. The prerequisite today is that any such religion shall appeal potentially to all mankind; and that its intellectual and rational sides shall not be incompatible with scientific knowledge but on the contrary based on it.

We humanists would not call ourselves humanists unless we were dissatisfied with official and traditional creeds and philosophies. But, we cannot be content with a negative attitude; we must have a constructive aim. Our humanism must have the wholeness and unity of a single pattern; but it must incorporate the diversity and variety of the different spheres of reality with which we are confronted in actual existence. Our humanism must allow for different levels of perfection in various spheres of achievement which human beings can reach in the course of their development.

"I recall the story of the philosopher and the theologian," Huxley once wrote. "The two were engaged in disputation and the theologian used the old quip about a philosopher resembling a blind man, in a dark room, looking for a black cat—which wasn't there. 'That may be,' said the philosopher, 'but a theologian would have found it.' . . . Though we can answer the question, 'What are the Gods of actual religions,' we can only do so by dissecting them into their components and showing their divinity to be a figment of human imagination, emotion, and rationalization. . . . But if God and immortality be repudiated, what is left? That is the question usually thrown at the atheist's head. The orthodox believer likes to think that nothing is left. That, however, is because he has only been accustomed to think in terms of his orthodoxy. In point of fact, a great deal is left....Buddhism in its uncorrupted form has no such belief in God nor in immortality, nor did the great nineteenth-century agnostics, nor do the orthodox Russian Communists, nor did the Stoics. Or course, the unbelievers have often been guilty of selfish or wicked actions; but so have the believers. . . . My final belief is in life."

Speaking in New York City at the New York Ethical Society in the late 1940s or early 1950s, the eminent scientist began but found that his microphone did not work. "What a wonder science is!" he expostulated (adding choice Christian curse words). When asked about the universe's origin, Huxley replied that he saw no logical reason why the universe had to have "originated." It is as easy to believe that there was nothing before there was something, he reasoned, than that there was something before there was nothing. He illustrated the short period of time mankind has figured in the universe's history: The Empire State Building, he explained, could symbolize the time the world has existed; and the time mankind has existed could be symbolized by picturing a postage stamp atop that skyscraper, which then was the world's tallest building. "Standing upright, or flat?" a Columbia University student pealed out, followed by Huxley's and the audience's laughter.

Upon heading UNESCO, from 1946 to 1948, Huxley stated that what should guide the newly formed United Nations should be "a scientific Humanism, global in extent and evolutionary in background." In 1962, he was named Humanist of the Year by the American Humanist Association. He signed Humanist Manifesto II. When Bertrand Russell was its president, Huxley was an honorary associate of the Rationalist Press Association. Many have forgotten, however, that not only was Huxley author with J.B.S. Haldane of *Animal Biology* (1927) and wrote *The Humanist Frame* (1962) and *Religion Without Revelation* (1967), with its call for an evolutionary and humanist religion, but also he was secretary of the Zoological Society of London and one of the world's leading experts on ants. {CE; CL; HM2; HNS; HNS2; RE; TYD; WAS, 26 April 1956}

Huxley, Leonard (1860—1933)

The son of Dr. Thomas Henry Huxley, Leonard was an agnostic like his father. He became a distinguished biographer and was an honorary associate of the Rationalist Press Association. {RAT; RE}

Huxley, Thomas Henry (1825—1895)

An English biologist and the principal exponent in England of Darwin's theory of evolution—he was called Darwin's bulldog—Huxley was not, like Darwin, from a family of the monied middle classes. The youngest son of an impecunious schoolmaster, he was born over a butcher's shop in Ealing but became one of the people who had a profound impact on 19th-century thought.

Upon becoming a member of the Metaphysical Society, he explained in *Science and the Christian Tradition* (1895),

Every variety of philosophical and theological opinion was represented there, and expressed itself with entire openness; most of my colleagues were *-ists* of one sort or another; and, however kind and friendly they might be, I, the man without a rag of a label to cover himself with, could not fail to have some of the uneasy feelings which must have beset the historical fox when, after leaving the trap in which his tail remained, he presented himself to his normally elongated companions. So I took thought, and invented what I conceived to be the appropriate title of "agnostic."

It came into my head as suggestively antithetic to the "gnostic" of Church history, who professed to know so much about the very things of which I was ignorant; and I took the earliest opportunity of parading it our Society, to show that I, too, had a tail, like the other foxes. To my great satisfaction, the term took; and when the *Spectator* had stood godfather to it, any suspicion in the minds of respectable people, that a knowledge of its parentage might have awakened, was, of course, completely lulled.

"Agnosticism," he explained, "is not a creed but a method, the essence of which lies in the vigorous application of a single principle....Positively the principle may be expressed as in matters of intellect, follow your reason as far as it can take you without other considerations. And negatively, in matters of the intellect, do not pretend conclusions are certain that are not demonstrated or demonstrable."

The meaning today, however, is that agnosticism holds that neither the existence nor the nature of God, nor the ultimate origin of the universe, is known or knowable. As Gordon Stein has pointed out, Huxley would be horrified at the violence done to his word by popular usage. Writing about Huxley, Mark Francis has stated, "The extent of the region of the uncertain varied according to the knowledge and the intellectual habits of the individual agnostic." However, Huxley said, "I do not very much care to speak of anything as 'Unknowable.' I confess that long ago, I once or twice made this mistake; even to the waste of a capital 'U.' "

His opponents enjoyed it when Bishop "Soapy Sam" Wilberforce asked him, "Are you descended from an ape, Mr. Huxley, from your mother's or your father's side?" Huxley's reply put Wilberforce's "science" into perspective. If such a question were to be put to me, Huxley replied, "would I rather have a miserable ape for a grandfather or a man highly endowed by nature and possessed of great influence and yet who employs these faculties and that influence for the mere purpose of introducing ridicule into a grave scientific discussion, I unhesitatingly affirm my preference for the ape."

Huxley, who often has been called "Darwin's bulldog" and the most versatile man of science in nineteenth-century England, later observed, "Men are very queer animals—a mixture of horse-nervousness, ass-stubbornness, and camel-malice."

Originally a naval surgeon, Huxley took cruises which afforded opportunities for his study of natural history. In 1860 he lectured on "The Relation of Man to the Lower Animals" and in 1863 published *Evidence as to Man's Place in Nature.* He also published *Physical Basis of Life* (1868), *Lay Sermons* (1870), *American Addresses* (1879), and *Evolution and Ethics* (1893). Huxley had some noted controversies with the Liberal Party's dominant personality, William Gladstone, and the Rev. Mr. Wace, during which he tried to demolish theological fictions while demonstrating scientific facts. His aims in life, Huxley said, were "the popularising of science and untiring opposition to that ecclesiastical spirit, that clericalism, which in England, as everywhere else, and to whatever denomination it may belong, is the deadly enemy of science."

Two of his sons—Leonard and Julian—were agnostics like their father. Leonard has written that, "Ten years before [T. H.] coined the word . . . he described the Agnostic position he had already reached" in a letter to Kingsley. According to McCabe, "but what [their] brilliant brother Aldous believes he alone knows—and I doubt if he does," a reference to Aldous's mysticism. A few months before Thomas Henry Huxley died he said to his son Leonard, "The most remarkable achievement of the Jew was to impose on Europe for eighteen centuries his own superstitions." Upon his death, scientists throughout the world sent their condolences to the family of one of the most decorated men of science of that time.

In 1997, Adrian Desmond published *Huxley: Evolution's High Priest,* the first volume of Huxley's biography. {BDF; CE; CL; EU, Mark Francis; FUK; JM; OEL; PUT; RAT; RE; TRI; TYD}

HUXLEY HERITAGE

A conference on "The Moral and Scientific Arts, the Huxleys in Context," was held at Westminster College, Oxford , in June 1997. Run by the Centre for Critical Inquiry, the conference discussed the Huxley family, its importance to humanism, and the significance of the Huxleys' ideas on science and philosophy. (See articles by Jim Herrick, Paul Kurtz, and Nicolas Walter in *New Humanist,* August 1997 and November 1997.)

Huysmans, Joris Karl (1848-1907)

Huysmans, a novelist of Dutch originborn in Paris, wrote *À Recours* (Against the Grain 1884), the aesthetic decadence of which influenced Oscar Wilde, and *Là-bas* (Down There, 1891), about devil-worship. In 1892 he wrote *En Route,* about his return to Catholicism. (See entry for Ben Hecht.)

HVMANIST BOOK CLVB

The Hvmanist Book Clvb [sic] advertised in a 1953 *The Humanist Newsletter* and featured 20% discounts on orders for all fiction and non-fiction. Founded by the newsletter editor, Warren Allen Smith, the club advertised books by Paul Blanshard, John Dewey, Corliss Lamont, Sidney Hook, Vashti McCollum, Charles Francis Potter, and Albert Schweitzer. For example, Schweitzer's *Psychiatric Study of Jesus,* which listed at $2.00, was sold for $1.60, postpaid.

Upon becoming book review editor of *The Humanist,* Smith continued the club but required that an applicant, to become a member, had to show proof (a mutilated IBM card, for example) of having resigned from the Book-of-the-Month Club or one of the other ubiquitous book clubs. Members also were prohibited from being required to purchase further books.

The return address contained Roman numerals. Whatever the large book clubs required, the Hvmanist Book Clvb satirized. *The Saturday Review of Literature* was sufficiently amused at such a marketing ploy that it carried an entire article about the founder and his eccentricities. The staff, for example, was headed by "Lvcretius," the only person authorized to sign the club's checks. "Jesus Vargas" was "in charge of having the public relations." "Jun Sczesnoczkawasm" sent correspondence with handwriting so large that the signature had to slant upwards into the right-hand margins. An Oregon university library did an extensive mail-order business with the club, which had several hundred members. The Harvard University Press found itself addressing letters as well as invoices to Lvcretius. (Although the club continued for several years in the 1950s, it was not a money-maker. So, taking a clue from Tom Sawyer's fence whitewashing idea, Smith sold the club for a profit.)

Hyde, Beverly (1916—1996)

Hyde was an active member of Humanists of Utah.

Hyde, Karl (1930—1995)

Hyde edited *The Freethinker* from 1967 to 1968 when it was a weekly. Afterwards, he worked in a full-time capacity for the British Humanist Association, eventually settling for many years in Penzance.

Hyde, Reynold (20th Century)

The Hydes, Reynolds and **Jennie**, were generous donors toward funding the Center for Inquiry—West in the Los Angeles, California, area.

Hyde, Vicki (20th Century)

Hyde, editor of the *New Zealand Science Monthly,* is a columnist for the *New Zealand Rationalist and Humanist.*

Hyman, Larry (1919-1999)

Hyman was president of the Humanists of New Jersey. In his group's newsletter (January 1999), he noted that "[a]lthough condemned as immoral by the majority of our fellow citizens in the first half of this century, the right of every individual to birth control, abortion, divorce, homosexuality, and pornography is accepted by most Americans today." A professor of English for thirty yearsat Brooklyn College, Hyman had interests that included John Milton, Andrew Marvell, and politics.

Hyman, Ray (20th Century)

Hyman, a professor of psychology at the University of Oregon, is on the executive committee of the Committee for the Scientific Investigation of Claims of the Paranormal, which publishes *Skeptical Inquirer.* He wrote *The Elusive Quarry* (1989).

Hynd, J. Hutton (Died 1970)

A Scottish Congregationalist who became a humanist with Stanton Coit, Hynd was forthright in his rejection of traditional religions. According to James F. Hornback, one of Hynd's favorite addresses was, "The Fundamentalists Are Right." While in St. Louis as a Leader from 1933 to 1950, he continued the Sheldon and Chubb heritage of sound institutionalism. Hynd was President of the American Humanist Association from 1947 to 1948. (See entry for Ethical Culture.) {EU, Howard B. Radest; HNS}

Hyndman, H. M. (1842—1921)

Hyndman, a freethinker, headed the Homerton Socialist Club (1881). He once forecast a bloodier revolution in England than the one who had occurred in France. {RAT; TRI}

Hypatia of Alexandria (355?—415)

Hypatia, the first notable woman in mathematics, wrote, "Fables should be taught as fables, myths as myths, and miracles as poetic fancies. To teach superstitions as truths is a most terrible thing. The child's mind accepts and believes them, and only through great pain and perhaps tragedy can the child be, in after years, relieved of them. In fact, men will fight for a superstition quite as quickly as for a living truth—often more so, since a superstition is so intangible you cannot get at it to refute it, but truth is a point of view, and so is changeable." Hypatia was renowned for her beauty and elegance, but little is known of her writing.

During Lent in 415 she was seized, dragged by Cyril's (later St. Cyril) strong-arm, church enforcers, the "parabolans," stripped, beaten, and stabbed to death with pieces of broken pottery. Then her body was hacked using oyster shells into pieces, was carried triumphantly through the streets, and later burned piecemeal by a band of monks. The monks allegedly had been encouraged by the archbishop, Cyril of Alexandria, who was a personal and political enemy of the prefect of Egypt, said to have been Hypatia's lover.

In a 1993 dramatic production, the Greek actress Irene Papas described Hypatia's death at the hands of the Christian mob more tersely: "They killed her with shells. They took her skin off."

Maria Dzielska, in *Hypatia of Alexandria* (1995), claimed that Hypatia was sixty when she died, adding that she was disliked by the local rabble for her elitist airs. She is said to have been less an Enlightenment *philosophe* than a transcendentalist astrologer and a Pythagorean mystic. Dzielska's research indicates that Hypatia died a virgin and found the body repugnant. She quotes Damascius to the effect that when one of Hypatia's regular students fell in love with her, Hypatia punished him by showing the student her sanitary napkin, stating, "This is what you really love, my young man, but you do not love beauty for its own sake." Dzielska, searching the original sources from the *Sud* lexicon to the correspondence of Synesius of Cyrene, states Hypatia was not devoted to Thoth, the baboon-headed god, and her aristocratic young men included more Christians than it did pagans. She concluded that Hypatia's martyrdom was "murder for a political purpose. . . . They killed a person who was the mainstay of the opposition against [the patriarch Cyril, a newly invested bishop of St. Mark's who expelled Novatians and Jews from the city], who through her authority and political connections provided support for the representative of the state authority in Alexandria contending against Cyril."

Commenting upon Dzielska's work, Gordon Stein has written of Hypatia's death, "It was an ugly scene, but not one carried out because of Hypatia's religious or philosophical beliefs. She had been said to be a witch by her enemies, but she was really only a non-vocal pagan. Whether we should continue to call her a freethought martyr is open to question. Also possibly open to question is whether this book is really Catholic apologetics. If it is, it does not do a good job of it, as the author *does* blame Cyril for Hypatia's death." (See entry for Maria Dzielska.) {*The American Rationalist*, March-April 1996; BDF; CE; CL; *Parade*, 5 Dec 1993; RE; TYD}

Hypes, Robert (20th Century)

Hypes, an atheist in Indiana, was a former Church of Christ preacher. His articles in *The Skeptical Review* relate how he was raised as a fundamentalist. However, upon engaging in serious Bible studies as an adult, Hypes found what it impossible to believe what he had been taught as a child. Hypes works in property management for an industrial manufacturer.

HYPOCRITE

• Hypocrite, n. One who, professing virtues that he does not respect, secures the advantage of seeming to be what he despises.

—**Ambrose Bierce**
The Devil's Dictionary

Hyslop, James Hervey. (Born 1845)

Hyslop was a psychologist who taught at Lake Forest, Smith, Bucknell, and Columbia. An editor of the *Journal* of the American Society for Psychical Research, Hyslop held that the psychic evidence is in favor of survival, but he stood entirely apart from the creeds. {RAT}

IAGO

Why, instead of always being equated with Good, is God not equated with Evil?

In Shakespeare's *Othello, the Moor of Venice* (c. 1602-1604), Iago is depicted as an older soldier, bitterly resentful of being passed over for promotion and now planning revenge. A villainous character, he exemplifes, in the words of Bertrand Russell, "how many of the villains in Shakespeare are Italians. Iago is perhaps the most prominent instance." Coleridge laments Iago's soliloquy, which reveals "the motive-hunting of a motiveless malignity—how awful it is!" Verdi's *Otello* (1887) further delineates Iago's evil character.

From a philosophic viewpoint, particularly in light of the obvious pain observed throughout the world, not only by humans but also by other animals, a case can be made that the concept of God the Creator is that God is the consummate Iago. Would a loving and omnipotent God allow the Holocaust? Murder? War? Disasters such as earthquakes? Physical imperfections? Inequalities? Pain and suffering?

Freethinkers who have been able to avoid being inculcated with the good-evil concept, or have somehow overcome its widespread acceptance, use a different terminology, one based upon ethics. (See entries for Ethics and for Pain.)

IBERO-AMERICAN COMMISSION

The Ibero-American Commission is a group of humanist leaders in Spanish-speaking countries of South, Central, and North America. On the Web: <http://idt.net/~wasm/asibehu>.

Ibn Al-Haytham [or Alhazen] (965-c. 1040)

An Arab mathematician born in Basra, Persia, Ibn al-Haytham made his career in Cairo, supporting himself by copying scientific manuscripts. Although he wrote extensively, only his works on optics, astronomy, and mathematics survive.

Optics, relying on experiment rather than on authority, introduced the idea that light rays emanate in straight lines in all directions from every point on a luminous surface. The work influenced Kepler and Descartes.

As a cosmologist, al-Haytham attempted to find mechanisms by which the heavenly bodies could be shown to follow the paths determined by Ptolemaic mathematics. Ptolemy had used math and reason to develop him views about vision, whereas Aristotle had only offered conjectures. Al-Haytham's findings, by shifting from authority to observation, devastated Aristotle's guesses on the subject. Doubters were simply asked to stare at the sun or any other bright object. Doing so resulted in their eyes being burned, and therefore without appeal to geometry or anything else he showed the light started outside the eye and reflected into it.

In mathematics Al-Haytham elucidated and extended Euclid's *Elements* and suggested a proof of the parallel postulate. {Richard Powers, *The New York Times Magazine*, 18 April 1999}

Ibn Rushd: See entry for Averroës.

Ibry, David (20th Century)

Ibry has written for *Humanist in Canada* and in 1994 gave a lecture concerning "How Humanist Started" to the Ethical Society of London (UK). He edited *Exodus to Humanism: Jewish Identity Without Religion* (1999). {*Humanist in Canada*, Spring 1997}

Ibsen, Henrik (1828—1906)

Ibsen, the Norwegian author of *The Enemy of the People* (1882) and *Hedda Gabler* (1890), was an open unbeliever who had written strong humanist materials in a country with such a strong Lutheran church. He discarded orthodoxy in his later teens but was quietly skeptical until 1871, when he met Georg Brandes. A few years later, to express his new militant mood, he wrote *The Emperor and the Galilaean*. Far in advance of his time, he was condemned by society for revealing truths which society preferred to keep hidden. *A Doll's House* (1879) is a powerful statement of feminism and women's rights. *An Enemy of the People* and *The Wild Duck* (1884) take up the effects of true and false idealism. Robertson cites all his later work as showing himself to be a thoroughgoing naturalist. Ibsen's influence upon 20th century drama is profound, and his dramas continue to be performed widely.

To the Danish critic Georg Brandes, Ibsen once wrote, "Bigger things than the state will fall. All religion will fall." At the time of his death, for he had become debilitated by a series of strokes, his masseur was asked about Ibsen's condition. "Not too bad. He's sworn a couple of times," the masseur noted. And when a nurse remarked to friends in his room that he seemed to be getting better, Ibsen spoke up: "On the contrary." According to biographer Michael Meyer, it was Ibsen's last correction. {BDF; CE; CL; JM; JMR; PUT; RAT; RE}

ICELANDIC HUMANISTS

An associate member of the IHEU is the Icelandic Ethical Humanist Association (*Sidmennt*), Aesufell 4 2F, 111 Reykjavik, Iceland. The president is Hope Knutsson, an American from New York who married an Icelander and has lived in the country for twenty-three years. The group publishes a newsletter. An estimated two-thirds of the population of Iceland wants a separation between the church and the state.

Frettabref Sidmenntar [the Sidmennt Newsletter] is on the Web in Icelandic: <www.islandia.is/sidmennt>.

Andrew Greeley, an outspoken Catholic priest, sociologist, and author of best-selling novels that by some have been termed "salacious," was asked about celibacy, whether priests have always practiced it. "For much of Catholic history," he responded, "celibacy was only a rule in theory. A friend of mine tells me a third of the population of Iceland are descendants of the last Catholic archbishop. [Laughs] Celibacy as a norm really only became typical after the Council of Trent."

Mikael Karlsson, of the University of Iceland, is on the Executive Committee of the Hume Society, a group that engages in scholarly activity concerning David Hume. {*Modern Maturity*, May-June 1996}

ICHTHUS

The fish symbol, also known as ichthus, appeared in the second century of the Common Era and was used as a secret sign of Christianity. The first Greek letters of the phrase "Jesus Christ, Son of God, Savior" spell out "fish" in Greek. Whatever or whoever feeds on fish is ichthyophagous, and serious students of fish are ichthyologists, not theologists.

ICONOCLAST

• Iconoclast, n. A breaker of idols, the worshipers whereof are imperfectly gratified by the performance, and most strenuously protest that he unbuildeth but doth not reëdify, that he pulleth down but pileth not up. For the poor things would have other idols in place of those he thwacketh upon the mazzard and dispelleth. But the iconoclast saith: "Ye shall have none at all, for ye need them not; and if the rebuilder fooleth round hereabout, behold I will depress the head of him and sit thereon till he squawk it."

—**Ambrose Bierce**
The Devil's Dictionary

ICUU: See entry for International Council of Unitarians and Universalists.

IDAHO HUMANISTS

• Humanists of Idaho, PO Box 44913, Boise, Idaho 83711. Contacts Chris Struble and John B. Harms.

E-mail: <hoi@pobox.com>. On the Web: <http://www.freeyellow.com/members3/humanists>.

Ide, Arthur Frederick (20th Century)

Ide is one of the editors of *Resurrection, Sex, and God: Essays on the Foundation of Faith* (1990). An ex-Catholic and ex-theologian, he has written, *Unzipped: The Popes Bare All* (1987), in which he details some of the perversions, greed, and corruption of Roman popes. He also wrote *The Qur'an on Woman, Marriage, Birth Control, and Divorce* (1996).

IDEALISM

• The idealist cannot be reformed; if he is driven out of his heaven, he makes an ideal out of his hell.

—Friedrich Nietzsche

• An idealist is one who, on noticing that a rose smells better than a cabbage, concludes that it will also make better soup.

—H. L. Mencken

• An idealist is a more dangerous animal than the Philistine just as a man is a more dangerous animal than a sheep.

—George Bernard Shaw

In philosophy, idealism is a view that mind and spiritual values are fundamental in the world as a whole. It is, therefore, opposed to naturalism and to materialism. Plato's early idealism conceived a world in which reality was constituted by eternal ideas.

George Berkeley in the eighteenth century referred the source of ideas to the individual's consciousness.

Immanuel Kant developed a transcendental idealism in which the phenomenal world of human understanding opposes a world of things-in-themselves.

Other idealists have been Benedetto Croce, Frances Herbert Bradley, Ernst Cassirer, Johann Gottlieb Fichte, Georg Wilhelm Friedrich Hegel, and Friedrich Wilhelm Joseph von Schelling. {CE; RE}

IDEOLOGY

Bertrand Russell, among others, has complained that the habit "of teaching some one orthodoxy, political, religious or moral, has all kinds of bad effects." As an example, he says that "the immense majority of intellectually eminent men disbelieve in Christian religion, but they conceal the fact in public, because they are afraid of losing their incomes." As to morals, "practically all men are unchaste at some time of their lives; clearly those who conceal this fact are worse than those who do not, since they add the guilt of hypocrisy." Thus, "It is only to the hypocrites that teaching posts are open. So much for the effect of orthodoxy upon the choice and character of teachers." Adding that ideology accompanies fanaticism, he laments that since 1914 there has been "anti-German fanaticism following the First World War, leading to the victory of the Nazis"; there was "anti-Semitic fanaticism, with the inevitable response of Zionist fanaticism"; and there was "Communist and anti-Communist fanaticism.

While mankind remains in this temper, Lord Russell wrote in 1951, "the sort of cooperation required for the inauguration of world government is clearly out of the question." {Lee Eisler, *The Quotable Bertrand Russell* (1993).

IDIOT

• Idiot, n. A member of a large and powerful tribe whose influence in human affairs has always been dominant and controlling. The Idiot's activity is not confined to any special field of thought or action, but "pervades and regulates the whole." He has the last word in everything; his decision is unappealable. He sets the fashions of opinion and taste, dictates the limitations of speech, and circumscribes conduct with a dead line.

—Ambrose Bierce
The Devil's Dictionary

Ignell, Nils (1806—1864)

Ignell, a Swedish rationalist, was brought up as a priest and his free views gave offense to many. He translated Renan's *Life of Jesus*, which many believed was an affront to orthodox Christianity. {BDF; RAT}

IGNORANCE

• I do not believe in the collective wisdom of individual ignorance.

—Thomas Carlyle

Rationalists are understandably concerned that "the cards have been stacked" against the scientific method of reasoning and free inquiry by historical developments and the control of religionists over much of citizenrys' everyday activities. Among the many examples which rationalists cite are

• superstition and ignorance
• believers' faith in what they call "sacred" scriptures
• pseudoscience that touts perpetual motion, parapsychology, U.F.O. abductions, quack medicine, ancient astronauts, bio-rhythm theories, cold fusion, astrology, psychic readings, fortune telling

Igwe, Leo (20th Century)

Igwe is general coordinator of the Nigerian Humanist Movement (PO Box 25269, Mapo Ibadan, Oyo State, Nigeria).

Ihering, Hermann von (Born 1850)

Ihering, a German zoologist, was director of the São Paolo Museum in Brazil. A special authority on the Mollusca, he was an editor of *Revista do Museu Paulista*. In *Was Wir Ernst Haeckel Verdanken*, Ihering records his high appreciation of Professor Haeckel and his *Riddle of the Universe*. {RAT}

IHEU: See entry for International Humanist and Ethical Union.

Ikhnaton (or Akhenaton) (Died c. 1354 B.C.E.)

The oldest known monotheist? In Egypt, Ikhnaton was king of Egypt of the XVIII dynasty, son and successor of Amenhotep III. Upon becoming king, he changed his name to honor the god Aton, and because of his religious innovations has been called "the heretic king of Egypt." First, he abandoned his early polytheism and became a monotheist. The sun, called Aton, was god, and god alone, and Ikhnaton declared he was Aton's son. The new capital was named Akhetaton [the modern Tel-El-Amarna}, and new provincial capitals were founded in Nubia and Syria. Because the sun nourished everything, artists to show the power of the sun turned to scenes from nature. Akhenaton, because of his fanaticism, defaced all statues on which the previously greatest god, Amon, had appeared. This so infuriated large numbers of Egyptians that the cult of Ikhnaton / Akhenaton died and, with it, Egypt lost Nubia and Syria, provinces which he had seriously neglected. Joy Collier, in *The Heretic Pharaoh* (1972), mentions the most familiar relic today of that time, a bust of Ikhaton's wife, Nefretete.

His successors, Sakere and Tutankhaton (Ikhnaton's son), inherited only Egypt and some of the upper valley, not Nubia and Syria. Tutankhaton, because his father had replaced Amon with Aton, changed his name to Tuthankamen, restored the name of Amon to monuments his father had defaced, and returned the capital to Thebes.

McCabe complains that it is remarkable how, when King Tut's tomb was discovered, apologists and others continued to pretend that the Hebrews had first introduced monotheism. However, it was Ikhnaten, five centuries before the first prophet appeared in Judaea, who first had imposed monotheism. {CE; RE}

Iles, George (1852—1942)

Iles, an American writer, was a Canadian who in New York was an admirer of Ingersoll. An agnostic, Iles was editor of *The Reader's Guide on Economic, Social, and Political Science*. He also edited *Little Masterpieces of Science* (6 volumes, 1902). {RAT}

Ilive, Jacob (c. 1705—1768)

Ilive was an English printer and letter founder. He was prosecuted for blasphemy in *Some Modest Remarks on the Late Bishop*

Sherlock's Sermon and sentenced to two years in prison. While confined in the Clerkenwell House of Correction, he published some pamphlets exposing the bad condition of the prison and suggested means for its improvement. {BDF; FUK; RAT; RE}

ILLEGITIMACY

"Illegitimacy," in a definition by Ernest R. Mowrer, a professor who taught sociology at Northwestern University in Evanston, Illinois, "is the act of giving birth to a child out of wedlock. Ordinarily the child conceived out of wedlock is the consequence of illicit sexual relations. However, in some cultures, sexual intercourse is looked upon as a normal part of courtship and conception is regarded as a guarantee of the potential fertility of the marriage. Under these circumstances, the marriage is consummated and the position of the child is no different from one born in wedlock."

Mowrer notes, however, that Christians place a stigma upon such mothers as well as their children, who are called "bastards." In Colonial America, for example, mothers like Hester Prynne in Hawthorne's *The Scarlet Letter* (1850) were required to wear a symbol, the letter A, to warn people they were seeing an adulteress, the mother of a bastard. Partly because of Hawthorne's novel, in which the bastard's father turned out to be a fictional Puritan —minister, the severity of treatment for mother and child has diminished considerably. Bastards are now called by a milder term: "illegitimate children of unmarried mothers." Nevertheless, particularly in smaller communities, pregnant unmarried women likely leave town in order to have their babies, some of whom are then placed for adoption and reared by foster parents. Some rural communities often sanction the compulsion of marriage between a couple about to give birth, and these have become colloquially known as "shot-gun" marriages.

Most secular humanists, freethinkers, Friends, Unitarians, Universalists, and others who ordinarily celebrate *all* human births are more apt to make no distinctions between "legitimate" and "illegitimate births." A number of states and communities sanction marriage without any initiating ceremony, so-called Common Law marriage, but this is considered an anachronism by the major organized religions. A sign of the change in attitude was French President François Mitterand's retort when asked if he had an illegitimate daughter in addition to his two legitimate sons from his fifty-year-old marriage to his wife, Danielle: "Yes, I have a natural daughter. So what?" (See entries for Miriam Allen deFord and Patricia Thompson.) {CE}

ILLINOIS ATHEISTS, HUMANISTS, AND FREETHINKERS

Illinois has the following groups:

• College of Lake County humanists are at <http://www.secularhumanism.org/cfa/orgs.html>.

• Dial An Atheist can be reached by telephoning (708) 506-9200.

• Ethical Humanist Society of Chicago (AEU), 1700 Maple, Evanston, Illinois.

• Free Inquiry Network (ASHS), POB 2668, Glen Ellyn, Illinois 60138; (630) 469-1111; Jim Zaluba is its founder. E-mail: <fin@freeinquirynetwork.com>. On the Web: <http://www.freeinquirynetwork.com>.

• Friends of Robert G. Ingersoll (Council for Secular Humanism), POB 5082, Peoria, Illinois 61601.

• Independent Atheist, 1127 North College, Decatur, Illinois 62522. Jeff Frankel is its contact.

• Humanist Association of Greater Chicago (AHA), 6439 Coach House Road, Lisle, Illinois 60532. Mike Werner is its contact. E-mail: <mwwerner@aol.com>.

• Midwest Committee for Rational Inquiry, MCR-1 B-2792, Des Plaines, Illinois 60017.

• Peoria Secular Humanists (ASHS), PO Box 994, Normal, Illinois 61761 (309) 452-8907; e-mail: <ahumanist@aol.com>.

• Secular Humanist Society of Chicago, 1023 West Vernon Park (Suite H), Chicago, IL 60607; (312) 226-0420. E-mail: <mocekwalker@mw.sisna.com>.

• Southern Illinois University at Carbondale: <http://www.secularhumanism.org/cfa/orgs.html>.

• University of Chicago humanists on the Web: <http://www.secularhumanism.org/cfa/orgs.html>.

ILPES

ILPES is a Costa Rican association, *Instituto Latino Americano de Prevencion y Education en Salud* (Latin American Institute for Health Education). Its director, Dr. Jacobo Schifter Sikora (Apartado 561, 1002 San Jose, Costa Rica), focuses on health problems, including sexually transmitted diseases, and AIDS.

Iltis, Hugh (1925-)

Iltis, a freethinker, is professor emeritus, University of Wisconsin, Madison. Concerned about the growing human population—when he was born the human population was 1.7 billion but has now become over 6 billion—Iltis in "Extinction Is Forever" in *Resurgence* wrote that

> we must abandon the fallacies of agricultural hope, for it is not a question of raising more food, but of raising fewer people! If population growth is not curtailed voluntarilty, the brutal powers of the state (as in China) or the brutal catastrophes of nature (as in Africa's Sahel) will surely do it for us.

IMAGINATION

• Were it not for imagination, a man would be as happy in the arms of a chambermaid as of a duchess.

—Samuel Johnson

• I never saw a purple cow,
I never hope to see one;
But I can tell you, anyhow,
I'd rather see than be one.

—Gelett Burgess
"The Purple Cow" (1895)

• Ah, yes, I wrote the "Purple Cow"—
I'm sorry, now, I wrote it!
But I can tell you, anyhow,
I'll kill you if you quote it.

—Gelett Burgess (1866-1951)
"Cinq Ans Aprés"

IMAGISM

Imagism was a successor to the French Symbolist movement. Its credo, inspired by the critical views of T. E. Hulme, was formulated around 1912 by Ezra Pound in conjunction with fellow poets Hilda Doolittle (H.D.), Richard Aldington, and F. S. Flint. In 1914 after Pound turned to "Vorticism, Amy Lowell, who scorned convention, took over the spiritual leadership of the group and became so influential Pound once referred to the group's "Amy-gism."

The movement influenced the poetry of Conrad Aiken, Marianne Moore, Wallace Stevens, D. H. Lawrence, and T. S. Eliot.

Concrete language and figures of speech, modern subject matter, freedom in the use of meter, and avoidance of romantic or mystical themes characterized imagist poetry. H. D., however, included mysticism in her work. {OEL}

Imgault-Huart, Clément (Born 1854)

Imbault-Huart was a French Orientalist with a knowledge of Arabic, Turkish, Persian, and modern Greek. He was appointed to the French embassies at Damascus and Constantinople. His *La Religion du Bab* (1889) is a study of Behaism. {RAT}

IMMACULATE ABIOGENESIS

Abiogenesis refers to the supposed spontaneous origination of living organisms directly from lifeless matter. Anything immaculate, as in the Immaculate Conception, has no stain. Anyone believing in the concept is directed to the entry herein for Zyp.

IMMACULATE CONCEPTION

The immaculate conception is a quaint theological invention. As defined by Leo Ward, who once taught at the University of Notre Dame in Indiana, it is "the doctrine that by Christ's merits and in view of the fact that she was to be his mother, the Blessed Virgin Mary was from the moment of her conception in St. Anne's womb kept free from original sin." Others, assuming that Joseph did not know who had impregnated his wife, find the theologians' explanation a self-evident bastardization of the facts.

In 1997, the Rev. Tissa Balasuriya in Sri Lanka was excommunicated by the Roman Catholic Church for his "relativism" and for challenging the Immaculate Conception in his preaching. (See entry for Catholic Relativism.)

IMMACULATE DECEPTION

• The Virgin Birth? Immaculate deception!

—Anonymous

Immerman, Karl Leberecht (1796—1840)

Immerman was a German poet and dramatist. For some years he was director of the Düsseldorf Theatre. Immerman followed Goethe in his pantheism, as shown in a poem "Merlin," in his novel, *Die Epigonon.* {RAT; RE}

IMMORALITY

• I wonder why murder is considered less immoral than fornication in literature.

—George Moore

• Immorality: the morality of those who are having a better time.

—H. L. Mencken

• Public schools are the nurseries of all vice and immorality.

—Henry Fielding

• Immoral, adj. Inexpedient. Whatever in the long run and with regard to the greater number of instances men find to be generally inexpedient comes to be considered wrong, wicked, immoral. If man's notions of right and wrong have any other basis than this of expedience; if they originated, or could have originated, in any other way; if actions have in themselves a moral character apart from, and nowise dependent on, their consequences—then all philosophy is a lie and reason a disorder of the mind.

—Ambrose Bierce
The Devil's Dictionary

In 1998 when the President of the United States was accused of immorality—allowing oral sex with a female intern in the White House—the Christian right cited the Bible and demanded not only Bill Clinton's impeachment but also his resignation. However, Menachem Z. Rosensaft, a New York City lawyer, disagreed with the Bible-quoting sexual McCarthyites (*Daily News*, 10 October 1998). "Nathan was brutal in his denunciation of King David for his adulterous affair with Bathsheba and for sending her husband, Uriah, to his death," he noted, then continued:

> When David admitted his guilt, Nathan told him God would spare his life but his unborn child would die. Nonetheless, God allowed David to remain king. After King Ahab had contrived to murder Naboth the Jezreelite to steal his vineyard, the prophet Elijah cursed him. Indeed, an unusual aside in Scriptures (*I King 21:25-26*) notes that "there never was anyone like Ahab, who committed himself to doing what was displeasing to the Lord. . . . He acted most abominably."
>
> Yet after Ahab rent his clothes, put on sackcloth, fasted and "walked about subdued," God told Elijah, "Because [Ahab] has humbled himself before Me, I will not bring distaster in his lifetime."

In other words, Rosensaft concluded, "the concept of high crimes and misdemeanors was well understood by the prophets. Disobeying God when the safety of the nation was at stake was the biblical equivalent of an impeachable offense. Mere human frailty or moral failing was not." Or, as freethinkers often say, "Beauty and immorality are in the eye of the beholder."

IMMORTALITY

• . . .the eternal life of the dead in our lives.

—Playwright **Harold Pinter**

• Millions long for immortality who do not know what do do with themselves on a rainy Sunday afternoon.

—Susan Ertz

• I don't want to achieve immortality through my work. I want to achieve it through not dying.

—Woody Allen

In many religions and philosophies, immortality is an attribute of deathlessness ascribed to the soul. It is rare to find belief of the body, but immortality of the soul is a cardinal tenet of Islam and, although not essentially a Jewish idea, is held generally in Judaism.

The ancient Greeks believed only the gods are truly immortal, although both they and the Romans believed in some possibility of an afterlife. The ancient Celts believed in immortality. Zoroastrianism posited immortality.

However, Hinduism, Buddhism, and Jainism generally considered individual immortality undesirable, believing instead in the reincarnation of men as a chain which eventually would lead to reunion with Nirvana, the infinite.

In Christianity, the resurrection of the body (in the sense of survival of personality) is believed in, as well as immortality of the soul. William Ernest Hocking's *The Meaning of Immortality in Human Existence* (1957) describes the Christian outlook.

Paul Edwards, in "Kierkegaard and the 'Truth' of Christianity" [in *A Modern Introduction to Philosophy* (1973)], is critical of the Christian concept of the "proof" of immortality, and most non-believers use the word only in observing the connection a person has with his parents and their ancestors: "How like her great-grandmother she looks and acts." Edwards also covers the subject in his *Immortality* (1992), as does Anthony Flew in the *Encyclopedia of Philosophy*, Vol. 4.

Lucretius, Hume, and Santayana held that the idea of nothingness *before* one's birth is in principle no more difficult to imagine than that of nothingness *after* one's living. "The fact of having been born," wrote Santayana, is a bad augury for immortality."

For decades it has been known that a body's mortality is mirrored on the cellular level of an immutable rule called the Hayflick limit. Dr. Leonard Hayflick, now of the University of California, San Francisco, discovered that when tissue cells are taken from the body and cultured in a laboratory dish, they grow and divide about fifty times—the number varies with the kind of tissue—then lapse into senescence. In 1998, Dr. Michael D. West of Geron and Advanced tell Technology announced that the Hayflick limit could be broken, leading to the speculation that biologists will one day be able to immortalize some of the body's cells using the Geron method. Some scientists, in short, see an immortality in endlessly dividing cells, a practical application of which could be using the cells for organ repair. {CE; Nicholas Wade, *The New York Times*, 17 November 1998}

IMPERIALISM: See entry for Islamic Imperialism.

IMPIETY (of which Socrates was accused)

• Impiety, n. Your irreverence toward my deity.

—Ambrose Bierce
The Devil's Dictionary

• Volumes might be written upon the impiety of the pious."

—Herbert Spencer

• When vice prevails, and impious men bear sway,
The post of honour is a private station.

—Joseph Addison

IMPOSSIBILITIES

• Some things are possible. Some things, like herding cats, are simply impossible.

—Anonymous

Imray, I. W. (Born 1802)

Imray was an author who wrote in Carlile's *Republican* and *Lion.* In 1828, his "Altamont," an atheistic drama, was published. {BDF}

"IN GOD WE TRUST"

"In God We Trust" was a phrase worn by Nazi God-fearing soldiers in Adolf Hitler's battles while they fought their God-fearing Allied Army enemies.

In 1996, in *Gaylor v. United States of America*, the United States Supreme Court ruled that it

would not review a case brought by the Colorado chapter of the Freedom from Religion Foundation. That group had argued that the nation's official motto implied a government endorsement of religion and sought to have the words removed from American coins and currency. A Federal trial judge and the 10th U.S. Circuit Court of Appeals earlier had rejected the suit, saying the words do not violate constitutional guidelines for the separation of church and state.

IN THE BEGINNING: See entries for Evolution, Genesis, Richard Hawkins, and RNA.

INCARNATION

Incarnation is a Christian belief devised by theologians to the effect that the Son (the second person of the Trinity) was incarnated, or made flesh, in the person of Jesus in order to save the world from Original Sin.

Freethinkers and humanists meet such a vapid concept with the utmost of incredulity.

INCEST

"The incest taboo," wrote Bertrand Russell in *New Hopes for a Changing World* (1951), "is perhaps the most successful example known of the victory of custom over instinct. The great majority of mankind at the present day go through life without at any moment experiencing any conscious impulse towards incest. There are, it is true, savage tribes where the impulse is still difficult to resist, and where adult brothers and sisters take pains not to meet. But in the main the prohibition has proved effective not only outwardly but inwardly, presumably because it is ancient and absolute and does not demand anything superhumanly difficult. To the social psychologist it is important, since it shows what custom can achieve."

In ancient Egypt and among the Inca, some royal families were involved in incestuous relationships. The subject is mentioned often in mythology and, as found in the Oedipus complex, in psychoanalytical speculation and theory.

A humanist "take" on the subject is illustrated by Sir Arnold Bax's (1883—1953) statement about life: "You should make a point of trying every experience once, excepting incest and folk-dancing."

INCUNABULIST

Humanists of all stripes have an interest in incunabulum, for example a book printed before 1501. Incanubula are works of art or of human industry of an early period. A person with original jazz materials from the latter part of the 19th century, as a further example, is an incunabulist.

INDEPENDENT ATHEIST

Jeff Rankel is editor of *Independent Atheist*, 1127 North College, Decatur, Illinois 62522.

INDEPENDENT PUBLICATIONS

Independent Publications (POB 102, Ridgefield, New Jersey 07657), publishes freethought literature.

INDEX LIBRORUM PROHIBITORUM

In a classic case of an attempt to censor books, The Holy See authorized a Congregation of the Index to compile a list of publications that Catholics should be forbidden to be read. If the purpose of the church was to preserve and propagate Christ's teachings, it was reasoned, no Catholic should be allowed publicly to contradict those teachings.

Any book disallowed from 1599 on was called "on the Index," and because it was made up only from decisions referred for judgment on specific works no consistency of inclusion followed; as a result, the failure of a book to appear in it did not imply that the book was in keeping with Christ's teachings. As a result, Cervantes, Descartes, Pascal, Stendhal, Swift, and hundreds of others landed "on the Index," a device that boomeranged somewhat inasmuch as non-Catholics used it as a "must" reading list.

The last edition of the Index was published in 1948. In 1966 the Congregation for the Doctrine of the Faith (formerly, the Holy Office) announced that the Index and its related penalties of excommunication would no longer have the force of law in the church. {CE; ER}

INDIA, RATIONALIST ASSOCIATION OF

The Indian Rationalist Association was founded in 1949 to "promote the spread of rationalism, defined as an attitude which unreservedly accepts the supremacy of reason and aims at establishing a system of philosophy and ethics verifiable by experience, independent of all arbitrary assumptions of authority." It was a successor to the Rationalist Association of India founded in 1930 and influenced by the British Rationalist Press Association. It was weakened by the Second World War and Quit India Movement, but re-formed in 1949. The Association has been active in undermining superstition and in defense of freedom of speech. Contacts are President R. Venkatadri; and Vice President N. Innaiah, A 60 Journalist Colony, Jubilee Hills, Hyderabad 500033, India. E-mail: <HU92@aol.com>. (See entries for N. Innaiah and Jyoti Shankar.) {*New Humanist*, February 1996}

INDIAN ATHEIST PUBLISHERS

In 1981 Sanal Edamaruku started Indian Atheist Publishers, which has published numerous rationalist books including several translations of western freethought classics and contemporary books.

INDIAN FREETHOUGHT: See entry for Jyoti Shankar. A history of Indian freethought is on the Web: <http://www.avana.net/~jshankar/hist0001.htm>.

INDIAN HUMANIST UNION

The Indian Humanist Union, an associate member of the International Humanist and Ethical Union, was founded by Narsingh Narain, a senior civil servant and magistrate. He retired from Government service to undertake social work and to promote freethought and the scientific approach to religion. The Society for the Promotion of Freedom of Thought was founded in 1954 and became the Humanist Union in 1960. *Humanist Outlook* is edited by his son, Prakash Narain, who leads the Humanist Union (PO Box 448, New Delhi 110 001, India). E-mail:<pnarain@ignca.ernet.in>.

INDIAN HUMANISTS, RATIONALISTS

In India, where more Indians speak English than do Englishmen, almost two hundred languages and over sixteen hundred dialects are to be heard. The influence of gurus, swamis, yogis, and others claiming mystical powers is great. Jawaharlal Nehru had a guru, as did his daughter, Indira Gandhi. Mrs. Gandhi's favorite was Dhirendra Brahmachari, who fell from favor when it was discovered that his holy messages appeared on blank sheets of paper but that this was because he had developed a new application of an old high school science experiment involving the use of invisible ink. When he attempted a comeback and greeted devotees with electric shocks, he was exposed as having a car battery with wires beneath his throne. Prime Minister P. V. Narasimha Rao was accused of having contacts with many swamis. One, Chandraswamy, is said to have been behind the showing of sacred idols which apparently drank milk, which strained the credulity of many Hindus but caused individuals throughout the country to stay away from work in 1995 and line up at temples to watch what they believed to be proof of a mystical miracle. Americans were reminded during the same period that the wife of their President Ronald Reagan consulted an astrologer. Britishers were reminded that their Duchess of York consulted Madame Vasso, a faith healer.

However, significant numbers of Indians are not mystics. For example, Prabhir Ghosh, president of the Science and Rationalists' Association of India, claims to have 86,000 members in 300 branches across India. But that is fewer than can be seen at dawn daily as they dip themselves along the banks of the muddy, garbage-strewn Hooghy River, a branch of the Ganges that flowers through the heart of Calcutta, believing that washing in the water cleanses the spirit.

B. Premanand, editor of *Indian Skeptic*, has written the following concerning an article, "Indian Guru Busters Debunk All That's Mystical," written by John F. Burns in *The New York Times* (10 October 1995):

- The Indian Science and Rationalist Association was started by Prabir Ghosh only in the 1980s, not in 1949. In the 1980s, I gave more than 200 lectures in West Bengal, and the people got inspired

and started the association. More than a dozen associations working in West Bengal are connected with *Indian Skeptic*. They are not, however, an All India Organisation and do not have 86,000 members and 300 centres in India. The largest state organisation in India is Dravida Kazhakam, or the Dravidian Association. They have about two million members in Tamilnadu.

• The Ganesha idols were not only of porous ceramics but also were of stones and metals. The trick of the gods drinking milk is explained in *Indian Skeptic* of November 1995: the milk simply flows down under the idol and is collected at the back side.

• It was not in 1993 but on 29th August 1992 at the inauguration of the Marriage Hall that Sai Baba produced a gold chain for presentation to the architect who built the hall where the Prime Minister, the Speaker, two state chief ministers, two governors, and two union ministers were present. This episode was to be incorporated with the propaganda film made by a Dutch film company on Sai Baba at an expense of $400,000 to show to people that even our Prime Minister was a witness to the creation of a gold necklace. Somehow, however, the trick got exposed in the film, and the government suppressed the video film produced by the Central Government corporation, Doordarshan. Before it was suppressed, I got a copy and now hundreds of copies are being shown to the people around India. One copy was given by me to the BBC for the documentary, "Guru Busters," shown on 10 September 1995.

• Mr. Prabir Ghosh has not travelled all over India, as mentioned in the article. It was I who gave more than 7,000 lectures and demonstrated "miracles" all over India.

• Dhirendra Brahmachari did not show any miracles. He only taught yoga. It was Balti Baba who showed the trick of how, if any question was written on a piece of paper and kept it in his pocket, the question would appear on another paper when immersed in milk. Answers did not appear on the paper, only the questions.

• It was not Dhirendra Brahmachari but Sadachari Sai Baba who, in the guise of raising or activating your sexual power (Kundalini power) gave electric shocks. He was exposed at Bombay, for I had demonstrated the equipment to our members there wherein six volts is transformed into 10,000 volts. He is now in jail for murdering his first wife and for running a prostitute den in the guise of training people in Tantra yoga (Kundalini Yoga).

• About 150 tricks of the godmen have been explained in my book, *Science Versus Miracles* (Vol. 1), and I propose to bring out nine more volumes in order to describe perhaps 1500 other tricks of the godmen which I have been able to explain since I started investigating them.

The National Council for Science and Technology Communication, Department of Science and Technology honored Premanand in 1998. It presented him with its national award for the Best Effort in Science Popularization during the period 1992—1996.

The many humanist groups in India, Jim Herrick has noted, are conscious of the problem of "communalism" as being a major issue with which humanists must deal. The Indian Radical Humanist Association (IRHA) and the related Indian Renaissance Institute (IRI) were largely responsible for organizing the IHEU's 14th World Congress in Mumbai in 1999. The two organizations were founded by M. N. Roy. The IRI seeks to provide the intellectual grounding for a renaissance of thought in Asian civilization. The IRHA works at a caompaigning grass-roots level. The Radical Humanists work with people in rural as well as urban areas to bring "awareness and confidence to common people so that they can change their conditions and [be] makers of their own world."

Other Indian humanist groups are the Atheist Centre (founded by Gora and his wife Saraswathi Gora), the Indian Secular Society (founded by A. B. Shah, an expert on Islam), and the Indian Rationalist Association.

Indians who signed Humanist Manifesto 2000 included G. R. R. Babu; Pushpa Mittra Bhargava; Amlan Datta; Sanal Edamaruku; Narisetti Innaiah; H. Narasimhaiah; Indumati Parikh; Avula Sambasiva Rao; Sibnarayan Ray; V. M. Tarkunde; and Ravipudi Venkatadri.

Humanists and rationalists and their organizations and publications in India include the following groups:

- *Age of Atheism, The* (a quarterly in English), Pithani Dibba, Visakhapatnam 530 002, Andhra Pradesh
- *Ambedkar Mission Patrika*, a Hindi monthly, Chitkohara P.O., Anishabad, Patna 800 002
- *Art Today*, Artsacre 37C, College Road, Calcutta 700 009
- *The Atheist*, an English Monthly, Atheist Centre, Benz Circle, Vijayawada 520 006
- *Ayudh* (The Weapon, a Marathi Monthly, Centre for Study of Social Change, c/o Dr. Indumati Parikh, 276, Telang Road, Matunga, Bombay 400 019
- *Bengali Monthly* of Bengal branch of IRHA, Renaissance Publishers, 15, Bankim Chatterjee Street, Calcutta 700 012
- *Bheem Patrika*, an Ambedkar journal published fortnightly in Hindi and English, ES - 393A Abadpura, Jalandhar - 144 003, Punjab, India
- Bihar Rationalist Society (IHEU), 216-A, S.K. Puri, Patna-800 001, Bihar
- *Buddhi wadi* (in Hindi, the Rationalist Quarterly of the Bihar Rationalist Society), 216-A, S. K. Puri, Patna-800001, Bihar
- *Charvakam*, a Telugu monthly, B. Ramakrishna, Nidamarru, Mangalagiri 522 503
- Dravidian Association, 50 EVK, Sampath Road, Madras 7
- *Free Thinker*—started by Sanal Edamaruku, the journal which was at 779 Pocket 5, Mayur Vihar, New Delhi 110 091, is published occasionally.
- *Freedom First*'s e-mail: <freedom@bom3.vsnl.net.in>.
- *Hetuvadi* (The Rationalist, Oriya monthly), 779, Pocket-5, Mayur Vihar-1, New Delhi 110 091
- *Hetuvadi* (The Rationalist, Telugu Rationalist monthly), 4-13-6, Ithanagar, Tenali, Andhra Pradesh 522201
- *Humanist Outlook*, PO Box 448, New Delhi 110 001 <pnarain@ignca.ernet.in>.
- Humanist-Rationalist Publications, publisher of books and *Rationalist Essays*, Chirala-523115, Andhra Pradesh
- Indian Human Union (IHEU) is at Kotwara House,Kaisarbagh, Lucknow U P
- Indian Radical Humanist Association (IRHA), 276 Telang Road, Matunga, Bombay 400 019. This is the important group founded by V. M. Tarkunde and presently led by Dr. Indumati Parikh.
- Indian Rationalist Association, contact is S. Edaramuku, 779, Pocket-5, Mayur Vihar-1, New Delhi, 110091.
- Indian Renaissance Institute in 1998 became an Associate Member of IHEU; its President is Dr. Gauri Malik. The group aims to rescue the positive contributions of Indian thought and learning from ancient to modern times in order that they may inspire an intellectual and cultural resurgence. It publishes the writings of M. N. Roy and the monthly *Radical Humanist*.
- Indian Secular Society (IHEU), 850/8A Shivaji Nagar, Off Bhandarkar Road, Pune 411004, Maharashtra State
- *Indian Skeptic*, 11/7, Chettipalayam Road, Podanur, Tamilnadu, 641 023, Tamilnadu
- *Jijnasa (Inquiry*, a Bengali Quarterly of Ideas, edited by Prof. Sib Narayan Ray, Renaissance Publishers, 15, Bankim Chatterjee Street, Calcutta 700 073

- *Misimi* (Golden Hue, Telugu Monthly of Humanist Ideas), Editor was the late Alapati Ravindranath; current editor is Venkateswarareddi; Plot No. 337A, Road No. 10, Jubilee Hills, Hyderabad 500 034
- *Modern Freethinker*, Pocket 5 Mayur Vihar-1, New Delhi
- *Modern Rationalist*, 50, E.V.K. Sampath Salai, Chennai (Madras) 600 007 <periyar@giasmd01.vsnl.net.in>.
- *Nasthika Yugam* (The Age of Atheism, a Telugu monthly), Pithani Dibba, Visakhapatnam 530 002, Andhra Pradesh
- *New Humanist*, Telugu Monthly of the A.P. branch of IRHA, Chirala 523 155
- *New Quest*, 850/8A, Shavaji Nagar, Off Bhandarkar Road, Pune 411 004, Maharasta State
- *Purogami* (Vanguard, a Bengali monthly), 15 Bankim Chatterjee Street, Calcutta 700 073
- *Radical Humanist,* a monthly; Sassoon Building, 1st Floor, 143 Mahatma Gandhi Road, Bombay 400 001

E-mail: <mrcssc@bom2.vsnl.net.in>.

- Satya Shodhak Sabha in 1998 became an Associate Member of the International Humanist and Ethical Union (IHEU). The group aims to popularize science and the scientific temper, to expose the so-called miracles of the godmen, to propagate humanism and atheism, to work for gender equality, and to mobilize opinion against religious exploitation of the masses.
- *Satyan Veshan* (Prabodh)(Gujarati monthly), 3 Abhinav Park, Ghod dod Road, Surat, Gujarat, 395001
- Science and Rationalist's Association of India, Calcutta—see entry for Prabhir Ghosh
- *Secularist, The* (bi-monthly in English), 15 Zapurza, Sahitya Sahawas, Bandra East, Bombay 400 051 <freedom@bom3.vsnl.net.in>.
- Self Respect Movement, Periyar Thidal 50 EVK Sampath R, Madras 600 007
- *Stree Swetcha* (Women's Liberation Telugu, monthly), Editor M. V. Subbamma, 9 MIGH, Mehdipatnam, Hyderabad 500 028
- *Tarakbodh*, Tarksheel Society Bharat, B-XI-413, Ram Bagh Road, Barnala - 148 101, Punjab, India
- *Tarkjyoty*, journal of the Rationalist Society of Haryana, G.H.S. Badsikri, The. & Distt. Kaithal, Haryana 136 027
- *Therali* (Malayalam monthly), 779, Pocket 5, Mayur Vihar-1, New Delhi 110 091
- *Vaishwik Manavvad* (Cosmopolitan Humanism, Gujarati Monthly of Gujarati Branch, IRHA, 4, Sanmitra Society, Jivraj Park Area, Opp. Malav Talav, Ahmedabad 380 051

(See entries for B. R. Ambedkar; G. R. R. Babu; G. M. Bazaz; P. N. Bazaz; Amlan Datta; T. L. S. Joshi; Maniben Kara; V. B. Karnik; H. Narasimbhaiah;Innaiah Narisetti; G. D. Parikh; Indumati Parikh; B. Premanand; M. V. Ramamurthy; Sibnarayan Ray; S. Rap; Ellen Roy; Evelyn Roy; M. N. Roy; A. B. Shaw; Abraham Solomon; D. K. Veeramani; Ravipudi Venkatadri; in *Free Inquiry* [Fall 1996], see "Humanism in India" by Matt Cherry, who describes fire walking, religious prostitution, combating Karma, and current developments in India; see entry for International Humanist and Ethical Union, which had its 14th Congress in Mumbai in 1998.)

INDIAN NATURALISM

Dale Riepe wrote *The Naturalistic Tradition in Indian Thought* (1961). In it he discusses the early Ajivikas and Carvakas views as well as the naturalistic elements of Jainism, Hinayana Buddhism, Samkhya, and Vaisesika.

INDIAN PHILOSOPHY: See the entry for Debiprasad Chattopadhyaya. Also, see the *Encyclopedia of Philosophy*, Vol. 4; and an extensive bibliography in *United Kingdom and the Commonwealth* by Gordon Stein.

INDIAN RADICAL HUMANIST ASSOCIATION (IRHA)

The Indian Radical Humanist Association started in 1920 and evolved with the evolution of M. N. Roy's intellectual development. Originally a Marxist, Roy during his imprisonment by the British in the 1931—1936 period announced that "a philosophical revolution must precede a social revolution" and founded the association. Initially, it was a political party taking part in the Indian National Congress and working for independence. The Radical Democratic Party, which was inaugurated n 1940, was disbanded in the belief that political parties would not bring about social change. The IRHA was formed in 1969 with the aim of bringing about change at the grass-roots level. (See article in *New Humanist*, February 1996)

INDIAN RELIGIONS: See entry for Riepe Dale.

INDIAN SKEPTIC

A monthly in English, *Indian Skeptic* is at 11/7 Chettipalayam Road, Podanur, Tamilnadu, 641 023, India.

INDIAN UNITARIANS

Not satisfied with traditional Christianity as taught by the missionaries, Hajor Kissor Singh learned about Unitarianism through contacts with Boston and London, preached the faith, walked all over the hills of Meghalaya, and established many congregations. In 1887 he founded the Indian Council of Unitarian Churches. The Khasi Unitarian Union of Meghalaya in the northeast corner of India presently has thirty-two congregations and five fellowships with about 9,000 members. Its minister was formerly the late Rev. Robert Steyn, a South African who was ordained after studying at Oxford and who served the group starting in 1981. It publishes *ICUC Bulletin*, a quarterly in English. The general secretary today is Mr. Carley Lyngdoh, Jowai, 793150, Meghalya, India.
Unitarianism was brought to Madras in the late 18th century by an Indian, William Roberts, who had been taken to England as a slave. While there he learned about Unitarianism and when his master died returned to India. The church provides education and religious services to ten or fifteen families in 1998. In 1995 it celebrated its 200th anniversary. The present leader-minister is Harrison Kingsley, 686 Mount Road, Madras 600 006. The Indian Council of Unitarian Churches (ICUC) held its fourth conference at Mahabalipurum (Madras) in 1995 with over one hundred delegates in attendance. In 1996, the 96th annual conference of the Unitarian Union of Northeast India was held at Shillong, Meghalaya, with over two thousand Unitarians in attendance. Unitarian congregations are also found in Hyderabad and Udaipur. On the Web: <http://www.uua.org/icuu/icuu-asia.html>

INDIANA HUMANISTS

- Humanist Friendship Group of Central Indiana, PO Box 254, Greenwood, IN 46142 (317) 885-1612.

INDIANS, AMERICAN: See entry for American Indians.

INDIFFERENCE

- Nothing matters to the man who says nothing matters.

—Lin Yutang

INDOCTRINATION

"I had to undergo at least 1,300 hours of heavy Christian indoctrination," Sir Ludovic Kennedy has estimated. "What a terrible waste of time."

INDUCTION

In logic, induction is the process of deriving general principles from particular facts or instances. In mathematics, it is a two-part method of proving a theorem involving a positive integral variable. First, the theorem is verified for the smallest admissible value of the integer. Then it is proven that if the theorem is true for any value of the integer, it is true for the next greater value. The final proof contains the two parts. {*American Heritage Dictionary*, 1992)

INDULGENCE

Sports cars can be an expensive indulgence, a gratification of a wish. Grandparents have been known to be fondly indulgent of their grandchildren, supplying them with gifts and attention. Pope John Paul II in 1998 declared 2000 to be a year for "millennial penitence" and a time to receive "early salvation." Penitents—people convinced they are "sinners"—who do a charitable deed such as giving up cigarettes or alcohol for a day, can earn an "indulgence" to eliminate punishment on earth or in purgatory. Indulgences for Catholics have long been a church-granted amnesty from certain forms of punishment, in this life or hereafter, for sin. Some liberal Catholics find themselves embarrassed by the practice, which seems to offer a shortcut to salvation. {Alessandra Stanley, *The New York Times*, 28 November 1998}

INDUSTRIALISM

Bertrand Russell wrote, "The aesthetic indictment of industrialism is perhaps the least serious. A much more serious feature is the way in which it forces men, women, and children to live a life against instinct, unnatural, unspontaneous, artificial. Where industry is thoroughly developed, men are deprived of the sight of green fields and the smell of earth after rain; they are cooped together in irksome proximity, surrounded by noise and dirt, compelled to spend many hours a day performing some utterly uninteresting and monotonous mechanical task. Women are, for the most part, obliged to work in factories, and to leave to others the care of their children. The children themselves, if they are preserved from work in the factories, are kept at work in school, with an intensity that is especially damaging to the best brains. The result of this life against instinct is that industrial populations tend to be listless and trivial, in constant search of excitement, delighted by a murder, and still more delighted by a war." {*Atlantic Monthly*, June 1921}

INEVITABLE

• Exploit the inevitable: one of my favorite pieces of advice.

—Arthur C. Clarke

INFALLIBILITY, PAPAL

Papal infallibility is a belief of the Roman Catholic Church that the Pope is kept by God from making a mistake when he speaks on a question of faith or morals. {DCL}

INFANTICIDE

• The killing of infants. Sanctioned by God as an appropriate punishment for the heathen. (*Psalm* 137:9)

—Carol C. Faulkenberrgy
Atlanta Freethought Society

Infeld, Leopold (1898—1968)

A Polish physicist, Infeld wrote with Albert Einstein *The Evolution of a Scientist* (1941). In 1950 he wrote *Albert Einstein, His Work and Its Influence Upon Our World*. In 1962, Prof. Infeld, of the Physics Institute in Warsaw, was elected an honorary associate of the Rationalist Press Association. {CE}

INFERENCE

An inference, in logic, is the deriving of one idea from another: Inference can proceed through either induction or deduction. {DCL}

INFIDEL

• Infidel, n. In New York, one who does not believe in the Christian religion; in Constantinople, one who does.

—Ambrose Bierce
The Devil's Dictionary

"Infidel," a word that comes from the Latin *infidelis*, or lacking in belief, denotes one who is not a believer. In Islam it is the Christians who are infidels. In Christianity anyone who is not a believer—e.g., Corneille, Molière, and Bayle (whom Calvin attacked)—are called infidels because they were known for their *esprit fort* and *libertin*. Tyndale in England added the Turkish infidels although they "knowledge one God," yet they "have erred and been faithless these eight hundred years," describing the Jews in a similar vein. Throughout Elizabeth I's reign, "infidel" signified only a "heathen" or Jew or"Muhammadan," and Jonson in his *New Inn* (1628—1629) has a phrase, "I did not expect / To meet an infidel, much less an atheist, / Here in Love's list." Infidel, atheist, rationalist, skeptic. In 1713, Anthony Collins's *Discourse of Freethinking, Occasion'd by the Rise and Growth of a Sect Called Freethinkers* led to Ambrose Philip's weekly journal, *The Freethinker*, along the lines of the *Spectator*. For Collins, "freethinker" was a name "for simple freedom from prejudice in secular affairs," but the orthodox were disturbed because if some men think more "freely" than others "they are (a) not terrorized by any veto on criticism, and (b) not hampered, or less hampered, by ignorant pre-suppositions." A freethinker's rationalism could easily lead to rejecting organized religion and, as pointed out by Bury's *History of Freedom of Thought* (1913), that is what happened.

INFIDEL NETWORK

The Infidel Network is on the Web: <http://infidels.org>.

INFIDEL SOCIETY: See the entry for James M. Beckett, a recording secretary of a New York group in the 1840s, the Infidel Society for the Promotion of Mental Liberty.

INFIDELITY

• The lover thinks of possessing his mistress more often than her husband thinks of guarding his wife.

—Stendhal

INFIDELS RECORDS

"My Name is Thomas" is a humanistic rock opera. It was recorded by a band called UniversalDice.com for Infidels Records. (See entry for Gerry Dantone.)

INFINITY

• Only two things are infinite, the universe and human stupidity, and I'm not sure about the former.

—Albert Einstein

To most, "the infinite" refers to having no boundaries or limits, something like X to the nth degree, that which is immeasurably great, world without end.

However, another kind of infinity is that of the infinitely small, the *infinitesimal*. Jim Holt, a writer about philosophy and science for *Lingua Franca* and *The Wall Street Journal*, has surveyed philosophers' views about the subject and in an article (*The New York Review of Books*, 20 May 1999), wrote,

> In his biography of Frederick the Great, Carlyle tells us that when Leibniz offered to explain the infinitely small to Queen Sophia Charlotte of Prussia, she replied that on that subject she needed no instruction: the behavior of her courtiers made her all too familiar with it. (About the only nonpejorative use of "infinitesimal" I have come across occurs in Truman Capote's unfinished novel *Answered Prayers*, when the narrator is talking about the exquisite vegetables served at the tables of the really rich: "The greenest petits pois, infinitesimal carrots. . . .")

Holt then relates the Greek debate over the nature of being:

> On the one side of this debate stood the monists—Parmenides and his followers—who argued that being was indivisible and that all change was illusion. On the other stood the pluralists—including Democritus and his fellow Atomists, as well as the Pythagoreans—who upheld the genuineness of change, which they understood as a rearrangement of the parts of reality. . . . But when you start parsing reality, breaking up the One into the Many, where do you stop? Democritus held that matter could be analyzed into tiny units—"atoms"—that, though finite in size, could not be further cut up. But space, the theater of change, was another questions. There seemed to be no reason why the process of dividing it up into smaller and smaller bits could not be carried on forever. Therefore its ultimate parts must be smaller than any finite size.

However, to imagine that it is possible to find something smaller than the smallest quark, and that there is still something smaller than that, *ad infinitum*, is analgous to imagining that out of nothing something came.

In his review of four current works on the subject, Holt explains the thinking of Zeno, Aristotle, Euclid, Saint Augustine, Kepler, Galileo, Fermat, Pascal, Newton, Bishop Berkeley, Voltaire, Lagrange, Laplace, d'Alembert, Hegel, Bergson, Bertrand Russell, Abraham Robinson, and others. His general conclusion is that the last word has not yet been written about so mammoth a topic as the infinitesimal.

INFRALAPSARIAN

• Infralapsarian, n. One who ventures to believe that Adam need not have sinned unless he had a mind to—in opposition to the Supralapsarians, who hold that that luckless person's fall was decreed from the beginning. Infralapsarians are sometimes called Sublapsarians without material effect upon the importance and lucidity of their views about Adam.

—Ambrose Bierce
The Devil's Dictionary

Ingersoll, Ralph (1900-1969): See entry for George Orwell, who considered the editor of *PM* a "dishonest demagogic type."

Ingersoll, Robert G. [Colonel] (1833—1899)

A famed lawyer and agnostic, the son of a Congregationalist clergyman, Ingersoll was inspired by Paine's fight for political and religious freedom. "To hate man and worship God exist without God just as well as he could exist without me. And I also feel that if there must be an orthodox God in heaven I am in favor of electing him ourselves." Roger E. Greeley, who impersonates Ingersoll in dramatic performances throughout the country, writes that Eugene Debs had called Ingersoll "the Shakespeare of oratory." Ingersoll became attorney general in Illinois shortly after the Civil War and might have become governor had he been willing to modify his strong anticlericalism and agnosticism. In 1876, he nominated James G. Blaine for President in what came to be called "the famous plumed knight speech."

In various lectures, he questioned the tenets of Christian belief, and these included "The Gods" (1872); "Some Mistakes of Moses" (1879); "Why I Am An Agnostic' (1896); and "Superstition" (1898). These drew huge audiences, with praise for his eloquence and irreverent wit as well as denunciations from the orthodox. In "Faith and Fact" (1887), he declared: "I know no more (of the immortality of the soul) than the lowest savage, no more than a doctor of divinity—that is to say, nothing." In "God and Man" (1888), he is emphatic concerning the worthlessness of what is called the Christian hope: "It offers no consolation to any good and loving man." In "Repairing the Idols" (1888), he pours all that refined scorn of which he was a master on the promise of a future life to the oppressed as compensation for their sufferings here. At the grave of the child, Harry Miller, speaking of the question, "Whither?" he said: "The poor barbarian weeping over his dead can answer the question as intelligently and satisfactorily as the robed priests of the most authentic creed." A partial reprint of his 1874 edition is *On the Gods and Other Essays* (1990). A biographies include Frank Smith's *Robert G. Ingersoll: A Life* (1990) and Mark A. Plummer's *Robert G. Ingersoll: Peoria's Pagan Politician* (1993).

As for his philosophic outlook,

> This is my creed:
> Reason is the only torch;
> Justice is the only worship;
> Humanity the only religion;
> Love the only priest;
> Happiness the only good.
> The time to be happy is now.
> The place to be happy is here.
> The way to be happy is to help make others so.

Many admirers praised Ingersoll:

• One of the constellations of our time . . . a bright magnificent constellation.

—Walt Whitman

• No finer personality ever existed.

—Thomas A. Edison

• How handsome he looked as he stood on that table, in the midst of those 500 shouting men and poured the molten silver from his lips! What an organ is human speech when it is employed by a master!

—Samuel Clemens

• His life and work have been an inspiration to the whole earth.

—Luther Burbank

• One of the bravest, grandest champions of human liberty the world has ever seen.

—Clarence Darrow

In the pages of the *North American Review*, Colonel Ingersoll defended freethought against Judge Black, the Rev. H. Field, Mr. Gladstone, and Cardinal Manning. What almost all observers have noted is that, although his printed speeches have been touched up since delivery, Ingersoll was one of the most eloquent speakers of his entire age. Often overlooked is that his wife, **Eva Parker Ingersoll**, was a freethinker. So was his daughter, **Eva Ingersoll-Brown**, as were her younger sister and aunt who lived with her.

Roger Greeley is honorary chairman of the Robert G. Ingersoll Memorial Committee, which is dedicated to restoring Ingersoll's birthplace in Dresden, New York, and to keeping his memory alive. At the house one can hear a wax cylinder recording which his friend Thomas Edison made in which Ingersoll states:

> While I am opposed to all orthodox creeds, I have a creed myself. Happiness is the only good. The time to be happy is now. The place to be happy is here. The way to be happy is to make others so. This creed is somewhat short, but it is long enough for this life, long enough for this world. If there is another world, when we get there we can make another creed. This creed will certainly do for this life.

The committee publishes a newsletter, *Ingersoll Report*. In addition, the Secular Humanists Society of New York have installed a plaque at the site of his home, now the Gramercy Park Hotel, 2 Lexington Avenue, in New York City. **Eva Ingersoll Wakefield**, his granddaughter, was once president of the New York City humanists.

Richard F. Stockton, a playwright whose work about Ingersoll has been performed in New York at La MaMa La Galleria, holds that there are four dramatic events that stand out in Ingersoll's life. First was the death of his father, the Reverend John Ingersoll. Stockton has written, "Despite their opposing religious views, the old revivalist on his deathbed asked Bob to read to him from the black book clutched to his chest. Bob relented, took the book, and was surprised to discover that it wasn't the Bible. It was Plato describing the noble death of the pagan Socrates: a moving gesture of reconciliation between father and son in parting. The second event was Bob's painful realization that his outspoken agnosticism not only invalidated his own political career but ended his brother Ebon's career in Congress, as well. Third was the exquisite anguish of seeing his supportive wife Eva and his young daughters made to suffer for his right to speak his own mind. And fourth was the dramatic tension of having to walk out alone on public stages, in a glaring spotlight, time after time with death threats jammed in his tuxedo pocket informing him that some armed bigot in that night's audience would see to it that he didn't leave the stage alive." However, at the age of sixty-six Ingersoll died of a heart ailment at his married daughter's estate up the Hudson River at Dobbs Ferry. His last lecture, titled "What Is Religion?" was delivered in Boston a few days earlier to the Free Religion Association. His last letter, written the day before he died, lamented Yankee imperialism in Cuba." The Council for Secular Humanism has made Ingersoll's birthplace in Dresden, New York, into a museum.

Ingersoll died of angina pectoris on 21 July 1899. He passed away peacefully, his last words reportedly being, "I am better now." His friend, W.J. Armstrong, was quoted in the *Los Angeles Times*: "He died unexpectedly and suddenly, after conversing cheerfully a few minutes before with the members of his family." {BDF; CE; CL; EU, Roger E. Greeley; *The Freethinker*, 4 October 1908; FUK; FUS; *Ingersoll Report*, Winter 1995-1996; HNS2; JM; JMR; *Northeast Atheist*, September-October 1997; PA; PUT; RAT; RE; TRI; TSV; TYD; U}

INGERSOLL REPORTER

Ingersoll Reporter is published three times per year by the Council for Secular Humanism, PO Box 664, Amherst, New York 14226-0664.

Ingham, Samuel (19th Century)

Ingham, a councilor, was a trustee in the 1860s of the National Secular Society in Manchester, England. {RSR}

Ingram, H. A. (19th Century)

Ingram wrote *Life and Character of Stephen Girard* (1885). {FUS}

Ingram, John Kells (1823—1907)

Ingram, an Irish economist, was a fiery patriot who wrote the rebel song, "Who Fears to Speak of Ninety-Eight?" A writer on economics, Ingram also wrote a work on slavery and serfdom, in which he did not spare the church. McCabe labels him a positivist. {JM; RAT; RE}

Inman, Thomas (1820—1876)

Inman was a physician and archaeologist known chiefly for his work on *Ancient Faiths Embodied in Ancient Names* (1869), in which he deals with the evidences of phallic worship in different nations and among the Jews. {BDF; RAT}

Innaiah: See entry for Innaiah Narisetti.

Inniss, Patrick (20th Century)

Formerly the Vice President of the Seattle, Washington, Rationalist Society, Inniss is an Advisory Board Member of African Americans for Humanism.

Innocent III (1161—1216)

Innocent III, Pope from 1198 to 1216, wrote in a letter to Count de Nevers, "The Jews, like Cain, are doomed to wander the earth as fugitives and vagabonds, and their faces are covered with shame. . . . Use against heretics the spiritual sword of excommunication, and if this does not prove effective, use the material sword." {CE; RE}

INQUIRER

The Inquirer is a British Unitarian fortnightly publication.

INQUIRY

• The crime of inquiry is one which religion never has forgiven.

—**Percy Bysshe Shelley**

INQUISITION

Gregory IX (1227—1241) instituted the Inquisition as a medieval ecclesiastical tribunal for the preservation of Christianity. Its purpose, according to the Very Reverend Raphael M. Huber, a professor of church history at the Catholic University in Washington, DC, was (a) to inquire into the spread of doctrines opposed to the Faith; (b) to call before its tribunals all Catholics suspected of heresy; and (c) to punish their infidelity, to convince them of error, and to exhort them to repentance. In the 16th century, a number of Protestant reformers (Calvin, Servetus, Bullinger) were treated with religious intolerance, and torture became a device used by the Inquisitors, who usually were selected from among the members of the Franciscan and Dominican Orders, preferably the latter, according to an anti-Catholic book, A *History of the Inquisition in the Middle Ages* (1887), by the American historian Henry Charles Lea.

Clifton points out that at its pinnacle of power in the late thirteenth century, the medieval Inquisition was largely staffed by Dominican monks. These monks, of a preaching order begun by St. Dominic in 1216, made a pun on their name in Latin: *domine cani*—loosely, "God's dogs"—a pack of black-and-white hounds pursuing heretics. He adds that by the 1220s some Franciscan monks "were also employed by the Inquisition for their skill in preaching and turning the people away from heretical doctrines; they were officially called to inquisitorial work by Pope Innocent IV in 1246." Today, "the modern equivalent of the Inquisition is a section of Vatican bureaucracy known as the Congregation for the Doctrine of the Faith, which periodically condemns certain Catholic theologians and professors for heretical tendencies. One example is the one year 'silencing' of the Dominican priest Matthew Fox of Holy Names College in Oakland, California, in 1988."

A 1995 work, Benzion Netanyahu's *The Origins of the Inquisition in Fifteenth-Century Spain*, contests the usual view that the Inquisition developed out of the religious tensions spawned by the conversion of thousands of Spanish Jews to Christianity. Rather, he holds that the Inquisition had little to do with religion, that only a few were "Judaizers," and that most were Christians to the core. During his eighteen years as the first Inquisitor General, Friar Tomás de Torquemada oversaw the "relaxing" to secular authorities of as many as two thousand *conversos*, and these were burned at the stake. Another three thousand were burned in effigy after they died in prison or escaped. Meanwhile, nearly forty thousand others were "reconciled" to the Church, first losing their property and then being sentenced to prison. Netanyahu's argument is that racial hatred previously reserved for Jews now was directed toward the *conversos*, and he develops the view that Spain's racists were hypocrites who knew the *conversos* were sincere Christians but deliberately led the Spanish clergy and the monarchy to institute an inquisition in order to combat the "Judaic heresy." (See entries for Tomás de Torquemada and Matthew Paris. Also see an extensive discussion by Joseph McCabe in his *Rationalist Encyclopedia*.) {CE; EH; ER; RE}

Inskip, Conrad (20th Century)

Inskip, a senior technical officer for the biological sciences department, is publicity chairman in New Zealand of the Auckland University Atheists. To taunt the anti-atheists, he wittily and sophomorically brags that he "keeps an excellent ritual sacrifice altar in his basement and endeavours to maintain a stock of black cats, virgins, and other important offerings." E-mail: <c.inskip@auckland.ac.nz>.

INSPIRATION

• The inspiration of the bible depends upon the ignorance of the gentleman.

—**Robert G. Ingersoll**

• All love is sweet,
Given or returned.
Common as light is love,
And its familiar voice wearies not ever. . . .
They who inspire it most are fortunate,
As I am now; but those who feel it most
Are happier still.

—**Percy Bysshe Shelley**

INSTITUTE FOR FIRST AMENDMENT STUDIES

The Institute for First Amendment Studies, POB 589, Great Barrington, Massachusetts 01230, is run by Skipp Porteous, author of *Jesus Doesn't Live Here Anymore* and *Challenging the Christian Right, an Activist's Handbook*. The Institute publishes a newsletter that defends the separation of church and state, and "Walk Away," a newsletter for ex-fundamentalists. On the Web: <http://apocalypse.berkshire.net/~ifas/>.

INSTITUTE FOR RATIONAL EMOTIVE THERAPY

The Institute for Rational Emotive Therapy, 45 East 65th Street, New York, NY 10021, is presided over by Dr. Albert Ellis. As president and founder, he has developed the psychological strategy used by Rational Recovery groups.

INSTRUMENTALISM

In philosophy, instrumentalism is the doctrine that scientific theories are not true descriptions of an unobservable reality. Rather, they are useful instruments that enable us to order and anticipate the observable world. Inasmuch as past scientific theories have been proved false, instrumentalists claim, present and future theories can possibly be proved false, also.

John Dewey advanced the doctrine by developing the pragmatism of William James. Instrumentalists, unlike realists, look for theories that work, rather than complete explanatory theories that are descriptively true—an intelligible but unattainable goal. (Denying instrumentalism are groups of realists, who hold that science *can* give an accurate description of an objective and fixed reality. See entry for Instrumentalism.) {AF; OCP; *The Economist*, 31 May 1997}

INTELLECTUAL

• An intellectual is a man who takes more words than necessary to tell more than he knows.

—**Adlai Stevenson**

To be intellectual is to be rational rather than emotional. An intellectual explores and evaluates new ideas. To intellectualize is to find a rational explanation. A religionist or freethinker who claims to have found "the truth," revealed or otherwise, whose mind is closed to alternative conclusions, is an anti-intellectual. In Russia, the élite of a society's intellectuals have been called members of the intelligentsia. Intellectuals generally avoid labeling their outlook, unless—as pointed out by a wag who went to Columbia University—the label is based upon their own name.

INTELLECTUALS

Nicolas Chauvin, a legendary French soldier known for his devotion to Napoleon, was the inspiration for "chauvinism," a belief in the superiority of one's own gender, group, or kind. Intellectuals often illustrate their chauvinism by claiming their gender, group, or kind was the first or is the best.

"*Contra los Franceses,*" a 1998 pamphlet by Manuel Arroyo Stephens, is a Spanish satirical broadside that takes French culture to task for numbers of faults including fraud, restraint of trade, and theft. Arroyo claims the French pilfered ideas from others and "sold them to the world" as examples of their home-bred genius. Corneille, for example, allegedly plagiarized his plots from 16th-century Spanish drama. Voltaire was an opportunist whose *Lettres philosophiques* rehashed mostly English ideas in vogue at that time.

Others accuse the French of being pretentious, superficial, priggish, bad-mannered, adding that their philosophy is a fad, their wine overrated, their novels unreadable, and they have not done anything since Matisse or Picasso, the latter of whom was not even French.

"Frog-bashing" is discussed in Jonathan Fenby's *On the Brink: The Trouble with France* (1998). He found that George III urged Etonians to hate the French, that the British still enjoy having fun at French expense. Fenby details what he believes are France's ills: a melancholy list that includes social division, widespread corruption, falling school standards, and an overweening state.

On the other hand, Tony Judt of New York University wonders if Arroyo's pamphlet should be read as a satire of Spanish inferiority and small-mindedness faced by the next-door riches of France with its art, its food, its countryside, and its writing.

As for American intellectuality, Europeans have been known to claim the phrase is an oxymoron. Depending upon the person's background, similar criticism is directed at Koreans, Japanese, Chinese, Australians, Southeast Asians, Africans, and at females vs. males, believers vs. non-believers, or others in such arbitrary divisions. (*The Economist*, 12 December 1998}

INTELLIGENCE

Although some have claimed that the more intelligent one is the more likely he or she will be a non-believer, no research is known to have proved or disproved this. Intelligence quotient (IQ) data show people differ in their mental ability, and that inequalities are largely inherited. Those who test low have substantially fewer options in life than those who test high. Daniel Seligman's *A Question of Intelligence: The IQ Debate in America* (1992) indicates that IQ tests are superior predictors of job success; that the rich average higher intelligence than the poor; that IQ scores have approximately the same predictive power for African Americans as for whites; that East Asians test higher than whites, with different structures; that men do better at quantitative tasks whereas women are somewhat better at verbal tests.

Dr. Catherine Cox, a psychologist, has made estimates of the IQs of famous people—pathologists conducting an autopsy say they can estimate, because there are more folds on the cerebral cortex of intelligent people, how smart a subject was based upon the convolutions. Although Cox's estimates have been highly criticized, partly because intelligence is thought to be an attribute of the entire personality and thus cannot be measured in isolation, and partly because her methodology is questioned, Seligman has documented some IQ test scores (shown in italics):

210 **Johann Wolfgang von Goethe**
190 **Sir Isaac Newton**; **Voltaire**
185 Galileo Galilei
180 Leonardo daVinci; René Descartes
175 Immanuel Kant
170 Martin Luther
165 **Wolfgang Amadeus Mozart**
160 **Benjamin Franklin**
155 Rembrandt Harmensz van Rijn
150 **Abraham Lincoln**
143 Richard M. Nixon
138 Hermann Goering (tested prior to Nuremberg Trials)
134 Franz von Papen (tested prior to Nuremberg Trials)
130 Ulysses S. Grant
119 John F. Kennedy
110 John Gotti (gangster)

---

100 Average score, from which deviations are figured

78 Muhammad Ali, also known as Cassius Clay (Because he was tested when he was eligible to be drafted into the Army, it has been alleged that, as did many others, he scored low in order to avoid service. Gerald Early, director of African and Afro-American Studies at Washington University in St. Louis, holds that the score was an honest reflection of his mental abilities, that he was neither literate nor analytical.)

In 1994, Charles Murray's and the late Richard J. Herrnstein's The *Bell Curve: Intelligence and Class Structure in American Life* suggested the alarmist interpretation of intelligence that blacks as a group score fifteen points lower than whites on IQ tests. (Meanwhile, Asians were said to score a few points higher than whites, and a brief mention was made that "Ashkenazi Jews of European origins . . . test higher than any other ethnic group.") Their study drew heavily on the National Longitudinal Survey of Youth, which studied 12,686 high school students who had graduated between 1980 and 1982. The findings were not particularly new, for William Shockley, winner in 1956 of the Nobel Prize in Physics, had in the late 1960s and 1970s lectured on his theory that, because blacks were intellectually inferior and reproduced faster than whites, blacks were causing a retrogression in human evolution. Low-IQ parents produce large families, Murray and Herrnstein argue with statistics, dragging average IQ's yet lower and leading to poverty, welfare dependency, crime, and out-of-wedlock births. High-IQ parents, on the other hand, have fewer children but better income and behavior. What this will lead to, they suggest, is a polarized world in which the IQ elite will separate themselves from the dumb poor, using totalitarian methods. In short, they paint a picture of an America which will be increasingly divided by race, one which will slide unavoidably into castes based on IQ.

The first humanists to react echoed the conclusion of an op-ed article by Frank Rich in *The New York Times*: "Such clever merchandising may make *The Bell Curve* the best-selling unread book since the last novel by Umberto Eco. Then again, Mr. Murray and Mr. Herrnstein may have outsmarted themselves. A book that blames low IQ's for what ails America may have tough sledding in a culture where even conservatives have been rushing to deify the 75 IQ of Forrest Gump," a reference to a movie directed by Robert Zemeckis and which features an idiot-savant. Humanists generally counter-argued that schools *can* overcome and alleged effects of hereditary determination and home environment on intelligence. Otherwise and among other points, if cognitive abilities cannot be changed, then schools could not be blamed for the blatant inequalities that *The Bell Curve* documents but never fully explains. Or, as pictured by E. D. Hirsch Jr., professor of education and humanities at the University of Virginia, "If we cast the net wider than our current programs by considering older studies and those from other countries, we find striking exceptions to [the book's] discouraging results. After all, an agronomist who confines his research to the desert is likely to conclude that cactuses are genetically superior to rice."

Editorialized *The Times*: "Mr. Murray's findings are not wrong because they are ugly. They are wrong because they blind us to more compelling interpretations and because they ignore the huge gaps in understanding the precise nature of intelligence. What is right about the book was already well known: skills have taken on increasing importance in the economy and they are difficult to acquire. What is new about the book—the fixation on genes as destiny—is surely unproved and almost surely wrong: programs here and abroad produce measurable, if unspectacular, results. These sobering lessons were clear before *The Bell Curve* was published."

Editorialized *The Nation*: "In the mid-nineteenth century, British craniologists 'proved' the inferiority of Africans and the Irish. And as Stephen Jay Gould wrote in 1973 during another periodic flare-up of these old arguments, 'What craniometry was to the nineteenth century, intelligence testing has been to the twentieth.'. It is tempting to shrug *The Bell Curve* off as a momentary blip on the country's racial radar. But it will be so only if its ideas are engaged and hooted out of respectable forums."

Alan Ryan, Princeton teacher of politics and a John Dewey expert, concludes in a lengthy critique in *The New York Review of Books* (17 November 1994), "*The Bell Curve* is not only sleazy; it is, intellectually, a mess." And Richard A. Gardner, of Columbia University's College of Physicians and Surgeons, has written that if IQ tests "were properly named, they would be called Tests That Predict Success or Failure in the School System From Which the Questions Have Been Derived."

As to why Albert Einstein was "so brilliant," *The Lancet* (June 1999) reported that the scientist's brain has been found to have had an inferior parietal lobe that was fifteen percent wider than normal because a groove that typically runs through the parietal area of the brain took an unusual course. This, according to pathologist Dr. Thomas Harvey and McMaster University neuroscientist Dr. Sandra F. Witelson, may have allowed more brain cells, or neurons, to establish connections between each other and work together more easily. Their findings astonished many about the man who did not speak until he was three. {CE; Gerald Early, *The New York Review of Books*, 28 May 1998; Lawrence K. Altman, *The New York Times*, 18 June 1999; PA}

INTELLIGENCE TESTING

Howard Gardner of Harvard has written the following:

> The most overrated idea is that our intelligence is an entity we can measure by sticking a mental dipstick into our mind/brain. We pull it out and we read 80 or 100 or whatever. Psychologists can tell us how smart we are, or maybe now geneticists. Then there's the "Bell Curve" twist that says society's problems are due to the dummies. The biological, psychological and anthropological evidence is strongly against this unitary notion of intelligence. There are many human intelligences, nobody is equally good at all, and cultural opportunities determine which are developed and to what extent. But there has been a conspiracy between the industry of psychometrics and the seductiveness of a familiar word. And that conspiracy yields this ubiquitous conviction that there's a single thing called smartness.
>
> {*The New York Times*, 31 October 1997}

INTERCOURSE

The Ancient Romans saw the body as the sensual, sometimes hard-to-control part of the spirit. The body, although it needed sensual gratification, had to be disciplined. The spirit was the body's friendly caretaker. Christianity, however, taught that the body is the enemy of the soul.

Clement of Alexandria held that sex is pure only if it is for procreation within marriage. Jesus the Christ said nothing of the kind, nor was St. Paul so harsh. By the 2nd century, Clement's view predominated, as did complementary views: no masturbation (very important), no sex if conception is unlikely (during lactation and menstruation), no sex in positions that preclude conception (anal, oral, etc.), no sex for the barren (it would only be pleasure), and no sex for homosexuals.

In the United States, twenty-four states ban humans from having sex with animals. {David Marr, *The Sydney Morning Herald*, 6 November 1999; *The Village Voice*, 28 December 1999}

INTERNATIONAL ACADEMY OF HUMANISM

In 1983, the Council for Secular Humanism established The International Academy of Humanism. It is composed of non-theists who are (1) devoted to the principle of free inquiry in all fields of human endeavor; (2) committed to the scientific outlook and the use of reason and the scientific methods in acquiring knowledge about nature; and (3) upholders of humanist ethical values and principles. It was founded with thirty members, the total membership is limited to sixty living individuals, and additional Humanist Laureates are nominated and elected by Academy members. Prospective Laureates must have demonstrated a commitment to the principles of humanism in order to be eligible for consideration. They should also have distinguished themselves by creative scholarship, scientific discovery, artistic or literary production, or other achievements of outstanding merit. They hold lifelong membership in the Academy. Humanists in the International Academy of Humanism reject supernaturalism or occult explanations of the universe, focus on the use of reason and science, and seek to encourage the moral growth and ethical development of the individual, based upon experience.

The activities of the Academy include the convening of seminars and congresses, the issuing of public statements, and the publication of articles, monographs, and books presenting the humanist outlook. In 1985, the Academy met at the University of Michigan; in 1986, at the University of Oslo; in 1988, at the State University of New York; in 1992 at Universiteit Voor Humanistick in Utrecht, The Netherlands; and in 1996 in Mexico City, Mexico.

Its Secretariat includes Paul Kurtz (President), Vern Bullough, Antony Flew, Gerald Larue, and Jean-Claude Pecker. Its membership in 1999 was as follows: **Pieter Admiraal**, medical doctor, The Netherlands; **Steve Allen**, author, humorist; **Shulamit Aloni**, Israeli Education Minister; **Ruben Ardila**, professor of psychology, *Universidad de Colombia*; **Kurt Baier**, professor of philosophy, U of Pittsburgh; **Sir Isaiah Berlin**, professor of philosophy, Oxford U; **Sir Hermann Bondi**, Fellow of the Royal Society, Past Master of Churchill College, London; **Yelena Bonner**, noted defender of human rights and wife of the late Andrei Sakharov; **Vern Bullough** (Secretariat), Historian, California State University at Northridge; **Mario Bunge**, professor of philosophy of science, McGill U; **Jean-Pierre Changeux**, *Collège de France* and *Institut Pasteur*; **Patricia Smith Churchland**, professor of philosophy, U of California at San Diego; **Sir Arthur C. Clarke, C.B.E.**, writer, Sri Lanka; **Bernard Crick**, professor of politics, U of London; **Francis Crick**, Nobel Laureate in Physiology, Salk Inst.; **Richard Dawkins**, Fellow of the New College, Oxford University; **José Delgado**, chairperson of the Dept. of Neuropsychiatry, U of Madrid; **Jean Dommanget**, astronomer, Belgium; **Umberto Eco**, Italian semiologist; **Paul Edwards**, professor of philosophy, New School for Social Research, New York; **Luc Ferry**, professor of philosophy at the Sorbonne and the University of Caen; **Sir Raymond Firth**, professor emeritus of anthropology, U of London; **Antony Flew** (Secretariat), professor emeritus of philosophy, Reading University; **Betty Friedan**, author, founder of the National Organization for Women (NOW); **Yves Galifret**, professor emeritus of physiology at the Sorbonne and General Secretary of *l'Union Rationaliste*; **John Galtung**, professor of sociology, U of Oslo; **Stephen Jay Gould**, Museum of Comparative Zoology, Harvard; **Adolf Grünbaum**, professor of philosophy, U of Pittsburgh; **Murray Gell-Mann**, Nobel Laureate in physics, California Institute of Technology; **Jürgen Habermas**, University of Frankfurt; **Herbert Hauptman**, Nobel Laureate in Medicine and professor of biophysical science, SUNY at Buffalo; **Alberto Hidalgo Tuñon**, president of the *Sociedad Asturiana de Filosofia*, Oviedo, Spain; **Donald Johanson**, Institute of Human Origins; **Sergei Kapitza**, Chairman of Physics at the Moscow Institute of Physics and Technology; **George Klein**, Swedish cancer researcher; **Gyorgy Konrad**, Hungarian novelist; **Paul Kurtz** (President of the Secretariat), professor emeritus of philosophy, SUNY at Buffalo; **Gerald Larue** (Secretariat), professor emeritus of archaeology and biblical studies, U of Southern California at Los Angeles; **Thelma Lavine**, president of the Society for the Advancement of American Philosophy; **Jolé Lombardi**, Organizer of the New University for the Third Age; **José Leite Lopes**, Director, *Centro Brasileiro de Pesquisas Fisicas*; **Paul MacCready**, president, AeroVironment, Inc.; **Adam Michnik**, Polish historian and writer; **Jonathan Miller**, theater and film director, physician, actor; **Taslima Nasrin**, Bangladeshi physician, novelist; **Conor Cruise O'Brien**, Irish author, statesman; **Indumati Parikh**, president, Radical Humanist Association of India; **John Passmore**, professor of philosophy, Australian National U; **Octavio Paz**, (deceased 1998) Nobel Laureate in Literature, Mexico; **Jean-Claude Pecker** (Secretariat), professor of astrophysics, *Collège de France, Académie des Sciences*; **Wardell Baxter Pomeroy**, psychotherapist and author; **W. V. Quine**, professor of philosophy, Harvard; **Marcel Roche**, emeritus researcher, *Instituto Venezolano de Investigaciones Científica* (IVIC), Venezuela; **Max Rood**, professor of law, former Minister of Justice in Holland; **Richard Rorty**, professor of philosophy, U of Virginia; **Arthur M. Schlesinger Jr.**, history educator; **Leopold**

Sedar Senghor, former president, Senegal; **J. J. C. Smart**, Australian philosopher; **Wole Soyinka**, Nobel Laureate in Literature, Nigeria; **Svetozar Stojanovic**, professor of philosophy, U of Belgrade; **Thomas Szasz**, professor of psychiatry, SUNY Medical School; **V. M. Tarkunde**, chairman, Indian Radical Humanist Association; **Richard Taylor**, professor of philosophy, Union College; **Sir Keith Thomas**, President, The British Academy; **Rob Tielman**, formerly, co-president, International Humanist and Ethical Union (IHEU); **Peter Ustinov**, noted actor, director, writer; **Mario Vargas Llosa**, Peruvian novelist, politician; **Simone Veil**, Deputy to European Parliament, France; **Gore Vidal**, novelist; **Kurt Vonnegut Jr.**, novelist; **Mourad Wahba**, professor of education, U of *Ain Shams*, Cairo; **Steven Weinberg**, Nobel Laureate in Physics; **G. A. Wells**, professor of German, U of London; **Edward O. Wilson**, professor of sociobiology, Harvard.

Deceased: **George O. Abell, Isaac Asimov, Sir Alfred J. Ayer, Dame R. Nita Barrow**; **Brand Blanshard, Bonnie Bullough; Milovan Djilas**; **Joseph Fletcher; Sidney Hook, Lawrence Kohlberg, Franco Lombardi, André Lwoff, Ernest Nagel, George Olincy, Chaim Perelman, Sir Karl Popper, Carl Sagan, Andrei Sakharov, Lady Barbara Wootton**.

INTL. ALLIANCE AGAINST FUNDAMENTALISM

In 1996 at the World Atheist Conference held in India, the International Alliance Against Fundamentalism was formed.

INTERNATIONAL ASSOCIATION FOR INTERCULTURAL EDUCATION

A cooperating organization of the IHEU is the International Association for Intercultural Education, c/o APBO 'Pieter Batelaan,' Sumatralaan 37, 1217 GP Hilversum, Netherlands.

INTL. ASSOCIATION FOR RELIGIOUS FREEDOM

The International Association for Religious Freedom, consisting of over 60 groups in more than twenty countries, includes liberal Christians, Buddhists, Shintoists, Hindus, Muslims, Sikhs, and Jews. It is supported by the Unitarian Universalist Association, is at 2 Market St., Oxford OX 1 3 EF, United Kingdom. E-mail: <iarf@interfaith_center.org>. On the Web: <http://www.interfaith-center.org/oxford/iarf>.

INTERNATIONAL ASSOCIATION OF HUMANIST EDUCATORS, COUNSELLORS, AND LEADERS

The International Association of Humanist Educators, Counsellors, and Leaders in 1994 was renamed the European Humanist Professionals.

INTERNATIONAL COUNCIL OF UNITARIANS AND UNIVERSALISTS (ICUU)

The International Council of Unitarians and Universalists is presided over by David Usher, Box 543, Peterborough, New Hampshire 03458. Member groups are found in Australia and New Zealand, Canada, Czech Republic, Denmark, European Unitarian-Universalists, Germany, Hungary, India, Pakistan, Philippines, Romania, Russia, South Africa, Sri Lanka, United Kingdom, and the United States of America. The group's newsletter is *The Global Chalice*. Its executive committee includes the following: Vice President, the Rev. Arpad Szabo of Romania; Secretary, the Rev. Clifford Reed of the United Kingdom; Treasurer, the Rev. Jill McAllister, of the United States of America; Member at large, Wolfgang Jantz of Germany. Program directors Polly and Ted Guild, 4 Kendal Common, Weston, Massachusetts 02193. E-mail: <73664.614@compuserve.com>.

The office mailing address is 1-6 Essex St., Strand, London WC2R 3HY, United Kingdom, phone 0171 240 2384. On the Web: <http://www.uua.org/icuu/>.

INTERNATIONAL DEVELOPMENT COMMITTEE

The Council for Secular Humanism's International Development Committee works with individuals and groups in various parts of the world, especially in developing countries. It assists them in spreading the humanist point of view and brings them into the International Humanist and Ethical Union (IHEU), headquartered in Utrecht, The Netherlands.

INTERNATIONAL FEDERATION OF SECULAR HUMANISTIC JEWS

Sherman Wine heads the International Federation of Secular Humanistic Jews at 28611 West Twelve Mile Road, Farmington Hills, Michigan 48334. {FD}

INTERNATIONAL HUMANIST AND ETHICAL UNION (IHEU)

The International Humanist and Ethical Union (IHEU) represents five million members of ninety organizations in thirty countries. It promotes non-theistic morality, has ninety-seven member organizations in thirty-five countries, and has consultative status with the United Nations, UNESCO, and UNICEF. The early sponsors, who founded IHEU in 1952, were also instrumental in the founding of the United Nations. They included **Lord Boyd Orr** (the first head of the World Food Organization), **Sir Julian Huxley** (the first head of UNESCO), and **Brock Chisholm** (the first head of the World Health Organization).

Many Humanist principles have already found expression in international human rights conventions; indeed, the Humanist attitude forms the philosophical basis of the concept of human rights as stated in the Universal Declaration of Human Rights. The IHEU has made submissions to the UN bodies on questions of environmental, economic, social, and cultural rights. Its concern for human rights and peace have been many and varied. The UN Convention on the Rights of the Child, the UN Convention on Torture, and the Geneva Convention on Refugees, for example, find strong support from IHEU Member Organizations.

In FAO, the UN's Food and Agriculture Organization, the IHEU has participated in the five-year Freedom from Hunger Campaign and is a founding member of the UNESCO NGO Working Group on Science and Ethics. The IHEU has been represented at major UN conferences such as World Population (Belgrade 1965; Bucharest 1974), Environment (Stockholm 1972); the UN World Conference on Women (Vienna 1994, and Beijing 1995); UNESCO's conference on the Power of Culture (Stockholm 1998), the Oslo Conference on Freedom of Religion or Belief (1998), of which the IHEU was a founding member, and others. It was an IHEU initiative that led to the adoption by the UN of the Right to Conscientious Objection to Military Service. The IHEU also raised with the UN bodies the issue of rights of religious and philosophical dissenters such as Taslima Nasrin of Bangladesh and Xiao Xuehui of China.

In collaboration with its Dutch Specialist Member HIVOS, the IHEU funds Member Organization activities in the third world through the Humanist Networking and Development Program, one which has supported the following:

- community development projects by Humanists in Bangladesh
- development of the Ibero-American and the South Asian Humanist networks

- Humanist groups in Africa
- Ibn Rushd and Enlightenment International Association's project Enlightenment in the Muslim World
- literacy and good citizenship youth programs for adolescents in Mumbai slums, and a Humanist school in Andhra Pradesh, India
- projects promoting the scientific outlook
- publication of Humanist books (Chinese) and magazines (Spanish, in Mexico)
- campaigns against blasphemy laws
- an expert committee examining the religious abuse of children

The IHEU facilitates the exchange of ideas of particular interest to humanists by publishing the journal *International Humanist News* (Bradlaugh House, 47 Theobald's Road, London WC1X 8SP), and by convening an international congress every two years. The first congress was at Amsterdam in 1951; the 14th in Mumbai in 1999; and the 15th will be in Melbourne, Australia.

As a federation of national and regional Humanist groups, IHEU coordinates activities of its Member Organizations, stimulates their policies, guides their strategies, fosters the growth of new humanist groups, and represents the interests of Humanists at the United Nations (New York, Geneva, and Vienna), UNICEF (New York), UNESCO (Paris), and the Council of Europe. It is a clearinghouse for information and inspiration as well as a forum where Humanist organizations and individuals can exchange thoughts and expertise for improving the impact of national activities. By representing Humanism to the world media, the IHEU ensures that an ever-greater number of people learn of the humanist alternative.

The IHEU is democratically organized and is funded by donations and membership dues from its Member Organizations and individual supporters. In 1993, IHEU had fifteen **ordinary members** (such as the Humanist associations of Canada, the United States, and India as well as the Council for Democratic and Secular Humanism in Buffalo). It had seven **specialist organizations** (such as the Rationalist Press Association in London and Prometheus Books in Buffalo, New York). There were sixty-one **specialist members** (representing groups of freethinkers, secularists, and atheists in numerous countries). There were four **cooperating organizations** (e.g., the Committee for the Scientific Investigation of Claims of the Paranormal, CSICOP); the Netherlands International Association for Intercultural Education; the Rationalist Association in Florissant, Missouri; and the Unitarian Universalist Association in Boston, Massachusetts).

In determining the eligibility of organizations that want to join, the IHEU requires acceptance of the following:

> Humanism is a democratic and ethical life stance, which affirms that human beings have the right and responsibility to give meaning and shape to their own lives. It stands for the building of a more humane society through an ethics based on human and other natural values in a spirit of reason and free enquiry through human capabilities. It is not theistic, and it does not accept supernatural views of reality.

When he resigned as co-president in 1994, Paul Kurtz recommended tapping the reservoir of humanist energies with a militant outreach, developing programs in moral education for children and education in science and critical thinking, and dropping "Ethical" in the union's title. In 1996 Babu Gogineni (of Hyderabad) was appointed Executive Director. Vice-presidents were Vern Bullough (U.S.); Fred Cook; Levi Fragell (Norway); and Jane Wynne Willson (U.K.). Treasurer was Robbi Robson (U.K.). Rob Tielman (Netherlands) led the organization until 1998.

In 1998 at a meeting in Heidelberg, a new structure was formalized. The Board (consisting of representatives of IHEU member organizations) renamed itself the General Assembly. The Executive Committee was redesignated the Board of Directors of the IHEU. The General Assembly (formerly the Board) was given a policy-setting function. The new officers are Levi Fragell, President; Jane Wynne Willson, John Leeson, Liesbeth Mulder, and Fred Cook, Vice Presidents; Robbi Robson, Treasurer; and Babu Gogineni, Executive Director. The IHEU, which was headquartered at Nieuwegracht 69A, 3512 LG Utrecht, The Netherlands, moved in 1996. It is now at Bradlaugh House, 47 Theobald's Road, London WC1X 8SP. Membership in 1996 cost $50 annual or $625 lifetime. For subscription only to the magazine, $15 per year. On the World Wide Web: <http://www.secularhumanism.org/iheu>. (See Mary and Lloyd Morain, "Reminiscences of IHEU's Founding from the U.S.A." in *International Humanist* July 1992) {*International Humanist News*, December 1996}

INTERNATIONAL HUMANIST AND ETHICAL UNION (IHEU), THE 1999 CONGRESS IN INDIA

In 1999 the 14th Congress of the International Humanist and Ethical Union was held in Mumbai, the first such held in the third world. Six hundred attended from twenty-three countries, of whom 450 were Indian. Dr. Indumati Parikh, President of the Indian Radical Humanist Association, was a key organizer. Speakers included Levi Fragell, President of the IHEU; Babu Gogineni, the Executive Director of IHEU; Professor Amlan Datta, who spoke on "The Finer Spirit of Humanism"; John Galtung, who was President of the Congress in Mumbai; Dr. H. Narasimhaiah, the former Vice-Chancellor of Bangalore University, who inaugurated the Congress; Justice V. M. Tarkunde; who gave a keynote address, stressing that humanism must reach out to the poor; Pekka Elo, a Finnish educator who spoke about the importance of teaching independent thinking; Babu Gogineni, who said that a chief aim of human development is the social and cultural fulfilment of the individual; Timo Airaksinen of Helsinki University, who looked at a range of philosophic theories of ethics and stressed the need to concentrate on facts and rational and logical conclusions; Rob Buitenberg from the Netherlands, who contrasted humanism as a public rights outlook and as an existential life stance; Professor Wahba from Cairo University, who described the tradition stemming from the Arab thinker, Averröes; Prof. R. Strinivassan, editor of *Freedom First* in India, who presented an account of rationalism in India; Jim Herrick of England, who discussed relations between British and Indian secularists; Hiranmay Karlekar, managing editor of the daily *Indian Express*; Fred Edwords, who discussed the problems connected with genetic modification, trans-hybrid species, neo-eugenics, pharmaceutical farming; Georges Liénard, who spoke about the ethical choices involved in the use of new biological possibilities; Jayant Narlikar, who spoke about the need to counter anti-scientific movements such as astrology and Feng Shu; Jean Claude Pecker, who addressed the importance of science's not becoming distorted to fit the prevailing views of the time; Joe Chuman of the United States; Alexander Cox of Costa Rica; Hugo Estrella of Argentina; Kjartan Selnes; R. M. Pal, a human rights compaigner; and others.

The congress took place at the M. N. Roy Human Development Campus. Ideas that were explored related to the future of humanism: fundamentalism and Islam; challenges to the global community; separating religion and the state; democracy and humanism; science and anti-science; education for social change. {*International Humanist News*, December 1998}

INTERNATIONAL HUMANIST NEWS

International Humanist News (Bradlaugh House, 47 Theobald's

Road, London WC 1X 8SP) was edited by Jim Herrick until 1999, at which time Babu Gogineni became its editor. A quarterly, it lists seventy-five or so humanist journals and a hundred or more organizations affiliated with the International Humanist and Ethical Union. E-mail: <im.rpa@humanism.org.uk>.

INTERNATIONAL HUMANIST AWARDS

The International Humanist and Ethical Union (IHEU), as of 1999, had awarded International Humanist Awards to the following: Elena Bonner, Alexander Dubcek, Sir Julian Huxley, Paul Kurtz, and Andrei Sakharov.

INTERNATIONAL HUMANIST PROFESSIONALS

The International Humanist Professionals (The Netherlands) have an e-mail address: <hsn@uvh.nl>.

INTERNATIONAL MULTIDISCIPLINARY CONFERENCE ON HUMAN BEHAVIOUR AND THE MEANING OF MODERN HUMANISM

The first International Multidisciplinary Conference on Human Behaviour and the Meaning of Modern Humanism was held at Delphi, Greece, in June 1995. Dennis V. Razis, a Greek physician specializing in oncology, served as head of the conference. (See entry for Dennis V. Razis.)

INTERNATIONAL NATURALIST CHURCH

The International Naturalist Church (PO Box 2469, Berkeley, California 94702-0469) is a secular church that calls itself "the only national non-profit membership organization that works to end supernaturalism and, instead, discover, teach, and promote religious Naturalism." Jeff Walther, who edits its newsletter, *Green Light*, says that "supernaturalism minus super equals naturalism." *Religious Naturalism* is a 325-page book that the group sells.

In addition to being pacifistic and in-your-face heretical, the newsletter favors stopping the drug war by endorsing hemp and making marijuana legal. This will provide

- a completely new tree-free, better source for unlimited, higher-quality paper;
- a completely new billions of dollars rescue crop and industry for our beleaguered family farmers and ranchers;
- a way to provide a completely new source of human, animal, and wildlife protein, food, for hemp seed is one of the world's best and cheapest sources of protein;
- a new source of agriculturally-produced fuel, methanol;
- a new and better fiber for clothing;
- the means to eliminate organized crime's primary source of income, power and the need for weapons;
- complete food and drug inspection for purity and safety for any drugs used;
- avoiding the primary negative trait of drug (ab)use—impoverishment, by cutting the cost to the user and supplier to a manageable small fraction of current prices;
- a new revenue source for taxation;
- for the elimination of prison overcrowding, for up to 40% of the current prison space is occupied by misadjudicated drug prohibition non-violent crimes;
- an analgesic, pain reliever, stress reliever, that is relatively as safe or safer than all other known alternatives for those in distress.

INTERNATIONALER BUND DER KONFESSIONSLOSEN UND ATHEISTEN

A German league of churchless individuals and atheists is *Internationaler Bund Der Konfessionslosen Und Atheisten* (IBKA), at Chausseestr, 8, D-10115 Berlin, Germany. Editor Rolf Heinrich publishes *Miz*.

INTERNET INFIDELS

Luree Dell-Bryan of Shawnee Lake, British Columbia, Canada, and Jeff Lowder of Colorado Springs, Colorado, are the promoters of Internet Infidels, a web site whose purpose is to provide a virtual library of information on nontheistic worldviews, including agnosticism, atheism, freethought, humanism, and secularism. For example, one can find entire books, can search for individual names, and can print the material without going to a library.

Internet Infidels is found on the World Wide Web: <http://www.infidels.org/>.

INTERNET WEBPAGES, HUMANISTIC: See entry for Web.

INTI

Inti in the Inca religion was the supreme god, the god of the sun. {LEE}

INUITS

Formerly called Eskimo people, the Inuits inhabit Arctic Canada and Greenland. Snowstorms with 75-miles-per-hour winds are common, as are days when it is minus 40 degrees Fahrenheit. The Inuit language is Inuktitut.

Baffin Island and the rest of the eastern portion of Canada's vast Northwest Territories in 1999 became Nunavut ("our land"), a region as big as Alaska and California combined. The Yukon census in 1996 listed 30,766 individuals; the Northwest Territories listed 64,401. The indigenous Indian and Inuit population accounts for only 1.5% of Canada's population.

In Nunavut and Igloolik, "the great darkness" is a time when the sun disappears and day becomes night for seven weeks. When the sun finally emerges from the horizon, it appears "like the nostrils of a bearded seal poking out of the ocean ice." It used to be the most important day of the year. "The first person who saw the sun would rush back to the sod houses or igloos to tell everyone," Rosie Iqualliyuqa, a ninety-six-year-old elder told reporter Anthony DePalma in the Northwest Territories. A great igloo would be built. Soapstone lamps that had provided the only illumination during the long night would be ceremoniously extinguished and relit from a single wick. Then, Mrs. Iqualliyuqa lamented, outsiders came from the south with their crosses and their schools and their strange notions about chopping up the day into small pieces called minutes, and the celebrations stopped. Now, with electric lights, alarm clocks and calendars, "the great darkness" came to mean almost nothing and young Inuits are now confronted with the tug of war going on between traditional culture and southern culture. {Anthony DePalma, *The New York Times*, 18 January 1999}

Ionesco, Eugène (1909—1994)

A Romanian-born French playwright, Ionesco is known for expressing the absurdity of bourgeois values and the futility of human endeavor in a universe ruled by chance. His *The Bald Soprano* (1950) was a classic of the theater of the absurd, leading him to observe upon seeing a production, "To incarnate phantasms, to give them life, is a prodigious, irreplaceable adventure." The play is still running in Paris after forty-eight continuous years.

Just as Dario Fo uses "grammelot," Ionesco before him lampooned the use of language as a means of communication. The very title of *The Bald Soprano* is nonsense—no soprano is in the play, bald or hirsute.

It was followed by *The Lesson* (1951), *The Chairs* (1952), and *Rhinoceros* (1959), the latter work involving an act of reverse anthropomorphism—on Broadway, Zero Mostel without changing his costume or makeup transformed himself into a credible beast. To *Esquire* (1974), Ionesco declared in a statement typical of his art of exaggeration and worded as if teasing metaphysicians, "In the name of religion, one tortures, persecutes, builds pyres." {CE; TYD}

IOWA HUMANISTS

• Humanists of Iowa (AHA) are at 2101 Hickory Lane, Cedar Falls, Iowa. Alan Levin is President; Richard Pieart is Vice President; and Betty McCollister is Treasurer. E-mail: <iowa@humanists.net>. Web: <http://humanists.net/iowa>.

• The Iowa Ethical Union is at 2660 Third Avenue, Marion, Iowa 52302. President is Marion Carson; Vice President is Larry Carter Center; and Secretary is Betty Woods.

IOWA SISTERHOOD: See entries for Mary Safford and Eleanor Gordon.

IOWA UNITARIANS AND UNIVERSALISTS

Iowa was once a "hotbed" of humanism. Unitarian ministers E. Burdette Backus, John Dietrich, and Curtis Reese were instrumental in encouraging "Unitarian humanism" to their congregations. Edwin H. Wilson's *The Genesis of a Humanist Manifesto* (1995) describes the Midwestern influence upon the early American Humanist Association. Backus, Dietrich, and Reese wrote widely—all three signed the 1933 Humanist Manifesto I.

Unitarian groups in Iowa tend to be more humanistic than theistic. Congregations with adherents more attuned to Universalism tend to be more theistic.

• Ames Fellowship, 1015 N. Hyland Ave., Ames, IA 50014; e-mail: <uufa@aol.com>.

• Burlington UU Fellowship, 625 North 6th St., Burlington, IA 52601; e-mail: <inspirit@earthling.net>.

• Cedar Falls-Waterloo, UU Society of Black Hawk County, 3912 Cedar Heights Drive, Cedar Falls, IA 50613; e-mail: <uu@cedarnet.org>.

Dorothy S. Grant of the Cedar Falls group wrote a manual for religious education directors, *Universalism in Iowa: 1830—1963, Symbols and Golden Rules of World Religions.* She also wrote *A Lay-Woman's Unitarian World.* In 1994, at the age of 89, she wrote *The Unitarian Universalist Society of Black Hawk County*, a 131-year history (1863—1994) with descriptive inventory of the group's acquisitions.

• Cedar Rapids, People's Church UU, 600 3rd Ave. SE, Cedar Rapids, IA 52401

• Clinton UU Fellowship, 309 30th Ave. N., Clinton, IA 52732

• Davenport Unitarian Church, 3707 Eastern Ave., Davenport, IA 52807; e-mail: <qcuu@juno.com>.

• Des Moines First Unitarian Church, 1800 Bell Ave., Des Moines, IA 50315; e-mail: <dsmuu@aol.com>.

• Dubuque UU Fellowship, Windsor Park 801 Davis, Dubuque, IA 52001; e-mail: <loguidice@uwplah.edu>.

• Iowa City UU Society, 10 S. Gilbert St., Iowa City, IA 52240; e-mail: <icuu@blue.weeg.uiowa.edu>.

• Mason City, UU Fellowship of North Central Iowa, 606 N. Monroe Ave., Mason City, IA 50401

• Sioux City, First Unitarian Church, 2508 Jackson St., Sioux City, IA 51104

(See entries for E. Burdette Backus, John Dietrich, Dorothy S. Grant, and Curtis Reese.)

IRELAND, HUMANISTS IN

• Association of Irish Humanists: Ellen Sides, 5 Ailesbury Gardens, Ballsbridge, Dublin 4 (00353) 1 269 3811

• Belfast Humanist Group: Les Reid (01232) 657060

• *Church and State*, a quarterly, care of P. Maloney, Box 159, Cork

• Ulster Humanist Association: Brian McClinton, 25 Riverside Drive, Lisburn BT27 4HE

Richard Boeke has reported that an estimated 4,000 members of the Non-subscribing Presbyterian Church of Northern Ireland contains many of whom are Unitarian and that there are Unitarian churches in Dublin and Cork. The Cork church rarely has services but the Dublin church meets regularly. Both are connected with the British Unitarians and the Northern Ireland Non-subscribing Church. Unitarians in Ireland are on the Web: <http://www.unitarian.org.uk/>.

(See entries for Mary McEvoy and Richard Spicer, authors of *The Humanist Philosophy—with an Irish Guide to Non-religious Ceremonies*)

Ireland, Alexander (1810—1894)

Ireland was a journalist and businessman. After meeting Emerson in 1833, he became a life-long friend and disciple. Ireland was appointed publisher and business manager of the *Manchester Examiner*, and he was one of the founders of the Manchester Free Library. He arranged Emerson's English tour in 1847—1848 and wrote a biography of Emerson that confesses his own ethical faith. {RAT}

Irion, Mary Jean (20th Century)

Irion, in *From the Ashes of Christianity* (1968), wrote, "Christianity was a great religion. It has been over for a hundred years now; whatever the twentieth century knows of it can be thought of as a lingering unreality preserved in the church. When something even so small as a lightbulb goes out, the eyes for a moment still see it; and a sound after it is made will have, in the right places, an echo. So it is not at all strange that when something so huge as a world religion goes out, there remains for a century or more in certain places some notion that it is still there. Irion also wrote *Yes, World: A Mosaic of Meditation* (1970). {TYD}

IRISH FREETHINKERS AND HUMANISTS: See entry for Ireland, Humanists In. Also, see a survey by Tony Akkermans in *The Freethinker* (June 1997), in which are cited John Toland as being described by Jonathan Swift as "the great Oracle of the anti-Christians"; William Lecky, the politician and historian; and John Bagnell Bury, a classical scholar who held professorships at Dublin and Cambridge.

Iron, Ralph: See entry for Olive Schreiner.

Ironside, Isaac (1808—1870)

Ironside was converted to freethought by listening to lectures of Frances Wright. He was a founding member in England of the Sheffield Mechanics' Institute. {VI}

IRONY

• One of my old formulas is to be an enthusiast in the front part of your heart and ironical in the back.

—Justice Oliver Wendell Holmes

IRRELIGION

• Irreligion, n. The principal one of the great faiths of the world.

—Ambrose Bierce
The Devil's Dictionary

Isaacs, Alan (1925—)

Isaacs, a freethinker, wrote *The Survival of God in the Scientific Age* (1966). {GS}

Isherwood, Christopher (1904—1986)

Because the novelist and playwright Isherwood, upon deserting his native England in 1939 for the safety of the United States, fell in with Thomas Mann and Bertrand Russell, some may have assumed he was interested in rationalism and a non-theist outlook. Actually, however, he also fell in with Swami Prabhavananda, with whom he produced a translation of the *Bhagavad-Gita*; and with Aldous Huxley, sharing his interest in mescaline. Vedanta as well as Hindu philosophy became important, much as for his friend W. H. Auden, with whom he co-authored *Journey to a War* (1939). Anglo-Catholicism was important.

Isherwood once argued with Russell and Julian Huxley, who were concerned about Aldous Huxley. Isherwood (in *Christopher Isherwood: Diaries, Volume One: 1939—1960*, published in 1997) wrote:

> "Did he—I mean—er, that is—do you mean to say he actually, er, really—*prays*?"
> "And why," asked Bertie, "does Aldous talk about Ulltimate Reality? Surely one kind of reality isn't any more or less real than another."

Isherwood's mysticism and Vedantism is featured in many of his writings. The frank description of the early days of his homosexuality is found in *Christopher and His Kind* (1976). His best-known work was the section "Sally Bowles" which John Van Druten dramatized in *I Am A Camera* (1951) and which was turned into a stage musical in 1968 as *Cabaret*. {OEL}

ISIS

Isis (*Ashet* in Egyptian), queen of the Egyptian gods, was worshipped throughout the late Roman Empire. As the major image of female divinity, states Clifton, "Isis became blended in devotion with the Virgin Mary." (See the entry for Christmas.) {EH}

Iska, Frank (20th Century)

From 1909 to 1921, Iska published *Vesmir*, first in Oklahoma City, then in Chicago.

ISLAM

In Arabic, Islam refers to submitting to, or having peace with, God. It is the religion of which Muhammad was the prophet. The adherents of Islam prefer to be called Muslims or Moslems rather than Muhammedans or Mohammedans, the latter two implying that Muhammed was a god (analogous to Jesus and the Christians) rather than a human. Muslims deny the divinity of Jesus, citing Jesus as another prophet, like Muhammad.

More than one billion adherents of Islam live in the present world of almost six billion. But they do not share a single history, language, culture, or tradition. Over the 1,400 years of the religion's existence, Islam has taken on many political, philosophical, theological, and mystical forms in a number of countries. Muslims are a diverse grouping of people who differ in gender, class, ethnicity, and experience. Although it may be thought to be a homogeneous group, it is not.

The Qur'an (Koran), believed to be a revelation of God to Muhammad, is held sacred throughout large portions of Asia and Africa, especially North Africa, the Middle East, Pakistan, Malaysia, and Indonesia. There are five essential duties, the Five Pillars, in Islam:

1. The Muslim must say, "There is no god but Allah, and Muhammad is His prophet."
2. Five times daily he must pray facing Mecca: at dawn, at noon, in midafternoon, at dusk, and after dark.
3. The Muslim must give alms generously.
4. The Muslim must keep the fast of Ramadan, which is the ninth month of the Muslim year.
5. Once in his life the Muslim male must, if he can, make the pilgrimage (Hajj) to Mecca.

Muslims follow injunctions against alcoholic beverages, touching or eating of pork, gambling, usury, fraud, slander, and the making of images. Although Islam permits polygamy—if a man can support four wives equally—it is not a typical practice in Islamic countries, except among clerics and the very wealthy. Islamic law includes prescriptions for family life, dress, commercial transactions, and diet. Like the Jews and Christians, Muhammadens revere the Old Testament of the Holy Bible.

Although some contemporary Muslims argue that Islam can regain strength by integrating Western notions of freedom and social reform, a more visible group of fundamentalist Muslims rejects Western and secular influences.

The demarcation between civil law and religious law is very difficult to make in an Islamic state. Further, there is no distinction between theology and philosophy.

In *Power* (1938), Bertrand Russell noted that "One of the arguments against democracy is that a nation of united fanatics has more chance of success in war than a nation containing a large proportion of sane men." The classic example he gives of power through fanaticism is the rise of Islam: "Mohammed added nothing to the knowledge or to the material resources of the Arabs, and yet, within a few years of his death, they had acquired a large empire by defeating their most powerful neighbors. Undoubtedly, the religion founded by the Prophet was an essential element in the success of his nation. At the very end of his life, he declared war on the Byzantine Empire. 'The Moslems were discouraged, they alleged the want of money, or horses, or provisions, the season of harvest, and the intolerable heat of the summer. "Hell is much hotter," said the indignant prophet. He disdained to compel their service; but on his return, he admonished the most guilty, by an excommunication of fifty days' (Gibbon, Chap. L). Fanaticism, while Mohammed lived, and for a few years after his death, united the Arab nation, gave it confidence in battle, and promoted courage by the promise of Paradise to those who fell fighting the infidel."

Lee Kuan Yew, senior minister of Singapore and the country's Prime Minister from 1959 to 1990, has written of predictions for Asia in the next century. He described Wang Chang, aged seventy, a fourth-generation Chinese Singaporean, who predicted the following: By the year 2150, Orthodox Islam will remain an all-embracing faith that will continue to lay down strict rules governing all aspects of a Muslim's life. Muslims, Wang holds, will not join any broad ecumenical movement, and he also believes that in 2150 there will be no world confederation of democracies—there will be a civil community of nations in which a tolerant live-and-let-live relationship prevails, but the Islamic world will remain separate. Wang's friend, Ali Alkaff, a fifth-generation Arab-Malay Singaporean, according to *The Economist* (11-17 September 1993), did not share Wang's faith that man's rationality will enable him to avoid obvious disasters. He did not, however, disagree with the viewpoint that the Islamic world will vary in its strict Koran-based religious practices.

Such a strictness in Afghanistan was shown in 1996 when music was banned on Kabul's radio stations and cinemas were closed because both lacked "suitably Islamic" material.

Most non-Muslims are unaware that Islam has taken so much from both Jewish and Christian traditions. Few know that according to Sura 4, Jesus was not crucified: the Jews "Killed him not, they did not crucify him, but it was made to appear that way to them." Thus, the heart of Christian doctrine is denied. Warraq and other critics point out that it was *despite* Islam that Islamic science developed, and he laments the fact that religion has so often been made the basis for perpetuating social injustices: the notion of a Holy War and making apostasy a capital offense are particularly intolerant. "In modern times," he wrote, blasphemy has simply become a tool for Muslim governments to silence opposition, or for individuals to settle personal scores."

"Muslims," wrote the philosopher Ernest Renan, "are the first victims of Islam. Many times I have observed in my travels in the Orient that fanaticism comes from a small number of dangerous men who maintain the others in the practice of religion by terror. To liberate the Muslim from his religion is the best service that one can render him." (See entries for Ibn Al-Rawandi, Civilization, Fatwa, Flat Earth Theory, Heaven—Muslim, Nation of Islam, and Ibn Warraq.) {CE; ER; RE}

ISLAMIC ASSOCIATIONS IN THE UNITED STATES AND CANADA

The Federation of Islamic Associations in the United States and Canada is at 25351 Five Mile Road, Redford Township, Michigan 48239. Estimates of the number of members exceed three million in the two nations.

ISLAMIC FUNDAMENTALISM

In Uzbekistan, according to *The Economist* (4 July 1998),

> The government uses the term *Wahhabism*, which refers to the puritanical Islamic creed of Saudi Arabia, to demonise all those who oppose the strict controls it is placing on Islam. The deferential parliament has obliged the president by rubber-stamping a "freedom of worship" law, which among other things makes it a crime to teach religion without official approval, bans unlicensed religious organisations and forbids religious dress in public.

(See entry for Taslima Nasrin, who is highly critical.)

ISLAMIC GAYS: See entry for Muslim Gays.

ISLAMIC IMPERIALISM

"The imperialism of Islam is indeed destructive," wrote Ian Buruma in London, who continued:

> [I]t deadens the human mind. But I'm not sure it is the worst we have seen. The cult of sacred places and native soil has been at the core of other forms of pseudoreligious political fundamentalism. State Shinto in pre-war Japan turned the entire nation into a sacred shrine. Nazism was built on worship of the German "race." The results were every bit as murderous and cruel as any Islamic revolution has been so far—indeed more so. The same is true of Communist imperialism, which is in some ways more comparable to Islamic fundamentalism."
>
> {Ian Buruma, "In the Empire of Islam," *The New York Review of Books*, 16 July 1998. Also see Ibn Warraq's *Why I Am Not A Muslim* [1995]}

ISLAMIC LAW

Bat Ye'or, in *The Decline of Eastern Christianity Under Islam: From Jihad to Dhimmitude, 7th to 20th Century* (1996), details how Muslims have been convinced of their own superiority over all non-Muslims and how this view is enshrined in law. Tariq Ismail, reviewing the book (*New Humanist*, December 1996), wrote: "In litigation between a Muslim and a dhimmi, the validity of the oath or testimony of the dhimmi was not recognised. Any fine imposed on a Muslim for a crime was automatically halved if the victim was a dhimmi. No Muslim could be executed for having committed any crime against a dhimmi. Accusations of blasphemy against dhimmis were quite frequent and the penalty was capital punishment. Since his testimony was not accepted in court, the dhimmi was forced to convert or die. The dhimmis had to wear distinctive clothing, was not permitted to build his house higher than that of a Muslim, forbidden to carry arms, and so on."

In the 19th and 20th centuries, Christians rebelled against the inferior position imposed upon them. Their struggle eventually led to the wars of national liberation for Greeks, Serbs, Bulgars, Rumanians, Armenians, and Zionists.

ISLAMIC PHILOSOPHY: See the *Encyclopedia of Philosophy*, Vol. 4. \

ISLAMIC SECULARIZATION

The International Society for Islamic Secularization (ISIS, PO Box 229, Buffalo, NY 14215) publishes *Separation of Mosque and State*. Its Executive Director is Ibn Warraq, its Chairperson is Marvin Zeyed, and its Vice-Chair is Taslima Nasrin. On the Web: <www.secularislam.org>.

Secular and religious rules can scarcely live side-by-side, the group holds, if the latter cannot allow compromise.

ISLAMIC WOMEN, RIGHTS OF

In 1997 a group of born Muslims, primarily from Iran and South Asia, signed "A Declaration of the Rights of Women in Islamic Societies. They declared the necessity "of publicly submitting an alternative to the mind-numbing religious certainties of Islamic fundamentalism, and the ineffectual vacillation and tinkering of Reformist Islam. The alternative is secularism: the secular voice is seldom if ever heard in debates on reforming Islamic society."

They formed the *Ar Razi Circle* to promote secularism in the Islamic world, saying oppression of women is a grave offense against all humanity; accused orthodox and fundamentalists religions of having devised claims of divine justification for the subordination of women to men; and named as goals such as the following:

- A woman should have freedom of action, should be able to travel alone, should be permitted to uncover her face, and should be allowed the same inheritance rights as a man.
- She should not be subject to gruesome ritual mutilations of her person.
- She should be free upon reaching the legal age to marry a man of her own choice without permission from a putative guardian or parent. She should be free to marry a non-Muslim. She should be free to divorce and be entitled to maintenance in the case of divorce.
- She should have equal access to education, equal opportunities for higher education, and be free to choose her subject of study.
- In Islamic societies, she should enjoy the same human rights as those guaranteed under International Human Rights legislation.

Signatories included the following:

Reza Afshari, *Iran, Political Scientist*
Sadik al Azm, Syria, Philosopher
Mahshid Amir-Shahy, Iran, Author, Social Critic, and Founder of the French Defense League for Rushdie
Masud Ansari, Iran, Physician, Author, United States
Bahram Azad, Iran, Scholar, Physician, United States
Parvin Darabi, Scholar, Homa Darabi Foundation, United States
Khalid Duran, Professor of Political Science, Editor and Founder of TransState Islam, Founder of the Ibn Khaldun Society, United States
Ranjana Hossain, Executive Director of the Assembly of Free Thinkers, Bangladesh
Mustafa Hussain, Sudan, Advisory Board, Ibn Khaldun Society, United States
Ramine Kamrane, Iran, Political Scientist, France
Ionna Kucaradi, Philosopher, Turkish Human Rights Commission and Secretary General, International Federation of Philosophical Societies, Turkey
Luma Musa, Palestine, Communications Researcher, United Kingdom
Taslima Nasrin, Bangladesh, Author, Physician, Social Critic
Hossainur Rahman, India, Social Historian, Columnist, Asiatic Society of Calcutta
Siddigur Rahman, Bangladesh, Former Research Fellow, Islamic Research Institute
Armen Saginian, Iran, Editor, Publisher, United States
Anwear Shaikh, Pakistan, Author, Social Critic, United Kingdom
Ibn Warraq, India, Author of *Why I am Not a Muslim*, United States

ISLAMISM: Islamism conveys the meaning of Islam as a political movement. Islamic fundamentalism does not.

Isnard, Felix (Born 1829)

Isnard was a French physician who wrote *Spiritualism and Materialism* (1879). {BDF}

Isnard, Maximin (1751—1830)

Isnard was a Girondin revolutionist who, upon becoming a member of the Assembly, declared, "The Law, behold my God. I know no other." He voted for the death of the King and was nominated president of the Convention. On the fall of the Girondins he made his escape, reappearing after Robespierre's fall. {BDF}

Isoard Delisle, Jean Baptiste Claude (1743—1816)

A French man of letters also called Delisle de Sales, Isoard left theology for literature. In 1769 he published the *Philosophy of Nature*, which in 1771 was discovered to be irreligious and he was condemned to perpetual banishment. While in prison he was visited by many philosophers. Voltaire gave five hundred francs for his benefit. Isoard went to the court of Frederick the Great and subsequently published many works of little importance. To the amusement of his friends, Isoard Delisle, a deist, jocularly wrote *A Memoir In Favor of God* (1802). {BDF; RAT}

Ison, Ralph E. (20th Century)

Ison is active in England with the Chiltern Humanists, and he was a director of the Rationalist Press Association until 1998. A biologist, he wrote "The Miraculous Birth of Jesus—A Biologist's View" (*The Freethinker*, December 1993), in which he questions how the Virgin Mary's eggs stimulated to divide and proceed to develop into a healthy male child. How, he asks, did a male set of chromosomes get inside Mary? And he questions God's omniscience in not setting Joseph's mind at rest by informing him *before* the event took place rather than after the deed had been committed. Joseph, according to *Matthew* I:19, presumably believed he was not the father of Jesus and also at first did not believe in miracles.

ISRAELI HUMANISTS

• The Israel Association for Secular Humanistic Judaism is at 14, Hatibonim Street, PO Box 4512, Jerusalem 92386.

• The Israel Secular Humanist Association (IHEU) is at POB 17141, Tel Aviv 61171, Israel.

• *Secular Humanistic Judaism,* 8 Itamar Ben Avi St., PO Box 4512, Jerusalem 91044

ITALIAN-AMERICAN FREETHINKERS: See *Freethought in the United States* by Gordon Stein.

ITALIAN FREETHINKERS: See entry for Beccaria. Also, see *Encyclopedia of Philosophy*, Vol. 4.

ITALIAN HUMANISTS AND FREETHINKERS

Italian freethought groups and publications include the following:

• *Ateo, Trimestrale di cultura laica* (The Atheist), an Italian quarterly published by the UAAR), is at C.P. 989, I-35100 Padover PD <uaarpd@tin.it>.

• *Centro Coscienza*, Corso di Porta Nuova, 16-20121, Milan

• *La Nuova Ragione*, Via dei Serpenti 35, 00184 Roma

• *Libero Pensiero*, 11 via Consolata, 10122 TO, Torino <roberto.laferla@agora.stm.it>.

• National Freethought Organization, 'Giordano Bruno,' 82, Via Teodosio, 20131 Milan <http://www.agora.stm.it/anlp/>

• Union of Italian Rationalists, Atheists, and Agnostics, c/o Lega Per l'Ambiente, Via Cornaro 1A, 35128 Padova. For information on the Webabout Unione degli Atei e degli Agnostici Razionalisti: <www.geocities.com/colosseum/8736/uaar.htm>

ITALIAN RENAISSANCE HUMANISTS: See entry for Cesare Beccaria.

ITHACA COLLEGE HUMANISTS

Humanists and freethinkers at Ithaca College, Ithaca, New York, can be found on the Web at:
<http://www.secularhumanism.org/cfa/orgs.html>.

Ito, Hirobumi (1841—1909)

Ito, a Japanese prime minister in the 1890s, declared, "I regard religion itself as quite unnecessary for a nation's life; science is far above superstition; and what is religion, Buddhism, or Christianity, but superstition, and therefore a possible source of weakness to a nation?" {TYD}

Ivers, Gregg (20th Century)

Ivers is author of *Lowering the Wall: Religion and the Supreme Court in the 1980s.* In 1992, he wrote *Redefining the First Freedom: The Supreme Court and the Consolidation of the State.*

Ives, Rosslyn (20th Century)

An Australian, Ives is President of the Humanist Society of Victoria. She spoke about "Putting the 'Who' Into Humanism: A Feminist Perspective" at the 1996 Humanist World Congress held in Mexico City. "An important feature of Humanism is the lack of dogma and an openness to change," she has written. "Thus Humanists never presume that an issue, such as gender, has been settled to everyone's satisfaction." Her e-mail:
<rosslyn@netspace.net.au>. {*Humanist in Canada*, Spring 1998}

Ivins, Molly (1944—)

Ivins, a Texas-born writer and columnist, has worked on *The Houston Chronicle*, the *Minneapolis Star Tribune*, *The Texas Observer*, and *The New York Times*. She wrote *Molly Ivins Can't Say That, Can She?* (1991) and *Nothin' But Good Times Ahead* (1993). Ivins has gone on record as being a non-theist. {E}

IXION

Ixion in Greek mythology was king of the Lapithes, the person who murdered his father-in-law in order to avoid paying a price for his bride. When no one on earth would purify him, Zeus took him to Olympus, where he was purified. However, there he tried to seduce Hera, resulting in Zeus's creating a phantom of her and by it Ixion became the father of the centaur monsters. Now, Zeus punished Ixion by having him chained eternally to a revolving, fiery wheel in Tartarus. (See entry for Tartarus.) {CE}

Izzi, John (20th Century)

Izzi, a freethinker, wrote *Fact is My Evidence* (1949). {GS}

Jabes, Jascha (20th Century)

Jabes, while a student at Queen's University in Ontario, Canada, was one of the founding members of Campus Freethought Alliance. {*International Humanist News*, December 1996}

Jack, Homer A. (1916—1993)

Jack, who founded the United Nations Non-Governmental Committee on Disarmament in the early 1970s and was its chairman until 1983, was a Unitarian minister. He founded the National Committee for a Sane Nuclear Policy (SANE), serving as executive director from 1960 to 1964. He was secretary general of the World Conference on Religion and Peace from 1970 to 1983. Further, he was a founder of the Congress on Racial Equality (CORE). Asked once why he had a doctorate in science but was involved in so many non-scientific ventures, Jack explained, "I became more interested in men than in mice."

A dynamic organizer, he assailed McCarthyism as well as Soviet totalitarianism and anti-Semitism. Dr. Jack supported China's entry to the United Nations. Among his books are *Wit and Wisdom of Gandhi* (1951), *The Gandhi Reader* (1955), and *Religion for Peace* (1973).

Jackanicz, Donald W. (20th Century)

Jackanicz was the long-time secretary of the Bertrand Russell Society. An archivist with the National Archives, Great Lakes Region, he has been editor of the *Russell Society News*. Jackanicz in addition to being a thoroughgoing administrator was supplier at Bertrand Russell Society meetings of Red Hackles, the hard-to-obtain Scottish whiskey favored by Sir Bertrand.

Jackson, Allan Cameron (1911—1990)

Jackson was an Australian atheist, rationalist, and philosopher. He studied in England at Cambridge, attending Wittgenstein's seminars, then taught at Melbourne University, finally moving in 1966 to a chair of philosophy at Monash University. Jackson played a significant role in the Australian philosophical community and was an active member of the Rationalist Society, becoming president and then a life member. His interest was in the intellectual questions raised by rationalism, not in converting people away from religion. Jackson favored an amalgamation or alliance of the various secular and humanist groups. {SWW}

Jackson, Arthur M. (20th Century)

When he signed Humanist Manifesto II, Jackson was the American Humanist Association treasurer. In San Jose, California, he currently heads "an empirical, predictive Science of Religion based on pure Humanism." Regretting that it is "of zero interest to the gatekeepers of current Humanist organizations, he deduces that this is "because they still believe that religion is about God and it is the enemy, not something to support." {HM2; HNS2; *Humanist in Canada*, Winter 1996-1997}

Jackson, Helen (Maria) Hunt (1830—1885)

Jackson, a writer of travel books, children's books, novels, and magazine articles, was a Unitarian and a transcendentalist. In her adult years, however, she had no church connection. Her *A Century of Dishonor* (1881) castigated the United States government for its treatment of the Indians, and her novel called *Ramona* (1884) merited much critical favor. *Mercy Philbrick's Choice* (1876) is said to be a fictional study of her friend, Emily Dickinson. Some of Jackson's earlier work was published under the pseudonyms of H. H. and Saxe Holm. {CE; U}

Jackson, John G. (1907—)

Jackson, an African American educator and historian, is an atheist. In his *Christianity Before Christ* (1938), he surveys historically the components of Christianity and shows that they existed before that religion was invented. Among the deities he cites are Adonis, Attis, Mithra, Prometheus, Krishna, and Buddha. *Ages of Gold and Silver* examines the origins of civilization, with his special emphasis on the long-ignored contributions of non-Caucasians.

Jackson has taught at the Black Studies Department of Rutgers University, at the University of New York, and at Northeastern Illinois University.

Jackson, Linda R. (20th Century)

When she signed Humanist Manifesto II, Jackson was a director of the American Humanist Association. {HM2}

Jacob, Alexandre Andre (1826—1878)

A French writer who used the pen name of Erdan, Jacob was the natural son of a distinguished prelate. After reading Proudhon, he refused to take holy orders. His *La France Mystique* (1855) was condemned for the skepticism that appears on every page. Sentenced to a year's imprisonment and a fine of three thousand francs, he took refuge in Italy, dying at Frascati, near Rome. {BDF}

Jacob, George (19th Century)

With Austin Holyoake, who also was anti-clerical, Jacob founded Holyoake & Co. in 1853.

Jacob, John (1812—1858)

Jacob served during the Indian Mutiny and became an English Brigadier-General in the Crimean War (1856). He wrote *Letters to a Lady on the Progress of Being in the Universe* (1855), a deistic work in which he dismisses Christian doctrines as nursery-tales. {RAT; RE}

Jacob, T. Evan (19th Century)

Jacob, a freethinker, is the author who wrote *Saladin the Little* (1887). {FUK; GS}

Jacobi, Friedrich Heinrich (1743—1819)

Jacobi became known in 1997 as the German philosopher who had a physical, homosexual relationship with Johann Wolfgang Goethe, or that was the revelation alleged in Karl Hugo Pruys's *The Caresses of the Tiger: An Erotic Goethe Biography*. Jacobi, a critic of Kant and Spinoza, held that reason is restricted to material subjects, that the ultimate reality is to be intuitively sensed. Employing "Humean skepticism," he defended the need for a "leap of faith," a concept denied by Hegel and Schelling. Jacobi's views influenced German Romanticism. {CE}

Jacobi, S. G. (20th Century)

Jacobi was a scientific humanist who warned that, although something was needed to replace orthodox religion, scientific humanism must be particularly cautious not to become "scientific inhumanism." {*Literary Guide*, April 1958}

Jacobs, Arthur David (1922—1996)

Jacobs, a musicologist, became an Honorary Associate of the Rationalist Press Association in 1995. He founded and edited the *British Music Yearbook* (1971—1979), wrote *Penguin Dictionary of Musical Performers* (1990), and contributed to the *New Grove*

Dictionary of Opera (1992). He wrote a biography in 1994 of Henry J. Wood, the maker of the Promenade Concerts in England.

Jacobs, Steven (20th Century)
A former president of the American Ethical Union, Jacobs signed Humanist Manifesto II. He is author of *The Hebrew Heritage of Black Africa* (1971). {HM2}

Jacobsen, Jens Peter (1847—1885)
Jacobsen, a Danish novelist and botanist, was instrumental in spreading Darwinian views in Scandinavia. He translated *The Origin of Species* and *The Descent of Man*. Among his novels were *Fru Marie Grubbe*, scenes from the 17th century, and *Niels Lyhne*, which includes his philosophy of atheism. {BDF; RAT}

Jacobsen, William (20th Century)
Jacobsen is executive director of the Humanist Community (AHA). (See entry for California Atheists, Humanists.) {FD}

Jacobson, Augustus (19th Century)
Jacobson was the American author of *Why I Do Not Believe* (1881) and *The Bible Inquirer*. {BDF}

Jacobson, Jens Peter (1847—1885)
A Danish poet and novelist, Jacobsen was a non-theist. (See entry for Scandinavian Unbelievers.)

Jacoby, Leopold (19th Century)
Jacoby was the German author of *The Idea of Development* (1874—1876). {BDF}

Jacolliot, Louis (1837?—1890)
Jacolliot was a French orientalist and a judge at Pondichery. He first aroused attention by his *The Bible in India* (1870), later writing *The Religious Legislators, Moses, Manu, and Muhammad* (1870) and *The Natural and Social History of Humanity* (1884). {BDF; RAT}

Jaffe, Eli (20th Century)
Jaffe is author of *Oklahoma Odyssey: A Memoir* (1993), which relates his youthful adventures working in community organizing during the depths of the depression. He is a Unitarian.

Jaffree, Ishmael (20th Century)
Jaffree is an African American attorney and church-state litigant before the U.S. Supreme Court. In "The Quest for Humanist Values" in *Free Inquiry* (Spring, 1990), he describes a 1982 complaint he filed to keep prayer and other religious activities out of the public schools of Mobile, Alabama. "As a lawyer and an agnostic who strongly believes in the separation of church and state," he wrote, "I was seeking to maintain the integrity of the Constitution and to keep public officials from making decisions about my children's spiritual upbringing." But what he thought was a simple enough request resulted in a 1983 U.S. District Court ruling against him, and the case set off a national controversy about the nature of secular humanism and the separation of church and state. Fellow blacks, he found, were hostile that he was not being a "good Christian." He was threatened, slandered, vilified by mail and phone, and his children were ostracized. But when the Supreme Court ruled in his favor, the negative criticism subsided. Still, he writes, "We African Americans are among the most repressed people, and religion helps us to cope with the everyday struggles of living. . . . I wish that people would be more open to the scientific method of inquiry and not so given to mysticism." Jaffree is an Advisory Board Member of African Americans for Humanism. {AAH}

Jahagirdar, R. A. [Justice] (20th Century)
Justice Jahagirdar from India addressed the Tenth International Humanist and Ethical Union (IHEU) World Congress held in Buffalo (1988). He is editor of *The Radical Humanist*, the journal formerly founded by M. N. Roy and called *Independent India*. The publication is devoted to scientific and rational thinking and to the promotion of a humanist view of life and social order. It is at Sassoon Building (1st Floor), Mahatma Gandhi Road near Kalaghoda, Fort, Mumbai 400 001.

JAHVE: See entry for God.

JAINISM
Jainism appeared in India about the same time as Buddhism, the sixth century B.C.E., and sprang from the same root: the atheistic Sankhya philosophy. At the time, there was a revolt against the religion of Brahma, whose priests had developed their speculations into so abstract a mass of verbiage that the warriors and others broke away, and Jainism became a popular alternative. Neither Jainism nor Buddhism was meant to become religions, but both did. Their atheistic monastic communities were founded seven or eight centuries before Christianity inspired such, and, editorializes McCabe, "in their longer history they never knew anything like the corruption of the monks and nuns of Europe." (See entry for Mahavira. For an estimate of the number of Jains worldwide, see the entry for Hell.) {RE}

James I: See entry for King James Bible.

James, Bob (20th Century)
James is on the board of directors of the Bertrand Russell Society and was one of its founding members.

James, Henry: See entry for William James.

James, Leslie (20th Century)
A retired barrister and former Chief Police Officer, James has written in *New Humanist* that "if the Church equates righteousness with uncomplaining acceptance of one's lot in a highly competitive society, it will make scant impression on the underprivileged criminal." Disagreeing with Harvard's John Rawls that the good things of life should be distributed on the hypothetical social contract accepted by all humanity sitting together in embryo in ignorance of their eventual genetic and environmental fortune, James responds, "Regrettably, such a solution to our criminological problem must remain a philosophical fantasy." In *The Freethinker* (June 1995), James wrote, "We are creatures of chance. Whether we were born in the First World or the Third, in England or in famine-torn Sudan, in a prosperous suburb or in a poverty-stricken inner-city, whether we were born male or female, white or black, strong or weak, clever or dull, mentally stable or unstable, and what environmental events befell us in our lives, all these circumstances are determined by chance, beyond our control." Such an attitude must have a profound effect upon our attitude to crime and punishment, James says as a retired barrister. "Dangerous criminals must be restrained and confined; sentences must be both deterrent and reformative, and sometimes compensatory; and the deterrent element may need to be manifestly disagreeable to deter the rest of us. But punishment for punishment's sake, for revenge or retribution, must be abandoned."

James, Marquis (1891—1955)
James wrote of Sam Houston's freethinking tendencies in *The Raven: A Biography of Sam Houston* (1929). {*Freethought History #15*, 1995}

James, Victor Montgomery Keeling (1897—1984)
James, after serving in the Royal Air Force during World War II, went to Melbourne, Australia, in 1947 to be co-minister with William Bottomley of the Unitarian Church. It was a time when secularism was convincing many Unitarians to move away from any theistic belief in the divinity of Jesus, leading to groups within Unitarianism who termed themselves Christian Humanists, religious rationalists, or even hymn-singing atheists. James served for twenty-two years, during which period his sermons became more rationalist and the hymns more secular. In 1961, he and W. Glanville Cook initiated a joint meeting of Unitarians and rationalists to create the Humanist Society of Victoria. James remained in the Unitarian ministry until his retirement in 1969. {SWW}

James, William (1842—1910)

"Religion is a monumental chapter in the history of human egotism," James once wrote. However, at a later time he did develop a form of personal religion and was sympathetic to mysticism and spiritualism.

William and Henry James were the sons of Henry James Sr., described by his biographer Alfred Habegger as a one-legged man who "reeked of turpentine, burned flesh, blood, pus, rot, agony, guilt, and endless waiting, and its fluids soaked so deeply into the folds of the boy's [Henry Jr.'s] mind that he was permanently altered." From time to time, a physician would cut bits of flesh away with a small, sharp knife, later finding it necessary to saw the leg off above the knee. But the stump did not heal, and yet another piece of the leg had to be sawed off, higher up. Henry Sr. had five children by three wives, and he lived a life of doom, guilt, and repentance, having been brought up in northern Ireland by his Presbyterian family. He turned to drink (then was able to stop), then turned to religion (from which he could not stop), enrolling in 1835 in the Princeton Theological Seminary. At this point he spoke out against Catholics and Spiritualists, believing that it is faith, not good works, which is the only hope of salvation. He then joined an obscure congregation inspired by the Scotsman Robert Sandeman, one that held the all clericalism and all ritual are corrupt, all doctrines superfluous, all men are depraved. In 1840, however, Henry Sr. married a woman whose small "Primitive Christian" community congregated in New York City's Canal Street. In time, he met Emerson and became interested in Swedenborg. It was Swedenborg who told him that God is not a cruel Calvinist father who sacrificed his son, that sin is not deep inside, and that sin is the result of spirits, a fact he knew because he had "talked" to the spirits. Meanwhile, Henry Sr. was an opponent of women's suffrage and held that woman is "inferior in passion, inferior in intellect, and inferior in physical strength." Her very inferiority, in fact, was what made her so appealing to man. It was from such a family that William and Henry James came. William he treated as a chosen one. Henry Jr. he considered sweet, not very bright, and his mother's favorite. The three younger children he considered as "extras."

Called an inspiration for many of the pragmatists who refined his philosophic outlooks, William James was a "radical empiricist." He greatly influenced John Dewey's instrumentalism, and he rejected transcendental principles, holding that the truth of a proposition is judged by its practical outcome. James joined the Harvard faculty in 1872 as a lecturer on anatomy and physiology and in 1880 he taught in the department of psychology and philosophy. His philosophy had three aspects—voluntarism, pragmatism, and radical empiricism. That which is true is "only the expedient in our way of thinking." He believed that ideas do not reproduce objects but prepare for, or lead the way to, them. An idea's function is to indicate "what conceivable effects of a practical kind the object may involve—what sensations we are to expect from it and what reactions we must prepare." This theory of knowledge he called pragmatism, a term already used by Charles S. Peirce. It rejects all transcendent principles and finds experience organized by means of "conjunctive relations" that are as much a matter of direct experience as things themselves. His philosophical writings include *The Will to Believe* (1897), *The Varieties of Religious Experience* (1902), *Pragmatism* (1907), and *Essays in Radical Empiricism* (1912). One of his students at Radcliffe College who was influenced by his views on pragmatism was Gertrude Stein, who at the time was greatly interested in psychology. At Harvard, one of his students was George Santayana, who later became a colleague.

When elected to the American Academy of Arts and Letters, James created a flurry by objecting to "the notion of an organization for the mere purpose of distinguishing certain individuals (with their own connivance) and enabling them to say to the world at large 'we are in and you are out.' . . . On the whole it seems to me that for a philosopher with my pretensions to austerity and righteousness, the only consistent course is to give up this particular vanity. . . . And I am more encouraged to this course by the fact that my younger and shallower and vainer brother is already in the Academy." Leon Edel commented that the two brothers could not "live under the same roof . . . and occupy seats side by side." At any rate, William quit the Institute, and Henry remained in the Academy.

Such a statement led wags to gossip about his brother Henry's (1843—1916) homoerotic stories and about their sister Alice's being, according to A. L. Rowse, "a Lesbian of a pronounced type." Henry also is alleged by Kaplan to have had homoerotic feelings toward William. Sibling rivalry was an easy case study for the eminent psychologist, whose youthful heterosexuality, according to biographer Fred Kaplan, included writing erotic poems of "phallic desires" penned to Alice. Lyndall Gordon, in *A Private Life of Henry James* (1999), wrote that Henry "never thought of himself as deviant, for the simple reason that the Edwardians drew a sharper line between sexual activity and tender friendship. Gordon suggests that the two women who inspired Henry the most—neither in a seriously sexual way—were Minny Temple (the prototype for Daisy Miller, Isabel Archer, and Milly Theale) and Constance Fenimore Woolson (the prototype for Maria Gostrey in *The Ambassadors* and for several character in his short stories).

Meanwhile, in *Cock and Bull* (1992), Will Self fictionally, although not necessarily historically, castigates Henry, saying he had "only half a cock. Not a lot of people know that. The poor man lost it chasing after a fire engine, trying to help out as an amateur fire fighter in his native Boston. He tripped and fell beneath the horses' hooves, only to emerge white and half unmanned. They carried him home to his exceptional family on a board. His brother William looked at poor Henry. He focused on the bloody patch that coated Henry's breeches, and challenged God, whomsoever he might be, to make his brother whole again. He was praying for all of us you see, he knew his brother. He knew that all we could look forward to was a series of thick, turgid novels; penis substitutes. Since poor Henters couldn't fuck anybody else, he resolved to fuck us all up with his serpentine sentences . . . uncoiling inside our minds like ever-lengthening weenies." In short, the Jameses had and continue to have their strong critics.

A postscript of *The Varieties of Religious Experience* and the last chapter of *Pragmatism* spell out James's religious views. These include a "piecemeal supernaturalism" that could be interpreted as a vague or "enlarged and tolerant naturalism," states William James Earle in the *Encyclopedia of Philosophy*, Vol. 4.

Under certain specified conditions, James wrote in his 1897 article, "The Will to Believe," we have a right to let our passional nature decide which of two alternative hypotheses to adopt. As summarized by the University of Edinburgh's T. L. S. Sprigge, "These are that the matter cannot be settled on intellectual grounds, and that the choice between them is *living* (we find each credible), *forced* (we must act in the light of one or the other), and *momentous* (really important). Examples are the choice between theism and atheism or free will and determinism."

R. W. B. Lewis, in *The Jameses: A Family Narrative* (1991) supports other academics' suspicions that James's "problems" included a belief that a link occurs between introspection and masturbation and between masturbation and insanity. The possibility that James was a compulsive masturbator is discussed but is generally denied.

McCabe found James's attitude to religion "peculiar" because he did not believe in a Supreme Being but was inclined to believe in a number of super-human beings. . . and said that therefore he was rather a polytheist than a theist. He also noted that the father had been a Swedenborgian minister, that Henry remained throughout life somewhat mystic though quite outside Christianity. Henry rejected the Swedenborgian and every other creed and had no sympathy with spiritualism. . . . In *A Pluralistic Universe* William James speaks very disdainfully about the God of the churches. In spite of his 'will to believe' and against the false claim of Spiritualists he never attained a belief in personal immortality, as he admits in his Ingersoll Lecture two years before he died. His brother Henry he found "had much the same position except that he (as he said) 'liked to think' that there was some ground (not Spiritualism) for believing in a future life."

Science writer and skeptic Martin Gardner points out that James was a theist who believed in an afterlife, which he defended with a clever model of the brain in his little book, *Human Immortality*. Gardner also argues that James was "too gullible and too ignorant of methods of deception to appreciate the ease with which intelligent persons can be deceived by crafty charlatans," and specifically he relates how James was conned by Mrs. Leonora Piper in an article, "Communicating With the Dead: William James and Mrs. Piper" (*Free Inquiry*, Spring 1992). (See entry for Eve Sedgwick.) {CE; CL; ER; GL; OCP; RE; TRI; TSV; TYD}

Jameson, Leander Storr [Sir] (1853—1917)

A physician and statesman, Jameson as a friend of Cecil Rhodes is remembered for his invasion of the Transvaal with six hundred men in 1895. But, notes McCabe, Dr. Jameson actually was a man of fine and serious character, one who was gravely deceived by South African friends. Jameson, although an agnostic, became Premier of Cape Colony. "With his natural fine character and his clear practical reasoning," wrote his biographer G. Seymour Fort, "he early divorced himself from any theological or metaphysical leanings." {JM; RAT; RE; TRI}

Jamieson, W. F. (Born 1837)

The Canadian-born Jamieson moved to Michigan after having been raised a Christian. In Michigan he had a famous debate with Moses Hull, then the renowned champion of Adventism, which resulted in Hull's conversion to Spiritualism. Jamieson held many debates with the clergy, and he wrote a pamphlet, "The Clergy, A Source of Danger to the American Republic." With Jacob Ditzler, he wrote *The Jamieson-Ditzler Debate* (c. 1878). {GS; PUT}

Jamison, A(lbert) Leland (1911—)

Jamison was co-editor with James Ward Smith of *Religious Perspectives in American Culture* (1961). {FUS}

Jammal, George (20th Century)

Jammal convinced producers of "The Amazing Discovery of Noah's Ark" that he had discovered part of the actual Biblical ark, which Sun International Inc. then televised to a national audience in 1993. Later, he confessed that it had all been a hoax, to the embarrassment of television executives. What he had done was to "cook" some California pine, then claim he had found it on Mt. Ararat. Some supernaturalists, who are unaware of Jammal's trickery, continue to cite the program as proof of the Ark's existence and the Bible's truth. Dr. Gerald Larue was in on the hoax, which illustrated how easily gullible people can be fooled. Jammal has since explained to agnostics and atheists that he believes television producers will be more wary in the future when they try to appeal to supernaturalists who want to believe such stories. Meanwhile, *Skeptical Inquirer*, *Free Inquiry*, and other journals have covered the story to the amusement of freethinkers in many countries.

Janes, Lewis (1844—1901)

Janes, who carried on a correspondence with Herbert Spencer, was active in the Brooklyn Ethical Association. (TRI)

Janne, Henri (20th Century)

A Belgian, Janne addressed the International Humanist and Ethical Union's (IHEU's) Second Moral Education Conference held in Brussels (1985). He is author of *Education and Youth Employment in Belgium* (1979).

Jannotta, Frank Skiff (20th Century)

Jannotta, with M. M. Mangasarian, wrote *Morality Without God* (1958). {GS}

Jannotta, Stella S. (20th Century)

Jannotta once was a director of the American Humanist Association.

Janowitz, Morris (20th Century)

A propaganda analyst for the Department of Justice during World War II, Janowitz was a professor of sociology at the University of Michigan. He is author of *Black Sociologists* (1974) and *Military Conflict* (1975).

Jansen, Cornelius (Cornelius Jansenius) (1585—1638)

During the French Revolution, Maréchal cited Jansenius as being the opposite of an atheist. The Dutch Roman Catholic theologian believed people should return to a greater personal holiness, and Jansenism was so controversial that the Vatican listed his works on their index of prohibited readings in 1641, 1642, and 1654. This was because Pope Innocent X objected to the extreme Augustinian positions on predestination and grace which Jansen, the Bishop of Ypres (1636—1638), was preaching. Edward Roach Hardy, in *The Encyclopedia of Religion*, declares that "in theology Jansenism led the Roman Catholic Church to reaffirm the Tridentine position on grace and free will; but its rigorism, though rejected as such, influenced the general development of moral theology." The Tridentine Profession of Faith, which was prescribed by Pius IV in 1564 to meet the requirements of the Council of Trent, spelled out what Catholic theology believed, particularly detailing information about points which were being assailed in the 16th century. {CE; ER; EU, Aram Vartanian}

Jantet, Charles (Born 1826) **and Jantet, Henry** (Born 1828)

Charles and Hector Jantet were two physicians, both freethinkers, from Lyons. They published *Aperçus Philosophiques on Rènan's Life of Jesus* (1864) and *Doctrine Medicale Matérialiste* (1866). {BDF}

Jantz, Wolfgang (20th Century)

Jantz, of Germany, is a Member At Large of the Executive Committee of the International Council of Unitarians and Universalists. (See entry for German Unitarians.)

JAPANESE AGNOSTICISM

> • Since most Japanese live as agnostics but choose to die as Buddhists, the [Japanese] funeral home will also take care of the complex religious rituals.
>
> —*The Economist*, 15 March 1997

JAPANESE PHILOSOPHY: See the *Encyclopedia of Philosophy*, Vol. 4. (Also, see entry for Yukio Mishima, a theist.)

JAPANESE UNITARIAN-UNIVERSALISTS

Shigetaro Akashi founded the Universalist Church in Nagoya in 1893. Akashi also founded the presently named Free Christian Church in 1953. One congregation meets in Tokyo. Contact: Shigeo Akashi, 5-14-10 Kitazawa, Setagaya-ku, Tokyo 155, Japan.

JAR-SUB

Jar-Sub, in an early Turkish religion, was God of the Universe. {LEE}

Jaroff, Leon (Morton) (1927—)

Jaroff, the founder as well as the managing editor of *Discover* (1980—1984), has written over twenty-nine cover stories for *Time*, of which he has been sciences editor. He wrote *The New Genetics* (1991). Jaroff is a Fellow of the Committee for the Scientific Investigation of Claims of the Paranormal (PSICOP), which publishes *Skeptical Inquirer*, and is an honorary member of the Secular Humanist Society of New York. In *Who's Who in the World*, he lists himself as being Jewish.

Jarrett, Claudia Jewett (20th Century)

A Unitarian, Jarrett wrote *Helping Children Cope with Separation and Loss* (1994), in which as a family therapist she discusses how children respond to unhappiness and what parents and others can do to help them.

Jarrett, James L(ouis) Jr. (1917—)

A member of the philosophy department at Columbia University in New York City, Jarrett was an associate editor of *The Humanist* in the 1950s. He is author of *Nietzsche's Zarathustra* (1988). He also wrote *The Teaching of Values* (1991). {HNS}

Jarry, Alfred (1873—1907)

A French playwright, founder of "pataphysics," a French absurdist concept of philosophy that included the science of laws governing exceptions, Jarry wrote: "If souls are independent, man is God." An illogician, he had a fictional character state, "God—or myself—created all possible worlds, they coexist, but men can hardly glimpse even one." {PA}

Jarvis, William (20th Century)

Chairman of the Department of Public Health Science at Loma Linda University in California, Jarvis is on the Council for Secular Humanism's Faith-Healing Investigation Project.

Jaspers, Karl (1883—1969)

Jaspers, a German philosopher generally placed within the orbit of existentialism, wrote *Man in the Modern Age* (1931) and *Philosophy* (1932). One's outlook, he held, should spring from the study of his individual existence, which he viewed as enclosed by an all-embracing, transcendental reality he called "the encompassing." In *Existentialism and Humanism* (1952), he included his pertinent views concerning both isms. {CE}

Jastrow, Joseph (1863—1944)

Jastrow and his brother, Morris, were sons of Marcus Jastrow, a Polish rabbi and editor of the Talmud material in *The Jewish Encyclopedia*. Joseph Jastrow became a psychologist, the President in 1900 of the American Psychological Association. For some years he was associate editor of the *Psychological Review*. In his *Psychology of Conviction* (1918), Jastrow expressed his rationalism and resented "the mist with which dogma has enveloped the atmosphere." {RAT; RE}

Jastrow, Morris (1861—1921)

Jastrow, an American Orientalist and brother of Joseph Jastrow, wrote *Study of Religion* (1901), a work which showed his independence of the creeds, Jewish or Christian. He scouts the idea that one religion is superior to another or that any is more than a purely natural development. {RAT}

Jastrow, Robert (1925—)

Jastrow is a physicist associated with the Mt. Wilson Observatory Hale Solar Lab in Pasadena, California. He wrote *The Evolution of Stars, Planets, and Life* (1967), *How to Make Nuclear Weapons Obsolete* (1985), and *God and the Astronomers* (1992). Jastrow, in an installment of Ben Wattenberg's "Think Tank," said,

> I'm a committed reductionist. I think that the whole is equal to the sum of the parts. But I also know that there is no way within my scientific discipline of finding out whether there is a larger purpose or design in the universe. So I remain an agnostic, and not an atheist. To profess a disbelief in the existence of design or of the deity is essentially, in itself, a theological statement which a scientist cannot make on the structure or on the strength of his own discipline. He can only make it as a personal belief.
>
> {CA; E}

Jaucourt, Louis de (1704—1779)

Jaucourt was a chevalier, French scholar, and member of the Royal Society of London and of the academies of Berlin and Stockholm. He furnished the *Encyclopédie* with many articles and conducted the *Bibliothèque Raisonnée*. {BDF}

Jaurès, Jean Leon (1859—1914)

A French Socialist leader, Jaurès was a cultivated man of a middle-class family who became a professor of philosophy, then took up politics. At one time he was Vice-President of the Chamber. An agnostic, Jaurès cordially supported all the legislation against the Church. In 1914, he was murdered by a fanatical Catholic. {JM}

Javeau, Claude (20th Century)

A Belgian, Javeau addressed the International Humanist and Ethical Union's (IHEU's) Second Moral Education Conference held in Brussels (1985). He writes on the subject of time management surveys.

Jaxon, J. L. (20th Century)

Jaxon is the publisher of *Atheist Nation* (PO Box 3217, Chicago, Illinois 60654).

Jayagopal (20th Century)

For the Atheist Society of India, Jayagopal edited *Age of Atheism* (1974—1979) and in Telugu *Nasthika Yugam* (1972—1979).

Jayawardena, Ben (20th Century)

A Sri Lankan freethinker, Jayawardena wrote *Book of Gems for Truth Seekers* (1953). {FUK; GS}

Jayewardene, Walter (20th Century)

Jayewardene heads the Unitarian Universalist Association of Sri Lanka (61/3 Old Road, Nawala, Rajagiriya, Sri Lanka). A social activist, he is General Secretary of the Green Earth Foundation; Chairman of the Sri Lanka Gem Miners Association; Vice President of the Sri Lanka Vegetable Farmers Movement; and President of the Sri Lanka-American Solidarity Foundation.

His wife, **Chandranie Wijetunga**, is Assistant Director of the Ministry of Finance.

JAZZ

Asked by a fan to define jazz, Louis Armstrong responded, "Man, if you gotta ask you'll never know."

Similarly, defining "humanism" or "democracy" or "love" is felt by many to be of limited value. (For a list of freethinking sentiments in popular music, see the entry for Andrew Charles.)

Jeans, James Hopwood [Sir] (1887—1946)

An English mathematician, physicist, and astronomer, Jeans in his *The Stars In Their Courses* (1931) wrote that there was a time when all planets of the solar system were part of the sun. This planetismal theory, taught by most astronomers of his day, held that nothing in the solar system can be called design and order. All came from unplanned catastrophes. "For the most part," Jeans wrote, "each [planetary] voyage is in splendid isolation, like a ship on the ocean. In a scale model on which the stars are ships, the average ship will be well over a million miles from its neighbor." A popularizer of science and the philosophy of science, Jeans was not a believer in the God of the theologians. The theologians, however, boasted how Jeans had demolished materialism. What they overlooked was that his theory equally demolished the Incarnation and most Christian doctrines. {CE; HNS2; RE}

Jefferies, Richard (1848—1887)

The Story of My Heart (1883) by Jefferies, the nature-lover, told how "In the march of time there fell away from my mind, as the leaves from the trees in autumn, the last traces and relics of superstitions acquired compulsorily in childhood. Always feebly adhering, they finally disappeared." This left him a Naturalist in every sense of the word.

Dying young after several years of suffering, he was said to have had a deathbed conversion. In a eulogy, Sir Walter Besant made it appear that Jefferies, at the end, returned to the Christian faith. A few years later, however, Sir Walter wrote to Mr. H. S. Salt: "I stated in my Eulogy that he died a Christian. This was true in the sense of outward conformity. His wife read to him the *Gospel of St. Luke*, and he acquiesced. But, I have since been informed, he was weak, too weak not to acquiesce, and his views never changed from the time that he wrote *The Story of My Heart*. You are, I am convinced, quite right. When a man gets as far as Jefferies did—when he has shed and scattered to the winds all sacerdotalism and authority—he does not go back. {BDF; FO; JM; JMR; RAT; RE; (H.S. Salt, *Company I Have Kept* (1930); TRI}

Jeffers, Robinson (1887—1962)

Jeffers, the famed poet and author of *Medea* (1946) wrote the present author about humanism:

> The word Humanism refers primarily to the Renaissance interest in art and literature rather than in theological doctrine; and personally I am content to leave it there. "Naturalistic Humanism"—in the modern sense—is no doubt a better philosophical attitude than many others; but the emphasis seems wrong; "human naturalism" would seem to me more satisfactory, with but little accent on the 'human.' Man is a part of nature, but a nearly infinitesimal part; the human race will cease after a while and leave no trace, but the great splendors of nature will go on.
>
> Meanwhile, most of our time and energy are necessarily spent on human affairs; that can't be prevented, though I think it should be minimized; but for philosophy, which is an endless research of truth, and for contemplation, which can be a sort of worship, I would suggest that the immense beauty of the earth and the outer universe, the divine "nature of things," is a more rewarding object. Certainly it is more pleasant to think of than the hopes and horrors of humanity, and more ennobling. It is a source of strength; the other of distraction.
>
> But I have said all these things more fully in my poems, and perhaps more clearly.

Jeffers attempted to include philosophic and scientific ideas in his work, with man being of trivial importance to the universe, which would be better off if man were driven out and the grass and the cliff would "enjoy wonderful vengeance and suck / The arteries and walk in triumph on the faces." Man, "the animals Christ was rumored to have died for," might well be cleansed through "kind" wars in order that nature can return to "the primal and the latter silences." An individual who found nature's stern beauty consoling, Jeffers considered nature of prime importance and man more a doomed and inverted animal within that pantheistic ideal. His adaptations of Greek tragedy brought him wide recognition, as did such works as *The Woman At Point Sur* (1927) and *Dear Judas* (1929). {CE; EU, William F. Ryan; WAS, 25 March 1951}

JEFFERSON BIBLE

The *Jefferson Bible* is on the Web: <angelfire.com/co/JeffersonBible/>. It is of particular interest inasmuch as Thomas Jefferson omits the tale about the supernatural birth of Jesus.

Jefferson, Thomas [President] (1743—1826)

The third U.S. President was the nation's most intellectual and philosophic chief of state. Jefferson established as well as designed the buildings of the University of Virginia. He believed in the trinity . . . but his was Francis Bacon, Isaac Newton, and John Locke. Jefferson's was the god of nature, not that of revelation or theology. The Declaration of Independence, except for minor alterations by John Adams, Benjamin Franklin, and others made on the floor of Congress, was his work. It took until 1786 for his bill establishing religious freedom in Virginia to pass, and it was grounded in the belief that man's opinions cannot be coerced—had it not been for his efforts, others might have established a United Protestant Church of America with who-knows-who as its "pope."

Of particular interest to humanists is *The Jefferson Bible*, in which Jefferson textually extracted the life and morals of Jesus of Nazareth from the Gospels in Greek, Latin, and French. Some religionists were alarmed that Jefferson had excised references to the supernatural. As a result and for protection, many buried their Holy Bibles in the ground, fearing the Jefferson text would be designated the only one allowed. In 1800, the *New England Palladium* wrote, "Should the infidel Jefferson be elected to the Presidency, the seal of death is that moment set on our holy religion, our churches will be prostrated, and some devoted to the worship of the most High." Such a viewpoint was known to Jefferson, who expressed in allusions to Connecticut, for example, that the New England clergy represented

> . . . the last retreat of monkish darkness, bigotry, and abhorrence of those advances of the mind which had carried the other States a century ahead of them.

To John Adams, Jefferson wrote that he longed for the time when "this den of the priesthood is at last broken up." To the Baptists in Danbury, Connecticut, in 1802, Jefferson wrote,

> I contemplate with sovereign reverence that act of the whole American People which declared that their legislators should make no law respecting an establishment of religion or prohibit the free exercise thereof, thus building a wall of separation between church and state.

In 1998 James H. Hutson, chief of the Library of Congress's manuscript division and a Presbyterian, questioned Jefferson's meaning, saying it "was never conceived by Jefferson to be a statement of fundamental principles; it was meant to be a political manifesto, nothing more." Conservative religionists claimed this was proof that Jefferson's "wall of separation between Church and State" metaphor should never have been interpreted as an overarching principle. Disagreeing, Barry Lynn, executive director of Americans United for Separation of Church and State, countered that Hutson's view was "merely one opinion" that most scholars do not hold.

The 6' 2 1/2" tall statesman, whose pet mockingbird pecked its food from its master's own lips, invented a revolving chair, a pedometer, a revolving music stand, a letter-copying press, and a hemp machine. Unlike Franklin, who wore plain clothes, Jefferson dressed like a dandy and was often seen wearing striped linen, a powdered wig, and a large topaz ring. Visitors to his home at Monticello see his skill as an architect. The "dumb waiters," according to Susan R. Stein's *The Worlds of Thomas Jefferson at Monticello* (1993), were private service trays that also were a fad in Paris, built to insure that servants could not overhear conversations. At a time when Paris was experiencing a revolution, Jefferson went on a buying spree, sending eighty-six large crates of goods back for his public and private use—these included seven busts by Houdon, forty-eight formal chairs, damask hangings, four full-length mirrors in gilt frames, and 120 porcelain plates. The Sèvres table sculptures had been made for Louis XVI (and it is not clear how Jefferson managed to obtain them). The Monticello home's entrance featured what he called "my Indian hall" and contained painted buffalo robes, moccasins, a head dress, and specimens such as mastodon bones, mounted moose, and elk antlers from the Lewis and Clark and other expeditions. One of the few items left, after his death and when his daughter had to sell everything in order to pay off his huge debts, was the famous clock in the entrance hall— it was not removable.

The best way to categorize such a complex thinker, remarked Eugene R. Sheridan, is to quote his letter to the Rev. Ezra Styles Ely (25 June 1819): "I am of a sect by myself, as far as I know." Jefferson also wrote to Benjamin Rush, "I am a Christian, in the only sense he [Jesus] wished any one to be; sincerely attached to his doctrines, in preference to all others; ascribing to himself every human excellence; and believing he never claimed any other." To Benjamin Waterhouse in 1811 he referred to the Revelation of St. John as "the ravings of a maniac," adding,

> The Christian priesthood, finding the doctrines of Christ levelled to every understanding and too plain to need explanation, saw, in the mysticisms of Plato, Materials with which they might build up an artificial system which might, from its indistinctness, admit everlasting controversy, give employment for their order, and introduce it to profit, power, and preeminence. The doctrines which flowed from the lips of Jesus himself are within the comprehension of a child; but thousands of volumes have not yet explained the Platonisms engrafted on them: and for this obvious reason that nonsense can never be explained.

In 1822, in another letter to Waterhouse, Jefferson wrote, ". . . that there is one only God, and he all perfect" (26 June 1822).

To John Adams, he wrote, "I have read his [Priestley's] *Corruptions of Christianity*, and *Early Opinions of Jesus*, over and over again; and I rest on them . . . as the basis of my own faith" (22 August 1813). In another letter to Adams (11 April 1823), Jefferson wrote, "And the day will come, when the mystical generation of Jesus, by the Supreme Being as His Father, in the womb of a virgin, will be classed with the fable of the generation of Minerva, in the brain of Jupiter."

Dr. J. Thomas in his *Dictionary of Biography* says that Jefferson "in religion is denominated a freethinker." He spoke in old age of "the hocus-pocus phantom of God, which like another Cerberus had one body and three heads." Religious liberals often quote his sentence, "The care of every man's soul belongs to himself. No man has the power to let another prescribe his faith." As a summary, and sounding like the deist of his time, he wrote of his hope that ". . . there is not a young man now living in the U.S. who will not die a Unitarian." Publicly, however, he remained a member of the Church of England, was a friend of the local priest, supported the priest's church, but made himself unavailable to become a godparent because of his not being a trinitarian. Jaroslav Pelikan, President of the American Academy of Arts and Sciences, has termed Jefferson a "rationalist Anglican." Robert S. Alley, professor of humanities emeritus at the University of Richmond, however, holds (*Free Inquiry*, Fall 1998) that "Any perusal of the Jefferson writings will establish that the Sage of Monticello was a Deist."

To the minister of the First Parish Church (Unitarian) in Portland, Maine, Jefferson once requested the services of a Unitarian minister for himself and for a small group of friends. The reply was that there was no one available to be sent so far away, to which a disappointed Jefferson is said to have remarked that he would have "to be a Unitarian by myself."

Meanwhile, Jefferson also wrote

> I am an Epicurean. I consider the genuine (not imputed) doctrines of Epicurus as containing everything rational in moral philosophy which Greek and Roman leave to us.

In 1815 when he listed his Albemarle County property for tax purposes, he included all the pictures, mirrors, chairs, and small items, but the list began with the big items:

> 5640. acres of land . . .
> 90. slaves of or about the age of 12 years
> 12. do. [ditto] of 9. and under 12 years
> 73. heads of cattle
> 27. horses, mares, mules and colts.

On the Fourth of July, 1826, the fiftieth anniversary of the signing of the Declaration of Independence, Jefferson was deathly ill. The day before, his pulse was barely perceptible but he had said he wanted so badly to live until the 4th as well as to outlive John Adams, who also was ill. "This is the Fourth?" he asked N. P. Trist, husband to one of Jefferson's granddaughters. It was only 11 PM, and Trist did not answer. Jefferson repeated the question, and Trist nodded yes, a forgivable white lie. Jefferson lived until the afternoon of the 4th, dying almost precisely at the time that John Adams did. The coincidence led a New York newspaper to report that the "like had never happened in the world, nor can it ever happen again, we may almost say with certainty." In Washington, D.C., the *National Intelligencer* agreed: "No language can exaggerate it—no reason account for it. It is one of those events which have no example on record, and as a beauteous moral must forever stand alone on the page of history."

Much of Virginia's Declaration of Human Rights, according to Massachusetts Institute of Technology historian Pauline Maier, was copied from George Mason's preliminary draft of Virginia's Declaration of Human Rights, including the words that "all men are created equal." In her *American Scripture: Making the Declaration of Independence*, Maier wrote that Jefferson's draft was wordy, that one-fourth was cut by Congress.

Jefferson's extravagant lifestyle and generosity to friends left him debt-ridden. In a will signed only a few months before his death at the age of eighty-three, he took notice that he was survived by only one of his six children, Martha, and her bankrupt husband, Thomas Mann Randolph.

Jefferson at one point was forced to sell part of his incomparable library to Congress for $23,950 in order to pay off some of his debts, and his bequest of the remaining collection of books to the University of Virginia greatly helped that school. To his grandson, Thomas Jefferson Randolph, Jefferson gave "my silver watch in preference to the golden one, because of its superior excellence, my papers of business going of course to him, as my executor, all others of a literary or other character I give to him as of his own property." And to James Madison he gave a gold-mounted walking staff of animal horn as "a token of the cordial and affectionate friendship which for nearly now an half century has united us in the same principles and pursuits of what we have deemed for the greatest good of our country."

A great debate has ensued concerning Jefferson's views about the Negroes of his time. Pulitzer-Prize-winning author David K. Shipler has noted the powerful contradiction of the Jefferson legacy. On the one hand, Jefferson was for individual liberty for everyone of every race. On the other, notes Shipler,

> He believed in the inferiority of black people, demonstrating how even a great thinker can remain captive of the racist stereotypes of his time. . . . In his only book, *Notes on the State of Virginia*, written in 1785, Jefferson observes his slaves and endorses virtually every stereotype—positive and negative—that today characterizes the system of prejudices about black people physically, mentally, sexually, emotional. . . . "They secrete less by the kidneys, and more by the glands of the skin, which gives them a very strong and disagreeable odor," he argues, adding that this "renders them more tolerant of heat, and less so of cold than the whites. They are at least as brave, and more adventuresome. But this may perhaps proceed from a want of forethought, which prevents their seeing a danger till it be present. . . . They are more ardent after their female; but love seems with them to be more an eager desire, than a tender delicate mixture of sentiment and sensation. Their griefs are transient. . . . In memory they are equal to the whites; in reason much inferior, as I think one could scarcely be found capable of tracing and comprehending the investigations of Euclid."

Jefferson, Shipler notes, "opposed racial mixing and intermarriage. His idea was to free the slaves, train them for self-sufficiency, and then deport them, for he saw no possibility that blacks and whites could live together. . . . There are two histories of Jefferson, the two histories of America. If we face Jefferson," Shipler declares, "we face ourselves."

Indicative of a possible new attitude toward Jefferson is that of Conor Cruise O'Brien, who, in *The Long Affair: Thomas Jefferson and the French Revolution, 1785—1800* (1996), has termed him a radical and a racist, one whose flaws are beyond redemption and whose reputation is undeserved. For O'Brien, Jefferson represents a liberal tradition which is intellectually, socially, and politically untenable. O'Brien is ferocious in his attack on the long affair with French revolutionaries and with Jefferson's handling of slaves, particularly one Jame Hubbard. Also, he predicted that

> . . . the American civil religion, official version—let me call it ACROV—will have to be reformed in a manner that will downgrade and eventually exclude Thomas Jefferson. Finally, I believe that Jefferson will nonetheless continue to be a power in America in the area where the mystical side of Jefferson really belongs: among the radical, violent, anti-federal libertarian fanatics." He adds, "I believe that the orthodox multiracial version of the American civil religion must eventually prevail—at whatever cost—against the neo-Jeffersonian racist schism. That the orthodox version should prevail is vital not only for America but also for the future of nonracial democracy, and of Enlightenment values generally, in those parts of the world where these are now dominant or where people are struggling to bring them into effective being.

O'Brien called attention to Jefferson's unethical link with *The National Gazette*, a newspaper he covertly supplied with pro-French-revolutionary editorial guidance while he was Secretary of State. And he cited Jefferson's "The tree of liberty must be refreshed from time to time with the blood of patriots and tyrants," words used to excuse much bloodshed.

Similarly, Michael Lind's *The Next American Nation* (1995) attacked Jefferson as "the greatest southern reactionary" in American history, adding, "Jefferson was obsessed, in particular, by the fear that his precious Anglo-Saxon nation would be corrupted by intermarriage with nonwhites. . . . Every major feature of the modern United States—from racial equality to Social Security, from Pentagon to the suburb—represents a repudiation of Jeffersonianism."

Further evidence of changing attitudes about Jefferson is found in Joseph J. Ellis's *American Sphinx: The Character of Thomas Jefferson* (1997). Ellis describes the person who drafted the Declaration of Independence as a foppish young man with limited political skill, a shy man of whom John Adams said, "During the whole time I sat with him in Congress, I never heard him utter three sentences together." As for Jefferson's character, Ellis wrote, "He was never a legend in his own time, always a controversial figure who combined great depth with great shallowness, massive learning with extraordinary naïveté, piercing insights into others with daunting powers of self-deception." Ellis, who read all 60,000 of Jefferson's letters, plus the letters of his friends and enemies, thinks that "the more you immerse yourself in the Jefferson papers, the more difficult it becomes to imagine a liaison between Jefferson and Sally Hemings. It's ironic, the more grounded you are, the more likely you are to get this wrong."

However, Jefferson's 1785 and 1787 negative views on blacks were set down when he was in his 30s. In 1809, he wrote a letter to Henri Grégroire that contained the following, which Shipler does not cite:

> Be assured that no person living wishes more sincerely than I do, to see a complete refutation of the doubts I have myself entertained and expressed on the grade of understanding allotted to them [blacks] by nature, and to find that in this respect they are on a par with ourselves. My doubts were the result of personal observation on the limited sphere of my own State, where the opportunities for the development of their genius were not favorable, and those of exercising it still less so. I expressed them therefore with great hesitation. . . . On this subject they are gaining daily in the opinions of nations, and hopeful advances are making towards their re-establishment on an equal footing with the other colors of the human family. I pray you therefore to accept my thanks for the many instances you have enabled me to observe of respectable intelligence in that race of men, which cannot fail to have effect in hastening the day of their relief.

(He never reversed his statement that sodomy should be punished by castration. See entry for homosexuality.)

Monroe Trotter, a leading black editor in the early 20th century, claimed that he was a direct descendant of Thomas Jefferson and Sally Hemings. Hemimgs was half-sister to Jefferson's wife, Martha, both having been fathered by the same owner of a plantation. By the age of fifteen, Sally had accompanied Jefferson's daughter on a voyage to join Jefferson in Paris, and many believe she became his concubine. Before returning to the United States, Hemings allegedly extracted the promise that he would free any children that she might bear him before they reached the age of twenty-one. Over the years, she gave birth to six children, some if not all of whom were thought by some to have been Jefferson's.

Willard Sterne Randall, however, called the Jefferson-Hemings sexual relationship fanciful: "She was only eight when Jefferson last resided at Monticello and was mourning his wife's death." The alleged "Congo Harem" which Jefferson was supposed to have had, Randall believes, was a politically motivated and preposterous rumor.

DNA tests in 1998, however, proved Randall and others wrong. Blood samples collected by Tufts University Professor Eugene A. Foster confirmed the oral tradition that, indeed, the nation's third President fathered at least one of Sally Hemings's children. Fifty-two-year-old John Jefferson of Norrisville, Pennsylvania, has been shown to be a direct descendant of Hemings through Eston Hemings Jefferson. His Y chromosome matched blood samples taken from the descendants of Jefferson's uncle, Field Jefferson. "I've known it practically all my life," Jefferson said in a public statement.

Commenting on the 1998 DNA evidence of miscegenation, Prof. Annette Gordon-Reed of New York Law School and author of *Thomas Jefferson and Sally Hemings: An American Controversy* said, "If people had accepted this story, he would never have become an icon. All these historians did him a favor until we could get past our primitive racism. I don't think he would have been on Mount Rushmore or on the nickel. The personification of America can't live thirty-eight years with a black woman." Prof. Gordon-Reed, however, may have revealed her own prejudgments, critics were quick to note.

Dr. Eugene A. Foster, the author of the original DNA analysisand a co-author of the *Nature* article that contained the test results, has complained that individuals have misunderstood his work. The retired pathologist, writing in *Nature* (January 1999), supported the view that any of several males in the Jefferson family could have fathered Eston Hemings, the child whose descendants bear the Jefferson Y chromosome. Foster believes it is more probable that Jefferson was Eston's father, rather than other individuals suspected at the time, two of Jefferson's nephews on his sister's side.

At a 1999 family reunion in Monticello, the eighty-sixth such, both the Jefferson and Hemings families met. Many of the two hundred Jefferson descendants were unwilling not only to open their arms to descendants of Jefferson's slave but also were unwilling to open the family cemetery. The six-member executive committee of the Monticello Association declared, according to their president, Robert M. Gillespie, "More evidence is coming forward, and we invited it. But let's make sure we make the correct decision, not a quick decision." As a result, the official organization of Jefferson's family went on record as not being prepared to accept the Hemings line as Jefferson descendants.

As the century ended, Daniel P. Jordan, now the Jefferson Memorial Foundation president, announced that "although paternity cannot be established with absolute certainy, our evaluation of the best evidence available suggests the strong likelihood that Thomas Jefferson and Sally Hemings had a relationship over time that led to the birth of one, and perhaps all, of the known children of Sally Hemings." James Truscott, president of the Monticello Association that previously had resisted the notion, declared his group would issue a report some time in 2000. For freethinkers, the DNA test results were easily accepted as fact. Individuals and events need to be seen in the context of their times. If Jefferson had sexual relations with a person considered little more than property by others, and if their relationship continued for a long time, this is not necessarily bad news. The findings are replete with humanistic overtones.

Jefferson's tombstone at Monticello, Virginia, is inscribed with "O.S." (old style calendar; the year began in March rather than January), not "A.D." (year of Our Lord):

Here was buried Thomas Jefferson,
Author of the Declaration of American Independence, Of the Statute of Virginia for Religious Freedom, and Father of the University of Virginia
Born April 2, 1743 O.S. Died July 4, 1826

(See entries for Church and State and Native Americans—Ethnic Cleansing. The entry for E. C. Vanderlaan contains Benjamin Rush's telling Jefferson that George Washington did not like to discuss his religious outlook. Roger E. Greeley offers a collection of the intellectual Jefferson's quotes in *Thomas Jefferson's Freethought Legacy* [1995].) {BDF; CE; CL; EU, Eugene Sheridan; FUS; HNS2; JM; Conor Cruise O'Brien, *The Atlantic Monthly*, October 1996; PA; RAT; RE; TRI; TYD; U; UU; Nicholas Wade, *The New York* Times, 7 January 1999; *Washline*, September 1997}

JEFFERSON, TERRITORY OF

From 1859 to 1861, residents of a region in what today is Colorado voted to establish the Territory of Jefferson and elected Robert W. Steele as provisional governor. Although never recognized by Congress, the territory passed laws and the franchise was denied to Native and African Americans. In 1861, Congress passed the Organic Act which created the Territory of Colorado. The provisional government soon dismantled, and William Gilpin replaced Steele as governor. {E}

Jeffrey, Francis [Lord] (1773—1850)

A Scottish judge, Jeffrey became Dean of the Faculty of Advocates in 1829, Lord Advocate in 1830, and Judge of the Court of Session in 1834. He helped to found, and for years edited, *The Edinburgh Review*. Although Hugh Miller in *The Treasury of Modern Biography* stated that although Jeffrey was "infected in youth and middle age by the widespread infidelity of the French Revolution," he later abandoned it. In Lord Cockburn's *Life and Letters of Lord Jeffrey* (1852), however, there was no such change. {RAT; RE}

JEHOVAH: See entry for God.

JEHOVAH'S WITNESSES

The Jehovah's Witnesses are a religious denomination that expects the Millennium to begin within a very few years. They call God by the name Jehovah and deny the doctrine of the Trinity. Jesus, however, they consider to be the greatest of the witnesses of Jehovah. The Bible, they believe, says that they are forbidden to accept blood transfusion, even to save their lives. A number of them, have, according to David A. Reed's *Blood on the Altar: Confessions of a Jehovah's Witness Minister* (1996), died, some at a young age, because of this belief. The Jehovah's Witnesses are at 25 Columbia Heights, Brooklyn, NY 11201.

Rikki Beadle-Blair, in the video entitled "Captivated," writes of the black Englishman who while in prison drools over the two "fuckable" Witnesses who visit his cell. But if they want to convert him, he explains, they are going to have to speak to him in his own street-trash lingo: "Don't say 'Let he who is without sin cast the first stone,' say 'If your shit don't stink, let me see you wear a turd as a moustache!' — you know, plain English, like." {DCL}

Jekyll, Walter (20th Century)

Jekyll, a freethinker, wrote *The Bible Untrustworthy* (1904). {GS}

Jellie, William (20th Century)

A Unitarian minister who moved from Auckland to England, Jellie in a 1910 sermon on *Genesis* said, according to John Maindonald,

> For what is Nature? Nature is only a comprehensive name, like God, meaning all things that are, and ever have been, and ever will be.

Jenkins, Clare (20th Century)

A Passion for Priests: Women Talk of Their Love for Roman Catholic Priests (1995), by Jenkins, includes interviews with individuals willing to reveal the greatest secret of their lives: having been emotionally involved with a priest. "Some had known their priests for twenty or more years," Jenkins reports, "longer than many marriages last. Others had had briefer affairs. One had married the man concerned. By no means all the relationships were sexual." Those most seriously affected were women with children fathered by their priests. The crux of the problem, Jenkins stated, is the 800-year-old rule of clerical celibacy and the unwillingness to permit the ordination of women.

A possible sequel, notes a Manhattan wag, could be *A Passion for Parishioners: Priests Talk of Their Love for Roman Catholic Parishioners.*

Jenkins, Hugh (Gater) (1908—)

Lord Jenkins of Putney is a Labour politician and campaigner for freedom of expression and the arts. A member of the House of Commons for Stoke Newington and Hackney North, Jenkins has been chairman of Victory for Socialism (1956—1960) and a member of the Arts Council (1968—1971). With others, he wrote *Essays in Local Government Enterprise* (1964). In 1995, he was named an Honorary Associate of the Rationalist Press Association.

Jenkins, Lydia Ann Moulton (1824?—1874)

One of the first women to preach as a Universalist, Jenkins was ordained by the Ontario Association of Universalists in Geneva, New York, in 1860, the first ordination of a woman by a denominational body in the nation. In the 1850s she spoke and wrote on women's rights issues and against what she had been taught in her Calvinist upbringing.

In 1858 the Ontario Association of Universalists granted her a letter of Fellowship (Fairport, New York). She and her husband became ministers of the Universalist Church in Clinton, NY, in 1860.

The Unitarian Universalist Women's Heritage Society has stated that "although Olympia Brown is generally recognized as the first woman minister (1863), Lydia's ordination may have been overlooked because of fear of potential controversy."

By giving the commencement address in 1859 at Lombard College, she was one of the first women, if not the first woman, to have given such a speech at any United States college. {U&U}

Jenkins, Norm (20th Century)

Jenkins is an Arizona humanist who thinks non-supernaturalists should advertise more.

He recommends automobile bumper stickers with signs such as

> Scientific Inquiry, The Only Path To Reality
> Arizona Secular Humanists. Call (602) 203-5328

Jenkins's E-mails: <eupraxopher@collegeclub.com> or <njenkins@genuity.com>. {*Secular Nation*, July-September 1998}

Jenkins, William P. (20th Century)

Jenkins has been an activist member of the American Humanist Association. {HNS}

Jenner, Edward (1749-1823)

> • A British physician and God's nemesis. His discovery of vaccination led to the eventual eradication of smallpox which, for countless centuries, had been God's favorite scourge for sinners.
>
> —**Carol C. Faulkenberry**, Atlanta Freethought Society

Jenney, Marie Hoffendahl (19th Century)

Jenney, who was graduated in 1897 by the Meadville Theological School, was a writer who was ordained as a Unitarian minister in 1898. {*World*, May-June 1995}

Jennings, Herbert Spencer (1868—1947)

A zoologist and one of the highest authorities on the science in the United States, Jennings in his 1933 Terry Lectures at Yale University (*The Universe and Life*) referred to a cheap symposium that had recently been published. It had had a catchy title, "Has Science Discovered God?" to which Jennings answered that in his own science the answer had to be No. "The progress of life," he insisted, "is not of the kind that would be anticipated if life were following a certain existing pattern, seeking a goal already set, or being guided by an all-knowing and all-powerful being." {JM; RE}

Jennings, Ivor (1903—1965)

Jennings, a freethinker, was a vice president of the National Council for Civil Liberties. {TRI}

Jennings, Robert L. (19th Century)

Jennings was an editor of *The Free Enquirer*, a New Harmony, Indiana, freethought paper in the 1820s and 1830s. {FUS}

Jensen, Johannes V. (1873—1950)

Jensen's Danish novel *The Fall of the King* (1900—1901) has been termed by Ingwersen a chilling masterpiece "in which all human aspirations seem ridiculous in view of the very brevity of human life. A human being's fate, as shown through the symbol of grinding millstones, is simply to be smashed to bits—into nothingness." Life, the author warns his readers, is to be accepted in all its beautiful banality, for that is all there is. Not only did Jensen reject Christianity but also he rejected the melancholy atheism that turns some people into fatalist or nihilists. Adds Ingwersen, Jensen "denounced Friedrich Nietzsche, as well, for being a grand and dangerous seducer who distracts the human mind from this very real world of facts." {CE; EU, Faith Ingwersen}

Jensen, J(ohn) Vernon (1922—)

Jensen, for his 1959 Ph. D. dissertation at the University of Minnesota, wrote on the rhetoric of Thomas H. Huxley and Robert G. Ingersoll in relation to the conflict between science and religion. {FUS}

Jensen, Peter Christian Albrecht (1861—1936)

Jensen, a leading German Orientalist, taught Semitic languages at Marburg University. He was an authority in Germany on Babylonia and Assyria. His rationalism is found in his *Moses, Jesus, Paulus* (1909—1910, 2 volumes) and *Hat der Jesus der Evangelien wirklich gelebt?* (1910). In the latter book, Jensen contents that the story of Jesus is a myth based upon the Epic of Gilgamesch. {RAT; RE}

Jensen, William (20th Century)

Jensen, a professor of the history of chemistry at the University of Cincinnati, told the Cincinatti Free Inquiry Group in 1999 about Baron Karl von Reichenbach, who around 1845 claimed to have discovered a new force which he named Od, a reference to Odin. Od, claimed the Baron, could only be seen by especially sensitive humans, whom he dubbed *sensitives*. William James, Jensen told the Cincinatti group, once divided the human race into two groups—the tough-minded and the soft-headed. Jensen suggested, in light of such charlatans, a third group—the soft-minded. (See entry for Zyp.) {*FIG Leaves*, March 1999}

Jersild, Per Christian (1935—)

Jersild is a Swedish physician, author, journalist, and debater. In *Darwin's Ofullbordade* (Darwin's Unfinished, 1997), he wrote

> The concept life stance has wider frames than the concept view of man—but since man puts himself in focus a life stance which does not embrace man as well is hardly possible. A religious person might claim that the conception of god is the essence of a life stance, but for myself as non-religious, as agnostic, as one who does not claim to have definite answers to the great questions, it is naturally to put the view of man in focus of my life stance. What is it that creates a decent order in the living room in my house of thoughts? For my part it is The Modern Project. The concept "modern" has many meanings, not the least in the arts, but The Modern Project is here another word for The Age of Enlightenment. . . . The complication with Christianity is that it to a high extent has been interested in life hereafter and left life on earth and politics at that. Thus, one can see . . . The Enlightenment as an attempt to practically and political implicate original Christian values of human dignity. But because the Enlightenment is anti-authoritative, tolerant, and run by reason, it tries to perform its project without the Bible's dictatorial image of God. One cuts the Ten Commandments from the first and the second dictates and keeps the rest. Christianity has become humanism.

Jersild, although not a member of the Swedish Humanist Association, is clearly a secular humanist, according to Fredrik Bendz.

JERUSALEM SYNDROME

The *British Medical Journal*, in an article about Jerusalem Syndrome, detailed Ms. Siegel-Itzkovich's statement that it has been known about by Israeli psychiatrists for decades and is "a temporary psychiatric condition characterised by patients believing they have become biblical figures such as Jesus, John the Baptist, or Moses. . . . It affects mainly Christian pilgrims, but is occasionally diagnosed in Jews who tour holy sites. Those affected begin to act strangely, sometimes proclaiming that they are ancient religious figures sent on a holy mission." (*The Freethinker*, April 1999)

Jervas, Charles (1675—1739)

Jervas was so distinguished an artist that he was appointed principal painter to George I and George II, yet his opulent house in London was one of the chief deistic centres. Walpole said that Jervas "piqued himself on total infidelity," an indication that Jervas was an avowed atheist. {RAT; RE}

Jesse, W. W. (19th Century)

Jesse, who was president of the Oregon State Secular Union, led his group, which included the following in the 1890s: J. Henry Schroeder, B. F. Hyland, D. W. Smith, vice-presidents; Katie Kehm Smith, secretary; and D. C. Stewart, treasurer. {RE}

Jesseph, Doug (20th Century)

Jesseph, of North Carolina State University, is a supporter of Internet Infidels.

JESUITS

If freethinkers or humanists were "forced" to join a church, the ideal order for them would likely be that of the Jesuits. The Jesuit order, the largest in the Roman Catholic Church, was founded by Ignatius of Loyola in 1540, its official name being the Society of Jesus. The Jesuits have a long tradition of vigorous missionary work and of intellectual and scholarly achievement. Some spend up to fifteen years in training. Behind the scenes, they are known for their influence in European politics and for their skill and resourcefulness in debate, characteristics that have led some—even several of the Popes—to mistrust them. Before the middle of the 18th century, a combination of publicists (including Voltaire) and the absolute monarchs of Catholic Europe undertook to destroy them. Portugal expelled the Jesuits in 1759. France suppressed them in 1764. The Spanish dominions were closed to them in 1767. In 1773, Clement XIV dissolved the order, but Frederick the Great and Catherine the Great refused to publish the brief suppressing them, so they continued to exist, mainly as educators, in Prussia and Russia. In 1814 Pius VII re-established them as a world order. *Jesuitical* as an adjective is used to describe devious argumentation. In the United States, the Jesuit schools include Fordham, Georgetown, and St. Louis University.

The period of 1965 to 1981, during which the Reverend Pedro Arrupe led the Jesuits, was known as the era of social activism. When he suffered a brain hemorrhage, the order's Superior General became the Very Reverend Peter-Hans Kolvenbach, a sixty-five-year-old Dutch Jesuit. The ranks of Jesuits have thinned since the mid-1960s when there were 36,000. It is estimated that there were 23,000 Jesuits in 1994.

In 1995 at a 34th General Congregation in Rome, the Jesuits although they "did not pretend or claim to speak for women" did declare their "personal concern" for the "unjust treatment and exploitation of women." They lamented that women have limited access to positions of influence, undergo female circumcision, have wage differences, are discriminated against in education, and as young girls are sometimes killed. The Jesuits stopped just short of recommending that women be ordained as priests. (See the section on Jesuits in McCabe's *Rationalist Encyclopedia*.) {DCL}

JESUS

G. A. Wells, professor of German at the University of London, is one of many who contend that Jesus was probably not a historical person. Rather, he holds, Jesus, William Tell, and King Arthur are legendary figures.

The dramatist Terrence McNally, in *Corpus Christi*, not only describes Jesus as a human but also refers to homosexuality among Jesus and his Apostles.

Jesus (4 B.C.E.?—29 C.E.?)

Approximately thirty centuries ago, the Chinese invented kites made of bamboo, silk, and paper. The individuals responsible may have been forgotten, but their positive contributions are still appreciated.

Long after that, a thousand or so years, a human being by the name of Jesus allegedly was born. Few agree as to when he, or He (for some claim he was God in disguise), was born. Many doubt that he even existed. Charles Francis Potter in the 1920s and 1930s suggested that because of changes in our present calendar, Jesus was born four years *before* B.C. (the Birth of Christ), that he died in 27 A.D. (*anno Domini*, in the year of the Lord). *The Cambridge Factfinder* lists Jesus as having been born "c. 5 BC" and being crucified in Jerusalem "c. 30 A.D." Other sources mention from 6 B.C.E. to 4 A.D., suggesting that he lived about thirty-three years. If He was the Christ, He was born B.C. (before Christ)! (See entry for Christmas, in which Wick Allison figures the date at 6 B.C.E.)

Tacitus in the 2nd century stated only what Christians believed about Jesus. The Jewish historian Josephus wrote about Jesus, but Wells and others declare that "no one can accept the glowing paragraph in Josephus' *Antiquities of the Jews* (C. E. 93) as coming from the hand of this orthodox Jew; it has to be regarded as at best a Christian reworking of a passage originally hostile to Jesus. That the non-Christian evidence is unhelpful has been conceded by many Christian scholars (e.g., Albert Schweitzer and D. P. Davies)." Meanwhile, Christians make the leap of faith and believe not only that Jesus the God existed but also that He, the Son, is the Second Person of the Trinity. The third is the Holy Ghost (or "Holy Spirit," for those who do not believe in any species of ghost).

Maréchal during the French Revolution cited Jesus as being the opposite of an atheist. Jesus was written about by biblical authors who did not know him during his lifetime. G. A. Wells, in *Encyclopedia of Unbelief*, lists various scholars who have written about and denied the historicity of Jesus: Guy Fau, Prosper Alfaric, W. B. Smith, and J. M. Allegro. Whether or not he lived, and who inseminated his mother, Mary, has been debated for centuries.

Roman Catholic priest Father Raymond E. Brown, emeritus professor of New York's Union Theological Seminary, has made new and often provocative interpretations of the New Testament. In *The Death of the Messiah* (1994), his 1,608-page commentary on the last days of Jesus, he favors John's opinion that some Jewish authorities wanted Jesus executed but merely questioned him after Jesus was arrested, this because he represented a blasphemer's threat to the temple. Such a view, that there was some Jewish involvement in the death of Jesus, helps fan controversies with Jews, who generally deny that Jesus was considered a blasphemer. Brown, however, points up the anti-Jewish sentiment easily found in the Gospels of Matthew and John. When John describes water and blood coming from the dying Jesus's body, Brown interprets this as symbolic of Jesus's pouring out the Holy Spirit on the early church. Orthodox Christians remain wary whenever any scholar such as Brown claims that their "divinely inspired Bible" is not literal history.

Jesus appears not to have been an "orthodox Jew," according to Gerald Larue (in *Skeptic*, Vol. 2, No. 3). The Gospels portray him as anything but that, for he associated with the wrong people—sinners and the hated tax collectors. According to *Luke* 8:1-3, Jesus and his disciples traveled with women who "provided for them out of their means" (and some manuscripts read "provided for him"). Further, no Jew living during the first thirty years of the first century of the Common Era could have lived according to the codified Mishnah. The codification of the Mishnah began following the destruction of the Temple in 70 and was completed during the early third century. Thus, first-century Jewish "orthodoxy" cannot be properly defined by reference to codes formulated in later eras.

Thousands were crucified around Jerusalem in the first century, according to John Dominic Crossan, a professor of biblical studies at DePaul University in Chicago. Unlike other scholars, Crossan holds that no one, including Joseph of Arimathea, buried Jesus. He thinks it likely that some Roman soldiers in deference to Jewish piety might have thrown the body into a shallow grave. In such a case, dogs would likely have eaten the body of Jesus. On Easter, then, there was no empty tomb. According to Crossan, there was not even a tomb. Meanwhile on the subject of the Jews having crucified Jesus, *Sura 4* of the Qur'an states, "Killed him not, they did not crucify him, but it was made to appear that way to them."

A pundit has said that Jesus was both original and inspiring: unfortunately, what was inspiring was not original, and what was original with Jesus was not inspiring. What caught the imagination of the masses, the pundit continued, was the spin added by the greatest public relations person of all time, Saul of Tarsis: "I am the way, the truth and the light. No man cometh unto the Father but by me."

Proof of Jesus's existence? His Omnipresence is on the Web: <http://members.aol.jesus316/index.htm>. (See entries for Christmas; Ganymede; Homosexuality; Immaculate Conception; Qualifications for a Leader; and Resurrection. Also, see the entry for Jesus in McCabe's *Rationalist Encyclopedia*. For details of his foreskin, see entry for Circumcision.) {CE; ER; EU, G. A. Wells; FUK}

JESUS, RESIGNATION OF

(Las Vegas) After a fortnight of vacation to "evaluate his life" and "reassess his goals" and career, Jesus Christ today announced his resignation. Sources say that he was probably under pressure to resign after failing to capitalize fully on his success.

While the religion he founded raked in billions each year, a significant number of people refused to buy into it, and earnings had been falling in recent years.

"I mean, my life just wasn't going anywhere," the 2,000-year-old Jerusalem-born saviour said in an interview. "I had a productive period a while back. "You know, walking around on water and shit. But to be honest since then I haven't gotten out much and haven't really gotten anything done."

Jesus, who answers prayer requests, admitted that he had been somewhat leisurely about his work in recent years. "I sometimes just drift off and can't seem to concentrate. I plain slept through the entire 1940s," mankind's Saviour told reporters, explaining how the Second World War was allowed to happen. . . .

Jesus said that his resignation was not due in any way to his arrest this February for stalking. Charges are still pending on that matter, after police realized that Jesus's omnipresence left him open to an estimated 50,000 counts of stalking. A police source, who wished to remain anonymous, stated that they were "still sorting out the paperwork" and estimated it would be at least another two centuries before all the charges were calculated, researched, and filed. . . .

The retirement, effective immediately, means that Christians who are seeking spiritual aid or guidance will no longer receive an answer to their prayers. . . . Jesus explained that, in order to minimize confusion in coming weeks and also to update prayer-answering to match today's technology he will be installing a voicemail system. . . . I don't want to bother with any of that shit while I'm on vacation." . . .

Archbishop Jim Carrey of Westminster Cathedral told reporters that "You can expect the same great service from our voicemail system that you've always gotten from Jesus." The response from Christians were varied although the changes were taken extremely well by the majority. "I just thank God for this," said Southern Baptist Chuck Whitman. "Getting up early on Sunday was just killing me, so I'm pretty glad actually."

The Fearsome Atheist Webzine
<http://fearsome.net/rants.htm>.

Jesus [Lee Jae-rok] (20th Century)

Jesus is alive and well in Seoul, South Korea. He is pastor of All Holiness Church. When a television station attempted to air a program exploring Jesus's "heretical" statements and his gambling habits, six church leaders stormed the network and interrupted the broadcast. Several hundred members of the church overpowered fifty guards, successfully cutting the program off the air, and 1,500 of its members protested in front of the television station, demanding that the network cancel any future programs.

The police sought arrest warrants for the six leaders. Meanwhile, the church was expelled from the Korean National Council of Churches, averring that its Jesus is not the Jesus who claims he is Jesus.

JESUS, SAYINGS OF: See entry for Q.

JESUS'S CHILDREN

The Cathari held that Jesus, instead of dying on the cross, married Mary Magdalen, settled in the Languedoc, and that their heirs founded the Merovingian dynasty that united Christian Europe under Charlemagne. (See Catharism.)

Jeter, Michael (1952—)

Jeter, a television star, won a Tony Award for his acting on "Evening Shade." He has appeared in "Boys in the Band," "The Naked Man," and "Jakob the Liar." Also, he appeared in the Milos Forman movie version of "Hair."

A person who can discuss Virginia Woolf, Tolstoy, Proust, Eudora Welty, Dame Maggie Smith, and the U. S. Constitution "without missing a beat," he has gone on record concerning the Bible:

> I defy the church's authority to tell me how I can be or how I can live. Anyway, I don't believe in that god. Because he's only had one bestseller. My god is the fucking Barbara Cartland of gods!

In 1996, Jeter was diagnosed as being HIV-positive and has been an AIDS activist. {Peter Kurth, *Poz*, January 1998}

JEW

Under Mosaic law and Israel's Law of Return (but not the Nuremberg Laws), an individual is not Jewish unless he or she came by it through the maternal line.

Christians and Muslims can be Christians and Muslims, however, even if their mother was an atheist, a Jew, a Hindu. What these two groups find confusing, then, is that some Jews say they are atheists, although one cannot logically be a Christian nor a Muslim atheist nor can one logically be both a believer in the Bible and a disbeliever in its contents.

Judaism, as a term, was coined by Greek-speaking Jews to designate their religious way of life in contrast with that of their neighbors, a way of life known as Hellenism. Many chose pagan Greek over religious Hebrew, sometimes calling themselves "cultural Jews."

During World War II, "the Jewish race" was a factor cited by some officials of the Axis alliance powers of Germany, Italy, and Japan, although they did not speak of "the Catholic race" or "the Methodist race."

The Union of Orthodox Rabbis in the United States and Canada, which has a membership of more than five hundred, declared in 1997 that the Reform and Conservative movements are "not Judaism" and urged Jews not to attend synagogues affiliated with those movements. In Israel Reform and Conservative movements have few members, the population being divided between a secular majority and a large Orthodox minority. In their announcement, the Orthodox Rabbis did not suggest that Jews in Reform and Conservative synagogues were any less Jewish than those in Orthodox synagogues. But the charge was that they are spiritually misleading their members by teaching "things contrary to the Torah." For example, religious law was being violated by rabbis' allowing Jews to drive on the Sabbath, and by the Reform movement's 1983 decision to recognize as Jews the offspring of interfaith marriages in which either the father or mother was Jewish. Previously, all branches had agreed that Jewish identity was solely derived from the mother. The Union's statement led to continuing differences between the groups, some accusing its leaders of "sheer chutzpah."

In contemporary Israel, according to Deborah Sontag (*The New York Times*, 27 January 1999), "Sephardic Jews constitute nearly half the population. . . . The rift between the Ashkenazi elite—Jews of Central and Eastern European descent—and the immigrants from North Africa and Arab countries is a fact of Israeli life. . . . What used to be considered a taboo, intermarriage—as it was called—between Ashkenazis and Sephardis, has lost its shock value. Pop music from North Africa, which used to be sold only at cassette stands at bus stations, dominates the radio airwaves. A quarter of the university students are Sephardic. And the army has become a path of social mobility."

[The present work takes the position that Judaism, like Christianity, is a religion, that its adherents are not classifiable by race, and that one can convert to Judaism, Islam, Christianity, or any other organized religion. Similarly, one can switch from any organized religion to non-theism. Entertainer Sammy Davis, a black whose lineage was African, converted to Judaism. The Roman Catholic Archbishop of Paris, Jean-Marie Cardinal Lustiger, was the son of Jewish parents. Isaac Asimov, whose parents were Jewish, became a non-theist and secular humanist. The U.S. Secretary of State, Madeline Albright, had Czech parents and grandparents who were Jewish, but her parents converted to Roman Catholicism in order to escape detection by the Nazis; Ms. Albright later converted to Protestant Episcopalianism. The son of atheist Madalyn Murray O'Hair converted to Christianity.]

Atheists like to point out that all humans, fortunately, are born without a belief in any organized religion's doctrines. Concerning the view that being a Jew is dependent upon his or her mother's being a Jew, a Manhattan wag has observed, "What an imaginative marketing program!"

JEW OF MALTA: See entry for Barabas.

JEW, AUTHENTIC

- In the popular vernacular, a Jew is a member of a widely dispersed group that originally descended from the ancient Hebrews and shares an ethnic heritage which is based on Judaism. Thus, someone whose grandparents were Jews but who is not a religious person is still considered by them to be a Jew, possibly even an atheistic Jew.

- But to those purists who distinguish between a Jew (a member of the religion) and a Hebrew (a member of or a descendant from one of a group of northern Semitic peoples including the Israelites), Einstein was a Hebrew, not a Jew. In short, not all Hebrews are Jews, just as not all Italians are Catholics. Nor are all Norwegians Evangelical Lutherans. The African American entertainer Sammy Davis was not a Hebrew but became a Jew. Einstein's parents, however, were Hebrews as well as Jews. This distinction is made throughout the present work to differentiate (a) the religious Jew who attends a synagogue regularly, (b) the non-religious Jew who feels a closeness to Judaism but does not participate actively, and (c) the Hebrew, whose ancestors were Jewish and who may or may not now be a religious or a non-religious Jew. Many people who are Hebrews, in short, are Jews as were their ancestors, just as many Norwegians are Lutherans, as were their ancestors. Other Hebrews as well as other Norwegians, however, are freethinkers, atheists, or uninterested either in religion or philosophy. The present work considers "atheistic Jew," "atheistic Catholic," and "atheistic Lutheran" oxymorons because of the contradictory terms.

- Only five "Jews" flatly turned down the chance to appear in a 1996 *Life* article which featured Frederic Brenner's photographic homage to American Jews. It was not clear if they objected to being labeled a Jew or whether they considered themselves just an American of Hebrew ethnicity: Woody Allen, Bob Dylan, Sandy Koufax, Paul Simon, and Barbara Walters. Those who did agree to be photographed included Barbra Streisand, Dustin Hoffman, Kirk Douglas, Steven Spielberg, Billy Wilder, Norman Mailer, Arthur Miller, Neil Simon, Walter Annenberg, Michael Milken, Michael Ovitz, Henry Kissinger, Leonard Nimoy, William Shatner, Elizabeth Taylor, and Beverly Sills.

- When French photographer Frédéric Brenner, author of *Jews/America/A Representation*, assembled Jews for a 1996 photo in New York City, he chose Lauren Bacall, Edgar Bronfman, Edgar Bronfman Jr., Charles Bronfman, Betty Friedan, Ruth Bader Ginsburg, Philip Glass, Edward I. Koch, Ralph Lauren, Roy Lichtenstein, Arthur Miller, Itzhak Perlman, Mark Spitz, Isaac Stern, Laurence and Preston Tisch, and Ruth Westheimer. Those unable to attend were Saul Bellow, Kirk Douglas, Allen Ginsberg, Dustin Hoffman, Henry Kissinger, Michael Milken, Philip Roth, Steven Spielberg, Michael Ovitz, and Barbra Streisand.

Jean-Paul Sartre distinguished between an "inauthentic Jew" and an "authentic Jew." The former suppressed his or her "Jewishness." The latter proclaimed it and fought against those who objected.

In 1997, Israeli Prime Minister Benjamin Netanyahu supported legislation that allowed Orthodox rabbis in Israel to define who is a "Jew." Also, he favored giving Orthodox rabbis even more control over Israel's religious life. Inasmuch as more than 90% of Jews in the United States belong to non-Orthodox branches of Judaism, Netanyahu's stand was protested.

JEW, CULTURAL

In the common vernacular, a person whose ethnic heritage is based on Judaism but who is not religious and likely is anti-religious can still think of himself or herself as being culturally Jewish. Similarly, a Louisianan whose ancestors were Catholic, French-speaking immigrants from Acadia might think of himself or herself as culturally Cajun even if being a Jew and unable to speak French.

However, many non-theists whose parents were Jews are adamantly opposed to being considered culturally Jewish, do not purchase "kosher food," and are as unwilling to display a menorah as a Christian icon.

JEW, THE VANISHING

Alan M. Dershowitz, in *The Vanishing American Jew* (1997) warned that if intermarriage trends continue, American Jewry would disappear. His book was written after his son Jamin married Barbara, a Roman Catholic. Raised an Orthodox Jew, Dershowitz surprised some by writing that Judaism need not be bound to revelation at Sinai or to Jewish law, a view similar to that of Mordechai Kaplan, to whom he alluded. "The great paradox of Jewish life is that virtually all of the positive values we identify with Jews—compassion, creativity, contributions to the world at large, charity, a quest for education—seem more characteristic of Jews who are closer to the secular end of the Jewish continuum than to the ultra-Orthodox end." Dershowitz considers Judaism as a civilization like "the American, Greek, or Roman civilizations." {See entry for Jew, Who Is A?}

JEW, WHO IS A?

Paul Kurtz is a secular humanist leader with an incisive view about "Who is A Jew?" In a work of that title (*Free Inquiry*, Summer 1997), he noted that Alan M. Dershowitz's *The Vanishing American Jew* (1997) writes that he is a thoroughly secularized Jew and a humanist, and he is agnostic about the existence of God. "Yet," Kurtz found, "he believes that it would be a tragedy if the American Jews were to decline or disappear." On the contrary, Kurtz defends assimilation of Jews into the mainstream:

> In reading Dershowitz I am struck by how deep-seated his own ethnic and tribal chauvinism is—and by his failure to appreciate the virtues of assimilation, the appeal of interreligious and/or interracial marriages. The United States (and Australia, New Zealand, Canada, and Western Europe to a lesser extent) are becoming truly universal societies, for they have taken steps beyond ancient ethnic, national, and racial chauvinism.
>
> Should we not applaud those couples (including Dershowitz's son and daughter-in-law) who are willing to transcend their ethnic backgrounds and transfer their affection to the broader human community, able to reach out and love "the aliens" in their midst? Rather than bemoan the loss of his grandchildren to Jewish identity, why not applaud the quest for a broader human identity?

Kurtz further discussed the concept that the Jewish people "represent a continuous line of descent of 3,500 years, traceable back to the original Jews or Hebrew who lived in Palestine." Citing Paul Wexler's *The Ashkenazic Jews: A Slavo-Turkic People in Search of a Jewish Identity* (1993), Kurtz found no "sacred chain" to uphold the view of any continuous line of descent. The implications of Wexler's study for the State of Israel, he states,

> are profound. Jewish nationalism and Zionist ideology are wedded to "the sacred chain" thesis. Wexler observes that, given the Israeli-Palestinian conflict today, the belief in an uninterrupted identity of the Jewish people and/or religion from the Palestinian period to the present impedes the systematic study of this historic Judaization process. If he is correct, this thesis need not justify the frenzied effort by Palestinian nationalists to throw the Jews into the sea, no more than that Native Americans need insist that the settlers in America and Canada return to Europe and Africa, or that the Australians give back Australia to the Aborigines.

From the secular humanist viewpoint, Kurtz concluded,

> . . . assimilation is a positive good and is not to be feared. The moral agenda for humanists is to persuade people that we need to go beyond the ancient divisive loyalties of the past and to attain a new ethical level in which all persons become a part of the community of humankind. This may be difficult. But if it is happening in America, why not elsewhere?

At the very end of 1998, a district judge in Jerusalem ordered the Israeli Government to recognize conversiions to Judaism performed by non-Orthodox rabbis. Minority Reform and Conservative leaders celebrated the decision. Orthodox leaders vowed to fight the ruling.

JEWISH ATHEISM

S. Levin, a South African pediatrician who has written (*New Humanist*, May 1995) about "Jewish Atheism," cites various biblical references to a non-caring, non-acting, not-there God. The Talmud does not feature God prominently, he notes, and he develops further evidence in the writing of Jewish authors that God could not exist or the Holocaust, for example, would never have been allowed.

From a semantic rather than an orthodox Jewish viewpoint, "Jewish atheism" and "Catholic atheism," which are analogous terms, appear to be illogical. Judaism is about a personal God, a chosen people, daily prayers and rituals, a sacred text, belief in a soul, and separation of the sacred from the secular. Those whose parents were Hebrews and who now do not accept Judaism could, however, consider themselves "cultural Jews" who, for example, like matzo ball soup and sad songs sung by a cantor. Similarly, those whose parents were Catholics and who now do not accept Christianity could, however, enjoy Gothic architecture and solemn liturgical music sung by castrati.

Shulamit Aloni, the Israeli minister of science during the Peres regime, has called herself an Israeli (whose parents were Hebrews), a Jew, and an atheist.

"A Jew by birth" is one whose mother was a Jew, according to Jewish religious law. Thus, if one's mother is a Jew and one later becomes a Catholic or an atheist the question of whether or not one is still a Jew remains a problem often debated in contemporary Israel. Orthodox rabbis, who in Israel control marriages and burials, may not recognize such individuals as Jews. Nat Henthoff, Wendy Lesser, and numerous others insist they are "atheistic Jews," *not* atheists whose parents were Jews.

Meanwhile, if one's mother is a Buddhist or a Baptist or an atheist, one is not automatically a Buddhist, Baptist, or atheist, for the person is expected to choose his religion or non-religion. Many, however, lazily continue without questioning their membership in their parents' religion. (See entry for Jews and Jews, Cultural.)

JEWISH AUTHORS

Many Jewish creative artists incorporate religious themes and references in their work. The British Commonwealth's chief rabbi, Jonathan Sacks, has written *Faith in the Future* (1995), and numbers of Jews over the centuries have produced not only novels, dramas, and poetry but also symphonies, paintings, and sculpture.

Hebrew literature starts with the Old Testament and the Apocrypha, parts of the Pseudepigrapha, and the Dead Sea Scrolls. The Talmud, the Midrash, the Targum, the Masora, the Zohar, the Aha of Shabcha, Saadia Ben Joseph Al-Fayumi, Dunash Den Tamin, Dunash Ben Labrat, Gershom Ben Judah, and Al-Fasi exemplify Hebrew literature up to the 14th century. Following the Crusades when the Jews were driven from country to country, they continued, often writing about mysticism and asceticism.

The modern period of Hebrew literature began with Moses Mendelssohn, the poet Jehuda (Leon) Gordon, and the novelist Solomon Yakob Abramovich. Other writers are the scholar Joseph Halévy, Ahad Ha-am (Asher Ginzberg), Hayyim Nahman Bialik, Abraham Shlonsky, Lea Goldberg, Nathan Alterman, Joseph H. Brenner, Salman Shneur, the Nobel laureate S. Y. Agnon, Moshe Shamir, Aron David Gordon, David Frishman, Yosef Klausner, Amos Oz, Abraham B. Yehoshua, Aharon Applefeld, Yehuda Amichai, et cetera.

Joseph Heller, the author of *Catch-22* (1961), has explained his view on being a Jewish author:

> Being Jewish informs everything I do. My books are getting more and more Jewish. But I write for everybody, and there is possibly something exotic about Jewish books for non-Jews, although fortunately Jews in America do buy books. New York, when I was growing up, was the biggest city in America, and consequently had more educated people than any other city, and had more Jews living there, so it is not surprising that there were so many books about Jews.

His *Good as Gold* (1979) is comically satirical about Jewish New York and Washington politics.

Max Frankel, in *Max Frankel, the Times of My Life* (1999), sounded almost like, and might even be, a secular humanist:

> Like my forebears in the shtetl, I understood my God to be an abstraction, without image, and I defined godliness as the pursuit of knowledge and good deeds. In my editorial combats with fellow Jews, I realize why I grew to define myself through journalism: because I shared the faith of the shtetl that "the word is threshold to the deed," and because I wanted always to escape the irrationality of the herd. Although I am sentimentally faithful to the tribe whose genes I carry, I know that my culture has been both diluted and enriched by a dozen other tribes. If my *Yiddishkayt* is to survive in America, it will be as a value system, not in a taste for bagels and log or a guilty twitch at the sight of bacon.

Other contemporary authors have made Judaism a part of their work. For example, Saul Bellow in *Herzog* (1964) tells of the inner life of a Jewish intellectual.

Arthur Miller, without specifically naming Judaism, includes his views on moralism and materialism in *Death of a Salesman* (1949), *All My Sons* (1947), *The Crucible* (1953), and *A View from the Bridge* (1955); his marriage to Marilyn Monroe, however, was performed by a Connecticut minister, a Unitarian.

Philip Roth in most of his works describes his complex relationship with his Jewish background, works which often have aroused controversy by his portrayal of contemporary Jewish life.

Norman Mailer, who has called himself an atheist, condemned Christianity in his *Christians and Cannibals*.

Irwin Shaw in *The Young Lions* (1948) describes two American soldiers, one a Jew, the other a Gentile, and tells how the Nazi who killed the first is killed by the second.

Herman Wouk in *Marjorie Morningstar* (1955) describes a Jewish girl's quest for romance and the career of acting, finally settling down as a New Jersey matron. Wouk, a rabbi, also wrote *This Is My God* (1959), a book about Judaism.

Alfred Kazin (1915—1998), author of *New York Jew* (1978), was a noted critic whose study of American prose literature starting with William Dean Howells was an important work entitled *On Native Grounds* (1942). Although thought perhaps to be a non-believer in the supernatural and afterlife, he wrote in *A Lifetime Burning in Every Moment* (1996), "We Jewish intellectuals are always looking for our cultural home." In *God & The American Writer* (1997), he discussed how writers of fiction make searches for the unexplainable, citing Emerson (who "began as a religion but ended as literature"), Harriet Beecher Stowe, Melville, Whitman, Lincoln (as a writer), Emily Dickinson, William James (who saw religion "as therapy"), Clemens, Eliot, Frost, Faulkner, and others. (See entries for Norman Mailer and Arthur Miller.) (CE; OEL}

JEWISH HUMANIST

On the staff of *The Jewish Humanist* (Birmingham Temple, 28611 West 12 Mile Road, Farmington Hills, Michigan 48335) are the following: Rabbi Sherman T. Wine; President Carolyn Borman; Vice President Michael Egren; Treasurer Mark Bulmash; and Secretary Edie Mellow. Past presidents have been Charles Paul, Stuart Rice, Lori Schechter, Judith Schneider, Nina Schneyer, and Robert Stone.

JEWISH NOSE

"... [T]he man on the cross had a Jewish nose," ex-Jesuit Peter de Rosa maliciously observed in 1988.

The Hittites, an ancient people of Asia Minor and Syria known for being one of the first to successfully smelt iron, are said by anatomists often to have had a "beaked nose." The Caucasoid race is said usually to have a high nose bridge, the Mongoloid race to have a medium or low nose bridge, and the Negroid race a low nose bridge.

Inasmuch as *race* is scientifically inappropriate when applied to national, religious, geographic, linguistic, or cultural groups, it is not clear how one would or could identify a Jewish, a Catholic, a Hindu, or a non-theistic nose. However, David Denby in *The New Yorker* 17 August 1998) described Leonard Bernstein as having "a virile Jewish beak."

"Even when the males are naked," a non-circumcised Manhattan atheist wag observed, "you can't be *sure* they're Jews. You can be fairly sure, however, if they're not." {CE}

JEWISH ORGANIZATIONS

Four major Jewish organizations are in the United States. The two largest, numbering around 1,500,000 each, are the Union of American Hebrew Congregations (Reform) and the United Synagogues of Conservative Judaism. An estimated 500,000 are members of the Union of Orthodox Jewish Congregations of America. The Jewish Reconstructionist Federation is at 165 East 56th Street, New York, NY 10022

JEWISH PHILOSOPHY: See entry in the *Encyclopedia of Philosophy*, Vol. 4.

JEWS

Jews are members of the tribe of Judah, whose religion is Judaism. By definition, Judaism is a religion developed among the ancient Hebrews, one that believes in one transcendent God who has revealed Himself to Abraham, Moses, and the Hebrew prophets. Although it is possible to convert to Judaism and become a Jew regardless of race or previous religion, it is lexicographically illogical to be an "atheistic Jew," just as, analogously, one is not an "atheistic Christian" or an "atheistic Muslim." However, many whose ancestors were Hebrews, including Nat Henthoff, persist in proclaiming that they are atheistic Jews rather than (as were Freud, Einstein, and others) "unbelieving Jews." Anne Frank's father, who served the Kaiser in World War I and who escaped to Holland when anti-Semitism became the national policy in Germany, was called a Jew by others although he did not call himself so—his family celebrated Christmas, not Chanukah; his family had not given him any religious instruction, and his children received no religious or theological instruction.

Nel Noddings, in *Educating for Intelligent Belief or Unbelief* (1993), remarks, "Christianity, it is said, focuses on belief more than most religions do. Judaism, for example, places more importance on ritual and practice. Indeed, some people today ignore the religious nature of Judaism entirely. In a letter to the *Village Voice* (9 June 1992), Nat Hentoff declared himself a 'Jewish atheist,' " adding that the present writer retorted, "Hentoff cannot be a Jewish atheist any more than one could be a 'black white,' that he might better call himself a secular humanist or just an atheist. Hentoff, who perhaps could better be described as a non-Jewish Jew, replied:

> I have now come full circle. Several rabbis once "excommunicated" me because I am for an independent Palestinian state. Now the secular humanists would censure me for calling myself Jewish. As I told the rabbis, I define myself, and it ain't nobody's business but my own.

Nodding observes, "Perhaps Hentoff should settle for the label 'existentialist.' In any case, the Hentoff-Smith exchange illustrates the fascinating mixture of belief, culture, politics, logic, and passion that is conjured up by the word *religion*. Even though few religions besides Christianity use belief as a basic test, belief is clearly involved in all religions. People do not engage in rituals and practices without believing in something that gives these rituals and practices meaning. At least, I am arguing here that such behavior would not be intelligent."

In 1995, Jean-Marie Cardinal Lustiger, who was "born a Jew" and converted at the age of fourteen to Roman Catholicism in 1940, created a furore when he visited Yad Vashem, a memorial in Jerusalem to the Holocaust. Now the Archbishop of Paris, he wore the red zucchetto of a prince of the Roman Catholic Church. But, he was met by Rabbi Yisrael Meir Lau's statement that Cardinal Lustiger had "betrayed his people and his faith during the most difficult and darkest of periods. If we were to accept Lustiger as a model," he said, "not one Jew would be left in the world to say Kaddish," the Jewish prayer for the dead. The Cardinal insisted that he had never repudiated his Jewish origins and even referred to "we Jews," adding, "To say that I am no longer a Jew is like denying my father and mother, my grandfathers and grandmothers. I am as Jewish as all the other members of my family who were butchered in Auschwitz or in the other camps." In short, instead of claiming he was from a Hebrew family, he said he was both a Jew and a Catholic. When asked if he thought he might become the next Pope, he answered "Crazy" in Yiddish, "*Meshuggeh!*"

The Reform branch of American Judaism in the 1980s renounced a principle which had guided Jews for 2,000 years: that in mixed marriages the religious status of children comes down through the mother. Thus, Peter Steinfels has explained, "the child of a Jewish woman and a non-Jewish man, therefore, was automatically Jewish, while the child of a Jewish man and a non-Jewish woman was not," possibly ordained because rabbis took pity on the Jewish women raped by Roman soldiers during the Jewish uprisings of 65-67 C.E. and 132-135 C.E. After all, had not Moses married Zipporah, a Midianite daughter of a foreign priest, and it was never suggested that her son Gershom or any other of her children were not Jews. Test cases include "a Carmelite monk who in the 1960s claimed Israeli citizenship inasmuch as he had been born a Jew. In 1970, an Israeli married to a gentile demanded that his children be recognized as Jewish by race but not by religion. In 1986, an American immigrant, converted to Judaism by a non-Orthodox rabbi, claimed a right to be recognised as Jewish," reported *The Economist* (14 August 1993). In the 1990s, a group of black Somali refugees encamped outside an Israeli embassy, describing themselves as Falasha Somali and asserting their own ancient Jewish lineage. Meanwhile, a black Ethiopian group called the Semitic People of Guihon and claiming to number four million have proclaimed their group's Jewishness. Opponents claim that such examples only prove that the Reform rule deepens the rift among Jews, blurring the boundary between Jews and non-Jews.

The main designations of Judaism are Conservative, Orthodox, Reform, and Reconstructionist. (See entries for Jew—Authentic, Judaism, Mankind., and Jew, Who is A? Also see entry for Sheldon F. Gottlieb, who declares that "Jews may relinquish the deistic aspects of the religion and still consider themselves to be culturally and ethnically Jewish." Also see the entry for Thomas Henry Huxley, who told his son Leonard, "The most remarkable achievement of the Jew was to impose on Europe for eighteen centuries his own superstitions." In addition, Joseph McCabe in the *Rationalist Encyclopedia* has a precise survey of Jews and Judaism. For an estimate of the number of Jews worldwide, see entry for Hell.) {CE; RE}

JEWS AND DNA

"DNA BACKS A TRIBE'S TRADITION OF EARLY DESCENT FROM THE JEWS" was the headline in the *New York Times* (9 May 1999). The reference was to Bantu-speaking, black people of southern Africa, the Lemba, who have a tradition of having been led out of Judea by a man named Buba. They practice circumcision, keep one day a week holy, and avoid eating pork or piglike animals "such as the hippopotamus."

A team of geneticists has found that many Lemba men carry in their male chromosome a set of DNA sequences that is distinctive of the cohanim, whom Jewish priests believe to be the descendants of Aaron. The theory of Dr. David Goldstein, a geneticist at Oxford University, is that the Lemba may have migrated to southern Africa from Senna in present-day Yemen.

Freethinkers, who hold that Jews are members of a religion, not a race, are hard put to explain how one's religion can be transmitted by one's D(eoxyribo) N(ucleic) A(cid). {Nicolas Wade, *The New York Times*, 9 May 1999}

JEWS AND MENSTRUATION

In 1648 there was a bizarre notion that Jewish men menstruated. Thomas Calvert claimed that Jews—men as well as females—are punished *curso menstruo sanguinis*—with a very frequent blood flux. This led to the blood-libel, a belief that Jews had to murder Christian children to provide themselves with blood for Passover matzos. Jewish men, in this belief that involved the subject of circumcision, collected blood to replace that lost through the perversion of their masculinity. (See entry for Jews, Blood Libel.) {James Shapiro, *Shakespeare and the Jews* (1997)}

JEWS FOR JESUS

Jews for Jesus is a group which cites the Bible for believing that it is God Himself who makes one Jewish. It holds that "Jewishness does not depend on what you know or what you don't believe or even on what you practice but on whether you follow the Jewish Messiah." To be Jewish, it holds, is to believe in Jesus. The most Jewish thing a person can do, it is claimed, is to believe in Y'shua as Messiah. Moses wrote about his coming in *Deuteronomy* 18:18. Micah predicted his birth in *Micah* 5:2. Isaiah described how he would die for our sins in *Isaiah 53*. And King David wrote that he would not stay dead in *Psalm* 16:10. "Believing in Jesus makes us all (Jews and Gentiles) more of who God wants us to be and that is what is most important," the San Francisco, California, based group preaches. On the Web: <http://www.jews-for-jesus.org>.

JEWS IN ISRAEL

Orthodoxy is the established religion in Israel. The Conservative and Reform denominations have no formal standing in the Jewish state. For historical reasons primarily, Israelis are either Orthodox or secular. The non-Orthodox movements, which flourished in pre-Holocaust Germany and continue to flourish in America, have failed to win many Israelis. This they attribute to their "second-class" legal status, "their traducers to their essentially alien and diasporic character," noted *The Economist* (21 June 1997). As a result, anyone converted in Israel by a non-Orthodox rabbi is not recognized as Jewish by the state—although, by a legal quirk, conversions done abroad are recognized.

JEWS, BLOOD LIBEL

During the Renaissance, a widely held bizarre notion held that Jewish men menstruated. Thomas Calvert, writing in 1648, reported the claim that "Jews, men as well as females, are punished *curso menstruo sanguinis*, with a very frequent blood flux." The blood-libel, the belief that Jews had to murder Christian children to provide themselves with the blood needed to make matzos for Passover, is bound up with this transgression of gender boundaries: Jewish men murder to collect blood to replace the blood they have lost through the perversion of their masculinity (circumcision). A similarly bizarre notion was that Jewish men were occasionally capable of breastfeeding. (See entry for Jews and Menstruation.) {Steven Orgel, *Impersonations: The Performance of Gender in Shakespeare's England* (1997)}

JEWS, FACTIOUSNESS OF

Three concepts of Jews are expressed in *Jews: The Essence and Character of a People* (1998) by Arthur Hertzberg and Aron Hirt-Manheimer: the Chosen, the Factious, and the Other. The authors do not hold that Jews were chosen by divine whim. Abraham "first chose God" when he broke the idols of his father Terah, a story that appears to be rabbinic lore and is found nowhere in *Genesi*. Rather, the authors say that Jews elected themselves. The authors decry their factiousness, or their proclivity for fighting among themselves. Their otherness, however, includes being "the obdurate outsider," both in their own minds and in the minds of others.

Exodus to Humanism: Jewish Identity Without Religion (1999), edited by David Ibry, points out that genetic research has not detected any special form of DNA in Jews, then cites individuals who have exited Judaism and become humanists.

JEWS, ULTRA-ORTHODOX

In 1997, when a group of Conservative and Reform Jews carried a Torah scroll to Jerusalem's West Wall to mark Shavuot, a holiday commemorating Moses's receiving of the Ten Commandments, ultra-Orthodox Jews were angered because of their belief that men and women must not pray and worship together. The wall is divided into prayer sections for men and women, with the view between the two sides blocked. When the one group of Jews arrived in front of the prayer area, the ultra-Orthodox Jews began shouting "Nazis! Christians! Whores! Goyim!" and hurled stones and bags of excrement at them from balconies of nearby yeshiva, a school of religious studies. {Associated Press, 12 June 1997}

Jeynes, Jennifer R. (20th Century)

Jeynes, the librarian for the South Place Ethical Society, has studied the history of philosophy and science, written on relativism, and reviewed books for *New Humanist*. In 1996 she was elected a member of the Council of Management of the National Secular Society.

JHWH: See entry for God.

JH-NIEUWSBRIEF

A humanistic publication for youths, *JH-Nieuwsbrief* is at P. O. Box 71, 1000 AB Amsterdam, The Netherlands

JIHAD

A jihad in Islam is a holy war, a war ordained by God. The Qur'an teaches that soldiers who die in jihad go immediately to Heaven. {DCL}

JIJNASA (Inquiry)

A Bengali quarterly, *Jijnasa* is at 15 Bankim Chatterjee Street, Calcutta 700 073, India.

Jillette, Penn Fraser (1955—)

Penn and Teller, magicians who have appeared on Broadway as well as throughout the nation, are known for including a touch of blasphemy in their performances. Teller, the quiet one who makes noise only when he plays the piano, is the partner of Penn, who delights in talking while the extraordinary tricks are performed to audiences unable to fathom how the magic is possible. From 1982 to 1984, he played bass in the New Christian Right Wing Band, at the same time sporting his "Team Satan 666" T-shirt. Told that *Time*'s cover featured "10 Top Scientists Talk About Why They Believe in God," Jillette joked, "How come these ten top scientists are all teaching at community colleges?"

Commented Joshua Quittner in *Wired*, "Penn is such an ardent atheist he refuses to go to weddings." In *PC Computing* (December 1991), Penn irked some readers with his freethinking. He described how a computer whiz has succeeded in producing a relatively complete text of the secret Dead Sea Scrolls by using a computer. Jillette concludes from this that the scrolls were authored by "some right-wing Jewish hermits" called Essenes. As for scholars needing forty years to release the contents of those scrolls, Jillette asks, "How long can it take to copy a few jugs full of smelly parchment?" As to who could be entrusted to receive the scrolls, Jillette quotes a UPI story that they *not* be turned over "to anyone who is circumcised." And what is it in the scrolls which is so controversial? Jillette has the answer: The text is mostly "rules for the religiously proper way to urinate in the desert." {CA; E; *Skeptical Inquirer*, Jan-Feb 1997}

Jimenez, Sheila (20th Century)

Jimenez is managing editor of *World*, the journal of the Unitarian Universalist Association.

"JINGLE BELLS": See entry for the composer, James Lord Pierpont.

Joad, C. E. M. (1891—1953)

Joad, a well-known radio personage, was a humanist who from 1941 to 1944 was a lecturer at South Place Ethical Society in London. He was a vocal advocate of scientific humanism. {FUK; TRI}

Joan [Pope]

McCabe relates in his *Rationalist Encyclopedia* the following: "In the Middle Ages, especially in the licentious period from the thirteenth to the seventeenth century, when every kind of sex-story was relished, the legend of a female Pope, who embarrassed the Papal Court by her pregnancy, was very popular. Her 'pontificate' was said to be from 855 to 858, which, we have every reason to believe, was, as stated in all lists of the Popes, the period of the pontificate of Benedict III. The Papal Court was in fact gross and half-barbaric, as is described by the monk-secretary of Charlemagne, Eginhard, in his *Annals*, but it was not until centuries later that the lascivious story of Joan appeared. The real interest of it is that it was extraordinarily popular during just those centuries when the Church is supposed to have kept Europe pious, virtuous, and devoted to the Papacy; so popular that Joan was included in the series of busts of Popes in Siena Cathedral. The statement that from 858 onward the cardinals took measures to verify the sex of a candidate for the Papacy just, like the legend of Joan, be regarded as popular fiction of the erotic later Middle Ages." {RE}

Joan of Arc

A 1996 poll concerning religious beliefs showed that 10% of Americans think that Joan of Arc was Noah's wife. (See entry for Dostoyevsky's Epilepsy.) {*The Economist*, 18 January 1997}

Jodl, Friedrich (1849—1914)

In 1894, with Marianne Hainisch, Jodl founded the Austrian ethical community. He was influenced by Mill and Comte and Spencer in his earlier years and remained agnostic in regard to the existence of higher powers. {RAT; TRI}

Joel, William Martin (Billy) (1929—)

Joel, a popular musician and recording artist once married to Christie Brinkley, has won several Grammy awards and is known for songs such as "Just the Way You Are," "Honesty," "Piano Man," "Streetlife Serenade," "Turnstiles," "The Stranger," "52nd Street," "Glass Houses," "Songs in the Attic," "The Nylon Curtain," "An Innocent Man," and "The Bridge." To a Knight-Ridder newspaper reporter, he said that his "River of Dreams" album (1993) is "the most personal writing I've ever done," that it "begins with a crisis of faith, a search for justice. In the end the guy realizes there's no justice, only faith." But, adding that he is an avowed atheist, Joel said he was not referring to a faith in God "but faith in humanity, judgment, your fellow man, in your ability to do your work, faith in the ground you walk on. Faith that you won't get shot when you walk out the door, that you won't drop dead." He also said that when he becomes depressed, he studies the classics and the serious piano works his father, a German-born survivor of concentration camps, had played and encouraged him to pursue.

Although his grandfather, Phillip Hyman, was a staunch atheist, Joel as a child was baptized at an evangelical church, the Church of Jesus Christ. When one day the preacher unfolded a dollar bill, saying, "This is the flag of the Jews," his family left the church. The best present he ever got at Christmastime, he has said, was Mark Twain's *Mysterious Stranger*, the tale in which Satan, appearing as a morally indifferent but life-enhancing visitor, reveals the hypocrisies and stupidities of a small town. Although freethinkers suspect Joel is an agnostic, not an atheist, they question his wishing people friendly God-bless-you's. {CA; E; OEL}

Jogand-Pages, Gabriel (20th Century)

A freethinker in the Netherlands, Jogand-Pages wrote *The Amusing Bible* (1950). {GS}

Johanson, Donald Carl (1943—)

A physical anthropologist, Johanson since 1981 has been president of the Institute of Human Origins in Berkeley, California. He taught anthropology at Stanford University (1983—1989), at Case Western Reserve University (1978—1981), and Kent State University (1978—1981). With M. A. Edey, he wrote *Lucy: The Beginnings of Humankind* (1982); with James Shreeve, *Lucy's Child: Discovering a Human Ancestor* (1989); and with Kevin O'Farrell, *Journey from the Dawn* (1990). In 1996 he wrote *From Lucy to Language*. Johanson was producer of the films "The First Family" (1981) and "Lucy in Disguise" (1982). In 1983 Johanson was named Humanist Laureate in Council for Secular Humanism's International Academy of Humanism.

John Paul I (Pope) (1912-1978)

An Italian named Albino Luciani, John Paul I died one month after succeeding to the papacy. According to Quentin Crisp, the pope died suspiciously because his tea had been poisoned by someone in the Vatican. A subsequent cover-up, he claimed, was successfully covered up. A 1984 book, *In God's Name* by David Yallop, alleged that the Italian mob killed the pope, noting that the Vatican's tradition of having no autopsy helped hide the fact. Cardinal Aloisio Lorschelder, the pontiff's choice to succeed him, questioned the death, saying in August 1998, "I have to say that a suspicion remains in our hearts."

In 1999 singer Elton John purchased rights to Yallop's best-selling work, saying he intended to make a movie about the mysterious death. (See entry for Quentin Crisp) {New York *Daily News*, 16 February 1999}

John Paul II: See entry for Stanislaw Lem.

John XII (Pope) (c. 937—964)

John XII was Pope from 955 to 964. In the historian Gibbon's words, "We read with some surprise that Pope John XII lived in public adultery with the matrons of Rome; that the Lateran palace was turned into a school for prostitution, and that his rapes of virgins and widows had deterred the female pilgrims from visiting the tomb of St. Peter, lest, in the devout act, they should be violated by his successor." John was mysteriously murdered.

John XXIII (Antipope) (c. 1370—1419)

Baldasarre Cossa, before entering the service of the Church and becoming the antipope John XXIII (1410-1415), was both a homosexual and a pirate. He had been made a cardinal by Boniface IX and was said to have been able, especially in financial matters. Held prisoner in Germany until released by Martin V in 1418, he died cardinal bishop of Tusculum. His reputation was one of unscrupulousness and self-aggrandizement. (See entry for Pirates.) {CE; *Lavender Lists*, Alyson Publications, 1990}

John, Roy (20th Century)

John has been an activist member of the American Humanist Association. {HNS}

John, Christian (20th Century)

John, a leader of German freethinkers, participated in the 1996 Humanist World Congress in Mexico City.

Johnny Rotten: See entry for John Lydon.

JOHNS HOPKINS UNIVERSITY ATHEISTS

Johns Hopkins University Atheists are on the Web: <http://www.secularhumanism.org/cfa/orgs.html>.

Johnson, Alvin Walter (1895—1958)

With Frank H. Yost, Johnson wrote *Separation of Church and State in the United States* (1948). {GS}

Johnson, B. C. (20th Century)

Johnson is author of *The Atheist Debater's Handbook* (1981). He provides many arguments against theism, presented particularly for debaters.

Johnson, Clara (20th Century)

Johnson is a retired chemist, a feminist, an atheist, a writer, and a part-time owner of the Prairie Moon Feminist Bookstore of Arlington Heights, Illinois. For *Freethought Today* (May 1998), she wrote "Pope John—or Joan?"

Johnson, Claude (20th Century)

A freethinker, Johnson wrote *Human Religion* (1917). {GS}

Johnson, David (20th Century)

A Marxist, Johnson wrote poetry that deals centrally with atheist and materialistic themes.

Johnson, Don (20th Century)

Johnson, the Senior Leader of the Society for Ethical Culture in New York City, took early retirement in 1998 and moved to his home in Asheville, North Carolina.

Johnson, Edna Ruth (20th Century)

Johnson is on the editorial board of *The Humanist*. {HNS2}

Johnson, Ellen (1955—)

When Jon Garth Murray mysteriously disappeared in August 1995, along with his mother Madalyn Murray O'Hair and her granddaughter Robin Murray O'Hair, Johnson became temporary president of American Atheist Inc. A homemaker with two children, she assumed "foul play was involved" and took charge of the organization, refusing, however, to believe they were escaping Federal income tax bills and hiding in luxury somewhere.

Johnson, with Ron Barrier, have a talk show, "Atheist Viewpoint," in which they call Christians "sheep" and "idiots," call television evangelists "bigots," and mock religious rituals and tenets. According to journalist Barbara Stewart, Johnson terms agnostics "wimps" and reads Jon Garth Murray's "Task of an Atheist" "as reverently as any Scripture quoting preacher." Stewart in an interview was told that Johnson was reared as an atheist, that her parents never railed against religion, "They just never talked about it." Johnson has supported O'Hair's many lawsuits against the government: to remove prayer from space capsules and Nativity scenes from public property and paid chaplains from the military and "in God We Trust" from coins, to name a few. 'Spike" Tyson, Atheist Inc.'s director, has said of her, "She's an inspiring speaker. We giggle a lot about this absurd religion based on a myth and its ridiculous followers."

Atheists, Johnson states, should come out of the closet, just as homosexuals are doing. "I want to see a movement," she has said. "I want atheists to do great things. I want them to get out and make a joyful noise for atheism." As a result, she revived the *American Atheist Newsletter* and headed American Atheists.

Meanwhile, Arnold Via told a *Time* reporter that "somebody's not telling the truth about things somewhere along the line." Of Johnson, Via added, "I can't imagine anybody inheriting the presidency of an organization because the previous president absconded with $630,000 and not filling out a police report." In 1999, she presided over an American Atheists Inc. meeting in Piscataway, New Jersey, the group's new headquarters. Mail address: Box 5733, Parsippany, NJ 07054-6733. Web: <http://www.atheist.org>. {*The New York Times*, 26 January 1997; *Time*, 10 February 1997}

Johnson, Heidi (20th Century)

Johnson, from Maryland, is on the board of the Freedom From Religion Foundation.

Johnson, James Hervey (1964—1988)

Johnson, an editor of *The Truth Seeker* following Charles Lee Smith, moved the magazine to San Diego, California, where it continued with Ian Hutton as editor. D. M. Bennett founded the magazine in 1873. Among Johnson's books were *Superior Men* (1949) and *Three Is No God* (1952). The generous James H. Johnson Charitable Trust (Box 16160, San Diego, California 92176) contributed large funds to Council for Secular Humanism's Center for Inquiry in Amherst, New York, as well as for the Center for Inquiry—West in Los Angeles, California.

Allegedly a tightwad and misanthrope, according to journalist Mimi Swartz, Johnson had a fortune estimated at from $15 to $20 million. Madalyn Murray O'Hair was unsuccessful in getting him to join her, and in 1983 she angrily wrote him, "You are a dying, defunct, discredited old man who will grow moldy in an unmarked grave." She then sent spies to infiltrate Johnson's organizations, staging a coup at a 1987 Truth Seeker shareholders' meeting and naming herself as chairman of the board. In 1988, he countersued but died the same year. {FUS}

Johnson, Jone (1951-)

Johnson, a Leader of the Northern Virginia Ethical Society (1997-), is active in the American Ethical Union (AEU). She is an ordained Unitarian Universalist minister and a member of the faculty of the Humanist Institute. She was Leader of the Ethical Humanist Society of Chicago (1991-1995) and minister in Michigan of the Berrien Unitarian Universalist Fellowship (1991-1993). Her humanistic inspirations include John Dietrich, Curtis Reese, and John Dewey, but also Anna Garlin Spencer, Elizabeth Cady Stanton, and Jane Addams.

Johnson has designed and maintains a number of websites related to humanism and "radical religion," Including the following:

• American Ethical Union <http://www.acu.org>
• The Transcendentalists <http://www.freereligion.com>
• Electronic Archives of Liberal Religion <http://www.jjnet.com/archives>
• Famous Unitarians and Universalists <http://www.jjnet.com/emerson>
• Notable Women with Liberal Religious Connections <http://www.geocities.com/~bread_n_roses>

Johnson's e-mail: <jj@pbat.com>. She is on the Web at <http://home.earthlink.net/~jone01/>.

Johnson, Matt: See entry for The The.

Johnson, Nic (20th Century)

Johnson is president of Harvard's Chaplaincy board.

Johnson, Oakley C. (20th Century)

Johnson wrote *Robert Owen in the United States* (1970). {FUS}

Johnson, Philip Cortelyou (1906—)

Johnson, a major American architect and historian, is known for his minimalist Glass House in New Canaan, Connecticut, and for Manhattan's Seagram Building, which he built with the collaboration of Miës van der Rohe. One biographer, Franz Shulze, has described Johnson's attraction to the Nazi philosophy (writing in a 1939 *The Examiner*, "Reduced to plain terms, Hitler's 'racism' is a perfectly simple though far-reaching idea. It is the myth of 'we the best,' which we find, more or less fully developed, in all vigorous cultures.") and to his homosexuality (Schulze found that Johnson was attracted to the homoerotic undertones of Nazism, "all those blond boys in black leather. . . . He who had sweated and sighed in the arms of lovers hastily picked on the streets of Weimar Berlin . . . could be the most fastidiously self-abnegating puritan in his glass palace in Connecticut.").

In his eighties, Johnson when interviewed by Hilary Lewis and John O'Connor, stated: "My philosophical outlook dates from a time and a way of thinking that differs from the liberal, acceptable, politically correct line that we all subscribe to today. To me, Plato was the worst—living the good and the true and the beautiful. There's no such thing as the good or the true or the beautiful. I'm a relativist. I'm a nihilist."

At the age of eighty-nine, he constructed near the Glass House an all-concrete, blood-red-and-black "Monsta," a building which looks more like a sculpture than like a house. "It's non-Euclidean . . . intuitive . . . all wiggly. It hasn't any back and front and sides. . . . I don't know how to describe it," he said, "and I'm glad I don't, because then I'd give it a silly name, like deconstructivism." The ceiling is nine feet high in one spot, twenty feet in another. Its lighting is set into the floor, leading him to observe, "If I didn't hate the term, I'd use the word 'spiritual' in this room."

In his nineties, Johnson posed for the cover of *Out*, a monthly gay and lesbian magazine. Previously, only a few knew that for over three decades he had shared his life with David Whitney, who when a 21-year-old college student had asked to see the Glass House and Johnson liked the idea. Whitney (who is not related to the New York family that founded the Whitney Museum of Art) moved in the day after he was graduated in 1963 by the Rhode Island School of Design, where he had studied architecture. With Johnson's help, Whitney got a job at the Museum of Modern Art (MOMA), later worked for Leo Castelli, then ran his own art gallery, and became an assistant to Jasper Johns. A performer in Claes Oldenburg's 1965 Happening, Whitney has said, it was my first nude scene. Everybody wanted to be the star, so I just decided to upstage them all and take my clothes off." The two did not go out socially for their first fifteen years together but, after television star Barbara Walters twitted Johnson in the 1970s, the two began attending functions together. Whitney has become a major figure in the installing of exhibitions as well as in collecting art. Asked in 1996 about their relationship, Johnson told reporters that, although he had some trepidation, "Why not? People know I'm gay, so what am I so scared of?"

Johnson was architect of the Cathedral of Hope, a gay and lesbian congregation in Dallas, Texas, that is part of the Universal Fellowship of Metropolitan Community Churches. "I love cathedrals, even though I'm not religious," he said. "Besides, I don't have too much work. Once you're 90, people don't tie you up for long-term projects."

Two months before his 90th birthday, Johnson, described as the cheerleader who had inspired so many young architects, was given a Gold Medal Award by the American Academy of Arts and Letters. His reaction to receiving the award, previously received by such as Cass Gilbert, Frank Lloyd Wright, and Ludwig Miës van der Rohe, was, "They made the rest of us look like a flock of pygmies." {*The New York Times*, 11 April 1996}

Johnson, R. S. (19th Century)

Johnson, a news agent, worked with John Bates as a secularist in Northampton in the 1860s. They formed an "Earnest and Thorough Radical Association," but found so little support that they "had no more than the twelve apostles." {RSR}

Johnson, Randall (20th Century)

Johnson is treasurer of Atheists and Agnostics of Wisconsin. E-mail: <rjohnson@igc.apc.org>.

Johnson, Reid (20th Century)

Johnson is Dean of the Center for Inquiry Institute (CFII). The institute offers a Certificate of Proficiency to students who have completed courses on Humanistic Studies, Critical Inquiry, or Science and the Paranormal. In 1999 courses were taught at the Center for Inquiry in Amherst, New York; the University of Oregon in Eugene, Oregon; and the University of North Carolina, in Chapel Hill, North Carolina. He signed Humanist Manifesto 2000.

Johnson, Richard Mentor (1781-1850)

Johnson was an American statesman. An Army colonel, he fought with distinction against the British and the Indians. He was a member of Congress from 1817 to 1819 and from 1829 to 1837, a Senator from 1819—1829, and Vice President from 1837 to 1840. Johnson issued a report against the suspension of Sunday mails, and he favored the rights of conscience. Although he never stated his position as regards religion, McCabe noted, "pious folk noted that he was always opposed to them in practical matters, as when they wanted to suppress the Sunday postal service or interfere with religious liberty." {BDF; FUS; JM; RAT; RE}

Johnson, Robert L. (20th Century)

Johnson edits *Think*!, a bimonthly published by the World Union of Deists (Box 47026, St. Petersburg, Florida 33743). The journal examines existence from the perspective of Thomas Paine and other deists.

Johnson, Samuel (1769-1784)

• Dr. Johnson, told by James Boswell that he was from Scotland, replied, "Sir, that, I find, is what a very great many of your countrymen cannot help." At their first meeting, Boswell had noted, "He is very slovenly in his dress and speaks with a most uncouth voice. Yet his great knowledge and strength of expression command vast respect and render him very excellent company. He has great humour and is a worthy man. But his dogmatical roughness of manners is disagreeable."

• When Hannah More told Johnson of "the pleasure and the instruction she had received from his writings," Johnson retorted, "Madam, before you flatter a man so grossly to his face, you should consider whether or not your flattery is worth his having."

• "A woman's preaching is like a dog's walking on his hinder legs," Johnson said in July 1763. "It is not done well, but you are surprized to find it done at all." In his poem "London" is a line, "And here a female Atheist talks you dead."

• At the time of his paralytic stroke in 1783, he told novelist Fanny Burney, that he had "composed in his own mind a Latin prayer to the Almighty, that whatever the sufferings for which he must prepare himself, it would please Him, through the grace and mediation of our blessed Saviour, to spare his intellects, and let them all fall upon his body."

• Shortly before his death Johnson told his friend William Adams about his fear of being considered one who was damned. Asked what he meant, he replied, according to Boswell, passionately and loudly, "Sent to Hell, Sir, and punished everlastingly." When Adams responded that he did not believe in Hell, Johnson brought the conversation to an abrupt end, saying, "I'll have no more on't." W. Jackson Bate's *Samuel Johnson* (1998) speculated as to why: "The truth is that for Johnson there was a far worse alternative to damnation. It could be expressed by a remark John Wesley once made in a letter to his brother Charles (1766): 'If I have any fear, it is not of falling into hell, but of falling into nothing.' " {Derek Jarrett, *The New York Review of Books*, 18 March 1999}

Dr. Johnson, as everyone called him and as he still is known, was the son of a bookseller who became a consummate lexicographer, the author in 1747 of the *Dictionary of the English Language*, upon which he had worked for eight years. He started a moralistic periodical, *The Rambler* (1750), wrote a prose tale of Abyssinia, *Rasselas* (1759), became a social figure in the Literary Club, and was given a crown pension that enabled him to figure as an arbiter of letters. In 1773 he accompanied his biographer JamesBoswell on a tour of Scotland. Although his literary reputation did not exceed that of his conversationalism, Dr. Johnson was a major figure of his age.

Johnson, Samuel (1822—1882)

Influenced by both the heritage of transcendentalism and the ferment of Free Religion in the Unitarian denomination, Johnson preached and lived a radical brand of individualism. A committed antislavery person—the English scholar Samuel Johnson (1709—1784) had a black servant, Francis Barber, for some thirty years, a person who married a white woman and inherited a large part of his fortune—he was requested by the Dorchester, Massachusetts, church "not to introduce any political subject into his next sermon," to which he responded, "I am accustomed to preach upon such subjects as I deem it my duty, and in the performance of that I will not be interfered with." In Lynn, Massachusetts, he persuaded the church to disassociate itself from the Unitarian denomination and become completely independent. In fact, he refused to join the Free Religious Association. Johnson looked beyond the Judeo-Christian tradition to the religions of the world for confirmation, and he was a pioneer in the study of Oriental religions, writing *Oriental Religions and Their Relation to Universal Religion* (1872—1885). Unitarians remember him particularly because with his friend Samuel Longfellow he produced the widely used *Hymns of the Spirit* (1864). {BDF; RAT; U&U}

Johnson, Sonia H. (1936—)

Johnson, a business consultant in California, is a freethinker who has written for *Truth Seeker*. She was excommunicated from the Church of Jesus Christ of Latter-day Saints in 1979 for having supported the proposed Equal Rights Amendment to the United States Constitution. The Feminist Caucus of the American Humanist Association named Johnson in 1982 the first "Humanist Heroine," and she responded that

> We know men's rights are worth laying down one's life for. Patrick Henry is considered an American hero because he said, 'Give me liberty or give me death.' No one doubts that, and the revolution was the result. Women must realize that women's rights are worth the same sacrifice. Human rights are never bestowed. They are wrested.

Johnson has written *From Housewife to Heretic* (1981) and *The Ship That Sailed Into the Living Room: Sex and Intimacy Reconsidered* (1991). (See entry for Steve Benson.) {WWS}

Johnson Jr., Thomas B. (20th Century)

When he signed Humanist Manifesto II, Johnson was a consulting psychologist. {HM2}

Johnson, William Harral (1834—1888)

Johnson was a secularist lecturer in London. He collaborated with W. S. Ross and C. R. Mackay in libeling Bradlaugh. {FUK; VI}

Johnson-Fay, Ellen (20th Century)

Johnson-Fay edited *Unitarian Universalism in the Home* (1982).

Johnston, Harry Hamilton [Sir] (1858—1927)

Johnston was an ethnologist and an administrator. He studied painting and exhibited at the Academy, then studied anatomy and zoology. Finally, he entered the British administration in Africa and rose to be a Special Commissioner. Johnston wrote works on the African peoples. In a symposium, *A Generation of Religious Progress* (1916), Johnston revealed his agnosticism and closed the article, "Let us serve man before we waste our time in genuflections and sacrifices to any force outside this planet." Johnston was an agnostic. {JM; RAT; RE}

Johnston, J. C. (20th Century)

Johnston is active in the Scottish Humanist movement and writes for *Scottish Humanist*.

Johnston, R. P. (20th Century)

Johnston, a freethinker, wrote *Letters to a Missionary* (1918). {GS}

Joja, Athanase (20th Century)

Joja, a Romanian, developed a philosophic outlook that he called socialistic humanism.

Jokinen, Ruth (1920—1996)

Jokinen for forty years ran an innovative private school and worked for civil rights and state-church separation. Her idols were church-state lawyer Leo Pfeffer, Thomas Paine, and Robert Green Ingersoll. When the Council for Secular Humanism purchased the Dresden, NY, Ingersoll birthplace in the mid-1980s, "Dixie" shocked Ingersoll fans by selling her home on Long Island and moving to Penn Yan, three miles from the Ingersoll birthplace. She became president of the Dresden, New York, chapter of the Robert G. Ingersoll Memorial Committee. In 1994 in Rochester, New York, she moderated a panel, "Elizabeth Cady Stanton Meets Susan B. Anthony," at that group's commemoration of Ingersoll's work on behalf of women's equality. "Her love of Ingersoll was legendary," Tim Madigan noted upon her death.

Joly, Robert (20th Century)

A professor of philosophy at the *Université de Mons* (Belgium), Joly is on the Council for Secular Humanism's Committee for the Scientific Examination of Religion. He is author of *Christianisme et philosophie* (1973).

JONAH

"The story of the whale swallowing Jonah, though a whale is large enough to do it, borders greatly on the marvelous," wrote Thomas Paine, "but it would have approached nearer to the idea of a miracle if Jonah had swallowed the whale." And which is more probable, added Paine, "that a man should have swallowed a whale or told a lie?"

Jonas, Carl (1913—1976)

The author of *Jefferson Selleck* (1953), Jonas wrote the present author as follows about humanism:

> What you ask appalls me. A fiction writer hates to say these things directly and prefers to say what he is in the corkscrew fashion of his profession, leaving the task of labeling to the academician. It had never occurred to me to ask myself whether I were a humanist at all. Of course I might be, and then again I might not be.
>
> I am a fallen Middlewestern Baptist which means that I don't go to church but have at least so my wife says a stern New England conscience; that I don't believe in God but am terribly in awe of something; that my theoretical morality is as loose as a goose in the sluice but my actual morality is as confining as a pair of high tight shoes; that the good life consists of doing very seriously more or less what one wants to plus paying up the bills more or less promptly; that people are fundamentally good; that science is a great thing but that perhaps the price we pay for our electric refrigerators, Hotpoint ranges, antihistamine pills, the cathartics is a little high; that ends do not justify means; that love is one of the best things there is but that a lot of people seem to have to get along pretty much without it; that the game's not over until the last ball's played; that we would all probably be better off if we stopped smoking cigarettes but that probably we won't; and that Scotch is considerably inferior to Bourbon. I also believe in the institution of marriage, in the United States Constitution, and in children, although I feel that, interesting as they are, they are considerably less interesting than adults. Oh

> yes, finally I believe that the Fifth Amendment should be changed, and that probably I am a Romantic… and that "Ah Love! could you and I with Him conspire /To grasp this sorry Scheme of Things entire, Would we not shatter it to bits, and then / Re-mould it nearer to the Heart's Desire!"
>
> {WAS, 29 July 1954}

Jones, Allan (20th Century)

Jones is a British activist in the Gay and Lesbian Humanist Association. {*Gay and Lesbian Humanist*, Winter 1998}

Jones, Chris (20th Century)

Jones is editor in Australia of *Victorian Humanist*.

Jones, Chris (1964—)

Jones heads the Miami chapter of Atheists of Florida. "Religion is a disease," he has said. "Plain and simple. Let's treat it like we treat any disease—locate it, learn its weaknesses, and vigorously aim to eradicate it." Christopher is a regional director of the Council for Secular Humanism.

Jones, David E. H. (20th Century)

Dr. Jones, of the University of Newcastle-upon-Tyne and better known by his pen name Daedalus, has written witty columns in the British scientific journal *Nature* since 1964. In one of his serious investigations, Jones concluded that arsenic in the wallpaper of the St. Helena house where Napoleon ended his days might have hastened the exiled French emperor's death. In one of his tongue-in-cheek columns, however, he has suggested that if the soul exists it should be possible to weight it. This could be accomplished, he proposes, by attaching piezoelectric transducers, inertial-navigation accelerometers, and other instruments to a dying person. This should make it possible to measure the direction, velocity, and spin of the soul as it leaves the body, causing the body to recoil slightly. The change in body weight would reveal the soul's mass. "Spin," explains journalist Malcolm W. Browne, "is a quantum property of subnuclear particles; the lepton and quark particles that make up matter have spins designated as one-half, while force-carrier particles like those of light have spins of zero, one, two, or other integer numbers."

Such an irreverent suggestion that "traditional theology is silent on the spin of the soul, though it may predict that the soul of a sinner would depart downward, and might weigh less than that of a righteous believer" predictably provoked a storm of criticism from theologians.

Jones is author of *The Inventions of Daedalus: A Compendium of Plausible Schemes* (1982). (See entry for soul.)

Jones, Ernest (1879—1958)

Dr. Jones, a noted psychoanalyst, was editor of *International Journal of Psychoanalysis* and author of *The Life and Work of Sigmund Freud* (3 volumes, 1953—1957). Invited to express his views on humanism, Jones wrote the present author:

> Are the following remarks of any use?
>
> (1) The exceedingly diverse senses in which the word "Humanism" is used prove conclusively that it is futile to seek for a unitary definition. The word can have no precise meaning if Christian existentialists and communistic humanists among others use it to express their particular ideals;
>
> (2) I fit myself easily into category 7, naturalistic humanism;
>
> (3) The writer who most influenced me in this direction was Thomas Henry Huxley.

A native of Wales, Jones was the only non-Continental and gentile member for many years of Freud's inner circle of followers. Also, Jones did not speak German. Some of his colleagues considered him an outsider and were concerned about his reputation for sexual misconduct with his patients. They also were upset by his having called Otto Rank a "swindling Jew," resulting in Jones's being criticized as illustrating "the arrogance and clumsiness of the British." Although Freud came to oppose and dislike Jones, Jones remained loyal to Freud. After Germany annexed Austria in 1938, Dr. Jones was instrumental in having Freud and his family taken to London, where Freud died the next year. His three-volume *The Life and Work of Sigmund Freud* upon its publication in 1953 was acclaimed as the authoritative work on the subject. Dr. Jones was an honorary associate of the British Rationalist Press Association when Bertrand Russell was its president. {CE; TRI; WAS, 12 May 1956}

Jones, Ernest Charles (1819—1869)

Jones was a barrister and political orator. His father was in the service of the King of Hanover, who became his godfather. A Chartist, he edited *People's Paper, Notes to the People*, and other Chartist periodicals. In 1848 he was tried for making a seditious speech and, during his two years in prison, wrote *Beldagon Church* and other poems. {BDF; RAT}

Jones, Jenkin Lloyd (1843—1918)

Jones led the *Unity* men, a radically modernist element in Midwest Unitarianism of the later 19th century. Stressing an absolutely creedless "ethical basis" as the common element in the churches he wanted to bring together, he was criticized negatively for ridding them of Christology as well as theology. As secretary of the Western Unitarian Conference, and founder of *Unity*, he encountered friction from the Boston Unitarians because of his independent course. In 1882 he reorganized the 4th Unitarian Society in Chicago as All Souls Church, and a decade later he played a central role in the World's Parliament of Religions. From 1905 to 1918 Jones was a director of the Abraham Lincoln Centre in Chicago and in opposition to World War I was a pacifist.

Garry Wills of Northwestern University has described Jenkins as follows: "The Welsh relative who had greater influence on [Frank Lloyd Wright] than anyone but his mother was the liberal Unitarian preacher, Jenkin Lloyd Jones, Wright's 'Uncle Jenk,' who became a surrogate father to him after his own father's defection. Jones was one of [Jane] Addams's principal allies, a regular presence at Hull House." (See entry for Frank Lloyd Wright.) {U&U}

Jones, John Gale (1771—1838)

Jones was a political orator. At the time of the French Revolution he became a leading member of the London Corresponding Society. Arrested at Birmingham for sedition, he obtained a verdict of acquittal. He was subsequently committed to Newgate in 1810 for having impugned the proceedings of the House of Commons, remaining there until liberated by the prorogation of Parliament. In 1811 he was again convicted for "a seditious and blasphemous libel." During the trials of Carlile and his shop men, Jones was a resolute advocate of the rights of free publication. {BDF}

Jones, John Percy (1872—1955)

When Jones, the Tasmanian-born son of Irish Catholics, met Henry George in 1890, he rejected Catholicism and developed an interest in social questions. A founding member of the Socialist Party, Fabian Society, and Labor Party in Victoria, he stood as Labor candidate in 1910 and won the Victorian Legislative Council seat for East Melbourne. In 1925 he became director of the Rationalist Association of Australia. When he supported the conservative

United Australia Party in 1934, he was expelled from the Labor Party. Jones's allegiance to the Rationalist Society of Australia continued until his death. {SWW}

Jones, John S. (20th Century)

Jones is on the editorial committee of New Zealand's *Rationalist and Humanist.* Although Jon Murray visited in 1994 to inquire about moving to New Zealand with his mother, Jones in 1997 claimed that they never applied for residency and he did not know where the O'Hairs, who had mysteriously disappeared, were. {*Time*, 10 February 1997}

Jones, LeRoi (20th Century): See entry for Imamu Amiri Baraka.

Jones, Larry (20th Century)

Jones is the Executive Director in Scotia, New York, of the Capital District Humanist Society. In 1996 he participated in the international conference of ethical humanists in Mexico City.

Jones, Llewellyn (1884—1961)

A critic and Harvard professor, Jones wrote the present author regarding humanism:

> As the first American "critic" to write about Johan Bojer, and the writer of the introduction to his works by Carl Gad, published when his American vogue was at its height, I have no hesitation in saying that at that time he was certainly a naturalistic humanist. I think it was at the end of *The Great Hunger* (1916) that the chief character says, when asked why he performed a chivalrous act, ". . . I sowed the corn in my enemy's field that God might exist." But this God is a humanly created God, and the same character expressly states that he does not believe in any resurrection, nor in Christ, but simply in human responsibility.

In 1954, Jones was program director of the Humanist Fellowship of Boston, a group affiliated with the American Humanist Association. From 1954 to 1962, he was literary editor of *The Humanist.* Jones signed Humanist Manifesto I. {FUS; HM1; HNS; WAS, 20 Aug 1956}

Jones, Lloyd (1811—1886)

Jones, the son of Catholic parents in County Cork, Ireland, came to Manchester in 1827 and joined the followers of Robert Owen. As "a social missionary," he had numerous debates with ministers, notably one in 1839 on "The Influence of Christianity" with J. Barker, then a Methodist. Jones contributed to a number of cooperative and trades-union publications. Upon his death, it was found he had written a *Life of Robert Owen.* {BDF; FUK; TRI}

Jones, Margaretha (20th Century)

An American ethical humanist, Jones spoke on the subject of "UNICEF and the Rights of Children" at the 1996 Humanist World Congress held in Mexico City. She is the IHEU's representative to UNICEF. Her e-mail: <aeugrowth@aol.com>.

Jones, Peter (20th Century)

Jones, in Scotland, is a corresponding secretary of The Hume Society, a group engaged in scholarly activity concerning David Hume.

Jones, Philip F. (1939—)

Jones was president of the Humanist Association of Canada (HAC) from 1989 to 1993, and he was the first president of the Coalition for Secular Humanist and Freethought (CSHAFT), serving from 1992 to 1994. Since 1962, he has been a member of the British Rationalist Press Association, and he has been a life member of the British Humanist Association since 1970. In 1994 at the Toronto conference of the Coalition for Secular Humanism, Atheism, and Freethought (CSHAFT), of which he is a former president, Jones spoke on "What Is the Good Life? A Humanist Perspective." Jones is a Secular Humanist Mentor of the Council for Secular Humanism.

Jones, Robert Edwards (Born 1927)

When he signed Humanist Manifesto II, Jones was executive director of the Joint Washington Office for Social Concern. An ordained Unitarian minister, Jones in 1960 was campaign press secretary to Governor Volpe of Massachusetts.

He has represented the Ethical Union, the American Humanist Association, and the Unitarian Universalist Association. In 1954, he was the Democratic Party's nominee for the Massachusetts House of Representatives, and in 1952 he was his party's delegate to the Democratic Convention. {HM2}

Jones, S. H. (20th Century)

Jones in 1936 published *Humanism*, explaining his Unitarian views concerning religious humanism.

Jones, Stanley (20th Century)

Jones, a freethinker, wrote *Genesis and Science* (c. 1910). {GS}

Jones, Tova (20th Century)

Jones is secretary of the Birmingham Humanist Group in England.

Jones, W. H. (19th Century)

With F. G. Jannaway, Jones wrote the *Immortal Soul Debate* (1895). {GS}

Jones, William (1819—1893)

Jones was an Australian freethinker, sculptor, and orator. He was president of the Central Cumberland Secular Society in 1886, one of the earliest of Sydney's groups. He lectured on theology and the Bible, becoming the only person in Australia to be convicted of blasphemy. In 1871 he was sentenced to two years in jail and a fine of £100 for lecturing against the Bible, but the fine was paid by public subscription and he was released on a two-year good-behavior bond. {RSR; SWW}

Jones, (William) Bill T(ass) (1952—)

Jones, the African American who is director of the Bill T. Jones / Arnie Zane Dance Company, met Zane at the State University of New York when nineteen and the two made a success of their venture. However, both were diagnosed as being HIV-positive in 1985, and Zane died from AIDS in 1988. Jones has continued to perform and to include social messages in his ballets. Anna Kisselgoff of The New York Times has described Jones as being "anything but your conventional social protest choreographer, and [is] a hot ticket on the international dance scene." Over five thousand attended a world première of his "Still/Here" in Lyons, France, September 1994.

"I have to be very clear about what I do with the time I have left—build my art," he has stated, adding that at this important time in human history our attitudes about death and sex are being brought to a head. "So I'd like to be recognized as being a major voice in the things Arnie and I stood for. . . . In 20 or 30 years, we'll be out from the Middle Ages, the Inquisition. This is a benign universe that exists on a level so far beyond the screams and cries of the Holocaust, my mother's tears, beyond lesions and sores and gasping for air in the last moments of life. I think if we look back, it'll be understood that we know what it feels for me to right now be saying, I am HIV positive, and I am all right. I am a homosexual man, and I have been promiscuous, and that too is all right."

As for the future, and knowing in 1994 that his physical condition was deteriorating, Jones has accepted his demise with a secular humanist's outlook (although he has not specifically addressed theism or non-theism):

> I will never grow old. My hands will never be discolored with the spots of age. I will never have varicose veins. My balls will never become pendulous, hanging down as old men's balls do. My penis will never be shriveled. My legs will never be spindly. My belly, never big and heavy. My shoulders never stooped, rounded, like my mother's shoulders are. . . . My face will never wrinkle. . . . My teeth will never yellow.

And how, he is asked by Henry Louis Gates Jr., does he envision his last night on earth? Jones hopes his affairs will be in order, that the dance foundation will be out of debt, that Bjorn Amelon (who, after Zane's death and Jones's five years with Arthur Aviles, became his present lover) will be healthy, that he will have a chance to send notes to all his friends, "and then I'd listen to music. On that day, it would be Nina Simone. It would be a long album. I'd hear the sound of the leaves outside. And I'd take pills and go to sleep. . . . I'd be by myself. I'd have to be by myself." (See Henry Louis Gates Jr., "The Body Politic," *The New Yorker*, 28 November 1994; and Larry Kaplan, "Bill T. Jones On Top," *Poz*, July 1994.)

Jones, William R(onald) (20th Century)

Jones, a lecturer on religious humanism, was named 1992 Humanist Pioneer by the American Humanist Association. An African American, once a fundamentalist, he is founder and director of the black studies program at Florida State University. Dr. Jones, who received his Master of Divinity degree at Harvard, edited *Black Theology*, a series of essays. He has held visiting professorships at Princeton and at Union Theological Seminary as well as at Brown and Howard. In South Africa, he has completed extensive fieldwork in conflict resolution. He is a contributing editor of *Religious Humanism*, a quarterly of the Fellowship for Religious Humanists.

Jones, Willie [Governor] (18th Century)

Jones, a post-Revolutionary politician, was a freethinker who stipulated in his will that no one was to insult his body by mumbling religious words over it. (See entry for North Carolina Freethinkers.)

Jonson, Ben (1572—1637)

Jonson, the English dramatist and poet who wrote *Volpone* (1606) and *The Alchemist* (1610) killed Gabriel Spencer, a well-known actor, in a duel. He escaped execution by claiming "right of the clergy," a term signifying that he could read and write. Jonson, a Christian, was buried in Westminster where his epitaph reads *O rare Ben Jonson*, evidently not a wry observation that to save space he had been buried standing up. {PA; TYD}

Jordan, David Starr (1851—1931)

A zoologist and President of the World Peace Congress in 1915, Jordan was a Unitarian Universalist, more specifically a non-Christian theist. "The creeds have no permanence in human history," he wrote in his *Stability of Truth*. {JM; RAT; RE; UU}

Jordan, Joseph Fletcher (1863—1929)

Although a presiding elder in the Methodist Church, Jordan was troubled by the doctrine of "hell and endless punishment." As a result and after hearing a sermon by Quillen H. Shinn, he converted to Universalism. One of the important early African American Universalist leaders, he was principal of the Suffolk Normal Training School in Virginia which had been started by Joseph H. Jordan (no relation). The school was supported until 1939 by the Universalist General Convention and the General Sunday School Convention. Although the school flourished, educating as many as three hundred students each year, membership at the church dwindled, and it closed in the 1930s. He wrote *The Distance Traveled* (1984?). {U; U&U}

Jordan, Joseph H. (1842—1901)

The first black to be ordained in the Universalist ministry, Jordan delivered in 1893 an address to the Universalist General Convention in Washington, DC, to ask support "for a mission to the Negroes in the South." {U&U}

Jordan, Stuart (20th Century)

Jordan is a past president and current board member of the Washington Area Secular Humanists. He is a senior staff scientist at the National Aeronautics and Space Administration Goddard Space Flight Center. {"E. O. Wilson's Consilience," *Free Inquiry*, Fall 1998).

Jordan, Terry G. (20th Century)

Jordan wrote "A Religious Geography of the Hill Country Germans of Texas," *Ethnicity on the Great Plains* (1980). He is a professor of geography at the University of Texas. {*Freethought History #15*, 1995}

Joseph II [Emperor] (1741—1790)

Joseph II was Emperor of Germany, the son of Francis I and Maria Theresa. In 1764 he was elected king of the Romans, and in the following year succeeded to the throne of Germany. He wrought many reforms, suppressed the Jesuits in 1773, traveled in France as Count Falkenstein, saw d'Alembert, but did not visit Voltaire. He abolished serfdom, allowed liberty of conscience, suppressed several convents, regulated others, abridged the power of the pope and the clergy, and mitigated the condition of the Jews.

Carlyle said, "A mighty reformer he had been, the greatest of his day. Austria gazed on him, its admiration not unmixed with terror. He rushed incessantly about, hardy as a Charles Twelfth; slept on his bearskin on the floor of any inn or hut;—flew at the throat of every absurdity, however broad and based or dangerously armed. 'Disappear I say.' A most prompt, severe, and yet beneficent and charitable kind of man. Immensely ambitious, that must be said withal. A great admirer of Friedrich [unidentified person, not Nietzsche]; bent to imitate him with profit. 'Very clever indeed,' says Friedrich, 'but has the fault' (a terribly grave one!) of generally taking the second step without having taken the first." {BDF}

Joseph, M. C. (20th Century)

In Iranjalakuda, India, Joseph became editor of *Yukthivadi* in 1929. {FUK}

Joseph, Newton (20th Century)

Joseph, a secular humanist, is a counselor on the staff of the non-profit San Fernando Valley Counseling Center in Northridge, California. He has written for *Freethought Perspective* (April 1999 and June 1999) and *Secular Nation* (April-June 1999).

Josephson, Matthew (1899—1977)

Josephson, a freethinker, wrote *Edison, A Biography* (1959) and *The Robber Barrons* (republished, 1995). {FS}

Josephus, Flavius (37—95?)

Josephus, a soldier who took part in the war between the Romans and the Jews, wrote several works of history. These include *The Jewish War*, *Antiguities of the Jews*, and *Against Aprion*, the latter a defense of the Jews. As Edmund Wilson and others have pointed out, Josephus was an apologist for the Romans and a cultural convert to Greco-Roman views.

Josephy, Walter (20th Century)

Josephy, an Ottawa humanist, is on the editorial committee of *Humanist in Canada*.

Joshi, Kumudben (20th Century)

Joshi was at the inauguration in 1990 of the Golden Jubilee of the Atheist Centre.

Joshi, Tarkateerth Lakshman Sastri (Deceased)

Joshi was known for his encyclopedic sweep of knowledge in Western and Eastern philosophy. He was editor of the Marathi language encyclopedia, *Vishwa Kosh*.

Joshua (Born 1895)

Joshua was an Indian humanist poet, one for whom a foundation has been named and which will present literary awards to writers in his humanist tradition.

The Telegu foundation encourages literature which "inspires humans to fix their sights on the heights of humanism and grow in moral stature and which helps them to master inner strength to march ahead in hope and which translates their dreams into reality. We need poets who rise above caste, religion, and politics and sing of truths about human welfare and Universal truth, and the Universal Human family. The poet's words should kindle hope in the minds of people, torn asunder by fear and violence." {*International Humanist News*, December 1993}

Jospin, Lionel [Prime Minister] (1937—)

Jospin, France's Education Minister from 1991 to 1992, was born into a Protestant family but has described himself as an atheist. His wife is Sylviane Agacinski, a professor of philosophy in Paris.

Jospin, a graduate of the Institute of Political Studies and National School of Administration in Paris, joined the Socialist Party when François Mitterrand revived it in 1971. The chairman of the Socialist Party (1981—1987), Jospin was his party's candidate for the French Presidency in 1995. He lost to Jacques Chirac but won a majority (52%) of the votes cast by 18- to 24-year-olds.
He became Prime Minister in 1997. {CA; E; *The Economist*, 18 April 1998}

Jouffroy, Theodore Simon (1796—1842)

Jouffroy, a French philosopher, followed Cousin, his master, in philosophy. After the 1830 Revolution, Jouffroy was appointed professor at the *École Normale*. He was a member of the Eclectic School and a member of the Academy of Moral and Political Science and the Educational Council. He wrote *Mélanges Philosophiques*. {RAT}

JOURNAL FOR THE CRITICAL STUDY OF RELIGION, ETHICS, AND SOCIETY

A bi-annual, the *Journal for the Critical Study of Religion, Ethics, and Society* is published by Prometheus Books, 59 John Glenn Drive, Amherst, New York 14228.

JOURNAL OF HUMANISM AND ETHICAL RELIGION

The *Journal of Humanism and Ethical Religion* is at 2 West 64th Street, New York, NY 10023.

JOURNAL OF RATIONAL RECOVERY

As an alternative to Alcoholics Anonymous publications, Jack Trimpey edits the *Journal of Rational Recovery*, Box 800, Lotus, California 95651.

JOURNALISM

• The difference between journalism and literature is that journalism is unreadable and literature is unread.

—Oscar Wilde

Jouy, Victor Joseph Etienne de (1764—1846)

Jouy was a French author who served as a soldier in India and afterwards in wars of the Republic. A disciple of Voltaire, to whom he erected a temple, Jouy was a prolific writer whose plays were much esteemed in his day. {BDF}

Jowett, Benjamin (1817—1892)

Jowett was Regius Professor of Greek at Oxford, Master of Balliol, and Vice-Chancellor of the University (1882—1886). He never rejected his clerical Orders, but he was important not only as one of the leading scholars of his time but also as a liberalizing influence in the University and the Church. He rejected not only the Christian creed but also the idea of a personal God. "The priests will always be too many for you," he observed. Furthermore, he was skeptical about immortality. In the *Life and Letters*, Jowett says that "Voltaire has done more good than all the Fathers of the Church put together" and "whether we shall recognize others in another life we cannot tell." To Sir R. Morier in a letter written a year before his death, Jowett wrote, "I fear that we are both rather tending to some degree of Agnosticism." {RAT; RE; TYD}

Joyce, James (Augustine) (Aloysius) (1882—1941)

According to David Tribe, Joyce was an outright freethinker. The famed Dublin-born novelist was educated at the Jesuit schools Clongowes Wood College and Belvedere College. In 1901 he wrote a letter of admiration in Dano-Norwegian to Ibsen, the philosophic naturalist and freethinker, and other early influences were Dante, George Moore, and Yeats. Disliking the narrowness and bigotry of Ireland ("that scullery maid of Christendom") and Irish Catholicism, Joyce went to Paris for a year in 1902, living in poverty and writing verse. Upon his mother's death, he returned to Dublin, stayed briefly, then left Ireland with Nora Barnacle, the woman with whom he spent the rest of his life and who bore him a son and a daughter. *Dubliners* (1941), *A Portrait of the Artist as a Young Man* (1916), and *Ulysses* (1914-1921) brought him much fame, although *Ulysses* was delayed by obscenity charges and did not appear in the United States until 1933. The novel, however, was received as a work of genius by writers as varied as T. S. Eliot, Hemingway, and Arnold Bennett. Less admiring were Claudel, Virginia Woolf, and Gertrude Stein. Often quoted is Joyce's reference to the Holy Ghost, Jesus's farewell to his Apostles on Mount Olivet:

> I'm the queerest young fellow that ever you heard.
> My mother's a Jew, my father's a bird. . . .
>
> What's bred in the bone cannot fail me to fly,
> And Olivet's breezy. . . . Goodbye, now, goodbye.

The photographer Andres Serrano tells the story that Joyce, sitting for a painter who said he wanted to capture Joyce's soul, was told, "Forget the soul. Just get the tie right."

After 1922, Joyce worked on *Finnegans Wake* (1939). He suffered greatly from eye trouble, and a severe attack of glaucoma in 1917 led to years of pain and several operations. In his later years, he was much troubled by his daughter's mental illness. Joyce died in Zürich in 1941. Critics often call Thomas Mann, Marcel Proust, and Joyce the major novelists of the twentieth century. Gossips accused him of being a misanthrope, a cocaine addict, a person who tested his failing eyesight by counting the number of lights on the Place de la Concorde when he took his evening walks.

Joyce is buried at the Fluntern Cemetery in Zurich, Switzerland. The gravestone is a flat marble slab inscribed only with name and vital dates in block lettering. Seated nearby is a statue of Joyce. {CE; OEL; TYD}

Joyner, Russell (20th Century)

Joyner has been on the editorial board of *The Humanist.*

Juarez, Benito Pablo [President] (1806—1872)

A full-blooded Indian, Juarez became President of the Republic of Mexico from 1858 to 1862 and again from 1867 to 1872. He previously had been Governor of Oaxaca, then Minister of Justice. A national hero, he fought a French attempt to establish a Mexican empire (1864—1867) under Maximilian. An atheist admired by Joseph McCabe, Juarez curtailed the clergy's privileges and checked their corruption. Upon being elected President, he said, "To finish the fratricidal war encouraged by the clergy, it is necessary to deprive them of the wherewithal for their resistance, to disarm them completely, and to attain this result is a real necessity to carry out the reform, separating the church from the state, suppressing convents, extinguishing all kinds of religious congregations, closing the novitiates, nationalizing the property of the clergy, allowing freedom of choice to the worshipper to support a cult and establishing freedom of thought."

The Reform Laws he instituted, which were the key to the separation of church and state, have been influential up to the 1990s. {CE; JM; RAT; RE}

JUCK-SHILLUCK

Juck-Shilluck, one of many African gods, is considered Creator of the World. {LEE}

Judah, Aaron (20th Century)

Judah, in *The Freethinker* (July 1996), suggests that Judaism originally was henotheistic but became monotheistic because of St. Paul's writings. "St. Paul should be in *The Guiness Book of Records*," he explains, "as the biggest cuckoo in the transcendental element for having laid his monotheistic egg in our henotheistic nest."

Judah, Samuel Benjamin Helbert (19th Century)

Judah, a freethinker, wrote *The Mystical Craft* (1844). {GS}

JUDAISM

Judaism, according to Samuel S. Cohon of the Hebrew Union College in Cincinnati, Ohio, was a term coined by Greek-speaking Jews "to designate their religious way of life in contrast with that of their neighbors, known as Hellenism." The religion of Israel, a reference to pre-exilic developments, and Judaism, a reference to post-exilic developments, is artificial. The terms describe successive stages of the same religious process. "Judaism represents," he continues, "the religious experience of the Jewish people, that is their consciousness of the sacred as embodied in the Torah both Written and Oral, or Scripture and Tradition. The stages of its growth correspond to the stages of Jewish political, cultural, and social evolution. Branching out of Semitic paganism, the religion of the early tribes of Israel was shaped by Moses at Sinai and Kadesh into the exclusive worship of Yahweh with a corresponding body of ritual and social legislation to meet the needs of the desert surroundings. In the agricultural economy of Canaan the nomadic religion acquired an elaborate sacrificial cult, festivals, sanctuaries, an organized priesthood, codes of laws, etc. It was greatly enriched by the institution of kingship and by the unique body of prophets, who advanced the monolatrous idea of Yahweh to the pure conception of ethical monotheism. The prophetic criticism of the cult and the subordination of ritual to righteousness affected priestly practice and resulted in the Deuteronomic Reformation, which centralized religious worship in Jerusalem and in the Zakodite priesthood."

In common usage, Judaism is the religion developed among the ancient Hebrews, one which holds that a transcendent God has revealed Himself to Abraham, Moses, and the Hebrew prophets, choosing them as "the Chosen People." One whose religion is Judaism is termed a Jew. Although some call themselves "atheistic Jews" or "non-Jewish Jews," the combination of terms is lexicographically illogical, as would be the analogous combinations of "theistic agnostic" or "Hindu Christian." However, writer Nat Henthoff and biologist Sheldon F. Gottlieb make a case for calling themselves atheists as well as Jews.

Ultra-Orthodox rabbis in Israel have been critical of a Steven Spielberg movie, "Jurassic Park," about dinosaurs which are brought back to life and which go wild. In 1993, Rabbi Zvi Gafner of the Agudath Israel Party, said, "It is inconceivable that we should give our seal of approval to a product that is imbuing Orthodox children with heresy. The dinosaur is presented in encyclopedias as an animal that is millions of years old, despite the fact that the world was created only 5,753 years ago."

In his *Selected Papers*, Bertrand Russell lists three sources of Western mentality: (1) Greek culture; e.g., Plato; (2) Jewish religion and ethics; e.g., the Old Testament; and (3) modern industrialism; e.g., Galileo, which itself is an outcome of modern science. "From the Jews we derive fanatical belief, which its friends call 'faith'; moral fervor, with the conception of sin; religious intolerance; and some part of our nationalism." (See entry for Jew. Also, see entry for Reconstructionism, which is different from Orthodox, Reform, and Conservative Judaism.) {CE; ER}

Judd, Ernest E. (1860?—1930?)

Judd was an early Australian freethinker, bookseller, and leader of the Socialist Labor Party. An anti-war activist and campaigner for the release of the "IWW Twelve" at the end of 1921, Judd regularly advertised freethought and birth control literature in *Liberator*, the secularist newspaper. {SWW}

Judkins, Larry (20th Century)

Judkins, a columnist in California for the *Sacramento Valley Mirror*, is a member of the Freedom From Religion Foundation and has written for *Freethought Today*.

Judkins, Makeda (20th Century)

Judkins is President of the National Association in Service to Mentally Stressed African American Families (NASMAF). She is an Advisory Board Member of African Americans for Humanism.

JUGGERNAUT

In Hinduism, a juggernaut is a deity, a deliverer from sin. His image is carried on a large wagon in an annual procession in India. According to legend, the wagon crushed worshippers who threw themselves under it. In common usage, a juggernaut is a force, an idea, or a system of beliefs that can overcome opposition—especially if it does so ruthlessly. {DCL; RE}

Julianus, Flavius Claudius [Emperor] (331?—363)

Julian the Apostate, Roman emperor from 361 to 363 and nephew of Constantine I, succeeded Constantius II, who had named him as his successor. In the massacre of his family by the sons of Constantine, he escaped. At an early age, he was entrusted to Christian monks but soon began contrasting the Greek view of life and its intellectual activities with the gloomy piety and the theological hairsplitting of his teachers. Sometime in the course of his studies, Julian abandoned Christianity for an eclectic paganism, writing "Refutation of the Christian Religion." He once declared, "No wild beasts are as hostile to men as Christian sects in general are to one another." The work, which was acutely critical of the absurd stories in the Old Testament and also of the life of Christ, was destroyed by the efforts of Theodosius II. Julian was unsuccessful in restoring paganism by issuing an edict of religious toleration. During a campaign against the Persians, he was killed in a skirmish. McCabe, however, denies any truth to the legend that when he fell in battle he cried, "Thou has conquered, Galilaean." This, states McCabe, is sheer Christian fabrication. The death of Julianus, wrote Wheeler, "was followed by the triumph of Christianity and the long night of the dark ages." {BDF; FO; JM}

Jung, Carl Gustav (1875—1961)

Jung, the famed Swiss psychiatrist, wrote about the psychology of religion in *Modern Man in Search of a Soul* (1933), and he wrote *Answer to Job* (1966). In 1954, he was asked to respond to the present author's categorization of seven humanisms. A. Jaffe, his secretary, replying that Prof. Jung had just left for his vacation, wrote the present author as follows:

> I should say that he most nearly belongs to the group 7 (naturalistic humanism). But in order to make your own judgment, read two of his works: *Psychology and Religion* and his work on Synchronicity (which will appear one of these days in the Pantheon Edition, Bollingen Series)."

However, Paul Edwards in *Immortality* states that Jung, along with Paul Tillich and Timothy Leary, admired the *Tibetan Book of the Dead*, a favorite book of those believing in reincarnation, which is opposed to naturalistic humanism. Jung also regarded unfavorably the rationalist tradition of scientific thought. Further, Jung was unafraid to speak of the soul and the spiritual.

In a 1959 letter to Ruth Topping, a Chicago social worker, Jung wrote, ". . . spiritual background has gone astray. Our Christian doctrine has lost its grip to an appalling extent, chiefly because people don't understand it any more. Thus one of the most important instinctual activities of our mind has lost its object. As these views deal with the world as a whole, they create also a wholeness of the individual, so much so, that for instance a primitive tribe loses its vitality, when it is deprived of its specific religious outlook. People are no more rooted in their world and lose their orientation. They just drift. That is very much our condition, too. The need for a meaning of their lives remains unanswered, because the rational, biological goals are unable to express the irrational wholeness of human life. Thus life loses its meaning. That is the problem of the 'religious outlook' in a nutshell. The problem itself cannot be settled by a few slogans. It demands concentrated attention, much mental work and, above all, patience, the rarest thing in our restless and crazy time." Gordon Stein, also, has written in *The American Rationalist* (October 1994) that Jung was no freethinker. Quite the opposite, in fact, for Freud's break with Jung was partly because of Jung's occultism and views concerning organized religion. Also, Jung is said to have been anti-Semitic and pro-Nazi up to the time the Nazis were defeated, after which he modified his stand. Freud further disapproved of Jung's having made a pass at Ms. Spielrein, one of his patients, after which she went to Freud for treatment.

A clinical psychologist, Richard Noll, wrote *The Jung Cult: Origins of a Charismatic Movement* (1994), in which he accused Jung of having falsified dates in relation to the theory of the collective unconscious. That theory holds that people share images, buried deep in their unconscious, which influence their thought and behavior. Jung cited the case known as the Solar Phallus Man, who had been a patient at the Burghölzli Mental Hospital in Zurich and claimed to have seen a vision of the sun with a phallus. Jung contended that the image came from the ancient Hellenic mystery cult of Mithras, a pagan god associated with sun worship. However, argues Noll, the person was the patient of Honegger, Jung's assistant. After Honegger committed suicide in 1911, Jung gradually took credit for the case. Noll holds that the Solar Phallus Man may have been a regurgitating of what popular books were reporting at the time, books about mythology, Mithras, paganism, and the occult. Jung, according to Noll, changed the dates of publication to show that the man could not have read such works. Noll further charges that Jung knowingly lied about the case as well as included anti-Semitic writings that formed the basis of Nazi ideology. Although Jung was admittedly never a Nazi, Noll claims there was a secret Jewish quota for the Analytical Psychology Club, an early Jungian association founded in 1916 in Zurich by Jung's followers. Jung is buried in the family plot of the Village Cemetery, Küsnacht, Switzerland. On the gravestone is an epitaph:

> First, the terrestrial man of the earth
> Second, the celestial man of heaven
> Called or not called.
> God is present

{CE; ER; TRI; WAS, 5 August 1954}

Junghuhn, Franz Wilhelm (1812—1864)

Junghuhn, son of a Prussian barber and surgeon, studied at Halle and Berlin, distinguishing himself by his love for botany and geology. In a duel with another student, he killed him and was sentenced to imprisonment at Ehrenbritster for twenty years. There he simulated madness, was removed to the asylum at Coblentz, and escaped to Algiers. In 1834 he joined the Dutch Army in the Malay Archipelago, traveling through the island of Java and making a botanical and geological survey. In 1854, he published his *Licht en Schaduwbulden uit de binnenlanden van Java* (Light and Shadow Pictures from the Interior of Java), which contains his ideas of God, religion, and science, together with sketches of nature and of the manners of the inhabitants. The pious were indignant, but freethinkers established *De Dageraad* (The Daybreak) as the organ of the Dutch Freethinkers Union. Junghuhn died in Java. {BDF}

JUPITER

Jupiter, the fifth planet from the sun, has four satellites which Galileo in 1610 discovered: Callisto, Ganymede, Europa, and Amalthea. Space probes starting in 1973 led in 1997 to photographs from the *Galileo* spacecraft of Europa, showing icy domes and ridges. Astronomers speculated that because of the ice Europa might actually be able to support some form of life. Arthur C. Clarke, whose *3001* was published before the photographic findings, had already anticipated that life existed on various planets. He also fictionalized that in 3001 a city of 41,000, Anubis City near Io's South Pole, had people "engaged in terraforming and scientific research."

JUSTICE

Bertrand Russell, in *Sceptical Essays* (1928), wrote that in a modern democratic society justice must prevail and justice must be the governing principle. "Such things as food, houses, and clothes are necessaries of life, about the need of which there is not much controversy or much difference between one man and another. . . . But [justice] would not mean equality in a community where there was a hierarchy of classes, recognized and accepted by inferiors as well as superiors. Even in modern England, a large majority of wage earners would be shocked if it were suggested that the King should have no more pomp than they have. I should therefore define justice as the arrangement producing the least envy. This would mean equality in a community free from superstition, but not in one which firmly believed in social inequality."

In *The Art of Philosophizing* (1968), Russell wrote: "The only way in which a society can live for any length of time without violent strife is by establishing social justice. Justice between classes is difficult where there is a class that believes itself to have a right to more than a proportionate share of power or wealth. Justice between nations is only possible through the power of neutrals, because each nation believes in its own superior excellent. Justice between creeds is even more difficult, since each creed is convinced that it has a monopoly of the truth of the most important of all subjects." (See Alan Ryan's "Politics of Dignity," *The New York Review of Books*, 11 July 1996, in which he discusses John Rawls's *Theory of Justice*, Robert Nozick's *Anarchy, State, and Utopia*, F. A. Hayek's *The Mirage of Social Justice*, and Avishai Margalit's *The Decent Society*.) {Lee Eisler, *The Quotable Bertrand Russell*}

JUSTICE BY GRACE, THROUGH FAITH

Justification by grace, in Christianity, is the belief that a person can achieve salvation only through faith and reliance on God's grace, not through good deeds. Paul wrote, "By grace are ye saved through faith; and that not of yourselves: it is the gift of God." By being friendly with God one is entitled to life with God in Heaven after death. During the Reformation, Luther's slogans were "Grace Alone" and "Faith Alone," which he urged against the common teaching of the Catholics, that people's good works, as well as their faith, helped to save them. Since the time of Luther, Protestants and Catholics have had few differences on the subject. {DCL}

Justice, Jeffrey A. (20th Century)

Justice is a commentator about Biblical inconsistencies. He has written for *The Skeptical Review*.

K. EXECUTIVE CLUB

In Uganda, the humanists are led by M. J. Collins's K. Executive Club, POB 3092, Kampala, Uganda. (See entry for Uganda, Humanists In.) {FD}

KA: See entry for Resurrection.

KADER KRINGLOOP KRANT

A Dutch publication, *Kader Kringloop Krant* is at Postbus 71, 1000 AB, The Netherlands.

Kadison, Alexander (20th Century)

A freethinker, Kadison wrote *Through Agnostic Spectacles* (1919). {GS; RAT}

Kaech, Jean (20th Century)

In Switzerland, Kaech coordinates a number of groups known as the World Union of Freethinkers (Postfach 6207, 3001 Bern, Switzerland). {FD}

Kafka, Dusan J. (20th Century)

The Rev. Dr. Dusan J. Kafka heads *Unitaria*, which, under Norbert Capek's leadership was a center of anti-Nazi resistance in Czechoslovakia. The small congregation of Unitarians had overpowering problems during rule by the Communists but is currently active. In 1923, the Liberal Fellowship became the Religious Society of Czechoslovakian Unitarians. Norbert Capek, at President Jan Masaryk's bidding, was instrumental in founding the church. The present group will change its name inasmuch as the Czechs and Slovaks have split Czechoslovakia into two parts.

Kafka, Franz (1883—1924)

Kafka, the Prague-born novelist who wrote in German, is one of the most influential of 20th century writers. Although he came from a middle-class Jewish family from Bohemia, he had a quadruple alienation, according to Martin Seymour-Smith:

(a) from his Jewishness;
(b) his Czech identity, as a German speaker);
(c) his family; and
(d) from his own potentiality to lead a full life.

As Seymour-Smith explains, Kafka and his near contemporary Rainer Maria Rilke were "torn between art (which reveals life) and life (which rejects the solitariness, selfishness, lovelessness of the dedicated artistic condition)." Unlike Rilke, however, Kafka could not find full faith in his writing and his life, except for a few moments, was even more wretched and guilt-ridden. Kafka's characters are functional but he is

> tragically uninterested in character: all are mysteriously in the right, trying him for the crime of human insufficiency, for dedication to inadequate words. Joseph K in *Der Prozess* (1925), *The Trial*, is being tried for nothing he can specify but he feels guilty and is executed. Karl Rossmann in *Amerika* (1927), *America*, is punished for *allowing himself to be seduced*; and despite the relatively comic surface of the book, it remained tragically unfinished because Kafka wanted to end it on a note of reconciliation and could not do it. As for the castle in the again unfinished novel of that name, Kafka's greatest: ultimately this, too, is reconciliation: the possibility of being a writer *and* being a full human being, who has a family and a human function.

The opening sentence of *The Trial* is exemplary of Kafka's portrayal of enigmatic reality:

> Someone must have slandered Joseph K., because one morning, without his having done anything wrong, he was arrested.

Das Schloss (1926, *The Castle*) was unfinished but contains the curious plot in which it is believed someone might be listening at the other end of a telephone line (God?) but no one responds (no God?). "Kafkaesque," as a result, has come to describe surreal distortion and a sense of impending danger.

Kafka's world is both dreamlike and real, as shown in *The Metamorphosis*, in which the character of Gregor Samsa, when the story is cross-read, lends himself to a kind of floating meaning. "I was Gregor Samsa," Paul Monette once confessed, adding, "It was not the last time I would take my life out of a book." Other gay writers have agreed, pointing out that the work is like a parable of closeted denial and coming out. Numbers of others have commented similarly about how they have felt the alienation from family that Kafka described so uniquely. Critics speak of Kafka's spinelessness against a strong-willed, self-made father, a man who would not comprehend his son although Kafka desperately desired his approval. Despite the "father = Father = God" equation and despite his bug-like dependence, Kafka never is able to find happiness, as shown in *Die Verwandlung*. Not with whores or girlfriends. He broke off an engagement with one girlfriend, then became engaged to her again, then became engaged in 1919 to another, then broke that off. In 1923 he met Dora Dymant, who was twenty years younger, and she stayed with him until his death in a sanatorium near Vienna, tragically unable ever to find what he had been searching for: personal salvation. His literary legacy was Kafka's sole concern. In his desk upon his death was a note to Max Brod, a friend:

> Here is my last will concerning everything I have written . . . the only books that can stand are . . . *The Judgment*, *The Stoker*, *Metamorphosis*, *Penal Colony*, *Country Doctor* . . . I do not mean that I wish them to be . . . handed down to posterity. On the contrary, should they disappear altogether that would please me best. . . . But everything else of mine . . . without exception is to be burned, and I beg you to do this as soon as possible.

Brod, however, not only failed to comply but edited *The Trial*, *The Castle*, and *America* for posthumous publication.

J. M. Coetzee, professor of General Literature at the University of Cape Town, South Africa, prefers the 1998 translation of *The Castle* by Mark Harman, explaining that Edwin Muir's translation is not nearly so good and suggesting that Muir because of his limited knowledge of German guessed at Kafka's meaning, often missing the point. Most critics do not find Kafka "a Jew," although his mother was a Jew and he learned from his parents about guilt, salvation, and the very concepts that made his life so miserable. Rather, he was not actively into any organized religion . . . none except art. {CE; GL; OCE; PA; J. M. Coetzee, *The New York Review of Books*, 14 May 1998; WWTCL}

Kagin, Ed (20th Century)

A Kentucky attorney and the son of a Presbyterian minister, Kagin is Vice President of the Cincinnati, Ohio, Free Inquiry Group. For its newsletter, *Fig Leaves*, he cited the following as proof there is no life after death: "For to him that is joined to all the living there is hope; for a living dog is better than a dead lion. For the living know that they shall die; but the dead know not any thing, neither have they any more a reward; for the memory of them is forgotten." *Ecclesiastes* 9:4-5, by God! Not forgotten, he added, is the person with an inscription on his tombstone, "Here lies an atheist, all dressed up and no place to go."

His wife, **Helen Kagin**, is secretary of the Cincinnati Free Inquiry Group.

Kahl, Joachim (1941—)

At the International Humanist and Ethical Union's (IHEU's) International Peace Conference in Zutphen (1983), Kahl of Marbury in Germany addressed the group. He wrote a moral critique of religion entitled *The Misery of Christianity* (1971). In 1981, he wrote, with Erich Warnig of Köln, *Freidenker, Gesohichte und Gegenuart*. {CA; E}

Kahle, Mitchell (20th Century)

Kahle is the Hawaii contact for American Atheists, Inc. E-mail: <mkahle@atheists.org>.

Kahlo, Frida (1907—1954)

A celebrated Mexican artist, often called a national treasure, Kahlo is known by many as the one who married Diego Rivera, divorced him, then remarried him. Her 1942 "Self-Portrait With Monkey and Parrot" was sold at Sotheby's in New York for $3,200,000., and her other works continue to have a wide following of admirers. Kahlo was the daughter of a lower-middle-class German-Jewish photographer, an epileptic, and a mother whom writer Amy Fine Collins has termed a "hysterically Catholic Spanish-Indian." In her youth, Kahlo sometimes dressed as a man, and she is said throughout life to have lovingly combed her noticeable mustache with a special brush. When Olga Campos leaned over, upon Kahlo's death, to kiss the corpse's cheek, Frida's mustache hairs bristled and for a moment the psychologist thought her friend was still alive.

In Mexico Kahlo is known as *la heroina del dolor*, a heroine of pain. This commenced when she was eighteen years old and was "technologically raped," the result of a hideous streetcar and bus accident in which her body was skewered by a thick metal bar which punctured her abdomen and ripped through her vagina. However, Collins has written, she was adored by such marginalized groups as "lesbians, gays, feminists, the handicapped, Chicanos, Communists (she professed Trotskyism and, later, Stalinism), hypochondriacs, substance abusers, and even Jews (despite her indigenous Mexican identify, she was in fact half Jewish and only one-quarter Indian)." Over eighty-seven publications have described her life and work, and her recently discovered diary had an initial print run of more than 150,000 and an introduction by Carlos Fuentes. When Rivera wanted a divorce to marry the Mexican film star, María Felíx, Kahlo overdosed on drugs. When they married, she had found him as irresistible as he was ugly, like "a boy frog standing on his hind legs," but even actress Paulette Goddard had gone to bed with him, and it was rumored sculptor Louise Nevelson also had. Meanwhile, Kahlo reportedly had affairs with Georgia O'Keeffe, Leon Trotsky, Trotsky's secretary Jean van Heijenoort, the painter Jacqueline Lamba, and others. Collins implies that Kahlo, who had at least thirty surgical operations, also had as many doctors as she had lovers. In 1953, after her right leg was amputated because of gangrene, Kahlo became particularly despondent. Rivera took a room next to hers, which improved her spirits greatly, and she entertained guests royally while in bed, also showing them her oozing sores. Toward the end of her life, when her atheism and Stalinism were strongest, her features coarsened and she took on somewhat the appearance of an effeminate boy.

Although her death certificate listed the cause of death as "pulmonary embolism," art historian Sarah Lowe and others felt Kahlo had decided that "enough was enough" and had committed suicide by overdose.

"Her paintings demand—fiercely—that you look at her," wrote biographer Hayden Herrera in *Frida*, a 1983 biography. Agreeing, Kirk Varnedoe, a chief curator of New York's Museum of Modern Art, wrote, "She clicks with today's sensibilities—her psycho-obsessive concern with herself, her creation of a personal alternative world carry a voltage."

In her vivid diary, Kahlo's last entry was "I hope for a happy exit and I hope never to come back." (See entry for Diego Rivera.) {Amy Fine Collins, "Diary of a Mad Artist," *Vanity Fair*, September 1995}

Kahn, Carol (20th Century)

At the Tenth International Humanist and Ethical Union (IHEU) World Congress held in Buffalo (1988), Kahn was a featured speaker. She is author of *Beyond the Helix* (1995).

Kahn, Marion (20th Century)

A signer of Humanist Manifesto II, Kahn has been president of the Humanist Society of Metropolitan New York. A retired art teacher, she is a member of Humanists of North Jersey and founder of Alliance Against Homelessness for the Mentally Ill of Bergen County, New Jersey. {HM 2}

Kaiser, Hilary (20th Century)

Kaiser, a Unitarian, wrote *Veteran Recall: Americans in France Remember the War* (1994). The book collects war stories, oral recollections, poems, and photographs of American World War II veterans living in Paris.

Kaiser, Michael (20th Century)

Kaiser is a student of philosophy and sociology at the University of Constance, Germany. In 1997 he was an intern at the International Humanist and Ethical Union headquarters in London. E-mail: <h0444hua@student.hu-berlin.de>.

KALAMAZOO COLLEGE FREETHINKERS

In Michigan the Kalamazoo College Freethinkers are at <http://www.secularhumanism.org/cfa/orgs.html>.

KALEVALA

The *Kalevala*, epic of the Finnish people, is a collection of poetic narratives that are at the root of a historicity of Finland. It was a shaper of the nation's language, much as Luther's Bible in Germany or the King James translation of the Bible in England. (See entry for Eino Friberg, a translator.)

Kalinicheva, Zoia Vasil'evna (20th Century)

A Moscow freethinker, Kalinicheva wrote *The Museum of the History of Religion and Atheism, A Short Guide* (1967). {GS}

Kalisch, Moritz Marcus (1825—1885)

Kalisch, born in Pomerania of Jewish parents, was educated at the University of Berlin, the came to England as a political refugee and tutor to the Rothschild family. His *Commentary on the Pentateuch*'s rational criticism anticipated the school of Wellhausen. Kalisch contributed to Scott's series of freethought tracts. {BDF; RAT}

Kallen, Horace (1892—1974)

A professor of aesthetics and philosophy at the New School for Social Research, Kallen wrote *Why Religion?* (1927); *Individualism—An American Way of Life* (1933); *Freedom and Experience* (1947); *Ideals and Experience* (1948); *Democracy's True Religion* (1951); *Freedom in the Modern World* (1952); and *A Study of Liberty* (1959).

As early as 1915 in *The Nation*, Kallen remarked that the "melting pot" concept is both a theoretical misconception and a practical failure. He suggested replacing it with "cultural pluralism."

A noted philosopher and writer, Kallen teamed with John Dewey in 1941 to edit *The Bertrand Russell Case*, detailing Lord Russell's inability to be hired to teach philosophy at City College of New York because of objections made by religious groups to his writings.

Asked in 1956 about humanism, Dr. Kallen wrote the present author:

> My Humanism may be called secular or human Humanism. Its specification is to be found in my *Secularism is the Will of God* (1954). It is the faith that human beings are all different from each other and are, as different, equally entitled to life, liberty, and the pursuit of happiness. This applies to supernaturalists as well as naturalists, atheists as well as theists, etc.
>
> The maxim *Homo sum nihil humanuum a me alienum puto* expresses it. So does the Protagorean aphorism, "Man is the measure of all things, of things that are that they are, of things that are not, that they are not." These two expressions imply one another and are systematically elaborated in the idea of Secularism as embracing all the attitudes and valuations of mankind without prejudice.

Dr. Kallen and the present writer once were invited to serve on the board of Protestants and Other Americans United for the Separation of Church and State (POAU), one aim of which was the attempt, for it was not successful, to keep Fordham University from acquiring New York City public land next to Lincoln Center in Manhattan. All the other board members were Protestant ministers, leading Dr. Kallen to remark, "You and I apparently are the 'other' Americans."

To the Euthanasia Society of America, he once declared that "voluntary death is an inalienable human right." His last work was *What I Believe and Why—Maybe* (1971). Kallen was a model humanist: kindly, secular, active, profound, a doer as well as a thinker. {CL; HNS; WAS, 11 May 1956}

Kallimachos (Ancient Greece)

Unlike the Hebrews, the Greeks such as Kallimachos thought of their major god, Zeus, as a lover, one who adored both sexes:

> Hate him O Zeus if he hates me—.
> Theokritos, my Theokritos, deliciously bronzed—
> Hate the boy four times as much as he hates me!
> Heavenly Zeus, by Ganymede I swear,
> The goldenhaired, you in your time have loved.
> I say no more.
>
> {Translations by Dudley Fitts}

Ganymede was the most beautiful of mortals. The father of the gods, Zeus, was attracted by this rosy-faced, bright-eyed boy, so he disguised himself as an eagle, seduced him, and carried him to Mount Olympus where Ganymede was the object of love—discreetly termed a cupbearer—among the other divinities. Zeus, as compensation to Ganymede's father for the loss of his son, gave him a team of beautiful, light-footed horses. The Hebrew Bible contains no such analogies.

Kallman, Chester (1921—1975)

Kallman, a poet, librettist, translator, and editor, has been depicted sensitively by Thekla Clark in her *Wystan and Chester: A Personal Memoir of W. H. Auden and Chester Kallman* (1996). The stepson of Dorothy Farnan, Kallman was a good-looking male described by Wystan Auden as "a Roumanian-Latvian-American Jew." Clark, however, termed Kallman an atheist. At a time when he was a lover of Harold Norse, Kallman met Auden and the two became lovers "mad with happiness." However, Kallman was not the monogamous kind, and he enraged the jealous Auden, once being choked by the poet. Although the two remained friends, they found that their relationship turned sexless. One of Kallman's many lovers, twenty-one-year-old Yannis Boras, was a Greek with whom he stayed for five years, until he was killed in an automobile accident. According to Clark, Kallman's libretto for the opera "Elegy for Young Lovers," was inspired by their relationship, after which he looked for other young Greeks as companions. Concerned as he grew older that he was losing his "Lana Turner looks," Kallman moved about, seldom informing Auden where he was. Clark depicts Kallman with affection, for she allowed him to stay at her home in Florence and he wrote to her extensively.

Of the fights Kallman had with Auden, Clark observed, "As a devout Christian, [Wystan] was satisfied . . . to let 'Miss God' pardon him. Chester, as a romantic atheist, couldn't." The two, she noted, got along best when they collaborated on librettos. Wystan, she noted, thought homosexuality was wrong whereas Kallman regarded it as both a moral lifestyle and beautiful. Wystan "wanted a certain blond beauty in his lovers." Kallman preferred "beetle brows." Although Kallman wrote the libretto for "The Tuscan Women," which was set to music by Carlos Chávez, he has become mainly remembered as a one-time lover of W. H. Auden.

Kalthoff, Albert (1850—1906)

Kalthoff, a freethinker, wrote *The Rise of Christianity* (1907). He joined Haeckel's Monist League and was its first President. {GS; RAT}

KAMA

In the Sanskrit language, Kama means sex as well as love indivisible. Swami Nostradamus Virato of the Church of Tantra (<tantra.org>) has introduced the subject of tantra—prolonged, ritualistic sexual pleasure as a path to the divine:

> Almost everyone is familiar with the Kama Sutra, a tantric treatise on lovemaking. Kama is also the name of the Hindu goddess of love. And love is what tantra encourages—total unconditional love, including the mind, the spirit, and the body. In tantra, the orgasm is with the universe.

As observed by one theist, "Kama is the non-theoretical Hindu concept of the Big Bang." {*Playboy*, July 1999}

Kamal, Alimul (1982—)

A teenager, Kamal was asked in a Flushing, New York, junior high school history class to write about "the religious holidays." To the teacher's surprise, he wrote that he was "not religious," then completed an essay about the winter solstice and secular humanism. Kamal, nephew of Taslima Nasrin, is one of a growing number of younger people who have become acquainted with, and do not fear to speak about, secular humanism.

Upon having to return to his native Bangladesh, however, he found many even in his own family were concerned about his "lack of religion." {WAS, numerous conversations}

Kamehameha, Maloka (20th Century)

Kamehameha wrote *An Atheist Goes to Church* (c. 1955). {GS}

Kamen, Henry Arthur (1936-)

Kamen, a Catholic, is author of *The Spanish Inquisition* (1965), adjudged by many critics to be a balanced view of the time. Kamen was born in Burma.

Kamenka, Eugene (1928—1994)

Kamenka, whose parents were Russian and Jewish, was born in Germany but educated in Australia. A professor and head of the History of Ideas Unit at the Australian National University, he wrote *The Ethical Foundations of Marxism* (1962), *Marxism and Ethics* (1969), *Intellectuals and Revolution* (1979), and *The Portable Karl Marx* (1982). Kamenka was an atheist who once wrote, "I fight, above all, the unnecessary waste of lives—not only by genocide, pointless wars, and blinkered terrorism, but by state, religious, or political oppression and brutality. I rail also against the elevation or deliberate preservation of ignorance and superstition to ward off fear of criticism, loss of privilege, and change." {SWW}

KAMI: See entry for Shinto.

Kaminer, Wendy (20th Century)

Kaminer, a Public Policy Fellow at Radcliffe College, wrote *I'm Dysfunctional, You're Dysfunctional* (1992), in which she described herself as a "liberal feminist Jewish atheist." She also wrote *True Love Waits: Essays and Criticism* and "The Last Taboo, Why America Needs Atheism." The latter *New Republic* (14 October 1996) article noted that today, with belief in guardian angels and creationism "becoming commonplace," it is as risky to make fun as "burning a flag in an American Legion hall." Almost all Americans, 95% she noted, profess a belief in God or some universal spirit, and 76% imagine Him as a heavenly father who actually pays attention to their prayers. Kaminer, herself an atheist, lamented that we have no Mark Twains and H. L. Menckens to counter today's Jimmy Swaggarts and born-again Christians. Readers complained that she had suggested religious belief is childish, that "worshiping a supernatural deity . . . is like worrying about monsters in the closet that find you tasty enough to eat." *The New York Times* called "offensive" her remark that the sacraments are "silly." Others, however, supported her wholeheartedly.

Sleeping with Extra-Terrestrials: The Rise of Irrationalism and Perils of Piety (1999) continues her deconstruction of pop culture and piety. She finds New Age spiritual practices "painful stupidities that people embrace to ease their fears of death," and she also laments our age's "blind antipathy to reason." {E; *Free Inquiry*, Fall 1999}

Kane, George (20th Century)

Kane wrote "The Atkins-Craig Debate on God's Existence: Points Not Made Are Points Lost," a critical review of religion for *Secular Nation* (July-September 1998).

Kane, Hal (20th Century)

Kane, a research associate at the Worldwatch Institute, has written for *The Humanist* concerning the world's desperate conditions concerning food production. Kane is author of *The Hour of Departure* (1995).

Kane, James Alexander (1912—1980)

Kane was a humanist, teacher, scholar, social reformer, linguist, and civil marriage celebrant. Raised a Roman Catholic, he renounced religion at maturity and was active in the Humanist Society of West Australia, of which he was prime founder. In addition he was involved with the Vietnam Moratorium Committee, the United Nations Association, the Australia-China Society (he visited China in 1978), and the Council for Civil Liberties. {SWW}

Kane, Sarah (1971-1999)

A provocative playwright, Kane committed suicide in a hospital room where she was being treated for depression. The daughter of a journalist, she grew up with a Christian-redemption outlook in a London suburb but rejected religion when seventeen, saying it involved "a spirit-filled, born-again lunacy." The Bible, she found, was full of rape, mutilation, war, and pestilence.

"Blasted," her first play, appeared to promote depravity. A rampaging soldier rapes another man, then gouges out his eyes, eats his tongue, and forces him to cannibalize a dead baby. *The Daily Mail* called the work "a disgusting feast of filth." "Cleansed" included a scene in which heroin is injected into an eyeball, amputation occurs, and a person is raped with a broom handle. Benedict Nightingale of *The Times* of London wrote in a review, "She is not the gloating opportunist that some reviewers of 'Blasted' thought. She has no less integrity than Pinter or Bond, but, God knows, I would hate to live in her head."

Her last play, "Crave," ended with a suicide. "Some people seem to find released at the end of it," the "enfante terrible of the British theater" said, "but I think it's only the release of death. In my other plays it was the release of deciding to go on living despite the fact that it's terrible." {Warren Hoge, *The New York Times*, 25 February 1999}

KANSAS HUMANISTS

• South Central Kansas Chapter of the Council for Secular Humanism, PO Box 3089, Wichita, Kansas 67201.

Kant, Immanuel (1724—1804)

Kant's critique of the proofs of God later contributed to forms of atheism. Although hardly a non-believer, Kant did disturb believers with his view that man and God are on the same level, and that our desire to please God is "a servile and pathological urge." As for God, who will always remain unknown, "We can no more extend our stock of theoretical insight by mere ideas, than a merchant can better his position by adding a few noughts to his cash account." Kant's *Kritik der reinen Vernunft* was added to the Vatican's list of prohibited reading in 1827. Zuckerstätter mentions that although Kant's "critical philosophy" is a complex synthesis of rationalist dogmatism and empiricist skepticism, Kant remained a believer. Also, he held with Plato that the mind will continue to exist after death, without any body. Ironically, his *Religion Within the Bounds of Pure* (i.e. *Mere*) *Reason* (1792—1794) indicates disbelief in every one of the standing Christian dogmas—Creation, Fall, Salvation, Miracles, and the supernatural basis of morals. Singing in the churches, he pronounced, was mere bawling. Prayer, whether public or private, was a form of superstition in that it addressed an unseen world: "To kneel or prostrate himself on the earth, even for the purpose of symbolizing to himself reverence for a heavenly object, is unworthy of man." In ethics, he was an extreme rationalist, holding that moral principles are objectively valid commands of the *a priori* reason. Like Plato, observes Robertson, Kant is finally occupied in discussing the "right fictions" for didactic purposes and ends "by sacrificing intellectual morality to what seems to him social security." McCabe called Kant "the ablest of the German philosophers," adding that he "did good service in showing that the scholastic philosophy which still dominated Europe was purely subjective (in other words, word-spinning), but his own theory soon died, and his ethical philosophy almost gave back to mysticism what he had taken away. He mistook the analysis of the puritanical mind of an old bachelor (himself) for a study of the moral sense generally and concluded that its 'categorical imperative' implied a God as law-given and a future life as a reward. He thus became a non-Christian theist and in his third chief work disowned all supernatural religion."

"Kant is generally considered the greatest of modern philosophers. I cannot myself agree with this estimate," Bertrand Russell wrote in his *History of Western Philosophy* (1945). "His philosophy allowed an appeal to the heart against the cold dictates of theoretical reason. In Kant . . . the subjectivist tendency that begins with Descartes was carried to new extremes. There is an emphasis upon mind as opposed to matter, which leads in the end to the assertion that only mind exists." {CE; CL; ER; EU, Rudolf Zuckerstätter; ILP; HNS2; JM; JMR; JMRH; PA; RAT; RE; TRI; TYD}

Kapila (6th Century B.C.E.)

Kapila was one of the earliest Hindu thinkers. His system is known as the Atheistic Philosophy. It is expounded in the *Sankhya Karika*, an important relic of bold rationalistic Indian thought. J. R. Ballantyne has translated his aphorisms. {BDF; CE}

Kapitza, Sergei (20th Century)

In 1993 Kapitza, a physicist at the Institute for Physical Problems, Moscow, and Chair of Physics at the Moscow Institute of Physics and Technology, was named a Humanist Laureate in the International Academy of Humanism by the Council for Secular Humanism. He signed Humanist Manifesto 2000.

Kaplan, Justin (1925—)

Kaplan, an author who is a member of the American Academy of Arts and Letters, won a Pulitzer Prize for biography in 1967. He has written *Mr. Clemens and Mark Twain* (1966), *Lincoln Steffens, A Biography* (1974), and *Mark Twain and His World* (1974). He has edited *Dialogues of Plato* and *The Pocket Aristotle* (1956). Asked about humanism, he responded to the present author:

> I'm uncomfortable with broad, over-used terms such as "humanism" (except in a purely historical sense) and even more uncomfortable with sub-species such as "theistic" and "secular." But if, on pain of death, I had to assign specific values to "humanism" in general I'd list free inquiry, tolerance, and concern and then pray for relief.
> {WAS, 10 April 1989}

Kaplan, Mordecai M. (1881—1983)

When he signed Humanist Manifesto II, Rabbi Kaplan was founder of the Jewish Reconstructionist Movement. This fourth branch of Judaism (the others being Conservative, Orthodox, and Reform) is closest to the philosophic movement of secular humanism. Kaplan wrote *Future of the American Jew* (1981). {ER; HM2; HNS}

Kara, Maniben (Died in the 1970s)

Kara, an associate of M. N. Roy, was a radical humanist and a leading trade union leader in Bombay. He was known for fighting for the rights of women at a time when that cause was not a popular one in India.

Karayan, Vagan (20th Century)

Karayan, while a student at University College in Los Angeles, California, was one of the founding members of Campus Freethought Alliance. {*International Humanist News*, December 1996}

Karim, Nehal (20th Century)

Karim, a sociologist at the University of Dhaka, is Secretary General of the Assembly of Freethinkers in Bangladesh. Although secularism was once a fundamental of the constitution there, he told a 1995 meeting of major Indian humanist organizations, a freethought movement has been weak although one was formed in the late 1920s. There are few human rights organizations in Bangladesh, he lamented, and the freethought movement there is in its infancy. Karim is author of *The Emergence of Nationalism in Bangladesh* (1992). He participated in the 1996 Humanist World Congress in Mexico City. {*New Humanist*, February 1996}

Karlekar, Hiranmay (20th Century)

Karlekar is managing editor of the daily *Indian Express*. At the International Humanist and Ethical Union's 1998 congress in Mumbai, he reviewed the century's humanistic developments, suggesting that it started as a philosophy and was now moving into action. Karlekar called for global disarmament and stated that freedom as discussed by Erich Fromm and Habermas is crucial to humanism. {*International Humanist News*, December 1998}

Karlfeldt, Erik Axel (1864—1931)

A Swedish poet and Nobel Prize winner, Karlfeldt was the rare Laureate who protested that he had no right to the prize because he was little known outside his own country. His *Arcadia Borealis* (1938) showed he was somewhat mystical but was an agnostic. In "A Vagrant," Karlfeldt wrote a couplet:

> What's your religion? What is your creed?
> I know only this: I know naught.
> {RE}

Karlin, Elizabeth (1944-1998)

A prominent physician who directed an abortion clinic in Madison, Wisconsin, Karlin was dogged for years by religionists who were anti-abortionists. She was followed and stalked, but upon her death she was eulogized by Secretary of Health and Human Services Secretary Donna Shalala, who said, "For years, day and night, she and her nurses endured harassment from demonstrators outside their clinic and their homes. She never wavered in her commitment to protect a woman's right to choose." Dr. Karlin was a donor to the Freedom From Religion Foundation. {*Freethought Today*, September 1998).

Karlsson, Mikael (20th Century)

Karlsson, of the University of Iceland, is on the Executive Committee of The Hume Society, a group that is engaged in scholarly activity concerning David Hume.

KARMA

A concept common to Hinduism, Buddhism, and Jainism, karma is a doctrine involving past and future reincarnations. For philosophic naturalists, it can neither be proved nor disproved and is a meaningless metaphysical concept, one incapable of being tested. However, in an apparently serious letter published in an April 1993 issue of Sri Lanka's *The Island*, Dr. C. Godamunne of Kandy wrote as follows:

> BEWARE
>
> Buddhists believe in rebirth. That is, a person can be born over and over again in this world (Samsara).
>
> It is due to your Karma. One can be born in the Animal World, Spirit World, Deva World, and Brahma Worlds. Lord Buddha was also born as a cobra, an elephant, a monkey, etc.
>
> So he was born in the Animal World, according to Jataka Katha (stories). So there is a chance that your parents may be born in the Animal World, due to their previous Karma. Say your father is born a bull and is slaughtered and its meat sold. If this meat is bought by your household and you eat it as a tasty dish then in short you are eating your own father's flesh. So beware, you Buddhists, lest you devour your own dear parents, your relatives, your friends.

Karmin, Otto (1881—1920)

Karmin was a Swiss freethinker and sociologist who was responsible for raising a monument to the Spanish freethought "martyr," Michael Servetus. {RAT; TRI}

Karnik, V. B. (Deceased in the 1970s)

Karnik, a humanist activist, edited the weekly *Radical Humanist* in India. He wrote *M. N. Roy, A Political Biography*; *Strikes in India*; and *Trade Unions in India*.

Karr, Barry (20th Century)

Karr is executive director of the Committee for the Scientific Investigation of Claims of the Paranormal, which publishes *Skeptical Inquirer*. E-mail: <skeptinq@aol.com>. On the Web: <http://www.csicop.org/>.

Karr, Steve (20th Century)

Karr, Barry Karr's brother, has been a director of public relations for *Free Inquiry*.

Karsten, Rafael (1879—1956)

Karsten, a Finnish non-theist, taught practical philosophy at the University of Helsinki. (See entry for Scandinavian Unbelievers.)

Karve, R. V. (20th Century)

In Bombay, India, Karve was an editor from 1931 to 1946 of *Reason*. A veteran rationalist and pioneer of family planning in India, he was prosecuted several times for his writings. {FUK}

Kasden, Lawrence Edward (20th Century)

Kasden is a film director and screenwriter. He co-wrote "The Empire Strikes Back" (1980) and "Return of the Jedi" (1982), and he wrote "Raiders of the Lost Ark" (1981). A videotape, "Larry Kasden, a Humanist in Hollywood," is available from the Society for Humanistic Judaism, 28611 West Twelve Mile Road, Farmington Hills, Michigan 48334.

Kasmar, Gene (1937—)

Kasmar is author of *All the Obscenities in the Bible* (1995), in which he focuses only on the King James version of the Bible. He includes such topics as prostitution, suicide, incest, homosexuality, and abortion (finding that the Bible is not against abortion). On the Web: <kerry@mtn.org>. {Gene Kasmar, *Humanist in Canada*, Autumn 1997; Gordon Stein, *The American Rationalist*, March-April 1996}

Kaspary, Joachim (19th Century)

Kaspary, a humanitarian deist, was assisted by the aptly named Epenetus Earwaker at the National Secular Society's outdoor meetings in London during the 1880s. {RSR}

Kato, Soichi (20th Century)

Kato was a member of the New York Humanist Society. As executive director of the International Committee for Breaking the Language Barrier, he worked with government and corporations to improve international communications through the use of uniform signs and symbols.

Kathan, Melvin L. (20th Century)

Kathan, a freethinker, wrote *Key to Creeds* (c. 1950). {GS}

Katz, Bernard (20th Century)

Katz is a senior writer for *The American Rationalist*, has written for *Truth Seeker*, and is the author of freethought pamphlets. He is associated with Humanists of South Jersey (AHA). Katz taught in the Philadelphia secondary schools and also was a stock and commodities broker.

His interest in religion, he has related, started when he tried to find the key to the irrationality of the stock market. As he examined religious beliefs, an area perhaps more irrational than the stock market, he drew parallels. The commonality he found was that they both work on high emotions, and neither is predictable. He found that there are few rationalities in either area.

Ibn Warraq has complained that Katz in *The Ways of an Atheist* (1999) has utilized some of his ideas, almost word for word, without citing his own *Why I Am Not A Muslim* (1995). (See entry for New Jersey Freethinkers, Humanists.) {FD}

Katz, Zev (20th Century)

With Renee Kogel, Katz edited *Judaism in a Secular Age—An Anthology of Secular Humanistic Jewish Thought*.

Kaufmann, Paul (1922—)

Kaufmann is an Australian humanist, rationalist, civil libertarian, and public servant. The descendant of four Jewish grandparents, he had left Austria for England, then served in the non-combatant part of the Australian Army. In the late 1960s he joined the Humanist Society of Canberra, eventually becoming President. With Geraldine Spencer, he campaigned to have the Australian census question on religion changed to read: "No religion, write none." Kaufmann contributed to humanist journals and newsletters and was active in civil liberties, human rights, and voluntary euthanasia organizations. {FUS}

Kaufmann, Walter (1918—1991)

One of the professors of philosophy at Princeton University whose popularity was proved by the immense number of students who chose his classes, Walter Kaufmann was raised a Lutheran. *Faith of a Heretic* (1963) described his inability to believe that Jesus was God, resulting in his becoming an orthodox Jew. He then left religion, toying with such terms as freethinker, atheist, and agnostic but preferring to be a heretic, one whose opinion "is contrary to the fundamental doctrine or creed of any particular church."

He wrote *Nietzsche* (1950), a work which fails adequately to describe Nietzsche's bad side, according to Paul Edwards. Kaufmann also wrote *From Shakespeare to Existentialism* (1959) and *Critique of Religion and Philosophy* (1961). Although he did not sign Humanist Manifesto II, he was one of fifty-eight who in 1980 signed its sequel, *A Secular Humanist Declaration*. Kaufmann once wrote, "Faith in immortality, like belief in Satan, leaves unanswered the ancient question: Is God unable to prevent suffering and thus not omnipotent? Or is he able but not willing to prevent it and thus not merciful? And is he just?" {SHD}

Kaula, William Mason (1926—)

Kaula, born in Australia of United States citizens, is an educator, geophysicist, and secular humanist. From 1963 to 1992, he taught geophysics and space physics at the University of California in Los Angeles. Kaula is a Fellow of the American Geophysical Union and a member of the National Academy of Sciences. He has written *Theory of Satellite Geodesy* (1966) and *Introduction to Planetary Physics* (1968).

Kaunda, Kenneth David [President] (1924—)

Kaunda, a former schoolteacher and Zambian politician, was president of Zambia from 1964—1991. In 1953 he opposed the formation of the Federation of Rhodesia and Nyassaland. His party was banned in 1959, he was imprisoned, but upon being released he formed a new independence party, the United National Independence Party.

In 1962 he rejected a British proposal for Northern Rhodesia that he said would perpetuate white supremacy. In 1963 he pressed for dissolution of the federation which had formed, and the following year he became president of the new nation and was re-elected five times. In the 1991 election, however, he lost. Kaunda has received the Nehru Award for International Understanding and the Knight of Collar Order of Pius XII. Among his books are *Black Government* (with C. M. Morris, 1960) and *Humanism in Africa and a Guide to Its Implementation* (1967).

A patriarch and an autocrat, Kauanda talks about "God's people" and his "philosophy of humanism" and "consciencism." Kaunda, who led his country for twenty-seven years, is said to have the cultural distinction of being an atheistic humanist and of preaching humanism, "a philosophy that synthesised Christian socialism and traditional African values."

Although Zambian Humanism was ideal in theory, it did not hide being a cover-up for Kaunda's one-man rule. His dictatorship was overthrown in 1992. {CE; DGC}

Kaur: See entry for Kaur Kawaljeet.

Kautsky, Karl (1854—1938)

Kautsky's *Foundations of Christianity* (1925) was highly negative and resulted in criticism by Christian leaders. {RAT}

Kavanaugh, James J. (20th Century)

Kavanaugh wrote *The Struggle of the Unbeliever* (1967) and *God Lives* (1993). {GS}

Kawaljeet, Kaur (1956-)

Kawaljeet is one of the editors and a regular contributor to *Buddhiwadi* (Rationalist), a Hindi quarterly published by Buddhiwadi Foundation. She lectures regularly on computer literacy and the scientific outlook at Priya Academy. Also, she manages Buddhiwadi Study and Research Center, organizations established by the Buddhiwadi Foundation. Kawaljeet participated in the 1999 Humanist World Congress at Mumbai, India, where she delivered a talk on Cultural Prerequisites of Freedom. She also attended the IHEU General Assembly at Mumbai as a representative of the Bihar Buddhiwadi Samaj. Her "How I Became a Rationalist" and her brief biography are available on the Internet.

E- mail: <bobsoft@vsnl.com> and <brs_patna@yahoo.com>. On the Web:http://www.myfreeoffice.com/buddhiwadi>. (See entry for Nath Ramendra, her husband.)

Kawamura, Matasuke (20th Century)

A member of the Japan Academy, Kawamura is Justice of the Supreme Court in Japan. He is a Unitarian.

Kawanzaa

Kawanzaa, a Kiswahill word that means "first," is a holiday based upon the African tradition of celebrating the harvesting of the first fruits. It was introduced for use by African Americans in 1966 by Dr. Ron Karenga. In a seven-day celebration (December 26th-January 1st), Nguzo Saba (Seven Principles) are taken up, one per day: Umoja (unity); kujichagulia (self-determination); ujima (collective work and responsibility); ujamaa (cooperative economics); nia (purpose); kuumba (creativity); and imani (faith). Symbols that are included are the straw mat (jkeka); the candle holder (kinara); the seven candles (mishumaa saba); corn (vibunzi or muhinki); a unity cup (kikombe); crops (mazao); and gifts (zawadi).

Kay, Robert E. (20th Century)

A psychiatrist, Kay is a Pennsylvania Life Member of the Freedom From Religion Foundation. He has written "Ten Basic Ideas for Raising Children" (*Freethought Today*, April 1999).

Kazantzakis, Nikos (1883—1957)

Kazantzakis, the Greek author of *Zorba the Greek* (1946), also wrote an ambitious work, *The Odyssey, a Modern Sequel* (1938), which includes the outlooks of Gautama, Jesus, Nietzsche, Lenin, and others. His *Die letzte Veruchung* was included on the Vatican's list of prohibited reading in 1953. {CE; ILP, Additus, 5 December 1961}

Kazi, Abdul Dadir (20th Century)

A freethinker in Karachi, Pakistan, Kazi wrote *Sartre and God* (1975), a study of Sartre's atheistic existentialism. {GS}

Kazin, Alfred (1915-1998)

Kazin's *God and the American Writer* (1997) states that he is not interested in a particular artist's profession of belief but, rather, "in the imagination he brings to his tale of religion in human affairs." The concept of God, he concludes, figures importantly in the American literary imagination, God and man "eternally watchful of the other."

He found Clemens and T. S. Eliot anti-Semitic. Hawthorne, he found, would not believe in God but could not escape the "power of blackness" that tormented his Calvinist ancestors: "In the depths of the heart," Hawthorne wrote, "is a tomb and a dungeon." Emerson, who was preceded by eight generations of clergymen, refused such a dungeon and overthrew organized religion altogether, proclaiming that divinity lies within: the "infinitude of the private mind." Whitman, although "drenched in religion," dared to come up with his own creed, a self-celebration and ecstatic, world-embracing sexuality in which God is one's bedfellow and "sleeps at my side all night."

Emily Dickinson thought Whitman was being "disgraceful" with such an idea. Kazin found that she "explained the religious quest better than anyone, and with justice to all, when she tossed off in a letter, 'It is true that the unknown is the largest need of intellect, although for this no one thinks to thank God.' " Although Kazin admired Dickinson as having "the most penetrating intellect," his favorites being Melville and Lincoln, two tortured souls who wanted to believe in God in the face of annihilation. Melville, Kazin held, retained a faith "even if he did not always know what and where and whom to believe." Lincoln, however, remained the rationalist who joined no church.

Kazin, who was not an observant Jew, arranged for his cremains to be given to Judith Dunford, who asked that his ashes be consigned to the East River in the shadow of the Brooklyn Bridge. (See entry for Jewish Authors.) {*The New York Times*, 23 July 1999}

Keane, Augustus Henry (1833—1912)

Keane, an anthropologist, was educated for the Catholic priesthood but discarded his orders and his creed, taking to travel and the study of ethnology. In 1883 he was appointed professor of Hindustani at University College. His works include *Man: Past and Present* (1899), *Ethnology* (1901), and *The World's Peoples* (1908). {RAT}

Keane, John (20th Century)

Tom Paine: A Political Life (1995) was written by the Australian-born John Keane, a professor of politics at the University of Westminster in England and director of the Centre for the Study of Democracy. In the biography, Keane found seventy new Paine selections that previously were not listed in other bibliographies. His new bibliography, *The Writings of Thomas Paine, 1737—1809*, contains over six hundred individual contributions by Paine.

Keane is critical of David Freeman Hawke, finding that he was guilty of "sniping." He wondered "why Hawke ever bothered to write a biography of Paine." Moncure Conway, although he wrote a valuable and fully documented sourcebook, is accused of "sermonising."

Although Jack Fruchtman Jr. found Paine "something of a country bumpkin," Keane disagrees, noting that "the world's chief public defender of republican democracy" mixed with individuals who may have had unorthodox religious views and were religious Dissenters. But, wrote Paine in the 18th century in what many find is a decidedly contemporary viewpoint, "I have always considered monarchy to be a silly contemptible thing. . . . I compare it to something kept behind a curtain, about which there is a great deal of bustle and fuss, and a wonderful air of seeming solemnity, but when, by any accident, the curtain happens to open, and the company see what it is, they burst into laughter." (See entry for Thomas Paine.) {Colin McCall, "Modern Messages—From the 18th Century," *The Freethinker*, June 1995; David Powell, "Books," *New Humanist*, May 1995}

Kearney, Sean (20th Century)

Kearney holds that "no one has made a greater and more lasting contribution to the development of Free Thought in Ireland than John Toland." {*New Humanist*, November 1997}

Keary, Charles Francis (1848—1917)

Keary was on the staff of the British Museum, and his rationalist views are set forth in *Pursuit of Reason* (1910). He put Christian doctrines disdainfully aside and believed only in the existence of the Absolute. {RAT}

Keats, John (1795—1821)

In his twenties, Keats decided against becoming a surgeon and became one of England's leading poets. The critics attacked his *Endymion* (1818), but his poems and sonnets are now considered consummate examples of romanticism. These include "Ode to a Nightingale," "Ode on a Grecian Urn," and the unfinished "Hyperion." Keats emphatically rejected Christianity, which in an 1816 work he said is "dying like an outburnt lamp."

Written in Disgust of Vulgar Superstition

The church bells toll a melancholy round,
Calling the people to some other prayers,
Some other gloominess, more dreadful cares,
More Hearkening to the sermon's horrid sound.
Surely the mind of man is closely bound
In some black spell; seeing that each one tears
Himself from fireside joys, and Lydian airs,
And converse high of those with glory crown'd.
Still, still they toll, and I should feel a damp—
A chill as from a tomb, did I not know
That they are going like an outburnt lamp;
That 'tis their sighing, wailing ere' they go
Into oblivion;—that fresh flowers will grow,
And many glories of immortal stamp.

The details of his death at such a young age are not widely known. In February 1820, he had entered his lodgings in Wentworth Place, staggering like a drunk. His friend, Charles Brown, heard Keats cough and say, "Bring me the candle, Brown, and let me see the blood." With his background in medicine, he looked at the blood for a moment, then said, "I know the color of that blood; it is arterial blood. I cannot be deceived in that color. That drop of blood is my death warrant. I must die." His diagnosis of tuberculosis was correct, and "he was to die the same slow and painful death he had witnessed his brother endure only a year before," Scott Slater and Alec Solomita have noted. He recovered somewhat but had relapses, suffering intermittently, they added, "from delusions of persecution—on the one hand, blaming his illness on literary critics and on the other, blaming Fanny Brawne, for not sleeping with him." Agreeing to go to Italy with a friend, painter Joseph Severn, Keats threatened suicide several times but became better by the time they reached Rome.

Several weeks before he died at the age of twenty-six, Keats told Severn he wanted no name engraved on his gravestone. He simply wanted the words, "Here lies one whose name was writ in water." On December 10th, upon suffering a hemorrhage, Keats staggered about his room crying, "This day shall be my last!" Severn previously had hidden all vehicles of self-destruction (knives, forks, drugs), and Keats was unable to kill himself. But every time the physician came Keats would ask, "How long is this posthumous life of mine to last?" On February 24th, Severn heard Keats calling out, "Lift me up for I am dying—I shall die easy—don't be frightened—thank God it has come." Severn then held Keats in his arms, their hands clasped for the next seven hours. After breaking out into a sweat, Keats whispered, "Don't breathe on me—it comes like ice." He then died very quietly. W. Sharp, who knew him well, said Keats, who did not believe in God and used the word only in a figurative sense, also had no belief in a future life. Like Shelley and Byron, Keats was not buried in England but near the pyramid of Cestius in Rome's old Protestant cemetery. Severn failed to follow the Keats request for a simple gravestone, choosing instead, "This grave contains all that was mortal, of a young English poet, who, on his death bed, in the bitterness of his heart, at the malicious power of his enemies, desired these words to be engraved on his tomb stone: "Here lies one whose name was writ in water.' " The Keats name is not on the gravestone, but it is found on the adjacent Severn gravestone: "devoted friend and death-bed companion of John Keats whom he lived to see numbered among the immortal poets of England." {CB; CE; JM; RAT; RE}

Keene, Charles Samuel (1823—1891)

Keene, one of the best-known *Punch* artists of his time, was a Gold Medalist of the 1890 Paris Exhibition. During his last illness, according to his biographer G. S. Layard, Holman Hunt tried to convince him of a future life. Keene, a thorough rationalist, replied, "Do you really believe this? I can't think so." {RAT; RE; TRI}

Keim, Karl Theodor (1825—1878)

Keim was a German rationalist and a professor of theology at Zürich. His rationalism hindered his promotion, and he was an invalid most of his days. He is chiefly known for the *History of Jesus of Nazara* (1867—1872) and *Primitive Christianity* (1878). {BDF}

Keiser, C. J. (20th Century)

Keiser, on the basis of his published views, was originally asked to sign Humanist Manifesto I. He never did. {EW}

Keith, Arthur [Sir] (1866—1955)

Sir Arthur Keith was a director of the Rationalist Press Association when Bertrand Russell was its president. He also became an honorary associate. Keith has critiqued Clifton Fadiman's editing of *I Believe* (1939). In that volume, twenty-two eminent thinkers had been asked in 1931 to summarize briefly their philosophic outlooks. Then, in 1939, they were asked to revise their comments: "Of the 22 men and women who contributed originally to these pages, only two [Hilaire Belloc, Dean Inge] regard the Creator—God, the One, omnipotent and personal—as having the form and properties set forth in the Book of Genesis. . . . Yet, I am far from claiming that the anthropomorphic God is dead; the most we can say is that he is dying. We humans are weak-kneed beings. Most of us still demand a God, cast in our own mold—one who can give succor when approached in prayer. An emotion has called Him into being." Keith wrote *The Place of Prejudice in Modern Civilization* (1931). (See entry for Spirit.) {CE; HNS; JM; RE; TRI}.

Keith, Brian (20th Century)

Keith is Vice President of the Humanist Association of Ottawa, Canada.

Keith, George [Earl Marischal] (1685—1778)

Keith, a Scottish soldier, 10th earl marischal (Lord Marshall), friend of David Hume, and Jacobite, was appointed captain of the Guard by Queen Anne. When his property was confiscated for aiding the Pretender, he fled to the Continent and was in high favor, as was his brother James, with Frederick the Great. Keith was appointed ambassador to Paris in 1751, governor of Neuchâtel (1752), and ambassador to Spain (1758). According to McCabe, Keith was "a very cultivated man, a friend of Voltaire, and a drastic deist. His biographer Mrs. Caithell says that 'in almost every letter he writes there is a jibe against some part or other of ecclesiastical lamas, as he called them.' " D'Alembert said in a funeral oration that Keith was "a man of pure and classic morals." Although eventually pardoned by George II of Britain, Keith remained for the rest of his life in Prussia. {BDF; CE; JM; RAT; RE}

Keith, James Francis Edward (1696—1758)

Keith was an eminent military commander. He joined the army of the Pretender and was wounded in 1715 at Sheriffmuir. Afterwards, he served with distinction in Spain and in Russia, rising to high favor under the Empress Elizabeth. In 1647 he took service with Frederick the Great as field-marshal and became Governor of Berlin. Carlyle calls him "a very clear-eyed, sound observer of men and things. Frederick, the more he knows him, likes him the better." From their correspondence it is evident Keith shared the skeptical opinions of Frederick. Marshal Keith fell in the battle of Hochkirch, 1758. {BDF; JM; RAT; RE}

Keleman, Lawrence (20th Century)

Keleman is author of *Permission to Believe: Four Rational Approaches to God's Existence* (1990). It is anti-atheist.

Kellam, Paul (20th Century)

Kellam, a founding editor of *Inc.* and a managing editor of *Consumer Reports*, is an active member of the Free Inquiry Society of Central Florida. His wife, **Eloise Roberts Kellam** (1928-1998), was also a secular humanist.

Keller, Harvey (20th Century)

Keller, Secretary of the Secular Humanist Society of San Antonio, Texas, is a regional director of the Council for Secular Humanism.

Keller, Helen Adams (1880—1968)

Blind and deaf since the age of two, Keller according to her mother had "not been ill a day since 'the illness,' " or so she told the governess, Annie Sullivan, when she took on the job of educating the six-year-old. Although the illness was called "brainfever," it might have been meningitis. Annie had the major problem of communicating with her charge and, as brought out by biographer Van Wyck Brooks in 1956, somehow was able to understand the connection between w-a-t-e-r and the water that was poured over her hand. "I understood," she explained later, "that it was possible for me to communicate with other people by these signs. Thoughts that ran forward and backward came to me quickly—thoughts that seemed to start in my brain and spread all over me." Nevertheless, she eventually graduated with honors in 1904 from Radcliffe and earned the world's attention for her accomplishments.

Keller's knowledge of religion depended heavily upon those who transmitted their own views on the subject, a condition similarly experienced by children reared to accept their parents' authoritative views. In *The Story of My Life* (1903), she wrote,

> There is much in the Bible against which every instinct of my being rebels, so much so that I regret the necessity which has compelled

> me to read through it from beginning to end. I do not think that the knowledge I have gained of its history and sources compensates me for the unpleasant details it has forced upon my attention.

In *The World I Live In*" (1908) Keller commented about smells:

> But, when advised by Alexander Graham Bell that "a day must come when love, which is more than friendship, will knock at the door of your heart and demand to be let in," Keller responded, "I can't imagine a man wanting to marry me. I should think it would seem like marrying a statue." To a 1922 proposal of marriage by mail, she responded,

In 1940 Keller wrote *Let Us Have Faith*, describing her faith in the future. That future included knowing about the 1957 William Gibson television play, "The Miracle Worker," describing her early life. The play enjoyed 700 performances beginning in 1959, following which a movie was made in 1962. In 1965, although she was incapacitated, she was one of twenty women elected to the Women's Hall of Fame at the New York World's Fair. She and Eleanor Roosevelt received the most votes.

In his review of Dorothy Herrmann's *Helen Keller: A Life* (1998), John Updike in *The New Yorker* (10 August 1998) relates the Alabama family's background: Helen's mother was related to the Massachusetts Adamses and to the orator Edward Everett. Her father was "a moody Confederate veteran and small-town newspaper editor of Swiss descent, a person who died deeply in debt in 1896. Whereas Annie was "a decidedly disaffected Catholic," Helen was "a rapt Swedenborgian," "a devotee of both Christ and Marx," "an ardent socialist, pacifist, and suffragist." The two, Annie told Herrmann, "had such fundamentally different conceptions of life that they would have loathed one another had they met under ordinary circumstances."

Although Updike is convinced that Keller was a Swedenborgian, Keller was on the advisory board of Charles Francis Potter's First Humanist Society of New York. Potter, who knew her and conversed with her, considered her a freethinker. {CE}

Keller, Paul (20th Century)

Gnostic atheism, writes Keller in *The American Rationalist* (January-February, 1994), goes one step further than atheism. Whereas atheism claims there is no defensible evidence for the claim that there is a God, gnostic atheism is the position that it is *known* that there is no God or other supernatural beings.

Keller, Robert (20th Century)

Keller is Treasurer of the Secular Humanist Association of San Antonio, Texas.

The world's population, at 5.7 billion in 1995, has exponentially increased more than two times since World War II. Kellert, in *The Value of Life: Biological Diversity and Human Society* (1996), lamented that it is ironically difficult to convince 5.7 billion people that we need to stop rather than increase our numbers. He added that we must stop converting our plains and forests to grazing and croplands and must stop our despoiling the world's oceanic systems.

He suggested several approaches to tackle the problem:

- naturalistic (we must again take pleasure in nature)
- ecologistic-scientific (we must make a systematic study of nature)
- esthetic (we must learn to appreciate the beauty of nature)
- symbolic (we must use nature in communication and thought)
- humanistic (we must combine the humanistic with the scientific when dealing with nature))
- moralistic (we must include the moralistic in our outlook toward nature)
- dominionistic (we must see the need to control nature)
- negativistic (we must show that even such creatures as snakes and spiders are good)

The more education people have, Keller states, the more they stress the importance of humanistic, moralistic, and scientific values. With E. O. Wilson, he is understandably alarmed that an estimated three species per hour are disappearing from Earth, the result being an ecological Armageddon.

Kelleher, Anne (20th Century)

Kelleher, a philosopher and broadcaster, took a leading part in defending humanism in England's Channel Four television program "Beyond Belief: Religion on Trial." She also has been an interviewer on "Choices, Choices" and a program for children, "Bright Sparks."

Kellerman, Lois (20th Century)

Kellerman was a young mother when she received intensive training in Ethical Leadership in the 1980s. She became a Leader in Queens, New York, in 1983. (See entry for Ethical Culture.)

Kelley, Alec E. (20th Century)

When he signed Humanist Manifesto II, Kelley was a professor at the University of Arizona. {HM2}

Kelley, George (20th Century)

Kelley is Co-Director with Margaret Downey of the Thomas Paine Pennsylvania Memorial Committee (Box 342, Pocopson, PA 19366).

Kelley, Pat (20th Century)

Kelley, a computer analyst, is the person who is webmaster of the Sacramento Freethought Web site: <http://www.rthoughtsrfree.org>.

Kellgren, Johan Henric (1751—1795)

Kellgren was the first Scandinavian author to take an explicit anti-Christian stance. He was a poet, critic, and editor. (See entry for Scandinavian Unbelievers.) {RAT}

Kelly, John (20th Century)

Kelley is active in the American Humanist Association chapter in Phoenix, Arizona. (See entry for Arizona Atheists, Humanists.)

Kelly, John E. (19th Century)

In Sydney, Australia, J. E. Kelly edited *Stockwhip* (1875—1877), which became *Satirist.* {FUK}

Kelly, Tim (20th Century)

Kelly in 1999 became a Board Member of Cincinnati's Free Inquiry Group. "I was originally reared in the Christian belief system (conservative)," he wrote for their newsletter, "but over time (over a course of some ten years), as a result of personal study and inquiry, left the Christian faith." He found the secular humanist group on the Internet. A researcher and writer, he owns and operates a corporate health facility center and teaches classes in the martial arts.

Kelso, John (19th Century)

A freethinker, Kelso wrote *Deity Analyzed in Six Lectures* (c. 1891). {GS}

Kemble, Frances Anne (Fanny) (1809—1893)

Kemble, an actress and playwright, was a Unitarian. She was an ardent writer against slavery. Kemble was the elder daughter of the famed English actor and manager, Charles Kemble, who in 1822 was manager of Covent Garden. Her aunt, Sarah Kemble Siddons, was the most distinguished actress of the Roger Kemble (1721—1802) family. In 1829 Fanny made her debut as Juliet under her father's management at Covent Garden, and she enjoyed such success that she went on to be the original Julia in Sheridan Knowles's *The Hunchback*, written expressly for her. In 1834 she married Pierce Butler, a Unitarian who owned plantations in Georgia with seven or eight hundred slaves to run them. But her feelings about slavery, particularly when she broke the law by teaching one to read, led her to write "Journal of a Residence on a Georgian Plantation in 1838-1839." In her diary she wrote, "The estate returned a full income under his [the overseer's] management, and such men have nothing to do with sick slaves; they are tools, to be mended only if they can be made available again; if not, to be flung by as useless, without further expense of money, time, or trouble." After several years of arguing about such issues, the Butlers separated. Fanny returned to England, wrote against slavery for the London *Times*, and finished her first novel at the age of 80. {CE; EG; U; UU}

Kemerling, Donald (20th Century)

Kemerling is vice president in Kansas City, Missouri, of the Eupraxophy Center.

Kemler, Edgar (20th Century)

Kemler wrote *The Irreverent Mr. Mencken* (1950). {GS}

Kempers, Anne Grimshaw (20th Century)

Kempers, a Unitarian, is author of *Heart of Lightness: Experiences of a Peace Corps Volunteer in Africa* (1993). She spent two years in Zaire.

Kennaway, Ernest Laurence [Sir] (1881—1958)

A pathologist, Kennaway wrote *Some Religious Illusions in Art, Literature, and Experience* (1953). {GS}

Kennedy, C. F. (20th Century)

Kennedy edits The Bibliofantasiac. E-mail: <tangle@interlog.com>.

Kennedy, Dan (20th Century)

A Unitarian, Kennedy covers media and politics for the *Boston Phoenix*. "From the Inside Out: Helping Ex-Prisoners Make the Transition" (*World*, June-August 1998) describes how volunteers helping prisoners "quickly found they were learning as much as they were teaching. They couldn't provide ex-convicts with the counseling and assistance they needed without stumbling into issues of class and of how the culture conspires against the despised and downtrodden."

Kennedy, Florynce (1916—)

Kennedy is an African American freethinker whose television programs frequently support liberal causes, including women's rights to have abortions. A lesbian and lawyer, she who co-wrote *Abortion Rap: Avortement Droit Des Femmes*. {Martin Duberman, *Stonewall*}

Kennedy, John F. (20th Century)

Kennedy, while a student at New Mexico State University, was one of the founding members of Campus Freethought Alliance. {*International Humanist News*, December 1996}

Kennedy, John Fitzgerald [President] (1917—1963)

The 35th United States President was his nation's first Catholic President, which was considered a milestone by many inasmuch as certain citizens had mistakenly believed that ours is "one nation under a Protestant God, indivisible, with liberty and justice for all." To his credit, at forty-three the youngest President to hold office, John F. Kennedy announced,

> Whatever one's religion in his private life may be, for the officeholder, nothing takes precedence over his oath to uphold the Constitution and all its parts—including the First Amendment and the strict separation of church and state.

As pointed out by Gore Vidal and others, President Kennedy did not separate the state from his love life, enjoying numerous eighteenth-century-like amoral sexual escapades within the White House. (See entry for Robert Frost.) {CE; Gore Vidal, *The New Yorker*, 1 December 1997}

Kennedy, Joseph Patrick II (1952—)

Kennedy, the son of Robert F. and Ethel Kennedy, is a Massachusetts congressman. Sheila Rauch Kennedy, whom he divorced, wrote in *Shattered Faith* (1997) that she had vomited when her ostensibly religious husband had asked for an annulment so he could marry a longtime aide, Beth Kelly, in a Catholic ceremony. She refused to accept an annulment, which would have meant their marriage had been invalid, because of the moral implications for their twin sons. Inasmuch as the Catholic Church does not recognize divorce, the only way to remarry is to declare the marriage invalid in the first place. "I don't actually believe this stuff," her book reports he told her. "It's just Catholic gobbledygook. . . . You can't be stupid enough to believe this." {*The New York Times* 24 April 1997}

Kennedy, Ludovic [Sir] (1919—)

A writer and broadcaster married to the Scottish ballerina Moira Shearer, Kennedy wrote an autobiography, *On My Way to the Club* (1989). He contributed to the BBC's "Panorama" (1960—1963) and produced a number of television series. "We're in an age where it's not possible to accept supernatural beliefs," he told a *Sunday Telegraph* interviewer in 1994. "In five hundred years God will simply be seen as myth and allegory. . . . There have been millions of gods in human history. This is just another one. We do not believe today in the gods the Greeks and Romans worshiped, but they did. I mean, why do people believe now there's just one? There could be hundreds up there watching us." Kennedy told the interviewer that he had discarded religion because he had wasted 1,300 hours on religious observances at school.

His preoccupation with euthanasia and "dying well," he explained, are not solely connected with atheism, for he knows many believers who are also interested in advancing the idea. "It's only the Catholics who are implacable enemies of euthanasia," he added. "That wicked old man the Pope," whereupon he quoted the Pope's words with feeling: "Suffering, especially during the last moments of life, has a special place in God's saving plan." To which Kennedy responded, "Unmitigated tosh!"

In 1986, Kennedy was elected an honorary associate of the Rationalist Press Association. In 1994, Queen Elizabeth II knighted him.

In 1996 Sir Ludovic was named President of the Voluntary Euthanasia Society, and in 1997 he became an Honorary Associate of the National Secular Society.

All in the Mind: a Farewell to God (1999) discusses how Margaret Knight's radio talks in the 1950s played a large part in secularizing Britain, swinging large numbers of people away from belief in God. Terry Sanderson found the book of interest but felt that it is no longer important to attack Christianity in the old ways, that Kennedy was, "regrettably, tilting at windmills that are already derelict—at least in Britain."

His *Testament: Reflections of a Born Again Heretic* confirmed what in 1996 he told the *Daily Telegraph*:

> I haven't believed in God since I first went to school. He exists only in the mind and is otherwise completely redundant. I had to undergo at least 1,300 hours of heavy Christian indoctrination—what a terrible waste of time.

{*The Freethinker*, July 1994 and February 1997; *The Freethinker*, July 1997}

Kenney, Anthony (20th Century)

See the entry for Richard Dawkins, who describes Kenney—the President of the British Academy—and his ability to renounce the Catholic orders and become an independent thinker.

Kenny, Courney (1847—1930)

Kenny was a university professor of law and a Member of Parliament who made an attempt to get his Religious Prosecution Abolition Bill (1887) passed in order to fight the blasphemy law. The attempt was unsuccessful. {GS}

Kenny, L. B. (20th Century)

Commencing in 1992, Dr. Kenny became chairperson of the Indian Rationalist Association.

Kenrick, John (19th Century)

Both Kenrick and Samuel Sharpe, historians of Egypt, were Unitarians. {JMR}

Kenrick, William (c. 1720—1779)

Under the name of Ontologos, Kenrick published a 1751 essay to prove that the soul is not immortal. His first poetic production was a volume of *Epistles, Philosophical and Moral* (1759), an avowed defense of skepticism and addressed to Lorenzo. In 1775 he commenced the *London Review*, and the following year he attacked Soame Jenyns's work on Christianity. Kenrick translated some of the works of Buffon, Rousseau, and Voltaire. {BDF; RAT}

Kent, Gordon (20th Century)

Kent, leader of a Humanist Society in Moline, Illinois, wrote *Humanism* (1944) and *Humanism for the Millions* (1951). {EW; GS; HNS}

Kent, Jack (20th Century)

A retired Unitarian minister, Kent is author of *The Psychological Origins of the Resurrection Myth* (1999). Antony Flew described the work: "Of all the accounts I know of the origin of the belief in the physical resurrection from the dead of Jesus, the son of Joseph, and hence of the rise of the Christian Church, the account here presented seems to me the most plausible." {*New Humanist*, September 1999}

Kent, Theodore C. (1923—)

Kent, a Unitarian minister, started a Humanist society in Moline, Illinois, in 1933. Edwin H. Wilson said Kent had a reputation "for certain sensational and erratic tendencies, such as dimming the lights with a rheostat during his meditational services and easing the lights back on when he got to the 'Amen." However, Wilson added that Kent was an excellent orator who was successful in reaching the hypothetical "man on the street." His paperback "Humanist for the Millions" was issued in several editions.

The author in 1995 of *Mapping the Human Genome: Reality, Morality, and Deity*, Kent wrote of the moral implications of the scientific effort to identify all the genes that make up DNA.

Kent, William (20th Century)

Kent wrote *Lift Up Your Heads, An Anthology for Freethinkers* (1948). {GS}

KENT (England) HUMANISTS

For information, write M. Rogers, 2 Lyndhurst Road, Broadstairs CT 10 1DD; telephone 01843 864506.

KENTUCKY HUMANISTS

Kentucky has the following groups:

• Louisville Association of Secular Humanists (ASHS), PO Box 91453, Louisville, Kentucky 40291; phone (502) 491-6693.

• Larry Reyka, POB 3208, Columbus, Ohio 43210, is the AHA coordinator of the north central region.

• University of Louisville humanists on the Web: <http://www.secularhumanism.org/cfa/orgs.html>.

Kepler, Johannes (1571—1630)

Kepler, the German astronomer whose "Kepler's laws" describe the revolutions of the planets around the sun, once professed Protestantism. However, he was excommunicated by the Tübingen Protestant authorities in 1612 because he had condemned the Lutheran doctrine that the body of Christ could be in several places at once. Kepler's mother, found guilty of witchcraft, was saved from harm because of her son's influence. Kepler eventually returned to Catholicism. {CE; ER; JMR; JMRH; TYD}

Keyser, Cassius Jackson (Born 1862)

Keyser was an American mathematician who was a member of the American Board of the *Hibbert Journal*. Keyser was a theist, but he rejected personal immortality. In *Humanism and Science* (1931) he discussed scientific humanism, arguing that "the spirit of Science" is "the soul of Humanism." {RAT}

Keracher, John (20th Century)

A materialist, Keracher wrote *How the Gods Were Made* (c. 1920). {GS}

Kerby, J. J. (19th Century)

Kerby's *Atheism and Socialism* (1905) was a provocative book in its time and showed the author's dedicated atheism.

Kerler, Dietrich Heinrich (1837—1907)

Writing to the German philosopher and phenomenologist Max Scheler, who believed that love is the great principle of human association and God is the source of all love, Kerler retorted, "Even if it could be proved by mathematics that God exists, I do not want him to exist, because he would set limits to my greatness."

Kern, Marc (20th Century)

Kern is the founding director and chief executive of Officer of Life Management Skills, which houses the Addiction Alternatives and Rational Life skills organizations. At the 14th annual HUMCON conference in 1994, which was sponsored by the Alliance of Humanist, Atheist, and Ethical Culture Organizations of Los Angeles County, California, Kern discussed rational coping skills, the Rational-Emotive behavior therapy of Dr. Albert Ellis, Rational Recovery, and other non-religious help for those with substance-dependence and related problems.

Kerns, Scott (20th Century)

Kerns once led the Texas chapter of American Atheists. At his wedding, Madalyn Murray O'Hair played the preacher and "took the ceremony very seriously," making sure that, unlike Texas justices of the peace, she would not slip a "God" or even a "Jesus" into the service.

Jon Murray, Kerns later found, was not up to heading the organization. "He had no special training, nor a great number of social skills, as well as a speech impediment. He was at an extreme disadvantage, and he was aware that he'd been put in a position beyond his abilities to handle." {*Time*, 10 February 1997}

Kerouac, Jack (1922—1969)

> • You have to believe in life before you can accomplish anything. That is why dour, regular-houred, rational-souled State Department diplomats have done nothing for mankind. Why live if not for excellence?
>
> —From Jack Kerouac's journals

Kerouac, an American novelist who became spokesman for the Beat generation, wrote *On the Road* (1957), which relates the wanderings of Sal Paradise and his friend, Dean Moriarty, across America. The two think they are getting somewhere and that they're looking for someone. Then it dawns upon them that they're already there, on the road, which is the sensible place to have a pad and for Dharma bums to be. He also wrote *Dharma Bums* (1958) and *The Subterraneans* (1958).

Of his confessional style of writing, Truman Capote once quipped, "That's not writing. That's typewriting."

Kerouac's chronic alcoholism led to his death from a stomach hemorrhage. During one of his breakdowns, he had hallucinated, thinking of himself as a prize in a war between angels and devils. He did not label his outlook, but although he was raised a Roman Catholic he developed views that were non-theistic with Zen and humanist overtones. (*The New Yorker*, 22-29 June 1998) {OEL}

Kerr, David (18th Century)

Kerr, a Fayetteville Presbyterian minister, became a passionate republican and skeptic upon accepting a professorship at Chapel Hill. (See entry for North Carolina Freethinkers.)

Kerr, Michael Crawford (1827—1876)

Kerr was an American statesman, a confirmed freethinker and materialist. He was a member of the Indiana legislature in 1856 and was elected to Congress in 1874. Kerr was known for trying to revise the tariff in the direction of free trade. {BDF}

Kesey, Ken (1935-)

Kesey, a hero of the countercultural revolution and the hippie movement of the 1960s, once was a paid volunteer at a Veterans Administration hospital in Menlo Park, California, where he took mind-altering drugs and reported on their effects. The job served as background *One Flew Over the Cuckoo's Nest* (1962; film, 1975), which is set in a mental hospital.

He also wrote *Sometimes a Great Notion* (1964), in which he examines values in conflict; *Little Tricker the Squirrel Meets Big Double the Bear* (1988), a children's book; and *Caverns* (1990), a mystery novel written with thirteen of his graduate students in creative writing at the University of Oregon and using the pseudonym of O. U. Levon, which read backwards is "novel U. O." [University of Oregon].

According to the American Library Association's *Banned Books* (1998), *One Flew Over the Cuckoo's Nest* is often banned because it is alleged to promote "secular humanism."

Kespohl, Julius (20th Century)

Kespohl has been an active member of the American Humanist Association. {HNS}

Kessler, John J. (20th Century)

Kessler, who worked on *The Humanist*, was a semanticist who wrote *The Three Hills of Semantika* (1955) and *Giordano Bruno, the Forgotten Philosopher* (c. 1960). {GS; HNS2}

Kessler, Julius (20th Century)

Kessler was on the advisory board of Charles Francis Potter's First Humanist Society of New York.

Ket (Kett, or Knight), Francis (16th Century)

Ket of Norfolk, a relative of the rebellious tanner, was prosecuted for heresy and was burned in a castle ditch. Stowe says he was burned in 1588 for "divers detestable opinions against Christ our Saviour." {BDF}

Ketkar, Kumar (20th Century)

Ketkar is editor in India of the *Maharashtra Times*, the only paper in the state of Maharashtra to oppose the Indian atomic explosions. At the 1998 congress of the International Humanist and Ethical Union in Mumbai, Ketkar discussed India's political problems as they related to humanism. {*International Humanist News*, December 1998}

Kevorkian, Murad (Jack) (1928—)

Michael Betzold, author of *Appointment With Doctor Death* (1993), once asked Dr. Kevorkian what he thought happened after one dies. "You rot," replied the retired pathologist who has achieved notoriety in the 1990s for having assisted more than 130 seriously ill individuals to kill themselves.

Although castigated by his opponents as "Dr. Death," Dr. Kevorkian believes euthanasia must be made legal through carefully designed physician-assisted suicide for individuals who have no hope of recovering from their illness. He has merited the wrath of various Christian officials but counters with the argument that religion and medicine should be completely divorced. Or, as his lawyer described it, "If the church is in charge, man, we might as well go back to the fucking Inquisition." In short, as a physician Kevorkian was trained to focus on and address the underlying problem, rather than be distracted by symptoms, and he had seen pointless suffering which could have and should have been ended to everyone's benefit.

Meanwhile, Michigan law outlaws physician-assisted suicide, and the state suspended Dr. Kevorkian's medical license because of his invention of "Mercitron," a machine that allows individuals to kill themselves painlessly at the flick of a switch. "The world knows I'm not a criminal," he has argued. "You've lost common sense in this society because of religious fanaticism and dogma. You're basing your laws, and your whole outlook of natural life, on mythology! It won't work!" His book on the subject, in which he argues for the goodness of planned death, is *Prescription: Medicine* (1993).

In a *Playboy* profile (August 1994), Kevorkian was asked if he was ever religious. "Not really," he replied. "I went to Sunday school until I got tired of the myths. Walk on water! You can't fool a kid."

An agnostic, Dr. Kevorkian addressed the annual convention in 1991 of the Freedom From Religion Foundation meeting in Ann Arbor. In 1994, the American Humanist Association named him Humanist Hero of the Year. In 1995, he assisted the Unitarian minister John Evans, who was suffering from pulmonary fibrosis, a terminal lung disease, to commit suicide. Evans was the twenty-second person of over forty Kevorkian, whom some began to call "Dr. Life," had assisted as of the end of 1996.

Asked if he would be present when the U.S. Supreme Court took up the issue of doctor-assisted suicide, Kevorkian responded, "Nothing good can come of this. Did anything good come out of [the abortion case of] *Roe v. Wade*? You got some doctors killed. What the Supreme Court does is irrelevant. . . . You want me to go down there and face nine religious kooks?" Meanwhile, Kevorkian is considered by many to be a *medical* kook. Betzold in "The Selling of Doctor Death" (*The New Republic*, 26 May 1997) details the many criticisms of Kevorkian's endeavors to pioneer the radical change in the way human beings die.

In what legal scholars considered a major mistake, Kevorkian chose to represent himself in a 1999 case brought against him for having helped end the life of Thomas Youk, a 52-year-old from a Detroit suburb who suffered from amyotrophic lateral sclerosis, or Lou Gehrig's disease. The incident was televised, Mr. Youk's family was present, Mr. Youk pleaded for medical help in ending his suffering, and Kevorkian was seen on film injecting the lethal chemicals. A jury, however, convicted him of murder. The Youk family, which was not allowed to speak at the trial, was disturbed by the jury's verdict, as was the Hemlock Society. However, a group of disabled people, called Not Dead Yet, was heartened, viewing the euthanasia movement as threatening to disabled people. Kevorkian responded by threatening to starve himself in jail, and his friends prepared to appeal the jury's decision. Found guilty by a Michigan judge, Kevorkian was sentenced in 1999 to ten to twenty-five years in prison despite pleas on his behalf from the widow and brother of the terminally ill man he was convicted of killing. He planned to appeal the conviction but was not allowed bail. Meanwhile, his supporters held that the Michigan lawmakers, not Kevorkian, should be jailed for having written such inhumanistic legislation. The doctor, they claimed, had now become a 20th century freethought martyr. Kevorkian is an honorary member of the Freedom From Religion Foundation. His hobbies include playing flute with a jazz quintet, composing ("A Very Still Life: the Kevorkian Suite" for flute and jazz quintet), and oil painting. A 1997 showing of thirteen paintings were said by critics to be those of an amateur, but they disturbed many viewers because they depicted severed heads, moldering skulls, rotting corpses, and a frame which was stained with his own blood. The doctor's fascination with the subject of death—even as a young physician, he photographed the eyes of dying patients, finding this "interesting"—has led to the speculation by his opponents that he would assist suicides not only for the terminally ill but also for people with "severe trauma" or "intense anxiety." (See entry for Derek Humphry.) {Associated Press, 6 January 1997; E; HNS2}

Key, Ellen Karolina Sofia (1849—1926)

The daughter of a Swedish countess, Key nevertheless came from an impoverished family. Through teaching and writing, she became a leading European female to write on social questions. Key joined Haeckel in his Monist (atheist) League, often writing for his monthly. Seven of her thirty works were translated into English. {JM; RAT; RE; WWS}

Khamarov, Eli (20th Century)

Khamarov, an author and social theorist, has gone on record as being a non-theist. He wrote *Surviving on Planet Reebok* and *Lives of the Cognoscenti*. {CA; E}

Khan, Akhtar Hameed (1915—)

Khan, according to Salman Rushdie, is a Pakistani poet who "is quoted as having said that while he admires Mohammed his real inspiration has been the Buddha. He denies saying this but nevertheless is accused of blasphemy by mullahs. In 1992, he was arrested for allegedly insulting the Prophet's descendants by writing a poem about animals that, the fundamentalists asserted, contained hidden allegorical meanings." In *The New York Times* op-ed article entitled "The Struggle for the Soul of Islam" (11 July 1993), Rushdie concludes, "He managed to beat that charge but now again his life is in danger. . . . We should understand that secularism is now the fanatics' most important target."

Khan, Seemin G. (20th Century)

An eye physician and surgeon in Chicago, Khan participated in the 1996 Humanist World Congress in Mexico City.

Khare, Nina (20th Century)

Khare was Secretary to the South Place Ethical Society from 1991 to 1996, at which time she left to join REFUGE, an organization that supports women seeking sanctuary from domestic violence. A fourth-generation freethinker, she comes from the Essex families of Warner and High. {*Freethinker*, August 1996}

Khayyám: See entry for Omar.

Khosla, Vinod (20th Century)

In the next one hundred years, Khosla tells friends, "traditional religion will be as relevant as witch doctors are today." The partner in Kleiner Perkins Caulfield & Byers, who was born in India and who co-founded Sun Microsystems in California's Silicon Valley, also holds that the pope, who "chooses to talk about gays, abortion and priests not being women . . . could use his power in better ways.

Kichanova, Inga (20th Century)

Kichanova, from the USSR, addressed the Fourth International Humanist and Ethical Union World Congress held in Paris (1966).

Kidneigh, John C. (20th Century)

When he signed Humanist Manifesto II, Kidneigh was professor of Social Work at the University of Minnesota. He wrote *Access to Medical Care* (1981). {HM2; HNS}

Kielland, Alexander Lange (1849—1906)

A Norwegian writer of novels, short stories, and plays, Kielland is a major writer of realism. With the purpose of encouraging social reform, he used wit and irony in such works as *Skipper Worse* (1882), *Tales of Two Countries* (1879), and *Norse Tales and Sketches* (1897). His *St. Hans Fest* (1887) attacked the hypocrisy of Christian morals. His humanistic novels succeeded in a country with a strong Lutheran church, forming an opposition counter-culture which has become more and more secular, according to Levi Fragell, a former executive director of Norway's humanist organization, *Human-Etisk Forbund*. {BDF; *Free Inquiry*, Winter, 1990-1991; RAT}

Kierkegaard, Søren (1813—1855)

According to Barnes, Kierkegaard was a Christian existentialist who believed that "the ultimate challenge for religious existentialism is to make the leap in faith, believing in God against reason and despite the absurd (or because of it)." During his lifetime, he was scarcely known outside Denmark and was not taken seriously by his compatriots. Born when his mother was forty-five and his father was fifty-six years of age, Kierkegaard had uneven legs, a hunched back, and frail health. In his journals, he remarked that "I was already an old man when I was born, delicate, slender and weak, deprived of almost every condition for holding my own with other boys, or even for passing as a complete human being in comparison with others." It was Karl Barth's interpreting him in his *Epistle to the Romans* that brought Kierkegaard's name to the larger audiences. Kierkegaard considered the Danish church "godless," which made him unhappy. Wanting to be an orthodox Lutheran, he hoped to commit himself to the claims of the Absolute without regard for the cost involved, according to Princeton's Otto A. Piper. Such an attitude is opposed to the "spectator attitude" of science and speculative philosophy. With emphasis, Kierkegaard pointed out that the hardships of such existential life were made tolerable only through the certainty of divine grace and forgiveness of sins. Such self-scrutiny was similar, he held, to that shown by Pascal and St. Augustine. He has greatly influenced contemporary Protestantism with his view that belief involves a leap of faith.

At Kierkegaard's religious funeral at a Viking church near Uppsala, Sweden, his nephew spoke up to complain that the Lutheran Church was appropriating the memorial of its most outspoken opponent, for his uncle had once written, "Pastors are royal officials, and royal officials have nothing to do with Christianity." Kierkegaard, however, was serene after suffering a fatal stroke, believing he soon would sit astride a cloud and sing Alleluia. {CE; ER; EU, Hazel E. Barnes; RAT; TRI}

KILLING

• Kill one man, and you are a murderer.
Kill millions, and you are a conqueror.
Kill all, and you are a God.

—**Jean Rostand**

Killip, A. E. (20th Century)

In Yorkshire in the early 1900s, Killip was a lecturer in Birkenhead for the British Secular League. {RSR}

Kilpatrick, William Heard (1871—1965)

Kilpatrick, the son of a Baptist minister, as a youth became a non-conformist who did not believe in report cards or pupil punishment. At the University of Chicago in 1898, after taking a course with John Dewey, Kilpatrick became determined to teach and to make schools different. At Mercer University, where he taught mathematics and became a vice president, he was found to be a nonbeliever in the Virgin birth. After a three-day theological trial, he was asked to resign. He then moved to Columbia University, where he became known as "the father of progressive education" and "the million dollar professor" for an estimated 34,000 students from 1909 to 1938. Although he praised Dewey, he differed educationally in some respects. At the present writer's request, he once spoke of his philosophic naturalism and humanism to New York City humanists, at which time he explained why he rejected organized class subjects that strictly followed a syllabus. He also visited the present writer's class of private school students at the progressive Bentley School in Manhattan, commenting that the teacher appeared to be following his own child-centered emphasis. "No," came a quick response, "I am just teaching the way I wish I'd been taught." Kilpatrick roared with laughter, for he confirmed that this echoed his own educational philosophy.

In 1953, as a subscriber to *The Humanist Newsletter*, Kilpatrick wrote his views about what a humanist's political views can be:

> A humanist may belong to any reputable party, provided that in his acceptance of this party affiliation he consistently maintains his respect for human personality and its full development, his acceptance of democratic freedom and equality joined with commitment to the common good, and his determination to find out by the free play of intelligence what to think and do as he faces the successive situations of life.

Adjacent was a copy of a *New Yorker* cartoon showing two men discussing politics, one saying, "As good Americans we should oppose McCarthyism, but if we do somebody'll say we're not very good Americans—see, that's McCarthyism!" {CE; HNS; HNS2}

Kim, Sang J. (20th Century)

Kim is an astronomer at the National Space Science Data Center at Goddard Space Flight Center / National Aeronautic and Space Administration in Greenbelt, Maryland. He laments the Korean Unification Church, which numbers less than 1% of Korean Christians but which has more Americans as members than it has Koreans. He also laments the Korean phenomenon of Jesus-worship. "Koreans have been bombarded only by Christian material for a long time," he writes. "We should educate and communicate with the religious. We should also show believers and unbelievers in Korea clear humanist visions and values that can be alternatives to religion, so that we and our descendants can live happily and prosperously without being abused by dogmatic religions." {*Free Inquiry*, Spring, 1992}

Kimberly, James (20th Century)

Kimberly is the chief development officer for the Council for Secular Humanism and for the Committee for the Scientific Investigation of Claims of the Paranormal.

Kimbrell, Lois (20th Century)

Kimbrell is associated with the Humanist Society of New Mexico (AHA). (See entry for New Mexico Humanists.) {FD}

Kincaid, Gerald (20th Century)

Kincaid in 1941 wrote his M.A. thesis at the University of Illinois on "The 'Lines of Argument' Used by Robert G. Ingersoll in His Lectures on Religion." {FUS}

Kindell, Roy (20th Century)

Kindell, a science and mathematics teacher, is associated with Humanists of Rogue Valley (AHA) in Oregon. (See entry for Oregon Rationalists, Humanists.) {FD}

KINDNESS

• One can always be kind to people about whom one cares nothing.

—Oscar Wilde

• Whoever you are—I have always depended on the kindness of strangers.

—Tennessee Williams

KING JAMES BIBLE

The year after James I (1566—1625) was born, he became titular king of Scotland. Although he married at the age of twenty-three and had several children, gossip of that time was that he had many liaisons with male lovers, beginning when thirteen with his cousin, Esmé Stuart. Upon succeeding Queen Elizabeth in 1603, the quip circulated that "Elizabeth was king, now James is queen." Among his lovers was the handsome Robert Carr, who was made a Gentleman of the Bedchamber. When Carr married, James wrote to him complaining of Carr's "withdrawing yourself from lying in my chamber, notwithstanding my many hundred times earnestly soliciting you to the contrary." A later favorite was George Villiers, the Earl of Buckingham, of whom James said, "You may be sure that I love the Earl of Buckingham more than anyone else. Christ had his John, and I have my George." James knew the Bible well, for during his twenty-two years as king (during which he had constant feuds with Parliament and ended by dissolving that body) the King James Version of the Bible was begun. Known as the Authorized Version, it had no rival among Protestants until the late nineteenth century, when the Revised Version was published in England. {AA; DCL; GL}

King, Baird (20th Century)

Lt. Colonel (Retired) King leads Humanists of Iowa (AHA).

King, Charles (1922—)

"Charlie" King is a freethinker and "soapbox orator." He left school when fourteen years of age. In 1961 he began speaking at the Sydney Domain forum, and in 1973 he formed and became president of the loosely structured Freethinkers Association of New South Wales. {SWW}

King, Florence (20th Century)

King, whose column "The Misanthropes Corner" is in *National Review*, wrote (Mid-March 1997) of her supporting a cause ". . . with every atheistic bone in my body." {CA}

King, Larry (Larry Zeiger) (1933—)

King is a noted American radio and television personality. In 1992 he was named to the Emerson Hall of Fame of the Broadcasters Hall of Fame. On the air, he has stated that he is a nontheist, that when he had a heart attack there was no bright light at the end of the tunnel "or anything like that." In *Powerful Prayers*, he ironically makes reference to his agnosticism toward the idea of God and the efficacy of prayer. {CA; E}

King, Margaret J. (20th Century)

King is arts editor of *Religious Humanism*, the quarterly of the Fellowship of Religious Humanists.

King, Patricia (20th Century)

King is a contributing editor to *Freethought Today*.

King, Peter (1776—1833)

A financier and a Whig member of the House of Lords, King voted for Catholic Emancipation and opposed the suggestion of a grant to the Society for the Propagation of the Gospel. "Of late years," reported *Gentleman's Magazine* in its obituary notice (1833), "Lord King has chiefly signalized himself as the bitter enemy of the Church, and particularly of the Episcopal Bench." King, the seventh Baron King, was a deist. {RE}

King, Thomas Starr (1824—1864)

King, a Universalist-Unitarian minister who spoke in California against slavery during the Civil War period, encouraged California to join the Union side. The Thomas Starr King School for Religious Leadership in Berkeley is named after him, for he is generally regarded as the most notable missionary of Unitarianism to the West Coast. King wrote *Christianity and Humanity*. Once asked the difference between the Unitarians and the Universalists, King, who had served both as a minister, quipped, "The one thinks God is too good to damn them forever, and the other thinks they are too good to be damned forever." {U; UU; U&U}

King, Victor (20th Century)

King is President of the Atheist Network's Board of Directors and edits its *Atheist Network Journal* (PO Box 130898, Houston, Texas 77219). He heads the Atheist Alliance that resulted when Madalyn Murray O'Hair's atheist chapters disbanded in 1991.

Kingdon, F. R. S. (1845—1879)

Kingdon, a British mathematician, was one of several scientists (Huxley, Darwin, Tyndall, etc.) who wrote about their freethought. His *Lectures and Essays* (published 1918) advised, "Keep your children away from the priest, or he will make them the enemies of mankind." {JM}

Kinglake, Alexander William (1809—1891)

Kinglake, a lawyer, made a reputation by his novel *Eothen*

(1844) and was commissioned to write the official history of the Crimean War (1863—1887, 8 volumes). In his novel, Kinglake had freely expressed his agnosticism, as he had in his personal letters, especially one published by Grant Duff in the *Spectator* (10 May 1919). {RAT; RE}

Kingsley, George Henry (1827—1892)

Kingsley, a traveler and writer, was brother of Canon Kingsley, who gave up the creed at an early date and took a part on the anti-clerical side in the French Revolution of 1848. In a memoir prefixed to his *Notes on Sport and Travel* (1900), his daughter Mary reproduced a letter of his expressing strong Rationalist sentiments and telling that he was an agnostic. In the book he severely criticized the churches, particularly resenting "the foul brutality and baseness" of the Roman Church. {RAT; RE}

Kingsley, Mary Henrietta (1862—1900)

Well-known as an African traveler, Kingsley startled many by her daring journeys and her trading in Africa. The daughter of George Henry Kingsley, also a traveler and an agnostic, she is quoted in Clodd's *Memories* as being an agnostic. Upon returning in 1900 to nurse wounded Boers, Kingsley died of enteric fever. {JM; RAT; RE}

Kinney, Paul (20th Century)

Kinney, with others, wrote "Should Public Schools Do Church Work?" (1947). {GS; HNS}

Kinnock, Neil [Rt. Honorable] (1942—)

Kinnock, a member of the House of Commons, has been on the National Executive Committee of England's Labour Party since 1978. From 1979 to 1983, he was chief Opposition Spokesman on Education. From 1980 to 1982 he was President of the Association of Liberal Education. In 1986, he wrote *Making Our Way*. He has stated publicly that he is an atheist. {CA; E; *New Humanist*, September 1996}

Kinsella, William Patrick (1935-)

Kinsella is the Canadian author of *Shoeless Joe Jackson Comes to Iowa* (1980) and numbers of other novels and works of poetry. In 1987 he was named Author of the Year by the Canadian Library Association. In 1994 he was decorated with the Order of Canada.

Kinsella is a member of American Atheists and the British Columbia Humanist Association. {CA}

Kinsey, Alfred (1854—1956)

An American biologist and noted sexologist, Kinsey was associated with the University of Indiana from 1920 until the time of his death. His early work dealt with the gall wasp. After receiving financial support from the university, the National Research Council, and the Rockefeller Foundation, Kinsey began a project of interviewing many thousands of individuals in a study which led to his publishing *Sexual Behavior of the Human Male* (1948) and *Sexual Behavior of the Human Female* (1953). The research immediately helped free American society of Victorian repression. His crusade to promote more enlightened sexual attitudes, according to James H. Jones's *Albert C. Kinsey: A Public/Private Life* (1997), led to the following:

> [I]n 1957, a year after his death, the Supreme Court's Roth decision narrowed the legal definition of obscenity, expanding the umbrella of constitutional protection to cover a broader range of works portraying sex in art, literature, and film. In 1960, the birth-control pill was introduced, offering a highly effective method of contraception. In 1961, Illinois became the first state to repeal its sodomy statutes. The next year, the Supreme Court ruled that a magazine featuring photographs of male nudes was not obscene and was therefore not subject to censorship. And in 1973, in a dramatic reversal, the American Psychiatric Association removed homosexuality from its list of psychopathologies.

Jones described Kinsey's finesse is developing and interviewing individuals, told of his interest in homosexuality (in fact, calls Kinsey—the father of four—a homosexual rather than a bisexual) and sadomasochism (who struggled as a youth with homoerotic feelings and punished himself by inserting a toothbrush up his urethra during masturbation); photographed his wife Clara masturbating; filmed writer Glenway Wescott and his companion Monroe Wheeler in order to document the former's "jackknifing" at the time of his orgasm; decreed that men could have sex with each other and that the wives, too, could be free to embrace whatever sexual partners they liked; even had himself photographed while engaged in masochistic masturbation. One of Kinsey's most provocative discoveries was that males of different social backgrounds and educational levels presented strongly dissimilar sexual histories. Many of his statistics were challenged, and he received considerable criticism from academic as well as religious sources for the scope of his research.

Martin Duberman, critiquing the Jones work, pointed out that he had ignored Kinsey's famous 0 to 6 scale (0 = exclusive heterosexuality; 6 = exclusive homosexuality). Insiders, he claimed, placed Kinsey at between a "1" and a "2"—more "straight" than "gay"—when younger, then shifting increasingly to the "homosexual" side of the scale as he aged, but never becoming an exclusive "6." In the final analysis, Duberman found the Jones book "never manages a coherent portrait—and personality contradictions *can* intelligible cohere."

Kinsey was the son of evangelical Methodists. His father had forbade dancing, tobacco, drink, and popular music in their household. Kinsey in his later years went public, according to Jones, declaring himself an atheist. He did not, however, become a member of any of the freethought associations. (James H. Jones, "Dr. Yes," *The New Yorker*, 25 August-1 September 1997)

Kinsley, Michael (1951—)

Kinsley was managing editor of *The New Republic* from 1976 to 1979 and its editor from 1979 to 1981. From 1981 to 1983 he edited *Harper's Magazine*. Now an internet editor of *Slate* with a World Wide Web following, Kinsley has gone on record as being a non-theist. {CA; E}

Kirby, Joe (20th Century)

Kirby wrote *The First Book of Atheist Humor* (1983). {GS}

Kirchoff, Chris (20th Century)

Kirchoff, who will graduate from Harvard in 2001, has been described by the *Humanist Association of Massachusetts Newsletter* "as the leading Humanist student at Harvard," succeeding Darek Araujo.

Kirk, John R. (20th Century)

When he wrote book reviews for *The Humanist* in the 1950s, Kirk was on the Michigan State University faculty and worked for WJIM-AM and WJIM-TV.

Kirkendall, Lester A. (1903—1991)

Kirkendall, who taught at Oregon State University, was the author of *Premarital Intercourse and Interpersonal Relationships* (1984). A co-editor of *The New Sexual Revolution*, he taught the first course on human sexuality on any campus in the United States. Kirkendall signed Humanist Manifesto II. In 1983, the American Humanist Association named him Humanist of the Year. {HM1; HNS2; PK}

Kirkhart, Roberta (20th Century)

Kirkhart is a teacher, writer, atheist activist, and defender of church and state separation. She addressed the 14th annual HUMCON conference in 1994 that was sponsored by the Alliance of Humanist, Atheist, and Ethical Culture Organizations of Los Angeles County.

Kirkman, T. P. (19th Century)

Kirkman, a freethinker, wrote *On the Infidelity of Orthodoxy* (1870). {GS}

Kirsch, Jonathan (20th Century)

Kirsch has found some stories in the Hebrew Bible that appear to have been played down by preachers. In *The Harlot by the Side of the Road* (1997), Kirsch recommends seven:

- Lot impregnates his daughters (*Genesis* 19:1-38)
- Hamor rapes Dinah with consequences (*Genesis* 34:1-31)
- Tamar, the harlot by the side of the road (*Genesis* 38:1-26)
- The bridegroom of blood: Zipporah circumcises (*Exodus* 4:24-26)
- Jephthah sacrifices his daughter (*Judges* 19:1-20)
- The traveler hacks up his concubine (*Judges* 19:1-30)
- Tamar is raped by her brother (2 *Samuel* 11:2-15; 12:9-25; 13:1-22)

{Wolf Roder, *FIG Leaves*, February 1999}

KISMET

Kismet is a Moslem expression of belief in a fate that rules the affairs of men. Not only a man's fortunes, but also his deeds with their future consequences are considered to be pre-ordained and inevitable. (See entry for Fate.) {ER}

KISSES

- A kiss can be a comma, a question mark, or an exclamation point.

—Mistinguett

Kisubi, Alfred (20th Century)

Kisubi, a professor of human services at the University of Wisconsin, is an Advisory Board Member of African Americans for Humanism.

Kitcher, Philip (20th Century)

Kitcher is a contributing editor of *Philo*.

Kittle, Rudolph (1853—1929): See entry for Harris Lenowitz.

Kittredge, Herman (20th Century)

Kittredge wrote *Ingersoll: A Biographical Appreciation* (1911). {GS}

Klacel, Francis Matthew (1808—1882)

Klacel was the first outright atheist among Bohemian authors. His *Ethics* (1847) was the first freethought work in Bohemia. Persecution drove him to America. {PUT}

Klaatsch, Hermann (1863—1916)

Klaatsch, a German anthropologist, was a leading German authority on primitive man and a distinguished anthropologist generally. A monist, Klaatsch contributed occasionally to the organ of the monist league, *Das Monistische Jahrhundert*. {RAT}

Klass, Philip Julian (1919—)

Klass, a technical journalist, an electrical engineer, and a former avionics editor of *Aviation Week and Space Technology*, is on the executive council and was a founding member of the Committee for the Scientific Investigation of Claims of the Paranormal, which publishes *Skeptical Inquirer*. He is author of *UFOs—Identified* (1968), *Secret Sentries in Space* (1971); *UFOs—Explained* (1975), *UFOs: The Public Deceived* (1983); and *UFO—Abductions: A Dangerous Game* (1988).

Klawans, Stuart (20th Century)

Klawans, a film critic for *The Nation*, found "Dogma," by the Catholic filmmaker Kevin Smith

> a movie that should not have offended so many Catholics. After all, it affirmed the divinity and unique salvific mission of Jesus, the efficacy of the sacraments in and of themselves and the Magisterium. The movie is therefore far more acceptable to Catholics than it is to Protestants, Jews, Muslims, Buddhists, Taoists, Hindus, Sikhs, Wiccans, animists of all nations and secular humanists.

Klawans then added that he was "a member of the latter group." {*The Nation*, 29 November 1999}

Kleber, John E. (1941—)

Kleber wrote his 1969 Ph. D. dissertation at the University of Kentucky on "The Magic of His Power: Robert G. Ingersoll and His Day." He wrote *Kentucky Encyclopedia* (1992). {FUS}

Kleberg, Carl-Johan (20th Century)

Kleberg, at the 1998 Congress of the International Humanist and Ethical Union in Mumbai, spoke about church-state separation in Sweden. Humanists, he explained, have argued for neutrality for religion in schools, but the church has constantly opposed such reform. In 1999 he is President of the Swedish Humanist Association. {*International Humanist News*, December 1998}

Klein, Dorothy (20th Century)

Klein, a freethinking activist, is on the Executive Board of the Humanist Society of Metropolitan New York.

Klein, Georg (20th Century)

Klein [the first name is pronounced yay-org], a Hungarian-Swedish secular humanist, is a researcher at the Department of Tumor Biology at Karolinska Institute in Stockholm, Sweden. A cell biologist and oncologist whose parents were Jewish, Klein in *The Atheist and the Holy City: Encounters and Reflections* (1990) is troubled by the perils inherent in religion. His book does not simply criticize religious systems, but he is concerned that religious bureaucracies built around the Jehovah-Jesus myths have resulted in many massacres of the innocent. "It is not enough merely to be 'anti-religious,'" he wrote. "One must build a positive force, humanism, that counteracts the religious influence in the schools, the army, and the government." Protesting that he is not an agnostic but an atheist, Klein added, "I am, indeed, an atheist. My attitude is based on faith. . . . The absence of a creator, the nonexistence of God is my childhood faith, my adult belief, unshakable and holy." The book describes what it was like to be a nonreligious doctor working in a Jerusalem clinic at a time when the world's major monotheistic religions were jockeying for position among the sacred sites. The book also relates his friendship with Leo Szilard, devoting two chapters to the "father of the atomic bomb."

In *Pieta* (1993), Klein addresses the age-old question, "Why is there suffering?" The book's hero is Arthur Schopenhauer, whose ethics of compassion is one that Klein embraces, and whose "unflinching pursuit of the truth" is one that Klein attempts to emulate. However, he also understands the dilemmas that arise when the two paths do not converge. Klein's interest in the Holocaust is not merely academic, for many of his Hungarian relatives perished in the death camps.

In 1993, Klein was named a Humanist Laureate in the International Academy of Humanism for Secular Humanism. He signed Humanist Manifesto 2000. (See entry for Christian de Duve.) {Fabiola Aguirre, "Science and Culture," *Free Inquiry* (Summer 1994); Timothy J. Madigan, "Searching for an Answer to Suffering," *Free Inquiry* (Summer 1994)}

Klein, Marty (20th Century)
Klein is on the editorial board of *The Humanist.*

Klein, Nettie (20th Century)
Klein, who had been the Secretary General of the International Humanist and Ethical Union, resigned at the 1996 conference of humanists in Mexico City, where she was given an award for more than thirty years' work as General Secretary. She first came into contact with the IHEU in Oslo in 1962, then attended conferences in Europe, India, and the United States. Klein spoke at the 1992 IHEU Congress in Amsterdam, receiving an award. A former humanist counselor, Klein wrote a regular column in *International Humanist News* up to the time of her retirement in 1996, at which time she announced she would be happily concentrating upon her grandchildren. {*International Humanist News,* December 1996}

Kleist, Heinrich von (1777—1811)
A German poet, Kleist was orphaned at eleven, enlisted in the army as a teenager, quit the army after four years in order to study, and from reading Kant he became a skeptic and freethinker. In 1800 he taught Kantian philosophy in Paris. His first gay relationships, according to Toronto critic Anna Sonser, were in the military and led to "lifelong associates with Ernst von Pfuel and Rühle von Lilenstern." He was plagued by moral and emotional upheavals, including a "Kant Crisis," which according to Sonser "undermined his faith in truth and knowledge and inaugurated a period of despondency and personal anguish." Upon becoming engaged to Wilhelmine von Zenge, he shortly thereafter went to Würzburg in search of treatment for what may have been a sexual disorder. Friends were aware that he fought against despair and desired death. Known chiefly for his dramas and a collection of tales, Kleist is also known for the suicide pact he arranged with Henriette Vogel. In Potsdam he shot her, then himself, when only thirty-four. {BDF; GL; RAT}

Klem, Tom (20th Century)
Klem chairs the Gay and Lesbian Atheists and Humanists in California. He spoke in 1994 at the 14th annual HUMCON conference sponsored by the Alliance of Humanist, Atheist, and Ethical Culture Organizations of Los Angeles County, California.

Klemm, Edward G. Jr. (1910—)
Klemm, a poet and a freethinker, wrote *I Wonder Why* (1977). {GS}

Kleveland, Åse (20th Century)
Kleveland, the Norwegian minister of culture, is a member of Norway's humanist organization, *Human-Etisk Forbund.*

Klinger, Friedrich Maxmilian von (1753—1831)
Klinger, a German writer, went to Russia in 1780 and became reader to the Grand Duke Paul. He published poems, dramas, and romances, exhibiting the revolt of nature against conventionality. Goethe called him "a true apostle of the Gospel of nature." {BDF}

Kluckhohn, Clyde K(ay) M(aben) (1905—1960)
A noted anthropologist on the Harvard faculty, Kluckhohn was a naturalist who wrote for *The Humanist.* His cousin was the Iowa novelist and Friend, Ruth Suckow. A particular interest of his was the culture of the Navaho Indians, as shown in *Navaho Withcraft* (1944). A humanistic 1949 work, *Mirror for Man,* popularized Kluckhohn's views. {HNS}

Klugman, Richard E. (1924—)
Klugman, who in 1938 arrived in Australia from Italy, is an atheist, humanist, politician, and medical practitioner. Upon becoming Labor Member of the House of Representatives in 1969, was one of three only who affirmed allegiance rather than to take the oath. By 1990, most of the Australian Labor Party members were affirming. Strongly anti-authoritarian, he has been active with the Council for Civil Liberties and the Humanist Society of New South Wales. Klugman has a special interest in Abortion Law Reform and education with particular emphasis on changing the syllabus on religious education in schools. {SWW}

Klugman, Werner (20th Century)
Klugman has been a president of the American Ethical Union. He is the Vice President and Treasurer in New York City of The Humanist Institute. {EU, Howard B. Radest}

Knapp, Wilfrid (20th Century)
Once a Korda Scholar in Paris, Knapp has taught government at Oberlin. She is a secular humanist. In 1977, she wrote *North West Africa, A Political and Economic Survey.*

Kneeland, Abner (1774—1844)
Kneeland was a Universalist minister who did not believe in God. The God-concept, he believed, was ". . . as much a fable and fiction as that of the god Prometheus." After serving a sixty-day sentence for blasphemy in Massachusetts, where adversaries were concerned by his freethinking successes, the former carpenter, journalist, and Baptist emerged as a national celebrity and a hero to freethinkers. Under the influence of radicals Robert D. Owen and Frances Wright, Kneeland publicly rejected the evidences of Christianity and left the Universalist denomination, saying he "did not believe in the God which the Universalists did." He then made a trek to the Iowa Territory, where he established for intellectuals a liberal community called Salubria, which did not prosper. He is buried in Farmington, Iowa. For many, Kneeland, who had journeyed from the Baptists to Universalists to presumed atheism, confirmed the warnings of many opponents of liberal religion that liberalism led to atheism and pantheism. He wrote the autobiographical *A Review of the Trial, Conviction, and Final Imprisonment . . . of Abner Kneeland for the Alleged Crime of Blasphemy* (1838). He also edited Voltaire's *Philosophical Dictionary.* In 1831, he was a founder of the weekly *Boston Investigator,* an early if not the oldest freethought journal. He eventually settled on a farm in Salubria, Iowa, dying there at an advanced age. {BDF; FUS; JM; Stephen Papa, *The Last Man Jailed for Blasphemy;* PUT; RAT; RE; TYD; U; U&U; UU}

Knezevic, Bozidar (1862—1905)
H. James Birx has described Knezevic, born in Ub, a small town in rural northwestern Serbia, as a lonely genius who wrote in Serbo-Croatian and who is little known. However, Knezevic "not only accepted the principles of both Darwinian and, with reservations, Spencerian evolutions but also combined and extended these frameworks along with his own penetrating insights into a cosmic vision that focused upon planetary history from a pananthropic perspective." In *Theories of Evolution* (1984), Birx describes Knezevic as a naturalist philosopher of cosmic evolution, a rationalist and an empiricist," one who, reminiscent of Spinoza and Bruno, was a freethinker, a humanist, and a pantheist who held God to be Nature. "Knezevic was neither encumbered nor shackled by a myopic and superannuated natural theology or archaic and obscure mysticism; he viewed science and reason as the instruments of a natural faith. . . . As a humanist, he firmly believed in the moral responsibility and value of individual as well as collective efforts," Birx added.

Knezevic wrote *History, the Anatomy of Time: the Final Phase of Sunlight* (1980. Translation by George V. Tomashevich in collaboration with Sherwood A. Wakeman); *The Principles of History*; and *Thoughts,* the latter consisting of 876 aphorisms.

Knight, Frank (20th Century)

Knight wrote "Absolutism or Absolutism!" in *The New Humanist* (May 1929).

Knight, Harry (20th Century)

Knight has been a general secretary in London of the South Place Ethical Society.

Knight, Margaret (1903—1983)

"I had been uneasy about religion throughout my adolescence, but I had not had the moral courage to throw off my beliefs until my third year at Cambridge," Knight wrote in the preface to *Morals Without Religion and Other Essays* (1955). After reading philosophers such as Russell, she added, "A fresh, cleansing wind swept through the stuffy room that contained the relics of my religious beliefs. I let them go with a profound sense of relief, and ever since I have lived happily without them." A teacher at the University of Aberdeen, Scotland, Knight signed Humanist Manifesto II. She edited *Humanist Anthology: From Confucius to Bertrand Russell* (1961), and *Humanist Anthology: From Confucius to Attenborough* (1995). In the latter work, which is a revision by James Herrick, writers who have been added are Mark Twain, E. M. Forster, J. Bronowski, Richard Dawkins, David Attenbourgh, A. J. Ayer, Antony Flew, Sidney Hook, and Paul Kurtz. She became a celebrity in Great Britain when she scored a first, giving a series of freethought lectures on the BBC radio in 1955, leading the *Sunday Graphic* to run a snapshot of her next to a headline with two-inch letters, THE UNHOLY MRS. KNIGHT. The story began, "Don't let this woman fool you. She looks—doesn't she—just like the typical housewife; cool, comfortable, harmless. But Mrs. Margaret Knight is a menace. A dangerous woman. Make no mistake about that." {HM2; WWS}

Knight, Richard Payne (1750—1820)

Knight, a patron of the arts and learning, wrote *Inquiry into the Principles of Taste* as well as works about the symbolic language of ancient art. What shocked his puritan contemporaries was *A Discourse on the Worship of Priapus and Its Connection with the Mystic Theology of the Ancients* (1786), in which he wrote that "Men are superstitious in proportion as they are ignorant, and . . . those who know least of the principles of religion are the most earnest and fervent."

In a 1957 preface to *Sexual Symbolism*, Ashley Montagu noted that Knight showed how phallic worship and phallic religions existed in Europe, not just among certain sects of the Chinese Tantrists and Taoists. Montagu added that it was not unexpected in the Age of Victoria that "the violence of the reaction to the publication of Knight's volume was such that the work had to be withdrawn upon publication." When Knight, a member of the Radical party in Parliament, died he bequeathed to the British Museum his collection of antiquities valued at £50,000. {CE; TYD}

Knight, Roger (20th Century)

Knight is an activist supporter of the Pink Triangle Trust in England. {*Gay and Lesbian Humanist*, Winter, 1998}

Knight, Van (20th Century)

Knight, a minister in Canada of the Victoria Church, has written,

> Never before have Unitarians been asked to tolerate, with good will, such radical diversity. If we are to continue to be a unifying religious presence, we have hard work to do. . . . Humanism remained the exclusive philosophy of most Unitarian congregations until the emergence of paganism around 1980. Paganism with its tradition of polytheism opened a Pandora's box.

KNIGHTS OF MALTA

Founded nine centuries ago, Knights of Malta began when a monk opened a hospital in Jerusalem for pilgrims who were attacked while making their way to the Holy Land. During the Crusades, it became a military organization celebrated for its defense of the islands of Rhodes and Malta. After the Crusades, it returned to its mainly medical work but kept the name. Now a charitable organization that is expensive to join, Knights of Malta includes in its goals to help the sick and the poor and to defend the teachings of the Roman Catholic Church. More than 12,000 are members of the Sovereign Military Order of Malta, the American Association of which includes 1,800 in its New York-based chapter. Other chapters are based in Washington and San Francisco. Members put K.M. (Knight of Malta) or D.M. (Dame of Malta) after their written names, make pilgrimages to Lourdes if they pay their own way, and may serve (without pay) on the boards of some Catholic charities. The Vatican newspaper has warned that dozens of groups use variations of the name but are simply profit-making organizations or scams. {Charles W. Bell, New York *Daily News*, 12 January 1999).

Knoblauch, Karl von (1757—1794)

A German author, Knoblauch was a friend of Mauvillon and published several works directed against supernaturalism and superstition. {BDF}

Knopf, Otto Heinrich Julius (Born 1856)

Knopf, a German astronomer, was director of the Jena University Observatory. He wrote many works on astronomy and was an active worker in the Monist League. In the tribute to Haeckel (*Was Wir Ernst Haeckel Verdanken*), Knopf expressed his thorough rationalism. He saw no "plan" in nature, and he thought that the old psychology, which taught a soul capable of living apart from the body is "struck out of the list of sciences." {RAT}

Knopfler, Mark (1949—)

Knopfler is a Scottish-born rock guitarist, singer, and composer. He founded and was lead guitarist, vocalist, and composer for the rock group Dire Straits. His albums include "Brothers in Arms" (1986, with Bob Dylan), and he received a Grammy Award in 1986 for best performance by a group. In 1983 he co-produced "Infidels." Knopfler has stated that he is not a theist. {CA; E}

Knower, Eve Tenney (20th Century)

Knower is a poet whose work included the following:

A TOAST

A toast to sceptics everywhere!
They breathe the clean and salty air
    Of doubt;
The spirit's smoth'ring feather beds,
Stitched carefully by wishful heads,
    They flout;
The sour wine of life they sip
And from the empty skins they rip
    The Truth;
If our poor, weakling hopes they blast,
They give to their own follies, past,
    No truth.
To them, whose flame can Nickie roast!
To their fine fire, we drink our toast:
    To doubt!
Drink deeply—all you sons of guile—
To man's good gift, the sceptic's smile!—
    To doubt!

KNOWLEDGE: See entry for Gravity.

• There are scores of thousands of human insects who are ready at a moment's notice to reveal the will of God on every possible subject.

—George Bernard Shaw

• Knowledge is a polite word for dead but not buried imagination.

—E. E. Cummings

Knowles, Cameo (1932—)

A sculptor and art therapist in Elkhart, Indiana, Knowles is a grandmother who is active in the Unitarian Universalist Fellowship. Her master's thesis at Indiana University develops the theory that through rigorous artistic training, people with Attention Deficit Disorder (ADD) can improve their fine motor control, develop their perceptual skills, increase their ability to concentrate, and thus "normalize" their behavior. Her works, in porcelain, bronze, cast hydrocal, and terra cotta, include depictions of Persephone, Aphrodite, Demeter, Bast, Athena, and Minerva. {*World*, November-December 1994}

Knowles, James (1831—1908)

Knowles founded *The Nineteenth Century*. He then edited *The Contemporary Review*. His letters to T. H. Huxley show that he shared Huxley's agnosticism. {RAT; RE}

Knowlton, Charles (1800—1850)

Believing that Christianity was the major obstacle to improvement in the quality of individual and social life, Knowlton was devoted to de-christianizing American culture. One of his books was *Elements of Modern Materialism* (1829). He was a pioneer of contraceptive medicine in America, and he believed that the then popular Robert Dale Owen's recommended method of coitus interruptus was inadequate. Writing *Fruits of Philosophy: The Private Companion of Young Married People, by a Physician*, he used a tone that was unpolemical. However, the book cost him fines and a three-month jail sentence at hard labor in Massachusetts.

Upon his release, he urged freethinkers not to relax simply because superstition had begun to "grow pale and totter away in the form of unitarianism, universalism, etc.," and he thought materialism to be the best way to root out religion. His influence was international, in that his marriage manual came to be imitated. {BDF; EU, Roderick S. French; FUK; FUS; TRI}

Knox, Robert (1791—1862)

Knox, an anatomist, was an outspoken deist and at times in his letters is closer to agnosticism. He was recognized as one of the ablest anatomical teachers in Britain. {RAT}

Knutsson, Hope (20th Century)

An American psychiatric occupational therapist from New York City who married an Icelander, Knutsson is president of the Icelandic Ethical Humanist Association (*Sidmennt*). In 1989, she introduced civil confirmation to Iceland, becoming one of the founders in 1990 of an organization that assists people with secular ceremonies, publishes and distributes a newsletter and booklets about such ceremonies, and has initiated a movement for the separation of church and state. E-mail: <hopeful@islandia.is>. On the Web: <www.islandia.is/sidmennt>. {*International Humanist News*, September 1997}

Knutzen, Matthias (Born 1645)

Knutzen was born in Holstein, lost his parents, and was brought to an uncle at Königsberg, where he studied philosophy. In 1674 he preached atheism publicly at Jena in Germany, and his followers were called *Gewissener* from their acknowledging no other authority but conscience. An estimated seven hundred were followers in Jena alone. Knutzen denied the existence of either God or Devil, deemed churches and priests useless, and held that there is no life beyond the present. For him, conscience is a sufficient guide, taking the place of the Bible, which contains great contradictions. {BDF; RAT}

Koch, Adrienne (1912—1971)

Koch wrote *Religion of the American Enlightenment* (1933), originally entitling it *Republican Religion*. She also wrote *The Philosophy of Thomas Jefferson* (1943). {GS}

Koch, Charlotte and Raymond (20th Century)

The Kochs wrote *Educational Commune: The Story of Commonwealth College* (1972). Freethinkers, they give a first-hand account of an independent school for workers that was established in the 1920s near Mena, Arkansas. {*Freethought History #14*, 1995}

Koch, G. Adolph (20th Century)

Koch's work about deism is *Republican Religion, the American Revolution, and the Cult of Reason* (1973). {FUS}

Koch, Heinrich (1800—1879)

A watchmaker who emigrated from Germany to the Midwest, Koch worked on *Der Antipfaff (The Anti-Priestling)*, one of the first rationalist papers in the West. One of his poems, which is pantheistic, is found in Whitehead and Muhrer's *Freethought on the American Frontier* (1992).

Koch, Leo Francis (20th Century)

A biologist on the faculty at the University of Illinois in Urbana, Koch called himself a scientific humanist and reviewed books for *The Humanist* in the 1950s. While a member of the American Humanist Association board, he voted for the termination of Priscilla Robertson as editor.

Kocol, Cleo (20th Century)

Kocol is the representative to the Atheist Alliance of the Sacramento-based Atheists and Other Freethinkers. She is on the board of the Atheist Alliance.

Kodish, Bruce I. (1952—)

A physical therapist and Alexander Technique teacher in private practice in Baltimore, Maryland, Kodish serves on the teaching staff of the Institute of General Semantics. He has a doctorate in applied epistemology from Union Institute Graduate School in Cincinnati, Ohio, having written on "The Adulthood of Humanity: General-Semantics and Secular Humanism."

Kodish, Susan Presby (20th Century)

Kodish is co-author with her husband, Bruce I. Kodish, of *Taking a Scientific Approach in Everyday Life*. A psychologist in private practice in Baltimore, Maryland, and education director of the Institute of General Semantics, she serves on the board of directors of the Washington Area Secular Humanists.

Koerbagh, Adriaan (1632 or 1633—1669)

Doerbagh was a Dutch martyr. After becoming a doctor of law and medicine, Koerbagh published *A Flower Garden of all Loveliness* (1668), a dictionary of definitions in which he gave bold explanations. The work was rigidly suppressed, and he fled to Culenborg. There he translated *De Trinate* and began a work entitled *A Light Shining in Dark Places* to illuminate the chief things of theology and religion by Vrederijk Waarmond, inquisitor of truth. When he was betrayed for a sum of money, Koerbagh was tried for blasphemy, heavily fined, sentenced to be imprisoned for ten years to be followed by ten years of banishment. Koerbagh died in prison. {BDF}

Koestler, Arthur (1905—1983)

A Hungarian-born English writer and a Communist in the 1930s, Koestler left the party over the Stalin purge trials, becoming a spokesman of the non-Communist left. His best-known novel, *Darkness at Noon* (1941), describes the purge of a Bolshevik "deviationist." In "The Lotus and the Robot" (1960), Koestler wrote of his conversation with a professor of comparative religion, an expert on Buddhism. Is it possible, he inquired, "to have a system of ethics divorced from any transcendental belief?" The question showed his sincere questioning as to how human life can be thought to be absolute or sacred, for we live in a world of evolutionary accidents?

According to Paul Edwards in *Immortality*, Koestler was favorably impressed by Emerson's view that after death we "lie in the lap of immense intelligence," or Absolute Mind, a "great reservoir of consciences."

Bernard Crick has written, "Like Koestler, I am 'a pious atheist,' " presumably with first-hand knowledge of the Hungarian-born writer's philosophic outlook.

In 1951, Koestler wrote about humanism to the present author:

> The term "supernaturalistic" begs the definition of nature. I believe this is not a problem of philosophy, but of semantics. If, however, your question refers to nineteenth-century materialism, that, of course, is dead as mutton. What will come after, I do not know. We live in an earthquake, and the new pattern of things has not crystallised.

His unusual personal affairs have been described in David Cesarani's *Arthur Koestler: The Homeless Mind* (1998). In 1951, for example, when he wrote the above about the meaning of humanism, Koestler was married to Mamaine Paget. But he thought the wife of Michael Foot, a well-known socialist, "had a bit of a yen for me" and when she was alone with him, according to Mme. Paget, he "suddenly grasped my hair, he pulled me down and banged my head on the floor. A lot." She managed to get away but was afraid to report the problem for fear it would lead to bad publicity. Daring to return after a time, she was again attacked and "I was overborne. I was terribly tired and weakened. There's a limit to how much strength one has and he was a very strong man. And that was it." Cesarani wrote that "Koestler had beaten and raped women before; over the next few years it would be almost a hallmark of his conduct."

At another time he refused to wear a condom, and when Elizabeth Jane Howard became pregnant and considered an abortion, she was told that "the idea of having children was anathema to him." After the abortion—in his *The Lotus and the Robot*, Koestler deplored "the slaughter of the unborn with its concomitant ill-effects on women"—and although she was having severe financial difficulties, he gave her little sympathy, adding "You'll get over it."

In their sitting room on Montpelier Square in London, Koestler and wife number three, Cynthia, swallowed honey laced with lethal quantities of barbiturates, dying during the night and were not found for two days. Koestler, who suffered with Parkinson's disease and terminal leukemia, was found in an armchair, a glass of brandy in his hand.

Cynthia, who had been in good health, typed a note added to his "farewell message" composed nine months prior. She wrote, apparently for Koestler's editor, Harold Harris, "I should have liked to finish my account of working for Arthur—a story which began when our paths happened to cross in 1949. However, I cannot live without Arthur, despite certain inner resources." The family dog lay dead nearby. {Bernard Avishai, *The New Yorker*, 6 January 1997; Alexander Cockburn, "The Rapist and the Snitch," *The Nation*, 23 November 1998; CE; TYD; WAS, 27 March 1951}

Kogel, Renee (20th Century)

With Zev Katz, Kogel edited *Judaism in a Secular Age—An Anthology of Secular Humanistic Jewish Thought.*

Kohl, Gim (20th Century)

At the 1999 convention of Humanists of Florida, Kohl co-led a think tank called "Who and Why Humanists of Florida Should Lead the Banner of Humanism."

Kohl, Marvin (1932—)

A professor emeritus of philosophy at the State University of New York at Fredonia, Kohl is visiting research scholar at the City University of New York Graduate Center. He was chairman of the board of directors of the Bertrand Russell Society for six years, 1989 to 1995. Kohl signed Humanist Manifesto II, is on the editorial board of *The Humanist*, and is a contributing editor for *Free Inquiry*. {HM2; SHD}

Kohlberg, Lawrence (1927—1987)

A professor of educational and social psychology at Harvard, Kohlberg was a Humanist Laureate in the Council for Secular Humanism's International Academy of Humanism. He wrote *Moral Development and Moral Education* (1973) and *Moral Stages* (1983). {*Free Inquiry*, Winter 1981}

Kohn, Alfie (20th Century)

Kohn is an author who signed a 1994 statement, "In Defense of Secularism," which was issued by the Council for Secular Humanism. He wrote *The Brighter Side of Human Nature* (1990) and *Beyond Discipline* (1996).

Kohn, Robert D. (20th Century)

An architect, Kohn became a leader in 1942 of the New York Ethical Culture Society. {EU, Howard B. Radest}

Kolb, Georg Friedrich (1805—1884)

Kolb was a German statistician and author of *History of Culture* (1869—1870). {BDF}

Kolbe, Hermann (1818—1884)

Kolbe was a leading organic chemist in Europe. Sir E. Frankland, who studied under him, wrote in *Sketches from the Life of E. Frankland* that Kolbe was an agnostic. {RAT; RE}

Kolenda, Konstantin (1923—1992)

The McManis Professor of Philosophy at Rice University, Kolenda had a regular "Philosopher's Column" in *The Humanist*. He wrote *Rorty's Humanistic Pragmatism: Philosophy Democratized* and *Religion Without God* (1976). {*Free Inquiry*, Winter 1981; HNS2}

Kollwitz, Käthe Schmidt (1867—1945)

A German graphic artist and sculptor, Kollwitz was an early artistic voice for feminism and an ardent pacifist and socialist. Her humanism included portraying the anguish being experienced by people suffering from hunger or other forms of misery. Her own suffering included losing one of two sons in World War I and a grandson in World War II. Kaiser Wilhelm II's entourage did not approve of the grim social conditions which she chronicled in her art, and during the Nazi period Kollwitz lost her teaching position and was prohibited from exhibiting her work. Kollwitz had an innate social conscience that was abetted by her husband, a physician who opened a clinic in 1891 in the Berlin slums—this is reflected both in her depiction of the urban poor as well as the depiction of peasants but also in her choice of medium: prints, because of the austerity of their tones. A 1905 etching, "Plowman With Standing Woman in Foreground," was critiqued by art critic Roberta Smith: "Kollwitz gives the tilled earth the soft, grainy darkness of a lithograph, while the sky is filled with light, airy scratches that resemble the faintest of brush strokes. Mediating between the two areas is the straining, nearly horizontal figure of a man harnessed to a plow. Reduced to a nearly unrecognizable beast of burden, his humanness is signaled more by an old woman watching him than by his actual form."

No expressionist and one who distanced herself from the avant-garde movements of her time, Kollwitz used a simplified, representational style in her lithographs and other works. {CE}

Kong, Dave (20th Century)

Kong is an activist with the San Francisco chapter of American Atheists, Inc. E-mail: <dksf@atheists.org>.

Kongfu-zi [Confucius; Kong Fuzi] (c. 571—479 B.C.E.)

K'ung Fu-tzu was a true humanist, said Lin Yutang. (His name was Latinized by missionaries and has since been spelled Kongfu-zi, using the simpler Pinyin system of transliteration): Lin had these observations:

> For the Chinese the end of life lies not in life after death—for the idea that we live in order to die, as taught by Christianity, is incomprehensible; nor in Nirvana, for that is too metaphysical; nor yet in the satisfaction of accomplishment, for that is too vainglorious; nor yet in progress for progress's sake, for that is meaningless.
>
> The true end, the Chinese have decided in a singularly clear manner, lies in the enjoyment of a simple life, especially the family life, and in harmonious social relationships. . . . There is no doubt that the Chinese are in love with life, in love with this earth, and will not forsake it for an invisible heaven.
>
> They are in love with life, which is so sad and yet so beautiful, and in which moments of happiness are so precious because they are so transient.

Kongfu-zi married at the age of nineteen, had one son, but after an unhappy marriage divorced his wife. A private school he commenced became so popular it is said to have had three thousand pupils. Teaching history, poetry, literature, the proprieties, music, natural science, and government, he avoided all references to the supernatural as well as deprecated feats of physical strength, according to Robert A. Ballou.

At the age of fifty-five, after having had a successful government position, he wandered from state to state with a group of pupils, spreading the principles which have given him worldwide immortality. Basically, he viewed the sociocultural context, rather than the supernatural, as the source and shaper of cultural change.

He is remembered for having rescued ancient Chinese classics from threatened oblivion, collecting and editing works such as the following: the *Wu Ching*, or *Canon of History*; the *Shu Ching*, or *Canon of Poetry*; the *I Ching*, or *Canon of Changes*—a mystical system of divination; the *Li Chi*, or *Book of Rites*; the *Ch'un Ch'iu*, or *Spring and Autumn Annals*—a local history which he himself wrote; and the *Shih Ching*, a book of odes. These constitute the six canonical classics of Confucianism. The *Shi Shu* of four books embody his major teachings, and his analects are found in *Lun Yü* (Collected Sayings: Analects). A 1997 translation, *Analects of Confucius*, is by Simon Leys.

Unlike the Christ and the Buddha, Kongfu-zi did not attempt to originate nor reform a religion. Instead, he organized the one that had existed in the land of his birth from time immemorial, giving form to its books, dignity to its formalities, and emphasis to its moral precepts. His way of life was one of formalism, of the proprieties, of a lack of extremes in all things.

Human behavior, not theology, was his chief interest. Asked about God, he would reply, "I prefer not speaking." (*Shang-Ti*, which means God, is a term Ballou documents that K'ung Fu-tzu used but once, preferring a more general and impersonal word *Tien*, meaning Heaven or the intangible order of goodness which rules the universe.)

Many of the sayings of Kongfu-zi are humanistic; for example:

- It is not truth that makes man great, but man that makes truth great.
- While you cannot serve men, how can you serve spirits? While you do not know life, what can you know about death?
- To give one's self earnestly to the duties due to men, and while respecting spiritual beings, to keep aloof from them, that may be called wisdom.
- If I do not associate with mankind, with whom shall I associate?
- By nature men are nearly alike.
- If we cannot serve man, how can we serve spirits?

Recently, American reference materials are becoming less Eurocentric and are incorporating international outlooks for balance; however, one goal of secular humanists has been to provide an objective humanities approach which includes all continents of mankind and which relegates national chauvinism to the past. Margaret Knight's *Humanist Anthology: From Confucius to Bertrand Russell* is an initial example. Russell, however, in *The Selected Papers of Bertrand Russell* (1927) wrote, "I must confess that I am unable to appreciate the merits of Confucius. His writings are largely occupied with trivial points of etiquette, and his main concern is to teach people how to behave correctly on various occasions. . . . His system, as developed by his followers, is one of pure ethics, without religious dogma; it has not given rise to a powerful priesthood, and has not led to persecution."

Confucianism, in short, is unique in the history of the survival of an ethic without religion. {CE; CL; ER; Pat Duffy Hutcheon, *Humanist in Canada*, Autumn 1997; JMR; JMRH; *New Humanist*, October 1998}

Konigsberg, Allen Stewart: See entry for Woody Allen.

Konner, Melvin (20th Century)

Konner, a physician, anthropologist, and author, has stated that he is a non-theist. On the faculty at Emory University, he also is affiliated with the Department of Psychiatry in the School of Medicine. He wrote *The Tangled Wing*, *Medicine at the Crossroads* and *Becoming a Doctor*, in the latter of which he explained,

> In general I was interested in the role of the chaplaincy in hospitals, and I came to believe it could be greatly expanded. This was ironic for an atheist, but logical for a professional anthropologist. . . . Although I had been religious as a teenager and could sympathize with all sorts of beliefs, I was now so skeptical that my sympathy seemed hollow. I thought that some patients could profit from talking with someone who at least took seriously the existence of an incorporeal realm, and who could discuss it in terms that would transcend my level of psychologizing.

{CA; E}

Konrád, György (1933—)

Author of *The Case Worker*, Konrád in 1990 was elected president of International P.E.N., the first Central European to hold this position in the organization for poets, essayists, and novelists. He is a Humanist Laureate in the Council for Secular Humanism's International Academy of Humanism. Konrád's father, the son of Ignac Kohn, changed the family name to that of an uncle, Konrád, who was a Talmudic scholar and owner of a bookstore.

In a 1992 novel, *A Feast in the Garden*, Konrád tells about David Kobra, an eleven-year-old who is clearly derived from the author's own experiences. Depicted are his siblings, parents, grandparents (the Kohns), friends, and neighbors as they perish or survive two World Wars, a Holocaust, a cold Hungarian police state, and all the confusion faced upon entering America. The plot cloys somewhat with all its details of simple domestic Hungarian pleasures, but the best anecdotes are those about the earlier generation, "whose mild skepticism and humanism Konrád/Kobra inherits," stated critic Suzanne Ruta. In 1995 he wrote *Varakozac* and *The Melancholy of Rebirth*.

Konrád is a member of the Hungarian Humanist Federation, an organization that arose following the fall of the "iron curtain." {WAS, conversation}

Koonz, John (20th Century)

Koonz, an Austin, Texas, middle school teacher, despite objections from parents who wanted him to teach creationism, has insisted on teaching evolution. "There is no compromise on this issue. Either we provide quality science education or we give in to religious fanatics," he declared.

Koonz is author of *A Guide Book to Parts of Our Universe from Planck Time to the Hominids.* {*Freethought Today*, September 1996}

Kopérnik, Nicholas (Copernicus) (1473—1543)

Although helping to open the era of modern science by his use of the scientific method, Kopérnik was held back greatly by his religious views. He doubted the Egyptian Ptolemy's complex calculations (2nd century of the Common Era) believing that Ptolemy's seventy-nine separate assumptions were "inconsistent with the perfection of God, who, he believed, operated through simple and harmonious laws. Here Copernicus was adumbrating, in religious terms, the scientific law of parsimony," stated Corliss Lamont. Later, Kepler (who believed in sun worship and astrology) and Galileo were to utilize empirical evidence to develop Copernicus's heliocentric theories of planetary motion. The Church, which Latinized his name, likely believes Copernicus is in Heaven, but scientists can make the case that Kopérnik found the heavens here on earth.

Many assume that the reason Copernicus refused to publish his book about the heliocentric system until he was dying was that he feared the Church would not like it, writes Ralph Estling (*Skeptical Inquirer*, November-December 1997). But he adds, "Very nearly everyone is wrong. Copernicus held back because he knew that his scientific colleagues wouldn't like it, and would have good reason not to. The calculations Copernicus made on where the planets should be in their paths around the sun were no better, and in many cases were worse than, what had been determined with the old, creaking geocentric system of Ptolemy. This because, while Ptolemy's preconceptions harked back to Aristotle, Copernicus's preconceptions went back a generation further, to Plato."

De Revolutionibus Orbius Coelestium [On the Movement of Heavenly Bodies, c. 1530] was denounced by the Vatican in 1616 and only removed from the Vatican's *Index Prohibitorum* two centuries later, in 1822. Modern astronomy was built upon the book's findings. In 1999 Pope John Paul II, in Torun, Poland, Kopérnik's birthplace, indulged in apologetics, stating, "Although Copernicus himself saw his discovery as giving rise to even greater amazement at the Creator of the world and the power of human reason, many people took it as a means of setting reason against faith."

Meanwhile, it was Aristarchus 1800 or so years earlier than Kopérnik who had discovered the movements of the planets around the sun, not the Latinized Copernicus, who erred in thinking the sun was the majestic symbol of God. (See entry for Aristarchus of Samos.) {CE; CL; ER; *The New York Times*, 8 June 1999; TYD}

KORAN (QUR'AN)

- Then I studied the Koran instead of reading it without knowing the meaning. I found it total bullshit.

—**Taslima Nasrin**
(See entries for Islam, Qur'an, and the Committee for the Study of Koranic Literature.

Korbol, Michael (20th Century)

"I self-discovered Catholic hypocrisy in 7th grade, but still was voted the parish's Catholic Youth Award in 8th grade. I then attended public high school and found the atmosphere refreshing," Korbol has written. He is a freethinker who is a doctor of podiatric medicine in Illinois. {*The Freethinker*, June-July 1997}

Korn, Bertram (20th Century)

Rabbi Korn has been an active member of the American Humanist Association. He wrote *American Jewry and the Civil War* (1951). {HNS}

Korn, Robert (20th Century)

Korn is author of "Were the Ten Commandments Written by God?" published in the May 1997 "Humanist News & Views" of the Humanist Association of Minneapolis and St. Paul.

Finding the commandments woefully deficient, Korn wrote, "I expect the average modern high school student could write a better set of commandments than these from the Bible. It is not reasonable to assume that the Ten Commandments were written by a being with godlike intelligence."

Korn, Selig (1804—1850)

Korn was a learned German Orientalist of Jewish birth. A convert to freethought, he wrote many works on mythology under the name of F. Nork, works listed in Fuerst's *Bibliotheca Judaica* and highly recommended for research by Wheeler. {BDF; RAT}

Kornbluth, C. M.: See entry for Science Fiction Writers on Philosophy.

Kors, Alan Charles (20th Century)

Kors is author of *Atheism in France 1650—1729* (1990), a definitive book about the orthodox sources of disbelief.

Korsch, Karl (20th Century)

Korsch, an unorthodox Marxist, called himself a humanist.

Korzybski, Alfred Habdank (1879—1950)

The eminent Polish linguist, a Count before his American naturalization and the creator of "General Semantics," Korzybski expanded semantics from its ordinary concern with only the meaning of words into a new system of understanding human behavior. "In the old construction of language," he held, "you cannot talk sense." Because of Aristotelian thinking habits, which he thought outmoded, men do not properly evaluate the world they talk about. As a consequence, words lose their accuracy as expressions of ideas, if ever they had such accuracy. Life, he explained, is composed of nonverbal facts, each differing from another and each forever changing. Too often, he contended, people get their thought-speech processes confused, so that they speak before observing and then react to their own remarks as if they were fact itself. General semantics, he explained, has to do with living, thinking, speaking, and the whole realm of human experiences. To say a rose "is" read," for example, is a delusion because the red color is only the vibration of light waves.

In 1921 his *Manhood of Humanity—The Science and Art of Human Engineer* caused a stir in the intellectual world. For one thing, his "time-binding theory" was explicitly non-theological in its premises. *Science and Sanity, An Introduction to Non-Aristotelian Systems and General Semantics* in 1933 is a landmark book.

> When I was five years old, my father, an engineer, gave me the feel of the world's most important scientific discoveries of the nineteenth century, which prepared the groundwork for the scientific achievements of the twentieth century and remain fundamentally valid today. The *feel* of the differential calculus, as well as non-euclidean and four-dimensional geometries, which he conveyed to me at that time shaped the future interests and orientations of my life, and became the foundation of my whole work.
>
> . . . A functional analysis, free from the old mythological and zoological assumptions, showed that humans, with the most highly developed nervous systems, are uniquely characterized by the capacity of an individual or a generation to begin where the former left off. I called this essential capacity "time-binding." This can be accomplished only by a class of life which uses symbols as means for time-binding. Such a capacity depends on and necessitates "intelligence," means of communication, etc. On this inherently human level of interdependence time-binding leads inevitably to feelings of responsibility, duty toward others and the future, and therefore to some type of ethics, morals, and similar social and/or socio-cultural reactions.
>
> . . . The mechanisms of time-binding are exhibited in most humans except those with severe psycho-biological illnesses. However, some *inaccessible* dogmatists in power, particularly dictators of every kind, have blocked this capacity considerably. Clearly police states of secrecy, withholding from the people knowledge of, and from, the world, or twisting that knowledge to suit their purposes, "iron curtains," etc., must be classified as saboteurs among time-binders, and certainly not a socio-cultural asset to the evolution of humanity. . . . .

> Metaphysicians of many kinds or many creeds since time immemorial tried to solve the . . . perplexities by postulating different "prime movers" or "final causes," beyond which the further "why" is ruled out as leading to the logically "verboten" "infinite regress." Originally religions were polytheistic. Later, in the attempt for unification, perhaps to strengthen the power of the priesthood, and also because of the increasing ability of humans to make generalizations, monotheisms were invented, which have led to the most cruel religious wars. Different rulers, dictators, "fuehrers," etc., have followed similar psycho-logical patterns with historically known destructive or constructive results. . . .
>
> Religions and sciences are both expressions of our human search for security, and so predictability, for solace, guidance, feelings of "belonging," etc., culminating in self-realization through a general "consciousness of abstracting," the main aim of my work.

Although Korzybski joined no freethought or naturalistic humanist groups, he illustrated by his outlook that he was a non-theist, in many ways an anti-theist. {HNS2}

KOSHER

• My soul is not my stomach, so it doesn't make a difference what I put there, so long as it is digestible."

—Rabbi Stephen Wise, Founder of Reform Judaism

Kosher is the descriptive term in Judaism for food and other objects that are "clean" according to laws contained in the Torah. Pork and shellfish, for example, are forbidden. Dairy products and meat may not be mixed.

In the slaughtering of animals, certain methods are prescribed. As an idiom, kosher means right, proper, or according to law as defined in the Torah.

Jewish comics tell the following:

> "Tell me, rabbi, have you ever tasted ham? Be truthful now," said the Catholic priest during a chess match.
>
> "Once," blushed the rabbi. "I was in college. Curiosity got the best of me. And, father, did you ever have sex with a girl? Be truthful now."
>
> "Once," blushed the priest. "I was in college before being ordained, and I did have sex with a girl."
>
> It was the move before checkmate, and a freethinking onlooker inquired of the priest, "It's better than ham, right?"

{DCL}

Kosik, Karel (20th Century)

Kosik in Czechoslovakia called his philosophic outlook "humanism."

Kosko, Bart (20th Century)

"Biology is not destiny," stated Kosko, an associate professor of electrical engineering at the University of Southern California. "It was never more than tendency. It was just nature's first quick and dirty way to compute with meat. Chips are destiny," he added, extrapolating how big a chip would be needed to replace the human brain. And he asked rhetorically, if such a chip *were* constructed, and an individual had the choice of "plugging" his brain into a chip that contained global thought or collective consciousness, what would this mean for humanity? In *Fuzzy Thinking* (1993), Kosko explained new and further ideas for programming computers. If the Aristotelian approach of "A or no-A" can be expanded to allow computers to work with vague, or fuzzy, concepts, for example, then the computer need not be limited to simple yes or no responses, Kosko pointed out.

Kostelanetz, Richard (1940—)

A writer and editor of many books about contemporary art, Kostelanetz wrote *John Cage* (1978), edited *Esthetics Contemporary* (1988), and wrote *Gertrude Stein Advanced* (1990). Kostelanetz signed Humanist Manifesto II and Humanist Manifesto 2000. {HM2; SHD}

Kotakowski, Leszek (20th Century)

Kotakowski in Poland once termed himself a Marxist humanist. Later, he turned against Marxism as well as naturalistic humanism.

Kotkin, Jean Somerville (20th Century)

Kotkin is executive secretary of the American Ethical Union. She is on the editorial board of *The Humanist* and is a contributing editor on *Free Inquiry*. After succeeding Howard Radest in the American Ethical Union office, she became a Leader for National Development. Said by James F. Hornback to be a "religious" humanist" with strong sympathies toward psychological humanism, Kotkin signed Humanist Manifesto II, is on the board of the American Humanist Association, and is Executive Director in New York City of the Humanist Institute. In addition, she is the IHEU's main representative to the United Nations. (See entry for Ethical Culture.) {CL; HM2; HNS2}

Kottinger, Herman Marcus (19th Century)

Kottinger wrote *The Youth's Liberal Guide for Their Moral Culture and Religious Enlightenment* (1877). {GS}

Kotula, Charline Kirkpatrick (Died 1995)

With her husband, Jo, Kotula was since its incorporation as a national group in 1978 the eastern vice-president of the Freedom from Religion Foundation (FFRF). The two were senior members of the Foundation's board of directors and its executive council. Also, they co-directed the New Jersey Freedom From Religion Foundation, the oldest and largest chapter.

Kotula, Jo (1910-1998)

Kotula was an aviation artist who during one month in 1931 had covers gracing four national magazines: *Popular Science*, *Air Trails*, *Model Airplane News*, and the *Saturday Evening Post*. Born in Poland, he came with his family when six months of age and lived in Pennsylvania, his father being a coal miner. Over a thirty-eight year span, he painted four hundred or so covers for *Model Airplane*, and during World War II he illustrated Air Force manuals.

One of five founders of the American Society of Aviation Artists, he along with his wife Charline was a co-founder of the Freedom From Religion Foundation. {*Freethought Today*, September 1998}

Kotaiah, Narra (20th Century)

Kotaiah, proprietor of Acme Tiles in Hyderabad, India, is an active member of the Andhra Pradesh Rationalists Association. He has been vice president of the Andhra Pradesh Chapter of the Indian Radical Humanist Association.

Kovács, Lajos (1909—1994)

Kovács was the twenty-eighth bishop of the Transylvanian Unitarian Church, the son of a Unitarian minister and the great-grandson of Janos Kriza, a 19th-century bishop. Kovács led the Unitarian church in Romania during dangerous times under a totalitarian regime. His wife of forty-five years, **Klára Vaska Kovács**, was also instrumental in helping train Romanian Unitarians and biblical scholars.

Kovoor, Abraham T. (1898—1978)

In Ceylon (Sri Lanka), Kovoor was President of the Ceylon Rationalist Association and edited the annual *Ceylon Rationalist Ambassador* (1966 to 1972). His writings helped expose god-men, and his influence was felt by B. Premanand and Dr. Narendra Dabholkar. Called "an atheist to the core," Dr. Kovoor was a rationalist who fought against unscientific beliefs. He rejected supernaturalism and asserted the essential dignity and worth of man and his capacity to achieve self-realization through the use of reason and scientific method. In 1998 a centenary memorial seminar was held in Delhi, according to *Modern Freethinker* (June 1998). (See entries for Premanand, Dabholkar, Ramendra, and G. Vijayam.) {FUK}

Kowalik, Pietr (20th Century)

Kowalik heads a Unitarian group, the Union of the Polish Brethren (Jednota Braci Polskich, SKR.POC2T.655, 50-950 Wroclaw, Poland).

Kraft, Michael (20th Century)

Kraft, while a member of the Humanists' Society at the University of British Columbia in Canada, was one of the founding members of Campus Freethought Alliance. E-mail: <mkraft@telus-planet.net>. {*International Humanist News*, December 1996}

Kraft-Lorenz, James (20th Century)

Kraft-Lorenz is a freethinker who actively supports the separation of church and state. He has written for *Truth Seeker*.

Kramer, Frederick (20th Century)

When he signed Humanist Manifesto II, Kramer was a humanist counselor. {HM2}

Kramer, Larry (1935-)

With Vitto Russo, author of *Celluloid Closet*, a work which exposed Hollywood hypocrisy about homosexuality, screenwriter-novelist Kramer in 1987 founded ACT UP (AIDS Coalition to Unleash Power). Kramer in 1969 had written the screenplay for D. H. Lawrence's *Women in Love* and. In 1985 he had written *The Normal Heart*, a play which first starred Richard Dreyfuss as a gay journalist seeking to publicize what was not yet realized to be a major international plague. The work was hailed by some as a successful work of political theater. Others complained that Kramer was too brash, that he had gone to such extreme limits that even many in the gay community, not just many in the heterosexual community, considered him an enemy. On the one hand, actress Elizabeth Taylor was saying that "Larry had shaken people up to AIDS awareness, whether they like it or not. He says it as it is." And on the other hand, Senator Jesse Helms was saying that "I'm not going to comment on Kramer. Remember he and that ACT UP put a giant condom on my house." Jeff Getty of ACT UP/Golden Gate was saying, "I'm fed up with him—PWAs [people with AIDS] need more hope and positive thinking. Larry Kramer's an old man who doesn't know when to shut up." And actress Barbra Streisand was saying, "His play, *The Norman Heart*, is a universal story about everyone's right to love. I'm proud that he has entrusted it to us to bring to the screen."

Kramer, author in 1987 of *Faggots*, was a founder of the Gay Men's Health Crisis (GMHC) but later he disagreed with its leaders and departed. He told writer Andrew Sullivan in 1995, "Evil has been the hardest thing I've ever had to research. I can't find anybody who writes about evil that makes any sense to me. I talk about evil as evil, not as evil in relationship to God, not evil as the opposite of good. Everybody brackets the two. I want to talk about evil. I want to talk about evil, per se. Nobody writes about it that way." He then allowed that Hanna Arendt had come closest to it. Kramer added, "I don't believe in God, so we have to leave him out of it. But I didn't think that the world was evil until the last few years. I've been unwilling to even think of that notion of evil. But I now think that the fact that this plague has been allowed to go on, that so many people have been allowed to die is just evil." Saying to Sullivan that he lives in Washington, DC, and knows how slow everything is, Kramer continued, "You know how fast everything can be made to go when you have someone who can make it go that fast and we're now on the third asshole in a row in the White House who simply doesn't want to do anything about it."

The award in literature given to him in 1996 by the American Academy of Arts and Letters was as follows: "Since his screenplay for D. H. Lawrence's *Women in Love* in 1969, Larry Kramer has been a prophet of psychic health and catastrophe among us—a prophet unmatched for the accuracy of his omens and the reliability of his anathemas and remedies. His uncannily foresighted novel *Faggots* appeared in 1978 just as the AIDS virus flooded whole wings of the American bloodstream; now its Swiftean portrait of all but vanished subculture stands as that culture's visible memorial. His later plays have been clear as firebells, memorable as tracer bullets."

Kramer has made no secret of the fact that he has AIDS and is aware that his life will be cut short before any cure is found. In a discussion of an NBC drama about AIDS, "An Early Frost," Kramer had said in 1985, "I'm so tired of us not being allowed to touch each other, kiss each other, as straight people are allowed to do, as black people are allowed to do, as anybody else is allowed to do on TV. Every other minority has been exposed and dramatized to the hilt. Why are we kept in such straitjackets?" {GL; *Poz*, April-May 1995}

Kramnick, Isaac (20th Century)

With R. Laurence Moore, Kramnick wrote *The Godless Constitution: The Case Against Religious Correctness* (1996). Kramnick is a Cornell University professor of history and government. In his writing he gives the ritually necessary nod to propriety: "One of the authors grew up in an Orthodox Jewish home. The other is descended from Irish and German Catholics on his mother's side and Calvinist Protestants on his father's."

Krassner, Paul (1932-)

At the age of twenty and upon learning about the New York Rationalist Society, Krassner came to believe that life is curiously askew inasmuch as it is next to impossible to find rationality anywhere in the world. From 1954 to 1958, he was managing editor of a controversial but humorous journal, *The Independent*, becoming known as an absurdist and an activist both in the New Left and the psychedelic subcultures.

In 1958, he wrote a guide for adolescents, *Guilt Without Sex*, and began publishing *The Realist*, "the hippest magazine in America." One of its outlandish covers depicted an Easter bunny nailed to a cross, which appealed to such of his friends as Lenny Bruce, Allen Ginsberg, Dick Gregory, Abbie Hoffman, Ken Kesey, Timothy Leary (1920—1996), and others he described as being "yippies," many of whom shared his use of Owsley White Lightning and other brands of lysergic acid diethylamide (LSD). Claiming to be an ordained minister of the Universal Life Church, with whatever tax advantages that provided, he preached in the radical 1960s that it is entirely rational to doubt God's inexistence: "I stand before you as an atheist, doing what men of the cloth should be doing."

Krassner, who edited Lenny Bruce's *How To Talk Dirty and Influence People*, was given his first big publishing break by the publisher Lyle Stuart.

Although comparatively unknown, Krassner is remembered as having been accused in 1969 of being one of the Chicago Seven who had disrupted the Democratic National Convention the previous year. Do you swear to tell the truth, the whole truth, and nothing but the truth, he was routinely asked. His response, which many fondly remember, was, "No."

In 1993, Krassner wrote about his unusual and irrational life in *Confessions of A Raving Unconfined Nut, Misadventures in the Counter-Culture*. "I had become an atheist at the age of thirteen," he stated, "when atomic bombs were dropped on Japan." Later, he added, "I stand before you as an atheist, doing what men of the cloth should be doing. . . . Since I was both an atheist and an absurdist, I had decided that the most absurd thing I could do would be to develop an intimate relationship with the God I didn't believe in." He also wrote *The Lighter Side of Unbelief.* "Atheism," Krassner declared in one of his albums, "We Have Ways of Making You Laugh" (1996), "is an extension of the reproductive urge." As proof, he includes noisy climaxes of his atheist girlfriends saying, "Ooh. Oh. No God! No God! No God!" Krassner signed a 1994 statement, "In Defense of Secularism," issued by the Council for Secular Humanism. {CA; E}

Kraus, Howard (20th Century)

Edwin H. Wilson has written of Kraus that he "appeared in Minneapolis and wanted to promote humanism on a commission basis—much the same as the Ku Klux Klan had been promoted. Harold Buschman responded to Kraus' proposal by remarking, 'That stinks!' Raymond Bragg also remembered being visited by Kraus at his Chicago office. 'He talked about promoting humanism by endorsing various commodities, including contraceptives,' Bragg recalled." {EW}

Kraus, Karl (1874—1936)

An Austrian satirist, Kraus declared, "When a culture feels that its end has come, it sends for a priest. {TYD}

Krause: See entry for Ernst H. Ludwig.

Krause, Karl Christian Friedrich (1781-1832)

Krause was a philosopher who, under the influence of Schelling and Fichte, became a pantheist. He taught at Jena, Göttingen, and Munich. Krause attempted to reconcile the absolutism of Hegel with the subjectivism of Fichte in a system that he called panentheism. (See entry for Charles Hartshorne.) {RAT}

Kreisner, Howard (20th Century)

Kreisner is editor of *Secular Nation*, a quarterly of the international Atheist Alliance which commenced in 1994 and of which he is vice-president. Also, he is president of the American Association for the Advancement of Atheism. He started the first atheist radio show at a public access station if Houston, Texas, and has been involved in several lawsuits involving religious displays on public property. In 1996, he was reported to have moved to Dallas, Texas, and to be in the process of an amicable divorce with Anna Voss. Both had moved from San Diego, where they were active in the Atheist Coalition. (See entry for California Atheists, Humanists.)

Krejei, Franz (1858—1909)

Krejei was a Bohemian psychologist, a professor of philosophy and psychology at the Czech University of Prague. An outspoken rationalist, he presided at the 14th Annual Congress of Freethinkers at Prague in 1907. He told those who attended, "Reaction is the real subversive element, and it shuts down the energy of motive forces until they accumulate and explode." {RAT; RE}

Krekel, Arnold (1815—1888)

Krekel was an American judge who had been born in Prussia but went with his parents in 1832 to America, settling in Missouri. He was elected in 1852 to the Missouri State Legislature, served as a colonel during the Civil War, was president of the Constitutional Convention of 1865, and signed the ordinance of emancipation by which the slaves of Missouri were set free. A pronounced agnostic, he was described in Putnam's *Four Hundred Years of Freethought.* Krekel when he realized he was about to die requested his wife not to wear mourning, saying that death was as natural as birth.

His wife, **Mattie Parry Krekel** (Born 1840), was also a freethinker. In a *Truth Seeker* (15 February 1890) article, she wrote, "Freethought means, first of all, mental self-assertion." {BDF; JM; PUT; RAT; RE; WWS}

Kreves, Eugene (20th Century)

When Kreves signed Humanist Manifesto II, he was minister of the DuPage Unitarian Church in Naperville, Illinois. {HM2}

Kreyche, Robert J. (20th Century)

A freethinker, Kreyche wrote *God and Reality* (1965). {GS}

Krikorian, Y(ervant) H(ovhannes) (Born 1892)

A respected naturalist in the philosophy department at the City College in New York, Krikorian reviewed books for *The Humanist* in the 1950s.

Krim, Mathilde (20th Century)

Krim addressed the Tenth International Humanist and Ethical Union (IHEU) World Congress held in Buffalo (1988). She is widely known for her work in studying human immunodeficiency viruses and their effects upon society. Dr. Krim co-founded the American Foundation for AIDS Research.

Kring, Walter Donald (1916-1999)

Kring was a Presbyterian-turned-Unitarian clergyman, author, ceramic artist, and sleuth into the secrets of Herman Melville's private life. He was minister of All Souls Unitarian Church in Manhattan for twenty-three years (1955-1978) before leading the Eliot Church in Natick, Massachusetts, until 1997.

He wrote *Religion is the Search for Meaning* (1955); *Across the Abyss to God* (1966); *Liberals Among the Orthodox: Unitarian Beginnings in New York City, 1819-1839* (1974); *Henry Whitney Bellows* (1979); *History of the Unitarian Church of All Souls, New York City, 1882-1978* (1991); and *Herman Melville's Religious Journey* (1997).

Kring is noted for having discovered that Melville may have been a wife beater and child abuser. During his writing about Henry Bellows, he came across a letter from Samuel Shaw, the half brother of Melville's wife, Lizzie, proposing that they fake a kidnapping to rescue her from Melville's sporadic violence.

The Melville Society elected Kring in 1979 as its first nonacademic president. He also was a past president of the Beacon Press of Boston, secretary of the American Unitarian Association, and president of the Harvard Divinity School Alumni Association and the Unitarian-Universalist Historical Society. {Wolfgang Saxon, *The New York Times*, 24 January 1999}

KRISHNA

Krishna, a popular deity in Hinduism, is the eighth incarnation (avatar) of Vishnu. Hindus, unlike those in the Judeo-Christian world, tolerate spectacular infidelity in their gods. For example, Krishna committed adultery with 16,000 married women. (See entry for Christmas. A Manhattan wag says Krishna's record with married women certainly beats Moses's or Jesus's.)

KRISTALL

Kristall, a quarterly associated with *Freigeistige Aktion*, is at Schillerstrasse 50, D-63263 Neu-Isenburg, Germany. E-mail: <ortrun.e.lenz@t-online.de>.

Kristeller, Paul (1905-1999)

Kristeller, a Columbia University professor, wrote more than eight hundred books and articles about the Renaissance, distinguishing humanism as a historical phenomenon. "Many people would say he was the greatest Renaissance scholar of the century," Professor James Hankins of Harvard has stated. A German Jewish refugee who came to the United States in the 1930s after having studied at the universities of Heidelberg, Berlin, and Freiberg, Kristeller was a founding member of the Renaissance Society of America and its president from 1957 to 1959.

His chief scholarly project was a seven-volume catalogue, *Iter Italicum* [Italian Journey], which was published between 1963 and 1996. An expert on Marsilio Ficino (1433-1499), an Italian philosopher who revived Platonism during the Renaissance, Kristeller was best known for his efforts on behalf of Renaissance humanism, as distinct from later forms. {Eric Pace, *The New York Times*, 10 June 1999}

Kristensen, Bjorn T. (20th Century)

In 1997 when 100,000 Norwegians were added to the state Evangelical Lutheran Church overnight because of a church-sponsored campaign to update its membership lists, Kristen noted, "What is happening here is terribly wrong. It is a federal abuse of the individual. The state church should do the same thing everybody else has to do—ask people to become members in a positive fashion." Kristensen is leader of the Human Ethical Association.

KRISTALL ZEITSCHRIFT FUR GEISTENSFREIHEIT UND HUMANISMUS

A German quarterly, *Kristall Zeintschrift fur Geistesfreiheit und Humanismus* is at Schillerstrasse 50, D-63263 Neu-Isenburg, Germany.

Kristol, Irving (1920—)

Kristol, a noted editor and social sciences educator, has stated in a telecast that he is "a non-believing Jew." He was co-founder and co-editor of *Encounter* and an editor of *Commentary* and *The Reporter*. With Nathan Glazer he wrote *The American Commonwealth* (1976) and with Stephen Spender and Melvin Lasky edited *Encounters*. Kristol is a senior fellow of the American Enterprise Institute, a fellow of the American Academy of Arts and Sciences, and a member of the Council on Foreign Relations. {William F. Buckley Jr., *New York Post*, 24 January 1998}

Krog, Helge (1889—1962)

Krog, a Norwegian critic and playwright, was a non-theist. (See entry for Scandinavian Unbelievers.)

Kroll, Leon (1884—1974)

Kroll, an eminent United States lithographer and painter, was a member of the American Academy of Arts and Letters. One of his murals is in the Justice Department, Washington, DC, and his paintings are found in major galleries throughout the United States. Asked about humanism in 1956, Kroll responded to the present author:

> I am neither a writer nor a philosopher, and I doubt whether my idea of humanism is of general interest. However, since my life is concerned with the search for truth and beauty as an artist-painter sees it, I will comment briefly. The artist is inevitably a lover of humanity. His work is based on that emotional quality. He gives it expression in terms of form and color. This is true even from the earliest records of painting and sculpture. The artist tries to express what he feels about what he sees and create a beautiful order through this visual perception. Technical experiments, while valuable and fascinating, are not enough, since they concentrate on too limited objectives and more often than not depart from aspects of life and nature to such an extent that they become academic.
>
> From my point of view, I can see no advantage in the elimination of the recognizable object. It serves, when sufficiently plausible, as a better universal language than arbitrary abstractions. The abstract element is inevitably present in a work of art whether the work is representational or not. It requires more mastery of design, more imagination, and a broad vision of humanity and nature to include man, his aspirations, and character in a work of art than to be satisfied with the comparative aridity of the abstract as a final expression. Some cultures, such as ancient Hebraic and Moslem, forbade the use of man as subject matter in art. The result, when compared to other art of the same period, resulted in mere decoration, some of it fabulously skillful but devoid of full expression of the human spirit. To me, man is more important than the atomic age or any other scientific contribution. Ever recurrent, yet always new and wonderful.

{WAS, 25 August 1956}

Kropotkin, Peter A. [Prince] (1842—1921)

Pyotor Alekseyevich Kropotkin, the foremost theorist of the anarchist movement, which he hoped to put on a scientific basis, was a philosopher of revolution. A geographer, and a naturalist in philosophy, he wrote *Paroles d'un révolt* (Words of a Rebel, 1885); *La Conquête du pain* (The Conquest of Bread, 1892); and *Etika* (1922, posthumously published, *Ethics*), in which he tried to present ethics as a science, except that he died before completing his work. One of his most controversial books was *Mutual Aid* (1902), in which he attacked T. H. Huxley and other Social Darwinists for their picture of nature and human society as essentially competitive. Kropotkin was consistently nonviolent in his anarchist beliefs, leading many non-anarchists to admire his outlook. McCabe describes him as "a pacifist anarchist of the Tolstoi type and an agnostic." A brother who translated Spencer's *Biology* into Russian died in Siberia in 1886. {CE; BDF; HNS2; JM; RAT; RE; TRI}

Kropp, Arthur (1957—1995)

A freethinker, Kropp was president of the 300,000-member civil liberties organization People for the American Way. He led the group through battles against the nomination of Judge Robert H. Bork to the Supreme Court and a proposed Constitutional amendment to prohibit flag burning and in favor of the Civil Rights Restoration Act of 1987 and the Civil Rights Act of 1991. He was instrumental in leading People for the American Way in its efforts on behalf of the Religious Freedom Restoration Act, the Freedom of Access to Clinic Entrances Act, and legislation allowing people to register to vote when they get their driver's licenses. According to his companion, Chris Bobowski, Kropp died of AIDS.

Kroto, Harold W. [Sir] (1939-)

Kroto, a signer of Humanist Manifesto 2000, was recipient in 1996 of the Nobel Prize in Chemistry. He teaches at the School of Chemical, Physical, and Environmental Science at Brighton in Sussex.

Krueger, Douglas E. (20th Century)

Krueger is author of *What Is Atheism? A Short Introduction* (1998). Christianity, he finds, "is just another religion with a host of grand promises, scary threats, and *no* evidence." Citing major sources, he makes a rational case for non-belief. A professor of philosophy at Northwest Arkansas Community College, Krueger has had much experience engaging in public debates.

Krumbein, Aaron (20th Century)

Krumbein wrote his 1943 M.A. thesis at Columbia University on "The Social Philosophy of Robert G. Ingersoll." {FUS}

Krutch, Joseph Wood (1893—1970)

Editor, teacher, naturalist, drama critic of *Nation*, Krutch in *The Modern Temper* (1929) wrote, "[P]oetry, mythology, and religion represent the world as a man would like to have it, while science represents the world as he gradually comes to discover it." Asked his views concerning humanism, Krutch wrote the present author:

> I suppose I would call myself some kind of a humanist, and if I have to fit into one of your categories, I suppose it would be into "naturalistic humanism," aware that the specifically human ought always to be seen against the background of all life. I am afraid I cannot be more specific than that without writing a book.

Krutch's books include *Comedy and Conscience after the Restoration* (1924), *Edgar Allan Poe: A Study in Genius* (1926), *The American Drama since 1918* (1939), *Samuel Johnson* (1944), *Henry David Thoreau* (1948, *The Measure of Man* (1954), and *The Human Nature and the Human Condition* (1959). Retiring to Arizona, he became not only the philosophic naturalist but also the scientific naturalist, focusing on *The Voice of the Desert: A Naturalist's Interpretation* (1955), in which he vividly describes the desert's insects and animals. {CE; HNS; TYD; WAS, 23 March 1949}

Krzyzanowski, Sigismund Julien Adolph (Born 1845)

Under the pen name of Sigismund Lacroix, Krzyzanowski with Yves Guyot wrote *The Social Doctrines of Christianity*. In 1877 he was sentenced to three months in prison for calling Jesus "*enfant adulterin*" in *Le Radical*. In 1881 he was elected president of the municipal council and in 1883 became deputy to the French Parliament. {BDF}

Ksarjian, Lena (20th Century)

Ksarjian is a member of the Council for Secular Humanism's Committee for the Scientific Examination of Religion (CSER). In "Religion as a Human Science" (*Free Inquiry*, Fall 1994), she stated, "I cannot consider myself an educated person without a formal understanding of how religion shapes culture and functions within it. As a humanist, I can participate in the human dramas shaped by Judaism and Christianity, with the understanding that religion is nothing more and nothing greater than the invention of the human imagination." In "Trying to Prove that the Bible is Pro-Woman" (*Free Inquiry*, Winter 1998-1999), Ksarjian writes that a Bible-based feminism actually promotes the patriarchy it tries to eliminate."

KU KLUX KLAN

The Ku Klux Klan is a designation mainly given to two distinct secret societies that played a part in American history, although the name has been used by other groups. A. W. Tourgées *Fool's Errand* (1880) and Thomas Dixon's *Clansman* (1905) were two works on which D. W. Griffith based his film, "The Birth of a Nation," which dealt with the organization.

David M. Chalmer's *Hooded Americanism* (1968) is one of several works listed by *The Columbia Encyclopedia* as a source about the group.

In the 1990s David Duke in Louisiana surprised many by representing a resurgence of a large public support for the KKK. He proposed dividing the country into racial "homelands," suggested that Manhattan and Long Island be declared "West Israel," and that the rest of the metropolitan area become "Minoria," an area set aside for Puerto Ricans, southern Italians, Greeks, and "other unassimilable minorities."

Some of the Klan's terminology is as follows:

Grand Dragon—head of State Klan	Kamelias—female members
King Kleagle—chief organizer	Klabee—treasurer
Klaliff—vice president	Klantoken—$10 initiation fee
Klanton—county organization	Klavern—local Klan lodge
Kleagle—organizer	Kligrapp—secretary
Kludd—chaplain	

{*AAH Examiner*, Summer 1998; CE; James Ridgeway, *Village Voice*, 3 March 1998}

Kübler-Ross, Elizabeth (1926—)

A psychiatrist, Kübler-Ross is cited by Paul Edwards as being a believer in reincarnation and "the most credulous person who ever lived."

Kubrick, Stanley (1928–1999)

Kubrick was a noted producer, director, and writer. His thirteen feature-length films are "Fear and Desire" (1953), "Killer's Kiss" (1955), "The Killing" (1956); "Paths of Glory" (1957); "Spartacus" (1960); "Lolita" (1962); "Dr. Strangelove" (1964); "2001: A Space Odyssey" (1968); "A Clockwork Orange" (1971); "Barry Lyndon" (1975); "The Shining" (1980); "Full Metal Jacket" (1987), and "Eyes Wide Shut" (1999).

To *Playboy*, he responded as to whether he thought "2001" is a religious film:

> I will say that the God concept is at the heart of "2001" but not any traditional, anthropomorphic image of God. I don't believe in any of Earth's monotheistic religions, but I do believe that one can construct an intriguing scientific definition of God, once you accept the fact that there are approximately 100 billion stars in our galaxy alone, that each star is a life-giving sun, and that there are approximately 100 billion galaxies in just the visible universe. Given a planet in a stable orbit, not too hot and not too cold, and given a few billion years of chance chemical reactions created by the interaction of a sun's energy on the planet's chemicals, it's fairly certain that life in one form or other will eventually emerge.

Interviewed by *American Cinematographer* (1969) and asked if there is an unseen cosmic intelligence, or god, in the movie, something responsible for the events depicted on the screen, Kubrick responded,

> The whole idea of god is absurd. If anything, "2001" shows that what some people call "god" is simply an acceptable term for their ignorance. What they don't understand, they call "god" . . . . Everything we know about the universe reveals that there is no god. I chose to do Dr. Clarke's story as a film because it highlights a critical factor necessary for human evolution; that is, beyond our present condition. This film is a rejection of the notion that there is a god; isn't that obvious?

So what did he say to people who find the movie spiritual and call it a "religious experience"?

> It's simply not there, religion and spirituality. Sufficiently advanced beings could be capable of things we might not even be able to understand—though these things would all make perfect sense to an advanced civilization, I suspect that these people to whom you refer are simply calling what they don't understand in my film "god."

Although the son of a physician, Kubrick was said by friends not to have consulted doctors, to have given himself medication if he did not feel well, and to have gotten insufficient sleep. Film was his life, but he loved to play chess, prepare meals, and be at home, from which he rarely traveled far. Although called secretive, reclusive, strange, mysterious, and cold, those who knew him well and worked with him found him the top man in his field. Of him Sydney Pollack the director said,

> I always think of Stanley literally on the edge of a smile. His eyes always had mischief in them. He always had this sense of the devil in him while he was very calmly asking questions. He read everything and knew absolutely all aspects of the business, including literally what the box-office receipts of every theater in the world were over the past few years.

Kubrick died in his sleep of a heart attack. Permission to bury him in his garden was arranged by the local authorities in Herefordshire—it was only the second time, the first having been for George Bernard Shaw. He is buried among his animals: dogs, cats, squirrels. {CA; E; Peter Bogdanovich, *The New York Times Magazine*, 4 July 1999}

Kuçuradi, Ioanna (20th Century)

Kuçuradi is head of the Department of Philosophy at Hacettepe University in Ankara, Turkey. She also is secretary general of the International Federation of Philosophic Societies. A secularist, she has described secularization in Turkey (*Free Inquiry*, Winter 1995-1996), including an analysis of Atatürk's contribution. "Compared with, for example, the French revolution," Kuçuradi states, "Atatürk's revolution shows the following striking specificity: the French revolution was an attempt to introduce into European social reality a historically new worldview—a concept of man and of what is valuable, which was created by the Enlightenment. . . . Atatürk's revolution was also an attempt to modernize Turkish society" with the aim to "introduce ideas and concepts, that were developed *not* in Turkey, but elsewhere and that proved to be more conducive to developing certain human potentialities. . . . Thus considered, Atatürk's was a cultural revolution, aimed at introducing the Enlightenment in Turkey and carried out through the modernization of the legal system." In 1996, she was moderator of a panel on secularism in the Middle East at the Humanist World Congress held in Mexico City.

Kuebler, Ernest William (1929—)

Working with Frederick May Eliot and Sophia L. Fahs, Kuebler became one of the most important forces in religious education in 20th century liberal religion. His approach was to move Unitarian religious education "from a Bible-centered to a child-centered approach." From 1937 to 1962, he was general editor of Beacon Books in Religious Education. {U&U}

Kuenen, A. (1829—1891)

Kuenen wrote *Christianity: Three Notices of the 'Speaker's Commentary.'* " (c. 1875) and *National Religion and Universal Religion* (republished 1979). {GS}

Kuenzli, Alfred E. (20th Century)

When he reviewed books for *The Humanist* in the 1950s, Kuenzli was on the faculty of the State University of New York, New York State College for Teachers in Albany.

Kuh, Edwin J. (20th Century)

Kuh, a freethinker, wrote *The Right to Disbelieve* (1910). {GS}

Kuhmerker, Lisa (Died 1998)

A founder of the Association for Moral Education and editor of *Moral Education Forum*, Kuhmerker addressed the Tenth International Humanist and Ethical Union (IHEU) World Congress held in Buffalo (1988). {*Free Inquiry*, Summer 1988}

Kuhn, Margaret (1905—)

In 1978, the American Humanist Association named Kuhn Humanist of the Year. Upon being forced to retire in 1970, she almost single-handedly created the Gray Panthers, a national organization dedicated to eradicating ageism and bringing about peace and social justice. In *Maggie Kuhn on Aging* (1977), she wrote, "We need to counter the old dehumanizing images of old age . . . . We are not 'senior citizens' or 'golden agers.' We are the elders, the experienced ones; we are maturing, growing adults responsible for the survival of our society. We are not wrinkled babies, succumbing to trivial, purposeless waste of our years and our time. We are a new breed of old people. There are more of us alive today than at any other time in history. We are better educated, healthier, with more at stake in this society. We are redefining goals, taking stock of our skills and experience, looking to the future." From 1978 to 1980, Kuhn served on President Jimmy Carter's Commission on Mental Health. {HNS2}

Kuhn, Thomas (Born 1922)

Kuhn's *The Structure of Scientific Revolutions* is a major work on the contemporary philosophy of science. Scientists, he argues, work within and against the background of beliefs that he characterizes as a "paradigm." No strictly logical reason for the change of a paradigm exists, although such changes occur, a view counter to that of Karl Popper, for whom science is the apotheosis of sound and logical defensible thought. Both Kuhn and Popper, however, are evolutionary epistemologists who see analogies between their views of scientific change and the evolution of organisms.

Richard Rorty, who holds that Bertrand Russell is "arguably the most influential philosopher to have written in English in this century," adds that John Dewey and Thomas Kuhn are "the only plausible rivals for that position." (See entry for Consilience.) {OCP}

Kuhr, Rudolf (20th Century)

Kuhr, an activist supporter of the International Humanist and Ethical Union, is associated with *Humaniste Aktion* in Germany. E-mail: <humanist.aktion@t-online.de>. On the Web: <http://home.t-online.de/home/humanist.aktion/>.

Kularatnam, K. (20th Century)

Prof. Kularatnam from Sri Lanka addressed the Sixth International Humanist and Ethical Union World Congress held in Amsterdam (1974).

KUMANI

Kumani, in an early Indian religion, was the virgin goddess. {LEE}

Kumar, Prem (20th Century)

Kumar, for *Humanist in Canada* (Autumn 1996), wrote "Canadian Multiculturalism."

Kumley, Lloyd (20th Century)

Kumley is Secretary of American Humanist Association. A lawyer, he is co-chairman of the AHA's Humanist Youth Club and edits several children's publications: *Sunrise Journal*, *Stargazer*, and *Star Walker*. His e-mail: <lloydk@teleport.com>. (See entry for Oregon Rationalists, Humanists.) {FD}

Kunchithapadam, Krishna (20th Century)

Kunchithapadam is the program chairperson and webmaster for Atheists and Agnostics of Wisconsin. E-mail: <krishna@cs.wisc.edu>.

Kundera, Milan (1929—)

A Czech novelist, Kundera studied at the Institute for Advanced Cinematographic Studies but left for Paris in 1968 when the Russians invaded. His first novel, *Zert* (*The Joke*, 1967), was followed by *The Farewell Party* (1976) and *The Book of Laughter and Forgetting* (1979). The latter, a semi-autobiographical view of postwar Europe, evoked cultural, political, and sexual lives of the "two or three new fictional characters baptized on earth every second." In *Testaments Betrayed*, Kundera has gone on record as being a non-theist. {CA; E; OCE}

K'ung Fu-Tzu: See entry for Kongfu-zi, which follows the simpler Pinyin system of transliterating Chinese.

Kunneman, Harry (20th Century)

Kunneman is a professor at the University of Humanist Studies in Utrecht. He is a member of the Dutch Humanist League.

Kunz, F. L. (20th Century)

Kunz, vice president of the Foundation for Integrated Education, is a naturalist. On the subject of the term, "humanism," he wrote the present author about his being a naturalist:

> However, I would like to say that I use the term in the sense as would a modern physicist, familiar with deductive-exact scientific method. Einstein would be my model here, and not Bertrand Russell. As you know, for such people—Einstein, Schrödinger, etc.—empiricism has a vital role in testing, winnowing, and proving out certain structures of thought which start with postulates, but end up as the finest kind of pragmatic science. One of the results of this development—which took strong hold at the time of James C. Maxwell—has been the physical and theoretical demonstration of the reality of the non-material. Thus we have established for us a view that inverts the 19th century mechanism, to which many 19th century people added a weak, inconsistent idealism.
>
> One of the important ingredients now, in 20th century thought, is a powerful *realistic* idealism. It is easy to show this, experimentally, in physics. Further, one can produce evidence which shows that the same *kind* of methodology and the same authoritative content of knowledge can be derived for biology, without submitting to reductionism. After that similar gains can be made (and are *prima facie* acceptable now) in human psychology and sociology. But what I have said above is only a small beginning and must not be taken to represent the whole of my own view.
>
> {WAS, 7 August 1956}

Kuralt, Charles Bishop (1934—1997)

Kuralt, a popular news correspondent and CBS television star, in one of his travels met an individual from the New York Secular Humanists who informed him that secular humanists are followers of Democritus and Protagoras, not Moses and St. Augustine. Also, that they hold nature as being paramount over humanity, not the other way around, for which reason they appreciate the way Kuralt closes his Sunday newscasts: with shots of birds, dew-wet flowers, quiet mountains, and assorted views of nature in the raw. Replied Kuralt, without admitting to being a philosophic naturalist, "I am a visceral, lower-case, secular humanist myself, and I wish you and the Secular Humanist Society equivalent of 'God-speed'!" Kuralt wrote *On the Road With Charles Kuralt* (1985).

Kuran, Timur (20th Century): See entry for Preference Falsification.

Kurdakul, Sukran (20th Century)

Kurdakul is president of Turkey's PEN, the organization of poets, essayists, and novelists. A dedicated secularist, he has actively tried to return from Moscow the body of Turkish poet Nazim Hikmet, an atheist and Communist. Kurdakul is a writer of poetry and literary history. {Stephen Kinzer, *The New York Times*, 27 February 1997}

Kurtz, Jonathan Jr. (1995—)

When ten weeks old, Kurtz, the grandson of philosopher Paul Kurtz and son of Jonathan Kurtz, Marketing Director of Prometheus Books, was the first to have a secular humanist Welcoming Celebration in the Center for Inquiry library in Amherst, New York. American humanists, following the lead of Jane Wynne Willson in Britain, have developed ceremonies for important moments in life—rites of passage such as birth, graduation, marriage, and death. With his grandparents (Claudine Kurtz, Paul Kurtz, Maria Curley, Robert Curley), aunt (Annie), and parents (Gretchen Kurtz and Jonathan Kurtz) participating, the Welcoming Celebration occurred 23 September 1995. Jonathan Jr. slept throughout the entire ceremony.

Kurtz, Paul (1925—)

A leading exponent of secular humanism, Kurtz is professor emeritus of philosophy at the State University of New York at Buffalo. An accomplished and versatile scholar, who is often called "unquestionably the most important atheist thinker and publicist in America today," Kurtz is all the following:

• editor-in-chief of the highly influential *Free Inquiry*, an international secular humanist magazine which is published quarterly (Box 664, Buffalo, NY 14226);

• an educator who has taught at Trinity College in Hartford, Connecticut; Vassar College in New York; the New School for Social Richard in New York City; Union College in New York; the University of Besacon in France;

• the President of the Secretariat of the Council for Secular Humanism's International Academy of Humanism, which he had helped to organize in 1983. Among those who have been elected are such political figures as Sakharov and Djilas, who were recognized for their defense of human rights and democracy;

• a member of the editorial board of *International Humanist*, a quarterly of the International Humanist and Ethical Union (IHEU), of which he was a co-president for eight years; in 1982 he addressed the Eighth IHEU World Congress in Hannover, as he did also at the Tenth in Buffalo in 1988;

• author of *Eupraxophy: Living Without Religion* (1989). He has introduced the term **eupraxophy**, or "good practice and wisdom," describing the movement of secular humanism as being an ethical, philosophical, and scientific one. Secular humanism, he emphasizes, is a nonreligious way of life and cosmic outlook;

• drafter in 1983 of Humanist Manifesto II and the individual who is at the center of criticism that it toned down the religious humanism of Humanist Manifesto I. After many attempts to contact Andrei Sakharov, who had been expelled from Moscow, Kurtz was able to contact him directly and got him to endorse the Manifesto, which became front-page news in *The New York Times*. Maintaining that secular humanism is a philosophic movement, not a religion, he argues that it is time for humanists to accomplish what most Enlightenment figures never did: abandon Deism and a belief in the supernatural, however that is defined. Humanism, he holds, should "break away from its ethnic foundations (the Society of Secular Humanistic Judaism) or its religious foundations (Unitarian Universalist Association, Ethical Culture, Fellowship of Religious Humanists, and the American Humanist Association). It should not be held hostage to Unitarian, Judaistic, or Adlerian institutional forms, but needs to develop its own identity and integrity." Now that the idea of God is dead, and only of minor literary interest, our major concern today is "to assert that humans are alive. This does not mean that we should exalt Reason, forget Passion, and not appeal to the whole person." In short, he favors a "thoroughly secular, atheist, or agnostic humanism . . . [that is] honest and truthful about who we are and what we stand for." "Isn't it time," he declares, "that we finally cut the umbilical cord of religion?"

• presenter to Andrei Sakharov of the International Humanist of the Year Prize in 1988, an honor which had been awarded *in absentia* earlier that year;

• Vice-President of the British Rationalist Press Association, to which in 1979 he was elected an honorary associate;

• a member of the Council for Secular Humanism's Committee for the Scientific Examination of Religion;

• an editor for Prometheus Books of *A Skeptic's Handbook of Parapsychology* (1985); *The Humanist Alternative* (1973); *Sidney Hook, Philosopher of Democracy and Humanism* (1982);

• the author of *The Fullness of Life* (1974); *Exuberance: A Philosophy of Happiness(1977); Forbidden Fruit, the Ethics of Humanism* (1988); *Philosophical Essays in Pragmatic Naturalism* (1990); *The Transcendental Temptation, a Critique of Religion and the Paranormal* (1991); and *The New Skepticism* (1992);

• a facilitator in setting up dozens of secular humanist chapters across the country and in establishing the movement's headquarters and building (at 3965 Rensch Road in Buffalo, New York 14228);

• the principal founder of the Committee for the Scientific Investigation of Claims of the Paranormal (CSICOP);

• a speaker on "The Future Course of Humanism" at the 3 November 1995 opening of the Centre for Critical Enquiry, Westminster College, Oxford.

• the publisher of *Philo*, a journal of the Society of Humanist Philosophers which commenced in 1998.

• recipient in 1998 of the International Humanist of the Year Award from the International Humanist and Ethical Union at a congress held in Mumbai.

• the individual mainly responsible for drafting and arranging signers for the important Humanist Manifesto 2000, of which he was a signer.

In 1988, the International Humanist and Ethical Union gave Kurtz a special Academy World Humanist Award for his far-reaching successes in expanding the influence of the philosophy of secular humanism. At the 9 June 1995 dedication of the Center for Inquiry in Amherst, New York, he was awarded a "Certificate of

Condemnation" signed by "the Horribly Reverend Pat Robertson" and "the Most Holy Johnnie Paul II," facetiously presented by the Committee of the Far Righteous for his being an igtheist, a denier of revealed truth, a discounter of creationism, and a skeptic.

In 1993, he spoke in Berlin at the European Humanist Federation, lamenting the rise of fundamentalism, which he found is associated with the weakening of the classical humanist tradition. Fundamentalism, he stated, is basically an authoritarian personality either in issuing commands (if a leader) or obeying them (if a disciple). Most often the fundamentalist doctrine is supported by nationalistic, racial, and ethnic chauvinism. It is intolerant of dissent and the greatest sin is heresy and blasphemy. Kurtz added, "The battle for rationality and freedom is never fully won, for waiting in the wings are new virtues and thus the courage to criticize nonsense and to defend rational humanism as an alternative." He suggested the following counter measures for humanists:

- Ally ourselves with forces which believe in democracy and tolerance, including liberal Christians;
- Produce serious criticism of the Qur'an and Bible and develop critical thinking in education;
- Develop visible humanist alternatives with a moral component.

In Toronto in 1994, he spoke at the conference of the Coalition for Secular Humanism, Atheism, and Freethought (CSHAFT) on "The Positive Reach of Humanism: An Agenda for the 21st Century." In 1995 in Madrid, he spoke to the Spanish Association of Rational Humanism concerning "Neo-Spirituality and the Paranormal."

In Delphi, Greece, he spoke at the first International Multidisciplinary Conference on Human Behaviour and the Meaning of Modern Humanism. Also, Kurtz has appeared in telecasts and on Public National Radio interviews.

Kurtz's critics have been many. Board members of the American Humanist Association were aghast when he accepted for *The Humanist* an advertisement from a sex-oriented magazine. Others have complained that "the Kurtz group" claims "secular humanism" is a philosophic movement worthy of being named as such in philosophy texts, but it is not. Herbert Tonne once objected to Kurtz' one-man rule, his "ownership of CODESH" combined with his financial interest in Prometheus Books. Although Prometheus Books supplies titles unavailable elsewhere, Tonne questioned its being owned by Kurtz's son and alleged that it was becoming a vanity press that preyed upon authors by charging them to accept their work or by paying scanty royalties. When Kurtz says, "Is it not time others work with us in establishing a new coalition?" what he really means, Tonne complained, is "It is time for the American Humanist Association, Freedom From Religion Foundation, and others, to do his bidding."

However, CODESH, now the Council for Secular Humanism, is currently run by a board of directors. Kurtz serves without salary or compensation as its chair. Kurtz claims he has personally committed some $600,000 toward the future of the organizations he founded.

Other critics have suggested that Kurtz is not up on a philosophic rung with Sidney Hook in the academic world although he pretends to be. Many have complained that his coinage, "eupraxophy," is ludicrous and unpronounceable, that it under-emphasizes the humanities. Nicolas Walter found his outlook as one filled with neologistic nostrums. Kurtz's retort is that the length and breadth of his leadership of the Council for Secular Humanism speaks for itself.

A compilation of his work, *Toward A New Enlightenment, The Philosophy of Paul Kurtz* (1994), focuses on central issues such as ethics, politics, education, religion, science, and pseudoscience which have concerned him throughout his career. *The Courage to Become: The Virtues of Humanism* (1997) is an affirmative perspective on Promethean humanism.

Kurtz's *Who's Who* entry:

> Two passions have dominated my intellectual and professional life: (1) a commitment to critical intelligence—I am skeptical of the false beliefs and mythologies that have motivated other men and women—and (2) a belief in the importance of human courage, particularly in defending reason in society and in attempting to reconstruct ethical values so that they are more democratic and humane.

In 1996 at the Humanist World Congress held in Mexico City, Kurtz was moderator of a panel discussion of science and superstition. He is an honorary associate of the New Zealand Association of Rationalists and Humanists. Kurtz's e-mail: <pksksh@aol.com>. The homepage on the Web: <http://www.secularhumanism.org/>. (His thorough agenda for 21st century humanism is found in *New Humanist*, February 1995; see entry for Humanists, Naturalistic.) {CA; E; *Free Inquiry*, Fall, 1991; FUK; FUS; HM2; HNS2; PK; SHD; TYD}

Kushner, Tony (20th Century)

Kushner, an agnostic with an interest in Marxism, was recipient in 1990 of the Whiting Foundation Writers Award. In 1992, for his epic "Angels in America," he received the London *Evening Standard* Award for Best Play, followed in 1993 by the Pulitzer Prize for drama and the Tony Award for best play of 1993.

"Angels in America" was the first part of the seven-hour production "Millennium Approaches," followed by the second part, "Perestroika" the Russian word for "rebuilding." In both, an angel appears as a genuine 20th century deus ex machina with a Message From on High. The work, a gay fantasia on national themes, has been praised by many of Kushner's contemporaries in the theater as being a universal metaphor from the facts of the historical moment. John Lahr, drama critic of *The New Yorker*, called it "a masterpiece. You'd be very hard-pressed to find a serious play of this dimension on Broadway in the last thirty years. It's talking about something [homosexuality] that American culture has had to adjust to."

Thomas M. Disch has written, " 'Angels in America' certainly has its quota of shock value—full frontal male nudity, simulated sex between men (who remain in their underwear), and any amount of inspired X-rated wisecracking. . . . Perhaps the most innovatively shocking element of 'Angels' is its complex portrait of right-wing power broker, and closet homosexual, Roy Cohn, who is dying of AIDS, delirious with rage and fear, haunted by the ghost of Ethel Rosenberg, and a villain to his last strangled breath. . . . When Cohn is dead at last, Kushner rises to a different kind of glory in one of Perestroika's greatest scenes, when Louis, a paragon of frazzled neoliberalism, says Kaddish over his archenemy's corpse, his rusty Hebrew cued by Ethel Rosenberg's ghost."

Although Kushner depicts an America of lies and cowardice, he also envisions an America of truth and beauty. "For me," Kushner has explained, "the bulk of it—the epic nature of it—becomes part of what it's about: this incredible struggle I feel people have to wage in order to be able to change themselves."

Kussman, Carmel (Died 1994)

Kussman, who had been on the Board of Directors of the American Humanist Association, was its treasurer at the time of her death. She was active in founding an American Humanist Association group in Brooklyn, New York, and she was a member of the Secular Humanist Society in Manhattan.

Kuvakin, Valerii (1939-)

Kuvakin, a professor of philosophy at Moscow State University, is Chairman of the Russian Humanist Association. He is associated with *The Humanist Alternative*, a quarterly, and *Zdravyi Smysl l* (Common Sense, Novatorov 18-2-2, Moscow 117421, Russia).

In 1997 he became head of the newly formed Center for Inquiry at Moscow State University. He is a contributing editor of *Philo* and signed Humanist Manifesto 2000. {*Free Inquiry*, Winter 1997-1998; *International Humanist Bulletin*, June 1995 and December 1997}

Kupyers, Janet (1970—)

Kuypers edits *Children, Churches and Daddies,* "the unreligious, non-family oriented literary and art magazine." She is author of *The Window* (1994). {*Freethought History*, #17, 1996}

Kwame, Nii Otto II [Chief] (20th Century)

Kwame, chief of the village of Pokuasi in Ghana, has given land for a Rational Centre of Ghana, the motto of which is "Down with Superstition." Working with Hope Tawiah, Kwame is a combination social worker, counselor, priest, and medicine man for the village's six thousand residents.

He has described how one of the villagers came to him with a child suffering from intestinal worms. Besides offering the traditional remedies, Kwame also went to the pharmacy and bought a vermifuge that he administered to the patient. After the patient recovered, Chief Kwame explained to the mother that the illness had been caused by worms and it was cured by medicine, an approach she accepted. "Such," observed his visitors Bonnie and Vern Bullough, "is the work of a rationalist in Ghana."

Kwasniewska, Aleksander [President] (1954-)

A Polish politician, Kwasniewska was a leader of the Polish youth movement including being chairman of the Polish Socialist Students' Union at Gdansk. He now is chairman of the Social Democracy of the Republic of Poland and leader of the Democratic Left Alliance Caucus. In 1995 he defeated Lech Walsea to become President of Poland.

Kwasniewska, an atheist, and his Catholic wife, Jolanta Kwasniewska, welcomed Pope John Paul on his 1999 visit to his native country.

Kwee, Swan Liat (20th Century)

A Dutch pamphleteer, Kwee wrote a "Bibliography of Humanism" (1957). {GS}

Kyd (or **Kid**), **Thomas** (1558—1594)

Kyd, the eminent dramatist, was suspected by many of being an atheist. He was closely associated with Marlowe, with whom he shared lodgings in 1591. Kyd's "atheistical" writings led to his being tortured and imprisoned. His *Spanish Tragedy* (1592) was published anonymously and was so popular that it passed through ten printed editions by 1633.

The only work published under his name was a translation from Robert Garnier, *Cornelia* (1594), re-issued in 1595 as *Pompey the Great, his faire Corneliaes Tragedie.* {OEL; TRI}

Kykhuizen, George (20th Century)

Kykhuizen is author of *The Life and Mind of John Dewey* (1973). (See entry for John Dewey.)

Laas, Ernst (1837–1885)

Laas was a German writer, a professor of philosophy at Strasbourg, who wrote and *Kant's Place in the History of the Conflict Between Faith and Science* (1882) and *Idealism and Positivism* (1879–1884). {BDF; RAT}

Labanca, Baldassarre (Born 1829)

Labanca was a professor of moral philosophy in the University of Pisa. He took part in the national movement of 1848, and in 1851 he was imprisoned, then expelled from Naples. Labanca, writing in 1886 on progress in philosophy and a study on primitive Christianity, dedicated his work to Giordano Bruno, the martyr of freethought. {BDF; RAT}

La Barre, Jean de: See entry for Weston La Barre

La Barre, Weston (1911–)

A Duke University anthropologist, author of *The Human Animal* (1954) and *Neurotic Defense Mechanisms in Supernatural Religion* (1970s), La Barre wrote the present author about humanism:

> Within the limits of your admirable definition—"that man through the manipulation of physical and social forces can attain the good life by means of a naturalistic, as contrasted with a supernaturalistic, philosophy"—I should say that, quite emphatically, I belong to the classification of "naturalistic humanism." I do not, however, like Ferm [editor of *The Encyclopedia of Religion*], consider that "religious humanism" is this at all, for religions in my view are invariably supernaturalistic, both *de jure* and *de facto*. How else can one be genuinely humanist except as a naturalist?
>
> Our experience since the Chevalier de La Barre was burned at the stake as a Voltairean radical in the Eighteenth century has been that the supernaturalists are distinctly inhumanists. [Voltaire wrote *Le Cri du Sang Innocent* (Cry of Innocent Blood) about François-Jean de la Barre, who was executed in Abbeville in 1766]. In my book, *The Human Animal*, I have attempted to be consistently naturalistic in my approach to the study of man.

Jean de La Barre's *Continuation de l'histoire universelle de Jacques-Bénigne Bossuet* was included in the Vatican's list of prohibited reading in 1745. "I wish I knew how to get my own books on the *Index Librorum Prohibitorum*," Weston La Barre wrote after *America*, the national Catholic weekly, panned his latest book and accused him of "objective blasphemy" and of being "flatly damnable.'" La Barre added,

> Discerning characters, these Jesuits!
>
> {TYD; WAS, 13 August 1954}

LABELING

Those with a philosophic bent are inclined toward being antinomenclaturists:

• You ask me whether I call myself a Scientific Humanist or a Naturalistic Humanist. I am not in the habit of giving myself labels, which I leave to others. I should not have any inclination to call myself humanist, as I think, on the whole, that the non-human part of the cosmos is much more interesting and satisfactory than the human part. But if anybody feels inclined to call me a Humanist, I shall not bring an action for libel.

–Bertrand Russell
in a 1951 letter to the present writer

Labiche, Eugène Marin (1815–1888)

Labiche, a French dramatist whose *La cuvette d'eau* brought him success and a successful career, wrote more than a hundred comedies. Jules Claretie described Labiche as "Voltairean." A member of the French Academy, he was an Officer of the Legion of Honour. {RAT}

Labouchere, Henry Du Pre (1831–1912)

Although of French extraction, Labouchere was a British editor and politician who rose high in the British diplomatic service, then founded and edited a radical weekly, *Truth*. According to his biographer, Thorold, Labouchere was "a strict agnostic . . . as completely non-religious as a man could be." When he lay slowly and placidly dying, a lamp in the room flickered. He raised his head and said, "Flames? . . . No, not yet." Others cite this as showing how hard it is to overcome what we are taught when young. Or, likely, he was simply showing he had a commendable sense of humor. {JM; RAT; RE}

Labregere, René (20th Century)

In Paris, Labregere started editing *Raison* in 1957.

La Bruyère, Jean de (1645–1696)

La Bruyère, a French writer who was tutor in the house of the prince de Condé, wrote *Les Caractères de Théophraste, traduits du grec; avec Les Caractères ou les Moeurs de ce siècle* (1688). He was a defender of classical writers in the "quarrel of the ancients and moderns." "A sanctimonious man is one who under an atheist king would be an atheist," he observed. He also wrote, "To what excesses will men not go for the sake of a religion in which they believe so little and which they practice so imperfectly." Le Bruyère was admitted to the French Academy in 1693. {CE; TYD}

Lacaita, James Philip [Sir] (1813–1895)

Lacaita was an Anglo-Italian statesman. The Revolutionaries of 1848 appointed him secretary to the Neapolitan Legation at London, but they failed, and the reactionaries canceled the appointment. It was mainly from Lacaita that Gladstone in 1850 got the information about the clerical-royalist horrors which he afterwards published in a Letter to Lord Aberdeen. Lacaita was imprisoned for a few days, but when the Letter was published (1852) he fled to Naples, then settled in England. Later, Lacaita was elected to the Italian Parliament. {RAT}

Lacépede, Bernard Germain Étienne de la Ville de [Count] (1756–1825)

Lacépede, a French naturalist and a friend of Voltaire and D'Alembert, composed operas and symphonies and wrote works on science. During the Revolution, he held office although he protested against the Terror. Napoleon made him Grand Chancellor of the Legion of Honor and Minister of State. Lacépede remained a deist and was stripped of his honors when royalty and the Church were restored. {JM; RAT}

Lachatre, Maurice (Born 1814)

Lachatre, a French writer, edited Library of Progress, in which has appeared his own *History of the Inquisition* and *History of the Popes* (1883). {BDF}

Lachs, John (1934–)

Lachs, who was born in Hungary, is an educator and philosopher who co-translated *Fichte, Science of Knowledge* (1970). An Episcopalian, he is a contributor to *American Philosophic Naturalism in the Twentieth Century* (1994). Lachs, an expert on Santayana, has written favorably about epiphenomenalism and the notion of cause.

La Clair, Paul L. (20th Century)

La Clair is a contributor to *Family Matters*, the newsletter of the Secular Family Network.

Lacour, Léopold (19th Century)

A French feminist, Lacour in *Humanisme intégral* (1897) called for equality of the sexes and "a humanism no longer virilist, but integral."

Lacroix, Sigismund: See entry for Adolph Krzyzanowski.

Lacy, George (19th Century)

In Sydney, Australia, Lacy and Charles Bright were editors of *Liberal* (1882–1884). {FUK}

Ladd, Parish B. (19th Century)

A freethinker, Ladd wrote *Commentaries on Hebrew and Christian Mythology* (1896) and *The Hebrews: Never in Egypt* (c. 1898). {GS}

Lader, Lawrence (1919–)

When he signed Humanist Manifesto II, Lader was chairman of the National Association for Repeal of Abortion Laws. In 1987, he wrote *Politics and the Church*. He also wrote *A Private Matter* (1995). {HM2}

Lafan, Tony (20th Century)

The Freethinker's Picnic: Newcastle's Secular Hall of Science 1884-1893 (1998) is Lafan's important description of the Australian city of Newcastle and how the laboring classes lived. He also wrote about how secularism came to flourish among them. {Fred Whitehead, *Freethought History #28*, 1998}

Lafargue, Paul (1842–1911)

A freethinker, Lafargue wrote *The Myth of Adam and Eve* (1928). {GS}

Lafayette, Marie Jean Paul [Marquis] (1757–1834)

Joseph McCabe, among others, points out that General Lafayette, who fought in the American army during the War of Independence, was a deist. Five barrels of soil from far off Boston Common New England were shipped to an obscure corner of Paris near the Place de la Nation, in which the general's body was buried. Overhead hangs an American flag, and nearby lies his son George-Washington de Lafayette.

On 4 July 1917 an American colonel, C. E. Stanton, traveled to the French site, observed the American soil, snapped to attention, and saluted while uttering the famous phrase, "Lafayette, we are here." {CE; JM; RAT; RE}

LaFerla, Roberto (20th Century)

In Italy, Dr. LaFerla, whose doctorate is in chemistry, is general secretary of the Central Committee of the Giordano Bruno National Freethought Association (29, via Bessarione, 1-20139 Milano M1, Italy) and of the Italian Committee for the Control of Claims about the Paranormal. During the first part of this century, his office—before the establishment of Vatican City—was intimidatingly opposite the Pope's Office. The two organizations collaborate with groups such as the Association for Religious Freedom in Italy.

LaFerla addressed the Eleventh International Humanist and Ethical Union (IHEU) World Congress held in Brussels (1990). {*Free Inquiry*, Winter 1990-1991}

Laffitte, Jacques (1767–1844)

Laffitte was a French statesman who, in 1814, became Governor of the Bank of France and President of the Chamber of Commerce. During the Restoration he was an anti-clerical member of the Chambre. He financed the Revolution of 1830 and was appointed Minister of Finance and Premier. But by supporting Polish and Italian revolutionaries, he annoyed the king, resigned in 1831, and by then had lost most of his fortune. {CE; RAT}

Laffitte, Pierre (1823–1903)

A mathematician who became Auguste Comte's successor as "director of positivism," Laffitte in 1892 was appointed to the newly created chair of the history of science at the *Collège de France*. Laffitte wrote *The General History of Humanity* (1859) and *The Great Types of Humanity* (1875–1876). In 1878 he founded *La Revue Occidentale*. {BDF; CE; EU, 516-517, Christopher Kent; RAT}

La Follette, Robert (Marion) [Governor] (1855–1925)

A Wisconsin governor and Congressman, La Follette founded the National Progressive Republican League and received nearly five million votes as U.S. President on the Progressive Party slate. He was a freethinker and a Unitarian. {CE, U, UU}

La Fontaine, Jean de (1621–1695)

La Fontaine, whose fables rightfully place him among the masters of world literature, wrote twelve books of some 230 fables drawn largely from Aesop. Popular with children, they are particularly appreciated for their wit and satirical views about French society and humanity in general.

Marc Fumaroli, in *Le Poète et le Roi: Jean de La Fontaine en son siècle* (1997), points out that, when sixty-two, La Fontaine was admitted to the *Académie Française*, taking the seat of Jean Baptiste Colbert, the prime minister who had died the year before. Praising his work, the pianist-critic takes issue on the point of La Fontaine's so-called "conversion" at the age of seventy-one and his repenting of past libertinism. Fumaroli credited Fénelon, the archbishop of Cambrai who is inclined to mysticism. Rosen felt no such intellectual inspiration was needed to explain the conversion. He credited a young abbé, Poujet, who was told by La Fontaine that "I have just been reading the Bible, and it is really a very good book." What he did not understand, however, was the idea of eternal damnation, particularly for infants. The abbé responded that it was not something to be understood; it is just an idea to be accepted. And when he insisted that the poet publicly condemn his past indecent stories because they had harmed people by corrupting readers, La Fontaine's housekeeper objected that "God would never have the courage to damn him. Stop tormenting him; he's much more stupid than wicked."

Nevertheless, the abbé won out and the poet, although insisting he had not been corrupted by writing such work, made a public and humiliating condemnation of his stories, even burning a comedy he had just written. For the last two years of his life he translated the *Psalms*. After his death, it was discovered that he wore a hairshirt and that he had been flagellating himself. According to Rosen,

> A conversion or reform of this sort in old age was commonplace during the sixteenth, seventeenth, and even eighteenth centuries. (When it did not take place, relatives and friends sometimes claimed that it had in order to save the reputation of the loved one.)

A year after his conversion and shortly before his death, La Fontaine wrote to a friend, "I would die of boredom if I had to stop writing verse." {CE; Charles Rosen, *The New York Review of Books*, 18 December 1997}

LaHaye, Tim (20th Century)

LaHaye, one of the leading negative critics of secular humanism, is author of *The Battle for the Mind* (1983).

Lagarrigue, Jorge (1854–1894)

Lagarrigue, a Chilean positivist, edited Comte's letters to Edger (1889) and wrote *La rôle de la France dans l'histoire de l'humanité, Positivisme, et Catholicisme*. {RAT}

Lagarrigue, Juan Enrique (Born 1852)

Lagarrigue, brother of Jorge Lagarrigue, was a Chilean positivist. He wrote *La religion de la Humanidad* (1893) and other positivist works besides a volume on Diderot and several pacifist pamphlets. {RAT}

Lagerborg, Robert (19th Century)

Lagerborg, a Finnish non-theist, wrote on freedom of religion in 1863. (See entry for Scandinavian Unbelievers.)

Lagerkvist, Pär Fabian (1891–1974)

The Swedish winner of the 1951 Nobel Prize in literature, Lagerkvist is said to have been a philosophic naturalist. *The Hangman* (1933) is concerned with good, evil, and man's search for God. Lagerkvist is an unbeliever who, although preoccupied with the plight of unbelievers, states Ingwersen, "turns a reassuring myth around to show the ludicrousness of its promise. The novel *Barabbas* (1950) may be, in fact, the ultimate characterization of the unbeliever who cannot transcend his own belief." (See letter from Walter Gustofson, above. Also, see entry for Scandinavian Unbelievers.) {CE; Faith Ingwersen, EU}

Lagerlof, Selma (1858–1940)

A Nobel Prize-winning Swedish novelist, Lagerlof in *Jerusalem* (1901) wrote, "Here [in Jerusalem], no mercy is shown. One hates one's fellow man to the glory of God." In 1909, she was the first gay woman, the first woman, and the first Swedish writer to receive the Nobel Prize for Literature. {TYD}

Lagrange, Joseph Louis [Comte] (1736–1813)

A French mathematician and astronomer, Lagrange was a freethinker during the Revolution. He solved isoperimetrical problems, on which the calculus of variations is based in part. He researched the nature and propagation of sound, studied the libration of the moon, and was influential in causing the adoption of the decimal base for the metric system. His *Analytical Mechanics* was called "one of the masterpieces of the human intellect" by Wheeler. Lagrange was a friend of D'Alembert, Diderot, Condorcet, and Delambre. Under Napoleon, Lagrange was made senator and count. Although an agnostic, he "was too famous for them to touch him," observed McCabe. Lagrange is buried in the Panthéon. {BDF; CE; JM; JMR; JMRH; RAT; RE}

La Grasserie, Raoul de (Born 1839)

La Grasserie was a French sociologist whose rationalism is expressed in his poetry (*Hommes et singes*, 1899) and work on the sociological aspect of religion (*Des religions comparées au point de vue sociologique*, 1899). {RAT}

La Hontan, Jean (1666–1715)

An early French traveler to Canada, La Hontan wrote *Dialogues With an American Savage* (1704), in which he states his objections to religion. {BDF}

Lahr, Bert (1895–1967)

Lahr, the American comic actor, first performed in burlesque and vaudeville, becoming known for his morose facial expressions. He appeared in many Broadway shows, in films, and on television. His 1956 performance in *Waiting for Godot* is considered the high point of his career, but he is best remembered as the Cowardly Lion in the film *The Wizard of Oz* (1939), with Judy Garland.

Lahr married a Ziegfield Follies girl, Mildred Schroeder. Theirs was an eventful twenty-seven-year marriage, according to a biography by his son, critic John Lahr, who, in "My Mother the Ziegfield Girl" (*The New Yorker* 13 May 1996), recalls the following concerning his mother:

> She once upbraided me for letting my friends call me Lahrheim, which was Dad's original name. (He changed it by deed poll in 1959.)
> "Your name is Lahr," Millie insisted over tea."
> "Face it, Mom," I said. "You were married to one of the great Jewish entertainers."
> Millie folded her napkin carefully in front of her and fixed me with a look. "John, your father was not Jewish," she said. "He was a star."

{CE}

Lainez, Alexandre (1650–1710)

Lainez was a French poet, of the same family with the general of the Jesuits. He lived a wandering Bohemian life, going to Holland where he met Bayle. {BDF}

Laing, R. D. (1927–1989)

Laing was a British psychiatrist who founded a therapeutic community in which the hierarchical distinction between physicians and patients was essentially eliminated. In his autobiography, *The Making of a Psychiatrist* (1985), and in his other writings, he developed what was termed Humanistic Psychology. {CE}

Laing, Samuel (Born 1812)

Laing was a Scottish-born politician and writer, the son of S. Laing of Orkney. After being secretary of the railway department of the Board of Trade, he became Liberal M.P. for Kirkwall in 1852 and helped repeal duty on advertisements in newspapers. In 1860 he became finance minister for India. His *Modern Science and Modern Thought* (1885) is an exposition of the incompatibility of the old and new view of the universe. In *Modern Zoroastrian* (1887), he gives the philosophy of polarity which, however, was anticipated by Crozier who in turn was anticipated by Emerson. Laing in 1888 entered into a friendly correspondence with Mr. Gladstone on the subject of agnosticism, his portion of which was published. {BDF; RAT; RE}

Laisant, Charles Ange (Born 1841)

A French mathematician who became President of the Mathematical Society of France, Laisant was an Officer of the Legion of Honour and Vice-President of the Astronomical Society. Laisant was an active rationalist and agnostic. {RAT}

Lakanal, Joseph (1762–1845)

Lakanal was a French educator who, giving up the career of priesthood, entered with ardor into the Revolution, was a member of the Convention (1792–1795), and worked to protect the interests of science. At the restoration in 1814 he retired to America, where he was welcomed by Jefferson and became president of the University of Louisiana. {BDF; RAT}

Lake, Greg (20th Century)

Lake, a lyricist, bassist, and lead singer for King Crimson, wrote in the recording entitled "Tarkus"

> Can you believe
> God makes you breathe
> Why did he lose
> Six million Jews

Lal, Surendra (20th Century)

Lal is a director in England of the National Secular Society.

Lalande, Joseph Jérôme Lefrançais de (1732–1807)

A French astronomer who became director of the Paris Observatory, Lalande was a freethinker during the Revolution. In his twentieth year, Lalande was made a member of the Academy of Sciences. In 1762 he became professor of astronomy at the *Collège de France*. In 1764 he published his *Treatise of Astronomy*, to which Dupuis subjoined a memoir, which formed the basis of his *Origin of All Religions*, an idea taken from Lalande. In 1793, Lalande hazarded his own life to save Dupont de Nemours and some priests whom he concealed in the observatory of Mazarin college. Upon Lalande's observations the Republican calendar was drawn up. At Lalande's instigation, Sylvain Maréchal published his *Dictionary of Atheists*, to which the astronomer contributed supplements after Maréchal's death. Lalande professed himself prouder of being an atheist than of being an astronomer. His *Histoire céleste française* (1801) included a catalog of over 47,000 stars. {BDF; CE; JM; JMR; JMRH; RAT; RE}

La Libre Pensée

In France, *La Libre Pensée* publishes the monthly *La Raison* and a philosophical journal, *L'Idée Libre*. (See entry for French Humanists.) {FD}

La Mothe Le Vayer, François de (1588–1672)

A French skeptical philosopher, La Mothe Le Vayer was patronized by Louis XIV and was preceptor to the Duke of Anjoy. His skepticism shows in *The Virtue of Pagans and Dialogues After the Manner of the Ancients*. {BDF}

LA NUOVA RAGIONE

An Italian humanist publication, *La Nuova Ragione* is at Via dei Serpenti 35, 00184 Roma, Italia.

LA PENSÉE ET LES HOMMES

La Pensée et les Hommes, an associate member of the IHEU, is at Avenue Adolphe Buyl 105, 1050 Brussels, Belgium.

LA RAISON

A French humanistic journal, *La Raison,* is at 10-12 rue des Fosses-Saint Jacques, 75005 Paris, France.

LA VOIX DE LA LIBRE PENSEE/DAS FREIE WORT

La Voix de la Libre Pensée/Das Freie Wort (Freethinker), is a quarterly in French and German of *La Libre Pensée Luxembourgeoise*, B. Postale 198, L-2011 Luxembourg.

LAMA

• Although both a lama and a llama are wooly, the latter is pronounced YAH-ma in Spanish and is not a "superior one," whereas the former is neither a beast of burden nor a ruminant.

–Warren Allen Smith

In the Buddhism of Tibet, a lama is a monk or priest. The chief of the lamas is the Dalai Lama.

Lamarck, Jean Baptiste Pierre Antoine de Monet [Chevalier de] (1744–1829)

An eminent natural philosopher, Lamarck compiled the first comprehensive theory of organic evolution and coined the word "biology." Originally trained as a Jesuit, he became a deist. His theory of acquired characteristics, that the giraffe's neck eventually extended out of need to reach high, for example, was rejected once the principles of heredity were established. His contribution mainly is that at a time when most naturalists advocated divine creation and the fixity of species, he championed the evolutionary framework which Charles Darwin later propounded. The two differed, especially in their view of the part played by "appetency" (organic changes resulting from environmental pressures) and the active exertion of the organism. According to McCabe, "*The Catholic Encyclopedia* claims that he was a Catholic but even the anti-evolutionary Quatrefages said that he was 'essentially deistic,' and no Catholic of Lamarck's time could be an evolutionist. In some passages, in fact, he is practically agnostic." Several years before his death, Lamarck became blind. {BDF; CE; EU, H. James Birx; JM; RAT; RE; TYD}

Lamarque, Pierre (20th Century)

Lamarque is a signer from France of Humanist Manifesto II. He was a tireless worker for the separation of church and state in France. His *Essai de topographia du Paris macconique* (1974) is about the Masonic Lodge. {HM2}

Lamarque-Osmin, Mireille (20th Century)

In 1978 at the Seventh International Humanist and Ethical Union (IHEU) World Congress held in London, Lamarque-Osmin of France addressed the group.

Lamb, Charles (1775–1834)

An essayist who wrote many children's books including *Tales from Shakespeare* (1807), Lamb was a boyhood friend of Samuel Taylor Coleridge. He was in Leigh Hunt's literary circle, along with William Hazlitt, John Keats, and Percy Bysshe Shelley. Suggesting that a final will contains the element of self-fulfillment, he playfully included in his own will, "I am not, therefore, going to die!"

Before leaving the Unitarians a few years before his death, he wrote, "O Southey, Southey, how long would it be before you would find one of us Unitarians propagating such unwarrantable scandal?" And to a Mr. Moxom, he wrote, "Did George Dyer send his tract to me to convert me to Unitarianism? Dear, blundering soul, Why, I am as old a One-God-ite as himself!"

McCabe tells that in a late edition of his *Essays of Elia*, Lamb "included a letter to the reactionary poet Southey in which he says: 'The last sect with which you can remember me to have made common profession were the Unitarians,' and E. V. Lucas in his authoritative life of Lamb quotes letters which show that he was an agnostic (October 1831)." {CE; JM; JMR; JMRH; RAT; RE; U; UU}

Lamb, Edward (20th Century)

When Lamb signed Humanist Manifesto II, he was president of Lamb Communications, Inc. He discusses lawyers and business in *The Sharing Society* (1979). {HM2}

Lamb, Gilbert D. (20th Century)

In the 1950s, Lamb was on the advisory board of Charles Francis Potter's First Humanist Society of New York.

Lamb, Helen Boyden (1906?–1975)

Helen Lamb [Lamont], an economist, was the second wife of philosopher Corliss Lamont. The author of *Studies on India and Vietnam* (1976), she signed Humanist Manifesto II. {HM2}

Lamb, William [Viscount Melbourne] (1779–1848)

An eminent British statesman, Lamb became Prime Minister of England (Whig, 1834; Whig, 1835–1841) and the chief counselor of the young queen, Victoria, granddaughter of George III. McCabe reports that Greville, who knew Lamb well and often discussed religion with him, was an atheist; and that Allen, who also knew him, said Lamb had "a perfect conviction of unbelief." All agreed that it was not a mere question of indifference, for Lord Melbourne was a serious student of religious matters all his life. {JM; RAT; RE}

LAMBETH CONFERENCE: See entry for Anglican Communion.

Lamborelle, Louis (Born 1874)

A Belgian author, Lamborelle wrote *The Good Old Times* (1874), *The Apostles and Martyrs of Liberty of Conscience* (1882), and other anti-clerical works. He lost a post under government because of his anti-clericalism, but Lamborelle was one of the council of the Belgian Freethought Party. {BDF}

Lamboy, Leo (20th Century)

Lamboy is president of the American Association for the Advancement of Atheism (AAAA). (See entry for California Atheists, Humanists.)

Lamennais, Hugues Felicite Robert de (1782–1854)

Lamennais was a French writer, one who described Rome as "the most hideous sewer that was ever opened up to the eye of man." Although Lady Blennerhassett cites his being a priest, from 1825 to 1835, the *Catholic Encyclopedia* states that Lamennais "died rejecting all religious ministration." {JM; RAT; RE}

La Mettrie, Julien Offray de (1709–1751)

During the French Revolution, Maréchal cited La Mettrie as one of the major atheists of all time. A philosopher and physician, he first studied theology, then switched to become surgeon to the Guards of Paris. His materialistic philosophy expounded in *L'Histoire naturelle de l'âme* (1745), which he wrote under the pretense of its being a translation from the English of Charp [Sharp], held that psychical phenomena can be explained as the effects of organic change in the brain and nervous system. His work was burned, and he fled to Leiden. When he wrote *L'Homme machine* (1747), he escaped under threat of arrest to Berlin, where Frederick II the Great of Prussia provided him protection. He then wrote *L'art de jour* (1751), a hedonistic work on ethics. Diderot and Holbach, who were influenced greatly by him, never acknowledged their indebtedness to his ideas. For La Mettrie, the only real pleasures are those of the senses, which he held are the only avenues to knowledge. The only god of life is pleasure, and it is absurd to assume a god to explain motion. Virtue is self-enlightened self-interest. The "soul" perishes with the body. Only under atheism will religious strife cease.

Unfortunately, La Mettrie died from something he ate. Frederick himself penned La Mettrie's biography, describing his life of hedonism and the death from food poisoning, which his opponents said was a providential punishment for such an atheist. La Mettrie is buried in the garden of Lord Tyrconnel. A recent intellectual history of his thought and its influence is Kathleen Wellman's *La Mettrie: Medicine, Philosophy, and Enlightenment* (1992). {BDF; CE; CL; EU, Aram Vartanian; JMR; JMRH; RAT; RE}

Lamm, Richard D. [Governor] (1935–)

Lamm, a former Governor of Colorado (elected in 1975), was named 1993 Humanist of the Year by the American Humanist Association. {HNS2}

Lamont, Beth K. (20th Century)

Corliss Lamont married his third wife, Beth Keehner, in 1986. A devoted humanist who cared for him in his final years and helped develop humanist telecasts, Lamont is on the Executive Board of the Corliss Lamont Chapter of the American Humanist Association. For *The Humanist* (November-December 1998), she wrote "Establishing an International Criminal Court," in which she argued that the United States was negligent in being one of seven nations—including China, Iraq, and Libya—which did not sign a Rome agreement to establish such a court.

Lamont is a program director for the Humanist Society of Metropolitan New York, which is on the Web at <http://www.corliss-lamont.org/hsmny/>. Her e-mail: <info.hsmny@corliss-lamont.org>. (See entry for Human Values Network.) {HNS2}

Lamont, Corliss (1902–1995)

A leading exponent of the philosophic movement of naturalistic humanism, Lamont was the son of J. P. Morgan's partner, Thomas William Lamont. Active on behalf of civil liberties, he left the American Civil Liberties Union (ACLU) over policy differences and became chairman of the National Emergency Civil Liberties Committee (NECLC).

In the 1940s and 1950s, he taught a class, naturalistic humanism, at Columbia University, the notes for which became the basis of his book, *The Philosophy of Humanism* (1949; reprinted 1990). It is considered by many a standard text on the subject. Known as a rebel at Columbia, he organized aid for Harvard scrubwomen who had been dismissed in a dispute over a new minimum-wage law. A key advisor and financial backer of the American Humanist Association, he wrote extensively about humanism, opposed the Vietnam War, and championed the Bill of Rights in numerous forums. In 1952 he was the candidate for U.S. Senate of the American Labor Party, receiving 10,000 votes. Six years later, on the Independent Socialist ticket, he received 49,000 votes.

Included among his works are the following: *Issues of Immortality* (1932); *The Illusion of Immortality* (1965); *You Might Like Socialism: A Way of Life for Modern Man* (1939); *Freedom Is As Freedom Does, Civil Liberties Today* (1942, 1956); *Freedom of Choice Affirmed* (1967); *A Humanist Funeral Service* (1947, 1977); *A Humanist Wedding Service* (1970); and *The Independent Mind.* He edited *Dialogue on John Dewey* (1959); *Dialogue on George Santayana* (1959); *Man Answers Death: An Anthology of Poetry* (1936, 1952); *Voices in the Wilderness: Collected Essays of Fifty Years* (1974); and *Yes To Life: Memoirs of Corliss Lamont* (1981). In the latter book, he wrote, "My final word is that in the battles that confront us today for America's freedom and welfare, our chief aim as public-spirited citizens must be neither to avoid trouble, nor to stay out of jail, nor even to preserve our lives, but to keep on fighting for our fundamental principals and ideals."

Several legal victories were dear to his heart. In the late 1950s, he won a case against the State Department, which had refused for nearly a decade to issue him a passport on the ground that his travel abroad "would be contrary to the best interests of the United States." And in 1965 he won a suit against the Postmaster General for violating his First Amendment rights by opening and withholding his mail, including propaganda from Peking. In 1961 the Supreme Court held a 1961 anti-propaganda mail law to be unconstitutional. In 1965, he won a lawsuit against the Central Intelligence Agency, which had opened letters mail or received by him, some from his wife. A Federal Court declared that "illegal prying into the shared intimacies of husband and wife is despicable."

Over the years, he was criticized negatively from all quarters. He was cited for contempt of Congress at the behest of Senator Joseph Mc Carthy. In 1956, however, he was exonerated of all charges by the U.S. Appeals Court and was editorially praised by *The New York Times* for his courageous stands on behalf of civil liberties. In 1956 he was quoted in the *Times*, "The truth is that I am an independent non-Communist radical closest in my thought to such British Socialists as Aneurin Bevan and the late Harold J. Laski. I have always done my own thinking and traveling; and am critical of Communist parties as well as the Soviet Union, without adopting the blinding anti-Communist and anti-Soviet obsession that is leading the West to destroy its own highest values."

For decades Lamont and Sidney Hook carried on a running battle, more political than philosophic. When shown Hook's letter, above, Lamont, then eighty-eight, responded:

> In the first place, let me say that I never praised or overpraised the Soviet Union without criticizing that country for its lack of democracy and civil liberties. In the second place, I never praised the tyrant Stalin when I was praising the Soviet Union. In the third place, Humanism as such does not support or criticize foreign political regimes. Our business is in the United States and the American Humanist Association does not expect its members to take correct positions on foreign affairs. Therefore, Hook had no right to denounce me as a Humanist because I admittedly made serious mistakes in judgment about the Soviet Union.
>
> Of course, in World War 2 it became necessary for Americans to cooperate with the Soviet Union, even though Stalin was still in power. And I in a patriotic way took part in the movement for the United States to aid the Soviet Union as an ally against Hitler and the Nazis.

James T. Farrell (quoted herein), like Hook, was critical of the political stands taken by Lamont. But Lamont insisted he had not been deceived or politically naive, that any nation transformed from feudalism to superpower in a few decades could not be expected immediately to develop democratic institutions like those in the West.

In 1977 Lamont was named Humanist of the Year by the American Humanist Association. He had said that his fusion of militancy and philosophy was based on humanist principles, "not Christian service to an improbable God, but service here and now to our fellow human beings." In 1981, he received the Gandhi Peace Award. In 1982, he was elected an honorary associate of the British Rationalist Press Association. He was a signer of Humanist Manifesto II and was on the editorial board of *The Humanist.* In 1988 at the Tenth International Humanist and Ethical Union (IHEU) World Congress, Lamont addressed the group. The American Humanist Chapter in New York City is named after him. Although attacked for his politics by many within the humanist movement, Lamont was a major influence, one who helped considerably in publicizing the goals of naturalistic humanism.

His 1928 marriage to Margaret Hayes Irish, a writer, ended in divorce. His second wife, Helen Lamb, whom he married in 1962, died in 1975. During his final years, he was happily married to his third wife, Beth Keehner, whom he married in 1986 and who is a devoted humanist. He is survived by a son, Hayes; three daughters—Margot Heap, Florence Antonides, Anne Jafferis; six grandchildren; one great-grandchild; fourteen step-children of his last two marriages; and fifty step-grandchildren.

A memorial held at Columbia University featured talks by family members Beth Lamont, Jonathan Heap, Edward M. Lamont Jr., Edward M. Lamont Sr., and Lansing Lamont.

On the Web: <http://www.corliss-lamont.org/>. (See entry for Helen B. Lamb. For negative views, see entries for James T. Farrell, Sidney Hook, and Priscilla Robertson.) {Fred Edwords, "Requiem for a Freedom Fighter," *The Humanist*, July-August 1995; FUS; HM2; HNS; PK; TYD; WAS, 22 September 1989 and numerous tête-a-têtes}

Lamptey, Micah (1966–)

When six years of age, Lamptey was baptized in Ghana as a Presbyterian. After being educated at Polytechnic, however, he wrote, "I realized that the larger portion of what the preachers said consisted of pure lies. They didn't apply to real-life situations, and I didn't feel that I would be losing anything if I never went to church again—and I haven't been back since. . . . When I told my friends about my disappointment with Christianity, they tried to convince me to become a Muslim. But I knew that Islam would have been worse, because the degree of tolerance I enjoyed in Christianity was nonexistent in Islam. Moreover, I knew that sooner or later I would be branded an infidel who would receive an infidel's punishment, and thus I did not accept Islam."

Lamptey considers himself typical of many Africans who find their neighbors have minds and hearts filled with fear, ignorance, and superstition. "I decided to find out," he has written, "if our belief in superstition and idolatry was worthwhile, and I eventually realized that belief in witches who were capable of siphoning off people's wealth and talents was not entirely true. The bulk of African superstitions can be violated with impunity. Many Africans go to good schools and universities to study science and perform scientific experiments, and then come out to practice superstition." Lamptey has become an active member of the Rational Centre in Accra, Ghana.

Lancelin, Pierre F. (c. 1770–1809)

Lancelin was a French materialist, a constructive engineer in the French Navy. He wrote *Introduction to the Analysis of Science* (1801–1803) and expressed original physico-mathematical theories. {BDF}

Land, Jan Pieter Nicolaus (1834–1897)

A Dutch writer, Land wrote critical studies on Spinoza and brought out an edition of the philosopher's work in conjunction with J. van Vloten. {BDF}

Landers, Caleb (20th Century)

Landers, a freethinker, wrote *The Skeptic's Defense Against All Christians and Other Priests* (1920). {GS}

Landor, Walter Savage (1775–1864)

Landor was an English poet, an ardent Republican who served as a volunteer colonel in the Spanish Army against Napoleon from 1808 to 1814. Termed the greatest English writer of his age, and one of the richest for he inherited a large fortune, Landor was nominally a Christian but scattered many freethought sentiments over his various works. He wrote the epic poem *Gebir* (1798) and *Imaginary Conversations* (1824–1853), which consists of nearly one hundred fifty dialogues between notables both ancient and modern. His other works include *Pericles and Aspasia* (1836), *Hellenics* (1847), and *Heroic Idylls* (1863). {BDF; CE; RAT; RE; TYD}

Landoy, Adèle Eugénie Sidonie: See entry for Jules-Joseph Colette.

Landry, Bolder (20th Century)

Landry, the founder of the Thomas Paine Foundation, is a freethinker and an anthropologist. He has written for *Truth Seeker*.

Lane, Margaret (20th Century)

Lane wrote *Frances Wright and the "Great Experiment"* (1971). {GS}

Lane, Ralph Norman Angell [Sir]: See entry for (Sir) Norman Angell, winner of the 1933 Nobel Peace Prize.

Lane, William (20th Century)

An American who migrated to Queensland, Lane became a leader of the Brisbane Socialists and edited the *Boomerang* and the *Worker*. In 1893 he led a party of Australians to Paraguay to found "New Australia," a Scottish colony which failed. Lane, a theist or a pantheist, was hostile to Christianity. {RAT}

Lanessan, Jean Louis de (Born 1843)

Lanessan was a French naturalist who at the age of nineteen became a naval physician. In 1879 he was elected as a Radical member of the Municipal Council of Paris. Dr. Lanessan founded *Le Reveil*, edited the *Marseillaise*, and started the International Biological Library, to which he contributed a study on the doctrine of Darwin. {BDF; RAT; RE}

Lanfrey, Pierre (1828–1877)

A French author and senator, Lanfrey wrote *The Church and the Philosophers of the Eighteenth Century* (1855) and *History of Napoleon I* (1867–1875). Lanfrey's *The Political History of the Popes* merited being placed on the Roman *Index*. {BDF; RAT}

Lang, Andrew (1844–1912)

Lang was a man of letters who translated *Odyssey* with Butcher and wrote *In the Wrong Paradise*. A disciple of E. B. Tylor, Lang upheld the evolutionary view of mythology. An authority on comparative religion, Lang from a theistic viewpoint wrote *Custom and Myth, Magic and Religion*. {BDF; JM; RAT; RE}

Lang, Arnold (1855–1927)

A Swiss zoologist, Lang taught phylogeny (evolution) at Jena and anatomy at Zurich, where he became Rector. His *Text-book of Comparative Anatomy* (1891) was a standard for years. In the symposium, *Was Wir E. Haeckel Verdanken* (1914), Lang pays a glowing tribute to Haeckel and described himself as "an Agnostic Freethinker." {RAT; RE}

Lang, Heinrich (1826–1876)

A German rationalist, Lang studied theology under Baur at Tübingen, then became a teacher at Zürich. {BDF}

Lang, J. Jack (20th Century)

Lang has been an active member of the American Humanist Association. {HNS}

Lang, Jerome D. (20th Century)

When he signed Humanist Manifesto II, Lang was president of the Humanist Association of Greater Miami, Florida. {HM2}

Lange, Bonnie (20th Century)

Lange has been President of the Truth Seeker Company in San Diego, California, and editor of *Truth Seeker*, the freethought journal.

Lange, Friedrich Albert (1828–1875)

Lange was a German neo-Kantian philosopher, author of *Geschhichte des Materialismus und Kritik senier Bedeutung in der Gegenwart* (1866; tr. *A History of Materialism,* 3rd ed., 1950). In its introduction, Bertrand Russell wrote that Lange was "an opposite of the Kantian view of the world." Lange held that materialism is unable to explain consciousness and is refuted, on scientific grounds, by the psychology and physiology of sensation, which shows that the world studied by physics is a world dependent upon our modes of perception, not a world existing independently on its own account.

Lange praised Nietzsche's first major work, *The Birth of Tragedy Out of the Spirit of Music* (1872), but, according to Gordon Stein, was unsympathetic to materialism. Lange's view on pantheism included the thought that some truths of nature are not only unknowable but also unverifiable. Consciousness he regarded as subjective experience, not just the effect of matter. (See entries for materialism and for Richard C. Vitzthum.) {BDF; CE; ER, George J. Stack; RAT; RE}

Lange, Fred E. Jr. (20th Century)

Lange is author of *Famous Unitarians/Universalists* (1987), which includes a listing of over one hundred noted individuals including five United States presidents who have been Unitarians or Universalists: John Adams, Thomas Jefferson, John Quincy Adams, Millard Fillmore, and William Howard Taft.

Lange, Richard H. (20th Century)

Chief of nuclear medicine at Ellis Hospital, Schenectady, New York, Lange is a member of the Council for Secularism's Faith-Healing Investigation Project.

Langfeldt, Gabriel (Born 1895)

A Norwegian who has written about novelist Knut Hamsun, Langfeldt presided over the Third International Humanist and Ethical Union Congress held in Oslo (1962). He wrote *Abnorme karakterer (psykopater)* 1976.

Langhorne, John (1735–1779)

An English poet, Langhorne in *The Country Justice* wrote, "Fanatic fools, that in those twilight times / With wild religion cloaked the worst of crimes!" {TYD}

Langley, John Samuel (1889–1959)

In Perth, Australia, Langley was secretary of the Rationalist Association of Western Australia in 1918 and in 1924 established *The Rationalist* as a monthly. Langley lectured throughout Australia and New Zealand and was an admirer of Thomas Paine. When his leadership was challenged by Walter D. Cookes, who he declared wished to use the rationalist movement as a distribution vehicle for pro-fascist propaganda, Langley objected but lost because the Rationalist Association of Australia, in need of Cookes's financial support, voted to appoint a new editor and secretary, William Glanville Cook. Langley has been incorrectly described as having had an "addiction to drunkenness," and he fought back by editing his own monthly *Freethought* from 1939 to 1944 and by writing *Why I Am Not a Rationalist* (1944).

Langley died a bitter and shattered man, disillusioned by those he believed loyal. {FUK; SWW}

Langley, Vera Lucy (1894–1978)

Mrs. John Langley was the only woman committee member of the Victorian Rationalist Association. {SWW}

Langley, Walter (Born 1852)

A painter, Langley won many gold medals for his pictures at Paris and Chicago, and he painted an autograph portrait for the gallery of the Uffizi at Florence. A rationalist, Langley was an admirer of Bradlaugh. {RAT}

Langsdorf, Karl Christian (1757–1834)

Langsdorf was a German deist, the author of *God and Nature*. In that work he discussed the immortality of the soul, and in other books he wrote on the subject of mathematics. {BDF}

LANGUAGE

• Cricketers assume that the cognoscenti know all about crosspieces, wickets, batsmen, and bowlers. Theists assume everyone should know about Jordan, Calvary, Original Sin, and Armageddon. Nontheists make no such assumptions, relying instead on the the scientific method of reasoning—first, observing phenomena, then formulating a hypothesis concerning the phenomena, then experimenting to determine the truth or falseness of the hypothesis, and finally making a conclusion that validates or modifies the hypothesis.

–**Allen Windsor**

Judeo-Christian theists, starting with the faulty major premise that in the beginning were Adam and Eve, assume that the first two humans logically spoke the same language. Later, Noah's descendants (who spoke one language) tried to build a tower (of Babel, the word in Hebrew meaning "confused") reaching up to heaven to make a name for themselves, but God "confounded" them so that each spoke a different language and all were scattered over the face of the earth. Some individuals assume language was given to man by God.

Anatole France's *Penguin Island* (1908) jocularly described Heaven's dilemma when on Earth a near-sighted priest erroneously baptized a group of penguins, whose language, if any, did not include French. His satiric approach to treating the evolution of the Church's institution—Are animals baptized with certain sacred words eligible for eternity in Heaven?—was not appreciated by theologians.

Freethinkers are aware that language is the systematic communication by vocal symbols, that it is a universal characteristic of the human species. Nothing is known of how language originated, but scientists generally hold that it has been so long in use that the length of time writing is known to cover (7,900 years at most) is trifling by comparison.

Today, there are between 3,000 and 4,000 speech communities, with numbers ranging from many millions of speakers down to a few dozen or even fewer. (See Martin Gardner, "Klingon and Other Artificial Languages," *Skeptical Inquirer*, July-August 1995.) {CE}

LANGUAGES AND HUMAN COMMUNICATION

• "I Saw the Pope," translated into Spanish by an American T-shirt maker, became "I saw the potato."

• When a beer company, Coors, used "Turn it loose" as its slogan, the Spanish translation became "Suffer from diarrhea."

• Clairol's curling iron, "Mist Stick," in German connoted "manure stick."

• Colgate introduced a toothpaste, Cue, in France, then found that *Cue* is the name of a French pornography magazine.

• "Come alive with the Pepsi Generation," translated into Chinese, became "Pepsi brings your ancestors back from the grave."

• The chicken slogan of Frank Perdue's American company, "It takes a strong man to make a tender chicken," when translated into Spanish, became "It takes an aroused man to make a chicken affectionate."

• Coca-Cola, advertised in China first as "Ke-kou-ke-la," actually meant "Bite the wax tadpole" or "Female horse stuffed with wax," depending on the dialect.

• Parker Pen marketed a ball-point pen in Mexico with an ad that was supposed to have read, "It won't leak in your pocket and embarrass you." Thinking *embarazar* (to impregnate) meant *to embarrass*, the ad then read, "It won't leak in your pocket and make you pregnant."

• The American car named Nova connoted to the Spanish it was a vehicle that "no go."

• . . . and religionists think God dotted every "i" and crossed ever "t" in the variously translated Bible?

Lankester, Edwin Ray (1847–1929)

Lankester was an English scientist who revised the translation of Haeckel's *History of Creation* and publicized evolutionary ideas. In

1876 he exposed the spiritist medium Slade, procuring his conviction. At the University of London, Lankester taught zoology and natural history.

According to McCabe, Lankester was "a virulent agnostic in private conversation though discreet in public utterances, but for many years before he died he was an Honorary Associate of the Rationalist Press Association." {BDF; JM; RAT; RE}

Lannstrand, Viktor (19th Century)

In 1888, Lannstrand founded the Utilitarian Society in Sweden.

Lanpher, Larry (20th Century)

Lanpher is treasurer of Humanist Association: St. Petersburg, Florida.

Lanson, Gustave (1857–1934)

Lanson was a French historian at the University of Paris. His *Histoire nationale de la littèrature Française* (1896) is useful to rationalists, and he edited Voltaire's *Letters philosophiques* (1908). Lanson is a Chevalier of the Legion of Honour. {RAT}

Lanza, Robert Paul (1956–)

Lanza contributes material to *The American Rationalist* as well as to *The Humanist*. He is an associate in surgery at the Harvard Medical School and senior scientist at BioHybrid Technologies in Shrewsbury, Massachusetts.

Lao-zi (Lao-tzu)(Lao-tse) (Born c. 604 B.C.E.)

Lao-zi is the Chinese philosopher who reputedly founded Taoism. If he actually lived, he likely knew Kongfu-zi [Confucius], who was younger, and neither was a religious supernaturalist. Both were freethinking conservatives. Lao-zi (which means "old philosopher") is, according to Robertson, "the first known philosopher who denied that men could form an idea of deity, that being the infinite"; and he avowed "the idea of a primordial and governing Reason (*Tau*), closely analogous to the *Logos* of later Platonism. . . . His system is one of rationalistic pantheism." He reduced religion to a minimum, denying superstition and teaching the rule of returning kindness for evil. However, Robertson laments, "the quietist and mystical philosophy of Lao-Tze and the practicality of Confucius alike failed to check the growth of superstition among the ever-increasing ignorant Chinese population." In fact, in a short time both men came to be worshiped as a God. Contemporary Taoism (Daoism), McCabe has remarked, "has as little relation to his teaching as the Roman Catholic system has to the teaching of Jesus."

Although some contemporary scholars think Lao-zi did not actually live, if he did he is credited with the poetic passages in the main Daoist text, *Dao De Jing* (Way and Virtue Classic). {CE; ER; HMS2; JM; JMR; JMRH; *New Humanist*, October 1998; RE}

Laplace, Pierre Simon (Marquis de) (1749–1827)

Laplace was the astronomer who, when asked by Napoleon why he did not mention God in his *Mecanique celeste,* reportedly replied, "Sire, I had no need of that hypothesis." With L. L. Lagrange, he is known for establishing, beyond a doubt, Newton's hypothesis of gravitation. In addition to his famous *Mécanique* (1799–1825), Laplace wrote the popular summary of the history of astronomy, *Exposition du système du monde* (1796). He was elected to the French Academy in 1816. Among Laplace's sayings was, "What we know is but little; what we know not is immense."

McCabe wrote a different description of Laplace:

> As he lived to the days of reaction in France, when a rebel against the Church could not be sure of a decent funeral, he formally returned to his practice of Catholicism and is counted amongst the pious. As a number of public men did this solely for the sake of peace, we do not know the state of his final opinions, which is doubtful. I have never found any authority for the statement that when Napoleon asked him (which he is not in the least likely to have done, since he was probably an atheist himself) where God came in in his theory of the volution of the solar system, he answered, 'Sir, I did without that hypothesis,' but it justly represents him in his prime."

{BDF; CE; CL; JMR; JMRH; RE; TYD}

Lappé, Frances Moore (20th Century)

Lappé, a Unitarian, is a nutritionist who wrote *Diet for a Small Planet.*

Lardner, Ring Wilmer Jr. (1915–)

Lardner, son and namesake of the American humorist and short-story writer, has been a reporter for the *New York Daily Mirror*, a press agent for Selznick International Pictures, and a renowned author. In 1942 he was recipient of the Academy of Motion Picture Arts and Sciences award for best original screenplay, "Woman of the Year."

In 1945, during the "Cold War" period of the 1940s and 1950s, the House Un-American Activities Committee (HUAC) was set up, a group that was to cause him much grief. Nineteen in the entertainment industry were subpoenaed by the committee, which was looking for Communists and for the possible injection of Communist propaganda into movie scripts. Appearing before a new Congressman, Richard Nixon, and the HUAC chairman, J. Parnell Thomas, Lardner was asked, for example, if he belonged to the Writers Guild. "I could answer the question, Mr. Chairman," Lardner responded, "but I'd hate myself in the morning." Whereupon Thomas had him removed from the stand.

Lardner, who came to be known as one of "the Hollywood 10," all of whom became blacklisted by the movie industry, reasoned that "If you were not a Communist you could say no to that question but you would be acknowledging the committee's right to ask the question. If you were a Communist and said yes, the next question was all about who else was, and asking you to name names where you had even less constitutional protection than about yourself." Refusing to cooperate further with the committee, he was cited for contempt and spent ten months of a one-year sentence at the Federal Correctional Institution in Danbury, Connecticut.

Imprisoned with Lester Cole, he found that Thomas, the Republican congressman from New Jersey, was already an inmate, having meanwhile been convicted of misappropriating Government funds. Seeing Thomas in the chicken yard, Cole made the memorable observation, "Oh, still handling the chicken shit, I see!"

Others who were blacklisted included Frances Chaney, an actress married to Lardner; Dalton Trumbo, author of "Spartacus"; Waldo Salt, who eventually won Oscars for "Midnight Cowboy" and "All the Way Home"; Merle Debuskey, a theatrical publicist; Madeline Lee Gilford, an actress and the widow of the actor Jack Gilford; and the actress Kim Hunter, all of whom found it next to impossible to find work because of the blacklisting. In 1970, however, Lardner received the award for the best screenplay, "M*A*S*H," adapted from another medium,

It was not until 1997 that the Screen Writers Guild West, representing more than seven thousand writers, restored screen credits on twenty-four films of "the Hollywood 10."

Lardner, who writes provocative articles such as "The Age of Reason, 1794–1994" in *The Nation* (21 February 1994), has been a member of the Secular Humanist Society of New York. He holds that censorship, not searching for Communists, is the new problem facing Americans in the 1990s. "The people behind it are basically the fundamentalists, the Christian right. And I think the First Amendment is being threatened in a great many ways from this censorship effort." (See Brandon M. Stickney, *Free Inquiry*, Summer, 1998, on how Lardner's work has been censored by the media.) {CA; WAS, 2 March 1998}

Larevellière-Lepaux, Louis Marie de (1753–1824

A French politician attached from youth to the ideas of Rousseau, Larevellière-Lepaux was a moderate Republican who defended the proscribed Girondins, was doomed himself but escaped by concealment, and distinguished himself by seeking to replace Catholicism with theophilanthropy, or "natural religion." He wrote *Reflections on Worship and the National Fêtes*. Larevellière-Lepaux became President of the Directory but refused to swear fealty to the empire, although he was offered a pension by Napoleon. {BDF; RAT; RE}

Larkin, Edgar Lucien (1847–1921)

An astronomer and the director from 1900 onward of the Lowe Observatory in California, Larkin wrote in the New York *Truthseeker* that "religion is totally useless in a universe based on law, and every creed and belief will be swept from the earth when men get out of infantile stages of growth." {JM; RAT; RE}

Larkin, Philip (1922–1985)

Larkin, a librarian at the University of Hull in England, and a poet and novelist, was a non-believer whose *Selected Letters* reveal that he lamented his inability to complete more than two poems a year. In his work, he chronicled England's post-1945 problems, and he was highly opinionated. Being a librarian, for example, involved handing out "tripey novels to morons." Literature needs no definition, for it is simply "what one thrills to." As for England, "God, what a hole [with its] witless crapulous people, delivered over gagged and bound to TV, motoring, and Mackeson's Stout!" As for parents: "They fuck you up, your mum and dad. They may not mean to, but they do. They fill you with faults they had, then add some new ones, just for you." A mordant humorist, he wrote shortly before his death, "How good the 1950s seem as far as rhyming and making sense and being clever go." Larkin has the distinction, according to Martin Seymour-Smith, "of being the last Englishman to write a viable non-expressionist body of poetry. We should be grateful to and for him."

A 1993 biography by Andrew Motion, however, points out that recently located Larkin's letters show him to have been an anti-Semite, a racist, and a misogynist. Anthony Thwaite, one of Larkin's literary executors, found the following ditty entitled "How To Win the Next Election": "Prison for the strikers / Bring back the cat / Kick out the niggers / How about that?" And in a 1985 letter written two months before he died, Larkin wrote to a childhood friend, Colin Gunner, "I find the 'state of the nation' quite terrifying. In 10 years' time we shall all be cowering under our beds as hordes of blacks steal anything they can lay their hands on." Larkin's father, Sydney, was known to have been openly sympathetic to Adolf Hitler, and Larkin is widely said to have "adopted and adapted" some of his father's views.

Larkin, Tom (20th Century)

A Boston school psychologist and political activist, Larkin has been a student at the Humanist Institute. {*Family Matters*, Fall 1998}

Laromiguière, Pierre (1756–1837)

Laromiguière, a French philosopher, joined the Congregation of the Christian Brothers, taught philosophy in their schools, then left the Church and wrote a *Projet d'éléments de métaphysique* (1793), which earned him the position of professor of philosophy at the Central School and later at the Faculty of Letters. Laromiguière, whose work was theistic but empirical, was "the father of university-philosophy in France." {RAT}

Larousse, Pierre Athanase (1817–1875)

François Diderot and the Encyclopedists were not the only lexicographers banned by the Vatican. In 1873, Larousse's *Grand dictionnaire Universel du XIXe siècle*, consisting of seventeen volumes (1866–1876), made the list of prohibited reading. According to Wheeler, most of Larousse's colleagues were also freethinkers. McCabe cites Larousse as being an atheist. {ILP; JM; RAT}

Larra, Mariano José de (1809–1837)

Disappointed in love, Larra shot himself. But before his early death, Larra was a distinguished Spanish author who, at eighteen, published a collection of poems, followed by *El Duende Satirica* (The Satirical Goblin). In 1831 his *Pobrecito Hablador* (Poor Gossip) newspaper unmercifully attacked the public affairs and men of Spain and was suppressed after its fourteenth issue. He then wrote for *Revista Espanola*, signing his articles "Figaro." A friend, describing Larra, wrote, "Larra could see too deep to possess any faith whatever. All the truths of this world, he was wont to say, can be wrapped on a cigarette paper!" {BDF; RAT; RE}

Larrabee, Harold A. (1894–1979)

A philosopher at Union College in Schenectady, New York, Larrabee wrote the present author about humanism:

> I have stated recently in a review in *The Journal of Philosophy* of Ralph Barton Perry's *The Humanity of Man* that it appears inevitable that any term derived from "man" or "human" should have meanings and interpretations almost as diverse as men themselves are. It is, therefore, rather presumptuous for any limited group of men to insist upon a monopoly of "human" or "humanism" for their own particular position.
>
> Nevertheless I find Naturalistic Humanism the label which comes the closest to my own views, for, while rejecting the supernatural as the ground and justification of human values, I should maintain that such values remain intact, unimpaired, and of great significance to man, although the cosmos may be indifferent to them. I sometimes refer to this sort of philosophy as "Aspiration Without Nonsense" or "Mythless Idealism." I should also emphasize as crucial for Naturalistic Humanism a moderating or a partial renunciation of familiar human demands, not only of the above demand for a cosmic warranty for human values, but also of the demand for absolute certainty in knowledge. These are the renunciations associated with scientific method. Naturalistic Humanism will obviously fail to satisfy those who insist upon having, or seeking, what it regards as beyond human finite knowing powers to supply. But I doubt that Naturalistic Humanists can wrest the label "Humanist" from those who claim it for other purposes.

Larrabee is author of *What Philosophy Is* (1928), and *Reliable Knowledge* (1945). He edited *Selections from Bergson* (1949); *Bentham's Handbook of Political Fallacies* (1952); and *In Quest of New Ethics* (1953). {CL; HNS; WAS, 8 September 1956}

Larroque, Patrice (1801–1879)

A French philosopher, Larroque was rector of the academies of Cahors, Limoges, and Lyons (1836–1849). But he was denounced for his opposition to clerical ideas and lost his position. Among his many works was *De l'Esclavage chez les Nations Chrétiennes* (1857), in which he proves that Christianity did not abolish slavery. His *Religious Renovation* (1859) proposed a moral system founded upon pure deism and was, for a time, prohibited in France. {BDF}

Larsen, Wayne Erik (1946–1996)

Larsen, an admirer of Ayn Rand as well as of secular humanism, was an honor graduate of Henry High School in Minneapolis, Minnesota, after which he was a Marine veteran who served in Vietnam. He conceived, organized, and worked as President of the

Sousa Society, an International Arts Olympics, but was unable to realize the group's successful completion because of his ill health.

Larsen, a graduate of Columbia University, was an active member of a New York support group—Agnostics, Atheists, and Secular Humanists Who Are Infected / Affected with AIDS/ HIV Illness (AASH). Upon his death from Kaposi's sarcoma (KS) and in keeping with his wishes, family members scattered his cremains in New York, Oregon, and Minnesota. {WAS, numerous conversations}

Larson, Edward J. (20th Century)

Larson, a Pulitzer Prize-winning author who wrote *Summer for the Gods: The Scopes Trial and America's Continuing Debate over Science and Religion*, was the featured speaker at a 1998 Freedom From Religion Foundation convention in Madison, Wisconsin. {*Freethought Today*, November 1998}

Larson, Martin Alfred (1897–1994)

Larson was a member of the National Advisory Council of Americans United. His early doctorate on the subject of Milton's theological concepts led him into teaching at Eastern Michigan University and the University of Idaho. A Unitarian, he wrote *Milton and Servetus* (1926); *Praise the Lord for Tax Exemption* (1969); *The Religion of the Occident* (1959); *The Story of Christian Origins* (1971); and *The Religious Empire in America* (1975). *The Essene Heritage* (1967) was an early study of its kind, and Larson postulated that, after Jesus left the Order of Essenes, he became a key figure of a new movement in which he attracted his own disciples. William B. Lindley in *Truth Seeker* (#2, 1994) wrote an obituary, lamenting the loss of such an important freethinker.

Larson, Orvin (20th Century)

Larson wrote *An Infidel: Robert G. Ingersoll* (1962, revised as *American Infidel: Robert G. Ingersoll*, 1995). {FUS}

Larue, Gerald Alfred (20th Century)

Larue is professor emeritus of archaeology and biblical studies at the University of Southern California in Los Angeles. He is a member of the Secretariat of the Council for Secular Humanism's International Academy of Humanism and president of the Council's committee for the Scientific Examination of Religion. Also, he is on the editorial board of *The Humanist*, is a senior editor of *Free Inquiry*, and signed Humanist Manifesto 2000.

He wrote *Homosexuality and the Bible* (1983), *Sex and the Bible* (1983), *Euthanasia and Religion* (1985); *The Way of Ethical Humanism* (1989); *The Way of Positive Humanism* (1989); and *Freethought Across the Centuries.*

The Supernatural, the Occult, and the Bible (1990) demonstrates that all belief systems have in common a dependence on magical thinking disguised as divine truth. In *Ancient Myth and Modern life*, Larue tells of the mythic origins and their acceptance as truth in the absence of science, then explains how the dysfunctional nature of religion is negatively affecting contemporary society.

Larue addressed the Tenth International Humanist and Ethical Union (IHEU) World Congress held in Buffalo (1988), and he helped dedicate the Council's Center for Inquiry in Amherst, New York, in 1995. In 1989, Larue was named Humanist of the Year by the American Humanist Association. In 1994, he became a Secular Humanist Mentor of the Council for Secular Humanism.

Reviewing Larue's *Freethought Across the Centuries: Toward a New Age of Enlightenment* (1996), Joe Barnhart wrote, "Its author is a humanist in the noblest sense of the world. He strives to find the common humanity in every culture and historical period. Most humanists are proud to identify in depth with the Enlightenment. Larue will help humanists today to sense their kinship with the struggling freethinkers of the past." (See entry for Soteriology.) {*Free Inquiry*, Winter 1996-1997; HMS2}

Laska, Andrew (20th Century)

Laska, of the North Texas Church of Freethought in Dallas-Fort Worth, Texas, wrote "Dissecting Dr. Laura" for *Secular Nation*(April-June 1999).

Laski, Harold J. (1891–1950)

A British Labour Party and Fabian Society official, one of the most famous speakers of his era, Laski was listed by Corliss Lamont as having been a philosophic naturalist. Nicolas Walter has called Laski "a leading freethinker, an Honorary Associate of the Rationalist Press Association and our second President from 1930 to 1933, and he was certainly a very popular writer and speaker among freethinkers."

Laski was chairman of the Labour Party in 1945 and 1946 and was a professor of political science at the London School of Economics from 1926 until the end of his life. He once wrote,

> The test, surely, of a creed is not the ability of those who accept it to announce their faith; its test is its ability to change their behavior in the ordinary round of daily life. . . . I cannot see, in the historic process, that the churches have been other than the enemies of reason in thought and of justice in social arrangements. Their concentration upon the life to come—for the reality of which I see no evidence—has, it seems to me, done more than most factors in history to deflect the attention of men from the realities of our life here and now. The result of the deflection has always been to the interest of those who live by privilege.

Despite his open rejection of all religion, Laski, according to Walter in *The New Humanist*, "remained very conscious of his Jewish identity—not surprisingly, in view of the personal anti-Semitism which he encountered and the terrible events which he witnessed." {CE; CL; FUK; TRI}

Laski, Margharita (1915–)

Laski, an author, is a freethinker, according to David Tribe. {TRI}

Lasley, Jack (20th Century)

Lasley edited *Priestcraft and the Slaughterhouse Religion* (1987). He also wrote *Threat of Radical Fundamentalism* (1995). {GS}

Lassalle, Ferdinand Johann Gottlieb (1825–1864)

Lassalle, who was born of Jewish parents, founded the German Social Democratic Party. A follower of Hegel and Feuerbach, he published a profound work on the philosophy of Heraclitus. Heine was charmed with him in 1846, and Humboldt called him "Wunderkind." McCabe wrote that Lassalle "might be described with Marx and Engels as one of the Three Musketeers of German atheistic Socialism."

For planning an insurrection against the Prussian Government, Lassalle was arrested but won his acquittal. In mid-career, he died in a duel. {BDF; JM; PUT; RAT; RE}

LAST WILL AND TESTAMENT

Wills often provide an insight into the mind of the deceased. Abraham Lincoln, a lawyer, had no final will, thereby dying "intestate." Lincoln's net worth of $110,295 was awarded by a court to his wife and two sons. The U.S. Congress, with strict observance of accounting rules, paid his salary only to the day of death. The purpose of a will is to allow the deceased to express one final wish for the disposition of his worldly goods.

Following are some of the recorded bequests:

- Nek'ure, Egyptian Pharoah's son who died c. 2601 B.C.E.
  His will, the oldest known to exist, provided for the disposition of fourteen towns and two estates. Its opening words pointed out that King Khafre's son had made the decisions about his property "while living upon his two feet and not ailing in any respect."
- Aristotle, who died 322 B.C.E.
  His will left three executors to handle his affairs until his chosen son-in-law, Nicanor, came of age. If Nicanor died prior to the time when Aristotle's daughter was old enough to marry him, Theophrastus was named as the second choice. He designated other individuals in the event Herpylis married.
- Vergil, died 19 B.C.E.
  Vergil asked that his *Aeneid* be burned with his death, a request he later canceled.
- Petrarch, died 1374
  The poet left 200 gold florins to Boccaccio, to buy a robe that would stave off the cold.
- Henry VIII, died 1547
  The much-married monarch in just under 7,000 words stated that he would not object if his cadaver were buried "in any place accustomed for Christian folke." However, he continued, "because we would be lothe in the reputation of the people to do injurie to the dignitie which we unworthilie are called unto," a better choice would be at Windsor, "midwaye between the Stalles and the high aulter."
- François Rabelais, died 1553
  His entire will read: "I have nothing. I owe much. The rest I leave to the poor."
- William Shakespeare, died 1616
  Shakespeare left considerable real estate holdings in and near Stratford to his two daughters, Susanna and Judith. Curiously, he gave his wife "my 2nd-best bed with the furniture."
- John Donne, died 1631
  The metaphysical poet left £500 to maintain his mother and a fifty-four-line poem entitled "The Will." Earlier in his *Devotions*, he wrote, "Any man's *death* diminishes me, because I am involved in *Mankind*; and therefore never send to know for whom the *bell* tolls; it tolls for *thee.*"
- **Peter the Great**, died 1725
  He advised his ministers to keep Russia continually at war for the good of the nation. In addition, he wrote a complete plan of strategy for a Russian conquest of Europe.
- Patrick Henry, died 1799
  Henry provided generously for his widow Dorothea unless she remarried, in which case he cut her off without a cent or "no more of my estate than she can recover by Law." She voted for freedom of choice and married his cousin, Judge Winston.
- **Marquis de Sade**, died 1814
  He gave Madame Quesnet 80,000 livres because "during the Reign of Terror, she saved me from the revolutionary blade all too surely suspended over my head." He insisted that his corpse be kept in an open coffin in the death chamber for a full 48 hours, "at the end of which period the said coffin shall be nailed shut." Only then, after he was found to be *definitely* dead, was he to be buried in the woods at Malmaison.
- Napoleon Bonaparte, died 1821
  His will, written twenty-one days before his demise, stated, "I die prematurely, assassinated by the English oligarchy." Although he left bequests that totaled six million francs, he had no funds for the purpose.
- **Jeremy Bentham**, died 1832
  Bentham's entire estate was given to London Hospital, provided that his preserved remains were permitted to preside over its board meetings. As a result, his body was turned over to Dr. Southward Smith, who performed the complete dissection and the anatomical lecture, for public and medical student alike that Bentham had stipulated. The bones were reassembled into a skeleton topped by a wax mask cast from the philosopher's expressionless face. The likeness was outfitted in Bentham's clothes and placed within a glass-fronted mahogany case, sitting upright in an armchair. For ninety-two years, the wax apparition was present, although duly noted as "not voting," at the meetings. The skeleton is on display at University College, London.
- Heinrich Heine, died 1856
  The German poet left his entire estate to his wife, provided she would marry again. "Because," his will read," then there will be at least one man to regret my death."
- **Charles Dickens**, died 1870
  Dickens left £80,000 to his family. He noted that he had paid to his wife, from whom he was separated, £600 annually, while assuming all expenses for the family. He asked that those who came to his funeral "wear no scarf, cloak, black bow, long hatband, or other such revolting absurdity."
- Brigham Young, died 1877
  The Mormon Church leader left $2.5 million in cash and real estate which was distributed to his seventeen wives and forty-eight children.
- **Karl Marx**, died 1883
  The founder of Marxism accumulated no personal wealth, leaving a scant £250.
- **Phineas T. Barnum**, died 1891
  The American showman left $4.1 million but gave his daughter Helen, whose notorious conduct he disliked, only some useless western property in return for a "quit claim" on his estate. The land proved to have valuable mineral deposits, which made Helen wealthier than all the other Barnum heirs put together.
- **Cecil Rhodes**, died 1902
  Rhodes in his first five wills called for a ". . . Secret Society, the true aim and object whereof shall be the extension of British rule throughout the world," and, eventually, "the ultimate recovery of the United States of America."
- **Florence Nightingale**, died 1910
  She refused burial in Westminister Abbey, giving her body "for dissection or postmortem examination for the purpose of Medical Science." Her wishes were ignored. She was buried at East Wello.
- Adolf Hitler, died 1945
  Mentioning that he and Eva Braun were marrying and then choosing to die "to escape the shame of overthrow or capitulation," the dictator wanted it clearly understood that his painting collection "bought by me during the years" had always been intended to establish a picture gallery in his hometown, Linz. Although a nominal Christian, he left nothing to the church.
- **George Bernard Shaw**, died 1950
  See entry for Shaw.
- **Albert Einstein**, died 1955
  After disposition of an estate of $65,000, Einstein left his manuscripts and royalties to Hebrew University, and his beloved violin to his grandson.
- **George Orwell**, died 1959
  Orwell requested that his grave be marked with his real name, Eric Arthur Blair. He left £9,909.
- Marilyn Monroe, died 1962
  She left over $1 million, although the estate was later declared insolvent.
- **Jawaharlal Nehru**, died 1964
  Following his cremation, Nehru asked that a handful of his ashes be scattered in the Ganges River. He took care to explain that his request bore no religious significance, noting, ". . . the Ganges has been to me a symbol and a memory of the past of India, running into the present, and flowing on to the great ocean of the future." To insure that no portion of his remaining ashes were preserved, he directed that they be disposed of by carrying them aloft ". . . in an airplane and scattered from that height over the fields where the peasants of India toil."

An estimated two-thirds of Americans die without leaving wills. But, in addition to Lincoln, they have historic company: Andrew Jackson, D. H. Lawrence, Howard Hughes, and Pablo Picasso. (See Herbert E. Nass, *Wills of the Rich and Famous*, NY, Warner Books, 1991.) {PA}

Lastarria, José Victorino (1812?–1888)

Lastarria was a Chilean statesman and a positivist. He founded several journals and literary societies and served as minister to Peru and Brazil. In 1873, he founded the Santiago Academy of Science and Literature. As a representative of the Chilean Congress, he helped promote the secularization of education, and he was active in trying to abolish the *fueros* (privileges) of the church. To Domingo Faustino Sarmiento in 1876, Lastarria wrote, "There is nothing worse for our societies than Catholic morality." Among his anticlerical works were *Investigaciones sobre la influencia social de la conquista i del sistema colonial de los españoles en Chile* (1844) and *Recuerdos literarios* (1868). {BDF; EU; RAT}

Laszecki, Karol (20th Century)

Laszecki, from Poland, addressed the 1966 Fourth International Humanist and Ethical Union World Congress held in Paris.

Latha, Chandra (20th Century)

Latha is a rationalist from Hyderabad, India, the author of *Seeds of Fertile Soil* and winner of a $3,000 prize by the Telugu Association of North America for her novel written in the Telugu language. The work is partly autobiographical, covers three generations of one family, and details a humanist hero's attempts to deal with superstitions and violence. {*International Humanist News*, September 1997}

Latham, John Greig [Sir] (1877–1964)

Latham, who represented Australia at the Versailles Peace Conference in 1919, was active in the Melbourne branch of the Rationalist Press Association and became president of the Rationalist Association of Victoria. From 1935 to 1952, he was Chief Justice. {SWW}

Latham, Robert (1812–1888)

Latham, an ethnologist, taught language and literature at London University College, then turned to medicine and lectured on forensic medicine at the Middlesex Hospital. In 1849 he abandoned medicine for philology and ethnology. Of him, Huxley wrote that "the existence of the Established Church was to his mind one of the best evidences of the recency of the evolution of the human type from the simian." Latham was a rationalist, "one who for brilliance of intellect and range of knowledge had scarcely an equal among his contemporaries," according to the *Dictionary of National Biography*. {RAT; RE}

Latimer, Donald (20th Century)

In 1978, when director of the Los Angeles Chapter of American Atheists, Latimer protested that public funds were being used to light and maintain a twenty-seven foot high Christian cross overlooking Cahuenga Pass, opposite the Hollywood Bowl, in Hollywood, California. He has been active in fighting for the separation of government and religion.

Latimer, Lewis H. (1848–1928)

Latimer, an inventor and a pioneer in the electric light, was the son of Virginia slaves. He had a difficult childhood inasmuch as his parents had escaped and were actively being pursued by James Gray, their owner. Fortunately, they succeeded in escaping and young Latimer secured work as a draftsman, although he had no experience. His drawings were so good that Alexander Graham Bell used his services. In addition, he was for a time an associate of Thomas Edison.

In 1890 Latimer wrote *Incandescent Electric Lighting*, the first book written on that subject. "Lights outside as well as in," he wrote, "are equally under control, and the coming or retiring guest may be lighted top the farthest point of the most extensive grounds without the necessity of the host being in any way exposed to the weather." This meant no more gaslights, and soon he was asked to set up lighting systems for buildings and streets in New York, London, Montreal, and Philadelphia.

Latimer was a founding member of a Unitarian church near his New York home in Flushing. For the *Encyclopedia of Religion*, he wrote the section on Latin American philosophy. In 1993, his granddaughter, Dr. Winifred Latimer Norman, wrote a biography, *Lewis H. Latimer, Scientist*. {EG; U}

LATIN AMERICAN MARXISM

Jorge J. E. Gracia and Iván Jaksic, in *Encyclopedia of Unbelief*, note that Marxism, like positivism, "interprets religion as superstition and an obstacle to social advancement. They also share en emphasis on science, a deterministic and materialistic view of reality, and the goal of social progress." Marxists generally are more antireligious and anticlerical than positivists, but Marxism was one of the forces in Latin America which challenged the predominance of Catholic thought and influence. "As a result," they note, "one can only conclude that orthodox Catholicism has perhaps seen its influence diminished through the efforts of these movements but that the bases of religious faith in the area, inspired by Catholic doctrine, remain strong."

Fidel Castro has at times called his philosophic outlook that of "communistic humanism." Raya Dunayesvskaya, former secretary to Leon Trotsky, stated the Karl Marx was a thoroughgoing naturalist in philosophy and that, at first, he had called his outlook "a new humanism." Sidney Hook, however, and other major figures in United States secular humanist circles predicted all along that communism and Marxism were doomed to fail because of their opposition to any beliefs not founded upon freedom, the significance of the individual, and political democracy.

LATIN AMERICAN UNITARIANS

A Unitarian minister, Lawrence Peers, heads *Luuna Luz*, a Latin-Unitarian Network Publication.

LATIN AMERICAN POSITIVISTS

Positivism, which was inspired by the writings of Comte, was found in various Latin American countries:

- Argentina—**J. Alfredo Ferreira** (1863–1935)
- Brazil—**Constant Botelho de Magalhaes** (1836-1891); **Luis Pereira Barreto** (1840–1923); **Miguel Lemos**; **Raimundo Teixera Méndez**; **Tobias Barreto** (1849–1923); **Silvio Romero**; **Clovis Brevilaqua**
- Chile—**Valentín Letelier** (1852–1919); **Jorge Lagarrigue** (died 1894); **Juan Enrique Lagarrigue** (died 1927); **Luis Lagarrigue** (died 1948)
- Cuba—**Enrique José Varona**—as minister of education, his reforms remained in place until Fidel Castro's revolution
- Honduras—**Ramón Rosa** (1848–1883) was minister general under President **Aurelio Soto**, and the two carried out ecclesiastical and educational reforms
- Mexico—**Gabino Barreda** (1818–1881); **Juso Sierra**
- Peru—**Mariano H. Cornejo** (1866–1942)
- Uruguay—**Alfredo Vázquez Acevedo**

(See entry for Positivism) {EU}

LATINUS: See entry for Roman Civilization.

Latourette, Keith Scott: See the entry for Theism.

LATTER-DAY SAINTS

The Reorganized Church of Jesus Christ of Latter-Day Saints is a denomination that separated from the Mormons in the 19th century. It rejects the name Mormon for itself. The Reorganized Church of Jesus Christ of Latter-day Saints, organized in 1830, is at PO Box 1059, Independence, Missouri 64051. {DCL}

LATVIAN UNITARIANS

Vija Vetra is founder of a Latvian congregation of Unitarians. They have no regular meeting place but can be reached by writing the International Council of Unitarians and Universalists, 1-6 Essex St., Strand, London WC2R 3HY, United Kingdom.

Lau, Theodor Ludwig (1670–1740)

Lau was a German philosopher. His *Philosophical Medications on God, the World, and Man* excited an outcry for its materialism, whereupon the work was suppressed. A follower of Spinoza, Lau held several official positions from which he was deposed because of his presumed atheism. {BDF}

Laubach, John Herbert (20th Century)

Laubach wrote *School Prayers, Congress, the Courts, and the Public* (1969). {FUS}

Laube, Heinrich (1806–1884)

Laube was a German dramatist and rationalist. In 1834 he was expelled from Saxony for his advanced opinions. In 1848 he sat in the National Assembly, and in the following year he became art director of the Vienna Court Theatre, which he raised to a high level. His novels, dramas, and literary works were published in sixteen volumes (1875–1882). {RAT}

Laubeuf, Maxime Alfred (Born 1864)

In the French *Qui est-ce?*, Laubeuf is described as the creator of the submersible submarine. He constructed the first boat of the type, the *Narval*, in 1898, then built a large number more for the French Navy. In his *Luttes maritimes prochaines* (1908), Laubeuf forecast naval wars. He was a chevalier of the Legion of Honour and an officer of the French Academy.

An agnostic, he wrote in 1920, "As to another world, I must declare myself unable to say anything, though it would, perhaps, be unphilosophical to deny everything a priori." {RAT}

LAUGHTER

• Laughter, n. An interior convulsion, producing a distortion of the features and accompanied by inarticulate noises. It is infectious and, though intermittent, incurable. Liability to attacks of laughter is one of the characteristics distinguishing man from the animals—these being not only inaccessible to the provocation of his example, but impregnable to the microbes having original jurisdiction in bestowal of the disease.

–Ambrose Bierce
The Devil's Dictionary

• [L]aughter is not a lack of seriousness. On the contrary, irony and lightness are one of the highest forms of intelligence.

–Dario Fo
commenting upon Roberto Benigni's winning an Oscar Award for his acting in the best foreign film of 1999, "Life Is Beautiful"

Freethinkers revel in laughter, some saying you can tell a religious person by the way his or her mouth turns downward, a non-religious person by the number of jokes that she or he tells. Even Krishna, Vishnu's avatar, amused himself by stealing the clothes of the goat-herd girls as they bathed in the river, Arthur Chappell happily relates in *Freethinker* (March 1999). Zeus seduced mortal women and turned men into donkeys. The Greek and Roman gods were known for their high jinks.

But the closest one comes to humor in the Bible is some children's referring to Elisha (*Kings 2*, 23-25), saying "unto him, go up, thou bald head, go up, thou bald head." But, as many a periwigged freethinker might complain unto them, "Dost thou find baldness is something laughable, ye intolerant louts?" The 1291 Council of Salzburg found it necessary to order that "the clergy must not be jesters, goliards, or buffoons; if they pursue such disgraceful accomplishments for a whole year, they are to be stripped of all ecclesiastical privileges." Better just to strip them of all their clothes, a freethinker might suggest . . . and listen, instead, to Phaedrus (the 1st Century Macedonian, born a slave, who translated Aesop's fables into Latin verse):

> A fly bit the bare pate of a bald man, who in endeavouring to crush it gave himself a hard slap. Then said the fly jeeringly, "You wanted to revenge the sting of a tiny insect with death; what will you do to yourself, who have added insult to injury?"

Laurence, Margaret [originally **Jean Margaret Wemyss**] (1926-):

A Canadian author, Laurence is best known for works depicting the lives of women struggling for self-realization in the male-dominated world of western Canada.

This Side Jordan (1960) describes her experiences in Ghana. *New Wind in a Dry Land* (1963) is an account of her years in Somaliland (now Somalia). *The Tomorrow Tamer* (1963) is a collection of short stories set in Ghana.

A fictional Canadian prairie town of Manawaka is the setting for *The Stone Angel* (1964), *A Jest of God* (1966), and *The Fire-Dwellers* (1959). A Unitarian, Laurence twice received the Governor General's Award for Fiction.

Laurence, James (1773–1841)

Laurence was a versatile writer, one who knew Goethe, Schiller, and other rationalists. His heterodox novel, *The Empire of the Nairs* (1807), was written in German, French, and English. When Robert Owen denounced "all the religions of the world" at the London Tavern in 1817, Laurence applauded him in a poem. {RAT}

Laurent, François (1810–1887)

Laurent was a Belgian jurisconsultant who was born in Luxembourg. His principal work is entitled *Studies in the History of Humanity*. He was a strong advocate of the separation of church and state, upon which subject he wrote (1858–1860). François also wrote *Letters on the Jesuits* (1865). {BDF; RAT}

Laurie, James Stuart (1773–1841)

Laurie was an educationist who at one time was Director of Public Education in Ceylon. His theistic views are given chiefly in *Religion and Bigotry* (1894) and *Gospel Christianity versus Dogma* (1900). {RAT}

Lauritsen, John (20th Century)

Lauritsen, author of *Religious Roots of the Taboo on Homosexuality* (1974) and *The AIDS War* (1993), is a thorn in the side of the American AIDS establishment, supporting molecular biologist Peter Duesberg's widely circulated assertion that the human immunodeficiency virus's relation to the acquired immune deficiency syndrome is one of "correlation but not causation." Lauritsen asserts that physicians and others are getting rich out of the present set-up, that some of the doctors who are now worth millions "were second-rate 'clap doctors' back in the 1970s" and for hundreds of individuals "the AIDS organizations have provided an opportunity for personal gain." Charities have little accountability, leading one AIDS worker to say, "There are more folk living off AIDS than dying from it here!" Lauritsen claims AZT is a poison-like substance which is toxic, and his disagreement with the more orthodox views leads him to liken his stand as similar to the child who uncovers the truth about Father Christmas, a truth they and their parents do not want to hear.

In "Hate Comes to Provincetown," Lauritsen has lamented how the Rev. Fred Phelps, pastor of the Westboro Baptist Church in Topeka, Kansas, preached hatred of homosexuals in his Massachusetts vacation town, which is known as a leading gay resort.

In 1998 Lauritsen, who describes himself as an atheist and an admirer of Voltaire, wrote *A Freethinker's Primer of Male Love*. {"My Atheism," *Freethinker*, January 2000; *Gay and Lesbian Humanist*, Spring 1998}

Lavan, Spencer (20th Century)

Lavan is author of *Unitarians and India: A Study in Encounter and Response* (1977).

Lavanam, Hemalata (20th Century)

In Vijayawada, India, Lavanam edited *Insaan* (1956–1962) and the monthly *Atheist* (1969 to the present). Sometimes described as "the Robert Ingersoll of India," "a Gandhian atheist," and "a most visionary and humanitarian human," Lavanam spoke in 1993 to Massachusetts humanists and, as head of India's Atheist Center, in 1996 she spoke on "Positive Atheism for a Positive Future" at the fourth World Atheist Conference which was held in India and of which she was a co-convener. She pointed to those pessimistic religious people who on the approach of the second millennium prophesied Armageddon and Doomsday and said that on the contrary we needed to give hope to humanity that the future would be bright and positive. Today's atheists, she advised, have a double role to play: they have to save humanity from pessimistic adventurism and to invent and promote tools to build a positive future in every walk of life. Now it is the responsibility of atheists to take positive strides toward promoting universal humanism and universal human identity without which it would become impossible to save even our physical and social environment. Atheists must work with liberal minded non-atheists in common cause, for they have a responsibility of restructuring the unjust and exploitive cultural, moral, social, political institutions and ideas and values, at local, national, and international levels. Mrs. Lavanam has an international following, is an honorary associate of the New Zealand Association of Rationalists and Humanists, and has traveled around the world several times. (See entry for G. Vijayam and for World Atheist Conference. For a 1995 interview in La Jolla, California, in which among other things he tells why he thinks Christians hate theists, see *Secular Nation*, Summer 1995.) {CA; E; FUK; *New Humanist*, February 1996}

Laveleye, Émile de (1822–1892)

A Belgian economist, Laveleye in 1864 received the chair of national economy at Liège University. He was elected a member of the *Institut* in 1869 and was associate editor of the *Revue de Belgique*. His rationalism is expressed in *Le parti clérical en Belgique* (1874). {RAT}

Lavender, Julia Margaret (Bella) (1858–1923)

Lavender was an Australian rationalist, feminist, and teacher. She was the first woman to graduate from an Australian University, receiving her B.A. in 1888. Lavender was described as a "witty, cogent, and instructive" commentator on social issues such as the rights of illegitimate children, sex discrimination, defense of English suffrage, anti-conscription, anti-militarism, and vindication of the rights of assembly and free speech.

Known also as Bella Guerin, she moved from Catholicism to rationalism and described her political evolution as from "imperialistic butterfly" to "democratic grub." {SWW}

Laveran, Charles Louis Alphonse (1845–1922)

The chief French authority on tropical diseases, Laveran was a Nobel Prize winner (1907) and a professor at the Pasteur Institute. While an army surgeon in Algiers he discovered (1880) the parasite that causes malaria. Asked by a French journal to comment about a report that Edison had adopted spiritualism, Laveran responded that he did not believe it. As a scientific man, Laveran added, he "did not believe in spirits." {CE; JM; RAT; RE}

Lavine, Thelma Zeno (20th Century)

Lavine, a philosophy educator, professor of philosophy at George Mason University, and president of the Society for the Advancement of American Philosophy, was named in 1993 a Humanist Laureate in the Council for Secular Humanism's International Academy of Humanism. She is a contributor to *American Philosophic Naturalism in the Twentieth Century* (1994). "The Case for a New American Pragmatism," which was originally printed in *Free Inquiry*, is reprinted in *Challenges to the Enlightenment* (1994). She has written *TV Course from Plato to Sartre* (1980), *From Socrates to Sartre: The Philosophic Quest* (1984); and was co-author of *History and Anti-History Philosophy* (1989).

A John Dewey scholar who wrote the introduction to the *Collected Works of John Dewey, Vol. 16* (1990), Lavine has also taught at the University of Maryland, George Washington University, and Inter-American Defense College. Lavine signed Humanist Manifesto 2000.

Lavisse, Ernest (1842–1922)

A leading French historian, Lavisse taught for many years at the Sorbonne. With Alfred Rambaud he edited *Histoire générale du 4e siècle à nos jours* (12 vols., 1893–1901) and, alone, edited *Histoire de France depuis les origines jusqu'à la révolution* (19 volumes, 1900–1922). His volumes are a synthesis of political, cultural, economic, and social history. In a biography of the historian Duruy, to whom he had once been secretary, Lavisse tells his agreement with him in freethinking. {CE; JM; RAT; RE}

Lavrov, Pytr Lavrovich (1823–1900)

Lavrov, a Russian mathematician, taught mathematics at the Artillery School but, because of his revolutionary opinions, was banished to the provinces. He escaped to Paris in 1870 and edited the revolutionary *Uperyod*. His chief work, *The Evolution and History of Human Thought* , was left unfinished at his death. Lavrov was a close student of philosophy and was an agnostic. {RAT}

LAW

• Lawful, adj. Compatible with the will of a judge having jurisdiction.
• Litigant, n. A person about to give up his skin for the hope of retaining his bones.
• Litigation, n. A machine which you go into as a pig and come out of as a sausage.

–Ambrose Bierce
The Devil's Dictionary

• "Are you trying to show contempt for this court?"
"No, your honor, I'm doing my best to conceal it."

–Mae West

The basis of law in Canada and the United States is English common law, which was imposed on England by a Frenchman, Henry II, in the 12th century. He had standardized local laws into a "common" law, adding some precepts from Roman law that had survived in the canon law of the medieval church.

The church played a great role in establishing our legal precepts, but it was by keeping alive Roman law, which survives today as civil law in much of Europe, Louisiana, and Quebec, not by promulgating the Judeo-Christian tradition via the Ten Commandments. In short, or at least as past Supreme Court justices have understood, the Holy Bible did not form the basis for law in Canada and the United States. Rome did.

For Christian fundamentalists to argue that the Ten Commandments formed the basis of the laws of the United States is, as noted by Canadian legalist Jerry Gilbert, patent nonsense. He has added, "To suggest that because early statute writers in the United States were Christian it is therefore a Christian state is like saying that because ancient Romans believed in a pantheon of gods Europeans should today bow at the feet of statues of Jupiter and Juno." Meanwhile, others point out that most of America's Founding Fathers were not, in fact, believers in the Christian Trinity. {*The New York Times*, 23 April 1997).

Law, David A. (20th Century)

With Corliss Lamont and Peter A. Angeles, Law wrote "Dewey's Idea of the Religious—Critical Evaluations" in *Religious Humanism* (Winter 1968).

Law, Harriet Teresa Frost (1831–1897)

An English freethinker, Law was a women's-rights lecturer who edited *Secular Chronicle*, a publication for which Karl Marx sometimes wrote. The journal was printed in Birmingham from 1872 to 1879. A lecturer, Law became engaged in numerous debates, aided by her husband, Alfred. The two organized the Walworth Association of Freethinkers. The only woman Secularist lecturer in England, she endured much insult as well as assault. Law, writes Royle, "had the distinction of being one of the few Secularists of whom Karl Marx approved." She was a member of the General Council of the International Working Men's Association and an advocate of women's rights. {BDF; EU, Gordon Stein; FUK; PUT; RAT; RSR; TRI; VI; WWS}

Law, Tim (20th Century)

Law, while a student at Temple University in Philadelphia, Pennsylvania, was one of the founders of Campus Freethought Alliance. {*International Humanist News*, December 1996}

LAW OF NON-CONTRADICTION

In logic, the law of non-contradiction is a basic principle: A sentence and the denial of the sentence cannot both be true—e.g., Jesus was a supernatural man, born by Immaculate Conception of a natural mother; Jesus was the son of Mary and an un-named human father, to whom she was not married. {DCL}

Lawler, James M. (20th Century)

Lawler, a professor of philosophy at the State University of New York at Buffalo, is author of *IQ, Heritability and Racism* and the *Existentialist Marxism of Jean-Paul Sartre* (1976).

Lawrence, D(avid) H(erbert) (1885–1930)

Lawrence, a novelist who held that industrial culture dehumanizes, preached a glorified union with nature and its corollary, sexual fulfillment. Although his *Sons and Lovers* was a success in 1913, it was not so until a publisher (Cambridge) bothered to print Lawrence's original version, the "naughty parts" of about 10% which had been cut by his original editor, Edward Garnett. What Garnett cut had to do with the hero putting on women's stockings and his references to "white, glistening globes" and other such descriptions of the female breast. Garnett had not, however, cut the part about the son's being in love with his mother and his failure to experience love with other women.

When Lawrence visited Mexico, to gain material for *The Plumed Serpent* (1926), he stayed with the humanist and poet, Witter Bynner. Bynner wrote an account of their stay, in which he described the skinny, bronchitic miner's son from Nottinghamshire and Emma Maria Frieda Johanna Baroness (Freiin) von Richthofen Weekley (a stoutly built, German noblewoman six years his senior whom he married, having eloped with her at a time when she was married to a Nottingham professor of etymology. Wags claimed she seduced him sexually within twenty minutes of their first meeting. They also related that in their numerous moves from southern Germany, Switzerland, Italy, Sicily, India, Australia, New Mexico, Mexico, England, and the south of France, it was Frieda who did the shopping and it was Lawrence who sewed the curtains as well as Frieda's underwear. Frieda was a cousin of von Richthofen, the German air-ace in World War I). The book was entitled *Journey With Genius: Recollections and Reflections Concerning the D. H. Lawrences* (1951). According to Bynner, Lawrence's horror at the Spanish obsession concerning blood (Jesus dripping on the cross) and their love of bullfighting (first plunging the *banderillas,* then adeptly stabbing with the sword) did not sit well with numbers of Latinos. When something was thrown at Bynner's house to show their dissatisfaction, Lawrence was so terrified that he jumped into Frieda's arms (she of the "big glistening globes"). Bynner withheld this and other tales until long after Lawrence's death.

Frieda was not Lawrence's only love, according to his biographer, Richard Aldington. Lawrence had written, "I believe the nearest I have come to perfect love was with a young coal miner when I was about sixteen," and Aldington added, "I should say Lawrence was about eighty-five percent hetero and fifteen percent homo." (Frieda never allowed a farmer's boy, William Henry, into their house, although Lawrence maintained relations.) *A Warden of All Souls*, however, failed to see that Lawrence was homosexual at all, leading A. L. Rowse to observe, "but there is nothing like an intellectual for obstinate obtuseness." Rowse added that in his rough mining community of Eastwood, Lawrence was laughed at and persecuted by schoolmates as girlish, "for he was refined and delicate. It was his fate to be persecuted by imperceptive fools most of his life, and it maddened him." Meanwhile, biographer Brenda Maddox in *D. H. Lawrence: The Story of a Marriage* (1994), doubts that Lawrence was unconsciously homosexual, despite his alleged attraction to anal penetration in lovemaking. She argues that what he longed for was the strong father missing from his childhood. At the time Lawrence met E. M. Forster, who was then thirty-six years of age and still a virgin, Maddox states, Lawrence was deeply attracted to men but was repelled by homosexuals.

According to his early poems, Lawrence also was attracted to his mother. Upon her death, he carried her downstairs, found her hairs on his jacket, and wrote of her being on her sickbed:

> My love looks like a girl to-night,
>   But she is old.
> The plaits that lie along her pillow
>   Aren't gold,
> But threaded with filigree silver
>   and uncanny cold.

A few lines later we discover she is, indeed, dead. "And her dead mouth sings/By its shape, like thrushes on clear evenings." His dead mother is called "my love," "the darling," "like a young maiden," "like a bride," and indeed the poem is called "The Bride," the groom clearly being Lawrence. Critic James Fenton, an Oxford Professor of Poetry, notes Lawrence's further indebtedness:

> You sweet love, my mother
> Twice you have blooded me,
> Once with your blood at birth-time
> Once with your misery.
> And twice you have washed me clean,
> Twice-wonderful things to see.

Lawrence's three great novels—*Sons and Lovers* (1913), *The Rainbow* (1915), and *Women in Love* (1921)—concern the consequences of trying to deny man's union with nature. Some critics found *The Plumed Serpent* fascistic in that Lawrence began to believe that mankind must be reorganized under one superhuman leader. But what really startled everyone was his *Lady Chatterley's Lover* (1928), in which readers exclaimed that he had described feminine sexual feelings better even than any woman had ever before been able to do. The book was banned in England and the United States for years. But copies were always somehow available and the intimate story of an English noblewoman who found love and sexual completion with her husband's gamekeeper became a topic of discussion of the intelligentsia for a long time. (Those in the cognoscenti were aware that the gamekeeper in the story was wish-fulfillment fantasy on Lawrence's part and, as Rowse points out, "It is significant that the double thrill the working-class fellow gives the sex-starved lady is not only sexual but also anal.) Lawrence inspired other writers to imitate his daring, and he became one of the primary molders of 20th-century fiction.

T. S. Eliot, writing about atheism, once stated, "There is the High Church Atheism of Matthew Arnold, there is the Auld Licht Atheism of our friend Mr. J. M. Robertson, there is the Tin Chapel Atheism of Mr. D. H. Lawrence. And there is the decidedly Low Church Atheism of Mr. [Bertrand] Russell." Lawrence would have agreed with the last, for he detested Russell's "arrogant rationalism," according to Rowse. Meanwhile, his biographer, H. Kingsmill, wrote in 1938 that Lawrence had a "home-made" religion which hovered between agnosticism and pantheism. "There is no God, but everything is Godly," Lawrence held. When Lawrence visited Ceylon, eight years before his death, he found "oriental mysticism" repellent, according to critic Simon Leys.

In *Phoenix: The Posthumous Papers of D. H. Lawrence* (1936) is found, "I know the greatness of Christianity; it is a past greatness....I live in 1924, and the Christian venture is done."

Although he openly had written and spoken about illicit sex, Lawrence seems never to have written or spoken about what he truly feared: tuberculosis. Lawrence died of consumption after years of a hacking cough. When Frieda was out of the room for a moment at the very end, he is said to have grasped Maria Huxley's wrists and said, "Maria, Maria, don't let me die." According to another version, his last words to Frieda were "Wind my watch."

Even before his death, Frieda had picked his successor: Angelo Ravagli, the husband of their landlady, an army lieutenant "with a well-known penchant for foreign women." During the last two years of Lawrence's life, Frieda found that Ravagli "gave her a feeling of being desired she had not had in years." Eventually, the two married. Janet Byrne's *A Genius for Living* (1995) writes of Frieda and Ravagli that they then lived a tranquil life despite his constant philandering.

Years after Lawrence's death, Frieda had his remains disinterred from their grave in Vence, France, cremated, and returned to San Cristobal, New Mexico. Catherine C. Robbins in *The New York Times* (6 August 1998) visited the site where the Lawrences had spent fifteen months on 160 wooded acres in the early 1920s and which his patron, Mabel Dodge Luhan, had given him in exchange for the original manuscript of *Sons and Lovers.*

In 1998 the shrine with its memorial had deteriorated allegedly because of neglect by the University of New Mexico, leading the D. H. Lawrence Center at Nottingham University in England to demand that the cremains be returned there for better safekeeping. However, Frieda—fearful that some of his admirers might find the cremains and scatter them across the ranch—had arranged for their being mixed into the concrete used to build the memorial. Moving the cremains and cement were therefore considered impractical. Meanwhile, the university claimed in 1998 that the site which in "St. Mawr" Lawrence described as "Ah! It was beauty, beauty absolute, at any hour of the day," had been carefully repaired. Lawrence had once complained that to protect furniture from gnawing rats they had hoisted it up to the ceiling on ropes, and Ms. Robbins confirmed visitors' complaints "of rat droppings in the shrine." {CE; James Fenton, *The New York Review of Books*, 22 October 1998; GL; HAB; RE; TRI; TYD}

Lawrence, Gil (20th Century)

Lawrence has a talk show on WALE Radio in Providence, Rhode Island, on which he features the atheist/agnostic point of view. (See entry for Rhode Island Atheists, Freethinkers.) {FD}

Lawrence, Harold T. (20th Century)

Lawrence edited "The Humanist Pulpit" in the early *The New Humanist* publication, and in 1929 he and A. Wakefield Slaten were succeeded by Edwin H. Wilson. {EW}

Lawrence, Jacob (1917–)

A painter, Lawrence was one of the Harlem Renaissance Group. His parents had migrated from the South, and he was born in Atlantic City. He lived for a time with foster parents in Philadelphia, then settled with his mother in 1930 in Harlem, where he met Langston Hughes, Alain Locke, Claude McKay, Augusta Savage, and others. "I remember hearing folks in the street in Harlem tell the stories of John Brown and Harriet Tubman in such a passionate way," he told a *New York Times Reporter*. When only twenty-three, he painted what has been called his masterpiece, the *Migration of the Negro* series. He is also known for his *Harlem* and *Coast Guard* series. Since the late 1930s, his subjects have included Toussaint L'Ouverture, the Haitian revolutionary; Harriet Tubman; John Brown; Frederick Douglass; and the migration of blacks to the North from the South after World War I. In New York's Whitney Museum of American Art are shown his *War* (1946–1947) and *Tombstones*.

Asked about the subject of humanism, Lawrence wrote to the present author:

> "Humanism" is to be human, to think, to analyze, and to probe. To respond and to be stimulated by all living things—beasts, fowl, and fishes. To respond through touch, sight, smell, and sound to all things in nature—both organic and inorganic—to colors, shapes, and textures—to not only look at a blade of grass but to really *see* a blade of grass. These things, to me, are what life and living are all about. I would call it "Humanism."

Lawrence is a member of the American Academy of Arts and Letters. {*The New York Times*, 12 April 1996; WAS, 7 July 1989}

Lawrence, James (1883–1941)

A Knight of Malta, Lawrence became acquainted with Schiller and Goethe at Stuttgart and Weimar and was detained with English prisoners at Verdun. In 1807 he published *The Empire of the Nairs, or the Rights of Women*, a free-love romance which he wrote in German, French, and English. Lawrence once addressed a poem on tolerance to Mr. Owen on the occasion of his having denounced the religions of the world, a poem that appeared in *The Etonian Out of Bounds*. {BDF}

Lawrence, Jerome (1915-)

Lawrence is an educator, director, and playwright. He directed "Auntie Mame" (1956); "The Gang's All Here" (1959); and "Inherit the Wind," the latter of which was translated and performed in three languages and was named best foreign play of the year by the London Critics Poll in 1960. According to the American Library Association's *Banned Books* (1998), the work is regularly banned because of its alleged "anti-religious nature." (See entry for Banned Books.)

Lawrence, Thomas Edward [Lawrence of Arabia] (1888–1935)

The illegitimate son of an Anglo-Irish landowner, Lawrence was educated at Jesus College, Oxford. He studied Arabic, traveled to Syria in 1909, and from 1910 to 1914 he worked on the excavation of Carchemish on the banks of the Euphrates. During this period, he became involved with British Intelligence, and the Arabs admired exploits he made during World War I. In 1918 he entered Damascus with the Arab forces after the Turks were defeated. Subsequently, his career was marked by mental breakdown, self-accusation, and anxiety about his own legend. Enlisting in the RAF in 1922, he then joined the tank corps under the legally adopted (1927) name of T. E. Shaw. In 1935, in a motorcycle accident near his home at Clouds Hill, Dorset, he was killed. The motorcycle had been a present of George Bernard Shaw, with whose wife [Charlotte] Lawrence is said to have confided his most intimate anxieties.

Known as "Lawrence of Arabia," a person who appeared to have a pathological aversion to publicity, Lawrence was cited as a man of action, a poet, ascetic, neurotic, and leader of men. E. M. Forster, from whom he had sought literary advice, found his style "granular." Auden based *The Ascent of F6* in part on the Lawrence legend. Lawrence appeared, complete with motorcycle, as Pvt. Meek in George Bernard Shaw's *Too True to be Good*. Robert Graves wrote the first authorized life in 1927.

In 1955 Aldington portrayed Lawrence as a hysterical homosexual, which outraged many inasmuch as no evidence exists that he ever was sexually involved with anyone. In *The Seven Pillars*, he wrote about being raped. However, it is speculated that this was connected with the passionate feelings he had for a handsome Arab youth, Dahoum, whom Lawrence called "Sheik Ahmed." Upon Dahoum's death during the war, Lawrence dedicated *The Seven Pillars of Wisdom* "to S.A." Many in gay circles speculate as to whether

Lawrence was "a top" or "a bottom" with his handsome Arab friends, and few go on record as believing he was a repressed homosexual.

Lawrence's biographer, V. Richards, wrote that Lawrence was an atheist and had at an early date "shaken free of the half-dead sentiments of formal religion." {CE; GL; JM; RE; TRI; TYD}

Lawrence, William [Sir] (1805–1867)

Sir William was professor of anatomy and surgery at the Royal College of Surgeons. While there, he delivered his "Lectures on Man," which when published roused a storm of bigotry. Although an earnest advocate of radical reform, he is said to have acquired a most lucrative practice. Lawrence denied the inspiration of the Bible, praised Voltaire, and made an open profession of deism. {BDF; RAT; RE}

Lawson, David (Deceased 1999)

When a visiting professor at Xi'an Teachers University in China, Lawson wrote as a secularist for *International Humanist*. His "Humanism in China" in *The Humanist* (May-June 1993) suggested that ancient Chinese humanism may be playing a larger role in the West than is ordinarily supposed. Lawson wrote about literary figures such as Wallace Stevens, John Reed, and Thomas Mann. {*Humanist in Canada*, Summer 1999}

Lawson, Louisa (1848–1920)

Lawson was an Australian freethinker, editor, and feminist. Starting as an Anglican, she was brought up a Methodist, then joined a Mudgee spiritualist group. After separating from her husband, she moved to Sydney with her son, Henry, a poet, and both came under the influence of the freethinker, Thomas Walker. Lawson established *Dawn*, Australia's first feminist journal, and helped found the Suffrage League in 1891. {SWW}

Lawson, Sarah (20th Century)

Lawson is a poet, a translator, and a regular contributor to the *New Humanist*. She has taught at Suzhou University in China and is author of a pamphlet, "Down Where the Willow is Washing Her Hair."

Lawton, Walter (20th Century)

Lawton has since 1958 been a leader of the Northern Westchester Ethical Culture Society. He was instrumental, in the American Ethical Union's Commission on Race and Equality, for taking on integrated projects in the South, and he led a much-publicized one in Birmingham, Alabama. Originally a Baptist minister turned businessman, Lawton also has been a Leader in Queens and Chicago. (See entry for Ethical Culture.) {EU, Howard B. Radest}

Layard, Austen Henry [Sir] (1817–1894)

A British Assyriologist, Layard combined archaeology with diplomacy, completing some excavations at Ninevah in Mesopotamia and serving as Minister to Spain (1869–1877) and Ambassador to Constantinople (1877–1880). He wrote *Discoveries in the Ruins of Nineveh and Babylon* (1853). In his autobiography (1903), Layard exposed the fraud of Palestine's "Holy Places." In an 1853 letter he wrote that "the best thing the Turks could do would be to turn all the Christians out of Jerusalem." Layard was a freethinker who explained in the autobiography that lectures he heard in early years "rapidly undermined the religious opinions in which I had been brought up." {CE; JM; RAT; RE}

Lavine, Thomas Z. (20th Century)

Lavine, a Robinson professor at George Mason University in Fairfax, Virginia, signed Humanist Manifesto 2000.

LAYING ON OF HANDS: See entry for Healing.

Laycock, Don (20th Century)

A professor of linguistics at the Australian National University, Laycock has written for *Free Inquiry*. He has edited *Linguistic Trends in Australia* (1970). {*Free Inquiry*, Summer, 1987}

Layton, Henry (1622–1705)

A lawyer, Layton wrote anonymous observations on Dr. Bentley's *Confutation of Atheism* (1693) and wrote a *Search After Souls, and Spiritual Observations in Man* (1700). {BDF; RAT}

Lazarus, Mark (c. 1868–1938)

Lazarus, a rationalist and barrister, was a member in England of the Rationalist Press Association and of the Rationalist Association of Australia. {SWW}

Lazarus, Moritz (1622–1705)

Lazarus was the son of a Yorkshire gentleman. Between 1692 and 1704 he published, anonymously, a series of quarto pamphlets (*Search After Souls*, etc.) in which he denied the immortality of the soul, bringing upon himself a violent controversy. Curiously, he believed in the divinity and Second Coming of Christ. {RAT}

Lazarus, William Paul (20th Century)

A Unitarian who is a biblical historian living in Florida, Lazarus has written *The Life of Jesus, History and Myth.*

LE LIBRE PENSEUR

Le Libre Penseur (The Freethinker), is the quarterly of the *Association Suisse des Libres Penseurs*, Case Postale 131, CH - 1000 Lausanne - 17, Switzerland.

Lea, Everett (20th Century)

A freethinker, Lea wrote *Straightening the Record on God, Man, and the Devil* (1955). {GS}

Leach, Edmund (Ronald) [Sir] (1910-1989)

A British anthropologist, Leach was an expert on the social anthropology of South Asia. A freethinker, he wrote *Rethinking Anthropology* (1961), *Lévi-Straus* (1970), and *Genesis as Myth* (1970). From 1966 to 1979, he was Provost of King's College at Cambridge. {Ibn Warraq, 1999}

Leach, Henry Goddard (1880–1970)

In the 1950s, Leach was on the advisory board of Charles Francis Potter's First Humanist Society of New York. He had been editor of *The Forum* (1923-1940) and had written *The Scandinavia of the Scandinavians* (1915).

Leake, Chauncey D. (1896–1978)

When he signed Humanist Manifesto II, Leake was a professor at the University of California, San Francisco. He also has been executive director of the University of Texas Medical Branch in Galveston. A pharmacologist, he wrote *Old Egyptian Medicine* (1952) and *Practical Philosophy: The Ethics* (1973), *The Logics* (1974), and *The Esthetics* (1976).

With Anatol Rapaport, Leake once approached the American Association for the Advancement of Science, suggesting that the American Humanist Association could appropriately be its philosophical branch. The proposal was declined on the basis that the humanists' membership did not include a high enough percentage of Ph. D's. {HMS2; HNS2}

Leakey, Richard Erskine (1944–)

Human evolution centered in East Africa, not Asia, the Leakey family of anthropologists and archaeologists has concluded. In 1931 **Louis Seymour Bazett Leakey**(1903–1972) began excavating at Olduvai Gorge, Tanzania.

With his wife, **Mary Leakey** (1913–1996), he discovered Zinjanthropus (1959; now regarded as Australopithecine), which has been dated at 1.75 million years of age, and Homo habilis (1961). Mary Leakey then discovered Homo fossils over 3.75 million years old. Their son, **Richard**, discovered another type of hominid skull, which he and Roger Lewin described in *Origins* (1979).

In 1993 Richard, who lost the bottom portion of his legs in a plane crash, was ousted as head of Kenya's wildlife service. In 1995 he was one of the founders of an opposition party with the aim of "cleaning up" Kenya. The Kenyan president accused him of being a white racist colonialist with foreign ties. In 1996, he entered wholeheartedly into politics, running as a candidate for the presidency.

With Lewin, Leakey wrote *Origins Reconsidered: In Search of What Makes Us Human* (1993), which holds that man was not created nor did he evolve by some grand design. Slight changes in climate, disasters from the sky, geological shifts: too many complexities exist for any god or gods to have arranged or even to have wanted to arrange. "I am not religious," Leakey wrote, "at least not in the formal sense. As a schoolboy I adopted a kind of personal atheism and was much ridiculed because my uncle was Archbishop of East Africa at the time. There developed a campaign to 'save' me, to which I reacted by being even more adamantly atheistic. I came to be critical of formal religion, particularly of the damage that missionaries were doing to the culture of the people of Kenya. I have no difficulty in accepting the notion that standards of ethics and morality could be derived in the absence of religion. And I now believe that such standards are an inevitable—and predictable—product of human evolution; altruism is part of the behavioral repertoire of social animals, so it can be expected to develop much further in intelligent and intensely social animals, like our human ancestors. This is the humanists' position."

In *One Life* (1983), he wrote, "I do not believe in a god who has or had a human form and to whom I owe an existence. I believe it is man who created God in his image and not the other way around; also, I see no reason to believe in life after death." In 1995, Richard Leakey became an Honorary Associate of the Rationalist Press Association. He is an honorary associate of the New Zealand Association of Rationalists and Humanists, and he signed Humanist Manifesto 2000. Of his outlook, Leakey has written,

> I am deeply influenced by what I see as the hypocrisy and negative influence of religion in people's lives and although I do see the positive contributions that the institutions of religion have made in the development of society, I am unashamedly irreligious myself.
>
> My paternal grand parents were CMS missionaries to East Africa and two of their four children married into church families. My father, as a successful human palaeontologist, was curiously ambivalent and, although he refused to have any of his children christened, he seemed to have a strong Christian sympathy. My mother, raised as a Catholic, had no time for religion of any kind and left her children in no doubt about her views.
>
> My own career has developed in Kenya where I have had modest success in my own work on human ancestry. I was fortunate to locate an important fossil site on the shores of Lake Turkana in 1968 and I spent a good number of years leading successful field expeditions.
>
> In 1989, I changed careers and became engaged in revamping Kenya's wildlife conservation programme. This work was a chance to gain insight into how corruption and greed in public institutions in Kenya was pulling the country to its knees and, without exception, the real villains were regular church-going Christians and prominent persons in the mosque. The ease with which people seem to pass on responsibility for their own failures and incompetence to their god is surely a handicap to progress. In Kenya, God's will is a frequent excuse and explanation for disasters that are simply the result of poor management, negligence, and professional incompetence. It seems to me that a rationalist approach which stresses personal responsibility in all actions would bring better results. Although I see religion as one of the greatest frauds, it is obvious that most people do need something that humanists can do without. We are a minority and perhaps we always will be. This we need to accommodate, especially where we are in public life where co-operation with various institutions seems to be essential for social if not socio-economic progress. Surely free thought and free speech is what we expect and so we must accept it too.

(See Genesis and Lucy for a Chinese view that mankind may not have begun in Africa.) {CA; E; *New Humanist*, November 1997}

LEAP DAY AND LEAP YEAR

Leap Day, February 29th, has been called Bachelor's Day because when St. Bridget and St. Patrick of Ireland agreed that women could propose marriage one year in every four, St. Patrick gave womankind the extra day. Leap Year happens only every four years except in centennial years not divisible by 400; for example, 1900. (See entry for Calendar.)

Lear, Norman (1922–)

In the 1995 Ware Lecture at the Unitarian Universalist General Assembly, Lear attacked the religious right's exclusivist theology. "Religious experience ought to bear a closer resemblance to 'love thy neighbor,' to the essence of the Sermon on the Mount," he said, "than to pietistic pistol-whipping." He is known as the television producer and founder of People for the American Way, the creator of television's Archie Bunker.

Holding a Doctorate of Humanities from Emerson College, Lear began in public relations, then became a comedy writer for television and films such as "Come Blow Your Horn" (1963) and "The Night They Raided Minsky's" (1968). He received four Emmy awards for the television show "All in the Family" and created "Maude" (1972). Lear has been named one of the top ten motion picture producers, and he has received numerous awards including the Mass Media award of the American Jewish Committee's Institute of Human Relations. In 1984, he was inducted into the TV Academy's Hall of Fame.

When asked to cite the American they dislike most, many religious fundamentalists have responded, "Norman Lear." Many rationalists and humanists, however, respond that Lear is one of the Americans they most admire.

Leatherbee, Brigham (19th Century)

A freethinker, Leatherbee wrote *The Christian Mythology* (c. 1885). {GS}

Lebed, Alexander Ivanovich [General] (1950-)

General Lebed served in Afghanistan (1981-1982) and the Caucasus (1988-1990), becoming in 1992 commander of the 14th Army in Moldova. In 1996 during the presidential elections, he finished third, receiving 15% of the vote. Yeltsin appointed him National Security Advisor, and he acted as chief negotiator in the Chechen conflict later in 1996.

No longer a Communist, he has said he is still an atheist although many former party members have expediently wrapped themselves in the patriotism of the Russian Orthodox Church. {CA}

Leblais, Alphonse (Born 1820)

Leblais was a French professor of mathematics, the author of a study in positivist philosophy entitled *Materialism and Spiritualism* (1865). Littré contributed the preface. {BDF}

Le Bon, Gustave (Born 1841)

A French sociologist, Le Bon wrote about medical and anthropological subjects. The Academy of Sciences and the Anthropological Society crowned one of his early works, and he made a research mission to India on behalf of the Government. He wrote *L'homme et les sociétés* (2 volumes, 1881) and a thoroughly rationalistic *Evolution of Matter* (1907) and *Evolution of Force* (1908). Le Bon was an Officer of the Legion of Honour and a member of the Belgian Royal Academy of Sciences. {RAT}

Lebowitz, Fran (20th Century)

Writer Lebowitz has gone on record: "I do not believe in God. I believe in cashmere." She has written columns for *Madamoiselle* and Andy Warhol's *Interview.* She is known for her biting, aphoristic commentary. (See entry for Afterlife, Speculations About.)

Lebrun, Harvey (20th Century)

When he signed Humanist Manifesto II, Lebrun was chairman of the Chapter Assembly, American Humanist Association. {HM2}

Lecky, William Edward Hartpole (1838–1903)

Lecky's *History of the Rise and Influence of the Spirit of Rationalism* (1865) is considered a classic study of rationalism. He also wrote *Democracy and Liberty* (1903). An Irish-born historian, Lecky had moderately liberal views and a dislike of democratic reforms, which colored his view of history. In *History of the Rise and Influence of the Spirit of Rationalism in Europe* (1866), he wrote, "When it began, Christianity was regarded as a system entirely beyond the range and scope of human reason; it was impious to question; it was impious to examine; it was impious to discriminate. On the other hand, it was visibly instinct with the supernatural. Miracles of every order and degree of magnitude were flashing forth incessantly from all its parts."

Other of his observations about religion:

- Almost all Europe, for many centuries, was inundated with blood, which was shed at the direct instigation or with the full approval of the ecclesiastical authorities.

- There is no wild beast so ferocious as Christians who differ concerning their faith.

- Whenever the clergy were at the elbow of the civil arm, no matter whether they were Catholic or Protestant, persecution was the result.

- The church fathers laid it down as a distinct proposition, that pious frauds are justifiable and even laudable.

- Fierce invectives against women form conspicuous and grotesque portion of the writings of the Church fathers.

McCabe, finding fault with some of his generalizations, says that Lecky's "compliments to Christianity are often so opposed to the facts he gives that George Eliot imagined him saying: 'It is true that 2 and 2 make 4 but one must not press these things too far.' Lecky was an agnostic . . . with an ethical regard for Christianity, but many of his tributes to it, and harsh censures of the Romans, which apologists quote, are refuted by other general statements and the facts in his own book. A critical edition would be useful." {BDF; CE; JM; RAT; RE; TRI; TYD}

Leclerc de Septchenes, N. (18th Century)

Leclerc was secretary to Louis XVI and translated the first three volumes of Gibbon. He also wrote an essay on the religion of the ancient Greeks (1787). A friend of Lalande, he prepared an edition of *Freret*, which was published after his death. {BDF}

Leconte, Joseph (1823–1901)

Leconte, an American geologist, is sometimes cited by religious writers as being orthodox. However, McCabe notes, Leconte's *Evolution and its Relation to Religious Thought* (1888) rejects all supernatural religion. Leconte described himself as a pantheist, recognizing "no test of truth but reason." {JM; RAT; RE}

Leconte de Lisle, Charles Marie René (1818–1894)

A French poet, Leconte de Lisle became a leading figure of a group known as the Parnassians when his *Poèmes barbares* (1872) was published. Anti-Christian and a pessimist, Leconte saw death as the only existing reality, and he drew inspiration from antiquity. A member of the French Academy, being elevated to the seat of Victor Hugo in 1887, he wrote *A Popular History of Christianity* (1871), which Robertson says would have delighted d'Holbach. Leconte did not delight Jews, however, when, upon taking the place of Victor Hugo at the Academy, he spoke of Moses as "the chief of a horde of ferocious nomads." {BDF; CE; JM; JMR; RAT; RE}

Lecount, Peter (19th Century)

Lecount was a lieutenant in the French navy. After the battle of Navarino, went to England as a mathematician in the construction of the London and Birmingham Railway, of which he wrote a history (1839). Lecount also wrote *A Few Hundred Bible Contradictions* and *A Hunt After the Devil, and Other Matters* (1843), citing himself as "the Rev. Peter Lecount." {BDF; FUK}

Le Dantec, Félix Alexandro (1869–1917)

Le Dantec was professor of biology at the Sorbonne. During the war, he "worked himself to death," McCabe states. *Nature* (16 August 1917) in its obituary notice said Le Dantec had "a passion for veracity" and "a hatred of superstitious and intellectual hypocrisy." He wrote in *Athéisme* (1906) that he believed in "the mysterious and universal agent which we call energy." {RAT; RE}

Lederman, Aleta and Karl (20th Century)

The Ledermans are activists with Rationalists of East Tennessee, 1036 Thompson Bridge Road, Maryville, Tennessee 37801.

Ledo, Michael (20th Century)

Bible Bloopers: Evidence That Demands a Verdict, Too! A Skeptic Answers Josh McDowell (1997) is a non-scholarly work that uses freethinking humor to make fun of religious views. A Hebrew midrash, he found, says that Canaan's children "shall be born ugly and black" and elsewhere warns that God will punish those who dared see his nakedness by swelling their lips and making their male members "shamefully elongated." *{Freethought History #26, 1998}*

Lee, Alfred McClung (1906–1992)

When he signed Humanist Manifesto II, Lee was professor emeritus of sociology-anthropology at the City University of New York. He worked with and wrote for Priscilla Robertson when she edited *The Humanist,* upon which he was an associate editor in the 1950s. His extensive books include *How to Understand Propaganda* (1952), *Toward Humanist Sociology* (1973), and *Race Riot* (1968). He edited and co-edited several textbooks in sociology. Throughout his career, Lee was involved in some of the most critical national and international issues of the time. During the late 1970s and early 1980s, he wrote extensively on the conflict between Catholics and Protestants in Northern Ireland. Among the many honors he received were the Distinguished Career Award of the American Sociological Association and the Distinguished Career Award of the Clinical Sociology Association. Lee was a Unitarian. {HM2; HNS}

Lee, Charles [General] (1731–1782)

Lee, whose father was a Major General in the British Army, settled in America in 1773 and became second in command to Washington in the War of Independence. He was a deist, as is shown in the "Memoir of J. Lee" which is appended to *The Correspondence of Sir. T. Hanmer.* {JM; RE}

Lee, Earl (20th Century)

A freethinker, Lee writes for *Truth Seeker*. He has listed three major myths of Christianity:

1. Christianity is important to our society because it serves as a moral rudder

> . . . but the ancient Greeks, among others, proved that it is possible to have an ethical culture without having a religiously "moral" culture;

2. Christianity is important as a patron of the arts and sciences, and of learning in general

> . . . but although this may have been partially true in the Medieval and Renaissance periods, today most religions are not particularly interested in art, except architecture; and "Christian rock music" shamelessly rips off the style and music of mainstream rock musicians.

3. Christianity, the religion of the Founding Fathers, is necessary as a bulwark of democracy around the world

> . . . but this is not a fact, for the movers and shakers of the Revolutionary war were Deists and members of liberal Protestant religions, and the Church in no way can be considered democratic.

Lee, author of *Drakulya* (1994), is an associate professor of library science at Pittsburg State University in Pittsburg, Kansas. He is a Unitarian. {*Truth Seeker*, #6, 1993}

Lee, Elizabeth Briant (1908–)

Lee, an author, signed Humanist Manifesto II. {HM2}

Lee, Gypsy Rose (Rose Lee Hovick) (1914–1970)

An internationally noted ecdysiast, Gypsy Rose Lee is quoted by E. Haldeman-Julius as having said, "Praying is like a rocking chair—it'll give you something to do, but it won't get you anywhere." As for the deity, "God is love, but get it in writing." She was known to have smiled that an ecdysiast, the term made popular during the 1940s for a stripteaser, depended upon audiences that had been taught by Puritans to enjoy thinking of sex as something bad. As she danced, she utilized large, colorful fans to conceal whether or not she had any clothes on.

Author Arthur Laurents (*The Advocate* 16 May 1995) states that in the memoirs of her sister, actress June Havoc, mention is made that both Gypsy's mother and Gypsy were lesbians. He added that he had been told that Rose "had a big fight with a hotel manager because she put too many people in her room. So she pushed him out the window and killed him." Laurents, who wrote "Gypsy," one of the greatest of Broadway musicals, said, "So how can you resist doing a musical based on a woman like that!"

Lee, Robert E. (1918–)

Lee, with Jerome Lawrence, wrote *Inherit the Wind* (1955) about Clarence Darrow. Lee is a Congregationalist. {FUS}

Lee, Tony (20th Century)

A secular humanist in Victoria, Australia, Lee has questioned how Noah managed to get to Australia to pick up a couple of Koalas, plus sufficient eucalyptus trees of a certain species upon which they feed.

Leedom, Tim C. (1945–)

Leedom is editor of *The Book Your Church Doesn't Want You To Read* (1993) (Box 5009, Balboa Island, California 92662), in which Kersey Graves tells of the sixteen known crucified saviors before Jesus, also of virgin birth, and other materials of interest to freethinkers. Contributors include Steve Allen, Dan Barker, Annie Gaylor, Gerald Larue, Skipp Porteous, and Sherwin Wine.

Gordon Stein, reviewing the book in *The American Rationalist*, cites errors in the research. For example, Catholic Bishop Mark Hurley is included as a freethinker, although he was part of the Vatican's Secretariat for [really *to*] Non-Believers." Alfred Russel Wallace was "as credulous a believer as there ever was" but is listed as a non-believer. Stein also was critical of a number of definitions of "freethought terms" which are given, and he states, "To call Siddhartha Gautama [the Buddha] an 'Indian philosopher' and Carl Jung a freethinker at all is amazing if not plain wrong." Nevertheless, Stein says, "it would be a good gift to give your wavering Christian friends." {LEE}

LEEDS (England) HUMANISTS

For information about the Leeds Humanists, contact Robert Tee by telephone: 0113 2577009.

Leenhof, Frederick van (Born 1647)

Leenhof, who was born in Zeeland, became a minister of Zwolle, the Netherlands, where he published *Heaven on Earth* (1703), which subjected him to accusations of atheism. {BDF}

Leeper, Geoffrey Winthrop (1903–1986)

Leeper, son of the warden of Trinity College, a lay cannon of St. Paul's Cathedral—five of his students became bishops in the Anglican Church—was a professor of agricultural chemistry, 1962 to 1969, then became dean of the agricultural science faculty at the University of Melbourne, Australia. A world authority on soil science, he gave lectures in which he said, "Human beings have evolved as temporary denizens of a second-rate planet of a fourth-rate star."

Leeper was a director of the Rationalist Association of Australia Ltd., and he became honorary vice president of the Humanist Society of Victoria in 1964. {SWW}

Leeson, John (20th Century)

Leeson was the first President of the European Humanist Federation/*Federation Humaniste Europèene* (EHF/FHE), which formed on 12 October 1991. He remains its networking officer. Founding organizations included those from Belgium, Germany, Hungary, Luxembourg, The Netherlands, Norway, and Britain. In 1993, its membership included 20 associations from 11 different countries. Its aims included the following:

- to carry out educational, scientific, and cultural action in order to promote a humanist vision of cultural, social, and ethical values in Europe;
- to promote exchanges among members and the circulation of information and experience which could contribute to the development of humanist values in Europe as well as to social and cultural progress;
- to propose such European legislation as it likely to facilitate the development and promotion of the activities of member organisations in Europe;
- to promote the development of cooperation among member organisations.

According to Leeson, EHF/FHE is a regional organization within the International Humanist and Ethical Union (IHEU). Leeson is Treasurer of the British Humanist Association.

In 1998 he was elected a Vice President of IHEU. E-mail: : <john.leeson@btinternet.com>.

Lefévre. André (1834–1904)

Lefévre was a French writer who, at the age of twenty-three, was one of the editors of *Magasin Pittoresque*. He translated *Lucretius* in verse (1876) and rote *Religions and Mythologies Compared* (1877).

Léfevre also edited the *Lettres Persanes* of Montesquieu, some *Dialogues* of Voltaire, and Diderot's *La Religieuse* (1886).

Lefebvre, Henri (20th Century)

In France, Lefebvre wrote about socialist humanism.

LeFevre, Edwin (Died 1994)

A former professor of mechanical engineering at Queen Mary College, London, LeFevre was a life member of humanist organizations. At his secular funeral, Nicolas Walter represented the humanists.

Lefkowitz, Mary R. (1935–)

Not Out of Africa: How Afrocentrism Became an Excuse to Teach Myth As History (1996) is Lefkowitz's convincing refutation of Martin Bernal's *Black Athena*. Lefkowitz, with Guy MacLean Rogers, edited *Black Athena Revisited* (1996), a work in which nineteen international scholars refute Bernal's thesis that "Dead White European Males" have erred purposely, refusing to admit that virtually all the creative contributions of Greece to the civilization of the West derive in reality from Egyptians, whom he claims were black. (See Jasper Griffin, "Anxieties of Influence," *The New York Review of Books*, 20 June 1996)

Lefort, César (19th Century)

Lefort was a disciple of Comte and author of a work on the method of modern science. {BDF}

LEFT-HANDEDNESS

Being left-handed, like being a homosexual or being red-haired, is a fact of life but is treated by some as worthy of being stigmatized. Although approximately 90% of humans are thought to be right-handed, not to be right-handed has been considered to be awkward and gauche (a French word meaning left, warped, clumsy). Psychologists have shown, however, that up to the age of one year infants will use either hand indiscriminately. It is between the ages of one and three that a preference appears and becomes established. Until recently, left-handed individuals were encouraged to become right-handed, much as homosexuals were encouraged to choose heterosexuality. The former often became stutterers, the latter became closeted in their behavior, sometimes siring a family, then exiting with a lover. ("No cure has been found for red-hairedness, either," a Manhattan comic has observed.)

Meanwhile, James A. Garfield, the twentieth president of the United States, was not merely the first ambidextrous chief executive. He was observed writing classical Greek with his left hand and classical Latin with his right. Simultaneously. {CE; PA}

LEGAL AID SOCIETY: See entry for Henry Booth.

Le Gallienne, Eva (1899–1991)

Le Gallienne, a grande dame of the theatre, died somewhat appropriately in 1991 on the night of the annual Tony Awards in New York City. In her prime she had earned a Tony, an Emmy, and an Oscar ("Resurrection," 1980), and some said she would have approved making her exit at the age of ninety-two at a time when others were now receiving applause. Her career as an actress commenced in 1914 in a London production of "Monna Vanna," ending in 1982 as a director-actress in New York of "Alice in Wonderland." On television, she had been in "Alice in Wonderland" (1955) and "St. Elsewhere—The Women" (1984). She was in a number of radio shows, and she recorded starting in 1943 with "The Rivals" for Harvard and including "Dick Cavett Talks with Le G" for CCS (1979). In 1918 she had supported Ethel Barrymore in "The Off Chance." In 1929 she was on *Time*'s cover, a recognition of her roles in "Hedda Gabbler," "Peter Pan," and other hits of the period. As Elizabeth I in a 1957 production of "Mary Stuart," she received critical acclaim.

But hers was a troubled life, one made difficult because she chose not to hide her lesbianism. She refused to arrange a convenient marriage, and she was public about the various companions who shared her life, one of whom was the poet May Sarton.

At New York's Hotel Algonquin, where she had her first apartment, Le Gallienne was known as one of "the four horsemen of the Algonquin," the others being Tallulah Bankhead, Estelle Wynwood, and Blyth Daly. After a falling out with Josephine Hutchinson, the consummate love throughout her years, LeGallienne was "so distressed and lonely at one point that she even turned to religion. She dressed like a nun, carried a beautifully bound missal, and attended mass daily," according to biographer Robert A. Shanke in *Shattered Applause* (1992). She liked to read the prayers of St. Thomas Aquinas or those of religious mystics such as Anchoress Juliana of Norwich. When she became very old, she was asked if she feared death and replied, "I don't think so. Of course this is something one cannot know for sure, but I don't feel any fear. It's part of life, part of the rhythm of the universe. And I am not a believer, so I don't fear anything that may come afterwards. I don't think that there is anything. Going to sleep is certainly not frightening. The very best thing is just going to sleep—eternal sleep. Remember, 'tis a consummation / Devoutly to be wish'd.' " Just the same, some years earlier she had taken instruction in the Roman Catholic faith in Westport, Connecticut. But the priest's lack of knowledge amused and disillusioned her, so she made it clear that the church was not to be allowed to bury her when she died. Commented Shanke, "LeG's range of acting was incredible. She went from the classic 'Trojan Women' to the contemporary 'Exit the King,' from sentimental 'Lilion' to the bare simplicity of 'Ghosts,' from the fantasy of 'Peter Pan' to the operatic bravado of 'Mary Stuart.' No other actress in her time, certainly not Katharine Cornell or Helen Hayes, could possibly boast such a colorful palette."

Le Gallienne, Richard (1866–1947)

LeGallienne was an English man of letters, the father of Eva Le Gallienne. He was associated with the fin-de-siècle aesthetes of the 1890s before becoming a resident of the United States. In his *Religion of a Literary Man* (1893), he rejected the belief in a future life and said that "organized Christianity has probably done more to retard the ideals that were its founder's than any other agency in the world." In *If I Were God* (1897), Le Gallienne professed a vague and unorthodox theism. {RAT; RE; TYD}

Legate, Bartholomew (c. 1572–1612)

Why is my King James Version of the Bible not dedicated to "Bartholomew Legate?" complained *Pique*'s New York City editor facetiously in 1992. The reference was to the anti-trinitarian native of Essex who, in 1611, was thrown into prison on a charge of heresy. Visited by King James in many personal interviews, Legate was asked if he prayed to Jesus Christ. Replied Legate, no, not for the last seven years but he had done so in the days of his ignorance. "Away, base fellow!" His Majesty had exclaimed. "It shall never be said that one stayeth in my presence who hath never prayed to the Savior for seven years together." The King then prepared a writ, *De Heretico Comburendo, 18 March 1612*, authorizing Legate to be burned at Smithfield, one of the last persons to be so punished in England. {BDF}

LeGoff, Jacques (20th Century)

LeGoff, who in France is a specialist in French Medieval Civilization and Literature, signed Humanist Manifesto 2000.

Leguin, Ursula Kroeber (1929–)

Leguin, in the introduction to *The Left Hand of Darkness*, wrote, "I am an atheist." However, the introduction is found in only some editions of the book.

Her many works include the following: *Rocannon's World* (1966); *The Word for World is Forest* (1967); *The Wizard of Earthsea* (1968); *The Lathe of Heaven* (1971); and *Unlocking the Air* (1996). She has received awards for her short stories, poems, criticism, science fiction, screenplays and, in 1995, Asimov's Reader's Award. {E}

LEGUMES

Without legumes, humanity would not have made it to the Dark Ages, Umberto Eco has argued.

Citing Jacques Le Goff's *La civilisation de l'Occident médiévale*, Eco notes that indigence, hunger, and insecurity confronted mankind prior to the year 1000. People were dying of tuberculosis, leprosy, ulcers, eczema, tumors, and by dread epidemics like the plague. Underpopulation combined with undercultivated land left nearly everyone undernourished. In the centuries before 1000, a new triennial system of crop rotation was slowly adopted, allowing the land to be more fruitful. In the second millennium, as a result, Europe's population doubled, maybe even tripled.

Without sufficient food, mankind could not have continued, let alone doubled. The poor did not eat meat, unless they happened to be able to raise a few chickens or did not get caught poaching lands owned by the lords. In short, Eco states, "Without beans, we would not number in the hundreds of millions and some of us, including even readers of this [material], would not exist. Some philosophers say that this would be better, but I am not sure everyone agrees."

As for the future? "We have all known for a long time that if the West ate unmilled brown rice, husks and all (delicious, by the way), we would consume less food, and better food," Eco advised. {Umberto Eco, *The New York Times Magazine*,18 April 1999}

Lehman, Karl (20th Century)

Lehman wrote *Thomas Jefferson: American Humanist* (1947). {FUS}

Lehn, Jean-Marie Pierre (1939–)

Lehn, who has contributed over five hundred articles to scientific publications, has received numbers of French as well as foreign honors.

He became a Nobel Laureate in chemistry (1987), and he signed Humanist Manifesto 2000.

Le Hon, Joseph (1809–1872)

Le Hon was a Belgian scientist, a captain in the Belgian army, professor of the military school of Brussels, and Chevalier of the Order of Leopold. Le Hon translated Professor Omboni's exposition of Darwinism and wrote *L'Homme Fossile en Europe* (1866). {BDF}

Lehrer, Thomas Andrew (1928–)

Lehrer, a songwriter, entertainer, and lecturer, wrote *Tom Lehrer Song Book* (1954) and numerous other works, including *An Evening Wasted With Tom Lehrer* (1959). A favorite of Isaac Asimov was Lehrer's "Vatican Rag":

> First you get down on your knees,
> Fiddle with your rosaries,
> Bow your head with great respect,
> And genuflect, genuflect, genuflect!
> Do whatever steps you want if
> You have cleared them with the Pontiff,
> Ev'rybody say his own
> Kyrie eleison,
> Doin' the Vatican Rag.
> Get in line in that processional,
> Step into that small confessional,
> There the guy who's got religion'll
> Tell you if your sin's original.
> If it is try playin' it safer,
> Drink the wine and chew the wafer,
> Two, four, six, eight,
> Time to transubstantiate!
>
> So you get down on your knees,
> Fiddle with your rosaries,
> Bow your head with great respect,
> And genuflect, genuflect, genuflect!
> Make a cross on your abdomen,
> When in Rome do like a Roman,
> Ave Maria,
> Gee, it's good to see ya,
> Gettin' ecstatic an' sorta dramatic an'
> Doin' the Vatican Rag.

In a 1996 interview online Lehrer was asked if he was an agnostic or an atheist. He responded:

> No one is more dangerous than someone who thinks he has The Truth. To be an atheist is almost as arrogant as to be a fundamentalist. But then again, I can get pretty arrogant.

So did he consider himself a fan of organized religion and is he a "spiritual" person? He responded

> To say that I am not a "fan" of organized religion is putting it mildly. My feeling about even disorganized religion is summed up in James Taylor's immortal line in "Sweet Baby James": "Maybe you can believe it if it helps you to sleep." I have no desire to promote secular insomnia. As for being "spiritual," not in the New Age sense, certainly. I find enough mystery in mathematics to satisfy my spiritual needs. I think, for example, that pi is mysterious enough (Don't get me started!) without having to worry about God. Or if pi isn't enough, how about fractals? Or quantum mechanics?

{CA}

Lehrman, Nathaniel (20th Century)

Lehrman is on the Executive Board of New York City's Corliss Lamont Chapter of the American Humanist Association.

Lei Yong-Sheng (20th Century)

Lei is professor of philosophy, dean of the Department of Social Sciences, and chief librarian at the Chinese Political College of the Young in Beijing, China. He is author of *The History of Western Epistemology*, among other works, and has written "The Hard Course of Humanism in China." He signed Humanist Manifesto 2000. (*Free Inquiry*, Summer 1996).

Leibniz, Gottfried Wilhelm von (1646–1716)

Leibniz's rationalistic philosophy was satirized in Voltaire's *Candide*. Little wonder, for Leibniz tried to use rationalism to prove the existence of God. His *Theodicy* (1710) should, according to one humanist, have been spelled *Idiocy*.

During the French Revolution, Maréchal cited Leibniz as one who seems atheist only from the standpoint of the strictest religious orthodoxy. Robertson has commented that Leibniz's philosophy, "with all its ingenuity, has the common stamp of the determination of the theist to find reasons for the God in whom he believed beforehand; and his principle that all is the best is the fatal rounding of his argumentative circle.

Thus his doctrine that that is true which is clear was turned to the account of an empiricism of which the "clearness" was really predetermined by the conviction of truth.

However, Bertrand Russell among others has pointed out that in some of the unpublished works Leibniz anticipated some of the ideas found in contemporary symbolic logic. When Leibniz died, his passing was scarcely noticed by the intellectuals and royal patrons of his day. {CE; CL; ER; EU, Aram Vartanian; HNS2; JMR; JMRH}

Leibowitz, Irwin (20th Century)

Leibowitz was a founder and is active with the Secular Humanists of South Florida. (See entry for Florida Atheists, Humanists.) {FD}

Leibson, Helen (20th Century)

When she signed Humanist Manifesto II, Leibson was president of the Philadelphia Ethical Society. {HM2}

LEICESTER (England) HUMANISTS

In 1995 Fred Whitehead visited the Secular Society Hall in Leicester and described the main meeting room, which can hold several hundred people. On the outside are terra cotta busts of Paine, Owen, Voltaire, Socrates, and (to the amusement of some) Jesus. At the building's opening on 6 March 1881, George Jacob Holyoake, who had coined the word "secularism," spoke on "Secularism, a religion which gives heaven no trouble."

For information about the oldest secular society in the world, write Secular Hall, 75 Humberstone Gate, Leicester LE 1 1WB; telephone 0116 2622250.

Leidy, Joseph (1823–1891)

Leidy, a physician and American naturalist, taught biology at the University of Philadelphia and was an eminent paleontologist. He received the Lyell Medal of the London Geological Society. Sir William Osler, who knew Leidy, thought him "one of the greatest naturalists of America" and said he was an agnostic: "I have often heard him say that the question of a future state had long ceased to interest him." {BDF; JM; RAT; RE}

Leigh, Henry Stone (19th Century)

Leigh was the English author of a deistic work, *The Religions of the World* (1869). {BDF}

Leigh, Mike (1943-)

An English film director, Leigh has directed plays ("Goose Pimples," 1981, winner of the Critics' Choice Best Comedy Award, *London Evening Standard*); numbers of feature films (including "Bleak Moments," 1971, Golden Hugo Award, Chicago Film Festival and Golden Leopard Award, Locarno Film Festival, 1972); and radio plays ("Too Much of a Good Thing," 1979). When his "Secrets and Lies" was nominated for an Oscar Award, he told biographer Michael Coveney, who inquired about his religious views, "I walked away from all that as early as I can remember and certainly, by the time of my bar-mitzvah, I did not believe in God. And I still don't." {CA}

Leigh, Richard (20th Century)

Leigh, with Michael Baigent and Henry Lincoln, wrote *Holy Blood, Holy Grail* (1982).

Leight, Jenna (20th Century)

Leight is an editor of *World*, the journal of the Unitarian Universalist Association.

Leighton, Frederic [Baron] (1830–1896)

A distinguished English painter and sculptor, Leighton was president of the Royal Academy and received numerous honors from many countries. His first picture, purchased by Queen Victoria in 1855, showed Cimabue's "Madonna" being carried through the streets of Florence. In *Addresses Delivered to the Students of the Royal Academy*, Leighton candidly refutes the common idea that Christianity inspired medieval art. On the contrary, the serious Christianity of the Middle Ages was a blight on art, he maintained. It was the Humanism of the Renaissance that delivered it. Although he sometimes used the language of theism, McCabe wrote, Leighton approaches agnosticism when he speaks of "the mysterious and eternal Fountain of all good things." {CE; JM; RAT; RE}

Leighton, J. A. (20th Century)

Leighton has been an active member of the American Humanist Association. {HNS}

Leiss, Fred (19th Century)

In New York, Leiss published *Freidenker* in 1872. It was a freethought publication printed in German.

Leitner, Gloria Jewel (1946)

Leitner, a freelance writer in Boulder, Colorado, contributes articles to *The Humanist*. She has written that humanists, who often mockingly poke holes in the New Age nostrums, need to come to terms with the scientifically oriented person who also embraces "spirituality," a word she defines to include what others say they experience during prayer, contemplation, meditation, and communal rituals of sanctity. "In its highest manifestation," she claims, "spiritual enrichment can result in a giving, loving, lucid life." {*The Humanist*, May-June 1996}

Leithauser, Gladys Garner (20th Century)

Leithauser, a retired teacher of writing and communication at the University of Michigan-Dearborn, is co-editor of *The World of Science: An Anthology for Writers* (1987). In 1994 she was a member of a panel discussing "What is the Good Life? A Humanist Perspective" at the 1994 conference of the Coalition for Secular Humanism, Atheism, and Freethought (CSHAFT) in Toronto.

Leland, Charles Godfrey (1824–1903)

An American author, Leland used the pseudonym of Hans Breitmann, writing poems with a German dialect while editor of *Graham's Magazine*. In 1869 he published *Hans Bresitman's Ballads*, and in 1862 he founded and edited in Boston the *Continental Monthly* in order to further the Union cause. Leland wrote more than fifty books, and in the 1880s he successfully introduced industrial and craft arts into American schools. He fought at the barricades in the French Revolution of 1848, translated Heine, and wrote a life of Abraham Lincoln. In his *Memoirs*, he speaks satirically of "the grandeur of monotheistic trinitarianism," wavering according to McCabe between theism and atheism. {CE; JM; RAT}

Leland, Lilian (Born 1857)

The daughter of Theron C. Leland, Ms. Leland said she never heard a prayer until she was six years old, when a religious woman undertook to teach her and her sister to say, "Now I lay me down to sleep" whereas her parents just before bedtime had played a game, "What are you going to give the old bachelor to keep house with?" A world traveler, Leland was a freethinker and a writer who married the son of Stephen Pearl Andrews, an abolitionist and freethinker. {PUT; WWS}

Leland, Theron C. (1821–1885)

Leland was an American journalist who edited with Wakeman a journal called *Man*. Leland was born in a log cabin in Cattaraugus County, New York, "amid the howling wolves and woods." Although he graduated with the highest honors from the Wesleyan Seminary at Lima, New York, he became interested in Fourierism and became a convert to that form of socialism. Leland was an advocate of phonography, which many at that time denounced as a humbug. But when he reported on the speeches of Daniel Webster and Kossuth and others for the New York *Tribune* and other papers, he began a reputation that placed him at the head of all stenographers.

At the fourth annual congress of the National Liberal League in 1880, Leland was elected secretary. Leland was a total disbeliever in Christianity. {BDF; PUT}

Lem, Kristin (20th Century)

A feminist folksinger and songwriter, Lem in 1996 was awarded the Charline Kotula Freethought Heroine Memorial Award at the convention of the Freedom From Religion Foundation in Madison, Wisconsin. Gloria Steinem has called Lem "a one-woman argument against the notion that the women's movement doesn't have a sense of humor."

Lem, Stanislaw (20th Century)

An estimated six million copies of Lem's novels, short stories, and plays can be found in print throughout East Europe and Russia. Over two dozen of his works have been translated into English, including *Solaris*(1970; the Soviets made a major film from this novel); *The Cyberiad* (1974); *The Futurological Congress* (1974); and *The Star Diaries* (1976).

Trained to be a physician and "brought up with the scientific outlook" by his father, also a physician, Lem subsequently "spent many hours over coffee arguing about God" with his friend Karol Wojtlya, who taught theology in Krackow (and is better known as Pope John Paul II).

As for religion, "For moral reasons I am an atheist—for moral reasons. I am of the opinion that you would recognize a creator by his creation, and the world appears to me to be put together in such a painful way that I prefer to believe that it was not created by anyone than to think that somebody created this intentionally." {CA}

Lemaire, Charles (19th Century)

A member of the Academical Society of Saint Quentin, Lemaire wrote an atheistic philosophical work entitled *Initiation to the Philosophy of Liberty* (2 volumes, 1842). {BDF}

Lemoine, Brett (20th Century)

With Jeffery Jay Lowder, Lemoine started Internet Infidels in 1995 and is its honorary president. Theirs is a major site for nontheistic materials: <http://www.infidels.org>.

Lemon, Alton (20th Century)

In *Lemon v. Kurtzman* (1971), named after the plaintiff, the Supreme Court set a standard for judging separation of church and state. The "Lemon Test" states that a law is in violation of the constitutional separation of church and state, unless it meets all the following criteria: (a) It must have a secular legislative purpose; (2) its principal or primary effect must be one that neither advances nor inhibits religion; and (c) it must not foster excessive entanglement with religion.

The Freethought Society of Greater Philadelphia honored Lemon and his wife, Augusta, in 1996 for their important efforts on behalf of the separation of church and state. He has been named an honorary officer of the Freedom From Religion Foundation.

Lemonnier, Camille (1845–1913)

Lemonnier was a Belgian writer, author of stories on hysteria, death, and other topics in which he evinces his freethought sentiments. In 1987, Lemonnier wrote *Le Mort.* {BDF}

Lenau, E. (19th Century)

Lenau edited from Chicago *The People's Press* from 1896 to 1905.

Lenau, Nicolaus (1802–1850)

Lenau, a Hungarian poet whose name was Nicolaus Franz Niembusch von Strehlenau, wrote in German. His poems were pessimistic and his constitutional melancholy deepened into insanity. A freethinker, he died near Vienna in Ober-Döbling. {BDF}

Lenbach, Franz von (1836–1904)

A German painter whose portraits were inspired by the models of Rembrandt and Velasquez, Lenbach used a fineness of coloring and was noted as an eminent German artist. He was ennobled by the Prince Regent of Bavaria and had many gold medals and orders. One of Lenbach's portraits is that of Haeckel, with whose philosophical outlook he agreed. {RAT}

Lenin [originally Vladimir Ilyich Ulyanov] (1870–1924)

"God-making is the worst way of spitting in one's own face," declared Lenin, the Bolshevik ideologist and founder of the USSR. He argued against the "God-building" of Lunacharski, Bogdanov, and Gorki. (Ironically, Lenin himself ended as somewhat of a godlike figure, entombed at Red Square.) Lenin believed that religion should be abolished, and he called for developing "the most widespread scientific education and antireligious propaganda," cautioning against "insulting the [religious] feelings of believers since this would only lead to the strengthening of religious fanaticism." "Religion," a fifty-six page pamphlet Lenin wrote, was not published in English until 1930.

Lenin's grandfather was Israel Blank, born around 1804 in Staro-Konstantynov, Ukraine, to Moshke (son of Isaac) Blank, a Jewish businessman. Isaac Blank had converted to the Russian Orthodox Church at one point, changing his name to Aleksandr Dmitrivich Blank and becoming a physician. His daughter, Mariya Aleksandrovna Blank, was the mother of Vladimir Ilyich Ulyanov, Lenin's actual name. Lenin's elder brother, Sasha, was hanged in 1887 for conspiring against the life of Tsar Alexander III.

Dimitri Volkogonov, in a biography, *Lenin* (1994), states that Lenin's maternal grandfather was Jewish and that Lenin had an affair with Inewssa Armand, his fellow revolutionary. A former Soviet general, Volkogonov was a believing communist who revered Stalin, then revered Lenin, then used secret Soviet documents to expose Lenin's iniquities. Lenin, he states, endorsed terror in general terms but avoided associating his name with any concrete acts of violence. During a kulak uprising in 1918, Lenin wrote, "Hang (and I mean *hang* so that the people can see) not less than 100 known kulaks, rich men, bloodsuckers. . . . Do this so that for hundreds of miles around the people can see, tremble, know, and cry: they are killing and will go on killing the bloodsucking kulaks." To punish Latvia and Estonia for declaring their independence in 1918, he wrote, "Cross the frontier somewhere, even if only to a depth of half a mile, and hang 100 [to] 1,000 of their civil servants and rich people." Concluded Volkogonov, once a disciple of Lenin and now accused by some of overstatement, it was Lenin who sowed "the seeds of the murderous collectivization . . . the appalling purges . . . and the postwar 'punishment' of entire nations." It was Lenin who was "the father of domestic Russian terrorism, merciless and totalitarian."

Contemporary humanists find that the flaw in Lenin's dialectic is that no democratic processes were in place, that the resultant "communistic humanism" did not include political democracy as it purported to work for the benefit of the masses.

Yuri Buranov, in *Lenin's Will, Falsified and Forbidden* (1994), claims that in 1922 and 1923, while Lenin lay incapacitated by severe strokes, the Central Committee of the Communist Party deliberately collaborated to falsify Lenin's last political testament, which led to Stalin's success in obtaining power. Revisionists such as the Harvard historian Richard Pipes place the blame for the evils of the Stalinist regime squarely on the shoulders of Lenin and his concept of the one-party state. Pipes and others hold that Lenin was the progenitor of modern revolutionary violence and radical, bloody social change, that he, not Stalin, gave the world a blueprint for the ideology-based terror state which Hitler and others would use to such deadly effect. According to Pipes's *The Unknown Lenin: From the Secret Archives*

(1996), Lenin was ruthless, mean, had a closed mind, and was ignorant of the world outside Russia. Not "Christ-like, at least in his compassion" nor "as excited and lovable as a little child," as viewed by the Australian Marxist historian Manning Clark.

Lenin's body was placed into a granite mausoleum on Red Square in Moscow, drawing huge crowds that could see the familiar face, now somewhat waxy in appearance. When the German army approached in 1941, the body was rushed to Siberia for safekeeping—minus his brain. The brain, pickled and sectioned, remained at the Soviet Academy of Sciences' Brain Institute, the 1926 academy which also has probed the brains of Stalin, Maxim Gorky, and Andrei Sakharov. The eventual disposition of Lenin's body, once the Soviet Union ceased, is uncertain. {CB; CE; CL; EU, Rolf H. W. Theen; JM; PA; RE}

Lennon, Ann (1906–)

Lennon, who during the 1940s was secretary of the Rationalist Association of South Australia, was once fined £10 for having said in a public park that God loved bloodshed and the smell of burning flesh. . . . This God of you Christians is a Jewish God, not an Aussie God, not a fair-dinkum Aussie God, just a Jewish god with money bags around his neck." Upon appeal, she was told by Judge Nield that despite Sir James Frazer's *The Golden Bough*, which showed that the gods of primitive races were neither the Christian nor the Jewish gods, rationalists of Miss Lennon's type still adhered to the view of the 1880s. He upheld the fine. Meanwhile, she continued as a rationalist and atheist lecturer at the Sydney Domain and Ingersoll Hall. {SWW}

Lennon, John (1940–1980)

Lennon was the rock 'n' roll superstar who, at the height of the group's fame, said the Beatles were "bigger than Jesus." During a drug episode when he was taking LSD, according to Mark Hertsgaard in *A Day in the Life*, Lennon allegedly thought he was Jesus Christ come back again. Hertsgaard claims Lennon continued the belief when he woke up the following day. However, Lennon later called himself an atheist, writing that "God is a concept by which we measure our pain."

His atheism is found in the song, "Imagine," perhaps written as an LSD reaction, in which he conjures up a world without countries or religion:

> Imagine there's no heaven—it's easy if you try;
> no Hell below us, above us only sky.
> Imagine all the people livin' for today.
>
> Imagine there's no countries—it's not hard to do;
> nothing to kill or die for and no religion too.
> Imagine all the people livin' life in peace.
>
> Imagine no possessions:
> I wonder if you can;
> no need for greed or hunger,
> a brotherhood of man,
> all the people sharing all the world.
>
> You may say I'm a dreamer,
> But I'm not the only one.
> I hope some day you'll join us,
> And the world will be as one.

Asked once if he was worried about the prospect of nuclear destruction, Lennon replied, "Well, like everyone else I don't want to end up a festering heap, but I don't stay up nights worrying. I'm preoccupied with life, not death."

His January 1981 interview in *Playboy* showed Lennon as something of a waverer. As for Dylan's having become a born-again Christian, Lennon replied,

> For whatever reason he's doing it, it is personal for him and he needs to do it. But the whole religion business suffers from the Onward, Christian Soldiers bit. There's too much talk about soldiers and marching and converting. I'm not pushing Buddhism, because I'm no more a Buddhist than I am a Christian, but there's one thing I admire about the religion: There's no proselytizing.

Lennon's very interest in cult leaders in India, however, was highly criticized by many non-theists. (See entries for Royston Ellis and Sam Phillips.) {PA; TYD}

Lennon, William F. Jr. (20th Century)

In the 1950s, Lennon was a director of the American Humanist Association's Humanist Fellowship of Boston.

Lennstrand, Viktor E. (1861–1895)

A lecturer and journalist, Lennstrand started in 1888 and was prosecuted for his anti-Christian propaganda. Twice he was fined 250 crowns and imprisoned, but he extended his influence with the general public, which discredited his opponents. He founded "Utilitarian Associations" which still survive in Sweden. Lennstrand wrote *What We Believe and What We Want* (1888), *Jehovah is Dead* (1891), and *The Republic, the Popular Vote and Freethinking* (1891). With A. Lindkvist, he founded the organ of Swedish freethought, *Fritankaren*. {BDF; EU, José M. F. Santana; JMR; PUT; TYD}

Lenowitz, Harris (20th Century)

Lenowitz wrote *A Big Jewish Book, Poems and Other Visions* (1978. He also wrote *Origins: Creation Texts from the Ancient Mediterranean; a Crestomathy* (1976). Lenowitz's translation of the familiar *Genesis* story in Rudolph Kittel's *Biblica Hebraica* (3rd Edition, 1937), is what might be called the "prick and hole" translation. Bernard Katz in *American Rationalist* (Sep-Oct 1991) reports the translator came up with the following:

> so the gods
> god made man as he looks
> looking like the gods
> they godmade them
> prick and hole
> they godmade them
> and the gods blessed them
> and the gods said to them:
> BREED A LOT AND FILL THE EARTH
> AND TAKE IT OVER. RULE. . . .
>
> at the first of the gods' godmaking skies and earth, the earth was all mixed up—darkness on top of deepness; so the gods' spirit swooped down on the waters. The gods said LIGHT so there was light, and the gods liked the light so they made it different from the darkness.
>
> they called the light Day
> called darkness night;
> so that was Evening
> and that was Morning
> the first Day. . . .
>
> Then the gods said,
> LET THE EARTH BRING OUT BREATHING
> LIFE OF ALL SORTS;
> CATTLE AND CRAWLER, EVERY EARTH LIFE
> and that's how it was:
>
> gods made all earth life
> cattle and red-dirt crawler too
> all of all kinds
> and liked it
>
> so the gods said
> LET'S MAKE SOME RED DIRT
> THAT'LL LOOK LIKE US, JUST LIKE US

IT'LL BOSS
THE FISH IN THE SEA
THE BIRD IN THE SKY
AND CATTLE
AND ALL THE EARTH
AND ALL THE CRAWLERS
CRAWLING THE EARTH

so the gods
godmade man as he looks
looking like the gods
they godmade them
prick and hole
they godmade them . . .
etc.

As noted, the original concept of monotheism (oneness of God) tacitly postulates that the original Original was bisexual.

When the document was written, according to a founding member of the New York secular humanists, "Individuals must not have been prudes and the author or authors did *not* need to bowdlerize. Their earthiness and their holes and pricks verily stuck out, being without benefit of the King James scholars who dressed the work up . . . a tad."

LENT

Borrowing from a celebration of spring, *lencten* in Old English and *lenzin* in Old High German, Lent in Christianity is a time of fasting and repentance of the sins (for example, "taking God's name in vain," masturbating, drinking too much alcohol) which the church fathers have conditioned the faithful to avoid. It begins on a holiday known as Ash Wednesday and ends several weeks later on another holiday known as Easter. "To give something up for Lent" is the way of abandoning a pleasurable habit, a practice freethinkers and humanists find masochistic.

The practice is observed by the Roman Catholic, Eastern, and some Protestant churches. Originally, the Lenten season was a period of preparation for baptism at Easter, and the imposition of ashes—adherents, for example, walk around all day with an incongruous, even disconcertingto freethinkers, dab of ashes on their foreheads–is a survival of a later practice. {DCL; ER}

Lenz, John (20th Century)

Lenz, a professor of classics at Drew University, became president of the Bertrand Russell Society in 1995. He is author of *Bertrand Russell and the Greeks*. Lenz has been critical of Martin Bernal's *Black Athena: The Afroasiatic Roots of Classical Civilization*. On the Web: http://daniel.drew.edu/~jlenz/brs.html {*Free Inquiry*, Fall, 1990}

Leo X, Pope (1475–1521)

See entry in Joseph McCabe's *Rationalist Encyclopedia*, which cites Leo as "a thoroughly vicious and unscrupulous man, and, in view of the position of the Church on the eve of the Reformation, one of the most scandalous Popes of the series."

Leo XIII, Pope (1810–1903)

The Pope from 1878 to 1903, Leo XIII in his *Quadragesimo anno* wrote, "To suffer and endure is the lot of humanity." In 1896 he issued an encyclical pronouncing Anglican orders invalid. {CE; ER; RE}

Leon, Herbert Samuel [Sir] (Born 1850)

Leon was the third Chairman of the Rationalist Press Association. He was M.P. for the Northern Division of Buckinghamshire from 1891 to 1895 and was created Baronet in 1911. {RAT}

Leonardo da Vinci (1452–1519)

The consummate Renaissance genius, the "love child of a peasant girl named Caterina and the respected notary Piero da Vinci, Leonardo was an architect, engineer, painter, musician, and sculptor. No longer painting the ideal human being as an ascetic monk, he as well as Michelangelo constructed the universal man who enjoyed life and reveled in existence. As such he represents one of the greatest humanistic minds of all time.

Robertson points out that Leonardo's passion for knowledge "is not Christian and that his reiterated rejection of the principle of authority in science and in literature tells of a spirit which, howsoever it might practise reticence, cannot have been inwardly docile to either priesthood or tradition." In addition to *Mona Lisa* and *The Last Supper*, Leonardo painted exquisite examples of the human form. Like the spirit of the Renaissance itself, Kenneth MacLeish has written, "the mind of this man destined to become its living symbol was fashioned in the quickening spring of the Western world's awakening from the shriveling darkness of the Middle Ages. He was free, as few human beings have ever been free, to become whatever his gifts might make of him. . . . A gracious person, pleasing if not loving, a singer, versifier, maker of marvelous illusions, he was both performer and showman. He devised puzzles and games, and jokes that made people 'roar with laughter.' He won the friendship of dukes and kings. Admirers called him 'the Divine Leonardo' and said he could do anything."

Born a Tuscan, he left for Milan at the age of thirty and subsequently wandered to Florence and Rome before dying an expatriate in France. But many facts concerning his life are sketchy, and it was left to the 16th-century critic Giorgio Vasari to invent much of what currently is known about his life. Vasari, for example, described Leonardo as a paragon of physical and spiritual beauty, a man who bought caged birds for the sole purpose of setting them free.

Vasari wrote that Leonardo died in the arms of King Francis I of France. Whether Vasari was objective or not, it is known that Leonardo was once imprisoned for two months, with four other Florentines (for sodomy with a seventeen-year-old boy). Also, Leonardo described his apprentice, Andrea Salaino [Salai], as "a thieving, lying glutton," a lovely lad with curly blond hair and the disposition of a weasel. Leonardo and Salaino remained inseparable for twenty-five years. In his will, Leonardo left Salai, now a fat and coarsened grown-up, a bequest as well as a dowry for Salai's sister.

Leonardo's book, *Treatise on Painting* (1651), reveals him to have been an artist and scientist united in one personality. {AA; CE; CL; JM; JMR; RE; TYD}

Leontium (c. 300 B.C.E.)

Leontium was a disciple and the mistress of Epicurus. An Athenian hetaera, she acquired distinction as a philosopher and wrote a treatise against Theophrastus, which Cicero praised as being written in an elegant manner. {BDF}

Leopardi, Giacomo Conte (1798–1837)

An Italian poet and scholar, Leopardi has been called "the supreme poet of modern Italy" and "one of the most definitely rationalistic as well as one of the greatest philosophic poets in literature." He also was called *Il Gobbo*, "the hunchback." Because of his spine's curvature and his melancholy he complained to his brother Carlo in 1822, "I need love, love, love, fire, enthusiasm, life. The world does not seem to be made for me."

A liberal and a freethinking agnostic at a time when independence of thought was dangerous in Italy, he wrote poetry deeply patriotic but contemptuous of the Italian rulers of his day. His fame rests primarily on his *Canti* [poetic songs]. Unfortunately, his short life was one long disease. McCabe called him "a deist without belief in immortality." {BDF; CE; JM; JMR; RAT; RE}

Leopold, Richard William (20th Century)

Leopold wrote *Robert Dale Owen, A Biography* (1940). {FUS}

LePoidevin, Robin (20th Century)

In *Defending Atheism: An Introduction to the Philosophy of Religion* (1996), LePoidevin in a scholarly way presented the arguments against belief. He is a contributing editor for *Philo*.

Lépine, Louis Jean Baptiste [Governor-General] (1846–1933)

Lépine, a French statesman, was Governor-General of Algeria in 1897. He wore the Grand Cross of the Legion of Honour and supported measures against the French Church. In Lyons, he was Prefect of Police. {RAT}

LePlongeon, Augustus (20th Century)

LePlongeon, in *Sacred Mysteries Among the Mayas and the Quiches* (1945), compares in an 1886 study the mysteries of the Mayas to those of Egypt, Greece, Chaldea, and India. The book also discusses Freemasonry.

Le Poidevin, Robin (1962-)

Le Poidevin wrote *Arguing for Atheism: An Introduction to the*

Philosophy of Religion (1996). According to Keith M. Parsons (*Philo*, Spring-Summer 1998), the book "is a logically deft and clearly written introduction to the philosophy of religion. It should be useful for undergraduate courses, though parts, such as the discussion of the modal ontological argument, are quite complex and certain to confuse beginners. The book is also a brief for atheism." Parsons critiques the book, pointing out places it could be improved, but he finds Le Poidevin a young "but already highly accomplished philosopher."

Lequinio, Joseph Marie (1740–1813)

A French writer and Conventionnel, once the mayor of Rennes (1790), Lequinio professed atheism. He voted for the death of Louis XVI, "regretting that the safety of the state did not permit his being condemned to penal servitude for life." In 1792 Lequinio published *Prejudices Destroyed*, which he signed "Citizen of the World" and in which he considered religion as a political chain. Liquinio took part in the Feasts of Reason and wrote *Philosophy of the People* (1796). {BDF}

Lerdo de Tejada, Sebastian [President] (1825–1889)

Lerdo de Tejada was in succession Minister of Foreign Affairs, President of Congress, President of the Supreme Court of Mexico, and, to the great anger of the clergy, President of Mexico (1872–1876). Like his friend Juarez, whom he succeeded, Lerdo de Tejada was, according to McCabe, "a drastic Rationalist." {RAT; RE}

Lermina, Jules Hippolyte (Born 1839)

Lermina, a French writer, founded the *Corsair* and *Satan* and published an illustrated biographical dictionary of France (1884–1885). {BDF; RAT}

Lermontov, Mikhail Yur'evich (1814–1840)

A major novelist and poet, Lermontov developed a reputation that is second in Russia only to Pushkin's. Lermontov began writing poetry when fourteen. His 1837 inflammatory poem, "On the Death of the Poet," protesting the death in a duel of Pushkin, resulted in his being temporarily banished to the Caucasus. Lermontov's family was said by Wheeler to have had some Scottish in its background and said that Lermontov studied at Moscow University, from which he was expelled.

Another rebel, Byron, influenced his early work. *The Demon* (1829–1841), which featured Satan, a fallen angel in love with a mortal, was the basis of an opera by Anton Rubinstein. *The Circassian Boy* (1875) reflects Lermontov's antireligious feeling and idealization of primitive life. *A Hero of Our Time* (1840), a novel that is partly autobiographical, is considered a classic of Russian psychological realism. Ironically, like Pushkin, Lermontov was killed in a duel. {BDF; RAT}

Lerner, Alan Jay (1918-1986)

An American lyricist and librettist, Lerner in an association with composer Frederick Loewe wrote popular musicals including *Brigadoon* (1947, film 1954), *Paint Your Wagon* (1951, film 1969), *Camelot* (1960, film 1967), and *Gigi* (1958), which won an Academy Award. Their *My Fair Lady* (1956, film 1964) ran for more than six years on Broadway. Lerner wrote *Love Life* (1948) with Kurt Weill and the book for the film *An American in Paris* (1951).

Lerner's will directed that he be cremated and that "there be no funeral and no religious ceremony of any kind in connection with my death. If God does not know me by now, no words by a stranger will help to inroduce me." {CE}

Lerner, Gerda (1920–)

Lerner's *The Creation of Feminist Consciousness: From the Middle Ages to 1870* (1993) tells of the many aspects of women's culture, development and history, and reflects a positive definition of feminine values which are implicit in belonging to a group with distinct characteristics and interests. From the outset, she shows, the Christian church has been a major factor in the oppression of women. Lerner credits Sarah Grimké, Mathilda Joslyn Gage, and Elizabeth Cady Stanton for the view that "the Bible and the orthodox church were the two greatest obstacles in the way of women's advancement."

She has described her experiences as a female Jewish atheist:

> More difficult and public was my refusal, four weeks before the appointed date, to go through with my Bar Mitzvah on the grounds that since I no longer believed in God nor in what was taught in religious instruction, it would be hypocritical for me to go through the ceremony. This provoked a family crisis, much noise, anger, and pressure of various sorts, but in the end I prevailed. But more—I refused to set foot in a synagogue again and kept to that refusal for over fifty years.

{CA; *Freethought History*, #10, 1994}

Lerner, Lawrence (20th Century)

Lerner is a contributor to *Freethought Today*, which is published by the Freedom From Religion Foundation.

Lerner, Leo (1907–1965)

A humanist, Lerner wrote *The Itch of Opinion* (1956) and co-wrote *Lincoln for the Ages* (1960). {HNS}

Lerner, Max(well) (Allen) (1902–1992)

Lerner was a noted journalist, syndicated columnist, and editor of *The Nation* (1936–1938). He wrote six thousand columns for the *New York Post* and was widely syndicated in *PM*, *The New Republic, and The Nation*. A rival of Walter Lippmann but a friend of Hugh Hefner ("I teach him sex," he joked, "and he teaches me politics."), Lerner was a classic immigrant who arrived at Ellis Island from Russia when he was five. His twin siblings did not survive, and the Lerners barely did so on money his father earned in the garment district and milk-delivery business.

He entered Yale in 1919, winning prizes in English, German, and patriotism, but was told when he neared graduation that "You ought to know that, as a Jew, you'll never get a teaching post in literature in any Ivy League college." Lerner's MA thesis adviser in economics, Isaac Lippincott, at Washington University, called him "the most capable graduate student I have had." He was granted a Ph. D. in 1927 solely "on the strength of the papers he had written."

Sanford Lakoff's *Max Lerner: Pilgrim in the Promised Land* (1999) relates how the 5' 7" Lerner became managing editor of the *Encyclopedia of the Social Sciences* as well as the first Jew appointed to the faculty at Williams College. He also relates his sexual escapades, including an affair with Elizabeth Taylor. Believing as a "neo-Marxian liberal" that collectivism was destined to replace individualism in the United States, he turned instead to Franklin Roosevelt's "level-headed American pragmatism," finding that it would be the best thing both for democracy and for whatever part of capitalism was worth retaining.

A friend of Harold Laski and Felix Frankfurther, Lerner was known as a spokesman for Popular Frontism before World War II and for favoring early American involvement against fascism. Lakoff thought Lerner was least attractive when, in the 1980s, he became more centrist.

In his last chapter of *Actions and Passions* (1949), Lerner wrote,

> I am speaking of an understanding frank enough to recognize that man is part of a naturalistic order, an animal with bestial impulses that can be multiplied by the multiple cunning of his brain. . . . I call this tragic humanism. I call it tragic because it must strip itself of the bar-

ren belief that men are wholly rational, and of the smug assumption that progress and happiness can come out of systems of power as such, whether capitalism, socialism, or communism. This is not a religion, or even a *mystique*. It is an idea to which the American creative thinker can dedicate himself with passion and wholeness. An idea with passion and wholeness behind it can move the world.

Of humanism, Lerner in 1951 wrote to the present author:

> Yes, I do consider myself—if anything—a kind of "naturalistic humanist." The phrase I use is "tragic humanist." You will find the closest approach to a deliberate formulation of in an editorial I did a few years back for the *American Scholar*, called "Toward A Tragic Humanism," and which I have included in my book of essays, *Actions and Passions* (1949), as an epilogue (pp. 258–259). I am now writing a brief book elaborating on this view and applying it to the war crisis.

In addition to a philosophic *Preface to Morals*, Lerner was the author of *It Is Later Than You* Think (1938), The *Portable Veblen* (1948), *The Essential Works of John Stuart Mill* (1961), and *Education and a Radical Humanism* (1962). A major work was a collection of the *PM* editorials, *America as a Civilization, Life and Thought in the United States Today* (1957).

Summing up his life for a *Who's Who in America* entry, Lerner wrote: "I have believed in love and work, and their linkage. I have believed that we are neither angels nor devils, but humans, with clusters of potentials in both directions. I am neither an optimist nor a pessimist, but a possibilist." (Lamont thought that Lerner, in calling his philosophy tragic humanism, "stresses too much the traumatic aspects of life.") {CL; WAS, 9 March 1951}

Leroux, Pierre (1797–1871)

Leroux was a French socialist and philosophic writer. At first a mason, then a typographer, he invented an early composing machine that he called the pianotype. In 1824 he became editor of the *Globe*, making it the organ of a Saint Simonian sect. Anti-Catholic, Leroux wrote author of *De l'Humanite* (1840). In 1848 he was elected to the Assembly. {BDF; RAT}

Lerroux y Garcia, Alejandro (1864–1949)

Lerroux y Garcia was a Spanish politician who for a quarter of a century fought for republicanism, socialism, and rationalism in Spain. He was editor and owner of *El Progreso* and thrice represented Barcelona in the Cortes. No fewer than three hundred times was he condemned for his press utterances, which resulted in his spending thirty years in prison and several years of being exiled. {RAT}

Leroy, Charles Georges (1723–1789)

Leroy, a lieutenant ranger of the park of Versailles, was one of the writers on the *Encyclopédie*. He defended the work of Helvetius on the Mind against Voltaire, and he wrote *Philosophical Letters on the Intelligence and Perfectibility of Animals* (1768). {BDF}

LES IDÉES EN MOUVEMENTS

A French humanistic journal, *Les Idées en Mouvement* is at 3 rue Recamier 75341 Paris, Cedex 07, France. <info-ligue@ligue.cie.fr>.

LESBIANISM

Lesbianism is a term to describe the sexual orientation of women to other women, one that comes from the putative homosexuality of Sappho, the lyric poet of Lesbos.

Some lesbian freethinkers—citing the mother of Jesus as a woman who allegedly gave birth to a child without a heterosexual act or the help of a man —have been known to use the argument, jocularly, to legalize lesbian marriages. (See entry for Homosexuality.)

Leslie, Charles (1650–1722)

Leslie's *Short and easie method with the deists* (1698) led Charles Gildon to forsake his Catholicism and become a leading deist. {FUK; HAB}

Lespinasse, Adolf Frederick Henri de (1819–1881)

Lespinasse was a Dutch writer who wrote in the *Dageraad* under the pen name of "Titus." In 1870 he emigrated to America and became director of a large farm, dying there in Orange City, Iowa. {BDF}

L'Espinasse, Julie Jeanne Elónore de (1732–1776)

A French beauty and wit, L'Espinasse became the protégé of Made du Deffand and gained the favor of D'Alembert. Her letters are models of sensibility and spirit. {BDF}

Lesser, Wendy (1952-)

Wesser is the founding editor of *The Threepenny Review*. A California-born writer who in 1988 became a Guggenhim fellow, she wrote *The Life Below the Ground* (1967); *His Other Half* (1991); *Pictures at an Execution* (1994); *A Director Calls* (1997); and *The Amateur: An Independent Life of Letters* (1998).

Reviewing an Annie Dillard novel about why, if God exists, wickedness is permitted, Lesser wrote

> As a Jewish atheist with little or no feel for nature, I am admittedly not the ideal reader of *For the Time Being*. (The Jewish part is important, for it means that Dillard's frequent references to the Baal Shem Tov and Rabbi Isaac Luria lack, for me, the appeal of exoticism).
> {*The New York Times*, 28 March 1999}

Lessing, Doris May (1919–)

Lessing, a novelist and short story writer who was born in Persia of British parents and who moved when she was five to a farm in Southern Rhodesia, knew by the age of twelve how to set a hen, raise rabbits, worm dogs, churn butter, cook and sew, go down mine shafts in a bucket, make cream cheese and ginger beer, drive cars, walk on stilts, and shoot pigeons and guinea fowl, all of which she said "is real happiness, a child's happiness: being enabled to do and to make, above all to know you are contributing to the family, you are valuable and valued."

Critic John Leonard has pointed out that Lessing, who left school at the age of fifteen, spent four years in a convent school "and was so admiring of holy water, rosary beads, Sanctus bells, and a coffin as pink as a cake, in the shape of a violin, she actually converted, for a couple of minutes, to Roman Catholicism." But when her mother explained the Inquisition, "she promptly quit religion."

Lessing was influential in assisting an entire generation to understand Africa as a continent in transition, particularly drawing attention to Southern Rhodesia (now Zimbabwe), where she lived for twenty-five years before moving to London. She wrote about Africa, communism, women, and global catastrophe in a series collectively titled *The Children of Violence* which included *Martha Quest* (1952), *A Proper Marriage* (1954), *A Ripple From the Storm* (1958), *Landlocked* (1965), and *The Four-Gated City* (1969). She is best known for *The Golden Notebook* (1962), an ambitious novel that was hailed as a landmark by the Women's Movement. Lessing was interested in the works of Idries Shah as well as Sufism, the Muslim philosophical and literary movement that emerged among the Shiites in the late 10th and early 11th centuries. Her *Collected Stories* (2 volumes, 1978) contain varied works including meditations on the material and spiritual life in "The Temptation of Jack Orkney."

In 1994, *Under My Skin*, volume one of her autobiography (to 1949), although it abounds, says Leonard, "with unpleasant smells from the past—horses, camphor, petrol, paraffin, chamber pots, dead fish, wet wool, the habits of nuns, her father's crotch—none is as redolent as the very *idea* of Anna's compulsive washing of herself in

The Golden Notebook, so that she won't smell of her own period." The work also abounds with tales of her life until she was thirty. She tells what she read, when the nuns let her; what music she enjoyed; where she went and what she thought. Presumably in volume two, she will tell how she became interested in Outer Space, for she wrote five volumes of the *Canopus in Argus: Archives* series. "Nothing in history," she writes in the autobiography, "suggests that we may expect anything but wars, tyrants, sickness, bad times, calamities, while good times are always temporary. Above all, history tells us nothing stays the same for long. We expect gold at the foot of always-renewable rainbows. I feel I have been part of some mass illusion or delusion. Certainly part of mass beliefs and convictions that now seem as lunatic as the fact that for centuries expeditions of God-lovers trekked across the Middle East to kill the infidel."

Walking in the Shade: Volume Two of My Autobiography, 1949-1962 (1998) relates obtaining her official Communist Party card in the 1950s at a time she had already become disillusioned by communism. Everyone was a communist in those days, she said—more would say, however, that intellectuals were left-wing. What Lessing disliked was the semi-dogmatism of her comrades' thinking, so the book attempts to evaluate her later views about society. Upon her return in 1956 to Africa, she was termed a "Prohibited Immigrant." Of her break with communism, she wrote:

> I knew that I had accepted the Marxist package for no deeper reason than that the communists I met in Southern Rhodesia had actually read the books I had, were in love with literature, and because they were the only people I knew who took it for granted that the white regime was doomed. . .
>
> I began a systematic search for something different.

{CE}

Lessing, Gotthold Ephraim (1729–1781)

A deist and aestheticist who was born in Kamenz, Saxony, where his father was a pastor in the Lutheran Church, Lessing studied at the University in Leipzig. He studied theology, medicine, and philosophy, but became particularly interested in literary criticism. Foote has written, "At an early age Lessing showed his independent nature, and this independence was especially noticeable in his views on religion. In his essay, 'How the Ancients Represented Death,' he contrasts the attitude of classical antiquity to death as the natural end of life with that of the Christian faith, which considers death a penalty for sin. Some of the posthumous essays of Hermann Samuel Reimarus, 'The Principal Truths of Natural Religion' and the 'Doctrines of Reason,' in which he subjects the important claims of Christianity to a profound examination and rejects them as untenable, were edited by Lessing, who took them with him to Wolfenbuettel. Lessing himself was greatly impressed by Reimarus's work, though he dissented from many of its conclusions. His part in circulating these heterodox views and his own ideas of the need of free discussion in religion, as expressed in 'The Education of the human Race,' were distasteful to the orthodox of the time, and Pastor Coeze pursued him as viciously as Talmage pursued Ingersoll a century later."

Lessing's *Nathan the Wise* (1779) spoke of the need for the peaceful coexistence of all religions. His *Education of the Human Race* (1780) spoke of the ideas of progress and evolution as related to religion. Rather than the French classical theatre, Lessing preferred Shakespeare as a model whom Germans should revere. A Mason and "a deist with a difference," unlike Voltaire he was profoundly interested in theology and confronted Christianity on its own grounds. Volker Dürr tells how in *A Rejoinder* Lessing formulated his credo and his legacy most eloquently: "If God were holding all the truth that exists in his right hand, and in his left just the one ever-active urge to find the truth, even if attached to it were the condition that I should always and forever be going astray, and said to me: 'Choose!' I should humbly fall upon his left hand and say: 'Father, give! Pure truth is surely for thee alone!" In his *Hamburgische Dramaturgie* (1767–1769), which concerned the Moslem faith in general and one Ismenor in particular, he observed that the Crusades, "which in their origin were a political stratagem of the popes, developed into the most inhuman persecutions of which Christian superstition has ever made itself guilty: the true religion had then the most and the bloodiest Ismenors." His *Origin of Revealed Religion* (c. 1760) professes to hold to a naturalist view of religion, for he believed that Christianity was established and propagated "by entirely natural means"—this before Gibbon.

In 1780, Lessing in a conversation with Jacoby expressed high appreciation of Goethe's *Prometheus*. "If I am a follower of anyone, it can only be Spinoza," he added. "There is no other philosophy but Spinoza's."

According to Robertson, Lessing with his versatile genius and vast reading was "a man of moods rather than a systematic thinker," that "in his strongest polemic there was always an element of mystification; and his final pantheism was only privately avowed." Although he did not array himself as a champion of rationalism, at the end he proved to be one of the strongest promoters of its reign. Heine called Lessing, after Luther, the greatest German emancipator. In contemporary times, Paul Edwards has cited Lessing's sympathy toward the idea of reincarnation.

Toward the end of his life, Lessing suffered severely from asthma. In February 1781, the malady became acute. According to Foote, he felt that the hand of death was upon him but conversed with his friends "with much of his old liveliness." To one of them who spoke of the annoyance which the clerics caused Voltaire on his deathbed, Lessing exclaimed: "When you see me about to die, call the notary; I will declare before him that I die in none of the prevailing religions." On February 15 he rallied "and joked with some of those who came to visit him," wrote his biographer James Sime. However, in the evening of the same day "a stroke of apoplexy followed, and after life's fitful fever he slept well." Meanwhile, Bishop J. F. Hurst's *History of Rationalism* (1865) reports that upon Lessing's death, some believed "the devil came and carried him away like a second Faust." (See the article by Karl Becker in the *Encyclopedia of Unbelief*.) {BDF; CE; CL; EU, Volker Dürr; FO; JM; JMR; JMRH; PE; PUT; RAT; RE}

Lessona, Michele (1823–1894)

Lessona was an Italian naturalist who translated some of Darwin's works. {BDF}

Lester, Toni P. (20th Century)

Lester, an associate professor of law and the Johnson Term Chair holder at Babson College, works as an employment discrimination law consultant. A Unitarian Universalist, she has been an at-large candidate for the board of directors of the Unitarian Universalist Service Committee.

L'Estrange, Thomas (Born 1822)

Thomas was an attorney and a writer. Having read F. A. Paley's introduction to *The Iliad*, he became convinced that the "cooking" process therein described had been undergone by all sacred books extant. He edited Hume's *Dialogues on Natural Religion*, was author of *The First Ten Alleged Persecutions*, and wrote various tracts. {BDF}

LeSueur, Meridel (1900–1996)

A Minnesota freethinker, LeSueur wrote *The Girl*, a collection of stories, and *North Star Country*, a folk history about the farmer-labor party. Before Voltairine de Cleyre's death in 1912, LeSueur met her and admired her beauty, brilliance, and ability to speak. Mencken, LeSueur declared, taught her the joy of going to taverns, "my first break with puritanism, with the rollicking midnight command of the wonderful midnight ride of Paul Revere, the great drunken carousel of American workers. The conversation of *The Girl* came from that," she added, "so don't let the new puritans throw any lace on him." Her library has been preserved at Augsburg College. {*Freethought History # 7, 1993;* and *#12,* 1994; WWS}

Le Sueur, William Dawson (1840–1917)

After Le Sueur, a freethinker, wrote a controversial biography of William Lyon Mackenzie (1795–1861), the work was suppressed by the Canadian rebel's grandson, William Lyon Mackenzie King. Le Sueur, a Canadian man of letters, has been called "the Sage of Ottawa." (See entry for his biographer, Clifford Holland.)

Letourneau, Charles Jean Marie (Born 1831)

A French scientist, Letourneau was educated as a physician. He wrote *La Penseé Nouvelle* and has published *Physiology of the Passons* (1868) and *Biology* (1875). Other of his works are *Science and Materialism* (1879), *Sociology Based on Ethnography* (1880), and *The Evolution of Marriage and the Family* (1885). Letourneau translated Büchner's *Man According to Science, Light, and Life* and *Mental Life of Animals;* Haeckel's *History of Creation* and *Letters of a Traveller in India;* and Herzen's *Physiology of the Will.* McCabe cites him as being an atheist and materialist who said, "We know that there is nothing in the whole universe except active matter." {BDF; JM; RAT; RE}

Leuba, James H(enry) (1868–1946)

A psychologist and an expert on religious mysticism, Leuba was on the advisory board of Charles Francis Potter's First Humanist Society of New York. Earlier, he had been a leader of the Ethical Culture Society. One of his provocative books is *The Belief in God and Immortality* (1916). He also wrote *A Psychological Study of Religion* (1912), in which his own agnosticism is explained, *The Psychology of Religious Mysticism* (1925), and *God or Man* (1933). Leuba once wrote,

> History is the record of the many dead that are still alive; and of the reasons why so many who expected to live on are dead.

{CL; EU, Howard B. Radest; FUS; HNS; HNS2; JM; RAT; RE; TRI}

Leucippus (5th Century B.C.E.)

Epicurus declared that Leucippus (Leukippos) was an imaginary person, but others say he was one of Protagoras's teachers. Aristotle believed it was Leucippus who originated the atomistic theory, although Democritus usually is credited. At any rate, Leucippus of Miletus is said to have demonstrated that matter is composed of tiny, indivisible properties in constant motion, an idea later developed by Lucretius. Two of his fragmentary works are believed to be *The Great World-system* and *On Mind,* although the latter may have been by Democritus. {BDF; CE; JMR; JMRH}

Leufstedt, G. J. (1830–1901)

Leufstedt was a Swedish non-theist. He sometimes was called "Lennstrand's predecessor" as well as "The Antichrist" for his lectures. (See entry for Scandinavian Unbelievers.)

Levallois, Jules (1829–1903)

Levallois, a French writer who in 1855 became secretary to Saint Beueve, wrote *Deism et Christianisme* (1866). His *Corneille inconnu* (1876) was crowned by the French Academy. Although a theist, he gave frank testimony to the agnosticism of Sainte Beuve, whose life he wrote (1872). {BDF; RAT}

Le Vayer, La Mothe (1588–1672)

A scholar, heretic, and rationalist, Le Vayer was tutor of Louis XIV's brother and one of the early members of the new Academy that had been founded by Richelieu. He was a skeptic of the school of Sextus Empiricus. Robertson believes that Le Vayer's influence upon Richelieu, who became Minister to Louis XIII in 1624, resulted in forty years of there being no burning of heretics or unbelievers in France. {JMR}

Levey, Michael Vincent [Sir] (1927–)

An art historian and author, Levey is a Fellow of the British Academy and a member of Ateneo Veneto. He has taught at Cambridge University, Oxford University, and New York University. Levey wrote *National Gallery Catalogues* (1956, 1959, 1971); *Painting in XVIIIth-Century Venice* (1959); *From Giotto to Cézanne* (1962); *The Life and Death of Mozart* (1971); and *Painting and Sculpture in France 1700–1789* (1992), among numerous books. He edited *Pater's Marius the Epicurean* (1985). Sir Michael is a Vice President of the Gay and Lesbian Humanist Association.

Of his philosophic outlook, Levey has written,

> I was brought up in an unostentatiously but fervently Roman Catholic household and fully reached a state of reason only after I rejected that faith in my twenties and on deciding that the child of my marriage to Brigid Brophy should receive no indoctrination comparable to mine, which had been onwards from birth. My wife (herself brought up a pious Christian) totally concurred, though she had scrupulously refrained from trying to influence my views. I then experienced the emotional havoc religion causes, since my decision about his grand-daughter nearly broke my affectionate father's heart. I have always felt how fortunate it was for me that my professional existence at the National Gallery and in London art-historical circles was blessedly secular. There were none of those academic-collegiate, pseudo-religious rituals, involving chapel and "grace," which human academics presumably endure—but should they? I believe that non-believers tend to be too politely passive in these matters, and in quietly conforming British intellectuals are often most at fault. God still gets a respectful nod at official dinner-tables where barely 1% of the diners can seriously suppose that he exists. My idea of a true feast of reason is one without thanks to him but also without the serving up, courtesy of Sainsbury's or Tesco, of once living slaughtered creatures. As I come towards the end of my life I feel the more passionately—yet rationally too, I would assert—that we must stop torturing (in the name of science) and killing (for mere love of it, or greed) the animal kingdom, inclusive of course of birds. Until humanists and rationalists start being humane and rational in treatment of species other than mankind, I shall continue to regard them as, in religious terminology, non-practising, whatever affirmations they may make about wanting to work for a civilised society. All my life I have been accused of absurd optimism, but on this score I feel the most profound and sad pessimism.

{*New Humanist,* March 1997}

Levee, Joseph R. (20th Century)

Levee, founder of thee Cincinnati-area Free Inquiry Group, is a Secular Humanist Mentor of the Council for Secular Humanism. In 1995 he became a member of the Council's board of directors, and in 1998 he became its treasurer. Levee, a fervent activist, is one of the more forward-looking secular humanists. {FD; WAS, conversations}

Levertov, Denise: See the entry for Theism.

Levett, Arthur (20th Century)

Levett, a freethinker, wrote *A Martian Examines Christianity* (1934). {GS}

Levi-Montalcini, Rita (1909—)

Levi-Montalcini, of the Institute of Neurobiology in Italy, won the Nobel Prize in physiology in 1986. She signed Humanist Manifesto 2000.

Levin, Alan (20th Century)

Levin and his wife, **Jane Wong Levin**, a professor at the University of Northern Iowa, are Unitarians. He is President of the American Humanist Association's Humanists of Iowa (2101 Hickory Lane, Cedar Falls, Iowa 50613). Long an activist, Levin also is the group's webmaster. E-mail: <alevin@cfu.net>. Web: <http://humanists.net/iowa>.

Levin, Benjamin H. (20th Century)

A freethinker, Levin wrote *To Spit Against the World* (1970), a novel about Thomas Paine. {GS}

Levin, Harry: See entry for Neo-Classical Humanism.

Levin, S. (20th Century)

Levin, a physician-pediatrician in Johannesburg, South Africa, writes on medical and psychological aspects of biblical and religious issues. He has coined "sinosis," which he defines as "a word I use to label people who suffer, yes, suffer, from a subjective and inchoate feeling of being in sin—not a state of wickedness, but of spiritual taint, blemish, defect, imperfection. This disorder is better known in Christian culture as the inevitable consequence of original sin, that is, Adam's primal disobedience and fall from divinely intended perfection. (In jocular terms we are dealing with Murphy's Flaw.)"

In "The Primal Dream: St. Paul's Vision" (*New Humanist*, February 1996), Levin examines the origins of Christianity, looks at the role of Paul in creating Christianity, and postulates a possible influence of hallucinogens. {"Sinosis," *New Humanist*, March, 1993; "Jewish Atheism," *New Humanist*, May 1995}

Levin, Simon S. (20th Century)

Levin is a freethinker who wrote *Jesus, Alias Christ* (1969). He also wrote *Adam's Rib* (1970), about medicine in the Bible. {GS}

Lévinas, Emmanuel (20th Century)

Lévinas in *Humanisme de l'autre homme* (Humanism of the Other Man, 1972) concerned Jewish humanism and called for an "alter-humanism."

Levine, Hermon M. (20th Century)

Levine's *The Naked Emperor* was published in Mexico in the 1970s. {GS}

Levine, Jack (1915–)

Levine, an American painter whose works treat social themes in a bitter, satirical vein, stated in 1953 that one of his paintings, "The Magician," expressed his fundamental opposition to anything which intellectually deludes large numbers of people. The painting appears to excoriate a world which, he held, is still deceived by magic. That magic might be superstition, fear, or political double-talk. Or it might be the abracadabra of spokesmen for fashionable art movements. In 1992, he responded to the present author about humanism:

> Writing is not my trade and I must take care that your question may not become obsessive and usurp my remaining years away from the easel. Many years ago I tended to use the term humanism in the sense of a predisposition towards the human image, as that approach which makes man the center of a work of art. This, most particularly, as a position countering abstractionism, concretism, and the like. A feeling grew on me that I was misusing the term and a term is all that it is. I now understand it as that new understanding of man in the universe which gave birth to the Renaissance, nearly overthrew church theology, and gave the arts a command of empirical phenomena that had not existed before (or since). All the above without once looking it up in the dictionary! I don't know where I stand in relation to the word and its meaning. Somewhere near, I hope.

Levine is a member of the American Academy of Arts and Letters. {WAS, 14 June 1992}

Levy, Ben (20th Century)

David Tribe has described Levy as an outright freethinker. (TRI)

Levy, Gabor (1914-1999)

A chemist who wrote editorials on humanistic morality as a consulting editor of *American Laboratory*, Levy in a last article wrote, "There is no Devil to blame, and no Supreme Power to forgive. . . . You must accept that there is no particular meaning or purpose to existence. {*Washline*, November 1999}

Levy, Irving (20th Century)

Levy, who assisted in the 1958 formation of the New York Chapter of the Rationalist Press Association, was a freethinker. To the New York City 42nd Street Library, he contributed an extensive collection of atheistic, agnostic, and freethought materials. The chapter's bulletin quoted his definition of a true rationalist as being one "who has divorced himself from supernatural beliefs and prevailing theologies." {FUK; FUS}

Levy, Janey (20th Century)

Levy, an art historian, has written for *Free Inquiry*.

Levy, J. H. (1838–1913)

Levy, writing in *National Reformer* as "Dialecticus," taught political economy at the City of London College. He became a regular contributor on politics, economics, ethics, psychology, philosophy, and religion. Levy was an anti-vaccinator and an anti-vivisectionist, activities related to his belief in individualism. He founded the Political Economy Circle of the National Liberal Club. {RAT; RSR}

Levy, Judith Anne Winstanley (1934–)

Levy is an Australian humanist and a politician. In 1986 she became the first woman to be president of any Australian legislature. Since 1975, she has been a member of the Legislative Council of South Australia. Since 1960 Levy has been a patron of the Humanist Society of South Australia. In 1986 she was named Humanist of the Year. {SWW}

Levy, Leonard W. (1923–)

Levy is author of *Blasphemy: Verbal Offense Against the Sacred, From Moses to Salman Rushdie* (1993), a massive history of blasphemy from ancient to modern times. He also wrote *Treason Against God* (1981). Levy is a scholar of Constitutional history. "At the time of the American Revolution," Levy wrote, "perhaps only four percent of the population belonged to churches." {*Freethought History #13*, 1995}

Lévy-Bruhl, Lucien (1857–1939)

A French writer, Lévy-Bruhl was a professor of literature at the Sorbonne and lecturer at the *École Libre des Sciences Politiques*. He edited *Letters of J. S. Mill to Comte* (1899). Although not a positivist, he was described by F. Harrison: "[N]o one abroad or at home has so truly grasped the assimilated Comte's ideas" as Lévy-Bruhl had done. {RAT}

Lewes, George Henry (1817–1878)

George Eliot had Lewes as her devoted companion for twenty-five years and, although he was a considerable writer in his own right, he has been described as being the main inspirer of her creative work. Lewes was one of the first to introduce English writers to the positivism of Auguste Comte and the evolutionism of Spencer and Darwin. Lewes was a close friend of G. J. Holyoake. In addition to being one of the founders of the *Leader*, he wrote about Aristotle and Goethe. A recent biography of the thoroughgoing empiricist is *G. H. Lewes: A Life* (1992) by Rosemary Ashton. {BDF; CE; FUK; RAT; RE; TRI}

Lewis, Arthur M. (20th Century)

Lewis is a freethinker who wrote *The Struggle Between Science and Superstition* (1934). {GS; FUS}

Lewis, Clarence Irving (1883–1964)

Lewis, a philosopher, combined symbolic logic with an essentially pragmatic epistemology. In opposition to the *Principia Mathematica* of Bertrand Russell and Alfred North Whitehead, Lewis developed his own system. In *Mind and the World-Order* (1929), he developed a position according to which the choice between logical (and thus philosophical) systems must be based on pragmatic grounds. Asked about humanism, Lewis responded to the present author:

> Classification sometimes involves over-simplification. I could not classify myself with those mentioned under any of your seven heads without disregarding some points, important to me, on which I would differ from each.
>
> {CE; WAS, 2 August 1954}

Lewis, C. Day (1904-1972): See entry for George Orwell, who considered the poet "not now completely reliable" because of his former membership in the Communist Party.

Lewis, C(larence) S(taples) (1898–1963)

A distinguished literary scholar, Lewis was a fellow of Magdalen College, Oxford, 1925–1954. Afterwards he was professor of Medieval and Renaissance English at Cambridge. His science fiction novels, such as *Out of the Silent Planet* (1938), contain obvious Christian overtones. His popular religious and moral writing included *The Problems of Pain* (1940), *The Screwtape Letters* (1940), and *The Four Loves* (1960). His spiritual autobiography is *Surprised by Joy* (1955). Lewis's close friend and intellectual sparring partner was Owen Barfield, a writer and philosopher of language. The two loved to hike, calling themselves "cretaceous perambulators." The two were key members of the Inklings, a group of Oxford intellectuals. It was Barfield who is credited with Lewis's celebrated transition from atheism to Christianity. {Sarah Lyall, *The New York Times*, 20 December 1997}

Lewis, H. H. (1901–1985)

A Missourian, Lewis wrote poetry which caught the attention of William Carlos Williams and others. A sampling of his freethought poetry, originally published in *New Masses*, can be found in Whitehead and Muhrer's *Freethought on the American Frontier* (1992).

Lewis, James R. (20th Century)

Lewis, chairman of the Department of Religious Studies at the World University of America, edited *The Encyclopedia of Cults, Sects, and New Religions* (1998). Included are references to the Branch Davidians; the Church of Scientology; the Church of Satan; Society for Krishna Consciousness; Heaven's Gate; the Solar Temple; the Church of All Worlds; Church of Jesus Christ at Armageddon; the Covenant, the Sword, and the Arm of the Lord; Commandment Keepers Congregation of the Living god; Church of the psychedelic Mystic; and the Nudist Christian Church of the Blessed Virgin Jesus.

Lewis, Joseph (1889–1968)

A major representative of atheistic thought, and a publisher of atheist and sex-education books, Lewis as a young person read Ingersoll and Paine. He was elected president of Freethinkers of America, which had first been organized in 1915. *The Bible Unmasked* (1926) was considered one of the most shocking books of the day. Obsessed by Paine, he called his freethought publication *Age of Reason* and arranged for statues of Paine to be placed in Paris; in Morristown, New Jersey; and at Thetford, England, in front of Paine's birthplace. His activism included trying to have the phrase "under God" stricken from the Pledge of Allegiance; protesting government celebrations of Thanksgiving; objecting to the annual Christmas stamps sold by the Post Office; and arguing against public-school children's "released time" for religious study.

In the Name of Humanity (1956) argued against the practice of circumcision. His Eugenics Publishing Co. published books on sexology which were inexpensive and generally unavailable elsewhere, and he distributed a book banned for many years in the United States, Marie Stopes's *Married Love.* Lewis easily was one of the better known atheists of his era. {EU, William F. Ryan; FUS; TRI}

Lewis, Michael (20th Century)

Lewis wrote *Liar's Poker* about his experiences as a bond trader on Wall Street. A senior editor of *New Republic*, he wrote in that publication (8 November 1993),

> Several months ago, I received a letter from the Bishop of Durham in England inviting me to participate in a public debate about God and religion. . . . I wrote back to say that God wasn't my line of work: that I did not believe in him, that I thought the church had done more harm than good.

As a journalist covering the 1996 Republican presidential primary campaign, he went to the First Annual Black Pro-Life Unity Conference in order to meet candidate Alan Keyes. While sitting at a table with two pastors who were Keyes's supporters,

> . . . it isn't five minutes before I am forced to admit that I am an atheist. The news is met as it always is: tell a Christian that you are an atheist, and he invariably responds with the uncomfortable smile of a man who thinks a joke is being played on him.
>
> {CA; E; *New Republic*, 8 July 1996; YD}

Lewis, Naomi (20th Century)

An English critic, Lewis attended the festive launch for Bradlaugh House in 1994. She is author of *The Emperor's New Clothes* (1997).

Lewis, Sinclair (1885–1951)

Lewis was a leading Midwestern author and Nobel Prize winner in literature. He wrote *Main Street* (1920), *Babbitt* (1922—originally, he had intended *Pumphrey* as the title), *Arrowsmith* (1925), and *Elmer Gantry* (1927), the last of which was a freethinking critique of the clergy. Will Durant's *On the Meaning of Life* (1932) quotes Lewis as having said, "It is, I think, an error to believe that there is any need of religion to make life seem worth living." In *Elmer Gantry,* Lewis used Birkhead as his technical advisor concerning ecclesiastical matters. What the novel turned out to be was a scathing satire of a Baptist-Methodist minister who changed into a voluptuous hypocrite, remarkably resembling most of the professing Christians in his congregation—a humanistic comment on the state of affairs of contemporary organized religion.

Lewis had long lambasted humanity for being what it is, rather than what it might be, as shown in *Main Street* and *Babbitt. Kingsblood Royal* (1947) is a powerful indictment of man for his cruel injustice to fellow men, another popular humanistic theme.

Of *Main Street*, H. L. Mencken wrote to George Jean Nathan: "Grab hold of the bar-rail, steady shock! I've just read the advance sheets of the book of that *Lump* (Nathan had described Lewis as "a tall, skinny, paprika-headed stranger") we met at Schmidt's and, by God, he has done the job! It's a genuinely excellent piece of work. Get it as soon as you can and take a look. I begin to believe that perhaps there isn't a God after all." The novel was inscribed to his first wife, born Grace Livingstone Hegger: "To Gracie [Lewis], who is all the good part of Carol," a reference to the work's heroine, Carol Kennicott.

When asked specifically about humanism just before his death, he wrote the present author:

> Just back from Italy. I find your letter. Yes, I think naturalistic humanism—with dislike for verbalistic philosophy—is my category.
>
> [Shown the postcard, Harrison Smith of *The Saturday Review of Literature* wrote that he had not known that while in Kansas City during the *Elmer Gantry* period, Lewis had accepted Unitarian minister Rev. L. M. Birkhead's offer to speak to some assembled Unitarians.

Lewis looked out over the pews and exclaimed, "Now if God exists, I'll give him exactly two minutes to prove it—to strike me dead!" Most of those present probably did not expect heavenly flashes of lightning to challenge his dare and, of course, he was applauded when the building remained intact. "Well, that settles that," he told those in the audience. Harrison Smith responded, "I did not know that he had labeled himself a humanist, a mild term for an angry crusader." But Smith promised to publicize the information. . . . Lewis may or may not have known the story that Charles Bradlaugh had done the same decades previously, giving God all of five minutes. George Bernard Shaw thought such a story fit Bradlaugh's character and was amused, adding if God *had* struck Bradlaugh dead it would prove "He is a savagely violent and vindictive idol like Blake's Nobodaddy."]

Lewis was elected to the American Academy's Institute in 1922, despite his scathing portrait of small-town America in *Main Street* and the resultant negative publicity. However, he politely declined. In 1930, he won the Nobel Prize, and during his acceptance speech he lambasted the American Academy, charging "It represents only Henry Wadsworth Longfellow" and naming twenty-one writers he considered were more deserving than members who were then in the Academy. He also attacked the "New Humanism" of Irving Babbitt, saying, "Of course *humanism* means so many things that it means nothing."

Lewis, on his deathbed, reportedly said to the Catholic nurse, "God bless you," leading to speculation that he had had "a death-bed conversion." But columnist Dorothy Thompson, once his wife, unequivocally denied such had taken place, and she cited such evidence as the above 3 June 1950 postcard. Lewis had been raised a Christian, she held, but became a non-believer after his sophomore year at Yale. (See entry for H. L. Mencken, who comments about Dorothy Thompson.) {CE; CL; EU, William F. Ryan; FUS; HNS; JM; RE; TRI; WAS, 3 June 1950—postcard was stolen and its whereabouts are unknown.}

Lewis, Stephen: See entry for Isabella Grigoroff concerning Lewis, who was Canada's former Ambassador to the United Nations.

Lewis, Teresa (19th Century)

Lewis wrote *Cremation* (c. 1875) at a time when the subject was quite unpopular. {GS}

LEWISHAM HUMANIST GROUP (England)

The Lewisham Humanist Group has discussions at the Unitarian Meeting House, 41 Bromley Road, Catford, London SE6.

Leyds, Willem Johannes (1859–1970)

Leyds, who was born in Java and educated at Amsterdam University, went to South Africa where in 1893 he became Secretary of State. In 1897 he came to Europe as representative of the Transvaal. A rationalist , he wrote a number of works on law and on South African history. {RAT}

Leykis, Tom (1956–)

A nationally syndicated talk-show host and radio director, Leykis has openly discussed his atheism while on the radio. "I'm an atheist. I don't subscribe to a belief in any god or deity," he has broadcast. A moderate who belongs to no political party, he bashes all sides when he feels they do something stupid. He has been associated with WBAI Radio and WABC Radio in New York City; WNWS Radio in Miami, Florida; WQBK Radio in Albany, New York; and KFYI Radio in Phoenix, Arizona. {CA; E}

Li Hung-chang (1823–1901)

A Chinese statesman and general, Li was viceroy of the capital province of Zhili (1870–1895) and controlled Chinese foreign affairs for the dowager empress Tz'u Hsi. During the Boxer Uprising (1900), he protected foreigners and was able to reduce the demands of the foreign powers for reparations. The British inventor Sir Hiram Stevens Maxim, who knew him, said Li was a disdainful atheist. {CE; JM}

Li, Virginia (20th Century)

Li, who is a professor of community health sciences at the University of California at Los Angeles School of Public Health, signed Humanist Manifesto 2000.

Li, Youzheng (20th Century)

Li, who is in the Institute of Philosophy, CASS, in Beijing, China, signed Humanist Manifesto 2000.

LIBERAL ARTS

In a college or university, the liberal arts are the areas of learning that cultivate general intellectual ability rather than technical or professional skills. The phrase is often used as a synonym for the humanities, although the liberal arts also include the sciences, languages, literature, history, philosophy, and mathematics. *Liberalis* in Latin means "suitable for a free man," as opposed to a slave, which liberals enjoy pointing out. {DCL}

Liberman, Norman (20th Century)

Liberman in 1972 was on the advisory board of the Humanist Society of Greater New York.

LIBERO PENSIERO

An Italian humanistic publication, *Libero Pensiero* is at 11 via Consolata, 10122 TO, Torino, Italy. <roberto.laferla@agora.stm.it>.

LIBERTARIANISM

A libertarian advocates the doctrine of free will and believes in absolute and unrestricted liberty, particularly of thought and action. Ayn Rand disavowed any connection, calling libertarians "hippies of the right."

LIBERATION THEOLOGY

Liberation theology, which is found particularly in the Roman Catholic Church in Latin America, emphasizes a Gospel call to free people from political, social, and material oppression. Among the leaders in liberation theology are Gustavo Gutierrez, Leonardo Boff, and Juan Luis Segundo. Richard McAfee Brown, a Christian theologian who taught at Pacific School of Religion, wrote *Liberation Theology and Its Critics*. Books in Spanish include some by José Miguel Bonino, an Argentinean Evangelical Methodist; and Tissa Balaysuriya, a Catholic priest.

LIBERTINAGE

Libertinage refers to freethinkers, or libertinism in religion. The word was coined in 1616 by theologians and continues to be used mainly by theologians.

LIBERTY

• The secret of liberty is courage.

–Pericles

Isaiah Berlin's view was that liberty essentially means that "I am not prevented by other persons from doing what I want." {*The Economist*, 13 June 1998}

LIBERTY

Liberty, an English quarterly of The Principality Publishers, is at PO Box 918, Cardiff CF2 4YP, United Kingdom.

LIBRARIES

A collection of clay tablets in Babylonia (21st century B.C.E.) is evidence of mankind's early interest in conserving information. The Ancient Egyptian temple libraries were described by Greek writers such as Diodorus Siculus, who wrote about the library of Ramses III (c. 1200 B.C.E.). In Ninevah the library of Assurbanipal (died 626 B.C.E.?) was the most noted before that of Alexandria, which was conceived by Ptolemy I (c. 306 B.C.E.). Alexandria became the center of scholarship, attracting Euclid and Archimedes and its library may well have achieved its goal of amassing a copy of every known book under a single roof, according to Douglas Jehl (*The New York Times*, 6 November 1999).

The Vatican Library—Platina was its first librarian—is the oldest public library in Europe. The Library of Congress in Washington, D.C., had as its prime mover Thomas Jefferson, who contributed his own library to Congress after the library burned in 1814. Among the chief modern libraries are the

Bibliothèque Nationale and the Mazarine in Paris; the British Museum, London; the Bodleian Library, Oxford; the Ambrosian Library, Milan; the Laurentian, Florence; the Lenin Library, Moscow; the Huntington Library, San Marison, California; the New York Public Library; and university libraries throughout the world.

The Bibliotheca Alexandrina, which will open in 2000, has been designed by a Norwegian firm and will have space for four million works, a French-designed computerized catalog, and five hundred built-in Internet ports. It represents the largest and most advanced in the Arab world.

Licher, Lloyd (20th Century)

Licher is active with the Secular Humanists of Marin and has written "A Test To Determine If You Are You Humanist." (See entry for California Atheists, Humanists.) {FD}

Lichtenberg, Georg Christoph (1742–1799)

Lichtenberg was a German satirical writer and scientist, a friend of G. Forster. He was a freethinker whose work showed his advanced opinions. "There is," he wrote in *Aphorisms*, "a sort of transcendental ventriloquy through which men can be made to believe that something which was said on earth came from heaven." {BDF; TYD}

Lichtenberger, Henri (1864–1941)

Lichtenberger, a French writer, followed the rationalism of Nietzsche, writing *La philosophie de Nietzsche*. He also wrote on Heine and on Wagner. {RAT}

Lick, James (1796–1876)

A freethinker, Lick is known as the individual who helped finance the Lick Observatory at Mt. Hamilton, California. A wealthy former piano maker, a flour miller, a political scientist, atheist, and materialist, Lick wrote *On Civil Liberty and Self Government* (1853). During the Civil War, he advised the U.S. Government about military law. {BDF; CE; GS; JM; PUT; RAT; RE}

Lidforss, Bengt (1868–1913)

Linforss, a Swedish botanist, was a non-theist. (See entry for Scandinavian Unbelievers.)

Lieberman, Jerome (20th Century)

At the 1999 convention of Humanists of Florida, Lieberman co-led a think tank discussion on "How and Why Humanists of Florida Should Lead the Banner of Humanism."

Liebknecht, Karl (1871–1919)

A German socialist and leader of the Spartacus Party, Liebknecht was an extreme left-wing member of the Social Democratic party, refusing to support the government during World War I. He and Rosa Luxemburg formed the Internationale, a revolutionary, antiwar socialist group.

The Spartacus Party became the German Communist party, and when in 1919 Liebknecht led an uprising against the government he was arrested and killed while being taken to prison. Liebknecht was an atheist and a materialist. In 1995, on the seventy-sixth anniversary of his death, legions of Berliners marched through eastern Berlin to honor his memory. {CE; JM; JMR; RAT}

Liebling, A. J. (1904-1963): See entry for George Orwell, who considered the *New Yorker* author a possible fellow traveler of the Communist Party in the 1940s.

Liénard, Georges (20th Century)

Liénard, vice president of the *Centre d'Action Laïque* in Belgium, spoke at the 1993 Congress of the European Humanist Federation in Berlin. He finds two opposing ways of approaching humanism. There is the idea of the secular—but the communist secular state has discredited that. Humanism cannot be represented as purely secularism, he explained, because it implies tolerance and democracy.

He represented the International Humanist and Ethical Union (IHEU) and the European Humanist Federation (EHF) at a 1997 International Symposium on Bio-Ethics, organized by the Council of Europe, and also one in 1998. (See entry for Belgian Humanists.)

Liening, John H. (Born 1818)

The son of a great-grandfather who had been a soldier in the Thirty Years' war, Liening emigrated from Germany to the United States when he was fourteen. Although educated as a Catholic, Liening became an atheist. When the war broke out, he enlisted and became a second lieutenant. Liening retired in California. {PUT}

LIES

A lie is an untrue statement that is made with the intent to deceive. An individual, for example, who claims to have spoken to God is, from a rationalist's viewpoint, a liar. In *Psalms* 116, it is written,

> I love the Lord, because he hath heard my voice and my supplications. Because he hath inclined his ear unto me, therefore will I call upon him as long as I live.

and

> I believed, therefore have I spoken: I was greatly afflicted: I said in my haste, All men are liars . . . etc.

Rationalists find amusing that "he hath inclined his ear [sic] unto me." They ask if the writer was telling the truth or telling a lie when he said, "All men are liars." Or in another context, when the Cretan said, "All Cretans are liars," was he being truthful or was *he* lying?

Lying is universal. The American judicial system presumes innocence until guilt beyond a reasonable doubt is proven, leading cynics to observe that guilty parties are practically required to plead "not guilty" when they stand before a judge and jury.

Freethinkers, knowing that children lie because they fear punishment, attempt to teach that many people make mistakes and do things they later are ashmaed of; but in telling the truth and admitting one's shame it is easier to avoid further lies. President George Washington, they are told by parents who know they are lying, could not tell a lie.

A case can be made that sometimes lies are permissible. Asked how he would respond in court if asked how old he is, the famed black baseball pitcher replied, "The goat ate the Bible with my birth certificate. That goat lived to be twenty-seven."

Children, however, find it difficult to understand why President Eisenhower lied about a U-2 spy plane that erroneously flew over the USSR; why President John F. Kennedy lied to his staff about the Bay of Pigs invasion in which numbers of Cuban patriots died; why President Lyndon B. Johnson lied about an American patrol boat's attack in the Bay of Tonkin, in which over forty thousand Americans lost their lives as did untold numbers of South Vietnames soldiers and civilians; why President Richard Nixon lied about the Watergate scandal, which involved abuse of power by public officials, violation of the public trust, contempt of Congress, and attempted obstruction of justice; why President William Jefferson Clinton lied about not having sex "with that woman," Monica Lewinsky, in the White House.

LIFE

• In the great game of human life one begins by being a dupe and ends by being a rogue.

–Voltaire

• Life is a hospital in which every patient is possessed by the desire of changing his bed. One would prefer to suffer near the fire, and another is certain he would get well if he were by the window.

–Charles Baudelaire

• Life does not cease to be funny when people die any more than it ceases to be serious when people laugh.

–George Bernard Shaw

• Why shouldn't things be largely absurd, futile, and transitory? They are so, and we are so, and they and we go very well together.

–George Santayana

• Life is a predicament which precedes death.

–Henry James

• Human life is a flash of occasional enjoyments lighting up a mass of pain and misery, a bagatelle of transient experience.

–Alfred North Whitehead

• The first half of our life is ruined by our parents, and the second half by our children.

–Clarence Darrow

• There are few things easier than to live badly and die well.

–Oscar Wilde

• The meaning of life is that it stops.

–Franz Kafka

• Life is a God-damned, stinking, treacherous game and nine hundred and ninety-nine men out of a thousand are bastards.

–Theodore Dreiser

• Life can little else supply
But a few good fucks and then we die.

–John Wilkes

• Life is divided into the horrible and the miserable.

–Woody Allen

LIFE AND EDUCATION IN FINLAND

A Finnish humanistic journal in English, *Life and Education in Finland,* is at Museokatu 18 A 2, 00100, Helsinki, Finland.

LIFE STANCE

"Life stance," a coinage in the 1970s and cited often by Harry Stopes-Roe, has been defined as follows:

> A life stance is an individual's (or a community's) relationship with what they accept as of ultimate importance, and the theory and practice of this in everyday living.

Jane Wynne Willson, who was a co-President of the International Humanist and Ethical Union, has commented, "The function of the term 'life stance' is to encompass both theistic and non-theistic positions without favouring one more than the other. Christianity (for example) is a theistic life stance; humanism (for example) is a non-theistic life stance. God is what is of ultimate importance to theists; the natural world and the people in it are what is of ultimate importance to humanists." (See entries for Harry Stopes-Roe and Nicolas Walter.) {*New Humanist*, February 1996}

LIFELINE: See entry for Long Distance Telephone Service.

Lightman, Bernard (1950)

Lightman, a believer and an associate professor of humanities at York University in Canada, is author of *The Origin of Agnosticism* (1987) and *Victorian Faith in Crisis* (1990). {GS}

Lightner, A. M. (20th Century): According to the American Library Association's *Banned Books* (1998), Lightner's *Gods or Demons?* "promotes a secular-humanistic belief in evolution and portrays the 'Bible as myth.' " (See entry for Banned Books.)

LIGUE FRANÇAISE DE L'ENSEIGNEMENT ET DE L'EDUCATION PERMANENTE

A specialist member of the IHEU is the *Ligue Française de l'Enseignement et de l'Education Permanente* at 3, Rue Récamier, 75341 Paris Cedex 07, France.

Lilienfeld, Paul von (1829–1903)

In 1867 Lilienfeld was appointed Vice-Governor of Petrograd. In 1885 he became Governor of Courland and Senator. Lilienfeld was one of the leaders of "organistic" sociology. Although he rejected supernatural claims and did not admit personal immortality, Lilienfeld was a theist who had an ethical regard for Christianity. {RAT}

Lilienthal, Alfred M. (20th Century)

Lilienthal is author of *The Zionist Connection: What Price Peace?* (1978)

Lilja, Nicolai (1808–1870)

Lilja was a Swedish writer who became parish clerk in the Lund diocese. He wrote *Man: His Life and Destiny.* {BDF}

Lima, Sebastião de Magalhaes (Born 1850)

An outstanding figure in Portuguese rationalism, Lima published *Priests and Kings* and *The Pope Before the World,* both of which were considered offensive by the clericalists. An enthusiastic republican and pacifist—he wrote *O livro da Paz,* 1896)—Lima published a Lisbon daily, *O Vanguarda,* which was often suspended before the Revolution. Lima is credited with helping Portugal obtain disestablishment of the church at the time of the Revolution. {RAT}

LIMBO

Limbo is a theological invention. In Roman Catholic theology, Limbo is located on the border (*limbus,* Latin for border) of Hell, and it is a place where "souls" remain that cannot enter. It has two parts: (a) the limbo of the Fathers—a place and state of rest wherein the souls of the just who died before Christ's ascension were detained until He re-opened Heaven to them, hitherto closed in consequence of Adam's fall; and (b) the limbo of the children—containing all children or adults who die without the baptism of water, blood, or desire and therefore in a state of original sin. St. Augustine taught that such children and unbaptized adults as are free from grievous actual sin eternally enjoyed a state of perfect natural happiness, knowing and loving God by the use of their natural powers, explained Joseph F. Thorning, who taught ethics in Mount St. Mary's Seminary and College, Emmitsburg, Maryland. In short, those in limbo do not suffer damnation, but they do not enjoy "the presence of God." In Limbo, according to Dante, are Socrates, Plato, Homer, Ovid, Horace, Democritus, Zeno, Thales, Anaxogoras, Heraclitus.

For freethinkers and humanists, *limbo* (from *limba,* to bend in Jamaica) is a colorful West Indian dance in which the dancers bend over backward, pass under a pole that is lowered slightly each time, and invite ectomorphic onlookers to join in. (See entry for Dante.) {CE; DCL}

Lin Yutang (1895–1976)

Lin, a Chinese-American, wrote a humanistic work, *The Importance of Living* (1937), which included the following:

> The pagan lives in this world like an orphan, without the benefit of that consoling feeling that there is always some one in heaven who cares and who will, when that spiritual relationship called prayer is established, attend to his private personal welfare. It is no doubt a less cheery world; but there is the benefit and dignity of being an orphan who by necessity has learned to be independent, to take care of himself, and to be more mature, as all orphans are. It was this feeling rather than any intellectual belief—this feeling of dropping into a world without the love of God—that really scared me until the very last moment of my conversion to paganism. I felt, like many born Christians, that if a personal God did not exist the bottom would be knocked out of this universe. . . . Finally my salvation came. "Why," I reasoned with a colleague, "if there were no God, people would not do good and the world would go topsy-turvy." "Why?" replied my Confucian colleague. "We should lead a decent human life simply because we are decent human beings," he said. This appeal to the dignity of human life cut off my last tie to Christianity, and from then I was a pagan. . . . A Chinese writer, Kung Tingan, said: "The Sage himself loved very much to argue! . . . The Sage talks about life, as he is directly aware of it; the Talented Ones talk about the Sage's words and the stupid ones argue about the words of the Talented Ones."

But no philosophy of life is complete, Lin noted, and "no conception of man's spiritual life is adequate, unless we bring ourselves into a satisfactory and harmonious relation with the life of the universe around us. Man is important enough; he is the most important topic of our studies: that is the essence of humanism."

When older, Lin was less favorable toward his earlier views of humanism. Many then no longer found him to be a naturalistic humanist, but the earlier views which led some to call Lin a "laughing humanist" included the following:

> • Religion in our country has so narrowed down to the contemplation of sin that a respectable man does not any longer dare to show his face in the church.

• Man wants to live, but he still must live upon this earth. All questions of living in heaven must be brushed aside. . . . The earth, after all, is real, as the heaven is unreal: how fortunate is man that he is born between the real earth and the unreal heaven!

• I sometimes think what a terrible punishment it would be for a ghost or an angel to have no body, to look at a stream of cool water and have no feet to plunge into it and get a delightful cooling sensation from it, to see a dish of Peking or Long Island duck and have no tongue to taste it, to see crumpets and have no teeth to chew them, to see the beloved faces of our dear ones and have no emotions to feel toward them.

• As for the superfine metaphysician who says that the teeth belong to the devil, and the Neo-Platonists who deny that individual teeth exist, I always get a satirical delight in seeing a philosopher suffering from a tooth-ache and an optimistic poet suffering from dyspepsia.

• So then, instead of holding on to the Biblical view that we are made in the image of God, we come to realize that we are made in the image of the monkey, and that we are as far removed form the perfect God, as, let us say, the ants are removed from ourselves.

• The difference between cannibals and civilized men seems to be that cannibals kill their enemies and eat them, while civilized men kill their foes and bury them, put a cross over their bodies, and offer up prayers for their souls. Thus we add stupidity to conceit and a bad temper.

• The average mind is charming rather than noble. Had the average mind been noble, we should be completely rational beings without sins or weaknesses or misconduct, and what an insipid world that would be! We should be so much less charming as creatures. I am such a Humanist that saints without sins don't interest me.

• There is still a greater philosophy than this naturalism, namely, the philosophy of Humanism. The highest ideal of Chinese thought is therefore a man who does not have to escape from human society and human life in order to preserve the original, happy nature.

• I should not presume that there must be necessarily a purpose, a meaning of human existence. As Walt Whitman says, "I am sufficient as I am." It is sufficient that I live—and am probably going to live for another few decades—and that human life exists. Viewed that way, the problem becomes amazingly simple and admits of no two answers. What can be the end of human life except the enjoyment of it.

• [On immortality]: Deprived of immortality, the proposition of living becomes a simple proposition. It is this: that we human beings have a limited span of life to live on this earth, rarely more than seventy years, and that therefore we have to arrange our lives so that we may live as happily as we can under a given set of circumstances.

• [On Adam]: If the writer of the Genesis story had been a Paoyü and knew what he was talking about, he would have written a different story. God took a handful of mud, molded it into human shape and breathed into its nostrils a breath, and there was Adam. But Adam began to crack and fall to pieces, and so He took some water, and with the water He molded the clay, and this water which entered into Adam's being was called Eve, and only in having Eve in his being was Adam's life complete. At least that seems to me to be the symbolic significance of marriage. Woman is water and man is clay, and water permeates and molds the clay, and the clay holds the water and gives it substance, in which water moves and lives and has its full being.

• [On food}: Our lives are not in the lap of the gods, but in the lap of our cooks. . . . Eventually we have to come to a conception of health and disease by which . . . men eat in order to prevent disease instead of taking medicine in order to cure it.

• [On writing]: The technique of writing is to literature as dogmas are to the church—the occupation with trivial things by trivial minds.

• [On Man]: So many people presume to know God and what God disapproves that it is impossible to take up this subject without opening oneself to attack as sacrilegious by some and as a prophet by others. We human creatures who individually are less than a billionth part of the earth's crust, which is less than a billionth part of the great universe, presume to know God! Yet no philosophy of life is complete, no conception of man's spiritual life is adquate, unless we bring ourselves into a satisfactory and harmonious relation with the life of the universe around us. Man is important enough; he is the most important topic of our studies: that is the essence of humanism!

[See entry for Laughing Humanists.) {CE; Warren Allen Smith, "Two Laughing Humanists: Lin Yutang, Carl Jonas," *Humanist World Digest*, August 1955}

Lin Zixin (20th Century)

Lin Zixin from China addressed the Tenth International Humanist and Ethical Union (IHEU) World Congress held in Buffalo (1988).

Lincoln, Abraham [President] (1809–1865)

President Lincoln's biographer, Douglas L. Wilson, found some rare details about the private man innumerable previous writers had not described. In *Honor's Voice: The Transformation of Abraham Lincoln* (1998), Wilson tells of Lincoln's having been raised a Baptist who never outgrew a sense of fatalism, even "a nameless sense of . . . doom." But upon reading a Paine work in which "a young woman engaged to be married, and while under this engagement she is, to speak plain language, debauched by a ghost," Lincoln developed a new take on the Virgin Mary.

Was Lincoln a religious man, or was he not? Each generation appears to reinvent Lincoln in its own image. Robert Ingersoll adulated our 16th President, and Ingersoll's granddaughter's husband, Sherman Wakefield, insisted that Lincoln was not "religious." In 1889, Wheeler quoted Lincoln's friend, Ward H. Lamon, as saying, "Lincoln read Volney and Paine and then wrote a deliberate and labored essay, wherein he reached conclusions similar to theirs. The essay was burnt, but he never denied or regretted its composition." Others, however, have called him a mystic. Lincoln himself wrote, "There was the strangest combination of church influence against me because I belonged to no church. Both northern and southern Christians read the same Bible and pray to the same God, and each invokes aid against the other." As a young man, Lincoln had the reputation of being an outspoken non-believer who read Thomas Paine, one who argued with friends against the tenets of organized religion. In his 1846 Congressional campaign, he found it necessary to say (in his high squeaky voice), "That I am not a member of any Christian Church is true, but I have never denied the truth of the Scriptures, and I have never spoken with intentional disrespect of religion in general or of any denomination of Christians in particular."

Some evidence exists, claims Michael R. Beschloss in *The New Yorker* (28 February 1994), that Lincoln's maternal grandmother was illegitimate and even that Lincoln was sired by someone other than his father of record. "The President's former law partner and eventual biographer, William H. Herndon, interviewed dozens of Kentuckians who had known the Lincoln family, and he became convinced that Thomas Lincoln was sterile and could not have been Abraham's father," Beschloss wrote. "As early as the eighteen-seventies, there was speculation that Lincoln's father had actually been, ironically, John C. Calhoun, the champion of states' rights, or perhaps even Samuel Davis, the father of the President of the Confederacy."

In *Lincoln at Gettysburg, The Words That Remade America*, Garry Wills terms Lincoln a Transcendentalist. At Gettysburg, Lincoln and

Edward Everett had been chosen to give an "Oration" and "Dedicatory Remarks" on the field where so many warriors had fallen. Everett, a transcendentalist trained in the classics in Germany and a professor of Greek at Harvard, orated for two hours. Lincoln followed with a 272-word address which, although he had never studied with Everett, attained a classical Greek *epitaphios* with its two essential and Periclean sections: *epainesis*, or praise for the fallen; and *parainesis*, or advice for the living. Remarked Wills, calling it the greatest of all political speeches, "The address does what all great art accomplishes. Like Keats's Grecian urn, it 'tease[s] us out of thought / As doth eternity.' " Lincoln was a member of no church, but he is called by Wills "a Transcendentalist without the fuzziness," one who drew on a shared philosophic tradition which Everett also honored. Lincoln's law partner, John T. Stuart, however, said "Lincoln was an avowed and open infidel whose beliefs sometimes bordered on atheism. . . . [He] went further against Christian beliefs . . . than any man I ever heard."

Another biographer, William Barton, has written, "Was Lincoln a Unitarian?" No, he knew the view of certain Unitarians, and these assisted him at important points in defining certain aspects of his faith. The Unitarian books which Mr. Lincoln read cursorily, the books by Parker and Channing, must have assisted him in this, but they gave assurance that there were forward-looking men who believed in God and in human freedom as he did, and who were quite as far from holding the teaching which he had taught to call orthodox as he was, yet who were not infidels, but counted themselves friends of God and disciples of Jesus." Barton also wrote, "Herndon asserts that Lincoln habitually spoke in his presence in terms of denial of the supernatural birth of Jesus. On a book of Lincoln's he had changed *John* 16:27 from 'Ye have loved me, and have believed that I came from God' to 'from nature.' "

Unitarians often do not realize that Lincoln's Vice President, Hannibal Hamlin, was a Unitarian—whether the two ever talked about their views is unknown.

McCabe cites the various authorities about Lincoln's religion: "As in the case of Washington, the evidence on the side of the angels is strained or tainted while there is ample evidence that he was at the most a deist. His partner and intimate friend [William H. Herndon] affirms it and quotes the support of Mrs. Lincoln in his life of the President. Colonel Lamon, another close friend who has written on him, says emphatically, 'He was not a Christian.' General Collis, the chief claimant of orthodoxy, can say no more than that he attended a church (which is a common ailment of politicians) and spoke about God (as, of course, every deist does). Rankin, the second principal claimant of orthodoxy, mainly relies on an old woman's recollection of a conversation with Lincoln. The most impartial biographer, C. G. Leland, says that 'as he grew older his intense melancholy and his emotional temperament inclined him towards reliance on an unseen Power and belief in a future state'—which is not far from agnosticism—and suggests that there is some political tinge in his public references to the deity. It is the way of all political flesh."

Still another biographer, Herbert Donald in *Lincoln* (1995), grants that Lincoln had early doubts about religion and that he wrote "in early life I was inclined to believe in what I understand is called the 'Doctrine of Necessity'—that is, that the human mind is impelled to action, or held in rest by some power, over which the mind itself has no control." But as Lincoln experienced war, by his Second Inaugural Address he—who had said that he "couldn't cut the head off of a chicken" and got sick "sick at the sight of blood"—turned to the Bible and theology for some justification of the need to lead the North in the killing of fellow Americans. He expressed the belief that "if God now wills the removal of a great wrong," then "the judgements of the Lord are true and righteous altogether."

Did Lincoln believe in racial equality? *The People's Almanac* (1975) responds: "Never a believer in true racial equality, Lincoln moved to free the slaves only after the overwhelming majority of his party had demanded it. Unlike the so-called 'Radical Republicans,' Lincoln never considered the possibility that the freed Negroes might some day function as full-fledged American citizens. Lincoln favored colonization in Central America as the 'final solution' to the Negro problem." On the one hand, as he wrote to Horace Greeley in 1862, "My paramount object in this struggle is to save the Union, and is not either to save or to destroy slavery. If I could save the Union without freeing any slave, I would do it; and if I could do it by freeing all the slaves, I would do it; and if I could save it by freeing some and leaving others alone, I would also do that." On the other hand, in an 1855 letter to Joshua F. Speed, he wrote, "How can any one who abhors the oppression of the Negroes be in favor of degrading classes of white people? Our progress in degeneracy appears to me to be pretty rapid. As a nation we began by declaring that 'All men are created equal.' We now practically read it 'All men are created equal, except Negroes.' When the Know-Nothings get control, it will read 'All are created equal, except Negroes and foreigners and Catholics.' When it comes to this, I shall prefer emigrating to some country where they make no pretense of loving liberty—to Russia, for instance, where despotism can be taken pure, and without the base alloy of hypocrisy."

Was Lincoln gay? Playwright Larry Kramer once asked novelist Gore Vidal why in his study, *Lincoln*, he had not included Lincoln's relationship with Joshua Fry Speed, which historian Jonathan Katz claims was a gay friendship. Vidal replied, "Well, I wasn't writing about that era of his life. It seems fairly obvious that he had this very close male relationship." Kramer proceeded to promise that he would write about "Abe's sleeping side by side in a double bed with another man every night for four years." What is known is that the lanky twenty-eight-year-old lawyer did not have enough money to buy bedding from Speed, a twenty-three-year-old merchant, who told Lincoln, "I have a large room with a double bed upstairs, which you are very welcome to share with me." For the next several years, the two men shared the Springfield, Illinois, bed. Kramer gave a speech in Wisconsin (*Advocate*, 30 March 1999) in which he previewed part of his forthcoming book, *The American People*. Quoting from diaries and letters of Joshua Speed, Kramer found such tidbits as "He often kisses me when I tease him, often to shut me up. He would grab me up by his long arms and hug and hug. Yes, our Abe is like a schoolgirl."

Eight people shared the one-room log cabin after Lincoln's mother died. During his lifetime and because of the lack of space and beds in many homes, it was not atypical for males to sleep in the same bed. Speed then moved home to Kentucky, marrying Fanny Henning a year later. A year following that, Lincoln married Mary Ann Todd. Martin Duberman, of the Graduate Center of the City University of New York, has cautioned that it is "irresponsible to quickly label someone from the past 'gay' or 'lesbian' unless we have very concrete evidence of genital activity and probably a romantic connection . . . and we almost never do."

As a young man, Lincoln was said to have enjoyed telling stories with sexual overtones and about beds. Wilson's *Honor's Voice* (1998) cites one such:

> Once when Mr. L. was surveying, he was put to bed in the same room with two girls, the head of his bed being next to the foot of the girls' bed. In the night he commenced tickling the feet of one of the girls with his fingers. As she seemed to enjoy it as much as he did he then tickled a little higher up; and as he would tickle higher the girl would shove down lower and the higher he tickled the lower she moved. Mr. L. would tell the story with evident enjoyment. He never told how the thing ended.

Wilson described an incident in which Lincoln visited a prostitute and, undressing, realized he had only $3., not the needed $5, whereupon he left the woman, who remained astonished at such integrity. Wilson adds that although this sounds like "a deliberate parody of the Honest Abe Lincoln legend," another biographer could claim the incident was evidence of the possibility of a bi- or homosexual young man.

Stephen B. Oates, in *Abraham Lincoln: The Man Behind the Myths* (1984), has pointed out that after Tad's birth in 1853, Mary contracted a gynecological disease that likely ended sexual intercourse between the Lincolns. The two had separate bedrooms installed when they remodeled their Springfield home.

Herndon wrote that his law partner told him about contracting syphilis in the 1830s during a "misadventure" in Beardstown, Illinois. However, Herndon may have told the story to irritate Mary Todd Lincoln, whom he did not like. Again, there is no concrete evidence that Lincoln ever had the disease that was common during his lifetime.

During his first term, in 1864, "In God We Trust" appeared on the two-cent coins. Ironically, when he was murdered he was found to have had a Confederate $5. bill in his wallet. The 6' 4" Lincoln's net worth of $110,295. was awarded at his death to his wife and two sons. The only U.S. President to die intestate (without a will), he has been claimed both by naturalists and supernaturalists. However, Robertson, writing that Lincoln "was certainly a non-Christian deist, and an agnostic deist at that," cites Lamon's *Life of Lincoln* and J. B. Remsburg's *Abraham Lincoln: Was He A Christian?* (1893).

Lincoln was assassinated 14 April 1865 while attending a performance at Ford's Theater in Washington, D.C., and sitting in a specially installed Victorian rocker. He was shot by the actor John Wilkes Booth, whose extravagant acting style Lincoln had admired so much that at one time he had invited Booth to the White House. (Booth declined the invitation, according to David S. Reynolds in *Walt Whitman's America*.) (In the audience the night of the assassination had been Peter Doyle, Whitman's intimate companion.) Mary Lincoln was so grief-stricken that she could not attend the funeral, crying out for Lincoln to take her with her, incredulous that he was dead. The White House which she had helped decorate was, at that very moment, being pillaged by souvenir hunters who cut pieces of the velvet carpet, stole china and silverware, and even carted off some of the furniture.

In 1876, more than a decade after Lincoln's burial in Springfield, Illinois, an attempt was made to steal the body for a $200,000 ransom. The coffin was then hidden, for safety, between the walls of his tomb. When in 1900 the old tomb was torn down and a new one was built, Robert worried that another attempted theft would be made and decided against a burglar alarm in favor of burying the remains in a ten-foot hole deep inside the tomb and covered with twenty inches of cement. On 26 September 1901, despite Robert's order that the coffin not be opened, local officials opened it to stop rumors that the body was not really there. When workers pried the lid open, the twenty-three witnesses smelled a pungent odor, then gaped at the body, which they recognized because of the beard, hair, and famous wart. His French kid gloves had rotted away on his hands. Fleetwood Lindly, a witness, remembered, "Yes, his face was chalky white. His clothes [were] mildewed, and I was allowed to hold one of the leather straps as we lowered the casket for the concrete to be poured. I was not scared at the time, but I slept with Lincoln for the next six months." Lindly, who died in 1963, was the last witness to Lincoln's last public appearance.

Of the four sons Mary Todd Lincoln bore (Robert Todd, Edward Baker, William Wallace, and Thomas or "Tad"), only Robert lived to manhood. In 1985, he died in a nursing home in Saluda, Virginia. An American lawyer and public official, Robert had his mother committed to a mental hospital after she was adjudged insane in 1875. Jean Baker, in *Mary Todd Lincoln: A Biography* (1987), claims that he had done this because he had designs on his mother's money and his desire to get her out of public view. According to Baker, after Mary managed to spring herself from the asylum, having been incarcerated for only four months, she threatened to kill Robert, her "monster of mankind son," that she demanded restitution for his "wickedness," on the ground that "you have tried your game of robbery long enough." But she did not change her will, resulting in Robert's inheriting $84,035 and her sixty-four trunks of dresses, jewelry, flatware, and other goods. In a biography of Myra Bradwell, *America's First Woman Lawyer* (1993), Jane M. Friedman describes Bradwell's correspondence with noted women's rights activist Susan B. Anthony, detailing her successful strategy to secure Mary Todd Lincoln's release from the mental hospital. (See entries for William H. Herndon and Oratory.) {CE; FUS; JM; JMR; PA; PUT; RAT; RE; TRI; TSV; TYD}

Lincoln, Alexander Jr. (20th Century)

Lincoln, a New Hampshire humanist, was devoted to farming, nature, ecology, and sound common sense. The Humanist Association of Massachusetts (AHA) names its lecture series after the Harvard 1932 graduate. Alexander Lincoln Jr. Lecturers have included Tom Ferrick, Judge of South Africa's Constitutional Court Richard J. Goldstone, and Bangladeshi physician-poet Taslima Nasrin.

Lincoln, Henry (20th Century)

Lincoln, with Michael Baigent and Richard Leigh, wrote *Holy Blood, Holy Grail Holy Grail* (1983).

Lindbergh, Charles Augustus (1902-1974)

Lindbergh was the American aviator who astounded the world in 1927 by making the first solo, nonstop transatlantic flight in a plane, *The Spirit of St. Louis*, described by one overly enthusiastic journalist as "the greatest event since the Resurrection." His plane's name also became the title in 1953 of his best-known work.

"Slim" Lindbergh married Anne Morrow, the daughter of the U.S. ambassador to Mexico, and the two made several long flights together, publicizing the growing importance of aviation.

In 1932 in a highly publicized kidnapping for ransom, their son Charles was kidnapped and killed by a blow to the head. Bruno Hauptman was convicted as the child's murderer and was electrocuted in 1936.

Lindbergh's father, Charles Augustus Lindbergh (1859-1924), was a Swedish-born congressman from Minnesota. He consistently attacked the methods of large industrial trusts and incurred vilification by his denunciation of war propaganda and war profits.

In 1938 after inspecting European air forces, the congressman's son favored isolationism with respect to the political and military struggle threatening in Europe, convinced that the Germans had air superiority. His anti-war speeches for the America First Committee led to his being branded pro-Nazi, and he resigned his reserve commission and quit the National Advisory Committee for Aeronautics.

Lindbergh was dubbed a fascist when in Des Moines, Iowa, he made a speech in which he said,

> The leaders of both the British and the Jewish races, for reasons which are as understandable from their viewpoint as they are inadvisable from ours, for reasons which are not American, wish to involve us in the war. . . . A few far-sighted Jewish people . . . stand opposed to intervention. But the majority still do not. Their greatest danger to this country lies in their large ownership and influence in our motion pictures, our press, our radio, and our Government." His wife warned him that he would be called anti-Semitic for saying this. However, he responded, "But I'm not!"

President Franklin Roosevelt, however, never allowed him to forget that he once had accepted a Nazi decoration.

With Alexis Carrel he worked in 1936 on the invention of a perfusion pump that could maintain organs outside the body. During World War II, Lindbergh offered his services to the air force, subsequently flying combat missions in the Pacific. In his later years he became a spokesman on conservation issues.

His wife's *Gift from the Seae*" outsold her husband's account of his flight over the Atlantic Ocean. Although Anne Lindbergh (1906-) is a Presbyterian, the celebrated aviator was described by his daughter Reeve (*The New Yorker*, 24-31 August 1998) as being a

> . . . deeply reserved, independent outdoorsman from the Midwest. All his life, he displayed a courteous indifference to convention, whether it was intellectual, religious, or political. He rarely attended church, and he hated school. His grandparents were Swedish immigrants on the American frontier, and he found his first love on a Minnesota farm, where he spent his boyhood, and in the natural world extending far beyond it—a child's infinity of river and field and forest. Above my father's head in those early days, and ever afterward, there stretched the even more compelling infinity of the sky.

(See entry for Race.) {CE}

Lindeman, Eduard C. (1885–1953)

A humanist, Lindeman edited *Emerson: The Basic Writings of America's* (1947). {HNS}

Lindet, Robert Thomas (1743–1823)

A French bishop, Lindet was elected to the States-General by the clergy of his district. He embraced Republican principles and was made Bishop of L'Eure. But in 1792, he publicly married, then renounced his bishopric and proposed that civil festivals should take the place of religious ones. Lindet became a member of the *Conseil des Anciens* and upon his death was buried without any religious service. {BDF}

Lindh, Anders Theodor (Born 1833)

Lindh was a Finnish lawyer and a poet who wrote in Swedish. He published freethought essays that brought him into considerable controversy with the clergy. {BDF; RAT}

Lindkvist, Alfred (Born 1869)

Lindkvist was a Swedish writer who, at the University of Uppsula, studied Mill, Darwin, and Spencer. He lost a stipend at the university by translating from the Danish a rationalistic life of Jesus entitled *The Reformer from Galilee.* In 1888 he joined Lennstrand in propagating freethought, for which he received a month in prison for having translated one of J. Symes's anti-Christian pamphlets. Lindkvist was an editor of *Fritankaren.* {BDF}

Lindley, Mark (20th Century)

Lindley, a humanist activist, has supported a fund-raising project for the Atheist Centre in India whereby locally woven fabric will be sold in the United States and at the Centre. A visiting professor at the University of Kerala (1997-1998) and Mahatma Gandhi University (1998-1999), Lindley is a member of the Humanist Association of Massachusetts.

Lindley, William B. (1933–)

Lindley is an editor for the freethinking journal, *Truth Seeker*. In one article, he pointed out that his reading of *Psalms* 51:5 is that whereas Christians believe in guilty babies, Catholics believe in guilty embryos. Lindley has degrees in physics from the California Institute of Technology. "The Bible is kinda like a high school band on the first day of school," he has observed. " 'Tain't easy to harmonize." (See entry for California Atheists, Humanists.) {FD}

Lindner, Ernst Otto Timotheus (1820–1867)

A German physician, Lindner was a friend of Schopenhauer, whose philosophy he maintained in several works on music. Lindner edited the *Vossische Zeitung* starting in 1863. {BDF; RAT}

Lindsay, (Nicholas) Vachel (1871–1931)

Although little evidence is available that Lindsay was a freethinker, he is included along with some of his poetry in Whitehead and Muhrer's *Freethought on the American Frontier*. Lindsay's Campbellite background, mixed with a touch of pantheism and romanticism and common sense, led him to preach the gospel of beauty. Few American schoolchildren have not been taught parts of *General Booth Enters into Heaven* (1913) or *The Congo* (1914), a rhythmic poem that has a dramatic conception and vivid imagery. In a 1935 biography, his friend Edgar Lee Masters recorded how Lindsay's "higher vaudeville" included the dramatic use of gesture and chant, and Lindsay was in great demand during his lifetime as a public reader of his own works, although eventually he tired of making money that way. His *Collected Poems* (1938) was published posthumously.

Rumor had it that he once lost his heart to Australian composer and pianist Percy Grainger, as had the Norwegian composer Edvard Grieg before him. Lindsay's poetry is noted for its virility.

His death in 1931 was reported as heart failure. However, biographer Eleanor Ruggles has described his final days. Lindsay was depressed by his financial situation, his declining reputation as a writer, and by some undiagnosed disease—perhaps idiopathic epilepsy. Like an insane person, he accused his wife Elizabeth of infidelity and her father of plotting to kill him. From moments of quietly reading poetry in bed, he would turn to weeping inconsolably. On December 4th, when she thought he was much calmer than usual, he left their bed and went downstairs. "Yes, dear," he told her, "I'll be up in a little while." But there was a terrific commotion, he ran upstairs, and she feared his mind had snapped and that he was going to murder their children. "I just tried to kill myself by drinking Lysol," he exclaimed. She started to run for a doctor, then heard him shout, "I got them before they could get me—they can just try to explain this, if they can!"

Ironically, the writer who had specialized in writing and speaking about beauty died in minutes, after having drunk the poisonous disinfectant. {CE}

Lindsay, Norman (1879–1969)

Lindsay, author of *The Curate in Bohemia*, was a noted freethinking painter in Australia. Much of his work was donated to the Australian National Trust. A biography by John Hetheringon, *Norman Lindsay: The Embattled Olympian* (1973), stated of his work,

> Whatever his rivals or professional critics might say for or against it, his work made an extraordinary impact on laymen. No artist had ever before stirred Australians in general as he did. Some marvelled and some fulminated; but they took notice. His riggish fauns and frolicking satyrs, bacchanals, bewigged gallants, wantoning nude ladies and all the rest captured the attention of people who had never heard of Rembrandt or Velasquez, never been inside an art gallery, never thought of a picture except as something to fill a blank space on a wall. They might not understand what he was driving at but the exuberance, verve, and gaiety of what he did excited and held them. More than anything else it was his treatment of sex that drew the public spotlight on to him and his work and kept it there. To Norman, sex was a wonderful and joyous thing. "Sex is not only the basis of life, it is the *reason* for life," he wrote. He was driven by an overmastering purpose to take sex out of the darkness.

Lindsay had been the son of a physician and the grandson of a Methodist minister. He once described his credo as "that the Greeks and Romans established all that the word civilization can mean, while Christianity, that communist uprising of the underworld, sought to destroy it and very nearly succeeded in doing so. All through my work I have maintained that theme, and that is the reason why it was attacked, although the attack took the crude device of denouncing it as indecent and immoral, because I took the nude human body as my symbol of the free spirit of man." Angered that the Tasmanian Public Library banned his work, Lindsay described the Australian national ego as "a crude and bastardly conglomeration of the basest contents of English nonconformism, Scottish Presbyterianism, and Irish Catholicism."

Lindsay was depicted in "Sirens," a movie which shows his wife, children, and an entourage which includes nude models. The work, directed by John Duigan, shows libertarianism winning out over a repressive form of Christianity. In Australia, the film was praised by freethinkers and attacked by religionists.

His freethinking son, **Jack Lindsay**, is an artist and a critic. {*Freethought History*, #10, 1994).

Lindsay, Ronald A. (20th Century)

An attorney, Lindsay is a contributing editor for *Free Inquiry*. He has represented the Council for Democratic and Secular Humanism in the federal courts, and he is on the Council for Secular Humanism's Committee for the Scientific Examination of Religion. {*Free Inquiry*, Fall, 1990, and Fall, 1993}

Lindsey, Ben (20th Century)

Judge Lindsey gave the address at the memorial service for Luther Burbank. As noted by Maynard Shipley, who was at the 1926 event, several Roman Catholic priests at the memorial were seen leaving, "offended in their narrow dogmatism by Lindsey's ringing challenges." (See entry for Luther Burbank) {*Freethought Today*, August 1993; TYD}

Lindsey, Theophilus (1723–1808)

Lindsey was one of the founders of the English Unitarian movement. He wrote *The Apology of Theophilus Lindsey, M.A., on resigning from the Vicarage of Catterwick, Yorkshire, 1775*. {U}

Lingås, Lars Gunnar (1947–)

Lingås was Secretary General of the Norwegian Humanist Association from 1993 to 1997. He has managed a university textbook division and been a social worker. A lecturer who has given seminars in ethics, professional ethics, and human rights, he has written textbooks on those subjects. Lingås is a life member of the International Humanist and Ethical Union. "I believe that the greater number of the 500,000 Norwegians who sympathise with us will join in," he has written. The Association in 1993 had 50,000 members, and in 1998 more than 60,000.

Lingås participated in the February 1995 European Humanist Seminar in Oslo. At the 1996 Humanist World Congress in Mexico City, he lamented that colonialists had destroyed so many beautiful cultures over the years. He emphasized that there is a need for an ethical dimension, which must be enlarged to create a common human identity. Humanists must examine whether they accept diversity within themselves. We must have our own tolerance and our own self-criticism. "We will not grow without an element of self-criticism and without the ability to have dialogue with other life stances," Lingås stated. His e-mail: <lingulv@online.no>. {*International Humanist News*, December 1996}

Lingeman, Richard Roberts (1931-)

An editor and writer, Lingeman was executive editor of *Monocle* (1960-1969), a columnist for the *New York Times Book Review* (1969-1978); and an editor of *Nation* since 1978. He wrote *Drugs from A to Z* (1969); *Small Town America* (1980); and *Theodore Dreiser: At the Gates of the City 1871-1907* (1986). Shown Sinclair Lewis's postcard about humanism, Lingeman, who was writing a book about Lewis, observed,

> [Regarding the Sinclair Lewis statement], it's good to have his belief in his own words—and late in his life. Though I'm not surprised at his self-characterization.
>
> As for myself, I lean toward naturalistic humanism but with some perhaps irrational faith that there is an unknowable creative spirit at the heart of it all.

(See entry for Sinclair Lewis) {WAS, 10 April 1999}

Lingwood, D. P. E. (20th Century)

In 1978, Lingwood wrote *Buddhism and Blasphemy* (1978). {GS}

Liniere, François Payot de (1628–1704)

A French satiric poet, Liniere was known as "the Atheist of Senlis." Boileau said the only act of piety Liniere ever did was drinking holy water because his mistress dipped her finger in it. In addition to writing many songs and smart epigrams, Liniere wrote a criticism of the New Testament. {BDF}

Link, Janet (1962–)

An artist in Raleigh, North Carolina, Link is a lifelong Unitarian. In her work, Link expresses her appreciation of beauty, once stating that "Every once in a while, say, in my figure-drawing class, the model will strike a pose, and the light will fall in and hit her just so, and it's just unspeakably beautiful. Then there's this frantic rush to get it all down on paper, to catch what exists in that moment only, and I never, ever do. But that's a lot like what I think about religion: It's the striving, the looking, the thinking that's important." {*World*, November-December 1994}

Linton, Eliza Lynn (1822–1898)

Linton, a novelist and journalist and the daughter of the vicar of Crosthwaite in Cumberland, was an agnostic who wrote for leading radical journals. In 1872 she published *The True History of Joshua Davidson, Christian and Communist*. On the subject of women's rights, she once wrote, "I think that the Christian religion has brought far more misery, crime, and suffering, far more tyranny and evil, than any other." She was married to William James Linton. {BDF; RE}

Linton, Eliza Lynn (1822–1898)

Linton was an English novelist and journalist, the author of *Azeth the Egyptian* (1846) and *Amymone* (1848), which she followed with many more successful novels. Her essays attacking feminism offended many of her female contemporaries. In a posthumously published memoir, *My Literary Life* (1899), she wrote a notably hostile portrait of George Eliot. Linton also was a frequent contributor to the *Agnostic Annual* and, according to Tribe, was an outright freethinker. {OEL; TRI; RAT}

Linton, William James (1812–1897)

Linton was a poet, engraver, and author. A Chartist in early life, he was acquainted with the chief political refugees. He wrote the *Reasoner* tract on "The Worth of Christianity." One of the founders of the *Leader*, Linton was an editor of *The Truthseeker*, the *National*, and the *English Republic*. According to McCabe, Linton's religious creed was "a large loose jumble of Christianity and Pantheism." {BDF; FUK; VI; RAT; TRI}

Lippard, James (20th Century)

A skeptic and activist freethinker, Lippard works for GlobalCenter on internet security and abuse issues. He is webmaster for "The Celebrity Atheist List" and a supporter of Internet Infidels. On the Web: <http://www.primenet.com/~lippard>.

Lippert, Julius (1839–1909)

A German scholar, Lippert wrote *Soul Worship* (1881), *The Universal History of Priesthoods* (1883), and *A Cultural History of Mankind* (1886–1887). {BDF; RAT}

Lippmann, Walter (1889–1974)

An eminent journalist, once secretary to muckraker Lincoln Steffans, Lippmann was a founder of *New Republic*. A syndicated columnist, he was also author of *A Preface to Politics* (1913) and *A Preface to Morals* (1929). Lippmann wrote the present author concerning humanism:

> The only way I can answer your question [about the connotations of humanism] is to tell you that Professor Mercier's comments [in *American Humanism and the New Age*, in which he stated that Lippmann had given up his naturalistic humanism in favor of theistic humanism] are based entirely on my published work and constitute, as I understand it, his interpretation of what I wrote in *The Good Society*, a book published about nine or ten years after *A Preface to Morals*. I should like to add that if there is any implication in your letter that I have recently changed my views profoundly, that is not the case. I delivered recently at the Episcopal Theological Seminary in Cambridge, Massachusetts, an address which in substance was prepared as part of a manuscript of a book which I plan to publish as a sequel to *A Preface to Morals*. In my view it marks the evolution of some of the ideas of *A Preface to Morals* but not a change in any fundamental sense.

In the above-mentioned address, Lippmann included the following:

> There are those who, if they had to describe their own religious condition, might say what Alexis de Tocqueville said of his friend Jean Jacques Ampere, the son of the great French physicist and mathematician. It was that his friend was not "a good Christian by belief," but that he was one, as de Tocqueville put it, "by intention, by taste, and, if I may so put it, by temperament." This would describe a great multitude in our western society today. They are those, you will recall, whom Dante placed in Limbo, reserving for them a special tenderness and compassion. . . .
>
> As long as the preacher expounds the law, he will be most successful if he is literal and concrete. He will be talking, as politicians and journalists do, to the old Adam in the language that the old Adam understands. But if the preacher is to go beyond this in an attempt to induce a transformation of the will, he will find that the very style of his discourse must be changed. He must go beyond the prosaic language of commonsense to metaphors and poetic parables. He is entering a realm where nothing can be made completely articulate or easily communicable. His words can convey only approximately, only by intimation, by suggestion, by analogy, what he means to say. For he is beyond the boundaries of the commonsense, where what is most poignant is inexact and the last things are ineffable. . . .
>
> He must, therefore, resort to metaphors, parables, and poetic fantasy. For the transcendent truths of the spirit are beyond the limits of commonsense and cannot be stated directly by language, which works within the limitations of commonsense. They can only be suggested to the imagination.
>
> Here, surely, we come upon the innermost problem of religious teaching in our age. For the transcendent experience is not easily evoked where there is not already a disposition to transcend experience and common sense. Yet the disposition to respond to revelation was, I think you will agree, greater in the ages of faith than it is in modern times. May I, venturing greatly, presume to say that the problem of irreligion has become so poignant because it has become necessary, as it was not in the ages of faith, to clear up the ambiguity between the supernatural and the eternal?
>
> "Ours is an age," says the English philosopher, C. E. M. Joad, "which has . . . no beliefs in regard to the existence of an order of reality other than that which we can see and touch"—that is to say an order of reality which, however abstrusely it may be described mathematically can nevertheless be verified by events. Now in the Ages of Faith the common sense of mankind took it for granted that the order of reality which men can actually see and touch was a small part of what we should now call a supernatural order. The old believer did not think of this supernatural order as being, in our sense of the term, supernatural. What we now call supernatural was for him the natural order of things. There was no conflict with his commonsense. Indeed to him it *was* commonsense to believe that the visible life of man on earth was the prelude to a larger and different life in an everlasting scheme of things. There was, therefore, an ambiguity in the old religion. Men did not have to distinguish between the supernatural and the eternal, between the Kingdom of God as having an existence in time and lace, and the Kingdom of God within them as an essence outside of time and place. . . .
>
> The critical change which has come in the Modern Age is an alteration of the commonsense of mankind. It is no longer natural to believe that the mundane experience of each individual is not his whole experience. In physics and the metaphysics of modern men, it is no longer self-evident, indeed it is not easily credible, that his experience continues in everlasting time and in some other place. He does not believe in the cosmic framework—as Dante for example visualized it—with its geography, its history, and its constitutional system. Thus for modern man the transcendent experience does not have the support of his common sense, and of his science, and of his cosmogony. If he is to attain it, he must reach it by a steeper and abrupter ascent from his mundane experience, and he must seize it in a much purer form. For the multitude there were the parables and in all the organized religions a much simpler and easier standard of religious life than that which the seers and the saints demanded of themselves. The alteration of commonsense by the development and popularization of science has not discredited the truth of religion. It has, however, left the churches and the preachers the task of making the harder standard of religious experience credible and convincing in itself—without the support of a supernatural physics and a supernatural history. They will have, I believe, to determine, after deep meditation and searching self-examination, how they can demonstrate that the life of the spirit is in fact the fulfillment of the nature of man. That demonstration, if it can be made, will become the support, as supernaturalism was in the Ages of Faith, of the religious life. . . .
>
> If the great hypothesis is valid, then there is no conflict, as the worldly believe, between the deepest needs of the old Adam and the idea of the New Man. Then we are so constituted that our paramount needs are identical with our moral obligations. In so far as we know the true needs of our natures and serve them, we do in fact fulfill the moral law. And as we understand the moral law truly and obey it, we live according to the dictates of our own natures. And so it can be argued, and perhaps in the end demonstrated, that the disorder which oppresses us comes because modern men do not transcend their immediate experience—that though they become educated, they do not become transformed. Today the moralists speak of this disorder as sin and vice. The statesmen speak of it as lawless and anti-social conduct. The physicians speak of it as maladjustment disclosed by symptoms of anxiety. Are they not talking about the same thing? Are they not talking about the person who has failed to understand and to live in the order to which man, as he is actually constituted, belongs? If that is so, then by the research and the meditations of dedicated men, and by the inspired disclosures of men of genius, the life of the spirit and the common sense of men may again be brought into harmony.

"When men can no longer be theists," wrote the author of *A Preface to Morals*, "they must, if they are civilized, become humanists. They must live by the premise that whatever is righteous is inherently desirable because experience will demonstrate its desirability. They must live, therefore, in the belief that the duty of man is not to make his will conform to the will of God but to the surest knowledge of the conditions of human happiness."

Haught quotes the following Lippmann views, found in *The Public Philosophy* (1955) and *A Preface to Morals* (1929):

> • There is no arguing with the pretenders to a divine knowledge and to a divine mission. They are possessed with the sin of pride, they have yielded to the perennial temptation. . . . No more than the kings before them should the people be hedged with divinity.
>
> • The radical novelty of modern science lies precisely in the rejection of the belief, which is at the heart of all popular religion, that the forces which move the stars and atoms are contingent upon the preferences of the human heart.

• Insofar as men have now lost their belief in a heavenly king, they have to find some other ground for their moral choices than the revelation of his will. It follows necessarily that they must find the tests of righteousness wholly within human experience.

• The greatest of all perplexities in theology has been to reconcile the infinite goodness of God with his omnipotence. Nothing puts a greater strain upon the faith of the common man than the existence of utterly irrational suffering in the universe.

{CE; CL; *Humanist Newsletter*, September-October 1953; TYD; WAS, 6 April 1949}

Lipps, Theodor (1851–1914)

A professor of aesthetics at the Royal Bavarian Academy, Lipps showed the influence of Hume, whose *Treatise on Human Nature* he edited in the German in 1895. He also showed the influence of Kant's pantheism, believing in "a divine world-I" or world-spirit. {RAT}

Liscow, Christian (1701–1760)

Liscow was one of the greatest of German satirists. His principal satires are *The Uselessness of Good Works for Our Salvation* and *The Excellence and Utility of Bad Writers*. He has been called the German Swift, and his writing shows him to have been an outspoken freethinker. {BDF; RAT}

Lisle, Lionel (19th Century)

Lisle wrote *The Two Tests: The Supernatural Claims of Christianity Tried by Two of Its Own Rules* (1877). {BDF}

Lismer, Arthur (1885–1969)

Lismer, a Canadian Unitarian, was an artist and an educator. {U}

Lisnoff, Howard (20th Century)

A college educator and counselor, Lisnoff has written for *The Humanist*.

Liston, Robert (20th Century)

Liston, in the *Saturday Evening Post* (11 July 1964), wrote an article about Madalyn Murray O'Hair, "Mrs. Murray's War on God." {GS}

Listowell (Richard Granville Hare) [4th Earl of] (1866–1931)

Listowell was a freethinker who served with the Yeomancy Cavalry in South Africa, receiving in 1900 the Queen's Medal, four clasps. He was president of England's Euthanasia Society.

His son, the **Earl of Listowell** (1907–), was a founding member in 1935 of the Voluntary Euthanasia Society. In 1996, he handed over the presidency to Sir Ludovic Kennedy, who remarked, "What a change in our fortunes there has been in the sixty years that Lord Listowell has been associated with our movement. The barriers against voluntary euthanasia are beginning to crumble, one after another." {TRI}

Liszinski (Lyszczynski) [Count] (17th Century)

Count Liszinski in 1688–1689 was found to have written that there is no God, or that man had made God out of nothing. As a result, the Polish bishops of Posen and Kioff investigated and found that not only did he deny the existence of God but also the doctrine of the Trinity and the Virgin Birth. He was then tortured and, according to Robertson, "the first step was to tear out his tongue, 'with which he had been cruel towards God'; the next to burn his hands at a slow fire. It is all told by Zulaski, the leading Inquisitionist." He then was beheaded, burned, and his ashes were scattered from a cannon.

Unitarianism may have been tolerated somewhat in the sixteenth century, but positive atheism was forbidden. King John Sobieski made no attempt to stop the execution, but later Pope Innocent XI bitterly censured the incident. At issue was Liszinski's statement that man was the creator of God, whom he had formed out of nothing. {BDF; JMR; JMRH}

LITANY

In many religions, litany is a ritual repeating of prayers. The shaman or clergyman or singer will chant some words, and the congregation will make a response. One such response is the Medieval litany, "Lord, have mercy." {DCL}

LITERARY REALISM, ROMANTICISM, AND NATURALISM: See entry for Naturalism.

LITERATURE AND SECULAR HUMANISM

Rejecting the pedestrian view that literature is boring, Lionel Trilling in "On the Modern Element in Modern Literature" wrote, "I have been read by Eliot's poems . . . and by *Ulysses* and by *Remembrance of Things Past* and by *The Castle*. . . . Some of these books at first rejected me; I bored them." Trilling, in short, bolstered W. H. Auden's view that *a real book reads us*.

For any philosophic movement to succeed, it ideally would be accompanied by supporting literary influences. Christian theism has its Bible, deism had its pamphleteers, transcendentalism had its poets, existentialism had its Sartre. A major weakness of naturalistic humanism has been its emphasis upon the academically abstruse writings of Homo academicus, professor-type philosophers. The author of a "Potpourri" column for *Free Inquiry*, who was critical of the journal's content, advised that for naturalistic humanism to succeed as a movement it must have the input as well as the output of critics, comics, satirists, poets, playwrights, and journalists as well as painters, sculptors, musicians: all who represent the humanities. [Not that there was a documentable connection, but "Potpourri" was soon thereafter discontinued by *Free Inquiry*.]

"What author or novels should I recommend to my growing young intellectual?" humanists are often asked. Maugham's *Of Human Bondage* and his *The Razor's Edge* are often cited as starters.

Little, Lawrence (20th Century)

Little wrote a useful bibliography for humanists, "Religion and Public Education" (1968). {GS}

Little, Shannon (20th Century)

Little has written about current films for *New Humanist*.

Littré, Maximilian Paul Émile (1801–1881)

Littré, a French philologist and philosopher, edited the works of Hippocrates (1839–1861), embraced the doctrines of Comte, and in 1845 published a lucid analysis of the philosophy of positivism. His *Dictionary of the French Language*, in which he applied the historical method to philology, was a colossal work. Although proposed for the Academy in 1883, he was bitterly opposed by Bishop Dupanloup, who successfully delayed his acceptance. But Littré was finally elected in 1871, at which time Dupanloup resigned. Under the Empire Littré twice refused the Legion of Honor. He was a positivist (agnostic) without any mysticism.

Littré's wife was an ardent Catholic. He did not interfere in her beliefs. According to Foote, however, she was less scrupulous than her husband. When he was dying, she excluded his friends from the deathbed, had him baptized, and secured his burial in consecrated ground with pious rites. Further, she said that her husband had recanted his heresy and died in the bosom of the Church. The Abbé Huvelin, her confessor who frequently visited Littré during his last illness, assisted her in the alleged fraud. At the funeral, according to a correspondent of *The Standard*, his friends were "very angry at this recantation in extremis, and claimed that dishonest priestcraft took advantage of the darkness cast over that clear intellect by the mist of approaching death to perform the rites of the Church over his semi-inanimate body." At the grave, M. Wyrouboff, editor of the Comtist review, *La Philosophie Positive*, which Littré had founded, delivered a brief address to the Freethinkers who remained, concluding,

> Littré proved by his example that it is possible for a man to possess a noble and generous heart, and at the same time espouse a doctrine which admits nothing beyond what is positively real and which prevents

any recantation. And, gentlemen, in spite of deceptive appearances, Littré died as be had lived, without contradictions or weakness. All those who knew that calm and serene mind—and I was of the number of those who did—are well aware that it was irrevocably closed to the "unknowable," and that it was thoroughly prepared to meet courageously the irresistible laws of nature. And now sleep in peace, proud and noble thinker!

You will not have the eternity of a world to come, which you never expected; but you leave behind you your country that you strove honestly to serve, the Republic which you always loved, a generation of disciples who will remain faithful to you; and last, but not least, you leave your thoughts and your virtues to the whole world. Social immortality, the only beneficent and fecund immortality, commences for you to-day.

However, the *Catholic Encyclopedia* counts him "amongst the lambs," states McCabe, who adds that—with blatant untruth—it says when Littré was near death that he "asked to be baptized, and he died a Catholic." Echoing this, the *Morning-Advertiser* wrote, "There can hardly be a doubt that M. Littré died a steadfast adherent to the principles be so powerfully advocated during his laborious and distinguished life. The Church may claim, as our Paris correspondent, in his interesting note on the subject, tells us she is already claiming, the death-bed conversion of the great unbeliever, who for the last thirty-five years was one of her most active and formidable enemies. She has attempted to take the same posthumous revenge on Voltaire, on Paine, and on many others, who were described by Roman Catholic writers as calling in the last dreadful hour for the spiritual support they held up to ridicule in the confidence of health and the presumption of their intellect."

Meanwhile, one year before his death, Littré was found to have written "*Pour La Dernière Fois*" (For the Very Last Time) for *The Comtist*. In it, he noted that he realized he did not have long to live: "For many months, my suffering have prostrated me with dreadful persistence. . . . Every morning when I have to be put to bed, my pains are exasperated, and often I have not the strength to stifle cries which are grievous to me and grievous to those who tend me."

Fearing the worst, he wrote to his friend, M. Caubert: "Last Saturday I swooned away for a long time. It is for that reason I send you, a little prematurely, my article for the Review. If I live, I will correct the proofs as usual. If I die, let it be printed and published in the Review as a posthumous article. It will be a last trouble which I venture to give you. The reader must do his best to follow the manuscript faithfully."

Referring to Charles Greville, Littré said, "I feel nothing of what he experienced. Like him, I find it impossible to accept the theory of the world, which Catholicism prescribes for all true believers; but I do not regret being without such doctrines, and I cannot discover in myself any wish to return to them." He concluded:

Positive Philosophy, which has so supported me since my thirtieth year, and which, in giving me an ideal, a craving for progress, the vision of history and care for humanity, has preserved me from being a simple negationist, accompanies me faithfully in these last trials. The questions it solves in its own way, the rules it prescribes by virtue of its principle, the beliefs it discountenances in the name of our ignorance of everything absolute; of these I have in the preceding pages made an examination, which I conclude with the supreme word of the commencement—for the last time.

In short, Littré's recanting never occurred. {BDF; FO; JM; RAT

Live (20th Century)

The recording artists known as Live have stated on one of their record jackets that they are non-theists. {E}

Livermore, Abiel A. (1811–1892)

Livermore, a Unitarian minister, was a 19th-century educator. He wrote *Liberal Christianity* (1886). {U}

Livermore, Mary Ashton Rice (1820–1905)

A Universalist and suffragist, Livermore became President of the American Woman Suffrage Association from 1875 to 1878. As a child brought up by the strict Calvinist doctrines taught in her devout Baptist home, she recalled (her) younger sisters," already admitting that "I expect to be lost." *The Story of My Life* (1897) further relates that she thought of God as "only a judge, who tried human beings, condemned or acquitted them, and sent them to reward or punishment." As a result, she directed her prayers to "Our Jesus who art in heaven."

Upon marrying a Universalist minister, she "was finally liberated from this religious torture" and felt that the "faith of the Universalist church is to be the faith of the church of the future." She helped her husband edit *New Covenant*, and she was active in the Temperance movement, which she characterized as "the anguished protest of hopeless and life-sick women against the drunkenness of the time, which threatened to fill the land with beggary and crime." {U; U&U; UU}

Livesay, Dorothy (1909-)

A Canadian lyric poet, Livesay shows in her work the influence of the French Symbolist poets and the impact of having participated in Montreal as a social worker during the Depression. She has acknowledged the affinity she has for the social gospel of such liberal poets as C. Day-Lewis, Stephen Spender, and W. H. Auden.

In 1944 and 1947 she received the Governor General's award for poetry. Two of her works are *Collected Poems* (1977) and *Selected Poems: The Self-Completing Tree* (1986). Livesay is a Unitarian.

Livingston, Bob (20th Century)

Livingston and his wife **Pat Livingston** are newsletter editors of *Atheists United*, published in Sherman Oaks, California.

Livingston, Herbert (20th Century)

Livingston has been president of Atheists United in California, and he has been active in fighting for the separation of church and state.

Livingston, Rosetta (20th Century)

Livingston, a member in California of the Freedom From Religion Foundation, wrote *Every Time We Say Goodbye* (1997), a novel with humanistic underpinnings.

Llewellyn, Jean (20th Century)

Llewellyn in Scotland is active with the Edinburgh Humanist Group.

Llorente, Juan Antonio (1756–1823)

A Spanish historian, Llorente wrote *A Critical History of the Spanish Inquisition* (1822, 10 volumes). Although Catholic writers have said Llorente was a superficial and untruthful critic of the Church, Llorente had been a canon of the Toledo Cathedral, Knight of the Caroline Order, and General Secretary of the Inquisition: an important cleric and a scholar. He became a Voltairean skeptic, moved to France where he published his history, and then was driven out when the restored Catholic royalty and Church returned. {JM; RAT; RE}

Lloyd, Caitlin (20th Century)

Lloyd is a contributor to *Family Matters*, the newsletter of the Secular Family Network.

Lloyd, G. J. Henry (20th Century)

Lloyd, a British rationalist and once head of the Humanist Council, was concerned about the semantic overtones and meanings of the words "rationalism" and "humanism."

Lloyd, John T. (1851–1928)

Lloyd, a Welshman born at Felin-y-wig, Denbighshire, was brought up in the Calvinistic faith, the form of Christianity handed down to him as a sacred legacy through a long line of ancestors. As a boy, he said, he was "resolutely ambitious to enter the ministry of the gospel." After studying for three years at Bala College, he spent twenty years as a Presbyterian minister in Johannesburg. A popular preacher, he officiated often in buildings that were too small to accommodate the crowds which flocked to hear him.

In a series of 1903 articles in the *Freethinker*, republished as *From Christian Pulpit to Secular Platform*, Lloyd told how he "converted" to freethought when fifty-two, discarding "God, Christ, and Immortality, with all the absurd dogmas concerning them." He rapidly became a stalwart of the freethought platform and an active member in England of the Rationalist Press Association. Lloyd wrote *God-Eating: A Study in Christianity and Cannibalism* (1921), a study of the superstitious history custom.

An attack of cerebral hemorrhage in 1927 prevented him from working further for freethought causes, but he was remembered for his activism, including his vigorous protest against the imprisonment in 1922 of J. W. Gott for blasphemy. He died calmly, simply losing consciousness. {FO; RAT; RSR}

Lloyd, John William (Born 1857)

Lloyd, of Welsh-English stock, was an American poet and writer. Although raised an orthodox Christian, Lloyd became an agnostic and anarchist, writing extensively in *Liberty* and *Lucifer*. {BDF}

Lloyd, Noel (1924-1998)

Lloyd, who was born in Liverpool, joined the RAF at the age of seventeen and served in Canada. With Geoffrey Palmer, who was to be his partner for fifty-three years, he was a member of the Rock Theatre Company. The two collaborated in writing more than thirty books, including a biography of E. F. Benson and *Father of the Bensons* (1998). A supporter of the Labour Party and gay rights, Lloyd was an activist humanist. {*Gay and Lesbian Humanist*, Winter 1998}

Lloyd, Richard (20th Century)

Lloyd in 1919 wrote an atheistic critique about an English curate at Midhurst, Robert Taylor. {GS}

Lloyd, Victor Henry (1921–)

Lloyd is an Australian humanist, teacher, lecturer, and writer. He was active with the Rationalist Society and became first president of the subsequent organization, the Humanist Society of Queensland. Lloyd has coordinated the society's policies on Civil Marriage Celebrants, Abortion Reform Movement, Homosexual Law Reform Movement, the Vasectomy Information Service, and the Sex Counseling Service. He led the group's opposition to Australia's involvement in Vietnam and the South African Tour. In 1989 he was named Humanist of the Year. {SWW}

Lloyd, William Watkiss (19th Century)

Lloyd was author of *Christianity in the Cartoons* (1865), in which he criticizes Rafael and the New Testament side by side. He also wrote *The Age of Pericles* and several works on Shakespeare. {BDF}

Llunas, D. José (19th Century)

In Barcelona, Spain, Llunas edited *Tramontana* from 1894 to 1895.

Locke, Alain Le Roy (1886–1954)

Locke, a major figure in the Harlem Renaissance, edited in 1924 a special edition of a magazine called *Survey Graphics,* which included Langston Hughes and other literary figures of the time. He then developed an anthology called *The New Negro* (1925), which included art by Winold Reiss and other black intellectuals. In an interview with Norm Allen Jr., Purdue philosopher Leonard Harris details how Locke attended Harvard, studying under William James, Josiah Royce, and Hugo Munsterberg; how he was the first black American to become a Rhodes Scholar; how, because Locke was black, many white scholars asked, "Could it be possible for a Negro to be that intelligent?"; and how he completed his doctoral degree under Ralph Barton Perry (1917), graduating from Harvard in 1918. He was a friend of Max Otto, Horace Bernard Stern, and Leeman Bryson.

Locke was part of the pluralist movement "which maintained that (1) there was something common among all humans, (2) various cultural orientations should be respected and that people ought to be given regard for their preferences, and (3) those preferences should not be prioritized." In his *The Philosophy of Alain Locke*, Harris looks "at what was behind his promotion of and associations with George Padmore, Paul Robeson, Richard Wright, Langston Hughes, Zora Neale Hurston, Claude McKay, Sterling Brown, Jean Toomer, Aaron Douglas, Wallace Thurmond, Roland Hayes, and the other literary giants of the era."

Locke taught philosophy at Howard University in Washington, D.C., for forty years. He is said to have used his connections to secure patronage for young, male writers deserving assistance, allegedly after they had shown their appreciation in the bedroom. Countee Cullen and Langston Hughes were so rewarded, and others in his circle of gay associates were Richard Bruce Nugent and Claude McKay. An apocryphal story has it that he graded women writers, regardless of talent, with an automatic "C," or average, on the first day of classes. Zora Neale Hurston, whom Locke liked, described him as "a malicious, spiteful little snot."

Locke clearly was a pragmatist with a scientific outlook, at a time when in the 1930s and 1940s, states Harris, many felt "Africans and African Americans were inferior because they were not scientific; that is to say, they were deemed inferior because they were not producers of scientific products. They were also seen as being emotional. Locke, in a way, reverses this whole process and rejects the foundation upon which these claims are made." In his *Who's Who* entry, Locke listed himself as an Episcopalian, but Allen claims Locke was a non-religious humanist, adding that it was common for freethinkers and rationalists and secularists to disguise their true beliefs within a community which itself was a minority. {AAH}

Locke, John (1632–1704)

Locke, the English founder of empiricism, although not a deist was related to deists in a variety of ways. He attempted to denude religion of all mystery. With Plato, he held that a human being on earth is a body and a mind, that upon death the mind will continue to exist without any body. His philosophic approach was used by deists who abandoned traditional jargon. In the main, however, Locke sought to defend and justify Christianity and in *Reasonableness of Christianity* (1695) he went so far as to show that belief in the revealed truths of the Christian faith is reasonable. During the French Revolution, Maréchal cited Locke as one who seems to be an atheist only from the standpoint of the strictest religious orthodoxy.

According to Robertson, the theism in Locke's *Essay Concerning Human Understanding* (1690) "undermined even his Unitarian Scripturalism, inasmuch as it denies, albeit confusedly, that revelation can ever override reason." But he adds that the effect of Locke's work, "especially of his naturalistic psychology, was to make for rationalism; and his compromises furthered instead of checking the movement of unbelief." His *Letters on Toleration* (1689) advocated religious freedom for all groups except atheists and Roman Catholics.

Locke died while Lady Masham was reading the *Psalms* to him, and she wrote, "His death was like his life, truly pious, yet natural, easy and unaffected." (See entry for Patrick Romanell.) {BDF; CE; ER; EU, Ross Rudolph and Aram Vartarian; FUK; HAB; JM; JMR; JMRH; RAT; RE; TYD}

Lockridge, Ross Jr. (1914-1948)

According to the American Library Association's *Banned Books* (1998), Lockridge's *Raintree Country* (1948) allegedly contains "1066 pages of blasphemy and sacrilege inimical to faith and morals and within the prohibition of the Catholic Index."

The Indian-born novelist taught at Simmons after doing graduate work at Harvard. His sole novel told with many flashbacks of a single day, 4 July 1892, in the life of a high school principal in a mythical Indiana county. The work obtained acclaim, in the midst of which Lockridge mysteriously committed suicide. (See entry for Banned Books.) {OCAL}

Lockroy, Étienne Auguste Édouard [Vice President] (1838–1913)

Lockroy was elected to the French National Assembly in 1871. From 1886–1887, he was Minister of Commerce and Industry, from 1902–1905 he was Vice President, and from 1895 to 1896 and 1898, and in 1898 he was Minister of War. Lockroy wrote a number of political and naval works. In *Au hazard de la vie,* Lockroy writes of his rationalistic outlook. {RAT}

Lockwood, Helen Drusilla (20th Century)

A staunch supporter of Priscilla Robertson's editorship of The Humanist, Lockwood headed the English department at Vassar College. She was a philosophic as well as botanical naturalist. In addition to being an outstanding scholar of the humanities, Lockwood with her brother invested in a young company (Eastman Kodak) which increased in value to such an extent that she was instrumental in setting up and paying for the Shakespeare Garden on the Vassar campus. {WAS, conversations}

Lockwood, Ingersoll (20th Century)

A freethinker, Lockwood wrote "Superstition" (1910). {GS}

Locurcio, Georgeia (20th Century)

Locurcio is on the staff of *Free Inquiry.*

Loeb, Jacques (1859–1924)

Loeb, an American physiologist, was an honorary associate of the Rationalist Press Association. He is best known for his tropism theory and for his experiments in inducting parthenogenesis and regeneration by chemical stimulus. He also propounded the mechanistic philosophy that all ethics were the outgrowth of man's inherited tropisms. He founded and edited the *Journal of General Physiology*. Loeb's *Organism as a Whole* was dedicated "to the group of Freethinkers, including D'Alembert, Diderot, Holbach, and Voltaire, who first dared to follow the consequences of a mechanistic science to the rules of human conduct." {JM; RAT; RE}

Loeb, John Langeloth (1902–1996)

In 1995, Harvard University received from banker-broker Loeb a $70.5-million gift, which ranked as one of the largest gifts ever given to higher education. The gift included a grant of $800,000 to endow the "humanist chaplaincy" at Memorial Church. Loeb has explained that he first became aware of Harvard's humanist chaplain, Thomas Ferrick, through an article in *The Harvard Gazette*, which said Ferrick lived on only $15,000 a year. "He had been a Jesuit and a Catholic priest, but had left the church and concentrated on good will among men," Loeb learned. "I sent him a gift out of the clear blue. It occurred to me that I wanted to make a statement while I was still alive. I didn't even discuss this with him, but I'm sure he can use it." Saying "I've always sort of been a humanist," Loeb explained further: "More crimes are being committed in the name of God every year. The humanistic approach of deeds, not creeds, appeals to me. This is a small step in having someone professors and students can talk to."

Loeb played a significant part in Loeb, Rhoades & Co.; Loeb, Rhoades, Hornblower & Co.; and Loeb Partners Corporation. From 1951–1954 he was governor of the New York Stock Exchange. (See entry for Thomas Ferrick.) {The New York Times, 9 Dec 1996}

Loewen, James W. (20th Century)

Loewen, a historian, is critical of the fact that United States high school history texts do not tell the truth, are chauvinistic, and exalt the country, right or wrong. In *Lies My Teacher Told Me: Everything Your American History Textbook Got Wrong* (1995), he details how the American Legion insists on celebrating past wars and how it holds that justice was always on our side. Southern states minimize the evils of slavery and brag about the glories of the Confederacy.

Students are never told that Helen Keller became a radical socialist agitator or that President Woodrow Wilson was personally racist and segregated the government and civil service. He notes that after World War II, the Allied Forces prohibited German schools from teaching German history until they could revise and censor the textbooks. Meanwhile, students suffer because of their lack of objective history texts.

Freethinkers would hail educational programs which include reference to individuals who are not theists rather than, as present, citing individuals as if they are all members of some organized religious group.

Lofmark, Carl (Died 1991)

Lofmark in 1986 was elected an honorary associate of the Rationalist Press Association. He was author of Bards and Heroes (1989), Does God Exist? (1990) and What is the Bible? (1990). The latter book is a short treatise in which Lofmark looks at the Bible's sources, its intentions, and what an unbeliever thinks is its value in the present age. Lofmark was a devoted secular humanist. {The Freethinker, May 1997}

Lofton, Saab (20th Century)

Lofton is the author of *A.D.* and *Battle Never-ending*, two works of science fiction. In "Faith vs. African Americans" (*Free Inquiry*, Summer 1999), he explains why as an African American he gave up faith:

> Africans had various tribal mythologies or Islam before being forcibly introduced to Moses and Jesus and the like, and unfortunately, all too many black nationalists out there are under the impression that, if blacks were to simply return to what was once worshiped, then "everything'll be alright." Well, it ain't that simple.

If you are going to be religious, he says tongue-in-cheek, "Be a part of the religious Left as Gandhi or Martin Luther King Junior or Pastors for Peace or those nuns who keep getting raped and massacred by graduates of our taxpayer-funded School of the Americas."

LOGIC

• Logic is like the sword: those who appeal to it shall perish by it.

–Samuel Butler

• Logic is the art of going wrong with confidence.

–Joseph Wood Krutch

Logic, the systematic study of valid inference, is concerned with the formal properties of an argument, not its factual accuracy. In the early 20th century, Bertrand Russell and Alfred North Whitehead worked to develop logical theory as the basis for mathematics. Logic, aesthetics, metaphysics, ethics, and epistemology are disciplines at the core of philosophy's pursuit of wisdom.

In 1945, in his *History of Western Philosophy*, Russell wrote of logic:

> I conclude that the Aristotelian doctrines with which we have been concerned are wholly false, with the exception of the formal theory of the syllogism, which is unimportant. Any person in the present day who wishes to learn logic will be wasting his time if he reads

Aristotle or any of his disciples. Nonetheless, Aristotle's logical writings show great ability, and would have been useful to mankind if they had appeared at a time when intellectual originality was still active. Unfortunately they appeared at the very end of the creative period of Greek thought, and therefore came to be accepted as authoritative. By the time that logical originality revived, a reign of two thousand years made Aristotle very difficult to dethrone. Throughout modern times, practically every advance in science, in logic, or in philosophy has had to be made in the teeth of the opposition from Aristotle's disciples.

In 1968, in *The Art of Philosophizing*, Russell wrote further on the subject:

> Logic was practically invented by Aristotle. For nearly two thousand years, his authority in logic was unquestioned. To this day teachers in Catholic educational institutions are not allowed to admit that his logic has defects, and any non-Catholic who criticizes it incurs the bitter hostility of the Roman Church. I once ventured to do so on the radio, and the organizers who had invited me were inundated with protests against the broadcasting of such heretical doctrines. Undue respect for Aristotle, however, is not confined to Catholic institutions. In most universities, the beginner in logic is still taught the doctrine of the syllogism, which is useless and complicated, and an obstacle to a sound understanding of logic. If you wish to become a logician, there is one piece of advice that I cannot urge too strongly, and that is, DO NOT learn the traditional formal logic. In Aristotle's day, it was a creditable effort, but so was Ptolemaic astronomy. To teach either in the present day is a ridiculous piece of antiquarianism.

An exercise in logic:

Any sentence within this rectangle is false.

If the sentence within the rectangle is true, then it is false? If it is false, then it is true? What is illustrated is the "double contradiction," also called the "paradox of the liar."

Typical of non-philosophy majors who enrolled in Charner Perry's University of Chicago class in logic was one who concluded, "Logically speaking, I didn't understand 49/64 of what Prof. Perry was saying." (See the *Encyclopedia of Philosophy*, volumes 4 and 5, for the international history of logic.) {CE}

LOGICAL ATOMISM

Although in 1951 Bertrand Russell wrote that he would not bring an action for libel if called a "naturalistic humanist," he responded, "When I have to describe my own philosophy I call myself a 'logical atomist.' " Later, both Russell and Wittgenstein abandoned the label.

Russell Wahl, of Idaho State University, in reviewing Ali Benmakhlouf's *Bertrand Russell: L'atomisme logique* (1996), warned that the work contains various errors and "should be approached somewhat sceptically by scholars or more advanced students." (See entry for Bertrand Russell.) {*Russell: the Journal of the Bertrand Russell Archives*, Winter 1998-1999; WAS, 24 February 1951}

LOGICAL PARADOXES

In his Principles of Mathematics (1903), Bertrand Russell evidenced great interest in statements which appear to be contradictory but actually have a basis in truth. Other logicians have shown a similar interest:

• I must be cruel only to be kind.
–*Hamlet*,Shakespeare

• I prefer to be a man of paradox than a man of prejudice.
–Jean-Jacques Rousseau

• War is peace. Freedom is slavery. Ignorance is strength.
–From *1984* by George Orwell

• Ignorance is like a delicate fruit; touch it and the bloom is gone.
–Oscar Wilde

• What is the answer? . . . In that case, what is the question?
–Gertrude Stein's alleged last words

• In novels one is forced to tell the truth . . . whereas in biography one can invent more freely. This will sound like a paradox only to those who do not practice either art. In fiction the accuracy and coherence of the imaginative narrative must be strong enough to impart a vision of truth to the reader; in biography the devices and tricks of historical narrative are so abundant that it is much easier to disguise lack of knowledge or less of comprehension. Biography is the art of concealment; fiction is that of revelation.
–Peter Ackroyd, novelist and biographer

Paradox forces the search for a deeper level of meaning, and many claim that it is not just a rhetorical or illustrative device but a basic aspect of all poetic language. Meanwhile, if a person insists that he is lying, is what he says true or false? (See the *Encyclopedia of Philosophy*, Vol. 5.) {CE}

LOGICAL POSITIVISM

Logical positivism is a 20th century philosophical movement, one holding that all meaningful statements are either analytic or conclusively verifiable or at least confirmable by observation and experiment. Also called logical empiricism, the movement is noted for showing that metaphysical theories are strictly meaningless. It began in the group called the Vienna Circle, forming in the 1920s around Moritz Schlick, and included Friedrich Waismann, Otto Neurat, Rudolf Carnap, Herbert Feigl, Victor Kraft, Hans Hahn, Carl G. Hempel, Karl Menger, and Kurt Godel. The Vienna Circle influenced A. J. Ayer and Gilbert Ryle.

In general, the logical positivists subscribed to Ludwig Wittgenstein's dictum in *Tractatus Logico-Philosophicus* (1921) that linguistic clarification is necessary in order to avoid meaningless questions. "Why" is meaningful, for example, in a question such as "Why is my piano pedal broken?", which according to the verification principle can be tested. But it is not meaningful, linguistically, in questions such as "Why did God create the universe?" or "Does God have blue eyes?", which according to the verification principle cannot be tested. The movement of logical positivism is now considered dead, but it influenced many as well as left its imprint on empiricism. (See entries for Carl G. Hempe, Verification Principle, and Principle of Verifiability. Also, see the *Encyclopedia of Philosophy*, Vol. 5.)

Lohman, Scott (20th Century)

Lohman is a contributor to The Freethought Observer, a Texas publication that commenced in 1994. He is president of the Humanist Association of Minneapolis and St. Paul.

Lohmann, Hartwic (Died 1642)

A native of Holstein, Lohmann occupied a good position in Flensburg in 1616 but, accused of atheism, fled to Copenhagen, where he practiced medicine. Lohmann wrote *Mirror of Faith*. {BDF}

Loisy, Alfred Firmin (1857–1940)

A French biblical critic and theologian, Loisy was ordained (1879) a Catholic priest. From 1881 to 1893, he was a professor at the Catholic Institute in Paris. Around the turn of the century, he became leader of a movement called Catholic Modernism, one that accepted theories of a higher criticism and defined a liberal type of humanitarianism. As a result, the Holy See condemned his books, and he was excommunicated in 1908. In *My Duel with the Vatican*, Loisy wrote, "I have given myself a lot of trouble in this world with small result. I took my own life and that of the Church seriously, and the consequence is that I have wasted the one and disturbed the other. The search for truth is not a trade by which a man can support himself; for a priest it is a supreme peril. For a long time now I have not really been a Catholic in the official sense of the word. I have strewn my intelligence and my activity to the four winds of an empty ideal. . . . Roman Catholicism, as such, is bound to perish, and it deserves no regrets."

John Ratté's *Three Modernists* (1968) describes Loisy's many attacks on the Church. The Vatican's 1948 *Index Librorum Prohibitorum* has fourteen entries for Loisy, including opera omnia (1932), starting with his Études évangeliques (1903). R. Joseph Hoffmann has written an introduction to a recently published edition of *The Gospel and the Church* (1988).

In 1927, Edwin H. Wilson interviewed Loisy, "the excommunicated leader of the modernist movement in Roman Catholicism. He showed me a thrice-edited manuscript containing a philosophy of religion which the modernists had hoped to use as a replacement for the thought of Thomas Aquinas. 'All we wanted,' said Loisy wistfully, 'was to have the church accept the fact of change.' " {CE; EW; JM; RAT; RE}

Lollard, Walter (14th Century)

Lollard was a heretic and martyr who was born in England. While preaching in Germany in 1315, he rejected the sacraments and ceremonies of the Church. Wheeler reports that Lollard was said to have chosen twelve apostles to propagate his doctrines and that he had many followers. But, arrested in Cologne, he was burned to death in 1322, "dying with great courage." {BDF; RE}

Loman, Abraham Dirk (Born 1823)

Loman was a Dutch rationalist. He held the entire New Testament to be un-historical and the Pauline Epistles to belong to the second century. Loman wrote many critical works of religion. {BDF}

Lombardi, Franco (1906-19--?)

A professor of philosophy at the University of Rome, Lombardi was a Humanist Laureate in the Council for Secular Humanism's International Humanist Academy. In 1941 he wrote *La Libertà del volere e l'individuo*. An anti-fascist, Lombardi wrote about Feuerbach, Kierkegaard, and Marx. His history of philosophy is *Dopo lo storicismo* (1970).

Lombardi, Jolé (20th Century)

An organizer of the New University for the Third Age, Lombardi is a Humanist Laureate in the Council for Secular Humanism's International Humanist Academy.

Lombroso, Cesare (1835–1909)

An Italian criminologist and physician, Lombroso in his *L'uomo delinquente* (3 volumes, 1896–1897) compared anthropological measurements and developed the concept of the atavistic, or born, criminal. Although this concept has been questioned by other criminologists, Lombroso continues to be credited with turning attention from the legalistic study of crime to the scientific study of the criminal. He also believed in humane treatment of criminals and felt limitations on the use of the death penalty are needed. Lombroso introduced Darwinism to Italy. He was honored by becoming an honorary associate of the British Rationalist Press Association, which Charles A. Watts founded in 1899. Even when in the last stage of his life he was duped by a Spiritualist medium, he clung to his materialism. His daughter in her biography of him states that by that time he was a physical and mental wreck, not at all in his prime. {BDF; CE; JM; RAT; RE}

LONDON (England) HUMANISTS

For information about Central London Humanists, phone Cherie Holt on 0171 916 3015 or Hilary Leighter on 01895 632096.

London, Jack (1876–1916)

London, who wrote *Call of the Wild* (1903), was a novelist with a humanist viewpoint, according to Corliss Lamont, who liked his socialistic outlook. The "bastard son of a wandering astrologer [William Chaney] whom he never saw" and of a Welsh farm girl [Flora Wellman, who later married John London, whose name was given to Jack], London started out as a gold-seeker in the first Klondike rush, a newspaper correspondent during the Russo-Japanese War, and in 1914 a war correspondent in Mexico. His crude *Call of the Wild* and *White Fang* (1906), both of which show empathy with animals, are more complex than some of his Soviet admirers appreciated or his English detractors granted. In the former, Buck—an offspring of a St. Bernard and a Scotch shepherd dog—is stolen in California and shipped to the Klondike where he is trained as a sledge dog. Loyal to his new master, John Thornton, Buck wins a wager by dragging a thousand-pound load on a sledge. But when Indians murder Thornton, Buck responds to the call of the wild, abandoning humans and returning to a wolf pack. The other novel tells the story of White Fang, offspring of an Indian wolf dog and a wolf, whose Indian owner had tormented him to make him more savage but whose new owner subdues him by kindness. London liked Marx as well as Nietzsche, finding their diametrically opposed theories of value both in his writing and in his personal outlook. London's freethought is most evident in *Before Adam* (1907).

"I am a hopeless materialist," London once declared. "I see the soul as nothing else than the sum of activities of the organism plus personal habits—plus inherited habits, memories, experiences, of the organism. I believe that when I am dead, I am dead. I believe that with my death I am just as much obliterated as the last mosquito you and I squashed."

Critic Scott L. Malcomson has written that "London wrestled with the implications of individualism. He wrote in a 1905 letter of having 'recently emerged' from the Nietzsche 'sickness.' The fight against individualism became an article of faith for him. 'I have been more stimulated by Nietzsche than by any other writer in the world. At the same time I have been an intellectual enemy to Nietzsche. Both *Martin Eden* and *The Sea Wolf* were indictments by me of the Nietzschean philosophy of the superman." Socialism, however, provided little more than a placebo for the Nietzsche sickness. In his "How I became a Socialist," London took the position that individuals would convert to socialism out of a terror of remaining in the lower class. Of this Malcomson remarks, "Hatred of one's class position is probably not the best way to build class solidarity."

When eighteen, London had experienced how strong men much like himself could be brutalized by an all-powerful, unforgiving system he called "John Law" and which punished poverty. He was arrested in Niagara Falls 29 June 1894 on a charge of vagrancy, for the police had commenced a crackdown on vagrants who were alleged to be giving the city a bad name. *The Buffalo Courier* headlined its story, "Swarms of Dude Hoboes," reporting that "[t]hese fellows are not deserving of charity as they wear good clothing and one fellow had a valuable gold watch and several gold rings. The authorities are bound to rid the city of these gentlemen." One of the thirteen cases cleared from the docket was "John Lunden." Young London was handcuffed to a tall black prisoner, shackled to the remainder of the troop of convicted vagrants, and unceremoniously led through the streets of Niagara Falls. After a thirty-day sentence, he and a fellow prisoner panhandled some change in Buffalo, went to a German saloon which his new friend wanted to rob, and London made a quick exit, jumping from the men's room window in the back of the saloon. He then hopped a freight train and returned to California. Until the day of his premature death, London maintained that he was not allowed to plead guilty or not guilty.

Reporter David Florek has speculated that London's jailing may have inspired his description of Buck, the canine hero of *Call of the Wild*:

> Then the rope was removed and he was flung into a cagelike crate. There he lay for the remainder of the weary night, nursing his wrath and wounded pride. He could not understand what it all meant. What did they want with him, these strange men? Why were they keeping him pent up in this narrow crate? He did not know why, but he felt oppressed by the vague sense of impending calamity. Several times during the night he sprang to his feet when the shed door rattled. . . .

According to the police docket, London said he was single, had a mother and father who were living, listed his occupation as "sailor," and said his religion was "atheist."

On another occasion, London was an arson suspect. In 1910 upon becoming famous but broken in health and frayed in spirit, he planned a house to be called Wolf House at Glen Ellen, a few miles north of San Francisco. Its two-story living room ran the length of the 15,000-square-foot U-shaped house, and it was built around a spring-fed pool stocked with fish. "It will be a happy house—or else I'll burn it down," he once wrote in an essay (published in *The House Beautiful*, 1960). Just days before he was to move in, the house went up in flames. London was one of several suspects. A few weeks prior he had insured the place for $6,000., a small amount inasmuch as it was estimated to have been worth $80,000 at the time. However, in 1980 Professor Robert N. Anderson of San Jose State University wrote that workers polishing a wooden mantle had left oil-soaked rags in the dining room, that deprived of circulating air they heated to the point that they started smoking, and that they eventually caught fire.

An alcoholic, London committed suicide at the age of forty.

THE STONE THE BUILDERS REJECTED

His plaintive epitaph, above, is near the burial plot in Sonoma, California. {*Buffalo News*, 26 June 1994; CE; CL; JM; RAT; TYD}

London, Rick (20th Century)

A cartoonist syndicated by Great Southern Writers Syndicate, London is an active Unitarian and considers himself an agnostic. {CA}

Long, Becky (20th Century)

In 1996 Long spoke at a conference of the Alabama Freethought Association about the continuing Virgin Mary apparition saga which occurs in her state, Georgia. {*Freethought Today*, May 1996}

Long, Gabrielle Margaret (Born 1888)

Long at the age of eighteen published an historical novel, *The Vampire of Milan* (1906), and under the pen-name of Marjorie Bowen or George R. Preedy has written about one hundred forty novels, biographies, historical works, or plays. She has been a director of the Rationalist Press Association. {RE}

Long, George (Born 1856)

Long was an American chemist who from 1913 to 1917 was Dean of the School of Pharmacy at Northwestern University Medical School. He was a rationalist who severely criticized all the church. {RAT}

Long, Marcus (20th Century)

When he reviewed books for *The Humanist* in the 1950s, Long was a member of the philosophy department at the University of Toronto.

LONG-DISTANCE TELEPHONE SERVICE

Lifeline is a long-distance telephone service, which according to one of its earthly co-founders Carl Thompson, was founded by Jesus Christ. The Oklahoma City company bills $6 million a month in the Lord's name, rents established lines, and prays that in four years it will have its own line in order not to use the Devil's line, American Telephone and Telegraph. AT&T, Thompson complains, "helps gays and lesbians." Lifeline donates 20% of profits to the Founder—to "conquer the world in the name of Jesus."

LONGEST WORD: See entry for Aristophanes.

Longet, François Achille (1811–1871)

Longet was a French physiologist who published a *Treatise on Physiology in* three volumes. A freethinker, he wrote several medical works. {BDF}

LONGEVITY

Longevity, n. Uncommon extension of the fear of death.

—**Ambrose Bierce**
The Devil's Dictionary

Longfellow, Henry Wadsworth (1807–1882)

A professor of modern languages at Harvard for eighteen years, Longfellow wrote "Song of Hiawatha" and other works. His daughter Alice is quoted as saying that her father was born a Unitarian and remained one all his life. William Dean Howells, in his *Literary Friends and Acquaintances*, says that at the most Longfellow was a non-Christian theist. "I think, he says, "that as he grew older his hold upon anything like a creed weakened, though he remained of the Unitarian philosophy concerning Christ." The poet, he added, "did not latterly go to church." {CE; JM; RAT; RE; U; UU}

Longfellow, Samuel (1819–1892)

Brother of the poet Henry, Samuel made his place in Unitarian history as a hymnist, collaborating with Samuel Johnson on the well-known collection, *Hymns of the Spirit* (1864). In contrast to many of the Transcendentalists, Longfellow was interested in the act of corporate worship as well as individual devotion. O. B. Frothingham characterized the hymns of the two men as reflections of their complementary personalities: "Johnson's were the more intellectual, Longfellow's the more tender; Johnson's the more aspiring, Longfellow's the more devout; Johnson's the more heroic and passionate, Longfellow's the more mystical and reflective." {TRI; U; U&U}

Longman, Heber Albert (1880–1954)

Longman, a freethinker, rationalist, and paleontologist in Australia, came to Australia from England in 1902. In Toowoomba, he met Irene, his wife-to-be who became the first woman to be elected to the Queensland parliament. Longman was foundation President of the Queensland Rationalist and Ethical Society in 1914. While he was director of the Queensland Museum from 1917 to 1945, it was said that the staff never celebrated Christmas Day because of the director's atheism. Longman achieved international recognition for his scientific work on vertebrate paleontology, and he was probably the first to give courses on vertebrate fossils at the university in the geology department. Longman wrote *Religion of A Naturalist* (1914). {SWW}

Longo, Gabriel (20th Century)

Longo is author of *Spoiled Priest: The Autobiography of an Ex-priest* (1966).

Longue, Louis Pierre de (18th Century)

Longue was a French deist. A writer in the service of the house of Conti, he completed *Les Princesses de Malabares*, in which he satirized religion. The work was condemned to be burned in 1734, but a new edition was published in Holland with the imprint of Tranquebar was made in 1735. {BDF}

Loomans, Diane (20th Century)

Loomans is a contributor to *Family Matters*, the newsletter of the Secular Humanist Family.

Loomer, Ralph (20th Century)

In 1980, Loomer was awarded the Canadian Humanist of the Year Award.

LOOMPANICS

Loompanics (Box 1197, Port Townsend, Washington 98368), is a company which resells and publishes off-beat books of a freethought nature. Its owner, according to David Briars, is a "libertarian-gun-nut, anarchist, and a sometimes misogynist." {FD}

Lopes, Jose Leite (20th Century)

A Humanist Laureate in the Council for Secular Humanism's International Academy of Humanism, Lopes is professor emeritus of *Centro Brasileiro de Pesquisas Fisicas* in Brazil. Two of his works are *La ciencio y el dilema de America Latino* (1975) and *Quantum Mechanics* (1977). An essay, "Science and the Making of Society in Latin America," is included in *Challenges to the Enlightenment, Essays in Defense of Reason and Science* (1994). Lopes signed Humanist Manifesto 2000.

Lopez Zaragoza, Patricia (20th Century)

Lopez is President of Mexico's *Asociación Mexicana Ética Rationalista*. She spoke at a 1992 inaugural meeting in Toronto of the Coalition for Secular Humanism and Freethought as well as in 1995 at the dedication of the Center for Inquiry in Amherst, New York. "Sowing the Seeds of Secular Humanism in Mexico" (*Free Inquiry*, Summer 1994) details the plan being evolved to promote humanism in a country of practicing Catholics, many under the influence of an extremist right-wing sect, the Opus Dei. Lopez's description of secular humanism in Mexico is found in English in *International Humanist News* (June 1995). Her original article was published in the Mexican quarterly, *Razonamientos*.

In 1996, speaking in India at the Fourth World Atheist Conference, Lopez said, "To spread humanism throughout our countries is a great responsibility, since we can see every day how fundamentalist and theist ideas try to take over the many facets of daily life. This is a great problem in underdeveloped countries like India and Mexico, that openly declare themselves as secular states. . . . We must work for freedom from irrationality and superstition for even the humblest and most marginalized of all human beings."

Also in 1996, she was instrumental in planning the Humanist World Congress in Mexico City, at which she was a participant as well as organizer. Her e-mail: <mendez@spin.com.mx>. {*New Humanist*, February 1996, April 1996, December 1996}

Loptson, Peter (20th Century)

Loptson, a professor of philosophy at the University of Saskatchewan and a member of the Hume Society, is author of *Theories of Human Nature* (1995). The work explores the idea of human nature and the many understandings of it put forward by such diverse figures as Aristotle, Rousseau, Marx, Freud, Darwin, and E. O. Wilson.

Lorand, Georges (1851–1918)

Lorand was a Belgian journalist, an active propagator of atheistic doctrines among the youth at the university of Bologna and in workmen associations. He edited *La Réforme* at Brussels, and he campaigned against standing armies and for pacifist causes. {BDF}

LORD OF FLIES: See entry for Beelzebub.

Lord's Prayer: See a critique in the entry for Harold Hillman.

Lorenz, Marguerite (20th Century)

Lorenz is president of the Freethinker's Society in California. (See entry for California Atheists, Humanists.) {FD}

Loria, Rudolf Hermann (1817–1881)

Loria was a professor of political economy at Turin University and a distinguished member of the *Accademia dei Lincei*, the Royal Economic Society, the Sociological Society, and the International Institute of Sociology. He was a positivist of the Ardigo school and had no place for religion. {RAT}

LOS ALAMITOS HIGH SCHOOL ATHEISTS

The Los Alamitos (California) High School Atheists are on the Web at <http://www.secularhumanism.org/cfa/orgs.html>.

Loti, Pierre (1850–1923)

"Pierre Loti" was the adopted name of Louis Marie Julien Viaud, a French novelist. In 1867 he entered the French navy, attaining the rank of lieutenant before his resignation in 1898, and he wrote novels about his experiences. *Aziyadë (*1879) and *Rarahu* (1880) established his reputation. He was admitted to the French Academy in 1891. Loti's romantic works contain his rationalist ideas. {RAT}

Lotze, Rudolf Hermann (1817–1881)

A German philosopher and psychologist, Lotze attempted to reconcile the views of mechanistic science with the principles of romantic idealism. All phenomena, he posited, are determined by the interaction of atoms. He saw the atoms as centers of force operating in a matrix of a more basic substance. By analogy from the immediate knowledge of spiritual existence in the self, Lotze argued that the centers of force are stages of development within the underlying substance of the world. His theory of space perception was an important contribution to philosophy. Lotze accepted no Christian doctrine and admitted God only in the impersonal form of the Absolute. {CE; JM; RAT; RE}

Loubet, Emile [President] (1838–1929)

Loubet was President of the French Republic (1900–1906), a lawyer who took up politics and was of the anti-clerical wing led by Gambetta. His hesitance as premier in 1892 to investigate the Panama Canal scandal forced his resignation, but he continued as minister of the interior until 1893, becoming president of the senate in 1896. During his presidency of the French Republic, Premiers René Waldeck-Rousseau and Émile Combes secured the limiting of Church privilege, culminating (1905) in the separation of church and state in France. {CE; JM; RAT; RE}

Loucks, Terry and Ursula Loucks (20th Century)

Mr. and Mrs. Loucks are the authors of *Burning Woods* (1998), a novel in which Christina Sheridan, an anthropologist, pursues the most important manuscript known to Christianity. Concerning their book, they have commented:

> There are more dangerous places to travel than Kashmir, Upper Egypt, and the West Bank in spite of the perils of religious strife in these blood soaked regions. The most dangerous places to travel these days are the pages of New Testament scholarship, where the origins of Christianity are under siege. The historicity of Jesus and his disciples is undoubtedly the most controversial subject in our times. The long held Christian beliefs of our society are being threatened by scholarly research on recently discovered manuscripts like the Dead Sea Scrolls and the Nag Hammadi codices. The debate raging between New Testament scholars and the orthodox clergy often erupts on television and our weekly new magazines.
>
> In the past few months Jesus has appeared on the covers of *Newsweek*, *Time*, and *Atlantic Monthly* almost as often as Princess Diana. Most of us, however, do not know enough about these manuscripts or the ongoing scholarly research to know whether or not they impact our most sacred beliefs. Is our New Testament Jesus preserved in these scrolls and codices? If not, what new picture of Jesus emerges? What impact does this have on our core beliefs about life, both now and hereafter?
>
> These questions and many more, including the impact of Eastern religions are addressed in *Burning Words*, as are the religious implications of recent physics discoveries. We are confident that the adventures of Christina Sheridan, an anthropologist who pursues the most important manuscript known to Christianity, will be so captivating that the reader will be unaware of how much they have learned until the smoke clears in the final scene of the chase.

Tom Flynn, however, found that the book shows "a New Age mix of quantum mysticism, the anthropic principle, and Eastern spirituality." {*Free Inquiry*, Summer 1999}

LOUISIANA HUMANISTS

• New Orleans Secular Humanist Association, 2905 Bryant St., Metairie, Lousiana 70003; (504) 456-6550

• Shreveport Secular Humanists (Council for Secular Humanism), 9476 Boxwood Drive, Shreveport, Louisiana 71118-4003; telephone (318) 687-8175. E-mail: <wwatkins40@aol.com> and <dan@softdisk.com>. Web: <http://www.softdisk.com/comp/shume/>.

Louÿs, Pierre (1870–1925)

A French poet and novelist, Louÿs (whose real name was Pierre Louis) translated the Greek poets and completed thoroughly pagan novels about ancient Greek life. *Aphrodite* (1896) has been presented on the stage and in 1906 was made into an opera. *Chansons de Bilitis* (1894) are lyrics in the manner of Sappho. {RAT}

LOVE

Love, the most humanistic of feelings, has been described variously over the centuries:

• She moves a goddess, and she looks a queen.

–Homer (around 850 B.C.E.)

• There are two days when a woman is a pleasure: the day one mar ries her and the day one buries her.

–Hipponax (c. 570–520 B.C.E.)

• Man's best possession is a sympathetic wife.

–**Euripides** (484–406 B.C.E.)

• Sometimes give your services for nothing, calling to mind a previous benefaction or present satisfaction. And if there be an opportunity of serving one who is a stranger in financial straits, give full assistance to all such. For where there is love of man, there is also love of the art. For some patients, though conscious that their condition is perilous, recover their health simply through their contentment with the goodness of the physician.

–**Hippocrates** (460–377 B.C.E.)

• I think I had better bathe before I drink the poison, and not give the women the trouble of washing my dead body.

–Socrates (470–399 B.C.E.)

• In childhood a woman must be subject to her father; in youth, to her husband; when her husband is dead, to her sons. A woman must never be free of subjugation.

–Hindu *Laws of Manu* (c. 200 B.C.E.–300 C.E.)

• Thy love to me was wonderful, passing the love of women.

–David, King of Judah and Israel (c. 1016–976 B.C.E.),
lamenting the death of Jonathan, *II Samuel* I:26

• Stay me with flagons, comfort me with apples: for I am sick of love. His left hand is under my head, and his right hand doth embrace me.

–*Song of Solomon* (3rd Century B.C.E.?)

• I hate and I love. Why I do so, perhaps you ask. I do not know, but I feel it and I am in torment.

–**Catullus** (84?–54? B.C.E)

• Love conquers all.

–Vergil (70–19 B.C.E)

• Greater love hath no man than this, that a man lay down his life for his friends.

–*St. John* 15:13 (2nd Century C.E.?)

• When you see a woman, consider that you face not a human being, but the devil himself. The woman's voice is the hiss of the snake.

–Saint Anthony, (251?–350)

• When Eve was created, Satan rejoiced.

–Muhammad (570?–632)

• Men are the supporters of women. . . . Good women are therefore obedient. . . . Admonish those women you fear will desert you, and leave them alone in the sleeping places, and beat them.

–*The Qur'an* (651–652)

• . . . in divine matrimony man receives by divine institution the faculty to use his wife for the begetting of children.

–Saint Thomas Aquinas (1225–1274)

• But love a womman that she woot it nought,
And she wol quyte it that thow shalt nat fele;
Unknowe, unkist, and lost, that is unsought.

–Geoffrey Chaucer (1340?–1400)

• Up from the earth I rose with his wings,
And death itself I could have found sweet.

–Michelangelo (1475–1564)
from a sonnet to Febo di Poggio,
a model and young male prostitute

• I live and love in God's peculiar light.

–Michelangelo (1475–1564)

• Love me, love my dog.

–John Heywood (1497–1580)

• Nature doth paint them [women] further to be weak, frail, impatient, feeble and foolish; and experience hath declared them to be unconstant, variable, cruel, and lacking the spirit of counsel.

–John Knox (c. 1514–1572)

• Nay, but to live
In the rank sweat of an enseamed bed,
Stew'd in corruption, honeying and making love
Over the nasty sty. . . .

–William Shakespeare (1564–1616)

• Absence is to love what wind is to fire; it extinguishes the small, it enkindles the great.

–Comte de Bussy-Rabutin (1618–1693)

• Whatever you do, stamp out abuses, and love those who love you.

–**Voltaire** (1694–1778)

• Friendship is Love without his wings.

–**Lord Byron** (1788–1824)

• Love's like the measles–all the worse when it comes late in life.

–Douglas Jerrold (1803–1857)

• How do I love thee? Let me count the ways.

–Elizabeth Barrett Browning (1806–1861)

• Faint heart never won fair lady!
Nothing venture, nothing win—
Blood is thick, but water's thin—
In for a penny, in for a pound—
It's Love that makes the world go round!

–William Schwenck Gilbert (1836–1911)

• Woman was God's second mistake. . . . Love is the state in which man sees things most decidedly as they are not.

–**Friedrich Nietzsche** (1844-1900)

• Religion has done love a great service by making it a sin.

–**Anatole France** (1844-1944)

• I delight in men over seventy. They always offer one the devotion of a lifetime.

–Oscar Wilde (1854-1900)

• Home is the girl's prison and the woman's workhouse.

–**George Bernard Shaw** (1856-1950)

• Married life presupposes the power of the husband over the wife and children, and subjection and obedience of the wife to the husband.

–Pope Pius XI (1857-1939)

• A pushing lady:
What are your views on love?
Mme. Leroi:
Love? I make it constantly but I never talk about it.

–**Marcel Proust** (1871–1922)

• The good life is one inspired by love and guided by knowledge.

–**Bertrand Russell** (1872–1970)

• Love consists in this, that two solitudes protect and touch and greet each other.

–Rainer Maria Rilke (1875–1926)

• Sappho wrote only of one theme, sang it, laughed it, sighed it, wept it, sobbed it. . . a song of love.

–**Willa Cather** (1876–1947)

• "Who was that lady I saw you with last night?"
"She ain't no lady; she's my wife."

–Joseph Weber and Lew Fields
in an 1887 vaudeville routine

• The program of our National Socialist women's movement contains really only one single point. This point is the child that must come into being that must thrive.

–Adolf Hitler (1889–1945)

• As the girl said, "A kiss on the wrist feels good, but a diamond bracelet lasts forever."

–**Adlai Stevenson** (1900–1965)

• Like all the very young we took it for granted that making love is child's play.

–Nancy Mitford (1904–1973)

• Three o'clock is always too late or too early for anything you want to do.

–**Jean-Paul Sartre** (1905–1980)

• Take my wife . . . please.

–Henny Youngman (1906–)

• It's not only this we praise,
it's the general love:
Let cat's mew rise to a scream
on the tool-shed roof.

–W. H. Auden (1907–1973)

• The female sex is in some respects inferior to the male sex, both as regards body and soul.

–*Roman Catholic Encyclopedia* (1912)

• Love is the extremely difficult realization that something other than oneself is real.

Iris Murdoch (1919-1999)

• Each of us who takes a wife does so only for the purpose of bringing children into the world. He is like the farmer who entrusts the soil with his seed and then patiently waits for the crop.

–Patriarch Athenagoras (20th Century)

• Love means never having to say you're sorry.

–Erich Segal (1937–)

• I get no kick from champagne.
Mere alcohol doesn't thrill me at all,
So tell me why should it be true
That I get a kick out of you.

–Cole Porter, 1934

• I *sleep* with Mr. Williams.

–Frank Merlo (1922–1963),
secretary to Tennessee Williams,
when asked by Hollywood mogul Jack Warner,
"And what do you do, young man?"

• Crucifixes are sexy because there's a naked man on them.

–Madonna, pop star in the 1990s

• Come on, baby, light my fire.

–The Doors, a 20th-Century rock and roll group

• I Wanna Sex You Up.

–Color Me Badd
(2 million music albums sold, 1993)

• So if you at a show in the front row
I'm a call you a bitch or a dirty-ass ho
You probably get mad like a bitch is supposed to . . .
So what about the bitch who got shot?
Fuck her. You think I give a damn about a bitch?

–N.W.A., "Straight Outta Compton" (1993),
an African American musical rap group

• Her body's beautiful so I'm thinkin' rape
Shouldn't have had her curtains open
so that's her fate . . . .
Slit her throat and watched her shake.

–The Geto Boys, "Mind of a Lunatic,"
(1993) an African American musical rap group

• In the ancient world, romantic love would seem to have been virtually unknown, and rarely celebrated. Our generic term "love" didn't exist. The sentiment of romantic love as we know it was the homoerotic love of older Greek men for boys; marital love, which surely existed, seems oddly not to have been much honored, at least in surviving literature. Plato's elaborately extended metaphor of the republic, or the perfectly balanced state, discusses marriage primarily as mating; by contrast, Plato's "Symposium" celebrates homoerotic love in the most blushingly romantic terms. How different this is from the extramarital erotic attraction of heterosexuals, which results in devastation and violent death. In Euripides' "Hippolytus," for instance, the young Queen Phaedra falls in love with her husband's illegitimate son, who rejects her, and causes her to commit suicide; Phaedra is no romantic, but rather the victim of an ungovernable, unwished-for passion imposed upon her by Aphrodite. Such sexual desire is akin to a curse. . . .

Just as the majority of humankind will continue to believe in gods of various denominations when no actual gods have been sighted, so men and women will continue to fall under the spell of romantic love and to shape, or misshape their lives to that end. Biologists may grimly describe for us the mammalian underpinnings of courtship, mating, bonding, fidelity (where there is in fact fidelity)—but, being human, knowing full well as the song warns us that "falling in love with love is falling for make-believe," we are the species that demands to be lied to, in the nicest ways.

–**Joyce Carol Oates**
The New York Times Magazine, 18 April 1999

• It starts when you sink in his arms and ends with your arms in his sink.

–Anonymous

• **love** *n* [ME, fr. OE *lufu*; akin to OHG *luba* love, OE *leof* dear, L *lubere, libere* to please] (bef. 12c) . . . (1) : strong affection for another arising out of kinship or personal ties; (2) : attraction based on sexual desire : affection and tenderness felt by lovers; (3) : affection based on admiration, benevolence, or common interests. . . . (8) a score of zero (as in tennis).

–*Merriam-Webster's Collegiate Dictionary, 10th Edition* (1993)

Love, John (1868–1947)

Love was a secularist and atheist. He supported Joseph Symes, secretary of the Australian Secularist Association during the time of a factional split and a fight for control of the Melbourne Hall of Science in 1888. {SWW}

Love, Stephen A. (20th Century)

Love wrote "And the Truth Shall Make You Free, An Atheist's Philosophy" (1965). {GS}

Lovecraft, H(oward) P(hillips) (1890–1937)

Lovecraft, called "The King of Weird" by Joyce Carol Oates, has been a generally overlooked American writer. Asexual and an atheist, he has been compared favorably with the gothicist Edgar Allan Poe for his grotesque tales.

His *The Shadow Out of Time* (1936) told of a researcher's body taken over by a member of an ancient race that had lived 150,000,000 years ago, one driven underground by the Great Race of giant living cones from the transgalactic world of Yith. One of the group, in the commandeered body and using ESP routinely, finds in the world he visits big airships and atomic-powered vehicles.

Lovecraft is said to have been proud of his life-long atheism, that the Cthulhu Mythos he wrote about was an "anti-mythology," described by Oates as "an ironic inversion of traditional religious faith. It constitutes an elaborate, detailed working-out of an early recurring fantasy of Lovecraft's that an entire alien civilization lurks on the underside of the known world: as a 'night-gaunt' may lurk beneath a child's bed in the darkness, or as mankind's tragically divided nature may lurk beneath civilization's veneer." In the Cthulhu Mythos were no "gods," just displaced extra-terrestrial beings, the Great Old Ones, leading to his view that deluded human beings mistake the Great Old Ones and their descendants for gods, worshiping them out of ignorance.

Like Poe, Oates has written, Lovecraft "set forth an aesthetics of the art to which, by temperament, and family history, he was fated. (Lovecraft's frequently updated essay 'Supernatural Horror in Literature' [1927] is a pioneering effort in tracing the history of the gothic sensibility from Ann Radcliffe, Hugh Walpole, 'Monk' Lewis, and Charles Maturin through Emily Brontë, Hawthorne, Poe, and Lovecraft's contemporaries Algernon Blackwood, Arthur Machen, Lord Dunsany, M. R. James, and others.) Both tried to sell their writing and editing skills in a debased and demeaning marketplace, with little financial reward, burning themselves out in the process. Both were beset by dreams, nightmares, 'visions.' Both entered upon brief, disastrous marriages (though there are bleakly comical overtones to Lovecraft's marriage to a woman seven years his elder.) Both left no heirs. Both died prematurely. Poe at forty, Lovecraft at forty-six, having egregiously mistreated their bodies."

For him, "weird fiction" is a product of an age that has ceased to believe collectively in the supernatural but still retaining the primitive instinct to do so. S. T. Joshi almost single-handedly has kept his work in the public eye. His *H. P. Lovecraft: A Life* (1996) was preceded by his editing of Lovecraft's fiction: *The Dunwich Horror and Others*; *At the Mountains of Madness and Other Novels*; *Dagon and Other Macabre Tales*; *Miscellaneous Writings*; and five volumes of *Selected Letters*.

Lovecraft was so unattractive that he is said to have hidden from everyone and did not like to walk where people would gaze at him. Following his father's death from syphilis, Lovecraft wore his deceased father's clothes. As a child he repudiated his mother's family's Baptist faith. Although he had stark, melancholy eyes, had a peculiar and stiff conduct, and wore "archaic" clothes, Sonia Greene, a writer-businesswoman, fell in love with him, and he consented to marry her. However, the marriage failed and after two years she asked for a divorce. Lovecraft is said to have been kind, patient, generous, unassuming, and gentlemanly in his personal relations, but in keeping with his Tory sensibility Oates found that he was an anti-Semite (despite his affection for Sonia Greene and other Jewish friends), racist, and an all-purpose Aryan bigot.

Like Poe, Lovecraft died with the self-estimate that his life had been a failure. Little could he have imagined that *Lovecraft's Best Supernatural Tales* would one day sell more than 67,000 copies in hardcover in a single year.

Lovecraft is buried in Providence, Rhode Island's Swan Point Cemetery, his granite monument simply inscribed with name and vital dates. {Joyce Carol Oates, "The King of Weird," *The New York Review of Books*, 31 October 1996}

Lovejoy, Arthur Oncken (1873–1962)

Lovejoy was an American philosopher and intellectual historian. He founded and was the first editor of the *Journal of the History of Ideas*. He made a distinction between the history of a philosophical system and the history of an idea—which may be shared by different systems and unlike the system may originate in or influence areas far removed from philosophy. His work argued for and encouraged an interdisciplinary approach in the study of philosophy, history, literature, and science. Lovejoy translated Bergson. His dissent from the creeds, which he wrote about in the *Hibbert Journal* (January 1907), stated that Christianity would be "invaluable" if it were stripped of its "historical elements," or characteristic doctrines. {CE; RAT}

Lovett, Robert Morss (1870–1956)

Morse was on the advisory board of Charles Francis Potter's First Humanist Society of New York. A University of Chicago professor of English, he wrote *Edith Wharton* (1950), a critical study. He also wrote *A Preface to Fiction* (1930), the play *Cowards* (1914), and an autobiography, *All Our Years* (1948). He edited *The Dial* (1919) and was long an associate editor of *The New Republic*. A distinguished literary figure, Lovett signed Humanist Manifesto I. {HM1; FUS}

Low, Clarence Harry (1884–1970?)

Low, who was treasurer of the New York Democratic State Committee from 1934 to 1941, was on the advisory board of Charles Francis Potter's First Humanist Society of New York. {HNS}

Low, David [Sir] (1891–1963)

Low, a freethinker, was a vice president in England of the National Council for Civil Liberties. {TRI}

Lowder, Jeffery Jay (20th Century)

Lowder, a freethinker and officer at the U.S. Air Force Academy in Colorado Springs, Colorado, spoke in 1996 at a meeting of the Alabama Freethought Association. He is a regional director of the Council for Secular Humanism.

An activist on behalf of freethought, he and Brett Lemoine in 1995 started Internet Infidels, a major site for nontheists on the World Wide Web: <http://www.infidels.org>.

Lowe, Ian (1942–)

Lowe is an Australian humanist and scientist. Since 1980 he has been director of the Science Policy Research Centre. Active in environmental groups, he is a member of the Council of Australian Consumers' Association and Scientists Against Nuclear Arms. In 1988, Lowe was awarded Humanist of the Year. {SWW}

Lowell, Amy (1874–1925)

An imagist poet, Lowell received a posthumous Pulitzer Prize in 1925 for *What's o'Clock.* Independent and defiant of social norms, the unmarried and lesbian poet enjoyed a good cigar and credited Ada Dwyer Russell, an actress, with giving her the emotional support she needed. A unitarian in her outlook, she was quite the nonconformist. In *What's o'Clock* (1925), she wrote, "I know that a creed is the shell of a lie." "Her confirmation as a member of Trinity Church did not last long," Jean Gould writes in the biography, *Amy* (1975). "She renounced conventional Christianity after a few years. . . . She would declare herself an atheist, although she was more of an agnostic. . . . Amy became convinced through her own sufferings and those of others that the god of this world, if there was one, was a devil and she did not hesitate to reject demonstration of deity." Further, she stipulated "that there be no formal funeral or gathering, and no religious service."

A collateral descendant of James Russell Lowell, she is identified with the literary movement of Imagism and, after Ezra Pound, became its main leader. Imagists advocated freedom in choosing subject matter, use of common speech, new rhythmic forms, concentration, and bringing about images in hard, clear common speech, precision, the creation of new rhythms, absolute freedom in choice of subject matter, the evocation of images in hard, clear poetry, and concentration. Its adherents wrote for *Poetry: A Magazine of Verse.*

Although D. H. Lawrence and others were attracted, language teachers in general have had trouble explaining to neophyte poets why a work has to have complete sentences, in order to communicate, when the imagists got by using fragments like . . .

> Heart-leaves of lilac all over New England,
> Roots of lilac under all the soil of New England,
> Lilac in me because I am New England.

Exceptionally obese and suffering ill health brought on by an injury suffered while lifting a buggy out of a ditch, Lowell died of a stroke. {CE; EG; GL; TYD; U; UU}

Lowell, C. Stanley (20th Century)

Lowell, a freethinker, wrote *The Great Church-State Fraud* (1973) and *The Religious Empire* (1976). {GS}

Lowell, James Russell (1819–1891)

A professor of modern languages at Harvard, an abolitionist, and a minister to Spain and Great Britain, Lowell was a Unitarian and the son of Unitarian minister Charles Lowell. "Toward no crimes," Lowell once wrote, "have men shown themselves so cold-bloodedly cruel as in punishing differences of belief." He also declared, "It seems to me that the bane of our country is a profession of faith either with no basis of real belief, or with no proper examination of the grounds on which the creed is supposed to rest."

While minister to London from 1877 to 1885, he influenced European opinion as to the growing stature of American letters and institutions. *A Fable for Critics* (1848), *The Bigelow Papers* (1848 and 1867), and *The Vision of Sir Launfal* (1848) are among his best works. Also, he was an editor of *The North American Review* and was the first editor of *Atlantic Monthly* (1857–1861). McCabe found that Lowell did not believe in a future life and, when Howells asked him whether he still believed in "a moral government of the universe," Lowell replied evasively that "the scale is so vast and we see so little of it," an admission of his agnosticism. {CE; JM; RAT; RE; TRI; TYD; U; UU}

Lowell, John A. (1798–1881)

Lowell, the founder of Boston's Lowell Institute, was a Unitarian. {U}

Lowell, Josephine Shaw (1843–1905)

Lowell was appointed by New York Governor Samuel Jones Tilden to the State Board of Charities, becoming its first woman commissioner. He had admired her interest in improving the conditions of mentally retarded women and women in trouble. Lowell came from a family of dedicated Unitarians and was friends with actress Fanny Kemble, poet Henry Wadsworth Longfellow, and Ralph Waldo Emerson. Her marriage in 1863 to Colonel Charles Russell Lowell ended a year later when he was killed in battle. General Sheridan had said of her husband, "He was the perfection of a man and a soldier." Mrs. Lowell's brother, Robert Gould Shaw, was leader of the black 54th Massachusetts Regiment. {EG}

Lowell, Maria White (19th Century)

Lowell, the wife of poet James Russell Lowell, was an ardent abolitionist and liberal who encouraged her husband in his work. She was a Unitarian.

Lowell, Percival (1855–1916)

A distinguished astronomer, Lowell spent ten years in Japan where he learned to disdain Christianity and became an agnostic. His sentiments are expressed in his *Soul of the Far East* (1886). {JM; RE}

Lowell, Robert (1917–1977)

According to David Tribe, Lowell became an outright freethinker. The American poet, whose work was richly symbolic and often autobiographical, was influenced by "new critic" John Crowe Ransom. "The kind of poet I am was largely determined by the fact that I grew up in the heyday of the New Criticism," Lowell wrote in the *Kenyon Collegian* (1974). "From the beginning I was preoccupied with technique, fascinated by the past, tempted by other languages."

Upon marrying his first wife, the novelist Jean Stafford, Lowell became a fanatical convert to Roman Catholicism, but his *Land of Unlikeness* (1944) betrays the conflict of Catholicism and his Boston ancestry. In the Second World War, he was jailed for six months as a conscientious objector. His second wife was Elizabeth Hardwick. Lowell reached the height of his public fame during his opposition to the Vietnam war and support of Senator Eugene McCarthy. He then married the writer Caroline Blackwood in 1973, and his later work is said to have indicated a philosophic acceptance of life and the world

In 1946 he received a Pulitzer Prize for *Lord Weary's Castle*, and he received another Pulitzer in 1973 for *The Dolphin.* Humanists have highly praised his translation of Aeschylus's *Prometheus Bound* (1969). {TRI}

Lowen, Jeanette (20th Century)

Lowen is a secularist who has written in *Free Inquiry* about the humanism of Albert Camus. She is author of *Imagine a World Without Boundaries* and *Anger in Twentieth-Century American Living.*
Löwith, Karl (20th Century)

Löwith wrote *Nietzsche's Philosophy of the Eternal Recurrence of the Same* (1935) during the days of National Socialist Germany. Harvey Lomax in 1997 translated the work, which H. James Birx (*Philo* Spring-Summer 1998) has called a key work that "presents a clear, focused, scholarly, and level-headed analysis and evaluation of the great philosopher's awesome and central concept of the eternal recurrence. Löwith often lets Nietzsche speak for himself, but this does not detract from a splendid presentation of the controversial thinker's system of ideas. Special attention is given to *Thus Spake Zarathustra* (1883-1885), which Löwith points out is Nietzsche's major work."

Lowry, Michael (20th Century)

Lowry, while a student at the University of Texas in Austin, was one of the founding members of Campus Freethought Alliance. {*International Humanist News*, December 1996}

Loynes, Paul E. (20th Century)

Loynes is a contributing editor to the *Secular Humanist Bulletin*.

Lozano, Fernando (19th Century)

In Madrid, Spain, Lozano edited *Dominicales del Libre Pensamiento* from 1894 to 1910. He used the pseudonym "Demófilo." He also wrote *Battles of Freethought*, *Possessed by the Devil*, and *The Church and Galeote*. {BDF; RAT}

Lubar, Katherine (20th Century)

Lubar is the women's contact for tht English Gay & Lesbian Humanist Association. E-mail: <KatLubar@compuserve.com>.

Lubbock, John [Sir] (1834–1913)

Lubbock was a banker, an archeologist, a scientist, and a statesman. He wrote *Prehistoric Times as Illustrated by Ancient Remains, and the Manners and Customs of Modern Savage* (1865) and *The Origin of Civilisation and the Primitive Condition of Man* (1870). {BDF; RAT}

Lucas, George W. Jr. (1944-)

Lucas is the film director whose financially successful works include being director of "Star Wars" (1977) and its companion films about the distant future. He told *Time* that he put the Force into "The Phantom Menace" (1999) "to try to awaken a certain kind of spirituality in young people." Asked if he believed in a higher being, he said, "I think there is a God. No question. What that God is or what we know about that God, I'm not sure." Edward Sorel, a freethinker known for his satire and art, was so amused by the answer that he wrote (*The Nation*, 7 June 1999), "Contrary to rumors that circulated before the film opened, God is *not* the phantom menace referred to in the movie title."

Lucas, H. (19th Century)

Lucas was a freethinker who wrote "The Revolution Which Began in Heaven, or Coela-Tartaraterra" (1850). {GS}

Lucas, Helen M. (20th Century)

Lucas wrote *A View of Lambert's "Notes on Ingersoll"* (1909). {GS}

Lucas, Jeff (20th Century)

Lucas is treasurer of Internet Infidels. E-mail: <jlucas@infidels.org>.

Luchaire, Achille (1846–1908)

Luchaire taught mediaeval history at Paris University. He wrote the six-volume *Innocent III* (1904-1908) and *France at the Time of Philippe Augustus* (1912), the latter work a refutation of the myth of mediaeval virtue, piety, and chivalry. Luchaire was a rationalist. {RE}

Lucian (c. 125–180)

A Greek prose writer, also called Lucianus, Lucian wrote masterly Attic prose in which he satirized Olympian fables and exposed the ineptitude of contemporary philosophers. Rabelais and Swift claimed they were greatly influenced by him.

The Montreal critic M. Morgan Holmes has pointed out that Lucian, in *Dialogues of the Gods*, describes Zeus's "pederastic infatuation with the lunkheaded Ganymede . . . in keeping with the sensuality of the heterosexual gods. *Lucius, or the Ass* includes a rollicking tale of priests who capture a village youth and force him to have sex with them, thus making a minor point on moral hypocrisy." In *A True Story*, Lucian describes a voyage to the moon where it is found there are no women and where marriage and procreation is between men under twenty-five. But moonmen do not have an anus, so intercourse is through an opening above the calf, and new men are thus conceived in the thigh. Alternately, 'tree people' emerge from acorns that grow on enormous penis-shaped trees of flesh produced by the planting of right testicles in the ground."

When Marcus Aurelius appointed the freethinking Lucian to a post of high authority in Egypt, Aurelius showed that Lucian's writings gave no great offense at court, where, reports Robertson, "religious seriousness was rare." According to Suidas, Lucian was named "the blasphemer" and torn to pieces by dogs for his impiety, but Wheeler reports Suidas was wishful-thinking. On the ground of his dialogue *Philopatris*, Lucian has been supposed an apostate Christian, but Wheeler states that work may not be genuine. What is known is that Lucian was skeptical, truth-loving, and an enemy of the superstition of the time, which he depicts in his account of Alexander, the false prophet. Thomas Wise in *A confutation of the reason and philosophy of atheism* (1706) attempted to repress the fact that Lucian was atheistic. His works have contemporary overtones:

- We were all drunk but Akindynos
  and so Akindynos
  seemed the only drunkard of us all.

- O lovely Whiskers O inspirational Mop!
  But if growing a beard, my friend,
  means acquiring wisdom,
  any old goat can be Plato.

{BDF; CE; GL; HAB; JMR; JMRH}

Luciani, Luigi (Born 1842)

Luciani succeeded Moleschott as professor of physiology at Rome University and Director of the Physiological Institute. His *Localizationi funzionali del cervello* (1885) was crowned by the Lombard Institute. A Senator, a Commander of the Orders of S. S. Lazarus and Maurice and the Crown of Italy, Luciani also is a member of the *Accademia dei Lincei*. His views resemble those of Moleschott and are of a materialist tendency. {RAT}

Lucifer

Lucifer is the planet Venus, or the morning star, "the bringer (or herald) of the light." In Latin, *luc-* and *lux* refer to light, and *-fer* means ferous. In addition, the word became a theological invention referring to an archangel who was cast from Heaven into Hell because he rebelled against God.

Lucifer is usually identified with Satan. Because the name Lucifer means "bearer of light" or "morning star," apologeticians explain that this refers to his *former* splendor as the greatest of the angels. Meanwhile, for freethinkers and humanists, Lucifer is the planet Venus. {DCL; RE}

Lucilius, Gaius (c 180–102 B.C.E.?)

Lucilius, the Latin satiric poet and founder of Latin satire, influenced Horace, Juvenal, and Persius. His works contain pungent wit and humanistic sentiment not unlike that heard in contemporary times (and as shown in a translation by Dudley Fitts):

- Darling, at the Beautician's you buy
  Your [a] hair
  [b] complexion
  [c] lips
  [d] dimples, &
  [e] teeth.
  For a like amount you could just as well buy a face.
- When as in sleep the slender Artemidôra lay,
  Demetrios fanned her with an ostrich-plume, &
  Blew her clean out of the house.
- Firmly, as with one voice,
  The entire Faculty of the College of Applied Astrology
  Foretold a healthy old age for my father's brother.
  Hermokleidês alone
  Maintained that he would die young;

but he made this statement
At the funeral service we held for my father's brother.

{CE}

Lucretius (Titus Lucretius Carus) (c. 96–c. 55 B.C.E.)

In *De Rerum Natura*, the Roman poet and philosopher Lucretius wrote, "Nothing can be created out of nothing" and "*Tantus religio potuit suadere malorum*" [So much wrong could religion induce]. Little is known of Lucretius, some of whose works were destroyed. St. Jerome alleges that Lucretius produced his didactic masterpiece—six books totaling 7,400 hexameter lines—in a fit of madness, culminating in suicide. Thoughtfully, states Antony Flew in the *Encyclopedia of Unbelief*, "the saint added that his affliction was the result of taking a poisoned love philtre." Flew explains that what Jerome held against Lucretius was that his work expounds the most coherent system of materialism in the ancient world, that of Epicurus. Hobbes agreed, that stuff is all there is and that everything which is not stuff is nonsense. Stuff consists of atoms. All our knowledge of all there is must, therefore, be based upon sensory perception. Although Aristotle did not accept his theory, Lucretius developed Leucippus's and Democritus's idea that matter is composed of tiny, indivisible particles in constant motion. It was not until the 18th century that the atomic theory was updated, and in 1808 John Dalton held that all the atoms of an element are of exactly the same size and weight.

During the French Revolution, Maréchal cited Lucretius as being one of the greatest atheists of all time. According to Robertson, *On the Nature of Things,* "with its enthusiastic exposition of the doctrine of Epicurus, remains to show to what a height of sincerity and ardour a Roman freethinker could rise. No Greek utterance that has come down to us makes so direct and forceful an attack as his on religion as a social institution. He is practically the first systematic freethinking propagandist; so full is he of his purpose that after his stately prologue to *alma Venus*, who is for him but a personification of the genetic forces of Nature, he plunges straight into his impeachment of religion as a foul tyranny from which thinking men were first freed by Epicurus."

A contemporary who has been significantly influenced by Lucretius is novelist Gore Vidal who, in *Palimpsest* (1995), told how Lucretius anticipated Darwin by two thousand years. Lucretius reasoned, "For it is not true as I think, that the race of mortal creatures [man] were let down from on high by some golden chain," to which Vidal added, "So much for the antique notion of Cadmus sowing dragon's teeth to create human beings or the peculiarly silly story of Adam and Eve believed by so many of my countrymen." Vidal continued: "Lucretius is aware—how, I wonder?—that we evolved. I've often quoted his law that nothing can come from nothing, but wonder about his corollary that nothing can go to nothing since, if the *it* is transitive—the going, that is—then it must be *some*thing and so, by definition, not *no*thing." Further, Vidal notes, Lucretius was a "proto-ecologist, fretting about overpopulation. Nature 'of her own accord first made for mortals the bright corn and the luxuriant vineyards of herself; she gave forth sweet fruits and luxuriant pasturage,' but now 'we exhaust our oxen and the strength of our farmers, we wear out the plow share, and then are scarce fed by our fields'; man seems congenitally unaware that 'all things gradually decay, and go to the reef of destruction, outworn by the ancient lapse of years.' Thus he anticipates," wrote Vidal, "the second law of thermodynamics, not to mention giddy entropy."

Christians generally frown upon Lucretius's work, calling it the ravings of a mad man. Many philosophers, however, are favorably impressed by his sociology or philosophy of history. Wheeler wrote of Lucretius, "Full of animation, dignity, and sublimity, he invests philosophy with the grace of genius."

McCabe, taking Lucretius literally rather than figuratively, finds it interesting "that Lucretius seems to take seriously Epicurus' idea of gods, more or less of the Olympian type but respectable, living a lotus-life in some remote part of space." Others take Lucretius' ideas figuratively, not literally. (See entries for Death and for Gore Vidal.) {BDF; CE; CL; EU; ER; HNS2; JM; JMR; JMRH; RE; TSV; TYD}

Lucy

The oldest known freethinking naturalistic humanist? That could be Lucy, the skeleton found in 1974 and estimated by geologists to be 3.2 million years old, plus or minus 10,000 years.

Named for the Beatles' song "Lucy in the Sky With Diamonds" and inarguably not a theist, Lucy has been exhibited in various galleries but rests permanently in a wooden box in a safe in Addis Ababa, Ethiopia. (See entries for Catopithecus, Donald Carl Johanson, and Paleontology.)

LUDDITES

Luddites oppose technical or technological changes. Named after Ned Ludd, or King Ludd, who allegedly destroyed knitting machines in an English industrial center, the group rioted between 1811 and 1816 in Nottinghamshire because of low wages and prevailing unemployment. This they attributed to machinery.

In the 1990s, some Luddites have fled to the woods and have replaced items in column one with those in column two, according to Bob Ickes in *New York* (24 July 1995):

voice mail	secretary
rollerblading	jogging
computer spellcheck	proofreaders
supermarkets	farmer greenmarkets
computer chess	chess
halogen lamps	beeswax candles
faxes	messengers
tele-democracy	town meetings
digital watches	watches that need winding
electric mowers	mowers that are pushed
touchtone telephones	rotary phones
cybersex	sex
laptop computers	typewriters with 43 gravity-controlled keys

Lüdemann, Gerd (20th Century)

Lüdemann is a professor of New Testament Studies at the University of Göttingen, Germany. In *The Great Deception, and What Jesus Really Said and Did* (1999), he charges that church authorities have long covered up historical evidence about Jesus. Jesus, he holds, was an inspiring person. However, those Christians who cannot separate what he authentically said and did are lending support to falsehoods that make traditional Christianity unbelievable.

The German Confederation of Protestant Churches in Lower Saxony demanded Lüdemann's dismissal from the theological faculty, and although he has retained his university post the chair he holds had to be renamed to disassociate him from the training program of German pastors.

Ludendorff, Erich (General) (1865–1937)

A German political leader, Ludendorff in a 1935 press interview stated, "I am not merely an opponent of Christianity; I am a heathen—and proud of it." {TYD}

Ludovici, Anthony (Born 1882)

Ludovici, an artist and illustrator, became interested in Nietzsche and translated six of Nietzsche's works. In 1910 he wrote *Nietzsche* and in 1911 *Nietzsche and Art*. Ludovici shared Nietzsche's view of religion. {RAT}

Ludvigh, Samuel (19th Century)

In New York and Baltimore, Ludvigh edited *Fackel* in the 1840s.

Ludwig, Emil (1881–1948)

Ludwig, a German biographer (said to have written unreliable portraits of Goethe, Napoleon, and Bismarck), wrote of his pantheism:

> Son of a naturalist and humanist, I was brought up in the precepts of neither Moses nor Jesus. Moral values were self-evident. . . . And why salvation? From what? The thought of man's fall and his original sin as the medium between God and myself, as well as the whole conception of a transfigured Son of God who will save me from the hell burning beneath paradise: this is alien to me. I have never disturbed this belief in others, nor have I envied them for it. To me Jesus—whom I later was to represent as a fighter and prophet—was as worthy of reverence as Socrates, because he died for truth, as men are doing again today. Goethe spoke the daring words, "The conviction of my continuation after death springs from my belief in action. For if I continue to work ceaselessly until my death, then nature is obliged to give me another form of existence when the present one can no longer house my spirit." The force of this argument impressed me even in my youth, and I have arrived at similar sources of a faith which rests, fundamentally, upon realistic forms.
>
> On this account my belief is all the more easily associated with a pantheism which sees God in all manifestations of nature, whether peopled with discrete gods or seen as one all-inherent spirit. . . . I recognize God in the logical construction of a crystal no less than in that of a Bach fugue. I see God in the pleading look of a dog as well as in the lovely bosom of a woman. I find him in the iridescent wings of a butterfly, and in the early-morning frost which means its death. . . . I see him in a playful kitten which seeks its play-fellow in the mirror, and in the murderous eyes with which it follows the movements of a robin. I recognize God in the inspiration which he sends me as if in a dream, and in the long labor by which I must carry it out. . . . {CE; GS}

Ludwig, Ernst Ludwig (1839–1903)

A German writer who used the pen name of "Carus Sterne," Ludwig [sometimes called Krause] became well-known for his scientific works on evolution, chiefly *Werden und Vergehen* (*Growth and Decay*, 1876). In 1863, he wrote *The Natural History of Ghosts*.

With Haeckel, Otto Caspari, and Gustav Jaeger, he established in 1877 the monthly magazine *Kosmos*, in which appeared the germ of his little book on *Erasmus Darwin* and to which Charles Darwin wrote a preliminary notice. BDF; RAT; RE}

Luetzelberger, Ernst Karl Julius (Born 1802)

Luetzelberger was a German controversialist, a friend of the Feuerbachs. He wrote on *The Church Tradition of the Apostle John* and a work on Jesus, which was translated in Ewerbeck's *Qu'est ce que la Religion*. In 1856, Luetzelberger was appointed town librarian at Nuremberg. {BDF}

Lugg, George Wilson (Born 1902)

Lugg was a freethinker who wrote *Religion? No! Good Living? Yes!* (1980). {GS}

Luik, John (20th Century)

A professor of philosophy at Brock University in St. Catharines, Ontario, Canada, Luik is one of the editors of *The Question of Humanism, Challenges and Possibilities* (1991).

Lukács, György (20th Century)

A Marxist, Lukács termed his outlook that of humanism.

Lumet, Sidney (1924–)

Lumet is a noted film director who was once married to Gloria Vanderbilt. As a child he appeared in "Dead End" (1935), "George Washington Slept Here" (1940–1941), and "My Heart's in the Highlands" (1939). He has directed over two hundred television plays and such movies as "Twelve Angry Men" (1957); "Stage Struck" (1958) "A View from the Bridge" (1961); "Long Days Journey into Night" (1962); "The Pawnbroker" (1965); "The Anderson Tapes" (1971); "Serpico" (1974); "Garbo Talks" (1984); and "Critical Care" (1997), the latter a satire about American medicine. With Alfred A. Knopf, he wrote *Making Movies* (1995).

Asked by reporter David Wallis, "When you die, how do you want to go out?", Lumet responded,

> I don't think about it. I'm not religious. I do know that I don't want to take up any space. Burn me up and scatter my ashes over Katz's Delicatessen.
>
> {*The New York Times Magazine*, 23 November 1997}

Lumis, Daylene (20th Century)

Lumis is secretary of the Humanist Association of Canada. She is a Montessori school administrator and teacher in Hamilton.

Lunacharsky, Anatole (1875–1933)

A member of the Union of Militant Atheists, Lunacharsky took part in the 1936 conference of the World Union of Freethinkers. {TRI}

Lundberg, George (20th Century)

Lundberg, who taught philosophy at the University of Washington, was a naturalist and a this-worldly rather than an other-worldly person.

Lundqvist, Alfred (Born 1860)

A Swedish writer, Lundqvist lost a scholarship at the university by translating from the Danish a rationalistic life of Christ. He then took to journalism and joined the active rationalist movement. For translating a pamphlet by Joseph Symes, Lundqvist was once imprisoned one month. {RAT}

Lundy, John (19th Century)

Lundy, in 1882, wrote *Monumental Christianity, or the Art and Symbolism of the Primitive Church* (1882). {GS}

Lunn, Arnold (20th Century)

With C. E. M. Joad, Lunn wrote *Is Christianity True?* (1933). {GS}

Lunn, Edwin (19th Century)

Lunn was an Owenite lecturer. He published pamphlets such as "On Prayer, Its Folly, Inutility, etc." (1839) and "Divine Revelation Examined" (1841). {BDF}

Luoma, Martti (20th Century)

Dr. Luoma, from Finland, addressed the Second European Conference of the International Humanist and Ethical Union (IHEU) held in Hannover (1968).

Lusky, Louis (20th Century)

An attorney in Louisville, Kentucky, Lusky was a reviewer of books for *The Humanist* when his friend Priscilla Robertson was the editor. He wrote *By What Right? A Commentary on the Supreme Court's Power to Reverse the Constitution* (1975) and worked valiantly on behalf of American Civil Liberties Union causes. {WAS, interview 1956}

LUST

Although freethinkers consider sexual craving normal, lust to some is a disordered desire for or inordinate enjoyment of sexual pleasure. The *Catechism of the Catholic Church* states that "sexual pleasure is morally disordered when sought for itself, isolated from its procreative and unitive purposes." President Jimmy Carter, in an ingenuous admission for a Baptist Sunday School teacher, stated that he, too, had lusted in his heart.

Freethinkers endearingly speak of their "lust for life" and feel no need to apologize for sizing up others' body parts or for fantasizing about what they might jocularly term "making the nasty." (See entry for Adultery.)

Lustig, Vera (20th Century)

Lustig, in "Holier Than Thou" (*New Humanist*, August 1994), notes that religious education "is of course both a politically and culturally sensitive issue; and one about which we seldom consult the young people themselves." The Belgians, she reported, have an anti-discrimination law that states that "Nobody should be forced to participate in any way in acts of worship." In England, however, Muslim girls are segregated. Lustig describes herself as "a secular Jew."

Lutes, Della (1872–1942)

Lutes, a little-known novelist, wrote a little-known work, *Gabriel's Search*, about a nineteenth century agnostic pioneer. *The Country Kitchen* (1936), about Michigan life in the 1870s and 1880s, was a best seller.

Luther, Martin (1483–1546)

Unable to convert the Jews to Protestantism, Luther described them as "this insufferable devilish burden." His solution was to encourage that their homes and synagogues be burned, their prayer books and property taken away, and their movements severely restricted. Meanwhile, in his 1513 study of the Scriptures, particularly St. Paul, Luther found a loving God who bestowed upon sinful humans the free gift of salvation, received by faith alone, and not by works. But as for man, "We have altogether a confounded, corrupt, and poisoned nature, both in body and soul; throughout the whole of man is nothing that is good," he pronounced. A 1994 statement by the Evangelical Lutheran Church in America admitted that "in 'The Jews and Their Lies' (1543), Luther called for Jewish homes and synagogues to be destroyed, for prayer books to be seized, and for rabbis to be forbidden to teach." The group, however, continued to honor his "bold stand for truth, his earthy and sublime words of wisdom and, above all, his witness to God's saving Word."

Erasmus's *Freedom of the World* (1524) contained an attack on Luther's doctrine of the enslaved will, leading to Luther's break with the humanists of the day.

Married (1525) to a former nun, Katharina von Bora, he raised six children. He was a bitter opponent of Desiderius Erasmus, who, unlike Luther, remained a Catholic. {CE; ER; RE}

LUTHERAN CHURCH–MISSOURI SYNOD

The Lutheran Church–Missouri Synod, organized in 1847, is at 1333 South Kirkwood Road, St. Louis, Missouri 63122 and represents over 2,500,000 members. (See entry for Evangelical Lutheran Church in America.)

Luttrell, Henry (1857–1918)

Luttrell entered the Irish Parliament in 1798, but in 1802 he went to the West Indies to manage his father's estates. A natural son of Earth Carhampton, he returned to London and was a frequent guest at Holland House. Greville said of him that he was "one of the most accomplished men of his time," an "honourable and high-minded gentleman," and "a sceptic in religion." {RAT}

LUXEMBOURG HUMANISTS AND JOURNALS

ADMD-L Bulletin, a quarterly in French and German of the *Association pour le Droit de Mourir dans la Dignité*, is at 50 Boulevard J. F. Kennedy, L-4170 Esch-Alzette, Luxembourg.

La Voix de la Libre Pensée/Das Freie Wort (Freethinker) is a publication in French and German of *La Libre Pensée Luxembourgeoise*, B. Postale 198, L-2011 Luxembourg.

The *Union Radical-Humaniste Luxembourgeoise* is at 39 Rue de Hollerich, 1741 Luxembourg, Grand Duchy of Luxembourg.

Luxemburg, Rosa (1871–1919)

Luxemburg, an atheist, was one of the founders of the Polish Socialist Party (1892). She acquired German citizenship through marriage and became a leader in the German Social Democratic Party. Upon becoming a Marxist, she was forced to flee to Switzerland.

In 1905, Luxemburg participated in the 1905 revolution in Russian Poland and was active in the Second International. With Karl Liebknecht, Luxemburg formed the German Spartacus Party. Both, while being taken to prison, were killed by soldiers. In 1995, legions of Berliners marched through eastern Berlin to honor the two martyrs of the left. Luxemburg is remembered as having been critical of Lenin in his triumph, foreseeing his dictatorship over the proletarian and predicting that his control would become permanent. {CE}

Luys, Jules Bernard (Born 1828)

Luys was a French alienist, a physician at *l'Hopital de la Charité* in Paris. He wrote *The Brain and Its Functions* in the International Scientific Series. {BDF}

Luz y Caballero, José (1812–1862)

Luz y Caballero, working with Father Félix Varela, is credited in Cuba with attacking scholasticism, promoting liberal principles, and introducing the rationalist philosophy that would enrich the intellectual life. {EU}

Lwoff, André Michel (1902–1994)

In 1965 Lwoff shared with Jacques Monod and François Jacob the Nobel Prize in physiology and medicine. The three were among the pioneers of modern molecular biology. They showed how some genes control the function of others in regulating the cell's metabolism. According to science editor Walter Sullivan, they found "that while one type of gene in the nucleus of a cell contains blueprints for the substances to be made, another type of gene regulates the rate of production of these substances."

Lwoff joined the Pasteur Institute in 1921, and he studied the role of vitamins, finding that some function as vital aids to enzymes. He also studied viruses that infect bacteria, helping lay the basis for much of modern biology.

From 1959 to 1968 Dr. Lwoff, who earned doctorates in both medicine and science, taught microbiology at the Sorbonne. Until 1972, he directed the Institute for Scientific Research on Cancer at Villejuif. He was known, according to *Le Monde*, as an opponent of capital punishment but a lover of painting, music, sculpture, and "those things that awaken the spirit."

Dr. Lwoff edited *Origins of Molecular Biology* (1979). The son of a father who was a psychiatrist and a mother who was a sculptor, both of whom had fled czarist Russia, Dr. Lwoff was a distinguished Humanist Laureate in the Council for Secular Humanism's International Academy of Humanism.

Lyall, Alfred Comyn [Sir] (1835–1911)

Lyall, a statesman, rose to the position of British Governor of the Northwest Provinces of India. His contact with Asia changed his earlier Christian belief, and he wrote a poem, "Theology in Extremis," which McCabe describes as "the highbrow way of saying 'The Church at its Wit's End.' "

In his retirement the Right Honorable Sir Alfred was a friend of the rationalist, Clodd, who tells in his memoirs that Lyall was an agnostic. {JM; RAT}

Lyczynski, Kazimierz (1634-1689)

A Polish atheist, Lyczynski wrote *De non existentia Dei* (Of God's Non-existence). For his non-belief, he was executed. {Finngeir Hiorth, *New Humanist*, December 1998}

Lydon, John [Johnny Rotten] (20th Century)

Lydon is a recording artist best known as Johnny Rotten of the Sex Pistols. On the liner notes of a 1992 single, "Cruel," he included,

> Where is God? I see no evidence of God.
> God is probably Barry Manilow.

{CA}

Lyell, Charles [Sir] (1797–1875)

A British geologist, Lyell influenced geologists of his time and also those of later periods. A popularizer of scientific ideas, he won general acceptance for James Hutton's theory of uniformitarianism, which is in opposition to catastrophism. The latter holds that at intervals in the earth's history all living things have been destroyed, as for example by floods or earthquakes, then replaced by an entirely different population—the theory correlated with some religious doctrines, such as the Mosaic account of the Flood. His work facilitated later acceptance of Darwin's theory of evolution, and among his important contributions was the division of the Tertiary period into the Eocene, Miocene, and Pliocene epochs.

Sir Charles was a member in London of the Unitarian Church called Little Portland Street. According to McCabe, Lyell was a theist until 1870, at which time he rejected all Christian doctrines and the belief in immortality and merely thought it "probable" that there was some sort of "Supreme Intelligence." But he had no tenderness for theology at any time, as is shown in the *Life, Letters, and Journals of Sir C. Lyell* (1881, 2 volumes). {BDF; CE; FUS; JM; RAT; TRI; U; UU}

Lyle-Wilson, Kimberly (20th Century)

Lyle-Wilson is president in Georgia of the Atlanta Freethought Society.

Lynch, Arthur (20th Century)

During the South African War, Lynch held a commission in the Boer forces and was prosecuted. He since has been M. P. for West Clare. In his *Religio Athletae* (1895), he disdains all religion but the cult of the beautiful. His chief work is *Psychology: A New System* (2 volumes, 1912). {RAT}

Lynch, Joe (20th Century)

Lynch, while a student at the University of Houston in Texas, was one of the founding members of Campus Freethought Alliance. {*International Humanist News*, December 1996}

Lyngzeidetson, Albert E. (20th Century)

Lyngzeidetson, who was a former chairman of the board of Atheists of Florida, spoke in Toronto at the 1994 Coalition for Secular Humanism, Atheism, and Freethought (CSHAFT) saying, "We need to face the destructive aspect of the Christian right." His advice was that humanists must take the moral high ground and proclaim that the principles of liberal democracy and tolerance are basic to society, that humanists need a positive message emphasizing that atheism *can* lead to a good life. A professor of philosophy and psychology at the Art Institute of Ft. Lauderdale, Florida, he is the author of *The Meaning of Atheism* and *The Challenge of the Christian Right* and "The Meaning and Purpose of Atheism" (*Secular Nation*, Fall 1994). (See "The Threat to the Atheists' Good Life," *Free Inquiry*, Winter 1995–1996.)

Lynn, Ken (20th Century)

Lynn and his wife **Monica Madden-Lynn** are active members of the Freedom from Religion Foundation. He is an Air Force officer who has written articles in *Freethought Today*. {*Freethought Today*, October 1997 and January-February 1998}

Lynn, Loretta (1935–)

Lynn is an entertainer cited by Paul Edwards in *Reincarnation* as being a believer in reincarnation.

Lyons, Lois (20th Century)

Lyons is president of the Humanist Association of Los Angeles.

Lyons, Sherrie (20th Century)

Lyons is a contributing editor on *Philo*.

LYSISTRATA

Lysistrata is a favorite fictional character among freethinkers and humanists. Aristophanes in 411 B.C.E. devised her character in order to encourage pacifism. In his satire, *Lysistrata*, Aristophanes suggested that women of Sparta and Athens could stop war by boycotting their husband-soldiers and not having sex until they agreed to stop fighting. Plato is said to have died with Aristophanes's works under his pillow. {CE; DCL}

Lyttle, Charles H(arold) (20th Century)

Lyttle was one of the first Unitarian ministers to use "humanist" in his sermons. He wrote *Humanist Sermons* (1917) and *Emerson's Self-Reliance* (1942) as well as edited *The Liberal Gospel (Channing Anthology)* in 1925. Lyttle's account of the Western Unitarian Conference is *Freedom Moves West* (1952). In that book, he writes of Humanist Manifesto I that it "sought to replace despondency and doubt of God's loving Providence by confidence in the power of human intelligence and co-operative good will to become its own Providence." {HNS}

Lyttleton, Edward (20th Century)

With C. Cohen, Lyttleton wrote *The Parson and the Atheist, A Friendly Discussion on Religion and Life* (1919). {GS}

MAAT

In Egyptian mythology, Maat was a goddess who personified truth and justice. Her laws were notably benevolent, not harsh as in the later patriarchal view described in *Deuteronomy* 28:15-68.

Mabu, Charles R. (20th Century)

Mabu in 1917 wrote *Nature Sufferage*, regarding the unfairness of not taxing church property.

MAC: Names starting with **MAC** or **MC** are listed as if they are spelled Mac.

McAndrews, Ed (20th Century)

McAndrews is on the Board in Ohio of Cincinnati's Free Inquiry Group.

MacArdle, Meredith (20th Century)

MacArdle was formerly the director of public relations for the British Humanist Association. She is now director of public relations for the Voluntary Euthanasia Society.

McBrien, Richard P. (20th Century)

The Rev. McBrien is author of *Catholicism* (1996), a survey of church teachings. Formerly the chairman of the theology department at the University of Notre Dame, he is one of the most outspoken liberal Roman Catholic theologians. The National Conference of Catholic Bishops attacked his book, complaining that it "raises no questions about the author's standing as a theologian and priest" but does not approve his inclusion of "inaccurate or at least misleading" statements about some doctrines. More important, the committee proclaimed, the book minimizes established church teachings by overemphasizing the plurality of viewpoints in the church and the importance of modern rather than traditional thinking. As such, it offers "a broad range of opinions on every topic with the apparent intention of allowing, or stimulating, the reader to make a choice. This places a heavy burden on the reader" who may not know which opinions are "part of the mainstream Catholic conversation" and which "are closer to the margins." {*The New York Times*, 11 April 1996}

McBride, Ellen (20th Century)

McBride is president of the American Ethical Union, the thirteen-member board of which is elected nationally.

McBryde, Mike (20th Century)

A freelance artist and writer in Pittsburgh, Pennsylvania, McBryde is an Advisory Board Member of African Americans for Humanism.

McCabe, Joseph (Martin) (1867–1955)

An English atheist, anticlericalist, and critic of the Catholic Church, McCabe described himself as a "pedlar of culture." E. Haldeman-Julius, his chief American publisher, called him the world's greatest scholar—his 121 Little Blue Books and 122 larger books totaling 7,600,000 words earned him $100,000. Ordained a Roman Catholic priest (Franciscan) at twenty-three and called Father Antony, he totaled the debits and credits of religion and concluded on one Christmas Eve that Christianity was bankrupt. Religion, particularly Roman Catholicism, he wrote, appealed to nonempirical, spiritual causes and thus was the chief opponent of materialism and, therefore, of science. His 1918 work, *The Popes and Their Church: A Candid Account,* resulted in much criticism. As John R. Burr has noted, McCabe's aggressive frankness and skepticism seem to have offended nearly everyone, including the British Rationalist Association, which expelled him in 1928.

McCabe was an editor of the *Joseph McCabe Magazine* (1930–1931) and *Militant Atheist* (1933). Of amusement to humanists is McCabe's novel, *The Pope's Favorite*, in which Lucrezia Borgia and Giulia, Pope Alexander VI's mistress, are featured. He wrote about two hundred books and thirty translations, delivered about two thousand lectures (including seven lecture tours in Australasia, the United States, and Canada), and held a score of public debates. McCabe, who described himself as an atheist and a materialist, wished his epitaph to be: "He was a rebel to his last breath." {EU, John R. Burr; FUK; FUS; RAT; RE; SWW; TRI}

McCabe, Steve (20th Century)

McCabe is cited by the Morains as having been "pivotal in maintaining the quality and accuracy of humanist publications." {HNS2}

McCall, Colin (20th Century)

McCall, in reviewing Antony Flew's *Atheistic Humanism* for the English *Freethinker* (June 1994), was in agreement with Flew's criticism of religion. However, he disagreed with Flew's using the term *race* in connection with Homo sapiens and his holding that "intelligence" can be "measurable" by humanly designed tests, a claim which even Alfred Binet did not make in 1905. "So," writes McCall, "I suppose it may be said that I go along with Antony Flew as an atheist but not as a geneticist." McCall, the son of parents who were officers of the Manchester branch of the National Secular Society during the presidency of Chapman Cohen, has been general secretary of the National Secular Society and a freethinker all his life. {FUK}

McCall, Fiona (1963–1995)

McCall, daughter of Colin and June McCall, was arts page secretary of *The Guardian*. Her obituary in that journal read,

> There are few pure people in the world. Fiona McCall was one of them. She was gentle and kind, funny and generous, a Marxist with a brilliant, non-dogmatic mind and a huge, quiet heart that caused her too much pain. She could have been a great critic—in film, theatre, art, opera, anything. . . .

Maccall, William (1812–1878)

A Scot, Maccall found his way to Unitarianism, then left it as being insufficiently broad. He wrote *Elements of Individualism* (1847), translated Spinoza's *Treatise on Politics* (1854), and contributed to *Secular Review* and other journals. Maccall was an idealistic pantheist. {BDF; RAT; VI; TRI}

McCallister, Mildred L. (1929–1994)

McCallister was president of the Humanist Association of the Greater Sacramento Area. She also was coordinator for the American Humanist Association's Northern California region. A published poet and author, she was active in the Sacramento Skeptics Society. (See entry for California Atheists, Humanists.) {FD}

McCann, Eamonn (1943–)

McCann, a freethinker living in Derry, holds that although the Vatican a decade ago would discuss certain controversial subjects, in 1996 it bristles with arrogant certainty. "The aspiration of Irish liberals has never been to extirpate the Catholic Church and end its influences," McCann noted. "What they've always wanted is a new accommodation with the Church. But all the indications are that this is no go. The furtive cabal that descended on Dundrum (17 February 1996) is not talking terms. Sooner or later we'll have to have it out with them." He would start by encouraging a campaign to have the Vatican lose its United Nations status. McCann wrote *War in an Irish Town* (1993). {*The Freethinker*, June 1996 and August 1999}

McCarroll, Tolbert H. [Brother Toby] (20th Century)

McCarroll was an attorney who helped prevent civil rights legislation from excluding atheists. He also was executive director of the American Humanist Association in the 1960s. He then became primarily interested in Humanistic Psychology, then in Catholicism, and finally became Brother Toby, head of a Catholic monastery. Although a large number of ex-Catholics become non-theistic freethinkers (e.g., Mary McCarthy), McCarroll is one of a handful of freethinkers who have made the reverse trip. (See entry for American Humanist Association.)

McCarthy, Mary (Therese) (1912–1989)

An acerbic and witty novelist, McCarthy described the Dickensian nightmare of her youth in *Memories of a Catholic Girlhood* (1935). She was a drama critic for *Partisan Review*, and her works include *The Groves of Academe* (1952), in which she satirized faculty life at a women's liberal arts college. She also wrote *The Group* (1963), about eight Vassar alumnae of 1933 for the thirty years following their graduation. Her posthumous *Intellectual Memoirs, New York 1936–1938* (1992) emphasized, according to Jean Strouse in *The Times* (24 May 1992), her lifelong crusades "against inaccuracy, cant, evasion, cliché, self-deception, bad writing, weak principles, and fraud—most famously when she said of Lillian Hellman, on Dick Cavett's television show, that 'every word she says is a lie, including *and* and *the*.' " (Hellman sued her but died before the case came to trial.)

Although as a youth McCarthy was convent-bred, she no longer considered herself a Catholic once she left her paternal grandparents' home. In her memoirs she reflects upon having had a maternal grandmother who was Jewish, but McCarthy the Trotskyite was a self-declared freethinker.

McCarthy wrote of her sexual exploits with Harold Johnsrud, John Porter, Philip Rahv, Max Eastman, even of three different men in the course of twenty-four hours. As for the males' sexual equipment, "there were amazing differences, in both length and massiveness. . . . [One married man had] a penis about the size and shape of a lead pencil," and tall men she found usually to be the most generously endowed. After she slept with the critic Edmund Wilson, in very short order the two married and she endured seven tempestuous years with him, bearing one child.

An outspoken atheist, McCarthy in *The Company She Keeps* (1942) has a character speak lovingly about a person to whom she is drawn sexually, " 'Oh my God,' she said, '. . . do not let them take this away from me. If the flesh must be blind, let the spirit see. Preserve me in disunity. '*A di*,' she said aloud, '*reddite me hoc pro pietate mea*.' (Oh gods, render me this in return for my devotion.). It was certainly a very small favor she was asking, but, like Catullus, she could not be too demanding, for, unfortunately, she did not believe in God." {CE}

McCarthy, Ngaire (20th Century)

McCarthy is President of the New Zealand Association of Rationalists and Humanists. She took office in 1998, the third female president in the Association's seventy-year history.

McCarthy, Timothy G. (20th Century)

McCarthy is author of *Christianity and Humanism* (1997), described by the publisher Loyola as being "an exploration of the hope of ecumenism, the promise of liberation theology, and the challenge and mission of Christian humanism as we approach the third millennium."

McCarthy, William (20th Century)

McCarthy, an atheist, wrote *Bible, Church, and God* (1946). {FUS}

McCartin, Brian (20th Century)

McCartin is administrator of the Thomas Paine Memorial Museum in New Rochelle, New York. The museum's website is at <www.midiapro.net/cdadesign/paine/>.

Macartney, James (1770–1843)

Macartney was an Irish anatomist who practiced as a surgeon in London and was professor of comparative anatomy and physiology at St. Bartholomew's Hospital. He also taught anatomy and surgery at Dublin University. Although the priests bitterly attacked him for his avowed Rationalism, he "did not formally commit himself to any creed" and held that "every revelation, no matter whether it be real or supposed, must produce hatred and persecution among mankind." Macartney was a deist. {RAT; RE}

Macaulay, Thomas Babington (1st Baron) (1800–1859)

Macaulay, an English historian and author, was elected to Parliament in 1830, where he distinguished himself as a Whig orator. He served in India as a member of the supreme council of the East India Company, helping to reform the Indian educational system. His greatest work was *The History of England from the Accession of James the Second* (5 volumes, 1849–1861). Criticized for being objective because of his Whig and Protestant bias, the work nevertheless was an unprecedented success. "The Church," he wrote, "is the handmaid of tyranny and the steady enemy of liberty." He also wrote, "With respect to the doctrine of a future life, a North American Indian knows just as much as any ancient or modern philosopher." {CE; TYD}

Macchi, Mauro (1818–1880)

An Italian writer, Macchi became professor of rhetoric at the age of twenty-four when, becoming obnoxious to the Austrians by the liberty of his opinions, he was soon deprived of his position. He then founded *l'Italia*, a Republican journal for which he was exiled. With Ausonio Franchi and Luigi Stefani, he worked on the *Libero Pensiero* and founded an Italian Association of Freethinkers. In 1861 he was elected deputy to Parliament for Cremona and, in 1879, was elevated to the Senate. One of his principal works is on the *Council of Ten*. {BDF; RAT}

McClain, Virgil (20th Century)

In South Bend, Indiana, McClain edited the monthly *Rip Saw* from 1955 to 1963. In 1963 it merged with *The Free Humanist*. {FUS}

McClelland, James Robert (1915–)

McClelland is an Australian atheist, a minister in the Whitlam government, a judge, and a journalist. Son of a Catholic mother and an agnostic father, he had a Catholic education but abandoned that faith at the age of seventeen. Active in civil libertarian causes, he practiced as a solicitor until elected in 1972 to the Senate. McClelland always insisted on affirming rather than swearing an oath, and after he resigned from the Senate in 1978 he became first Chief Judge of the New South Wales Land and Environment Court.

He was President in the 1950s of the Royal Commission into British Nuclear Weapons Tests in Australia, and since 1986 has written weekly columns for *Sydney Morning Herald*. McClelland's autobiography is *Stirring the Possum*. {SWW}

McClinton, Brian (20th Century)

McClinton in Ulster is secretary of the Ulster Humanist Association. That group's publication, *The Humanist*, has stated that a new core syllabus for religious education in Ulster schools will do nothing to alleviate the tension between Catholics and Protestants. The Minister of Education, McClinton holds, needs to work toward a more humane and humanist attitude in the educating of Irish students. However, in 1998 when an agreement was reached for peace in Northern Island, McClinton said, "The agreement is the best chance for peace that Northern Ireland has had." He added, "Compromise is, in fact, a humanist virtue." According to him, the "peace process" has been dominated by the two absolutist belief systems of Orange and Green, which have so far steadfastly refused a compromise.

McClinton is author of *Ulster's Third Way: The Humanist Alternative Beyond Orange and Green* (1998). {*International Humanist News*, June 1995 and December 1998; *New Humanist*, December 1997}

Maccoby, Hyam (20th Century)

Maccoby's *A Pariah People: The Anthropology of Antisemitism* (1996) found evidence of anti-Semitism in the Greek and Greco-Roman Empires for the 3rd Century B.C.E., and also in Gnosticism and Islam. But it was the Christians who first treated the Jews as pariahs. This was because, as St. Augustine had preached, the Jews had to be punished for their having rejected Jesus and caused a deicide. Although the Albigenses had to be exterminated, the Jews "were spared this fate because they were considered to have an important contribution to make to Christian society." Maccoby notes that Protestants such as Luther had diatribes against the Jews as bitter as did the Nazis. His view of the Holocaust: "If a people has been subjected to constant vilification and demonisation over a period of centuries, so that a popular loathing has been instilled so deeply as to operate like an instinct, it is no surprise that eventually a movement will arise that has as its aim the extermination of this alleged pest and enemy of humanity."

As his research shows, Maccoby clearly laments anti-Semitism. {Colin McCall, *The Freethinker*, December 1996}

McCollister, Betty (1920–)

An Iowan newspaper columnist, McCollister has written for *Free Inquiry*, *Skeptic*, and *The Humanist*. She is a former member of the board of directors of the American Humanist Association, has six children and fifteen grandchildren, and is particularly interested in evolution, church-state separation, and women's issues.

McCollister, who has been President of Humanists of Iowa, became that group's treasurer. She wrote *Voices for Evolution* (1989). {*Free Inquiry*, Winter, 1986-1987}

McCollum, James T. (20th Century)

When he signed Humanist Manifesto II, McCollum was a humanist counselor. The son of Vashti McCollum, he performed as a humanist counselor the first humanist wedding service ever conducted at West Point Military Academy. {HM2; HNS2}

McCollum, Scot (20th Century)

McCollum, from Wisconsin, is on the board of directors of the Freedom From Religion Foundation.

McCollum, Vashti (Cromwell) (1912–)

President of American Humanist Association from 1962 to 1965, McCollum took a case to the Supreme Court which insured that students do not have to receive religious education in public schools. Justice Felix Frankfurter, in his written opinion, said, "Designed to serve as perhaps the most powerful agency for promoting cohesion among a heterogeneous democratic people, the public school must keep scrupulously free from entanglement in the strife of sects." In that 1948 case, Justice Hugo Black wrote, "[T]he First Amendment rests upon the premise that both religion and government can best work to achieve their lofty aims if each is left free from the other within its respective sphere." He added, "[E]very State admitted into the Union since 1876 was compelled by Congress to write into its constitution a requirement that it maintain a school system 'free from sectarian control.' "

McCollum signed Humanist Manifesto II. Her autobiographical story is *One Woman's Fight* (1950). In it she tells how *McCollum v. Board of Education, 333 U.S. 203, 212 (1948)* struck down religious instruction in public schools.

In 1993, McCollum spoke at the Freedom From Religion Foundation's annual convention in Huntsville, Alabama. She is in the Women's Hall of Fame in Seneca Falls, New York. {FUS; HM2; HNS; HNS2; WAS, conversations; WWS}

McConnell, Francis J. (1871–1953)

McConnell has a chapter on Thomas Paine in his *Evangelicals, Revolutionists, and Idealists*. {FUS}

McConnell, Joy (20th Century)

McConnell, who had been the American Ethical Union's Director of Growth and Development and Religious Education, resigned at the end of 1998.

McCord, Barney (20th Century)

McCord, from Alabama, is on the board of the Freedom From Religion Foundation.

McCord, Melody (20th Century)

McCord, from Alabama, is on the board of the Freedom From Religion Foundation.

McCorkel, James (20th Century)

McCorkel is the vice president for academic affairs at Jersey Shore Medical Center of Meridian Health System in Neptune, New Jersey. He is on the board of directors of the UU Service Committee.

MacCorquodale, Kenneth (20th Century)

A professor of philosophy at the University of Minnesota, MacCorquodale was one of the writers of *Modern Learning Theory* and was editor of the Century Psychology Series. {PK}

McCoy, Guy and **Victoria** (20th Century)

The McCoys are co-founders of Atheists of Northern Colorado. Guy is the gorup's treasurer and his wife Victoria edits their newsletter. E-mail: <vgmccoy@juno.com>.

McCoy, Robert (20th Century)

McCoy was President of the American Humanist Association from 1966 to 1968. He is president of Minnesota Skeptics.

MacCready, Paul Beattie (1925–)

A Humanist Laureate in the Council for Secular Humanism's International Academy of Humanism, MacCready is president of AeroVironment, Inc. He wrote *Investigation of Atmospheric Turbulence* (1952). In 1979, he was leader of the team that developed Gossamer Albatross for human-powered flight across the English Channel. In 1981, he was on the team that developed the Solar Challenger, an ultralight aircraft powered by solar cells; in 1987, the General Motors Sunraycer; and in 1990 the General Motors Impact. The American Society of Mechanical Engineers in 1980 named him "Engineer of the Century." MacCready signed Humanist Manifesto 2000 and is described in the biographical work by Richard L. Taylor, *The First Human-Powered Flight* (1995).

McCrimmon, Ian (20th Century)

McCrimmon is an Illinois freethinker. He has written for *Freethought Perspective* (June 1999).

McCrone (20th Century)

McCrone, of the McCrone Research Institute, signed Humanist Manifesto 2000.

McCurdie, Jim (20th Century)

McCurdie has written about how Robert G. Ingersoll discovered Robert Burns while still a teenager. McCurdie, who discovered Ingersoll's work when secretary of the Rationalist Press Association in Glasgow (now the Glasgow Humanist Society), has noted that Ingersoll in 1878 made a pilgrimage to Burns's birthplace. He is active with the Scottish humanist groups. {*Freethought History*, #23, 1997}

McDermott, John Joseph (1932–)

McDermott, an educator who has taught at Queens College in Flushing, New York, the State University of New York at Stony Brook, and Union Theological Seminary, edited *Writings of William James* (1967), *Basic Writings of Josiah Royce* (2 vols., 1969), and *The Philosophy of John Dewey* (2 vols., 1973). He is a contributor to *American Philosophic Naturalism in the Twentieth Century* (1994).

Macdonald, E. Stewart (20th Century)

Macdonald was a director in the 1950s of the American Humanist Association.

Macdonald, Eugene Montague (1855–1909)

Macdonald was an editor of the atheistic *Truthseeker* from 1883 to 1909, succeeding D. M. Bennett. Macdonald's brother, George, succeeded him. He wrote *Col. Robert G. Ingersoll as He Is*, *A Defense of Ingersoll*, and *Design Argument Fallacies* (1896). {BDF; FUS; PUT; RAT; RE}

Macdonald, George E. (1857–1943)

Macdonald was an editor of the atheistic *Truthseeker* from 1909 to 1926. With S. P. Putnam, he had edited the San Francisco journal,

Freethought (1888–1891). His "Thumbscrew and Rack: Torture Instruments Employed in the 15th and 16th Centuries" (1904) has been reprinted and contains descriptions of how the church used not only racks and thumbscrews but also the wheel and the cruel spider, which was devised to rip off a woman's breast. Such devices, he claims, were powerful tools to get individuals to conform to religious dogma. {BDF; FUS; PUT; RAT}

MacDonald, John Francis (c. 1897–1970)

"Jack" MacDonald was a public servant and long-time president of the Rationalist Association of New South Wales. {SWW}

MacDonald, Norman (20th Century)

MacDonald, a Scottish poet who wrote *Vox Humana*, which opens with "A Humanist Anthem." He writes on such other subjects as apartheid, animal rights, and ecology. MacDonald has been an active member of the Glasgow Humanist Society.

McDonald, Ramsay (1866–1937)

McDonald was associated with a labour church-ethical society affiliated with the English Ethical Union. {TRI}

McDonnell, William (19th Century)

McDonnell's *Heathens of the Heath* (1874) and *Exeter Hall* (1873) are little-known freethought novels. The author was born in Cork, Ireland, but moved to Canada. {BDF; PUT}

Mc Dowell, Jean Thelma (20th Century)

In 1930 for her M.A. thesis at Northwestern University, McDowell wrote on the oratory of Robert G. Ingersoll. {FUS}

MacDowell, Mary (20th Century)

MacDowell, a contemporary of Jane Addams and one who was involved in Chicago social work, was invited to sign Humanist Manifesto I, the only female so asked. She failed to sign. {EW}

McEldowney, David (20th Century)

In the 1950s, McEldowney was managing editor of *The Humanist.*

McElroy, Wendy (20th Century)

McElroy, a contributing editor for *Free Inquiry*, is author of *XXX: A Woman's Right to Pornography* (1996) and *Sexual Correctness* (1996). Active in libertarian circles, she holds that pornography does not deserve simply to be tolerated but, rather, it deserves celebration. "Pornography is the explicit artistic description of men and/or women as sexual beings," she states, and she laments that religious fundamentalists define the explicit depiction of sex as evil. Also, she laments that leftists define it as violence against women, which she holds is equally illogical. "Pornography benefits women, both personally and politically," she states in her campaign to make pornography legitimate. *True Love Waits: Essays and Criticism* (1999) contains witty social comments particularly about feminism.

MacEnulty Jr., John F. (20th Century)

When he signed Humanist Manifesto II, MacEnulty was president of the Humanist Society of Jacksonville, Florida {HM2}

McEvoy, John G. (1942–)

With A. Truman Schwartz, McEvoy edited *Motion Toward Perfection: The Achievement of Joseph Priestley* (1989).

McEvoy, Mary (20th Century)

McEvoy, A popular Irish soap opera star of "Glenroe," has been described by James F. Clarity as a religious skeptic. A Dublin telecast, it has tackled the subject of religious disaffection, an issue that in the 1980s would have been "too touchy." {*The New York Times*, 1 April 1997}

MacEwan, Douglas M. C. (1917–)

At the Second European Conference of the International Humanist and Ethical Union held in Hannover (1968), MacEwanof the UK Conservation Society addressed the group.

McFadyen, Ted (20th Century)

A retired journalist and broadcaster, McFadyen was secretary from 1993 to 1996 of the Brighton Lesbian and Gay Switchboard. A secular humanist, he represented the Gay and Lesbian Humanist Association at a 1997 conference in Brighton, England, regarding the policing of lesbian and gay communities. He has written for *Gay & Lesbian Humanist.*

McFarlane, Todd (20th Century)

McFarlane is a writer and comic book artist. When criticized by his heavily satire-laden portrayal of religion and God, he explained in the letters page of his comic book, *Spawn*, that "I go on record by stating that I do not believe in God." {CA; E}

McGaha, James E. (20th Century)

McGaha is a regional director in Arizona of the Council for Secular Humanism.

McGary, Keith (20th Century)

In the 1950s when he was a member of the philosophy department at the University of Wisconsin, McGary was an associate editor of *The Humanist.* {HNS}

McGaw, Howard F. (1911–1997)

McGaw directed the library at Ohio Wesleyan (1946–1949), at the University of Houston (1950–1961), and Western Washington State College (1963–1967). He was professor of library science at Western Washington University from 1963 until his retirement in 1977. A Unitarian and life member of the Freedom From Religion Foundation, he once reported, "If I had had any reservations about a life in the hereafter, such reservations would have been dispelled years ago when I read Corliss Lamont's *The Illusion of Immortality.* {*Freethought Today*, January-February 1998}

McGee, John (20th Century)

McGee wrote *A History of the British Secular Movement* (1948).

McGee, Lewis A. (20th Century)

A liberal minister, McGee once was a director of the American Humanist Association.

MC GILL UNIVERSITY FREETHINKERS

In Montreal, Quebec, Canada, the McGill University Atheist, Agnostic, and Secular Humanist Society is on the Web at <http://www.secularhumanism.org/cfa/orgs.html>.

McGill, Charles (20th Century)

McGill is Treasurer of the Scottish Humanists.

McGinley, Phyllis (1905–1978)

She may or may not have gone on record concerning her religious or philosophical preference, but the Oregon-born 1960 Pulitzer Prize winner wrote the following freethought poem:

Lament For A Wavering Viewpoint

Ah, snug lie those that slumber
Beneath conviction's roof.

Their floors are sturdy lumber,
Their windows weather-proof.

But I sleep cold forever
And cold sleep all my kind.

For I was born to shiver
In the draft from an open mind!

{TYD}

McGlynn, Montana (20th Century)

A student of archeology at Hunter College in New York City, McGlynn said on MTV's "Real World Boston," "Christianity is the single worst thing that has happened to women. I believe in Darwin, not God. Science is my religion." {CA}

McGovern, Edythe M. (20th Century)

A professor of English at Los Angeles Valley College, Mc Govern specializes in children's literature. She is author of *They're Never Too Young for Books* (1993). A Secular Humanist Mentor of the Council for Secular Humanism, McGovern was a founder of Secular Humanists of Los Angeles (SHOLA). (See entry for California Atheists, Humanists.) {FD; *Free Inquiry*, Winter, 1989-1990}

McGowan, Christopher (20th Century)

McGowan is author of *In the Beginning: A Scientist Shows Why the Creationists Are Wrong* (1984).

McGrath, Thomas (1916–1990)

A Midwesterner born on a South Dakota farm, McGrath is said by Whitehead and Muhrer, in their *Freethought on the American Frontier* (1992), to have been a freethinker. His *Letter to an Imaginary Friend* is a take-off of Christmas in the remote farms and villages of North Dakota, and McGrath is said to have been one of the most eminent of American atheist poets. A video about the atheist poet, called "The Movie at the End of the World, is available from Mike Hazard (344 Ramsey St., St. Paul, Minnesota 55102). {*Freethought History* #26, 1998}

McGrory, Jim (20th Century)

McGrory, a member of the Cincinnati, Ohio, Free Inquiry Group, writes for its newsletter, *Fig Leaves*.

Mach, Ernst von (1838–1916)

Mach was Rector of Prague University (1879–1880) and professor at Vienna University (1895–1901). He was ennobled and admitted to the Austrian House of Peers on his retirement in the latter year. Mach studied the relation of physics to psychology, and the development of his views brought him to an advanced rationalist position. He maintained that there was no essential difference between the physical and the psychic—that both consisted of elements—thus cutting the root of the Christian doctrines. All knowledge comes from the senses, he taught, and he was relentless in campaigning against anything metaphysical in science.

Mach, whose name is used to describe the scale by which supersonic speeds are measured, wrote *The Analysis of Sensations* (1886) and *The Science of Mechanics* (1893). {RAT}

Machado, Bernadino [President] (1851–1922)

Machado, the third president of the Republic of Portugal (1915–1917), was an agnostic as were his two predecessors. He took an open part in International Freethought Congresses. Because of the demoralization in Portugal following World War II, Machada was deposed. But during his guidance, the old power of the Roman Church was broken and so remained until a few years after his death. {JM; RAT; RE; TRI}

Machan, Tibor (20th Century)

Machan, a professor of philosophy at Auburn University in Alabama, is a contributing editor for *Free Inquiry*. He wrote *Introduction to Philosophic Inquiries* (1985). Machan is active in libertarian circles.

Machiavelli, Niccolò (1469–1527)

Machiavelli was "the standing proof of the divorce of the higher intelligence of Italy from the faith as well as from the cause of the Church before the Reformation," according to Robertson. To him the Church "was the supreme evil in Italian politics," and in his time he was considered no religionist although he never avowed atheism.

He did not believe in a prayer-answering deity, but like the superstitious of his time he believed that "all great political changes are heralded by prodigies, celestial signs, prophecies, or revelations." He did not hold that wickedness is to be preferred over goodness; rather than being interested in evil and good, he was concerned with political efficiency. Because Christianity preached meekness and selflessness and could weaken a political society, he frowned upon such. The political man, he felt, needed not virtues but vitality (*virtù*).

Machiavelli's belief in the method of science, at a time when Aristotle was always invoked to maintain the status quo rather than to experiment with completely free inquiry, helped influence future freethinkers in Italy, including Vico the sociologist. However, in contemporary usage, a "Machiavellian" leader is one who cunningly subordinates moral principle to political goals. (See the *Encyclopedia of Philosophy*, Vol. 5.) {CE; DCL; ER; FUK; JMR; JMRH; TYD}

McHugh, Linda Beyer (20th Century)

McHugh is Editor-in-Chief of *World*, the journal of the Unitarian Universalist Association.

McIlroy, William (1928–)

McIlroy, who once was general secretary of the National Secular Society, has a column, "Down to Earth," in the British secular humanist monthly, *The Freethinker*, of which he was once editor. He is author of a pamphlet published by the Sheffield Humanist Society, "Foundations of Modern Humanism" (1995). As for the claim that building temples builds bridges, McIlroy wrote to *The Star* (31 January 1996) in Sheffield, "Temples, churches, synagogues, and mosques are centres of religious superstition. Historically and contemporaneously, religion has been a divisive, not a bridge-building, influence."

His *Foundations of Modern Humanism* (1995), is the text of a lecture delivered to the Sheffield Humanist Society. {*Freethought History* #18, 1996; FUK; TRI}

Macin Andrade, Raúl (20th Century)

Macin was a participant on a panel discussing religious fundamentalism in Mexico at the 1996 Humanist World Conference held in Mexico City.

McInnis, Grace (20th Century)

McKinnis, a member of the Canadian Parliament, was awarded the Canadian Humanist of the Year Award in 1974.

MacIntire, Roger W. (20th Century)

MacIntire, a Unitarian, is author of *Enjoy Successful Parenting* (1996) and *Teenagers and Parents: 10 Steps for a Better Relationship* (1996).

McIntosh, Janet (20th Century)

McIntosh, a graduate student in ethnology at the University of Michigan" is a critic of creationism, writing that "[t]he secular creationist standpoint not only commits biological errors but defies common sense." {*Free Inquiry*, Spring 1998}

Mac Intyre, Alasdair (20th Century)

Mac Intyre in 1957 wrote *Difficulties in Christian Belief.* With Paul Ricocur, Mac Intyre wrote *The Religious Significance of Atheism* (1969). A Catholic and professor of philosophy at Duke University, Mac Intyre is a critic of humanism. His most noted work is *After Virtue.* {GS}

McIntyre, Jane (20th Century)

McIntyre, of Cleveland State University, is on the Executive Committee of The Hume Society, a group engaged in scholarly activity concerning David Hume.

Maciocha, Teresa (20th Century)
Maciocha edited Edwin H. Wilson's *The Genesis of a Humanist Manifesto* (1996). She has worked for social change agencies including Community Jobs and Greenpeace. Also, she worked for the Buffalo Coalition for Common Ground and the Western New York Peace Center in an alternatives-to-violence program. {EW}

Mack, Burton (20th Century)
Mack is a biblical scholar. In *Who Wrote the New Testament? The Making of the Christian Myth* (1993) and *The Book of Q and Christian Origins* (1995), he indicates that most Christians have a completely mistaken idea as to how the books of the Bible came to be written.

Mack, Frank (20th Century)
Frank is author of *Yuletide Sunshine Carols* (1978). {GS}

Mackay, Charles (1814–1889)
Mackay was sub-editor of the *Morning Chronicle* from 1835 to 1844, editor of the *Glasgow Argus* from 1844 to 1847, and editor of the *Illustrated London News* from 1852 to 1858. Known as the writer of songs, such as "There's a Good Time Coming, Boys," Mackay was sympathetic to rationalist causes. {RAT}

McKay, Claude (1890–1948)
A leading African-American poet of the Harlem Renaissance, McKay wrote revolutionary rhetoric. According to Norm Allen Jr., McKay was a progressive freethinker. Following is typical of his outlook:

The white man is a tiger at my throat,
Drinking my blood as my life ebbs away,
And muttering that his terrible striped coat
Is Freedom's and portends the Light of Day.
Oh white man, you may suck up all my blood
And throw my carcass into potter's field,
But never will I say with you that mud
Is bread for Negroes! Never will I yield. . . .

{AAH}

McKay, Fred (1914–1997)
McKay was one of the longest-serving members of the National Secular Society, having joined in 1941 and remained until his death in 1997.

Mackay, Robert William (19th Century)
Mackay wrote *The Progress of the Intellect* (1850), *Sketch of the Rise and Progress of Christianity* (1853), and *The Tubingen School* (1863). {BDF; RAT}

McKellen, Ian [Sir] (1939–)
The English-born actor, McKellen, has been decorated as a Commander of the Order of the British Empire and a Knight Bachelor. He has appeared in numbers of classical plays from "Hamlet" and "Macbeth" to "Six Degrees of Separation" and "The Band Played On." On Broadway, he received a Tony Award. In Los Angeles and New York City in 1984, he appeared in a one-man show, "A Knight Out at the Lyceum," which was devised especially for a Gay Games IV tour in the United Kingdom and South Africa.

"I was brought up a Christian, low church, and I like the community of churchgoing. That's rather been replaced for me by the community of people I work with. I like a sense of family, of people working together. But I'm an atheist. So God, if She exists, isn't really a part of my life." {Tim Appelo, *Mr. Showbiz, 19 January 1996;* CA; E}

McKelvic, C. (20th Century)
McKelvic, a freethinker, wrote *Fear and Religion* (1935). {GS}

McKenna, Peter (20th Century)
McKenna, writing in the English *Freethinker* (February 1994), complains in "The Dreadful Secret of Little Bible Stories" that children are being given Bible stories which contain brutality such as a crucifixion; Elisha cursing children for saying to him "go up, thou bald head," whereupon a gang of bears tears forty-two of them to pieces; Ahab's seventy sons are killed at God's command; "the angel of the Lord" slaughters 185,000 Assyrians; and on and on. He suggests that his son's state school should not be distributing these "horrible little books" published by Collins, which ironically also publishes the Bible.

McKenzie, Elizabeth (1973–)
McKenzie has served as President of the Auckland University Atheists. She is a Councillor of New Zealand's Rationalist Council.

Mackenzie, G. L (19th Century)
Mackenzie was a freethinker who wrote *Brimstone Ballads and Other Verse* (1899). {GS}

McKenzie, John Grant (Born 1882)
McKenzie, a freethinker, wrote *Nervous Orders and Religion* (1951). {GS}

Mackenzie, John Stuart (1860–1937)
A professor of logic and philosophy at the University College of South Wales (1895–1915), Mackenzie was active with the Ethical Movement and the Moral Education League. In 1907, he wrote *Lectures on Humanism* (1907), in which he discussed pragmatism, naturalism, and ethical religion. An intuitionist in ethics, but entirely outside Christianity, he wrote in his *Manual of Ethics* (1893) that we must reject Christian doctrines, that "what remains essential to religion is the reality of the moral life." In *A Generation of Religious Progress* (1916), Mackenzie observes that religious creeds "have the disadvantage of having to be accepted without definite proof." {RAT; RE}

Mackenzie, William Lyon (1795–1861)
Mackenzie was an early 19th century Canadian journalist, freethinker, and insurgent leader who had been born in Scotland. His *Colonial Advocate* had attacked the government, resulting in his printing office's being partly demolished. After being elected (1820) to the Legislative Assembly of Upper Canada, Mackenzie was five times expelled for "libel" and five times reelected by his constituency. In 1834 he became the first mayor of Toronto, and in 1837 when his Reform party was defeated, Mackenzie and a group of insurgents unsuccessfully attempted to seize Toronto. Fleeing to the United States, he set up a provisional government but was imprisoned for eighteen months by the U.S. authorities for having violated the neutrality laws. In 1849, after a proclamation of general amnesty, he became a member (1851–1859) of the Legislative Assembly of United Canada (Upper and Lower Canada). "His aspiration to a cosmic moral order owed something to Christian humanism, though his clerical critics were far too myopic to perceive this," observed Clifford Holland in a biography of William Dawson Le Sueur. (See entry for William Dawson Le Sueur.)

Mackey, Sampson Arnold (Died 1846)
Mackey was an astronomer and shoemaker who is said to have constructed an orrery, a mechanical model of the solar system, out of leather. He wrote *The Mythological Astronomy of the Ancients* (1822–1824), *Pious Frauds* (1826), and a rare book, *Sphinxiad.* {BDF}

Mackie, John Leslie (1917–1981)
Mackie was an Australian atheist and philosopher. His published

works included *The Cement of the Universe* (1974) and *Ethics: Inventing Right and Wrong* (1977). His last, *The Miracle of Theism* (1982), discussed the main arguments for and against the existence of God. He concluded that those against theism outweigh those in its favor. {SWW}

Mackie, Ross (Died 1994)

Mackie was a key figure in New Zealand rationalism. In 1978 with Dave Miller he managed the *New Zealand Rationalist and Humanist*, advocating the myth theory of Jesus and following rationalist authorities such as J. R. Robertson and G. A. Wells. {SWW}

McKinney, Arthur L. (20th Century)

McKinney, a freethinker, wrote *An Endless Day Awaits Us?* (1959). {GS}

McKinney, John L. (20th Century)

When he reviewed books for *The Humanist* in the 1950s, McKinney was in the department of philosophy at the University of Arkansas.

MacKinnon, Ian (20th Century)

MacKinnon is author of "The History of Freethought in Australia" (*American Rationalist*, January-February, 1990).

MacKinnon, John (20th Century)

MacKinnon has been a member of the American Humanist Association. {HNS}

McKinsey, C. Dennis (20th Century)

McKinsey edits the monthly *Biblical Errancy* (1983 to the present). In his *Encyclopedia of Biblical Errancy* (1995), he challenges the common view that the Bible is a good book filled with good material. Voltaire had said that the gospels contain almost as many errors as words. McKinsey shows this also applies to other parts of the Bible. He maintains that the Bible's negative teachings must be corrected and its inadequacies exposed. Readers of the Bible seem unaware, he holds, of its deceptively inaccurate conglomeration of mythology and folklore masquerading as a valid picture of historical reality, and this leads to their detached stupor. He offers twenty-four reasons why it is bad *not* to challenge "the Bible-pounders."

Mackintosh, James [Sir] (1765–1832)

A Scottish philosopher, Mackintosh in his youth settled amongst London radicals and rose to the important offices for which he was knighted. He wrote about moral philosophy, and his *Vindiciae Gallicae* (1791) was a reply to Edmund Burke's *Reflections on the French Revolution.* Sir James's work was the leading Whig statement in favor of the French Revolution, but from 1796 on he grew hostile to French radicalism. As a member of Parliament, Mackintosh supported penal and parliamentary reform. According to Greville Mackintosh "had never believed at all during life." However, McCabe calls Mackintosh a liberal theist who, when his son tried to induce him on his deathbed to make a profession of Christianity, refused. {JM; RAT; RE}

Mackintosh, John R. (1833–1907)

A freethinker, Mackintosh wrote *The Basis of Faith* (1894). {GS}

Mackintosh, Thomas Simmons (Died 1850)

Mackintosh wrote *The Electrical Theory of the Universe* (1848) and *An Inquiry into the Nature of Responsibility.* {BDF}

MacKnight, James W. (20th Century)

A minister, MacKnight has been a member of the American Humanist Association. {HNS}

McKnight, Russell L. (20th Century)

When he signed Humanist Manifesto II, Mc Knight was president of the Humanist Association of Los Angeles. {HM2}

McKown, Delos B(anning) (20th Century)

McKown, head of the philosophy department at Auburn University in Alabama, is the secularist author of *The Classical Marxist Critiques of Religion: Marx, Engels, Lenin, and Kautsky* (1975). He also wrote *With Faith and Fury* (1985), a tragicomic novel concerning American religion. In *The Mythmaker's Magic, Behind the Illusion of Creation Science* (1993), McKown satirizes the "Creation Scientists." He holds that although our Constitution is utterly secular, the practice of religion enjoys stronger legal guarantees than does the dissemination of scientific knowledge. Americans are often led to believe that science and religion do not conflict, he writes, but this is false whenever a religion based on scriptural inerrancy arises.

McKown is on the Council for Secular Humanism's Committee for the Scientific Examination of Religion. In addition, he is a contributing editor for *Free Inquiry* and a supporter of Internet Infidels. In 1993, he spoke at the Freedom From Religion Foundation's annual convention held in Huntsville, Alabama. His subject: "Why the Religiously Liberated Languish and Fundagelicals Flourish and What To Do About It!" {HNS2}

McLachlan, Sarah (20th Century)

McLachlan, who reportedly has said she is an agnostic, once performed for the Pope. Her atheistic "Dear God," is in a 1996 XTC tribute CD, *A Testimonial Dinner*, but she was not the author. "I don't follow any organized religion," she told a reporter (*Spring Chat*, 28 May 1996), "but I do believe in the idea of god as a verb—being love and light and that we are part of everything as everything is part of us. {CA; A}

MacLaine, Shirley (1934–)

A bodacious movie actress, MacLaine believes in reincarnation as well as remembers some of her past embodiments (and, as such, is a subject for many jokes by comedians).

McLaren, Alexander Duncan (1868–1947)

McLaren, a writer, secularist, and freethinker, was born in Tasmania. He was secretary of the Australian Secular Association in 1890 and spoke at the 1892 opening of the Sydney Lyceum (Freethought Hall). Between 1906 and 1933, McLaren had sixty-six articles published in the *Freethinker.* Also, he revised G. W. Foote's *Infidel Death Beds* (1933). From 1916 to 1947 he lived in England. {FUK; SWW}

MacLean, Angus (1909–)

MacLean is author of *The Wind in Both Ears* (1987), which concerns Unitarian Universalist religious education.

MacLean, Kenneth Torquil (20th Century)

MacLean was the Unitarian Universalist Association's special assistant to the President for International and Interfaith Relations. He wrote *Problems of the Planet* (1975) and *World Environmental Problems* (1981). In 1999 he became minister of the Unitarian Fellowship of the Desert in Palm Desert, California. (See *World*, July-August 1995.)

MacLeish, Archibald (1892–1982)

An American poet and public official, Mac Leish wrote *Conquistador* (1932), which describes in poetic form the conquest of Mexico, for which he received a Pulitzer Prize. A New Deal advocate, he was Librarian of Congress (1939–1944) and Undersecretary of State (1944–1945) during Franklin D. Roosevelt's administration. From 1949 to the 1960s, he taught at Harvard. Son of a prosperous businessman whose convictions were fixed, and who was not outwardly affectionate, Mac Leish once described his father's lack of pity thusly: "God was father's father." In 1958, he retold the story of Job in a modern setting, entitling it *J. B.* and winning a second Pulitzer Prize. Some critics resented his retelling of the Biblical story, objecting to its humanistic overtones; others claimed it improved upon the original.

In 1944, MacLeish had an article in *Atlantic Monthly* (November) entitled, "Humanism and the Belief in Man." First, he found classical humanism impractical. The trouble with it, he wrote, was that it was formulated at a time when "the sickness of the soul was dogma and superstition," when "humanism considered as an intellectual discipline-for-discipline's sake, or as a regimen to free the mind of prejudice and infatuation, or as an aristocratic training of the taste, or as a cult of the classic past, or as the appreciation of fine arts and beautiful letters, [was] a prime specific for such ills as bigotry and puritanism and jesuitry and vulgarity and Victorianism and the complacency of the bourgeois mind." But the problem in 1944, he added, is not *excess* of belief. It is *lack* of belief.

He then blasts the neo-humanists such as Irving Babbitt and Paul Elmer More, who are crying out for a "great conversion of the world, a vast revival, a wind from beyond the planet and the stars, to fill us in spite of ourselves, and without our effort, by some miracle of faith, like the miracle they imagine to have happened when Christianity first took the world, or when the religion of the Prophet took it." He continued:

> There is a definition of humanism by which humanism becomes a belief in the one thing in which man has greatest need now to believe—himself, and the dignity and importance of the place he fills in the world he lives in. There is a definition of humanism by which humanism becomes precisely the belief of man in his own dignity, in his essential worth as a man, in what Ralph Barton Perry calls "his characteristic perfection": a belief not in the potentiality of man, but in the actuality of man; a belief not in the classic perfection of the beautiful letters men have written in the distant past, but in the human perfection of the men who wrote those letters and of others like them, whether writers or other writers, and whether living in the past or in the present or not yet born; a belief not in the thing a man may become if he reads the right books and develops the right tastes and undergoes the right discipline, but a belief in the thing he is.

Then, characteristic of other naturalistic humanists whose total philosophy of life must necessarily include political and economic views, MacLeish added:

> If the fundamental proposition upon which the government of the world was based were the proposition that man, because he is man, and in his essential quality as man, has worth and value which governments exist to serve and to protect, regardless of race and regardless of color or religion, there would be little room for the play of international politics which, under color of realism or under color of necessity, puts power first or oil first or gold first, and men second or nowhere, preparing thus for the wars of power or of oil or gold.

Concluding with advice to the generation which has "lost its sense of the place of man in the universe" and which should learn to teach men to believe in themselves and thereby assure their freedom, MacLeish summed up his case: "It is man whom the humanist values, and man is in all men—is all men."

Asked in 1951 to elaborate further, he replied to the present author:

> My difficulty is that although I know what I believe, I do not know what word you put to it. I have never called myself a humanist, though if that is the word which applies to my beliefs, then I suppose I am one. However, I do not like labels—even good ones.

His lines from "Geography of This Time" are part of the liturgy of the Unitarian Universalist churches:

> What is required of us, Companions, is the recognition of the frontiers
> across this history, and to take heart
> and cross over.
>
> To persist and cross over and survive.
> But to survive
> To cross over.

{CE; CL; TYD; WAS, 30 May 1951}

McLeod, John (19th Century)
McLeod is author of *Religion: Its Place in Human Culture* (1873). {GS}

McLoughlin, Emmett (20th Century)

McLaughlin is author of *American Culture and Catholic Schools* (1960), *Crime and Immorality in the Catholic Church* (1962), and *People's Padre* (1952). The latter book was an autobiography in which he described leaving the priesthood and becoming a freethinker. McLoughlin maintained that the doctrine of probabilism justifies the birth control pill. {FUS}

McMahan, Marjorie and **Richard** (20th Century)

The McMahans are activists with the Capital District Humanist Society, PO Box 2148, Scotia, New York 12302. Richard is editor of the group's *Humanist Monthly*.

McMahan, R. H. Jr. (20th Century)

When he heard a radio advice-giver say that you cannot be moral without God and said one could logically be frightened if approached by a group of men in jeans and leather jackets but would not be "if these young men were carrying Bibles," McMahan jocularly devised these scenarios:

- You're a Palestinian in Jerusalem.
- You're a Protestant in Dublin
  and their Bibles are wrapped in rosary beads.
- You're black, and those lads are white.
- You're white, and those lads are black.
- You're leaving a gay bar,
  and those Bible-toting lads are wearing jackets
  with the BornAgain University logo.
- You're wearing a yarmulke in Redneckville, Arkasippi,
  or in the "wrong" neighborhood in Anytown;
  those Bibles are New Testaments.
- You're a Muslim girl being approach by a mullah
  carrying the Qur'an *and* the knife he's about to use
  to assure that you will never enjoy the sex
  that will be the right of the man whose property you will be.

{*The* Humanist Monthly, newsletter of the Capital District Humanist Society}

McMillan, Robert (c. 1880–1940?)

McMillan, a journalist, was a long-time president of the Rationalist Association of New South Wales, Australia. He wrote *The Great Secret* and *The Origin of the World.*

McMurran, Stella (Died 1998)

A Canadian who was the central fitgure in Ottawa's movement for the rights of dying people, McMurran and her husband Don founded the Ottawa branch of Dying with Dignity in 1986 and, subsequently, Choice in Dying—Ottawa. "70 per cent of Canadians," she declared, agree with television personalities like David Suzuki and Robert Buckman in their belief in individual freedom of choice, up to and including the end of life.

McNally, Terrence (1939-)

A controversial playwright who is Catholic, McNally won an Obie in 1971 for "Bad Habits"; an Obie in 1974 for best play, "The Ritz"; a Tony in 1990 for "Kiss of the Spider Woman," best book of a musical; an Emmy in 1990 for "André's Mother"; a Pulitzer prize for drama nomination in 1994 for "A Perfect Ganesh"; and a 1995 Outer Critics' Circle award for best Broadway play, "Love! Valour! Compassion!"

Raised a Catholic, McNally infuriated the Catholic League for Religious and Civil Rights in 1998 with his play, "Corpus Christi," described as his unique view of "the greatest story every told." The plot is about a Jesus-like figure born in a Texas flea-bag hotel in which the noise of violent sex next door greets little Joshua. The chap grows into a charismatic person who has gay lovers including a long-running affair with Judas and other of his apostle-like friends. One scene is nonexplicit but is of a sexual encounter with an HIV-positive street hustler.

The Manhattan Theater Club, which planned to stage the play, received a telephoned bomb threat that promised the "extermination of every member of the theater." The caller of the threat, identifying himself as being from an unknown group called the National Security Movement of America, said, "Again, message is for Jew guilty homosexual Terrence McNally. Because of you we will exterminate every member of the theater and burn the place to the ground. Death to the Jews worldwide." Deciding first to cancel the play because of the possibility of violence, the club's administrators reversed themselves and opted for free expression combined with tight security. Praising the decision to allow the play to be seen were thirty of the nation's leading playwrights, including Tony Kushner, Arthur Miller, Christopher Durang, A. R. Gurney, Stephen Sondheim, and Wendy Wasserstein.

McNamara, Matilda Emilie Bertha (1853–1931)

McNamara, formerly Bredt, was a bookseller, feminist, and socialist who had been born in Poland. Her book shop was a meeting place for freethinkers, feminists, and other radicals. Her daughter Bertha married poet Henry Lawson, and her daughter Hilda married politician J. T. Lang. A plaque at the entrance of the Sydney Trades Hall commemorates her rationalism:

> Kindly and gracious in her splendid way
> She knew no nationhood
> And her religion each and every day
> Was that of doing good.

{SWW}

McNamara, William Henry Thomas (1852–1906)

McNamara married the widow Bertha Bredt, and together they operated a book shop which sold socialist, freethought, and radical literature. Some described it as a "democratic rendezvous" with an international reading room of imported newspapers, which could be consulted for one penny. The McNamaras felt that socialism could be achieved by workers voluntarily forming cooperatives and gradually assuming social control from privately owned industries. {SWW}

McNeese, S. J. (20th Century)

McNeese was a freethinker who wrote *An Appeal to Reason, or Sanity Versus Faith* (1924). {GS}

Macon, Nathaniel (1757–1837)

Macon, a statesman and a deist, said that if a Hindu were to come to North Carolina and aspire to an office to which merit would entitle him, his religion should not be a bar. He helped during the Constitutional Convention of 1835 to open public office to North Carolina Catholics and set the precedent for further opening of citizenship privileges to persons of all faiths and none. (See entry for North Carolina Freethinkers.)

McQueen, Albert J. (20th Century)

McQueen has been an assistant professor of sociology at Eastern Michigan University.

McQueen, Alexander (20th Century)

Dubbed "British Designer of the Year" in 1996, McQueen was asked by David Bowie in *Dazed and Confused* (November 1996) who he would like to dress more than anyone else in the world. "I can't think of anyone who deserves such a privilege," McQueen joked. Then "the sub-headline there!" said Bowie. McQueen answered, "Oh my God no, 'cause I'm an atheist and an anti-royalist, so why would I put anyone on a pedestal?" {CA}

McQueen, Thelma (Butterfly) (1911–1995)

McQueen, the personable African American actress who played Prissy in "Gone With The Wind" (which Margaret Mitchell originally had intended to entitle *Pansy*), is remembered for her distinctively high voice (and the confession to her mistress that "Lawdy, Miss Scarlett, I don't know nuthin' 'bout birthing babies"). In that movie, she performed the part of a dim-witted maid prone to outbursts of hysteria, being bitterly criticized for playing such a racial stereotype. She, however, retorted that she had refused to eat watermelon in the movie and had particularly objected to being slapped by Scarlett.

It became increasingly difficult for McQueen to find work in film or the theater following "Gone With The Wind," partly because the audience associated her voice with that of Prissy. At the age of sixty-four, McQueen, who had never completed college, graduated with a degree in political science from the City College of New York. She worked with antipoverty groups, taking a job as a waitress in a soul food restaurant, and she gave tap dance and ballet lessons at Harlem's Mount Morris Park Recreation Center in order, in her words, to help her "black family."

"I'm an atheist," she once declared, "and Christianity appears to me to be the most absurd imposture of all the religions, and I'm puzzled that so many people can't see through a religion that encourages irresponsibility and bigotry."

In 1989, the Freedom from Religion Foundation honored her with its Freethought Heroine Award. She told a reporter for the *Atlanta Journal and Constitution* (8 October 1989), "As my ancestors are free from slavery, I am free from the slavery of religion." She also lamented that humans had not put the energy on earth and on people that had been put on mythology and on Jesus Christ, for if we had there would be less hunger and homelessness. "They say the streets are going to be beautiful in Heaven. Well, I'm trying to make the streets beautiful here. . . . When it's clean and beautiful, I think America is heaven. And some people are hell."

Burned over 70% of her body in a 1995 accident at her home, she died after telling firefighters how her clothes had caught fire from a faulty kerosene heater. When a Christian neighbor observed the incident, however, she told the *Atlanta Constitution*, "I believe she [Thelma] made it into Heaven. She threw up both her hands as she was coming out of that burning house, and made it in with Jesus." On the contrary, the atheistic McQueen had been a Life Member of the Freedom From Religion Foundation since 1981 and had included the foundation in her will. {*Freethought Today*, January-February 1996; TYD; WAS, conversation; WWS}

Macrae, Gordon (20th Century)

Writing "Abusive Priests" in *The New Zealand Rationalist and Humanist* (Winter, 1998), Macrae cites a study which indicates that "up to 15% of the clergy were abusers." His response: "What's really frightening is that they seriously believe that it is only 'up to 15%.' Anyone ready to wager on it being significantly higher?"

Macrobius, Ambrosius Theodosius (c. 400–423)

Macrobius, a Roman pagan official believed to have been Proconsul in Africa, resisted Christianity to the end. His *Saturnalia* describes patricians he knew, and it illustrates the high character of the last generation of Roman gentlemen. Macrobius made one of the earliest attempts to resolve religion into solar myths. {RE}

MACROCOSM

The macrocosm, as distinguished from the microcosm, is the entire world, the universe. During the Renaissance, *microcosm* (from the Greek *mikros*, small, and *kosmos*, order) was applied specifically to human beings, who were considered to be small-scale models of the macrocosm, with all its variety and contradiction. {DCL}

MacSweeney, Myles (1814–1881)

A mythologist, MacSweeney upon coming to London from Enniskillen heard Robert Taylor at the Rotunda in 1830 and adopted his views. He held that Jesus never existed, wrote in the *National Reformer* as well as *Secular Chronicle*, and published "Moses and Bacchus" (1874). {BDF}

McTaggart, John (20th Century)

McTaggart is assistant professor of sociology at the Kings University College, Edmonton, Alberta, Canada. He has written on "Organised Humanism in Canada and The Netherlands" in *New Humanist* (March 1997).

M'Taggart, John M'Taggart Ellis (1866–1925)

"G. E. Moore, John Ellis McTaggart, and Bertrand Russell are the first three academic atheists of note," writes Berman. A student of Hegel, M'Taggart (Mc Taggart) believed that the ultimate reality is spiritual, and he denied the real existence of the material, of space, and of time. A determinist, he held that determinism is not incompatible with moral obligation. With Moore and Russell, McTaggart was a member of the Apostles, a Cambridge Society with a distinctively irreverent attitude toward God and religion. His own atheism is found in *Some Dogmas of Religion* (1906), *Studies in Hegelian Cosmology* (1918), and *The Nature of Existence* (1921 and 1927). As for Hegel's cosmology, McTaggart claimed that "the Absolute is not God and in consequence there is no God."

In *Some Dogmas of Religion*, he saw "no reason to think that positive belief in immortality is true" or "to suppose that God exists." As for Christianity, McTaggart wrote, "If one was a Christian one would have to worship Christ, and I don't like him much. If you take what he said in the first three gospels (for St. John's has no historical value I believe) it is a horribly one-sided and imperfect ideal. Would you like a man or a girl who really imitated Christ? I think most of the people I know are living far finer lives than anything you could get out of the gospels. The best thing about him was his pluck at the Crucifixion, and other people have shown as much." Although Ducasse and McTaggart did not believe in God, both believed in reincarnation, according to Paul Edwards, whose *Immortality* (1992) and *Reincarnation* (1996) humorously critiques such nonsense. {CE; HAB; JM; PE; RAT; RE}

McWilliams, Peter (20th Century)

McWilliams, in *Ain't Nobody's Business If You Do: The Absurdity of Consensual Crimes in a Free Society* (1993), accuses organized religion of making consensual acts a crime. He holds that any activity, which does not harm the person or property of another, should not be illegal.

Macy, Christopher (20th Century)

When he signed Humanist Manifesto II, Macy was director of the Rationalist Press Association, Great Britain. He wrote *Marriage and Divorce* (1969) and *The Arts in a Permissive Society* (1971). In 1977, he edited "Rationalism and Humanism in the New Europe." {FUK; HM2}

Madach, Imré (1823–1880)

Madach was a Hungarian patriot and poet. In 1852 he was incarcerated for one year for having given asylum at his castle to a political refugee. In 1862 he became a delegate at Pesth, the same year he wrote a poem, "*Az Ember Tragédiaja*" (The Human Tragedy), a free-thinking work in which mankind is personified as Adam, with Lucifer in his company. {BDF; RAT}

Maddoux, Martin (20th Century)

Maddoux wrote *Humanism Exposed* (1983) and *America Betrayed* (1984).

Maddox, John Royden [Sir] (1925–)

In 1986, Maddox was elected an honorary associate of the Rationalist Press Association, and in 1994 Queen Elizabeth II knighted him. Kennedy has been editor of *Nature* since 1980 and held that post also between 1966 and 1973. In spite of (or perhaps because of) having been sent to Sunday school as a child, he has said, he has always been offended by the hypocrisy of the religious. An even greater offense, the chemist and physicist and naturalist believes, is confusing important issues by the telling of fairy stories. Maddox has written *Revolutions in Biology* (1964), *The Doomsday Syndrome* (1972), and *Beyond the Energy Crisis* (1975).

Madigan, Timothy J(oseph) (1962–)

Madigan was the Executive Editor (1987–1997) and Editor (1997-1999) of *Free Inquiry*. Also, he was co-editor of *The Secular Humanist Bulletin* until 1997. He has taught philosophy at several Western New York institutions, including Monroe Community College, Medaille College, Erie Community College, Houghton College, Daemen College, Canisius College, and the State University of New York at Buffalo. He graduated summa cum laude in 1985 from the latter university, receiving his Ph. D. in 1999. Since 1999 he has been the editorial director for the University of Rochester Press.

Madigan is one of the youngest as well as one of the best-recognized faces in the secular humanist movement, for he has traveled widely and speaks extensively. He has given presentations at Harvard University, Princeton University, Yale University, Louisiana State University, California State University-Northridge, Southeastern Louisiana University, University of South Alabama, Drew University, University of Richmond, Hofstra University, Youngstown State University, Brock University, University of Minnesota, and Hiram College. He has also spoken at conferences in Moscow and St. Petersburg, Russia; Madrid, Spain; Delphi, Greece; Warsaw, Poland; Amsterdam, The Netherlands; London, England; San Jose, Costa Rica; Toronto, Canada; Edinburgh, Scotland; and Cairo, Egypt.

A writer on extensive subjects, including the singer Al Jolson, Madigan co-wrote (with Glenn Odden) such plays as *The Knife Before Christmas*, *Unnecessary Roughness*, *Forever Hold Your Piece*, and *Primary Suspect*. He was co-editor of *On the Barricades: The Best of Free Inquiry* (1989); *The Question of Humanism* (1991), and *Toward a New Enlightenment: The Philosophy of Paul Kurtz* (1993) and edited *"The Ethics of Belief" and other Essays by W. K. Clifford* (1999). Also, he has been associate editor of *Moody Street Irregulars: The Jack Kerouac Newsletter*; and editor of *The Brontë Newsletter*. Also, he is a United States editor of *Philosophy* Now (London).

A Secular Humanist Mentor of the Council for Secular Humanism, Madigan was active as an assistant to Paul Kurtz in the establishment of secular humanist societies throughout the nation.

He is an honorary associate of the New Zealand Association of Rationalists and Humanists. Also, he is a member of the American Philosophical Association, the Society for Advancement of American Philosophy, the Bertrand Russell Society (on the board of directors, 1993–present), the John Dewey Society, the David Hume Society, the International Brontë Society, and the International Primate Protection League. He is Executive Director of the Society of Humanist Philosophers.

In "*Legor et Legar*: Schopenhauer's Atheistic Morality" (*Philo*, Fall-Winter 1998), Madigan states that Nietzsche referred to Arthur

Schopenhauer as the first inexorable atheist among German philosophers. "Yet Schopenhauer's philosophy—in particular his discussion of 'compassion' as the basis of morality—can serve as a starting point for dialogue among Hindus, Buddhists, Jews, Christians, Muslims, and atheistic humanists, all of whom need to address what Raimundo Panikkar calls 'The Silence of God.' " Schopenhauer, "this friendless and bad-tempered philosopher," has much to teach about the nature of morality, he writes.

"Like many people," Madigan has written, "I was named after a relative. But in my case, the relative in question was a Roman Catholic nun—my mother's cousin, Sister Timothy." Nuns, until fairly recently, assumed a male name when taking up the wimple. As a young Catholic, Madigan read in *The Acts of the Apostles* that the biblical Paul "wanted Timothy to accompany him, and he took him and circumcised him because of the Jews that were in those places, for they knew all that his father was a Greek." But then the Church Fathers changed their minds, thanks to a revelation from God, and Christians did *not* have to have their foreskins removed. Observed Madigan after becoming an atheist, "And after this cruel joke, the guy *still* honored God? What a schmuck."

In his introduction to W. K. Clifford's *The Ethics of Belief*, Madigan notes that Clifford chose for his epitaph a statement from Epictetus: "I was not, and was conceived; I loved, and did a little work; I am not, and grieve not." Dr. Madigan signed Humanist Manifesto 2000. His e-mail: <timothymad@aol.com>. (See entry for New York Atheists, Freethinkers, Humanists.) {FD; HNS2; *Secular Humanist Bulletin*, Summer 1994}

Madison, James [President] (1751–1826)

The "master builder of the Constitution," our 4th United States President had a wife, Dolley, who has the distinction of having been an official White House hostess for two presidents: She served also for Thomas Jefferson, then a widower. Madison learned Hebrew and made a thorough study of theology after being graduated by Princeton, at which time he gave up his beliefs. He helped draft the constitution of Virginia, insisting that it include protections for religious freedom. He effectively protested against a proposal to make contributions compulsory in Virginia to religion, and he got church and state completely separated there. In his letters, he shows that all his life he opposed the churches. In one (19 May 1823), he insists that the university shall not become "an Arena of Theological Gladiators."

The 5' 4" one-hundred-pound Madison was reserved, dressed conservatively, enjoyed a risqué story, but according to his letters to Jefferson was a chronic worrier, always afraid that the worst was soon to happen.

Richard K. Matthews, in *If Men Were Angels: James Madison and the Heartless Empire of Reason* (1995), argues that Madison deserves more credit for being an accurate symbol of America. "Think of who he was and what he achieved," Gordon S. Wood of Princeton has written in critiquing the Matthews thesis:

> The major architect of the Constitution; the father of the Bill of Rights and one of the strongest proponents of the rights of conscience and religious liberty in American history; co-author of *The Federalist*, surely the most significant work of political theory in American history; the leader and most important members of the first House of Representative since 1789; co-founder of the Democratic-Republican party in the 1790s; secretary of state in Jefferson's administration; and the fourth president of the United States—all this, and still he does not have the popular standing of the other founding fathers, especially that of his closest friend, Thomas Jefferson.

Madison, whose wife Dolley was a lapsed Quaker, in 1785 wrote to William Bradford Jr., "During almost fifteen centuries has the legal establishment of Christianity been on trial. What have been Christianity's fruits? Superstition, bigotry, and persecution." He added, "Religious bondage shackles and debilitates the mind, and unfits it for every noble purpose." Madison was one of the few statesmen who did not sprinkle speeches with references to God. McCabe calls Madison a "freethinker like his three predecessors." Washington, Lincoln, and Madison never spoke about God in their letters. {CE; FUK; FUS; JM; RAT; RE; TRI; TYD}

Mädler, Johann Heinrich (1794–1874)

Mädler, a German astronomer, was appointed in 1836 Observer at the Berlin Royal Observatory, and in 1840 he became professor of astronomy and director of the observatory at Dorpat. His *Populäre Astronomie* (1841) and *Die Fixternhimmel* (1858) were highly regarded. A pantheist, Mädler once wrote a poem in which he emphatically rejected Christianity and confined his belief to a pantheist conception of God. {RAT}

MADONNA

Madonna is a picture, statue, or other image of Jesus's mother. She generally is pictured with the baby Jesus in her arms. If Joseph had spoken Latin, he would have referred to his wife, Mary, as *mea domina*, "my lady," although she allegedly did not give birth to his baby but, rather, was supernaturally inseminated. (A Manhattan wag suggests she was inseminated not by the Holy Ghost but by theologians.)

In the 1990s people spoke of Madonna Louise Veronica Ciccone (1958–) as the lady who was naturally inseminated. A pop icon, singer, and actress, Madonna became known for her albums *Madonna* (1983) and *Like A Virgin* (1984). A Roman Catholic, she wrote *Sex* (1992) and embarrassed many church officials of various faiths by her views as well as by her actions. Called the "Material Girl," she appeared in movies, such as "Desperately Seeking Susan, Truth or Dare," a revealing backstage performance that brought her much publicity. Her "Papa Don't Preach" took a strict Catholic position, that if you are going to have a baby you should not abort it.

Madonna infuriated many by making obscene gestures with a crucifix during performances. She wore huge crosses and turned them from religious ornaments into fashion statements as well as sex accessories. Once, she called Catholicism "disgusting" and "hypocritical," leading the Vatican to denounce her for not being a model Catholic woman. Her very first words upon meeting basketball star Dennis Rodman, for example, were, "Are you going to eat my pussy first? I like someone to eat me out and get me loose." In 1996, after several public figures described their sexual experiences with her, Madonna although not married to Carlos Leon had a baby, Lourdes Maria Ciccone Leon, by him, and the child was sent to the Catholic Church for schooling.

In 1996, Madonna starred as Evita Peron in the movie "Evita." One of the quick-change artists of her generation, Madonna upon releasing a 1998 album, "Ray of Light," told of her interest in *sivasana*—a yoga-like totally prone corpse pose—in Sanskrit, and the Jewish mystical art of the cabala. Andrew M. Greeley has observed that Madonna has an obvious "God hunger." As to having become a Buddhist, Madonna told journalist Andrew Smith (*Daily News*, 3 May 998), "No, I've studied Buddhism and I suppose in some ways I'm practicing it. But I wouldn't say I'm anything specific. These are just things and ideas that I find useful. I feel like I'm just now figuring out who I am and what I want. And the more you know, the more you realize you don't know. I feel like I'm on this journey and I'm searching for answers, but I couldn't say what I am or what I'm not in terms of some religious dogma, or affiliating myself with a group of thought. I really shy away from that." {Dennis Rodman, *Bad As I Want to Be* (1996); *The New York Times*, 1 March 1998; *Vanity Fair*, June 1996}

Maeterlinck, Maurice (1862–1949)

The Belgian author of *Pelléas and Mélisande* (1892) liked the mysticism of Emerson and Novalis, and the sixty works he wrote can be considered a symbolist manifesto. In 1911, he received the Nobel Prize in Literature, for his work about impending doom, life's mystery, and ennui was popular with the reading public. Although not a naturalistic humanist, he was enough of a non-believer to rate having all his works prohibited by the Vatican's Index in 1914. "There is a vein of mysticism in his ethical conceptions," noted McCabe, "but he was outside all churches and apparently not even a theist. In a work on the question of a future life (*La Morte*), he leaves it open and is not, as is sometimes said, a Spiritualist." {CE; ILP; JM; RAT; RE}

Magee, Bryan (20th Century)

Confessions of a Philosopher: A Journey Through Western Philosophy (1999) reveals that Magee is not religious but is fascinated by studying philosophers' works, particularly those by Schopenhauer, Hume, Bertrand Russell, and Kant.

Colin McCall objected to Magee's statement that atheists know there is not a God, saying atheists simply find no evidence for a God, that in Laplace's famous phrase, we have "no need of that hypothesis." But he liked the 600-page book which, he said, was written by a liberal socialist and Labour MP who became a "liberal non-socialist." {*The Freethinker*, April 1999}

Magee, William Connor (1822–1891)

Magee, a freethinker, wrote *Christianity in Relation to Freethought, Scepticism, and Faith* (1892). {GS}

Magellan, Ferdinand (Fernão de Magalhães) (c. 1480–1521)

"The church says the earth is flat, but I know that it is round, for I have seen the shadow on the moon, and I have more faith in a shadow than in the church," Magellan declared. A Portuguese navigator with unusual determination, he began the first voyage around the world in 1519. Prior to that, he had served in Portuguese India, in Morocco, in Spain, in South America, and after putting down a mutiny of some of his officers in Patagonia he discovered and entered the strait that bears his name, later reaching the Pacific Ocean. Traveling onward, his fleet of three vessels sighted no land for nearly two months, but eventually it reached the Philippines where he was killed supporting one group of natives against another. His crew, however, was able to complete the trip in 1522, proving the roundness of the earth and revolutionizing ideas of the relative proportions of land and water. Equally important, it revealed the Americas as a new world, separate from Asia. Had it not been for Magellan's faith, in astronomy rather than theology, the New World would not have been understood as quickly by Europeans. {CE; TYD}

Magellan, Jean Hyacinthe de (1723–1790)

João Jacinte de Magalhaes, as he was originally named, was Portuguese, a descendant of explorer Ferdinand Magellan. He entered the monastic order of St. Augustine, then left the Order and the Church of Rome without entering any other branch of Christianity. Magellan made astronomical and other scientific instruments and was admitted to the Royal Society (1774) and was a corresponding member of the Academies of Science of Paris and Madrid. {RAT}

MAGI: See the entry for Christmas.

MAGIC: See entry for Fertility Rites.

MAGIC REALISM

Magic realism (*magischer Realismus*) is a term coined by Franz Roy to describe tendencies in the work of certain German artists of the new objectivity (*neue Sachlichkeit*), characterized, according to the *Oxford Companion to English Literature*, "by clear, cool, static, thinly-painted, sharp-focus images, frequently portraying the imaginary, the improbable, or the fantastic in a realistic or rational manner."

The term was used in the United States with the 1943 exhibition of artworks by Charles Sheeler and Edward Hopper. It subsequently has been used to describe the works of such Latin American authors as Jorge Luis Borges, Gabriel Garcia Márquez, and Alejo Carpentier.

Magic realist works typically have a strong narrative drive in which the recognizably realistic mingles with the unexpected and the inexplicable. Dreams, fairy-stories, or mythology combine with the everyday and, sometimes, the irrational. (See entry for Jorge Luis Borges.) {OCE}

Maginnis, Patricia (20th Century)

Maginnis was named the American Humanist Association's Humanist Pioneer in 1978 for her fighting on behalf of birth control. {HNS2}

Magistro, Charles (20th Century)

Magistro has been a liberal Unitarian Universalist minister in Brooklyn, New York; Stamford, Connecticut; and Garden City, New York.

Maglia, Adolfo de (Born 1859)

A Spanish journalist, Maglia founded the freethinking group *El Independiente* and edited *El Clamor Setabense* and *El Pueblo Soberano*. {BDF}

Magnani-Torelli, E. (20th Century)

At the Second European Conference of the International Humanist and Ethical Union held in Hannover (1968), Magnani-Torelli of Italy addressed the group.

Mahan Jr., Ludlow P. (20th Century)

When he signed Humanist Manifesto II, Mahan was president of the Humanist Chapter of Rhode Island. He is associated with the Rhode Island Atheists. (See entry for Rhode Island Atheists, Freethinkers.) {FD; HM2}

MAHASKTI

In India, Mahaskti was considered the Divine Mother, supreme creator of the universe. {LEE}

Mahavira (c. 560–483 B.C.E.)

In Jainism, practiced by perhaps two million people in India, it is believed that a succession of twenty-four tirthankaras (saints) originated the religion. The last was Vardhamana, called Mahavira (the great hero) and Jina (the victor). Mahavira, who, like Gautama, was not a theist, taught a rigid asceticism and solicitude, holding that life is a means of escaping the cycle of rebirth, or the transmigration of souls. Released from the rule of Karma, the total consequences of past acts, the soul can then attain Nirvana, and hence salvation. The brotherhood of monks he organized took vows of celibacy, nudity, self-mortification, and fasting. Jainism has appealed to many of India's most prominent industrialists, bankers, and politicians, who are known for their charity. They have, for example, established asylums for diseased and decrepit animals. {RE}

Mahfouz, Naguib (Nagib Mahfuz) (1911–)

Mahfouz, winner of the 1988 Nobel Prize for Literature, wrote *The Children of Gebelawi* (1959), which was banned in Egypt because it allegedly scoffed at religion and insulted the Prophet Mohammed. In 1994, a group of young Egyptian fundamentalists ambushed and stabbed the Egyptian novelist outside his home. Many linked the attack to a newspaper's plan to publish the novel, which theologians at Al Azhar University had condemned in a *fatwa*. Mahfouz wrote *The World of God* 1962), *God's World: An Anthology of Short Stories* (1973), *Satan Preaches* (1979), *One Act Plays* (1989), and *Children of the Alley* (1996). (See entry for Fatwa.)

Mahler, Gustav (1860–1911)

A major composer and conductor who was born in Austrian Bohemia of Jewish parentage, Mahler had a distinguished career. As described in *Columbia Encyclopedia*, Mahler

> followed Bruckner in the Viennese symphonic tradition. He added folk elements to the symphony and expanded it in terms of length, emotional contrast, and orchestral size. He used choral or solo voices in four symphonies; the Second, Third, Fourth, and Eighth; the Eighth is known as the Symphony of a Thousand because of the enormous performing forces required. The thinner texture, wide-ranging melodies, and taut, intense emotionalism of Mahler's late works strongly influenced the next generation of Austrian composers, especially Arnold Schoenberg and Alban Berg.

Terry Sanderson in *Gay & Lesbian Humanist* (Spring, 1998) praised the 1997 Albert Hall performance of the gigantic "Symphony of a Thousand," adding that although it is set to a religious text, Mahler "refused steadfastly to attach himself to any organized religion. He was born a Jew but has been described as a life-long agnostic. At one point he converted to Catholicism, purely for the purpose of obtaining a job that he coveted—director of the Court Opera of Vienna. It was unthinkable for a Jew to hold such a prestigious position, hence the utilitarian conversion to the state religion. After the confirmation service was over, he came out of the church and remarked to a friend: 'I've just changed my coat.' The Austrians' famous anti-Semitism, however, was not to be quenched by such a token gesture, and he was eventually driven out of the country an anti-Semitic press campaign."

Mahler, a morbid person by nature, one who brooded upon the inevitability of death, saw Dr. Sigmund Freud briefly. But he never overcame his fears, not even after comforting his daughter with his music. "Madness seizes me, annihilates me," he told friends who said he appealed to the Devil to take possession of his soul. He was never, however, adjudged clinically insane.

Mahler died of a heart attack brought on by a bacterial infection. {CE; *Current Biography*}

MAHOMET: See entry for Muhammad.

Mailer, Norman (1923–)

Playwright, short-story writer, versifier, literary critic, journalist, and self-publicist, Mailer is the Pulitzer Prize-winning novelist of *The Naked and the Dead* (1948). His work is known for its neurotic sexuality, and some believe it reveals its author's complex feelings toward women and his own tendencies toward violence. In 1941 he wrote the present author concerning humanism,

> I find it rather astonishing that your categories fail to include Marxism, which is the only philosophical system whose end is truly man himself. I suppose that I would have to list myself under *atheistic humanism* with a demurrer at being bedded down with Sartre.

Because Mailer is known for changing his viewpoints, he may or may not still hold what he then wrote. In *Christians and Cannibals*, Mailer wrote,

> What characterizes the Cannibals is that most of them are born Christians, think of Jesus as Love, and get an erection from the thought of whippings, blood, burning crosses, burning bodies, and screams in mass graves. Whereas their counterpart, the Christians—the ones who are not Christian but whom we choose to call Christians—are utterly opposed to the destruction of human life and succeed within themselves in starting all the wars of our own time.

Mailer's two Pulitzer Prizes were for *An American Dream* (1968) and *The Executioner's Song* (1979). *Oswald's Tale: An American Mystery* (1995), utilizing KGB files in Belarus and concerning the person who assassinated President John F. Kennedy, was described as "a masterpiece" by *The Economist*.

The second of his six wives, Adele Mailer, wrote *The Last Party: Scenes From My Life With Norman Mailer* (1997). It describes how their marriage started as a "trip into the light fantastic with a nice Jewish boy genius, newly famous and rich, my fatal attraction." In detail she then describes their sex life together, as well as with others (one four-way of which resulted in a stock-broker's smashing his cigarette "on Norman's mechanically gyrating rear"). She related how on 20 November 1962 he stabbed her two times but, lying to the grand jury, she claimed that she did not know who stabbed her. Her husband later pleaded guilty to third-degree assault, was given probation, and never went to jail.

The Gospel According to the Son tells the story of Jesus Christ, but not the Christ of Christian orthodoxy. "I'm one of the fifty or one hundred novelists in the world who could rewrite the New Testament," Mailer told people. In doing so, he wrote the life of Christ as if the Christ is telling the story. And, like the Christ, he is half man and half something else, leading critic James Wood to observe that Mailer comes off as "a kind of celebrity-centaur. The work has the Second of the Trinity receiving messages from the First of the Trinity which come at quite low frequency. By fusing the four gospels, Mailer tries to resolve C. S. Lewis's observation that either Christ was who he was or else he was a total madman." Remarked critic Michiko Kakutani, "Indeed Mr. Mailer's Father and Son have a lot in common: both are full of themselves, both are fond of self-dramatization, and both tend to feel put upon by their public responsibilities."

> For those who would ask how my words have come to this page, I would tell them to look upon it as a small miracle. (My gospel, after all, will speak of miracles.)

Mailer's odd change of viewpoints is apparent, also, in his interview in *Time* (30 September 1991):

> I happen to believe in it [reincarnation]. . . . It just seems to me that if we lead our lives with all that goes wrong with them, and then we die and that's the end of us, that doesn't make much sense.

Sometimes referred to "as one of the heftiest egos ever to hit the printed page," Mailer is a member of the American Academy of Arts and Letters. (See entry for Michael Novak, who claims that Mailer in 1998, by writing "Religion to me is now the last frontier," recognizes the importance of religion and has changed his former views. One of Mailer's former friends, Norman Podhoretz, writes in *Ex-Friends* [1999] that Mailer is a coward.) {CE; WAS, 20 February 1951}

Maillet, Benôit de (1656–1738)

Maillet was a French author who was successively consul in Egypt and at Leghorn. After his death was published "Telliamed," the anagram of his name, in which he maintained that all land was originally covered with water and that every species of animal, man included, owes its origin to the sea. {BDF}

Maillot, Arthur François Ève (1747–1814)

First a soldier, then an actor, eventually a French dramatist, Maillot embraced the Revolution with enthusiasm and was nominated a Commissary of the Convention. Although several times imprisoned under Napoleon I, he was a known rationalist and writer of comedies. {RAT}

Maimonides (Moses ben Maimon) (1135-1204)

A Jewish scholar, physician, and philosopher, Maimonides wrote *Moreh Nevukhim* (tr., *Guide for the Perplexed*) in Arabic and explained his proof of the existence of God, expounded the principles of creation, and elucidated metaphysical and religious problems. His thinking exerted a profound influence upon Christian thinkers.

However, Israel Shahak wrote in *Jewish History, Jewish Religion*,

> [Maimonides] was a racist and his attitude toward blacks and Mongols was worse than the attitude of Aquinas toward the Jews. The latter attitude was acknowledged by Catholics only after a long and severe struggle against a previous cover-up. . . . Maimonides' attitude toward non-Jews, whatever their race, is hardly better than his views about blacks and Mongols. One example: According to Maimonides (and all his commentators) in his monumental compendium of Talmudic law, *Mishneh Torah*: "If a Jew has a coitus with a Gentile woman, whether she be a child or three or an adult, whether married or unmarried, and even if he is a minor aged only nine years and one day—because he had willful coitus with her, she must be killed, as is the case with a beast, because through her a Jew got into trouble" ("Prohibitions on Sexual Intercourse"). It is obvious a person who could promulgate such a horrible law, and many similar ones, could also compare human beings to half-apes.
> {*The Nation*, 6 July 1998}

Main, Margaret Huntley (20th Century)

Main is a freethinker who writes for *Truth Seeker*. She is author of *A Rose Queen is Forever* (1989) and articles in various journals.

Maindonald, John (20th Century)

Maindonald is the President of the Australia and New Zealand Unitarian Association. E-mail: <john@maths.newcastle.edu.au>.

Maine, Colin (20th Century)

An Australian freethinker, Maine wrote *The Unpleasant Personality of Jesus Christ* (c. 1977). {GS}

Mainlaender, Philipp (Philipp Batz) (19th Century)

A pseudonym of Philipp Batz, Mainlaender wrote *Philosophy of Redemption*, the first part of which was published in 1876. A German pessimist, he held that polytheism gives place to monotheism and pantheism, and these again to atheism. "God is dead," he wrote, "and his death was the life of the world." {BDF}

Maitland, Edward (1824–1897)

A freethinker, Maitland wrote *How to Complete the Reformation* (c. 1872). He also wrote *By and By: An Historical Romance of the Future* (1977). {GS}

Maitland, Frederick William (1850–1906)

Maitland was an English legal historian, a professor at Cambridge University and a leading authority of his time on English law. He wrote *Domesday Book and Beyond* (1897), a model for the use of a source; and, with Sir Frederick Pollock, *The History of English Law Before the Time of Edward* (1895). Maitland was secretary of a group of freethinking scholars who gathered round Sir Leslie Stephen and shared his agnosticism.

"Then, as always, he was a dissenter from all the churches, " wrote his biographer, H. A. L. Fisher. {CE; JM; RAT; RE}

Maizels, Albert (20th Century)

Maizels is president of Humanists of the Gold Coast. (See entry for Florida Atheists, Humanists.) {FD}

Major, Charles Edwin (1859–1954)

Major was the first president of the New Zealand Rationalist Association, from 1927 to 1930. He reportedly was against "creeping socialism" but was for the kind of rationalism represented by the evolutionist and laissez-faire liberal, Herbert Spencer. His other accomplishments have been listed in David Harner's *The New Zealand Liberals* (1988). {SWW}

MAKE HAPPY

The desire to make someone happy is a humanistic one. A humanist, in a basic sense, is one devoted to positive human interests. Best-selling American author Stephen King told a gathering at the University of Maine, his alma mater, "The desire to please—or try to—seems hard-wired into my system. When I was a kid, my mother sometimes used to say, 'Stevie, if you were a girl, you'd always be pregnant.' " (See entry for Stephen King.) {Mark Singer, *The New Yorker*, 7 September 1998}

Malachi, Martin (20th Century)

Malachi, a Catholic and Jesuit, is author of *The Final Conclave* (1978), a work concerning the Vatican.

Malathi, A. (20th Century)

Ms. Malathi is assistant director of the Atheist Centre in Vijayawada, India.

Malebranche, Nicolas (1628–1715)

During the French Revolution, Maréchal cited Malebranche as one who seems to be an atheist only from the standpoint of the strictest religious orthodoxy. His philosophy, a synthesis of Cartesian and Augustinian thought, tried to reconcile the new science with Christian theology. Some of his ideas influenced Leibniz, Berkeley, and John Norris, but his theism was always paramount. He thought eternal truths are contained in a divine intellect, that the soul is part of that intellect. {Aram Vartanian, EU; CE; ER}

MALE

• Male, n. A member of the unconsidered, or negligible, sex. The male of the human race is commonly known (to the female) as Mere Man. The genus has two varieties: good providers and bad providers.

–**Ambrose Bierce**
The Devil's Dictionary

Malherbe, François de (1555–1628)

Malherbe was a French poet who served in the civil wars of the League and enjoyed the patronage of Henry IV. He was called the prince of poets and the poet of princes. He enjoyed skeptical raillery. When told upon his deathbed of paradise and hell, he said he had lived like others and would go where others went. {BDF; RAT; RE}

Malik, Gauri Bazaz (20th Century)

Malik is President of the Indian Renaissance Institute.

At a 1995 conference of humanists in India, Dr. Malik spoke of women's issues in South Asia. She thought that the world was awakening to the position of the poor and illiterate, of which women with their children are the major part. This region has been a male-dominated part of the world. "Crushing poverty," she explained, "overlaid with longstanding patterns of discrimination create conditions for women which threaten their well-being, curtail their social, political, economic rights, and limit their opportunities." As a result, she reported that agriculture constitutes the livelihood of eighty to ninety percent of South Asia and women undertake the greater part of this work.

Because of a tradition of women's playing a full part in the Vedic tradition and in the early part of the nationalist movement, there has been a continuing loss of women's status. The dowry system means that mothers abort or kill girl children to avoid a large payment on marriage. Population control is necessary but should be brought about in an enlightened way. She said, "A mass campaign for literacy, land reform, health education, which would have ensured an overall development and education, would check the population in a natural way." Quoting Gandhi, she continued, " 'Prejudices cannot be removed by legislation. They yield only to patient toil and education.' The Beijing U.N. Conference for women in September 1995 identified and highlighted education as the field for NGOs who work at the grassroots level. It is only through them," she concluded, "that integrated human development can have a future." {*New Humanist*, February 1996}

Malinowski, Bronislaw (1884–1942)

Malinowski was a Polish-born English anthropologist who founded "functionalism," a movement with the theory that cultures should be studied in terms of their particular internal dynamics. He studied the Trobriand Islanders (1914–1918), and he did research in Africa and the Americas. At the time Malinowski wrote *Magic, Science, and Religion* (published 1948), he dropped the comment that he did not love science because of his agnosticism. "I, personally," he declared, "am unable to accept any revealed religion, Christian or not." {TRI; TYD}

Malkin, Yaakov (20th Century)

Malkin is a dean of the International Federation of Secular Humanistic Jews.

Malladi, Ramamurthy (20th Century)

Malladi is an active member of the Indian Rationalist Humanist Association.

Malleson, Andrew (1931–)

A signer of Humanist Manifesto, Dr. Malleson is a psychiatrist. He wrote *Need Your Doctor Be So Useless?* (1973). {HM2}

Malleson, Miles (Born 1888)

Malleson, an author, was a freethinker, according to David Tribe. {TRI}

Mallet, David (1705–1765)

Mallet was a Scottish poet who became under-secretary to the Prince of Wales. He edited Bolingbroke's works and was a close friend of Hume and Gibbon. Those who knew him described him as being "a great declaimer in all the London coffee-houses against Christianity." {FUK; RAT; RE}

Mallett, Josephine (19th Century)

A French author, Mme. Mallet wrote a work on *The Bible* (1882), taking on its origin, errors, and contradictions. {BDF}

MALLEUS MALEFICARUM

A far-reaching document of the papal Inquisition was *Malleus Maleficarum*, written in the 1480s by two Dominican inquisitors, Heinrich Krämer and Jakob Sprenger. In 1484 Pope Innocent VIII issued the bull *Summus desiderantes affectibus*, which gave the Inquisition, not the secular courts, jurisdiction over witchcraft as heresy. Sprenger, the dean of Cologne University, and Krämer had served as inquisitors in parts of Germany. The document allowed inquisitors to handle almost any probability. It even suggested judgments which could be used: "We have exerted our utmost endeavor by various fitting methods to convert you to salvation, but you have been given up to your sin and led away and seduced by an evil spirit and have chosen to be tortured with fearful and eternal torment in hell, and that your body should here be consumed in flames." {EH}

Mallock, William Hurrell (19th Century)

Mallock was a freethinker who wrote *Atheism and the Value of Life* (1884) and *The Individualist* (1899). In his *Is Life Worth Living* (1879), he wrote, "Whatever may be God's future, we cannot forget His past." {GS; TYD}

Malon, Benoît (1841–1893)

Malon was a French socialist, one of the founders of the *International*. He was editor of *L'Intransigeant* and wrote on the religion and morality of the Socialists. {BDF; RAT}

Malone, Dumas (Born 1892)

Malone wrote *The Public Life of Thomas Cooper, 1783–1839* (1926). {FUS}

Malone, Tom (20th Century)

Malone has been a contributing editor to *Freethought Today*. As President of Humanists of Georgia, he stated that the American Humanist Association "has become irrelevant" and its leaders "simply want AHA to become a warned-over Unitarian-type society. The world doesn't need another Unitarian church." An activist, Malone teaches history and coaches boys' varsity soccer in a public high school. However, in an about-face and feeling that Madalyn O'Hair's virulent attacks on religion have strengthened the opposition to the freethought cause, Malone became no longer associated with the Atlanta Freethought Society and was elected in 1994 to the board of the American Humanist Association. He is chairman of their Commission for the Defense of Humanism.

In 1996, citing marital problems which required him to "reexamine my priorities," Malone resigned as President of Humanists of Georgia. (See entry for Georgia Freethinkers, Humanists.) {FD}

Malot, Hector Henri (1830–1907)

Malot was the French author of a trilogy (*Les amants*, 1859; *Les epoux*, 1865); *Les enfants*, 1866), works which brought him dramatic fame. He was known for the delicate moral tone and purely humanitarian character of his novels. The French Academy crowned his *Sans Famille* (1878). {RAT}

Malraux, André (1901–1976)

A major French man of letters, author of *La Condition humaine* (1933, *Man's Fate*), which won the 1933 Goncourt literary prize. Malraux once wrote, "To the absurd myths of God and an immortal soul, the modern world in its radical impotence has only succeeded in opposing the ridiculous myths of science and progress."

"The individuality of Malraux's hero," Thweatt writes, "is integrated into the 'virile fraternity' of the Communist cause; and *La Condition humaine* effects a syncretism of communism and existentialism that is similar in many respects to Montaigne's syncretism of Christianity and classical philosophy. At the same time, Malraux's work presents a study of the degrees and variety of authentic action, set against the panorama of the 1927 repression of Communist insurgency by the Kuomintang."

Under Charles DeGaulle, Malraux served (1945, 1958) as minister of information, and in 1959 he became DeGaulle's minister of cultural affairs. His arbitrariness irritated his former left-wing allies, despite his decision to persuade Marc Chagall to paint the ceiling of the Opéra Garnier. Similarly, his independence irritated the Gaullists, as when he resisted pressure to have an iconoclastic play by Jean Genet banned. "One must always choose freedom, even when it has dirty hands," he said."

In *Signé Malraux* (1996), French philosopher Jean-François Lyotard described how Malraux was self-taught but falsely said he had studied at the *École du Louvre*. Or how, although brought up in a grocery shop, he had falsely told his rich first wife, Clara, that his mother had belonged to the haute bourgeoisie. In 1923 when he and Clara went to Indochina to steal Khmer statues, he was arrested, then expelled, then returned to found an anti-colonialist newspaper.

Asia provided the setting of his early novels, in which, as described by *The Economist* (30 November 1996), "characters are transcended by the cause they choose to kill and die for." In Spain's civil war, Malraux commanded a squadron in the Republican air force. In 1945 he changed from his former pro-Marxism to embrace Charles de Gaulle but was fascinated by revolutionary leaders who placed themselves beyond the pale of social convention, such as T. E. Lawrence or Mao Zedong. His companion was the novelist Louise de Vilmorin.

In 1996, Malraux' remains were transferred to the Pantheon, France's final resting place for illustrious men (and one woman, Marie Curie). President Jacques Chirac, on that occasion, described Malraux as "neither of the right, nor of the left, but of France." {CE; EU, Vivien Thweatt; PA}

Malte-Bruun, Konrad (1775–1826)

Malte-Bruun was one of the first geographers of his time. In 1800 he was banished from Denmark on account of his advanced opinions. Settling in Paris, he collaborated with Mentelle in publishing a large geographical work (16 volumes, 1804–1807), and in 1808 he founded the *Annales des Voyages*. Malte-Bruun's chief work was his *Précis de géographie et de l'histoire* (8 volumes, 1810–1829). {RAT}

MALTHUSIAN THEORY

The British economist Thomas Robert Malthus (1766-1834) wrote *An Essay on the Principle of Population* (1978). He argued that human population tends to increase faster than food supply and can be checked only by moral restraints or by war, famine, and disease.

The 1998 Nobel Award in Economics was given to Amartya Sen, who believes the Malthusian Theory is wrong. {See entry for Amartya Sen.}

Malvezin, Pierre (Born 1841)

Malvezin was a French journalist. *La Bible Farce* (1879) was condemned and suppressed in 1880 and he was sentenced to three months in prison. Malvezin conducted the review, *La Fraternité*. {BDF}

Mamiani Della Rovere (Count Terenzio) (1865–1867)

Mamiani Della Rovere was Pius IX's Minister of the Interior and in 1857 was appointed professor of the philosophy of history at Turin University. He entered the Italian Camera, was Minister of Education in 1861, ambassador at Berne, and Vice-President of the Senate (1867). Mamiani was disliked by most of the Italian rationalists and was a non-Christian theist. His philosophy was largely built upon the ideas of Hegel, and he talked of a reconciliation of the Catholic Church with modern culture. In *La Religione dell' Avvenire* (1880), however, he showed that he meant a religion without revelation or miracles or dogmas. {RAT}

MAN

> • Man, n. An animal so lost in rapturous contemplation of what he thinks he is as to overlook what he indubitably ought to be. His chief occupation is extermination of other animals and his own species, which, however, multiplies with such insistent rapidity as to infest the whole habitable earth and Canada.
>
> **–Ambrose Bierce**
> *The Devil's Dictionary*

Man, the result of evolutionary processes, came about utterly by chance. No "unseen hand" created the species. Mankind is a lucky accident that lives in a universe which is 13 or so billion years old. Our insignificant little planet did not even exist for two-thirds of that universal history.

Magnum miraculum est homo: Man is a great miracle—these were the words said to have been the inspiration for Renaissance philosophers. But *is* "man the measure of all things"? And what about "The proper study of mankind is man"? Such a statement sounds somewhat arrogant. Just the same, mankind exists, and we humans are a part. It is important for us to determine what we are without over-valuing our species, which goes back only about 200,000 years. Mankind is the *measurer*, if not the measure. The proper study of mankind must include the scientific outlook if we are to understand our species as well as our universe.

Evolutionary concepts appeared in some early Greek writings, such as those of Thales, Empedocles, Anaximander, and Aristotle. For the fifteen centuries that the Catholic Church enjoyed a restraining influence, evolutionary theories did not develop whatsoever and *Genesis* was taught as fact. In the middle 1990s, bipeds were thought to have existed 5.5 million years ago, and Homo erectus existed between 1.6 million and 250,000 years ago.

Paleontologists, however, will undoubtedly make new findings, some of which may even challenge the commonly held view that Homo erectus originated in Africa. In 1995, for example, bones and stone tools were found in the Longgupo cave in central (Sichuan) China which indicate that perhaps 1.9 million years ago hominids existed. Although this may or may not alter the view that Homo sapiens probably emerged in Africa no more than 200,000 years ago, the Chinese discoveries may well indicate an earlier date for migrations out of Africa. The earliest recognizable member of the Homo genus, currently known as Homo rudolfensis, is generally dated as having lived 2.5 million years ago in the Rift Valley of East Africa.

A 1999 study indicated that the modern Homo sapiens likely interbred with Neanderthals. (See entries for Neanderthal Man and for Woman.) {CE}

MAN AND HIS CREATIONS

Humans are bipedal mammals of the Primate order. Anatomically, they are related to the great apes, but they differ in the notable development of the brain and the capacity to speak, to reason, and to form and freely interbreed races.

At one time, it was believed that the first three mythical kings of Sumer—A-lulum, Alagar, and En Men Lu Anna—had reigned for 28,000 years, 36,000 years, and 43,200 years respectively. Biblical figures, despite the illogical dating, did not live so long: Adam, 930 years; Seth, 912; Enos, 905; Jared, 962; Methusaleh, 969; Noah, 950. Noah's son lived a mere 600 years; Abraham, 175; Isaac, 180; Jacob, 147; Joseph, 110.

Thomas Parr of England is said to have lived 152 years. Eagles and swans live the longest lives among birds, and some carp and pike may live as long as 150 years. Japanese women have been estimated to have an expected longevity of over 81 years. Whales live an average of only 60.

Antipater of Sidon in the second century B.C.E. drew up a list of the seven wonders of the world which humans had created:

- the Great Pyramid of Khufu or all the pyramids with or without the Sphinx
- the Hanging Gardens of Babylon, with or without the walls
- the statue of Zeus by Phidias at Olympia
- the temple of Artemis at Ephesus
- the Mausoleum of Halicarnassus
- the Pharos at Alexandria
- the Colossus of Rhodes

Of these, only the pyramids remain, although damaged by nature and by man.

In 1994, the editors of *The Economist* produced a rival list:

- the microprocessor, invented by Ted Hoff and which brought together the transistor (1947) and the integrated circuit (1959
- the pill, which in 1963 turned a Mexican yam into an oral contraceptive that "tells the brain not to ask the ovaries to release more eggs"
- the telephone network, started by Alexander Graham Bell in 1876 and presently allowing any of over 580,000,000 subscribers anywhere on the planet to converse "usually within ten seconds of dialing"
- the jumbo jet whose Boeing 747 planes are manufactured in "the largest building, by volume, in the world, encompassing 13.4 million cubic meters (472 million cubic feet) of space—enough room to accommodate about 550 Westminster Abbeys"—and which can carry up to 570 passengers with a range of over 8,000 miles. Boeing 747s have carried over 1.4 billion passengers a total of over 18 billion miles, "almost 200 times the distance from the earth to the sun"
- the offshore oil platform, which since 1947 has allowed drilling under the world's seas. In 1989, a platform weighing 1,500,000 tons and named Gullfaks C became the largest object ever to have been moved by mankind. Eleven tugboats moved the 860-feet high platform which contained 245,000 cubic meters of concrete and 80,000 tons of reinforcing steel—enough to build ten Eiffel Towers. The platform accommodates 330 individuals and cost $2 billion to build.
- the hydrogen bomb, which was first exploded in 1952 at Eniwetok by the United States and the second in 1953 by the USSR, has changed the nature of international conflict, for nuclear weapons now exist which can destroy all of Earth's 286 cities of more than a million people, many times over and in a matter of moments. Hydrogen bombs on intercontinental missiles launched from hidden submarines have made possible "a completely different kind of war, one in which anything on the earth could be destroyed in a matter of minutes." The most modern are accurate to within about 100 metres.
- Tranquility Base, a patch of the moon upon which landed Neil Armstrong and Buzz Aldrin in their spacecraft, the *Eagle,* at 22:18 (Greenwich mean time), 20 July 1969. It was the first time in the moon's four billion years of existence that human footprints had touched its dust. Now, plans are afoot for basing a permanently crewed moon-base in order to obtain raw materials for export to Earth.

Some, however, are curmudgeons on the subject:

• The earth has a skin and that skin has diseases; one of its diseases is called man.

–Friedrich Wilhelm Nietzsche

• I believe the best definition of man is "the ungrateful biped."

–Feodor Mikhailovich Dostoevsky

• Man is a dog's ideal of what God should be.

–Holbrook Jackson

• Perhaps the only true dignity of man is his capacity to despise himself.

–George Santayana

• What is man, when you come to think upon him but a minutely set, ingenious machine for turning, with infinite artfulness, the red wine of Shiraz into urine?

–Isak Dinesen (Karen Blixen)

"Man" in Old English or Anglo-Saxon was universal and referred to all humans equally. *Waepman* was the word for a male human, *wifman* for the female human. Although some contemporary feminists object to the use of "man" to include women as well as men, the objection is not to its historical origins, which were gender-free. The newly coined pronoun "(s)he" is considered by many to be redundant.

With some chariness, women who lead a group choose to be called a "chair," but it is believed more prefer "chairwoman," "chairperson," or the original "chairman." (See entry for Mankind. For the oldest ancestor of man, see entry for Catopithecus.)

MAN IN EARLY AMERICA

In 1996 two college students watching a hydroplane race on the Columbia River in Kennewick, Washington, found a skeleton that was more than 9,000 years old. If the first findings by forensic anthropologist James Chatters prove true, the skeleton was a "Male, Caucasian," not racially or culturally associated with any existing American Indian group.

In that case, and a radiocarbon test showed one bone to be between 9,300 and 9,600 years old, the remains indicate that the earliest Americans may have reached Washington because 16,000 years ago the North Atlantic was frozen from Norway to Newfoundland. The "Native Americans," in short, might *not* have originated in Asia. {Douglas Preston, "The Lost Man," *The New Yorker,* 16 June 1997}

MANA: See entry for animism.

MANCHESTER (England) HUMANISTS

For information about the Manchester, England, humanists, telephone 0161 681 7607.

Manchester, William (20th Century)

Manchester wrote *Disturber of the Peace: The Life of H. L. Mencken* (1950). He also described in *A World Lit Only by Fire: The Medieval Mind and the Renaissance* the wild parties held by Pope Alexander VI. (See entry for Alexander VI.) {FUS}

MANDEAN, also MANDAEAN

Mandeans are members of a Gnostic sect that originated in Jordan and presently exists in Iraq. Mandean is a form of Aramaic used by the Mandeans. (For an estimate of the number of Mandeans worldwide, see entry for Hell.)

Mandell, Terri (20th Century)

Mandell is on the Board of Directors of the American Humanist Association. She is author of *Power Schmoozing* (1996).

Mander, Alfred Ernest (1894–c. 1960)

Mander was an Australian rationalist, writer, and lecturer. His free-thinking books included *Common Cause: The Christian God*, and *Life After Death.* He also wrote *Psychology for Everyman (and Woman)*

(1935) and *Clearer Thinking (Logic for Everyman)* (1936). During the 1920s he lectured widely in New Zealand. {SWW}

Mandeville, Bernard de (1670–1733)

A Dutch-born English author and physician, Mandeville wrote on ethical subjects, his most famous being *The Fable of the Bees* (1714), a work which Adam Smith praised. He said the self-seeking effort of individuals is the mainspring of an industrial society that religious or legal restraints are mere fictions invented by rulers and clergymen to put men under domination. "Private vices," he wrote in his satire on the principles of morality, "are public virtues." Another of his works was *Usefulness of Christianity in War* (1731). Mandeville was one of the main deists in eighteenth-century England and, according to McCabe, "one of the freest of the many freethinking Englishmen of the 18th century." {BDF; CE; FUK; JM; JMR; JMRH; *New Humanist*, August 1997; RAT}

Manekin, Ted (20th Century)

For a brief time in 1999, Manekin was Executive Director of the Center for Inquiry Institute in Amherst, New York.

Manen, Willem Christian van (1842–1905)

Manen, who for twenty years was a pastor of the Reformed Church, taught theology at Groningen University and ancient Christian literature and New Testament exegesis at Leydon. His chief work, *Paulus* (1890–1896, 3 volumes), made a sensation because he rejected all the Pauline Epistles as spurious, a view which was little adopted. In 1904 Manen became an honorary associate of the Rationalist Press Association. {RAT; RE}

Manfred [King of Sicily] (1232–1266)

The natural (illegitimate) son of Frederic II, Manfred was the King of Sicily who took over the Kingdom as Regent when Frederic died and refused to yield it to Pope Innocent IV and his successors, Alexander IV and Urban IV. In 1254, papal forces invaded Sicily, and Manfred was forced to restore the kingdom to the papacy, retaining only the duchy of Taranto in fief from the pope. In a battle in which Charles I defeated him at Benevento (1266), Manfred was killed. According to the Florentine historian Villani, Manfred was a notorious skeptic as well as a gifted prince of high ideals. {CE; JM; RE}

Mangasarian, M(angasar) M(ugurdital) (1859–1943)

In Chicago, Mangasarian edited *Liberal Review* and *Rationalist*. He is the author of *A New Catechism* (1902) and *Humanism, A Religion for Americans* (1925). He founded the Chicago Society of Ethical Culture, later the (Rationalist) Independent Religious Society.

Mangasarian wrote at least two dozen pamphlets. In *The Rationalist* (15 May 1915), he wrote, "Christianity . . . made, for nearly 1,500 years, persecution, religious wars, massacres, theological feuds and bloodshed, heresy huntings and heretic burnings, prisons, dungeons, anathemas, curses, opposition to science, hatred of liberty, spiritual bondage, the life without love or laughter. " {FUS; RAT; RE; TYD}

Mangialetti, Nada (20th Century)

Mangialetti is a clinical psychologist who has been a member of Humanists of Hawaii and Educational Vice President of the New York Area Skeptics. She has written for *Free Inquiry* and *The Secular Humanist Bulletin*.

Mangione, Jerre (1909–)

Mangione has been on the editorial board of *The Humanist* and was a staff writer for *Time* (1931), an acting director of Yaddo (1977–1978), and an acting director of the Italian Studies Center (1978–1980). He wrote *An Ethic at Large, a Memoir of America in the Thirties and Forties* (1978).

Manhattan, Avro (1914–1990)

Manhattan's *The Vatican in World Politics* was a bestseller in 1949. He was a friend to Picasso, George Bernard Shaw, and H. G. Wells. Said to be a deist, he promoted the "still, small voice inside people, believing all children are born with great creative potential which is crushed by vulgar entertainment, modern educational shortcomings, and the lack of time to create something out of nothing." He also wrote *Catholic Imperialism and World Freedom* (1952) and *The Dollar and the Vatican*. In 1953 the King of Italy conferred on him the title of Baron. In 1971, he wrote *Religious Terror in Ireland*. In *The Vatican's Holocaust*, he describes how 700,000 perished when Croatia was an independent Catholic state. In 1976 he received the Pioneer Award from the American Atheists, for world-wide education in the matter of theo-politics. In 1981 he was named, to some people's amusement, Knight Commander of the Knights of Malta.

Dawn of Man: An Epic of Our Ancestors Before Man's Discovery of Fire (1986) took forty years to complete, and Manhattan's satire of USSR and USA politics, entitled *The Presidential Web*, took twenty years. His other works include *The Catholic Church Against the Twentieth Century* (1946), *Catholic Imperialism and World Freedom* (1972), *The Dollar and the Vatican* (1956), *The Vatican Billions: 2000 Years of Wealth Accumulation* (1972), and *The Vatican Holocaust: The Sensational Account of the Most Horrifying Massacre of the Twentieth Century* (1986). (See *Freethought Today* [Winter, 1990] for a discussion of Manhattan's philosophic outlook.) {TRI}

MANIBOZHO

Manibozho, in an Algonquin Indian religion, was the god who created earth and mortals out of clay. {LEE}

MANICHAEISM

> • Manicheism, n. The ancient Persian doctrine of an incessant warfare between Good and Evil. When Good gave up the fight the Persians joined the victorious Opposition.
>
> –**Ambrose Bierce**
> *The Devil's Dictionary*

Manichaeism (or Manicheism, Manichaeanism, Manicheanism, Manicheeism) is an invented theological term referring to a syncretistic religious dualism which originated in Persia and was widely held in the Roman Empire during the 3rd and 4th centuries. Merriam-Webster's unabridged dictionary defines it as having also been found "in central and eastern Asia for a longer period, and teaching as a saving wisdom given through the Hebrew prophets, Jesus, and Mani that a cosmic conflict exists between a good realm of light and an evil realm of darkness, that matter and flesh are in the realm of darkness, and that man's duty is to aid the forces of good by practicing asceticism, especially by avoiding procreation and animal food." In short, Manichaeism is di-theistic, not mono-theistic. It divides the world between good and evil powers or regards matter as inherently evil.

Manickham, Poopathi (20th Century)

Manickham, who lives now in Seattle, Washington, was once a Saivite but is now a Dalit, which he says by default makes him a rationalist and humanist. Saivam and Dalit, he claims, are not at all similar. Some temples in South India still discourage Dalits from entering, he has written, "and if you manage to sneak in they smell your caste by chance and you know how they speed up their pooja—I received the same kind of treatment from a white-only Episcopalian church in Seattle."

He is interested "in a collective effort in the pursuit of total liberation of the oppressed people in the name of caste, religion, and race worldwide." {E-mail to WAS, 7 April 1998}

Manikin, Lewis (20th Century)

Manikin's *Scientific Humanism, or The Religion of Humanity* (1940) continued using the term "God" in his attempt to merge his views of humanism and the sciences.

Mankiewicz, Herman (1897–1953)

Mankiewicz was one of the famed Algonquin Round Table wits—the Algonquin was a Manhattan hotel where a group of noted intellectuals dined and drank Mankiewicz wrote such major screenplays as "Citizen Kane" (except that how much was his and how much was Orson Welles's is the subject of endless dispute), "Girl Crazy," and "Dinner at Eight."

At the end of his life he suffered from edema, his physicians had given up hope, and the family had gathered. To his brother Frank who had on a brand-new, dark blue suit, Mankiewicz complained, "Your suit is much too black and absolutely appropriate for a funeral." To another brother, Don, he discussed details of his funeral: "Assuming the ceremony will be held indoors, hats will not be worn. You won't have any trouble, except that Dore Schary will wear his hat. You are to go up to him and tap him on the shoulder and say, 'Dore, I have a message for you from the deceased: Take off your hat, you're in the house.' " His biographer, Richard Meryman, describes how a rabbi entered the room to provide solace during the final moments. "Get the hell out of here," exclaimed the screenwriter. "I never had any use for you when I was living, and I've got no use for you now." His last words were with his brother Joe, with whom he had been co-makers on loans for films. "Well that finishes everything I've got to take care of before I go to meet my maker. Or . . ." and he chose his last words, ". . . should I say 'co-maker'?"

Manilow, Barry (1946)

Manilow is a singer, composer, and arranger. Starting in the mailroom at CBS, he has worked his way up to receiving numbers of musical awards. In 1979, he earned a Grammy Award for "At the Copa" and, in 1977, a special Tony Award. Other of his hits include "I Write the Songs," "Mandy," "Looks Like We Made It." A UK correspondent for *The Independent* (18 November 1998), asked Manilow if he believed in God and was told, "Yes. His name is Clive Davis, and he's the head of my record company." Asked then how important his Judaism is, he responded, "It isn't. My humanism is." {CA}

MANKIND (HUMANKIND)

People are only one of an estimated 1,394,000 identified animal species. Since the 17th century, when scholars began to separate types of flora and fauna, classifications of the mutations of people into races have been made. Scholars generally hold that a common evolution of races occurred, that the differentiation of races occurred relatively late in history. Although some dislike categorizing, most anthropologists agree that three distinct races exist: the Caucasoid, Negroid, and Mongoloid. Each of these broad groups can be divided into subgroups—for example, the Negroid group includes the peoples of Africa south of the Sahara, the Pygmy groups of Indonesia, and the inhabitants of New Guinea and Melanesia. Lacking, however, is general agreement as to the classification of such people as the aborigines of Australia, the Dravidian people of South India, the Polynesians, and the Ainu of North Japan.

When a supposed superiority of their own kind of culture or nationality occurs, in which cultural and psychological values to race are attributed, such an approach is called racism. The racial doctrines of Nazi Germany, for example, resulted in a vicious anti-Semitism that proclaimed that "the Jews are a race." Racism has complicated the integration movement in the United States and was the basis of segregation polices known as apartheid in the Republic of South Africa. (Bishop Desmond Tutu has explained how correctly to pronounce the Dutch word *apartheid*: uh-PART-hate, and he calls attention to the last syllable.) At what has been called the present "century of the common man," women have insisted "man" be replaced by "people." Many writers have chosen to unsex "mankind" and use "humankind." Wole Soyinka, noting suggestions to replace "history" with "herstory," has mused about any need for such a political correctness "hersterectomy." {CE}

Mann, Bryon and **Diana** (20th Century)

The Manns are Scots who moved to New Zealand in 1968. Bryon was a humanist activist at Glasgow University in the second half of the 1960s. {*Glasgow Group Newsletter*, September 1997}

Mann, Heinrich Landes (Born 1821)

Mann was a German pessimistic poet who wrote under the penname of "Lorm (Hieronymus)." In addition to many philosophical poems, he wrote a volume of essays entitled *Nature and Spirit* (1884). {BDF}

Mann, Horace (1796–1859)

An American educator who helped found the first public school at Lexington, Massachusetts, Mann was president of Antioch College. He was active in many Unitarian churches and founded, with others, the First Unitarian Society in West Newton, Massachusetts. *The Dictionary of American Biography* described him as "a Puritan without a theology." Mann was attacked by many, who felt state schools should not teach religion, and he eventually won the fight to keep sectarian religion out of the schools. School libraries which he commenced had no books based upon strict religious beliefs, which represented a large change inasmuch as in the early days of Massachusetts there was a state supported church. As a result, the church views had been taught. Mann believed only in an impersonal God, and he rejected immortality. Just before his death, he told some students, "Be ashamed to die until you have won some victory for humanity." {CE; EG; JM; RE; U; UU}

Mann, Mary Tyler Peabody (1806–1887)

Mann, the sister of Elizabeth Palmer Peabody and the wife of Horace Mann, was a Unitarian. She and her sister established a school for girls in what is now Brookline, Massachusetts. {CE}

Mann, Thomas (1875–1955)

Mann, the Nobel Prize-winning novelist, author of *Buddenbrooks* (1901), *Dr. Faustus* (1947), and *The Magic Mountain* (*Der Zauberberg* 1924, translated 1927), discussed the subject of humanism as early as 1938, when he wrote:

> For me and my kind the religious is lodged in the human. Not that my humanism springs from a deification of humanity—verily, there is small occasion for that! Who could find the heart, contemplating this crack-daily given the lie by the bitter and harsh facts? Daily we see it commit all the crimes in the Decalogue; daily we despair of its future; all too well we understand why the angels in heaven from the day of its creation have turned up their noses at sight of the Creator's incomprehensible partiality for this so doubtful handiwork of his.
>
> And yet—today more than ever—I feel we must not, however well-founded our doubts, be betrayed into mere cynicism and contempt for the human race. We must not—despite all the evidence of its fantastic vileness—forget its great and honorable traits, revealed in the shape of art, science, the quest for truth, the creation of beauty, the conception of justice. Yes, it is true, we succumb to spiritual death when we show ourselves callous to that great mystery on which we are touching whenever we utter the words "man" and "humanity."
>
> . . . What Christians call "original sin" is more than just a piece of priestly trickery devised to keep men under the Church's thumb. It is a profound awareness in man as a spiritual being of his own natural infirmity and proneness to err, and of his rising in spirit above it. Is that disloyalty to nature? Not at all. It is a response to her own deepest desire. For it was to the end of her own spiritualization that she brought man forth. . . .
>
> I believe in the coming of a new, a third humanism, distinct, in complexion and fundamental temper, from its predecessors. It will not flatter mankind, looking at it through rose-colored glasses, for it will have had experiences of which the others knew not. It will have stouthearted knowledge of man's dark, daemonic, radically 'natural' side; united with reverence for his superbiological, spiritual worth. The new humanity will be universal—and it will have the artist's attitude: that is, it will recognize that the immense value and beauty of the human being lie precisely in that he belongs to the two kingdoms, of nature and spirit. It will realize that no romantic conflict or tragic dualism is inherent in the fact; but rather a fruitful and engaging combination of destiny and free choice. Upon that it will base a love for humanity in which its pessimism and its optimism will cancel each other out.

In *Dr. Faustus*, the character of Serenus Zeitblom is pictured as the extreme academic type of humanist. Zeitblom describes his humanism on page one of the novel, and presumably this also is Mann's view of a classical humanist:

> I am by nature wholly moderate, of a temper, I may say, both healthy and humane, addressed to reason and harmony; a scholar and *conjuratus* of the "Latin host," not lacking all contact with the arts (I play the viola d'amore) but a son of the Muses in that academic sense which by preference regards itself as descended from the German humanists of the time of the "Poets."

He continued,

> As for my Catholic origin, it did of course mould and influence my inner man. Yet that lifelong impress never resulted in any conflict with my humanistic attitude in general, my love of the "liberal arts" as one used to call them.

Zeitblom, like the neo-humanists Paul Elmer More, L. J. A. Mercier, and Jacques Maritain, deplores "liberal theology," which he considers a *contradictio in adjecto*:

> The scientific superiority of liberal theology, it is now said, is indeed incontestable, but its theological position is weak, for its moralism and humanism lack insight into the daemonic character of human existence. Cultured indeed it is, but shallow; of the true understanding of human nature and the tragic nature of life the conservative tradition has at bottom preserved far more; for that very reason it has a profounder, more significant relation to culture than has progressive bourgeois ideology.

Are we to conclude, inasmuch as the character of Adrian Leverkuhn is obviously not in accord with Mann's personal beliefs, that Thomas Mann is speaking his thoughts through the person of Zeitblom? That Mann, who used the German equivalent of the word "humanist" over a score of times in the book, is a classical humanist in sympathy with Zeitblom? That in using the first person throughout the book to describe Zeitblom's humanism, Mann was in fact seeing through the "faustian" character of Germany's many Leverkuhns and was suggesting that Germany's only salvation was that of rejecting the materialism of science which had brought about her downfall and accepting the spiritual approach of classical humanism?

The answers are not found in *Dr. Faustus*, a scene of which is based upon his own sister's suicide. When the reader finishes the book, he not only sees the defects of Leverkuhn's thinking but also finds Zeitblom's philosophy distasteful. The two appear to be extremes, and the reader is forced at times to agree with both, though eventually disagreeing with both. In Chapter XXV, the reader finds himself agreeing with the Devil in his reference to theology:

> I hope you do not marvel that "the Great Adversary" speaks to you of religion. God's nails! Who else, I should like to know, is to speak of it today? Surely not the liberal theologian! After all I am by now its sole custodian! In whom will you recognize theological existence if not in me? And who can lead a theological existence without me? The religious is certainly my line: as certainly as it is not the line of bourgeois culture. Since culture fell away from the cult and made a cult of itself, it has become nothing else than a falling away; and all the world after a mere five hundred years is as sick and tired of it as though, *salva venia*, they had ladled it in with cooking-spoons.

Here, Mann has given an indication of his own personal view. Like his great grandfather, a freethinker and rationalist, Mann is no supernaturalist but, rather, is a naturalist who, amused, looks at the various theological devices such as heavens, hells, angels, devils, original sins, and other-worldly speculations. Or, as he explained in a speech of Dr. Breisacher:

> In the genuine religion of a genuine folk such colourless theological conceptions as sin and punishment never occurred, in their merely ethical causal connection. What we had here was the causality of error, a working accident. Religion and ethics represented the decline of religion. All morality was "a purely intellectual" mis-understanding of the ritual. Was there anything more god-forsaken than the "purely intellectual?" It had remained for the characterless world-religion, out of "prayer"—*sit venis verbo*—to make a begging appeal for mercy, an "O Lord," "God have mercy," a "Help" and "Give" and "Be so good." Our so-called prayer . . . is the vulgarized and rationalistically watered-down late form of something very vital, active and strong: the magic invocation, the coercion of God.

It is between the lines of *Dr. Faustus* that one finds Mann's personal beliefs. After he finished the novel in 1947, he wrote the present author in 1948:

> In my opinion I do not belong to any philosophical school, and I gladly leave it to you to classify me. It has been said of the "Faustus"-novel that I had split myself therein, and that both, the narrator as well as the hero, bore a resemblance to myself. There is some truth in that, and I especially have to admit that Zeitblom displays many traits of my own intellectual form and existence. This is not altered by the fact that he is treated with some irony at the beginning of the book and that, in general, he to a certain extent plays the role of Famulus Wagner in Goethe's "Faust." I don't believe that I may call myself a classical humanist. This intellectual form seems hardly possible any longer today. You are familiar with my comments on the subject and know that my hopes are aimed at the development of a new humanism which is no longer purely optimistic, but religiously tinted and deeply experienced in all dark aspects of life, a humanism which derives its pride from the unique and mysterious position of man between nature and mind.
>
> As I said before, I leave it to you to put a name to this my proud sympathy for the secret of man.

As pointed out by Alex Ross, *Doctor Faustus*, born of a close study of earlier composers, went on to influence later ones. Theodor Adorno, a philosopher, was Mann's "musical adviser," giving advice on technical details and lending his own manuscripts for perusal. Mann cut and pasted Adorno's and others' writings into the text. At the time he wrote the work, he was socially friendly with Schoenberg, Stravinsky, Otto Klemperer, Arthur Schnabel, Arthur Rubinstein, Ernst Krenek, and Hanna Eisler. The work, Ross has written, "is not simply a parable of the artistic life; it is a grand realist novel of music, a monument to the culture in which Mann came of age."

Life's dark sides were depicted in *Die Bekenntnisse des Hochstaplers Felix Krull* (1954), a work said to have been influenced by his guilt feelings about having been a poor husband and a father. Several of Mann's works, including *The Holy Sinner* (1951), show people who need to be creative but who, in practice, experience the concept of evil, leading to a form of artist-guilt.

Der Zauberberg (The Magic Mountain) concerns a fanatical Freemason and a fanatical Jesuit, the implication being that neither extreme is preferable to a humanistic naturalism.

Although Mann undoubtedly is one of the giants of the century, he received much negative criticism for *Doctor Faustus*, which to many elevated Germany's Nazi era to a kind of demonic myth, not attacking it analytically from a social or political point of view. He also was faulted for exploring sibling incest (Katia and her twin brother, Klaus Pringsheim) in *The Blood of the Walsungs*; caricaturing his parents and friends in *Buddenbrooks*; and including platonic homosexuality and the culture of decline in *Death in Venice* (1925). Many criticized the support he gave to the German cause in the First World War. However, his supporters point out that he fled Germany, became a US citizen in 1944, and has been recognized as an outstanding German literary figure of the 20th century.

In 1941, according to W. H. Auden, he and his lover Chester Kallman visited Mann's California home. "At the Manns, we took turns screwing a friend on Thomas's big bed when the family was away," he wrote. Mann was generally known in artistic circles as being bisexual, and his son, Klaus (1906-1949), was openly homosexual. Critic Gordon A. Craig, in fact, has listed the names of Mann's young men who, like Horace's Ligurinus, he "yearned for." (Of Ligurinus, Horace wrote, ". . . In dreams at night/I hold you in my arms, or toil/behind your flight/Across the Martian Field,/Or chase through yielding waves/the boy who will not yield.")

Mann's loves were Lübeck schoolmates Armin Martens and Willri Timpe; the art student Paul Ehrenberg, "with whom he became a close friend in 1899, during his first years in Munich"; then, later in life, the seventeen-year-old Klaus Heuser, "whom he met while vacationing on the island of Sylt in 1927, when he was fifty-two"; and Franzl Westermeier, "a waiter in the Grand Hotel Dolder near Zürich, with whom he became infatuated while staying there in 1950." The latter was immortalized in *Felix Krull.* In each case, according to Craig, "the passion with which he was affected was powerful, brought him moments of exaltation and despair, and, in the case of Ehrenberg at least, to open declarations of love." However, Craig notes that so far as we can tell there is no proof that the Mann's love was reciprocated, let alone consummated.

Mann left the United States in 1954, hounded by McCarthyites and disenchanted with American politics. He spent his last years in Switzerland. In his *Diary*, Mann had directed that he wanted his gravestone to stand in a land where German-language poets reposed. The cemetery is next to a church at Kilchberg near Zurich, Switzerland. On his marker are his name and dates as well as the name and dates of his wife Katia (died 1980), who was the daughter of a wealthy mathematics professor who came from a Jewish family that had converted to Protestantism. Adjacent is Erika (died 1969), their eldest daughter, who had given up a career as a journalist and cabaret performer to manage his affairs. Nearby is an obelisk that marks the grave of Swiss writer Conrad Ferdinand Meyer, as well as the snow-capped Alps and a fragment of Lake Zurich. (One of Mann's critics has been James T. Farrell—see the entry for Farrell. Also, see entry for Van Meter Ames. Ronald Hayman, in *Thomas Mann, A Biography* (1995) states that Mann was deeply influenced as a young man by the writings of Nietzsche. Hayman alleges that Mann had a fiercely competitive relationship with his older brother, had a secret attraction to young boys as well as to his son Klaus, and scolded his son Klaus for disturbing his tranquillity by once attempting suicide. When Klaus did successfully commit suicide, Mann chose to continue a lecture tour and did not attend the funeral. Mann's son Michael also committed suicide. Mann's diaries detail not only his attacks of hypochondria but also, while in his seventies, his flirting with hotel waiters and observing muscular young men on beaches. Although an admittedly heartless egocentric, Mann continues to rate more positive than negative literary criticisms.) {CB; CE; CL; GL; HNS; HNS2; Alex Ross, *The New York Times*, 6 April 1997; WAS, 23 December 1948}

Mann, Walter (20th Century)

A freethinker, Mann wrote *Pagan and Christian Morality* (1917) and *Christianity in China: An Exposure of Foreign Missions* (1927). In *The Religion of Famous Men* (1926), he wrote, "Science has gone on from strength to strength; position after position, once occupied by religion, has been captured until the whole of science has been emancipated from the bondage of the supernatural." {FUK; GS; TYD}

Mansholt, Sicco Leendert (Born 1908)

In 1974, Mansholt, who was Vice-President and later President of the European Community (ECC), said, "We as Humanists have to make clear that any durable society must be developed on the basis of justice and in a democratic way." The Council of Europe had been formed in 1949 as a consultative body to stand for democracy in Europe after World War II, and in 1950 it became the parent of NATO.

In 1968 at the Second European Conference of the International Humanist and Ethical Union, Dr. Mansholt addressed the group. In 1974 at the Sixth IHEU World Congress, he presided. Mansholt's study of Albert Schweitzer is entitled *Eerbied voor het leven* (1975).

Manson, Julius (1903-1998)

Manson was President and NGO Representative in New York City of the Corliss Lamont Chapter of the American Humanist Association.

Manson, Marilyn (1969-)

Manson [a/k/a Brian Warner], a recording artist, has publicly bragged about being an in-your-face atheist. A rock star who onstage has hoisted a flaming cross made of television sets and ripped pages from a Bible as he performed, Manson upsets many with his "foul mouth" but turns just as many viewers on with his zany antics. On MTV he once said he wanted to be known as the person who brought an end to Christianity, at another time saying, "Do you really want to go to a place filled with a bunch of assholes."

Numerous freethinkers have found his performances violent, intemperate, sophomoric, and inhumanistic. {E}

Mantegazza, Paolo (1831–1910)

An Italian anthropologist, Mantegazza wrote *The Physiology of Pleasure* (1854). He also wrote on the physiology of pain, spontaneous generation, ecstasy, and love. In 1876, he wrote a romance, *Il Dio Ignoto* (The Unknown God). {BDF; RAT}

Manton, Rita (20th Century)

Manton in Britain is active with the Havering and District Humanist Society.

Manuel, Frank Edward (20th Century)

Manuel was editor of *The Enlightenment* (1965). He wrote *Religion of Isaac Newton* (1974), *Age of Reason* (1982), and *Requiem for Karl Marx* (1995).

Manvell, (Arnold) Roger (1909–1987)

Manvell, who was born in Leicester and has a doctorate in literature from the University of London, has written widely about film, theater, and the history of the Third Reich. At Boston University, he was visiting professor of films (1975–1981). His book about freethinkers is *The Trial of Annie Besant and Charles Bradlaugh* (1976).

Manzoni, Romeo (Born 1847)

An Italian physician, Manzoni wrote on the doctrine of love of Bruno and Schopenhauer. He also wrote *A Life of Jesus.* {BDF}

Mao Zedong [President of the Republic; Chairman of the Communist Party] (1893–1976)

Mao Zedong (Tse-tung), founder of the People's Republic of China, was one of the original members of the Chinese Communist Party. An ardent atheist, he differed greatly with leaders of the Union of Soviet Socialist Republics, but the Third World was highly influenced by his revolutionary theories. According to Nicholas D. Kristof in *The New York Times* (2 June 1992), it is ironic that an atheist such as Mao has been turned into a something of a god by great numbers of Chinese people. They dangle his portrait like an amulet from taxi rear-view mirrors, much as the Catholic St. Christopher dangles from Western taxi rear-view mirrors as good-luck charms. "I heard there was a convoy of 15 cars," said one Beijing driver, "and every one got in a bad accident except the two that had Chairman Mao's picture." Mao, like Stalin, represents a communistic humanism in which life was undemocratic but at least seemed infused with order and purpose. Kristof adds, "Sociologists have written of how some people, disoriented by the new chaos of pluralism, seek to 'escape from freedom' to the womb of authoritarianism, and that perspective may help explain the Mao portraits in China and the Stalin portraits displayed in some Russian vehicles."

Mao organized Kuomintang-sponsored peasant and industrial unions in the 1920s and, after the Kuomintang-Communist split in 1927 led the disastrous "Autumn Harvest Uprisings" in Hunan. In 1958 his "Great Leap Forward" was such a failure that an estimated twenty million people starved, and Mao withdrew temporarily from public view. In 1969 he reasserted his leadership, violently purging his opponents. Mao's ideas on revolutionary struggle and guerrilla warfare have been influential, particularly among Third World revolutionaries, and in death as in life Mao has continued as one of China's most powerful figures.

In 1994, Dr. Li Zhisui (1920–1995) wrote *The Private Life of Chairman Mao*, detailing from his viewpoint as Mao's personal physician what China's "Great Helmsman" was really like. According to Dr. Li, Mao was an irritable, manipulative egotist incapable of human feeling. He surrounded himself with sycophants and pretty young women (and was not above groping his male bodyguards). He refused to be treated for a sexually transmitted disease, genital herpes, although he knew he was spreading it to the women who shared his bed. "If it's not hurting me, then it doesn't matter. Why are you getting so excited about it?" Mao asked his physician, who had suggested he was a carrier of a disease giving *trichomonas vaginalis* to his sexual partners. Meanwhile, added Dr. Li, "The young women were proud to be infected. The illness, transmitted by Mao, was a badge of honor, testimony to their close relations with the Chairman." The doctor further reported that Mao had an undescended testicle, suffered from bouts of impotency, became infertile for undetermined reasons in midlife, and did not bathe his face and hands, which were washed by his bodyguards.

Further evidence that he was one atheist others would not care to imitate, Mao did not brush his teeth, washing his mouth in the morning with tea and then eating the tea leaves, which left his teeth coated with a green patina. When it was suggested he should use a toothbrush, Mao replied, "A tiger never brushes his teeth." In Dr. Li's voluminous description, wrote journalist Richard Bernstein, "Mao emerges as a kind of Chinese Caligula, whose bohemian and decadent life contrasted utterly with the images of it so carefully fashioned by Chinese propaganda." (See Mao's views about Hegel and Feurebach in the entry for Marxism.) {CE; *The New York Times*, 2 October 1994}

Mapanje, Jack: See entry for Poets.

Maple, Eric (1915–)

Maple, an author, is a freethinker, according to David Tribe. {TRI}

Maple, William H. (20th Century)

In Chicago, Maple edited the monthly *Ingersoll Memorial Beacon* from 1904 to 1913. He wrote *No "Beginning," or the Fundamental Fallacy* (1899). {GS}

Mapplethorpe, Robert (1946–1989)

Mapplethorpe, one of the more controversial of 20th-century U.S. artists, encountered strong flak from the religious right because of his homoerotic photographs. Although denied grants and funds by the National Endowment for the Arts, he expressed unfavorable remarks concerning organized religion and successfully pursued his endeavors with little concern about any detractors before dying from AIDS in his early forties. "Everything in life to him, from Catholicism to militarism, seemed like a lie. He was court photographer to the liars," his friend Joel-Peter Witkin said. Even the crucifixion obsessed him, Witkin added, saying that if ever he received the last rites of the Church he would do it "as an insurance policy." Mapplethorpe's philosophy was fundamentally to forgive and be unjudgmental, to be peaceful and encourage coexistence, in short to be humanistic.

Among his works are *Certain People: A Book of Portraits* (1985) and *Black Book* (1986), a collection of erotic photos featuring African Americans. Patricia Morrisroe, in *Mapplethorpe: A Biography* (1995), points out that Sam Wagstaff, a man of aristocratic good looks, found Mapplethorpe the "someone to spoil" for whom he had searched both sexually and intellectually. Rocker Patti Smith was the artist's significant other before he vainly and sado-masochistically searched for the ideal black man—a "God." Morrisroe relates how Mapplethorpe then found Milton Moore, a Tennessee bumpkin who had been AWOL from the Navy. Moore's black penis, which aesthetically was an artistic gem, jutted from his unzippered Sunday suit, looking like a baby elephant's trunk, and was featured in "Man in Polyester Suit."

One of Mapplethorpe's commercial assignments was a high-heeled shoe, sleek in purple satin, propped on the cushioning mounds of a black man's buttocks. During foreplay with his several black lovers, he would diabolically address them as "nigger" and would punish them for their crime in having caused him to desire them by requesting they become coprophagous. "Is there any difference in approaching a black man who doesn't have clothes on," Mapplethorpe once asked, "and a white man who doesn't have clothes on? Not really. It's form."

When the wife of arch conservative Senator Jesse Helms reportedly saw his photograph of a man fisting another's anus ("Helmut and Brooks, N.Y.C., 1978"), she is said to have ejaculated, "Lord have mercy, Jesse!" But the critic Janet Kardon praised the same photo's composition, particularly "the centrality of the forearm." It was not reported whether the Senator's wife ever observed the photo of Mapplethorpe's Jim urinating into the mouth of Tom ("Jim and Tom, Sausalito, 1977") as he knelt before him in an abandoned bunker in Sausalito. To many, the photo symbolized a holy communion, with the donor standing over a kneeling supplicant, his eyes reverently closed.

"What is finally Catholic," wrote Arthur C. Danto of Mapplethorpe's work, "is the abiding mystery of spirit and flesh," to which the secularist could agree, particularly if Catholic were not capitalized.

The photographer's devout Catholic mother once sent her son to worship in a Quonset hut consecrated to Our Lady of the Sorrows. This led to his first drawings, of Madonnas with cubistically rearranged faces. Later he transferred what he called the "magic and mystery" of the Church into the exquisite agonies and hieratic rituals of sadomasochism. Visiting London when he was in his twenties, Mapplethorpe met the English filmmaker Derek Jarman, with whom he spent several days in bed. Jarman later likened Mapplethorpe to Faust, saying he had been corrupted by the offer from the Prince of Darkness to fulfill his fantasies. True, the monkey Mapplethorpe had kept in his student days was called Scratch, borrowing one of the Fallen Angel's nicknames. True, when it starved to death, Mapplethorpe lopped off its head and sculpted its skull into a musical instrument, eating part of its flesh in a voodoo ritual. And true, he told his bedmates that every sexual act had a third participant: over their two sweating bodies, the Devil spectrally presided. "True to Georges Bataille's theory about erotic behavior, Mapplethorpe mocked the missionary piety of heterosexual coupling and praised libertinism as a seizure of forbidden knowledge, a career of research conducted along the border between good and evil, life and death," added Peter Conrad. Conrad, in *The New Yorker* (5 June 1995), called him "the Devil's disciple."

Mapplethorpe was accused of taking on an upper-class anti-Semitism and an unseemly snobbism. "I've always been honest with people. I've never lied. I think I've lived a moral life," he told a priest at a time he knew he would die of AIDS. This might have been said as an objection to false rumors that he had purposely had sex with blacks in order to transmit his illness to them, revengeful and with the belief a black had infected him with the virus.

Three months before his mother died and at a time when he had lost considerable weight and looked much older than he actually was, Mapplethorpe succumbed to AIDS, paralysis having set in on the left side of his face. His black model, Milton Moore, whose physical attributes approximated his ideal, did not attend a memorial held at the Whitney Museum, nor did any of the gay crowd that had been his major support. Those who attended, ironically, were art dealers, dressed in suits much as if they were attending an auction at Christies.

Mapplethorpe's ashes were later buried in his mother's coffin. Mapplethorpe's father did not allow his son's name to be engraved on the tombstone. Meanwhile, books have proliferated about him, one of the best being Arthur C. Danto's *Playing with the Edge: The Photographic Achievement of Robert Mapplethorpe* (1995).

Maradani, Subba Rao (20th Century)

Maradani heads the twin cities chapter (Hyderabad and Secunderabad) of the Andhra Pradesh Rationalist Association.

Marat, Jean Paul (1743–1793)

Marat was a French revolutionist. Although usually depicted in odious colors, McCabe states, Marat actually was a cultivated man trained in medicine and the author of several scientific works of an atheistic and materialistic character. Voltaire complained that Marat's *Philosophical Essay on Man* (1773) was too materialistic. Twice he fled to England because he had been outlawed in France for his incendiary diatribes and calls for violence. In 1792 he was elected to the Convention, where he led the attack against the Girondists. "His truculence," McCabe writes, "had a purely patriotic root. It is interesting to note that Charlotte Corday, the young woman who assassinated him, also was a freethinker but of a rival political school." Corday, a royalist sympathizer, stabbed Marat to death in his bath. {CE; JM; RAT}

Marchena, José (1768–1821)

A Spanish writer, Marchena read the writings of French philosophers and then fled Spain when threatened by the Inquisition. Becoming a friend of Brissot and the Girondins, Marchena wrote *Essai de Théologie* (1797) and translated into Spanish Molière's *Tartuffe* and some works of Voltaire. In addition, he translated Dupuis' *Origine de tous les Cultes*. Marchena became secretary to Murat. {BDF; RAT}

Marchesini, Giovanni (Born 1868)

Marchesini was an enthusiastic positivist of the school of Ardigó. He taught philosophy and pedagogy at the University of Padua. His various works are as rigorously opposed to theology or theism as those of Ardigó. Among his works are *Morale Positiva* (1892), *Crisi del Positivismo* (1898) and *Simbolismo nella Conoscenza e nella Morale* (1901). {RAT}

Marcó del Pont, Luis (1938–)

An attorney and human rights advocate, Marcó del Pont spent ten years in exile for defending political prisoners in Argentina. He is a member of the Argentine Humanist Society and has published books concerning university reform and leading freethinking Argentineans.

Marcus Aurelius (121–180)

Marcus Aelius Aurelius Antoninus, the Roman emperor, was originally named Marcus Annius Versus. A zealous Stoic, he tried to decrease the brutality at gladiatorial shows. However, he regarded Christians as natural enemies of the empire and persecuted them for their obstinancy and their crimes. "I learned from Diognetus," he declared, "not to give credit to what was said by miracle-workers, and about the driving away of demons and such things." His *Meditations* expresses a humanistic philosophy and, according to Wheeler, the ideas "breathe a lofty morality and are a standing refutation of the view that pure ethics depend upon Christian belief." {BDF; CE; JM; TYD}

Marcus, Cyril (1904–1994)

Marcus, a Scot who became a market gardener in the South of France, was the son of Jewish parents. In his early thirties, he developed multiple sclerosis and returned to England, forced to use a wheelchair for the remainder of his life. A member of the Brighton and Hove Humanist Group, Marcus was memorialized by a tribute in *The Freethinker* (November 1994).

MARDUK

Marduk, in an early Babylonian religion, was the sun god, the supreme god. {LEE}

Maréchal, Pierre Sylvain (1750–1803)

Maréchal was an articulate and militant atheist at the time of the French Revolution. Known as *"l'homme sans Dieu,"* he listed three main categories of atheism:

- true atheists–
  Bruno, Diderot, d'Holbach, Epicurus, Hobbes, Hume, La Mettrie, Lucretius, Meslier, Vanini,
- possible atheists–
  Averroës, Bayle, Campanella, Cicero, Descartes, Molière, Montaigne, Spinoza
- those who seem atheists only from the standpoint of the strictest religious orthodoxy–
  Aristotle, Bacon, Gassendi, Leibniz, Locke, Malebranche, Newton, Plato, Rousseau

As opposites of atheists, he lists these:

St. Augustine, Jacques Bénigne Bossuet, Jansenius, Jesus, François de la Mothe-Fénelon, Pascal

Maréchal's *Dictionnaire des athées* (1798) was the first biographical dictionary of skeptics. According to J. M. Robertson, it is one of the best examples of a general historic treatment of the subject, along with Joseph Mazzini Wheeler's *Biographical Dictionary of Freethinkers* (1889). Robertson prefers Wheeler's work, for Maréchal's work "exhibits much learning, but is made partly fantastic by its sardonic plan of including a number of typical religionists (including Job, John, and Jesus Christ!), some of whose utterances are held to lead logically to atheism." McCabe, however, found Maréchal both a scholar and a man of great learning, adding that the book was the result of strong persuasion by the mathematician Lalande.

Maréchal's *Almanach des honnêtes gens* (1788), which was not an attack upon religion but which on a calendar substituted the names of renowned laymen for saints, was instantly denounced by the *Parlement de Paris*. Its printer was prosecuted, Maréchal was imprisoned for four months, and the censor who had passed the book was exiled thirty leagues from Paris.

Although a major figure in his time, Maréchal is seldom included today in standard reference books. However, Gordon Stein wrote "Pierre Sylvain Maréchal" in *American Rationalist* (July-August 1991), praising him. {BDF; EU, Aram Vartanian; JMR; JMRH; RAT}

Maresse-Smith, Edgar (19th Century)

In Trinidad in the 1890s, Maresse-Smith was president of the National Secular Society branch. {FUK; GS}

Maret, Henry (Born 1838)

Maret was a French journalist and deputy. He combated against the Empire, edited *Le Radical*, and was elected deputy in 1881. {BDF}

Marett, Robert Randolph (Born 1866)

Marett, a Jersey lawyer who became lecturer in philosophy at Exeter College (Oxford), became Dean of Exeter College. He is one of the chief authors of the pre-animistic theory of the origin of religion, and he believed in an impersonal God and rejected Christian doctrines.

His books include *Personal Idealism* (1902) and *The Threshold of Religion* (1909). {RAT; RE}

Margarot, Maurice (1745–1815)

Margarot was a republican and a freethinker. He also was a convict, having been so outspoken in debate that he was tried for sedition and sentenced as one of a group of "Scottish Martyrs" in 1794. Upon being transported to New South Wales, he demanded his freedom, which was refused. At his home, a meeting place for radicals, he condemned colonial voracity, resulting in his servitude at the Norfolk Island and Newcastle penal settlements. Upon being pardoned, he returned in 1810 to England, where he continued to harass the Colonial Office and never wavered in his zeal for social freedom. {SWW}

Margolis, Clorinda G. (20th Century)

When she signed Humanist Manifesto II, Margolis was associated with the Jefferson Community Mental Health Center in Philadelphia, Pennsylvania. She wrote *Manual of Stress Management* (1982). {HM2}

Margolis, Joseph (1924–)

When he signed Humanist Manifesto II, Margolis was professor of philosophy of Temple University. He is author of *The Truth About Relativism* (1991). {HM2; SHD}

Marguerite (Queen) (1553–1615)

Marguerite of Valois, Queen of Navarre and sister to Francis I, was included as a freethinker by Wheeler because she protected too many religious reformers. She was the daughter of King Henry II and of Catherine de Medici, and her marriage to Henry, the Protestant king of Navarre (later Henry IV of France), was intended to mark the peace between Roman Catholics and Protestants. Instead, the marriage was a prelude to the massacre of Protestants on St. Bartholomew's Day. {BDF}

Marguerite, Victor (Born 1866)

Marguerite, a member of the French Academy, was a novelist. He was an Officer of the Legion of Honour, President of the *Société des Gens de Lettres* and of the *Ligue Républicaine d'Action Nationale*, and Vice-President of the Commission of the National Fund for Literary Travel. A rationalist, he wrote *Disaster* (1898), *The Commune* (1904), *Vanity* (1907), and *Frontiers of the Heart* (1913). {RAT}

Marietta, Don (20th Century)

"The Goodness of the Godless" was the subject of Marietta's lecture at the 1999 convention of Humanists of Florida.

Marietta, O. (20th Century)

Marietta wrote the *Paine Memorial* (1908). {GS}

Mariette, François Auguste Ferdinand (1821–1881)

A French Egyptologist, Mariette spent thirty years in Egypt in the archeological service of the French government, during which time he reportedly acquired more foreign decorations and honors than any other archeologist that had lived up to that time. In Egypt, he received the titles of bey and later of pasha. In 1863 he founded at Bulak (now part of Cairo) the Egyptian national museum. Some today know Mariette as having suggested the story for the libretto of the opera, "Aîda." Mariette's brother in a biography described him as a decided atheist, saying he never entered a church and "found no charm in the pastorals and fictions of which we have a prodigious heap in Christianity." {JM; RAT; RE}

MARIJUANA: See entries for drugs and for International Naturist Church.

Marillier, Léon (1842–1901

Marillier lectured on the religions of non-civilized peoples at the *École des Hautes Études* and was professor of psychology and ethics at the *Sèvres École Normale Supérieure des Jeunes Fille*s. An authority on the psychology of religion, he translated into French Andrew Lang's *Myths, Cults, and Religions* (1896). Marillier was also joint editor of the *Revue de l'histoire des religions*. {RAT}

Mario, Alberto (Born 1825)

Mario was an Italian patriot, the editor of the *Tribune* and *Free Italy*. He became aide-de-camp to Garibaldi and married an English lady, Jessie White. In 1860 he wrote *Slavery and Thought*, a polemic against the papacy. {BDF; RAT}

Mario, Jessie White (1832–1906)

A daughter of the ship-builder Thomas White, Mario wrote *Alice Lane*, a novel published in 1853. In Paris she adopted the views of Lamennais, and in Italy she became a follower of Mazzini and Garibaldi. Mario translated Garibaldi's memoirs. Her *Birth of Modern Italy* (1909) was well received. By her command, her funeral was designed to be purely secular. {RAT}

Marischal [Lord]: See entry for David Hume, who called Lord Marischal an atheist.

Maritain, Jacques (1882–1973)

Maritain, a French neo-Thomist philosopher, urged Christian involvement in secular affairs and was the French ambassador to the Vatican (1945–1948). In *True Humanism* (1936), he described *l'Humanisme intégral:* "Such a humanism, considering man in the integrality of his natural and his supernatural being and setting no limits *a priori* or the descent of divinity into man, can also be called Humanism of the Incarnation." (See entry for Theism.) {CE}

Mark, Charles (20th Century)

Mark, of Wolsingham in England, was a Chartist. His obituary describes him as "the father and founder of Freethought principles in this locality." He had been active in freethought and secular circles. {RSR}

Mark, Edward Laurens (Born 1847)

Mark became the Hersey professor of anatomy at Harvard and Director of the Bermuda Biological Staff of Research. His *Was Wir Ernst Haeckel Verdanken* showed his high regard for Haeckel. Mark believed that Haeckel's monistic philosophy "will in time deeply influence all thoughtful and impartial people." {RAT}

Marke, Ronald (1936–)

An Australian atheist, rationalist, and editor, Marke emigrated to

Australia from England in 1962. In Chippendale, Australia, he has edited the bi-monthly *Rationalist News* (1967 to date). {FUK}

MARKETING . . . OF ORGANIZED RELIGION

God's Total Quality Management Questionnaire has appeared on the World Wide Web. Stating, tongue-in-cheek, that God asks that you take a few moments to answer a few questions and adding that He thanks you in advance for your time and effort, the test includes the following:

1. How did you find out about God? (Circle as many as are applicable.) divine inspiration; friend or relative; near-death experience; newspaper; personal visit; television; word of mouth; Torah; Holy Bible; Qur'an; *Playboy*; *Why I Am Not A Christian*; other book (please specify title): ______other:
2. What other sources of inspiration in addition to God are you currently using? (Circle) Alcohol or drugs; Ann Landers advice column; biorhythms; fortune cookies; horoscope; insurance policies; Jimmy Swaggert; lottery; mantras; self-help books; sex; tarot; television; none; other (specify):
3. God employs a limited degree of Divine Intervention to preserve the balanced level of felt presence and blind faith. Which do you prefer (circle one): more Divine Intervention; less Divine Intervention; current level of Divine intervention is just right; don't know
4. God also attempts to maintain a balanced level of disasters and miracles. Rate on a scale of 1 (unsatisfactory) to 5 (excellent) His handling of the following:
   a. disasters (flood, famine, earthquake, war)
   b. miracles (rescues, spontaneous remission of disease; sports upsets

THANK YOU, AND GOD BLESS!

Markham, Edwin (1852–1940)

Markham, once the superintendent of a California school, wrote humanistic poems such as "Brotherhood" and "Earth Is Enough." His Universalism shows in "Outwitted":

He drew a circle that shut me out—
Heretic, rebel, a thing to flout.
But Love and I had the wit to win:
We drew a circle that took him in.

Markham's popularity grew when, inspired by Millet's famous painting, he wrote a poem, "The Man with the Hoe" (1899), in which he protested against the degradation and exploitation of labor, including child labor. {CE; U}

Markovic, Mihailo (1923–)

Markovic, a professor of philosophy at the University of Belgrade and the Serbian Academy of Science and Arts, has been a co-president of the International Humanist and Ethical Union. Some remember his felt criticism of Stalinism in the name of a Humanist Marxism. In 1978 at the Seventh International Humanist and Ethical Union (IHEU) World Congress in London, Prof. Markovic addressed the group, as he did also at the Eighth held in Hannover (1982). Markovic wrote *The Contemporary Marx: Essays on Humanist Communism* (1974) and *Democratic Socialism* (1982). For the *Encyclopedia of Philosophy*, Markovic wrote the section on Yugoslav philosophy.

Although he once was named a Humanist Laureate in the Council of Secular Humanism's International Academy of Humanism, the honor was revoked at the recommendation of Paul Kurtz because of Markovic's political views concerning genocide in Yugoslavia, views about Serbian nationalism which were considered anti-humanistic. (See entry for Ethical Culture.) {SHD}

Markovic, Svetozar (1846–1875)

A Serbian socialist, Markovic was a philosopher who wrote on aesthetics in "Reality in Poetry," which was published in *Matica* (1870), and on his atheism in "The Realistic Trend in Science and Life," in *Letopis Matice Srpske* (1871–1872).

Marks, Erich (Born 1861)

Marks, a German historian, taught at Berlin University, Freiburg, and Leipzig. He wrote a study of Queen Elizabeth and other historical works. He occasionally lectured for the German Ethical societies {RAT}

Marks, Murray (1840–1918)

Marks, a dealer in art treasures, advised Rossetti and Whistler concerning their purchases. His obituary in the *Times* stressed his "probity" as well as his high artistic skill. Marks gave generously to museums and public collections. He followed the creed of Spinoza, of whom he was a close student. {RAT}

Marks, Raube (20th Century)

A board member of the Freedom From Religion Foundation, Marks of Illinois operated H. H. Waldo Booksellers, a leading mail-order supplier of vintage humanist and freethought books. In 1997, the company's title became Robb Marks (Box 350, Rockton, Illinois 61072; telephone (815) 624-4593).

Marley, Harold P. (20th Century)

Marley, a Unitarian minister, signed both Humanist Manifesto I and II. {FUS; HM1; HM2}

Marlowe, Christopher (1564–1593)

Often described as being the greatest English playwright before Shakespeare, Marlowe belongs to the genre known in French literature as *poète maudit*, one of the "accursed poets" who like Rimbaud, Verlaine, Poe, or Dylan Thomas, went to the "bad." Marlowe is known for *The Tragical History of Doctor Faustus* (c. 1588). In it, and in exchange for twenty-four years of power and pleasure, Faust forfeits his soul to Mephistopheles, a theme also used by Goethe, Charles François Gounod, Thomas Mann, Steven Vincent Benét, and others.

On the subject of religion, Marlowe wrote,

- I count religion but a childish toy,
  and hold there is no sin but ignorance.
- Religion hides many mischiefs from suspicion.
- Both law and physic are for petty wits.
  Divinity is basest of the three,
  Unpleasant, harsh, contemptible, and vile.

Marlowe was a member of "the School of Night," a group of free-thinking intellectuals. As for his atheism, in *Doctor Faustus* Marlowe makes Mephistopheles affirm that "Hell hath no limits . . . but where we are is hell," which is a common view today but was original in his time. In private talk, Robertson writes, Marlowe is said to have gone into much more detail as to his unbelief. For example, he claimed that Jesus had sex with his disciple John: "Christ did love him with an extraordinary love," he wrote. In "Edward II," Marlowe wrote about the 14th-century British king who was killed in part because he lavished so many royal favors on his male lover.

His death before he reached the age of thirty was caused by accidental manslaughter, for which Marlowe himself was to blame. In a tavern brawl, Marlowe when only twenty-nine was stabbed in the eye and killed, allegedly in a quarrel over a boy. Characteristically, he died swearing.

Marlowe once had written, "All they that love not tobacco and boys are fools." Charles Nicholl, in *The Reckoning, The Murder of Christopher Marlowe* (1994), contends that Marlowe's death was not an accidental killing that involved a youth, that it was an act of murder which resulted from Marlowe's political and intelligence affiliations. Nicoll suggests that when efforts to slander Marlowe as a dangerous atheist failed, it was Nicholas Skeres, not the man who claimed he had killed Marlowe in self defense—Ingram Frizer—who was the villain responsible for Marlowe's death. Skeres allegedly worked for a faction which supported the Earl of Essex and wished to discredit Marlowe as a way of discrediting Marlowe's friend Sir Walter Raleigh.

Marlowe lived at a time when personal fighting and duels were common. The longevity of writers and poets who were his contemporaries was short—as A. L. Rowse has pointed out, George Peele died of syphilis, Robert Greene was horribly diseased, and both

Thomas Kyd and Thomas Nashe died in their thirties. Within a few years of Marlowe's death, Ben Jonson would duel and kill the well-known actor Gabriel Spencer. Although further specific evidence is lacking for his reputed atheism, Marlowe admittedly had an eventful death. {CE; GL; JM; JMR; JMRH; RAT; PUT; RE; TYD}

Marmontel, Jean François (1723–1799)

A priest who was educated by the Jesuits and who taught in a Toulouse seminary, Marmontel adopted deism and settled as a writer in Paris. His novel, *Bélisaire*, was condemned for heresy. He wrote many articles for Diderot's *Encyclopaedia*. Marmontel, whose complete works fill nineteen volumes, was appointed Historiographer of France and became a member of the French Academy. {RAT; RE}

Marquand, John (Phillips) (1893–1960)

Marquand was a Pulitzer Prize-winning author whose great aunt, on his mother's side, was the transcendentalist Margaret Fuller. She would not, he joked to friends, have liked his work. *The Late George Apley* (1937) is an amusing tale told by Mr. Willing, a friend of the late Mr. Apley, who is asked by Apley's son John to describe his father. Willing uses family letters to describe how Apley marries Catherine Bosworth out of a somewhat Puritan sense of duty and tells of his Brahmin life and his idealism as it conflicts with social prudence, showing how compromises are a big part of life.

Marquand also wrote detective stories about Mr. Moto, a Japanese sleuth, and *H. J. Pulham, Esq.* (1941) told the life of a New Englander twenty-five years out of college.

Point of No Return (1949) concerned a banker who in middle age found he was no longer able to turn from the path of materialism.

Life at Happy Knoll (1958) has sketches in epistolary form which describe a country club's problems.

Asked about humanism, he responded to the present author,

> I should honestly try to oblige you if I were not completely involved at present in trying to finish a novel. In this unhappy situation, I feel that tilting with philosophical windmills would throw me completely off the track, if I am not off the trolley already.

That novel was *Melville Goodwin, U. S. A.*, about how stultifying is the life of an Army officer.

Tim Marquand, his grandson who is a record company executive, was raised a Unitarian, as was his grandfather. Tim's father, **John Phillips Marquand Jr.**, was cited in Edward Klein's *All Too Human: The Love Story of Jack and Jackie Kennedy* (1996), as being the one to whom the future wife of President John F. Kennedy was once madly in love. According to Klein, she "chain-smoked aromatic French cigarettes, drank grasshoppers, and listened to Jack talk about the novel he was writing. They made love in the fashion of the day, groping and fumbling and going almost all the way. It left Marquand, as the American saying went, 'with blue balls.' It left Jackie, as the French put it with more delicacy, *une demi-vierge*, a half-virgin."

Then the shocker: One night as the two went up to Marquand's apartment on the slow, creaky French elevator, "Jackie let herself get carried away. She was in Marquand's arms, her skirt bunched above her hips, the backs of her thighs pressed against the decorative open grillwork. And by the time the elevator jolted to a stop, she was no longer a *demi-vierge*."

Gore Vidal, in *Palimpsest* (1995), had previously related the story, writing only that the good Catholic Jackie had lost her virginity to an unnamed friend of his "in a lift that he had installed in a pension on Paris's Left Bank. They had discussed marriage. He came from a better family than hers, as we used, quaintly, to say, but he had no money. He was also Protestant." Then, in Vidal's words, "suddenly a fellow Roman Catholic, also on the make for glory if not money, came her way." It was Kennedy. When Jackie told the un-named "lift-lover," he was appalled and said, "You can't marry that . . . that Mick!" Whereupon Jackie told him, "He has money and you don't." Although they argued, Marquand lost. An inveterate reader, he died of a heart attack while reading *In Her Sister's Shadow*, Diana DuBois's story about Lee Radziwill, a work in which he is mentioned several places.

The elder Marquand, known particularly for detective stories about Mr. Moto, a Japanese sleuth, was said to have been something of an Apley himself, one with a "kindly harassed face." He enjoyed satire, particularly that by Sinclair Lewis, and he wrote satirically about the affluent middle class. {*Dictionary of American Biography*; WAS, 27 February 1951}

Marquis, Don (1878–1937)

Marquis, an American journalist and humorist, wrote in a poetic work, "Transient,"

> Give up the dream that Love may trick the fates
> To live again somewhere beyond the gleam
> Of dying stars, or shatter the strong gates
> Some god has builded high; give up the dream.

{TYD}

Marr, Wilhelm (1818–1904)

Marr was a German socialist. He wrote *Religious Excursions* (1876) and several anti-Semitic tracts. {BDF}

MARRIAGE

- Were Adam and Eve married? If so, by whom?
- What if rabbis required that Christians marrying Jewish women had to get circumcised?
- The Universal Declaration of Human Rights places no restriction on the gender or sexuality of any persons marrying.

In Israel, the Orthodox rabbinate has a government monopoly on the performing of marriage ceremonies. Non-Orthodox ceremonies constitute a small fraction of the number of marriages conducted by the Orthodox rabbinate. In 1993, only 200 of 26,000 marriages were performed for the non-Orthodox. As a result, hundreds of Israeli couples get around the rabbinate each year by going to Cyprus to obtain their marriages, according to journalist Joel Greenberg in *The New York Times* (27 April 1994). Others are married by proxy in Paraguay, receiving their certificates by mail. Secular civil-rights advocates object to such a situation, and Rabbi Ehud Bandel of the Conservative movement in Israel has observed, "The absurdity is that the only place in the free world where Jews are denied religious freedom is the Jewish state. The state does not claim to set religious standards for Muslims and Christians, but it does determine that for Jews the only way is Orthodox Judaism, which is a minority in the Jewish world."

Many in Western society assume that romantic love has always been the outcome of romantic love. Not so, writes Bertrand Russell in *Marriage and Morals* (1959), who says it is only since about the period of the French Revolution that a "proper" marriage was arranged by parents. "The novels and plays of a hundred years ago deal largely with the struggle of the younger generation to establish this new basis for marriage as opposed to the traditional marriage of parental choice," he writes. Russell continues, "Whether the effect has been as good as the innovators hoped may be doubted. There is something to be said for Mrs. Malaprop's principle, that love and aversion both wear off in matrimony so that it is better to begin with a little aversion." In America, Lord Russell says, the romantic view of marriage has been taken more seriously than anywhere else, "and where law and custom alike are based upon the dreams of spinsters, the result has been an extreme prevalence of divorce and an extreme rarity of happy marriages." Children, of course, are what make a marriage important "but for children there would be no need for any institution concerned with sex, but as soon as children enter in, the husband and wife, if they have any sense of responsibility or any affection for their offspring, are compelled to realize that their feelings towards each other are no longer what is of most importance."

"The triumph of Christian teaching," Russell notes, "is when a man and a woman marry without either having had previous sexual experience. In nine cases out of ten where this occurs, the results are unfortunate. Sexual behavior among human beings is not instinctive, so that the inexperienced bridge and bridegroom, who are probably not aware of this fact, find themselves overwhelmed with shame and discomfort. It is little better when the woman alone is innocent but the man has acquired his knowledge from prostitutes. . . . All this could be put right by better sexual education, and is in fact very much better with the generation now young than it was with their parents and grandparents."

Lord Russell's ideas sound commonplace in the 1990s, but in the 1940s his views on sex and marriage led to his being refused a teaching position at City College of New York. That city, he complained in a book edited by John Dewey and Horace M. Kallen, *The Bertrand Russell Case*, "was virtually a satellite of the Vatican. . . . An Anglican bishop was incited to protest against me, and priests lectured the police, who were practically all Irish Catholics, on my responsibility for the local criminals. A lady, whose daughter attended some section of the City College with which I should never be brought in contact, was induced to bring a suit, saying that my presence in that institution would be dangerous to her daughter's virtue . . . [and my works were pronounced] lecherous, libidinous, lustful, venerous, erotomaniac, aphrodisiac, irreverent, narrow-minded, untruthful, and bereft of moral fiber. . . . I was thought wicked for saying that very young infants should not be punished for masturbation." In fact, the Registrar of New York County said publicly that Russell should be "tarred and feathered and driven out of the country."

The "row" ended, Russell explained, when Dr. Albert C. Barnes, the inventor of Argyrol, gave him a five-year appointment to lecture on philosophy at his Barnes Foundation, "where I lectured in a gallery of modern French paintings, mostly of nudes, which seemed somewhat incongruous for academic philosophy." Although Russell had been warned that Barnes quickly tired of people and demanded constant flattery, and although Russell had exacted a five-year contract from him, Barnes terminated the appointment at the end of 1942. To Lucy Donnelly, Russell wrote concerning the Barnes episode, "I used, when excited, to calm myself by reciting the three factors of $a^3 + b^3 + c^3 - 3abc$; I must revert to this practice. I find it more effective than thoughts of the Ice Age or the goodness of God."

"The most extraordinary" invitation to marriage, so described by Sotheby's when auctioned in 1942 according to *The Oxford Book of Letters*, was sent in 1861 by a prolific Victorian novelist:

> My dearest Miss Dorothea Sankey
>
> My affectionate & most excellent wife is as you are aware still living—and I am proud to say her health is good. Nevertheless it is always well to take time by the forelock and be prepared for all events. Should anything happen to her, will you supply her place—as soon as the proper period for decent mourning is over.
>
> Till then I am your devoted Servant
>
> Anthony Trollope

John Boswell, in *Same-Sex Unions in Pre-Modern Europe* (1994), identified seven ceremonies marking same-sex unions before the 12th century, seventeen in the 12th century, and more than a score from the 13th to the 16th centuries. As to whether the unions constituted marriage, Boswell concluded that some of them did so long as marriage is defined as "a permanent emotional union acknowledged in some way by the community." Whether or not an erotic element existed, evidence is incomplete and it is not clear if the two were supposed to live together forever or could subsequently marry somebody of the opposite sex.

Toward the end of the century, many intellectuals questioned whether marriage is, in fact, a "failing institution." If half or more, depending upon the country, end in divorce, is marriage a failure? And is marriage really a marathon in which the whole point is to arrive at a predetermined finish line: namely, the death of one partner? If a marriage lasts for thirty years and both partners were perfectly happy for the first twenty-eight, is the entire marriage a loss if the couple chooses to separate before dying? Analogously, if a person is a professional accountant for twenty-eight years, then chooses to be a journalist, is this evidence of a career failure?

In short, some argue, dogmatic fundamentalists and Judeo-Christians and moral conservatives can be expected to disapprove of divorce but secularists need not attach a stigma to divorce. On the contrary, the fluidity of a marriage which results in divorce and re-marriage can be progressive and positive for all concerned.

The Catholic Church grants an estimated 60,000 annulments each year in the United States and, according to Robert H. Vasoli's *What God Has Joined Together* (1998), more than eighty percent of those seeking annulments obtain them. Inasmuch as it does not recognize divorce, the only way for Catholics to be free to marry again in the church is to have the marriage declared invalid in the first place. Sheila Rauch Kennedy, in *Shattered Faith: A Woman's Struggle to Stop the Catholic Church From Annulling Her Marriage* (1997), calls that "hypocrisy" and "nonsense."

In the 20th century, Denmark, Iceland, Norway, and Sweden have been the first to grant legal recognition of gay marriages. Canada, however, became the first country whose Supreme Court ruled that "spouse" includes homosexuals. In an 8-to-1 decision in 1999, it struck down the heterosexual definition, ruling that "The exclusion of same-sex partners from the benefits of" the Ontario Family Law Act "promotes the view that M [a letter standing for one of the two lesbians who had brought the case] and individuals in same-sex relationships generally, [is] less worthy of recognition and protection." The court stressed that its decision might well affect "many other statutes that rely on a similar definition of the word 'spouse.' "

Meanwhile, freethinkers are those for whom marriages are not made in Heaven—they're made here on Earth. (See entries for Christian Marriage, Divorce, [St.] Peter, and Bertrand Russell,.) {Bertrand Russell, *Autobiography* (1967); *The Economist*, 23 March 1996}

MARRIAGE, A DEFINITION

• Marriage, n. The state or condition of a community consisting of a master, a mistress, and two slaves, making in all, two.

–Ambrose Bierce
The Devil's Dictionary

MARRIAGE, FORMS OF

• Bigamy refers to unlawful polygamy, or the entering into another marriage when already legally married to another. A bigamist, according to strict church teaching, is one who marries someone who already is carnally known by another. For anyone in the Catholic holy orders, a person who is under a vow of continence who marries anyone, even for the first time, is guilty of bigamy—the person has, it is reasoned, already married the church.

• Common law marriages are those that are entered into between a man and a women without ecclesiastical or civil ceremony. They are not recognized as legal in many jurisdictions and often must be followed by cohabitation to be legally valid in other jurisdictions. Further, the common law arrangement likely will need to be provable by the writings, declarations, or conduct of the parties.

• Digamy (also called deuterogamy) refers to a legal second marriage after a first marriage ends—for example, by death or divorce of the spouse.

• Monogamy, in the past, referred to the custom of marrying one person for a lifetime. It has come to mean marriage with but one person at a time, as contrasted with bigamy.

• Polygamy is a marriage form in which a person of either sex possesses a plurality of mates at the same time.

• Monandry is a woman's having one husband at a time.

• Polyandry is a marriage form in which one woman has two or more husbands at the same time, as contrasted with polygamy. Fraternal polyandry is a marriage in which several brothers share one wife. Sororal polyandry is the sharing by sisters of one husband.

• The dissolution of any valid marriage by a court or other body having competent authority is called a divorce, or *divorce a vinculo matrimonii*, as distinguished from annulment (a judicial pronouncement declaring the invalidity of a marriage—some poor people complain that the church charges too much for such), and distinguished from judicial separation (the cessation of cohabitation by mutual agreement).

• Among some non-Christians, divorce is defined as being a formal separation of man and wife by the act of one party or by consent according to established custom—for example, as in a *talak* (the Muslim divorce that is effected by the simple act of the husband's rejecting the wife).

• None of the above terms apply to the sexual gettings-together of non-humans. (See entry for Divorce.)

Marris, Robin (1924–)

Marris, who is from the United Kingdom, addressed the Second International Humanist and Ethical Union World Congress held in London (1957). In 1974 Morris wrote *The Corporate Society.*

Marryatt, Thomas (1730–1792)

Marryatt, who could read any Greek or Latin author before he was nine, abandoned his Presbyterianism for deism. He studied medicine at Edinburgh and from 1766 practiced in various Irish and English towns.

Besides medical works, he wrote a rationalistic *Philosophy of Masons.* Although commonly regarded as an atheist, Marryatt was a deist. {RAT}

MARS

Toward the end of the 20th century, evidence appeared to suggest past life on Mars. By testing twelve or so meteorites from Mars that were found in Antarctica, British as well as American scientists have speculated that Mars could have been inhabited for quite a long period and could even have some life today. One meteorite, called 79001, was considered the "Rosetta stone" of the British studies inasmuch as an analysis of trapped gases within the rock were almost identical in composition to atmospheric samples gathered by the Viking spacecraft in 1976.

Scientists predict that in the 21st century samples will be collected by robotic landers on Mars, returned to Earth, and analyzed by international bodies of scientists to come up with definitive conclusions.

Marsalek, Kenneth (1951–)

Marsalek is a founding member and president of Washington Area Secular Humanists. He is a Secular Humanist Mentor of the Council for Secular Humanism, a regional director of the Council, a member of the Council's board of directors, and a contributing editor of the *Secular Humanist Bulletin.*

In "'Star Trek': Humanism of the Future" (*Free Inquiry*, Fall 1992), he points out that religion has always prompted belief in gods, devils, angels, and the afterlife. In "Star Trek," however, when Captain Kirk tells a space alien to "Go to the Devil," the alien replies, "We have no Devil, Kirk." Exposure to the idea that religious beliefs are not universal enables us to recognize our own beliefs as a product of our culture, rather than as sacred truths. "Mr. Spock shows us," explains Marsalek, "that there is some alien in all of us. He makes the alien more familiar, more acceptable, and even likable. This helps to overcome what Carl Sagan has called 'human chauvinism.' Through science fiction such as 'Star Trek,' we gain perspective not only from different cultures, but from different planets, different species, and different times. . . . It plants small seeds of doubt that may germinate, grow, and ultimately blossom into humanism." (See entry for Washington [DC] Humanists.) {FD}

Marsden, E. C. (20th Century)

Marsden, a freethinker, wrote *Some Religious Terms Simply Defined* (1914). {GS}

Marsden, George M. (1939–)

Marsden, in *The Soul of the American University, From Protestant Establishment to Established Nonbelief* (1994), laments that freedom of religion has become freedom *from* religion on the campus. Religion, he holds was driven from campuses as being utterly scientific. Now, he adds, science has lost its own credentials, a conclusion which many find questionable. He wrote *The Outrageous Idea of Christian Scholarship* (1996).

Marselli, Niccola (Born 1832)

Marselli was an Italian writer, the author of advanced works on the science of history: *Nature and Civilisation, The Origin of Humanity,* and *Great Races of Humanity.* (BDF)

Marshak, David (20th Century)

Marshak, with M. Elizabeth Anastos, wrote *Philosophy-Making for Unitarian Universalist Religious Growth and Learning: A Process Guide.*

MARSHALL UNIVERSITY FREETHINKERS

Rationalists United for Secular Humanism is a group at Marshall University in Huntington, West Virginia. On the Web: <www.secularhumanism.org/cfa/orgs.html>.

Marshall, Alan John (1911–1967)

"Jock" Marshall was an Australian rationalist, zoologist, and author. Although one-armed because of a shooting accident when he was sixteen, he had a distinguished career at Oxford and London Universities, which led to appointment as the Foundation Chair of Zoology and Comparative Physiology at Monash University. He wrote *The Great Extermination* (1968) and *Darwin and Huxley in Australia* (1970). In a posthumous accolade, Russell Drysdale said Marshall "challenged ideas, apathy, entrenched attitudes, and lack of imaginative thinking. He disposed of sacred cows without requiem and tore to shreds the cloak of our improper conceits." {SWW}

Marshall, Franklin (20th Century)

In 1995, Marshall was elected co-president of the Northeast Atheist Association.

Marshall, George N. (1916–1993)

From 1960 to 1985, Marshall led the Unitarian church's most unconventional body, the Church of the Larger Fellowship. From its office in Boston, Marshall reached Unitarians around the world who did not live near a church, an estimated 4,000 members. He communicated with them by mail, computer network, fax, audio and videotaped sermons, publications, and toll-free telephone numbers for counseling. A friend of Albert Schweitzer, Marshall was a founding member of the American Friends of Albert Schweitzer. In addition to two books about Schweitzer, he wrote eight volumes on religious and social themes, including *Facing Death and Grief* (1981) and *Challenge of a Liberal Faith* (1970).

Marshall took part in civil rights marches in Selma, Alabama, was an outspoken advocate of the separation of church and state, and opposed prayer in public schools as well as tax aid to religious schools. He once had been minister of the historic First Church in Plymouth, Massachusetts, founded by the Pilgrims who landed at Plymouth Rock.

Marshall, Henry Rutgers (1852–1927)

Marshall, an architect and writer, was a lecturer on aesthetics at Columbia and Yale. He was president of the American Psychological Association, a member of the American Philosophical Society, and the author of *Pain, Pleasure, and Aesthetics.* In *Consciousness,* Marshall professed pantheism and rejected the idea of personal immortality as "a crude and inadequate expression of the whole truth. . . . . As much of myself as is of the Eternal will join with it in death," he stated. {JM; RAT}

Marshall, John [Supreme Court Judge] (1755–1835)

Marshall, a statesman and jurist, is known for expanding Federal power while serving as the 4th Chief Justice of the Supreme Court. A Unitarian, born in a log cabin and the eldest of fifteen children, he spent his youth in primitive surroundings, but through his mother he was related to the Lees and the Randolphs and to Thomas Jefferson, who later was to become his great antagonist.

A University of Toronto teacher of political science, Jean Edward Smith, described in *John Marshall, Definer of a Nation* (1996) how Marshall was the first Chief Justice to locate and define the real powers of the office. Marshall had led a company of backwoods riflemen through many of the major battles of the Revolutionary War and had spent the winter at Valley Forge with George Washington, his lifelong hero. Like Washington, Marshall distrusted local and state governments which often failed to support the federal government once battles moved beyond their borders. He became convinced that state governments' provincialism needed the discipline of Federal law, Professor Joseph J. Ellis of Mount Holyoke College has pointed out, if the American republic was to endure.

Marshall resented Jefferson's avoidance of military service, and the two did not get along although they respected each other, with qualifications. "I never admit anything," said Jefferson of Marshall. "So sure as you admit any position to be good, no matter how remote from the conclusion he seeks to establish, you are gone. So great is his sophistry you must never give him an affirmative answer or you will be forced to grant his conclusion. Why, if he were to ask me if it were daylight or not, I'd replay, 'Sir, I don't know. I can't tell.' "

Marshall had a semi-invalid wife, Polly, and eleven children. Although his parents, wife, children, and other relatives were Episcopalians, Marshall was an independent Unitarian. {CE; U; UU; *The New York Times Book Review*, 1 December 1996}

Marston, John (1576–1634)

Whether or not he was a Calvinist, or whether he was serious, Marston the satirist and dramatist once wrote, "Man is the slime of the dung-pit." {CE}

Marston, Philip Bourke (1850–1887)

Marston was an English poet who, blind in childhood, became devoted to poetry. A friend of Rossetti, Swinburne, and Thomson, he wrote poems which were sad and sincere. In accordance with his wishes, Marston was buried in unconsecrated ground at Highgate, and without religious service. {BDF; RAT}

Marsy, François Marie de (1714–1763)

Marsy was a freethinker who had been educated as a Jesuit. When he brought out an analysis of Bayle in 1755, he was confined to the Bastille. {BDF; RAT}

Marten, Henry (1619–1680)

Marten, who was elected to Parliament in 1640, was expelled for his republican sentiments in 1643. Resuming his seat in 1646, he took part in the civil war, sat the civil war, sat as one of King Charles's judges, and became one of the Council of State. He proposed the repeal of the statute of banishment against the Jews, and when it was sought to expel all profane persons, proposed to add the words "and all fools." Tried for regicide in 1660, he was kept in Chepstow Castle until his death. Carlyle called him "sworn foe of Cant in all its figures; an indomitable little Pagan if no better." Wood's *Athenae Oxonienses* states that Marten "never entered upon religion but with design to laugh both at it and morality." {BDF; JM; RAT; RE}

Marthaler, John Andrew (1918–1995)

Marthaler, a boat captain and radar technician who was a member of the Unitarian Universalist Association, was an outspoken and unintimidated freethinker. His automobile carried a large atheistic slogan, "Just Say No To Religion."

In 1994 he was interviewed by Fred Whitehead, in which he told of years of writing letters to local newspapers and attending conventions of the American Atheists. "I actually see people run when they see me coming," he said. "The get to where they can't be near me. There is something about an atheist. See, a Christian believes in devils and they believe that if they interfere with this devil he will do something to them. This is Christianity at its best. They believe in devils; you have to believe in devils to be a Christian. There would never be any Christianity without that Christian devil."

On Easter Sunday in 1995, he died. *The Mississippi Press* reported that John had converted to Christianity on his deathbed, through the efforts of his sister, Mrs. Anna Presley. A letter to the editor from Hank Shiver soon afterwards, however, said, "From my personal observations, John was in a diminished mental capacity shortly before his death. John had low oxygen levels to the brain, suffered a stroke, difficulty breathing, heart attacks, and was on life support." {*Freethought History #14*, 1995}

Martin, Alfred Wilhelm (1862–1933)

Martin was a Jewish-Christian-Unitarian theist who left his Free Church in Seattle to write and teach comparative religions in New York, 1907 to 1931. In 1907 he was assistant leader of New York's Ethical Culture Society and lecturer for the Brooklyn Institute of Arts and Sciences. He had been ordained as a Unitarian minister in 1888. In his *A Generation of Religious Progress* (1946), Martin remarked that astronomers have "banished from the firmament the divinities with which a superstitious reverence had endowed the planets and stars." (See Ethical Culture.) {RAT}

Martin, Bon Louis Henri (1810–1883)

Martin was a French historian, whose nineteen-volume *History of France* (1838–1853) was a monumental work of erudition. A confirmed Republican, he opposed the Second Empire and, after its fall, became a member of the National Assembly in 1871 and a senator in 1876. Martin became an elected member of the Academy in 1878. In addition to his historical works he contribute to *Le Siecle, la Liberté de Penser*, and *l'Encyclopédie Nouvelle*. {BDF; RAT}

Martin, Clem (20th Century)

Martin, a physician, signed Humanist Manifesto II. {HM2}

Martin, Dexter (20th Century)

Martin, a retired professor of literature, is a freethinker who has written widely and with a distinctive sense of humor. To close friends, Martin confesses that he is head of Outcast College for the "unaccredited and contented." Among his pamphlets are " 'Dirty Words' In The Bible"; "Why Blacks Should Burn the Bible," for its God sanctions slavery, as does Jesus; "Craziness of the Catholic Mass," about eating the body and drinking the blood of God; and "Masturbation in the Bible"; and "Asking God to Cheat in Sports," suggesting that God would be breaking rules if He favored one team over the other. "Would a decent father like to see some of his children defeat his other ones and make them feel miserable? If you beg God to give your team a victory, aren't you unconsciously hoping He'll be unlawful, unjust, and unpaternal? If you thank Him afterwards, shouldn't you also say, 'I'm grateful to you, God, for granting us an unfair advantage by Your invisible presence and influence. I'm happy You didn't believe as a father should'?" In 1993, he wrote, "Skeptical Essays About Religious Question," five works showing his continued irreverence.

Martin, Emma (1812–1851)

Martin wrote a freethought tract in 1844, "Baptism a Pagan Rite," followed in 1848 by "The Bible: No Revelation" and "Reasons for Renouncing Christianity." She is known mainly as a lecturer, "a handsome woman, of brilliant talent and courage." An ex-Baptist, she was fined but not jailed for her activism upon behalf of freethought. It had been the trials of Holyoake and Southwell for blasphemy that had led her to inquire about and embrace the freethought cause. While Holyoake and Paterson were in jail, Mrs. Martin went about committing the "crime" for which they were imprisoned.

Underwood states that Martin did not live to reach her fortieth birthday, dying of consumption "just as she was beginning to develop the full strength of her intellect and to realize the full value of life." She passed away "calmly, undismayed by any superstitious fears, conscious of that integrity of soul and clearness of conscience, which proves ever an armor of defense in every supreme hour of life." Funeral services were conducted "on strictly rationalistic principles, in accordance with her own express desire, her personal friend and admirer, George Jacob Holyoake, making the address, and speaking to the friends present in behalf of the deceased." Holyoake in the address said, "In courage of advocacy and thoroughness of view, no woman, except Frances Wright, is to be compared with her, and only one, Harriet Martineau (greater, indeed, in order of power), resembles Mrs. Martin in largeness and sameness of speculation, and her capacity to treat purely social questions, and those relating to woman. She had an affectionate nature, which astonished those who knew her in private, as much as her resolution astonished those who knew her in public. Indeed, she was the most womanly woman of all the public advocates of Woman's Rights."

In 1848 a circumstantial account of her death-bed recantation was circulated in Scotland at a time when, actually, she was lecturing in London. Three years later she did die after severe suffering. Eight days prior to her death, G. J. Holyoake visited and found her reading Strauss's *Life of Jesus*. She requested that he speak at her graveside, which he did. His address was published as "The Last Days of Mrs. Emma Martin." Although she had endured her suffering with great fortitude, the Rev. Brewin Grant, in the spirit of evangelical Christianity, described her death as a "dreadful tragedy" and agony as "the eloquent and fitting requiem" for it. {BDF; EU, Victor E. Neuburg; FO; FUK; PUT; SAU; VI; WWS}

Martin, Herbert (20th Century)

Martin, once head of the philosophy department at the University of Iowa in Iowa City, wrote "The Religion of Humanity":

> To serve the present age as best I may
> Is my imperative, moral and religious.
> My country is Humanity, its service my
> Religion. To see my fellows strive for what will
> Satisfy their need, struggling, unavailing oft,
> Rising anew, girded by hope and will to win,
> Defying fate's frustrations to the end—
> All this fills me with reverence, awe,
> and worship.

Martin, James R. (20th Century)

When he signed Humanist Manifesto II, Martin was a humanist counselor. {HM2}

Martin, Jay (20th Century)

Martin is active in the Humanist Community of San Francisco. (See entry for California Atheists, Humanists.) {FD}

Martin, Joanne (20th Century)

In 1995 Martin was elected Vice President of the Northeast Atheist Association.

Martin, Kingsley (1897–1969)

Martin, a writer and editor, in 1958 became an honorary associate of the Rationalist Press Association. His autobiography, published posthumously, is Editor*: New Statesman Years, 1931–1945* (1970). {TRI}

Martin, Louis (19th Century)

Martin, who described himself as an atheist socialist, wrote *Les Evangiles Sans Dieu* (1887). Victor Hugo praised it. {BDF}

Martin, Louis Auguste (1811–1875)

In Paris, Martin edited *Morale Independente* in 1855. One of his works is *Histoire de la femme* (1862). For having written *True and False Catholics* (1858), he was fined three thousand francs and imprisoned for six months. {BDF}

Martin, Michael (20th Century)

Martin is Professor of Philosophy Emeritus, Boston University. In New York, Martin edited *Exit* from 1969 to 1972 and *Repartée* from 1968 to 1972. He is author of *The Case Against Christianity* (1991), in which he critiques the Apostles' Creed, the Nicene Creed, the Athanasian Creed, and other theological concepts.

Also, he wrote *Atheism: A Philosophical Justification* (1990), in which he distinguishes

negative atheism
(that there are no good reasons for belief in God, or that the term "God exists" is not factually meaningful)

from

positive atheism
(the position that "God exists" is a false although meaningful statement).

He cites Voltaire, a deist, as being a nonbeliever. He also cites Upton Sinclair as a being a nonbeliever, although Sinclair was basically a spiritualist. (Note Sinclair's letter herein.)

Martin attempted to revive Joseph Lewis's freethought ventures after Lewis's death in 1968, to limited success. Antony Flew, reviewing *Atheism,* finds it "not a book to put into the hands of someone deliberating whether to become or remain an atheist or a theist." It is, however, satisfactory for someone who has worked "in some other area of philosophy and now wanted to learn what had been happening in the philosophy of religion during the last forty or so years." He adds, "Such a reader would not be put off by the amount of formalism in which Martin indulges, and would not require an explanation—which Martin neglects to provide—of the symbol "IFF." [IFF = if and only if] On the other hand even the reader would presumably need some indication—which is again not provided—of the contents of Antony Flew's well known "Theology and Falsification."

A contributing editor for *Free Inquiry*, Martin also wrote *The Big Domino in the Sky, and Other Atheistic Tales* (1996), stories which reveal the fallacies of traditional arguments for the existence of God and the improbability of God's existence given the evil in the universe. He is an honorary associate of the New Zealand Association of Rationalists and Humanists.

Martin, who signed Humanist Manifesto 2000, is a supporter of Internet Infidels and a contributing editor of *Philo*. On the Web: <http://www.infidels.org/library/modern/michael_martin/martin-bio.html> {E; *Free Inquiry*, Fall, 1990 and Fall 1997; GS; Antony Flew, *New Humanist*, February 1995}

Martin, Oscar (20th Century)

A New Zealand student of commerce and computer science, Martin is vice-president of Auckland University Atheists. After graduating, he sophomorically taunted opponents of atheism, "I intend to go on a church-burning psychotic rampage." E-Mail: <peacenet@ihug.co.nz>.

Martin-Diaz, James Robert (20th Century)

Martin-Diaz is an editorial associate for *Free Inquiry*. In 1982, he edited *Engineers for the Public Good*.

Martinaud, M. (19th Century)

Martinaud was an ex-abbé who refused ordination and wrote to his bishop *Letters of a Young Priest, who is an Atheist and Materialist* (1868). In it, he stated, "Religion is the infancy of peoples, atheism their maturity." {BDF}

Martineau, Harriet (1802–1876)

"From the moment a man desires to find the truth on one side rather than another, it is all over with him as a philosopher," wrote Martineau in her "Letters on the Laws of Man's Nature and Development." The youngest of eight children of a Norwich (England) silk manufacturer, she was a sister of the Rev. James Martineau, who attained a celebrity nearly equal to her own and was nearest to her in age. Her family had once been driven with thousands of their fellow Huguenots from France to England, a story she heard often from her parents. In spite of her increasing deafness as a child, she was sent to singing schools and became an accomplished performer upon the piano until her infirmity caused her to lose interest. As for her health, "I have never," she once wrote, "had the sense of smell, nor, therefore, much sense of taste; and before I was twenty I had lost the greater part of my hearing. When my companions give me notice of distant objects by means of any of these senses—when they tell me what is growing in an invisible field or garden, or where there is music, or what people are saying on the farther side of a reach of the lake on a calm summer evening, I feel a sort of start, as if I were in company with sorcerers."

Lacking the exercise of her senses, however, she developed an interest in writing, according to Underwood. "When the great comet of 1811 appeared, I was nine years old," Martineau wrote. "Night after night that autumn the whole family went up to the long range of windows in my father's warehouse to see the comet. I was obliged to go with them, but I never once saw it! My heart used to swell with disappointment and mortification. No effort was wanting on my part; and parents, brothers, and sisters used to point and say, 'Why, there! Why, it is as large as a saucer! You might as well say you cannot see the moon!' I could not help it; I never saw it, and I have not got over it yet."

Martineau's religious education had been in the Unitarian faith, and her first work, published in 1823, was "Devotions for Young People." Her next was a religious novel, *Christmas Day*. In 1930 when the British and Foreign Unitarian Association offered prizes for the three best tracts—"On the Introduction and Promotion of Christian Unitarianism among the Roman Catholics, the Jews, and Mohammedans"—Martineau competed for all three. Although there were three separate sets of judges, Martineau won all three prizes.

From 1839 to 1844, Martineau was a confirmed invalid. But she continued to write, even when prostrate in bed with illness. Somehow, with the aid of mesmerism, her health improved to the point that in 1840, ear trumpet in hand, she toured Egypt, Palestine, and Arabia, writing an account of her the friends she made and finishing an essay on the life and purposes of Moses and his dealings with the Israelites of old. "It is my deliberate opinion that the one essential requisite of human welfare in all ways is scientific knowledge of human nature," wrote Martineau, whose collections of stories interpreted economics to the laymen of her time.

In her youth, Martineau had attended services at the Octagon Chapel, and she had an article published in *Monthly Repository*, which she described as "a poor little Unitarian periodical." She wrote *Illustrations of Political Economy* (9 volumes) and *Illustrations of Taxation* (1834). Her unflattering description of the United States in *Society in America* (1837) was accompanied by her becoming an advocate for the abolition of slavery.

When she openly avowed her unbelief concerning religion, even her brother, James, censured her publicly for her atheism. One Christian reviewer remarked that her work "is exceedingly interesting, but it is marred by the mocking spirit of Infidelity which she allows for the first time to darken her pages and testify to the world her disbelieve in the Divine revelation." Even her friend, Charlotte Brontë, "grieved sadly over this declension on the part of one whom she admired as combining the highest mental culture with the nicest discharge of feminine duties. The book (*Eastern Life*), Brontë said, was the first exposition of avowed atheism and materialism she had ever read—the first unequivocal declaration of a disbelief of God or a future life. Hundreds, she said, had deserted Miss Martineau on account of this book." Martineau, however, denied losing any friends whatever by her book and, in fact, said she had gained a new world of sympathy. And she persisted: "There is no theory of a God, of an author of Nature, of an origin of the Universe, which is not utterly repugnant to my faculties; which is not (to my feelings) so irreverent as to make me blush; so misleading as to make me mourn. I can now hardly believe that it was I who once read Milton with scarcely any recoil from the theology; or Paley's *Natural Theology* with pleasure at the ingenuity of the mechanic-god he thought he was recommending to the admiration of his readers. . . . What an emancipation it is—to have escaped from the little enclosure of dogma, and to stand—far indeed from being wise—but free to learn!"

Nathaniel Hawthorne described her as follows: "She is a large, robust, elderly woman, and plainly dressed; but, withal, she has so kind, cheerful, and intelligent a face that she is pleasanter to look at than most beauties. . . . All her talk was about herself and her affairs; but it did not seem like egotism, because it was so cheerful and free from morbidness. And this woman is an atheist, and thinks that the principle of life will become extinct when her body is laid in the grave! I will not think so, were it only for her sake."

Martineau's *Autobiography*, published after her death, shows the full extent of her unbelief, for she had also repudiated her Unitarianism. In it she described herself as "an atheist in the regular sense—that of rejecting the popular theology—but not in the philosophic sense of denying a First Cause." However, adds McCabe, "her First Cause was impersonal and she rejected immortality." Martin Greif has praised her for her feminism and alleged lesbianism, although no specific names of her loves were cited.

Fewer than six weeks before her death, Martineau wrote her last letter, to H. G. Atkinson, which included the following:

> I cannot think of any future as at all probable, except the "annihilation" from which some people recoil with so much horror. I find myself here in the universe—I know not how, whence or why. I see everything in the universe go out and disappear, and I see no reason for supposing that it is not an actual and entire death. And for my part, I have no objection to such an extinction.
>
> I well remember the passion with which W. E. Forster said to me, "I had rather be damned than annihilated." If he once felt five minutes' damnation, he would be thankful for extinction in preference. The truth is, I care little about it any way. Now that the event draws near, and that I see how fully my household expect my death pretty soon, the universe opens so widely before my view, and I see the old notions of death, and scenes to follow so merely human—so impossible to be true, when once glanced through the range of science—that I see nothing to be done but to wait, without fear or hope for future experience, nor have I any fear of it. Under the weariness of illness I long to be asleep.

Martineau's funeral was entirely private and free from religious ceremonial. {BDF; CE; EG; *Freethought History #9*, 1994; Pat Duffy Hutcheon, "Harriet Martineau, The Woman Who Thought Like a Man," *Humanist in Canada*, Summer 1996; JM; Harriet Martineau, *Autobiography* (1877); JMR; RAT; RE; SAU; TRI; WWS}

Martineau, James (1804–1900)

Martineau, a Unitarian and the brother of Harriet Martineau, was an English theologian who upheld the theist position against the negations of physical science. He wrote *A Study of Spinoza* (1881) and *Types of Ethical Theory* (1885). Robertson terms him a philosopher who was rather a coadjutor than a champion of the Unitarian sect. {CE; JMR; JMRH; U}

Martins, Charles Frédéric (1806–1889)

In 1863 Martins became corresponding member of the Academy of Sciences. A botanist, he wrote an introduction to Lamarck's *Philosophie Zoologique* (2 vols., 1873), in which he professed agnosticism, rejected materialism and spiritualism, and was negative in his views of myths and churches. {RAT}

Marty, Martin E. (1928–)

Marty wrote *The Infidel: Freethought and American Religion* (1961), an anti-freethought book according to Gordon Stein. Affiliated with the University of Chicago, Marty headed up the Fundamentalist Project.

In 1998 at a symposium, "The Role of Religion in Public Life" sponsored by Minnesota Public Radio (MPR), however, he said, "It is the role of unbelievers to force religions to be benign," a comment which Marie Castle found was analogous to Steve Allen's suggestion that the task of atheists is to civilize the Christians. Castle found Marty "a long way from being religious in the sense of believing biblical mythology. He may be closer to being a deist than anything." Nominally, he is a Lutheran. {GS; *Secular Nation*, July-September 1998}

MARTYR

• To die for an idea is to set a rather high price upon guesswork.

—**Anatole France**

• A thing is not necessarily true because a man dies for it.

–Oscar Wilde

Religious martyrs are willing to suffer persecution for their faith, including undergoing torture or death. In the days of the Romans, martyrs who became victims were revered to the point that even any object associated with them was venerated. Relics came in three classes: (a) the body of a saint, or any part thereof; (b) any part of his clothing; and (c) a prayerbook. Chaucer has described how animal bones were sold as saints' bones to gullible country parsons, pointing up the fact that the Papacy long has had a problem authenticating relics.

In the 1990s, "living martyrs" have videotaped goodbye messages before committing suicide. Saleh Abdel Rahim al-Souwi, for example, carried an estimated forty pounds of explosives onto an Israeli bus, killing himself and over twenty Jews as well as injuring dozens more. In the videotape he had made beforehand, he said, "It is good to die as a martyr for Allah." Holding a rifle and using quotations from the Qur'an, he added, "Sages end up in paradise." A young Palestinian, he left behind his family and parents. His father, although giving his condolences to the victims' families, said his son "is lucky to be a martyr."

Marvin, Burdette K. (20th Century)

Marvin wrote *Christian Teaching: An Inquiry* (1949). {GS}

Marvin, F. S. (20th Century)

Marvin has been an active member of the American Humanist Association. {HNS}

Marvin Francis Sydney (1863–1943)

Marvin, a positivist writer, wrote *The Living Past* (1913). He was an inspector of schools and was a divisional inspector and inspector of training colleges. He wrote *The Unity of Western Civilization* (1970). {RAT}

Marx, Karl (1818–1883)

"The first requisite for the happiness of the people is the abolition of religion," wrote Marx, a philosopher and revolutionary theorist who was descended from a line of rabbis and brought up as a Lutheran. He came to believe that "The proofs of the existence of God are nothing but proofs for the existence of the essentially human self-consciousness. . . . Man is the supreme being for man. . . . Atheism and communism . . . are but the first real coming-to-be, the realization become real for man, of man's essence."

According to Stack, Marx began and ended his productive life with a few basic assumptions: "(1) that religious beliefs channel human energy and hope into another, ethereal world and thereby divert man's efforts from the improvement of his earthly estate; (2) that the capitalist economy, especially in the form of political economy, is unjust and encourages egoism and selfishness, breeding 'social atoms' that are only interested in their own welfare; (3) that there are 'laws' governing human history, principles of economic evolution, and dialectical opposition that derive from the historical pattern of 'class conflict'; (4) that a truly human society of communal cooperation toward a common end is possible; (5) that man must overcome both religious and economic alienation if he would attain genuine emancipation; and (6) that the capitalist system of economy entails basic 'contradictions' (especially that engendered by the collective production of goods and the unequal benefits of the distribution of these goods) that will eventually lead to its negation."

Leon Trotsky's former secretary, Raya Dunayevskaya, described Marx's philosophy in *The Humanist Alternative* (1973) as "a new Humanism." Dunayevskaya adds that Karl Marx was a thoroughgoing naturalist who at first had called his outlook "a new humanism," by which he meant a Marxist rather than a communistic humanism. McCabe, saying that Marx is often credited with having said that religion is "the opium of the people," wrote that that description might initially have been written by the Rev. Charles Kingsley, a Christian Socialist. In his *Criticism of the Hegelian Philosophy of Right* (1844), Marx wrote, "Religion is the sigh of the oppressed creature, the feelings of a heartless world, just as it is the spirit of unspiritual conditions." He then added, "It is the opium of the people."

Marx declared that "the workers have nothing to lose in this [revolution] but their chains. They have a world to gain. Workers of the world, unite!" He claimed that the phrase "dictatorship of the proletariat" was coined by Louis Auguste Blanqui (1805–1881), and at one point he said, according to Engels in a letter to C. Schmidt, "All I know is that I am not a Marxist." Nevertheless, in an 1852 letter he summarized his achievements: "What I did that was new was to prove…that the class struggle necessarily leads to the dictatorship of the proletariat." In his *Theses on Feuerbach* (published 1888), Marx wrote, "The philosophers have only interpreted the world in various ways; the point is to change it."

Corliss Lamont considered Marx a dialectical materialist who differed from naturalistic humanists by his ambiguous attitude toward democracy and his acceptance of determinism.

Bertrand Russell objected to Marx for two reasons: "one, that he was muddle-headed; and the other, that his thinking was almost entirely inspired by hatred." Russell added, in his *Portraits From Memory* (1956), "The doctrine of surplus value, which is supposed to demonstrate the exploitation of wage earners under capitalism, is arrived at, (a) by surreptitiously accepting Malthus's doctrine of population, which Marx and all his disciples explicitly repudiate; (b) by applying Ricardo's theory of value to wages, but not to the prices of manufactured articles. . . . His belief that there is a cosmic force called Dialectical Materialism which governs human history independently of human volitions, is mere mythology. His theoretical errors, however, would not have mattered so much but for the fact that, like Tertullian and Carlyle, his chief desire was to see his enemies punished, and he cared little what happened to his friends in the process."

One of his works, *On Religion* (translated into English by the USSR, 1975) greatly disturbed leaders of the various organized religions. Socialism was greatly affected by political Marxism, but many Socialists following the 1917 Russian Revolution disassociated themselves from Soviet Communism. Although some ensuing Communist regimes claimed to be orthodox Marxists, they often interpreted the views of Marx in greatly different ways. With the dramatic fall of the USSR and other communist nations in the 1990s, Marx's influence has dwindled but not disappeared.

Marx died in his sixties while writing at his worktable. Allegedly, among his last words were these: "Get out of here and leave me alone. Last words are for fools who haven't said enough already." At Marx's funeral, Stephen Jay Gould noted, "Only nine people were there." Marx is buried in London's Highgate cemetery. A bronze bust perches atop a stone block with the words,

> Workers of all lands unite.
> The philosophers have only interpreted the world
> in various ways;
> the point is to change it

His wife Jenny (died 1881) and daughter Eleanor (died 1898) lie adjacent. Just across the way lies social reformer Herbert Spencer. (See entry for Louis Blanc, author of the phrase "Let each produce according to his aptitudes . . . let each consume according to his need." Also see entries for Communistic Humanism and Communistic Christian Settlements.) {CE; CB; EU; FUK; JM; PA; RAT; RE; *The New York Times*, 26 June 1999; TRI}

MARXISM À LA MAO AND KISSINGER [TOP SECRET]

> Chairman Mao [of China]: Do you pay attention or not to one of the subjects of Hegel's philosophy, that is the unity of opposites?
>
> Henry Kissinger[United States Secretary of State]: Very much. I was much influenced by Hegel in my philosophic thinking.
>
> Mao: Both Hegel and Feuerbach who came a little later after him. They were both great thinkers. And Marxism came partially from them. They were predecessors of Marx. If it were not for Hegel and Feuerbach there would not be Marxism.
>
> Kissinger: Yes, Marx reversed the tendency of Hegel, but he adopted the basic theory.
>
> Mao: What kind of doctor are you? Are you a doctor of philosophy?
>
> Kissinger: Yes. (laughter) . . . . I can't read German in its original form. I must translate into English, because it is too complicated in its original form. This is quite true. Some of the points of Hegel—quite seriously—I understand better in English than in German, even though German is my mother language.
>
> –from *The Kissinger Transcripts: The Top-Secret Talks with Beijing and Moscow* (1998)

MARY

> • There is no God, and Mary is his mother.
>
> –Gore Vidal in *Palimpsest*, quoting a statement George Santayana is said to have made (See entry for Virgin Mary.)

Mary Magdalen

The Cathari held that Jesus did not die on the cross, that he married Mary Magdalen, that they settled in the Languedoc, and that their heirs founded the Merovingian dynasty that united Christian Europe under Charlemagne. (See entry for Catharism.)

MARY, THE VIRGIN: See entry for Great Mother Goddess.

MARYLAND HUMANISTS

Maryland has the following humanist groups:

• Atheist Students' Association (ASA), University of Maryland at College Park. It was founded by Ali Aliabadi and Brie Waters in 1995. Keith Augustine, a philosophy major, is its secretary.

• Baltimore Secular Humanists (ASHS; a chapter of WASH), PO Box 24115, Baltimore, Maryland 21227; telephone Ken Marsalek (410) 467-3225. Contact: Don Evans at <don.evans@cwix.com>.

• District of Columbia Chapter (WASH), PO Box 15319, Washington, DC 20003; (202) 546.7430. E-mail: <lgporter@erols.com>.

• Frederick Secular Humanists (ASHS; a chapter of WASH), 123 West 2nd St., Frederick MD 21701; (301) 631-5982). E-mail: <frank_greene@compuserve.com> and <jewell_kross@ftdetrck-ccmail.army.mil>. 18 South Jefferson St., Frederick, Maryland 21901; (301) 619-3680.

E-mail: <jewell_kross@ftdetrck:ccmail.army.mil>.

• Humanist Association of the National Capital Area (AHA), POB 2465, Wheaton, Maryland 20902. Roy Toracaso is its contact.

• Johns Hopkins University Atheists are at <http://www.secularhumanism.org/cfa/orgs.html>.

• Maryland-District of Columbia Secular Humanist Chapter of WASH (ASHS), PO Box 15319, Washington, DC 20003; (202) 298-0921.

• Mid Atlantic Region (AHA), 3708 Brightview Street, Wheaton, Maryland 20902. Roy Torcaso is coordinator for the District of Columbia, Delaware, Maryland, and Virginia.

• University of Maryland Atheist Students Association is on the Web: <http://www.secularhumanism.org/cfa/orgs.html>.

Masaryk, Jan (1886–1948)

Jan, the son of Tomás Masaryk, followed in his father's political footsteps. During World War II, he became foreign minister of the Czech government-in-exile, continuing until 1945, at which time and shortly after the Communist coup in 1948 he committed suicide. His death, for he leaped from a window and the news media publicized the event, was alleged to have been his final act of defying the Communists. Others allege he was killed. Masaryk was a Unitarian. {CE; JM; UU}

Masaryk, Tomás Garrigue [President] (1850–1937)

Masaryk, a Czech patriot, statesman, sociologist, and philosopher, believed that philosophy should not only contemplate the world but also should try to change it. He cared little for epistemology, but he accepted Hume's empiricism and Comte's positivism. After being professor of philosophy at the University of Prague, he led the independence movement from 1907 on, becoming Czechoslovakia's first president (1918–1935) following World War I. In 1923, the Liberal Fellowship was formed, and that led to the establishment of the Religious Society of Czechoslovakian Unitarians. More a positivist than a freethinker, he believed in "the supreme moral and religious command to love men."

Although not a Unitarian himself, he was said to have found his wife's Unitarianism congenial. In his *Ideale der Humanitat* (1902), Masaryk professed agnosticism, according to McCabe, and he took part openly in the international freethought movement. In 1938, Masaryk wrote *Modern Man and Religion* (1938). {RAT; RE; TRI}

Mascagni, Pietro (1863–1945)

Mascagni's "Cavalleria Rusticana" (1890) gave him a worldwide reputation as an excellent Italian composer. Although he wrote church music, Mascagni according to his biographer, G. Bastianelli was a pagan even in his religious compositions and had "no religion." {JM; RAT; RE}

Masci, Filippo (1844–1901)

Masci, an Italian philosopher, was a Commander of the Crown of Italy, Rector of Naples University, Secretary of the Royal Society of Naples, and member of the Council of Higher Education. In his writings such as *Psicologia religiosa* and *Elementi filosofici*, he held that matter and spirit are two aspects of one evolving reality. {RAT}

Maslow, Abraham H. (1908–1970)

Maslow is regarded as the founder of humanistic psychology. In 1927 at City College of New York, when introduced to William Graham Summer's *Folkways*, Maslow found that the book freed him from his "simple, unquestioning ethnocentrism" and changed the way he saw the world. As described by Richard J. Lowery in *A. H. Maslow: An Intellectual Portrait*, Maslow came to believe the following:

> Man has a higher nature and . . . this is part of his essence. . . . We need not take refuge in supernatural gods to explain our saints and

sages and heroes and statesmen, as if to explain our disbelief that mere unaided human beings could be that good or wise.

Maslow, who taught at Brandeis University and New York University, was named Humanist of the Year by the American Humanist Association in 1967. With B. Mittelmann, he wrote *Principles of Abnormal Psychology* (1941). Also, he wrote *Motivation and Personality* (1954) and *Religion, Values, and Peak Experiences* (1964).

Maslow was a key influence in Betty Friedan's turn toward secular humanism, she wrote as well as told friends.

Mason, Gabriel Richard (20th Century)

"What I Believe" by Mason appeared in Joseph Lewis's freethought publication, *Age of Reason* (March, 1964). For that magazine he also wrote "Existentialism for Freethinkers" (March, 1965). In 1956 he wrote *Great American Liberals* and, in 1965, *Existentialism for Freethinkers*. With Arthur Burton in 1969, Mason wrote *William James and Religion*.

Mason, Haydn Trevor (1929–)

Prof. Mason in 1988 was elected an honorary associate of the Rationalist Press Association. In 1994, he was the subject of a festschrift, *The Secular City*, edited by T. D. Hemming, E. Freeman, and D. Meakin. The work was subtitled "Studies in the Enlightenment Presented to Haydn Mason" and contained essays in honor of the leading authority in England on Voltaire and eighteenth-century France.

Mason, Josiah [Sir] (1795–1881)

Mason, a British philanthropist, was a Birmingham manufacturer who began life by hawking on the streets at the age of eight. He gave a considerable amount of money to charities, including an orphanage and a college of science. Although his biographer reported that Mason was "not a religious man according to the views of any sect or party" and forbade Christian teaching in his foundations, Mason's wishes were not carried out. The college of science, now incorporated as part of Birmingham University, began with what McCabe calls "the usual clerical influence." Mason was a theist but "the dogmatic ecclesiastical aspects of religion were repugnant to him." {JM; RAT; RE}

Mason, Leonard (20th Century)

Mason is a contributing editor of *Religious Humanism*, a quarterly published by the Fellowship of Religious Humanists.

Mason, Marylin (20th Century)

Mason is the education officer for the British Humanist Association.

MASONIC LODGE, MASONRY: See entry for Freemasons.

MASORETIC

Of the number of ancient versions of the Holy Bible, the Masoretic translation was by the Masoretes, people who tried to preserve unchanged the text of the Hebrew Bible and in so doing provided it with vowel points and copious annotations. The Masorah notes, enumerations of the occurrences of words or concern with their orthography, accumulated from c. 500 to c. 1100. (See entry for Bible.)

Masquerier, Lewis (1802–1888)

An American land reformer of Huguenot descent, Masquerier wrote *The Sataniad*, established *Greenpoint Gazette*, and contributed to the *Boston Investigator*. {BDF}

MASS

For freethinkers and humanists, mass refers to a unified body of matter with no specific shape, as in "a mass of bull dung." But for Christians, Mass (or mass) is a public celebration of the Eucharist, a theological invention having to do with "the Last Supper" and "communion." In England during the Middle Ages, a mass was in honor of a specific person—Michaelmas was the feast day of Michael the angel; Christmas was the feast day of Christ; and so on. (See entries for Universe and Neutrino.) {DCL}

MASSACHUSETTS ATHEISTS, HUMANISTS

Massachusetts has the following groups:

• Amherst College Atheists, Agnostics, Rationalists, and Godless Humanists. On the Web: <www.secularhumanism.org/cfa/orgs.html>

• Coalition of Humanists, Atheists, and Ethical Organizations of New England. Joseph Gerstein is its contact.

• Harvard Secular Society is on the Web: <www.secularhumanism.org/cfa/orgs.html>.

• Humanist Association of Massachusetts (AHA), POB 38-1125, Cambridge, Massachusetts. Joseph Gerstein is President. Executive Director and editor of the newsletter is Tom Ferrick. E-mail: <thomas_ferrick@harvard.edu>. (See entry for Alexander Lincoln Jr.)

• Massachusetts Institute of Technology Atheists, Agnostics, and Humanists on the Web: <www.secularhumanism.org/cfa/orgs.html>.

• Williams College's Doubting Club is at <www.secularhumanism.org/cfa/orgs.html>.

Massen, John B. (1915–)

Massen, the founder, first President, and assistant treasurer of the Atheist Alliance, spoke in 1994 at the Toronto conference of the Coalition for Secular Humanism, Atheism, and Freethought (CSHAFT). He actively publicizes OABITAR (**O**bjectivity, **A**ccuracy and **B**alance **I**n **T**eaching **A**bout **R**eligion, Inc., 1525-A Day Avenue, San Mateo, California 94403). In *Secular Nation*'s first issue (Fall 1994), Massen tells that the new alliance formed "as an alternative to atheist organizations that are totally controlled by a single family," an obvious reference to Madalyn Murray O'Hair. His e-mail: <athalsfj@aol.com>.

Massenet, Jules Emile Frédric (1842–1912)

Massenet, an important French composer, composed more than twenty operas, one of the best known being "Manon" (1884), which exemplifies his sensual style and contains accompanied spoken dialogue rather than the traditional recitative. A freethinker, Massenet also wrote a daring and popular oratorio on "Mary Magdeleine" and an opera, "Herodiade." {BDF; CE; JM; RAT; RE; TYD}

Massey, Gerald (1829–1907)

Massey was an Egyptologist who published *A Book of Beginnings, Natural Genesis*, and *Ancient Egypt: The Light of the World* (1907). George Eliot, impressed by what she had read about him, cast Massey as the character of Felix Holt in her novel of the same name. In *Natural Genesis* he had a chapter on "The Historical Jesus and Mythical Christ," which has appealed to contemporary freethinkers. Massey was born of poor parents and was sent to a factory at the age of eight to earn a miserable pittance. At fifteen, he left Tring for London, was an errand boy, and after reading widely became a freethinker and political reformer. The *Spirit of Freedom* that he started in 1849 cost him five situations in eleven months. Massey lectured widely on such subjects as "Why Don't God Kill the Devil?" and "The Historical Jesus and the Mythical Christ." {BDF; RAT}

Massol, Marie Alexandre (1805–1875)

Massol was a French writer who studied under Raspail, then went to Paris and became a Saint Simonian. In 1848 he wrote on Lamennais's *La Réforme* and worked on the *Voix du Peuple* (Voice of the People) with his friend Proudhon, to whom he became executor. In 1865 he established *La Morale Independante* with the object of showing that morality has nothing to do with theology. {BDF; RAT}

Masterman, Patrick (20th Century)

A theist who is anti-atheistic, Masterman is author of *Atheism and Alienation: A Study of the Philosophical Sources of Contemporary Atheism* (1971). {*Freethought History #9*, 1994}

Masters, Edgar Lee (1869–1950)

Author of the best-selling *Spoon River Anthology* (1915), Masters amused a large audience by his collection of free-verse epitaphs in which the sins and scandals of small-town folks were bared. But his was an anti-democratic outlook filled with a bleak view about man. If there is a God, and he didn't believe there is, then God gets the blame for the catastrophes which both the good and evil people must endure. His cynicism is anti-humanistic, and his view élitist to many; to others he was a cynic but also a secularist and a humanist. *Lincoln, the Man* (1931) expresses the viewpoint that Lincoln was no friend of liberty. His *Serpent in the Wilderness* (1933) contained his poetry. Masters, a friend of Vachel Lindsay, was a law partner of Clarence Darrow.

Jefferson Howard, one of the individuals depicted in *Spoon River Anthology*, is likely a picture of Masters himself, according to May Swenson. Thomas Jefferson was an idol of Masters, and Howard's epitaph read

> Foe of the church with its charnel dankness,
> Friend of the human touch of the tavern. . . .

In a 1942 interview by Robert van Gelder of *The New York Times*, Masters said,

> I am a Hellenist. . . . The great marvel of the world is Greek civilization. They thought in universals, as did the Elizabethans. We are provincial in our thoughts.

He previously had declared,

> Many books have been written to show that Christianity has emasculated the world, that it shoved aside the enlightenment and wisdom of Hellas for a doctrine of superstition and ignorance.... Hebraic and Christian anthropomorphism . . . has done so much to curse the world.

Masters had a sense of humor, as shown in the following poem entitled "The Convert":

> Friend in China write me letter of great missionary
> Who convert many Chinese people.
> And say if they believe they can eat poison,
> And handle serpents, as written in Holy Scripture.
> Chan Chou accept Jesus, and is baptized.
> Then handle cobra to prove he believe.
> Cobra bite Chan Chou, and he die.
> Missionary say Chan Chou die because he did not believe.
> I say he believe or would not handle cobra.

According to Swenson, "In *Spoon River*, Masters borrowed the mouths of the dead to give outlet to all his grudges, beliefs, indignations, insights, prophesies, discoveries of glaring injustice, revelations of life's mysteries and paradoxes—and his own eccentric philosophy. Miraculously he also created and bequeathed to us a world in microcosm, new in form, timeless in essence." {CE; CL; EU, William F. Ryan; May Swenson, Introduction to *Spoon River Anthology*, 1962; TYD}

Mastroianni, Marcello (1923–1996)

Mastroianni, an Italian movie actor noted for his good looks and introspective air, was directed by Federico Fellini in "La Dolce Vita" (1959), "8 1/2" (1963), and "City of Women" (1978). "I loved life, and I was loved back," the son of a cabinetmaker was once quoted as saying.

Upon his death, his former lover, Catherine Deneuve; their daughter Chiara Mastroianni; and Anna-Maria Tato, his companion of the last twenty-two years, attended a funeral at the St.-Sulpice Church in Rome. The church benediction—no Mass was offered—was a compromise between Ms. Deneuve, a practicing Roman Catholic, and Ms. Tato, who opposed it because the actor was not religious. The coffin with his body was then brought from Paris to Rome, where it was received by Flora Carabella, whom he had married in 1948, and their daughter, Barbara. Both had arranged for the secular service, stating that the actor had made it clear he did not want a religious burial. Thousands, including fellow actor Sophia Loren, attended the outdoor funeral.

MASTURBATION

• Masturbate: to read X-rated material with one hand.

–Anonymous

The *Catechism of the Catholic Church* (1994) states that the deliberate stimulation of the genital organs in order to derive sexual pleasure "is an intrinsically and gravely disordered action. . . . The deliberate use of the sexual faculty, for whatever reason, outside of marriage is essentially contrary to its purpose."

A 1741 pamphlet by a Swiss physician, S. A. D. Tissot, "Onanism, or a Treatise on the Disorders of Masturbation," sounded a general alarm that masturbation was not only immoral but also it was dangerous, that it drained the body of vital fluids and caused neuroses which could damage the nervous system. A few years later, Benjamin Rush, a signer of the Declaration of Independence and a physician who bled and purged patients, wrote that masturbation caused poor eyesight, epilepsy, memory loss, and tuberculosis, that masturbators were easy to spot because they looked sickly and repugnant. Charles Dickens in 1850 continued the idea, describing Uriah Heep as a pale creature who lacked eyebrows and had red eyes and clammy hands which he chafed together constantly, and "everyone knew he was a masturbator." (As further evidence of non-scientific declarations at that time, Dr. William Finley Semple of Mount Vernon, Ohio, in 1869 warned that using "the rubbery abomination" of chewing gum, "would exhaust the salivary glands and cause the intestines to stick together.")

J. H. Kellogg, who invented corn flakes, informed parents in *Plain Facts for Young and Old Embracing the Natural History and Hygiene of Organic Life* (1888), that among the thirty-nine signs of masturbation were acne, bashfulness, boldness, nail biting, use of tobacco, and bed wetting. He recommended bandaging children's genitals, or enclosing them in a cage, or simply tying the children's hands. Kellogg recommended circumcising boys without an anesthetic, and he recommended applying carbolic acid on the girls' clitorises . . . adding without documentation that eating corn flakes daily would prevent the vile practice.

Mark Twain had a comment about masturbation which is believed to be similar to that of other non-believers who prefer the Ancient Greek over the Ancient Hebrew viewpoint: "The signs of excessive indulgence in this destructive pastime are easily detectable. They are these: A disposition to eat, to drink, to smoke, to meet together convivially, to laugh, to joke, and tell indelicate stories—and mainly a yearning to paint pictures."

Journalist Gina Kolata has written, "Some 19th-century inventors patented devices to stop masturbation, including a genital cage that held a boy's penis and scrotum with springs, an alarm sounding when an erection occurred. Though later reformers like Sigmund Freud later denounced these remedies, they believed that the act could cause impotence, premature ejaculation, and a dislike of intercourse."

The dancer Vaslav Nijinsky, at the time that he was found by the psychiatrist Eugen Bleuler to be "a confused schizophrenic with mild manic excitement," not only believed he had become God; he also believed that he would now convert the world back to feeling rather than thinking, that his servants were having sex with animals, and that his four-year-old daughter Kyra's masturbating would cause her mental and physical breakdown. According to Peter Ostwald's *Vaslav Nijinsky: A Leap into Madness* (1991), Nijinsky was repeating a common assumption of the 1910s.

Meanwhile, surveys show that 60% of adult men and 40% of adult women masturbated in the past year and that 90% of teen-age boys and 65% to 70% of teen-age girls masturbated, leading Kolata to add, "Today, Americans presumably know better." In short, smart children learn from each other that the cause of it all is their parents' ignorance in believing the Old Testament "sin of Onan," the spilling of seed on barren ground. The not-so-smart parrot the perverse view that masturbation (and, for some, all sex) is bad for your health. The great majority are aware that masturbation is but one small facet of healthy sex.

Sometimes called "the last taboo," masturbation in 1994 was mentioned favorably by the African American Surgeon General, Joycelyn Elders. Her clumsily improvised answer to a question at a United Nations conference was misconstrued to mean she favored *instructing* students how to masturbate, whereas she had merely said the subject was one about which schools should *inform* and not necessarily be excluded from sex education discussion in schools.

Commented journalist Frank Rich when the Surgeon General was forced to leave office, "Surely the President knows that anyone who needs masturbation lessons is unlikely to meet the minimal intellectual requirements for school attendance anyway." Rich added, after comedians brought the subject further out of the closet, "The more people talk about masturbation, the more fears can be dispelled among those young people who still worry that the act turns one into "a confirmed and degraded idiot" —which was the serious concern of Sylvester Graham, inventor of the graham cracker, from his popular 1834 book, *A Lecture to a Young Man*." (Rich and Elders could not have known that the President in 1998 would himself be described by Monica Lewinsky as having engaged in oral sex with him in the White House but that he had finished himself off in the bathroom, a tale that titillated individuals around the world.)

Meanwhile in the 1990s, the comic Woody Allen cautioned individuals, "Don't knock masturbation—it's sex with someone I love."

Mata, Pedro (1875–1946)

Mato was a Spanish physician, a professor at the University of Madrid. He wrote *Glory and Martyrdom* (1851), poetry, as well as *A Treatise on Human Reason* (1858-1864) and *On Moral Liberty and Free Will* (1868). {BDF}

MATERIALISM

Materialism is a widely held system of thought that explains the nature of the world as entirely dependent on matter, the final reality. Early materialists such as Democritus, Epicurus, and the proponents of Stoicism, conceived of reality as material in nature. In the 17th century the theory continued, and in the 18th century Locke's investigations were adapted to the materialist position. In the 19th century, it developed in the form of dialectical materialism and in the formulations of logical positivism.

In *Humanist Sermons* (1927), John Dietrich and Curtis Reese wrote

> Humanism is not Materialism. Humanism holds the organic, not the mechanistic or materialistic, view of life. . . . Humanism encourages research in the realm of the spirit.

Thus countering the link of materialism to a deterministic, mechanistic view of the universe and reality, the two early Unitarian religious humanists used "spirit" in the old sense, much as we talk of "team spirit" or a "spirited person" or even "keeping one's spirits up" when ill or suffering, Jone Johnson has noted. Organic views, such as the naturalism of Dewey, were not meant to isolate the so-called spiritual issues.

As a term, materialism often implies a narrow reductionist view that is not a necessary prerequisite for either a naturalist or a humanistic approach, Alan Levin has observed. "The term has received a black eye because of Marx's 'dialectic materialism.' When Marx used the phrase, he implied a hidden unmeasurable mechanism, thus violating the principle of materialism."

Extreme materialism, according to Keith Campbell in the *Encyclopedia of Philosophy*, "is the view that the real world consists of material things, varying in their states and relations, and nothing else." One 20th century religious leader, Harlem's Reverend Ike in New York City, used to illustrate his faith in "materialism": "I wear $500 suits because the Lord *wants* me to wear $500 suits." Materialists deny the existence of spirit and look for physical explanations for all phenomena. A materialist traces mental states to the brain or nervous system, not to the spirit or the soul. (See entry for Frederick Albert Lange, whose philosophic position was the opposite of the Kantian view of the world. Also, see the entry for Richard C. Vitzthum, whose work on materialism was more favorable than that of Lange. For one view as to how materialism differs from humanism, see the entry for Humanism Per Curtis Reese.) {CE; DCL; RE; WAS, e-mail from Jone Johnson, 23 May 1999 and Alan Levin 23 May 1999}

MATHEMATICS

Science's top unanswered questions:

- How did life begin?
- What is consciousness?
- Why does the universe appear to follow mathematical laws?

Pythagoras dealt with the last question by declaring that numbers are the basic elements of the universe. Some have since assumed that God is the great mathematician, the one who declared, "Let there be numbers" before declaring "Let there be light." Such a view, mathematician George Johnson explains, uses the notion of God metaphorically but embraces the philosophy of Plato "who proposed, rather unscientifically, that numbers and mathematical laws are ethereal ideals, existing outside of space and time in a realm beyond the reach of humankind."

The point of science, however, is to describe the universe without invoking the supernatural. Reuben Hersh in *What is Mathematics Really?* (1997) wrote that "Ideal entities independent of human consciousness violate the empiricism of modern science," insisting that mathematics is more of a human creation, like literature, religion, or banking. Rather than being some ethereal essence, it comes from people who invented, not discovered it.

At the end of the twentieth century, such a human-centered mathematics has gained force and respect. Stanislas Dehaene, in *The Number Sense: How the Mind Creates Mathematics* (1997), [provides experimental evidence to show that the brains of humans—and even of chimpanzees and rats—may come equipped at birth with an innate, wired-in aptitude for mathematics. Gregory J. Chaitin's *The Limits of Mathematics* (1997) takes an anti-Platonist stance. Other contemporary mathematicians no longer take for granted the Platonic creed. Rather than being a Universal Truth, mathematics is a useful invention.

If humans ever were to encounter an alien civilization, would they understand concepts like pi, the ratio of a circle's circumference to its diameter? Platonists assume yes, according to John D. Barrow in *Pi in the Sky* (1992). The anti-Platonists such as Jean-Pierre Changeux, the French neurobiologist, argue against such. "The Platonist claim that every intelligence must produce prime numbers, pi, and the continuum hypothesis," insists Hersh, "is an example of simple anthropomorphism."

When does mathematics start for a human being? Some say it starts with one's heartbeat in the womb, that it is the basis for all music, that its lack of importance in academic circles is lamentable.

Anyone who can explain why the following is the correct answer deserves to be called a mathematician:

```
          .111,111,111
           111,111,111 [multiplied by]
12,345,678,987,654,321
```

(See entries for Population, Human; Population Explosion; and Six Degrees of Separation.) {George Johnson, *The New York Times*, 10 February 1998}

Mather, Cotton (1663–1728)

One of the most celebrated of all New England Puritan ministers, he wrote *Magnalia Christi Americana* (1702), which vaguely shows how the history of Massachusetts demonstrated the working of God's will. He is often depicted as the archetype of the narrow, intolerant, and severe Puritan. He played an important part in the Salem witchcraft trials of 1692. (CE; OCAL; OEL)

Mather, David (19th Century)

In Whitehead and Muhrer's *Freethought on the American Frontier* (1992), Robert M. Wright relates a story about Dodge City, Kansas, which was told by Wright. Mather, or Mathews as Wright called him, was city marshal of Dodge at a time when an itinerant preacher was drawing large crowds to hear his sermons. Hearing that Mather was a wicked man, a killer of killers, so bad that he had killed seven one night in one house and all at one sitting, the preacher was ecstatic one Sunday upon finding Mather in a seat of honor in front of the evangelist. How the preacher rejoiced, how happy he was that in front of the large assemblage he could say he had converted the wickedest man in the county! He was so happy, in fact, he was now willing to die, certain that he would be rewarded by a place in heaven. Whereupon, large numbers agreed, declaring they wanted to die so they too could go to heaven rejoicing together. Then Mather rose. He said at last religion had been poured into him. He could feel it in his fingertips. He was sure that he, too, would go to heaven now that he had experienced the spirit. Then, he pulled out his two six-shooters, saying he would shoot the preacher and them and then himself to insure they all departed together. "I will send you first," he said, firing a shot over the preacher's head. Then he fired several shots in the direction of the faithful. Everyone fell to the floor, afraid. It was at this point that Mather declared, "You are all a set of liars and frauds. You don't want to go to heaven with me at all," whereupon he shot the place up and left. The now powerless preacher left town, too, departing for new fields. Wright ended the story much as fellow Midwesterner Mark Twain would have: "And I am sorry to relate, the people went back to their backsliding and wickedness."

Mather, Increase (1639–1723)

Cotton Mather's father, in *The Mystery of Israel's Salvation*, set the stage for America's apparent need for strong religious leaders as well as for its bibliolatrous future:

> Consider . . . that some of us are under special advantage to understand these mysterious truths of God: that is to say, such of us as are in an exiled condition in this wilderness.... God hath led us into a wilderness, and surely it was not because the Lord hated us but because he loved us that he brought us into this Jeshimon.

Mather was the president of Harvard College (1685–1701) but spent little time in Cambridge. He and his son were outstanding upholders of the old Puritan theocracy and of the established order in church and state. {CE; OCAL; OEL}

Mathewson, Debra (20th Century)

Mathewson is Secretary of Atheists of Northern Colorado. E-mail: <mark_m@sprynet.com>.

Mathiesen, Marius (20th Century)

Mathiesen is an active member of the Norwegian Humanist Association and maintains their web page. E-mail: <mathiesen@human.no>.

Mathews, Harold Victor (1903–)

Mathews is an Australian humanist and educational innovator. He arrived in Australia from South Africa in 1912. In 1946 he became head of Australia's first and only major experimental school. He holds that "speed reading" claims are questionable. Active in Rotary, View, Probus, and Skeptics, he co-authored *Sex for Modern Teenagers* (1968). {SWW}

Matisse, Henri (1869–1954)

Matisse, the French painter, sculptor, and lithographer who along with Picasso is considered one of the two foremost artists of the modern era, was of Flemish descent—the name sometimes was spelled **Mathis** or **Mathisse**. When twenty-nine, he married Amélie Parayre, but it was with his first mistress, Camille Joblaud, that Matisse had his first child. The story of his difficulties in first becoming an artist, and of a "Humbert scandal" involving the Parayre family's finances, has been detailed by Hilary Spurling in *The Unknown Matisse: A Life of Henry Matisse, The Early Years, 1869-1908* (1998). The scandal made Parayre one of the most vilified names of that time, but once the Humberts were found guilty and sentenced to five years' solitary confinement with hard labor both the Parayre and Matisse families felt exonerated. This allowed Matisse to continue his painting, which had been cut short by the "dark period" in his life.

Matisse once wrote, "Ever since there have been men, man has given himself over to too little joy. That alone, my brothers, is our original sin. I should believe only in a God who understood how to dance."

Henry Spurling's *The Unknown Matisse* (1998), confirmed not only that Matisse was "a staunch atheist" but also an anarchist. {TRI; TYD}

Matoub, Lounes (1956-1998)

Matoub, an activist in the Berber cultural movement, was co-founder in 1976 of the Algerian Human Rights League. In 1994 Islamists kidnapped him and repeatedly threatened his life. In 1998 he was murdered in Algeria "for his freethinking and his defiant mountain music.

"They'll never kill him," the singer's sister was quoted as having said. "He has left his songs, which will speak for him." {*The Freethinker*, August 1998}

MATRIARCHY: See entry for Patriarchy.

Matrix-Holt, Cherie (20th Century)

Matrix-Holt, a member of the Central London Humanist Group and a former employee of the British Humanist Association, has written in *New Humanist* (May 1994) about a case in which a number of gay men were imprisoned for consensual sado-masochistic activities. Sado-masochism is not illegal in England and a person cannot consent to assault. But, according to Matrix-Holt, "there are exceptions: casual fighting, ritual circumcision, and beatings for religious purposes (no matter how severe) are allowed. A person can consent to being injured by a medical practitioner. Tattooing and piercing are allowed, yet only for decoration."

Matson, David E. (20th Century)

Matson, a Biblical scholar, has written for *The Skeptical Review*, pointing out many of the theologians' inconsistencies in their attempt to "harmonize" the Bible. Matson, a computer programmer, is editor of the Oak Hill Free Press (PO Box 61274, Pasadena, CA 91116). He has written for *Freethought Perspective*. On the Web: <www.rthoughtsrfree.org/sfw/books.htm>.

Matson, Floyd W(illiam) (1921–)

A professor of American Studies at the University of Hawaii and a former president of the American Association for Humanistic Psychology, Matson is author of *The Broken Image* and *Becoming and Behaviour*. He signed Humanist Manifesto II. {HM2; PK; SHD}

Matson, Rosemary (20th Century)

Matson is a California representative of the National Women's Political Caucus. An activist on behalf of eco-feminist, civil liberties, women's rights, and world peace causes, she was named 1995 Humanist Heroine by the American Humanist Association's Feminist Caucus. {HNS2; *The Humanist*, Nov-Dec 1995}

Matson, Wallace I. (20th Century)

Matson, a freethinker, wrote *The Existence of God* (1965). He wrote *Sentience* (1987). {GS}

Matsumura, Ken (20th Century)

Matsumura is chairman of the Northern California Council of Humanist Organizations (NOCCHO), and he is a director of Secular Humanists of the East Bay (SHEB) in Berkeley, California.

Matsumura, Molleen (20th Century)

Matsumura is a local humanist group leader in East Bay, Berkeley, California, the Network Project Director of the National Center for Science Education, an associate editor of *Free Inquiry*, a Secular Humanist Mentor of the Council for Secular Humanism, and a contributing editor of the *Secular Humanist Bulletin*. In 1991, she collaborated with Fang Fu Ruan, writing *Sex in China*. She also wrote *Voices for Evolution* (1995), a collection of the official position of many groups with regard to the teaching of evolution and creationism. Matsumura is associate director of the National Center for Science Education. In her position, she has blamed America's decentralized education system, which allows countless small decisions on what is taught in schools to be made at the local level. Matsumura signed Humanist Manifesto 2000. {*The Economist*, 17 August 1996; FD; Molleen Matsumura, "Pornography: A Business Like Any Other," *Free Inquiry*, Fall 1997}

Matthews, Dave (20th Century)

On the death of Matthews's sister, the recording artist said he no longer was a believer. "I'm glad some people have that faith. I don't have that faith. If there is a God, a caring God, then we have to figure he's done an extraordinary job of making a very cruel world." {CA}

Mattill, A. J. Jr. (1924–)

In a pamphlet, "Ingersoll Attacks the Bible," Mattill synthesizes a number of Ingersoll's comments about the Bible. Other of his works include *The Seven Mighty Blows to Traditional Beliefs* and *Jesus and the Last Things: The Story of Jesus the Suffering Servant.* He also has written a critique of freethought, *The Art of Reading the Bible*, and a study of Universalism, *The Evolution of American Universalism.* Originally ordained to the ministry of the Evangelical United Brethren Church in 1952, he transferred to Churches of God in North America in 1966, then dropped his ordination and membership to be ordained a Unitarian in 1979. He translated Albert Schweitzer's *The Problem of the Lord's Last Supper* (1982) and wrote *Ingersoll Attacks the Bible* (1987) and *A New Universalism for a New Century* (1989).

Mattill has described his works as "free-thought studies that seek to show the inadequacy of traditional religions and set forth the basic elements of a rational religion." He has written for *Free Inquiry* and is a contributing editor of *The American Rationalist.* {*Free Inquiry*, Spring, 1981; GS}

Mattson, Esther (20th Century)

Mattson was one of the plaintiffs in the lawsuit, *Freedom From Religion Foundation v. Ozaukee County, Wisconsin*, which led that county to abandon its official Good Friday holy day. She received the Freedom From Religion Foundation's 1998 Freethinker of the Year Award. {*Freethought Today*, April 1997}

Matulis, Sherry (1931–)

"I was born an atheist (aren't we all?) in the small town of Nevada, Iowa," Matulis has written. She is a contributor of poetry and articles to *Freethought Today*, which is published by Freedom From Religion Foundation. In 1991 at the 50th annual convention of the American Humanist Association, Matulis was named "Humanist Heroine." In 1954, she experienced a life-threatening illegal abortion sought after she was raped. Often called "the village atheist," Matulis has written,

> Rumor has it that I'm the love child of a clandestine affair between Elizabeth Cady Stanton and Jules Verne, but don't you believe it for a moment. Actually, I'm a libertarian feminist who has devoted the first fifty years of her life primarily to the children of her body, five in number, and who is intent on devoting at least the next fifty to the children of her mind, which at last count number somewhere in the gazillions. {WWS}

Maubert de Gouvest, Jean Henri (1721–1767)

Brought up as a monk, Maubert de Gouvest fled and took service in the Saxon army. He was thrown into prison by the King of Poland, but the Papal nuncio procured his release on condition of his retaking his habit. This he did and went to Rome to be relieved of his vows. Failing this, he went to Switzerland and England, where he was well received by Lord Bolingbroke. Maubert de Gouvest published *Lettres Iroquoises* (1752) and other anonymous works, but in 1764 he was arrested as a fugitive monk and vagabond in Frankfort, where he was imprisoned for eleven months. {BDF}

Maude, Aylmer (1858–1908)

While on business in Moscow from 1880 to 1897, Maude met Tolstoi, whose mysticism he did not share. He collaborated in translating Tolstoi's works and wrote *Tolstoi and his Friends* (1901) and *Life of Tolstoi* (1908–1910). {RAT}

Maudsley, Henry (1835–1916)

Maudsley, who was born in Yorkshire, was educated in London, took mental pathology as his specialty, and reached eminence in his profession. He wrote many works, among them *The Physiology and Pathology of the Mind* (1867) and *Body and Mind* (1870). His *Natural Laws and Supernatural Seemings* (1880) was a powerful exposure of the essence of all superstition. {BDF; RAT; RE}

Maugham, John (Died 1875)

Maugham was a freethought leader in London. He was an opponent of Holyoake and of Bradlaugh's neo-Malthusian policies. {VI}

Maugham, W(illiam) Somerset (1874–1965)

Maugham, an expert storyteller and a master of fictional technique, was orphaned at ten and sent to live with his uncle, a stern vicar. *Of Human Bondage* (1915) describes some of the bondages in life that a person with a clubfoot has—Maugham was a stammerer who empathized with such problems. Another bondage which he described was that of being born into some organized religion, as if the geographical accident must remain permanent. "A Unitarian," he wrote in the novel, "very earnestly disbelieves in almost everything that anybody else believes, and he has a very lively sustaining faith in he doesn't quite know what." (Any rationalist looking for a novel to recommend might well start with this book.)

The Moon and Sixpence (1919) is based on the life of the French painter Paul Gauguin—asked what the title meant, Maugham has been quoted as saying, "People tell me it's a good title but they don't know what it means. It means reaching for the moon and missing the sixpence at one's feet."

One of his better known works is a short story, "Miss Thompson," which reached a wide audience when made into a movie. Maugham wrote with wit and irony, frequently showing a resigned agnosticism combined with a cynical attitude toward life.

Summing Up (1939) includes the following: "The arguments for immortality, weak when you take them one by one, are no more cogent when you take them together. . . . For my part, I cannot see how consciousness can persist when its physical basis has been destroyed, and I am too sure of the interconnection of my body and my mind to think that any survival of my consciousness apart from my body would be in any sense a survival of myself. . . . It has been said that metaphysics is the finding of bad reasons for what we believe on instinct." After discussing religion, he declared "I remain an Agnostic."

The Razor's Edge (1943) is a humanistic account, one that deals with Laurence Darrell, a young American, and his search for "spiritual" fulfillment. Darrell, it could be argued, is the leading fictional proponent of humanistic naturalism. In his search for truths, not Truth, he found,

> I wanted to believe, but I couldn't believe in a God who wasn't better than the ordinary decent man.

He further comes to doubt all the basic tenets of Christian theology; is not satisfied with theologians' answers to his question that, if an all-good and all-powerful God created the world, why did he create evil; and finds interesting the Katha-Upanishad's statement, "The sharp edge of a razor is difficult to pass over; thus the wise say the path to

Salvation is hard." Any rationalist will understand the feeling that Darrell experiences when in India he at last senses why he needs neither a nirvana nor a heaven: the sharp edge of reason had shown him that the ecstasy of life is not dependent upon retiring to a cloister and accepting the various theological explanations but, rather, is connected with understanding the joys of living in *this* world, in loving the objects of *this* world, "not indeed for themselves, but for the Infinite that is in them."

Maugham in 1914 had met Gerald Haxton, a young American who remained his companion until dying in 1944. Maugham is said to have believed that early nights would keep him young, and he used this as an excuse to decline certain invitations. But there is the story that at one party, when a friend encouraged him to stay a little longer, Maugham declined, saying, "I want to keep my youth." Whereupon his bitchy friends, knowing of his bisexuality, chimed in, "Then why didn't you bring him with you so we could meet him?" Maugham was not amused. His son's later accounts of his own and his father's homosexual escapades have dazzled gossips for decades. One story, told by Martin Greif, is that Maugham was injected with cells from sheep fetuses (as allegedly Merle Oberon and also Pope Pius XII had been), and "he delighted in demonstrating to uncomfortable guests his ability to achieve a rampant erection." Another story is that on his deathbed, the elder Maugham grabbed Alan Searle's hand and, whispering to his lover Searle, said, "I want to shake your hand and thank you for all that you've done for me." In another version, his last words were, "Dying is a very dull, dreary affair. And my advice to you is to have nothing whatever to do with it."

In 1949, in *A Writer's Notebook*, Maugham wrote, "What mean and cruel things men do for the love of god." Two years later he wrote the present author concerning humanism:

> The fact is that I know nothing about the philosophy of naturalistic humanism, and so there is nothing I can say about it.

However, soon afterwards he apparently completed some research, for he became associated with the *New Humanist*, a publication of the British Rationalist Press Association (RPA), of which Bertrand Russell was president. Maugham also accepted an honorary associateship from the Rationalist Press Association. {CE; CL; GL; JM; RE; TYD; WAS, 24 March 1951}

MAUI

In Polynesia, the Maui gods were sons of the sun. {LEE}

Maupassant, Guy de (1850–1893)

Maupassant was described by Corliss Lamont as a humanist, an author who is an exemplar of French psychological realism. Before going mad in 1891, Maupassant—whose full name was Henri René Albert Guy de Maupassant—wrote prodigiously about characters that were unhappy victims of their greed, their desire, their vanity. But he describes the sordidness without sermonizing.

Although his short stories are masterpieces and include "The Necklace," "The Piece of String," and "Mlle. Fifi," he is also known for *A Life* (1883), *Bel-Ami* (1885), and *Pierre And Jean* (1880), the latter a study of two brothers and their hatred. The influence of Maupassant upon other writers has been significant. {CE; CL; JMR; RAT; RE; TRI; TYD}

Maupertuis, Pierre Louis Moreau de (1698–1759)

Maupertuis was a French mathematician, geometrician to the Paris Academy of Sciences and one of the chief experts engaged to measure a degree of the meridian. Maupertuis was a friend of Frederic the Great and Voltaire. Besides his many works on mathematics and astronomy, Maupertuis published a rationalist work on religion (in Latin, 1750). He was a member of the French Academy. {RE}

Maurer, George (20th Century)

Maurer, who has been the Treasurer of the Cincinnati, Ohio, Free Inquiry Group, became President in 1998.

Maurois, André: See entry for Charles Mayer.

MAUSOLEUM

• Mausoleum, n. The final and funniest folly of the rich.

—**Ambrose Bierce**
The Devil's Dictionary

Mauvillon, Jakob Von (1743–1794)

Secretary to the King of Poland, Mauvillon wrote several histories. Besides translating and writing intelligently on matters of economic and military science, he became a pronounced heretic, carefully hiding his unbeliefs. A friend and admirer of Mirabeau, he defended the French Revolution in Germany. One of Mauvillon's anonymous works was *The Only True System of the Christian Religion* (1767), which first had the title of *False Reasonings of the Christian Religion*. {BDF; JMR; JMRH; RAT}

Maverick, Maury Jr. (20th Century)

Maverick, a journalist for the *San Antonio Express-News* and a former Texas legislator, wrote *Texas Iconoclast*. He is an activist member of the Freedom From Religion Foundation.

Mawer, W. (19th Century)

Mawer was a freethinker who wrote "Plain Reasons Why Prosecution for Blasphemy Should be Abolished" (1884). {GS}

Maxim, Hiram Stevens [Sir] (1840–1916)

Maxim, the inventor of the Maxim machine gun, was an American who moved to England. Among his inventions were a smokeless powder, a delayed-action fuse, and an airplane. In 1900 he became a British subject and in 1901 he was knighted. His brother Hudson and his son Hiram Percy Maxim were all scientists. McCabe, who knew him well, said that in private Maxim was a virulent atheist. Maxim gave expression to it by making a large collection of criticisms of religion which were arranged in a volume he called *Li Hung-chang's Scrap-Book* (1913). The Chinese statesman, whom he had known, was dead, but Maxim had said he would have agreed for he, also, was a disdainful atheist. He also wrote *My Life* (1915). {JM; RAT; RE}

Max Müller, Friedrich (1823–1900)

Max Müller, a philologist, became the highest authority in Europe on Sanskrit. However, the clergy kept him out because of his advanced rationalism. Max Müller's pantheist views are seen in his *Origin and Growth of Religion* (1878). {RAT; RE}

Maxse, Frederick Augustus (1833–1900)

Maxse's distinguished career in the navy won him the appointment of Rear Admiral. After he retired, he worked for progressive movements, especially rationalism. Maxse was an atheist and, according to George Meredith, a fiery one. {RAT; RE}

Maxwell, Jordan (20th Century)

Maxwell is a freethinker who lectures on astromythology and astrotheology. He has written, "Christians today do not orient themselves to new knowledge or existing factual evidence. They stubbornly cling to these stories and myths that are over 6,000 years old which they have been led to believe, and thus lead others to believe." Jordan appeared on over two hundred radio and television programs across the country, speaking about ancient mysteries of the Bible and similar topics.

Maxwell, Stephen (1953–)

Maxwell is an Australian rationalist, atheist, and plumber. By the age of twelve, he claims to have become an unbeliever despite his and his family's being nominally Catholic. In the 1980s Maxwell joined the Rationalist Association of New South Wales, became treasurer in 1992, and is a regular contributor to *The Rationalist News*. He is author of *The History of Soapbox Oratory, Part One: Prominent Speakers of the Sydney Domain*. {*Freethought History*, #23, 1997; SWW}

May, Samuel (1810–1899)

A Unitarian minister, May was an Abolitionist who wrote *The Fugitive Slave Law and Its Victims* (1856). {U}

May, Samuel Joseph (1797–1871

May, a Unitarian minister, was a prominent Abolitionist. He wrote *On Redemption By Jesus Christ* (1847) and *What Do Unitarians Believe?* (1869). Though both were married, May and educational leader George Barrell Emerson (1797-1881) maintained an intimate sexual friendship for their entire years. {*Improper Bostonians: Lesbian and Gay History from the Puritans to Playland* (1998); U}

May, Walter Victor (Born 1868)

May, a German zoologist, edited the Socialist *Beobachter*. He was imprisoned for twenty-two months for blasphemy. He wrote, besides zoological works, *Goethe, Humboldt, Darwin, Haeckel* (1904), *E. Haeckel* (1909), and other volumes on evolution. In *Wir Ernst Haeckel Verdanken*, May explains that he does not strictly follow Haeckel but is "as far removed as ever from any ecclesiastical creed." {RAT}

Mayabb, Stanley E. (20th Century)

When he signed Humanist Manifesto II, Mayabb was co-founder of the Humanist Group of Vacaville and Men's Colony in San Luis Obispo, California. {HM2}

Mayakovsky, Vladimir (Vladimirovich) (1893–1930)

Stalin admired Mayakovsky's fiction, but the poet-dramatist-activist revealed in *The Bathhouse* his contempt for political developments in Stalin's time. Called "the leading poet of the Revolution," Mayakovsky became a leading Russian futurist, attacking all of his country's literary past, and calling for a radical linguistic experiment. He loved to bait the bourgeoisie, and two of his satirical plays are *Klop* (1928, translated as *The Bedbug*) and *Banya* (1930, *The Bathhouse*). Although known for his propaganda (*agitka*), he was admired by William Carlos Williams for his "stepped lines."

Once, he wrote an impassioned poem criticizing Esenin for having committed suicide, but after an unhappy love affair with Lili, the wife of Osip Brik, Mayakovsky shot himself to death. According to Martin Seymour-Smith, Mayakovsky "at heart was a religious (non-Christian) modernist but with his roots more firmly in tradition than many of his contemporaries." {CE; TRI}

Maybeck, Bernard (1862–1973?)

Maybeck, a Unitarian, is the architect who designed in 1939 the Palace of Arts in San Francisco for the Golden Gate Exposition Frank Lloyd Wright, when invited to deliver the first Maybeck lecture at the University of California in Berkeley during the 1950s, was asked if he had ever met Maybeck. To his hearers' surprise, he answered no, adding he did not think much of Maybeck's architecture, according to Alan Parcells in *World* (Sep-Oct 1992). {UU}

Mayer, A. W. F. (20th Century)

Writing in *Freethinker* (August 1999), Mayer laments the fact that "there are whole cultures in other countries and cultural groups in this country today in which a woman is considered better dead than defiled. Fathers and brothers will pursue and kill daughters or sisters for disobeying or being forced to disobey their cultural rules. Marital or sexual 'crimes' can lead to women being beaten, imprisoned, maimed, or outcast from their families."

Mayer, Charles (Born 1881)

A French scientist, Mayer is author of *In Quest of A New Ethics* (translation by Harold Larrabee). In 1951, he wrote the present author:

Je suis en possession de votre lettre me demandant si je connais actuellement des personnages importants en France dont la philosophie est l'équivalent de ce qu'aux États-Unis vous appelez 'humanisme naturaliste.' Il est très difficile de vous preciser des noms parce qu'en France l'appellation d'humaniste n'a pas le sens relativement précis qu'elle possède aux États-Unis. C'est ainsi que Maritain, écrivain catholique, se réclame tout autant de l'humanisme que Sartre, écrivain athée.

Je suis donc bien embarrasé pour vous citer quelques noms. George Duhamel, André Siegfried, Jules Romains, Emile Henriot, et aussi bien entendu Édouard Herriot son des Humanistes mais comme l'a remarque très justement le Professeur Harold Larrabee pour André Maurois je serais surpris qu'ils acceptent de se placer sous une denomination philosophique quelconque. Espérant que ces quelques renseignements répondent à peu près à l'objet de votre lettre, je vous prie de croire, Cher Monsieur, à mes bien sympathiques sentiments.

The letter states that although "naturalistic humanist" is not a commonly used term in France, Mayer considers that the phrase generally describes the outlooks of Duhamel, Siegfried, Romains, Henriot, and Herriot. However, Maurois likely would not have listed himself as such. In the 1950s, Mayer was a correspondent (France) for *The Humanist*. {HNS; WAS, 25 July 1951}

Mayer, Jean (1920–1993)

Mayer, who was president of Tufts University from 1976 to 1992, was a visionary, nutritionist, and recipient of three Croix de Guerre and nearly a dozen other French military honors. While a French second lieutenant in the field artillery, he was captured by German forces during World War II but shot a guard and then served with the French underground. In 1950 he joined the faculty of Harvard University, where he taught nutrition and public health. He became an adviser to Presidents Nixon, Ford, and Carter, as well as to Congress, the UN's Food and Agriculture Organization, the World Health Organization, and the United Nations Children's Fund. In 1966, he was one of the first scientists to speak out against the use of herbicides in the Vietnam War.

Mayer was a member of Boston's King's Chapel and was proud of Tufts' Universalist past.

Mayer, Philip (20th Century)

A liberal minister, Mayer wrote *The Nature Spirit: Religion Without Supernatural Hopes* (1987). {GS; HNS}

Mayer, William V. (20th Century)

Director of the Biological Sciences Curriculum Study at the University of Colorado, Mayer is on the Council for Secular Humanism's Committee for the Scientific Examination of Religion. In 1980, he wrote *Perspective on the Educational Uses of Animals*.

Mayfield, William H. (20th Century)

Mayfield was a freethinker who wrote "A Brief Summary of Fundamentals Relating to Life, Death, Religion, and Philosophy" (1951). {GS}

Mayhew, Jonathan (1720–1766)

An important 18th century liberal, Mayhew was called by Conrad Wright one of "the two great leaders (with Charles Chauncy) of the first generation of New England Arminians." Minister of West Church in Boston, he was a strong opponent of creeds in any form, and he led in the attack on the doctrines of "original sin," laying the groundwork for the affirmation of human nature that would eventually develop in the thought of William Ellery Channing and others.

In the funeral sermon for Mayhew, Chauncy said, "He nobly claimed that which he esteemed equally the right of others—the liberty of thinking for himself." {TYD; U; U&U}

MAYLASIAN FREETHOUGHT

• Nakkeeran Parry, in Kuala Lumpur, belongs to an atheist organization called Periyar Paguthariyu Pasarai. Phone (603) 4456781.

• A Dravidar Association at Kuala Lumpur is modeled upon the Dravidian groups of India. (See *Freethought in the United Kingdom and the Commonwealth* by Gordon Stein.)

Maylone, W. Edgar (20th Century)

A freethinker, Maylone wrote *Thrown At the Atheist's Head* (1973). {FUS; GS}

Maynard Smith, John (1920–)

In 1986, Prof. Maynard Smith, professor of biology at the University of Sussex, was elected an honorary associate of the Rationalist Press Association. His works include *On Evolution*, (1972), *The Evolution of Sex* (1978), *Evolution and the Theory of Games* (1982), *Evolutionary Genetics* (1989), and, with Eörs Szathmáry, *The Major Transitions in Evolution* (1995).

Smith shares Daniel C. Dennett's strong supporter of Darwinism. (See his critique of Darwinism in the entry for Dennett.)

Mayo, E. L.: See entry for Theism.

MAYONNAISE

• Mayonnaise, n. One of the sauces which serve the French in place of a state religion.

–Ambrose Bierce
The Devil's Dictionary

Mayor, Osborne Henry: See the entry for James Bridie.

Mayr, Ernst (1904–)

Mayr is a retired zoology educator who is associated with the Museum of Comparative Zoology at Harvard University. He was a member of the Rothschild expedition to Dutch New Guinea in 1928, to New Guinea 1928–1929, and various other places. He has written about New Guinea birds, systematic zoology, animal species, and evolution.

He was president of the XIII International Ornithology Congress in 1962, recipient of the Wallace Darwin medal in 1958, and editor of *Evolution* (1947–1949). Mayr has received honors from Australian, British, New Zealand, German, and Russian organizations.

Because of his 1997 article in which the words "by God" appeared, he was asked if he was a theist and responded,

> I am definitely a non-theist. When I used the expression "by God," it was merely an expletive.
>
> When I got my first employment contract in 1926 at the University of Berlin, I had to make a formal declaration to be exempted from paying the 10% church tax.
>
> My views are obvious to anyone reading my recent book, *This is Biology* (Harvard University Press, 1997).
>
> {WAS 12 May 1997}

Mayr, Jack (20th Century)

Mayr is an atheist-humanist activist in Milwaukee, Wisconsin.

Mayur, Rshmi (20th Century)

Mahur, director of the International Institute for a Sustainable Future and President of Global Futures Network, signed Humanist Manifesto 2000.

MAZDA

See entry for Zoroastrianism. Mazdaism is an Iranian religion that evolved about the fifth century B.C.E., succeeding the prophetism (Zoroastrianism) of an earlier period. {ER}

Mazlish, Bruce (1923-)

A historian and educator at the Massachusetts Institute of Technology, Mazlish (with Jacob Bronowski) wrote *The Western Intellectual Tradition* (1960). His other works include *James and John Stuart Mill: Father and Son in the 19 Century* (1975; *The Co-Evolution of Humans and Machines* (1993); and *The Uncertain Sciences* (1998). He edited *Psychoanalysis and History* (1963, revised 1971).

In *The Uncertain Sciences* Mazlish urges science and the humanities to work on understanding their relationship. So long as religion slows the process, humanity will continue to have difficulty discarding religion unless scientists and humanists combine their efforts. Unfortunately, people will continue to "espouse and act in accordance with religious beliefs, rather than the laws and methods of the human sciences," he laments. He is alarmed that one poll reports that 70% of Americans "belong to a church of some sort."

Mazhar, Isma'il (20th Century)

In Cairo, Egypt, Mazhar edited in Arabic *al-'Usur* from 1927 to 1931. One of his works published in the 1960s on the subject of Arab philosophy is *Tarikh al-fikr al Arabi*.

Mazlish, Bruce (1923–)

"A human is that animal who breaks out of the animal kingdom by creating machines," Mazlish has written in *The Fourth Discontinuity: The Co-Evolution of Humans and Machines* (1993). A professor of history at Massachusetts Institute of Technology, Mazlish warns humanists that they must not let machines dominate them, that machines "can pose a real threat if we don't understand that they are an extension of ourselves that can be used to better or worse purposes." Machines can be good, of course, such as telescopes and microscopes and eyeglasses that are extensions of our sensory apparatus. We increasingly acquire artificial hips, knees, and pacemakers. We merge our mental faculties with a computer. But, Mazlish states, in the human quest for perfection we have developed the computer robot that will take on a life of its own. This, he warns, is scary.

Mazlish is author (with J. Bronowsky) *The Western Intellectual Tradition* (1960). He also wrote *The Riddle of History* (1966), *Meaning of Karl Marx* (1984), and *The Leader, the Led, and the Psyche* (1990). Mazlish is associate editor of *Journal of Interdisciplinary History*. (See an interview with Mazlish by Timothy J. Madigan in *Free Inquiry*, Fall 1994.)

Mazzini, Giuseppe (1805–1872)

Mazzini was a revolutionist and Italian patriot, whose secret society *Giovine Italia* (Young Italy) campaigned for Italian unity under a republican government. A supporter of Giuseppe Garibaldi's expedition to Sicily, Mazzini like Garibaldi was a member of the Masonic Lodge, an organization disapproved of by the Vatican because of its being a secret lodge that was non-theistic and pro-deistic. Carlyle called Mazzini, the deist, "a man of genius and virtue, a man of sterling veracity, humanity, and nobleness of mind." McCabe, rather than emphasizing Mazzini's deism, said Mazzini praised Christ, criticized Christian doctrines, and had an emphatic belief in a deistic God. {BDF; CE; JM; RE; Denis Mack Smith, *Mazzini*, 1995}

Mc: Names starting with **Mac** or **Mc** are listed as if they are spelled Mac.

Mead, George Herbert (1863–1931)

An American philosopher and psychologist, Mead studied the development of the mind and the self, and he regarded mind as the natural emergent from the interaction of the human organism and its social environment. Within this biosocial structure the gap between impulse and reason is bridged by the use of language. Man, to master language, sets up assumptions as to his role in life, and self and consciousness-of-self emerge, giving intelligence a historical development that is both natural and moral. Mead called his position social behaviorism, using conduct—both social and biological—as an approach to all experience.

The Columbia Encyclopedia states that the work of John Dewey and of Mead may be regarded as complementary.

Mead wrote *The Philosophy of the Present, Mind, Self, and Society*;

and *The Philosophy of the Act*, all published posthumously. Not a member of an organized religion, Mead was a freethinker and non-supernaturalist. {CE; HNS2}

Mead, Margaret (1901–1978)

Mead, the American anthropologist who was affiliated with the American Museum of Natural History from 1926 until her death, won world fame through studies of child rearing, personality, and culture. Among her books are *Coming of Age in Samoa* (1928), *Growing Up in New Guinea* (1930), *Male and Female* (1949), and the autobiographical *Blackberry Winter* (1972).

Asked about humanism, she responded to the present author:

> I can't classify myself under any of the headings in any known fashion. I suspect that we are on the verge of a new religious integration. This is going to owe a great deal to technical advances on the one hand, i.e., developments like "Cybernetics," Gray Walter's *The Living Brain*, and things of that sort, and a rapprochement between Eastern and Western historical religions on the other—the sort of thing that is foreshadowed in Neville Shute's *Round the Bend*, or Edmund Taylor's chapter, "Journey Into Morning," in *Richer By Asia*. I also suspect that in what is at present called the "neo-orthodoxy," young people are handling traditional religious symbols of all sorts including traditional atheism on a deutero level, which most religious leaders are unwilling or unable to deal with. So I'm afraid I don't fit in any way.

Mead did not fit in with Hannah Arendt, either. In *Between Friends* (1995), her letter to Mary McCarthy illustrates this: "I was away from New York, an idiotic affair at Baltimore, honorary degree together with Margaret Mead, a monster, and Marianne Moore, an angel. . . . Mead (one better call her only by her second name, not because she is a man, but because she certainly is not a woman)." Although Mead had been married three times, she was described by one of her friends as one who "fell in love with women's souls and men's bodies. She was spiritually homosexual, psychologically bisexual, and physically heterosexual." When she was asked what she thought of homosexuals, Mead—who when she gave birth at the age of forty to her child had insisted on having the delivery filmed in order to study the film—once replied, "They make the best companions in the world." And in 1976, speaking before the Washington Press Club, Mead told the reporters, "I think extreme heterosexuality is a perversion."

Mary Catherine Bateson, her daughter, was once chastised by Mead for having had a romance with another woman. Then, six years after her mother's death, Bateson disclosed in her memoirs that Mead and anthropologist Ruth Benedict had had a long affair, commencing in the summer of 1925 when the two took a trip together to the Grand Canyon. Fearing an openly lesbian relationship would damage her career, Mead remained closeted. In fact, both she and the married Benedict were once romantically interested in linguist Edward Sapir. {AA; Margaret Mead, *An Anthropologist at Work* [1959]; WAS, 16 August 1954}

Mead, Sidney Earl (1904–)

A distinguished American church historian, Mead wrote, "When the overwhelming bulk of American Protestantism turned 'right' in a flight from Reason (during the early 1800s), Unitarianism turned 'left' in defense of Reason." He described a "typical Unitarian" as "one for whom the standard religious formulas have failed, who lives therefore on the verge of a belief vacuum." He was president of Meadville Theological School from 1956 to 1960, after which he taught at Southern California School of Theology and at the University of Iowa. Among his works are *The Old Religion in the Brave New World* (1977) and *History and Identity* (1979). {U&U}

Meade, Robert D. (20th Century)

Meade, in "The Gods and Medical Practice" (*The American Rationalist*, January-February 1996), describes some scenes of cross-cultural psychology in which he observed the following:

> • In Nepal, he was prevented from helping a holy man who was clearly having an epileptic fit. Next day near a bodi tree, his followers rejoiced that the holy man had been taken into death by God.
>
> • In Northern India, he observed a village where smallpox was rampant and the natives had erected statues to Sheetala, the goddess of smallpox. Residents prayed that they would receive the blessings of Sheetala and have as evidence the disease's scars, which in the rest of the world are met with great dread.
>
> • In Central Africa, he found a young woman lying on the ground, bewitched, receiving sacrifices of scarce and precious foodstuffs that were burned to obtain the gods' help in her recovery. She died a short time later.
>
> • In another place, chanting noises were made by women dressed in dark colors while in the front of the room a man in a long, white robe was leading the chants. In his hand he had a long stick, on which was perched a carving of a nearly naked figure, his grimacing face contorted and twisted as if in great pain. Candles cast an eerie glow, and the room was filled with the fetid stench of rancid burning wax. The place was a small town in the State of Washington, and the Catholic parishioners "were engaging in a primitive, superstitious ritual and praying to yet another god that their leader, the Pope, would recover from surgery, which had removed a tumor from his colon."

Meades, Jonathan (20th Century)

Meades, a British novelist, was named an Honorary Associate of the National Secular Society in 1997. On his television program, "Modern Times," he has attacked some of the directions of recent leaders of organized religion, saying, "The churches got it wrong. The punters wanted more mumbo-jumbo, not less." {CA}

Meador, Andrew J. (20th Century)

Meador was a freethinker who wrote *The Christ of Prophecy* (1953). {GS}

MEANING

• The meaning of life is that it stops.

–Franz Kafka

• There is an old bon mot, sometimes ascribed to Sir Hamilton A. R. Gibb of Oxford . . . that every Arab word has its primary meaning, then its opposite meaning, then something to do with a camel, and lastly something obscene. Similarly, it was said at Harvard, when I was there in the '60s, that every Sanskrit word means itself, its opposite, a name of God, and a position in sexual intercourse.

–Wendy Doniger, *The Implied Spider*

MEANINGLESSNESS: See entry for Walter Burkert.

MECCA: See entry for Islam.

MEDICINE

• Like a celestial chaperon, the placebo leads us through the uncharted passageways of mind and gives us a greater sense of infinity than if we were to spend all our days with our eyes hypnotically glued to the giant telescope at Mt. Palomar.

–Norman Cousins

Gerald W. Friedland and Meyer Friedman in *Medicine's 10 Greatest Discoveries* (1998) list the following:

- 1543: Andreas Vesalius's *De Humani Corporis Fabrica* (The Structure of the Human Body) illustrated why without bones our bodies would be mushy blobs.
- 1628: William Harvey's *De Motu Cordis* (On the Motion of the Heart) introduced the discovery of circulation, saying that his findings were "of so novel and unheard-of character, that I not only fear injury to myself from the envy of a few, but I tremble lest I have mankind at large for my enemies."
- 1675: Anton Leeuwenhoek, looking under a microscope at a drop of rainwater, found "little animals," bacteria that cause all kinds of diseases.
- 1796: Edward Jenner, using cowpox to cause a mild disease to protect from the deadlier smallpox, led to injecting dead bacteria to help eradicate smallpox and protect against bubonic plague, chickenpox, cholera, diphtheria, influenza, measles, mumps, rabies, typhoid fever, tetanus, and other diseases.
- 1842: Crawford Long used ether to prevent the feeling of pain, developing surgical anesthesia.
- 1895: Wilhelm Roentgen discovered the X-ray beam, leading to the development of the most important diagnostic tools.
- 1907: Ross Harrison grew living cells outside the body, making it possible to search for the causes of diseases including cancer.
- 1912: Nikolai Anichkov discovered that cholesterol is responsible for coronary artery disease.
- 1928: Alexander Fleming discovered penicillin, leading the way for the development of other antibiotics to treat infections.
- 1950-1953: Maurice Wilkins did pioneer work to isolate a single

fiber of DNA, leading James Watson and Francis Crick to develop their own double helix model of DNA, the heredity-bearing molecule. All three shared the Nobel Prize.

MEDICINE AND RELIGION: See entry for Robert D. Meade.

MEDIEVAL PHILOSOPHY: See entry for classical humanism. Also, see the *Encyclopedia of Philosophy,* Vol. 5.

MEDITATION: See entry for Bliss.

Medow, Louis E. (20th Century)

Medow was one of fifty-three charter members in 1991 of Atheists of Florida. He is a member of the South Florida Chapter of American Atheists.

Medvedev, Zhores A. (1925–)

When he signed Humanist Manifesto II, Medvedev, a Soviet dissident, was associated with the Medical Research Council. In 1986 he wrote *Gorbachev* and in 1990 *The Legacy of Chernobyl.* {HM2; SHD}

Medwin, Thomas (1788–1869)

In 1810, Medwin collaborated with Shelley, his cousin, in writing *Ahasuerus the Wanderer,* which publishers rejected as "atheistic." It was finally published in 1823. Medwin in 1824 published a *Journal of the Conversations of Lord Byron* and, after Shelley's death, wrote *A Memoir of P. B. Shelley* (1833), which he later expanded into *The Life of P. B. Shelley* (2 volumes, 1847). {RAT}

Meercx, Joep (20th Century)

A Dutch conscientious objector, Meercx is full-time secretary of the International Humanist and Ethical Union's Human Rights Commissioner's *ombudsteam.* An anthropologist with experience in Argentina, he has worked as a volunteer for Amnesty International. Jim Herrick wrote about Meercx's work in the *New Humanist* (June 1988).

Meehl, Joanne H. (20th Century)

Meehl, an employment counselor with the South Coastal Worker Assistance Center, is author of *The Recovering Catholic: Personal Journeys of Women Who Left the Church* (1995). The book tells of the reasons women begin to question their faith, the heavy burden of religious guilt, the attitudes of the hierarchy toward women, and the escalating amount of sexual abuse cases involving priests. Meehl is, herself, a recovering Catholic.

Meeker, Kevin (20th Century)

Meeker in 1996 won the Graduate Student Award for submitted papers at the Pacific Division meetings of the American Philosophical Association. His subject was "Hume's Scepticism about Reason and Naturalized Epistemology."

Meeker, Mindy (20th Century)

Meeker is Vice President for Programs of the Secular Humanist Association of San Antonio, Texas.

Megahey, Leslie (20th Century)

Megahey in 1994 wrote and directed "The Advocate," a movie that commences showing a man fitted with a noose, about to be executed for having had "carnal knowledge of the she-ass here present." At his side is the complicit donkey, also about to be hanged.

According to Megahey, in 15th Century France animals and inanimate objects could be tried under civil law. Rats could be summoned as courtroom witnesses, but because of the church's influence a Jewish doctor could not. The story, which begins in 1452, is said to take place just thirty years after cohabiting with a Jew ceased to be a capital crime. In the script, the advocate of the title serves as a public defender, and his first client is a woman accused of witchcraft. He loses. His second is a pig, the property of some roving Gypsies. The pig has been accused of killing and partially devouring a Jewish boy from the village—thus, a double crime, because the Catholic Church has an injunction against eating meat on Fridays. He loses again.

Janet Maslin, reviewing the medieval shenanigans in *The New York Times* (24 August 1994), notes that a last-minute pardon arrives, not for the man and his ass but for his impassive-looking consort. "She is released without stain to her character," intones a solemn magistrate, who then presides over the man's execution. Whereupon the local peasants watch eagerly as justice is done. Megahey's wit in detailing theological niceties is clearly in the tradition of freethought.

Megata, E. M. (20th Century)

In the 1950s, Megata was a correspondent (Japan) for *The Humanist.*

Mehring, Darryl (20th Century)

Mehring is active with the Humanists of Boulder, Colorado. (See entry for Colorado Humanists.) {FD}

Mehta, Ved (Parkash): See entry for Samuel Taylor Coleridge.

Meier, Jürg (20th Century)

At the Eighth International Humanist and Ethical Union (IHEU) World Congress held in Hannover, Meier of Switzerland addressed the group. Meier is a historian of goldsmithing.

Meier, Richard Louis (20th Century)

Meier is a planner, a futurist, and a behavioral scientist. He has written *Science and Economic Development* (1956), *Modern Science and the Human Fertility Problem* (1959), *Resource-Conserving Urbanism for South Asia* (1968), and *Ecological Planning and Design* (1991). Meier has taught at the Institute for Mental Health at the University of Michigan and is professor emeritus at the University of California.

Meighan, Roland (20th Century)

Meighan is author of *The Freethinker's Guide to the Educational Universe* (1994). It is a selection of quotations on education. Among other noted individuals, Paul and Goodman and Bertrand Russell included, Meighan quotes Carl Rogers: "I deeply believe that traditional teaching is an almost completely futile, wasteful, overrated function in today's changing world. It is successful mostly in giving children, who can't grasp the material, a sense of failure."

Meijer, Theo (20th Century)

Meijer is President of the British Columbia Humanist Association.

Meissner, Alfred (1822–1885)

Meissner was a German poet and freethinker, the author of *Recollections of Heine,* among other works. Heine called Meissner "the heir apparent of Schiller." {BDF; RAT}

Meister, Jacques Henri (1744–1826)

Meister was a Swiss writer who, although intended for a religious career, met D'Holbach and Diderot, of whom he wrote a short life. He was secretary to Grimm. Meister wrote *Origin of Religious Principles* (1762) and *Natural Morality* (1787). {BDF; RAT}

Melcher, Frederic G. (Born 1879)

Melcher, a noted publisher and editor, was a Unitarian. {U}

Meldrum, Max (Duncan) (1875–1955)

A Scot who arrived in Australia in 1889, Meldrum was a rationalist and freethinker. In art, he was a controversial figure who used "tonal realism" and who claimed that anyone who believed in religion would never be a great painter.

Meleagros (Ancient Greece)

Meleagros, whose work is quoted by Dudley Fitts in the Greek anthology, sings his humanism poetically:

• I swear it, by Love I swear it!
More sweet to me is Hêliodôra's voice
Than the holy harp of Lêto's golden Son.

• O Night, O sleepless tossing, longing for Hêliodôra!
Poor eyes hot with tears in the lingering white dawn!
Is she lonely too?
Is she dreaming of how I kissed her,
And dreaming so, does she turn to kiss
the dream of me?—or a new love? a newer toy?
Forbid it, lamp!
See it never!
Did I not set you to guard her?

• Squealshrilling Mosquitoes, fraternity lost to shame,
Obscene vampires, chittering riders of the night:
Let her sleep, I beg you!, and come
(If you must come) feed on this flesh of mine.

(Oh useless prayer! Must not her body charm
The wildest, most heartless, most insensate beasts?)

Yet hear me, devils, I have warned you:
No more of your daring,
Or you shall smart from the strength
of my jealous hands

• O Fingernail of Hêliodôra,
Surely Love sharpened you,
surely Love made you grow:
Does not your lightest touch transfix my heart?

• Fair are the boys of Tyre, by Love I swear it!
But Myiskos
Sweeps the bright stars from the sky, that bursting sun.

Méline, Félix Jules (Born 1838)

Méline was a French statesman who worked with the anti-clerical Gambettists. He was President of the Chambre (1888–1889) and Premier and Minister of Agriculture (1896–1898). Upon quitting the Chambre, Méline supported all measures against the Church, and became a Senator in 1903. Méline was an Officer of the Legion of Honour. {RAT}

Melissos (fl. 444 B.C.E.)

A man of action, Melissos led a successful sally to capture the Athenian fleet, according to Plutarch. Melissos was a freethinker who said of the gods that "there was no need to define them, since there is no knowledge of them." But, as in the case of Parmenides and Zeno and others of the Eleatic school, writes Robertson, Melissos of Samos turned first "to deep metaphysic and then to verbal dialectic, to discussion on being and not being, the impossibility of motion, and the trick-problem of Achilles and the tortoise." {JMR; JMRH}

Mellen, Ida M. (Born 1877)

Mellen wrote to the present author her views about humanism:

> I list myself in *Who's Who* as a rationalist and feel that liberals who commonly avoid mentioning their convictions in such a record do serious wrong to liberalism. Incidentally, I believe it is more fashionable now to say non-theism rather than atheism.
>
> Dr. Potter's definition of Humanism for Webster's permanently prevents me from becoming a Humanist. Self-perfectibility has been superseded by self-improvement, which is more reasonable, since perfection, at least in the Occident, is out of the question. Also, I consider character more important than personality and draw a sharp line of demarcation between the two. This bars me as well from embracing Humanism.
>
> Dr. [Carleton] Coon's definition of humanism is wholly wrong in saying that "Every scientist has to be a humanist as well, if he wants anyone to read and understand his stuff." Apparently he forgets there are other sciences in the world than anthropology. I have been writing books in the field of popular science for thirty years, and it would be ridiculous to suggest that I would need to become a Humanist in order to be understood.
>
> {WAS, 4 June 1957}

Mellen, Richard (20th Century)

Mellen, who heads the American Society of Freethinkers, is known for distributing freethought materials, including REASON IS THE ANSWER bumperstickers. (See entry for American Society of Freethinkers.) {FD}

Melly, George (1926–)

For *New Humanist* (July 1993), Melly wrote about his outlook:

> I came from a middle-class Liverpool family and was born in 1926. My mother was Jewish by birth, but had converted to the Church of England at the age of fourteen shortly after her Orthodox father had died. My father was of Unitarian stock. I was sent to what was called The Children's Service at the local Church; a middle-class affair—working-class children attended Sunday School in the afternoon—and then when I reached a suitable age, attended normal services and was eventually confirmed at the age of fourteen or so. My mother believed vaguely in an after-life. My father, as I discovered later, just paid the minimum lip-service to religion and went to church only on Christmas Day. When I was about sixteen I discovered Surrealism and with its adamant atheism and my "conversion" followed. I have never seen any reason to deviate and it is now fifty years later.
>
> It seems to me that religion of whatever complexion has been responsible for more misery and violence in the course of history than any other factor, and among religions I include a faith in extreme nationalism or any rigid system. I view my death with no qualms. I shall not hesitate to take Pascal's wager. Our only contribution, or so I believe, to the world is through our genes. I find it a mixture of panic, self-importance, and superstition to insist on personal survival. I've had a very full and interesting life, adore both nature and art, have been blessed with many friends, have laughed a great deal and wept mercifully little. At no time have I felt even the least temptation to lift my hat to any form of unseen power.

In 1970 he wrote *Revolt Into Style: The Pop Arts in Britain.* He also wrote an autobiography, *Scouse Mouse, Or, I Never Got Over It,* as well as *Paris and the Surrealists* (1991). In 1986, Melly was elected an honorary associate of the British Rationalist Press Association. He also is an honorary associate of the National Secular Society and a Vice President of the Gay and Lesbian Humanist Association (GALHA).

Melly, Sarah (20th Century)

In Nottingham, Melly is active with the Nottingham Humanist Group.

Mellow, Edie (20th Century)

Mellow in secretary in Michigan of *The Jewish Humanist.*

Melton, Nancy (20th Century)

Melton is on the staff of the freethinker magazine, *Truth Seeker.*

Melville, Arthur (20th Century)

Melville, who has a B.A. in philosophy, an M.A. in religious education, and a Ph. D. in clinical psychology, is author of *With Eyes To See: A Journey From Religion to Spirituality* (1942). Ordained as a Maryknoll priest in 1961, he ministered in Guatemala from 1961 to 1968 in an area without roads, electricity, or running water. After establishing clinics, a birth control program, cooperatives, credit unions, and literacy programs, he converted the parochial school into a public school and turned church property into a cooperative vegetable garden for the poorest families. Finding that the oppressed Mayan people were permitted no legal means for advancing, he joined the revolutionary movement and was expelled. Going underground in Mexico, he was arrested, jailed, almost beaten to death, and put back into the United States.

Melville the priest then married, did counseling in California prisons, and has written critiques of the established systems that guide the lives of most people. For *Truth Seeker* (#123: 1), he wrote, "Pope on the Carpet in Guatemala."

Melville, Herman (1819–1891)

An internationally respected, major U.S. author, Melville was the son of Alan Melvill (as the family name was spelled when Herman was born). His father imported French dry goods as well as spent the family inheritance, having borrowed $20,000 from his father and from his parents-in-law. His mother, Maria, was a stern Calvinist of the Reformed Dutch Church variety. She believed that all children are born in Original Sin, that they must be "sanctified in Christ," and they must be baptized. We are predestined, she would relay to her family, by God's free grace to be chosen, or not be chosen, into the elect. Even a life of "good works" could not persuade God to choose an individual . . . which might explain a line in *Pierre* (1852), according to biographer Hershel Parker, that if our actions are "foreordained...we are Russian serfs to Fate."

Upon his father's death, when Herman was twelve, the family was in deep debt and Herman was sent to work in a bank for over a year at $150 per year. He then worked in his brother's store as a clerk, taught school, and at the age of twenty joined a whaling ship, signing on as a cabin boy on a ship bound for Liverpool, which he wrote about in *Redburn* (1849). Spending eighteen months on a whaler in 1841-1842, he found such intolerable hardships on board that he and a companion escaped from the ship at the Marquesas Islands. Here, the two were captured by a tribe of cannibals, then rescued by an Australian whaler, about which he wrote *Typee: A Peep at Polynesian Life* (1846) and *Omoo: A Narrative of Adventures in the South Seas* (1847). Robertson points out that in Chapter 24 of *Typee*, Melville recounts how some of the natives he met were unafraid of their gods, not only abusing them but also challenging them to fight. Melville's unsympathetic view of Christian missionaries in Polynesia was met with a hostile reaction from church journals. And from this point on, his skepticism about religion was shown in his various works.

Laurie Robertson-Lorant in a biographical work, *Melville* (1996), tells of his first time crossing the ocean as a passenger, for he was journeying to England to sell the rights to *White-Jacket*. Walking out onto the ship's deck one evening, he was shocked to see a man in the water, and he shouted for crew members. The drowning man, however, refused any help and disappeared below the waves. In his journal, Melville recalled the man's expression: "it was merry," he wrote. The experience was an upsetting one, but the captain later explained that passengers jumping overboard was not all unusual, that often their loved ones were often on hand to see them leap.

After marrying Elizabeth Shaw, daughter of the Chief Justice of Massachusetts, Melville bought a farm near Pittsfield, Massachusetts, befriending his neighbor Nathaniel Hawthorne and being one of the first to appreciate his genius. In fact, it is said that Mrs. Hawthorne found the emotional attachment between Melville and her husband a bit much, and she was pleased when her husband was appointed by his friend, President Franklin Pierce, to the post of consul at Liverpool, England, requiring that they move from the Tanglewood area. (Melville had written, after meeting Hawthorne and reviewing in 1850 his *Mosses from an Old Manse* for *The Literary World*, "Already I feel that this Hawthorne has dropped germinous seeds into my soul. He expands and deepens down, the more I contemplate him; and further and further, shoots his strong New England roots into the hot soil in my Southern soul." Although he tried to disguise his identity by signing the review, "By a Virginian Spending July in Vermont," Melville and his extended metaphor of insemination were easily detectable. Meanwhile, Mrs. Hawthorne has been quoted as saying of her husband, "He hates to be touched more than anyone I know.")

Melville's masterpiece is *Moby-Dick; or, The Whale* (1851), a symbolic account of a deranged whaling captain's obsessive voyage to find and destroy the great white whale that had ripped off his leg. On one level, it can be read as a sociological critique of various American class and racial prejudices, on another a repository of information about whales and whaling, and on another a philosophical inquiry into the nature of good and evil, of man and his fate. On yet another, the work is an exposé of the sordidness of the business of butchering whales. Why, Melville speculated, do we follow certain of our desires even when we logically deduce that these desires hurt us? Why is what we call "evil" actually evil? Why if we know something is dangerous do we persist in pursuing it?

Billy Budd, Foretopman (written during the last five years of his life but published in 1924) features Billy, a handsome sailor who, because of his innocence and beauty, is hated by Claggart, a dark, demon-haunted petty officer. Billy, in his simplicity, cannot understand why Claggart should hate him, why, in short, evil should desire to destroy good. When Claggart concocts a story that Billy wants to start a mutiny, Billy in his only act of rebellion strikes Claggart, who after the blow dies as he falls and his head hits a hard surface. Although the ship's captain sympathizes with Billy and recognizes his essential innocence, he is forced to condemn him to death. Following Billy's hanging, he lives on as a legend among sailors. The book was dedicated to Hawthorne. Its homosexual overtones inspired Benjamin Britten to write an opera, "Billy Budd," an idea developed by George Steiner in *New Yorker* (5 July 1993).

Pierre, or the Ambiguities, was a critical and financial disaster. A Gothic romance with Shelleyan overtones and a satire on the literary profession, it touches upon a variety of controversial subjects. The title character is doted upon by a mother whose "playfulness of . . . unclouded love" implies a perverse sexuality. He then falls in love with Isabel, who it turns out is his illegitimate sister; yet, "he imprinted repeated burning kisses upon her . . . . They coiled together, and entangledly stood mute." Mr. Falsgrave, the family clergyman, is as hypocritical and deceitful as everyone else in the community. His cousin Glen, with whom he had felt "an ardent sentiment" when the two were lads and had explored "the preliminary love-friendship of boys," steals Lucy, the person to whom he is engaged, Pierre murders him in a rage and is imprisoned. Lucy and Pierre's mother die of grief. Pierre and Isabel, who now are incestuously in love, commit suicide in his prison cell. In short, Pierre, who had hoped to find a way to set the universe aright, is undone by his ideals and becomes "the fool of Truth, the fool of Virtue, the fool of Fate." The New York *Day Book* commented upon *Pierre* with the headline, HERMAN MELVILLE CRAZY.

Crazy was not Hawthorne's analysis of Melville. As Parker points out, Hawthorne wrote that Melville was into metaphysics. In his November 1856 journal Hawthorne had written:

> Melville, as he always does, began to reason of Providence and futurity, and of everything that lies beyond human ken, and informed me that he had "pretty much made up his mind to be annihilated"; but still he does not seem to rest in that anticipation; and, I think, will never rest until he gets hold of a definite belief. It is strange how he persists—and has persisted ever since I knew him, and probably long before—in wandering to-and-fro over these deserts, as dismal and monotonous as the sand hills amid which we were sitting (during his visit with Hawthorne in Liverpool).
>
> He can neither believe, nor be comfortable in his unbelief; and he is too honest and courageous not to try to do one or the other. If he were a religious man, he would be one of the most truly religious and reverential; he has a very high and noble nature, and better worth immortality than most of us.

James Wood, noting Hawthorne's analysis, wrote that Melville "was tormented by God's 'inscrutable' silence—this is clear from the work. Moby-Dick, who is both God and Devil, flaunts his unhelpful silence as God does to Job: 'Canst thou draw out leviathan with a hook?' In the chapter 'The Tail,' Ishmael admits that if he cannot really comprehend the whale's rear, then he can hardly see his face: 'Thou shalt see my back parts, my tail, he seems to say, but my face shall not be seen,' an appropriate of the verse in *Exodus* in which God tells Moses that 'thou shalt see my back parts: but my face shall not be seen.' "

"Most people, Melville tells Hawthorne, "fear God, and *at bottom dislike* Him . . . because they rather distrust His heart, and fancy Him all brain like a watch. . . . You perceive I employ a capital initial in the pronoun referring to the Deity; don't you think there is a slight dash of flunkeyism in that usage?" The lines exemplify, wrote Wood, that Melville "could not help playing the infidel: he was one of the most delvingly sacrilegious writers who ever existed. . . . He slapped at God; but, in some way, he could not do without the idea of being slapped by God in return. . . .Ahab's monomaniacal hunt of the whale is not so far from Ishmael's multiple tolerance of it."

In 1866, when forty-seven, Melville became an outdoor customs inspector in New York City (at the Hudson River on Gansevoort Street, named after his mother's maternal family), a position he held for nineteen years. During this time he was relatively unknown. It was not until 1920 that literary scholars recognized his genius; in fact, his *New York Times* obituary referred to him as Henry, not Herman.

Now one of America's most written about authors, Melville has a large number of supporters as well as detractors. He has been described by Ohio State University professor Elizabeth Renker as a drunken wife-beater who once pushed his wife down a flight of stairs. Donald Kring, when he wrote a biography of Henry Whitney Bellows, came across an 1867 letter from Samuel Shaw, the half brother of Melville's wife, Lizzie, that proposed they fake a kidnapping to rescue her from Melville's sporadic violence. The University of Delaware's Hershel Parker, however, in a 1996 biography, *Herman Melville: A Biography, Volume 1, 1819–1883*, disbelieves the allegation. But although many scholars may have overlooked Melville's weaknesses, three of four Melville children had plainly led unhappy lives. His oldest son committed suicide. And the five women in his family who survived him looked on him at times as a "beast," in the words of Eleanor Metcalf's son Paul.

Stan Goldman's *Melville's Protest Theism, The Hidden and Silent God in "Clarel"* (1994), challenges past views that Melville was an agnostic. However, he was a member in New York City of the Church of All Souls (Unitarian), whose minister Walter Donald Kring in *Herman Melville's Religious Journey* (1997) has described Melville's turning from Calvinism to Unitarianism.

Melville is buried at the Woodlawn Cemetery in the Bronx, where also buried are composer Irving Berlin, musician Miles Davis, and former New York City Mayor Fiorello LaGuardia. (See entries for Moby-Dick, Ethan Allen, and for James Wood, who holds that Melville was not a Christian theist and did not believe in a supernatural God. Also see entry for Alfred Kazin, who wrote that Melville retained his faith despite knowing in what and where and whom to believe.) {CE; CL; GL; JM; JMR; JMRH; OCAL; OEL; RAT; TRI; TYD; Philip Weiss, *The New York Times Magazine*, 15 December 1996; U; UU}

MEME

In 1976 the biologist Richard Dawkins coined the word "meme" to describe an element of culture: a word, a song, an attitude, a religious belief, a mealtime ritual, a technology. Much of what people do depends upon memes which have changed their human nature, such as being served cranberry juice by a friend, then serving it to other friends later on because of one's memory of how pleasant the occasion was. Reviewing Susan Blackmore's *The Meme Machine* (1999), Robert Wright remarked that, "Like genes, memes pass from person to person, and over time some memes prove more prolific than others. So vast bodies of memes evolve—ideologies or religions or industries or musical genres. 'Memeplexes,' that is." Dawkins holds that culture evolves in Darwinian fashion. Whereas memes formerly traveled largely from parent to child, today through television, radio, and the Internet they travel almost instantaneously. In a foreword to the Blackmore book, Dawkins proudly reported that "memetic" had appeared at least 5,042 times on the World Wide Web at the time he last checked.

Memmi, Albert (20th Century)

Memmi is an honorary president of the International Federation of Secular Humanistic Jews.

MEMORIAL SOCIETIES

"Why Bury $5,000 In A Hole?" asked Heather Anderson in an article in *World* (July-August 1996). Instead of incurring huge burial costs, many prefer joining memorial societies and giving the savings to the remaining family members rather than to professional morticians. Traditional burials include the purchase of a casket, embalming, several days' use of the funeral home for visitation and service, and a hodge-podge of additional services from the funeral director (salmon-color caps behind the eyelids, dentures, wires to shut the jaw, clipping of the frenula so the mouth will close, haircuts, shaves, etc.). Addresses of memorial societies and crematoriums are available from most Unitarian, freethought, or humanist societies.

Mena, Abelardo (20th Century)

When he signed Humanist Manifesto II, Dr. Mena was senior psychiatrist of the Veterans Administration Hospital, Miami, Florida {HM2}

Ménard, Louis (1822–1901)

Ménard, a French painter and author, wrote *Prologue of a Revolution*, for which he was obliged to leave France. He also wrote *Morality Before the Philosophers* (1860), *Studies on the Origin of Christianity* (1867), and *Freethinkers' Religious Catechism* (1875). {BDF}

Mencius: See entry for Meng-zi.

Mencken, Henry (Louis) (1880–1956)

"As for religion, I am quite devoid of it," Mencken declared in *Minority Report* (1956). "The act of worship, as carried on by Christians, seems to me to be debasing rather than ennobling. It involves groveling before a Being who, if He really exists, deserves to be denounced instead of respected." He also wrote,

> The chief contribution of Protestantism to human thought is its massive proof that God is a bore.

Mencken, one of the best-known journalists of his day, wrote, "The effort to reconcile science and religion is almost always made by scientists unable to shake off altogether the piety absorbed with their mother's milk." In *Smart Set* (1920), he explained, "To sum up: (1)

The cosmos is a gigantic flywheel making 10,000 revolutions a minute; (2) Man is a sick fly taking a dizzy ride on it; (3) Religion is the theory that the wheel was designed and set spinning to give him the ride." His skepticism about religion is scattered through nearly all of his writings, and his most important works are *The Philosophy of Friedrich Nietzsche* (1908), *Treatise on the Gods* (1930), and *Treatise on Right and Wrong* (1934). The second of the three discussed Huxley, who was one of his heroes, and agnosticism.

Mencken—the curmudgeon, anti-Semite, and Prussophile—is not the household name he once was, but in 1992 Marion Elizabeth Rodgers, who had edited *Mencken and Sara: A Life in Letters* (1988), published *The Impossible H. L. Mencken: A Selection of His Best Newspaper Stories* (Doubleday, 1992). John Updike, known to some as the stereotypical Anglo-Saxon Protestant, reviewed it in *The New Yorker*, much as in earlier times it would have been covered by an ASP (White Anglo Saxon Protestant is now considered redundant). Updike, for example, negatively criticized the following Mencken observation: "The popularity of Fundamentalism among the inferior orders of men is explicable. . . . The cosmogonies that educated men toy with are all inordinately complex. To comprehend their veriest outlines requires an immense stock of knowledge, and a habit of thought. It would be as vain to try to teach to peasants or to the city proletariat as it would be to try to teach them to streptococci." What this all amounts to, he continued, "is that the human race is divided into two sharply differentiated and mutually antagonistic classes . . . a small minority that plays with ideas and is capable of taking them in, and a vast majority that finds them painful, and is thus arrayed against them. . . . The intellectual heritage of the race belongs to the minority, and to the minority only."

Two posthumous works, *Thirty-five Years of Newspaper Work* and *My Life as Author and Editor* (1993), were not published at his specific request until thirty-five years after his death. The latter contained not only his impressions of Theodore Dreiser, James Joyce, Ezra Pound, Eugene O'Neill, Frank Harris, George Jean Nathan, Anita Loos, and Scott Fitzgerald but also included ethnic slurs, usually about Jews, for which he had long been known. Of Alfred Knopf, he wrote that the publisher "showed a certain amount of the obnoxious tactlessness of his race." He described Stelle Golde, who was *Smart Set's* editorial secretary, as "a grotesque Brooklyn Jewess."

Of Dorothy Thompson, Sinclair Lewis's second wife, Mencken wrote, "She was the true daughter of her Methodist pa—a tinpot messiah with an inflamed egoism that was wholly unameliorated by humor." Yet, Mencken was the one who exposed a Baltimore hotel's refusal to permit the African American poet Countee Cullen to speak. He fought against injustice wherever he found it, as in the execution of Sacco and Vanzetti or the deportation of Emma Goldman and other Jewish radicals following World War I when the Great Red Scare occurred.

Mencken coined many neologisms, including *Bible Belt*, *booboisie*, *smuthound*, and *Boobus americanus*. He so delighted in skewering Baptists and Methodists that he was dubbed "the Anti-Christ of Baltimore," although he was more "the Anti-Christian of Baltimore" and held that what Christians needed to do was practice the teachings of their Christ. He also targeted American society, with which he maintained a love-hate relationship: "There's no underestimating the intelligence of the American public" and "Democracy is the art of running the circus from the monkey cage." Asked why he stayed in the country if he found so much that was unworthy of reverence here, he quipped, "Why do men go to zoos?"

As for God, Mencken the caustic rationalist wrote, "It is impossible to imagine the universe run by a wise, just, and omnipotent God." As for his early religious experiences, he stated, "What I got in Sunday School . . . was simply a firm conviction that the Christian faith was full of palpable absurdities and the Christian God preposterous." And as for his faith, he said, "Faith may be defined briefly as an illogical belief in the occurrence of the improbable." (See entry for Neo-Humanism, which Mencken attacked.) {CE; CL; EU, John R. Burr; FUS; PA; RE; TRI; TYD}

Mendel, (Abbot) Gregor Johann (1822–1884)

An Austrian monk known for his work on heredity, Mendel had been forgotten until other botanists repeated his experiments and gave his name to the new theory of heredity. N. Iltis, a relative who wrote *Life of Mendel* (1932), states that Mendel was violently anti-Christian right up to the time when he entered the monastery. In fact, he wrote a poem in which he speaks of "the gloomy powers of superstition, which now oppress the world." A poor man, Mendel had entered the monastery because it offered a chance of study. As a priest, said McCabe, "he shirked his functions as far as possible, and even as abbot he bought Darwin's *Origin of Species* and accepted evolution, which was then anathema to all Catholics." Mendel's experiments became the basic tenets of genetics and were a notable influence in plant and animal breeding. {JM; RE}

Mendelsohn, Jack (1918–)

A Unitarian minister, Mendelsohn is author of *God, Allah, and Ju Ju: Religions in Africa Today* (1962) and *Being Liberal in an Illiberal Age: Why I Am A Unitarian Universalist.* In 1971 he wrote *Channing: The Reluctant Radical*, concerning the major nineteenth century Unitarian leader. In 1997 the Unitarian Universalist Association presented Mendelsohn with its Award for Distinguished Service to the cause of Unitarian Universalism.

Mendelsohn, Oscar Adolf (1896–1978)

Mendelsohn was a humanist, public analyst, musician, and writer. He wrote *The Earnest Drinker; Liars and Letters Anonymous*; *Drinking With Pepys*, and *Outrageous Liars*. In 1964 he was appointed honorary vice president of the Humanist Society of Victoria. Upon his death, he bequeathed to Monash University funds for presenting in perpetuity a free public lecture to promote the study of humanism, materialism, positivism, and other effects of the application of the scientific attitude to human affairs and thought. As a result, some of Australia's leading freethinkers have given lectures; e.g, Professor Sir Macfarlane Burnet, Professor John A. Passmore, and Sir Mark Oliphant. {SWW}

Mendelssohn, Moses (1729–1786)

Mendelssohn, a Jewish philosopher who was a leader in the movement for cultural assimilation, had a high repute in Germany for his philosophical works, and some were crowned by the Berlin Academy. In later years he had a more definite belief in God and immortality but not Judaism or Christianity. "He lived entirely in the sphere of deism and natural religion," McCabe quotes Baur as having written. He translated *The Psalms* and *The Pentateuch* into German. {CE; JM; RAT; RE}

Mendenhall, J. H. (19th Century)

Mendenhall, a freethinker, wrote *Christianity, A Fiction* (1892). {GS}

Mendes, Catulle (1841–1909)

A French-Jewish novelist, Mendes at the age of nineteen founded the *Revue fantaisiste* at Paris and was prosecuted for articles he wrote for it. In his volume of verse, *Pour dire devant le monde* (1891), Mendes gives free expression to his caustic atheism. {RAT; RE}

Mendez -Acosta, Mario (20th Century)

A television news commentator in Mexico City, Mendez-Acosta has written for *Free Inquiry*. At the Tenth International Humanist and Ethical Union (IHEU) World Congress held in Buffalo (1988), Mendez-Acosta addressed the gathering. He is a member of the Ibero-American Commission, a group of humanist leaders in

Spanish-speaking countries. In 1995, he spoke at the dedication of the Center for Inquiry in Amherst, New York, and in 1996 he was a key organizer with his wife, Patricia López Zaragoza, of the 1996 Humanist World Congress held in Mexico City. {*Free Inquiry*, Winter, 1986}

Mendizabal, Juan Alvarez (1790–1853)

Mendizabal, the son of a Jew named Mendez, was a Liberal Spanish statesman, a minister during the reign of Cristina. During the brief spell of power of the Voltairean liberals, Mendizabal contributed to the subjugation of Spain's clerical party and abolished the religious orders, proclaiming their goods as national property. According to McCabe, he "checked the monastic bodies of Spain, and enriched the national treasury from their swollen coffers." {BDF; RAT}

Mendoça, Pedro (20th Century)

A Brazilian, Mendoça spoke on the unification and the need for expansion of humanism at the Humanist World Congress held in Mexico City in 1996. Mendoça is a philosophic positivist.

Mendoza, Antonio (20th Century)

"I grew up as a Catholic," Mendoz said when asked about the religious images in his artwork, "but early on I gave up any sort of belief and stopped going to church. I don't particularly have any problem with the church since it has no effect on my life whatsoever. It upsets my mother that I am an atheist, but that's an issue she has to resolve herself." {CA}

Mendoza, Diego Hurtado de (1503–1575)

Mendoza was a famous and learnèd Spanish author. After studying Latin, Greek, Arabic, and Hebrew at the university, he joined the army. While at school he wrote the comic novel, *Lazarillo de Tormes*, which was condemned by the Inquisition. When sent on an embassy to Pope Paul III, the latter was greatly shocked at Mendoza's audacity and vehemence of speech. Because of the intolerant policy of Philip II, Mendoza's chief work, *History of the Moorish Wars*, remained unprinted for thirty years. The Inquisition also prohibited Mendoza's satires and burlesques. He commented on Aristotle, translating his *Mechanics*. {BDF}

Mendum, Ernest (Born 1853)

The son of Josiah P. Mendum, Mendum worked with his father at the Boston *Investigator*. He assisted in the organizing of the Paine Memorial Corporation and was an organizer of the Ingersoll Secular Society. {RAT; RE}

Mendum, Josiah P. (1811–1891)

Mendum, a publisher and the proprietor of the *Boston Investigator*, had become acquainted with Abner Kneeland in 1833. When Kneeland left Boston for the West for reasons of health, Mendum continued the paper together with Horace Seaver. Mendum was one of the founders of the Paine Memorial Hall in Boston and was a chief support of freethought there.

Among the titles he sold: *Theological Works of Thomas Paine* ($1); Thomas Paine, *The Age of Reason* ($3 per dozen); *Hume's Essays* ($1); *Speech of Abner Kneeland* (12¢); *Baron d'Holbach's System of Nature* ($1.25); Abner Kneeland, "A review of the Evidence of Christianity" (50¢); Ethan Allen, *Oracle of Reason* (37¢). {BDF; PUT; RAT}

Menendez, Albert J. (20th Century)

A contributing editor to *Americans for Religious Liberty*, Menendez is author or co-writer of more than twenty books including *Religion at the Polls* (1977), *Church Schools and Public Money* (1991), and *Church and State in Canada* (1997). His concerns are that states have generous give-aways to sectarian schools, which leads to a serious problem: keeping church and state separate. He edited *The Best of Church and State: 1948–1975* (1975). In 1978, he wrote *John F. Kennedy, Catholic and Humanist*. In 1993, his *Visions of Reality, What Fundamentalist Schools Teach*, examines the various textbooks used in fundamentalist schools, documenting that the schools promote prejudice against people of other faiths, distort history, derogate our literary heritage, cast science in a bad light, and otherwise indoctrinate children with "visions of reality" that are incompatible with public tax support. In *The December Wars* (1993), Menendez discusses religious symbols and ceremonies in the public square, tracing the celebration of Christmas as far back as the fourth century, when Catholic orthodoxy used Christmas as a major propaganda tool and a political issue as well as a religious observance. With Edd Doerr, Menendez has compiled *Religious Liberty and State Constitutions* (1993), in which are listed the religious liberty and church-state provisions of the fifty state constitutions. {FUS}

Meng-zi (Mencius; Meng Tzu) (371?–288? B.C.E.)

A great teacher, Meng-zi is memorable for his insistence on advancing Kongfu-zi's (Confucius's) view that man is by nature good and that humans are the main part of the state, so it follows that it is the ruler's fault if they go astray. Some rulers apparently were exemplary, for one rationalistic duke who lived earlier than 250 B.C.E. refused to permit the sacrifice of a man as a scapegoat on his behalf. In 166 B.C.E., also, the Han Emperor Wen permanently abolished such sacrifices. Meng-zi, a better sociologist than Lao-zi (Lao-tzu) or Kongfu-zi (K'ung Fu-tzu), taught that "it is only men of education who, without a certain livelihood, are able to maintain a fixed heart. As to the people, if they have not a certain livelihood, it follows that they will not have a fixed heart." Alas, laments Robertson, despite such a clear outlook, "the Chinese mass always pullulated on cheap food, at a low standard of comfort, and in a state of utter ignorance. . . . Centuries before our era, the Chinese had a rationalistic literature, an ethic no less earnest and far more sane than that of the Hebrews, and a line of known teachers as remarkable in their way as those of ancient Greece who flourished about the same period." But supernaturalism and superstition flourished just the same, for, as Robertson concludes, "there is an inherent tendency in all systematized and instituted religion to degenerate intellectually and morally, save for the constant corrective activity of freethought."

McCabe wrote that although Meng-zi "is much less frequently quoted than K'ung Fu-tzu, of whom he professed to be merely a disciple, he was in some respects greater and much more interesting. Like K'ung Fu-tzu he was an atheist, but he had not the conservatism of the older sage. There was a great ferment of thought in China at the time, and almost every fundamental theory of life had its apostle. Meng-tsu advocated the full social application of the ethic of K'ung Fu-tzu, especially his Golden Rule (Reciprocity). He denounced war and social injustice and was the first Chinese democrat. The modern Chinese writer Yuan Cho-ying well shows both his atheism and his very modern sentiments in *Le philosophie morale et politique de Mencius* (1927)." {CE; JM; JMR; RE}

Menninger, Karl A. (1893–1990)

Menninger was an eminent psychiatrist who had been a subscriber to *The Humanist*. A nominal Presbyterian, he wrote *Whatever Became of Sin?* (1988) and *The Human Mind Revisited* (1978). He is one of three sons of Dr. Charles Frederick Menninger, who founded the Menninger Foundation, which has had a major influence on treatment of the mentally ill. {HNS}

MENNONITES

Non-believers who tour in Israel or even in New York City are sometimes startled upon seeing Jews dressed in black and appearing to be at a rehearsal for some movie about life in the distant past. In Pennsylvania and elsewhere—for example, in Belize on large farms—they are similarly startled upon seeing Christians who appear as if they also are on a movie set, individuals who do not drive cars, use electricity from public utilities, accept Social Security or Medicare, or go to war.

Examples of the latter group are the American Mennonites, who are directly descended from three sects that originated in the European Reformation: the Swiss Brethren, Obenites, and Hutterites. The larger groups in America are the Old Mennonites, General Conference Mennonites, Mennonite Brethren in Christ, Mennoniten Brüder Gemeinde, Reformed Mennonites, and Old Order Amish.

The Old Mennonites are found in Lancaster County, Pennsylvania, and stress strict discipline, baptism by immersion of believers only, and widespread home missions. The movement is led by an unsalaried lay-clergy. They practice foot-washing, the anointing of the sick, and the kiss of charity (a salutation known as the holy kiss—*Romans* 16:16; *I Corinthians* 16:20; and *I Thessalonians* 5:26—which Professor William M. Beahm of the Bethany Biblical Seminary in Chicago, thinks was practiced "promiscuously among early Christians, but [is] now limited to the same sex and found only among certain religious groups like the Dunkers and others."

The Mennoniten Brüder Gemeinde is divided into two parts, the larger branch that immerses the applicant for baptism forward, the smaller that insists on backward immersion.

The Old Order Amish oppose all ritualism, do not allow church buildings, meet in houses or barns, conduct several-hour services in German, forbid pictures and insurance, and dress very plainly.

Menno Simons (1492-1559) was a Dutch Anabaptist (a re-baptizer) who had been a Roman Catholic priest. He rejected any state church and preached against religious persecution, oaths, the taking of life, and infant baptism. {ER}

Menocchio, Giacamo (1532–1607)

"Creation: All was chaos . . . and out of that bulk a mass formed—just as cheese is made out of milk—and worms appeared in it, and these were the angels . . . and among that number of angels, there was also God, he too having been created out of that mass at the same time." For penning this statement, Menocchio, a 16th century miller, was regarded as a heretic, a threat to the Church, and, as a result, he was burned at the stake, according to Florence Grippe in *The New York Times* (15 December 1991).

Mensah, Emmanuel Kofi (20th Century)

The chairman of Action for Humanism in Ikeja, Lagos State, Nigeria, Mensah has been studying for his doctorate in philosophy at the Adventist Seminary of West Africa in Nigeria. "Religion is the brainchild of fear, and fear is the parent of cruelty," he writes in an essay found in Norm Allen Jr.'s book. Although conversant with the ways of witch doctors, he also cites Thomas Paine and Bertrand Russell. Accused of being an Antichrist by an office worker, Mensah responds, "I am not an Antichrist. I am a humanist who is committed to the utilization of the fundamental faculties of reason and objectivity." To which the accuser cries, "Go, go, go away! You devil!" As for the future, he hopes extensive education will be possible. But humanism must not remain Eurocentric. On the second largest continent of the world, Mensah says it will be difficult to reach a population where only 20 percent can read. But songs, poetry, dramas, plays, and the media can logically be utilized to what he hopes to see, "the bright morning when Africa's problems will be solved through education and self-reliance rather than spirituality, astrology, numerology, magic, and other paranormal beliefs."

In 1997 he had returned to his native Ghana, where he planned to resume the editorship of *Sunways*, a humanist newsletter he edited in 1991. (See entry for Action for Humanism.) {AAH}

Mentelle, Edme (1730–1815)

Mentelle was a French geographer and historian. He wrote *Précis de l'Histoire des Hébreux* (1798) and *Précisde l'Histoire Universelle*, both of which are thoroughly anti-Christian. In fact, Mentelle doubted if Jesus ever existed. He was a member of the Institute and Chevalier of the Legion of Honor. {BDF; RAT}

Menuhin, Yehudi (1916–)

Menuhin, the renowned New York-born violinist, has won ten Grammy Awards and appeared throughout the world in concerts featuring both classical and modern composers. He wrote an autobiography, *Unfinished Business* (1977, and was co-writer of *The Music of Man* (1979, which is autobiographical. Menuhin is a member of the British Humanist Association. In 1993, Queen Elizabeth honored him by making him a Life Peer.

Mepham, George (1916–1995)

Mepham in Britain was secretary of the Sutton Humanist Group. With his wife, he co-founded the group in 1955 and was active for many years on the Executive Committee of the British Humanist Association. Barbara Smoker, president of the National Secular Society, presided over Mepham's funeral ceremony at the North East Surrey Crematorium.

MEPHISTOPHELES

In *Faust*, Goethe depicts a devil, Mephistopheles, who tempts Faust into selling his soul to the "powers of darkness." Marlowe, in his *Doctor Faustus*, spelled it Mephistophilis. {DCL}

Mercado Domenech, Serafin J. (20th Century)

A Mexican, Mercado spoke on education for the cyber-age at the 1996 Humanist World Congress held in Mexico City.

Mercer, Beryl (20th Century)

In Cornwall, Mercer is active with the Cornwall Humanists.

Mercier, Charles Arthur (1852–1919)

Although he began life as a cabin boy, Mercier ended as a distinguished authority on mental diseases, the author of *Conduct and Its Disorders* (1911). When Spiritualism became popular during the war of 1914–1918, he wrote a caustic criticism, *Spiritualism and Sir O. Lodge* (1917). Mercier was an agnostic. {RAT; RE}

Mercier, L. A. (19th Century)

Mercier wrote *La Libre Pensée*, which was published in Brussels in 1879. {BDF}

Meredith, Evan Powell (1811–1880)

Meredith was a Welsh writer, once a Baptist minister and an eloquent preacher in the Welsh tongue. He translated the Bible into Welsh. However, his investigation into the claims of Christianity made him resign his ministry. In *The Prophet of Nazareth* (1864), Meredith mentions a purpose of writing a work on the gospels but failed to include it. He did, however, expose the prophecies of Jesus. His *Amphilogia* (1867) was a reply to the Bishop of Landaff and the Rev. J. F. Francklin. {BDF; RAT}

Meredith, George (1829–1909)

One of England's greatest novelists, Meredith wrote cerebral works that contained psychological character studies. *Ordeal of Richard Feverel* (1859) is one of the Hampshire-born writer's best-known works. Even in his "late boyhood," he "detested religion," but not, according to his biographer R. E. Sencourt, Christianity as he interpreted it for himself. In his novels as well as in his poetry, he includes his belief in evolution—in life as a process of becoming. Of Meredith, Wheeler in 1889 said, "Deep thought and fine grace characterise his writings. As a poet Mr. Meredith is not popular, but his volumes of verse are marked by the highest qualities and give him a place apart from the throng of contemporary singers."

Meredith made numerous references to Darwin, Swinburne, and Renan as well as emphasized "the creative activity of nature" as the sole source of life and energy. He was one of the earliest members of the General Council of the Secular Education League, according to *Nineteenth Century* (April 1911), and he corresponded with freethinker G. W. Foote as well as "gave his name as well as his cheque" to the support of the *Freethinker*. In 1883, he protested against

Foote's imprisonment for blasphemy, and in one of his letters spoke of the fight against the priests as the best of causes.

Contemporary critics praise Meredith for his joyful belief in life as a process of evolution. Edward Clodd, who knew Meredith well, wrote in his *Memories* that Meredith wrote to him, "When I was quite a boy I had a spasm of religion that lasted six weeks, but I never since have swallowed the Christian fable."

On 13 April 1909, Meredith wrote a letter to Theodore Watts-Dunton on the death of Swinburne, which had taken place three days previously. "He was the greatest of our lyric poets—of the world, I could say, considering what a language he had to wield." On April 23, he wrote to Foote, enclosing a contribution to the *Freethinker* fund, and this was almost certainly the last letter he ever wrote.

On May 4, he said: "Nature is my God and I trust in her." His remains were cremated at Woking. There was no religious service, but when the ashes were buried at Darking Cemetery, Foote reported, "a clergyman muttered some Anglican prayers." That same day, in Westminster Abbey, "the Dean conducted with great ceremony a requiem service."

Freethinkers, however, have been most inspired by Meredith's own thought about finality:

> Into the Earth that gives the rose
> Shall I with shuddering fall?

{BDF; CE; CL; FO; *Freethinker* (20 October 1912); *Freethinker*, January 1998; JM; RE; TRI; TYD}

Mérimée, Prosper (1803–1870)

Mérimée was a cultivated gentleman, a painstaking student of archaeology, a linguist who translated Russian authors into French, a senator under the Empire, and a member of the Academy. *The Chronicle of the Reign of Charles IX* (1829) has an objectivity and psychological penetration called rare among the romanticists. According to Robertson, he—like Flaubert, Zola, Daudet, Maupassant, and the De Goncourts—was a rationalist. In his anonymous brochure on H(enri) B(eyle), "Eleutheropolis," there is an open profession of atheism. {BDF; CE; JM; JMR; RAT; RE}

Merleau-Ponty, Maurice (20th Century)

Merleau-Ponty, in *Humanism and Terror* (1947), discussed humanism in terms of his distaste for Communism.

Mero, Ralph (20th Century)

Mero is a Unitarian minister who is executive director of Compassion in Dying. The group has assisted a number of people who wanted to commit suicide, offering guidance and suggestions on how to end a life. Members say, however, they do not administer lethal drugs, but refer patients to doctors for prescriptions that taken in sufficient doses can be fatal. His group praised a 1994 decision by Federal Judge Barbara Rothstein that struck down a 140-year-old Washington State ban on assisted suicide. (See entry for suicide. Also see "On Their Own Timetable," *The World*, January/February 1995.)

Merrell, Lloyd Frank (20th Century)

The Humanist (Spring, 1941) contained Merrell's "Look Within," which one scientific humanist says is commendably humanistic but, notes a wag, shows a questionable command of anatomy:

> We seek for God through age on age
> Outside of man with futile quest.
> The God of every pilgrimage
> Is deep within the pregnant breast.

Merrill, Walter (20th Century)

Merrill wrote *From Statesman to Philosopher: A Study of Bolingbroke's Deism* (1949). {FUK; FUS}

Merritt, Henry (1822–1877)

An English painter and writer from Oxford, Merritt on coming to London lived with Holyoake and contributed to the *Reasoner*, using the signature "Christopher." Merritt wrote on *Dirt and Pictures* and *Robert Dalby and His World of Troubles*, among other works. {BDF; RAT}

Merton, Thomas (1915–1968)

An American religious writer and poet, Merton was a Roman Catholic convert who became a Trappist monk in 1941 and was later ordained a priest. In 1965 when a refrigerator was delivered to his hermitage, he was bothered with the idea that he had chosen to live the life of a hermit but should a hermit have a refrigerator? He decided that the solitary life could be judged only by the interior, not by the external surroundings. Or, as *The Economist* (20 July 1996) observed, "Trappings have little to do with Trappists." Merton died in an accident in Thailand. {CE}

Merwin, W(illiam) S(tanley) (1927–)

Merwin, a poet and member of the American Academy of Arts and Letters, is known for his translation of *The Cid* (1959) and for such poetry such as *A Mask for Janus* (1952), *Drunk in the Furnace* (1960), *The Carrier of Ladders* (1970, for which he received a Pulitzer award), and *The Compass Flower* (1977).

Responding about humanism, Merwin wrote the present author:

> "Humanism" *tout court*, as in your first category, is a term that I would not have made a point of quarrelling with, at one time, if it had been applied to me, though I would never have laid claim to it on my own and have always been uncomfortable with "isms" and that one is no exception. But I have come to have and to recognize further misgivings about the word and what strike me as the assumptions around it, which seem serious enough for me to avoid the use of it insofar as possible, and to feel that I do not at all fit the ascriptions that it implies.
>
> What I hear in the word "humanist" now is the suggestion of a "devotion to humanity and human interests" exclusively of, or in preference to, or *as against* any and all other forms of life. At its least it connotes to me a rather smug and stuffy club, content with its membership policy, and at its worst a comfortable platform from which to justify the current proliferation of human fabrication, convenience, and self-importance, at the expense of every non-human living being.
>
> What I value most about my own species, what I take to be singular about it, is the craving to see, beyond immediate comfort, advantage, and condition, the nature of life as a whole in each of its forms and in its full mystery, and the ability to recognize itself as a gifted part of that undefinable and unqualifiable totality. I think of that as our true and only place, and I believe that any values we may arrogate to ourselves that do not arise from such a recognition and its sobering demands for proportion and responsibility, are simply egotism writ large—and the great classical "humanists" themselves, as well as the events of our age, have made plain enough the consequences of that.

{WAS, 19 May 1989}

Meslier, Jean (1664–1729)

Meslier was a French atheist, a critic of popular superstition. During the French Revolution, Maréchal cited Meslier as being one of the greatest atheists of all time. To him, all religions are nothing but "*erreurs, abus, illusions, et impostures.*" However, he had been a curé of Etrépigny, in Champagne, and was known as a charitable priest, a champion of animal rights, and a religious man. Surprisingly, at his death he left two autographed copies of *Testament*, in which he wrote his personal views about life. These have been called "one of the most notorious examples of apostasy." A third copy was to have been deposited in the archives of the jurisdiction of Sainte-Menehould. But by some strange chance one of the books circulated, and then one hundred copies appeared on the market in Paris, selling at ten louis apiece.

On the copy he left for his parishioners, he wrote, "I have not dared to say it during my life, but I will say it at least in dying or after my death." He said that although some men before him had impugned miracles, some gospels, some dogma, some the conception of deity, some the tyranny of kings, he impugned them all. And whereas most deists had eulogized the character of the Gospel Jesus, Meslier envelops it in his harshest invective. His writing style was slow and heavy—the style of a carthorse, Voltaire called it. Robertson has commented that although Voltaire, d'Holbach, and Diderot were slow in publicizing Meslier's work, "the entire group of fighting freethinkers of the age was in some sense inspired by the old priest's legacy." Writing in *Freethought History* (#3, 1992), Gordon Stein explains a commonly held misconception that Anna Knoop's translation—*Superstition in All Ages by Jean Meslier . . . Translated from the French*—

is by Meslier. However, Stein explains, the book is a translation of Baron d'Holbach's *Le Bon Sens* (*The Good Sense*).

Except for the excerpts from his will, in which he requested to be buried in his own garden, Meslier's work have never been translated into English. In his will, Meslier left his property to his parishioners. {BDF; EU, Aram Vartanian; JMR; JMRH; RAT; RE; TRI}

Messadié, Gerald (20th Century)

Messadié, an atheist, grew up in Egypt and is the author of fifteen books. *A History of the Devil* (1997) carries the message that belief in the Devil actually leads one to evil. {George Rowell, *Pique*, March 1999}

Messenger, Dally (1938–)

Messenger is an Australian civil celebrant, humanist, and educationalist. In 1970, he was the first ever to apply to become an independent, authorized, civil celebrant in Australia. One reason the clergy accepted the concept is that they objected to having been "forced" previously to officiate at inappropriate ceremonies.

For Messenger, all humans are deserving of such ceremonies, even those whom the clergy do not like. {SWW}

Messer, William (20th Century)

Messer, an activist member of the Free Inquiry Group in Cincinatti, Ohio, is on the board of that city's American Civil Liberties Union.

MESSIAH

Although the word is not found in the Old Testament as a proper name or as a technical term, "messiah" appears in Apocalyptic literature such as *Enoch* 48:10 and refers to men, principally kings and high priests whose consecration to their high office was symbolized by the ceremony of pouring oil on their heads. Such a rite gave what was considered a divine afflatus. Saul was designated "the Meshiach Yahweh," or anointed of the Lord. Others were David, Solomon, John, Jehoahaz and, when there were no longer kings over Israel, reference is made in *Ezekiel* and *Leviticus* to the anointing of high priests. Because of their role in history as "a kingdom of priests and a holy nation," the Jewish people are frequently spoken of as "God's anointed."

Following the destruction of Judea in 586 B.C.E., the Jews entertained the hope of an early restoration of their independence and the re-establishment of the monarchy under a scion of the Davidic dynasty whose throne would endure forever. Zerubbabel was seen as a possible fulfillment of this hope. The prophets of Israel projected the vision of the coming of the Great Day of the Lord, when God's kingdom would be universally established. The longing for the coming of a personal Messiah assumed greater and greater prominence whenever the Jewish religion was threatened, and in the year 5000 of the Creation Calendar it was believed a Messiah would appear and inaugurate the millennium.

Jesus, according to Frederick Clifton Grant who once taught at Union Theological Seminary, "did not proclaim himself as Messiah nor did he undertake to gather a group of followers whom he could lead in a revolt against the Roman authority." Grant adds that the Christian story of the last days of Jesus "was never looked upon as a documentary account of the proceedings. . . . It is difficult to maintain the traditional view that Jesus claimed, in the presence of the high priest and his satellites, to be either the Messiah or the Son of Man who was expected to come upon the clouds of heaven."

In the 20th century, the Grand Rabbi Menachem Mendel Schneerson was believed to be the Messiah by many Lubavitchers. A pluralist, he steadfastly believed that traditional Judaism was the only Judaism, but he welcomed the non-Orthodox even if they only visited in order to sample what he had to offer. Over 1,500 Chabad houses, or Lubavitch centers, were opened from Morocco and Hong Kong to Kiev and Seattle, and the organization allegedly took in one hundred million dollars a year in contributions. In 1991 when Schneerson prophesied to Hasidic groups that they were living in the messianic era, other rabbis rejoiced and proclaimed that "Schneerson *is* the Messiah," some even stepping up campaigns to do good deeds in order that the arrival of the Messianic era might be hastened. Despite his having two strokes and being on his deathbed, he was aware that his followers fervently believed he would not die. When he succumbed, however, his followers were so sure he would not die that they had made no preparations whatsoever for his burial. "Once he is out of the body," a rabbi rationalized, "it is the soul and you have no more limitations. Hopefully, he can accomplish everything he wanted to now." Many believe Menachem Schneerson will rise from the grave and declare himself the Messiah, but others showed concern that he had left no directions as to who would control the movements five hundred million dollar budget in the event he was unable to do so.

Psychologists note that when events challenge beliefs, the response can be reinterpretations that allow believers to weather periods of doubt. "Indeed," observed *New York Times* reporter David Gonzalez (14 June 1994), "the thousands of mourners that have descended upon the city can help to strengthen the ties of faith that bind the Lubavitcher movement's estimated 200,000 members worldwide." In short, the Messiah "cannot" die . . . but, if he does, there is a reason. (See entry for Sabbatai, who was married to a Christian prostitute and proclaimed himself the Messiah. For the view that Isaiah's "sign" had nothing to do with a messiah, see entry for Kenneth E. Nahigian.) {ER}

METAPHYSICAL SOCIETY

The Metaphysical Society was a debating group that met in London nine times a year to discuss issues pertaining to philosophical ideas and religious beliefs. The members, some of the most notable figures of Victorian Society, included theists as well as non-theists. Included in the 1870s were William Kingdon Clifford, William Gladstone, Thomas Henry Huxley, Archbishop Henry Manning, John Ruskin, and Alfred Lord Tennyson. {Tim Madigan, numerous conversations.}

METAPHYSICS

Metaphysics is a division of philosophy which is concerned with the fundamental nature of reality and being. It includes ontology, cosmology, and often epistemology. Metaphysics, therefore, goes beyond or transcends the natural science of physics. The source of the word is *Metaphysica*, the title of Aristotle's treatise on the subject.

Since the middle of the 19th century, however, the dominant philosophical trend has been in the direction of positivism, which denies metaphysical assertions. The logical positivists, for example, by using the verification principle find that metaphysical questions are meaningless, unable to be tested. Philosophic naturalists such as A. J. Ayer and Bertrand Russell were anti-metaphysics in their writing, but some contemporary supernaturalists are known to continue speculating that if God is all-powerful He is capable of arranging for a number of angels to dance upon the point of a pin.

Writers of fiction enjoy questioning whether things are genuinely real, as in Franz Kafka's *The Metamorphosis*, in which Gregor Samsa wakes up one morning to find himself transformed into a giant insect. A literalist would assume Gregor actually did so; figuratively, Kafka was writing a tale of psychological terror.

Schopenhauer said that humans are doomed by nature to be metaphysical creatures. However, according to Michael J. Dee's *Conclusions* (1917),"There are no more metaphysicians among the educated Japanese. Why should there be among us?" (See the entry for verification principle. Also see the *Encyclopedia of Philosophy*, Vol. 5.) {CE; DCL; ER; TYD}

Metcalf, John (20th Century)

Metcalf in 1995 was appointed company secretary of the Rationalist Press Association. In 1996 he was named Administrative Director of the RPA.

Metcalf, Paul (1918-1999)

Metcalf's mother was Eleanor Thomas Metcalf, a granddaughter of Herman Melville and his literary executor. His father, Henry Knight Metcalf, was a descendant of Roger Williams. Although Metcalf said he had thought little about his famous ancestors, in his 1965 book, *Genoa*, he acknowledged his relationship to Melville and told his hometown newspaper, *The Berkshire Eagle*, that the book "was a way of getting the Melville monkey off my back." Metcalf was instrumental in furthering Melville studies. In 1921 the manuscript of Melville's *Billy Budd* was discovered in a tin box in his family's home. Just before his death, two more boxes of family papers were discovered.

Metchnikov, Élie (1845–1916)

Metchnikov was a Russian writer in French, the author of many works including one on Japan. After working with Pasteur, Metchnikoff became deputy director of the Pasteur Institute in Paris. He introduced the theory of phagocytosis, that certain white blood cells are able to engulf and destroy harmful substances such as bacteria. In 1908, he shared with Paul Ehrlich the Nobel Prize in Physiology. Metchnikov also developed a theory that lactic-acid bacteria in the digestive tract could, by preventing putrefaction, prolong life. And with P. P. É. Roux, he experimented with calomel ointment as a treatment for syphilis. In *The Nature of Man* (1904) Metchnikov expressed his atheism, according to McCabe. He also wrote a critical article on Christian communion in *Revue Internationale des Sciences Biologiques*. {BDF; CE; JM; RAT; RE}

Metrodoros (4th or 5th Century B.C.E. ?)

According to Robertson, there were three freethinking Metrodoroses: Metrodoros of Lampsakos, a friend of Epicurus; Metrodoros of Chios; and another Metrodoros of Lampsakos. The latter was a disciple of Anaxagoras and zealously carried out his master's teaching as to the deities and heroes of Homer, "resolving them into mere elemental combinations and physical agencies, and making Zeus stand for mind, and Athenê for art." James Hemming has written of the 4th Century Metrodoros, an Epicurean philosopher, who wrote: "to consider the Earth the only populated world in infinite space is as absurd as to assert that, in an entire field sown with millet, only one grain will grow." {JMR; JMRH; *New Humanist*, November 1993}

METROPOLITAN COMMUNITY CHURCH: See entry for Gay.

Mettrie, Julien de la: See La Mettrie, Julien de.

Metzger, Bruce M. (20th Century)

Metzger with Michael D. Coggan edited *The Oxford Companion to the Bible* (1993). The work is written in a scholarly, not necessarily skeptical, point of view.

Metzger, Tom (20th Century)

Metzger is a white racist leaders who is an atheist. He founded WAR (White Aryan Resistance) and is active on the radical and racial right. According to *Soldiers of God: White Supremacists and Their Holy War for America* by Howard L. Bushart, John R. Craig, and Myra Barnes, Metzger originally was a part of Christian Identity. His rejection of religion is thought not to be based upon science but, rather, on aesthetics—he feels that Christianity is not suited for the white man. "Break out of your death cell, White man!" he has editorialized on the Web. "Your race and only your race must be your religion." {CA}

Meunier, Amédée Victor (Born 1817)

Meunier was a French writer who popularized science. He wrote *Scientific Essays* (1851–1858) and the *Ancestors of Adam* (1875). {BDF}

MEXICAN FREETHINKERS, HUMANISTS

The Mexican Ethical Rationalist Association (*Asociacion Mexicana Ética Racionalista*, Apdo 19-546, Mexico City DF 0-3900, Mexico) is a leading ethical rationalist group in Central America and publishes a quarterly, *Razonamientos*. It is an associate member of the International Humanist and Ethical Union. (See entry for its quarterly, *Razonamientos*. Also see entries for José Luis María Mora and Ignacio Ramirez.)

MEXICAN POSITIVISTS

Gabino Barreda (1818–1881) introduced a Comtean variety of positivism in Mexico. Upon being put in charge of educational reform in 1867, he introduced changes that reflected his antischolastic views. Later, during the dictatorship of Porfirio Díaz, Justo Sierra led the intellectual life and was more inspired by Mill and Spencer than by Comte. Upon being named minister of education, Sierra reestablished the National University, which had been abolished earlier as a result of a church-state controversy. Like most positivists, Sierra based his anticlericalism on what he regarded as the religious superstition. In 1974, Leopoldo Zea wrote *Positivism in Mexico*. {EU}

Meyer, George J. (20th Century)

A physician, Meyer is a member of the freedom From Religion Foundation who lives in Florida. For *Freethought Today* (August 1998), he wrote, "Science and Religion Never Friendly."

Meyer, Hans (Born 1858)

Meyer, a writer who traveled around the world, climbed some of the highest ranges of Asia, Africa, and America, and wrote various travel works. In 1884 he joined his father in a publishing firm and edited the *Konversations-Lexikon*, an important German encyclopedia. In 1891 he married Haeckel's daughter Lisbeth, and he shared the views of his father-in-law. {RAT}

Meyer, John J. (20th Century)

Meyer, a freethinker, wrote *20,000 Trails Under the Universe With a Cerebroscope* (1917). {GS}

Meyer, Lodewijk (17th Century)

A Dutch physician, Meyer was a friend and follower of Spinoza. He published *Exercitatio Paradoxa* (1666) on the philosophical interpretation of scripture, a work Wheeler avers has wrongly been ascribed to Spinoza. {BDF}

Meyer, Sophie (20th Century)

Meyer, president of the Residents Association at Pennswood Village in Newtown, Pennsylvania, participated in the 1996 Humanist World Congress in Mexico City. Her e-mail: <smyr@aol.com>.

Meyers, Carol (20th Century)

A professor of religion at Duke University, Meyers is on the Council for Secular Humanism's Biblical Criticism Research Project.

Meyerson, Barbara (20th Century)

Meyerson is an Adjunct Leader of the Society for Ethical Culture in New York City.

Mezentius [King] (Ancient Rome)

In *The Aeneid*, Vergil's writing of the Roman national epic in the 1st Century B.C.E., Mezentius, King of the Etruscans, is depicted as a classic type of freethinker, doubtless drawn from barbaric life. A *divum contemptor*, he calls his right arm his god and in dying declares that he appeals to no deity. He does not, however, deny that gods exist. {JMR; JMRH}

Mialhe, Hippolyte (Born 1834)

Mialhe was a French writer who, from 1860 to 1862, was with the French army of occupation at Rome. He organized federations of freethinkers in France, edited *L'Union des Libres-Penseurs*, and wrote *Mémoires d'un libre Penseur* (1888). {BDF}

Miall, Louis Compton (Born 1842)

A biologist who had taught at Leeds University, Miall was Fullerian professor of physiology at the Royal Institution (1904–1905) and President of the Zoological Section of the British Association in 1897. His *History of Biology* was published by the Rationalist Press Association in 1911. {RAT}

Michaels, Barbara (20th Century)

Michaels is on the Board of Governors of The Humanist Institute.

Michaud, Yves (20th Century)

Michaud, in France, is a corresponding member of The Hume Society, a group engaged in scholarly activity concerning David Hume.

Michelangelo Buonarroti (1475–1564)

As did Leonardo da Vinci, Michelangelo typified the ideal in art of "a new type—the universal man—the many-sided personality, delighting in every kind of this-earthly achievement" rather than the old type, the ascetic monk as ideal human. The Sistine Chapel ceiling and the homoerotic sculpture of *David* are his best-known works. The latter scandalized Australian authorities, who even in the present century have sent police to seize coffee-table books containing photos of the nude statue. His poems and sonnets were not published until 1960, having been altered for centuries to show that the love poems were addressed to women, not men (as was his original intent).

Although his "Pieta" and "Moses" earned high praise from church officials, he was aware that *Deuteronomy* IV: 16-18, specifically prohibits "the likeness of male or female, the likeness of any beast that is on the earth, the likeness of any winged fowl that flieth in the air, the likeness of anything that creepeth on the ground, the likeness of any fish that is in the waters beneath the earth." Both the Old Testament and the Qur'an are scathing about idolatry, and Michelangelo (along with other artists of his time) was aware that religious Jews could not even make or own statues or busts.

Michelangelo never married, but according to *The Advocate* (19 August 1997) he likely was "intimate" with a Roman nobleman named Tommaso Cavalieri and, perhaps, with Pope Julius III. {CE; CL; GL}

Michelet, Jules (1798–1874)

Michelet was a French historian, author of *History of France* and *The French Revolution*, and the greatest historian of the romantic school. With his friend Quinet, he wrote *The Jesuits* (1843).

In 1851, refusing the oath of allegiance to Louis Napoleon (later Napoleon III), Michelet lost his position as professor of history at the *Collège de France*. In 1867, upon publication of his major work, the *Histoire de France* (1833–1867), he traced the biography of the nation as a whole, rather than concentrating on persons or groups of people. His work was allegedly marred by emotional bias against the clergy, the nobility, and the monarchic institutions, but his critics were complaining against his atheism. *Sorceress* (1862) dealt with witchcraft in the Middle Ages, a work which like his other works provoked Christian critics.

"Man," Michelet once wrote, "is his own Prometheus," to which he added that he had "no faith but humanity." {BDF; CE; JM; RAT; RE}

Michener, James (1907–1997)

Michener, the Pulitzer Prize-winning author of *Tales of the South Pacific* (1984), was one of the few major American authors to publicly acknowledge his secular humanism. In 1989, while a guest lecturer on a Star Princess Cruise shop plowing Alaskan waters, the writer of numerous novels gave a talk to the ship's auditorium-packed crowd during which he recounted his being a foundling who had never had skates, a wagon, or a sled. His clothes, he said, were always somebody else's. And he added, "I never felt in a position to reject anyone. I could be Jewish, part Negro, almost everything else. I am a Humanist, a knee-jerk liberal. I am a Humanist because I think humanity can, with moral guidance, create a decent society."

In a popular essay he refuted critics who attacked his humanistic credo, one that supported secular and liberal values. In *Parade* (24 November 1991):

> I was raised as an orphan by a farm couple and took their name. I know nothing of my parents so I never felt in a position to reject anybody. I could be Jewish, part Negro, probably not an Oriental, but almost anything else. This has loomed large in my thoughts.
>
> . . . . I decided (after listening to a "talk radio" commentator who abused, vilified, and scorned every noble cause to which I had devoted my entire life that) I was both a Humanist and a liberal, each of the most dangerous and vilified type. I am a Humanist because I think humanity can, with constant moral guidance, crate a reasonably decent society. I am terrified of restrictive religious doctrine, having learned from history that when men who adhere to any form of it are in control, common men like me are in peril. I do not believe that pure reason can solve the perceptual problems unless it is modified by poetry and art and social vision. So I am a Humanist. And if you want to charge me with being the most virulent kind—a *secular humanist*—I accept the accusation. But I do not want to be accused of atheism. No man who loves the book of *Deuteronomy* and the first chapter of the *Epistle of James*, as I do, can be totally non-religious. . . .

In *The World is My Home: A Memoir* (1992), Michener again described his philosophy as being a kind of "liberal humanism" in the vein of Thomas More, Thomas Jefferson, and John Dewey.

Although unsure of his parentage and his birthdate, Michener thought he had been born in New York and had arrived in Doylestown, Pennsylvania, when he was about two weeks old. Mabel Haddock Michener, a poor young widow, he wrote in his autobiography, "made her living by taking in orphaned children and doing other families' laundry."

When ninety and suffering from poor health, he chose to discontinue his life-saving kidney dialysis treatment and died of complications following renal failure. John Kings, a longtime friend and assistant, explained Michener's personally choosing to end his life. "He felt he had accomplished what he wanted to accomplish in terms of his life's work. He did not want to suffer a long series of complications." (See entry for Hernan Rodriguez, who quotes from Michener's *Iberia*.) {CE; HNS2; Thaila Daley Kleinoeder, *The Pen Woman*, March-April 1998; TYD}

MICHIGAN HUMANISTS AND FREETHINKERS

Michigan has the following groups:

- American Atheists, Inc., PO Box 96, Wayne, Michigan 48184-0096. Henry Schmuck is a contact; E-mail: <hmorgan@oeonline.com>.
- Freethought Association of West Michigan (ASHS), PO Box 9873, Wyoming, Michigan 49509
- Great Lakes Humanist Society, PO Box 1183, Mt. Pleasant, MI 48804. E-mail: <humanist@netscape.net>.
- Humanist Community of Central Michigan (AHA), 2401 Wellington Road, Lansing, Michigan 48910. Ron Clement is its contact. Larry Reyka is the coordinator of the north central region of the AHA.
- Humanist Ethical Church, 6033 Hopkins Road, Flint, Michigan 48506. The Rev. Paul O'Brien is the leader. E-mail: <paul@tir.com>
- Humanist Fellowship of West Michigan (AHA), 6647 Noffke Drive, Caledonia, Michigan 49316. Dirk Nebbeling is a contact. The group's homepage on the Web: <http://members.aol.com/faowm>.
- Humanists of South East Michigan (AHA), POB 432191, Pontiac, Michigan 48343. T. L. Hall is its contact.
- Kalamazoo College Freethinkers are at: <www.secularhumanism.org/cfa/orgs.html>.
- Michigan Technological University's Freethinker, Atheists, and Rationalists Organization are on the Web at: <www.secularhumanism.org/cfa/orgs.html>.
- Monroe County Community College Humanists are found on the Web at: <www.secularhumanism.org/cfa/orgs.html>.
- Secular Humanists of Detroit (ASHS), POB 432191, Pontiac, Michigan 48343; 220 Bagley, Room 908, Detroit, Michigan 48226 (313) 962-1777. Contact: Steve Walker. E-mail: <avhogan@dhol.com>.
- Society for Humanistic Judaism, 28611 West 12 Mile Road, Farmington Hills, Michigan 48334.
- University of Michigan at Flint Humanists: <www.secularhumanism.org/cfa/orgs.html>.
- Western Michigan University's Atheists, Heathens, and Agnostics group is on the Web: <www.secularhumanism.org/cfa/orgs.html>.

MICHIGAN TECHNOLOGICAL UNIVERSITY

In Houghton, Michigan, the Michigan Technological University's Freethinker, Atheists, and Rationalists Organization is on the Web: <http://www.secularhumanism.org/cfa/orgs.html>.

Michnik, Adam (20th Century)

Michnik is editor of *Gazeta Wyborcza*, Poland's leading newspaper. In 1993 he was named a Humanist Laureate in the Council for Secular Humanism's International Academy of Humanism. He is a political writer and co-founder of KOR (Workers' Defense Committee), the organization of dissident intellectuals that helped to end communist rule in Poland. His essay, "The Church and the

Marty's Stake in Poland," is included in *Challenges to the Enlightenment, Essays in Defense of Reason and Science* (1994).

Micklewright, F.M. Amphlett (1908–)

A freethinker, Micklewright wrote *Rationalism and Culture* (19–?) and *The New Orthodoxy* (1943). {FUK; GS}

MICROBES

• We live in evolutionary competition with microbes. There is no guarantee that we will win.

—Dr. Joshua Lederberg, Nobel Prize Winner, 1958

Before birth, the human fetus is germ-free. But as the newborn passes through the birth canal or is delivered by Cesarean operation, bacteria inhabit the body. Few places in nature, in fact, harbor populations as diverse and numerous as those found in the human body. Microbiologist Dr. Jeffrey Gordon of Washington University in St. Louis estimates that at least four hundred species set up housekeeping in the baby's gut, and many more reside on the skin, the mouth, and elsewhere. For the most part, however, they work on their hosts' behalf and in subtle and intriguing ways. In a Darwinian struggle for survival they not only feed their hosts but also help synthesize vitamins. "The colon almost looks like it evolved for the purpose of harboring bacteria," Dr. Abigail Salyers, a microbiologist at the University of Illinois, has noted. The microbes, which have been evolving for billions of years and are always seeking new niches such as the plaque on human teeth, "want a free lunch," Dr. Salyers has stated. "We want to survive in their world and take advantage of it. Thus our bodies have evolved to accommodate microbes. We should love them. They're like our mother. They clean up our messes."

In fact, Dr. Carl R. Woese, an evolutionary microbiologist at the University of Illinois in Urbana, has observed, "If you wiped all multicellular life forms off the face of the earth, microbial life might shift a tiny bit [but] if microbial life were to disappear, that would be it—instant death for the planet!" {*The New York Times*, 15 October 1996}

MICROCOSM: See entry for macrocosm.

Middlebrooks, Dennis (20th Century)

Middlebrooks, who works in New York City for Bank Leumi, jokingly describes himself as one of the Jewish-owned bank's "Saturday men," explaining that by being a freethinker he can work on others' sabbath. Formerly president of the Secular Humanist Society of New York, he joined in 1998 with Warren Allen Smith, another former president, to found FANNY (Freethinking Activist Nonbelieving New Yorkers).

Middlebrooks is one of the Civil War and Robert G. Ingersoll cognoscenti. He has been published widely in letters-to-the-editor columns. A courageously independent thinker, he is an active rather than a passive nonbeliever. (See entry for Freethinking Activist Nonbelieving New Yorkers.)

Middleton, Conyers (1683–1750)

Middleton, a fellow of Trinity College, Cambridge, wrote *Letter from Rome, Showing an Exact Conformity between Popery and Paganism* (1729), in which, according to Robertson, "the part of paganism in Christianity is so set forth as to carry inference further than the argument ostensibly goes." His proclamation did nothing to check the spread of open deism among students at Oxford University, the university officials publicly lamented. Middleton is considered to be one of the earliest English rationalistic theologians. He as a latitudinarian advocated opening the church to a broad spectrum of beliefs. Middleton wrote a classic *Life of Cicero*. {BDF; CE; FUK; JMR; JMRH}

Middleton, Hannah Elina (1942–)

Middleton is an Australian atheist and Marxist anthropologist. Asked to describe her life's stance, she replied with a quotation from the Russian dramatist Aleksandr Nikolayevitch Ostrovsky (1823–1886): "Man's dearest possession is life and since it is given to him to live but once he must so live as to suffer no torturing regrets for years without purpose, so live as not to be seared with the shame of a cowardly and trivial past, so live that dying he can say all my life and my strength has been given to the finest cause in the world: the liberation of mankind." {SWW}

Miescher, Friedrich (19th Century)

Miescher isolated a substance which he called nuclein (now known as DNA, or deoxyribo nucleic acid) in 1869. Not until the last half of the 20th Century did research reveal its significance as the material of which the gene is composed. Philosophers have generally overlooked the importance of Miescher's discovery. {CE}

Mignacca, Marge (20th Century)

Mignacca is a contributing editor of *The American Rationalist.*

Mignardi, G. (19th Century)

Mignardi was an Italian writer, a freethinker who published *Memorie di un Nuovo Credente* (Memoirs of a New Believer, 1884). {BDF}

MIHRAB

Muslims who must face Mecca, but who cannot tell in which direction Mecca is, look for a mihrab, a niche in the wall of a mosque or a room that indicates the direction.

Analogously, freethinkers who cannot tell in which direction Amherst, New York, is consult an atlas, use a compass, or inquire at a petrol station.

Milbrath, Lester W. (20th Century)

Milbrath is professor emeritus of environmental studies at the State University of New York at Buffalo. He addressed the Tenth International Humanist and Ethical Union (IHEU) World Congress held in Buffalo (1988) and is author of *Learning to Think Environmentally* (1996).

Milelli, Domenico (Born 1841)

Milelli was an Italian poet whose family intended to make him a priest. However, turned out to be a rank pagan, as shown by his *Odi Pagane* (1879), *Canzonieri* (1884), and other works. {BDF; RAT}

Miles, Austin (1933–)

Miles's *Don't Call Me Brother* (1989) describes how he went from circus ringmaster to Pentecostal televangelist and back again. His experiences with the born-again are detailed. In *Setting the Captives Free* (1990), he has members of the Assemblies of God and other Pentecostal churches tell how they were victimized.

Miles, Jack (1942–)

Miles is author of the controversial *God: A Biography* (1995). An Episcopalian who once was a member of the Jesuit order and studied at both the Gregorian College in Rome and Hebrew University in Jerusalem, Miles treats God as a character in a literary work, the Bible. Just as Hamlet and Don Quixote are "real," so is God. "No character . . . on stage, page, or screen," Miles says, "has ever had the reception that God has had." God, he writes, is a male with multiple personalities. First, he created the world in order to make a self-image, which, explained Phyllis Trible in a *New York Times* review (14 May 1995), indicates that "He does not fully understand who He is but discovers Himself through interaction with humanity. Immediately the focus narrows to the man and the woman in the garden. When they disobey their creator, He responds vindictively and so reveals His own inner conflict. Called God in *Genesis I*, he is lofty, powerful, and bountiful; called Lord God in *Genesis II* and *III*, he is intimate and volatile. Ambivalent about His image, the creator becomes the destroyer: the floor descends. A radical fault runs through the character of God."

The work infuriated religious fundamentalists but was found refreshing by religious liberals. (See review of *God* by Robert Gorham Davis in *Free Inquiry*, Summer 1996.)

Miles, William John (1871–1942)

Miles in 1912 was secretary of the Rationalist Press Association of New South Wales, Australia. He was a rationalist, public accountant, businessman, and eccentric. In 1914 he published the *Sydney Rationalist Annual*. When his Australia First and right-wing *Independent Sydney Secularist* ceased in 1940 after forty-nine issues, Miles wrote that censorship had caused him to suspend publication. However, a new group continued the journal, saying that it now was being put out "by a few atheists who do not favour the Communistic Propaganda which has become a feature with the Rationalist Association of New South Wales (although many of the members are certainly not Communists)."

Milk, Harvey (1930–1978)

Milk, a political conservative who became an ardent liberal, was elected in 1977 to the San Francisco Board of Supervisors. A gay activist, he along with San Francisco Mayor George Moscone were shot and killed by former city supervisor Dan White, a rabid opponent of gay rights. When White was sentenced to only seven years and eight months, although the murder of public officials was subject to the death penalty in California, a riot followed and over one hundred individuals were injured. White later committed suicide.

Milk once wrote, according to the gay journal, *The Advocate*, "I want *nothing* even smacking, or smelling, or hinting of religion."

MILKY WAY

Although many in organized religion still speak of a three-tiered universe (Heaven, above; Earth, in the middle; Hell, below), any rationalist is aware that we are in the large aggregation of gas, dust, and stars held together by the gravitational attraction between its parts and which is known as the Milky Way. Our galaxy, which is one of innumerable others, contains a sun and perhaps one hundred billion stars.

Cosmologist David N. Schramm, reviewing Robert Osserman's *Poetry of the Universe* (1995), exclaims how well the book helps us "stretch our minds so that we can see expanding space curved somewhat like the surface of Earth, but in three dimensions rather than Earth's two, and with the added fourth dimension, time. What we know from modern astronomy is this: Other galaxies are moving away from our Milky way galaxy and, no matter which direction they are moving in, the farther away they are the faster they move. Our view when we look out at the galaxies is what a raisin might see in a rising loaf of raisin bread; the more distant raisins have more rising dough between them and thus move faster while nearby raisins have less dough separating them and thus move apart more slowly."

Schramm continues, "In the universe, it is space itself that is expanding (rising) and the galaxies, like the raisins, remain the same size. The elegant simplicity of the expansion of the universe is pointed up by Mr. Osserman's observation that a person anywhere, in any galaxy at any time, could make an egocentric map of the universe, with himself or herself at the center of the map, and come to exactly the same conclusion about the shape and evolution of the universe (his section on egocentric maps is revealing and quite amusing)." Osserman, a mathematician, is one of many who attempt to make the cosmos meaningful. (See entry for Extraterrestrial Life.)

Mill, James (1773–1836)

Mill was a philosopher and historian who, the son of a poor Scottish shoemaker, was educated by patrons for the church. He took up the study of Greek philosophy and became licensed as a preacher in the Scottish Church, but he moved instead to London and became editor of the *Literary Review*. He would have entered the pulpit as a Presbyterian preacher had he not, according to his son, by his "own studies and reflections been led to reject not only the belief in Revelation, but the foundations of what is commonly called Natural Religion." Further, "He came to the conviction that 'concerning the origin of things nothing whatever can be known.' " Mill looked upon religion as "the greatest enemy of morality," and he regarded the God of Christianity as an embodiment of the "ne plus ultra of wickedness."

In 1819, he published his *History of British India* (3 volumes). For the fifth edition of the *Encyclopedia Britannica*, Mill wrote many articles. A friend of Bentham, he also wrote in the *Westminster Review*, forwarding the views of philosophic radicalism. In religion he became a skeptic and, after reading Bishop Butler's *Analogy*, became interested in atheism.

Mrs. Grote, commenting upon Mill's death, said, "He died without any pain or struggle, of long-standing pulmonary phthisis." A few days earlier, Francis Place wrote to Mrs. Grote, "Stayed too long with poor Mill, who showed much more sympathy and affection than ever before in all our long friendship. But he was all the time as much of a bright reasoning man as ever he was—reconciled to his fate, brave, and calm to an extent which I never before witnessed, except in another old friend, Thomas Holeroft, the day before the day of his death." {BDF; FO; JM; RAT; RE}

Mill, John Stuart (1806–1873)

The son of James Mill, John was so severely educated by his father that he read Greek at the age of seven. At the age of twelve, he was well acquainted with the classics and had begun to study logic. Becoming one of the most learned writers of his generation, he was respected throughout the country. A founder of utilitarianism along with Jeremy Bentham, Mill stressed the method of empiricism as the source of all knowledge. He was a strong advocate of proportional representation, labor unions, and farm cooperation. He favored women's rights and was not averse to Comte's religion of humanity. In 1856, his *Principles of Political Economy with Some of Their Applications* (1848) was included on the index of prohibited reading. According to Delos B. McKown, Mill wished to win over to his skeptical position on religion only those of superior intelligence and character. He did not wish to deprive lesser mortals of their religion, hoping instead to improve their religious outlook through education. Neither did he suggest Nature as an alternative to supernatural religion, according to the *Encyclopedia of Philosophy* (Vol. 5).

Mill wrote that "Christian morality (so-called) has all the characters of a reaction; . . . Its ideal is negative rather than positive; passive rather than active; Innocence rather than Nobleness; Abstinence from Evil, rather than energetic Pursuit of Good. . . . It holds out the hope of heaven and the threat of hell, as the appointed and appropriate motives to a virtuous life; in this falling far below the best of the ancients, and doing what lies in it to give to human morality an essentially selfish character. . . . It is essentially the doctrine of passive obedience; it inculcates submission to all authorities found established."

He also wrote, "It is conceivable that religion may be morally useful without being intellectually sustainable." Also, "God is a word to express, not our ideas, but the want of them."

Mill, who was in his forties and after having loved her for twenty years, married Harriet Taylor in 1851 when her husband died. But she died in 1858 and, profoundly affected, he dedicated to her the famous *On Liberty* (1859), which they had worked on together. It is a major work revered by rationalists because of its pro-democratic, liberal stand.

According to Robertson, Mill's *Three Essays on Religion*—"Nature," "The Utility of Religion," and "Theism" (1859, 1875, in *Dissertations and Discussions)*—exhibit not only that Mill was not a Christian but that he had never been one. Equally important, Mill "cleared the air of the hell-fire and the God who prospered on fear. More than any other event," Berman maintains, Mill "shifted the onus of proof from the atheist to the believer." With Viscount Morley, he agrees that "probably no English writer has done so much as Mr. Mill to cut at the root of the theological spirit." What he believed in was a finite God, one who exists but is not as the traditionalists claim necessarily all-powerful, perfectly good, and entirely omniscient. Prof. Bain, his intimate friend and biographer, once said of Mill that "in everything characteristic of the creed of Christendom he was a thorough-going negationist. He admitted neither its truth nor its utility." Bain also wrote that Mill "absented himself during his whole life from religious services." Mill's important philosophical work is the *System of Logic* (1843), in which he treats philosophy comprehensively and from the viewpoint of an empiricist.

In his *Three Essays on Religion*, Mill admittedly mellowed his agnosticism with a view of a finite and impersonal God. But, wrote Paul Edwards in *Immortality*, Mill remained agnostic concerning the subject of life after death, or immortality.

In 1871, accepting under great pressure the office of pall-bearer at Grote's funeral, Mill on walking out of Westminster Abbey remarked to Bain, "In no very long time, I shall be laid in the ground with a very different ceremonial from that." Bain then noted, "It so happened, however, that a prayer was delivered at his own interment by the Protestant pastor at Avignon, who thereby got himself into trouble, from Mill's known scepticism, and had to write an exculpation in the local newspaper. The pastor, Bain found, was "a very intelligent and liberal-minded man." However, when the *Democratie du Midi* announced that Mill had received "the last consolations of religion" on his death-bed, "M. Rey honourably denied the statement and said, "*Il n'y avait point de pasteur pres du lit de M. Mill*" (There was no clergyman at Mr. Mill's bedside.)

After a fall, Mill died of erysipelas. Three days before his death in 1873, he had walked fifteen miles. Dr. Gurney described his last hours:

> Mr. Mill suffered but little, except in swallowing, and from the heat and weight of the enormous swelling, which, by the time I arrived from Nice, had already spread over his face and neck; and yet he learned from me on my arrival the fatal nature of the attack with calmness and resignation. His express desire that he might not lose his mental faculties was gratified, for his great intellect remained clear to the last moment. His wish that his funeral might be quiet and simple, as indeed, his every wish, was attended to by his loving step-daughter with devoted solicitude. (New York *Daily News*, 12 May 1873)

One English Christian journal, which itself went out of business soon afterwards, declared its opinion that Mill's soul was burning in hell and expressed a hearty wish that his disciples would soon follow him. (See entry for Helen Taylor.) {BDF; CE; ER; EU, Delos B. McKown; FO; FUK; HAB; ILP; HNS2; JM; JMR; JMRH; RAT; TRI; TSV; TYD}

Millar, John (1735–1801)

Millar was a jurist who was intended for the Church, but discussion on religion with inventor James Watt and economist Adam Smith undermined his religious beliefs. He became tutor to the son of Lord Kames, at whose house he met Hume and adopted his philosophy. In 1760 Millar became an advocate and the following year he became a professor of law at Glasgow University. His *Origin of the Distinctions of Ranks* (1806) is discreetly rationalistic. {RAT}

Millard, Killick (1870–1952)

In 1936, Millard founded the Euthanasia Society in England.

Millay, Edna St. Vincent (1892–1950)

Millay is sometimes remembered as the American poet who was known for the bohemian freedom of her life style, the one who wrote

> My candle burns at both ends;
>   It will not last the night;
> But, ah, my foes, and, oh, my friends—
>   It gives a lovely light.

To which Dorothy Parker respectfully remarked, "We all wandered in after Miss Millay. We were all being dashing and gallant, declaring that we weren't virgins, whether we were or not. Beautiful as she was, Miss Millay did a great deal of harm with her double-burning candles . . . made poetry seem so easy that we could all do it. But, of course, we couldn't."

Millay was born in Maine and was given her middle name to honor a New York City site, Greenwich Village's St. Vincent Hospital, in which one of her relatives had once been taken and had recovered. She graduated from Vassar College (and had tried to commit suicide there by jumping from her dormitory window). Millay moved to Greenwich Village in the 1920s (to "the smallest house in New York City," 9 1/2' wide, at 75 1/2 Bedford Street, which at various times was inhabited also by matinee idol John Barrymore, film actor Cary Grant, and composer-critic Deems Taylor). In the Village she became associated with the Provincetown Players, writing one-act satirical fantasies for them such as *Two Slatterns and a King* (1921). *A Few Figs from Thistles* (1920) established her as a reckless, romantic, cynical, "naughty" New Woman, and her impact became great upon writers of her time.

In 1923, Millay married Eugene Jan Boissevain, a Dutch coffee importer, and moved to "Steepletop," a farm near Austerlitz, New York. That same year, she won the Pulitzer Prize for *Harp-Weaver and Other Poems*. Critics found her work contained a disillusioned bitterness and remarked about her technical ability, particularly in her sonnets.

Millay wrote the libretto for Deems Taylor's opera, *The King's Henchman* (1927) and, with George Dillon, she translated Baudelaire's *Flowers of Evil* (1936).

Jennifer S. Wilson of the University of Minnesota relates that at a cocktail party Millay once discussed her recurrent headaches with a psychologist who asked her about her attraction to women. "Oh, you mean I'm homosexual!" Millay responded. "Of course I am, and heterosexual too, but what's that got to do with my headache?"

Although, like many poets, she used the word "God," she did not appear to mean it in an orthodox sense. In her "Conversation at Midnight," Millay wrote,

> There is no God.
> But it does not matter.
> Man is enough.

In 1949, her husband died, and Millay died less than a year later of heart failure. {CE; GL; OEL; OCAL}

Millé, Constantin (19th Century)

A Romanian writer, Millé lectured at Jassy and Bucharest on the history of philosophy, from a materialistic point of view. He was also active with Codreano and, after the latter's death, in spreading socialism. Millé, who contributed to the *Revista Sociala* and the *Vütoral* edited by C. Pilitis, has been active in the International Freethought Federation. {BDF; PUT; RAT}

MILLENNIUM

Revelation:20 refers to the thousand years during which holiness is to prevail and Christ is to reign on earth, which will be a period of great happiness because the devil will be cast into a bottomless pit. The idea possibly derives from the Zoroastrians of ancient Persia, who conceived of the history of the world in thousand-year periods, culminating in the final defeat of evil and triumph of good.

According to many biblical passages, one day for God equals 1,000 earthly years. Using this analogy, if God created in six and rested for one, the Earth can endure for 6,000 years and must then rest for the final 1000 years. Inasmuch as Anglican Archbishop James Ussher stated in 1650 that the world began on 23 October 4004 B. C., something apparently has not worked out: The world did *not* end 6000 years later, or on 23 October 1996. Ergo, even Dionysius Exiguus's miscalculation of the date of Jesus' birth by at least four years is wrong. Millennialists persist in believing that Jesus Christ will return to rule the Earth with his saints and cast the devil into a bottomless pit. At midnight on 31 December 1999, millennialists again despaired.

Naturalists and humanists, on the contrary, looked to the new millennium as an arbitrary period of time during which people will be united by their humanity, not by their faith. Also, they do not consider "millennium" to be a Christian occurrence, pointing out that on 31 December 1999 in Jerusalem the calendar year there will read 5758. (See Nicolas Walter on Pre-Millennial Tension in *The Freethinker*, October 1996. A cogent discussion of "the millenial itch" is in *The Economist*, 4 January 1997) {Stephen Jay Gould, *USA Weekend*, 19-21 September 1997}

Miller, Arnold (20th Century)

Miller, associate professor of geology at the University of Cincinnati, is editor of *Paleobiology*, a quarterly journal of the Paleontological Society. His expertise is in evaluating trends in global diversity through geologic time. Miller has spoken to the Cincinnati secular humanists about ways to combat the unscientific views known as creationism.

Miller, Arthur (1915–)

Miller, who was married to Marilyn Monroe after her marriage to baseball player Joe DiMaggio, is a major American playwright. For many, he is as well known for being Monroe's husband as for having invented the character of Willy Loman, the "ordinary" person in *Death of a Salesman* (1949) who is destroyed by hollow materialistic values. Miller's work, which deals with moral and political issues, includes *All My Sons* (1947), and *A View from the Bridge* (1955), the latter of which gained the censors' wrath because one of the male characters "contemptuously" kisses another man.

The Crucible (1953), which was a powerful depiction of religious paranoia and its resulting mayhem, was made into a 1997 movie. Its director, Nicholas Hytner, said, "The sad truth about this story is that it will always be topical. It speaks directly about the bigotry of religious fundamentalists across the globe, about communities torn apart by accusations of child abuse, about the rigid intellectual orthodoxies of college campuses. There is no shortage of contemporary Salems ready to cry witchcraft." *After the Fall* (1964) is a thinly disguised story of his marriage to Monroe (whom he married in Connecticut in a ceremony presided over by a Unitarian minister). The work appears to say that we are all, indeed, fumbling around in a godless world, so what responsibility do we have to others!

In 1989, he wrote the present author:

> Humanism? I don't know, I guess it has to be the opposite of inhumanism, and we all know what that is.

In 1992, still unwilling to be labeled, he wrote concerning which kind of humanist he might be:

> Depends on the day. I'd call myself a secular humanist, excepting when the mystery of life is overwhelming and some semi-insane directing force seems undeniable.

When the Sydney Theatre Company produced his "Broken Glass," Miller was quoted in 1995:

> I have no formal religion but there's a space in my head for it. Maybe I would believe in God if he believed in me. But we're living in a reality that's so hard to understand. In the last seventy-five years the human race has been humiliated in a way we've never known before.

(See entry for David Diamond, who disagrees with Miller's 1992 statement.)

{CA; CE; E; RI; TYD; WAS, 1 May 1989 and 15 June 1992}

Miller, Cecil H. (20th Century)

Miller was on the executive committee of the Southwestern Philosophical Conference when in the 1950s he wrote book reviews for *The Humanist*.

Miller, D. M. (20th Century)

Miller wrote *The Evolution of God: The Origins of Moral Behavior* (1998). Our goals, he holds, are set by our emotions, not by our intellect. The existence of God is a lie told by our genes to compel us to act in ways that promote our welfare and their survival. The reason we are imperfect is that while a certain amount of goodness is good for us, too much is bad for us. Miller's book includes his observations on society's evolution. {Jim Cox, Midwest Book Review}

Miller, David (20th Century)

Miller was a key figure in 1978 of the Manawatu branch that took over the management of *The New Zealand Rationalist and Humanist.*

Miller, Dusty (20th Century)

In Britain, Miller is active with the York Humanist Group and is author of *Women Who Hurt Themselves* (1994).

Miller, Emma (1839–1917)

Miller was an Australian freethinker and women's activist. Born in England to a Unitarian and Chartist family, she emigrated to Queensland in 1878 and became an advocate of women's right to suffrage, to form trade unions, and to freedom from exploitation in houses of work. An admirer of Thomas Paine, she was foundation president of the Women's Equal Franchise Association. Miller also was a founding member of the Australian Labor Party. {SWW}

Miller, Florence Fenwick (Born 1854)

A writer, Miss Miller retained her maiden name with her husband's consent. She published *The House of Life* (1878), and from 1876 to 1882 sat on the London School Board. In 1877, speaking of Harriet Martineau, Miller repudiated "superstition and priestcraft" and declared herself an agnostic like Miss Martineau. {RAT}

Miller, Irene L. (20th Century)

Miller is an actor who portrays Margaret Sanger in one-woman shows.

Miller, James (Died 1989)

Miller, a folk-singer better known as Ewan MacColl, was the joint founder of the Theatre Workshop. A Communist, he also was a humanist, according to Nicolas Walter. In 1985, when he realized he was approaching the end of his life, Miller wrote a song for his companion Peggy Seeger called "The Joy of Living," which he contributed to a BBC Radio 4 program about humanism in 1987:

> Take me to some high place
> Of heather, rock and ling;
> And the sundew hung with diamonds.
> Feed me to the wind:
> So that I will be
> Part of all you see,
> The air you are breathing.
>
> I'll be part of the curlew's cry
> And the soaring hawk, the blue milkwort
> Scatter my dust and ashes,
> I'll be riding the gentle wind
> That blows through your hair,
> Reminding you of how we shared
> In the joy of living.

Miller, James Alexander (1915–)

A professor emeritus of oncology at the University of Wisconsin, Miller, a naturalist, reviewed in the 1950s Julian Huxley's book on cancer in *The Humanist.* Miller has won a large number of awards for his cancer research, including in 1980 the Mott award of the General Motors Cancer Research Foundation.

Miller, Jeanne (20th Century)

Miller, whose son was preyed upon by a Chicago-area priest in 1982, founded VOCAL (Victims of Clergy Abuse Linkup, Inc.), a national advocacy group which since its formation in 1991 has received much attention by the media. At the 1993 Freedom From Religion Foundation's annual convention in Huntsville, Alabama, Miller spoke on "Clergy Sexual Abuse and the Moral Bankruptcy of Institutional Religion."

Miller, Jonathan Wolfe (1934–)

Miller is the London-born physician, actor, theater and film director known to Americans particularly for his co-authoring and acting in "Beyond the Fringe" (1961–1964) and for his 1986 directing on Broadway of "Long Day's Journey Into Night." He was associate director of the National Theatre (1973–1975) and artistic director of Old Vic (1988–1990). He has directed many dramas and operas, including works by Shakespeare, Marston, Wilde, Henry James, Beethoven, Mozart, and Verdi. Miller, a physician who was a research fellow in the history of medicine at University College, London University (1970–1973), is author of *Freud: The Man, His World, His Influence* (1972) and *The Don Giovanni Book* (1990).

Miller has been decorated with the Order of the British Empire (OBE) and in 1996 was admitted into the Council for Secular Humanism's Humanist Academy. Also, he is an Honorary Associate of the National Secular Society.

Miller, Montague David (1839–1920)

Miller, called "Monty," was an atheist, carpenter, socialist veteran, and a "Eureka Stockader." To the grief of his mother and the disgust of his Wesleyan father, he became an atheist at the age of 15. Arguing that Christianity was scientifically unsound and that atheism provided a superior moral code for society, Miller became a leading lecturer for the Australian Secular Association. *Ross's Magazine* described him as "The Tolstoi of Australia," and he was elected the first chairman of the Melbourne branch of the Industrial Workers of the World.

On his deathbed, Miller said he would die with "atheistic fortitude." Thomas Walker spoke at the graveside while mourners sang "The Red Flag." {SWW}

Miller, O. W. (20th Century)

Miller, who was an associate professor of psychology and assistant in philosophy at Nebraska Wesleyan University, wrote *The Kantian Thing-in-itself* (1956). Asked his views on humanism, he responded to the present author:

> Relative to Religious Humanism, as I think of it, it is inclined to be too superficial. It fails to recognize man as being profoundly related to the rest of Reality. It may not over-emphasize the humanistic element in Christianity, but it under-estimates the divinity of man. The 25th chapter of *Matthew*, the *Book of James*, and many other sections of the Scriptures stress the humanistic aspects of religion. But the 17th Chapter of *John* and numerous other scriptures stress the fact that man is more than a social being. Furthermore, Humanism is a religion without a theology. I would prefer a theology without a religion. That is, if I had a choice. But when we come to Renaissance Humanism, that is a horse of another color. I am in hearty accord with Petrarch, Erasmus, Rabelais, Sir Thomas More, and Cervantes, for the reason that they stress man, learning, knowledge, reason, and scholarship.
>
> So far as Naturalistic Humanism is concerned, I have given it considerable attention. And I am inclined to believe that this Philosophy of Reality is moving in the right direction. As I teach it, this Philosophy correlates with Naturalistic Theism or Theistic Naturalism as set out by five or six outstanding thinkers, and as found in E. S. Brightman's book on the philosophy of religion, and elsewhere. When it comes to Supernaturalism, in the accepted sense of the term, we are on dangerous ground, unless we understand how to differentiate between Metaphysics and Logic.
>
> As for myself, Leibnitz, Immanuel Kant, and others help me over the bumps, or out of the mud, of this system of thought. If this world in which we live is not real, then nothing is real. Relative to this point, *The Realm of Ends* by James Ward gives me my direction. Kant, Ward, and other philosophers of like mind bring us back from our Transcendental Tangent. Ward, especially, points out, in other words, of course, that man, ignoring the whole of his nature, tends to yield himself to the Centrifugal forces of life and thought, when a much more reasonable and satisfactory view might be arrived at if man would attempt to see himself in terms of both the Centrifugal and the Centripetal. If man would only check on himself in terms of Metaphysics and Logic, he might then realize that his natural Logical Tendencies have carried him entirely too far from the center of Theological Gravity.
>
> {WAS, 25 April 1956}

Miller, Olin (20th Century)

Miller, a freethinker, wrote "400 Bible Errors" (c. 1970). {GS}

Miller, Perry (1905–1963)

Miller edited *The Transcendentalists* (1950). A towering figure in the field of American intellectual history, he held in *The New England Mind* (1939) that religion rather than economics was the prime motive behind the settling of New England. He wrote *The American Puritans* (1956) and edited *The Works of Jonathan Edwards* (1957). {CE}

Miller, Rachel Seabolt (20th Century)

Miller is treasurer of Rationalists United for Secular Humanism.

Miller, Russell E. (1917–1993)

Miller wrote *The Larger Hope: History of the Universalist Church in America* (2 volumes, 1979–1985), the definitive history of Universalism's origins in 1770 and its history until its merger with the American Unitarian Association in 1961. He also wrote a comprehensive history of Tufts University, *Light on the Hill,* describing its history including its having been chartered by a group of Universalist clergy in 1852. Miller, who joined the Tufts faculty in 1948, served as chairman of the history department from 1975 to 1980.

Millerand, Alexandre (Premier) (1859–1943)

Millerand in 1883 joined the staff of Clemenceau's paper, *La Justice*. Later, he edited *La Petite République*. In 1885 he entered the Chambre as a Radical-Socialist, breaking with the extreme Socialists in 1899. In 1920 he was elected Premier of France. {RAT}

MILLERSVILLE UNIVERSITY HUMANISTS

Humanists in Pennsylvania at Millersville University are found on the Web at <http://www.secularhumanism.org/cfa/orgs.html>.

Millholland, Jean (20th Century)

Millholland is the Executive Director Emeritus of the Council for Secular Humanism. She has been an active director of humanist activities since the formation of the group, and she signed Humanist Manifesto 2000.

Millière, Jean Baptiste (1817–1871)

Millière was born of poor French parents, became an advocate, and founded the *Proletaire* at Clermont Ferrand. For writing *Revolutionary Studies*, he was, after the *coup d'état,* banished to Algeria until the amnesty of 1859. In 1869 Millière started, with Rochefort, the *Marseillaise*, of which he became one of the principal directors. At the election for the National Assembly, he was elected for Paris. Although he took no part in the Commune, but sought to act as an intermediary, he was arrested and summarily shot near the Pantheon. Millière died exclaiming, "*Vive l'humanité!*" {BDF; RAT}

Millikan, Robert Andrew (1868–1953)

Millikan, an American physicist and educator, won the 1923 Nobel Prize for Physics, which was awarded for his measurement of the electron's charge. He also made important studies of cosmic rays (which he named), X rays, and physical and electric constants.

Millikan also lectured on the reconciliation of science and religion. At a time when Leuba showed that more than 80% of the greater scientific men of America did not believe in God, Millikan said he had "never known a thinking man who did not believe in God." {CE; RE}

Mills, C. Wright (1916–1962)

An eminent American sociologist, Mills was controversial because he advocated comparative world sociology. He criticized intellectuals for not using their freedom responsibly by working for social change. *The Power Elite* (1956) referred to the power structure of post-war American society in terms of an oligarchy. *The Nation* (8 March 1958) wrote,

> As a social and as a personal force, religion has become a dependent variable. It does not originate; it reacts. It does not denounce; it adapts. It does not set forth new models of conduct and sensibility; it imitates. Its rhetoric is without deep appeal; the worship it organizes is without piety. It has become less a revitalization of the spirit in permanent tension with the world than a respectable distraction from the sourness of life.

{CE; TYD}

Mills, David (20th Century)

Mills, a freethinker, wrote *Overcoming Religion* (1981). The work originally was entitled *Holy Hypnosis*. {GS}

Mills, Jeanne (20th Century)

Mills is author of *Six Years With God: Life Inside Rev. Jim Jones's People's Temple* (1979).

Mills, Mike (20th Century)

Mills, the bassist for the group R. E. M., was asked by *Q Magazine* if he believed in God. Mills responded, "No." {CA}

Mills, William (Deceased 1999)

Mills was a Unitarian humanist in Montreal, a staunch supporter of non-believers.

Milne, A. A. (1882–1956)

Milne, a freethinker according to David Tribe, is known for his verse collections for children, particularly *Winnie-the-Pooh* (1926) and *The House at Pooh Corner* (1928). From 1906 to 1914 he had been an assistant editor of *Punch*, and after the First World War he had begun a career as playwright with *Mr. Pim Passes By* (1919). "The Old Testament," he declared, "is responsible for more atheism, agnosticism, disbelief—call it what you will—than any book ever written; it has emptied more churches than all the counter attractions of cinema, motor bicycle, and golf course." {OEL; TRI; TYD}

Milnes, Richard Monckton (Baron Houghton) (1809–1885)

Milnes was a poet and a politician. A Liberal M.P., he was conspicuous in the support of reform. He was President of the Social Science Congress, the Foreign Secretary of the Academy, and Trustee of the British Museum. Milnes described himself as "a Puseyite sceptic," explaining that "Christianity is the consummation, the perfection, of idolatry." {RAT; RE}

Milos, Marilyn Fayre (20th Century)

Milos, a nurse, is founder and executive director of the National Organization of Circumcision Information Resource Centers. She is co-founder of the International Symposia on Circumcision. An atheist, she is outspoken in her opposition to genital mutilation of males and females. Circumcision, she holds, was originally practiced for religious reasons, as a punitive measure, as a puberty or premarital rite, as an absolution against the feared toxic influences of vaginal (hymeneal) blood, and as a mark of slavery.

Milton, John (1608–1674)

Milton, whom Corliss Lamont referred to as "the Protestant poet," wrote *Areopagitica* (1644), a classic statement on human rights and freedom of thought which non-believers revere, along with Mill's *On Liberty*. His is the superlative argument for freedom of the press. *Paradise Lost* (1667) with its story of Satan's rebellion against God is an amusing literary addition to the Bible, taken literally by many, along with Adam and Eve's expulsion from the Garden of Eden. A listing in the Vatican's index of prohibited reading is as follows:

> ***Miltonus****, Ioannes. Literae pseudo-senatus anglicani, Cromwellii reliquorumque perduellium nomine ac iussu conscriptae. Decr. 23 nov. 1694.*

As a young man, Milton visited the aging Galileo and left Italy with a lasting hatred for all forms of tyranny. His *Areopagitica* became the first defense of freedom of speech and press in the English language, and although not a nominal Unitarian he was a vocal anti-trinitarian. It can be assumed that the Pope did not appreciate Milton's referring to him as "the triple tyrant."

Paradise Regained incorporates a homosexual temptation into the famous banquet scene, the University of Michigan's Claude J. Summers has pointed out. The scene includes "allusions to Alexander the Great, Scipio Africanus, Ganymede, and Hylas." After citing Alexander and Scipio as examples of individuals unsusceptible to heterosexual temptations, Satan tempts Christ with a seductive *tableau vivant t*hat includes "Tall stripling youths rich clad, of fairer hew / Then Ganymede or Hylas."

Those who have only read his *Paradise Lost* label Milton an orthodox Christian, McCabe objects, adding that the same is true for Chaucer. "In other works," McCabe states, "he clearly shows himself a freethinker. The historian Macaulay drew attention to the 'heterodox views on the nature of the deity and the eternity of matter' in Milton's Latin treatise, *Christiana Doctrine*, and said that he was obviously 'emancipated from the influence of authority.' Even *Paradise Lost* is rather a rationalization of a Christian legend than an acceptance of it in the church sense." "The finest thing about this Paradise," said Taine, "is its hell."

A philosopher who liked Milton was Bertrand Russell who, in *Fact and Fiction* (1961), wrote: "Above all, I admired *Areopagitica.* I treasured such sentences as, 'As good almost kill a man as kill a good book, who kills a man kills a reasonable creature, God's image; but he who destroys a good book, kills reason itself.' This was an inspiring sentiment for an intending writer who devoutly hoped that his books would be 'good books.' And more especially, encouraging to a budding philosopher was the statement, 'Where there is much desire to learn, there of necessity will be much arguing, much writing, many opinions; for opinion in good men is but knowledge in the making.' This might almost be taken as the sacred text for free speech and free discussion. 'Opinion in good men is but knowledge in the making' says in a few words what is essential for the condemnation of censorship. Alas, I did not know in those days that to cure Milton of opposing censorship, they made him a censor. This is the almost invariable logic of revolutions, while in the making, they praise liberty; but when successful, they establish tyranny."

Contemporaries cite Milton's having had three wives and of being no champion of women's rights. His blindness, according to biographer John Philipps, came from a *gutta serena* or *amaurosis*, a condition of loss of sight from disease of the optic nerve, retina, or brain without any perceptible external change in the eye. Phillips added that Milton died in "a fit of the Gout, but with so little pain or emotion that the time of his expiring was not perceived by those in the room." {CE; CL; ER: EU, Paul H. Beattie; Lee Eisler, *The Quotable Bertrand Russell*; GL; ILP; JM; RE; TYD}

Milyukov, Pavel Nikolaevitch (Born 1859)

Milyukov was a Russian historian who was banished for his liberal views at Moscow University and who then accepted the chair of history at Sofia University (1897–1898). From 1901 to 1905, he was on the staff of Chicago University. In 1905 he was elected to the Duma. Milyukov edited the *Free Nation* and *Popular Rights* and was one of the Liberal leaders who effected the Revolution of 1917. When the Bolshevists seized power, he moved to England. Milyukov was a rationalist. {RAT}

MIND

• The human mind is like a parachute: it works best when it's open.

–**Jun Sczesnoczkawasm**

Miner, Alonzo Ames (1814–1895)

A temperance crusader and an opponent of slavery, Miner reached public prominence as president of Tufts College (1862–1874). He was one of Boston's most prominent representatives of Universalism in the late 19th century. {U&U}

MINERVA

The Roman goddess identified with the Olympian Athena, Minerva was worshiped in various places. Her Aventine Hill temple was a meeting place for skilled craftsmen, actors, and writers. {CE}

MINISTER

• Minister, n. An agent of a higher power with a lower responsibility. In diplomacy an officer sent into a foreign country as the visible embodiment of his sovereign's hostility. His principal qualification is a degree of plausible inveracity next below that of an ambassador.

–**Ambrose Bierce**
The Devil's Dictionary

MINNESOTA ATHEISTS, HUMANISTS

• Friends Free of Theism, 7227 Park Avenue, Richfield, Minnesota 55423. Rob Nienkerk and Charles French are contacts.

• Humanist Association of Minneapolis and St. Paul (AHA), 4418 Josephine Lane, Robbinsdale, Minnesota 55422-1328; (612) 321-9050. E-mail: <hieror@aol.com>. On the Web: <http://humanist-msp.org>.

• Minnesota Atheists (Atheist Alliance) (ASHS), POB 6261, Minneapolis, Minnesota 55406. (612) 588-1597. Steve Petesen and Marie Castle are its co-chairpersons. E-mail: <mac@min.org>. On the Web: <http://www.mnatheists.org>.

• University of Minnesota Atheists and Unbelievers (ASHS), 300 Washington Avenue SE, Minneapolis, Minnesota 55455; telephone (612) 731-1543. Officers in 1996 were Stephanie Erickson and Jason Erickson, [unrelated] co-presidents; Jodi Gustafson, activities and discussion group leader; Mike Fritsche, activities coordinator; and Nick Rezmerski, publicist.
<http://www.secularhumanism.org/cfa/orgs.html>.

Minsås, Unni (20th Century)

Minsås, who is vice-president of the Norwegian *Human Etisk Forgund*, is a member of the Executive Committee of the International Humanist and Ethical Union.

Minsberg, David (1920–)

Born in Poland, Minsberg came to the United States at the age of four, was raised in an orthodox Jewish family, moved to the Philippines where he married a Filipina, taught, and sold as well as published books. In *The Agnostic Mystique, A Guide for the Unperplexed* (1996), he states that humans are metaphors for god, that this helps make possible the development of a humanistic outlook, one that involves having no canon, no council, and no infallible or fallible authority. Theists and atheists are two sides of a coin, he holds. Agnostics, however, are a coin standing on edge. The agnostic is his own authority, Minsberg maintains after delving into subjects such as education, morality, paradox, humor, government, religions, and how we bumble and stumble in order to accomplish our humanistic dreams.

Minsky, Marvin (20th Century)

Minsky is Toshiba professor of media arts and sciences and professor of electrical engineering and computer sciences at the Massachusetts Institute of Technology. He is one of the world's leading theorists of artificial intelligence. Life, he has stated, is as much about knowing how to avoid mistakes as knowing about what is right. Past myths may have made people feel good, but in the world of cyberspace some individuals unfortunately are clinging to the old instead of growing with the new. "People," he appeals on behalf of activism, "need to grumble that the world does not make sense . . . but could."

Minsky is best known for research on knowledge representation, machine vision, robotics, computational complexity, and confocal microscopy. He has written *The Society of Mind* (1987) and in 1992, with Harry Harrison, *The Turing Option*, a novel about the future of artificial intelligence. As to whether machines can ever deal with the intangibles of humanness, Minsky told *New York Times* reporter Claudia Dreifus (28 July 1998),

> It's very tangible, what I'm talking about. For example, you can push something with a stick, but you can't pull it. You can pull something with a string, but you can't push it. That's common sense. And no computer knows it. Right now, I'm writing a book, a sequel to *The Society of Mind*, and I am looking at some of this. What is pain? What is common sense? What is falling in love?
>
> What are emotions? Emotions are big switches, and there are hundreds of these. . . . If you look at a book about the brain, the brain just looks like switches. . . . You can think of the brain as a big supermarket of goodies that you can use for different purposes. Falling in love is turning on some 20 or 30 of these and turning a lot of the others off. It's some particular arrangement. To understand it, one has to get some theory of what are the resources in the brain, what kind of arrangements are compatible, and what happens when you turn several on and they get into conflict. Being angry is another collection of switches. In this book, I'm trying to give examples of how these things work.

He then praised Stanley Kubrick and Arthur C. Clark, whose "2001: A Space Odyssey" predictions were just about right in everything except for the date. His favorite sci-fi authors are Robert Heinlein, the late Isaac Asimov, Gregory Benford, David Brin, and Larry Niven. Also, Mary Shelley, who he said "was right in predicting how people would not understand the poor thing [Dr. Frankenstein's creation]. "That's *such* a sad story! By the way, I've gone through that book very carefully to see if she left any hints explaining how the robot worked. But alas, no clues and the funny part is when you read it, you don't mind."

A thoroughgoing philosophic naturalist, Minsky—unlike too many secular humanists—has a rollicking sense of humor. On the Web: <www.ai.mit.edu/people/minsky/minsky.html>. {CA; E; WAS 17 January 1997}

Miosa, Frank T. (20th Century)

At the Tenth International Humanist and Ethical Union (IHEU) World Congress held in Buffalo (1988), Miosa addressed the group. A Canadian who directs the Toronto Learning Centre, he spoke on "Humanism and Ethics" at the 1994 Toronto conference of the Coalition for Secular Humanism, Atheism, and Freethought.

Mirabaud, Jean Baptiste de (1675–1760)

Mirabaud was a French writer who translated Tasso and Ariosto and became perpetual secretary to the French Academy. He wrote *Opinions of the Ancients on the Jews, a Critical Examination of the New Testament* (under the name of Fréret); *The World: Its Origin and Antiquity* (1751); and *Sentiments of a Philosopher on the Nature of the*

Soul (1743). *The System of Nature*, which was attributed to Mirabaud, was written by d'Holbach. {BDF; RAT}

Mirabeau, Honoré Gabriel Riquetti [Comte de] (1749–1791)

Mirabeau was a famed French statesman and orator. He inherited from his family a passionate nature, a frank strong will, generous temper, and a mind of prodigious activity. He entered the army in 1767 but, by an amorous intrigue that provoked the ire of his father, was imprisoned. In fact, he was jailed several times on the request of his father, Victor de Mirabeau, with whom he carried on a public quarrel. In 1783 his *Erotika Biblion* anonymously appeared and dealt with the Bible's obscenity. In 1785 he fled to England in exile, where he moved in Whig circles. When sent in 1786 on a secret mission to Prussia, he betrayed his government's trust by publishing his unedited reports to Paris, containing accounts of scandal and intrigue in the Prussian court and leading many to regard him as having an unsavory reputation. When the king ordered the States-General to leave the hall after the day's session was declared closed, Mirabeau replied (with words which have been variously reported): "We shall not leave our places save by the force of bayonets." The assembly remained in session and adopted Mirabeau's motion that its members were inviolable.

In 1791 Mirabeau was chosen President of the National Assembly and became leader of the Revolution. He actually had sought to create a strong constitutional monarchy on the British model, which would permit him to play a decisive role as prime minister. However, members of the Assembly were barred for cabinet posts by a 1789 decree specifically directed against him. Mirabeau then began secret dealings with the court, entered the pay of the king and queen, and his political position became untenable. He advocated the abolition of the double aristocracy of lords and bishops as well as the spoliation of the church and the national guard. Carlyle called him "far the strongest, best practical intellect of that time."

In January, 1791, he sat as President of the Assembly, with his neck bandaged after the application of leeches. Foote reports that at parting Mirabeau said to Dumont, "I am dying, my friend; dying as by slow fire." On the 27th of March he stood in the tribune for the last time. Four days later he was on his death-bed. Crowds beset the street, anxious but silent, and stopping all traffic so that their hero might not be disturbed. A bulletin was issued every three hours. "On Saturday, the second day of April," says Carlyle, "Mirabeau feels that the last of the Days has risen for him; that on this day he has to depart and be no more. His death is Titanic, as his life has been. Lit up, for the last time, in the glare of the coming dissolution, the mind of the man is all glowing and burning; utters itself in sayings, such as men long remember. He longs to live, yet acquiesces in death, argues not with the inexorable."

Although Mirabeau is sometimes classed as a deist, McCabe wrote, "Carlyle tells in his *French Revolution* that when he was dying he said, pointing to the sun, 'If that isn't God it is at least his Cousin.' He rejected the idea of immortality and seems rather to have been an atheist." Power of speech gone, Mirabeau made signs for paper and pen, and wrote the word *dormir*, "to sleep." Cabanis, the great physician, who stood beside him, pretended not to understand this passionate request for opium. Thereupon, writes the doctor, "He made a sign for the pen and paper to be brought to him again, and wrote, 'Do you think that Death is dangerous?' Seeing that I did not comply with his demand, he wrote again, 'How can you leave your friend on the wheel, perhaps for days?' " Cabanis and Dr. Petit decided to give him a sedative. While it was sent for "the pains became atrocious." Recovering speech a little under the torture, he turned to M. de la Marek, saying, "You deceive me." "No," replied his friend, "we are not deceiving you, the remedy is coming, we all saw it ordered." "Ah, the doctors, the doctors!" he muttered. Then, turning to Cabanis, with a look of mingled anger and tenderness, he said, "Were you not my doctor and my friend? Did you not promise to spare me the agonies of such a death? Do you wish me to expire with a regret that I trusted you?" "Those words," says Cabinis, "the last that he uttered, ring incessantly in my ears. He turned over on the right side with a convulsive movement, and at half-past eight in the morning he expired in our arms." Dr. Petit, standing at the foot of the bed, said, "His sufferings are ended." "So dies," wrote Carlyle, "a gigantic Heathen and Titan; stumbling blindly, undismayed, down to his rest."

Upon his death in 1791, impressive manifestations of public sorrow and respect were shown, for he had gained wide popularity with the masses. A procession a league in length wended its way. The Church of Sainte-Geneviève was turned into a Pantheon, and he was buried in the Panthéon. But when his dealings with the court were discovered, the body was later removed. {BDF; CE; FO; JM; RAT}

MIRACLES

> • Miracle, n. An act or event out of the order of nature and unaccountable, as beating a normal hand of four kings and an ace with four aces and a king.
>
> **–Ambrose Bierce**
> *The Devil's Dictionary*

Anthony Flew in the *Encyclopedia of Philosophy*, Vol. 5, states that the term, like the word "nice," is often used to refer primarily to the responses of the user. Believers think of a miracle as a preternatural occurrence that is viewed as the expression of a divine will, for its cause is hidden. Non-believers, who are naturalists in philosophy, hold that if the sun stood still, or Lazarus rose from the dead, or Jesus walked on the top of water, or the crippled suddenly became no longer crippled, these cases would not be what they appeared to be on the surface. As a result, investigations would be commenced to determine the actual cause. If someone appears to walk atop water, at what distance and at what angle did observers see this, and could the water level have been so low it only appeared the individual was walking on water? If a blind person suddenly sees, what degree of blindness had he had and under what conditions did the situation seem to change?

The Catholic Church requires rigid attestation of supposed miracles before canonizing a person (making the individual an officially recognized saint), but the church does not require belief in other than biblical miracles.

At the end of the millennium, the "faithful" have been seeking miracles and finding them—they believe—in unlikely forms and places. These include, wrote Joe Nickell in "Miracles or Deception?" (*Skeptical Inquirer*, September-October 1999), apparitions of the Virgin Mary (for example in the Bosnian village of Medjugorje, beginning in 1981), bleeding statues and crucifixes (e.g., in Quebec in 1985), and miraculously appearing images, such as the portrait of Mary seen in a splotch on a tree in Los Angeles in 1992. "People seem to hunger," Nickell added, "for some tangible religious experience, and wherever there is such profound want there is the opportunity for what may be called 'pious fraud.' Money is rarely the primary motive, the usual impetus being to seemingly triumph over adversity, renew the faith of believers, and confound the doubters. An end-justifies-the-means attitude may prevail, but the genuinely religious and the devoutly skeptical may agree on one thing, that the truth must serve as both the means and the end. Ultimately, neither science nor religion can be served by dishonesty." (For a possible explanation of why some think a miracle has occurred, see entry for Healing Effect. Also see entry for David Hume.) {CE}

Miralta, Constancio (Born c. 1849)

Miralta was the pen name of a popular Spanish writer who had been a priest and doctor of theology. He wrote for *Las Dominicales*. His most notable works are *Memoirs of a Poor Clerical*; *The Secrets of Confession*; and *The Sacrament Exposed*. Miralta's work, *The Doctrine of Catholicism upon Matrimony*, greatly encouraged civil marriages. {BDF}

Miranda, Don Francisco (1750–1816)

Miranda was a South American patriot and general, a Venezuelan who aided the Americans in the War of Independence.

Reportedly, Miranda was a skeptic and follower of James Mill. Mill himself described Miranda as an atheist. A hero of the struggle for independence from Spain, Miranda is sometimes called the Precursor to distinguish him from Simón de Bolívar, who completed the task of liberation.

In France Miranda fought in the French Revolutionary Wars but, running afoul of the Jacobins, fled to England, where he was helped by William Pitt. Miranda sought foreign aid and led in 1806 an unsuccessful expedition to the Venezuelan coast. He was dictator of the country for a short time but in 1812 surrendered to the Spanish.

Bolívar and others, angered by his capitulation, seized him and turned him over to the Spanish, who deported him to Cádiz and kept him in a dungeon of the Inquisition for the rest of his life. {BDF; CE; JM; RAT; RE}

Mirbeau, Octave (1850–1917)

Mirbeau, a French novelist, was an atheist who defined religions as "the monstrous flowers and the hideous instruments of the eternal suffering of man." {JM; RAT; RE}

MISCEGENATION

Cohabitation, sexual relations, or marriage between members of different races is called miscegenation.

Although unofficially miscegenation may be frowned upon, one author—Dorothy West, a patrician black writer, daughter of a slave, and the longest surviving member of the Harlem Renaissance of the 1920s—wrote in *The Wedding* (1995) that class, good manners, and a good education are important, not color: "Color was a false distinction; love was not."

A classic case of miscegenation is the pairing of President Thomas Jefferson—or his close relative—and his young black slave, Sally Hemings. DNA tests in 1998 indicated that fifty-two-year-old John Jefferson of Norrisville, Pennsylvania, is a direct descendant of Hemings through Eston Hemings Jefferson. Mr. Jefferson's Y chromosome matched blood samples taken from the descendants of Jefferson's uncle, Field Jefferson. {*The New York Times*, 1 November 1998}

Mishima, Yukio (1925–1970)

Mishima, the first Japanese novelist to win a Nobel prize, was called by *Life* "the Japanese Hemingway." He had been born Kimitake Hiraoka of a samurai family, worked in an aircraft factory during World War II, and practiced physical fitness and the ancient arts of the samurai as a member of his Tatenokai (Shield Society). *Temple of the Golden Pavilion* (1956) depicted a psychopathic monk who destroys the temple he loves. Other of his works are the semiautobiographical *Confessions of a Mask* (1949) *The Sound of Waves* (1954), and *The Sailor Who Fell From Grace With the Sea* (1963).

A homosexual, he and one of his student acolytes committed ritual suicide (*seppuku*), cutting open their bellies, after an unsuccessful demonstration against the army for its alleged lack of power under the Japanese constitution. On the eve of his death, Mishima wrote two Columbia University professors, hoping they would judge his work sympathetically.

Mishima, with his militia of students, was a theist devoted to the restoration of the Japanese emperor's divinity. {*The Economist*, 11 November 1995}.

MISCREANT

• Miscreant, n. A person of the highest degree of unworth. Etymologically, the word means *unbeliever*, and its present signification may be regarded as theology's noblest contribution to the development of our language.

–Ambrose Bierce
The Devil's Dictionary

Mishra, Aditya: See entry for Hindu Skeptic.

Mishra, Nirmal K. (20th Century)

Mishra, a California humanist, participated in 1996 in the international congress of humanists in Mexico City. E-mail: <nmishra@ecs.csun.edu>.

MISIMI

A Telugu humanistic monthly, *Misimi* is at Plot No. 337A, Road No. 10, Jubilee Hills, Hyderabad 500 034, India.

MISSIONARIES, RELIGIOUS

• Missionaries are going to reform the world whether it wants to be reformed or not.
–Oscar Wilde

• Missionaries, my dear! Don't you realize that missionaries are the divinely provided food for destitute and underfed cannibals? Whenever they are on the brink of starvation, Heaven in its infinite mercy sends them a nice plump missionary.
—Oscar Wilde

(See entry for Electronic Ministries, which in 1996 took in an estimated $3.5 billion)

MISSISSIPPI HUMANISTS

The Humanist Association of Mississippi (AHA) is at Route 1 Box 170, Enterprise, Mississippi 39330. Charles L. Graham is its contact. Phone: (601) 693-1244. {FD}

MISSOURI HUMANISTS AND FREETHINKERS

Missouri has the following groups:

• Ethical Society of St. Louis (IHEU), 9001 Clayton Road, St. Louis, Missouri 63117.

• Family Freethought Alliance (ASHS), PO Box 260067, St. Louis, MO 63126; (314) 825-6422. The group is on the Web at: <http://www.geocities.com/Tokyo/Temple/9917/ffc/index.html>. E-mail: <nonbelief1@aol.com>.

• Humanists Mid-Continent (AHA), 5828 Cherry St., Kansas City, Missouri 64110. Contacts are Audra and Delta Gier.

• Kansas City Eupraxophy Center (ASHS), 6301 Rockhill Road (Suite 412), Kansas City, Missouri 64131; (816) 822-9840. Verle Muhrer, its head, has arranged for a special euphraxophy building to provide a variety of programs for area humanists and freethinkers (816) 822-9840. E-mail: <uprax@sound.net>.

• Rationalist Society of St. Louis (ASHS), PO Box 2931, St. Louis, Missouri 63130; telephone (314) 664-4424. Their site on the Web is at: <http://www.geocities.com/Tokyo/Temple/9917/rss/.html>. E-mail: <rsslbarb@aol.com> and <smiling@infidels.org>.

• The Voice of Reason in Kansas City, Missouri, sponsors a radio talk show on KKFI-FM which is geared toward the interests of skeptics and humanists.

• University of Missouri at Kansas City Humanists: <http://www.secularhumanism.org/cfa/orgs.html>.

• Washington University in St. Louis's League of Freethinkers is on the Web at <http://www.secularhumanism.org/cfa/orgs.html>.

Mitchell, J. Barr (19th Century)

Mitchell was the anonymous author of *Dates and Data* (1876) and *Chrestos, A Religious Epithet* (1880). Dr. Mitchell also wrote in the *National Reformer*, using only his initials. {BDF}

Mitchell, Katrina (1972–)

Mitchell is a photographer known for her attempts to plumb the depths of female identity. "I spent my whole childhood and adolescence thinking about religious ideas. I don't think I can express all of my beliefs in words just yet, but I feel, as a Unitarian Universalist, that whatever I end up believing, it's okay. Besides, I feel like everything I do is spiritual. When I make the time and the place to create, that's a very spiritual exercise." Among her works are black and white nude photos she took of herself, in motion and splattered with mud. "There is a mirror on the floor and I'm standing over it. Everything is blurry, except my genitals, and there's dark mud everywhere. Afterward, everyone who saw the photos said, 'This is about menstruation,' and I saw then what they saw: The photos feel very ritualistic, very secret, very private. It's about something mysterious that men can't ever understand, a time women can use to reflect on what is happening to our bodies and in our lives." {*World*, November-December 1994}

Mitchell, Logan (Died 1841)

Mitchell was author of lectures published as *The Christian Mythology Unveiled* (1881), also called *Superstition Besieged.* Reportedly a suicide, he left by his will a sum of £500 to any bookseller who had the courage to publish his book, an offer taken up by B. Cousens. {BDF}

Mitchell, Maria (1818–1889)

Mitchell was an astronomer and educator. Raised a Friend, she was critical of that group's strictness and began to go to Unitarian services. Here, she found that she could be more independent, but she did not abandon the use of "thee" and "thou" in her speech. Her interest in astronomy led to her finding what she claimed was a comet, a discovery confirmed by other astronomers. As a result, she was awarded a gold medal by the King of Denmark and became known as America's first woman astronomer. Later, she taught at Vassar and became the first woman member of the American Academy of Arts and Sciences. {U}

Mitchell, Peter Chalmers [Sir] (1864–1945)

Mitchell, who became one of Britain's leading zoologists, was uncompromising in his freethought, according to McCabe. An atheist and a materialist, he described himself in Evolution *and the War* (1915) as "one who dislikes all forms of supernaturalism and who does not shrink from the implications even of the phrase that thought is a secretion of the brain, as bile is a secretion of the liver." Mitchell was an honorary associate of the Rationalist Press Association (RPA). {JM; RAT; RE}

Mitchell, Steven (20th Century)

Mitchell has been a vice president and editorial director of Prometheus Books as well as an editorial associate of *Free Inquiry.*

Mitchell, Violet (1900–1994)

Mitchell, an English lady from Hertfordshire, was passionately committed to the causes of radical freethought and animal rights. A friend of President Chapman Cohen of the National Secular Society, she was anti-Christian because "it propagates the idea that animals are lower than humans; they are 'different' but not lower. Like the Government, Christians assure me they are against inflicting 'unnecessary' pain; like some trade unionists, they uphold justice but do not demand justice for all sentient creatures. For me, Justice is indivisible—it is not logical to confine it to *homo sapiens.* Upon her death, her friend George Mepham noted that "Violet was an atheist—she insisted that 'Humanist' did not adequately define her non-belief." {*The Freethinker*, February 1994}

Mitchell, Warren (20th Century)

The actor who played the role of the irascible Alf Garnett in "Till Death Do Us Par," Mitchell is an atheist. {*Freethinker*, January 2000}

Mitchison, Naomi (Mary Margaret) [Lady] (1897–1999)

In 1984, Lady Mitchison was elected an honorary associate of the Rationalist Press Association. At the time of her death, she not only was the oldest member of the organization but also had been involved with it longer than anyone else. Among her dozens of books are *Cloud Cuckoo Land* (1925), *Comments on Birth Control* (1930), and an autobiography entitled *All Change Here* (1975).

Mitchison's father was the physiologist and philosopher J. S. Haldane. Her mother was the hostess Kathleen Trotter. Her brother was the pioneering geneticist J. B. S. Haldane. Her uncle was R. B. Haldane (Lord Haldane of Cloan), the Liberal and then Labour Lord Chancellor. When her husband, Gilbert Richard Mitchison, was wounded in action while serving in the army in France, she nursed him back to health, he became a barrister, and the two formed the nucleus of a largely left-wing intellectual circle.

Mitchison was an active supporter of birth control, but she had seven children over twenty-two years. Her first son's death from meningitis was cruelly described in Aldous Huxley's *Point Counter Point.* Her other three sons became distinguished scientists and Fellows of the Royal Society. Her daughters became writers.

A radical in religion as well as politics, she supported the freethought movement, joined the Rationalist Press Association, and served as a director of the short-lived paper of "scientific humanism," *The Realist* (1929). She visited the Soviet Union in 1934 but was never a fellow traveler. She supported the Scottish Nationalists and became involved in 1963 with the Bakgatla tribe in Bechuanaland (later Botswana). During a career of seventy years, she contributed thousands of articles and letters to scores of papers as well as produced books at a rate of more than one a year.

In 1997, a birthday party was held in Carradale, near Campbeltown in southwest Scotland, for the 100-year-old socialist, feminist, anti-militarist, anti-racists, Scottish nationalist, internationalist, writer, lover, parent, and grandparent. {Nicolas Walter, *New Humanist*, November 1997; *New Humanist*, March 1999; TRI}

Mitford, Jessica (1917–1996)

Mitford, an incisive critic of her British upbringing and of American ways, made her reputation with *The American Way of Death* (1963; *The American Way of Death Revisited*, 1998), a scathing indictment of the funeral industry in which undertakers had "successfully turned the tables in recent years to perpetrate a huge, macabre, and expensive practical joke on the American public." Undertakers, who now called themselves "funeral directors" and "morticians," sold coffins which had become "caskets," supplied hearses which had become "professional cars," flowers which had become "floral tributes," for corpses which had become "loved ones." They did not, however, like cremation's being referred to as "bake and shake" nor to her description of what went on backstage, where the body . . .

> is in short order sprayed, sliced, pierced, pickled, trussed, trimmed, creamed, waxed, painted, roughed, and neatly dressed—transformed from a common corpse into a Beautiful Memory Picture.

She also revealed information about neighborhood undertakers, to the dismay of the trade, and included a list of anatomy departments and medical schools that have better uses for dead bodies than being embalmed. When she questioned the prices on some of the items being charged, she was told by an undertaker, "How much would it cost you to stay in a good motel for three days?"

As to the Dr. Thomas Holmes who, she wrote, is often affectionately referred to as "the father of American embalming" and who followed early Judaeo-Christian belierfs as to the nature of God, man, and the hereafter, Mitford denied the idea. Instead, she said, embalming "originated with the pagan Egyptians and reached its high point in the second millennium B.C. Thereafter, [it] suffered a decline from which it did not recover until it was made part of the standard funeral service in twentieth-century America."

Journalist Richard Severo reported that Mitford's work led to an investigation by the Federal Trade Commission but that California Congressman James B. Utt, whose state is known "for its Pharaonic funerals and ornate cemeteries," denounced Miss Mitford as "pro-Communist, anti-American" and speculated that she would donate profits from the book to "the coffers of the Communist Party, U.S.A." Mitford had been a Communist in the 1940s.

The youngest daughter born to Lord Redesdale (David Mitford) and Lady Redesdale, the former Sydney Bowles, she came from an eccentric family. Her sister Pamela aspired as a child to be a horse. Her sister Diana wanted to be a Fascist and, eventually, became the wife of England's ranking Fascist, Sir Oswald Mosley. Her sister Unity became a disciple of Hitler, shot herself, then died nine years later in a nursing home. (In the sitting room they shared as children, Unity had adorned her side with swastikas while Jessica responded by carving small hammers and sickles into the windowpanes on her side of the room.) Her sister Nancy became a novelist, best known for her *Pursuit of Love* and *Love in a Cold Climate*.

When nineteen, she ran away from home with a second cousin, Esmond Romilly, a nephew of Winston Churchill, getting cut out of her father's will. Romilly, who joined the Canadian Air Force, was killed in action in 1941. She then married a Brooklyn lawyer in 1943, moving to Oakland, California. In addition to writing *The Trial of Dr. Spock, William Sloan Coffin Jr., Michael Ferber, Mitchell Goodman, and Marcus Raskin* (1969), five who were accused of aiding and abetting those who sought to violate the Selective Service Act, she wrote *Kind and Unusual Punishment: The Prison Business* (1973), finding prisons are wanting in almost everything except brutality; *A Fine Old Conflict* (1977), about her Communist days; *Poison Penmanship: The Gentle Art of Muckraking* (1979); and *The American Way of Birth* (1992), in which she accused doctors of doing too many Caesareans and of not paying attention to the possibilities offered by midwifery.

The Letters of Nancy Mitford and Evelyn Waugh (1997) include her tweaking Waugh about religion. She compared the resurrection of the body to "finding your motor car after a party," and expressions such as "she must be in Heaven by now" were equated with "she'd caught the 4:45." Waugh's displeasure resulted: "Would it not be best always to avoid any reference to the Church or to your Creator? Your intrusions into this strange world are always fatuous." Not swayed by such reasoning, she continued her mirthful ways, describing, for example, a mix-up at a florist's and a French lesbian artist's saying, "My wreath was the kind of thing a trades union sends to the Pres. of the Republic. It took two men to carry it. All the old lesbians looked absolutely astounded & I was treated like the widow by the undertakers." Although Mitford was nominally an Anglican, she was actually an agnostic, as shown in her letters to Waugh.

Late in life, asked what sort of funeral she wanted, she replied an elaborate one that had "six black horses with plumes and one of those marvelous jobs of embalming that take 20 years off." She added that she wanted "streets to be blocked off, dignitaries to declaim sobbingly over the flower-smothered bier, proclamations to be issued—that sort of thing." Shortly before her death, Ms. Mitford said to her friend and fellow non-theist Molly Ivins, "Well, I had a good run, didn't I?" {Richard Severo, *The New York Times*, 24 July 1996; Molly Ivins, *The New York Times*, 25 August 1996; *Vanity Fair*, March 1997}

MITHRA or MITRA

• The Mithraists were the first to teach that strength is gentleness. All of this is rather better than the Christian hysteria which vacillates between the murder of heretics on one hand and the cringing rejection of this world on the other.

–**Gore Vidal**, *Julian*

(See entries for Christmas and for Zoroastrianism.)

Mitrokhin, Lev W. (20th Century)

Editor of *Social Science*, a leading publication in the former USSR, Mitrokhin also is deputy editor in Moscow of *Problems of Philosophy*. At the Eleventh International Humanist and Ethical Union (IHEU) World Congress held in Brussels (1990), Mitrokhin addressed the group. {*Free Inquiry*, Winter, 1990-1991}.

Mitterrand, François Maurice Marie [President] (1916–1996)

Mitterrand, a president of France, became a prisoner of war during the Second World War, escaped, then became active in the French Resistance. In the 1950s, he held several cabinet posts, joined the weak Socialist party, then became its secretary in 1971. In 1981, Mitterrand became the first Socialist president of the French Fifth Republic. Jean Lacouture's *Mitterand* (1998) not only describes his eloquence, his brilliance at stragegy, his being a master of timing, a leader of men, a charmer of women, but also tells how in his later life he could be arrogant, cynical, cruel, vindictive, a schemer who liked to divide and rule.

The courageous leader of the French Resistance, after his dubious beginning as a Vichyite, was author of a number of books, including *Le coup d'état permanent* (1964), *Un socialisme du possible* (1970), and *Politique II* (1981). It was not until 1995 that he divulged some secrets about his past: that he had worked for the collaborationist Vichy regime before joining the Resistance during World War II; in 1940, while serving in the Vichy army of Marshall Philippe Pétain, he wrote *First Agreement*, a novel about Elsa and Philippe, a couple madly in love and living together, which was a shocking notion at that time; and that until 1986 he had remained friends with René Bousquet, the Vichy official charged in 1989 with crimes against humanity for his role in deporting Jews from France to Nazi death camps. Later, he joined the Resistance. Alan Riding, of *The New York Times*, has suggested that because Mitterrand had stunned his wide circle of Jewish friends with such disclosures, he chose to collaborate on a work with Elie Wiesel, *Memoir in Two Voices* (1996). To Wiesel he explained that he had been unaware of Vichy's anti-Semitic policies and that he had thought Bousquet was only a respectable businessman. Wiesel does not state in the book whether he found these explanations valid ones.

Progressive freethinkers were shocked when, in 1994, Mitterrand as the President of France said of Rwanda, "In such countries, genocide is not too important."

In 1994, when the world press announced his prostate cancer (he kept it a secret for fifteen years!), Mitterrand, a declared atheist, met with a devoutly Catholic French philosopher to discuss death. The philosopher, Jean Guillot, 93, told reporters that Mitterrand confided that the doctors had given him no more than six months to live, that his major goal was to live until at least 7 May 1995 in order to complete his second seven-year term. In a television interview, asked what he would say when he arrived "who knows where," Mitterrand replied drily, "Eternity is a long time." (In fact, he did live out his term of office.)

Mitterrand ended his own life by halting the drug treatment against the cancer that killed him. Roland Dumas, a close friend and a former Foreign Minister, said over television, "A few days before his death, he told me, 'Now I have my philosophy.' " He had asked his physician, Jean-Pierre Tarot, what would happen if he stopped taking all drugs except painkillers, and the physician told him he would be dead in three days. The day Mitterrand stopped the treatments, he died. In flowing African robes, Arab Headdresses, and sober mourning clothes, numbers of notables assembled for a requiem Mass in Notre Dame Cathedral while his family 250 miles away in Jarnac conducted a small funeral. In Paris, Jean-Marie Cardinal Lustiger said that Mitterrand was "more agnostic than anything else," adding,

"May François Mitterrand find in the company of saints the help, forgiveness, and courage finally to open his eyes to the invisible," a comment that angered many and surprised some of the sixty world leaders and thirteen hundred other dignitaries who had gathered. Maurice Duruflé's "Requiem" was played.

Meanwhile, in Jarnac, in a small Romanesque Church of St. Peter, the entering procession started with the former President's widow, Danielle, their two sons, and his longtime mistress, Anne Pingeot, and their daughter, Mazarine Pingeot. Mrs. Mitterrand had invited both women to the interment next to his parents' graves in the church graveyard. "A sceptical free-thinker, he had a religious feel for nature," reported *The Economist* in an obituary. "His stature rests . . . on a grasp of the limitations of politics, on being a catalyst, on knowing when to do nothing. He was an exceptional leader in a time when France was ceasing to be an exception."

Among others, journalist Adam Gopnik has commented upon how Mitterrand orchestrated his own afterlife. For example, *Paris-Match* published a photo of Mitterrand on his deathbed, one that looked as if he himself might have photographed his final minute. He had chosen to die not on a hospital or state bed but a medium-sized married couple's bed with white bedspread, looking as if it had just been smoothed out by the *femme de ménage*. Dressed for a Sunday promenade, in a dark-gray suit and shoes, "he looked the way the French like their leaders to look—dignified and serene without trying too hard for that effect." Gopnik, after saying that by American standards Mitterrand was a relatively weak leader, observed that "the French love authoritarian leaders and pine for them when they're gone." They were amused upon finding that their President had kept an entire separate second family, "like a character in the fifties French comedy. Anne Pingeot, Mazarine's (their "illegitimate" daughter) mother, who is a scholar of nineteenth-century sculpture, was not really his mistress; she was a second wife. He spent the weeks with Danielle at the Élysée, and the weekends with Anne and Mazarine at the château of Souzy-la-Briche, another *propriété de la nation* that the French President had at his disposal." Gopnik continues: "One day, he would be found with Danielle on the Rue de Bièvre, in the Fifth Arrondissement, and the next, chez Anne on the Rue Jacob, in the Sixth. He had two country residences, too: one at Latche, in the Landes, for Danielle, their two sons, and the Labradors; one in Gordes, in Provence, for Anne, Mazarine, and the cats. He spent Christmas with Anne and Mazarine and New Year's Day with Danielle and his sons. These arrangements were widely known yet never made public. (He had other liaisons. He loved women, particularly their feet. He asked his conquests to take their shoes off in front of him, so that he could caress their insteps.)"

After Mitterrand's death, Dr. Claude Gubler wrote *The Great Secret* (1996), in which he revealed that Mitterrand had sworn his doctors to silence when they had found prostate cancer that had spread to most of the rest of his body by November 1981. Many condemned Dr. Gubler for betraying a confidence, although others were surprised that Mitterrand had been able to dupe them about such a basic issue as his health for more than a decade.

However, according to Gopnik, "In Mitterrand, the French got what they want: not so much an authoritarian figure as a romantic one, and romantic in both the strict and the popular senses. . . . For most of the past two hundred years, it has been the passionate unspoken conviction of the French people that History, in Mitterrand's sense—the high, romantic, sometimes even tragic sense—was happening here. Not happening here in just the modest, decent sense in which history always happens everywhere but in the grand, Hegelian sense: the spirit of the time kept its court in Paris." {CE}

Mittermaier, Karl Joseph Anton von (1787–1867)

Mittermaier was a German jurisconsult whose works on law gained him a high reputation. He obtained a chair at the Heidelberg University, and in 1831 he represented Baden in Parliament. A free-thinker, he wrote about the need for freedom in all areas. {BDF; RAT}

Mittie, Stanilas (19th Century)

Mittie in 1789 proposed the taking of church bells to make money and cannon. During the revolution he distinguished himself by other anti-clerical suggestions. {BDF}

MIZ

A German humanistic journal, *Miz* is at Wurzberger Strasse 18a, 63739 Aschaffenburg, Germany.

MIZUAGE

Geisha girls in Japan are unavailable for brief sexual encounters. However, in the past young girls were sold to a highest bidder for the purpose of deflowering. The rite was known as mizuage. Meanwhile, a geisha can be supported by a wealthy man interested in a long-term sexual relationship.

MOBY-DICK

Herman Melville's masterpiece, *Moby-Dick; or, The Whale* (1851), is a symbolic account of the conflict between man and his fate. Or of Man's love for, but conflicts with, Nature.

Critics disagree concerning the symbolism of Moby-Dick, a white whale that attacks the whaling ship *Pequod* and tears away Captain Ahab's leg. Ahab then becomes monomaniacal, his one purpose in life being that of capturing the fierce and cunning whale. His crew—Americans that include Asians, American Indians, Africans, and whites—endures storms, lightning, loss of the compass, the drowning of a man, and the insanity of Ahab's favorite, a lad named Pip. When the white whale again attacks and the captain's ivory leg is snapped off, Ahab eventually is able to harpoon the whale but gets fouled in the line and is pinioned to the whale.

The ship is sunk and, as the final spars settle in the water, one of the crew nails to the mast a sky-hawk that pecks at the flag he is placing as a signal. The ship,

> like Satan, would not sink to hell till she had dragged a living part of heaven along with her, and helmeted herself with it.

The sole survivor is Ishmael, narrator of the tale (and named after the Biblical Ishmael, Abraham's son who was cast out after the birth of Isaac and is sometimes considered to be the forebear of the Arabs). In the opening scenes Ishmael needs to spend a night in New Bedford, the inn is crowded, and he has to share the inn's wedding bed with a harpooner and cannibal, Queequeg. Reluctantly going to bed under such circumstances (the pagan had no objection, free-thinkers note, to sharing a bed with another human being), Ishmael awakens in the morning to find his bedmate's arm "thrown over me in the most loving and affectionate manner. You had almost thought I had been his wife." The two maintain a close friendship up to the end of the work.

Robert K. Martin, professor of English at the *Université de Montréal*, wrote in *Social Critique and Literary Form in the Sea Novels of Herman Melville* about the "imagery of marriage as well as with a sense of sexual and racial transgression" in the early scenes. Ishmael's religious outlook is that it is "unbecoming" to be "hugging a fellow male in that matrimonial sort of way." Ishmael, however, comes across as not at all being another Christian homophobe.

When Father Mapple, in a sermon, reinforces Ishmael's fear of otherness and particularly of male friendship as preached in Christianity, Ishmael concludes humanistically, "I'll try a pagan friend . . . since Christian kindness has proved but hollow courtesy." At the plot's end, Ishmael is saved from drowning by using Queequeg's coffin (saved not by "the blood of the lamb" but by a pagan, no less!).

Martin states that "One of Melville's most daring insights in *Moby-Dick* is the recognition of homophobia as a force linked to racism and required by patriarchal society just as much as the suppression of women." For critic Alfred Kazin, Ahab is a self-conscious Prometheus dedicated to "[striking] the sun if it wronged me." But of those who held that the whale is God and Fate, mindless and cruel, few noted that Melville's hero set out to kill God. Also, few at the time recognized the work's humanistic brilliance and Melville's statement about how puny are man's attempts to fight against, not just live with, nature. Today, *Moby-Dick* is as close a work as any other to being America's prose epic. {CE; OCAL; OEL}

Mocenicus, Philippus (16th Century)

Mocenicus, although the Archbishop of Nicosia in Cyprus, wrote as a Venetian philosopher such heretical works as *Contemplations* (1588), *Peripatetic Question of Coesalpinus*, and the books of Telesio on *The Nature of Things* in a volume entitled *Tractationum Philosophicarum*. {BDF}

Mockus, Michael (20th Century)

In 1916, attorney Theodore Schroeder, a freethinker, defended Mockus on a blasphemy charge. {FUS}

MODERN FREETHINKER

An Indian publication in English, *Modern Freethinker* is at 779 Pocket 5 Mayur Vihar-1, New Delhi 110 091, India. <mahesh@del1.vsnl.net.in>.

MODERN RATIONALIST

A monthly in English, *Modern Rationalist* is at 50, E. V. K. Salai, Chennai (Madras) 600 007, India. E-mail: <periyar@giasmod01.vsnl.net.in>.

MODESTY

• Modesty died when clothes were born.

–Mark Twain

Modisett, Mitchell (20th Century)

Modisett is the Past President of Humanists of Florida. He was a participant at the 3rd Annual Atheist Alliance Convention and at the 1999 convention of Humanists of Florida.

Moehlman, Arthur B. (1889–1952)

Moehlman was a member of the American Humanist Association. In 1970, he wrote *School Administration*. {HNS}

Moehlman, Conrad Henry (Born 1879)

Moehlman, an educator, wrote *The Wall of Separation Between Church and State* (1951). {FUS; HNS}

MOHAMMEDAN

Muslims object to the word Mohammedan, which implies that the man called Muhammed, like the Christ called Jesus, was a supernatural being. (See entries for Islam, Muhammed, and Muslim.

Moia, Nelly (20th Century)

Moia is a head teacher in Luxembourg. In 1988 she resigned in disgust from the National Working Party on Lay Moral Education, after much constructive work in assembling course materials. She did so to protest against a bill to abolish the right to abstain from religious and lay moral instruction in schools.

Three of her works with theses of humanist morality are *For Animals* (1992), *For Women* (1993), and *Geint d'Pafen* (Against the Holy Joes) (1994).

Moiseev, Nikita (20th Century)

Moiseev, a Russian professor of mathematics, signed Humanist Manifesto 2000.

Moleschott, Jacob (1822–1893)

Moleschott, a Dutch born scientific materialist, became a popularizer of science. He was a professor of physiology at Zurich and afterwards at Turin. Moleschott wrote *Circulation of Life*, *Light and Life*, *Physiological Sketches*, and other medical and scientific works. Lange called him "the father of the modern materialistic movement," a view also affirmed by Finngeir Hiorth (*New Humanist*, February 1994). Moleschott's best known work, *Force and Matter* (1855), had in its day much the same success as Haeckel's *Riddle of the Universe*, McCabe wrote, adding, "It was translated into every European language and sold by the hundred thousand. Moleschott did not refuse the label Materialist—and he was, of course, an atheist—though like Haeckel (and modern physics) he held that matter and energy are two aspects of the ultimate reality. In youth he had studied philosophy and had more inclination for poetry than science. He was a man of warm sentiments and high ideals. He was virtually driven out of Germany for his heresies and rose to high honors in Italy, where freethought was general in the academic world fifty years ago." {BDF; JM; PUT; RAT; RE}

Molesworth, Robert (1656–1725)

The Right Honourable Robert Molesworth supported the Prince of Orange in the Revolution of 1688, after which he was called to the Privy Council and employed at London. He sat in the Irish Parliament from 1695 to 1699 and in the English Parliament from 1705–1708 and 1714–1725. The Royal Society admitted him in 1698, and he was created Baron and Viscount in 1719. An intimate friend of Toland and Shaftesbury, he shared their deistic views openly, as illustrated in his *Account of Denmark as it was in the year 1692* (1694). {RAT}

Molesworth, William [Sir] (1810–1855)

Molesworth was a statesman and man of letters, the eighth baronet of his family. In 1855 he was Secretary for the Colonies. For some time, he was proprietor and conductor of the *Westminster Review*, in which he wrote many articles. Molesworth produced an edition of Hobbes at his own expense, and he contributed to the support of Auguste Comte. He was a deist. {BDF; RAT; RE}

Molière, Jean Baptiste Poquelin (1622–1673)

Molière was a French playwright and actor, the creator of high French comedy, the forerunner of the *Comédie Français*. An upholsterer, he joined the Béjan troupe of actors when young, toured the provinces for thirteen years, and received the patronage of Louis XIV. His farces, comedies, masques, and ballets ridiculed a vice or a type of excess by caricaturing a person who incarnates it: *Tartuffe* (1664), the religious hypocrite; *Le Misanthrope* (1666), the antisocial man; *The Would-be Gentleman* (1670), the parvenu; *The Learned Women* (1672), affected intellectuals; *The Imaginary Invalid* (1673), the hypochondriac. When he produced *Don Juan*, a religious writer described it as "a school of atheism in which, after making a clever atheist say the most horrible impieties he entrusts the cause of God to a valet who says ridiculous things." Similarly, *Tartuffe*, a satire on religious fanatics and hypocrites, resulted in the clergy's demands that Molière be burned as a heretic and led to his excommunication. Molière's father had been valet to the King, and this as well as his skill in writing comedies got him royal protection. His farces, contemporaries also find, remain uproariously amusing.

During the French Revolution, Maréchal cited Molière as being only a "possible" atheist. McCabe labeled Molière a freethinker.

Martin Greif relates that when Molière was in his own late forties, he fell in love with fifteen-year-old Michel Baron, "the talented young actor whom he had taken into his own home after removing him from a company of child actors of which he was the star." Molière's wife, twenty-one years his junior, screamed bloody murder. The boy, not exactly dumb, moved out. Molière ordered him back. The wife said, "Choose! It's either him or me."

According to Greif, Molière chose and "three years later, when the playwright died, Michel Baron was at his side." Curtain . . . except that there was a Catholic funeral despite any last confession and without his ever repudiating his profession of being a comedian.

Molière was buried at night, for no priest in Paris would escort the body to the cemetery and no cemetery would accept him. Louis XIV, however, intervened, pointing out that Church law defined burial to be four feet and asking that Molière, then, be buried five feet but without pomp or scandal. As a result, a non-religious ceremony resulted. The casket was covered with the upholsterers' embroidered banner, not something related to comedy. When 150 gathered and became noisy, Madame Molière dispensed coins and requested that those present escort the body to the cemetery. Here, the playwright was buried in a section reserved for suicides and unbaptized children. Later, the body was moved, and today Molière's tomb is in the huge Père-Lachaise cemetery in eastern Paris, near the tombs of Chopin, Bizet, Proust, and Oscar Wilde.

The *Catholic Encyclopedia* blandly describes Molière as a Catholic, yet he died as McCabe points out, excommunicated, and the priests whom his wife summoned refused to come, giving in only when the King said that some sort of burial service should be arranged. {CB; CE; EU, Aram Vartarian; JM; RAT}

Molina, Mario José (1943–)

Molina came to the United States from Mexico in 1968. He won the Nobel Prize in Chemistry in 1995, his achievements including the discovery that fluorocarbons deplete the ozone layer of stratosphere. Molina signed Humanist Manifesto 2000. "We have to understand our environment," he wrote in his *Who's Who in America* entry, "to find out if we are tampering with it. One of our accomplishments has been to call attention to society's potential altering of the atmosphere."

Moll, Shirley R. (20th Century)

A Minnesota atheist, Moll is treasurer of the Atheist Alliance. E-mail: <smoll175@aol.com>.

Molnar, Alex (20th Century)

Molnar, a professor at the University of Wisconsin-Milwaukee, is an activist who supports public schools and opposes vouchers for religious and private schools. He is consulting editor of *Educational Leadership*, the journal of the Association for Supervision and Curriculum Development. In 1996, he spoke in Madison, Wisconsin, at the Freedom From Religion Foundation conference.

Molnar, Thomas Steven (20th Century)

Molnar wrote *Theists and Atheists* (c. 1980) and *Giving Kids the Business* (1996). {GS}

Molony, Daniel D. (20th Century)

Molony was instrumental in helping form the 1958 New York Chapter of the Rationalist Press Association. Molony lived in Staten Island, New York.

Molteno, John Charles [Sir] [Premier] (1814–1886)

Molteno, the Premier of Cape Colony, was a poor boy of Italian extraction who had been born in England. In South Africa, he made a fortune and rose in politics to become Premier. His son and biographer stated that his father had shed at an early age the Catholic belief in which he had been reared, that although his life was "in the highest sense religious" he was "above the narrow formularies of any sect." {JM; RAT}

Momerie, Alfred Williams (1848–1900)

A theologian, Momerie taught logic and mental philosophy at King's College and in 1883 was preacher to the Foundling Hospital. He wrote *The Defects of Modern Christianity* (1882) and *Agnosticism* (1884), which led to accusations of his heresy and his eventually being deprived of his positions. In *The Fate of Religion* (1893), Momerie wrote that "the orthodoxy common to all the Churches is a monstrous outgrowth of ecclesiasticism." Momerie retained his clerical title and remained a theist. {RAT}

Mommsen, Theodor (1817–1903)

A historian, Mommsen studied at Kiel, then became professor of law in Leipzig, Zürich, and Berlin. He wrote *History of Rome* (1853–1885), in which he expressed the opinion that it is doubtful if the world was improved by Christianity. His chief biographer, L. M. Hartmann, says in *Theodor Mommsen* (1908) that he "left Christianity for Deism and Deism for Atheism." He disliked Kaplanokratie (the rule of priests), and Hartmann says that one of the reasons Mommsen left his *History of Rome* unfinished was that "he found no pleasure in describing the substitution of the Nazarene for the ancient spirit." Mommsen was Perpetual Secretary of the Berlin Academy of Sciences. In 1902 Mommsen won the Nobel Prize in literature. {BDF; JM; RAT; RE}

Mon, Stormy (1945-)

Although raised a Methodist, Mon is an Oregonian freethinker, a "free spirit" and not a joiner. *Imagine Freedom from Governments and Churches* is an entire work that is uncopyrighted and free on the Web: <http://www.stormy.org>. Included are topics such as libertarianism; Mormons ("history of a fraud"); the Bible (a book review); the Koran (about Mohammed's insecurity); and religious dogmas (which are responsible for the second-class treatment of women throughout history). E-mail: <stormy@stormy.org>.

"Mona Lisa": See entry for Homoeroticism.

Mondale, R. Lester (20th Century)

The half-brother of former Vice President Walter Mondale, Lester Mondale was the youngest signer of Humanist Manifesto I and a spokesman for humanism in Unitarianism and Ethical Culture for many years. In 1933 he led the Philadelphia Ethical Culture Society. He wrote *Three Unitarian Philosophies of Religion* (1946, 1952) and *The New Man of Religious Humanism* (1973). Mondale once was president of the Fellowship of Religious Humanists, and he signed both Humanist Manifesto I and II. He is on the editorial board of *The Humanist.* In 1998 Mondale was given a Lifetime Achievement Award at the Fourth Annual Atheist Alliance Convention, and it was noted that he was the sole surviving signer of the 1933 Humanist Manifesto. In 1999 he signed Humanist Manifesto 2000. (Walter Mondale, when a Senator, addressed the Fifth International Humanist and Ethical Union World Congress held in Boston (1970). See entry for Ethical Culture.) {HM1; HM2; HSN2; EU, Howard B. Radest; EW; FUS; HNS}

Moneta, Ernesto Teodoro (1838–1918)

Moneta was a Nobel Prize winner (1907), a journalist who fought "the Papal troops" in the war for the liberation of Italy and afterwards edited the anti-Papal *Secolo* for thirty years. Moneta was one of the leading workers in Italy for peace and reform. He founded *La Vita Internazionale* and the Lombard Union for Peace and Arbitration. Moneta was a rationalist. {RE}

MONEY

• What's the answer to 99 questions out of 100, son? Money.

–Malcolm Forbes Sr., a billionaire, to Malcolm Forbes Jr

The first paper money was issued by China in 1024. In 1661 a Swedish bank printed paper money. All organized religions, including philosophic associations, are quite agreeable to accepting money . . . and credit cards. {*The Economist*, 31 December 1999}

Money, John (1921–)

A sexologist at Johns Hopkins University, and one of the pioneers in the field, Money has written for *Free Inquiry.* He addressed the Tenth International Humanist and Ethical Union (IHEU) World Congress held in Buffalo (1988). That year, he wrote *Gay, Straight, and "In Between": The Sexology of Erotic Orientation.*

Rolling Stone in an article described Money: "Having lost his faith in his early 20s, Money increasingly reacted against what he saw as the repressive religious strictures of his upbringing and, in particular, the anti-masturbatory, anti-sexual fervor that went with them. The academic study of sexuality, which removed even the most outlandish practices from moral considerations and placed them in the 'pure' realm of scientific inquiry, was for Money an emancipation." {CA; *Free Inquiry*, Summer, 1988}

Monette, Paul (1945–1995)

Monette is the author of *Borrowed Time: An AIDS Memoir* (1988), which describes the death of a lover, attorney Paul Horwitz, "46 now and dying by inches." A complementary work, *Love Alone: Eighteen Elegies for Rog* (1988), is a book of poetry. His National Book Award-winning *Becoming A Man, Half a Life Story* (1992) describes his life as a homosexual. In December 1991, Monette himself was diagnosed with AIDS, and in his remaining life he stated as a goal that he would continue his pleas for humanistic justice. *Halfway Home* is narrated by a performer who has AIDS and who transforms himself into a deity named Miss Jesus, one who fights with his athletic brother. It is about the dying performance artist who retreats to a friend's California estate to confront his mortality.

"One hundred percent tolerance is possible," he has written. "Everyone is capable of healing the hate in their heart." Reminiscing, he describes his having been a closeted homosexual teacher, sometimes raging against a "straight" world that had made his life so dangerous. "We laugh together then and dance in the giddy circle of freedom. . . . And every time we dance, our enemies writhe like the Witch in Oz, melting, melting—the Nazi Popes and all their brocaded minions, the rat-brain politicians, the wacko fundamentalists and their Book of Lies." Monette added that he did not believe in any afterlife.

In 1994, Monette issued *Last Watch of the Night: Essays Too Personal and Otherwise.* In it, he discusses the hypocrisy of the Catholic Church as well as the 1993 march by homosexuals on Washington. He also tells of the difficulties and occasional ironies of gay writers trying to "get covered" by the mainstream press. One of Monette's strengths is that of explaining what it is like to live with AIDS. His radiation treatments for a form of cancer, KS, or Kaposi's sarcoma, are "Arcadian compared to the exigencies of chemo," he writes in vivid prose. In 1983 he and Horwitz visited Keats's grave in Rome, and later he tells how he shopped for his own as well as his lovers' burial plots. In the 1994 work, which was an essay, "My Priests," contains his atheistic ruminations on "the Vatican Nazis," "bloodsucker convents," and "The Vatican's Minister of Hate (Cardinal Ratzinger)." Whether writing about the "Nazi popes" or the "shit-eating Republicans," Monette is nothing if not opinionated.

Another of his lovers, casting agent Stephen Kolzak, died of AIDS. Monette's obituary in *The New York Times* (12 February 1995) mentioned his winning the 1992 National Book Award for nonfiction, which he reportedly said had "literally kept me alive" after contracting AIDS. Monette said the award had appropriately sent a message that gay and lesbian literature "is significant." Ned Rorem set to music Monette's "Live Alone" for a male chorus. {GL}

Monge, Gaspard [Conte de Paluse] (1746–1818)

Monge, the French physicist, was so precocious that the priests who educated him set him to teach physics and mathematics at the age of sixteen. Later he became so distinguished in both sciences that Napoleon made him not only a senator but created him Count of Pelusium. He became a member of the Academy of Sciences in 1780 and, through the influence of Condorcet, was made Minister of the Marine in 1792. Napoleon gave him an estate for his many services to the French nation. Maréchal and Lalande include Monge's name in their list of atheists. {BDF; JM; RAT; RE}

Mongez, Antoine (1747–1835)

Mongez was a French archaeologist, a member of the Academy of inscriptions and of the Institute, before which he said he "had the honor to be an atheist." Mongez, one of the most ardent members of the Convention, wrote many memoirs. {BDF; RAT; RE}

Mongold, Harry E. (20th Century)

Mongold contributes material to *The American Rationalist*, one article of which (July 1992) states there were two Christianities in the time of Paul. There was the Judaistic one taught by James, John, and Peter, in which a Messiah had arrived to bring glory to Israel. Also, there was Paul's Hellenistic one, in which all mankind was freed from the rule of the elemental spirits. Paul derives his from Greek ideas, whereas the former "is mainly the Jewish religion except for the belief that the Messiah had come and been executed."

Mongold finds that the book of *Acts*, which evidently was written to reconcile the two, is filled with inconsistencies and fails to convince that there was only one religion of Jesus. More and more, he finds, "science is making it harder and harder to distinguish between the Hebrew religion and that of other peoples. In other words, early history in the Bible seems less and less reliable."

MONGOLIAN ATHEISM

Atheists abound in former republics of the USSR. B. Batbayar, a member of the Mongolian Parliament, was quoted in the press as explaining why a late 1990s Christian-oriented television program was tolerable: "I'm very happy in Mongolia to introduce news without commentary. Personally, I'm an atheist." {*The New York Times*, 26 January 1997}

MONISM

Monism, in metaphysics, is a term applied from the 18th century to any theory that explains phenomena by one unifying principle or as the manifestation of a single substance. Monists stress the *oneness* of reality. Hegel identified this oneness as spirit, or mind. Spinoza identified it as an all-pervasive deity. On the question of whether people's minds are distinct from their bodies, for example, a monist would hold either that mental conditions are essentially physical conditions (materialism) or that bodies depend on minds for their existence (idealism). A form of rationalism introduced by Haeckel, monism was meant to replace the usual German "freethought" as a positive philosophy of reality. Haeckel disliked the term "agnostic," which had little support in Germany, and thought atheism too negative and materialism too weak in recognizing the importance of energy. The British jibed at his philosophy as "out of date," said McCabe, who added that the complaint looks foolish in the light of modern developments in physics. Alternatives to monism are dualism (for example, matter and spirit, or good and evil) and pluralism (the explanation of the universe in terms of many principles). Bertrand Russell, for example, was a pluralist. (See a discussion of monism by Roland Hall in the *Encyclopedia of Philosophy*, Vol. 5.) {CE; DCL; RE.}

MONK

Men under religious vows who live in community and whose work is usually centered on their community, often called a monastery, are monks. Buddhism and Christianity have notable groups of monks. Freethinkers and humanists, stated a Manhattan wag, "are not in the business of monkery." (For Maria Monk, see entry for Hoaxes, Religious.) {DCL}

Monk, Maria (Born 1850)

Monk wrote *The Awful Disclosures of the Hotel Dieu Nunnery of Montreal* (1836), which is an anti-Catholic classic.

Monk, Ray (20th Century)

Monk wrote *Bertrand Russell: The Spirit of Solitude* (1996), in which he details Russell's weaknesses as well as his greatness.

MONKEY

- Monkey, n. An arboreal animal which makes itself at home in genealogical trees.

–**Ambrose Bierce,** *The Devil's Dictionary*

MONKEY'S UNCLE

Monkey's Uncle is published by Ed Babinski at 109 Burwood Drive, Simpsonville, South Carolina 29681. {FD}

Monod, Jacques (1910–1976)

In 1965, Monod shared with Andrew Lwoff the Nobel Prize in physiology. The author of *Chance and Necessity* (1971), he was associated with the French *Institut Pasteur*. Monod signed Humanist Manifesto II. In his *Le Hasard et la necessité*, Monod wrote, "The scientific attitude implies . . . the postulate of objectivity—that is to say, the fundamental postulate that there is no plan; that there is no intention in the universe." {HM2}

MONOGAMY

• I am a strict monogamist: it is 20 years since I last went to bed with two women at once, and then I was in my cups and not myself.

–H. L. Mencken

• In this society, we view monogamy like we view virginity—one incident and it's over, the relationship is destroyed—but we should view monogamy like we view sobriety. You're sober. You might get completely drunk one night, but you can get sober again. You can get monogamous again.

–Dan Savage
gay syndicated columnist

• All sex is a power play. We like to deny it. We like to pretend that sex is birds and bunnies and bubbling brooks, that sex can't be evil, nasty power dynamics, but that's what makes it hot for people, whether they cop to it or not. Even the most vanilla sexual scenario has a subtle interplay of power back and forth. In the leather S&M scene, they take those seeds and exaggerate it until it's laughable. You watch people having S&M sex and it's the most ridiculous thing you've ever seen. It's like cops and robbers or Indians and cowboys with your pants down.

–Dan Savage

• Sexual boredom is the most pandemic dysfunction in this country. Think of sex as an appetite. Now think about having to eat the exact same meal every day for the rest of your life—of course you'd get bored.

–Judith Seifer, Past President,
American Association of Sex Educators, Counselors and Therapists

• I don't know if monogamy is a natural way to live,. It's a product of social organization, but it's essential for the way our society is organized, both emotionally and for the passage of property. In my practice I rarely find people who have had affairs say they would do it again.

–Judith Seifer

• I'm not made for a monogamous world. Monogamy is an Anglo concept. To most Latin European men, or Iberian men, the whole notion is hopelessly archaic. It's not that I disagree with it philosophically. It's just that under the rules I choose to live by—because they are the rules of the game I'm playing, the game of life in Anglo Saxon America—you are not allowed to cheat. And my wife wouldn't permit it. She wouldn't be married to me if I did. So you make choices and you sacrifice.

–Geraldo Rivera
{*Playboy*, October 1998}

• It's a medical fact that monogamy and intimacy are what make people happy.

–Drew Pinsky, M. D. a/k/a Dr. Drew,
co-host of MTV's "Love Line"

In all societies, the family is one in which the choice of partners is generally guided by the rules of **exogamy** (one must marry outside a group) and, in more complex societies, by rules of **endogamy** (one must marry within a group). Incest is a taboo and is proscriptive. Rules concerning marriage are usually prescriptive, and marriage is usually heterosexual and entails exclusive rights and duties of sexual performance. However, the Nayar women of India ritually marry men of a superior caste and are allowed to enjoy sexual relations with any number of other men and bear legitimate children. Among the Dahomey of West Africa, a woman can marry another—the first woman becomes legal father of the children (by other men) of the second.

Polyandry (having several husbands) is found where the value of a woman's labor is high and can result in limited births. A **levirate** (in Latin, *levir* = husband's brother) marriage is one between a widow and her late husband's brother, as described in the *Book of Ruth*. Other variations of marriages are found in past as well as in present societies.

Monogamy, particularly in Judeo-Christian societies, is considered the normal practice in marriage. Others find it "unnatural" although one of the oldest expressions of the egalitarian spirit: even if you are rich and powerful, you still get only one wife. As a result, some upper-class men claim multiple wives by philandering or, possibly, by having serial, not parallel, marriages. Although monogamy works for many, freethinkers recognize, it does not work for others.

Sea horses are monogamous. They have no teeth, stomach, or ribs. Their eyes move independently of each other. The male endures pregnancy, holding the eggs the female deposits in his brood pouch until they develop into babies. Just before sunrise, seahorses "dance" together, linking their tails in an elaborate tango. The male emits musical sounds as the female deposits the eggs into his pouch, possibly because among males throughout the world he is the only one certain he is the babies' father.

The author of *Monogamy*, Dr. Adam Phillips, has written that many Americans mistakenly believe there is a predictor of personality—that some key fact about a person, an essential microdot of information, makes everything else intelligible; for example, the person's being gay, a transvestite, or a "normal" heterosexual. Beware, Phillips as a psychoanalyst adds, of judging a complex being by a simple standard. "If you discover that your employee is gay, your partner is a transvestite, your best friend is a "normal" heterosexual, what have you actually discovered about them?" he asks. "What can you predict about their parenting skills, their eating habits or indeed their ability to be President of the United States? These seemingly intimate details about people's lives make us jump to unlikely conclusions because so few reliable conclusions are available. It is one thing to believe that sexuality is intimately revealing, quite another to believe we know what it reveals. Even the oracle always needs interpretation." Part of the complex of moral life, Phillips avers, is that people can do good things for bad reasons, and vice versa. Many are shocked to learn that someone in a monogamous relationship is found to have been unfaithful. Phillips added:

> Perhaps it is not fidelity that we really believe in. What we really believe in, what we are committed to, is how disappointing we are to ourselves, and how we can use our ideals to humiliate ourselves and others. It seems as though our preferred state of mind is righteous indignation, and so our preferred political act is scapegoating. And in a democracy, scapegoating is always a failure of the political imagination.

(See anthropologist Laura Betzig's *Despotism and Differential Reproduction* [1986]; and entry for Polygamy.) {Adam Phillips, "How Much Does Monogamy Tell Us? *The New York Times*, 2 October 1998; Barbara Johnson, "Sex Advice for the Clinton Age," *The New York Times Magazine*, 4 October 1998}

MONOPHYSITISM: For an explanation of monophysitism, a form of heresy, see the entries for Eutyches and for Christianity.

MONOTHEISM

The concept of monotheism, non-theists hold, has been a major stumbling block to freethinking about philosophic ideas. It is a doctrine or belief that there is one God. James Henry Breasted, an American Egyptologist, held that Pharaoh Ikhnaton (1375–1358 B.C.E.) was a monotheist. Diop and Freud similarly claimed that monotheism was not original with the Jews. Zoroastrianism in its early stages was monotheistic, and in its later stages Greek religion became monotheistic. The belief was introduced in Israel first by *II Isaiah* in the exile about 440 B.C.E., and it became increasingly popular until it was fully established in the course of post-exilic days. For Gore Vidal and some other freethinkers, monotheism is a curse, the enemy of pleasure and the foe of rational inquiry. (See entry for Egyptian Religion.) {CE; ER}

MONROE COUNTY (MICHIGAN) COMMUNITY COLLEGE

Monroe County Community College has a humanist group. On the Web: <http://www.secularhumanism.org/cfa/orgs.html>.

Monroe, Jasper R. (1825–1891)

Monroe edited the weekly *Iron-Clad Age* (1881–1898) in Indianapolis, Indiana. According to Fred Whitehead's *Freethought History* (#2, 1992), Monroe was a novelist, playwright, and poet noted for his freethinking. Monroe had started the *Rockford Herald* (1855) and the *Seymour Times* (1857). He wrote *Origin of Man, or The Early Reformers* (1885). During the Civil War he was appointed surgeon to the 150th regiment. Following his death, his daughter, **Lulie Monroe Powers** (1850–1895), continued publishing of *Iron-Clad Age*. P. H. and Pearl A. Powers edited it until 1898, after which it eventually was absorbed by *The Truth Seeker*. {BDF; FUS; JM; PUT; TRI}

Monsey, Messenger (1693–1788)

Messenger was an English physician, an intimate friend of Sir Robert Walpole, Lord Chesterfield, and other leading skeptics. The *Roll of the Royal College of Physicians* states that Monsey "shook off the manacles of superstition and fell into the comfortless bigotry of scepticism." {RE}

MONSIGNOR

Monsignor, n. A high ecclesiastical title, of which the Founder of our religion overlooked the advantages.

–**Ambrose Bierce**, *The Devil's Dictionary*

Montagna, Donald (20th Century)

Montagna, a business trainee and a member of the New York Society for Ethical Culture, worked briefly with Arthur Dobrin on Long Island, then took his skills in organizational development and psychology into leadership of the Washington Society in 1972. (See entry for Ethical Culture.) {EU, Howard B. Radest}

Montagu, Ashley (1905–1999)

An anthropologist and social biologist, Montagu wrote *On Being Human* (1950), *The Natural Superiority of Women* (1953), *The Cultured Man* (1958), *The Humanization of Man* (1962), *Immortality, Religion, and Morals* (1971), and *The Elephant Man* (1971). A consultant for UNESCO on matters pertaining to race, he edited the National Historical Society Series. He produced, financed, wrote, and directed the film, "One World or None" (1946). Montagu, a Unitarian, once declared, "The Good Book—one of the most remarkable euphemisms ever coined."

To *The New York Times* (9 Dec 1993), Montagu wrote:

> Why cannot we abolish all guns? In Japan it is a crime to own a gun, and the murder rate is spectacularly low. There is no reason for owning a gun, not even by the police. Guns are made to kill. The freedom to own a gun constitutes the freedom and the license to use it. Can we not begin the control and prevention of violence by the control and prevention of gun ownership? This would be a first significant step toward a healthier America and the recognition that civilization is a race between education and catastrophe.

Montagu was named the American Humanist Association's 1995 Humanist of the Year. {CE; HNS2; TYD}

Montagu, Basil (1770–1851)

The natural ("illegitimate") son of the Earl of Sandwich, Montague became Commissioner in Bankruptcy and later Accountant-General in Bankruptcy. He secured many reforms of the law, edited the works of Bacon (1825–1857, 16 volumes), and wrote a number of works on law and philosophy.

According to Harriet Martineau, Montagu before his death "distinctly declared in a message to me his approbation of the avowal his friend W. Atkinson and I made of opinions like his own," opinions which were atheistic. {RAT; RE}

Montagu, Edward [Earl of Sandwich] (1625–1672)

A British admiral, Montagu was a friend and supporter of Cromwell. He accepted the restoration of Charles II and became Admiral of the Fleet, Knight of the Garter, and Master of Trinity House. Pepys, the famed diarist and son of one of the earl's cousins, was his secretary and often mentions his master's heresies: "I found him to be a perfect skeptic," Pepys wrote on 7 October 1660. On another page he describes the earl composing an anthem during service in the royal chapel, all the while muttering heavy curses over the work. The Earl of Sandwich negotiated (1661) the marriage between Charles and Catherine of Braganza, secured English possession of Tangier as part of her dowry, and brought Catherine to England. At the battle of Lowestoft (1665) in the second Dutch War, he fought with distinction and was killed in the battle of Southwold Bay in the third war. {CE; JM; RAT; RE}

Montagu, Mary Wortley [Lady] (1689–1762)

Born Lady Mary Pierrepont, daughter of Evelyn Pierrepont, later Duke of Kingston, Montagu became the wife of Britain's ambassador to Turkey. She is remembered for her quarrel with Pope, who then attacked her viciously in his poems: with "gendered hatred," according to Isobel Grundy's biography, *Lady Mary Wortley Montagu: Comet of the Enlightenment* (1999). Horace Walpole also disliked her, depicting her as a greedy, heartless eccentric. Her letters, however, show her to have been a brilliant woman struggling for emancipation.

While in Turkey, she learned about the practice of inoculation. On her return home she grafted a small amount of the smallpox germ into her young daughter, the practice caught on among her friends, and by 1718 she was working to educate the general public in the use of inoculation against smallpox.

Wal Sichel, however, disliked her because of "her aversion to the Church and to everything that transcended her own faculties." He objected to her freethinking and such of her remarks as "Either the papists are guilty of idolatry or the pagans never were so." She had, in fact, been a freethinker all her life. Others found her difficult, prone to quarreling, somewhat lacking in care about her clothes, and having in Horace Walpole's words an "old, foul, tawdry, painted, plastered visage."

At the age of nineteen she not only translated Epictetus but also married the skeptical grandson of the skeptical Edward Montagu, the Earl of Sandwich. Pope, Lord Hervey, and other Deists met in her salon. Her five volumes of letters were free about her opinions. For example, she wrote that "Priests can lie, and the mob believe, all over the world." For that reason she scorned "the quackery of all the Churches . . . and all creeds and theological shimsies." {JM; JMR; JMRH; RAT; RE; *The Economist*, 5 June 1999}

Montaigne, Michel Euqie (Seigneur de) (1533–1592)

A stoic, skeptic, and Epicurean, Montaigne once wrote, "O senseless man, who cannot possibly make a worm and yet will make gods by the dozens!" Of the witty essayist, Saint-Beuve reportedly observed that Montaigne was a good Catholic, only he was not a Christian. Lamont and others have pointed out that Montaigne never rejected Christian supernaturalism. During the French Revolution, Maréchal cited him as being only a "possible" atheist. Thweatt notes that Montaigne's skepticism in his own time was viewed "not as a covert attack on faith but as a legitimate defense of Christian doctrine." McCabe labels him "clearly a deist with a great disdain of the churches and their quarrels, but his expressions are necessarily so guarded that his Essays have only a literary interest today."

Freethinkers respect Montaigne because he expressed natural thoughts in common language, recognizing that all religious opinions are the result of custom. Also, his *Essays* opened the era of freethinking in France. At the end, no one was sure whether Montaigne was a secret atheist or whether he was a Christian. Emerson had said, "Montaigne is the frankest and honestest of all writers," admiring his motto, "*Que sais je?*" (What know I?). {BDF; CE; CL; ER; EU, Aram Vartarian and Vivien Thweatt; HNS2; JM; PA; RAT; RE; TYD}

Montalvo, Juan (1832–1889)

Montalvo was sharply critical in Ecuador of the regime of Gabriel Garcia Moreno (1860–1875) and his alliance with the church. Montalvo's *Siete trados* and *Mercurial eclesiástica* were both called heretical, and he was accused of being anticlerical. {EU}

MONTANA FREETHINKERS

The E Club, 600 Chestnut, Anaconda, Montana 59711 is run by Frank and Marie Skiles. The group publishes *Slant Press* and appeals to secular humanists, freethinkers, agnostics, and atheists. The title's E stands for empiricist. {FD}

Monteil, Charles François Louis Edgar (Born 1845)

Monteil was a French journalist who fought against the Empire, writing in *Le Rappel*. For his *Histoire d'un Frère Ignorantin* (1874), he was prosecuted by the Christian Brothers and condemned to a year in prison, fined two thousand francs plus an additional fine of ten thousand francs in damages. In 1877, Monteil wrote a *Freethinker's Catechism*. In 1883, he was made Chevalier of the Legion of Honor. {BDF; RAT}

Monteiro, J. P. (20th Century)

Monteiro is the Brazilian and Portuguese corresponding member of The Hume Society, a group engaged in scholarly activity concerning David Hume.

Montesquieu, Charles Louis de Secondat [Baron de Bréde et de] (1689–1755)

A French jurist and political philosopher, Montesquieu gained a seat in the French Academy in 1728, although there was dissent by many because of his alleged irreligion, which most called deism. His *Persian Letters* (1721), supposedly written by Persian tourists in Europe, satirized and criticized French institutions. The work had to be printed in Rouen and published at Amsterdam. In his posthumous *Pensées Diverses: De la religion*, his anti-clericalism is emphatic. "Churchmen," he wrote, "are interested in keeping the people ignorant." He expressed himself both as a convinced deist and, with no great air of conviction, as a believer in immortality. But he said, "I call piety a malady of the heart, which plants in the soul a malady of the most ineradicable kind. . . . The false notion of miracles comes of our vanity, which makes us believe we are important enough for the Supreme Being to upset Nature on our behalf. . . . Three incredibilities among incredibilities: the pure mechanism of animals [the doctrine of Descartes]; passive obedience; and the infallibility of the Pope." As for immortality, he declared, "The religion of Confucius denies the immortality of the soul, and the sect of Zeno did not believe in it."

The clergy denounced him and his work was placed on the Roman *Index*. Others called him a deist in his heart and an Erastian in his politics, or one who approved of state supremacy in ecclesiastical affairs. *L'Esprit des lois (The Spirit of the Laws,* 1748) studies comparatively three types of government—republican, monarchic, and despotic. His conclusion that the powers of government should be separated and balanced in order to guarantee the freedom of the individual greatly influenced the formation of the American Constitution. Montesquieu hailed the *Encyclopédie*'s writers at a time when the clergy was calling them atheists. His own work, particularly his *Thoughts*, was deistic. Under pressure, according to McCabe, Montesquieu admitted a priest to his deathbed, "so Catholics now claim him." {BDF; CE; JM; JMR; JMRH; RE; TYD}

Montgolfier, Joseph Michel (1740–1810)

The inventor of the passenger-carrying balloon, Montgolfier was a French chemist and paper-manufacturer. In 1783, he and his brother Jacques Étienne Montgolfier sent up at Annonay, near Lyons, a large linen bag inflated with hot air. Its flight covered more than a mile and lasted ten minutes. Also that year, a Montgolfier balloon sailed over Paris in the first manned free balloon flight. Montgolfier served the Revolution with zeal and was much honored. Lalande, who knew him well, wrote that Montgolfier was an atheist. {BDF; CE; JM; RE}

Montgomery, Edmund (Born 1835)

Montgomery, a philosopher whose parents were Scottish, lived as a youth in Frankfort, where he saw Schopenhauer and became a friend of Feuerbach. Dr. Montgomery holds not only that there is no evidence of a God but that there is evidence to the contrary. {BDF; RAT}

Montherlant, Henri de (1896–1972)

Montherlant, a French novelist and dramatist of decadent and egotistical novels that glorify force and masculinity, fought in World War I. Later, he was an athlete and a bullfighter. Among his works are *Les Bestiaires* (1926, tr. *The Bullfighters*, 1927), *Le Cardinal d'Espagne* (1960), and *La Guerre civile* (1965, tr. 1967 in *Theatre of War*). "Religion," Montherlant wrote, "is the venereal disease of mankind." {CE}

Moodie, Sara E. (20th Century)

Moodie, while at student at Brock University, St. Catherines, Ontario, Canada, was one of the founding members of Campus Freethought Alliance. {*International Humanist News*, December 1996}

Moody, Joel (19th Century)

In *Science of Evil* (1871), Moody observed, "Men of generous culture or of great learning, and women of eminent piety and virtue, from the humble cottage to the throne, have been led out for matters of conscience and butchered before a mad rabble lusting after God. The limbs of men and women have been torn from their bodies, their eyes gouged out, their flesh mangled and slowly roasted, their children barbarously tortured before their eyes, because of religious opinion." {TYD}

Mook, Friedrich (1844–1880)

Mook, a German freethinker, became lecturer to a free congregation at Nürenberg and wrote a popular *Life of Jesus* (1872–1873). While traveling abroad, Mook drowned in the River Jordan. {BDF; RAT}

MOON

Earth's single natural satellite is called the Moon. It rotates elliptically about the earth each 27.322 days and is about 240,000 miles (385,000 kilometers) away. The accepted wisdom in planetary science, according to John Noble Wilford of *The New York Times* (29 July 1997), is "that a massive object sideswiped Earth 4.5 billion years ago, in the heavy bombardment of planets and planetary fragments during the solar system's formative period. The collision scattered crustal debris that later coalesced in orbit to form the Moon." Wilford added, "Scientists at Harvard University even calculated that the object that collided with Earth must have been as massive as Mars."

Believing that the Moon is the home of the gods, some American Indians objected strongly in 1969 when astronaut Neil Armstrong landed there and, irreligiously to them, exclaimed, "That's one small step for man, one giant leap for mankind." (He had meant to say, ". . . one small step for a man. . . .") According to Armstrong, the Moon "has a stark beauty all its own. It's like much of the high desert areas of the United States. It's different, but it's very pretty."

However, despite man's having stepped on the moon and despite the various scientific tests which have made, astronomers generally agree that our closest celestial neighbor remains a mystery. {PA}

Moon, Sun Myung (20th Century)

The Korean-born Moon, who in 1954 established the Holy Spirit Association for the Unification of World Christianity, heads what today are the 10,000+ members of the Unification Church. His followers, called "Moonies" by most, are not supposed to tape-record or take photographs during his sermons, one of which lasted sixteen hours and forty minutes. Journalists are generally prohibited from attending services. He has not granted an interview in two decades.

Peter Maass (*The New Yorker*, 14 September 1998) has described the group's views:

> The core of Moon's beliefs, expressed in "Divine Principle," a four-hundred-and-eleven-page book, is that Eve was seduced by Satan in the Garden of Eden and had illicit sexual relations with Adam. This violated God's desire that Adam and Eve await His blessing of their union before becoming intimate and having children. Their offspring were thus tainted by Satan's influence; evil invaded the human spirit. God later sent Jesus to establish a pure family on earth, free of evil, but Jesus was crucified before He could marry and have children. Moon sees the essence of his own mission as completing the one given to Jesus—establishing a "true family" untouched by Satan while teaching all people to lead a God-centered life under his spiritual leadership.

Some parents have hired professional "deprogrammers" to return their children from what they allege is Moonie brain-washing, fearful that their son or daughter would be married in one of the group mass wedding ceremonies Moon arranges for couples who are not acquainted with each other before the occasion.

At least two of the thirteen children Moon had with his current wife (his first marriage ended in divorce) have reportedly rebelled against him. According to Maass, the wife of Moon's eldest son by his current wife and his onetime heir apparent fled from their family compound in Irvington, New York, taking her five children. She obtained a restraining order against Moon and accused Moon's son, Hyo Jin, of "secreting himself in the master bedroom, sometimes for hours, sometimes for days, drinking alcohol, using cocaine and watching pornographic films." Her account of the marriage and divorce are found in a tell-all memoir, *In the Shadow of the Moons* (1998). Included are allegations of money laundering, cocaine abuse, infidelity, incest, and sexual abuse.

The Washington Post (10 March 1999) reported that Moon's enterprise—Kahr Arms—specializes in manufacturing lethal, concealable six-inch guns, adding that it has purchased the company that manufactures the gangsters' favorite weapons: tommy guns.

Moondog: See entry for Louis Hardin.

Mooney, Jo Ann (1959-)

Mooney from 1998 to 1999 was the Council for Secular Humanism's Director of Humanist Community Development.

Moor, Edmund (1771–1848)

Moor was a major in the East Indian Company. He wrote of *The Hindu Pantheon* (1810) and *Oriental Fragments* (1834). {BDF}

Moore, Basil (20th Century)

In Wales, Moore is active with the Mid-Wales Humanists.

Moore, Brian (1921–1999)

The Belfast-born Moore, whose parents were Catholic with republican sympathies, emigrated in 1948 to Canada and subsequently moved to the United States. The first of his nineteen novels were published pseudonymously under the name of Michael Bryan. His works include *Judith Hearne* (1955; published in the US as *The Lonely Passion of Judith Hearne*, 1956), about a lonely Belfast spinster who becomes alcoholic; *The Luck of Ginger Coffey* (1960), about the misfortunes of an Irish immigrant in Canada; *I Am Mary Dunne* (1968), a first-person female narration; *Catholics* (1972), in which a papal representative visiting an Irish religious community some time in the future; and *The Mangan Inheritance* (1979), about an American journalist in search of his Irish heritage. Although he had left Ireland, he remained a distinctly Irish novelist. His father had been a distinguished physician and member of the Senate of Queen's University. Moore, in later life, was pleased to have received an honorary degree from the university with which his father had been associated.

Graham Greene was an admirer and had some of the same skill at creating a location and the struggle between atheism and Catholicism. In 1995, Moore became an Honorary Associate of the Rationalist Press Association. {*New Humanist*, March 1999}

Moore, Charles C(hilton) (Born 1872)

From Lexington, Kentucky, Moore edited the weekly *Blue Grass Blade* from 1884 to 1905. He was imprisoned for sending atheistic material through the mail, then received a hero's welcome in 1899 upon returning home—he described his experiences in *Behind the Bars* (1899). Michael Adcock, in an article in *American Rationalist* (October 1992), claims that Kentucky may have had many notable freethinkers, but none was quite like Moore. For one thing, he was an imprisoned freethinker who was able to convert his warden, E. G. Coffin, to freethought. *The Rational View* (1890) exposed many of the Bible's contradictions, and his final book, *Dog Fennel in the Orient*, debunked all the "holy places" he visited on a tour to Palestine. Moore is the last known person to go to prison for blasphemy in the United States. {Cincinnati, Ohio, *Fig Leaves*, May 1995; FUS}

Moore, George Augustus (1852–1933)

A novelist, Moore was educated in a Catholic college but abandoned the Church while studying art in Paris, as shown in his first work, *Flowers of Passion* (1877). *A Modern Lover* (1883), set in artistic Bohemian society, was banned by the circulating libraries, a fact that confirmed Moore in his outspoken battle against prudery and censorship. In his *Confessions of a Young Man* (1888), he observed, "Women have never invented a religion; they are untainted with that madness, and they are not moralists." Moore told McCabe he called himself a Protestant for political reasons but that he actually was an agnostic. In his literary drama, *The Apostle* (1911), Moore made Paul strike Jesus dead on finding him alive years after his supposed resurrection, and Catholics tried to get him prosecuted for *Brook Kerith* (1916), which presented Jesus as an Essenian monk. Moore was instrumental in the planning of the Irish National Theatre, which Yeats acknowledged "could not have been done at all without Moore's knowledge of the stage." {RAT; RE; TYD}

Moore, Benjamin (20th Century)

Moore, a physiologist, taught at University College, London, and at Yale and Liverpool universities. A theist, he was a dissenter from creeds. In his *Origin and Nature of Life*, he spoke of the God of theology as "a perfect superman," although the beauty of the world suggested to him "an infinite intelligence." He may have been agnostic as to immortality and was not displeased that what he called the dogmas of a century ago are "now buried in a merciful oblivion." {RAT}

Moore, G(eorge) E(dward) (1873–1958)

"G. E. Moore, John Ellis McTaggart, and Bertrand Russell are the first three academic atheists of note," writes Berman. Moore edited *Mind* (1921–1947), which showed his change from an early influence by the idealism of F. H. Bradley and the transcendental epistemology of Immanuel Kant to a new and critical epistemology. "The Refutation of Idealism" and *Principia Ethica* distinguish between acts of consciousness and their possible objects, and between the ways in which we can be said to know and the things we can know. Although he did not consider linguistic analysis the main interest of philosophy, notes *Columbia Encyclopedia*, he was concerned along with Bertrand Russell and Ludwig Wittgenstein in philosophical problems that are caused by the imprecisions of ordinary language. Moore, McTaggart, and Russell were prominent members of the Apostles, a Cambridge Society with a distinctively irreverent attitude toward God and religion. In one of his essays, Moore wrote, "I am an infidel, and do not believe that God exists; and I think the evidence will justify my disbelief. But just as I think there is no evidence for his existence, I think there is also no evidence that he does not exist. I am not an atheist in one sense: I do not deny that God exists. My arguments will only urge that there is no reason for thinking that he does: they will *not* urge that there is reason for thinking he does not. I do *not* believe that he does exist, but also I do *not* believe that he does not exist." Elsewhere, he admitted that he had not been "a good answerer of philosophical questions" but he did endeavor to place truth before consistency or the desire for an answer. Moore was a Fellow of the British Academy. McCabe, who was his friend, told him that Jesus was probably an Essenian monk to about the age of thirty. Moore wrote a play, *The Apostle*, and a novel, *The Brooke Kerith*, in which he rejected the Christian view of Jesus. He was an agnostic, McCabe wrote, but said he preferred to be regarded as a Protestant for reasons of Irish politics and to express his abhorrence of the Roman Church. Meanwhile, McCabe added, Protestants shuddered at his blasphemies about Jesus.

In 1954, asked his views of humanism rather than of atheism, Moore responded,

> None of the titles you mention seems to me suitable to cover my philosophical position. I should say that my position cannot properly be called a "Humanism" at all, since I regard philosophy as not dealing specially with mankind at all, but with the whole universe.
> {CE; HAB; JM; RAT; RE; TRI; WAS, 5 August 1954}

Moore, Howard W. (1889–1993)

When interviewed by *The New York Times* on the occasion of his 102nd birthday, he said he was asked what, inasmuch as he did not believe in God, sustained him, and he answered, "My own sense of moral responsibility. To accept an authority outside oneself is to deny oneself the right to make an ultimate decision. Understanding that and the consequences likely to follow is to know freedom in the deepest sense."

During World War I, Moore had been a pacifist and was sentenced to five years at hard labor for refusing to serve in the Army. "War was futile and its use as an instrument of national policy a confession of moral bankruptcy," he stated in *Plowing My Own Furrow* (1985), a book written at the age of ninety-five from his stone house north of Cherry Valley, New York. He and other conscientious objectors had been sent to Fort Leavenworth in Kansas, where he said they were beaten, taunted, and tortured for two years. The World War I resister and atheist died at the age of 104.

Moore, James (20th Century)

An American scholar who lectures in the history of science and technology at the Open University in England, Moore with Adrian Desmond wrote *Darwin* (1991). He also produced *The Darwin Legend* (1994), in which he tells of the legend of Darwin's alleged conversion to Christianity at the end of his life, repeatedly told by religious propagandists but denied by the Darwin family. Moore tells of Darwin's evasive views of religion and irreligion as well as his family's disingenuous treatment of them. {Nicolas Walter, "Rationally Speaking," *New Humanist*, May 1995}

Moore, James Proctor (20th Century)

Moore wrote *This Strange Town, Liberal, Missouri* (1963). {GS}

Moore, John Howard (Born 1862)

Moore was an American writer. In his *Better-World Philosophy* (1899), he wrote with a humanitarian idealism. In *Savage Survivals* (1916) he is more directly rationalistic. {RAT}

Moore, Marianne (1877–1972)

Moore, the Pulitzer Prize-winning poet for *Collected Poems* (1951) and author of *Predilections* (1955), wrote wittily, intellectually, and satirically. Asked her view of humanism, Moore, a Presbyterian, responded to the present author:

> I have not thought of myself as a humanist—was asked recently if I might not be called a moralist and perhaps I could be.
>
> I am much concerned about the irresponsibility of man for man. Casuists who are despots violate the rights of man, confused by the apparent triumph of other despots, unintentionally testifying to the fact that there is a moral law and that it is not transgressed with impunity—unconsciously emphasizing verities of the Apostle Paul in which they take no interest—that the servant of righteousness is made free and the wages of sin is death.
> {WAS, 17 June 1956}

Moore, Michael (20th Century)

In 1996, at the 2nd Annual Atheist Alliance Convention, held in Minneapolis, Moore spoke on the subject, "Truly Free: Civil Rights and Civil Duties."

Moore, R. Laurence (20th Century)

Moore, a professor of history and government at Cornell University, co-wrote with Isaac Kramnick *The Godless Constitution: The Case Against Religious Correctness* (1996). In his writing he gives the ritually necessary nod to propriety: "One of the authors grew up in an Orthodox Jewish home. The other is descended from Irish and German Catholics on his mother's side and Calvinist Protestants on his father's."

Moore, Samuel D. (19th Century)

Moore, a freethinker in Adrian, Michigan, was a supporter of *The Truth Seeker* during the time Bennett was arrested and imprisoned. He regularly attended freethought conventions. {PUT}

Moorehead, Caroline (20th Century)

Moorehead is author of *Bertrand Russell: A Life* (1993). Although she covers much of the material already contained in Russell's autobiography, Moorehead tells how Lady Ottoline Morrell, who became Russell's mistress in 1910 and fueled his passion for sexual enlightenment, did not much care to have sex with him. It was his mind she fell in love with. The work does not emphasize Russell's non-belief, slightly mentioning his work for Haldeman-Julius and his writing *Religion and Science* and *Why I Am Not a Christian*.

Mooren, Jan Hein (20th Century)

Mooren, at a 1997 seminar of the European Humanist Professionals in London, spoke of research done on the victims of violence. A psychologist at the Humanist University in Utrecht, he described how trauma is experienced on an emotional, cognitive, and behavioral level. Because those who have experienced post-trauma stress lose control of their live, humanist counselors are needed to insure that they receive treatment.

Mor, Barbara (20th Century)

With Monica Sjöö, Mor wrote *The Great Cosmic Mother* (1991).

Mora Poltronieri, Hugo (20th Century)

Mora, who is president of the Costa Rican Association of Esperanto, participated in the 1996 Humanist World Congress in Mexico City. Mora is an ethical humanist activist.

E-mail: <miaumiau@sol.racsa.co.cr>.

Mora, José Luis Maria (1794–1850)

Mora was a liberal reformer in Mexico, one critical of church power. He held that the Mexican Republic was being held back by the corporate interests of the church. For example, its many franchises and *fueros* prevented any serious attempt at creating national unity, and he suggested that both the church and the army weakened public morality. Mora wrote *México y sus revoluciones* (1836). His efforts influenced later liberals, including Ignacio Ramírez, who passed the reform laws that suppressed monasteries in Mexico. (See entry for Ignacio Ramírez.) {EU}

Morain, Lloyd (1917–)

Morain was president of the Illinois Gas Company when he signed Humanist Manifesto II. From 1951 to 1955, he was President of the American Humanist Association, a position he again had from 1969 to 1972.

With his wife Mary in 1954, Morain co-wrote *Humanism as the Next Step*. He served as editor of *The Humanist* for more than ten years, during which time he was criticized for not having included an obituary for Priscilla Robertson, a previous editor. Upon his retirement, he remained on the editorial board. The Morains were on the Board of Directors of the International Humanist and Ethical Union (IHEU), and Lloyd was one of four directors responsible for incorporating that group. In 1994, the American Humanist Association named the two Morains Humanists of the Year.

Lloyd Morain signed Humanist Manifesto 2000. (See entry for Priscilla Robertson. For a negative criticism of his updating of *Humanism as the Next Step*, see the bibliography herein.) {FUS; HM2; PK}

Morain, Mary (1911–1999)

Mary Morain, co-writer of *Humanism as the Next Step* (1954), was on the editorial board of *The Humanist* and of the International Society for General Semantics. In 1952, she was on the first Board of Directors of the International Humanist and Ethical Union (IHEU). "Humanism is practical," she has written. "It helps us to understand complex situations, to solve problems, and to make decisions. . . . It teaches that there is an intrinsic, inalienable value in all human beings. . . . It teaches us to look for courage, for comfort, to one another, our fellow humans. . . . A sense of belonging comes to those who realize that we are in every respect a part of nature—a nature far larger, far older, than ourselves."

While president of the International Society for General Semantics, she edited two books of tested classroom exercises in general semantics, *Teaching General Semantics* and *Classroom Exercises in General Semantics*. She also edited two anthologies of articles from *ETC., Bridging Worlds Through General Semantics* and *Enriching Professional Skills Through General Semantics*.

In 1994, the American Humanist Association named her and her husband, Lloyd, Humanists of the Year. {HM2; PK}

Morais, Herbert M. (1905–1970)

Morais wrote *Deism in Eighteenth Century America* (1934). {GS}

Moraita, Miguel (Born 1845)

A Spanish historian, Moraita taught at Madrid and was an ardent enemy of clericalism. He wrote the voluminous *History of Spain*. When in 1884 he made a discourse at the university against the pretended antiquity of the Mosaic legends, several bishops excommunicated him. The students, against whom the military were employed, supported Moraita.

Moraita was Grand Master of the Spanish Freemasons. {BDF; RAT}

MORAL MAJORITY

Moral Majority is an organization of conservative Christians. Paul W. Weyrich, a longtime moral crusader, suggested to its leader, the Rev. Jerry Falwell, the name of the far right group. Weyrich heads the Free Congress Foundation. Both groups support *The Weekly Standard*, a conservative magazine. Conservatives have pressured the Republican Party to work toward raising the general public's "moral standards." Annoyed that President Bill Clinton's standing in the polls did not suffer during his impeachment trial, Weyrich said that while he was "not suggesting that we all become Amish or move to Idaho, he believed that "we have to look at what we can do to separate ourselves from this hostile culture. What steps can we take to make sure that we and our children are not infected? We need some sort of quarantine." (Richard L. Berke, *The New York Times*, 21 February 1999}

MORAL THEOLOGY: For the change from the Catholic Church's concentrating on sin, its causes, its characteristics, its degrees, and consequences to emphasizing love, see the entry for Bernard Häring.

MORALITY

• Act only on that maximum through which you can at the same time will that it should become universal law.

–Immanuel Kant (1724-1804)

• Do unto the other feller the way he'd like to do unto you an' do it fust.

–Edward Noyes Westcott (1846-1898), *David Harum*

• That indeed were a world fit to perish, wherein the moralist had set up the ignoble maxim: Safety first.

–Havelock Ellis (1859-1939)

• Bourgeois morality is largely a system of making cheap virtues a cloak for expensive vices.

–George Bernard Shaw

• Don't look down on *any* human being . . . unless it's to help him up.

—Donald Robert Perry Marquis (1878-1937)

So far, about morals, I know only that what is moral is what you feel good after and what is immoral is what you feel bad after.

–Ernest Hemingway (1899-1961)

• Morality is the theory that every human act must be either right or wrong, and that 99% of them are wrong.

–H. L. Mencken

• A dog licks his balls . . . because he can.

–A Teton Valley, Wyoming, B-K cowboy's observation

"Morality does not depend on religion," John Ruskin declared, one of the many who came to the same conclusion.

"The infliction of cruelty with a good conscience is a delight to moralists—that is why they invented hell," wrote Bertrand Russell. Lord Russell wrote that there is something better than traditional morality, and it involves learning how to lead a happy life. But he added that a way of life "cannot be successful as long as it is a mere intellectual conviction. It must be deeply felt, deeply believed, dominant even in dreams. I do not think that the best kind of life is possible in our day for those who, below the level of consciousness, are still obsessed by the load of sin. It is obvious that there are things that had better not be done, but I do not think the best way to avoid the doing of such things is to label them sin and represent them as almost irresistibly attractive." He also wrote, "We need a morality based upon love of life, upon pleasure in growth and positive achievement, not upon repression and prohibition."

For John Dewey, morality lies within the individual and is relative to his experience. G. E. Moore's intuitionalism postulated that individuals receive an immediate awareness of the morally good. Kant found moral law in the categorical imperative. Relatively speaking, morality or what ideally is right human conduct differs from community to community, depending upon what value judgments have been accepted by its inhabitants.

Sir Ron Dearing, the chief curriculum adviser in England, is known for his view that a renaissance of moral education is needed to deal with the violence of modern society.

"World Scientists' Warning to Humanity" is a statement signed by more than 1,600 leading scientists, including more than 100 Nobel laureates in science. Signatories included Carl Sagan, James Watson, Stephen Jay Gould, Paul Ehrlich, Murray Gell-Mann, Roger Penrose, Stephen Hawking, and E. O. Wilson. In preparation for the millennium, they called for a moral manifesto: "We the undersigned, senior members of the world's scientific community, hereby warn all humanity of what lies ahead," the document read. "No more than one or a few decades remain before the chance to avert the threats we now confront will be lost and the prospects for humanity immeasurably diminished." As a result, "A new ethic is required. . . . This ethic must motivate a great movement, convincing reluctant leaders and reluctant governments and reluctant peoples themselves to effect the needed changes." (See Lee Eisler's *The Quotable Bertrand Russell* for more of Lord Russell's many views on the subject. In his *New Hopes for a Changing World* (1951), Russell explains what he believes is better than traditional. Also see Paul Kurtz's view in the entry for Common Moral Decency.) {Roger Bingham, "Toward a Science of Morality"; and John Hartung, "Prospects for Existence: Morality and Genetic Engineering" in *Skeptic*, Vol. 4, No. 2, 1996; CE}

MORALITY, GENITAL-BASED

Genital-based morality, according to Edwin Kagin in a tongue-in-cheek article (*FIG Leaves*, February 1999),

> is an infantile system of primitive simplistic thinking involving magical make-believe, and is thus quite easy to understand. Abortion, homosexuality, pornography, prostitution, unmarried sex, oral sex, sodomy (maybe gomorra, too), non-monogamous sex, 'adult' videos, nudist clubs, nude beaches, nude dancing—anything that touches upon, views, uses, or has anything whatsoever to do with, genitals, is immoral and bad.

However, if the preacher meets the deacon in a whorehouse, lawyer Kagin observes, both are expected to lie about sex, even under oath.

Morandini, D. Michael (20th Century)

Morandini has been an active member of the American Humanist Association. {HNS}

Moravec, Hans (20th Century)

Moravec, who has gone on record as being a non-theist, is a researcher into artificial intelligence and robotics.

Moravia, Alberto (Alberto Pincherle) (1907–)

Son of an architect, Moravia was a Roman-born Jew who became an eminent critic, playwright, film critic, journalist, and writer of fiction. Spiritual ennui is the theme of his *Time of Indifference* (1929), which depicted his own humanistic outlook and his concern about a middle-class society that favored the rise of Fascism. His early criticism of bourgeois "bad faith" and moral decadence led some to accuse him of "Jansenism" for his stand on moral determinism.

Moravia spent much of World War II on the run, having depicted Mussolini comically in *The Fancy Dress Party* (*La mascherata*, 1941). Some critics objected to *Woman of Rome* (1947), calling it immoral, lewd, and sexually over-obsessed; the prostitute he describes is a strong symbol of the power of femininity. The novel's Adriana observes that "everything was love and everything depended on love . . . and if you did not have it you could not love anyone or anything."

The freethinking Moravia also wrote *Two Women* (1957), *The Empathy Canvas* (1960), *Time of Desecration* (1980), and *The Conformist* (1951), the latter of which explored the psycho-sexual basis of politics.

In 1952, all his writing was placed on the Vatican's index of prohibited reading.

Sartre is said to have been influenced by Moravia's early work. In Germany, one publisher refused to publish any of "the Jew's books," but *Time* (15 December 1961) called him one of the century's best writers. {CE; ILP, Additus; OCE}

MORAVIAN CHURCH

The Moravian Church's origin can be traced to the evangelical movement in Bohemia led by John Hus, who suffered martyrdom in 1415 after being burned at the stake. In a conflict with Archbishop Zbynek over a papal schism, he had sided with Pope Alexander V rather than with Pope Gregory.

In 1457 followers of Hus formed an organization called *Unitas Fratrum* (Unity of Brethren). The union of followers included four principles as the basis for their church: (1) the Bible as the only source of Christian doctrine; (b) public worship to be conducted on the model of the Apostolic Church, (c) the Lord's Supper to be received in faith and defined in the language of Scripture, and (d) true Christian life as essential evidence of saving faith.

A contemporary affected by Moravian mysticism was the poet Hilda Doolittle. {See entries for Hilda Doolittle and John Hus.} {ER}

Moravec, Hans (20th Century)

An artificial intelligence and robotics researcher, Moravec was described in *Mondo 2000*: "He's rife with contradictions. He's married to an evangelist, though he is himself an atheist." {CA}

Morazán, Francisco [President, Central American Federation; President, Costa Rica] (1799–1842)

Morazán, a Central American statesman, led the Honduran revolutionary army that overthrew (1829) the regime of Manuel José Arce and was proclaimed president of the Central American Federation in 1830. Because of opponents who complained that Guatemala dominated the group, Morazán moved the capital to San Salvador.

A liberal, he promoted education, abolished most monastic orders, and established freedom of worship. Opposed by an increasing number of conservatives, he eventually went into voluntary exile until recalled in 1842 by Costa Rica and was proclaimed president there. In 1842, his own partisans shot him. {CE; EU}

More, Byron (20th Century)

More, a freethinker, wrote *Is the Bible Authentic?* (c. 1901). {GS}

More, Max (20th Century)

More is a Californian who is president of the Extropy Institute. Also, he is editor of *Extropy: The Journal of Transhumanist Thought*. More holds that humanists need not fear "their own Promethean urge to challenge the gods," and he thinks humanists should be activists: "No more gods, no more faith, no more timid holding back. Let us blast out of our old forms, our ignorance, our weakness, and our mortality. The future belongs to posthumanity." (See Max More, "On Becoming Posthuman," *Free Inquiry*, Fall 1994.) {CA}

More, Paul Elmer (1864–1937)

More, who with Irving Babbitt is associated with the movement of New Humanism or neohumanism, wrote *On Being Human* (1936).

More, Thomas (Sir) (1480–1535)

McCabe is skeptical about More's being a "saint" of the Roman Church. "One of his chief biographers," McCabe notes, "says that he was 'a bundle of contradictions,' but the evidence suggests that he was sceptical in his youth and prime, and very sincere in his later sacrifice for his faith. The Catholic argument that he was not serious in writing the sceptical second part–as published: it was written first–of the *Utopia* is frivolous." That part is plainly skeptical and anti-clerical, however, and McCabe continues that "no Catholic could have written as he did about religion."

A highly intelligent person, More was a ruthless interrogator. He hunted heretics, burned books, and contested those who believed they could find God directly and without utilizing priests and popes.

As for the canonization, "Like that of Joan of Arc, and others in modern times, it was a political and financial move. British priests–the fact was concealed from the laity–were outraged to find at the close that they had to pay Rome £15,000, besides £4,000 for a present to the Pope." {RE; TYD}

Moreau, Hégésippe (1810–1838)

Moreau was a French poet, a radical and a freethinker who fought in the barricades in 1830. He wrote *The Mistletoe and the Oak*, and his entire works were collected with an introduction by Sainte-Beuve. {BDF; RAT}

Moreau, Jacques Joseph (1804–1884)

Moreau, a physician, became a distinguished alienist of the materialist school. He wrote on moral faculties from a medical point of view. {BDF; RAT}

Morehead, Robert (19th Century)

A freethinker, Morehead wrote *Philosophical Dialogues* (1845). {GS}

Morellet, André (1727–1819)

The Jesuits educated Morellet, a French encyclopedist, and all his life he kept the title of the Abbé Morellet. Yet, according to the *Grande Encyclopédie,* he "did more than any in spreading the views of the philosophers." Morellet was friends with Voltaire, Diderot, D'Alembert, and Franklin. {RAT; RE}

Morelli, Giovanni (1816–1891)

Morelli was an Italian writer, politician, and rationalist. The rebellion against the Papacy and Austria drew him into active life in 1848, and at the collapse of the Republic he returned to his interests in art, writing several volumes on the Italian and foreign galleries. In 1859 he was commander of the National Guard at Magenta. From 1860 to 1870 he sat in Parliament for Bergamo, and in 1873 he passed to the Senate. {RAT}

Morelly, N. (18 Century)

Morelly was a French socialist, author of *Code de la Nature*, a work sometimes attributed to Diderot. It was published in 1755 and urged that man should find circumstances in which depravity is minimized. Little is known of him, but it is believe he was a priest who turned rationalist and drew upon himself the zeal of the orthodox by his writings. {BDF}

Morem, Sally (20th Century)

Morem, a science writer, is secretary of the Humanist Association of Minneapolis and St. Paul. For *Secular Nation* she has written "Peering at Faces in the Clouds" (September-October 1996) and "Does God Exist?" (October-December 1998). E-mail: <sjmorem@juno.com>.

MORES

Mores is a bi-monthly in Dutch of *Humanistisch Verbond Belgie* at Lange Leemstraat 57, 2018 Antwerpen, Belgium.

Moreton, Stephen (20th Century)

Moreton has reviewed books for the *Gay and Lesbian Humanist.*

Morfill, William Richard (1834–1909)

A philologist, Morfill in 1900 was a professor of Russian and Slavonic languages. He composed grammars of the Russian, Polish, Serb, Tchek, and Bulgar languages, and he was familiar with Turkish, Irish, and Welsh. His rationalist sentiments appear in his article on Slav religion in *Religious Systems of the World.* {RAT}

Morgan, Angela (20th Century)

Morgan, a poet who wrote *Gold On Your Pillow* (1952), wrote the present author concerning humanism:

> I have read a brochure of the American Humanist Association, "Ten Points" or divisions of the Humanist idea, and it rejoices me to find the propositions so convincingly stated. . . . It is a great step forward in human history to throw away the old superstitions as to the nature of man. Someone had to explode that stupid doctrine of Original Sin before humanity could stand on its feet and draw a wholesome breath. . . .
>
> There must be, somewhere, a cosmic or celestial reality which is drawing the human being up toward a nobler destiny. . . . How could man grow, how could he evolve, how could he become better and greater without this unseen but plausible power or force for good, drawing him forward and up? . . . The gods of primitive man are to be discredited; the God of vengeance who throws his disobedient children into hell fire is too preposterous to consider; the God of theology is not too popular with modern thinkers. But First Cause, or Source, or Creator–how can we get away from that logical need? Do I fall into the general classification of naturalistic humanism?

Morgan, a Unitarian, did most of her research on such subjects as deism and transcendentalism. {WAS, 17 February 1951}

Morgan, Anna (20th Century)

In Britain, Morgan is active with the Lichfield Humanist Group.

Morgan, Arthur E. (1878–1975)

Morgan was president of Antioch College (1920–1936) and chairman of the Tennessee Valley Authority (1933–1938). Among his works are *My World* (1927), *The Philosophy of Edward Bellamy* (1945), *The Search for Purpose* (1955), *The Community of the Future* (1956), *Dams and Disasters* (1970), and *The Making of the TVA* (1974). In the 1950s, he reviewed books for *The Humanist* and was active in promoting Friends' and humanist causes. {EW; HNS, U}

Morgan, Conway Lloyd (1852–1936)

Morgan taught zoology and geology at Bristol University College. When that school became a university, he was Vice-Chancellor but resigned to take the chair of psychology.

McCabe calls Morgan "a more advanced Rationalist than Voltaire and Paine," adding that Morgan rejected the belief in immortality, admitted only an impersonal "First Cause," and said that "the general trend of Haeckel's constructive scheme of scientific interpretation is on lines which are winning or have won acceptance." {RAT; RE}

Morgan, Dermot (1953-1998)

Morgan, who was known as Father Ted in England's Channel 4 sit-com, was an atheist who, as Rory Carroll reported in *The Guardian* (7 March 1998), "savaged the Church throughout his career." Upon his death and at the request of his family, communion was held at St. Theresa's church, Mount Merrion, Dublin, after which the body was cremated. Father Michael Paul Gallagher, who had tutored Morgan at University College, Dublin, told a congregation, which included the Irish President and government ministers, that it was part of Morgan's vocation "to be hard to take at times." He did not mention that in Morgan's last interview, a few days before his death, he called the clergy "ju-ju men." {*The Freethinker*, May 1998}

Morgan, Ernest (20th Century)

During the 1960s, Morgan was a director of the American Humanist Association. He was co-founder of the Arthur Morgan School and published *A Manual of Simple Burial* which helped lead to the development of memorial and cooperative burial societies across the nation. {HNS2}

Morgan, James (20th Century)

Morgan's "The Measure of a Man" was printed in *Humanist in Canada* (Summer 1997). He is an Ontarian psychotherapist who specializes in men's issues.

Morgan, Martin (20th Century)

Morgan is associated with the Humanist Fellowship of Brooklyn (AHA). (See entry for New York Atheists, Freethinkers, Humanists.) {FD}

Morgan, Richard (20th Century)

Morgan is an Episcopalian who has written *The Supreme Court and Religion* (1972). {GS}

Morgan, Thomas (Died 1743)

Morgan was a Welsh deist, known for his *The Moral Philosopher* (1737). A Presbyterian, he was deposed for his Arianism about 1723, at which time he was a physician in Bristol. Morgan, who edited Radicati's "Dissertation on Death" (1731), called Moses "a more fabulous romantic writer than Homer or Ovid," and he attacked the evidence of miracles and prophecy. Lechler called Morgan "the modern Marcion." {BDF; FUK; RAT}

Morgan, Thomas Charles [Sir] (1783–1843)

Morgan was made a baronet in 1811. A warm friend of civil and religious liberty, he was a skeptic who wrote *Sketches of the Philosophy of Life* (1818) and *Philosophy of Morals* (1819). The *Examiner* wrote of him, "He was never at a loss for a witty or wise passage from Rabelais or Bayle." He did lose clients, however, for through clerical persecution many refused to use him as their physician. {BDF; RAT}

Morgenbesser, Sidney (1921–)

Dr. Morgenbesser was John Dewey Professor of Philosophy at Columbia University. He has edited *Philosophy, Science, and Method: Essays in Honor of Ernest Nagel* (1969) and *Philosophy, Morality, and International Affairs* (1974). {CL}

Morgenroth, Florence (20th Century)

Morgenroth is president of Humanists of the Suncoast in Florida.

Morgentaler, Henry (1923–)

Morgentaler was one of the founders in 1968 of the Humanist Association of Canada, and he served as its first president. He spent the last nine months of World War II in German concentration camps, moving to Montreal in 1950. He is a leading campaigner in Canada for the legalization of abortion, and he has expressed pride in having performed 65,000 abortions. Eight clinics in major cities across Canada bear his name. In 1992 his first clinic, in Toronto, exploded in a fiery blast. Members of the Campaign Life Coalition, he said, pray for him daily: "They think I'm the embodiment of the devil." Inasmuch as surgeons have been threatened and even killed, he wears a bulletproof vest to work.

At the 1990 Humanist World Congress, Morgentaler said,

"Humanism is not just an intellectual philosophy, but also has practical implications in its aim to create the full realisation of all human potential. . . . Humankind is facing unresolved Humanist problems: population, environment, nuclear risks, ethnic and tribal conflicts. Humanism is devoted to human welfare, to the acceptance of democracy and the peaceful resolution of conflict by a constructive rational solution to problems."

In 1973, he was named the first Humanist of the Year by the Canadian Humanist Association. In 1975 he was so named by the American Humanist Association. In 1999 he received the annual award of the Bertrand Russell Society, saying, "I have been a great admirer of Bertrand Russell and consider him one of my mentors, the man who deeply influenced my philosophy of life. As founder of the Humanist Association of Canada, I have often quoted Bertrand Russell, especially his saying that 'the good life is based on love guided by reason.' "

A physician who was born in Poland, Dr. Morgentaler spent six years in Nazi concentration camps before going to Canada. He has written *Abortion and Contraception* (1982).

In an article, "Secular Humanism Versus Christianity" in *Humanist in Canada* (Spring 1990), Morgentaler states, "I believe people should be made aware that it is possible to develop a life-style and a commitment to human values without the necessity of believing in God or the illusions of immortality. . . . It is this commitment to the values of secular humanism, embodying the desire for justice and a better society, that is the origin of my twenty-year-old struggle for women's right to safe medical abortions. . . . It is time we all change our attitudes and learn to live in peace and harmony in spite of religious or ideological differences."

Morgentaler, who is on the Board of Governors of The Humanist Institute, signed Humanist Manifesto II and Humanist Manifesto 2000. At the Tenth International Humanist and Ethical Union (IHEU) World Congress held in Buffalo (1988), Morgentaler addressed the group. In 1990, he presided over the Eleventh World Congress held in Brussels. Also in 1990, at Carleton University, he debated Michael Horner on the subject, "Secular Humanism vs. Christian Humanism: Which is the Superior World View?" A biography by Catherine Dunphy, *Morgentaler: A Difficult Hero* (1996) details his extraordinary life.

An honorary president of the Humanist Association of Canada, Morgentaler in 1992 addressed the Toronto conference of the Coalition for Secular Humanism, Atheism, and Freethought (CSHAFT).

A biography by journalist Catherine Dunphy, *Morgentaler: A Difficult Hero* (1997), showed Morgentaler as being at times impatient and stubborn, a difficult person to work with. However, he has many Canadians, particularly women, who support his efforts, and he is an important personage in Canadian humanism. {Anthony DePalma, *The New York Times*, 10 November 1998; E; HM2; HNS2; Henry Morgentaler, "The Moral Case for Abortion," *Free Inquiry*, Summer 1996; *Humanist in Canada*, Winter 1997-1998; SHD}

Mories, A. S. (20th Century)

Mories wrote *Haeckel's Contribution to Religion* (1904). {GS}

Morin, André Saturnin (1807–1888)

A French advocate and writer, Morin in 1830 wrote defending the revolution against the restoration. In 1848, he was made sous-prefet of Nogent. During the Empire he combated vigorously for Republicanism and freethought, writing under the signature "Miron" in the *Rationaliste* of Geneva, the *Libre Pensée of Paris*, and *Libero-Pensiero* of Milan. Morin was associated with Ausonio Franchi, Trezza, Stefanoni, and the Italian freethinkers. His principal work is *An Examination of Christianity* (1862, 3 volumes).

His *Jesus Reduced to His True Value* went through several editions. Morin was one of the founders of the *Bibliothèque Démocratique*, to which he contributed several anti-clerical volumes. In 1876 he was elected to the Municipal Council of Paris, where he brought forward the question of establishing a crematorium. {BDF; RAT}

Morison, James Augustus Cotter (1831–1888)

Morison was an English positivist and man of letters. In 1863 he published *The Life and Times of Saint Bernard.* He was one of the founders of *Fortnightly Review*, in which he wrote, as well as in the *Athenaeum.* In 1886 he published "The Service of Man," an essay toward the religion of the future, which shows that the benefits of Christianity have been much exaggerated and its evils palpable. George Meredith once dedicated to Morison a volume of poems. {BDF; RAT; RE}

Morley, John [Viscount Morley of Blackburn] (1838–1923)

A statesman, man of letters, and editor of the liberal *Fortnightly Review*, Viscount Morley wrote lives of Voltaire (1872), Rousseau (1873), and *Diderot and the Encyclopedists* (1878). "All religions die of one disease," he reportedly said, "that of being found out." He also observed in *Critical Miscellanies* (1872) that "Where it is the duty to worship the sun, it is pretty sure to be a crime to examine the laws of heat."

In 1886, Morley was appointed by Mr. Gladstone Chief Secretary for Ireland. He was a friend of McCabe, who said he was an admirer of the freethought opinions of Voltaire, Diderot, and other heretics, as shown in his *Diderot and the Encyclopedists* (1878). McCabe added, "His political associations and high social position restrained him, and he once begged me, almost tearfully, not to publish a letter of his in which he said that Gladstone was far inferior, both morally and intellectually, to J. S. Mill. But he was a man of fine and universally respected character–'Honest John' he was often called–and in his autobiography (*Recollections*, 1917) he again avowed himself an agnostic." In 1919 Morley became an honorary associate of the Rationalist Press Association. {BDF; FUK; JM; RAT; RE; TRI}

MORMON, BOOK OF

The Church of Jesus Christ of Latter-day Saints claims that its founder, Joseph Smith, was visited by God and Jesus Christ, who told him not to join any established church. Later in a revelation he was instructed to form the church and was directed to a hill in Palmyra, New York, where golden tablets contained a revealed book. Smith translated *The Book of Mormon* from these tablets that allegedly gave God's historical account of the Western Hemisphere from about 600 B.C.E. to 421 C.E. After the Christ was crucified, according to the revelations Smith received, he appeared in North America and ministered to its inhabitants, who were believed to be descendants of immigrants from Jerusalem. Mormons using the book hold that theirs is the only true Christian faith. Through proxy they baptize the dead, whom they believe were denied an opportunity to join the church. They believe that God dwells near the planet Kolob, with his many wives and countless spirit children, whom He sends to Earth as humans to be tested. Marriage and family relationships last for eternity, according to the revealed "truths." {Andrew Jacobs, *The New York Times*, 31 May 1998}

MORMON CHURCH

The Mormons originated in the United States in the nineteenth century, with teachings based on the Bible and the *Book of Mormon.* The latter was allegedly revealed by angels to Joseph Smith, a poor, half-literate seventeen-year-old, who was told to look for some golden plates bearing a history of ancient America which God had hidden on Hill Cumorah, near his father's farm in upstate Manchester, New York. He went, he saw, but the angel he talked to would not let him possess the plates. Finally in 1827 the angel allowed him to take the gold book, and in time he decoded the book's "Reformed Egyptian" hieroglyphics and dictated his translations to a scribe. At one time Joseph gave 116 pages of the translation to a follower who lost them. Angry angels punished him by repossessing the plates. After months of prayer and meditation, he got the text back and in 1830 published the *Book of Mormon*, but he was left empty-handed and could not keep the plates. Under the leadership of Brigham Young, the Mormons moved to Utah and laid stress on hard work, loyal family life, and abstinence from alcohol and tobacco. Mormonism was once controversial because of polygamy, but the church repudiated the practice in 1890 and no longer sanctions it. It also closed the priesthood to blacks, who, according to Mormon doctrine, carried the mark of Cain. That policy, however was reversed in 1978 because the church's President said he had "a revelation."

John L. Brooke in T*he Refiner's Fire: The Making of Mormon Cosmology, 1644–1844* (1995) tells how on his father's side Smith was descended from a line of village magicians. In the wake of

Salem witchcraft trials in the 1690s, the Smiths had practiced white witchcraft. On his mother's side, Smith inherited a mix of sectarianism and hermeticism (an interest in alchemy, magic, and the occult). Brooke's goal was to explore "the particular affinities, latent and manifest, running between the religious culture of prophesy and restoration and the occult cultures of popular conjuring and esoteric hermeticism." How it was possible for an ignorant farm boy to have come up with a religion that now claims nine million members or more remains the most astonishing of Joseph Smith's alchemical achievements. (See entry for Steve Benson, grandchild of Mormon President Ezra Taft Benson. Also, see entries for Church of Jesus Christ of Latter-Day Saints, Gentile, and Reorganized Church of Jesus Christ of Latter-Day Saints. As to how Virgil Thomson was turned onto marijuana by the Mormons' President, see entry for Thomson.) {CE; DCL}

MORMON HOMOSEXUALS

D. Michael Quinn in *Same-Sex Dynamics Among Nineteenth-Century Americans: A Mormon Example* (1996) wrote of being a closeted gay Mormon who was excommunicated by his church but still considers himself a true Mormon.

Vern L. Bullough, reviewing the work, wrote, "I long ago ceased to regard myself as a Mormon and believe religion is a matter of choice, not of biology. I regard Quinn's interpretation of Mormonism as a major flaw in his work." {*Free Inquiry*, Winter 1996-1997}

MORMON MISSIONARIES

"Where did you serve your mission?" Mormon girls are said to ask men asking for a date. Depending upon the men's answer, Andrew Jacobs has written, "they won't even date you." The pressure to serve a mission is intense, young Mormons find, "and those who don't can find themselves on the fringes of Mormon life."

A two-year mission is considered a rite of passage for Mormon men who reach the age of nineteen. Women, who make up only 17% of the missionary force, must wait until they are twenty-one and are not pressured to become missionaries the way men are. Their focus is more upon marriage and having families, and they are not allowed to hold the priesthood, perform baptisms, or supervise confirmations. Upon their nineteenth birthday, however, men must interrupt whatever else they are doing and go out into the world to proselytize. Although church officials claim there is no pressure to win converts, many missionaries say that those with a prodigious tally, not just five to seven people a year, can expect a hero's welcome upon their return home and promotions in the church hierarchy.

Citing examples of Mormons who quit the church, Jacobs noted that in Mormonism "You either believe everything or nothing: there is no gray area." As a result some quitters who have "lost the fire" confess that they worried about becoming an apostate. But they sometimes question the church's doctrines or become disillusioned upon discovering that potential converts are offered access to the church's generous welfare program. Disapproving of such, they become lapsed Mormons despite the pressure they feel from their Mormon neighbors against anyone "who wants out."

Although the Salt Lake City "Temple Square" brand of Mormonism does not practice polygamy, pious Mormons are advised, according to K. L. Johnson (*New York Times Magazine,* 21 March 1999), "that they will have the opportunity to take on more than one wife after death so that they may become head of their own expansive patriarchies."

In New York City, the number of members has more than doubled from 1990 to 1997, almost entirely because of people who have converted to the faith. An estimated two hundred forty Mormon missionaries operate in the city, and 20,123 individuals were converted in 1997 because of their efforts. Worldwide, the church's membership has grown from four million in 1978 to ten million in 1998. Whereas the Roman Catholic Church has 6,000 missionaries around the world, Mormons have 60,000 working in 160 countries. {Andrew Jacobs, *The New York Times*, 31 May 1998)

MOROCCAN HUMANISM: See entry for Mohammed Choukri.

Moroz, Andrew (20th Century)

Moroz wrote "The Inconsistency of Theism" (*Secular Nation*, July-September 1998), pointing out that philosophy is a human endeavor that entails no assumptions. "And if through logical argument and rational debate the impossibility of a god is revealed, however much our sentiment of nostalgia calls for a divine caretaker to walk our world, the falsehood must be cast off so we may enjoy the ultimate freedom that only truth can bring.

Morrell, R. M. (19th Century)

Morrell was a secularist who founded the National Sunday League in 1856. It pioneered Sunday lectures at St. Marin's Hall and other London centers, and it campaigned against the restrictions on Sunday entertainments imposed by the Act of 1781. Annie Besant was its vice-president.

Morrell, Robert W. (20th Century)

In Nottingham, England, Morrell has edited the *Thomas Paine Society Bulletin*. He wrote *The God of the Twilight* (1980). {FUK; GS}

Morris, Charles (19th Century)

Morris wrote *Aryan Sun-Myths: The Origin of Religions* (1899), in which he showed that all Indo-Germanic nations have worshiped crucified saviors. He held that the sun-myths of the ancient Aryans were the origin of the religions in all of the countries peopled by the Aryans. {CE}

Morris, Charles W. (1901–)

When he signed Humanist Manifesto II, Morris was professor emeritus of the University of Florida. He also taught in the philosophy department at the University of Chicago and the University of Denver. {HM2; HNS; HNS2}

Morris, Desmond (20th Century)

An zoologist, Morris wrote *Biology of Art* (1961), *Apes and Monkeys* (1965), *The Naked* Ape (1967), *The Art of Ancient Cyprus* (1985), *The Illustrated Naked Ape* (1986), and with Ramona Morris *Men and Apes* (1965).

In *The Naked Ape* he included the following:

> [Religion] has led to a number of bizarre by-products, such as belief in "another life" where we will at last meet up with god figures. . . . In a sense, we still believe in an after-life, because part of the reward obtained from our creative works is the feeling that, through them, we will "live on" after we are dead.

In 1994, Morris wrote *The Human Animal*, which contains the following:

> There have been many arguments about the location of the immortal human soul. Could it be in the heart, in the head, or perhaps diffused throughout the whole body–an all-pervading spiritual quality unique to the human being? The answer, it seems to me as a zoologist, is obvious enough: a man's soul is located in his testicles; a woman's in her ovaries. For it is here that we find the truly immortal elements in our constitution–our genes.

{CA; E}

Morris, Edward (20th Century)

Morris is associated with the Humanist Association of Middle Tennessee. (See entry for Tennessee Humanists.) {FD}

Morris, Ethel (20th Century)

A Unitarian minister in Auckland from 1948–1957, Morris moved to England where, although eschewing little of the traditional Christian language, was a religious humanist, according to John Maindonald.

Morris, Gordon (20th Century)

Morris is a regional director in Minnesota of the Council for Secular Humanism.

Morris, Gouverneur (1752–1816)

Morris, who helped draft the Constitution of New York State, was Minister to France from 1792 to 1794. He retired in disgust at the excesses. Morris detested Paine, according to McCabe, and "is responsible for much of the libel of him, but he was himself a Deist. Jefferson, a close friend, wrote, 'Morris often told me that General Washington believed no more of that system (Christianity) than he himself did.' " {RAT; RE}

Morris, Steven (20th Century)

Morris, a professor of physics at Los Angeles Harbor College in Wilmington, California, wrote "The Founding Fathers Were *Not* Christians" in *Free Inquiry* (Fall 1995). He cites the non-Christians Thomas Paine, George Washington, John Adams, Thomas Jefferson, James Madison, Ethan Allen, and Benjamin Franklin. Morris spent one year at the South Pole, running a seismometer. He has written widely about astronomy and has been an active member of the Los Angeles-based Atheists United.

Morris, William (1834–1896)

An English poet, artist, architect, interior decorator, book illuminator, furniture maker, lecturer, businessman, translator, essayist, printer, craftsman, Socialist campaigner, publisher, and painter, Morris is considered one of the great Victorians. An early interest in the ritual and architecture of the Middle Ages led, after he read Ruskin, to the ideas on aestheticism and social progress in his work. His *News from Nowhere* (1891), according to Corliss Lamont, "sketched a Humanist Utopia in terms of a simple and secularized village economy in which crowded cities and grimy factories are both eliminated and where regular work merges with applied art and the creation of beauty." Art is the expression of joy in labor rather than an exclusive luxury. He made no distinction between art and craft and saw fine design and workmanship as the salvation of the industrial society.

Life and Death of Jason (1867 was a poem in heroic couplets based on the story of Jason, Medea, and the Argonauts. It and *Earthly Paradise* (1868–1870) established Morris as one of the most popular poets of his day. From 1876 onward, Morris took a fervent interest in social questions, and in 1883 he joined the Socialists. W. Allingham, his friend, wrote that by this time he had quite ceased to take an interest in theology. "It's so unimportant, it seems to me," he told Allingham. From this nonchalant attitude, Morris passed to atheism, and his friends tell how he used to declaim with great zest a certain scornfully anti-Christian couplet of Swinburne's.

The personal and family troubles Morris experienced are detailed in Norman Kelvin's edition of *The Collected Letters of William Morris* (1995) and in Fiona MacCarthy's *William Morris: A Life for Our Time* (1995). Jane, the daughter of an Oxford stable hand who became his wife, openly had an affair with Dante Gabriel Rossetti, who once described Morris as an exhausted wombat. His wife, it is documented, never really loved Morris and married him only to rise from the working class. She witnessed his many temper tantrums and reacted coldly toward him. Max Beerbohm recalled Morris as "a wonderful all-round man, but the act of walking round him has always tired me."

Even fellow socialist George Bernard Shaw, noting Morris's extreme fits of rage, speculated that Morris suffered from some form of epilepsy. Jenny, their daughter, was diagnosed at the age of sixteen as epileptic, and her grand mal seizures frightened both of her parents, who tied her to her bed in order to protect themselves as well as her. William Butler Yeats, however, said of Morris, "If some angel offered me the choice, I would choose to live his life, poetry and all, rather than my own or any other man's." Morris believed in the "abolition of private property" and "the struggle against Capitalism." His acquaintances included Eleanor Marx, the youngest daughter of Karl, and Friedrich Engels. A friend of the leading anarchists of his day, Morris was arrested for public disorder and he founded the Hammersmith Socialist Society.

According to R. Page Arnot's *William Morris: The Man and the Myth*, Morris, despite having his views distorted by his Christian Socialist friend Bruce Glasier, who claimed Morris was a religionist, stated, "I am what is called bluntly an atheist." Peter Faulkner, an editor of the *Journal of the William Morris Society*, has written extensively about Morris's "socialist humanism."

On his death, Morris was widely mourned as "our best man" by his fellow socialists, by whom he was deeply revered. His view that "the true incentive to useful and happy labour is, and must be, pleasure in the work itself" links his political and artistic aspirations, both of which have remained profoundly influential. (See entry for Frank Lloyd Wright.) {CE; CL; OEL; Peter Faulkner, *New Humanist*, September 1996; PUT; RAT; RE; TRI}

Morrissey (20th Century)

Morrissey, a recording artist, has gone on record as being a non-theist. {E}

Morrison, Dan (20th Century)

Morrison is on the editorial committee of *Humanist in Canada*.

Morrison, George Ernest (1862–1920)

Morrison was an Australian writer who had crossed Australia on foot from the Gulf of Carpentaria to Melbourne and the following year he traveled from Shanghai to Rangoon. For the *Times*, he became the Pekin correspondent. The Chinese decorated him with their Order of the Excellent Crop. In his *Australian in China* (1895), Morrison showed personal regard for the missionaries but revealed the utter futility and hypocrisy of their work. He estimated that they converted "nine-tenths of a Chinaman per worker per annum," and was disdainful of the Christian effort. {RAT}

Morrison, Jim (1943–1971)

The noted musician Morrison, as well as his wife, **Patricia Kennealy-Morrison**, were non-theists. Both, she has written, were attracted to

> the most ancient faith in which he and I were married and which we both ardently espoused. I refer to paganism, also known as witchcraft or wicca. Today, the Craft (the pre-Christian religion of Celtic Europe) is enjoying a resurgence.
> {*The New York Times Magazine*, 28 December 1997}

Morrison-Reed, Mark D. (1949–)

Morrison-Reed is author of *Black Pioneers in a White Denomination*, a study of Unitarian Universalists.

Morrow, David (20th Century)

Morrow contributes material to *The American Rationalist*, one article of which (July 1992) laments the fact that astrology is more popular than psychology in the United States.

Morrow, James (20th Century)

According to Celebrity Atheists, Morrow, an author, is a non-theist. {E}

Morrow, Lance (1939–)

Morrow, of *Time*, wrote in that magazine, "If you scratch any aggressive tribalism, or nationalism, you usually find beneath its surface a religious core, some older binding energy of belief or superstition . . . that is capable of transforming itself into a death-force, with the peculiar annihilating energies of belief. Faith, the sweetest refuge and consolation, may harden, by perverse miracle, into a sword–or anyway into a club or a torch or an assault rifle. Religious hatreds tend to be merciless and absolute." {TYD}

Morrow, Marguerite (20th Century)

Morrow in Scotland is active with the Glasgow Humanist Society.

Morse, Edward Sylvester (1838–1925)

Morse, an American zoologist and art expert, was director of the Peabody Museum at Salem, Massachusetts. In an article in *Knowledge* (1898), he was reported as saying, "I have not yet seen anything in the discoveries of science which would in the slightest degree support or strengthen a belief in immortality." {RAT}

Morse, Philip M. (20th Century)

Brought up as a Methodist, Morse was an airline pilot, then worked in computer publications, printing, inventory control, and distribution for a computer company. He has written, "I have always been a skeptic but not an atheist until my 50s in a gradual process of self-awareness." On the subject of Earth's overpopulation, he has published an article in *Freethought Today*.

Morse, Sidney H. (19th Century)

Morse in Boston, Massachusetts, edited *The Radical* in the 1860s. In 1892, he wrote *Ethics of the Homestead Strike.*

Morselli, Enrico Agostino (Born 1852)

Morselli was an Italian physician and scientist. He wrote many works on anthropology, including one on "Suicide" in the International Scientific Series. Morselli edited *Revista di Filosofia Scientifica,* and he translated Herbert Spencer on the past and future of religion. {BDF; RAT}

MORTAL SIN

In Roman Catholic theology, a sin is mortal when it is serious enough to subject the sinner to damnation. For example, willful murder is a mortal sin. Less serious sins are called venial.

Secular humanists consider "sin" a device particularly for psychiatrists who are trying to address a cure for clients who have been misled by their religious shepherds. But they prefer the secular terminology used—for example on the subject of murder, vice, or crime, etc.—in the various international legal codes. (See entry for venial sin.) {DCL}

Mortier, Roland (20th Century)

Mortier, a cultural historian from Belgium, has been cited by Michel Delon in the Parisian *Les Cahiers Rationalistes* as being a rationalist. Mortier is author of *Diderot on Allemagne 1750–1870* (1986).

Mortillet, Adrien de (Born 1853)

Mortillet, the son of Louis Mortillet, sustained his father's views and became professor at the School of Anthropology founded by him (largely, according to McCabe, for the correction of theology) at Paris. He edited the review, *L'Homme Préhistorique.* {RAT}

Mortillet, Louis Laurent Gabriel de (1821–1890)

Mortillet was a French scientist who had been educated by the Jesuits but was condemned in 1849 for his political writings, forcing him to take refuge in Switzerland. Mortillet wrote *A Contribution to the History of Superstition* and other works that showed his freethought.

He was curator of the Museum of St. Germain and was elected Deputy in 1885. An atheist, Mortillet fought the Church while a member of the Chambre. {BDF; RAT; RE}

Mortimer, James (20th Century)

In *Murders and Other Friends: Another Part of Life* (1994), Mortimer describes himself as an "atheist for Christ." In the book's last chapter he presents himself as an unbeliever who is sympathetic to the ethical and cultural aspects of Christianity. {CA; E}

Mortimer, John Clifford (1923–)

A novelist, barrister, and playwright, Mortimer at one time was married to Penelope Mortimer (1918–), the novelist who wrote *The Pumpkin Eater* (1962), *The House* (1971), *Long Distance* (1974), and an autobiography, *About Time* (1970). He married his second wife, also a Penelope, on his forty-ninth birthday. The son of Kathleen, an artist, and Clifford Mortimer, a lawyer known for his expertise concerning divorce law, he wrote *A Voyage Round My Father* (1971), which is an autobiographical portrait of his blind and histrionic father.

Mortimer's plays include *The Dock Brief* (1958, which was produced for both radio and television in 1957). In 1982, Mortimer wrote an autobiographical work, *Clinging to the Wreckage.* His films include "The Innocents" (1961); "The Dock Brief" (1962, and called "Trial and Error" in the United States); "The Running Man" (1963), a translation of Feydeau's "A Flea in Her Ear" (1968); and "John and Mary" (1969). The latter starred Dustin Hoffman and Mia Farrow. In 1971 Mortimer became famous for explaining to an Old Bailey jury why Rupert Bear, a children's comic-strip character, had an extraordinarily large erection.

Ian Parker, in *The New Yorker* (20 March 1995), states that Mortimer has been captive to the success of "Rumpole of the Bailey," a reference to Horace Rumpole, a Dickensian-like character. A captive to the memory of his father, Mortimer says of him, "He and Rumpole are both objects of my invention," admitting that much of his work can be traced directly to his own life experiences.

Mortimer is a conservative as well as a socialist. Some have said that, if Britain were ever to become a Republic, they could envision Mortimer as its ideal first President. Parker adds that Mortimer "took theatre into court, as judges sometimes observed, and he took the court into the world of letters–into theatre, films, television, and journalism." Parker also reported that upon interviewing Mick Jagger for a newspaper profile, Mortimer asked him, "Do you believe in immortality?" Jagger's response: "What a question to throw me in the middle of the World Cup!" Mortimer's response, an indication of his interest in the gods of celebrities, was, "But *do* you?"

Mortimer is an atheist who, according to Parker, "is nonetheless indebted to the Christian tradition."

Morton, A. L. (Born 1903)

Morton, a freethinker, wrote *The Life and Ideas of Robert Owen* (1967). {FUS}

Morton, Francis Torrey (20th Century)

A freethinker, Morton wrote *The Proven Continuity of Life, Its Relation to Jesuitism and the Christian Religion* (1913). {GS}

Morton, James Ferdinand Jr. (20th Century)

Morton wrote "The American Secular Union" (1910) and "Exempting the Churches" (1916). {GS}

Mortyn, Frank (20th Century)

Since 1980 Mortyn in San Diego, California, has edited *Humanist Century.* A physicist, Mortyn lectures widely on humanism and freethought. Mortyn is a senior writer for *The American Rationalist.*

Moscheles, Felix (1883–1917)

Moscheles, a painter and the son of pianist Ignaz Moscheles, was a friend of Whistler and DuMaurier. An agnostic, he at one time was President of the International Arbitration and Peace Association. {RAT; RE}

Moser, Elwood (20th Century)

Moser was a freethinker who wrote *Evolution and Man, Natural Morality, the Church of the Future, and Other Essays* (1919). {GS}

Moser, Gerald (20th Century)

Moser is author of *Seven Essays on Joseph Priestley* (1994). A founding member of the Unitarian Universalist Fellowship of Centre County, Pennsylvania.

Moses

There is general agreement, according to McCabe, that "the Hebrews got the story of the baby in the bulrushes from an ancient Sumerian record about the birth of Sargon, whose mother put him in a basket of reeds by the river, where he was found and adopted. . . . Persistent search in the abundant remains has discovered no evidence that the Hebrews ever were in Egypt, and it is now the more common opinion that they were not a united people before the tribes straggled into Syria. This and the wholly fabulous character of the Moses story do not dispose us to look for even 'a kernel of truth' in it," McCabe concluded. Arthur M. Davis, among others, has wondered if Moses could read. He allegedly walked down from Mt. Sinai with two stone tablets, on one of which "Thou shalt not Kill" was allegedly inscribed. Yet later on Moses ordered his army to butcher thousands of men, women, and male children (*Numbers* 31: 14, 17-18). {RE}

Moses, George (19th Century)

A Canadian, Moses in 1871 became the first Native North

American to be ordained as a Universalist minister.

MOSLEM

Moslem is a dated form of Muslim. See entry for Islam.

MOSQUE

A mosque is an Islamic meeting house.

Moss, Arthur B. (1855–1937)

Moss, a lecturer and writer, wrote numerous pamphlets, a number of which are collected in *Waves of Freethought* (1885). He was a contributor to the *Secular Chronicle, Secular Review, Freethinker, Truthseeker*, and other journals. Moss, a devout Christian until the age of sixteen, became a freethinker after reading Paine's *Age of Reason*. A school board officer, he was for a time prohibited from lecturing on Sundays. Moss was a pillar of the Camberwell Secular Society until his death. {BDF; FUK; PUT; RAT; RSR; TRI}

Moss, Harry Walter Sr. (20th Century–deceased)

Moss wrote *The Book of the Few–Genesis: A Secular Interpretation of Biblical Creation* (1997?). We were meant, he concludes to eat fruit from the Tree of Knowledge. We were not, however, meant to eat from the Tree of Life, which means that we will not live forever. But knowledge is immortal, Moss illustrated, so long as we pass it to the next generation.

Moss, J. (19th Century)

In 1869, Moss of Bristol started a West of England and South Wales Secular Union. This led to the formation of a society at Cardiff. {RSR}

Moss, James (20th Century)

Moss, a New York City psychiatrist, is an Advisory Board Member of African Americans for Humanism.

Mossner, Ernest Campbell (1907–)

When he reviewed books in the 1950s for *The Humanist*, Mossner taught English at the University of Texas in Austin. He wrote *David Hume* (1962) and was on the editorial board of the *Encyclopedia of Philosophy* from 1963 to 1967. {FUS}

Mosso, Angelo (1846–1910)

Mosso, an Italian physiologist, was an agnostic. He was appointed assistant to Moleschott at Turin University. Mosso was a Commander of the Order of S. S. Maurice and Lazarus and of the Crown of Italy. His funeral, at which learned societies were represented, was purely secular. {RAT}.

Most, Johann Joseph (1846–1906)

A German anarchist, Most was a bookbinder by trade and edited German as well as Austrian newspapers. His work was frequently suppressed, and he was imprisoned for his public denunciation of religion, patriotism, and accepted moral standards. When elected to the Reichstag (1874–1878), he became disillusioned with government and was deported. In England, he was deported after serving a sixteen-month sentence for glorifying the assassination of Russia's Alexander II. In 1882 he emigrated to the United States, where he was jailed many times for his writings. In New York, his circle frequented Justus Schwab's 51st Street saloon, an establishment so shocking that men and women entered by the same door. Emma Goldman came under his influence, and he received the dubious honor one day of being publicly whipped by her because of a disagreement they had about anarchy.

Most once wrote, "God is merely a specter, fabricated by designing scoundrels, through which mankind is tyrannized and kept in constant dread. But the phantom instantly dissolves when examined under the glass of sober reflection." *The God Pestilence* (1902) states,

> Among all mental diseases that have been systematically inoculated into the human cranium, the religious pest is the most abominable. . . . The more man clings to religion, the more he believes. The more he believes, the less he knows. The less he knows, the more stupid he is; the more stupid, the easier he is governed. The easier to govern, the better he may be exploited; the more exploited, the poorer he gets.

{CE; FUS; PA}

Mostel, Zero (Samuel Joel) (1915-1977)

An actor known for his expressive face, large body, but graceful movement, Mostel made his Broadway debut in *Keep 'Em Laughing* (1941). He also was featured in *Ulysses in Nighttown* (1958 and 1974), *Rhinoceros* (1961; film, 1973), *A Funny Thing Happened on the Way to the Forum* (1962; film, 1966), and *Fiddler on the Roof* (1964). His 1965 autobiography was titled *Zero by Mostel*.

Mostel's last wish, told to his wife, was that he wanted to be cremated "like Einstein" with no funeral or memorial service. {CE}

Mosterin, Jesús (20th Century)

Mosterin, who teaches logic at the University of Barcelona in Spain, is a member of the Ibero-American Commission, a group of humanist leaders in Spanish-speaking countries.

MOTHERS

• All women become like their mothers. That is their tragedy. No man does. That's his.

–Oscar Wilde

• The only regret I have is giving you birth.

–The mother of composer Stephen Sondheim, in a note to the son she abandoned and just before she underwent life-threatening heart surgery.

Mothersill, Mary (20th Century)

When she signed Humanist Manifesto II, Mothersill was chairman of the philosophy department of Barnard College, which was affiliated with Columbia University. In 1984, she wrote *Beauty Restored*. Prof. Mothersill spoke at Corliss Lamont's memorial service in 1995. {CL; HM2}

Motley, John Lothrop (1814–1877)

A Unitarian who was highly negative about Catholicism, Motley wrote *The Rise of the Dutch*. He was a minister to Great Britain and Austria.

Oliver Wendell Holmes reported in his *John Lothrop Motley* (1889) that William Lewis, one of Motley's critics, wrote, "It is understood, and he makes no mystery of it that he inclines towards the vague and undecided doctrine of the Unitarians." {CE; RAT; RE; U; UU}

Mott, Lucretia (1793–1800)

Mott was a Quaker who from 1818 on became well-known as a lecturer for temperance, peace, the rights of labor, and the abolition of slavery. Delegated to the World's Anti-Slavery Convention in London in 1840, she was excluded on account of her gender. In 1848, she organized the first woman's rights convention in the United States, at Seneca Falls, New York.

Although a Quaker, she was said by Wheeler to have preferred conscience to revelation. Mott was a friend of Mrs. Rose and Mrs. Stanton. Her husband, James, attended the 1840 London conference on slavery, presided over the 1848 conference, and aided in the founding (1864) of Swarthmore College. A renegade Quaker who was thrown out of her church for her radical views, Mott was socially ostracized for her humanistic outlook concerning slavery, and a rioting mob once almost burned her in her home. She was associated with the Free Religious Association. {CE; PUT; BDF; TYD}

Mouat, Kit (20th Century)

Mouat founded the Humanist Letter Network (International) in 1962. He wrote *What Humanism is About* (1963) and *An Introduction to Secular Humanism* (c. 1973). {FUK; TRI}

Mounier, Emmanuel (1903–1950)

Mounier founded *Esprit*, a journal of Personalism.

MOUNTAINS

Early Christians believed mountains were ugly excrescences, that human depravity had brought them about, and that they were the land's punishment for having accepted Abel's murdered blood. English writers, living with hills but not mountains, ordinarily described them negatively. Hamlet, bragging of his love for the dead and about-to-be buried Ophelia, declares, "[L]et them throw/millions of acres on us, till our ground,/singeing his pate against the burning zone,/make Ossa [a Greek 6,489 ft. high peak] like a wart!" The English "divine" and metaphysical poet, John Donne, called mountains "warts, and pock-holes in the face of th' earth."

Geologists vividly describe how some mountains are remains of plateaus dissected by erosion, while others are cones of volcanoes or intrusions of igneous rock that form domes. The concept of plate tectonics is the first reasonable unifying theory, hypothesizing that the earth's crust is broken into several plates that sideswipe each other or collide. Not until recent times has it been understood that Africa was joined with what now are the Americas. In 1953 when Sir Edmund Hillary and Tenzing Norkay of Nepal reached the summit of Earth's highest elevation, Mount Everest on the border of Tibet and Nepal, a new and romantic view of mountains occurred. As to why mankind had the desire to climb such dangerous objects, humanistic mountaineers reply, "Because they're there." {CE}

MOVEMENTS

In the political realm, the four major movements of the latter part of the 20th Century have been, according to editorials in newsletters of several freethought organizations,

- the civil rights movement;
- the anti-war movement;
- the women's movement; and
- the gay and lesbian movement.

Mowat, Robin (1925-1998)

Mowat was a New Zealand rationalist known to many as an itinerant, or man with no address. From time to time he would call into Rationalist House and pick up his mail. Upon his death it was learned that he had served in the British Merchant Service and the Royal Navy during World War II.

Moya, Francisco Xavier (Born c. 1825)

Moya was a Spanish statistician who became deputy to the Cortes of 1869. He wrote several works on the infallibility of the Pope and on the temporal power. {BDF}

Moynihan, Patrick Berkeley [Lord] (1906–1965)

Moynihan, the 2nd Baron of Leeds, was the second president of the English Euthanasia Society. He was chairman of the Liberal Party Executives from 1949–1950.

Mozart, Wolfgang Amadeus (1756–1791)

Mozart, the Austrian composer, represents one of the great peaks in the history of music. His works, written in almost every conceivable genre, combine beauty of sound with classical grace and technical perfection.

A prodigy, he was taught to play the harpsichord, violin, and organ by his father, Leopold, and began composing before he was five. When Mozart was six, he and his older sister performed a concert for the Empress Maria Theresa in Vienna. By the age of thirteen, he had written concertos, sonatas, symphonies, a German operetta, and an Italian opera.

The Pope made him a Knight of the Golden Spur, and for ten years he was concertmaster to the archbishop of Salzburg, a position in which he was restless because of his doubts about Catholicism. Two leading biographers are in agreement that Mozart was a non-Christian theist, but the *Catholic Encyclopedia* claims him as being a Catholic.

Mozart became a Freemason in 1784 and took his Freemasonry seriously. His *Kleine Freimaurer Kantate* (K.623), "A Small Freemason Cantata," for chorus, two tenors, bass, and chamber orchestra has the following recitative:

> For the first time, noble brothers,
> We are met in this great seat of virtue, wisdom, and truth,
> We consecrate ourselves to the sanctity of our labor,
> Which is to discover for ourselves the great mysterious truth.
> Joyful are all brethren on this day,
> This happy day of holy dedication
> By which the brotherhood is bound in unity.
> Let us be thankful that human kindness
> Reigns among men once again upon earth.

"The Magic Flute" is permeated by Masonic imagery, themes, and motifs. Also, Mozart wrote *Maurerische Trauermusik* (K. 477), the "Masonic Funeral Music," about which Paul Nettl has written: "The low, threatening notes of the winds anticipate the serious mood. Several chords serve as an introduction, then a plaintive, rhapsodic melody is played by the solo violin. This juxtaposition of winds and strings corresponds to the dialectic of life and inexorable death. . . . The dotted rhythms in the bass accompany the sobbing of the strings which, toward the middle of the piece, rear up in sudden anguish and then return to a gentle but serious lament. His famous 'Requiem Mass' was composed for Count Walsegg, who paid Mozart but put his own name on the composition. Ulibichov, the second leading biographer, gives further evidence that he abandoned the Church."

Mozart had worked feverishly on the requiem, with the foreboding that it would commemorate his own death. Meanwhile, he died at the age of thirty-five without finishing it. One of his pupils, Franz Süssmayr, did finish the requiem.

Freemasonry was sternly condemned by the Catholic Church. To his father Mozart in 1778 explained that Masonry was his only creed. "The orthodoxy of my youth is all over," he explained, "and will never come back." McCabe quotes the biographer Wilder as saying that "on his death bed [Mozart] refused to ask for a priest and when his wife nevertheless sent for one, it was refused, and he was buried without service in the common grave of the poor."

Common myth has it that at Mozart's funeral snow fell. However, Nicolas Slonimsky, author of *Music Since 1909* and *My First Hundred Years*–he lived to be 102–checked with the Austrian weather bureau and learned that it was a clear day there on 7 December 1791. {CE; *Freethought History #9* 1994; JM; RAT; RE}

Mthembu, Ayida S. (20th Century)

The Assistant Dean of Student Affairs at the Massachusetts Institute of Technology, Mthembu is an Advisory Board Member of African Americans for Humanism.

Muavia (510–585)

McCabe has written of Muavia, the first caliph of Syria, "His name will hardly be found in any encyclopedia of general history because religious influence has always restrained historians from doing justice to the brilliance of the Arab civilization of the Middle Ages while Christendom was semi-barbarous. Muavia, in particular, is ignored because, while theologians plead that it necessarily took the Church many centuries to raise the Teutonic barbarians to civilization, Muavia thus raised the equally barbaric Arabs in a single generation." McCabe labels Muavia, the son of opponents of Muhammad who were convinced that he was an imposter, "a skeptic with the formal title of Caliph." McCabe included him in his *Hundred Men Who Moved the World.* (See entry for Muawiya,) {JM; RE}

Muawiya (Died 680)

Muawiya (also spelled Moawiyah) was the first Ummayad caliph (661–680) and one of the greatest Muslim statesmen. Under Umar he became the able governor of Syria. As caliph he made Islam an autocracy. His administration was tolerant, and he displayed an enlightened point of view in his dealings. McCabe might have mistaken Muavia for Muawiya, for Muavia's parents were allegedly opponents of Muhammad, who was born around 570 and died in 632. {CE}

Mudaliar, Murugesa (19th Century)

In Madras, India, Mudaliar edited *Philosophical Inquirer* from 1878 to 1888. {FUK}

Muehl, Siegmar (20th Century)

Muehl is author of "Hermann's 'Free Men': 1850s German-American Religious Rationalism," in *Missouri Historical Review* (July 1991). A descendent of Eduard Mühl, publisher of Herman, Missouri's first newspaper, *Lichtfreund*, Muehl has taught in the College of Education at the University of Iowa. He has written for *Freethought History* and has translated freethought authors such as the German-American Friedrich Muench.

Muench, Friedrich (1799–1881)

Muench was a significant figure in German-American and Missouri history. Formerly a Lutheran pastor in his native Germany, Muench exchanged his orthodox views about miracles and revelation for a faith in "natural" religion based on reason.

During the Civil War years, he served a term in the Missouri legislature, during which time his anti-slavery views resulted in threats against his life, property, and family. An account of his views can be found in *Freethought History* (#6, 1993), edited by Fred Whitehead. Muench's brother, Georg, established the Mount Pleasant Vineyards in Augusta, Missouri, where his winery continues.

Muhammad (Mohammad, Mahomet) (570?–632)

Muhammad, the Prophet of Islam, was born in Mecca of the tribe of Kuraish. Scholars are unsure whether he was born in the early 7th century or, as Lawrence Conrad has suggested, "well into the second century A.H.," which is 570 of the Christian Era, a difference of eighty-five years.

One of the most famous humans in history, he at the age of forty felt that Allah had selected him to be the Arab prophet of true religion, the "revelations" and teachings of which are recorded in the Qur'an and which are the basis of Islam. Although his early successes were few and in 622–the date is confirmed by dated coinage which marked the beginning of a new era–he was almost murdered by enemies, Muhammad escaped to Yathrib in a flight, or Hegira, upon which Islam counts its dates. The city, henceforth called Medina, or City of the Prophet, became a model theocratic state, and by 630 Muhammad had won all Arabia.

Although he had assumed Jews and Christians would welcome him for having converted so many and for being the last of the prophets, a successor of Jesus the Christ, he became disappointed in their refusal to do so and enmity commenced despite the common use by the three religious groups of the Old Testament. In a short time, he began persecuting the Jews who refused to accept his religion, and he reduced Christians to dependency in areas that his zealous armies had conquered on three continents.

"The Koran accuses the Jews of corrupting the Scriptures and the Christians of worshipping Christ as the son of God, although He had expressly commanded them to worship none but Him," writes N. J. Dawood in his translation of *The Koran* (Penguin, 1956). "Having thus gone astray, they must be brought back to the right path, to the true religion preached by Abraham. This was absolute submission or resignation to the will of Allah."

Unlike Jesus, whom Christian followers believed was the supernatural Christ and Son of God, Muhammad was a human being born to Abdallah ibn Abd-al-Muttalib and his wife Armina. Muhammad was raised by a grandfather, then by an uncle, for both his parents had died by the time he was six years of age. At the age of twenty-five, he was the chief merchant and camel driver of a rich widow, Khadija, whom he married three years later. Upon her death, he provided himself with a harem, which brought a variety of problems, and he had several wives. One of his daughters, Fatima, had offspring to whom contemporaries boast of being related. And in 632, after several decades of successful preaching, Muhammad died in the arms of his last favorite wife, Aisha.

Muhammad, which in Arabic means "the praised one," disliked having his followers called Muhammadans. This, he reasoned, made it sound as if he was a supernatural being, like the Christ after whom the Christians had named themselves. Instead, he was but a prophet, like the man Jesus, except that Muhammad preached that he was the last and the greatest of the prophets. Other prophets he recognized were Adam, Abraham, and Moses. The Qur'an, he declared came to him during a vision when a voice said "*Iqra*" (recite), "Recite in the name of your Lord, the Creator, who created man from clots of blood. Recite! Your Lord is the Most Bounteous One, who by the pen has taught mankind things they did not know." When Muhammad awoke, he found the words "inscribed upon his heart" and he recited a series of messages from Allah, the *Qur'an*, in revelations which came to him over a period of twenty-three years. The popular belief in idols he disliked intensely, and he made his followers discard them, preaching, "There is no god but Allah, and Muhammad is His prophet." He disclaimed power to perform miracles but emphasized that he was the messenger of Allah who was sent forth to confirm previous scriptures.

Muhammad specified the exact size of the stick with which a man may beat his wife: It should be no thicker than one man's thumb—contemporary feminists are infuriate by such an idea, however. For his millions of followers, Muhammad is a prophet who saw a vision of one god and one brotherhood of the faith. He courageously attacked evil. He proclaimed his message vigorously. He organized followers into a compact moral force. And they proudly continue the force of his personality. Non-Muslim scholars, however, hold that the Muslims were not much interested in Muhammad at the beginning, that the concept of *sunna* (the right or established way of doings things) began as a general idea.

For example, Ibn Al Rawandi has written (*New Humanist*, February 1995) that there "was the *sunna* of a region, the *sunna* of a group of persons, or the *sunna* of some particular distinguished person such as David or Solomon or the Caliph, even the *sunna* of Allah. It was not until the manufacture of hadiths (prophetic traditions) got under way in the second Islamic century that all these vague notions were absorbed and particularised in the detailed *sunnat-an-nabi* (the *sunna* of the Prophet). . . . In fact, rather than seeking to extract a biography of Muhammad from the Quran on the assumption that it is a record of what he said, it could just as well be argued that there is no necessary connection between Muhammad and the Quran at all. Why could not Muhammad have been simply a military leader of monotheist persuasion, as indicated in the 'Constitution of Medina,' who stirred up the Arab tribes to conquest? Once they had acquired an empire they needed a religion to hold it together and justify their rule. In accordance with the Jewish and Christian models available this meant they needed a 'revelation' and a 'revealer.' Hence the Qur'an and 'the Prophet' were contrived and conjoined," Ibn Al Rawandi argues, "over a period of a couple of centuries." (See entries for Islam, *Qur'an*, and Dostoyevsky's Epilepsy. Three rationalistic studies of Muhammad are by W. M. Watt, *Muhammad at Mecca* [1953]; W. M. Watt, *Muhammad at Medina* [1956]; and *Muhammad and the Origins of Islam* [1994]. A particularly devastating critique of the Muslim religion can be found in a review by Ibn Al-Rawandi of Ibn Warraq's *Why I Am Not A Muslim* in *New Humanist*, December [1995]. For other critics of Muhammad, see the entries for Taslima Nasrin and Anwar Shaikh.) {CE; ER}

Muhammad, Khallid Abdul (20th Century)

In 1993 at Kean College in New Jersey, Muhammad as National Spokesman of the Nation of Islam said (Nat Hentoff, *Village Voice*, 26 November 1996) the following:

- Everybody always talk about what Hitler did to the Jews. But don't nobody ever ask, "What did the Jews do to Hitler?" The Jews had undermined the very fabric of society of that society. The way they do wherever they go.

- Go to the Vatican in Rome where the old, no-good Pope, you know that cracker. Somebody need to raise that dress up and see what's really under there.

- In South Africa, if they don't get out of town by sundown, we kill the white women. We kill the children. We kill the babies. We kill the blind. We kill the cripples. We kill the faggot. We kill the lesbian. We kill 'em all.

"If you say you're white, goddammit I'm against you. If you're a Jew, I'm against you. Whatever the hell you want to call yourself, I'm against you," Muhaddad said in September 1997. During a 1998 "Million Youth March" at which fewer than ten thousand showed up, Muhammad reiterated his outlook: "Stop asking me about the Jews being the bloodsuckers of the black nation. . . . They *are* the bloodsuckers of the black community." A subsequent 1999 "Million Youth March" was attended by even fewer individuals.

Muhammad ibn al Hudail *al Basri* (Died c. 849)

Muhammad was a philosopher of Asia Minor, founder of the Muhammadan Freethinking sect of Mutazilah around 757. {BDF}

Muhrer, John (20th Century)

Muhrer, while a Webster University student, was one of the founding members of Campus Freethought Alliance. {*International Humanist News*, December 1996}

Muhrer, Verle (20th Century)

Muhrer is a professor of philosophy at Penn Valley Community College (Kansas City, Missouri). A humanist activist, he is co-editor with Fred Whitehead of *Freethought on the American Frontier* (1992). Muhrer is a Secular Humanist Mentor of the Council for Secular Humanism and heads the Center for Inquiry–Midwest. (See entry for Missouri Humanists.) {FD}

Muir, John (1838–1914)

An American naturalist born in Scotland, Muir was a conservationist and crusader for national parks and reservations. He traveled, often by foot, throughout the country. The glacier he discovered in Alaska is called Muir glacier. The Muir Woods National Monument is also named for him.

John of the Mountains (1938) describes his scientific naturalism, although he did not use that terminology.

Muirden, Bruce (1928–1991)

In Adelaide, Australia, Muirden edited the quarterly *Australian Humanist* from 1968 to 1975. His *Diggers Who Signed On For More* (1990) is about Australia's part in the wars of intervention. Muirden was a humanist, journalist, author, and political press secretary. He served as Labor press secretary under eight ministers in the Dunstan,

Corcoran, and Bannon governments.

The Puzzled Patriots, which told the story of the Australian First Movement, painted a disquieting picture of what can happen to civil liberties when legal processes are suspended on grounds of "security." {FUK; SWW}

Muirhead, John Henry (1855–1940)

Muirhead was a member of the London Ethical Society and wrote of its founding. However, he belonged rather (like Bosanquet) to the school of Absolute Idealists. His views are chiefly given in his *Philosophy and Life* (1902), *Elements of Ethics* (1910, and *Social Purpose* (1918).

At an Ethical symposium, Muirhead stated, "The claims of priests and Churches to be the depositories and administrators of a system of divinely-given commands are groundless." {TRI; RAT}

Mújica, Armando (20th Century)

Mújica, a Mexican economist, spoke on the subject of a need for a humanistic economics program in Latin America at the Humanist World Congress held in Mexico City in 1996.

Mulder, Liesbeth (20th Century)

Mulder, a music teacher who is professionally active in Dutch Public Education policy initiatives, is acting President of the Dutch Humanist League.

In 1998 she was elected a Vice President of the International Humanist and Ethical Union.

Mullen, Frank (20th Century)

A recording artist who plays with the band Suffocation, Mullen, when asked where he got ideas for his lyrics, responded, "Basically, a lot of it comes from my own thoughts. A lot of it has to do with government, the way we see it. It deals with a lot of stuff that's just the way we see the world and we see what's happening, is where a lot of our lyrics come from. I'm not really satanic, I don't really believe in that. I have my own religious views and stuff, I don't believe in [the various organized religions]. So my religious views are on, I guess, an atheist point." {CA}

Mullen, Shirley Annette (20th Century)

Mullen organized *Freethought* (1987) and was an active freethinker.

Müller, F. Max: See entry for Max Müller, F.

Muller, H. C. (Born 1855)

A Dutch writer, Muller contributed articles to De *Dageraad* (the Daybreak) and taught modern Greek at the University of Amsterdam. {BDF}

Muller, Helen D. (20th Century)

Muller, with Edythe M. McGovern, wrote *They're Never Too Young for Books* (1993).

Muller, Herbert J. (1905–)

When he signed Humanist Manifesto II, Muller was a professor of literature at the University of Indiana. He is author of *Uses of the Past* (1952) and is brother of Hermann Muller. "The First Crusade," he once observed, "set off on its two-thousand-mile jaunt by massacring Jews, plundering and slaughtering all the way from the Rhine to the Jordan. 'In the temple of Solomon,' wrote the ecstatic cleric Raimundus de Agiles, 'one rode in blood up to the knees and even to the horses' bridles, by the just and marvelous judgment of God.' "

Asked specifically for his views concerning humanism, Muller wrote to the present author:

> I am working on a couple of books, one on the subject of Tragedy which may be of some interest in connection with your inquiry about the humanistic implications of literature. But your definition No. 7, naturalistic humanism, fits my position closely enough.

Some of Dr. Muller's other books are *The Spirit of Tragedy* (1956), *Freedom in the Ancient World* (1961), and *Adlai Stevenson: A Study in Values* (1968). {HM2; HNS; TYD; WAS, 23 March 1956}

Muller, Hermann Joseph (1890–1967)

Muller was a Nobel Prize-winning (1946) geneticist at the University of Indiana. He was developer of the theory that genes are life's basis inasmuch as they can replicate as well as any alterations which may arise in them. He wrote the present author concerning humanism,

> The statement of about 1000 words that I gave as President-elect of the American Humanist Association at their annual meeting, on March 10, 1956, in Chicago, represents my viewpoints.

Muller, who wrote more than 350 articles and four books, was president of the American Humanist Association from 1956 to 1958 and was named their Humanist of the Year in 1963. {CE; HNS2; WAS, 25 March 1956}

Muller, Robert (20th Century)

Muller joined the United Nations in 1948 as an intern. He rose through the ranks to become Assistant Secretary General to three Secretaries General. He was one of the main architects of the U. N. institutional system in economics and social fields. Awarded the UNESCO Peace Education Prize in 1989, he currently is Chancellor Emeritus of The University for Peace in Costa Rica, which was created in 1980 by the U.N.

In an interview, Muller stated that "Many world conflicts, even the Middle East conflict, are basically religious conflicts. They are the most difficult to resolve, because all involve fundamentalist believers. They have found the total and absolute truth, and you cannot even discuss any alternatives with them."

But his is a positive humanistic outlook: "The whole biology on this planet—as I see when walking in the woods of Costa Rica—is creation, reproduction, and an incredible diversity that is part of the totality. Unity in diversity is the role of evolution, which we understand as humans, but we must not kill each other in the name of diverse religions, diverse customs, and diverse languages. We must see the planet as our home, and this is another great change in our worldview that is now taking place." {"1995: The United Nations' Year for Tolerance," *Free Inquiry*, Winter 1995-1996}

Mulliam, Tom (20th Century)

Mulliam is co-editor with Ben Price of *Groundswell*, a monthly that supports individual freedoms.

Mullin, Ross (20th Century)

Mullin is a freethinker who writes for *Truth Seeker*.

Mullins, Edwin (1933–)

Mullins, an art critic, became an Honorary Associate of the Rationalist Press Association in 1995. A journalist and filmmaker, he wrote *Songs* (1962), *The Royal Collection* (1993), and a novel, *Angels on the Point of a Pin* (1979).

Mullins, Terry (20th Century)

Mullins was secretary of England's National Secular Society from 1979 until 1996, at which time the position went to Keith Porteous Wood.

MULTICULTURALISM

Individuals who emphasize the importance of multiculturalism do so to call attention to the differing intellectual and artistic activities which otherwise would be overlooked. As Michael Lind of *Harper's* has pointed out, however, "One may debate the definition of Western civilization, but no one can dispute that postclassical Euro-American societies share traditions that they do not share with Middle Eastern, South Asian, African, or East Asian nations. 'Unmasking' and 'deconstructing' all concepts leads to paranoia and solipsism. Societies cannot function without grand narratives any more than individuals can function without memory and foresight." {Michael Lind, "Western Civ Fights Back," *The New York Times*, 6 September 1998}

MUMBAI

Mumbai is the contemporary name of Bombay, the city in India. It was the site of the 1999 International Humanist and Ethical Union Congress.

Mumcu, Ugur (20th Century)

One of Turkey's most respected secular journalists, Mumcu was gunned down in the street because "secularism is now the fanatics' most important target," according to Salman Rushdie in an op-ed article, "The Struggle for the Soul of Islam" in *The New York Times* (11 July 1993). Turkey's Interior Minister reportedly said that at least three other previous killings had been carried out by a group called Islamic Movement whose members have been trained in assassination techniques "at an official Iranian facility between Teheran and Qom." Rushdie added that in July 1993 when thirty-six secularist writers and artists gathered for a conference in the town of Sivas, all were burned to death in their hotel by a mob of Islamic fundamentalists that accused them of being atheists and therefore were deserving of being burned alive.

Mumford, Lewis (1895–1990)

Mumford, a social philosopher and educator at the University of Pennsylvania (1951–1959), wrote *Conditions of Man* (1944) and *Conduct of Life* (1951). Asked about humanism, he responded to the present author:

> The question put to me about humanism is one that I attempted to answer a year or two ago in response to a UNESCO inquiry; but it is a difficult subject to define in a brief manner. Perhaps the negative approach is the most accurate one. Certainly I am not a classical humanist in the original historic sense, for I do not believe that Greece and Rome were the sole repositories of human culture, nor do I believe that the valid insights of Christianity can be left out of a humanist synthesis. Neither am I a humanist in the sense that Paul Elmer More was, because, though he included the insights of oriental philosophy and even religion in his concept of humanism, he treated science with the same contempt that his brethren in the sixteenth century did; whereas science itself, for me, is a human instrument, important for man's further development: In this regard I would depart from Socrates's believe that stars and trees could teach him nothing, and would ally myself with Aristotle's fuller humanism.
>
> Again, my humanism is not theistic in the sense of accepting the sanctions of the church for the goods of humanism: But my humanism does not exclude a concern for a more cosmic order, in which man's existence is a transitory, not a final term; nor does it exclude a concern for those ultimate problems with which religion has dealt. Certain, I would reject Sartre's atheistic humanism, as I reject his existentialism: For me existentialism is a form of philosophic illiteracy, just as, existentially speaking, it is a final step in the devaluation and degradation of man. To call it humanism is like calling absolutism democracy.
>
> These negatives would seem to put me, by exclusion, among the naturalistic humanists: Yet I do not find that classification altogether satisfactory; for thinkers like Dewey give the scientific and objective view of life exclusive validity; and disparage other modes of apprehension and intuition, overlooking or misinterpreting the subjective roles of language, art, and dream. For this reason, I have sometimes used the adjective "organic" to describe my effort to embrace every kind of existence, cosmic, mechanical, biological, social, personal, and divine.
>
> What this means concretely is demonstrated partly in *The Condition of Man*; but the volume that will follow it, *The Conduct of Life* (Autumn 1951), will bring out my conception of humanism even more fully. Perhaps holistic humanism would be a better description of my brand: Yet there is such an accretion of meanings around the very word humanism, it is so encrusted with barnacles, that I would gladly drop it altogether if one could find a more adequate term. . . . I have a philosophic reason for keeping aloof. You will find it, should you be curious, in *The Conduct of Life*, in the section of "The Fallacy of Systems."

(See entry for James T. Farrell.)
{WAS, 27 March 1949, 15 February 1951, and 28 April 1956}

Mumford, Stephen D. (20th Century)

Mumford, president of the Center for Research on Population and Security, wrote *The Pope and the New Apocalypse: The Holy War Against Family Planning* (1986). He has been a frequent speaker at humanist meetings, at which he describes the relationship between world population growth and national and global security. Mumford was a participant at the 3rd Annual Atheist Alliance Convention. {HNS2}

Münch, Friedrich (1799–1881)

A rationalist, writer of the first book on American grape varieties, an abolitionist, and an elected state senator, Münch was known as a liberal in religion. Theodore Parker published his *Treatise on Religion and Christianity* (1847), which shows his having been influenced by German "higher criticism." Excerpts from his work, including a photograph, can be found in Whitehead and Muhrer's *Freethought on the American Frontier*. The authors conclude that basically Münch was a theist. A part of "*Wer ist ein Freidenker?* (Who is a Freethinker?)," taken from his *Gesammelte Schriften*, is quoted in *Freethought History* (#7, 1993).

Munday, Diane (20th Century)

For thirty years, Munday has been a leading campaigner in Britain for a woman's right to choose an abortion. During that time, she writes, "the rationalist and humanist movement has been steadfast in its support for legal abortion, whilst individual humanists and rationalists have played predominant roles. I believe that while there is a Roman Catholic Church there will be an aggressive anti-abortion movement. I hope that humanists will continue to oppose it with vigour and rational argument for as long as is necessary." (*New Humanist*, October, 1990).

Munsch, Robert (20th Century)

Munsch, a Unitarian, has written children's books including *Alligator Baby*, *Stepheanie's Pony Tail*, *Paper Bag Princess*, and *Love You Forever*. Web: <http://bookzone.scholastic.ca/fauthor_musch.html>. {CA}

Münsterberg, Hugo (1863–1916)

Münsterberg was an American psychologist who was director of the psychological laboratories at Harvard University. He resigned in 1914, when a wealthy American offered $10,000,000 to the university if it would dismiss him (for defending German's action in the War). Münsterberg disdainfully rejected the idea of *personal* immortality and thought it could be desirable "only to a cheap curiosity," but contended for "eternal life" in a vague, impersonal sense. {RAT}

Munullog (19th Century)

Munullog in Manchester, England, wrote *Hymns and Songs for the Church of Man* (1890). {GS}

Murad, Ferid (1936–)

A physician, Murad co-edited *The Pharmacological Basis of Therapeutics* (1985). He is a teacher in the University of Texas Medical School's Department of Integrative biology, Pharmacology, and Physiology. In 1998, with Robert F. Furchgott and Louis J.

Ignarro, Murad won the Nobel Prize in Physiology or Medicine. They shared the prize for discovering the role of nitric oxide as a signaling molecule in the cardiovascular system—their work paved the way for several medical breakthroughs, including the anti-impotence drug Viagra. Murad signed Humanist Manifesto 2000.

Murchison, Roderick Impey [Sir] (1792–1871)

A famed British geologist, Murchison served in the Napoléonic wars but after the peace turned his attention to science. He established the Silurian as a new geologic system and, with Adam Sedgwick, collaborated on the establishment of the Devonian system. Murchison also defined and named the Permian Period. In 1855 he was appointed director general of the Geological Survey of Great Britain. When Murchison was near the end of his life, a fellow geologist said he hoped that God would give him back his Christian faith and hope. Sir Roderick had long been known for his heresies, and he did nothing to satisfy his friend's hopes. {JM; RAT; RE}

Murdoch, (Jean) Iris [Dame] (1919–1999)

Murdoch, a member of the Irish Academy, was a novelist and a philosopher. Her novels have been described as "subtle, witty, convoluted, puzzling, and often wildly comic," in which she views man "as an 'accidental' creature thinking of himself as free but actually constricted by the boundaries of self, society, and the natural world." Her works often show an individual's finding that he lacks freedom as well as the lack of capacity for self-knowledge. Among her writings are *The Flight from the Enchanter* (1956), *An Accidental Man* (1972), *The Sacred and the Love Machine* (1974), and *Nuns and Soldiers* (1980). In *Metaphysics as a Guide to Morals* (1992), she develops her version of Platonism, stating that mankind has imperfect apprehensions concerning morality, apprehensions which we can never fully understand. In her view, Christianity needed to be demythologized, that its claims concerning incarnation and divine existence are philosophically incredible. We may need the idea of the Good for the moral life, but do we need any ontological proof of the existence of God? The figure of Christ may be religiously significant, but can Jesus, like Gautama, be both real and mystical without the old god-man mythology? Murdoch was influenced by the German phenomenologist Edmund Husserl as well as Husserl's Zen Buddhist critic Katsuki Sekida. She found fault with much in Wittgenstein's thought, preferring the dualism she has modified from the thinking of Plato and Schopenhauer.

One of her concerns, reported *New Economist* (25 Sep 1993), "has been religion and its role in the modern world. She herself does not believe in God and, in the specific case of Christianity of the more orthodox sort, has a problem with the picture of God as a person up in Heaven, and Christ as his son, a magical, spiritual being. But she thinks that the maintenance of religion is essential; that it must be preserved. She notes that many are comforted by the belief that they will meet their loved ones after death but, in her opinion, such beliefs are, literally considered untrue." Buddhists and Hindus do not have this problem, she noted, for what matters to Gautama is a "mystical" matter, mystical not as something magic but what Meister Eckhart taught, that what matters is the soul, the spirit, and what is meant by these. An Anglican who became a Marxist then a non-Marxist, Murdoch has written that although philosophy is not itself religion it can teach people much about religion: "To lose Christianity would be a most terrible thing. The figure of Christ is so compelling. That is what we're so lucky to have, as it were. . . . I daresay anything can be made holy by being sincerely worshipped."

In a review of her *Metaphysics as a Guide to Morals*, Peter Heales in *New Humanist* concluded that "we shall delude ourselves if we look here for the philosopher's stone. Perhaps the most rational response would be a 'flight from the enchantress.' "

Colin McCall, in *Freethinker*, June 1996), noted Murdoch had been included in *Women Philosophers* (1996) but, added, "I certainly cannot go along with Iris Murdoch in her belief in transcendent 'beauty.' The statue is broken, the flower fades, the experience ceases,' she says, 'but something has not suffered from decay and mortality.' " According to Jim Herrick, Murdoch once declined being a vice-president of the Gay and Lesbian Humanist Association because she did not share what she felt was the "anti-religion" in some humanistic outlooks. She had, in fact, once described herself as being a Christian Buddhist.

In 1987 she was made a Dame of the Order of the British Empire. In 1997, her husband, Prof. John Bayley, reported that his wife was suffering from Alzheimer's disease. As her death approached, Bayley wrote *Iris: A Memoir of Iris Murdoch* (1998), in which he describes his attempt to understand his wife's physical condition. She had told a friend that she was "sailing into the darkness," but of their last years together, he wrote that "we are physically closer. . . . She is not sailing into the dark. The voyage is over, and under the dark escort of Alzheimer's, she has arrived somewhere. So have I." {CE; TRI; TYD}

Murdoch, Marion (1850–1943)

The first woman to receive a Bachelor of Divinity degree from Meadville Theological School, Murdoch was a key member of the Iowa Sisterhood. With her life partner, Florence Buck, she served as a co-pastor of Unitarian churches.

In 1893, she was a featured speaker at the World's Parliament of Religions, where she recommended the ministry as an appropriate profession for women.

Murger, Henri (1822–1861)

A French author, Murger contributed poems and dramas to the *Revue des Deux Mondes*. In the poem "*Le Testament*," he states in answer to an inquiring priest, "*Reponds lui que j'ai lu Voltaire*" (Tell him I have read Voltaire). Murger's most popular work was *Scenes of Bohemian Life*. {BDF; RAT}

Murillo, Bartolomé (1617?–1682)

Murillo, a famous Spanish religious and portrait painter, once incurred the wrath of the Spanish Inquisition. He had followed the generally accepted rules for Christian art: The Virgin Mary must be on the right of the cross, St. John on the left; God, Jesus, angels, and the apostles could be shown with bare feet; but the feet of the saints and of the Virgin Mary could not be shown bare. Murillo was condemned by the Inquisition for having painted one scene "suggesting that the Madonna had toes." He escaped serious punishment, but in Cádiz while working on "The Marriage of St. Catherine" for the Capuchin church, he fell from a scaffold and died as a result of his injuries. {CE}

Murphy, Audie (1924-1971)

Murphy, the most celebrated, most decorated soldier of World War II, was not known to believe in the supernatural nor in an afterlife. He killed some 240 German and Italian soldiers and was awarded numerous medals including the Medal of Honor. His will provided that there be "no funeral service and only my sons in attendance at my burial at the graveside of my family plot at Forest Lawn Cemetery. If Pamela is then my wife, she shall also be present." He wanted only a medium-priced funeral and a "simple, plain and ordinary burial ceremony." The memorial in Los Angeles was attended by six other Medal of Honor winners and over six hundred people, after which the body was flown to Arlington National Cemetery in Virginia. There, he was buried with full military honors, with then U. S. Ambassador to the United Nations George Bush in attendance. So much for wills!

Murphy, Howard A.: See entry for Theism.

Murphy, John Patrick Michael (20th Century)

A Colorado activist and freethinker, Murphy is an attorney and member of the Freedom From Religion Foundation, Inc. He has appeared on various news programs to argue his tax-the-church initiative and was a participant at the 3rd Annual Atheist Alliance Convention. "Hitler Was *Not* an Atheist," Murphy's article in *Free Inquiry* (Spring 1999), confirms that Hitler was a member in good standing of the Church of Rome, his troops were often sprinkled with holy water by the priests, he liked corporeal punishment in home and school, he openly despised homosexuality and criminalized it and, "if past is prologue, we know what to expect if liberty becomes license" and political and ecclesiastical authority figures take over.

Murphy, Lionel Keith (1922–1986)

The Honorable Mr. Justice Lionel Murphy was Justice of the Australian High Court. He was a delegate in 1968 to the UN Conference on Human Rights in Teheran. As Attorney-General in the Whitlam government, he was responsible for reform of divorce law, trade practices, legal aid, and racial discrimination. He had been a Senator until his resignation in 1975 to become High Court Judge. In 1983 he received the Humanist of the Year Award. {SWW}

Murphy, Robin (20th Century)

Murphy has been on the editorial committee of *Humanist in Canada*.

Murray, (George) Gilbert (Aimé) (1866–1957)

Murray, the Australian-born British classical scholar, is best known as a Greek scholar, a translator of Greek drama. He wrote *The Rise of the Greek Epic* (1907) and *Hellenism and the Modern World* (1953). McCabe describ ed Murray as being one of the chief "appeasers" in British public life and, as such, not only never attacked the churches but at times appeared to be against freethinkers. But in an address to the Classical Association, he once confessed that he was an agnostic. To the present writer, Murray wrote concerning humanism,

> My secretary, who misdirected my other letter to you, has now left, so I cannot repeat it. What I must have said, in general, is not to make any such elaborate distinctions between the different kinds of humanism, but one great distinction between that which man can know and what he cannot know; let him act according to his knowledge, but I would say not quite neglect certain things to which he is sensible but cannot at present have certain knowledge.
>
> Practically, this puts me on much the same level as Julian Huxley, but with more emphasis on the higher nature of man in regions where the mere animal does not reach.

According to Hector Hawton, Murray preferred the term "Freethinker" to either "Humanist" or "Rationalist." {CE; CL; HNS; HNS2; JM; RAT; RE; TRI; WAS, 19 August 1956}

Murray, John (1741–1815)

The Universalist movement in America began when John Murray's boat from England ran aground in 1770 at Cranberry Inlet, New Jersey. He had been brought up as a strict Calvinist, but the influence of John Wesley relieved that fear in some respects. It was his reading of James Reilly's *Union* (1759) which greatly influenced him, for Reilly argued that all humanity actually achieved union with Christ in his death and therefore had already paid the price for sin. Espousing such an outlook, he was ostracized and had other tragedies in his life. He lost his child as well as his wife; was beset by economic difficulties; served time in debtor's prison; and resolved the problems by moving to America. While preaching, he endured persecution: rotten eggs and stones were hurled at him. In Boston, he picked up one such stone and remarked, "This argument is solid and weighty, but it is neither rational nor convincing." In 1775, he was chaplain in the American Revolutionary army. In 1788 he married Judith Sargent Stevens (Murray), the widowed daughter of Winthrop Sargent, whose literary career complemented Murray's religious work. In 1779 he formed the Gloucester Universalist Church with Sargent's help. Objecting to the payment of taxes to support the Congregational church in their area, his group won in a landmark case their right to support the church of their choice. As such, the Universalists helped to move American society away from enforced religious obligations. In 1793, he moved to the Boston Universalist Society. (See entry for Caleb Rich.) {CE; EU, Paul H. Beattie; FUS; U; U&U; UU}

Murray, Jon Garth (1954–1996?)

Murray was managing editor of *American Atheist*, the magazine once edited by Madalyn Murray O'Hair. He became President of American Atheists. However, according to David Travis, an editorial, financial, and clerical worker who ended his association with the O'Hair group in 1995, Jon did not "even know when to be polite." Travis called him a "screaming madman running around the office, shouting obscenities about everyone and everything." Scott Kerns, another member, lamented that Jon "had no special training, nor a great number of social skills, as well as a speech impediment. He was at an extreme disadvantage, and he was aware that he'd been put in a position beyond his abilities to handle." Allegedly, Murray alienated many atheist chapters so badly that they seceded, and those which did not were dissolved by 1991.

Murray disappeared, along with his mother and sister Robin, in 1996. Although his body had not been found as of the end of 1999, the FBI was investigating whether David Waters and Gary Karr had anything to do with the disappearances. (See entries for Robin Murray-O'Hair and Madalyn O'Hair.) {*Time*, 20 February 1997}

Murray, Judith Sargent Stevens (1751–1820)

Wife of John Murray, the founder of American Universalism, Judith Murray was the first native-born woman dramatist to have her plays professionally performed. Also, she was among the first to have published statements on women's rights in the United States, for she wrote "On the Equality of the Sexes (1790). Daughter of the prominent Gloucester sea captain Winthrop Sargent, she wrote *The Gleaner* (3 volumes, 1798), a series of her essays, plays, and poems. That publication was subscribed to by George and Martha Washington. Murray's pseudonym was Constantia. {U; U&U}

Murray, Norman (20th Century)

In Montreal, Murray wrote a freethought work, *Eye-Opener* (19–?). {GS}

Murray, Orson S. (19th Century)

In Fruit Hills, Ohio, Murray from 1844 to 1848 edited *Regenerator*.

Murray-O'Hair, Robin (1965–1996?)

The adopted granddaughter of Madalyn O'Hair, Robin Murray-O'Hair succeeded her mother as editor of *American Atheist*. In 1995, she along with her Uncle Jon and Madalyn mysteriously disappeared. Although assumed to have been killed, Robin had not been found as of the end of 1999. (See entries for Robin Murray-O'Hair and Madalyn O'Hair.)

Murray, William J. Jr. (20th Century)

A wealthy Roman Catholic and an Eighth Army officer, Murray met Madalyn Murray O'Hair during World War II. He refused to admit paternity of her son, William J. III., and refused to divorce his wife. {*Vanity Fair*, March 1997}

Murray, William J. III (1946–)

Murray, with his mother Madalyn Murray O'Hair, joined Lewis Schempp in the lawsuit against the School District of Abington, Pennsylvania. They took the case all the way to the

Supreme Court and won a 1963 ruling that the Bible could not be read aloud nor could the Lord's Prayer be allowed in a public school inasmuch as this constituted a religious exercise and was unconstitutional under the First and Fourteenth Amendments. He later became a born-again Christian, runs a Texas ministry called the William Murray Faith Foundation, and wrote *My Life Without God* (1982)

Murry, John Middleton (1889–1957)

Murry, husband of Katherine Mansfield and friend of the D. H. Lawrences, edited the *Athenaeum* (1919–1921). He published Virginia Woolf, T. S. Eliot, Paul Vallѐry, and other important writers.

Murry wrote critical works of Dostoevsky, Keats, Shakespeare, D. H. Lawrence, establishing himself as a well-known critic. He and Lawrence were interested in pacifism and in planning a Utopian community called "Rananim." (See entry for G. K. Chesterton, who wrote humorously about Murry's atheism.)

MUSIC

The first heartbeats when we are in the womb introduce us to musical rhythm. Later, we distinguish sounds, melody, harmony, and timbre, utilizing mathematics to help notate our feelings and moods, not our thoughts. Those not in the cognoscenti, however, think music can connote thoughts.

MUSIC, FREETHOUGHT AND HUMANIST: See entries for Andrew Charles and The Residents.

MUSIC OF THE SPHERES

The ancient Greeks believed that the music of the spheres—a beautiful sound, inaudible to the human ear—was made by the stars and planets as they moved through the heavens. The "spheres" were not the planets themselves, but invisible globes to which the planets were believed to be attached. (See entry for Ptolemaic Universe.)

Musil, Robert Elder von (1880–1942)

Musil's *The Man Without Qualities* (1953–1960) has been described as satirical, expressionistic, and the last work of the classical tradition. Critic George Steiner places the German Musil and the French Proust on the same profound level, adding that Musil was a highly trained and qualified mechanical engineer with a keen grasp of mathematics and mathematical logic.

Musil, whose wife was Jewish, was particularly interested in philosophy. He did not, however, argue by precept or example for the radical unison of the philosophical and the poetic.

Steiner suggests that "qualities" is not the best translation of Musil's best work. A more exact title, he explains, would be *The Man Whose "I" Is in Search of His "Me."*

MUSLIM: See entry for Islam. Note that *Muslim* is not interchangeable with *Arab* or *Arabian*: not all Muslims are Arab, and not all Arabs are Muslim. For critics of the Muslim religion, see entries for Taslima Nasrin, Anwar Shaikh, and Ibn Warraq. For an estimate of the number of Muslims worldwide, see entry for Hell.

MUSLIM GAYS

Following is a 1999 Reuters report from Istanbul, Turkey:

> Turkish men: macho, Muslim, and mustachioed. But behind the oh-so-masculine facade thrives a tradition of cross-dressing and homosexuality that harks back to Ottoman times.
>
> Switch on a Turkish television set and videos of girlish male pop singers in full makeup and flamboyant clothes top the local charts. A popular talk show is hosted by the Irritable Virgin, a loud-mouthed man with a penchant for blonde wigs and sequined dresses.
>
> And the country's best-loved classical music diva, Bulent Ersoy, is a voluptuous transsexual whose recent marriage to a man caused a stir more because the groom was half her age than for other lurid details.
>
> To even the most casual observer, gender-bending and gayness are an open secret in this predominantly Muslim society. But talking about it is strictly taboo, so even though everyone knows otherwise closeted male pop stars appear in the tabloids with female models on their arms.
>
> ``There is this silent consensus: you can be gay as long as you don't come out and give it a name," columnist and cultural commentator Perihan Magden said.
>
> It was not always so. The Ottoman Empire was renowned for liberal sexual practices including transvestite dancers and infamous harems often housed young boys as well as women.
>
> "In the Ottoman Empire everything was completely in the open. It was the Tanzimat (Westernization process) in the 19th century that changed all that," historian Murat Bardakci said.

The first international conference of gay Muslims was held in New York City, May 1999, by Al-Fatiha Foundation (405 Park Avenue, Suite 1500, New York, NY 10022). That foundation was formed in 1997 by Faisal Alam, who admitted that he had not fully reconciled his sexuality and his faith. "But when you face God and the Prophet on the day of judgment, the first question he'll ask is not whether you are gay or how many sex partners you had, but did you believe in me?" Alam rationalized. The sixty or so attendees included blond-haired and blue-eyed European Americans as well as olive-skinned Americans and Europeans of Arab and South Asian descent.

In addition to the references in the Qur'an about Lut (Lot), hadith (sayings attributed to the Prophet Muhammad) such as the following are problems for gay Muslims who are literalistic:

- When a man mounts another man, the throne of God shakes.
- Kill the one that is doing it [having intercourse] and also kill the one that it is being done to.
- Cursed are those men who wear women's clothing and those women who wear men's clothing.

However, no record appears to exist that in the Prophet's time anyone was executed for same-sex acts. The third Caliph, Omar, ordered a homosexual man to be burned alive. According to Alam, the Hanafite school (predominant in South Asia and Eastern Asia today) maintains that same-gender sex does not merit any physical punishment. The Hanabalities (predominant in the Arab world) believe, however, that sex between males must be punished severely. The Sha'fi school (also predominant in the Arab world) argues that punishment for sodomy can only be carried out if there are four adult male witnesses who actually see the penetration "as though the key is going into the key hole." The Ismaili sect (also known as the Agha Khani movement, with a population of approximately two million) believes Islam is a continuously evolving faith that must be reinterpreted to adapt to modern-day society and culture.

The Prince Agha Khan, thought to be a direct descendent of the Prophet Muhammad, was thought to have been open to dialogue and communication with progressive movements within Islam.

Nevertheless, it is widely held that Muslims who are Western-style homosexuals will *never* be allowed to enter Paradise. {WAS, conversations with Faisal Alam, a Pakastini Muslim, and Ibn Warraq, author of *Why I Am Not A Muslim*.}

MUSLIM RELIGION, CRITICISM OF

Ibn Warraq's *Why I Am Not A Muslim* (1995) discusses the totalitarian nature of Islam and its law, Islamic colonialism, how Islam treats heretics and freethinkers, the status of women, the undemocratic pressures applied by Islamic immigrants in the West, and its taboos (wine, pork, and homosexuality). G. A. Wells, professor of German at the University of London, has praised the book not only for being "courageous" but also for scrutinizing the fundamental tenets of Islam so uncompromisingly.

Religion, Warraq found, "is largely a reshuffling of ideas of a yesterday, and to this Islam is no exception. It has taken a great deal from both Jewish and Christian traditions, but I doubt whether many Christians are aware of in what strange guise Christianity figures in the Qur'an. According to Sura 4, Jesus was not crucified: the Jews '[k]illed him not, they did not crucify him, but it was made to appear that way to them.' This strikes at the heart of what is now established as Christian doctrine. If there was no atoning death, there is no redemption, through such a death." What is in the Qur'an about Christianity, Warraq claims, "derives from heretical sects." The Qur'an looks more authentic than the Gospels, Wells noted, "in that its author works no miracles and makes no claim to divinity. . . . Also, there are so many variant readings that it is misleading to speak of the Koran: 'The definitive text still had not been achieved as late as the ninth century."

Islam never really encouraged science, if by science is meant "disinterested inquiry," according to Warraq. What Islam means by "knowledge" is religious knowledge, for all other knowledge is dangerous to the faith. Whatever real science occurred under Islam occurred despite, not because of, the religion. Further, he holds, the Muslim world has been indebted from the beginning to the Greeks and is indebted now to science for understanding its own intellectual and cultural history.

Warraq concludes that he is "convinced that despite all the shortcomings of Western liberal democracy, it is far preferable to the authoritarian, mind-numbing certitudes of Islamic theocracy." Few other works have dared touch such subjects, and like Salmon Rushdie he is afraid to reveal his exact whereabouts for fear of being assassinated.

Various intellectuals are concerned that within a few decades Muslim authoritarianism will have become so widespread that opposition will form and that "crusades" against Islam will result in the loss of enormous amounts of human lives. (See entries for Anwar Shaikh and Ibn Warraq.)

MUSLIM WOMEN, PLIGHT OF

Muslim heterosexual men read in the Qur'an (II.223), "Your wives are a tilth for you, so go into your tilth when you like." A man's wife's vagina, in short, is solely his to cultivate, and it is her duty to satisfy his sexual needs. (See entries for Homosexuals, Muslim, and Homa Darabi.)

MUSLIMS IN AMERICA

The first Muslims in America who were black were brought in slave ships. Approximately a fifth of the slaves brought to America from West Africa were Muslims. Some black Muslims say that "Islam is part of the genetic memory of blacks."

Diana Eck, a teacher of comparaative religion at Harvard University, points out that in 1998 there are more Muslims than Episcopalians in the United States and more Buddhist temples in suburban backyards than is generally realized.

It is estimated that by the year 2016 Muslims will overtake Jews as America's largest religious minority. {*The Economist*, 24 August 1996}

MUSLIMS, BLACK

Wali Farad, whom his followers believed was "Allah in person," founded the Black Muslim group in Detroit in 1930. When he mysteriously disappeared in 1934, Elijah Muhammad assumed leadership and preached, in addition to the Qur'an's teachings, that white men are devils and that blacks are God's chosen people. Upon his death his son, Wallace D. Muhammad became the leader. In 1976 a group led by Louis Farrakhan split off from Wallace D. Muhammad's group. One of the better-known ministers was Malcolm X. Moderates stress the Islamic principles of universal brotherhood and social justice. {CE}

MUSLIMS, NON—IN MUSLIM COUNTRIES: See entry for Bat Yóer.

Musset, Charles Alfred de (1810–1857)

A French romantic poet, whose infatuation with George Sand also resulted in disillusionment, Musset was published first in *Revue des Deux Mondes. Confession d'un enfant du siècle* (1836) is an account of his affair with Sand and reflects the disillusioned mood of many of his contemporaries. According to Robertson, Musset like Béranger was a rationalist. In 1853, Musset was admitted into the Academy.

McCabe says of Musset, "His early poems are full of skepticism, but after his rupture with George Sand he fell into a morbid state and wrote a religious book. In his later work he returned to his first position—a non-Christian theist with no belief in immortality. His art was exquisite but his character weak, and he vacillated as poets so often do." {BDF; CE; JM; JMR}

Musset, Louis Charles Alfred de (1810–1857)

A French poet and dramatist, Musset completed a free translation of De Quincey's *Opium Eater* (1828). His career as a littérateur was interrupted by his painful liaison with George Sand, with whom he was infatuated but who did not return his affection. Musset's work is known for its melancholy and anxiety, which was known as the *mal du siècle*. His *Espoir en Dieu* shows what Lanson has termed its "banal religiosity." McCabe states that Musset was plainly agnostic as to a future life and was far removed from Christian doctrines, though always a theist. {RAT}

Mussolini, Benito [Il Duce] (1883–1945)

Mussolini, who was a freethinker and a socialist before becoming Italy's fascist dictator during the Second World War, had the following observations concerning religion:

• Religion is a species of mental disease. It has always had a pathological reaction on mankind.

• The God of the theologians is the creation of their empty heads.

• The history of the saints is mainly the history of insane people.

• When we claim that "God does not exist," we mean to deny by this declaration the personal God of theology, the God worshiped in various ways and diverse modes by believers the world over . . . that God of absurd attributes who is an affront to human reason.

• Science is now in the process of destroying religious dogma. The dogma of the divine creation is recognized as absurd.

• Religious morality shows the original stigmata of authoritarianism precisely because it pretends to be the revelation of divine authority. In order to translate this authoritarianism into action and impose it upon humanity, the priestly caste of revealers has sprung up and with it the most atrocious intolerance.

The king dismissed Mussolini when the Allies invaded the mainland, leading to a rebellion within Mussolini's Fascist Party. Both Mussolini and Hitler had at one time used "new humanism" as descriptions of their views, to the embarrassment of many humanists.

The Germans made him a puppet ruler in Northern Italy, but upon the German collapse Mussolini was captured by Italian partisans, summarily tried, and executed. The remains were finally buried in 1957, at the San Cassiano Cemetery, Predappio, Italy. He first had been buried in a Capuchin monastery cemetery in Cerro Maggiore. {PCE; TYD}

Muzzey, David Saville (1870–1965)

Muzzey was a Yankee seminarian turned American historian, who taught part time at Columbia University and Barnard. His textbooks have been widely used throughout the nation. Muzzey joined the Ethical Culture Society Leadership in 1898, serving for the long period to 1965. His works include *Life of Thomas Jefferson* (1918) and *Ethics as a Religion* (1951). Muzzey's *Political Idol of Other Days* (1939) received an honorable mention by the Pulitzer Prize committee. {EU, Howard B. Radest}

Myers, Francis (20th Century)

A member of the department of philosophy at the University of Denver, Myers in the 1950s was an associate editor of *The Humanist*. He wrote "Comments on George Axtelle's 'John Dewey's Concept of the Religious' " in *Religious Humanism* (Summer 1967). {HNS}

Myers, Lonny (20th Century)

In 1999 the American Humanist Association made Myers its Humanist Distinguished Service Awardee. An activist in the fields of human sexuality and sexually transmitted disease, she is a staunch defender of abortion rights. Also, she works to educate people about the dangers of sexually transmitted diseases (particularly in regards to women and infants), teaches medical assistants, and actively tries to eradicate the practice of female genital mutilation in the United States and elsewhere. {*The Humanist*, March-April 1999}

Myers, William (20th Century)

Dr. Myers, a Florida anesthesiologist, is a member of the board of Freethinkers, Inc.

Myler, Harley (1953–)

Myler, who is a professor of electrical and computer engineering at the University of Central Florida, is secretary in Winter Park, Florida, of Freethinkers, Inc. He has also taught at Florida Institute of Technology and New Mexico State University in addition to having had industrial experience with General Instrument Corporation and with the US Army Air Defense Artillery as missile systems officer. In addition to writing over thirty technical articles, he is author (with A. R. Weeks) of *Computing Imaging Recipes in C* (1993) and *The Pocket Handbook of Image Processing Algorithms in C* (1993).

Myler, Robert J. (20th Century)

When he signed Humanist Manifesto II, Myler was title officer of Title Insurance & Trust Company. {HM2}

Myrdal, Gunnar (1898–1987)

An eminent Swedish economist, Myrdal was a public official and a sociologist. His *Crisis in the Population Question* (1934), written with his wife, Alva, stimulated general welfare measures, and he headed Carnegie Corporation of America from 1938–1942, writing an exhaustively detailed study of African Americans in a book entitled *An American Dilemma* (1944). When he signed Humanist Manifesto II, he was a professor at the University of Stockholm, Sweden. Myrdal was considered the foremost expert on the Swedish economy. {HM2; CE}

MYSTERY AND MYSTERIES

• Three great mysteries there are in the lives of mortal beings: the mystery of birth at the beginning; the mystery of death at the end; and, greater than either, the mystery of love. Everything that is most precious in life is a form of love. Art is a form of love, if it be noble; labor is a form of love, if it be worthy, thought is a form of love, if it be inspired.

Supreme Court Justice Benjamin Nathan Cardozo,
at a 1931 wedding at which he officiated

As explained in *The Columbia Encyclopedia*, secret cults existed in Greek and Roman religion: "The conventional religions of both Greeks and Romans were alike in consisting principally of propitiation and prayers for the good of the city-state, the tribe, or the family, and only secondarily of the person. Individuals sought a more emotional religion that would fulfill their desires for personal salvation and immortality. Secret societies were formed, usually headed by a priest or a hierophant.

By the 5th cent. B.C. mysteries were an important part of the fabric of Hellenic life. Although the mystic rites were kept secret, it was known that they required elaborate initiations, including purification rites, beholding sacred objects, accepting occult knowledge, and acting out a sacred drama. . . . The most important mystery cults in Greece were the Eluesinian, the Orphic, and the Andanian. Since the mystery deities were associated primarily with fertility, many scholars believe that these cults were based on unrecorded primitive fertility rites. The popularity of mystery cults spread in the Hellenistic age and still more widely in Roman times."

The mystery—also called miracle—play was a form of medieval drama, one that started in the 10th century by dramatizing the liturgy of the Roman

Catholic Church. It reached its height in the 15th century. One problem, the church found, was that too much of the play was devoted to dramatizing the tantalizing sinning, too little at the very end to resolving the sin.

Mystery—detective—stories involve solutions to crimes based upon the logical interpretation of the evidence presented. Although Aesop's fables, Chaucer's *Canterbury Tales*, and the Apocrypha contain elements of mystery stories, Edgar Allan Poe's "The Murders in the Rue Morgue" and his other "tales of ratiocination" involving the chevalier C. Auguste Dupin started the present genre. Other writers have been Wilkie Collins, Charles Dickens, and Arthur Conan Doyle. When Doyle was sent to a Roman Catholic public school, he became revulsed by Christianity, according to Christopher Hitchens (*The New York Review of Books*, 4 November 1999). But later in life Doyle turned to spiritualism.

MYSTICISM

• Mysticism is not religion, but a religious disease.

–George Santayana

Mysticism is the practice of putting oneself into, and remaining in, direct relation with God, the Absolute, or any unifying principle of life. Christian mystics are numerous: Clement of Alexandria; Origen; St. Augustine; Cassian; St. Gregory I; Erigena; St. Peter Damian; St. Anselm; St. Bernard of Clairvaux . . . and the *Columbia Encyclopedia* lists many others, including Swedenborg. Books on the topic include William James's *The Varieties of Religious Experience* (1902); Friedrich von Hügel's *The Mystical Element of Religion* (1923); and Henri Bergson's *The Two Sources of Religion and Morality* (1935). There are no known freethinker-mystics.

Bertrand Russell has noted that mystics have conceived of numbers as "God's thoughts," that mathematics is "the chief source of the belief in eternal and exact truth, as well as in a supersensible intelligible world." But Lord Russell has no interest in mysticism nor in "intuition," which he said Bergson had raised

> to the position of sole arbiter of metaphysical truth. But in fact, the opposite of instinct and reason is mainly illusory. Instinct, intuition, or insight is what first leads to the beliefs which subsequent reason confirms or confutes; but the confirmation, where it is possible, consists, in the last analysis, of agreement with other beliefs no less instinctive. Reason is a harmonizing, controlling force rather than a creative one. Even in the most purely logical realms, it is insight that first arrives at what is new.

(See the *Encyclopedia of Philosophy*, Vol. 5, for the history, nature, and assessment of mysticism.) {CE; ER}

MYTHOLOGY

• Mythology, n. The body of a primitive people's beliefs concerning its origin, early history, heroes, deities, and so forth, as distinguished from the true accounts which it invents later.

–Ambrose Bierce
The Devil's Dictionary

• Mythology is what grown-ups believe; folk-lore is what they tell their children; and religion is both.

–Cedric Whitman

• History is facts which become lies in the end; legends are lies which become history in the end.

–Jean Cocteau

MYTHS

• Why do we continue to find myths so fascinating? The ascendancy of science and the triumphs of modern Western thought leave a large gap, an unsatisfied need, which we attempt to meet with beliefs of very different kinds and very different origins. The Hubble telescope has not killed astrology; antibiotics have to contend with herbal remedies and acupuncture; men and women are still carried off by mysterious creatures from other worlds (though nowadays in interplanetary flying machines rather than in fiery chariots) and return after undergoing experiences which ordinary language is powerless to convey. And the study of myth flourishes as never before. The word "Western," of course, gives a clue. We enjoy the practical benefits of those triumphs, but we flinch from the triumphalism—rational, patriarchal, colonialist—that often accompanies them, and we hope that comfort and meaning can be found in the very different wisdom of other times and other places.

—Jasper Griffin,
"The Myth of Myths,"
The New York Review of Books, 4 November 1999

MYTHS, SCIENTIFIC: See entry for Science, Myths of.

Naber, Samuel Adriaan (Born 1828)

Naber, a learnèd Dutch writer, became rector of the Haarlem gymnasium and head teacher at the Amsterdam Athenaeum. With Dr. A. Pierson of Verisimilia, he wrote a Latin work showing the fragmentary and disjointed character of the Epistles attributed to Paul. {BDF}

j

NACH: See entry for the North American Committee for Humanism.

NACH NEWSLETTER

A publication three times per year of the North American Committee for Humanism, *Nach Newsletter* is at Box 191, 5901-J, Wyoming NE, Albuquerque, New Mexico 87109.

Nachtigal, Gustav (1834–1885)

Nachtigal, a German traveler who became private physician to the Bey of Tunis, explored North Africa and wrote *Sakara und Sudan*. A freethinker, Nachtigal became German Consul General at Tunis. {BDF}

Naczelna, Rada (20th Century)

Naczelna is associated with Wspolnota Unitarian Universalistow w Rzeczypospolitej Polskiej. (See entry for Polish Unitarians.)

Naden, Constance Caroline Woodhill (1858–1889)

Naden was a follower of Hinton's pantheistic mysticism. After seriously studying science, she moved to a position closer to Spencer's agnosticism. Naden in 1885 won the Paxton Prize for a geological essay. She also was a respected poet. {RAT; RE}

Naewiger, G. E. Conrad (19th Century)

A freethinker, Naewiger wrote "God Is Love: Is It True?" (1890). {GS}

Nagel, Ernest (1901–1985)

An outspoken atheist and the John Dewey Professor of Philosophy at Columbia University, Nagel was author of *Logic Without Metaphysics* (1956) and, with Morris Raphael Cohen, *An Introduction to Logic and Scientific Method* (1934). In the former book, according to Anthony Flew, Nagel contends that (a) the familiar universe, sometimes called nature, is in truth all there is; and its manifest plurality is no sort of false front for any hidden or transcendental unit; and (b) "Organized matter" is primary "in the executive order of nature." In short, Nagel's naturalism admits no incorporeal, purely spiritual agents. Nagel was, with Hook, one of the two philosophically most distinguished former pupils and lifelong admirers of John Dewey.

He was editor of the *Journal of Philosophy* (1940–1956), of *Philosophy of Science* (1956–1959), and *Journal of Symbolic Logic* (1939–1945). Dewey, Hook, and Nagel all were atheistic and, in philosophy, naturalists.

Nagel preferred the labels "materialist" and "contextual naturalist." His naturalism, wrote H. S. Thayer in the *Encyclopedia of Philosophy* (Vol. 5), included "a place for imagination, liberal values, and human wisdom." Nagel was a Humanist Laureate in the Council for Secular Humanism's International Academy of Humanism. {CE; CL; EU, Antony Flew; SHD}

Nagel, H. Kyle (20th Century)

When he signed Humanist Manifesto II, Nagel was a minister of the Unitarian Universalist Church of Kinston, North Carolina. He is associated with the Humanists of Houston, Texas. (See entry for Texas Atheists, Freethinkers, Humanists.) {FD; HM2}

Nagy, Peter Tibor (20th Century)

Nagy spoke in Berlin at a 1995 meeting arranged by the International Humanist and Ethical Union (IHEU). He said that in Hungary, unlike in Poland, only about 13 to 17% are actively involved in the churches, the Christian Church being in a minority. An estimated 20% of Hungarians clearly reject religion. (See entry for Hungarian Humanists.)

Nahigian, Kenneth E. (20th Century)

Nahigian, a biblical scholar, in "Isaiah's Prophecy" (*Truth Seeker*, #2, 1993), wrote that prophecy is a muddy science, that Bible prophecy is muddier than most. For example, he cites that most Christians take at face value the prophecy of the child Immanuel as presented in *Matthew* 1: 22-23:

> Now all this was done that it might be fulfilled which was spoken of the Lord by the prophet, saying, Behold, a virgin shall be with child, and shall bring forth a son, and they shall call his name Emmanuel, which being interpreted is, God with us.

But in the Masoretic text of the Holy Bible, *Isaiah* 7:14 reads

> Therefore the Lord himself shall give you a sign; Behold [the *ha'almah*] shall conceive, and bear a son, and shall call his name Immanuel.

Explains Nahigian, "The Matthew interpretation of Isaiah has several problems, the largest hanging on the Hebrew word *'almah*. Writing in Greek, the gospel author turned *'almah* into *parthenos*, a word usually (but not always) meaning 'virgin.' In fact he had a precedent for this: the Septuagint, a translation of the Old Testament used by Greek-speaking Jews of the day, did indeed use *parthenos* in the Isaiah passage. But the Septuagint was for the most part a notoriously sloppy translation, and its version of Isaiah was more error-ridden than the rest. By the Middle Ages the Jews had abandoned the Septuagint, and other Greek translations, by Aquila, Theodotion, Lucien, and others, did not use the word *parthenos*." Nahigian concludes, " *'almah* is an adolescent female, virgin or not." Further, he declares that nearly all modern commentaries agree with Talmudic scholars that Isaiah's "sign" had nothing to do with a messiah.

Naigeon, Jacques André (1728–1810)

A French atheist, Naigeon was first an art student, then a disciple and imitator of Diderot. He became copyist to and collaborator with Holbach, conveying his works to Amsterdam to be printed. A contributor to the *Encyclopédie*, he also published *Recuëil Philosophique* (1770) and edited Holbach's essay on prejudices and his *Morale Universelle*. In addition, Naigeon edited the works of Diderot, the essays of Montaigne, and a translation of Toland's philosophical letters. His principal work is the Dictionary of Ancient and Modern Philosophy in the *Encyclopédie Méthodique* (1791–1794). In 1790 he addressed the National Assembly on "Liberty of Opinion," asking them to withhold the name of God and religion from their declaration of the rights of man. Describing himself as an atheist, Naigeon defined the morality of the Church as an order "to love above all things a god whom we do not know and priests whom we know too well." {BDF; RAT; RE}

Naiman, Dorothy N. (20th Century)

When she signed Humanist Manifesto II, Naiman was a professor emerita at Lehman College, City University of New York. {HM2}

Naimark, Rick (20th Century)

Naimark is President of the Society for Humanistic Judaism.

Naipaul, V(idiadhar) S(urajprasad) (1932-)

A Trinidian essayist and writer of Indian descent, Naipaul is known for works that examine exile as well as alienation. The son of Hindu Indians who immigrated to Trinidad as indentured servants, he attended the University of Oxford in 1950, subsequently settling in England. *A House for Mr. Biswas* (1961) brought him critical acclaim and examined the disintegration of a family in a postcolonial nation—his own father was an inspiration for the hero, whose life from the job of sign-writer to that of journalist includes seeing younger members of his family depart for opportunities in Europe. *A Bend in the River* (1979) was set in central Africa and included a horrifying portrait of emergent Africa. *A Way in the World* (1994) was an autobiography in the form of a novel. His non-fiction includes *An Area of Darkness* (1965), a highly controversial and critical account of India; *India: A Wounded Civilization* (1977); *India: A Million Mutinies Now* (1990); *The Middle Passages* (1962); and *The Return of Eva Peron* (1980).

A freethinker, Naipaul in his recurrent themes of violence, homelessness, and alienation has been compared to Joseph Conrad. (For Naipaul's comments on Islam, see entry for Pakistan.) {OEL; Ibn Warraq, 1999}

Nakens, José (Born 1846)

The founder and editor of *El Motin*, Nakens was a Spanish journalist. His Republican and freethought paper functioned in connection with a library. Nakens also wrote for *La Piqueta* (The Pick-axe). {BDF}

Nalladaroo, Soonnu M. (1969-)

Nalladaroo, in Pune and Mumbai, India, is a humanist interested in establishing an electronic office or clearinghouse of liberal ideas worldwide. On the Web: <www.geocities.com/Athens/Rhodes/3318/>.

Nampudiribad, Unny (20th Century)

Nampudiribad is a publicity chairman for an activist member of the University of Minnesota Atheists and Humanists.

Nansen, Fridtjof (1861–1930)

Nansen, a Norwegian, won the Nobel Peace Prize in 1922. After his 1882 trip to the Arctic, he became curator of the natural history collection of the Bergen Museum. His expedition, the first to cross Greenland, laid the basis for all future Arctic work. After World War I, he received international acclaim for his work to repatriate war prisoners and to help famine-stricken Russia. In 1921, he was appointed High Commissioner for Refugees by the League of Nations. An agnostic, he wrote in *Science and the Purpose of Life*, "The religion of one age is the literary entertainment of the next." {CE; *Free Inquiry*, Winter, 1990-1991; JM; RAT; RE}

Napier, Charles James [Sir] (1782–1853)

Napier was a British general who served with distinction in the Napoléonic Wars. While stationed in Cephalonia, he met Lord Byron and was asked, although he declined, to command the Greek independence forces. "I would rather have finished the roads in Cephalonia," he explained in his private journal, "than have fought Austerlitz or Waterloo." In dealing with the Chartist unrest in Northern England, General Napier was a moderate. In 1841 he went to India, undertaking the conquest in 1843 of Sind. He then served as governor of Sind until 1847. In *Life and Opinions*, Napier although he believed in God was skeptical about a future life—" 'Tis an idle waste of thought thus to dwell on what no thought can tell us," he said—and he was disdainful of Christianity: "Jesus of Nazareth! The thing's impossible," he wrote. {JM; RAT; RE}

Napoléon I (1769–1821)

Napoléon Bonaparte, the son of Carlo and Letizia Bonaparte (or Buonaparte), may have been caricatured by Gillray in England as but a deformed megalomaniacal dwarf. But in France he has always been an icon.

Known as "the Little Corporal," the Corsican-born future emperor of the French first attracted notice by his part in dislodging the British from Toulon (1793); thereafter, he had a series of major military and political victories. The Napoléonic legend, the picture of a liberal conqueror spreading the French Revolution throughout Europe, was a potent factor in French history and helped make his nephew French emperor as Napoléon III. Few will deny that Napoléon was one of the greatest military leaders in history, that he dominated European history between 1800 and 1815, a period known as the Napoléonic Era. But as noted by Alan Schom in *Napoléon Bonaparte* (1997), Napoléon was such a war-maker that he disillusioned many. Beethoven, for example, removed the dedication of the "Eroica" after Napoléon declared himself Emperor, in 1804.

In Catholic France, he made peace with the Church by the Concordat of 1801, which reestablished the church in France. This neutralized the anti-revolutionary priests who had encouraged peasant unrest. Meanwhile, Napoléon declared that France had finished with the "romance of the revolution." Lord Rosebery, who made a study, *The Last Phase*, of Napoléon's position as regards religion showed that especially in his later years Napoléon did not believe in the divinity of Christ or in a future life. McCabe remarks of this, "Catholics boast that at the end he asked for the sacraments. In doing so, however, he gave his friends the excuse that 'there is so much that one does not know.' "

Haugh holds that Napoléon "was an agnostic during his years of triumph, but that as he neared death, broken by captivity, he uttered religious declarations." Prior to that, he had these views:

- I would believe in a religion if it existed ever since the beginning of time, but when I consider Socrates, Plato, Mahomet, I no longer believe. All religions have been made by men.
- A soul? Give my watch to a savage, and he will think it has a soul. . . . If I have a soul, then pigs and dogs also have souls.
- If I had believed in a God of rewards and punishments, I might have lost courage in battle.
- I do not think Jesus Christ ever existed.
- It remains an open question whether Christ ever lived.

Napoléon died of cancer on St. Helena and was buried there. In 1840, he body was returned to France, first being checked by a physician, Dr. Guillard, who found "the features of the Emperor were so little changed that his face was instantly recognized by those who had known him when alive. His entire person presented the appearance of one recently interred." The beard and nails had grown after death, however, his face was puffy, and the skin was "soft and supple." His heart and entrails were preserved in two silver vessels in the coffin.

Although many called him "the Little Corporal"—he was 5' 6"—many democrats called him "the Little Prick." Dr. John K. Lattimer, a retired urologist at the Columbia-Presbyterian Medical Center in New York City, is something of an expert on the latter accusation. When Lattimer was contacted by the descendants of Ange Paul Vignali, a priest and doctor who had attended Napoléon on St. Helena and who conducted the autopsy when the Emperor died in 1821, he learned that in exile Napoléon had scorned Vignali, a fellow Corsican and "about twenty years ago I bought several things from the family, including the urological relic." That relic, explained the eighty-year-old urologist, is Napoléon's phallus. {CE; JM; PA; *The New York Times*, 9 July 1994; TYD}

Napoleon, Jérôme (1822–1891)

Napoleon, said by Tribe to be the generally distrusted relative to the hated Louis, was a freethinker and a republican. {TRI}

Naquet, Joseph Alfred (Born 1834)

Naquet, a French materialist, became a physician in 1859. In 1867 he was imprisoned for fifteen months for belonging to a secret society. With M. Regnard, he founded the *Revue Encyclopédique*, which was suppressed at once for containing an attack on theism. After being a professor of chemistry at Paris and Palermo, Naquet upon returning to Paris expressed so openly the advanced views he had cultivated among the Garibaldians that in 1867 he received fifteen months in prison. In 1869, however, he continued the attack with a book, *Religion, Propriété, Famille*, this time being fined five hundred francs and sentenced to four months' imprisonment and the loss of civil rights for life.

From 1871 to 1882 he was in the Chambre, passing to the Senate in 1882. During that time, he secured the passing of liberal divorce laws. A leading champion at Paris of the innocence of F. Ferrer, Naquet was an agnostic. In 1883 he was elected to the Senate. Naquet represented Vaueluse in the National Assembly, where he voted with the extreme left. The divorce law in France was passed chiefly through his advocacy. {BDF; RAT; RE}

Narain, Narsingh (1897–1972)

Narain in 1960 founded the Indian Humanist Union (IHU) in Naini Tal, Uttar Pradesh State, in northern India. He has pointed out that although Nehru used the word "spiritual" in the sense that many humanists do, there was no indication that he had turned a "theist" and had ceased to be an agnostic. E-mail: <pnarain@ignca.ernet.in>. (See entry for Ramendra.) {For his views on humanism and religion, see *International Humanist News*, November 1996; *New Humanist*, December 1996}

Narain, Prakash (20th Century)

Narain, son of Narsingh Narain, was chairman of the Railway Board, secretary of Surface Transport, and Secretary of Urban Development for the Government of India. He edits *Humanist Outlook* and leads the Humanist Union in India. As its leader, he spoke at a 1995 conference of major humanist groups in India of the need to find a balance between traditional and modern societies: "The balance to be struck between continuity and change is a delicate one," he stated. The caste system, which had begun as a tool for division of labor, has led to injustices and atrocities. Further, the denial of the rights of women and the mistreatment of Hindu widows demonstrates, he holds, the damage of religion to the community.

Narain participated as a moderator in the 1996 Humanist World Congress in Mexico City. His concern was that the information revolution can be an instrument for the dissemination of humanist values but that caution needs to be paid to insure that humanist values not be hindered by this new cyber-revolution. He is one of the members of the IHEU's Committee on religious Extremism and Rational Inquiry. E-mail: <pnarain@ignca.ernet.in>. {FUK; *International Humanist News*, December 1996; *New Humanist*, February 1996; December 1996}

Narasimhaiah, H. (20th Century)

Narasimhaiah is a nuclear physicist, a household name in Karnataka State. He was formerly the Vice Chancellor of Bangalore University. Narasimhaiah inaugurated the International Humanist and Ethical Union India Congress. He signed Humanist Manifesto 2000.

Narayan, P. K. (20th Century)

Narayan, a hypnotist, assisted Abraham T. Kovoor, President of the Ceylon Rationalist Association in helping spread rationalism in India. He educated the audience as to how suggestion swayed devotees into getting into trance, thereby helping expose the tricks of Satya Sai Baba.

Narisetti, Innaiah (1937–)

Innaiah, as he is generally known in Hyderabad, did his doctoral work researching the subject of thesis and anti-thesis by the media. His degree was delayed because his university ineptly ruled that, despite his having passed the thesis in writing, he had to receive a unanimity of examiners' votes in order to pass his oral exams. Eventually, the nation's high court ruled that the university had been in error for demanding the examining committee's unanimity of favorable votes. Meanwhile, his thesis was examined in detail by three committees over a ten-year period, from 1969 to 1979.

In 1992 and 1994 he addressed the American Humanist Association conference in Washington, D.C., and in 1994 that group's conference in Detroit. From 1992 to 1994 he was President of the Andhra Pradesh Rationalists Association, and in 1995 he became an executive member of the Indian Radical Humanist Association. In 1996 he was elected Vice President of the Rationalist Association of India. A former lecturer in philosophy at Osmania University, he is a journalist and author.

Narisetti has written about Agehananda Bharati's *Ochre Robe*, which he translated into Telugu, describing the book's being banned in India. The work had recorded Bharati's memoirs about editing Vivekananda's eight volumes, finding nonsense in Vivekananda's views and mischievously pleading that inasmuch as the views had been allegedly expressed by a divine person nothing should be deleted or edited. The swamis in the Ashram detected the mischief and denied Bharati's plea, also asking him to quit. Later he wrote further negative views about Vivekananda, who at the time was considered an influential nationalist and a modern spiritualist whose Yoga system was touted by many. Ramakrishna Ashram put pressure on the Indian government, and the book was banned in 1967. Later Bharati added a few pages, the work was published in the United States, and Narisetti translated it into Telugu as well as had it serialized in the daily *Andhra Prabha*.

In addition to being author of many books in Telugu, Narisetti has written *Inside Andhra Pradesh (*1980); *The Philosophical Consequences of Modern Science* (1982); *The Birth and Death of Political Parties in India* (1982); *Politics for Power—Study of Contemporary Andhra Pradesh Politics* (1982); *Between Charisma and Corruption* (1991); and *M. N. Roy, Evelyn, Ellen: A Bibliography* (1996). For the *Encyclopedia of Unbelief*, he wrote "Unbelief in India."

Narisetti has written for Delhi's *Radical Humanist* and Hyderabad's *Indian Rationalist* as well as translated many works from English to Telugu, including M. N. Roy's *Reason, Romanticism, and Revolution*. He signed Humanist Manifesto 2000.

His wife, **Komala**, is a retired assistant professor of English at Dr. Ambedkar Open University in Hyderabad. His daughter is a Washington, D. C., psychiatrist, and his son is a business writer for *The Wall Street Journal*. Dr. Narisetti's e-mail: <hu92@aol.com>. His address: A-60, Journalists' Colony, Jubilee Hills, Hyderabad 500 033, Andhra Pradesh, India. (See entry for Agehananda Bharati.) {WAS, numerous conversations.)

Narla, V. R. (1908-1985)

Popularly known as Narla Venkateswararoa, Narla edited two

Telugu daily newspapers for thirty years, producing voluminous iconoclastic writings in Telugu. Influenced by M. N. Roy and humanistic thought, he became an ardent skeptic who lectured in several Indian universities. "The Poverty of Intellectualism in India" was one lecture given in Mysore, in which he explained how India had rejected the open mind of an ancient seer, Uddalaka. The seer felt that India had failed to accept the path of Henry Louis Vivian Derozio (1809-1831), instead following the path of Gandhi and his "inner voice." According to Narla, Vedanta helped kill India's vitality, denying reason as the way to discover truths.

Narla also lectured on "East and West: Myth of Dichotomy" and "The Truth about the Gita." The Gita, he complained, encourages and justifies violent killings of kith and kin and proudly declares that that the four-caste system (called Varna) is a noble creation. Gita, said Narla, has been tragic for India, and he appealed to contemporary Indians to discard Gita along with its rebirth and Karma concepts. The caste system, he complained, even included birds and animals. Instead, he spoke up for a humanism and rationalism that emphasized human values in all walks of life. His aphoristic sayings are found in *Gods, Goblins, and Men*.

Narla had been a member of Rajya Sabha, the central legislative body in India, from 1958 to 1970. Upon his death, his library of thousands of books in English and Telugu was donated to the Ambedkar Open University in Hyderabad. {I. Narisetti to WAS, 13 July 1999}

Narlikar, Jayant (20th Century)

Narlikar spoke at the 1998 Congress of the International Humanist and Ethical Union in Mumbai. Ignorance, he lamented, often produces anti-science. People in high office consult astrologers or become interested in Feng Shui (geomancy), and an understanding of science needs to be a key part of educating the general public. {*International Humanist News*, December 1998}

Narveson, Jan (1936–)

Narveson, a professor of philosophy at the University of Waterloo in Canada, is author of *The Libertarian Idea*. His article, "Humanism Is For Humans" (*Free Inquiry*, Spring, 1993), was challenged in the following issue (Summer, 1993) by Wolf Roder, of the Cincinnati, Ohio, McMicke College of Arts and Sciences. In 1993 Narveson wrote *Moral Matters*.

Nascimento, Francisco Manuel do (1734–1819)

Nascimento was a Portuguese poet who entered the Church but, having been the translator of Molière's *Tartuffe*, was accused in 1778 of heresy. As a result, he had to flee for his life from the Inquisition. Nascimento wrote many poems and satires under the name of "Filinto Elysio." {BDF; RAT}

Nash, David (20th Century)

Nash's *Secularism, Art, and Freedom* (1992) is a history of the Leicester Secular Society, one of the oldest surviving British freethought organizations.

Nash, J. V. (20th Century)

In the 1920s, Nash wrote "Homosexuality in Lives of the Great," which E. Haldeman-Julius published as Little Blue Book No. 1564. Nash reportedly was a non-theist.

Nasrin, Taslima (1962–)

Nasrin (also, **Nasreen**), a Bangladesh novelist, was attacked in print after writing *Lajja* (Shame, 1992, 1997). Hundreds of members of the Council of Soldiers of Islam demanded her death. In the novel, she depicts Bangladesh's Hindu minority as having been picked out for revenge by Muslims after the incident in December 1992 in which a Hindu mob destroyed an ancient mosque in Ayodhya, northern India. Her work depicts a Hindu family attacked by Muslims in the aftermath of the razing of the Babri mosque in Ayodhya by Hindu extremists. A reward of 50,000 taka (£850) was immediately offered to anyone who would kill the thirty-one-year-old former gynecologist, daughter of Dr. Rojab Ali, a government physician and practitioner of the Sufi tradition of Islam.

In December 1993, 5,000 zealots marched through Dhaka, demanding her death. A general strike there resulted in clashes in which one man was killed and more than two hundred were injured.

"She is worse than a prostitute," complained Maulana Azizul Haque, the mullah who has called for her execution. "She demands 'freedom of the vagina.' She says that if a man can have four wives, a woman should have the right to four husbands. Even within marriage, she says a woman should have the right to other men. This is against the Qur'an and Allah. It is blasphemy!" Although quoted as having said that "the Qur'an should be thoroughly revised," she countered that her purpose was to suggest that "we have to move beyond these ancient texts if we want progress," a comment which deepened the controversy.

Muslim militants say *Nirbachito Kolum*, a collection of some of her newspaper columns, is blasphemous, and they publicize her separation after a few years from Bangladeshi poet Rudra Mohammad Shahidullah.

Meanwhile, some publishers who fear Muslim fundamentalists stopped picturing pigs in children's books, horse-riding and ballet are kept out because they are symbols of the wealthy, and witches are excluded for fear of satanism and the occult.

Nasrin has been a bold advocate of sexual freedom in her newspaper columns, poems, and novels. Like Salman Rushdie of India, who rallied prominent writers to support her feminism, Nasrin was forced into a life of hiding. She fled to Sweden 1994 after the twelve nations of the European Union made a formal offer of asylum to the writer. Once there, she said, "The fundamentalists are destroying our society. The silent majority is afraid of them. They will do anything in the name of God. The progressives are not so organized, for they cannot bring together 300,000 people at one time." As for the Muslim clergy: "The country is infected with them. Their long hair, beards, and robes conceal their insatiable lust for wealth and women."

Interviewed by Mary Anne Weaver for *New Yorker* (12 September 1994), Nasrin was described as "utterly ordinary," a shy Marxist professor and poet who became an atheist at the age of eleven or twelve. She reiterated that she had never, never said the Qur'an (Koran) should be revised.

> No, how many times do I have to say it? I've said it over and over again. I said that *Shariat* law should be revised. I want a modern, civilized law, where women are given equal rights. I want no religious law that discriminates, none, period—no Hindu law, no Christian law, no Islamic law. Why should a man be entitled to have four wives? Why should a son get two-thirds of his parents' property when a daughter can inherit only a third? Should I be *killed* for saying this?

Bangladesh mullahs, giving no reasons, declared one woman's second marriage was contrary to Islamic law and she was led to a fundamentalist stronghold where a pit had been dug overnight. She was lowered into the pit and buried waist deep. Then, slowly and methodically, the woman was stoned—a hundred and one times. Her death was said to have horrified even the Dhaka's élite. In another town, a woman who was condemned by a *fatwa* for adultery was doused with kerosene and burned to death. Women everywhere, Nasrin declared, are humiliated and driven out of their villages by fundamentalist mullahs.

In Stockholm, Nasrin remained secreted for several years. "They've taken everything from me," she said. "My innocence, my youth, now my freedom. I know if I ever go back that I'll have to keep silent, stay inside my house. I'll never lead a normal life in my country, until my death."

Asked in an interview with Sara Whyatt (*Index*, September-October 1994) if she still thought herself a Muslim, Nasrin responded, "No, I am an atheist. All forms of religion are anachronistic to me. I dream of a world without religion. Religion gives birth to fundamentalism as surely as the seed gives birth to the tree. We can tear the tree down, but if the seed remains it will produce another tree. While the seed remains, we cannot root out fundamentalism."

In *The Guardian* (14 December 1994) when journalist Linda Grant mentioned that Muslim fundamentalists say that humanism is an import from the West, Nasrin responded,

> Humanism is not western or eastern or southern or northern. It is just humanism. They protest against me, but I am surprised that they don't protest against inequality and injustice. What I have done is protested against the system which is against women. I have seen that, in the name of tradition, society wants to keep women in ignorance and slavery. . . . I realised from childhood that women were treated as childbearing machines or decorations, not human beings.

A 1995 poem, "Self Portrait," appears in *New Humanist* (December, 1995) and commences

> I don't believe in God.
> I look upon Nature with wondering eyes,
> However much I move forward grasping the hands of progress
> society's hindrances take hold of my sleeve
> and gradually pull me backwards.
> I wish I could walk all through the city
> in the middle of the night,
> sitting down anywhere alone to cry. . . .

It ends

> Throughout the world,
> religion has extended its eighteen talons.
> In my lone brandishing,
> how many of its bones can I shatter.
> How much can I rip
> discrimination's farspreading net?

"Taslima," Salman Rushdie wrote in an open letter published in *The New York Times* (14 July 1994), "I know there must be a storm inside you now. . . . You have done nothing wrong. The wrong is committed by others against you. You have done nothing wrong, and I am sure that one day soon you will be free."

In her Oxford Amnesty Lecture of 1995, Nasrin said

> Again I dare to write against male-made religion. I believe that women are oppressed by every religion. If any religion allows the persecution of people of different faiths, if any religion keeps people in ignorance, if any religion keeps women in slavery, then I cannot accept that religion. Freedom for women will never be possible until they cross the barrier of religion and patriarchy.

In 1995, she wrote The *Game in Reverse*. Nasrin has published fifteen books, including *Nirbachita Column* (1991), which portrays the predicament of women in a male-dominated society.

In 1996, Nasrin was elected a Humanist Laureate in the Council for Secular Humanism's International Academy of Humanism. She is an honorary associate of the New Zealand Association of Rationalists and Humanists and is the Vice-Chair of the International Society for Islamic Secularization (PO Box 229, Buffalo, NY 14215).

At the 1996 Mexico City conference of humanists, Jim Herrick described her as being "an atheist from personal experience. She grew up in a country where people were forced there by the partition of India on religious grounds. She accepted that religion could cause great art, but said that it also did too much damage. She began to apply her powers of observation, analysis and reason to religion and found she could not accept it at all. She used her writings to expose the crimes of religion, which teaches people to hate one another and glorifies poverty. The position of women concerned her and she questioned why women in the East should be deprived of education. Democracy and secularism should be put in practice throughout the world."

Like Antigone and putting family above state, Dr. Nasrin alarmed her friends by returning in 1998 to Bangladesh after a forced four-year exile. She returned with her dying mother, whom she had brought to New York City for medical treatment. Upon her arrival, the religious fundamentalists immediately demanded her death. Again she was forced into hiding; again diplomatic overtures had to be made to rescue her for a return to Sweden. Her plight was described in *Free Inquiry* (Winter 1998-1999), with letters of support from Sir Arthur C. Clarke, Wole Soyinka, Sir Hermann Bondi, Steven Weinberg, Sir Raymond Firth, Edward O. Wilson, and Mario Bunge. Included was an interview, "One Brave Woman vs. Religious Fundamentalism," by Matt Cherry and Warren Allen Smith, in which she said:

> • When I began to study the Qur'an, the holy book of Islam, I found many unreasonable ideas. The women in the Qur'an were treated as slaves. They were nothing but sexual objects.
>
> • I don't find any difference between Islam and Islamic fundamentalists. I believe religion is the root, and from the root fundamentalism grows as a poisonous stem. If we remove fundamentalism and keep religion, then one day or another fundamentalism will grow again. I need to say that because some liberals always defend Islam and blame fundamentalists for creating problems. But Islam itself oppresses women. Islam itself doesn't permit democracy and it violates human rights.
>
> • When I was 14 or 15 years old, I found the Bengali translation of the Qur'an, and I learned what God says in the verses. I was surprised to read wrong information about the solar system in the Qur'an—for example, that the sun is moving around the earth and the earth is not moving but standing still because of the support of the mountains.
>
> • [Religion] does not often teach people to love one another. On the contrary, it often teaches them to hate people of a different faith. Religion also leads people to depend on fate and thus lose self-confidence. It unnecessarily glorifies poverty and sacrifice and thus serves the vested interests of the wealthy few. In all countries and through all ages, conscientious people have exposed these unethical aspects of religion and educated people to see religion with the eyes of reason and logic.
>
> • Nothing will be achieved by reforming Muslim scriptural tenets. What is needed is a change of the *sharia*, the code of laws based on the Qur'an. I want a uniform civil code that is equally applicable to men and women.
>
> • I am an atheist. I do not believe in prayers. I believe in work. And my work is that of an author. My pen is my weapon.

Amar Meebela (My Girlhood Days, published as *Enfance, au*

Féminin, 1998, in a translation from Bengali by Philippe Benoît) was immediately banned in Bangladesh because "its contents might hurt the existing social system and religious sentiment of the people and could also create adverse reaction in the country."

Time (the Asian edition) described her as "one of the 20 most influential women in the 20th century," and she became noted throughout the world. As of the end of 1999, Nasrin had moved from her hiding place in Sweden to one in Europe. She signed Humanist Manifesto 2000.

On the Web: <http://nasrin.humanists.net>. E-mail: "Taslima" <wasm@idt.net>. (See Taslima Nasrin, "On Islamic Fundamentalism," *The Humanist*, July-August 1996, which is an adaptation of her speech 28 April 1996 at Harvard University, sponsored by the Humanist Chaplaincy; on the Web, details of her legal problems are found at <http://www.pen.org>. Nasrin has expressed to the present author her dissatisfaction with the English translation of her *Shame*.) {CA; E; "An Interview with Matt Cherry and Warren Allen Smith," *Free Inquiry*, Winter 1998; *Freethought History #13*, 1995; HNS2; *International Humanist News*, March 1994 and December 1996; *New Humanist*, December 1996; WAS, "Taslima Nasrin: An Intereview," in *Humanist in Canada*, Summer 1998, and numerous conversations; WWS}

NASTHIKA YUGAM (The Age of Atheism)

A Telugu monthly of the Atheist Society of India, Nasthika *Yugam* is at Pithani Dibba, Visakhapatnam 530 002, Andhra Pradesh, India.

NASTIKA MARGAM (The Atheist Way)

A Telugu monthly, *Nastika Margam* is at Nastika Kendram, Benz Circle, Vijayawada, India.

Natanson, Maurice (1924–1996)

Natanson helped introduce the work of Jean-Paul Sartre and Edmund Husserl in the United States. His many books include *Phenomenology and Special Reality, an Essay in Memory of Alfred Schutz* (1970); *Phenomenology, Role and Reason* (1974); *Edmund Husserl, Philosopher of Infinite Tasks* (1973); *Anonymity: A Study in the Philosophy of Alfred Schutz* (1986); and *Edmund Husserl*, which won a 1974 National Book Award. His *The Erotic Bird: Phenomenology in Literature* will be published posthumously.

When he reviewed books for *The Humanist* in the 1950s, Natanson was a member of the philosophy department faculty at the University of Houston. Afterwards, he taught at the University of North Carolina and the University of California at Santa Cruz. From 1976 until 1995, he taught at Yale. Natanson died of prostate cancer.

Nath, Ramendra (1957-)

Since 1983, Ramendra has been teaching philosophy at Patna University, from which he received his Ph. D. and his D. Litt. The dissertation for the former degree was written on the subject, "Bertrand Russell's Ethical Philosophy," for the latter, "M. N. Roy's New Humanism and Materialism."

Ramendra is the founder-president of Bihar Buddhiwadi Samaj (Bihar Rationalist Society, an Associate Member of the IHEU) and founder- trustee of Buddhiwadi Foundation, a registered, non-profit, educational trust for promoting rationalism and humanism.

He has written many books, booklets, papers and articles in Hindi and English including *Why I am Not a Hindu* and *Is God Dead?* These and some of his other writings as well as his brief biography are available on the Internet.

At the 1995 conference of humanists in India, he said, "Communalism and the caste-system are, in my opinion, two major obstacles that prevent integrated human development in the South Asian region." He added, "Because communalism is linked to fundamentalism and religious identities, promotion of rationalism and humanism alone can provide a lasting solution to the problem of communalism. We must attack the fundamentalism of all religions in order to destroy the root cause of communalism."

Ramendra is a supporter of Internet Infidels. His E- mail addresses: <bobsoft@vsnl.com> and <brs_patna@yahoo.com>. On the Web: <www.myfreeoffice.com/buddhiwadi> and <www.geocities.com/Athens/Aegean/2035>. (See entry for his wife, Kawaljeet Kaur.) {*New Humanist*, February 1996; WASM, 1 March 1999}

Nath, Shivendra (20th Century)

Nath is a trustee of the Buddhiwadi Foundation. (See entry for Buddhiwadi Foundation).

Nathanson, Jerome (1908–1975)

Nathanson, a journalist and student of philosophy, followed Algernon D. Black in 1940 as a leader of the New York Ethical Culture Society. He remained until 1975, continuing his predecessor's emphasis on activism. From 1943 to 1945, he secured the help of John Dewey in organizing the Conferences on Science and Democracy and was authorized by him to write a work that contains few direct quotations or phrases, *John Dewey: The Reconstruction of the Democratic Life* (1951).

In 1952, he was on the first board of directors of the International Humanist and Ethical Union (IHEU). Also in the 1950s, Nathanson worked with Priscilla Robertson, editor of *The Humanist*, resigning with her and her staff when a dispute with Corliss Lamont and the American Humanist Association board of directors arose concerning her rights of editorial freedom. (See entry for Ethical Culture.) {HM2; EU, Howard B. Radest; HNS2}

NATION OF ISLAM

The Lost-Found Nation of Islam was established by Wallace D. Fard in 1930. Calling himself Prophet, Fard stated his mission: "to restore and to resurrect his lost and found people, who were identified as the original members of the Tribe of Shabazz from the Lost Nation of Asia." In the 1930s he chose Elijah Poole of Detroit, Michigan, to be his "divine representative," and Poole transformed into the Honorable Elijah Muhammad who, for forty-four years, suffered persecution and rejection from the very people among whom he was appointed as a Servant of God, not surprisingly because he renounced whites and preached a form of apartheid.

In 1946 a black separatist organization was promoted by Malcolm X who broke away in 1964 and founded his own Organization for Afro-American Unity, preaching "active self-defence." He persuaded teacher and singer Louis Farrakhan to join the organization, and when the group dissolved in 1985 Farrakhan formed the Nation of Islam.

In 1986 Farrakhan was denied entry into the United Kingdom because of his inflammatory speeches against, among others, Jews and homosexuals. In 1995 Farrakhan organized a "Million Men March" of around 400,000 black men in Washington. {Barry Duke, *The Freethinker*, July 1998}

NATIONAL CENTER FOR SCIENCE EDUCATION

The National Center for Science Education, B-9477, Berkeley, California 94709, was founded in 1982 to counter the creationist threat to science education in the public schools. Eugenie C. Scott is its leader. On the Web: <http://www.natcenscied.org>.

NATIONAL COMMITTEE FOR PUBLIC EDUCATION AND RELIGIOUS LIBERTY (PEARL)

The National Committee for Public Education and Religious Liberty (PEARL, 165 East 56th Street, New York, NY 10022) is dedicated to preserving public schools and church-state separation. The Council for Secular Humanism is one of the member organizations. (See "The Campaign to Overturn *Felton v. Aguilar* in *Free Inquiry*, Winter 1996-1997)

NATIONAL COUNCIL AGAINST HEALTH FRAUD

The National Council Against Health Fraud, POB 33008, Kansas City, Missouri 64114, is a group that fights quack remedies, including divine healing. On the Web: <http://www.primenet.com/~ncahf>. {FD}

NATIONAL FREETHOUGHT ORGANISATION

The National Freethought Organisation, *Giordano Bruno*, is at 82, Via Teodosio, 30131 Milan, Italy.

NATIONAL LEAGUE FOR THE SEPARATION OF CHURCH AND STATE

The National League for the Separation of Church and State, POB 2832, San Diego, California 93112, was founded in 1876. It has published *Truth Seeker* and was connected with the James H. Johnson Charitable Trust.

NATIONAL SECULAR SOCIETY (NSS)

The National Secular Society, which publishes *The Freethinker*, a secular humanist monthly, was founded in 1866 by Charles Bradlaugh before he embarked on his parliamentary career as a radical Liberal.

It was formed to unite the various secular societies that had developed from the Owenite and Chartist movements. During the late nineteenth century, it was the main freethought organization in England. At first it attracted mostly self-educated working-class people, and it still retains some of its traditional forthright and down-to-earth character as the most militant element in the humanist movement. In 1881, G. W. Foote started *The Freethinker*, which is one of England's boldest and liveliest progressive periodicals.

Barbara Smoker served as the society's president, according to Nicolas Walter's tabulation, for twenty-four years and five months. Foote was president for twenty-five years and eight months. The longest serving president, however, was Chapman Cohen, from 1915 to 1949.

The NSS is headquartered at Bradlaugh House, 47 Theobald's Road, London WC1X8SP, England. Dan O'Hara was succeeded as President by Denis Cobell, the current president. Vice presidents are Peter Brearey and Jim Herrick.

E-mail: <kpw@secularism.org.uk.> (Telephone 0171-404 3126; fax 0171-430 1271) {*The Freethinker*, February 1998}

NATIONAL SERVICE CONFERENCE OF THE AMERICAN ETHICAL UNION

The National Service Conference of the American Ethical Union is at 2 West 64th Street, New York, NY 10023.

NATIONAL SUNDAY LEAGUE

The National Sunday League, formed in 1856 by secularist R. M. Morrell, campaigned against the restrictions on Sunday entertainments imposed in England by the Act of 1781. Annie Besant was its vice-president. A similar organization, the Free Sunday Society, supported P. A. Taylor's opposition to Thomas Hughes's Sunday Trading Bill in 1872. Secularists took a leading part in the group, aiming to show that Sunday legislation was, in fact, aimed only at the poor. {RSR}

NATIVE AMERICAN RELIGION

Native Americans, also known as American Indians, do not have a religion with a deity, Gayle Morse of the Akwesasne Mohawk Group told a secular humanist group in Upstate New York in 1993. The individual is dominated by the feeling of being part of a greater whole: the family, the tribe, the reservation. Concern for the group's welfare is good, he said, but individual strivings for advancement or betterment relative to or at the expense of others is not. At the same meeting, Dr. Ron Hoskins of the Cherokee Nation identified the cardinal values associated with the traditional medicine wheel ("the symbol of how two-leggeds view the world") as wisdom, vision, passion, trust, compassion, and thoughtful reflection. The universe and right behavior within it, he says, are governed by the original knowledge that lies deep in each individual at birth. Although the various Native American tribes differ in their views, they are generally pantheistic, emphasizing that they are a part of nature, not a special being above nature or one whose purpose is to exploit nature.

Native Americans, in fact, were considered less than human when Europeans arrived on the continent from Christian Spain. In 1516 Pietro Martire d'Anghiera's *De Orbo Nova* was published and described Vasco Núñez de Balboa's killing the leader of the Indians of Quarequa, Panama, and six hundred of his warriors. Balboa fed to his dogs forty more Indians whom he accused of sodomy. Peter Martyr's *Decades* (1555), the anglicized version of Martire's work, depicts the following:

> [Balboa] founde the house of this kynge infected with most abhominable and unnaturall lechery. For he founde the kynges brother and many other younge men in womens apparell, smoth & effeminately decked, which by the report of such as dwelte abowte hym, he abused with preposterous venus. Of these abowte the number of fortie, he commaunded to bee gyven for a pray to his dogges.

"Preposterous" refers to a confusion of before and behind, "venus" to sexual acts. In the battle that precedes the slaughter of the forty Panamanian sodomites, according to Jonathan Goldberg's *Sodometries* (1994), there are no "good" Indians, all are sodomitical animals, and it was a religious duty that they be "hewed . . . in pieses as the butchers doo flesshe . . . , from one an arme, from an other a legge, from hym a buttocke, from an other a shulder, and from sume the necke from the bodye at one stroke." Goldberg observes, "After the sodomites are fed to the dogs, there are two kinds of Indians in the text, sodomitical ones, and noble savages. As the latter lift their hands to heaven, it's as if they're proto-Christians, at the very least testifying to the universality of the Judeo-Christian condemnation of 'unnatural' sexuality. Serving as a mirror of European belief, this split representation of Indians permits the covering over of divisions within the invading troops. . . . . Balboa is not only the righter of sexual wrongs, the restorer of proper gender, he's also the universal liberator of the underclasses."

The Carib Indians were the native people who formerly inhabited the Lesser Antilles, West Indies. Fewer than five hundred still survive on a reservation in Dominica, and many are half-breeds. A century before the arrival of Christopher Columbus, the Caribs overran the Lesser Antilles and drove out the Arawak Indians. The original name by which the Caribs were known, *Galibi* or *Calibi*, was corrupted by the Spanish to *Caníbal*. It is said that Columbus, upon hearing of *Caníba* mistakenly associated the word with *Grand K'han*, for whom he was searching. When on a Sunday Columbus discovered an island with these people, he called the island Dominica, an "islande of the Canibales." Cubans also told him they were *Canibáles*, and when he landed on "Hayti," Columbus heard the name of the people as *Caribes*, their country *Carib*. They were described as being brave and daring, and rightfully or wrongfully they have been compared to the warlike Spartans whereas the Arawaks were Athenian-like and artistic. Because of their fierceness the Caribs gained the reputation of being anthropophagi, or eaters of human flesh, thus the English word *cannibal*. In 1525 Tomás Ortiz claimed that the Caribs were not merely cannibals (as Columbus first has declared) but "were sodomites more than any other race." In 1526 Gonzalo Fernández de Oviedo repeated the formula, "The Indians eat human flesh and are sodomites." However, In 1542, Las Casas wrote in *Brevisima relacion de la destruccion de las Indias* that although a "few" sodomites might be found among the Indians, "for whose sakes nevertheless all that world is not to be condemned. We may say as much of the eating of man's flesh." In short, he found diabolical the Spanish accusation that the Indians "all were polluted with the abhominable sinne against nature: which is a wretched and false slaunder." Such a sentiment ran counter to the view that in New Spain the conquerors had every right to extirpate the pagans who, according to Cortez's translator Aguilar,

> pierce their ears and put very large and ugly objects in them; others pierce their nostrils down to the lip and put in them large round stones which look like mirrors; and others will split their lower lips as far as the gums and hang there some large stones or gold ornaments so heavy that they drag the lips down, giving a most deformed appearance.

Alvar Núñez Cabeza de Vaca in 1527 went to Florida and for a two-year stretch lived "alone among the Indians and naked like them," sometimes as their slave, sometimes as their "medicine man." He finally reported that "in the 2,000 leagues we sojourned by land and sea . . . we found no sacrifices and no idolatry." Nor any native cannibalism. As an outsider, he was respected by the various Indian groups he met, and in his "preaching" he tells them that the god they pray to is the same as the one he calls *Dios*. What disturbed the Spaniards back home when they learned of it was that on Galveston Island Cabeza de Vaca had found some Spaniards ate each other, the very act they had accused the Indians of doing: "The Indians were so shocked at this cannibalism that, if they had seen it sometime earlier, they surely would have killed every one of us." Cabeza de Vaca by this time knew six Indian languages and had become a shaman—he reported trying the native practice of sucking and cauterizing wounds "with good results."

The Native Americans fared no better further north. William Bradford (1590–1657), governor of Plymouth Colony, wrote *History of Plymouth Plantation*, which vividly describes the burning of the Pequot Indians at Mystic, in Connecticut:

> All was quickly on a flame, and thereby more were burnt to death than was otherwise slain; It burnt their bowstrings and made them unserviceable; those that scaped the fire were slain with the sword, some hewed to pieces, others run through with their rapiers, so as they were quickly dispatched and very few escaped. It was conceived they thus destroyed about 400 at this time. It was a fearful sight to see them thus frying in the fire and the streams of blood quenching the same, and horrible was the stink and scent thereof; but the victory seemed a sweet sacrifice, and they gave the praise thereof to God, who had wrought so wonderfully for them, thus to enclose their enemies in their hands and give them so speedy a victory over so proud and insulting an enemy.

The Native Americans, it transpired, "deserved" to be killed for the sake of Christianity. However, any Indians who somehow escaped death were fair bait to be converted to their conquerors' religion . . . of love.

The Native American Church, which claims to have at least 200,000 loosely organized members, call their religious orientation "the Peyote Road" and over fifty tribes in the United States and Canada utilized peyote by 1890. Although the use of the drug has been challenged in the courts, the rights of peyotists to religious freedom have generally been upheld. (See Jonathan Goldberg, *Sodometries: Renaissance Texts, Modern Sexualities* (1994. See the entry for Hopi, whose placed a large emphasis upon Nature.) {CE; DGC}

NATIVE AMERICANS: See entry for American Indians.

NATIVE AMERICANS, ETHNIC CLEANSING

In the 1990s, when American newspapers described in detail the "ethnic cleansing" of Balkan groups which seek to gain a geographical area and kill or move all those who are ethnically different—Muslim-dominated Bosnians, Serbs, Croats, etc. —American history books continued to overlook the "near cleansing" of Native Americans by the whites who were forefathers of the country's majority.

Columbus was at the helm when the original cleansing began, except that his approach utilized forced labor more than genocide. The Massachusetts and Virginia colonists were far more successful, aided by disease and starvation, which almost killed themselves as well as the Native Americans. The mis-named Indians feared John Smith would kill them all, although historians downplay the fact.

Played up is the story of Squanto and the Wampanoags who befriended the Pilgrims, helping them avert starvation and joining them in the first Thanksgiving. Omitted is the fact that, soon afterwards, the English settlers wiped out every tribe within striking distance. William Bradford, in a 1636 search-and-destroy raid, happily reported that "It was a fearful sight to see them thus frying in the fyer . . . but the victory seemed a sweete sacrifice, and they gave prayers thereof to God . . . ."

Benjamin Franklin sponsored a Pennsylvania act that paid a bounty for Indian scalps. The Louisiana Purchase arranged by Thomas Jefferson resulted in eviction notices for the Indians. Andrew Jackson and Martin Van Buren favored "removal" of Indians, resulting in the deadly forced march known as the "Trail of Tears" in 1836.

The justification for believing that the entire continent belonged to the United States was termed "manifest destiny," or a carrying out of the Divine Providence. The concept encouraged expansionism and was connected with slavery—both the North and the South wanted to admit those new states that supported its section's economic, political, and slave policies. By the end of the 19th century, the belief was used to support expansion in the Caribbean and the Pacific.

After the war between the states, battles against the American Indians continued, as did broken treaties between the two sides. There was a brutal war against the Apache; Custer's Last Stand; the removal of the Nez Perce from the Northwest in 1877; the massacre of hundreds of surrendering men, women, and children at Wounded Knee, South Dakota, in 1890; and, in addition, the corrupt paternalism of the Bureau of Indian Affairs.

Defenders point out that Japanese historians fail to tell the story of the rape of Nanking; that Soviet books leave out the Stalinist terror; that Iraqi children are not given the facts of the Gulf War. Meanwhile, until multicultural textbooks address the situation, Indians continue to be romantically depicted as ecologically sensitive "noble savages." {Kenneth C. Davis, "Ethnic Cleansing Didn't Start in Bosnia," *The New York Times*, 3 September 1995}

NATURAL LAW

Natural law is the doctrine that human affairs should be governed by ethical principles that are part of the very nature of things and that can be understood by reason. The first two paragraphs of the American "Declaration of Independence" contain a clear statement of the doctrine. {DCL}

NATURALISM

• Naturalism, in philosophy,

> is a position that attempts to explain all phenomena and account for all values using strictly natural (not supernatural) categories. The opposite of idealism, it is sometimes equated with empiricism and positivism.
>
> In a broad sense, naturalism has been maintained in diverse forms by Aristotle, the Cynics, the Stoics, **Giordano Bruno**, **Spinoza**, **Thomas Hobbes**, **Auguste Comte**, **Jean Jacques Rousseau**, **Friedrich Nietzsche**, **Karl Marx**, William James, **John Dewey**, and Alfred North Whitehead. These philosophers, however, differed widely on specific questions. Comte and Nietzsche, for example, were professed atheists whereas Aristotle, James, and **Dewey** attempted to explain phenomena in terms of biological processes of perception. Spinoza and the idealists emphasized metaphysics.
>
> **Peter H. Hare** has written about the American naturalist tradition: "The Enlightenment naturalism found in **Cadwallader Colden**, **Franklin**, **Jefferson**, and others was enriched in the nineteenth century by German and British idealism—the concept of experience in American naturalism was much broadened by wrestling with idealism; the same sources contributed process logic to American naturalism. As is widely recognized, Darwinian biology also enriched American naturalism; to mention still another example, medieval logic enriched **Charles Sanders Peirce**'s naturalism. In the twentieth century, the close study of Aristotle enriched the naturalism of **John Herman Randall Jr.**, **C. I. Lewis**'s naturalism was enriched by lifelong study of Kant. Marxism enriched the naturalisms of **Roy Wood Sellars** and **Marvin Faber**. **W. V. O. Quine**'s naturalism has been enriched by Rudolf Carnap's linguistic philosophy, Alfred Tarski's philosophy of logic, and Pierre Duhem's philosophy of science." Hare also cites the naturalism of **Murray Murphey**, **Hilary Kornblith**, **James Gouinlock**, **Arnold Berleant**, **Peter Manicas**, **Wilfrid Sellars**, and **Paul Kurtz.**
>
> Contemporary naturalists place an emphasis upon unifying the scientific viewpoint with an all-encompassing reality. Some resources on the subject are Marvin Farber's *Naturalism and Subjectivism* (1959), V. C. Punzo's *Reflective Naturalism* (1969), Jamie M. Ferreira's *Skepticism and Reasonable Doubt* (1987), and P. F. Strawson's *Skepticism and Naturalism: Some Varieties* (1987).

Thomas Clark has material on the Web about naturalism: <http://www.naturalism.org>.

• Naturalism, in literature,

> includes an analysis of reality in terms of natural forces—heredity, environment, physical drives. **Émile Zola** in his *Le Roman expérimental* (1880) said that like a scientist a novelist should examine various phenomena in life and draw indisputable conclusions. Other literary naturalists were **the Goncourt brothers**, J. K. Huysmans, **Guy de Maupassant**, **George Moore**, **George Gissing**, **Theodore Dreiser**, Frank Norris, Stephen Crane, **James T. Farrell**, and James Jones. In the late 19th century, naturalism became associated with André Antoine, Otto Brahm, Constantin Stanislavsky and the Moscow Art Theatre, and dramatists such as Henry François Becque, **Gerhart Hauptmann**, Count Leo Tolstoy, and **Maxim Gorky.**

• One teacher has illustrated for laymen the nuances of the meaning of naturalism in philosophic circles:

For the **theistic supernaturalist**,
"in the beginning" means *Genesis*.

For the **philosophic naturalist**,
"in the beginning" means "the Big Bang" and "RNA."

For the **scientific naturalist**,
as John Muir said, "I find that if I touch anything, it's connected to everything else in the universe."

. . . and in literary and artistic circles:

The **literary realist**
sees a wastebasket which is rectangular, black, 2 feet wide by 3 feet high, and costs $30.83 postpaid, tax included.

The **literary romantic**
sees the same item as an elegant, contemporary, Danish-designed receptacle which matches any decor and costs a mere $30.83

The **literary naturalist**
sees a cheap, rectangular, black hospital container with pus and stains on one side, discarded bandages at the bottom, and an unidentified three-pound chunk of bone and flesh dripping with blood in the center.

The **artistic naturalist** sees an elegant woman seated on a porch overlooking a tree-shaded pond, a black Burmese kitten at her feet, an Apple Macintosh laptop perched on her skirt, her inexpensive wastebasket partly filled with discarded, unwrinkled drafts of sonnets.

(See entry for James Thrower, whose *Short History of Western Atheism* describes non-and anti-theistic developments in pre-Socratic, Socratic, and Hellenistic times. See a discussion of naturalism by Arthur C. Danto in the *Encyclopedia of Philosophy*, Vol. 5. See *American Philosophic Naturalism in the Twentieth Century*, edited by John Ryder (1993); and "The Significance of American Philosophic Naturalism" by Patrick Romanell, *Free Inquiry*, Winter 1995-1996. See the entry for Humanistic Naturalism, a term John Dewey and others preferred.) {CE}

NATURALIST CHURCH: See entry for the "Supernaturalism minus super equals Naturalism" International Naturalist Church.

NATURALISTIC HUMANISM: See entry for Humanists, Naturalistic.

NATURALISTIC HUMANISM MOVEMENT

An attempt to start a "naturalistic humanism movement" began in 1953 at the Rienzi, a roué's hangout in New York City's Greenwich Village. The attempt died the following year.

Commenced by John Collins and Warren Allen Smith as a European-style student philosophic movement, it appealed to intelligentsia who were against the existentialism propounded by Jean-Paul Sartre and for naturalistic humanism, the philosophic outlook of Corliss Lamont. Although it was unable to appeal to large numbers who would have stormed St. Patrick's and St. John's cathedrals demanding an end to their tax-exempt status, or paraded on various campuses to stir up collegiates' interest in philosophy, the group did form the Greenwich Village Humanist Club and worked with the American Humanist Association's New York City chapter. (See entries for John Collins; Greenwich Village Humanist Club; Humanists, Naturalistic; and Warren Allen Smith.)

NATURALISTIC HUMANIST, THE OLDEST: See entry for Lucy.

NATURE

• Nature is a perpetual circulatory worker, generating fluids out of solids, and solids out of fluids, fixed things out of volatile, & volatile out of fixed.

–Isaac Newton

To some, nature is what God created in six days, an entity over which man was to be lord. Adam, the creation chosen to be lord and whose name is derived from *adamah*, or earth, developed a depraved nature, or so Paul taught in the Bible, and not only did Adam lose the original righteousness insofar as the supernatural gift of divine grace was concerned but also he transmitted this sin to all his descendants. Theologians then, as well as now, have found it difficult to explain how the sin of Adam could be transmitted that way. Present-day Protestants tend to reject the theory of the origin of sin as being in Adam's "fall."

In 1925, Bertrand Russell in *What I Believe* wrote, "The philosophy of nature should not be unduly terrestrial; the earth is merely one of the smaller planets of one of the smaller stars of the Milky Way. Vitalism as a philosophy, and evolutionism, show, in this respect, a lack of sense of proportion and logical relevance. They regard the facts of life, which are personally interesting to us, as having a cosmic significance, not a significance confined to the earth's surface. Optimism and pessimism, as cosmic philosophies, show the same naive humanism; the great world, so far as we know it from the philosophy of nature, is neither good nor bad, and is not concerned to make us happy or unhappy. All such philosophies spring from self-importance, and are best corrected by a little astronomy."

Arthur C. Clarke, in *3001*, tells of a future space trip in which Nature is re-named:

> When they were fifty thousand kilometers out, [Poole] was about to view the whole of Star City, as a narrow ellipse enclosing the Earth. Though the far side was barely visible, as a hairline of light against the stars, it was awe-inspiring to think that the human race had now set this sign upon the heavens.
>
> Then Poole remembered the rings of Saturn, infinitely more glorious. The astronautical engineers still had a long, long way to go before they could match the achievements of Nature.
>
> Or, if that was the right word, Deus.

(For a contemporary theory about the origin of life in nature, see the entry for Richard Dawkins.) {Lee Eisler, *The Quotable Bertrand Russell*; John Updike, "Immortal Isaac," *The New Yorker*, 30 March 1998}

Naudé, Gabriel (1600–1653)

A scholar, heretic, and skeptic, Naudé is cited by Robertson as one of the freethinkers in seventeenth-century France, along with La Mothe le Vayer and Gui Patin. Naudé, however, sided with the Catholics in politics. Because of his forensic defense of the Massacre, a brutal religious slaughter of that time, he is, along with Patin, sometimes claimed as a believer. {JMR; JMRH}

Navarro, Antonio (20th Century)

Navarro has been the director of Radio and TV Marti and a senior vice president of W. R. Grace. In 1990 he was appointed director of the U.S. Information Agency's Office of Cuba Broadcasting, overseeing the operation of Radio and TV Marti. From 1985 to 1990 he served on the Presidential Advisory Board for Cuba Broadcasting. In *Tocayo* (1981), he wrote of two suspenseful years of his life during the onset of Fidel Castro's dictatorship. In his underground resistance movement against Castro, he was known by the code name "Tocayo" (namesake).

In 1986, he received the New York City Liberty Medal, awarded to foreign-born citizens who have made a contribution to the city. And he has directed in Lima, Peru, the foundation of a graduate school of business in association with Stanford University. Navarro is a freethinker, as evidenced by an op ed article he wrote for the *Miami Herald* (9 February 1995):

> I submit that a rightful life—not out of fear of eternal punishment or hope of eternal reward, but out of self-respect and love for your fellow human beings—is the true mark of an honorable man or woman. . . . Religion is necessary for many, and properly so. It is comforting, relieves anxiety, provides meaning to life. But some others, the silent minority, simply—and most of them quietly—accept our unexplainable world for what it is: unexplainable. Count me in.

{*Freethought Today*, June-July 1997}

Navarro, Osvaldo (20th Century)

Navarro, a Cuban, spoke on "Man, Naturalism, and Literature" at the 1996 Humanist World Congress held in Mexico City.

Navarro de Francisco, Cesar (20th Century)

Dr. Navarro de Francisco is a former president of the *Ateneo* of Madrid, a headquarters that was built in 1884. The *Ateneos* (The Atheneums) were founded in the nineteenth century, stimulated by classical Athens, and devoted to humanist values and freethought.

Navez, Napoleon (19th Century)

Navez was a Belgian freethinker. He became the president of Antwerp's *Libre Pensée*. Also, he was an active member of the Council of the International Federation of Freethinkers. {BDF}

Navias, Eugene B. (20th Century)

Navias wrote *Parish Ministry and Pedagogy 1823–1983: A Past and Future Look at Religious Education* (1983).

Nayar, Kuldip (20th Century)

Nayar delivered the M. N. Roy Memorial Lecture under the auspices of the Indian Renaissance Institute at New Delhi in 1999. In "Prospects of India-Pakistan Relations," he detailed the problems between the two countries. {*The Radical Humanist*, June 1999}

Nayler, James (1617?–1660)

A Quaker, Nayler was a disciple of George Fox. Gradually, however, he gained his own following and in 1656 rode into Bristol, his group crying, "Holy, holy, holy, Lord God of Israel." A parliamentary trial in 1656 was told that his disciples were worshiping, not Nayler, but the "Christ within him." However, he was sentenced, whipped through the streets, pilloried, bored through the tongue with a hot iron, branded in the forehead, and sent to hard labor in prison. Nayler is typical of the many hundreds of Quaker "unbelievers" who were imprisoned and more or less cruelly handled during the 17th century. {CE; JMR; JMRH}

Naylor, B. S. (19th Century)

In Australia, Naylor edited a spiritualist and freethought monthly, *Glow-Worm* (1869 to 1870). {FUK}

NAZARETH See entry for Christmas.

NCCL: See the entry for Brian Dyson, who wrote *Liberty in Britain 1934–1994, A Diamond Jubilee History of the National Council for Civil Liberties*. The National Council for Civil Liberties' (NCCL's) first president was the freethinker and novelist E. M. Forster.

NEANDERTHAL MAN

Although students of prehistory have speculated that Neanderthal man had some part in the evolution of modern humanity, a 1997 study of Neanderthal DNA suggested it has no such connection, that interbreeding was not possible. The study of bones found in Germany that were over 30,000 years old also indicated that the Neanderthals split off much earlier from the hominid line than modern humans did. This left chimpanzees, the study found, as mankind's closest living relatives.

Not so, reported Dr. Erik Trinkaus, a paleonthropologist at Washington University in St. Louis. His mid-1999 study alleged that Neanderthals and modern humans not only coexisted for thousands of years but also that they cohabited. Upon examining a 24,500-year-old skeleton of a young boy discovered in a shallow Portuguese grave, Trinkaus found not only that the boy was a hybrid but also that the discovey "refutes strict replacement models of modern human origins" and also seemed to undermine interpretations of the 1997 study, done by Dr. Svante Paabo of the University of Munich in Germany. The Paabo study was wrong because all that it showed "is that Neanderthal biology is outside the range of living humans, not modern Homo sapiens back then." Scientists at the end of the century found the differing studies intriguing and only tentative. "But if you look deep enough in evolutionary time," said Dr. Alan Templeton at Washington University, "you find a lot of interbreeding. That is what humanity is all about: we interbreed a lot." {*The Economist*, 112 July 1997; *The New York Times*, 25 April 1999}

Nearing, Scott (183-1983): See entry for George Orwell, who considered the leftwing journalist and writer a possible member of the Communist Party.

Nebbeling, Dirk (20th Century)

Nebbeling is active with the Humanist Fellowship of West Michigan. (See entry for Michigan Humanists.) {FD}

NEBRASKA HUMANISTS

• Reason, PO Box 24358, Omaha, NE 68124; (402) 553-5607

NECROMANCY

Necromancy, a word with its roots in the Greek *nekros*, corpse, includes black magic, sorcery, magic qualities, and predicting the future by communicating with the spirits of the dead.

NECROPHAGIA

Necrophagia (eating of parts of a corpse, a practice followed in some primitive religions), necrophilia (an erotic interest in corpses), and theophagy (eating of a god) have figured in some religious beliefs. (See entries for Death and Corpse Worship. A 1997 movie in which necophilia is used as an erotic theme is David Cronenberg's "Crash.")

NECROPHILIA

Necrophilia is an obsessive fascination with corpses and with death. (See entry for theophagy, the "eating of God.")

Neale, Edward Vansittart (1810–1892)

A freethinker, Neale wrote "Reason, Religion, and Revelation" (1875). {GS}

Needham, (Noel) Joseph [Terence Montgomery] (1900–1995)

A scientist and China scholar, the "Erasmus of the Twentieth Century," Needham is known for his *Clerks and Craftsmen in China and the West* (1970). Dubbed an eccentric who in his middle age was a Morris dancer, the author of *Molly Dancing in East Anglia*, Needham became one of the few holders of fellowships both of the Royal Society (for scientists) and the British Academy (for the rest).

He was a sociologist who edited *Science, Religion, and Reality* (1955) and wrote *Science and Civilisation in China* (6 volumes, 1954–1985). Needham had conceived the latter book when he traveled to China in 1942 and began wondering how the West could have overlooked such Chinese scientific inventions as printing, pest control, the magnetic compass, the casting of iron, stirrups, efficient horse harnesses, wheelbarrows, and gunpowder. The project became so extensive that he and dozens of associates worked on it for the next five decades. Experts often compare his work to that of Darwin and Gibbon for its size and scope.

His interest in biochemistry at Cambridge University led him to write the three-volume *Chemical Embryology*, the lengthy forward of which was later published as a separate book, *A History of Embryology*, which is still regarded as a definitive work. Needham argued that a fundamental difference between Western and Chinese approaches to scientific advancement is the West's preoccupation with natural law. The West follows scientific principles developed by Galileo and others, whereas the Chinese Taoist and Confucian tradition is more concerned with social ethics and the direct implications of science. "A wise ancient counselor advised against gunpowder," Needham observed, "for it singed beards, burned houses, and brought Taoism into discredit." An admirer of Taoism, regarding its initiates as primitive communists, Needham was a champion of China to the end of his life.

At Cambridge, Needham was almost as well known for his left-wing beliefs as for his scientific achievements. An avowed Marxist, he along with J. D. Bernal and Julian Huxley charged America with using germ warfare during the Korean War, resulting in his being barred from entering the United States. During World War II, he called for the formation of a new international scientific agency, and he is sometimes credited with putting the "s" in UNESCO. From 1946 to 1948, Needham served as the group's director of natural sciences. He was associated with Cambridge University for seventy years, and he and his first wife, Dorothy, were the first married couple (besides Queen Victoria and Prince Albert) to become Fellows of the Royal Society. After his first wife's death, Needham married his longtime colleague, Lu Gwei Djen, who died in 1991.

"I have always been an Anglican and a socialist," Needham has written, for he admitted to liking William Laud (1573–1645), the archbishop who was hostile to Puritanism and who believed that the Anglican ritual should be strictly followed. "I have always been a rationalist in the sense that I think it is very good for the Church to be criticised and I suspect that some of the Fellows thought it peculiar, to say the least of it, on account of my reputation, that I was the one who introduced the *New Humanist* to the Senior Combination Room at Caius College. One of the most liberating experiences of my life was when I found that about a quarter of humanity (the Chinese and their congeners) have no need for the doctrine of a benevolent creator God. I therefore became, without giving up my Christianity, an 'honorary Taoist' because the Tao might be described as the order of nature and the way in which everything works. I even became a Lay Reader attached to the church of Thaxted in Essex where I served for many years. . . . Thus I have not been what is normally called a rationalist in all my life, but defined in my own way I am one, really."

In 1941 Needham was elected an honorary associate of the Rationalist Press Association. {CE; TRI}

Nees von Esenbeck, Christian Gottfried (1776–1858)

A German naturalist, Nees von Esenbeck first became a doctor of medicine, then a professor of botany at Bonn (1819) and Breslau (1831). He was leader of the free religious movement in Silesia and, in 1848, took part in the political agitations and was deprived of his chair. Nees von Esenbeck wrote several works on natural philosophy. {BDF}

Nefertiti or **Nefretete**: See entry for Ikhnaton.

Negri, Gaetano (1838–1902)

An eminent Italian historian, Negri as a youth fought against the Papal troops but then became leader of the Conservatives at Milan. In the Senate, he was so lenient to the Church in his later works that he is claimed as being orthodox. His best known work, *Julian the Apostate*, speaks of Christianity as "an irrational illusion" and in the preface Villari describes Negri as "a confirmed Rationalist." {JM; RAT; RE}

Negri, Maxine (20th Century)

In 1990 Negri arranged with the Humanist Society of Friends to share American Humanist Association facilities for the performing of weddings, memorial services, and personal counseling. Negri is on the editorial board of *The Humanist*, and, in 1981, was named Humanist Pioneer of the Year. She has been published in New Zealand's *Rationalist and Humanist*.

"I consider humanism to be the hope of the world," she said in 1994. "Scientific data led by human reasoning and human-created ethics is the future of our planet. Our job is to get the message and concept out—loud and clear—to every inhabited corner of Earth. The world's greatest challenge at present is to defeat the fanaticism of religious fundamentalism. . . . America's is in safeguarding our Constitution's guarantee of separation of church and state." {HNS2; *The Humanist*, March-April 1999}

Negri, Vitali (20th Century)

Negri, a contributor of freethought articles to *The American Rationalist*, wrote *The Creator and the Created* (1933).

Negri-Garlanda, Ada (1870–1945)

Negri-Garlanda was an Italian poet of works such as *Fatalita* (1892), *Tempeste* (1895), and *Maternita* (1896). In 1896 she married Garlanda, a merchant. Negri-Garlanda was a Socialist and rationalist. {RAT}.

Nehru, Jawaharlal [Prime Minister] (1889–1964)

India's first Prime Minister, Nehru was the son of a devoted Hindu mother and a humanistic father. Nehru, who thought spiritualism absurd and the belief in a personal god "very odd" indeed, wrote, "I am interested in this world, in this life, not in some other world or a future life." Sibnarayan Ray, a lecturer in English literature at City College, Calcutta University, wrote the present author in 1949 about Nehru,

> His mind is a queer ensemble of scientific ideas and primitive beliefs; he lives in the Western style, speaks and writes excellent English, talks rationalism and democracy, and then observes all the ancient superannuated rituals of Hindu society. Take for example the custom of Sradh, of offering sacrifices to the dead. Nehru observed it when his father died some years before. He comes of a Kashmir Brahmin family and is quite openly fanatical about preserving the blood-purity of his caste. Most journalists and admirers from the West do not seem to have any guess about this facet of his personality. But what is more surprising is that they refuse to recognise by common consent what is patent and obvious—his insufferable arrogance, his messy thinking and wooliness, his fondness for self-exhibition, and his dictatorial temper. Quite recently (1949) an American journalist, Mr. Martin Ebon of McGraw Hill Co., interviewed him and had some taste of his greatness—ask him for his impression." Ray adds that the real humanists in India have been Jyotirao Phule and Isvar Chandra Vidyasagar but that their work, unlike Nehru's, has not been translated from Maharashtrian and Bengali, respectively.
>
> His will, read in part on All India Radio by his sister Madame Pandit, included the following: "My desire to have a handful of my ashes thrown into the Ganga at Allahabad has no religious significance, so far as I am concerned. I have no religious sentiment in the matter. I have been attached to the Ganga and the Jumna rivers in Allahabad ever since my childhood and, as I have grown older, this attachment has also grown. . . . The Ganga, especially, is the river of India, beloved of her people, round which are intertwined her racial memories, her hopes and fears, her songs of triumph, her victories and her defeats. . . . And though I have discarded much of past tradition and custom, and am anxious that India should rid herself of all shackles that bind and constrain her and divide her people, and suppress vast numbers of them, and prevent the free development of the body and the spirit; though I seek all this, yet I do not wish to cut myself off from the past completely. . . . The major portion of my ashes should, however, be disposed of otherwise. I want these to be carried high up into the air in an aeroplane and scattered from that height over the fields where the peasants of India toil, so that they might mingle with the dust and soil of India and become an indistinguishable part of India.

Stanley Wolpert's *Nehru: A Trust With Destiny* (1996) provides a negative view. For him, Nehru was a Fabian with an undying belief in the "benevolent despotism" of strong socialist government. Wolpert claims that Nehru did not understand the tension between India's religious groups, and this allegedly led to the country's double partition, Punjab and Bengal. He also has outraged certain sections of the Indian intelligentsia because, from the University of California in Los Angeles where he teaches Indian history, he wrote to *The Indian Express* (5 February 1997), explaining his suggestion that Nehru may have had homosexual experiences. According to the newspaper, Wolpert said he did not broach the subject during his three meetings with Nehru in 1957–1958. However, Nehru enjoyed dressing in drag:

> Wearing his wig, made up with lipstick, powder and eye shadow, his body draped in silks and satins, Jawahar most willingly offered himself up night after night to those endless rehearsals for the Gaekwar's At Home as a beautiful young girl, holding out her jug of wine and loaf seductively to her poet lover, Omar.

Wolpert claims that Nehru's first attachment was with a young man called Ferdinand Brooks, his French teacher. A theosophist, the "handsome" man was a disciple and lover of Charles Webster Leadbeater, a renegade Anglican curate who was accused of child molestation and pederasty on several continents. Leadbeater openly advocated mutual masturbation among young boys. Wolpert also suggested that Nehru may have had a gay relationship in Harrow and he made much of Panditji's admiration for Oscar Wilde. As a result, many Indians have generally been aghast at the accusation, but not Ashok Row Kavi of the Humsafar Trust, which publishes India's only registered gay and lesbian magazine.

Prakash Narain of the Indian Humanist Union has pointed out that although Nehru used the word "spiritual," he did so in the sense that many humanists do and had not turned a "theist" nor ceased to be an agnostic. (See entries Prakash Narain and for Sibnarayan Ray. Also see "What Is Religion," *New Humanist*, November 1989.) {CB; CE; CL; *The Economist*, 18 January 1997; HNS2; TRI; TYD; WAS, Sibnarayan Ray, 1949}

Neider, Charles (20th Century)

Neider edited "Mark Twain—Reflections on Religion" in *Hudson Review #16* (1963). {GS}

Neidig, H. (19th Century)

A freethinker, Neidig wrote *Mistakes in the Teaching of Jesus* (1892). {GS}

Neill, A(lexander) S(utherland) (1883–1973)

Neill, a Scottish headmaster of the Summerhill School in Leiston, Suffolk, England, was internationally known for his *Summerhill: A Radical Approach to Child Rearing* (1960, with a foreword by Erich Fromm). Other of his works were *The Problem Teacher* (1939), *Hearts, Not Heads* (1945), *The Problem Family* (1948), *The Free Child* (1953); and *Talking of Summerhill* (1967, its American title being *Freedom, Not License*).

Neill's progressive coeducational Summerhill School at Leiston, England, included optional attendance, a school parliament, and no religious instruction. Some educators continue to debate his philosophy.

A friend of Wilhelm Reich, Neill accompanied Reich's wife, Ilse Ollendorff, to the public school in New Canaan, Connecticut, where she and the present writer were teachers in the 1960s. Neill was nonplused by the elaborate and air-conditioned facilities, the comfortable chairs, the imposing library, the planetarium, the audio-visual studio which piped programs to classrooms, the science laboratories, the athletic rooms and fields. "How can you teach in such a place!" he marveled, stating that his own school had only the most elementary facilities. Told of the influence of John Dewey and William Heard Kilpatrick upon the art and English department's educational philosophy, Neill continued to marvel, highly approving of what he observed. Over coffee, he told of some of his "radical" ideas, adding that "radical" comes from *radix*, root, and his educational philosophy aimed at the roots of teaching. Asked about his philosophic outlook, he scoffed at organized religion and stated that he was continually formulating his philosophy, that he did not expect to finish the task nor did he think that that would be desirable. {TRI; WAS, conversation}

Neilson, John Shaw (1872–1942)

Neilson was a South Australian freethinker and poet. In 1893, he won the Australian Natives Association Literary Prize.

Nelson, B. J. (20th Century)

Nelson is secretary-treasurer of the Humanist Association of New Hampshire-Vermont. (See entry for New Hampshire Humanists.) {FD}

Nelson, Gustave (19th Century)

Nelson wrote for the New York *Truthseeker* and is conjectured to be the author of *Bible Myths and Their Parallels in Other Religions*, a learned work that shows how much of Christianity has been taken from paganism. Born in Denmark, Nelson moved to America, eventually becoming a physician. {BDF; PUT; RAT}

Nelson, Jon (20th Century)

Nelson reviewed *The Book Your Church Doesn't Want You To Read* for *Humanist in Canada* (Spring 1997), finding it "the most talked-about book in the freethought movement."

Nelson, Margaret (20th Century)

In Britain, Nelson is active with the Suffolk and North Essex Humanists.

Nelson, Richard (20th Century)

Nelson, a Texas freethinker, was one of the planners of a January 1999 Humanist and Freethought Conference in Arlington, Texas.

Nelson, Ron (20th Century)

In Culver City, California, Nelson edited the monthly *Atheist Connection* (1982 to 1983).

Nelson, Theodor (Ted) Holm (1938?–)

In 1960, Nelson created a computer project called Xanadu, one which resulted in his being called the "hypertext guru and design genius" of cyberspace, "one of the seminal thinkers of our century," and "the greatest computer visionary of our time." He predicted the universal knowledge repository known today as the World Wide Web. Xanadu as a software product changed its specifications a number of times. But it has been described as an ultimate vision of the "docuverse" and involves all documents in the world accessible to all people in the world, with a way to see and create connections among all the documents and their parts.

His Project Xanadu is devoted to the idea that, in or out of cyberspace, we need freedom and availability of information. His dream is of a global hypertext publishing system, a universal library, a system to resolve copyright disputes, and a meritocratic forum for discussion and debate. By putting all such information within reach of all people, Xanadu is meant to eliminate scientific ignorance and help cure political misunderstandings. It links virtual documents from text or audio-visual elements widely dispersed on a computer network with easy version tracking. It also provides for micropayment of authors' royalties nd coordinates copyright, ownership, and quotations functions. His concept of hypertext has made Nelson legendary in programming circles.

Nelson in 1959 earned a B.A. in philosophy from Swarthmore College but was almost expelled for his arguments in favor of sexual liberation. In 1963 he earned an M.A. in sociology from Harvard. *Computer Lib/Dream Machines: You Can and Must Understand Computers NOW* (1974) was published four months prior to the unveiling of the first commercial available personal computer.

In "The Curse of Xanadu" (*Wired*, June 1995), Gary Wolf wrote,

> Nelson's hatred of conventional structure made him difficult to educate. Bored and disgusted by school, he once plotted to stab his seventh-grade teacher with a sharpened screwdriver, but lost his nerve at the last minute and walked out of the classroom, never to return. On his long walk home, he came up with the four maxims that have guided his life: most people are fools, most authority is malignant, God does not exist, and everything is wrong.

Nelson is the son of actress Celeste Holm and playwright Ralph Nelson (1916–1987), who directed the 1962 movie "Requiem for a Heavyweight" and "Lilies of the Field" (1963). A designer, generalist, and contrarian, Nelson holds that "transclusive hypermedia will be the publishing medium of the future" and in his *Literary Machines* has called himself a "Systems Humanist." "I identify as a card-carrying atheist," he has written, "but I can't find anyone to issue me a card."

He is author of *Computer Lib: Dream Machines* (1987), an unusual book which *Wired* and other publications cite as indicating that he was the designer in 1965 of HTTP (Hyper Text Transfer Protocol). A developer of software and zipper lists, he teaches at Keio University Shonan Fujisawa Campus.

Explaining his coinages hypertex (http) and hypermedia, Nelson has told his students at Japan's Keio University and others via <http://www.sfc.keio.ac.jp/~ted/> that

- Hypertext is Literature, not Technology.
- Literature is a Two-God System.
- There is a philosophy of interconnection behind Xanadu.
- Xanadu is a Three-God System.
- Xanadu may be a Four-God System.
- Xanalogical Structure Is the Manifest Destiny of Literature.

From the early 1980s until 1998, he worked on a design for ZigZag, a software program that uses no metaphors, no icons, no applications, "a Tinkertoy world for users to share, explore, and reconfigure." An Australian, Andrew Pam, wrote a demo version of the program which uses a Perl 5 code and runs under the Linux operating system which Nelson describes as "the sexual revolution brought to the spreadsheet. In a spreadsheet, society required that a cell have an up connection, a downconnection, a left connection, and a right connection. In this system each cell's connections are its own business."

When fifteen, Nelson wrote the following:

YES

There are apparently people
To whom a small bier
From the bartender of the First Cause
Signifies the ultimate binge.

{CA; E; WAS, 1950–1998; *Technology Review*, September-October 1998; *Wired*, June 1995 and September 1995}

Nelson, Wallace (1856–1943)

In 1892, Wallace was a lecturer in Queensland, Australia, of the Gympie Secular Society. Scottish-born, he was a rationalist, journalist, and politician. Only 4' 8" tall, he was editor of *Stockwhip* (Sydney), *People's Newspaper* (Rockhampton), and *Westralian Worker* (Kalgoorlie). In 1883 he wrote *The Death of Adam*. On his death, he was cremated and the obituary notice in *The Rationalist* included that he "never wavered in opposition to superstition." {SWW}

Nemerov, Howard (1920–1991)

Nemerov, an American author who writes poetry, fiction, criticism, often with a philosophic viewpoint, received a Pulitzer in 1977 for his *Collected Poems*. Asked about humanism, he responded to the present author:

> I have not myself had much occasion to use the word *humanism* or its curricular form *humanities*. The latter probably began as an administrative convenience for separating what was science from whatever was not, but the tail soon began wagging the dog—as if the sciences were somehow not a human endeavor! —and people accordingly began treating the verbal distinction as a real border, or maybe a better chasm.
>
> Your investigation has as a side-effect the illustration of what happens when people meet the demand to define their terms, the demand is a sign of unease, possibly of disease, a crisis of faith in which what is demanded is demanded precisely because it has become impossible: the result is a splitting into orthodoxies and heresies of just that sectarian sort that has ever been characteristic of religion and its disputes, wranglings, hair-splittings, and burnings at the stake; the sort, maybe, that the term humanism was in the first place designed to evade. This is a Laodician response on my part, and I have long regarded the trimmers as the nicest people in hell. To be at home in one's language is to be happy with its splendid inability to stick to one subject or to say only one thing about it.
>
> I'll settle for being comfortably, or what others will call ignobly, vague.

{WAS, 24 March 1989}

NEO-CLASSICAL HUMANISM—THE GREAT WORD WAR

For several hundred years after the Renaissance period, there was not much concern for nor interest in classical humanism, and it was in the latter 19th and early 20th centuries that an adherent such as Matthew Arnold took center stage. He looked at the world of his day and decided that its "barbarians, Philistines, and the populace in general" suffered a great need in their intellectual life for Hellenism. He suggested that, to satisfy this need for intellectual nourishment, the world should look backward. It should look backward to the highest and best ideas which were available from the past and which could advantageously be imitated. The new Renaissance he envisioned was a "Renascence," a word that never became popularly used.

A quarter of a century after Arnold died, his concepts of culture were taken up and advanced by William C. Brownell, Irving Babbitt, and Paul Elmer More. These neo-classical humanists, "neo-humanists," maintained that man cannot hope to go forward unless he looks backward for models of perfection. They argued that faith in science alone would never be sufficient to solve man's problems, and they pointed to the unbridled arrogance of science and the unchecked dreaming of romanticism which they claimed had combined to give man a most dangerous and conceitful notion—that of the idea of progress. Science, they pointed out, only led men into the dens of naturalism and materialism and from there into the caverns of a decadent culture. Something more than science was needed, they said, and that something was close to a need for culture in the Arnoldian sense of the word.

In 1929, over one dozen books and articles were written concerning "new humanism." In 1930, no fewer than six books and over fifty articles appeared in *Saturday Review of Literature, Bookman, New Republic, Yale Review, Commonweal, Scribner's, Forum,* and *Christian Century*.

From 1928 to 1933, the movement was in its heyday. Support came from T. S. Eliot and Norman Foerster as well as from Stuart P. Sherman, L. T. More, G. E. Elliott, E. J. Mather, A. R. Thompson, Robert Shafer, H. H. Clark, G. B. Munson, S. B. Gass, R. L. Brown, and L. J. A. Mercier. Together, they turned out and defined their positions toward humanism in what amounted to thousands of paragraphs, barrels of printer's ink, and tons of paper, leading one wag to describe the movement as "Word War I." Of the many books on the subject, those by Babbitt and More are the most authoritative and Foerster's *Humanism and America* (1930) the most representative.

In 1989, Harry Levin, the Irving Babbitt professor of comparative literature emeritus at Harvard University, wrote, "Two generations ago my old teacher and Harvard predecessor, Irving Babbitt, was calling for a New Humanism. He had been protesting against certain modernistic tendencies that he—not I—thought were undermining the classical canons of literature. But culture itself was still focused upon the traditional habits of reading and writing, and more particularly upon great books. Subsequent developments in technology, leading toward audiovisual dependence and artificial intelligence, seem to be shifting away from humanism of any kind."

By 1930, however, the "new humanists" were being called "neo-humanists" and were being attacked by such influential writers as Mary M. Colum, Henry Seidel Canby, Max Eastman, C. H. Grattan, Henry Hazlitt, Lewis Mumford, G. N. Shuster, Edmund Wilson, and Rebecca West. Their main line of attack was on the cultural approach of neo-humanism. Allen Tate and other Catholics, as well as Charles Francis Potter and many liberal ministers, assailed the movement on religious grounds. In addition, it was attacked by philosophers and scientists who did not agree with the neo-humanist opinion concerning naturalism. Representative of the attacks was *Critique of Humanism*, edited by C. H. Grattan, a direct reply to the claims made in Foerster's *Humanism and America*.

Although the average man in the bread lines knew little about the great word war, many of the nation's intellectuals were preoccupied with humanism from 1930 to 1933. Spectacular verbal battles were waged, some quite personal and disagreeable. Babbitt came in for the most criticism, and he fought back valiantly, never giving in on a point, especially in regard to his personal dislike of Rousseau. In one bout, Babbitt called H. L. Mencken an author whose writings were "nearer to intellectual vaudeville than to serious criticism." Mencken replied that the new humanism was but "a somewhat sickly and shamefaced Christian mysticism." Grattan accused the neo-humanists of being merely "skilled practitioners of the literary racket."

Other fights receiving top billing were O. W. Firkins vs. Edmund Wilson; Hazlitt vs. T. S. Eliot; and Tate vs. Shafer. Shafer called Tate a contemptible creature possessed of "self-confident readiness in the art of misrepresentation." Canby criticized Babbitt and neo-humanism as being but examples of a narrow sectarianism, and Hazlitt accused the movement of trying to revive an outworn and discredited metaphysics. Rebecca West warned that anyone who followed More as a critic and guide of modern literature did so at his own heavy cost. She granted that the only man of genius whom the neo-humanists could claim was T. S. Eliot, but she added that all the rest of their supporters would hardly make an even exchange for Proust, Joyce, Lawrence, Aldous Huxley, and Virginia Moore. Struggles such as these were commonplace in 1930 magazine columns.

Their emphasis upon the literary gave the neo-humanists the reputation of being "literary humanists," but they neither liked the title nor that of "neo-humanist." In literature they were opposed to such writers as Dreiser, Sinclair

Lewis, Mencken, and James Branch Cabell because of these authors' "futile idealism." Rousseau received the greatest part of the blame for this allegedly futile idealism, especially from the pen of Babbitt. Agreeing with Babbitt, William L. Sperry wrote that Rousseau was the arch-enemy and "We are not to forget those angels of darkness who have given his (Rousseau's) heresy a local habitation: Cooper; Poe; Melville; Emerson; Whitman; Masters; Dreiser; and all their kind." Sperry continued, adding Einstein, Eddington, and Walter Lippmann.

In 1933, when L. J. A. Mercier's *Challenge of Humanism* was published, neo-humanism was all but dead. A Catholic and a Harvard professor, he originally had published the book in 1928 as *Mouvement Humaniste aux États-Unis*. Upon its publication, however, wags described his efforts as analogous to those of a doctor giving a blood transfusion to a centenarian with collapsed lungs. Worse, Babbitt died in 1933. T. S. Eliot, the obvious leader to take over the movement, had other projects to finish. This left Mercier who, like a guerrilla, was attacking as late as 1948, saying the University of Chicago's Chancellor Robert Hutchins was his type of humanist. In short, what started as "new humanism" and became "neo-humanism" died with its leaders. {For a discussion of the neo-humanists and their scorn of the determinism of Taine, of any form of "impressionism"—the term they loosely applied to theories such as those of Walter Pater and Benedetto Croce that accepted Immanuel Kant's separation of aesthetic experience from practical life—see the article by Stephen C. Brennan of Louisiana State University in *The Johns Hopkins Guide to Literary Theory & Criticism* (1994). Also, see entries for Norman Foerester, theism, and Charles Trinkaus.}

NEO-HUMANISM: See entries for Neo-Classical Humanism and for Harold Bloom.

NEO-MARXISM: See entry for Consilience.

NEONATICIDE

Neonaticide, a reference to the killing of a newborn, has been practiced and accepted in most cultures throughout history. As to whether it is immoral or an illness, professor of psychology Steven Pinker at the Massachusetts Institute of Technology holds that it is difficult to call it an illness. In fact, neonaticide may be a product of "maternal wiring." Mammalian mothers, he holds, must "decide" whether to allot their energy and food to their newborn or to their current and future offspring. If a newborn is sickly, or if its survival is not promising, "they may cut their losses and favor the healthiest in the litter or try again later on." The religious orthodox would find substituting "neonaticide" for "infanticide" unacceptable, either for humans or, apparently, for other animals. {Steven Pinker, "Why They Kill Their Newborns," *The New York Times Book Review*, 2 November 1997}

NEO-RELIGIONISTS: For an estimate of the number of neo-religionists worldwide, see the entry for Hell.

NEPAL HUMANISTS

Nepal is known for having the world's tallest mountain, Mt. Everest. It also is known for its apostle of peace, Raja Jayaprithvi Bahadur Singh (Raja Jaya Prithvi), an intellectual and secular humanist who in 1928 founded Humanistic Club in Europe, Asia, and America. The club's objectives were as follows:

- to open Humanistic Clubs in as many places of every country as possible so that the ideals of unity, peace, and cooperation may be with us even in our play, in our recreation, and in our light-heartedness;
- to conduct research in sociology, philosophy, and psychic phenomena and other disciplines so as to get into the inner truth of every aspect in life;
- to spread the ideals of truth to all contending parties and classes and, thus, make it possible to bring mutual goodwill and understanding among them;
- to exchange ideas on human interest with other sister organizations of the world; but in doing so one ought to strictly avoid controversial themes like religion and political propaganda;
- to build linkages of the Club with other social and philanthropic bodies.

In 1929 he started extensive travels to various countries to organize branches:

- a Geneva, Switzerland, club was formed at #3, Chemin de l'Escalade, Champel, Geneva, with Lady Blomfield, Baroness Tanfani, Myers Stolt (treasurer), Madam Myers, Hale White (secretary), Sindey [Cindy?] Brown, Mr. and Mrs. Rao;
- the Berlin, Germany, lecture took place under the auspices of the Mittwoch-Gesellschaft, whose President, Dr. Ludwig Stein, chaired the meeting;
- the Prague, Czechoslovakia, lecture took place at Sal Gregur Obseen Dum, with Dr. Professor Lesney chairing the meeting;
- In Vienna, Austria, the lecture took place in Industrishaus, the chair being Dr. Greiger of the University of Vienna;
- the Budapest, Hungary, meeting was held under the auspices of the Hungarian Club with many members of the Hungarian parliament present; Dr. Vamberi translated the lecture into the Hungarian language;
- The Belgrade, Yugoslavia, meeting was chaired by Alexander Yovicic, formerly Charge de Affairs in the Serbian Legation in London and held under the auspices of the Anglo-Jugoslav Club. Speakers included Dr. Brana Petronijevic, formerly professor of philosophy in the University of Belgrade; Dr. Sibe Melicic, a poet and member of the Ministry of Affairs. The lecture was translated by Dr. Vladeta Popovic of the University of Belgrade;
- In Bucharest, Romania, the lecture took place in Femme Casse, arranged for by Princess Kanta Kusino;
- In Warsaw, Poland, the lecture took place under the auspices of The Intellectual Union in Karmienica Duke's Mansion. Prof. Liebinski chaired the meeting;
- A second meeting in Berlin took place in Hotel Esplanade under the auspices of the League of Meera Mundam. The chair was Graff Bedandroff, the League's president;
- In Paris, France, the lecture took place in Salle des Fêtes du Grans Orient de France. The chair was Dr. P. Charpy and the speech was given as a poem:

  Asantushtaa dwijaa nashtaah
  Santushtaa iva paatrhivaah,
  Salajjaa ganikaa nashtaah,
  nirlajjaashca kulastriyah. . . .

- The first lecture was held in one of the committee rooms of the House of Commons during the occasion of the anniversary of the International Peace Society. The second took place in Coxton Hall, 12 Palmer Street, under the auspices of the Three-fold Movement—Union of East and West, League of Neighbours, and Fellowship of Faiths. Speakers besides the Raja were Annie Besant, president of the Theosophical Society; Cecil H. Wilson, Member of Parliament; Charles Frederick Weller, the American founder of the League of Neighbours; and Kedar Nath Das Gupta, founder of the Union of East and West in India, England, and America. The meeting was chaired by Sir Francis Young Husband.

The Raja then traveled to Venice, Iceland, Rome, Egypt, Sri Lanka, Singapore, Thailand, Hong Kong, Shanghai, and Japan during the year. His further trips included the following:

- 1931: Ram Dutta Awasthi from Askota was appointed as a teacher to start Satayavadi Primary School in Bajhang.
- 1931: In America, one of the Raja's lectures was broadcast in Chicago by the National Broadcasting Company.
- 1935: the Raja procured 5,000 masks from Japan and visited Abyssinia to serve war victims.
- 1936: the Raja established a free army hospital, a nursery school, and a primary school; he visited Burma to establish a basic school

about humanism, the Jaya Prithvi Institute, at Memio Rangoon.

• 1936: a Humanist Club was activated at Banglore and talks were given to oppose English rule in India and Rana rule in Nepal; the Raja expressed the view that the League of Nations was utterly failing to solve a rising threat of war and was not bringing peace into the world.

• 1938: a Satyavadi school in Bajhang was granted form approval by the director of schools, a royal a priest.

• 1939: Jaya Prithvi was perceived by the English rulers of India and the Rana rulers of Nepal as a trouble-maker and a threat to the status quo; he was kept under house arrest for one year in his Jai Bhawan Banglore, India, residence.

In Nepal, the Research Academica for Humanism & J. P. B. Singh, Nepal (RAFHAJ) is at PO Box 11201, Central Office, Kathmandu. Officers are as follows:

• Executive Committee
  President: Mr. Min Bdr. Singh
  Vice President: Mr. Dharma Bdr. Chand
  Treasurer: Mr. Narendra Bdr. Singh
  Member: Mr. Prem Bdr. Singh
  Member: Dr. Raja Ram Subedi
  Member: Ram Pd. Mishra

• Advisory Board
  Dr. Trailokya Nath Upreti
  Dr. Durga Pd. Bhandari
  Dr. Prem Raman Upreti
  Prof. B. C. Malla
  Mr. Yadav Kant Silwal

In 1998 the Humanist Association of Nepal (HUMAN) became an Associate Member of the International Humanist and Ethical Union. The group's aims include the fight against social injustice, the struggle for moral and mental improvement by the advancement of humanism, and the study and dissemination of the principles of humanism. Ganga Prasad Subedi is the association's secretary.

Gopi Upreti, a Nepalese professor, is the humanist contact in Nepal. Ganga Prasad Subedi signed Humanist Manifesto 2000. (See entries for Jai Prithvi Bahadur Singh and Gopo Upreti.)

Nerlich, Graham (20th Century)

Prof. Nerlich, of the University of Adelaide, is a patron of the Humanist Society of South Australia.

NERO: For a reference to Nero's "husband," see the entry for Alexander Pope.

Nerren, Dan (20th Century)

Nerren is president of the Humanist Association of Tulsa and is an activist on issues concerning church-state separation. He wrote "Prayer Just Doesn't Work" for *Freethought Today* (June-July 1996), a description of the sign he and some Tulsa, Ohio, citizens displayed in their opposition to that city's National Day of Prayer observance. E-mail: <gphil@ix.netcom.co>. {*Freethought Today*, June-July 1996 and June-July 1997}

Nesbit, Wilbur D. (1871–1927)

A Midwesterner, Nesbit published volumes of poetry that contained his liberal outlook, according to Whitehead and Muhrer's *Freethought on the American Frontier* (1992). They include one example from *The Cry for Justice: An Anthology of the Literature of Social Protest* (1921), which had been edited by Upton Sinclair with an introduction by Jack London.

Nesin, Aziz (1915–1995)

A prominent leftist author and newspaper editor in Turkey, Nesin in a July 1993 conference was accused by Muslim militants of being an atheist. They were upset that in Sivas at the conference of writers Nesin had praised Pir Sultan Abdal, a 16th-century poet who preached rebellion against oppression. Also, they were angry that his newspaper had published excerpts from Salman Rushdie's *The Satanic Verses*, which in 1989 Ayatollah Ruhollah Khomeini of Iran had condemned as blasphemous, imposing a death sentence upon Mr. Rushdie. As their anger increased, a group of religious fundamentalists congregated and set fire to the hotel in central Turkey, killing thirty-seven of his colleagues who were inside.

Neslin had said he did not need God "because I want neither paradise nor hell." Although in bad health during the 1980s, he was director of the Union of Turkish Authors from 1975 to 1989. He had a heart attack while visiting Moscow in 1982 and a stroke in 1983. His vision gradually worsened and before he died he was partially blind. A week before he died, he announced he was going to organize an anti-fundamentalist conference that would have taken place in Istanbul in 1996. He was survived by four children from two marriages and a female companion of his final years. Nesin was buried by friends without a religious ceremony in an unmarked, undisclosed location on the property of the Nesin Vakfi." {*Freethought History* #9, 1994; and #17, 1996}

NESTORIANISM

Nestorianism was a heretical view ascribed to Nestorius and ecclesiastically condemned in 431 CE. Ibas, the Bishop of Edessa in Syria (435–457), welcomed Nestorianism and established a famous Nestorian School at Edessa. This led some Syrian churches within the Empire to become Monophyite while others were Nestorian. It was mainly from Nestorian monasteries in Syria that the Arabs recovered what was left of Greek philosophy. (See entries for Monophysitism and for Christianity. Also, see a description by Joseph McCabe in his *Rationalist Encyclopedia*.) {ER; RE}

Netanyahu, Benzion: See entry for Anti-Semitism.

Nethercot, Arthur H(obart) (Born 1895)

Nethercot's *The First Five Lives of Annie Besant* (1960) and *The Last Four Lives of Annie Besant* (1963) depict the struggles of English atheists in the nineteenth century. {FUK}

NETHERLANDS, THE: See entry for Dutch.

Neufeld, Muriel (20th Century)

When she signed Humanist Manifesto II, Neufeld was on the executive committee of the American Ethical Union. {HM2}

Neuhoff, Ralph R. (20th Century)

When he reviewed books for *The Humanist* in the 1950s, Neuhoff was a St. Louis attorney.

Neumann, Henry (20th Century)

Neumann, a college teacher of English and education, became a Leader of the Brooklyn Ethical Society from 1911 to 1966. A humanist and an octogenarian, he was highly regarded in liberal circles. (See entry for Ethical Culture.) {EU, Howard B. Radest}

Neumann, Johannes (20th Century)

At the Eleventh International Humanist and Ethical Union (IHEU) World Congress held in Brussels (1990), Prof. Neumann of Germany addressed the group. Neumann, an educator, has written about the mentally handicapped, marriage, and mixed marriages.

Neumann, Walter B. (20th Century)

When he signed Humanist Manifesto II, Neumann was an American Ethical Union treasurer. {HM2}

Neureiter, Anton (20th Century)

Neureiter is Secretary General of the Antiklerikaler Arbeitskreis, which was founded in 1985 in Austria. Its *Teuflischer Almanach* (The

Devil's Almanac) was under investigation by Austrian authorities, who charged the Austrian atheists with blasphemy for organizing a 1985 Salzburg Anticlerical Week.

NEUTRINOS

Although the neutrino was known to be any of three electrically neutral subatomic particles in the lepton family, it was not until 1998 that neutrinos were found to have mass. At the Institute for Cosmic Ray Research of Tokyo University, Dr. Takaaki Kajita announced in June of 1998 the startling evidence that neutrinos can change form and therefore must have mass. Even a minuscule mass would amount for much or all of the so-called dark matter of the universe, In so doing, he and his group of fellow scientists challenged the existing theory about all matter.

If neutrinos do have sufficient mass, physicists were quick to point out, the overall mass of the universe would increase, possibly slowing the universe's present expansion. However, the elusive particles cannot be seen. Therefore, the evidence that they have mass is indirect and still not fully verified or understood. Nevertheless, the discovery appeared to have far-reaching consequences for all future investigations of the nature of matter.

Wolfgang Pauli in 1930 had hypothesized the neutrino's existence, and in 1956 the particle was finally discovered by Dr. Frederick Reines and the late Dr. Clyde Cowan of Los Alamos National Laboratory. For the discovery, Dr. Reines awarded a Nobel Prize.

In comments about the discovery, Dr. Yoji Totsuka, leader of the Kamioka Neutrino Observatory in Japan, said that although the neutrinos are now known to have some mass, that mass must be very small. The difference between the masses of muon nutrinos (as distinct from the two other neutrinos, named electron and tau) is about 0.07 electron volts (a measure of particle mass). Although this does not yield a value of the masses themselves, only of the difference between those of muon neutrinos and other types, the mass of the neutrino is admittedly small. However, at any given moment every teaspoon worth of volume of space throughout the universe contains an average of 300 neutrinos, so their aggregate number is staggering.

The early thinking about neutrinos, however, was entirely elementary. "The solar neutrino issue is far from settled," according to Dr. John Learned of the University of Hawaii. It is possible that a fourth, a fifth, and even a sixth kind of neutrino will be found. Whereas in the 1930s there were just neutrons, protons, and electrons, physicists theorizing about the sun at the end of the century were increasingly puzzled by what they were finding.

On the day the startling scientific discovery was announced, 224 members of the United States House of Representatives voted to amend the Constitution to allow organized prayer in public schools. The count was sixty-one votes short of the two-thirds necessary to pass a constitutional amendment. Freethinkers lamented that when the legislation lost, the bill's sponsor, Oklahoma Republican Ernest Istook Jr., remarked, "It's time we put the emphasis on what we believe, and almost every American believes in God." Observers were quick to note that the Representative and his ilk had no comprehension whatsoever of neutrinos, only of how to replace science with a Bible-inspired "creation science." {Malcolm W. Browne, *The New York Times*, 5 June 1998; *The Economist*, 13 June 1998}

NEUTRUM

Neutrum, an associate member of the International Humanist and Ethical Union, can be reached at UL. Zlota 72 M I, 00-821 Warsaw, Poland.

NEVADA HUMANISTS

The Secular Humanist Society of Las Vegas (ASHS) is at 240 North Jones Boulevard (Suite 106), Las Vegas, Nevada 89107. Loretta Cardaronell is a contact. (702) 594-1125

Neville, Frank (20th Century)

Neville, of Dundee, Scotland, is international officer of the Humanist Society of Scotland, for which he is Agenda 21 Officer. Originally in the Non-Combatant Corps during World War II, he later served with the Heavy Anti-Aircraft Artillery in North Africa, Sicily, and Italy until the end of hostilities, at which time he was sent as an interpreter to Austria for one year. From 1939 his civilian career has been in various roles, including an active interest in Green Politics. He favors a civilian peace service in which conscientious objectors to military conscription could be trained for non-violent conciliation work. {*Humanism Scotland*, Autumn 1997; *International Humanist News*, October 1995}

Nevins, Allan (1890–1971)

Nevins, following a career in journalism, became a professor of American history at Columbia University (1931–1958), following which he became senior research associate at the Huntington Library. He won two Pulitzer Prizes in biography, one on Grover Cleveland and the other on Hamilton Fish. Nevins was a Unitarian. {CE}

Nevinson, Henry W. (1856–1941)

A respected and idealistic British journalist, Nevinson after a 1904–1905 visit to Africa was indignant about the surviving traffic in slaves. The following year, he visited Russia and exposed Tsarism. An agnostic, he wrote in *Essays in Rebellion* (1913) about Maeterlinck's speculation concerning a future life, saying that "talk of that kind rests on no sounder basis than the old assertions about the houris and the happy hunting-grounds." {RAT; RE}

NEW AGE

A 1980s movement relating to a complex of spiritual and consciousness-raising, New Age adherents in the 1990s sounded like evangelical Christians when they complained about how badly they were being caricatured. Joan Duncan Oliver, editor of *New Age Journal*, complained that some wanted to flee the label because it "has a very flaky load on it," one of "crystals, and Shirley MacLaine, and Ouiji boards." As Peter Steinfels has pointed out, "Drawing on humanistic psychology, Asian religions, occult practices, and subterranean religious traditions in the West, as well as the shamanism and nature worship, the movement assembled a smorgasbord of concepts and techniques for achieving personal peace and stretching capacities. Its defenders are quick to distinguish 'fringe' expressions like healing through crystals or channeling messages from extraterrestrial spiritual masters from its major concerns: cultivating awareness of every person's tremendous inner potential, overcoming the dualisms and sharp distinctions that have marked Western culture—between body and mind, the divine and the human—and strengthening intuition and imagination over analytic reason."

Some Judeo-Christian thinkers, such as Doug Groothuis who teaches philosophy and ethics at Denver Seminary, find the varying degrees of New Age pantheism incompatible with their insistence on a personal God who cannot be identified with His creation. Integrating practices like yoga into Christianity "simply can't be done," he holds, and New Age activities are "dangerous because of the possibility of demonic intervention." Others, such as Richard Kyle who teaches religion and history at the Mennonites' Tabor College in Kansas, embrace some New Age concepts and practices as ways of correcting what they consider the unduly cerebral and masculine emphases of their traditions. Kyle likes the movement's criticism of reductionism in science and materialism in the economy, and he welcomes its environmentalism and emphasis on equality of the sexes. In terms of underlying principles, however, "Christianity and the New Age are totally at odds." Still others condemn the New Age movement as a sign of the Anti-Christ. Eugene Kennedy, a former priest and a Roman Catholic psychologist, calls summer school institutes and workshops catering to religious educators "McSpirituality, junk food for the soul. . . . . History, learning, and the vast poignant drama of human longing and suffering can be set aside. In matters of religious faith, this is Disneyland posing as Chartres." James Kullander, a graduate student at Union Theological Seminary, believes New Age is no threat to religion. To the contrary, he wrote (*The New York Times*, 26 October 1998), "I'll be the first to admit that the New Age is full of charlatans and misguided prophets. But it also offers guidance to people whose spiritual longings are not being met by traditional Christian teachings."

Freethinkers are more apt to view the movement as anti-intellectual, unable to utilize the hard-edged tests of scientific rationality. For a secular humanist, Paul Kurtz has pointed out in his varied writings, New Age involves fuzzy thinking which is unworthy of a rational person's involvement. {*The New York Times*, 13 July 1996}

NEW HAMPSHIRE HUMANISTS

New Hampshire has the following groups:

• Humanist Association of New Hampshire-Vermont, POB 23, Keene, New Hampshire. B. J. Nelson, Arpad Toth, and Valerie White are contacts.

• Secular Humanists of Merrimack Valley (ASHS), POB 368, Londonderry, New Hampshire 03053; (603) 434-4195. Margaret Bennett is a contact at <margbennet@aol.com>.

NEW HUMANIST (United States)

In the 1930s, religious (or naturalistic) humanism had developed within and without religions—in particular, Unitarianism. In Chicago *The New Humanist* was a bimonthly (cost: $1/year) published in Chicago at a time when that city was a hotbed of humanism. "From 1930 through 1934," Edwin H. Wilson has written, "Harold Buschman and I privately owned and published *The New Humanist*—an ownership necessary to obtain second-class mailing privileges. None of the several churches or churchmen who were trying to set up schismatic (Unitarian) humanist societies along church lines tried to establish a national organization. On paper, the New Humanist Associates was formed—persons privileged to help meet printers' bills." Raymond Bragg and Edwin H. Wilson were instrumental not only in running the magazine but also in doing the groundwork for arranging Humanist Manifesto I. {EW; Edwin H. Wilson's *The Genesis of a Humanist Manifesto* (1995)}

NEW HUMANIST (United Kingdom)

New Humanist, the quarterly journal of the Rationalist Press Association, is edited by Jim Herrick at Bradlaugh House, 47 Theobald's Road, London WC1X 8SP. Numerous naturalistic, rationalistic, and secular humanists evaluate the publication as one of the most important humanistic journals of the time.

A 1997 survey of its readership found that 91% were members of the Rationalist Press Association and 34% were members of the British Humanist Association. Only 16% attended 5 or more humanist meetings in the last year, and 66% attended none. As to the terms subscribers preferred in describing their outlooks:

33%	Humanist
29%	Atheist
14%	Rationalist
5%	Freethinker
4%	Agnostic
2%	Scientific Humanist
1%	Ethical, Religious, or Secular Humanist

Only 4% found "Religious Humanist" an acceptable term whereas 63% voted for "Rationalist." E-mail: <jim.rpa@humanism.org.uk>. (See entry for Rationalist Press Association.

NEW JERSEY FREETHINKERS, HUMANISTS New Jersey has the following groups:

• American Atheists Inc., PO Box 709, Holmdel, NJ 07733; <http://www.atheists.org/>.

• Bertrand Russell Society, c/o 38B Loantaka Way, Madison, NJ 07940. (201) 765-0776. Allen Schwerin is the contact. E-mail: <aschweri@mondec.monmouth.edu>. On the World Wide Web: <http://daniel.drew.edu/njlenz/brs.html>

• Essex County Ethical Culture Society, 516 Prospect St., Maplewood, New Jersey 07040

• First Unitarian Fellowship of Hunterdon County, Box 122, Baptistown, NJ 08803. Contact is the Rev. Mary Tiebaut (215) 766-9486.

• *Focus*, a monthly, 687 Larch Avenue, Teaneck, New Jersey 07666 <rca001@aol.com>.

• Freedom from Religion Foundation, NJ Chapter, 10 Westminster Place, Morristown, NJ 07960. (201) 984-6236. Allie Fuentes is the contact.

• Freethought Commentary, POB 162 Park Station, Paterson, New Jersey 07513.

• Hudson Humanists, pO Box 111, 113 Pavonia Ave., East Jersey City, NJ 07310; (201) 792-9434. Contact: Brian Lemaire t<lemaire.3@worldnet.att.net>.

• Humanists of North Jersey (AHA), 27 Bedford Place, Glen Rock, New Jersey 07452. (201) 444-6627. Robert Drake was President up to 1999; Carol Sorce is Vice President; Martin Alboum is secretary; and Herbert Honig is Treasurer. Its new officers in 1999 are Maddy Urken, President; Joe Walinski, Vice President; Marty Alboum, Secretary; Herb Honig, Treasurer; and members-at-large are Fred Brack, Myrna Pelta, and Carol Sorce. Carl Shapiro is the contact at <rbgarber@aol.com>.

• Humanists of South Jersey, 105 Maplewood Drive, Mapleshade, NJ 08052 (609) 482-2261. Marvin Zimmerman is President.

• Jewish Cultural School and Society, PO Box 7038, West Orange, NJ 07052. Contact is Rhea Seagull at (201) 325-7247. The group operates a Sunday educational program for children aged 4 to 14 at the Jewish Community Center. The group is a member of the Congress of Secular Jewish organizations (CSJO) and the International Federation of Secular Humanist Jews.

• New Jersey Humanist Network (ASHS), PO Box 51, Washington, New Jersey 07882; telephone (908) 689-2813. E-mail: <hbrown@nac.net>. Contact is Harley Brown.

• New Jersey Secular Society; contact is Jim Mac Iver (973) 655-9054

• Princeton Ethical Humanist Fellowship, PO Box 3286, Princeton, NJ 08543. President is Gene Queval at (609) 588-8694; secretary is Dick Reichart at (609) 924-6492.

• Princeton Freethought Association can be found on the Web: <daraujo@fas.harvard.edu> and <http://www.secularhumanism.org/cfa/orgs.html>.

• Princeton Memorial Association, 48 Roper Road, Princeton, NJ 08540 (609) 924-5525. Contact is Durinda Putnam

• Sect of Zarathustra, 30 Stockton St., Bloomfield, NJ 07003; (973) 748-8166

• Unitarian Universalist Church at Washington Crossing, 268 Washington Crossing Pennington Road, Titusville, NJ 08560. Contact is Paul Tuerf at (609) 737-0515.

• Unitarian Universalist Fellowship of Sussex County, 1 West Nelson St., Newton, NJ 07860

(See entry for Charles B. Reynolds.)

NEW MEXICO HUMANISTS AND SKEPTICS

Following are groups and publications in New Mexico:

• *American Rationalist*, a bi-monthly, is edited at PO Box 80182, Albuquerque 87198-0182

• *Humanism Today*, an annual, is published at Box 191, 5901-J Wyoming NE, Albuquerque, New Mexico 87109.

• Humanist Society of New Mexico (AHA), POB 4756, Albuquerque, New Mexico 87196, has as its contacts Lois Kimbrell and Leland Franks. Phone (505) 265-7203.

• North American Council of Humanism (NACH), Box 191, 5901-J Wyoming NE, Albuquerque, New Mexico 87109. It publishes *Dialogue* quarterly. E-mail: <conachi@aol.com>.

• *Skeptical Inquirer*, a bi-monthly, is edited at 944 Deer Drive NE, Albuquerque 87122

NEW YORK HUMANISTS, ATHEISTS, FREETHINKERS

New York State has the following groups and publications:

• *AAH Examiner*, PO Box 664, Buffalo, NY 14226, a quarterly newsletter published by African Americans for Humanism. E-mail: <cfiflynn@aol.com>.

• American Humanist Association, Northeast Region (AHA), POB 1256, Fair Lawn, NJ 07410. Theodora Dolores Trent is coordinator for New York, Pennsylvania, and New Jersey.

• Capital District Humanist Society (ASHS), POB 2148, Scotia, New York 12302. Larry Jones is Executive Director; Rick Gottesman is secretary; Lois Lewis is treasurer; Dennis Bender is the contact at (518) 381-6239. E-mail: <myrnabeckr@aol.com> and <cdhs@ global2000.net>.

On the Web: <www.global2000.net/org/cdhs>.

• Cornell University humanists are at: <www.secularhumanism.org/cfa/orgs.html>.

• *Dialogue*, American Ethical Union, 2 West 64th Street, New York, NY 10023

• *Family Matters*, P. O. Box 664, Amherst, NY 14226-0664. <familynews@secularhumanism.org>.

• *Free Inquiry*, a quarterly of secular humanism, is at PO Box 644, Amherst, NY 14226-0664 <freeinquiry@secularhumanism.org>.

• *Free Mind*, 7 Harwood Drive, PO Box 146, Amherst, NY 14226

• Freethining-Activist-Nonbelieving New Yorkers (FANNY), 31 Jane St. (10-D), New York, NY 10014. Dennis Middlebrooks and Warren Allen Smith, both of whom once presided over the Secular Humanist Society of New York, are co-directors. E-mail: <wasm@idt.net>

• Harlem Atheist Association, 424 Vanderbilt Avenue, Brooklyn, NY 11238. Eugene Charrington was the director of this group that is inactive.

• *Humanist, The*, a bi-monthly of the American Humanist Association, is published at 7 Harwood Drive, Amherst, NY 14226. <thehumanist@juno.com>.

• Humanist Activists, Box 10-D, 31 Jane Street, New York, NY 10014. (212) 366-6481

• Humanist Fellowship of Brooklyn (AHA), A-2E, 334 Howard Avenue, Brooklyn, NY 11233. Martin Morgan is the contact.

• Humanist Society of Metropolitan New York (AHA), Corliss Lamont Chapter, 777 United Nations Plaza (lobby floor), New York, NY 10017-3521. (212) 353-2213. Dr. Julius Manson is President; Sala E. Farber is Executive Director; Beth K. Lamont is Humanist Advocate. Before his death, Jesse Gordon was its leader. On the Web: <http://www.corliss-lamont.org/>.

• Humanist Society of Western New York (AHA), 7 Harwood Drive, POB 1188, Amherst, NY 14226. Fred Edwords is the contact.

• Independent Rationalists, 31 Jane Street (10-D), New York, NY 10014 <wasm@idt.net>

• Ithaca College freethinkers are at: <www.secularhumanism.org/cfa/orgs.html>.

• *Journal of Humanism and Ethical Religion* is no longer published by the Ethical Society at 2 West 64th Street, New York, NY 10023

• Long Island Secular Humanists, Box 119, Greenlaw, NY 11740. Contact is Gerry Dantone, fax (516) 742-4618; E-mail: <infidelsre@aol.com>.

• Northeast Atheist Association, RR-1 B-1090, Athens, NY 12015. Robert Blokesberg-Fireovid is the contact person.

• New York Society for Ethical Culture, 2 West 64th Street, New York, NY 10023. The humanistic group publishes *New York Society for Ethical Culture Newsletter*. E-mail: <revbob@ix.netcom.com>.

• New York University Humanists on the Web: <http://www.secularhumanism.org/cfa/orgs.html>.

• *Philo*, PO Box 664, Amherst, NY 14226 <fivaughn@aol.com>.

• *Platform*, 4450 Fieldston Road, Bronx, NY 10471

• Rationalists NY, Box 10-A, 31 Jane Street, New York, NY 10014; <wasm@idt.net>.

• Rensselaer Individuals for Freethought (RIFT), Rensselaer Polytchnic Institute, Troy, NY 12180.

• *Secular Humanist Bulletin* is published quarterly at PO Box 664, Amherst, NY 14226-0664 <shb-editor @ secularhumanism.org>.

• Secular Humanist Society of New York (ASHS), POB 7661, FDR Station, New York, NY 10150. The group was founded by Warren Allen Smith, its president, who later resigned. It meets irregularly and publishes *Pique*. E-mail: <jarents@bestweb.net>.

• *Skeptical Beliefs*, a bi-monthly, is at PO Box 703, Buffalo, NY 104226-0703

• State University of New York at Albany: <http://www.secularhumanism.org/cfa/orgs.html>.

• State University of New York at Buffalo: <www.secularhumanism.org/cfa/orgs.html>.

• Western New York Secular Humanists (ASHS), POB 664, Amherst, NY 14226. {FD}

NEW YORK CHAPTER, AMERICAN HUMANIST ASSOCIATION (AHA)

The New York Humanists, founded by its President Warren Allen Smith, voted in 1953 to affiliate with the American Humanist Association. Eva Ingersoll Wakefield was Vice-President, and Dorothea Thayer was Secretary-Treasurer. The chapter had a Humanist Action Committee and a Greenwich Village Humanist Club. Its original plans were to form proposed clubs in Brooklyn and Morningside Heights. The present contact of the New York Chapter (AHA) is Beth Lamont, 315 West 106th St., New York, NY 10025. On the Web: <http://www.corliss-lamont.org/>. {*The Humanist Newsletter*, Summer 1953}

NEW YORK CHAPTER, COUNCIL FOR SECULAR HUMANISM: See entry for Secular Humanist Association of New York.

NEW YORK INTELLECTUALS: See entry for Irving Howe.

NEW YORK UNIVERSITY HUMANISTS

New York University humanists are on the Web: <http://www.secularhumanism.org/cfa/orgs.html>.

NEW ZEALAND ASSOCIATION OF RATIONALISTS AND HUMANISTS

Officers in 1998 were as follows: President, Ngaire McCarthy; Vice President, Peter Hansen; Secretary, David Ross; Treasurer, Nick Pullar; and Councillors: Rachael Callender, Bill Cooke, Liz McKenzie, Marta McKenzie, Peter Russell.

Honorary Associates are as follows: Gianni Bartocci; H. James Birx; Sir Hermann Bondi; Steve Cooper; Richard Dawkins; Warwick Don; Zoë During; Denis Dutton; Brian Edwards; Antony Flew; Ida Gaskin; Maurice Gee; Dame Barbara Goodman; Finngeir Hiorth; Bernard Howard; Paul Kurtz; Lavanam; Richard Leakey; Tim Madigan; Michael Martin; Taslima Nasrin; Ian Plimer; Barbara Smoker; Dame Catherine Tizard; David Tribe; Ibn Warraq; and Lewis Wolpert.

NEW ZEALAND ATHEISTS AND HUMANISTS

• The Auckland University Atheists, c/o Rationalist House, 64 Symonds St., Auckland, New Zealand, was founded in 1990. Web: <crash.ihug.co.nz/~remk/fnz/aua/index.html>; <www.secularhumanism.org/cfa/orgs.html>.

• Christchurch Branch, NZ Association of Rationalists and Humanists, c/o TMA Hooper, 42 Harris Crescent, Christchurch, New Zealand.

• Christchurch Humanist Fellowship, 158 Panorama Road, Christchurch, New Zealand.

• Hawke's Bay Freethinkers, c/o Robyn Church, 2 Millar St., Napier, New Zealand.

• New Zealand Association of Rationalists & Humanists Inc., Rationalist House, 64 Symonds Street, Auckland 1001, New Zealand. On the Web: <http://www.freethought.org.nz>.

• *New Zealand Humanist*, a quarterly, PO Box 3372, Wellington, New Zealand. E-mail: <iain-middleton@clear.net.nz>.

• New Zealand Humanist Society (IHEU), is at POB 3372, Wellington. Attempts in 1998 were made in 1998 to merge the group with the New Zealand Association of Rationalists & Humanists

• *New Zealand Rationalist and Humanist*, a quarterly, 64 Symonds Street, Auckland 1001 <bill@freethought.org.nz>.

• *New Zealand Rationalist & Humanist Newsletter*, 64 Symonds Street, Auckland 1001; e-mail: <nzarh@freethought.org.nz>.

• Northland Freethinkers, c/o Peter Murphy, Box 5453, Hamilton, New Zealand.

• The Skeptics (NZCSICOP), the New Zealand Committee for the Scientific Investigation of Claims of the Paranormal, 150 Dyer's Pass Road, Christchurch 2, New Zealand.

• South Taranaki Freethinkers, c/o Dr. D. S. Devadhar, 7 Kowhai St. Hawera, 4800 South Taranald, New Zealand

• Waikato Freethinkers, c/o Peter Murphy, Box 5453, Hamilton

• Bill Cooke, a lecturer at Manakau Institute of Technology, signed Humanist Manifesto 2000.

{FD}

NEW ZEALAND HUMANIST

A quarterly, *New Zealand Humanist* is at PO Box 3372, Wellington, New Zealand. E-mail: <iain-middleton@clear.net.nz>.

NEW ZEALAND RATIONALIST AND HUMANIST

The *New Zealand Rationalist and Humanist* (64 Symonds Street, Auckland 1, New Zealand) is edited by David Ross. E-mail: <bill@freethought.org.nz>.

NEW ZEALAND RATIONALIST COUNCIL

The Rationalist Council is a group of nine, elected by the body of members of the New Zealand Rationalist Association, for two-year durations. Bill Cooke is President; Ngaire McCarthy is Vice President; and Peter Hansen is Secretary. The group's councillors are Carl Brett; Rembrandt Kuipers; Elizabeth McKenzie; George Pirie; Nick Pullar; and David Ross. The Rationalist Council is found on the Web: <crash.ihug.co.nz/~remk/fnz/nzrats/index.html>. (See entry for William Cooke, author of *Heathen in Godzone: Seventy Years of Rationalism in New Zealand.*)

NEW ZEALAND UNBELIEVERS

See an extensive article by Harry H. Pearce in the *Encyclopedia of Unbelief.* Also see *Freethought in the United Kingdom and the Commonwealth* by Gordon Stein, which cites 1857 as the date of Charles Southwell's *Auckland Examiner*. Unitarian groups are active in Auckland, Blenheim, and Wellington.

NEW ZEALAND UNITARIANS

John Maindonald (28 Alexis Avenue, Mt. Albert, Auckland 1003, New Zealand) is the contact for Australian and New Zealand Unitarians. (See entry for Gayle Feeney, head of the Australian and New Zealand Unitarian Association.)

Newcomb, Rexford (1866–1968)

Newcomb, who has been a member of the American Humanist Association, wrote *Spanish Colonial Architecture in the United States* (1937). {HNS}

Newcomb, Simon (1835–1909)

An American astronomer born in Nova Scotia, Newcomb worked on the *Nautical Almanack* and in 1877 became senior professor of mathematics in the U. S. Navy. He has been associated with the equipment of the Lick Observatory and wrote *Principles of Political Economy* (1885). The British astronomer, Proctor, quotes Newcomb as rejecting the idea of immortality, and according to McCabe Newcomb never made any secret in America of his freethought views. {BDF; JM; RE}

Newcomb, Steven (20th Century)

A Shawnee/Lenape legal scholar, Newcomb has pointed out the role of Christianity in the historic oppression of American Indians. "Indian people are denied their rights in United States laws," he wrote, "simply because they were not Christians at the time of European arrival." Newcomb has proposed writing a book to be entitled *Pagans in the Promised Land: Religion, Law, and the American Indian*. {*Freethought History #9*, 1994}

Newkirk, Ingrid (20th Century)

A non-theist, Newkirk is an animal rights advocate associated with People for the Ethical Treatment of Animals (PETA, PO Box 42516, Washington, DC 20015).

Newland, H. Osman (Died 1920)

A sociologist, Newland wrote *A Short History of Citizenship* (1904) and *The Model Citizen* (1908). He lectured in English literature, history, and sociology to the London County Council when the war broke out in 1914. In the army, he rose to the rank of captain. He then went to Mesopotamia, where he became President of the Baghdad Literary Society but succumbed to dysentery. Newland wrote *Sierre Leone* (1916), *West Africa* (1920), and articles on religion in the *Literary Guide*. He founded the British West African Association. Newland was an agnostic. {RAT}

Newman, Bobby (20th Century)

Newman is author of *The Reluctant Alliance: Behaviorism and Humanism* (1992).

Newman, Charles Robert (19th Century)

Newman wrote "Essays in Rationalism" (1891). {GS}

Newman, Ernest (1868–1959)

Newman was a music critic on the *Manchester Guardian*, the *Birmingham Post*, the *Observer*, and *Sunday Times*. He wrote with particular authority on Wagner, and in his *Study of Wagner* (1899) rejects even the sentimental Christianity of the master, according to McCabe. Newman translated Albert Schweitzer's *J. S. Bach* and Romain Rolland's *Beethoven the Creator*. {RAT; RE; TRI}

Newman, Francis William (1805–1897)

Cardinal Newman's brother was an atheist. As a young man he went to Baghdad with the object of assisting a Christian mission, but his further studies convinced him he could not conscientiously undertake the work. Returning to England, he became classical teacher in Bristol College and, subsequently, Latin professor at London University. In *The Soul: Its Sorrows and Aspirations* (1849), Newman states his theistic position. In *Phases of Faith* (1856), he explains how he came to give up Christianity, how he became a Unitarian. He also wrote *A History of the Hebrew Monarchy* (1847); *Theism: Doctrinal and Practical* (1858); *What is Christianity Without Christ?* (1881); and *Life After Death* (1886). In *Mature Thoughts on Christianity* (1897), he passed beyond conservative Unitarianism when he discarded belief in a future life. He also wrote a number of tracts on the defective morality of the New Testament, the historical deprivation of Christianity, and the religious weakness of Protestantism.

Charles Robert Newman, a younger brother, was an agnostic. {BDF; RAT; RE; VI; TRI}

Newman, Henry (20th Century)

Newman was organizer and leader of the Brooklyn Society for Ethical Culture. He was a non-theistically oriented humanist. The group had much support among professional secularized Jews into the 1940s, according to present member Eric Freudenthal. During World War II, despite the Society's support of the war, Newman was an outspoken pacifist.

Newman, Michael (20th Century)

Newman, a secondary school teacher and an atheist, was arrested under England's blasphemy law for selling the video, "Visions of Ecstasy." He has worked to correct the inequities of the 1988 Education Reform Act, but he had to resign from his school position. As a result, he has been a subject of discussion in the media, including an appearance on Channel Four's "Comment" program in England.

Newman, Paul (1925–)

Newman, actor, professional race-car driver, and food company executive, responded to a question put to him by television interviewer Barbara Walters that he does not believe in an afterlife. The 1986 recipient of an honorary Academy Award for career achievement, however, was not asked specifically if he is non-theistic. He is a Unitarian.

Newman, Ralph A. (20th Century)

Newman is author of *The Evolution of Conscience* (1981). {GS}

Newman, Randy (1943–)

A singer, songwriter, and musician, Newman in 1984 received a Grammy Award for the best instrumental composition. He appeared in "Ragtime," a 1981 film, and he wrote "Sail Again" (1979), "Trouble in Paradise" (1983), "Land of Dreams" (1988), and "Faust" (1995), a rock musical. A professed atheist in the last work, he sings the part of the Devil in a retelling of the Goethe story and revels in telling God that He is a figment of the human imagination.

His father also was an atheist. Visiting in a hospital with his son, he lampooned the idea of a benevolent and merciful deity: "That's God will over there, and that's God's will over there, and that's God's will over there," he said, pointing to the ill. In "Old Man," he includes the lines, "Don't need no god to comfort you,/ You taught me not to believe that lie."

But his son came to the view that people should be allowed to believe what they think they need to believe, that although he "never had faith," still "I have respect for the idea. There's no joy being an atheist." {CA; E}

Newnes, George [Sir] (1851–1910)

A newspaper and magazine projector, Newnes was given his baronetcy for being "a pioneer of clean popular literature." He applied much of his wealth to public purposes, including the building of a cable railway for use by invalids. Although he was the son of a clergyman, and married a clergyman's daughter, he rejected Christianity and was merely a theist. Hulda Friedrichs, in her *Life of Sir G. Newnes* (1911), wrote that in regard to the idea of a future life Newnes was "a reverent and open-minded agnostic." {RAT}

Newton, Isaac [Sir] (1642–1727)

Called by some the greatest scientist of all time, Newton was President of the Royal Society from 1703 until his death. In addition to discovering the universal law of gravitation and developing the calculus, he built the first reflecting telescope. Along with Voltaire in France, Lessing in Germany, and Franklin, Jefferson, and Paine in America, Newton was a deist, one who had no interest in pantheism. Maréchal's 1799 *Dictionnaire des athés anciens et modernes* listed Newton as one who seems an atheist from the standpoint of the strictest religious orthodoxy. Robertson, however, finds Newton "was always pathologically prepossessed on the side of his religion, and subordinated his science to his theology even in the *Principial*." The economist John Maynard Keynes, speaking in 1947 at the Royal Society's Newton Tercentenary Celebration, said he had gone through some million of Newton's words on alchemy and found them "wholly devoid of scientific value."

A non-trinitarian, Newton expressly formulates the propositions: (a) that "there is one God the father . . . and one mediator between God and man, the man Christ Jesus"; (b) that "the Father is the invisible God whom no eye hath seen or can see. All other beings are sometimes visible"; and (c) that "the Father *hath* life in himself, and hath *given* the Son to have life in himself." He believed that God was somehow behind the influence of gravitation, keeping stars from collapsing into one mass. From time to time, Newton felt, although supplying no documentation, God stepped in to adjust the orbits of planets. Basically, his discovery of the universal law of gravitation did not directly undermine religious faith—Newton regarded his discovery, according to *The Economist* (16 March 1996) as being "not merely consistent with God's existence, but tantamount to proof of it." The power of his work was "that it demonstrated (or appeared to demonstrate) the staggering power of science and the susceptibility of the physical world to human understanding. In that way, Newton inspired later thinkers to demand ever more of reason. If the intellect could comprehend the universe, in its seemingly limitless complexity, then surely it could also comprehend justice, authority, right and wrong. It was in the face of these new demands, rather than in response to Newton's discoveries in their own right, that faith retreated."

Had such thoughts been published, Newton under the Act of 1697 could have been liable to loss of office and all civil rights. Newton also wrote, "Atheism is so senseless and odious to mankind that it never had many professors. *Can it be by accident* that all birds, beats, and men have their right side and left side alike shaped (except in their bowels), and just two eyes, and no more, on either side of the face?" For Robertson, Newton was "some kind of Unitarian."

Michael White's *Isaac Newton: the Last Sorcerer* (1997) describes his Arianism and how, between 1672 and 1675 he set out twelve points of faith that formed the foundations of Arianism. Newton in 1669 had promised to take holy orders as a requirement of the Lucasian professorship. When his friend Aston applied for an exemption from taking holy orders, the request was seen as setting a precedent that would destroy Trinity College's reputation. In 1675 when he visited London to apply for a special dispensation, His Majesty granted the Lucasian professor and all subsequent holders of the chair exemption from holy orders and was willing "to give all just encouragement to learned men who are & shall be elected" to it.

Martin Gardner, pointing out Newton's belief in alchemy, terms Newton a fundamentalist. "Newton's passion for alchemy," he wrote, "was exceeded only by his passion for Biblical prophecy. Incredible amounts of intellectual energy were spent trying to interpret the prophecies of Daniel in the Old Testament, and the Book of Revelation in the New. He left more than a million words on these subjects, seeing himself as one who for the first time was correctly judging both books. Having been so successful in solving some of the riddles of God's universe, he turned his talents toward trying to answer riddles posed by God's Holy Word."

But Newton, as described by John Updike,

> spent hours poring over the Bible, compiling charts and dictionaries...of his own, dangerously anti-Trinitarian views, and for the *prisca sapientia*—the wisdom that he, with the Rosicrucians, believed the ancients possessed and had secreted in their documents. The Middle Ages had, in truth, erased some ancient knowledge. The Greek astronomer Eratosthenes, in the third century B.C., calculated the circumference of the round earth to be twenty-four thousand miles (less than a thousand miles off the true value) and the distance to the sun to be ninety-two million miles, a stunningly close estimation. But the Old and New Testaments did not hold such mathematical wisdom; Newton researched the prophetic utterances of Daniel and St. John for a chronology of the future, and carefully concluded that Satan's spell over the world would be broken in the year 1867. He did not know that his own science had excused God from running the universe, allowing Him merely the initial push—a push, astronomers recently concluded, that will carry everything infinitely outward, into darkness and heat death.

As for his personal life, "Newton had no interest in music or art, and once dismissed poetry as 'ingenious fiddle-faddle.' He never exercised, had no recreational hobbies, no interest in games, and was so preoccupied with his work that he frequently forgot to eat or would eat standing up to save time. He had few friends, and even to them he was often quarrelsome and vindictive." Following the publication of *Principia*, Newton suffered a massive mental breakdown marked by severe insomnia, deep depression, amnesia, loss of mental ability, and paranoid delusions of persecution.

Gardner speculates that Newton may have suffered from mercurial and other toxic metal poisoning caused by his alchemical experiments. Or, he adds, "Others have conjectured that throughout his life he was a manic-depressive with alternating moods of melancholy and happy activity. His breakdown was only the worst of such episodes." (See entries for Gravity and for E. O. Wilson.) {CE; CL; ER; Martin Gardner, *Skeptical Inquirer*, September-October 1996; JMR; JMRH; John Updike, "Immortal Isaac," *The New Yorker*, 30 March 1998}

Newton, Jeremiah (20th Century)

Newton, who calls himself an "atheist priest," is a Stonewall Veteran and a humanist activist. (See entries for AASH and Herbert Huncke.)

Newton, Tyre (20th Century)

Newton is associated with the Humanist Association of Palouse (AHA). He is professor emeritus of mathematics at Washington Sate University. (See entry for Washington Atheists, Humanists.) {FD; *Freethought Today*, January-February 1999}

Neymann, Clara (19th Century)

Neymann was a German-American freethought lecturer, a friend and colleague of Fran Hedwig Henrich Wilhelmi. {BDF}

Ngugi wa Thiong'o (1938–)

A writer in Kenya, Ngugi once began an address to the Fifth General Assembly of the Presbyterian Church of East Africa by saying, "I am not a man of the church. I am not even a Christian." His point was to censure the church for its role in the colonizing of his native land, and when he finished he was denounced for blasphemy. His novels include *Weep Not, Child* (1964), *The River Between* (1965), and *A Grain of Wheat* (1967). Theodore Pelton in *The Humanist* (March-April 1993) has written about Ngugi's teaching at the University of Nairobi, his being imprisoned because of his differences with the Kenyan government, and his willingness to use literature in order to stir people to revolt.

NICENE CREED

The creed, which begins, "I believe in one God," asserts that Jesus was "of one substance with the Father." The Arians contended that the Son was created and only the Father was eternal. The creed has been expanded from one that was issued in Nicaea (Nice) by the first Nicene Council in 325 CE. Most Christians who repeat the words are entirely unaware of the difficulties which have been involved in wording the material to satisfy the ecumenical, Eastern Catholic, Western Catholic, Provincial Church, confessional Protestant, democratic declarations, and American Protestant, sects and cults. The Apostles' Creed, which merely said that Jesus was the Son of God the Father, conceived by the Holy Spirit and born of the Virgin Mary, has been popular in both the Catholic and Protestant churches. (See entries for Arius and for Christianity.) {ER}

Nichol, Charles Ready (Born 1876)

With A. S. Bradley, Nichol wrote *The Nichol-Bradley Debate* (1907). {GS}

Nichol, John (1833–1894)

Nichol, the son of John Nichol, shared his father's rationalism, refused to graduate until the theological tests were abolished, then passed with first-class honors. In a biography by Knight, Nichol was described as follows: "Neither he nor his father ever belonged to the Unitarian community," as had been claimed. Nichol was skeptical about immortality and rejected the Christian idea of God: "An omnipotent beneficence is flatly contradicted by the facts of the universe every hour." Nichol professed only an ethical regard for Christianity. {RAT}

Nichol, John Pringle (1804–1859)

Nichol was an astronomer who had been licensed as a preacher. After a few sermons, however, "his mind was turned away from the Church of Scotland," his son stated. "In religion he thought for himself, and, of course, arrived at his own conclusion."

In 1836 Nichol was appointed Regius Professor of Astronomy at Glasgow University. His chief work was *A Cyclopaedia of the Physical Sciences* (1857). An earnest theist and idealist, Nichol was a friend of Martineau and J. S. Mill. {RAT}

Nichols, Billy Joe (20th Century)

When he signed Humanist Manifesto II, Nichols was minister of the Richardson Unitarian Church in Texas. {HM2}

Nicholson, Jack (1937–)

Nicholson is a noted actor, director, and producer. His acting debut in Hollywood was in a stage production of "Tea and Sympathy." He has appeared in numerous films, including the following: "Cry-Baby Killer" (1958); "Studs Lonigan" (1960); "Easy Rider" (for which he received an Academy Award nomination for best supporting actor, 1969); and "One Flew Over the Cuckoo's Nest" (Academy Award for Best Actor, 1975).

"I don't believe in God now," Nicholson told a 1992 *Vanity Fair* interviewer. But "I can still work up an envy for someone who has a faith. I can see how that could be a deeply soothing experience." {A; CA}

Nicholson, Katherine Conway (1907–)

"It was only by chance that I learned I had a great-uncle, Moncure," Nicholson has stated. "When I asked about him I was told, 'We never speak of him.' In other words, he was the black sheep of the family."

Despite having a famous apostate in the family, she and her cousins were raised as Episcopalians, "but I am happy to say that four of us, entirely on our own, found the Unitarians and are Humanists, as well." {*Freethought Today*, April 1997}

Nicholson, William (1753–1815)

Nicholson was an English writer on chemistry and natural philosophy. At an early age, he went to India, then returned to London as a mathematics teacher. He published useful introductions to chemistry and natural philosophy, and he wrote *The Doubts of the Infidels, Submitted to the Bench of Bishops by a Weak Christian* (1871), a work that was republished both by Carlile and by Watson. His rationalist views are given in his *Doubts of the Infidels* (1781). Nicholson died in poor circumstances. {BDF; FUK; RAT}

Nickell, Joe (1944–)

A technical writer, Nickell is the author of *Inquest on the Shroud of Turin* (1987). With John F. Fischer, he wrote *Mysterious Realms* (1993). In *Looking for a Miracle* (1993), Nickell examines miracle claims, weeping icons, relics, snake handling, speaking in tongues, stigmata, visions, and healing cures. He also is author of *Weeping Icons, Relics, Stigmata, Visions and Healing Cures* (1993) and *Entities*: Angels, Spirits, Demons, and Other Alien Beings(1995), in the latter of which he discusses the controversial claims of those who say they have experienced guardian angels, demonic spirits, and extraterrestrial visitors. A former stage magician and private detective, Nickell is on the editorial board of *Skeptical Inquirer* and has written for *Free Inquiry*. In 1995 he was named a senior research fellow of the Center for Inquiry in Amherst, New York. Nickell signed Humanist Manifesto 2000. (See entry for Spontaneous Human Combustion.)

Nichols, John (20th Century)

Nichols, a general practitioner in Surrey, England, has written for *New Humanist*. His expertise includes the relationship between Darwinism and physical healing.

Nichol, Brian (20th Century)

Nichol is Chair of the Mid-Warwickshire branch of Amnesty International and a member of Coventry & Warwickshire Humanists. (See entry for Buddhism and Secular Humanism.)

Nicolai, Cristoph Friedrich Wilhelm (1733–1811

The most persistent spokesman of the Enlightenment in Germany, Nicolai advocated a "natural religion" in keeping with his neologist views. He opposed Pietism, mysticism, Protestant orthodoxy, crypto-Catholicism, and the Jesuits. His publishing of *The General German Library* (founded 1765) ran to 106 volumes and was praised by Heine. As a publication, it was instrumental in spreading a deistic rationalism, labeled *Aufklärung*, or enlightenment, through Germany's middle class. Among the authors he published were Andreas Riem (1749–1807), who wrote anonymously against priestcraft as no other priest had yet done; Georg Schade (1712–1795), who although he believed in the immortality of animals, was a believer in Natural Religion on the lines of Tindal (1760), stating that "all who assert a supernatural religion are godless imposters"; J. B. Basedow (1723–1790), an active deist and educational reformer who liked Rousseau's *Émile*. {BDF; EU, Volker Dürr; JMR; JMRH; RAT}

Nicolle, Charles Jules Henri (1866–1936)

Nicolle, a French physician and microbiologist, won the Nobel Prize in 1928 for his work on typhus. His rationalism is found in *La destinée humaine* (1936), in which he treats sympathetically the ideas of God and immortality but confesses that he is an agnostic. {RE}

Niebuhr, Barthold Georg (1776–1831)

An eminent Copenhagen-born German historian, Niebuhr read twenty languages and had an extraordinarily wide knowledge. From 1816 to 1823, he was the Prussian ambassador to the Holy See. His history of Rome (3 volumes, 1811–1832) is said to have inaugurated modern scientific historical method. Niebuhr related individual events to the political and social institutions of ancient Rome, seeking to recreate the past in terms understandable to the modern reader. His liberalism was antirevolutionary and he admired the Roman republic, favoring agrarianism as the basis of a well-balanced state. Niebuhr's biographer, Winkworth, showed that while he refused in his later years to discuss religion—Niebuhr had been an aggressive skeptic in earlier years—he always rejected Christianity: "I would not overthrow the dead Church, but if she were to fall it would give me no uneasiness." {CE; JM; JMRH; RAT; RE}

Niebuhr, Reinhold: See entries for George Orwell and for Theism.

Niel, André (1913–)

At the Second European Conference of the International Humanist and Ethical Union (IHEU) held in Hannover (1968), Niel from France addressed the group. He writes on such subjects as publicity, literary analysis, and structuralism.

Niel, Mathilde (1926–)

A contributor to Erich Fromm's *Socialist Humanism*, Niel is associated with *L'Institut de L'Homme* in Paris. She has written *Psychanalyse du Marxisme* (1967). {PK}

Nielsen, Kai (1926–)

When he signed Humanist Manifesto II, Nielsen was a professor of philosophy at the University of Calgary in Canada. Now emeritus, he has been called one of the century's leading atheists.

Nielsen is the author of *Philosophy and Atheism: In Defense of Atheism* (1985) and *Ethics Without God* (1990). In 1989, he wrote *God, Skepticism, and Modernity*, followed in 1990 by *Does God Exist?: The Great Debate*, in which he debates J. P. Moreland, a Christian and professor of philosophy at Biola University. Nielsen calls God a figment of human inspiration and states that disbelief in a god does not mean that an individual is immoral or will be unethical. In 1996 he published *Naturalism Without Foundations*, expressing the view that naturalism can avoid the pitfalls of both absolutism and relativism and showing what he terms the playful but still corrosive skepticism of post-modernism.

Nielsen, a supporter of Internet Infidels, is a contributing editor on *Philo*, for which he wrote "Naturalism and Religion: Must Naturalistic Explanations Explain Religion Away?" (Spring-Summer 1998) and "On Being a Secularist All the Way Down" (Fall-Winter 1998). "The atheism I articulate and defend is a naturalism in that it rejects all forms of supernaturalism," he states. It is a social naturalism that can also be termed a nonscientistic naturalism and a form of historicism. (See Nielsen's entry for "Agnosticism" in the *Dictionary of the History of Ideas* and for "Atheism" in *Encyclopedia Britannica* 1983.) {CA; E; HM2; SHD}

Niemojewski, André (1864–1921)

Niemojewski's chief work, *Legends* (1902) was suppressed in Austria and Russia, but after a prolonged struggle he won the right to continue its circulation. Deported from his native Poland for assiduous rationalist lecturing, he passed to Austria, narrowly escaping a sentence of ten years in prison. He returned to Poland in 1906 and was a leader among the rationalists. Niemojewski edited *Wolny Mysl* from 1906 to 1908. {RAT}

Nienkerk, Robert (20th Century)

Nienkerk is active with Friends Free of Theism in Richfield, Minnesota. (See entry for Minnesota Atheists, Humanists.) {FD}

Nietzsche, Friedrich Wilhelm (1844–1900)

Nietzsche is the German philosopher credited with the phrase, "God is dead." In fact, he wrote, "philosophers and 'free spirits' feel ourselves irradiated by a new dawn by the report that the 'old God is dead'; our hearts overflow with gratitude, hearts overflow with gratitude, astonishment, presentiment, and expectation. . . . You say you believe in the necessity of religion. Be sincere! You believe in the necessity of the police."

"What is it: is man only a blunder of God's," he asked, "or God only a blunder of man's?"

In his passionate opposition to Christianity, Nietzsche developed the concept of the *Ubermensch* (translated by some as "superman" and by others as "overman"). Since God is dead, in short, man is free to invent his own "values." As to labels, he insisted, "There are no philosophies, only philosophers."

Lamont wrote of Nietzsche,

> One is repelled by the cruel, egoistic, hard-boiled sort of Superman that Nietzsche had in mind, but the idea of a new species beyond man is invigorating . . . an eventual Superman who will surpass present-day man as much as man does the highest species of animals.

Nietzsche's *Ecce Homo* (1889) suggests that atheism came instinctively to him. In *The Gay Science* (1882), a madman announces that "God is dead," then realizes he has come too soon—for Nietzsche, the death of God is a liberating idea that sets man free to explore vast possibilities. However, as noted by George J. Stack, the consequences of the loss of religious faith in God will be a 100-year period of "nihilism." Nietzsche called God (if conceived of as a "providential" being) "the greatest immoralist in deeds that has ever existed." In 1887, he wrote *The Genealogy of Morals*. His *The Antichrist* (1889) expresses his various anti-Christian sentiments and ideas, finding that Christendom had a "vampiric" effect on the Roman Empire and castigating its reversal of the "noble" values of the Greco-Roman world.

As for Richard Wagner's sentimental return to the Christian faith, Nietzsche passed up no chance to mock him. Joachim Köhler, in *Nietzsche and Wagner* (1998), found Nietzsche as anti-Semitic as Wagner. Both lived a comfortable bourgeois life but thought the bourgeois society would end in bloodshed and be replaced by warlike heroes who would be contemptuous of the masses.

Most secular humanists shy away from Nietzsche, because he so inspired the German Nazis under Adolph Hitler and because of his condemnation of *Mensch* (Man). "Thus Spake Zarathustra" became a Hitler Youth motto. Although there is little if any reliable evidence to support Nietzsche's alleged anti-Semitism, his sister Elisabeth Forster-Nietzsche was outspokenly anti-Semitic. In presiding over his archives from 1900 until her death in 1935, through selective editing, outright forgery, and toadying to Hitler, she recast her "beloved Fritz" as a Teutonic superman, according to journalist Ferdinand Protzman.

Nietzsche's philosophic views are discussed in *Theories of Evolution* (1984) by H. James Birx, who considers him a secularist but not a secular humanist. Bertrand Russell, himself a non-theist, denounced fellow non-theist Nietzsche. Although Nietzsche denied that he was a Social Darwinist, "this is precisely what he was," Paul Edwards wrote in *God and the Philosophers*. Russell was also critical of other Social Darwinists and power-worshipers.

Nietzsche's last eleven years were spent in total mental darkness, first in an asylum in Basel, then in his mother's and later his sister's care in Röcken, Germany, where he is said to have been fond of playing the piano and splashing in the bathtub. McCabe said of this period, "His mind gave way under the strain of his fierce indignation against stupidity and hypocrisy but the clerical charge that this mental unbalance may be traced in his works is ludicrous. They are masterly indictments of the developing faults of the new age which have so fatally revealed themselves since death. His chief mistake was to assume that Christianity had introduced humanitarianism into the world and to fail to hold the balance in his mind between the need for virility and the need to help the weaker members of society."

Lesley Chamberlain's *Nietzsche in Turin* (1998), a friendly work, mentions not only that Nietzsche's father and grandfather were parsons but also that his mother's father was a parson. She wrote that Nietzsche carried an umbrella when he went walking in order to shade his sensitive eyes from light. Children were known to have filled it with pebbles that showered down on his head when he opened the umbrella. She also notes that when he walked his steps were oddly short and high—his myopia made him afraid of tripping.

In 1865, taken by friends to a brothel, he may have infected himself with syphilis. In 1867 he was treated for a syphilitic infection. As to his last days, Chamberlain wrote:

> As for the drama of ill-health, it never left him after he reached his mid-twenties. Even in childhood he had suffered headaches and myopia, and the weakness seemed to run in the family since it also afflicted Elisabeth, and their father Carl Ludwig, who had died at thirty-six of a brain disease. Nietzsche gave out never to know quite what was wrong with himself, though he suspected a hereditary problem and congratulated himself on surviving beyond his father's age. Yet how can he not have known he had syphilis, with a scar close to his foreskin and a history, albeit brief, of treatment? He surely lied to Wagner's doctor, Otto Eiser. The syphilis caught from prostitutes in his student days was complicated by diphtheria and dysentery contracted as a medical orderly in the 1870 Franco-Prussian War. Nietzsche was left with a delicate stomach and poor digestion and a recurring migraine, with constant vomiting and retching maximizing the pain in his head and the disruption [of] work. For days he could do nothing but lie in a dark room. . . .

From a clinical viewpoint, Dr. Archinto P. Anzil (*The New York Times Book Review*, 14 February 1999) has described the problem:

> Friedrich Nietzsche suffered from a tertiary form of neuro-syphilis, namely, from general paresis of the insane or dementia paralytica. This is an inflammation of the brain tissue, i.e., an encephalitis caused by or at least etiologically related to the microbial agent of syphilis. A typical and early manifestation of dementia paralytica is the development of paranoid ideas, usually notions of grandeur: patients think of themselves as being one of the paramount historical figures of their time or of times past. Characteristically, Nietzsche, imbued as he was in classic pre-Christian antiquity, thought he was the god Dionysus. As for Carl Nietzsche, the philosopher's father, he died of a stroke, a very common condition that as a rule has nothing to do with syphilis.

At the end, according to John Banville (*The New York Review of Books*, 13 August 1998),

> His handwriting began to decay, to such a degree that only his mother could read his script. A fragment of one of the *Dionysus Dithyrambs* of this time comes through her: Lesley Chamberlain describes it, accurately, as being of "Rilkean purity and inwardness":
>
> > Solitude is
> > Not pain but ripening–
> > For which the sun must be your friend.
>
> The sun was the only friend left to him now. There was, as Kleist had said of himself, no help for him upon this earth. He suffered prostrating attacks of weeping, accompanied by trembling and facial grimaces. He hid in his room on the Via Carlo Alberto, watching the winter harden. Christmas came and went, and on January 3 in the

Via Po he embraced a cabman's nag and collapsed on the pavement. The police had already been called when his kindly landlord Davide Fino arrived. Nietzsche recognized him, and Fino brought him home, where behind the locked door of his room he raved and ranted and danced naked in the private bacchanal of his dementia.

(See entries for George Eliot, Ernst Horneffer, and Karl Löwith. Also, see *Theories of Evolution* (1984) by H. James Birx and a discussion of Nietzsche's philosophy by Walter Kaufmann in the *Encyclopedia of Philosophy*, Vol. 5.) {BDF; CE; CL; DCL; ER; EU, George J. Stack; JM; PA; RAT; RE; TRI; TSV; TYD}

Nieuwenhuis, Ferdinand Jakob Domela (Born 1848)

A Dutch publisher, Nieuwenhuis at first was a Lutheran minister. But one Sunday in 1877 he resigned, telling his congregation that he had ceased to believe in Christianity. Stunned, they accepted his resignation but commended him for his honesty. He then contributed to *De Banier* (Banner), *de Dageraad* (Dawn), and *de Vragen des Tijds* (Questions of the Time). In 1879 he started a socialist paper, *Recht coor Allen*, which became an important daily organ of socialism and freethought. His principle writings were *With Jesus; For Or Against Socialism; The Religious Oath Question; The Religion of Reason;* and *The Religion of Humanity*. In 1887 he was sentenced to a year of solitary confinement for an article he had not written, and he was harshly treated until the pressure of public opinion secured his release. {BDF; RAT}

Niezing, Johan (20th Century)

At the International Humanist and Ethical Union's (IHEU's) International Peace Conference (1983), Niezing of the Netherlands addressed the gathering. He is the author of *Sociology, War, and Disarmament* (1970) and *Strategy and Structure—Studies in Peace Research* (1978).

NIGERIAN HUMANISTS

The Humanist Friendship Center presided over by Charles Ufomadu is at Omuoma Onicha Ezinihitte Mbaise, Imo State.

Action for Humanism is at PO Box 91, Ilishan Remo, Ogun State.

General coordinator of the Nigerian Humanist Movement is Leo Igwe, PO Box 25269, Mapo Ibadan, Oyo State, Nigeria.

NIGERIAN RATIONALISM: See *Freethought in the United Kingdom and the Commonwealth*, by Gordon Stein, which describes that country's rationalist association.

Nigg, Walter (20th Century)

Nigg wrote *The Heretics, Heresy Through the Ages*, in which he describes rebels within the Christian community.

Nightingale, Florence (1820–1910)

A nurse, a reformer, famous as the "Lady with the Lamp," Nightingale influenced military hospital cleanliness and raised nursing standards. "I have lived and slept in the same bed with English countesses and Prussian farm women. . . . No woman has excited passions among women more than I have," she wrote late in life to the surprise of those who considered her a conventional Victorian conformist. Nightingale, according to biographers Martha Vicinus and Bea Nergaard, who edited *Ever Yours, Florence Nightingale* (1990), was attracted to Roman Catholic religious orders because of their commendable social work. But she "always distrusted dogma" and "throughout her life Nightingale remained a critical member of the Church of England, continually seeking to adapt its tenets to her emotional and religious needs."

Meanwhile, some Unitarians have claimed that her viewpoint was that of a theistic Unitarianism. She had, however, written W. G. Tarrant, "I am so glad that my God is not the God of the High Church or of the Low; that he is not a Romanist or an Anglican—or a Unitarian." From 1857 on, she lived as an invalid, corresponded widely, received countless visitors, became generally renowned as the founder of nursing, and was the first woman to receive the British Order of Merit (1907), three years before her death. "The Church," she once wrote, "is now more like the Scribes and Pharisees than like Christ. . . . What are now called the essential doctrines of the Christian religion, Christ does not even mention." {CE; EG; JM; RAT; RE; TYD; UU; WWS}

Nigro, Anthony (20th Century)

Nigro is on the staff of *Free Inquiry*.

NIHILISM

• Nihilist, n. A Russian who denies the existence of anything but Tolstoi. The leader of the school is Tolstoi.

–Ambrose Bierce
The Devil's Dictionary

Ivan Turgenev, in *Fathers and Children* (1861), has a character named Bazarov who holds that everything is so bad at that time that all should be destroyed in order that a better system can be constructed. Such a person, called a nihilist, had strong feelings against both the church and the state. Nihilists held that human life is meaningless, and therefore all religions, laws, moral codes, and political systems are thoroughly empty and false.

According to Robert G. Olson in the *Encyclopedia of Philosophy*, Vol. 5, Nietzsche was an early user of the term and was "one of the first of the atheists to dispute the existence of a necessary link between atheism and nihilism." Nietzsche disagreed with Ivan, in Dostoyevsky's *Brothers Karamazov* (1880), that "If God does not exist, everything is permitted." Nihilism was somewhat popular among Russian extremists until the fall of the Czarist government in 1917.

Nihilism is apparent in Gaspar Noé's 1999 film, "I Stand Alone," one in which a middle-aged man is driven to despair by unemployment, rejection, and lack of love. "You are always alone, alone when you're born, alone when you die, alone, always alone," a character laments. "The older you get, the lonelier you are, alone with a few memories that life steadily destroys. Life is like a tunnel. Everyone has his little tunnel. But at the end of the tunnel, there is no light. There is nothing." {DCL; Alan Riding, *The New York times*, 14 March 1999}

Nijinsky, Vaslav (1890-1950): See entry for masturbation, which the famous dancer believed, after becoming interested in Tolstoy's religious philosophy and becoming schizophrenic, caused mental and physical breakdown. Also see Peter Ostwald's *Vaslav Nijinsky: A Leap into Madness* (1991).

Nikarchos (Ancient Greece)

Nikarchos illustrated an ancient Greek and humanistic sense of humor (Translation by Dudley Fitts):

• Yesterday Dr. Marcus went to see the statue of Zeus.
Though Zeus,
& though marble,
we're burying the statue today.

• Fortunatus the portrait-painter got twenty sons
but never one likeness.

• To ease his rumbling stomach our Kritôn
[the miser] sniffs
not mint,
but the product of the Mint.

• Fatal, fatal is the song of the dire night-raven:
but when Demophilos [the popular tenor]
sings
even the dire night-raven blenches & dies.

Nikolaevsky, Boris Ivanovich

Nikolaevsky, the famed archivist and Russian historian, was a Menshevik who was known by many to be a non-theist. {*The New York Review of Books*, 28 May 1998)

NILE DELTA: See entry for Delta and its connection with the pudenda.

Nilsen, Steinar (20th Century)

A Norwegian, Nilsen wrote "Beyond the University—Humanism as a Popular Movement" in *International Humanist* (October, 1990). He is the former President of the Human-Etisk Forbund (Human Ethical Association), one of the largest humanist organizations in the world in ratio to the size of its population. About one quarter of the Norwegian population of 4.3 million attends a humanist ceremony of some kind every ten years, he reports. Once challenged by a Lutheran minister, who lamented that humanists have stolen the ceremony of confirmation by tagging the word "civil" to it, Nilsen countered by offering to give the confirmation ceremony back to the church "if the church would agree to return the Winter Solstice Celebration to us ordinary people and stop calling it Christmas!" In 1994, Nilsen was named President of the European Humanist Federation. E-mail: <steinar.nilsen@mimer.no>. (See entry for European Humanist Federation.) {*International Humanist News*, March 1994}

Nin, Anaïs (1903–1977)

The daughter of the Spanish composer Joaquin Nin, Anaïs was a writer whose fiction contained searching portraits of women. A patient of Jung, she included much in her fiction about erotica and the subconscious. Nin is best known for her correspondence with Henry Miller (1965) and her six volumes of diaries (1966–1976). Upon her death, and knowing of her non-interest in religion, Rupert William Pole took her cremains over Santa Monica Bay in California to Mermaid Cove. "I told the pilot to fly there," he explained, "and I let go of the blanket containing her ashes just as a ray of sunlight broke through the overcast sky."

NIRVANA

• Nirvana, n. In the Buddhist religion, a state of pleasurable annihilation awarded to the wise, particularly to those wise enough to understand it.

–Ambrose Bierce
The Devil's Dictionary

In Buddhism, Jainism, and Hinduism, nirvana is the highest state of consciousness. The soul is freed from all desires and attachments. Many non-Buddhists inaccurately cite Heaven or Paradise as synonyms for nirvana. One can attain Nirvana in life, however, and the death of one who has attained it is termed *parinirvana*, or complete nirvanah, a goal that is beyond description. Some in their search for nirvana utilize yoga in order to obtain the extinction of all attachment and ignorance.

Freethinkers have been known to achieve nirvana, sometimes while listening to a cello, or cuddled up close to a mate on a wintry morning, or watching the skies on a moonlit night, or even while masticating. {CE; DCL}

Nisbet, Lee (20th Century)

A professor of philosophy at Medaille College in Buffalo, New York, Nisbet is a contributing editor for *Free Inquiry.* Also, he is on the executive council of the Committee for the Scientific Investigation of Claims of the Paranormal and is special projects director for *Skeptical Inquirer*. Nisbet is author of *The Gun Control Debate* (1990). {SHD}

NITRIC ACID

A poisonous air pollutant, nitric acid contains properties that are used by the human immune system to kill disease organisms and destroy cancers. Also, the acid dilates the blood vessels leading to the erectile spaces in the penis, allowing the penis to become engorged with blood.

As one Manhattan humanist observed, "One man's poison is also his pleasure."

NITROGEN

Excluding water vapor, about 78% of air around us is made up of nitrogen. Oxygen comes second, with 21%. The remaining 1% consists of argon, carbon dioxide, and hydrogen. Up to a height of almost fifty miles, where the mesosphere ends, this mixture of gases remains the same. Nitrogen is very important for plants.

Nitschke, Philip (20th Century)

Nitschke was awarded the title of 1998 Australian Humanist of the Year for his pioneering work for the terminally ill. He invented the coma machine in order legally to assist the death of patients who had made their own choice to end their lives. Even in extremis, patients could operate the machine themselves.

As a supporter of voluntary euthanasia, Dr. Nitschke claims that he sees little evidence that there is a god: "I haven't seen any miracles at those last moments. People in their final moments, while I am expecting them to say something profound, rarely do." {*International Humanist News*, May 1998}

Niven, Larry (20th Century)

Niven is a science fiction author. In *N-space*, a collection of narrations and short stories, he writes of his agnosticism. {CA; E}

Nkrumah, Kwame (1909–1972)

Nkrumah, Ghana's president (1960–1966), wrote *Consciencism* (1964), in which he outlined what he called a humanistic philosophy. However, he has allegedly suppressed numbers of political opponents and, after a series of strikes in 1961, made himself supreme commander of the armed forces as well as assumed absolute control of the Convention People's party. While on a trip to Peking in 1966, his government was overthrown and he took refuge in Guinea. {CE}

NOAH (or Noe)

In the Bible, Noah built an ark when divinely directed to do so, and this saved human and animal life from "the deluge." Afterwards, God established a covenant with Noah, whose three sons—Shem, Ham, and Japheth—are eponymous ancestors of races as mankind is divided in the Bible, according to *Genesis* 6-10.

Critic James Fenton has pointed out that Noah, when Ham once accidentally saw his nakedness, laid a curse not upon Ham but upon Ham's son: "Accursed be Canaan. He shall be his brothers' meanest slave. . . . Blessed be Yahweh, God of Shem. Let Canaan be his slave. May God make space for Japheth. May he live in the tents of Shem, and let Canaan be his slave." (*Genesis* 9:20-27). In short, Fenton explains, because Ham accidentally went into his tent and saw his father's nakedness, thereby breaking a taboo, this explains how, "despite the single common origin of Man, some peoples of the world live together on unequal terms." John Block Friedman's *The Monstrous Races in Medieval Art and Thought* (1981) shows more about Ham's misdeed. He *mocked* Noah's nakedness as well as unsuccessfully tried to get his brothers to do the same. But Ham also had sinned on the ark, failing to follow Noah's rule to be sexually continent. With the aid of a magic demon, however, Ham slept with his wife, resulting in his being punished by being given a black skin. Thus, when the world was divided up, Japheth received Europe, Shem got Asia, and Ham was given Africa. Further, Fenton adds,

> Ham became father to all the monsters of legend—including all the monsters of classical legend, the giants, the anthropophagi, the people with heads growing beneath their shoulders, and so forth. In some versions there was nothing necessarily bad about these monsters—they were after all a part of God's creation—it was just that their ancestry had to be accounted for.

Freethinkers are appalled at the overtones of such a tale and hold that the resultant anti-Hamitism hurt race relations because of its unsound theories.

Peter Gomes's *The Good Book* (1996) cites a poll finding that 10% of those quizzed thought that Joan of Arc was Noah's wife. (For Bruce Bagemihl's disproving that Noah's Ark contained an all-heterosexual group, see entry for Animal.) {*The Economist*, 18 January 1997}

NOBEL PRIZE WINNERS

Alfred B. Nobel (1833–1896) was a Swedish chemist who made a large fortune by the invention and manufacture of explosives. He left the bulk of it for a foundation that would dispense prizes to the most distinguished workers in science, letters, and the peace movement.

McCabe in the 1940s found that not more than three out of more than two hundred Nobel Prize winners are claimed in the voluminous *Catholic Encyclopaedia*—Carrel is one example. However, about one hundred fifty of the recipients did not write about or speak on religion, which McCabe noted squares with the findings of Leuba that seventy per cent of American scientists (including teachers in institutions under sectarian influence) are atheists or agnostics.

He found that of the five definite Christians, two (Kipling and Mistral) are of doubtful orthodoxy, one (Eucken) is a theologian of no literary merit, one (Pearl Buck) had a serious quarrel with her Church, and one (Selma Lagerlof) is a sentimental writer of little more than local repute.

Meanwhile, the following international rationalist writers received the prize: **Björnstjerne Björnson**, **Anatole France**, **John Galsworthy**, **Sinclair Lewis**, **Maurice Maeterlinck**, **Theodor Mommsen**, **Eugene O'Neill**, **Luigi Pirandello**, **Romain Rolland**, **George Bernard Shaw**, and **Rabindranath Tagore**.

The following did not: **Bertold Brecht**; **Joseph Conrad**; **Anton Chekhov**; **E. M. Forster**; **Maxim Gorky**; **Henrik Ibsen**; **James Joyce**; **D. H. Lawrence**; **Marcel Proust**; **August Strindberg**; **H. G. Wells**; and **Virginia Woolf**.

Few rationalists, McCabe notes, "seem to be aware of the strength of their position, while the strength of the Churches is now in the less educated Fundamentalist masses." He qualifies this by saying that "we must, however, take certain circumstances into account. The judges and their academic advisers are for the most part conventional Christians, and are apt to understand the qualification 'of an idealist tendency' in their own way, while, as men of one of the smaller States, they—as the awards show—are apt to strain matters in favour of small nations or to be swayed by broad political considerations.

Thus, while the literary prize has been awarded repeatedly to men and women who are almost unknown outside their own small countries—G. Deledda, Gjellerup, Selma Lagerlof, Pontoppidan, Sigrid Undset, etc.—or to Christian writers of no literary distinction like Eucken, world-figures, mostly of a decided idealist (but Rationalist) tendency, like Wells, Conrad, Zola, D'Annunzio, Capek, Galdòs, Ibañez, Santayana, Gorki, Tolstoy, Sudermann, Sinclair, and Russell, etc., have been passed over. (**Bertrand Russell** in 1950 received the Prize in Literature). Further, the award for humanitarian work has occasionally been rather parochial (Archbishop Soderblom) or very questionable (Elihu Root, Theodore Roosevelt, Austen Chamberlain, A. Henderson, Gen. Dawes, or paid officials at Geneva). Of the recipients of the scientific awards, in fine, not one in five has ever declared his views on religion." {RE}

Nobel-winning unbelievers listed herein are **Jane Addams**, **(Sir) Norman Angell**, **Klas Pontus Arnoldson**, **Svante August Arrhenius**, **Samuel Beckett**, **Albert Camus**, **Frances Crick**, **Christian René De Duve**, **William Faulkner**, **Edward H. Fisher**, **Dario Fo**, **Murray Gell-Mann**, **Herbert Hauptman**, **Ernest Hemingway**, **Pär Lagerkvist**, **Selma Lagerlof**, **Charles Laveran**, Jean-Marie Lehn, Sinclair Lewis, **André Lwoff**, Naguid Mahfouz, **Thomas Mann**, Mario José Molina, Theodor Mommsen, **Hermann J. Muller**, Ferad Murad, **Alva Myrdal**, Fridtjof Nansen, Eugene O'Neill, Carl von Ossietzky, **Linus C. Pauling**, **Octavio Paz**, Henrik Pontoppidan, Ludwig Quidde, Charles Richet, Ronald Ross, **Bertrand Russell**, **Andre Sakharov**, **José Saramago**, **Jean-Paul Sartre** (who, however, refused out of principle—when his surviving relatives demanded the money that went with the prize, they were rebuffed), Erwin Schrödinger, **Albert Schweitzer**, George Bernard Shaw, Charles Scott Sherrington, Jens Christian Skou, **Michael Smith**, **Wole Soyinka**, **John Steinbeck**, Jack Steinberger, **James Dewey Watson**, and **Steven Weinberg**. Also, **Emily Greene Balch**, a Unitarian and Quaker, won the 1946 prize for founding, along with **Jane Addams**, the Women's International League for Peace and Freedom.

Although the Prize has gone to many of the finest writers of the century—e.g., **Beckett**, **Faulkner**, Hamsun, **Mann**, Yeats—neither James Joyce nor Vladimir Nabokov were so honored. Boris Pasternak, pressured by the Soviet government, rejected the prize.

The 1998 Nobel Prizes in the sciences were $978,000 each. Meanwhile, the Templeton Prize for Progress in Religion in 1999 became the world's richest award, $1,240,000.

Noble, Iris (20th Century)

Noble, a freethinker, wrote *Clarence Darrow, Defense Attorney* (1958). {FUS}

NOBLE SAVAGE

Primitivism has been shown as a revolt against luxury (Goldsmith's *The Deserted Village*), against sophistication (Richard Cumberland's *The West Indian*), and against neo-classicism. Primitivism supposed a belief in man's natural goodness and in the inevitable corruptions of civilization. Boswell found a visiting Tahitian "elegant." Readers delighted in books such as Burroughs's Tarzan and Kipling's Mowgli or with the Truffaut film, "*L'Enfant sauvage.*" The ideas of primitivism were in many ways continued in the Romantic movement, with its stress on Nature, freedom (both political and artistic), and the natural man. Jean-Jacques Rousseau advanced the idea that people who live within civilization are no more "civilized" and perhaps not so "civilized" as those worthy people who live in non-civilized places. Often the "noble savage," another term for the primitive man, lived close to nature, not as a lord over nature, and the simple innocence of his desires inspired numbers of writers and thinkers, particularly those who were concerned about the excesses of the Industrial Revolution. {DCL}

Noelle, David C. (20th Century)

Noelle is on the faculties of the Department of Cognitive Science and the Department of Computer Science and Engineering at the University of California, San Diego. He is chairman of the San Diego Association of Secular Humanists (SANDASH); is vice president of the Freethinkers' Society, which operates the Thomas Paine Coffeehouse in San Diego; and was one of the initial members of the Secular Humanists of Los Angeles (SHOLA); and in Pennsylvania is a regional director of the Council for Secular Humanism.

On Easter of 1996, he was a speaker at the Mount Soledad Cross protest. For *Free Inquiry*, he interviewed Patricia Churchland. Noelle is the webmaster and internet coordinator of SANDASH; the San Diego Association for Rational Inquiry (SDARI, a group of skeptics); and the Council for Secular Humanism. On the Web: <www.cse.ucsd.edu/users/dnoelle/>. E-mail: <admin@secularhumanism.org> and <dnoelle@cs.ucsd.edu>.

Noffs, Theodore Delwin (1926–)

The Reverend "Ted" Noffs is an individualistic Australian theologian and social reformer. In 1974 he founded the Wayside Chapel, Kings Cross, Sydney. During the 1970s he established Australia's first Life Education Centre, a rehabilitation program for young drug addicts, one which has been copied around the world. The Centre also establishes contact with the aged, lonely, migrants, and Aborigines. "All religious, political problems must be given a human face," he once said, declining to join the humanists but claiming to be a non-believer in the Bible. In 1985 he received the Humanist of the Year award. {SWW}

Noiré, Ludwig (1829–1889)

Noiré was a German monist whose works show the influence of Spinoza and Schopenhauer. He was the author of *Aphorisms on the Monist Philosophy* (1877) and a work on the *Origin of Speech* (1877). Noir contended, according to Wheeler, that "language originates in instinctive sounds accompanying will in associative actions." {BDF; RAT}

Nokes, G. D. (20th Century)

Nokes wrote *History of the Crime of Blasphemy* (1928). {GS}

Nöldeke, Theodor (1836–1930)

Nöldeke, a German orientalist, taught theology at Kiel University in 1864 and in 1872 became professor of Semitic philology at Strasbourg University. The chief works he published were *A History of the Koran* (1856), *Geschichte des Korans* (1860) and *Das Leben Muhammads* (A Life of Muhomet, 1863), which show a divergence from Christianity. In addition to writing *A Literary History of the Old Testament,* Nöldeke wrote an estimated six hundred scholarly works, pamphlets, and articles. {BDF; RAT}

Nolte, Nick (1941-)

Nolte, an actor, has appeared in numerous plays and movies. During the 1960s he made money by selling phony draft cards to college students, saying he did it only to help underage kids get served in bars. The FBI, however, arrested him for dealing in counterfeit government documents and he was given forty-five years in jail, since suspended—as a result, he is now a felon, was not drafted into the armed services, and can never vote. Nolte has been married (and divorced) three times. Asked in a *Playboy* (April 1999) interview if he believed in God, Nolte responded, "I have difficulty with God and with beliefs. You have to ask the question, If God created man in his own image, what kind of an image is God?" If there is a God, the interviewer continued, what do you hope he overlooks about you? "I hope," Nolte answered, "God would overlook that he made me in his image, because he sure fucked up."

NOMA (Non-Overlapping Magisteria): See entry for Stephen J. Gould.

NONADORANTES

The followers of Ferenc David in Transylvania were called Nonadorantes because they refused to accord "adoration" to Christ.

NONBELIEVERS: For statistics showing that non-believers outnumber believers, see entry for Hell.

NONCONFORMISTS

Protestants in England in the 17th century and afterwards were called non-conformists if they refused to belong to the Church of England, which was the established church. They were also called dissenters. Freethinkers who do not conform to or refuse to be bound by accepted beliefs, customs, or practices, are also called nonconformists. {DCL}

NONCONFORMITY

• How conventional all you unconventional people are!

–**George Bernard Shaw**

NON-OVERLAPPING MAGISTERIA: See entry for Stephen Gould.

NON-REALISTS

• Most Unitarians in Britain do not believe in a transcendent Deity who is really out there somewhere. Those who feel this way ("non-realist" is the trendy term over here) and who tend to emphasise religion as being about human relationships may well describe themselves as "religious humanists." I have never heard a congregation here in Britain describe themselves as being "secular humanist," but this is not to say that there aren't any.

—Matthew Smith, a British Unitarian <matjanros@aol.com>.

NON-RELIGIONISTS: For an estimate of the number of non-religionists worldwide, see the entry for Hell.

NONSENSE

• When a mathematical or philosophical author writes with a misty profundity, he is talking nonsense.

–Alfred North Whitehead

Noon, Richard (20th Century)

Noon in 1996 was an unsuccessful candidate for membership in the National Secular Society's Council of Management.

Noordenbos, D. (1896–1978)

Noordenbos is author in the Netherlands of *Het Atheisme in Nederland in De Negentiende Eeuw.*

Noorthouck, John (19th Century)

Noorthouck wrote a *History of London* (1773) and an *Historical and Classical Dictionary* (1776). He also has been credited with the *Life of the Man After God's Own Heart.* {BDF; FUK}

Nordau, Max Simon (1849–1923)

Nordau, a physician born of Jewish parents at Pesth, wrote several books of travels and earned much negative criticism for his trenchant work, *Economic Lies of Our Civilisation* (1978) and *Degeneration* (1993). {BDF; RAT}

Nordenfeldt, Johan (20th Century)

Nordenfeldt, director of the United Nations Center Against Apartheid, addressed the Tenth International Humanist and Ethical Union (IHEU) World Congress held in Buffalo (1988).

Norman, Andrew (20th Century)

The Andrew Norman Foundation was an early donor to help fund the Center for Inquiry–West in the Los Angeles, California, area.

Norman, C. H. (20th Century)

Norman wrote *The Neutrality of God* (1931). {GS}

Norman, Winifred Latimer (20th Century)

Norman, granddaughter of the African American scientist, Lewis H. Latimer, is author of *Lewis H. Latimer, Scientist* (1994). Dr. Norman has been a trustee of the Unitarian Universalist Association and is a member of the Fourth Universalist Society in New York City.

Norris, Henry Hadley (1771–1850)

Norris in 1839 wrote *Principles of the Jesuits, Developed in a Collection of Extracts from Their Own Authors to Which are Prefixed a Brief Account of the Origin of the Order and a Sketch of Its Institute.* In the work, he described murder, deceit, intrigue, political chicanery, and bribery which he alleged Jesuits used to accomplish their goals.

Norris, Julie (20th Century)

Norris in Britain is active with the West Glamorgan Humanist Group in Uplands, Swansea.

North, Luke (20th Century)

North wrote *Why I Am An Atheist* (1916). {GS}

NORTH AMERICAN COMMITTEE FOR HUMANISM (NACH)

The North American Committee for Humanism (NACH), which was promoted by Sherwin T. Wine, was formed to provide humanist leaders a forum for resolving mutual problems and planning mutual goals.

On its founding board were humanist leaders affiliated with the American Ethical Union; the American Humanist Association; the Council for Democratic and Secular Humanism (now the Council for Secular Humanism); the Fellowship of Religious Humanists (now Friends of Religious Humanism), an affiliate of the Unitarian Universalist Association the Humanist Association of Canada; and the Society for Humanistic Judaism.

Its first project was the establishment of the Humanist Institute, which enrolled its first class in 1984. Howard Radest served as the Institute's founding Dean. The Institutes annual journal is called *Humanism Today.*

In 1997, sixty-eight had been graduated, and four of the Institutes graduates and students sit on the current board of directors of the American Humanist Association. Seven are Ethical Culture leaders. Eleven are Unitarian-Universalist ministers. The present dean is Robert B. Tapp.

A specialist member of the International Humanist and Ethical Union, the Committee is at Box 191, 5901-J Wyoming NE, Albuquerque, New Mexico 87109. (See entries for Jean Kotkin and Alfred W. Cook.) {*The Humanist,* January-February 1998}

NORTH AMERICAN FREETHOUGHT: See *Freethought in the United States,* which discusses the subject in detail, by Gordon Stein.

NORTH CAROLINA ATHEISTS

Wayne Aiken is a contact for American Theists, Inc. E-mail: <waiken@atheists.org>.

NORTH CAROLINA FREETHINKERS

Charles Alfred Human Jr., in "Pioneers of Freethought in North Carolina," has noted that as early as 1761 complaints were being made about freethinkers. "One of them declared that the money he is obliged to give to a minister, he would rather give to a kind girl," John MacDowell, a minister for the Society for the Propagation of the Gospel complained. "Another believes there is neither Hell nor Devil, and there is here one gentleman of fortune in particular; he is not of the vestry, but strives to influence them as much as he can, whom I heard myself declare he could not believe in Jesus Christ & he despised the holy sacrament of the Lord's Supper. To him, with two (sic) other gentlemen in the St. James Parish, a young phisician (sic) who was reputed to be an Atheist and (sic) who died since I came here, left Lord Bolingbroke's works. What can a minister of God expect from these?"

Human then cites an early alleged "coterie of infidels" by name: **Ezekiel Polk** (grandfather of President James K. Polk); **Charles Polk**, son of Colonel Thomas Polk; **Charles and Ezra Alexander**, two signers of the Mecklenburg Declaration of Independence of 1775; **Moses Winslow**; and **James Brandon**.

Governor **Willie Jones**, a post-Revolutionary governor, was a freethinker who stipulated in his will that no one was to insult his body by mumbling religious words over it.

North Carolina academia included the University of North Carolina's co-founder, **William Davie**, who brought Continental ideas of dancing and polite society as well as religious skepticism.

Dr. **David Kerr**, a Fayetteville Presbyterian minister, became a passionate republican and skeptic upon becoming a professor at Chapel Hill. Another professor, **Delvaux**, was a skeptical French ex-monk. Still another, Professor **Richards**, had a profession detested by the Puritans: He was a strolling actor.

Samuel Allen Holmes was nihilistic and held that honesty and integrity were "deceptions and injurious pretenses" and incited a riot on campus in 1799.

Joseph Gales, an early 19th century deist was a leading newspaperman who owned *The Raleigh Register*.

Another deist, **Nathaniel Macon**, said that if a Hindu were to come to North Carolina and aspire to an office to which merit would entitle him, his religion should not be a bar.

The avowed deist **Christopher Dudley** served seven times as State Senator for Onslow County. {*Truth Seeker*, Vol. 123:1}

NORTH CAROLINA HUMANISTS

• American Humanist Association, Mid-Atlantic Region (AHA), A-140, 1 College Row, Brevard, North Carolina 28712. O. Andrews Ferguson is coordinator.

• Duke University Humanist Society is at <http://www.secularhumanism.org/cfa/orgs.html>.

• Humanists of North Carolina (AHA), POB 1491, Pisgah Forest, North Carolina 28768. Marge Glanzman is a contact.

• Onslow Freethought Society, 704 Ireland Court, Jacksonville, North Carolina (810) 353-9362.

NORTH DAKOTA HUMANISTS

• Bernie Schatz is the American Humanist Association coordinator of the northern part of the United States. (See entry for Minnesota Atheists, Humanists.)

• Sheri Anderson, RR, Fargo, North Dakota, is coordinator for North Dakota Humanists. {FD}

NORTH TEXAS CHURCH OF FREETHOUGHT

The North Texas Church of Freethought (PO Box 111894, Carrolton, Texas 76011) was founded in 1995 by Mike and Marilyn Sullivan, Deborah A. Boak, and Tim Gorski. On the Web: <http://webs.airmail.net/~freethgt/>.

NORTH-EAST HUMANIST NEWSLETTER

A quarterly, *North-East Humanist Newsletter*, is at 58 Garmondsway Road, West Cornforth, Ferryhill, County Durham DL17 9HD, United Kingdom.

NORTHERN IRELAND HUMANISTS

For information about the Ulster Humanist Association, contact Brian McClinton, 25 Riverside Drive, Lisburn, Northern Ireland BT27 4HE; telephone 01846 677 264

Northcote, Orford (19th Century)

Northcote, a freethinker, wrote *Ruled by the Tomb* (1899). {GS}

Norton, Andrews (1786–1853)

While Dexter Professor of Sacred Literature at Harvard, Norton was characterized by Perry Miller as "the perfect summation of Unitarian scholarship." His *The Evidences of the Genuineness of the Gospels* (1837–1844) was a rational interpretation of the Bible which sought to sweep away Calvinist orthodoxy and argue against Trinitarianism. In his later career, however, he became an agent of conservative reaction against Transcendentalism, remembered chiefly for his attacks on George Ripley and Ralph Waldo Emerson. Their doctrine of religious intuition rejected not only the miracles but the need for any empirical justification for religious ideas, thus throwing Norton's entire program out the window. Norton countered that the self and its intuitions were untrustworthy bases for a religious faith, and he saw in Transcendentalism the danger of self taking precedence over things of deeper importance. {U; U&U}

Norton, Charles Eliot (1827–1908)

Norton, an American scholar and teacher, was professor of the history of art at Harvard from 1875 to 1898. As a man of letters, he had a stimulating influence on his time. "One may sigh for all that one loses in giving up the old religion," he wrote in a 1905 letter to Goldwin Smith. "But the new irreligion is the manlier, honester, and simpler thing, and affords a better theory of life and a more solid basis for morality." With James Russell Lowell, he edited (1864–1868) the *North American Review* and was a founder (1865) of the *Nation*. Although Norton was reticent about his skepticism, Sir Leslie Stephen, the British agnostic leader, dedicates his *Essays on Freethinking* to him and in his letters frequently describes Norton, of whom he was a close friend, as an agnostic. {JM; RAT; RE; TYD}

Norton, David (1930–1995)

In the 1960s, Norton was an associate leader with Jeff Hornback of the Ethical Society of St. Louis. His books include *Personal Destinies* and *Democracy and Moral Development*.

Norton, W. L. (19th Century)

Norton, a freethinker, wrote *Try-Square, or The Church of Practical Religion* (1887). {GS}

NORWEGIAN HEATHEN SOCIETY

"Our goal is to contribute to reduction of the superior force the church and christianity has in Norway, with its exceptional position in Norwegian laws, school, and culture," states the mission of *Det norske Hedningsamfunn Collettsg* on the Web: <http://www.hedning.no/hedning/e-index.html>.

NORWEGIAN HUMANISM

Kristian Horn, who founded the Norwegian Humanist Association (**Etisk-Forbund**), did so because of his interest in fighting for the rights of Norwegian unbelievers. The association of academics that he started was then helped when Levi Fragell became its director and chose to make the movement strong by fighting against the state church. In 1995, out of a population of four million, Norway had 52,600 humanists. The humanist "coming-of-age ceremony" which is provided has been attended by 120,000 a year, and one study shows that of the several thousand new members per year more than one-half are less than thirty-four years old.

The Norwegians, one of whom has boasted that for their leaders they have no philosophers but many working class people, at a February 1995 meeting in Oslo were optimistic as to the future of their group.

Fri Tanke, a publication which comes out seven times per year, is at Boks 6744, St. Olavs pl. 0130 Oslo. At the same address is *Humanist*, a bi-monthly in English.

Humanist in Norway can be e-mailed: <humanist@human.no>.

Humanist Tidsskrift for Livssyndebatt, is a bi-monthly of Human-Etisk Forbund at Boks 6744, St. Olavs pl. 0130 Oslo. <skaara@human.no>.

Lorentz Stavrum is the current president of the Norwegian Humanist Association. On the Web: <http://nettvik.no/forenings-gaarden/human_etisk/> and <http://nettvik.no/human_etisk>.

Norwegians who signed Humanist Manifesto 2000 included Levi Fragell, Bernt Hagtvet, and Tove Beate Pedersen. (See entries for Lars Gunner Lingås and *Det Norske Hedningsamfunn* [Society of Norwegian Heathens and for Scandinavian Unbelievers].)

NORWEGIAN SKEPTICS

On the Web, the Norwegian skeptical organization is at <http://www.skepsis.no/>.

NORWICH (England) HUMANISTS

For information write Vincent G. Chainey, Le Chene, 4 Mill St., Bradenham, Thetford IP25 7PN; or telephone 01362 820982.

NOTHING (1)

No such thing as "nothing" exists. Even the vacuum of empty space, devoid of even a single atom of matter, seethes with subtle activity. As described in *Physical Review Letters*, Dr. Steve K. Lamoreaux, an atomic physicist now at Los Alamos National Laboratory, it is possible to measure the force exerted by fleeting fluctuations in the vacuum that pace the universal pulse of existence. Such a view leads to the fact that the universe may have sprung from a virtual particle. {*The New York Times*, 21 January 1997}

NOTHING (2)

NOTHING (3)

According to "Nothing (1)" above, "Nothing (2)" is in error.

NOTRE DAME

The exceptionally beautiful Notre Dame cathedral in Paris, built by masons for the Catholic hierarchy, was home for the fictional hunchback Quasimodo. According to Emmanuel Le Roy Ladurie in *The Beggar and the Professor* (1997), the Gothic building's splendor included a choir full of pimps and madams, its bays sheltered foundlings, and in front were endless, irritating processions of priestlings and monks.

Nott, Josiah Clark (1804–1873)

Nott was an American ethnologist who had been born in South Carolina. He wrote *The Physical History of the Jewish Race, Types of Mankind* (1854) and *Indigenous Races of the Earth* (1855). His purpose was to disprove the theory of the unity of the human race. {BDF}

Nott, Kathleen (1910–1999)

Nott, whose father was a printer and whose mother ran a boarding house, displayed early intellectual brilliance and moved from King's College London to Somerville College, Oxford. The prose work which brought her into the public eye was *The Emperor's Clothes* (1953), a study of the dominant Christianity of writers such as Graham Greene, Dorothy Sayers, and T. S. Eliot and how current theological standards of Christian orthodoxy affected literature and literary criticism. Although her critique could be harsh, she adhered to positive humanist values. She wrote *Philosophy and Human Nature* (1970). Another of her works, *The Good Want Power* (1977), examined the problem that politicians are never good and the good never become politicians. Active in PEN, the international organization to support writers in prison or under threat, she edited its journal *Pen International* for twenty-seven years and was briefly elected President of the English Pen.

While a student at Oxford, she became depressed by contemporary philosophy, "its contempt for ethics and hence for living. I went down with a strong dislike of the world I was entering. It appeared to be run by an alliance of force and fraud and there was something fraudulent about even philosophy's linguistic exclusiveness."

In 1979, Nott was elected an honorary associate of the Rationalist Press Association, about which she commented,

> I was much honoured to become an Associate of the RPA, but I sometimes wonder whether I am a Rationalist or a Humanist. However, I believe that I am human and I try to be reasonable and to know myself.

During the 1950s, she reviewed books for *The Humanist*, although she asked in the 1960s if a humanist was someone "who was rude to God or else someone who was kind to animals." What she lamented was that writers like T. E. Hulme (1883-1917) and T. S. Eliot (1888-1965) disliked science more than they disliked totalitarianism.

Francis King, a friend, wrote in *The Independent* (11 March 1999) that Nott was "a poet sadly underrated by those swept hither and thither on choppy tides of fashion, a prose writer who combines vigour with self-discipline, and a philosopher with a rare gift for exegesis not only of her own ideas but of the ideas of others." {*The* Freethinker, April 1999; New *Humanist*, March 1999; TRI}

Noun, Paul (19th Century)

Noun was the French author of *The Scientific Errors of the Bible* (1881). {BDF}

Novak, John (20th Century)

Novak, professor of education at Brock University in St. Catharines, Ontario, Canada, is editor of *Insights*, the newsletter of the John Dewey Society. A Secular Humanist Mentor of the Council for Secular Humanism, Novak has written for *Free Inquiry*. At the 1994 Toronto conference of the Coalition for Secular Humanism, Atheism, and Freethought (CSHAFT), Novak spoke on "John Dewey vs. Bertrand Russell on Religious Belief." (See "Transatlantic Dewey," *Free Inquiry*, Winter 1995-1996.)

Novak, Michael (20th Century)

A theologian of the American Enterprise Institute, Novak is a vocal critic of secular humanism. He is the author with his daughter Jana of *Tell Me Why: A Father Answers His Daughter's Questions About God* (1998).

"Secular humanism," he has lamented, "gave us answers for 500 years that no longer seem adequate even to many who tried hard to be faithful to them. That is why so many far-seeing souls announced that we have come to the edge of the Enlightenment and are stepping forth into something new, untried, not yet transparent." He cited authors Norman Mailer and Vaclav Havel as examples of individuals in 1998 who recognize that "reason and faith spring from the same stream. The death of either reason or liberty means death for them, too." {*The New York Times*, 24 May 1998}

Novikov, Yakov (Born 1849)

Novikov was a Russian sociologist, the President of the first International Sociological Congress and a leading Russian pacifist. His rationalist views appear in his *La justice et l'expansion de la vie* (1905), and he has taken part in various International Freethought Congresses. {RAT}

Novoselic, Krist (20th Century)

A recording artist who is the bassist for Nirvana, Novoselic participated in a Yahoo chat online in June 1998 for his new band, Sweet 75. Asked if he believe in God, he replied, "What is God?" {CA}

Nowell-Smith, Patrick Horace (1914–)

A professor of philosophy, York University, Canada, Nowell-Smith signed Humanist Manifesto II. In 1986, he was elected an honorary associate of the British Rationalist Press Association. His first and only book, *Ethics*, was published in 1954. In Toronto in 1980, he helped to found and became the first President of Dying with Dignity. He was President of the World Federation of Right-to-Die Societies from 1986 to 1988. Nowell-Smith is a member of the Voluntary Euthanasia Society's London committee. {HM2}

Nowicki, Andrzej (20th Century)

At a 1996 Polish Humanist Conference on Integration, Nowicki commented that the Catholic Church wielded power without authority, even though it exercised power indirectly. It has power without democratic control. He said, however, that it is important that religious teaching in Poland be replaced by the teaching of philosophy. {*New Humanist*, September 1996}

Nowlan, William (19th Century)

Nowlan, who became Charles Watts's father-in-law, was a secularist in Northampton at a time when in 1875 the town had both a National Secular Society branch and a separate Secular Propagandist Society. {RSR}

Noyes, Rufus King (Born 1853)

Noyes spent his early years upon a farm in New Hampshire, then became a physician. He was house surgeon at Boston City Hospital, and he was known for holding that diseases can be cured without alcoholic liquors and that diseases can be cured without using poisonous drugs. A materialist, he found great satisfaction in the opinions of Haeckel, Darwin, and Spencer, but he was anti-vaccination. Noyes wrote *Views on Religion* (1906). {PUT; RAT}

Noyes, Thomas Herbert (19th Century)

Noyes wrote *Hymns of Modern Man* (1870). {BDF}

Nozick, Robert (1938–)

Nozick, a professor of philosophy at Harvard University, has been described as being one of the most important of the contemporary secular philosophers. An unbeliever, he wrote *Anarchy, State, and Utopia* (1974); *Philosophical Explanations* (1981); *The Nature of Rationality* (1993), called by Prof. Russell Hardin of the University of Chicago, "an articulate defence of a barebones libertarianism"; and *Socratic Puzzles* (1997). Hardin has written that Nozick is notable for his cogent work on decision theory, epistemology, theory of value, and the good life. The state cannot have a very large role in the economy and society if the libertarian rights of individuals are to prevail, he holds. Nozick was President of the Eastern Division of the American Philosophic Association 1997-1998. {CA; OCP}

Nozzi, Dom (20th Century)

Nozzi is active with the Humanist Society of Gainesville, Florida. (See entry for Florida Atheists, Humanists.) {FD}

NUCLEAR FUSION: See entry for Science and Non-Science.

NUDITY

• Clothes make the man; naked people have little or no influence in society.

–Mark Twain

Freethinkers are quick to point out that all humans are, when born, atheists as well as nudists. Ethnologists, in explaining how, why, and when societal mores operate for or against such conditions, note that forces within Western civilization, mainly male, have particularly been successful in clothing the males and hypocritically speaking out against premarital intercourse. This may or may not, according to a Manhattan wag (and "size-queen"), have inspired French artist Sylvie Blocher to paint "The Bride, Disappointed, Gets Dressed Again." (See entry for Christian Nudists.)

Nuland, Sherwin B. (1930–)

The physician who wrote *How We Die* (1994), Nuland has called himself "a Jewish agnostic." In his "reflections on life's final chapter," Dr. Nuland states that "Man is an obligate aerobe," which maxim he says has "the simple directness of any of the most quoted aphorisms of the ancient Hippocrates." He challenges the medical establishment to improve the quality of life for older people, "not to prolong its duration." In doing so, he recalls Harvard's Nobel-Prize-winning physicist, Percy Bridgman, who at the age of seventy-nine faced up to the laws concerning suicide by shooting himself. Dr. Bridgman's left a note: "It is not decent for Society to make a man do this to himself. Probably, this is the last day I will be able to do it myself." The present U.S. laws do not permit the expedient end of life for those who are in pain and have no chance of surviving. However, Nuland admits to having helped some who were in pain to "ease a patient's going." The Reformed Church in the Netherlands, he points out, recently took the position that "the natural order of things is not necessarily to be equated with the will of God."

Nuland also wrote *Origins of Anesthesia* (1983), *Doctors: Biography of Medicine* (1992), and *The Face of Mercy* (1993).

NULLIFIDIAN

A nullifidian, according to *Webster's Third International Dictionary*, is

1. a person of no faith or religion**:** skeptic, unbeliever
2. one lacking in faith **:** disbeliever.

Naturalistic and secular humanists, in short, are nullifidians. (See entry for Greg Erwin.)

Numan, Gary (1958–)

Numan is a British-born vocalist and musician. His albums include "The Pleasure Principle" (1979) and "I, Assassin" (1982). His singles include "Cars" (1979) and "She's Got Claws" (1981).

"I am not religious, quite the opposite," he wrote in a mailing list digest. "It would seem, particularly at the moment, that in certain countries to deny having faith is virtually to admit to being a worshipper of the devil. Such is the fear, hate, and hostility created by the believers of this so-called all-forgiving God. I worship nothing. Not a good lie nor a dark one. If nature is proof of God's amazing creation, then I have truly seen the light, and the light is black. Nature is genius at its most cruel and savage. No benevolent God could have come up with such an outrage." Newman's album, "Exile," focuses on such ideas. {CA; E}

Numbers, Ronald (20th Century)

Numbers, a professor of history, was "born and reared in a fundamentalist Seventh-day Adventist family of ministers." In a preface to one of his books, Numbers continues,

> I learned Price's version of earth history at my parents' knees. I subsequently attended Adventist church schools from first grade to college, and though I majored in science I saw no reason to question the claims of strict creationism. In fact, I do not recall ever doubting the recent appearance of life on the earth until the late 1960's, while studying the history of science at the University of California, Berkeley. I vividly remember the evening I attended an illustrated lecture on the famous sequence of fossil forests in Yellowstone National Park and then stayed up much of the night with a biologist friend of like mind, Joe Willey, first agonizing over, then finally accepting, the disturbing likelihood that the earth was at least thirty thousand years old. Having thus decided to follow science rather than Scripture on the subject of origins, I quickly, though not painlessly, slid down the proverbial slippery slope towards unbelief. In 1982, when attorneys for both sides in the Louisiana creation-evolution trial requested my services as a possible expert witness, I elected to join the ACLU team in defending the Constitutional wall separating church and state. In taking my pretrial deposition, Wendell R. Bird, the creationists' lawyer who had tried to recruit me for his side, devoted two lengthy sessions to probing the limits of my historical knowledge and the thinness of my religious beliefs. On the basis of this inquisition, Bird publicly labeled me an "Agnostic." The tag still feels foreign and uncomfortable

to me, but it accurately reflects my theological uncertainty.
{A; CA}

NUMEROLOGY

• Numerology is an entertaining, sociable superstition like astrology—benign except to paranoid schizophrenics. It pretends that the inevitable, predictable, clockwork behavior of Arabic numerals locked into the decimal system can, on occasion, give us occult messages we should not ignore. If a year number 2000 isn't an all-points bulletin from on high, what is? Any excuse for a party. That the odometer is slightly out of whack, that Jesus was born in 5, 6, or 7 B.C., shouldn't be allowed to spoil the party. Jesus was born a few years before himself? Chalk that up as another miracle and party on.

–**Kurt Vonnegut Jr.**
"Last Words for a Century,"
Playboy, January 1999

NUN

• A Manhattan test-maker holds that "a deceased nun" is analogous to "Nun of the Above."

A nun is a woman belonging to a religious order and is one under solemn vows of poverty, chastity, and obedience. Numbers of believers have confessed that they have more love for nuns than for priests or other members of the hierarchy.

Freethinkers particularly like the Sisters of Perpetual Indulgence, an "order" of drag performance artists who, clad in nuns' habits and vibrant facepaint, have been damned by the Catholic Archdiocese of San Francisco since the 1980s.

Lavender Lists (1990) lists the following ten nuns who were lesbians:

• Benedetta Carlini—Judith Brown, in *Immodest Acts*, describes how Benedetta, born in the Tuscan mountains of Italy in 1590, had a sexual relationship with another nun, then spent her last thirty-five years in prison.
• Virginia Apuzzo—When she entered a convent at the age of twenty-six, few could have predicted that she would leave and in 1982 become head of the National Gay Task Force.
• Mary Kregar—She was charged with having seduced a married woman and breaking up a twelve-year marriage, for which the husband was awarded $1,500,000 in damages. Mary was a nun in Our Lady of the Sea Church in Port Isabel, Texas.
• Jeanne Cordova—She did not enter the Immaculate Heart of Mary order for entirely spiritual reasons, and in *Kicking the Habit* she tells of her having had a crush on one of the nuns.
• Marge Helenchild—After finding existence as a nun too regimented, Marge left the order and played tackle for a women's pro football team, then co-founded the Radical, Lesbian, Feminist, Terrorist Comedy Group.
• Diana DiPrima—DiPrima left her convent after onlyeighteen months, displeased that she and other nuns had to gather in the chapel and whip themselves or one another to atone for the sins of people who were out of town.
• Mary Mendola—Mary, first a newswriter in the Women's Army Corps, then a nun, left the order to become author of *The Mendola Report*, a far-reaching look at gay and lesbian couples.
• Jean O'Leary—Soon after graduating from high school, O'Leary entered a convent, had eight lesbian relationships while in the convent, then left and became executive director of the National Gay Rights Advocates.
• Rosemary Curb and Nancy Manahan—an anthology about lesbian nuns.

Nuñez, Rafael [President] (1825–1894)

President Nudes of Colombia wrote many poems and political articles. In philosophy, he was a follower of Mill and Spencer. During his presidency, a new constitution created the centralized Republic of Colombia in 1886. {CE; BDF}

Nureyev, Rudolf (1938-1993)

A Russian ballet dancer who defected from the Soviet Union in 1961 while on tour in Paris, Nureyev was one of the leading classical ballet dancers of his generation. His major roles included the leads in "La Bayadère," "Les Sylphides," "Giselle," "Swan Lake," "Romeo and Juliet," "Le Corsaire," "Raymonda," and "Sleeping Beauty." He often danced with Margot Fonteyn and because of his virtuosity and expressiveness was one of the greatest male dancers of the 1960s. In 1982 he became an Austrian citizen

Like the Russian-American dancer Mikhail Baryshnikov, Nureyev focused on the humanities, not on religion. He conducted orchestras in America, Europe, and the former Soviety Union. When Nureyev was accused of being anti-Semitic, Baryshnikov angrily denied the accusation. Nureyev, well-known in gay circles, died in his mid-fifties of AIDS. His autobiography, *Nureyev*, appeared in 1962. {CE}

Nussbaum, Martha C. (20th Century)

Nussbaum's *Cultivating Humanity* is an important philosophic defense of the need to be a "citizen of the world." The book's title comes from the Roman philosopher Seneca: "Soon we shall breathe our last. Meanwhile, while we live, while we are among human beings, let us cultivate our humanity." {*Free Inquiry*, Winter 1997-1998}

Nute, Ephraim (1819–1897)

Nute, who had been a Unitarian minister in Chicopee, Massachusetts, moved to Kansas and was granted $3,500 by the Boston Unitarians to build a church in Lawrence. But fighting between pro- and anti-slavery forces resulted in the Kansas Territory's being a frightening place for settlers. "The condition of affairs in the Territory is on the whole far worse than I expected to find," he wrote. "Bands of robbers are prowling about and every night some outrage is committed. Men are fired upon, knocked down, plundered, and left for dead. Houses are burned." When Nute's brother-in-law was "shot and scalped by the Border Ruffians," according to an 1856 account in the Boston *Evening Transcript.* Nute himself was captured by proslavery sympathizers, and he "was prevented from leaving on the ground that he was 'obnoxious.' " He was, however, released after two weeks. The building of the church was delayed for a long time, and not until 1861 was Kansas admitted to the Union as a free state. {EG}

Nuytz, Louis André: See entry for Louis André-Nuytz.

Nyblaus, Claes Gudmund (Born 1817)

Nyblaus, a Swedish bookseller, published a number of anti-Christian pamphlets. {BDF}

Nygaard, Karl-Henrik (20th Century)

Nygaard is President of the Norwegian Humanist Association. At a February 1995 Humanist European Seminar in Oslo, he spoke on "Death in the Humanist Tradition." First quoting Wittgenstein, "Death is not an event of Life. Death is not lived through," he said that, "It is difficult to demand that doctors who are bound by their Hippocratic Oath should kill other people. There is a risk that we might consider the value of human life as not necessary or too expensive to sustain."

Nyström, Anton Christen (1842–1931)

Nyström was a Swedish positivist. A medical doctor, he served as assistant and field doctor in the Dano-Prussian War of 1867. In Stockholm, he established a Positivist Society and a Workmen's Institute, and he was a member of the Freethought Federation of Sweden. Nyström wrote *History of Civilisation*. {BDF; PUT; RAT; RE}

OABITAR: See entries for John B. Massen; and for **O**bjectivity, **A**ccuracy, and **B**alance **i**n **T**eaching **A**bout **R**eligion, Inc.

OAK HILL FREE PRESS

Dave E. Matson operates the Oak Hill Free Press (PO Box 61274, Pasadena, California 91116). Two of the company's publications are "Common Sense and the Bible" and "Common Sense Versus the Bible."

Oates, Joyce Carol (1938–)

Oates, a writer of realistic novels tinged with surrealism, is known for describing the connection between violence and love as she finds it in American life. She has written *A Garden of Earthly Delights* (1967), *Childwold* (1976), and *Solstice* (1985). Her interests are catholic, as evidenced by her writing about religious fanaticism in *Son of the Morning*, about brutality in *On Boxing*, and college faculties in *Unholy Love*. Twenty-seven or more of her novels have been published, as well as seventeen or more collections of short stories, seven or more books of poetry, five or more volumes of essays, fifteen plays, and more than two dozen works published by small, independent presses.

When her grandfather died of emphysema, Oates described in a *Playboy* (November 1993) interview, her family became religious. "My parents had been Catholic and they had lapsed. That's a joke to other people, but to Catholics you are never not a Catholic. You're born Catholic and you're baptized, then you become a lapsed Catholic for the next ninety years. It's like an alcoholic—you're never not an alcoholic. I'm not a person who feels very friendly toward organized religion. I think people have been brainwashed through the centuries. The churches, particularly the Catholic Church, are patriarchal organizations that have been invested with power for the sake of the people in power, who happen to be men. It breeds corruption. I found going to church every Sunday and on holy days an exercise in extreme boredom. I never felt that the priest had any kind of connection with God. I've never felt that anyone who stands up and says 'Look, I have the answers' has the answers. I would look around in church and see people praying and sometimes crying and genuflecting, saying the rosary, and I never felt any identification. I never felt that I was experiencing what they were experiencing. I couldn't figure out whether or not they were pretending. . . . Organized religions such as the Catholic Church are the antithesis of religious experience.... The persistence of crackpots, pseudoscientists like astrologers, suggests the failure of science and education. How can people still be superstitious, still believe in nonsense and astrology and grotesque demonic religions of every kind, every fundamentalist religion crowding us on all sides? How can we have these phenomena and say that science and education have not failed? That's embarrassing."

In a similar vein, during a conversation reported in *The New York Times Magazine* (25 December 1994) with fellow novelist Bebe Moore Campbell, Oates stated, "I was never very religious, so I look upon the phenomenon of religion as interesting. But religion has been used by people in power for their own ends, which are pretty transparent, and they are men. So there are different ways of experiencing religion. I mean, obviously, the inner and the spiritual are very different from what I'm talking about."

Oates has written so many articles, essays, and books that her friends wonder where she finds all the time. *With Shuddering Fall* tells a story that is analogous to the biblical myth of Abraham and Isaac. But "merely having faith" in a supernatural reality," she has written, "leaves one really nowhere." Her own favorite short story, she has stated, is her "Where Are You Going, Where Have You Been?" That work has been made into a movie, "Smooth Talk."

Greg Johnson's *Invisible Writer, a Biography of Joyce Carol Oates* (1998), similarly confirms Oates's distaste for religion. At any early age she was furious that a group of cardinals had proclaimed that abortion was unacceptable under any circumstance, reasoning that the fetus might be male.

Oates, Thomas (19th Century)

Oates in the 1860s was a leading secularist in the central northern English community of Middleton. He was active in the Lancashire Secular Union. {RSR}

Oberoi, Harjot (20th Century)

A Punjabi-born academic, Oberoi gave up his appointment to the chair of Sikh studies at the University of British Columbia after his book on Sikh history, *The Construction of Religious Boundaries*, was criticized by fundamentalist Sikh leaders. He had suggested that their religion had its roots in Hinduism and Islam rather than being a completely separate divine revelation. As a result, he joined the university's faculty of arts.

OBERLIN COLLEGE FREETHINKERS

In Ohio the Oberlin College Freethought Alliance is on the Web at <www.secularhumanism.org/cfa/orgs.html>.

OBITUARIES

• There's no bad publicity, except an obituary notice.

–Brendan Behan

OBJECTIVE CORRELATIVE

"Objective correlative" became a fashionable term after neo-humanist T. S. Eliot in an essay, "Hamlet and his Problems" (1920), used it. *Hamlet* was an "artistic failure," he alleged, because Hamlet himself is "dominated by an emotion which is inexpressible, because it is in *excess* of the facts as they appear. . . . The only way of expressing emotion in the form of art is by finding an 'objective correlative'; in other words, a set of objects, a situation, a chain of events which shall be the formula of that *particular* emotion." The view was not widely accepted, particularly by naturalistic humanists in the humanities. (See entry for Hamlet.) {OEL}

OBJECTIVISM

In philosophy objectivism holds that all reality is objective and external to the mind, that knowledge is reliably based on observed objects and events. An emphasis is placed on objects, not feelings or thoughts, in literature or art. Rand is a key individual in the objectivist movement. On the Web: <www.geocities.com/Athena/6234>. {See entry for Ayn Rand.}

OBJECTIVITY, ACCURACY, AND BALANCE IN TEACHING ABOUT RELIGION

Objective, Accuracy, and Balance in Teaching About Religion (1525-A Day Avenue, San Mateo, California 94403) is led by John B. Massen. His coalition called OABITAR seeks addition to public school history textbooks, when they "teach about religion" by text on major religions, of text about the vital contributions to the advancement of civilization by "non-religion" (skepticism, unbelief, rationalism, humanism, freethought, and atheism). The group hopes to prevent educational censorship by the deliberate exclusion of "non-religion." Members of the group are the American Humanist Association (AHA), the Council for Secular Humanism, and the Atheist Alliance (AA). {FD}

Obregón, Álvaro [President] (1880–1928)

General Obregón, who was President of Mexico from 1920 to

1924, has been described as having been "one of the most enlightened generals in the revolution" of 1913. At a time when peonage was rampant, he advanced agrarian and labor reforms. Obregón was involved in a long, bitter quarrel with the church and in 1928, when again chosen president, he was assassinated by a fanatical Roman Catholic who did so "in order that religion may prevail.". Obregón wrote *Ocho mil kilómetros en campaña* (1917). {TRI}

O'Brien, Conor Cruise (1917–)

In 1972, O'Brien was elected an honorary associate of the Rationalist Press Association and, in 1996, a Humanist Laureate in the Council for Secular Humanism's International Academy of Humanism. A writer and a diplomat, O'Brien has been vice chancellor of the University of Ghana, a member of the Dail Eireann in Dublin, a senator of Dublin University (1977–1979), editor in chief of the London *Observer* (1978–1981), and pro-chancellor of the University of Dublin. Among his books are *To Katanga and Back* (1962, which contains his version of why he was forced to resign as special UN representative of Secretary-General Däg Hammerskjöld), *Camus* (1969), *Edmund Burke's Reflections on the Revolution in France* (1969), *God Land: Reflections In Religion and Nationalism* (1988), *The Great Melody* (1992, a study of Edmund Burke), and *Ancestral Voices* (1994), the latter book being an analysis of the progressively Catholic nature of modern Irish nationalism. In 1988 he was recipient of the Valiant for Truth Media award.

Donald Harman Akenson, in *Conor: A Biography of Conor Cruise O'Brien* (1995), states that, contrary to the analysis of the British Left, Conor regarded the Irish Republic's irredentist claim on Northern Ireland, not the British presence in Ulster, as the real form of imperialism in modern Ireland. O'Brien is a member of the Royal Irish Academy.

O'Brien's "Thomas Jefferson: Radical and Racist" (*Atlantic Monthly*, October 1996) called the American president a prophet of a "civil religion," which is in error and apparently was written without a knowledge of Jefferson's Virginia Statute for Religious Freedom and other of his writings, according to Merrill D. Petersen, author of *The Jefferson Image in the American Mind*. O'Brien denied this and has retorted that Jefferson's racism was purposely overlooked by using the inscription on his monument in Washington, an inscription which quotes Jefferson's contention that the slaves "are to be free" while omitting the immediately following statement: "Nor is it less certain that the two races, equally free, cannot live in the same government." This, he holds, shows that the slaves, if freed, are to be deported.

In an interview with Timothy J. Madigan (*Free Inquiry*, Spring 1998}, O'Brien elaborated upon his having judged Jefferson by current concepts of liberty and freedom. He cited one of Jefferson's slaves, Jame Hubburd, who repeatedly attempted to escape and was severely flogged in the presence of his companions. "I don't think a man who flogged a slave for seeking his liberty is likely to long remain a hero in [America's increasingly] multi-racial society." O'Brien is one of the few debunkers of Jefferson, calling him a wild-eyed anarchist who was a died-in-the-wool racist. (See entry for Thomas Jefferson.) {*Atlantic Monthly*, January 1997; CE}

O'Brien, James (1805–1864)

O'Brien was an Irish orator, famous as a barrister and Chartist agitator. In 1840 he was punished by being sent to prison for eighteen months. Although sometimes described as a Catholic, O'Brien wrote to Robert Owen after his famous rejection of all religion in the London Tavern, "If I mistake not, your ideas and mine are the same, or nearly so, on these subjects." {RAT; RE}

O'Brien, Paul (20th Century)

O'Brien, who calls himself a reverend, heads the Humanist Ethical Church (6033 Hopkins Road, Flint, Michigan 48506). E-mail: <paul@tir.com>.

OBSCENITY

• Damn all expurgated books; the dirtiest book of all is the expurgated book.

–Walt Whitman

• Obscenity is whatever happens to shock some elderly and ignorant magistrate.

–Bertrand Russell

• Nothing risqué, nothing gained.

–Alexander Woollcott

In the United States, courts have ruled that material which appeals to prurient interest in sex and which does not have serious literary, artistic, political, or scientific value can be banned as obscene. The legal determination that material falls within a definition of obscenity is usually made by a jury. In some communities, pornography is vigorously attacked as being obscene. In others, nudity of any kind is deemed obscene. Americans are said to be more conscious of obscenity than are Europeans.

A Greenwich Village humanist in New York City has defined obscenity as "whatever gives a male judge an erection." (*All the Obscenities in the Bible*, by Gene Kasmar, is available from 6066 Shingle Creek Parkway #182, Brooklyn Center, Minnesota 55430. The work includes references to human sacrifice, child cruelty, human cannibalism, incest, scatology, harlotry, suicide, slavery, violence, etc.) {CE}

O'Casey, Sean (John) (Casey) (1880–1964)

O'Casey was an outright freethinker, according to David Tribe. In six volumes, O'Casey was autobiographical, beginning with *I Knock at the Door* (1939) and ending with *Sunset and Evening Star* (1954). He was a Dublin-born Protestant who first wrote under the name of Sean O Cathasaigh. *Juno and the Paycock* (1924) brought him much recognition, as did *The Plough and the Stars* (1926), which, however, provoked nationalist riots at the Abbey Theatre in 1926. He moved to England in 1926, settling there permanently and remaining alienated from Ireland. His various works have been grim, satirical, and not always kind to the Irish people.

According to George Orwell, O'Casey the playwright was "very stupid" and possibly a member of the Communist Party. (See entry for George Orwell.) {CE; OEL; TRI; TYD}

OCCAM'S RAZOR

William of Occam, an English philosopher of the fourteenth century, spoke of a principle that "entities are not to be multiplied beyond necessity" (*entia non sunt multiplicanda praeter necessitate*), meaning that explanations in philosophy should be kept as simple as possible. The principle is known as Occam's (also, Ockham's) Razor. Albert Einstein warned that one should not shave too much, that "Everything should be made as simple as possible, but not simpler."

William (c. 1285-c. 1349), a Franciscan logician, was known as "doctor invincibilities" by fellow friars. His writing as a monk on the character of knowledge—making a distinction between the name of a thing and the thing itself—was an epistemological study, one that angered Pope John XXII, then in Avignon. (See entry for William of Occam [Ockham].) {CE; DCL; William Safire, *The New York Times Magazine*, 31 January 1999}

OCCULTISM

Occultism is the study of the supernatural and involves a belief in the possibility of bringing occult "powers" under human control. Believers have invested much time and money into such non-scientific ventures.

Ocellus Lucanus (7th Century B. C. E.)

An early Greek philosopher, Ocellus Lucanus maintained the eternity of the cosmos. An edition of his work was published with a translation by the Marquis d'Argens. Thomas Taylor published an English version. {BDF}

Ochino, Bernardino Tommasini (1487–1564)

An Italian reformer and a popular preacher, Ochino was chosen general of the Capuchins. He then was converted to the Reformation by Jean Valdez, being forced to flee to Geneva in 1542. Invited to England by Cranmer, Ochino became prebend of Canterbury, preaching in London until the accession of Mary, at which time he was expelled and went to Zürich. Here he became an anti-trinitarian and was banished about 1562 for *Thirty Dialogues*, in one of which he shows that neither in the Bible nor the Fathers is there any express prohibition of polygamy. Ochino then went to Poland and joined the Socinians. Banished from Poland also, Ochino died in Moravia. Beza, the French Calvinist theologian, ascribed the misfortunes of Ochino, and particularly the accidental death of his wife, to the special interposition of God on account of his erroneous opinions. {BDF}

Ochs, Philip (20th Century)

Ochs, a non-believer, illustrates his outlook in the lyrics he has written and the songs he has sung. He is a popular entertainer.

OCKHAM'S RAZOR: See entry for Occam's Razor.

O'Connor, Arthur (afterwards **Condorcet**) (1768–1852)

O'Connor, who was born in Cork, joined the United Irishmen and went to negotiate for military aid. In 1798 he was tried for treason, but acquitted. He entered the French service and rose to distinction. In 1807, he married Elisa, the only daughter of Condorcet, whose name he took and whose works he edited. O'Connor also defiantly edited the freethinking *Journal of Religious Freedom* during the restoration. {BDF; JM; RAT; RE}

O'Connor, (Mary) Flannery (1925–1964)

O'Connor is an American author who portrayed contemporary Southern life as a grotesque and gothic combination of brutal comedy and violent tragedy. In *Wise Blood* (1949), a character declares, "I'm going to preach there was no Fall because there was nothing to fall from, and no Redemption because there was no Fall, and no Judgment because there wasn't the first two. Nothing matters but that Jesus was a liar." In *Everything That Rises Must Converge*, published posthumously in 1965, is a story, "Greenleaf." It contains the description, "She was a good Christian woman with a large respect for religion, though she did not, of course, believe any of it was true." {TYD}

O'Connor, Richard (20th Century)

O'Connor wrote *Sinclair Lewis* (1971). {GS}

O'Connor, Sinead (20th Century)

O'Connor, a singer known for having a shaved head, enraged Catholics when she tore up a picture of Pope John Paul on a "Saturday Night Live" television program in the 1990s. In 1994, when a priest helped her kick her marijuana habit, she told *The Irish Times* that he had restored her faith in the Church. But, she added without further explanation, she still did not think the Church is good for young people.

In 1999 the Irish rocker claimed she had become a priest, a member of a Catholic splinter group known as the Latin Tridentine Church, that she intended to administer "sacraments" including last rites, would wear a clerical shirt (and a dog collar), and would now be known as Mother Bernadette Mary.

O'Connor, Tom (20th Century)

In the 1950s, O'Connor was a member of the board of directors of the American Humanist Association's Humanist Fellowship of Boston.

Od: See entry for Zyp.

Odden, Glenn (20th Century)

A Presbyterian, an occupational therapist, and playwright, Odden has written in *Free Inquiry* (Fall 1996), "Religion was a favorite target of (Ambrose) Bierce. He saw the hypocrisy of many religious institutions and clergy with a clarity that he maliciously exploited."

O'Dell, George E. (1874–1970?)

O'Dell, a British empiricist and humanist, was trustee and then president of National Union of Clerks and Administrative Workers (1906–1913), assistant to Stanton Coit in the British Ethical Union (1903–1913), then executive secretary of the American Ethical Union and editor of *The Standard* (1913–1947). In the 1950s he was on the advisory board of Charles Francis Potter's First Humanist Society of New York. James F. Hornback has written that O'Dell was "a Humanist never really accepted by Felix Adler as a leader." O'Dell wrote *Aspects of Ethical Religion* (1926). (See entry for Ethical Culture.) {HNS}

O'Dell, Robin (20th Century)

O'Dell and Tom Barfield wrote "A Humanist Glossary" (1967). {GS}

Odenkirk, Bob (20th Century)

Odenkirk, a comedian, said on Comedy Central's "The Daily Show" (27 October 1998), "I was raised Catholic, so of course I'm now an atheist." Along with his comedy partner David Cross, Odenkirk is behind "Mr Show," an HBO production.

Odger, George (1813–1877)

Odger was an agitator, the son of a Cornish miner and a shoemaker in his youth. He was secretary of the London Trade Council from 1862 to 1872. He organized the English welcome to Garibaldi in 1864 and was one of the most anti-clerical of the Labour leaders, although he never wrote on religion. {RAT}

Odgers, W(illiam) Blake (1849–1924)

Odgers was a freethinker who wrote "Should the Existing Laws as to Blasphemy Be Amended And, If So, In What Direction?" (1883). {GS}

ODIN: See entry for Zyp.

O'Donaghue, Alfred H. (Born 1840)

O'Donaghue was an Irish-American counselor at law. Although educated for the Episcopal ministry at Trinity College, Dublin, he became a skeptic and published *Theology and Mythology* (1880), an inquiry into the claims of Biblical inspiration and the supernatural element in religion (1880). {BDF}

O'Donnell, Thomas F. (20th Century)

With Hoyt Franchere, O'Donnell wrote *Harold Frederic* (1961). {FUS}

O'Dowd, Bernard (Patrick) (1866–1953)

O'Dowd, an Australian secularist, poet, librarian, and parliamentary draftsman, was head teacher of a Catholic boys' school when seventeen, but his open advocacy of freethought doctrines made that position untenable. He was editor of the *Australian Secular Lyceum Tutor* (1888) and wrote a book of verse, *Poetry Militant* (1909). When eighty-three, O'Dowd gave an address at the Unitarian Church: "I am one who has perhaps, under the influence of what Goethe or someone has called the World Spirit, drifted often over perilous seas, from Roman Catholicism through Spiritualism, Secularism (now called Rationalism), Mysticism, Theosophy, New Thought, and so on . . . but at one stage or another on my pilgrimage I had made contact with the Unitarian movement and, at long last, what I hope is permanent contact." Upon his death, some in his family tried to arrange Catholic rites for him, but his wishes prevailed and the Unitarian service was conducted by Victor James. {FUK; SWW}

OEDIPUS

In Greek mythology, Oedipus was son of King Laius of Thebes and Queen Jocasta. But as dramatized in Sophocles's *Oedipus Rex*, he unknowingly kills his father during an incident in which on a narrow road the two become enraged when neither will give the right-of-way. As the result, and after solving the "riddle of the Sphinx," Oedipus, who had grown up thinking he was the adopted son of the King of Korinth, became Queen Jocasta's husband. Upon learning the truth, that he had married his own mother, who then committed suicide, Oedipus in horror made the tragic and inspiring decision to blind, not kill, himself. The drama has a universal interest, involving as it does human accidents, rage, adoption, and love.

Many contemporary philosophers and psychologists are critical of the Freudian concept of the "Oedipus complex," holding that, like the term God, the concept has some use as a symbol but not as a verifiable fact. For Freud, the play shows us the fulfillment of our childhood wishes and the resultant guilt feelings. Boys have an ambivalence toward their father, erotic wishes toward their mother, and "the bisexuality originally present in children" with a "corresponding jealousy and hostility" toward their mother. For Melanie Klein and other critics, however, Freud needs to be amended by showing that hostility begins at birth and is directed not solely at the father but also at the mother. Jacques Lacan suggests further that if the child fails to obtain satisfaction from his mother, he blames a symbolic father, then wields language to get what he wants.

Philosopher Jonathan Lear has pointed out that "We cannot begin to appreciate the meaning of Oedipus if we continue to think that Oedipus was oedipal," this because the central point Sophocles made is *not* that Oedipus discovered that in killing his father and sleeping with his mother he surrendered to his unconscious wishes. Rather, the work illustrated how fathers can be violent, how nature can be perverse, and how society suffers when the state is authoritarian and patriarchal.

Woody Allen, in the movie entitled "Mighty Aphrodite" (1995), includes a Greek chorus along with Jocasta, to whom he gives the wittily bitchy line, "I hate to tell you what they call my son in Harlem." {Sarah Boxer, *The New York Times*, 6 Dec 1997; CE}

Oelberg, Sarah (20th Century)

Oelberg is minister in Hanska, Minnesota, of the Nora Church Unitarian Universalist. She has written,

> I am a humanist because I cannot be otherwise. It is the only way that makes sense to me; I am compelled to be a humanist by the dictates of my mind. It's what my search for truth and meaning tells me is real. My humanism allows me to be the chief agent of spiritual force and intellectual freedom in my life. It affirms my power to carve out my own destiny and to derive standards and values form my own experience, in light of others' experience. It guides my lifelong commitment to the disciplined and responsible search for meaning. It requires me to ask, with respect to beliefs, "Is it reasonable to believe this? Does it make sense in terms of what I know about the world and the universe?"
>
> . . . [H]umanism is the core of my religion. It is grounded in the three Rs—reason, rationality, and responsibility. It is my rock, upon which I stand proudly and joyously.
>
> {*World*, November-December 1997}

Oersted, Hans Christian (1777–1851)

Oersted, a Danish physicist whose name became a classic in the literature of science, was, like Goethe, a pantheist. This he shows in his *Aanden i Naturen* (1849, 2 volumes). In 1819 he discovered that a magnetic needle is deflected at right angles to a conductor carrying an electric current. This established a relationship between magnetism and electricity and initiated the study of electromagnetics. Oersted also was the first to isolate aluminum, and a unit of magnetic field strength is named for him. {JM; RAT; RE}

Oest, Johann Heinrich (18th Century)

Oest was a German poet. Because of the poems he published at Hamburg in 1751, he was accused of materialism. {BDF}

Offen, Benjamin (1772–1848)

Offen was an American freethinker who had been born in England. In New York Offen became lecturer to the Society of Moral Philanthropists at Tammany Hall and was associated with the Free Discussion Society. He wrote *Biblical Criticism* and a critical review of the Bible, *A Legacy to the Friends of Free Discussion* (1846). Offen supported the *Correspondent*, *Free Inquirer*, and *Boston Investigator*. {BDF; FUS}

Ofili, Chris (20th Century)

"The Holy Virgin Mary, which artist Ofili painted, includes a large image collaged with lumps of elephant dung and close-up photographs of female genitalia. The work was shown at the Royal Academy in London in 1997. When it was scheduled to appear in a show, "Sensation: Young British Artists From the Saatchi Collection," at the Brooklyn Museum of Art, New York City's Catholic mayor, Rudy Giuliani, threatened to cut off the museum's city subsidity and remove its board if the show with Ofili's "sick stuff" was not canceled. The resultant furore over First Amendment rights had the city's Catholic archbishop siding with the mayor but had artists and others rebuking those who try to censor artists.

"I was brought up a Catholic and was an altar boy," the British-born African artist told reporters from his London home. "I believe in God, but I'm not dominated by it. We all studied math, but we don't go around spewing numbers. Religion should be used in the appropriate way. The church is not made up of one person but a whole congregation, and they should be able to interact with art without being told what to think. This is all about control. We've seen it before in history. Sadly, I thought we'd moved on."

Ofili obtained the elephant dung from the London Zoo. "There's something incredibly simple but incredibly basic about it," he said. "It attracts a multiple of meanings and interpretations." He places clumps of the dung carefully on each canvas. On one a clump of dung is a jeweled brooch encrusted with gold sparkles on a goddess. In another it is an abstract element floating in a densely painted background. In yet another, five balls of dung descend in a line, each with a letter formed from colored pins spelling out the name Rodin. Many of the works rest on two large clumps of dung, which act almost as feet. "It's a way of raising the paintings up from the ground and giving them a feeling that they've come from the earth rather than simply being hung on a wall," explained the winner of a 1998 Turner Prize for young British artists. {Carol Vogel, "Holding Fast to His Inspiration," *The New York Times*, 28 September 1999}

Ogbonna, Dominic I. (20th Century)

Ogbonna, a graduate student of philosophy at the University of Nigeria in Nsukka, is actively involved with the Nigerian Humanist Movement. Works which he has cited as convincing him not to become a priest are Morton Prince's *Dissociation of Personality*, Bertrand Russell's *Skeptical Essays*, Charles Darwin's *Origin of Species*, and works by Carl Sagan on astronomy.

Ogwurike, Chijioke (20th Century)

Dr. Ogwurike, from Nigeria, addressed the Fourth International Humanist and Ethical Union World Congress held in Paris (1966). He is author of *Concept of Law in English-Speaking Africa* (1979).

O'Hair, Madalyn Murray (1919–1996?)

O'Hair is the activist atheist who triggered the 1963 Supreme Court decision that eliminated prayer in the public schools. Her efforts later blocked Buzz Aldrin from taking communion during the Apollo 11 flight to the moon, and she was instrumental in the striking down of a part of the Texas constitution requiring officeholders to believe in a supreme being. When she refused to take an oath upon being called for jury duty in Austin, Texas, she was jailed. But the US Court of Appeals for the Fifth Circuit in New Orleans in a two-to-one ruling found she had been jailed illegally, that jurors who are atheists are not required to swear an oath or any other religion-based premise that might violate their beliefs.

"I want to be able to walk down any street in America and not see a cross or a sign of religion," she has said. "I won't stop 'til the Pope—or whoever the highest religious authority is—says that atheists have a right to breathe in this world."

Details of her life vary. In her 1970 autobiography, *An Atheist Epic*, O'Hair revealed that, when twenty-two, she married John Roths. During World War II, he joined the Marines, and she joined the Women's Army Corps (claiming, in fact, to have been on Eisenhower's staff). She had a son by an Eighth Army officer, William J. Murray Jr., a wealthy Roman Catholic who denied paternity of the son. She called the son Bill and raised him. Divorcing Roths, she attended South Texas College of Law, dabbled in Communism and socialism, then had another son, Jon Garth. She married an ex-FBI informer, a hard drinker by the name of Richard O'Hair. They lived in Texas with Bill and Bill's daughter Robin, who had been born in Hawaii in 1965.

"Basically," her son Bill told Mimi Swartz in a 1997 interview, "this family was so dysfunctional anything could have happened. . . . She was a Marxist, I was a laissez-faireist." In his 1982 *My Life Without God*, he detailed his differences with his mother and told of her hatred for her father. Madalyn, he revealed, once asked him to murder the old man. Murray, now a "born-again" Christian, runs a Texas ministry called the William Murray Faith Foundation, one which favors "pro-life, pro-family, anti-violence, anti-pornography, and creation science."

With Bill gone from her family, the trinity of atheism became Madalyn, Jon, and Robin. They set up as many as twelve organizations, including the American Atheists and the Society of Separationists. Also, there were the American Atheist General Headquarters, the Charles E. Stevens American Atheist Library and Archives, Inc., and United World Atheists. Her organizations received funds from around the nation, and numerous atheist chapters formed. In the late 1970s she claimed 70,000 families were on the mailing list of American Atheists.

In her childhood, O'Hair said she picked up the Bible "and read it from cover to cover one weekend—just as if it were a novel—very rapidly and I've never gotten over the shock of it. The miracles, the inconsistencies, the improbabilities, the impossibilities, the wretched history, the sordid sex, the sadism. . . . I looked in the kitchen at my mother and father and I thought, Can they really *believe* in all that?"

Of her many critics, Jane Kathryn Conrad was one of the most outspoken. She published a highly critical pamphlet, "Mad Madalyn," divulging that Madalyn's father had keeled over the night after the morning she told him to drop dead. Conrad provided other details, alleging that Madalyn received her Ph. D. from a mail order school called the Minnesota Institute of Philosophy, one that was operated by an atheist. Conrad described how Madalyn allegedly mistreated her second husband, O'Hair. And Madalyn's atheism, Conrad claimed, actually was entirely a business-oriented entity, adding that Madalyn skimmed cash from contributions, fought with absolutely everyone and trusted no one, liked homosexuals only if they contributed money (and accused one of trying "to make a gay Atheist a day"), arranged for about fifty or sixty wills with a value of about $3 million to develop a Center, did not comply with the terms of gifts made to the Center enjoyed expensive travels, and enjoyed telling tasteless stories about Jews, Christians, and humanists. (Angry that James Hervey Johnson was not going to bequeath over $15 million to her, she wrote him, "You are a dying, defunct, discredited old man who will grow moldy in an unmarked grave." He never gave in to her.) To one of her homosexual associates who complained to her, she said, "I would expect this kind of literature to issue from a misogomist [*sic*]. I am a *female* head of an American atheist group. You are a sock-sucker."

Certainly she achieved journalists' attention. In a 1965 *Playboy* interview she said, concerning sex, "I need somebody who can . . . slug it out, toe to toe, and I don't mean a physical battle. I mean a man who would lay me, and when he was done I'd say 'Oh brother, I've been *laid*.' . . . . You think *I've* got wild ideas about sex? Think of those poor old dried up women lying there on their solitary pallets yearning for Christ to come to them in a vision." When a believer challenged her to explain how she could possibly have been born without God's help, Madalyn retorted, "My mother and father were fucking in bed one night."

In her *Why I Am An Atheist*, O'Hair wrote, "Is mankind advanced or retarded by faith in god? Well, if history, with the crimes of the Inquisition, with the crusades, with all the religious wars, if this does not answer the question, we could demolish it by asking if a belief in Santa Claus would not do just as well. . . . Religion has caused more misery to all men in every stage of human history than any other single idea."

In a 1990 speech, she declared, "Religion has ever been anti-human, anti-woman, anti-life, anti-peace, anti-reason, and anti-science. The god idea has been detrimental not only to humankind but to the earth. It is time now for reason, education, and science to take over."

Barbara Bernstein, Executive Director of the New York Civil Liberties Union, Nassau Chapter, has pointed out that O'Hair had no role in the school prayer decision of 1962, despite journalistic accounts to the contrary. "That 8-to-1 ruling in *Engel v. Vitale*," Bernstein declared, "was a result of a suit brought by the New York Civil Liberties Union on behalf of five families in New Hyde Park, N.Y., who objected to a prayer composed by state officials for daily recitation. The Court ruled that even a nondenominational prayer was religious and that 'it is no part of the business of government to compose official prayers for any group of the American people to recite."

Another critic, Lawrence Wright, wrote in *Saints and Sinners* (1993) that O'Hair is a liar and a highly frightened person. She resembles, he said, "a bowling ball looking for new pins to scatter." Her critics as well as her supporters, in short, are numerous and include many whom she "excommunicated."

From 1962 to 1964, O'Hair edited *Free Humanist* and was briefly on the board of the American Humanist Association. In 1976, she wrote the present author concerning humanism,

> The [Naturalistic] Humanists deserve one another. I know that group and know them well. I don't want any part of the warped thinking that goes on with them.

Phil Donahue invited her to be on the first episode of his pioneering talk show, and she was on many other talk-shows, saying such things as

> I love a good fight. I guess fighting God and God's spokesmen is sort of the ultimate, isn't it?

and

> We have to live now. No one gets a second chance. There is no heaven and no hell. . . . You either make the best or the worst of what you have now, or there is nothing. Laugh at it. Hug it to you. Drain it. Build it. Have it.

Orin "Spike" Tyson said of her, "She went out in public and made it acceptable to at least say the A word. She put it on the map.

One of O'Hair's provocative works was *All the Questions You Ever Wanted to Ask American Atheists, With All the Answers* (1986). Long the editor of *American Atheist*, she was succeeded by Robin Murray-O'Hair, but the financial problems continued, the Internal Revenue Service investigated the various associations, and Madalyn eventually cut all ties with the atheist chapters she had worked to form. At a 1993 Atheist Convention in Sacramento, O'Hair was televised on C-Span for national coverage. She spoke on behalf of atheism's being taught in schools and lamented the hold on education which organized religion has had over the years.

Mysteriously, O'Hair simply disappeared from public view in 1996. Left unanswered was whether she was kidnapped, killed, or had hidden because of her health, fiscal, or legal problems. An ex-employee, David Travis, has claimed that he accidentally opened an envelope from New Zealand Guardian Trust that contained a bank statement showing more than $900,000 had been deposited. Meanwhile, the *San Antonio Express-News* in December 1996 revealed that the United Secularists of America and American Atheists Inc. listed $627,500 in missing assets, "assets believed to be in the possession of Jon Murray, former secretary."

Mimi Swartz in *Vanity Fair* (March 1997) wrote that Madalyn and Robin were spotted near the end of 1996 in Auckland, close to the New Zealand Guardian Trust, and that a receptionist identified Madalyn as a client. Schwartz concluded, "If the Murray O'Hairs are not in Auckland, they are most likely close by, or certainly have been in the past." However, *The New Zealand Herald* claimed the O'Hairs were not in New Zealand as of January 1997, and Ellen Johnson claimed their passports were still in the United States on her desk.

In 1998, however, son Jon believed his mother and Robin had been forcibly taken from their home—they had left an unfinished meal and pets. For some reason $500,000 was spent on gold coins at the time of their disappearance. Police were said to be looking into a possible link that Danny Fry may have had in their disappearance, for he disappeared at about the same time. Fry's nude, headless, and handless body was found in 1995 east of Dallas, Texas.

In a 1999 breakthrough, two of the office managers—Gary P. Karr, a former convict who previously had been an accessory to four homicides in Texas including one in which a corpse was mutilated; and David Waters—were arrested. They were suspected of being part of a plot to rob and murder Ms. O'Hair. A lawyer representing Waters, however, said that although Waters had served several years in an Illinois penitentiary on a murder conviction and later had pleaded guilty in 1994 to having stolen $54,000 from American Atheists Inc., he did not have the $500,000 in gold coins that belonged to the O'Hair family, that in fact Waters was about to be evicted from his apartment because of lack of funds. Karr admitted to helping to dispose of four homicide victims in Texas, including one with its head and hands hacked off.

Karr and Waters were indicted, but the case remains unsolved. Until the three bodies can be located—those of O'Hair, her son Jon Murray, and her granddaughter Robin Murray—the case as of the end of 1999 had not been closed.

"I have told Jon and Robin," Madalyn O'Hair was quoted in a 1986 atheist newspaper, "that when I die they should gather me up in a sheet, unwashed . . . and put me on a pyre in the back yard. . . . I don't want any damn Christer praying over the body. . . . I don't want some religious nut to shove a rosary up the ass of my body." (Assuming Madalyn did die, some jokers in her American Atheists group, whose membership dipped to 2,400 from 50,000 or more, began making bets as to the date of her "Second Coming." See entries for John Vinson, the lawyer O'Hair allegedly bankrupted, for David Travis, and for Ellen Johnson. Also, see entries for Jon Garth Murray; and for Arnold Via, the last to see Madalyn before her disappearance.) {CA; E; EU, Gordon Stein; FUS; PA; *The New York* Times, 26 March 1999; Time, 10 February 1997; TYD; *Vanity Fair*, March 1997; WAS, 21 January 1976}

O'Hair, Richard (20th Century): For the second husband of Madalyn Murray O'Hair, see entry for her.

O'Hair, Robin (1965–1996?): See entry for Robin Murray-O'Hair.

O'Hara, Daniel (20th Century)

O'Hara, a former Anglican curate (1968–1970), is a past president of the National Secular Society (1996–1997) and of the Gay and Lesbian Humanist Association. He is a member of the South Place Ethical Society and the British Humanist Association. In addition, he has been on the Board of the Rationalist Press Association, resigning as director in 1998. He writes for England's *New Humanist* and *The Freethinker*.

O'Hara has estimated that, worldwide, in 1996, "Humanists in the modern sense would probably be far short of one million, whereas those who identify as Christians well exceed one billion." He holds that non-believers have an excellent record despite their small size for contributing to the relief of ignorance, poverty, and disease. {*The Freethinker*, May and December 1996}

O'Hara, Frank (1926–1966)

An American poet of note, O'Hara founded the Poet's Theatre and later the center of the New York School of Poets. *Collected Poems* (1971) is his best-known work, but also he was a major art critic during the late 1950s and early 1960s. His poetry contains subjects and images frequently drawn from the world of urban gay male culture. "Biotherm (For Bill Berkson)" is a collage which combines scenes of Fire Island, restaurant menus, and classic Hollywood cinema. The cognoscenti recognized the title as a reference to a sunscreen brand name. O'Hara's influence upon gay poetry was great, as was his taste for liver-damaging liquor.

O'Hara was killed when his Fire Island dune buggy was struck by a twenty-three-year-old summer worker taking a joyride with a young woman. He died intestate, whereupon Kenneth Koch arrived at his apartment with two suitcases "to get the poems to make sure nothing happens to them," which he managed to do. Those who attended the funeral were concerned that the sixty-year-old Scottish pastor from a Presbyterian church in East Hampton, who did not know O'Hara, would turn the event into a religious ceremony, but he did not. O'Hara's lovers included Larry Rivers; Joe Le Sueur; Lawrence Osgood; and John Ashberry.

O'Hara, a renegade Catholic of an extreme sort, once wrote, "It's well-known that God and I don't get along together." (O'Hara was reportedly concerned about his impotence, a fact the present author confirmed following a drinking bout at New York's Golden Pheasant on 48th Street in the 1950s.) {CE; GL}

O'Higgins, Bernardo [General] (1778–1842)

A Chilean soldier and statesman, O'Higgins was the illegitimate son of Marquis O'Higgins, an Irish Catholic who settled in South America and was Governor of Chile for the Spaniards. A revolutionary leader chosen to replace José Miguel Carrera, O'Higgins lost a battle at Rancagua and fled with the remnant of his army to Argentina, where he joined forces with San Martín. The combined forces defeated the Spaniards at Chacabuco, and O'Higgins was named supreme director of Chile, whose independence he proclaimed in 1818.

In 1823, after his financial reforms aroused much opposition, he was deposed and exiled to Peru, where he died. Like his friend General Miranda, General O'Higgins was an atheist. {CE; JM; RAT; RE}

O'Higgins, James (20th Century)

O'Higgins wrote *Anthony Collins: The Man and His Works* (1970). {FUK; GS}

OHIO HUMANISTS, ATHEISTS

• American Atheist TV Forum, Columbus, Ohio. Contact is Frank Zindler, who hosts a program on Channel 21.

• Ann B. Pratt founded Central Ohioans for Rational Inquiry.

• Dial An Atheist, Columbus, Ohio, has the telephone (614) 294-0300.

• Free Inquirers of Northestern Ohio (ASHS), PO Box 2379, Akron, Ohio 44309; (330) 869-2025. Brent Bowen is President. Web: <http://home.neo.lrun.com/fino/home.html>. E-mail: <mvye@uakron.edu>.

• Free Inquiry Group (ASHS), POB 8128, Cincinnati, Ohio 45208. (513) 557-3836. George Maurer and Joe Levee are contacts: <joelevee@aol.com>. Web: <http://gofigger.org/>.

• *Freethought Perspective*, 833 Orchard St., Toledo, Ohio 43609

• Humanist Association of Ohio (ASHS), 2637 Home Acre Dr., Columbus, OH 43231; (614) 890-0653. Earl Wurdlow is the contact.

• Humanist Chapter of Miami Valley (AHA), A-4, 809 McCleary, Dayton, Ohio 45406. Karen A. Price is the contact.

• Humanist Community of Central Ohio (AHA), POB 141383, Columbus, Ohio 43214. Derrick Strobl is President. Phone: (614) 470-0811. Larry Reyka is the coordinator of the north central region of the AHA. E-mail: <info@hcco.org>. Web: <http://www.hcco.org/>.

• Humanists of Northwest Ohio (AHA), 4126 Nantucket Drive, Toledo, Ohio 43623. Phyllis C. Cauffiel is the contact.

• Oberlin College Freethought Alliance Web: <http://www.secularhumanism.org/cfa/orgs.html>.

• Ohio State University's Students for Freethought are on the Web at: <www.secularhumanism.org/cfa/orgs.html>.

OHIO STATE UNIVERSITY FREETHINKERS

Students for Freethought at Ohio State University are on the Web: <www.secularhumanism.org/cfa/orgs.html>.

Ohlinger, F. W. (20th Century)

Ohlinger wrote "Natural Religion or Revealed Religion" (1924). {GS}

Öhrwall, Hjalmar (1851–1929)

Öhrwall, a professor of physiology at Uppsala in Sweden, was a non-theist. (See entry for Scandinavian Unbelievers.)

O'Keefe, J. A. (19th Century)

O'Keefe was educated in Germany and was the author of an essay, "On the Progress of the Human Understanding" (1795), in which he speaks disparagingly of Christianity. O'Keefe was a follower of Kant and in 1816 was listed in *Living Authors of Great Britain.* {BDF}

O'Kelly, Edmund de Pentheny (19th Century)

O'Kelly wrote *Consciousness, or the Age of Reason* (1853); *Theological Papers*, which Holyoake published; and *Theology for the People* (1855), a series of short papers suggestive of religious theism. {BDF}

Oken, Lorenz (1779–1851)

Oken was a German morphologist and philosopher. In his *Sketch of Natural Philosophy* (1802), he advanced a scheme of evolution. He developed his system in *Generation* (1805) and in *A Manual of Natural Philosophy* (1809). Oken was a professor at Jena but was dismissed because of his liberal views. From 1817 to 1848 he edited *Isis*, a scientific journal. In 1832 he became a professor at Zürich, where he died. Oken shared the philosophical pantheism of Schelling. {BDF; RAT; RE}

OKLAHOMA HUMANISTS

• Humanist Association of Tulsa (AHA), POB 904182, Tulsa, Oklahoma 74105; Dan Nerren is President. (918) 742-8826. On the Web: <http://www.geocities.com/Athens/Forum/8666/>. E-mail: <gphil@ix.netcom.co>.

• Humanist Society of Payne County (AHA), Route 1, Box 656-2, 617 North Washington Street, Stillwater, Oklahoma 74075. Phone (405) 372-2381. Dr. Harry K. Brobst is the contact. E-mail: <102651.3373@compuserve.com>.

• Humanists of Central Oklahoma (AHA), POB 94043, Oklahoma City, Oklahoma 73143. Frank Titus is the contact.

• Oklahoma Atheists, PO Box 23022, Oklahoma City, OK 73123.

OKLAHOMA STATE UNIVERSITY

The student group at Oklahoma State University is on the Web at <http://www.secularhumanism.org/cfa/orgs.html>.

OLD AGE

• Strength of body, and that character of countenance which the French term *physionomie*, women do not acquire before thirty, any more than men.

–**Mary Wollstonecraft**

• I have everything now I had twenty years ago . . . except now it's all lower.

–**Gypsy Rose Lee**

• The best years are the forties; after fifty a man begins to deteriorate, but in the forties he is at the maximum of his villainy.

–**H. L. Mencken**

• A man is as old as the woman he feels.

–Groucho Marx

• Did you ever see a hearse with a luggage rack on top?

–**Fernando Vargas**,
asked why he was not
saving up for his old age

OLD TESTAMENT

Strict Jews are said to say "Hebrew Bible" rather than Old Testament. However, parts of that collection are written in Aramaic, not Hebrew.

Meanwhile, others use "Tanakh," an acronym for the three divisions: Torah (the five books of Moses); Nebiim (the books of the prophets); and Ketubim (other sacred writings).

Oldfield, Josiah (20th Century)

A physician and reformer, Oldfield founded the Humanitarian Hospital of St. Francis at London. He also founded the Society for the Abolition of Capital Punishment (1901) and raised and commanded a casualty Clearing Station and a Field Ambulance during World War I. In the compilation *Do We Believe?* (1905), he wrote, "We all need a wider conception [than the Christian] of God as the basis of our creed." Oldfield was a theist and had mystic ideas about the soul. {RAT}

Oldham, J. H. (20th Century)

Oldham, a theist, wrote *Christian Humanism* (1944).

Oldiges, Elizabeth (20th Century)

Oldiges is a former president of the Cincinnati, Ohio, Free Inquiry Group. She is an active participant in the humanistic Camp Quest.

Olmstead, Clifton F. (20th Century)

Olmstead wrote *History of Religion in the United States* (1960). {GS}

Olds, Mason (20th Century)

Olds, of the Department of Humanities at Springfield College, Springfield, Massachusetts, is editor of the journal, *Religious Humanism*. Olds wrote *American Religious Humanism* (1996), in which he explained that religious humanists are not theists. He avers that religious humanists constitute the largest percentage of organizationally active humanists in the United States, a fact that many secular humanists say is unsupported.

Olds, Nettie (19th Century)

Olds succeeded Katie Smith as director of the First Secular Church in Portland. She wrote *The Truth Seeker* (26 January 1895), "Secularism must be built upon the social plain . . . . Enlist the young in our ranks and the Christian churches will be compelled to go out of business for want of converts." {WWS}

Olincy, Dan (20th Century)

Olincy is a tax and estate planning attorney in Los Angeles. He is a former chairman of the California State Bar Tax Committee. He has written for *Free Inquiry*.

Olincy, George (20th Century)

A lawyer, Olincy is a Humanist Laureate and a member of the Academy of Humanism. {SHD}

Olincy, Virginia (20th Century)

The wife of George Olincy, Virginia Olincy is active in secular humanist causes. {SHD}

Oliphant, Marcus Laurance Elwin [Sir] (1901–)

Oliphant is an Australian physicist and humanist. He worked with the Manhattan Nuclear Weapons Project in the United States during 1943 to 1945 but has since campaigned for the peaceful use of atomic energy and against the secrecy surrounding the development of the atomic bomb. Oliphant is an outspoken advocate of voluntary euthanasia and other social issues. {SWW}

Oliver, Henry (1820?–1900?)

Oliver was an Australian secularist, freethinker, and furniture maker. He helped found the Adelaide Secular and Free Discussion Society in 1876. Oliver edited their *Review* (1878–1879), and during the 1880s distributed *Liberator* for the Australian Secular Association. {FUK; SWW}

Oliver, Phillip B. (20th Century)

In the 1950s, Oliver was an editorial associate for *Humanist World Digest, a Quarterly of Liberal Religion.*

Oliver, Robert (20th Century)

Oliver reviewed Michael Martin's *The Domino in the Sky and Other Atheistic Tales* in *New Humanist* (November 1997).

Oliver, William (Died 1764)

Oliver, a physician who lived in Bath, was accused of atheism and may likely have been a non-theist. {BDF}

Oljelund, Ivan (20th Century)

In Sweden, Oljelund wrote *Humanismen: Nagra Synpunkter* (Humanism: Some Views, 1919), in which he included a Humanist Manifesto.

Olson, Culbert L. [Governor] (1876–1962)

Once a Governor of California, Olson was a spokesperson for atheists. He wrote *My Views on Religion* (1950?), which included the following:

• The thousands of gods that man has worshiped are myths born of his fears and his imagination.

• I wouldn't say that religion has promoted the social progress of mankind. I say that it has been a detriment to the progress of civilization, and I would also say this: that the emancipation of the mind from religious superstition is as essential to the progress of civilization as is emancipation from physical slavery.

• I don't see how anybody can read the Bible and believe it's the word of God, or believe that it is anything but a barbarous story of a barbaric people.

{GS; TYD}

Olson, Floyd (20th Century)

Olson, a retired landscaper, was one of the plaintiffs in *Freedom From Religion Foundation v. Ozaukee County, Wisconsin.* The suit ended in that county's abandoning their official Good Friday holy day, and he received the 1998 Freedom From Religion Foundation's "Freethinker of the Year Award." {*Freethought Today*, April 1997}

OLYMPIAN, OLYMPIUS

• Olympian, adj. Relating to a mountain in Thessaly, once inhabited by gods, now a repository of yellowing newspapers, beer bottles, and mutilated sardine cans, attesting the presence of the tourist and his appetite.

–Ambrose Bierce
The Devil's Dictionary

Mount Olympus, in Greek mythology, had a peak shielded from human view by clouds and which was home of the Olympian gods. Olympus was the name given to the remote heavenly palace of the various gods. The site is located in northern Greece between the regions of Thessaly and Macedonia.

Olympia, not to be confused with Olympus, is a city in the southern Greek region of the Peloponnesus. It is a center of the worship of Zeus and was the scene of the Olympic Games. The great temple of Zeus was celebrated for the ivory, gold-adorned statue of Zeus by Phidias, one of the seven wonders of the world. {CE}

Omar Khayyám (Born 18 May 1048)

The most famous of Eastern freethinkers, Omar Khayyám came from Khorassan, a province (now in northeast Iran) which had long been known for its rationalism. One of the ablest mathematicians of his age, he designed a calendar which Gibbon has noted surpasses the Julian and approaches the accuracy of the Gregorian calendar. According to Robertson, Omar was anything but devout. One of Omar's contemporaries wrote, "I did not observe that he had any great belief in astrological predictions; nor have I seen or heard of any of the great (scientists) who had such belief." He is said to have gone on pilgrimages not from piety but from fear, for he dreaded the hostility that he would receive if his agnosticism was found out. He placed ethic above creed and was given to the praise of wine, which helps explain why he was never very popular in the Moslem world.

Many scholars hold that some of the quatrains attributed to Omar Khayyám were actually written by others, individuals who were venting their freethinking without danger of being accused.

Edward FitzGerald's translations include the following:

• The cycle which includes our coming and going
Has no discernible beginning nor end;
Nobody has got this matter straight,
Where we come from and where we go to.

• Oh, threats of hell and hopes of paradise!
One thing at least is certain—*this* life flies;
One thing is certain, and the rest is lies;
The flower that once has blown forever dies.

• The moving finger writes, and having writ
Moves on: nor all thy piety nor wit
Shall lure it back to cancel half a line
Nor all the tears wash out a word of it
And that inverted bowl we call the sky
Whereunder crawling coop'd we live and die
Lift not your hands to it for help—for it
Rolls impotently on as thou and I.

• Ah, Love, could thou and I with fate conspire
To grasp this sorry scheme of things entire
Would we not shatter it to bits, and then
Remold it nearer to the heart's desire!

(See entries for Edward FitzGerald and Pat Duffy Hutcheon)
{BDF; CE; JM; JMR; JMRH; TYD}

Omboni, Giovanni (Born 1829)

Omboni was a Lombard naturalist. A professor of geology at Padua, he wrote many scientific works. In 1848 he interrupted his studies to take part in the war against Austria and the Papacy. {BDF; RAT}

OMBUDSMAN FOR HUMANISTS: See the entry for I. Samkelden.

OMNIPOTENCY

• I think that I shall never see
A poem lovely as a tree.
A tree whose hungry mouth is prest
Against the earth's sweet flowing breast. . . .
Poems are made by fools like me,
But only God can make a tree.

–Joyce Kilmer (1886–1918), "Trees"

• "Trees" [by Kilmer] maddens me, because it contains the most insincere line ever written by mortal man. Surely the Kilmer tongue must have been not far from the Kilmer cheek when he wrote, "Poems are made by fools like me."

–Heywood Broun (1888–1939),
It Seems To Me (1935)

• God can create three creatures such that A is taller than B; B is taller than C; and C is, uh, taller than A.

–Anonymous

• "In English," said the professor, "a double negative forms a positive.

In some languages, though, such as Russian, a double negative is still a negative. However, not even God can cite an example in which a double positive can form a negative." From the back of the classroom someone piped up, "Yeah, right!"

–Internet

OMNIPRESENCE

In Terrence McNally's "Corpus Christi," a drama performed in New York City in 1998, God after conversing with His son announces that He is leaving, at which the character representing Jesus remonstrates," You are supposed to be everywhere all the time!"

Responds God: "*That* is a very big misunderstanding."

ONANISM

Onan, the son of Judah in *Genesis* 38:9, "spilled it," the seed, on the ground. This was the King James translators' euphemism for "masturbating." Because "the Lord" was displeased and killed Onan, Jews, Muslims, and Christians cite the chapter and verse to teach that exciting one's genital organ is enough to send Jill or Jack off to Hell.

The comic, Woody Allen, has countered such irrational nonsense by saying, "Don't knock masturbation—it's sex with someone I love."

O'Neill, Eugene Gladstone (1888–1953)

O'Neill, a foremost creative playwright of his century, was the son of actor James O'Neill and was born in a New York City hotel room. (A plaque in his honor was mistakenly installed by Mayor Abe Beame and other dignitaries on the same block but at the northeast, rather than the southeast, corner of Manhattan's 44th and Broadway. Tennessee Williams had arrived at the correct corner before discovering the officials' mistake.)

O'Neill attended a Catholic boarding school and Princeton, hunted for gold and contracted malaria in Honduras (1909), worked for a time in Argentina and South Africa, reported for a Connecticut newspaper, and was confined to a sanatorium for six months because of a physical breakdown. His first play, *The Web* (1913–1914), was followed by managing with Robert Edmond Jones the Greenwich Village Theatre (1923–1927) and being director of the Provincetown Players. At that 133 MacDougal Street playhouse where his one-act plays were produced, troupes took turns being star, usher, and ticket-taker. O'Neill won Pulitzer prizes for *Beyond the Horizon* (1920), *Anna Christie* (1921); *Strange Interlude* (1928); and *Long Day's Journey Into Night* (produced 1956). In *The Dynamo,* O'Neill clearly shows that he had rejected the Catholic faith in which he was reared. He also is known to have been influenced strongly by Schopenhauer. In 1936, O'Neill received the Nobel Prize in literature.

O'Neill's work described the plight of oppressed people in many places; it used stream-of-consciousness, literary realism, naturalism, and (chiefly Freudian) expressionism; *The Great God Brown* (1926) affirmed a pagan idealism combined with a tragic view of contemporary materialism; *Mourning Becomes Electra* (1931) adapted a Greek theme and used fate in its theme. The religion-rationalism conflict was taken up in two works: *Dynamo* (1929) depicts an electrical dynamo which replaces the old God but which destroys its worshippers; and the hero of *Days Without End* (1934) is irresistibly attracted to Catholicism. *The Iceman Cometh* (1946) is deliberately pessimistic, presenting man as possessor merely of hopeless illusions and the certainty of death. Of his various works, *Long Day's Journey into Night* is the most autobiographical, describing as it does his addictive mother who was an ex-matinée idol, his drunk brother, and himself Freudianly depicted as trapped in such a brooding family.

In 1953, suffering from a disease that affected the coordination between the nerves and the muscles, which was leading to a steady deterioration of his bodily functions, O'Neill on several occasions informed his wife Carlotta that he was going to jump from his hotel window into the Charles River, which flowed below.

According to biographer Louis Sheaffer, O'Neill about two months before his death told his wife, "When I'm dying, don't let a priest or Protestant minister or Salvation Army captain near me. Let me die in dignity. Keep it as simple and brief as possible. No fuss, no man of God there. If there is a God, I'll see him and we'll talk things over." At the end of November, an infection set in and close to the end O'Neill cried out, "I knew it! I knew it! Born in a hotel room and, goddamn it, dying in a hotel room!" {CE; JM; TYD}

Onimus, Ernest Nicolas Joseph (Born 1840)

Onimus was a French positivist. He studied medicine at Strasburg and Paris, and he wrote a treatise on *The Dynamical Theory of Heat in Biological Science* (1866). In 1873 he was one of the jury of the Vienna Exhibition and obtained the Cross of the Legion of Honor. Onimus wrote *Psychology in the Plays of Shakespeare* (1878) and has written in periodicals including *Revue Positive.* {BDF}

ONION

• Life is like an onion: you peel it off one layer at a time, and sometimes you weep.

–Carl Sandburg

ONION

Onion is an American Midwest publication. It is one of the few that regularly deals satirically with religion.

In one issue is what appears to be a heartwarming story about a little paralyzed boy who prays for recovery. However, the sub-heading of the story is "NO," SAYS GOD. Another story:

> VANIMO, PAPUA NEW GUINEA—In His first official statement since the July 17 tsunami that claimed the lives of an estimated 3,000 Papua New Guineans, the Lord announced Monday that He killed the island villagers as part of His longtime "moving in ysterious ways" policy, calling the natural disaster "part of My unknowable, divine plan for mankind."

Similar stories in the Wisconsin publication concern the unmerited suffering in a world supposedly ruled by a beneficent Providence. Other satirical accounts are illustrated by such as the following headlines: DRUGS WIN DRUG WAR, about public-policy shortfalls; FROG WITH HUMAN HEAD WARNS AGAINST DANGERS OF GENETIC ENGINEERING, about the era of scientific wonders; ANIMAL-RIGHTS ACTIVISTS RELEASE 71,000 COWS INTO WILD, about activists. In addition to publishing on paper, *Onion* is found on the Web: <http://www.theonion.com>. {Hendrik Hertzberg, *The New Yorker*, 10 May 1999}

ONTOLOGY

Ontology is a branch of metaphysics that is concerned with the nature and relations of being. The ontological argument is an argument for the existence of God based upon the meaning of the term *God.* Logical positivists, however, use the verifiability principle to show the meaningless of ontological arguments. A thing cannot be proved by its definition, they hold. A centaur can be defined and even depicted as being a creature which is half man and half horse; however, centaurs do not "exist." To define God as "the Being perfect in power, wisdom, and goodness whom men worship as creator and ruler of the universe" does not prove that God "exists," for according to the verifiability principle there is nothing to test. A carrot, a triangle, and a dog all "exist," for they are subjects, not predicates. But "God exists and is all-powerful" is not grammatically similar to "Carrots exist and are red."

As illustrated by Paul Edwards in *A Modern Introduction to Philosophy* (1973), "Since existence is not a characteristic or quality it follows that it cannot be part of any concept. It cannot be part of the concept of God any more than of the concept of cat or gangle (a coinage). It may well be true that God exists, but this conclusion cannot be derived from the concept of the all-perfect Being any more than the existence of centaurs or hippogriffs (a coinage) or leprechauns could be deduced from an analysis of the corresponding concepts. It has also been pointed out that if the ontological argument were sound we could, with equal justice, prove the existence of a perfect scientist, a perfect singer, and any other number of perfect beings. This alone is sufficient to indicate that there is something drastically wrong with the ontological argument." (See the *Encyclopedia of Philosophy*.) {CE; ER}

"ONWARD, CHRISTIAN SOLDIERS"

Words for the popular hymn, "Onward, Christian Soldiers" (1865), by the Anglican Sabine Baring-Gould (1834–1924), were revised in 1908 by the Unitarian minister Frederick Lucian Hosmer (1840–1929) to "Forward through the ages/in unbroken line/move the faithful spirits/at the call divine."

Freethinkers with a pacifist leaning lean to changing the words still further . . . to "Backward, Christian Soldiers."

Oort, Henricus (Born 1836)

Oort was a Dutch rationalist who studied theology at Leyden. Among his many works are *The Worship of Baalim in Israel* (1865) and *The Bible for Young People*, written with Drs. Hooykaas and Kuenen (1873–1879). {BDF}

OPEN COURT

Open Court was a liberal periodical published in Chicago as a monthly (1887–1933) and a quarterly (1934–1936). After its first editor, B. F. Underwood, Paul Carus was its editor for most of his life. Open Court remains a noted publishing house. {FUS}

Oppenheim, Josie (19th Century)

A freethinker, Oppenheim wrote *Personal Immortality and Other Papers* (1877). {GS}

Oppenheimer, David (1914–1991)

In 1986, Oppenheimer was elected an honorary associate of the Rationalist Press Association. A distinguished neuropathologist, a gifted musician, and a rationalist, he has written music for productions of *Oedipus* and *Alcestis*, and he co-writer with Margaret Esiri the *Diagnostic Neuropathology* (1989). {CE}

Oppert, Julius (1825–1905)

Oppert, a French-Jewish Orientalist, felt there was no career for a Jew in Germany, then settled in France. He shared with Rawlinson (another rationalist) the honor of having found the key to the cuneiform characters in Mesopatamia. He was appointed professor of Sanskrit, later of Assyrian philology and archaeology, at Paris University. In his youth, he abandoned the Jewish faith and never adopted any other. {RAT; RE}

Oppy, Graham (20th Century)

Oppy, an Australian, is a contributing editor on *Philo* and a supporter of Internet Infidels.

OPTIMISM

• Optimism is the madness of maintaining that everything is right when it is wrong.

–**Voltaire**

• Optimism, n. The doctrine or belief that everything is beautiful, including what is ugly.

–**Ambrose Bierce**

• The basis of optimism is sheer terror.

–Oscar Wilde

• The optimist thinks that this is the best of all possible worlds, and the pessimist knows it.

–J. Robert Oppenheimer

Orage, Alfred Richard (1873–1934)

Orage was editor of the *New Age*. He wrote several sympathetic works on Nietzsche. {RAT}

ORATORY: See the entry for Edward Everett concerning epitaphios, epainesis, and parainesis.

Orbok, Ilona St. Ivanyi (20th Century)

Orbok is Deputy Bishop of the Unitarian Church in Budapest. (See entry for Hungarian Unitarians.)

OREGON HUMANISTS, RATIONALISTS

• Center For Rational Thought, 415 SW 13th Avenue, Portland, Oregon 05826. Lanny Swerdlow is the president; telephone (503) 241-9268

• Corvallis Secular Society (ASHS), 126 N.W. 21st Street, Corvallis, Oregon 97330; telephone (503) 754-2557. E-mail addresses: <byersr@peak.org>and <dearing@peak.org>. Web: <http://css.peak.org/>.

• Family of Humanists (AHA, IHEU), POB 4153, Salem, Oregon 97302. Devin Carroll is president and Lloyd Kumley is editor of the chapter newsletter. (503) 391-6810. On the Web: <http://www.teleport.com/~lloydk/humanist.htm> and <lloydk@teleport.com>.

• Humanist Association of Salem (ASHS), PO Box 4153, Salem, OR 97302; (503) 371-1255. Lloyd Kumley is President. E-mail: <lloydk@teleport.com>. On the Web: <www.teleport.com/~lloydk/humanist.htm>.

•Humanists of Portland-Vancouver Metro Area (AHA), POB 3936, Portland, Oregon 97208. Pat Burnet is the contact. Ellis Dunn has succeeded Don Baham as president. E-mail: <kerflouie@aol.com>. On the Web: <www.teleport.com/~brownd/humanist.html>.

• Humanists of Rogue Valley (AHA), POB 648, Talent, Oregon 97540. Phone: (503) 535-2723. Roy Kindell is President. .

• Oregon State University at Corvallis has a Society for Logic and Reason. On the Web: <www.secularhumanism.org/cfa/orgs.html> and <http://osu.orst.edu/groups/slr>. President is Daisy Peel.

• University of Oregon's Students for Freedom From Religion is on the Web: <http://www.secularhumanism.org/cfa/orgs.html>.

Orelli, Johann Kaspar von (1789–1849)

Orelli was a learned Swiss critic. He edited many classics and wrote letters in favor of Strauss at a time when there was an outcry at his being appointed professor of Zürich. {BDF; RAT}

Orendorff, Charles (19th Century)

Orendorff wrote *The Pantheist* (1865). {GS}

Orense, José Maria [Marquis d'Albaida] (1800–1880)

A soldier of a noble family, Orense took part in the struggle against the Church and despotism, for which he was expelled from Spain several times. After the Revolution of 1868, he became President of the Cortes. For many years he was the leader of the anticlericals and was heavily denounced by the Church. {RAT; RE}

Origen (Origines Adamantius) (185?–254?)

Origen, the Christian who cut off his own penis, declared that he did so out of his Christian zeal for purity. He was not allowed to be ordained as a priest, but the famed ascetic, philosopher, and Egyptian-born scholar was allowed to preach. His lectures won him wide acclaim, and around 230 the bishops of Jerusalem and Caesarea ordained him. However, his own bishop, Demetrius, banished him and ordered him deposed. In 231 Origen founded in Alexandria the Catechetical

School, one of his pupils being St. Gregory Thaumaturgus. Around 250, during the persecution of Decius, Origen was put in prison, tortured, and pilloried. He died soon after being released.

Origen knew Greek philosophy and wrote, according to St. Jerome, eight hundred works, in some of which he attempted to synthesize the fundamental principles of Greek philosophy, particularly those of neoplatonism and stoicism, with the Christianity of creed and Scripture. This, he held, proved the Christian view of the universe to be compatible with Greek thought. Because he blended pagan philosophy with Christian theology, he was condemned by Justinian in the Monophysite controversy. Origen has been called the "grandfather" of Arianism (the *castrated* grandfather, some hasten to add), and his thinking led to the idea of an eternal and immanent Trinity. {CE; ER}

ORIGIN OF LIFE: See entries for Genesis and for RNA.

"Origin of the World"

Most freethinkers, rather than finding the work of French painter Gustave Courbet (1819–1877) repulsive or offensive—the Louvre has his controversial "Wounded Man"—particularly have appreciated his "Origin of the World." A provocative study of a woman with her legs spread, the work was owned by the French psychoanalyst, Jacques Lacan.

ORIGINAL SIN

Original sin is a quaint theological device to explain what is called "the graceless nature of man requiring redemption to save himself." Christian theology generally has sought to derive sin from man's abuse of the freedom with which he was created. But how to explain man's ability to misuse his freedom so that as a sinner he will set himself against God? The answer is given in the doctrine of *peccatum originis,* original sin, or the sin which caused Adam's fall from God's grace and his expulsion from paradise, which meant that the sin was transmitted from generation to generation and all of Adam's descendants must be regarded as being of a "perverted" or "depraved" nature. Such an interpretation, given by the apostle Paul, worked its way into Christian thinking, and to rid oneself of sin it was necessary to be baptized. Baptism washed away the original sin and restored man to his innocent state, except that after baptism original sin still leaves a tendency to sin. The German term, *Erbsunde,* is more explanatory than the English one, for it means "inherited sin."

For challenging the basic Roman Catholic belief about original sin, the Rev. Tissa Balasuriya in Sri Lanka was excommunicated in 1997 for his "relativism."

One Manhattanite reports that Original Sin is his favorite drink—it is a hard cider which contains 6% alcohol and is distributed by New York Beverages (Telephone: (212) 874-3381). (See entry for Robert Gorham Davis, who has a negative criticism of Original Sin. Also see entries for Catholic Relativism and Bernard Vonnegut.) {CE; DCL; ER}

ORIGINAL VIRTUE: See entry for Bernard Vonnegut.

Orme, Richard McAllister (1797–1869)

With the Rev. David Devine, Orme wrote *David Devine and the Devil; or the Devil in His Own Defence* (1894). {GS}

Ormsby, R.K.M. (19th Century)

Ormsby edited from Kentucky in 1838 the *Louisville Skeptic.*

Orozco, José Clemente (1883–1949)

A Mexican muralist who "concentrated on Humanist themes," according to Corliss Lamont, Orozco was a genre painter. At New York's New School for Social Research, he completed true fresco painting, executed directly on the wet plaster. In 1923 he completed a controversial mural entitled "Christ Destroying His Cross." His other work includes *Prometheus* (1930), at Frary Hall, Pomona College, California, and mural paintings in the university at Guadalajara. Much of his work illustrates the theme of man versus machine. In Mexico, Orozco was one of the leaders of the Mexican resistance and, with Rivera, one of the leaders of Mexican renaissance. {CE; CL}

Orr: See entry for Boyd Orr, John.

Orr, Hugh Robert (20th Century)

Orr edited *Progressive World,* a bi-monthly of the United Secularists of America from 1947 to 1981. Upon his death, his wife, **Frances Orr**, became editor. {FUS}

Orr, M. A. (19th Century)

A freethinker, Orr wrote "Two Letters Addressed to the Bishop of Repos" (1876). {GS}

Orr, Robert (20th Century)

Orr has been an activist member of the American Humanist Association. {HNS}

ORTHODOX CHURCH IN AMERICA

The Orthodox Church in America, an Eastern Orthodox church organized in 1794, is at PO Box 675, Syoset, New York 11791.

ORTHODOX JEWISH CONGREGATIONS IN AMERICA

The Union of Orthodox Jewish Congregations in America is at 333 Seventh Avenue, New York, NY 10001.

ORTHODOXY

• Orthodox, n. An ox wearing the popular religious yoke.

–Ambrose Bierce
The Devil's Dictionary

Orthodoxy refers to "correctness" of religious belief according to some arbitrary, authoritative standard. Unlike heterodoxy, in which an individual chooses to be at odds with the accepted or authoritative view, orthodoxy conforms to the official formulation of truth. To choose otherwise would be heretical.

Orthodox Judaism, according to Rabbi D. de Sola Pool of Shearith Israel in New York City, involves "the total Jewish tradition of living as determined by the basic Pentateuchal code of Moses, amplified by three thousand years of Jewish life in Biblical and post-Biblical ages." Orthodox Jews, for example, do not "violate the Sabbath." They cannot use hotel keys but can use electronic card-keys to enter their rooms. Not at all interested in assimilating, the men sport *tzitzis,* the fringes to remind him of his 613 religious obligations. Women even on college campuses are seen with skirts worn to the ankle and sleeves to the wrist.

Roman Catholicism, with its dogma as defined by the Church in its creeds and by the deliverances of the Pope, is such that all its members—whether liberal, conservative, radical, reactionary, saints or sinners—are orthodox. Otherwise, they would be charged with heresy or excommunicated.

Trinitarian Protestants look upon themselves as orthodox with respect to Unitarians.

The Christ was heterodox, according to Boston University School of Theology's Francis Gerald Ensley, "with respect to the Judaism of his day and yet was to become the founder of a new orthodoxy." Orthodoxy varies depending upon the time—what is heterodox at one period may be orthodox in a later one. (See entries for Jews and for Judaism.) {ER}

Ortmann, Arnold Edward (Born 1863)

Ortmann was an American zoologist born in Magdeburg. After serving in the German army (1882–1883), he made a zoological and paleontological scientific expedition to Zanzibar. In 1894 he migrated to the United States, becoming curator of invertebrate paleontology at Princeton. In 1899 he was a member of the Princeton Arctic Exhibition, and he was associate editor of *The American Naturalist.* In *Was Wir Ernst Haeckel Verdanken,* Ortmann told that he had never departed from the teaching of his old master at Jena. {RAT}

Orwell, George (pseudonym of Eric Arthur Blair) (1903–1950)

A British novelist born in India, Orwell is remembered for his satirical novels, *Animal Farm* (1946), about the failure of communism, and *Nineteen Eighty- Four* (1949), a prophetic work which describes the dehumanization of man in a time when sociopolitical conditions are making human freedom difficult to achieve. Orwell's fiction deals with the problems of human freedom. He was seriously wounded in 1936, fighting with the Republicans in the Spanish Civil War. In Sweden, his *Essays* were published by the Verdandi Students' Association and Hjalmar Öhrwall, included along with Claes-Adam Wachtmeister's *The Atheist Manual.*

Arthur C. Danto has commented on *Animal Farm*'s symbolism:

> "A Fairy Story" is Orwell's subtitle for the book, and it is made to order for a certain kind of illustration in which pigs can be shown as ridiculous, taking on more and more human attributes; and as evil, since they can, with a few wicked touches, serve as caricatures of various easily represented figures in Soviet history, which Orwell in part meant as the target of his allegory. The proportion that Orwell quite clearly had in mind—Soviet dictators are to human beings as human beings are to animals—makes *Animal Farm* a pessimistic book only if dictatorship is the inevitable result of political revolution, and if, again, revolutions are inevitably, as the word implies, circular. Orwell's message was not to beware of revolution but to watch out for the pigs, who may try to take it over. Even then, had the animals' revolution fallen into the hands of Snowball [the Trotsky figure] rather than the Stalin character in the book [Napoleon]—life might have been as rosy as its promise in the speech of old Major [the utopian idealist], which ignited the misanthropy and the discontent of the proletarian beasts who made the revolution and endured its bitter consequences.

One character in *Animal Farm* is Moses, the tame raven who represents Orwell's satirical view of organized religion in dictatorships:

> Moses, who was Mr. Jones's especial pet, was a spy and a tale-bearer, but he was also a clever talker. He claimed to know of the existence of a mysterious country called Sugarcandy Mountain, to which all animals went when they died. It was situated somewhere up in the sky, a little distance beyond the clouds, Moses said. In Sugarcandy Mountain it was Sunday seven days a week, clover was in season all the year round and lump sugar and linseed cake grew on the hedgerows. The animals hated Moses because he told tales and did no work, but some of them believed in Sugarcandy Mountain, and the pigs had to argue very hard to persuade them that there was no such place.

Orwell has been criticized for having provided names of suspected Communists to M16, the Secret Intelligence Service. He also was on record for his suspicions of Jews: Deutscher (Polish Jew); Driberg, Tom (English Jew); Chaplin, Charles (Jewish?); homosexuals ("pansies"); blacks (Paul Robeson, "very anti-white. [Henry] Wallace supporter"); vegetarians, peaceniks, women in tweed skirts and, in Alexander Cockburn's words, "others athwart the British Way.").

Although he was not a member of the British Humanist Association, he is generally revered by rationalists, freethinkers, and secular humanists. He reviewed some Rationalist Press Association books, but Anatole France's and Mark Twain's books he found to have been written by "bigoted atheists." Nietzsche was right, he wrote in 1940, about Christianity: "You can smell it—it stinks." In one of his notebooks, not published until after his death, Orwell wrote, "Recently I was reading somewhere or other [about] an Italian curio-dealer who attempted to sell a 17th-century crucifix to J. P. Morgan. Inside it was concealed a stiletto. What a perfect symbol of the Christian religion."

Timothy Garton Ash, reviewing *The Complete Works of George Orwell* (20 volumes, edited by Peter Davison, 1998), commented upon Orwell's Englishness, his love of what the English poet Craig Raine "memorably calls 'the beauty of facts.' If he had a God, it was Kipling's 'the God of Things as They are.' " Koestler called Orwell a "reverent atheist." Bernard Crick called him "a clear Humanist, even a Rationalist with a pronounced anti-Catholicism, even though one with an ironic attachment to the liturgy, the humane political compromises and the traditions of the Church of England." Flew wrote that "anyone seeking a paradigm of Humanist values can scarcely do better than to look to Orwell."

"I direct that my body shall be buried (not cremated) according to the rites of the Church of England in the nearest convenient cemetery," he wrote in a will made three days before his death. "Here," wrote Nicolas Walter, "Orwell follows the familiar pattern of so many freethinkers who were brought up in the Church of England, may have lost all belief in its doctrines and all respect for its practices, but still keep a nostalgic affection for the Authorised Version of the Bible, the Book of Common Prayer, and Humans Ancient and Modern." {Timothy Garton Ash, "Orwell in 1988," *New York Review of Books*, 22 October 1998; CE; Arthur C. Danto, " 'Animal Farm' at 50," *New York Times Book Review*, 14 April 1996; TRI; TYD; Walter, *New Humanist*, December 1998}

Ory, Georges (20th Century)
Ory wrote *An Analysis of Christian Origins* (1961) and *A La Recherche des Esseniens* (1975). {GS}

Osborn, Reuben (20th Century)
Osborn wrote *Humanism and Moral Theory* (1970), a humanistic work.

Osborne, Francis (1589–1659)
An English writer, Osborne was an adherent of Cromwell in the Civil War. His *Advice to A Son* (1656) was popular though much censured by the Puritans, who complained and proposed that the works be burned. They passed an order 27 July 1658 forbidding the works to be sold. {BDF}

Osborne, John (1929–1994)
Osborne, the English dramatist known as one of the "angry young men," first received attention not as an actor but as author of *Look Back in Anger* (1956). His plays generally describe the frustration of living without hope in a world filled with false values and include *The Entertainer* (1957), *Luther* (1961) and *A Subject of Scandal and Concern* (1961), which has freethought overtones, according to Gordon Stein and David Tribe. Osborne also wrote the screenplay for *Tom Jones* (1963). Osborne died on Christmas Eve, 1944, "an unexpected Christian," according to critic John Mortimer. {CE; GS; TRI; TYD}

Osborne, William Alexander (1873–1967)
Osborne, an Australian rationalist, physiologist, and educationalist, taught physiology and histology at the University of Melbourne from 1903 to 1939. He described himself as an evolutionist and referred to Christmas as the season of "Mithraic festivities." {SWW}

Oscapella, Eugene (20th Century)
Oscapella in an Ottawa, Ontario, lawyer and former chairman of the Drug Policy Group of the Law Reform Commission of Canada. He wrote "Witch Hunts and Chemical McCarthyism," for *Humanist in Canada* (Autumn 1996).

Oscar, L. (19th Century)
Oscar was a Swiss writer, author of *Religion Traced Back to Its Source* (1874). He considered religion "a belief in conflict with experience and resting on exaggerated fancies" of animism and mythology. One of the chapters was entitled, "The Crucifixion of the Son of God as Christian Mythology." {BDF}

Oser, Scott (20th Century)
Oser, while a student at the University of Chicago, was one of the founding members of Campus Freethought Alliance. {*International Humanist News*, December 1996}

Osgood, William Fogg (1864–1943)
An accomplished mathematician, Osgood was a Unitarian. Among his works are *Advanced Calculus* (1925) and *Functions of Complex Variables* (1936). {U; UU}

OSIRIS: See entry for Christmas.

Osler, William [Sir] (1849–1919)
A Canadian physician, Osler was renowned as a medical historian and as one of the most brilliant and influential teachers of medicine in his day. He was professor at McGill (1875–1884), the University of Pennsylvania (1884–1889), Johns Hopkins (1889–1904), and Oxford (from 1905). In 1911 he was knighted. In several of his works, he was clearly an agnostic with tenderness to religion, reports McCabe. In his Ingersoll Lecture, "Science and Immortality," he shows how science demolishes the myth and then professes a sentimental attachment to it. He also says, "It may be questioned whether more comfort or sorrow has come to the race since man peopled the unseen world with spirits to bless and demons to damn him." {CE; JM; RAT; RE}

Ossietzky, Carl von (1889–1938)
Ossietzky, a German pacifist, was the Nobel Prize winner in 1935. Following World War I, Ossietzky edited the antimilitarist weekly *Weltbühne* from 1927. In 1932, he was imprisoned for articles in that publication. After Adolf Hitler's rise to power, he was removed (1936) to a prison hospital shortly before the announcement that he had been awarded the Nobel Prize. The German government protested and barred all Germans from future acceptance of a Nobel Prize. Ossietzky died two years later. Originally a Catholic, Ossietzky had quit the church. {RE}

Ostlind, Robert (1920–1997)
Ostlind, who served in the Army Air Corps during World War II,

did regular clerical work with the Freedom From Religion Foundation. His memorial was held at Freethought Hall in Sauk City, Wisconsin. {*Freethought Today*, January-February 1998}

Ostwald, Wilhelm (1853–1932)

Ostwald, who was born in Riga, for a time was a professor of physical chemistry at Leipzig University, earning international fame as a chemist. In 1906 he retired as a Privy Councillor and joined Haeckel in promoting the Monist League, the most power Rationalist body of that time. In *Individuality and Immortality* (1906), Ostwald said that death is not an evil but, rather, is a necessary factor in the existence of the race. He had, he said, no desire whatever for a future life. He published three volumes of *Monistic Sunday Sermons* (1911) and paid a glowing tribute to Haeckel in *Was Wir Ernst Haeckel Verdanken*. Long before the "new physics" was developed, Ostwald insisted that energy is the fundamental reality.

When he died, a pastor in clerical gown appeared at the funeral and in an address declared that "as a scientist Ostwald had not trodden the pathway of theology." Friends of the deceased were amazed and, after several others had spoken, a representative of the Monists' Union was allowed to speak for a few minutes after promising the relatives not to say anything against the Church or religion. {FO; RAT; RE}

O'Sullivan, Gerry (20th Century)

O'Sullivan, who became editor of *The Humanist* in 1994, is author with Edward S. Herman of *The "Terrorism" Industry*. During a flare-up in 1994 with American Humanist Association president Michael Werner, O'Sullivan was dismissed as *The Humanist*'s editor. Werner had asked O'Sullivan to intervene in an argument over Rick Szykowny's final editorial, and O'Sullivan had refused, citing editorial autonomy. He then was dismissed in a scene reminiscent of previous editors' (e.g., Paul Kurtz and Priscilla Robertson's) dismissals. O'Sullivan is a book review editor of *Z*, a journal.

Oswald, Eugene (Died 1912)

Oswald fled the Grand Duchy of Baden, compelled to leave on account of his share in the revolutionary movement of 1848. For a time he was a journalist in Paris, contributing to the rationalistic *Liberté de Penser*. In England he became President of the Carlyle Society, Secretary of the Goethe Society, and author of a positivist study, *Der Positivissmus in England* (1884). {RAT}

Oswald, Felix Leopold (Born 1845)

Oswald was a Belgian-born American author. Educated as a physician, Oswald devoted his attention to natural history. He contributed to the *Popular Science Monthly*, *The Truthseeker*, and other journals. Oswald published a work describing his travels in Mexico and Central America, *Summerland Sketches* (1881). Other of his books are *The Secrets of the East* (1883), in which he argues that Christianity is derived from Buddhism, and *The Bible of Nature* (1888), or principles of secularism. Dr. Oswald became Curator of Natural History in Brazil. {BDF; GS; PUT; RAT}

Oswald, John (Died 1793)

Oswald's early life is obscure. He came of poor Scottish parents, bought a commission in the 42nd Highlanders, served in America and India, taught himself Greek, Latin, and Arabic, and after abandoning Christianity mixed with the Brahmins in India. A republican by conviction, he entered the French revolutionary Army and was killed in the Vendean War. He left some poetry and wrote an anti-religious pamphlet, "Ranae Comica Evangelizantes, or the Comic Frogs Turned Methodists." {RAT}

Otakpor, Nkeonye (20th Century)

A senior lecturer in philosophy at the University of Benin, Nigeria, Otakpor is a member of the Executive Board of the Nigerian Philosophical Association. In any diagnosis of the politics of the Western God, Otakpor states, one notes that what is meant by "God" is culturally determined. Thus, there is Allah of Islam; Brahman of Hinduism; Tao of Taoism; Yahweh of the Jews; Chiukwu of the Igo; Olorun of the Yoruba; Leve of the Mende; Juok of the Shilluk; Nzambe of the Bakongo; and God of the Western man. For the Igbo, as an example, Chiukwu was never born, never died, never had human parents or siblings. To them, the Western God is a selfish, colonial God. To them, also, historians and the world press have been Eurocentric, relegating much of the world including theirs to the "primitive" or "Third World." "While the Western God is *supposed* to have died for all men," he writes, "the Western man is metaphorically dying mainly because of his sins of exploitation, domination, and destruction of non-Western peoples. In being humanized, the Western God died. In being divinized, in playing God to other peoples and cultures, dissolving them, ceaselessly unmaking them, making it impossible for such people to create and recreate their positivity, the death of Western man is chronicled." At the same time, he claims, Western man overlooks Egypt's ancient past (implying Egyptians were black, which is a point of controversy), although its pyramids are excellent reminders, as are the Ife, Benin, Nok, and Igbo-Ukwu cultures in Nigeria which are as old as the Roman culture. Similarly, the Indian and Chinese cultures and civilizations are overlooked. In short, the West has categorized the world into three parts: the first is theirs; the second belongs to their siblings; the third is reserved mainly for marginalized Africans, Asians, and Latin Americans. Instead of *one* human race, there are *three* worlds inhabited by different human races "and this segmenting has obviously been intended as a convenient vehicle for racial segregation." He continues: "Parallel to the acceptance of one Western God is also the acceptance of one religious system, one marriage system, one philosophical system, one system of governance and political economy, and one model of reality as constructed from Western European prisms." It follows that non-Europeans will distrust such an outlook, which has resulted in the depopulation of the African continent by slave traders "in order to create the wealth of modern Europe."

In short, the Western God has no appeal whatsoever to many Africans, who consider it blasphemous for the West annually to celebrate a humanized dead God. "An African God, whether of the Mende, Shilluk, Bakongo, Igbo, Yoruba, or Kasai, is neither one-dimensional nor selfish. No African God is worshiped alone nor is there any injunction that Africans should worship only that which is recognized as God. Indeed, while recognizing African Gods in their individual cultures as the ultimate ONE, Africans worship a plurality of spirits that are not on the same pedestal with whatever is taken as a God in the different traditions."

What lesson does he feel is to be learned by Western humanists? That "the inherent pluralism in African lifestyles, the emphasis on the community rather than the atomized self, etc., are indices of the African abiding faith in the worthwhile coexistence of the ONE and the MANY." And that "to the extent that no African God is a predatory being, none of them permitted or sanctioned (overtly or covertly) colonialism, imperialism, and apartheid. Chiukwu (God) of the Igbo, for example, never encouraged the destruction, pillaging, and despoliation of other peoples and their cultures."

Otakpor makes a strong case for the importance of a complacent and prosperous Western minority to take seriously the ethos of the peasantry in Nigeria, Brazil, Angola, Burma, India, and other parts of the non-European world. {AAH}

Otárola Pacheco, Ricardo (20th Century)

Otárola is a Costa Rican lawyer who is active in the Costa Rican as well as the Iberoamerican humanist associations. He was instrumental in starting *Asociación Iberoamericana Ético Humanista* (ASIBEHU) and in developing its World Wide Web home page. In 1996 he was a moderator of a panel on organizing humanism in a cybernetic era at the Humanist World Conference held in Mexico City.

Otárola has been instrumental in developing and hosting webpages, his own being at <www.geocities.com/WestHollywood/5553>. His e-mail: <bettedavis@geocities.com>. Otárola has hosted the homepage of ASIBEHU: <http://idt.net/~wasm/asibehu>.

Otis, Harrison Gray (1765–1848)

Otis, nephew of the American colonial political leader James Otis, was a staunch Federalist. A leader of the Hartford Convention, he was a U.S. senator (1817–1822) and mayor of Boston (1829–1831). In a biography, Samuel Eliot Morison describes how Otis and his wife joined Dr. Peter Thacher's Brattle Street Church, which became Unitarian: "Most, under the guidance of liberal Congregational clergymen, became Unitarians. The Otises belonged to the Brattle Street Church, which John Adams described as the 'politest' in Boston, under four successive liberal ministers: J. S. Buckminister, Edward Everett, John G. Palfrey, and Samuel K. Lothrop." In 1860, Otis's relative and namesake—Harrison Gray Otis—nominated Abraham Lincoln for President. {EG; CE}

O'Toole, Adam Duff (14th Century)

O'Toole was an Irish freethought martyr, burned to death in 1327 at Hogging (now College) Green in Dublin. Holinshead wrote that O'Toole "denied obstinatelie the incarnation of our savior, the trinitie of persons in the vnitie of the Godhead and the resurrection of the flesh; as for the Holie Scripture, he said it was but a fable; the Virgin Marie he affirmed to be a woman of dissolute life, and the Apostolike see erronious." {BDF}

O'Toole, Fintan (20th Century)

O'Toole's biography of the fellow Irish-born Richard Sheridan led to his conclusion that the extent of political tolerance relates to the level of social order in a society. O'Toole currently is a theatre reviewer in New York. {*New Humanist*, March 1998}

Otto, Max (1876–1968)

A distinguished professor of philosophy at the University of Wisconsin, Otto co-wrote with Henry Nelson Wieman *Is There A God? A Conversation* (1932). He also wrote *Things and Ideals* (1924), *Natural Laws and Human Hopes* (1926), and *Science and the Moral Life* (1949). In the 1950s, Otto wrote book reviews for *The Humanist.*

Otto argued that unless we insist on limiting in some manner the acceptable meaning of God, it is easy to prove the existence of God by "dilution into vagueness"; through reducing the definition of the term "until it means no more than everyone, even the confessed atheist, will have to admit to exist. Thus the definition of God virtually proves his existence. . . . The word *God* is made to stand for so much that it loses all distinctive meaning. . . . Belief bought at this price costs too much. It not only impoverishes the religious life...but it tends to dissipate the mental discipline so laboriously and slowly achieved by men."

At John Dewey's memorial service, held at the Community Church (Unitarian) in Manhattan, Dr. Otto told how he once had asked Dewey a question as they were walking on the campus. Dewey stopped. Dewey cogitated quietly. Time passed. More time passed. *Much* more time passed. Otto wondered after a few minutes if Dewey might be experiencing some physical problem. A stroke? Worse? Finally, and just as Otto started to interrupt Dewey's seemingly comatose state, Dewey came to life and gave a thorough and profound answer to the question he had just been asked. The response took a long, *long* time, and it was painstakingly complete, logical, replete with examples, spoken without a pause. Otto observed, as everyone present chuckled, that he was very, *very* careful, from then on, what he asked Dewey. "Ask a question, and you deserve an answer, not just a response!" (See entries for John Dewey and for the American Humanist Association.) {CL; HNS; U}

Otway, Thomas (1652–1685)

Otway wrote *The Atheist* (1683), a comedy. At one point, Otway stated, "These are rogues that pretend to be of a religion now! Well, all I say is, honest atheism for my money." {E}

Otwell, Anne (20th Century)

Otwell, called by some the Prophet Serpentfoot, has had many problems with Floyd County, Georgia, officials. She has been charged with public indecency for disrobing and of disrupting a lawful meeting because of her objections to prayers being said at the Floyd County Commission meetings. When she asked to be allowed to pray on the grounds of "equal time," she prayed to "my God (who is) here tonight in person," at which the audience of more than fifty filed into the hallway in order to avoid what she had to say. An eccentric who has lived in a teepee alongside a highway, she has been described by Fred Whitehead as the kind of activist freethinkers and humanists should support inasmuch as she is on the firing line in small communities which term her a "village atheist" although, he adds, she is closer to being a pantheist.

Her voicemail starts, "This is Serpentfoot for the NNNWM, the Church of Nudists, Natives, and Naturalists with a Mission." {*Freethought History* #16, 1995}

OUDEREN WEKKRANT

A Dutch humanist journal, *Ouderen Wekkrant* is no longer published.

Ouida: See entry for Ramée, Marie Louise de la.

Ouvry, Henry Aimé (19th Century)

Ouvry was translator of *Dietetics of the Soul* by Feuchterslebens and *Unsectarian Catechism* by Rau. Ouvry wrote several works on the land question. {BDF}

Överland, Arnulf (20th Century)

Överland was a Norwegian non-theist, a member of the Rationalist Press Association (RPA) in England. (See entry for Scandinavian Unbelievers.)

Overmann, Roy (20th Century)

At the Fourth Annual Atheist Alliance Convention, held in St. Louis and hosted in 1998 by the Rationalist Society, Overmann addressed the group on "Humanism: The Logical Conclusion to Atheism."

Overstreet, Harry Allen (1875–1970)

Chairman of the philosophy department at the City College of New York (1911–1939), Overstreet was author of a very popular book in its day, *The Mature Mind.* On the subject of religion, he stated, "I have long since learned that a man can believe in a perfectly cockeyed theology and still be a royally fine person."

On the subject of humanism, he wrote the present author in 1951, "I list myself as a naturalistic humanist for the following reasons:

• The new naturalism assumes that nature includes for more than any of our systems of knowledge has ever included or now includes. This means that to a naturalistic humanist there are no limits that can now be set to the possibilities inherent in the nature that includes human nature. This removes all dogmatic certainties whether of the 'materialistic' or the 'spiritual' sort. The destiny of man is apparently as limitless as the nature of which he is part.

• The new naturalism further assumes that the only way of knowing is through the natural processes of the mind. All supernatural deliverances and guarantees, therefore, are out.

• Humanism assumes that the goal of human development lies in the greatest possible fulfillment of human powers. Man does not live to serve some supernatural being. He lives to bring to fruition the powers with which nature has endowed him. As of today, this fruition would seem to lie in a life of widely shared friendliness, understanding, and cooperation.

In the *Hibbert Journal* (1913–1914), Overstreet rejected the idea of God as a father, creator, person, or "ideally perfect being," and accepted only "a god that is ourselves and grows with the world." He also declared, "Christianity as an institutionalized religion has laid no stress on the pursuit of truth. Indeed, for the most part it has been suspicious of the truthseeking process. The truthseeker might overturn accepted beliefs." {RAT; TYD; WAS, 28 August 1951}

Overton, Richard (17th Century)

Overton was an English Republican who wrote a satire on relics (1642) and a treatise on *Man's Mortality* (1643), which was anti-Christian enough to say that "the present [belief in the] going of the soul into heaven and hell is a mere fiction," though Overton did believe in a general resurrection at the end of the world. The book was much attacked, and Parliament was moved to institute an inquiry as to the authorship. After satirizing the Episcopal Church, Overton in 1646 turned upon the Presbyterian clergy, warmly denouncing all religious persecution. He was arrested (on a political charge) and imprisoned, but the army obtained his release. He continued his campaign, and in 1649 he was lodged in the Tower, from which he maintained his output of fiery and critical pamphlets. Upon being released, he was again imprisoned from 1659 to 1663. {BDF; RAT}

Ovid (Publius Ovidius Naso) (43 B.C.E.–18 C.E.)

The Latin poet Ovid (Naso, his last name, is apparently a familial inheritance, a reference to a big nose) was admired by Shakespeare, was distrusted in the nineteenth century as an immoralist, and was dismissed for most of the present century as being but a lightweight. But, adds the critic Bernard Knox, Ovid is now back in favor.

In his own time he was all the fashion. Ovid's was, as Knox notes (*The New York Review of Books*, 15 Jan 1998), "an age of peace that succeeded generations of war and also one that saw the obsolescence of the stern moral code that had made the early Roman republic a nation of dedicated farmer-soldiers and faithful fertile wives."

Ovid's work falls into three categories: erotic poems, mythological poems, and poems of exile. *Amores* contains forty-nine short love poems. *Metamorphosis*, one of Chaucer's favorite books, concerned myths and is his greatest work. The poems of exile include *Tristia*, because for some reason in the year 8 of the Christian Era he was abruptly exiled to Tomis, a Black Sea outpost, where he later died. His work was written not to teach morals or lofty edification but, rather, to give pleasure. He shows his expertise, particularly when discussing women and how to appreciate their charms.

As for religion, "It is expedient that gods should exist," he observed in *Ars amatoria*. "Since it is expedient, let us believe they do." However, Ovid "had no faith in personal survival after death," Lamont reports.

According to Robertson, Ovid "could satirize the dishonest merchant who prayed to the Gods to absolve his frauds; but he hailed Augustus as the sacred founder and restorer of temples, prayed for him as such, busied himself with the archaeology of the cults, and made it, not quite without irony, a maxim to 'spare an accepted belief.' " (See entry for Poets.) {CE; CL; JMR; JMRH; TYD}

Owen, John (19th Century)

Owen wrote *The Religious Aspects of Scepticism* (1891). {GS}

Owen, Robert (1771–1858)

Owen, a Scot who had owned a cotton-spinning mill, moved to Indiana, where he started a socialist experiment in New Harmony. His "Declaration of Mental Independence," delivered on the 50th anniversary of the Declaration of Independence, is found in Whitehead and Muhrer's *Freethought on the American Frontier*. Two of his works were *Debate on the Evidence of Christianity* (1829) and *Threading My Way: Twenty-seven Years of Autobiography* (1874). Phyllis Palmer in the *Encyclopedia of Unbelief* notes that "he was not a caricature philanthropist devoted more to an idea than to actual people" and "he could not accept religious tenets that rationalized poor planning and justified the poverty that accompanied early industrialization." McCabe wrote that Owen believed that "man's character is made for him and not by him" and that "all the religions of the world are false." For a time he had the Royal family among his public supporters, but religious opponents forced him into a public declaration of atheism. He then founded a movement known as Socialism (not State Socialism) and later an ethical movement which he called Rational Religion. The latter had 100,000 members, who may or may not have been agnostics, and in the trade unions he is said to have had influence over more than a million. In his Autobiography, Owen found that "one and all had emanated from the same source, and their varieties from the same false imaginations of our early ancestors."

Robertson admired him because "from an early age he had lost all belief in the prevailing forms of religion. . . . He had come to his rationalism through the influence rather of Rousseau than of Voltaire; and he had assimilated the philosophic doctrine of determinism—of all ideals the most difficult to realize in conduct—with a thoroughness of which the flawed Rousseau was incapable." Owen during a debate on religion once said, "When we use the term Lord, God, or Deity we use a term without annexing to it any definite idea." Further, he said, "All the religions of the world are false."

Somehow, when he was eighty-four and his mind was failing, Owen was duped by a spiritualist medium, who convinced him that spirit communication represented "a great moral evolution . . . about to be effected for the human race," and spiritualist socialism, a kind of "socialism of eternity." Wheeler says of Owen that he "profoundly influenced the thought of his time in the direction of social amelioration, and he is justly respected for his energy, integrity, and disinterested philanthropy."

At the age of eighty-eight, Owen died. His son, Robert Dale Owen, was quoted as follows in the newspapers, which noted that Owen's name had at one time been a terror to the clergy and to the privileged classes: "My dear father passed away this morning, at a quarter before seven, and passed away as gently and quietly as if he had fallen asleep. There was not the least struggle, not a contraction of a limb, of a muscle, not an expression of pain on his face. His breathing gradually became slower and slower, until at last it ceased so unperceptibly, that, even as I held his hand, I could scarcely tell the moment when he no longer breathed. His last words distinctly pronounced about twenty minutes before his death, were 'Relief has come.' About half an hour before he said , 'Very easy and comfortable.'"

Owen's remains were interred in the churchyard of St. Mary's, Newtown. Inasmuch as the law allowed the minister had a right to read the Church of England burial service over the heretic's coffin, according to Foote, the Freethinkers who stood round the grave had to bear the mockery as quietly as possible. (See entry for Robert Dale Owen, his son.) {BDF; CE; EU, Phyllis Palmer; FUK; FUS; JM; PUT; RAT; RE; VI; TRI}

Owen, Robert Dale (1800–1877)

The son of Robert Owen, one without his father's charisma but with his interest in the New Harmony experiment, Robert Dale Owen was a writer, a communitarian, and a Democratic member of the Indiana legislature. Owen's early freethought principles changed in his later life. In *Footfalls on the Boundary of Another World* (1859), inspired perhaps by the death of his wife, he turned to spiritualism. He once was an editor of the New Harmony, Indiana, *Free Enquirer*. {EU, Phyllis Palmer; FUK; FUS; RAT; VI; TRI}

Owen, T. E. (19th Century)

Owen, in what was considered a rare event in the 1880s, wrote in Welsh in *Secular Review* about a freethought group at Rhybydd. {RSR}

Owen-Towle, Tom (20th Century)

Owen-Towle is author of *The Gospel of Universalism* (1993), reflections on the people and history of American Universalism. He also wrote *O. Eugene Pickett* (1996).

Owens, Karen (20th Century)

Owens is a regional director in California of the Council for Secular Humanism.

Owens, Jesse (1913–1980)

An African American who won four gold medals at the 1936 Olympics, Owens was a Universalist who had been a Baptist. He is remembered partly because at the 1936 Olympic games in Berlin, he astounded the world and upset Hitler's "Aryan" theories by equaling the world mark (10.3 seconds) in the 100-meter race, by breaking world records in the 200-meter race (20.7 seconds) and in the broad jump (26 feet 5 3/8 inches / 8.07 meters), and by winning also (along with Ralph Metcalfe) the 400-meter relay race. Owens wrote *Blackthink: My Life as Black Man and White Man*. {CE}

Oxlee, John (1779–1864)

A freethinker, Oxlee wrote *A Confutation of the Diabolarchy* (c. 1875), consisting of letters to the Lord Archbishop of Canterbury. As early as 1843, Oxlee went on record as believing in "the inexpediency and futility of any attempt to convert the Jews to Christianity." {GS}

OXYGEN

Oxygen, which is a colorless, odorless, tasteless gas, is the most abundant element on earth. Evolutionists point out that for early forms of life, however, oxygen was a poison. (See entry for nitric acid.)

OXYMORON

Rhetorical figures in which incongruous or contradictory terms—oxymorons—are combined include the following:

deafening silence	childproof
Christian Science	legally drunk
clearly misunderstood	same difference
Now, then . . . (hesitating)	found missing
religious tolerance	pretty ugly

Oyama, Y. (20th Century)

In Yokahama, Japan, Oyama edited *Iunri* in the 1910s.

Ozawa, Seiji (1935-)

A noted conductor of orchestras, Ozawa was born in Hoten, China. After being trained in Japan, Paris, and the United States, he conducted the Toronto and San Francisco symphonies. In 1973 he began a long tenure as conductor of the Boston Symphony. During a televised interview, Ozawa explained that although he directed religious music he was not at all religious. {Dennis Middlebrooks, July 1999}

Ozon, François (1968-)

A French filmmaker, the homosexual Ozon has been said to be heir to the satirical surrealist Luis Buñuel. "I'm happy to have had a Catholic education," he told an *Advocate* (1 September 1998) reporter, "because I know what's wrong and what's good—and I prefer what's wrong."

"A Summer Dress" depicts a young gay man on vacation whose clothes are stolen while he is having a mid-day dalliance with a woman, after which he bicycles home in the woman's dress. The film, he said, says you *can* have sex but have to protect yourself. "It's a film about not being guilty about your own sexuality."

Paalzow, Christian Ludwig (1753–1824)

Paalzow was a German jurist who translated Voltaire's commentaries on *The Spirit of the Laws* and Burigny's *Examination of the Apologists of Christianity* (1793). He also wrote *A History of Religious Cruelty* (1800). {BDF; RAT}

PACHACAMUC

The Yuncas called Pachacamac the supreme god, the creator of all. {LEE}

PACIFISM

Man is kept from being his best, according to Bertrand Russell, by his pugnaciousness. *Free Man's Worship* tells of his pacifism during World War II. "If I could give to others what has come to me in this way," Lord Russell writes, "I could make them too feel the futility of fighting. But I do not know how to communicate it; when I speak, they stare, applaud, or smile, but do not understand." In former times, he explained, "when two wished to live on the produce of a piece of land which only yielded enough for one, they must either both starve or fight till one was killed. In practice, it was not single men who fought, but groups of men, called successively tribes, nations, coalitions, or United Nations. In spite of Christianity, when enjoined peace before the necessary industrial technique had been invented, sheer necessity drove men into conflict." In his various works, Russell discusses the consequences of war over various historical periods, and he laments that war between men and nations will continue in the future, remarking that "In England, Germany, and the United States (in 1917), no government could have withstood the popular demand for war. A popular demand of this sort must have an instinctive basis, and for my part, I believe that the modern increased in warlike instinct is attributable to the dissatisfaction (mostly unconscious) caused by the regularity, monotony, and tameness of modern life."

Devoted pacifists as well as many former soldiers devoted to the cause of war admit the utter inhumanness of killing. They were outraged in 1937 when German planes bombed Guernica during the Spanish Civil War, an incident during which women and children who were killed were memorialized by Pablo Picasso's painting, "Guernica." They also lamented the bombing of Dresden, Germany, in which at least 35,000 Germans died—the humanist Kurt Vonnegut Jr. wrote *Slaughterhouse-Five; or The Children's Crusade* (1969), a novel inspired by his experience of the bombing while an American prisoner-of-war in that city. Others have lamented the bombing by Americans of Nagasaki and Hiroshima during World War II. John Hersey wrote *Hiroshima* (1946) to detail the conflagration, in which 90% of Hiroshima was leveled and as many as 140,000 casualties occurred. An estimated 100,000 were killed when Tokyo was firebombed in 1945, an event described hyperbolically by American General Curtis LeMay: "We scorched and boiled and baked to death more people in Tokyo on that night of March 9-10 than went up in vapor at Hiroshima and Nagasaki combined."

Katsumoto Saotome, a Japanese antiwar campaigner observed that "[t]he firebombing probably led to an earlier end of the war. But I think killing noncombatants was an unforgivable violation of human morality. But in fact it was Japan that was the first to kill noncombatants, when it bombed cities like Chongquing [Chungking] in China." In many respects, observed journalist Nicholas D. Kristof on the firebombing's fiftieth anniversary, "the firebombing of Tokyo was the top step in a spiral staircase in the capacity of conventional arms and the willingness to use them." (See entry for War.) {Lee Eisler, *The Quotable Bertrand Russell*}

Pack, Ernest (20th Century)

In London during the early 1900s, Pack was a lecturer for the British Secular League. He wrote *The Parson's Doom* (1900?) and *The Trial and Imprisonment of J. W. Gott for Blasphemy* (c. 1920). {FUK; RSR}

Padia, Chandrakala (20th Century)

Padia is on the board of directors of the Bertrand Russell Society.

PAEDICATIO

Paedicatio is a prudish way to refer, using Latin, to anal penetration, whether male/female, female/male, female/female, or male/male.

PAGAN

If you are "irreligious" or a hedonist, according to *Webster's Collegiate Dictionary*, you are a pagan:

> **pagan** *n* [ME. fr LL *paganus*, fr. L, country dweller, fr *pagus* country district; akin to L *pangere* to fix] (14th Century) **1 :** HEATHEN **1;** *esp* : a follower of a polytheistic religion (as in ancient Rome) **2** : one who has little or no religion and who delights in sensual pleasures and material goods : an irreligious or hedonistic person or a heathen

> **heathen** *n pl* [ME *hethen* fr. OE *haethen*; akin to OHG *heidan* heathen, and prob. to OE *haeth* heath] **1** : an unconverted member of a people or nation that does not acknowledge the God of the Bible **2** : an uncivilized or irreligious person

To a Christian, Moslem, or Jew, a pagan is not one of the fellow believers. Although semantically a "snarl word" with negative overtones, pagan to non-believers has positive overtones. Tacitus and Juvenal indicated that in their time the pagans, or rustics, were those who were not called up for military service and did not take the military oath. Inasmuch as the Christians deemed themselves the soldiers of Christ, they called those who did not take *their* oath "pagans." Augustine, in his *City of God* thought of the pagans as the best-educated men of the African cities.

Leaders of an American pagan organization that includes the Covenant of Unitarian Universalist Pagans (CUUPS) have urged dictionary publishers to adopt the following definition:

> **neo-paganism** n A collection of diverse contemporary religions rooted in indigenous traditions or deriving inspirqation therefrom, characterized by a belief in the interconnection of all life, personal autonomy, and immanent divinities. Often nature-centered and supportive of gender equality.

Kafiristan, in northeast Afghanistan on the southern sz of the Hindu Kush, was a region named after the Arabic word *kafir*, which mean "the country of unbelievers, the pagans." Its 60,000 or so residents practiced animism until about 1895–1896, at which time they were forced to convert to Islam. The area is now called Nuristan, which in Persian means "land of light or the enlightened." The Kafiri language belongs to the Indo-European family and, some have suggested, Greek settlers were the founders. During the 1979–1989 occupation by Soviet forces, some of the heaviest guerrilla fighting occurred here.

Contemporary secular humanists, agnostics, atheists, and freethinkers—none soldiers of Christ—are, gratefully, pagans and heathens. Also, they likely are pacifists who do wholly disapprove of the religious wars found throughout Earth. They likely are not, however, members of the pagan-worshiping Wiccan religionists. Those Wiccans consider themselves witches whose ethics are "to harm no one, do what you will." Wiccans do not, however, recognize the concept of Satan and base their beliefs on pre-Christian religion, when people celebrated the waxing and the waning of the moon, the solstices, the equinoxes. On the Web: <http://www.bloomington.in.us/~pen>. (See entries for Halloween, Wicca, and Witchcraft.) {CE; RE}

PAGAN PRACTICES

Since Neolithic times, pagans have enjoyed various "religious" practices. For example, trees have been considered symbols of birth, fertility, and good fortune. To alert the tree gods inside that we need their help, we "knock wood."

Druids hung gilded apples and candles onto oak trees to please the god of the sun, Balder.

Celts celebrated the solstice with bunches of mistletoe, the berries of which supposedly held the seeds of the sun's fire. Scandinavians added the myth that promised a kiss underneath would bring good luck, or at least heat things up.

Saturnalia was the ancient Roman wildly licentious holiday for Saturn, god of agriculture who was said to be returning from his exile. Not a few orgies were held under trees from which candles were displayed.

Pope Gregory I wrote to St. Augustine, the first Archbishop of

Canterbury, that the best way to convert the Anglo-Saxons could be to adapt some of their customs. Ergo, Jesus's alleged birth date was moved to December 25th to coincide with the solstice. And many of the pagan practices, including the use of fir trees, were incorporated. Germans, who had displayed fir trees for the solstice, began displaying them to celebrate the Christ's birth. In 1605 a Strasbourg scribe observed the first such tree,

> At Christmas they set up fir trees in the parlors and hang upon them roses cut from many colored paper, apples, wafers, spangle-gold, sweets, etc.

Puritans in America, however, considered Christmas Day one of penance and fined anyone caught feasting 5 shillings. By 1856, however, President Franklin Pierce inaugurated the custom of the White House Christmas tree. By 1997, according to the National Christmas Tree Association, an estimated 30,000,000 trees (and untold needles) were dragged into America's living rooms. Scotch pine has been the most popular breed, followed by the Douglas and balsam firs. (See entry for Thomas W. Flynn.) {Lenore Skenazy, New York *Daily News*, 29 November 1997}

Paganini, Niccolo (1782–1840)

Paganini was an Italian violinist whose virtuosity became a legend. He perfected the use of double and triple stops and revived the practice of *scordatura*, the diverse tunings of the strings. As a child prodigy in 1793, Paganini made his debut at Genoa. When he retired in 1835, he lost his voice and, later, died from cancer of the larynx. According to his biographer, Count Conestabili, Paganini was orthodox but admitted "religious indifferentism." He received neither the last sacrament nor had any religious service at his funeral, and McCabe says Paganini's friends knew he was an atheist. {CE; JM; RAT; RE}

Pagano, Francisco Mario Saverio Antonio Carlo Pasquale (1748–1800)

Pagano was an Italian jurist, philosopher, and patriot. A friend of Filangieri, he became a professor of criminal law in 1787. For his *Political Essays* in three volumes (1783–1792) he was accused of atheism and impiety. He wrote on *Criminal Process* and *On God and Nature*. Taking part in the Provisional Government of the Neapolitan Republic in 1791, he was taken prisoner by the royalists and executed 6 October 1800. {BDF; RAT}

Page, David (1814–1879)

Page was a Scottish geologist, author of introductory and advanced textbooks on geology. His *Man: Where, Whence, and Whither?* (1867) advocated Darwinian views and received mixed reviews in Scotland. A friend of Robert Chambers, Page was for some time credited with his *Vestiges of Creation* because of the scientific details he had supplied. {BDF; RAT}

Page, Don (20th Century)

In 1968, Page was among the founders of the Humanist Association of Canada, editing *Humanist in Canada* from 1982 to 1987. He then edited the International Humanist and Ethical Union's *International Humanist*. In October of 1992 he was appointed editor of *The Humanist*, the bi-monthly publication of the American Humanist Association with headquarters in Amherst, New York. But the following June he resigned, stating that he was "unwilling to assume responsibility for certain editorial arrangements that predate the beginning of my mandate last October." In a farewell editorial, he remarked that the European Humanist Federation gives a strong voice for humanist values within the political and social councils of an increasingly unified Europe, representing "a *pluralistic* but *unified* humanism." "Surely," Page writes, "we should aim at no less on this continent." Except for the long period during which Edwin Wilson edited *The Humanist*, the Board of Directors of the American Humanist Association has had little luck in holding on to its editors. (See entry for Priscilla Robertson.)

Page, Martin Richard (1938–)

Page is the author of *Britain's Unknown Genius: The Life-Work of J. M. Robertson* (1984). {FUK}

Page, Preston (20th Century)

Page is president of Humanists of the Jefferson Tradition (AHA). (See entry for Virginia Freethinkers, Humanists.) {FD}

Page, Ra (20th Century)

Page, the literary editor of *City Life* in Manchester, England, is a freelance writer for the *Guardian*. In "Cyberphobia: the Ethics of Computer Evolution," Page related his concern with the central dilemma between the utilitarian worth of the computer, its service to mankind, and its threat to the integrity of human thought. {*New Humanist*, September 1996}

Pagels, Elaine Heisy (1941–)

Pagels, a historian of religion, is an Episcopalian. She wrote *The Johannine Gospel in Gnostic Exogesis* (1973), *The Gnostic Paul* (1975), *The Gnostic Gospels* (1979), and *Adam, Eve, and the Serpent* (1988). Her *Origin of Satan* (1995) takes up the dichotomy of how Christianity (within the basic gospel message of love and good works) demonizes its enemies. Originally, Satan had been a servant of God, one who obstructed human mischief; for instance, he stood in the path of Balaam's ass, not allowing Balaam to proceed because God did not want him to proceed. Around the 7th century B.C.E., however, some Jewish scribes pictured Satan in a sinister way, using him as a device to explain division in the house of Israel. Christians have continued the concept, down to the present. By calling its opposition "the devil's work," Christianity attacked whatever it wished, from abortion to prayer in the schools to gays to family values.

In *The Origin of Satan, Pagels wrote,*

> Such visions (of Satan) have been incorporated into Christian tradition and have served, among other things, to confirm for Christians their own identification with God and to demonize their opponents—first other Jews, then pagans, and later dissident Christians called heretics.

The early Christians, she states, had a unique view of life and faith as a cosmic battle of good vs. evil, and from this they introduced an evil being (Satan) who opposed the great good (God). She shows how the gospels put the Jews in the devil's camp. Romans fare better, for they were the political power of the time and were prime converts. Pagels gets across the idea that it is not wrong that Christians aim for a victory over evil. But so long as they treat others as evil incarnate, she sees little hope for any Christian peace.

Meanwhile, other scholarship more and more confirms that Satan originated as a Judaized version of the Zoroastrian spirit of evil, Ahriman. (See entries for Gnosticism and Devil.) {TYD}

Paget, James (Sir) (1814–1899)

Paget was a surgeon, pathologist, and friend of Darwin, Huxley, Pasteur, Prime Minister Gladstone, and writers Tennyson, Browning, and Eliot. He declared, "I know of no book which has been a source of brutality and sadistic conduct, both public and private, that can compare with the Bible." {TYD}

Paget, Violet (19th Century)

An English author using the pen name of "Vernon Lee," Paget wrote such works as *Studies of the Eighteenth Century in Italy* and *Baldwin*, which were dialogues on her 1886 views and aspirations. In 1883 she had written "Responsibilities of Unbelief" in *Contemporary* and was outspokenly aggressive concerning her agnosticism, as she also was in her *Vital Lies: Studies of Some Varieties of Recent Obscurantism* (1912, two volumes). {BDF; RAT; RE}

Pageze, L. (19th Century)

Pageze was a French socialist who wrote on the *Concordat* and the *Budget des Cultes*. In 1887 he wrote *Separation of Church and State*. {BDF}

Paglia, Camille (1947–)

Paglia, an intellectual, democrat, and libertarian who is thoroughly conversant with the humanities, sizzles, whether on the printed page or during appearances on television. A professor of humanities at the Philadelphia University of the Arts, she does not hesitate in her rebelliousness to object to the Establishment's wrong goals or society's weaknesses, and when she takes aim she levels her cannons with precision. For example, she is known for her view that a prostitute is "the ultimate liberated woman, who lives on the edge and whose sexuality belongs to no one."

A lesbian and an atheist, she minces no words. "I do not believe in God," she writes in *Vamps and Tramps* (1994), "but I believe God is man's greatest idea. Those incapable of religious feeling or those (like hardcore gay activists) who profane sacred ground do not have the imagination to educate the young. Flicking the radio dial in America, one hears bursts of beautiful, spellbinding poetry. But it is neither academics nor contemporary writers who are filling the air with dazzling imagery and profound spiritual truths. Alas for progressive politics, these are the voices of white and black Christian ministers, reading form the Bible. Why have intellectuals abandoned the people? This is the shame of modernism. High Romanticism at least gave poetry as the prize of rebellion and, turning from God, put nature in his place."

Paglia added, "Everyone in the world should know all the great religions of the world: Hinduism; Buddhism; Greco-Roman and Near Eastern paganism; Judeo-Christianity; Islam, African, North American, and Oceanic tribal cults, pre-Columbia imperial myth. Art, history, and philosophy are intertwined with the evolution of religion. This is the true multiculturalism. The secularism of the Enlightenment was meant to free the mind, not kill the soul. In the spirit of the eighteenth-century encyclopedists and revolutionaries, we must keep church and state separate, even while we preserve the eternal insights and metaphors of religion. Authority belongs to the classroom, not the pulpit."

Her *Sexual Personae, Art and Decadence from Nefertiti to Emily Dickinson* (1991), explains that art is a pagan background between male and female, form and chaos, civilization and demonic nature. She followed this with *Sex, Art, and American Culture* (1992), in which she denounced the women's movement's descent into Puritanism. The artist Mapplethorpe, she holds, was the contemporary pagan priest of art.

Of her, Gloria Steinem has said, "Twenty years ago, feminism was blamed for the beef boycott. Now divorce. Feminism isn't responsible for divorce; marriage is responsible for divorce. What's important is that we have progressed enough that being a feminist is no longer seen as some fringe activity. It is mainstream enough for anti-feminists like Camille Paglia to need to say they are feminists."

Paglia is particularly eloquent on the subject of feminism: "To rescue feminism, we must give religion its due but require it to stay in its place. Again, Judeo-Christianity is only half our tradition. Paganism has other paradigms to offer. The militant virgin goddesses, Athena and Artemis, with their cold autonomy, are heroines of mine. Plato speaks of two Aphrodites, a common one of physical childbirth and the other, the Uranian, patron of spiritual and intellectual influence, specially associated with homoerotic relations. Evasions of nature's biological imperative are distinctly human. I take the extreme view of that Enlightenment neopagan, the Marquis de Sade, who lauds abortion and sodomy for their bold frustration of mother nature's relentless fertility. My code of modern Amazonism says that nature's fascist scheme of menstruation and procreation *should* be defied, as a gross infringement of woman's free will."

In many respects, Paglia is the most eloquent speaker on behalf of contemporary secular humanism, although she does not align herself with any particular philosophic movement. A 1960s free speech militant, she alarms prudes and fundamentalists with her enlightened logic, aesthetics, and ethics.

In an uplifting 1995 interview with Tim Madigan, Paglia went on record concerning many subjects:

> I hate dogma in any form. I hate it in the Roman Catholic church, which is why I left it twenty-five years ago. I hate it in gay activism and feminism now. Dogma has also taken over the humanities departments in elite schools–poststructuralism and so forth. . . . There's nothing more dangerous to a liberal democracy than fixed dogma. . . .
>
> I'm an atheist but we people of the sixties were very spiritual in our own ways. That is, we abandoned organized religions, but we sought out Hinduism and Buddhism. We were very interested in cross-cultural spiritual experiences. A passage to India, as it were. . . . The Enlightenment turned away from organized religion, but put reason and science in its place. Romanticism rebelled against organized religion, but put nature and art in its place. What has modernism done? It turned against organized religion, and given nothing in its place. . . . There's two thousand years of developed thought behind Christianity. There's three thousand years behind Judaism. So, better Jehovah than Foucault. Jehovah at least brings along this incredible work, the Bible. What a great collection of poetry, *magnificent*, filled with things of spiritual use, whether you believe in God or not. The grandeur and intellectual development of Catholic theology is staggering. Foucault is a fraud; and that's the diet our best kinds in the elite schools are being fed. It is appalling. The man knew nothing. . . .
>
> The overall theme of my work is this: Judeo-Christianity never defeated paganism. Instead, paganism, after the fall of Rome, was driven underground. . . . *Postmodernism* is a big fancy word for nothing. It is so *passé*. Let's get past Beckett's *Waiting for Godot*. . . . Most of the women in academe who pretend to be feminists are not. They do not know the history of feminism. . . . My feminism predates the feminism of Gloria Steinem. I go way back. . . . It's not male hatred of women, but male fear of woman that is the great universal. . . .
>
> I have a peculiar way of looking at things, through male eyes. It's probably because of my bisexual experience. Many of the things I'm saying are obvious, but feminism is so stuck behind its own blinders. One of the worst of these is to constantly see misogyny everywhere. I'm called a misogynist! Does that make any sense? Someone who's an open lesbian, who's written on Madonna and Diana and Elizabeth Taylor and Jackie Kennedy Onassis? I'm constantly writing evocatively of women. . . .

{E; *Free Inquiry*, Spring 1995}

Pahl, Stewart V. (20th Century)

During the 1960s, Pahl was a director of the American Humanist Association. He wrote *Humanism is Now!* (1972).

PAIN

• Pain: the essential ingredient of art.

–Allen Windsor

(See entries for Evil and Iago.)

Paine, Robert Treat (1731–1814)

Paine, one of the signers of the Declaration of Independence, was a member of the Continental Congress (1774–1778), eventually becoming attorney general of Massachusetts and then (1790–1804) the state's supreme court justice. Paine was active in his later years as a Unitarian. {EG}

Paine, Thomas (1737–1809)

Paine was a major American revolutionary and one of the country's inspiring founders. Paine's father was a Quaker and a staymaker (who manufactured women's undergarments). He attended the local grammar school in Thetford, England, where, Paine recalled, "it was my good fortune to have an exceedingly good moral education, and a tolerable stock of learning."

Just before arriving in America, he was felled by typhus and had to be carried off the ship on a stretcher, but he lived to fight against despotism and become one of the country's best-known defenders. He infuriated Thetford citizens with his advocacy during the French Revolution of an invasion of Britain by France. However, Thetford today sports a statue by Sir Charles Wheeler of its famous citizen.

Wheeler, approving of Paine's views, wrote that *Common Sense* (1776) advocated absolute independence for America and "did more than anything else to precipitate the great events of that year. Each number of the *Crisis*, which appeared during the war, was read by Washington's order to each regiment in the service. Paine subscribed largely to the army and served for a short time himself."

Paine in 1787 went to London to sell his invention of an iron bridge. His *Rights of Man* (1791–1792), written as a reply to Edmund Burke's *Reflections on the Revolution in France*, brought him a sentence of outlawry because it was a defense of the French Revolution. Paine then fled to Paris where, although he could not speak French, he was elected a member of the Convention. When he protested against the execution of King Louis XVI and the Terror, however, he was imprisoned for nearly a year and narrowly escaped the guillotine. While in jail, he wrote his deistic *Age of Reason* (1793–1794), a powerful attack on Christianity and the Bible.

In *Age of Reason*, he wrote, "The idea man can affix to the name of God is that of a first cause of all things," a concept basic to his belief in deism. Son of Quaker parents, he was called "a man steeped in sin" and a "hater of Christ" by his enemies, but his "Common Sense" still appeals to contemporary rationalists interested in deism. Morrell in the *Encyclopedia of Unbelief* details Paine's religious views: Paine held Jesus in high regard. He disbelieved in revealed religion, believing instead in that which makes common sense and is in accord with science. Revealed religion, he reasoned, was harmful and needed to be rejected. His deism postulated a God that had created everything but then had left mankind to get on with things themselves. Not only refuting the divinity of Christ, he said of the four gospels, "It is, I believe, impossible to find so many and such glaring absurdities, contradictions, and falsehoods as are in these books." In England, notes Robertson, Paine's views were much discussed. Paine was instrumental in "laying deep and wide the English foundations of a new democratic freethought; and the upper-class reaction in the nature of the case was doomed to impermanency, though it was to arrest English intellectual progress for over a generation. The French Revolution had re-introduced freethought as a vital issue, even in causing it to be banned as a danger."

"I do not believe," he wrote in *The Age of Reason*, "in the creed professed by the Jewish church, by the Roman church, by the Greek church, by the Turkish church, by the Protestant church, nor by any church that I know of. . . . Each of those churches accuse the other of unbelief; and for my own part, I disbelieve them all." He further elaborated: "All national institutions of churches, whether Jewish, Christian, or Turkish, appear to me no other than human inventions, set up to terrify and enslave mankind and monopolize power and profit."

In 1797, Paine founded in Paris the little "Church of Theo-philanthropy," beginning his inaugural discourse with these words: "Religion has two principal enemies, Fanaticism and Infidelity, or that which is called atheism. The first requires to be combated by reason and morality; the other by natural philosophy." Paine was no scholar. As a result, and because champions of the "religion of Galilee" enjoy disparaging any unlearned person who meddles with religion, Paine was considered an antagonist. However, his astute Biblical criticism jarred them, and his approach became a forerunner of later scholastic research. Robertson laments the fact that Paine "lived to find himself shunned and vilified, in the name of religion, in the country whose freedom he had so puissantly wrought to win." He received sympathy and fair play, ironically, "only from the atheists whom he distrusted and opposed, or from thinkers who no longer hold by deism." Robertson adds, "There is reason to think that in his last years the deistic optimism which survived the deep disappointments of the French Revolution began to give way before deeper reflection on the cosmic problem [citing Conway's *Life of Paine*], if not before the treatment he had undergone at the hands of Unitarians and Trinitarians alike."

Paine's *Discourse to the Society of Theo-philanthropists* (1798), Berman found, discredits atheism and is clearly deistic. However, President Theodore Roosevelt in an illogical outburst mistakenly called Paine a "filthy little atheist." Paine was clearly not an atheist; he was a deist, believing in a God of moral truth, a Supreme Architect of the universe who had no further control over his creation and to whom petitionary prayers are redundant. "I believe," he wrote, "that God is too good to kill his son when he couldn't revenge himself in any other way, and also too mighty to be under any necessity of doing it. Any system of religion that has anything in it which shakes the mind of a child cannot be a true religion or system. . . . I do not believe in the creeds of any other church; my own mind is my own church." He also wrote, "I believe in one God and no more: and I hope for happiness beyond this life."

In England, his effigy was burned, as were his books, and he was attacked in print by Bishop Richard Watson of Llandaff, among others. In 1802 he returned to America, where his views on religion and his opposition to Washington made him unpopular. His last years were saddened by ill health and neglect. In 1806, William Carver found him in such a bad state that he scrubbed Paine from head to toe: three times. Carver also cut his nails, some of which had grown around his toes "nearly as far under they extended on top," and shaved him and cut his hair. Carver for five months took him to his own home but, after five months, found Paine was "not house-trained" and sometimes drank as much as a quart of brandy at a sitting. Meanwhile, Paine never earned money from his publications, requesting, for example, that the money be given to buy mittens for American soldiers. When Paine demanded something for his "selfless" services, the State of New York gave him a 300-acre farm at New Rochelle and the Pennsylvania Assembly and the Continental Congress gave him some cash grants. But Paine was not a good manager, was always in need, and was attacked by Americans who believed his *Age of Reason* was anti-Christian, although in fact the tract affirmed Paine's deism and his belief in an afterlife. Paine, unlike the other Founding Fathers, was regarded as one with "no connections" but one who made the others uneasy because he wrote for ordinary people and his fiery language was easily able to stir them up.

Two early works about him, better than most which have followed, are Crane Brinton's bibliographical essay in *The Dictionary of American Biography* (1934) and Eric Foner's *Tom Paine and Revolutionary America* (1976). They point out that Paine, who had participated in the major American and French revolutions, favored revolutions elsewhere. Although other revolutionaries had worked in their own countries, Paine favored Toussaint L'Ourverture's black republic of revolutionary Haiti.

Jack Fruchtman Jr., in *Thomas Paine: Apostle of Freedom*, tells of Paine's view on miracles: "The story of the whale swallowing Jonah, though a whale is large enough to do it, borders greatly on the marvelous but it would have approached nearer to the idea of a miracle if Jonah had swallowed the whale." And which is more probable, Paine asked, "that a man should have swallowed a whale or told a lie?" Fruchtman repeats the story that "no one could stand to be in the same room with Paine for very long," because he was unclean and had "the brimstone odour." John Keane, however, takes exception to Fruchtman's describing Paine as "something of a country bumpkin," saying that Paine "found himself in familiar company. The men and women who attended the lectures of Ferguson and Martin were mainly self-educated shopkeepers and artisans, many of whom leaned towards unorthodox religious views, and religious Dissenters, with strong leanings towards political radicalism. . . . These audiences were decidedly modern in outlook."

In 1995, John Keane in *Tom Paine*, estimated to be the fiftieth biography of the pamphleteer, wrote how—when forty-four and part of an American mission to France—Paine was described by an interpreter as of "dirty appearance and brimstone odor," so smelly that he needed very hot water (*bien bouiilli*) to be bathed of his stench. Others have commented that Franklin was frequently unwashed and unshaven.

Although said to have been the first to call his country the United States of America, he was only one of the first, having written the phrase on 13 January 1777. On 21 June 1776 Thomas Jefferson asked Benjamin Franklin to review his draft of "A Declaration by the Representiaves on the United States of America." John Dickinson on 17 June 1776 in a draft of some articles of confederation used "the United States of America." Linguist William Safire concludes that eighteen on three committees, including Roger Sherman, were aware of the phrase but that Jefferson usually is credited. Paine was a popularizer of the phrase, not the coiner.

Biographer David Freeman Hawke compiled an extensive bibliography of Paine's works, one which, however, has been criticized by Keane. Hawke described Paine's final days. Although in great pain, he had a sense of humor and his mind was clear. His doctor referred one day to his distended abdomen saying, "Your belly diminishes." "And yours augments," replied Paine.

Paine's last years were full of pain, caused by an abscess in the side, which was brought on by his imprisonment in Paris. He expired, after intense suffering, on June 8, 1809, placidly and without a struggle. Pious visitors hoping to "save his immortal soul from the wrath of God," however, disturbed even his last hours. Foote supplies some examples:

> • One afternoon a very old lady, dressed in a large scarlet-hooded cloak, knocked at the door and inquired for Thomas Paine. Mr. Jarvis, with whom Mr. Paine resided, told her he was asleep. "I am very sorry," she said, "for that, for I want to see him particularly." Thinking it a pity to make an old woman call twice, Mr. Jarvis took her into Mr. Paine's bedroom and awoke him. He rose upon one elbow; then, with an expression of eye that made the old woman stagger back a step or two, he asked, "What do you want?" "Is your name Paine?" "Yes." "Well, then, I come from Almighty God to tell you, that if you do not repent of your sins, and believe in our blessed Savior Jesus Christ, you will be damned and . . . ." "Poh, poh, it is not true; you were not sent with any such impertinent message: Jarvis make her go away. Pshaw! he would not send such a foolish old woman about his messages; go away, go back, shut the door."
>
> • Two weeks before his death, his conversion was attempted by two Christian ministers, the Rev. Mr. Milledollar and the Rev. Mr. Cunningham. The latter said, "Mr. Paine, we visit you as friends and neighbors; you have now a full view of death, you cannot live long, and whoever does not believe in Jesus Christ will assuredly be damned." "Let me," said Mr. Paine, "have none of your popish stuff; get away with you, good morning, good morning." The Rev. Mr. Milledollar attempted to address him, but he was interrupted in the same language. When they were gone he said to Mrs. Heddon, his housekeeper, "Do not let them come here again; they intrude upon me." They soon renewed their visit, but Mrs. Heddon told them they could not be admitted, and that she thought the attempt useless, for if God did not change his mind, she was sure no human power could.
>
> • Another of these busybodies was the Rev. Mr. Hargrove, a Swedenborgian or New Jerusalemite minister. This gentleman told Paine that his sect had found the key for interpreting the Scriptures, which had been lost for four thousand years. "Then," said Paine, "it must have been very rusty."
>
> • Even his medical attendant did not scruple to assist in this pious enterprise. Dr. Manley's letter to Cheetham, one of Paine's biographers, says that he visited the dying skeptic at midnight, June 5–6, two days before he expired. After tormenting him with many questions, to which he made no answer, Dr. Manley proceeded as follows: "Mr. Paine, you have not answered my questions; will you answer them? Allow me to ask again, do you believe, or—let me qualify the question—do you wish to believe that Jesus Christ is the Son of God?" After a pause of some minutes he answered, "I have no wish to believe on that subject." I then left him, and know not whether he afterwards spoke to any person on the subject. Sherwin confirms this statement. He prints a letter from Mr. Clark, who spoke to Dr. Manley on the subject. "I asked him plainly," said Mr. Clark. "Did Mr. Paine recant his religious sentiments? I would thank you for an explicit answer, sir." He said, "No, he did not."
>
> • Mr. Willet Hicks, a Quaker gentleman who frequently called on Paine in his last illness, as a friend and not as a soul-snatcher, bears similar testimony. "In some serious conversation I had with him a short time before his death," declared Mr. Hicks, "he said his sentiments respecting the Christian religion were precisely the same as they were when he wrote *The Age of Reason*."
>
> • Cheetham, who was compelled to apologize for libeling Paine during his life, confirmed that Paine "died as he had lived, an enemy to the Christian religion."

Meanwhile, children in Sunday schools were told what was published by the Religious Tract Society, that Paine had recanted. According to William Cobbett, the source of the mischief was Mary Hinsdale, who had formerly been a servant to Mr. Willet Hicks. This gentleman sent Paine many little delicacies in his last illness, and Mary Hinsdale had conveyed them. According to her story, Paine made a recantation in her presence and assured her that if ever the Devil had an agent on earth, he who wrote *The Age of Reason* was undoubtedly that person. When Hinsdale was hunted out by Cobbett, however, "she shuffled, she evaded, she affected not to understand," and finally said she had "no recollection of any person or thing she saw at Thomas Paine's house."

One of Paine's intimate friends, Colonel Fellows, was met by Walt Whitman, the American poet, soon after 1840 in New York. Whitman became well acquainted with the Colonel, who was then about seventy-eight years of age, and described him as "a remarkably fine old man." From conversations with him, Whitman became convinced that Paine had been greatly calumniated in respect to his views. Thirty-five years later, addressing a meeting at Lincoln Hall, Philadelphia, on Sunday, 28 January 1887, the democratic poet said, "Thomas Paine had a noble personality, as exhibited in presence, face, voice, dress, manner, and what may be called his atmosphere and magnetism, especially the later years of his life. I am sure of it. Of the foul and foolish fictions yet told about the circumstances of his decease, the absolute fact is that as he lived a good life, after its kind, he died calmly and philosophically, as became him."

Upon his death, Paine was refused interment in a Quaker cemetery and was buried in a plot on a New Rochelle, New York, farm given him by New York State to reward him for his Revolutionary writings. Few people attended the funeral of the person who was the first to use the expression, "the religion of humanity," Morrell reports. And of these "none represented the U.S. government. Ten years later William Cobbett removed Paine's remains and took them to England, but their whereabouts are unknown." His death mask, however, is on display at the public library in Thetford, England. (See entries for John Keane, author; Brian McCartin, administrator of the Thomas Paine Memorial Museum; and Reason Street. Also, see entry for Extraterrestrial Life, for Paine was one of the first in Colonial America to extrapolate about the subject.) {BDF; CE; CL; ER; EU, Robert W. Morrell; FUK; FUS; HAB; HNS2; JM; OEL; PA; RAT; RE; William Safire, *The New York Times Magazine*, 5 July 1998; TSV; TYD; UU; VI; TRI}

Painlevé, Paul (1863–1933)

Painlevé was professor of general mathematics at Paris University. Few Frenchmen of his time had so many national and international honors. He was an outspoken rationalist who supported the erection of a statue to Servetus. {RAT; RE}

Painter, Nell Irvin (20th Century)

Painter, a freethinker, wrote *The Narrative of Hosea Hudson: His Life as a Negro Communist in the South* (1979). Hudson, although a Communist, sang in his church choir and served as a deacon, but the work contains an account of theological conflicts in the black community in 1930s Birmingham. Many of the black "Reds" were Christians, but others were orthodox Marxist atheists. In 1996, Painter wrote *Sojourner Truth* 1996). {*Freethought History #14*, 1995}

PAKISTAN HUMANISTS

The founding father of Pakistan, M. A. Jinnah, according to Ian Buruma,

> a lawyer with fastidious Anglophile habits, was a secular man who ate ham—in private. He had no desire to found a religious state, let alone a theocratic state. He just didn't want to be dominated by Hindus. To him, the Congress Party of Gandhi and Nehru was inevitably a Hindu party, and a rather vulgar one at that, and since Congress would rule India, the only alternative was to create a separate, secular state for Muslims.

The other founding father, Sir Mohammed Iqbal, a convert of Kashmiri Brahmin stock, was a poet and an intellectual who, Buruma relates,

> . . . . made a speech in 1930 in which he promoted the ideal of an Islamic state in India. Naipul describes Iqbal's dream as a tribal one, a longing for a world that is "neatly parceled out, every tribe in his corner." It is indeed a dangerous dream, as we know from recent Balkan events where Muslims are the victims of orthodox Christian zealots.
>
> But Iqbal was a more complicated character than Naipaul makes him out to be. Nehru saw him as an exponent not of religious zealotry but of modern nationalism. His Urdu poetry was full of nationalist sentiments. Part of his vision of a Muslim state in India was a desire for Islam to "rid itself of the stamp that Arabian imperialism was forced to give it. . . . " Nehru observed [in *The Discovery of India*] that since "Indian nationalism was dominated by Hindus and had a Hinduised look . . . a conflict arose in the Moslem mind." In fact, Iqbal later seems to have changed his mind about the Muslim state, and came to believe that it would be harmful to India and Muslims too. According to Nehru, Iqbal turned to socialism in his last years, inspired by the splendid achievements of the Soviet Union.

In Pakistan, Dr. Yunis Shaikh has founded a group that holds public meetings about religion and women's rights. Called the Enlightenment, the group has lobbied the Government and Senators and MPs, criticizing the use of the Sharia law. The group has challenged Muslims to a debate, saying that they will change their minds if convinced and if the Muslims agree to do the same. Shaikh has not been attacked directly, but threats have been made against his parents and he has had to give up two jobs. E-mail: <pakhumanist@hotmail.com>.

Meanwhile, V. S. Naipaul, in *Beyond Belief: Islamic Excursions Among the Converted Peoples* (1998), is "enraged" by the fundamentalist Islam he has found in Pakistan and other predominantly Islamic countries. A Pakistani journalist, Asawal D. Sardar, has written a detailed criticism of the country's blesphemy law, finding it a pretext for persecution. (See Ibn Warraq's *Why I Am Not A Muslim*.) {*International Humanist News*, December 1998; M. A. Jinnah, *In the Empire of Islam, The New York Review of Books*, 16 July 1998; Asawal D. Sardar, The International Association for Religious Freedom: <iarfna@nywork2.undp.org>.}

PAKISTAN UNITARIANS

In 1991 Indirius Dominic Bhatti discovered Unitarianism in a dictionary of religions. The definition described his own religious ideas, and he told others as well as organized the Unitarian Universalist Christians of Pakistan (UUP). In 1994 UUP became a member of the Unitarian Universalist Association.

UUP's aims and objectives are

- to promote justice, peace, human dignity, and social development;
- to mobilize communities against cruelty/ies and slavery/ies of all sorts;
- to prepare people to get social, administering therapy to the socio-religiously confused and disturbed;
- to work for social, economic, educational, environmen tal, cultural, and religious uplifting;
- to offer a form of religious liberalism and social justice to demoralized people.

The Unitarian Universalist Christians of Pakistan have sold land in Lahore to build a church for its 100 members. The group can be reached by contacting Indirius Dominic Bhatti, PO Box 6127, Lahore Cantt, Pakistan. On the Web: <http://www.uua.org/icuu/icuu-asia.html>.

Pal, R. M. (20th Century)

Pal spoke at the 1998 congress of the International Humanist and Ethical Union that was held in Mumbai. He stated that the religious division of the partition of India had as a goal to end communal problems, but India today is faced with majority communalism, not minority communalism. Pal holds that it is a myth that India has a tradition of tolerance. There has been flexibility and pluralism, but not real tolerance. He wrote "Fascism and Its Continuing Appeal" for *Radical Humanist* (June 1999). {*International Humanist News*, December 1998}

Paleario, Aonio (c. 1500–1570)

Paleario was an Italian humanist and martyr. In 1520 he went to Rome and took his place among the brilliant men of letters of the court of Leo X. After the taking of Rome by Charles V, he retired to Sienna. In 1536 he published at Lyons an elegant poem on the mortality of the soul, one modeled on Lucretius.

While a professor of eloquence at Milan, he was accused of heresy. He had called the Inquisition a poignard directed against all men of letters. On 3 July 1570, he was hanged by religious authorities, who then threw his body into flames. {BDF}

PALEONTOLOGY

Paleontology, the study of early beings, is of the utmost importance to freethinkers who develop their philosophical outlook. Basically a science of the life of past geologic periods based on fossil remains, it is closer to geology than to biology. This is so because the environment of animals and plants cannot be understood and reconstructed without knowledge of the age, structure, and composition of the rocks in which their remains are found.

Paleontology can be subdivided into paleobotany (the study of ancient plants, also called paleophytology); palynology (the study of ancient spores, pollen, and microorganisms); and paleozoology (the study of ancient animals, which includes the invertebrate such as clams and the vertebrate such as dinosaurs.

Richard Fortey's *Life* (1998) is a paleontological study of what else besides dinosaurs has occupied the earth in the last four billion years. Less than one percent of all the species that ever lived are known to us through fossils, he explains. As to why dinosaurs disappeared, Fortey discusses Stephen Jay Gould's conclusions about the creatures of the Burgess Shale, which Gould felt died without issue and illustrated the blind and random pruning of an earlier and vastly more diverse world. Fortey, however, notes that the Burgess Shale animals are now believed to be forerunners of existing species which, as pointed out by ecologist Jerry A. Coyne, undermines "Gould's claim that if evolution were replayed, the vagaries of chance would populate the modern world with creatures substantially different from those we know."

In 1999 paleontologists reported in *Science* (23 April 1999) that a team, headed by Dr. Berhane Asfaw in Ethiopia, had named a newly found species Australopithecus garhi (the latter word meaning "surprise" in the language spoken by the Afar people). "This species is descended from Australopithecus afarensis and is a candidate ancestor for early Homo," the scientists stated. Characteristics of the skull, teeth, and limb bones seemed to mark the species as a descendant of A. afarensis, which lived from 3.7 million to 3 million years ago and are represented by the "Lucy" skeleton from Ethiopia. Even earlier species of australopithecines, found in Kenya, have been dated back to 4.2 million years. The hominids are thought to have split from the ape lineages more than 5 million years ago. (See entries for Stephen Jay Gould and Lucy.) {CE; *The New York Times Book Review*, 12 April 1998; John Noble Wilford, *The New York Times*, 23 April 1999}

Palevitz, Barry A. (20th Century)

A professor in the botany department at the University of Georgia in Athens, Georgia, Palevitz in "Science and the Versus of Religion" (*Skeptical Inquirer*, July-August 1999) warns that science and religion are different spheres, that "religion and science are equally valid *at what they do individually, but not in each other's sphere*." He resents the implication "that scientists have no spiritual dimension," citing how awed he becomes when snorkeling on a coral reef, "humbled by a crisp December night full of stars, forever amazed by a dividing cell, and inspired by human creativity."

Palfrey, John Gorham (Born 1796)

Palfrey, a Unitarian minister, was a politician, writer, and 18th century theologian.

Palfrey, Sarah Hammond (1823-1914)

The daughter of John Palfrey, Sarah was a Unitarian and an author.

Palladas (Ancient Greece)

Palladas wrote humanistically . . . but not for feminists:

- To the man who has married an ugly wife
  Lamp-light's an even deeper darkness.

- Only twice is womankind
  Anything but an affliction:
  [1] in bride-bed
  &
  [2] in the grave.

- Praise, of course, is best:
  plain speech breeds hate.
  But ah the Attic honey
  Of telling a man exactly what you think of him!
- In silence walk your wretched span; in silence
  Be like Time, that passes silently.
  And live unheeded:
  You shall be so, once dead.

(Translation by Dudley Fitts found in *Poems from the Greek Anthology*)

Paley, William (1743–1805)

Paley, an English theologian, wrote *Horae Paulinae* (1790) to prove that the New Testament is not "a cunningly devised fable." He believed that all living things were created by "a divine watchmaker," a viewpoint which Darwin later showed was erroneous. {CE}

Pallas, Peter Simon (1741–1811)

Pallas was a German naturalist and traveler. Invited by Catherine II to become professor of natural history at St. Petersburg, he traveled through Siberia and settled in the Crimea. In 1769 he was a member of an expedition to observe the transit of Venus, and until 1774 he explored the upper Amur, the Caspian Sea, and the Ural and Atlas mountains, collecting valuable specimens in natural history. In 1810 he returned to Berlin, where he died. Lalande spoke highly of him, and Cuvier considered him the founder of modern geology. A rationalist, he was equally distinguished in geology, zoology, and anthropology. {BDF; CE; RAT}

Pallavicino, Ferrante (1616–1644)

Pallavicino was an Italian poet and wit. He was a canon of the Lateran congregation, but for composing some satirical pieces against Pope Urban VIII he had a price set on his head. Fleeing to Venice, he was betrayed by a false friend, and the Inquisition had Pallavicino beheaded at Avignon on 5 March 1644. {BDF}

Palmaer, Bernhard Henrik (1801–1854)

Palmaer was a Swedish satirist, the author of *The Last Judgment in the Crow Corner*. {BDF}

Palmen, Ernst [Baron] (1849–1919)

Palmen was a Finnish historian, a professor of history at Helsingfors University. A monist and atheist, he strongly supported Haeckel, whom he hailed as "a second Prometheus" who was "like every bringer of truth and light." {RAT; RE}

Palmer, Charles (20th Century)

Palmer is associated with the Atheist League of the State of Washington. (See entry for Washington Atheists, Humanists.) {FD}

Palmer, Courtlandt (1843–1888)

An American reformer, Palmer had been brought up in the Dutch Reformed Church but became a freethinker while young. In 1880 he established and became president of the Nineteenth Century Club, dedicated to the utmost liberty of public discussion. Among its members was Colonel Robert G. Ingersoll. He contributed to the *Freethinker's Magazine*, *Truthseeker*, and other journals.

After bidding the members of his family an affectionate farewell, Palmer, aware that he was dying, said: "The general impression is that Freethinkers are afraid of death. I want you one and all to tell the whole world that you have seen a Freethinker die without the least fear of what the hereafter may be." Upon his death, Colonel Ingersoll delivered the eulogium. Mrs. Palmer did not share her husband's agnosticism. She felt some liberal Christian minister should say a few words over her husband's corpse and, out of tenderness to her feelings, Ingersoll consented to the proposal. The Rev. R. H. Newton then spoke, refraining from any pious allusions to the dead agnostic and confining his words entirely to Palmer's character. {BDF; FUS; RAT; RE}

Palmer, Edwina (1904-1999)

Palmer joined the South Place Ethical Society in 1927 and was one of its most active workers. At the time of her death, she had been a member of the Rationalist Press Association for thirty years. {*New Humanist*, March 1999}

Palmer, Elihu (1764–1806)

During the time of Paine and Jefferson, Palmer was the most notorious of the militant American freethinkers. According to Roderick S. French, Palmer was of a philosophic mind and carried his scientific rationalism beyond deism, becoming, "one of the first tentative voices of philosophic naturalism in America. His views were unified by the anthropology of his confident humanism. His thought and work were inspired by the conviction that the powers of man are competent to all the great purposes of human existence.' " Palmer was blind from an attack of yellow fever, yet he initiated organized unbelief in the U.S. by founding a deistic society in New York in 1796, leading it until his death in 1806. He dictated to a secretary his *Principles of Nature* (1802) and "The Immoral Teachings of Jesus," the latter of which is found in Gaskin's *Varieties of Unbelief: From Epicurus to Sartre* (1989). "The crimes of ecclesiastical despots," he cried, "are still corroding upon the very vitals of human society." {BDF; EU, Roderick S. French and Gordon Stein; *Freethought History #9*, 1994; FUK; FUS; JM; RAT; TYD}

Palmer, Harold (20th Century)

Palmer in 1995 was elected co-president of the Northeast Atheist Association.

Palmer, John (20th Century)

In 1995, Palmer was elected treasurer of the Northeast Atheist Association.

Palmer, William Scott (20th Century)

Palmer, a freethinker, wrote *An Agnostic's Progress* (1905). {GS}

Palmerston, Henry John [Viscount] (1784–1865)

Palmerston was a British statesman. His viscountcy, to which he succeeded in 1802, was in the Irish peerage and therefore did not prevent him from entering the House of Commons in 1807. Initially a Tory, he served (1809–1818) as secretary of war but then joined the Whig government as foreign minister.

A firm believer in liberal constitutionalism, Palmerston was instrumental in securing the independence of Belgium (1830–1831), and in 1834 he formed a quadruple alliance with France, Spain, and Portugal to help the Iberian countries put down rebellions aimed at restoring absolutist rule. Viscount Palmerston vigorously prosecuted the Crimean War, facilitated the unification of Italy, and suppressed the Indian Mutiny.

Although his diplomacy has been described as having been reckless, it did advance British prestige. McCabe says Palmerston was either a skeptic or an atheist and that Morley in his *Life of Gladstone* wrote of Palmerston, "The Church in all its denominations was on terms of cool and reciprocated indifference with one who was above all else the man of the world." {CE; JM; RAT; RE}

Panaetius (Died 111 B.C.E.)

Panaetius was a Stoic philosopher, a pupil of Diogenes and perhaps of Carneades. About 150 B.C.E. he visited Rome and taught a moderate stoicism, denying the doctrine of the conflagration of the world, and placing physics before dialectics. Panaetius wrote *On Duties*, to which Cicero expressed his indebtedness in his *De Officiis*. {BDF}

Pancholi, N. D. (20th Century)

At the 1998 congress of the International Humanist and Ethical Union in Mumbai, Pancholi talked about religious separatism and terrorism in Kashmir. The movement for separation in Kashmir, he reported, is not primarily a religious movement but is one for democratic rights that many feel have been denied. {*International Humanist News*, December 1998}

Pancoucke, Charles Joseph (1736–1798)

An eminent French publisher, Pancoucke was acquainted with d'Alembert, Garat, and others, and was a correspondent of Rousseau, Buffon, and Voltaire, whose works he brought out. Pancoucke translated Lucretius in 1768, brought out the *Mercure de France*, projected in 1781 the *Encyclopédie Méthodique* (of which there are 106 volumes), and founded the *Moniteur* (1789). {BDF; RAT}

PANENTHEISM: See entry for Charles Hartshorne.

Panizza, Mario (19th Century)

Panizza was an Italian physiologist and philosopher. He wrote a materialist work, *The Philosophy of the Nervous System* (1887). Panizza rejected the idea of a spiritual soul. His *Anniversario del supplizio di Giordano Bruno* (1890) was a eulogy of Bruno, whom he admired. {BDF; RAT}

Pankhurst, Richard (1839–1898)

Pankhurst was a radical skeptic and feminist. He drafted the 1882 Married Women's Property Act, which gave the wife the right to her own property which, previously, had passed into the absolute control of the husband. {TRI}

Pankhurst, Sylvia P. (20th Century)

In 1920 Pankhurst called her Worker's Socialist Federation the Communist Party. It was the first Marxist use of "communism" in England. {TRI}

Pannill, H. Burrell (20th Century)

Pannill wrote *The Religion of John Fiske* (1957). {FUS}

Panosch, Martin (20th Century)

Panosch, of the Austrian *Freidenkerbund Oesterreichs*, was a participant in 1996 of the humanist conference in Mexico City. His e-mail: <mpan@fc.alpin.or.at>.

Pantano, Eduardo (19th Century)

An Italian author, Pantano wrote a book on the Sicilian Vespers and the Commune (1882). {BDF}

PANTHEISM

• Pantheism, n. The doctrine that everything is God, in contradistinction to the doctrine that God is everything.

–Ambrose Bierce
The Devil's Dictionary

Pantheism identifies the universe with God or God with the Universe. John Toland in the 18th century used it, although ancient thinkers also had ideas of "God is all, and all is God." Xenophan, the ancient Hindus, the Stoics, Erigena, Eckhart, Boehme, Bruno, Fichte, Schelling, Hegel, Schleiermacher, W. P. Montague, Alfred North Whitehead—all were interested in the concept and devised different interpretations of its meaning.

McCabe defined pantheism as "any theory that admits the existence of a God but denies that he is distinct from nature. The word (literally meaning 'the All is God') was introduced in the eighteenth century but covers a great variety of philosophies, from ancient Brahmanism or the theories of the Eleatic School in Greece to those of Spinoza, Goethe, Schelling, etc." He adds that "It was a natural reaction against the old idea of a God or gods creating the world and then working miracles and giving relations to improve the work they had performed; but the nature of the union of God and the world, the spiritual and material, the infinite and the finite, etc., could not be contemplated in exact thought, and the system was more apt to appeal to poets."

A contemporary who thinks of the totality of all the galaxies and all within that known and unknown space as being the Ultimate, a kind of super-Mother Nature, might label herself or himself as a pantheist. Particularly, adds a Manhattan wag, when viewing a beautiful sunrise or sunset.

A United Kingdom web page about pantheism is at <http://members.aol.com/Heraklit1/index.htm>.

A compact disk, "Song of the Pantheist" with words by Judson M. Savage and music by freethinker Warren Allen Smith, was once available from Box 10-D, 31 Jane Street, New York, NY 10014. (See entries for Charles Hartshorne, Minot Savage, and John Toland. Also, see Alasdair Mac Intyre's article on pantheism in the *Encyclopedia of Philosophy*, Vol. 6.) {CE, ER}

PANTHEON

Originally, the pantheon was a temple to all gods. The Pantheon in Rome (built in 27 B.C.E., destroyed, and rebuilt in the 2nd Century by Hadrian) was made of brick with a large hemispherical dome. In 609 it became a Christian church.

In Paris the Panthéon, which was designed by J. G. Soufflot, was built between 1764 and 1781. Several times secularized and reconsecrated, it became a national mausoleum. Among the early honorees were François Voltaire and Jean-Jacques Rousseau. Also honored are authors Victor Hugo and Emile Zola; resistance hero Jean Moulin; and Louis Braille, who invented the reading system for the blind. The 70th and 71st people whose remains were enshrined in the Panthéon, in 1995, were Marie and Pierre Curie. {CE}

Papa, Stephan (20th Century)

Papa, a Unitarian, wrote *The Last Man Jailed for Blasphemy* (1998). He tells the story of Universalist minister Abner Kneeland, who became infamous by the 1830s for his outspoken and, for the times, unorthodox public writings and views on religion. (*World*, July-August 1999)

PAPACY: For a caustic critique, see Joseph McCabe's *A Rationalist Encyclopedia*.

PAPAL BULL

A papal bull is the Vatican's mascot, or so freethinkers assume.

Papillon, J. Henry Fernand (1847–1873)

Papillon was a French philosophic writer who wrote *An Introduction to Chemical Philosophy* (1865). He contributed to the *Revue de Philosophie Positive* and the *Revue des Deux Mondes*. His principle work was *Nature and Life* (1873). Although he leaned to a rationalism of the spiritual kind in his later years, he never embraced Christianity. {BDF; RAT}

Papp, Gabor (20th Century)

Papp is leader of the Hungarian humanist organization, *Magyar Humanista Egyesulet*. The association has held seminars about philosophical and theoretical problems of abortion and euthanasia. Papp edits a 440-year-old ethical monthly magazine that regularly represents humanist values and reprints articles from international and national magazines.

Paps, George (20th Century)

In the 1950s, Paps was a director of the American Humanist Association.

Paquet, Henri Remi René (Born 1845)

Paquet was a French writer who, after studying under the Jesuits, went to Paris, became an advocate, but devoted his attention to literature. Under the anagram of "Nérée Quépat," he published *La Lorgnette Philosophique* (1872), a dictionary of the great and little philosophers of the time. He also wrote a study of La Mettrie entitled *Materialist Philosophy in the Eighteenth Century*. {BDF; RAT}

PARADISE

For Christians, paradise is a state of pure happiness, which is associated with the Garden of Eden and with Heaven. The word has a pagan (Zoroastrian) rather than Judeo-Christian source: *pairi-daëza* is a garden, an enclosed park, a paradise in the Avestan view.

For non-theists, paradise is more apt to be associated with a pleasant place or state of ideal beauty, like one's bed on a sleepy Sunday morning and afternoon.

PARADOX: See entry for Logical Paradoxes.

PARAGUAYAN FREETHOUGHT

Augusto Roa Bastos, who was born in 1917, a prominent author in Paraguay. He is one of the few there to express himself in non-supernaturalistic terms.

Forced because of his democratic views to live in exile in France for forty years, he was able at last to return in 1997. Twice during his long exile he had reentered the country secretly, and both times he was expelled for being a dangerous agitator who preached subversion. This was because Roa Bastos had written a surreal portrait of a paranoid dictator, *I, The Supreme*.

Asked for his views by a reporter, he lamented that Paraguay is not yet a democracy, that it "is still a 19th-century country, not having advanced much in its culture. It continues to be an island surrounded by land." The less educated peasants "know me as a myth," he found, "created by circumstances [of exile] rather than by my own action."

Asked about his early influences, he replied, "When I came from the countryside to Asunción, I lived in the house of a bishop, who was my uncle, where there were only church books, which of course I did not read, and the classics. I did read the classics. My uncle had a complete set of Flaubert, for example. The cultured priests, in those days, were censors and were charged with confiscating prohibited books. The first book I read in my life was *Don Quixote*, just because it was there."

"It is a fact," he observed when asked if writers are creative in order to be remembered even after they die, "that there is a progressive invasion of the shadow of death on the work of people who had very strong drives in their youth. They enter old age and become reactionary—this is the case with Octavio Paz. Now we can speak of him as a terminated case, a closed proceeding. All in all, I believe he was a really great poet."

And does he believe in God? Roa Bastos's response:

> The important thing is faith–and you have to have faith in someone or something–independent of the question of the existence of God. I condemn those who try to strip others of their faith: it is like extracting their inner force. There is a need to believe. I always resist the idea of a crusade to do away with the believers. I have always taken great care not to dispossess others of their faith. It may be the only wealth that they have.

By inference, then, Roa Bastos is a typical freethinker.

A Country Behind the Rain, which he is working on, will attempt "to look at societies from all parts of the world. When I sit down to write, I am surrounded by an unstoppable stream of memories of my wanderings through the world: a small village in India, in Venezuela, in Paraguay, or in Sicily. There are always two or three central themes, emerging from dreams and central obsessions." {Silvia Soler in *Búsqueda*, Montevideo, 7 May 1998; *World Press Review*, August 1998}

Paranjpye, Raghunath P. [Sir] (1876–1966)

The Indian Rationalist Association (IRA) was formed in Madras in December at a conference inaugurated by the late Sir Raghunath P. Paranjpye, who had been a founding member of the Rationalist Association of India and was an honorary associate of the Rationalist Press Association of London. He wrote *Religion on the Indian Problem* (1943). {FUK}

PARANORMAL

The paranormal, or supernatural, is that which is not scientifically explainable. Asked about the subject, philosopher Paul Kurtz, chairman of the Committee for the Scientific Investigation of Claims of the Paranormal (Box 703, Buffalo, New York 14226), remarked, "Far more exciting and constructive than the paranormal is astrophysics."

PARANORMAL HOAXES: See entry for Hoaxes, Paranormal.

PARAPRAXIS

Parapraxis is a Freudian term to describe a slip of the tongue that reveals a subconscious motive.

Paul Edwards gives the example of having attended a dull party and, leaving early, was told by the hostess, "Oh, it's so good of you to leave." She had meant to say "to have come."

Pardee, Caroline J. (1911–)

With Robert H. Jones, Pardee wrote *My Dear Carrie: The Civil War Letters of George K. Pardee and Family* (1994). An Ohio Unitarian, Pardee discovered in her attic the letters written by her grandfather to her grandmother while he served in the 42nd Ohio Volunteer Infantry during the Civil War.

Pardon, P. H. (20th Century)

Mlle. Pardon, in 1947, was elected as an honorary associate of the Rationalist Press Association.

Pare, William (1805–1873)

Pare was an Owenite social reformer. He wrote an abridgment of Thompson's *Distribution of Wealth*. Also, he wrote *Capital and Labor* (1854), *Cooperative Agriculture* (1870), and Vol 1 of the *Biography of Robert Owen*. {BDF; RAT}

Parfait, Noel (Born 1814)

Parfait was a French writer and politician. He took part in the revolution of 1830 and wrote many radical brochures. After the coup d'état he took refuge in Belgium. In 1871 Parfait was elected deputy and sat on the extreme left. {BDF}

PARICA

In Peru, Parica was considered to have been a god who flooded the earth. {LEE}

Parikh, G. D. (Deceased)

Parikh, who was the rector of Bombay University, produced the People's Economic Plan for the Indian Rationalist Humanist Association.

Parikh, Indumati (20th Century)

The president of the Radical Humanist Association of India and a physician Dr. Parikh signed Humanist Manifesto II. In 1988, the Council for Secular Humanism's International Academy of Humanism elected her a Humanist Laureate. She is internationally noted for the work she has done in a Bombay slum area by organizing clinics for family planning, maternal and child-care services, educational programs for women, and day nurseries. Her main goal, she says, is helping women to help themselves.

A signer of Humanist Manifesto II, she was married to Prof. Parikh who, before his death, wrote "People's Plan 1," a Radical Humanist contribution to the Economic Reconstruction of post-independent India. He had taught at Ruia College and was Rector of Bombay University.

At the Second International Humanist and Ethical Union World Congress held in London (1952) and also at the Tenth held in Buffalo, she addressed the gathering. In 1992 at the 40th Anniversary IHEU Congress in Amsterdam, she was presented with a Distinguished Humanist Service Award for "her unparalleled charitable services to the needy and ill in India, and her inspiring exemplification of the ideals of humanism." In a revealing interview by Levi Fragell, the Norwegian editor of *Human-Etisk*, Parikh was asked her views of Mother Teresa, the Nobel Peace Prize winner. She remained discreetly quiet, but Abe Solomon, president of the Indian Secular Society, said, "Mother Teresa has been a disaster for India." It was then that Dr. Parikh said, "Yes," that she agreed with Solomon's wisdom. This is because, in her words, "Contraception, information about sexual matters, abortion—the keys to some of the greatest social problems of our world–are regarded by mainstream religions as precipitating a shameful decline and lack of morality. They include not only Hindu and Muslim traditions but also the Christian churches who are supplying medical assistance to India. The Roman Catholic church is influential in this connection and has a very negative influence, perhaps fatal."

In 1994 her essay, "The Need for the Third World of Humanism," was included in *Challenges to the Enlightenment, Essays in Defense of Reason and Science.*

In 1996, she welcomed humanists to the M. N. Roy Memorial Development Campus and told about the launching of the South Asian Humanist Centre. "We need interdisciplinary research," she explained, "to discover our rational heritage; we have to launch a massive drive for non-formal education for our masses. . . . To my mind South Asian people are moving in a vicious circle of ignorance, poverty, primitive and ritual-ridden religious fundamentalism, fatalistic attitudes and population explosion. The result is the erosion of democratic and human values, which is leading us to authoritarian, bureaucratic power politics." Parikh signed Humanist Manifesto 2000.

On the Web: <mrcssc@bom2.vsnl.net.in>. (See entry for G. Vijayam.) {HM2}

Paris, Bruno Paulin Gaston (1839–1903)

Paris was a director of the *École des Hautes Études* and then professor of the French language and literature at the *Collège de France* (Paris University). In its obituary notice the *Athenaeum* described Paris as being "one of the most distinguished and most learned Frenchmen of modern times," a reference to his writing works on medieval literature. Paris shared Renan's views, as shown in his discourse on that writer and in his *Penseurs et poètes* (1896). {RAT; RE}

Paris, Erna (20th Century)

An award-winning journalist in Toronto, Paris has won six awards for feature writing and is the author of a variety of books: *Stepfamilies* (1984); *Unhealed Wounds: France and The Klaus Barbie Affair* (1985); and *The Garden and the Gun: A Journey Inside Israel* (1988). Her *The End of Days: A Story of Tolerance, Tyranny, and the Expulsion of the Jews from Spain* (1995) not only describes Spain during the Inquisition but also relates social upheavals in nineteenth and twentieth century France and Germany.

Paris, Matthew (of) (Died 1259)

Paris recorded that in 1249 a total of 443 heretics were burned in Saxony and Pomerania. Previously, multitudes had been burned by the Inquisitor Conrad, who was himself finally murdered in revenge. He was the confessor of Saint Elizabeth of Hungary, and he taught her among other things, "Be merciful to your neighbor" and "Do to others whatsoever you would they should do to you." His praises as recorded by Montalembert are cited by Robertson. Matthew of Paris was an English historian, a monk of St. Albans. {CE; JMRH}

Parisot, Jean Patrocle (17th Century)

Parisot was a Frenchman who wrote *La Foy devoilée par la raison (1681,* Faith Unveiled By Reason), a work whose title led it to be suppressed. {BDF}

Park, Charles Edwards (1873–1962)

Called by *Time* "the Grand Old Man of U.S. liberal pulpits," Park was minister of Boston's First Unitarian Church for forty years. In contrast to many of the currents of modernism and Humanism among Unitarians, Park preached a Christian message based on the religion of Jesus, preaching that the central quest of Christianity is to "know Christ in his human character, as a man among men." This was not a supernatural view, because Park attributed to Paul, not

Jesus, many of the supernatural elements of the Christian tradition. But for him Jesus was a teacher whose mysticism was "the key to the whole personality." As expected, others found his approach anything but liberal. {U&U}

Park, James (20th Century)

Park is the Humanist Campus Minister at the University of Minnesota. He participated in the 1996 discussion, "Is There Life After Death?", at the University of Minnesota campus.

Parke, David (20th Century)

Parke is author of *The Historical and Religious Antecedents of the New Beacon Series in Religious Education* (1978). He edited *The Epic of Unitarianism* (1957). {GS}

Parke, W. H. (19th Century)

Parke was a freethinker who wrote "Salvation Without Saviours—the Route of the Divinities" (1800?). {GS}

Parker, Dorothy (Rothchild) (1893–1967)

The witty Parker once wrote, "I went to a convent in New York and was fired finally for my insistence that the Immaculate Conception was a spontaneous combustion." She was drama critic for *Vanity Fair* (1916–1917) and book critic for *The New Yorker* (1927). Her *bons mots* were legendary:

- Men seldom make passes
  At girls that wear glasses.
- The affair between Margot Asquith and Margot Asquith will live as one of the prettiest love stories in all literature.
- Look at him, a rhinestone in the rough.
- His body has gone to his head.
- If all the girls in attendance (at the Yale prom) were laid end to end—I wouldn't be a bit surprised.
- I was the toast of two continents: Greenland and Australia.
- (Asked to use the word *horticulture*)
  You can lead a horticulture,
  but you can't make her think.
- (Told that Clare Boothe Luce was kind to her inferiors):
  And where does she find them?
- (Informed that President Calvin Coolidge was dead):
  How could they tell?
- (A 1933 review of "The Lake," starring Katharine Hepburn):
  Miss Hepburn runs the gamut of motions from A to B.
- (At a party): One more drink and I'll be under the host.
- All I want is a little room where I can lay my hat and a few friends.
- Brevity is the soul of lingerie.
- This is not a novel to be tossed aside lightly. It should be thrown with great force.
- "The House Beautiful" is the play lousy.
- Tonstant Weader fwowed up.
  (in a review of "The House at Pooh Corner")
- Salary is no object: I want only enough to keep body and soul apart.

Critic Brendan Gill calls her "a blatant homophobe." However, Parker is often cited for her humanistic sentiment:

The man she had was kind and clean
And well enough for every day,
But, oh, dear friends, you should have seen
The one that got away!

Parker, one of the better-known wits who were members of the Algonquin Round Table (Alexander Woollcott, Robert Benchley, Harpo Marx, Irving Berlin, George S. Kaufman were others), once described her bisexual husband and screenwriting partner, Alan Campbell, as "the wickedest woman in Paris." An alcoholic who was unhappy in several love affairs and who had three marriages, she made at least four attempts at suicide, once by swallowing a bottle of shoe polish. Not unsurprisingly, she suggested EXCUSE MY DUST as the epitaph for her gravestone.

Her final death "was anti-climactic and painfully lonely," Stephen M. Silverman wrote (*Where's There's a Will*, 1991). "She became a drunk in later years, and increasingly reclusive. She had settled into the Volney Hotel on Manhattan's East 74th Street, inhabited principally by widows and divorcees. . . . [One night] she got drunk with an old friend, returned home to the Volney, and telephoned the friend to say goodnight once more in a slurred and sentimental speech. They found her the next morning in a pile on the floor, C'est Tout [her dog] whimpering in a corner." She left an estate worth about $90,000 in 1990 dollars. After expenses, the remaining $20,000 was given to Dr. Martin Luther King Jr., which she had directed although they had never met. The money went to his organization, the NAACP, and within a year King was murdered.

Parker's will had stated that no service of any kind should be held, but Lillian Hellman took charge and 150 attended. Parker was cremated in a yellow satin gown that had been given to her by Gloria Vanderbilt. At Manhattan's Frank E. Campbell Chapel, where the body lay, Kate Mostel stayed overnight, saying she felt a body should not be left alone. Her husband, actor Zero Mostel, gave a eulogy, suggesting that the last thing Parker would have wanted was this formal ceremony. "If she had her way," he added to everyone's amusement, "I suspect she would not be here at all." Hellman's eulogy included "She was part of nothing and nobody except herself."

Afterwards it was found that Parker owed the Volney $385., a drug store $24., a newspaper delivery service $95., and the Internal Revenue Service $65. In her apartment was $350. worth of uncashed royalty checks, some of them seven years old. Also lying around was a $10,000 check from Hellman, which represented the sum obtained from selling a Picasso gouache Parker once had given Hellman and which she had sold upon hearing in 1965 that Parker was destitute.

Parker, according to Christopher Hitchens (*Vanity Fair*, October 1999), "had never been very affirmatively Jewish—she disliked her father's piety and always insisted that her hatred of Hitler and fascism was, so to say, secular." {CE}

Parker, Edward Harker (1849–1926)

When Parker returned from trade in China to study law in London, he was called to the bar but, instead, joined the Consular Service in China and Burma. In 1896 he was appointed reader in Chinese literature at Liverpool University College, and in 1901 professor at Manchester.

His works on China do not conceal his rationalism. "The Chinese intellect," he wrote in *Studies in Chinese Religion* (1910), "is quite robust enough to take care of itself, and it is not likely that it will ever surrender itself to the dogmatic teaching of any Christian sect." {RAT; RE}

Parker, Eva: See the entry for her husband, Robert G. Ingersoll.

Parker, John C. (19th Century)

Parker is author of an essay in *Prolegomena to the History of the Religion of Israel* (1878) in which he demonstrated the various human patterns of authorship in the Old Testament. {FD}

Parker, John C. (1926–)

When a teenager, Parker became convinced that he was the only Democrat and atheist in Vermont, then moved to Connecticut where he worked as a nurse's aide in a state mental hospital. In the late

1940s, he remembers, "I went to a dinner celebration sponsored by Charles Smith of *The Truth Seeker*, honoring Vashti McCollum—who was a real beauty. Woolsey Teller also spoke." Parker edits *The Northeast Atheist* (PO Box 63, Simsburg, Connecticut 06070. (WAS, 20 July 1997)

Parker, Theodore (1810–1860)

A Unitarian minister of note, Parker was brought up in poverty and who acquired a university education while laboring on the farm. A famed orator he was opposed to slavery (to the point of sheltering slaves in his own house), contributed to *The Dial*, and was a transcendentalist. His *Discourse on Matters Pertaining to Religion* was considered a "radical" viewpoint in 1842, and he agreed: *radix* is a word-root that describes getting down to the *roots* of matters. Not only did Parker deny miracles but also he introduced Unitarians to the new German scientific criticism of the Bible. He was an early example of the preacher who used his pulpit as a platform for constantly urging social reform. For him, most of the traditional supports of Christian belief such as the biblical miracles, the inspiration of the scriptures, and the divinity of Jesus were *transient* rather than permanent and necessary parts of religion. Such an outlook made him a rebel, an iconoclast, among fellow Unitarians, and "Parkerism" became a shorthand phrase for modernist and reformist stances within Unitarianism. Parker, who bequeathed his library of 13,000 volumes to the Boston Public Library, is described in Edward J. Renehan Jr.'s *The Secret Six* (1995) as one of the men who conspired with John Brown. (See entry for Frances Power Cobbe.) {BDF; CE; ER; EU, Paul H. Beattie; FUS; JMR; JMRH; U; U&U; UU}

Parkman, Francis Sr. (Born 1788)

Parkman, a Unitarian minister, was a teacher and writer. He was pastor of the New North Church in Boston. {U}

Parkman, Francis (1823–1893)

Parkman, a historian and a horticulturist, wrote *The Oregon Trail* (1849), describing how the West was opened up in 1846. The son of the Rev. Francis Parkman Sr., Parkman remained a Unitarian all his life. {U; UU; CE}

Parmelee, Maurice (1882–1969)

Parmelee, whose expertise was economics and sociology, taught at Syracuse, Kansas, Minnesota, Michigan, and New York universities. A materialist, he described his *Science and Human Behaviour* (1913) as "an attempt to explain human behaviour on a purely mechanistic and materialistic basis." {RAT; RE}

Parmenides (500 B.C.E.)

A pupil of Xenophanes and a leading figure of the Eleatic school, Parmenides contributed to philosophy the method of reasoned proof for assertions. First, being is the material substance of which the universe is composed. Being, then, is the sole and eternal reality. Using dialectic, he destroyed the possibility of generation, destruction, change, and motion. Change and motion, he held, are illusions of the senses. There is no empty space, logically, because being is spatially extended. Therefore, motion is impossible. He was reverenced but feared by Plato, according to Theaetetus. But Plato derived from Parmenides, according to Bertrand Russell, "the belief that reality is eternal and timeless and that, on logical grounds, all change must be illusory." Parmenides "made short work of the counter-sense of not being" but, states Robertson, "does not seem to have dealt at close quarters with popular creeds." (CE; BDF; JMR; JMRH; Bertrand Russell, *History of Philosophy*)

Parny, Evariste Désire de Forges de (1753–1814)

Parny was a French poet. A disappointed passion for a Creole inspired his "Amatory Poems," after which he wrote the audacious *War of the Gods*, *Paradise Lost* and *The Gallantries of the Bible*. His poems were erotic and full of charm, leading to his being addressed by Voltaire as "*mon cher Tibullus*." Although the Revolution swept away his fortune, he accepted it, even wrote fiery poems to support it. His long poem, *La guerre des dieux* (1799) is a scathing parody of the Bible. In 1803, Parny was admitted into the French Academy. {BDF; RAT; RE}

Parris, Thomas Collins Touzeau (1839–1907)

Although educated at the Bristol Baptist College, Parris became a Unitarian minister, patronized by Samuel Courtauld. Parris helped his father sell books in Bristol, then moved to London where he joined Bradlaugh during the 1877 crisis. In his later years he joined the anti-Foote Freethought Federation, and he was a friend of William Morris at Kelmscott House. More a teacher than a lecturer, he spoke for the National Secular Society in the 1870s but did not enter into debates, working mainly in the South West of England. Parris was active as a secularist until infirmity compelled his retirement shortly before his death. {RSR; TRI}

PARROT

The common name for the order Psittaciformes, which is comprised of 315 species of colorful birds, is parrot. Some species can be taught to imitate the human voice. Supernaturalists are known to have taught pet parrots to say "Amen"; naturalists, "God is dead, haha."

In 1998 a parrot's fossil found in Wyoming was thought to be between sixty-five million and seventh million years old, thereby living at the same time as dinosaurs.

Parry, Brian (1949–1996)

Parry, with his partner Barry Duke, served on the Council of Management of the National Secular Society. He helped found the Gay and Lesbian Humanist Association. Denis Cobell conducted a secular humanist funeral ceremony for Parry. {*The Freethinker*, February 1997}

Parry, Charles Humbert Hastings [Sir] (1848–1918)

A British composer, Parry wrote many oratorios, concertos, choral odes, and works of a religious character. But, according to McCabe, Parry was a freethinker. In the obituary notice, *The Times* reported, "From his earliest years Parry had had no sympathy with dogmatic theology, but as his mind concentrated more and more upon the problem of human struggle and aspiration of life and death, failure and conquest, he found his thoughts most perfectly expressed in the language of the Bible." {JM; RAT; RE; TRI}

Parry, Nakkeeran (20th Century)

Parry is an atheist who in Kuala Lumpur, Maylasia, belongs to Periyar Pagutharivu Pasarai. Phone: (603) 4456781.

Parsons, Jack (1920–)

Parsons, a population expert, became an Honorary Associate of the Rationalist Press Association in 1994. He wrote *Population vs. Liberty* (1971), *Changing Directions* (1974), *Population Fallacies* (1977), and *Human Population Competition: A Study of the Pursuit of Power Through Numbers* (1999). Parsons is a member of the Fabian Society and of the British Humanist Association.

Parsons, Keith (20th Century)

Parsons, a supporter of Internet Infidels, is an assistant professor of philosophy at the University of Houston–Clear Lake. He wrote *God and the Burden* of Proof. Parsons is the head of the Council for

Secular Humanism's Society of Humanist Philosophers and editor of its journal, *Philo*, which commenced in 1998.

Philo, in David Hume's *Dialogues Concerning Natural Religion*, was the character who braved the religious temperament of the times in order to provide rational grounds for being skeptical of religious assertions concerning god, reality, and ethics. The journal named *Philo*, in his words, offers "high-quality, critical examinations of theistic and religious claims, conducts useful explorations of issues in humanistic and naturalistic ethics, and facilitates meaningful discussions in these areas." Its first contributors included Paul Kurtz, Adolf Grünbaum, Richard Gale, Kai Nielsen, Michael Martin, Quentin Smith, Theodore Schick Jr., Theodore M. Drange, Keith M. Parsons, and H. James Birx.

Parsons, Lucy E. (1853–1942)

Parsons was the widow of Albert Parsons, a Haymarket martyr who, although innocent was one of four to hang in 1887, singing "Annie Laurie" shortly before his execution. When twenty, she fled Ku Klux Klan-riddled Texas with her husband, describing herself as Indian and Spanish, although she appeared to be African American and a former slave. She gave birth to a son, Albert, in 1879 and to a daughter, Lulu Eda, in 1881. Some official designated the daughter "nigger" on her birth certificate. Once arrested for leading a Hunger Demonstration in 1915, Parsons was bailed out by Jane Addams. In her late eighties, nearly blind, she died in a house fire. According to Carole Gray, "Lucy survived many disabilities, including being a black woman married to a white man at the turn of the century, having two children to raise alone after her husband's murder, being an atheist, and supporting the unpopular cause of labor rights." {*Free Inquiry*, Spring 1995}

Partington, Anna (20th Century)

Partington, who was educated at the University of Manchester in England, has written for *The American Rationalist*.

Parton, James (1822–1890)

Parton, who was born in England but educated in New York, was an author. He wrote many biographies, including those of Jefferson (1874) and of Voltaire (1881). He also has written *Topics of the Time* (1871), *On Church Taxation*, and "The Immortality of Religious Capitals" (1883). William Dean Howells said of Parton, "In the days when to be an agnostic was to be almost an outcast, he had the heart to say of the Mysteries that he did not know." {BDF; JM; RAT; RE}

Partridge, Andy (20th Century)

Partridge, a songwriter and recording artist, is lead singer of XTC. "Basically, I don't believe in God," Partridge told an interviewer. "I don't think there's a stately British actor in a white sheet looking down on us all and deciding that *you're* going to get run over, and *you're* going to win the pool." Heaven and Hell are states of mind, he holds but adds, "If you can create heaven for yourself without creating hell for somebody else, fine. That's a good enough code. Try and create heaven for somebody else as well, but don't create hell for anyone 'cos that's less than animal." {CA}

Partzsch, Kurt (20th Century)

At the Eighth International Humanist and Ethical Union (IHEU) World Congress in Hannover (1982), Partzsch from Germany was given a Humanist Award for his contribution to social welfare in Germany.

Parvish, Samuel (18th Century)

A deist, Parvish wrote *An Inquiry Into the Jewish and Christian Revelation* (1739), of which a second edition was issued in 1746. {BDF; FUK}

Pascal, Blaise (1623–1662)

During the French Revolution, Maréchal cited Pascal as being the opposite of an atheist, pointing out that he thought reason was impotent in resolving man's problems and satisfying his hopes. Instead, Pascal believed in the necessity of a mystic faith, holding that man needed faith in order to understand the universe. With Plato, he believed that the mind, after the body dies, continues to exist without *any* body. He did write, however, that "men never do evil so completely and cheerfully as when they do it from religious conviction."

At the age of thirty-two he retired to a monastery, gave up his life of pleasure, fasted, wore a girdle of sharp nails, and in seven years he died. {CE; ER; EU, Aram Vartanian; RE; TYD}

PASCAL'S WAGER

Pascal had the idea that it is prudent to believe in God's existence, for if there is no God little will be lost, and if there is a God then eternal happiness can be gained. The flaw in his thinking, however, is that he assumed there is only one god. If there is more than one, then selecting one would annoy the others. If the one god were the kind to penalize someone who had no evidence of its existence, then how to explain that "God is a God of love."

The rationalists' approach is to remain neutral—if there is one or more gods, let *them* recruit *you*. Meanwhile, Pascal instead of asking "Is there a god?" might better have asked, "Is there exactly one god, or are there many?" (See entry for Blaise Pascal.)

Pascoli, Giovanni (1855–1912)

An Italian poet, Pascoli translated Homer's *Iliad* and *Odyssey*, which resulted in his being termed in the *Athanaeum* as "the first rank of living Italian poets." Some Italian authorities regarded him as "the greatest Latin poet since the Augustan Age." Pascoli was anti-Papal, and in much of his verse he rejoices at the triumph of Garibaldi and the liberators of Italy. However, he was a theist with a certain moral tenderness for Christianity. He called upon the clergy to "get rid of the ashes and scum [of dogma and ritual' upon their souls and present Christianity as a torrent of love." {RAT}

Pasek, Michael (20th Century)

Pasek is membership secretary of the Humanist Association of Canada. {HAC}

Pashinski, Alexander (20th Century)

Pashinski, a lecturer at Moscow State University in Russia, spoke at the 1993 Congress in Berlin of the European Humanist Federation (EHF). Racism, he lamented, is an alternative ideology to humanism: "Racism is a way of life, the way without love of people for their own selves, without love of other people as humans. Racism does not want people to represent themselves as humans, enjoy the freedom of sharing their relationships, and develop their interaction with other humans in an harmonious way. They cannot accept democracy as an institution to govern racial and national relations, because it is human-based."

Pasolini, Pier Paolo (1922–1975)

Pasolini, a former Roman Catholic and a Marxist, was an Italian writer and film director. His "Decameron" (1971) depicted nuns reveling in copulation. Crotch shots and close-ups of penises abound, and his "The Gospel According to St. Matthew" (1964), "The Canterbury Tales" (1972), and other films show that as an atheist he had no reverence for the Church. Some, however, consider "The Gospel According to St. Matthew" to be the best film every made of the life of Jesus. In 1975, a male street hustler mysteriously murdered Pasolini. {Tim Madigan, *Free Inquiry*, Spring 1991}

Pasquarello, Tony (20th Century)

An emeritus philosopher at Ohio State University at Mansfield, Pasquarello successfully pursued a second career as a pop-jazz-classical musician and performer. He has investigated, in "Humanism's Thorn: The Case of the Bright Believers," why it is that intelligent people can be believers. Certainly, he notes, bright people do not believe in nonsense. Yet, traditional theism *is* nonsense. Ergo, how to explain Augustine, Aquinas, Erasmus, and Erigina! Either God exists or he doesn't. Either there is or there isn't an elephant in my bedroom. Perhaps, Pasquarello infers, if humanists could learn why so many intelligent people are turned on to religion humanism itself will profit. In the final analysis, he writes wittily, "It's comforting to know that Smith, the neighbor to my left, thinks the Earth is round. But it's positively demoralizing to know that Jones, my other neighbor, thinks it is flat. Particularly if Jones holds a doctorate in geodetic sciences."

In *The Altar Boy Chronicles* (1999), he describes what it was like to grow up in a Catholic Little Italy during World War II. (*Free Inquiry*, Winter, 1992-1993)

Pasquier, Étienne (1529–1615)

Pasquier was a French journalist. He defended the universities against the Jesuits, whom he also attacked in a bitter satire, *Catéchisme des Jesuits*. {BDF}

Passerani, Alberto Radicati di (Died 1737)

Passerani, an Italian philosopher and a count attached to the court of Victor Amedée II, wrote some pamphlets against the Papal power. The Inquisition pursued him and seized his goods. He fled to England, making the acquaintance of Collins, and to France and Holland. In the year of his death he published *Recueil de Pièces curieuses sur les matieres les plus intéressantes* and containing *A Parallel Between Mahomet and Sosem* (an anagram of Moses), *an Abridged History of the Sacerdotal Profession*. He also wrote *A Faithful and Comic Recital of the Religion of Modern Cannibals*, reportedly by Zelin Moslem. Passerani had one work that pretended to be a translation from an Arabic work on Mohammedanism, satirizing the Bible, and with a pretended sermon by Elwall the Quaker. Passerani died in Holland, believing in no afterlife and leaving his goods to the poor. {BDF; RE}

Passmore, John (1914–)

Passmore, an emeritus professor of philosophy at the Australian National University, is a Humanist Laureate in the Council for Secular Humanism's International Academy of Humanism. He is a researcher in the History of Ideas Programme at Canberra's Australian National University and a corresponding member of The Hume Society. He signed Humanist Manifesto 2000.

Passmore, who is president of the Australian Academy of Science, is an atheist and author of various philosophical works including *A Hundred Years of Philosophy* (1957), *Philosophical Reasoning* (1961), *Man's Responsibility for Nature* (1974), and *Recent Philosophers* (1985). In 1994 Passmore wrote "Hostility to Science" in *Challenges to the Enlightenment, In Defense of Reason and Science*. {CA; SWW}

Pasteur, Louis (1822–1895)

The famed French scientist Pasteur, father of modern hygiene and public health, made research on fermentation, at one time claiming to disprove the theory of spontaneous generation in his experiments with bacteria. In a lecture in the Sorbonne's grand amphitheatre, Pasteur linked spontaneous generation to the kind of materialism that needed no divine creator. Said Pasteur, "neither religion, nor philosophy, nor atheism, nor materialism, nor spiritualism has any place here. . . . It is a question of fact. I have approached it without preconceived idea." This led to his germ theory of infection, and in his work on wine, vinegar, and beer he developed the process of pasteurization. He also found a solution for the control of silkworm disease, and his technique of vaccination against anthrax led to a successful treatment against rabies in 1885. Pasteur was elected to the Academy as a successor of Littré, and he gave his name as Vice-President of the British Secular Union. Wheeler in his *Dictionary of Freethinkers* confirms that in his prime Pasteur was vice-president of the British Secular (Atheist) Union, and Wheeler was the chief secularist writer of the time.

In *The Private Science of Louis Pasteur* (1995), Gerald L. Geison claims that Pasteur did not claim that nonliving matter can spontaneously organize itself into living matter, that he did not even believe in spontaneous generation, and that when his experiments gave wrong results Pasteur simply lied by giving an alternative explanation. He was, Geison hastens to add, a truly great scientist. But when Pasteur treated several victims who had been bitten by a rabid dog and announced he had discovered a treatment for rabies in humans, based on experiments on dogs, Pasteur as a matter of fact had only studied some thirty dogs, a third of which had succumbed to rabies. However, Nobel Prize winner M. F. Perutz, in *The New York Review of Books* (21 Dec 1995), declares that Geison is entirely wrong about Pasteur's alleged unsavory and unethical conduct, then deconstructs Geison's deconstruction in order to restore Pasteur's "rightly dominant image."

In an edition of the *Encyclopedia Britannica*, an article about Pasteur describes him as "this simple and devout Catholic," changing the content to the contrary in earlier editions. The anonymous Catholic author quotes as his authority the standard biography by Vallery-Radot. However, states McCabe, that biography describes Pasteur as a freethinker "and this is confirmed in the preface to the English translation by Sir W. Osler, who knew Pasteur personally. Vallery-Radot was himself a Catholic, yet admits that Pasteur believed only in 'an Infinite' and 'hoped' for a future life." In his Academy speech in 1822, Pasteur said, "The idea of God is a form of the idea of the Infinite whether it is called Brahma, Allah, Jehovah, or Jesus." Pasteur did not receive the sacraments at death. Relatives put rosary beads in his hands, and the *Catholic Encyclopedia* claims him. {BDF; RE; TRI}

Pastor, Joseph (19th Century)

Pastor was the first editor of *Pokrok* in Chicago and Racine, Wisconsin. The Czech journal lasted from 1867 to 1878. {FUS}

Pastoret, Claude Emmanuel Joseph Pierre de (1756–1840)

Pastoret was a marquis, French statesman, and writer. His *Zoroaster, Confucius, and Mahomet* (1787) and *Moses Considered as Legislator and Moralist* (1788) were written at a time when comparative religion was a study in its infancy. His principal work is a learned *History of Legislation* (11 volumes, 1817–1837), in which he passes in review all the ancient codes. Pastoret embraced the Revolution and became President of the Legislative Assembly. He proposed the erection of the Column of July on the Place of the Bastille and the conversion of the church of Ste. Geneviève into the Pantheon. In 1792 he presented a motion for the complete separation of the state from religion. During the Terror, he fled but returned as deputy in 1795. In 1820 Pastoret succeeded his friend Volney as a member of the French Academy. In 1823 he received the cross the Legion of Honor, and in 1829 Pastoret became Chancellor of France. {BDF; RAT; RE}

PATAPHYSICS

Pataphysics has as its purpose the parodying of the methods and theories of modern science. A French absurdist concept of a philosophy or science dedicated to studying what lies beyond the realm of metaphysics, it often expresses ideas in nonsensical language. For example, Alfred Jarry wrote, "If souls are independent, man is God." Absurdists neither confirm nor deny that pataphysics is the science of shit, a Manhattan wag has noted, choosing to remain silent about that which they have thoroughly tested in laboratories.

Pater, Walter (Horatio) (1839–1894)

The *Dictionary of National Biography*, citing his agnosticism, states that Pater had "lost all belief in the Christian religion." "By the time he arrived at Oxford as an undergraduate," Peter Ackroyd has observed, Pater "had no more faith in Christianity than in Ovid's Metamorphoses."

Ackroyd, calling Pater the meek mentor of Oscar Wilde, described him as being ugly but intriguing, the "Caliban of letters." Pater is said to have searched for academic preferment, not for a wife. Although he said, "I would give ten years of my life to be handsome," the mustache he grew made matters worse. His peers are said by Ackroyd to have considered him a somewhat overrefined Oxford tutor who lived with his cat and was cared for by his two sisters. Henry James, remarking about Pater's reserve and his diffidence, wrote that Pater was "the mask without the face."

At Braenose College, Oxford, where he taught philosophy, Pater was known for its "hearties"–athletic young men with more profile than prose style–and the poet A. C. Benson, who shared Pater's tastes, said, "That a man should be ardently disposed to athletic pursuits was no obstacle to Pater's friendship, though he was himself entirely averse to games; it rather constituted an additional reason for admiring one with whom he felt otherwise in sympathy." Pater is said to have lectured on philosophy, usually without mentioning any particular philosopher, and in his private quarters he had a bust of Hercules (which he termed a "coquetry"), becoming one of the first of Oxford dons "to bring a carefully studied taste to the arrangement and decoration of his rooms." In his thirty years there, he never received any other lectureship or professorship. Denis Donaghue, in *Walter Pater: Lover of Strange Souls* (1995), wrote that Pater had a high receding forehead and eyes bright but perhaps a little too close together. He wore a frock coat very correctly, but he sported an apple-green tie, which in some eyes, at least, was equivalent to wearing a dress.

Among his friends were Swinburne, Rossetti, the Humphry Wards, and the Mark Pattisons. His *Studies in the History of the Renaissance* (1873) included essays on Johann Joachim Winckelmann, the eighteenth century German scholar who pursued Hellenism in more than a scholarly sense, causing Pater to remark about Winckelmann's "romantic, fervid friendships with young men" which "perfected his reconciliation with the spirit of Greek sculpture." The work established Pater's reputation. He also wrote about Botticelli. In an essay on Leonardo da Vinci (1869) he described Mona Lisa as one "who had learned the secrets of the grave." In an essay (1868) on the poetry of William Morris, Pater, searching for a conclusion, concluded with a memorable statement, "To burn always with this hard gem-like flame, to maintain this ecstasy, is success in life." (Ackroyd has written, "How *does* one burn with a hard, gem-like flame?")

In a fictional biography, *Marius the Epicurean* (1885), which described a young intellectual in the time of Marcus Aurelius, Pater described his responses to paganism, Christianity, and Rome, leading Mrs. Humphry Ward to comment that "No one can fail to catch the autobiographical note." Pater, an unbeliever, directly faced the question of what one may lie for in a world devoid of God. He believed that one must devote oneself to the improvement of the quality of one's individual consciousness during the brief moments of existence that mortality allows. In his posthumous and unfinished *Gaston de Latour* (1896), Pater reveals a preoccupation with the cruelty, beauty, and religious sensibility of a largely imaginary "impassioned past."

From time to time, Pater gave public lectures. "Did you hear me?" he asked Oscar Wilde after one such event. "We overheard you," Wilde replied. Remarked Ackroyd, "Reading Pater is like listening to Wilde through a conch shell." When he heard that Pater had died in his fifty-fifth year, Wilde asked, "Was he ever alive?" Death, however, Pater thought of as "the last curiosity," and wags have said that it is somehow appropriate that Pater should have been buried at Oxford during the summer vacation.

Many attacked him as being unscholarly and morbid, but Pater had a profound influence on the undergraduates of the day and was acclaimed by Oscar Wilde as "the holy writ of beauty." Because of Pater's influence, Paananen states, "Victorian earnestness—reflected in the efforts of writers like Eliot, Carlyle, and Arnold to hold to morality and hard work even in a godless universe—went out of fashion." Oscar Wilde named Pater as the key influence on his life. {Peter Ackroyd, "Pomp and Circumstances," *The New Yorker*, 15 May 1995; BDF; CE; EU, Victor N. Paananen; GL; JM; OEL; RAT; RE}

Paterson, Katherine (20th Century)

According to the American Library Association's *Banned Books* (1998), Paterson's *The Great Gilly Hopkins* is often banned because allegedly "Christians are portrayed as being dumb and stupid." (See entry for Banned Books).

Paterson, Thomas (19th Century)

Paterson, after the imprisonment of Southwell and Holyoake, edited the *Oracle of Reason*. For exhibiting profane placards he was arrested and sentenced 27 January 1843 to three months in prison. His trial was docketed as *God v. Paterson* (1843). Paterson then insisted on considering God as the plaintiff and, by quoting from "the Jew book," testified concerning the plaintiff's bad character. When released, he went to Scotland to uphold the right of free publication. There, he was sentenced to fifteen months in prison for selling "blasphemous" publications. On his release he was presented with a testimonial 6 April 1845, with H. Hetherington presiding. Paterson, who had been the only Scottish atheistical publisher, then moved to America. (See Forgotten Freethinkers #10, *The American Rationalist*, January-February 1995.) {BDF; FUK; RAT; VI}

Paterson, William Romaine (Born 1871)

A novelist who wrote under the name of Benjamin Swift, Paterson wrote *Nancy Noon* (1896) as his first novel. His rationalism is found in a pamphlet, "The Credentials of Faith," which he published in his own name in 1918. It is a searching criticism of Christianity in the form of a dialogue. {RAT}

PATHOS: See entry for Tragedy, for the two terms are commonly mis-used.

Patin, Gui (1601–1671)

Patin, the admiring friend of French philosopher and scientist Pierre Gassendi, was never explicitly heretical. He may have written of Socinianism as a pestilent doctrine, but he was constantly anti-clerical. The Society of Jesus, he felt, was "that black Loyolitic scum from Spain." He was not a wholehearted freethinker, however, ending one of his 836 letters with *Credo in Deum, Christum crucifixum, etc.* The other 835, however, did not so end. Larousse said of him, "*C'était un libre penseur de la famille de Rabelais*," that he was a freethinker of the Rabelaisian family. {BDF; JMR; JMRH}

Patri, Umesh (20th Century)

Patri appeared with Lavanam, the Indian atheist, at the San Joaquin Valley, California, Center for Nonviolence in 1994. Dr. Patri, who wrote *Hindu Scriptures and American Transcendentalists*, is an authority concerning the influence of Renaissance philosophy on contemporary Indian humanism.

PATRIARCHY

• God is for men, and religion for women.

–Joseph Conrad

• This is where the family honor lies!

—a high school biology teacher in Egypt, sketching the female reproductive system and pointing out the entrance to the vagina, according to Egyptian journalist Abeer Allam

Anthropologists speak of patriarchy as being a familial and political social system in which a father is the head and descent is traced through his side of the family. In the latter part of the present century, feminists around the world have objected to the acceptance of such a concept.

A matriarchy, in which a woman has dominated the family clan or tribe, allegedly existed in ancient times but usually failed. Iroquois women could nominate and depose members of their ruling council, but male members enjoyed a veto over women. Crow women took ritual offices, but their power was limited by menstrual taboos. Myths regarding matriarchies and matriarchates are thought by many to be the result of males' rationalization to continue their dominance.

Taslima Nasrin is an example of a contemporary who opposes patriarchy and, in fact, laments that it enjoys a success because it was males, not God or gods, who wrote the allegedly "sacred" books that decreed male dominance over females. She, and many others, refuse to take their father's last name. Therefore, inasmuch as she represents a major danger to the continued dominance of patriarchy in Islamic societies, a fatwa was placed on her head and Muslim fundamentalists in Bangladesh demanded that her writings be burned and that she be hanged. As a result, she was forced to flee not once but twice to safety in Sweden.

Reports of the negative effects of patriarchy on females fill many newspaper columns. In Afghanistan, the Taliban not only require that all women be covered from head to feet but also can be flogged or killed for the slightest infractions of male-written laws. In Morocco, a woman who has been raped and is now an unmarried mother becomes an outcast in her conservative Islamic society. Treated as being inferior under Morocco's Koranic laws, such women are legal minors, inherit only half a share, need permission from a male relative to marry, and can simply be repudiated without recourse by their husbands. A woman who has a child out of wedlock is treated with even more disdain. Asked who fathered her baby, a middle-aged lady by the name of Zara told a reporter matter-of-factly, "Hariba is the daughter of a policeman who took me by force at the cemetery." Although rich or educated women might successfully obtain an abortion, which is illegal, poor young women cannot.

"In many Islamic countries people deal with unwanted pregnancy by pretending it doesn't exist. It's a taboo subject," Wassyla Tamzali, a specialist in women's rights at Unesco said in 1999.

The killing of "unchaste" girls and women by their relatives is condoned in Arab parts of Jordan, Egypt, Syria, Lebanon, Yemen, and Israel. Douglas Jehl, writing in Jordan (*The New York Times*, 20 June 1999), described how female chastity is seen in the Arab world "as an indelible line, the boundary between respect and shame. An unchaste woman, it is sometimes said, is worse than a murderer, affecting not just one victim, but her family and her tribe." He relates how a teenage brother by killing his "unchaste" sister thereby earned his family's respect as well as that of the community's.

Patriarchy exists, similarly, in Jewish and Christian countries, leaders often citing the Holy Bible as God's wishes on the subject. A woman has no chance, in short, of ever becoming a Pope or a Jewish leader. Freethinkers, on the other hand, cite many instances of their leaders' co-equality. (See entry for and books by Taslima Nasrin.) {CE; Marlise Simons, "After the Rape, a Lifetime of Shame. It's Morocco," *The New York Times*, 1 February 1999}

Patterson, Dorothy Smith (20th Century)

Patterson is president of the board of the Unitarian Universalist Service Committee.

Patton, Dennis (1943–)

Patton, a sculptor, is an active member of the People's Unitarian Universalist Church in Cedar Rapids, Iowa. His works include "In Transit," consisting of sixteen-foot-high figures, striding, baggage in hand, perhaps toward a commuter flight at the Cedar Rapids Airport, where it was installed in 1993. Many of his works are constructed of stainless steel and painted in vibrant colors. {*World*, November-December 1994}

Patton, George Smith Jr. [General] (1885–1945)

An American major general who received much publicity for his spectacular sweep of U.S. forces from Normandy through Brittany and Northern France, Patton is one of those cited by Paul Edwards as having believed in reincarnation.

Patton, Kenneth L(ee) (1911–1994)

Patton, the author of *Hello Man* (1945) has been a Unitarian Universalist minister in his emphasis upon the importance of the symbolic resources of world religion. In his Madison, Wisconsin, church, designed by Frank Lloyd Wright, Patton started to develop his view that "religion cannot operate without symbols." At the Charles Street Meeting House (Universalist) in Boston, he combined art, symbols, and words, writing *Man's Hidden Search: An Inquiry in Naturalistic Mysticism* (1954), *A Religion for One World* (1964), and *Services and Songs for the Celebration of Life* (1967). Patton once was a director of the American Humanist Association. He wrote to the present author that he is a Naturalistic Humanist,

> . . . although I would prefer to call it Humanistic Naturalism, for I believe naturalism is the larger and more definitive term for the position I hold, and humanism only modifies it. I would not quarrel with the basic concern of Humanism with human values and development, but I believe we have been, not too much concerned with man, but too little concerned about the other-than-human creatures and elements of the natural world. It is here that the mystical naturalism of the more radical schools of Zen Buddhism has much to teach us. Humanists still tend to consider themselves as somewhat set over against nature, whereas the Chinese and Japanese naturalists have for many centuries placed man completely within the realm of nature, as one creature among many others. They have a delightful sense of "at home-ness" in the natural world. Through Zen Buddhism they have developed a profoundly mystical (in a completely this-worldly sense) and aesthetic appreciation of the human and natural condition, which I believe will go far to correct the overly utilitarian and positivistic trends in the pragmatic and scientific humanist of the west. Not that these latter issues should be slighted, but rather that they should be supplemented by the artistic and poetical dimensions of humanism and naturalism which the Orient has demonstrated are potential within a naturalistic philosophy.
>
> The men who have most influenced my thinking have been John Dewey, Max C. Otto, and A. Eustace Haydon. In addition to Zen Buddhism, I should also refer to Existentialism, with whose metaphysics I would quarrel, but with whose emphasis upon the emotional and aesthetic aspects of the human situation I believe are a corrective to the overly bland estimates of the Scientific Humanism of America. I believe that Humanism is now emerging into something approaching maturity, through the interaction of various strands of world naturalism such as those referred to above.

In *A Religion for One World*, he underlined the meaning of the word *universalism* as being a religion which draws from all the religions. His Charles Street Meeting House in Boston features a variety of symbols, for the poet Patton insisted that "religion cannot operate without symbols." Included is a bookcase of world scriptures, a mural of the Great Nebula in Andromeda, and a sculpture symbolizing the atom. Patton's humanistic poems are found in *Hello Man* (1945) and *Strange Seed* (1946). {CL; EU, Paul H. Beattie; HNS; WAS, 28 May 1956; U&U}

Patwari, A.B.M. Mafizul Islam (20th Century)

Patwari is president of the Humanist and Ethical Society of Bangladesh. He wrote *Fundamental Rights and Personal Liberty* (1988) and *Humanism and Human Rights in the Third World* (1992).

PAUL (Saint)

> • The conversion of Paul was no conversion at all: it was Paul who converted the religion that has raised one man above sin and death into a religion that delivered millions of men so completely into their dominion that their own common nature became a horror to them, and the religious life became a denial of life.
>
> –**George Bernard Shaw** (1856-1950)

Some scholars hold that anti-Semitism arose because St. Paul, the apostle to the Gentiles and the earliest Christian writer, encouraged it. He may or may not have been born of orthodox Jewish parentage. Hyman Maccoby, for example, states that Paul claimed to be a Jew and even a Pharisee but possibly was a non-Jew who converted and became disaffected. Similarly, Betty McCollister in *The Humanist* (July-Aug 1993) finds that anti-Semitism "infects the first three gospels, especially the passage in Matthew in which Jews accept blood guilt in perpetuity, and permeates the fourth gospel, attributed to John, whose author (whoever he was) was obviously not a Jew." Meanwhile,

Episcopal Bishop John S. Spong in *Rescuing the Bible from Fundamentalism* (1991) describes St. Paul as a "self-loathing and repressed gay male." S. Levin, in "The Primal Dream: St. Paul's Vision" (*New Humanist*, February 1996), postulates that if Paul participated in an Eleusis experience or in another of similar type, he hallucinated a Jesus figure (*Galatians* 1:12, 16), adding that "the use of the word hallucination does not necessarily brand him as psychiatrically disturbed. Hallucinations can be no more than misperceptions, visual, auditory, olfactory, tactile. But they can also be pathological." (See reference to his alleged "Dostoyevsky's epilepsy" under Dostoyevsky, Fëodor.)

Paul, Alice (1885–1977)

Paul wrote the Equal Rights Amendment and in 1928 founded the World Party for Equal Rights for Women. The daughter of Quakers, Paul was a freethinker.

Paul, Charles (20th Century)

Paul is a past president of *The Jewish Humanist*. He is the journal's editor, along with Rabbi Sherwin T. Wine, and is a member of the humanistic Birmingham Temple.

Paul, M. Eden (20th Century)

Paul wrote *Rationalism* (19–?). {GS}

Paul, Susanne J. (20th Century)

Paul is on the editorial board of *The Humanist* and was President of the Board of Directors of the American Humanist Association.

Paulett, Robert C. (Died 1998)

Paulett, a Freedom From Religion Foundation member from Virginia, was a freethinking activist.

Paulhan, Jean: See entry for Dominique Aury. Paulhan was a member of the French Academy.

Pauli, Gregorius (16th Century)

An Italian who was a minister in Cracow, Pauli declared Jesus to be "a mere man." Further, he preached community of goods, promised a speedy millennium, and condemned the bearing of arms. Inspired, a group of Unitarian ministers and nobles in 1562 formally renounced the doctrine of the Trinity. With forty-two subscribing ministers, they formed a Unitarian Church in Poland, opposing infant baptism. Remarks Robertson about the church, "Ethically, its doctrine was humane and pacificatory, its members being forbidden to go to law or to take oaths; and for a time the community made great progress, the national Diet being, by one account, 'filled with Arians' for a time." {JMR; JMRH}

Pauli, Karl E. (20th Century)

In Erie, Michigan, Pauli edited *Granpappy's Almanac* from 1962 to 1963. It was an unbelievers' journal. Among his works were "Philosophy of Atheism" (1915) and "State of Ohio vs. Karl E. Pauli, et al." (1923). {GS}

Pauline, Mark (20th Century)

Pauline, a performance artist, is the leading force behind Survival Research Laboratories. His group of machinists has performed internationally and been featured in *Wired*, *The Mondo 2000 Users' Guide to the New Edge*, and on a CBS show concerning cyberculture. In an interview in *Re/Search* (#5/6), Pauline describes the conflicts that as a child he had about religion. "Then," he states, "I quit believing in god." {CA; E}

Pauling, Linus Paul (1901–1994)

A chemist, Pauling is the only person to have received two Nobel Prizes, the chemistry prize in 1954 and the peace prize in 1962. He was active in promoting peace, world disarmament, and the cessation of nuclear weapon testing. Many know of him because of his advocacy of taking large quantities of Vitamin C in order to fortify the body against colds, for his announcement resulted in pharmacies being immediately unable to maintain adequate supplies. During World War II, ignoring the widespread resentment against Japanese-Americans, he hired as his gardener a young man whose parent had been born in Japan–in retaliation, vandals defaced Pauling's house to show contempt for his brand of social conscience. In 1952, Pauling was denied a passport, partly because he had incurred the suspicion of Sen. Joseph R. McCarthy, who had accused him of having a "well nigh incredible" record of membership in Communist front organizations. Pauling denied under oath that he had ever been a Communist, and it turned out that he had applied for a passport in order to go with his wife, Ava, to participate in a London conference on the structure of proteins. Meanwhile, Pauling's *The Nature of the Chemical Bond* was regarded as hostile to the dialectical materialism of Marx, Engels, and Lenin, and when the Soviets criticized his work Pauling countered by calling Stalinist science distorted.

A Unitarian and son of an Oregon druggist, Pauling dropped out of his Portland high school as a form of protest against taking courses that he regarded as pointless. Gaining entrance to Oregon Agricultural College without a high school diploma, he majored in chemical engineering, was quickly recognized as a prodigy, and eventually became a fellow of the Linus Pauling Institute of Science and Medicine. When a professor at the California Institute of Technology, he had said there were "many aspects" of religion that offered no conflict with science. But he said there was some question as to the extent to which a "good scientist" could accept religious dogma. Challenged about this on the NBC TV program, "Youth Wants to Know," he was told that Dr. Robert A. Millikan of the same school had declared that "the more he read and the more he studied, the more he was sure about the existence of God." Pauling commented: "My experience has been different, in a sense almost opposite, of Professor Millikan."

In 1961 the American Humanist Association named Pauling Humanist of the Year. For him, "Humanism is a rational philosophy...a philosophy of service for the good of all humanity, of application of new ideas of scientific progress, for the benefit of all humankind." In 1972 he won the Lenin Peace Prize, and in 1974 he won the U.S. National Medal of Science. For three decades or more, Pauling was a member of the First Unitarian Church in Los Angeles. He wrote *No More War!* (1962) and *How To Live Longer and Feel Better* (1987). Often photographed with his beret atop his head, Pauling remained to the end irreverent, iconoclastic, and outspoken. {CE; CL; HNS2; U; UU}

Paulson, Philip K. (20th Century)

Paulson is head of the Humanist Association of San Diego (AHA). In "I Was an Atheist in a Foxhole" (*Secular Nation*, Fall 1995), he tells of his experiences in Vietnam when other soldiers in a panic screamed out for God to help them. "To hell with God!" he insisted. "You help us! You radio back for mortar and artillery fire support!" Ironically, when his group pulled through, he was told, "See, Paulson, God answers prayers." In 1973 Paulson joined the American Humanist Association: "I needed to belong to a group of nontheists who shared my visions of hope and who inculcated rational methods of reasoning, social sympathy, and cooperative skills." (See entry for California Atheists, Humanists.) {FD}

Pauw, Cornelius (1730–1799)

Pauw was a learned Dutch writer who wrote philosophical researches on the Americans, Egyptians, Chinese, and Greeks. Frederick the Great esteemed him for his ingenuity and penetration. Pauw was the uncle of Anacharsis Clootz. {BDF}

Pavlov, Ivan Petrovich (1849–1936)

A Nobel Prize winning physiologist, Pavlov is internationally known for his experiments with dogs. According to Joseph McCabe, Pavlov was a materialist and an atheist. The first son of the village priest and the grandson of the village sexton, Pavlov was an honorary associate of the Rationalist Press Association (RPA). He has said, however, that he envied his wife's belief in religion. {CE; JM; TRI}

Pawelek, John (1942–)

A senior research scientist in dermatology and a lecturer in pharmacology at Yale University, Pawelek was raised a Lutheran but is an active member of the Unitarian Society of New Haven, Connecticut.

One of his inventions is a sunblock that doubles as a medication for vitiligo, a blotchy-skin condition that results from the failure of some melanin cells to produce pigment. Pawelek has called himself "an optimistic agnostic." {*World*, July-August 1999}

Payne, George (19th Century)

Payne, a leading Manchester, England, secularist in the 1880s, was instrumental in forming an Electoral Rights Defence Association, which had ninety branches in fifty-eight towns, mainly in Lancashire. {RSR}

Payne, John (1842–1916)

Between the ages of thirteen and nineteen, Payne translated the whole of Dante, much of Goethe, Lessing, and Calderon, and parts of other French, German, Spanish, Italian, Portuguese, Turkish, Persian, Arabian, Greek, and Latin writers. Payne became a poet in his leisure, never went to church, and thought Christianity "of no practical value as a moral agent." He added that "the best Church is that without a priest, a faith that is pure of the poisonous parasite." His work consists of two volumes of collected works and includes his *Songs of Life and Death* (1902). {RAT; RE}

Paz, Octavio (1914–1998)

An educator and winner of the 1990 Nobel Prize in Literature, Paz was the Mexican Ambassador to Afghanistan, Pakistan, Nepal and Ceylon (from which post he resigned because of his Government's 1968 massacre of student demonstrators). In the early 1950s he was an attaché in the Mexican embassy in Delhi, later returning as ambassador. In a 1952 poem, "Mutra," he wrote about Mathura, a Hindu holy city said to have been the birthplace of the god Krishna. Paz, a one-time Catholic, became an atheist.

Among his works are *Raiz del Hombre* (1937), *A la Orilla del Mundo* (1943), and *Piedra de Sol* (1957). He also has written *The Monkey Grammarian* (1981). In 1988, he wrote *Sor Juana* (The Traps of Faith). Paz's work is distinguished for its insight, elegance, and erudition. Of his *Sunstone (Piedra de Sol)*, the Swedish Academy of Letters said, "This suggestive work, with its many layers of meaning, seems to incorporate, interpret, and reconstrue major existential questions, death, time, love, and reality." The Academy quoted one of his poems as his literary credo:

> Between what I see and what I say
> Between what I say and what I keep silent
> Between what I keep silent and what I dream
> Between what I dream and what I forget:
> Poetry.

In 1979 in *The New Yorker*, he commented upon the chasm separating Americans and Mexicans: "In general, Americans have not looked for Mexico in Mexico; they have looked for their obsessions, enthusiasms, phobias, hopes, interests—and these are what they have found. In short, the history of our relationship is the history of a mutual and stubborn deceit."

In 1983 he told Alan Riding of *The New Yorik Times*, "Intellectuals have a semireligious attitude, so it's difficult for them to criticize their own religion. Therefore, they hate me as they would a heretic. If they could, they'd send me to the stake."

In 1992, Paz became a Humanist Laureate in the Council for Secular Humanism's International Academy of Humanism. His work shows that he has been influenced by surrealism, existentialism, Buddhism, Hinduism, and most recently by erotic love and artistic creativity. In a 1992 *New York Times* article, he spoke of capitalism: "The market, blind and deaf, is not fond of literature or of risk, and it does not know how to choose. Its censorship is not ideological: it has no ideas. It knows all about prices, but nothing about values."

In 1994 in an interview in *New Perspectives Quarterly*, he asserted that Mexico was "condemned to modernize" its economy and society: "I say condemned because seeing the United States, Europe, and Japan, I think modernization is not a benediction. It is a kind of air-conditioned hell."

Two of his works on India were published in 1997: *In Light of India* and *A Tale of Two Gardens, Poems from India 1952–1995*. Like Gandhi, Paz was anti-materialism. He found distasteful the demon of money, the doctrines of envy, and the vulgarity in popular entertainment. Fundamentalism, he held, should be called by its true name: fanaticism. Returning to India in 1968 and viewing Shiva and Parvati, the divine couple depicted as the ultimate in happiness, Paz wrote, "It was as though we were leaving ourselves. Shiva and Parvati: we worship you not as gods but as images of the divinity of man." The work about India surveys its society, its politics, and its art and literature.

He had been sick for years with what he called a "long and wretched" illness, cancer. When a European news agency prematurely reported his death, Paz telephoned to the station, "It pains me that those who insist on killing me are in such a hurry."

When Paz died, observers commented upon his appeal to young intellectuals, but they also called attention to his cerebral jousting with Carlos Fuentes, who opposed Paz's political conservatism. Paz's critics accused him of tepid, bourgeois reformism for his views against Fidel Castro and Che Guevara, to which he retorted, "The 'progressive' intellectuals, almost all of whom wanted to establish a totalitarian socialist regime, attacked me vehemently."

Carlos Fuentes was conspicuously absent from the funeral rites, held at the Palace of Fine Arts in Mexico City where the body had lain in state. The rites were entirely secular, and Paz's body was cremated. Citing the loss of such a Promethean figure whose poetry, literary criticism, cultural essays, and political polemics had won a Nobel Prize, literary critic Christopher Dominguez Michael said, "The death of Paz closes a chapter in our history. It is the end of the age of the intellectual as the master of his era." {*The New York Times*, 21 and 25 April 1998}

Paz y Miño, Manuel Abraham (20th Century)

Paz, a Peruvian who teaches applied philosophy, is a member of the Ibero-American Commission, a group of humanist leaders in Spanish-speaking countries. He was a participant in the 1996 Humanist World Congress held in Mexico City. Paz wrote *No existe Dios?* (Does God Not Exist?, 1995) *and* publishes *Revista Peruana de Filosofia Aplicada* (RFPA; Peruvian Journal of Applied Philosophy, El Corregidor 318, Lima 25, Peru). E-mail: <rpfa@yahoo.com>. On the Web: <RPFA@www.computextos.com.pe>.

Peabody, Elizabeth Palmer (1804–1894)

Peabody's West Street Book Shop in Boston became the gathering place for transcendentalists and other reformers. Margaret Fuller's conversations for women were held there in the early 1840s, and Peabody became one of the most prominent women among the transcendentalists. She organized in 1860 the first kindergarten in Boston. In close connection with William Ellery Channing, Ralph Waldo Emerson, and Bronson Alcott, she emphasized in her thoughts and works the possibility of the nurture and full development of a child's, or any individual's, inherent capacity for good, based on what her mentor Channing called a "likeness to God."

Peabody published Fuller's transcendental magazine, the *Dial*, as well as pamphlets of the Anti-Slavery Society and several of Hawthorne's early works. She was greatly respected by religious and philosophic liberals of her day. (See Enrique Krause's "In Memory of Octavio Paz," *The New York Review of Books*, 28 May 1998.) {CE; FUS; U; U&U; UU}

Peabody, Francis Greenwood (1847–1936)

The son of Ephraim Peabody, minister of King's Chapel in Boston, Peabody as a Harvard teacher emphasized ethics. He taught that the modern economic conditions were threatening the foundations of the old social order, including family, property, and the state. This made political and economic questions into ethical ones and demanded a new spirit of service and self-sacrifice in the marketplace. A liberal rather than a radical, Peabody did not advocate a change in existing structures of society, except insofar as changed personal behavior might alter them. His *Jesus Christ and the Social Question* (1900) was "a pioneer statement of Christian social principles" and helped move liberal thinking away from a concentration on individualism and personal development toward a sense of the ethical imperative in social life. As for his schooling at Harvard College and Divinity School, Peabody wryly remarked, "I cannot remember attaining in seven years of Harvard classrooms anything that could be fairly described as an idea." {U&U}

Peacock, E. P. (19th Century)

Peacock was a president of the American Secular Union. {FUS}

Peacock, John Macleay (1817–1877)

Peacock was a Scottish poet who wrote in the *National Reformer* and other publications. In 1867 he published *Hours of Reverie*. {BDF; RAT}

Peacock (or Pecock), Reginald (c. 1390–1460)

Peacock may have been "the father of English rationalism." He was successively Bishop of St. Asaph (1444) and Chichester (1450), by the favor of Humphrey, the Duke of Gloster. Peacock declared that Scripture must in all cases be "the doom of reason," and he questioned the genuineness of the Apostles' Creed. In 1457 he was accused of heresy, recanted from fear of martyrdom, was deprived of his bishopric, and imprisoned in a monastery at Canterbury. Here, when visited, he would repeat

> Wit hath wonder, that reason cannot skan,
> How a Moder is Mayd, and God is Man.

Peacock's books were publicly burned at Oxford. Wheeler declares that Peacock's influence contributed to the Reformation. {BDF}

Peacock, Samuel (1839–1933?)

Peacock, a physician, was a land investor and secularist. He was an adviser and supporter of Joseph Symes. In 1911, he was legally involved in an "Anti-Abortion" termination of pregnancy homicide action, but the jury failed to agree at the second trial. At the third, Peacock was acquitted. (See entry for Ghosts.) {SWW}

Peale, Norman Vincent (1898–1993)

Peale, a Methodist, wrote *The Power of Positive Thinking* (1952), which contained such help-yourself advice as (1) read and memorize verses from the Bible and say them before bedtime, when you get up, and at odd moments during the day; (2) put yourself in the hands of God and think of Him as your unseen partner; (3) draw on Higher Power by yielding to it, saturating your mind with the Bible; etc.

However, in a 1995 issue of *Lutheran Quarterly*, two ministers argued that Peale clearly based his self-help prescriptions not on the Bible but on a book by an obscure 1920s mystic, Florence Scovel Shinn. John Allen, Peale's son-in-law who is president of the board of the Peale Center for Christian Living, has denied any plagiarism had taken place. {*World*, November-December 1995}

Pearce, George (c. 1850–c. 1925)

Pearce was the first secretary of the Rationalist Press Association in Brisbane, and he was an active reporter of Queensland rationalist news to *Ross's*, an Australian magazine. {SWW}

Pearce, Harold Herbert (1926–1993)

Pearce was an Australian atheist, rationalist, humanist, and electrical fitter. At Sydney University, he was a Rationalist Atheist speaker, and he was a regular Sydney Domain lecturer. A foundation member of the Australian Party and Defense of Government Schools, Pearce also was president of the Rationalist Association of New South Wales from 1970 to 1978. {SWW}

Pearce, Harry Hastings (1897–1984)

Pearce is one of Australia's best-known rationalists, freethinkers, and secularists. Over a period of sixty years, he set up or revived rationalist groups, engaged in press controversies, and presented papers to cultural societies on literary, scientific, philosophical, and religious matters. Pearce collected an estimated 15,000 titles of freethought and radical publications, which he willed to libraries in Canberra and Melbourne. Upon his death he was given a secular funeral, and his body was carried out for cremation to the strains of Australia's "Waltzing Matilda" and New Zealand's "*Po Atarau*" (Now Is the Hour). He is author of articles on non-believers in Australia and New Zealand in the *Encyclopedia of Unbelief*. He wrote *Failure of Christian Morality* (1943) and *Back to the Bible and What* (1945). {FUK; GS; SWW}

Pearce, John (20th Century)

Pearce was once chair of the British Humanist Association's Ceremonies Sub-Committee. In "A Future for British Humanism" (*New Humanist*, June 1999), he suggested that as the largest body of non-believers the British Humanist Association needs to lead the way to help an amalgamation of the various groups.

PEARL: See entry for National Committee for Public Education and Religious Liberty.

Pearson, Charles Henry (1830–1894)

Pearson was an Australian secularist, academic, journalist, politician, and education reformer. He was the first headmaster of a school for girls afterwards called the Presbyterian Ladies College, but because of his controversial speeches on free trade and land tax he was asked for his resignation. Supported by David Syme, Pearson wrote regularly for *The Age*. Using the language and values of enlightened Protestantism, he emphasized ways to move a society previously unified by faith to one joined in citizenship. If teachers could not speak what they believed, he argued, it was impractical to teach Christianity. Pearson propounded the reforming power of education based on the principles of such education being secular, compulsory, and free. {SWW}

Pearson, Hesketh (1887–1964)

Pearson, a freethinker, wrote *Tom Paine, Friend of Mankind* (1937). {GS}

Pearson, Karl (1857–1936)

Pearson wrote *Matter and Soul* (1886), *The Positive Creed of Freethought* (c. 1888), and a volume of essays entitled *The Ethic of Freethought* (1888), in which he advocates "a concrete religion which places entirely on one side [that is, excludes] the existence of God and the hope of immortality." A mathematician, he took up the eugenics movement, wrote a life of Sir F. Galton, and was appointed Galton Professor of Eugenics and Director of the Laboratory for National Eugenics at London University. {BDF; RAT; RE}

Peart, Neil (20th Century)

Peart, a lyricist and drummer, is quoted online at a Rush fan site as saying he is a "linear-thinking agnostic, but not an atheist, folks." In a 1980 interview, he mentioned his views by referring to the Rush songs "High Water," "Roll the Bones," "Presto," "Ghost of a Chance," and "The Big Wheel." {CA; E}

Pebody, James (19th Century)

Pebody, with his brother Edward, were leading Northampton secularists in the 1860s. They met at the Admiral Nelson public house on The Green. {RSR}

Pechmeja, Jean de (Died 1785)

A French writer, Pechmeja was a friend of Raynal and wrote a socialistic romance in twelve books. He used the style of Telemachus. {BDF}

Peck, John (Born 1819)

Peck was raised in a log cabin in the Canandaigua Lake region of New York State. He said, "I have stood for hours watching the eagles as they soared over the waters, or swooped down to bring up a big fish. I used to start up the wild deer to see them bound through the forest and thought them the most beautiful and graceful in the world. But my chief delight was on the waves. As soon as the fury of a storm had subsided I was out in a boat and spent hours on the bounding waves." A smithy interested in astronomy, Peck found that "the more I studied the laws of nature, the less use I found for a God. I have studied the systems of religion a good deal, and there is so much absurdity in all of them that, in spite of myself, the ridiculous side is constantly turning up." Peck lectured widely but was considered a blasphemer, particularly because he had become convinced "that the Christian scheme was the most stupendous fraud; and against this superstition I have spent the best energies of my life." Peck wrote *Miracles and Miracle Workers* (1896). {FUS; PUT}

Peck, Robert: The American Library Association's *Banned Books* (1998) cites Peck's *A Day No Pigs Would Die* as often banned because the book "is bigoted against Baptists." (See entry for Banned Books.)

Pecker, Jean-Claude (20th Century)

Pecker, a member of the Secretariat of the Council for Secular Humanism's International Academy of Humanism, is a professor of astrophysics at *the Collège de France, Académie des Sciences*, holding the chair of theoretical astrophysics for twenty-five years. He is an active member of *Union Rationaliste* and is the permanent representative of the International Humanist and Ethical Union (IHEU) at UNESCO. At the Tenth International Humanist and Ethical Union World Congress held in Buffalo (1988), Prof. Pecker addressed the group. In 1970, he wrote *Space Observatories* and in 1992 *The Future of the Sun* (*Le promeneur du ciel*). His essay, "From Aristotle to the New Age," is in *Challenges to the New Enlightenment, Essays in Defense of Reason and Science* (1994).

In 1995 in Delphi, Greece, Pecker spoke at the first International Multidisciplinary Conference on Human Behaviour and the Meaning of Modern Humanism.

In 1996 he was a participant at the Humanist World Conference held in Mexico City. Jim Herrick described Pecker's asking if laicity in France, 1789–1996, was an obsolete model. "The basic religiosity of the French exists beside an essential scepticism," he stated. "Laicity was the fight to separate church and state. There has been a pressure from the political Right for money to be contributed toward Catholic schools (outside the state system). Muslims were largely found in the state schools and there had been the "Islamic scarf" debate where the question of the right of Muslim girls to wear the Islamic scarf at school became an issue." Pecker then described the 1905 laws that established separation of church and state. "The attitude of the French government at that time made France more radically free from Church influence than any other European country, even in the symbols of power." French humanists, he concluded, have the job of making sure that the State remains neutral about religion. Pecker's father, incidentally, was a rabbi.

In 1998 at the congress of the International Humanist and Ethical Union held in Mumbai, Pecker spoke on "Science and the Paranormal," lamenting that so many are not aware that St. Teresa levitating and the image of Christ on the Shroud of Turiun have no basis whatsoever in science. He signed Humanist Manifesto 2000. (See entry for Tolerance.) {SHD; *International Humanist News*, December 1996 and December 1998}

Peden, W. Creighton (1935–)

Peden is a contributing editor for *Religious Humanism*, the quarterly of the Fellowship of Religious Humanists.

Pedersen, Tove Beate (20th Century)

Pedersen is the General Secretary for the Human-Etisk-Forbundel I Norge, which is the largest membership humanist organization (60,000 members in a country of four million).

A psychologist and feminist, she left the church when at high school she was provoked by seeing a bishop blessing weapons in Vietnam. She signed Humanist Manifesto 2000. {*International Humanist News*, October 1998}

PEDOPHILIA

In the mid-1980s stories commenced about lascivious Catholics priests who preferred children as their sex object, thus reanimating age-old stereotypes of the priesthood. Apologists complained about such anti-Catholic prejudice, but Philip Jenkins's *Pedophiles and Priests, Anatomy of a Contemporary Crisis* (1996) makes the case that the "social construction" of the crisis arose from within Roman Catholicism itself. He also holds that the incidence of pedophilia among Catholic clergymen is similar to that found in other denominations. No known study compares the incidence of pedophilia between non-theists and theists. (See entries for Horatio Alger and Priests.)

Peebles, J. M. (1822–1922)

Peebles wrote *The Christ Question Settled, of Jesus, Mary, Medium, Martyr* (1909) and *To Dance With Angels* (1990). {GS}

Peel, Daisy (20th Century)

Peel is president of Oregon State University's Society for Logic and Reason in Corvallis.

Peikoff, Leonard (20th Century)

Peikoff is a writer of objectivist philosophy. In *Objectivism: The Philosophy of Ayn Rand* (1993), he wrote, "Every argument commonly offered for the notion of God leads to a contradiction of the axiomatic concepts of philosophy. At every point, the notion clashes with the facts of reality and with the preconditions of thought." He also is author of *Introduction to Objectivist Philosophy* (1990). {CA; E}

Peirce, Charles Sanders (1839–1914)

Virtually unknown during his lifetime, Peirce greatly influenced William James and John Dewey with his view that logic is the beginning of all philosophic study, and what an idea means is to be found in examining its consequences. He coined the term "pragmatism," which James used with acknowledgment, although it is reported that originally James had chosen to use the word "humanism." Peirce was a scientist. But, according to Charles Hartshorne, Peirce held matter to be " 'mind hide-bound by habit,' the portion of nature in which creative spontaneity is slight, hence largely without consciousness, though not without feeling. There is a continuum of all possible (thought not of all actual) forms and qualities, so that differences commonly regarded as of kind (such as that between a color sensation and a sound sensation) are really differences of degree (theory of Synechism). The whole of evolution is a 'divine poem.' In a few passages of Peirce's writings it seems to be suggested that God is in some manner enriched by the world process, himself a temporal being, but in others God is referred to in traditional fashion as wholly independent of time and the world." For those who find such a view metaphysical, Hartshorne the metaphysician continued: "Primarily a logician, Peirce thoroughly revised many portions of logic and was one of the chief creators of symbolic logic. Among the matters best worked out in his fragmentary and often difficult writings are his frequency theory of probable reasoning, his theory of the categories (also called Phenomenology), and his studies of the kinds and uses of signs.

Peirce lost his position at Johns Hopkins because of allegations that he had seduced his colleagues' wives. As a result, he spent his last days in poverty and obscurity.

After Peirce's death, Morris R. Cohen edited Peirce's major essays, entitling them *Chance, Love, and Logic* (1923). For further evidence that Peirce was theistic, see Hartshorne's 1941 article, "A Critique of Peirce's Idea of God." Peirce's collected papers total eight volumes and were published from 1931 to 1958. A 1993 biography by Joseph Brent points out that it was William James, in a lecture at Berkeley, who named Peirce as the founder of pragmatism, although Peirce himself never used the term in print until afterwards, then favoring the term "pragmaticism." (Those in the cognoscenti pronounce his name PURSE, which rhymes with nurse. See an article about Peirce by Murray G. Murphey in the *Encyclopedia of Philosophy*, Vol. 6. Also see the entry by Leroy F. Searle of the University of Washington in *The Johns Hopkins Guide to Literary Theory & Criticism* which discusses Peirce's pragmaticist maxim that "the entire intellectual purport of any symbol consists in the total of all general modes of rational conduct that, conditionally upon all the possible different circumstances and desires, would ensue upon the acceptance of the symbol." Peirce held that it is by inquiry and experiment that we seek the "fixation of belief," while the ethics of the process is profoundly summarized in the slogan that Peirce would have on "every wall of the city of philosophy: Do not block the way of inquiry." Writes Searle, this means that "no belief is ever ultimate, and no one ever gets the last word.") {CE; CL; ER; TRI}

Pekar, Harvey (20th Century)

Pekar, writer of *American Splendor* (1986) comics, has written, "There are plenty of people who, based on the evidence they perceive, are agnostics, not believing they have answers as to what the purpose of life is and if and when it ends. You can't force them, including me, to be spiritual."

PEKING MAN

In 1995, Prof. Huang Peihua of the Chinese University of Science and Technology reported that, after using electronic spin resonance, it had been determined that the remains of the pre-historic "Peking Man," which had thought to have existed from 700,000 to 200,000 years ago, was not as old as previously thought. He placed the Peking Man as having been active about 585,000 to 250,000 years ago.

In 1996, however, Richard Ku, a researcher at the University of Southern California, announced that the bones, from a cavern at Zhoukoudian near Beijing were at least 400,000 years old and perhaps considerably older. If this is the case, the research contradicts the contentions that the Peking Man deposits were so recent that they suggest that primitive hominids coexisted with the direct ancestors of anatomically modern humans.

"The Zhoukoudian deposits have really stood as evidence of late survival of the species in the Far East," said Philip Rightmire, an anthropologist at the State University of New York at Binghamton. "If you push even the latest levels back to 400,000 years ago, then a claim for overlap begins to fall away. It begins to look more like a gradual evolution from one form to the next, rather than an overlap." The remains of the Peking Man were discovered in 1921, and at least forty hominids that were unearthed reveal that they used stone axes and fire. {*The New York Times*, 2 May 1996}

Pelagius (5th Century C.E.)

A British monk, Pelagius believed in the freedom of the human will, denying that "Original Sin" made man incapable of self-reform. He emphasized human effort in spiritual salvation. For him, human nature was not, in other words, incorrigibly corrupt. Such a view led Pelagius into a controversy with St. Augustine, who won. As a result, and ever since, Christianity has taught that human nature is corrupt and dependent upon God for salvation. The Pelagian heresy foreshadowed the Unitarian belief in human freedom and the positive qualities of human nature. {CE; ER; EU, Paul H. Beattie; JMR; JMRH}

Pelin, Gabriel (19th Century)

Pelin was the French author of works on *Spiritism Explained and Destroyed* (1864) and *God or Science* (1867). {BDF}

Pell, John (20th Century)

Pell, a freethinker, wrote *Ethan Allen* (1929). {FUS}

Pelletan, Pierre Clement Eugène (1813–1884)

A French writer, Pelletan as a journalist wrote in *La Presse* under the name of "*Un Inconnu*," articles distinguished by their love of liberty and progress. In 1852 he published his *Profession of Faith of the Nineteenth Century* and in 1857 *The Law of Progress* and *The Philosophical Kings*. From 1853 to 1855 he opposed Napoléon in the *Siècle* and, afterwards, established *La Tribune Française*. Although elected deputy in 1863, the election was annulled. He was re-elected in 1864. In 1883 he wrote *Is God Dead?* {BDF; RAT; RE}

Pellett, Thomas (Born 1671)

A Fellow of the Royal College of Physicians, Pellett was a Censor in 1717, 1720, and 1727. He edited Newton's *Chronology of Ancient Kingdoms* (1728) and was said to have been one of the most studious and learned physicians of the day. Viscount Percival said in his *Diary:* "Dr. Holmes told me that now Dr. Tyndal [Tindal] is dead and the head of the unbelievers is Dr. Pellett, the physician, who, though he never published anything, is a man of the best learning and the coolest speculative infidel of the whole pack." {RAT}

Pelli, Cesar (1926–)

Pelli, the architect born in Argentina but who became an American citizen, has an international reputation and is a member of the American Academy of Arts and Letters. Named one of the top ten of living American architects, he was dean of Yale's School of Architecture (1977–1984.

His works include the Pacific Design Center in Los Angeles; the U.S. Embassy in Tokyo; the Museum of Modern Art in New York City; the Expansion and Residential Tower of New York City's World Financial Center; New York's Carnegie Hall Tower; Plaza Tower in Costa Mesa, California; Docklands Light Railway Station in London; and the New Main Terminal at Washington National Airport. He had the Kuala Lumpur commission to build the tallest two towers in the world, the Petronas Towers 1 and 2, which were are 1,483 feet or 88 stories each. His first sacred building, a Catholic church at St. John's University in New York, was designed as "a distillation of visiting thousands of churches. It was, however, in line with directives of the Second Vatican Council, he told reporter David W. Dunlap (*The New York Times*, 31 October 1999). "From a philosophical point of view, I'm very much in sympathy with those views," he explained, saying they include "democratic views of what a church should be." Worshipers facing the altar see a slice of sky, framed by the cross. "We want people to see the sky and sense that nature is where we are; that this is God's world." Whether Pelli is as much a freethinker as Frank Lloyd Wright, who also designed churches, is unclear. In 1992, asked about the present author's description of seven humanisms, Pelli wrote,

> Secular Humanism defines our moment, but all its other forms continue to affect us.
>
> {WAS, 15 June 1992}

Pelrine, Eleanor Wright (20th Century)

A Canadian author, Pelrine signed Humanist Manifesto II. He wrote *Abortion in Canada* (1971). {HM2}

Pelton, William (20th Century)

Pelton is active with the Humanists of Denver. (See entry for Colorado Humanists.) {FD}

Pemberton, Charles Reece (1790–1840)

Pemberton was an English actor, author, and freethinker. He traveled throughout the world and, in 1843, wrote *The Autobiography of Pel Verjuice*. {BDF; RAT}

PEMBERTON PUBLISHING COMPANY LTD.

Pemberton Books in England, a publisher of many freethought works, was a precursor to America's Prometheus Books. Trading as Human Horizons and wholly owned by the Rationalist Press Association, it has a special interest in the production of radio and television programs.

Penelhum, Terence (1929–)

Penelhum is a corresponding member in Canada of The Hume Society, a group engaged in scholarly activity concerning David Hume. He wrote *David Hume* (1992) and *Reason and Religious Faith* (1995).

Pengelley, Eric T. (20th Century)

Pengelley, a retired professor of evolution and ecology at the University of California, is a naturalist who holds that religion warps one's mind. The Bible "has been used throughout the ages," he has noted, "to justify everything from slavery to genocide, misogyny to child abuse, and other delectable absolute Christian ethics."

Born to an "areligious" family in Canada, he moved as a toddler with his family to Jamaica, then spent his formative years at a boarding school in England. He spent five years in the Canadian Air Force during World War II. Pengelley is author of *Sex and Human Life* (1978). {*Free Inquiry*, Summer 1996}

PENIS

> • I've seen an awful lot of them, and if you put all the Kennedys together, you wouldn't have a good one.
>
> –Truman Capote,
> musing about the size of the Kennedy brothers' penises
> {*RFK, A Candid Biographyof Robert F. Kennedy* (1998)}

Religionists have been known to express shock when "intimate" body parts are discussed. Although female breast sizes are more readily observable, males historically have hidden their "wedding kit" or "family jewels"—Americans in general find the subject of penis sizes "taboo." Women about to be married, those who have been inculcated by the patriarchal system with the idea that pre-marital sex is bad and hearing "until death do us part," fear "the honeymoon night" for a variety of reasons.

From before 1400 to the mid-sixteenth century, European religious art emphasized the genitals of the infant Jesus and the dead Christ. As pointed out by Leo Steinberg in *The Sexuality of Christ in Renaissance Art and in Modern Oblivion* (1996), such an *ostentatio genitalium* enforced the doctrine of the divine incarnation. God, in short, was all man. Only later were the fig leaves and gravity-defying loincloths added.

In 1995, a secular discussion about penises by Jack McAninch, M.D., chief of urology at San Francisco General Hospital, revealed findings of his study involving eighty men. He found that when erect, the average penis is 5.1 inches in length and 4.9 inches in circumference. When flaccid, the average penis is 3.5 inches in length and 3.9 inches in circumference. His research indicated that an erect penis should be considered "subnormal" only when it is 2.8 inches or less in length and/or 3.5 inches or less in girth. His study shows that only 2% of men fell into that category.

Earlier, the Alfred C. Kinsey Institute for Sex Research had found that the erect penises of college males in its study measured as follows: .2% had 3.75 inches; .3 % had 4 inches; .2 percent had 4.25 inches; 1.7% had 4.5 inches; .8% had 4.75 inches; 4.2% had 5 inches; 4.4% had 5.25 inches; 10.7% had 5.5 inches; 8% had 5.75 inches; 23.9% had 6 inches; 8.8% had 6.25 inches; 14.3% had 6.5 inches; 5.7% had 6.75 inches; 9.5% had 7 inches; 1.8% had 7.25 inches; 2.9% had 7.5 inches; 1% had 7.75 inches; 1% had 8 inches; .3% had 8.25 inches; .3% had 8.5 inches; .1 percent had 8.75 inches; and .1% had 9 inches. According to this, the median erect male penis is 6 inches, not 5.1 inches as in Dr. McAninch's study.

In 1990, the Mariposa Foundation (3123 Schweitzer Drive, Topanga, California 90290) measured circumference as well as length of erect penises in its study on condoms. The median length of erect penises—both white college as well as non-college students—was 6 inches; the median of black college students was 6.25 inches. The circumference of erect penises for whites as well as blacks in its study was between 4.75 and 5 inches. More black college and white non-college students had larger circumference figures than did white college students. The study also indicated that non-college whites have, of those who exceed the average, longer erect penises than college whites. It also indicated that black college students have, of those who exceed the average, longer erect penises than white college students do.

As to whether penis size comes from the father's or the mother's side, Charles Panati in *Sexy Origins & Intimate Things* suggests that "Penile size, as with many male characteristics, is largely a matter of heredity. If Dad is hung, there's a good probability his sons will be too." *Playboy* (June 1998) playfully added to Panati's opinion, "The length of a man's penis has nothing to do with his height or the size of his nose, feet, or hands. There is an inverse correlation, however, to the price of his automobile."

Herman Melville is only one of many writers intrigued by the subject. In *Moby-Dick*, Melville wrote of the whale's penis as being "grandissimus." Northern Italian boatmen along the Po River speak of their *remo ghignante* (tricky oar), according to Alberto Bevilacqua's *Eros* (1996). The carters of Arginotto call it *Alberobello* (beautiful tree), and Mirasole smugglers call their penis *Fratello Branca* (sharp shooter). Men as well as women of other nations often ascribe a pet name to the male's penis.

Until the 1960s, little was discussed in the media about the male genitalia. Groucho Marx brought down the wrath of ABC Radio censors in the late 1940s when he asked a Mrs. Story, the mother of nineteen kids, why she had so many. "Because I love my husband," she reponded. "I love my cigar too," said the comic, "but I take it out of my mouth once in a while."

In 1961 the Barbie doll was given a male partner, Ken, whose penis was a discreet but unbiological bump. In 1971 *Cosmopolitan* pictured a naked man (actor Burt Reynolds). The penis became a part of "The Crying Game," and John Bobbit's was cut off by his angry girlfriend (an act allegedly common in South America), after which Bobbit appeared in pornographic movies with his sewed-on body part. On television, a widely seen "Seinfeld" episode had a worried male concerned that his date had seen his naked penis in a shrunken state and would no longer be interested in him. In 1993 *The New York Times* accepted the word, according to Gay Talese, author of *Thy Neighbor's Wife*. "There's Something About Mary," a movie, teems with references to masturbation, castration, oral sex, and a five-minute sequence in which Ben Stiller gets his penis snagged in his zipper. Female rappers Salt 'N' Pepa can be heard on "Shoop" singing about "What's up with that thang / I wanna know how does it hang / Straight up, wait up . . . ." *Billboard*'s 1997 modern-rock hit was Third Eye Blind's "Semi-Charmed Life," about "snorting speed and getting blow jobs." In the space of a generation, in short, the male organ moved from being a taboo to becoming a public piece of conversation.

When a woman claimed that Bill Clinton, the newly elected President of the United States, had as the Governor of Oklahoma dropped his trousers and demanded oral sex, she cited in a lawsuit brought against Clinton that she had been forced to witness his "distinguishing characteristic" known as Peyronie's disease. Journalists had trouble in choosing the wording for their

Puritanical readers to show that the allegation referred to a sharp curvature when the penis is erect.

A 1999 movie, "American Pie," depicts a teenager boy defiling a just-baked pie, the ads showing the pastry with a hole in the crust where he had masturbated. A 1999 comedy telecast, "Action," has a prostitute putting her hand down the trousers of a movie star and, later, a father discussing the size of his sex organ with his pre-treen daughter. Also in 1999, one of the Presidential candidates—Elizabeth Dole—and 272 million other Americans saw advertisements for Viagra (a sex-enhancing pill for the estimated 30 million men who suffer from impotence). The ads featured her husband, former Senate majority leader and himself once a Presidential candidate from the State of Kansas, Robert Dole.

There is no known study that compares the penis sizes of theists with non-theists or, for that matter, that correlates penis sizes (length, width) with breast and/or feet sizes. Some individuals, in fact, are embarrassed to discuss such, except with strangers. Others, who erroneously believe you can tell a person's religion by the length of his nose, have been known to continue making assumptions about male penis sizes or female breast sizes by referring to their race. (Concerning phallocentrism, see entries for Adamastor, Origen, and John Allegro) {*The Economist*, 10 July 1999; Scott Turow, "Something's Up," *Vanity Fair*, September 1999}

PENIS MODIFICATIONS

For adherents of Judaism and Islam, circumcision is a religious ceremony in which the prepuce of the male child is amputated (*milah*), the glans is bared (*periah*), and the flow of blood is stanched (*metuitzah*). Benedictions (invocations of "divine" blessings) are recited before and after the circumcision, and the child is given a name at this time. Afterwards a festive meal is arranged. Similar ceremonies are found among some Egyptians, Polynesians, Indian tribes of the New World, and primitive tribes of Africa and Australia.

Circumcision, although termed "genital mutilation" by some, came about according to Louis Finkelstein, then the President of the Jewish Theological Seminary of America in New York City, for a variety of possible reasons: (a) for hygienic purposes; (b) as a mark of tribal affiliation; (c) as a preparation for sexual life; (d) as an initiation test of courage before acceptance into the tribe; (e) as a means of sanctifying the generative faculties; and (f) as a sacrifice redeeming the male from the god who gave him life. For Jews circumcision is one of the most important of the 613 commandments.

Raven Rowanchilde of the University of Toronto's sociology department has speculated that men of many cultures alter their penises despite the pain involved in order to augment their appeal as mates. Natalie Angier in *The New York Times* has described some of Rowanchilde's views:

> In Australia and New Guinea, a number of traditional peoples practice subincision, in which a cut is made to the underside of the penis that makes the organ look wider without, apparently, affecting its capacity to perform. According to anthropologists who study these groups, the women consider intercourse with a subincised man to be superior to sex with a non-incised partner.
>
> In twenty cultures of Southeast Asia, men ritually insert objects like bells, balls, pins, rings, or marbles made of ground shells under the skin of the genitals. The To Saloe-maoge women of Sulawesi may even demand to know the number of penile marbles a man possesses before they will consider a proposal of marriage. The Dyak men of Borneo use a palang, a smooth bar with rounded ends made of bone or metal, to transect the head of the phallus; Dyak women, according to anthropologists, say that sex without a palang is like rice, "but with it, it tastes like rice spiced with salt."

{ER; Natalie Angier, *The New York Times*, 7 July 1998}

Penn, Sean (1960-)

An actor, Penn married Madonna Louise Ciccone in 1985, but the two are now divorced. He has been in a variety of Broadway plays and films, receiving an Academy Award in 1996 for "Dead Man Walking." In an interview in *George* (December 1998), he told writer Nick Toches that he is an agnostic. {CA}

Pennetier, Georges (Born 1836)

Pennetier was director of the Museum of Natural History at Rome. He wrote *Origin of Life* (1868), in which he argued the concept of spontaneous generation. {BDF}

PENNSYLVANIA HUMANISTS AND JOURNALS

Pennsylvania has the following groups:

- American Humanist Association, Northeast Region (AHA), POB 1256, Fair Lawn, NJ 07410. Theodora Dolores Trent is coordinator for New York, Pennsylvania, and New Jersey.
- Freethought Society of Greater Philadelphia (FSGP, A chapter of FFRF Inc)., PO Box 242, Pocopson, PA 19366. Margaret Downey and Joe Zemel are the contacts at <downey1@cris.com>
- *Greater Philadelphia Story*, bi-monthly of the Freethought Society of Greater Philadelphia, Chapter of the Freedom From Religion Foundation, PO Box 242, Pocopson, Pennsylvania 19366-0242
- Humanist Association of Greater Philadelphia (AHA), 1702 Sheffield Drive, Blue Bell, Pennsylvania 19422. William Proctor and Gabriel Elias are contact members. Phone: (215) 635-0305.
- Humanist Community of Pittsburgh (AHA), 735 Summeriea Avenue, Washington, Pennsylvania 15301. Stephen Yelanich is the contact.
- Millersville University Humanists on the Web: <www.secularhumanism.org/cfa/orgs.html>.
- Pennsylvania State University humanists are at <http://www.secularhumanism.org/cfa/orgs.html>.
- Philadelphia Gay and Lesbian Secular Humanists, PO Box 2141, Philadelphia, PA 19103 (215) 602-2245. E-mail: <pglsh@hotmail.com>. On the Web: <members.aol.com/pglsh>.
- Pittsburgh Secular Humanists (ASHS), 5003 Impala Drive, Murrysville, PA 15239; (412) 476-5694. E-mail: <jimsioux@sgi.net>. On the Web: <http://www.geocities.com/~shiwpa/PSHMain.html>
- Temple University humanists and freethinkers: <http://www.secularhumanism.org/cfa/orgs.html>.

PENNSYLVANIA STATE UNIVERSITY

Pennsylvania State University humanists are at <http://www.secularhumanism.org/cfa/orgs.html>.

PENTATEUCH

The five books Moses allegedly wrote at God's command—*Genesis*, *Exodus*, *Leviticus*, *Numbers*, and *Deuteronomy*—are known as the Pentateuch. Some contemporary scholars have proposed that the books actually are a compilation of four separate narratives, woven together by ancient editors, or redactors, to create a single text.

The four narratives have been identified by the letters J, E, P, and D–J (the first letter of the German spelling of the name Yahweh), E, for Elohim, the Hebrew word for God; P, for the priestly source, referring to passages concerned with religious law; and D, signifying Deuteronomy.

Richard Elliott Friedman, a professor of Hebrew and comparative literature at the University of California at San Diego, has argued that the D-J narrative is far longer than the three others and comprises a "hidden book," one which runs from *Genesis* to the *First Book of Kings* and is nearly three thousand years old. Thus, he claims, it is the world's first book-length prose work. Harold Bloom's *The Book of J* argued that J's author was a woman.

Religious fundamentalists, however, believe that the Pentateuch was "revealed" by God, who dotted each "i" and crossed each "t." Secular humanists, after analyzing the various books, find God's creation lacking in literary quality when compared to works by such authors as Sophocles, Shakespeare, Goethe, or Victor Hugo. {Gustav Niebuhr, *The New York Times*, 23 January 1999}

PENTECOST: See entry for Holy Ghost.

Pentecost, Hugh (19th Century)

Pentecost, who was a freethinker, wrote *What I Believe* (189-?). {GS}

PENTECOSTAL CHURCHES

In the United States, the Assemblies of God organization numbers over 2,400,000. Pentecostal Assemblies of the World, which represents an estimated 1,000,000, is at 3939 Meadows Drive, Indianapolis, Indiana 46205. The United Pentecostal Rhuch Internation, which numbers an estimated 700,000, is at 8855 Dunn Road, Hazelwood, Missouri.

PENTECOSTALISM

A contemporary movement in religion, Pentecostalism is based on direct personal appeal and power rather than dependence upon polity and doctrines. The Pentecostalism which is found in the

United States began with such ministers as Charles Fox Parham, who preached to his Topeka congregation in 1901 that speaking in tongues was objective evidence of baptism in the Spirit, and William Joseph Seymour, a self-educated African American who in 1906 said that if people prayed with sufficient fervor God would send "a new Pentecost," one like the miracle described in *Acts*. *Pentecost*, a word which derives from the Greek, is a name for the Jewish Feast of Weeks, which falls on the fiftieth day after Passover. Worldwide, it is growing rapidly, gaining an estimated twenty million members a year. The Yoido Full Gospel (Pentecostal) Church in Seoul, South Korea, has 800,000 members. The various Pentecostal groups in 1994 were estimated to total as many as 410 million.

Harvey Cox, in *Fire From Heaven: The Rise of Pentecostal Spirituality and the Reshaping of Religion in the Twenty-first Century* (1994), distinguishes between Pentecostalism and fundamentalism: "[They are not the same. Fundamentalists attach such unique authority to the letter of the verbally inspired Scripture that they are suspicious of the Pentecostals' stress on the immediate experience of the Spirit of God. . . . [W]hile the beliefs of the fundamentalists, and of many other religious groups, are enshrined in formal theological systems, those of Pentecostalism are embedded in testimonies, ecstatic speech, and bodily movement. But it *is* a theology, a full-blown religious cosmos, an intricate system of symbols that respond to the perennial questions of human meaning and values."

"Speaking in tongues" (glossolalia) is observed at meetings. In 1906 after Seymour and his followers began speaking in tongues, which they held is a sign of the coming of the end of the world as predicted in the *Book of Revelation*, San Francisco was shaken a few days later by the great earthquake. Seymour, who had been shunned by most up until this time, now found himself surrounded by flocks of blacks and whites who uncharacteristically joined together despite that era's racial separation. "God was now assembling a new and racially inclusive people to glorify his name and to save a Jim Crow nation lost in sin," Cox wrote. Although whites soon split off into their own congregations, Cox found that Pentecostalism is "one of the least segregated forms of Christianity" in a religion which allegedly preaches brotherhood.

Oral Roberts in the 1960s encouraged a Pentecostal revival organized by faith-healing. The formal origin of the *new* Pentecostalism or *charismatic* movement is traced to Dennis Bennett, an Episcopal minister whose methods influenced many Protestant denominations, the Roman Catholic church, and, to a lesser extent, Eastern Orthodox communions.

Another type of Pentecostalism consists of sects which adopt or tolerate beliefs and practices such as ancestor worship and polygamy. These are found mostly among non-whites in Africa, Latin America, and Asia.

Pentecostalism is just one more form of a supernaturalistic religion to rationalists or freethinkers, who nevertheless are impressed by the growth of the movement among the poor, the dispossessed, the less education, and minorities. (See entry for Tongues.) {S. M. Burgess and G. B. McGee, eds., *Dictionary of Pentecostal and Charismatic Movements* (1988); CE; Dan Wakefield, "Speaking in Tongues," *The Nation*, 23 January 1995}

Penter, John (20th Century)

Penter is author of *Circumstantial Evidence* (1981). {GS}

Penzig, Rudolph (Born 1855)

Penzig, a German educationist, wrote *Arthur Schopenhauer und menschliche Willensfreiheit* (1879) and edited *Ethische Kultur*. Active in the Monist League, Penzig showed his rationalism in *Laienpredigten* (1905, a collection of ethical addresses). {RAT}

PEOPLE

• It is absurd to divide people into good and bad. People are either charming or tedious.

–Oscar Wilde

• When there are two conflicting versions of the story, the wise course is to believe the one in which people appear at their worst.

–H. Allen Smith

• The devil is an optimist if he thinks he can make people meaner.

–Karl Kraus

• People who have no faults are terrible; there is no way of taking advantage of them.

–Anatole France

PEOPLE FOR THE AMERICAN WAY

People for the American Way (2000 M St NW, Washington, DC 20036) is an organization dedicated to separation of church and state. It specifically is not anti-religion.

PEOPLE FOR THE ETHICAL TREATMENT OF ANIMALS

People for the Ethical Treatment of Animals (PETA) is at PO Box 42516, Washington, DC 20015. (See entry for Ingrid Newkirk.)

Perelman, Chaim (Born 1912; Deceased)

Perelman, a Polish-born professor of philosophy at the University of Brussels, Belgium, and dean of the faculty of philosophy of letters at the Free University of Brussels, was a Humanist Laureate in the Council for Secular Humanism's International Academy of Humanism. He signed Humanist Manifesto II. Perelman wrote *New Rhetoric and the Humanities* (1979) and *Justice, Law and Argument: Essays on Moral and Legal Reasoning (1980)*. Perelman had been a member of the board of directors of Hebrew University. {HM2}

Pérez, Allen (20th Century)

Pérez, formerly a Costa Rican lawyer, is the Unitarian Universalist Service Committee's Latin America-Caribbean associate. He and his wife, **Debbie Duquay Pérez**, have been active in the *Asociación Ético Humanista Costarricense* (ASEHUCO). In the State of Washington and in Costa Rica, the two have fought for human rights. He currently works on behalf of the Unitarian Universalist Service Committee in Cuba, Haiti, and Central America.

Pérez-Escalarin, Antonio (20th Century)

Perez-Escalarin is the author of *Atheism and Liberation* (1978). {GS}

Pérez Galdós, Benito (1843–1920)

Pérez Galdós has been called the greatest Spanish novelist since Cervantes. He wrote a cycle of forty-six historical novels, *Episodios nacionales*, which recount episodes in Spanish history from 1805 to the end of the century. He also wrote *Doña Perfecta* (1876); an attack on clericalism and religious intolerance, *La familia de León Roch* (1878), and a four-volume work contrasting the lives of two women of widely different classes, *Fortunata and Jacinta* (1886–1887). Elected to the Royal Academy in 1897, Pérez Galdós became deputy of the republican party in Madrid. Upon becoming blind in 1912, he continued to dictate his books until his death. In the words of McCabe, "No other man did as much as this distinguished atheist for the emancipation of Spain." He added that the British Royal Society of Literature presented its gold medal to him as "the most distinguished living representative of Spanish literature." {BDF; CE; JM; RAT}

PERFECTIBILITY OF MAN

• Out of timber so crooked as that from which man is made, nothing entirely straight can be built.

–Immanuel Kant

Rousseau and others advanced the doctrine of the perfectibility of man, saying that people are capable of achieving perfection on earth through natural means, without the grace of God. Inasmuch as "perfectibility" is logically impossible to attain, it has been recommended that the concept might better be termed "the improvability of man." (See entry for Charles Francis Potter who regretted using "perfectibility" rather than "improvability" of man.)

Perfitt, Philip William (Born 1820)

Perfitt was a liberal minister at South Place and elsewhere. He founded the Free Church on London's Newman Street and edited the *Path-finder* (1859–1861). {VI}

Pericles (c. 495–429 B.C.E.)

Under the tutelage of Pericles, Athens reached its zenith. The famed "Funeral Oration of Pericles," as told by Thucydides, includes the following: "Our constitution is named a democracy, because it is in the hands not of a few but of the many. Our laws secure equal justice for all in their private disputes, and our public opinion welcomes and honors talent in every branch of achievement, not for any sectional reason, but on grounds of excellence alone. . . . We are lovers of beauty without extravagance, and lovers of wisdom without unmanliness." Nowhere is he cited as having mentioned the name of a single god, nor does he mention some future existence for the fallen Athenian soldiers who have died. The *Encyclopedia Britannica* states that Pericles was "unpopular on account of his rationalism in religious matters," to which McCabe responds that it is clear Pericles shared the atheism that had then become common in Greece. Humanists find it difficult to locate an analogous contemporary in a high government position.

When Pericles was married, around forty, and with two adolescent sons, he met twenty-five-year-old Aspasia, a golden-haired lass from Megara who managed a brothel and conducted a school for elocution and philosophy, intended principally for young ladies. She then withdrew from teaching and resumed the role of courtesan, became his new mistress, and was already pregnant by him. Inasmuch as she was from Megara and not an Athenian citizen, he could not marry her. But he arranged another marriage for his former wife, brought Aspasia into his house, and willed his fortune to their son, Pericles II.

Pericles himself is believed to have died of a combination of flu and toxic shock syndrome, during an Athenian plague that lasted from 430 to 427 B.C.E. The condition was one in which a maddening fever was followed by bloodshot eyes, inexplicable vomiting and bleeding, followed by skin lesions and diarrhea. Medical historians have been unable to cite the exact cause, inasmuch as Thucydides's accounts lacked even rudimentary medical vocabulary. He wrote that the disease was African, from somewhere south of Ethiopia. His *phlyktainai* could, however, be translated as blisters, which have fluid, or as calluses, which do not. Blisters might suggest smallpox, but bubonic plague is a possibility. (See entry for Plague.) {CE; CL; JM; Anthony Ramirez, *The New York Times*, 18 August 1996; PA; RE; TYD}

Perier, Casimir (1777–1832)

Although he had a clerical education, Perier became a wealthy banker who entered politics as a moderate anti-clerical. He was Minister of Finance and Commerce under the restored monarchy, but he resigned and supported the Revolution of 1830. Later he was President of the Chambre, President of the Council, and Minister of the Interior. Perier, whose deism is found in his *Opinions et discours* (1838), was the grandfather of President Casimir-Perier. {RAT; RE}

Peris, Daniel (20th Century)

In *Storming the Heavens: The Soviet League of the Militant Godless* (1998), Peris details the history of atheism in the Soviet Union. The Bolsheviks, he mentions that Lenin once said, were the "Jacobins, plus the proletariat." Their League of the Godless turned out posters by the thousands that proclaimed "Religion is poison. Protect your children." To counter a widespread folk belief that the corpses of particularly holy persons did not decay, the Bolsheviks opened the tombs to demonstrate that they rotted like the rest of mankind. *The Godless*, Peris found in his research, was a weekly with a circulation ranging from two to five hundred thousand. {Fred Whitehead, *Freethought History* #26, 1998}

Periyar (Erode V. Ramaswami) (1879–1973)

Periyar (which means "great leader") was a controversial leader of social reform and of atheism in modern India. He used the pseudonym Erode V. Ramaswami. Periyar was greatly influenced by Robert G. Ingersoll and had much of his writing translated into Tamil. Deodhekar notes the complex political struggles he endured, and at his death he was buried in a simple wooden coffin, not cremated as is the Hindu custom. Vast crowds gathered in Madras to pay homage. His grave is now a monument to atheism and to Tamil aspiration. Periyar was an editor of *Kudi Arasu* and *Pakutharivu*, both in Telugu.

Delegates to the fourth World Atheist Conference in Vijayawada also attended a one-day State Rationalist Conference held by the Periyar organization. In the center of their multi-building compound is a statue of Periyar with one of his sayings on the base. On seeing it, several Americans read it, shouting at the top of their lungs, "There is no God. There is no God. There is no God at all. He who invented God is a fool. He who propagates God is a scoundrel. He who worships God is a barbarian." (See entries for Ramendra, K. Veeramanim, and G. Vijayam.) {EU, Govind N. Deodhekar; FUK; HNS2; Jerry Rauser, *The Free Mind*, February 1996}

PERIYAR PAGUTHARIVU PASARAI

Periyar Pagutharivu Pasarai is an atheist organization in Kuala Lumpur, Malaysia. Phone (603) 4456781. (See entry for Nakkeeran Parry).

Perkins, A(lice) J. G. (20th Century

Perkins, with Theresa Wolfson, wrote *Frances Wright: Free Enquirer* (1939). {GS}

Perkins, Erasmus (19th Century)

Perkins, the publisher of a periodical, *The Theological Inquirer* (1815), reprinted Shelley's *Refutation of Deism* as well as other essays and letters sympathetic to letters sympathetic to atheism. Berman finds that Perkins lacked Richard Carlile's dynamism and publicizing genius and that his periodical had little circulation or impact. Further, Perkins neither avowed nor defended atheism. {HAB}

Perkins, Frederick W. (20th Century)

A Universalist minister, Perkins once wrote, "The traditional idea has been, and in the minds of many Christians it still persists, that religious truth must be certified by some external authority. The Catholic or High Church Anglican says, 'I believe because the church or the bishop or long-established tradition says so.' The orthodox Protestant, who yet craves some substitute for the ancient authorities to determine what to believe, says, 'I believe because Jesus says so.' The true liberal says, 'I believe because reason and conscience say so.' This does not mean that the liberal must discard all external helps. Only a consummate intellectual egotist would be so lacking in spiritual humility."

Perkins, Palfrey (1883–1976)

Perkins, a Unitarian activist and minister, was a supporter of the Harvard Divinity School, was chairman of the Board of Trustees of Wellesley College, encouraged the Boston Symphony Orchestra, and helped form the Unitarian Service Committee. {U&U}

Perkins, Thomas Handasyd (1764–1854)

A prominent member of the Federalist Party, Perkins was elected eight times to the Senate and three times to the lower house of the Massachusetts legislature. His philanthropy included the Boston Athenaeum and the New England Asylum for the Blind. A Unitarian, Perkins worshipped at the Church of the Rev. Dr. Ezra Stiles Gannett, and that is where his funeral was held, according to Thomas G. Cary's *Memoir of Thomas Handasyd Perkins* (1856). {EG}

Perón, Eva Duarte de (1919–1952)

The wife of Argentine's President Juan Domingo Perón, Eva, a devout Catholic, became something of a worldly saint to her countrymen. *Santa Evita* by Tomás Dujovne Ortiz tells what happens to Eva, three years after her death at a time when plans to overthrow Perón were underway and a new junta decided to insure that she remain dead, both physically and symbolically. An Army colonel who as a spy lectured about secrecy and rumor and who was an admirer of Kant and Edmund Burke, hijacked Eva's mummified body. The corpse was first hidden behind a movie theater's screen, a place that often played Abbott and Costello movies. (The theater's owner had called the body "Sweetie.") Moved various other places, it was then detected by an Army officer's wife in her husband's attic, leading to his shooting his pregnant wife in a panic and ending up as a destitute drunk who came to believe Evita, as Eva was affectionately known, had been stolen from him and buried on the moon. (See Sarah Kerr, "Working Girl," *The New York Review of Books*, 20 February 1997.)

Perot, Jean Marie Albert (19th Century)

A French banker, Perot wrote *Man and God* (1881) and *Moral and Philosophical Allegories* (1883). {BDF}

Perrier, Jean Octave Edmond (Born 1844)

Perrier, a French zoologist, was curator at the Museum of Natural History in Paris. He wrote numerous works on natural history and one on *Transformisme* (1888). An agnostic, Perrier stated in a symposium on spiritualism, "I believe that when one is dead, one is dead for a very long time." {BDF; RAT}

Perrin, Raymond S. (19th Century)

Perrin wrote *The Religion of Philosophy*, an attempt to unify knowledge and compare the chief philosophical and religious systems of the world. {BDF}

Perrons, François Tommy (1822–1901)

Perrons was a French historian, a professor of rhetoric at the Polytechnic and inspector for the Paris Academy. He wrote *Jérome Savanarole* (2 volumes, 1853), *L'église et l'état sous le règne de Henri IV* (2 volumes, 1872), and *La démocratie en France au moyen age* (2 volumes, 1873). These were crowned by the Academy. His chief work is *Histoire de Florence* (6 volumes, 1877–1884), but the work of particular interest to rationalists is his *Les Libertins en France au XVII siècle* (1896). {RAT; RE}

Perry, Charles M. (20th Century)

Perry wrote *The Ironic Humanist* (1924). {GS}

Perry, David (20th Century)

A public school teacher, Perry asked his class one day if they knew where snakes came from. Amidst the cries of "God made them," he heard a lone voice utter, "They evolved from fish."

His goal, he has said, is not to create juvenile humanists but, rather, to teach individuals to think rationally. {*Secular Nation*, July-September 1998}

Perry, Ralph Barton (1876–1957)

Perry was a philosopher at Harvard University (1876–1957) and the Pulitzer Prize-winner in 1936 for *The Thought and Character of William James* (1935). Asked for his views on humanism, Perry wrote that at the age of eighty he was confined to a hospital bed but recommended that his new work, *The Humanity of Man* (1956) be consulted. In a review of that book in *The Journal of Philosophy* (16 August 1956), Harold A. Larrabee wrote, "A weakness for which the author is not responsible, but which the book does little to remedy, lies in the multiple and confusing meanings of 'humanism.' The ancient classicists, the Renaissance scholars, the followers of More and Babbitt, and the scientific anti-supernaturalists each have firm holds on separate corners of the label, and have torn it to shreds. How can any small group of men make good an exclusive claim to so broad a classification? Professor Perry's own 'humanism,' which includes and excludes something of each of them, only complicates further an already intolerable imbroglio in semantics. The humanity of man, as freedom of choice, is bountifully manifested in the diverse and conflicting ways in which men lay claim to the title of human." [WAS, 1 May 1956}

Perry, Thomas Ryley (19th Century)

Perry, one of Carlile's shopmen, was sentenced in 1824 to three years in Newgate Prison for having sold Palmer's *Principles of Nature.* He became a chemist at Leicester and in 1844 petitioned Parliament for two prisoners Paterson and Roalfe, who were imprisoned for blasphemy. Perry stated to the judge that his own imprisonment had not fulfilled the judge's hope of his recantation. {BDF}

Perry, William Graves Jr. (1913–)

Director of the Bureau of Study Counsel at Harvard University and author with C. P. Whitlock of the *Harvard Reading Course* (1948), Perry contributed humanistic works to Priscilla Robertson when she was editor of *The Humanist.* One of his books was *Forms of Intellectual and Ethical Development in the College Years* (1968). Students remember Dr. Perry as the scholarly gentleman, the superlative professor with a prominent hearing aid in each ear.

Perry, William J. [Admiral] (1927–)

Perry, the son of a grocer who became a teacher at Stanford University, was appointed in 1977 to be President Jimmy Carter's Under-Secretary of Defense for research and engineering. A person who emphasized technological solutions to military problems, he was appointed in 1994 by President Bill Clinton to head the Pentagon as Secretary of Defense. In 1995 he was Vice President of Hambrecht & Quist, a San Francisco-based investment banking firm that specializes in high-tech companies. Admiral Perry is a Unitarian. {*Current Biography* 1995}

Perrycoate, Frank Hill (20th Century)

A freethinker, Perrycoate wrote *On the Influence of Religion Upon Truthfulness* (1913) and *Religion and Moral Civilisation* (1915). {GS}

Persons, Stow (1913–)

Persons is author of *Free Religion: An American Faith* (1947), which studied the free religious movement that emerged from Unitarianism following the Civil War. {FUS}

PERUVIAN HUMANISTS

Manuel Abraham Paz y Miño is president in Peru of *Asociación Ediciones, Revista Peruana de Filosofía Aplicada.* His *Peruvian Journal of Applied Philosophy* (El Corregidor 318, Lima 25, Peru) is on the Web: <RPFA@www.computextos.com.pe>. His e-mail: <rpfa@geocities.com>.

PERVERSION

- A pervert is one who denies the pleasure of sex.

–Anonymous

- *Nicht Der Homosexuelle Ist Pervers, Sondern Die Situation In Der Er Lebt"* ("It's Not the Homosexual Who is Perverse but the Situation in Which He Lives"

–A 1970 German movie directed by Rosa von Praunheim.)

Peshkov, Alexei Maximovitch: See entry for Maxim Gorky.

PESSIMISM

- Pessimism, n. A philosophy forced upon the convictions of the observer by the disheartening prevalence of the optimist with his scarcrow hope and his unsightly smile.

–Ambrose Bierce
The Devil's Dictionary

- Pessimist: one who, when he has the choice of two evils, chooses both.

–Oscar Wilde

- A pessimist thinks everybody is as nasty as himself, and hates them for it.

–George Bernard Shaw

Pestalozzi, Johann Heinrich (1746–1827)

Pestalozzi was a Swiss educational reformer. His theories laid the foundation of modern elementary education. After studying theology at the University of Zurich, he conducted a school for poor children, then directed the experimental institute at Yverdon, which was established on Pestalozzian principles. His theory was based on the importance of a pedagogical method that corresponded to the natural order of individual development and of concrete experiences. He held that the individuality of each child is paramount and something that has to be cultivated actively through education. He opposed the prevailing system of memorization learning and strict discipline, replacing it with a system based on love and an understanding of the child's world. Running through much of Pestalozzi's writing is the idea that education should be moral as well as intellectual. "No other Italian, and few Frenchmen, wrote French as well as he," said Larousse. In 1871, at the triumph of the moderates, Pestalozzi was expelled from France and ceased to be a friend of that country.

A deist like Rousseau, Pestalozzi kept theological instruction out of his schools, despite the heavy pressure of the clergy. "We seek the foundations of dogma and of all religious opinions in human nature," he wrote in a "Report to Parents." E. Langner, in a detailed study of his views, concludes that Pestalozzi "rejects all sectarian claims." {CE; JM; RAT; TRI}

PETER

Peter is a name conferred by Jesus on Simon, his closest disciple. Matthew contains a passage in which Jesus acclaims Peter as the rock on which he will build his church. Robert Gorham Davis points out, in connection with the Roman Catholic view that ordaining married men would be a drastic departure from the tradition of the Roman church, "It depends on how early a tradition begins. All three synoptic Gospels agree that Peter, the rock on which Jesus founded his church, was married, with a mother-in-law that Jesus cured of a fever. Paul exclaims in his anguished first letter to the Corinthians, 'Have I no right to take a Christian wife about with me, like the rest of the apostles and the Lord's brothers and Cephas?' 'Cephas,' meaning 'rock,' is the Aramaic equivalent of Peter, whose inheritors the popes profess to be. If he was married, why not they?"

Peter I (Peter the Great) (1672–1725)

Peter, czar of Russia (1682–1725), was a major figure in the development of imperial Russia. After visiting Europe, he returned to Russia and started ruthless reforms in order to change what he considered were the country's backward ways. Before actually outlawing beards, he imposed a tax on them, later personally cutting some of the beards himself. Also, he ordered Russians to wear Western dress henceforth. He introduced territorial conscription, enlarged and modernized the army, founded a navy, and set up military-technical schools. He increased the number of nobles owing service to the state, forced nobles' sons to attend military-technical schools, and created a bureaucratic hierarchy in which promotion depended on merit rather than birth. The Academy of Sciences was founded, the calendar reformed, and the alphabet simplified.

Although the discontented looked to Peter's son, Alexis, the son was tried for treason and tortured to death in 1718, followed by Peter's proclaiming himself "emperor of all Russia" in 1721. Peter's second wife, crowned as Catherine I in 1724, succeeded him. Those who regard Russia as essentially European praise him for his policy of Westernization, and others who consider Russia a unique civilization attack him for turning Russia from its special path of development.

Peter was known for having convulsive fits. He had, states the *Columbia Encyclopedia*, "a bearlike constitution, was of gigantic stature, and possessed herculean physical prowess. He drank himself into stupors and indulged in all conceivable vices but could rouse himself at a moment's notice, and he was willing to undergo all the physical exertions and privations that he exacted from his subjects."

"That Peter rejected and mercilessly mocked the Orthodox Catholic religion is well known," McCabe wrote, adding, "As French Deism had not at that time reached Russia it is clear that he and his leading companions at court were atheists. His favorite type of orgy was to travesty and insult the only religion he knew. In considering these orgies and the intemperance of his character we have to remember that Peter did not introduce them into Russian life. It had in moral respects remained barbaric during centuries of church domination, and Peter's breaches in its isolation, on which the clergy insisted, led to the beginning of an improvement of life and character."

Alexei Gostev, however, labels Peter as one who "inclined to Protestantism." For example, he tried to close all monasteries. The mockery of church rituals, Gostev adds, is not the result of his and his companions' atheism but more a desire to challenge the value system of the period. (WAS, interview with Alexei Gosteve, 1998) {CE; JM}

Péters, Laurent (20th Century)

A French journalist, Péters is with the Association for the Mohsen Hachtroudi Foundation. In 1996 he was a participant at the Humanist World Congress in Mexico City.

Petersen, Bill (20th Century)

At the Fourth Annual Atheist Convention hosted in 1998 by the St. Louis Rationalist Society, Petersen spoke about "Activism Against the Boy Scouts."

Petersen, Steve (20th Century)

Petersen is co-chairman of the Minnesota Atheists. He wrote "The Death of Each of Us Is in the Order of Things" for *Secular Nation* (Summer 1995}.

Peterson, David (20th Century)

Peterson is editor of *The Separationist*, the newsletter of the Secular Humanists of the Low Country in South Carolina. He is on the Web: <http://www.serve.com/sechumlo>. Peterson's E-mail: <sechumlo@mail.serve.com>.

Peterson, James (20th Century)

Peterson is active with the Humanists of Tallahassee. (See entry for Florida Atheists, Humanists.) {FD}

Peterson, R. (19th Century)

Dublin-born, Peterson at the age of twelve was sent by his father to New York to learn the mercantile business. Not liking this, he began life on his own as a newsboy sleeping under stoops and in crockery crates on the docks. Emigrating to Ohio, he learned the printer's business, became a lawyer in Texas, and published that state's second Republican newspaper. His editorials attracted the attention of the Ku Klux Klan which, one midnight, surrounded his house, bullied and threatened, then rode away. Peterson published *Common Sense*, a freethought journal "devoted to the rise of reason and the downfall of faith." {PUT}

Petrarch, Francesco (Petrarca) (1304–1374)

One of the great figures of Italian literature, the poet Petrarch was among the first to realize that Platonic thought and Greek studies provided a new cultural framework. A friend of Boccaccio, he can be termed a freethinker, according to Robertson, in that "with less aggressiveness but also without recoil, stood for independent culture and a rational habit of mind as against the dogmatics and tyrannies of the Church." Petrarch was in the main a practical humanist, "not in accord with the verbalizing scholastic philosophy of his time, and disposed to find his intellectual guide in the skeptical yet conservative Cicero."

Called "the first modern man" and "the founder of modern criticism, Petrarch earned a name for resisting all dogmatisms. . . . For himself, having little speculative power, he was disposed to fall back on a simple and tolerant Christianity. Thus he is quite unsympathetic in his references to those scholars of his day who privately indicated their unbelief."

Although he knew nothing of the teaching of Averroës, for example, he spoke of him as "that mad dog who, moved by an execrable rage, barks against his Lord Christ and the Catholic faith." Such a statement is ironic inasmuch as Averroës was a *Muslim* scholar. (See entry for Classical Humanism.) {CE; ER; HNS2; JMR; JMRH; RE}

Petit, Claude (17th Century)

Petit was a French poet who, being accused of having written some impious pieces, was burned on the Place de Grève in 1665. {BDF}

Petrini, Henrik (1863–1957)

Petrini, a professor of physics in Sweden, was a non-theist. (See entry for Scandinavian Unbelievers.)

Petronius Arbiter, Gaius (c. 27–66)

A Roman satirist (whose original name was Titus Petronius Niger according to Plutarch and Pliny but Gaius according to Tacitus), Petronius was one of the first authors to utilize humor extensively. He used a literary device, *petroni arbitri satyricon*, which satirized manners of a place at a particular time and which used colloquial language. Known as the *arbiter elegantiae* in Nero's court, he had the reputation of being a luxurious profligate. When caught in an intrigue and arrested with no hope of being freed, he called his friends. In their presence, he slit his veins and bled to death in leisurely fashion while they observed the tragic scene. "It is fear," he declared in *Satyricon*, his satire of excesses in Nero's Rome, "that first brought gods into the world."

A generation ago, John Sullivan and William Arrowsmith provided the standard translation of *Satyricon*. Today, according to Peter Green of the University of Texas at Austin, R. Bracht Branham and Daniel Kinney have supplied the standard translation. Scholars still discuss whether *The Satyricon* is a genitive plural with *libri*—books—understood, in which case the work is "a recital of lecherous happenings." Or is it a neuter plural, *Satyrica*, which Branham and Kinney state is "a heuristic metaphor for the moral ambiance of the fictional world Petronius has created"? What is apparent is that Petronius has pleased centuries of audiences with his descriptions of homosexual rape; dildoes spruced up with oil, pepper, and crushed nettle seeds; incestuous voyeurism; heterosexual cornholing; and energetic pederasty.

In *The Satyricon* is a character, Encolpius (a well-endowed stud whose name means "crotch"), and scenes such as the following:

> After serving up these verses he befouled me [the narrator is male] with a slobbery kiss. Then he got up on my bed and in spite of my resistance forced the covers off me. He labored long and hard over my groin—in vain! The make-up caked on his face melted and streamed off in rivulets; there was so much rouge in his wrinkles you'd have thought of an old wall battered by a rainstorm.

> There are just two things that keep him from being one in a million: he's circumcised and he snores. Now I don't mind that he's cross-eyed. So's Venus. That's why he's never quiet: one eye is always on the move. I only paid three hundred for him.

> He persuaded the girl to sit down on top of his [penis], and ordered Corax to get under the bed he was lying on and keep his master in motion by putting his hands on the ground and thrusting his own loins against the bottom of the bed. He obeyed the command reluctantly and the girl was skillful enough to match him, thrust for thrust. When the business was nearing a climax, Eumolpus ordered Corax in a loud voice to redouble his efforts. So old Eumolpus, sandwiched between his valet and his mistress, was riding a kind of seesaw.

For Green, the Branham and Kinney translation makes clear that as a philosophical Sceptic, Petronius pens verses on the deceptiveness of dreams and the senses. And, like Epicurus, he thinks that fear created gods.

The controversial 1968 film version of *The Satyricon* was by Federico Fellini. {BDF; GL; JMR; JMRH; Peter Green, "Bigus Dickus," *The New Republic* (28 October 1996; TYD}

Petrosyan, Maria (20th Century)

Petrosyan's *Humanism* (1972) is a Marxist discussion of what is needed as an alternative to religious education.

Petrowski, Marc (20th Century)

After receiving his doctorate in gerontology and the sociology of knowledge, Petrowski taught at East Central University in Oklahoma. A non-theist, he wrote "Prayer and Healing" for *Freethought Today* (March 1996).

Petruccelli della Gattina, Ferdinando (1813–1890)

Petruccelli was an Italian writer and historian. A deputy to the Naples Parliament in 1848, he took part in the anti-Papal Revolution and was driven to France and his property confiscated at its failure. His history of the Papal elections, *Histoire diplomatique des Conclaves* (1864–1865, 4 volumes) was put on the Vatican's *Index*. {BDF; RE}

Petrus de Abano: See entry for Abano.

Petty, William [Marquis] (1737–1807)

Petty, a British statesman who became Premier, had the titles of the Marquis of Lansdowne, Viscount Colne, Earl Wycombe, and Earl of Shelburne. He opposed the American war and, as Premier, was happy to bring it to a close. Later, he opposed the French War and, in cooperation with Bentham, supported reform at home. Sir John Bowring, in his *Memoir of Bentham*, wrote that "Lord Shelburne avoided talking on religious subjects for fear, he hinted, of getting into a scrape, but he avowed to Bentham that his opinions were what is called skeptical." {JM; RAT; RE}

Petzoldt, Joseph (1862–1929)

Petzoldt was President of the German Society of Positive Philosophers. Like Mach, and more or less following Avenarius, Petzoldt pleaded for a psychophysical parallelism, holding that the psychic and the physical, or what are commonly called spirit and matter, are two aspects of a monistic reality. He described himself as an Empirio-critical Positivist. {RAT}

Pevey, Richard (20th Century)

Pevey is active with the Shreveport Secular Humanists. (See entry for Louisiana Humanists.) {FD}

Peypers, H.F.A. (Born 1856)

Peypers, a Dutch writer, was an Amsterdam physician. He contributed to *De Dageraad* and was one of the five editors of that freethought monthly. {BDF}

Peyrard, François (1760–1822)

Peyrard, a French mathematician, was a warm partisan of the revolution and was one of those who in 1793 incited Bishop Gobel to abjure his religion. An intimate friend of Sylvian Maréchal, Peyrard furnished him with notes for his *Dictionnaire des Athées*. Peyrard wrote a work on *Nature and Its Laws* (1793–1794) and translated the works of Euclid and Archimedes. Peyrard proposed the piercing of the Isthmus of Suez. {BDF; RAT}

Peyrat, Alphonse (Born 1812)

Peyrat was a French writer who fought against the Second Empire. He founded *l'Avenir National*, which was condemned several times because of its controversial content. In 1871 he was elected deputy of the Seine and proposed the proclamation of the Republic. Among other works, he wrote a *History of the Dogma of the Immaculate Conception* (1855), *History and Religion* (1858), and *Elementary and Critical History of Jesus* (1864). {BDF; RAT}

Peyrefitte, Roger (1907–)

An openly gay French novelist, Peyrefitte is no favorite among Catholic officials. *The Red Cassock* is a parody about the murders of Pope Paul VI and Pope John Paul I. *The Keys of St. Peter* is about corruption in the Vatican. *This Special Friendship* (1945) takes place in a Jesuit school for boys, where the youths are counseled daily to guard themselves against impure friendship, yet where sex abounds. When a French film based on the book was released in 1963, the film was considered scandalous by showing sixteen-year-old George failing head-over-heels for Alexandre, a twelve-year-old, exchanging poems, swearing eternal friendship in a blood ceremony, and meeting in secret.

In one of his tales, Peyrefitte told about a marquis who discovered when he was forty-five, and "with fright," that he was gay. "Then," he continued, "he realized he had lost forty years of his life. One should never lose hope. Homosexuality can strike any straight man at any age." *The Exile of Capri* (1961) is a fictional account of Baron Jacques d'Adelswärd Fersen (1880-1923), a pederast.

Peyrefitte won the 1991-1992 Prize of the Balzac Academy for his work as a whole.

Peyrère, Isaac de la (1594–1676)

A French writer, Peyrère was brought up as a Protestant. In *Praeadamitae*, because he had maintained that men lived before Adam, the bishop of Namur censured it, the hangman in Paris burned the book, and la Peyrère was arrested at Brussels by order of the Archbishop of Malines. He escaped, however, by favor of the Prince of Condé on the condition he would retract his book at Rome. According to his epitaph, he never did. {BDF}

Pfalzner, Paul M. (20th Century)

Pfalzner, a Canadian freethinker in Ottawa, has written for the English *Freethinker*, including a tragi-comic satire, "The Perils of Perfection, or a Plague on Pleroma." The article spoofs God's alleged perfection. He is on the editorial committee of *Humanist in Canada*.

In "Why I Am Immune to Mystics" (*Free Inquiry*, Summer 1995), Pfalzner traces his antipathy to mysticism and irrationalism to his youthful experiences in his native Austria during the time of its Anschluss with Nazi Germany."

Pfalzner has served as President of the Humanist Association of Canada. {CA; HAC}.

Pfalzner, Paul (20th Century)

Pfalzner, a medical physicist, is a non-theist who is on the editorial committee of *Humanist in Canada*. {E}

Pfannstiel, Harvey (20th Century)

Pfannstiel is Vice President of the Secular Humanist Association of San Antonio, Texas.

Pfeffer, Leo (1910–1993)

Author of *Church, State, and Freedom* (1953), *The Liberties of an American: The Supreme Court Speaks (1956),* and *God, Caesar, and the Constitution* (1975), Pfeffer had a legal career that included defending many church-state separation cases. He was with the American Jewish Congress from 1945 to 1964, becoming director of its Commission on Law and Social Action in 1957. Pfeffer represented Roy R. Torcaso, a notary public from Wheaton, Maryland, whose commission was withheld because he refused to take an oath declaring belief in God. He was elated when the Supreme Court in 1961 ruled that states could not compel officeholders to declare a belief in God. The Court in a unanimous ruling struck down a provision of the Maryland Constitution on the ground that it was a "religious test for public office," a provision which stated, "No religious test ought ever to be required as a qualification for any office of profit or trust in this state, other than a declaration of belief in the existence of God."

Pfeffer was the founder of Public Education and Religious Liberty (PEARL). In 1972, Pfeffer in *PEARL v. Levitt*, argued before a U.S. District Court, which invalidated a law which allocated state funds to pay for a portion of the salaries of parochial school teachers and other so-called secular services in parochial schools. In 1973, in the U.S. Supreme Court, he argued the *Pearl v. Nyquist* case, and the court ruled that direct grants to religious schools for building maintenance and repair, tuition reimbursement to parents, and tax credits for tuition at religious schools are unconstitutional.

Alan, his son and a professor of law at Skidmore College, has reported that his father had started out to become a high school English teacher. Under New York law at the time, however, he could not be certified unless he passed a course in public speaking. He took the course, but failed it. Twice. Law school was his second choice. Later, while professor of Constitutional Law and chair of the political science department at Long Island University professor, Pfeffer was remembered as a punster—whenever anyone referred to tanks, tongs, or tents, Pfeffer would reply, "You're welcome." Although the university had no award to give outstanding teachers, they devised one, and Prof. Pfeffer became the first recipient. In 1988, the American Humanist Association named him Humanist of the Year. Pfeffer's funeral was secular in content but was held in a synagogue. {FUS; HNS2}

Pfeiff, Johan Gustaf Viktor (Born 1829)

Pfeiff was a Swedish baron, the editor in 1822 of *The Truthseeker*. He translated some of the writings of Herbert Spencer into Swedish. {BDF}

PHALLICISM

The emphasis upon sex is found in a wide range of religions. In the Yucatan are gigantic phalli in the ruins of temples. In Egypt are ithyphallic (showing an erect penis) carvings on the walls of temples, and Herodotus described phallic statues of Osiris in the country's fifth century B.C.E. villages. In India, combined representations (*lingam* and *yoni*) were found by Christian missionaries, who tried to rid the country of them although the objects had long ago spread to the East Indies and Japan. In Japan, phallic worship was incorporated into Shinto. The *phallos*, the male organ or a model of it, was prominent in the religious life of Arabia before Muhammed.

Frazer's *The Golden Bough* described how it was the main feature of religions which spread from the Aegean Sea to Mesopotamia and from the Black Sea to Egypt. In the Middle Ages, an exaggerated and exposed *pudenda* formed the key-stone of the arch over many church doors, acting as a charm against devils or the evil eye. One such, which was over the door of Cloyne cathedral, is preserved in the Royal Irish Academy at Dublin, for priests had such "obscenities" removed and began to boast of the exceptional chastity of Irish women. In a Norman church in Hertfordshire, England, such a specimen was found. The custom—in France, where the phalli of saintly men were in some places preserved and kissed; and Italy, where traces were preserved all through the Middle Ages—was noted by Voltaire, who ridiculed how priests blessed phallic models on the feast of Saints Cosmas and Damian, then sold them to the women. In the Hebrew religion, a phallic element lasted until the Captivity, although it is disguised in English translations by using such euphemisms as "loins" or "rock." In Syria, priests and people adopted a phallic religion and had phallic images and sacred prostitutes (of both sexes) in the temple and on the "high places."

Clifford Howard's *Sex Worship* (1902) and H. Cutner's *A Short History of Sex Worship* (1940) were earlier works this century on the subject, and in the contemporary literature are dozens of volumes, including Reay Tannahill's *Sex in History* (1982). In her book, Tannahill holds that the old primate mating position had man with only a back view of his sexual partner, enjoying an esthetic satisfaction in opulent, rounded buttocks. Women had no view at all. She not only tells of the phallic symbols but also includes a photograph of a Greek urn, upon which is depicted an individual carrying in a Dionysiac procession a phallic object in the form of a fish.

Non-believers also "worship" a penis, often describing it as a treasure (a part of "the family jewels"). They are apt to speculate occasionally about historical figures and how small, for example, Napoléon really was or how many penises a drunken Alcibiades may have knocked off statues. Women on television talk-shows gain their fifteen minutes of fame discussing penises they have felt and compared, sometimes adding blow-by-blow descriptions of their encounters.

The New Yorker once referred to rugged actor John Wayne's "p.i.," later explaining that the tough symbol of masculinity suffered from "penis insufficiency." In San Francisco and other cities touted for their sexual excesses, artists find that "the bigger the sculpture's dong, the more the work's worth." Some Haitians and Africans carve erotic, "big-dick" statues, sometimes with a shield that, upon being removed, exposes a well-proportioned penis, which appeals to a portion of the general public.

Many urbanites are entranced by underwear ads, at the same time swallowing the Victorian view that sexual display is bad . . . and therefore sinful. One non-believer, asked about phallicism in New York City's Greenwich Village, observed, "Sorry, I'm a breast man."

Few seem aware that in ancient Greece phallic worship was entirely normal and centered around Priapus (the son of Aphrodite). Or that in Rome the cult of Cybele and Attis with its festive excess and annual "Day of Blood" took place in order that admittance into the priest caste could take place upon showing self-inflicted castration.

One penis of which there is no further record is that of a well-known Christian with a zeal for purity: Origen. He cut *his* off. (See entries for Napoléon and Origen.) {CE; RE}

Phanu, Y. (20th Century)

Phanu has since 1979 edited *Nasthika Yugam* in Vijayawada, India, a publication in Telugu. {FUK}

Pharmacopulo, A.P. (19th Century)

Pharmacopulo was the Greek translator of Büchner's *Force and Matter*. He was a corresponding member of the International Federation of Freethinkers. {BDF}

Phatak, N. R. (20th Century)

In India, Phatak wrote *Rationalists of Maharashtra* (1962). {FUK; GS}

Pheidias: See entry for Phidias.

Phelips, Vivian (1860–1939)

After a full term in the Indian Civil Service (engineering), Phelips retired to England and wrote *Churches and Modern Thought* (1906). The Bishop of London called it "that most dangerous of books." {FUK; RAT; RE}

Phelps, Christopher (20th Century)

Phelps's *Young Sidney Hook: Marxist and Pragmatist* (1997) includes an attack on the post-revolutionary Hook, particularly from 1938 onwards. Hook is excoriated for accepting the Medal of Freedom from President Ronald Reagan in 1985 and condemned for helping to lead an "anticommunist crusade." The work is patently biased, according to Paul Kurtz (*Free Inquiry*, Fall 1998).

Phelps, J. A. P. (20th Century)

In Durban, Phelps has written for *The Freethinker* (August 1996) about how, indirectly, the odd urge to "worship" cropped up. His reference is to the word *glory*, in which members of a community share—without verbal expression—the glory and wonder of the return of spring, or of sunshine after storm, or the discovery of new edible roots or nuts, or the birth of a precious child. Those memorable moments, such as looking into the sky and unexpectedly seeing two hundred wild geese in formation, fill one with glory, a word he prefers to "wonder" or "awe." {*The Freethinker*, August 1996}

Phenix, Philip Henry (1915–)

Phenix, a philosopher, worked on and wrote for *The Humanist*. He wrote *Realms of Meaning* (1975) and *Education and the Common Good* (1977). {HNS}

PHENOMENOLOGY

Edmund Husserl founded a philosophical method that was known as phenomenology, one that was supposedly devoid of presuppositions and which focused purely on phenomena. The aim was to elucidate meaning through intuition. The school of thought influenced existentialism. (For a discussion by Richard Salmite, see the *Encyclopedia of Philosophy*, Vol. 6, which mentions Heidegger, Sartre, and Merleau-Ponty.) {CE}

Phidias (c. 500– c. 432 B.C.E.)

Phidias, the Greek sculptor, was one of the greatest sculptors of ancient Greece. No original in existence can be attributed to him with certainty, but numerous Roman copies of supposed fidelity exist. His greatest achievements were the "Athena Parthenos" at Athens and the "Zeus" (one of the Seven Wonders of the World) in the temple of Olympia, both colossal figures of chryselephantine workmanship (draperies of beaten gold, flesh parts encrusted with ivory). The "Athena," which was dedicated in the Parthenon (c. 447–429 B.C.E.), was the chief treasure of Athens. It was destroyed in antiquity, but several copies are preserved. McCabe wrote of Phidias that "he was in the end prosecuted for impiety by the Athenian democracy and died in prison. Much is obscure in the matter, but it is agreed that it was the priests who pressed the prosecution of the great artist." {CE; JM}

Phifer, Kenneth (20th Century)

An author, Phifer wrote *The Faith of a Humanist* and *A Book of Uncommon. Faith* (1991).

PHILANTHROPINISTS: See entry for Johann Bernhard Basedow.

PHILANTHROPY

• Take egotism out, and you would castrate the benefactors.

–Ralph Waldo Emerson

Philip, Ambrose: See entry for Infidel.

Philp, H. L. (20th Century)

Philp wrote *Freud and Religious Belief* (1974). {GS}

Philipon, Marie Jeanne (18th Century): See entry for Roland de la Platière. At the time of her execution, she exclaimed, "O Liberty, what crimes are committed in thy name!"

Phillip, Arthur (1738–1814)

Phillip was an early Australian secularist. {SWW}

PHILIPPINE UNITARIANS

The Unitarian Universalist Church of the Philippines (UUCP), which has five churches and ten fellowships, has between four hundred and one thousand members.

The Rev. Toribio Quimada, who preached the Universalist concept concerning "salvation for all," started the Universalist Church of the Philippines in 1954. He held that God is love and it would be illogical that a place such as Hell would be reserved for sinners. He held that the Bible's contradictions prove that the Bible is not the word of God. For him, Jesus was the son of Mary and Joseph, not God, that Jesus was a person who preached love, peace, equality, and justice for the oppressed. In 1988 Quimada was murdered, the same year UUCP was admitted as a member congregation of the Unitarian Universalist Association.

The Unitarian Universalist Church of the Philippines held its 41st annual convention in 1996. Rebecca Sienes was elected President, and Josephine Espartero was elected president of their Women's Association. Their treasurer, the Rev. Eddie Espartero, was drowned in a 1996 flood while visiting one of his churches.

According to Marlin Lavanhar, the UUCP has succeeded through faith healing to cure chronic and supposedly terminal illnesses. They accept no money for their services.

Contact: Roberto Cagadas Sr., 065 Rovira Road, Bantayan, Dumaguete City 6200, Negros, The Philippines.

Phillippo, William Skinner (19th Century)

Phillippo was an English farmer, a deist who wrote an *Essay on Political and Religious Meditations* (1868). {BDF}

Phillips, Bernard (20th Century)

A professor of religion at Temple, Phillips in *The Humanist Alternative* (1973) explains the relationship of Zen and Buddhism with humanism. He is author of *The Essentials of Zen Buddhism, an Anthology of the Writings of Daisetz T. Suzuki* (1963). {PK}

Phillips, Julia Miller (1944–)

Phillips has produced such films as "Steelyard Blues" (1972); "The Sting" (which received an Academy Award for best picture of the year in 1973); "Taxi Driver" (1976); "Close Encounters of the Third Kind" (1977); and "The Beat" (1988). She received the Katherine McFarland Short Story award in 1964.

In *You'll Never Eat Lunch in This Town Again*, she states, "I'm a third generation atheistic Jew." {CA; E}

Phillips, Richard [Sir] (1767–1840)

An industrious English writer, Phillips was a hosier, bookseller, printer, publisher, republican, Sheriff of London (1807–1808), and knight. He compiled many schoolbooks, chiefly under pseudonyms such as the Rev. J. Goldsmith and the Rev. D. Blair. His own opinions are found in his *Millions of Facts*. In *Golden Rules and Social Philosophy* (1826), Phillips expressed his rationalism and dedicated the book to Simon Bolívar. {BDF; RAT; RE}

Phillips, Sam (20th Century)

Once a big star in Christian music, Phillips has now rejected what she considers to be its narrow and often-bigoted worldview. On her album, *Martinis and Bikinis*, Phillips sings a rousing version of Lennon's scathing song, "Just Gimme Some Truth":

> I'm sick and tired of hearing things
> From uptight, shortsighted, narrow-minded hypocrites;
> All I want is the truth;
> Just gimme some truth.

Phillips, Stephen (1868–1915)

In 1897, Phillips's *Poems* was awarded the Academy Prize as best book of the year. *Christ in Hades and Other Poems* (1896) and *Paolo and Francesca* (1899) show Phillips's advanced Rationalism. The latter book was received enthusiastically, and Phillips was compared by serious critics to Sophocles and Shakespeare. Phillips was both a poet and an actor. {RAT; RE}

Phillips, Thomas Trewin (c. 1840–1920?)

Phillips was an Australian secularist, boarding house proprietor, and temperance worker. An itinerant lecturer for the Australian Secular Association, he was involved in the 1891 take-over of the Melbourne Hall of Science. {SWW}

Phillips, Wendell (1811–1884)

Phillips, the American reformer often ranked with Edward Everett and Daniel Webster as an orator, was a delegate to the World Anti-Slavery Convention in London (1840). He opposed the Mexican War, the annexation of Texas, and slaveholding everywhere. The black slave, he argued, was owed not only freedom but also land, education, and full civil rights. When the 15th amendment to the United States Constitution did enfranchise blacks, Phillips agitated for social reforms, prohibition of liquor, woman suffrage, abolition of capital punishment, currency reform, and labor rights. Phillips was a freethinker. {TRI}

Phillpotts, Eden (1862–1960)

Phillpotts, a prolific and popular British novelist, playwright, and poet, did not discuss his personal views on religion in his work. Joseph McCabe, however, was his personal friend and states that he found "no man nearer to me in his opinions on religion, but though he remains an agnostic, in recent years he has become milder and more conservative." Phillpotts was an honorary associate of the Rationalist Press Association. {JM; RAT; RE; TRI}

PHILO

Philo is a biannual publication of the Society of Humanist Philosophers. It commenced in 1998. Paul Kurtz is publisher and Keith Parsons is Editor.

The character Philo, in David Hume's *Dialogues Concerning Natural Religion*, braves the religious temperament of the times to provide rational grounds for being skeptical of religious assertions concerning God, reality, and ethics.

Contributing editors are Kurt Baier; H. James Birx; Mario Bunge; Daniel C. Dennett; Theodore M. Drange; Paul Edwards; Antony Flew; Richard Gale; Adolf Grünbaum; Peter H. Hare; Ted Honderich; Philip Kitcher; Valerii Kuvakin; Robin LePoidevin; Sherrie Lyons; Michael Martin; Kai Nielsen; Graham Oppy; W. V. Quine; John Searle, J. J. C. Smart; Theodore Schick Jr.; Quentin Smith; and Svetozar Stojanovic.

Executive Editor Lewis Vaughan is at PO Box 664, Amherst, NY 14226-0664. E-mail: <fivaughn@aol.com>.

Philodemus (1st Century B.C.E.)

A prominent Epicurean philosopher in Greece, Philodemus wrote on central philosophical questions such as the fear of death and the nature of happiness. Some of his treatises were found at Herculaneum in 1997, along with portions of Epicurus's *On Nature*. {Tim O'Keefe, *The New York Times*, 28 July 1997}

PHILOSOPHER-KING

In Plato's *Republic*, the ideal ruler was one who had the virtue and wisdom of the philosopher.

PHILOSOPHER'S STONE

Practitioners of alchemy thought they could change other metals into gold. Figuratively, the "philosopher's stone" is a substance thought to be capable of regenerating man "spiritually." It appears in the alchemical literature under hundreds of different and fanciful names. {AF}

PHILOSOPHERS, FEMALE

"Most philosophers these days are attached to university teaching or research departments," Colin has noted. "Not so in the past; and before the end of the nineteenth century there were no women academic philosophers, because there were no women academics."

Mary Warnock in *Women Philosophers* (1996) includes women of merit who were "concerned with matters of a high degree of generality, and . . . at home among abstract ideas." Her work presented the "generalising, explanatory, and argumentative aspects of their works.

Included among the seventeen she describes are the following:

> Anne Conway (1631–1679); Mary Wollstonecraft (1759–1797); Harriet Martineau (1802–1876); Victoria Lady Welby (1837–1912); Mary Whiton Calkins (1863–1930); Susan Stebbing (1885–1943); Hannah Arendt (1906–1975); Simone de Beauvoir (1908–1986); and Iris Murdoch (1919–1999).

PHILOSOPHERS, PLAGIARISM BY

Philosophers, all of whom are trained in ethics, have never plagiarized others' material or ideas. One or two, perchance, have been known, however, to *wander* into others' texts.

PHILOSOPHERS, TENDENCIES OF

Philosophers as an entire group, frequently hesitate to go on record with direct statements which contradict other philosophers. They do, however, feel free to "tend" toward the view that . . . .

PHILOSOPHES

In France during the eighteenth century, a group of radical thinkers and writers, including Voltaire and Jean-Jacques Rousseau, were called *Philosophes*, a word taken from Old French rather than from the Latin *philosophus* or the Greek *philosophos*. The *philosophes* stressed the use of human reason and were critical of established religious and political practices in France. {DCL}

PHILOSOPHIES, SOCIOLOGY OF

The Sociology of Philosophies: A Global Theory of Intellectual Change (1999), by Randall Collins, makes the point that the development of philosophy is determined by the social structure of the philosophical profession. At any one time and in any one community, philosophers are almost universally members of a comparatively small number of competing groups. These last for some time, until absorbed or extinguished by other groups. Self-sufficient philosophers—"isolates"—are exceptional. The macrohistorical work by Collins, according to Anthony Quinton in *The New York Review of Books* (8 April 1999), is in a league with the works of Spengler and Toynbee.

Collins divided the philosophical universe into seven: Greek (with its Roman attachment); medieval European (and Jewish); Islamic; modern Western; Chinese; Indian; and Japanese. According to Quinton, Collins "rightly observes that religion is not the enemy of philosophy but commonly its stimulant. Religious authorities often seek to suppress independent thinking. But dogmas have to be defined, clarified, and defended, and that generates creative philosophy, as the intellectual efflorescence of the European Middle Ages makes evident." However, Quinton finds weaknesses in the approach, which although it is enormously detailed, learned, and comprehensive does not take up the relative importance of the ideas over which the various philosophers conflict.

PHILOSOPHY

Philosophy attempts to discover the fundamental principles of the sciences, the arts, and the world that the sciences and arts deal with. The word *philosophy* is from the Greek for "love of wisdom." Philosophy has subdisciplines that explore principles of specific areas, such as knowledge (**epistemology**), reasoning (**logic**), being in general (**metaphysics**), beauty (**aesthetics**) and human conduct (**ethics**).

The shortest definition of philosophy, that it is thinking about thinking, is a basic one. However, as noted in *The Oxford Companion to Philosophy*, most definitions of philosophy are controversial, and the subject has changed in the course of history.`

Bertrand Russell in his 1927 *Selected Papers* found three principal types of philosophy:

> • The first of these, which I shall call **the classical tradition**, descends in the main from Kant and Hegel; it represents the attempt to adapt to present needs the methods and results of the great constructive philosophers from Plato downwards.
>
> • The second type, which may be called called **evolutionism**, derived its prominence from Darwin, and must be reckoned as having had Herbert Spencer for its first philosophical representative, but in recent times it has become, chiefly through William James and M. Bergson, far bolder and more searching in its innovations than it was in the hands of Herbert Spencer.
>
> • The third type, which may be called "**logical atomism**" for want of a better name, has gradually crept into philosophers through the critical scrutiny of mathematics. This type of philosophy, which is the one that I wish to advocate, has not as yet many wholehearted adherents, but the "new realism" which owes its inception to Harvard is very largely impregnated with its spirit. It represents, I believe, the same kind of advance as was introduced into physics by Galileo: the substitution of piecemeal, detailed, and verifiable results for large untested generalities recommended only by a certain appeal to imagination.

Others have expressed varying views of philosophy and philosophers:

> • Our quaint metaphysical opinions, in an hour of anguish, are like playthings by the bedside of a child deathly sick.
>
> **–Samuel Taylor Coleridge**
>
> • If you wish to understand a philosopher, do not ask what he says, but find out what he wants.
>
> **–Friedrich Wilhelm Nietzsche**
>
> • Philosophy, n. A route of many roads leading from nowhere to nothing.
>
> **–Ambrose Bierce**
>
> • All are lunatics, but he who can analyze his delusions is called a philosopher.
>
> **–Ambrose Bierce**
>
> • I think I think; therefore, I think I am.
>
> **–Ambrose Bierce**
>
> • Philosophy teaches us to bear with equanimity the misfortunes of others.
>
> –Oscar Wilde
>
> • The business of philosophy is to show that we are not fools for doing what we do.
>
> **–Oliver Wendel Holmes**
>
> • Philosophy consists very largely of one philosopher arguing that all others are jackasses.
>
> **–H. L. Mencken**
>
> • Those who lack the courage will always find a philosophy to justify it.
>
> **–Albert Camus**

John Casti (*Skeptic*, Vol. 4, No. 3, 1996) lists "Big Questions" that philosophers currently ask:

1. How did life originate on Earth?
2. Are human social behavioral patterns determined by our genes?
3. How do humans acquire language?
4. Is it possible to build a computing machine that will think, just like you and me?
5. Do there exist intelligent, extraterrestrial life forms in the Milky Way galaxy?
6. Does there exist an objective reality independent of human observers?

(See entry for Purpose of Life. Also, *The Encyclopedia of Philosophy*, Vol. 6, has informative entries concerning the anthropology of philosophy, bibliographies, dictionaries, encyclopedias, journals, educational philosophy, the philosophy of history, law, religion, and science.) {DCL}

PHILOSOPHY, DICTIONARIES AND ENCYCLOPEDIAS OF

In mid-1998 the *Routledge Encyclopedia of Philosophy,* edited by Edward Craig and containing ten volumes, was published. Prior to that, the leading such reference works were as follows:

Audi, Robert, General Editor, *The Cambridge Dictionary of Philosophy* (1995)

Edwards, Paul, ed., *Encyclopedia of Philosophy* (1967), four volumes

Flew, Antony, *A Dictionary of Philosophy* (1979)

Honderich, Ted, *The Oxford Companion to Philosophy* (1995)

Phips, William [Sir] (1651–1695)

Governor Phips, the first royal governor of the Colony of Massachusetts, declared that as of 12 October 1692 "spectral evidence" would no longer be admissible in court. As a result, the infamous Salem Witch Trials came to an end.

Prior to the declaration, an estimated nineteen were hanged and one was pressed to death. Phips stated that he stopped the proceedings "because I saw many innocent people might otherwise perish," including fifty-two people with pending cases of witchcraft—all of whom were released within three months of his ruling. Whether or not Governor Phips was a believer is unclear, although he likely made the ruling for humanitarian as well as for political reasons. Sir William was knighted because, backed by the Duke of Albermarle, he found a considerable treasure in a sunken vessel off Hispaniola (Haiti). His decisions irked many in the religious community, and he died while being investigated on charges of maladministration. {CE}

PHOBIAS

Phobias are intense fears that a person develops concerning a specific thing or situation. They sometimes are classified as severe neuroses that represent or are symbolic of repressed anxiety or fear. Achluophobia, fear of the dark, is sometimes traced to an individual's upbringing by supernaturalists who believe in ghosts and demons. Triskaidekaphobia, fear of the number 13, is similarly triggered by superstition. Xenophobia or zenophobia, fear of strangers, has a connection as shown in *Judges 12: 4-6* with how Hebrews pronounced the word "shibboleth" differently from others. {CE}

Photius (c 820–892?)

A Greek churchman and theologian, Photius was one of the most learned men of his time. As a leader of the orthodox faction, he wished to treat the repentant iconoclasts indulgently. Although he was chosen to be a patriarch, the pope refused to recognize him. In 867, Photius retaliated by calling a synod that challenged the pope in Bulgaria. Later, he became a patriarch when Pope John VIII recognized him, but in 886 he was forced to resign under imperial pressure, and he died in exile. According to Robertson, Photius was something of a freethinker, declaring from the pulpit that earthquakes were produced by earthly causes and not by divine wrath. But he was an image worshipper, as were large numbers at that time. Many reckon the deep cleavage between East and West from the schism of Photius, although the final schism did not occur until the 11th century. Photius is venerated as a saint in the Eastern Orthodox Church. {CE; ER; JMR; JMRH}

PHRENOLOGY

• Phrenology, n. The science of picking the pocket through the scalp. It consists in locating and exploiting the organ that one is a dupe with.

–**Ambrose Bierce**
The Devil's Dictionary

Although phrenology (cranioscopy), a study of the shape of the human skull, was of interest to followers of the 18th century founder, Franz Joseph Gall (1758–1828), today's neurologists and anthropologists have refuted the theory and call it a form of quackery. In ancient times, the heart was believed to be the center of human intellect and emotion. The brain was thought of more as the body's cooling system. Gall taught that certain parts of the brain had specific tasks, for example to handle the physical or emotional or intellectual. Henry Clark informed the New York Area Skeptics (27 February 1996) that Gall mapped each of the areas upon discovering them. A slight forehead bulge, for example, represented people who show up on time for appointments and who remember to pay their bills. However, a corresponding depression in the skull represented people who were characteristically forgetful. Not only is the memory located in the front of the brain, Gall believed, but also a swelling over the corresponding area of the brain indicated an enhanced characteristic whereas a depression indicated a reduced characteristic. Church leaders, complaining that his assertions were at odds with religious teachings and did not allow room for the human "soul" asked him to leave Austria. By 1804 he and Johann Spurzheim had identified ten more areas of the brain, and many of Europe's élite hailed this new "science." In France, he became famous as well as wealthy. Soon after going to the United States to lecture at Harvard, Gall died.

In 1835 Orson, Lorenzo, Charlotte, and other members of a Fowler family "picked up the torch of Phrenology," treating it like a real business. They founded a publishing house and issued various books. Also, they supported causes like women's suffrage and even published a book written by Susan B. Anthony. In the 1850s, a Fowler phrenological reading cost between $1 and $3. When in the 1930s the last of the Fowler family died, phrenology also died. {CE}

Phule, Jyotirao (1827–1890)

According to Sibnarayan Ray of City College, Calcutta University, Phule was one of the outstanding secular humanists of the 19th century in India. His name stands out among the non-Brahmin reformers of Maharashira, and he led a revolt against Brahmin domination and subjugation of the non-Brahmins. He criticized all the social evils and the inimical acts of the Brahmins in particular, starting the Satyashodhak movement after the Sepoy Mutiny in order to carry on further agitation against Brahminism. He was a clear-thinking rationalist and did not accept any organized religion or models of worship. His work, however, has not been translated from Maharashtrian into English. (See further comments in the entries for Nehru and Sibnarayan Ray.)

Phunkel, Oscar (20th Century)

Phunkel was a freethinker who wrote *Where Is God?* (1979). {GS}

PHYSICS

The two pillars of 20th Century physics—quantum mechanics and general relativity—have both been confirmed by experiment. But, according to New York University physicist Alan Sokal, "they are based on incompatible conceptual structures: they cannot both be exactly correct." Sokal, who became noted for pulling a hoax in *Social Context* about "postmodernism in the humanities," was serious when he continued, "the central unsolved problem of theoretical physics is to find a logically consistent theory that would reduce to quantum mechanics and general relativity in their respective domains while superseding them conceptually. Superstring theory is one candidate for such a unified theory of quantum gravity."

However, superstring theory may or may not turn out to be the correct theory of quantum gravity. "Unfortunately," Sokal continues, "the clash between quantum mechanics and general relativity occurs only at energies a million billion times higher than those achievable in present-day accelerators. A direct experimental test of superstring theory—or of any theory of quantum gravity—is thus out of the question. Nevertheless, these theories may well have experimentally testable consequences at lower energies. They may predict, for example, the masses and interactions of the various fundamental particles (quarks, leptons, and so forth). We won't know whether this is the case until these theories are better understood, and it is in this direction that superstring theorists are working." His conclusion is that we should not reject superstring theory prematurely, using spurious philosophical grounds.

"The total energy of the universe appears to be zero," physicist Victor J. Stenger has written. Therefore, and counter to religionists' views, "no miracle of energy created 'from nothing' was required to produce it. Similar, no miracle was needed for the appearance of order. Order can and does occur spontaneously in physical systems." (See entries for *Genesis*, Hoaxes, String Theory, and Steven Weinberg.) {CE; Vixtor Stenger, *Free Inquiry* Winter 1998-1999; *The New York Times*, 22 July 1996}

Pi y Margall, Francisco (1824–1901)

A Spanish philosopher and republican statesman, Pi y Margall said that the first book he learned to read was Volney's *Ruins*. A translator of Proudhon, he also introduced to Spain the writings and philosophy of Comte. Pi y Margall was associated with Castelar and Figueras in the attempt to establish a Spanish Republic, and he became Minister of the Interior as well as, in 1873, the President. {BDF; PUT; RAT}

Piatt, Donald A. (20th Century)

Piatt, an editor, has been a staff member of *The Humanist*. {HNS}

Picasso, Pablo Ruiz y (1881–1973)

Picasso, the world-famous Spanish painter, settled in Paris in 1901. He and Braque developed cubism, in which three-dimensional subjects were fragmented and redefined from different points of view, simultaneously. In 1917 he designed ballets for Diaghilev, after which came a period of monumental nudes which developed in the 1930s into terrifyingly distorted forms. William Rubin, in *Les Demoiselles d'Avignon* (1995), claimed that Picasso created personal fetishistic symbols in order to resolve his conflicts with the world. He expressed his atheism, his willingness to risk anarchy for freedom, his fear of disease and illness, and "his deep-seated fear and loathing of the female body, which existed side by side with his craving for and ecstatic idealization of it." David Tribe, similarly, terms Picasso a nonbeliever, an outright freethinker.

"Guernica" (1936), often called the most powerful outcry of the age, was a painting symbolizing a fleet of Adolf Hitler's bombers which General Francisco Franco of Spain requested and which destroyed the Spanish town. In 1974, as stunned visitors looked on helplessly, a vandal drew a can of spray paint from his pocket and scrawled the words "Kill Lies All" on the masterpiece. Fortunately, a heavy coat of varnish acted as a transparent shield and the lettering was removed without damage.

Picasso's secret, "a childhood vow to God," was explained by John Richardson, in "At the Court of Picasso" (*Vanity Fair*, November 1999): "When his younger sister Conchita had been dying of diphtheria in Corunna in 1895, young Pablo vowed that he would never paint again if his sister's life was spared. He *did* paint again, and her life was not spared. Hence Picasso's identification with the Minotaur, to whom woman after woman would have to be sacrificed."

Picasso had two wives, a succession of mistresses (when he separated from Fernande Olivier, Picasso is said by Rubin to have had a sexual fascination with the thirteen-year-old girl he and Fernande had adopted, at which time Fernande retrieved the child), a number of whores (Rubin claimed Picasso got a venereal disease during his visits to a brothel), and his children—legitimate and otherwise [with model Marie-Thérésèe Waltger, he had a daughter, Maïa]—were subjects of sensational reports by the world's popular press.

His ability to work even when a nonagenarian, according to Richardson, was due in great part to his wife Jacqueline's "solicitude, patience, and sacrificial ardor that sustained the artist in the face of declining health and his greatest enemy, death, [for this] enabled him to be more productive than ever before and go on working into his 92nd year." She was distraught from the day he died but lived thirteen more years to the age of fifty-nine, at which time she shot herself. "A young priest presided over the minimal rites that were compatible with a ceremony in an unconsecrated place," Richardson described. "Although spacious, the guardroom, where the ceremony took place, was unseasonably hot and airless, and crammed with flowers. Four gravediggers carried Jacqueline's coffin—a very fancy one in the Empire style, which Picasso would have appreciated for its inappropriateness." {CE; OEL; PA; TYD}

Picchioni, Anthony (20th Century)

Picchioni is clinical director of an adult psychiatric unit at Charter Hospital of Grapevine, Texas. He is author of *A Comprehensive History of Guidance in the United States*. {*Free Inquiry*, Fall, 1992}

Pichard, Prosper (19th Century)

A French positivist, Pichard wrote *Doctrine of Reality* (1873), "a catechism for the use of people who do not pay themselves with words." Littré wrote a preface. {BDF}

Pickett, O. Eugene (1925–)

Pickett, the fourth president of the Unitarian Universalist Association, led 1000 churches and fellowships with a membership of 170,000. He presided from 1979 to 1983. {CL; U}

PICKPOCKETS, DIDDLERS, AND GRIFTERS

• A crow thieves; a fox cheats; a weasel outwits; a man diddles. To diddle is his destiny. "Man was made to mourn," says the poet. But not so:—he was made to diddle. This is his aim—his object—his *end*. And for this reason when a man's diddled we say he's "*done*"

—Edgar Allen Poe.

• When Egypt's King Farouk was wedded in 1938, Cairo's pickpockets dutifully declared a moratorium for the day in honor of the person who appeared to be a latterday Tutankhamun.

–Max Rodenbeck, *Cairo*, 1998

If evil is a theological term, diddling is a freethinker's. A rational person is well aware that a coin has three sides, that confronted with a decision one has more than one choice and it *could* be the edge. Choices are not so much *between* good and evil but *among* several.

A choice many people have made over the centuries is to diddle. As David L. Maurer pointed out in *The Big Con* (1955), diddling goes back to Egyptian and Mesopotamian times, and to Reynard the Fox by way of the Elizabethan coney-catachers and the Spanish picaresque. It has intrigued not only Edgar Allan Poe ("Diddling") but also H. L. Mencken (who described the lingo of pickpockets in *The American Language*); S. J. Perelman; Pruence Crowther; Stuart Berg Flexner; George Roy Hill (*The Sting*, 1973); Preston Sturges ("The Lady Eve" (1941); Herman Melville (*The Confidence Man: His Masquerade* (1857); Samuel Clemens (the King and the Duke in *Huckleberry Finn*); and others.

The parson may choose *between* righteousness and lust, but the freethinker chooses *among* being an honest banker, or a banker who "fudges" in the way he accounts financial sums, or perhaps being a banker who is a grifter, a moonshiner, a shell-game hustler, a forger, a pot smoker, a safecracker, an internet scamster.

As pointed out by Luc Sante (*The Big Con*, 1999), diddlers who are big cons sometimes work in pairs: the roper and the inside man—the archetypal Punch and Judy, or Mr. Tambo and Mr. Bones in minstrelsy. Losers to big cons hesitate to admit they have been "taken" by the likes of such grifters as Limehouse Chappie, Yellow Kid Weil, the Square-Faced Kid, Slobbering Bob, the Hashouse Kid, the High Ass Kid, the Indiana Wonder, Wildfire John, or the Christ Kid.

One Manhattan recording studio owner who had known all along that a client—an African American Christian bishop—was a grifter, nevertheless got taken. Not only did the bishop "stiff" him with a worthless check at the last of numerous sessions but also he stiffed an entire church that had advanced him several thousand dollars to record their choir, then failed to show up or pay the studio. That same bishop recorded Sunday radio services in which a statement "Be sure to read *John* 3:5 and don't forget the old bishop" actually was a demand for money after following his advice to bet on the fifth horse in the third race. The "service" included "canned" music, "canned" applause, and "canned" audience participation. No one who heard the weekly services, broadcast in Philadelphia and New York City, could have guessed that the bishop arrived in a blue Cadillac with two fellow homosexual helpers, who supplied him and themselves with beer and cocaine as the service was "patched" together by studio engineers. (See entry for Stanley Walker.) {Fernando Vargas, numerous conversations}

Picton, J. Allanson (1832–1910)

Picton wrote *The Bible in School: A Question of Ethics* (1907). He originally had been a minister for the Cheetham Hill Congregational Church (1856–1862), but upon being accused of heresy, moved to a more liberal congregation at Leicester. He then entered public life and was M.P. for Leicester from 1884-1894. Picton was an advocate of secular education and ended his own religious development as a pantheist, writing *The Religion of the Universe* (1904) and *Pantheism* (1905). {GS; RAT}

Pieart, Richard (20th Century)

Pieart is Vice President of Humanists of Iowa. E-mail: <iowa@humanists.net>.

Piech, Ferdinand (1937–)

Piech, an automotive executive, is a recipient of the Austrian Badge of Honor for Achievements in Science and the Arts. He has worked for Porsche and Audi and in 1993 became chief executive officer of the Volkswagen management board.

In a German atheist magazine, *Miz* (April 1996), the Volkswagen CEO is asked what it is he believes:

> My persuasion is that one must have such a lifestyle, that the end can come every day, and then one's conscience is clear. That is connected with the fact that I'm an atheist. One should always have a clear conscience concerning one's environment and the people. This is my attitude.

{CA; E}

Pierce, Benjamin (Born 1809)

A Unitarian, Pierce was a prominent mathematician and an astronomer in the 19th Century. {U}

Pierce, Richard D. (1915–1973)

When he reviewed books for *The Humanist* in the 1950s, Pierce was chairman of the social studies department at Emerson College in Boston.

Pierce, Ulysses G. B. (20th Century)

Pierce, who was chaplain of the United States Senate from 1909 to 1913, once stated, "It is a colossal conceit to suppose that man is the acme of all creation, and that in its boundless ranges no higher type of life is reached. I think few of us have ever read an argument for immortality that did not fail to satisfy us." Contemporary secularists understandably wonder how he ever got approved for the job. {CE}

Piercy, Blodwen (20th Century)

A former president of the Humanist Association of Canada, Blodwen Piercy is married to Joe Piercy. The two have been co-editors of *Humanist in Canada*. E-mail: <jepiercy@cyberus.ca>

Piercy, Joe (20th Century)

Piercy, a Canadian, is on the editorial board of *International Humanist.* He is President of Canadian Humanist Publications (CHP) and, with his wife Blodwen Piercy, is co-editor of *Humanist in Canada*. E-mail: <jepiercy@cyberus.ca>

Pierpont, James Lord (1822–1893)

"Jingle Bells," the winter song, was composed by Pierpont, an organist at the Unitarian Church in Savannah, George. His brother, John Jr., was the pastor, and his father, John Sr., was a poet, a prominent Abolitionist, and a founder of the American Unitarian Association. Pierpont was uncle of the financier John Pierpont Morgan. On the Web: <http://www3.pair.com/montrsmu/carolshist/jingleb.html>.

Pierson, Allard (1831–1896)

Pierson was a Dutch rationalist critic. At first, he was minister to the Evangelical congregation at Leuven, afterwards at Rotterdam, and finally became a professor at Heidelberg. He resigned his connection with the Church in 1864. Pierson wrote many works, including *Poems* (1882), *New Studies on Calvin* (1883), and *Verisimilia* (1886), written in conjunction with S. A. Naber. {BDF; RAT}

Pietrantonio, Ann Marie (20th Century)

In 1996, Pietrantonio won a Freedom From Religion Foundation contest for an essay describing her experiences of being forced to pray in a public school. {*Freethought Today*, October 1996}

Pigault-Lebrun, Guillaume Charles Antoine (1753–1835)

Pigault-Lebrun was a witty French author of comedies and romances. His *Le Citateur* (1803) was a collection of objections to Christianity, borrowed in part from Voltaire, whose spirit he largely shared. In 1811 Napoléon threatened the priests he would issue this work wholesale. Under the Restoration, the book was suppressed but has been frequently reprinted. Pigault-Lebrun became secretary to King Jerome Napoléon. {BDF; RAT}

Pike, E. Royston (Born 1896)

Pike wrote *Slayers of Superstition: A Popular Account of the Leading Personalities of the Deist Movement* (1931). He disliked "humanism" as a term describing various degrees of unbelief. {FUK; FUS}

Pike, J. W. (Born 1826)

Pike was an American lecturer who wrote *My Religious Experience* and *What I Found in the Bible* (1867). {BDF}

Pikkusaari, Jussi (1939–)

In the 1980s, Pikkusaari was chairman of the Humanist Union of Finland. He had helped enable regional centers to form humanist associations, following which he arranged for the nine separate associations in 1987 to form the Union. (See entry for Finnish Freethinkers, Humanists.)

Pilcher, Edward John (Born 1862)

Pilcher grew up among the Wesleyan Methodists, but the study of Biblical prophecy, especially in *Daniel* and *Revelation*, convinced him of "the baselessness of Christianity." He published a translation of the Babylonian code of law, *The Hammurabi Code* (1904). A well-known Assyriologist, Pilcher contributed to the *Reformer*, *Freethinker*, and *Literary Guide*. {RAT}

PILEGASH: See entry for concubines.

PILGRIM

• Pilgrim, n. A traveler that is taken seriously. A Pilgrim Father was one who, leaving Europe in 1620 because not permitted to sing psalms through his nose, followed it to Massachusetts, where he could personate God according to the dictates of his conscience.

—**Ambrose Bierce**
The Devil's Dictionary

Pillai, Omchery N. N. (20th Century)

Pillai spoke at the 1995 conference of major Indian humanist organizations, telling about the model of society in Kerala (South India). He told of his personal encounter with an "untouchable" which led him to campaign against the caste system. Kerala, which has a high level of education, is experiencing humanistic changes. {*New Humanist*, February 1996}

Pillsbury, Parker (1809–1898)

Pillsbury was an American reformer who, after being a Congregational minister for one year, perceived that the churches were the bulwark of slavery and abandoned the ministry. He became an abolitionist lecturer, edited the *Herald of Freedom*, *National Anti-Slavery Standard*, and the *Revolution*. He also preached for free religious societies. His principal work is *Acts of the Anti-Slavery Apostles* (1883). *The Church as It Is* (1885) contains his non-Christian views on theism, as does his autobiography. {BDF; JM; PUT; RAT; RE}

PILTDOWN MAN

In 1908, an amazing discovery was made at Piltdown in Sussex: human remains in the form of a fossil. In 1911–1913 the parts of a broken cranium and jaw of a primitive man were found. In 1915 another skull of the same type was found. "Sir Arthur Keith thinks that the race may have been ancestral to Modern Man," Joseph McCabe reported in his 1940 work. He added, "The race to which the specimens belonged is intermediate between Pekin Man and Neanderthal or Mousterian Man and is generally regarded as having lived in southern England (which was an extension of Europe) at least 250,000 years ago."

In the 1950s, however, fluorine tests were made which showed that the fossil was no more than 50,000 years old, and an X-ray analysis proved that the jaw was from a chimpanzee. Further tests showed the jaw and tooth were of modern origin. What had been hailed as the "missing link" in the evolutionary chain was, in fact, a ruse. Who had been responsible, however, was not known. The novelist Sir Arthur Conan Doyle lived nearby and visited the site, unsure who the hoaxer could have been. Scientist Stephen Jay Gould speculated that scholar Pierre Teilhard de Chardin was a prime suspect. But what became clear to everyone was that even rationalists can be "taken" and for a period of several decades.

In 1953, when Kenneth P. Oakley made chemical tests, the bones were found to have been those of a recently dead human and the jaw of a recently dead orangutan, both cleverly treated to appear old. According to Gardiner, a trunk found in the mid-1970s in the southwest tower of the Natural History Museum contained irrefutable physical evidence that Hinton was the hoaxer. In the trunk were many vials of rodent remains along with hippopotamus fossils, elephant teeth, and assorted bones that were stained with the same mix of chemicals used on the Piltdown bones. "These two stupid men, Dawson and Smith Woodward, really believed that the elephant bone went with the man that was two feet above in the gravel bed," Gardiner concluded. "In a way, the last piece of evidence was to show what fools they were."

Chris Stringer, a paleoanthropologist at the Natural History Museum, has said that although Gardiner's hypothesis is "very convincing," he is still unwilling to rule out the possibility that Dawson, who had found the bones, might have been involved in the hoax as well.

Dr. Ian Langham in Australia and Frank Spencer of Queens College, New York City, studied the hoax independently and Spencer's *Piltdown, a Scientific Forgery* (1990) named the two culprits as being Sir Arthur Keith, who provided the technical expertise and possibly the bones, which were stained to look prehistoric, and Charles Dawson, who planted them in the gravel pit where he then led others, including Teilhard, on fossil hunts.

In 1996, Prof. Brian Gardiner, a paleontologist at King's College in London, reported (*Nature*, 23 May 1996) he had found the hoaxer: Martin A. C. Hinton, a paleontological prodigy whose specialty was rodent bones and who was an expert in Sussex geology. Gardiner held that Hinton had planted some specially stained human and orangutan remains in a gravel pit in Piltdown in order to discredit his boss, Arthur Smith Woodward, the paleontologist at the Natural History Museum in London. Angry that Smith Woodward had refused to pay his wages weekly instead of in a lump sum upon completion of his work, Hinton devised the scheme of placing the bones where Charles Dawson would find them. Dawson, a lawyer and amateur scientist, discovered the Piltdown bones per Hinton's plan, took them to Smith Woodward, and Smith Woodward was appropriately fooled. When he died in 1948, Smith Woodward apparently still believed in the authenticity of the bones. (See entries for Ralph Waldo Emerson, who had been fooled into believing in the authenticity of a 2,900-pound Cardiff, New York, giant, and Frank Spencer. Also, see entry for Peking Man. In a 1996 work, *Unraveling Piltdown: The Science Fraud of the Century and Its Solution*, John Evangelist Walsh details why and how Charles Dawson is believed to have been the definite perpetrator.) {RE}

Pincherle, Alberto: See entry for Alberto Moravia.

Pinel, Carl (20th Century)

Pinel, a nurse, wrote "Whatever Happened to Lazarus," in which he discusses "near-death experiences." But death, he points out, is like virginity: Both are absolute conditions. Either Lazarus died, or he did not. Pinel also asks why no one inquired of Lazarus what his alleged death was like, and he speculates as to why Jesus would so cruelly want to return Lazarus to this harsh world of suffering. "The most likely explanation," Pinel wrote, "is that the story was made up when the Gospels were written about a century after the deaths of their alleged authors. St. John may not have heard of Lazarus, who may not even have existed anyway."

Although James Hemming argued in *New Humanist* (June 1998) that Jesus was a humanist, Pinel countered that Jesus, so far as we can tell "was a fanatic." As an example, he cites the parable of the unmerciful servant, who is forgiven a debt by his master but, in turn, fails to cancel a debt owed to him and is handed over to be tortured. Jesus warns his listeners: "This is how my heavenly Father will treat each of you unless you forgive your brother from your heart." "Those," Pinel points out, "are not the words of a gentle person, but of a megalomaniac obsessed with sadistic power fantasies." {*The Freethinker*, July 1995; *New Humanist*, October 1998}

Pinel, Philippe (1745–1826)

Pinel was director of the Bicêtre Hospital and then of La Salpetrière. Under Napoléon he was professor of physics and hygiene, then of pathology, at the Paris School of Medicine. At a time when gross medieval theories, based upon the Gospels, held that insanity was due to diabolical possession, Pinel anticipated a medical theory and became a leader in the treatment of insanity. Pinel was a materialist and a humanitarian. {RAT; RE}

Pinkham, Daniel (20th Century)

Pinkham, the music director of Boston's King's Chapel, is a Unitarian who teaches at the New England Conservatory of Music.

Pinkham, Lydia (1819–1883)

Pinkham was the tenth of twelve children born to a strong-minded Quaker woman. As a girl in Lynn, Massachusetts, she and her sister Gulielma helped escort the ex-slave Frederick Douglass who was scheduled to speak in their town. Although the crowd jeered as they and some other drably dressed Quaker girls accompanied Douglass, no harm came to anyone. As a young lady, the fiercely independent Pinkham developed an interest in pharmacology, once copying a formula that was supposed to improve one's health. Eventually, she developed the product into Lydia E. Pinkham's Vegetable Compound, which she advertised as "the greatest medical discovery since the dawn of history." The product was a success, and women who had been too shy to go to male doctors began writing her for advice about their medical problems. Pinkham then wrote a small book for women, distributed it free, and helped many with good advice about puberty, conception, birth, and other subjects considered delicate at the time. Surprisingly, the Women's Christian Temperance Union, which fought against the use of liquor, endorsed her "vegetable compound," unaware that one of its ingredients was alcohol. Lydia and some of her children attended Unitarian and Universalist churches. {EG}

Pinn, Anthony B. (20th Century)

Pinn, who teaches religious studies at Macalester College in Minnesota, is author of *Why, Lord? Suffering and Evil in Black Theology*. The work explores failed efforts by Christian apologists to reconcile the existence of Black suffering with the belief in an omnipotent, just, and loving God. Pinn, who signed Humanist Manifesto 2000, offers "strong" humanism as an alternative to theistic religions. {*International Humanist News*, December 1997}

Pinsker, Michael (20th Century)

Pinsker is a director of the National Secular Society.

Pinter, Harold (1930–)

Pinter, according to David Tribe, is an outright freethinker. The English dramatist, in his "comedies of menace," invests the commonplace with tension and mystery, often through the use of silence. Among his best-known plays are *The Dumbwaiter* (1957), *The Birthday Party* (1958), *The Caretaker* (1960), *The Homecoming* (1965), and *No Man's Land* (1975). Pinter's inspiration for *Betrayal* (1978) was autobiographical, describing how, while he was married to the actress Vivien Merchant, he had an affair from 1963 to 1969 with Joan Bakewell, a British television news broadcaster and journalist who was married to television producer Michael Bakewell. {TRI; TYD}

PIQUE

Pique, the newsletter of the Secular Humanist Society of New York, was named in 1990 by its editor, Warren Allen Smith. In 1993, in a fit of pique over differences with the chapter's board, he resigned. From a circulation of over 800, *Pique* then dropped dramatically in quality and in loss of the chapter's members. In 1998 John Arents revived the newsletter.

Pirandello, Luigi (1867–1936)

Pirandello, one of the great figures in 20th century European theater, was grotesquely humorous but intellectually pessimistic. He was blacklisted for sympathetically portraying homosexuals in "Six Characters in Search of An Author" (1921), but he received the 1934 Nobel Prize in Literature. Using a central theme, man's attempts to distinguish between reality and illusion, Pirandello saw reality as an intangible, and what is thought to be reality he saw only as a series of illusions. Basically a rationalist, he wrote such works as *Right You Are If You Think You Are* (1917), *Henry IV* (1922), and *Tonight We Improvise* (1930). Dr. W. S. Starkie, an orthodox biographer, laments that "God is too absent from his work, and there is no trace of the wonderful balm of mysticism." The Italian philosopher, Croce, has a book on Pirandello's poetry and remarks that "his conception of reality is the exact opposite to the religious." Some have suggested that at the root of Pirandello's pessimism was a marriage in which his wife for fourteen years was insane. {CE; JM; RE}

PIRATES

Piracy is considered a crime against mankind and, except during times of war, pirates can be executed without trial. In the 1st Century B.C.E. pirates preyed upon Phoenician and Greek commerce, intercepting grain convoys and almost starving Rome itself. Unlike *privateering*, piracy involves no commission and receives the protection of no national flag. H. A. Ormerod's

Piracy in the Ancient World (1924) and Philip Gosse's *The History of Piracy* (1968) are classic studies of piracy. Sir William Gilbert, however, ridiculed romantic pirate stories in his *Pirates of Penzance* (1879).

Baldasarre Cossa (c. 1370–1419), before entering the service of the Church and becoming the antipope John XXIII, was a pirate. He also was a homosexual, as were such other pirates as Bartholomew Sharp (fl. 1680); Edward Teach (died 1718 and was known as Blackbeard); and Anne Bonney (fl. 1718) and Mary Read (born 1690). {CE; *Lavender Lists*, 1990}

Pirie, George (20th Century)

Pirie in 1998 retired as President of the New Zealand Association of Rationalists and Humanists. He is author of "An Essay on Humanism," a work that can be found on the Web: <crash.ihug.co.nz/~remk/fnz/nzhum/essayhum.html>.

Piron, Alexis (1689–1773)

"His pieces were full of wit and gaiety, and many anecdotes are told of his profanity," wrote Wheeler. "Among his sallies was his reply to a reproof for being drunk on Good Friday, that failing must be excused on a day when even deity succumbed." Piron was a French comic poet. In his old age, he became blind. Worried about a Bible in the margin of which he had written parodies and epigrams, Piron jocularly threw the whole book in the fire. Asked on his death-bed if he believed in God, he responded, "Parbleu, I believe even in the Virgin." {BDF}

Pisacane, Carlo (1818–1857)

Pisacane, the Italian son of the Duke of San Giovanni, served in the army in Algeria and joined the revolutionary forces against Austria and the Papacy. He was the chief organizer of Mazzini's army. When the Roman Republic fell, he fled to Switzerland and then to England. In 1857 he led a small venture against the reactionary Neapolitan power, but it failed and Pisacane fell in the fight. Pisacane dissented strongly from Mazzini's theism and was an agnostic who was scornful of all religion. {RAT}

Pisarev, Dmitri Ivanovich (1840–1868)

Pisarev was a Russian critic, journalist, and materialist. His successes included a criticism on the scholastics of the nineteenth century, and his works were published in ten volumes. {BDF; RAT}

Pitcher, Edwin Hoffman (20th Century)

Pitcher wrote "A Definition of Truth" (1945). {GS}

Pitkin, Royce S. (20th Century):

Pitkin, when he reviewed books for *The Humanist* in the 1950s, was President of Goddard College. An estimated one-third of the Goddard students then were Unitarian Universalists. For ten years Pitkin was president of the Vermont-Quebec Unitarian Universalist Convention.

Pitt, Marie Elizabeth Josephine (1869–1948)

An Australian journalist, poet, and freethinker, Pitt published controversial verse in the *Socialist* which "criticised the press, the Church, and the State." In 1911, she was one of the editors of the *Socialist*. Pitt was a Unitarian.

Pitt, William [1st Earl of Chatham] (1708–1778)

Pitt, a British statesman, was called "the Great Commoner" because of his services to his country. He criticized the War of the Austrian Succession which, in 1742, led to the downfall of Robert Walpole. He denounced government policy in the Seven Years War, then became head of a coalition government in 1757. His shrewd policy led to the defeat of the French in India and Canada. Although he formed another ministry in 1766, he was forced to retire in 1768 because of mental illness. Pitt ardently opposed the American War and particularly the use of Indians against the colonists. It is disputed whether he wrote a certain "Letter on Superstition," a letter first published in the *London Journal* (1733), and which contained the deistic views that "the more superstitious people are, always the more vicious; and the more they *believe*, the less they practice. Atheism furnishes no man with arguments to be vicious; but superstition, or what the world made by religion, is the greatest possible encouragement to vice, by setting up something as religion, which shall atone and commute for the want of virtue." The letter ends with the words, "We need a religion of humanity. The only true divinity is humanity."

In 1819, Pitt wrote "A Letter on Superstition." His biographer, Basil Williams, denies it but gives other evidence that Pitt was a deist having only "a simple faith in God" but no belief in the Christian God. Wilberforce, the pious abolitionist who was intimate with the younger Pitt, said, "Lord C. died, I fear, without the smallest thought of God." Instead of a parson at his deathbed, Chatham had Pitt's son read Homer to him. {BDF; JM; RAT; RE; TYD}

Pitt, William (1759–1806)

Pitt "the Younger," a British statesman who was made prime minister by George III, instituted lower customs duties in accordance with Adam Smith's theories, and his liberal policies continued until Great Britain became involved in the French Revolutionary Wars, followed by the Napoléonic Wars. Pitt resigned in 1801 when the king refused to approve Catholic Emancipation. Although Horatio Nelson's great naval victory at Trafalgar pleased him, he was upset by the defeat of Britain's allies at Austerlitz (1805) and died soon afterwards. William Pitt the younger, according to Robertson, was "an agnostic deist. Whether or not the elder Pitt was a deist, the younger gave very plain signs of being at least no more." He adds that Pitt's illustrious rival, Charles James Fox, also was an unbeliever, "though equally careful to make no profession of unbelief." Macaulay, Rosebery, and others apparently accepted a story by the Bishop of Lincoln that Pitt had had a deathbed conversion. But the best-informed witness, Lady Hester Stanhope, Pitt's niece and intimate friend, who kept house for him until he died (Pitt possibly was gay), bluntly pronounced the clerical story "a lie," saying that Pitt "never went to church in his life." {BDF; CE; JMR; JMRH; RAT}

Pittman, Jason (20th Century)

Pittman, while a student at Kalamazoo College, was one of the founding members of Campus Freethought Alliance. {*International Humanist News*, December 1996}

Pitzer, Donald E. (20th Century)

Pitzer wrote *Robert Owen's Legacy* (1972). {FUS}

Place, Francis (1771–1854)

Place, an English radical reformer, was active in the trade-union movement. Because of his efforts, the anti-union Combination Acts of 1799–1800 were repealed in 1824. An early leader of the Chartists, he helped draft the "People's Charter." Place wrote *Illustrations and Proofs of the Principle of Population* (1822), one of the earliest tracts on birth control. Jeremy Bentham told John Quincy Adams in 1817 that Place was an atheist, a fact documented in the *Reasoner* (26 March 1854). His biographer, Graham Wallis, called him an agnostic, but the word was unknown in Place's time. Meanwhile, Lord Morley in his *Recollections* states that Place was "regarded as an atheist by his friends." {BDF; CE; FUK; HAB; JM; RAT; RE; TRI}

PLACEBO EFFECT: See entry for Healing.

PLAGUE

Religionists often ascribe an individual's illness to her or his having "sinned" or somehow gone against God's will. God, the omnipotent one, then punishes the person or an entire group by sending a contagious, malignant, epidemic disease or other form of illness. Giovanni Villani, who died of the pestilence in 1348, had argued that the plague was divine punishment for the current sins of the Florentines: "avarice, greed, and usurious oppression of the poor."

The Judeo-Christian Bible tells of the ten plagues of Egypt, during which the waters were turned to blood, frogs and lice and flies and boils and hail and locusts and darkness affected the earth and its living creatures.

In Athens in 429–430 B.C.E. a plague occurred, killing Pericles among others.

In Rome in the 3rd Century a disastrous epidemic occurred, during which 5,000 persons reportedly succumbed daily.

In Constantinople in 1334, a widespread epidemic spread throughout Europe, aided by returning Crusaders who carried the disease back home and causing an estimated three-quarters of the population of Europe and Asia to die.

According to David Herlihy's *The Black Death and the Transformation of the West* (1998), the infectious agent of the Black Death that struck Europe might not have been bubonic plague. Had it been, then outbreaks in the human population should have been preceded by extensive deaths among local rodents. No such lethal outbreak of mortal disease (or epizootic) among rodents has been recorded, however. Herlihy describes how the Church had to conduct trials when petitioners described having been miraculously cured and petitioned to be canonized. A seventy-volume hagiographic collection (*Acta Sanctorum* published in Antwerp starting in 1643) shows that the "sign of the plague" was frequently described as petechiae, or spots, characteristic of anthrax and some other diseases (but rare with bubonic plague). Herlihy estimated that the population of Europe was reduced by two thirds between 1320 and 1420. In England, some cities and villages fell by seventy or eighty percent in the late decades of the 14th Century.

In London in 1665 a great plague occurred.

In 1918-1919 an influenza pandemic became a global horror the scope of which rivaled that of the Black Death of the Middle Ages.

At the end of the 20th century a plague, called AIDS and caused by HIV (Human Immuno-deficiency Virus), had killed over fourteen million throughout the world and infected another forty-seven million. In 1959 the first known AIDS-like case was believed to be that of a Bantu man who lived in Leopoldville, Belgian Congo (now Kinshasa in the Democratic Republic of Congo). As of 1998 an estimated one in four adults in Botswana Namibia, Swaziland, and Zimbabwe had become infected by the virus, as well as almost one in five adults in several other African countries. Although prevention programs stressing health education and condom use helped some nations slow transmission of the virus, no effective vaccine had been found to prevent infection.

The causes of such diseases may eventually be determined, but large numbers of "believers" hold that an all-loving God is behind the illnesses. Many leaders of organized religious groups and individuals, such as Catholicism's Mother Teresa, preached out against the use of condoms. People who were entirely ignorant of HIV were told the bromide, "Sex is sinful. Just don't do it."

Meanwhile, scientists continued working to halt the spread of the frightening epidemic. J. Claiborne Stephens and thirty-eight others wrote "Dating the Origin of the CCR5-Δ32 AIDS-Resistance Allele by the Coalescence of Haplotypes," *The American Journal of Human Genetics*, Vol. 62, No. 6 (June 1998). The group studied a mutant gene, one that obliterates the receptor site where the HIV-1 virus attaches to lymphoid cells of the immune system. They estimated, using mathematical models to analyze the data, that this mutant gene in 4,166 individuals from thirty-eight ethnic groups in Europe, Asia, the Middle East, and North America first appeared in European populations about 700 years ago (with a plausible range of uncertainty of 275 to 1,875 years in the past). The data, they suggested, provided "considerable, albeit indirect, support for the scenario that the . . . [mutant gene] has rapidly increased in its frequency by a strong selective pressure, possibly an ancient plague, the nature of which is currently undetermined." (See entries for AIDS and HIV.) {CE; Joel E. Cohen, *The New York Review of* Books, 4 March 1999; The *New York Times*, 4 February 1998}

Planck, Max (1858–1947)

Planck, a German physicist, sought to explain the experimental spectrum of black body radiation, and he introduced the hypothesis (1900) that oscillating atoms absorb and emit energy only in discrete bundles (called quanta) instead of continuously, as assumed in classical physics. The success of his work and subsequent developments by Albert Einstein, Niels Bohr, Werner Heisenberg, Erwin Schrödinger, and others established the revolutionary Quantum Theory of modern physics, of which Planck is justly regarded as the father. In 1918, he received the Nobel Prize in physics. His biographer, H. Hartmann, said that Planck was "far removed from all dogmatic, mystery-mongering beings" and recognized God only as "the ideal Spirit," adding that Planck believed in no future life. "Religion," he wrote in *Where Is Science Going?* (1932), "belongs to that realm that is inviolable before the law of causation and therefore is closed to science." {CE; JM; RE; TRI; TYD}

PLANETS

Although he did not explicitly predict the existence of planets around stars other than the Sun, Epicurus "believed in an infinity of worlds, meaning other ordered systems beyond the visible universe as it was then conceived," according to science writer John Noble Wilford. "This contrasted to the Earth-centered cosmos of the contemporary Aristotle, whose cosmology prevailed in Western thought for more than two millennia."

In 1999 the discovery of planets around other stars has made Epicureans of astronomers, Wilford has written. "Only in the last three years have astronomers established the reality of latter-day Epicurean speculations about a plurality of worlds, which in recent centuries came to mean planets beyond the solar system, some possibly inhabited. But while astornomers tip their hats to Epicurus, they just wish he had advised them how to make sense of the distant planets being detected by their telescopes." {*The New York Times*, 2 March 1999}

Plate, Ludwig (Born 1862)

Plate was a German zoologist, a teacher of zoology at Marburg, a curator of the Institute of Marine Science at Berlin University, and a director of the Phyletic Museum at Jena University. One of the founders of the Monist League, he publicly debated in defense of Monism against Christianity (*Ultramontane Weltanschauung und Modern Lebenskunde* (1907).

PLATFORM

Platform is published by the Ethical Culture Society at 4450 Fieldston Road, Bronx, NY 10471.

Plato (427?–347 B.C.E.)

During the French Revolution, Maréchal cited Plato as one who seems to be an atheist only from the standpoint of the strictest religious orthodoxy. But, like Aristotle, he is no freethinker and, instead, is one who inspires theists. "Not one of them," Plato wrote, "who took up in his youth with this opinion that there are no gods ever continued until old age faithful to his conviction." In Christian history, he is the typical philosopher of dualism. As such, according to Robertson, "he came to be *par excellence* the philosopher of theism, as against Aristotle and those of the Pythagoreans who affirmed the eternity of the universe."

What freethinkers admire about Plato, however, was his early love of ratiocination, of "the rendering and receiving of reasons."

"Platonic love" has come to mean a kind of sexless friendship. Although Phaedrus praised pederasty, not homosexual intercourse in general, Plato condemned homosexual intercourse in both the *Laws* (Book VIII) and the *Republic*. In the former, he wrote that it should be punished by a deprivation of civil rights, which was a severe penalty. He also stated that adultery, fornication, and the use of prostitutes should not be engaged in; but, if engaged in, it should be kept private or closeted.

The *Symposium* (384 B.C.E.?) speaks of the philosophical life as being an ongoing quest for ennobling beauty. Such a quest can result in a type of immortality in which one can leave beautiful memorials of words and deeds. The work describes male love:

> . . . if any device could be found whereby a state or an army were made up only of lovers and beloved, there would be no better way of living, since lovers would abstain from all ugly things and would be ambitious in pursuing honor and truth toward each other; and in battle side by side, such troops, although few, would conquer most of the world, since a man would be less willing to be seen by his beloved than by all the rest of the world, fleeing the ranks during a fight or

throwing away his arms; he would choose to die many times rather than that.

In fact, when the Sacred Battalion of Thebes, entirely composed of pairs of lovers, fought the battle of Chaeronea, according to Reay Tannahill, "all 300 of its members fell dead or mortally wounded." Elsewhere, Plato wrote, "Through the nightly loving of boys, a man, on arising, begins to see the true nature of beauty." So although in his *Laws* he writes one thing, in his private life he practices another. Apologists explain he was merely relating the attitudes of his time, attitudes which were not his own.

Bertrand Russell, in *History of Philosophy*, has called Plato one of philosophy's misfortunes: "Plato possessed the art to dress up illiberal suggestions in such a way that they deceived future ages, which admired the *Republic* without ever becoming aware of what was involved in its proposals. It has always been correct to praise Plato, but not to understand him. This is the common fate of great men. My object is the opposite. I wish to understand him, but to treat him with as little reverence as if he were a contemporary English or American advocate of totalitarianism." {CE; ER; Lee Eisler, *The Quotable Bertrand Russell*; EU, Aram Vartanian; GL; HNS2; JM; JMR; JMRH; Reay Tannahill, *Sex in History*; RE; TYD}

PLATONISM: See the entry for Platonism by Gilbert Ryle in the *Encyclopedia of Philosophy*, Vol. 6. Bertrand Russell, in *History of Philosophy*, details the weaknesses of Platonism.

Platt, James (19th Century)

Platt was a woolen merchant, the deistic author of *Business* (1875), *Morality* (1878), *Progress* (1880), *Life* (1881); and *God and Mammon*. {BDF}

Platt, Robert [Lord] (1900–1978)

Platt, a physician, wrote *Private and Controversial* (1972). The *Dictionary of National Biography* praised the book "with its frank and penetrating views of medicine and music (his two great loves), his interesting family background, his experiences in wartime, medical ethics, religion—which he approached negatively—statistics, and enthusiasm." Platt was president in England of the Eugenics Society. {TRI}

PLEASURE: See entry for Schadenfreude.

PLEDGES

Freethinkers are not into pledging, except to pledge allegiance to their government, family, or friends, as well as to pledge a liquid toast when honoring someone.

A major part of church, synagogue, and temple financing, once members have been securely indoctrinated about guilt (or the need for self-reproaching in the event of any inadequacy in following doctrine), is the pledge. Although in the United States religious groups have arranged to be tax exempt, and in some countries they even receive money from the national government, money is needed to build, to pay salaries, to pay for various religious projects. Members are encouraged to make weekly, monthly, quarterly, or annual pledges of money. The pledges are solemn binding promises to support the religious organization by helping to finance their programs. (An unlikely church T-shirt, described in Ken Alley's *Once Upon a Pew*, proclaims, "I UPPED MY PLEDGE. UP YOURS.)

PLEONISM

• Pleonism, n. An army of words escorting a corporal of thought.

–Ambrose Bierce
The Devil's Dictionary

Plimer, Ian (20th Century)

Plimer is professor of earth sciences at the University of Melbourne and author of *Telling Lies for God* (1994). He is an honorary associate of the New Zealand Association of Rationalists and Humanists.

Pliny the Elder (c. 23–79 CE)

A Roman naturalist whose extensive work lacks scientific authority, Gaius Plinius Secundus "had no faith in personal survival after death," Lamont has written. "From the moment of death onward, the body and soul feel as little as they did before birth," Pliny wrote. In his *Natural History*, he wrote, "It is ridiculous to suppose that the great head of things, whatever it may be, pays any regard to human affairs."

Shelley's *A Refutation of Deism* (1814) cites Pliny as being an atheist. By the end of the seventeenth century, Pliny's *Natural History* (77 CE) had been universally rejected because of his pseudoscientific methods. According to James Wynbrandt's *Toothsome Tales & Oral Oddities from Babylon to Braces* (1998), Pindar advised eating a mouse twice a month in order to prevent toothache.

When Mt. Vesuvius erupted, Pliny went to the site in order to calm the people. Volcanic fumes overcame him there. {BDF; CE; CL; TYD}

Pliss, Pat (20th Century)

Pliss has been business manager of *The Humanist*.

Plotina (c. 70–121)

Plotina, a Roman Empress, was the wife of Trojan and, in conjunction with Hadrian, did much of the work that is credited to the so-called "Stoic Emperors." Pliny described her as "the embodiment of all the virtues," and the historian Dio said she was of the highest character. Like Hadrian, but more seriously, she was a follower of Epicurus, according to one of her letters reproduced in Henderson's *Life of Hadrian*. McCabe laments that "our literary traditions about ancient Rome completely ignore the existence of such fine Empresses as Livia, Plotina, Sabina, Julia, etc." {JM; RE}

Plotinus (250–270)

A native of Egypt who was perhaps of Roman descent, Plotinus studied the philosophies of India and Persia and became known as a neoplatonist. Although he opposed Christianity, his theories had a considerable influence on Christian theologians. His idea of emanation, a view of origination as being a series of hierarchically descending radiations from the Godhead through intermediate stages to matter, was more developed than that of the Stoics and of Philo. Reaching God through thought is not possible, he reasoned, but it is attainable when the soul, in an ecstatic state and in a mystical fashion, loses the restraint of the body and allows a person "to know God." Plotinus allowed no one to paint his portrait, although one Roman artist did so from memory), and he refused to celebrate his own birthday, but only the birthdays of Plato and Socrates.

Plotinus's pupil Porphyry collected his teacher's writings under the title *The Enneads*. Reportedly, his last words were, "Try to bring back the god in you to the divine in the All," which has also been translated as, "I am trying to bring back the divine in us to the divine in the All." {CE; EH; ER}

Plumacher, Olga (19th Century)

Plumacher was a German pessimist, a follower of Hartmann. She wrote *Pessimism in the Past and Future* (1884) and has defended her views in *Mind*. {BDF}

Plumer, William [Governor] (1759–1850)

An American senator, Plumer in 1780 became a Baptist preacher, then resigned because of his skepticism. A deist, he served in the New Hampshire legislature for eight terms, during two of which he was Speaker. From 1812 to 1818, Plumer was Governor of New Hampshire. {BDF; RAT}

Plumptre, Constance (20th Century)

Plumptre wrote *Studies in Little-Known Subjects and Other Essays* (1903). {GS}

PLURALISM

Pluralism is a conviction that various religious, ethical, racial, and political groups should be allowed to thrive in a single society. In metaphysics, pluralism can also mean an alternative to dualism and monism. A pluralist asserts that there are more than two kinds of principles, whereas the dualist maintains there are only two and a monist only one.

Philosophers generally considered as pluralistic are Empedocles, Gottfried Wilhelm von Leibniz, William James, and Bertrand Russell. {CE; DCL}

Plutarch (46?–120)

A Greek essayist and biographer, Plutarch after traveling widely became a priest in his native Boeotia, a region of ancient Greece. In *The Parallel Lives* (translated by Sir Thomas North in 1579), he paired biographies of Greeks and Romans and influenced many, supplying Shakespeare with material for *Julius Caesar* and *Antony and Cleopatra* but also supplying Rousseau with doctrines and Alexander Hamilton with his heroes and ambitions. "The superstitious man," he wrote, "wishes he did not believe in gods, as the atheist does not, but fears to disbelieve in them."

Bertrand Russell found Plutarch interestingly gossipy. Plutarch told how Mark Antony, before he pursued Queens, traveled with a third-rate actress, inflicting her talent upon respectable provincials. He also tells how Caesar as a young man got into trouble "for reading a love letter from Brutus's mother during a meeting of the Senate, where no one was allowed to read anything." For Plutarch, who condemned the vulgar notions of deity, he would rather men said there was no Plutarch than traduce his character—in other words, superstition is more impious than atheism. Comments Lord Russell, "His heroes are not statuesque figures of perfection; they are concrete men, who could have existed even if they never in fact did." {BDF; Lee Eisler, *The Quotable Bertrand Russell*; GL; HNS2; Bertrand Russell, *Understanding History*; TYD}

PLUTO: See entry for its discoverer, Clyde Tombaugh.

Pobo, Kenneth (1954-)

A professor of English at Widener University in Chester, Pennsylvania, Pobo has taught at the University of Wisconsin and was poetry editor of *Cream City Review* (1980-1981). He wrote *Musings from the Porchlit Sea* (1979), *Postcards from America* (1980), *Billions of Lit Cigarettes* (1980), and *Yes, Irises* (1992).

Pobo feels his poetry is in the tradition of Eliot, Pound, William Carlos Williams, and Auden. What he dislikes is "the boring 'I' poems of contemporary writing," and he is committed to the gay rights and feminist movements. Is there any hope for the human race? "No," he responds. But is there any hope for individuals? "Yes."

Asked about humanism, Pobo responded:

> I consider myself a humanist in the tradition of E. M. Forster who opens his great novel *Howards End* with the phrase "Only connect." I do not think of the word "humanist" as soft and gushy but a word which is as exact as the point of a diamond. A humanist must care about social justice issues. For me, Forster's only connect starts in our homes but extends beyond the borders of concepts like the nation-state. Humanists can be believers in a Supreme Being or Beings or not. As of now, I see little evidence which supports a belief in a Supreme Being who "cares" about us. We must care for each other—as much as we can—as it is a bleak world. And such caring is an active verb. It means trying to wake up. As a writer who is gay, I feel particularly driven to use my time, and my writing life, to advance a greater awareness of a simple fact: gay people are people and not just "things" to be controlled and/or eliminated by a vicious society.
>
> Likewise, I see little evidence that there is a life after death. I certainly hope that heaven, were there to be such a place, would have nothing to do with all-day sunlight and gold streets and glitzy mansions. I'd like to go to a heaven with my lover. It's called a bedroom. It's here on earth. Another easy-to-get-to heaven is my garden. Why strive for a heaven with too much sun and not enough darkness? Plans need darkness to thrive. As for Hell, oh brother, don't I wish there were a big nasty one waiting for Pat Buchanan, Jerry Falwell, and Ronald Reagan. But those dull boys needn't worry too much. Worms will eat them and finally they'll make the world more beautiful when they fertilize flowers. Hell is usually conceived of as hot. If it exists, it probably would be hot. I so prefer Uranus, Neptune, and Pluto—free of humankind, they're already much warmer than Earth. Since I write poems, stories, and essays, sure, I'd love them "to live on" but even if they don't (and they probably won't) I had a blast writing them and think it's a pretty cool way to spend a lifetime.
>
> {WAS, 5 Mar 1999}

Podmore, Frank (1855–1910)

While at Oxford, Podmore became a Spiritualist, but in 1880 he disturbed the National Association of Spiritualists by informing them that he had become a skeptic. He was a member of the Council of the Society for Psychical Research from 1882 to 1909. Podmore collaborated with Gurney and Myers in compiling *Phantasms of the Living* (1886) and believed strongly in telepathy. McCabe holds that the two finest exposures of Spiritualism are Podmore's *Modern Spiritualism* (1902) and *The Newer Spiritualism* (1910). Podmore also worked in the Fabian Society and was an agnostic. {RAT}

Poe, Charlotte (1953-)

Poe, married and the mother of three children, is founder and president of FTVC, a freethinkers group in Ventura, California. She also edits that organization's monthly newsletter. Formerly a chemical engineer, she owns and operates a promotional products company that includes a line of freethought merchandise produced and distributed by freethinkers. E-mail: <FrThVC@aol.com>. Poe Specialties is on the Web at <http://members.aol.com/PoeSpecs/>.

Poe, Edgar Allan (1809–1849)

Although one of America's major writers, the grandfather of the detective novel, Poe is often dismissed as being an alcoholic and a failure. He was the son of actor parents: an alcoholic father who deserted his family shortly after Edgar was born and a mother who died of consumption soon after that. Raised and adopted by a wealthy Virginia merchant John Allan and his wife, Poe at the age of seventeen entered the University of Virginia, withdrawing after a term because of his excessive drinking and gambling. The Army dismissed him for having disobeyed an order.

When twenty-seven, Poe married his tubercular cousin, Virginia Clemm, a plump girl who was only thirteen. The two lived in poverty, with Virginia sleeping on a straw mattress wrapped in Poe's old army coat and using Poe's cat as a bed-warmer. When Virginia died during the winter, Poe removed the coat from the body and wore it to the cemetery. The cat, incidentally, died of starvation when deserted by Maria Clemm, Poe's aunt/mother-in-law, after Poe's death.

His biographer R. W. Griswold is accused of overemphasizing Poe's personal faults and distorting his letters, a jealous man who was envious. Others, however, emphasize Poe's greatness as a writer and say he was a complex person, tormented and alcoholic, yet also considerate, humorous, a good friend, and an affectionate husband. In France, Poe is particularly liked, partly because he was introduced through superior translations by Baudelaire, who, many feel, improved upon Poe.

Poe, who wrote "The Premature Burial" and the stream-of-consciousness "The Tell-Tale Heart," was known always to have been fearful of being prematurely buried. He wrote the compelling "Masque of the Red Death" and "The Fall of the House of Usher, as well as "The Murders in the Rue Morgue" and "The Raven."

Wheeler cites Poe's "Eureka, A Prose Poem" (1848) as indicating his pantheistic views of the universe. The work is generally overlooked but is an attempt to establish an all-embracing theory of cosmogony. He jeered at Aristotle, calling him Aries Tottle, and Bacon, whom he called Hog. Both he called "intellectual grovellers." Further, he claimed that his own description of the operation of gravity was better than Newton's. Biographer Kenneth Silverman in *Edgar A. Poe: Mournful and Never-Ending Remembrance* (1991) further explained:

> What Poe revealed, to capsulize his treatise, was that in the beginning, Divine Volition willed into being a "primordial Particle" and diffused it as atoms into a limited part of Space, the Universe of Stars. Owing to a tendency to regain their original oneness (gravity), the atoms began to agglomerate, forming clusters of nebulous matter.

> The condensation and rotation of one such cluster gave rise to the solar system, whose planets represent the coalescings of ring after ring of matter whirled off by the shrinking sun at the center. The planets have continued the same revolutionary movements (orbits) around the sun that characterized them as rings. Innumerable similar systems exist. In a necessary reaction to the originating divine diffusion of atoms, they will one day draw together into an almost infinitely less number of vast spheres, the "ingathering of the orbs" proceeding until the spheres themselves collapse into "the final globe of globes." Being rather nonmatter than matter, this ultimate globe will instantaneously disappear, leaving God to remain "all in all." The entire process if likely repeated forever and forever, "a novel Universe swelling into existence, and then subsiding into nothingness, at every throb of the Heart Divine.

"No thinking being lives who, at some luminous point of his life of thought, has not felt himself lost amid the surges of futile efforts at understanding, or believing, that anything exists *greater than his own soul*," Poe added. But for him, Silverman continued, such a feeling of personal infinitude . . .

> is but the residue of an original identity between ourselves and God, for the universe consists simply of fragments of diffused godhead, "infinite individualizations of Himself." The "Heart Divine" that gives birth to the universe is "*our own*"; each soul is "in part, its own God—its own Creator." God presently exists as the Universe of Stars, whose reunion is but his reconstitution as Individual. As the clusters ingather, we will become more conscious of our identity with Him and at least blend into the one God. Then our awareness of individual identity will gradually be merged in the "general consciousness." Our distress in considering that we shall lose our person-ality dissolves in the realization that at the epoch of final condensation our consciousness will be identical with Divinity. Then the self knows: "he shall recognize his existence as that of Jehovah." After dying, we eventually become God.

For him, God was a term representing a sense of the Ideal, not some anthropomorphic being. In "Al Aaraaf" Poe has God commanding the angel Nesace, "ruler" of Al Aaraaf, to convey a message to other worlds. The angel Ligeia is roused by Nesace and asked to awaken a thousand seraphs to perform God's embassy. Two souls, Ianthe and Angelo, fail to respond. Silverman comments that the incomplete and unusual work shows Poe trying to combine Tycho Brahe's nova with a repository for souls in the Koran, explaining that Al Aaraaf is the heaven for art and artists, the "birth-place of young Beauty."

Such an outlook about God did not please a young theological student named John Henry Hopkins, son of Vermont's Episcopal bishop. He objected to Poe's cynicism toward formal Christianity. He also recalled hearing Poe praise the "highly cultivated" Jesuit fathers at nearby St. John's College, because they "smoked, drank, and played cards like gentlemen, and never said a word about religion."

When Hopkins saw the manuscript copy of *Eureka* at the publisher's office, he was appalled that Poe included the vision of a never-dying self, coextensive and identical with God, "a system of complete and pure pantheism." This Hopkins called unscientific and predicted that Christians would consider such a pantheism a damnable heresy which would place Poe's "great discovery" in with "the empty chimaeras of infidelity."

Soon after the book was published a review appeared in the *Literary World* which lumped Poe with the Transcendentalists, rated Poe's account of planet formation a rehash of Laplace, and generally described the work as being "arrant fudge." Poe, the reviewer lamented, thinks nothing exists greater than his own soul, which is "extraordinary nonsense, if not blasphemy; and it may very possibly be both."

Poe responded with a long retort, claiming that what Laplace covered "compares with that covered by my theory as a bubble compares with the ocean on which it floats." He said the "Student of Theology," which he assumed to be Hopkins, used mis-quotations, faulty grammar, and a tone of "*turn-down-shirt-collar-ness*." As for being accused of pantheism, or polytheism, or paganism, or "God knows what," he offered that he cared only that he not be accused of being a "Student of Theology."

McCabe said *Eureka* was written the year before Poe died and is a combination pantheistic-agnostic profession of faith. The idea of God, Poe said, "stands for the possible attempt at an impossible conception," adding that we know nothing about the nature of God, that Nature and God are one and the same, and there is no such thing as personal immortality.

The main mention of organized religion in Poe's entire life, his biographer Woodberry wrote, was that the Bible was read to him while he was dying. However, Poe had written the following, in addition to referring to a "great celestial Oneness" and to explaining in detail his oneness with the Oneness in *Eureka*:

- The idea of God, infinity, or spirit stands for the possible attempt at an impossible conception.
- The pioneers and missionaries of religion have been the real cause of more trouble and war than all other classes of mankind.
- No man who ever lived knows any more about the hereafter . . . than you and I; and all religion . . . is simply evolved out of chicanery, fear, greed, imagination, and poetry.

One story has it that Poe attempted suicide by an overdose of opium and it was on a drinking spree that he died. Joseph Walker, a Baltimore printer, found him delirious in a Baltimore tavern. Talking to specters "that withered and loomed on the walls," he stopped breathing, or so the story went.

However, Dr. R. Michael Benitez, a cardiologist and assistant professor of medicine at the University of Maryland Medical Center, holds that Poe was not drunk at the end of his life, that by the time he died at the age of forty Poe almost always avoided alcohol, that even a glass of wine made him violently ill for days. What happened, Dr. Benitez holds, is that Poe entered Washington College Hospital comatose. By the next day he was perspiring heavily, hallucinating and shouting at imaginary companions. The next day, he improved but could not remember having fallen ill. On his fourth day at the hospital, he again grew confused and belligerent, then became quiet and died. This, the doctor concluded in *The Maryland Medical Journal* (September 1996), is a classic case of rabies. Rabies victims frequently exhibit hydrophobia because it is painful to swallow, and when Poe was calm and awake he refused alcohol and could drink water only with great difficulty.

Agreeing, Dr. Henry Wilde of Chulalongkorn University Hospital in Bangkok, Thailand, stated that Poe "had all the features of encephalitic rabies." No, most authorities counter, there was never any evidence of a bite or scratch, which would have been the case had he developed rabies.

When taken to a hospital because he was delirious, Poe was unable to communicate rationally with the physician there, Dr. John J. Moran, who had heard of the author but did not know him. Poe's funeral was arranged by the physician, who located a relative, the Rev. W. T. D. Clemm, one of Virginia's cousins, to conduct the service. The body was buried the next day, long before news of the death reached New York and other places.

Only eight persons attended the burial on a forbidding October day in Baltimore's Westminster Presbyterian Cemetery, and the ceremony lasted no more than three minutes, according to one who attended. Dr. Moran had purchased the wooden coffin, and Poe was buried next to his grandfather, Major David Poe, the only marker being "No. 80." The grave went unmarked for twenty-six years. It took ten years to raise the necessary one thousand dollars to erect a tombstone, at the unveiling of which the only literary notable present was Walt Whitman. Before the reburial, Poe was exhumed and Dr. Henry Shepherd reported that the "skull was in excellent condition—the shape of the forehead, one of Poe's striking features, was easily discerned. The teeth were perfect and white as pearl." The body was transferred to a sturdy casket and buried by George Spence, a gravedigger who had known Poe and had buried him the first time, also. The epitaph on the Baltimore monument:

QUOTH THE RAVEN NEVERMORE

At the time of the reburial, his deceased aunt, Mrs. William Clemm, was laid nearby. Her daughter, Poe's teenage wife, Virginia, joined them in 1885. She had been exhumed years earlier when her graveyard had been disturbed by developers. William Fearing Gill, an early admirer of Poe, had placed Virginia's bones in a box and kept them under his bed.

{BDF; CE; JM; *The New York Times*, 15 September 1996; PA; PUT; RAT; RE; TYD}

POEM, THE BEST IN 1000 YEARS: See entry for *Hamlet*.

POETS

> • In Plato's republic, poets were considered subversive, a danger to the republic. I kind of relish that role. So I see my present role as a gadfly, to use as a soapbox to promote my various ideas and obsessions.
>
> **–Lawrence Ferlinghetti**
> Upon being named San Francisco's first poet laureate in 1998

Poets have been banned since time immemorial. Publius Ovidius Naso was exiled in 8 CE by Augustus Caesar to Tomi, a bleak fishing village on the Black Sea coast, where he died nine years later. Ovid was banned because he showed a lack of reverence for authority. He brought out "The Art of Love" just at a time when Augustus's daughter was shipped off to Pandataria for her adulterous liaisons. In Hungary today, according to Donald Harrington, people are more apt to cite poets rather than statesmen or historical figures.

Recent poets cited by the 25th anniversary issue of *Index on Censorship* (1997) include the following:

• Jack Mapanje, punished by Dr. Hastings Banda, the dictator of Malawi, for "Of Chameleons and Gods"

• Ken Saro-Wiwa, hanged in Nigeria for founding the Movement for the Survival of the Ogoni People

• Allen Ginsberg, whose poetry was banned on national public radio in the United States on the grounds that it contained "indecent language"

• Miroslav Holub, a Czech poet whose work did not celebrate the glories of Stalinism

• Liu Hong Bin and Yang Lian of China, who have lived in exile since the Tiananmen massacre

• Samih Al-Qasim and Mahmoud Darwish of Palestine, who are persecuted by Israeli authorities

• Shams Langaroudi of Iran, whose four-volume history of modern poetry has been banned from publication in Iran

In the words of Mark Doty, an American poet, poets are "true guarantors of individuality," which makes them the antithesis of the repressive authoritarian spirit. (*The Economist*, 11 October 1997)

Poey, Andrés (Born 1826)

Poey was a Cuban meteorologist and positivist of French and Spanish descent. He wrote in the *Modern Thinker* and is author of many scientific memoirs as well as a popular exposition of positivism (1876), in which he has a chapter on Darwinism and Comtism. {BDF}

Pohl, David C. (20th Century)

Pohl, a Unitarian minister, has been the Unitarian director of the Department of Ministry. He retired in 1993, having been a minister of liberal religion for almost four decades.

Poincaré, Jules Henry (1854–1912)

Poincaré was a French mathematician, a forerunner of Einstein, who won eight gold medals, nine honorary degrees, and forty diplomas from foreign academies. In his last words, *Last Thoughts* (published 1913), Poincaré entirely rejected Christianity and believed in God only in the sense that he is the moral ideal. He wrote,

> We know how cruel the truth often is, and we wonder whether delusion is not more consoling.
>
> {*Humanism Scotland*, Autumn 1997}

Poincaré, Lucien (Born 1862)

Poincaré was a French physicist who taught at Paris University and Sèvres and was an Officer of the Legion of Honour. A rationalist, he wrote *The New Physics and its Evolution* (1907) and *Electricity, Present and Future* (1909). {RAT}

Poincaré, Raymond [President] (1860–1934)

The cousin of Jules Poincaré, Raymond Poincaré became President of the French Republic (1913–1920). He was an atheist who reportedly had developed a strong moral sense. {JM; RAT; RE; TRI}

Pojman, Louis (20th Century)

Pojman's *Ethics: Discovering Right and Wrong* (1995), discusses many ethical theories, most of which do not require a god or God. The work is often used in college-level introductory courses in ethics.

Polak-Schwartz, H. A. (20th Century)

In the 1950s, Madame Polak-Schwartz of the Netherlands was a correspondent for *The Humanist*. In 1952, she was Organizing Secretary of the newly founded International Humanist and Ethical Union (IHEU).

Polanski, Roman (1933–)

Polanski is a noted film director, writer, and actor. Accused of sexual improprieties, he has been barred from coming to the United States from his native France. His 1962 "Knife in the Water" won a Venice Film Festival award, and his "Cul-de-Sac" in 1966 won a Berlin Film Festival award. "Rosemary's Baby" (1968) won him much fame, and he intentionally included ambiguities so that it can be interpreted as having no genuine supernatural events; i.e., those are all in Mia Farrow's head, not real events. His opera, "Lulu," won him a 1974 award at the Spoletta Festival. Polanski's autobiography, written in 1984, is *Roman* and reveals his atheism. {CA; E}

Polansky, Joseph A. Jr. (20th Century)

Once a seminarian and a Trappist monk, Polansky joined the Benedictine order for five years. In *Prick the Bubble* (1999), he tells how, at the age of twenty-nine, he lost his sight because of diabetes. Earning an M. A. in Systematic Theology at Duquesne University, he continued post-graduate work at the University of Notre Dame.

Hired as a religious education coordinator at a parish in Coldwater, Michigan, he began to realize, in his words,

> that I was not making sense. I thought I spoke the English language, but I was talking the artificial language of theology and might have been babbling in tongues. I became violently religious—the beginning of my last-ditch stand for my faith. Actually I was clinging to an empty shell and was so much happier when I let it go. I proceeded to

analyze myth, symbol, ritual, sacrament, idols, miracles, and other facts of religion, and realized that religion was an illusion.

Married for over two decades and a member of the Freedom From Religion Foundation, Polansky is active in Altoona, Pennsylvania, community concerns and addresses local organizations on the importance of the Leader Dog program. {*Freethought Today*, September 1998}

Polansky, Lorie (20th Century)

The wife of Joseph A. Polansky Jr., Lorie has written for *Freethought Perspective* (April 1999).

POLEMICS

Polemics (with its linguistic roots in Greek of *polemikos*, hostile, and *polemos*, war) involves arguments among professing Christians in an effort to determine the "true" Christian view with regard to specific questions.

In everyday usage, to polemicize is to write or deliver an argument, or to engage in disputation or controversy. (See entry for Apologetics.)

Polet, Theo (20th Century)

Polet has been a representative of the International Humanist and Ethical Union (IHEU) at UNESCO. In 1958, the United Nations allowed the group non-governmental organization (NGO) status.

POLISH HUMANISM

A "Law of the Infinite Cornucopia" has been described by a Polish philosopher, Leszek Kolakowski, who explained that there never is a shortage of arguments to support whatever doctrine you want to believe in. Causes, in short, can invariably be found for any event, however extraordinary or unexpected, and whatever happens will be explained. When 1995 elections resulted in a loss for the candidates of the Catholic Church, the Primate of Poland, Jozef Glemp, credited the "neo-pagans." However, critics have suggested that the Church's choices lost basically because the majority of Polish voters did not approve of the Church's trying to influence the voting. Primate Glemp had called on the faithful to pray for "the elections, President Walesa, and the fatherland." Walesa lost. The winner was Aleksander Kwasniewska, an atheist whose wife is Catholic and whose platform included economic reform and a pragmatic approach to solving governmental problems.

More than one dozen small Polish humanist groups reportedly existed in Poland in 1994. Professor Barbara Stanosz—who signed Humanist Manifesto 2000—has worked with the German *Humanistischer Verband Deutschlands* to obtain funds for their magazine, *Bez Dogmati*. Two other active leaders are Jan Wolenski and Bohdan Chwedenczuk. There are these groups and publications:

• Association for Humanism, c/o Prof. Dolowy, is at UL. Rackowiecka 39A M 10, 02-521 Warsaw

• *Bez Dogmatu* (Without Dogma) is a quarterly at Instytut Wydawniczy "Ksiazka I Prasa," ul. Twarda 60, 00-818 Warszawa

• Culture Secular Society, an associate member of the IHEU, is at Rada Krajowa, UL. Koszykowa 24, 00-553 Warsaw

• Neutrum AL Jerozolimskie Marszalsowska 13, 13-PL 0026 Warsaw

• Neutrum, UL. Zlota 72 M I, 00-821 Warsaw

• Polish Freethinkers Society, U1, Jaroslawa Dabrowskiego 17A M 1, 02-561 Warsaw

• *Res Humana*, a quarterly, 00-553 Warszawa, ul. Koszykowa 24

(See entries for Andrzej Dominicrat, Leszek Kotakowski, and for Society for Humanism and Independent Ethics.)

POLISH PHILOSOPHY: See *Encyclopedia of Philosophy*, Vol. 6.

POLISH UNITARIANS

The Unitarian Universalist Community in Poland (UUCP) has 150 members and friends. Congregations are found in Chorzow, Katowice, Myslowice, Zabrze, Bytom, and Warczawa.

In the 16th and 17th centuries the Polish Brethren were condemned to banishment and in 1658 were involved in the Counter-Reformation.

In the first thirty years of the present century in Krakow, Pastor Grycz-Smilowski achieved a restoration of the Unitarian movement, but his death in 1959 resulted in a lack of interest in Unitarianism.

Today Unitarian groups are acknowledged by the Polish Government and collaborate with religious and humanistic groups to protect religious freedom and human rights.

Contacts include Rada Naczelna of Wspolnota Unitarian Universalistow w Rzeczypospolitej Polskiej; and Dr. Helmut Iwa, ul. Wolskiego 10/5 41-500 Chorzow, Poland.

Pietr Kowalik heads the Union of the Polish Brethren (Jednota Braci Polskich, SKR.POC2T.655, 50-950 Wroclaw, Poland). The presiding council of a Unitarian group in Chorzow consists of Helmut Iwa, President of the Community; treasurer Marek Ziolkowski; and secretary Zbigniew Strombirski. Contact is the Rev. Michael Gozdzik, ul Weilka Skotnica 38/44 41-400 Myslowice, Poland.

POLISH-AMERICAN FREETHOUGHT

Freethought in the United States, by Gordon Stein, discusses various American freethought groups.

POLITICS

• Politics, n. A strife of interests masquerading as a contest of principles.

–Ambrose Bierce, *The Devil's Dictionary*

POLITICAL PHILOSOPHY: See *Encyclopedia of Philosophy*, Vol. 6.

POLITICAL RESEARCH ASSOCIATES

A group that monitors the political far right and the fundamentalist-religious right is Political Research Associates, 120 Beacon Street (Suite 202), Somerville, Massachusetts.

Polk, Charles (18th Century)

Polk, son of Colonel Thomas Polk, was a freethinker. (See entry for North Carolina Freethinkers.)

Polk, Ezekiel (18th Century)

Polk, the grandfather of President James K. Polk, was a freethinker. (See entry for North Carolina Freethinkers.)

Pollard, Robert (1907–)

Pollard wrote "Abolish the Blasphemy Laws" (1957). {TRI}

Pollitt, Katha (1949–)

"For me, religion is serious business," Pollitt wrote in *The Nation*, "a farrago of authoritarian nonsense, misogyny and humble pie, the eternal enemy of human happiness and freedom." Her column, "Subject To Debate," is in *The Nation* (26 December 1994), for which she is an associate editor. In her columns she has written that for some reasons "my left-wing, cosmopolitan parents—he the agnostic Episcopalian, she the atheistic Jew—sent me to a private nondenominational Protestant school for girls. Prayer in the schools? For nine years I had chapel *every* day: three hymns, the doxology, the Lord's Prayer, a Bible reading (or was it two Bible readings?) and, on Fridays, a sacred-music solo from Mr. Crandall, the organist. Never mind that one-third of the student body was Jewish and another third Roman or Eastern-rite Catholic. You don't have to say the prayers, our teachers used to tell us, but you should bow your head as a mark of respect. Not praying was easy, not bowing somewhat less so. It was not singing that was the real challenge. I loved choral singing, which is surely one of life's great pleasures, but since I didn't believe in God, to take part was to participate in falsehood. Truth or beauty? Principled isolation or join the fun? Reign in Hell observe in Heaven? These questions obsessed me for years and, indeed, still do."

Pollitt wryly recommends that students be *forced* to endure school prayer, at least until "it will become clear that prayer in schools does nothing to lower crime or teen pregnancy, much less raise S.A.T. [educational] scores. The religious kids will still be devout, but the others—the ones from nonobservant homes, who supposedly need to be forced into piety—will have been moved from apathy to disgust" and the message to the youth will have become clear, that "we have nothing for you here, start thinking about the hereafter."

After mentioning on a television program, "Crossfire," that she, as a representative of the secular humanist viewpoint, did not believe in God, Pollitt was awarded the Freedom From Religion Foundation's (FFRF) Freethought Heroine of 1995 award. (Her acceptance speech was published in *Freethought Today* [April 1996].) {CA; E; WWS}

Pollock, David (20th Century)

Pollock is Chairman of the Board of Directors of the Rationalist Press Association. E-mail: <david.pollock@virgin.net>.

Pollock, Frederick [Sir] (1845–1937)

Pollock, an English jurist, succeeded to his baronetcy in 1888. He was a professor of jurisprudence at Oxford and, after 1914, was judge of the admiralty court of the Cinque Ports. In addition to numerous works on law, Pollock wrote monographs on Spinoza (1880). His correspondence with Oliver Wendell Holmes was published as *The Holmes-Pollock Letters* (1941). Sir Frederick was a Fellow of the British Academy, Correspondent of the French Institute, and Associate of the Royal Academy of Belgium. He considered that "man's life and thought will not be fixed," that "our ideals themselves are shifting and changing shape," and that superstition is "a great and deadly serpent." {JM; RAT; RE}

POLTERGEISTS: See entry for Ghosts.

Polybius (c. 203–120 B.C.E.)

A leader of the Achaean League, Polybius the historian was influential in Greek politics. Of his forty books, only the first five survive. Following is a sample from *Histories*:

> Since the masses of the people are inconstant, full of unruly desires, passionate, and reckless of consequence, they must be filled with fears to keep them in order. The ancients did well, therefore, to invent gods, and the belief in punishment after death.
>
> {CE; *Humanism Scotland*, Autumn 1997; TYD}

POLYGAMY

> • Polygamy, n. A house of atonement, or expiatory chapel, fitted with several stools of repentance, as distinguished from monogamy, which has but one.
>
> **–Ambrose Bierce**
> *The Devil's Dictionary*

> • Brigham Young originated mass production, but Henry Ford was the one who improved on it.
>
> –Will Rogers

Of 1,154 societies studied by anthropologists, 980 have been openly polygamous. For example, the four Incan offices from petty chief to full chief were given ceilings of seven, eight, fifteen, and thirty women, respectively.

Although Catholic teaching specifically holds that polygamy is sinful, the practice forms a central part of the traditional social structure of millions of Africans in every region. One Catholic president, Félix Houphouët-Boigny, who built in the Ivory Coast the world's second largest basilica after St. Peter's in the Vatican, is known to have several wives. Africa has more than ninety million Catholics and is one of the most fertile recruiting grounds for new believers. Although Cardinal Poupard of the Ivory Coast states the church will never endorse polygamy, he acknowledges that it exists but vows to attempt to replace it gradually with monogamy.

Joseph Smith continues to inspire some polygamists, who believe in original divine revelations including plural, or celestial, marriage. The official Church of Jesus Christ of Latter-day Saints, when Wilford Woodruff was its president, renounced polygamy in 1890, particularly in order to gain political acceptance for Utah's becoming a state. It now excommunicates polygamists. However, Ogden Kraut, a fundamentalist publisher and historian in Salt Lake City, estimates that there are 30,000 to 35,000 practicing polygamists, counting all family members, in the United States, a number estimated to be four or five times greater than in the 1880s. Timothy Egan in 1999 put the figure at anywhere from 20,000 to 60,000 people living in families where one man is married to two, three, five, as many as thirty women. "No one has been prosecuted for polygamy in Utah for nearly fifty years," he claims. At a 1999 trial of David Ortell Kingston, the polygamist who was convicted of incest with his sixteen-year-old niece, the Kingston clan was said to have about one thousand members and $150 million in assets. The number of polygmaists was estimated at between 20,000 and 30,000. Brigham Young is believed to have had twenty-seven to fifty-five wives, sixteen of whom bore him fifty-seven children.

Journalist Florence Williams (*The New York Times*, 11 December 1997) interviewed one polygamist's household, which belonged to a financier in his forties. It was a 35,000-square-foot motel-like structure "with 37 bathrooms and 31 bedrooms, this for 10 wives and 28 children." All the wives shared a central kitchen. By schedule, they rotated child-care duties, cooking, cleaning, yard work, and gardening. The house was shaped like an airplane propeller with three radiating blades. Two of the blades housed bedrooms for wives and children (the latter grouped by age and sharing bedrooms with half-siblings). Some wives were said to get along better than others, one wife saying, "We have to want to get along." "We're a 24-hour restaurant," said another, noting the four refrigerators, two dishwashers, and fourteen counter stools. Rooms just off the hub contained a home theater, a computer room, and several bathrooms with specially designed child-height counters. "There are cheaper ways to have sex," the polygamist explained but added, "We feel it's the best deal on earth to live together and work together, and the architecture absolutely shows that."

On the subject of polygamy, Bertrand Russell in *Political Ideals* (1961), wrote: "It is generally assumed without question that the state has a right to punish certain kinds of sexual irregularity. No one doubts that the Mormons sincerely believed polygamy to be a desirable practice, yet the United States required them to abandon its legal recognition, and probably any other Christian country would have done likewise." However, he notes that the prohibition might not have been wise. After all, polygamy is legally permitted elsewhere in the world and, had it been allowed in Europe or in Utah, "the world would have acquired a piece of knowledge it is now unable to possess. I think in all such cases, the law should only intervene when there is some injury inflicted without the consent of the injured person." (See entries for Ochino, Mormon Church, and Pentecostalism.) {CE; Lee Eisler, *The Quotable Bertrand Russell*; *The New York Times*, 4 June 1999}

POLYGYNY

Women, it is claimed, need men to protect them. But because a man's sexual needs often exceed a woman's, the solution is to allow polygny: the practice of having more than one wife at a time. Many refute this, claiming that it is not possible for a man with multiple spouses to give each the equal treatment that is required, for example, by the Qur'an.

POLYTHEISM

Polytheism is the belief in more than one god. The ancient Greeks were polytheists whose gods included Apollo, Athena, Dionysus, and Zeus. {DCL}

Pombal, Sebastião José de Carvalho e Melo [Marquis de] (1699–1782)

Pombal was a Portuguese statesman who, after serving as ambassador to England and Austria, became secretary for foreign affairs and war for King Joseph. In 1736, he became chief minister. A dynamic Portuguese political figure, he was a zealous organizer and was notoriously anti-clerical. Pombal curbed the Inquisition by subordinating it to the king's authority, then expelled the Jesuits from Portugal and its colonies as well as redrafted the property laws to prevent the accumulation of great wealth by the church. Prior to this, an estimated ten percent of the population had been priests and the Inquisition was still burning heretics at the stake. Inasmuch as there were few or no Protestants, those who suffered were either Jews or so-called "New Christians," formerly Jewish families that had converted but were thought to still have Jewish affiliations.

An enlightened despot, Pombal ended slavery in Portugal, reorganized the educational and military systems, and encouraged agriculture and industry. He was instrumental in building up Brazil with increased production of minerals, tobacco, and sugar, but in his actions he was admittedly ruthless in suppressing all opposition. (See review by Derek Beales of Kenneth Maxwell's *Pombal: Paradox of the Enlightenment* in *The New York Review of Books*, 18 April 1996.) {CE; Tim Egan, *The New York Times Magazine*, 28 February 1999}

Pomerantz, Alfred (20th Century)

"The Messiah" by Pomerantz was published in an April 1959 *Age of Reason,* Joseph Lewis's freethought magazine. Pomerantz also wrote "Trinity," in the February 1960 issue.

Pomeroy, Ernest Arthur George (Born 1867)

Pomeroy, the seventh Viscount Haberton, served in the army and succeeded to the title in 1912. He wrote a number of advanced rationalist works and, in *Idol of Fear* (1905), he drastically criticized Christianity, defended Judas, and included discourses about Jesus which were along Voltairean lines. {RAT; RE}

Pomeroy, Wardell Baxter (1913–)

A psychotherapist, Pomeroy is a Humanist Laureate in the Council for Secular Humanism's International Academy of Humanism. He received much recognition for his work with Alfred Kinsey and others on *Sexual Behavior in the Human Male* (1948) and *Sexual Behavior in the Human Female* (1953). He has written *Boys and Sex* (1968) and *Girls and Sex* (1969) as well as *Dr. Kinsey and the Institute for Sex Research* (1972).

Pompery, Edouard (1812–1895)

Pompery was a French publicist. A follower of Fourier, he wrote on Blanquism, on opportunism (1879), and on Voltaire (1880). {BDF}

Pomponazzi, Pietro (1462–1525)

One of the Renaissance thinkers, Pomponazzi did not believe in immortality or a future existence. He questioned St. Thomas Aquinas's interpretation of Aristotle. Church officials disliked his view that the soul is mortal, that to believe it is immortal requires acceptance simply on faith. Not only did he deny immortality but also he held that ethics could do very well without the belief (adding, however, that mankind is "brutish and materialized" and needs the belief in heaven and hell to make them moral). In Venice, the Inquisition burned Pomponazzi's book on immortality, highlighting how devastating his critique really was. In spite of his philosophical views, he insisted on his readiness to submit all his tenets to the judgment of the Church. {BDF; CE; CL; ER; JMR; JMRH}

De Ponnat [Baron] (1810–1884)

De Ponnat was a French writer, educated by the Jesuits but later a thorough freethinker and democrat. A baron, he collaborated with A. S. Morin on the *Rationaliste* of Geneva. He was imprisoned for a year because of articles in *Le Candide* and other publications, and he wrote *The Cross of Death*, a discourse to the bishops who assisted at the Ecumenical Council of Rome (1862). His principal work is a history of the variations and contradictions of the Roman Church. {BDF}

Ponsonby, Arthur Augustus William Harry (1871–1946)

Ponsonby was the first Baron of Shulbrede, the son of General Sir Henry Ponsonby. He became Under-Secretary for Foreign Affairs in 1924 and for the Dominions in 1929. In his *Conflict of Opinion* (1919, Ponsonby rejected Christianity and admitted God only as "the spirit of perfection outside of us. . . . We may conceivably in time succeed in creating God more definitely." {RE}

Pontiac [Chief] (Flourished 1760–1766)

Chief Pontiac of the Ottawa Indian tribe reportedly said, of Robert Rogers who was on his way to taking possession of the Western forts for the English, "They came with a Bible and their religion—stole our land, crushed our spirit . . . and now tell us we should be thankful to the 'Lord' for being saved."

Pontoppidan, Henrik (1857-1929)

A Danish novelist and Nobel Prize winner, Pontoppidan early in life was a journalist. In 1880 he was prosecuted for blasphemy. He later became a minister but reverted to Rationalism, writing a series of satirical novels. Tennyson was inspired by his description of a mythical sea-monster, the *kraken*, which slept in the depths of the sea, an "ancient dreamless, uninvaded sleep" which Tennyson described as a "pained fascination with the thought of a life which somehow is not life at all." Pontoppidan had described the *kraken* in his *Gesta et vestigia Danorum extra Daniam* (1740) and a *Natural History of Norway* (1755). {RE}

Pontius, James (20th Century)

Pontius, a freethinker, wrote *The Holy Bible in a Nutshell* (c. 1910). {GS}

Pool, Gary (20th Century)

Pool, an editor in Indiana, has written about Amnesty International for *The Humanist* (USA).

Pool, Elijah: See entry for Nation of Islam.

POPE

The head of the Roman Catholic Church is the pope, who is believed by his church to be the successor of the apostle Peter. He is Bishop of Rome, president of the College of Cardinals, and monarch of the 108.7-acre Vatican city state, which is a small nation within Rome. The corporate finances have never been made public. Fewer than 500 residents live there, but the Vatican has diplomatic relations with 130 nations.

In *Saints and Sinners: A History of the Popes* (1997), Eamon Duffy points out that one-third of the popes elected between 872 and 1012 died under unusual circumstances; for example:

- John VIII (872–882) was bludgeoned to death by his own entourage;
- Stephen VI (896–897) was strangled;
- Leo V (903) was murdered by his successor, Sergius III (904–911);
- John X (914–928) suffocated;
- Stephen VIII (934–942) was horribly mutilated.

Meanwhile, the Greek antipope John XVI (997–998) had his eyes, nose, lips, tongue, and hands removed but failed to die.

Pius II (1458-1464), according to William Manchester, as bishop "fathered several children by various mistresses." Quentin Crisp theorizes that Pope John Paul I "died so suspiciously soon after his enthronement [that he was] rumored to have been poisoned with lethal cups of tea." (See entry for the notoriously immoral John XII, pope from 955 to 964. For a description of his wild parties, see the entry for Alexander VI. For Pope Joan, see entry for Hoaxes, Religious. Also see Papal Bull. A recent book on the politics of the Vatican and how the church's leaders wish their followers would follow, not complain, see Thomas Reese's *Inside the Vatican*, 1997. See entry for Quentin Crisp.) {DCL}

Pope, Alexander (1688–1744)

Pope's *Essay on Man* (1734) contains the celebrated couplet:

> Know then thyself, presume not God to scan;
> The proper study of mankind is man.

He is generally conceded to be the leading 18th century English poet. According to Voltaire, Pope's "The Universal Prayer," attached to "An Essay on Man," was mainly influenced by the philosophy of Lord Shaftesbury, and that prayer has often been called the deists' prayer. As a child born of Roman Catholic parents, whose father was a prosperous Roman Catholic linen draper, Pope was debarred from a Protestant education. As a result, he was almost entirely self-taught. Only 4' 6" tall (1.4 meters), he was afflicted by a tubercular condition, Pott's disease, which left him with a pronounced spinal curvature starting in his later childhood. In addition, as can be discerned in his *Eloisa to Abelard* (1717), Pope's genital apparatus was dysfunctional and his romantic life was thus thwarted.

Joseph Addison attacked Pope for his Tory leanings, but Pope called Addison and his *Tatler* friend Richard Steele "hermaphrodites" (homosexuals). William Wycherly and the poet-critic William Walsh, among others, liked Pope. Pope prospered by publishing his translations of Homer, which have been said to be magnificent but somewhat inaccurate. With the money earned, he bought a lease on a house in Twickenham, where he and his mother lived for the rest of their lives.

The Popes, appropriate family name that it was, were Catholic. Or were they? McCabe states that Pope was one of a large and brilliant circle of Deists in London, that although many quote the words about the proper study of mankind they often forget to quote the preceding "presume not God to scan." Lord Chesterfield described Pope in one of his letters as "a Deist believing in a future life." The *Catholic Encyclopedia* claims him on the ground that he "willingly yielded" to a friend's suggestion that he should receive the sacrament when he was dying. It is another of the constructive untruths of that flower of Catholic culture," McCabe complains. "What Pope said was, 'I do not suppose that it is essential, but it will look right,' " which McCabe finds strange language for a man who had been an "apostate" for a quarter of a century. McCabe cites Pope's "Universal Prayer" as an indication that Pope actually had entirely deserted Catholicism and was a deist.

Alexander Pope, according to Martin Greif, had something else in common with some of the Vatican Popes: He had strong homoerotic desires. A member of the "Scriblerians," an all-male club that included homosexuals such as John Arbuthnot, John Gay, Robert Harley, Jonathan Swift. In the 1730s Pope engaged in one of the most famous and venomous literary feuds in history, according to Martin Greif in *The Gay Book of Days*: "Pope, supposedly jealous that his friend Lady Mary Wortley Montagu had taken up with John Hervey, Baron Hervey of Ickworth, began satirizing Hervey's effeminacy in his poetry, most notably as "Lord Fanny" in *Imitations of Horace* (1733–1738) and as "Sporus" in the *Epistle to Dr. Arbuthnot* (1734). If Pope's picture of the mincing Lord Fanny had not set London laughing, the reference to Sporus had literate London holding its sides, since Sporus was the boy 'bride' of Nero who would bare his rear for the emperor to attack in public." Greif continues, "At the same time, Nero's 'husband' was Doryphorus, who would return the favor in kind—also in public. Hervey, understandably upset by these jibes, responded with verses of his own that ridiculed the crippled poet's hideous hump and his less than noble birth. London wags found this hilarious, too. Eventually, the feud died down and was forgotten." {CE; A. Owen Aldridge, EU, G. S. Rousseau, "Scriblerians," GL; RAT; RE; TYD}

POPE JOHN PAUL I

John Paul I (1912-1978) died or was murdered one month after he took office in 1978, being succeeded by John Paul II.

Reviewing "The Godfather" in *Christopher Street* (Issue #153), Crisp advised moviegoers about the movie: "This picture stops just short of being blasphemous, but viewers should be warned that it denounces Catholicism at least as vigorously as it attacks the Mafia. In one early scene, we are shown a Vatican official offering Mr. Pacino the control of a vast conglomerate enterprise in exchange for sufficient money to cover its own ill-advised investments. The narrative also manages to drag in Pope John Paul I who, in real life, died so suspiciously soon after his enthronement and who was rumored to have been poisoned with lethal cups of tea."

A 1984 book, *In God's Name* by David Yallop alleged that the Italian mob killed the pope, a charge which the Vatican denounced as "shocking and deplorable." The Church explained that the strain of office had proved too much for the 65-year-old pope and that he had suffered a heart attack. However, no autopsy was performed, according to Vatican tradition.

Cardinal Aloisio Lorschelder, the late pontiff's choice to succeed him, also questioned the death, saying in August 1998, "I have to say that a suspicion remains in our hearts." In 1999 singer Elton John purchased rights to Yallop's best-selling novel, saying he intended to make a movie about the mysterious death. {CE; New York *Daily News*, 16 February 1999}

POPE JOHN PAUL II: See entry for Stanislaw Lem.

POPÉ (died c. 1690)

Popé was a Pueblo medicine man who practiced his traditional religion. He was anti-Spanish rule and in 1680 organized a revolt during which attacks on Sante Fe, the capital city, killed some 400 colonists and missionaries and forced survivors to retreat down the Rio Grande to El Paso. Assuming a despotic role, Popé attempted to wipe out all traces of the Spanish conquerors, their language, their culture, their churches—he even washed clean anyone whom the Spaniards had baptized. In 1692 shortly after Popés death, the Spaniards reconquered the area and rebuilt the Catholicism he had wiped out. {CE}

Pope, John (20th Century)

Pope wrote *The Hellions* (1987). {GS}

Pope, Liston (20th Century)

A Southern freethinker, Pope wrote *Millhands and Preachers* (1942), which tells about the role of the church in social affairs and its frequent vassalage to economic leaders. {*Freethought History #14* 1995}

Popper, Karl Raimund [Sir] (1902–1994)

Popper, a philosopher and a defender of democratic systems of government, was born in Vienna. His father, Simon Popper, a doctor of law at the University of Vienna, was a prominent liberal lawyer, and his mother, Jenny Schiff Popper, was a pianist. Although his parents were Jews, Popper was christened in a Protestant church. For a few months, Popper considered himself a Communist, but upon witnessing a confrontation between Vienna police and young unarmed socialists trying to rescue some Communists from the police station, he saw the police fatally shoot several of the young people. Although a Marxist would have accepted that such deaths might be necessary on the road to revolution, Popper decided he could not. As World War II approached, he and his wife, Josefine, left for New Zealand. There, he was a lecturer in philosophy at Canterbury College in Christchurch. In 1945, Popper went to London to teach at the London School of Economics. At the time of his death, Popper was professor emeritus of logic and scientific method at the University of London, where he had taught from 1949 to 1969.

In a 1934 work, *The Logic of Scientific Discovery*, he argued that science does not proceed through verification. Rather, it makes bold, competing conjectures, exposing them to rigorous tests and eliminating those which have been refuted. "Next to music and art," Popper has stated, "science is the greatest, most beautiful, and most enlightening achievement of the human spirit."

Popper's *The Open Society and Its Enemies* (1945) has been called one of the most influential books of the century. It was the inspiration for the widespread use of the phrase "open society." He argued that communism and fascism are philosophically linked, and in *The Poverty of Historicism* (1957), another attack on Marxism, he questioned the idea that there are inexorable laws of human history. Rather, he believed, history is influenced by the growth of knowledge, which is unpredictable. "Erroneous beliefs may have an astonishing power to survive," he wrote, "for thousands of years, in defiance of experience and without the aid of any conspiracy. . . . One example is the general conspiracy theory itself . . . the erroneous view that whenever something evil happens it must be the evil will of an evil power."

His simple idea that anyone could understand was that man makes progress by making mistakes. In science, he held, the mark of a good theory is that it should be easily falsifiable and open to correction. The origin of "falsification" was, according to I. Grattan-Guinness (*Russell: The Journal of the Bertrand Russell Archives*, Summer 1998),

> In Vienna at that time, at least in the bourgeoisie to which Popper's family belonged, there operated the *Dienstmädchen* system of "slave labour," as he described it to me. A woman worked as servant to a family for thirteen days per fortnight, from a Sunday to the following Saturday week; then her employment would continue unless the head of the household decided that it be terminated at the end of the next fortnight. When Popper was about nine years old (around 1911, therefore) his father accused their servant of stealing an amount equivalent to £15, and dismissed her under this rule. Upon asking his father about the woman's prospects, "I did not receive a satisfactory reply." Thus the influence of his father was negative—in his own later terms, a falsification. In response to my query, he confirmed that *The Open Society* had been written to oppose that sort of system as well as the ones which the Nazis and the Communists were trying to impose in the 1940s. . . . "Communism will always revive," Popper said to me on another occasion.

Freudianism, Popper complained, was not genuinely scientific, unable to be refuted because it is so all-encompassing. In politics, he held that the mark of a good system of government was that it should be open to criticism, something lacking in the political utopianism of Plato, Hegel, and Marx. His difference with Wittgenstein was that he thought scientific theories can be proved false but cannot be proved true, that genuine philosophical problems exist; Wittgenstein, on the other hand, argued that puzzles caused by language's imprecision exist, not genuine philosophical problems, that the puzzles could be "dissolved" through a better understanding of language.

Rejecting the certainty of knowledge, Popper held that knowing is an individual, unpredictable act of genius. Unlike the logical positivists, he believed that knowing is not limited to verifiable statements. For him, psychology, astrology, metaphysics, Marxist history, and Freudian psychoanalysis are all pseudo-sciences, and he rejected them as "myths."

In Search of a Better World (1992) contains a selection of thirty years of Popper's lectures and essays. *Challenges To The Enlightenment,*

In Defense of Reason and Science (1994) contains a translation of "Emancipation Through Knowledge," which he had delivered in German on the Bavarian Broadcasting Network in a 1961 series of broadcasts on the meaning of history.

Critics have pointed out that Popper claimed to have solved one of the great philosophical puzzles, David Hume's "problems of induction." But he did not and, according to his own theories, should have welcomed the fact when his error was pointed out. He did not, however, ever admit he was wrong, leading some to accuse him of being un-Popperian.

In 1979, Prof. Popper was elected an honorary associate of the British Rationalist Press Association. Also, he was a Humanist Laureate in the Council for Secular Humanism's International Academy of Humanism. He refused, however, to sign their *Secular Humanist Declaration* (1980) if B. F. Skinner signed it.

In a 1992 interview with *The Sunday Times* in London, when Popper was asked to comment on the collapse of the Marxist states of Eastern Europe: "I will not except to say, 'I told you so.' I just knew that these were beastly regimes and I kept saying so. That is all."

Sir Karl's wife, Josefine, died in 1985. They had no children. (See *New Humanist*, November 1994, in which Andrew Ferguson states that Popper is as effective as F. R. H. (Ronald) Englefield "in showing that most of what Hegel wrote is meaningless rubbish (except in so far as it serves as a rationale for the state exercising absolute power)." Also, see the entry for Richard Bailey, who found that Popper was active in Austrian politics and social reform; and see Anthony Quinton's article on Popper in the *Encyclopedia of Philosophy*, Vol. 6) {CE; Sarah Lyall, *The New York Times*, 21 March 1998}

POPULATION, HUMAN

Demographer Nathan Keyfitz in a 1991 letter to the historian Justin Kaplan wrote that

> The dead outnumber the living, in a ratio that could be as high as 20 to 1. Credible estimates of the number of people who have ever lived on the earth run from 70 billion to over 100 billion.

If in 1997 an estimated 5.8 billion humans were alive, and averaging the above figures to put the total persons ever born at about 85 billion, we can extrapolate that the dead outnumber us about fourteen to one. The dead will always outnumber us.

Two thousand years ago, the Earth had an estimated one-quarter of a billion people (the population of the United States in 1990). That figure doubled to a half- billion people by 1650. By 1830 the human population passed one billion, by 1930 two billion, and by 1973 four billion. Around 1965-1970 the global population growth rate reached an all-time peak, according to Joel E. Cohen, author of *How Many People Can the Earth Support?* (1995). "In Africa," Cohen added, "contrary to the world trend, the absolute number of chronically undernourished increased by two-thirds between 1970 and 1990. Africa also had the highest population growth rates during that period—and still does."

Writer Annie Dillard (*Harper's Magazine*, January 1998), after presenting the above figures, continues:

> One tenth of the land on earth is tundra. At any time, it is raining on only 5 percent of the planet's surface. Lightning strikes the planet about a hundred times every second. The insects outweigh us. Our chickens outnumber us four to one. One fifth of us are Muslims. One fifth of us live in China. And every seventh person is a Chinese peasant. Almost one tenth of us live within range of an active volcano. More than 2 percent of us are mentally retarded. We humans drink tea—over a billion cups a day. Among us we speak 10,000 languages.
>
> We are civilized generation number 500 or so, counting from 10,000 years ago, when we settled down. We are *Homo sapiens* generation number 7,500, counting from 150,000 years ago, when our species presumably arose; and we are human generation number 125,000, counting from the earliest forms of *Homo*.
>
> Every 110 hours a million more humans arrive on the planet than die into the planet. A hundred million of us are children who live on the streets. Over a hundred million of us live in countries where we hold no citizenship. Twenty-three million of us are refugees. Sixteen million of us live in Cairo. Twelve million fish for a living from small boats. Seven and a half million of us are Uygurs. One million of us crew on freezer trawlers. Nearly a thousand of us a day commit suicide.

Dillard then notes Joseph Stalin's observation, "A single death is a tragedy, a million deaths is a statistic." Included among the statistics: Mao in China starved 30 million. Eleven million children under five die each year now. In Bangladesh in 1991, waves drowned 138,000.

As to how important, relatively, all this is, Dillard noted

> Ten years ago we thought there were two galaxies for each of us alive. Lately, since we loosed the Hubble Space Telescope, we have revised our figures. There are nine galaxies for each of us. Each galaxy harbors an average of 100 billion suns. In our galaxy, the Milky Way, there are sixty-nine suns for each person alive. The Hubble shows, says a report, that the universe "is at least 15 billion years old." Two galaxies, nine galaxies . . . sixty-nine suns, 100 billion suns. . . .
>
> These astronomers are nickel-and-diming us to death.

POPULATION EXPLOSION

Priscilla Robertson in the 1950s was only one of many humanists who issued an alarm in the pages of *The Humanist* concerning the troubling increase in the human population. In the 19th century, Lord Richie Calder was one of many who had sounded a similar alarm. Meanwhile, some major church organizations have, contrarily, fought birth control measures and planned parenthood programs.

Thomas Robert Malthus had predicted that the population would eventually outstrip the food supply. Karl Marx rejected that view, arguing that the problem was not one of overpopulation but of unequal distribution of goods, a problem that even a declining population would not solve.

Family planning has succeeded in some countries—Japan, the republics of the former Soviet Union, and most of Europe—and in some developing countries, such as India, China, Kenya, Pakistan, Taiwan, Turkey, Egypt, and Chile. In the United States, however, birth control and abortion are bitterly debated. Zero Population Growth, an educational group founded in 1970, has aimed to stop population growth, first in the United States and then in other countries. On the international level, besides the International Planned Parenthood Federation, the United Nations Economic and Social Council provides birth control aid to underdeveloped nations.

During the Roman Empire, an estimated quarter to a half billion humans existed. By the mid-19th Century, the number had increased to one billion. By 1930 the number had increased to 2 billion. In 1992, the world's population was about 5.4 billion. In 1995, the population had increased to 5.7 billion. The U. S. Department of Commerce has estimated that by 2010 the number will increase to 7 billion and by 2020 to 7.9 billion. The United Nations has estimated that the population in 1990 will have doubled by 2050. By the year 2150, one estimate has the human population as high as an incredible 694 billion. Theists may ignominiously welcome the latter number as a bullish sign for church finances. But non-theist organizations such as the International Humanist and Ethical Union (IHEU) and the Council for Secular Humanism have reacted with horror when they extrapolate as to what such a future will bring.

Of particular interests to freethinkers and rationalists is "punctuated equilibrium," an idea developed by Niles Eldredge and Stephen Jay Gould, one which recognizes that although the theory of evolution satisfactorily describes the past it cannot predict the future. The negative conclusion which they have developed, for example, states first that only at times of speciation, when one evolutionary lineage splits into two, does evolutionary change occur. Speciation, however, requires the geographical isolation of subpopulations of a species. With 5.7 billion humans interbreeding and possessing easy mobility to all parts of the Earth, isolation has now become next to impossible. Thus, evolutionary changes will come to a stop, and the species we now have will not increase as they were able to do in the distant past. By over-populating the Earth, in short, humans are tragically leading to their own demise as well as that of other species. Arthur C. Clarke's *3001* extrapolates that long before 3001 Earth will not be habitable. (See entry for Paul Ehrlich, who predicts that with the globe's population heading toward ten billion by the middle of the 21st century, Western countries will gobble up the resources needed by the impoverished throngs of Asia, Africa, and Latin America. Also see entries for Hugh Iltis and Priscilla Robertson.) {CE; *Free Inquiry*, Spring, 1999, has an entire issue containing alarming population growth figures—articles are by Philip Appleman, Diana Brown, Lester R. Brown, Roy W. Brown, Frances Kissling, Craig Lesher, and Carl Wahren.}

Porath, Alan (20th Century)

A Wisconsin freethinker, Porath is a retired chemical engineer. He was one of the plaintiffs in a successful environment lawsuit and also in a successful suit for Ozaukee County, Wisconsin, to abandon their official Good Friday holy day. He received the Freedom From Religion Foundation's 1998 Freethinker of the Year Award. {*Freethought Today*, April 1997}

Porath, Mary (20th Century)

A retired Wisconsin teacher and children's librarian, Porath and her husband, Alan, were plaintiffs in a successful lawsuit, *Freedom From Religion Foundation v. Ozaukee County, Wisconsin*, that ended in the county's abandoning their official Good Friday holy day. She received the Freedom From Religion Foundation's 1998 Freethinker of the Year Award. {*Freethought Today*, April 1997}

PORNOGRAPHY

In his *Forbidden Knowledge: From Prometheus to Pornography* (1996), Roger Shattuck discussed what kinds of knowledge that are not now strenuously forbidden which really ought to be forbidden. Milton's *Paradise Lost* warned against undue curiosity, repeating the view that to eat of the forbidden fruit resulted in having knowledge that one would be better not to know. "Know to know no more," Milton advised Adam and Eve. Augustine and other church leaders were in agreement.

Shattuck advised "a wise agnosticism" in dealing with the subject of pornography. It is not the forbidding of knowledge which is the solution; the important thing is for people to learn how to handle what formerly was forbidden but which can no longer be beyond the scope of our studying.

Anthony Comstock (1844–1915) was an American censor who banned as pornographic *Fanny Hill* (1750), *The Lustful Turk, Peep Behind the Curtains of a Female Seminary, A Night in a Moorish Harem, Love on the Sly*, Whitman's *Leaves of Grass*, Shaw's *Mrs. Warren's Profession*, and an estimated 500,000 reproductions of drawings or paintings. "Anything which tends to destroy the dignity of womanhood or to display the female form in an irreverent manner is immoral," he stated. Although he expressed a reverence for the female form, "the place for a woman's body to be—denuded—is in the privacy of her own apartments with the blinds down."

In 1934 when Henry Miller's *The Tropic of Cancer* was printed in Paris, the poet Ezra Pound rejoiced, "an unprintable book that is fit to read."

In 1963 the New York publishing firm of G. P. Putnam's Sons was taken to trial for printing John Cleland's *Fanny Hill*. The firm won, lost an intermediate appeal, and in 1964 won gain in New York's Court of Appeals, 4 votes to 3. {PA}

Porphyry (c. 242–c. 305)

Porphyry, a Greek scholar and Neoplatonic philosopher, was a follower of and editor of *The Enneads* of Plotinus. He made sharper attacks on Christianity than had his teacher in a work titled *Against the Christians*. Church leaders who could find any copies destroyed them, for they objected to his criticism that the *Book of Daniel* was written during the Maccabean period, centuries later than the time it describes. He also listed other discrepancies, such as the various accounts of Jesus's resurrection, and he questioned how Paul could tell fellow Christians to "Bless and curse not" but so bitterly denounce his opponents in the early church. Porphyry avoided gambling, the theater, horse racing, and public games. He was a vegetarian, believing that the less-developed souls of animals entered those who ate their flesh. Porphyry's *Isagoge*, an introduction to Aristotle's logic, became a standard medieval text. In *Porphyry's Against the Christians: The Literary Remains* (1994), R. Joseph Hoffmann has edited and newly translated the pagan critic's work. {BDF; CE; EH; HNS2}

Porteous, Skipp (1944–)

A Fundamentalist preacher turned humanist, Porteous is editor of *The Freedom Writer*, a First Amendment newsletter. He also edits *Walk Away*, a newsletter for people leaving fundamentalism. In *Jesus Doesn't Live Here Anymore* (1991), Porteous describes how he was "saved" at the age of eleven and how he was able to walk away. Since 1984, he has served as President and National Director of the Institute for First Amendment Studies.

Porteous, who had been a Unitarian Universalist, converted to Judaism in 1996. On Chanukah Sunday, before some eighty friends and family at the Hevreh of Southern Berkshire in Massachusetts, he observed, after being with his wife of fourteen years, Barbara Simon, "The formal conversion does make a difference, because you feel like you have the whole Jewish community behind you. "Barbara never tried to convert me," he stated to the *Jewish Forward*, but "in July I decided I was really Jewish at heart. Right away I started observing Shabbat" and chose as his Hebrew name Avi ben Avraham. {*Free Inquiry*, Fall, 1990; *World*, March/April, 1994}

Porter, Bernard (20th Century)

When he signed Humanist Manifesto II, Porter was president of the Toronto Humanist Association. {HM2}

Porter, Burton F(rederick) (20th Century)

Porter wrote *Deity and Morality With Regard to the Naturalistic Fallacy* (1968). {GS}

Porter, George (20th Century)

Porter, who is newsletter editor of the Washington (District of Columbia) Area Secular Humanist *WASHline*, is a Secular Humanist Mentor of the Council for Secular Humanism.

Porter, Lois (20th Century)

Porter, a founding member and first president of the Washington Area Secular Humanists in Washington, D. C., is author of "Fanny Wright: Free Enquirer" and "Matilda Joslyn Gage, Feminist and Secular Humanist." She is a Secular Humanist Mentor of the Council for Secular Humanism and an Associate Editor of *Free Inquiry*. In 1994 in Rochester, New York, Porter spoke on "Female Freethinkers" at a Robert G. Ingersoll memorial in commemoration of Ingersoll's work on behalf of women's equality. He is Vice-President of the Washington Area Secular Humanists. {*Free Inquiry*, Fall, 1990 and winter 1996-1997}

Porter, Samuel P. (19th Century)

From 1892 to 1894, Porter was secretary in New York of the Freethought Federation of America.

PORTUGUESE FREETHINKERS: See entry for Pombal.

Porzio, Simone (1496–1554)

Porzio was a disciple of Pomponazzi. When lecturing at Pisa and asked about the soul, he echoed what he had written in *De Mente Humana*, that the human soul differed in no essential point from the soul of a lion or plant, that those who thought otherwise were prompted by pity for man's mean estate. {BDF}

Poser, Ernest G. (20th Century)

Poser, an emeritus professor of psychology at the University of British Columbia, wrote "Reflections of a 'Born Again' Humanist" in *Humanist in Canada* (Summer 1997). He is a founder of organized humanism in Canada.

Posidonius (c. 125–51 B.C.E.)

A Greek Stoic philosopher, Posidonius of Apameia wrote copiously, but all his works have been lost. Those on ethics and physics contributed greatly to the Stoic outlook. Posidonius held that a vital force emanates from the sun and permeates the world, which was his doctrine of cosmic sympathy showing that man and all else in the universe are united. He calculated the circumference of the earth, drew a map of the earth, and showed it to be a sphere. Similarly, many ancient Greeks thought that the earth's land mass is ocean-circled. His suggestion that India could be reached by sailing westward across the Atlantic, rather than eastward, erred only by stating that India was 70,000 stadia away. {CE}

POSITIVISM

• Positivism, n. A philosophy that denies our knowledge of the Real and affirms our ignorance of the Apparent. Its longest exponent is Comte, its broadest Mill, and its thickest Spencer.

–Ambroce Bierce
The Devil's Dictionary

Positivism is an approach to philosophy frequently found in the twentieth century. Positivists usually hold that all meaningful statements must be either logical inferences or sense descriptions, and usually argue that the statements found in metaphysics, such as "Human beings are free" or "Human beings are not free," are meaningless because they cannot possibly be verified by the senses.

The works of Francis Bacon, George Berkeley, and David Hume contain in an implicit form the basic tenets of positivism. The term is specifically applied to the system of Auguste Comte, who developed its coherent doctrine and who then influenced various trends of contemporary thought, including the movement of logical positivism. (See entries for Comte; Latin American Positivism; Humanism, per Curtis Reese; and Leopoldo Zea, author of *Positivism in Mexico*. Nicola Abbagnano wrote about positivism in the *Encyclopedia of Philosophy*, Vol. 6; also see "The London Positivists" in *The London Heretics* by Warren Sylvester Smith; and the entry for Pedro Mendoça, a Brazilian positivist.) {CE; DCL; RE}

Posner, Gary P. (20th Century)

Posner, a Florida physician and critic of faith healing, is on Council for Secular Humanism's Faith-Healing Investigation Project. He founded Tampa Bay Skeptics in 1988. {*Free Inquiry*, Winter, 1986-1987}

"Posos, Juan de" (18th Century)

An undiscovered author using the name Posos expressed atheistic opinions in a book of imaginary travels, published in Dutch at Amsterdam in 1708 and translated into German at Leipzig in 1721. {BDF}

Post, Albert (20th Century)

Post wrote *Popular Freethought in America, 1825–1850* (1943). {FUS}

Post, Amy (1803–1889)

Post was an American reformer, a leading advocate of slavery abolition, temperance, woman's suffrage, and religious reform from as early as 1828. {BDF}

POST-CHRISTIAN

Post-Christian is a term that began to be used in the latter part of the 20th Century. Freethinkers admit that the term is an overly optimistic expression that denotes a hoped-for wish-fulfillment. (See entry for Post-Human.)

POSTERITY

• Do you have a desire to be remembered?
"I don't think so."
I mean, do you think about posterity?
"What did posterity ever do for me?"

–Alfred Hitchcock,
answering questions by
Peter Bogdanovich in *Who the Devil Made It*

Postgate, John Raymond (1922–)

Postgate, a microbiologist, became an Honorary Associate of the Rationalist Press Association in 1994. He wrote *Microbes and Man* (1969), *The Sulfate-Reducing Bacteria* (1979), and *A Plain Man's Guide to Jazz* (1973). He has written,

> I was born in Pimlico in 1922 and grew up in Hendon and Finchley, North London. My parents were political animals. Raymond Postgate, my father, was a socialist historian, writer, and propagandist (the fame he derived from founding the *Good Food Guide* came late in life), and my mother was Daisy, daughter and later private secretary of George Lansbury, sometime leader of the Labour Party.
>
> Although politically active in my undergraduate days at Oxford—I led a group of Labour sympathisers in the University's Communist-dominated Labour Club during the Second World War—I was distracted by girls, jazz music, and science, in that order, and politics became a minor though still abiding interest. I remain a jazz enthusiast, writer, and musician, and am married with three grown-up daughters, but my career was in science: I took First Class Honours in Chemistry from Balliol, followed by a D. Phil. for research in Chemical Microbiology, and became a professional research scientist.
>
> Happily I was successful. I had become fascinated by microbes, especially bacteria, because they can live in extraordinarily harsh environments (air-free, boiling hot, sub-zero, hyper-saline), can feed on poisonous or seemingly intractable substances, can conduct remarkable chemical processes. My research gained me Fellowship of the Royal Society, a D. Sc. from Oxford, a couple of Visiting Professorships in the USA; in due course I became Director of a personal research unit at the University of Sussex, where I was also Professor (now Emeritus) of Microbiology: I was President of the Institute of Biology and of the Society for General Microbiology. As well as numerous research papers and some technical books I have also published a couple of reasonably successful popular science books, *Microbes and Man* and *The Outer Reaches of Life*, and articles on popular science.
>
> I became atheistic as a ten-year-old, to the discomposure of my Cub-master, whom I stopped in the street to announce brightly that, there being no God, I could no longer be a Cub. (Pages 146-8 of my wife's and my biography of my father, *A Stomach for Dissent*, describe how he aided my liberation from religion).
>
> Being a scientist, becoming aware of the astonishing scope of microbial existence, has re-enforced my disbelief. In addition, the strong social conscience (inherited) has made me acutely aware of the appalling cruelties and injustices inflicted in the name of God, today as much as in the past. Not that there have not been comparable atrocities inflicted in the name of Karl Marx, even of Darwin. I know and regret that a large part of humanity seems to require a system of prescriptive beliefs, usually a religion. It is a requirement that mankind must grow out of. I try when I can to show that enlightenment and reason can provide awe, wonder, delight, escape, even social and moral imperatives, without calling for mysticism, hatred, revenge, or retribution. {*New Humanist*, September 1996}

POST-HUMAN

N. Katherine Hayles, mindful of Donna Maraway's 1985 "A Manifesto for Cyborgs," has been concerned about the trend of humans to depend upon machines. In *How We Became Posthuman: Virtual Bodies in Cybernetics, Literature, and Informatics* (1999), she as a leader in cybertheoryland discussed cybernetics, the interdisciplinary postwar science devoted to analyzing both the animal and mechanical kingdoms as self-organizing systems based around information flows and feedback loops. A new subjectivity exists, she has found, one that undercuts the centrality of consciousness and erodes the distinction between humans and machines.

According to her, today's "third wavers" largely spurn such philosophical reflections, being more interested in programming Darwinian computer simulations that, following the archetype of Artificial Life, attempt to reproduce the logic of organic life by allowing codes to "evolve" inside the petri dish of a personal computer. Future generations, she extrapolates, will be stupefied by "the postmodern orghodoxy that the body is primarily, if not entirely, a linguistic and discursive construction." If already we have become posthuman, she asks, what kind of posthumans will we be? (See entry for Cybernetics and Cyberspace.) {Erik Davis, "The Posthuman Touch, *Village Voice*, 23 March 1999}

Postma, Paul (20th Century)

Postma served as treasurer of the International Humanist and Ethical Union (IHEU) for twenty years. In 1998 at their congress in Mumbai, Postma was given a distinguished service award. {*International Humanist News*, December 1998}

POST-MODERNISM AND THE POST-MODERNIST CRITICISM OF HUMANISM

Commencing as early as 1949, a postmodernist movement began which reacted against the theory and practice of modern art or literature. Paul Kurtz finds that postmodernists are critical of "modernity," which in part is equated with the Enlightenment—thinkers like Descartes, Bacon, Locke, Voltaire, Diderot, Condorcet, d'Holbach, the Encyclopedists, Kant, Goethe, Bentham, Mill, Marx, Darwin, Freud, Jefferson, Madison, Franklin, and Paine. These were individuals who had confidence in mankind's ability to control its destiny, who declared that humans are free and rational agents, and who believed mankind is responsible in some measure for its future.

But in the 1960s a group of anti-humanists spoke about "the death of man," with Theodor Adorno critical of humanism's optimism, stating that after Auschwitz we can no longer write hymns "to the grandeur of man" (quoted in *French Philosophy of the Sixties: An Essay on Anti-Humanism*, 1990). The French postmodernists included Louis Althusser, Jacques Derrida, Jacques Lacan, Michel Foucault, and Jean-François Lyotard. Drawing upon Heidegger's philosophy, they deplore the growth of technology, maintain that language is a veil masking Being, state that every text should be deconstructed, and hold that objective scientific knowledge is a myth. They hold the anti-humanist views that human beings are *not* capable of free and autonomous choice; that they are *not* rational and responsible; that universal ethical norms can *not* be discovered; and that the ideals of liberal democracy and of human rights do *not* have genuine authenticity. The postmodernists pushed the Sartre generation aside, concentrating upon their own new rebellions—against humanism, against literature, against the shape of a printed page, against the idea of progress, sometimes even against clarity of expression itself.

Victor Farias in *Heidegger and Nazism* (1989) points out that Heidegger joined the Nazi Party in 1933 and in 1935 reaffirmed the "inner truth and greatness of National Socialism," believing the Party was Germany's only hope for grasping "the problem of technology." Incredibly, states Kurtz, Philippe Lacoue Labarthe, a disciple of Derrida, has defended Heidegger by maintaining that "Nazism is a humanism" because "it rests on a determination of *Humanitas* which is, in its eyes, more powerful, i.e., more effective, than any other." Although Luc Ferry and Alain Renaut have negatively criticized the postmodernist Heideggerians, their influence persists but only in a minor way.

Paul Kurtz declared in opposition to the anti-humanists that "we need a *re*-enchantment with the ideals of humanism, a *re*-enlightenment. We need a new Enlightenment. For those who say it is not possible, I say it is, and indeed, the humanist stream of culture is making headway in spite of its critics." Postmodernism, its critics state, is over-reliant on technology-assisted instruction. It resists the misapplication of technology to teaching, which depends upon human contact and teachers and the interaction of students as well as of other teachers. Belgian philosopher Paul Cliteur is in agreement, stating that postmodernism rejects the Enlightenment, that although many postmodernists may be atheists it behooves the secular humanists to refute their methodology.

Richard Rorty of the University of Virginia has the view that post-modernism is

> one of these terms that has been used so much that nobody has the foggiest idea what it means. It means one thing in philosophy, another thing in architecture, and nothing in literature. It would be nice to get rid of it. It isn't exactly an idea; it's a word that pretends to stand for an idea. Or maybe the idea that one ought to get rid of is that there is any need to get beyond modernity.

Jean Bricmont, Vern L. Bullough, Xiaorong Li, Theodore Schick Jr., John Searle, Harvey Siegel, and E. O. Wilson have discussed postmodernism in a series of articles edited by Matt Cherry (*Free Inquiry*, Fall 1998). Cherry pointed out that postmodernism questions accepted standards and emphasizes how social context affects beliefs and theories, therefore trying to "deconstruct" the assumptions underlying truth claims. It encourages openness to the points of view of those outside the mainstream. Although it is to be welcomed that postmodernism provides an antidote to complacent claims of certainty, Cherry points out that, in their finding it difficult to get at the truth, postmodernists reject the very notion of "truth" itself. This leads to a view that there is no "objective knowledge" and no "facts," only personal interpretation. Therefore, "reason" and "science" are no better than any other "myth," "narrative," or "magical explanation." Were such theories taken seriously, they would, for example, destroy support for science, social reform, and universal human rights.

For most, postmodernism is already passé. What will be the intellectual fashion of the near future is always unclear. (See entry for Deconstruction. A first-rate discussion of the topic is found in Tony Judt's *Past Imperfect: French Intellectuals, 1944–1956* (1993). Also, see the article by John McGowan of the University of North Carolina in *The Johns Hopkins Guide to Literary Theory & Criticism*, who points out that the term *postmodernism* was first used in reference to architecture as early as 1947 and is best understood as "marking the site of several related, but not identical, debates among intellectuals in the last four decades of the twentieth century. These debates revolve around the relation of artworks to social context, the relation of art and of theory to political action and to the dominant social order, the relation of cultural practices to the transformation or maintenance of society in all its aspects, the relation of the collapse of traditional philosophical foundations to the possibility of critical distance from and effective critique of the status quo, the relation of an image-dominated consumer society to artistic practice, and the future of a Western tradition that now appears more heterogeneous than previously thought even while it appears insufficiently tolerant of [open to] multiplicity." Finally, see "Why Postmodernism is Not Progressive: If You Seek Understanding or Social Change, Don't Go There," by Barbara Epstein, *Free Inquiry*, Spring 1999.) {Paul Cliteur, "The Challenge of Postmodernism to Humanism," *New Humanist*, August 1995; Paul Kurtz, *Free Inquiry*, Winter, 1992-1993}

POSTULATE

A postulate is a statement accepted as true for the purposes of argument or scientific investigation; e.g., "No human has survived death." {DCL}

Pott, Joseph Holder (18th Century)

A freethinker, Pott wrote, "A Charge Delivered to the Clergy of the Archdeaconry of St. Alban's at the Visitation" (1796). {GS}

Potter, Charles Francis (1885–1962)

Potter, author of *The Story of Religion* (1929), founded in 1929 the First Humanist Society of New York City, which met Sundays in Manhattan's Steinway Hall on 57th Street. Included on its advisory board were Harry Elmer Barnes, L. M. Birkhead, E. A. Burtt, John Dewey, John H. Dietrich, Will Durant, William Floyd, Edwin Franko Goldman, Helen Keller, James H. Leuba, Robert Morss Lovett, George E. O'Dell, John Herman Randall Jr., Oliver L. Reiser, Roy Wood Sellars, Herbert Bayard Swope, and Oswald Garrison Villard. Dr. Potter wrote extensively concerning his philosophy, about which he wrote the following: "Humanism is not only belief in the possibility of the slow and steady self-improvement of the would-be-human race, individually and socially, without any assistance from alleged celestial super-persons, but it is also the intelligent implementation of that belief by co-operation with groups and agencies working toward that end." A tireless popularizer of the Humanist movement and publicist for the liberal cause generally, he started as a Baptist but, when church leaders questioned his theological views, found it necessary to convert to Unitarianism.

In 1923–1924, he came into national prominence by engaging in a series of debates with the Baptist fundamentalist leader John R. Straton over the issues of biblical fundamentalism. Soon thereafter he served as a defense team expert in the famous Scopes trial on evolution, for the theological war between liberalism and fundamentalism expanded in the 1920s. Potter rejected the doctrine that "the chief end of man is to glorify God" and declared instead that man should strive "to improve himself, both as an individual and as a race."

His ethically centered religion of growth rejected supernaturalism in religion. The weddings he performed were unique at that time in that the bride and groom, rather than repeating others' vows, had to devise their own. When Potter mentioned the cross, he referred to Benjamin Franklin's kite: "One symbol typifies salvation by sacrifice; the other, service by science." Individuals attending his lectures for the first time were warned, "What I will say will be devoid of fairy-tales about angels, demons, devils, or gods, for mine is a faith in man and a belief in man's capabilities for improving individuals and society as a whole by the slow, steady improvement of human personality."

In 1938, he was a founder of the Euthanasia Society of America. Potter's works included *Was Christ Both God and Man?* (1924), *Humanist Sermons* (1927), *Humanism, A New Religion* (1930), *Humanist Religion* (1931), *Humanizing Religion* (1933), *The Meaning of Humanism* (1945, 1972),*The Lost Years of Jesus Revealed* (1948), *Creative Personality: The Next Step in Evolution* (1950), and *The Preacher and I: An Autobiography* (1951).

As a contributing editor to *The Humanist Newsletter* (September-October 1953), Potter wrote:

> Humanism is an adult American religion for mature minds. The humanist has outgrown belief in fairy-tales about angels, demons, devils, or gods. In place of faith in miracles and the supernatural, his interest is in the slow steady improvement of human personality, both his own and that of other people. He recognizes that theology has been superseded by psychology, sociology, creative art, and scientific education.
>
> He has long since abandoned the idea of the creation of the world and man by a primitive tribal deity 4000 years ago, and believes instead in evolution, not as a mere scientific theory, but as a life process of which he is a part and which he and his fellow men are learning to direct intelligently in order to produce a better world.
>
> Humanism is a new positive constructive emphasis in religion. Whether a man believes or disbelieves n God is not so important today as to believe in man.

Edwin H. Wilson credited Potter with realizing the worldwide potential of humanism and of the value of obtaining prestigious names. "I had a talk about humanism with Sec'y [Cordell] Hull in February," Potter might say casually in a letter, "an appointment arranged by F.D.R. himself after he read my sermon in the N.Y. Times. Dr. Borchard of Yale, exert on International Law often consulted by Hull and Roosevelt, who went to Lima and back with Hull, is a member of our society here, and has been talking humanism to them. Several other administration men are humanists," Potter added. In the same letter to Wilson he said, "Dr. Har Dayal of India and London, a splendid scholar who could lecture fluently in eight languages, spoke for me here on 'Why I Am A Humanist,' and joined our society, but, alas, he just died of a heart attack. Auer was down last week and we had a long session, discussing the manifesto. Burtt is speaking for me next Sunday, and I will talk with him about it. Aronson speaks for me the 30th. . . ." Potter was well acquainted with many, and his zeal for humanism was apparent to all. However, Wilson includes caustic references to Potter by some of the "meticulous academic men" involved with the writing of Humanist Manifesto I. Raymond Bragg, for example, were concerned that because of Potter's "flare for publicity" humanism might become too exclusively identified with him rather than with the American Humanist Association.

For the Merriam-Webster company, Potter wrote several definitions, including one for "humanism" which the dictionary used. Unfortunately, he reported later, he had used the words "perfectibility of mankind" rather than "improvability of mankind" as a humanistic goal. (See the entry for Ida M. Mellen. To the present writer's surprise, the charismatic and jovial Dr. Potter and his wife enjoyed putting on ESP demonstrations at their Hotel Ansonia apartment in Manhattan, she in an adjacent room and unable to see certain cards drawn from a deck. Whether or not she bettered the mathematical odds for such, their interest in the subject was unexpected. It was a time when even the dedicated skeptics were intrigued by parapsychologist Joseph Banks Rhine's experiments.) {CL; FUS; HM 1; HNS; HNS2; U; U&U; WAS, 16 October 1956}

Potter, Dennis (Christopher) (George) (1935–1994)

Potter, a playwright, an author, and a freelance journalist on the *Daily Herald*, *The Sun*, and the *Sunday Times*. He wrote plays and novels but devoted his professional life to television. Some of his controversial BBC works were "Pennies From Heaven" (1978, remade as a Hollywood film), "The Singing Detective" (1986), and "Lipstick on Your Collar" (1993). When asked by Melvin Bragg of Channel 4 in England about his once having said he'd "never quite thrown off the idea of believing in God," Potter responded, "Well, I don't know. God's a rumor, if you like. Christianity or indeed any other religion that is a religion because of fear of death or hope that there is something beyond death does not interest me. What kind of cruel old bugger is God if it's terror that is the ruling edifice, the structure of religion? And too often, for too many people, it is, Now that to me isn't religion. Religion has always been . . . the wound, not the bandage. I don't see the point of not acknowledging the pain and the misery and the grief of the world, and if you say, 'Ah, but God understands' or through that you come to a greater appreciation, I then think, 'That's not God, that's not my God, that's not how I see God.' I see God in us or with us, if I see God at all, as shreds and particles and rumors, some knowledge that we have, some feeling why we sing and dance and act, why we paint, why we love, why make art. All the things that separate us from the purely animal in us are palpably there, and you can call them what you like, and you can theologize about them, and you can build great structures of belief about them. The fact is they are there and I have no means of knowing whether that thereness in some sense doesn't cling to what I call me."

Upon learning in 1994 that he had cancer that had spread to his liver, Potter christened the cancer Rupert, after the publisher Rupert Murdoch, whom he detested for allegedly polluting the body politic. "I would shoot the bugger if I could," he exclaimed. Instead of wasting the bullet, however, and when his wife herself died of cancer, Potter rushed to write a final work. "My only regret," he said, "would be to die four pages too soon. If I can finish, then I'm quite happy to go. I don't mind. I am quite serene. I haven't had a single moment of terror since they told me. I know I'm going to die, whether it's in four weeks' time, five, six. It might be longer—I might make eight, nine, ten, who knows?" Potter died fourteen weeks later, a week after Margaret, who had been his nurse, ally, and comrade for thirty-five years.

Potter, (Helen) Beatrix (1866–1943)

A British Unitarian, Potter was born in Kensington, was never sent to school, and grew up a lonely child. She became self-taught and invented a cipher so elaborate that the half-million words she wrote in it were not deciphered until Leslie Linder broke the code and published *The Journal of Beatrix Potter* (1966). *The Tale of Peter Rabbit* (1893) began as a letter to the son of a former governess and was published at her own expense in 1901.

In 1913 she married a Lakeland solicitor, William Heelis, and for the remainder of her life devoted herself amost entirely to her farms and the new National Trust.

Potter identified with Unitarianism more because of family loyalties than acceptance of the Unitarian outlook. She has written, "I shall always call myself a Unitarian because of my father and grandmother, but for the Unitarians as a Dissenting body, as I have known them in London, I have no respect. Their creed is apt to be a timid, illogical compromise, and their forms of Service, a badly performed imitation of the Church." The relatives she named were friends of James Martineau, whose writings emphasized the primary role of the conscience of the individual. Her father, Rupert, had studied under Martineau at New College (Unitarian) in Manchester, England.

As pointed out by Stephenie Pierson, Peter Rabbit, now a century old, has been "analyzed by child psychiatrists, scrutinized by scientists and botanists, lionized by authors and poets (Graham Greene, W. H. Auden, Maurice Sendak), parsed by philologists and linguists. He's been held and chewed and read and loved by generations of small children on large laps. And he's come out with his charm, his dignity, and his little blue waistcoat intact." {CE; EG; OEL; U; UU}

Potter, Van Renssalaer II (20th Century)

Potter, an emeritus professor of oncology at the University of Wisconsin, signed Humanist Manifesto 2000.

Potter, Wendall (20th Century)

Potter, an African American who lives in the Detroit area, wrote "After Years of Searching I Remain A Staunch Atheist" for *Secular Nation* (Fall 1995). His parents had told him about the god who they said lived in the sky, and they also lied about Santa Claus and the Easter Bunny. As a child, he wrote,

> I watched with amazement and sometimes fear, my parents go to church and "get happy." But how could this be? My mother nearly always cried and there was nothing happy about it—not only did the whole event distress me for 14 years, it was totally unbelievable. It seemed discrediting to any god who would sanction that kind of "emotional overdosing." That kind of emotionality was no different than what I saw at sports events or red hot parties. I was a teen before I figured out that no god could have such an effect on a person at 11:30 a.m. and by 7 p.m. hostility and sometimes violence dominated the same person. Rather than believe that god allowed this, I knew at 16 years old that he couldn't exist. And everything I've seen in the last 10 years has validated my belief.

Potter, Thomas (1718–1759)

In 1770, when John Murray landed at Good Luck on Barnegat Bay, New Jersey, he was given hospitality by a Universalist, Thomas Potter. It was Potter who urged Murray to preach once again, and nine years later Murray organized the First Universalist Church in America at Gloucester, Massachusetts.

Potter, William James (1829–1893)

The idea of the Free Religious Association can be traced to Potter's desire to form a "spiritual anti-slavery society" in the wake of the dispute over the formation and principles of the National Conference in 1866. Potter thought "the New Protestantism" should be a radical movement, in essence the latest expression of the core of the Protestant tradition, the resistance to theological authority. He refused to label himself "Christian," and he persuaded his New Bedford, Massachusetts, First Congregational (Unitarian) Society to allow him *not* to administer the Lord's Supper. During the tensions between radicals and Unitarian moderates in the 1870s and 1880s, Potter was dropped from the American Unitarian Association yearbook in 1873. His last book was *Lectures and Sermons, with a Biographical Sketch* (1895). {FUS; U&U}

Potts, Richard (20th Century)

In Dallas, Texas, Potts edited *Common Herd*, a non-believers' journal, from 1909 to 1940. {FUS}

Potvin, Charles (1818–1902)

A Belgian author, Potvin was a member of the Royal Academy of Letters and a professor of the history of literature at Brussels. He wrote anonymously *Poesie et Amour* (1858) and *Rome and the Family.* Under the name of "Dom Jacobus," Potvin wrote *The Church and Morality* and *Tablets of a Freethinker*. He was president of *La Libre Pensée* of Brussels and was director of the *Revue de Belgique*. {BDF}

Pouchet, Felix Archimède (1800–1872)

Pouchet was a French naturalist who studied medicine under Dr. Flaubert, father of the author of *Madame Bovary* and became a physician in 1827. While a professor of natural history at the Museum of Rouen, Pouchet by his experiments enriched science with many discoveries. He wrote *The Universe* (1865). {BDF}

Pouchet, Henri Charles George (1833–1894)

Pouchet, a French naturalist, was the son of Felix Pouchet. Also a physician, he became a professor of comparative anatomy in the museum of Natural History at Paris. In 1880 he received the Legion of Honor. He wrote *The Plurality of the Human Race* (1858). {BDF}

Pougens, Marie Charles Joseph de (1755–1833)

Pougens was a French author, a natural son of the Prince of Conti. When twenty-four, he was blinded by smallpox. Pougens was an intimate friend of philosophers, and he embraced the revolution with ardor although it ruined his fortunes. He wrote *Philosophical Researches* (1786), edited the posthumous works of d'Alembert (1799), and worked at a dictionary of the French language. His *Jocko* was the tale of a monkey and showed his sympathy with animal intelligence. In his *Philosophical Letters* (1826), he gives anecdotes of Voltaire, Rousseau, d'Alembert, Pechmeja, and Franklin. {BDF}

Poulin, Paul (19th Century)

Poulin was a Belgian follower of Baron Colins and was the author of *What Is God? What Is Man?* (1865), a scientific solution of the religious problem. He maintained that man and God exclude each other, that the only divinity is moral harmony. {BDF}

Poulsen, Kenneth (20th Century)

Poulsen is active with the Humanists of the Sun Coast in Tarpon Springs, Florida, of which he once was President. In 1995, he was honored as Humanist of the Year at the All-Florida Humanist Conference held in Clearwater. An atheist who is a member of Atheists and Agnostics of Wisconsin, he has written

> I am an atheist because I value the preciousness of life and believe in the earth sciences and nature. Neither gods, supernaturals, nor spirits are necessary for a crutch in the atheist dedication to a moral and ethical life.

(See entry for Florida Atheists, Humanists.) {FD; *Freethought History #13*, 1995; *Humanists of the Palm BeachesNewsletter*, October 1997}

Poultier d'Elmolte, François Martin (1753–1821)

At the Revolution, Poultier d'Elmolte cast aside his Benedictine frock, married, and became chief of a battalion of volunteers. Elected to the Convention, he voted for the death of the King. Exiled in 1816, he died at Tournay in Belgium. He wrote *Morceau Philosophiques* in the *Journal Encyclopédique*; *Victoire* [Confessions of a Benedictine]; *Discours Décadaires*, for the use of Theophilantropists; and *Conjectures on the Nature and Origin of Things* (1821). {BDF; RAT}

Pound, Louise (1872–1958)

When she reviewed books for *The Humanist* in the 1950s, Pound was a member of the English department at the University of Nebraska. A sister of Dr. Roscoe Pound, the noted former Dean of the Harvard Law School, she was state tennis champion of Nebraska in 1891–1892 and state golf champion in 1916. Her specialty was regional American slang and folklore, she contributed articles to the *Encyclopedia Britannica*, and she was on the advisory board of *American Literature, College English*, and the *Bulletin of the American Association of University Professors*. Pound edited *American Speech*.

Asked about humanism, Pound responded to the present author:

> *Human, humane, humanism, humanist, humanitarian, humanitarianism*—here is a cluster of related words for lexicographers to watch, to define, and to modify their definitions when and as necessary. To follow the history of significant words, their rise and expansions of meaning, is always of interest, and preferably it is from the basic historical meaning that start should be made.
>
> It was in the fifteenth and sixteenth centuries, the period of the English renaissance, with its rediscovery of the cultural and philosophical legacies of Greece and Rome, that the term humanism entered our language. It had about the same meaning as the Latin *humanitas* as used by Cicero and his contemporaries, that is, culture of the mind. Lists of the early English and European humanists are rarely identical, although to all humanism meant, no doubt, a break with the past. Some historians viewed early humanism as a revolt against the theological preconceptions of the mediaeval mind, a turn, as it were, to the earth and those dwelling on it. But surely on the whole it maintained for its users the tradition of religious orthodoxy while taking on the meaning it has retained into our own time, that of liberal cultural acquirement befitting human beings. To the humanist such acquirement was to be gained through knowledge of poetry, drama, history, rhetoric, logic, with especial emphasis on the ancient literatures. The latter seemed a storehouse of wisdom having permanent values for the conduct of life; and, further, Latin, the language of the church, gave unity to Christian Renaissance civilization. Hence the educated youth should be trained in the 'humanities' (French *les humanites*). Emerson writes in this tradition when he speaks in *English Traits*, 1856, of "an Eton youth learned in all the humanities," that is, learned in the traditions of humanism, though by his time the word might also imply devotion to human interests and to systems of thought or action concerned with them.
>
> Today with the lessening of emphasis on the culture of ancient civilizations and with the rise of science to dimensions incredible in older days, the meaning of humanism is enlarging. As it turns still more to the physical world and those dwelling in it, it seems to be taking to itself some of the qualities of humanitarianism. The latter word is an extension from humane, which means gentle, kindly, sympathetic. The humanist who was concerned with the ideal world of thought and valued cultural education derived from the study of the humanities may now be a person interested in the actual world of human life, sympathetic with the human race and conscious of man's obligations to society. The new devotion to the study of the natural world makes the old limitations seem impractical. As I hear the word humanism used today it seems to have connotations of human welfare, helpfulness, and progress. The humanist may be a cultivated man who practices humanity and humanitarianism. And he believes that to attain their best possibilities human beings must rely on themselves, not on the natural or on the supernatural.
>
> I have no new classifications to offer or proposals to try to further. On the whole, for me too the meaning of the term humanism is changing or has changed. It is enlarging from that of concern for the enhancement of mental culture, ability, and outlook into a wider naturalistic concern for general human welfare. It now implies devotion not only to the mind of man but to humanity and human interests in general. It is this meaning that as time passes will no doubt enlist most supporters.

One of Willa Cather's biographers, Sharon O'Brien, writes that while at Duke University she came across Cather's letters to Pound, her friend at the University of Nebraska, "romantic letters in which Cather agreed that relationships like theirs were 'unnatural,' " which one secular humanist has interpreted as being a reference to the two's specific rather than general humanistic interests. {WAS, 4 January 1952}

Poundstone, Paula (20th Century)

Poundstone, a comedian, is a non-theist, according to Celebrity Atheists. She has said, "Although raised a conservative Methodist, I am, in fact, a liberal atheist. Many people mistake me for Irish." The nice thing about being an atheist, she tells audiences is that

> you don't feel compelled to try to convert everybody. Can you just see a couple of atheists going door to door on Sunday morning and saying to people who come to the door in their bathrobes, "We have no word. Here's a book of blank pages we'd like you to take a look at."
>
> {CA; E}

Powell, B. F. (19th Century)

Powell was a compiler of the *Bible of Reason* (1837), or scriptures of ancient moralists. {BDF}

Powell, David (20th Century)

Powell has reviewed books for *New Humanist*.

Powell, Frederick York (1850–1904)

The historical works Powell wrote allowed him to succeed Froude as Regius Professor of Modern History at Christ's Church (Oxford). He knew Irish, Maori, Gypsy, and Persian and was an agnostic when he went to Oxford, calling himself "a decent heathen Aryan." Of Gladstone, Powell said to Edward Clodd, "What an extraordinary thing it is that a man with such brains for finance shouldn't be able to throw off the superstitious absurdities of the past." {RAT; RE}

Powell, Thomas (Died 1862)

Powell was a Chartist leader who was secretary of the London Atheistical Society. He emigrated to Trinidad. {VI}

POWER

• The strong do what they can; the weak do what they must.

–Thucydides

• [T]he only purpose for which poweer can be rightfully exercised over any member of a civilised community, against his will, is to prevent harm to others. . . . He cannot rightfully be compelled to do or forbear because it will be better for him to do so, because it will make him happier, because in the opinions of others, to do so would be wise or even right.

–John Stuart Mill
"On Liberty"

• I didn't understand that there were two things vastly more important than orgasm to most people, and that's power and its handmaiden, money.

–Norman Mailer
commenting about his having proposed the hipster, in *Advertisements for Myself*, as contemporary hero, a psychopath, utterly selfish, who exorcises the dread of the atomic age by existing for the intensity and immediacy of his pleasure—an immediacy embodied in the Negro, who had always lived with violence and had developed a proud indifference to respectability.

{David Denby, *The New Yorker*, 20 April 1998}

Powers, J(ames) F. (1917–)

An author, Powers wrote the present author concerning humanism:

> I'm not educated enough to classify myself as allied with any of the kinds of humanism you list unless it would be No. 4 (theistic humanism), but I have an instinct against definitions, which may be attributed to my lack of education, and against abstractions. I am not bragging, nor am I confessing, but just telling it as it is, to the extent that I can truthfully *tell*. This won't be any help, probably, but may be better than no reply at all.

In 1963, his *Morte d'Urban* won the National Book Award. His 1975 book of short stories is *How The Fish Live*. Powers is a member of the American Academy of Arts and Letters. {WAS, 15 June 1992}

Powers, LeGrand (20th Century)
Powers, a Universalist minister, was the first state labor conciliator in the United States, having been appointed by the Governor of Minnesota.

Powers, Lulie Monroe: See entry for J. R. Monroe.

Powers, Richard W. (20th Century)
Powers is a contributor to *Freethought Today*, which is published by Freedom From Religion Foundation.

Powys, Llewelyn (1884–1940)
Powys was a prolific essayist and journalist, and his *Skin for Skin* (1925) described somberly the course of his own tuberculosis and the idyllic Dorset interludes when it seemed he was being cured. *Impassioned Clay* (1931) was a personal account of the human predicament, the Epicurean ethic, and his confrontation with death. *Damnable Opinions* (1935) presented radical and iconoclastic views he shared with his brothers, John Cowper Powys and Theodore Powys. {FUK; RE}

Poynter, J. W. (20th Century)
Poynter wrote *The Popes and Social Problems* (1949). {GS}

Pozner, Vladimir (20th Century)
A Russian journalist and former spokesman for the Soviet Union, Pozner on a CNBC talk show with Phil Donahue stated that he is an atheist. He wrote *Remembering War* (1990) and *Eyewitness* (1992). {CA; E}

Prades, Jean Martin de (1720–1782)
A French theologian, de Prades was an intimate with Diderot and contributed the article on "Certitude" to the *Encyclopédie*. In 1751 in the first open attack on Christianity by a French theologian, de Prades presented to the Sorbonne his thesis for the doctorate. He maintained many propositions on the soul, the origin of society, the laws of Moses, miracles, all views contrary to the dogmas of the Church. His thesis made a great scandal, and Pope Benedict XIV condemned it. As a result, de Prades fled to Holland for safety. Recommended to Frederick the Great by d'Alembert de Prades was received with favor and became reader to that monarch. Frederick wrote an anti-Christian preface to de Prades's work on ecclesiastical history, published as *Abrége de l'Histoire ecclesiastique de Fleury* (1766). {BDF; RAT}

PRAGMATISM
In philosophy, pragmatism is a method in which the truth of a proposition is measured by its correspondence with experimental results and by its practical outcome. "What difference will it make to practice if this philosophical claim is true?" asked the pragmatists. Truth, then, is tested by the practical consequences of belief. Originators of the system were C. S. Peirce and William James. John Dewey was influenced by the pragmatic outlook. Dewey held that as new discoveries are made, truth is modified, that truth is relative to time and place and purpose of inquiry.

The Revival of Pragmatism (1999), edited by Morris Dickstein, includes essays by Richard Rorty, Hilary Putnam, Judge Richard Posner, Stanley Fish, Richard Poirier, and Ross Posnock. Alan Ryan, in a *The New York Times Book Review* (4 April 1999), noted that the contributors divided along familiar lines:

> Rorty says that we should see pragmatism as a form of "romantic polytheism." Rorty's longstanding distaste for philosophers who unproductively go on and on about whether what we believe is really true has a predictable result here. The romantic polytheist does not believe that there really are innumerable gods to be worshiped and obeyed. Rather the polytheist has bought Dewey's thought that "God" is a plausible name for whatever we most mind about.
>
> Posner offers a different perspective; his conception of pragmatism owes as much to the everyday understanding of the word as to anything more philosophically strenuous. But his essay is a very readable, and indeed a rather elegant, discussion of the ways an appellate judge goes about deciding what the law requires. Just as Richard Rorty provides us with John Dewey rather dramatically loosened up, so Judge Posner provides us with something like Benjamin Cardozo in his shirtsleeves. . . .
>
> Ray Carney's account of the paintings of Thomas Eakins is perhaps the farthest removed from the work of the philosophers and lawyers, and it is certainly the most self-conscious about going back into the 19th century rather than promoting pragmatism as a branch of late-20th-century avant-gardism. But Carney takes off from one of Dewey's pregnant remarks in *Art as Experience*—that "mind is primarily a verb"—and Eakins's paintings of the surgeon at work in "The Surgical Clinic of Professor Gross" and "The Clinic of Professor Agnew" provide him with just the platform he needs.

(See H. S. Thayer in the *Encyclopedia of Philosophy*, Vol. 6, for discussions of Peirce, James, Dewey, and others. Also see the entry for Richard Rorty and a 1994 work, *Recovering Pragmatism's Voice: The Classical Tradition, Rorty, and the Philosophy of Communication*.) {CE; RE}

Prahl, Frank (20th Century)
Prahl at the 1993 Freedom From Religion Foundation's annual convention in Huntsville, Alabama, spoke on "Library Censorship: What You Can Do." He is a member of the American Humanist Association and is secretary of Humanists of Houston, Texas. Prahl was one of the organizers of a January 1999 Humanist and Freethought Conference in Arlington, Texas.

Prairie, Alexander (20th Century)
Prairie was a President of Atheists United in Sherman Oaks, California. He resigned in 1993.

PRAKTISCHE HUMANISTIEK
A Dutch quarterly for humanist counselors, *Praktische Humanistiek* is at Postbus 470, 3500 AL Utrecht, The Netherlands; <mg@uvh.nl>.

Pratchett, Terry (20th Century)
Pratchett is a science fiction and writer of humorous materials. His Discworld series contains an article entitled "A Life in the Day of Terry Pratchett," in which he remarks, "I think I'm probably an atheist, but rather angry with God for not existing." {CA; E}

Prater, Horatio (Died 1885)
Prater wrote *Physiology of the Blood* (1832), *Letters to the American People*, and *Literary Essays* (published 1856). A gentleman of fortune, he left the bulk of his money to benevolent objects. Because of his knowledge of physiology and to insure that he was really dead, Prater ordered that a deep wound be made in his arm. {BDF}

Pratt, Ann B. (20th Century)
Pratt founded the Central Ohioans for Rational Inquiry group.

Pratt, Enoch (Born 1810)
Pratt, a Unitarian, was a 19th century financier and philanthropist. {U}

Praxiteles (c. 370–330 B.C.E.): See entry for Beauty.

PRAYER

• Prayers are to men as dolls are to children. They are not without use and comfort, but it is not easy to take them seriously.

—**Sir Francis Galton**

• It is best to read the weather forecast before praying for rain.

—**Mark Twain**

• Pray, n. To ask the laws of the universe be annulled on behalf of a single petitioner confessedly unworthy.

–Ambrose Bierce

• The English . . . obviously regarded praying much as they did a necessary physical function, something best done in private.

–Baroness James of Holland Park

• Hands that help are better than lips that pray.

–Robert Ingersoll

• Some freethinker solutions as to Whom to pray to
–the great French goddess, Mais Oui
–the vegetation god, Lettuce
–Who Knows (as in, why oh why did it rain?)

–Anonymous

• E-mail #1 to God
If I pray to You, will You listen?

<wasm@idt.net>

You can waste your time, if you wish. However, I'd appreciate it if you'd get off my back and let me finesse programming 9001-beta for HAL.

<God@eden.com>

• E-mail #2 to God
Why, dear God, did the Age of Miracles end?

<secularhum@aol.com>

That was the development phase of the project.
Now we're in the maintenance phrase.

<God@eden.com>

• E-mail #3 to God
O, Heavenly Lord of Us All, why did You allow Satan and evil?

<RevDoodoo@aol.com>

Believe me, Satan is simply an MIS director who takes credit for more powers than he actually possesses. Nonprogrammers become scared of him. He's irritating, but irrelevant. I had thought I eliminated evil in one of the earlier revs, so you'll just have to put up with the problem until I devise an update of the program.

<God@eden.com>

PRAYER FOR FORGIVENESS

In Louisiana, Shreveport humanists tell the story about the boy who prayed for a bicycle. When it did not come in time for his birthday, he prayed for one at Christmas. When none arrived at Christmas, he realized that is not how things worked. Next day he stole one . . . and prayed for forgiveness.

PRAYER IN PUBLIC SCHOOLS: See entry for Katha Pollitt.

PRAYER WHEEL

In Buddhism, a prayer wheel is a cylinder with prayers written on it. The wheel is turned by some worshipers during prayer, or the turning may be used as a substitute for spoken prayers. {DCL}

Preda, Pietro (19th Century)

Preda was an Italian who wrote *Revelation and Reason* (1865) under the pseudonym of "Padre Pietro." {BDF}

PREDESTINATION

In theology, predestination is a doctrine asserting that God has pre-planned from eternity the salvation of certain souls. Calvinism even developed double predestination, asserting that God has foreordained some people to damnation. The Roman Catholic Church teaches that predestination is consistent with free will inasmuch as God moves the soul according to its nature. Calvinism, however, rejects the role of free will. Naturalists find such a doctrine impossible to test and meaningless. (See entries for determinism and for Jacobus Arminius.) {CE}

PREFERENCE FALSIFICATION

Timur Kuran, in *Private Truths, Public Lies: The Social Consequences of Preference Falsification* (1995), holds that social pressures can make people say that they want and believe something that they really do not want or believe. As an illustration, individuals in a dictatorship may speak highly of their leaders but privately call them scoundrels and fools. People in small American towns may attend church regularly and pray with everyone else, even though they are unsure whether they actually believe in God or understand their church's doctrines. "Falsified preferences," of course, could simply be labeled as lies, but he notes that they are lies with certain social implications. Usually, they are the result of perceiving what the opinions of others presently are or will be. Unwilling to disagree with the majority, individuals protect their reputation by declining to say anything that people might deem bizarre or offensive. As people's thoughts about other people's thoughts change, Kuran notes, people's public preferences are affected. When the shifts are rapid, there can be a bandwagon effect. He gives as examples the changing norms involving smoking, discrimination, sneaker wear, the use of "Ms.," surprise best-sellers, the use of "African American," and recycling.

Public pressures, it follows, affect private preferences as well as public pressures. He gives the example that "Hindu ideology has contributed to the untouchables' acceptance of their deprivations as fair, that it has made many treat their wretched existence as natural, and that it has facilitated their complicity in an order that degrades them." Thoughts that are generally considered "unthinkable" eventually become "unthought," illustrating that social pressures can make certain ideas disappear from public discussion. Kuran discusses how the possibilities of law involve an inherent mystery. Laws often are rarely enforced—those requiring people to clean up after their dogs, those banning littering, those directing where people can smoke, for example—but have an effect on people's perceptions of other people's attitudes.

Kuran's thesis bears on why "the village atheist" is disliked, why the moral majority makes cogent attacks upon homosexuals, hippies, and unwed mothers, as well as why social pressures can be serious obstacles to liberty but why, in the face of such obstacles, governmental efforts might actually promote freedom.

PREJUDICE

"Children," said Sir Peter Ustinov, the Goodwill Ambassador-at-Large for Unicef, "are the one strata of life which have absolutely no prejudice. None of us, and this is a message of hope, are born with prejudice. You often see children playing with someone who is hideously deformed by some caprice of nature, and the only people appalled are the adults who are wondering whether the children should be allowed to play together. Unfortunately, prejudice comes from education and with family life and all the things that are praised by religious orthodoxy. Every good bottle of wine has to have some residue. Similarly, life comes with prejudice, and there's little one can do. I am still learning things that I learned in my first school, for example. Why do I think that? I ask myself and then trace it back to some idiotic history book or patriotic idea." {WAS, Conversation 22 April 1995}

PRELATE

• Prelate, n. A church officer having a superior degree of holiness and a fat preferment. One of Heaven's aristocracy. A gentleman of God.

–Ambrose Bierce
The Devil's Dictionary

• . . .an ecclesiastical oxymoron.

Johnny Hart
in "B.C.," a cartoon strip

Preller, Ludwig (1809–1861)

Preller began to study for the Church but became a rationalist and turned to philology, which he taught at Jena. Preller wrote about Greek and Roman religion (*Griechische Mythologie* and *Romische Mythologie*, 1854–1858) and was an agnostic. {RE}

Premanand, B. (20th Century)

Premanand is an Indian famous for his debunking of the miracle men in India. As a devout Hindu twelve-year-old, he believed those men and longed to possess their powers. In a *New Humanist* interview with Jim Herrick (June 1992), he smiled upon hearing that in the West European psychics and spiritualists are thought of as fraudulent whereas Indian gurus are believed to be basically honest. "They want something new and they think that new powers come from these gurus," he explained. "In India," he added, "you can take action against people who make false advertisements." Premanand has toured the State of Maharashtra to expose god-men by repeating their tricks, James Randi-style, in front of large audiences. "I would be really happy to see a true miracle," he said when interviewed. "It is one of my ambitions before I die." But, reported Herrick, "there is a twinkle in his eye at this point."

In addition to being convenor of India's Committee for the Scientific Investigation of Claims of the Paranormal (CSICOP), he edits *Indian Skeptic*, a monthly in English. In his *Science Versus Miracles* (1994), Premanand explains 150 or so tricks of the godmen, and he proposes bringing out nine more volumes in order to explain an additional 1500 of the godmen's tricks.

For his popularizing of science, he was given an award in 1998 of

100,000 rupees by the National Council for Science and Technology Communication of the Indian Government's Department of Science and Technology. (See entries for Narendra Dabholkar and Govind N. Deodhekar.)

Premontval, André Pierre Le Guay de (1716–1767)

When nineteen, Premontval in the college of Plessis Sorbonne composed a work against the dogma of the Eucharist. He was a member of the Academy of Sciences at Berlin. He wrote *Le Diogene de d'Alembert* (1754, Freethoughts on Man), *Panangiana Panurgica* (1757, The False Evangelist), and *Vues Philosophiques* (1757). In *De la Théologie de L'Etre*, Premontval denied many of the ordinary proofs of the existence of a God. {BDF}

Prentice, Ruth (20th Century)

Prentice is historian of Internet Infidels. On the Web: <rprentice@infidels.org>.

PRESBYTERIAN

• Presbyterian, n. One who holds the conviction that the governing authorities of the Church should be called presbyters.

—**Ambrose Bierce**
The Devil's Dictionary

PRESBYTERIAN CHURCH

The Presbyterian Church (USA), organized in 1983, is at 100 Witherspoon Street, Louisville, Kentucky. It reports having 3,600,000 or so adherents. Andrew W. Rule, once professor of church history and apologetics in the Louisville Presbyterian Theological Seminary, Louisville, Kentucky, gave the following description in the 1940s:

> A Church is presbyterian when it acknowledges in its polity no higher office than that of "presbyter" or elder, and when its highest courts, therefore, are composed of presbyters. It is Protestant in the sense that it claims historical continuity with the Protestant Reformation, and adheres to the basic Reformation principles. It is catholic in the sense that it recognizes, and is proud to claim membership along with other non-Presbyterian bodies in one, universal Church, the body of Christ is that Head, constituted by Him "from above."

{ER}

Prescott, James W. (20th Century)

When he signed Humanist Manifesto II, Prescott was with the National Institute of Child Health and Human Development. Prescott edited San Diego's *Truth Seeker* from 1989 to 1990. He is founder and director of the Institute of Humanistic Science. His e-mail: <dpresco1@san.rr.com>. {FD; HM2}

Prescott, William Hickling (1796–1859)

Prescott, a historian, wrote histories of Mexico, Peru, and Spain. In 1904, W. H. Munro edited twenty-two volumes of his works. When he visited London in 1850, at the house of the Bishop of Oxford, he met the daughter of a Bishop who said she had never before heard the name of Dr. William Ellery Channing. According to his friend George Ticknor, Prescott replied, "I gave her a great shock by telling her I was a Unitarian. The term is absolutely synonymous, in a large party here, with infidel, Jew, Mohammedan; worse even, because [a Unitarian was] regarded as a wolf in sheep's clothing." Like many leading families of Boston, according to his biographer C. Harvey Gardiner, the Prescotts shifted to Unitarianism. "Like Susan [his wife], William could not turn his back on his church, so they compromised. A compact between them provided for their alternating between the Unitarian and Episcopal churches." {CE; EG; U; UU}

PRESIDENTS, RELIGIOUS AFFILIATIONS OF THE U.S.: See entry for Franklin Steiner.

Presley, Sharon (20th Century)

Presley, the director of the Institute for Critical Thinking, is author of *Belief Style Traps—Tyranny of the Mind*. She spoke at the 1995 Atheist Alliance Convention in North Hollywood, California.

Press, Jacques (20th Century)

A noted Hollywood composer, Press was an associate of Arthur Fiedler and the Boston Pops Orchestra. In 1972 to the New York Humanist Chapter (AHA), Press discussed "Humanism and Creative Imagination in Music."

Preston, S. Tolver (Born 1844)

A freethinker, Preston wrote *Science and Sectarian Religion* (1883). {GS}

PRESTON (England) HUMANISTS

For information, telephone Peter Howells at 01257 265276.

Prévost, Eugène Marcel (Born 1862)

Prévost, a novelist, wrote a successful novel, *Le scorpion* (1887), which was based on his negative experiences of the Jesuits as teachers. Prévost was admitted to the French Academy in 1909, was an Officer of the Legion of Honour, and the Honorary President of the *Société des Gens de Lettres*. He wrote *De la prostitution des enfants* (1909). {RAT}

Prévost, Louis Constant (1787–1856)

Prévost taught geology at Paris University. McCabe says of Prévost that "his work in ridding the science of Biblical adulterations and establishing the principle of uniformity raised him to the position in France which Lyell occupied in England." {RAT; RE}

Prévost-Paradol, Lucien Anatole (1829–1870)

Once a professor of French literature at Aix in 1855, Prévost-Paradol resigned in 1856 and joined the staff of the *Journal des Débats* and the *Courrier du Dimanche*. He was a spirited opponent of the clerical-imperialists, was sent to prison in 1866, and the *Courrier* was suppressed. In 1870 he became French Ambassador at Washington, for which his advanced colleagues blamed him. The Franco-Prussian War, which at once broke out, so depressed him that he shot himself in America, which, according to McCabe, at least proved that in accepting the Empire he had not embraced its theology. Prévost-Paradol was a member of the French Academy. {RAT}

Preyer, Wilhelm Thierry (1841–1897)

Preyer's *The Soul of the Child* (1889) was the German physiologist's well-known work. Preyer was one of the first German professors to welcome evolution and apply it to physiology and psychology. He wrote a Rationalist appreciation of Darwin, *Darwin: Sein Leben und Wirken* (1896). {RAT; RE}

Price, Ben (20th Century)

Price is co-editor with Tom Mulliam of *Groundswell*, a freethought monthly devoted to individual freedoms.

Price, Karen A. (20th Century)

Price is associated with the Humanist Chapter of Miami Valley (AHA) in Ohio. (See entry for Ohio Atheists, Humanists.) {FD}

Price, Lawrence M. (Born 1881)

Price wrote *The Reception of English Literature in Germany* (1968). Asked for his views of humanism, he responded to the present author:

> Your inclusion of me probably indicates that you wish to know what the non-philosopher pictures to himself under the term "humanism." I am under the impression that philosophy is concerned in great part with the relation of the human mind to the outside material world. I find the hypothesis of the existence of the mind of man no bolder than the hypothesis of the existence of matter. The humanist, I would say, considers the impact of the material world upon the mind as the most important thing about matter. His view of the universe is therefore homocentric. This illusion I regard as highly healthful. Man thus feels he is an actor of a bit part in a universe drama. Most humanists prefer to think that the drama will have a happy end of some sort. Most humans are humanists, although

some of them are not aware of it. A motor mechanic thinks that the machine is what is important to him. He is not aware of the fact that the importance of the machine consists in the fact that it stimulates his curiosity.

If I am a humanist I do not know to which group I belong. I do not disagree with any paragraphs of the [Harry] Overstreet letter. The Webster definition is somewhat random. The terms ancient humanism, classical humanism, and neo-humanism seem useful for the library or the historian. Theistic humanism seems to me a contradiction of terms. I have no opinion, for lack of a clear conception, of atheistic humanism and communistic humanism.

(See entry for Harry Overstreet) {WAS, 15 October 1951}

Price, Robert M. (1954-)

Price, who has taught New Testament, theology, and mythology at Drew University, Montclair State University, and Unification Theological Seminary, edits *The Journal of Higher Criticism* and writes fiction. He commenced as a fundamentalist Baptist, then became interested in the theology of Paul Tillich, briefly flirted with Unitarian Universalism, and is now a freethinker. He hosts Heretics Anonymous at his New Jersey home and is a supporter of Internet Infidels. Price signed Humanist Manifesto 2000.

In 1999 he was named Executive Director of the Council for Secular Humanism. "I take quite seriously the likelihood that there was no historical Jesus in the first place," he wrote in *World* (Winter 1998-1999), a thesis he will develop in *Deconstructing Jesus* (2000). E-mail: <criticus@aol.com>.

"PRICK AND HOLE" BIBLE: See entry for Harris Lenowitz.

PRIDE

On the subject of pride, Bertrand Russell observed:

> The men who think out administrative reforms and schemes of social amelioration are for the most part earnest men who are no longer young. Too often they have forgotten that to most people, not only spontaneity but some kind of personal pride is necessary to happiness. The pride of a great conqueror is not one that a well-regulated world can allow, but the pride of the artist, of the discoverer, of the man who has turned a wilderness into a garden or has brought happiness where, but for him, there would be misery—such pride is good, and our social system should make it possible, not only for the few, but for the many.

But as for those who are proud of their having accepted some organized religious group's views, Russell wrote,

> There is something feeble, and a little contemptible, about a man who cannot face the perils of life without the help of comfortable myths.

(See entry for Richard Taylor, who has written a defense of Pride.)

{Lee Eisler, *The Quotable Bertrand Russell*}

Priest, John F. (20th Century)

A professor of religion at Florida State University, Priest is on the Council for Secular Humanism's Committee for the Scientific Examination of Religion. At the Tenth International Humanist and Ethical Union (IHEU) World Congress held in Buffalo (1988), Priest addressed the group. {*Free Inquiry*, Summer, 1982}

Priestley, J. B.: See entry for Theism. Also see the entry for George Orwell, who suspected Priestley of Communist ties because he made so much money in the USSR.

Priestley, Joseph (1733–1804)

Priestley, a chemist who was in the Royal Society, was co-discoverer of oxygen with Swedish pharmacist Karl Wilhelm Scheele (1742–1786). In his *History of Electricity* (1767), Priestley explained the rings (now known as Priestley's rings) formed by a discharge upon a metallic surface. The importance of his discovery of "dephlogisticated air," the gas Lavoisier later named oxygen, Priestley did not fully appreciate. In 1774, Priestley published his *Examination of Scottish Philosophy*, followed in 1782 by *History of the Corruptions of Christianity*. The latter book was considered blasphemous and was burned in public, for it rejected predestination and the Trinity, and it refused to accept the view that the Bible is divinely revealed. In 1786, he published *History of Early Opinions Concerning Jesus Christ*. In 1790 he wrote two volumes of *A General History of the Christian Church to the Fall of the Western Empire* and in 1803 finished another four volumes. At one time he wrote of his regret that Benjamin Franklin was not only an "unbeliever in Christianity" but also refused to read books and pamphlets purporting to "prove" the truth of Christianity. Priestley, according to *Motion Toward Perfection: The Achievement of Joseph Priestley* (1990), read Jefferson but did not share his theology, . He opposed the slave trade and favored the French Revolution, which led in 1791 to people storming his house, wrecking his library, and destroying his scientific apparatus. As a result, Priestley—once a Presbyterian and now a convert to Unitarianism—fled in 1794 to the United States, residing the rest of his life in Northumberland, Pennsylvania, where his sons lived. Here, he received a warm welcome, continuing his scientific experiments and becoming the last defender of the phlogiston theory, one which postulates that in all flammable materials a substance (phlogiston) without color, odor, taste, or weight is given off in burning. He also was critical of Benjamin Franklin, writing, "It is much to be lamented that a man of Dr. Franklin's general good character and great influence, should have been an unbeliever in Christianity, and also have done so much as he did to make others unbelievers."

Priestley, who despite a problem with stammering had been a Unitarian preacher in England at Needham Market, Leeds, Birmingham, and Hackney, also preached from 1794 to 1804 in Northumberland. A lecture he gave in Philadelphia led to the establishment of that city's first Unitarian Church and, in 1796, the first church so named in the Americas. Berman relates the reaction by Matthew Turner to Priestley's *Letters to a Philosophical Unbeliever*—the two discussed deism, atheism, and Unitarianism. Priestley hoped that his *History of the Corruptions of Christianity*, which concluded that much accepted Christian dogma was in fact a "corruption" of the original Christian truth, would clear away theological error to exhibit the version of Unitarianism that he thought would eventually predominate as the Christian faith. Although his definition of "God" was unorthodox, Priestley believed in *human* survival after death; in fact, he reasoned that inasmuch as animals live in such misery here, "a merciful God will make them some recompense for it hereafter."

In England, Priestley is revered as a founder of the Unitarian movement. In the United States, his version of Enlightenment Unitarianism became a significant part of the American liberal heritage. However, as can be seen from his criticism of Franklin, he was anything but a liberal in the current meaning of that word. (See entry for John Clifford.) {BDF; CE; EG; FUS; HAB; HNS2; JMR; JMRH; TYD; U; U&U; UU}

PRIESTS

- . . . the priest in his surplice, who resembles a dangerous rhinoceros.

–Vincent Van Gogh, upon his arrival in Arles after recovering from a bout of religious fervor {*The Letters of Vincent Van Gogh*, 1996}

The Kansas City Star, at the end of 1999, sent questionnaires to 3,000 of the 46,000 priests in the United States, asking about their sexuality. Of 801 responses received, 75% of the priests said they were heterosexual, 15% were homosexual, and 5% were bisexual. The paper found that Catholic priests are dying from AIDS-related illnesses at a rate four times higher than the general population and that the cause is often concealed on their death certificates.

Prillaman, Lexro Bernard (20th Century)

In 1931 for his M.A. thesis at Northwestern University in Illinois, Prillaman wrote on the subject of the figures of speech which Robert G. Ingersoll used. {FUS}

PRIMATE

• Primate, n. The head of a church, especially a State church supported by involuntary contributions. The Primate of England is the Archbishop of Canterbury, an amiable old gentleman, who occupies Lambeth Palace when living and Westminister Abbey when dead. He is commonly dead.

–Ambrose Bierce
The Devil's Dictionary

Primm, Sarah (20th Century)

Primm is active in the Humanist Association of Pikes Peak. (See entry for Colorado Humanists.) {FD}

PRINCETON UNIVERSITY FREETHINKERS

Princeton University in New Jersey has a freethinkers' group which can be found on the Web: <http://www.secularhumanism.org/cfa/orgs.html>.

PRINCIPLE OF EMERGENCE: See the entry for Determinism.

PRINCIPLE OF VERIFIABILITY

The Logical Positivists held that the Principle of Verifiability is a claim about what meaningfulness is: "at its simplest, a sentence is meaningful provided there is a method for verifying it. Therefore, if a sentence has no such method, i.e., if it does not have associated with it a way of telling whether it is conclusively true or conclusively false, then it is meaningless."

In the 1920s it was hoped this would strip "metaphysical discourse" of its pretensions of factuality. Thus, "Dominica has 365 rivers" is verifiable, therefore meaningful. "St. Peter used to flap his wings in my apple tree" is unverifiable and meaningless. " 'Twas brillig, and the slithy toves did gyre and gimble in the wabe" is both meaningless and nonsensical. "In the beginning God created the heaven and the earth" is unverfiable and therefore meaningless. (For discussions of the principle, see entry by R. W. Ashby in *Encyclopedia of Philosophy*, Vol. 8; and by Ernest LePore of Rutgers University in *The Cambridge Dictionary of Philosophy*.)

Pringle, Allen (19th Century)

Pringle was a Canadian freethinker, author of *Ingersoll in Canada* (1880). {BDF; FUK}

Pringle-Pattison, Andrew Seth (20th Century)

Pringle-Pattison, in Australia, wrote *Awake! Theological Addresses and the Clergy* (1922). {GS}

Prins, Marie P. (20th Century)

Prins, a Dutch secular humanist, has written, "Why is it necessary to have such a heavy philosophical discussion about whether people need God to be moral? Let us look at the practice. After all there have been quite a few atheists all through a large part of recorded history—for instance the Confucians and the Buddhists. I may be missing something," she added, "but I am not aware that their morals are any worse nor any better than those of mono- or poly-theists of whatever kind." {*Free Inquiry*, Summer 1996}

PRINTING

"Printing," according to Pulitzer-Prize winner Dared Diamond, is "the best single 'invention' of this millennium." Without its invention, people would not have read quickly the Bible, Martin Luther's 95 Theses, the Declaration of Independence, the Communist Manifesto, or other world-changing texts.

But Johannes Gutenberg (1400-1468) is only partly responsible:

> Gutenberg played a major practical and symbolic role in independently reinventing, in a greatly improved form and within a more receptive society, a printing technique previously developed in Minoan Crete around 1700 B.C., if not long before that.

Chinese printing is known to go back to around the 2nd Century C.E., Diamond continues, "when Buddhist texts on marble pillars began to be transferred to the new Chinese invention of paper via smeared ink. By the year 868, China was printing books. But most Chinese printers carved or otherwise wrote out a text on a wooden block instead of assembling it letter by letter as Gutenberg did (and as almost all subsequent printers using alphabetic scripts have also done). Hence the credit for what Gutenberg invented is also corrected from 'printing' to 'printing with movable type': that is, printing with individual letters that can be composed into texts, printed, disassembled, and reused." The Minoans had created a disk covered on both sides with spiraling arrays of 241 symbols constituting 45 different "letters" (actually, syllabic signs), which were not deciphered until recently. The disk was discovered in the ruins of a 1700 B.C.E. palace at Phaistos on Crete. {Jared Diamond, *The New York Times Magazine*, 18 April 1999}

Priscillian (Died 385?)

A Spanish churchman, the bishop of Avila, Priscillian was suspected of Manichaean and Gnostic leanings because he stressed puristic ideals, sought perfection in asceticism, and dabbled in astrology. The Roman Emperor Maximum ordered that Priscillian be put to death for practicing magic, and he was executed despite protests from such of his former opponents in the church as St. Ambrose, St. Martin, and the pope. In a council held at Brago (563?), Priscillianism was finally condemned and disappeared from Spain. {CE; TYD}

PRISON INMATES

A study in England's *The Guardian* (2 Feb 1998) reported that inmates in British prisons numbered as follows:

34,506 were Christians of various denominations
4,758 were members of others faiths;
85 were agnostics
76 were atheists.

Pritt, D. N. (Born 1887)

Pritt was a barrister and freethinker. He was vice president of the National Council for Civil Liberties in England. {TRI}

PRIVACY

The right to privacy is a fundamental right, according to Levi Fragell, President, and Babu R. R. Gogineni, Executive Director of the International Humanist and Ethical Union. *La vie privée* is, for freethinkers, to be cherished above every other right.

In 1998 when the United States President William Jefferson Clinton was threatened with impeachment, the IHEU went on record in a letter to President Clinton:

> We write as President of the International Humanist and Ethical Union (which has 100 member organisations in over 35 countries including the USA) to express our deep concern at the invasion of your life, and Ms. Lewinsky's [a White House employee who admitted to having had oral sex with him], privacy.
>
> We consider quite unacceptable the gross interference of both State and judiciary in what are essentially matters of personal morality. Whether the person involved is a private citizen or the President of the United States is immaterial. The public persecution and humiliation to which you are being subjected reminds us humanists of the terrible practices carried out by the Church in the Dark Ages—and of the cruelties perpetrated by some theocratic regimes in today's world.
>
> Protection of privacy, when matters do not attract the provisions of the criminal law is a fundamental human right. If privacy were violated by society's official institutions, we can none of us feel safe in our private lives, and therefore commiserate with you at the public violation of your rights.
>
> As human beings we all rely on a reciprocal sense of solidarity and common humanity from our fellow citizens, and we deeply regret that this has not been available to you, as Congress prepares to initiate impeachment proceedings against you.
>
> {*International Humanist*, October 1998}

PROCESS PHILOSOPHY: See entry for Charles Hartshorne.

Proctor, Richard Anthony (1837–1888)

Proctor, an English astronomer, spoke out against religion as being irreconcilable with the facts of science. The honorable secretary of the Royal Astronomical Society, he maintained in 1869 the since-established theory of the solar corona. Attracted by Newman, Proctor for a time was a Catholic, but when he thought out the question of Catholicism and science he formally renounced religion in a letter to the *New York Tribune* (November 1875), calling the two irreconcilable. Further heretical views were shown in his remarks on the so-called Star of Bethlehem in *The Universe of Suns, and Other Science*

Gleanings. Proctor entirely rejected the miraculous elements of the gospels, which he considered largely a *rechauffé* of solar myths. He pointed out the coincidence between the Christian stories and solar myths, and also with stories found in Josephus. According to his friend Edward Clodd, Proctor was an agnostic to the end of his life. The very last article that Proctor published was a vindication of Colonel Ingersoll in his controversy with Gladstone in the *North American Review*. Proctor contracted yellow fever and died in New York. {BDF; JM; RAT; RE}

Proctor Jr., William Earl (20th Century)

When he signed Humanist Manifesto II, Proctor was president of the Philadelphia Area American Humanist Association. {FD; HM2}

PROFESSORIAL ACADEMESE

Roy Bhaskar's *Plato etc: The Problems of Philosophy and Their Resolution* (1994) includes the following sentence:

> Indeed dialectical critical realism may be seen under the aspect of Foucauldian strategic reversal of the unholy trinity of Parmenedian/Platonic/ Aristotelian provenance; of the Cartesian-Lockean-Humea-Kantian paradigm, of foundationalisms (in practice, fideistic foundationalisms) and irrationalisms (in practice, capricious exercises of the will-to-power or some other ideologically and/or psycho-somatically buried source) new and old alike; of the primordial failing of western philosophy, ontological monavalence, and its close ally, the epistemic fallacy with its ontic dual; of the analytic problematic laid down by Plato, which Hegel served only to replicate in his actualist monovalent analytic reinstatement in transfigurative reconciling dialectical connection, while in his hubristic claims for absolute idealism he inaugurated the Comtean/Kierkegaardian and Nietzschean eclipses of reason, replicating the fundaments of positivism through its transmutation route to the superidealism of a Baudrillard.
>
> {*Skeptic* Vol. 4, No. 2, 1996}

PROGRESS

• Signs of one who is making progress are: He censures no one, praises no one, blames no one, finds fault with no one, says nothing about himself as though he were somebody or knew something. When he is hampered or prevented, he blames himself. And if anyone compliments him, he smiles to himself at the person complimenting; while if anyone censures him, he makes no defense. He has put away from himself his every desire, and has transferred his aversion to those things only, of what is under our control, which are contrary to nature. In a word, he keeps guard against himself as though he were his own enemy lying in wait.

–**Epictetus**

PROGRESSIVE LEAGUE

The Progressive League in England was formed in 1932 to bring together various progressive societies and individuals. It specializes in social activities, organizes conferences, produces the monthly *Plan*, and is headed by Dorothy Forsyth, 39 Belsize Court, Lyndhurst Gardens, London NW 3 5QP.

PROMETHEUS

In Greek mythology, Prometheus is the Titan who was man's benefactor. He stole fire from the gods, gave it to man, and taught man many arts and sciences. Zeus, in retaliation, plagued man with Pandora and her box of evils, then chained Prometheus to a mountain, where an eagle preyed on his ravaged liver, which was daily reconstituted so it could be daily re-ravaged. Aeschylus's *Prometheus Bound*, Goethe's "Prometheus," Byron's "Prometheus," and Shelley's *Prometheus Unbound* relate the myth, pointing out that the gods were less angry at Prometheus for giving man fire than they were about his having given man *hope*.

Paul Kurtz, in his *Toward a New Enlightenment* (1994), emphasizes the Promethean myth as being Hellenistic in origin, a myth which "has inspired countless generations of protesters, atheists, secularists, and humanists who herald Prometheus's heroic virtues. Pitted against this myth are the Mosaic, Christian, and Islamic revelatory myths, Hebraic in origin and inspiration. One difference is that the Greeks, at least by the time of the pre-Socratic philosophers, knew that the Homeric legends were only mythological" whereas "Judeo-Christian theologians and philosophers, still today, have not accepted the fact that their Gospels are likewise only confused mythical fictions spun out of the human imagination." Kurtz submits that Prometheus is particularly relevant today, that "Promethean men and women have audacity and the stubbornness and determination to create and realize their own ideals. They are self-generating free spirits, thinkers, and doers. Prometheus thus emphasizes the heroic virtues. . . . The human being by definition is a Promethean animal and human history began when men and women set out on their own without Zeus to create a better, more interesting, morally meaningful, and exciting life." (See entry for Greek and Roman gods.) {CL}

PROMETHEUS-SPRAVODAI SPOLOCNOSTI PROMETHEUS

A quarterly Slovak publication with English summaries, *Prometheus-Spravodai Spolocnosti Prometheus* is at Palovicova 14, 82 1 08 Bratislava, Slovakia.

PROMETHEUS BOOKS

Prometheus Books, a publisher (59 John Glenn Drive, Amherst, New York 14228), is the largest publishing company in upstate New York. It has more than one thousand titles and has specialized in books on secular humanism, atheism, skepticism and the paranormal, science, philosophy, the social sciences, sexology, education, and history.

Run by Paul Kurtz's son, Jonathan, the company has published works by Peter Ustinov, Martin Gardner, Sidney Hook, Thomas Szasz, Isaac Asimov, Steve Alan Kennedy Taylor, James T. Farrell, Bertrand Russell, Susan Blackmore, and Stefan Heym. It also publishes classical authors, including Descartes, Kant, Paine, Darwin, Dewey, Huxley, Adam Smith, and others.

Some of its published authors have complained that the company is partly a vanity press, others that it is nepotistically allied with the Council for Secular Humanism. However, Prometheus remains one of the largest printers of freethought books., titles which other companies often are fearful of publishing. On the Web: <pbooks6205@aol.com>.

PROMETHEUS SOCIETY

The Prometheus Society (IHEU) is at Osadna 3, 831 03 Bratislava, Slovac Republic. (See entry for Jaroslav Celko.)

PROMISCUITY

• What I have seen of the love affairs of other people has not led me to regret that deficiency in my experience.

–**George Bernard Shaw**

• Save a boyfriend for a rainy day, and another in case it doesn't rain.

–Mae West

PROOF

The love of truth is admirable. But veracity, as defined by John Locke, is "not entertaining any proposition with greater assurance than the proofs it is built upon will warrant." Bertrand Russell adds, "What sort of thing is it reasonable to believe without proof? I should reply: The facts of sense experience and the principles of mathematics and logic–including the inductive logic employed in science. These are things which we can hardly bring ourselves to doubt, and as to which there is a large measure of agreement among mankind. But in matters as to which men disagree, or as to which our own convictions are wavering, we should look for proofs, or, if proofs cannot be found, we should be content to confess ignorance." {Lee Eisler, *The Quotable Bertrand Russell*}

Proper, Matt (20th Century)

Proper, who is from Niskayuna and goes to Yale, is president of the Yale University Humanists and Secularists.

PROPHET

A prophet is one who utters "divinely" inspired revelations. The word is not a useful term in philosophy. According to R. B. Y. Scott, professor of Old Testament Literature and Exegesis in the United Theological College of Montreal in Canada, "The first prophets so-called were dervish ecstatics, like the prophets of Baal (*I Kings* 18:25-29) and other contemporary groups whose psychopathic acts and cries were attributed to divine possession (*I Samuel* 10: 5, 6)." The prophets were not forecasters or philosophers "but mystics, preachers, moralists, poets, and men of action who felt themselves to be mouthpieces of Yahweh." Major Prophets are said to have been Isaiah, Jeremiah, Ezekiel, and Daniel. Minor Prophets were Hosea, Joel, Amos, Obodiah, Jonah, Micah, Nahum, Habbakuk, Zephaniah, Haggai, Zechariah, and Malachi. Emanuel Swedenborg and Joseph Smith are self-proclaimed prophets who came out of Protestant backgrounds. Muhammad declared he was the last and greatest of the prophets. In Greece, the prophets were called poets.

PROSTITUTION

• Prostitutes are a necessity: without them, men would assault respectable women in the streets.

–Napoleon

Joseph McCabe points out that prostitution was no less frequent in Christian than in pagan times. He cites a French priest who had a most extensive knowledge of classical and medieval literature and who found "that while the wicked Greeks had about fifty words for the sex act, and the Romans (including Dr. Sanger's Martial) about the same number, the French of the Middle Ages had 300. Compare Rabelais. And the evil had a brazenness that would never have been tolerated in Athens, Alexandria, or Rome. In 1189, ships took 300 prostitutes to the Crusaders in Palestine, and St. Louis complained bitterly of the same traffic in the Sixth Crusade. Thousands of them—the Swiss, in 1476, found 2,000 left behind in one camp after the defeat of the Emperor—accompanied armies, and hundreds flocked to important Church Councils."

McCabe's *Story of the World's Oldest Profession* (1932) analyzes the subject, including sacred prostitution. Humanists Bonnie and Vern L. Bullough have written *Women and Prostitution, A Social History*, in which they discuss the historical, sociological, and anthropological background of the "world's oldest profession." Novelist Emily Hahn told the present author that prostitution, both male and female, entirely "natural."

Pierre Bayle has pointed out that prostitutes are seldom atheists. Agreeing, a recent editor of *Free Inquiry* found when he attended a 1997 prostitutes' conference in California, "I did meet some sacred whores when I was at the conference," jocularly adding, "but my atheism repelled them. I can't even get laid at a prostitution convention!" (See entry for Australian and New Zealand Humanists.) {RE}

Protagoras (c 481–411 B.C.E.)

"As to the gods, I have no means of knowing either that they exist or do not exist. For many are the obstacles that impede knowledge, both the obscurity of the question and the shortness of human life," wrote Protagoras. He is "the first notable Humanist of whom there is reliable record," according to Corliss Lamont, and formulated the famous dictum, 'Man is the measure of all things, of things that are that they are, and of things that are not that they are not.' " Protagoras's agnosticism was archetypal . McCabe called it an obvious screen for his atheism, led to the Sophistic tradition of agnosticism. It incited Athenians to banish him and burn his books in the market place. {CE; CL; HNS2; JM; RE; TYD}

PROTESTANT WORK ETHIC

The Protestant work ethic is a view of life that promotes hard work and self-discipline as a means to material prosperity. It is called Protestant because some Protestant groups believe that such prosperity is a sign of God's "grace." {DCL}

PROTESTANTISM

• Definition of Protestantism: hemiplegic paralysis of Christianity—and of reason.

—Friedrich Wilhelm Nietzsche

• The chief contribution of Protestantism to human thought is its massive proof that God is a bore.

—H. L. Mencken

PROTESTANTS AND OTHERS UNITED FOR THE SEPARATION OF CHURCH AND STATE

Horace Kallen and Warren Allen Smith once served on the Board of Protestants and Other Americans United for the Separation of Church State (POAU). One aim of the group, composed mainly of clerics except for the two naturalistic humanists, was to keep Fordham University from acquiring New York City public land next to Lincoln Center in Manhattan. The goal was unsuccessful. Commenting upon the group's title, Kallen, a professor of aesthetic at the New School for Social Research, remarked to Smith, "You and I apparently are the 'other' Americans." (See entry for Church and State.)

PROTOCOLS OF THE ELDERS OF ZION: See entry for Hoaxes, Religious.

Proudhon, Pierre Joseph (1809–1865)

Proudhon was a French social theorist and anarchist. In 1840 in a memoir, "What Is Property?", he gave the celebrated answer, "*C'est le vol!*" (It's theft!"). Asked about God, he replied with the aphorism, *"Dieu, c'est le mal"* (God, God is evil). As for humanism, he wrote, "I can be neither spiritualist, nor materialist, nor atheist, nor humanist. . . . Humanism is a false religion."

After the Revolution of 1848 he was elected a member of the constituent assembly and tried unsuccessfully to establish a national bank for reorganization of credit in the interest of the workers. He attacked Louis Bonaparte when President, resulting in a sentence of three years in jail and a fine of 10,000 francs. For his \ work \ on *Justice in the Revolution and in the Church*, he was condemned to three years in prison and 4,000 francs fine in 1858. Proudhon escaped to Belgium. Among his posthumous works was *The Gospels Annotated* (1866). His complete works totaled twenty-six volumes and often express his anarchistic views. {BDF; HNS2; RAT; RE}

Proust, Marcel (1871–1922)

Called by some one of the three major authors of the century (along with Thomas Mann and James Joyce, who also were freethinkers), Proust was a novelist, essayist, and critic, the author of *A la recherche du temps perdu* (1913–1937; English translation, *Remembrance of Things Past*, 1922–1931; however, *In Search of Lost Time* is a less careless translation). His parents were wealthy, and one of his cousins married Henry Bergson. His father, Dr. Adrien Proust, was a writer of thirty-four books. His younger brother, Dr. Robert Proust, wrote *The Surgery of the Female Genitalia*, a work about prostatectomies so well-known that some physicians referred to them as "proustatectomies."

Proust was actively involved on the side of Dreyfus, in the Dreyfus case of 1897–1899. In Proust's view, time mocks man's intelligence and his endeavors. Memory synthesizes yet distorts past experience. Most experience causes inner pain, and the objects of man's desires are the chief causes of his suffering. In Proust's scheme, man is isolated, society is false and ruled by snobbery, and artistic endeavor is raised to a religion and is superior to nature. His ability to interpret man's innermost experience in terms of such eternal forces as time and death created a profound and protean world view, inspiring wide discussion.

A sickly child, Proust endured a lifelong bout with asthma. He was allergic to flowers, pollen, dust, perfume, smoke, dampness, and cold, and his attacks could also be triggered by emotional upsets. Some of his attacks were largely psychosomatic, and in the winter he slept fully clothed. Even in summer he wore sweaters, mufflers, stockings, gloves, and a nightcap to bed. He became so obsessed with his asthmatic condition that he often used more than twenty towels after bathing to avoid having a damp towel touch his body. His skin, he felt, was so sensitive that instead of using soap, described writer Alain de Botton, he would wash with "finely woven, moistened towels, then pat himself dry with fresh linen (an average wash requires twenty towels, which Proust specifics must be taken to the only laundry that uses the right non-irritant powder, the blanchisserie Lavigne, which also does Jean Cocteau's laundry." Truman Capote, ever the gossip, wrote that Colette had told him that she wore the same perfume that Empress Eugénie had worn, adding that Cocteau had told her Proust wore that same perfume, too. Proust never married. He had such an attachment to his mother that although over thirty years old he would tell her about his "peeing" and bowel movements and how he had slept the night before.

Many assumed that Proust had sexual relationships with a number of men. However, the Baron de Charlus, the principal homosexual character in his *A Race Accursed*, is one of the most grotesque of the many characters he depicted. Meanwhile, according to Edward

White's *Marcel Proust* (1998), Proust did have a major lover, a young waiter from the Ritz, a person who lived with him for two years.

By 1912 Proust was living in bed. In 1922 he suffered uremia, vertigo, speech difficulty, and an attack of bronchitis. While struggling for breath on 18 November 1922, he hallucinated that a large black woman was chasing him and, shortly afterwards, succumbed to the illness that had plagued him all of his life.

As for any afterlife, Proust once wrote to the editor of *L'Intransigeant,*

> I think that life would suddenly seem wonderful to us if we were threatened to die as you say. Just think of how many projects, travels, love affairs, studies, it—our life—hides from us, made invisible by our laziness which, certain of a future, delays them incessantly. . . . But let all this threaten to become impossible for ever, how beautiful it would become again! Ah! If only the cataclysm doesn't happen this time, we won't miss visiting the new galleries of the Louvre, throwing ourselves at the feet of Miss X, making a trip to India. The cataclysm doesn't happen, we don't do any of it, because we find ourselves back in the heart of normal life, where negligence deadens desire. And yet we shouldn't have needed the cataclysm to love life today. It would have been enough to think that we are humans, and that death may come this evening.

Proust, according to David Tribe, was an outright freethinker. {AA; CE; GL; OEL; TYD}

Provenza, Paul (20th Century)

Provenza is an actor and a comedian. Online, he has written,

> I did about ten minutes of anti-religion material on a special on Comedy Central called "Pulp Comics," in which I have a priest hitting on a 13-year-old boy in a confessional, and the Last Supper done as a Friar's Roast. . . . In my [standup] act, I do a half hour or so of the ridiculousness of religion and lambaste the Catholic Church in particular. I point to how irrational it is to have any reverence for religion at all. We look at the ancient Greeks with their gods on a mountain top, throwing lightning bolts, and say, "Those ancient Greeks. They were so silly. So primitive and naïve. Not like our religions. We have burning bushes talking to people and guys walking on water. We're . . . sophisticated.

{CA}

PROVIDENCE

• Mussolini: a gift from providence.

–Pope Pius XI

(However, see entry for Mussolini.)

Provine, William (20th Century)

In 1995, Professor William Provine of Cornell University, a historian of science and a firm adherent of Darwinian evolution, stated, "To my mind, evolutionary biology leads straight to a vision which is equivalent to atheism," which leaves at most a distant God "of no comfort whatsoever." He added that when biological organisms die, "they are really and truly dead. There simply is no such thing as immortality or life after death." Continuing during a symposium at Vanderbilt University, Provine said, "Mammals don't have virgin birth, and none has ever happened. Resurrection doesn't exist in the natural world." Life is produced, he added, "by a process that gives not one damn about us. It simply plops us here as humans on the earth the same way it does chimpanzees or gorillas or the AIDS virus or anything else."

PRUDE

• Prude, n. A bawd hiding behind the back of her demeanor.

–**Ambrose Bierce**, *The Devil's Dictionary*

Prusak, Peter (20th Century)

Writing in *Prometheus,* a humanistic journal published in Bratislava, Prusak advised the nation of Slovakia, new in 1993, that the most democratic system is to separate state and religion. "In the current post-totalitarian society," he notes, "the churches, especially the Roman Catholic Church, enjoy support, subsidies, and biased preference from several politicians and parties, despite the fact that in the recent census 27 per cent of the population claimed to be non-denominational or atheists." Prusak is concerned that the Slovak Republic's new constitution does not separate church and state and that this "leaves room for unhealthy efforts for domination instead of mutual understanding, tolerance, respect, and cooperation for the benefit of the whole community."

PSEUDONYMS

A pseudonym is a fictitious name which authors sometimes assume as their pen name. Freethinkers and atheists, for example, have often used pseudonyms in order to avoid conflicts and public disapproval, even hangings or guillotinings, because of their individualistic views. (For a key to such, see Gordon Stein's listing in *God Pro and Con* [1990]. Also, see entry for Jun Sczesnoczkawasm.)

Psichari, Jean (Born 1854)

Psichari (Joannes Psuchares) was a French Hellenist and novelist of Greek extraction. In 1903 he taught modern Greek at the *École des Langues Orientales Vivantes.* His *Essai de grammaire historique néo-grecque* (1887) won the Volney Prize of the *Institu*t, and his *Autour de la Grèce* (1895) was crowned by the Academy. Psichari married Renan's daughter. In his novel, *Soeur Anselme* (1919), he gave an account of Renan's last days. {RAT}

PSYCHE: See entry for Eros.

PSYCHICS

Psychics claim to be capable of extraordinary mental processes, such as extra-sensory perception and mental telepathy. In 1997 singer Dionne Warwick's "Psychic Friends Network" reportedly logged about 4,000,000 minutes monthly at $4 per minute but apparently could not foresee its forthcoming bankruptcy. {*American Rationalist, May*-June 1997}

PSYCHOANALYSIS

• Psychoanalysis? It's that science which probes the history of one's infancy to see how it affects one's adultery.

—Bruce Wright

Sigmund Freud gave the name, psychoanalysis, to a system of interpretation and therapeutic treatment of psychological disorders. It began after he studied (1885-1886) with the French neurologist J. M. Charcot and became convinced that hysteria was caused not by organic symptoms in the nervous system but by emotional disturbance. It involved free association, dream interpretation, and analysis of resistance and transference in order to explore repressed or unconscious impulses, anxieties, and internal conflicts. (In *Encyclopedia of Unbelief,* see Paul Edwards's section on Wilhelm Reich. He and other non-theists have been negatively critical about some of the claims of psychoanalysis. Note that some psychiatrists are also psychoanalysts: for example, Mrs. Isaac [Janet] Asimov, a non-theist.) {CE]

PSYCHOKINESIS

Psychokinesis, according to psychics, is the production or control of motion by the exercise of psychic powers. A Manhattan secular humanist, when asked for money from several psychics, decided to test psychokinesis: "All those who believe in psychokinesis, please raise my hand."

Ptah-Hotep (2nd or 3rd Century B.C.E.?)

McCabe described Ptah-Hotep as being an ancient Egyptian moralist whose *Maxims* survived but whose date is variously assigned to the second or the third millennium. Breasted speculates that the work may date to 2,000 B.C.E. The work shows a cultivated middle-class in ancient Egypt, one with moral sentiments remarkably like those of our contemporary times and openly ignoring the Egyptian religion. It never mentions an Egyptian deity but speaks throughout of "God" in the monotheistic sense. Other literature of the second millennium (or earlier), such as *The Song of the Harper*, shows a widespread and flippant skepticism about a future life and some, according to McCabe, is atheistic. If so, the alleged "oldest book in the world" is atheistic. {JM; RE}

PTOLEMAIC UNIVERSE

Ptolemy, the Greek astronomer, put forth a model of the universe in which the Earth was the center, with the sun, moon, planets, and stars revolving around it. The Ptolemaic system prevailed in astronomy for nearly fifteen hundred years, until the model of the solar system proposed by Nicolaus Copernicus (with the sun, not the earth, at the center) was accepted. Church authorities forced Galileo to declare belief in the earth-centered universe. {DCL}

Ptolemy II (c. 308–246 B.C.E.)

Ptolemy II, son of Ptolemy I and Berenice of the Macedonian dynasty, was king of ancient Egypt from 285 to 246 B.C.E. He continued his father's efforts to make Alexandria the cultural center of the Greek world, completed the Pharos, and encouraged the translation of the Pentateuch into the Greek Septuagint. During his reign, a canal was built from the Nile to the Red Sea. Ptolemy warred against Syria until he married his daughter Berenice to the Syrian Antiochus II. He repudiated his wife Arsinoë in order to marry his sister, who was also named Arsinoë.

According to McCabe, most around Ptolemy were skeptics who had no pressure of either Greek or Egyptian priests, and Alexandria did become the world's greatest center of freethought as well as of art, science, and all culture. Ptolemy's learned tutor is known in Greek literature as "Theodorus the Atheist." {JM}

PUBIC HAIR: SEE ENTRY FOR RED HACKLE.

Puccinelli, Blanche Lee (20th Century)

In the 1950s, freethinkers were smiling about such of Puccinelli's provocative booklets as "My Convent Daze" and "Deaf, Dumb and Blind."

Pueckler Muskau, Hermann Ludwig Heinrich (1785–1871)

A prince and freethinker, Pueckler Muskau was a German who traveled widely and wrote his observations in a work entitled *Letters of a Defunct* (1830). He also wrote *Tutti Frutti* (1832) and *Semilasso in Africa* (1836). {BDF}

Puertas Fuertes, Jesús Antonio (20th Century)

Puertas Fuertes, a teacher of ethics in a Zaragoza, Spain, *collegio*, attended the 1994 CSHAFT meeting in Toronto. On Costa Rican television in 1995, Puertas Fuertes was interviewed about secular humanism and spoke at the founding of *Asociación Iberoamericana Ético Humanista* (ASIBEHU), an association to encourage ethical humanism in South and Central America. In 1996, Puertas was moderator of a panel discussion on intolerance at the Humanist World Congress in Mexico City.

PUGWASH CONFERENCE: See entry for Cyrus Eaton.

PULITZER PRIZES

Joseph Pulitzer (1847–1911) left funds to found what now is the Columbia University graduate school of journalism and endowed the Pulitzer Prizes, awards given annually for achievements in American journalism. Of the $375 million in 1990 dollars which he was worth at the time of his death, no money was left to churches. {CE}

Pullar, Nick (20th Century)

Pullar is Treasurer of the New Zealand Association of Rationalists and Humanists.

Pulley, Marie Harlowe (20th Century)

Pulley wrote *Christianity, the Greatest Misfortune* (1948). {GS}

Pullman, George (1831–1897)

A Universalist, Pullman invented the railroad sleeping car that revolutionized dull nighttime travel, an improvement often lamented by Puritans, who imagined dire happenings within such cramped and open sleeping quarters. In 1868, he introduced dining cars. His first parlor car, the Pioneer, was used in President Abraham Lincoln's funeral train. {CE; U}

Pullman, Tracy (20th Century)

Pullman was a member of the American Humanist Association. {HNS}

PULSARS

Pulsars, which are remnants of stellar explosions known as supernovae, rotate rapidly and emit beams of radio waves that can be detected by radio telescopes. Since 1968 more than five hundred have been observed.

Four types of pulsars have been located. A millisecond pulsar is the most extreme type. If a neutron star spins fast enough—once every 100 seconds or so—and also has a strong magnetic field, it emits pulses of radio waves intense enough to reach the earth. Such a bleeper is a radio pulsar, first discovered in 1967. A second type is the x-ray pulsar that spins at the same rate as a radio pulsar but emits x-rays instead. A third is the millisecond pulsar, of which more than fifty have been spotted. In 1998 a fourth type was found, an x-ray millisecond pulsar called SAX J1808.43658 after its coordinates in the sky. Astronomers have long wondered why the fastest-spinning stars in the universe, "millisecond pulsars," came to rotate so fast. The 1998 discovery is satisfying astronomers that by using an orbiting x-ray detector, the Rossi X-Ray Timing Explorer, they have finally caught one in the act of being spun and have analyzed its motion. {CE; *The Economist*, 25 July 1998}

Pulszky, Franz Aurel (1814–1897)

Pulszky was a Hungarian writer and politician. His account of England (*Aus dem Tagebuch eines in Grossbritannien reisenden Ungarn*, 1837) opened the doors of the Hungarian Academy to him. He was elected to the Diet in 1839 and in 1848 was appointed Under-Secretary of State in the Ministry of Finance. For his involvement in the revolutionary movement of 1849, he was compelled to fly to England, where he became a friend of G. J. Holyoake. The Austrian Government condemned him to death. After 1860 he lived in Italy, taking part in the work of liberation, until 1866, when he was allowed to return to his country to serve in the Diet. {RAT}

PUNISHMENT

To punish is to inflict some kind of a penalty for an offense, a sin, or a fault. The religionists' ultimate punishment is to consign a sinner to Hell. Secular societies often imprison individuals for their offenses. In the United States, the number of people locked up since 1980 has tripled. One in every 163 Americans is in jail or prison, a rate six times the average in Europe. {*The Economist*, 13 February 1999}

PURGATORY

Roman Catholics believe that souls who have died "in grace" must expiate their "sins." They do this in "purgatory," a place or condition of suffering. Purgatory is not mentioned in the Bible. It is, therefore, a quaint concept devised by its theologians, who have been known to spend time arguing whether it is possible to commit a "venial sin," for example, in Purgatory.

PURITAN

• A Puritan is a man, in a black frock, sitting on a rock, reading Scripture, sucking a lemon—and contemplating adultery.

–Anonymous

• The puritan is one who uses the cross as a hammer to knock in the heads of sinners.

–H. L. Mencken

• People blame our Puritan [background for our attitudes about sex], but a scholarly study some years back showed that *most* children in the early New England colonies were born out of wedlock. It seems that available land was extremely limited, the hostile Indians being so close by, and a landless suitor could not support a wife. So girls will be girls and boys likewise, and so on. The Puritan tradition, in brief, is sex.

–Arthur Miller

PURITAN ETHICS

Puritan ethics, according to Mrs. Ethyn W. Kirby, formerly a history professor in Wells College, Providence, Rhode Island, "stressed the virtues of sobriety, honesty, and thrift. An outstanding element was moral fervor, which is shown in Edward Dering's rebuking Queen Elizabeth and in William Prynne's attacks on bishops and theatres, and which gave to Puritanism a dogged strength and vigor." When Nathaniel Hawthorne wrote *The Scarlet Letter* and exposed the weakness of Puritan ethics in practice, he used Prynne as the last name of the bastard daughter of the Puritan minister who had sired her. Jonathan Edwards is one of the better known United States Puritans, celebrated for his sermon, "Sinners in the Hands of an Angry God." (1741).

Researching her family history, Dorothy Greninger found much that she had not expected:

> The Puritans arrived in Massachusetts in 1630 with a Royal Charter. Instead of setting up a branch of the Church of England, as expected, they set up First Church, a sort of combination church-state. To join the church, you had to agree with the official theology. Otherwise you could be banished, even in midwinter. This could be a death sentence. Not only errant Puritans were banished. Anabaptists were banished. Quakers were banished; they were also abused physically (ears cut off, whippings). When supply ships were delayed, Fast Days were decreed to save food. Minister John Wheelwright preached that fasting was not necessary; he and his supporters were banished. Anne Hutchinson was tried for holding a discussion in her home on [a question of theology]. Her crime seems to have been that, as a woman, she had no right to be making such judgments. When Indians later killed Anne and other members of her family, Governor John Winthrop Sr. was said to have regarded this as punishment for her incorrect theology. [To anyone suggesting that Puritans were] "almost exactly like all other human beings at all times," which people could be meant: Adolf Hitler? Torquemada?
>
> {ER; *Mensa Bulletin* December 1998}

PUROGAMI (Vanguard)

A Bengali monthly, *Purogami* is at 15 Bankim Chatterjee Street, Calcutta 700 073, India

PURPOSE OF LIFE

Who am I? What am I? Where am I? Why am I? When in time am I?

Philosophy, a study which investigates causes of reality and synthesizes learning, has developed answers utilizing logic, ethics, aesthetics, metaphysics, and epistemology in order to address such questions.

Humanists, rationalists, and freethinkers in general reject the ancient answers. Astronomy and the various other sciences are consulted for contemporary and empirical answers. Richard Dawkins, for example, in 1995 published *River Out of Eden*, a radically different picture than that depicted in the biblical Garden of Eden. From his viewpoint as an evolutionary biologist, Dawkins posits that the central purpose of evolution is the survival of DNA, not of the beings that are the DNA's temporary expression. Life perhaps began when the first molecule of RNA, DNA's elder cousin, got itself more or less accurately replicated in some natural stew of chemicals on the primitive earth. The first living cells, the first plants and animals, emerged merely because they were better mechanisms for repeating that first ancient accident of replication." In short, the purpose of life is for DNA to endure, not for humans to bow to one of the various supernatural divinities. According to Dawkins, DNA is not just a human's way of making another human: "The universe we observe has precisely the properties we should expect if there is, at bottom, no design, no purpose, no evil and no good, nothing but blind, pitiless indifference."

Nobel Prize winner Christian de Duve, differing from others who hold that the universe is meaningless, wrote in *Vital Dust, Life as a Cosmic Imperative* (1995): "For me, this meaning is to be found in the structure of the universe, which happens to be such as to produce thought by way of life and mind. Thought, in turn, is a faculty whereby the universe can reflect upon itself, discover its own structure, and apprehend such immanent entities as truth, beauty, goodness, and love. Such is the meaning of the universe as I see it." (See entries for Christian de Duve, Bertrand Russell, and the various other secular humanists and rationalists listed herein.)

Pushkin, Aleksandr Sergyevich (1799–1837)

Hailed even in his own time as Russia's greatest poet, Pushkin was known for his fairy romance *Ruslan and Lyudmila* (1820) and his novels, *Eugene Onegin* (1828) and *Boris Godunov* (1831). Although he entered government service, he was exiled to the south of Russia because of his liberalism, during which time he read Voltaire and Byron, authors whose outlooks he liked. After the accession of Nicholas I (1826), he was allowed to return to Moscow.

Hugh McLean alleges that Pushkin was an atheist when young. An energetic and self-consciously Byronic type of person, according to Serena Vitale's *Pushkin's Button* (1999), "When, as a youth, he pirouetted in a waltz or mazurka, provincial ladies took him for a foreigner, a demon, or a Freemason." In Odessa he once wrote that he was taking lessons in atheism from a deaf English philosopher. However, most Russian authors of his time were nominally Orthodox, attending services only when they had to and remaining generally unconcerned about religious matters.

Although he denied writing the blasphemous *Gavriiliada* (The Gabrieliad), in which God and Zeus are depicted as sexual creatures, intellectuals at the time were certain he was the author.

Pushkin's mother's grandfather was Abram Hannibal, who was Peter the Great's Africa-born and black general, "the blackamoor of Peter the Great" in Pushkin's words. Pushkin's African heritage is rarely mentioned.

According to Vitale, Pushkin's marriage in 1831 to Nikolayevna Goncharova proved to be an unhappy one. Georges d'Anthès—a Frenchman who was formally adopted by a wealthy and homosexual Dutch Ambassador to the court of Czar Nicholas I, Jacob van Heeckeren—publicly showed affection for the poet's wife, possibly to hurt van Heeckeren, and Pushkin began receiving anonymous letters concerning their intimate dance-floor conversations. But whether or not anything more than some stolen kisses was concerned, Pushkin and d'Anthès scheduled a duel on a snow-covered field outside St. Petersburg.

A skilled duelist, Pushkin had the strategy of allowing d'Anthès to fire first in order that he would have to stand without moving when it was Pushkin's turn to fire. But it was Pushkin who received the mortal shot and, carried home, he died two days later in what *The New Leader*'s assistant editor Richard Lamb has called "the most tragically unnecessary death of any great writer." Tsar Nicholas wrote Pushkin on his deathbed, expressing his "forgiveness." However, Lermontov, among others, accused government officials of complicity in the affair.

Pushkin's large debts were paid by the government, his children's education was paid for, and his widow was given a pension. She, in fact a brief favorite of the Tsar, later married a general. D'Anthès was expelled from Russia but had a successful political career in France and died in 1895, at eighty-three, surrounded by children, grandchildren, and great-grandchildren. {BDF; CE; EU, Hugh McLean; JM; d Lamb, *The New York Times Book Review*, 7 March 1999; RAT; RE}

Putnam, George Haven (1844–1930)

Putnam, an author and the son of G. P. Putnam, founded a well-known publishing house. In 1864 during the Civil War, he was captured by the Confederates, then retired with the rank of major. Active in many civic and social causes, Putnam organized the American Publishers' Copyright League in 1887 and led the successful battle for passage of an international copyright law in 1891. McCabe, who knew him well, says he "often scolded him for his appeasement policy as regards the churches, but he did not conceal his skepticism and was a member of the British Rationalist Press Association." {JM; RAT; RE}

Putnam, Hilary (1926–)

Putnam. a Harvard philosopher, has been described as being one of the most important of contemporary secular philosophers. Trained in the tradition of Rudolph Carnap's Logical Positivism, he later came under the influence of such philosophers as W. V. Quine, Ludwig Wittgenstein, and Nelson Goodman. In the process, states Nicholas G. Fotion of Emory University, Putnam became a critic of positivism, arguing that "there is no privileged foundation to our knowledge, no fixed principle of verifiability, no fact-value distinction as the positivists characterized it, and that sentences (our beliefs) cannot be assessed as true or false individually (i.e., holism rather than atomism is correct)." Putnam is also critical of another foundationalist position, which he calls metaphysical realism. Of late, adds Fotion, Putnam "has rejected functionalism, the theory that mental states are computational states—a theory he himself founded earlier in his career. Of late he has also written about matters of ethics and politics. Like his views in metaphysics and epistemology, he tends to want to hold a middle, yet somewhat liberal, position between two extremes—although he confesses there were times (e.g. during the Vietnam War) when he flirted with Marxism, a position he now finds extreme." His major works are *Representation and Reality* (1988), *Realism with a Human Face* (1990), and *Renewing Philosophy* (1992).

Some freethinkers question why, as an atheist, Putnam observes the Jewish holidays and feels that such traditions are important. {CA; OCP}

Putnam, Samuel Porter (1839–1896)

An American freethought lecturer and author, Putnam was a Congregational, then a Unitarian minister for a time but left the ministry and became in 1892 the president of the Freethought Federation of America. One of its accomplishments was keeping the World's Fair in Chicago (1893) open on Sunday, for at that time all public "amusements" had to be closed on Sundays. His major work was *400 Years of Freethought* (1894), which included over 140 portraits. In San Francisco from 1888 to 1891 he edited *Freethought* with George E. Macdonald, the brother of the editor of the *Truth Seeker* who later became editor of that publication himself.

In *My Religious Experience* (1891), Putnam declared, "The last superstition of the human mind is the superstition that religion in itself is a good thing, though it might be free from dogma. I believe, however, that the religious feeling, as feeling, is wrong, and the civilized man will have nothing to do with it. . . . [When the] shadow of religion disappeared forever . . . I felt that I was free from a disease." He added, "The moment that one loses confidence in God, or immortality in the universe, [one becomes] more self-reliant, more courageous, and the more solicitous of aid where only human aid is possible."

"On the night of December 11-12, 1896," Gordon Stein has written (*The American Rationalist*, September-October 1995), "freethought lecturer and author Samuel Porter Putnam and rising freethought star May Collins were found dead in her guest room in Boston. Immediately, rumors began circulating in the religious press that there had been some sort of 'hanky-panky' going on between the 58-year-old Putnam and the 20-year-old Miss Collins, who was on her first freethought lecturing tour away from her native Kentucky." Both, however, were found fully clothed. A coroner found their deaths were due to accidental asphyxiation by illuminating gas. For some unexplained reason, Putnam took pains to conceal from friends that he was a divorced man with two children. {BDF; EU, Gordon Stein; FUS; RAT; RE; TRI; TYD}

Putsage, Jules (19th Century)

Putsage was a Belgian follower of Baron Colins, the founder of the Colins Philosophical Society at Mons. Putsage wrote *Determinism and Rational Science* (1885) along with many essays in *La Philosophie de L'Avenir* of Paris and *La Societe Nouvelle* of Brussels. {BDF}

Putz, Paul (20th Century)

Putz is Treasurer of Arizona Secular Humanists, PO Box 3738, Scottsdale, Arizona 85271.

Pyat, Felix (1810–1889)

Pyat was a French socialist, writer, and orator. His religious father had sent him to a Jesuit college at Bourges, where Pyat secretly read the writings of Beranger and Courier. Pyat wrote popular dramas, such as *The Rag-Picker of Paris* (1847). In 1871 he founded *Le Combat*. Elected to the National Assembly, Pyat protested against the treaty of peace, was named member of the Commune, and was condemned to death in 1873. Returning to France after the armistice, he sat as deputy for Marseilles. {BDF; RAT}

Pycroft, S. (18th Century)

Pycroft wrote *A Brief Inquiry into Free Thinking in Matters of Religion, and Some Pretended Obstructions To It* (1713). {GS}

Pyeshkov, Aleksey Maximovich: See entry for Maxim Gorky.

Pyke, James G. (1874–1930)

Pyke was an Australian freethinker, Esperantist, and bookseller. A pioneer president of the Melbourne Esperanto Club, he used the pen name "Ezoko," the Esperanto word for the pike fish and a play on his own name. Owner of Carrolton's Bookshop in Melbourne, he obtained the franchise for Haldeman-Julius's Little Blue Books. While returning from an Esperanto conference in Malta, he disappeared from the ship, *Balranald.* {SWW}

Pyke, William Thomas (1859–c. 1940)

Pyke was an Australian freethinker, rationalist, and bookseller. In 1929 he was described as "probably the most knowledgeable bookseller Australia has ever produced." His freethinking family views were endorsed by his grandson, Frank, who bequeathed a substantial portfolio of stocks and money to advance "the aims and objects of Rationalism." {SWW}

Pynchon, John (1937–)

Pynchon, an American novelist noted for his wild sense of humor, is often grouped with authors of black humor, such as Vonnegut and Heller. In describing 20th century life, he turns to fantasy, as shown in *V* (1963), which features mythical albino alligators in New York City sewers; in *The Crying of Lot 49* (1966), a satirization of California life; and in his masterpiece, *Gravity's Rainbow* (1973), in which he discusses war and death in World War II London.

Like a Kerouac character, Pynchon has next to dropped out of the public's sight. The most recent photograph available is one in the 1953 Oyster Bay High School yearbook, although his back was photographed in 1996 for a magazine story stating he lives in Manhattan with his wife and their son. Shunning personal appearances, he asked the comedian "Professor" Irwin Corey to accept a National Book Award for *Gravity's Rainbow*, and the humorist complied by delivering one of his pseudo-academic doubletalk lectures while dressed in tuxedo and tennis shoes.

Mason & Dixon (1997) reveals Pynchon's early skills in engineering physics as he tells the tale of Charles Mason and Jeremiah Dixon, British astronomers in the 1760s who established the southern boundary of Pennsylvania, the Mason-Dixon line which eventually became the border between the slave states and the free states. Louis Menand, of the Graduate Center of the City University of New York, notes that the novel really is about modernity and entropy, the latter a thermodynamic term referring to systems which run down because of a loss of available energy as all molecules reach the same temperature. Entropy, Menand explains, leads to the standardization and universalization of time and space, to an attempt to get everyone on the planet on the same wavelength. But "Once it is established that the density of the earth makes it impossible for there to be a society of people living under its surface, that possible world will disappear.

This example is fantastic. The examples of the American Indians and the native South Africans are not."

Pynchon, like Kerouac, never labeled his outlook, but it is nontheistic. {CE; Louis Menand, *The New York Review of Books*, 12 June 1997; OEL}

Pyrrho of Elis (c. 360 –c. 170 B.C.E.)

The father of skepticism, Pyrrho found that the contradictory of any statement can be entirely plausible, also. Therefore, the best philosophic attitude is to be imperturbable and to suspend judgment, to be a skeptic and doubter about everything. The concept arrived after his trip to India with Alexander's army, during which he accompanied the philosopher Anaxarchus and became acquainted with the philosophy of the Magi and the Indian Gymnosophists. As they traveled, they noticed that different peoples disagreed on a variety of matters, and Pyrrho realized that this is so because we are confined to our own impressions of what is truth. Rational principles are not what govern life but, rather, conventions and instincts govern life. It is related that in his personal life he kept house with his sister, sharing with her in all domestic duties. Pyrrho, who lived to be ninety, left no written work, but his principles were perpetuated by Timon of Philius, his pupil, and his general outlook was developed by Sextus Empiricus.

C. E. Pulos in *The Deep Truth, A Study of Shelley's Scepticism* (1962) notes that Pyrrho by not developing the positive side of his scepticism "seemed to deprive men of their motives for action and to inculcate an attitude of indifference." The positive side of scepticism was emphasized, however, by Sextus Empiricus. For him, the academic sceptic is free to shun the improbable and to pursue the probable with as much intensity as is desired. Bertrand Russell in his *History of Philosophy* (1945) observes that "Scepticism as a philosophy is not merely doubt, but what may be called dogmatic doubt. The man of science says 'I think it is so-and-so, but I am not sure.' The man of intellectual curiosity says 'I don't know how it is, but I hope to find out.' The philosophical Sceptic says 'nobody knows, and nobody ever can know.' It is this element of dogmatism that makes the system vulnerable. Sceptics, of course, deny that they assert the impossibility of knowledge dogmatically, but their denials are not very convincing." {BDF; CE; RE}

PYRRHONISM

• Pyrrhonism, n. An ancient philosophy, named for its inventor. It consisted of an absolute disbelief in everything but Pyrrhonism. Its modern professors have added that.

–Ambrose Bierce
The Devil's Dictionary

Pythagoras (c. 582–c. 507 B.C.E.)

According to Robertson, the elusive Pythagoras "is not so much a rationalistic as a theosophic freethinker; but to freethought his name belongs insofar as the system connected with it did rationalize, and discarded mythology."

Little is known about his life inasmuch as some of his disciples came to worship him as a demigod, and it is impossible to differentiate his teachings from those of his followers. The Pythagoreans taught that numbers constitute the true nature of things, performed purification rites, and believed in the transmigration of souls. Shelley's *A Refutation of Deism* cited Pythagoras as a theist, along with Plato and Anaxagoras. {CE; HNS2; JMR; JMRH; RE}

Q

"Q," a reconstructed Greek text of the Bible, is a hypothetical first-century work composed mostly of the alleged sayings of Jesus. First published in Belgium as *Documenta Q,* it is believed by some scholars that Q, which is short for *Quelle,* the German word for source, is a literary source for the Gospels of Matthew and Luke. Other scholars, however, believe the work never existed. (See Charlotte Allen's "Q: The Search for a No-Frills Jesus," *The Atlantic Monthly,* December 1996)

Quakers (Society of Friends)

Members of the Religious Society of Friends, according to the journal of George Fox, were first called Quakers "because we bid him (Justice Gervase Bennett of Derby) tremble at the word of God, and this was in the year 1650." The name, which at first was used in scorn, at once became popular. Fox's preaching made converts among Seekers, Independents, Baptists, and other sectarians, and the new faith spread through the British Isles to the Continent to Barbados and in 1656 to America. Hangings in Boston by fellow Christians and imprisonment in Cromwellian and Restoration England failed to discourage the group. Rhode Island was the greatest mainland stronghold until in 1681 Pennsylvania was granted by Charles II to the distinguished Quaker convert, William Penn.

Elias Hicks (1748–1830), a Quaker from Hempstead, New York, was one of the most able preachers of his time. He worked against slavery and in 1811 published his *Observations on Slavery.* When a division in the Society of Friends occurred in 1827, he was a leader of the liberal separation party, to which the name Hickside was unofficially given. Hicks, a neighbor and friend of Walt Whitman's father, was unitarian in his view of Jesus, a position which was different from most others in the Society of Friends. His followers have been called Hicksite Quakers.

When no longer persecuted, Friends lived as a people apart, and they became known for their humanitarianism. They renounced war, favored improved Indian relations, were against Negro slavery to the point that some shared in the activities of the Underground Railroad, and worked for prison reform, temperance, and Indian aid. Quakers believe in great simplicity in daily life and in worship. Their services consist mainly of silent meditation. Although in the past they wore distinctive clothing, Friends no longer do. Throughout the world and since the first World War, the American Friends Service Committee has been a well-known force for improving the plight of peoples without the accompanying missionarying common among most other religious service groups, except the Unitarian.

Edwin H. Wilson, in "Humanism Among the Quakers," cited the following Quakers as being Humanists: Jesse H. Holmes, professor emeritus of philosophy at Swarthmore College; Roscoe Pound, a professor at the University of Harvard College; Paul H. Douglas, professor of economics at the University of Chicago; J. Russell Smith, professor of economic geography at Columbia University; and Albert T. Mills, professor of history and political science at James Millikin University. {DCL; ER; EW}

QUALIFICATIONS FOR A LEADER

- 0 Number of times Jesus exhorted his followers to pray in public
- 0 Number of times Jesus urged followers to aspire to public office
- 0 Number of times Jesus advocated rebellion against the Roman Empire
- 0 Number of times Jesus demanded the abolition of slavery, abortion, pornography, gladiatorial combat, war, and child abuse
- 0 Number of times the Bible prohibits or even mentions the word "abortion"
- 0 Number of times the Bible calls for establishment of democracy, jury trials, freedom of speech, freedom of religion, freedom of assembly:
- 0 Number of times Jesus advocated strong close-knit families
- 0 Number of times Jesus urged equal rights and fair treatment of women

{From the Internet}

QUANTUM THEORY

"Quantum theory, which has been evolving since the beginning of the century, is a mathematical framework describing the behavior of extra-small objects, including atoms," Malcolm W. Browne explained in a *New York Times* article (14 October 1998) about the 1998 Nobel Prizes in Physics and Chemistry.

The theory is, simply, that radiant energy is transmitted in the form of discrete units, "quantum" referring to the quantity or specific portion that can be measured. Together with the theory of relativity, quantum theory is the theoretical basis of modern physics. The former assumes importance in the special situation where very large speeds are involved, the latter for the special situation where very small quantities are involved. Older theories treated energy solely as a continuous phenomenon, and matter was assumed to occupy a very specific region of space and to move in a continuous manner.

Dr. Robert B. Laughlin of Stanford University, one of the Nobel Prize winners, told reporters that the fractional quantum Hall effect ("the generation of an electric potential perpendicular to both an electric current flowing along a conducting material and an external magnetic field applied at right angles to the current upon application of the magnetic field," according to the *American Heritage Dictionary*) would likely have no immediate applications. "It's more of cosmological than practical interest at the moment," Laughlin said, adding

> Potentially, it can help us understand the quantum structure of the vacuum throughout the space-time of the universe. There are two great tends in physics: Newtonian reductionism, in which you look for the wheels and cogs that make the big mechanism work, and the opposite, in which you take little things like the equations of motion and see how they make the big mechanism work. The latter is [my] approach.

A difficult theory, particularly to humanists whose forte often is the humanities, it was described by Browne:

> All very small objects—molecules, atoms, subnuclear particles, photons of light—obey the rules of quantum mechanics. Quantum mechanics deals with large assemblages of particles and calculates probabilities rather than certainties. Viewed quantum mechanically, all objects are said to have "wave functions" that include all their possible conditions. For instance, it is possible, because a wave function includes all possibilities, for an object to be in two places at the same time.
>
> Since the electrons that orbit atoms are quantum particles, the mathematical of quantum mechanics apply to them, and physicists and chemists have long known that it is theoretically possible to predict the interactions of atoms by calculating the wave functions of their orbital electrons.

The five quantum theorists who won Nobel Prizes in 1998 besides Laughlin were Dr. Walter Kohn of the University of California at Santa Barbara; Dr. John A. Pople, a mathematician at Northwestern University in Evanston, Illinois; Dr. Horst L. Störmer of Columbia University In New York City; and Dr. Daniel C. Tsui of Princeton University in New Jersey. (See entry for String Theory.) {CE; *The New York Times,* 14 October 1998}

QUASARS

Quasars, or quasi-stellar objects, are the most distant and most luminous objects in the universe. Astronomers in space, uninterested in ancient explanations of the universe's genesis, have in the 1990s detected a quasar an estimated sixty sextillion miles away. A quasar is 10 billion light years away, or 60 sextillion miles—60 followed by 21 zeros. Astronomers are working on the assumption that a few minutes after the "big bang," an immense explosion created the universe. That explosion probably spread lots of hydrogen gas and much less helium gas between galaxies. Using the Hubble Space Telescope, they continue to make new discoveries, one being that most quasars are presumably powered by black holes—extremely dense regions at the center of many galaxies where gravity is so strong that light cannot escape—and that the bulk of quasar formation appears to have occurred about 2.5 billion years after the Big Bang. Before 1.9 billion years and after 3 billion, the creation of quasars was exceedingly rare. However, astronomers continue to develop new findings, and what presently is known about quasars is regularly modified. {CE}

Quatrefages, Jean Louis Armande, de Breau (1810–1892)

Quatrefages, a French zoologist, at first opposed theories of evolution, then got Darwin nominated a corresponding member of the French Academy. He is frequently quoted as "one of the great Christian scientists," but after being raised a Protestant he gave up Christianity for deism early in life. In *Les Emules de Darwin* (The Rivals of Darwin, published 1894, 12 volumes), Quatrefages continued to reject Darwinism but also rejected the Christian version. For him, the origin of life and similar problems remained "a mystery." {JM; RAT; RE}

QUEENS UNIVERSITY

Queens University humanists are found on the Web: <www.secularhumanism.org/cfa/orgs.html>.

QUEENSLAND HUMANIST

An Australian publication, *Queensland Humanist is* at GPO Box 2041, Brisbane 4001, Australia.

QUEER THEORY

Queer Theory, as understood on campuses, is a prism through which scholars examine literary texts. Such theorists scorn traditional definitions of "homosexual" and "heterosexual," making no strict demarcation between male and female. Instead, and as Foucault pointed out, sexuality is that which exists on a continuum, with some people preferring sex partners of the opposite sex, others enjoying partners of both sexes. "Only since the 19th century," journalist-critic Dinitia Smith has written, "have sexual definitions become rigid. And along with this rigidity . . . has come anxiety, panic, and intensifying homophobic attitudes."

By looking at literary works through the prism of queer theory, queer theorists attempt to clarify them and explain their mysteries. At the forefront of the outlook, Smith has pointed out, are Eve Kosofsky Sedgwick, a Duke University professor who does not like being called "the straight woman who does queer studies," and Judith Butler, a professor at the University of California, Berkeley.

In provocatively titled essays like "Jane Austen and the Masturbating Girl," "How to Bring Your Kids Up Gay," and "Is the Rectum Straight?: Identification and Identity in *The Wings of the Dove*," Sedgwick has taken texts traditionally seen as heterosexual and exposes what she says are their homoerotic themes. Desire and repression, she agrees with Foucault, are at the root of all politics. "You can't," she holds, "understand relations between men and women characters unless you understand the relationship between people of the same gender. Also important is the way homophobia is aroused in a particular cultural setting." For example, in the case of Dickens's *Our Mutual Friend*, with its "cultural setting" that of England of the mid-1800's, a strong attraction between two men would not necessarily culminate in sex but would lead to a kind of "homosexual panic."

Disagreeing with queer theory, the critic and Catholic Andrew Sullivan has regarded such theorists "as a sect restricted to the academy, which they control as a cartel. Their essential argument is that the whole notion of gender is wrong, there is no such thing as responsibility, and any attempt to go by the rules is oppressive." Sedgwick has countered, "I think it's ridiculous to say 'queer theory' is not about ethical responsibility. There is an ethical urgency about queer theory that is directed at the damage that sexual prohibitions and discriminations do to people." (See entry for Eve Kosofsky Sedwick.) {Dinitia Smith, *The New York Times*, 17 January 1998}

Quental, Antero de (1842–1891)

Said by Wheeler to be one of the most advanced minds in Portugal, Quentel published poetry and prose that showed him to be a student of Hartmann, Proudhon, and Rénan. In his *Os Sonetos Completos* (1886), Quental showed how his early mysticism passed into a rather pessimistic atheism, then to a tranquil agnosticism. Quental was a socialist who led the Coimbra dissidents in their opposition to the monarchy and to romanticism. {BDF; CE; JM; RAT; RE}

Quering, Wanda (20th Century)

Quering, from Nebraska, is on the board of directors of the Freedom From Religion Foundation.

Quesnay, François (1694–1774)

Quesnay was a French economist who is noted for his *Tableau Economique* (1708) and his doctrine of *Laissez Faire*. Quesnay, a physician, derived moral and social rules from physical laws. A peasant boy, he had not been taught to read until he was twelve years old, but he learned Latin and Greek, studied medicine, surgery, philosophy, and mathematics, winning a high repute as a surgeon. He founded the Physiocratic School of political economy. Although he did not specify his own views, he associated with Diderot and wrote articles for the *Encyclopédie*. {BDF; JM; RAT; RE}

QUEST & CONTROVERSEY

Quest & Controversy, a quarterly of Humanist of Inland Communities, is at PO Box 1001, San Jacinto, California 92581.

QUESTIONING

• Judge a man by his questions rather than his answers. . . . He must be very ignorant for he answers every question he is asked.

–Voltaire

• No man really becomes a fool until he stops asking questions.

–Charles P. Steinmetz

Quételet, Lambert Adolphe Jacques (1796–1874)

Quételet was director of the Brussels *Observator* and a professor of astronomy, geodesy, and mathematics at the Military School. He was eight times President of the International Statistical Congress and is counted as one of the founders of statistical science as well as of meteorology. His advanced rationalism is seen in *Sur l'homme et le développement de ses facultiés* (1835, 2 volumes). {RAT; RE}

Qufu

Qufu is the birth and burial place in China of K'ung-Fu-Tze (Confucius).

Quidde, Ludwig (1858–1929)

Quidde, a German historian, was the Nobel Prize winner in 1927. A professor of history at Munich University and Vice-President of the International Peace Conference, he had in 1894 caused a sensation with *Caligula*, which was understood to be an attack on the Kaiser. Quidde in his writings approvingly quoted Frederick the Great's negative comments on Christianity. {RE}

Quigley, Harold J. (20th Century)

When he signed Humanist Manifesto II, Quigley was a leader of the Ethical Humanist Society of Chicago. A Presbyterian dismissed for heresy, he became a Leader of Ethical Culture Societies in Cleveland, Los Angeles, and Chicago (1962–1981). (See entry for Ethical Culture.) {HM2}

Quimada, Toribio (Died 1988)

Quimada founded the Universalist Church of the Philippines in 1954. His outlook included the idea that salvation is for all; that God is love and therefore Hell for sinners is illogical; that Jesus was a son of Mary and Joseph, not a god; that Jesus preached love, peace, equality, and justice. In 1988 he was brutally murdered.

Quin, Malcolm (19th Century)

Quin was a secular leader in Leicester, England, during the 1870s. He helped supply hymns, saying, "People who believed in nothing else believed in hymns." {RSR; WSS}

Quinn, Thom (20th Century)

Quinn, a professor at the University of Wisconsin, signed Humanist Manifesto 2000.

Quincy, Josiah (1772–1864)

Quincy was son of Josiah Quincy Sr. (1744–1775), the eminent political leader during the American Revolution who, along with John Adams, defended the British soldiers in their trial following the Boston Massacre. Like his father, Quincy was a political leader, serving as a Federalist in the state senate. He then became minority leader in the U.S. House of Representatives, arguing against admitting Louisiana as a state unless the original thirteen states all voted in favor. Quincy opposed the War of 1812, left Congress, became mayor of Boston, and in 1829 became president of Harvard, where he served until 1845. Quincy wrote *The History of Harvard University* (1840). Robert A. McCaughey, in *Josiah Quincy, 1772–1864, The Last Federalist* (1974), cites Quincy as being a Unitarian. {U}

Quine, Willard Van Orman (1908–)

Quine, a professor of philosophy emeritus at Harvard University, is a Humanist Laureate in the Council for Secular Humanism's International Academy of Humanism. He is a contributing editor on *Philo*. Among his works are *Methods of Logic* (1950); *From A Logical Point of View* (1953), *Word and Object* (1960); *Set Theory and Its Logic* (1963); *The Ways of Paradox* (1966); *Ontological Relativity* (1969); and *From Stimulus to Science* (1995).

In 1992, Harvard University Press issued a new edition of his *Pursuit of Truth,* in which he states: "I am of that large minority or small majority who repudiate the Cartesian dream of a foundation for scientific certainty firmer than scientific method itself. But I remain occupied, we see, with what has been central to traditional epistemology, namely the relation of science to its sensory data. I approach it as an input-output relation within flesh-and-blood denizens of an antecedently acknowledged external world, a relation open to inquiry as a chapter of the science of that world. . . . I call the pursuit naturalized epistemology. . . .

"The most notable norm of naturalized epistemology actually coincides with that of traditional epistemology. It is simply the watch-word of empiricism: *nihil in mente quod non prius in sensu.* This is a prime specimen of naturalized epistemology, for it is a finding of natural science itself, however fallible, that our information about the world comes only through impacts on our sensory receptors. And still the point is normative, warning us against telepaths and soothsayers. . . .

"The science game is not committed to the physical, whatever that means. Bodies have long since diffused into swarms of particles, and the Bose-Einstein statistic has challenged the particularity of the particle. Even telepathy and clairvoyance are scientific options, however moribund. It would take some extraordinary evidence to enliven them, but, if that were to happen, then empiricism itself—the crowning norm, we saw, of naturalized epistemology—would go by the board. . . . The collapse of empiricism would admit extra input by telepathy or revelation, but the test of the resulting science would still be predicted sensation."

"In other words," observes Prof. Eric Walther of C. W. Post College, "science really is the Pope who declares himself to be fallible. All that religion or spirituality *or any hypothesis whatsoever* needs to do, to win our allegiance, is to predict our sensations more accurately than can be done without it." (See the discussion about Quine by C. F. Presley in the *Encyclopedia of Philosophy*, Vol. 7.) {CA; CE; E; SHD}

Quinet, Edgar (1803–1875)

After an attack on the Church (*Le génie des religions*) in 1842, Quinet roused such enthusiasm that he was appointed professor of history at Paris University. He was then deposed, however, for attacking religion in his lectures. For his share in the Revolution of 1848 he was exiled, during which time he wrote a number of Rationalist works in Belgium. In 1871, Quinet returned to France and sat with the anti-clericals in the Chambre. His twenty-eight volumes of work advanced rationalism both in France and in Belgium. {RAT; RE}

Quintin, Jean (Died 1530)

"The heretic of Picardy," Quintin allegedly founded the *Libertines*. He is said in 1525 to have preached in Holland that religion is a human invention. He was arrested and burned at Tournay, Belgium, in 1530. {BDF}

Quiogue, Gonzalo (20th Century)

When he signed Humanist Manifesto II, Quiogue was vice president of the Humanist Association of the Philippines. He wrote *Thought-Provoking Essays of Humanists, Rationalists, and Freethinkers* (1978). {GS; HM2}

QUR'AN (also called *Alcoran*; previously spelled Koran)

• Koran, n. A book which the Mohammedans foolishly believe to have been written by divine inspiration, but which Christians know to be a wicked imposture, contradictory to the Holy Scripture.

–Ambrose Bierce
The Devil's Dictionary

The Qur'an is Islam's sacred text, considered by Muslims to contain the "revelations" of Allah which were delivered to Muhammed by Gabriel. In addition to humans, the work speaks of three classes of creatures:

- angels (*malaika*), the messengers and slaves of God are commanded by four archangels: Jibril (Gabriel), Mikail, Izrail, and Israfil;
- jinns, which probably represent the old animistic gods, have been created by fire, are intelligent, and have a connection with magic and talismans—they can be made to serve man;
- devils, such as Shaitan (Satan) and Shayatiyn (several shaitan), do not reside in Hell but will end up there at the end of time. One of their weapons against men is disease, especially the plague. Shaitan is the power in man's heart that is opposed to God.

The Qur'an teaches an uncompromising monotheism, is completely patriarchal in its outlook, and urges absolute submission to the one God: Allah. Written in classical Arabic, it gives "guidance for the pious who believe in the mysteries of the faith, perform their prayers, give alms." A 1734 translation was made by G. Sale, an 1861 translation was made by J. M. Rodwell, and numerous later editions are available.

The book contains as much violence as the other sacred books; e.g.,

Sura 89.17: God killed them, and those shafts were God's, not yours.
Sura 14.4: God misleads whom he will and whom he will he guides.
Sura 32.32: If we had so willed, we could have given every soul its guidance, but now my Word is realized: 'I shall fill Hell with jinn and men together.' "
Sura 19.72: There is not one of you who will not go down to it [hell], that is settled and decided by the Lord.
Sura 97.5: For Laza [the fires of hell] dragging by the scalp, shall claim him who turned his back and went away, and amassed and hoarded.
Sura 104.4: "It is God's kindled fire, which shall mount above the hearts of the damned.
Sura 54:45: The sinners are in error and excitement. On the day when they shall be dragged into fire on their faces.

No secular-style Voltaire or Thomas Paine has ever spoken out in the Muslim world or, at any rate, was openly allowed to live on in such a society. (See Ibn Warraq's *Why I Am Not A Muslim.*) {ER; Qur'an}

Quris, Charles (19th Century)

A French advocate of Angers, Quris published some works on law and *La Défense Catholique et la Critique* (1864). {BDF}

RA, or RE

Ra, the Egyptian sun god and chief deity, was considered creator and father of all things. By day, he sailed across the sky in a celestial barge, and by night he attacked the forces of evil and darkness. Early kings of Egypt claimed to have been Ra's descendants. The pyramid is a symbol of Ra, and the hawk and the lion are manifestations of his existence. Amon and Aton frequently are identified with Ra. The chief deity of Egypt in the second millennium B.C.E., Ra was the center of the cult being Heliopolis (the City of the Sun), a cult not native to Egypt and which may have been introduced from the East. Ra's followers, represented today by Rastafarians, for example, use a variety of fetishes. In Jamaica, they venerate Haile Selassie as a god, teaching the eventual redemption of blacks and their return to Africa. Marijuana is used in their rituals. Haile Selassie, born Tafari Makonnen and the grandnephew of Emperor Menelik II of Ethiopia, became emperor when the empress mysteriously died. He then claimed to be the 111th descendant of King Solomon and the Queen of Sheba to rule Ethiopia. {CE}

RABBI

A rabbi in Judaism is a teacher and leader of worship. Jesus is referred to as a rabbi. The title of ordination for authoritative teachers of Judaism began in the period after the destruction of the Temple in 70. Rabbinism is the religious discipline by which the teachers of post-Biblical (Old Testament) Judaism implemented Biblical religion to the needs of their day. {ER}

Rabelais, François (c. 1490–1533)

Rabelais, the French writer and physician, is one of the great comic geniuses in world literature. "The grand jester of France," Bacon called him. As a Franciscan novice, he studied Greek, Latin, science, law, philosophy, and letters, becoming respected by the humanists of his time, including Budé and the Franciscan humanist, Pierre Amy. Pope Clement VII at one time granted him permission to enter the Benedictine monastery of Maillezais. His heretical humor brought him into trouble, and he was once rescued by a military friend from the "in Pace," a form of burying alive. But this did not dampen his spirits, though it made him cautious; for he dreaded the idea of being burnt alive "like a herring," saying he was "dry enough already by nature."

The attacks he made on astrology disturbed many, for he even scoffed at the astrological leanings of the new Pope, Paul III. Calvin, who once had been his friend, attacked Rabelais in *De Scandalis,* accusing him of *libertinage,* profanity, and atheism. It is not clear whether Rabelais purposely, and three times, substituted an "n" for an "m" in *âme,* making "ass" [*âne*] out of the word for "soul" . . . or whether it truly was a printer's error. Fortunately for Rabelais, the king laughed along with other readers. But not the scholars at the Sorbonne, about whom he had made jibes in his work.

Wheeler mentions that Rabelais was denounced as heretical by the clergy for his satires, not only on their order but on their creed. Coleridge said of him, "Beyond a doubt he was among the deepest as well as boldest thinkers of his age." McCabe notes that when Rabelais was "at last condemned, the Pope was induced to overlook his terrible crime on the ground of what are now said to be the most obscene books in European literature, and on condition that he promised to return to the monastery (which he never did)." McCabe continues that it "is now generally said that his works should not be regarded as obscene because he merely wished to laugh the world out of its murderous religious passion. As if he could not get men to laugh at less gross jokes! He did not care a pin about religion and its moral code." Robertson suggests that a reasonable inference as to his general creed is that Rabelais was a deist or a unitarian. However, and to save him from being persecuted as a heretic, Cardinal Jean du Bellay arranged for Rabelais to spend his last years as curate at Meudon (1550–1552).

"All attempts have been made," Walter Besant has written, "to prove that Rabelais was a Christian," which Besant denied. Rather, he stated, "the old man, now that life was drawing to its close, now that his friends were dead, dispersed, and in exile, discerned at last the wickedness of continuing to say masses, which were to him empty forms, in the cause of a Church which was full of absurdities and corruptions."

Many of his friends had perished in prison or at the stake. Rabelais, however, died a natural death in his bed, Foote has described. His end came at a house in the Rue des Jardins, Paris. Many stories were told of his death-bed, and may be found in the bibliophile Jacob's (Paul Lacroix) introduction to the Charpentier edition of Rabelais' works. When he had received the extreme unction, he said aloud that they had greased his boots for the great journey. When the priest in attendance asked if he believed in the real presence of Jesus Christ in the holy wafer, he replied meekly "I believe in it, and I rejoice therein; for I think I see my God as he was when he entered Jerusalem triumphant and seated on an ass." Toward the end they put on his Benedictine robe, whereupon he punned upon a Psalm: *Beati qui moriuntur in Domino* [Blessed are they who die in the Lord). When a messenger from Cardinal du Bellay arrived, Rabelais said in a feeble voice, "Tell monsignor I am going to seek the great Perhaps." Gathering his strength for a last effort, he cried out in a burst of laughter, "Draw the curtain, the farce is over."

Although the story may be apocryphal, Jacob remarks, they are "in keeping with the character of Rabelais and the spirit of his writings." {BDF; CE; FO; JM; JMR; JMRH; RE}

Rabl, Carl (1853–1917)

Rabl taught anatomy, in succession, at Vienna, Prague, and Leipzig universities. He was director of the Anatomical Institute at Leipzig, a member of the Privy Council, and recipient of many national and international honors. He was one of the first to defend Haeckel against the charge of "forgery," and in *Was Wir Ernst Haeckel Verdanken* Rabl tells how Haeckel had converted him to rationalism in his youth. {RAT; RE}

RACE, RACISM

• It's good that there are yellow Frenchmen, black Frenchmen, brown Frenchmen. They show that France is open to all races—but so long as they remain a small minority. Otherwise France would no longer be France.

–Charles deGaulle,
First President of France's Fifth Republic, in 1959

• [Aviation is] a gift from heaven . . . a tool specially shaped for Western hands . . . one of those priceless possessions which permit the White race to live at all in a pressing sea of Yellow, Black and Brown."

–Charles Lindbergh
in a *Readers Digest* (1939) article

Genesis explains how Noah, after the deluge, divided the world among his three sons. Japheth received Europe, Shem got Asia, and Ham was given Africa. Ham got the worst of the property for two reasons: first, he had accidentally seen his father's nakedness when he walked into a tent; and second, he had disobeyed Noah's order that on the ark everyone was supposed to be sexually continent—Ham, however, with the aid of a magic demon had slept with his wife, and the punishment was that Ham and all his offspring were given a black skin. The black race, in short, is a symbol of Ham's having broken a taboo, according to the author or authors of *Genesis.*

The ancient Greeks, however, had no word for race. A slave could be of any color, depending on who had been captured. Herodotus described Thracians as having blue eyes and Egyptians as being dark-skinner and woolly haired. Egyptian men were described as liking cats and as urinating while sitting down rather than standing up. It is only recently that the growing biological evidence indicates that race has virtually no scientific meaning at all.

The idea of race, according to David R. Roediger's *Black on White: Black Writers on What It Means to be White* (1998), came about because social meaning became attached to physical differences. White Europeans gave such meaning an inherent, God-given origin, and Americans kept up the tradition. Roediger's and other scholars' work holds that the label of race evolved recently as a tool of the vanquished as well as the victors. Race formerly was thought to be inborn, journalist Ethan Bronner has suggested (*The New York Times,* 10 January 1998), with some arguing that skin color or facial structure was a window on internal characteristics like wile or listlessness or intelligence. Now, scholars tend to argue the opposite, that race is a tool invented by white Europeans to justify their conquests.

The losers, meanwhile, thought of their conquerors in racial terms. In the 17th century, for example, the Chinese often depicted Europeans as having tails. Nancy Shoemaker in an *American Historical Review* article showed that the Cherokee Indians, especially those of the Southeast, called themselves red out of pride, eager to differentiate themselves from black slaves.

In the past, some Americans have erroneously used the word "race" to refer to "religion or nationality," speaking, for example, about the Catholic race, the Jewish race, the French race, the German race. Today, however, the word is almost exclusively used to refer to the purported major biological divisions of humanity—the Caucasoid, Mongoloid, and Negroid. Inasmuch as a number of groups—the Australian aborigines, the Dravidian people of South India, the Polynesians, and the Ainu of Northern Japan, to name four—do not fit into the three arbitrary groups, some anthropologists reject the concept of race outright. They stress, instead, the heterogeneity of the world's population.

The *Columbia Encyclopedia*, surveying the subject, states that it is inappropriate to apply *race* to national, religious, geographic, linguistic, or cultural groups, nor can the biological criteria of race be equated with any mental characteristics such as intelligence, personality, or character.

In the 17th century, after scholars first began to separate types of flora and fauna, Johann Friedrich Blumenbach was the first to divide mankind according to skin color. In the 19th and early 20th century, Joseph Arthur Gobineau and Houston Stewart Chamberlain held that some groups are superior to others and attributed cultural and psychological values to race. Such an approach, called racism, culminated in the vicious racial doctrines of Nazi Germany, and especially in anti-Semitism. The same approach complicated the integration movement in the United States and was the foundation of South Africa's segregation policies. Numbers of individuals continue to refer to the "Jewish race," as if the black entertainer Sammy Davis Jr. and

Rabbi Herman Wouk are of the same race. Commentators are heard to refer to "fighting between Latinos and Jews."

Racism in Canada has been described in Cecil Foster's *A Place Called Heaven: The Meaning of Being Black in Canada* (1996) and in Frances Henry's *The Caribbean Diaspora in Toronto: Learning to Live with Racism* (1994).

The international as well as the national humanist organizations are united in their total abhorrence of racism. In 1993 the International Humanist and Ethical Union (IHEU) board went on record:

> Humanists disagree with and reject any kind of racism and Nazism. . . . As humanists we hold the opinion that an active fight for values is the best way of counteracting the indifference among people, which enables racists and neo-nazis to get approval of their outlook towards people with a different colour or a different ethnic or cultural background. We do not believe that this problem can be solved by keeping it in the dark. . . .

Race comes in colors, according to Henry Louis Gates's *Colored People* (1995), who calls himself colored rather than African American: dark chocolate, coffee, café au lait, cherrywood, light-yellow, almost orange, tan, beige, blue-black, slate, and octoroon ("light and bright and damn near white").

Yale geneticist Kenneth K. Kidd, however, says,

> In lectures, I now say that human races do not exist if by race you mean a discrete category, a qualitatively different subgroup of humanity. When I look at DNA, I see no racial differences. There tend to be more DNA variations within each population group than between groups, and such variation is present broadly around the world within every population. This contradicts conventional wisdom of earlier this century when there was a tendency to think of population as monomorphic with rare variants.

"All in the Family," an American television program, spoofed two WASPs [White Anglo-Saxon Protestants] who might be called the pigment-hewed as contrasted with the melanin-impaired:

Archie Bunker: And that's why they aren't white, meat-head! That's why you never see a white gorilla or a white chimpanzee!

Mike: Oh yeah? I think I'm looking at one right now.

(See entries for Jewish Nose; Man; Khalid Muhhamad; Noah; and Alexander Pashinski.) {CE; *Humanist in Canada*, Winter 1998-1999}

Rachel, Julia (20th Century)

Rachel is Vice President in Georgia for Internal Communications of the Atlanta Freethought Society.

Rachmaninoff, Sergei Vasilyevich (1873-1943)

A pianist, composer, and conductor, Rachmaninoff was one of the greatest pianists of his generation. He conducted the Imperial Opera (1905-1906). In 1917 he left Russia, never to return, moving to Switzerland and immigrating to the United States, living in Manhattan on West End Avenue, and becoming a citizen shortly before his death. His compositions' massive chords and dramatic chord progressions make his work popular. The second (1901) of his four piano concertos and the "Prelude in C Sharp Minor" (1892) are his best-known works. He also wrote "Rhapsody on a Theme of Paganini" (1934) and many other works.

Neither he nor his friend Tchaikovsky, according to the program notes when the Kirov Opera Chorus performed in 1998 in New York City, "expressed anything approaching religious fervor." {CE}

Radcliffe, Elizabeth (20th Century)

Radcliffe, of Santa Clara University, is on the Executive Committee of The Hume Society, a group engaged in scholarly activity concerning David Hume.

Radenhausen, Christian (Born 1813)

Radenhausen was a German philosopher, at first a merchant, then a lithographer who lived in Hamburg. He published his *Isis, Mankind and the World* (4 volumes, 1870–1872); *Osiris* (1874); *Christianity is Heathenism* (1881); and *The True Bible and the False* (1887). {BDF}

Radest, Howard (1928–)

Radest, a graduate of New York City public schools and Columbia College, became Leader of the Bergen, New Jersey, Ethical Society in 1956. He signed Humanist Manifesto II and from 1971 to 1973 was a professor of philosophy at Ramapo College in New Jersey. He became a director of Ethical Culture Schools in 1979. He also is Dean of the Leadership-Training Institute of the Northern American Committee for Humanism (NACH) and is one of the "Troika" of co-chairmen of the IHEU, which includes Bert Schwarz of Holland and Mihaelo Markovic of Yugoslavia. Radest's *Toward Common Ground: The Story of the Ethical Societies in the United States* (1969) is the definitive work to date on the topic.

Radest is the founding dean of the Humanist Institute and also founded Columbia University's Seminar on Moral Education. He is on the editorial board of *The Humanist* and is a contributing editor of *Free Inquiry*. He once was secretary general of the International Humanist and Ethical Union (IHEU), and from 1964 to 1970 was executive director of the American Ethical Union. The proceedings of the 1970 International Humanist Congress he edited as *To Seek a Humane World.*

The Devil and Secular Humanism: The Children of the Enlightenment (1990) is somewhat pessimistic, lamenting that humanists are committed to anti-clericalism, reason, progress, science, and democracy but fail to supply individuals with their heartfelt needs. Heir to the legacy of Felix Adler, Radest holds that somewhere around 1973, with the issuance of *Humanist Manifesto II*, the humanist movement toned down the religious humanism which had been an early influence going back to the 1941 founding of the American Humanist Association. He laments secular humanists' being "raucous" and "strident" in their protests, believing that anti-clericalism is in "bad taste" and is apt to "alienate liberal allies." Radest believes that "It is the radical claim of humanism that we can live rich and full lives while denying eternity. It is the even more radical claim that such lives are more satisfying precisely because they come closer to truthfulness and do not rely on illusions." However, he differs with the Council for Secular Humanism and *Free Inquiry* that what is now needed is a thoroughly secular, atheist, or agnostic humanism, one that cuts the umbilical cord of religion and religiosity. Radest is on the editorial advisory board of *Religious Humanism*, the quarterly published by the Fellowship of Religious Humanists.

At the Seventh International Humanist and Ethical Union (IHEU) World Congress held in London (1978) and at the Tenth held in Buffalo (1988), Prof. Radest addressed the groups. Two of his books are *Understanding Ethical Religion* (1958) and *On Life and Meaning* (1963). He has retired as Director of the Ethical Culture Schools in New York. In 1993, he received the American Humanist Association's Distinguished Service Award. Radest signed Humanist Manifesto 2000. (See entry for Ethical Culture. {CL; EU; *Free Inquiry*, Fall, 1991; FUS, HSN2}

RADFORD UNIVERSITY HUMANISTS

Radford University (Virginia) humanists and freethinkers are on the Web: <www.secularhumanism.org/cfa/orgs.html>.

Radhakrishnan, Sarvepalli [Sir] (1888–1975)

An Indian statesman and philosopher, Radhakrishnan declared, "It is not God that is worshiped but the group or authority that claims to speak in His name. Sin becomes disobedience to authority, not violation of integrity." {TYD}

RADICAL

Radical, a word the Latin root of which (*radix*) means *root*, is used by many conservatives to depict some kind of scary revolutionary whose nihilism might include blowing up buildings—if an idea is different from the usual, to them it is *radical.*

Radical, however, is used by rationalists to describe going to the root of a problem; e.g., "Choose the radical solution of starting all over again."

Radix is the root of *radish*, a plant the roots of which are preferred by diners over the upper portions. Rationalists, those known for going to the roots of problems, can rightfully be called radicals, individuals who prefer going to primary sources rather than simply accepting what appears on the surface.

RADICAL HUMANIST

Radical Humanist, a journal in English of the Indian Radical Humanist Association, is in Mumbai [formerly Bombay] at Sassoon Building, 1st Floor, 143 Mahatma Gandhi Road near Kalaghoda, Fort, Mumbai 400 001, India. R. A. Jahagirdar is editor and V. M. Tarkunde is Editor Emeritus. <mrcssc@bom2.vsnl.net.in>. (See entry for M. N. Roy.)

RADICALISM

• Radicalism, n. The conservation of to-morrow injected into the affairs of today.

–Ambrose Bierce
The Devil's Dictionary

Radicati, Albert (18th Century)

Radicati, Count of Passeron, was an Italian who lived for a time in England. His *Twelve discourses concerning Religion and Government* (1734) states, ". . . to say that Deists are Atheists is false; for they that are so called by the Vulgar, and by those whose interest it is to decry them, admit a first cause under the names of God, Nature, Eternal Being, Matter, universal Motion, or Soul. Such were Democritus, Epicurus, Diagoras, Lucian, Socrates, Anaxagoras, Seneca, Hobbes, Blount, Spinoza, Vanini, St. Évremond, Bayle, Collins, and in general all that go under the name of Speculative Atheists; and none but fools or madmen can ever deny it."

Radicati's philosophical dissertation reveals his pantheistic materialism. He shocked his contemporaries by openly advocating suicide and free love. He also held that men "are not blamable for the crimes they commit, since they are always forced either by education or habit to commit them." Deists and moderate freethinkers alike attacked much of his thought. {BDF; HAB}

RADOGAST

In an early Slavic religion, Radogast was the god of the sun. {LEE}

Rafferty, James A. (1921–)

Rafferty, when he signed Humanist Manifesto II, was a lecturer at the USIU School of Human Behavior. {HM2}

Rafton, Harold R. (20th Century)

A scientist, Rafton in 1954 was President of the Humanist Fellowship of Boston, as well as a member of its board of directors. He was vice president of the American Humanist Association at the time Priscilla Robertson was fired as editor of *The Humanist*. In fact, he and John Kirk were the ones who moved that she be terminated. It was a time during which the board was concerned that the magazine was moving in a more topical or issues-oriented direction rather than being philosophically oriented and featuring articles which explained the principles of humanism.

Whenever asked if he believed in a Supreme Being, Rafton was known to answer, "Yes, Mankind." {HNS; HNS2}

Rafton, Helen (20th Century)

Mrs. Helen Rafton, wife of Harold Rafton, was a member of the American Humanist Association. {HNS}

Raglan (John Somerset FitzRoy) [5th Baron] (20th Century)

Lord Raglan is an Honorary Associate of the National Secular Society. He was president of the United Kingdom Housing Trust from 1983 to 1989 and is Chairman of the Bugatti Owners Club.

Those who look him up in *Who's Who* are amused that he lists his avocation as being that of a mechanic for his Bugatti.

Ragon, Jean Marie de (1781–1862)

Ragon was a French Freemason, by profession a civil engineer at Nancy. He became Chief of Bureau to the Minister of the Interior. Author of many books on Freemasonry, he wrote *The Mass and Its Mysteries Compared with the Ancient Mysteries* (1844). {BDF}

Ragsdale, J. Arthur (20th Century)

Ragsdale edited *The Story of a Humanist Church* (c. 1970). {GS}

Raines, Barbara (20th Century)

Raines, a teacher of science long active in Ethical Society groups, became in 1960 the Leader of the West Coast Council for Ethical Culture, where she specialized in humanistic psychology. She returned briefly to leadership in Northern Westchester in 1970. (See entry for Ethical Culture.)

RAISON PRÉSENTE

A French quarterly, *Raison Présente* is at 14 rue de l'Ecole-Polytechnique, 75005 Paris, France.

Rajala, Eric (20th Century)

Rajala is a case manager at Transitional Living Services, which helps people with a diagnosed mental illness. The editor of *Chile Verde*, the newsletter of New Mexico's Green Party, he has written about freethought in a variety of journals. In 1997 he became a senior writer for *The American Rationalist.*

Raj-Gauthier, Rupert (20th Century)

Raj-Gauthier has been Secretary of the Humanist Association of Canada. Also, he was a contributing editor of *Qwer Quarterly*, newsletter of North America's lesbian and gay secular humanist group. At the 1994 Toronto Conference of the Coalition for Secular Humanism, Atheism, and Freethought (CSHAFT), Raj-Gauthier spoke on "Humanism and Spirituality."

Raleigh or Ralegh, Walter [Sir] (1554?–1618)

A courtier, poet, and adventurer, Raleigh was a leading soldier and explorer of his time. He served (1569) as a volunteer in the Huguenot army in France. His 1592 expedition returned to England with a richly loaded Portuguese sailing ship known as a carrack. In 1592, he searched for El Dorado on an expedition up the Orinoco River in Guiana. Later, he sat in Parliament.

Because of his connection with the poetic group known as the "school of night," led by Thomas Harriot and including Christopher Marlowe and George Chapman, he was accused by many, including the Jesuits, of being an atheist. In The Lie Raleigh had written self-defensively, "Go tell the Church it shows what's good, and doth no good."

Robertson, after researching Raleigh's writings, considers Raleigh "a deist, given to free discussion." But in Raleigh's History of the World (1614), written in the Tower, if it is authentic, Raleigh makes clear his belief in deity and repudiates atheism and pantheism: "I do also account it an impiety monstrous, to confound God and Nature, be it but in terms." Queen Elizabeth, however, reportedly called Raleigh an atheist. In 1899 papers by Thomas Kyd were found in which Kyd, who had been arrested for atheism, said he got the papers from Marlowe and denied all sympathy with the views expressed. However, F. S. Boas in *Fortnightly Review* (1899) concluded that the material was a vehement Unitarian argument on Scriptural grounds and was much more likely to have been written by Francis Kett than by Marlowe. Whatever the facts, it was a time when rationalism was becoming more and more popular and a time when persecution of non-believers increased the zeal of those who objected to such persecutions.

Accused of treason, Raleigh in a relaxed manner approached the scaffold, spoke to the crowd of the charges against him and explained why they were flimsy, then asked the executioner to show the ax. "Dost thou think I am afraid of it?" he said, running his hand along the blade. Biographers H. D. Selincourt and E. Thompson then report that he said of the ax, "This is a sharp medicine, but it is a physician for all diseases. When I stretch forth my hands, dispatch me." Lying down, he stretched out his arms, and when the executioner hesitated Raleigh cried, "Strike, man, strike!" It took two blows, and all was finished. {CE; JMR; JMRH; TRI; TYD}

Rall, Ted (20th Century)

A columnist and a cartoonist, Rall wrote *Revenge of the Lathchkey Kids* (1998), which contains a chapter on his non-religious views. On the Web: <http://www.rall.com>. {CA}

Ram, Joachim Gerhard (17th Century)

Ram was a Holstein philosopher who was accused of being an atheist. {BDF}

RAMADAN: See entry for Islam.

Ramaer, Anton Gerard Willem (1812–1867)

Ramaer was a Dutch writer, an officer in the Dutch army in 1829. He wrote on Schopenhauer and others, contributed to *De Dageraad*, and often used the pseudonym of "Laçhmé." {BDF}

Ramamurthi, M. V. (Died 1998)

In Hyderabad, Ramamurthi was editor of the monthly *Vikasam* in Telugu from 1975 until his death. Also, he published widely in English and Telugu on humanism, rationalism, and secularism. He was a lawyer, one of India's early radical humanists who worked along with M. N. Roy, and one of his country's leading radical humanists. Ramamurthy was a president of the Indian Radical Humanist Association, and he was chairperson of the Indian Rationalist Association. (See entry for his wife, Malladi Subbamma.) {FUK}

Ramanthan, S. (20th Century)

Ramanthan, who was minister for information in Rajaji's Congress Cabinet of Madras Presidency in 1937, strengthened the rationalists' Self-Respect Movement, which formed part and parcel of the Non-Brahmin Movement of South India. Famed as a rationalist in the Madras State Government in the 1950s, Ramanthan was a founding member of the Indian Rationalist Association and acted as its president until 1958.

Ramaswamy, E. V. (20th Century): See entry for G. Vijayam.

Rambaud, Alfred Nicolas (1842–1905)

Rambaud was an authority on Russian, entrusted by France with Government missions. He was a key person in bringing about the Franco-Russian *entente*. Rambaud during the period of secularization taught contemporary history at Paris University, and he wrote *Histoire de la civilization générale français* (1887, 2 volumes). A rationalist, Rambaud worked cordially against the Church. {RAM; RE}

Ramée, Marie Louise de la (Ouida) (1839–1908)

Although the family name was **Ramé**, Ramée changed her name to de la Ramée. She moved from France to London in 1859, where she adopted the pen name of "Ouida," a reference to a child's lisping pronunciation of Louisa. She was an ardent humanitarian, an anti-vivisectionist, and a disdainful opponent of Christianity. "Of all powerless things on earth," she wrote, "Christianity is the most useless. . . . Christianity has made of death a terror which was unknown to the gay calmness of the pagan." She spared neither Catholic nor Protestant and was caustic about the "cant" to which they give birth. Her *Views and Opinions* (1895) has a chapter entitled "The Failure of Christianity." She moved to Italy from 1860 and in 1874 settled in Florence, where she wrote *Under Two Flags* (1867). Her *Folle-Farine* (1871), according to Bulwer-Lytton was "a triumph of modern English fiction." All told, de la Ramée wrote forty-five novels, often set in a world far removed from reality and showing a spirit of rebellion against the moral ideals reflected in much of the fiction of the time. When her literary profits declined and she fell into debt, de la Ramée in 1894 moved to Lucca, then until her death lived in destitution in Viareggio. David Tribe has classified her as an outright freethinker. {BDF; OEL, RAT; RE; TRI; TYD}

Ramée, Pierre de la (1515–1572)

Called Ramus, Ramée was a French humanist. He attacked the doctrines of Aristotle, was accused of impiety, and his work was suppressed in 1543. Ramée lost his life in the massacre of St. Bartholomew, 26 August 1572. {BDF; WWS}

Ramendra (20th Century)

Dr. Ramendra, a reader in the department of philosophy at Patna College, Patna University, founded the Bihar Buddhiwadi [Rationalist] Samaj [Society] with his wife Dr. **Kawaljeet** in 1985. In 1996 he founded the Buddhiwadi Foundation, a non-profit, tax-exempt educational trust that promotes rationalist-humanism and works to eradicate blind faith and superstition. Dr. Kawaljeet is the managing trustee of the organization.

The two are writing *Rationalist, Humanist, and Atheistic Trends in Twentieth Century Indian Thought*, a work which will contain life-sketches and philosophies of eight thinkers: Periyar, M. N. Roy, Ambedkar, Gora, Kovoor, A. B. Shaw, Narsingh Narain, and Ramswaroop Verma.

He is author of *Why I Am Not a Hindu and Why I Do Not Want Ramrajya* (1995) and *Is God Dead?* (*Kya Ishwar Mar Chuka Hai?* 1998). The latter work defends atheism by showing that the idea of "god" obstructs the growth of knowledge and morality. Ramendra can be found on the Web at <www.myfreeoffice.com/buddhiwadi>.

Ramírez, Ignacio (1818–1879)

Ramirez, who was influenced by José Luis Maria Mora, was a liberal who led attacks on the power and influence of the church in Mexico. He passed the reform laws that suppressed monasteries in Mexico, which earned him the name *El nigromante* (the necromancer) for his alleged atheism. {EU}

Ramon y Cajal, Santiago (1852–1934)

A Spanish histologist, Ramon y Cajal won the Nobel Prize in 1906. He taught anatomy at Valencia, Barcelona, and Madrid universities. In spite of his position, Ramon y Cajal was an outspoken materialist and wrote a manual of science for Ferrer's atheistic schools. Inasmuch as his research chiefly concerned brain and nerve tissue, he played a part in expelling mysticism from physiology and psychology. {RAT; RE}

Rampal, Jean-Pierre Louis (1922–)

Rampal, the distinguished French flutist, has appeared throughout the world. In 1956 he received the *Oscar du Premier Virtuose Français*; in 1969, Prix Edison; and in 1978, Prix Leonie Sonning. Rampal wrote a children's book, *La flûte* (1978), and in autobiographical materials he cited his atheism. {CA; E}

Ramsay, William [Sir] (1852–1916)

The discoverer of helium, Ramsay was a Scottish chemist whose early experiments showed that the alkaloids are related to pyridine, which he synthesized (1876) from acetylene and prussic acid. With Rayleigh, he discovered argon, and, with M. W. Travers, krypton, neon, and xenon. Ramsay also carried on research concerning radium emanation. In 1902 he was knighted and in 1904 he received the Nobel Prize in Chemistry. His Christian biographer, Filden, admitted that Sir William was an agnostic with a tinge of mysticism and no belief in a future life. However, he used theistic phrases and in 1908 wrote to a friend, "Life has been pretty good to us—perhaps I should say 'God.' I feel inclined to." {CE; JM; RAT; RE}

Ramsey, William James (1844–1916)

Ramsey became a freethinker early in life, for he was the son of a freethinking, Chartist shoemaker. But when his family moved to Norwich, he sang in the cathedral choir. Upon hearing Bradlaugh in Norwich in 1859, Ramsey returned to being a freethinker and joined the Reform League in London, being present at the "storming" of Hyde Park in 1866. He was a founding member at the Old Street Hall of Science, where he was a regular chairman at Sunday lectures. In 1877 after having been a shoemaker, he became manager of the Freethought Publishing Company for Bradlaugh and Besant. Charged with blasphemy in 1883, he was sentenced along with Foote to nine months in the jail at Holloway. In the 1890s he founded the Freethought Federation, then edited the *Jerusalem Star* (1895–1896) under the pseudonym "Le Vitty Cuss." In 1906 he worked to secure the return of his old Reform League colleague, W. R. Cremer, as M.P. for Hackney. {BDF; FUK; RAT; RSR; TRI; WSS}

Ranc, Arthur (1831–1908)

Ranc was a French writer and deputy who had been brought up by his parents as a freethinker and Republican. He took the prize for philosophy at the College of Poitiers and studied law at Paris. Upon conspiring with C. Delescluze against the Second Empire, he was imprisoned but escaped to Geneva. Ranc collaborated on *La Marseillaise*, was elected on the Municipal Council of Paris in 1871, and became a Deputy in 1873. Ranc wrote *Under the Empire* and other political works. {BDF; RAT}

Rancie, Norman (1888–1968)

Rancie was an Australian freethinker, atheist, and anarcho-syndicalist. Like his father, J. R. Rancie, he was a member of the Australasian Secular Association. In the early Free Speech battles, Rancie was one of the first to be arrested. He joined the Industrial Workers of the World in 1915 and edited their journal, *Direct Action*, for two years. Rancie was critical of all politicians, maintained a militant atheism, and upheld his individual brand of idealism throughout his life. {SWW}

Rand, Anthony F. (20th Century)

Rand, when he signed Humanist Manifesto II, was president of the Humanist Society of Greater Detroit. {HM2}

Rand, Ayn (1905–1982)

Alice Rosenbaum was born in St. Petersburg to a nonobservant Jewish family. Upon arriving in the United States, she renamed herself Ayn (rhymes with "nine") after a Finnish woman whose work she had read. Later, living in Chicago, she decided to change her last name but keep the initials. Looking at her Remington-Rand typewriter, she decided upon Ayn Remington, later choosing Rand.

An atheist at the age of thirteen, Rand became *the* philosopher of objectivism—she appropriated the term "objective" from the Marxist regime she had fled. Many defined it as a dog-eat-dog outlook, Gore Vidal describing her philosophy as "nearly perfect in its immorality." Rand was best known for her novels, *The Fountainhead* (1943) and *Atlas Shrugged* (1957). For college students in the 1950s and 1960s Rand became something of a cult figure. By 1965 courses on her books and ideas were offered in eighty cities, and many started subscribing to her newsletter, *The Objectivist*.

She opposed the altruism of welfare states and espoused a rational self-interest that included a woman's right to have an abortion. As for underdogs, she once told an audience at West Point,

> Today's mawkish concern with and compassion for the feeble, the flawed, the suffering, the guilty is a cover for the profoundly Kantian hatred of the innocent, the strong, the able, the successful, the virtuous, the confident, the happy.

Basically, she believed that selfishness is a virtue, that altruism is a vice, that laissez-faire capitalism is our best possible choice:

> Since politics is a branch of philosophy, objectivism advocates certain political principles—specifically those of laissez-faire capitalism.

According to Corliss Lamont, in this outlook she suffers from "the reductive fallacy," in which philosophers or others oversimplify by illegitimately classifying certain multiple phenomena under one category. Rand's self-interest fallacy, he says, makes this popular novelist an individual "with philosophic pretensions and semantic naiveté." Others have noted that the "Me Generation" of the 1970s found appealing her "rational selfishness," and she has a large following among many atheists. One who definitely disliked her was the architect, Frank Lloyd Wright, whom she allegedly depicted in *The Fountainhead.* (Some insist, however, that it was another architect that she had in mind). John Galt, the heroic fictional architect in *Atlas Shrugged* complained that

> We are on strike against self-immolation. We are on strike against the creed of unearned rewards and unrewarded duties. We are on strike against the dogma that the pursuit of one's happiness is evil. We are on strike against the doctrine that life is guilt.

Of religion, she wrote much, including the following:

> Religion . . . is the first enemy of the ability to think. That ability is not used by men to one-tenth of its possibility, yet before they learn to think they are discouraged by being ordered to take things on faith. Faith is the worse curse of mankind, as the exact antithesis and enemy of thought.
>
> For centuries, the mystics of spirit had existed by running a protection racket—by making life on earth unbearable, then charging you for consolation and relief, by forbidding all the virtues that make existence possible, then riding on the shoulders of your guilt, by declaring production and joy to be sins, then collecting blackmail from the sinners.

Martin Seymour-Smith, a critic, is quite explicit: "Unfortunately her crypto-totalitarian and ultra-simplistic ideas have had some influence on the conservatively bred young, since they allow people to be ruthless without a bad conscience. Her 'philosophy' is capitalistic-Superman (as in the figure in the comics): the 'great' men are those who use others, in the name of 'reason,' with an enlightened ruthlessness." As icing on the cake, he adds, *The Fountainhead*—like her other books—is offensively ill written ('pedestrian, pockmarked with short, clipped staccato sentences')."

While working on a Cecil B. DeMille set, she encountered an extra, Frank O'Connor, with whom she reportedly had a sexy relationship. Their eventual marriage included her calling him "Cubbyhole" and his calling her "Kitten Fluff," details brought out in "Ayn Rand: A Sense of Life," a movie produced and directed in 1998 by Michael Paxton. The movie shows her as being a histrionically proud figure who loved attention, "tiddlywink music," and movie star Gary Cooper.

Atlas Shrugged was dedicated to Nathaniel Branden, who she told both her husband and Branden's wife that they were going to sleep together. Branden, who became her principal heir, reportedly lost interest in Rand sexually—she was 61 and he was 36—and began a relationship with a younger woman. According to Stephen M. Silverman (*Where There's a Will*, 1991), Rand found out about it in 1967 and not only cut him and his wife out of her life but also cut him out of the will. The final estate was valued at $877,000., all of which went to a close associate, Leonard Peikoff, a disciple who had kept in touch with her daily for the last four years of her life.

Rand's *New York Times* obituary was written by Edwin McDowell, who described her belief that "selfishness was good and altruism evil," and that the welfare of society must always be subordinate to individual self-interest. Objectivism was described as a belief in "the concept of man as a heroic being, with his own happiness as the moral purpose of life."

Rand's final services were held in Manhattan's Frank E. Campbell Funeral Home, where she was laid out next to a six-foot-high dollar sign, her favorite symbol. The services were followed by a private burial at which mourners dropped flowers into the grave. Kipling's "If" was read, as it had also been read at her husband Frank's memorial. (See entries for Libertarian, Leonard Peikoff, and Jeff Walker.) {CE; CL; EU, William F. Ryan; *Objectivist Newsletter*, Issue #1, 1962; Stephen M. Silverman, *Where There's a Will*, 1991; TYD; WWS}

Randall, James A. (20th Century)

Randall wrote "A Paper on the Life and Character of Mr. Thomas Paine" (1909). {GS}

Randall, James G. (20th Century)

Randall is a contributing editor to *Freethought Today*. At the 14th annual HUMCON conference sponsored in 1994 by the Alliance of Humanist, Atheist, and Ethical Culture Organizations of Los Angeles County, California, he told of his lawsuits against the Boy Scouts, charging the organization with religious discrimination. A lawyer, he has defended cases for individuals who have been forced to pray in schools or otherwise been forced into religious conformity.

Randall Jr., John Herman (1899–1980)

A professor of philosophy at Columbia University and a former editor of the *Journal of Philosophy*, Randall signed both Humanist Manifesto I and II. In the 1950s, he was on the advisory board of Charles Francis Potter's First Humanist Society of New York and of the Ethical Culture Society. Among his books are *The Problem of Group Responsibility* (1922), *Making of the Modern Mind* (1926), *The Philosophy of Paul Tillich* (1952), *The Role of Knowledge in Western Religion* (1958), and *The Meaning of Religion for Man* (1968). Randall was President from 1966 to 1967 of the Metaphysics Society of America, editor of the *Journal of History of Ideas*, and joint editor of the *Journal of Philosophy*.

Edwin H. Wilson in *The Genesis of a Humanist Manifesto* (1995) has described Randall's significant contributions and tells of his correspondence with both Bragg and Wilson. {CL; HM1; HM2; HNS; HNS2; PK}

Randello, Cosimo (19th Century)

Author of *The Simple Story of a Great Fraud*, Randello was an Italian critic of the origin of Christianity. His book was directed against Pauline theology and was published in Milan in 1882. {BDF}

Rane, M. A. (20th Century)

Rane was secretary of the Indian Rationalist Association from 1957 to 1958.

Randi, James (1928–)

Randi is a Canadian-born writer, educator, and magician whose given name is Randall James Hamilton Zwinge. With Bert Sugar, he wrote *Houdini, His Life and Art* (1976). An internationally known conjurer and a skeptic, Randi lectures on paranormal subjects. *Flim-Flam* (1981) and *The Truth About Uri Geller* (1975) are two of his books. His work in exposing fraudulent faith healers has won him awards from the Council for Democratic and Secular Humanism, and he is a fellow of the Committee for the Scientific Investigation of Claims of the Paranormal. In 1989, he wrote *The Faith Healers*, an exposé, in which he offered to give $1,000. to anyone providing evidence of healing through prayer. His criteria for a cure by faith:

- The disease must not be normally self-terminating.
- The recovery must be complete.
- The recovery must take place in the absence of any medical treatment that might normally be expected to affect the disease.
- There must be adequate medical opinion that the disease was present before the application of whatever means were used to bring about the miracle.
- There must be adequate medical opinion that the disease is not present after the application of whatever means were used to bring about the miracle.

No one yet has claimed this money despite its having been successively augmented by others. When he informs believers that he is not a believer, he finds they usually are "infuriated by such a response....{They} usually turn away and leave ringing in the air a declaration that there is just no point in trying to reason with me and that I will be 'prayed for.' I have no need of this patronization, nor of such a condescending attutide, and I resent it. I consider such an action to be a feeble defense for a baseless superstition and a retreat from reality."

In *The Mask of Nostradamus* (1990), Randi unmasks the 16th-century astrologer, including among other points that in the prophecy game it is important to make *lots* of predictions and hope that at least some of them come true. In addition to being on the editorial board of *The Humanist*, the "Amazing Randi" is principal investigator of the Council for Secular Humanism's Faith-Healing Investigation Project.

Arthur C. Clarke wrote an introduction to Randi's *An Encyclopedia of Claims, Frauds, and Hoaxes of the Occult and Supernatural* (1995), a volume that alphabetically presents hundreds of entries, with cross-references, on topics such as the paranormal, supernatural, occult and mysticism, and fringes of science. On the Web: <http://www.randi.org>. {CA; E}

Randolph, A(sa) Philip (1889–1979)

Son of a Methodist minister, Randolph was influenced by Karl Marx and the Socialist Party's vision of the nobility of the masses. In 1917 as editor of *The Messenger*, he called upon black men to refuse military service, leading President Woodrow Wilson to call him the most dangerous Negro in America. Although never a porter himself, Randolph became the formidable chief of the International Brotherhood of Sleeping Car Porters, won wage increases, won shorter hours, and in 1935 obtained the group's admission to the American Federation of Labor.

In 1941 when Randolph announced that he would lead tens of thousands of his constituents in a protest march on the White House, President Franklin D. Roosevelt told him, "Questions like this have sociological implications. They can't be gotten at with hammer and tongs. They can't be settled with marches." Randolph remained unswayed. "You can't bring 100,000 Negroes to Washington. We can't have that," said Roosevelt. Randolph remained unswayed. So Roosevelt sighed, picked up a pen and signed an order establishing the Fair Employment Practices Commission, arguably the single most important decree since the 13th Amendment.

According to Norm Allen Jr., Randolph may have listed himself in *Who's Who* as a Methodist, but he did so to avoid public criticism of his outlook of secularism and humanism. He also listed himself as a Mason. "We consider prayer as nothing but a fervent wish," he declared while being the civil rights leader and founder of the railway porters union. Malcolm X, who once alleged that all leaders of black communities are muddled, added that he found Randolph "the least confused." Randolph's photo was once on the cover of the Black Muslim's *Muhammad Speaks* (1963).

Randolph signed Humanist Manifesto II. In 1970, the American Humanist Association named Randolph Humanist of the Year. {HM2; HNS2; Jae Maeder, New York *Daily News*, 15 March 1999; TYD}

Randolph, Vance (1892–1980)

A Midwesterner and an authority on Ozark culture and folklore, Randolph worked in Girard, Kansas, at the newspaper, *Appeal to Reason*. Some of his off-color Ozark folk stories are found in *Pissing in the Snow* (1976). Whitehead and Muhrer, in their *Freethought on the American Frontier*, include "The Infidel's Grave," a story from Randolph's *The Devil's Pretty Daughter and Other Ozark Folk Tales* (1955).

Ranke-Heinemann, Uta (1927–)

In *Eunuchs for the Kingdom of Heaven* (1990), Ranke-Heinemann, a German, claims that "the whole of church history adds up to one long arbitrary, narrow-minded masculine despotism over the female sex." She describes the cultural domination of women that a celibate governing elite of the Catholic Church has perpetuated. John Cardinal O'Connor attacked the book upon its publication, objecting to its statement that homosexuality is so pronounced that many religious orders and diocesan seminaries require men to pass an HIV test. The author also attacks St. Thomas Aquinas's view that women are an inferior form of man and declares that "celibate hatred of sex is hatred of women." Celibacy, it is noted, was not a Catholic rule until Pope Gregory VII in the 11th Century fought clerical marriages. He feared, because of the German emperor's edicts, that priests' progeny would inherit ecclesiastical property. "I am tired," writes Ranke-Heinemann, "of the hair-splitting nonsense of the white bachelors of the Church who are defining sexual intercourse."

In 1994 she has written *Putting Away Childish Things: The Virgin Birth, the Empty Tomb, and Other Fair Tales You Don't Have to Believe to Have a Living Faith*. Ranke-Heinemann is qualified to write on such a subject, for she is one of the few women ever to qualify as a university professor in Catholic theology. However, she lost her academic chair when the Pope withdraw her permission to teach. Ironically, Ranke-Heinemann professes a faith in God and religion. She interprets Jesus speaking for God's love, for mercy and for compassion, not for the dead, but to the living.

Rankel, Jeff (20th Century)

Rankel published *Independent Atheist* (1127 North College, Decatur, Illinois 62522). {FD}

Rankin, David O. (20th Century)

Rankin, a senior minister at the Fountain Street Church in Cedar Rapids, Michigan, has more than two thousand parishioners. He has also served Unitarian Universalist churches in Watertown and New Bedford, Massachusetts, as well as in San Francisco and Atlanta. In "We All Burn Out" (*World* , Sep-Oct 1995), Rankin describes some of the hazards as well as the glories of being a minister.

Ransleben, Guido E. (20th Century)

Ransleben wrote *100 Years of Comfort in Texas* (1954). {*Freethought History #15*, 1995}

Ranson, Allan O. (20th Century)

In 1935 for his M. A. thesis at the University of Wisconsin, Ranson wrote on the "Persuasive Methods used by Robert G. Ingersoll." {FUS}

Ransom, George F. (19th Century)

Ransom, a freethinker, wrote *Shall We Live Again?* (1895). {GS}

Rao, Avula Sambasiva [Chief Justice] (20th Century)

Mr. Justice (retired) Rao has been chief justice of the Andhra Pradesh High Court in India, the vice chancellor of Andhra University, and a former chairperson of the Indian Radical Humanist Association. He has been a vocal critic of India's religious organizations and their influence in detracting from the democratic goals of secularism and rationalism.

Rao, Badrinath Krushna (20th Century)

Rao, a student of sociology at the University of Alberta in Canada, has written about South Asia and the Kashmir imbroglio for *Humanist in Canada* (Spring 1999). The current problem has to do with the internal contradictions of Hindu society, he wrote.

Rao, Kotapati Murahari (20th Century)

Rao, a rationalist, is President of the Academy of Rural Development and Research in Hyderabad, India.

Rao, P. V. S. (20th Century)

Rao, the recipient in 1987 of the Padma Shri in India, is a rationalist. Dr. Rao is senior professor and head of the computer systems and communications group at the Tata Institute of Fundamental Research in Bombay.

Rao, K. Ranganatha (20th Century)

Rao, a retired additional director of medical science, Government of Andhra Pradesh in India, teaches biochemistry. Dr. Rao is a rationalist.

Raphael, Sally Jessy (1943–)

Raphael, a noted U.S. talk-show host, has stated, "I don't believe in God. Although it isn't what most people think, I believe this is all there is. No heaven. No reincarnation. Once it's over, it's over. Once you believe that, it causes you to live every day of your life to the fullest. Every morning I wake up and say, 'If this is the only day I have left, what can I do to make it mean the most?' . . . If you believe in an afterlife, I think it makes living a lot easier. Unfortunately, I've had to find another way to define my existence. Immortality for me comes from trying to do the most you can for your fellow man. I do extensive charity work to make an impact with my life. My form of prayer is meditation. It's been a part of my life for thirty years. I meditate for ten minutes to half an hour every day, morning and night. Meditation focuses you so you can come out relaxed and with an enormous amount of energy." In 1988, Raphael received the television industry's Emmy Award for being the outstanding daytime talk-show host. {Celebrity Atheists on the Web}

Rapisardi, Mario (1844–1912)

Rapisardi was an Italian poet, born in Sicily. He translated Lucretius in 1880 and published poems on *Lucifer*, which chants the victory of the devil over the Christian God, and *The Last Prayer of Pius IX* (1871). {BDF}

Rapoport, Anatol (1911–)

Rapoport, a neuropsychiatrist at the University of Michigan and author of *Science and the Goals of Man* (1950) and *Operational Philosophy* (1953), wrote to the present author about humanism:

> "Humanism" to me is an orientation which places man's aspirations at the center of a system of values. The possibility of doing so derives from two assumptions: (1) that no outside agency need be considered which *prescribes* values for man regardless of what man's aspirations may be; (2) that it is possible to distill from the variety of special forms in which human aspirations are expressed (as exemplified in diverse cultures, religions, value systems) a number of basic aspirations characteristic of man as a biological organism.
>
> The first of these assumptions can be made by default, as it

were, there being no objective evidence to the contrary. The second can be disputed, for it is quite possible that no common human aspirations are discernible, i.e., that conflicting value systems are irreconcilable. Therefore adherence to this second assumption is an act of faith, perhaps the only article of faith to which a humanist subscribes. There is a methodological advantage (from the point of view of ethical theory) to making the two assumptions of humanism. If one can be objective, empirical methods arrive at conclusions as to what the common denominator of human aspirations is and if one takes this common denominator as the ultimate measure of value, one is spared the necessity of grappling with unanswerable questions, such as "What does God want of Man?" The ultimate human values, if they can be found, become not imperatives (signifying what must be) but discoveries (signifying what is) and cannot be altered, or escaped from, any more than the other laws of nature.

The humanist, therefore, wishes to know what man as man must do, because he cannot do otherwise, and seeks to define human aspirations in those terms. All other problems of value seeking then become practical ones, that is, one seeks means to enable man to achieve these (human) ends. This, to my way of thinking, is the extension of scientific orientation to ethics. The scientist too discovers what (are the laws of nature). To the extent that he tries to apply science to pre-conceived ends, he works within the framework of the *necessary* and has abandoned questions beginning with 'Why?' where they have no meaning. The scientist also tries to work with the fewest possible arbitrary assumptions. For the same reason the humanist avoids assumptions concerning extra-human prime movers, coercers, frustrators, or evaluators of human aspirations. Further comments on these matters can be found in my articles, "Religion and Salvation" in *The Humanist*, and "How Relative Are Values?" in *ETC., A Review of General Semantics.*

In the 1950s, Rapoport reviewed books for *The Humanist.* In 1989, he was professor of peace studies at the University of Toronto. His field of research is mathematical biography. {WAS, 29 March 1956}

Rapp, Sandy (20th Century)

Rapp is author of *God's Country: A Case Against Theocracy* (1991).

Rapp, William Jourdan (1895–1942)

Rapp was on the advisory board of Charles Francis Potter's First Humanist Society of New York. A playwright and an editor of *True Story*, he was a nominal Episcopalian.

Rappleyea, George W. (20th Century)

In the 1950s, Rappleyea was on the advisory board of Charles Francis Potter's First Humanist Society of New York.

Rappoport, John (20th Century)

Rappoport, in *The Most Hated Woman in America* (1998), tells of the disappearance and possible murder of the O'Hair family.

Raso, Jack (20th Century)

Raso is editor and managing editor of the *Nutrition and Health Forum* newsletter and a consultant to Prometheus Books. He wrote *The Dictionary of Metaphysical Healthcare: Alternative Medicine, Paranormal Healing, and Related Methods* (1996), warning about "alternativism," an ill-defined, ragtag, quasi-religious movement which is displacing, and in some cases supplementing, organized religion. An atheist, he believes that belief in God facilitates belief in alternative healthcare, which he opposes. {*Freethought Today*, March 1997}

Raspail, François Vincent (1794–1878)

Raspail was a French chemist and politician who had been brought up by ecclesiastics and intended for the Church. While quite young, he became professor of philosophy at the theological seminary of Avignon but, being examined on theological dogmas, was rejected. He went to Paris, became a scientific lecturer, took part in the Revolution of 1830, and refused an offer from Louis Philippe of the Legion of Honor. Frequently imprisoned, Raspail nevertheless was finally elected to the chamber in 1869, where he sat on the extreme left. {BDF; RAT; RE}

Rasputin, Grigori Yefimovich (1872–1916)

A Russian "holy man with peculiar eyes," Rasputin (the name given him by fellow villagers meant "the debauched one") was a semi-literate peasant who preached and practiced a doctrine of salvation that mixed religious fervor with sexual indulgence. As a young man, he had joined a heretical sect called The Flagellants, whose all-night orgies of incantations, wild dances, provocative switchings, and indiscriminate copulations were practiced as sinful prerequisites of redemption. In public baths he displayed his body to admiring young women. (His penis when erect measured 13" according to his daughter Maria. His wife, Praskovia Fedorovna Dubrovina, a blond, blue-eyed village girl whom he married about 1891 and the mother of his three legitimate children, said, "He has enough for all.") Rasputin would urge women to debase themselves and "try the flesh," would fondle their breasts until they confused sexual excitation with religious fervor, and would then convince husbands that intercourse with their wives was an act of redemption willed by God. Hordes of peasants were said to have thrown themselves at his feet, kissing the hemline of his black caftan, crying "Father Grigori, our Savior!" His bedroom was called "the holy of holies," and the number of his illegitimate children is unknown.

In Czar Nicholas II's court, Rasputin gained a powerful hold over Czarina Alexandra Feodorovna and, through her, over the czar. He became a member of the royal family, convincing them that he was able to heal the emperor's only son, Alexis. His influence over the Russian state was enormous. He was known to obtain huge "fees" from the rich for political favors, then empty his pockets during the same day to the poor and needy. Although he preferred sex with aristocratic beauties because "they smelled better," he never improved his own peasant odors and scooped up his food with his hands. His disciples, however, saw in him the reincarnation of Christ.

Prince Felix Youssupov, using his beautiful wife as bait, arranged a midnight party at which Rasputin drank several glasses of poisoned wine and ate enough cakes filled with potassium cyanide to kill a cow. When these did not kill him, the Prince shot him with a pistol. Rasputin staggered out into the courtyard where another conspirator shot him again. Rasputin was then stabbed many times. Two days later, the official account stated, his trussed-up body was found under the ice of the Neva River, one arm half-free and his lungs filled with water. Rasputin had still been alive when submerged and he had died by drowning. "If I die," Rasputin once correctly prophesied, "the Emperor will soon lose his crown."

Alexander Cockburn's grandmother entertained Prince Felix Youssupov in the years following the Russian revolution of 1917. She told relatives a slightly different story of how Youssupov had compulsively described to her again and again the scene as it took place in his palace in St. Petersburg:

> Determined to finish off this charismatic monk who held such sway over the Romanovs, particularly the Czarina, Youssupov had invited Rasputin to dinner. They'd served him a poisonous brew that he had tossed down with relish. Then they'd shot him. Finally they'd dragged him down to the edge of the canal that flowed past the bottom of the garden, and stuffed him under the ice. The next morning they found he'd crawled back up the bank before finally expiring. And all through the killing, Youssupov told Joan, the phonograph had been playing "Yankee Doodle Dandy."

By the 1990s, Rasputin was no longer the media figure he once had been. But in the 1970s, a rock group called Boney M had a hit song entitled, "Rasputin, Rasputin, Russia's Greatest Love Machine."

{CE; Alexander Cockburn, *NY Press*, 26 Mar 1997–1 Apr 1997; PA}

Rastern, Richard (20th Century)

An American living in Costa Rica, Rastern is the person who helped found *Triangulo Rosa*. That group successfully defied the nation's public health system by insisting that all, not just pregnant women, be given the latest medications for the treatment of those who are HIV-positive. The Supreme Court ruled in 1998 that, indeed, the country could not afford *not* to spend the needed funds.

Rastern currently is director of Agua Buena Human Rights Association, Apartado 366-2200, Coronado, Costa Rica. That group supports the formation of strong advocacy groups run for and by People Living with HIV/AIDS throughout the Latin American region. Panama followed the Costa Rican model in 1999, agreeing to supply the cocktail of medications to HIV-plus individuals and those with AIDS. E-mail: <rastern@sol.racsa.co.cr>.

Ratcliffe, C. E. (20th Century)

A Scot, Ratcliffe wrote "Reflections" (1920) and *Fact and Fiction—Secular Poems* (1956). {GS}

Ratcliffe, Samuel Kerkham (Born 1868)

Ratcliffe, a journalist and lecturer, was one of the regular lecturers for the Ethical Societies at London. He edited the *Echo* in 1900 and from 1903 to 1906 was acting editor of the Calcutta *Statesman.*

He was a secretary of the Sociological Society and the London representative of the New York *New Republic*. In 1915, he was appointed a lecturer at the South Place Ethical Society. In *A Generation of Religious Progress* (1916), Ratcliffe contributed a chapter. He concluded that "the very revival of superstition and the manufacture of new creeds are evidence of profound dissatisfaction with the established orthodoxies, and of the determination of the human spirit to find a satisfying means of expression for the craving after reality." Writing about Charles A. Watts, Ratcliffe stated, "I have always associated the name of Charles A. Watts with causes the advocacy of which demanded courage and tenacity and unremitting watchfulness, and we could always be sure of finding him at his post. The Rationalist Press Association stands as a most unusual monument to his memory."

Ratcliffe's grandson is Nicolas Walter, of the Rationalist Press Association. {FUK; RAT}

RATIOCINATION

To ratiocinate (ra-tee-OS-uh-nate) is to reason logically and methodically. The process of reasoning is such that one re-traces thoughts, understanding the steps used in order to arrive at some conclusion. For example, the direction to find the white house had been to go north past the second stoplight, then turn right. But upon arriving, we find no white house. Using ratiocination, we re-think the steps we took (much like slowly reversing movie frames on a film, one by one, returning to the particular frame at which we were given the original direction) and see the mistake: we went south, not north. Cartoonists often illustrate this by drawing an electric light bulb above the person's head, symbolizing "the moment of understanding."

A Connecticut teacher has given the following to test the ratiocinative processes of students:

1. The Hundred Years War lasted how long?
2. In which month do the Russians celebrate the October revolution?
3. In which country are Panama hats made?
4. From what animal do we get catgut?
5. Where do Chinese gooseberries come from?
6. Louis XVIII was the last one, but how many previous kings of France were called Louis?
7. What was King George VI's first name?
8. What color is a purple finch?
9. What kind of creatures were the Canary Islands named after?
10. How long did the Thirty Years' War last?

Answers given by Dennis Berson in *People's Almanac*:

1. From 1337 to 1453 is 116 years.
2. November (7th). The Russian calendar was 13 days behind.
3. Ecuador.
4. The sheep.
5. New Zealand.
6. Sixteen, for Louis XVII died in prison during the Revolution and never reached the throne.
7. Albert.
8. The distinctively colored parts are crimson.
9. A breed of large dogs. The Latin name was *Canariae insulae*, Island of the Dogs.
10. 30 years, of course, from 1618 to 1648.

Some additional questions to test one's ratiocination:

1. When was Jesus born?
2. If there is no god but Allah, and Muhammad is His prophet, what will happen to non-believers when they die?
3. If a baby dies before it is baptized, will its soul go to limbo or to purgatory?
4. In order to insure peace in outer space, the individuals chosen to inhabit the place should all be members of what organized religion?
5. Is common sense uncommon?

RATIONAL

• Rational, adj., Devoid of all delusions save those of observation, experience, and reflection.

–**Ambrose Bierce,** *The Devil's Dictionary*

RATIONAL CENTRE

In Ghana, the Rational Centre, led by Hope N. Tawiah, is at POB 01132, Osu-Accra, Ghana. (See entries for Ghanian Humanists and Tawiah, Hope N.) {FD}

RATIONAL RECOVERY RESIDENTIAL FACILITIES

The Rational Recovery Residential Facilities, at Placerville, California, can be reached by telephoning (916) 621-4374. {FD}

RATIONAL RECOVERY SELF-HELP NETWORK

An alternative to Alcoholics Anonymous, Rational Recovery Self-Help Network is at Box 800, Lotus, California 95651. For chapters in various cities and states, a listing can be obtained from the headquarters or found in "Freethinkers Directory." (See entry for Secular Organizations for Sobriet and for James Taylor) {FD}

RATIONAL RELIGION

In 1839, Robert Owen united the various bodies of his followers in "The Universal Community Society of Rational Religionists." In 1817 he had declared that "all the religions of the world are false," and the 100,000 members of the new group were fellow agnostics who, by religion, meant devotion to moral and social ideals. The movement broke into fragments, Secularism taking over the criticism of religion, and later attempts to organize non-theists on the basis of "rational religion" had had no large or permanent success. {RE}

RATIONAL THINKER JOURNAL

Rational Thinker Journal, an Illinois internet organization for freethinkers, is found at <www.geocities.com/athens/forum/1906>.

RATIONALISM

In philosophy, rationalism is a theory that holds that reason alone, unaided by experience, can arrive at basic truth regarding the world. It is opposed to empiricism on the question of the source of knowledge and the techniques for verification of knowledge. René Descartes, G. W. von Leibniz, and Baruch Spinoza all represent the rationalist position whereas John Locke represents the empirical. Specifically, according to Edgar Sheffield Brightman, who once taught at Boston University in Massachusetts, rationalism is as follows: (a) the deductive [Cartesian, mathematical] method of drawing logical inferences from elementary concepts [intuitions, axioms, innate, or a priori truths], as opposed to the empirical method; (b) the doctrine (opposed to sensationalism) that reason is a higher source of knowledge, independent of sense [when Locke said that "there is nothing in the intellect that was not first in sense," Leibniz added "except the intellect itself"]; or (c) the appeal to coherent thought [as opposed to irrationalism] as a criterion of truth.

McCabe states that the word *rationalism* came into use in the seventeenth century. Bacon spoke of "Rationals who in the manner of spiders, spin webs from their own substance," but he was referring to the Aristotelian philosophers who disdained empirical science and claimed that reason was the source of truth. In Germany, at the time, they were sometimes called Rationalists. McCabe continues, "About the middle of the century the Clarendon State Papers recorded the appearance of 'a new sect calling themselves Rationalists,' who follow 'what their reason dictates to them in Church or State.' In 1661 Comenius applied the name to the Socinians (unitarians) and Deists. The word was rarely used, and was not adopted by any body of sceptics. It was usually applied to Christians who tried to prove that their faith is in harmony with reason, or to philosophers who slighted the empirical method of investigations. What are now called

'Rationalists' were sceptics, infidels, Atheists, Freethinkers, or Naturalists. Kant, in the latter part of the eighteenth century, used the word in both senses, but in Great Britain it was Owen's foundation of Rational Religion which led the public to call his followers 'Rationals,' or 'Rationalists,' that made the name popular. In 1845 George Holyoake published a booklet with the title *Rationalism: A Treatise for the Times*, but later preferred the word 'Secularism.' Others called themselves Freethinkers, Agnostics, or Atheists. The group of Agnostics, with a few liberal Theists, who were associated with C. A. Watts in 1887, adopted the word, and in 1893 founded the Rationalist Press Committee in order to 'circulate Rationalist publications,' and the name was later changed to Rationalist Press Association. It defined Rationalism as 'the mental attitude which unreservedly accepts the supremacy of reason and aims at establishing a system of philosophy and ethics verifiable by experience and independent of all arbitrary assumptions or authority.' "

McCabe then notes that rationalists became, "in the common usage of the term, men and women who by this use of reasoning have become convinced that religious beliefs are false. Since it would obviously be absurd to refuse the title of 'Rationalist' to men like Voltaire and Paine, the name is in historical retrospect extended to Deists and Theists who rejected all Christian doctrines or who today declare their rejection of the teaching of every branch of the Christian Church." Organized Rationalists, he added, include members of the Rationalist Press Association (which has no doctrinal or philosophical tests) and similar bodies, and they "usually reject also the belief in God and Immortality and subscribe for the propagation of their opinions."

For Bertrand Russell in his 1928 *Sceptical Essays*, rationality in opinion is "the habit of taking account of all relevant evidence in arriving at a belief. Where certainty is unattainable, a rational man will give most weight to the most probable opinion, while retaining others which have an appreciable probability, in his mind, as hypotheses which subsequent evidence may show to be preferable. This, of course, assumes that it is possible in many cases to ascertain facts and probabilities by an objective method—i.e., a method which will lead any two careful people to the same result." (For one view of how rationalism differs from humanism, see the entry for Humanism, Per Curtis Reese. See a detailed discussion by Bernard Williams in the *Encyclopedia of Philosophy*, Vol. 7.) {CE; ER; RE}

Rationalist Annual

The Rationalist Press Association's *Rationalist Annual* ceased in 1968 and was replaced by *Question*, which ceased in 1980.

RATIONALIST ASSOCIATION

The Rationalist Association, POB 994, St. Louis, Missouri 63188, publishes *The American Rationalist.* Dr. Gordon Stein was its long-time editor, and Barbara Stocker its managing editor. Upon Stein's death in 1996, Dr. Kaz Dziamka of Albuquerque, New Mexico, was named the editor.

RATIONALIST PRESS ASSOCIATION (RPA)

The Rationalist Press Association (RPA) began in 1890 as the Propagandist Press Committee. On 26 May 1899, an association of rationalists that grew out of a Rationalist Press Committee established by C. A. Watts, who had already founded the *Agnostic Annual* (1884) and the *Literary Guide* (1885). The original directors were R. B. Anderson, J. S. Dryden, C. T. Gorham, Clair Grece, G. J. Holyoake, Joseph McCabe, C. A. Watts, and A. G. Whyte. Watts's printing and publishing business belonged to a line going back to Richard Carlile in 1817. In 1902 the RPA began to publish the R.P.A. Reprints and sold four million copies in twenty-five years.

In 1940, the honorary associates listed by McCabe were as follows: Arnold Bennett, Prof. Berthelot, B. Björnson, Sir John Boyd Orr, G. Brandes, Prof. Breasted, Prof. Buisson, Prof. Bury, G. Clemenceau, the Hon. J. Collier, C. Darrow, Prof. J. Dewey, Dr. Einstein, Dr. Sigmund Freud, Sir P. Geddes, Sir R. Gregory, J.B.S. Haldane, Prof. Haddon, E. Haeckel, Sir J. Hammerton, Lord Horder, Sir T. A. Hunter, Julian Huxley, L. Huxley, Sir A. Keith, Sir E. Ray Lankester, J. Loeb, C. Lombroso, Somerset Maugham, Sir P. C. Mitchell, Lord Morley, Prof. Pavlov, Eden Phillpotts, T. Reinach, Earl Russell, Bertrand Russell, Sir E. S. Schafer, Sir C. Sherrington, Sir G. Elliot Smith, Sir L. Stephen, H. G. Wells, and Sir H. Wood. Mc Cabe added, caustically, "All the Churches in Great Britain put together could not, from their 8,000,000 members, compile a list which would be half as impressive."

Other honorary associates have included the following: Edward Brabuck, James Bridie, Jacob Bronowski, Basil Chamberlain, Robert Chorley, George Cole, William W. Collins, Joseph Fletcher, Alfred Foster, Frederick Furnivali, Charles Guignebert, Jane Harrison, Edwin Hartland, Édouard Herriot, Leopold Infeld, Ernest Jones, Harold Laski, Carl Lofmark, Willem Manen, Kingsley Martin, David Oppenheimer, Raghunath Paranjpye, P. H. Pardon, Karl Popper, Albert Rivett, Margaret Schlauch, B. F. Skinner, Grafton Smith, Robert Stout, Alan Taylor, George Trevelyan, Edward Westermarck, Edward Willis, Barbara Wootton, and Emile Zola.

In 1998, the honorary associates were as follows: Dr. Peter Atkins; H. J. Blackham; Professor Colin Blakemore; Professor Marcel Boll; Professor Sir Hermann Bondi; Alan Brownjohn; Dr. Colin Campbell; Noam Chomsky; Professor Bernard Crick; Professor Francis Crick; Dr. Richard Dawkins; Lord Dormand; Professor Paul Edwards; Professor Lionel Elvin; Professor Sir Raymond Firth; Professor Antony Flew; Lord Foot; Right Honorable Michael Foot; Tony Harrison; Dr. James Hemming; Dr. Christopher Hill; Prof. Eric Hobsbawm; Richard Hoggart; Professor Ted Honderich; Professor Sir Fred Hoyle; Prof. Leopold Infeld; Lord Jenkins of Putney (Hugh Jenkins); Ludovic Kennedy; Professor Paul Kurtz; Richard Leakey; Sir Michael Levey; John Maddox; Professor Haydn Mason; Professor John Maynard Smith; George Melly; Naomi Mitchison; Brian Moore; Edwin Mullins; Professor Patrick Nowell-Smith; Dr. Conor Cruise O'Brien; Jack Parsons; Prof. John Postgate; Claire Rayner; Professor the Earl Russell; Lord Sefton of Garston; Mrs. Renée Short; Dr. David Starkey; Dr. D. J. Stewart; Dr. V. M. Tarkunde; David Tribe; Baroness Turner of Camden; Professor G. A. Wells; Arnold Wesker; Professor Lewis Wolpert; Baron Young of Darlington; and Professor J. Z. Young.

The Rationalist Press Association is at Bradlaugh House, 47 Theobald's Road, London WC1X 8SP. In 1998 its directors were Ivor Russell (Chairman); Antony Chapman; Nigel Collins (appointed March 1998); Jim Herrick; Ralph Ison (retired March 1998); John Metcalf; Daniel O'Hara (retired March 1998); David Pollock; Jonathan Stopes-Roe; Nicolas Walter; and Jane Wynne Willson (Vice-chairman). Metcalf and Willson retired in 1998 and with Russell offered themselves for re-election at the Annual General Meeting to be held 12 July 1999. The number of members was about 900. (See entry for Frederick James Gould, author of a history of the Rationalist Press Association from 1899 on. {RE; Nicolas Walter, "A Century of Reason," *New Humanist* #2 and #4, 1999, summarizes the RPA's century of existence. Explained is the connection between the RPA and the British Humanist Association.}

RATIONALIST PRESS ASSOCIATION, CENTENARY OF

The centenary of the Rationalist Press Association, which formerly was *Watts' Literary Guide*, was celebrated by its quarterly journal, *New Humanist*, in June 1999. Officers and honorary associates sending their greetings included the following:

Peter Atkins, Professor of Chemistry at Oxford University
Alan Brownjohn, poet and novelist
Bernard Crick, professor emeritus of politics London University
Sir Hermann Bondi, Chairman, RPA
Lord Dormand, the Labour MP for Easington from 1970-1987
Lionel Elvin, former director of the London Institute of Education
James Hemming, educational psychologist
Paul Kurtz, Vice-President, RPA
Ludovic Kennedy, TV presenter and author
Richard Leakey, paleo-anthropologist
Michael Levey, art historian
Haydn Mason, chairman of the board of the Voltaire Foundation
George Melly, jazz singer, entertainer
Patrick Nowell-Smith, professor emeritus of Philosophy
David Pollock, RPA director
John Postgate, professor of microbiology, the University of Sussex
Claire Rayner, writer and chair of the Patients' Association
Conrad Russell, historian; active in the House of Lords as a Liberal Democrat
Ivor Russell, Chairman, RPA
D. J. Stewart, former chairman of the British Humanist Association and also the Rationalist Press Association
David Tribe, former president of the National Secular Society
Lewis Wolpert, professor of biology as applied to medicine at University College, London

RATIONALIST RECOVERY ORGANIZATION: See entry for SOS.

Rationalist Reporter

The Rationalist Reporter was a monthly bulletin of the New York Chapter of the Rationalist Press Association in 1958. (See entries for E. L. Gruber and Louis Hayden.)

RATIONALISTS NEW YORK

Rationalists New York (Box 10-A, 31 Jane Street, New York, NY 10014) publishes and/or distributes material about freethought, rationalism, and secular humanism. E-mail: <wasm@idt.net>.

RATIONALISTS UNITED FOR SECULAR HUMANISM (RUSH)

Deidre C. Conn is President of Rationalists United for Secular Humanism. The group's founder was Chad Docterman, and its other officers include David Fellinton, Vice President; David Anderson, Secretary; and Rachel Seabolt Miller, Treasurer. E-mail: <Conn3@marshall.edu>. On the Web: <www.marshall.edu/rush/>.

Ratner, Joseph (1901?–1979)

Ratner was a scientific humanist. With John Dewey, he edited *Education Today* (1940). Ratner edited Dewey's *Characters and Events*. His most noted books were *The Philosophy of Spinoza* and *Spinoza on God*. Ratner died of a heart attack. {HNS}

Ratner, Sidney (1908–1996)

Ratner was an editor who wrote for *The Humanist* in the 1950s. With Arthur F. Bentley, he edited *Inquiry Into Inquiries: Essays in Social History* (1954). He also wrote *Taxation and Democracy in America*, *The Tariff in American History*, and *The Evolution of the American Economy*. Ratner taught at Rutgers University and specialized in economic history. His wide range of interests led him to write a history of the Supreme Court and one of John Dewey, and he published a series of essays about Dewey. In 1989, the Society for the Advancement of American Philosophy awarded him its Herbert Schneider Award.

During World War II, Ratner served as an economist for the Government's Board of Economic Warfare and the Foreign Economic Administration, following which he became a principal economist in the planning division of the State Department. When the Swedes complained of a lack of ball bearings during the war, items that were necessary for the manufacture of Allied landing craft, Ratner suggested that the bearing industry was controlled by an international cartel. The cartel, which included Germany, had put pressure on the Swedes to limit the supply. When the United States initiated diplomatic efforts with Sweden, the shortage disappeared in two weeks.

Ratner was influential in President Franklin D. Roosevelt's attempt to expand the size of the Supreme Court, for he found a precedent in President Ulysses S. Grant's appointments to the Court. Ratner was married to the scholar **Louise M. Rosenblatt**, also a distinguished humanist. {HNS; Reed Abelson, *The New York Times*, 17 January 1996}

Rau, Herbert (1813–1876)

Rau was a German rationalist who studied theology and became a preacher to free congregations in Stuttgart and Mannheim. Rau wrote *Gospel of Nature, A Catechism of the Religion of the Future,* and other works. {BDF; RAT}

Rauser, Jerry (20th Century)

Rauser, an atheist activist in Minnesota, attended the 1996 fourth World Atheist Conference in Vijayawada, India. His experiences were recorded in *The Free Mind*, newsletter of the University of Minnesota Atheists and Humanists (February 1996) and in *Secular Nation* (September-October 1996).

Ravindranath, Alapati (20th Century)

Ravindranath, a rationalist, is editor of *Misimi* in Hyderabad, India.

Rawlinson, Henry Creswick [Sir] (1810–1895)

An English Orientalist and administrator, brother of the Orientalist George Rawlinson, Rawlinson served as a consul at Baghdad and became interested in deciphering the cuneiform of the Behistun inscriptions of Darius I. He published his results in *Journal of the Royal Asiatic Society* (1846). Also, Rawlinson, a Major-General, helped prepare *The Cuneiform Inscriptions of Western Asia* (1861–1884, 5 volumes) for the British Museum. His brother was a clerical dignitary who stated that Sir Henry was a non-Christian theist who never went to church. The brother remarked, "Not committed to the daily performance of those religious acts and practices which to many are the essentials of an upright life, he held the broad way of doing good because it was good." McCabe retorted, "One would have thought that in the mind of a priest the 'broad way' did not lead to doing good. In plain English, the famous Assyriologist was a liberal Theist who accepted no creed and (unofficially) did not go to church." {JM; RAT; RE}

Rawson, Albert Leighton (1829–1902)

Rawson was an American traveler and author. After studying law, art, and theology, he made four visits to the East. In 1851–1852 he made a pilgrimage from Cairo to Mecca, disguised as a Moslem student of medicine. Rawson illustrated Beecher's *Life of Jesus*. In the *Freethinkers' Magazine*, Rawson maintained that the Bible account of the twelve tribes of Israel is non-historical. {BDF}

Rawson, Roy Robert (1898–1971)

Rawson was an Australian freethinker, Esperantist, parliamentarian, and radical bookseller. A partner of James G. Pyke in Pyke's bookshop, he was in charge of the Haldeman-Julius Little Blue

Books. The shop was the center of the Melbourne Branch of the Left Book Club and the Book Censorship Abolition League. In 1952, Rawson was elected as Australian Labor Party member to the Legislative council for six years. {SWW}

Ray, Sibnarayan (1921–)

Ray, once one of the editors of *The Radical Humanist* along with Ellen Roy, edited the writings of M. N. Roy, which Oxford University Press has published (3 volumes). In 1949 when at Calcutta University, he described humanism to the present author:

> To most Humanists in India the question whether Nehru believes in a soul or not is rather unexciting if not irrelevant. Personally I know that his mind is a queer ensemble of scientific ideas and primitive beliefs; he lives in the Western style, speaks and writes excellent English, talks rationalism and democracy, and he observes all the ancient superannuated rituals of Hindu society. Take for example the custom of Sradh, of offering sacrifices to the dead. Nehru observed it when his father died some years back. He comes of a Kashmir Brahmin family and is quite openly fanatical about preserving the blood-purity of his caste. Most journalists and admirers from the West do not seem to have any guess about this facet of his personality. But what is more surprising is that they refuse to recognise by common consent what is patent and obvious—his insufferable arrogance, his messy thinking and wooliness, his fondness for self-exhibition, and his dictatorial temper. Quite recently an American journalist, Mr. Martin Ebon of McGraw Hill Co., interviewed him and had some taste of his "greatness"—if you chance to meet him, ask him for his impression. . . . There has not been much of a humanist movement in India during the present century. Apart from the publications of Renaissance Publishing, Tagore's latter-day writings are the only considerable literature on the subject. Humanism in India has been mostly of a religious orientation. Its chief content was social reform with God's fatherhood and man's inherent divinity as the chief moral mainsprings. Nanak, Dadu, Chaitanya, Kabir, and all our medieval social reformers preached varieties of religious humanism comparable to the work and ideas of St. Francis. In the 19th century, due largely to the impact of Western ideas, a secular social reform movement started in Bengal, Maharashtra, and certain parts of South India. But the rise of Nationalism and Gandhi's influence in the present century completely swamped that process.
>
> The two most outstanding secular humanists of the 19th century are Jyotirao Phule and Isvar Chandra Vidyasager. Unfortunately, no English translations of their works have so far been made; they wrote exclusively in their mother languages, the former in Maharashtrian, the latter in Bengali. . . . Our own movement is expressly secular. It started as a political movement with the Radical Democratic Party as its central organisation. In our 1948 Conference, however, we decided to dissolve the Party organisation and transform our activities into a more flexible and comprehensive socio-cultural movement. The chief research centre of our movement is the Indian Renaissance Institute (13 Mohini Road, Dehradun). The Renaissance Publishers (15 Bankim Chatterji Street, Calcutta) publish our *The Humanist Way* (quarterly; previously, it was called *The Marxian Way*) and *The Radical Humanist* (weekly, 8 Parekh St., Ratilal Mansions, Bombay). For a comprehensive idea of our philosophy, read M. N. Roy's *New Humanism*, his *Beyond Communism*, his *New Orientation*, and his *Science and Philosophy*. Also my own *Radicalism*. And with Ellen Roy I wrote *In Man's Own Image*.

At the Third International Humanist and Ethical Union World Congress held in Oslo (1962), Ray addressed the group and was acclaimed as one of India's leading intellectuals, In *A New Renaissance* (1998), he describes his concerns as to how the social group known as the intelligentsia has developed or failed to develop in different periods and different Asian societies. A global renaissance is needed, he argues, to address the problems of global pollution, global cretinization, global inequality, and the amassing of destructive weapons. Ray signed Humanist Manifesto 2000. {Jim Herrick, *International Humanist News*, October 1998; WAS, 2 July 1949}

Raynal, Guillaume Thomas François (1713–1796)

Raynal, a French historian and philosopher, was brought up as a priest but renounced that profession soon after moving in 1747 to Paris. There, he befriended Helvetius, Holbach, Diderot, Mechmeja, and others, compiling a philosophical history of European establishments in the two Indies, a work full of reflections on the religions and political institutions of France. The work was censured by the Sorbonne and burned by the hangman by order of Parliament in 1781. Raynal escaped and spent six years in exile, part of the time to the court of Catherine the Great. {BDF; RAT; RE}

Raymo, Chet (20th Century)

Raymo is author of *Skeptics and True Believers, the Exhilarating Connection Between Science and Faith*. A professor of physics and astronomy at Stonehill College in Northaston, Massachusetts, he writes a science column in the Boston *Globe*. He has spoken to the Humanist Association of Massachusetts about why so many see the face of Jesus in a nebula, sea monsters in Loch Ness, flying saucers in the sky. It is because we yearn to be part of something greater than ourselves, he holds. We learn by hard experience that miracles do not happen: "Yearning and learning are integral parts of being human (the first may be genetic; the second we must work at). We cannot be fully human without both. Finding the proper balance between yearning and learning can keep us occupied for a lifetime."

Rayner, Claire Berenice (20th Century)

Rayner, a writer and broadcaster, became an Honorary Associate of the Rationalist Press Association in 1995. Similarly, she is an Honorary Associate of the National Secular Society. Also, she is a Vice President of the Gay and Lesbian Humanist Association (GALHA). Rayner has written numerous BBC programs, and among her eighty or so books are *Mothers and Midwives* (1962), *Everything Your Doctor Would Tell You if He Had Time* (1980), *Safe Sex* (1987), and *Dangerous Things* (1993). "Children should be made to realise," she has said concerning the superstitions youngsters are forced to grow up with, "that only five of the biblical ten commandments have any relevance today." {*Gay and Lesbian Humanist*, Winter 1998)

Razi, Ar (865–925)

Razi was the greatest physician of the Middle Ages. He upheld the values of rationalist, religious skepticism, belief in science, the application of human reason to the problems besetting mankind, empiricism, a lack of dogmatism, and a mistrust of blind tradition. As such, he is highly regarded by contemporary rationalists. (See entry for Al Razi Circle) {*International Humanist News*, December 1997}

Razin, Alexander V. (20th Century)

Razin, a professor of ethics at Moscow State University, signed Humanist Manifesto 2000.

Razis, Dennis V. (20th Century)

Razis, a Greek physician specializing in oncology, headed the first International Multidisciplinary Conference on Human Behaviour and the Meaning of Modern Humanism. The conference was co-sponsored by the International Humanist and Ethical Union and was held June 1995 in Delphi, Greece. Convinced of the need for humans to pull together to work for solutions to the predicament of humanity in today's world, Razis set out to organize scientists and scholars. He had been encouraged by the late Melini Mercouri, then the Minister of Culture in Greece. After her death, he was able to find funding from a variety of Greek governmental and private organizations. Present at the conference were Mercouri's husband, Jules Dassin; the Greek Minister of Defence, G. Arsenis; the Metropolite of Amphissa (a church official over the Delphi area), and numerous academics, scientists, and representatives of the IHEU.

In 1996, Razis was a participant in the Humanist World Congress held in Mexico City. In 1998 he edited *The Human Predicament*, a collection of articles about the survival and fulfillment of our planetary and ethical species. He signed Humanist Manifesto 2000. {*International Humanist News*, October 1995}

RAZONAMIENTOS

Razonamientos is a Mexican quarterly published by the *Asociacion Mexicana Ética Racionalista*, Apdo. Postal 19-546, Mexico, DF 03900, Mexico. It was first published in 1995, and its editorial board consists of humanists from Argentina, Canada, Colombia, Mexico, the Netherlands, Peru, Spain, and the United States of America.

E-mail: <mendezm@spin.com.mx>.

Read, Allen Walker (1906–)

A distinguished lexicographer and professor emeritus of English at Columbia University, Read has written, "The word 'god' is not needed in an explanation of human or nonhuman affairs. All sentences in which the word 'god' is used in first-order usage are either invalid or obfuscatory in the same way that all calculations in which zero is multiplied result in zero."

The ex-Iowan scholar is known for being an expert on British and United States slang as well as having pinpointed the first usage of "O.K.," for which William Safire and other linguists often cite his scholarship. He is cited by the *Oxford Companion to the English Language* (1992) for also having traced the origin of "Dixie," "Podunk," and "Rebel Yell." He has traced "You know," the ubiquitous interjection used when an individual is searching for what to say next, to 1835, citing evidence that it was "a phrase an Englishman throws in at the turn of every sentence, when he is hunting for a new idea, or the words to fill the coming one." His research has shown that the word *gay* did not exist in its contemporary meaning of homosexual before the 1950s.

Classic American Graffiti, Lexical Evidence from Folk Epigraphy in Western North America (1935) was Read's first work, published in Paris and issued privately in seventy-five copies. A glossarial study of the low element in the English vocabulary, it is a masterpiece of latrinalia. For example, in a Banff, Alberta, latrine in 1928 he recorded the following:

> Oh! I wish I had the balls of a stallion
> and a prick of a fellow I know.
> I would flee to the highest church steeple
> and I would piss on the people below.

Read's study includes the shocking-for-some four-letter Anglo-Saxon words, along with such others as balls, clap, puss, bone, dose, hose. It included a quote from a Pompeii wall (around 79 C.E.): *Hic ego puellas multas futui*. The author's unembarrassed reporting as to how folks folksily communicate on a vulgar, not just a formal and informal level, caught the appreciative eye of lexicographers as well as the disapproving eye of bluenoses.

Read has been president of the Dictionary Society of North America and the Linguistic Association of Canada and the United States. Married to the Alfred Korzybski expert Charlotte Read, he is a longtime advocate of secular humanism and is a member of the Secular Humanist Society of New York. {HNS; HNS2}

Read, Carveth (1848–1931)

Read was Grote professor of philosophy and lecturer on comparative psychology at London University College. He wrote *Natural and Social Morals* (1909), in which he argues for a humanist ethic and rejects "all shades of religion." Read added, "With the spread of civilization, the religious spirit declined because so much strength of character exists as to make civilization possible." {RAT; RE}

Read, Herbert [Sir] (1893–1968)

An adviser to the publishing firm Routledge and Kegan Paul, Read once described himself as "an anarchist, romanticist and agnostic." He was an eminent critic of both art and literature. Charlotte Franklin, writing in *New Humanist* (December, 1990), disagrees with *The Economist's* view that he was "prescient, acute, intelligent and honourable; but also cold, egotistical and unforgivably self-righteous." She holds that his exploring of utopian themes in *The Green Child* and his philosophic views in *The Contrary Experience* (1974) deserve a wider audience, saying he is a humanist in her eyes. Read is also author of *Naked Warriors* (1919), about war's horrors, *Alienation: The Role of the Artist in Society* (1967), and a collection of essays called *The Cult of Sincerity* (1969). {CE; TRI}

Reade, William Winwood (1824–1875)

Reade, a nephew of the novelist Charles Reade, was an English traveler and writer. Born in Scotland, he studied at Oxford, then journeyed to Africa, writing *Savage Africa* (1863), *The African Sketch Book* (1873), and *The Story of Ashantee Campaign*, which event he accompanied as *Times* correspondent. In the *Martyrdom of Man* (1872), Reade rejects the doctrine of a personal creator—the work enjoyed eighteen editions. It surveyed ancient and medieval history, telling of the growth of religion from savage beginnings and leading up to a definitely anti-theistic presentation of the future of human life with the claim to have shown "that the destruction of Christianity is essential to the interests of civilization." His last work, *The Outcast*, was a freethought novel that describes the harsh experiences of a skeptic who had rejected Christianity and any belief in a future life. McCabe states that although in the *Dictionary of National Biography* Reade is described as an atheist, actually he was an agnostic of the Spencerian school, one who recognized God as "the First Cause and Inscrutable Mystery."

His obituary, written by Charles Reade in the *London Daily Telegraph*, included, "He wrote his last work, *The Outcast*, with the hand of death upon him. Two zealous friends carried him out to Wimbledon, and there, for a day or two, the air seemed to revive him; but on Friday night he began to sink, and on Saturday afternoon died in the arms of his beloved uncle, Mr. Charles Reade." Winwood Reade not only rejected belief in immortality, but he regarded it as making many men and women, and even nations, "spiritual prisoners of the Shadow of Death, even while living." Moncure D. Conway, at the gravesite, said that Read "warned these life-long victims that the only victory over death is to concentrate themselves on life." {BDF; FUK; FUS; JM; JMR; JMRH; RAT; RE; TRI}

Reagan, Ronald Jr. (1958–)

Reagan is son of the 40th United States President, a Presbyterian. While interviewing the self-proclaimed messiah Charles Manson for a media program, Reagan was preached to by the man who allegedly had a "spell" over a "family" of followers who were found guilty of murdering actress Sharon Tate and her four guests. When Manson, explaining his "message" on the recorded program, asked the President's son if he believed in God, Reagan responded, "No, I do not." {CA; E}

Réage, Pauline (20th Century)

Réage was a pen name for the author of *The Story of O* (1954). (See the entry for Dominique Aury.)

REAL ACADEMIA ESPAÑOLA

The Royal Academy of Spain, which as *Real Academia Espaōla* was founded in 1713 to advance the study of the Castilian language, is located at Felipe IV 4, 28014 Madrid, Spain.

Its most recent dictionary in 1992 accepted about 600 new words from Mexico, but the academy's motto states that it "cleanses, fixes, and adds splendor" to Spanish, protecting it from debasing infiltrators. In 1868 when Feliz Ramos i Duarte printed a first dictionary of "Mexicanism," he termed it as a compendium of "tainted" terminology, in keeping with the academy's purposes. In 1997 at the First International Congress on the Spanish Language, held in Mexico, Mexicans made it clear that their country is the largest Spanish-speaking nation in the world, and they presented a 561-page list of 69,566 words and phrases which originated in Mexico. *La Real Academia Espanōla*, however, complained that it was not invited to the conference and did not intend to allow its branches overseas to become equal partners with headquarters in Madrid.

García Márquez scandalized the Iberian conservatives with his proposal "to simplify grammar before grammar simplifies us," and he suggested dropping the accent marks and either the letter "b" or "v" from written Spanish, since they sound the same. But Camilo José Cela, the Nobel Prize winner from Spain, issued a call to arms to defend the language from being extinguished by other more aggressive competitors, like English. {Julia Preston, *The New York Times*, 16 April 1997}

REALISM

In medieval philosophy, realism was a position that universals or general concepts have existence independent of both the human mind and individual objects. As such, it was directly opposite to nominalism (which holds that universal words or concepts have no objective reality outside the mind, that events exist objectively).

In epistemology, realism holds that individual things exist independently of the mind's perception of them. As such, it is opposed to idealism (which holds that reality exists only in the mind).

In literature, it is a movement in contradistinction to naturalism, expressionism, or surrealism that attempts to portray life as it is. Balzac and Stendhal were precursors of realism. Somerset Maugham's *Liza of Lambet* is exemplary, and the author uses proletarian or lower-middle-class settings.

David Deutsch's *The Fabric of Reality* (1997) makes a current case for realism. In his view of the philosophy of science, he disagrees with instrumentalism, for which science is a tool for anticipating what can be done and then using technology to control it. Instead, Deutsch portrays science as the means for giving and understanding an accurate description of an objective and fixed reality. Current theories, he holds, give real insights into the nature of reality. What is already known about evolution, computation, and human knowledge—combined with the deepest physical theory, namely quantum physics—shows what the universe is like. *The Economist* (31 May 1997) suggests several flaws in his arguments. First, he fails to persuade people that realism is right, that instrumentalism is wrong. Second, the various strands of his arguments illustrate "Popperian epistemology [which] is in poor odour among philosophers." And third, he assumes without showing that quantum physics and theories of life and knowledge belong to the same explanatory realm. Meanwhile, many realists insist Deutsch is on the right track. (See Bertrand Russell's *Problems of Philosophy* (1912) and the *Encyclopedia of Philosophy*, Vol. 7. Also, see entry for Magic Realism.) {AF; CE; DCL; OCP}

REALITY

• Reality is that which, when you stop believing in it, doesn't go away.

–Phillip K. Dick
{*The Eupraxopher* November-December 1997}

Reams, Ruth Dickinson (20th Century)

When she signed Humanist Manifesto II, Reams was President of the National Capital Area's Humanist Association. {HM2}

REASON

• Reason is the greatest enemy faith has. Whoever wants to be Christian should tear the eyes out of his reason.

–Martin Luther

• Reason is always a kind of brute force; those who appeal to the head rather than the heart, however pallid and polite, are necessarily men of violence. We speak of "touching" a man's heart, but we can do nothing to his head but hit it.

–G. K. Chesterton

Freethinkers and rationalists have a differing viewpoint: "No sensible man, however agnostic, has 'faith in reason alone.' Reason is concerned with matters of fact, some observed, some inferred," wrote Bertrand Russell (*Bertrand Russell on God and Religion*). "The question whether there is a future life and the question whether there is a God concern matters of fact, and the agnostic will hold that they should be investigated in the same ways as the question, 'Will there be an eclipse of the moon tomorrow?' But matters of fact alone are not sufficient to determine action, since they do not tell us what ends we ought to pursue. In the realm of ends, we need something other than reason. The agnostic will find his ends in his own heart and not in an external command." As an example, he says that a railroad timetable will dispense reasonable information about when trains run from one city to another; but no timetable tells a person that it is wise to travel to that city. In *The Rationalist Annual*, Russell stated that "the question is how to arrive at your opinions and not what your opinions are. The thing in which we believe is the supremacy of reason. If reason should lead you to orthodox conclusions, well and good; you are still a Rationalist. . . . Not to be absolutely certain is, I think, one of the essential things in rationality."

REASON STREET

Reason Street in New York City honored Thomas Paine's "Age of Reason" (1795) and its uncompromising attack on the Bible. The name became corrupted to Raisin Street, "raisin" being a colloquial term for a slave. When the street became city property in 1809, it was rechristened Barrow Street in honor of an artist and Trinity Church vestryman, Thomas Barrow. Barrow Street runs parallel and a block south of Grove Street, where Paine died. {Daniel B. Schneider, *The New York Times*, 2 May 1999}

REASONINGS

Reasonings is a monthly of Atheists & Agnostics of Wisconsin, 278 Orchard Drive, Oregon, Wisconsin 53575. E-mail: <mbr@execpc.com>.

Reber, George (19th Century)

Reber was the American author of *The Christ of Paul, or the Enigmas of Christianity* (1876), a work which exposes the frauds and follies of the early fathers. {BDF}

RECANTATION

To recant is to repudiate a previous belief, formally and publicly. Interestingly, some theistic individuals or families are so fearful that a person will not go to Heaven, to be joined at some later time, they fraudulently arrange last-minute recantations, baptisms, and the like. Meanwhile, some non-believers have been known to recant on their deathbeds, or so clericals have reported. (See entries for Kay Boyle, Sinclair Lewis, Maximilian Littré, Emma Martin, Thomas Paine, and Voltaire, among many others.)

Reccord, Augustus Phineas (1870–1946)

Reccord, a Unitarian minister, was author of *Who Are the Unitarians?* (1920). During World War II, and after his retirement, he served as a minister of the Louisville (Kentucky) Unitarian Society. An early publicist for Unitarianism, he once wrote: "Much of the prevalent indifference to the church is because of the impression that it demands that we make a choice between an unintelligent faith and an irreligious culture." Soldiers who heard his lectures could have heard his "Good Men in Hell," a lecture in which he explained why all good Unitarians should aim *not* for Heaven but for Hell; he then cited Mark Twain, Emerson, Diderot, and all the other good company who would be found there. In short, Reccord made it clear that he believed not in Heaven or Hell but in heaven and hell: in purely intellectual entities.

Some soldiers were nonplussed upon seeing the septuagenarian Bostonian, during his Kentucky church's fair, plunk down a quarter at a "kissing booth" in order to raise money for the war effort. One, a Bible Belt Methodist who had been avoiding his church's services because he complained they "missionaried" him, asked Reccord how and if he might join the Unitarians quickly before leaving for battle. Reccord's response, quite shocking to the Methodist whose church continually campaigns for new members, was, "Goodness, I have no idea!" With a little research, however, he located a membership book, and, with no further proselytizing, the soldier was allowed the following Sunday to join the non-Christian Unitarian church, after which he had his Army identification tag changed to list his religion as "None." In a short time, Reccord received a postcard from that soldier in France who had led his company up the hill at Omaha Beach: "Greetings and love, from an atheist in his foxhole!" {WAS, conversations}

Reclus, Élie Michel (1827–1904)

A brother of Jean Reclus and the son of a Protestant minister, Reclus fought in the Revolution of 1848 and was driven to Brussels, where he taught comparative mythology. He wrote many works on ethnology, including *Primitive Folk* (1891). Reclus was an atheist. {RAT; RE}

Reclus, Jean Jacques Elisée (1830–1905)

Reclus, a French geographer and socialist, was the son of a Protestant minister. The Moravian brethren educated him. Reclus left France after the 1851 coup, traveling in England, Ireland, and North and South America. Reclus upheld the cause of the North during the American civil war and in 1871 supported the Commune, being taken prisoner and sentenced to transportation for life. Receiving amnesty in 1879, he returned to Paris and published a standard *Universal Geography* in thirteen volumes. Reclus, who gave his two daughters in marriage without either religious or civil ceremony, wrote a preface to Bakounin's *God and the State*. {BDF;RAT; RE}

Reclus, Paul (1847–1914)

Reclus, a Protestant minister, had three noted sons who became atheists: **Élie**, **Jean**, and **Paul Reclus**. Paul was a professor of clinical surgery at Paris University and, unlike his brothers, took no part in advanced politics nor was he so aggressive as they were. {RAT; RE}

RECONSTRUCTIONISM

Reconstructionism in Judaism is a 20th century American movement that advocates a creative adjustment to contemporary conditions for Jews. It differs from Orthodox, Reform, and Conservative Judaism. Reconstructionist Judaism accepts all forms of Jewish practice, regarding Judaism as a culture rather than a theological system. In its redefinition of Judaism, reconstructionism refers not only to religion but also to Judaism as a civilization that includes language, customs, and culture. The movement was founded in 1922. In a 1934 book, *Judaism as a Civilization*, Rabbi Mordecai M. Kaplan wrote that the Jewish spirit is nourished through art, literature, and music. To him, God was not the personal deity portrayed by tradition. Rather, God is a symbol of the source of meaning, or the creative force found in the universe.

An estimated 15,000 Reconstructionist households existed in 1996. Rabbi Mordechai Liebling, executive director of the Jewish Reconstructionist Federation in Philadelphia, has described the typical Reconstructionist synagogue as having 300 families. Most synagogues are found in the Northeast, but a 350-family congregation exists in Eugene, Oregon. (See entries for Mordecai M. Kaplan and A. Walter Socolow.) {CE; *The New York Times*, 20 January 1997}

RECTOR

• Rector, n. In the Church of England, the Third Person of the parochial Trinity, the Curate and the Vicar being the other two.

–**Ambrose Bierce**
The Devil's Dictionary

RED HACKLE

Bertrand Russell preferred Lapsang Suchong tea and Red Hackle whisky. Discussing his preferences with Robert C. Marsh, Russell remarked about "red" that "there is nothing rarer than a red-headed woman who is not a bitch." He explained that dark pubic hair did not excite him erotically, that blonde pubic hair was almost invisible, but red pubic hair was highly arousing sexually. Just not in his tea or whisky, one might infer. {*Russell: the Journal of the Bertrand Russell Archives*, Summer 1995}

Red Hot Chili Peppers (20th Century)

The Red Hot Chili Peppers, a musical group, had in its album "One Hot Minute" the lyrics, "I was not created / In the likeness of a fraud." This clear rejection of biblical fundamentalism was accompanied by the group's admitted paganism and hedonism. Other of their works called for honesty, equality, and peace while praising the joys of sex. {*Free Inquiry*, Winter 1995-1996}

Red Jacket (c. 1758–1830)

A chief and a famed orator of the Seneca tribe in upstate New York, Red Jacket was so called because he wore red jackets first given him by the British. However, his original name was Otetiani, and he was also called Sagoyewatha. He is included by Whitehead and Muhrer in their *Freethought on the American Frontier* (1992) because of his vehemence in opposing missionaries who lived on reservations and his speech to one of those Christian missionaries.

The speech explained the Indians' view, and when at the end Red Jacket said he hoped the Great Spirit would protect him on his journey home, the missionary replied, "There [is] no fellowship between the religion of God and the works of the Devil, and, therefore, [I cannot] join hands. . . ." When this was interpreted to Red Jacket, he and his fellow Senecans smiled at the Christian's negativism and hate, then retired in a peaceable manner. {CE}

Reddals, George Holland (1846–1875)

An English secularist, Reddals was a compositor on the Birmingham *Daily Post*, then started the *Secular Chronicle* (1873), which was continued by Francis Neale, H. V. Mayer, and G. Standring. {BDF; FUK}

Rediess, Paul (20th Century)

In "The Power of Prayer," Rediess describes a Christian neighbor whose car slams into another's. "God damn, holy ghost, jesus christ, great god almighty, god damn," the neighbor was overheard to say.

Then a juvenile, Rediess reasoned, "If he had used intuition to pre-time the request, he would not have needed to express the request and could have saved money on a new bumper and parking light." His father, however, responded, "Sonofabitch!" To which Rediess observed, "I don't know what a male puppy had to do with it." {*Secular Nation*, July-September 1998}

REDEMPTION

• Redemption, n. Deliverance of sinners from the penalty of their sin, through their murder of the deity against whom they sinned. The doctrine of Redemption is the fundamental mystery of our holy religion, and whose believeth in it shall not perish, but have everlasting life in which to try to understand it.

–**Ambrose Bierce**
The Devil's Dictionary

Freethinkers who make a mistake which harms others either deny they have erred or, inspiringly, redeem themselves by apologizing or otherwise making up for having erred.

Redman, Edward (20th Century)

A minister of the First Unitarian Church of Ann Arbor, Michigan, Redman in 1957 addressed the Ann Arbor Regional Humanist Conference.

REDUNDANCY

• Redundant true sentences are true. Redundant false sentences are false . . . except this one.

–**Ted Nelson**

Redwood, John (20th Century)

Redwood is author of *Reason, Ridicule, and Religion—The Age of Enlightenment in England 1660–1750* (1976). He holds that the mockeries of a few witty skeptics interacted with reason and faith to produce a wide range of opinions, books, and controversies. The period, he adds, was more an age of ridicule than of reason.

Reeb, James (1927–1965)

Reeb, a Unitarian Universalist minister, was murdered in 1965 in Selma, Alabama, while working in a civil rights protest organized by Martin Luther King Jr. An account of his life is found in Duncan Howlett's *No Greater Love: The James Reeb Story* (1966). {U}

Reece, Gordon (20th Century)

Reece, a senior lecturer in engineering mathematics at the University of Bristol, has described himself as "a Jewish atheist" in *New Humanist*. By this he explains, "It means that the God I don't believe in is the Jewish God. The others don't even rate the honour of incredibility."

Reed, Clarence (20th Century)

Reed was a Unitarian who wrote "The Greatest Modern Discovery" (19–?). {GS}

Reed, Clifford (20th Century)

The Rev. Reed, of the United Kingdom, is Secretary of the International Council of Unitarians and Universalists.

Reed, David (Born 1790)

Reed founded the Unitarian Universalist journal, then called *The Christian Register*. {U; UU}

Reed, Esau (20th Century)

Reed edits a World Wide Web homepage that lists notable individuals who have been public about their lack of belief in deities. The list is a collaborative effort, for which he provides documentation. On the Web: <http://www.infidels.org:80/infidels>.

Reed, John (1887–1920)

Reed, a radical leader and journalist, wrote *Ten Days That Shook the World* (1919), an eyewitness account of the revolution that put the Bolsheviks in power. In 1919, expelled from the Socialist convention, he helped form a Socialist splinter party, the Communist Labor Party. Although he had made a name in journalism, writing from Mexico about Pancho Villa, Reed went to the USSR and worked for the Soviet Bureau of Propaganda. Reed died of typhus and was buried at the Kremlin. Reed was against all organized religions. {CE}

Reed, Lewis (19th Century)

Reed was a freethinker who wrote *Jingles or Humor, Sarcasm and Fact to Tingle the Present* (1894). {GS}

Rees, Lloyd Frederick (1895–1988)

Rees was an Australian humanist and artist. In Sydney, he lectured and taught art history, drawing, and painting. Traditionalists as well as modernists critically accepted him. Rees was a member of the Humanist Society of New South Wales. {SWW}

Rees, Malcolm (20th Century)

Rees has reviewed books for *The Freethinker*, including "H. J. Blackham and the Upshot of History." {*The Freethinker*, May 1996}

Rees, Martin [Sir] (1943-)

Sir Martin, holder in England of an honorary post that allows him to be called the Astronomer Royal of England, wrote *Before the Beginning: Our Universe and Others* (1997). As an astrophysicist, he says that to understand where atoms come from we first must understand the stars. "Did the creator magically turn ninety-two different knobs to make the different elements?" he told Claudia Dreifus (*The New York Times*, 28 April 1998):

> Or is there a reason why the earth contains a lot of carbon, oxygen, and iron, but not much gold and uranium? The explanation is that all the atoms were once inside a star. When our Milky Way galaxy was first formed about ten billion years ago, it contained the simplest atoms: hydrogen and helium. Then, the first stars were formed and the nuclear fuel that kept those stars shining converted hydrogen into helium through nuclear fusion and then converted helium into other atoms: carbon, oxygen, and the rest of the periodic table. Later, the stars ran out of fuel, they exploded, threw back all that debris into interstellar space and it all eventually condensed into new stars. One of which was our sun.

People, Rees has concluded, are but "the dust of long, dead stars." He doubts that intelligent life exists elsewhere but has little doubt that our species one day will propagate out through the galaxy.

Reese, Curtis W. (1887–1956)

A Southern Baptist turned Unitarian minister, Reese served in Alton, Illinois, and Des Moines, Iowa. In his post as executive director of the Western Conference Office (Unitarian) located in Chicago, Reese encouraged the organization of Unitarian churches and the acceptance of Humanism. He was a key figure in relocating Meadville Theological School to Chicago. An editor of *Unity*, he was an early leader of the Humanist movement within Unitarianism and was the successor to Western radical leader Jenkin Lloyd Jones as dean from 1930 to 1957 of Chicago's Abraham Lincoln Center.

In 1944, when Frederick M. Eliot, a humanist by not a doctrinaire one, according to Edwin H. Wilson, rejected the candidacy of Curtis Reese for the presidency of Meadville Theological School, Eliot explained that his decision had not been a personal one but, rather, he did not want Meadville to be perceived as having fallen into humanist hands. From 1949 to 1950, he was President of the American Humanist Association.

Concerning the present author's categorization of seven humanisms, Reese wrote:

> Category No. 7, naturalistic humanism, would come nearer indicating my position in the classification of humanist types. I have, however, at times in the past styled my position **Organic Humanism**, since I have made an effort to weave into my position strands from the various classifications of Humanism. I arrived at my original humanist position without any traceable influence from any other person, but I was very soon thereafter greatly influenced by the writings of F. S. C. Schiller, Roy Wood Sellars, William James, and John Dewey.
>
> I think that Classical Humanism properly belongs in the tradition of Modern Humanism, although it does not move out vigorously into the main stream of Humanism. Theistic Humanism, while better than Humanistic Theism, does not seem to me to be a very fruitful concept.
>
> Atheistic Humanism is more dogmatic about the nature of the universe than I care to be. Communistic Humanism I do not regard as a satisfactory designation because to me Humanism with its emphasis on freedom and the possibility of the intelligent control of natural processes is contradicted by the Communist ideology.

Reese, who signed Humanist Manifesto I, wrote *Humanist Sermons* (1927) and *The Meaning of Humanism* (1945).

Describing Midwestern humanism, Warren R. Ross wrote in *World* (November-December 1997) of Reese's importance:

> What was later to be called religious humanism first gained strength in the late 19th century in the Western Unitarian Conference. The Rev. Mary Safford preached what she called a "religion of morality on fire with love for humanity" from the pulpit of the Des Moines Unitarian Church, where she was followed by the Rev. Curtis Reese and his "religion of democracy." It was the Rev. John Dietrich in

Minneapolis who gave this reason- and ethics-based science-loving faith the name of humanism."

Reese's family, all devout Southern Baptists, declared they would rather see Reese burn in hell, as he surely would, if he left the Baptist Church at Tiffin, Ohio, and became minister of the Unitarian Church at Alton, Illinois, which he did. Edwin H. Wilson, learning this at a much later date, said even Reese's sister, who previously had named her son for Curtis, legally changed the child's name to that of a Baptist evangelist. Wilson observed, "I understood for the first time the painful pressure that had produced the terrific productivity and dynamic leadership of Curtis Reese." (See entry for Humanism, per Curtis Reese) {CL; HM1; EU, Paul H. Beattie; EW; FUS; HNS; HNS2; U; U&U; WAS, 28 April 1956}

Reeve, Christopher (1952–)

Reeve is the actor known for playing the title role in "Superman" (1978). He has performed in over one hundred plays, telecasts, and movies. An accident while riding a horse has confined him to a wheelchair, but he inspiringly, valiantly, and successfully continued to continue acting and directing. In Minneapolis, speaking at the Courage Center to the disabled on 27 October 1996, he was asked, "Do you believe in the Lord?" Reeve responded, "Even though I don't personally believe in the Lord, I try to behave as though he was watching." The Minneapolis *Star-Tribune* reported that the audience responded with "huge applause for a moment that was typical for its simplicity and candor." *Cinemania* (24 April 1997) had a column by Roger Friedman about where Reeve gets his undaunted courage, and Reeve's brother Ben Reeve, a nonpracticing Massachusetts lawyer, replied that it wasn't from God: "We're devout atheists, so that wasn't it."

On a Larry King telecast in 1998, Reeve was asked about his religious views, and Reeve responded,

> Well, believe it or not, I think that, y'know, God is not an entity that you find when you go to church and pray to God Almighty, you know, and I always remembered that going to church as a kid, you know, and they talk about the vengeance of His terrible swift sword and His army, I said, 'Well, that's kind of a scary guy.' But I think that—while I don't believe in God per se, I believe in spirituality. And I believe that spirituality actually is automatically within ourselves, but we have to learn how to access it, and what that is, is realizing there is a higher power; there is {King suggested "So it's not atheism?"] more than just us, there is an inner strength, there is something, y'know, that comes from—I don't know where exactly it comes from, but it's—it really is the best that humans can be and perhaps what it is—perhaps really what it is is love.

Asked online (7 May 1998) what he meant when at one point in his book he said it seemed that his spirit and left his body and looked down on it from the corner of the hospital room, Reeve explained,

> I feel strongly that we are not our bodies. In fact, if a person says "my body," who is the "me" that is being referred to? Clearly, the spirit and body are two different things. And beyond that, I'm still searching for the meaning of it all.

{CA; E}

Reeve, F. D. (20th Century)

Reeve, in *American Poetry Review* (Spring, 1994), uses the poet's approach in describing his religious non-belief. He writes, "In most of the forty wars on the surface of the earth today, the antagonistic nationalisms are underwritten by religious allegiance—Jew against Arab, Christian against Jew, Catholic against Muslim, Suni against Shiite. Some of the finest art and poetry of the Greeks was characterized by religious unity; much was not. In a secularized, overpopulated world, our cultural goal cannot be Arnold's 'to make reason and the will of God prevail.' From an individual's point of view, earthly life is very chancy; one's free will is restricted by luck, by the nature of the society one is born into, and by one's own nature. The ancient ideals of heroism and of transcendent immortality are incredible. The competitive haste to line one's pockets by exploiting the natural world threatens to expunge human life long before the earth itself goes out in fire and ice. History proves some men to have been reasonable; mankind, to have been irrational. Or, we might put it simply, clearly no one is in charge. Both god and the devil exist only in the mind of man."

Reeves, Joseph (1881–1969)

Reeves, who once was a chairman of the Rationalist Press Association (RPA), was a freethinker who supported innumerable causes, such as the Federal Union (1938) and the Parliamentary Group for World Government (1945). {TRI}

Reeves, William Pember (19th Century)

Reeves, an unbeliever and Fabian, married Maud Reeves, a prominent activist for the vote and for women's rights at the turn of the century. Their daughter, Amber, shocked the Fabian set by having an affair with historian H. G. Wells, with whom she had a daughter. Ruth Fry in *Maud and Amber* (1992) describes the family, relating how Amber wrote a short work, *Ethics for Unbelievers*.

REFORM

• Reform, n. A thing that mostly satisfies reformers opposed to reformation.

—**Ambrose Bierce**
The Devil's Dictionary

REFORM JUDAISM

As explained by Samuel Cohon, once a professor of Jewish theology at Cincinnati's Hebrew Union College, Reform Judaism "stems from the endeavor on the part of Jews in Western Europe to adjust themselves spiritually to the changed order introduced by the Enlightenment, on the one hand, and by the political and social upheaval at the turn of the eighteenth century, on the other. The doctrine of the rights of man," he added, "culminating in the French Revolution, broke down the barriers wherewith both Church and State kept the Jews apart from their neighbors. In 1791 the National Assembly enfranchised all the Jews of France. Four years earlier the U.S.A. adopted its Constitution based on the principles of equality and of liberty of conscience. For the first time since their dispersion the Jews found themselves the equals of their fellowmen." However, when a humanist congregation, Congregation Beth Adam, tried in 1994 to join the national Reform Jewish organization, the 220-member "temple without God" led by Rabbi Robert Barr had difficulty. Congregation Beth Adam does not explicitly acknowledge something bigger than them all: God. As a result, local synagogues and the Reform movement's regional board voted against including the humanistic group, and the Union of American Hebrew Congregations voted 115 to 13 to reject them. Rabbi Alexander M. Schindler, speaking for the Reform group reasoned that "Reform allows for a wide spectrum of belief. Yet some common understanding is necessary."

Meanwhile, Dr. Eugene Mihaly of Hebrew Union College warned that "Exclusion, ostracism, mindless stringency to appease the traditionalists, institutional coercion are alien to Reform Judaism. They chill and kill. They are the death knell of liberal religion." Commented Rabbi Barr concerning the rejection, "Clearly, the contemporary liturgy isn't speaking to most people at this point. The unaffiliated rate is high, and the attendance of the affiliated is quite low."

The founder of Reform Judaism in the United States was Isaac Mayer Wise. He oversaw its spread across the country. In the United States, Reform Jewish congregations have more members than other branches of Judaism. In 1995, Rabbi Eric H. Yoffie, who had pushed for greater rights for the Reform and Conservative Jewish movements in Israel, was elected president of the Union of American Hebrew Congregations, the main body of North American Reform Judaism. {DCL}

Rege, Meghasyama Pundalika (20th Century)

Rege is vice president of the Indian Secular Society. He wrote *Concepts of Justice and Equality in the Indian Tradition* (1985). {*Free Inquiry*, Summer, 1986}

Regenbrecht, Michael Eduard (1792–1849)

Regenbrecht, a German rationalist, left the Church with Johannes Ronge, becoming a leader of the free religious movement at Breslau. {BDF}

Reghillini de Schio, Mario (1760–1853)

Born of Venetian parents, Reghillini de Schio was professor of chemistry and mathematics. He wrote *Masonry* (1833) in French, tracing the lodge to Egypt. He also wrote *An Examination of Mosaism and Christianity* (1834). Also, he published a number of books on Freemasonry. Mixed in the troubles of Venice in 1848, he fled to Belgium, dying there in poverty. {BDF}

Regnard, Albert Adrien (Born 1836)

Regnard, a French physician and publicist, wrote *Essais d'Histoire et de Critique Scientifique* (1856), which he published himself after finding no suitable publisher that would print the work on scientific materialism. He started, with Naquet and Clemenceau, the *Revue Encyclopédique.* When its first issue was suppressed, he started *La Libre Pensée with Asseline and Condereau.* His articles in this publication netted him four months in prison. He wrote *New Researches on Cerebral Congestion* (1868), *Atheism* (1878), and *A History of England Since 1815.*

Regnard translated Büchner's *Force and Matter* in 1884 and was delegate to the Freethinkers' International Congress at Antwerp in 1885. {BDF; PUT; RAT}

Regnard, Jean François (1655–1709)

A French comic poet, Regnard went to Italy about 1676 and, on returning home, was captured by an Algerian corsair and sold as a slave. Caught in an intrigue with one of the women, Regnard turned Moslem. The French consul paid his ransom, and he returned to France about 1681. Regnard wrote a number of successful comedies and poems. He was made a treasurer of France and, according to Wheeler, died an Epicurean. {BDF}

Regnaud de Saint-Jean D'Angély, Michel Louis Étienne [Count] (Born 1761)

Regnaud de Saint-Jean D'Angély was prominent in the National Convention, and it was at his demand that Voltaire's remains were removed to the Pantheon and a statue was erected to him at Paris. He edited the *Journal de Versailles.* Napoléon admitted him to the Council of State, making him Secretary of State in 1810 for the Imperial Family. In 1816 he was proscribed and sailed for America. In 1819, he was allowed to return. {RAT}

Regnier, Mathurin (1573–1613)

Regnier was a French satirical poet, brought up in Chartres for the Church but showing little inclination for its austerities. A devoted pagan, Regnier did obtain a canonry in the cathedral of his native place. {BDF}

Rehák, Alexander (20th Century)

Rehák, an emeritus professor in Slovakia, signed Humanist Manifesto 2000.

Rehan, Khursid Rehan (20th Century)

In "Jama't-e-Tableegh—A New Sect in the Making" (*The Radical Humanist,* June 1999), Rehan names the four major sects within the Sunni denomination of Islam: Hanafi, Shafayi, Hambali, and Maliki, all named after four Imans. A new sect, he finds, is in the making: Jama't-e-Tableegh [group of campaigners], which discards the existence of orders and their interpretations as well as the interpretations given by the other four Imans. The movement was launched in 1930 by Maulana Mohammed Ilyas of Delhi with a view to purifying Islam, which was felt to be infected with the Hinduistic and Western cultures.

Reich, David (20th Century)

Reich is editor of *World,* the journal of the Unitarian Universalist Association. He is author of "Fighting the Right on Civil Rights for Lesbians, Gays, and Bisexuals." *{The World,* July-August 1994}

Reich, Eduard (Born 1839)

A German physician and anthropologist, Reich studied at Jena, traveled much, and published over thirty volumes besides editing the *Athenaeum* of Jena (1875) and *Universities* of Grossenbain (1883). Dr. Reich, a freethinker, wrote *Man and the Soul* (1872), *The Church of Humanity* (1874), *History of the Soul* (1884); and *The Emancipation of Women* (1884). {BDF}

Reich, Wilhelm (1897–1957)

Reich, who was born into an Austrian Jewish family, became a noted as well as controversial psychoanalyst. His life was one long series of problems. A student of Freud, he eventually broke with his master, as had Jung and Adler—he developed his own theories of neurosis, including a concept about "character armoring" and another about the centrality of "genital" potency. Because of his radical politics, he was expelled from the International Psychoanalytic Association. The German Communist Party also expelled him, complaining about his bourgeois views concerning psychiatry. Moving to the United States he was jailed for several weeks, suspected of being a possible German spy. However, he was one of the first leftists to see the weaknesses of Soviet Marxism, and he developed a following in the 1920s that considered him a prophetic genius.

His first wife, Annie, was a former patient. Although he said he was a devoted husband, he accused Annie of driving away their two daughters by poisoning them against him. Ilse Ollendorff Reich, his wife and the mother of Reich's son, Peter, wrote *Wilhelm Reich, A Personal Biography* (1969). Of the famed Austrian psychiatrist who was hostile to religion, she has written the present author concerning her ex-husband:

> Reich never belonged to any organized religious community and, until the time he went to prison, he never went to any kind of religious services. I don't know what he would have called himself, probably an agnostic or a humanist. His funeral was secular. He identified with Christ / Jesus the human, and I think he accepted not the Christianity of the Church but the teachings of Jesus. Dr. Elsworth Baker, who in my book was named as the person who gave a brief eulogy at the memorial service and ended with Reich's version of the Lord's Prayer from his *Murder of Christ,* was a psychiatrist who practiced Reich's orgone therapy. He was a devoted "disciple" of Reich, and he organized after Reich's death a group of orgone therapists into the "College of Orgonomy," feuding with all those who in their own way believed they were the only true followers. Baker died a few years ago.
>
> Reich's version of the Lord's Prayer is only different from the original in the start: "Our Love / Life, who art from Heaven," and he substituted "guilt" for debts and in the last two lines "and lead us not into distortion of love, but deliver us from our perversions." He mentions "God-Father is the basic cosmic energy from which all being stems, and which streams through (the) body as through anything else in existence." *Murder of Christ* was written in 1952.

"I don't know," continued Ilse, herself a Quaker,

> whether he distinguished between Christ the supernatural and Jesus the natural. I do think that the concept of Christ was for him a universal concept, continuing through the ages, but that Jesus was for him *the* natural, exceptional human being who, because of his message of love and his understanding of human nature, had to be murdered. I do know that during his imprisonment and until shortly before his death he attended the Protestant services in prison. He sent our son Peter some prayers that he must have found in those services. This "conversion" seemed to me utterly strange, almost unbelievable in view of his past anti-church attitude. I had, of course, no way to find out why and how this change came about.

Paul Edwards in the *Encyclopedia of Unbelief* described Reich as a "psychiatrist with enormous influence on current therapeutic techniques, second perhaps only to that of Sigmund Freud, and one of the most outspoken opponents of religion, especially its harmful effects on character and mental health. As a psychological rather than a philosophical critic of religion, Reich continued the work of Friedrich Nietzsche and Freud, developing this critique more systematically and in greater detail than his predecessors." Unfortunately, in his later years Reich began to believe all kinds of absurd things, saw Communist conspiracies everywhere, asserted the existence of UFOs, toyed with the idea that he himself was the son of a spaceman, and was jailed by the government because of his orgone box, a contraption in which one was supposed to sit naked in order to boost one's energy, especially one's erotic vigor. The Food and Drug Administration in 1956 declared the orgone box a fraud. Reich wrote in *The Mass Psychology of Fascism* (1933), "What religion calls freedom from the outside world really means fantasized substitute gratification for actual gratification. . . . Every form of mysticism is reactionary, and the reactionary man is mystical." Convicted of contempt of court, Reich died in prison.

Gaskin, pointing out that one defect of Marx's and Lenin's analyses of religion is that they give no account of why religious belief persists in situations in which it is not of assistance to the ruling classes in upholding the status quo. But Reich, stated Gaskin, "takes the analysis in a different and more radical direction. In the *Mass Psychology of Fascism* (1933), Reich suggests that the *energy* that underlies religious emotions can be seen as displaced or redirected sexual energy." Reich, who once joined the Communist Party, was expelled by the party for writing that book. However, he remained a Marxist.

In 1994, Mary Boyd Higgins edited Reich's *Beyond Psychology: Letters and Journals, 1934–1939*. She includes private writings from Reich's pivotal period, a time when he used such jargon as "vegetative," "vasovegative," and "Sexpol." Henry H. Bauer, professor of chemistry and science studies at Virginia Polytechnic Institute and State University, Blacksburg, Virginia, wrote that the book reveals Reich's ignorance of much of the science in which he regarded himself as competent. He adds, "This book provides copious support for those who would debunk Reich's scientific pretensions, and Reich's attitude—especially perhaps toward women–as he comes across as notably self-centered and altogether not very nice. Yet the book was put together for publication by an admirer, as the introduction plainly shows. So we get insight not only into Reich but also into his followers, and into how skeptical perspective is lost once allegiance has been lent."

"There's a therapist Jerry travels to New York to see every two weeks, a practitioner of Wilhelm Reich's theories of orgonomy," wrote Joyce Maynard when describing her nine-month affair with novelist J. D. Salinger. "Jerry never goes into it much with me, except to say that this therapy involves working with a person's muscles, and using one's voice in a certain way that releases blocked energy. This is not the kind of therapist with whom you talk about your childhood, or the kind with whom you might discuss the fact that the young woman you are living with is unable to have intercourse."

An eloquent supporter of Reichian therapy is philosopher Paul Edwards. In 1995, he spoke to overflowing crowds three successive weekends at the New School for Social Research, where Reich had once taught a course that served as the basis for his *Function of the Orgone*. Overbearing, jealous, crafty (he stole his friend Myron Sharaf's wife), and a martinet whose rages terrified his friends, Reich nevertheless was an excellent psychiatrist. Unlike Freud, who stood out of sight of his patients, Reich met his nude patients and as a physician probed their bodies for tenseness and other problems. For him, the mind anchors itself in the body and, for example, we might keep our fear down by arching our shoulder. Certain parts of the body were pressed in order to treat the patient, and exercising was recommended. Instead of treating symptoms, which will only reoccur, Reich tried to get at the underlying character traits and worked on them. Whereas Freudian therapists used words rather than physical contact and kept patients for years (Diana and Lionel Trilling had analysis for decades), Reich aimed to keep his patients for a short time. If Karen Horney could not help a patient, it was alleged, she sent him to a Reichian, not a Freudian. Edwards holds that Freud's therapy does not help much but that Reich's does.

Edwards noted that Reich when young had found his mother in a tutor's arms, had revealed this to his father, and when his mother later committed suicide the experience greatly affected him. Edwards approved much about Reich's views, including his opposition to lifelong marriages and his acceptance of masturbation as being entirely natural. Religion goes hand-in-hand with sexual repression, Reich held. That energy might well have gone into sex, and the inference could be made that if one has a good sex life he will not need religion badly. (See the entries by Paul Edwards in *Encyclopedia of Philosophy*, Vol. 7, The *Encyclopedia of Unbelief*, and *Oxford Companion to Philosophy*.) {Henry H. Bauer, *Skeptical Inquirer*, September-October 1995; CE; EU, Paul Edwards; Richard Gilman, "Orgonization Man," *The New York Times Book review*, 5 September 1999; Joyce Maynard, "Salinger in Love," Vanity *Fair*, September 1998; Ilse Ollendorff Reich to WAS, 21 November 1991}

Reichenbach, Hans (1897–1953)

Reichenbach, whose name is associated with the Logical Positivist movement but who was critical of the narrow scope of its verificationism, termed himself a "logical empiricist." His *Selected Writings, 1909–1953* was about space and time. {HNS; HNS2; OCP}

Reichwald, E. C. (19th Century)

Reichwald was secretary starting in 1883 of Chicago's American Secular Union. Chicago's Half Century of Progress featured "an old and established representative house engaged in the Chicago fruit and vegetable trade" of "Messrs. Reichwald & Bro., which was established in 1865 by Jones & Reichwald, who were succeeded in 1868 by E. C. Reichwald & Co." Both E. C. and his brother W. G. Reichwald were radical freethinkers. {PUT}

Reid, Alastair (1926–)

Although born in Scotland, Reid has chosen to live mainly in Hispanic countries. The son of a minister, he is a poet, translator, essayist, and author of books for children. *Ounce, Dice, Trice* (1958) is a collection of puns and odd-sounding "nonsense" words. *Weathering* (1978) is a collection of his poems. Reid translated Neruda's *Isla Negra Notebook* (1982) and Borges's *Gold of the Tigers* (1977).

In "Remembering Robert Graves," Reid tells of his long friendship with Graves, "a first-rate classicist" who, in the course of writing the two Claudius novels, "had immersed himself in Roman history" and who taught him much about writing. Graves, he wrote, "was a deicide [one who kills or destroys a god]; he had made from the great tangle of his existence a religion that he could feel true to, and which could resolve the contradictions and oppositions in his thinking. As a devotee, he was privy to the Goddess's will. He always bowed solemnly nine times at the first sight of the new moon. To the supplanting of the Goddess by a Father God he attributed all the ills of the modern world." Since the Bronze Age, Reid explained, an all-embracing female deity—Moon Goddess, an Earth Mother, controlling seasons, fertility, and the cycle of birth and death—had been worshipped throughout Europe until challenged by the male gods of the Greco-Roman world. With Christianity, goddess worship disappeared, preserved, according to Graves, by poets alone as a divine secret—or through the worship of a muse. From his vast reading, Graves created a monomyth that gave order to his deepest convictions and restored to poetry some of the sanctity he felt it had lost by neglecting myth for reason." Commented Reid, "I never believed in the Goddess, any more than I believed in a Christian God. I realized, however, that Robert did believe, insistently so, and that the belief sustained and justified him." {*The New Yorker*, 4 September 1995}

Reid, George Archdall O'Brien [Sir] (Born 1860)

Reid once summed up his early career, saying he had been in succession a schoolmaster, a Kauri-gum digger, a stockman, a hunter, and joint-editor of *Bedrock*. As a scientific writer, particularly on questions of heredity, he first won attention by his *Present Evolution of Man* (1896). He also wrote *Alcoholism* (1901) and *The Principles of Heredity* (1905, in which he expressed his rationalism: "Almost without exception, religions have restrained the instinct of curiosity—hence the prolonged intellectual and social stagnation in which so many races have sunk." He added, "Probably in all history there is no instance of a society in which ecclesiastical power was dominant which was not at once stagnant, corrupt, and brutal." {RAT}

Reid, W. Nichol (20th Century)

Reid wrote *The Supremacy of Reason* (1924). {GS}

Reil, Johann Christian (1758–1813)

Reil was a German physician who, although intended for the Church, turned instead to medicine. He wrote many medical works, displacing some old ideas in a way which brought on him the accusation of pantheism. While attending a case of typhus fever at Halle, he was attacked by the malady and succumbed. {BDF; RAT}

Reilly, Patricia Lynn (20th Century)

Reilly, a Unitarian, is co-director of a women's theology center in Berkeley, California, and author of *A God Who Looks Like Me* (1995). "In the very beginning was the Mother," she corrects *Genesis*, taking issue with what she considers the sexist, patriarchal, and out-of-touch theology of mainstream churches. "Our search for God who looks like us," she holds, "begins in our own lives. She will be found there."

Reimarus, Hermann Samuel (1694–1768)

Reimarus's *Apology or Defence of the Reasonable Worshipers of God* and his *Fragments* (1774–1778) revealed Reimarus's views that religion can be based on common sense. One does not need revelation, dogmas, and church doctrines, reasoned one of the most radical of the German rationalists. He thought the Old Testament was a weak religious achievement, that biblical stories are full of humbug and deceit. Jesus, he noted, did not teach the idea of the Trinity nor claim that he was God's chosen son. Reimarus wrote *The Principle Truths of Natural Religion* (1754) and left behind the *Wolfenbültel Fragments*, which were published by Lessing in 1777. Reimarus professed "natural religion," or deism. {EU, 286, Karl Becker; BDF; RAT; RE}

Reinach, Joseph (1856–1921)

Reinach was of a German-Jewish family that settled in France. He practiced law until his friend Gambetta made him *chef de cabinet*, and he entered the Chambre as an anti-clerical. On the Dreyfus case, Reinach powerfully opposed the Church. He gave his own Rationalist views in a life of Diderot (1894), and he wrote the life and edited the speeches of Gambetta. Reinach was an honorary associate of the Rationalist Press Association (RPA). {RAT; RE}

Reinach, Salomon (1858–1932)

Reinach, the younger brother of Joseph, was a professor of archaeology at the Louvre. His *Apollo* (1904), *Cultes, mythes, et religions* (1905–1908, 3 volumes), and *Orpheus* (1909), are standard works on the evolution of religion. {RAT; RE}

Reinach, Théodore (1860–1928)

Reinach, an agnostic, wrote *Religions et sociétés* (1905), in which he stated that "all the hypotheses which have become beliefs, all the hopes of a beyond and the moral laws which piety has raised, have been shattered," but "the Unknowable remains." {RE}

REINCARNATION

For those not content just with living on Earth in their present existence, the dream of reincarnation, or a rebirth or embodiment in some other form, is an alternative. Several religions, including Hinduism, believe that the human spirit returns to earth in different forms again and again as it strives for perfection. If reincarnation usually means rebirth in another body of the same species, especially the human, transmigration has the broader meaning of passage back and forth across the boundaries of all forms—plant, animal, human, demonic, and divine. Thus, an individual born with a physical defect might dream of becoming a beautiful butterfly one day. Presumably, porcine creatures aspire also, although it is not clear to what ends nor exactly who or what executes the changes. Jesus has been identified by some as having been reincarnated as the wife of Julius Caesar. Paul Edwards in *Reincarnation: A Critical Examination* (1996) thoroughly and incisively refutes karma, reincarnation, and related topics. With wit and humor, he attacks J. M. E. McTaggart, C. J. Ducasse, Ian Stevenson, Shirley MacLaine, and others who have fallen for what secular humanists and freethinkers term as nonsense. The Law of Karma, for example, offers only *post hoc* explanations. Reincarnationists cannot explain credibly how the mind could make its transition from a dead body into the womb of the mother of its next incarnation. Edwards is the first philosopher to have critically examined reincarnation, then shown in depth the theory's inconsistencies. Mercilessly attacked are Elisabeth Kübler-Ross; Raymond Moody, author of the best-selling *Life After Life*; Karlis Osis and Erlandur Haraldsson, specialists in deathbed visions; and Stanislav Grof and Joan Halifax, who have attempted to support reincarnation and other supernaturalistic theories by citing certain experiences during LSD sessions. Edwards exposes their illogic. Although Mory Bernstein in *The Search for Bridey Murphy* claims that Julius Caesar, Spinoza, and T. H. Huxley believed in reincarnation, Edwards disproves the allegation. Neither, Edwards wrote, were David Hume or many others cited by various authors proponents of reincarnation.

Christopher Hitchens has summarized Edwards's arguments:

- No reincarnationist has ever attempted to answer the question first proposed by Tertullian: "How happens it that a man who dies in old age returns to life as an infant?"

- Reincarnation beliefs predate the findings of evolution. They can give no account of the act that human bodies descended from nonhuman species. And those extremists who postulate human souls in animal or insect bodies obviously cannot describe the experience in any known language.

- Unless a reincarnationist is willing to say there was a "first generation" of souls created with the first humans, he is exposed to absurdity by the recency of human life on the planet.

- Since all births are defined by reincarnationists as "rebirths," there has either not been a vast explosion in the human population, or souls from "astral bodies" are being mobilized to make up the spiraling deficit. An ingenious solution put forward in some reincarnationist circles—the idea of a single soul inhabiting many bodies at once—destroys the essential claim that any form of individual identity can survive death.

Martin Gardner (*Free Inquiry*, Summer 1997) reviewed Edwards's *Reincarnation* favorably, adding, "One reason Edwards's book is such a pleasant read is that he has a sense of humor and sarcasm worthy of Voltaire or H. L. Mencken."

{DCL; ER; Christopher Hitchens, *The Nation*, 12 May 1997; PE; RE}

Reinders, Clarence (20th Century)

Reinders, who was raised in the Roman Catholic religion and entered a seminary when he was sixteen, became disillusioned with religion by the time he was twenty-one, rejecting church rituals such as communion—which he regards as cannibalism—and rejecting belief in the Bible—which he considers fiction.

In 1998 Reinders, joined by the Freedom From Religion Foundation, filed a lawsuit against the City of Marshfield, Wisconsin, seeking to remove a sixteen-foot religious shrine from a public park. The city, in order to skirt the issue, reportedly planned to sell 7,500 square feet of the park to a religious group in order to maintain the shrine in its location. Reinders received the Foundations "Emperor Has No Clothes" award.

Reiner, Albert L. (20th Century)

Reiner is author of *Shabbat Commentaries, Torah Commentaries.* Instead of viewing belief in God, practice of ritual, or observance of *halakha* as the *sine qua non* of Jewishness, he views the Torah as a source of the ideals, humanity, and idiom that are the heritage of Judaistic Humanists.

Reinfeldt, Sebastian (20th Century)

At the Eighth International Humanist and Ethical Union (IHEU) World Congress held in Hannover (1982), Reinfeldt of Germany addressed the group.

Reinhardt, Aurelia (1877–1947)

Reinhardt was a Unitarian educator, the president of Mills

College. She was the first woman to serve as moderator of the American Unitarian Association. {U}

Reinhold, Ernst Christian Gottlieb (1793–1855)

Reinhold was a German philosopher who taught at Kiel University and Jena University. In the main, he followed the ideas of his father, Karl Reinhold, but in some respects he was nearer to Kant. Reinhold called himself a "Speculative Theist."

Reinhold, Karl Leonhard (1758–1825)

Reinhold, father of Ernst Reinhold, was a German philosopher. In 1772 he became a Jesuit, but the Society was suppressed in the following year, so he taught philosophy at a Barnabite College. Adopting the rationalist ideas which were current in Vienna under Joseph II, Reinhold abandoned Catholicism. He joined the Freemasons and a Rationalist Society called *Zur Wahren Eintracht*. Reinhold collaborated on Wieland's *Deutsche Mercur* and married Wieland's daughter. In his last work, *Die alte Frage, Was ist Wahreit?* (1820), he returned to a rationalistic theism. {RAT}

Reiser, Armin (20th Century)

At the Tenth International Humanist and Ethical Union (IHEU) World Congress held in Buffalo (1988), Reiser from Germany addressed the group.

Reiser, Oliver L. (1895–1974)

Reiser taught philosophy at the University of Wisconsin and the University of Pittsburgh. He is well-known in humanist circles because of his *Promise of Scientific Humanism* (1940). In addition, he founded the International Committee on Scientific Humanism in the 1950s. In describing his own humanism, Reiser has written,

> The one great hope for democracy lies in the development of a non-supernaturalistic religion which, unlike other intellectual movements, will be non-academic in its appeal to all civilized individuals. This new foundation for a coming world-order must be the emergent outcome of the thought-content of a universalized culture. In providing this unification of man's intellectual-emotional make-up, through a synthesis of the world of facts with the world of values, scientific humanism rediscovers democracy in man's creative cooperation for a better world. The major contribution of a coming philosophy will be the answer to the cry of people everywhere groping toward a view which will give them at once a confidence in the future, a motive for work, and a goal. The god of this coming world-religion, that is the object of reverence of scientific humanism, is the spirit of humanity in its upward striving—the fearful and wonderful quest to explore the depths and shoals of the cosmic environment and tame the universe for social weal and further human adventure.

Included among Reiser's books are *Humanistic Logic for the Mind in Action* (1930), and an introduction to scientific humanism entitled *Planetary Democracy* (1933). In the 1950s, Reiser was on the advisory board of Charles Francis Potter's First Humanist Society of New York. {FUS; HM1; HM2; HNS; HNS2}

Reisman, David (20th Century)

Reisman wrote *The Lonely Crowd* (1950). {EW}

Reiss, Harriet M. (20th Century) and Ira L. Reiss (1925–)

In their book, *An End to Shame: Shaping Our Next Sexual Revolution* (1993), the Reisses denounce America's present sexual climate. They also outline what steps they believe should be taken to change that climate. He lists his religion in *Who's Who* as Jewish.

Reiss, Ira (20th Century)

In 1996, at the 2nd Annual Atheist Alliance Convention, held in Minneapolis, Reiss spoke on the subject, "Sexuality in America: Walking Backwards into the 21st Century."

Reiss, Mike (20th Century)

Reiss, a producer for the telecast, "The Simpsons," has described himself as being both a humanist and a humorist. "The humanists," he has written, "have never produced an artist like that religious ceiling-painter Michelangelo. We've never spawned a musician like that hymn-scribbler Bach. But we have produced the brightest, most biting wits: Twain and Voltaire, Swift and Bierce. Let's keep the humanist movement funny. It's what we do best." (See examples of his wit in the entry for Humanist Humor.) {*Secular Humanist Bulletin*, Summer 1996}

Reitmeister, Louis Aaron (Born 1903)

Reitmeister wrote "A Brief Essay About the Gods and My Friends" (1948). {GS}

Reitzel, Robert (1849–1898)

Reitzel was a German-American revolutionary. Born in Baden, he studied theology, went to America, walked from New York to Baltimore, and became minister to an independent Protestant church. Resigning that job, he became a speaker of a freethought congregation at Washington for seven years. In Detroit he edited *Der Arme Teufel*, informing his readers that he "shall be a poor man and a Revolutionaire all my life." {BDF}

REKENSCHAP

A Dutch cultural-scientific quarterly in Dutch and English, *Rekenschap* is at Postbus 75490, 1070 AL Amsterdam, The Netherlands. E-mail: <hv@euronet.nl>.

RELATIVISM

In philosophy, relativism is the doctrine that no ideas or beliefs are universally true but that all are, instead, "relative." That is, their validity depends on the circumstances in which they are applied. Conceptions of truth and moral values are not absolute but are, instead, relative to the persons or groups holding them. Thus, the moon is not "up," unless one clearly maps what is "down." Abortion to some is absolutely bad in all cases, but to others it is permissible in some, many, or even in all cases. John Dewey and his school are credited by their critics of being ethical relativists. {DCL; ER}

RELIGION

"There is not enough religion in the world," Nietzsche once lamented, "to destroy the world's religions."

As to what religion is, Bertrand Russell explained, "By religion, I mean a set of beliefs held as dogmas, dominating the conduct of life, going beyond or contrary to evidence, and inculcated by methods which are emotional or authoritarian, not intellectual." "Religion is based," Lord Russell also believed, "primarily and mainly on fear. It is partly the terror of the unknown, and partly the wish to feel that you have a kind of elder brother who will stand by you in all your troubles and disputes. Fear is the basis of the whole thing—fear of the mysterious, fear of defeat, fear of death. Fear is the parent of cruelty, and therefore it is no wonder if cruelty and religion go hand in hand." But religion has attracted many, he added, because "belief in God serves to humanize the world of nature, and to make men feel that physical forces [of nature] are their allies. In like manner immortality removes the terror from death. People who believe that when they die they will inherit eternal bliss may be expected to view death without horror. It does soothe men's fears somewhat even when it cannot allay them wholly."

Writing in 1969, Russell lamented that religion, "as embodied in the Churches, discourages honest thinking, in the main, and gives importance to things that are not very important. Its sense of importance seems to be quite wrong. [In ancient times] when the Roman Empire was falling, the Fathers of the Church didn't bother much with the fall of the Roman Empire. What they bothered about was how to preserve virginity. That was what they thought important. In the present day, when the human race is falling, I find that eminent divines think it's much more important to prevent artificial insemination than it is to prevent the kind of world war that will exterminate the whole lot of us. That seems to me to show a lack of sense of proportion." {Lee Eisler, *The Quotable Bertrand Russell*}

• Religion? Superstitious crap!

–Carl Pinel of Stockport, England

• The idea of a good society is something you do not need a religion and eternal punishment to buttress; you need religion if you are terrified of death.

—Gore Vidal

• People who are no longer religious are more able to be honest with themselves and with others, about how they feel, whatever that feeling is.

—W. W. Watters

{See "The Secular Sphinx: The Riddle of Ethics Without Religion," by Michael Shermer in *Skeptic*, Vol. 4, No. 2, 1996; *The Freethinker*, January 1997)

RELIGION AND SCIENCE

In the 1990s, many freethinkers and secular humanists accused religious liberals—such as the theistic Unitarians—of reducing theology to vacuousness in their attempt to reconcile a theistic religion with science. That attempt at reconciliation, however, has been a strong one. In the 1970s attempts were made to link Eastern religion with science.

"Theology is not some airy-fairy form of metaphysical speculation," Cambridge University particle physicist turned Anglican priest John C. Polkinghorne has written. His *Belief in God in an Age of Science* (1998) claims that science and religion both are rooted in encounters with reality. But, countered Harvard biologist E. O. Wilson, author of *Consilience* (1998), "If history and science have taught us anything, it is that passion and desire are not the same as truth. The human mind evolved to believe in the gods. It did not evolve to believe in biology."

RELIGION AND SCIENCE, CONFLICT OF (AND NOMA)

Stephen Jay Gould, writing of the supposed "conflict" or "warfare" between science and religion, has a scientific humanist's—he cagily calls it a Jewish agnostic's—viewpoint:

> No such conflict should exist because each subject has a legitimate magisterium, or domain of teaching authority—and these magisteria do not overlap (the principle that I would like to designate as NOMA, or "nonoverlapping magisteria"). The net of science covers the empirical realm: what is the universe made of (fact) and why does it work this way (theory). The net of religion extends over questions of moral meaning and value. These two magisteria do not overlap, nor do they encompass all inquiry (consider, for starters, the magisterium of art and the meaning of beauty). To cite the usual clichés, we get the age of rocks, and religion retains the rock of ages; we study how the heavens go, and they determine how to go to heaven.

Richard Dawkins, also a secular humanist—but an outright atheist—disagrees with Gould. In "You Can't Have It Both Ways: Irreconcilable Differences?" he denies Gould's views:

> [I]t is completely unrealistic to claim, as Gould and many others do, that religion keeps itself away from science's turf, restricting itself to morals and values. A universe with a supernatural presence would be a fundamentally and qualitatively different kind of unvierse from one without. The difference is, inescapably, a scientific difference. Religions make existence claims, and this means scientific claims.
> {*Skeptical Inquirer*, July-August 1999}

RELIGION-FREE

Religion-Free (R-F, or Ruff!) is a designation suggested by James L. Sanders to be placed on correspondence, envelopes, lapel pins, etc., as a way of identifying fellow non-believers. Religion-Free's address is 413 West Navajo Road, Flagstaff, Arizona 86001. {FD}

RELIGION, ADHERENTS OF

Of the 5,929,839,000 humans in mid-1999, an estimated 66% are *not* Christians and a total of 34% *are* Christians, according to the *1998 Encyclopaedia Britannica Book of the Year*. According to Pres. Bill Clinton, who proudly cited figures supplied by Prof. Robert Putnam of Harvard University, America has more houses of worship per head than any other country. Freethinkers cite similar figures, but lament the way the houses are utilized. (See documentation in the entry for Hell.)

RELIGION, GOOD AND BAD

"Those who take pride in their religious observance, whether at Easter services or celebrating the haj, may this week wish to ponder the company they keep," wrote *The Economist* at the time of Easter (11 April 1998). Agreeing with those Germans who are skeptical about Scientology, "which tries to turn its followers' minds and part them from their money, the journal defines religion as "any system of belief in a higher unseen controlling power."

> All right, you may say, Scientology may be a religion, but if so what about all the cults that meet the same dictionary definition? Are the Branch Davidian, of Waco-massacre fame, and suicide-promoting Heaven's Gate, and metro-gassing Aum Shinrikyo, also to qualify as religions? Well, yes. They may direct their message at the weak and susceptible, but so do other religions. They may hold views that are offensive, but so do other religions (many are founded on a heresy). They may even promote violence, but violence is often the handmaiden of strong religious belief. If you doubt it, go to Bosnia, or Northern Ireland, or the Middle East or countless other places where, even today, men fight their neighbours apparently irrationally. That is ethnic strife, you will be told, but in truth it is religious: Bosnians, whether Muslim or Orthodox, are ethnically identical; so are Ulster's Catholics and Protestants; Arabs and Jews alike are Semites. It is religion, not race, that fires them up.

RELIGION, WARS OF

The Wars of Religion, from 1562–1598, spread following the Saint Bartholomew's Day Massacre in 1572. (See entry for Saint Bartholomew's Day Massacre.) {CE}

RELIGIONS

Non-Christians totaled 66% and Christians only 34% in a recent study. (See entry for Hell.)

RELIGIONS, ORIGIN OF: See entry for Walter Burkert.

RELIGIOUS

In part because of criticism that "religion" (from the Latin *religare*, to restrain) is only a set of beliefs whereas "faith" (from *fidere*, to trust) is an unquestioning trust in those beliefs, many with a vested interest in organized religion have substituted "faith-based" for "religious." {William Safire, *The New York Times Magazine*, 27 June 1999}

RELIGIOUS HUMANISM: See entry for Humanism, Religious

RELIGIOUS HUMANISM

Religious Humanism is a quarterly at 7 Harwood Drive, PO Box Box 1188, Amherst, NY 14226-7188.

RELIGIOUS IDENTITY

Collective religious identity is a given in many parts of the world. If you are in Bangladesh, it is expected that you are a Muslim. In Bosnia, if you are a Catholic you are a Croat. In fact, adds Jack Miles, author of *God: A Biography*, ". . . and vice versa, to the point that if you change your religion from Catholicism to Orthodoxy or Islam, you will feel as if you have also changed your nationality to Serb or 'Turk.' " In America, however, one may be any religion or none and still be fully an American. Collective religious identity is weakened and individual religious autonomy is strengthened by the separation of religion and nationality in American culture.

RELIGIOUS RIGHT: See entry for Christian Right.

RELIGIOUS SOCIETY OF FRIENDS: See entry for Quakers.

Relly, James (Died 1778)

Relly was an associate of the evangelist George Whitefield who, with John and Charles Wesley, co-founded the Evangelical Revival. But Relly withdrew from this connection, becoming an independent preacher of Universalism. In 1759, he published *Union*, a theological treatise on universal salvation. {U}

Remsburg, John E. (1848–1919)

Remsburg, who wrote *Six Great Americans*, was a rationalist and critic of morality as found in the Holy Bible. Although he lived in Atchison, Kansas, that town's library has no copies of his work, according to Fred Whitehead in *Freethought History* (#2, 1992). In *Bible Morals* (1885), he cited twenty crimes and vices sanctioned by scripture. In his *The Bible* (1905), he condemns as pernicious and false such Biblical views as the following: Blessed are the poor in spirit; Blessed are the meek, for they shall inherit the earth; If thy right eye offend thee, pluck it out; If thy right hand offend thee, cut it off; Whosoever shall marry her that is divorced committeth adultery; Resist not evil; Whosoever shall smite thee on the right cheek, turn to him the other also; Love your enemies; Lay not up for yourselves treasurers upon earth; Take no thought for your life, what ye shall eat, or what he shall drink, nor yet for your body, what ye shall put on; Take therefore no thought for the morrow. Such views, combined with the name of Christ, Remsburg held, have caused more persecutions, wars, and miseries than any other name has caused.

In 1994, *The Christ: A Critical Review and Analysis of the Evidence of His existence* was reprinted. It is a classic in American freethought although, as Gordon Stein has pointed out, Remsburg in speaking for a mythological Christ makes the error of interchanging "Christ" when "Jesus" is meant. "Remsberg says that the two terms are interchangeable," writes Stein (*The American Rationalist*, November-December 1994), "but that is only true if you are a convinced Christian who believes that Jesus *was* the Christ. Since Remsburg does not believe this, he should distinguish the possibly historical Jesus from the *concept* of Christ (Messiah)." {BDF; FUS; PUT}

Rémusat, Charles François [Count] (1831–1897)

Rémusat taught Chinese at Paris University and was one of the first to win recognition for Lao-tse and the Buddha. In his works, Rémusat severely criticized the Christian missionaries. {RAT; RE}

Rémusat, Jean Pierre Abel (1788–1832)

Rémusat was a French Orientalist, appointed in 1814 professor of Chinese at the *Collège de France*. Rémusat was one of the first to vindicate the high morality of Lao Tzu and Buddha, and he severely criticized the missionaries for their Chinese translation of the Bible. He was an Officer of the Legion of Honour. {RAT}

RENAISSANCE HUMANISM: See entries for Classical Humanism, Marsilio Ficino, Paul Kristeller, and Charles Trinkaus. During the 1940s and 1950s Trinkaus criticized past academic views of Renaissance humanism.

RENAISSANCE HUMANISM AND ITS UNITARIAN OFFSHOOT

Pat Duffy Hutcheon, in "Renaissance Humanism and Its Unitarian Offshoot" (*Humanist in Canada*, Summer 1998), describes how the naturalism of the ancient Greeks surged again in Renaissance times, then evolved further into both the humanism and Unitarianism of today. "The defining feature of modern humanism—what distinguishes it from all other world views—is its underlying philosophy of evolutionary naturalism," she writes. "Naturalistic humanists are committed to the evidence of communicable, joint, publicly testable observation—combined with our precious human reason as the means of making connections among experienced regularities."

RENAISSANCE PUBLISHERS

In India, Renaissance Publishers is a leading publisher of M. N. Roy and atheist materials.

Renan, Henriette (1811–1861)

Renan was the sister of J. Ernest Renan. She abandoned Catholicism while young. She is said to have inspired her brother to write a life of Christ and she accompanied him to Syria, copying out his notes. In the East she contracted a fatal illness, never returning to the Church and helping Renan with his *Vie de Jesus* until a few days before her death. {RAT}

Renan, Joseph Ernest (1823–1892)

Renan's *Life of Jesus* (1863) gave a Humanist interpretation of the Christ as "an incomparable man" and created an international sensation. He has the distinction of having nineteen specific works included on the Vatican's index of prohibited reading. In addition, the Pope personally attacked Renan as a "French blasphemer." *Vie de Jésus* made the list in 1863, *L'antechrist* in 1881, and *L'église chrétienne* in 1881. His faith, Renan claimed, was destroyed neither by metaphysics nor philosophy but by historical criticism. In 1848 he gained the Volney prize for a memoir on the Semitic languages, and in 1852 published his work on Averroës and Averroîsm. In 1856 he was elected member of the Academy of Inscriptions.

In his *Life of Jesus,* Renan wrote, "No miracle has ever taken place under conditions which science can accept. Experience shows, without exception, that miracles occur only in times and in countries in which miracles are believed in, and in the presence of persons who are disposed to believe them." Being a professor of Hebrew in the Institute of France, Renan was denounced by the bishops, who deprived him of his chair which, incidentally, was restored in 1870.

McCabe accused one work, Barry's *Renan* (1905), of being "a Catholic libel." Renan's sister Henriette was his invaluable assistant and, like him, never returned to the Church. Canon Barry's life of Renan states that she received the last sacraments from "a good Maronite priest" when she was dying. Renan, however, said that the man was "a sort of fool" who forced his way to Henriette when brother and sister were unconscious with fever in Syria, and that the priest had daubed her with his holy oil.

In Psichari's *Soeur Anselmine*, his son-in-law wrote that Renan's last days were tranquil, that he told him, "I know that when I am dead nothing of me will remain." {BDF; CE; CL; ER; FUK; ILP; JM; PUT; RE; TYD}

Renand, Paul (19th Century)

Renand was a Belgian author who wrote *Nouvelle Symbolique* (1861), which discussed the identity of Christianity and paganism. {BDF; RAT}

Renard, Georges (19th Century)

A French professor at the *Academie de Lausanne*, Renard wrote *Man, Is He Free?* (1881) and *A Life of Voltaire* (1883). {BDF}

Renard, Jules (1864–1910)

A French writer, Renard wittily observed, "The Heavenly Father feedeth the fowls of the air'—and in winter He letteth them starve to death." He also remarked, "I don't know if God exists, but it would be better for His reputation if He didn't." {TYD}

Renfro, Henry (1831–1885)

Renfro was an ordained Baptist minister who lived near Waco, Texas. By the early 1880s, he had read the works of Paine, Ingersoll, and other freethinkers. When his Baptist denomination ordered him stripped of his ministerial credentials, Renfro joined a fellow Waco minister, J. D. Shaw, a freethinker who announced his own infidel views and started publishing the *Independent Pulpit*.

The story of the two freethinkers was written by Renfro's great-great-grandson, William Clark Griggs: *Parson Henry Renfro: Free Thinking on the Texas Frontier* (1994). {*American Rationalist*, September-October 1995; *Freethought History #15*, 1995}

Rengart, Karl (19th Century)

Rengart was a German democrat and freethought friend of C. Deubler. {BDF}

Renner, Gerald (20th Century)

Renner is a contributor to *Family Matters*, the newsletter of the Secular Family Network.

Renouvier, Charles Bernard (1815–1903)

A French philosopher, Renouvier was an ardent Radical and follower of the critical philosophy. Among his works are *Manual of Ancient Philosophy* (2 volumes, 1844); *Republican Manual* (1848); *Science of Morals* (1869); and *A Sketch of a Systematic Classification of Philosophical Doctrines* (1885). With F. Pillon, he translated Hume's *Psychology* (1878). {BDF}

RENSSALAER INDIVIDUALS FOR FREETHOUGHT (RIFT)

In Troy, New York, Will Bobrowski and Marshall Vandegrift founded Renssalaer Individuals for Freethought (RIFT) in 1999. The student group is a member of the Campus Freethought Alliance.

Renton, Nicholas Edwin (1931–)

Renton, who was born in England, is an Australian humanist and business consultant. Since 1962 he has been a member of the Humanist Society of Victoria, and in 1987 he became national president of the Council of Australian Humanists. During his term of office he persuaded the American Broadcasting Corporation (ABC) to treat humanism as a "religion" in their religious broadcasting departments, and he participated in television debates on subjects such as "Does Man Need God?" and "Is Marriage Really Necessary?" "Nick" Renton is the author of some twenty books, and his *Guide For Meetings and Organisations* (1961) has been widely used as a reference work. {SWW}

Renton, William (Born 1852)

Renton was an English writer who was educated in Germany. At Keswick he published *Jesus* (1876), a psychological estimate. He has also written a romance of the last generation, *Bishopspool* (1883). {BDF}

REORGANIZED CHURCH OF JESUS CHRIST OF LATTER-DAY SAINTS

A break-off, separatist group of Mormons, the Reorganized Church of Jesus Christ of Latter-Day Saints, was organized in the 1800s and has its headquarters at Box 1059, Independence, Missouri 64051. (See entry for Church of Jesus Christ of Latter-Day Saints.)

REPRESSION

Repression is a Freudian concept that describes the unconscious exclusion from the conscious mind of painful impulses or fears or desire. A person who sexually molests a child, whether a priest or a non-theist, might be suspected of attempting to repress the memory.

REPUBLIC, THE

The Republic is the best-known dialogue of Plato. In it, Socrates is shown outlining an ideal state ruled by philosopher-kings. (See entries for Poets and for Utopia.) {DCL}

REQUIEM

• Requiem, n. A mass for the dead which the minor poets assure us the winds sing o'er the graves of their favorites. Sometimes, by way of providing a varied entertainment, they sing a dirge.

–**Ambrose Bierce**
The Devil's Dictionary

RES HUMANA

A Polish quarterly, *Res Humana* is at 00-553 Warszawa, ul. Koszykowa 24, Poland.

Residents, The (20th Century)

The Residents are a 26-year-old San Francisco-based band whose members' identities have never been divulged. In photographs and performances, they appear with giant, veiny eyeballs on their heads, crowned with top hats.

Their CD-ROM album, "Wormwood" (1999), turns the most violent and cruel Bible stories into songs. Singing a bit of "Jesus Loves Me," a figure in a skull mask comes out in a puff of smoke and says, "The idea here is not to insult Jesus but maybe to shine a little light into some dark corners and show that the Good Book is also the *bad* book." A song follows about Jeremiah ("They call me Mr. Misery/they laugh and dump decay on me") and John the Baptist, which offers a good excuse for a severed-head prop. Circumcision is a major theme.

The marriage of Dinah, the woman in *Genesis*, causes her brothers-in-law to kill all the men and enslave all the women of her town. And God's brutality is sung about: Abraham kills his son, rejects Cain's offering of grain, and transforms Lot's wife into a pillar of salt. The group's female singer, as the daughter of Jephthah, who is sacrificed by her father to win a war, intones, "I'm gonna die with no tears in my eyes, 'cause God digs my daddy!" "Judas Saves" offers an alternative theory: "Just as Dorothy needed the Wicked Witch to get over the rainbow,' the skull head sings by way of introduction, "where would Jesus be without his Judas?"

"Give Me That Old Time Religion" has new lyrics that include, "It was good for making millions/selling platitudes to pilgrims," and ending, "Even if it's just a token/it was good for giving home to/human spirits that were broken/so it's good enough for me." That The Residents has been so successful with younger people is a sign of freethinkers' inroads via popular music. {Ben Ratliff, *The New York Times*, 7 April 1999}

Restrepo, Antonio José (Ñito) {Ambassador] (1855–1933)

In spite of his atheism, Restrepo became the Ambassador to the League of Nations from Colombia. In this capacity he negotiated the treaty that ended the war between Finland and Russia, for which a street in Helsinki is named after him. {WAS, letter from Dr. Joe Vikin, 13 September 1997}

RESURRECTION

In keeping with the Logical Positivists' Principle of Verification, resurrection is a meaningless concept unless interpreted psychoanalytically as wishful thinking. To a naturalist, any form of life that dies is *dead* and by definition never returns to life. Brain death, which involves the final cessation of activity only in the central nervous system, is not the total death of an individual—such a condition involves a flat electroencephalogram for some length of time, and it shows only that one function of a body has died. Death of an individual occurs when there is cessation of *all* life (metabolic processes), and no living creature has ever "risen" from the dead. Once dead, a body becomes rigid (rigor mortis), discolors because of settling of blood (livor mortis), it cools (algor mortis), there is a breakdown of tissue by enzymes liberated by that tissue after death (autolysis), and there is an invasion of the body by organisms from the gastrointestinal tract (putrefaction).

Wishful thinking, however, about loved ones leads to hoping that the deceased will somehow return, or continue in some future existence. For example, in Egyptian religion when the state cult grew and pharaohs became powerful, huge and splendid temples were constructed to the gods, leading to powerful priesthoods. The populace found expression of religious feeling in the funerary cults. The Egyptian *Book of the Dead* describes how the deceased were provided with food and drink, weapons, and articles of toilet. Tombs were visited by the family, who brought new offerings. Although the ancient Egyptian strongly believed in life after death, his idea of passing from his life on earth to life in the hereafter is somewhat obscure, according to the *Columbia Encyclopedia*, and the concepts concerning the afterlife were complex. Individuals hoped not only to extend their life beyond the grave, but to become part of the perennial life of nature. The *ka* was a kind of double or other self, not an element of the personality, but a detached part of the self which was sometimes said to guide the fortunes of the individual in life. When a man died he was said to join with his *ka*. The *ba*, on the other hand, was the manifestation of an individual after his death, usually thought to be represented in the form of a bird. Also, there was *akh*, the transformation of some of the noble dead into eternal objects, such as stars or other objects in the changeless rhythm of the universe.

For the Hebrews, the body was essential to full life. The soul in itself had no force or substance, and must be reunited with the body if the actual man was to exist after death. *Daniel* 12:2, 13 suggests that those who have remained faithful through persecution will be raised up hereafter. *Job* 19:25 states that Job is convinced that after he dies and is buried he will appear in his flesh before God, who will vindicate him. Ernest Findlay Scott, who once taught at Union Theological Seminary in New York City, explained that "for the most part, however, the Old Testament accepts the primitive view that after death the soul survives only as a ghost in Sheol, the world of shadows underneath the earth. The idea of immortality is by no means absent form the Old Testament, but it expresses itself in the purely religious faith that fellowship with God must needs be for ever. . . . The doctrine of resurrection first becomes prominent in the apocalyptic books, which take their departure from the Old Testament idea of the 'day of Jahveh,' when the new age will be ushered in by a general Judgment. On this day, according to the apocalyptists, the dead of past ages will be raised up to receive sentence of acquittal or of condemnation. Much of the detail in this conception can be traced to Persian sources."

Christian belief in the resurrection of Jesus involves seven, or perhaps eight, different accounts in the New Testament: *Matthew* 28; *Mark* 16; *John* 20; *John* 21; *I Corinthians* 15: 3-8; *Acts* 1: 2,3; *Luke* 24: 13-32. The accounts often are in conflict with one another. In Paul's narrative, eye-witnesses are cited who were fully convinced that they had seen "the risen Lord," and they were in a mood of ecstasy, in which they were conscious only of the momentary impression.

In *Kings* II 4:32-35, the child was dead . . . and Elisha . . . lay upon the child . . . and the child sneezed seven times, and . . . opened his eyes. Later, in Chapter 13, they were burying a man . . . . They cast the man into the sepulchre of Elisha; and when the man was let down, and touched the bones of Elisha, he revived, and stood upon his feet.

In *Mark* 5, Jesus took the damsel by the hand, and said unto her . . . Damsel, I say unto thee, arise. And straightway the damsel arose, and walked. Jesus arranged some other resurrections in *John* and *Luke*, and in *Acts* 9:40 St. Peter also achieves a resurrection.

In all such cases of resurrections, believers are blissfully ignorant about the realities of rigor mortis, livor mortis, algor mortis, and autolysis. Or, for that matter, putrefaction. (See the entries for Adonis and for Jesus. For the most thorough discussion of the subject by a secular humanist, see *Immortality*, edited by Paul Edwards. Or consult Joseph McCabe's *Rationalist Encyclopedia*, which states that "although all Catholics, and the great majority of Protestants, still believe it, argument about it is a waste of time, especially as immortality of any sort is now so easily refuted.") {CE; ER}

Rethore, François (Born 1822)

A French professor of philosophy at the Lyceum of Marseilles, Rethore wrote *Condillac, or Empiricism and Rationalism* (1864). He translated Spencer's *Classification of Sciences*. {BDF}

Reuschle, Karl Gustav (1812–1875)

Reuschle, a German geographer, wrote *Kepler and Astronomy* in 1871. He dedicated to D. F. Strauss his *Philosophy and Natural Science* (1874). {BDF; RAT}

Revel, Jean-François (20th Century)

Revel, a French journalist, signed Humanist Manifesto II. He is author of *Descartes, inutile et incertain* (1976) and *How Democracies Perish* (1983). {HM2}

REVELATION

• It looks as though modern science has been holding back a revelation quite as momentous as Copernicus's: it is Earth, not sky, that is heavenly.

–Vincent Cronin, *The View From Planet Earth*

In theology, revelation is a manifestation of divine will or truth. *Revelation*, one of the books of the Judeo-Christian Bible, ironically reveals nothing from God in the way of any factual information, previously unknown, nor does it reveal any scientific information at all. "Revealed religions" are founded primarily on the revelations of God to man.

As to how freethinkers trick the gullible, magicians such as Randi sometimes purposely provide revelations, explaining that nothing supernatural is involved.

Revere, Paul (1735–1818)

A silversmith and American patriot, Revere participated in the Boston Tea Party, making a famous ride to warn everyone about an approaching British attack. He was christened and remained active throughout his life in the New Brick Church in Boston, one which merged with the Old North and Second Church in 1776 and in 1802 became Unitarian under the Rev. John Lathrop. {CE; U; UU}

REVERENCE

• Reverence, n. The spiritual attitude of a man to a god and a dog to a man.

–**Ambrose Bierce**
The Devil's Dictionary

Revillon, Antoine (Born 1832)

A French journalist, "Tony" Revillon was a lawyer, a writer for many journals, an author of romances, and in 1881 an elected deputy. {BDF}

REVISTA PERUANA DE FILOSOFIA APLICADO

Revista Peruana de Filosofia Aplicada, a Peruvian quarterly for the Journal of Applied Philosophy, is at El Corregidor 318, Rimac, Lima 25, Peru. E-mail: <rpfa@geocities.com>.

REVOLUTION

A revolution consists of the overthrow of a government by one group and its replacement with another. America's deist-inspired Founding Fathers favored revolution and in the Constitution devised a way for future Americans to have a peaceful revolution, constitutionally. Other forms of government, even anarchism, do not welcome revolution.

Rey, Marc Michel (19th Century)

Rey, an Amsterdam printer and bookseller, printed all the works of d'Holbach and Rousseau and some of Voltaire's. Rey conducted the *Journal des Savans*. {BDF}

Reybaud, Marie Roch Louis (1799–1879)

Reybaud was an economist and politician. He worked on the *Tribune*, *Corsaire*, *National*, and other papers. He wrote a history of the French Expedition to Egypt (10 volumes, 1830–1836). In 1846 he was elected to the Chambre and in 1848 to the Legislative Assembly. Reybaud was politically more conservative in his later decades, but he retained his rationalism. {RAT}

Reyka, Larry (20th Century)

Reyka heads a Mensa special interest group (SIG) called HUM-SIG that promotes humanist values, democracy, and reason. His e-mail: <lreyka@beol.net>.

Reynaud, Antoine Andre Louis (1777–1844)

Baron Reynaud, a French mathematician, became one of the National Guard of Paris in 1790. A friend of Lalande, Reynaud was a teacher and examiner for about thirty years in the Polytechnic School. {BDF}

Reynaud, Jean Ernest (1806–1863)

Reynaud was a French philosopher. For a time he was a Saint Simonian. In 1836 with P. Leroux he edited the *Encyclopédie Nouvelle*. A moderate Democrat in the Assembly of 1848, Reynaud had great success with an 1854 work, *Earth and Heaven*. But a clerical council held at Périgueux formally condemned it. {BDF; RAT}

Reynolds, Charles B. (Born 1832)

Reynolds was an American lecturer. Brought up religiously and becoming a Seventh Day Baptist preacher, he then converted to freethought. In Boonton, New Jersey, he convened a "free thought" conference in a tent but came into conflict with the neighbors, who pelted him "with ancient eggs and vegetables." *The New York Times* reported, "They chopped away the guy ropes of the tent and slashed the canvas with their knives. When the tent collapsed, the crowd rushed for the speaker to inflict further punishment by plunging him in the duck pond." Whereupon Reynolds moved on to Morristown, New Jersey, where residents began "clamoring for his indictment for blasphemy."

In the only blasphemy trial ever held in the United States, Reynolds in 1886 was defended by Colonel Robert Ingersoll. "No jury has yet, in the state of New Jersey," Ingersoll intoned in a speech which covered forty-four pages, "decided that honest men are not free, that there is a manacle on the brain. . . . Say to the world that New Jersey shares in the spirit of this age, that New Jersey is not a survival of the Dark Ages, that New Jersey does not still regard the thumbscrew as an instrument of progress, that New Jersey needs no dungeon to answer the arguments of a free man, and does not send to the penitentiary men who think and men who speak." However, Reynolds was found guilty and fined seventy-five dollars.

Reynolds wrote articles in the *Boston Investigator*, *Truthseeker*, and *Ironclad Age*.

The New Jersey statute forbidding "cursing, scoffing at or denying the existence of God or Jesus" remained on the books until 1979, at which time the code was changed. {BDF; FUS; *The New York Times*, 26 January 1997; PUT; RAT}

Reynolds, George William MacArthur (19th Century)

An English writer of many novels, Reynolds wrote *Errors of the Christian Religion* (1832). {BDF}

Reynolds, Malvina (Born 1900)

Reynolds was a writer of songs and a Unitarian. She sang her own songs in appearances throughout the United States, Japan, and England. Many of her works were recorded on Folkway albums. Included among her compositions are "Malvina Reynolds Sings the Truth" (1967; "What Have They Done to the Rain?" (1962); "From Way Up Here" (1962); "Bury Me in My Overalls" (1956); "Willow Tree" (1956); and "Tweedles and Foodles for Young Noodles" (1970). {U}

Reynolds, Rick (20th Century)

A monologist and comedian, Reynolds was in a hit show, "Only the Truth is Funny," from 1990 to 1992. "I don't believe in God," he said on the show, adding, "I hope he doesn't hold that against me." In his show, "All Grown Up and No Place to Go," Reynolds includes, "I don't use the term 'miracle' lightly. I don't believe in God, or reincarnation, or destiny, or the Publishers' Clearinghouse Sweepstakes." {CA; E}

Rezmerski, Nick (20th Century)

In 1995, Rezmerski became secretary of the University of Minnesota Atheists and Humanists (UMAH). He was a founder of Campus Freethought Alliance. {*International Humanist News*, December 1996}

Rhodes, Cecil John [Prime Minister] (1853–1902)

Rhodes was a British imperialist, business magnate, and the Prime Minister of the Cape Colony, South Africa. He developed the country which bore his name, Rhodesia (now Zimbabwe).

McCabe wrote of Rhodes, "Apart from his imperial policy in Africa, which at least had no taint of greed, he was a man of high ideals and left nearly the whole of his fortune of about $30,000,000 for educational and philanthropic purposes. Marcus Aurelius and Gibbon were his favorite authors, and he had an immense admiration of Reade's *Martyrdom of Man*. His biographer, Sir T. F. Fuller, shows that he was an agnostic." {CE; JM; RE; TRI}

Rhoades, Don (20th Century)

Rhodes is co-chair of the Atheist Community of Austin, Texas.

He has written for *Secular Nation* (October-December 1998). E-mail: <donrodz@swbell.net>.

Rhoads, Cornelius P. (20th Century)

When he reviewed George D. Stoddard's *Krebiozen, The Great Cancer Mystery* for *The Humanist* in 1956, Dr. Rhoads, whose nickname was "Dusty," was scientific director of the Sloan-Kettering Institute for Cancer Research. In 1956 he was given the Walker Prize for Cancer Research, which is awarded every five years by the Royal College of Surgeons of Britain for the "best work in advancing the knowledge of the pathology and therapeutics of cancer."

He was specifically cited for having found the presence of a "cancer-immune mechanism" in human cells which, in turn, led to chemotherapeutic studies.

RHODE ISLAND ATHEISTS, FREETHINKERS

• Rhode Island Atheists, POB 22, Coventry, Rhode Island 02816. Ludlow Mahan is the contact for the group, which helped start Gil Lawrence's show on WALE radio.

• WALE Radio, Providence, Rhode Island. Gil Lawrence's radio talk show features the atheist/agnostic point of view.

Rhys, Jocelyn (20th Century)

Rhys wrote *Shaken Creeds: The Resurrection Doctrines* (1922). {GS}

Rhys, John [Sir] (1840–1915)

Rhys was a professor of Celtic at Oxford and, in 1895, Principal of Jesus College, Hibbert Lecturer, and Fellow of the British Academy. When Mrs. Humphrey Ward tried to force the Church of England to admit ministers who denied the Virgin Birth, Rhys wrote to Edward Clodd, "If they were only called by the same name of Christians it matters not that they are ritualists or agnostics; the name is the great thing that would enable them to enjoy the Church together." {RAT; RE}

Rialle, J. Girard de (Born 1841)

Rialle was a French anthropologist. He wrote in *La Pensée Nouvelle,* conducted the *Revue de Linguistique et de Philologie comparée,* and has written on how fetishism is dealt with in *Comparative Mythology* (1878). Rialle also wrote works on ethnology. {BDF}

Riback, Bernard L. (20th Century)

Riback, when he signed Humanist Manifesto II, was a humanist counselor. {HM2}

Ribelt, Léonce (19th Century)

Ribelt was a French publicist, author of several political works and collaborator on *La Morale Indépendante.* {BDF}

Ribeyrolles, Charles de (1812–1861)

Ribeyrolles was a French politician. Intended for the Church, he chose instead to become a social democrat and edited the *Emancipation of Toulouse* and *La Réforme* in 1848. A friend of Victor Hugo, he shared in his exile at Jersey but died at Rio Janeiro. {BDF; RAT}

Ribonucleic acid (RNA): See entries for RNA and *Genesis.*

Ribot, Alexandre Felix Joseph (1842–1923)

During his three times as Premier of France, Ribot struggled with the Church. An agnostic, Ribot was a member of the French Academy. {RAT; RE}

Ribot, Théodule A. (1839–1917)

Ribot was a French philosopher, the author of *Contemporary English Psychology* (1870) and resumés of the views of Mill, Bain, and Spencer, whose *Principles of Psychology* he has translated. Ribot also wrote *On Heredity* (1873); *The Philosophy of Schopenhauer* (1874); and *Contemporary German Psychology.* Ribot conducted the *Revue Philosophique.* {BDF; RAT; RE}

Ricardo, David (1772–1823)

Ricardo, a British economist of Dutch-Jewish parentage, entered business as a stockbroker at the age of twenty and within five years had amassed a large fortune. After reading Adam Smith's *The Wealth of Nations,* he began to study political economy. His major work, *The Principles of Political Economy and Taxation* (1817) contained his important theories on the determination of wages and value. He held that wages tend to stabilize around the subsistence level and that the value of almost any good is a function of the labor needed to produce it. His thinking greatly influenced the development of classical economics. According to the *Dictionary of National Biography,* Ricardo abjured Judaism in his youth and never returned to it or adopted any other creed. {JM; RAT; RE; TRI}

Ricci, Paul (20th Century)

Ricci, who is professor emeritus of philosophy at Cypress College in California, addressed in 1994 the 14th annual HUMCON conference sponsored by the Alliance of Humanist, Atheist, and Ethical Culture Organizations of Los Angeles County. His lecture, "Does the Complexity of the Universe Imply the Christian God as Creator?", made the point that new ideas in the fields of cosmology and physics are of no help in bolstering the discredited Design Argument for the existence of God. He is highly critical of *The Fingerprint of God* by astronomer and evangelist Hugh Ross. Ricci is author of *Fundamentals of Critical Thinking.*

Ricciardi, Gerry (20th Century)

Ricciardi, while at student at Boston University in 1998, signed the Campus Freethought Alliance's "Bill of Rights for Unbelievers."

Ricciardi, Guiseppe Napoléone [Count] (1808–1885)

Count Ricciardi, an Italian patriot, was son of Francesco Ricciardi, Count of Camaldoli (1758–1842). After the age of nineteen, he said, he never kneeled to a priest. In 1832 he founded at Naples *Il Progresso,* a review of science, literature, and art. Arrested in 1834 as a Republican conspirator, Ricciardi was imprisoned for eight months, then lived in exile in France until 1848. There he wrote in the *Revue Indépendante,* pointing out that the Papacy from its very essence was incompatible with liberty. He was elected deputy to the Neapolitan Parliament, sitting on the extreme left. In 1849, *A History of the Revolution of Italy in 1848* was printed. Condemned to death in 1853, he was seized and his fortune was taken. At the time of the Ecumenical Council, he called an Anti-Council of Freethinkers at Naples in 1869. The Italian government dissolved this, however, but the organization led to the formation of an International Federation of Freethinkers. Count Ricciardi's final work was a life of his friend, Mauro Macchi (1882). {BDF; RAT; RE}

Rice, Ann (1941–)

Rice is author of *Interview with the Vampire* (1976), *The Feast of All Saints* (1980), *Cry to Heaven* (1982), and *Exit to Eden* (1985). She also writes as A. N. Roquelaure and Anne Rampling. According to Atheist Celebrities on the Internet, Rice is a non-believer.

Rice, Madeleine Hook (20th Century)

Rice wrote *Federal Street Pastor: The Life of William Ellery Channing* (1961). {GS}

Rice, Robert M. (1902–1993)

Rice was a Universalist who had pastorates in Maine,

Massachusetts, and the Oak Park, Illinois, Unitarian church which was designed by Frank Lloyd Wright. When he ended his ministry there, the church made Rice minister emeritus.

Rice, Stuart (20th Century)
Rice is a past president of *The Jewish Humanist.*

Rice, Thomas Jefferson (19th Century)
Rice wrote *Departure, or Selections from the Jottings of Twenty Years* (1875). {GS}

Rice, William Brooks (1905–1970)
As chairman of the Joint Merger Commission, the body through which the groundwork was laid for the merger of the American Unitarian Association (AUA) and the Universalist Church of America (UCA) in 1961, Rice played an important role in modern religious liberalism. He was a Unitarian minister in Dover and Wellesley Hills, Massachusetts. {U&U}

Rice, William G. (20th Century)
Rice was a member of the American Humanist Association. In 1967 he wrote *A Tale of Two Courts: Judicial Settlement of Controversies Between the States of the Swiss and American Federations.* {HNS}

Rich, Caleb (1750–1821)
Although John Murray's Gloucester Church is considered the first officially recognized Universalist Church, Caleb Rich's church founded in Warwick, Massachusetts, in 1773 predates Murray's church, although it had no official legal recognition. When twenty-one, Rich became a Baptist but began to believe that a fear of hell is a selfish (and therefore tainted) motive for religious experience and moral action. His rebellion against the use of hell as a motive for conversion grew and was supplemented by visionary religious experiences confirming in him the doctrines of universal salvation. The Baptists then excluded him, which led to his forming the Warwick church. One of Rich's converts to Universalism was Hosea Ballou. {U; U&U}

Richards, William (18th Century)
Richards wrote *Reflection on French Atheism and On English Christianity* (1796). {GS}

Richardson, Benjamin Ward [Sir] (1828–1896)
The son of an eminent British physician, Richardson introduced fourteen new anesthetics into medical and surgical practice and took a deep interest in popular education, often on freethought lines.

In his autobiography, *Vita Medica* (1897), Richardson stated that "man is no more immortal than the thing on which he writes his learning" and admits only an impersonal vital spirit in the universe. {JM; RAT; RE}

Richardson, Eliot Lee (1920–)
Richardson, an eminent lawyer who has served in more cabinet positions than any other person in American history, comes from a family whose forebears were Unitarians since the early 19th century. He attended Milton Academy and at Harvard received his B.A. in Philosophy *magna cum laude*. After being in the Normandy invasion, where he won a bronze star and two purple hearts, he got his law degree from Harvard (again *magna cum laude*).

Moving into government, he served as a Senate aide, then as acting secretary of health, education, and welfare; became US attorney for Massachusetts; was Massachusetts Lieutenant Governor and Attorney General; was secretary of Health, Education, and Welfare (under President Eisenhower); was Attorney General under President Nixon; was Ambassador to Great Britain and Commerce Secretary (under President Ford); and headed the US delegation to the Third International Law of the Sea Conference (under President Carter). During the Watergate scandal, after President Richard Nixon demanded that he fire special prosecutor Archibald Cox, Richardson received plaudits from around the world for resigning as Attorney General in protest. {*World*, January-February 1997}

Richardson, J. P. (Born 1821)
Richardson, the son of Puritan parents, was taught to believe that the world was coming to an end in 1843. When it did not, he began to read freethought literature and met Horace Seaver and J. P. Mendum, becoming a subscriber to the Boston *Investigator*. Richardson became an ardent opponent of slavery, and when the Civil War broke out he enlisted, raising the first company (Cambridge, Massachusetts, 1861) "in all the loyal North" for the war. After the war, he became a judge in Texas and was a president of the Liberal Association of Texas. {PUT}

Richardson, Nancy (20th Century)
Richardson, while a student at the University of Puget Sound in Tacoma, Washington, was one of the founders of Campus Freethought Alliance. {*International Humanist News*, December 1996}

Richardson, Peter Tufts (20th Century)
Richardson, a Unitarian, wrote *Four Spiritualities* (1996). The minister of the Unitarian Universalist Congregation of Andover, Massachusetts, he divides the world's spiritual traditions into the Journey of Unity, of Devotion, of Works, and Harmony.

Richardson, Robert Dale Jr. (1934–)
Richardson, a Unitarian, is author of *Henry Thoreau: A Life of the Mind* (1986) and *The Mind on Fire* (1995). His father, **Robert Dale Richardson Sr.**, who wrote the introduction to the Beacon Press edition of Abraham Lincoln's autobiography, had served Unitarian parishes around New England, later becoming a chaplain at a Boston mental hospital. {*World*, January-February 1997}

Richberg, Donald Randall (20th Century)
Richberg, a freethinker, wrote "G. Hovah Explains" (1940). {GS}

Richelieu, Armand Jean du Plessis, [Duc de] [Cardinal] (1585–1642)
McCabe cites Richelieu as one of two statesmen—the other was Colbert—who made France great in spite of its corrupt Church and tainted monarchy. Rarely noticed is that Richelieu was highly independent in religious matters. He angered Rome by his alliance with the Protestants instead of the Catholics in the Thirty Years War. He drove the Papal troops out of Switzerland, induced the King to break off relations with the Vatican, and, as Bayle reports in his dictionary, threatened to sever the connection with Rome and unite with the Protestants in a French National Church. Although there is no evidence that Richelieu was a skeptic, he had little depth in his religious views, McCabe insists. {RE}

Richepin, Jean (1849–1926)
Richepin was a French poet, novelist, and dramatist born in Algeria. He began his life as a physician, and during the Franco-German war he took to journalism. In 1876 he published the *Son of the Beggars*, which was suppressed.

His *Les Blasphèmes* (1884) appeared in several editions. He also wrote *The Atheist's Prayer and Other Poems*, which was published posthumously in 1934. {BDF; RAT}

Richer, Leon (Born 1824)
Richer was a French deist and journalist. With A. Guéroult, he edited *l'Opinion Nationale*, and in 1869 he founded and edited *L'Avenir des Femmes.* In 1868 he published *Letters of a Freethinker to a Village Priest* and has written volumes in favor of the emancipation of women, collaborating with Mlle. Desraismes in the Women's Rights congresses held in Paris. {BDF}

Richert, Robert (20th Century)
Richert, who is president and co-founder of Freethinkers

Toastmasters Club, led a freethought workshop in 1994 at the 14th annual HUMCON conference sponsored by the Alliance of Humanist, Atheist, and Ethical Culture Organizations of Los Angeles County, California.

Richet, Charles (1850–1935)

Richet was a 1913 Nobel Prize winner in physiology. His special study was anaphylaxis, a term he used to describe a phenomenon noted earlier by Theobald Smith and which referred to a hypersensitive reaction (akin to allergy) to injections of foreign proteins such as serums. Richet also discovered that hydrochloric acid is the base of gastric juice. Conan Doyle and others erroneously label him a Catholic or a spiritualist, but as president of the French Society for Psychical Research Richet repeatedly explained that he did not believe that the phenomena were due to spirits. Richet also said he was not hostile to religion, that he had never written about the subject. The Catholic *Revue des Deux Mondes*, after his death, described him as "the greatest physiologist that France has had since Pasteur," overlooking the fact that Richet was a non-theist, not a Catholic. He had contributed to the organ of Haeckel's Monist League because, Richet explained, he "has the misfortune to believe more in science than theology" and was convinced that man's future is not in belief in "childish dogmas." {CE; JM; RAT; RE}

Richler, Mordecai (20th Century)

A comic writer, Richler tells of his non-religious views in Douglas Todd's *Brave Souls: Writers and Artists Wrestle with God, Love, Death, and the Things That Matter* (1996). {CA}

Richter, Johann Paul Friedrich (1763–1825)

Jean Paul, as he was known, was the most widely read novelist in Goethe's time. As to whether Richter was a believer, an answer can be found in the title he chose for a chapter in his *Siebenkäs* (1796–1797): "The Dead Christ Proclaims from the Top of the World Edifice That There Is No God." Although rejecting Christianity, he accepted the idea of immortality. In his lifetime, he was a popular writer who was admired for the idealism and warm portrayals of simple life as shown in his novels. Two other of his works are *Titan* (1800–1803) and *Levana* (1807), the latter a treatise on education. Richter's biographer described his position as "a sentimental Deism" like that of Rousseau. {CE; EU, Volker Dürr; JM; RE}

Rickard, Alan (1929–)

Rickard is an Australian rationalist, atheist, travel agent, writer, and philosophical anarchist. With Frederick W. Swann and Laurence F. Bullock he co-founded the Atheist Society of Australia. He was editor of *The Atheist Journal* until 1981. {FUK}

Rickards, D. A. (20th Century)

During the 1960s, Rickards was a director of the American Humanist Association. He is a veterinarian and song writer, noted for his satires of religious belief.

Ricker, Marilla Marks (1840–1920)

Ricker, an American freethinker and attorney, was a frequent contributor to *Truth Seeker*. Her major work was *I'm Not Afraid, Are You?* (1912). In 1910 she ran unsuccessfully for governor of New Hampshire, for the Attorney General ruled her ineligible to run. She also wrote *Four Gospels* (1911), favorably comparing Paine and Ingersoll with John Calvin and Puritan Jonathan Edwards.

When Christians pray, she quipped, they spell it with an *e.* {EU, Gordon Stein; WWS}

Rickman, Thomas (Clio) (1761–1834)

Rickman was an English radical who published several volumes of poems and in 1819 a life of his friend Thomas Paine. He also published a portrait of Paine by Romney that was engraved by Sharpe. A Quaker who wrote poetry under the name of "Clio," Rickman was prosecuted several times for selling Paine's works and his house was a center for the leading London heretics.

Rickman was an aggressive deist. {BDF; FUK; RAT; RE}

Riddle, Oscar (1877–1968)

Riddle was a biologist and author of a major work on the conflict of science and religion, *The Unleashing of Evolutionary Thought* (1954). Asked about humanism, Riddle replied to the present author:

> After fifty years spent in biological research I can have no doubt that this research, above all else, led to the *naturalistic humanism* described below. Naturalistic humanism sees the truly admirable in the already attained form and functioning of the human being; and finds the truly hopeful in the near certainty that the same or like impulses to growth or change will persist indefinitely. It seeks perfection and absolutes neither in humankind nor elsewhere in a universe of flow and flux. It rejects the view that all ages are alike in fortune or other respects, though it grants that crucial problems of personal and mental freedom have faced man in every age.
>
> Man's severest tests probably lie ahead. The changing framework and essence of society—above all else that exists—are surely, solely, and securely in human hands. In this newest and most involved sphere of reality neither the inevitable nor the Providential can intrude. Here—in emerging majesty well mixed with latent cruelty and bulging desire—man is both builder and creator. This form of humanism can come only as a halting, step-wise growth to each person that acquires it. Its roots seem to rest in inquiry, atheism, and experience; its purely personal fruits clearly range from the calms of comprehension to the revels of the mind. Eventually it puts leadership above instinct, logic and test above too-free emotion, and fellowship above faith. It channels the prized distillates of human brains toward undivided service to human beings.

From 1959 to 1960, he was President of the American Rationalist Federation. In 1958, Riddle was named Humanist of the Year by the American Humanist Association. {FUS; HNS2; WAS, 8 May 1956}

Ridgeway, Nathaniel (19th Century)

In the 1870s, Ridgeway was an active leader in Manchester, England, of the Lancashire Secular Union. {RSR}

Ridings, Elijah Francis Ambrose (19th Century)

Ridings wrote "A Reply to Atheism Weighed in the Ballance and Found Wanting"(1823). {GS}

Ridley, Francis Ambrose (1897–1994)

Ridley, who was born in Wales, was "a great Victorian freethinker" who in the 1920s after receiving a Licentiate of Theology at Durham University became one of Hyde Park's colorful left-wing orators and confessed atheist. Once a Trotskyite, Ridley was expelled by Trotsky himself. He wrote for *New Leader* (later the *Socialist Leader*) in 1941 and was a member of its National Council in 1943. From 1947 he was co-editor (with George Stone) of the *Socialist Leader* for two years and editor of *Left* for five. He wrote *Mussolini Over Africa* (1935), *Next Year's War* (1936), *The Papacy and Fascism* (1937), *Julian the Apostate and the Rise of Christianity* (1937), and *The United Socialist States of Europe* (1944). Many secularists were not radical, he noted, let alone revolutionary, and many socialists were not secularists, either because they were Christian Socialist or because they regarded the "religious issue" as needlessly divisive. But when Chapman Cohen retired as editor of *The Freethinker* in 1951, Ridley directed the journal toward a secular humanist outlook. At one time Ridley debated with Marcus Garvey, the American pioneer of "black power," and an unfounded story depicted him in the British Museum Reading Room occupying the chair of Marx or Lenin. Ridley was a colorful individual, "almost a revolutionary saint," according to Ellis Hillman. His funeral was officiated by Terry Mullins and assisted by Barbara Smoker. At the ceremony, Martin Page declared, "Let the world know that there was no deathbed conversion, no recantation, no renunciation of the freethought and socialist ideals that had sustained him through seven decades." {*The Freethinker*, May 1994; FUK; TRI}

Ridley, Matt (20th Century)

Ridley, a journalist on scientific subjects, wrote *The Red Queen* and *The Origins of Virtue*. He states in the latter book that he is a nonbeliever. {CA}

Ridout, Ronald (Died 1994)

Ridout, cited in the *Guiness Book of Records* for producing more English textbooks than anyone else, was a member of the Rationalist Press Association.

Riehl, Aloys (Born 1844)

Riehl was an Austrian philosopher who taught at Gratz University, Kiel, Halle, and Berlin. He described himself as a philosophical Monist and advocated psycho-physical parallelism, rejecting the idea of a separable spiritual principle. His chief work is *Der philosophische Criticismus und seine Bedeutung für die positive Wissenschaft* (2 volumes, 1876–1887). His rationalism is plainer in his *Giordano Bruno* (1900) and *Friedrich Nietzsche* (1905). {RAT}

Riehemann, Robert (20th Century)

Riehemann is an adjunct faculty member in the mathematics department at Thomas More College. Also, he is a systems specialist at Cincinnati Bell Information Systems, and he has taught astronomy to humanist children at Camp Quest. For *Free Inquiry* (Spring 1997), he wrote, "Family Friendly Libraries," wondering why some libraries continue to forbid children to see certain harmless material. Riehemann in 1998 became a board member of Cincinnati's Free Inquiry Group, also serving as its program director. He wrote "Science at Home" for *Family Matters* (Fall 1998).

Riem, Andreas (1749–1807)

Riem was a German rationalist who, at first a Christian preacher, was appointed by Frederick the Great as chaplain of a hospital at Berlin. He quit, however, in order to become secretary of the Academy of Painting. Riem wrote anonymously on the *Aufklaring*. {BDF}

Riepe, Dale (20th Century)

Riepe, professor emeritus of philosophy at the State University of New York at Buffalo, wrote *The Naturalistic Tradition in Indian Thought* (1961). The work discusses the early Ajivikas and Carvakas views of the naturalistic elements of Jainism, Hinayana Buddhism, Samkhya, and Vaisesika. (See entry for Indian Naturalism.)

Rignano, Eugenio (20th Century)

Rignano, an Italian writer, edited an international scientific review, *Scientia*. In his *Essays in Scientific Synthesis* (1918), he predicted the gradual disappearance of religion and wrote that "we may regard it with tranquil security" as it "no longer responds to our needs." {RAT}

Riley, Isaac Woodbridge (20th Century)

Riley wrote "Early Freethinking Societies in America" in the *Harvard Theological Review* (1918). {FUS}

Rilke, Rainer Maria (1875–1926)

The acknowledged greatest lyric poet of modern Germany, Rilke had an unhappy childhood. Born to German-speaking parents in Prague, he had a father who after a failed military career turned to the railroad. His socially frustrated mother had difficulty recovering from the death of her first child, a girl who died in infancy a year before he was born. She called Rilke Sophie and dressed him like a girl. Until he was five, he had braided long hair. Fearing that his son would become feminine, his father sent him to a military school, which Rilke soon disliked. With the help of an uncle, he attended the University of Prague. Married but briefly, he preferred an unsettled, wandering life among literary people and aristocrats who gave him shelter. Greatly influenced by his extensive travels, he met sculptor Rodin, who hired him briefly as his secretary and taught him much about creativity. World War I drove Rilke back to Germany, after his having been to Italy, North Africa, France, and elsewhere. War service and chronic ill health constantly frustrated his work.

Rilke's verse was often mystical and prophetic. His use of symbolism led to poetry which resembled that of medieval verse. He was antipathetic to large modern cities, and he probed into emotional and spiritual issues, frequently being absorbed with death as a poetic theme. In *Stories of God* (1904), he expressed a mysticism that was continued in *Das Stundenbuch* (1905, tr. *Poems from the Book of Hours*), a work in which he treated God as an evolutionary concept.

Since his death, Rilke's reputation has grown greatly, despite his favorable views of political strongmen like Mussolini. Critics such as William H. Gass of Washington University in St. Louis have noted his "belief" in animism (that all things, as well as the parts of all things, are filled with life) and "the notion that we grow our death inside us like a talent or a tumor; that we are here to realize the world, to raise it, like Lazarus, from its sullen numbness into consciousness; that differences are never absolute, but that everything lies on a continuum as colors do (life and death, for instance); that simple people have an understanding of life and an insight into the secret rhythms of nature. These themes are like tides that rise and fall inside him, as if he were just their bay and receptive shoreline."

Commenting about Ralph Freedman's *Life of a Poet* (1996) and Edward Snow's selection and translation of *Uncollected Poems: Rainer Marie Rilke* (1996), Gass wrote, "Rilke proclaimed the poet's saintly need to accept reality in all its aspects, meanwhile welcoming only those parts of the world for which he could compose an ennobling description. He was venomous about organized religion, yet there are more Virgin Marys, Saints and Angels in his work than in many cathedrals." Gass calls Rilke a priest of the poet's art who "takes the European lyric to new levels of achievement, forming, with Valéry and Yeats perhaps, a true triune god, and the texts of a worthy religion at last—one that we may wholeheartedly admire, in part because we are not required to believe."

Rilke, following a reluctantly diagnosed case of leukemia, died in the arms of his doctor of blood poisoning. The myth concerning his illness is that he had been gathering some roses from his garden in order to honor the Egyptian beauty Nimet Eloui, had pricked his hand on a thorn, and the wound not only failed to heal but both his arms became swollen. Ulcerous sores developed in his mouth and the pain in his stomach and intestines contributed to his gloomy and depressed state. {CE}

Rimbaud, Arthur (1854–1891)

A French poet, Rimbaud wrote hallucinatory and dreamlike verse which anticipated the symbolists. *Les illuminations*, written over an undetermined time period and possibly finished before he was nineteen, consisted of prose poems which transcended all traditional syntax and narrative elements. His interests were anything but religion in this period of his life. A. L. Rowse's *Homosexuals in History* cites a work Rimbaud wrote at the age of sixteen, after having been picked up by some soldiers and brutally initiated into sex:

Mon triste coeur bave à la poupe . . .
Mon coeur couvert de caporal . . .
Ithyphalliques et pioupiesques . . .
Leurs insultes l'on dépravé. . .

From 1872 to 1873, he and Paul Verlaine lived the bohemian *dansons-la-gigue* life together, much to Madame Verlaine's disgust. During a drunken brawl, Verlaine fired a pistol, wounding Rimbaud in the wrist, and the resultant scandal led to the end of their relationship, whereupon Verlaine fell in love with nineteen-year-old Lucien Letinois. (Verlaine was sentenced to two years' imprisonment, 1873 to 1875.) In his confessional autobiography, *Saison en enfer* (Season in Hell, 1873), Rimbaud renounced his former hellish life and his work, saying he had reached God and that his illuminations had been hallucinations after all. He then set off for Cyprus and beyond, dying at the age of thirty-seven after having become a trader in Abyssinia and, according to Martin Greif, "with the name of his faithful native boy Djani on his lips." He died with only his sister Isabelle at his side, and she returned to Ardennes "with the mortal remains of the brother whose soul she had entrusted to God."

Rimbaud, according to Rowse, had a deathbed conversion to Catholicism, one arranged by Rimbaud's mother. {CE; GL}

Rimmer, Robert (1917–)

The author of *The Harrad Experiment* and other novels, Rimmer has stated he believes that Bhagwan Shree Rajneesh is an enlightened humanist. However, this led Ronald O. Clarke, professor of religious studies at Oregon State University, to label the Bhagwan as "the product of a delusional system associated with a narcissistic personality disorder."

The Bhagwan replied that, yes, like Jesus he is a narcissist. In response, Robert Basil, editor of *Not Necessarily the New Age: Critical Essays,* ridicules both Rimmer and the Bhagwan. In 1995, Rimmer published *Let's Really Make Love*, in which he advocated a change of views about how our "lust for life" should be an integral part of a family's education for the 21st century.

Rimmer for a time was on the editorial board of *Free Inquiry,* which is evidence of how varied are that journal's viewpoints. On the Web: <http: www.harrad2000.com>. {SHD; *Free Inquiry*, Summer, 1989}

Rimsky-Korsakov, Nicolai Andreyevich (1844–1908)

"The Five," a group of late 19th-century Russian composers, were

Balakirev, the leader; Cui; Moussorgsky; Borodin; and Rimsky-Korsakov. Although Rimsky originally had intended to have a naval career, he turned seriously to composing after meeting Balakirev in 1861. In 1871 he became professor of composition at the St. Petersburg Conservatory, retiring from the navy in 1873. In 1861 he became assistant to Balakirev, the director of the imperial Chapel, and conducted the St. Petersburg Symphony Concerts (1886–1900). His symphonic poem *Sadko* (1867) and his first symphony (1865) were the first works in these forms by a Russian, but it was Rimsky's operas which brought him fame. His best-known orchestral work is *Scheherezade* (1888), which was used by the Diaghilev ballet. Among his pupils were Glazunov, Gretchanin, and Stravinsky. He once spent an evening at Lev Tolstoy's estate near Moscow at a time when the novelist had given up art for religion and who vainly as well as unsuccessfully exhorted Rimsky-Korsakov to do likewise. When the composer apologized for having exasperated his host, Tolstoy reassured him, "Not at all. For me it's been very interesting to come face to face with gloom."

Stravinsky referred to his teacher's "bourgeois atheism," recalling in one of his conversation books how Rimsky at a dinner table pooh-poohed the idea of "resurrection . . . drawing a zero on the tablecloth as he said, 'There is nothing after death; death is the end.' " Meanwhile, Rimsky was not above churning out church choruses for performance by the Imperial Court Chapel Choir, at whose school he taught part time exactly until he qualified for a pension.

Ironically, the atheist Rimsky's "The Invisible City of Kitezh" overflows with heart-rending religious lyricism and portrays the title character Fevronia's bodily resurrection. Critic Richard Taruskin observed that the religion in the opera, while nominally Christian, "is really a pantheistic pagan folk religion. And that enabled Rimsky to draw inspiration from musical folklore, his eternal well, and also from that other great 19th-century pagan, Richard Wagner, whose nominally Christian 'Parsifal,' together with the avowedly pagan 'Ring' cycle, served as Rimsky's chief model in ways both overt and well hidden." {Richard Taruskin, " 'Kitezh': Religious Art of an Atheist" *The New York Times*, 25 February 1995}

Ring, Ken (20th Century)

Ring is author of a humorous "Interview With God" (*New Zealand Rationalist and Humanist* (April 1994), in which He claimed no knowledge whatsoever of the Pope or even what a pope is. As for Mary's being a virgin, "Course not! She worked the bar in the old Stable and Manger. She did this bit where she came in on the donkey. . . ."

As for his views of contemporary problems on Earth, God seemed to be somewhat disappointed. "Just look," He lamented, "at what the competition is doing, you know; Gambling never did deliver; neither did Rampant Sex; now we're getting people who are even turning away from Rugby!"

Rios, Etienne (20th Century)

Rios is a Spanish-speaking member of *Free Inquiry*'s staff. At the 1996 Humanist World Conference held in Mexico City, he was moderator of the Humanism in Latin America panel.

Rios was one of the founders of Campus Freethought Alliance. {*International Humanist News*, December 1996}

R. I. P.

R.I.P. A careless abbreviation of *requiescat in pace*, attesting an indolent goodwill to the dead. According to the learnèd Dr. Drigge, however, the letters originally meant nothing more than *reductus in pulvis*.

–Ambrose Bierce
The Devil's Dictionary

Ripley, George (1802–1880)

A Unitarian minister, Ripley first became well-known as the writer of essays in the *Christian Examiner*, in which he rejected the necessity of the biblical miracles as an underpinning for Christianity and in which he defended Emerson's Transcendentalism against the attacks of Andrew Norton. Wanting to translate Transcendental ideals into social reality, he founded the Brook Farm Community (1841–1847) and became perhaps the leading controversialist for the Transcendentalists.

He was attracted to the utopian views of Charles Fourier. But a disastrous fire at the farm in 1846 resulted in the commune's no longer being able to continue, and Ripley moved to New York, dispirited and debt-ridden. An intellectual interested in the German views of Johann Gottfried von Herder and Friedrich Schleiermacher as well as the English theologian James Martineau, Ripley was among the most learnèd of the Transcendentalists.

An 1870 letter from William Henry Channing to J. H. Noyes includes the following: "It was George Ripley, and Ripley alone, who truly originated Brook Farm, and his should be the honor through all time. And a very high honor it will be, sooner or later." {CE; FUS; U; U&U; UU}

Ripley, Robert L(eroy) (1893–1949)

Ripley used mathematics to prove that even if Heaven existed, he would choose not to go there. A popular journalist whose "Believe It Or Not" column, including artwork to illustrate, was found in leading newspapers, Ripley was the subject of a biography, *Ripley: The Modern Marco Polo*, by Bob Considine. In 1929, Ripley's own book, *Believe It Or Not*, was published. Among Ripley's items: (a) During the Mexican War, a certain Señor Lascurain served for 37 minutes as President of Mexico before being impeached; (b) A postage stamp built the Panama Canal, a reference to a Nicaraguan stamp that featured a volcano; its depiction of one of the nation's small volcanoes in full eruption was used to encourage Congress to choose Panama over Nicaragua; and (c) When Neils Paulsen, of Uppsala, Sweden, died in 1907 at the age of 160, he left two sons—one nine years old, the other 103. (See entry for Heaven.)

Ripley, Sarah Alden Bradford (1793-1867)

The wife of Unitarian minister Samuel Ripley, Sarah Ripley was a friend of Emerson, Thoreau, Fuller, and Hawthorne. Although sympathetic to the Transcendentalist movement, she was more of a religious skeptic, science having displaced theology as her principal authority. (See Joan W. Goodwin's *The Remarkable Mrs. Ripley* [1999].)

Ris, Hania W. (1914–)

A physician, Ris wrote "Agnostics Do Not Need To Apologize For Their Lack Of Belief" in *Freethought Today* (June-July 1996). Whenever she told individuals she was an agnostic, she reports, they almost invariably try to change her mind, unsuccessfully.

Risk, Robert G. (20th Century)

Risk, president of the Leadville Corporation, was a vice president of the A.H.A. and was chairman of its Committee on Publications. He signed Humanist Manifesto II. When Priscilla Robertson resigned over differences with the American Humanist Association (AHA) board, he resigned, also. {HM2; HNS}

Ritchie, Brian (20th Century)

Ritchie, a recording artist, is a bassist with Violent Femmes. "We don't really think it's our job to provide a consistent viewpoint," Ritchie said of the group's 1994 album, "New Times." "People are not consistent. Why should we be? We're not interested in selling people a message. We think it's better to just be ourselves, and if people are confused, that's fine. We're confused." But not about religion. Ritchie is a devout atheist. {CA; E}

Ritchie, David George (1853–1903)

Ritchie taught logic and metaphysics at St. Andrews University and was president of the Aristotelian Society (1898–1899). In his posthumously published *Philosophical Studies* (1905), Ritchie complained that his academic position closed his lips about religion. He did not believe in a personal God—his God was "the highest or ideal good"—or immortality. {RAT; RE}

Ritchie-Calder, Peter Ritchie [Lord] (20th Century)

Lord Ritchie-Calder, formerly of the University of Edinburgh when he signed Humanist Manifesto II, has been President of the British Rationalist Association. He signed Humanist Manifesto II. {HM2; FUK; SHD}

RITES

• Rite, n. A religious or semi-religious ceremony fixed by law, precept, or custom, with the essential oil of sincerity carefully squeezed out of it.

–**Ambrose Bierce,** *The Devil's Dictionary*

A criticism of the rationalist and secular humanist groups is that they have no rites, no solemn ceremonies to celebrate a person's birth, coming of age, marriage (as well as divorce), and death. To counter this, Corliss Lamont and Jane Wynne Willson are among those who have developed suitable wedding and funeral services that can be adapted for individual non-believers. Their approach is entirely unlike that of the Catholics, whose holy rites include the Eucharist, Baptism, Confirmation, Penance, Ordination, Marriage, and Extreme Unction. (See entries for Humanist Ceremonies, Corliss Lamont, and Jane Wynne Willson .)

Ritter, Charles (Born 1838)

A Swiss writer, Ritter translated into French Strauss's *Essay of Religious History*; George Eliot's *Fragments and Thoughts*, and Zeller's *Christian Baur and the Tübingen School.* {BDF}

Rivas, Aida (1919–)

Rivas is author of "Memoirs of a Godless Sinner" in *Freethought Today* (May 1995). She had been raised in Uruguay, was an atheist whose parents were tolerant, and came to the United States as an immigrant. Rivas is a member of the Freedom From Religion Foundation.

Rivera, Diego (1886–1957)

Rivera was a controversial Mexican muralist. A declared atheist, he was a Communist who mixed with rich capitalists. Patrick Marnham's *Dreaming with his Eyes Open* (1998) depicts Rivera as a person who for a time and for effect wore a gun and holster. He was an overweight person who reached three hundred pounds, a Marxist who chummed in Mexico with Trotsky and André Breton, and a pal in 1914 with Picasso in Montparnasse and in the 1930s with the Rockefellers in Manhattan.

At a time when his first wife was pregnant, Marnham wrote, Rivera was sleeping with the photographer and Soviet agent Tina Modotti. When the mother of his first child was delivering their baby, he was sleeping with her friend, never acknowledging the daughter they had together. When married to the noted artist Frida Kahlo, he allegedly slept with her younger sister Cristina as well as with Paulette Goddard, Louise Nevelson, and others.

Rivera is said by Marnham to have exaggerated many personal stories, concluding that he was a dreamer "with his eyes open": for example, averring that he was so sickly at birth he was discarded into a bucket of dung but miraculously somehow recovered; that he lived for two years with the Tarascan Indian wet nurse who had carried him off into a forest; that as a boy he lectured to Christians in their church about the falsity of their religion; that he once recommended eating "women's brains in vinaigrette"; and that he was related on his mother's side to the Emperor Maximilian's wife, Carlotta.

Rivera "concentrated on Humanist themes," according to Corliss Lamont. His "Man at the Crossroads" mural for Rockefeller Center in New York City (1933) depicted Lenin along with working class individuals—when Rivera refused to remove the likeness of Lenin, in the resultant furor the work was destroyed.

Murals of his in the Detroit Institute of Arts as well as in numerous buildings in Mexico City typify his interpretation of industrial America and the importance of revolution. Marnham noted in 1932 at the time Edsel Ford was paying Rivera for the Detroit work, over 300,000 workers were being laid off and the remaining workers were receiving pay cuts from $33 to $22 per week: "At City Hall there was talk of closing the museum and selling its collection, and there on the platform of the central railway station stood a 'foreign artist' being greeted by the Mexican vice consul and the German-born museum director, an artist who was due to be paid $10,000 to cover a perfectly decent wall with Communist paintings."

Rivera's impact was wide, particularly upon artists such as Jackson Pollock. He was "emblematic," *The New York Times* critic Michael Kimmelman wrote (20 December 1998), "in the debates about national or indigenous art versus art in the International style. And, Picasso aside, he was perhaps the only artist of the century whose popularity made him a global diplomat. Rivera became the cherubic public face of revolutionary, postcolonial Mexico." (See entry for Rivera's wife, Frida Kahlo.) {CE; CL}

Rivera, Geraldo (1943-)

A television personality and journalist, Rivera lists himself as Jewish in *Who's Who in America*. Previously, he allegedly said on one of his television programs that he did not "believe in faith." {Celebrity Atheists}

Rivero, Jesús (20th Century)

Rivero was a participant in 1996 at the Humanist World Congress in Mexico City. He spoke on the subject, "*Los Idolos y los medios masivos de comunición.*"

Rivers, Fred M. (20th Century)

In 1970 for his Ph. D. dissertation at the University of Maryland, Rivers wrote "Francis Ellingwood Abbott: Free Religionist and Cosmic Philosopher." {FUS}

Riverso, Emanuele (1928–)

At the Eighth International Humanist and Ethical Union World Congress at Hannover (1982), Prof. Riverso addressed the group.

Rivet, Gustave (Born 1848)

Rivet was a French writer and politician. He taught rhetoric at Dieppe and was deposed for writing, under the influence of Victor Hugo, poetry of an advanced character. In 1877 he turned to journalism, writing in the *Homme Libre*, the *Voltaire*, and other rationalist papers. In 1879 he became *chef de cabinet* in the Ministry of Fine Arts. He was elected to the *Chambre* in 1883 and was its *Questeur* from 1898 to 1903. It was Rivet who proposed the abolition of the oath in France. In the Senate in 1903, Rivet supported the legislation against the Church. {RAT}

Rivett, Albert Cherbury David [Sir] (1885–1961)

Rivett was an Australian rationalist, secularist, administrator, scientist, and chemist. After obtaining a Rhodes scholarship (1907), he was appointed a Melbourne University lecturer in chemistry (1911), then a professor (1924). In 1948, he was made an Honorary Associate of the Rationalist Association of Australia, Ltd. {SWW}

Rivadavia, Bernardino [President] (1780-1845)

An Argentine statesman and diplomat, the first president of the United Provinces of La Plata (1826-1827), Rivadavia was a liberal largely responsible for Argentina's independence and for progressive measures that led to its centralistic government. When a unitarian constitution, adopted in 1826, was rejected, Rivadavia resigned and went into exile. Hugo Estrella, head of the Argentine humanist group, claims that Rivadavia's life is in the tradition of secular humanism. {See entry for Argentine Freethinkers, Humanists.}

Rizal, José (1861–1896)

Rizal was a Philippine nationalist, author, poet, and physician. After studying at a Jesuit school in Manila, he studied at the University of Madrid and in Paris, Berlin, Heidelberg, and Leipzig. In Berlin he published his first novel, *Noli me tangere* (1886, The Lost Eden), which was a diatribe against the Spanish administration and the religious orders in the Philippines. Because of this attack, he was compelled by the Spanish to leave the Philippines, and Rizal then lived successively in China, Japan, the United States, England, France, and finally Hong Kong, where he practiced medicine. Upon returning to Manila in 1892, he was arrested as a revolutionary agitator and was banished to Dapitan. On his way to Cuba in 1896, he was arrested and returned to Manila. After being exiled twice, he had great influence with natives in the Philippines. But, according to McCabe, he was given a farcical trial and was charged with being an instigator of insurrection and founder of secret revolutionary societies. As a result, Rizal was murderously shot. {CE; JM; RAT; RE}

RNA (Ribonucleic Acid)

The origin of life is closely connected with RNA, or ribonucleic acid, the polymeric constituent of all living cells and many viruses. Toward the end of the 20th Century, the origin of life remained shrouded in mystery. RNA, however, was the popular candidate mentioned by biologists searching for a single molecule that could replicate itself. Douglas Philp, at the University of Birmingham in Britain, worked with molecules simpler than RNA. According to *The Economist* (4 May 1996), Philp and his colleagues "found four families of dimer (and about a dozen different chemical combinations) that look promising as autocatalysts—an impressive advance considering that a few years ago none, other than the nucleic acids, were known. Whether any of them could form the basis of an alternative genetic system is a moot point. Their shortness is partly a deliberate constraint imposed by the experimenters. Nevertheless, a genetic molecule would almost certainly have to be a polymer if it were going to carry a significant amount of information."

It also would have to be more chemically variable than anything Dr. Philip's team had come up with. Their work suggests first, stated *The Economist*, "that RNA may not have had such an easy time of it at the beginning, and second that living systems based on radically different biochemistries from that which emerged on earth some 4 billion years ago are conceivable. It also suggests that it might be possible to achieve a profound change in the way that chemical engineering is done. If recognition sites can be engineered into useful molecules, such as drugs, without altering their function, the external catalysts needed to make them could be scrapped. That would be radical." (See entries for DNA, Genesis, and Purpose of Life.)

Roa Bastos, Augusto: See entry for Paraguayan Freethought.

Roalfe, Matilda (1813–1880)

An English freethinking bookseller, Roalfe served two months in jail for purposely defying the English blasphemy laws by selling Paine's *The Age of Reason* and Southwell's *The Oracle of Reason.* Upon her release, she again deliberately sold the proscribed works but, for some reason, was not again prosecuted. Roalfe wrote *Law Breaking Justified* in 1844, the same year that she edited in Edinburgh *The Plebian.* {BDF; EU, Gordon Stein; FUK; RAT; TRI; WWS}

Roan, Michael (20th Century)

Roan is director of the Tandem Project, a non-sectarian, nonprofit international human rights organization founded in 1985 to promote, implement, and monitor the 1981 United Nations Declaration on the Elimination of All Forms of Intolerance and Discrimination Based on Religion or Belief. In *Free Inquiry* (Winter 1995-1996), Roan described the involvement by secular humanists in a 1995 London conference sponsored by the Tandem Project and the Human Rights Centre at the University of Essex.

Robbins, Richard (20th Century)

Robbins, when he reviewed books for *The Humanist* in the 1950s, was in the department of sociology and anthropology at Wellesley College.

Robbins, Tom (1936–)

Robbins is an author who has written a biography, *Guy Anderson* (1965); and fiction such as *Another Roadside Attraction* (1971), *Even Cowgirls Get the Blues* (1976), and *Half Asleep in Frog Pajamas* (1994). In *Skinny Legs and All*, he wrote that "Religion is not merely the opium of the masses, it's the cyanide." {CA; E}

Robert, Pierre François Joseph (1763–1826)

Robert was a French *conventionnel* and friend of Brissot and Danton. A professor of public law, he was nominated deputy for Paris. After writing *Republicanism Adapted to France* (1790), Robert became secretary to Danton and voted for the death of the king. He wrote in Prudhomme's *Révolutions de Paris.* {BDF}

Robert, Roberto (1817–1870)

Robert was a Spanish anti-clerical satirist. His mordant style is illustrated in such of his works as *The Rogues of Antonio*, *The Times of Mari Casania*, and *The Skimmer of the Centuries.* {BDF}

Roberts, Brad (20th Century)

Roberts, who as a singer fronts the rock group, Crash Test Dummies, holds a degree in philosophy. He is known for a song, "God Shuffled His Feet," which is an evocation of the inscrutability of the Almighty, with its refrain, "God shuffled his feet and glanced around at them. / The people cleared their throats and stared right back at him."

Roberts, F. A. (20th Century)

Roberts is an active supporter of New Zealand's *Rationalist and Humanist.*

Roberts, George W. (20th Century)

Roberts was editor of the *Bertrand Russell Memorial Volume* (1979). {GS}

Roberts, Isaac (1829–1908)

A businessman and astronomer, Roberts took photographs with his twenty-inch reflector and won the Gold Medal of the Royal Astronomical Society as being the best available at that time. In a letter to Holyoake, Roberts stated, "We seem to be now as ever the playthings of some being that permits us to blunder into the maximum discomfort of life and at the end has arranged that we must return to the state of unconscious atoms." Roberts was an agnostic. {RAT; RE}

Roberts, John Emerson (Born 1853)

After serving a number of Baptist churches, Roberts became a Unitarian in 1884. In 1887 he served the All Souls Unitarian Church in Kansas City. Finding the Unitarians were too "spiritual" for him, he withdrew two-thirds of the Unitarian congregation to form "The Church of This World." The *Grand Rapids Herald* in Michigan described him (9 June 1899) as follows:

> Mr. Roberts (he objects strongly to be called reverend) is a talented speaker and a man of the most advanced character, holding extremely radical views. He is filling the pulpit of a church which is unique in many of its characteristics. Its pastors receive the splendid salary of $12,000 per year, and what is more strange still, the church is not compelled to resort to any of the usual methods to raise the sum necessary for the running expenses of the church, the rent for the pews proving to be ample for all purposes. It is peculiar also in the character of its services. The pastor delivers a weekly address, or lecture; he scorns the name of sermon. The music of the service is rendered by a full orchestra of 18 pieces, and as he expresses it, "they don't have any fooling with phantoms or with things they don't know anything

about." Such a thing as a public prayer is unknown to its members, and the minister of this odd flock says that he can conceive of nothing more vulgar than a public prayer.

Roberts wrote *The Inevitable Surrender of Orthodoxy* (1895). {*Freethought History #7*, 1993; GS}

Roberts, Morley (Born 1857)

Morley, a novelist, moved from England to Australia, working on railways and farms. Migrating to America, he again took to railroad and farming work. About fifty novels, a volume of verse, a volume of plays, and a collection of essays followed his first novel, *The Western Avernus* (1887). In one essay, he expressed his agnosticism and his disdain of theology: "God must be very young, and that is his only excuse. . . . When I say God I mean the common conception of Him. It certainly is not mine, if I have any." {RAT}

Roberts, Paul William (20th Century)

Roberts is the Canadian author of *In Search of the Birth of Jesus, the Real Journey of the Magi* (1995). Intrigued by references to the Magi in the Bible, he set out on his own travels. The book discusses his view that the Dead Sea Scrolls do not confirm the Vatican's version of Christianity but, actually, reveal a "bitter conflict between rival factions and the warning of a coming schism that would rend the religion in two." Critic Christopher Lehmann-Haupt relates more of Roberts's findings: "Jesus was born the prophet of a religion involving the individual's inner knowledge, not faith in an earthly institution. This religion was heavily influenced by Zoroastrianism, the system founded in Persia by Zoroaster teaching the worship of Ormaz in the context of a universal struggle between the forces of light and darkness. As Mr. Roberts says he learned, the wise men from the East were Zoroastrian Magi. . . . The purpose of their journey . . . was essentially to avert a situation in which 'good works or spiritual improvement' would become irrelevant and in which faith alone would get you to Heaven." In short, without Zoroaster there would be no Christ. He was the bridge, and the Romans burned it. {"Books of the Times," *The New York Times*, 14 December 1995}

Roberts, R. (Born 1843)

After studying for the ministry at the Bala Welsh Calvinistic Methodist College, Roberts was expelled for heresy and became a Congregationalist minister. Serving for some years at Guisbrough and Leeds, he then joined the Unitarians, serving as minister at Hunslet and Bradford. Then he abandoned every shade of Christianity and established an Ethical Society at Bradford. An agnostic, Roberts contributed to the *Literary Guide*. {RAT}

Roberts, Robert Rewalt (20th Century)

In 1957 for his M.A. thesis at the University of Chicago, Roberts wrote "The Freethought Movement of Chicago." {FUS}

Robertson, A. D. (19th Century)

Robertson is New York edited the *Free Enquirer* in 1835. {BDF}

Robertson, Alexander (19th Century)

In 1865, Robertson wrote *Theistic and Atheistic Philosophy*. {GS}

Robertson, Archibald (Robert Arch) (20th Century)

Robertson, a humanist, wrote *Anglican Shipwreck* (1945), *Jesus: Myth or History* (1946); and *Man His Own Master, An Essay in Humanism* (1948). {FUK; TRI}

Robertson, D. P. (20th Century)

Robertson wrote *Should Churches Be Taxed?* (1968). {FUS}

Robertson, George Croom (1842–1892)

Robertson, the son of an Aberdeen tradesman, was appointed assistant to Professor Geddes and in 1866 professor of mental philosophy and logic at London University College. In 1876 Bain, a friend and admirer, got him appointed editor of *Mind* (a title suggested by Robertson for the new philosophical review). Robertson was a member of the Metaphysical Society and took an interest in women suffrage, the education of women, and other reforms. He wrote on Hobbes (1886) and, although never writing about religion, agreed with his friends Sir L. Stephen and Bain. {RAT}

Robertson, James (20th Century)

At the Seventh International Humanist and Ethical Union (IHEU) World Congress held in London (1978), Robertson from the United Kingdom addressed the group.

Robertson, John B. (20th Century)

Robertson edited *Philosophical Works of Francis Bacon* (1905). {EW}

Robertson, John M(acKinnon) (1856–1933)

Robertson, who was born on the Isle of Arran, has been called "the most successful of all the [freethought] leaders at making his way in the world." At first a railroad telegraph clerk, then a clerk in an insurance office, he became active in the 1880s in the Edinburgh Secular Society. In 1884, he moved to London to work on the *National Reformer*, of which he became editor on Bradlaugh's death. Robertson is credited with having led Annie Besant to socialism, although he himself became a "New Liberal." In 1906 he was elected Liberal M.P. for Tynemouth, having previously failed to win Northampton. In 1911 he was appointed Parliamentary Under-Secretary to the Board of Trade, a position he held until the fall of Asquith's government in 1915. Losing his seat as an Asquithian Liberal in 1918, he devoted himself to freethought literature until his death. The breadth of his writings on both freethought and political topics was enormous, and he became one of the most important of latter-day Liberals and Secularists.

Robertson believed that Jesus never existed, and he wrote a five-volume series on the subject. The Gospels, he reasoned, were actually derived from morality plays. Although few historians and scholars now agree, his concepts stirred much discussion. He used "freethought" almost as a synonym for progress in the liberalization of the philosophy of religion, states Gordon Stein. His editorship of *Reformer* was from 1893 to 1904, prior to which he had been an editor of *The National Reformer*, upon which Charles Bradlaugh and Joseph Barker had also been editors. During his time with Bradlaugh, Robertson professed atheism but later, according to McCabe, preferred to be called an agnostic. Following Moncure Conway's departure from the South Place Ethical Society in 1899, he along with Herbert Burrows and J. A. Hobson served as a panel of lecturers there.

In 1895, Robertson wrote *Modern Humanists*. He then wrote *Short History of Freethought, Ancient and Modern* (1915), which is a major and authoritative book on the subject. His two-volume *History of Freethought* and his *History of Freethought in the Nineteenth Century* (1929) are major reference works. Robertson's wide interests included Walt Whitman, about whom he published a study in the "Round Table Series," Mithraism, socialism, Toryism, and barbarism. He also wrote a pamphlet, "Thomas Paine: An Investigation," a scathing exposure in 1900 of Christian calumnies regarding Paine's alleged deathbed recantation.

For some months before his death, Robertson's health had been failing. He attended a meeting of the Bradlaugh Centenary Committee in December. On Thursday January 5, 1933, he was at work on two books which he was writing, and in the evening was listening to a wireless talk on "Saving," a subject in which he had long been keenly interested. Shortly afterward he had a "stroke" and died. His remains were cremated on January 7, and in accordance with his own often-expressed wish there was no ceremony of any kind at the funeral. (See the entry for D. H. Lawrence.) {BDF; EU, Gordon Stein; FO; FUK; JM; RAT; RE}

Robertson, Marion Gordon (20th Century)

The Rev. "Pat" Robertson founded and leads a powerful grass-roots movement, the Christian Coalition. In his *The New World Order* (1995), he writes that "What Christians have got to do is take back this country, one precinct at a time, one neighborhood at a time, and one state at a time." Robertson is anti-evolution, anti-abortion, anti-gay rights, and anti-liberal religion. Because war profits the "monopoly bankers," he implies that the Rothschilds and their agents (including "the Rothschild publication, *The Economist*) have incited World War I, the cold war, and the Gulf War in order that military spending by various governments would increase the need for compound-interest loans, the "eighth wonder of the world." Robertson does not argue that international Jewish high finance was behind Hitler's war against the Jews, and he treats the Holocaust as Satan's work, a sign of the coming holocaust of American Christians at the hands of diabolical liberals.

Robertson, Priscilla Smith (1910–1989)

A scientific humanist, historian, civil libertarian, and author, Priscilla Robertson was editor of *The Humanist* in the 1950s, that magazine's "Golden Age" according to the present author and numbers of intellectuals who wrote about, subscribed to, and contributed to the quarterly and its causes. When she and Corliss Lamont had a tiff over her rights as an editor to, or not to, publish one of his articles, the board of directors of the American Humanist Association dismissed her. As described by philosopher Harold A. Larrabee at the time (2 March 1959), "In a ruthless and even brutal exercise of majority power by the AHA Board of Directors . . . Priscilla Robertson was dismissed as Editor and Gerald Wendt was appointed to replace her on a caretaker basis." Prof. Larrabee added, "It became quite apparent that a narrow majority of the Directors were strongly opposed to the way in which the magazine has attempted to challenge its readers with new ideas for the Humanism of the future, and prefer to flog the dead horses of past controversial issues in a sectarian spirit."

As a consequence, the magazine's staff (including Vassar's English Department Chairman Helen Lockwood, Ethical Culture leader Jerome Nathanson, book review editor Warren Allen Smith) resigned en masse to show their support for her. She never again was active as a humanist, despite encouragement from a group of intellectuals in Taminent, Sidney Hook, numbers of writers who vowed never again to submit articles to the magazine, and others. She did, however, chair the Kentucky Civil Liberties Union during a particularly active time for civil-rights cases.

Robertson was the only child of historian Preservèd Smith, the Cornell historian of note who amused scholars by writing a work about theophagy (the eating of God, or communion). A heretic like her father, she wrote *Revolutions of 1848* (1952) which was described by Crane Brinton in *The New York Times* as "in the best tradition of what, in a word perhaps significantly beginning to be overworked, we must call humanism." *An Experience of Women* (1982), about the "new woman" on the eve of the twentieth century, she stressed the cross-cultural relationships of female life in nineteenth-century Britain, France, Germany, and Italy. *Lewis Farm*, which describes growing up on her father's Massachusetts farm won an award in 1968 from the American Academy and Institute of Arts and Letters.

The Humanist carried no obituary following its former editor's stroke in 1989, although the then editor Lloyd Morain knew of her death. Meanwhile, *Free Inquiry* described her extensive contributions to the humanist movement, and eminent humanists went on record as to her massive efforts upon behalf of humanism. {HNS; HNS2}

Roberty de la Cerda, Eugène de (Born 1843)

Roberty was a French positivist writer of Russian birth. He wrote works on sociology, and he completed an essay, "The Old and the New Philosophy" (1887) as well as *The Unknowable* (1889). {BDF; RAT}

Robeson, Paul (1898–1976)

Robeson, the American actor, bass, and controversial humanitarian, was an All-American football player at Rutgers (1919; he was a valedictorian in what then was a Jim Crow-era white college), after which he went to Columbia University law school (1923) and began an acting career with the Provincetown Players in 1924. In 1925 he made his debut as a concert singer. With a resonant voice and the ability to project a humane spirit, he won acclaim by creating the title role in Eugene O'Neill's *Emperor Jones* (1925; film, 1933).

Known popularly for his rendition of "Ol' Man River" in Jerome Kern's *Show Boat* (1928; film, 1936) and for his interpretations of Negro spirituals, Robeson was assumed to have continued the Protestantism of his youth. However, after his association with Communist causes and his winning of the International Stalin Peace Prize (1952), he was suspected of being a non-theist and became a pariah in his native country. To avoid trouble after being blacklisted by Hollywood because of his political leanings, he moved to England in 1958 and continued appearing in concerts in Europe and the Soviet Union. George Orwell, alleging that Robeson was "very anti-white" and a Henry Wallace supporter, questioned whether or not Robeson actually was a member of the Communist Party.

A polyglot (ten languages, from Chinese to Swahili), he spoke out against man's inhumanity to man and utilized naturalistic rather than supernaturalistic terms in arguing his outlook. His outspokenness, however, left him not only defiant but also frustrated and disillusioned. Like the Emperor in O'Neill's play, he became a take-no-shit Negro who was lucky enough to obtain the empty title of King of Jamaica but also who, as critic Gary Dauphin has noted, "hit a ceiling" and "settled uncomfortably in a throne that did not quite fit, his crown slightly askew and his eyes gone a little desperate from the need for constant vigilance." In 1961 when found in a Moscow hotel bathroom after having slashed his wrists, he was said to have made a "suicide attempt," a charge Paul Robeson Jr. has always denied.

Called by some "the Black Colossus," Robeson has received more favorable attention now that the Soviet Union has fallen. At a private party, searching for someone to sing like her husband some years after his death, Mrs. Robeson chose Gilbert Price, Langston Hughes's protégé. Price, a Catholic and winner of four Tony Award nominations, idolized Robeson as well as knew of his non-theism. In 1998, Robeson was granted a lifetime achievement award as part of the Grammy Awards ceremony, being honored along with musicians Roy Orbison, Bo Diddley, and the Mills Brothers. A homepage is on the Web: <www.motownmagic.com/robeson.html>. (See entry for George Orwell.) {CE; Gary Dauphin, *The Village Voice*, 20 January 1998; Gilbert Price to WAS, numerous conversations, 1980s}

Robespierre, Maximilien François Marie Isidore de (1758–1794)

Robespierre was one of the leading figures of the French Revolution. A lawyer, he became attached to the democratic and deistic theories of J. J. Rousseau. Elected to the States-General (1789) and the National Convention (1792), he became leader of the Jacobins in their struggle with the Girondists. In 1793 he was elected to the Committee of Public Safety, which he dominated throughout the Reign of Terror. Called "the incorruptible," he overthrew both the extreme left and the moderates in the Convention and instituted a new civic religion. In 1793 when rightists joined the Plain in a rising in the Convention, Robespierre was arrested, tried, and guillotined.

McCabe writes of Robespierre's role as President of the Convention: "As such he was mainly responsible for the second and most bloody part of the Terror. Against the stupid but common idea that at the French revolution atheism led to horrible outrages, it is important to point out that Robespierre, who was responsible for the worst excesses, was a dogmatic believer in God and simultaneously imposed the worship of God—at its inauguration he publicly burned an ugly effigy of atheism—and the regime which led to thousands of executions (mostly atheists) without proper trial." In short, McCabe insists that Robespierre was a "fanatical believer in God—practically a Unitarian—who hated Atheism and persuaded the French Government, at the height of the Terror, to recognize the existence of the Supreme Being and declare it the established religion." Meanwhile, many claim Robespierre was a deist who liked the theories of Rousseau. McCabe observes that following the revolution, "as soon as Robespierre was killed and his religion abolished," the subsequent period of atheism, the Directorate, found Paris orderly and well behaved. {JM; RAT; RE}

Robin, Charles Philippe (Born 1821)

Robin was a French physician, a senator, and a member of the Institute and of the Academy of Medicine. In company with Littré he refounded Nysten's *Dictionary of Medicine*. In 1872 his name was struck out of the list of jurors on the ground of his unbelief in God, and despite many protests it remained until 1876, the year he was elected Senator. One of the Republic left, he received the Legion of Honor. {BDF; RAT; RE}

Robin, Édouard Charles Albert (Born 1847)

Robin was a French chemist and physician. He was a professor of therapeutic clinics at the Paris University and scientific editor of the *Bulletin Général de Thérapeutique* and the *New York Herald*. In a symposium on spiritualism, Robin declared, "Communicate with the spirits of the dead! To do that it is necessary that they exist, and we have no reason whatever to suppose that our life is prolonged under another form beyond the grave. Let us put aside these dreams." {RAT}

Robinet, Jean Baptiste René (Born 1825)

Robinet was a French physician who became Comte's doctor and one of his executors. During the war of 1870 Robinet was made Mayor of the Sixth Arrondissement of Paris.

He wrote *Notice of the Work and Life of A. Comte* (1860), a memoir of the private life of Danton (1865), and contributed an account of the *Positive Philosophy of A. Comte and P. Lafitte* to the "*Biblioteque Utile*" (1881). Robinet opened a shop for the sale of deistic literature. {BDF; RAT; RE}

Robinson, Alson (20th Century)

Robinson, a liberal minister, was asked to sign Humanist Manifesto I and did so, but too late to be included in the original publishing. {EW}

Robinson, Charles E. (20th Century)

Robinson wrote "The 'Dear Bill' Letter" (1951). {GS}

Robinson, Chris (20th Century)

Robinson is the lead singer and lyricist for the Black Crowes. From a profile by Kim Neely in *Rolling Stone* (24 January 1991):

> Chris . . . contends that the Crowes' interest in voodoo paraphernalia springs from nothing more than a love of the exotic. . . . Some, however, didn't find it so comical. The piece spawned a panicky rash of LP-and-concert-ticket bonfires organized by alarmed Christian parents in Texas and Virginia. Naturally, Robinson is eager to share his views on that sector of society. "Jesus Christ loved everyone," he says bluntly. "Jesus Christ probably loved Satan. I mean, I don't believe that God and Satan are real, but if you're a Christian, then you love everyone. And if you're a Christian and you think I'm fucked up, then fuck you!
>
> {CA}

Robinson, David (1947–)

Robinson wrote *The Unitarians and the Universalists* (1985). In 1982, he was author of *The Apostle of Culture: Emerson As Preacher and Lecturer.*

Robinson, Frank Bruce (20th Century)

Robinson wrote *Crucified Gods Galore* (1933) and *Your God-Power* (1943. {GS}

Robinson, H. D. (H. M. Duhesquet) (19th Century)

With S. J. W. Taber from 1832 to 1833, Robinson edited a New York freethought publication called *Comet.*

Robinson, Harriet Hanson (1825–1911)

Robinson, the first woman to testify before the United States Committee on Woman Suffrage, as a girl had been excommunicated by a Congregational Church. A teenager, she had joined after asking permission from her mother, a Universalist. "If you think it will make you any happier, do so," her mother had told her, "but I do not believe you will be satisfied."

That prediction came true because the new church said that her mother was an unbeliever, that her mother would not go to Heaven. Forced to choose, the daughter wrote later, "I mustered up courage to say, with shaking voice, 'I do not believe; I cannot go to your church, even if you do excommunicate me.' " She was to become active in fighting for women's rights, and with money she earned she helped send her brother John to study to become a Universalist minister.

Harriet married William Hanson, a Unitarian and a journalist, and the two bought a plot in Sleepy Hollow Cemetery. The plot, she wrote in her diary, was next to the famous Hawthornes except for one. The one she did not name, because she felt the famous writer did not live up to his abilities, was that of Thoreau. {EG}

Robinson, Henry Crabb (1775–1867)

Robinson was a writer who met Goethe and Schiller at Weimar and who in London was a friend of Coleridge, Wordsworth, Southey, and Lamb. His posthumous papers (1869, 3 volumes) show him to have been a rationalist. {RAT; RE}

Robinson, James (20th Century)

Director of the Institute for Christianity and Antiquity at Claremont College, Robinson is on Council for Secular Humanism's Committee for the Scientific Examination of Religion.

Robinson, James Hervey (20th Century)

Robinson wrote *The Mind in the Making* (1921), *The Humanizing of Knowledge* (1924, 1926), and *The Human Comedy: As Devised and Directed by Mankind Itself* (1937). {EW; GS}

Robinson, Richard (1902–1996)

Robinson, who taught philosophy at Cornell University for nearly twenty years and taught another twenty at Oriel College, wrote *The Province of Logic* (1931) and *Definition* (1950). His moral critique of religion, *An Atheist's Values* (1964), was written in a popular style and does not contain technical language or abstract speculation. {*New Humanist*, June 1996}

Robinson, Svend [Member of Parliament] (20th Century)

Robinson, a member of the Canadian Parliament, has publicly announced that he is gay and that he is a non-theist.

Robinson, Thomas C. (20th Century)

Robinson is a freethinker who was refused a position at a Dade County high school because of his atheism. Although he sued the University of Miami, he lost in the 1950s. {*Freethought Today*, September 1997}

Robinson, Wade (20th Century)

Robinson, of the Rochester Institute of Technology, is President of the Hume Society.

Robinson, William J. (20th Century)

Robinson wrote *If I Were God—A Freethinker's Faith* (1930). {GS}

Robson, Robbi (20th Century)

Robson represented the International Humanist and Ethical Union (IHEU) in 1995 at the UN's Fourth World Conference held in Beijing, China. Although somewhat disappointed at the objections advanced by members from some of the "religiously oriented" states, she found that the conference did help the cause of attacking women's inequality.

Robson cited these achievements:

> affirmation that women's rights are human rights; recognition that

"culture" is not a reason to deny women their fundamental rights; agreement of the importance of eliminating discrimination against the girl child; commitments to review punitive measures against women who undergo an abortion; recognition of the need for action against the feminization of poverty; declaration against violence against women; rape acknowledged as a war crime; agreement to recognize the economic contributions of women's unpaid work; agreement of the need to address women's unequal share of education and power; recognition of women's contribution toward sustainable development; holding the United Nations accountable for women's equality within its own structures.

In 1996, Robson spoke about a proposed new agenda for feminism at the Humanist World Conference held in Mexico City. She is chairman of the British Humanist Association and treasurer of the International Humanist and Ethical Union (IHEU). {*International Humanist News*, October 1995}

Roca, Deodoro (1890-1942)

In Argentina Roca was author of the University Reform Manifesto (1918). A polemicist, writer, libertarian, and iconoclast, he was admired by Waldo Frank, José Ortega y Gasset, Stefan Zweig, and Rafael Alberti. His courageous writings and activities made him unpopular among the upper class in which he was born, but youth admired him, calling him a beloved teacher.

The Argentine Humanist Society is named after Roca.

Rocca Jr., Bernard T. (20th Century)

Rocca, when he signed Humanist Manifesto II, was a consultant to International Trade and Commodities. He wrote *Fitting in the Pieces* (1964) and *Faith, Fact, and Reason* (1973). {FUS; HM2}

Rocca Sr., Bernard T. (Born 1892)

When he signed Humanist Manifesto II, Rocca was president of the United Secularists of America. He is author of *Fitting In the Pieces* (1961), a collection of essays on humanism, evolution and religion, miracles, dogma, and immortality. {HM2}

Roche, Marcel (1920)

Roche, a permanent delegate to UNESCO from Venezuela, is a Humanist Laureate in the Council for Secular Humanism's International Academy of Humanism. A bacteriologist, he wrote *La investigacion cientifica en Venezuela* (1967). Roche is editor of *Interciencia.*

Rochelle, Paula (20th Century)

Rochelle is on the Executive Committee of the American Humanist Association's Board of Directors. A resident of Saratoga, California, she attended the 1996 Humanist World Congress in Mexico City. Her e-mail: <prochelle1@aol.com>.

Rockefeller, Steven C. (1936–)

Rockefeller is author of *John Dewey: Religious Faith and Democratic Humanism* (1991). A humanist and Buddhist, Rockefeller details Dewey's move from a Congregationalist rearing to his interest in a neo-Hegelian realism to his eventual naturalistic humanism.

Rocker, Rudolf (1873–1958)

A German anarchist and historian, Rocker in his *Nationalism and Culture* wrote, "The sense of dependence on a higher power, that source of all brighter future, will yield place to an enlightenment which makes man himself the master of his fate. . . . Only when man shall have overcome the belief in his dependence on a higher power will the chains fall away that up to now have bowed the people beneath the yoke of spiritual and social slavery."

Rockler, Michael (20th Century)

Rockler, a professor of education at National-Louis University, became Chairman of the Board of Directors of the Bertrand Russell Society in 1995. In addition, he edited the group's newsletter, *The Bertrand Russell Society Quarterly*. Rockler is a Secular Humanist Mentor of the Council for Secular Humanism. In Toronto at the 1994 conference of the Coalition for Secular Humanism, Atheism, and Freethought, Rockler spoke on "John Dewey vs. Bertrand Russell on Religious Belief." He is author of *Innovative Teaching Strategies* (1988).

Rockoff, Mark (20th Century)

Rockoff is secretary of Atheists United, which publishes a monthly newsletter in Sherman Oaks, California.

Rockwell, W. Teed (20th Century)

Rockwell sometimes writes for *Truth Seeker.* To Nietzsche's and Ayn Rand's denial of the value of altruism and pity he suggests there is a closely related third virtue: compassion. It is compassion, he states, which is a necessary part of what it means to be a good person.

Rod, Louis Édouard (1857–1910)

Rod was a Swiss novelist who edited *La Revue Contemporaine* in 1884. From 1886 to 1893 he was a professor at Geneva University. In France he wore the Cross of the Legion of Honour and the decoration of the Crown of Italy. Until about 1889, when he wrote a pamphlet in defense Zola's *Assommoir*, he belonged to the naturalist and more boldly rationalistic school. He then fell under the influence of Tolstoy, joining what he called the intuitionist school.

In one work, entitled "Religion," he closes with a drastic piece of prose poetry which he called an "Atheistic Hymn to the Lord." Although Lanson called him a neo-Christian, the Catholic Delfour quoted Rod as saying, "In reality I have the soul of a believer who has fallen into scepticism." {RAT}

Roddenberry, Eugene Wesley (Gene) (1921–1991)

One of the best-known science fiction writers, Roddenberry wrote *Star Trek* (1980) and, with Susan Sackett, *Star Trek: The First 25 Years* (1991), in both of which he shows that humans through critical thinking and cooperative effort will progress.

A March-April 1991 interview in *The Humanist*, on which he was a member of the editorial board, details his humanistic philosophy.

On the subject of religion, he has written,

> My family was from the South. My mother was very religious. Every Sunday we went to church—Baptist church. . . . I guess I was around fourteen and emerging as a personality. . . . I listened to the sermon, and I remember complete astonishment because what they were talking about were things that were just crazy. It was communion time, where you eat this wafer and are supposed to be eating the body of Christ and drinking his blood. My first impression was, "This is a bunch of cannibals. . . ." I guess from that time it was clear to me that religion was largely nonsense—largely magical, superstitious things. In my own teen life, I just couldn't see any point in adopting something based on magic, which was obviously phony and superstitious.
>
> My brother and sister are nonreligious. In fact, the whole family is. You don't see religious stuff in my family when you are around them. This, in a family that fifteen years before had Tuesday prayer meetings in the house. Mom began that in her early twenties and just drifted out of it in later years.

His *Who's Who* entry:

> To be different is not necessarily to be ugly; to have a different idea is not necessarily to be wrong. The worst possible thing that can happen to humanity is for all of us to begin to look and talk and act and think alike. The best measure of maturity and wisdom in a human is the recognition of value received on hearing another say: "I disagree with you, for the following reasons. . . ."

In 1997, 0.2 ounces of his cremains, along with the ashes of Timothy Leary and twenty-two others whose families paid $4,800., were placed on a Pegasus rocket, launched from a Lockheed L1011 jet, and shot three hundred miles into orbit. It was the first such burial in space. The "ashtronauts" were expected to orbit the Earth between eighteen months to ten years before gravity would yank them back into the atmosphere and vaporize them. (See entry for Arthur Chappell.) {HNS2; *The New York Times*, 22 April 1997; TYD}

Roddenberry, Majel (Leigh Hudec) (20th Century)

Mrs. Eugene Roddenberry, known as the "First Lady of Star Trek," starred as Nurse Christine Chapel in the original "Star Trek" series and two of the films. In 1995, she accepted the Humanist Arts Award of the American Humanist Association upon behalf of her late husband. "Gene," she said, "was a man who loved humanity unconditionally, fearlessly—from rabbis to agnostics, from university professors to the functionally illiterate . . . and, if he had had a chance, from earth person to alien. Humanity—and beyond humanity, people." She is author of *Human Adjustment to Kainji Servoir in Nigeria* (1994).

Roder, Wolf (20th Century)

Roder teaches at the McMicke College of Arts and Sciences in Cincinnati, Ohio. For the spring, 1993, *Free Inquiry*, he challenged an earlier article by Jan Narveson about the growing human population problem. Roder, an active member of the Cincinnati Free Inquiry Group, reviews books succinctly for various freethought journals.

Rodes, Jean and **Richard Rodes** (20th Century)

Jean and Richard Rodes head a Unitarian group, Friends of Russia and the Ukraine (5250 Patriot Lane, Columbia, Maryland 21045).

Rodger, George (20th Century)

In Scotland, George Rodger is secretary of the Humanist Society of Scotland, which publishes the *Scottish Humanist*. He has headed the training of funeral officiants, a group that uses *Funerals Without God* in their training.

Rodin, Auguste (1840–1917)

Rodin "created some of the most stirring of modern statuary, giving impassioned, if somewhat theatrical, expression to the radiant actualities of life on earth," Corliss Lamont has written of the well-known sculptor. A huge bronze door for the *Musée des Arts* décoratifs was never finished, but he said it was inspired by Dante's *Inferno* and was to have been called "Gate of Hell." "The Thinker" (1879–1900), "The Kiss" (1886), and "The Bather" are among his better-known works. He also completed "The Hand of God" (1897–1898), which is in the Parisian Rodin Museum. Rodin's biographer, Mauclair, said that, as his work suggests, Rodin was "independent of all religious doctrine" and that his favorite authors were Rousseau and Baudelaire. {CE; CL; JM; RAT; RE; TYD}

Rodriguez Cobo, Mario: See entry for Humanist Movement.

Rodriguez, Hernan (20th Century)

Rodriguez was born in Buenos Aires, Argentina, came in 1976 to the United States, where he works as a translator, and is a member of Minnesota Atheists. In their newsletter (July-August 1995), Rodriguez discusses his surprise in high school upon learning that Columbus, whom he previously had thought was sent to enslave the Indians, had not been allowed to enslave them. That, in fact, when Bobadilla, the special envoy of the Crown inspected Columbus's governorship in Santo Domingo, he had sent Columbus back to Spain *in chains* from his third voyage for having done so. Rodriguez cites a work by a Spanish priest, *History of the Indies* by Bartolom de las Casas, which argues that, wanting to save the Indians from slavery by the Spaniards, he had recommended the introduction of black African slaves in order to spare the indigenous people from the hard labor. Because Queen Isabella did not want her own subjects to be enslaved, and these included the Indians, it was considered permissible to use blacks inasmuch as they came from other dominions.

Rodriguez then cites James Michener's postulates in *Iberia*, which complement de las Casas:

1. Catholicism captured Spain and adopted a policy of keeping the country in darkness.
2. Using Spain as a base, Catholicism intended to enslave the world.
3. In order to police its conquests, Spanish Catholicism invented the Inquisition, which it proposed to install in subdued territories.
4. The archpriest of these designs was King Felipe II. He was personally evil and committed many crimes in furtherance of his aims.

De las Casas, at the end of his life, recognized his mistake and condemned the importation of African slaves, Rodriguez notes. The British abolished slavery in 1833, and Spain and Portugal ended it in 1840. Today, Rodriguez states, Latin-America has formed societies based more on the interrelation of human beings as the fundamental organization of life rather than on the production and distribution of goods.

Rodriguez, Sue (20th Century)

Rodriguez in 1993 was given the Canadian Humanist of the Year Award. The citation included the following: "Sue Rodriguez, with the support of the Right to Die Society of Canada, is currently engaged in a court battle to win the right to a doctor-assisted suicide when she determines that her deteriorating condition, as a result of amyotrophic lateral sclerosis, no longer makes her life worth living. Whatever the outcome of this legal action, Sue Rodriguez is to be thanked for her public example of bringing a new degree of honesty to the dying process on behalf of all Canadians."

Roelker, Edith (20th Century)

Roelker wrote *A Season in Utopia, the Story of Brook Farm* (1961). {GS}

Roell, Hermann Alexander (1653–1718)

Roell was a German theologian, author of a deistic dissertation on natural religion that was published at Frankfort in 1700. {BDF}

Roes, David (20th Century)

Roes is New Zealand editor of the *New Zealand Rationalist and Humanist*.

Roesch, Michael (20th Century)

Roesch is active with the Siskiyou Secular Humanists. (See entry for California Atheists, Humanists.) {FD}

Rogeard, Louis Auguste (1820–1896)

A French publicist, Rogeard became a teacher but was dismissed for refusing to attend mass. In 1849 upon moving from Chartres to Paris, he took part in the revolutionary movement. Under the Empire, he was sentenced to five years for writing *Les Propos de Labienus* (1865). Rogeard fled to Belgium, where he wrote a criticism on the Bible in the *Rive Gauche*. In 1871 he assisted Pyat on *Le Vengeur* and was elected to the Commune but declined to sit. An incisive writer, he signed himself "Atheist." {BDF; RAT}

Rogers, Carl Ransom (1902–1987)

Rogers is one of the founders of humanistic psychology, a movement fundamentalists dislike because of its emphasis on autonomy, not on self-surrender and obedience as is the Judeo-Christian emphasis. He wrote *Becoming Partners: Marriage and Its Alternatives* (1977). In 1964, the American Humanist Association named Rogers Humanist of the Year. {HNS2; TRI}

Rogers, Gerald F. (20th Century)

Rogers, a poet, writer, and philosopher, is author of "Confucius, The First 'Teacher' of Humanism?" (*Free Inquiry*, Spring, 1993). He holds that many people are misled by the later works of Confucian revisionists who have infused mysticism and abstract speculations into Confucian thought, contrary to its original naturalism.

Rogers, Gordon (20th Century)

If there is no god, does life have a purpose? Asking the question, Rogers concludes that if there is any purpose in the universe, it is what we humans (and any other conscious life forms, if any) put there (*New Humanist*, October, 1990). Dr. Rogers has held the Chair in Engineering Thermodynamics at the University of Bristol and also been a Pro-Vice Chancellor.

Rogers, James Edwin Thorold (1823–1890)

Until 1859, Rogers was an enthusiastic High Church priest. Later he became professor of statistics and economics at King's College and Drummond Professor of Political Economy at Oxford, as well as a member of Parliament. Rogers, a rationalist, wrote *The History of Agriculture and Prices* (1866–1887, 8 volumes). {RAT; RE}

Rogers, Joel Augustus (1883–1966)

Rogers was an African American historian, a scholar, a thinker, a motivator. According to McBryde, his research "did much to combat the feelings of white superiority." His revolt against Christianity "was based largely on his observation that racism and Christianity go hand in hand. A case in point is the segregation of black and white churches. He found the Mormon religion to be especially racist. There are Mormons who still harbor the notion that blacks cannot go to heaven because of their race." The miracles of the Bible, his father also believed, were "rubbish." In *Nature Knows No Color Line*, he gave evidence "of the origin of color prejudice which began when Nordic or fair-skinned whites imposed their standards of beauty on the darker Spaniards, Portuguese, Greeks, and Italians. The color white had become equated with purity, cleanliness, and Godliness. Conversely, blacks were forced to believe that everything associated with the color black was trivial or inferior." Although Rogers allegedly was an atheist, he was well-versed in many of the world's religions. {AAH, Mike McBryde}

Rogers, John (1500–1555?)

An English Protestant, Rogers started out as a Roman Catholic priest. But William Tyndale converted him to Protestantism, after which Rogers worked on an English translation of the Bible, using the name of Thomas Matthew and eventually being burned as a heretic. Catherine D. Bowen tells the story that when Oliver Wendell Holmes's brother John was dying, those present asked the nurse if Holmes was still alive. She reached under the sheets, felt some warm feet, and whispered, 'Nobody ever died with their feet warm." John Holmes looked up suddenly and, in the last words he was ever to speak, said, "John Rogers did." {CE}

Rogers, Neil (20th Century)

Rogers, a radio talk show host in the Miami, Florida, area, has broadcast that he is a non-theist despite his Jewish heritage. {E}

Rogers, W. S. (20th Century)

Rogers wrote "The Search for Truth Outlined in Letters from a Rationalist" (c. 1923). {GS}

Rogers, Walter Lacy (19th Century)

Rogers wrote "A Review of a Paper Called 'The Fallacies of Unbelief' " (1875). {GS}

Rojas, Fernando de (1465?–1541?)

La Celestina (1499) by Rojas has been termed the greatest work of world literature between Dante's *Divine Comedy* and the rise of Tudor drama. Devlin calls it a profound study of unbelief, saying Rojas saved himself from the Spanish Inquisition by his mendacious, medieval moralizing. {CE; EU, John Devlin}

Rokitansky, Karl (1804–1878)

Rokitansky was a German physician and scientist who had been born in Bohemia. He founded the Viennese school in medicine. His principal work is *A Manual of Practical Anatomy* (1842–1846). {BDF; RAT}

Roland de la Platière, Jeanne Manon Philipon (1754–1793)

A French patriot, the daughter of a drunken engraver, Mme. Roland (Marie Jeanne Philipon, also spelled Phlipon) was fond even at the age of nine of reading Plutarch's *Lives*. When twelve and taken to visit the palace at Versailles, she surprised her parents by disliking the place because the royalist splendor "made me feel injustice and look upon absurdity." For the remainder of her life, she continued her distaste for fashionable society. While at a convent she noted the names of skeptics and, after reading their works, she became in turn a Jansenist, a stoic, a skeptic, an atheist, and a deist. Philip and Grace Wharton, in their *Queens of Society*, while confessing that "from Cartesian, Madame Roland became Stoic, from Stoic Deist, and from that she never returned," are candid enough to add that "her life was morally faultless." Another Christian writer says of her, "the only God she invoked was the future.

After her marriage in 1779 with **Jean Marie Roland de la Platière** (1734–1793), she became interested in the Revolution "of another France, a new American Republic, a republic void of aristocratic distinctions, where merit and not rank should demand and receive homage." She sensed the danger of such a stand, once writing that "we must be ready for everything, even to die without regret! . . . The insolence of the rich and the misery of the people excite my hatred against injustice and oppression, and I no longer ask for anything but the triumph of truth and the success of the Revolution. I am glad there is danger. I see nothing else capable of goading you on. It is impossible to rise to freedom from the midst of corruption without strong convulsions. They are the salutary crises of a serious disease." However, her husband, however, was appointed minister of the interior and they became part of the establishment. King Louis XVI dismissed him in 1792, but he was restored to office after the overthrow of the monarchy. When he became filled with horror at the shocking massacres of September, Roland wrote an address of remonstrance to the Assembly, one that offended the Robespierrean party that had come into power. Danton, Robespierre, and Marat at this time became bitter enemies of the Rolands. Accused of royalism in 1793, Jean resigned and fled Paris.

When friends begged Mme. Roland to escape, she replied, "I am ashamed of the part you would have me play. I will neither disguise myself nor leave the house. If they wish to assassinate me, it shall be in my own home." To her own home, indeed, the mob came, hooting and shouting derisively around the carriage into which she had been placed. Asked if she wanted the blinds pulled, she replied, "No, gentlemen. I do not fear the eyes of the populace. Innocence should never assume the guise of crime." To which the officer in charge remarked that she had more strength of mind than many men, that "you wait patiently for justice." "Justice!" she exclaimed. "Were justice done I should not be here. But if I am destined for the scaffold, I shall walk to it with the same firmness and tranquility with which I now go to prison. I never feared anything but guilt." Imprisoned for five months, she spent much of her time writing memoirs, but the friend to whom she had entrusted the work, fearful it would be discovered, destroyed it.

On the day of her execution, her carriage moved slowly amid a jeering crowd. The historian Carlyle described her: "A noble white vision, with its high queenly face, its soft proud eyes, long black hair flowing down to her girdle, and as brave a heart as ever beat in woman's bosom. Like a white Grecian statue, serenely complete she shines in that black wreck of things. Graceful to the eye, more so to the mind; genuine, the creature of sincerity and nature in an age of artificiality, pollution, and cant; there, in her still completeness, she, if thou knew it, is the noblest of all French women."

Underwood describes what followed:

> There was a pause—a stir, at the foot of the guillotine. Would she faint, this brave woman, at the horrors prepared for her—at the headsman's basket and sharp hungry machine of death? She bent reverently to the statue of Liberty which with strange mockery was set up near the guillotine; uttered her world-famed apostrophe to it, "O Liberty! what crimes are committed in thy name!"; spoke a few cheering words to the old man, La Marche, who shared her fate; begged the executioner to spare those aged eyes the horror of witnessing her death; asked, as her face grew eloquent with the sublime thoughts which this supreme hour of her life evoked, for pen and paper to which to commit them: asked only to be brutally refused. With unfaltering step, unblanched face, and serene eyes, she stepped upon the scaffold, and stepped a moment later into the unknowable, and, through that cruel death, into at least an earthly immortality. So perished, at the age of thirty-nine, one of the purest, if not the purest character evoked by the French Revolution.

Foote supplies a similar description, saying that feeling she was doomed, she determined to go before the Revolutionary Tribunal alone. M. Chaveau-Lagarde, a lawyer, wished to defend her, but she declined his services. "You should lose your life," she said, "without saving mine. I know my doom. Tomorrow I shall cease to exist." On October 9 she was driven in the tumbril to the guillotine, clad in white, with her long black hair hanging down to her girdle. With her was a prisoner named Lamarche, whom she endeavored to cheer. She renounced her right to be executed first, so that her dejected companion might be spared the pain of seeing her blood. Samson would not consent to this. "Will you," she gaily asked, "refuse a lady her last request?" and he yielded. "*O Liberté, que de crimes on commet en ton nom!*" (O Liberty, what crimes are committed in thy name!"), she exclaimed, but she bowed before the statue nevertheless, knowing that Liberty was holy though worshipped mistakenly with cruel rites.

Her husband, then in hiding in Rouen and hearing of her death, deliberately stabbed himself to death. His body was found at the foot of a tree on the road to Paris. He had thrust a cane-sword into his own heart. Beside him was a letter, in which he said that he died, as he lived, "virtuous and honest," refusing to "remain longer on an earth polluted with crimes." As a result of his death, and anticipating the Tribunal, he secured his property to his daughter.

Margaret Fuller wrote of her, "Madame Roland is the fairest specimen we yet have of her class; as clear to discern her aim, as valiant to pursue it, as Spenser's Britomarte; austerely set apart from all that did not belong to her, whether as woman or as mind. She is an antetype of a class to which the coming time will afford a field—the Spartan matron, brought by the culture of the age of books to intellectual consciousness and expansion. Self-sufficingness, strength, and clear-sightedness were in her combined with a power of deep and calm affection." {CE; BDF; FO; RAT; RE; SAU; WWS}

Roles, John (20th Century)

Roles served in the Royal Signals Corps in the Far East during the final stages of World War II. He was depicted in James Gardiner's *Who's A Pretty Boy Then?* Roles, a gay humanist, had been in the antiquarian book business. {*Gay and Lesbian Humanist*, Autumn 1999}

Rolland, Romain (1866–1944)

Rolland, a French novelist, biographer, playwright, and musicologist, spent two crucial years in Rome, where he was influenced by German intellectuals. He wrote biographies of Beethoven (1903), Michelangelo (1905), Tolstoy (1911), and Mahatma Gandhi (1924). His ten-volume novel, *Jean-Christophe* (1904–1912), established his reputation in the literary world. In 1915 Rolland received the Nobel Prize in Literature. His genuine pacifistic philosophy and the courage of his convictions led to his self-exile in Switzerland, where he remained until 1938. According to McCabe, Rolland used the word God occasionally "but he explains that what he means by God is 'vague and indefinite.' " {JM; RAT; RE; TRI}

Rollason, Atheist Evolution (1994–)

Babies by the thousands are named Jesus, Mohammed, Mary, and Christian or Christine, but George and Tina Rollason of Pennsylvania claim to be the first ever to name a baby girl "Atheist Evolution Rollason," born 20 July 1994. (A Manhattan wag has speculated about the slim odds that one day she will marry a chap named Jesús or Gautama.)

Rolleston, Thomas William (Born 1857)

Rolleston edited the *Dublin University Review* (1885–1886) and was an assistant editor of the New Irish Library. He wrote *The Encheiridion of Epictetus* (1881) and *The Teaching of Epictetus* (1888). His rationalism is developed in *Parallel Paths*), in which he adopted impersonal theism and left the question of immortality open. {RAT}

ROLLINS COLLEGE FREETHINKERS

Rollins College, Florida, humanists are on the Web: <www.secularhumanism.org/cfa/orgs.html>.

Rollins, Henry (20th Century)

Rollins, a vocalist and actor, in a spoken word video, "Talking from the Box," says he is not a spiritual person and does not believe in an afterlife. {E}

Rollins, Jim (20th Century)

Rollins is a St. Louis, Missouri, rationalist activist. E-mail: <smiling@infidels.org>.

Rolls, Montgomery (20th Century)

Rolls, a freethinker, wrote *Come Out of the Madhouse* (1932). {GS}

Rolph, C. H.: See entry for Cecil Rolph Hewitt.

Rolph, William Henry (1847–1883)

Rolph was a German philosopher, the son of an English father. He wrote *On Biological Problems* (1884), in which he accepted evolution, discarded theology, and placed ethics on a natural basis. {BDF}

ROMA (GYPSIES)

- Bury me standing. I've been on my knees all my life.

–Manush Romanov

Uncapitalized, a gypsy is one who prefers an unconventional life. A temporary member on a college faculty is called a gypsy, and in the theatre a gypsy is a member of a chorus line.

The Gypsies, inaccurately called such because they were thought to have come from a so-called Little Egypt, prefer the name **Roma**. Originally they came from a low caste tribe in central India, the Dom, one noted for its singing and dancing. To escape Muslim invaders, they fled and Dom became corrupted into Rom. They speak Romany, a unique language sometimes traced to northwest India, and an estimated six to ten million are found on every continent and in forty countries. Often, they travel in small caravans and make their living as fortune tellers, singers, metalworkers, dancers, musicians, horse dealers, and auto mechanics. Sometimes, they do settle down with non-gypsies but have continued to cling to their identity and customs. Their spiritual life consists of a mixture of animism, deism, fear of ghostly ancestors, and the adoption of the religion of their country of residence.

Many Roma are Roman Catholic, Orthodox Eastern Christian, or Islamic. They are said by Fonseca to have no heroes or myths of origin, "of a great liberation, of the founding of the 'nation,' of a promised land. They have no Romulus and Remus, no wandering, battling Aeneas. They have no monuments, no anthem, no ruins, and no Book. Instead of a sense of a great historical past, they have a collective unease, and an instinctive cleaving to the tribe." And, unlike the other great diaspora, the Jews, the Gypsies have never desired their own nation state.

In 1997, Ion Cioaba, the self-styled king of all Roma, died in Bucharest of a heart attack. He had agitated for Gypsy rights during the dictatorship of

Nicolae Ceausescu, being jailed in 1986. When the Ceausescu regime toppled in 1989, Cioaba had a solid gold, thirteen-pound crown placed on his head at a coronation that attracted 5,000 followers. Meanwhile, in Prague President Vaclav Havel, a champion of human rights, lectured Czechs about their unfair discrimination against Roma. Numbers of Czech Roma had left for Canada and other countries, and Havel lamented their being forced out by public pressure. An estimated 200,000 to 300,000 members of the Roma underclass live in the country, and Czech authorities estimated that from seven to twelve million Gypsies lived in Europe.

Roma are known as the Sinti in Germany and the Roma in Eastern Europe. During World War II, they were treated as racially inferior and were rounded up, deported to camps, and subjected to the Nazis' "extermination through labor" program under which slaves survived ninety days on average. Romani Rose, the current chief of the Central Council of German Sinti and Roma, believes that 500,000 European Gypsies were robbed, exploited as slaves, and murdered in the Nazi *Porraimos* (the Devouring, or Holocaust. Auschwitz had its own Gypsy section.

Of the estimated one million living in the United States, only 5,406 were found by the 1990 Census—those who responded probably said they were Romanian, Mexican, or Greek. They usually get along without birth certificates, Social Security numbers, bank accounts, Medicare, and public assistance of any kind. "We've grown up fearing documents. Hiding one's identity is a tragedy, but it's necessary," said Ian Hancock, who revealed his Roma ethnicity after receiving tenure as professor of linguistics at the University of Texas in Austin, Texas. "Discrimination against Roma," he added about the group he called "the most discriminated against ethnic population" in America. "It is widespread in this country. It's not just police, it's landlords, funeral parlors, sometimes restaurants."

Like the Jewish Hasidim, Roma maintain strong boundaries to ward off the outside world. Associating with the non-Roma, or *Gadje*, is strictly avoided by following rules and rituals. According to Hancock, "You must remember Gypsy culture rests solidly on the idea of pollution and purity. *Gadje* are not clean in a ritual way. Socializing too intimately with *Gadje* contaminates you. Being in their world, you start to suffer and have to go back with Roma to get your balance back. We don't have a physical country, so this movable border is our national frontier."

Andrew Blythe, who was related to the last "king" of the Gypsies in Great Britain, emigrated from Scotland to America to escape harassment during the 1800s. According to *The Economist* (30 May 1998), a man said to be Blythe's great-grandson, William Blythe, died in a car crash, but not before fathering a son. When his mother remarried that lad changed his name . . . to Bill Clinton. {CE; *The Economist*, 8 March 1997; *The New York Times*, 27 February 1997 and 24 February 1999; Isabel Fonseca, "Among the Gypsies," *The New Yorker*; Christine Popp, New York *Daily News*, 7 March 1999}

Romagnosi, Giovanni Domenico (1761–1835)

Romagnosi was an Italian philosopher and jurist. In 1791 he published *Genesis of Penal Law*, many pages of which are borrowed from d'Holbach's *System of Nature*. Romagnosi became professor of law in Parma, Milan, and Pavia. A member of the Italian Academy, he wrote *Elements of Philosophy* (1821), *What Is a Sound Mind?* (1827), and *Ancient Moral Philosophy* (1832). Wheeler described him as "a somewhat obscure writer" who, nevertheless, "contributed to the positive study of sociology." {BDF; RAT; RE}

Romains, Jules (1885–1972)

Romains was a French playwright and author, a chief exponent of "unanimism," a literary theory positing the collective spirit or personality. For example, the spirit of a city might be described. He is author of *Men of Good Will* (27 volumes, 1932–1946), an attempt to give a panoramic view of French life. Also, he wrote poems, *La Vie unanime* (1908); a masterful play, *Cromedeyre-le-Vieil* (1920); and a satirical farce, *Doctor Knock* (1923). (See letter from Charles Mayer, who describes Romains as being a naturalistic humanist.) {CE; HNS}

ROMAN CATHOLIC CHURCH

The National Conference of Catholic Bishops is at 3211 Fourth St., Washington, DC 20017. The church has around 22,700 groups numbering over 61,000,000.

ROMAN CIVILIZATION

Latins claim an association with Latinus, whom they identify as a son of Odysseus by the goddess Circe. With Circe, Latinus had a celebrated amour in the *Odyssey*. Jasper Griffin, professor of Classical Literature and Public Orator at Oxford University, is a fellow of Balliol College and makes the point that the Latins wanted to attach themselves to the Greek genealogical legends, which explains their invention of Latinus. {"Anxieties of Influence," *The New York Review of Books*, 20 June 1996}

ROMAN GODS: See the entry for Greek and Roman Gods.

Romanell, Patrick (1912–)

Romanell, an educator and philosopher, was born in Bari, Italy, and when a teenager became a naturalized citizen of the United States. He has taught philosophy in Panama, Ecuador, and Italy. He was chairman of the philosophy department at Wells College, taught medical philosophy at the University of Texas, and also taught at the University of Oklahoma, the University of Texas, and the University of Arizona. Romanell wrote *The Philosophy of Giovanni Gentile* (1938), *La Polémica entre Croce y Gentile* (1946); *Locke's Letter Concerning Toleration* (1950); *Making of the Mexican Mind* (1952); *El Neo-Naturalismo Norteamericano* (1956); *Para um Naturalismo Dialéctico* (1967); *Humanistic Perspectives in Medical Ethics* (1972); *John Locke and Medicine: A New Key to Locke* (1984); and, with C. D. Leake, *Can We Agree?* (1950). He was book editor of *The Journal of Philosophy* (1939–1951) and wrote book reviews for *The Humanist* in the 1950s.

A noted naturalist, he is particularly known for his *Toward A Critical Naturalism* (1958). For Giovanni Be Crescenzo's *Patrick Romanell and Present-Day American Naturalism* (1966), the leading Italian existentialist, Nicola Abbagnano, wrote the preface.

An annual Romanell–Phi Beta Kappa Professorship in Philosophy is awarded, and the American Philosophical Association sponsors an annual Patrick Romanell Lecture on Philosophical Naturalism, the first lecture of which was given in 1986 by Abraham Edel.

In "The Significance of American Philosophic Naturalism," Romanell makes a strong case for naturalism: "Everything so far lends weight to our overall assessment of American naturalism as a tenable philosophy, except for one important matter, namely, its incomplete analysis of life's conflicts, the very stuff that human life is made of, basically and ultimately." Dewey, he points out, was aware that "the problem of evil is a well-recognized problem, while we rarely or never hear of a problem of good." This points up the philosophic need to distinguish between tragedy and pathos, to pay "serious attention to the tragic dimension of life and to the Problem of Good that goes with it." For Romanell, "historically viewed, philosophical naturalism from its pre-Socratic to its American varieties in the twentieth century belongs to the oldest tradition in Western philosophy. Inasmuch as this venerable tradition would have much more relevance and strength if it were to develop an adequate analysis of the tragic side of life, the most significant contribution that a thorough-going critical naturalism can make, at present, may well consist precisely in teaching the success-oriented people of America in particular that the disconcerting clash of life's equally good things brings unavoidable failure in its train from time to time, as a consequence of which there is no real solution to the tragic choices at stake, let alone a quick or happy one." Further, "since problems of evil and problems of better are resolvable in theory at least, it is indeed fortunate that the tragic problems of good are the only type in human existence that have no solution in principle. The sooner American philosophical naturalism recognizes them candidly as insoluble by nature, the sooner it can address them appropriate for the benefit of humanity's endless pursuit of wisdom."

Asked by the present author in 1995 if in his eighties he was still a naturalist, Romanell confirmed the point, adding, "I'm still a *damn* naturalist on earth, not a *damned* one in Dante's inferno!" Romanell has donated his extensive collection of philosophy books to the Council for Secular Humanism's Library of American Philosophical Naturalism. {Patrick Romanell, "The Significance of American Philosophical Naturalism," *Free Inquiry*, Winter 1995-1996; WAS, 17 February 1995}

Romanes, George John (1848–1894)

A zoologist, a friend of Darwin, and a stout champion of Darwinism, Romanes has been called "a great scientist who deserted Rationalism for religion." McCabe, however, states that the "conversion" has been misrepresented, that "his last years were saddened by a grave illness which admittedly lowered the vigour of his mind, and his very zealous wife induced him to die in the Anglican communion. She then, with the co-operation of Bishop Gore, published, with the title *Thoughts on Religion*, what purported to be his new ideas. The book, even as it left their devout hands, does *not* show a belief in the leading Christian dogmas, or even in the orthodox conception of God. What it does painfully show is the wreck of a scientific mind. It makes the friend of Darwin and Huxley declare that 'the nature of man without God is thoroughly miserable,' and 'unbelief is usually due to indolence, often to prejudice, and never a thing to be proud of.' If these are the actual words of a man who for twenty years had known all the great Victorian Rationalists, it was tragic to publish them." {RE}

ROMANIAN HUMANISTS, UNITARIANS

Unitarianism began in Romania within the liberal wing of the Protestant Reformation in the second half of the 16th century, at the Diet of Torda (1568). At that time King John Sigismund, inspired by the preaching of Francis David, declared liberty of conscience and religion for the first time. At the end of the 16th century there were 400 congregations. Because of 400 years of subsequent persecutions, there were in 1998 around 125 congregations with settled ministers and about fifty small fellowship, with a total membership of approximately 80,000.

The headquarters is in Cluj (Kolosvar), the capital of Transylvania, and Transylvanian Unitarians are ethnic Hungarians whose services are conducted in Hungarian.

Bishop Janos Erdo has headed the Unitarian Church in Romania (Bd. 21 Decembrie Nr. 9, 3400 Cluj-Napoca, Romania). *World* (January-February 1996) contained a photograph of the first new Unitarian church building built in Romania this century, one which stands at Baròt. Its minister is Alpar Kiss. The Rev. Arpad Szabo now heads the Romanian Unitarians, who number around 80,000. As Bishop of the Unitarian Church of Romania, he was elected for a five-year term.

Romanian Unitarians, according to Scott Gerard Prinster of the *Institutul Teologic Protestant* in Club-Napoca, Romania, do not hesitate to call themselves Christians, "although members of other denominations might quibble with that." Most agree that the Resurrection was spiritual, not physical, but remain unsure how to make that information relevant. Complete religious freedom did not exist as of 1997. Individuals do not leave their denomination and remain of whatever religion their parents are. Religious humanism, as in the United States, is unknown, although most Romanian Unitarians would not object to the idea that the promise and potential of humanity is desirable. "*Principiile umanitariste*" (1922) included Eugen Relgis's view that humanism is needed to deify and humanize Man.

E-mail: <steve@ldpa.demon.co.uk>. On the Web: <http://www.uua.org/icuu/icuu-europe.html>. (See entries for Mircea Eliade, the Rev. Ferencz Sebe, and Arpad Szabo.) {WAS, 2 June 1997}

Romano, Ray (20th Century)

At the Fourth Annual Convention of Atheists hosted in 1998 by the St. Louis Rationalist Society, Romano spoke on "The Death of Judas."

ROMANTICISM

Romantics are known for breaking the rules laid down by the Classicists. Romanticism was an artistic and intellectual movement originating in Europe in the late 18th century. It emphasized nature, placed an emphasis on the individual's expression of emotion and imagination, and rebelled against established social rules and conventions. Among the leaders, all non-believers, were Johann Wolfgang von Goethe, Victor Hugo, and Johann Friedrich von Schiller. {DCL}

Romilly, Samuel [Sir] (1757–1818)

Romilly was an English law reformer. He was in sympathy with Rousseau's views, and he was a friend with Diderot and with Jean d'Alembert. Romilly's enthusiasm for the French Revolution inspired his *Letters Containing an Account of the Late Revolution in France* (1792). His work in reforming criminal law began with his *Thoughts on Executive Justice* (1786). Sir Samuel was particularly interested in the reform of law, the abolition of slavery, and opposition to the feudal monarchs of Europe. During Queen Victoria's reign, many of Romilly's proposals were adopted. According to the *Dictionary of National Biography*, "He early lost all faith in Christianity but embraced with ardour the gospel of Rousseau." The writer of the notice added that Romilly's "principles were austere to the verge of Puritanism." {CE; JM; RAT; RE}

Romiti, Guglielmo (19th Century)

An Italian positivist, Romiti was professor of anatomy in the University of Siena. His *Anatomic Notes* was disapproved by many theologians. {BDF}

Romme, Gilbert (1750–1795)

Romme was a French mathematician who became deputy to the Legislative Assembly in 1791 and a member of the Convention in 1792. In 1793 he introduced the new Republican Calendar, the plan for which was drawn by Lalande, the names having been assigned by Fabre d'Eglantine. Romme advocated the Fêtes of Reason. Upon being condemned to death, Romme committed suicide. {BDF; RAT}

Ronge, Johannes (1813–1887)

Ronge was a German religious reformer. A Catholic priest in 1840, he was suspended because of his views. In 1844 he denounced in a letter the worship of "the holy coat," which led to his excommunication from the church. He then preached at free congregations but was proscribed after the Revolution of 1849. Taking refuge in England, Ronge issued a revolutionary manifesto in 1851. In 1861 he returned to Frankfort and in 1873 settled at Darmstadt. {BDF; TRI}

Ronsard, Pierre (1524–1585)

Ronsard was a French poet. He became page to the Duke of Orleans and, afterwards, to James V of Scotland. Ronsard, a freethinker, was a favorite at the French Court. {BDF}

Rood, Max (20th Century)

Rood is a professor of law at Rujksuniversiteitte Leiden and former Minister of Justice in Holland. A Humanist Laureate in the Council for Secular Humanism's International Academy of Humanism, he wrote *Fifty Years of Labour Law and Social Security* (1986) and *Procesrecht in arbeidszaken* (1994). Rood signed Humanist Manifesto 2000.

Rood-de Boer, Madzy (20th Century)

Mrs. Rood-de Boer, a professor of family law and juvenile delinquency, is President of the Socrates Foundation. Founded in 1950, it stimulates humanist influence on science and culture in the Netherlands by founding humanist chairs at the Dutch State Universities; by editing a quarterly on science and culture called *Rekenschap* (PO Box 114, 3500 AC Utrecht, the Netherlands); and by organizing yearly philosophical Socrates lectures. His book on child welfare is *Stroomversnelligen in de kinderbescherming* (1973).

Roofe, Paul G. (20th Century)

Roofe, when he reviewed books for *The Humanist* in the 1950s, was chairman of the anatomy department at the University of Kansas.

Rooney, Andrew (Andy) Aitken (1919–)

• My wife's from the Midwest. Very nice people there. Very wholesome. They use words like "Cripes." For Cripes sake! Who would that be—Jesus Cripes? Son of Gosh? Of the church of the Holy Moly? I'm not making fun of it—you think I want to burn in Heck?

A writer, columnist, and television commentator appearing on the CBS program, "60 Minutes," Rooney has worked with CBS since 1959. In 1968, and again in 1978, 1981, and 1982, he won an Emmy Award. Rooney is author of *The Story of Stars and Stripes* (1946), *Pieces of My Mind* (1984), and *Not That You Asked* (1989).

In Paul Rifkin's *The God Letters* (1986), Rifkin tells of posing as a fifth grade student who asked noted individuals if they believed in God. Rooney responded, "No, of course I don't [believe in God] and anyone who tells you that there is a god who makes his or her presence known to him or her is hallucinating or not telling the truth."

Rooney told Sam Donaldson on ABC's "Prime Time Live" (May 1995) that he was critical of anyone who even claims to know whether or not a god exists." And in a 1996 interview with Arthur Unger in *TV Quarterly*, he was asked if people really knew him. "The only thing I hide from people," Rooney responded, "that I have never said so far as being blunt and honest goes, is that I am not a religious person. I'm not sure the American public would accept from me that fact. I don't think that would please them or that it would attract a lot of people to me. And I take the position that it is sort of a personal matter, so I do not ever make an issue of it." {CA; E}

Roorda van Eysinga, Sicco Ernst Willem (1825–1887)

A Dutch positivist, Roorda van Eysinga served as engineer in Java but was expelled about 1864 for writing on behalf of the Javanese. He contributed to the *De Dageraad* and *Revue Positive*, eventually moving to Switzerland, where he died. {BDF; RAT}

Roosevelt, Eleanor and Franklin Roosevelt: See entry for Adlai Stevenson.

Roosevelt, Sara Delano (19th Century)

The mother of Franklin Roosevelt and an important influence on his life, Sara Roosevelt was raised a Unitarian, later becoming an Episcopalian. She once was a member of the New York City Unitarian Church of All Souls.

Roquetaillade, Jean de la (14th Century)

Roquetaillade, who was also known as Rupescina and was an early French reformer of Auvergne, entered the Franciscan order. His bold discourses, however, led to his imprisonment in 1356 by order of Innocent VI. Nostradamus said Roquetaillade had been accused of magic and was burned at Avignon in 1362, but Wheeler reports this has been disputed. {BDF}

Rorem, Ned (1923–)

Rorem is sometimes described as music's elder statesman but also its enfant terrible. "Swords and Plowshares," which he wrote for the Boston Symphony in 1990, has pacifism as its theme—Rorem is outspoken in his own views concerning pacifism. For twenty-seven years, Rorem has lived monogamously with James Holmes, an organist and choir director in New York, and he believes that gay-rights groups should seek to abolish the military, not to achieve fuller representation in it. A member of the American Academy, Rorem in 1976 won the Pulitzer prize in music. In addition to writing journals, he is best known for his vocal works such as "Air Music" (1975) and *5 Prayers for the Young* (1977). His *Paris Diary* (1966) shocked many with its revelations about his and others' sexual escapades as, for example, "I can't sleep with famous people. Or for that matter with rich people, or people in power, used to being the center of attention. I have been in bed with four *Time* covers—Lenny Bernstein, Tennessee Williams, Noel Coward, and John Cheever (included among 3,000 proportionately anonymous souls, including one woman)—and I performed out of a combination of duress and politeness."

In *Setting the Score* (1988), Rorem went on record as not believing in God nor in an after-life. Asked specifically about his views concerning humanism, Rorem responded to the present author in 1996,

> I have gone on record dozens of times in my thirteen books (and specifically in the essay, "Notes on Sacred Music" in the collection *Settling the Score*) that I do not believe in God, nor in an after-life. I do, however, believe in Belief, which is why I have made so many musical settings of good poetry (and prose) about God. I am a Quaker "by inheritance." My parents converted before my birth, not for religious but for philosophical purposes, and hoped to ally themselves with a group that believed in pacifism. For better or worse I believe that all war is wrong at all times. But I never go to meeti . . . any more than to Alcoholics Anonymous meetings, the tenets of which I nonetheless observe.

To *New York Times* reporter Anthony Tommasini, he responded similarly:

> I don't think life has a purpose. We invent purposes to get through life. I feel basically good, but I am surrounded by death, the deaths of friends, and friends' mates, and every time it is unbearable. I don't believe in God, and I know there is no afterlife. Yet I do believe in belief. I'm not moved by the belief of the Moonies, but I am by the belief of Michelangelo, King David, Paul Goodman.

{GL; *The New York Times*, 20 January 1998; WAS, 2 November 1996}

Roretz, Karl (1881–1967)

Roretz, an Austrian, was on the first Board of Directors in 1952 of the International Humanist and Ethical Union (IHEU). At their initial meeting, Roretz addressed the group.

Rorty, Richard (1931–)

Rorty, a Humanist Laureate in the Council for Secular Humanisms' International Academy of Humanism, left the University of Virginia in 1998 to become professor of comparative literature at Stanford University. A leading gadfly of contemporary philosophy, he was the son of parents who were atheists and Trotskyites. His maternal grandfather was Walter Rauschenbusch, the theological genius of the Social Gospel.

Reviewing his *Achieving Our Country: Leftist Thought in Twentieth-Century America* (1998), philosopher Alan Ryan wrote

> Richard Rorty is a scandal to his profession. He is a philosopher who thinks that philosophy is a distraction from more important matters. He has for years argued that the pursuit of Truth—as distinct from the humbler search for usable truths—is fueled by self-deception. He has insisted that even if humanity all too often behaves cruelly and sadistically, we would be better off without a sense of sin. Nevertheless, Rorty has a substantial streak of filial piety. It was his hero, John Dewey, who first scandalized his philosophical readers almost a century ago by urging them to turn away from "the problems of philoso-

> phy" to "the problems of men." *Achieving Our Country* is an appeal to American intellectuals to abandon the intransigent cynicism of the academic, cultural left and to return to the political ambitions of Emerson, Dewey, Herbert Croly and their allies.

Ryan praises Rorty's favoring of the kind of "participatory" grasp of the world celebrated by Whitman and Dewey, and finds few thinkers other than American pragmatists "have had the courage to insist that it is life itself that justifies our ideas about what is true, good, or beautiful."

In *Achieving Our Country*, Rorty credits the New Left for helping end American involvement in Vietnam but blames it for retreating from pragmatism into theory. As a result, members of the left "give cultural politics preference over real politics, and to mock the very idea that democratic institutions might once again be made to serve social justice. . . . It leads them to prefer knowledge to hope." Although not ruling out a place for religious forces in any reformist coalition, Rorty simply makes no reference to them.

Rorty's other works include *Consequences of Pragmatism* (1982), *Pragmatism from Pierce to Davidson* (1990), and *Essays on Heidegger and Others* (1991). In 1994 he wrote "After Philosophy, Democracy" in *The American Philosopher*, a collection of conversations with Quine, Danto, and others edited by Giovanna Borradori. Also, he was a contributor to *American Philosophic Naturalism in the Twentieth Century* (1994).

His 1994 "Trotsky and the Wild Orchids" is found in *Challenge to the Enlightenment, In Defense of Reason and Science*. Included is his complaint about right-wing conservatives who assume that he is a moral relativist because of his atheism:

> The orthodox tend to think that people who, like the postmodernists and me, believe neither in God nor in some suitable substitute, must feel that everything is permitted, that everybody can do what they like.

At the 1994 Toronto conference of the Coalition for Secular Humanism, Atheism, and Freethought (CSHAFT), Paul Kurtz described Rorty as perhaps *the* leading United States philosopher. Richard Shusterman of Temple University calls Rorty "probably the most influential contemporary American philosopher on literary theory," citing the two volumes of his *Philosophical Papers* written between 1980 and 1989. These, adds Shusterman in an article in *The Johns Hopkins Guide to Literary Theory & Criticism* (1994), "include articles defending pragmatist views of interpretation and scientific inquiry against varieties of representationalism, as well as articles connecting pragmatism with Heidegger and others in the Continental tradition of philosophy and literary theory."

In 1994, David L. Hall wrote *Richard Rorty, Prophet and Poet of the New Pragmatism*, in which he contrasts Rorty's thought with that of Donald Davidson, W. V. O. Quine, Jürgen Habermas, Michel Foucault, Martin Heidegger, Jacques Derrida, and others. The State University of New York in 1994 also published a work, *Recovering Pragmatism's Voice: The Classical Tradition, Rorty, and the Philosophy of Communication*, in which various authors show that pragmatism fosters inquiry and pluralism by rejecting strategies for closure, questioning prevailing metanarratives, and encouraging the development of new habits of conduct through a critical practice that is fundamentally self-reflective.

"During the quarter century in which various forms of imported eliminitivist analytic philosophy had much institutional power in American academe," Peter H. Hare has written, "many naturalists were unfairly treated. This unjust treatment caused understandable bitterness and resentment. Although these feelings are understandable, hypersensitivity to any philosophy deeply critical of American naturalism has unfortunate consequences. Year after year of intense preoccupation with Richard Rorty, for example, is—at the very least—distracting. Shortly after Rorty's book *Philosophy and the Mirror of Nature* was published in 1979, it was quite adequately shown that Rorty's so-called pragmatism was radically inconsistent with the pragmatism of American naturalism and not a genuine threat. But today hypersensitive naturalists continue refuting Rorty. Rorty, who enjoys cleverly baiting his critics, encourages this pointless activity. *Neglect* is what Rorty's philosophy now calls for, in my view," Hare states. He then adds that fifty years from now "when historians look back at this period in American philosophy they will consider that Rorty played a significant role only because the discussion of his charming prose stimulated useful clarification of the character of American naturalism. The American naturalist tradition is too resilient and resourceful to be seriously threatened by Rorty. In the long run, Rorty is enriching the tradition he is laboring to discredit."

That 1979 work, *Philosophy and the Mirror of Nature*, argued against the idea that it is possible to pass judgment on what we believe based upon some objective, transcendental standpoint. What Rorty has tried to show is that no belief is more fundamental than any other and that philosophy, which cannot establish anything, should be understood as a conversation with, in the words of Trinity College's (Oxford) Right Honorable Lord Quinton, "the same sort of claim to finality as the conversations of cultural and literary critics. Heidegger, Wittgenstein, and Dewey are invoked as a kind of pantheon for this undermining of the conception philosophers have ordinarily held of their philosophical activity."

"Suppose," Rorty wrote in a witty book review (*The New York Times* (22 September 1996), "some newly discovered scrolls provided good reason to think that Christianity was a fraud perpetrated by a con man named Paul (formerly Saul). Seeing a commercial opportunity in the resentment of the poor and downtrodden, Paul invented a religion teaching that God's only wish is that we should love one another, and commissioned hacks to write the Gospels and the Epistles. After putting this discovery together with what we already know about the forged Donation of Constantine, the Spanish Inquisition and the televangelists, and with the absence of scientific evidence for the claim that Jesus was both God and man, should we conclude that we ought to cleanse our minds and our culture of Christianity?"

No, he continues, "we might reflect that bad men occasionally come up with good ideas, and that the egalitarian and altruistic strains in Christianity have done a lot for liberal democracy and human rights. So we might decide to throw away only the rotten parts of Christianity (the creeds and the clergy, perhaps), while keeping the good bits." Analogously, he added, although Freud may have been in error about many things, we "can continue to explain our quirks, fantasies and neurotic miseries by reference to unconscious beliefs and desires—especially beliefs about our parents and desires for offbeat sex." (See Richard Rorty, "Remembering John Dewey and Sidney Hook," *Free Inquiry*, Winter 1995-1996) {CA; E; OCP; *The New York Times*, 16 May 1998; Peter Steinfels, *The New York Times*, 11 July 1998}

Rosa, Peter (de) (1932–)

Rosa, a Jesuit theologian who left the priesthood, wrote the following in *Vicars of Christ: The Dark Side of the Papacy* (1988):

> [Catholicism's] disastrous theology had prepared the way for Hitler and his "final solution." [The Church published] over a hundred anti-Semitic documents. Not one conciliar decree, not one papal encyclical, bull, or pastoral directive suggests that Jesus's command, "love your neighbor as yourself," applied to Jews. Jews were hounded

> from one land to another. One pope gave them a month to quit their homes in Italy, leaving them only two places of refuge. During the Crusades, they were slaughtered in the thousands, out of devotion to Christ. A Jew who showed his nose on Good Friday was virtually committing suicide, even though the man on the cross had a Jewish nose. . . . There is, tragically, an undeniable link between . . . the papal legislation, the pogroms—and the gas chambers and crematoria of the Nazi death camps.
>
> ("A Jewish nose" was not explained. See entry for Jewish Nose.) {TYD}

Rose, Charles H. (19th Century)

Rose, an Australian, wrote *A Light To Lighten the Gentiles* (1881). {BDF}

Rose, Edward B. (19th Century)

An emigrant to Port Elizabeth in 1887, Rose founded a small independent freethought movement in South Africa. His audiences were small, and Royle wrote that Rose's lectures "resulted in no lasting success." {FUK; RSR}

Rose, Ernestine Louise Susmond (Polowsky) (1810–1892)

Rose, the Polish-born daughter of a Jewish rabbi, wrote *A Defense of Atheism* (1851) and lectured widely on behalf of freethought. She founded *Agnostic Journal*, which replaced the *Secular Review*. She spoke out in favor of the abolition of slavery, of civil rights, and of equal opportunities for education. Rose, one of the inaugurators of the Woman's Rights Movement, was a constant champion of freethought. In 1838 she had given the first petition to permit married women the right to hold real estate. In 1869, Rose joined Elizabeth Cady Stanton, Lucy Stone, and Susan B. Anthony to form the National Woman Suffrage Association. An Owenite, she was called by Owen his "daughter." In 1853 Rose was elected president of the National Women's Rights Convention.

Moncure Conway tells this of her, that "she went down South, and after being there a little time, her soul was stirred at what she saw going on in the fair city of Charleston. So she advertised that she would publicly lecture the Charlestonians. The novelty of a woman appearing in public attracted a large audience, who were amazed and overwhelmed to hear her rate them about slavery in a way that could hardly have been surpassed by that Mr. Garrison on whose head they had set a price. It was due partly to her sex, and partly to the paralysis caused by her audacity, that she was not torn to pieces; as it was, it required considerable influence to get her safely out of the city."

In her last hours, she asked her friend Hypatia Bonner to insure that no one would try to get her to recant her past atheism, and Bonner reported that Rose died "quite untroubled by any thoughts of religion." At her funeral, Jacob Holyoake said

> More than comely in features, which had dignity of contour, Mrs. Rose had a voice which at once arrested attention by its strength and melody. She spoke with easy accuracy, and with eloquence and reason. . . . Like her great co-worker in the anti-slavery movement, Lucretia Mott, Mrs. Rose took truth for authority, not authority for truth. . . . The slave she helped to free from the bondage of ownership, and the minds she had set free from the bondage of authority were the glad and proud remembrance of her last days.
>
> {BDF; EU, Victor E. Neuburg; FUS; JM; PUT; RAT; RE; SAU; TRI; WWS}

Rose, John (19th Century)

In 1894, Rose led the Progressive Lyceum in Sydney, Australia.

Rose, Olin (20th Century)

Rose wrote *Anti-Christian Addresses (1919–1921).* {GS}

Rosenblatt, Louise Michelle (20th Century)

Rosenblatt, who was a professor of education at New York University, taught a course entitled "Literature and the Crisis in Values." A naturalist in philosophy, she married a fellow humanist, Sidney Ratner. Rosenblatt wrote *Transactions with Literature* (1990) and *Literature as Exploration* (1995).

Rosenfeld, Herbert T. (20th Century)

With Harry Elmer Barnes, Rosenfeld wrote *Is Humanism A New Religion?* (1962). {TRI}

Rosenkranz, Johann Karl Friedrich (1805–1879)

Rosenkranz was a German philosophy who taught at Königsberg University. During the Revolution of 1848, he was Councillor to the Minister of Cults, and at the failure of the Revolution he resumed his chair, holding it until he became totally blind. A follower of Hegel, he organized an encyclopedia of learning on a Hegelian basis, edited the works of Kant, and wrote many volumes of philosophy. His rationalism is found in *Naturreligion* (1831) and a work on Diderot (1866). {RAT}

Rosenow, Albert (Born 1855)

Rosenow was born in Germany of Jewish parents but, upon reading the work of Ludwig Büchner, became a freethinker. In Walla Walla, Washington, he helped organize the Liberal Society and the Washington Secular Union. {PUT}

Rosenthal, M. L. (1917–)

Rosenthal, when he signed Humanist Manifesto II, taught at New York University. {HM2}

ROSICRUCIANS

A secret society, the Rosicrucians have successfully remained so because its members are not allowed to disclose the movement's secrets, and exceptions over the years have been difficult to find. Allegedly, it was founded by Christian Rosenkreus about 1420, although some consider him but a legendary figure. He is supposed to have received his wisdom and philosophy from ancient sources in various places he visited, Palestine, Damascus, Egypt, and Spain. Those with kabbalistic, mystical, astrological, alchemical, and esoteric interests were attracted and are found in Europe, England, Scotland, South Africa, Australia, New Zealand, South America, India, and elsewhere.

Fama fraternitatis (1614) and *Confessio rosae crucis* (1615), both probably written by Johan Valentin Andreä (1586–1654), described Rosenkreus's travels and the development of the Rosicrucian society, which has variously been called Brothers of the Rosy Cross, Rosy-Cross Knights, and Rosy-Cross Philosophers.

William Butler Yeats's collection of poems, *The Rose* (1895), illustrates his Rosicrucianism. William York Tindall, in a Columbia University literature class, described how Yeats placed a rose in a glass container, somehow pumped all the air out, sealed the top, and held the rose upwards toward a full moon, expecting to see its "soul" waft away. When nothing transpired, Yeats retried, this time being more diligent about getting the rose into a vacuum. This and succeeding attempts failed, however. Yeats continued to focus on using cipher methods learned from the Rosicrucians; that, for example, 9 is a symbol of fertility; ergo "nine bean rows" connoted more to those in the Rosicrucian cognoscenti than to hoi polloi.

The Rosicrucian Fellowship in America has described its outlook as

> a mystical philosophy, founded upon Christian principles and based upon the reality of Christ and the work he came to earth to do.

It holds that a sixth sense is latent in man which, when developed, enables one to investigate the realm of the super-physical where dwell the dead. Spiritualistic methods of making contact with the dead, however, are not approved. Rosicrucians make much use of astrology and believe in the principle of re-birth, according to Charles S. Braden, who was chairman of the Department of History and Literature of Religion at Northwestern University, Evanston, Illinois. {CE; ER}

Roskoff, George Gustav (Born 1814)

Roskoff was a German rationalist. He studied theology and philosophy at Halle and wrote *Hebrew Antiquity* (1857), *The Samson Legend and Herakles Myth* (1860), and a standard *History of the Devil* (2 volumes, 1869). {BDF; RAT}

Rosny, Joseph Henri (Born 1856)

Rosny was a French novelist who rejected all theistic belief. He was an Officer of the Legion of Honour. Somewhat influenced by Tolstoi and repelled by Zola's conception of naturalist art, he turned to social idealism and with his brother, **Justin Rosny**, also an agnostic, developed a style said to have been hampered "by their introduction of so much erudition and moral philosophy." {RAT}

Rosny, Louis Léon Lucien Prunol de (1837–1916)

Rosny taught Japanese at Paris University. His research on Buddhism and Confucianism was profound. He founded the Orientalist Congress, the Ethnographical Society, the Oriental Athenaeum, and the Society for Japanese Studies. Rosny was a theist, but his research on Orientology was of great value to rationalists. {RE}

Ross, Charles (20th Century)

Ross is treasurer of Atheists of Florida. E-mail: <athalflc@aol.com>.

Ross, David (1972–)

Ross has been Vice President of the Auckland University Atheists and is Secretary of the New Zealand Association of Rationalists and Humanists. He edits *The New Zealand Rationalist & Humanist Newsletter*.

Ross, Edward Alsworth (1866–1951)

An American sociologist, Ross taught economics at Stanford University, from which he was ousted in a controversy over academic freedom. He had opposed the use of migrant Chinese labor in the building of the railroads—the Stanfords, who were involved in the building of the Union Pacific Railroad, were disturbed by his stand. He then taught at the University of Wisconsin. Ross wrote *Social Control* (1901), *Principles of Sociology* (1921), and his autobiography, *Seventy Years of It* (1937). In *Changing America* (1912), Ross states that "the religion a hierarchy ladles out to its dupes is chloroform" and that "the end of clericalism is in sight." {CE; JM; RAT; RE}

Ross, Harold Wallace (1892–1951)

In France during World War I, Ross edited the servicemen's newspaper, *Stars and Stripes*. In 1925, he founded *The New Yorker* and remained its managing editor until his death. Ross, a freethinker, was successful in featuring such sophisticated authors as Dorothy Parker, James Thurber, and Wolcott Gibbs and in obtaining cartoons showing Peter Arno's urban characterizations, Charles Addams's macabre scenes, and Helen Hokinson's satirized clubwomen. Upon his death, a private service was held at Manhattan's Frank E. Campbell Funeral Chapel. His ashes were strewn over the emerald mountains of his native Aspen, Colorado.

Ross, James M. (20th Century)

Ross is an active member of the Humanist Society of Scotland. He is author of a proposal that Scotland should have a Senate.

Ross, John (19th Century)

Ross in 1867 was one of the leaders in Australia of the Eclectic Association of Victoria.

Ross, Robert Samuel (1873–1931)

Ross was an Australian rationalist, publisher, editor, and Socialist. His interest in the writings of the American rationalist, Robert Green Ingersoll, led him to the Free Thought Society where he met Wallace Nelson. In 1903 he was appointed editor of the Broken Hill *Barrier Truth*, but within a year his anti-religious stance and public advocacy of birth control and the violation of the holy Sabbath Day developed an opposition that resulted in his dismissal. In 1908 he became secretary of the Victorian Socialist Party and editor of its paper, the *Socialist*. {SWW}

Ross, Ronald [Sir] (1857–1932)

Ross was a physician who won the Nobel Prize in 1902 for his work on malaria. He was knighted in 1911. He had been a member (1881–1899) of the Indian Medical Service, and he was a professor of tropical medicine at University College, Liverpool. In a volume of poems and a book of literary plays, Ross expounded his Theistic Rationalism. In one poem, "Dogma," he rejected all Churches and creeds and wanted "no priest but conscience, and no lord but law." {RAT; RE}

Ross, Warren R. (20th Century)

Ross is a contributing editor of *World*, the journal of the Unitarian Universalist Association in Boston. He is author of "The Marginalized Majority: UU Humanism in the 1990s" (*World*, November-December 1997}, in which he looks into humanist history from the mid-1800s to the 1990s.

Ross, William Stewart ("**Saladin**") (1844–1906)

A Scottish freethinker, the son of orthodox Presbyterians, Ross at the age of twenty went to Glasgow University to study for the Church. Finding his university interests were more literary than theological, he set out to make his name as a poet, entered a publishing house, then managed the Thomas Laurie branch store in London. At the university he had come to doubt the orthodox creeds, and his freethinking grew after reading the poetry of Burns and the philosophy of Thomas Carlyle. His first involvement with the Secularists came in 1880 when, as president of the Lambeth Radical Association, he chaired a lecture from Bradlaugh which had been organized by the South West London branch of the National Secular Society. Caring neither for Bradlaugh nor Mrs. Besant, he had the support of C. A. Watts. However, the elder Watts must have had some trouble controlling his writing articles under the "Saladin" pseudonym, according to Royle. Ross hated the hypocrisy of his age: "Ours is the Era of Dissimulation," he told F. J. Gould in a 1900 interview. His outlook showed him to be a man of public hates.

Ross wrote many essays on secularism, his most famous book being *Roses and Rue* (1891). He edited the *Agnostic Journal* (1888) which joined with *Secular Review* to form a joint title, *Agnostic Journal (& Secular Review)* that was published from 1889 until his death in 1906.

The end of his life was tragic, for he concealed that he was suffering from an illness that impaired his walking. Because of sclerosis, which he admitted in 1904, he had edited the *Agnostic Journal* from his bed, scarcely able to write except with two hands. After his death, wrote Royle, Ross's influence continued as an inspiration to those rebels whom freethought inevitable attracted. He had built up an alternative school of thought to the official one of Bradlaugh, Besant, and Foote, and this had resulted in attracting old hands such as W. H. Johnson and young enthusiasts like C. R. Mackay, Ernest Pack, and Guy Aldred. "Even freethought, apparently, needed its guru," Royle observed. {BDF; EU, Victor E. Neuburg; RAT; RE; RSR}

Rosseau, Leon (Died 1870)

Rosseau was a French writer for *The Rationalist* of Geneva, writing under the name of L. Russelli. He wrote *Female Followers of Jesus*, founded *The Horizon*, contributed to *La Libre Pensée*, and was editor of *l'Athée*. {BDF}

Rossellini, Roberto (1906–1977)

An Italian film director and producer, Rossellini made the key film of the neo-realist movement, "Open City," in 1946. His "Miracle" (1948, in which Anna Magnani plays a peasant made pregnant by a shepherd she believes is St. Joseph, is said to illustrate that sacrilege was a stimulant for many Italian film makers, including Pier Paolo Pasolini. An affair Rossellini had with actress Ingrid Bergman caused an international scandal; later, he married her.

Rossetti, Dante Gabriel (1828–1882)

An English poet and painter, son of Gabriele Rossetti and brother of Christina Rossetti (1830–1894, who worshiped at Christ Church, having been swept up into the Anglo-Catholic movement in the Church of England), was one of the founders of the Pre-

Raphaelite movement. John Ruskin championed the Pre-Raphaelites, buying many of Rossetti's works. Rossetti was a master of the sonnet form, and his poetry is considered superior to his painting, which is sensuous and somewhat two-dimensional. In 1860 Rossetti married his model Elizabeth Siddal, whom he loved and had been more or less engaged to for nearly ten years. She, however, was melancholic and tubercular and died from an overdose of laudanum in 1862. In a fit of guilt, Rossetti buried with her a manuscript containing many of his poems. Some years later he permitted her body to be exhumed and the poems recovered. Wheeler cites Rossetti as a freethinker. Jan Marsh, in *Christina Rossetti* (1995), terms him "an irreligious libertine" and Christina "an Anglo-Catholic, and, among Anglo-Catholics, a Puritan" but "decidedly hostile to Roman Catholicism." In a memoir prefixed to his *Works*, Rossetti wrote that he was "a decided skeptic . . . professed no religious faith, and practiced no regular religious observances." {BDF; JM; RAT; RE; TRI; TYD}

Rossetti, William Michael (1829–1818)

Rossetti was a critic, man of letters, and brother of Dante Rossetti. He edited Shelley's work in 1870, with a memoir and numerous notes. Rossetti, a rationalist, became chairman of the Committee of the Shelley Society. {BDF; RAT; RE}

Rossmässler, Emil Adolf (1806–1867)

Rossmässler was a German naturalist who had studied theology but abandoned it for science. Among his writings are *Man in the Mirror of Nature* (1849–1855) and *The History of the Earth* (1868). {BDF; RAT}

Rost, Jacob Leo (1921–1997)

Rost, who was born in Canada, served in the United States Army during World War II. In Key West, he once won a first-prize contest for resembling Hemingway in his physical appearance. A producer of plays and movies in Hollywood, New York, and London, Rost arranged with humanist friends to scatter his ashes around a tree in Boca Raton that he had gazed at while working and thinking. {*Humanists of the Palm Beaches Newsletter*, October 1997}

Rostand, Edmond (1868–1918)

Rostand was a French poet and dramatist who is known particularly for his *Cyrano de Bergerac* (1897). *La Princesse lointaine* (1895, *The Princess Faraway*) was written for Sarah Bernhardt. In 1900 Rostand wrote *L'Aiglon*, whose central figure is the pathetic duke of Reichstadt (Napoléon II), a role long played by Sarah Bernhardt. Maude Adams played his barnyard fable *Chantecler* (1910) in the United States. Jules Harasazti, a Catholic, wrote his biography in which, states McCabe, he "blushes to tell that he believed that the time for churches is over and 'It is now only in the theater that souls can feel their wings.' " Rostand had adopted rationalism in his youth, and in mature life he held that it was the destiny of the theatre to supersede the Churches. "It is now only in the theatre that souls can feel their wings," he believed. (See entry for Gerald Wendt, who cites Rostand as a humanist.) {CE; JM; RAT; RE; TYD}

Rostand, Jean (Born 1894)

Rostand, a French biologist, presided over the Fourth International Humanist and Ethical Union World Congress held in Paris (1966). In 1978 he wrote *Pensées d'un biologiste*. A biography, *Jean Rostand, un homme du future* (1988), was written by Andrée Tetry.

ROSWELL INCIDENT

The first United States Air Force (USAF) Roswell Report in 1995 and a second one in 1997 exploded any myth that a UFO from outer space landed in Roswell, New Mexico, in 1947, according to *Skeptical Inquirer* (May-June 1998). That town's residents are said generally to regard the hoopla as harmless fun, a sign of tourist gullibility, and source of welcome dollars. {See the 1997 work by Philip J. Klass, *The Real Roswell Crashed Saucer Coverup*}

Roth, Julius (19th Century)

Roth was the German author of *Religion and Priestcraft* (1869) and *Jesuitism* (1871). {BDF}

Rothenbuecher, Adolph (19th Century)

Rothenbuecher was the author of *Handbook of Morals* (1884), which was written from the secular standpoint. {BDF}

Rothman, Milton A. (1919–)

Rothman in *A Physicist's Guide to Skepticism* (1988) prescribes intellectual ammunition as a way to cure, or at least diminish, prejudice and superstition. He also is author of *The Science Gap: Dispelling the Myths and Understanding the Reality of Science* (1984). In light of data from the Cosmic Background Explorer (COBE) satellite, which has prompted a reassessment of metaphysics, Rothman holds that "Theories saying that the big bang was caused by God answer no realistic questions. They simply push the questions back to an earlier period and make the questions impossible to answer. A realistic theory such as the big bang theory is the only kind that permits questions to be answered in an empirical manner so that we may understand the answers if we are prepared." Rothman, who notes a certain amount of dissatisfaction with the term *secular humanism* has suggested substituting the term *realistic humanism*. We live, he states, in a time when the magnet of illusion is stronger than the pull of realism. The USSR tried to indoctrinate several generations into the worldview of atheism, but Russian visitors to other countries are found rushing to see the nearest Russian Orthodox church. "The magnet," he writes, "is the feeling of comfort experienced in any group setting. Whether it is a therapy group, an Alcoholics Anonymous-type group, or a church, the feeling is powerful. If secular or realistic humanism is going to extend its influence beyond a tiny minority of the population, it will have to provide a similar setting." {*Free Inquiry*, Summer, 1993}

Roths, John (20th Century): For the first husband of Madalyn Murray O'Hair, see her entry.

Rothstein, Arnold M. (1923–)

Rothstein, an adjunct professor in the Division of Humanities at New College, Hofstra University in Hempstead, New York, is author of *The Jesus Idea* (1993). His study examines Jesus as an idea (of salvation) which gradually was constructed and modified over a considerable span of time in the absence of historical evidence.

Rotteck, Karl Wenceslaus (1775–1840)

Rotteck was a German historian and statesman. In 1819 he represented the Freiburg university in the States of Baden, where he was known for his liberal views. The government, however, disapproved of those views and forbade him to edit any paper and he was then deprived of his chair. His *General History of the World* (9 volumes, 1827) gave one of the broadest views of history which had then appeared, but Wheeler reports Rotteck's death was hastened by constant governmental persecution. {BDF; RAT}

Rotten, Johnny: See entry for John Lydon.

Rouchard, Robert (20th Century)

Rouchard is a North Hollywood, California, freethinker who has written for *Freethought Perspective* (June 1999).

Roumain, Jacques (20th Century)

A Haitian socialist who wrote about *Négritude*, Roumain referred to his outlook as being that of humanism.

Rousseau, Jean Jacques (1712–1778)

An author, political theorist, and philosopher, Rousseau was a controversial figure in his time. One of his books, *Emile* (1762), was burned in Paris, and later Rousseau himself was burned in effigy in his native Switzerland by Geneva by ecclesiastics. Although Voltaire said he resembled a philosopher "as a monkey resembles a man," the anti-intellectual Rousseau did advocate a better life for humanity and a more democratic organization of society: "Man is born free and everywhere he is in irons!" Humanists, he held, need to include human emotion in their outlooks. Meanwhile, he lamented that "The less reasonable a cult is, the more men seek to establish it by force."

His *Social Contract* (1762) is a notable document concerning human rights in a society which contains unjustifiable inequalities. *Émile* made the Vatican's index of prohibited books in 1762, *Du contract social, ou principes du droit politique* in 1766, and three other of his works from 1766 to 1806: *Lettre à Christophe de Beaumont Archevêque de Paris; Lettres écrites de la montagne;* and *Julie ou la nouvelle Héloise, lettres de deux amans, habitans d'une petite ville au pied des Alpes.* Pope Clement XVIII fulminated against *Emile*. That work contained his "Confession of Faith of a Savoyard Vicar," in which the supernatural element in Christianity are discarded.

In his *Confessions* (1781), the great romantic described how he enjoyed being spanked by Mlle. Goton, as well as masturbating while fantasizing over the spankings meted out by his foster mother; told of having *des ménages à trois;* wrote of flashing his buttocks in dark alleys to the horrified delight of a number of spankingly innocent maidens; and philosophized about a malformed nipple on Mlle. Zulietta, one of the prostitutes he employed and whom, up to this conclusive point, he had considered absolutely perfect.

Rationalists everywhere welcomed Rousseau's statement, "As long as people believe in absurdities they will continue to commit atrocities." And he was a favorite of revolutionaries. According to Mallet du Pan, Rousseau was the great fomenter of the Revolution: "He had a hundred times more readers than Voltaire in the middle and lower classes. . . . No one has more openly attacked the right of property in declaring it a usurpation. . . . It is he alone who has inoculated the French with the doctrine of the sovereignty of the people, and with its most extreme consequences." The critic also gives credit to freethinkers Diderot and Condorcet.

During the French Revolution, Maréchal cited Rousseau as one who seems to be an atheist only from the standpoint of the strictest religious orthodoxy. Rousseau believed in life after death and immortality. Of this, Bertrand Russell has remarked that Rousseau's hope for an afterlife was based upon "the heart" rather than upon reason: "In Rousseau's environment, reason, as represented by Voltaire, was opposed to religion, therefore away with reason! There is no law of nature guaranteeing that mankind should be happy. Everybody can see that this is true of our life here on earth, but by a curious twist, our very sufferings in this life are made into an argument for a better life hereafter. We should not employ such an argument in any other connection. If you had bought ten dozen eggs from a man, and the first dozen were all rotten, you would not infer that the remaining nine dozen must be of surpassing excellence; yet this is the kind of reasoning that 'the heart' encourages as a consolation for our sufferings here below." Russell also observed Pythagoras and Orphic religion had tainted the views of Plato and later the Christian theologians and, "from them, in a new form, to Rousseau and the romantics and the myriad purveyors of nonsense who flourish wherever men and women are tired of the truth." Russell countered that a powerful antidote to such nonsense, which hardly existed in earlier times, is science.

In 1778, learning that Rousseau was living in poverty in Paris and trying to finish his last book, *Reveries of the Solitary Walker*, René-Louis de Giradin invited him as well as his companion, Thérèse Le Vasseur, to live on his 2,500-acre estate at Ermenonville, north of Paris. They were given a cottage in exchange for music lessons (Rameau snubbed Rousseau's musicianship, saying Rousseau was a musician of little talent but great influence), and Rousseau was often seen sitting on a rustic bench, dispensing his wisdom to the children of the unworldly Marquis de Giradin. He also entertained intellectuals who came to pay him honor. Upon Rousseau's death, a midnight burial was arranged and a white marble tomb was constructed. Later, the body was transferred to the Panthéon in Paris. {BDF; CE; CL; Lee Eisler, *The Quotable Bertrand Russell*; ER; HNS2; JM; JMR; JMRH; RAT; RE; TYD}

Rousseau, Rita (20th Century)

Rousseau, who belongs to the Unitarian Church of Evanston, Illinois, wrote "Bicultural Marriage" in *World* (March-April 1999) about her and others' marriages with people of other backgrounds.

Rousseau, Wyman (20th Century)

At the time of his graduation from New Canaan High School in Connecticut, Rousseau refused to attend the Baccalaureate service, leading his English teacher to predict accurately that his thoughtful student would likely succeed as a liberal minister. In 1994, the Rev. Wyman Rousseau was honored by the Piedmont, North Carolina, Unitarian Universalist Church in celebration of his twenty-five years of service to the denomination.

Rout, Ettie Annie: See entry for Ettie Annie Rout Hornibrook.

Rouvier, Pierre Maurice (1842–1911)

Rouvier, a French statesman, was elected to the National Assembly in 1871 and strongly supported Gambetta. He held a number of offices. From 1902 to 1905, when he was Minister of Finance in the Combes Cabinet, the disestablishment of the Church was effected. Rouvier was Premier from 1905 to 1906. He passed to the Senate in 1903. An able financier, Rouvier took a prominent part in the anti-clerical opposition and in the various stages of the secularization of France. {RAT}

Roux, Edward (1903–1966)

An ex-Communist who was one of the founders of the Liberal Party, Roux was forced by the government to stop lecturing, writing, editing, and attending meetings. He formed the Humanist Association of Johannesburg, South Africa, editing its *Rationalist*. {FUK; TRI}

Rouzade, Leonie (19th Century)

Rouzade was a French lecturer on freethought. She wrote several brochures and novels, notably *Le Monde Renversé* (1872) and *Ci et Ca, Ca et La*, ideas upon moral philosophy and social progress. She also wrote for Malon's *Revue Socialiste* and was one of the editors of *Les Droits des Femmes*. {BDF}

Rowen, Margaret W. (Died in the 1940s): See Martin Gardner's "The Incredible Flimflams of Margaret Rowen: Seventh-day Adventists and the Second Coming," *Free Inquiry*, Spring 1996.

Rowland, Anne (20th Century)

Rowland, a West Redding, Connecticut, artist, in a 1991 "*Dictu Santificare*" show at the Greg Kucera Gallery in Seattle, Washington, used her talent as an artist "to sanctify by saying." Central to her work are issues surrounding religious faith in representation, the relationship between representation and claims made about it, and the conflict between the contemporary understanding of the physical world and elements of Christian doctrine. Building on Voltaire's quip, "If God did not exist, it would be necessary to invent him," she painted the God people have invented: a wise, old, masculine, bearded being. But she reasoned that if we assign a gender to God, we must accept the deity as a sexual being, with all the ramifications that entails. Thus, she painted what other artists have omitted: "God's Penis," "God's Skin," "God's Brain," "God's Skeleton, "Jesus When He Was Just An Embryo," "Mary Magdalene's Hair," "Jesus's Penis," and a number of other works. Non-believers are both amused and inspired by Rowland's verve, irony, and humor as shown in her postmodern art. (See entry for Christ's Penis.)

Rowland, Peter (20th Century)

Rowland, a retired chemist, made a discovery in the field of crystallography which became known as the "Rowland Transformation." At one stage in his career, he worked for an International Project on Nuclear Safety.

As to why people believe in God, Rowland has written they do so for several reasons: (a) the God-Parent effect—an "imprinting" occurs in the young and then continues in various species; e.g., wolves as well as dogs learn at an early age about a pecking order, and the pack and its leader are their gods; similarly, children who learn how they were fathered and how their fathers were fathered assume irrationally that all humans have been fathered by some original father; (b) tribal cohesion—humanity evolved as a tribal animal, and there is a pecking order and hierarchy; e.g., the British monarch is still—symbolically at least—the "anointed of God"; and the instinct to worship a line of command and carry that right up to a god-head clearly has survival value, giving the tribe cohesion; (c) survival instinct—children do not believe they will ever die, and a belief in immortality helps reinforce this self-image as the stuff of which dreams are made; (d) and dreams—in past ages, dreams appeared to support the idea of the human spirit with its tribal God-Parent imagery; e.g., we dream of the dead so they must still be alive somewhere; however, this is contrary to the evidence from Electro-encephalography, Rapid Eye Movement sleep studies and brain scanning techniques such as Magnetic Resonance and Positron Emission Tomography that dreams have a physico-chemical basis. "Religion," Rowland concludes, "is a genetic disease." {Peter Rowland, *New Humanist*, August 1995}

Rowlandson, Mary (White) (c. 1635–c. 1678)

Rowlandson, wife of a Congregational minister, was abducted along with her two children by the Indians during King Philip's War. She wrote *The Sovereignty & Goodness of God, Together with the Faithfulness of His Promises Displayed; Being a Narrative of the Captivity and Restauration of Mrs. Mary Rowlandson.* A popular example of 17th-century American prose, it became America's first international best seller and described the dangers endured by settlers, their contempt for the non-Christian Indians, and the importance of a devout dependence upon the Bible during enforced captivities.

In the work she wrote of her having been guilty of pride, which is why God apparently put her through such misery and took her baby's life and separated her from her elder child. "I have seen the extreme vanity of the world," she confessed in a style still considered typical of how a Christian should respond to adversity.

Rowley, Henry (Born 1855)

Rowley spoke on behalf of freethought in various English communities, and as a young man became friends of G. J. Holyoake, Lloyd Jones, E. O. Greening, E. V. Neale, and Benjamin Jones. When he arrived in Brooklyn in 1888, Rowley joined the Brooklyn Philosophical Society and was its secretary and president. Rowley was a materialist whose favorite philosopher was Spinoza, his favorite poet Shelley. {PUT}

Rowland, Raymond (20th Century)

A freethinker, Rowland was chairman of the League Against Cruel Sports, which he formed in England in 1924. {TRI}

Rowse, A(lfred) L(eslie) (1903–1997)

Rowse was a poet, biographer, and Tudor historian who wrote some ninety books. In his several works about Shakespeare (1963, 1973, and 1977), he argued that Emilia Bassano Lanier, daughter of an Italian court musician, was the "dark lady" of Shakespeare's sonnets. He also argued that Shakespeare was "a strongly sexed heterosexual" and a man "more than a little interested in women—for an Englishman," denying that any of the sonnets were written for a male lover. Rowse himself was homosexual. His 1942 memoir, *A Cornish Childhood*, was a best seller and made him a bona fide scholar celebrity.

Rowse is not known to have been a theist nor an active member of any organized religion. His not having been accorded any honors by the Crown until he was ninety, at which time he was made a Companion of Honor, has been ascribed to Isaiah Berlin, who was the Crown's chief but unofficial adviser on academic honors and who had negative views about him. {OEL, Paul Johnson, *The New York Times*, 12 November 1997}

Roy, Arundhati (20th Century)

Roy wrote *The God of Small Things* (1998), leading London Observer Service reporter Kate Kellaway to ask if he thought that there is a god overseeing his life. "No," he responded. I am just like an animal. I have no religion." So when you die, that's it? "Yes . . . something even before you die, that's it." {CA; E; *Raleigh News and Observer* 29 July 1998}

Roy, Ellen Gottschalk (1904–1961)

The second wife of M. N. Roy, Ellen Roy—a German by birth—was one of the leaders in India of a radical or secular humanism. She wrote *Radical Democracy* and, with Sib Narayan Ray, *In Man's Own Image*. On a 1955 visit to New York City, she was entertained by New York University Professor George Axtelle, spoke of her editorship of the weekly *The Radical Humanist*, and confided that she regretted having been unable to have voted for Adlai Stevenson, the Democratic Party nominee for President, whom she admired for his philosophic outlook.

Roy was the one who broke a story about the Communist (Chinese) invasion and was murdered soon afterwards. At one time the Communists were an important radical force in the country, and some suspected she had been murdered by them. However, a police investigation ruled that she was murdered by a common thief attracted by her artificial jewelry.

Roy, Evelyn Trent (1892-1970)

The first wife of M. N. Roy, Evelyn Roy was a Stanford Uniersity graduate who worked in the international Communist movement and in 1922 was a founding member of the Indian Communist Party in exile (in Tashkent). With M. N. Roy, she wrote *One Year of Non-Cooperation* and *The Communist Manifesto*. She was divorced from him in 1927.

Roy, Joseph (19th Century)

Roy was the French translator of Feuerbach's *Essence of Christianity* (1864) and *Religion, Death, Immortality* (1866). He also has translated Marx's *Capital*. {BDF}

Roy, M(anabendra) N(ath) (1887–1954)

Norwegian philosopher Finngeir Hiorth calls Roy one of India's best-known atheists, along with Gora, Periyar, and A. B. Shaw. Roy founded the Communist Party of India and was its principal theorist and inspirer during the 1920s. Later, he broke with the communists and in 1937 started the journal, *Independent India.* In 1940 he founded the Radical Democratic Party, which was intended as an alternative, among others, to the Communists. In the 1950s, he was a correspondent (India) for *The Humanist*, and he edited in India the *Radical Humanist.* Also, he was on the first Board of Directors in 1952 of the International Humanist and Ethical Union, addressing the group at their initial Congress in Amsterdam. Among his many books, all published by the Renaissance Press, are *Radical Democracy, New Humanism, Science and Philosophy, Beyond Communism* (1987), *and Reason, Romanticism and Revolution* (1989).

Dr. Innaiah Narisetti, the author of "Unbelief in India" in the *Encyclopedia of Unbelief*, has translated into Telugu several of Roy's works. In 1992, Innaiah, who was teaching at the Dr. Ambedkar Open University, wrote to the present author about Roy, whose original name was Narendranath Bhattacharya:

> India missed the Renaissance movement during British rule. When the nationalist spirit was at its peak, the fundamentalist revivalism swept the minds of intellectuals. At that juncture M. N. Roy raised the Renaissance slogan in 1938, but it went unheard. Later, after independence, he launched the Renaissance movement for the attainment of a rational and humanist society. His attempt was against the religious flow, and he had hard times swimming against the current. Roy trained few intellectuals to further the cause of rationalism in India, dying in 1955, but seeds of his thought are slowly but firmly growing in India. The Indian constitution has incorporated the need for scientific temper as a fundamental duty of the citizens.
>
> M. N. Roy started his youth as a national-terrorist against Britishers, and in his attempt to acquire German arms he landed in the United States of America in 1916. There, he met Evelyn Trent at Stanford University, who helped transform him from a nationalist to an internationalist. The two married in New York in 1917, lived in New York's Greenwich Village for a time, but eventually were forced to flee to Mexico. There, they played a historical role and were invited to Moscow for the Second International Communist Congress. While working with Lenin, both Roys trained young communists for Asian revolution and also established an emigré Indian Communist Party. In 1926 and 1927, Stalin sent him to China to help advise the movement there. Later, Roy differed with the Russian leaders, resenting their bossism. While working with Brandleir, he was expelled from the party. Returning to India, he was arrested by the British rulers and jailed for six years. During that time, he studied and developed his ideas and wrote volumes about rationalism. Thereafter, he never looked back and pleaded with others to adopt the scientific study of history. History, philosophy, and theology in India had been full of myths and stories, and Roy believed such subjects should use the historical method of reasoning as their method.
>
> Indian society at that time was absorbed with religion, from birth to death. The very idea of secularism was alien to Hindus. Roy discussed the problem thoroughly, defining secularism as being based upon the separation of state and church. Roy's stand ultimately led to non-religious society in public life. The Indian constitution incorporated secular ideas, which were never implemented inasmuch as the rulers continued to be afraid of the nation's fundamentalists. Religious codes have yet to be replaced with uniform civil codes. Ambedkar, the depressed class leader who once studied at Columbia University and who was an ardent admirer of Roy's ideas, fought in vain for a uniform civil code.
>
> Roy went through the irrational politics of parties and decided that politics are possible without such parties. He therefore abolished his own Radical Democratic Party and in 1948 commenced India's humanist movement. Erich Fromm's *The Sane Society* (1955) recommended Roy's *Reason, Romanticism, and Revolution* in order to understand the European renaissance. In that book, Roy developed a philosophy which was scientific and which was the first of its kind in India inasmuch as he used the scientific method as his tool.
>
> Roy's rationalism, scientific to the core, inspired certain intellectuals to study philosophy, theology, history, and sociology using rationalism and the scientific method. Laxman Sastri Joshi, for example, studied Indian philosophy and produced volumes using such a rationalist approach. Similarly, Shib Narayan Ray wrote on Indian literature. V. M. Tarkunde developed thoughts on secularism, civil liberties, and human rights. Gora, the atheist, conducted a movement against irrational theology, acknowledging his indebtedness to Roy's thoughts but facing many hardships.
>
> In addition to writing several books, Roy also edited journals such as *The Humanist Way, The Radical Humanist*, and *Independent India.* His articles found enthusiastic readers among the young. Placing man in the center of his New Humanism, he developed a value system without religion, giving the utmost importance to freedom and saying that other values flow from freedom. A person need not be afraid of supernatural forces, he taught, because they are creations of man. Humans can be rational and cooperative as well as moral in a natural way, without benefit of the divine. He derived his premises on the basis of the physical and the biological sciences. In addition, he tried to connect law with man's rationality. Although the late A. B. Shah did not agree with Roy's logic, he accepted the essential nature of man as being rationally based.
>
> In India, Roy's attempts to build a philosophical system along scientific lines represented a first, and his general outlook is gaining a gradual acceptance in academic circles. He evolved twenty-two theses as the basic principles of his Integral Humanism, saying that as the scientific progress takes place philosophy must remain subject to scientific scrutiny and that principles which cannot stand the test should be discarded rather than retained. He disapproved of 'ultimate truths' and tried to reconcile determinism with the new quantum theory. The laws of probability, he felt, yield results which are proof for causality in the broad sense. But his writing, between 1931 and 1936, has not been updated and in light of new findings deserves to be edited.

"In his last days," continued Narisetti, Roy "was associated with the International Humanist and Ethical Union, being its vice president from the IHEU's inception. He laid firm foundations in his lifetime for humanist, rationalist, secularist, and atheist movements in India, training hundreds of persons in study camps. Although these movements are still weak, they have been built on solid philosophic grounds and most surely will one day have a bright future." (See entry for Ramendra.) {FUK; HNS; HNS2; WAS, 1992}

Royall, Anne Newport (1769–1854)

Royall was a contentious freethinker, according to a biography, *Anne Royall's U.S.A.*, by Bessie Rowland James. She wrote *Sketches of History* (1826), followed by *The Black Book*, which was about "the black deeds of evil doers," resulting in one newspaper calling her "a poor, crazy vagrant." She piqued quite a few different individuals, as pointed out by Kansas freethought editor Fred Whitehead.

In Saratoga Springs, New York, where she stayed in the same Saratoga Springs boarding house as Theodore Dwight, a newspaper editor, James noted, "At every meal while Dwight said grace Anne muttered complaints, such as 'Our meals grow cold under these prayers of hypocrisy.' The diners tittered. . . . She called attention to the 'venom in his eye' and to his 'austere countenance heavily charged with puritanical frigidness.' "

> • She opposed missionaries: "Under the name of *foreign* missions, *home* missions, *Bible* societies, *children's* societies, *rag-bag* societies, and *Sunday School* societies, the missionaries have laid the whole country under tribute. This is done under the pretense of spreading the Gospel. The gospel has nothing to do with it. . . . Either the country must put down these men, or they will put down the country. Their object and their interest is to plunge mankind into ignorance, to make him a bigot, a fanatic, a hypocrite, a heathen, to hate every sect but his own, to shut his eyes against the truth, harden his heart against the distress of his fellowman, and purchase heaven with money."

• She opposed the campaign to stop the Sunday mails: "The Third Presbyterian Church [in Philadelphia] even went an annoying step farther. On the Sabbath a chain was stretched across the street in front to prevent traffic from passing." [This subsequently was forbidden by law.]

• In Burlington, Vermont, a storekeeper named Samuel Hickok threw her down the front steps into snow, resulting in "a contusion, a dislocated ankle, a fracture of the larger bone of the leg, a smaller bone broken above the ankle, knee badly sprained, and the flesh much bruised."

• She once declared that she wanted to "drill an army of women and shoot every Presbyterian I can find!" Meanwhile, Freemasons were generally said to have welcomed and supported her.

• When the Pennsylvania Senate and House honored her with a banquet, she noted the "Hon. Logan who is keen for uniting Church and State; he openly avows it and is a warm friend of Dr. Ezra Stiles Ely. May both their *heads* be severed before we see the day." She then gave a toast: "Blue-skins: May all their throats be cut!"

• In Washington, children of Christian fanatics broke her windows, and the parents carried "loads of tracts to my door, crying out, 'Who wants to go to heaven? Here is your passport.' " The "commander-in-chief" who had led the nocturnal vigil, John Coyle Sr., reported Mrs. Royall called him a "d—d [damned] old bald headed son of a b—h [bitch]." Not once, but three times! Meanwhile, "Holy mobs of boys (black and white)" arrived "to shower the house with stones, yell, and blow horns." Charged with disturbing the peace, she was convicted and fined $50., which was paid by two newspaper reporters, who wanted to defend the principle of freedom of the press.

• To a mob of students at the "celebrated University of Vagabonds," her description of the University of Virginia, she decided, "The Presbyterians have the whole of Virginia under their thumbs."

• In Washington, D.C., she started a newspaper called *Paul Pry*. When finally closing it she claimed her editorials had been the first to proclaim the abandonment of reform by General Jackson, the first to challenge the Post Office loans and the Post Office frauds, the first to challenge the Indian land frauds of the great land companies, and the first to put a stop to the enormous swindling of a knot of "God's people, as they impiously call themselves." She then started *The Huntress*, which favored states rights in opposition to the encroachments of the general government. She attacked celebrations of the landing at Plymouth Rock, pointing out the slaughter of the Pequot Indians and the torture of their people during witch-hunts.

In 1854, she died and was buried in the Congressional Cemetery in a grave that remained unmarked until 1914, when a small monument was erected. Except for the James biography and publicizing of Mrs. Royall by Fred Whitehead, few are aware of her place in freethought history. {Alice S. Maxwell and Marion B. Dunlevy, *Virago—The Story of Anne Newport Royall (1769–1854)* [1985]; WWS}

Royce, Josiah (1855–1916)

A professor of philosophy at Harvard University, Royce has been described as a theist, a pantheist, and a Christian. Some hold that he believed in immortality, but in the *Hibbert Journal* (1907) he wrote, "I pretend to no knowledge about my future fortunes." McCabe thinks it incorrect to class Royce as a Christian thinker, but Royce is regarded as a leading metaphysician, an idealist, a believer that reality is the life of an absolute mind. We know truth beyond ourselves, he held, because we are a part of the logos, or world-mind. {CE; RAT; RE}

Royer, Cleménce Auguste (1830–1902)

Royer, born of a Catholic royalist family, was a French author. In Switzerland she opened at Lausanne a course of logic and philosophy for women. In 1860 she shared with Proudhon in a prize competition on the subject of taxation. In 1862 she translated Darwin's *Origin of Species*, including a bold preface and notes. Her philosophical romance *The Twins of Hells* was inderdicted in France. In *The Origin of Man and of Societies* (1869) she states a scientific view of human evolution and challenges the Christian creed. Her many other books and articles in liberal journals evidenced her freethought. {BDF; RAT}

Royle, Edward (20th Century)

Royle wrote *The Infidel Tradition from Paine to Bradlaugh* (1976). Called by Nicolas Walter "the best-known historian of the freethought movement," Royle has a chapter on Secularism, Rationalism, Positivism, and Ethicism in *A History of Religion in Britain*, edited by Sheridan Gilley. He also wrote *Radical Politics* 1790–1900; *Religion and Unbelief* (1971); *Victorian Infidels* (1974); and *Radicals, Secularists, and Republicans* (1980). {*Freethought History* #18, 1996, contains Fred Whitehead's evaluation of Royle's work.}

Rubáiyát (11th Century)

Edward FitzGerald in 1859 translated the Persian poet Omar Khayyam's *Rubáiyát*, which contains a particularly humanistic sentiment:

> A Book of Verses underneath the Bough,
> A Jug of Wine, a Loaf of Bread – and Thou
> Beside me singing in the Wilderness –
> Oh, Wilderness were Paradise enow!

(See entry for Omar Khayyam.)

RUBBISH

> Rubbish, n. Worthless matter, such as the religions, philosophies, literatures, arts, and sciences of the tribes infesting the regions lying due south from Boreaplas.
>
> –**Ambrose Bierce**
> *The Devil's Dictionary*

Rubenstein, Jack C. (20th Century)

When he signed Humanist Manifesto II, Rubenstein was on the executive committee of the American Ethical Union. {HM2}

Ruble, Leland W. (20th Century)

Ruble edits *Freethought Perspective* (833 Orchard St., Toledo, Ohio 43609), a monthly bulletin "dedicated to a discussion of freethought and other related subjects of interests to skeptics, atheists, deists, agnostics, humanists, and freethinkers.

Rudis-Jicinsky, J. (20th Century)

Rudis-Jicinsky wrote *Historical Sketch of the Bohemian Freethought in the United States* (191–?). {GS}

Rudnick, Paul (20th Century)

Rudnick is a dramatist who has helped topple several taboos. "Jeffrey" was a comedy about AIDS. His movie script for "In & Out" had actor Tom Selleck kissing actor Kevin Kline, both heterosexuals. "The Most Fabulous Story Ever Told" in 1998 was described as "a queering of the Bible—a sort of Queen James version—beginning with Adam and Steve in the Garden of Eden, replacing Cain and Abel with lesbians Jane and Mabel.

A gay man himself, Rudnick is not put off by ministers who preach against homosexuality, adding, "I don't think gay people should ever allow themselves to be suckered into those kinds of bogus debates with a minister who has a flock of three and a half people." They have, however, helped inspire him by some of their prudish arguments:

> I thought, What if God *did* make Adam and Steve? But beyond just the idea of a gay take on the Bible, I wanted to explore everyone's attitude toward God nowadays. In an odd way, *that* has become the final taboo. Everyone's talking about anal sex and their lubricant of choice, but if you ask someone if they believe in God, it actually will make them uncomfortable.

Asked if he was ever bar mitzvahed, Rudnick told *Out* (December 1998) reporter Steven Drukman,

> You bet I was. I learned Hebrew phonetically, from a record that was,

like, *The Greatest Hits of Rabbi Shlomo*, and I had no idea what I was saying. I could have been chanting "Kill the Jews!" and would not have known. I was the first child at my temple to be bar mitzvahed in sportswear—a rust-colored double-breasted blazer and coordinated brown slacks. When I walked down the aisle, I heard statues crumble and Rabbi Schneerson weep.

When asked if he believed in God, Rudnick replied,

> I think of myself as an atheist who reads his horoscope—a superstitious atheist. But then on some level, God is the largest superstition of all time.

Asked the same by another interviewer, Stephen Holt (*LGNY*, 6 May 1999), Rudnick replied,

> I believe in Comedy. I believe in Theater. I believe in transcendent experiences. I think that working on a play and watching a comedy on a hot night, that is what strikes me as deeply spiritual and as possessing a higher level of pleasure than just ice cream . . . though I don't mean to ice-cream bash in any way.

Ruedt, P. A. (Born 1844)

Ruedt was a German lecturer known as the "apostle of unbelief." With Lassalle he started *Die Waffe* and was imprisoned in 1870 for participation in social democratic agitation. Ruedt wrote widely on the subject of freethought. {BDF}

Ruelle, Charles Claude (19th Century)

Ruelle was a French writer, the author of *The History of Christianity* (1866) and *La Schmita* (1869). {BDF}

Ruether, Rosemary Radford (20th Century)

Ruether edited *Religion and Sexism: Images of Women in the Jewish and Christian Traditions* (1974). She wrote *Womanguides* (1996).

Ruge, Arnold (1802–1880)

A German reformer and member of the Tugenbund, Ruge was imprisoned for six years. After his liberation, he became professor at Halle and, with Echtermeyer, founded the Hallische Jahrbücher (1838), which opposed church and state. Elected to the Frankfort Assembly, he sat on the extreme left. Compelled to flee because of his viewpoints, he went to England, where he wrote *New Germany* and translated Buckle's *History of Civilisation*. Ruge's expectation was that "theoretical Humanism" would lead to "practical Humanism," that as soon as [the] meaning of Christianism is discovered, the whole Christian heaven falls to the earth, and a new religion is originated, the religion of Humanism." He advocated "the transcendence of Patriotism in Humanism." {BDF; RAT}

Ruggieri, Cosmo (Died 1615)

Ruggieri was a Florentine philosopher and astrologer who was patronized by Catherine de Medicis. He published *Almanachs* in 1604, then issued it annually. At the time of his death in Paris, Ruggieri declared himself an atheist and, in consequence, his corpse was denied a Christian burial, and the people dragged his body through the mud. {BDF; RAT; RE}

Ruiz, Angel (20th Century)

Ruiz, who is a professor of mathematics at the Universidad de Costa Rica, signed Humanist Manifesto 2000.

Ruja, Harry (1912–)

Ruja, a past chairman of the Bertrand Russell Society, is on the board of directors of that group. He is generally considered to be one of the leading Russell scholars. In 1933, Ruja was graduated with honors from the University of California at Los Angeles, where he majored in philosophy. In 1934, he received his M.A. from the University of Chicago and in 1936 his Ph. D. from Princeton University. Ruja's encounter with Russell began in 1930 when assigned to read *The Free Man's Worship*, and in 1939, after sitting in on a session of Russell's graduate seminar at the University of Chicago, he interviewed Russell.

In addition to writing *Psychology for Life* (1955), Ruja edited *Mortals and Others, Bertrand Russell's American Essays* (1975); and co-authored, with Kenneth Blackwell, two volumes entitled *A Bibliography of Bertrand Russell*. In 1984 Ruja received the Bertrand Russell Society's Lifetime Service Award. In 1993, he received its award for his "distinguished contributions to Russell scholarship, devotion to the ideal of rationality, and his inspirational fortitude." (See Ruja's "Bertrand Russell's Life in Pictures" in *Russell: The Journal of the Bertrand Russell Archives, Winter 1995-1996.*)

Rule, Jane (20th Century)

Rule is a writer, a lesbian, and an atheist, according to *Brave Souls: Writers and Artists Wrestle with God, Love, Death, and the Things that Matter* (1996). {CA}

RUMOR

• Rumor, n. A favorite weapon of the assassins of character.

–**Ambrose Bierce**
The Devil's Dictionary

Rumpf, Johann Wilhelm (19th Century)

Rumpf was the Swiss author of *Church, Faith, and Progress* and a critical *The Bible and Christ* (1858). In Geneva, Rumpf edited *Das Freire Wort* (1856). {BDF}

Rumi, Jalaluddin: See entry for Dervish.

Runyon, G. Vincent (20th Century)

Runyon, along with D. M. Bennett and James Hervey Johnson, is a subject of *Freethought By Three Men*. Formerly a Methodist minister, Runyon became an atheist, which he described in *Why I Left the Ministry and Became An Atheist* (1961). His seminary, he wrote, had educated him to be a quack, which he defined:

> A quack in short is one who pretends to have an inside wire or track. No priest, rabbi, minister, or bishop or cardinal or pope has inside knowledge about heaven, hell, and god, but to hear me exhort you would have thought that I had influence with God. This is how all ministers sound when they pray (bray) with that old paranoia voice of divine authority, which so many clergymen quickly develop, while thundering and reechoing their god's fiendish and diabolical warnings of future punishment. Pause and listen some Sunday to these circus freaks peddling their wares over the radio, and please notice at the same time how subtly yet how brazenly they beg for gold to carry on their quackery.

{FUS}

Rupp, Julius (Born 1809)

A German reformer, Rupp studied philosophy and theology, becoming a minister in 1842. Upon protesting the creeds, he became leader of the free religious movement in East Prussia. {BDF}

Rusden, Henry Keylock (19th Century)

Rusden was an Australian atheist, rationalist, accountant, and author. Son of a clergyman, he became a freethinker and founded in 1867 the Eclectic Association. From 1866 onwards, he issued a series of pamphlets assailing Christianity as an affront to reason and an obstacle to progress. His books—*Paul* in 1871 and *The Person, Character, and Teaching of Jesus* in 1872—were notable for their unremitting dogmatism, Darwinian social evolution, and Spencerian individualism. Rusden was a member of the Rationalist Society of Victoria, the Yorick Club, and the Cremation Society. {SWW}

Ruse, Michael (20th Century)

Ruse, professor of philosophy and zoology at the University of Guelph in Canada, is author of *Homosexuality: A Philosophical Inquiry* (1990) and believes that "the war against prejudice can be won" but regrets that many who say they are believers in democracy do not believe that "a free society means letting people do what they want because they want to, and not because society approves."

Rush, Benjamin (1745–1813)

Rush, a signer of the Declaration of Independence, was involved in a scheme to remove George Washington as commander-in-chief. One of the leading physicians in America during his lifetime, Rush was an extreme advocate of bleeding as a cure for almost all diseases. But his controversial cure was shown during the 1793 yellow-fever epidemic in Philadelphia to have had a deleterious effect on the victims. He developed advanced theories for the treatment of mental disorder later in his career. A product of the Enlightenment, part of the intellectual milieu associated with Benjamin Franklin and others, Rush was one of the earliest American opponents of slavery. Formerly a Presbyterian and an Episcopalian, in 1790, much influenced by Elhanan Winchester, who advocated the doctrine of universal salvation, Rush helped establish the Universalist Church. (See entry for E. C. Vanderlaan.) {U; U&U; UU}

Rush, Reuben (Born 1868)

When ten years old, Rush heard Charles Bradlaugh and Annie Besant, and he became a lifelong freethinker as a result. At the International Congress of Freethinkers, he spoke in the 1890s concerning the imperative need for making this world a better world than he had found it to be. {PUT}

Rushdie, (Ahmed) Salman (1947–)

From a strict Muslim viewpoint, Rushdie is a non-believer, which he does not deny. His *Satanic Verses* (1988) satirizes Muhammad and all his works (as well as satirizes British police, American Christians, Margaret Thatcher, and others). Rushdie, who signed Humanist Manifesto 2000, has not been overly successful arguing that fiction is not fact, and his religious outlook is questioned by many commentators. However, he did write the following in *The Independent on Sunday* (4 February 1990):

> And I would like to say this: Life without God seems to believers to be an idiocy, pointless, beneath contempt. It does not seem so to non-believers. To accept that the world, here, is all there is; to go through it, towards and into death, without the consolations of religion seems, well, at least as courageous and rigorous to us as the espousal of faith seems to you. Secularism and its works deserve your respect, not your contempt. . . . To be an Indian of my generation was also to be convinced of the vital importance of Jawaharlal Nehru's vision of a secular India. If what Indians call 'communalism,' sectarian religious politics, were to be allowed to take control of the policy, the results would be too horrifying to imagine. . . .

Some of his severest critics, non-Muslims, have been disappointed by the alleged retraction of some of his earlier views, which predictably failed to move the Muslim authorities. They hold that he should fight *all* forms of fundamentalism, difficult as his existence has become.

In 1994, to mark the fifth anniversary of the *fatwa* against Rushdie, an Iranian foundation increased its £1.4 million reward an unspecified amount for anyone who will kill him. In addition, the 15 Khordad [5 June] Foundation offered to foot the bill for any expenses incurred in executing Ayatollah Khomeini's decree, who ruled that because of Rushdie's blasphemy he must die. Undaunted, Rushdie in 1995 came out with *The Moor's Last Sigh*, his first novel in seven years and one which tells of a tragic riff in 1492 when the Arab sultan Boabdil gives up his beloved Alhambra to Ferdinand and Isabella, which leads to a humiliation that puts an end to centuries of Moorish rule in Europe. Beneath the surface, the work protests the rise of Hindu fundamentalism.

The Ground Beneath Her Feet (1999) broke new ground, its post-modern theme being that the "ground" beneath humankind's feet is constantly shifting, meanings are constantly changing, reality exists on several levels, and "the principle of uncertainty" rules. The work is surreal, telling as it does an Orpheus-like tale about Ormus Cama and a Eurydice-like Vina Apsara, a singer who is both a sex goddess and an icon of the celebrity age.

In a Public Broadcasting System interview with David Frost, Rushdie replied, when asked if he believed in God, "I do not need the idea of God to explain the world I live in." In 1985 he had said similarly,

> God, Satan, Paradise, and Hell all vanished one day in my fifteenth year, when I quite abruptly lost my faith . . . and afterwards, to prove my new-found atheism, I bought myself a rather tasteless ham sandwich, and so partook for the first time of the forbidden flesh of the swine. No thunderbolt arrived to strike me down. . . . From that day to this I have thought of myself as a wholly secular person.

(For a freethinker's view about Islam, see Ibn Warraq's *Why I Am Not a Muslim*.) {CA; E; TYD}

Rushton, Cecilie (20th Century)

Rushton, a senior female district court judge in New Zealand, is author of "Realising Women's Rights—The Constraints," in *The New Zealand Rationalist and Humanist* (December 1993). She questions whether, inasmuch as New Zealand is a signatory to the 1979 United Nations Convention on the Elimination of All Forms of Discrimination Against Women, religionists may continue to impose their discriminatory practices in the name of religious freedom.

She also opposes respecting practices of indigenous peoples when they are discriminatory against women. In the article she finds that "religion has not been kind to women. Ironically in Christian countries the most devout adherents of the faith are women. Women, 'liberated' from religion by Marxism, now flock back to the church."

The Talmud, she notes, "launches an all-out attack on women. The *Testament of Reuben* 5:1-2 sees women as intrinsically evil:

> For women are evil. . . and since they have no power or strength over men, they use wiles by outward attractions, that they may drawn him to themselves. And whom they cannot bewitch by outward attractions, him they overcome by craft.

Jubilee 25:1 states:

> Let the words of torah rather be destroyed by fire than imparted to women.

Other writings of Judaism similarly depict masculinity as normal and femininity as a deviation.

Christianity similarly has an anti-female bias, particularly because of St. Paul's teachings, and she cites numerous examples.

Islam, which she estimates as having close to half a billion women adherents, is the most detrimental of the major religions to women. Although Mohammed was not misogynistic, the interpretation of Islamic writings have disadvantaged women not only in Saudi Arabia but in other countries, she claims. Separateness and veiling are practices which discourage feminism, and *Surah* 2 of the Qur'an states that "Your wives are as a tilth unto you, so approach your tilth when and how you will," equating women with cultivated land and leading to masculine views that they have the right to impregnate their wives at will.

"Custom, often inextricably mixed with religion," she writes, "is again used to exclude women from decision-making roles and positions of influence. This is exemplified in many of the Pacific Island countries, although much of the genuine custom has been destroyed by missionaries and replaced by rules and mores imported from the narrower aspects of other cultures." She describes how the Maori women in New Zealand are forbidden to speak at tribal meeting grounds, and even the television game shows exclude women as moderators for to do otherwise, the director of production at Television New Zealand has stated, "would mean a great break with tradition."

Rusk, Ralph (Leslie) (1888–1962)

Rusk, who taught literature at Columbia University, wrote *Literature of the Middle Western Frontier* (1925), *The Letters of Ralph Waldo Emerson* (6 volumes, 1939), and *The Life of Ralph Waldo Emerson* (1950). His own outlook in class lectures was that of a modified Emersonianism, except that Rusk was a naturalist, not a transcendentalist, in philosophy.

Ruskin, John (1819–1900)

Ruskin, a distinguished English critic and social theorist, was the virtual dictator of artistic opinion in England during the mid-19th century. His first work, *Modern Painters* (1843–1860, 5 volumes) began as a defense of J. M. W. Turner and held that art is a "universal language" based on national and individual integrity and morality. He applied the idea to architecture in *The Stones of Venice* (1851–1853). He also attacked the ugliness and waste of modern industrial England, proposing social reforms, some of which—old-age pensions, nationalization of education, organization of labor—are now widely accepted. In 1870 Ruskin was appointed Slade Professor at Oxford, the first professor of art in England.

"I know few Christians so convinced of the splendor of the rooms in their Father's house, as to be happier when their friends are called to those mansions," Ruskin declared. "Nor has the Church's ardent 'desire to depart, and be with Christ,' ever cured it of the singular habit of putting on mourning for every person summoned to such departure."

In 1860 Ruskin told Augustus Hare that he "believed nothing." In later years he called himself "a Christian Catholic" (as distinct from the pagan Roman Catholics, but he included Huxley). Although he never went to church, he said he took "the Lord's Supper." According to his biographer, Sir E. Z. Cook, what Ruskin meant was that he dined at his own table. According to McCabe, Ruskin was never a Christian and, in fact, lost his mental balance occasionally in later years. {CE; JM; RAT; RE; TRI; TYD}

Russel, Lucy Channing (19th Century)

In 1819 Russel, Catherine Sedgwick, and other transplanted New Englanders, founded the Unitarian Church of All Souls in New York City. In 1994, that church celebrated its 175th year. Russel's brother was William Ellery Channing.

RUSSELL: THE JOURNAL OF THE BERTRAND RUSSELL ARCHIVES

Russell: the Journal of the Bertrand Russell Archives is published by McMaster University Press twice a year, in the summer and the winter. The editor is Kenneth Blackwell, whose e-mail is <blackwk@mcmaster.ca>. The journal has an extensive homepage on the Web: <bookstore.services.mcmaster.ca/mupress/journals/russell/journal.htm>.

Russell, Bertrand (Arthur) (William) [3rd Earl] (1872–1970)

Lord Russell was a mathematician, philosopher, and social critic. In 1950 he won the Nobel Prize winner for Literature (1950), inasmuch as there is no prize for philosophy, leading some critics to joke that the judges must never have read his *Collected Stories*. *Principia Mathematica* (1903), which he co-wrote with Alfred North Whitehead, is generally considered the major work on the subject of mathematical logic. "I personally cannot see," Paul Edwards has wittily remarked, "how *Principia Mathematica* could ever have been completed if Russell and Whitehead had not started on it long before they were born."

In 1905, Russell became a president of the prestigious Rationalist Press Association. His election to the Royal Society particularly pleased him, as did his becoming one of the dozen distinguished British personalities who received the Order of Merit. In his later years, he invariably added FRS and OM to his letterheads.

Russell came from a distinguished family. One of his ancestors had died on the scaffold, accused of having plotted the assassination of Charles II and his brother, the future James II. His grandfather, Lord John Russell, was twice prime minister (1846–1852; 1865–1866) and author of the Reform Bill of 1832. His father (John, Viscount Amberley) was a Liberal, but both his grandfather and father had died by the time he was six, so it is his grandmother who was the major adult influence in his life. His life was a model of liberalism, one in which he fought for such causes as those of women's suffrage, birth control information for the poor, free trade, defense of the civil rights of conscientious objectors, eliminating the scourge of imperialistic war, and combating governmental tyranny.

In his three-volume *Autobiography* (1967–1969), Russell wrote that as a boy he rejected personal immortality, that after reading John Stuart Mill he abandoned the first-cause argument and with it all belief in God. "I see no reason whatsoever to believe in immortality," he wrote to Lord Milford (19 May 1952). "I think that a person is an organization like a cricket club and that one might just as well expect a cricket club to go to heaven when it is dissolved as expect the same thing about oneself." In the same letter, he commented about his use of his title: "Like Lord Trent I avoid it for trade purposes as my old name has a certain monetary value. Except for trade purposes, I use my title."

In the *Hibbert Journal* (October, 1912), Russell used the word "God" as his concept of a sort of world-soul, but thereafter he regretted using the term and discarded all religious language from then on. Russell wrote *A History of Western Philosophy* (1945), one of his best-known works. His dissident moral and religious views, besides being found in *Why I Am Not A Christian* (1927), are contained in *The Analysis of Mind* (1921), *The Analysis of Matter* (1927), *Skeptical Essays* (1928), *Marriage and Morals* (1928), and "Greek Exercises" in *The Collected Papers of Bertrand Russell*, Volume 1.

Not accepting that Jesus was the most perfect of men, he wrote, "I cannot myself feel that either in the matter of wisdom or in the matter of virtue Christ stands quite as high as some other people known to history. I think I should put the Buddha and Socrates above him in those respects." In "Has Religion Made Useful Contributions to Civilization?", he stated in 1930, "My own view on religion is that of Lucretius. I regard it as a disease born of fear and as a source of untold misery to the human race." For him, "The whole conception of God is a conception derived from the ancient Oriental despotisms. It is a conception quite unworthy of free man. . . . A good world needs knowledge, kindliness, and courage; it does not need a regretful hankering after the past or a fettering of the free intelligence by the words uttered long ago by ignorant men." In a 1947 broadcast, "The Faith of a Rationalist," he decried "hatred of Jews, oppression of Negroes, contempt for all who are not white," concluding that it is important that "no supernatural reasons are needed to make men kind and to prove that only through kindness can the human race achieve happiness." In his essay, "The Free Man's Worship," he wrote: "Three passions, simple but overwhelmingly strong, have governed my life: the longing for love, the search for knowledge, and unbearable pity for the suffering of mankind." For Russell, "The good life is one inspired by love and guided by knowledge."

Russell's first marriage in 1894 to an American Quaker friend of Walt Whitman, Alys Pearsall Smith, was a simple London Quaker meeting, "without being congratulated by a host of silly fools who don't think in their hearts that we are to be congratulated." None of the Russells attended, and Lady Russell in a cool letter announced she had disinherited him. Although divorced in 1921, and despite his three other marriages, Alys arranged his 78th birthday party in 1950 and wrote him, "I am utterly devoted to thee, and have been for over 50 years."

Russell's marriage to Ottoline Morrell had been expected to bring him some degree of sexual happiness, for he told friends of his having been disappointed sexually with Alys Pearsall Smith. Russell later wrote that his pyorrhea and bad breath were in part responsible for their breakup. With Ottoline, he tore up "dusty old growths in my mind" and lovingly refused to let her "hide under shady sentimental willow trees," their little problem being that she believed in God and he did not. At one time, according to *Ottoline Morrell: Life on the Grand Scale* (1993) by Miranda Seymour, she tried convincing Russell that God existed, and in his determination to explain their differences on the subject he started to write a book, *The Religion of Contemplation*. It was about reverential atheism, but when Wittgenstein told him the book was rubbish and its first chapters on the theory of knowledge were untenable, Russell tried to suppress the book. Ottoline, who found much she liked in both Wittgenstein and in Siegfried Sassoon, also discovered they were not interested in her sexuality, both being homosexual. She then became lovers with "Tiger" Gomme, who had been working on plinths in the garden at a time when she and Russell were not on speaking terms. (Seymour speculates that D. H. Lawrence may have had her in mind when he wrote *Lady Chatterley*.)

His belief in open marriage led him to Lady Constance Malleson, whose stage name was Colette O'Niel. Although they scarcely knew each other, he wrote, "The first time that I was ever in bed with her (we did not go to bed the first time we were lovers, as there was too much to say), we heard suddenly a shout of bestial triumph in the street. I leapt out of bed and saw a Zeppelin falling in flames." The war, he found, had further distracted him, and in 1915 he recalled the moment: "The thought of brave men dying in agony was what caused the triumph in the street. Colette's love was in that moment a refuge to me, not from cruelty itself, which was unescapable, but from the agonising pain of realising that that is what men are."

Russell later married Dora Black (1920) and became a father, following which he married Edith Finch, who had taught at Bryn Mawr (where his first wife, Alys, had been a cousin of one of its presidents). With Dora, he founded the Beacon Hill School, which was progressive in avoiding authoritarianism along with democratic in encouraging students' individuality.

Caroline Moorehead's biography, *Bertrand Russell, A Life* (1933), states that his most enduring lovers were Lady Ottoline Morrell and Lady Constance Malleson but that he had slept with Miriam Brudno, Helen Dudley, Celeste Holden, Katherine Mansfield, and (probably) Barry Fox and T. S. Eliot's wife, Vivienne.

His multiple marriages and controversial views led to his being denied a teaching position at the City College of New York (CCNY), for he was challenged by a parent, the Episcopal bishop, and the Roman Catholic hierarchy as one who likely would undermine the "health and morals" of his students. In his later years, he was active for nuclear disarmament, using civil disobedience to draw attention to his campaigns.

In 1967 he organized an international tribunal, with Jean-Paul Sartre as chairman, which tried the U.S. government on charges of participating in war crimes in Vietnam. The tribunal found the United States government guilty, and Russell regarded American foreign policy as a detriment to world peace. As his biographer, Alan Wood, has said, the world was never again the same once Russell had set the minds of men on the march. Moorehead, however, tells how Russell in 1960 was "Svengalied" by Ralph Schoenman, an American graduate student at the London school of Economics, who she describes made Russell into something of a puppet for his own causes. Schoenman was a left-wing graduate student at the London School of Economics, managed Russell's affairs for eight years, wasted large amounts of money, destroyed a number of old friendships, and led to a decline in Russell's reputation among many scholars. As for Russell's ever being a Communist, he was not. In China he described himself as a "Marxist," never a Communist, Royden Harrison has pointed out in *Russell: the Journal of the Bertrand Russell Archives* (Summer 1995).

Nicholas Griffin, of McMaster University in Canada, has edited Russell's letters, volume I (1992) of which contains tales of his "ferocious" longing for Lady Ottoline, thoughts to Santayana, and Ludwig Wittgenstein's devastating criticism of Russell's theory of knowledge.

T. S. Eliot, reviewing Russell's *Why I Am Not a Christian,* remarked, "Mr. Russell supposes that he is not a Christian, because he is an Atheist. . . . As we become used to Atheism, we recognize that Atheism is often merely a variety of Christianity. In fact, several varieties. There is the High Church Atheism of Matthew Arnold, there is the Auld Licht Atheism of our friend Mr. J. M. Robertson, there is the Tin Chapel Atheism of Mr. D. H. Lawrence. And there is the decidedly Low Church Atheism of Mr. Russell," concluding that Russell's book "is a curious, and a pathetic, document." James Thrower, however, expresses the popular view in his *Short History of Western Atheism* (1971): "Russell's atheism is classic, not to say monumental."

In 1951, when asked specifically about humanism, he wrote the present author:

> You ask me whether I call myself a Scientific Humanist or a Naturalistic Humanist. I am not in the habit of giving myself labels, which I leave to others. I should not have any inclination to call myself humanist, as I think, on the whole, that the non-human part of the cosmos is much more interesting and satisfactory than the human part. But if anybody feels inclined to call me a Humanist, I shall not bring an action for libel.

In 1956, he added:

> I do not object to your classifying me as a "naturalistic humanist," though it is not a description I should ever think of calling myself. When I have to describe my own philosophy I call myself a "logical atomist." I have read the material that you sent with your letter, but I have nothing to add except that my reason for not liking the word "humanist" is that I regard human beings as a trivial accident which would be regrettable if it were not so unimportant.
>
> (Antony Flew in *A Dictionary of Philosophy*, noted that both Wittgenstein and Russell later abandoned the logical atomist label.)

As for belief, Russell wrote, "I wish to propose for the reader's favourable consideration a doctrine which may, I fear, appear wildly paradoxical and subversive. The doctrine in question is this: that it is undesirable to believe a proposition when there is no ground whatever for supposing it true."

Critics have lamented certain of Russell's views. In 1918, for example, he wrote to Ottoline Morrell, "I hate being all tidy like a book in a library where no one reads. Prison is horribly like that. Imagine if you knew you were a delicious book and some Jew millionaire bought you and bound you uniform with a lot of others." Caroline Moorehead has pointed out that his opinions on Blacks were equally disagreeable. As for another minority, he had "little but contempt for homosexuals. . . . Like [D. H.] Lawrence, Russell came to dislike and disapprove of homosexuality: 'Lawrence has the same feeling against sodomy as I have,' he wrote to Ottoline in 1915. 'You had nearly made me believe there is no great harm in it, but I have reverted; and all the examples I know confirm me in thinking it sterilizing.' The examples were Strachey and Keynes; and they knew it."

Richard Rorty has written that Russell "is arguably the most influential philosopher to have written in English in this century," adding that John Dewey and Thomas Kuhn are his only plausible rivals for that position. However, in light of Wittgenstein's, Quine's, and Sellars's undermining of Russell's logical atomism, Rorty has written that "historians are more likely to describe [Russell] not as the Galileo of his discipline, but as the founder of a relatively short-lived and provincial school of thought."

An indication that future critics will continue to find fault with Russell is found in a 1996 work by Ray Monk, *Bertrand Russell, The Spirit of Solitude, 1872–1921*, in which the author presents the sage as a sage but one who was disturbed, not merely egoistical and cold, was blind to others' sufferings, and wore out his lovers with his obsessions. Monk's second volume will take up Russell's later life.

In keeping with one of his statements, "What is wanted is not the will to believe, but the wish to find out, which is the exact opposite," a group of devotees publishes the Bertrand Russell Society Newsletter (3802 North Kenneth Avenue, Chicago, Illinois 60641). They also meet annually, toasting "Bertie" with his favorite scotch, Red Hackles. In addition, *Russell: The Journal of the Bertrand Russell Archives* is published twice a year by the McMaster University Library Press. The Russell Archives are at MacMaster in Hamilton, Ontario, Canada.

The Bertrand Russell Society homepage is at <http://daniel.drew.edu/~jlenz/brs.html>. (See entry regarding T. S. Eliot's criticism of Russell under D. H. Lawrence. Also, see entries for Logical Atomism, Marriage, and Alan Ryan. For articles by Paul Edwards, William P. Alston, and A. N. Prior, see the *Encyclopedia of Philosophy*, Vol. 7. See the Conrad Russell entry for information about Marjorie "Peter" Spence, Sir Bertrand's third wife.) {CE; CL; Lee Eisler, *The Quotable Bertrand Russell*; EU, John L. McKenney; FUK; HAB; HNS2; JM; PA; RAT; RE; Richard Rorty, *The New Republic*, 2 December 1996;TRI; TSV; TYD; WAS, 24 February 1951 and 9 May 1956}

Russell, Bertrand—Humor of

The late Trevor Banks opined that Russell was "by far the wittiest of the major philosophers," admitting with a smile that this "is a bit like saying Margaret Thatcher was the prettiest of the British Prime Ministers." Examples he gave of Lord Russell's humor during some of his stage monologues entitled "Bertie" are as follows:

- Solemnity is a condition precedent to believing anything without evidence.

- When you take from a man all sense of humor there will only be enough left to make a bigot.

- It is not surprising then that Whitehead once observed: "The total absence of humor from the Bible is one of the most singular things in all literature."

- What a queer work the Bible is. Abraham (who is a pattern of all the virtues) twice over, when he is going abroad, says to his wife, "Sarah my dear, you are a very good-looking person, and the King is very likely to fall in love with you. If he thinks I am your husband, he will put me to death, so as to be able to marry you, so you shall travel as my sister, which you are, by the way."

- So far as I can remember, there is not one word in the Gospels in praise of intelligence; in this respect ministers of religion follow gospel authority more closely than in some others.

- Children should be sent to boarding schools to get them away from mother love.

- The people who are regarded as moral luminaries are those who deny themselves ordinary pleasures and seek compensation in interfering with the pleasures of others.

- There was supposed to be some mystic virtue about gold that made it worthwhile to dig it up in the Transvaal and put it underground again in bank vaults in America.

- Some of the Gnostics held that the world was made by the devil while God wasn't looking. There is a good deal to be said for that theory, and I am not concerned to refute it.

- Truly high-minded people are indifferent to happiness, especially other people's.

- An honest politician will not be tolerated by a democracy unless he is very stupid . . . because only a very stupid man can honestly share the prejudices of more than half the nation.

- I was told that the Chinese said they would bury me by the Western Lake and build a shrine to my memory. I have some slight regret that this did not happen, as I might have become a god, which would have been very chic for an atheist.

- I heard Lytton Strachey read his *Eminent Victorians*, which he considered a very serious historical work . . . and I read it again to myself in prison. It caused me to laugh so loud that the officer came round to my cell, saying I must remember that prison is a place of punishment.

- [G. E.] Moore was the most honest person I have ever met. I only once succeeded in making him tell a lie, and that was by a subterfuge. "Moore," I said, "do you always speak the truth?" "No," he replied. I believe this was the only lie he had ever told.

- There are nuns who never take a bath without wearing a bathrobe. When asked why, since no man can see them, they reply: "Oh, but you forget the good God." Apparently they conceive of the deity as a Peeping Tom whose omnipotence enables him to see through bathroom walls, but who is foiled by bathrobes."

- Many Chinese have that refinement of humor which consists in enjoying a joke more when the other person cannot see it.

- Leibniz wished to be thought well of, so he published only his second-rate work. All his best work remained in manuscript.

- It is sometimes said that a very large part of my writing has been about sexual relations. Actually only about 1% of my writings are concerned with sex, but the conventional public is so obsessed with sex that they haven't noticed the other 99%.

• Protestants tell us . . . that it is contrary to the will of God to work on Sundays. But Jews say that it is on Saturdays that God objects to work. Disagreement on this point has persisted for 19 centuries, and I know no method of putting an end to the disagreement except Hitler's lethal chambers, which would not generally be regarded as a legitimate method in scientific controversy.

• If you wish to be happy yourself, you must resign yourself to seeing others happy.

Russell, Conrad Sebastian Robert [Earl] (1937–)

Earl Russell, Bertrand Russell's younger son, was elected an honorary associate of the British Rationalist Press Association in 1988. Previously, his uncle Frank Russell and his father were honorary associates. In the House of Lords during a discussion of the Education Reform Bill, he was one of the few who opposed strengthening of religious education in schools. The Fifth Earl Russell, whose mother was Marjorie ("Peter") Spence, remarked, "Let me say first that I am in profound agreement with the remarks made by the most reverend Primate the Archbishop of Canterbury about the importance of Christianity for an understanding of history. . . . But it is one thing to tell people what Christianity says, another thing to teach them by the authority of the state that it is right. . . . I know the right to withdraw is there. That right is vital, but it does not altogether confer what I should like, with the voice of an honest atheist, to ask for—that is equality before the law."

In 1993, his *Academic Freedom* was published, in which he points out that, although the ideal of academic freedom is the cornerstone of higher education, state control often encroaches upon the traditional freedoms of universities. Professor the Earl Russell, a member of the House of Lords, teaches at King's College, University of London, England.

"My early memories," he wrote in *New Humanist* about not having been brought up a Christian, "include such things as listening to my father's debate with Father Coplestone, when I was eight. I remember, too, my father's amusement at a fan letter which claimed that 'the Jesuit's morbid pronunciation of "God" robbed me of all belief in said being." I was familiar, from an early age, with such awkward questions as where Cain's wife came from. Yet, at the same time, I grew up aware of religion as a language in which people have described experience which is not confined to the religious, and with a good working knowledge of the Bible as a document to be read in the same spirit as Herodotus or Homer. I have known for as long as I can remember that the Devil can quote scripture." Earl Russell was tempted around the age of fifteen by religion, he added, but did not succumb.

In *Academic Freedom* (1993), Russell makes a lucid case for an academic world exempt from government interference. Although professors swear to no Hippocratic oath, they do have professional values not only to maintain but also to defend, he reasons, adding that "the taking of money for teaching and research also imposes a duty to engage in those activities."

In 1994, *The* (London) *Sunday Times* (24 July 1994) carried a news article, "Missing Wife of Bertrand Russell Found 25 Years On." Caroline Moorehead, a Russell biographer, had tracked down the pipe-smoking third wife of Bertrand Russell, whom friends called "Peter" and whom at age sixty-three he had married when she was twenty-five. Peter had changed her name to Patricia, was living alone with a pet sheepdog, had little to do with her neighbors, had left her husband in the early 1950s after fifteen years of marriage because she could no longer tolerate his womanizing, and had done so after an unhappy holiday in Sicily when during a picnic he declared, "I am as drunk as a lord, but then I am one."

The couple divorced within two years and Conrad, then fifteen, initially went to live with his mother in a remote Cornish mill. For more than twenty years, however, Conrad had lost track of his mother. {*New Humanist*, November 1993}

Russell, Dora (Winfred) (Black) (1894–1986)

With her husband, Bertrand Russell, Dora Russell ran the Beacon Hill School from 1927 on. They had approximately twenty boys and girls, ages four to eleven. The students were given no religious instruction, could read whatever they wished, bathed together freely, and had their questions answered openly and freely.

"In humanism," she has written, "I have always felt the warmth of association with all organic life, with our roots in the productive soil of our earth. My dissent from god and religion arose from its denial of this very life which animates plants, birds, animals, and humans. If god created all this, then why are his worshippers commanded to reject it all as savage, bestial, lust and sin. . . . Without falling into a mystical vitalism that reverences organic nature as sacred, we can at least try to serve rather than subdue the prancing seas of life."

A feminist who has been described as being perhaps fifty years ahead of her time, she comes alive in Dale Spender's *The Dora Russell Reader: 57 Years of Writing and Journalism, 1925–1982* (1985). Her own outlook is found in *The Tamarisk Tree: My Quest for Liberty and Love*.

In addition to working on behalf of birth control and nuclear disarmament, she was a founding member of the League of Progressive Societies and Individuals, the National Council for Civil Liberties, and the Abortion Law Association. In 1958, she organized a women's peace caravan which toured Europe in an early attempt to break down Cold War barriers. Ronald Clark, among others, has suggested that her husband Bertrand's militantly irreligious phase, which began somewhat abruptly in 1925, was partly the result of his (second) wife Dora's influence. {EU, John L. McKenney; HNS2; SHD; WWS}

Russell, I. R. (20th Century)

Russell is Vice-Chairman of the Board of Directors of the Rationalist Press Association.

Russell, Ivor (20th Century)

Russell, the president in Scotland of the West Glamorgan Humanists, is chairman of the Rationalist Press Association.

Russell, John [Viscount Amberly] (1842–1876)

Russell, son of the first Earl Russell, was described by J. S. Mill in a letter to Carlyle as "one of the best of our rising politicians." He was a Spencerian agnostic and gave his eldest son a Rationalist tutor, but the Court of Chancery canceled the appointment.

His son, **John Francis Stanley Russell**, second Earl Russell (1865–1931), nevertheless grew up an agnostic and a supporter of the Rationalist Press Association. Russell died when his son, Bertrand, was four and was remembered by him only as being "philosophical, studious, unworldly, morose, and priggish." {RAT; RE}

Russell, John (Born 1855)

Russell wrote *The Task of Rationalism in Retrospect and Prospect* (1910). He has been the foreign editor of the *Journal of Education*. {GS}

Russell, John Francis [Second Earl] (Born 1865)

Russell, son of Viscount Amberley, was a lawyer and writer. His

Lay Sermons (1902) and *Divorce* (1912) departed from the views in which his father educated him. A Fabian Socialist, he was one of the first to list his religion in *Who's Who* as being "Agnostic." {RAT}

Russell, Phillips (20th Century)

Russell wrote *Jefferson, Champion of the Free Mind* (1956). {GS}

Russell, Richard S. (20th Century)

Russell, secretary of Atheist Alliance, Inc., writes for *The Freethought Observer* and *Secular Nation*. He is the Hotline contact for Atheists and Agnostics of Wisconsin. E-mail: <rsrmadison@aol.com>.

Russell, Thomas (19th Century)

Russell wrote *Testimony of Atheists* (1857). {GS}

RUSSIA

"The Russian Sphinx" by Aileen Kelly (*The New York Review of Books*, 20 May 1999) contains the following:

Western visions of Russia as an alien civilization, by turns threatening and alluring, are rooted in its anomalous history. The schism of 1054 between the Byzantine and Roman Churches detached it from the culture of Western Christendom, and the Mongol invasion two centuries later completed its isolation. It knew nothing of the Renaissance, the Reformation, and the first flowering of secular thought in the West; the Muscovite state that emerged in the fifteenth century under the despot Ivan IV resembled the civilization of medieval Europe rather than the contemporary West. In the early eighteenth century Peter the Great's reforms brought into the community of European nations a vast and backward country (even as late as 1917, 80 percent of the Russian Empire's population were classified as peasants). Yet this lumbering land established itself as a great power when, in 1814, the Russian Tsar rode into Paris at the head of his army after the victorious campaign against Napoleon.

England's Winston Churchill was later to say that the Soviet regime's unparalleled, terror-driven feats made it appear to the West as "a riddle, wrapped in a mystery, inside an enigma."

Martin Malia's *Russia Under Western Eyes: From the Bronze Horseman to the Lenin Mausoleum* (1999) is an end-of-the-century evaluation of what historically has transpired in Russia over the centuries.

RUSSIAN HUMANISTS AND FREETHINKERS

• The Russian Center for Inquiry was inaugurated in 1997 in a ceremony attended by Paul Kurtz, its prime mover; Timothy J. Madigan of the *Free Inquiry* staff; Jan Eisler of the St. Petersburg (Florida) Humanist Society; and Jim Herrick of the Rationalist Press Association. Fifty distinguished scientists and philosophers spoke, many deploring the rising level of irrationality in Russia and the world.

The center aims to transcend the intolerance of ancient religious, nationalistic, and ethnic differences by encouraging each individual to become a citizen of the world community. "Above all," Kurtz challenged those who are working upon behalf of secular humanism in Russia, the group needs to attempt "to give meaning to life by answering the basic existential questions that had largely been ignored by Marxist ideology."

The Center cooperates with the Committee for the Scientific Investigation of Claims of the Paranormal (PSICOP), developing scientific critiques of psychic phenomena, UFOlogy, astrology, and other pseudo-sciences. It continues some of the goals of the Institute for the Scientific Study of Atheism, which closed down in 1991.

However, as pointed out by Herrick, "Dogmatic, ideological atheism is obviously no help to humanism (though humanists may often be atheists)." Key figures in the Russian Center for Inquiry's initial conference were Dr. A. Panin, Acad N. Moiseev, Dr. Tazhurizina, Dr. Chang, Valerii Kuvakin, and professors Abelev, Frolov, Gretsky, Mezhuev, Razin, and Volchenko.

Russians who signed Humanist Manifesto 2000 included Garry I. Abelev; Yuri Nikolaevich Efremov; Vitalii Ginzburg; Valerii Kuvakin; and Alexander V. Razin.

• Ethical Dialogues has become an associate member of the International Humanist and Ethical Union (IHEU).

• *Zdravyi Smysl* (Common Sense) is the Russian Humanist Society's quarterly and is published at 119899 Moscow Vorobjovi Gory, Moscow University, Philosophy Department, Moscow B-234. In 1996, a Russian Humanist Society (RHS) held its third general meeting at the Moscow State University. Its chairman is Professor Kuvakin. In 1998 the society became an Associate Member of the International Humanist and Ethical Union (IHEU). In 1997 it was estimated at a humanist conference in Moscow that 60% of Russians are religious believers, 15 to 20% are unbelievers, and 20 to 25 % are undecided. Of these only about 7% would identify as atheists. Observed Jim Herrick, "So much for seventy years of atheist indoctrination! Humanists must emphasise that humanism should be presented in the context of individual freedom and open dialogue." (See entries for Mikhail Gorbachev and Valery Kuvakin.) {"Ethical Dialogues in Moscow," *New Humanist*, December 1995; Jim Herrick, "Humanism in Russia," *New Humanist*, November 1997; Jim Herrick, *International Humanist News*, December 1997}

RUSSIAN PHILOSOPHY

Vladimir Fedorvich Titov was chairman of the department of Marxist-Leninist philosophy at Moscow State University until, in 1991, his faculty voted, as he put it, to "liquidate completely" his department. He regrets the decision, saying that for seventy years Marxism-Leninism *was* Russian philosophy, that "Marx was a great thinker. Without him you can't do philosophy." (See the *Encyclopedia of Philosophy*, Vol. 7. Also see Z. V. Kalinicheva's "The Museum of the History of Religion and Atheism" (1967), a guide to the museum. Also, see entries for Valerii Kuvakin and Alexey Sokolow.) {Patricia Cohen, *The New York Times*, 13 March 1999, writes of current professors' complaints.}

RUSSIAN UNITARIANS

In 1993 a Unitarian group was founded following the collapse of the Soviet Union. Congregations in 1998 included one in Moscow and one in St. Petersburgh. Paul Sawyer and his family have been active in helping the two congregations, spending time in 1994 working with people who showed interest. Contact in Moscow is Vitaly Verigan, A/J 667, OTD/Sv 5, Zhukovske, Moskow, OBL Russia 140160. Contact in St. Petersburgh is Yevgeni Schlacter (Eugene Schlacter), 197341, St. Petersbourg Serebristy Blvd., 37, ap 8. Jean and Dick Rodes head a Unitarian group, Friends of Russia a and the Ukraine (5250 Patriot Lane, Columbia, MD 21045).

Rusterholtz, Wallace P. (20th Century)

Rusterholtz wrote *American Heretics and Saints* (1938). {GS}

Rustin, Bayard (1910–1987)

Rustin, a nominal member of the Society of Friends, was not technically a theist and is not known to have believed in an afterlife although he could sing Gospel music and knew the Bible because of his early background in religious circles. An African American, he is best remembered for his role in organizing the giant 1963 civil rights march on Washington and for his continuing involvement in that cause.

His advocacy of gay rights, although often overlooked, was another of his basic interests. To *The Washington Blade* in 1986, he said he had informed his civil rights colleagues that he was gay and had never concealed his homosexuality. In fact, he encouraged young people to come out, saying, "Although it's going to make problems, those problems are not so dangerous as the problems of lying to yourself, to your friends, and missing many opportunities." {AA}

Ruth, J. (20th Century)
Ruth wrote *What Is the Bible?* (1904). {GS}

Ryall, Maltus Questall (1809–1846)

Ryall was secretary of the Anti-Persecution Union in 1842 and assisted his friend, Holyoake, on *The Oracle of Reason* and *The Movement*. He died in poverty. {BDF; FUK; VI}

Ryan, Alan (1940–)

Ryan is a philosopher who wrote *John Stuart Mill* (1970), *Bertrand Russell: A Political Life* (1993), and *John Dewey and the High Tide of American Liberalism* (1995). He has been a lecturer in philosophy at New College, Oxford University, in his native England, was a visiting professor of political science at the City University of New York, and since 1988 has taught at Princeton. Ryan lists his religion as "none."

In *John Dewey and the High Tide of American Liberalism* (1995), Ryan argued that the thought of John Dewey is more relevant today than ever before, that a revival of his ideas is needed. He was not, Ryan found, as far left politically as some had claimed, and his philosophic style was to "reconstruct" the institutions and linguistic habits we had grown accustomed to. His *Liberal Anxieties and Liberal Education* (1998) is concerned with evaluating contemporary higher education in the United States. The work shows the influence of Dewey, Mill, and Russell, three about whom he has written extensively. Ryan has been described as a self-acknowledged, aggressive atheist of the Bertrand Russell vein, a Mill, Dewey, and T. H. Green scholar. {*The Nation*, 25 September 1995}

Ryan, William F. (1925–)

Ryan wrote *Haldeman-Julius and the Blue Academy* (1978). {GS}

Ryberg, Y. E. (Born 1828)

A Swedish merchant captain, Ryberg translated several of Bradlaugh's pamphlets and other secular literature. {BDF}

Rydberg, Abraham Viktor (1828–1895)

Rydberg taught the history of civilization at Stockholm University, and he was instrumental in influencing the spread of Rationalism in Sweden. Two of his works are *Bilbeln's Lära om Kristus* (1862) and *Romeska sägner om Paulus och Kristus* (1874). {RAT; RE}

Ryder, John (20th Century)

Ryder, an associate professor of philosophy at the State University of New York College at Cortland, is editor of *American Philosophic Naturalism in the Twentieth Century* (1995). Naturalism, he explains, holds that nature is objective and can be studied to gain knowledge that is not determined by methodology, perspective, belief, or theory.

Contributors on the subject of naturalism included Justus Buchler, Morris Cohen, John Dewey, Abraham Edel, Marvin Farber, Sidney Hook, Paul Kurtz, John Lachs, Corliss Lamont, Thelma Lavine, John McDermott, Ernest Nagel, W.V.O. Quine, John Herman Randall Jr., Richard Rorty, George Santayana, Meyer Schapiro, Roy Wood Sellars, Evelyn Shirk, and F.J.E. Woodbridge.

Rylande, C. G. (20th Century)

A freethinker, Rylande wrote *Did Jesus Ever Live?* (1935). {GS}

Ryle, Gilbert (1900–1976)

Ryle wrote about the phenomenology of Husserl and Heidegger's *Sein und Zeit* and was a friend of Wittgenstein. In his "Systematically Misleading Expressions" (1932), he focused on linguistics and held that a main part of philosophy must be "the detection of the sources in linguistic idioms of recurrent misconstructions and absurd theories." The editor of *Mind* (1948–1971), Ryle was an influential figure among British philosophers. (See entry for Richard C. Vitzthum.) {AF; OCP}

S. A. HUMANIST POST

An Australian monthly, *S. A. Humanist Post* is at GPO Box 177, Adelaide, 5001, Australia.

Saatkomp, Herbert J. (20th Century)

A professor at Texas A & M, Saatkomp is an authority on Santayana.

Sabbatai Zevi (also, Shabbatai Zvi and Shabbatai Sevi) (1626–1676)

At the height of the Ottoman rule, Sabbatai Zevi proclaimed himself the Messiah, named the year 1666 as the millennium, and gathered a host of followers. A Jewish mystic and founder of the Sabbatean sect, he attempted to land in Constantinople, was captured, and to escape death embraced Islam. Although he was married to a Christian prostitute, he appealed to a following in the hundreds of thousands for his doctrine of universal sin. In the 18th century, the Sabbatean movement was revived under Jacob Frank. {CE}

SABBATARIANS

Sabbatarians insist that the Sabbath be observed in a strict way. In the United States, Sabbatarian laws, known as "blue laws," barred certain business and sporting activities on Sunday. The term is also used to apply to those who observe the seventh day (Saturday) as the Sabbath, such as certain Adventists and Seventh-Day Baptists. {CE}

SABBATH

• Sabbath, n. A weekly festival having its origin in the fact that God made the world in six days and was arrested on the seventh. Among the Jews observance of the day was enforced by a Commandment of which this is the Christian version: "Remember the seventh day to make thy neighbor keep it wholly." To the Creator it seemed fit and expedient that the Sabbath should be the last day of the week, but the Early Fathers of the Church held other views.

–Ambrose Bierce
The Devil's Dictionary

The Babylonians were likely not the first to have a day of rest, usually at fixed periods, and they had a seven-day week, on the seventh day of which they considered it unlucky to work although they did not suspend work on that day. Because their festival at the full moon was called Sabattu, it is quite possible the Jews adopted the name from them during the Exile, according to McCabe. The Muslims followed the Jews, except they are not compelled to abstain from work except during the hours of service. By the fourth century Rome had a day's holiday, with free entertainments, on more than half the days of the year. In fact, they resisted Constantine's attempt to introduce Sunday. The claim of some apologists that Christianity, which changed the day of rest to "the Sun's Day" in honor of Christ, conferred a great boon on the poor workers of Rome by bringing them one day's rest in seven, reflects their abysmal ignorance of Roman history. In Islam, Friday is the weekly day of public prayer. {CE; RE}

Sabin, Ibn (c. 1218–c. 1271)

Sabin, Al Mursi, was a Spanish Arabian philosopher born of a noble family at Murcia. About 1249 he corresponded with Frederick II, replying to his philosophic questions. Sabin committed suicide about 1271. {BDF}

SACERDOTALIST

• Sacerdotalist, n. One who holds the belief that a clergyman is a priest. Denial of this momentous doctrine is the hardiest challenge that is now flung into the teeth of the Episcopalian church by the Neo-Dictionarians.

–Ambrose Bierce
e Devil's Dictionary

Sachse, Heinrich Ernst (1812–1883)

A German atheist, Sachse worked upon behalf of forethought causes in Magdeburg. {BDF}

Sachs, B. (20th Century)

Sachs was on the advisory board of Charles Francis Potter's First Humanist Society of New York.

Sackett, Susan (20th Century)

Sackett is Vice President of the Arizona Secular Humanists, PO Box 3738, Scottsdale, Arizona 85271. She also is a regional director of the Council for Secular Humanism.

SACRAMENT

• Sacrament, n. A solemn religious ceremony to which several degrees of authority and significance are attached. Rome has seven sacraments, but the Protestant churches, being less prosperous, feel that they can afford only two, and these of inferior sanctity. Some of the smaller sects have no sacraments at all–for which mean economy they will indubitably be damned.

–Ambrose Bierce
The Devil's Dictionary

SACRED

• Sacred, adj. Dedicated to some religious purpose; having a divine character; inspiring solemn thoughts or emotions; as, the Dalai Lama of Thibet; the Moogum of M'bwango; the temple of Apes in Ceylon; the Cow in India; the Crocodile, the Cat, and the Onion of ancient Egypt; the Mufti of Moosh; the hair of the dog that bit Noah, etc.

–Ambrose Bierce
The Devil's Dictionary

SADDUCEES: See entry for Sadoc.

Sade, Donatien Alphonse François [Comte de] (1740–1814)

Sade was author of *Justine, Juliette, Philosophy in the Bedroom* (1791), which admittedly is pornographic. However, his work has been considered a part of the pantheon of such French authors as Rousseau, Balzac, Racine, and Proust, and is included as part of the French canon in the Bibliothèque de la Pléiade series.

Sade described himself as "atheistic to the point of fanaticism." He also wrote, "Anything beyond the limits and grasp of the human mind is either illusion or futility; and because your god having to be one or the other of the two, in the first instance I should be made to believe in him, and in the second a fool."

Sade is known mainly as **the Marquis de Sade**, a title he held before becoming count when his father died in 1767. After fighting in the Seven Years War and marrying, he was imprisoned because of his allegedly scandalous conduct (for example, persuading Rose Keller, an unemployed widow, not a whore, to come to his villa in 1768, where he tied her to the bedposts, gagged her with a fur muff, whipped her until she bled, then poured sealing wax into her wounds, etc.). *Philosophy in the Bedroom* (1795), in which he declared that "Religions are the cradles of despotism," has a daughter sodomize her mother with a dildo. Worse, so the mother will further agonize, Sade has the mother raped by a syphilitic servant, her orifices are sewn, and she cannot excrete, causing her body the utmost of pain.

Psychologists, as pointed out by Laurence L. Bongie's *Sade: A Biographical Essay* (1998), have had wide discussions as to what must have been Sade's hateful feelings toward his mother as well as his mother-in-law. A French critic, Pierre Klossowski in 1933, suggested that the root of Sade's malignant condition was a "negative Oedipal complex," involving an inability to work through a normal rivalry with his father, whom he considered a weakling, and by identifying with his father turned his libido against his mother by punishing her in his fictional mother-torture fantasies. Others, however, claim Sade's mother did not abandon him nor his father.

In 1771, three years after his liberation from Pierre-Encize, the Sades and their three children moved to La Coste in an attempt to avoid his reputation and his creditors.

In 1772 dressed in a vest of marigold-yellow satin with matching breeches, a plumed hat on his head and a gold-knobbed cane in his hand, he organized a party in Marseilles that was held in a prostitute's room. His valet, Latour, assembled four girls for his pleasure, and de Sade not only had active and passive sodomy with Latour but also copulated with the prostitutes, whipped them, and was whipped by them. The Aix-en-Provence parlement, after convicting him of sodomy and an attempt to poison–actually, he had fed the women Spanish fly that looked like candy and they became so sick they called the police–sentenced him in absentia to death to death, then had him beheaded and burned in effigy. Sade understandably fled to Italy.

For twenty-seven years he was confined in places such as the Bastille (by some, Sade was credited with causing the Bastille riot), the dungeon at Vincennes, and at Charenton asylum. During this time he wrote ribald romances and, released during the revolution, had some of his plays produced by the *Comédie Française.* De Sade believed that inasmuch as both sexual deviation and criminal acts exist in nature, they are natural, a premise which the Church fought strenuously. His notion may have come from his reading of d'Holbach and libertine literature, according to Robert Darnton (*The New York Review* of Books, 14 January 1998). He also believed that sex that involves pain is not necessarily bad and can, in fact, be gratifying. This, however, was considered perversion, and because of such "sadism" (the term was first included in a dictionary in 1834) his work was banned for its obscenity. He also was put in prison and later sent to an insane asylum for having written a pornographic novel, *Zoloe and Her Two Acolytes,* in which the chief characters were based on Napoleon and Josephine. In addition to his many affairs with women, he preached in his novels the superiority of male attractions and he had homosexual relations, according to his helpful and cooperative valet.

Aldous Huxley termed Sade "the one complete and thoroughgoing revolutionary of history." Sade's depictions of horror, although revolutionary, were not particularly colorful or picturesque. They included matter-of-fact descriptions of acts which both church and state have committed throughout history, allegedly to enforce good behavior in keeping with judicial standards which had been set by the religious and governmental leaders. What other authors had not done so well, however, was to describe the humiliation which humans have experienced. Charles Rosen, author of *The Romantic Generation*, has observed that Sade knew that all sexual intercourse is basically an act of violence and rape. Further, Rosen suggests, "Sade is impressive because he makes hypocrisy almost impossible to sustain in considering the erotic imagination. There are many reasons for thinking that pornography does not actually stimulate or inspire sadistic acts, and if this is the case, Sade's work might reasonably be made required reading for high school students (he is perhaps a bit strong for the elementary level)."

Maurice Lever, in a biography entitled *Sade* (1993), wrote that the Marquis richly deserves his terrible reputation. For example, his *120 Days of Sodom*, written while Sade was in the Bastille, describes the possibility of multiple incest: a nobleman programs three generations so that he is able to show that, "in fucking [his daughter], he fucked his sister . . . and his daughter-in-law, and . . . also constrained his son to fuck his own sister and mother-in-law." Imprisoned, he did more than just imagine: He sent his wife, which humiliated her, to arrange for and deliver pastries and some custom-made wooden ebony dildos ("six inches in circumference by eight or nine inches long"), then recorded 6,536 "introductions" (to sodomize himself) in order to obtain *prestiges*, or orgasms, by stuffing himself at both ends. Lever's book reads like a surrealist creation, including Sade's taunt to his enemies: "Kill me or take me as I am, because I will not change."

Francine du Plessix Gray, in *At Home With the Marquis de Sade* (1998), noted that Sade and his wife, Renée-Pélagie, were married for twenty-seven years, fifteen of which he was running from the police or was in jail. On the evening he was released from the Bastille she obtained a formal separation: "Having survived greater measures of passion and devotion than most women experience in ten lifetimes, she returned to being the placid, conventional creature she had been before she met Donatien de Sade. Reclusion, religious devotion, the petty groveling of a provincial Catholic life, would now be the measure of her days." Under the Directory he sank into poverty, was returned to Charenton as a criminal and insane madman, and at age seventy-three bought the sexual services of Madeleine Leclerc, daughter of an employee at Charenton. He was with her until a week before his death, 2 December 1814. Ms. Du Plessix Gray, in summing him up, writing,

> He never grasped the fundamentals of civilised life: which have to do with accepting, with a measure of serenity, the ultimate necessity of compromise.

That, however, could explain people's continued fascination with him.

Although as a young man Octavio Paz was enthusiastic about de Sade, after examining the ontological impossibilities and philosophic weakanesses of Sade's views Paz finally found his youthful admiration had vanished. In *An Erotic Beyond: Sade* (1998) he came to view the infamous libertine as a philosophically tyrannical bore.

"Let us renounce," Sade wrote, "the ridiculous theory of the immortality of the soul, made to be scorned as relentlessly as that of a God as false and as ridiculous as it is. Let us abjure with equal courage both of these absurd fables, the fruits of fear, ignorance, and superstition."

Upon his father's death, Sade's son burned at least two volumes of a projected ten-volume novel, *The Days of Florabelle, or Nature Revealed.* His remains were scattered, for his 1806 will requested that "all traces of my grave disappear from the face of the earth, as I flatter myself that my memory will be effaced from the minds of men." (Angela Carter wrote a feminist defense, *The Sadean Woman*; in 1989 Arlette Farge's *Le Goût de l'archive* related that in 1766, furious that a horse and carriage would not allow his own carriage to pass through a narrow street, Sade buried his sword in the horse of the carriage blocking his way.) {CE; GL; PA; TYD}

Sadi, Marie François (19th Century)

Sadi, the grandson of Count Lazare Carnot, was an atheist. He became President of the French Republic. (See entry for Count Lazare Carnot.)

Sadler, Gilbert T. (20th Century)

Sadler wrote *Behind the New Testament* (1921). {GS}

Sadler, Laetitia (20th Century)

Sadler is the lead singer of a band called Stereolab. In an interview in the *Minnesota Daily* (May 1996), she was asked if she was a Marxist and replied, "I'm not for ideologies and religions. You have to think for yourself. Things have to make sense in your head and have to correspond to a reality or a possibility. It's good to see what could happen rather than just be fatalistic." {CA}

Sadoc (3rd Century B.C.E.)

Sadoc was a learned Jewish doctor. He denied the resurrection, the existence of angels, and the doctrine of predestination. He opposed the idea of future rewards and punishments. His followers, named after him, were Sadducees. {BDF}

Saffi, Aurelio (1819–1890)

Saffi was one of the triumvirs, or three heads, of the Roman Republic of 1848. He fled to Switzerland, then to England, when it was crushed, then returned to Italy in 1860 when Garibaldi offered him a position. Saffi wrote many historical and legal works in which his anti-Papal sentiments found expression. {RAT; RE}

Safford, Mary Augusta (1851–1927)

An important woman in the 19th-century Unitarian ministry, Safford was a leader of what came to be known as the "Iowa Sisterhood' or the "Iowa Band." She preached what she called a "religion of morality on fire with love for humanity." This group of women ministers actively promoted liberal religion in the Midwest. She was minister in Humboldt, Sioux City, and Des Moines, Iowa, as well as secretary of the Iowa Unitarian Association. {U; U&U, *World*, November-December 1997}

Safford, Victoria (20th Century)

Safford is minister in Northampton and Florence, Massachusetts, of the Unitarian Society. She has written of her humanism,

> To the extent that I know no personal god and acknowledge no First Cause or Creator; to the extent that I love and struggle in and weep for the human condition and hold it not separate from the other natural drama we are all caught in; to the extent that I expect no afterlife but am busy enough trying to live rightly now; to the extent that human freedom and the defense of this freedom against human evil are somewhat of a mission for me, I suppose I am a humanist
>
> Yet what if I say that art is as clarifying, as satisfying, as much a portal to the truth for me as science ever can be? What if I claim that they are two expressions of the same deep human longing to see? What if I say that a story or an image, even a biblical one, can sometimes hold for me more wisdom than a set of proven facts? What if I know that certain rituals, certain rites, certain symbols, even Christian or Jewish or Muslim ones, are as likely to transform me as certain reasoned arguments? What if I get as much or much more out of watching the ocean rush in and out, and hearing it at night, and swimming in its salt, than out of any human discourse? To the extent that metaphor and myth live for me; to the extent that as a minister I'm more curious about how people feel than about what they know; to the extent that human limitations make me daily doubt human grandeur, I suppose my humanism is in question.
>
> I'm not an "ist" at all. I'm a human being, trying to discern and describe the beautiful, the good, the true, and to effect these, to the extent that I can, in the world.
>
> {*World*, November-December 1997}

Saga, Francesco De Rovigo (Died 1566)

Saga was an Italian heretic, put to death at Venice for his antitrinitarianism on 25 February 1566. {BDF}

Sagan, Carl (1934–1996)

Sagan, who was the director of Cornell's Laboratory for Planetary Studies, once wrote, "The idea that God is an oversized white male with a flowing beard who sits in the sky and tallies the fall of every sparrow is ludicrous. But if by 'God' one means the set of physical laws that are found in the universe, then clearly there is such a God. This God is emotionally unsatisfying. It does not make much sense to pray to the law of gravity." His publications include *The Dragons of Eden* (1977), for which he received a Pulitzer Prize. In 1980 he created and was host of the public-television science series "Cosmos." In 1981, the American Humanist Association named him Humanist of the Year. Also, he was a Humanist Laureate in the Council for Secular Humanism's International Academy of Humanism. Sagan's essay, "Real American Patriots Ask Questions," written with his third wife Ann Druyan, is included in *Challenges to the Enlightenment, Essays in Defense of Reason and Science* (1994).

In *The Demon-Haunted World* (1996), Sagan protested against superstition and people's uncritical acceptance of pseudo-scientific claims. Richard Lewontin has pointed out that Sagan regretted the fact that most of us do not have control of the intellectual apparatus needed to explain manifest reality in material terms. In place of scientific (i.e., correct material) explanations, we substitute demons.

Religions, Sagan wrote, are the "nurseries of pseudo-science." "I worry," he added, "that, especially as the millennium edges nearer, pseudo-science and superstition will seem year by year more tempting, the siren song of unreason more sonorous and attractive. Where have we heard it before? Whenever our ethnic or national prejudices are aroused, in times of scarcity, during challenges to national self-esteem or nerve, when we agonize about our diminished cosmic place and purpose, or when fanaticism is bubbling up around us–then, habits of thought familiar from ages past reach for the controls. The candle flame gutters. Its little pool of light trembles. Darkness gathers. The demons begin to stir."

He was concerned about doomsday asteroids that are rumored to soon hit the Earth, although he admits there is always the possibility. Reports of alien abductions are complete nonsense. He also writes about repressed memories, creationism, belief in miracles, and the claims of tobacco companies that cigarettes have not been shown to be harmful. In a March-April 1996 cover story for *Skeptical Inquirer*, Sagan recommends science as a source of spirituality. "It has beauty, power, and majesty that can provide spiritual as well as practical fulfillment," he explains. At the same time, he laments the fact that "superstition and pseudoscience keep getting in the way, providing easy answers, casually pressing our awe buttons, and cheapening the experience."

In *The Demon-Haunted World: Science as a Candle in the Dark* (1996), he commented on a variety of topics:

> If some good evidence for life after death were announced, I'd be eager to examine it; but it would have to be real scientific data, not mere anecdote. . . . Better the hard truth, I say, than the comforting fantasy. . . . If you want to save your child from polio, you can pray or you can inoculate. . . . Try science. . . . Since World War II, Japan has spawned enormous numbers of new religions featuring the supernatural. . . . In Thailand, diseases are treated with pills manufactured from pulverized sacred Scripture. "Witches" are today being burned in South Africa. . . . The worldwide TM [Transcendental Meditation] organization has an estimated valuation of $3 billion. For a fee, they promise to make you invisible, to enable you to fly. . . . It is morally as bad not to care whether a thing is true or not, so long as it makes you feel good, as it is not to care how you got your money, so long as you have got it.

Sagan's memorial service was held in New York's Cathedral Church of St. John the Divine, the structure that features a statue of God (a bearded Caucasian with His arms outstretched) on the front. Church officials referred to "Carl the great atheist" and explained that the site was chosen because of Sagan's record of having successfully worked with national church leaders on environmental matters. Speakers included MIT physicist Philip Morrison; Harvard paleontologist Stephen Jay Gould; the former director of the USSR's Space Research Institute, Ronald Sagedeev; Vice President Al Gore; and Sagan's daughter, Sasha; son, Jeremy; and third wife, Ann Druyan, who is secretary of the Federation of American Scientists. Druyan told of his and her exuberance at having included an interstellar message along with Bach, Beethoven, and other composer's music in two NASA Voyager spacecrafts now beyond the outer solar system. At a speed of 40,000 miles per hour, the objects are traveling in space and have a projected shelf life of a billion years. How, they mused, would some finder in the distant future interpret all this, perhaps even after Earth no longer had humans. The memorial ended with Sagan's recording of an excerpt of "Pale Blue Dot: A Vision of the Human Future in Space." The powerful and life-like voice resounded eerily throughout the immense Gothic structure. (See "A Battle-Cry for Reason and Rationality," *Skeptical Inquirer*, July-August 1996; also see entry for Ann Druyan.) {CE; HNS2; Richard Lewontin, *The New York Review of Books*, 9 January 1997; TYD; Warren Allen Smith, *Skeptical Inquirer*, July-August 1997}

Saginian, Armen A. (20th Century)

Saginian, the executive director of New Horizons, signed Humanist Manifesto 2000.

Sahlin, Mona (1957–)

Sahlin is a Swedish government official. She was Minister of Labor (1990–1991), Chairman of the Commission on Labor Market (1991–1992), and deputy prime minister, minority equality issues (1994 to date). Sahlin, a Social Democrat, has been on the executive committee of her party since 1990 and its secretary since 1992. According to Celebrity Atheists, Sahlin is a non-theist who, asked on national radio if she believed in God, responded in the negative. {CA; E}

Sahula-Dycke, Ignatz (20th Century)

Sahula-Dycke wrote *The God Business: Polemic Essays About Religion and Its Effect on Western Behavior* (1973).

Saich, Roy (20th Century)

Saich in Britain is active with the Coventry and Warwickshire Humanists. He also is a member of the National Secular Society and of the Gay and Lesbian Humanist Association (GALHA).

Saigey, Emile (Died 1875)

Saigey was a French inspector of telegraph wires. He wrote *Modern Physics* (1867) and *The Sciences in the Eighteenth Century: Physics of Voltaire* (1874). {BDF}

Saillard, F. (19th Century)

Saillard was a French author who wrote *The Revolution and the Church* (1869) and *The Organisation of the Republic* (1883). {BDF}

SAINT

• Saint, n. A dead sinner revised and edited.

–**Ambrose Bierce**

• Saints should always be judged guilty until they are proved innocent.

–**George Orwell**

• "Ah, my lord, it is only the first yard that *really* matters."

–**Marie Deffand**,
who had been told that St. Denis carried his head twenty or thirty yards after it had been cut off.

A "saint" is "canonized" by having the Pope proclaim that the individual is deemed worthy of being "venerated," or respectfully revered. The papal statement is made after "beatification," a decree that the person can be honored in a limited way and after at least two miracles are "authenticated" that the "blessed one's intercession" has completed.

Pope John Paul II in 1998 canonized Edith Stein (1891-1942), a Jewish intellectual, philosopher, and atheist who became a Carmelite nun. Numbers of Jews, including the World Jewish Congress, immediately objected to the Vatican's logic and sensitivity, saying Stein had been gassed during the Holocaust because she was Jewish, not because she had become a Carmelite nun. Stein, upon becoming a nun, took the name Teresia Benedicta of the Cross The miracle which elevated her to sainthood occurred because a two-year-old namesake survived an accidental overdose of aspirin-like Tylenol. After Teresia Benedicta McCarthy of Brockton, Massachusetts, suffered from severe liver damage, she is said to have recovered overnight after her family prayed to Teresia Benedicta of the Cross.

Saint Vitus, a 3rd century Christian martyr, suffered from what today is called Sydenham's chorea (named after a physician, Thomas Sydenham [1624-1689]). The affliction, involving jerky and involuntary movements of the body, was called St. Vitus's Dance. The condition is not hereditary, whereas Huntington's disease–also a disturbance of the nervous system–is. {ER}

Saint Bartholomew's Day Massacre

Beginning 24 August 1572, French Protestants, or Huguenots, were systematically murdered by Roman Catholics. Many Huguenots had come to Paris for the wedding of Henri of Navarre (later Henri IV) to Marguerite of Valois–a Catholic, Marguerite had been forced into the marriage in an attempt by Catherine de' Medici (the regent from 1560 to 1563 and adviser from 1563 to 1574) to reconcile the Protestants and Catholics. With so many Protestants in Paris, Catherine and her son, King Charles IX, successfully carried out a general massacre which spread throughout France and caused the resumption of the Wars of Religion (1562–1598). Alexandre Dumas *père* wrote a vivid description of the event, which in 1993 was turned into a movie, "Queen Margot," by Patrice Cherneau. {CE}

Saint-Évremond, Charles de Marguetel de Saint-Denis de (1613?–1703)

Saint-Évremond was a major-general, a writer, an amateur moralist, and a critic. He served under Condé and Nördlingen. For satirizing Cardinal Mazarin he was once confined in the Bastille. He was exiled, however, for his hostility to the 1658 Peace of the Pyrenees, which set the Franco-Spanish border, and he died in England, where he was buried in Westminster Abbey. His writing contributed to the skeptical, freethinking current of his century, and his *Comédie des académistes* showed him to be the most famous Epicurean and hedonist of his day. He influenced young men like Bolingbroke, according to Robertson, and he was known as a Deist. Asked on his deathbed if he wished to reconcile himself to God, Saint-Évremond replied that, no, he desired to reconcile himself to appetite (or, in another translation, "Certainly, with my stomach."). {CE; BDF; JMR; JMRH; RAT; RE}

St. Gaudens, Augustus (1848–1907)

St. Gaudens, an Irish-born US sculptor, is described as being the foremost sculptor of the late nineteenth century. His most famous work, often called "Grief," depicts a mysterious figure with a face that is shadowed. But he had another title in mind: either "Peace" or "Nirvana." In 1897 in Boston, he built a monument to Robert Gould Shaw, a colonel in a Negro regiment in the Civil War. St. Gaudens was "firm in his principles and a great admirer of Mr. O. B. Frothingham, with whom he agrees," his daughter has said, referring to the leader of the radical wing of late 19th-century Unitarianism. Louise Hall Tharp Little has written of his religious views in *Saint-Gaudens and the Gilded Era* (1969). {CE; UU}

Saint-Glain, Dominique de (Born c. 1620)

Saint-Glain was a French Spinozist who went to Holland in order to profess the Protestant religion more freely. He assisted on the Rotterdam *Gazette*. Upon reading Spinoza, he espoused the system and translated into French the *Tractatus Theologico-Politicus* under the title of *La Clef du Sanctuaire* (1678). When he was violently attacked for this, Saint-Glain changed the title to *Ceremonies Superstitieuses des Juifs* (*Superstitious Jewish Ceremonies)* and also to *Reflexions Curieuses d'un Esprit Desintéressé* (*Curious Reflections of a Disinterested Soul*). {BDF}

Saint-Hyacinthe, Themiseul de Cordonnier de (1684–1746)

Saint-Hyacinthe was a French writer, the author of *Philosophical Researches* (1743). Voltaire published his *Diner Du Comte de Boulainvilliers* under the name of St. Hyacinthe. {BDF}

St. John, Henry [Viscount Bolingbroke] (1678–1751)

One of the most provocative British statesmen, admired by Voltaire for his wit, Viscount Bolingbroke was a conservative, pro-Church, English aristocrat. However, his writings show him to have been, in fact, a deist. He believed that God does not intervene in history, has never revealed Himself, and it is man's reason alone that is paramount in living a meaningful life. Said to be more a debater than a thinker, he had a much greater influence than Samuel Johnson was willing to admit. Voltaire had been his intimate, often acknowledging his debt, and St. John supplied Pope with the material for his *Essay on Man*. Although his outlook had assimilated part of the Spinozistic and the atheistic case against anthropomorphism, he used anthropomorphic language on the score that "we must speak of God after the manner of men." McCabe says that St. John was one of the most important of the Deists, "though he concealed his views." Robertson believes the weak side of Bolingbroke's polemic was its inconsistency. {BDF; CE; EU, E. Graham Waring; FUK; FUS; JM; JMR; RAT; RE; TRI}

ST. JOHN'S CATHEDRAL, NEW YORK CITY

Although in Reims it is declared that their cathedral is the largest Gothic cathedral in the world, the Manhattan Episcopalians claim that theirs, St. John the Divine with a statue of God on the front, is.

Virgil Thomson, although not a theist, recognized the panache involved in having one's memorial in a noted place. He ordered that his memorial be held in New York at "the St. John the Too-Too Divine" Cathedral.

Saint-Just, Louis Antoine (1767–1794)

Saint-Just was a prominent figure during the French Revolution, a student of philosophy and a commissary to the army. McCabe wrote that his enemies had gotten him arrested and guillotined during the Terror. However, Saint-Just was a leading member of the dreaded Committee of Public Safety and, later, president of the Convention. A supporter of Robespierre in the destruction of the Hébertists and Dantonists, Saint-Just believed in the perfect state, one based on rigorous Spartan virtue, and he allowed no opposition. When Robespierre was overthrown and Saint-Just was prevented from delivering a speech in his defense, Saint-Just was arrested and both were guillotined. McCabe listed Saint-Juste as an atheist, one who "died at the age of 27, with great serenity." {CE; RAT; RE}

Saint Lambert, (Charles) Jean François de (1717–1803)

Saint Lambert was a French writer who, after being educated among the Jesuits, entered the army. He became a devoted adherent of Voltaire and an admirer of Madame du Chatelet. Saint Lambert wrote some articles in the *Encyclopédie*. His poem, "The Seasons" (1769), gained him admission to the French Academy. His *Philosophical Works* were published in 1801. {BDF; RAT; RE}

Saint Mary's Duluth Clinic

When a hematologist told Dr. Van Druten he was headed for the St. Mary's Duluth Clinic, Druten responded, "Oh, the clinic of the unwed mother Mary!" {*Secular Nation*, July-September 1998}

Saint Nicholas: See entry for Santa Claus.

Saint Paul: See entry for Paul, Saint.

Saint Pierre, Jacques Henri Bernardin de: See entry for Bernardin de Saint-Pierre, Jacques Henri.

Saint Priest, Alexis Guignard [Count] (1805–1851)

Saint Priest was the son of the Russian Princess Sophia Galitzer. He took part in the Revolution of 1830 and later was French Plenipotentiary Minister in Brazil, Portugal, and Denmark. Among his works was a history of the suppression of the Jesuits (1844), and at the time of Saint Priest's death he was writing a biography of Voltaire. {RAT; RE}

Saint-Saëns, (Charles) Camille (1835–1921)

Saint-Saëns, an eminent French composer, was an outright freethinker, according to David Tribe. He is best known for the opera "Samson et Dalila" (1877), which Caruso sang. Saint-Saëns also wrote symphonies, concertos, and symphonic poems. Franz Liszt called him "the finest organist in the world." Indicative of his outlook, Saint-Saëns once wrote, "When Art was born, Religion took possession of it. Religion did not create Art." {TRI}

St. Sebastian: See entry for Sebastian.

Saint-Simon, Claude Henri de Rouvroy [Comte de] (1760–1825)

Saint-Simon, a French courtier and writer of memoirs, was founder of the semi-Socialist Saint Simonians. A noble who traveled extensively in America, Germany, and Britain, he acquired a humanitarian zeal which he crystallized into what he called a New Christian sect (*Nouveau Christianisme*) for social service. However, he rejected all Christian doctrines. Saint-Simon made a fortune through land speculation, then lavished his wealth on a salon for scientists and spent his later years in poverty, sustained by the faith that he had a message for humanity. The message was that brotherhood must accompany scientific organization, and his writings contain certain ideas foreshadowing the positivism of Auguste Comte, who for a time was his pupil. After his death, Barthélemy Prosper Enfantin and Saint-Armand Bazard led a group of Saint-Simonians. The group called for abolition of individual inheritance rights, public control of the means of production, and gradual emancipation of women. By 1833, the movement had disintegrated, but it exerted much influence upon later socialist thought. {CE; JM; RAT; RE; TRI}

St. Teresa of Avila

"Visions of Ecstasy," a film by Nigel Wingrove, depicts St. Teresa of Avila having a sexual fantasy about a nun and an imagined erotic relationship with Jesus. {*New Humanist*, December 1996}

St. Vitus: See entry for Saint.

Sainte Croix, Geoffrey Ernest Maurice de (1910-2000)

A Marxist historian of ancient Greece and Rome, de Ste. Croix wrote*The Origins of the Peloponnesian War* (1972) and *The Class Struggle in the Ancient World* (1981). "He revived the pro-Athenian, pro-democratic stance of earlier scholars like George Grote," said Victor Bers of Yale. His loathing of Christianity and the Roman Catholic Church—it was a source of intolerance and cruelty, he thought, particularly to women—led him to denounce God, whom he called Yahweh. In 1972 he was elected a fellow of the British Academy. Although some historians disagreed with him, others found his work outstandingly written and based on exact detail.

Sainte-Beuve, Charles Augustin (1804–1869)

Sainte-Beueve was a French literary historian and critic. The first major professional literary critic, he developed the appreciation of literature through psychological and biographical insight. First a student of medicine, then of literature, he contributed reviews to the *Globe* in 1824. A favorable review of Hugo's *Odes and Ballades* gained him the attention of the Romantic school. He made his mark in 1828 with his *Historical and Critical Picture of French Poetry in the Sixteenth Century*. He also published some poetry and a semi-autobiographical psychological novel, *Volupté* (1834), which was inspired by his love for Mme. Victor Hugo. He considered his great work to be *Port-Royal* (1840–1859), a six-volume history not only of Jansenism but also including a section of 17th-century French society. In 1844 Sainte-Beuve was made a member of the French Academy, and he became a senator. According to McCabe, the more famous "Sainte-Beef" became, the more advanced and outspoken he became in his skepticism. In *Pensées d'aout*, he abandoned all beliefs. The *Grand Encyclopédie* states that as Saint-Beueve grew older he became more and more hostile to religion and was "the protector of Freethought in the Senate."

Dan Hofstadter, in *The Love Affair as a Work of Art* (1996), holds that Proust, as shown in *Contre Sainte-Beuve*, unpublished writings brought out in 1954, had a long-cherished plan to write an attack on the critic whose famous "method" was allegedly wrong. However, he never finished the project, instead writing *A la recherche du temps perdu*. Proust disagreed that in studying literary works one essentially was understanding an author, that therefore he would need to know the person's religion, his background, his friends, his ideas. No, Proust held, a work is the product of another "I" than the one we list "in our habits, in society, and in our vices." To understand an author, then, one does not need to speak to his friends but, rather, needs to plumb the work by introspection. Diderot scholar P. N. Furbank, citing Robert Calasso's *The Ruin of Kasch*, says that Proust had more in common with Sainte-Beuve than he liked to pretend. "Where Proust wanted to offer a devastating description of Sainte-Beuve's 'method,' " writes Calasso, "he revealed its secret, which was in fact very close to his own." The New Critics, similarly, held that readers and critics should focus not on authors but on works. Sainte-Beueve would not have agreed, of course, with T. S. Eliot and the other New Critics. {BDF; CE; JM; RAT; RE; TRI}

Saisset, Émile Edmond (1814–1863)

Saisset, a French philosopher, belonged to the eclectic and pantheistic school of Victor Cousin. He taught at the Sorbonne in 1862 and was a member of the *Académie des Sciences Morales*. Saisset's views on religion are seen in his *Le scepticisme* (1865). {RAT}

Sakala (20th Century)

Dr. Sakala of the Atheist Centre in Vijayawada, India, addressed the 1992 IHEU Congress in the Netherlands. On the subject of social action in India, she described how the Centre gives medical assistance as well as socio-psychological counseling for women, some of whom have married at the age of thirteen and are deserted after a period of time. For years, she reports, the Atheist Centre has championed inter-caste and inter-religious marriages in order to break down some of the barriers in Indian society.

Sakamoto, Tatsuya (20th Century)

Sakamoto, of Japan's Keio University, is a 1997 Hume Conference Director of The Hume Society, a group engaged in scholarly activity concerning David Hume.

Sakharov, Andrei D(mietrievich) (1921–1989)

Sakharov, the outspoken Soviet advocate of human rights and nuclear physicist who from 1948 to 1956 helped develop the USSR's hydrogen bomb, was a member of the Academy of Sciences in Moscow. When in the late 1960s he became a critic of Soviet repression and the world arms race, he was imprisoned. Further, he was excluded from participating in Academy of Science matters, and he was banished to Gorky, where he was prohibited from speaking freely and which called the world's attention to the problem of dissidents in the USSR.

Sakharov was the first Soviet citizen to win the Nobel Peace Prize, in 1990. In his acceptance speech, Sakharov said that mankind's goal is to "make good the demands of reason and create a life worthy of ourselves and of the goals we only dimly perceive."

During his imprisonment and confinement, he worked on *Moscow and Beyond: 1986 to 1989* and *Memoirs* (posthumously published, 1992), the latter a chronicle of his life until 1986 and written despite K.G.B. (secret police) interference during an eleven-year period in which he was exiled to Gorky (which now is called Nizhny Novgorod and to which thousands of visitors annually trek, finding on a window of the door to his study that Sakharov had printed with a blue marker, "*Per aspera ad astra* [Through perseverance, to the stars].).

In 1980, the American Humanist Association named Sakharov Humanist of the Year. In 1988, he was awarded the Humanist Award by the International Humanist and Ethical Union "for his long-standing contributions to the cause of human rights." This was presented to him in the United States, when finally Soviet politicians allowed him to travel. Paul Kurtz presented the award "in recognition of his long-standing contributions to the cause of human rights, the scientific outlook, and the ideals of humanism." In accepting, Dr. Sakharov commented that he had a deep affection for the international humanist movement. In addition, Sakharov was a member of the Council for Secular Humanism's International Academy of Humanism.

At his memorial, David Remnick, author of *Lenin's Tomb: The Last Days of the Soviet Empire* (1993), walked in the funeral cortege of, in his estimation, "the most fearless martyr of the regime." Said one of Sakharov's old friends in a metaphor reminiscent of religious legend and the story of Saint George, "I'm only glad that before he died Sakharov dealt the system a mortal blow. If God sent Jesus to pay for the sins of humankind, then a Marxist God somewhere sent Andrei Sakharov to pay for the sins of our system." Upon hearing this, John Bayley remarked that "even then no one could know that the blow was mortal, least of all that courageous populist Boris Yeltsin, whose towering figure was just ahead of Remnick in the funeral procession." (See entry for Elena Bonner.) {CE; HM2; HNS2}

Salacrou, Armand (Born 1899)

Salacron's "*Certitudes et Incertitudes*" in *Theatre* (1943), observed, "The existence of a world without God seems to me less absurd than the presence of a God, existing in all his perfection, creating an imperfect man in order to make him run the risk of Hell." {TYD}

Saladin: See entry for William Stewart Ross.

Saladin (Salah ad-Din) (1137?–1195)

Christopher Hitchins has called Saladin, the Muslim warrior and Ayyubid sultan of Egypt, "the greatest Kurd in history." He, the opponent of the Christian Crusaders, conquered Jerusalem among other sites. The Christians never recovered from their loss to his army. {CE}

Saladin, Kenneth (20th Century)

Saladin, who once sued to have Christian symbols removed from the city seal of Milledgeville, Georgia, is a professor of biology and an activist on behalf of church-state separation. {*Free Inquiry*, Fall, 1984}

Salaville, Severien (1755–1832)

Salaville, a French journalist during the 18th century, was, according to Robertson, "the one convinced and reasoning atheist among the publicists of the Revolution [who] opposed the Cult of Reason with sound and serious and persuasive argument, and strongly blamed all forcible interference with worship, while at the same time calmly maintaining atheism as against theism." {JMR; JMRH; RAT}

Saldaña, Jorge (20th Century)

Saldaña participated in the 1996 Humanist World Congress held in Mexico City. He spoke on "Telecracia y Dictadura," noting how Mexican radio and television coverage has been instrumental, unfortunately, in keeping one political party in power for sixty-five years.

Sale, George (1680–1736)

Sale was an English Oriental scholar. He was one of a society that undertook to publish a *Universal History* and was one of the compilers of the *General Dictionary*. With a preliminary discourse and explanatory notes, he translated the *Qur'an*. Sale was one of the founders of the Society for the Encouragement of Learning. {BDF}

Sales y Ferre, Manuel (Born c. 1839)

A Spanish scientist, Sales y Ferre was a professor at the University of Seville. A freethinker, he published several works on geology.

Salgadão, Sebastiao (20th Century)

Salgadão, a noted photographer, when asked by *Photographer's Forum* interviewer Ken Lassiter if he believed in God, responded in the negative:

> KL: Sometimes the words "compassion, empathy, humanity, dignity, and tenderness" are used to describe your photographs. Is that how you feel about the people?
>
> SS: People sometimes ask if I am a religious person. I am not a religious person. I don't believe in God, that there is only one superior who directs all things in the universe. No, I believe one kind of that is in man–the human god. {CA; E}

Saliers, A. (19th Century)

Saliers was a contributor to *l'Athée*. He wrote *On Patriotism* (1881). {BDF}

Salisbury, Harrison E(vans) (1908–)

Salisbury, an author and journalist, responded to the present author concerning humanism:

> If I have to be categorized, put me in Class One ["to the lexicographer, a term denoting devotion to human interests as well as one referring to the study of the humanities"]. I have no relationship to humanism as a religion or sect. I simply fit, I think, your definition. I try to have a regard for my fellow human beings, I try to have sympathy for the mixed bag of the human condition, and I try to keep my fellow man in mind when I am acting or writing. If not, I would declare out of the human race, of which I have no intention. It is always surprising to me to find people who seem to regard the human race as a Party of One.
>
> {WAS, 9 July 1992}

Salisbury, Lee (20th Century)

Salisbury, of Shakopee, Minnesota, wrote "Leading Scientists Still Reject God" for *Secular Nation* (January-March 1999).

Saleeby, Caleb Williams (Born 1878)

After being assistant to Sir Jonathan Hutchinson at the Polyclinic, Saleeby wrote the Spencerian *Evolution, the Master Key* (1906), in which he described himself as "a camp follower of those who believe that we cannot know reality." Although an agnostic, he was chiefly occupied with Eugenist propaganda and was a member of the National Birth-rate Commission. He edited *The New Library of Medicine* and sat on various national and scientific commissions. {RAT}

Salk, Jonas Edward (1914–1995)

Dr. Salk, an American physician and microbiologist who developed a vaccine against poliomyelitis, was one of America's all-time leading scientists. In the 1960s he developed the first successful vaccine against poliomyelitis, the viral illness that had gripped the nation in fear with images of children doomed to death or paralysis. His 1955 announcement that the new polio vaccine was safe and effective became a turning point in the fight against a disease which, wrote journalist Harold M. Schmeck Jr., "condemned some victims to live the rest of their lives in tanklike breathing machines called iron lungs and placed sunny swimming holes off limits to children because of parents' fears of contagion." In the five years before 1955, when mass inoculations with the vaccine began, cases of paralytic polio averaged about 25,000 a year in the United States. A few years after polio vaccination became routine, the annual number of cases dropped to a dozen or so, sometimes fewer. In 1969 not a single death from polio was reported in the nation, the first such year on record, and by the time of his death the disease was on the verge of being eradicated worldwide.

Some eminent virologists insisted, right up to the first field trial, that the killed virus vaccine should be withheld in favor of a live virus vaccine concurrently under development. The live virus vaccine, developed by Dr. Albert Sabin, was first licensed in 1961. The live virus is modified in the laboratory so that it stimulates immunity but causes no damage. After the polio vaccine was proved successful in the field trials, Dr. Salk became a hero to the public with opinion polls ranking him, Schmeck added, roughly between Churchill and Gandhi as a revered figure of modern history.

In 1976 the American Humanist Association named Dr. Salk Humanist of the Year. In 1977 in Washington, DC, he received the Presidential Medal of Freedom. At the time of his death, from a heart attack, Dr. Salk had a conviction that he lived at the crucial time at which the graph of world population growth changed its slope, a harbinger of future leveling-off and decline. From 1970 on, he also lived with and was married to Françoise Gilot, a French painter and the former mistress of Pablo Picasso. {CE; HSN2}

Sallet, Friedrich von (1812–1843)

Sallet was a German poet of French descent. An officer in the army, he was imprisoned for writing a satire on the life of a trooper. In 1834 he attended Hegel's lectures at Berlin, and in 1838 he quit the army. In a poem, "The Layman's Gospel," Sallet takes New Testament texts and expounds them pantheistically; the God who is made flesh is replaced by the man who becomes God. {BDF; RAT}

Salmeron y Alonso, Nicolas (1838–1881)

Salmeron y Alonso was a Spanish statesman who studied law and became a Democratic journalist. During the Revolution of 1873, he became President to the Cortes. Salmeron y Alonso wrote a prologue to the work of Giner on *Philosophy and Arts* (1878), and his own works were issued in 1881. Salmeron, an outspoken agnostic who took part in the 1892 International Freethought Congress at Madrid, was a great force in the growth of Spanish rationalism. {BDF; PUT; RAT; RE}

SALON

During the Enlightenment, periodic gatherings of persons noted in literature, philosophy, the fine arts, or similar areas were held at one person's home and were known as salons. {DCL}

Salt, Henry Stephens (1851–1939)

Salt was an English writer who had been born in India and was educated at Eton. A contributor to *Progress*, Salt wrote *Literary Sketches* (1888) and *A Life of James Thomson* (1889). He was a member of the Rationalist Press Association. {BDF; FUK; RAT; TRI}

Salt, Lorraine (20th Century)

Salt has been on the editorial committee of *Humanist in Canada*.

Salter, William Mackintire (1853–1931)

An Ethical Culture leader of note in Chicago (1882–1883), Salter along with Judge Henry Booth founded the Bureau of Justice, which grew into the Legal Aid Society. Salter had trained in Iowa at Knox College, and later he studied at Harvard Divinity School. In 1902, he wrote *Society and Its Children, With Special Reference to Child Labor.* {EU, Howard B. Radest; RAT}

Salters, Edgar Evertson (Born 1858)

Salters was an American author who studied at Concord, Paris, Munich, and Heidelberg. In 1884 he published a sketch, *Balzac*, followed by *The Philosophy of Disenchantment*, concerning Schopenhauer and Hartmann. In *The Anatomy of Negation*, Saltus gives an account of some atheists and skeptics from Kapila to Leconte de Lisle (1886). Salters (called Saltus by Wheeler) also wrote novels. His brother Francis was a poet, the author of *Honey and Gall.* {BDF}

SALVATION

In Christianity, salvation is a union or friendship with God and a deliverance from Original Sin and damnation. Jesus promised salvation to his followers. The Salvation Army, a Protestant denomination organized along military lines and headed by a general, is known for its charitable works and streetcorner bands featuring tubas, accordions, and blissfully non-professional singers. "Deliverance of evil" is a theological invention which has nothing to do with freethought, rationalism, and secular humanism.

SALVATION ARMY

The Salvation Army, organized in 1865, is at 615 Slaters Lane, Alexandria, Virginia 22313.

Salverte, Anne Joseph Eusèbe Baconniere de (1771–1839)

Salverte was a French philosopher who studied among the Oratorians. He contributed to Maréchal's *Dictionnaire des Athées* in 1793, published an elegy on Diderot in 1801, and as an elected deputy demanded that Catholicism not be recognized as the state religion. He is remembered for his work on *The Occult Sciences* (1829). On his deathbed, Salverte refused religious offices. {BDF; RAT}

Salvianus (5th Century)

"Apart from a very few who avoid evil, what is nearly the whole body of Christians but a sink of vice?' Those words, by a Marseilles priest, gave a picture of the moral condition of the Christian world that he saw at the middle of the fifth century. Salvianus's work, *De Gubernatione Dei (On the Providence of God)*, like other critical documents of the time, was not translated. For Africa he gives an appalling picture, confirmed by Augustine's sermons that Africa is "the cesspool of the world." Some observers have noted that, judging by his work, the Christians seem not to have bettered the Romans the way they had claimed. {RE}

Samaram: See entry for G. Vijayam.

SAME-SEX MARRIAGES

Is the legalization of same-sex marriage desirable? According to almost all the leaders of organized religions, no. However, Vern L. Bullough, a *Free Inquiry* senior editor and prominent secular humanist, replies yes, "because the benefits that come from legal marriage are substantial" and he finds no moral or ethical reason that individuals in such relationships should be discriminated against. (See entry for Spouse.) {*Free Inquiry*, Winter 1997-1998}

Samkalden, I. (20th Century)

Samkalden, former professor of the Law of International Organisation and former Minister of Justice for the Netherlands, was the first Commissioner for Human Rights of the International Humanist and Ethical Union. As an ombudsman, her main duty is to act on behalf of persons "who are the victims of discrimination on account of their conviction or personal disposition, with special reference to the humanist philosophy of life." Also, the Commissioner deals with "infringements on the principle of separation of church and state in concrete cases." As such, Dr. Samkalden, also the former Lord Mayor of Amsterdam, and Minister of State, served from 1983 to 1986. In the June 1988 *New Humanist*, Jim Herrick has described the history of this group. Humanists anywhere in the world who might need its services should write the Commissioner for Human Rights, Plompetorengracht 19, 3512 CB, Utrecht, Holland.

Samper, José María (1828–1888)

At first a militant anticlericalist in Colombia, Samper as a representative of the "Generation of 1849" helped create the Liberal party and brought José Hilario López to power. The López administration enacted sweeping anticlerical reforms, the first that truly separated church and state in Latin America. "Until 1848," Samper wrote in *Apuntamientos para la historia politica y social de la Nueva Granada desde 1810* (1853), "Bogotá had been held in almost complete subjection by the clergy. The Jesuits and the other friars and clerics dominated most of the families with the power of superstition, and they had been able to fanaticize the masses and make them into blind instruments of absolutistic propaganda." However, when the liberal reforms did not achieve the support of the masses, Samper became a devout Catholic and held that liberalism and Catholicism were not incompatible. {EU}

Sampson, Wallace I. (20th Century)

Dr. Sampson, a physician at Stanford, is on the Council for Secular Humanism's Faith-Healing Investigation Project.

Samson, Leon (20th Century)

Samson was a dialectical materialist who wrote *The New Humanism* (1930).

Samson, Peter H. (1914–1992)

Samson, who was born in Utrecht, the Netherlands, was an assistant minister at the First Unitarian Church of Los Angeles from 1938 to 1940, where he was ordained in 1939. As an accredited interim minister from 1983 to 1992, he served nine churches, from Honolulu, Hawaii, to Adelaide, Australia, to Paramus, New Jersey. Samson's booklets, "The Living Sources of Free Religion" (1949) and "What It Means to Be a Unitarian" (1951), were extensively distributed in Unitarian and Universalist societies.

SAN DIEGO STATE UNIVERITY ATHEISTS

San Diego State University Atheists on the Web: <http://www.secularhumanism.org/cfa/orgs.html>.

Sand, George (Amandine Aurore Lucile [Lucie] Dudevant, née Dupin, Baronne Dudevant) (1804–1876)

Sand came from an old and aristocratic family. Her father, Maurice Dupin, had been an officer in the Imperial Army. Upon his death at the age of thirty from a fall off his horse, her mother had to raise the family, all boys but Aurore, who was raised by her grandparents. At the age of fifteen, she was sent to a convent in Paris to finish her education, and the following year when her grandmother died she was left heiress of the Dupin estate at Nohant. There were not many eligible men of her own class in the vicinity, but she met and married Baron Dudevant, a young neighbor of twenty-seven and an officer in the Imperial Army. They separated when she was but twenty-four, she retained her estate, and when twenty-seven she and her little children went to Paris (possibly to be with Jules Sandeau, a young journalist she had once met). At first trying to be a painter, then a writer, she chose to appear before the public under a masculine guise for, as explained by Underwood, "already she had learned that the world is more lenient in its criticism and judgment of a man than it is of a woman. The petty, superficial homage paid to youth and beauty in a woman did not deceive her." She chose George as her first name, and presumably Sand was inspired by her friendship with Sandeau.

A romantic by nature, Sand shocked the Parisian *literati* and became its center. Her iconoclastic opinions and daring mode of life caused many rumors during the period in which she wrote eighty novels, all of which made the Vatican's list of prohibited reading from 1840 to 1863. Sand was a strong believer in women's rights. Often wearing male attire, she was said to have had female as well as male lovers. Her notorious liaisons included Jules Sandeau, Alfred de Musset, Prosper Mérimée, and Frédéric Chopin, giving her the reputation of being a nymphomaniac. However, the philosopher she most admired—Pierre Lerous—was not her lover. Nor was the philosopher Rousseau, whose work had led to her dropping Catholicism—he had died in 1778.

The Goncourts, "who believed genius to be exclusively a male possession, put it with a gloating coarseness: an autopsy of any famous female writer, Mme. Sand or Mme. de Staël, would reveal a clitoris growing enviously toward the size of a penis," according to Julian Barnes in a review of Barbara Bray's *Flaubert-Sand: The Correspondence (The New York Review of Books*, 10 June 1993). A restaurateur once told the Goncourts, "It's a funny thing, but when she's dressed as a man I call her Madame, and when she's dressed as a woman I call her monsieur."

Sand once wrote concerning the Prussian invasion of 1870 and the Commune of 1871 that the Communards "have ruined and will continue to ruin the republic, exactly as the priests have ruined Christianity." After Balzac, Robertson notes, it is difficult to find a great French novelist who is not frankly rationalistic. He claims Sand will not be claimed by the orthodox. However, in her correspondence with Flaubert she has an open mind about the afterlife, writing, "When I'm no longer useful or agreeable to other people, I'd like to depart peacefully without a sigh, or at least with no more than a sign over the poor human race: it doesn't amount to much, but I'm a part of it, and perhaps I don't amount to much either." As for her using the word "God," she explained that "it is an avatar of which the meaning is often an enigma."

In *Flaubert-Sand: The Correspondence* (1993), *The Economist* (5 June 1993) remarks of the letters to her literary friend in France, "They had their differences. Flaubert was a vehemently reactionary anti-Christian, arguing always against the need to assist or promote the weak and meek. Sand was a true daughter of the French revolution; Flaubert, examining it with his head rather than his heart, saw dismal proof of human stupidity, the failing he excoriated in *Bouvard et Pécuchet*. He was appalled by modern life; Sand, although older, embraced it wholeheartedly. But life was, as Henry James shrewdly observed, her greatest talent; she was "a supreme case of the successful practice of life itself." The English, who once had thought of her as an assailant of marriage and religion, eventually came to appreciate her work and genius, Wheeler observed.

Of religion, she wrote to a friend, "If I make use of the expression 'God,' it is only to refer to one of the loveliest of hypotheses which the human mind has ever conceived, and which expresses only the complete *good* which we all seek. I appreciate and respect your faith (theism) but cannot share it with you. In the future, my friend, make up your mind to respect those who love the truth, even if they seek it in a light that you consider deceptive."

Upon her death and in accordance with her wishes, no religious ceremonies were performed, according to Underwood, "save a short prayer, which was insisted upon by the Catholic priest of the diocese, as essential to his permission to allow the body to be buried in consecrated ground.

Victor Hugo delivered the funeral oration over her grave, in the course of which he thus eulogized her: "She is the one great woman in this century whose mission it was to finish the French Revolution and commence the revolution of Humanity. Equality of the sexes being a branch of the equality of men, a great woman was necessary. It was for a woman to prove that her mind might possess all gifts, without losing a particle of her angelic nature—might at once be strong and gentle. George Sand was that woman. She is one of the glories of our age and country. She had a great heart like Barbes, a great mind like Balzac, and a great soul like Lamartine. She was good, and accordingly she had detractors, but the insults to her were of that kind which posterity will count as glories."

Upon her death Turgenev wrote to Flaubert, "What a good man she was, and what a kind woman." Flaubert had addressed her as "*chere maître*."

Plauchat, in his *Galerie Contemporaine*, had said that Sand believed in God, but "certainly not in the vengeful and merciless God of the orthodox." Her last work was a critical notice of Renan's "*Dialogues et Fragments Philosophiques*" in *Le Temps* only a month before her decease. Toward the end of May she took to her bed, suffering from internal paralysis, from which she never rose again. Up until the day of her death she remained lucid, one of the last directions being, "*Ne touchez pas à la verdure*," which her children understood to mean that she wished that the tree in the village cemetery where she was soon to be buried should not be disturbed. On 8 June, at nine in the morning, Foote reported, she "expired in calmness and serenity." (See entry for Flaubert.) {BDF; CE; FO; PUT; RE; SAU; TRI; TYD}

Sandburg, Carl (1878–1967)

Winner of a Pulitzer Prize in 1940 for his biography of Abraham Lincoln, Sandburg featured Chicago in many of his poems. A Universalist, he voiced the long-range optimism characteristic of humanists, as in his "The People, Yes": And man the stumbler and finder, goes on,

> man the dreamer of deep dreams,
> man the shaper and maker,
> man the answerer. . . .
>
> Man is a long time coming.
> Man will yet win.

Sandburg's recollection of what it was like to attend Lombard, a Universalist-founded college in Galesburg, Illinois, at which he was a member of the 1898–1899 basketball team, is found in his *Ever the Winds of Chance* (1983). He had been raised a Lutheran but said he subscribed to Unitarian Universalism "a little more definitely than to any other denomination." In addition to his Pulitzer Prize for the six-volume Lincoln work, Sandburg won Pulitzers for *Cornhuskers* (1918) and *Complete Poems* (1950). His autobiography is *Always the Young Strangers* (1953). In *The People, Yes* (1936), Sandburg reasoned, "To work hard, to live hard, to die hard, and then to go to Hell after all would be too damned hard."

At the request of Mrs. Sandburg, the Rev. George C. B. Tolleson, minister of the Unitarian Church in Charleston, South Carolina, conducted her husband's funeral. She and two of the Sandburg daughters conferred with Mr. Tolleson prior to the service and told him about a little red notebook in which Sandburg had copied out a passage from Walt Whitman in memory of Lincoln. Tolleson used that excerpt in the service, the lines beginning, "Come, lovely and soothing Death," as well as Sandburg's own "Finish," which begins, "Death comes once; let it be easy." {CE; CL; TYD; UU}

Sanders, Donald R. (1951–1995)

Sanders has been described by journalist Mimi Swartz as "a pornographer with a penchant for alienating others and a phone-sex business." He became something of a surrogate son to atheist Madalyn Murray O'Hair and a brother to Jon Garth Murray. In the mid-1980s he was placed on the board of American Atheists and worked in a number of capacities, the last as its executive vice president. He also served on the boards of directors of the Society of Separationists and was the National Chapter Coordinator for American Atheists. In 1989 he received the "Atheist of the Year" award. In 1992 in Houston, Sanders helped organize the American Atheist's picketing of George Bush's church, and he was an activist upon behalf of gay as well as atheist causes. According to Sanders's close friend, Leslie Perez, a transsexual and former death-row denizen once known as Leslie Douglas Ashley, it was Sanders who helped the O'Hairs in their alleged escape to New Zealand. "They were transferring money abroad for a time," Perez told journalist Mimi Swartz. "I know 'cause Don told me about it."

Upon his death from AIDS, Sanders's cremains were mixed with those of his deceased partner-in-life, Mark Franceschini, who had died in 1992. Inasmuch as Franceshini's Roman Catholic family wants to remove his remains for a religious ceremony, the interment of their ashes has remained undisclosed. {*Vanity Fair*, March 1997}

Sanders, James L. (20th Century)

Sanders founded Religion-Free (R-F, or Ruff!), 413 West Navajo Road, Flagstaff, Arizona 86001. He proposes that the designation by placed on correspondence, envelopes, lapel pins, etc., as a way of identifying fellow non-believers. He wrote "Leaving Religion and Anti-Religion" for *The American Rationalist* (March-April 1997). {FD}

Sanders, Joseph R(oosevelt) (20th Century)

When he signed Humanist Manifesto II, Sanders was a professor at the University of West Florida. He wrote *Aristotle and Kierkegaard* (1972). {HM2}

Sanderson, John Scott Burdon [Sir] (1828–1905)

Sanderson was a master of epidemic diseases. "His Rationalist views were so well known," McCabe reported, "that when (1859) he applied for positions at hospitals he was asked for testimonials to his orthodoxy, though the testimonials which were accepted referred only to his high character and ability." Sanderson taught physiology and histology at London University College and was professor of medicine at Oxford. In 1893 he was President of the British Association. Sir John was Anti-Vitalist, and he joined in the public rebuke of Lord Kelvin, in 1903, for saying that science was returning to a belief in a Vital Principle. {RAT; RE}

Sanderson, Terry (20th Century)

Sanderson is a British rationalist, journalist, and member of the National Secular Society, the author of *Making Gay Relationships Work* (1990) and *How To Be A Happy Homosexual* (1989). "Religion," he has written, is "a potent enemy of the lesbian and gay community," and he has urged the Humanist movement to take a firmer stand on gay and lesbian rights. *The Potts Papers* (1996) has been described as being a beguiling satire, a story "packed with perverted sex, gambling, random violence, and a great deal of hoovering."

Sandhu, Ranjit (20th Century)

Sandhu, philosopher Paul Kurtz's secretary, is on the staff of *Free Inquiry* and *Skeptical Inquirer*. Son of a Hindu father and a Greek Orthodox mother, he has been instrumental in organizing Dr. Kurtz's office at the Council of Secular Humanism's Buffalo address.

Sands, Maniel (20th Century)

Sands wrote *Lessons from the Creator, the Image of God* (1903). {GS}

Sandvig, Bente (20th Century)

Sandvig is head of the Research Department for the Human-Etisk Forbund in Norway. He has fought against a law which Parliament passed, one which removed the right of exemption from religious education and ensuring that religious education is preponderantly Lutheran. Holding that the Norwegian Parliament is thereby ignoring the international obligations of human rights conventions, Sandvig is one of the leaders of the Norwegian humanists who are demanding that the law be changed. His e-mail: <sandvig@human.no>. {*International Humanist News*, April 1996}

Sandwich, John Montagu [Earl of]: See John Montagu.

Sanger, Margaret (1879–1966)

Sanger, the leader in the birth-control movement, was the daughter of a pious Catholic mother who died at age forty-nine after having had eleven babies and seven miscarriages. Her father was a freethinking, socialist Irishman.

She was jailed in 1915 because the Comstock Act classified birth control data as obscene and not fit for the US mails and she had mailed such material. Her clinic at 46 Amboy Street in Brooklyn was closed in 1916 when a policewoman posed as a patient. In 1917, given a choice of a fine or thirty days in the workhouse, she chose the jail time. Refusing to be fingerprinted, proclaiming she was a political prisoner, she also refused a physical examination. During her thirty days in jail, she read aloud to the thirty-seven women in her cellblock, giving them birth-control advice. Upon her release, she was met by society women, working mothers, and militant feminists singing the "*Marseillaise*," joined in by female prisoners still inside.

A believer in "free love" and sensual, spiritual sex, Sanger had many lovers. (She called sexologist Havelock Ellis "King" but enjoyed sex more with historian H. G. Wells, according to Irving Wallace's *The Intimate Sex Lives of Famous People* [1981].)

To her sixteen-year-old granddaughter, she once advised, "Kissing, petting, and even intercourse are all right as long as they are sincere. I have never given a kiss in my life that wasn't sincere. As for intercourse, I'd say three times a day was about right."

In 1957, the American Humanist Association named her Humanist of the Year. One reason for her nomination was that the nominating committee (Harold R. Rafton, Edwin H. Wilson, Malcolm H. Bissell, Sherman D. Wakefield, and Warren Allen Smith) recognized that honors to women had woefully been overlooked in past years. According to Wakefield, Sanger's father was a great admirer of Robert G. Ingersoll, and when Margaret was a young girl in Corning, New York, her father took her to welcome Ingersoll to town for a lecture that her father had arranged. Her admiration for Ingersoll is shown in *Margaret Sanger, An Autobiography* (1938).

In 1992, Ellen Chesler's *Woman of Valor* sympathetically details her sex-without-fear views. Judie Brown, president of the American Life League, disliked Sanger, saying her "legacy is fifty-seven types of sexually transmitted disease." Others who disliked her pointed to her 1922 book, *Pivot of Civilization*, in which she urged the segregation of "morons, misfits, and the maladjusted" and called for sterilization of "genetically inferior races." Later and in her autobiography, she singled out "the Asiatic races," lamenting that "the incessant fertility of [the Chinese] millions spread like a plague."

Alexander Cockburn is one of her few negative critics, writing (*New York Press*, 23-29 September 1998) that she "was a monster, racist, and not much discomfited by Nazi 'family planning' in the Dachau manner."

As for religion, Sanger stated, "No gods, no masters." {CE; HNS2; TRI; TYD; WWS}

Sanguinetti, Horacio (1935-)

Sanguinetti is the current President of the Argentine Humanist Society. A lawyer, teacher, and writer, he was rector of the National College of Buenos Aires and first Secretary of Education of the Autonomous City of Buenos Aires (1996-1997). Sanguinetti has written about liberal leaders like Robespierre and books on the University Reform of 1918's influence in Latin America.

Sankar, Jyothi (20th Century)

In 1971, Sankar and A. Suryanarayana founded a monthly, *Free Thought*, for the Indian Rationalist Association.

Sansom, Peter (20th Century)

Sansom is a liberal minister who was a member of the American Humanist Association. {HNS}

SANTA CLAUS

Santa Claus is not required to visit all 2,000,000,000 children under the age of eighteen, for he does not (appear to) handle the Muslim, Hindu, Jewish, and Buddhist children on Earth. This reduces his workload to perhaps 15% of the total, or 378,000,000, which based upon 3.5 children per household averages down to 91,800,000 homes. With thirty-one hours of Christmas to work with, according to John Michael Keller in *Skeptic* (Vol. 2, No. 3), thanks to the different time zones and the rotation of Earth, assuming he travels east to west (which seems logical), this works out to 822.6 visits per second. Assuming one good child in each household, this leaves Santa 1/1000th of a second to park, hop out of the sleigh, jump down the chimney, fill the stockings, distribute the remaining presents under the tree, eat whatever snacks have been left, get back up the chimney, get back into the sleigh, and move on to the next house. This means that Santa's sleigh moves at 650 miles per second, or 3,000 times the speed of sound. On land, conventional reindeer can pull no more than 300 pounds, but, assuming each child gets at least two pounds, the sleigh carries 321,300 tons, not counting the overweight Santa. Instead of only eight or nine reindeer, he needs 214,200 for such a payload, which must tote 353,430 tons (or four times the weight of the *Queen Elizabeth*). It follows that 353,430 tons traveling at 650 miles per second will create enormous air resistance. The lead pair of reindeer will absorb 14.3 quintillion joules of energy per second, each. In short, they will burst into flame almost instantaneously, exposing the reindeer behind them and creating deafening sonic booms in their wake. The entire team will be vaporized within 4.26 thousandths of a second, and Santa will be subjected to centrifugal forces 17,500.06 times greater than gravity. Thus, a 250-pound Santa would be pinned to the back of his sleigh by 4,315,015 pounds of force. This, of course, is entirely credible to Christian children, who also believe God is in Heaven and one day if they are good little boys and girls they will be rewarded by seeing Him.

In Russia, Grandfather Frost is called *Ded Moroz* (pronounced, incredibly, "dead morose").

Freethinkers tell their children the Santa myth but make it clear that the story is truly make-believe, that Santa symbolizes goodness, surprises, and sharing. (See entry for Tom W. Flynn, whom his friends call the anti-Santa Claus.)

Santa Maria, Domingo [President] (1825–1885)

In 1846 Santa Maria edited *El Orden* and from 1847 to 1850 he was Governor of Province of Colchagua, Chile. When the clericals were in power from 1851 to 1853, he had to live in Peru, and from 1858 to 1861 he was in exile, mainly in England. From 1881 to 1885 he became President of the Republic of Chile, during which time laws of divorce and civil marriage were passed and the privileges of the corrupt Church were restricted. An attempt was made to assassinate him, but at the close of his term of office Santa Maria became President of the Senate. {RAT}

Santana, José M. F. (20th Century)

Santana created a non-believer's calendar, *Uskonnottomien Kalenteri* (1983) in Swedish, and he was active in freethought affairs in Sweden. A lawyer, he helped establish the Humanist and Ethical Union of Sweden in 1979. (See entry for Scandinavian Unbelievers.)

Santayana, George (1863–1952)

Santayana, a Spanish-born U.S. philosopher and critic at Harvard University (1889–1912), is author of *The Life of Reason* (1905–1906), *Scepticism and Animal Faith* (1923), and *The Last Puritan* (1935). According to John Gouinlock, Santayana's mother was a deist, his father an atheist. Both regarded religion as a form of superstition but believed in conforming to its outward requirements. His early *The Life of Reason* (1905–1906) used the Aristotelian principle to distinguish what is ideal in human life–in art and science, society and the moral life, and religion. Reason's aim is harmony. Life teaches the lesson of human finitude, not of existence without end. If there were but one God, He would be responsible for evil as well as good. In polytheism, with its many gods which celebrate different ideal ends, religion is more robust, complete, and poetic. The Jews were the first to deny authenticity to other religions, and Christians and Muslims perpetuated this intolerance, making it a virtue. Calling himself a pessimist and one disillusioned, he meant that one must be free of illusion if he is to have a clear conception of the ideal; and to be pessimistic means to regard the universe as functioning according to laws that are indifferent to human interest and independent of human will, which explains his liking Spinoza, also one who was disillusioned and pessimistic. His naturalism was not consistently elaborated but, as Gouinlock notes, "Few philosophers have done so much to show how religion can become obscure and debased when it pretends to science; and no philosopher has argued so well that religion can be a poetic expression and celebration of temporal life."

Santayana did not fully acknowledge his homosexuality until fairly late in life. According to editor and critic Scott McLemee, Santayana told his secretary Daniel Cory after a 1929 conversation with a gay A. E. Housman that, "I think I must have been that way in my Harvard days, though I was unconscious of it at the time." McLemee added,

> One finds Santayana's clearest homophile expression in a set of four elegiac sonnets for Warwick Potter, a young man Santayana called his "last real friend," who died of cholera following a boating accident in 1893. The sequence, "To W. P." (1894) inevitably recalls Milton's "Lycidas," though Santayana's poem is much less an exercise in literary and mythological allusion than Milton's. More than "Lycidas," it seems a genuine outpouring of grief—though the sense of loss is transformed by the poet into resignation and even acceptance: "For time a sadder mask may spread / Over the face that ever should be young." The sequence ends on a note of transcendence, with his grieving friends vowing to Potter to "Keep you in whatso'ever things are good, and rear / In our weak virtues monuments to you." Even so, Santayana's most powerful lines convey the wounding permanence of loss: "And I scarce know which part may greater be— / What I keep of you, or you rob from me."

(A gay Manhattan wag has speculated as to what intended when he wrote, "My humanism was entirely confined to man.")

Santayana once wrote of his parents' influence upon his thinking:

> I had heard many Unitarian sermons (being taken to hear them lest I should become too Catholic) and had been interested in them so far as they were rationalistic and informative, or even amusingly irreligious, as I often thought them to be; but neither in these discourses nor in Harvard philosophy was it easy for me to understand the Protestant combination of earnestness with waywardness. . . . My mother, like her father before her, was a Deist: she was sure there was a God, for who else could have made the world? But God was too great to take special thought for man: sacrifices, prayers, churches, and tales of immortality were invented by rascally priests in order to dominate the foolish. My father, except for the Deism, was emphatically of the same opinion.
>
> Thus, although I learned my prayers and catechism by rote, as was then inevitable in Spain, I knew that my parents regarded all religion as a work of human imaginations, and I agreed, and still agree, with them there. . . . The necessity of naturalism as a foundation for all further serious opinions was clear to me from the beginning.

In *The Life of Reason* he explained that religion is not something to be taken as being literally true. It is merely symbolic and thoroughly human, it aims at the "life of reason," but it largely fails in attaining it. As for the gods, fear created them; but this fear and the mythology that it produces only half deceives the thinker. What is needed, he writes, is a paganizing of Christianity. It should take as its standard of value the human in life. Otherwise, it will continue with its mythology, the price of which is superstition, and although mythology and magic have their imaginative values, neither has succeeded: The Life of Reason, insofar as it is life, contains the mystic's primordial assurances, and his rudimentary joys; but in so far as it is rational it has discovered what those assurances rest on, in what direction they may be trusted to support action and thought; and it has given those joys distinction and connexion, turning a dumb momentary ecstasy into a man-colored and natural happiness."

In 1951, while convalescing at the Convent of the Blue Nuns in Italy, he wrote to the present author:

> In my old-fashioned terminology, Humanist means a person saturated by the humanities: Humanism is something cultural: an accomplishment, not a doctrine. This might be something like what you call "classical humanism." But unfortunately there is also a metaphysical or cosmological humanism or moralism which maintains that the world is governed by human interests and an alleged universal moral sense. This cosmic humanism for realists, who believe that knowledge has a prior and independent object which sense or thought signify, might be some religious orthodoxy, for idealists and phenomenalists an oracular destiny or dialectical evolution dominating the dream of life.
>
> This "humanism" is what I call egotism or moralism, and reject altogether. Naturalism, on the contrary, is something to which I am so thoroughly wedded that I like to call it materialism, so as to prevent all confusion from *romantic* naturalism like Goethe's for instance, or that of Bergson. Mine is the hard, non-humanistic naturalism of the Ionian philosophers, of Democritus, Lucretius, and Spinoza. Those professors at Columbia who tell you that in my *Idea of Christ in the Gospels* I incline to theism have not read that book sympathetically.

They forget that my naturalism is fundamental and includes man, his mind, and all his works, products of the generative order of Nature. Christ in the Gospels is a legendary figure. Spirit in him recognizes its dependence on the Father, and not monarchical government; i.e., the order of nature; and the animal will in man being thus devised, the spirit in man is freed and identified with that of the Father. My early *Lucifer,* which you mention, has the same doctrine.

Santayana in *Soliloquies in England* (1922) wrote, "Skepticism is the chastity of the intellect, and it is shameful to surrender it too soon or to the first comer. . . . My atheism, like that of Spinoza, is true piety toward the universe and denies only gods fashioned by men in their own image, to be servants of their human interests." He also wrote, in his *Reason in Science,* "A thorough Materialist, one born to the faith and not half plunged into it by an unexpected christening in cold water, will be, like the superb Democritus, a laughing philosopher."

Martin Greif has called *The Last Puritan* the best novel ever written by a philosopher. It also is one of the saddest, for it relates the story, according to A. L. Rowse, of Santayana's own unrequited love for Bertrand Russell's heterosexual brother Frank. The attraction began when Santayana was invited to go for a cruise on the Russell yacht and, although Frank had no trouble crossing the narrow plank to the boat, George almost fell into the water and had to be helped over with the aid of Frank's strong, manly arms. Even when Frank was later imprisoned for bigamy, the two maintained a correspondence. It is possible that the relationship was not totally unrequited, an allegation which came up later when Frank was sued for divorce by his wife.

Forty years later, Santayana was writing to his first inspiration, his one and only love, "You now say more than you ever 'said' to me, even in our young days, about being 'attached' . . . to me; you must have been, in some way which . . . I don't pretend to understand. In that case, why drop me now, when certainly there has been no change on my side except that involved in passing from twenty to sixty?"

Of the defects of the Russell character, for Frank once forgot George's name and called him Sargeant, Santayana wrote of Bertrand Russell: "There is a strange mixture in him, as in his brother, of great ability and great disability; prodigious capacity and brilliance here—astonishing unconsciousness and want of perception there. They are like creatures of a species somewhat different from man."

Frank appears as the anti-hero Lord Jim Darnley in *The Last Puritan,* leading Rowse to conclude that "the story may have demanded it, but there is an element of wish-fulfillment here, perfectly understandable in the circumstances."

At his request, and because of his long residence in Italy, Santayana was buried in a plot reserved for Spanish nationals in the Catholic cemetery in Rome. (See the section by Frederick A. Olafson on Santayana in the *Encyclopedia of Philosophy,* Vol. 7.) {CE; CL; EU, John Gouinlock; GL; HNS; PA; RE; TRI; TYD; WAS, 9 February 1951}

Sante, Luc (20th Century)

A leading expert on con artists, Sante is author of the introduction to David W. Maurer's *The Big Con* (1999). He also wrote *Low Life, Evidence*, and *The Factory of Facts.* (See entry for Pickpocketry, which explains how Sante's introduction helps support the view that diddling is an alternative to black-and-white/either-or choices.)

SANTERIA

Santeria has mistakenly been called "the Latin voodoo." More correctly, it is a religious outlook which originated in West Africa, one tempered in Cuba and other Caribbean countries as well as in some cities of the United States. In *casas* (houses), autonomous priests administer to their initiates, or godchildren. As *babalawos* of the Yoruba religion, the leaders—petitioning *orishas,* divine spirits—advise in matters such as love, work, and health. They feed the *orishas* sacrificial animals, such as chickens, goats, or lambs, fulfilling revelations by *iyaloshas,* or priestesses. In 1993, when Hialeah, Florida, banned such ritual animal sacrifice, the United States Supreme Court ruled unanimously that such a ban violated the Santeristas's freedom of religion. As a result, the secretive Afro-Cuban faith has become more open and has an estimated ten thousand adherents in the country, with three hundred Santeria priests in South Florida alone. Leaders claim many of their adherents are Catholics in addition to being Santeristas.

According to Russell Miller, *botánicas,* the herbal pharmacies which stock Santeria sundries, are patronized by many Puerto Ricans, Cubans, and people from the Dominican Republic who are living in the United States. When lurid news reports appear of animal parts found in parks and on street corners, animal-rights groups including the Humane Society have complained loudly that Santeristas are responsible. Although attempts are being made to form various churches, such as the Lukumi Babalu Aye in Miami, most Santeristas are said to prefer meeting in families' houses.

Lizette Alvarez has quoted Anthony Cabrera Mondesire, a Santeria priest and author, as describing Santeria:

In the Beginning

Oloddumare, the supreme being, created the universe and sent the orishas, or deities, to create life out of the elements. Therea re two master orishas: Obatala, who created human life and consciousness out of the substance of the earth, and Orumila, who governs an individual's destiny.

The Meaning of Life

The world is a place for the soul to evolve. Santeros strive to be of service to others, to develop good character and to keep a cool head. There are two other types of people: bystanders and those who are destructive. All humans go to heaven—ikole orun—when they die, but destructive people live in hell on earth and suffer in heaven.

Good and evil

The terms are too subjective, since what can be good for one person can be evil for another. Instead, forces in the universe are either constructive or destructive for humanity. In either case, they are controlled by orishas.

Affecting Fate

With the help of priests, who can divine the past, present, and future, individuals can appeal to the orishas through prayers, music, proper behavior, and offerings of food, flowers, or other items and, in initiations or dire straits, animal blood.

Priesthood

Women can become priests, but only men can become high priests. Priests are the only ones who can interpret the laws expressed in the 256 symbols of the Ifa Corpus, a codification of Santeria tradition. Each priest receives an individualized set of taboos, which can include prohibitions on alcohol use, promiscuity, or illegal activities, for example.

Following is a printed set of directions given to a person who told his priestess that he was having personal problems:

Read Psalm 20 THREE TIMES over black and red candle
Light black candle at 11 PM
Light red candle at 6 AM
Put mix into basin of water and read Psalm 20 THREE TIMES over it
In the morning put the clothes that you are wearing on the WRONG SIDE and sprinkle mix lightly unto them
While sprinkling mix say: IN THE NAME OF GOD THE FATHER, IN THE NAME OF GOD THE SON, AND IN THE NAME OF GOD THE HOLY GHOST
Shake clothes 3 TIMES and put them back on RIGHT SIDE
Then put clothes on bed and use the remaining water to clean your face.
Then put clothes on.
Get A GLASS OF RUM AND 3 CIGARETTES, light the cigarettes, and put behind the door
When leaving the house open the door and throw the rum outside and say: ST. MICHAEL! ST. MICHAEL! ST. MICHAEL! PLEASE DEFEND ME
Take a little Bible with you and read PSALM 4

The individual said that the fivc differently colored candles had cost over $15 each. He did not mention the cost of a variety of liquids in small vials which he was supposed to mix.

{Russell Miller, "A Leap of Faith," *The New York Times,* 30 January 1994; Lizette Alvarez, *The New York Times,* 27 January 1997; WAS}

Saphin, Edward C. (20th Century)

Saphin, a freethinker, wrote "What Does the Bible Conceal?" (19–?). {GS}

Sapir, Louis (20th Century)

Sapir was a President of the Society for Ethical Culture in New York City.

Saposnekow, Jacob (20th Century)

Saposnekow, whose alma mater was City College of New York, was a naturalistic humanist. {HNS}

Sappho (c. 630 B.C.E.)

Sappho, who was the greatest of the early Greek lyric poets and the earliest woman author whose work survives, was an aristocrat, a teacher, and an extensive writer of poetry. Plato called her "the tenth Muse." Inasmuch as her island home was Lesbos and her circle of friends were mostly but not exclusively women, she has become the archetypal lesbian and symbolic mother of lesbians. Little of her total output of writing still survives. Legend has it that when church father Tatian branded Sappho a whore in 140 C.E., her books were burned by the Christians. One version of the legend claims it was in 380 at the time of Gregory Nazianzen, whereas others set the burning in Constantinople and Rome in 1073.

Sappho freely wrote about the gods and called upon Aphrodite not as a fearsome deity but as a mentor and confidante, the translator Anita George has pointed out. George added, "To perhaps overenthusiastic lesbians and feminists, Sappho represents a utopian dream: a socially prominent woman of influence and genius dwelling in a matriarchal society." However, George holds that Sappho's very real accomplishment was that "she lived proudly as a lesbian and achieved everlasting fame as a poet in spite of the severe obstacles posed by her society." {GL}

Saramago, José (1922-)

Saramago in 1998 became the first Portuguese-language writer to win the Nobel Prize in Literature. The Swedish Academy praised Saramago "who with parables sustained by imagination, compassion, and irony continually enable us once again to apprehend an illusory reality."

A 1989 work, *The History of the Siege of Lisbon*, has an humble publishing house proofreader inserting a "not" into a history of Portugal, leading to the work's affirming that the Crusaders did *not* help liberate 12-century Lisbon from Moorish occupation.

Critics have praised his use of the supernatural, the allegorical, the paradoxical, and the irrational in his questioning of faith and existence. In a satire, *The Gospel According to Jesus Christ* (1991), God mixes his seed with Joseph's, resulting in Jesus's decidedly nonvirgin conception. Further, God shows the innocent human Jesus how to create a religion that will spawn violence and intolerance. Using unusual punctuation and leaps in time, the story not only gives Saramago's version of Jesus's life but also refers to what has happened to Christianity in the interim. "It is apparent," Alan Riding has written, "that he knows his Bible, and he treats the figure of Jesus with compassion, as a victim of a power struggle between God and the Devil. But his underlying message is that religion has turned man against man in wars, massacres, exterminations, autos-da-fé, and the like, 'all in the name of God.' " The country's center-right Government vetoed the novel's choice as a 1992 European literary prize and called the work blasphemous. Furious, he left Lisbon and moved to the Canary Islands with his wife, Pilar del Rio, a Spanish journalist.

In *Blindness* (1998), blindness overcomes all the human population but one person, a woman. While anarchy and bestiality abound all around, the streets filling with filth, this one woman becomes a mother and a god to all around her. She helps guide. She illustrates how humanity is achieved through suffering. She uses tenderness to help the blind see again, the novelist implying that it is illogical for mankind to wait until horrors occur, that humans are fully able to see how to overcome their figurative blindness.

Saramago, who because of poverty left school to become a car mechanic, has a working man's outlook. He is a member of Portugal's outlawed Communist Party and was a journalist until the revolution of 1974. An atheist in a Roman Catholic and conservative land, he was temporarily amused when for the second year running the Nobel had gone to someone the Vatican perceives to be anti-religious. "Why does the Vatican get involved in these things?" he asked. "Why doesn't it keep itself busy with prayers? Why doesn't it instead open its cupboards and reveal the skeletons it has inside?"

When journalists approached, he told them, "If the Pope were on the jury, they [Nobel Committee] wouldn't have given me anything. The Vatican is easily scandalized, especially by people from outside. They should just focus on their prayers and leave people in peace. I respect those who believe, but I have no respect for the institution."

Saramago signed Humanist Manifesto 2000. {CA; Tim Parks, "Sightgeist," *The New York Review of Books*, 18 February 1999; Alan Riding, *The New York Times*, 9 and 12 October 1998 and 3 December 1998}

Sarandon, Susan (1946-)

Sarandon, an actress seen in the movie "Thelma and Louise," has been quoted as saying, "I'm really a Humanist," adding to the *Los Angeles Times* reporter that her role as Louise was not to present men in a negative light and that she rejects the "feminist" label.

Sarcey, Fracisque (1827–1899)

Sarcey was a French critic, the editor of *Le XIXe. Siècle*. He wrote plays, novels, and many anti-clerical articles. In his *Souvenirs de jeunesse* (1884) and *Souvenirs d'âge mûr*, Sarcey tells of his rejection of all religious beliefs. {BDF; RAT; RE}

Sardou, Victorien (1831–1908)

Sardou became one of the best dramatists of the nineteenth century, and he wrote more than seventy plays. His farce comedy is *Divorçons!* (1880). In *Fédora* (1882), Sarah Bernhardt made her triumphant return to the Paris stage. Two plays were written for Sir Henry Irving, *Robespierre* (1899) and *Dante* (1903), but were never given in French. Sardou had abandoned Catholicism early in life, and although Spiritualists quote him as one of their conquests McCabe states that he was not, that he was a rationalist. Sardou was elected to the French Academy. {RAT; RE; TRI}

Sargent, Denny (20th Century)

Sargent wrote *Global Ritualism: Myth and Magic Around the World*, a non-theological discussion by a freethinker about the value and use of ritual.

Sargent, Doris E. (20th Century)

Sargent was secretary and a member of the board of directors in 1954 of the Humanist Fellowship of Boston.

Sargent, Mike (20th Century)

Sargent in Britain is active with the Worthing Humanist Group.

Sargent, Pamela (1948–)

Sargent, an author, wrote *Cloned Lives* (1976), *The Golden Space* (1982), and *Ruler of the Sky* (1983). She has edited an anthology, *Women of Wonder* (1975) and received numerous awards for her writing.

Asked by interviewer Jill Engle which books had influenced her as a child, she listed some by E. B. White, Grimm, Bulfinch, Walter Farley, Fred Hoyle's *The Nature of the Universe*, Betty Friedan's *The Feminine Mystique*. "Oh, and the Bible, believe it or not, even though I was brought up as an atheist," she added. "The Old Testament's full of good stories, my personal favorites being those of David and Esther. I never could get into the New Testament." {CA; E}

Sargent, Porter (1872–1951)

A publisher of handbooks concerning private schools, Sargent in 1935 wrote *The New Immoralities: Clearing the Way for a New Ethics.* {HNS}

Sarlin, Alfred Bernhard (1860–1919)

A Finnish writer, Sarlin was an influential journalist who wrote two controversial books, *Rules by the Grace of God* (1908) and *Russia in the Light of the Facts* (1908). He was condemned to four months in prison for translating Kropotkin's *Terror in Russia*, and in 1912 he began a large work, *Humbug as Lord of the World*, which was to consist of twenty parts and deal drastically with religious shams. Only nine parts were published at the time of his death. They were aggressively rationalistic, and Sarlin was condemned to six more months in prison. {RAT}

Sarma, Armadeo (20th Century)

Sarma is the convenor of the Society for the Scientific Examination of Para-Science (GWUP) in Rossdorf, Germany. He also is a representative of Euroskeptics.

Sarmiento, Domingo Faustino [President] (1811–1888)

Sarmiento was an Argentine leader who opposed Catholic doctrine. A predecessor of positivism, he believed Catholicism could best be opposed by removing its economic foundations—which were based on feudal structures—and by promoting free enterprise and laissez-faire economics. An opponent of Juan Manuel de Rosas, Sarmiento spent years of exile in Chile, becoming known as a journalist and an educational reformer. He helped overthrow Rosas in 1852.

Alberdi was the main architect of the constitution in 1853, and Sarmiento was president of Argentina from 1868–1874. During Sarmiento's term of office, a law was passed establishing civil marriage as the only legal marriage in Argentina. His administration was also marked by the conclusion of the War of the Triple Alliance against Paraguay, by material progress, and, especially, by the organization of schools and the reform of educational methods. Sarmiento wrote *Facundo, o Civilización i barbarie* (1845; translated as *Life in the Argentine Republic in the Days of the Tyrant*, nominally a biography of Juan Facundo Quiroga but actually a criticism of *caudillismo*, personalism in politics. {CE; EU}

Saro-Wiwa, Ken: See entry for Poets.

Saroyan, William (1908–1981)

A prolific writer, Saroyan wrote *The Time of Your Life* (1939), for which he received a Pulitzer prize. He also is known for *The Human Comedy* (1942) and short stories such as "My Name is Aram" (1940). Asked for his views of humanism, Saroyan responded to the present author in what some say was his typical fashion:

> The fellows from whom you have received comments are the fellows for the job, I'm not. First of all, I don't understand what any of it's about. I think living is an animal event, although the animal has become quite sophisticated, artistic, cunning, and/or phoney. I am not, however, as some fools allege anti-intellectual. I can exchange ideas with anybody and have always found doing so a fine animal pleasure, especially when I do most or all of the talking, which is the case very nearly every time. I think man's soul has been probed so deeply and humorlessly that all of the probing has become boring and virtually meaningless. It appears to be—this probing, that is—a substitute for actual living or an escape from a sense of guilt and failure for having lived poorly or ineffectually. (Refer to the first sentence of this paragraph and let me quickly get the hell out of here.)
>
> I am opposed to the latter four kinds of humanism you mention—theistic humanism, atheistic humanism, communistic humanism, naturalistic humanism. I am glad I didn't write any of the books you mention and glad I wrote the ones I wrote. And I wish you every success because I expect that will make you glad.
>
> {WAS, 3 April 1951}

Sarraga de Ferrero, Belén (20th Century)

A Spanish educationist, Sarraga in Malaga edited a rationalist and feminist organ, *Conciencia Libre*. In Montevideo, Uruguay, in 1910, she edited *Liberal*. Sarraga attended the International Freethought Congresses at Rome (1904) and Paris (1905). {RAT; WWS}

"Sarrasi" (19th Century)

Sarrasi was a pseudonym of A. de C., a French Orientalist who wrote *L'Orient Devoilé* (1880), in which he shows the mythical elements in Christianity although remaining anonymous. {BDF}

Sars, Georg Ossian (1837–1927)

Sars taught zoology at Christiania University and was one of the eminent Norwegian scientists of his time. He supported Haeckel's Monism. On Haeckel's eightieth birthday, Sars described the much-derided *Riddle of the Universe* as "the stately structure of the Monistic philosophy" and declared that "progress can be promoted no longer by metaphysical speculations and antiquated theological dogmas." {RAT; RE}

Sarton, George (1884–1955)

Sarton, a Harvard historian, wrote in his *History of Science*, "The most malicious kind of hatred is that which is built upon a theological foundation." He was author of *The Faith of a Humanist* (1912) and *The History of Science and the New Humanism* (1931). {TYD}

Sarton, May (1912–1995)

Sarton was born in Belgium but moved to Massachusetts at the age of four when her father became a Harvard professor. By the age of eighteen she had had two poems accepted by Harriet Monroe's *Poetry*. *Encounter in April* (1936), her first book of lyrics, was followed by several volumes of poetry. *The Single Hound* (1938) was published by Elizabeth Bowen, by that time her lover. When thirty-four, Sarton fell in love with a Simmons College English teacher, Judy Matlack, moving in with her.

Margot Peters, in *May Sarton: A Biography* (1997), details the literary bad girl's love affairs with numbers of individuals from Muriel Rukeyser to her own shrink. Included are the drunken brawls, her father's paying for girlfriends' ship tickets, her mediocre reviews, her teaching at Wellesley, and her winning a Guggenheim. Included are details of her intense relationships, her compelling hunger for affection, and her disappointments at not being known for her work but, rather, for being a spokeswoman for lesbian coming out.

Sarton's novels include *Faithful Are the Wounds* (1955), which describes a distinguished Harvard professor's life and suicide; *I Knew a Phoenix* (1959), which were sketches for an autobiography; *Mrs. Stevens Hears the Mermaids Singing* (1965), an openly lesbian novel in which she revealed her homosexuality; and *At Seventy: A Journal* (1985), which received the American Book Award. Published posthumously in 1995 was *At Eighty-Two*, based upon the journal she kept up to her death and containing her annoyance at being old: uncertain balance, clumsy fingers, mislaid names and objects, inadequate strength, frequent pain, and the admission that "words do not obey me anymore."

Although in the 1990s the National Endowment of the Arts frowned upon giving financial grants to anyone who was homosexual or lesbian, Sarton in 1967 had received NEA grant money. She stated she was "proud of the fact that I came out as a lesbian in 1965" but that she had done so only after her parents' deaths. "I'm not sure I would have done it if they had been alive." She objected to being labeled a "lesbian writer," adding, "I think my work is universal, and I think my value is as a maker of bridges between two worlds—homosexuals and heterosexuals, between old and young, between men and women."

A Unitarian, she taught or lectured at Harvard, Wellesley, the University of Chicago, the University of Iowa, Colorado College, Beloit College, the University of Kansas, and Dennison University. In 1993 at the First Parish Unitarian Church in Brookline, Massachusetts, where funeral services were held for a 100-year-old elm tree, felled to make room for constructing a school, Sarton's poetry was featured. She had written, "Is there a more unnerving sound than the hideous mechanistic screech of a buzz saw at work? It is an anti-sound; it does not fit with any landscape."

Sarton was a long-time friend of the actress Eva le Gallienne, with whom she studied acting and who also a non-believer. Upon becoming an octogenarian in 1993, Sarton wrote *Encore: A Journal of the 80th Year*, discreetly making no further mention, as she had in a 1973 journal, that she, like the Mrs. Stevens of the 1965 novel, was a woman homosexual who is not a sex maniac, a drunkard, a drug-taker, or in any way repulsive . . . a homosexual who is neither pitiable nor disgusting, without sentimentality. Such a revelation by so stellar a poet made her an immediate heroine to feminists. Although ignored by most critics, Sarton was described by Enid Nemy as "a commanding, no-nonsense figure with clear blue eyes and a shock of white hair," a woman who lived in "self-imposed loneliness" in a weathered clapboard house on the Maine coast. She had had, she admitted, a difficult life being a seeker after truths, an ardent explorer of life's important questions.

An individualistic and stoical figure, Sarton died of breast cancer. Asked before her death how she would like to be remembered, she replied, "As wholly human." {CE; GL; U}

Sartre, Jean-Paul (1905–1980)

A French existentialist, a philosopher greatly influenced by Heidegger, and a 1964 Nobel Prize winner (he declined the honor), Sartre once wrote, "Thus the passion of man is the reverse of that of Christ, for man loses himself as man in order that God may be born. But the idea of God is contradictory and we lose ourselves in vain. Man is a useless passion." Sartre's entire body of works made the Vatican's list of prohibited reading in 1948.

His mother was a Schweitzer from Alsace, and the 5' 4" Sartre was first cousin to Albert Schweitzer. The two dominant personalities, both of whom had been reared as Lutherans, were almost polar opposites in their philosophic outlooks.

Sartre's 1938 novel, *Nausea*, describes the hero's discovery of the meaningless contingency of all existents, human and nonhuman. His *Being and Nothingness* in 1943 became the central work of humanistic existentialism. It described the plight of the individual in a God-less world without objective meaning, one in which humans had to make their own values. *No Exit* in 1944 contains the line, "So that's what Hell is. I'd never have believed it. . . . Do you remember, brimstone, the stake, the gridiron, [when it comes to] hell, it's other people!"

Typical of his atheistic humanism are these statements: "The doctrine I am presenting is the very opposite of quietism, since it declares that there is no reality except in action. It goes further and adds that Man is nothing else than his plan; he exists only to the extent that he fulfills himself; he is therefore nothing else than his life. . . . Man is anguish. He lives forlornly in a world without God. He has nothing to cling to within himself, nor without. . . . Existentialism is nothing else than an attempt to draw all the consequences of a coherent atheistic position. It isn't trying to plunge man into despair. It declares that even if God did exist that would change nothing. Not that we believe God exists, but we think that the problem of His existence is not the point. In this sense Existentialism is optimistic, a doctrine of action. Man cannot start making excuses for himself. There is no determinism. Man is free. The coward makes himself cowardly. The hero makes himself heroic. What counts is total involvement."

In his *Existentialism as a Humanism* (1946), Sartre rejected theism because, according to Paul Edwards in *God and the Philosophers*,

> It is incompatible with free will in the somewhat peculiar sense in which he takes it to be a basic fact about human beings. If there were a God, he would create human beings with a "nature" or "essence," and this is incompatible with Sartre's view that in man existence precedes essence. This seems to mean that human beings do not have an essence until they have chosen their initial "fundamental projects," Sartre's term for character traits. Sartre maintains that at the age of five or six a child makes his first fundamental choice which gives him his early character. This choice can at any time be undone so that the person acquires a different character or essence. The initial fundamental choice was not even in principle predictable. Even God, if there were a God, could not have known it in advance.

In 1966–1967, although he and Bertrand Russell differed on philosophic questions, Sartre joined the International War Crimes Tribunal which found the United States guilty of genocide during the war with North Vietnam.

Upon Sartre's death, no public ceremonies were planned, but an estimated 25,000 to 50,000 people came spontaneously to pay tribute at his funeral. In Moscow, *Izvestia* noted the death with only five lines. Sartre is one of the many celebrities buried at Montparnasse (for example, André Citroën, Guy de Maupassant, the Iowan actress Jean Seberg, Pierre Laval, Alfred Dreyfus).

The following year, Simone de Beauvoir published *Adieux: A Farewell to Sartre* (1981), in which she told of his last months, his being incontinent, his young companions, and his stashing of whisky bottles, rather than his interest in evaluating his political legacy. Some of what she failed to include, Bianca Lamblin added in *A Disgraceful Affair: Simone de Beauvoir, Jean-Paul Sartre, & Bianca Lamblin* (1996). Lamblin, a redheaded Polish-born Jew who had come to France with her parents as a baby in 1922, had become hopelessly infatuated with Beauvoir, her high school teacher with whom she had sex. She then had sex after Beauvoir introduced her to Sartre, then thirty-three, who also became her teacher at the Sorbonne. In 1940, when Lamblin was dropped by Sartre, then by Beauvoir, she was infuriated and the following year married Bernard Lamblin, a fellow student. Mrs. Lamblin wrote in her book that she would never have written her memoirs except that Beauvoir had written pettily and vengefully about her and, "nauseated and disgusted when I discovered the true personality of the woman I had loved all my life," she published the work, entitled *Mémoires d'Une Jeune Fille Dérangée*, a play on Beauvoir's *Mémoires d'Une Jeune Fille Rangée*. Lamblin holds that Beauvoir had introduced her and others to Sartre in order to satisfy his "need for romantic conquests," particularly after his own interest in Beauvoir had cooled. Although Lamblin faced danger as a Jew, Sartre and Beauvoir "never worried about my fate or tried to get news of me" from the end of 1940 until the liberation in 1944.

In *Past Imperfect, French Intellectuals, 1944–1956*, Tony Judt damns Sartre as being a national embarrassment, not an asset, because he failed to test his political thoughts against political realities. Sartre, Judt declares, argued away the brutalities of Stalinism, was deluded or perverse, and thought too much but saw too little. Judt, however, does not attack other intellectuals, such as political commentator Raymond Aron, Catholic novelist François Mauriac, publisher Jean Paulhan, and the humanist Albert Camus. (See the article by Frederick A. Olafson on Sartre in the *Encyclopedia of Philosophy*, Vol. 7.) {CB; CE; CL; EU, Hazel E. Barnes; ILP, Additus, 15 December 1961; PA; TYD; TRI}

Sass, F. (20th Century)

In the 1950s, Sass was a Uruguayan correspondent for *The Humanist*.

SASTRIYA HETUVADAM

A Telugu monthly about scientific rationalism, *Sastriya Hetuvadam* is at 3-15 A.P. Housing Board Colony, Moula Ali 500 040, India

SATAN

To believers within Judaism and Christianity, Satan is God's adversary and is the lord of evil. In pre-exilic Jewish thought the figure of Satan was not known, and Judaism held that there was but one divine power, one God. The Zoroastrian view held that in life there are two ways of life which are in conflict: the good, and the evil. This ancient Persian belief, which pre-dated Judaism, was that earthly as well as spiritual beings must choose the good or the evil side in the battle. Evidence of the Zoroastrian influence is found in *Zechariah* 3:1-2, *Job*, I:1; and *I Corinthians* 21:1.

As explained in the *Encyclopedia of Religion* by Julian Morgenstern, then the President of Hebrew Union College in Cincinnati, Ohio, "The absolute monotheism of normative Judaism affirmed that there was only one divine power, one God, and, in purposed refutation of the dominant Persian dualism of the day, that He was the creator of both light and darkness, the source of evil as well as good (*Isaiah* 45: 6-7). But to the popular Jewish mind of that day dualism seemed to solve conveniently one of the baffling problems of existence, the problem of good and evil, and so, contrary to the tenets of official Judaism, evolved the figure of Satan, patterned obviously after the Zoroastrian power of evil, Ahriman. Actually Satan never had any place in the theology of normative Judaism. The name, *Satan*, in Hebrew means "adversary; accuser"; and just this role Satan plays in the Old Testament and in subsequent Jewish apocalyptic literature. He is the adversary of God and man. He seeks to frustrate God's purposes of good and to entice men to defy God and do evil. Then he accuses them before God and brings about their punishment and destruction. However in Jewish thought and legend Satan was never more than a figure of secondary rank and power, always subordinate to God and subject to discipline by Him. Only in Christianity, as it emerged from Judaism, did Satan come to be regarded as a divine being; altogether independent of and hostile to God, the malevolent worker of evil in the world, and thus to be identified with the Devil."

The Yazidis, part of Iraq's Kurdish minority, have been branded by many Christians and Muslims as devil worshipers. Chris Hedges, writing from Sheik Adi, Iraq, for *The New York Times* (31 May 1993), said the Yazidis believe that Satan, "whose name they are forbidden to pronounced, is actively malevolent, while God is passively benevolent. To ward off evil, as well as use the powers of the Prince of Darkness to their own advantage, they propitiate Satan's representative, known as the Peacock Angel, in their religious rites." The sect follows the teachings of Sheik Adi, a holy man who died in 1162, whose crypt lies in the shrine in the Lalish Valley, about 15 miles east of Mosul. Writes Hedges, "Yazidis are not allowed to harm plants or animals in the valley. And pilgrims reverently wash themselves in the streams in purification rites before visiting the shrine. Yazidis have no public places for worship outside of the sacred valley, where believers gather to celebrate the four yearly festivals. Like Zoroastrians they venerate fire, the sun, and the mulberry tree. They believe in the transmigration of souls, often into animals. The sect does not accept converts and banishes anyone who marries outside the faith. Yazidis are forbidden to disclose most of their rituals and beliefs to nonbelievers." Sheik Adi's coffin is draped with green and white silk sheets in a sanctuary that contains a stone carving of a six-foot-high snake on the right side of the front door. The snake is blackened each day with shoe polish and venerated by worshipers. "We are not allowed to kill black snakes," said Baba Shaweesh, who wears dreadlocks and has a scraggly beard. "The snakes have magical powers it is best not to challenge." Baba Shaweesh became a eunuch, one of the last ceremonial eunuchs in the Middle East, "to resist the temptation of the flesh." He carried out the operation himself with a knife and the juice from some medicinal plants to heal the wound. To the reporter he stated that he can divine the future but will not relate everything he sees to his followers because, "I receive wisdom in my dreams. I see when men will die and days later preside over their funerals. I am visited by Sheik Adi, who tells me what will take place in the weeks and months ahead. But there is a lot I do not tell to others. How much can people accept? It is often best in this world to be ignorant."

Nonbelievers find ludicrous such imaginative inventions as Satan and the Devil. Many believers, however, speak of both with fear. A 1997 study by the Barna Research Group in Oxnard, California, found that an estimated two-thirds of Americans do not believe in the Devil as a living entity, that Satan is "not a living being, but is a symbol of evil," this despite Jesus's declaration to "Get thee hence, Satan" (*Matthew* 4:10).

(See entries for Ahriman, Beelzebub, Devil, and Elaine Pagels. McCabe's *Rationalist Encyclopedia* suggests that the concept of Satan was "borrowed" by the Jews in the second century from the Babylonian mythology which was then current. Other scholars, such as Norman Cohn, a Fellow of the British Academy, hold that Satan originated as a Judaized version of the Zoroastrian spirit of evil, Ahriman.) {CE; ER}

SATAN, CHURCH OF

The Church of Satan was founded by Anton Szandor La Vey (1930–1997). Called the "Black Pope," he became noted in the 1960s for using a "Satanic Bible," a work said to have been based on a Spenserian tract by the pseudonymous Ragnar Redbeard and entitled *Might is Right*.

La Vey held that the cardinal principle of Satanism was indulgence, that there is no need for any God in one's outlook, and the best way to show contempt for God is to enjoy people.

In Los Angeles his daughter Zeena operates an occult-oriented and true-crime book store called Hellhouse, one which had Adolf Hitler PEZ dispensers and (convicted killer) Charles Manson lunchboxes. Estranged from her father, Zeena drives around Los Angeles in a hearse.

When La Vey's wife, Diane, filed for divorce, the settlement forced him to liquidate his assets, which included the Church of Satan. Journalist Alan Cabal (*New York Press*, 12–18 November 1997) observed, "It was dissolved in bankruptcy court, a fitting end for an organization that never had the slightest meaning beyond shock value. Various tinpot wannabes have attempted to keep the name going, but the cognoscenti of the Satanic tradition abandoned it decades ago when it became apparent that the Church was nothing more than a cash cow."

SATANISM

Satanism is a term invented by religious fundamentalists, one which implies that a living Satan exists and that profoundly wicked people choose to worship Satan instead of God. These Satanists allegedly abduct innocent children, burn houses of worship, are responsible for morally bad events, use 13 and 666 as secret passwords, and are dedicated to anti-religious causes.

In 1995, the Proctor & Gamble Company sued a distributor of Amway, a competitor, alleging that it was spreading rumors linking the company to Satanism. For over fifteen years the company had been fighting a rumor that its president had spoken in support of Satanism on a nationally televised talk show and that the company's moon-and-stars trademark is a Satanic symbol. No one from the company had ever discussed Satanism on a talk show, Proctor & Gamble argued, and its trademark dates from the mid-1800's, when a man in the moon was a popular design and when its thirteen stars in the logo design was chosen to honor the thirteen original colonies.

SATORI

Satori is the Japanese word for the state of enlightenment sought in Zen Buddhism.

SATYAN VESHAN (Prabodh)

A Gujarati monthly, *Satyan Veshan (Prabodh)* is at 3 Abhinav Park, Ghod dod Road, Surat, Gujarat, 395001, India.

Saul, John Ralston (20th Century)

Saul, who in 1995 was designated Canadian Humanist of the Year by the Humanist Association of Canada, wrote *Voltaire's Bastards* (1993) and *The Doubter's Companion* (1994). In the latter book, subtitled "A Dictionary of Aggressive Common Sense," Saul writes in a style reminiscent of Bierce. He has given the prestigious Massey Lectures in Toronto. {CA; E}

Saul, Marjorie Joan (1923–)

Saul, who arrived in Australia in 1924 from England, is a humanist, agnostic, secretary, and journalist. Although reared in the Church of England, she left the church when a student at Sydney University. From 1980 to 1981, she was president of the Humanist Society of New South Wales, and she was convenor of the humanist sub-committee investigating the incidence of female genital mutilation in Australia. She contacted Muslim women's groups and disseminated information to women's health organizations in order to eradicate the practice. During the late 1970s and early 1980s she was the sexist advertising contact for the Women's Electoral Lobby investigating the stereotyped portrayal of women in advertising. {SWW}

Saull, William Devonshire (1783–1855)

Saull was an English geologist who established a free geological museum, contributed to the erection of the John Street Institute, and was principally instrumental in opening the old Hall of Science, City Road. Saull wrote about the connection between astronomy and geology. He is buried in Kensal Green, near his friends Allen Davenport and Henry Hetherington. {BDF; RAT; VI}

Saumur, Lucien (20th Century)

Saumur wrote *The Humanist Evangel* (1982). {GS}

Saunders, Thomas Bailey (Born 1860)

Saunders, a lawyer and writer, translated into English many works of Schopenhauer. He also translated Harnack and *The Maxims and Reflections of Goethe* (1893). His own rationalism is shown in *Quest of Faith* (1899), where he rejected the creeds and accepted only "a co-ordinating Power." {RAT}

Saunderson, Nicholas (1682–1739)

Saunderson, an English mathematician, lost both his eyes and his sight by smallpox when but a year old, yet he became conversant with Euclid, Archimedes, and Diophantus when read to him in Greek. He lectured at Cambridge University, explaining Newton's Mathematical Principles of Natural Philosophy, even his works on light and color. It was said, Wheeler reports, "They have turned out Whiston (a Unitarian) for believing in but one God, and put in Saunderson, who believes in no God at all." The same author was pained that a man who experienced "the kindness of Providence throughout his extraordinary life [should be guilty of] the obtrusion of infidel opinions," apparently unaware that Saunderson was blind for fifty-five years. Saunderson said that to believe in God he must first touch him. {BDF; RAT; RE}

Sauvestre, Charles (1818–1883)

Sauvestre was a French journalist, one of the editors of *L'Opinion Nationale*. He wrote *The Clergy and Education* (1861), *Secret*

Instructions of the Jesuits (1865), *Religious Congregations Unveiled* (1870), and other anti-clerical works. {BDF}

Savage, Dan (20th Century)

Savage writes a sex advice column, formerly called "Hey, Faggot," now called "Savage Love," in *Village Voice* and other alternative weeklies. Typical of his hilarious but rational advice is what he responded to a gay man who, when he was with another man, said he felt as if he was "being watched . . . by God or angels in the room."

Advised Savage, "Let me walk you through this: If there were such things as angels—which there are not—and if there were such a thing as God—which there is not—God and his heavenly host would have more important things to do than stand at the foot of your bed and watch you get fucked in the ass." {CA}

Savage, Maxwell (20th Century)

A Unitarian minister, Savage wrote, "Since Christ was human, born within the circle of history, he becomes of true value to us who are human, for now, in the light of the full spiritual and moral stature of his life we can try to live our own lives as truly as he lived his; not imitating him, but inspired by him. The Christ, a God, is outside our circle since we are not superhuman. Need for him has ceased. He should be allowed to join the line of lesser gods who have gone into oblivion."

Savage, Minot Judson (1841–1918)

At first a Congregational minister in Framingham, Massachusetts, Savage after a long process of growth toward liberalism converted to Unitarianism. His *Religion of Evolution* (1876) was one of the earliest attempts to extract religiously satisfying and optimistic conclusions from evolutionary theory, and his sermons on the subject found an enormously responsive audience in Chicago, Boston, and New York. As an orator, he was considered one of the great preachers of his era.

The Beacon Press's 1937 *Hymns of the Spirit* contained Savage's words for a pantheistic hymn (which has been modified as "Why Seek Afar For Beauty?" Although unpublished, the hymn has been taped by Warren Allen Smith with his somewhat modified words and performed with his music):

> Why seek afar for beauty? Look, it glows
> In dew-wet grasses all about your feet;
> In birds, in sunshine, childish faces sweet,
> In stars and mountain summits topped with snows.
>
> Go not abroad for happiness. For, see,
> It is a flower blooming at your door.
> Bring love and justice home, and then no more
> Will you wonder in what dwelling joy may be.
>
> In wonder-workings, or some bush aflame,
> Men look for God and fancy him concealed.
> But in Earth's beauty nature stands revealed,
> While grass and flowers and stars spell out her name.

{CE; U; U&U}

Savage, Rick (20th Century)

Savage is a director of the National Secular Society.

Savonarola, Girolamo (1452–1498)

Savonarola was an Italian religious reformer, a Dominican who was popular in Florence because of his eloquent attacks on moral laxity. Pope Alexander VI excommunicated him (1497) because Savonarola ignored his order to stop preaching. Savonarola was finally executed as a false prophet. (See entry for Pierre van Paassen.)

SAVANT OF VIRGINIA

Abraham B. Carter has published *Savant of Virginia*, a work which includes many writers who were members of the Society of Evangelical Agnostics. {FD}

Savary, Anne Jean Marie René [Duc de Rovigo] (1774–1833)

Savary, a French soldier, joined the army in 1790, fought with distinction in the German and Egyptian campaigns, and was made a brigadier-general after Marengo by Napoleon. In 1807 he was created Duc de Rovigo and appointed Governor of East Prussia. He then commanded an army in Spain, and in 1831 was given the supreme command in Algeria by Louis Philippe. Savary's *Memoirs* are evidence of his rationalism. {RAT}

Savelle, Max (20th Century)

Savelle wrote *Seeds of Liberty: The Genesis of the American Mind* (1948), a study of how deism developed in the United States prior to the American Revolution. {FUS}

Savile, George: See entry for Charles Halifax.

Sawtelle, C. M. (19th Century)

Sawtelle was the American author of *Reflections on the Science of Ignorance* (1868), or as he explained, how to teach others what you do not know yourself. {BDF}

Sawyer, Caroline (Born 1812)

Sawyer, a Unitarian, was a 19th-century poet and writer. {U}

Sawyer, Robert J. (20th Century)

A Canadian science fiction writer, Sawyer in 1996 responded to questions some readers had submitted to *Science Fiction Weekly*. One reader asked about *The Terminal Experiment*, in which Sawyer introduced the concept of the "Soulwave" and wondered if this idea was born out of hope or personal belief. Sawyer responded,

> The idea of the soulwave isn't really born of either hope or personal belief. I believe that when we die, we're eaten by worms—end of story. That's one of the reasons why *The Terminal Experiment* debunks the so-called near-death experience. But I do think that questions of immortality fascinate writers—they crop up again in my latest novel, *Starplex*. After all, we write so that something of ourselves will survive our death.

{CA}

Sawyer, Thomas Jefferson (1804–1899)

One of the greatest of the pioneer educators of 19th century, Sawyer founded *The Christian Messenger* (1831), helped found the Universalist Historical Society 1834), and was dean of Tufts Divinity School (1882–1890). {U; U&U}

Sax, Karl (Born 1892)

Sax, a naturalistic humanist, was a scientist and member of the American Humanist Association. Concerned about the world's food supply and Earth's diminishing natural resources, he wrote in *Standing Room Only, the World's Exploding Population* (1955). The work had a profound influence upon Priscilla Robertson, then editor of *The Humanist,* who developed a strategy for encouraging international efforts to publicize one of mankind's greatest dilemmas, one that became exponentially worse in the 1990s. {HNS; HNS2}

Say, Jean Baptiste Léon (1826–1896)

Say was a pioneer of the Cooperative Movement and was France's Minister of Finance after 1871. He also became President of the Senate. Like his friend President Thiers, Say was an agnostic. {RAT; RE}

Sayers, Dorothy L.: See entry for Theism.

Sayles, John (1950–)

Sayles is a film director, writer, and actor. He wrote *Pride of the*

Bimbos (1975), *The Anarchists Convention* (1979), and "Los Gusanos" (1991). He is a MacArthur Foundation grantee and works for Paramount Pictures. According to Celebrity Atheists, Sayles's politics is "survivalist" and his religion is "Roman Catholic Atheist." {CA; E}

Sayre-McCord, Geoffrey (1956–)

Sayre-McCord, of the University of North Carolina, is on the Executive Committee of The Hume Society, a group engaged in scholarly activity concerning David Hume.

Sbarbaro, Pietro (Born 1838)

Sbarbaro was an Italian publicist and reformer. He published a work on *The Philosophy of Research* (1866), dedicated to Mauro Macchi a book on *The Task of the Nineteenth Century*, and presided at a congress of Freethinkers held at Loreto. {BDF}

'SBLOOD

A slang expression which refers to Jesus's dripping blood on the cross, *'sblood* is found in Hamlet's retort to Guildenstern, " 'Sblood, do you think that I am easier to be played on than a pipe? Call me what instrument you will, though you can fret me, yet you cannot play upon me."

A similar slang expression of that time was " 'Swounds," a reference to Jesus's discomfiture caused by nails used to pin him onto the cross. Individuals of that time apparently believed that the body could be held up by nails.

Scales, Peter (20th Century)

Scales, a secular humanist, is a social-political scientist who has written for *Free Inquiry*. {Summer, 1981}

Scambini, Henry (20th Century)

Scambini, a freethinker comedian, entertained at the First Annual Atheist Alliance Conference in 1995.

"'Beauty may be only skin-deep, but ugly goes to the bone': I made that joke up," he says, adding that he helped train both Lenny Bruce and Richard Pryor.

SCANDINAVIAN PHILOSOPHY: See the article by Justus Hartnack in the *Encyclopedia of Philosophy*, Vol. 7.

SCANDINAVIAN UNBELIEVERS

José M. F. Santana in *Encyclopedia of Unbelief* has an extensive listing of unbelievers in Sweden, Finland, Norway, and Denmark. Faith Ingwersen follows with a study of unbelief in Scandinavian literature. From the year 1000 when the Scandinavian countries were Christianized, they mixed the Christian and the pagan. The first openly militant atheist in Sweden was **Viktor Lennstrand** (1861–1895), who held that no true social reform can come about if people "are blinded, weakened, imprisoned, and stupefied by Christine doctrine." The first Scandinavian author to take an explicit anti-Christian stance was the Swedish poet, critic and editor **Johan Henric Kellgren** (1751–1795).

Noted Swedish unbelievers include **Per de Grytnäs**, who in 1619 was hanged as a renegade for denying "pure evangelical doctrine"; **Olof Von Dalin** (1708–1763), poet; **Johan Tobias Sergel** (1740–1814), painter and cartoonist; **Carl Michael Bellman** (1740–1795), poet; **Johan Henric Kellgren** (1751–1795), poet, publicist, and a member of the Swedish Academy; **F. W. C. Areschoug** (1830–1908), a botanist; **G. J. Leufstedt** (1830–1901), called "Lennstrand's predecessor" and "the Antichrist" for his lectures; **Anton Nyström** (1842–1931, who introduced the ideas of Comte into Sweden; **Karl Staaff**, a prime minister; **Hjalmar Öhrwall** (1851–1929), a professor of physiology at Uppsala; **Knut Wicksell** (1851–1926), who followed Lennstrand as editor of the *Freethinker* and *Think for Yourself!*; **Svante Arrhenius** (1859–1927), recipient of the Nobel Prize in chemistry and a declared atheist; **Hinke Bergegren** (1861–1936), journalist; **Anna B. Wicksell** (1862–1928), pacifist and a member of a League of Nations committee; **Allen Vannerus** (1862–1946), author of *Atheism Versus Theism*; **Henrik Petrini** (1863–1957), professor of physics; **Bengt Lidforss** (1868–1913), botanist; **Hjalmar Söderberg** (1869–1941), novelist; **Ingemar Hedenius** (born 1908), a professor of philosophy at Uppsala University; and **José M. F. Santana**, a Spanish lawyer living in Sweden, who helped establish the Humanist and Ethical Union of Sweden in 1979).

Noted Finnish unbelievers include **Anders Chydenius** and **Robert Lagerborg**, who wrote on freedom of religion in 1863; **Viktor Heikel** and **Mathilda Asp**, who in 1887 founded the first nonbelievers' organization; **Rolf Lagerborg**, a philosopher; **Edward Westermarck** (1862–1939), founder of Finnish sociology; **Rafael Karsten**, a professor of practical philosophy at the University of Helsinki; and **Errikki Hartikainen**, secretary general of the Union of Freethinkers' Associations of Finland.

Norwegian unbelievers include poet and playwright **Bjornstjerne Bjørnson** (1832–1910; novelist **Alexander Kielland** (1849–1906), whose *St. Hans Fest* (1887) attacks the hypocrisy of Christian morals; critic and playwright **Helge Krog** (1889–1962); **Arnulf Överland**, a member of the Rationalist Press Association of London; **Fridtjof Nansen** (1861–1930), zoologist who was the Nobel Peace Prize in 1923; botanist **Kristian Horn** (1903–1981); **Erik and Dagfinn Eckhoff**, founders of the Pagan Society; and critic of religion and theology **Andreas Edwien** (born 1921). Edwien wrote *Is Christianity a Danger to World Peace?* (1977) and *Jesus in Conflict with Human Rights* (1979).

In Denmark, unbelievers include **Frederik Dreier** (1827–1853), author of *Spiritual Belief and Freethinking*; **Rudolf Varberg**; **Georg Brandes** (1842–1927), literary critic; **Jens Peter Jacobsen** (1847–1885), poet and novelist; **Johannes V. Jensen** (1873–1950), writer and journalist; and **Jeppe Aakjaer** (1866–1930).

The Dane **Karen Blixen** (1885–1962), who wrote under the pen name "Isak Dinesen," declared in *Out of Africa* (1937) that God and Satan are equally glorious, equally eternal, necessitating human courage to accept such a fate and live dutifully in pride and with honor.

Ingwersen considers **Pär Lagerkvist** (1891–1974) as "an unbeliever preoccupied with the plight of the unbeliever. He often turns a reassuring myth around to show the ludicrousness of its promise. The novel *Barabbas* (1950) may be, in fact, the ultimate characterization of the unbeliever who cannot transcend his own belief." {EU, José M. F. Santana; EU, Faith Ingwersen}

Scarbrough, Allan (Died 1998)

"It's Lonely Being An Atheist," wrote Scarbrough in *Freethought Today* (June-July 1998). An Arizonan with an accounting degree, he found while studying at Bob Jones University that the dictatorial structure and intolerance of fundamentalism was not for him. By reading Bertrand Russell, Jean-Paul Sartre, and Ayn Rand, he began to have serious doubts about Christianity and became a freethinker.

SCARABAEUS

• Scarabaeus, n. The sacred beetle of the ancient Egyptians, allied to our familiar "tumble-bug." It was supposed to symbolize immortality, the fact that God knew why giving it its peculiar sanctity. Its habit of incubating its eggs in a ball of ordure [shit] may also have commended it to the favor of the priesthood, and may some day assure it an equal reverence among ourselves. True, the American beetle is an inferior beetle, but the American priest is an inferior priest.

–Ambrose Bierce
The Devil's Dictionary

Scargill, Daniel (17th Century)

Scargill is an example of one who recanted his atheism. In 1669, he wrote *Recantation* . . .

publickly made before the University of Cambridge (of which he was formerly a member). Scargill described how he once had been a Hobbesian atheist: "I do profess . . . that the openly professed atheism of some, and the secret atheism of others, is the accursed root of all the abounding wickedness. . . . in the present age." His recanting made it difficult for Hobbes, who was trying to protect himself against the accusation that he was an atheist and a spreader of atheism. {HAB}

SCATOLOGY

Scatology, a study of fecal excrement, can lead to an obsession with anything involving excretary functions. Coprology (using scatalogical findings) is the science of solid waste products. *Merde: Excursions in Scientific, Cultural, and Sociohistorical Coprology* (1999) is a work by marine biologist Ralph A. Lewin in which human, sloth, prairie dog, and even Guatemalan jumping viper excrement is studied scientifically. Such studies expand human understanding of the environment.

SCEPTIC

Sceptic is a United Kingdom journal at <toby@cs.man.ac.uk>. (See entry for *Skeptic* and Skepticism.)

Scepticus: See entry for Britannicus, Scepticus.

Schade, Georg (1712–1795)

Schade was a German deist who believed in the immortality of brutes. In 1770 he was imprisoned on the Isle of Christiansoe for his opinions. He left, settling at Kiel, Holstein, in 1775, where he died in 1795. {BDF}

SCHADENFREUDE

A German word, *schadenfreude* refers to taking pleasure from the misfortunes of others. Freethinkers, for example, should not take pleasure upon reading that churches lose lawsuits of child molestation by priests and are required to pay out huge sums of money. The real issue is that of the damage done to the children.

Schadewald, Robert (20th Century)

Schadewald was formerly head of the National Center for Science Education, a group founded in 1982 to counter the creationist threat to science education in the public schools.

Schafer, David (20th Century)

Schafer is President of the Humanist Association of Central Connecticut (HACC), of which he was a co-founder. He signed Humanist Manifesto 2000. E-mail: <djschaf@compuserve.com>. (See entry for Connecticut Atheists, Humanists.)

Schäfer, Edward Albert Sharpey [Sir] (1850–1936)

Schäfer, who taught physiology at University College in London and at Edinburgh University, edited the *Quarterly Journal of Experimental Physiology*. He was President of the British Association in 1912 and gave an address on the origin of life which was materialistic. Schäfer was an honorary associate of the Rationalist Press Association and was an agnostic. In that group's *Annual* for 1914 he rejected all "interventions of the Deity" in biology and said, "The churchgoer still prays but he would be astonished if his prayers were answered." {RAT; RE}

Schafersman, Steven (20th Century)

Schafersman is associated with the American Humanist Association's Houston, Texas, chapter. At the Fourth Annual Atheist Convention hosted in 1998 by the St. Louis, Missouri, Rationalist Society, he spoke on "Spreading Humanism Through the Web." (See entry for Texas Atheists, Freethinkers, Humanists.) {FD}

Schaff, Adam (20th Century)

Schaff, from Poland, partook in a Marxist—non-Marxist Humanist Dialogue in Vienna in 1968, at which A. J. Ayer from Britain also participated. Unfortunately, Russian tanks entered Prague just before the Dialogue was to convene, but the conference continued just the same. In attendance were about sixty thinkers from both Eastern European and Western countries, and according to Paul Kurtz the Dialogue eventually degenerated into a shouting match because of the Soviet invasion of Czechoslovakia. In 1977, he wrote *Structuralism and Marxism*. In 1995, he wrote *The Polish Challenge*.

Schaffer, Hal (1931–)

When a professor at Adelphia University in New York, Schaffer as varsity soccer coach took his team to the NCAA Finals. He was Dean of Admissions and Records at State University College at Cortland, New York, and he has been a board member of the American Movement for World Government, the American Civil Liberties Union, and Humanists of the Palm Beaches in Florida. Schaffer, although retired, has served as a USTA Tennis Umpire.

Schantz, B. T. (20th Century)

Schantz wrote "Ethan Allen's Religious Ideas" in the *Journal of Religion* (1938). {FUS}

Schaper, Bertus W(illem) (20th Century)

At the Second International Humanist and Ethical Union Congress, which was held in London (1957), Dr. Schaper of the Netherlands addressed the group. In 1976 he wrote about the Munich four-power agreement in *Het trauma van Munchen*.

Schapiro, Herbert (20th Century)

Schapiro is a local humanist activist in Tuscon, Arizona, and a former board member of the Freedom From Religion Foundation. He has a journalistic clipping service, which has proved invaluable to many freethought societies by providing them with news sources. {SHD}

Scharf, Ed (20th Century)

Scharf is a Texan freethinker. His accounts of freethought in Comfort, Texas, during the 1800s have been published in *Freethought Today*. {*Freethought History* #20, 1996; *Freethought Today*, April 1998}

Schatz, Bernie (20th Century)

Schatz is the American Humanist Association coordinator of the northern part of the United States. (See entry for Minnesota Atheists, Humanists.) {FD}

Schatzman, Evry (20th Century)

Schatzman, an astronomer who is the former president of the French Physics Association and a member of the Academy of Sciences, signed Humanist Manifesto 2000.

Schechter, Lori (20th Century)

Schechter is a past president of *The Jewish Humanist*.

Scheffer, Ary (1795–1858)

A French painter of the romanticist movement, Scheffer painted religious pictures and was often assumed to be a Catholic. He was, however, a Deist who in his youth had joined the Carbonari and always opposed the Bourbons and the Church in France. Scheffer was a friend of Renan, who married his niece. {RAT; RE}

Scheiber, Béla (20th Century)

Scheiber is president of the Rocky Mountain Skeptics and is on the executive council of the Committee for the Scientific Investigation of Claims of the Paranormal.

Scheick, William J. (20th Century)

Scheick, with Edward H. Davidson, wrote *Paine, Scripture and Authority: The Age of Reason as Religious and Political Idea* (1994). The book, according to Gordon Stein, claims "that *The Age of Reason* was not written so much to express Paine's views on religion as it was to tell his views on the political system that was dependent upon religion for its survival." {*The American Rationalist*, July-August 1994}

Schell, A. (1817–1894)

In 1849 Schell sailed from New York via Cape Horn to San Francisco, and he made seven trips across the Isthmus of Panama, and twenty-seven trips by rail across America. Schell was an active freethinker. {PUT}

Schelling, Friedrich Wilhelm Joseph von (1775–1854)

Schelling taught philosophy at Jena, Wurzburg, and Munich. He is counted third (after Kant and Fichte) in the dynasty of German philosophers, according to McCabe, and was a pantheist who rejected the ideas of a personal God and immortality as well as Christian dogmas. {RAT; RE}

Scheman, Naomi (20th Century)

A professor of philosophy at the University of Minnesota, Scheman is author of *Engenderings: Constructions of Knowledge, Authority, and Privilege* (1993). There are moral reasons not to believe in an all-powerful, all-knowing god, she said in a 1996 speech to University of Minnesota Atheists and Humanists. Further, many of the attitudes of believers about God's role in the world are morally troubling, which is why her speech was entitled, "Quarreling With a God I Don't Believe In: On the Moral Grounds for Atheism."

Schempp, Ed (1908–)

Schempp was joined by Madalyn Murray O'Hair in the historic lawsuit in which the Supreme Court ruled that Bible readings were illegal in U.S. schools. Reciting the Lord's Prayer in the School District of Abington Township, Pennsylvania, because of their efforts was ruled a violation of the First and Fourteenth Amendments. In 1993, Schempp told *Church and State* that he and his wife Sidney has raised their three children in a church-affiliated with the Unitarian Universalists, that his son Ellory had been sixteen at the time his high school was mandating ten Bible Verses to be announced over the public address system at the start of the day, and that Ellory had rebelled by reading the Qur'an instead of standing for the daily recitation of the Lord's Prayer. His infuriated teacher had sent Ellory to the principal, the principal was speechless when young Schempp would not relent, and the result in 1963 was *Abington Township School District v. Schempp*. The principal, a Methodist minister, wrote letters to universities where Ellory had applied, labeling him a "troublemaker" and appealing to Tufts University in Boston even after it had accepted him. Ellory later earned a doctorate in physics at Brown University and today manages a high technology superconductor firm. Commenting upon the prayer and Bible reading problem in 1993, Ellory Schempp has said,

> It's a sad thing that school prayer continues to be so divisive. There are some groups in the country that feel very strongly that symbolic acts of this kind are very important to them. But what these people don't understand is that this kind of religion by rote does not foster Christian values. I think it is important that [separationists] continue to take these cases on. . . . We have to realize there is a proper sphere for religion and a proper sphere for public schools. I wish we would focus on providing a proper education in the schools rather than worry about providing a little Bible reading.

Scher, Ted (20th Century)

Scher is a chapter contact for the *Humanist Quest of Milwaukee , Wisconsin, Newsletter.*

Schérer, Edmond (Henri) (Adolphe) (1815–1889)

According to Robertson, Schérer, a French poet, "was an unbeliever almost against his will." Like Béranger and Taine, he was a rationalist at a time when most of the French poets were theists. One of his works is *Etudes Critiques sur la littérature contemporaine* (1863–1889). He originally had come from a Protestant family, but his views were too free for him to retain his position as a professor of exegesis at Geneva, so he went to Strasbourg. Here, he became chief of the School of Liberal Protestants. When he wrote *Revue de Théologie et de Philosophie Chrétienne* (1850–1860), his views "drew down a tempest from the orthodox." When elected deputy in 1871, Schérer sat with the Republicans of the left. {BDF; JMR; JMRH; RAT; RE}

Scherer, Paul: See entry for Theism.

Scherr, Johannes (1817–1886)

Scherr was a German author who, with his brother Thomas, wrote *A Popular History of Religious and Philosophical Ideas* (1843) and *History of Religion* (1857). In 1860 he became professor of history and literature at Zürich. {BDF}

Scheuer, Sidney H. (20th Century)

When he signed Humanist Manifesto II, Scheuer was chairman of the Committee for an Effective Congress. He was on the first National Board of Directors in 1952 of the International Humanist and Ethical Union (IHEU) and at the 1957 Congress addressed the group. In 1978 he received a special award "for 25 years of devoted service to IHEU." Scheuer is the author of *Ethics of International Economics* (1980). {HM2}

Schick, Theodore Jr. (20th Century)

Schick is a professor of philosophy at Muhlenberg College in Allentown, Pennsylvania. He wrote *How To Think About Weird Things*. A professor of philosophy at Muhlenberg College in Allentown, Pennsylvania, he is author of "Can A Robot Have Moral Rights?" an amusing exercise in *Free Inquiry* (Winter 1997-1998). Schick was an instructor of "The History and Philosophy of Skepticism" at the January 1998 Center for Inquiry Institute in San Diego, California.

"Can You Go to Heaven? he asks in *Free Inquiry* (Fall, 1999), and he answers in the negative. In fact anyone looking forward to eternal bliss, he explains, should get prepared for the bad news.

In *Philo*, of which he is a contributing editor, he wrote "The 'Big Bang' Argument for the Existence of God" (Spring-Summer 1998). He signed Humanist Manifesto 2000. {*Free Inquiry*, Spring 1998}

Schievella, Pasqual S. (20th Century)

A non-theist, Schievella wrote *Hey! It That You, God?* (1985). {GS}

Schiff, Johan Moriz (Born 1823)

Schiff was a German physiologist, a professor of comparative anatomy at Berne (1854–1863); of physiology at Florence (1863–1876); and at Genoa. He wrote many physiological treatises which were attacked as being materialistic. {BDF}

Schifter, Jacobo (1952–)

Schifter is a Costa Rican who founded the *Instituto Latino Americano de Prevencion y Education en Salud* (ILPES) (Latin-American Institute for Health Education, Apartado 561, 1002 San Jose, Costa Rica). A freethinker, he set up an association for educating Central Americans concerning sexually transmitted diseases. {WAS, conversations]

Schiller, Ferdinand (Canning Scott) (1864–1937)

Schiller, the British philosopher who called his philosophic system "humanism," wrote *Humanism: Philosophical Essays* (1903, 1912), *Riddles of the Sphinx: A Study in the Philosophy of Humanism* (1910),

Studies in Humanism 1912), *Tantalus* (1924), *Problems of Belief* (1924), and *Our Human Truths*, published posthumously in 1939. Schiller's humanism, closely related to the pragmatism of William James, held that "man is the measure of all things." (See the article by Reuben Abel on Schiller in the *Encyclopedia of Philosophy*, Vol. 7.) {CE; CL; HNS2; TRI; TYD}

Schiller, Johann Christoph Friedrich von (1759–1805)

Schiller has been called, after Goethe, the greatest of the German poets. He was raised in a religious atmosphere, but he appeared to have little respect for Christianity's influence as a factor in cultural progress. Although called "the representative of the rationalism of his age," Schiller in *Robbers* (c. 1779) makes his worst villains freethinkers and champions religion against all assailants although seldom giving favorable portraits of priests. That play was one of the great plays of the "*sturm und drang*" period. Schiller often wrote as if a deist but for a time professed to be a Kantian.

Like his friend Goethe, according to Robertson, "he sought to reduce the Biblical supernatural to the plane of possibility. . . ; he does not hesitate to say that a healthy nature (which Goethe had said needed no morality, no *Natur-recht,* and no political metaphysic) required neither deity nor immortality to sustain it." He once wrote Goethe, "A healthy poetic nature wants, as you yourself say, no moral law, no rights of man, no political metaphysics. You might have added, as well, it wants no deity, immortality, to stay and support itself withal."

His *Gods of Greece*, to which Elizabeth Barrett Browning replied in *Pan Is Dead*, gave offense to many of the orthodox, and Schiller afterwards erased part of it. The Greek gods, he felt, had vanished from the world and had taken with them all that was fairest in color and sound, leaving the husk of the word. In "Resignation," he poetically makes the unbeliever say that the illusions of superstition are holy only because they are covered by the giant shadow of our own fears.

Schiller was a member of the Masonic Lodge, a non-theistic secret organization with deistic rituals. Schiller was ennobled in 1802.

As for immortality, he declared, "A healthy nature needs no God or immortality. There must be a morality which suffices without this faith." Carlyle, writing of Schiller's final illness, stated, "Feeling that his end was come, be addressed himself to meet it as became him; not with affected carelessness or superstitious fear, but with the quiet unpretending manliness which had marked the tenor of his life. Of his friends and family be took a touching, but a tranquil farewell; he ordered that his funeral should be private, without pomp or parade. To someone inquiring how be felt, he said, "Calmer and calmer"; simple but memorable words, expressive of the mild heroism of the man. About six, he sank into a deep sleep; once for a moment he looked up with a lively air, and said, 'Many things were growing plain and clear to him!' Again be closed his eyes; and his sleep deepened and deepened, till it changed into the sleep from which there is no awakening; and all that remained of Schiller was a lifeless form, soon to be mingled with the clods of the valley. (See the article by Julius Elias on Schiller in the *Encyclopedia of Philosophy*, Vol. 7.) {BDF; CE; EU, Volker Dürr; FO; JMR; JMRH; RAT; RE; TYD}

Schilpp, Paul A. (1897–1993)

Schilpp, the editor of the twenty-one-volume Library of Living Philosophers and who had been associate editor of *Religious Humanism*, wrote the present author concerning humanism:

> *Humanism*, to me, connotes an emphasis on man as both the end and goal of all human endeavor as well as upon the essential dependence of man upon himself in the processes of individual growth and of social development and progress. I believe, in other words, that man has to work out his own (individual and social) salvation with fear and trembling, yes, but also with courage, insight, and caring. Such working out need not preclude, however, man's making use, in this process, of any and all avenues of approach open to him: the use of nature and of natural laws as he comes increasingly to understand these, as well as the use of his intellectual, moral, aesthetic and spiritual powers as he learns to develop and understand these. In terms of method and procedure I suppose I would fit mostly into the category of *naturalistic humanism*.
>
> But, in terms of metaphysical considerations, I would rank as a *theistic humanist.* So long as man is—in the area of ultimates—still as largely ignorant as he is today, and in view of man's obviously finite nature and even more finite (and limited) knowledge and comprehension, it seems to me the height of human arrogance for finite man to want to rule out God. Such procedure reminds me of the attempt, on the part of a mosquito, to rule out the possibility of man because the mosquito never has met a man and, if it had met one, could, obviously, neither explain nor understand man. But I cannot grant that theistic humanism of necessity must be held "within the framework of a supernaturalistic philosophy." If there is a God, He must have some nature, which will be "natural" to Him as human nature is natural to man (or dog-nature is natural to a dog). God, in order to *be* God, must, I suppose, be thought of as *superhuman*; but this implies no more that He is supernatural than the fact that man is supervegetative implies that man is supernatural. God is merely beyond finite man's finite grasp—as, indeed are many natural phenomena events yet in this atomic age. I would insist, therefore, that my theistic humanism is a type of naturalistic humanism.
>
> Everything that has ever been achieved in human history has been achieved by man (from the sub-beastly atrocities of war and other forms of head-hunting to the highest achievements of human hands, heart, mind, and spirit). Though man is finite, the latent capacities of his nature are so nearly limitless that no man can actually imagine or even dream what man may yet be able to achieve: *If* he will marshal and use the best powers of his rational, moral, and spiritual capacities in the building of a better world of human understanding, appreciation, freedom, and love. More detailed statements of the writer's theistic humanism are found in *This Is My Faith* (1956) and in his Tully Cleon Knoles Lectures in Philosophy, *Human Nature and Progress* (1954).

{WAS, 27 August 1956}

Schirmer, Greta B. (20th Century)

Schirmer was treasurer and a member of the board of directors in 1954 of the Humanist Fellowship of Boston, a group affiliated with the American Humanist Association.

Schisler, Charles (20th Century)

Schisler is a life member of Atheists of Florida and is that group's President. His "Some Principles of Rationalism" appeared in *The American Rationalist* (January-February 1997). Schisler wrote a booklet, "The Necessity of Atheism" (337 Golfview Road, Box 306, North Palm Beach, Florida 33408), in which he affirms atheism "as an antidote to theologies of perversion and ideologies of hate." E-mail: <schisler@earthlink.net>.

SCHISM

Church groups have long had a record of disunions and discord. When a formal breach of union occurs within a church it is called a schism. Divisions have occurred sometimes because of personality conflicts among the leaders or because of arguments over organization or content. A main schism was the "Great Schism" of 1054, which produced a separation of the four Eastern and the Roman patriarchates which exists to the present time. Pope Leo IX, inspired by the ideals of the Cluniac Reform and under provocation from the aggressive Patriarch of Constantinople, Michael Cerularius (1043–1058), demanded that the latter acknowledge the supreme jurisdiction of the Holy See in the church universal. The causes of the schism were deep-seated and comprised political, cultural, as well as religious differences. (See McCabe's *Rationalist Encyclopedia*, which reports that "The Popes were brought back to Rome from their luxurious and vicious court at Avignon, not by a neurotic nun, as Catholics represent, but by the threat of the Romans to repudiate their allegiance, as they had often done." He details the Great Schism, including its end in 1414 at the Council of Constance, at which 1,000 prostitutes allegedly attended.) {ER; RE}

Schlacter, Yevgeni (Eugene) (20th Century)

Schlacter is associated in Russia with the St. Petersburgh

Unitarian group at 197341, St. Petersbourg, Serebristy Blvd., 37, ap 8. E-mail: <eugene@uua.spb.su>.

Schlauch, Margaret (1898–1986)

In 1962, Prof. Schlauch was elected an honorary associate of the Rationalist Press Association. She was the author of *Gifts and Tongues* (1942) and *English Medieval Literature and the Social Foundations* (1956). Born in New York City's Greenwich Village, she taught at New York University (1927–1951) and became known as an educator, author, philologist, and specialist in Anglo-Saxon and Viking literature. In 1951 she moved to Poland, where she became a citizen, a member of the Communist Party, and a professor at Warsaw University.

Schleiermacher, Friedrich Daniel Ernst (1768–1834)

A Protestant theologian, Schleiermacher excelled as one who helped secure the liberation of the church from the state. His translations of Plato and his interest in the Romantic movement led him to define religion as an absolute dependence on a monotheistic God, reached through intuition and independent of dogma. His *Religion: Speeches to its Cultured Despisers* (1893) and *The Christian Faith* (1821–1822) strongly influenced liberal Protestant theology. Robertson points out, however, that Schleiermacher's friend Sach, "who had passed the Discourses in manuscript, woke up to denounce them as unchristian, pantheistic, and denuded of the ideas of God, immortality, and morality." Others called him "godless," pointing to his view that civil marriage should precede religious marriage, and be alone obligatory.

Robertson calls him "at bottom a pantheist, and the secret of his attraction for so many German preachers and theologians then and since is that he offered them in eloquent and moving diction a kind of profession of faith which avoided alike the fatal undertaking of the old religious rationalism to reduce the sacred narratives to terms of reason, and the dogged refusal of orthodoxy to admit that there was anything to explain away." {CE; ER; JMR; JMRH; RAT; RE}

Schlesinger, Annette (20th Century)

Schlesinger, from Indiana, is on the board of the Freedom From Religion Foundation.

Schlesinger Jr., Arthur M(eier) (1917–)

Schlesinger, whose *The Age of Jackson* (1946) and *A Thousand Days* (1965) won Pulitzer Prizes, wrote the present author about humanism:

> I am not sure that I can contribute anything very useful. My own views on the problem are rudimentary. It seems to me that most important for the preservation of civilization is a belief in moral standards. That belief is really most solid when it is founded upon a fervent belief in a supernatural order. For those of us who lack a belief in supernatural religion, we must base the standards as securely as possible on our own conception of man. For my own part, I find the Christian interpretation (as in Reinhold Niebuhr) of the incompleteness of merely human experience and the inadequacy of merely human resources entirely convincing; but I cannot go along with the belief that this incompleteness and this inadequacy are to be perfected by an infusion of the supernatural. I do not know where this puts me in your categories, but I do think that any great literature must be based on an understanding of the weakness and fallibility, the misery as well as the grandeur, of man.

Schlesinger (which he pronounces SCHLAY-sing-er) elsewhere has written, "My general belief is that Augustinian Christianity is fine up to the point where belief in God comes in. In other words, I find the Christian interpretation of experience more illuminating than any humanist interpretation, though I agree with the humanists in being unable to take the supernatural seriously." Elsewhere, Schlesinger has identified one of the problems in our country to be that we have "too much pluribus, and not enough unum."

In a *Wall Street Journal* article (22 November 1995), Schlesinger lamented the murder of Israeli Prime Minister Yitzhak Rabin, saying it was "only the latest outrage committed by people who think they are executing the will of God." Noting that pollsters find that "more than a third of American adults claim that God speaks to them directly," Schlesinger asked, "Am I alone in finding this a scary statistic? What in the world do they mean? How does God talk to them? Do they hear voices, like Joan of Arc? And what does God say to them? He continued, "Fundamentalism in one form or another has been the scourge of the 20th century. Fundamentalists are absolutists—people who believe they are appointed carriers of a sacred gospel and feel so sure they are right that they have no compunction about killing heretics or doing anything else to advance their cause. . . . Unrebuked and unchecked, fundamentalists of all faiths will continue to believe that they are serving God by mayhem and murder."

Schlesinger in the *Who's Who* volumes lists himself as a Unitarian. In 1996 he was elected a Humanist Laureate in the Council for Secular Humanism's International Academy of Humanism. He was President of the American Academy and Institute of Arts and Letters (1981–1984) and has been its Chancellor. (In a 22 June 1992 Op-Ed column of *The New York Times*, Schlesinger relates how he first heard Niebuhr preach in the winter of 1940-1941. The preacher "cast an intellectual spell on my generation," he wrote. "He persuaded me and many of my contemporaries that original sin provides a far stronger foundation for freedom and self-government than illusions about human perfectibility.") {CE; TYD; WAS, 24 February 1951 and 2 May 1956; conversation, 19 April 1995}

Schlesinger, Melvin (1916-1999)

Schlesinger was named "Freethinker of the Year" in 1994 by the Freedom From Religion Foundation (FFRF), of which group he was a member of the board of directors. This was in recognition of his role as successful plaintiff in a significant state-church challenge. The 7th Circuit Court of Appeals in Chicago had ordered a township to remove a huge Catholic crucifix from a public park in 1993, which represented a legal victory that had taken over ten years to obtain. During the Coolidge Administration, the Knights of Columbus had donated a "war memorial" to the park, a work which turned out to be this crucifix. It has since been moved to a Catholic rather than a public property. Owner of a real estate firm, he had been treasurer of the Freedom From Religion Foundation. {*Freethought Today*, January-February 1999}

Schlick, Moritz (1882–1936)

Schlick, founder of the Vienna Circle, was a professor of philosophy at the University of Vienna. A leading figure in the development of logical positivism, he wrote *Space and Time in Modern Physics* (1920) and *The Problems of Ethics* (1931). "How men know what they know," he believed, could be ascertained by using the methods of the sciences. At the age of fifty-four, Schlick was murdered by a paranoid student. (See entry for logical positivism. Also see the article by Béla Juhos in the *Encyclopedia of Philosophy*, Vol. 7.) {CE; TRI}

Schmidt, Eduard Oskar (1823–1886)

Schmidt was a German zoologist who traveled widely and became professor of natural history at Jena. Among the first of Germans to accept Darwinism, he illustrated its application in many directions and published *The Doctrine of Descent and Darwinism* in the "International Scientific Series." {BDF; RAT}

Schmidt, Fred (20th Century)

Schmidt, a retired journalist for the *San Antonio Express-News*, is a Texas labor leader and an assistant to U. S. Representative Henry B. Gonzalez. He is an activist for Freedom From Religion Foundation.

Schmidt, Kaspar (1806–1856)

Schmidt, a German philosopher, wrote a system of individualism in *The Only One, and His Possession* (1845). He also wrote *A History of Reaction* (1852) and translated Adam Smith's *Wealth of Nations* and Say's *Textbook of Political Economy.* {BDF; RAT}

Schmidt, Nathaniel (1862–1939)

Schmidt was one of the early leaders of the Ethical Culture

Society. A scholar, he wrote *The Coming Religion* (1930). {EU, Howard B. Radest}

Schmitz, Al (20th Century)

Schmitz was coordinator of the 1998 World Congress held in Luxembourg of the World Union of Freethinkers.

Schmuck, Henry (20th Century)

Schmuck, the former state director of Michigan's American Atheists Inc. can be e-mailed at <hmorgan@oeonline.com>.

Schneeberger, F. J. (Born 1827)

Schneeberger was an Austrian writer who used the name "Arthur Storch" for some of his popular novels. He was one of the founders of the German Freethinkers' Union. {BDF}

Schneider, Amy (20th Century)

Schneider is manager of *Le Salon*, a coffeehouse that opened in October 1997 at the Center for Inquiry International in Amherst, New York.

Schneider, Georg Heinrich (19th Century)

A German naturalist, Schneider wrote *The Human Will From the Standpoint of the New Development Theory* (1882) and other works. {BDF}

Schneider, Herbert W(allace) (1892–1984)

Schneider, an associate of John Dewey and a professor of philosophy at Columbia University, was author of *History of American Philosophy* (1946) and *Religion in Twentieth Century America* (1952, 1964), in the latter of which he characterized humanists as follows:

> There are among the humanists left-wing Unitarians who do not reflect the liberalism of Emerson and who do not wish to be confined to Christian limitations. There are materialists who are no longer "doctrinaire" materialists but who are suspicious of the theologians who use terms like "soul," "immortal," transcendental," "God," and "spirit"; they prefer more secular language for their secular truths. There are naturalists who are disgusted by the use of . . . supernatural symbols and myths . . . who find no use for organized religions, but who have a "religious" concern for the life of reason. There are still a few old-fashioned rationalists, free-thinkers or professional atheists . . . . And there are many individuals who cannot be labeled. . . .

On the subject of humanism Schneider, who was a signer of Humanist Manifesto II, wrote the present author:

> You state the important types of humanism very well and if I had to choose I would certainly belong in the seventh, naturalistic humanism. But I am interested in giving a humanistic account of theism without supernaturalism. To me it seems pretty close to the position of Feuerbach in his *Essence of Christianity*.
>
> {CL; HM2; PK; SHD; WAS, 5 March 1951}

Schneider, Martin (1921-1999)

Schneider, a major in the Marine Corps in the South Pacific during World War II, was a Life Member of the Freedom From Religion Foundation.

Schnitzler, Arthur (1862–1931)

An Austrian playwright, Schnitzler in *Buch der Sprüche und Bedenken* (1927), wrote, "Martyrdom has always been a proof of the intensity, never of the correctness of a belief. . . . Martyrdom has always been a proof of the intensity, never of the correctness, of a belief." {TYD}

Schoelcher, Victor (1804–1893)

Schoelcher was a French philosopher who devoted himself from about 1826 to advocating the abolition of slavery. In 1848 he was made Under Secretary of the Navy and caused a decree to be issued by the Provisional Government enfranchising all slaves on French territory. Schoelcher was elected Deputy for Martinique in 1848 and 1849. Having opposed the coup d'état of Louis Napoleon (later Napoleon III) in 1851, Schoelcher was forced into exile in England until Napoleon's fall in 1870. In London, he wrote occasionally in the *Reasoner* and *National Reformer*. Returning to Martinique in 1871, Schoelcher was elected a life senator in 1875. {BDF; CE; RAT}

Schoenig, Richard (20th Century)

Schoenig, in "The Truth About Faith" (*American Rationalist*, May-June 1997), concluded that faith (a) contradicts reason; (b) is not a path to knowledge; (c) cannot objectively adjudicate its conflicting claims; (d) cannot be justified on the basis of strength of internal conviction; and (e) is not found in all people.

Schoenman, Ralph (20th Century)

Schoenman, who had been a graduate student at the London school of Economics, managed Bertrand Russell's affairs for eight years. According to Moorehead and others, Schoenman "Svengalied" Russell, wasted large amounts of his money, was responsible for destroying a number of Russell's old friendships, and tried to make the elderly Russell into a puppet for his own personal causes. (See entry for Bertrand Russell.)

SCHOLASTICISM

Christian thinkers in Europe during the Middle Ages encouraged scholasticism, which was marked by careful argumentation. Central to scholastic thought was the idea that reason and faith are compatible. Thomas Aquinas tried to show that ancient philosophy, especially that of Aristotle, supported and illuminated Christian faith.

A freethinkers' scholasticism focuses on free inquiry, the erudite, and a profound search for knowledge. {DCL}

Scholl, Aurélien (Born 1833)

Born in Bordeaux, Scholl was a French journalist who wrote for *Corsaire*, founded *Satan*, *Le Nain Jaune*, and wrote on*l'Evénement*. In addition to writing several novels, Scholl wrote *Le Procès de Jésus Christ* (1877). {BDF; RAT}

Scholl, Eldon (1918–1990)

Scholl was an editor and was one of the founders of the *American Rationalist*. A lifelong rationalist and freethinker, he worked for environmental and other causes, sometimes under the pseudonym of Arthur Stahl. After the demise in 1956 of the United Secularists of America, Scholl and a group started the *American Rationalist*, which continues to be published. In 1948 in St. Louis, Missouri, he started *Secular Subjects*. {EU, Eldon Scholl; HNS}

Scholl, Karl (Born 1820)

Scholl was a German writer and preacher to the free religious bodies of Mannheim and Heidelberg. Because of his opinions, he was suspended as a minister in 1844. He wrote *Messiah Legend of the East* (1852) and in 1861 a volume on *Free Speech*, in which he extracts writings by English, French, and American freethinkers. In 1870 he started a monthly journal of the Religion of Humanity. In 1879, Scholl wrote *Judaism and the Religion of Humanity*. {BDF}

Scholtz, Jud R. (20th Century)

Scholtz has been a member of the American Humanist Association. {HNS}

Schonfield, Hugh J. (20th Century)

Schonfield is author of *The Passover Plot: Did Jesus Really Die On the Cross* (1965).

SCHOOL

• God has no place in public schools, just as facts have no place in organized religion.

School Principal in the teleseries "The Simpsons"

Schopenhauer, Adele (1797–1849)

An accomplished woman and the sister of Arthur Schopenhauer, Adela Schopenhauer sided with her brother when his rationalism alienated their mother, and she relieved his pessimistic melancholy. In her *Diary* (1909, 2 volumes) are numerous rationalistic passages. She is said to have been an incredibly ugly woman, miserable for much of her life. She may have committed suicide, as her father was rumored to have done. {RE}

Schopenhauer, Arthur (1788–1860)

Schopenhauer, a German who was the "philosopher of pessimism," was among the first of avowed atheists. Theism is incompatible with the responsibility of a "moral being," he wrote, "because in theism responsibility always falls back on the Creator of that being. . . . If our will is free it is also original being, and vice versa." Touted as the pre-eminent pessimist, he believed that the prime mover of human life is "the will to live," but it also is the basic cause of human suffering. When he became infected with syphilis, Schopenhauer feared he would lose what he valued most: his mind. One of views, on tetragamy rather than monogamy, was that two men should share a women as a wife until she was past childbearing age and then should marry a second young woman, continuing to care for the first. His *Parerga and Paralipomena* (1851) highlighted his deep hatred of woman, which was related to his philosophic pessimism.

Schopenhauer's main significance lies in his original conception of reality and in his compellingly argued and terrifying bleak and pessimistic vision of human existence as a meaningless, unceasing, and futile struggle, full of torment and suffering, in a hostile and godless universe. This vision still stands as a disturbing and powerful challenge to anyone of a more optimistic persuasion. In a chapter of *Parerga*, "Religion, A Dialogue," he wrote, "Faith and knowledge are related as the two scales of a balance; when the one goes up, the other goes down. . . . The power of religious dogma, when inculcated early, is such as to stifle conscience, compassion, and finally every feeling of humanity. . . . For, as you know, religions are like glow worms; they shine only when it's dark. A certain amount of ignorance is the condition of all religions, the element in which alone they can exist. . . . To free a man from error is to give, not take away." As pointed out by Gaskin and others, Schopenhauer thought religion is superfluous to the enforcement of morality, that "it is not *true* in any but a 'flowery or allegorical' sense. But religion is "needed" by ordinary people to give direction and form to their lives. The philosophical person may transcend religion, but he or she should not expect others to do so."

"The fruits of Christianity," Schopenhauer declared, "were religious wars, butcheries, crusades, inquisitions, extermination of the natives in America, and the introduction of African slaves in their place."

Lamont, observing that although Schopenhauer may have been an atheist, "In his own way, Schopenhauer was as anthropomorphic as anyone else. For he ascribed to the cosmos the human attributes of mind, will, and evil. Instead of postulating a good Mind or an all-inclusive God at the very heart of things, he postulated an evil Will, in essence an all-inclusive Devil. The excellent lesson that Schopenhauer's pan-Satanism teaches is that if we indulge in the pathetic fallacy of imputing to the universe qualities that emerge only in living forms, there is at least as much of a case for imputing the bad qualities as the good."

In Frankfort am Main, the Schopenhauer Society founded in 1911 continues to meet and study his views. (See the article by Patrick Gardiner on Schopenhauer in the *Encyclopedia of Philosophy*, Vol. 7.) {BDF; CE; CL; ER; EU, Rudolf Suckerstätter; PA; RAT; TYD}

Schorer, Mark (20th Century)

Schorer wrote *Sinclair Lewis: An American Life* (1961). {GS}

Schoumans, Jan (20th Century)

Schoumans was awarded the Yad Vashem medal in 1999, the highest civilian award offered by the State of Israel. A member of Humanist Association of Canada, Schoumans had hid people of a Jewish background from the Nazis during the occupation of Holland through the Second World War. {*Humanist in Canada*, Summer 1999}

Schreiber, H. E. (Ernie) (20th Century)

Schreiber, a former President of the Humanist Association of Canada (HAC), is on the editorial committee of *Humanist in Canada*. He is a Secular Humanist Mentor of the Council for Secular Humanism.

E-mail: <heesnaps@magi.com>. On the Web, his page for European Union North American Communicators (EUNACOM) expresses secular and atheist views: <http://www.eunacom.net>.

Schreiner, Olive (1855–1920)

Schreiner, whose pseudonym was **Ralph Iron**, was the daughter of a German missionary and was born in Basutoland (now Lesotho). She wrote *The Story of an African Farm* (1883), which has been likened to Emily Brontë's *Wuthering Heights* and which relates the story of two children living in the African veldt. It describes how her father had been a missionary to the natives of Basutoland and how the harshly pious home had driven her to atheism. The book was so virile that few suspected the author was a woman. Because of its feminist and anti-Christian sentiments, the work was highly controversial. In 1889, she wrote *The Search for Truth*. Schreiner, a champion of liberalism, was married to S. C. Cronwright-Schreiner, who wrote her biography (1923). Edward Carpenter wrote of her, "I have seen her shake her little fist at the Lord in heaven and curse him down from his throne." {BDF; CE; GS; RAT; RE; WWS}

Schrödinger, Erwin (1887–1961)

A 1933 Nobel Prize winner in physics, with P. A. M. Dirac, Schrödinger was a non-believer. He is noted for developing wave mechanics (1926), which is a form of quantum mechanics. The Schrödinger equation is a widely used mathematical tool of the modern quantum theory. In *What Is Life?* (1944), Schrödinger speaks of his having turned against religion although it "has never done me any harm." {CE}

Schroeder, J. Henry (Born 1840)

Schroeder worked at mill-wrighting, mining, saw-milling, farming, and dairying, building the first creamery in Coos County, Oregon. A freethinker and a materialist, he was elected to the Oregon House of Representatives in 1878. He also was elected president of the Oregon State Secular Union. {PUT}

Schroeder, Theodore (1864–1953)

Schroeder, a libertarian crusader and publicist, was influenced by the works of Thomas Paine, Robert G. Ingersoll, and Ludwig Feuerbach to become a freethinker. He particularly liked Feuerbach's *The Essence of Christianity*. Schroeder, a lawyer in Salt Lake City, Utah, called polygamy "sanctified lust," and he perceived the Mormon theocracy as a threat to the separation of church and state. His erotogenetic theory of religion was refuted by William James but was defended by Chapman Cohen and Havelock Ellis. Religion, Schroeder came to believe, "is the most pernicious single influence in human society; without one redeeming feature." But he distinguished between religion and theology, which he considered a worthy intellectual pursuit; and he consistently defended a person's right to hold and expound religious views. In 1911, Schroeder founded the Free Speech League, and he wrote for *Truth Seeker*. {EU, Ralph E. McCoy; FUS; TYD}

Schroeter, Eduard (1810–1888)

Schroeter was a German-American writer who studied theology at Jena and entered the freethought religious communion in 1845. In 1850 he moved to America, speaking in Sauk City, Minnesota, and other places concerning the merits of freethought. In 1881 he attended the International Conference of Freethinkers at Brussels. Schroeter was a contributor to the Milwaukee *Freidenker*. {BDF; RAT}

Schroot, A. (19th Century)

A German author, Schroot wrote *Visions and Ideas* (1865), *Natural Law and Human Will, Creation and Man*, and *Science and Life* (1873). {BDF}

Schubert, Franz Peter (1797–1828)

Schubert, the Austrian composer who was one of the most gifted musicians of the 19th century, wrote his first symphony in 1813. Except for a circle of admirers who were among the leading artists of the period, Schubert received little recognition before his death. Although he taught music to the children of a Hungarian nobleman, he basically lived in poverty.

Although his father and uncle were educated by Jesuits and remained devout, his brother Ignaz Schubert was described as a "freethinker," and according to Daniel O'Hara the brothers shared an "anti-clericalism and contempt for orthodox piety." Wrote Franz to Ignaz,

> You have no idea what a gang the priesthood is here: bigoted as mucky old cattle, stupid as arch-donkeys, and boorish as bisons.

He further described a ceremony to observe the festival of St. Francis, a part of which involved kissing a relic of the saint: "[S]everal of the adults crept out of the door, having no desire, perhaps, to share in this privilege."

As a youth, Schubert was educated in Catholic schools. By his mid-teens, he led a Bohemian life and had close friendships with wealthy young men who were allegedly bisexual or homosexual. Terry Teachout (*Commentary*, March 1997) cited one of these friends:

> Anyone who knew Schubert knows how he was made of two natures, foreign to each other, how powerfully the craving for pleasure dragged his soul down to the slough of moral degradation. . . . His body, strong as it was, succumbed to the cleavage of his—I would like to say souls, of which the one pressed heavenwards and the other wallowed in slime; perhaps, too, it succumbed to lack of recognition which some of his larger efforts suffered and to bitterness at the meanness of his publishers.

Elizabeth McKay, a biographer, held that Schubert might have suffered from cyclothymia, a form of manic-depressive disease, citing how his music often ranged between the *extremely* joyous, then the *extremely* tragic. Toward the end of 1822 when he was but twenty-five, Schubert was diagnosed with syphilis. He would have to have known that medical treatments at the time usually did not work, and commentators have suggested that the theme of intense but doomed love of life, which appears in his work, must have arisen from such a realization. Although he composed several Masses, Schubert never made a public break with the Church, as pointed out by Daniel O'Hara (*Ethical Record* of the South Place Ethical Society, February 1997). He always omitted the phrase "I believe in one holy catholic and apostolic church," and according to O'Hara "clearly rejected the exclusivist pretensions of the Roman church, though Protestantism held no attractions for him." Other Masses omitted "references to the Virgin Birth, the resurrection of the body, and the session of the risen Christ at the right hand of the father."

O'Hara holds that Schubert's religion was "art, love, and friendship," that a key concept was also his love of nature. In his final days, Schubert made no call for a priest or for devotional literature, and he received extreme unction only when he was no longer conscious. As his father wished, Schubert was buried with a traditional Catholic funeral and is entombed near Beethoven, whom he never met even though they lived nearby each other for years. {CE; Fred Whitehead, *Freethought History* #22, 1997}

Schueneman-Pott, Friederich (1826–1892)

Although he studied for the Lutheran ministry, Schueneman-Pott renounced the Christian religion and became a lecturer for the Free Religious Society in Germany. In 1848 he fought against the government, was indicted for high treason, was imprisoned, was tried, and was acquitted. He went to the United States in 1854 and edited *Blätter für Freies Religiöses*, a German freethought publication that was published from 1856 to 1877. He also made lecturing tours throughout the country. Schueneman, who had been adopted by Baron Ernst von Pott, wrote widely on ethical and freethought subjects. {PUT}

Schug, Philip (20th Century)

In the 1950s when he was minister of the First Unitarian Church in San Antonio, Schug was an associate editor of *The Humanist* and a director of the American Humanist Association. {HNS}

Schüklenk, Udo (20th Century)

An academic, Schüklenk has written on such subjects as "Deathly Doctrine: Christian Churches and AIDS" and Ethics, Research, and the Public Understanding of Science," in the latter of which he argues that "religious beliefs or good intentions are no viable substitute for a rational ethical analysis." On the Web: <www.uclan.ac.uk/facs/ethics/udopage.htm>.

Schultes, Richard Evans (1915–)

A leading ethnobotanist, Schultes is an expert on hallucinogens and drugs as well an eminent museum director. A popular Harvard professor and an expert on Richard Spruce, Schultes has spent months in various jungles to complete his botanical studies. In 1992 he received the Linnean Gold Medal from the Linnean Society. A thorough description of the provocative scientist, a Unitarian, has been written by E. J. Kahn Jr. in *New Yorker* (1 June 1992).

Schultz, Werner (20th Century)

Schultz, the editor of *Diesseits*, signed Humanist Manifesto 2000.

Schultz, William Alan ("Bill") (1947–)

Schultz is a senior software engineer. He is Vice President of Internet Infidels. E-mail: <pope@agnostic.org> and <bill@infidels.org>. On the Web: <http://www.agnostic.org/>.

Schultz, Werner (20th Century)

Schultz, who is active with the *Humanistischer Verband Deutschlands*, is one of many Europeans who has objected to the hanging of a crucifix on the wall of every classroom in all Bavarian schools. "What would happen," he writes in *International Humanist News* (October 1995), "if it were decided in a class with 70% Muslim pupils to hang a Koran Sura next to the blackboard? There would be a storm of protest roaring through the Christian West—even though one line written in Arabic would nowhere near have the same effect on little children as does a tortured man on a cross."

Schultz is one of the members of the IHEU's Committee on Religious Extremism and Rational Inquiry.

Schultz, William (1949–)

When he signed Humanist Manifesto II, Schulz was a Ph. D. candidate at Meadville/Lombard, the University of Chicago. For his 1954 doctoral dissertation, he wrote "Making the Manifesto: A History of Early Religious Humanism," published as a hardcover book in 1975. He interviewed many of those who had written *Humanist Manifesto I* and observed about the John Dewey philosophy that, coming as it did

> . . . on the explosive heels of the technological revolution, it quite readily reinforced the "rumor" already spreading for several decades (since Huxley's time and before) that science could transform Being. Man was flexing his muscles in Nature's face; intelligence, judgment, and the scientific input could regulate and direct her. Lacking the obstacles which a deity might provide, and confident that the universe (matter) was just waiting to be exploited for man's benefit, humanity stood in awe before the possibilities with which its new Weltanschauung presented it. Religious humanism institutionalized that awe.

At the Tenth International Humanist and Ethical Union (IHEU) World Congress held in Buffalo (1988), Schulz addressed the group. In 1985, he was elected the fifth President of the American Unitarian Universalist Association, a position he held from 1985 to 1993. He then was named executive director of Amnesty International U.S.A., the human rights organization which received the Nobel Prize for Peace in 1977. {EW; HM2; U}

Schultze, Karl August (Born 1846)

Schultze was a German writer who studied at Jena, Göttinger, and Münich. He wrote *On Fetishism* (1871), *A History of the Philosophy of the Renaissance* (1874), and *Kant on Darwin* (1875). In 1876 Schultze became professor of philosophy in Jena, and in 1883 wrote *Elements of Spiritualism*. {BDF}

Schumacher, Mary (20th Century)

Schumacher heads the Friendly Lesbian Atheist Group of Atheists and Agnostics of Wisconsin.

Schumaker, John (20th Century)

Schumaker, who is concerned about the origins of religion, has written for *Free Inquiry*. He is a lecturer in psychology at the University of Newcastle and is author of *Wings of Illusion* and *The Corruption of Reality*. In "Can Religion Make You Happy?" (*Free Inquiry*, Summer 1998), Schumaker wrote that "Modern religion is failing as a vehicle of transcendence" but that without religion "[t]o be very good at what one loves to do is the best prescription for a satisfying life."

Schumann, Robert Alexander (1810–1856)

A noted German musical composer, Schumann had studied law at Leipzig but decided instead on a career in music. Because of a hand injury which resulted in his abandoning any career as a pianist, he served as editor of the *Newe Zeitschrift für Musik* from its inception in 1834 until 1844, championing younger composers, particularly Chopin and Brahms. In his lieder he set to music lyrics by such poets as Heine, Goethe, Eichendorff, and Kerner. Schumann wrote a "profane" oratorio, *Paradise and the Peri* (1840), and his *Letters* reveal his freethought and liking of Goethe's pantheism and Jean Paul Richter's rationalism. In 1854 after a nervous breakdown, Schumann entered a sanitarium, where he died two years later. {CE; BDF; RAT; RE}

Schummer, David (20th Century)

Schummer is coordinator of Campus Freethought Alliance, which represented at the end of 1997 forty-two freethought campus groups. In 1998 while a student at the State University of New York at Buffalo, he signed the Alliance's "Bill of Rights for Unbelievers."

Schurz, Carl (1829–1906)

A Missouri Senator, Schurz worked with German freethinkers in a group called *Ethische Kultur* (Ethical Culture) and having a newsletter, *Westliche Post*. Ethical Culturist Felix Adler was invited to give them "his episcopal benediction," but upon visiting he monopolized the large audience and spoke at great length only on his own views. {See entry for Ethical Culture.}

Schütte, Frank L. (20th Century)

A Berliner, Schütte is a spokesman of the board of the International League of Non-Believers and Atheists (ILNA), which he had founded in 1976.

Schuyler, Louisa Lee (19th Century)

Schuyler, a member of the New York Unitarian Church of All Souls, founded that city's Bellevue Hospital's school of nursing.

Schwalb, Isaak (20th Century)

Schwalb wrote "A Fraud Masked by Religion" (1976). {GS}

Schwalbe, Gustav (1844–1916)

Schwalbe, a German anthropologist and physician, served as military surgeon in the Franco-German War, after which he taught at Leipzig, Jena, Königsberg, and Strasbourg. His anthropological works include *Studien über den Pithecanthropus Erectus* (1899) and *Die Vorgeschichte des Menschen* (1904). Schwalbe was an agnostic. {RAT}

Schwaner, Wilhelm (Born 1863)

Schwaner, a German writer, was editor of the *Berliner Reform* (1896–1897) and edited and published the *Volkserzieher* and *Upland*. Some of his rationalist works, which had a large circulation, were *Germanenbibel* and *Gottsuchen der Völker*. Schwaner was a pantheist of the Goethe school, with a sentimental regard for Christianity and a disdain of its doctrines and clergy. {RAT}

Schwartz, A. Truman (20th Century)

Schwartz, with John G. McEvoy, edited *Motion Toward Perfection: The Achievement of Joseph Priestley*.

Schwartz, Delmore (1913–1966)

Schwartz was a poet, editor, and author of *In Dreams Begin Responsibilities* (1938). Asked for his views on humanism, he responded, "I'm sorry to have to say that my own views, such as they are, can't be formulated in terms of the seven kinds of humanism you mention." {WAS, 11 March 1951}

Schwartz, Mauricio-José (20th Century)

Schwartz, at the 1996 Humanist World Congress held in Mexico City, spoke about Mexican cybernetics and democratic participation.

Schwartz, Tony (20th Century)

Schwartz, who has been a *New York Times* and *Newsweek* correspondent, is author of *What Really Matters: Search for Wisdom in America* and *Trump, The Art of the Deal*. A member of Manhattan's All Souls Unitarian Church, Schwartz is a theist who makes no apologies for using the word *God*. {He wrote *The Media, the Second God* (1981). {*World*, Sep-Oct 1995}

Schwartz, Walter G. (20th Century)

When he signed Humanist Manifesto II, Schwartz was director of the Humanist Committee of San Francisco. {HM2}

Schwarz, Bert (20th Century)

A former co-chairman of the International Humanist and Ethical Union, Schwarz has also been a member of the Dutch parliament. A retired businessman, he is a professional masseur in The Hague. (See entry for Ethical Culture.)

Schweichel, Georg Julius Robert (Born 1821)

Schweichel was a German writer who, first studying jurisprudence, took up literature. He took part in the events of 1848, then moved to Switzerland where he wrote *Life of Auerbach*, a novel, and wrote a preface to Dulk's *Irrgang des lebens Jesu* (1884). {BDF}

Schweikher, Paul (20th Century)

Schweikher, a scientist, has been a member of the American Humanist Association. {HNS}

Schweitzer, Albert (1875–1965)

An Alsatian theologian, physician, and organist, Schweitzer wrote *Von Reimarus zu Wrede* (1906, tr. *Quest of the Historical Jesus, 1910*); *The Psychiatric Study of Jesus* (1913; 1948); and *Civilization and Ethics* (1923). His ethical philosophy was developed in *Philosophy of Civilization* (1923), which contained his concept of "reverence for life." For that concept, he received the Nobel Prize for Peace in 1952.

Reared a Lutheran, Schweitzer was an unorthodox Protestant, rejecting as he did the historical infallibility of Jesus although admiring the spiritual Jesus. Sacrificing a comfortable life in Europe, where in 1905 he had written a biography of Bach, co-edited his music (1912–1914), and enjoyed a reputation as being an organist who excelled playing Bach's compositions, Schweitzer moved in 1913 to Lambaréné in Africa. There, he founded a hospital to which people feared coming until the word went out that Dr. Schweitzer never surgically removed any body parts. Some critics accused him of administering dictatorially, but specialists and notables visited him from all over the world to observe his successful hospital.

In the mid-1940s, and after having had trouble with Protestant sources in obtaining hospital funds because of certain fears he was not preaching an infallible Jesus, he joined the Church of the Larger Fellowship (Unitarian). Vilma Szantho Harrington, wife of the New York Unitarian minister Donald Harrington, has written that Schweitzer ". . . told me personally that he was a Unitarian when I visited him with my husband in Lambaréné."

Norman Cousins, writing of his visit, admired the physician's workmanship, productiveness, and applied humanism, remarking that on Schweitzer's daughter's birthday Schweitzer showed his sense of humor by playing a boogie-woogie tune for her on the organ. Schweitzer admired not only Cousins but also wrote friendly letters to Romain Rolland, Gandhi, Hermann Hesse (to whom in 1915 he wrote, "I feel a bond with you in the ideal of humanity. Both of us remained loyal to this ideal in an age when it lost prestige"), Einstein, Thomas Mann, Pablo Casals, and Bertrand Russell.

From his African hospital, he wrote the present author in 1951 concerning humanism:

> I find the articles [in *The Humanist*] very interesting and my full sympathy is given to the movement which it represents: Humanism. The world thinks it must raise itself above humanism; that it must look for a more profound spirituality. It has taken a false road. Humanism in all its simplicity is the only genuine spirituality. Only ethics and religion which include in themselves the humanitarian ideal have true value. And humanism is the most precious result of rational meditation upon our existence and that of the world.
> (Translated from the French by Warren Allen Smith).

In 1956, he wrote again:

> I kindly ask you to excuse me for writing after such a long time. But I am so overburdened with work and so tired also, as my eyes are overtired. It also is impossible for me to write something about my Humanism. I must be very concentrated on my work, the medical and the literary work. I think your study, as you term it, very interesting. Please give only your opinion about me as you think it and feel it after the thoughts that I lay down in my works. That will be the best. When you will send me a copy of your work, it will greatly be appreciated. But please do not send it to Lambaréné (where the termites eat my books) but to my address at Gunsbach, Alsace, France.

The above is a translation from the German by A. Silver, nurse, who added:

> Dr. Schweitzer asked me to express to you his regret for not having answered your letter dated 26 April 1956. He is very much interested indeed in your study of Humanism and in former years he surely would have contributed more to this study. But now it is no more possible. The hospital grew to a greater importance than he had ever intended, the hospital administration is much more complicated than before, and the correspondence is tremendous. Dr. Schweitzer works in general on the hospital ground from 7 a.m. till sunset and has to write often till midnight. This is his life week after week and year after year, without ever having some time for himself, to finish his manuscripts, which he wants so much to finish before it may be too late. Many letters remain unanswered, as our time for correspondence is rather limited. He asked me to thank you for the honor you showed him in inviting him to contribute his thinking about humanism, and to thank you for your sympathy.

In 1961, Schweitzer wrote to George N. Marshall of the Unitarian Church of the Larger Fellowship,

> I thank you cordially for your offer to make me an honored member of the Unitarian Church. I accept with pleasure. Even as a student I worked on the problem and history of the Unitarian Church and developed a sympathy for your affirmation of Christian freedom at a time when it resulted in persecution. Gradually I established a closer contact with Unitarian communities and became familiar with their faith-in-action. Therefore, I think you that through you I have been made an honored member of this church.

Norman Cousins, who like Marshall had visited with and written about Schweitzer in Africa, said that he shared Schweitzer's humanistic outlook and his interest in the historical Jesus, the man-not-a-god, as well as his profound belief in applied ethics, in *applying* humanism, not just talking about it. Schweitzer's critics, however, focused on his dictatorial rule of the African hospital, his helping blacks but allegedly considering them inferior, his failing to pass on any skills to the natives in order that one day they could replace the foreigners who had come, and his insufficiently applying his philosophy to the social realm.

Schweitzer had designed a simple stone cross for his gravestone, and he was buried on the hospital grounds in Lambaréné. The inscription, "Here Lies Dr. Albert Schweitzer," is in French only. {CE; CL; HSN2; U; UU; WAS, 15 April 1951 and 1956}

Schweitzer, Jean Baptista von (1833–1875)

A German socialist poet, Schweitzer studied law in Berlin and Heidelberg. After Lassalle's death, he became president of the German Workmen's Union and was sent to Parliament in 1867. He wrote the *Zeitgeist and Christianity* (1862) and *The Darwinians* (1875). {BDF; RAT}

Schweninger, Ernst (Born 1850)

Schweninger was a German pathologist, once the private physician to Prince Bismarck. He later became professor and director of the chief clinic at Berlin. In the Haeckel Memorial Volume (*Was Wir Ernst Haeckel Verdanken*, 1914), Schweninger wrote a cordial appreciation of the great monist, whose rationalism he fully endorsed. Haeckel, he wrote, had raised for himself, in the record of enlightenment, "a monument *memoriá et aere perennius.*" {RAT}

SCIENCE

Naturalists in philosophy use science and the scientific method when they reason. As Bertrand Russell wrote in *The Art of Philosophizing* (1968), "Whoever wishes to become a philosopher will do well to pay attention to the history of science, and particularly to its warfare with theology." He then explains his criticism of the Catholic Church: "With the exception of pure mathematics, every science has had to begin by fighting to establish its right to exist. Astronomy was condemned in the person of Galileo, geology in the person of Buffon. Scientific medicine was, for a long time, made almost impossible by the opposition of the Church to the dissection of dead bodies. Darwin came too late to suffer penalties, but Catholics and the Legislature of Tennessee still regard evolution with abhorrence. Each step has been won with difficulty and each new step is still opposed, as if nothing were to be learnt from past defeats. In our day, it is the newest science, psychology, that encounters opposition, particularly when it seems in danger of interfering with the doctrine of 'sin.' The conception of 'sin' was the Church's way of preventing anti-social behavior. If the police failed, the sinner could not congratulate himself on his escape, for God would punish him. In ethics, equally, the old obscurantism continues. No one is injured when a man marries his deceased wife's sister, yet the Church is still shocked by such wicked behavior, since it defines 'sin' not as what does harm, but as what the Bible or the Church condemns."

Addressing the historical conflict between religion and science, the

Catechism of the Catholic Church (1994) states that basic scientific research, as well as applied research, "is a significant expression of man's dominion over creation. Science and technology are precious resources when placed at the service of man and promote his integral development for the benefit of all. By themselves, however, they cannot disclose the meaning of existence and of human progress. Science and technology are ordered to man, from whom they take their origin and development; hence they find in the person and in his moral values both evidence of their purpose and awareness of their limits." Science, the catechism continues, "must be at the service of the human person, of his inalienable rights, of his true and integral good, in conformity with the plan and the will of God."

However, Isaac Asimov in *The Encyclopedia of Unbelief*, makes it clear that what scientists do *not* believe "are the tenets of religion, in particular those of the Judeo-Christian belief-system." He adds that "the scientific view is that fundamentalism is a form of religion that clings to Babylonian science of twenty-five centuries ago and by modern standards is nothing but superstition. Fundamentalists, on the other hand, wish to appropriate the respect given to science, and wish to have their views taught in the public schools as 'science.' This cannot constitutionally be done if their views are backed only by biblical evidence and nothing more, since that would violate the principle of separation of church and state. Therefore, they present their fundamentalist views without mention of the Bible, surround it with a potpourri of undigested scientific terminology, and call it 'scientific creationism.' However, calling a horse a golden-haired princess doesn't make it any the less a horse, and 'scientific creationism' is merely fundamentalism." (See McCabe's *Rationalist Encyclopedia* for a discussion of Science and Religion and Scientists and Religion.) {EU; Lee Eisler, *The Quotable Bertrand Russell*}

SCIENCE AND GOD: See entry for "Do Scientists Believe in God?"

SCIENCE AND NON-SCIENCE

The scientific method involves observation, induction of laws, formation of hypotheses predicting yet unobserved phenomena, and observations to test these hypotheses. Ted Debiak, President of New York Area Skeptics, adds two more principles:

- A hypothesis must be falsifiable: that is, its proponent must be able to specify what evidence would lead him to abandon it.

- "Double-blind" experiments are preferable, as in medical experiments where neither the patient nor the examining physician knows what treatment has been administered. More generally, an observer should not know the "correct" or "expected answer" answer.

Other requirements of good science are communication with others in the field and reproduction of results in other laboratories.

Debiak in an 18 March 1998 speech to the New York Area Skeptics provided some examples of non-science:

- Margaret and Kate in 1848, abetted by their aunt, pretended that sounds they were able to make with their joints were made by the spirits of the dead, with whom they could communicate. Thirty years later they admitted the hoax, but Spiritualism by then had grown into a new religion and mere facts were not going to destroy their claim.

- The "N-rays" of René Blondot in 1903 appeared to emanate from an iron container enclosing a hot platinum filament. Blondot, attempting to find a filter for polarized X-rays, noticed that radiation seemed to pass through an aluminum window and was diffracted by an aluminum prism. The spectrum was observed as a fluorescent thread. However, the experiments could not be reproduced elsewhere. In 1904, Robert Wood, an American physicist, visited the university of Nancy (for which the rays were named) and in the dark room removed the prism without the knowledge of Blondot or his assistant. Blondot still saw the spectrum. When Wood surreptitiously replaced the prism, the assistant, thinking there was no prism, saw no spectrum. Blondot had to admit that it was all an illusion.

- The 1908 Piltdown Man was later shown to have been a hoax after fluorine tests indicated the alleged remains were not over 200,000 years old but, rather, consisted according to X-rays of a chimpanzee jaw and a tooth of modern origin. The usual suspect for the forgery is Charles Dawson.

- R. Ron Hubbard, the founder of Scientology, claimed to be the only person who could remember all his past lives, including one as Piltdown Man.

- In 1966 Boris Derjaguin claimed that when water vapor condenses in a fine quartz capillary it takes a new form, with density, viscosity, and boiling point greater, and freezing point less, than for ordinary water. Scientists outside of Russia later determined that polywater is really a colloidal dispersion of silica (quartz) in water.

- In 1989 B. Stanley Pons and Martin Fleischmann claimed they had achieved nuclear fusion, not at the usual millions of degrees, but at room temperature. However, scientists now see cold fusion as an illusion despite the fact that conferences continue to debate the subject.

Irving Langmuir has suggested the following laws of bad science: (1) The maximum effect is produced by a barely detectable change in conditions; (2) effects are close to the limit of detectability; (3) there are claims of great accuracy; (4) fantastic theories, contrary to experience, are suggested; (5) *ad hoc* explanations are always provided for disappointing results; and (6) the percentage of scientists who accept the results rises to about 50%, then falls to zero.

{John Arents, "When Science Goes Wrong, *The New York Area Skeptic*, Summer 1998}

SCIENCE EDUCATION

Freethinkers and secular humanists strongly favor science education. However, schools are populated by students whose vocabulary includes such words as creationism, faith, heaven, hell, holy ghost, soul, spirit, virgin birth. And religions, as Carl Sagan pointed out, currently are "nurseries of pseudoscience." Meanwhile, many science teachers use the scientific method of reasoning most of the time but, because of their religious faith, they believe Jesus once literally rose from the dead; that the Ten Commandments or the Book of Mormon or the Qur'an were personally delivered by God or by angels to Moses or Joseph Smith or Muhammad; that upon their death they will go to Heaven; etc. A 1997 survey by Edward J. Larson of the University of Georgia reported that of the 600 of 1000 American scientists who responded to a query, about 40% believed in a God who, by the survey's strict definition, actively communicated with humankind and to whom one may pray "in expectation of receiving an answer."

Dr. Alan Hale, the co-discoverer of Comet Hale-Bopp while the comet was still visible in 1997, stated that unless drastic changes are made he would not recommend that young people seek careers in science. This was because he deplored the limited career options and the widespread superstitious beliefs spawned by "scientific illiteracy," two of the main causes he perceived of a malaise in science. He specifically worried about antiscientific attitudes based on belief rather than reason and cited hundreds of "vicious hate letters" he had received after he publicly scoffed at the belief by superstitious skywatchers that a bright star visible near the Hale-Bopp comet was a "companion" carrying extraterrestrial visitors to the solar system.

SCIENCE FICTION WRITERS ON PHILOSOPHY

- To me however, death is merely death, and a person who was alive is gone, and although sorrow and loneliness may devour you as a result, it should not be put on public display, any more than it must. I realize this is not a popular view and will not prevail.

–**Isaac Asimov**, *I. Asimov*

- It makes, in the upshot, no difference from which direction one approaches the central question of our time: will we, or will we not, survive the consequences of our own ingenuity? Both alternatives remain open.

–**John Brunner**,
The Evolution of a Science Fiction Writer

- Gods can do anything. They fear nothing: they are gods. But there is one rule, one Seal of Solomon that can confound a god, and to which all gods pay service, to the letter: When belief in a god dies, the god dies. . . .To be replaced by newer, more relevant gods.

–**Harlan Ellison**
from the introduction to *Deathbird Stories*

• History has the relation to truth that theology has to religion—i.e., none to speak of.

–Lazarus Long
in **Robert A. Heinlein**'s *Time Enough For Love*

• The most important Manhattan Projects of the future will be vast government-sponsored enquiries into what the politicians and the participating scientists will call "the problem of happiness"—in other words, the problem of making people love their servitude. . . . The love of servitude cannot be established except as the result of a deep, personal revolution in human minds and bodies.

–Aldous Huxley
from the Foreword to *Brave New World*

• After 20 generations of shilly-shallying and "we'll" cross that bridge when we come to it," genus homo had bred itself into an impasse. . . . Mental subnormals were outbreeding mental normals and supernormals, and the process was occurring on an exponential curve. . . . If you think that had any effect on breeding practices, you do not know genus homo.

–C. M. Kornbluth
from "The Little Black Bag"

• For me, it is far better to grasp the Universe as it really is than to persist in delusion, however, satisfying and reassuring.

–Carl Sagan
The Demon-Haunted World
(See the entries for Aliens from Outer Space and for Voltaire, who was the first to use the expression. Also, critics have noted that an inordinate number of science fiction writers, named herein, are non-theists.) {*The American Rationalist*, September-October 1997}

SCIENCE, MYTHS OF

Gina Kolata laments that some scientific myths are too good to die. In *The New York Times* (6 December 1998), she listed two examples:

• the "Hawthorne Effect" was a much touted 1927-1933 study of factory workers at Western Electric's Hawthorne Plant in Illinois, one which showed that regardless of the changes made in working conditions productivity increased. However, as Stanford University's Dr. Lee Ross has shown, only five workers took part in that study, and two of these were replaced partway through for gross insubordination and low output. The University of Michigan's Dr. Richard Nisbett calls the Hawthorne effect "a glorified anecdote. Once you've got the aanecdote, you can throw away the data."

• A 25 June 1990 study by Dr. Bernard Siegel told of two oncologists who tested a combination of four chemotherapy drugs, which had the initials EPHO. When one doctor's patients did well, but only a fourth of the others' patients improved, the first doctor explained that he had simply rearranged the letters of the drugs so they spelled HOPE. The test was challenged by the University of Toronto's Dr. Robert Buckman, who traced the Siegel story to a book by Norman Cousins, who had referred to an article published in a 1988 *Western Journal of Medicine*, the writer of which said the story was simply a parable meant to tell doctors that there is more to treating cancer than merely doling out drugs.

SCIENTIFIC HUMANISM: See entry for Secular Humanism.

SCIENTIFIC MATERIALISM: See entries for Lucretius, Hobbes, and Materialism.

SCIENTIFIC METHOD

Scientists are aware that questions are not settled. Provisional answers are given to such questions; later, other scientists are invited to provide more illuminating answers. Scientists, according to David Baltimore of the Massachusetts Institute of Technology, "are different from artists in that they give primacy to logic and evidence, but the most fundamental progress in science is achieved through hunch, analogy, insight, and creativity. The culture of science is one that allows for both rigor and fluidity, an amalgam that, though quite different from nonscientific culture, is no less valuable."

In their investigations, scientists observe phenomena and come up with a hypothesis, experiment to demonstrate the truth or falseness of that hypothesis, then make conclusions which validate or modify the hypothesis. {*The New Yorker*, 27 January 1997}

SCIENTIFIC THEORY

• [Do not] put too much confidence in experimental results until they have been confirmed by theory.

–Sir Arthur Eddington

SCIENTOLOGY

The Church of Scientology is a religious sect which was founded in 1954 by science fiction writer L. Ron Hubbard (1911–1986). His *Dianetics: The Modern Science of Mental Health* (1950) formed the basis of a philosophic outlook which allegedly offers an alternative path to overcoming physical and mental stress. The soul, it is claimed, can be cleaned of its negative energy through a ceremony called "processing." Each person, it is taught, creates his or her own problems. The common man is smarter than the educated elite. We all possess Godlike powers and un-tapped, unlimited potential (which can be accessed through techniques which cost money).

Challenged in the 1950s by the American Medical Association and the American Psychological Association, and investigated in the 1960s by the governments of England, Australia, and the United States, the church had its tax-exempt status temporarily questioned. Hubbard moved to England in 1959 and lived the rest of his life as a recluse. The group's leadership denies that it is a cult, and they have claimed a membership of eight million, although others put the figure as low as fifty thousand. The church in 1995 had a paid staff of 13,000.

Many celebrities have been attracted to Scientology, a feat attributable to its three-decade efforts that are unusual for a religious group. Included are musician Elvis Presley's daughter, Lisa Marie; musicians Isaac Hayes and Chick Corea; television legal analyst Greta Van Susteren; and actors John Travolta and Tom Cruise. "Through Scientology," Travolta said at an award from the public works commission for a renovation project in Los Angeles, "you learn to examine your life and be more productive. You can make sure you avoid any pitfalls and you can face your challenges and handle them." The church operates a Celebrity Centre near Hollywood Hills, a place which caters to artists and actors and where they can stay while being counseled.

In 1995, several dissidents electronically posted on computer bulletin boards a 136-page text that could be copied for free. Some Scientologists are required to pay thousands of dollars to the church for their copy. As a result, the "free" text was copied in Finland, Germany, China, and elsewhere around the world. Charging that the dissidents had infringed on copyrights and had misappropriated "trade secrets," United States marshals seized their computers and files. Meanwhile, the posting underlined the ease with which individuals on the global computer network could by-pass national laws to oppose religions and, in addition, could also freely criticize governments. "A church that won't tell you what they teach until you pay them?" That question echoed throughout the cyberspatial network, but church officials countered by saying their membership remained faithful.

The church sued a major magazine, *Time*, because of a 1991 article that described the Scientology movement as a "global racket" and claiming that it had had questionable dealings on the Vancouver Stock Exchange. The $416,000,000 libel suit was dismissed by a Federal judge in 1996, and the writer of the article countersued, accusing the church of harassment and improperly obtaining his credit reports.

In 1996, the southern state of Bavaria in Germany required all state employees to fill out a questionnaire detailing any tie to the Church of Scientology. The leaders of Germany's sixteen regional states also debated whether to place the Scientologists under government surveillance. They charged that the self-help movement is a profit-making scheme and should be denied the tax breaks ordinarily given to churches and charities. French as well as German governments have questioned whether Scientology is a religion, claiming that it is a money-making enterprise because of the high fees it charges members.

Although Hubbard died, Scientologists take comfort in the writings he left behind and believe he currently is doing research "in some other place." Annual birthday parties are held in his honor. (See entries for L. Ron Hubbard as well as for Science and Non-Science.) {CE; *New York*, 29 July 1996 and 13 February 1998

Scobie, Richard S. (20th Century)

For twenty-seven years, Scobie was executive director of the Unitarian Universalist Service Committee, a humanitarian group that engages in social action, education, and service as well as supports the development of local democratic institutions and leadership in Africa, the Caribbean, Central America, India, and the Philippines. Scobie retired in 1998, saying that

> [T]he bipolar balance of terror has given way to the chaos of ethnic, religious, and racial warfare in Europe, Asia, and Africa. Globally, the gap between rich and poor, north and south, is growing with savage implications for the ever more vulnerable majorities. The marginalizations of indigenous people in Mexico, Burma, and South Dakota, the marketing of women in Thailand, India, and the streets of Los Angeles, and the disenfranchisement of poor mothers and children by structural adjustment in the Third World and welfare reform in the United States all ensure that UUSC will continue to be needed, and busy.

Scopes, John T(homas) (20th Century)

Scopes wrote *Center of the Storm: Memoirs of John T. Scopes* (1966).

He had been a biology teacher who was tried in 1925 for teaching Darwinism in a Dayton, Tennessee, public school. Clarence Darrow was one of his attorneys while William Jennings Bryan aided the state prosecutor. On the first day of the trial when Judge John T. Raulston bowed his head and began to pray, Darrow objected to the prayer but was overruled. Darrow also objected to a sign proclaiming, "Read Your Bible," and it was removed. During the trial, Bryan admitted that he knew nothing of ancient civilization or other religions. In what became known as the "Monkey Trial," the jury, one member of which was illiterate, found Scopes guilty, for the defense had never denied that Scopes had taught the doctrine of evolution. Also, the trial was lost partly because of the defense, which refused to plead any of the technical defenses available, fearing an acquittal on a technical rather than a constitutional basis. Scopes was fined $100. Later, however, he was released by the state supreme court on a technicality. Although the case tended to discourage enactment of similar legislation in other states, the law was not repealed until 1967. {CE; GS; PA; TYD}

Scot, Reginald (1584–1599)

Scot was an English rationalist, author of *The Discoverie of Witchcraft* (1584), the first English work to question the existence of witches. King James I had the book burned, but it was republished in 1886. {BDF}

Scott, Amy (19th Century)

Scott was the first recorded African American to join a Universalist church, the one in Philadelphia.

Scott, Bill (20th Century)

Scott is Vice President (programming) of Free Inquirers of Northeastern Ohio. {*FINO*, 1 Jan 1998}

Scott, Clinton Lee (Born 1890)

Scott, a Universalist minister at St. Petersburg, Florida, signed Humanist Manifesto I as well as Humanist Manifesto II. He wrote *The Universalist Church of America: A Short History* (1957). Of the first manifesto, Scott said it probably represents as well as any one statement could a cross section of the thought of the number of persons included," adding that "One of the primary virtues of a Humanist is his intellectual modesty. Whether the universe is 'self-existing' or 'created,' and whether or not there is a cosmic end beyond the fulfillment of man's life here and now are matters about which even a Theist can make but a poor guess. However, I like the positive character of the statement and especially the recognition of the economic factors." {EW; HM1; HM2; HNS; U}

Scott, Ernest (1967–1939)

Scott, who married Mabel Besant, daughter of the militant feminist Annie Besant, changed his name on Mabel's insistence to Besant-Scott. The two moved to Australia, where he became a reporter for *The Herald* in Melbourne. During Annie Besant's 1894 lecture tour of Australia, they assisted in the establishment of the Australasian section of the Theosophical Society. Ernest edited the *Australia Theosophist*, but his wife converted to Roman Catholicism and the marriage broke up. In 1913 he was invited to the Chair of History at the University of Melbourne, where he maintained his earlier freethought attitudes and where "religious belief was to him simply a delusion." {SWW}

Scott, Eugenie C. (20th Century)

Scott, an anthropologist, is executive director of the National Center for Science Education. She is a Fellow of the Committee for the Scientific Investigation of Claims of the Paranorma, which publishes *The Skeptical Inquirer*. In 1994 she addressed the 14th annual HUMCON conference sponsored in Long Beach, California, of the Alliance of Humanist, Atheist, and Ethical Culture Organizations of Los Angeles County.

She has gone on record in *Skeptical Inquirer* (July-August 1999) as being concerned about any "theistic science movement," the growth of which would be detrimental to pure science. Polls, she further laments, "show that almost half of Americans deny that evolution occurred. About 40 percent think that evolution occurred, and was guided by God, and an additional 10 percent or so agree that evolution occurred, but deny any role for God."

Scott, George Campbell (1927–)

Scott, an actor and director who in 1971 refused an Oscar for his performance in the film, "Patton," but accepted a 1971 Emmy Award for "The Price," was asked by CNN's Larry King if he believed in life after death. Scott replied in the negative but was not asked if he also was a non-theist.

Scott, Harold (20th Century)

A Unitarian minister, Scott was a contributing editor to *The Humanist* in the 1950s. {HNS}

Scott, Peter (20th Century)

Scott in Britain is active with the Berkshire Humanists.

Scott, Richard (20th Century)

Scott's *A Game of Chess* (1954) refutes the existence of God and the truth of Christianity. {FUS}

Scott, Robert H. (20th Century)

Scott is author of "An Atheist Speaks." He wrote a critical survey in 1949 of the Federal Communications Commission's decision on atheistic religious programs.

Scott, Thomas (1808–1878)

Scott was an English scholar who traveled widely, lived with Indians, and was a page to Charles X of France. Having investigated Christianity, he later devoted himself to freethought propaganda by sending scholarly pamphlets among the clergy and cultured classes. From 1862 to 1877 he issued from Mount Pleasant, Ramsgate, over a hundred different pamphlets and challenged the Christian Evidence Society to debate his freethought viewpoints. With Sir G. W. Cox, he wrote *The English Life of Jesus* (1871). Scott also wrote *A Farewell Address* (c. 1875). {BDF; FUK; RAT; RE; TRI}

SCOTTISH HUMANISM

In the 1960s, an active Humanist group at Glasgow University included Bryon and Diana Mann, John Milburn, Anna McLaren, Jessie Brooks, Jim McCurdie, and Floris Greenlaw.

The United Kingdom Christian Handbook 1992–1993 contains statistics compiled by Fergus Watt concerning the incidence of religious non-belief in Scotland. He estimated a total of 3.2 million adult believers over fifteen years of age, of whom 2,900,000 are Trinitarians and 300,000 are non-Trinitarian or "other." From 1985 to 1990, Watt found a decline in membership of 15% among Roman Catholics, 8% among Presbyterians, 4% among both Methodists and Baptists, and 3% among Anglicans. However, Pentecostals made a 39% increase and Afro-Caribbeans increased 67% (although they had but 385 members as of 1990). Watt estimates that non-believers in Scotland number around 500,000.

Scottish humanist contacts include the following:

Alloa: Charles McGill, 33 Balfour St., Alloa, FK10 1RU

Angus: Bob Watson, Fairfield Mains, Arbroath Angus, DD11 3RX

Banff/Moray: Geoff Armitage, Norheim, Church St., Dufftown, Banffshire

Dumfries and Galloway: Charles Douglas, Midpark, Balmaclellan, Castle Douglas, Galloway DG7 3PX

Dundee: John Duncan, 10 Barnes Ave., Dundee

East Neuk of Fife: Sandy Edwards, 11A Strathkinness High Road, St. Andrews KY 16 9UA

Gourock: J. C. Johnston, 7 McPherson Drive, Gourock, PA19 1LJ

Mid-Fife: Campbell Brown, Croft Cottage, Croft Road, Markinch KY 7 6EQ

Lochaber: Hector M. Rogers, Tigh Na Car Ruadh, Invergarry, Invernesshire

Mid-Borders: Fergus Watt, Plesandis, Main St., Denholm, Roxburghshire TD 9 8NU

North Ayshire: Robin Wood, 37 Inchmurrin Drive, Kilmarnock KA 3 2JD

Orkney: Eric Stockon, West Cottage, Sanday Orkney KW17 0HB

South Ayshire: John Watson, Park Farm, Turnberry, Ayrshire KA26 9ND

Scottish humanist groups include the following:

- *Humanist Scotland* is at <ahenness@aol.com>.
- Humanist Society of Scotland: George Rodger, 17 Howburn Place, Aberdeen AB11 6XT, United Kingdom (01224) 573034. Their newsletter is edited by Alex Scott, 51 Inveroran Drive, Glasgow G61 2PJ. Their secretary is Alan Henness, 138 Lumley Street, Grangemouth FK38BL On the Web: <http://visitweb.com/hss>.
- HSS Aberdeen Group: Rosalind Cheyne, 9 Westfield Terrace, Aberdeen (01224) 635675.
- HSS Edinburgh Group: Mrs. Jean Llewellyn, 2 Saville Terrace, Edinburgh EH 9 3AD (0131) 667 8389. Steuart Campbell is on the contact. <explicit@cix.co.uk>
- HSS Glasgow Group: Alan Henness, 138 Lumley St., Grangemouth FK3 8BL (01324) 485152.

Scotland has four Unitarian congregations. The oldest, in Edinburgh, was started in the 1770s as a "congregation of Universalist dissenters," and it adopted the Unitarian label around 1815. Its one hundred members include agnostic humanists as well as liberal Christians. Glasgow, Dundee, and Aberdeen each have from fifty to seventy members. According to John Clifford, Dundee is largely chrstocentric in its worship, Glasgow and Aberdeen much less so. The four comprise the Scottish Unitarian Association.

(See entries for Humanism in Scotland, Humanist Society of Scotland, and Humanist Society of Scotland, Glasgow Group.)

{*Glasgow Group Newsletter*, September 1997}

SCOTTISH HUMANIST PUBLICATIONS

Scottish Humanist was published by the Scottish Humanist Council, c/o Robin Wood, at 37 Inchmurrin Drive, Kilmarnock, Scotland.

Humanism Scotland, edited by Jane Fox, is the official organ of the Humanist Society of Scotland at 11A Strathkinness High Road, St. Andrews, KY16 9UA, United Kingdom.

E-mail: <Ahenness@aol.com>. {FD}

SCOTTISH UNITARIANS

On the Web: <http://www.ednet.co.uk/~hill> and <http://www.unitarian.org.uk/>.

Scotus, John Duns: See entry for Aureol.

Scrase, Leslie (20th Century)

Scrase is the editor and publisher of *The Humanist Theme* and author of *Coping with Death*, which complements the British Humanist Association's *Funerals Without God*. His *The Sunlight Glances Through Poems* (1996) includes wry humor, reaction to public events, and a humanistic philosophy.

In *Some Ancestors of Humanism* (1997), Scrase found significant aspects of humanism in Jainism, in Buddhism, in the ancient Chinese religions and teachings of Confucius, and the Ancient Greeks. Although none can specifically be termed "humanism," he notes, "to come anywhere near to modern humanism, all these strands are needed."

Scribe, Augustin Eugène (1791–1861)

Scribe's first play, *Le Prétender sans le savoir* (1810) was a failure and was followed by a dozen other failures. But in 1815 his *Une Nuit de la Garde Nationale* inaugurated a success for the French playwright. He wrote one hundred and fifty plays for one theatre; his works fill seventy-six volumes (1874–1885). Scribe was admitted to the French Academy in 1836. He avoided politics and controversy, and he had no religious membership. His work, however, contained liberal religious ideas. {CE; RAT}

Scriven, Michael: See entry for Atheistic Humanism.

SCRUPULOSITY

William Van Ornum, a professor of clinical psychology at the Marist College in Poughkeepsie, New York, defines scrupulosity as a disorder that shows itself through obsessive-compulsive worship and irrational religious belief. "Even though it's about faith, scrupulosity is a terrible, terrible disease," he has written in *A Thousand Frightening Fantasies: Understanding and Healing Scrupulosity and Obsessive Compulsive Disorder* (1998).

He cites examples: a woman with scrupulosity sits through three or four Roman Catholic Masses before she believes the priest said the final prayer the right way; an elderly woman fears she has sinned by giving germs to others after she has used a toilet; a computer programmer stays late at work daily as restitution because she feels she has not given 100% to her employer. Van Ornum has stated that "Martin Luther had it awful. He couldn't say Mass. If he said one word wrong, he had to say the whole Mass over again."

Commenting on the subject, the Rev. Thomas Santa in a *Scrupulosity Anonymous Newsletter* mailed from Liguori, Mississippi, wrote, "Scrupulosity at its basis is not a religious disorder. It's an obsessive-compulsive disorder. But therapists have a tendency to jump to the conclusion that someone with religious problems is screwed up because of their religion and not because of a disorder." The newsletter is mailed to more than 13,000 subscribers. {Associated Press, 22 February 1998}

SCYLLA

In Greek mythology Scylla was the female sea monster who devoured sailors.

The idiom, "to be between Scylla and Charybdis," means that by avoiding one danger it is possible to be exposed to yet another danger. Charybdis was a ship-devouring sea monster who resided just opposite Scylla's cave.

Scylla betrayed her father to his enemy Minos in order to seek Minos's love, but he then scorned her. {CE}

SCYTHIA

An ancient region from the Danube to the borders of China, Scythia was occupied by warlike mounted nomads who came from Russia in the 1st millennium B.C.E. Early Scythians believed they sprang from a union of the Greek hero Heracles with a sexually aggressive snake-woman in a Scythian cave.

Before the 9th century B.C.E., they formed a kingdom in the East Crimea, and during the 7th century B.C.E. they invaded Mesopotamia, Syria, and the Balkans. Thereafter, they survived attacks by Darius I of Persia (512 B.C.E.) and Alexander the Great (c. 325 B.C.E.), but after 300 B.C.E. they were driven back to South Russia and were displaced there in the 2nd or 1st century B.C.E. by a related group, the Sarmatians. {CE; Jasper Griffin, "Anxieties of Influence," *The New York Review of Books*, 20 June 1996}

Sczesny, Gerhard (20th Century)

A German, Sczesny addressed the Third International Humanist and Ethical Union World Congress held in Oslo (1962).

Sczesnoczkawasm, Jun (20th Century)

Sczesnoczkawasm is a pseudonym for an ex-English department chairman who taught at Bentley School in New York City and at New Canaan High School in Connecticut. A rationalist of dubious parentage, Sczesnoczkawasm is the life companion of Allen Windsor. Sczesnoczkawasm, once on the staff of the Hvmanist Book Clvb [*sic*], was designated as the individual "in charge of (unspecified) relations with the public."

"The bad thing about having my name," Sczesnoczkawasm once wrote, "is that no one can figure out my gender, religion, or nationality. The good thing is that no one can figure out my gender, religion, or nationality." (See entry for Hvmanist Book Clvb and Allen Windsor.)

SEA OF FAITH

Sea of Faith is a network of those who, while remaining within the Christian churches, hold broadly humanist ideas. David Boulton, who edits a magazine of the same name, finds that sea-of-faith humanists have much in common with others in the humanist movement. {David Boulton, *New Humanist*, November 1997}

Seabolt, Rachel: See entry for Rachel Seabolt Miller.

Seabrook, Gabriel (20th Century)

Seabrook, an anthropologist and author, is a secular humanist.

Seaburg, Hugh F. (20th Century)

In 1933 for his M.A. thesis at the University of Iowa, Seaburg wrote on the subject of Robert G. Ingersoll's speeches. {GS}

Séailles, Gabriel (1852–1906)

Séailles taught philosophy and was dean of the philosophical faculty at the Sorbonne. Apart from rationalist passages in his *Ernest Renan* (1895) and *Les affirmations de la conscience moderne* (1903), he wrote a letter which was read at the International Congress of Freethinkers at Rome in 1904. In it he said, "The human mind can conceive of no ideas more extravagant or ridiculous than it [the Church] has invented to fool and cheat the ignorant multitude and to awe and suppress the intellectual minority." {RAT; RE}

Searle, John R. (1932–)

Searle has been described as being one of the most important of the contemporary secular philosophers. A professor of mind and language at the University of California at Berkeley, Searle wrote *The Rediscovery of the Mind* (1992) and *Mind, Language, and Society* (1999). According to Nicholas G. Fotion of Emory University, "The mind, for Searle, is intentional (à la Brentano) in that perceptions, memories, imaginings, desires, and many other mental states take objects (e.g., I see *the car* and I remember *Aunt Fanny*)." Fotion adds, "For Searle, although the mind emerges from the body, it possesses an ineliminable subjective character with which materialistic accounts cannot adequately deal. In religion to this claim, he uses his famous Chinese room argument to show that even though a 'system' (a computer and a person) inside a room can manipulate Chinese symbols, it does not necessarily operate on the level of meaning. To do that, mental (intentional) concepts need to be introduced into the system."

In "Consciousness and the Philosophers" (*The New York Review of Books*, 6 March 1997), Searle attacks functionalism and David J. Chalmers's *The Conscious Mind: In Search of a Fundamental Theory.* He is a contributing editor for *Philo.* (See entry for Richard C. Vitzthum.) {OCP}

Sears, Catherine (20th Century)

Sears, from 1971 to 1973, edited *Progressive World.* {GS}

Sears, John W. (20th Century)

Sears, a clinical psychologist, signed Humanist Manifesto II. {HM2}

Seaton-Tiedemann, (Mrs.) M. L. (1858–1948)

In *Freethinker* (16 June 1918), Seaton-Tiedemann, the founder of the Divorce Law Reform Union in England, wrote, "Every measure for the true welfare of the community has been opposed by the Churches." {TRI}

Seaver, Horace Holley (1810–1889)

The Investigator was a radical periodical founded by Abner Kneeland, and some of its incisive articles had been written by "Z." This proved to be Seaver's signature, and when Seaver became editor he continued the publication for fifty years, until it merged with the *Truth Seeker.* Seaver was a zealous member of the "producing classes," and in his magazine he pointed out the connection between skepticism and social reform. He wrote *Occasional Thoughts of Horace Seaver From Fifty Years of Freethinking* (1888), which illustrated his atheism and materialism. With Josiah P. Mendum, he helped in the erection of the Paine Memorial Hall. Seaver's funeral oration was delivered by Colonel Robert Ingersoll. {BDF; EU, Roderick S. French; FUS; PUT; RAT}

Sebald, Hans (20th Century)

Sebald, professor emeritus of sociology at Arizona State University in Tempe, has documented in *Free Inquiry* (Winter 1993) that in contemporary Germany "secular humanism has a hard time to oppose a church structure that has extended its tentacles into every nook and niche of society." Germany, he finds, "is an anomaly among modern nation states insofar as the government functions as the church's tax collector," passing the collection plate not only for Catholics and Protestants but also nonbelievers may support humanist or freethinker organizations. Such an agreement was part of the 1933 *Concordat*, the treaty between the Third Reich and the Vatican, "personally signed by the pope and Hitler (the latter himself a Catholic who was never excommunicated) and in fact the first significant international treaty Hitler signed upon coming into power." Such an arrangement, Sebald notes, "so convenient and lucrative for the church, contributed to the minimal opposition shown by German Catholicism against the Nazi state—after all, who wants to have a falling out with an agent who so reliably fills one's treasury?"

He is author of *Witch-Children From Salem Witch-Hunts to Modern Courtrooms* (1995). {*Free Inquiry*, Spring 1997}

Sebastian, St. (Died 287)

A Roman martyr, Sebastian is known as the homosexual's saint. Shakespeare, Walter Pater, Oscar Wilde (who adopted the pseudonym "Sebastian Melmoth" on his release from prison), Claude Debussy, Jean Cocteau, T. S. Eliot, Wallace Stevens, Mishima, Thomas Mann (whose Aschenbach in *Death in Venice* worships Sebastian as a "new type of hero"), and others have shown an interest in the man. {GL}

Sebe, Ferencz (20th Century)

Sebe, who is Unitarian district minister for northwestern Romania, is an expert about the origins of Unitarianism in 16th century Transylvania. (Note that the ancient province of Dacia, now Romania, was Romanized in the 2 and 3rd centuries and was overrun successively by the Goths, Huns, Avars, Bulgars, Magyars, and Mongols.)

Sebille, Adolphe (19th Century)

Sebille was a French writer who, under the pseudonym of "Dr. Fabricus," published *God, Man, and His Latter End* (1868), which was a medico-psychological study. He also wrote *Letters from a Materialist to Monsignor Dupanloup* (1868–1869). {BDF}

Sechenov, Ivan (19th Century)

Sechenov (or Setchenoff) was a Russian philosopher who, in 1863, published *Psychological Studies*, explaining the mind by its physiology. {BDF}

Seckel, Al (20th Century)

A humanist and member of the Bertrand Russell Society, Seckel is author of *Bertrand Russell on Ethics, Sex, and Marriage* (1987) and *Bertrand Russell on God and Religion* (1991).

SECRET INSTRUCTIONS OF THE JESUITS: See entry for Hoaxes, Religious.

SECRETS

• When anyone says to me, "Can you keep a secret?" I say, "Why should I, if you can't?

–**Gore Vidal**
Playboy, December 1998

SECRETARIAT FOR GROWTH AND DEVELOPMENT

The Secretariat for Growth and Development works to support the creation and growth of new humanist groups. It is located at the Center for Inquiry International in Amherst, New York, and is supported by the Council for Secular Humanism and Prometheus Books.

Grants have been given to humanist groups in Bangladesh, China, Costa Rica, Egypt, India, Indonesia, Mexico, and Peru from the Humanist Network Development Program. {*International Humanist News*, October 1998}

SECRETS

• There are two secrets to success:

1. Never tell everything you know.

SECT

A sect is a religious group, often one which has separated from a larger denomination. The word often implies disapproval, as exemplified by the observation in the 1830s of the astute French visitor, Alexis de Tocqueville: "From time to time strange sects arise that endeavor to strike out extraordinary paths to eternal happiness. Religious insanity is very common in the United States."

SECT OF ZARATHUSTRA

A freethought group, The Sect of Zarathustra is at 30 Stockton Street, Bloomfield, New Jersey 07003.

SECULAR ALTERNATIVE

The Atheist League of Washington (POB 1785, Seattle, Washington 98111), published *Secular Alternative.* {FD}

SECULAR EDUCATION LEAGUE

The Secular Education League was formed in 1907 for the purpose of removing all teaching of religion from all state-funded schools in England. "After nearly a century," laments Nicolas Walter, "its work still needs to be done." {*New Humanist*, February 1996}

SECULAR FAMILY NETWORK

Family Matters, edited by Jan Loeb Eisler, began with a winter 1997 issue and provided secular humanist resources and viewpoints for parents, children, and families. E-mail: <hasp@gte.net>

SECULAR HUMANISM, A SURVEY OF

Variously called scientific, naturalistic, ethical, or even religious, the movement of secular humanism has succeeded in making an impact upon philosophic as well as religious thought. Although secular humanism draws its supporters from a variety of viewpoints, most secular humanists in order to attain the good life discard all dependence upon anything outside man himself. They are content with life's exciting uncertainties. Some like John Dewey have emphasized instrumentalism; some like Curtis W. Reese have incorporated Unitarianism; some like Corliss Lamont stress philosophic naturalism; some like Nobel Laureates Francis Crick, Murray Gell-Mann, Herbert Hauptman, André Lwoff, and Steven Weinberg emphasize the scientific method; some like Carl Sagan join astronomy with humanism; Paul Kurtz has coined *eupraxophy*, or "good practice and wisdom," to describe the movement's being ethical, philosophical, and scientific.

In 1899, Charles Watts founded the Rationalist Press Association (RPA) in Great Britain, a group of agnostics whose goal was to "circulate Rationalist publications." They defined rationalism as "the mental attitude which unreservedly accepts the supremacy of reason and aims at establishing a system of philosophy and ethics verifiable by experience and independent of all arbitrary assumption of authority." The RPA has no doctrinal or philosophical tests, but its members usually reject a belief in God and immortality, are both secular and humanistic in their outlooks, and prefer the rationalist label.

In 1928 Jai Prithvi Bahadur Singh of Nepal founded a Humanistic Club, and in the following year traveled throughout Europe in order to encourage the setting up of other such club which, following the aftermath of World War I, he felt were needed to inspire intellectuals. Europe at the time had sunk into bankruptcy, and the resultant internal chaos had, he felt, plunged the intellectuals of the world into a state of shock. To resolve this "state of nightmare," he proposed turning to humanistic principles and values that could improve the governance of the relationship between men and nations. He included among his humanistic tenets the following:

• Instead of entering into unhealthy competition and dogmatic contradictions, humans should direct their behavior toward a path of reconciliation so that security, privileges, and prosperity can be insured through mutual understanding.
• The general public needs an organization through which it can interact, exchange ideas, and solve common problems.
• If the doctrine of self-security is based on humanitarian grounds, the path leading to a peaceful society will automatically open.
• Whatever is done to destroy human civilization is, lamentably, a symbol of animalistic instinct.
• Humanism is a philosophic outlook which human beings, creatures who are distinct from other animals, choose to observe as a duty and not as a religion.

Singh's lecturing led to conferences in Switzerland, Germany, Czechoslovakia, Austria, Hungary, Yugoslavia, Romania, Poland, Russia, France, Iceland, Italy, Egypt, Sri Lanka, Singapore, Thailand, Hong Kong, China, Japan, and England, following which several humanistic clubs were founded.

In the United States, the secular movement of humanism commenced just before the 1920s and greatly expanded in the 1930s when the philosophy of naturalistic humanism was nurtured in Unitarian societies in the Midwest, West, and East. Edwin H. Wilson in 1930 wrote in *The New Humanist* that adult education in England and the United States was evidence that what is now called *secular humanism* was beyond authoritarian church control.

Most Ethical Culture and some Universalist societies also helped publicize the beliefs. By 1933 the movement had become sufficiently popular and had gained enough adherents that a group of thirty-four philosophers and scholars formulated a "clarion call" for its wholehearted support. The document they agreed upon is known as **A Humanist Manifesto**, and it was signed, along with others, by Reese and Dewey. Over half the signers were or have been ministers of Unitarian, Universalist, and Ethical Culture societies. The manifesto appeared in the May-June, 1933, issue of *New Humanist* with a note by Raymond B. Bragg, editor, stating that it was a product of many minds, was designed to represent a developing point of view, and was not in any sense a new creed. Had the signatories written individual statements of belief, he added, they undoubtedly would have stated the propositions differently. He continued, "The importance of the document is that more than thirty men have come to general agreement on matters of final concern and that these men are undoubtedly representative of a larger number who are forging a new philosophy out of the materials of the modern world."

Signers of Humanist Manifesto I included literary people such as **Llewellyn Jones** and **Robert Morss Lovett**. There were educators such as **W. Frank Swift** and **V. T. Thayer**. Journalists included **Harry Elmer Barnes**, **William Floyd**, and **Albert C. Dieffenbach**. An imposing group of philosophers was represented: **John Dewey**, **Edwin A. Burtt**, **John Herman Randall Jr.**, **Oliver L. Reiser**, and **Roy Wood Sellars**. There were economists such as **F. H. Hankins** and scientists such as **A. J. Carlson**, **Maynard Shipley**, and **Bernard Fantus**. There was **Rabbi Jacob J. Weinstein** and such Unitarian and Universalist ministers as **J.A.C. Fagginger Auer**, **E. Burdette Backus**, **Ernest Caldecott**, **A. Eustace Haydon**, **Harold P. Marley**, **R. Lester Mondale**, **Charles Francis Potter**, and **Edwin H. Wilson**. Wilson, who was the guiding force behind the formulation of the manifesto and who became a particularly effective organizer for the American Humanist Association, edited its journal, *The Humanist*, and as a Unitarian minister was helpful in bringing together the religious as well as the naturalistic humanists.

Four years prior to the manifesto, **Charles Francis Potter** had founded a Humanist Society in New York City, the first "church" of its kind in the nation. It served as a precedent for the formation of other such organizations, which now are found nationwide. Potter replaced sermons by lectures. His society had no paid clergy, no creed, no prayers, and no baptisms. Wedding ceremonies were unique in that the bride and groom, rather than repeating a vow devised by someone else, composed their own. As to God and immortality, Potter and his group were agnostic. The purpose of the society was to provide a place where mature minds could meet and discuss an adult American religion, one "devoid of fairy-tales" about angels, demons, devils, or gods; one based upon a faith in man and a belief in man's capabilities for improving individuals and society as a whole by the slow, steady improvement of human personality. Potter's ultimate hope was that his church with its philosophy of humanism and its utilization of common sense and the scientific method would serve as a model for others, and that eventually all or at least the majority of churches would merge into a humanistic, not a supernaturalistic, union which could be imitated in other nations.

John Dewey has been considered the unofficial dean of the movement, although he preferred the phrase "humanistic naturalism" to "naturalistic humanism." His *Reconstruction in Philosophy* (1920) indicted metaphysics as "the product of an aristocratic and leisure class, the expression of a desire to escape into another world instead of facing the responsibilities of the here and now." Other early leaders whose books supported and outlined the meaning and purpose of this secular movement of humanism included James H. Leuba, a psychologist; Max C. Otto, professor of philosophy at the University of Wisconsin; Julian S. Huxley; Bertrand Russell; and H. G. Wells.

George Santayana's *Genteel Tradition at Bay* (1931) served as a powerful attack on the neo-humanism of Babbitt and Moore—his book strongly supported naturalism. He wrote that "the principle of morality is naturalistic. Call it humanism or not, only a morality frankly relative to man's nature is worthy of man, being at once vital and rational, martial and generous; whereas absolutism smells of fustiness and faggots [burned sticks]." His *The Life of Reason* (1905–1906) explained that religion is not something to be taken as being literally true; it is merely symbolic and thoroughly human, it aims at the "life of reason," but it largely fails in attaining it. As for the gods, fear created them; but this fear and the mythology that it produces only half deceives the thinker. What is needed, he insisted, is a paganizing of Christianity.

Walter Lippmann provided further support. In his *A Preface to Morals* (1931), he described how the "acids of modernity" have eaten away traditional theology with its beliefs in a personal God, Original Sin, and the resurrection of Jesus. Stating that there is nothing absolute in the morals as laid down by traditional theology, he asserted that the new naturalism which based its faith on reason considered morals as being common sense observations, that they are arrived at objectively rather than subjectively, and that they naturally conclude that love is good and hate is bad, that beauty is a quality above ugliness, and that pleasure is above pain.

Irwin Edman in his *Four Ways of Philosophy* (1937) wrote that the naturalist admits some religious impulse in man but "the supernaturalist insists that this impulse which nature generates cannot be satisfied by nature save as seen in a supernatural context. To which the naturalist retorts that nature generates some impulses, possibly, which cannot be satisfied, as a man may be hungry without proving thereby that food is in his neighborhood or his reach."

To the growing number who wrote or spoke about naturalistic humanism, or joined the American Humanist Association, more and more new names appeared. **Sherman D. Wakefield**, husband of Robert Ingersoll's granddaughter (**Eva Ingersoll Wakefield**), edited a monthly *Progressive World*, which was a more "folksy" journal than the American Humanist Association's *The Humanist*. Other journals began. *Free Inquiry* was formed by **Paul Kurtz** to represent the secular humanism of the Council for Secular Humanism (formerly CODESH, the Council for Democratic and Secular Humanism), which now represents the largest number of secular humanists in the United States. At least thirteen humanist journals are published in The Netherlands, where an estimated 25% of the population are secular humanists. There is the *Australian Humanist*; the French *Espace de Libertés*; the English *Ethical Record*; the English *Family of Humanists* which publishes *Sunrise Journal* for youth up to 9 years and *Starwalker* for youth 9 to 15 years of age; the English *Freethinker*; the English *Gay and Lesbian Humanist*, a quarterly; the Swedish bimonthly *Human-Etiska Förbundet*; the Belgian *Het Vrije Woord*; the Norwegian *Humanist*; the German *Der Humanist*; *The Humanist in Canada*; the English *Humanist News*; the Indian *Humanist Outlook*; the Israeli *Humanist Review*; the American *Journal of Humanism and Ethical Religion*; the English *New Humanist*; the New Zealand *Humanist*; *The Scottish Humanist*; the Israeli *Secular Humanistic Judaism*; the Indian *Radical Humanist*; the Indian Secularist; the Finnish *Vapaa Ajattelija (Free Thinker)*; *Bengali Monthly*; the Telugu humanist monthly for Women's Liberation *Stree Swetcha*; and *Misimi*, a Telugu monthly of humanist ideas; to name but a few. In the 1980s, humanist groups were formed not only in Central America but also in South America.

The apparent success of secular humanism, however, has not been matched by its membership rolls. Although an estimated 25% in The Netherlands are humanists, fewer than 150,000 Americans subscribe to the various humanist publications. Philosophy professors as a group are not active members, choosing to avoid being "labeled." But the **International Humanist and Ethical Union (IHEU)** and its journal, *International Humanist News* (47 Theobald's Road, London WC1X 8SP, England) continue making valiant efforts to publicize the movement, believing that it represents the world's "hope" in the 21st century. Entirely in disagreement are religious fundamentalists.

In 1993, *Merriam-Webster's Tenth New Collegiate Dictionary* finally included the following:

> **secular humanism** n (1933) : HUMANISM 3; *esp* : humanistic philosophy viewed as a nontheistic religion antagonistic to traditional religion
> **secular humanist** *n or adj*

In 1992, Houghton Mifflin's *American Dictionary of the English Language*, Third Edition, had the following:

> **secular humanism** n. 1. An outlook or a philosophy that advocates human rather than religious values.
> 2. Secularism.

No major reference book cites humanistic naturalism, the term used by Kenneth L. Patton, John Dewey, James Gutmann, and the present author.

In 1996, Presidential candidate Patrick Buchanan was quoted at a rally of supporters in Des Moines, Iowa: "We see a cultural war going on for the soul of America. We see the God of the Bible expelled from our public schools and replaced by all the false gods of secular humanism. Easter is out, but we can celebrate Earth Day. We can now worship dirt." (The Ninth Circuit Court of Appeals has ruled that secular humanism is *not* a religion. See the entries for Hugo L. Black and for teratology.) {EW; RE}

SECULAR HUMANIST ASSOCIATION OF ISRAEL

An associate member of the International Humanist and Ethical Union is the Secular Humanist Association of Israel, PO Box 18200, Tel Aviv-Jaffa 61 280, Israel.

SECULAR HUMANIST BULLETIN

The *Secular Humanist Bulletin* (Box 664, Amherst, NY 14226; telephone (716) 636-7571) is an associate members' quarterly newsletter of the Council for Secular Humanism. It is edited by Tom Flynn and Tim Madigan. Contributing editors are Brent Bailey and Farrell Till. Flynn includes a distinctive column, "Secular Humorist." His e-mail: <SHB-Editor@secularhumanism.org>.

SECULAR HUMANIST SOCIETY OF NEW YORK

The Secular Humanist Society of New York (SHSNY) was founded by Warren Allen Smith, who in 1990 entitled its newsletter *Pique*. Present at the initial meeting were Tim Madigan and Paul Kurtz of the Council for Secular Humanism. The meeting was held in Variety Recording Studio, 130 West 42nd Street, its first members being the studio's co-owners Fernando Vargas and Smith.

Honorary members secured by Smith were Isaac Asimov, Paul Cadmus, Arthur C. Clarke, Paul Edwards, Albert Ellis, Sidney Hook, Ring Lardner Jr., and Allen Walker Read. *Pique* he chose as its newsletter's title in order to signal that as editor he wished to be an activist and stir up interest about the group's objectives. Dennis Middlebrooks succeeded him as presiding officer.

Although Smith left the group, the newsletter continues and the group's board of directors in 1999 is John Arents, Conrad Claborne (Vice President), Artur Harris, Hugh Rance (President), George Rowell, and Roger Sorrentino.

SECULAR HUMANISTIC JUDAISM

Secular Humanistic Judaism, a journal written in English, is at 8 Itamar Ben Avi St, PO Box 4512, Jerusalem 91044, Israel.

SECULAR HUMANISTIC MUSIC: See entry for Andrew Charles.

SECULAR JEWS

A number of Jews say they are agnostic or atheistic but are "secular Jews," by which they identify with the Jewish religion of their ancestors but disbelieve in any supernatural deity. Journalist Nat Henthoff and biologist Sheldon F. Gottlieb both call themselves atheistic Jews. "I define myself," Henthoff has explained when informed that it appears to be illogical to call oneself an atheistic Jew or an atheistic Catholic, "and it ain't nobody's business but my own."

Meanwhile, others call themselves non-Jewish Jews, which appears to many to be analogous to calling oneself a non-Christian Christian, a non-Spanish Spaniard, or a non-African African. However, if one's mother is Jewish, one is automatically Jewish according to strict Jewish theologians. Meanwhile, if one's mother is a Congregationalist or an atheist, one is not automatically a Congregationalist. A 1969 reward of $19.69 offered by Jun Sczesnoczkawasm to any baby who, within two weeks of birth, verified that he or she was born a member of any religious group had—as of the end of 1999—gone uncollected.

SECULAR JOURNAL

The stated purpose of *Secular Journal*, an online newsletter, is

> to provide a journal in conjunction with a communications network on a bilingual English/German basis (to be expanded into multilingual services as more cooperators offer their support and expertise). American English is being used since most continental European countries use it as a second language. The German language parts are accepted in the styles currently common in Austria, Germany, and Switzerland. Articles and essays reproduced here originate from various atheist, secular, and secular humanist publications. Original individual submissions are welcome, as long as they concern themselves with those, or closely associated subjects. No hate mail or pornography (including pictures) will be accepted or distributed, but sarcasm is welcome, within the limits of common decency.

SECULAR NATION

Secular Nation, the International Atheist Alliance Magazine was edited by Howard Kreisner. Marie A. Castle and Anna Voss had been counselors. In 1996, however, it merged with *The Freethought Observer* at the same address and in 1997 Castle became its editor. Its address: Box 6261, Minneapolis, Minnesota 55406. E-mail: <mac@mtn.org>.

SECULAR ORGANIZATIONS FOR SOBRIETY

Secular Organizations for Sobriety (SOS), a Council for Secular Humanism support group for recovering substance abusers, has more than one thousand local groups throughout North America and several in Britain. It is located at 5521 Grosvenor Boulevard, Los Angeles, California 90066. For details about the Central London Group, write 42A Marler Road, London SE23 2AD or telephone (0181 291 5572); or 28 Newgate Close, St. Albans AL 4 9JE (0172 7851266). (See entries for James Christopher, Rationalist Recovery Organizations for Self Help, and SOS.)

SECULAR WEB

The Secular Web is a product of Internet Infidels, Inc., a non-profit organization dedicated to providing information over the Internet about the existence of a god, church/state separation, the possibility of life after death, mysticism and the paranormal, and the interface between science and religion. Included are thousands of historical and contemporary articles. For example, one can find Joseph Mc Cabe's *Biographical Dictionary of Ancient, Medieval, and Modern Freethinkers*, can search for individual names or listings, and then can print the material.

It is the largest site on the Web that is dedicated to the promotion of secular viewpoints, including agnosticism, atheism, freethought, humanism, and rationalism. On the Web: <http://www.infidels.org/>.

SECULARISM

As formulated in 1841 by **G. J. Holyoake** (1817–1906), secularism is a variety of utilitarian social ethic which seeks human improvement without reference to religion. It does so without reference to religion and turns exclusively to human reason, science, and social organization to solve problems. It appeals partly as a protest against the dominance and control of human life by ecclesiastical bodies, or by religious faith and dogma which had its new birth at the Renaissance, according to Robert Worth Frank, who taught religion and ethics in the Presbyterian Theological Seminary in Chicago, Illinois. According to Frank, the word is used derogatively by religionists because it leads to a "pursuit of specialized interests without any sense of the unity of life and which has initiated a crisis in the religious and cultural life of modern man."

Holyoake, however, felt that "Secularist" had a positive meaning, one which indicated that the rejection of religion was accompanied by humanitarian feeling and endeavor. Thus, it was thought to be preferable to the words in current use: Atheist, Freethinker, Skeptic, Infidel. In 1852, a conference of twenty-two secular societies convened in Manchester, and many of the groups built Halls of Science or schools. In 1858 Charles Bradlaugh succeeded Holyoake as president of the London Secular Society, and in 1866 he and Austin Holyoake founded the National Secular Society. Holyoake described his aims in the *Origin and Nature of Secularism* (1896).

Other writers about the subject include Horace Kallen, author of *Secularism is the Will of God* (1954); and Edward Royle, author of *Radicals, Secularists, and Republicans: Popular Freethought in Britain, 1866–1915* (1980) and *Victorian Infidels: The Origins of the British Secularist Movement, 1791–1866* (1974).

One of the most outspoken contemporary critics of "secularism" is Pope John Paul II, who often utters condemnations of secularist stands that differ from his own. "Resist secularism, free love, and the culture of death," he warns, the last a term he uses instead of abortion. {ER; EU, Gordon Stein; RE}

SECULARIST

A bi-monthly in English of the Indian Secular Society, *Secularist* is at 15 Zapurza, Sahitya Sahawas, Bandra East, Bombay 400 051, India; <freedom@bom3.vsnl.net.in>.

Sedgmore, Brian (20th Century)

Sedgmore, a Member of the United Kingdom Parliament, has expressed his secularism in radio broadcasts. He is an honorary associate of the National Secular society. {*The Freethinker*, February 1999}

Sedgwick, Catharine Maria (1789–1867)

Sedgwick, a Unitarian, wrote fiction about the simple domestic virtues of the American home, which she considered the safeguard of the Republic. She depicted early 19th century social customs in such of her romantic novels as *A New-England Tale* (1822) and *Redwood* (1824). The romantic adventures of Colonial settlers who experienced Indian captivities and massacres were described in *Hope Leslie, or Early Times in the Massachusetts* (1827). Sedgwick was active in the Unitarian Church and as a feminist, but she did not participate in radical reform movements. She and William Ellery Channing's sister, Lucy Channing Russel, are credited with founding in 1819 All Souls Unitarian Church in New York City. {U}

Sedgwick, Ellery (1872–1960)
Sedgwick wrote *Thomas Paine* (1899). {GS}

Sedgwick, Eve Kosofsky (20th Century)

Sedgwick was raised in a traditional assimilated Jewish family. Her father was a scientist for the National Aeronautics and Space Administration, and her mother was a high school English teacher. In 1975, after being graduated by Yale ("a very frigid place [in which] there wasn't even feminism, let alone gay and lesbian studies"), she was hired by Hamilton College and began what she termed a study in "queer theory," a new approach in literary analysis.

Applying the analysis to Henry James's short story "The Beast in the Jungle," she found that ordinarily the work is read as a heterosexual love story about John Marcher, who cannot return the love of a woman and upon her death he realizes the extent of his life. But Sedgwick points out that in the final paragraphs, as Marcher hurls himself on the grave he looks up and sees a stranger, a man: "There was a kind of hunger in his look," James wrote. Marcher was conscious of "the image of a scarred passion . . . something that profaned the air: and in the second that, roused, startled, shocked, he was yet the next moment looking after it, as it went, with envy." Her interpretation is that the stranger is looking for a homosexual encounter in the cemetery, that the beast in the jungle is a "man's desire for man—and the denial of that desire."

The American Academy of Arts and Letters in 1995 presented her with its Morton Dauwen Zabel Award:

> Eve Sedgwick has turned a piercing yet affectionate poet's eye on a vast body of English and American poetry and fiction that has famously secreted itself in layers of carapace and veiling—the world of high passion and passionate friendship, especially that large but half-mute department called the love of man for man. Her elaborate and quite astonishing discoveries constitute not merely a large addition to our understanding of great and lesser writers, they likewise stand as powerful statements in one of our century's, our nation's, last debates—the right, or denial, of adult human mind to choose its willing partner.

Sedgwick is married to Hal Sedgwick, a professor of visual perception at the City University of New York's College of Optometry. In 1991 Sedgwick found she had breast cancer. To reporter Dinitia Smith in 1998 she said, "I have lived over a year with knowing I will probably die of this disease. And I have been interested in what it's all going to be like." A non-theist, she has studied Buddhism. "In Buddhism," she added, "gender seems very ephemeral." {Dinitia Smith, *The New York Times*, 17 January 1998; WAS conversation, 17 May 1995}

Seeger, Daniel Andrew (20th Century)

A 1964 Federal Appeals Court in New York City ruled in Seeger's favor after he objected to the U.S. Selective Service Act's limitation of draft exemptions to those who have faith in a Supreme Being. In 1965 the Supreme Court upheld the Appeals Court by a slim margin. {CL}

Seeger, Pete (1919–)

Seeger is a noted folksinger and composer, a controversial activist known for using music to struggle against war, racism, poverty, and pollution. In the 1940s he organized the Almanac Singers, touring the nation with the group, then teamed with Woody Guthrie in writing labor and anti-Fascist songs. He once toured with Progressive Party candidate Henry Wallace, and he organized a group, the Weavers. Seeger takes pride in having been one of the first Yankee college students who fell in love with Southern folk music, performing in hundreds of concerts, completing many recordings and writings, and getting others interested in the idea of making their own music as well as reviving old music of many types. Among his songs are "Where Have All the Flowers Gone" (1961); "If I Had a Hammer," in collaboration with Lee Hayes; "Kisses Sweeter than Wine," in collaboration with the Weavers; and "Turn, Turn, Turn." For a time, the various broadcasting networks blacklisted him, stating that his work was too controversial.

When a member of the Community (Unitarian) Church of New York, Seeger wrote that "It is fine to think of Unitarian-Universalism as a world religion. Now, how about reaching out to sing more songs (in our services) that are not in English, like '*De Colores*'; '*Nkosi Sikelele Africa*' (the South African national anthem), '*Ragupati Ragavi*'; etc."

His idea of the ideal church: "It would be like a water tower. I would put the congregation on a platform at the very top, where they could see all around, without walls. My church has always been the outdoors." And of liturgy: "I am no longer leery of using the word 'God,' though I have my own definition. I particularly like what a French mystic said: 'The eye through which I see God is the same eye through which God sees me.' "

In 1994 President Clinton presented Seeger with an award for outstanding contributions to American culture. {*World*, November-December 1995, and July-August 1996}

Seeley, John R. (20th Century)

Seeley in 1952 was a director of the American Humanist Association. {HNS}

Seeley, John Robert (1834–1895)

Seeley was an English historian and man of letters. In 1863 he was a professor of Latin in London University. In 1866 appeared his *Ecce Homo*, a survey of the life and work of Jesus Christ—it was published anonymously, and Lord Shaftesbury denounced it in unmeasured terms as "vomitted from the pit of hell." In 1869, Seeley became professor of modern history at Cambridge. In 1882 he wrote *Natural Religion.* Prof. Seeley, a president of the Ethical Society, accepted God and immortality but not Christianity, which he regarded as "the original Ethical Society." The Bible he regarded as "an ancient text-book." {BDF; RAT; RE}

Sefton, William Henry [Baron Sefton of Garston] (1915–)

In 1989 Lord Sefton was elected an honorary associate of the Rationalist Press Association. In the House of Lords, he once moved an amendment to ensure that religious education should promote "an understanding of various religious beliefs and living beliefs such as humanist and secular points of view, but does not promote any particular religion or belief." He defended such a proposal to protect the integrity of teachers, adding that he resented being told that "as a pagan I was responsible for the moral anarchy which is now so rampant and pernicious." The House of Lords rejected his motion, 120 votes to 31. "To summarise why I have become a rationalist is a difficult task for one not educated in formal writing," he wrote in *New Humanist*, "but I think it can be boiled down to a belief that a person should be honest and have the courage to speak out at all times. In all the debates on TV and radio, very rarely does one hear mention of the real villains in the piece." For Lord Sefton, the main opposition to a peaceful and rewarding life here and now is superstitious religion. He, however, prefers Thomas Paine's view: "I am a citizen of the world and my religion is to do good." {*New Humanist*, November 1993}

Segarelli, Gherardo (13th Century)

In the 1260s when there was an outbreak of Flagellants, a religious order of self-scourgers, Segarelli came forward as a new Christ. According to Robertson, he "had himself circumcised, swaddled, cradled, and suckled; and proceeded to found a new order of 'Apostolicals,' after the manner of a sect of the previous century, known by the same name, who professed to return to primitive simplicity and to chastity, and reproduced what they supposed to be the morals of the early Church, including the profession of ascetic cohabitation. Some of their missionaries got as far as Germany; but Segarelli was caught, imprisoned, reduced to the status of a bishop's jester, and at length, after saving his life for a time by abjuration, burned at Parma, in the year 1300." Two of his followers, Fra Dolcino and Margherita di Trank, set up an armed movement which held out in the southern Alps for two years, until the Apostolicals were reduced to cannibalism. But in 1307 when they were overpowered, Dolcino was forced to watch his beautiful companion Margherita burn to death before his eyes. Refusing to abjure, Segarelli was gradually tortured to death, uttering no cry. {JMR; JMRH}

Segond, Louis Auguste (19th Century)

Segond was a French physician and positivist. In 1849, he wrote a plan of a positivist school to regenerate medicine. {BDF}

Seibel, George (20th Century)

Seibel wrote *The Religion of Shakespeare* (1924). {GS}

Seidel, Anton (1850–1898)

An eminent Hungarian conductor, Seidel after working in Europe came to the United States where in New York he conducted the American premiere of "*Die Meistersinger von Nürnberg*" (1876), "*Triston und Isolde* (1887), and the Ring cycle (1889). His wife was Austrian soprano Auguste Kraus. He was director of the New York Philharmonic Orchestra from 1891 until his death. Seidel, an atheist, died of ptomaine poisoning. {H. Krebbiel, *Anton Seidel* (1898); H. Finck, *Anton Seidel, A Memorial by His Friends* (1899)}

Seidel, Martin (16th Century)

Seidel was a Silesian deist who held that Jesus was not the predicted Messiah. He tried to propagate his opinion among the Polish Socinians, explaining in *The Foundations of the Christian Religion* that the Old and New Testaments are inconsistent. {BDF}

Seidel, Peter (20th Century)

Seidel, an active member of the Cincinnati, Ohio, Free Inquiry Group, is author of *Invisible Walls* (1998). "Our failure to react to planet-imperiling circumstances," he writes regarding the human exploitation of our natural surroundings, "does not lie in our not knowing what is wrong or not knowing what to do about it, but rather in our failure to take this knowledge seriously enough to act on it. We need to understand this failure and to do something about it." An environmental architect and planner who studied with architect Mies van der Rohe, he has taught architecture at Virginia Polytechnic Institute, University of Michigan, Miami University, and Central China University of Science and Technology.

Seiden, Rita (20th Century)

At the International Humanist and Ethical Union's (IHEU's) Second Moral Education Conference held in Brussels (1985), Seiden of the United States addressed the group.

Seider, Rose (20th Century)

In 1972 Seider was financial secretary of the Humanist Society of Greater New York.

Seidl, Anton (20th Century)

Seidl followed Theodore Thomas, who died in 1905, as director of the New York Philharmonic Orchestra. Hungarian by birth, he was rumored to be the illegitimate son of Franz Liszt. This, as well as the rumor he was an atheist and a freethinker, was to his advantage in public relations. "For an ordinary American citizen it might have been reprehensible," wrote Howard Shanet in *Philharmonic: A History of New York's Orchestra* (1975), "but for a Hungarian artist it seemed romantically in character. Besides, he had such personal fire that many who disagreed with him nevertheless admitted his fascination. Dvorak, who criticized him as a 'wild rebel and an atheist,' became his fast friend during his stay in New York." Seidl, after leaving the Leipzig Conservatory in 1872, actually had lived in the household of Richard Wagner for a number of years and was his disciple.

Seigneuret, H. J. (19th Century)

Seigneuret, a freethinker, wrote *Moses Before the Court, or the Forgery of the Old Testament* (c. 1880). {GS}

Seignobos, Charles (1854–1942)

Seignobos, a French historian who taught at Paris University and the Sorbonne, wrote *Histoire de la civilisation* (1886) and *Cours d'histoire* (9 volumes, 1903–1906), in which his rationalist views appear. He was an Officer of the Legion of Honour and of Public Instruction. {RAT}

Seiple, David I. (20th Century)

With Casey Haskins, Seiple edited *Dewey Reconfigured: Essays on Deweyan Pragmatism* (1999).

Selassie, Haile: See entry for Ra.

Selden, John (1584–1654)

An English scholar and jurist, Selden in *Table-Talk* (1689) wrote, "The clergy would have us believe them against our own reason, as the woman would have had her husband against his own eyes." He also wrote, "*Scrutamini scripturas* [Let us examine the scriptures]: These two words have undone the world." {TYD}

Seldes, George (Henry) (1890–1995)

A muckraker and agnostic who wrote for *The Nation*, Seldes liked to expose official and unofficial censorship of the press. In 1939 he wrote *The Catholic Crisis* and in 1938 *Lords of the Press: The Facts About the Most Powerful Anonymous Group of Men in America*. On his 100th birthday he told a *Nation* reporter: "I've never been asked about religion. Father thought that it was totally wrong, the whole world system of inculcating religion in young people 5, 6, 7, and 8 years old, you know. . . . So his idea was to keep you away from anything religious until you were 15 or 16—in the teens—and then you could study all the religions, and you might want to choose to be a Mohammedan. He said the main thing is that we [the Seldes family] are all deists; we believe in God. We are not atheists, none of us. We may be agnostic—that's a good healthy way to be, my father would say—but we're certainly not atheists. We're religious people. That's the only religion we had in the family for generations." Seldes, who died at the age of 104, was an honorary member of the Freedom From Religion Foundation.

Seleveld, Elizabeth (20th Century)

A Norwegian, Seleveld was a participant in a science and superstition panel at the 1996 Humanist World Congress held in Mexico City.

SELF-IMPROVEMENT

• It makes little difference how many university courses or degrees a person may own. If he cannot use words to move an idea from one point to another, his education is incomplete.

–**Norman Cousins**

SELF-RELIANCE

Freethinkers aim to rely upon their own capabilities, judgment, resources, and independence. Few if any would object to the ideas found in Ralph Waldo Emerson's essay, "Self-Reliance."

SELF RESPECT MOVEMENT

K. Veeramani in India leads a socio-political and atheistic movement in Tamil Nadu in southern India known as Self Respect Movement, Periyar Thidal 50 EVK Sampath R, Madras 600 007, India. {FD}

Self, Will (1961–)

Self, a freethinking British writer with decidedly unorthodox heroes involved in incidences of black humor, has become a countercultural icon. *Cock and Bull* (1993) features a woman who sprouts a penis and a man who grows a vagina. Self, who as a teenager used marijuana, amphetamines, and cocaine and later used heroin, informed *Vanity Fair* that the work was written to voice "anger at the way gender-based sexuality is so predetermined, the way we fit into our sex roles as surely as if we had cut them off the back of a cereal packet and pasted them onto ourselves."

My Idea of Fun (1994) features a boy who apprentices himself to the Devil and learns how to commit cold-blooded murder, or at least he says he learns how. A leading satirist, Self constructs a new Mephistophelean bargain, for in order to obtain the magical powers of penetrating the past and having lots of fun and money, the boy must avoid any sexual intercourse with a woman. In fact, his penis will fall off if he achieves penetration, he is warned, so he resorts to masturbation until his mysterious guide, called the Fat Controller and apparently a metaphor for capitalism run amok in the 1980s, disappears. He then meets another would-be mentor, a sinister psychiatrist named Dr. Gyggle who tells him Fat Controller is a manifestation of his "delusionary apparatus" and a lonely boy's delusion constructed "to compensate for the lack of a father" and to "punish himself for his own Oedipal crime." Cured of his fantasies by Dr. Gyggle, the boy falls in love and becomes a successful marketing entrepreneur in a world of fun where junkies are businessmen and businessmen are the Devil's servants, where babies play with razor blades and animals serve as sex partners for humans. Until the Fat Controller resurfaces, that is.

My Idea of Fun has been described by *The New York Times* book reviewer Michiko Kakutani as "a genuinely ambitious and accomplished novel, a novel that reads like an original and often willfully perverse Cuisinart mix of William Burroughs, William Gaddis, Thomas Pynchon, and Lewis Carroll. One reads the book with a combination of fascination and nausea, intellectual curiosity and emotional horror, impressed by Mr. Self's virtuosic skills with language and satire even while being repelled by his images of necrophilia, mutilation and torture."

Great Apes (1997) describes a world of ten-second orgies, parents humping their children, and sign language before the alpha male: "I worship your adamant penis" or "the refulgence of your anal scrag." Evolution has taken a different turn, with chimpanzees ruling the cities while subhuman humans are roaming the African savanna and are caged in zoos. Simon Dykes, the thirty-nine-year-old in the story, is now a transformed man, an insane chimp in a psycho ward. The "what if?" plot describes how he is psychologically treated to restore his humanity.

Of contemporary authors, Self is one of the most irreverent. In a foreword to *Book of Revelation* (Pocket Canons), he called the work a "sick text" and a "guignol of tedium." (See entry for Mikhail Bakunin.) {Tad Friend, *New York*, 1 September 1997}

Seligman, Joseph (20th Century)

Seligman, a railroad-banking tycoon, endowed a lectureship for Felix Adler at the new and liberal Cornell University, where President Andrew D. White defended his wide-ranging lectures on "Oriental

Language and Literature" from Christian and orthodox critics. Seligman greatly assisted Adler at a time just before Adler founded the Ethical Culture movement.

Sellars, Roy Wood (1880–1973)

Sellars, a philosopher who wrote *Evolutionary Naturalism* (1922), signed Humanist Manifesto I in 1933. His 1918 *Next Step in Religion* rejected H. G. Wells's God as well as the Christian: "I challenge any one to develop a really tenable system of theology," to which he added that he wanted to see a "human faith" with "no tottering creed to sustain." He also wrote *Evolutionary Naturalism* (1922), *Religion Coming of Age* (1928), *The Philosophy of Physical Realism* (1932), "Religious Humanism" in *The New Humanist* (May-June 1933), and "In Defense of the Manifesto" in *The New Humanist* (May-June 1933).

Expanding on his ideas concerning humanism, Sellars in 1956 wrote to the present author:

> The direction to be taken in the use of the term humanism, according to my way of thinking, is along naturalistic and empirical lines. It concerns itself with the achievement of human values and with the purposes and endeavors which give meaning to human life. Meaning is embedded in activities which give lasting satisfaction and a retrospective justifiability. And these, so far as I can see, are sufficient unto themselves and require no supernatural framework. Such an added framework strikes me as essentially traditional in character and of the stuff of which mythology is made.
>
> I prefer to speak of naturalistic humanism rather than of scientific humanism. This is, of course, a minor point. The term scientific calls up, in my mind, the ways of testing knowledge about ourselves and the world. And so far as that goes it is all to the good. But life is more than knowledge. It is an affair of imagination and values as well, of finding out what is good and beautiful and worth while. In naturalistic humanism we have the meeting-point of philosophy and religion in that both concern themselves with the interpreting of human life, though their historical genius has been different. On the whole, religions have taken the path of special revelations and sacred literature. All this immersed in ritual and liturgy. Philosophy has emphasized thought and clarification. This element has not been absent from past religion but it has been used dependently and subordinately. The humanist feels that it is both the most courageous and the wisest thing to face up to the human situation as the sciences have disclosed it and to aim at enriching human life in its various dimensions, social, familial, political, and artistic, to mention but a few of those dimensions. He takes it that the meaning of life can be spelled out in this frame which, after all, has always been with us, though under some condemnation to the mysteries held by faith. The transition will not be easy for many, for the rhetoric and mental pictures involved will be different. As I see it, it will be an affair of gradual shifting of perspective and emphasis.
>
> It is my conviction that it will be better for man when he recognizes and admits his actual status and standing as a creature of this planet and determiner of his own destiny. The humanist does not regard himself as romantic when he cherishes the hope that, out of this recognition, there will come an enforcement of the ideals of mutual understanding and fellowship in both their personal and their institutional forms. And, in these days, the debate will be a world-wide affair.

In the 1950s, Sellars was on the advisory board of Charles Francis Potter's First Humanist Society of New York, and he has been an official of the American Humanist Association. During the 1950s, he reviewed books for *The Humanist.*

His son, **Wilfred Sellars**, is a noted philosopher whose Empiricism *and the Philosophy of Mind* (1956) is a study in analytic philosophy. He attacked the "myth of the given" in empiricism and helped turn analytic philosophy away from the foundationalist motives of the logical empiricists. The very idea of "epistemology" was, in fact, questioned. A 1997 edition includes an introduction by Richard Rorty. (See entry for American Humanist Association.) {CL; EW; FUS; HNS; HNS2; PK; RAT; U; WAS, 2 September 1956}

Sellevold, Elizabeth (20th Century)

A Norwegian humanist, Sellevold attended the 1996 international conference of humanists in Mexico City. Her e-mail: <forlag@human.no>.

Sellon, Edward (19th Century)

Sellon was an English archaeologist, the author of *The Monolithic Temples of India: Annotations on the Sacred Writings of the Hindus* (1865), and other scarce works which were privately printed. {BDF}

Selnes, Kjartan (20th Century)

A Norwegian, Selnes spoke about the media in a cybernetic era at the 1996 Humanist World Conference held in Mexico City. Noting that the media help considerably to shape events, he cited the three news agencies (in France, Germany, and England) which in 1840 divided the world into spheres. In the 1990s, the major news sources are Reuters, the Associated Press, FPI, and UPI. The media, he noted, does not simply show us the world, it plays a part in changing it. This has been seen in the power of the media to disillusion the Americans in the Vietnam War and the impact of pictures of war in Bosnia. In the third world the mass media are seen as elite agents. Left to itself the market does not necessarily encourage diversity.

Selnes holds that the markets should be more regulated by humanist values. His e-mail: <selnes@human.no>. {*International Humanist News*, December 1996}

Selous, Frederick Courteney [Sir] (1851–1917)

Selous, a professional elephant-hunter in Africa, wrote *A Hunter's Wanderings* (1881), winning the Royal Geographical Society's Gold Medal. In a symposium on immortality in the *Christian Commonwealth* (1915), Selous wrote, "I have no confidence that I shall survive bodily death; nor, until I know what my future state would be if I did so, do I hope for survival." He further said he did not believe in "some power, which is known to civilized man as God."

During World War I, he volunteered for service, although he was in his sixties, and was killed in action. E-mail: <selnes@human.no>. {RAT; RE}

SEMANTICS

Semantics is a scientific or philosophical study of the relations of words and their meanings. "To argue whether the medication killed the patient or contributed to her death is to argue over semantics," it has been said. But the semanticist has shown that certain words used at certain times carry positive, or perhaps negative, overtones.

For example, an automobile named Nova would be difficult to market in countries where *no-va* means "it doesn't go." "Navel" is preferred to "belly button" upon formal occasions. "The Gay 90s" connoted something different in the 1870s as contrasted with its meaning in the 1900s.

ETC: A Review of General Semantics is published quarterly by the International Society for General Semantics (2465 A & B Salvio St., Concord, California 94520). The organization was formulated by Alfred Korzybski (1879–1950) and was founded by S. I. Hayakawa (1906–1992) in 1943.

Sembat, Marcel Étienne (Born 1862)

Sembat was an agnostic and a politician. He was elected to the French Chambre in 1893. For a time he edited *La Petite République* and, later, was one of the editors of *L'Humanité.* In 1914 he was Minister of Public Works in Viviani's cabinet. {RAT}

Semerari, Giuseppe (20th Century)

Semerari, in Italy, is a corresponding member of The Hume Society, a group engaged in scholarly activity concerning David Hume.

Sémérie, Eugène (1832–1884)

Sémérie was a French positivist. Becoming a physician, he studied mental maladies and in 1867 published *Intellectual Symptoms of Madness*, in which he maintained that the disordered mind went back from positivism to metaphysics, theology, and then to fetishism. The work was denounced by the Bishop of Orleans. A friend of Pierre Lafitte, Sémérie edited the *Politique Positive* and wrote *Positivists and Catholics* (1873) and *The Law of the Three States* (1875). {BDF; RAT}

Semier, Doug (20th Century)

Semier, while a student at the University of California in Irvine, was one of the founding members of Campus Freethought Alliance. {*International Humanist News*, December 1996}

Semler, Johann Salome (1725–1791)

Semler was a German critic, a professor of theology at Halle and founder of historical Biblical criticism there. He translated Simon's *Critical History of the New Testament*, and by asserting the right of free discussion drew down the wrath of the orthodox. {BDF}

Semple, Etta Donaldson (1855–1914)

An American freethinker, Semple published in her newspaper, *The Free-Thought Vindicator*, on the front page: "A Reward of $1,000 will be Given to the Man, Woman or Child, who will Furnish Positive Proof Of A God, the Holy Ghost, Jesus Christ (as a savior), the Soul, the Devil, Heaven or Hell, or the Truth of the Bible." No takers appeared, but her unpopularity led to her attempted assassination (another woman was killed instead).

A photograph and excerpts of Semple's freethinking are found in Whitehead and Muhrer's *Freethought on the American Frontier* (1992).

She wrote in 1898,

> If I deny the existence of a God—if I deny the idea of a gold-paved city with pearly walls and jasper gates somewhere out of knowledge and space and prefer to die and trust to the unfaltering laws of nature—if, in plain words I don't want to go to heaven. whose business is it but my own?
>
> {EU; E. Graham Waring; WWS}

Sen, Amartya (20th Century)

Winner of the 1998 Nobel Memorial Prize in Economic Science, Sen was honored partly for proving that Thomas Malthus was wrong with his prediction that too many people and too little food will necessarily lead to worldwide starvation. The Master of Trinity College, Cambridge, Sen has been called "the conscience of the profession" by another Nobel laureate, Robert Solow. He has merged philosophy with economics in such of his works as *Poverty and Famines: An Essay on Entitlement and Deprivation* (1981). His view is that the "poverty index" takes into account not only the proportion of a society living below the poverty line but also the degree of poverty among the most destitute.

In 1994 Sen was President of the American Economics Association, and he teaches part-time at Harvard University. {*The New York Times*, 15 Oct 1998; *The Economist*, 17 Oct 1998}

Senancour, Étienne Pivery de (1770–1846)

Although his parents wanted him to become a priest, Senancour escaped to Geneva, where he adopted the deism of Rousseau and devoted himself to literature. His *Overmann* (1804) was received favorably by the critics, and it was admired by Sainte-Beueve and Matthew Arnold. The work was a lightly fictionalized series of letters in which the author discusses man, his own melancholy, and intellectual matters.

Although Brinton described Senancour as "not at all religious," McCabe labeled him a theist. {CE; RAT; RE}

Seneca, Lucius Annaeus (the younger) (c. 3 B.C.E.–65 C.E.)

Seneca, a Roman philosopher, dramatist, and statesman, wrote *Dialogi*, essays on anger, on divine providence, on Stoic impassivity, and on peace of soul.

Robertson reports that his monotheistic aversion to the popular superstitions of his day represents the elevating power of the higher Greek Stoicism: "On this score he belongs to the freethinking age, while his theistic a priorism belongs to the next." Of religion, he wrote, "Religion is regarded by the common people as true, by the wise as false, and by the rulers as useful." As for immortality, Seneca wrote, "After death, nothing is. . . . Let the ambitious zealot lay aside his hope of heaven, whose faith is but his pride. . . . Naught's after death, and death itself is naught. . . . Then may the saints lose all their hope of heaven, and sinners quit their racky fears of hell." {CE; ER; JMR; JMRH; RE; TYD}

Senghor, Léopold Sédar [President] (1906–)

Senghor, the son of a Senegalese landowner, won a scholarship to study in Paris, where he met other writers and formulated the concept of negritude. That concept asserted the importance of African heritage. Serving with the French army in World War II, Senghor represented Senegal (1945–1958) in the French legislature, then became president of the Senegalese republic, serving from 1960 to 1980.

Although a secular humanist, Senghor ruled a nation that is said to be over 59% Moslem. Among Senghor's works are *Chants d'Ombré* (1945), *Éthiopiques* (1956), *On African Socialism* (1959, 1964), *Selected Poems* (1964), and *Freedom 1, Negritude and Humanism* (1974). A distinguished intellectual, he wrote many essays in French. He instructed that his distinctive poetry should be accompanied by musical instruments. In 1984, he became the first black member of the French Academy.

Senghor, who lives in France, is a Humanist Laureate in the Council for Secular Humanism's International Academy of Humanism. (CE)

Senior, Clarence (1903–1974)

When he reviewed books for *The Humanist* in the 1950s, Senior was Chief of the Commonwealth of Puerto Rico's Department of Labor, Migration Division. A professor of sociology at Brooklyn College, Senior wrote *The Puerto Ricans* (1965) and *The Assault on Poverty* (1966). {HNS}

SENSA: See Bertrand Russell's *Problems of Philosophy* (1912) and the *Encyclopedia of Philosophy*, Vol. 7.

Sensible, Captain (20th Century)

Captain Sensible is a guitarist, the founding member of a punk band called The Damned. He e-mailed the following to an onliner:

> When Cliff Richard, a celibate born-again Christian, refused to introduce the group, arguing that the band and punk music in general are evil], Bloody cheek! I've got three kids, and they think I'm okay. How dare the uptight buffoon bad-mouth people he doesn't even know. I'll tell ya what I think is evil, though. It's not using yer dangly bits for what they're there for . . . love, procreation, and, dare I say . . . a bit of bloody fun along the way!
>
> How many times have religions of the world been damaged by some discovery or other only to move the goalposts and carry on as before as though nothing had happened? They gave Galileo a hard time for saying the world was round. Somehow God seems to have forgotten to tell his "flock" about our planet revolving 'round the sun and all that. Then there was the theory of evolution, the teaching about which in school was fought against in a courtroom in the USA and is still disbelieved by a majority of Americans, incredibly. There's also no mention of dinosaurs in the Bible, either. Perhaps it's not inspired by an all-knowing being after all and is, after all, just a cracking good work of fiction? No, I'm afraid none of that faith things holds any water for me.

On the Web: <www.geocities.com/SunsetStrip/Towers/4962>

{CA}

SEPARATION OF CHURCH AND STATE

• I believe in an America where the separation of church and state is absolute.

–President John F. Kennedy

An organization devoted to keeping church and state separate is on the World Wide Web: <www.louisville.edu/~tnpeteol/church/index.htm>. (See entries for Church and State and also for Protestants and Other Americans United for the Separation of Church and State.)

SEPTUAGINT

The Septuagint version of the Holy Bible was made in Alexandria, Egypt, by various translators who worked from about the 3rd to the 1st century before the Christian era. It varies widely in its degree of literalness and in its linguistic level. Kenneth E. Nahagian, for example, calls it a "sloppy" translation. (See entries for Bible and Yoel Wasserman.) {ER; CE}

Serafini, Maria Alimonda (19th Century)

Serafini was an Italian who wrote *A Catechism for Female Freethinkers* 1869). She also wrote *Marriage and Divorce* (1873). {BDF}

SERBIAN-AMERICAN FREETHINKERS: See *Freethought in the United States*, by Gordon Stein, for a discussion of Serbian-American freethinkers in the United States.

Sercombe, Parker (20th Century)

Sercombe wrote "God's Principle Jokes" (c. 1900), not a memorably lengthy work. {GS}

SERENITY

Serenity, according to Bertrand Russell's *Understanding History* (1957), is not, as pedants try to convince us, a quality of the truly great men "who see how, in mysterious ways, good comes out of evil, and that, speaking generally, they help us to bear with fortitude the misfortunes of others. The generous young, exposed in almost every university of the world to this desiccated abomination, are apt to reject with scorn all the conventionally great names." As examples of those whose supposed "serenity" is the theme of "endless academic nonsense," Lord Russell cites Shakespeare's lines:

As flies to us are we to the gods.
They kill us for their sport.

And

You taught me language, and my profit on't
Is, I know how to curse.

"No," continues Russell, "the greatest men have not been 'serene.' They have had, it is true, an ultimate courage, a power of creating beauty where nature has put only horror, which may, to a petty mind, appear like serenity. But their courage has had to surpass that of common men, because they have seen deeper into the indifference of nature and the cruelty of man. To cover up these things with comfortable lies is the business of cowards; the business of great men is to see them with inflexible clarity, and yet to think and feel nobly. And in the degree in which we can all be great, this is the business of each of us."

Sergi, Giuseppe (1841–1936)

Sergi taught anthropology and experimental psychology at Rome University and was director of the Roman Museum of Anthropology. He wrote more than a hundred books and two hundred academic articles, for which he has been dubbed "the Grand Old Man of Italian Rationalism as well as science." At the International Congress of Freethinkers in Rome (1904), Sergi gave a fiery atheist address, saying that "the conceptions of a soul, a future life, a God, are all superstitious errors which have clouded the human mind and given a false direction to human conduct." {RAT; RE}

Sergi, Johan Tobias (1740–1814)

Sergi, a Swedish painter and cartoonist, was a non-theist. (See entry for Scandinavian Unbelievers.)

Serling, Rod (1924–1975)

Serling, a television writer who produced "The Twilight Zone," was a winner of eight Emmy Awards. He was a Unitarian Universalist. {EG}

SERMONS

• Homilophobia is what keeps me in bed on Sunday mornings.

—Anonymous
[Homilophibia denotes "fear of sermons"]

• "Better to see a sermon than hear one.

—Anonymous

Serrano, Andres (1950–)

Serrano is the controversial artist whose "Piss Christ" depicts a photograph of a crucifix immersed in urine. The work is Serrano's statement concerning art's lack of limitations in conveying artistic symbolism. A high school dropout at fifteen, a drug dealer and addict at twenty, this son of an African-Cuban mother and a Honduran father strongly defends his right to depict whatever an artist feels. Other of his works include photographs taken in a morgue and entitled "Rat Poison Suicide," "Infectious Pneumonia," "AIDS Related Death," and so forth. Since right-wing protests against financing of his art catapulted him to martyrdom, Serrano has enjoyed the ensuing publicity.

"You can't have the sacred without the profane," Serrano has said. I wouldn't be so obsessed with Christianity if I didn't have a feeling for it, and I find it strange when people call me an anti-Christian bigot. What is wrong is to make something that isn't beautiful." Some critics, however, complain that his work, artistically, is less than compelling. Sister Wendy Beckett, however, likes it. The sixty-two-year-old Catholic nun, who lives in a Carmelite order in England and stars in a British Broadcasting Corporation art show called "Sister Wendy's Grand Tour," finds a religious meaning in Serrano's "Piss Christ." "You could regard it as a moving meditation on what we do to the figure of Christ," she has said in 1993 over the radio. "To say it is blasphemous says more about the person looking at it." Sister Wendy appeared to be directing her thoughts at such as U.S. Senator Jesse A. Helms, the Republican from North Carolina, who has called the work blasphemous. Helms had been instrumental in voting against funds for the United States National Endowment for the Arts whenever it supported such controversial artists as Serrano.

Serrano has explained that his photographs of religious tableaux are informed by "unresolved feelings about my own Catholic upbringing, which help me redefine and personalize my relationship with God. For me, art is a moral and spiritual obligation that cuts across all manner of pretense and speaks directly to the Soul." He belies the fundamentalist view of his work as "anti-Christian bigotry," arguing that "[as] a former Catholic and as someone who even today is not opposed to being called a Christian, I feel I had every right to use the symbols of the Church, and resented being told not to." Further, Serrano has written that he is indebted to Renaissance and medieval religious paintings, and that by using blood, piss, semen, and milk in his work he is merely creating abstract images. In 1987 he did abstract photographs entitled *Blood, Milk*, and *Piss*. His *Ejaculate in Trajectory* was completed in 1989.

Critic Holland Cotter has observed that a crucifix brought the artist to light, and religion seems to be his métier. Critic Mark Stevens has quoted Serrano as saying his "use of bodily fluids, especially in connection with Christianity, has been a way of trying to personalize and redefine [my] relationship with Christ." Serrano has also said that his use of urine was "meant to question the whole notion of what is acceptable and unacceptable. There's a duality here, of good and evil, life and death." Stevens stated that Serrano, like many artists, enjoyed violating a taboo., "a provocateur working in familiar Western traditions not only of art but of religion, where anticlericalism and an iconoclastic attack upon idols are common." He added, "In fact, Serrano is provocative less because he violates taboos or criticizes the Catholic Church than because he is at bottom so palpably, so classically, religious. He is a hair-shirt Catholic, one obsessed with putting great pressure on the body in order to feel the spirit. Serrano, in his way, is outrageously old-fashioned."

The artist lives in a downtown Brooklyn apartment which contains a shower of over one hundred crucifixes in his bathroom, dragon sconces he found in a Parisian flea market, a bishop's bed, crimson stoles, a photo of a prostitute, a skeleton, a pickled human brain in a jar, numerous skulls and religious objects. "I'm not a practicing Catholic, but I like the Catholic *aesthetic*, Serrano explained to a *New York* reporter (14 October 1996) in 1996. "What's going on here (in the decor of the apartment) has nothing to do with spirituality. I like the sense of theater, the sense of drama."

A 1997 show of his large photographs includes one of a priest who has been pleasantly tied up, apparently a ready masochist; an Asian woman also tied and seemingly ready for rough sex; a woman holding a horse's penis; a white man on his knees, orally sucking a black man; a woman "receiving head" while dressed as a clown; a female midget about to be penetrated by an appendage at least one-fourth her height; and similar other scenes. The show is entitled, enigmatically, "A History of Sex."

Serre, de la (18th Century)

De la Serre wrote *Examination of Religion* (1745), a work attributed to Saint Évremond and condemned to be burned by the Parliament of Paris. {BDF}

Sertl, Franz (20th Century)

Sertl is author of the history of freethought in Austria, *Die Freidenkerbewegung in Österreich im zwanzigsten jarhundert*. The work recounts the history of organized freethought from 1848 to date. (See entry for Austrian Freethinkers.)

Servetus, Michael (Miguel Serveto) (1511–1553)

A Spanish physician and Unitarian theologian, Servetus was the first to publish an account of how the blood circulates in the body. In 1531, his *On the Errors of the Trinity* was published, and he became the most famous of the sixteenth-century anti-Trinitarians, hated by Catholics and Protestants alike. Luther called the book horribly wicked. Servetus sent a copy of his *Christianismi Restitatio* to Calvin, who denounced him to the Catholic authorities at Lyons, where Servetus was imprisoned but escaped. Melanchthon in 1539 warned the Venetian Senate against allowing the book to be sold. Servetus himself was said to have been an astrologer (at a time when Martin Luther on Biblical grounds rejected astrology and the Copernican astronomy alike, holding devoutly to a belief in witchcraft). "Your Trinity is the product of subtlety and madness. The Gospel knows nothing of it. God is one and indivisible." Declared a heretic on charges brought by the Protestant leader John Calvin, Servetus refused to recant and was caught heading for Italy via Geneva. There he was burned alive, in what has been described as "a slow fire," along with some of his allegedly odious writings, to the delight of Protestants and Catholics alike. (See entry for Otto Karmin.) {BDF; CE; CL; ER; EU, Paul H. Beattie; HNS2; JM; JMR; JMRH; RE; TRI; TYD; U, UU}

Service, Robert (19th Century)

In 1870, Service founded in Melbourne, Australia, the Sunday Free Discussion Society.

Service, Robert W. (1874–1958)

"The Shooting of Dan McGrew" and "The Cremation of Sam McGee" were two long works which made Service famous in the 1910s and 1920s. An Englishman raised largely in Scotland but a poet who made the Yukon famous, Service described the wild northwest frontier in all its ruggedness. Poor Sam, for example, in the middle of his cremation alarmed his buddies by coming unfrozen and exclaiming he had not felt so warm in ages. "The Ballad of Blasphemous Bill" tells how his buddies, to fulfill his final wish, were able to fit him into his coffin only by sawing up his frozen body. Whitehead and Muhrer contain some of Service's poems in their *Freethought on the American Frontier* (1992), adding that in his later years Service wrote religious poetry which was somewhat orthodox. {CE}

SETI

SETI, the search for extraterrestrial intelligence, aims radio telescopes at thousands of target start systems in the hope of receiving signals from "out there." (See entry for Extraterrestrial Life.)

Settle, John (1842–1915)

Settle was a Lancashire miner who late in life became a rationalist and made the Rationalist Press Association the residuary legatee of his estate, on condition that the money should be used for the delivery of lectures in Wigan. {RAT}

Settle, Mary L. (20th Century)

Settle wrote *The Scopes Trial* (1972). {GS}

Seume, Johann Gottfried (1763–1810)

Seume was a German poet who, sent to Leipzig to become a theologian, became disgusted by the dogmas and left for Paris. He lived an adventurous life, traveled extensively, and wrote *Promenade to Syracuse* (1802) A deist, Seume was highly critical of orthodox Christianity, writing that "Grotius and the Bible are the best supports of despotism." {BDF; RAT}

SEVEN DEADLY SINS

In the Middle Ages, the sins that led to "damnation" were pride, covetousness (greed), lust, anger, gluttony, envy, and sloth.

SEVEN WONDERS OF THE WORLD: See entry for Man.

SEVENTH DAY ADVENTISTS: See Martin Gardner's "The Incredible Flimflams of Margaret Rowen, Seventh-day Adventists and the Second Coming," *Free Inquiry*, Spring 1996 and Spring 1997. Gardner also discusses "the comic pratfalls of Robert Reidt."

Severance, Caroline (19th Century)

Severance was vice president of the Free Religious Associates when Octavius Brooks Frothingham was its president. {FUS}

Severance, Channing (20th Century)

Severance, a freethinker, wrote *The Failure of Christianity* (1921). {FUS}

Severn, Joseph (1793–1879)

As a youth, Severn won the Gold Medal of the Royal Academy for his art, at which time he became a friend of Keats and accompanied the doomed poet to Italy and cared for him. After Rome "was taken from the Pope," to quote McCabe, Severn remained in Italy and became British Consul. Severn shared Keats's Rationalism and followed the struggle against the Church with enthusiasm. {RAT; RE}

Sewards, Colin (20th Century)

Sewards, of Metroplex Atheists in Texas, is a board member of the Atheist Alliance.

SEX

• In your sex life preserve purity as far as you can before marriage, and if you indulge, take only those privileges that are lawful. However, do not make yourself offensive or censorious to those who do indulge, and do not make frequent mention of the fact that you do not yourself indulge.

–Epictetus

• As far as sex is concerned, I don't think the American man gives his woman a fair shake. There's not enough quantity and certainly not enough quality. People talk the game, but they don't play it very well.

–Frank Sinatra, singer

The sexual attitudes of non-believers as compared to those of believers have never been definitively studied. Because of many of the organized churches' teachings it is likely, however, that the former are more apt to enjoy sex, experimenting with different positions and partners, whereas the latter are more apt to suffer needless anxiety about sex and to feel guilty even when finding their left testicle is larger than their right (which they may not know is a universal characteristic) or when they have a pleasurable orgasm (which many women regrettably never achieve). *Sex in America* (1994) does state that Christian churchgoers likely have fewer partners than "heathens," but one of the facets of studying sex is that humans have difficulty talking about it, particularly *during* it.

The sex life of early man is a mystery. Reay Tannahill, in her *Sex in History* (1980), remarks that "polygamy has been far more widespread than monogamy during most of the five thousand years of recorded history." Erotic Stone Age drawings exist, and there is much evidence that it was not always known how human births came about, that "it is not altogether easy to accept that *homo sapiens*, after more than 100,000 years of fully-fledged existence, may still have been unaware of the biological facts of life when the Neolithic revolution began." Evidence exists that some thought *man* can become pregnant (for instance, by eating possum) and die in childbirth. Some women denied that men had anything whatsoever to do with their being pregnant. Men, meanwhile, viewed themselves as superior in all ways to women, and they dominated the world's earliest civilizations in the Near East.

In Greece, where dildos were used and where masturbation was considered an emotional safety valve, Demosthenes observed, "We have hetairai for our pleasure, concubines for our daily needs, and wives to give us legitimate children and look after the housekeeping." Hetairai were successful women in a man's world, sometimes very successful; they also were experienced in anal intercourse. As for pederasty, "the bloom of a twelve-year old boy," said Straton, "is desirable, but at thirteen he is much more delightful. Sweeter still is the flower of love that blossoms at fourteen, and its charm increases at fifteen. Sixteen is the divine age." The Greeks, however, considered intercourse with a boy who had not reached the age of puberty as evil and as illegal as in other civilizations; homosexuality in the modern sense is seldom attested to in ancient Athens.

As Tannahill among others points out, "It was the monotheistic strand of Near Eastern culture that won in the end, that of the Hebrews, who had no need to compromise between religious and secular law. The Pentateuch was a mixture of Near Eastern customs and ordinances handed down from Sinai, but both had the authority of Yahweh and were thus mandatory. So the attitudes born of the Neolithic era were preserved, and when the Christian Church, solidly based on Hebrew foundations, took over the Western world as successor to Rome, social and sexual relationships became fossilized in the amber of ancient Hebrew custom. To Near Eastern prejudices, the Church Fathers added their own. Sex was transformed into a sin and homosexuality into a danger to the state." The Church proscribed adultery, abortion, homosexuality, infanticide, zoophilia, and masturbation. Whereas Solon had suggested "three times a month" for marital intercourse and the Jewish *Mishnah* prescribed, "Every day for the unemployed, twice a week for laborers, once a week for ass drivers," the Church said *never*, unless children were the object. Whereas other societies regarded sex as pleasurable, in any position, to the Church sexual pleasure was a sin "and only the man-superior position was acceptable." Meanwhile, while the Church encouraged monogamy, others compared the practice to that of a person voluntarily choosing a lifetime diet of one cup of rice per day for sustenance.

Tannahill has written that Asia and the Arab world added a new dimension to "pure love" that was to influence not only poets and troubadours of courtly love but also the whole image of woman in the West. "The Victorian resurrection of courtly love was largely responsible for transforming middle-class ladies into sweet, untouchable guardians of morality, whose distaste for sex led to an explosive increase in prostitution, an epidemic spread of venereal disease, and a morbid taste for masochism," she notes. "The artificial ideal of the Victorian family was sustained until well into the twentieth century, most influentially by Hollywood rather than the Church, but the published researches of Kinsey and others, increasing familiarity with psychoanalytic theory, and simple economic reality ultimately helped to undermine it. Even so, it still survives, despite the revulsion against traditional relationships expressed in women's liberation, gay liberation, and the free sex movement, and despite the fact that, in legal terms, the sexes have in many countries been brought almost into equilibrium." If so, and in social terms, much remains to be accomplished, feminists will argue.

Georgian England's most popular sex manual in the 1690s, *Aristotle's Master-Piece*, remained in print for several centuries. It avoided anything that was considered to be at all problematic—homosexuality, sadomasochism, masturbation—as well as "any dialectic of sex with neurosis."

In nine states of the United States it was illegal in 1933 for unmarried sex between consenting heterosexuals. Oral sex (giving and receiving) was illegal in twenty states for heterosexuals, twenty-seven states for homosexuals, leading activists to complain that few remember what Jefferson said in his first inaugural address in 1801: "A wise and frugal government, which shall restrain men from injuring one another, shall leave them otherwise free to regulate their own pursuits of industry and improvement."

Bertrand Russell, in 1969, wrote, "I should deal with sexual morality exactly as I should with everything else. I should say that if what you're doing does no harm to anybody, there's no reason to condemn it. And you shouldn't condemn it merely because some ancient taboo has said that this is wrong."

Views on sex are almost as varied as sexual positions:

- The pleasure is momentary, the position ridiculous, and the expense damnable.

  –Lord Chesterfield

- Sex: the thing that takes up the least amount of time and causes the most amount of trouble.

  –John Barrymore

- Is sex dirty? Only if it's done right.

  –Woody Allen

- Men and women, women and men. It will never work.

  –Erica Jong

- Why should we take advice on sex from the Pope? If he knows anything about it, he shouldn't.

  –George Bernard Shaw

- Nothing in our culture, not even home computers, is more overrated than the epidermal felicity of two featherless bipeds in desperate congress.

  –Quentin Crisp

In 1992, a study of the sexual practices of Americans was compiled, one involving 3,432 men and women aged 18 to 59. Their study found that 22.8% of the women had been forced by men to do something sexually that they did not want to do; however, only 2.8% of the men said they had ever forced a woman into a sexual act. While only 2.8% of men and 1.4% of women in the study identified themselves as homosexual or bisexual, 10.1% of men and 8.6% of women reported they had had same-sex desires or experiences—this finding was quite different from the 1-in-10 figure that came from the 1948 Kinsey study. The statistics include how many like to watch a partner undress, receive oral sex, give oral sex, have anal intercourse, have group sex, etc. More than 80% of Americans are said to have had one sexual partner, or no partner at all, in the preceding year, and that number rises to 96% among the married. Half the population is said to have no more than three different partners, the median for men being six and for women was two, in an entire lifetime. A total of 90% of the women and more than 75% of the men claim they have never had extramarital sex. The survey findings were published in two books: *Sex in America: A Definitive Survey* (1994) and *The Social Organization of Sexuality* (1994), the latter going far beyond Kinsey and being one of the most comprehensive tour of our bedrooms ever published.

However, critics were fast to note flaws in the study's methodology. For example, the average man was said to have had six sex partners while the average woman had had two—logically, these numbers should be equal (and imply that men exaggerate or women understate). Also, those interviewed in the presence of a spouse or a sex partner responded differently when interviewed alone. The study, which had wanted to obtain a sample of about 400 homosexuals, had fewer than 100 because the Bush Administration had agreed with conservative pressure and withdrew the project's financing. The original survey, which was to have been paid for by the Federal Government, was opposed by religious and ultra-conservative leaders, leading to its discontinuance. Because the Government was afraid to ask, someone else found out: the National Opinion Research Center at the University of Chicago.

A government can be quite effective in setting an ideological fashion. For example, and as evidence of the efficacy of the prudery of Chairman Mao's teachings, the Chinese *Legal Daily* in 1994 told of two highly educated university lecturers who, after months of trying to conceive a child, sought the advice of a physician. The physician, finding the wife was still a virgin, learned that the couple thought that sleeping together, literally just sleeping in the same bed, was a reproductive act. (See entries for Adamastor, Arthur Danto, fucking, sex education, sexuality, and sodomy. Also, see Joseph McCabe's *Rationalist Encyclopedia* concerning sex and religion. He points out that of the 600 religious sects that are included in a *Dictionary of Religion*, only seven were founded by women. **Wardell Baxter Pomeroy**, a leading sexologist and one of the authors of the Kinsey Report, is a Humanist Laureate in the Council for Democratic and Secular Humanism's Academy of Humanism. **Vern L. Bullough**, among other secular humanists noted herein, has written extensively on the topic.) {CE; Lee Eisler, *The Quotable Bertrand Russell*}

SEX ACT: See entry for Calvinism, with E. L. Doctorow's comments.

SEX EDUCATION

Annie Besant was an advocate of birth control, and she toured and lectured widely. In her time, however, most of the uneducated learned about birth control through advertisements in urinals and drug stores, and on posters. In 1877, when she stood trial for advocating birth control and was acquitted, manufacturers launched a sales drive. Michael Mason, in *The Making of Victorian Sexuality* (1995), reasons that abstinence did not find favor with wives. One York wife was quoted as saying, "Self-restraint? . . . not much! If my husband started on self-restraint, I should jolly well know there was another woman in the case."

Mason found that rationalist W. R. Greg regarded celibacy as a "social gangrene." The Reverend Charles Kingsley celebrated the joys of physical lovemaking with his wife; but if it was not so enjoyable, how on earth could frailer creatures be restrained? So although the Anglican clergy deplored celibacy—a Roman practice—they backed restraint and later marriage, and deplored sensuality. On this the high-minded agnostics, such as George Eliot, were their allies.

George Drysdale, a precursor of Havelock Ellis, argued in the 1880s that sexual abstinence could cause lesions in the sexual organs. Mason denies that

Victorian women were ignorant or joyless, but he admits that many doctors were opposed to birth control, and they were enraged when Bertrand Russell's father declared in 1868 that they ought to favor it. They were too scared of a charge of impropriety to make a vaginal examination. They also feared their patients would desert them for quacks—and on sexual matters quacks have abounded. {Noel Annan, "Under the Victorian Bed," *The New York Review of Books*, 22 June 1995}

SEX IN ISLAM

Muslims generally understand sexual fulfillment within marriage for both parties to be the ideal state of affairs. One's sexual needs must be understood and satisfied. Licensed sex is neither sinful nor restricted solely to procreation: it serves as a means of communication and a source of solace.

Muslims complain that others misinterpret their teachings, for it would be a corruption of Muslim practice if women within the marriage institution were considered a degradation. On the contrary, Muslim leaders insist, but virginity is highly valued for girls. To control impregnation (*aze*), the Prophet recommended *coitus interruptus*. Most Muslims disapprove of abortion, unless the mother's life is severely medically compromised.

Female circumcision is practiced in many parts of Africa in order to control female sexuality and insure virginity at the time of marriage. As for polygamy, a man's needs often exceed a woman's, according to the patriarchal outlook. The man must not take more wives, however, than he can afford.

Homosexuality is either considered unlawful, abnormal, punishable under the *shariah*, or tolerated in those areas where homosexuals are viewed as a "third sex," neither men nor women. (See entry for Heaven–Muslim, for sex continues even after one's death. Also see Ibn Warraq's *Why I Am Not A Muslim*.)

SEX SYMBOLS

The Christian cross has been interpreted as a sex symbol. "Just as the sun was the father," wrote B. Z. Goldberg in *The Sacred Fire* (1958), "so was man's lingam [a stylized phallic symbol of the masculine cosmic principle and of the Hindu god Siva] the father; and just as the moon was the mother, so was the yoni [the stylized representation of the female genitalia symbolized in the Hindu cosmology]. . . . The lingam is in the shape of a rod with a round head; so any object of this form, stone or wood, might become such a symbol. The yoni is an oval opening; so any oval figure might represent the female divinity of sex. By further simplification it was enough to draw a vertical line to suggest the lingam and a horizontal one to signify the yoni, while the union of the two was represented by the cross." Goldberg details many sex symbols found in Africa, Australia, Asia, Europe, and the Americas.

SEX, ORAL

I mind how once we lay such a transparent
summer morning
How you settled your head athwart my hips and
Gently turn'd over upon me. . . .

—**Walt Whitman**
"Song of Myself," *Leaves of Grass*

SEX-CHANGE OPERATIONS

In 1952, George Jorgensen became Christine by having a sex-change operation in Denmark. An estimated 25,000 Americans have had sex-changing surgery to date, according to *New York Times* reporter James Brooke (8 November 1998).

Through the 1980s, when few surgeons would perform the operations, about two-thirds of the nation's sex-change surgeries were done at Mount San Rafael Hospital.

In Trinidad, Colorado, of the 3,800 patients Dr. Stanley H. Biber treated, the pioneering surgeon claimed that over the years only three, all men, had been unhappy in their new sex.

Because of unfavorable publicity in the 1970s, Dr. Biber and other surgeons drew up guidelines to eliminate the surgery on demand. Most candidates now must go through two psychiatric evaluations, live and dress in their new role for at least a year, and undergo nine months of hormone treatments: testosterone for women and estrogen for men. Toward the end of 1998, Dr. Biber found a major shift in the sex of his patients, from overwhelmingly male to 50-50 now.

Sextus Empiricus (around 200 CE)

Sextus's *Outlines of Pyrrhonism* and his treatises against the dogmatists began with ten tropes attributed to Aenesidemus, "ways of skeptical argumentation leading to suspense of judgment about what is not evident. . . . He showed how our moral beliefs are relative to the customs of our society. The result of all of this was not to deny that knowledge is possible but to lead the seeker after knowledge to suspend judgment on all non-evident questions. By so doing, people will achieve *ataxaria*, a state of being unperturbed, and they can then live undogmatically following the dictates of nature and custom and acting on how things appear to be." Robertson points out that Sextus Empiricus was one of the freethinkers of antiquity who passed down the view that "all religious doctrine had been invented by politicians in order to control the people." (See entry for Pyrrho.) {BDF; CE; EU, Richard H. Popkin; JMR; JMRH}

SEXUAL ACTS OF HETEROSEXUALS

A report on the sexual practices of British men (*The Economist*, 9 May 1998) reveals that 7.8% have twenty-one or more heterosexual partners over a lifetime. The same study showed men in the United States had 12.7%. Women in Britain with that many partners claimed 1.2% whereas American women claimed 2.4%.

Slightly less than 5% of men in the two places claimed to have had extramarital sex within the past year, as compared with slightly less than 3% of the women.

Only 8% to 11% of Britishers found pre-marital sex "almost always wrong" whereas 24% to 32.7% of Americans found it sinful. Similarly fewer Britishers (76% to 83%) found extra-marital sex "always or almost always wrong" whereas 93.5% of American women and 88.9% of American men thought so.

"Unsurprisingly," wrote *The Economist* editors, "Americans are less likely to use a condom despite engaging in riskier sex. They pay a price: the incidence of AIDS is ten times as high as it is in Britain. The authors [of the study published in the *American Journal of Public Health*] conclude that 'Our public health may be the high price we pay for our public opinion.' "

SEXUAL ACTS OF THE BONOBO

The bonobo, animals inaccurately called pygmy chimpanzees, lubricate the gears of social harmony with sex in all possible permutations and combinations: males with females, males with males, females with females, and even infants with adults. The sexual acts include intercourse, genital-to-genital rubbing, oral sex, mutual masturbation, and "French-kissing." Frans de Waal, a primatologist at Emory University in Atlanta, Georgia and author of *Bonobo: The Forgotten Ape* (1997), has said that

> Sex is there, it's pervasive, it's critical, and bonobo society would collapse without it. But it's not what people think it is. It's not driven by orgasm or seeking release. Nor is it often reproductively driven. Sex for a bonobo is casual, it's quick, and once you're used to watching it, it begins to look like any other social interaction.

In his book, de Waal found that, "The chimpanzee resolves sexual issues with power; the bonobo resolves power issues with sex." {*The New York Times*, 22 April 1997}

SEXUAL DYSFUNCTION

Pioneering sex therapists William Masters and Virginia Johnson have stated that if children early on are trained that sex is bad or dirty, such training has been identified as one of the primary causes of sexual dysfunction in married couples. Organized religions include no sex education classes in their sabbath schools, and critics claim this leads children to consider sex as something bad rather than as something basic to human happiness.

SEXUAL ORIENTATION

"Sexual orientation" is favored over the term "sexual preference" because it indicates an identity that cannot be changed or cast aside lightly, like a preference. One could be a male brunet with a preference for doughtnuts and for being a beautiful blonde female but still be a doughtnut-eating brunet male.

One's sexual identification is commonly defined as homosexual, heterosexual, or bisexual, depending on a person's sexual relationship.

SEXUALITY, ANIMAL: For a deconstruction of the Noah's Ark myth, see entry for Animal.

SEXUALITY

Jerome Beadle and Bruce Falton, mindful that organized religion's stand on sex has always stood in the way of people's enjoyment of sex, have compiled the following instances. For their complete listings, see *People's Almanac #2*.

• 14 CE. Emperor Tiberius of Rome forbade the execution of virgins, whereby virgins were deflowered by the executioner before the sentence was carried out.

• c. 875. The Scottish King Ewen III established the rights of "the First Night": "Wives of common men shall be free to the nobles; and the Lord of the ground shall have the maidenheads of all the virgins dwelling in the same." The practice may have continued up to the beginning of the Middle Ages.

• 1072. Pietro Damiana, an Italian reformer who was son of a prostitute, preached inside brothels that virginity should be preserved and that girls should abstain from sex.

• 1191. When King Richard the Lion-Hearted arrived at Marseilles in his first holy crusade against the infidels, he was horrified to discover that his advance party of trusty Christian knights had spent all the campaign funds on prostitutes.

• 1274. St. Thomas Aquinas, who called sex "lust," preached that *any* sexual activity other than that intended for procreation was a sin against nature. His four other offending categories were, in descending order: (a) bestiality; (b) homosexuality; (c) using any position other than face to face, with the woman on her back; and (d) masturbation, which he considered effeminate in men.

• 1275. Angela de Labarthe of Toulouse was burned at the stake for having sexual intercourse with the Devil. Reportedly, she had given birth to a child with a wolf's head and a snake's tail.

• 1300. The Lothardi sect in Russia believed in Christian morality so long as members were twenty-seven inches below ground; hence, their meetings were held in subterranean caves and featured riotous orgies.

• 1382. *Sex* made its first appearance in a John Wycliffe translation of the Bible: "Of alle thing is havynge sowle of ony flesh, two thow shalt brynge into the ark, that maal sex and femaal lyven with thee."

• 1415. [The original] Pope John XXIII was deposed for "notorious incest, adultery, defilement, homicide, and atheism." While still a chamberlain, he had openly kept his brother's wife as a mistress. While a cardinal in Bologna, "two hundred maids, matrons, and widows, including a few nuns, fell victim to his brutal lust." (John was the original Pope John XXIII, but of the Pisan Line. At the same time, Pope Gregory XII was pope but of the Roman Line. Meanwhile, a third pope, Pope Benedict XIII, was pope but of the Avignon Line. This was during the Great Schism, 1378-1417.)

• 1484. Pope Innocent VIII was nicknamed "the Honest," because he was the first pope to acknowledge his illegitimate children publicly.

• 1529. During Cardinal Thomas Wolsey's trial for treason, he was accused of giving Henry VIII syphilis by whispering in the king's ear.

• 1535. Father Valdelamar, a priest in Toledo, Spain, was found guilty of rape, blasphemy, consorting with prostitutes, and extorting the favors of a young woman in exchange for absolution. He was sentenced to a mere thirty-day house arrest and a fine of two ducats.

• 1542. Andrew Boorde in his *Dyetary of Helth* warned solemnly that eating lettuce killed sexual desire. Later, and upon becoming Bishop of Chichester, he was publicly defrocked for keeping three prostitutes in his chambers.

• 1555. Pope Paul IV, who organized the Inquisition which had been set up by Paul III, ordered the removal of Michelangelo's paintings from the Sistine Chapel on the grounds that they were obscene. Michelangelo's pupil, Daniele da Volterra, was ordered to add clothes to all the naked figures (including all the angels and the Virgin Mary) in *The Last Judgment*, after which de Volterra was nicknamed "the Breeches Maker."

• 1559. Pope Paul IV began compiling the *Index Librorum Prohibitorum*, the list of books deemed to have blasphemous or profane content. Over 4,000 titles, including the total output of Balzac, Dumas, Stendhal, and Alberto Moravia, were included. In 1966, the Catholic Church stopped publishing the *Index*.

• 1565. Mass-scale erotic convulsions swept the Convent of Nazareth in Cologne. A German doctor De Weier found that the nuns were throwing themselves on their backs, shutting their eyes, raising their abdomens erotically, and thrusting forward their pudenda.

• 1585. St. Mary Magdalene de Pazzi ran madly about the convent, masochistically rolling around on thorns and burrs, whipping herself, and begging other nuns to hurl globules of hot wax at her. She was canonized in 1671.

• 1611. Two unmarried women found to be pregnant upon arrival in Virginia were returned to England in an attempt to stamp out the risk of promiscuity in the colony.

• 1624. Richard Cornish was hanged for forcing a young man into "unnatural" sexual relations. Two who complained were later pilloried and had their ears sliced off for protesting this first homosexual hanging in America and for alleging that Cornish "was put to death through a scurvie boys meanes & no other came against him."

• 1634. In France, Jeanne des Anges, a nun, suffered nightmarish erotic hallucinations and convulsions after being spurned by the Curé Grandier. The curé was put to death, providing the basis for Aldous Huxley's *The Devils of Loudun* (1952) and Ken Russell's 1970 film, "The Devils."

• 1634. Mary Mandame was charged in Plymouth, Massachusetts with "dallyance diverse tymes with Tinsin, an Indian" and "committing the act of uncleanse with him." She was sentenced to be whipped and to wear at all times a badge of shame on her left sleeve. Tinsin was whipped at the pillory for "allurement & enticement."

• 1653. An eighty-two-year-old man was executed in England for adultery.

• 1656. Captain Kemble of Boston was found guilty of "lewd and unseemly behavior," having kissed his wife in public on the Sabbath after a three years' sojourn at sea.

• 1658. Plymouth, Massachusetts, Puritans passed an adultery law which required a female offender not only to be whipped but to bear for the remainder of her life the letter A on her breast. Failure to comply made her liable to having the A branded on her face with a red-hot iron. The law was portrayed by Nathaniel Hawthorne in *The Scarlet Letter* (1850).

• 1665. *Condom* first appeared in a work by John Wilmot, Earl of Rochester. The word may come from the Latin *cunnus* (the female pudenda) and *dum* (implying an inability to function), not from the legendary but mythical Dr. Condom; however, its origin is uncertain.

• 1672. Women shipped out of England to Virginia for the express purpose of helping to populate the new colonies were priced not in currency but in tobacco, sometimes being valued at 120 pounds of tobacco per female.

• 1680. Maiden Lane in downtown New York was so named, according to *People's Almanac*, because so many maidens lost their maidenheads there.

• 1684. A sex manual published in London under the title *Aristotle's Masterpiece, or the Secrets of Generation Displayed in All Parts Thereof*, advised extensive sexual foreplay and emphasized the value of clitoral massage, saying "blowing the coals of these amorous fires" pleased women.

• 1702. Lord Cornbury, a governor of New York and New Jersey, performed most of his official duties in women's clothes. He was recalled in 1708 after landing in jail for debt.

• 1708. Edmund Curll was indicted for having sold *Venus in the Cloister, or the Nun in Her Smock*, a blasphemous tale of lesbian nuns first published in France in 1682.

• 1714. The Roman Catholic Church banned the confessional requirement that men name their partners in fornication when it was discovered that priests might be making carnal use of the information.

• 1723. In Montpellier, France, police raided a meeting of the Multiplicants, a sect in which twenty-four-hour-only marriages were consummated publicly on the altar, followed by orgies. Its leaders were hanged, and the women—after having their heads shaved—were placed in nunneries.

• 1729. Sir Francis Dashwood masqueraded as King Charles XII of Sweden, thereby seducing Empress Anne of Russia.

• 1750. John Cleland wrote the erotic novel, *Fanny Hill, or the Memoirs of a Woman of Pleasure*, called by Anthony Comstock "the most obscene book ever written" but one which never made the Vatican's *Index*.

• 1768. *The Encyclopedia Britannica* was first issued. The entry for "Woman" stated, "The female of man. See Homo."

• 1770. Pope Clement XIV outlawed the 200-year-old practice of using castrati in papal choirs. Persons performing such operations on young boys were excommunicated, though the boys were made very welcome into the choirs thereafter.

• 1782. Dr. John Hunter, assisting a couple incapable of having children, got the man to masturbate, then took the semen in a warm syringe and injected it into the posterior part of the wife's vagina. The result was a bouncing success, the first child of artificial insemination. Church officials expressed their outrage at such a perversion.

• 1798. The Bishop of Durham warned Britain's House of Lords that France was trying to defeat England morally, not militarily, by smuggling in hordes of ballet dancers.

• 1821. The first American obscenity trial found printer Peter Holmes guilty of smut-peddling. He had published *Fanny Hill.*

• 1822. A statue of Achilles representing the invincibility of the Duke of Wellington, commissioned and paid for by the women of England, was unveiled in Hyde Park. At the unveiling, witnesses realized this was London's first nude statue . . . and within a few days the statue miraculously grew a fig leaf.

• 1829. The British banned the Hindu practice of suttee in India and elsewhere throughout the Empire, although it continued until at least 1905. Suttee was the enforced immolation of a widow on her husband's funeral pyre.

• 1834. Sylvester Graham (1794–1851), best remembered for inventing the graham cracker, wrote "A Lecture to Young Men on Chastity, Intended Also for the Serious Consideration of Parents and Guardians." He warned that "high seasoned food, rich dishes, and the free use of flesh" led to insanity. He advised married couples that overdoing it sexually led to, among other problems, "chilliness, headache, melancholy, hypochondria, hysterics, feebleness of all the senses, impaired vision, loss of sight, weakness of the lungs, nervous cough, pulmonary consumption, disorders of the liver and kidneys, urinary difficulties, disorders of the genital organs, spinal diseases, weakness of the brain, loss of memory, epilepsy, insanity, apoplexy, abortions, premature births, and extreme feebleness, morbid predispositions, and an early death of offspring." Further, he warned that every ejaculation lowered a male's life expectancy.

• 1843. Joseph Smith, founder of Mormonism, first exhorted his followers to practice polygamy.

• 1847. A British physician named Simpson angered churchmen when he administered the newly discovered chloroform to a woman in childbirth. The church claimed that the Bible commands that women should bring forth their children in sorrow.

• 1869. The term *homosexuality* was coined by Dr. Benkert, a Hungarian physician.

• 1873. The U.S. Congress passed the Comstock Act, banning obscene materials—including rubber prophylactics—from the mails. This caused George Bernard Shaw to coin the word *comstockery.*

• 1881. Henry James, in *Washington Square*: "He wanted to abuse somebody, and he began, cautiously—for he was always cautious—with himself."

• 1882. Aletta Jacobs opened the world's first birth-control clinic, in Holland. She popularized the diaphragm, which was known as the "Dutch cap."

• 1895. Striptease shows began in Paris with *Le Coucher d'Yvette* showing a girl gradually removing her clothes as she vainly searched for a flea.

• 1900. Sigmund Freud's *The Interpretation of Dreams* underscored the importance of repressed sexual desires in human behavior.

• 1913. The world's first nude calendar was published, and it contained "September Morn," a painting by French artist Paul Chabas (1869–1937). Antipornography crusader Anthony Comstock complained, "There's too little morn and too much maid."

• 1916. Margaret Sanger opened America's first birth-control clinic (a phrase she coined) at 46 Amboy Street in Brooklyn, New York. After a policewoman posed as a patient to obtain evidence, the establishment was closed.

• 1924. André Gide in his autobiographical novel *If It Die* became the first important modern public figure to declare publicly that he was a homosexual.

• 1934. Upon reading Henry Miller's *The Tropic of Cancer*, poet Ezra Pound remarked, "At last, an unprintable book that is fit to read."

• 1938. The Roman Catholic-oriented National Organization for Decent Literature was founded. In the years to come it would condemn such works as C. S. Forester's *The African Queen*, Ernest Hemingway's *A Farewell to Arms*, James Michener's *Tales of the South Pacific*, and Christopher Morley's *Kitty Foyle.*

• 1946. Mahatma Gandhi, the Indian leader, publicly confessed that he had been taking naked girls to bed with him for many years—to test his mastery of celibacy.

• 1946. Massachusetts, charging Kathleen Winsor's *Forever Amber* with being obscene, made an attempt to ban its sale because of the following: 70 references to sexual intercourse; 39 illegitimate pregnancies; 7 abortions; 10 descriptions of women dressing, undressing, or bathing in the presence of gentlemen; 5 references to incest; 13 references ridiculing marriage; and another 49 "miscellaneous objectionable passages." Afterwards, a radio comedian was censured for suggesting that Miss Winsor should have called her book *Forever Under.*

• 1948. Dr. Alfred Kinsey and associates published *Sexual Behavior in the Human Male*, to be followed five years later by *Sexual Behavior in the Human Female.*

• 1951. A nationwide census in India indicated there were nearly 3 million husbands and more than 6 million wives between 5 and 14 years old.

• 1952. Surgeon Christian Hamburger in Denmark performed successful sex-change surgery on ex-American soldier George Jorgensen. The fame achieved by then Christine Jorgensen led to the Danish surgeon's being so swamped with applications for the operation that the Danish government had to restrict the operation to Danish patients only.

• 1953. Hugh Hefner published the first *Playboy*, which was undated because Hefner did not know whether there would be a second issue. The first playmate was Marilyn Monroe. The magazine infuriated leaders of organized religion, for it was aimed at "that select group of urbane fellows who were less concerned with hunting, fishing, and climbing mountains than with good food, drink, proper dress, and the pleasure of female company."

• 1961. USSR leader Nikita Khruschev expressed his outrage upon visiting Hollywood and finding the "indecencies" of the film "Can Can."

• 1966. William H. Masters and Virginia E. Johnson published *Human Sexual Response*, the first detailed description and analysis of the physiological aspects of sexual excitation and orgasm.

• 1967. "I Am Curious (Yellow)," a Swedish film, became one of the first popularly distributed movies in the U.S. to portray sex explicitly.

• 1971. The world's first commercial sperm bank was opened in New York City.

• 1973. Robert A. Martin, a twenty-eight-year-old Quaker pacifist, was arrested during a peace march on the White House. Refusing to pay a $10 bond, he was moved to a District of Columbia jail where prisoners with records for violence were kept. In two days, he was raped 50 times.

• 1977. The first female-to-male transsexual operation was performed on a female University of Missouri student. Reported *The New York Times*, "The doctors said the penis contained a tiny hydraulic system that permitted a fluid to be pumped from a reservoir in the abdomen into the penis to cause erection. Investigation shows that the penis-erection device has been used in more than 200 operations in the country to date, most performed by the device's inventor, Dr. F. Brantley Scott, a urologist affiliated with the Baylor College of Medicine in Houston." {PA}

Seymour, Edward Adolphus (1804–1885)

A British statesman, Seymour was a commoner who rose to be First Lord of the Treasury. He was made Duke of Somerset and Earl St. Maur for his services. In his retirement he wrote *Christian Theology and Modern Skepticism*, in which he rejected all supernaturalism. Seymour believed in a "Supreme Intelligence" which, if it did exist, he felt throws "a ray of light beyond the mystery of the grave." {JM; RAT; RE}

Seymour, Nick (20th Century)

Seymour, a recording artist, was a member of the disbanded New Zealand/Australian band called Crowded House. When asked in an interview on MTV Europe (30 September 1993) if the band's members believed in God, Paul Hester responded, "No! My father used to try to get me to go to Sunday school, but I wouldn't." Seymour said, "No, not anymore. I am a bit of a lapsed Catholic." {CA}

Shadwell, Thomas (1640–1692)

Shadwell was an English dramatist. Some of his work illustrates the days of Charles II and were damned by Dryden in his *Mac Flecknoe*. {BDF}

Shaen, William (1821–1887)

A Unitarian, Shaen arbitrated in the *National Reformer* the dispute between Holyoake and Bradlaugh. {VI}

Shaftesbury, Anthony Ashley Cooper [1st Earl of] (1621–1682)

Earl Shaftesbury supported religious toleration during the Oliver Cromwell period, but in 1673 he renounced his earlier position because he was suspicious of the king's favoring the Roman Catholics. A founder of the Whigs, he pressed for the exclusion bill to keep the Roman Catholic duke of York (later James II) from becoming king. When Charles dissolved the 1681 Parliament, Shaftesbury found it expedient to flee to Holland. He is considered one of the most skillful and influential politicians of his day. According to Voltaire, the dominant influence on Pope came from Shaftesbury, particularly his deists' prayer, "The Universal Prayer." The Earl did not parade his unbelief, for to do so would have been dangerous. But he was a champion of the deists because of his *Letter Concerning Enthusiasm* (1708), his *Essay on the Freedom of Wit and Humour* (1709), and his treatise *The Moralists* (1709). The anecdote is told that he was overheard by a scrubwoman as he remarked to a number of friends that "All wise men have the same religion." When the scrubwoman eagerly inquired what this religion of all wise men was, Lord Shaftesbury is said to have replied: "Wise men, madam, never tell."

Shaftesbury, Anthony Ashley Cooper [3rd Earl of] (1671–1713)

The third Earl of Shaftesbury was educated privately under Locke's supervision. He entered Parliament but quit because of health problems. In Holland, he met Bayle and in 1711 published *Characteristicks*. Although he attended church and took the Sacrament, Cooper held a deistic view of the Bible and gave a yearly pension to the deist Toland. In philosophy, he deserted Locke for Platonism, and he held an intuitionist ethic. {BDF; CE; CL; EU, A. Owen Aldridge; FUK; HAB; JM; JMR; JMRH; RAT; RE; TYD}

Shah, A. B. (1920–1981)

At his death, Shah was director of the Institute for the Study of Indian Traditions and honorary professor at the Indian Institute of Education, both at Pune in India's State of Maharashtra. According to Norwegian philosopher Finngeir Hiorth in *The Secularist* (India, January-February 1991), Shah along with M. N. Roy, Gora, and Periyar was among India's most interesting atheists. In 1968, he founded the Indian Secular Society. He was also founder-editor of *New Quest*, a journal of criticism, creative writing, and ideas. And he was an indefatigable crusader for secular humanism. "Secularism," he wrote in 1968, "primarily means the separation of religion from man's secular life," a definition which shows George Jacob Holyoake as the source for his concept. In 1966, he addressed the Fourth International Humanist and Ethical Union World Congress held in Paris. When he signed Humanist Manifesto II, Shah was president of the Indian Secular Society, which he had founded in 1969, and was director of the Institute for the Study of Indian Traditions. Shah died of a heart attack. (See entry for Ramendra.) {FUK; HM2; SHD}

Shahan, Mark (20th Century)

Shahan heads the membership committee of Atheists and Agnostics of Wisconsin

Shaikh, Anwar (1928-)

Shaikh's *Islam: The Arab Imperialism* (1998) starts by pointing out the inherent absurdities in the concept of prophethood. The Prophet started by being politically weak and claiming to be a mortal and humble servant of Allah. Once becoming strong, after his move from Mecca to Medina, "he began changing his tone, until he was able to claim himself to be Allah's Superior." Muhammmed's arrogance is expressed, claims Shaikh, in the arrogance of the religion he invented toward all non-Arabs, especially the Jews.

Ibn al Rawandi, in commenting about Shaikh's work, has written,

> The notorious episode of the Jewish tribe of the Banu Quraiza, in which Mohammed is supposed to have overseen the slaughter of 800 Jewish men, is seen by Shaikh as "a pathetic model of ethnic cleansing. The Jews suffered this fate when they refused to become Arabs. We cannot find an example of such extreme nationalism so early in history. Yet the Muslims believe that Islam does not recognise nationalism. They insist that it is a message of international brotherhood."

As regards history this is not quite true, of course. It was routine in the ancient world that when a city was conquered the men were killed and the women and children sold into slavery.

Shaikh is editor of a humanist journal, *Liberty*. Born a Muslim in the Indian city of Gujarat (now Pakistan), he lives in England. In Pakistan the Muslim clergy have demanded his extradition in order that he may be publicly hanged.

In an interview with Ibn Al Warrag in *The Radical Humanist* (June 1999), Shaikh told how after being born near the city of Gujrat (in present-day Pakistan), he was circumcised and brought up "breathing Islam." In his twenties, however, he began to be skeptical about Islam. He has detailed his becoming a "liberal humanist" in books which he published at his own expense: *Islam: The Arab Imperialism*; *Eternity*; *Faith and Deception*; and *Taxation and Liberty*, all available from Principality Publishers (PO Box 9181 Cardiff, Great Britain CF2 4YP). Shaikh signed Humanist Manifesto 2000. *The Freethinker*, November-December 1998}

Shaikh, Younis (20th Century)

Shaikh started a group, the Enlightenment, in Pakistan in the early 1990s. It holds public meetings that raise questions about religion and women's rights. The group has lobbied the Government and Senators and MPs, criticizing the use of the Sharia law. Although he has not been attacked directly, threats have been made against his parents and he has had to give up two jobs. *{International Humanist News, December 1998}*

SHAKESPEARE AND BARDOLATRY: For "the worship of Shakespeare" as a substitute for Christianity, see the entry for Bardolatry.

SHAKESPEARE, SHAKE-SPEARE, SHAKSPERE

Doubt continues as to the authorship of the greatest dramatic pieces and works in the English language—e.g., "Hamlet," "Macbeth," "King Lear," "Romeo and Juliet," "As You Like It," "The Comedy of Errors," the "Sonnets," and others:

- **Baconian Theory** holds that the son of a Warwickshire husbandman would not likely have had the skill to write such magnificent works, whereas Francis Bacon (1561-1626) did. Doubters think such a view sounds like social snobbery.
- **Oxfordian Theory** holds that the 17th Earl of Oxford, Edward de Vere (1550-1604), wrote some or all of the plays. T. J. Looney identified him in 1920, but doubters call his theory "looney." At the start of the 21st Century, however, more and more are leaning toward the theory's credibility.
- **John Fletcher** (1570-1625) is thought to have been the collaborator on "Henry VIII," "Cardenio," and "The Two Noble Kinsmen," the latter work which may have derived in part from a 1613 masque by Sir Francis Beaumont (1584-1616).
- **Stratfordian Theory** holds that William Shakspere (1564-1616 was the author. Charles Chaplin in *My Autobiography* (1964) and Sigmund Freud (1856-1939) in a letter to Arnold Zweig (2 April 1937) are just two of many who do not think so. Henry James (1843-1916) wrote in a letter to Violet Hunt (26 August 1903) that he found it "*almost* as impossible to conceive that Bacon wrote the plays as to conceive that the man from Stratford, as we know the man from Stratford, did."

The present work will follow the plan of the editors of *Harper's Magazine* (April 1999), which describes the two viewpoints:

The Oxfordian Theory was advanced by Mark K. Anderson, author of *Prospero's Bible: The Secret History and Spiritual Biography of the Man who was "Shake-speare"*; Tom Bethell, author of *The Noblest Triumph*; Joseph Sobran, author of *Alias Shakespeare*; Richard F. Whalen, *author of* Shakespeare: Who Was He?" and Daniel Wright, co-patron with Sir Derek Jacobi of the De Vere Society of Great Britain.

The Stratfordian Theory was advanced by Jonathan Bate, author of *The Genius of Shakespeare*; Harold Bloom, author of *Shakespeare: The Invention of the Human*; Marjorie Garber, author of *Shakespeare's Ghost Writers*; Irvin Matus, author of *Shakespeare, in Fact*; and Gail Kern Paster, editor of *The Shakespeare Quarterly*

In light of such diverse viewpoints, in the present work,

Shakespeare will refer to whoever *really* was the author of the greatest dramatic pieces and work in the English language (whether or not we ever determine for sure who wrote them.

Shake-speare will refer to Roger Stritmatter's research, which indicates that the pen name for Edward de Vere, Earl of Oxford (1550-1604), was Shakespeare, that he wrote under that name because as an earl he could not risk using his own name, and that he was the actual author of most if not all the works ascribed to William Shakspere. Stritmatter, in an eight-year study of an annotation by de Vere of the Bible, found that more than a quarter of the 1,066 annotations and marked passages in the de Vere work appear in Shakespeare. The parallels range from the thematic—sharing a motif, idea, or trope—to the verbal—using names, phrases, or wordings that suggest a specific biblical passage. Stritmatter found the correlation between Shake-speare's favorite biblical verses and de Vere's Bible is high: .439 compared with .054, .068, and .020 for Spenser, Marlowe, and Bacon.

Shakspere will refer to William Shakspere (1564-1616), whom most have come to think, perhaps erroneously, wrote the works.

Shakespeare, Sonnets of

"Shall I Compare Thee to a Summer's Day?" was, in the past, said to have been written for a fair-haired, wealthy young woman, Viola de Lesseps.

However, as pointed out by Harvard professor Stephen Greenblatt, the editor of *The Norton Shakespeare*, it was one of a group of 126 sonnets written to a fair-haired, wealthy young man, whom he once described as "the master mistress of my passion." The first seventeen of the sonnets clearly address a man, and not until the 127 does "the Dark Lady" appear. Greenblatt in response to the question, "How is it that a miserably undemocratic, unenlightened culture 400 years ago could be more tolerant of expressions of same-sex love, or the appearance of it, than our own?", responded that

> Elizabethan England was not in fact more tolerant; our laws on sexual relations, inadequate though they may be, are models of sweet reasonableness compared with the viciously punitive statutes on the books in the 1590's. But there is considerable evidence that those statutes were rarely, if ever, enforced: charges were rarely brought, juries were consistently unwilling to convict, and many of the most politically powerful figures in the realm were altogether comfortable with expressions of same-sex desire. We, by contract, have prominent politicians like the Senate majority leader, Trent Lott, who voice the opinion that homosexuality is akin to alcoholism and kleptomania.

(See entry for Shakspere—the Oxford Argument, in which the homosexual Richard de Vere is thought to have written the sonnets.)

{The New York Times, 6 February 1999}

Shakspere, William (1564–1616)

The greatest playwright and author in the English language–if indeed he wrote all the works ascribed to him–Shakspere was the person who pointed out that "Modest doubt is called the beacon of the wise." Santayana in "The Absence of Religion in Shakespeare" indicates that Shakspere was not into supernaturalism. The German critic Gervinus declared that Shakspere "wholly discarded from his works . . . that which religion enjoins as to faith and opinion." He also wrote that "Just as Bacon banished religion from science, so did Shakespeare from art. . . . From Bacon's example it seems clear that Shakspere left religious matters unnoticed on the same grounds." Robertson commented, "While there is no record of his having privately avowed unbelief, and certainly no explicit utterance of it in his plays, in no genuine work of his is there any more than bare dramatic conformity to current habits of religious speech; and there is often significantly less. In *Measure for Measure* the Duke, counseling as a friar the condemned Claudio, discusses the ultimate issues of life and death without a hint of Christian credence." Prof. J. R. Green in the 19th century wrote, "Often [Shakspere's] questionings turned to the riddle of life and death, and he leaves it a riddle to the last without heeding the common theological solutions around him." But, because of his being the best known of all writers in English, and never unequivocally having gone on record concerning his philosophic outlook, Shakspere has been claimed by believers and non-believers alike.

Secular humanists empathize with the man born where a Roman road (*strata via*) crossed an *afon* (Welsh for the river Avon) near a *ford*: Stratford-on-Avon. As pointed out by Princeton's Thomas Marc Parrott, town records show that John, his father, a glover, had been fined twelve pence for failing to remove a dirt heap in front of his house. But the father's fortunes rose in 1552 when he married Mary Arden, daughter of his father's landlord. Now the father became the town's first ale-taster (who supervised the price and quality of ale as well as bread). He continued advancing, becoming a town councilor, chamberlain (keeper of borough accounts), alderman, and in 1568 the bailiff or presiding officer of the Corporation. In such a capacity he granted licenses starting in 1568 to traveling companies of players, leading one to envision that he might have taken the four-year-old William to his first stage play in some guild hall, possibly utilizing complimentary tickets. By 1578, in a turn of fortune, John's finances were such that he was unable to pay the weekly sum of four-pence for the relief of the poor, and by 1586 he was deposed from his office as alderman because of continued absences from meetings. In 1592, John was reported a "recusant," one who failed to attend the parish church for fear of being arrested for debt, and one can imagine the effect this had on his family. Mary, William's mother, had come from a family whose landed gentry included a Robert Arden, who in 1438 had been sheriff of the county; and his descendant, Edward Arden, also once high sheriff, who was executed in 1583 for alleged complicity in a Roman Catholic plot against the life of Queen Elizabeth. William's mother, in the opinion of Princeton's Thomas Marc Parrott, likely adhered in secret to her father's faith.

William was baptized as *Gulielmus filius Johannes Shakspere* on Wednesday, April 16th, 1564. The oldest surviving child, he studied in a guild school that taught subjects entirely in Latin, including *Aesop's Fables*, Cicero, Vergil, Ovid, Terence, Plautus, Seneca, and the Geneva version of the Bible. In what must have embarrassed the family, the son William at age nineteen informed his parents of his need for a speedy marriage to Anne Hathaway, eight years his elder. On November 28th, 1582, friends filed a bond with the Bishop of Worcester, in whose diocese the town of Stratford lay, in order that the couple could marry without the customary delay of a triple announcing of the banns in church. For any such delay would have carried them into the Advent season and by the old church law marriage was forbidden from Advent Sunday until about the middle of January (apparently so as not to distract from the celebration by Christians of Jesus's alleged birthday). The Bishop granted the license, and Anne's child Susanna was baptized May 26th, 1583, only six or so months after the revelation. John took no part in the marriage and possibly did not approve of his son's marrying a poor girl eight years the boy's elder, but Susanna arrived soon after the marriage ceremony. Two years later Anne presented William with twins, Hamnet and Judith. Thereupon, and perhaps because his wife had "gotten religion" on account of her "sin" that resulted in daughter Susanna, William left the family to make his name and fortune in the evil theatre world of the evil city of London, which Puritans had preached so much against and which obviously attracted the twenty-something writer.

Although his references to religion were many and varied, following are a few:

- In religion, what damned error but some sober brow will bless it, and approve it with a text, hiding the grossness with fair ornament?
  –*The Merchant of Venice*

- Thrust your head into the public street, to gaze on Christian fools with varnish'd faces.
  –*The Merchant of Venice*

- Methinks sometimes I have no more wit than a Christian.
  –*Twelfth Night*

- His worst fault is, he's given to prayer; he is something peevish that way.
  –*The Merry Wives of Windsor*

- Scurvy jack-dog priest! By gar, me vill cut his ears.
  –*The Merry Wives of Windsor*

- Modest doubt is call'd the beacon of the wise.
  –*Troilus and Cressida*

- Thou art a proud traitor, priest . . . gleaning all of the land's wealth into one, into your own hands, cardinal, by extortion. . . . I'll startle you worse than the sacring bell, when the brown wench lay kissing in your arms, lord cardinal.
  –*King Henry VIII*

- We are such stuff as dreams are made of, and our little life is rounded with a sleep.
  –*The Tempest*

- I tell thee, churlish priest, a ministering angel shall my sister be, when thou liest howling.
  –*Hamlet*

His 154 sonnets are cryptic in their description of his relations with a rival poet, a dark woman, and a handsome man. No one is certain as to who these three, if they were real, actually were. A. L. Rowse, himself a homosexual, claimed Shakspere had no male lover, that he was "a strongly sexed heterosexual" and a man "more than a little interested in women—for an Englishman." Rowse claimed the Dark Lady was Emilia Bassano Lanier, the daughter of an Italian court musician. (See entry for Shakespeare, Sonnets of.)

Many point to atheistic overtones in "The Tempest":

> Our revels now are ended. These our actors,
> As I foretold you, were all spirits, and
> Are melted into air, into thin air;
> And, like the baseless fabric of this vision
> The cloud-capped towers, the gorgeous palaces,
> The solemn temples, the great globe itself,
> Yea, all which is inherent, shall dissolve,
> And, like this insubstantial pageant folded,
> Leave not a rack behind: We are such stuff
> As dreams are made of, and our little life
> Is rounded with a sleep.

Shakspere's successes are internationally known, but not so well-known is that he stayed away from his family in Stratford until his final years, returning as likely the wealthiest man in town. He must have been disturbed by the slander that was circulated about his daughter Susanna, and still more by the imprudent marriage of Judith who, in 1616, married Thomas Quiney in February, the "closed season," without a special license, resulting in their excommunication.

McCabe notes that Shakspere's work is entirely objective, "his pagan characters using pagan language, his Christian characters Christian, and we have no expression of personal opinion or evidence of contemporaries" about his personal beliefs. "It is therefore impossible to reach a definite conclusion. We may say with the historian Green that there is no depth in 'the religious phrases which are thinly scattered over his work' and that in the serious and more or less didactic plays of his last phase he does not apply to the problems of life 'the common theological solutions'; in other words he gives us the impression of being a simple humanist in his maturity. We can say only that the skeptical interpretation seems more probable than the Christian."

In 1616 William had called for his lawyer, Francis Collins, to make certain changes in his will. The opening paragraph of his will included the following: "I commend my soul unto the hands of God my Creator, hoping, and assuredly believing through the merits of Jesus Christ, my Savior, to be made partaker of life everlasting," words typical of the time and likely were those of his lawyer. In fact, George Bernard Shaw researched the material and concluded, "Shakespeare had no conscious religion." Shakspere arranged for a marriage portion for Judith, canceled his gift of plate (silver) to her in favor of his little grandchild, Elizabeth (who had become his darling in his last days); left memorial rings to Burbage, Heminges, and Condell; left little or nothing to the just-excommunicated Judith; and left his "second best bed" to his wife, apparently a recognition that their hasty wedding had not resulted in a congenial and happy marriage. He left nothing to any church. The next month, according to the Vicar of Stratford, "Shakespeare, Drayton, and Ben Jonson had a merry meeting and it seems drank too hard for Shakspere died of a fever there contracted."

When Virginia Woolf visited Shakspere's grave at Stratford-upon-Avon in 1934, she noted in *A Writer's Diary* (1934) her feelings about how "down there one foot from me lay the little bones that had spread over the world this vast illumination."

In *Shakespeare, the Invention of the Human* (1998), Harold Bloom concluded that Shakespeare's religious sentiments will never be known, because "Shakespeare maintained his usual ambiguity in this dangerous area." He also noted that *Hamlet* is neither a Protestant nor a Catholic work: "It seems to me indeed neither Christian nor non-Christian, since Hamlet's skepticism does not merely exceed its possible origin in Montaigne but passes into something rich and strong in Act V, something for which we have no name."

Inasmuch as his only son had died in childhood, and Susanna's only child, Elizabeth, died childless in 1670, and the three sons of Judith had died long before, Shakspere's descendants were soon extinct. He achieved his immortality as have all productive humanists: by living on in his works. (See George Santayana's "The Absence of Religion in Shakespeare; and Les Reid's "Shakespeare and the Wars of Religion," *New Humanist*, December 1995, in which he considers the possibility that Shakespeare was a Catholic. Also, see entry for A. L. Rowse.) {CB; CE; FUK; GL; JMR; JMRH; TRI; TYD}

SHAKSPERE—THE OXFORD ARGUMENTS

Tom Bethell, and others who have argued the Oxford Theory in *Harper's Magazine*, April 1999, makes the case that no evidence exists to prove that Shakspere wrote anything at all, "let alone the erudite works of 'Shakespeare.' " Yes, the man found work minding the horses of theatergoers, he became an actor as did his young brother Edmund, but he left London in 1604 at the age of forty and soon thereafter sued a neighbor for a malt debt of 35 shillings. Are we, at the height of his powers, led to suppose that "England's greatest writer threw down his pen, perhaps in mid-play, and headed back to Warwickshire, preferring the milieu of Stratford's small-claims court and its conveyance office to literary London [?]. Even his will makes no mention of any literary remains.

Daniel Wright agrees, pointing out that in the early 1780s, the Reverend Dr. James Wilmot, a friend of Dr. Johnson, researched Shakspere and found he had lived a fairly nondescript life, had no major connection to the literary world, and after an uneventful life was buried without ceremony in a grave that failed even to identify its occupant by name.

It was an age during which writers anonymously published pamphlets, books, plays, essays, tracts, and other texts including unflattering satires under a pseudonym in order to escape being hauled before the Privy Council (as was Samuel Daniel for his *Philotas*). Some were imprisoned (as were George Chapman and Ben Jonson for *Eastward Ho*); others were mutilated (as were John Stubbs, Alexander Leighton, and William Prynne). Some may even have been assassinated (as was, perhaps, Christopher Marlowe). Princeton's Gerald E. Bentley attests that "the large majority of all English plays before the reign of Elizabeth are anonymous, and even from 1558 to 1590 the authors of most plays are unknown." For seven years after the Shakespeare plays began to be printed, they were published without any name at all affixed to them. Not until the end of the sixteenth century did any plays begin to appear in print under the name of "William Shakespeare," a name that Wright points out "might have been adopted by almost any writer who desired to conceal his title, office, or baptismal name yet wished to assert his identity as a playwright."

Mark K. Anderson points out that Orson Welles and Roger Stritmatter think Oxford wrote the works. Citing "Hamlet," he notes that the Prince enacts entire portions of Oxford's life story: "Oxford's two military cousins, Horace and Francis Vere, appear as Hamlet's comrade-at-arms Horatio and the soldier Francisco. Oxford satirizes his guardian and father-in-law, the officious bumbling royal adviser Lord Burghley (nicknamed 'Polus'), as the officious, bumbling royal adviser Polonius. The parallels between Burghley and Polonius are so vast and detailed that even the staunch Stratfordian A. L. Rowse admitted that 'there is nothing original' anymore in asserting this widely recognized connection. Furthermore, like Polonius, Burghley had a daughter." Anderson thoroughly advances similar "proof" that the details of Oxford's life, not that of Shakspere, had similarly close connections with "Helena," "Falstaff," "King Lear," and "Prospero."

Joseph Sobran makes a convincing argument: Oxford was homosexual, had been accused of "buggering boys," and he did not put his name to the love sonnets, for "no common poet would have dared make amorous advances to an earl, but another earl might." The reference is to the Earth of Southampton. The Sonnets were published in 1609, five years after Oxford's death, their cryptic dedication supplied by the publisher, the dedicatee described as "the only begetter of these ensuing sonnets, Mr. W. H." —the initials, reversed, of Henry Wriothesley, third Earl of Southampton. "By praising the poet in such terms while presuming to dedicate his poems for him," Sobran continues, "the publisher invites the inference that the real author was no longer able to speak for himself: he was already dead. (William of Stratford still had seven years to live.) The poet's self-revelations match Oxford and nobody else in Elizabethan England. If the Sonnets and the other works of Shakespeare had been ascribed to Oxford from the start, it's hard to imagine that anyone would doubt his authorship today."

Richard F. Whalen, developing the view that Oxford was an excellent writer and had connections with the theatrical world, mentions that research on Oxford has only recently begun, that although it is unlikely "that much more will be found about the Stratford man," we are left with a choice as to the real author: "The Stratford merchant and theater investor, a simple man of mundane inconsequence? Or the recognized poet, patron of acting companies, and playwright, known at the time to be writing under a pseudonym,; a complex, mercurial nobleman in Queen Elizabeth's court whose life is mirrored in Shakespeare's works; a man with direct personal links to the publishers of the First folio? The choice seems obvious."

SHAMAN

Siberian tribes had shamans ("they who know") who, because of an alleged ability to achieve a communion with the spirit world, guided people with their mystical wisdom. A shaman was said to have been born to his job, having been chosen by a spirit to be a tribe's magician, medium, or healer. Similar to the African witch doctor and the American Indian medicine man, the shaman shielded mankind from spirits which might be harmful. Ancestor worship is related in that spirits of the dead are believed to continue dwelling in the natural world and can influence the living. Ancestor worship has been ritualized in West Africa and in ancient China, as well as in the Shinto faith and among Melanesians. Somewhat related is the raising of a person, once alive, to the level of a god—some Roman emperors were so elevated in a deification known as apotheosis. (See entry for Emperor worship.)

SHAME

• Fool me once, shame on you. Fool me twice, shame on me.

–Anonymous

Shange, Ntozake (1948–)

Shange (born Paulette Williams in Trenton, New Jersey) is a playwright and poet. Her "For Colored Girls Who Have Considered Suicide When the Rainbow is Enuf" (1976) is a feminist drama which describes the psychological, emotional, and physical pain some African American women receive from insensitive black men as well as an often hostile environment. Religious liberals quote her poem,

i was cold
i was burning up
a child & endlessly weaving garments
for the moon with my tears
I found god in myself
& i loved her
i loved her fiercely.

Shank, Michael (20th Century)

Shank's family was raised by his mother "to be straight-and-narrow, Bible-believing Christians." She saw to it that her children went to the local Baptist church each Sunday. "But it didn't work! I was under the influence of two opposing forces: the inquisitiveness I learned from my grandfather and the religious conservatism of my mother's church. Eventually, the rational side won over my mind, but

Mother's life and deeds won over my heart."

Now an activist Unitarian in Des Moines, Iowa, Shanks (E-mail: <seeker@dwx.com>) has written that, to him, humanism

> means that it's up to people to solve the world's problems. God will not do it for us. It also means that our differences—whether they are about religion, race, gender, affectional orientation, politics, or whatever—are miniscule compared to what we have in common as human beings. If I diminish the humanity of someone else, through racism, sexism, religion, or in any other way, I diminish my own humanity.

Shankar, G. N. Jyoti (20th Century)

Shankar wrote *God–Bubble Pricked* (1973) and *How to Secularize India?* (1977). The son of a Baptist minister in India, he became the general secretary of the Indian Rationalist Association before moving to the United States. Living by the motto of "Goodness is necessary—God is not," he is webmaster of "Bubbles," a freethought page on the Web at <http://www.avana.net/~jshankar/index.htm>.

Shankar, to illustrate his approval of cremation, went to the Wisconsin Memorial Park in 1978 and with his wife reserved two boxes on the wall "to avoid going six feet under!"

His history of freethought in India is on the Web: <http://www.avana.net/~jshankar/hist0001.htm>. E-mail: <jshankar@avana.net>. {CA; E; GS; e-mail to WAS}

Shannon, Julie (20th Century)

Shannon, a Unitarian Universalist, is a composer whose musical, "Stones," won Phoenix, Arizona, Maxie awards in 1994 for best musical, best direction, best actress, best actor, best supporting actress, best supporting actor, best musical direction, and best scenic designs. The play is about the Chicago African American community of the 1920s.

Shapiro, Carl (20th Century)

Shapiro wrote *Freethought versus Religion* (1977), *Freethought Works* (1979), and *Saner Living Through Atheism* (1978). He is associated with *Freethought Commentary* in Paterson, New Jersey. (See entry for New Jersey Freethinkers, Humanists.) {FD; GS}

Shapiro, Karl: See entry for Theism.

Shapley, Harlow (1885–1972)

Shapley, the former director of the Harvard Observatory, once offered this observation: "Biochemistry and microbiology, with assistance from geophysics, astronomy and other sciences, have gone so far in bridging the gap between the inanimate and the living that we can no longer doubt but that whenever the physics, chemistry and climates are right on a planet's surface, life will emerge and persist." Among his writings are *Star Clusters* (1930), *Galaxies* (1943), and *Of Stars and Men* (1958). {CE; CL}

SHARIA

The Islamic *sharia* law in Mogadishu, when carried out, involved fitting the crime to the punishment. In one six-month period in 1995, there were eight hand and foot amputations, and three executions, one by stoning and two by firing squad. The stated authority for the law is the Qur'an.

Sharif, Ahmed (20th Century)

Sharif, a professor of English literature, is a Bangladeshi who is an atheist.

Sharma, Bhogendra (20th Century)

Sharma, a Nepalese humanist leader, heads the International Humanist and Ethical Union's (IHEU's) Centre for Victims of Torture. E-mail: <cvict@mos.com.np>.

Sharp, S. (19th Century)

Sharp was an old-time anti-slavery reformer in Ohio. A successful businessman, he gave generously to aid freethought causes. {PUT}

Sharpe, Lynn (20th Century)

Sharpe is the wife of R. A. Sharpe, who has described her as "a militant atheist . . . who has never been willing to acknowledge that there is more to religion than a collection of fairy-tales."

Sharpe, R. A. (20th Century)

Sharpe, who has described himself as a "Post-Christian," wrote *The Moral Case Against Christian Theism* (1997). The work, commented Daniel O'Hara, "finds more to admire in the character and teaching of Jesus than [Carl] Lofmark, George Wells, or Margaret Knight would have allowed." However, O'Hara adds, "It is refreshing to have such a clear and unanswerable case against moral theism so well and briefly presented: it is amazing that it emanates from the SCM Press," which formerly was the publishing arm of the Student Christian Movement. {*The Freethinker*, May 1997}

Sharpe, Samuel (1799–1881)

Both Sharpe and John Kenrick, major historians of Egypt, were Unitarians. Sharpe in 1863 wrote *Egyptian Mythology and Egyptian Christianity*, and in 1871 he wrote *The Rosetta Stone*. {JMR; JMRH}

Shattuck, Roger (20th Century)

Shattuck, author of *Forbidden Knowledge: From Prometheus to Pornography* (1996), is a senior professor of French and Literature. His work challenges academics and others to resolve the problem of the cultural divide between the humanities and science. Scientifically informed humanists and humane scientists: these are the desired goals, he states. (See entry for Pornography.)

Shaughnessy, P. (19th Century)

A Scot and a freethinker, Shaughnessy wrote *Is God Knowable?* (c. 1880). {GS}

Shaw, George Bernard (1856–1950)

In his early London years Shaw boldly proclaimed himself "like Shelley, a socialist, an atheist, and a vegetarian." He told McCabe that for a time he had to live on twelve cents a day. When Charles Bradlaugh died in 1891, leaving the National Secular Society without a leader, Shaw was asked to take on the leadership. However, he called them the fundamentalists of the secularist movement, and they withdrew their offer to make him Bradlaugh's successor, accusing Shaw of having an outlook that relied on purely mystical assumptions.

Shaw had many careers—playwright, critic, journalist, platform spellbinder, protester against censorship, unpopular critic of Britain's war policies, producer and director of many of his own plays, champion of the rights of women. He had a twenty-five-year exchange with a nun, Dame Laurentia McLachlan, during which both tried and failed to convert the other. She never forgave him for his blasphemous picture of Jesus as "the conjurer" in his fable, *The Adventures of the Black Girl in Her Search for God* (1932). Although he would never allow himself to be called a Christian, he can be classed as an unbeliever only in the sense that there was, as he said at the end of his life, no church in the world that would receive him, or any in which he could consent to be received. Shaw has written, "The fact that a believer is happier than a skeptic is no more to the point than the fact that a drunken man is happier than a sober one. The happiness of credulity is a cheap and dangerous quality of happiness, and by no means a necessity of life. Whether Socrates got as much out of life as Wesley [John Wesley, the founder of Methodism] is an unanswerable question, but a nation of Socrateses would be much safer and happier than a nation of Wesleys."

Not everyone appreciated Shaw's wit nor his dramatic plots.

Frank Harris described him as "the first man to have cut a swathe through the theater and left it strewn with virgins." Oscar Wilde observed, "Bernard Shaw has no enemies but is intensely disliked by his friends." H. L. Mencken wrote of Shaw, "It is his life work to announce the obvious in terms of the scandalous." McCabe wrote, "He virulently criticizes Christianity and suggests that Jesus was of unbalanced mind—and equally criticizes Rationalism (and science), following Samuel Butler in the belief that a Vital Principle animates the living universe and that instinct (or the inspiration of this) is the guide, not reason." George Orwell thought Shaw was probably not a Communist but was "reliably pro-Russian on all major issues."

Shaw was turned down several times before he was awarded the Nobel Prize in 1925. *St. Joan* was published in 1924. The prize was not awarded until 1926, leading to the author's Shavian comment, "I wrote nothing in 1925, and that is probably why they gave it to me."

In *Bernard Shaw, The Ascent of the Superman* (1996), Sally Peters claims the playwright was a gender bender, a Uranian or Urning, terms made fashionable by the Marquess of Queensberry to derogate "queer" people. Although her proofs are not entirely convincing to other scholars, she told of Shaw's woolly yellow Jaeger one-piece suits which he thought contained one's body odors. He was a neurotic washer, and he felt his body excrements would be odorless if he stuck to a vegetarian diet. Vaccinations, he held, killed people and should be avoided.

Shaw the socialist author left a capitalist estate of $1,028,252. Reaffirming his belief in creative evolution rather than in any specific church creed, he asked that memorials to him that took "the form of a cross or any other instrument of torture or symbol of blood sacrifice" be omitted. His ashes were to be sprinkled at Ayot St. Lawrence. "Personally," he wrote in his final instructions, "I prefer the garden to the cloister." After making numerous small bequests, Shaw left the bulk of his sizable fortune for the development of a British alphabet having forty letters. In court, however, the request was lowered to a £500 prize being offered in a competition to select a letter design.

At the age of ninety-four, Shaw was lucid but tired during his final days. Biographer St. John G. Ervine has written that to a few close friends Shaw said he was ready, if not longing, for his final rest. On the last day of his life an hour before he died and when visited by a friend, Ellen O'Casey, he said wryly, "Well, it will be a new experience anyway." (Shaw's acquaintance with many leading freethinkers is described in *The London Heretics* by Warren Sylvester Smith. See entry for George Orwell.) {CE; EU, Warren Sylvester Smith; FUK; HNS2; JM; PA; RAT; RE; TRI; TYD; WSS}

Shaw, James Dickson (1841–1926)

Shaw, an American writer brought up on a cattle farm in Texas, joined the Southern army during the American Civil War and was wounded. He became a Methodist Episcopal minister, but upon studying biblical criticism in order to answer the skeptics his own faith gave way. He then started the *Independent Pulpit* at Waco, Texas, the only freethought paper in the South, with subscribers in every state and several other countries. Shaw rejected all supernaturalism and wrote *The Bible, What Is It?* (1892)) as well as *The Bible Against Itself*. {BDF; *Freethought History #15*, 1995; PUT}

Shaw, Naomi (20th Century)

When Shaw signed Humanist Manifesto II, she was president of the National Women's Conference, American Ethical Union. {HM2}

Shaw, Robert (1927-1978)

Shaw, an author and actor, appeared in various West End productions and as Rosenkrantz in "Hamlet" (1951). He had parts in such movies as "From Russia with Love," "The Battle of the Bulge," "A Man for All Seasons," and "A Town Called Bastard." On Broadway he was in "Elmer Gantry." Shaw was a Unitarian.

Shaw, Robert Gould (1837–1863)

Shaw, a Union hero in the American Civil War, was the white colonel of the 54th Massachusetts Regiment, the first body of black troops organized in any of the free states. It was a time when so many opposed black troops that the authorities sent the troops by ship rather than by train. But Colonel Shaw had the satisfaction of marching his troops up Beacon Hill in Boston, where at the State House Governor John Albion Andrew proudly cheered them on. In the attack on Fort Wagner in Charleston, South Carolina, Shaw was killed. The Boston Commons today has a sculptured figure of him by Augustus Saint-Gaudens who, like Shaw, was a Unitarian. {CE; EG}

Shawn, William (1907–1992)

The son of Benjamin and Anna Bransky Chon, Shawn changed his name by 1932 because "Chon sounded too Chinese." After dropping out of the University of Michigan when twenty, he worked for six months at $30 a week for a Las Vegas, New Mexico, newspaper called *Daily Optic*. In 1929 he got a job in Chicago with *International Illustrated News*. Cecille, his wife and also a journalist, got freelance work with *The New Yorker*, and Shawn secured a job as reporter for the "Talk of the Town" section. By 1935 he had become associate editor of the magazine, in 1939 became managing editor, and from 1952 until he was fired in 1987 by S. I. Newhouse was *The New Yorker*'s editor. One hundred seventy writers, artists, and editors, including J. D. Salinger, petitioned to have Shawn rehired, to no avail, this despite the magazine's never having had a year in which it lost money. Under Shawn's leadership the magazine was, in fact, the most successful of any in the nation. Newhouse chose, however, to hire Robert Gottlieb.

The five-foot-five Shawn was noted for his phobias: he would not live above the second floor because he was afraid of heights; at the theater he sat toward the back, fearing a fire might erupt; he avoided all tunnels and elevators. Rumor had it that he carried a hatchet in his briefcase in the event he got stuck in an elevator.

A private public figure who was married for sixty-three years, Shawn was revealed in 1998 by reporter Lillian Ross's book to have carried on a surprising decades-long affair, a "shadow marriage" in which he had even raised a child (an adopted Norwegian boy, Eric) with her.

Following his death in Manhattan of a heart attack in his Fifth Avenue apartment bed, and in accordance with his wishes, he was cremated with no memorial or religious service. His son Allen read John Donne's poem "A Valediction: Forbidding Mourning" at the cremation. Also present were wife Cecille, son Warren, and writer Jamaica Kincaid. (Paul Alexander, *New York*, 27 April 1998)

Sheen, Martin (Ramos Estevez) (1940–)

Sheen, an actor who has appeared in numerous films, in television shows, and on Broadway, has stated, "I'm one of those cliff-hanging Catholics. I don't believe in God, but I do believe that Mary was his mother." According to Atheist Celebrities on the internet, Sheen is a non-believer. {TYD}

SHEFFIELD (England) HUMANISTS

For information, write Gordon Sinclair, 9 South View Road, Barnsley S74 9EB; telephone 01226 743070.

Shields, Jill (20th Century)

Shields is secretary of the Free Inquirers of Northeastern Ohio.

Shields, Susan (20th Century)

For nearly a decade, Shields was a Missionaries of Charity sister who played a key role in Mother Teresa's organization. How the nun harmed her helpers as well as those they "helped" is described in "Mother Teresa's House of Illusions," a damaging article in *Free Inquiry* (Winter 1997-1998).

According to Shields, while huge donations were being amassed, one summer the sisters were given more crates of tomatoes than they could distribute. As an example of Mother Teresa's thinking, she scolded the sisters for canning the tomatoes, saying that "storing things showed lack of trust in Divine Providence." Shields cites other examples in her explanation of how she decided to leave whereas others, who had no education beyond what they brought with them when they joined, did not have the courage to walk away.

Sheldon, Lurana (20th Century)

Sheldon, a freethinker, wrote *Is That You, God?* (1900). {GS}

Sheldon, Walter Lorenzo (1858–1907)

Sheldon founded the St. Louis Ethical Culture Society in 1886. He had disagreed heavily over what he considered Felix Adler's anti-scientific attitudes, for he had adopted the scientific method of reasoning in his own attempt to overcome his earlier Fundamentalism. In the *Journal of Speculative Philosophy*, Jeff Hornback has written, Sheldon had an article on the common fallacy of "Agnostic Realism" (1885), in which he contended that "we may not assume that as unknowable which we *use* as real and knowable." Hornback adds, "The journal was published by the famous St. Louis Hegelians, who made the city one of America's two philosophic capitals—the other was Concord, with Emerson and the Transcendentalists, who were closer to the Ethical founders. The Hegelians brought the leading European philosophers to the United States, in translation, and were much too urbane and convivial for the ploddingly moralistic New Englander, Sheldon."

In his diary jottings, Sheldon wrote on 18 May 1888, "Remark. The three different elements to be met in my Society (1) the radical German (2) the conservative American & (3) the Hebrew—how to blend them. . . .! Baffled, baffled by this Hebrew question! cramped by it and never can get away from it. . . . Now I am a stranger among H's and G's [Hegelians and Germans]. . . . Resolution. Stop letting Salter, Adler, and the rest treat me as a youth and an apprentice. . . . I have not the worldly tact of Professor A, nor the personal sweetness of W, nor the objective personality of C. . . . Salter is too much in the air, Adler is too much in himself, Weston too much with ladies, Mangasarian too much in Constantinople, Gizycki [George von Gizycki, a German philosopher] too much in the Utilitarianism, Black is too much and too long at one station, Coit alone is amenable to experience." (See entry for Ethical Culture.)

Shelley, Mary Wollstonecraft (1797–1851)

Shelley, best known for her science-fiction novel, *Frankenstein* (1818), was the daughter of philosopher William Godwin (who must have marveled at the creature he, who had a doctorate, had created). Like her husband Percy, whom she had married after his first wife Harriet committed suicide by drowning herself, Shelley was a freethinking deist, an early example of a female who had no compunction about admitting she was an unbeliever. She and Shelley had one child, Percy Florence Shelley.

Underwood has supplied details about the unusual life the Shelleys led: "In 1814, Shelley, not yet separated from his first wife, meeting Mary at the grave of her mother, whither she often fled to escape the scoldings of her step-mother, declared his love for her. The scene, their peculiar circumstances, their daring faith in each other, their youth, their beauty, made for them a romance which was irresistible. On the 14th of July, Harriet, Shelley's wife, came to London, and Godwin called on her and endeavored to reconcile Shelley to her, not dreaming of the drama going on under his own roof. On the 28th of July, Mary Godwin, aided, abetted, and accompanied by her step-mother's daughter, Jane Claremont, ran away with Shelley. Mrs. Godwin pursued the party, but could not make them return. Godwin held little or no communication with them until the death of Shelley's first wife, and their legal marriage. 'The three,' says K. Paul in his biography of Godwin, 'went to Paris, where they bought a donkey and rode him in turn to Geneva, the others walking. He was bought for Mary, as the weakest of the party, but Shelley's feet were soon blistered, and he was glad to ride now and then, not without the jeers of the passersby. Sleeping now in a cabaret, and now in a cottage, they at last finished the strange honeymoon, and the strangest sentimental journey ever undertaken since Adam and Eve."

When the first Mrs. Shelley drowned herself in 1817, Shelley had hastened home to England to claim the two children of his first marriage. Mr. Westerbrook, the children's maternal grandfather, however, refused him the custody, and the claims of the father were set aside on the grounds of his "infidelity," whereupon the children "were sent to be educated in a clergyman's family, the more surely to save them from any hereditary taint of skepticism." Death, however, "stilled the hearts of the two eldest of their little children, who had grown so dear to them: taking first William, and then Clara, only the youngest, named for his father, Percy, remaining to them."

One evening when Lord Byron visited them at their Italian villa, only Byron, Polidori, Shelley, and Mary being present, the subject of ghosts, goblins, and wraiths came up. Underwood adds, "The subject had a weird fascination for those poetic, mystic natures, and it held them with its half-defined sense of the horrible until far into the night. As they at last rose to retire, Byron in one of his sudden impulses, said, 'Let us each write a ghost story!' All eagerly agreed, and made a compact there and then to do so. No one was to see any part of the others' manuscript, will all were completed. Like most sudden compacts of the kind, it was only partly carried out." Mary, who having been brought up in Scotland, the land of "bogles," "brownies," and witchcraft, and despite her father's philosophic teachings had an interest in the "uncanny." Although the others never carried out the compact, Shelley was delighted with his wife's specimen, in which Victor Frankenstein says, "With how many things are we upon the brink of becoming acquainted, if cowardice or carelessness did not restrain our inquiries"; and "For the first time, also, I felt what the duties of a Creator toward his creature were, and that I ought to render him happy before I complained of his wickedness."

Colin McCall has pointed out that the 1935 film, "Bride of Frankenstein," contained an unfortunate prologue in which Mary Shelley tells her husband and Byron, "My purpose was to write a moral lesson of the punishment that befell a mortal man who dared to emulate God." Nonsense, McCall rejoinders! "Mary Shelley's 'monster' was 'fashioned to be susceptible of love and sympathy'; he becomes violent because he is rejected. 'I am malicious,' he says, 'because I am miserable; am I not shunned and hated by all mankind?' "

Stephen Jay Gould has pointed out that Percy Bysshe Shelley, in his preface to *Frankenstein*, "had, in order to justify Dr. Frankenstein's experiment, alluded to Erasmus Darwin's atheistical view on the possibility of quickening matter by electricity." Gould in his *Dinosaur in a Haystack* says of the monster that his misery arises "from the moral failure of other humans, not from his own inherent and unchangeable constitution."

Shelley wrote six novels, five volumes of biographical essays, two "mythological dramas" in verse, a score of short stories, and two volumes of engaging travelogue, *Rambles in Germany and Italy* (1844). In 1997 the British biographer Claire Tomalin came across a handbound manuscript of a long-lost story that Shelley had written for Lady Mountcashell's daughter Laurette, a thirty-nine page happy children's story that had lain forgotten for over 170 years.

Upon Mary's death, what was said to be her husband Percy's heart was found wrapped in her copy of *Adonais*—however, some skeptics believe the salvaged organ was more likely Shelley's liver. Although she had wanted to repose in Rome next to her husband, she was buried in the family vault at St. Peter's church in Bournemouth, along with her husband's heart, or liver, and their son (Sir Percy Florence Shelley). Also buried there are her parents (William and Mary Wollstonecraft Godwin, who were moved from Old St. Pancras in London). Toward the end of her life, she became somewhat interested in religion. (See entries for Mary Wollstonecraft Godwin and for Cloning.) {CB; CE; Stephen Jay Gould, "Why Darwin?" *New York Review of Books*, 4 April 1996; Richard Holmes, *The New York Review of Books*, 22 April 1999; JMR; RAT; SAU; TSV; TYD}

Shelley, Percy Bysshe (1792–1822)

Many are the tales about Shelley. He switched from Eton, where he refused to fag (a Briticism to describe English public school boys who are required to act as servant to an older schoolmate), to Oxford. There in a school essay, Shelley wrote that so long as there is theism there needs logically to be the antithesis. But his essay, "The Necessity of Atheism," (1811), earned no A+. On the contrary, Oxford expelled him. His father, Sir Timothy Shelley, also forbade him his house. Shelley then went to London, wrote *Queen Mab*, and met Miss Westbrook, marrying her in 1811 and separating after two children had been born. In 1816 he learned that his wife had drowned herself, so he claimed the custody of his children. Lord Chancellor Eldon, however, decided against him, largely because of Shelley's heretical opinions, which were considered radical in his day but are mild today. Shelley previously had written *A Letter to Lord Ellenborough,* indignantly attacking the sentence the judge passed on E. I. Eaton for publishing Thomas Paine's *Age of Reason.* In 1816 Shelley married Mary, daughter of William Godwin and Mary Wollstonecraft. In 1818, fearing their son might also be taken from him, Shelley left England never to return . . . and never to live to the age of thirty-one.

Lamont described Shelley's outlook as having "a vague pantheistic belief." His bisexuality and anti-establishment views shocked Europe more than wife Mary's *Frankenstein.* His *Queen Mab* (1813) tells how he wept when his mother took him "to see an atheist burned. . . . The thirsty fire crept round his manly limbs; his resolute eyes were scorched to blindness soon; his death pang rent my heart! The insensate mob uttered a cry of triumph, and I wept. 'Weep not, child!' cried my mother, 'for that man has said, "There is no God!" ' " On the contrary, Shelley believed "the being called God bears every mark of a veil woven by philosophical conceit, to hide the ignorance of the philosophers even from themselves." For Shelley, classical Greece had seen the highest fulfillment of man as a free being; the introduction of Christianity, however, withered man's spirit and constrained his estimate of himself. For Shelley, "Every reflecting mind must allow that there is no proof of the existence of a Deity." *Queen Mab* contains the following:

How ludicrous the priest's dogmatic roar!
The weight of his exterminating curses,
How light! and his affected charity,
To suit the pressure of the changing times,
What palpable deceit!—but for thy aid,
Religion! but for thee, prolific fiend,
Who peopleth earth with demons, hell with men,
And heaven with slaves!

In 1812 Shelley wrote to Elizabeth Hitchener, "I have lately had some conversation with Southey which has elicited my true opinions of God—he says I ought not to call myself an Atheist, since in reality I believe that the Universe is God." Remarks Berman: "So for Southey the universe (in Shelley's thought) is another name for God; whereas for Shelley God is another name for the universe. The distinction is not unimportant." Berman has written a particularly thorough description of Shelley's views, finding his philosophical method "is closer to that of Hammon, Turner, and Collins than it is to Scepticus's. It is epistemological rather than metaphysical. Shelley is more interested in the nature of our knowledge and belief in God than in the nature of God *per se.*"

Shelley's little known "A Refutation of Deism" (1814) has been reprinted in J. C. A. Gaskin's *Varieties of Unbelief* (1989). In it, the young Shelley not only rejects the existence of God but also rejects Judeo-Christian revelation, citing its immoral character and suspect historicity. His arguments against "deism" also apply to traditional "theism." Shelley cites as atheists Epicurus, Democritus, Pliny, Lucretius, and Euripides. He also lists Anaxagoras, Pythagoras, and Plato as being theists.

Shelley accidentally drowned off Leghorn while returning in a small yacht from an 1822 visit to his friend, the bisexual Lord Byron. Sharing his fate were his friend Williams and a sailor lad, all of whom had unsuccessfully faced a squall which submerged them. When Shelley's body washed ashore near Viareggio, its face was so disfigured that his body had to be identified by the copies of Aeschylus and John Keats's poems doubled back in his jacket. "The face and hands, and parts of the body not protected by the dress, were fleshless," wrote the poet's friend Edward Trelawny. Because of Italian law and a plague at that time, the body had to be cremated on the spot. Trelawny and poets Byron and Leigh Hunt, called by Tom Weil, "perhaps the most literate team of undertakers in history," performed the ritual. An iron mattock was used to crack Shelley's skull, which Byron had requested be saved for him. Trelawny said "more wine was poured over Shelley's dead body than he had consumed during his life," after which Trelawny tossed salt and frankincense onto the flames and poured wine and oil over the cadaver, leading to dancing flames as Shelley cooked. Hunt recalled the "inconceivable beauty" of the flickering flame-sheet. Presently, continued Trelawny, "the corpse fell open and the heart was laid bare. The frontal bone of the skull, where it had been struck with the mattock, fell off; and, as the back of the head rested on the red-hot bottom bars of the furnace, the brains literally seethed, bubbled, and boiled as in a cauldron, for a very long time. . . but what surprised us all was that the heart remained entire. In snatching this relic from the fiery furnace, my hand was severely burnt." Arthur Norman, in a 1955 article in *The Journal of the History of Medicine*, suggested that Shelley may have suffered from "a progressively calcifying heart . . . which indeed would have resisted cremation as readily as a skull, a jaw, or fragments of bone." Later, Trelawny—who said Shelley was an atheist to the last—presented Shelley's heart (some say it was his liver) to the poet's wife, Mary, for burial in Bournemouth, England. In 1889, sixty-seven years after his death, the heart (or liver) was buried with the body of his son, Sir Percy Florence Shelley. However, Trelawny did not give the skull to Byron, for, ". . . remembering that he had formerly used one as a drinking cup, I was determined Shelley's should be so profaned."

Shelley's ashes, contained in an oak casket, were delivered to the British consul in Rome who, because the Vatican had closed the old section of the Protestant Cemetery, stored the remains in his wine cellar. At Mary's request, they tried to rebury their son William, who had been buried in the same cemetery three years before, with his father. However, beneath the child's stone they found, instead, the skeleton of a grown man. So Shelley was buried alone for a time, then moved by Trelawny to a better plot near the rear wall. Byron, despite having a clubfoot and who once swam the Bosporus, swam to the site where Shelley had died, symbolically leaving a flower. Instead of the marble statue of a nude Shelley spread supine, just washed ashore from the fatal shipwreck, which is found in the first quadrangle at Oxford's University College (where Shelley was "sent down" in 1811 for his freshman tract in favor of atheism), a simple marker decorates the poet's grave. A white slab embedded in the ground, it contains only his name, the words *cor cordium* (heart of hearts), the dates of his birth and death in Latin, and Trelawny's lines from *The Tempest:*

PERCY BYSSHE SHELLEY
Cor Cordium
Natus iv. Aug MDCCXCII
Obit. vii. Jul. MDCCCXXII

Nothing of him that doth fade
But doth suffer a sea-change
Into something rich and strange.

Today both Trelawny and Keats now lie nearby. Trelawny once wrote, "The principal fault I have to find is that the Shelleyan writers, being Christians themselves, seem to think that a man of genius cannot be an Atheist, and so they strain their own faculties to disprove what Shelley asserted from the very earliest stage of his career to the last day of his life. He ignored all religions as superstitions. . . . A clergyman wrote in the visitors' book at the Mer de Glace, Chamourni, something to the following effect: 'No one can view this sublime scene and deny the existence of God.' Under which Shelley, using a Greek phrase, wrote, "P. B. Shelley, Atheist," thereby proclaiming his opinion to all the world. And he never regretted having done so." {BDF; CB; CE; CL; EU, Terry L. Meyers; FO; HAB; JM; PUT; RAT; RE; TRI; TSV; TYD}

Shepherd, James (1904–)

A freethinker, Shepherd was on the executive committee of the National Secular Society in England and worked for civil liberty causes. {TRI}

Shepherd, Luke (19th Century)

In 1836 Shepherd edited a freethought publication from Rochester, NY, *The World As It Is*.

Sheppard, Hugh Richard Laurie (20th Century)

Sheppard is the author of *What Can We Believe?* (1939). {GS}

Sherer, Naomi (20th Century)

Sherer is on the Board of Directors of the American Humanist Association.

Sherman, Marian (1892–1975)

Sherman was born and educated in England but emigrated with her parents to Canada and worked as a medical missionary in India from 1922 to 1934. A physician, she was a co-founder of the Victoria Humanist Fellowship and told *The Star* (Victoria, 17 March 1955), "The concepts of personal immortality and a personal deity are irrational. That which cannot be made clear in words (e.g., God) cannot exist." Commenting upon how people hate the word atheist, she said, "They think there is something evil about it. It only means a person who doesn't believe in a supernatural being over us."

Sherman, a physician, in 1975 was given the Canadian Humanist of the Year Award. {WWS}

Sherman, Robert I. (20th Century)

Sherman, a radio talk host and an atheist activist, is heard on AM Radio WKTA, Chicago. "My notoriety," he has written, "comes from attacking virtually every state/church separation violation within shouting distance of Chicago. Victories include: Removal of Christian crosses from city seals in numerous nearby municipalities. Enging Buffalo Gorve, Illinois, Police Department exclusion of atheists from their public education program, formerly known as 'Boy Scouts Explorers Post' but now known as 'Police Cadets.' Ending forced acknowledgement of the Judeo-Christian god in compulsory recitation of pledge of allegiance in Illinois public schools. Removal of Christian crosses that adorned the Kane County, Illinois, government center." {CA}

Sherman, William Tecumseh [Union General] (1820–1891)

Sherman was a Union general in the American Civil War. A banker in San Francisco and New York and a lawyer in Leavenworth, Kansas, he became superintendent of what today is Louisiana State University at Baton Rouge. When Louisiana seceded, he resigned the university post, rejoined the U. S. Army as a colonel, and commanded a brigade in the first battle of Bull Run. He distinguished himself in the Vicksburg and Chattanooga campaigns and took Atlanta in 1864, burning the city. After capturing Savannah, he wreaked havoc through South Carolina and received the surrender of General J. E. Johnston in 1865. Sherman's statement that "war is hell" expressed his belief in the need for ruthlessness in modern warfare.

He "did not believe that God was molding events in response to human petition, conduct, or spiritual state," stated Charles Royster in *The Destructive War W. T. Sherman, Stonewall Jackson, and the Americans* (1991). He cites David F. Boyd as recalling that Sherman's "only peculiarity about religion was that he was such an advocate for *individual* religious *freedom*, that he thought it wrong ever to attempt to influence any one's religious convictions. I have often heard him about this: if I could I would *not* change the religion of a Hottentot or Feejee Islander, etc. etc." Sherman was married for almost forty years to a devout Roman Catholic, and although their children were reared as Catholics Sherman joined no church. "He regarded organized religion as a human invention and dismissed the doctrines of the Trinity and of transubstantiation as 'mathematical impossibilities.' He prefaced mention of the immorality of the soul with the word 'if.' Sherman," Boyd continued, "did not oppose belief or the practice of Christianity. Chaplains accompanied his army, and revival meetings among soldiers went on during the George and Carolina campaigns."

When religious ministers sought permission to ride the railroad to the front lines, Sherman responded, "Certainly not; crackers and oats are more necessary to my army than any moral or religious agency." According to Royster, "To Sherman war was a natural phenomenon, guided by nature's laws, which God had created but which operated with the consistency of mathematics, not by God's 'mere fiat.' As for an afterlife, Sherman remained an agnostic. Royster added that

Sherman "mistrusted metaphysics, philosophy, and religious or ethical systems that tried to change what he took to be human nature."

Shermer, Michael (20th Century)

Shermer, editor of *Skeptic*, wrote *Why People Believe in Weird Things*. He is a non-believer. {CA}

Sherrington, Charles Scott [Sir] (1857–1952)

Sherrington was an English neurophysiologist who was educated at Cambridge. As a physician, he did important work in the study of cholera and of diphtheria and tetanus antitoxins, resulting in the improvement of health and safety conditions in British factories during World War I. He was knighted in 1922. With E. D. Adrian Sherrington shared the 1932 Nobel Prize in Physiology or Medicine for their discoveries regarding the function of the neuron. Although he did not call himself a materialist, he virtually recommends it in his works. In *The Brain and Its Mechanism* (1933), Sherrington holds that in time science will show "how the brain does its thinking." Sherrington was an honorary associate of the Rationalist Press Association. {CE; JM; RE}

Shinn, Quillen Hamilton (1845–1907)

Shinn, a West Virginian who fought for the Union and who spent time in a Confederate prisoner of war camp, studied with Ebenezer Fisher at St. Lawrence University and became one of the greatest builders of Universalist churches of his time. He traveled over 25,000 miles a year, preached in every state, and started "about fifty" churches and the same number of Sunday schools. {U; U&U}

SHINTO

The ancient Japanese native religion of Shinto had no one god who ruled over the other gods, but the sun goddess was exalted above the others. Kami, meaning above or superior, was a word designating deities, supernatural beings who originated after chaos gave birth to heaven and earth. At first, there were three rulers of the Heavenly Plain (which one should not confuse with the Christian or Jewish "Heaven"). More followed, and eventually a pair—Izanagi and Izanami—ruled the "bridge of heaven," stood on the rainbow, and created, after piercing with a jeweled spear, the island now known as Japan, to which they descended. The sun goddess Amaterasu-o-mi-kami and her brother Susa-no-wo, the storm god, have been claimed to be the direct ancestors of Jimmu, who in 660 B.C.E. was also claimed to have been the first Emperor of Japan. For Asian children, the myth was a constructive way to explain origins as well as ethics and morality. For example, Susa-no-wo was known for his disorder, roughness, and evil, and parents used his symbolic traits in discussing bad behavior with their sons and daughters. (See entry for Fukuzawa. For an estimate of the number of Shintoists worldwide, see the entry for Hell.) {CE; ER}

Shipley, Maynard (1872–1934)

Shipley, husband of writer Miriam Allen deFord, was a signer of Humanist Manifesto I. A lecturer on astronomy and evolution, he wrote thirty-three "Little Blue Books" and was founder and president of the Science League of America. Shipley died thirteen months after signing the manifesto and, following her husband's request for cremation, de Ford then spread his ashes in the San Francisco Bay he had so deeply loved, an unusual act and one which disturbed some Californians at that time. Shipley, a popular public and radio lecturer wrote *The Key to Evolution* (1927) and *The War on Modern Science* (1929). {EW; FUS; HM1}

Shirley, Ralph B. (20th Century)

Shirley, a freethinker, wrote *God, the Greatest Hoax* (1971). {GS}

Shisler, Charles (20th Century)

Shisler, a humanist, has written in *The American Rationalist* that humanism needs to include the following principles:

> Whereas the Universe is the sum total of *everything* existing in infinite space, we know that whatever entities exist, they are part of the Universe and that there can be nothing *external* to the Universe, causative or otherwise.
>
> We recognize we must master our own destiny, using unique powers of reason and methods of science to comprehend the Universe and solve problems, and we vigorously oppose all efforts to denigrate human intelligence.

He also finds that humanism as a philosophy differs from other outlooks, that as humanists, in his opinion,

> We value our sense of humor—that antidote to pomposity—whose acid wit can erode foundations of majestic memorials to enshrined error.
>
> We affirm humanism as a realistic alternative to theologies of perversion and ideologies of violence—and as a source of rich personal significance and genuine satisfaction in ennobling service to others.
>
> We believe in optimistic hope rather than despair, learning in place of dogma, truth instead of ignorance, joy and beauty rather than guilt or sin, tolerance in place of fear, love instead of hatred, reason over blind faith.

SHIT

The uses of human defecation or excrement, vulgarly called shit, are positively described by J. C. Jenkins in *The Humanure Handbook: A Guide to Composting Human Manure* (1998).

Shockley, Patricia (20th Century

Shockley is Secretary of the Board of Directors of the American Humanist Association. She is a co-founder of the Columbus chapter of that association.

Shoemaker, Lene Lund (20th Century)

Shoemaker is a leader of the Danish Unitarian Church. (See entry for Danish Unitarian Church.)

Shook, Eric (20th Century)

Shook, while a student at the University of Wisconsin in Milwaukee, was one of the founding members of the Campus Freethought Alliance. {*International Humanist News*, December 1996}

Shor, Morton (20th Century)

Shor, an atheist, is co-author with Rabbi William E. Kaufman of *A Question of Faith: An Atheist and a Rabbi Debate the Existence of God* (1993). The letters quoted, in which each develops his points, show that the rabbi refuses to listen to the atheist and Shor is left trying to show how shallow and false are the rabbi's arguments.

Short, Renée (20th Century)

In 1986, Mrs. Short was elected an honorary associate of the Rationalist Press Association. A member of Parliament, she was instrumental in getting the Abortion Law Reform Act placed on the Statute Book in England. She was a Labour MP from 1964 to 1987. In 1978 she presided over the Seventh International Humanist and Ethical Union (IHEU) World Congress in London. In 1979 she wrote *The Case of Long-term Prisoners*.

Shosky, John Edwin (1955–)

Shosky, assistant professor of philosophy at American University in Washington, D.C., addressed the 1994 Toronto conference of the Coalition for Secular Humanism, Atheism, and Freethought (CSHAFT), speaking about "Propositions Without Proof." A communication consultant and speechwriter, he has been a senior policy analyst at the White House's Office Publication Affairs (1988). From 1995 to 1997, he was Vice President of the Bertrand Russell Society.

Shosky edited *Philosophical Essays: Antony Flew* (1998), collecting twelve essays by the renowned atheist philosopher.

Shotwell, David A. (20th Century)

Shotwell is a freethinker who has written "Knowledge, Truth, and Science" for *The American Rationalist* (September-October 1995).

Shotwell, James Thomson (1874–1965)

Shotwell was assistant general editor of the *Encyclopedia Britannica* (1904–1905) and from 1907 onward taught history at Columbia University. His rationalism is expressed in *Religious Revolution of To-day* (1913), in which Shotwell includes a naturalistic theory of the origin of religion as well as an account of the dissolution of Christianity. {RAT}

SHROUD OF TURIN: See entries for Turin Shroud and for Hoaxes, Religious.

SHS

SHS is an abbreviation for Secular Humanist Society, and many such groups meet regularly in American cities, usually publishing their own newsletters. They have banded into an Alliance of Secular Humanist Societies (ASHS), a network for mutual support. All are associated with the Council for Secular Humanism, Box 664, Buffalo, NY 14226.

Shuemaker, Harry R. (1938–)

Shuemaker, a 13th generation Unitarian Universalist, traces his ancestry from John and Priscilla Alden and the *Mayflower*. His great, great, grandfather joined the Universalist church of Avon, Illinois, in the 1880s, the minister being the Rev. Miss Anna Flemming. Shuemaker, a retired high school social studies teacher, is an active member of the Unitarian Universalist Society of Geneva, Illinois, a church that dates to 1842.

He claims to be a "humanistic/naturalistic/theistic/ Christian/plus a tiny pinch of pagan UU."

"Non-believers," he holds, "seems to say that we don't believe anything when, in fact, we believe so much that it cannot be easily written down. I like such phrases or labels as 'Believers in the Free Spirit,' 'the Free Mind,' and 'the Open, Loving Heart," or something like that. Or just Unitarian Universalist will do." E-mail: <hs4rocky@interaccess.com>.

Shuford III, R. L. (20th Century)

When Shuford signed Humanist Manifesto II, he was an instructor at the Charlotte Country Day School. {HM2}

Shute, J. Ray (20th Century)

The Hon. J. Ray Shute from North Carolina in 1952 was a director of the American Humanist Association. {HNS}

Siano, Brian (20th Century)

Siano, a freelance writer in Philadelphia, writes about skepticism, UFOs, and similar subjects for various publications, including *The Humanist*, of which he has been a senior editor.

Sibbern, Gabriel (19th Century)

Sibbern, a Danish philosopher, wrote *Om Humanisme* (On Humanism, 1858), which was rationalistic and emphasized humanism as "a view of life."

Siciliano, Pietro (1835–1885)

Siciliano, who had been professor in the University of Bologna, wrote *Positive Philosophy, Socialism, Darwinism* and *Modern Sociology* (1879). He wrote the rationalistic *Modern Psychogeny*, with a preface by J. Soury (1882). {BDF; RAT}

SIDDHARTHA: See entry for Gautama.

Sides, Ellen (20th Century)

Sides is a member of the Committee of the Association of Irish Humanists, County Wicklow, Ireland. In *New Humanist* (February 1995), she made the point that "the case of humanism is not best served by speaking of those with religious beliefs." Sides is editor of the *Newsletter* of the Association of Irish Humanists.

Sidgwick, Henry (1838–1900)

Sidgwick was the son of a clergyman and cousin of Archbishop Benson, but when he took a course at Cambridge he became a Rationalist. In 1869 he was appointed professor of moral philosophy, resigning on account of the religious tests. When these were abolished two years later, he became a lecturer on moral and political philosophy and later Knightsbridge Professor.

The basis of Sidgwick's thought was British utilitarianism, and he held that the doctrine of common sense rests on the principles of utilitarianism. Morley's *Recollections* (1917) states that Sidgwick "broke with orthodox Christianity in an early stage of his life and seems to have made no return to it." Mrs. Sidgwick confirmed this in a biography (1906), saying that "half a dozen bishops tried hard to get him to die as a Christian" and gave him Christian burial, but "his old hope of returning to the Church of his fathers had not been fulfilled." Sidgwick was a theist, McCabe notes. {RAT; RE}

Sidney, Algernon (1617–1678)

Sidney was an English Republican, the second son of Robert, Earl of Leicester. He became a colonel in the Army of Parliament and a member of the House of Commons. Sidney's liberal ideas were set forth in his *Discourses Concerning Government* (published 1698), a treatise that had great influence on the 18th-century political thought, particularly in the American colonies. On the Restoration, he remained abroad until 1677 but, being implicated in the Rye House Plot, was condemned by Judge Jeffreys to be executed on Tower Hill 7 December 1678. On the scaffold, Sidney refused the aid of any minister of religion. {BDF; RAT; RE}

Siebold, John (20th Century)

"Curricula in universities are decidedly naturalist in character if not outright atheist in content," Siebold has noted (*Free Inquiry*, Spring 1999).

Siegal, Sue (20th Century)

Siegal is an editor of the newsletter of the Capital District Humanist Society, PO Box 2148, Scotia, NY 12302.

Siegel, Hannah L. (20th Century)

Siegel in 1954 was a member of the board of directors of the Humanist Fellowship of Boston, a group affiliated with the American Humanist Association.

Siegfried, Andre (1875–1959)

A French economist, historian, and academician, Siegfried is said by Charles Mayer to have been a naturalistic humanist. One of Siegfried's works was *America in Mid-Century* (1955). (See entry for Charles Mayer.)

Sierichs, William Jr. (20th Century)

Sierichs is a Biblical scholar. He has written "The Pagan Origins of Biblical Morality, or Where Did Moses *Really* Get Those Commandments From?" in *The American Rationalist* (January/February 1995). His "Daniel in the Historians' Den" was written for *The Skeptical Review* (July-August 1996). Sierichs writes of the influence of Egyptians, Mesopotamians, and others. (See entry for Freedom of Religion.)

Sieyès, Emmanuel Joseph [Count] (1748–1836)

Sieyès was a French revolutionary and statesman. A clergyman before the Revolution, he was known as Abbé Sieyès. He advocated the formation of the national assembly and participated in the writing of the Declaration of the Rights of Man and Citizen and the constitution of 1791. As a member of the Convention, he voted for the execution of King Louis XVI. His prudent silence enabled him to live through the Reign of Terror, and in 1794 he became active in the government again. In 1799 he entered the Directory, then conspired with Napoleon Bonaparte in the overthrow of the Directory by a coup d'état. After the Bourbon restoration, he lived in exile in

Brussels. Although named as one of the few priests who took a prominent part in the Revolution, Sieyès wrote that he "evaded every occasion of clerical work" before that time and was a freethinker who never returned to the Church after taking part in the Revolution. {CE; JM; RAT; RE}

Sifakis, Carl (20th Century)

Sifakis is author of *Hoaxes and Scams* (1995), in which he finds "considerable evidence" that, although many find it hard to understand why so many people fall for a hoax or fraud, financial or other gain is an important factor and it is the victims who often are "the dishonest." The work details alphabetically all kinds of scams. He describes the fake Piltdown Man, various evidences for Bigfoot, hoaxes connected with "spirit rappings," poltergeists, ghosts, and claims by religious messiahs. Ghosts, Sifarkis states, are embedded in British culture. In the United States, "messiahs" are more common.

Siffle, Alexander François (1801–1872)

Siffle was a Dutch writer who studied law at Leyden and became notary at Middleburg. A contributor to *De Dageraad*, Siffle was a man of wide reading. {BDF}

Sigismund, John [King] (16th Century)

The first Unitarian king in history, King John of Transylvania called the Diet of Torda in 1568, at which time his court preacher Francis David spoke in favor of religious toleration for *all* religious groups. The king then issued the first edict of religious toleration in modern Western history. It read in part, "Preachers shall be allowed to preach the Gospel everywhere, each according to his own good, if not they shall not be compelled. . . . No one shall be made to suffer on account of his religion, since faith is the gift of God." Upon the king's death, the new ruling prince confiscated churches and schools, giving them to the Roman Catholic church. He also imprisoned the first Unitarian bishop, David Ferenc, who died in 1579. In 1948, the Communist regime also confiscated schools and church properties. However, a Unitarian church still exists in Romania, although it since has had to withstand the intolerance of Roman Catholics, Protestants, and Communists. {CE; EU, Paul H. Beattie}

Sigward, M. (Born 1817)

Sigward was an active French democrat and freethinker, the compiler of a Republican calendar. He took part in the International Congress at Paris in 1889 and was one of the editors of *Le Danton*. {BDF}

Sik, Toma (20th Century)

Sik is secretary of the Israel Secular Humanist Association in Tel Aviv, Israel.

Sikes, Mary Ellen (20th Century)

Sikes founded and is coordinator of the Central Virginia Secular Humanists, a chapter of Washington Area Secular Humanists. Also, she is a regional director of the Council for Secular Humanism and a contributing editor to the *Secular Humanist Bulletin*.

SIKH

A Sikh is an adherent of Sikhism, a monotheistic religion founded by the guru Nanek in northern India in the 16th century, one which combines elements of Islam and Hinduism. Sikhs refuse to recognize the Hindu caste system, forbid idolatry and pilgrimages, and believe that the soul goes through several cycles of death and rebirth before becoming liberated.

They are known for five distinctive K's: the kesh (uncut hair covered, in the case of men, by a turban); the kanga (comb, to keep the hair neat); the kachera (short trousers worn under outer garments); the kirpan (or sword, usually worn in a small version on a key chain or elsewhere); and the kara (an iron bangle worn on the wrist). (For an estimate of the number of Sikhs worldwide, see entry for Hell.)

Silk, Joseph (1942–)

Silk and John D. Barrow wrote *The Left Hand of Creation* (1994), in which they explain the most recent findings in cosmology.

Siller, Sidney (20th Century)

Siller, when he signed Humanist Manifesto II, was chairman of the Committee for Fair Divorce and Alimony Laws. {HM2}

Sillman, Jerry (20th Century)

Sillman is an activist with Rationalists of East Tennessee, 1036 Thompson Bridge Road, Maryville, Tennessee 37801.

SILOISM: See entry for Humanist Movement, which is distinct from and often antithetical to the movement represented by the International Humanist and Ethical Union.

Silone, Ignazio (Secondo Tranquilli) (1900–1978)

An humanist, novelist, and journalist, Silone founded the Italian Communist Party in 1921. As an anti-Fascist lived in exile in Switzerland from 1930 to 1945. He wrote *Fontamara* 91933), *Bread and Wine* (1937), and *A Handful of Blackberries* (1952). His memoir in *The God That Failed* (1950) illustrated how a European ex-Communist changed. {CE; OEL}

Silson, Roy (20th Century)

Silson, who has written for *New Humanist*, had an early interest in Mendelian principles, leading to his having specialized in the more complex genetics of those utility and fitness qualities important in evolution and practical breeding.

Silver, Queen (1910–1998)

By the age of seven, Silver had read Darwin and Haeckel, and less than two years later she delivered a series of lectures in Los Angeles on such subjects as Darwin, human nature in the animal world, Mexico, and Peru. When eleven, she publicly challenged William Jennings Bryan to a debate on evolution. Bryan declined. In Inglewood, California, from 1923 to 1932, Silver published *Queen Silver's Magazine*. She helped to found a Los Angeles group which later became Atheist United, and she has been a member of many freethought and humanist organizations. Her journals and personal papers were left to the Center for Inquiry libraries. {*Free* Inquiry, Winter 1998-1999; Freethought *Today*, January-February 1998; WWS}

Silverman, Carl (1956-)

An agnostic and freethinker whose parents were Jewish, Silverman of Waynesboro, Pennsylvania, challenged the owner of the Hagerstown, Maryland, Suns, a Class A affiliate baseball team of the Toronto Blue Jays. The owner was giving church-themed discounts to Sunday games if individuals brought a bulletin from their church. Inasmuch as the city of Hagerstown owns the stadium, Silverman took his case to the Maryland Commission on Human Relations, which found "probable cause" that the promotion violated state antidiscrimination laws.

Silverman told the press, "It irked me that if you bring a church bulletin, you are treated better, you get a better deal." Saying he rejects all religion as being a brand of mental illness, he formerly had waged a successful battle with his local school district to keep the Gideons from distributing Bibles throughout the public schools. Also, he forced the State of Pennsylvania to remove crosses from two state parks. {*The New York Times*, 2 May 1999}

Silverman, David (1966–)

Silverman, a professional inventor who works for American Telephone and Telegraph, has filed more than eighty patents. He has compiled an American Atheist mailing list and can be reached at <hdiweb@gtminet.net>.

Silverman, Herbert (20th Century)

Silverman, a professor of mathematics at the College of Charleston, is an active secular humanist in the Greenville, South Carolina, area, where he is a regional director of the Council for Secular Humanism. In 1992 when he applied to become a notary public, he struck "God" out of the phase "so help me God" on the application. South Carolina's Governor Carroll A. Campbell Jr. and its Secretary of State Jim Miles rejected the application. But in 1995, Fifth Circuit Judge Thomas L. Hughston Jr. ruled (Order 94-CP-40-3594, 2 August 1995) that state laws requiring officeholders to sign oaths affirming the existence of a deity are unconstitutional. *The Wall Street Journal* (9 August 1995) recognized Silverman's achievement by placing him in their "winners" column.

Commented *The Economist*, "Mr. Silverman, raised in the Jewish faith, says he will enjoy being a notary public if he wins his case. He hopes it will 'change the hearts and minds of some of my fellow South Carolinians who don't believe that atheists can be moral and ethical people.' "

Silverman signed Humanist Manifesto 2000. His homepage can be seen at <http://math.cofc.edu:8080/~kunkle/herb.html>. {"In (blank) we trust," *The Economist*, 12 October 1996; *Freethought Today*, September 1995}

Silverman, Joell (20th Century)

When Silverman signed Humanist Manifesto II, he was chairman of the Religious Education Committee, American Ethical Union. {HM2}

Simcox, Edith (1844–1901)

Simcox was author of *Natural Law*, and she wrote on the Design Argument in the *Fortnightly Review*, using the signature "H. Lawrenny." Simcox was a rationalist and non-theist. {BDF}

Simcox, George Augustus (1841–1885)

Simcox was an English poet who brought out editions of Juvenal, Thucydides, Demosthenes, and others. He wrote *History of Latin Literature* (1883). Simcox, who was influenced by Swinburne and Morris, wrote about such rationalists as Renan, Shelley, and Harriet Martineau. His own skepticism is seen in *Poems and Romances* (1869) and in a drama, *Prometheus Unbound* (1867). {RAT}

Simcox, John V. (20th Century)

With Warren Sandel and Raymond Winch, Simcox wrote *Is the Roman Catholic Church a Secret Society?* (1946). {GS}

Simmermacher, Donald G. (20th Century)

A New Mexican social worker, Simmermacher is a secular humanist who has written for *Free Inquiry* (Spring, 1986).

Simmons, Albert (20th Century)

Simmons, who used the pseudonym "Ignotus," wrote *Agnostic First Principles* (c. 1900). {GS}

Simmons, Bayard (20th Century)

Simmons was the first "suffra-gent" imprisoned for female suffrage (1906). His poems are found in *Fanfare for Freethought* (1938). {TRI}

Simmons, J. W. (20th Century)

A freethinker, Simmons wrote *Checking Up on the Bible By Facts of Science* (1947). {GS}

Simmons, Philip (20th Century)

Simmons, an English professor at Lake Forest College, is author of *Deep Surface* (1997). A Unitarian Universalist, he has written about nature's "Wild Things—e.g., grouse, turkey, rabbit, squirrel, fox, ferret, beaver, bobcat—that so many of us overlook. {*World*, November-December 1998}

Simms, Carolyne (20th Century)

Simms wrote *Letters from a Roman Catholic* (1976). {GS}

Simon de Tournai (13th Century)

Simon de Tournai was a professor at Paris University early in the 13th century. He reportedly said that "three seducers"—Moses, Jesus, and Muhammad–"have mystified mankind with their doctrines." As a result, he was said by unnamed Christian authorities to have been punished by God for his impiety. {BDF}

Simon, Barbara (20th Century)

Simon is a lawyer married to Skipp Porteous. The two have made their Institute for First Amendment Studies, which is based in Great Barrington, Massachusetts, into a major organization that studies individuals and groups—including religious—violate the First Amendment of the United States Constitution. Both Simon and her husband are Jewish.

Simon, François Jules (1814–1896)

Simon taught philosophy at the Sorbonne but was deposed for protesting against Napoleon's *coup d'état* in 1851. In 1871, Simon became Minister of Public Instruction, Life-Senator, President of the Council, and a member of the French Academy. Although French Rationalists disliked his leniency to the Church, he was an outspoken non-Christian theist in his *La religion naturelle* (1856) and *Dieu, patrie, liberté* (1883). {RAT; RE}

Simon, John Ivan (1925–)

Simon is a film and drama critic known for his acerbity, judiciousness, censoriousness, approbation, nit-picking, affirmativeness, and a variety of other disparate qualities which have made him loved as well as feared by individuals throughout the world of theatre. "Since 'Sacrilege' is a Catholic play," he thundered in a typical *New York* critique (13 November 1995) about a nun who challenges the Vatican to open the priesthood to women, "let me make my confession. I have no use for organized religion of any kind, and don't give a rap whether Sister Grace, who so fervently desires it, makes it from nun to priest. Consequently, all the thrashing about in Diane Shaffer's play leaves me out."

Born in Yugoslavia, Simon came to the United States when he was sixteen. A graduate of Harvard, he has been a film and drama critic on the staffs of a variety of magazines. He is author of *Acid Test* (1963), *Paradigms Lost: Reflections on Literacy and Its Decline* (1980), and *The Sheep from the Goats: Selected Literary Essays* (1989).

Simon, Maud (20th Century)

A freethinker, Simon wrote *Speaking For Myself, or Some Personal Points of View* (1945). {GS}

Simon, Neil (1927-)

In a biography, *Neil Simon Rewrites*, he reminisced about religion's indelible mark:

> So there I sat at the party drinking anything they put before me. I was completely stunned, not from liquor but from emotion. I knew how it felt to be drunk but I didn't know how to feel success. Was there something inside of me which allowed me to enjoy my moment but not be elated or overcome with it? I had been taught somewhere in my backgound that Jews did not gather around a campfire talking about the possessions they had with them, for they would surely be gone in the morning.
>
> You did not boast about your good fortune because God would certainly punish a boaster. I was not overly religious, in fact hardly religious at all, but your culture, by osmosis, or what you hear around the dinner table as a boy, brands fears and superstitions into your mind forever.

{CA}

Simon, Richard (1638–1712)

A devout Catholic who refuted Protestantism, Simon was a champion of the Bible against Spinoza. But then, in his *L'histoire critique du Vieux Testament* (1678), he impugned the Mosaic authorship of the Pentateuch. As a result, his French translation of the New Testament, a four-volume work called *Bibliothèque Critique*, was suppressed and the translation was condemned by Bossuet and the Archbishop of Paris. Simon wrote always as an avowed believer, but his work gave a new breadth of footing to the deistic arguments. {BDF; ER; JMR; JMRH}

Simonides of Ceos (c. 556–468? B.C.E.)

Simonides, a Greek lyric poet, wrote much which was lost, but his encomia, epinicia, and dirges were excellent. Two of his finest epitaphs are on the fallen at Marathon and at Thermopylae. "The longer I consider the subject of God," he declared, "the more obscure it becomes." {TYD}

Simonis (16th Century)

Simonis was a Polish physician who was persecuted for his opinions given in an atheistic work entitled *Simonis Religio*, published at Cracow in 1588. {BDF}

Simons, John (20th Century)

While a student at Western Washington University, Simons was one of the founding members of Campus Freethought Alliance. {*International Humanist News*, December 1996}

Simons, Minot (20th Century)

A Unitarian minister, Simons once stated, "The theory of evolution has removed the entire foundation of the doctrine of the fall of man and of the inherent depravity of human nature."

Simpson, George (Died c. 1844)

Simpson, of the Glasgow Zetetic Society, put forward a *Refutation of the Argument a priori for the Being and Attributes of God* (1838). It was a reply to two Scots, Clarke and Gillespie, in which he used the signature "Antitheos." {BDF}

Simpson, George Gaylord (1902–1984)

Simpson, a paleontologist, anthropologist, and a chairman of the Department of Geology and Paleontology, The American Museum of Natural History, New York City, wrote *This World of Life: The View of an Evolutionist* (1964), *The Meaning of Evolution* (1967), and *Biology and Man* (1969).

Asked to comment on humanism, Simpson wrote to the present author:

> Naturalistic Humanism, as I understand and accept it, is the view that all that we can possibly know or verify exists or occurs in nature, that is, in the physical universe. The supernatural is not philosophically excluded; it is simply unknowable. Supposed knowledge of the supernatural, when not merely bogus, is an error as to the significance of certain natural activities of the human mind and emotions. These activities, generally labeled as religious, are real and may be profoundly valuable, but they are a part of human *nature*, not a contact with the supernatural. There is no proved limit to what we may know within the framework of naturalism. It follows that what we now believe is always provisional and relative to the progress of knowledge in general. A believer in naturalism cannot be dogmatic even on this point, but the whole history of mankind testifies that acceptance on faith of supernatural, or of non-natural, postulates or hypotheses is stultifying at best.
>
> My concept of naturalism further includes these beliefs: that men and mankind are worthy both individually and as a whole; that they are responsible to and for themselves and to and for each other; that they have legitimate natural (not supernatural) values and morals; and that they are perfectible through their own resources. I take it that these views make my naturalism also humanistic in some sense of that abused word. Of course all this must here be said too briefly to be unambiguous. For instance, it is imperative to add that perfectibility, as I mean it, does not imply a single, static, and definable state of perfection or beatitude. It implies, rather, a relative goal, always receding, constantly to be redefined, and not necessarily or even desirably the same for all of us.

After his death, his daughter, Joan Simpson Burns, while rummaging through some of his papers came across a novella, *The Dechronization of Sam Magruder*, which she published in 1996. It is about a mid-22nd-century scientist who experiments with the quantum theory of time and accidentally gets caught between two particles of time, disappearing but reappearing eighty million years in the past. That made Magruder the only Homo sapiens on earth, and the novella goes into how he made tools, survived on dinosaur meat, eggs, and figs, and carved onto stone slabs a record of his experiences. Eighty million years later, in the Rocky Mountains, the slabs are located. Finding a tyrannosaur, Magruder writes that "it was a reptile, a dinosaur 15 feet high as it poised on its ponderous hind legs, 30 feet long from its obscene snout to the end of its great, tapered tail. . . . Its small, two-toed hands were held up beneath its tremendous jaw in a way that might have seemed ludicrously ladylike if the intention had not been so obviously grim. Its teeth were six-inch daggers and gleamed white as it swung its ponderous head to face me." Despite such pedagogical language, Prof. Alan Lightman and Stephen Jay Gould see another level of meaning to the story, for Simpson appears to have felt that he was a lonely person whose work would be dismissed or ignored by future generations.

"I wanted to shake him," Gould wrote in an afterword, "and tell him how much we all loved him. . . . But no one could . . . please him." {CE; HNS; WAS, 10 April 1956}

Simpson, James (20th Century)

Simpson is on the editorial board of *The Humanist.*

Simpson, James Young (1873–1934)

Simpson wrote *Landmarks in the Struggle Between Science and Religion* (1926). {GS}

Simpson, Lyle L. (20th Century)

An Iowa attorney, once President of the American Humanist Association, Simpson is a naturalistic humanist. He is President of the American Humanist Association's Endowment Fund. {CL; HNS2}

Simson, John (1668–1740)

Simson, a theologian, was librarian at Glasgow University, then decided to preach, but his lectures drew upon him the suspicion of heresy. In 1715 the General Assembly of the Scottish Church referred his case to a committee of thirty ministers and six elders, and he was warned to be more careful. In 1726 he was again impeached, on the ground that he denied the divinity of Christ. Simson never wrote his views, and it is not clear what he really believed., but he appears to have been ahead of his time with his view that reason is "the foundation of theology." {RAT}

SIN

Although "sin," as distinguished from crime and vice, is not a meaningful concept to secular humanists—the Greeks and Romans had no word for the concept—it is of major importance to Judeo-Christians. Secular humanists find that belief in such a concept can lead to unhealthy and harmful guilt complexes, feelings of "having sinned," with the resultant fears concerning how best to "acquire forgiveness" lest the sinner "be punished by the wrath of God." Although humanists may study the religionists' interest in this injurious concept, they often do so in order to provide therapy to those who suffer from the repercussions of believing in such a concept.

"There would be no point to sin if it were not the corridor to pleasure," novelist Mary Gordon has written. Whereas pleasure may be avoided by orthodox believers in sin, non-believers feel no guilt whatsoever in seeking sensual gratification nor frivolous amusement and are amused that anyone should believe that "what does not come from faith is sin," as explained by the Christian apostle Paul, who greatly influenced Augustine, Luther, Kierkegaard, and others in their own affirmation of the concept.

Sin is ever-present and is ever-tempting. Five decades ago in the 1940s,

Wilhelm Pauck of the University of Chicago wrote about the never-changing transgression of the "law of God": "The most adequate definitions of sin as developed by Christian theology (in harmony with its identification with unfaith) were those in which it is interpreted as *superbia* (pride) and *concupiscentia* (selfish desire and, in the narrower sense, sensuous lust). Sin as pride is in the last resort the refusal on man's part to acknowledge God as God. It is imbued with the attitude of *hybris* by which man tries to deify, absolutize himself as if he could be self-sufficient. Sin as concupiscence is every expression of egotism and selfishness in which an utter disregard of both God's sovereignty and love is shown." In short, believers if they are conscientious believers must not yield to sin. To do so is to be egotistic, non-theistic, and anthropocentric.

Contemporary Protestants introduced a definition of sin that was determined by the insights of the natural and social sciences in the moral development of mankind and of human groups and individuals. Some liberal Protestants, however, have come to regard the term *sin* as practically meaningless. Others are rediscovering the Biblical, particularly Pauline, teaching concerning sin. Roman Catholicism makes the distinction between *mortal* and *venial* sins. *Mortal* sin, according to Dr. Pauck, "is regarded as that transgression of God's law which causes the sinner to lose the effect of grace, thus rendering him subject to eternal punishment in hell. A *venial* sin is a violation of God's law which does not alienate the sinner from God, entailing no loss of grace, but requiring submission to penitential discipline. A mortal sinner can acquire forgiveness only by fulfilling the requirements of the sacrament of penance through which grace is restored in him."

Non-believers, although considered sinners by believers, do not condone crime (violation of the civil law) or vice (immorality resulting from the disregard of the social and ethical standards of society). Non-believers do, however, take an active interest in defining crime and vice. As a result, they take great interest in such questions as, Is euthanasia a crime? Is the exclusion of religious institutions from taxes a crime? Is allowing animal sacrifice, or the handling of poisonous snakes, in a religious service a crime? Is nudism a crime? Is teaching the need for the illusion of divinity or immortality a crime? What vices, such as the presently illegal pleasures which are provided by organized crime groups, are not crimes?

In 1993, according to Peter McWilliams in *Ain't Nobody's Business If You Do*, more than 350,000 people are in jail for something they did—something that did not physically harm another's person or property. In Michigan, he states, "More than 135 people are currently serving life sentences without possibility of parole for the mere possession of illegal drugs. . . . In addition, more than 1.5 million people are on parole or probation for consensual crimes. And more than four million people are arrested each year for doing something that hurts no one except, potentially, themselves." McWilliams estimates that, because of this, "every man, woman, and child in this country is paying $800 per year to destroy the lives of six million fellow citizens involved in the tangled web of consensual acts, crime, and punishment. And moving the underground economy that is associated with consensual crimes above ground would create six million tax paying jobs."

Sin, according to Bertrand Russell, is called that as an excuse for cruelty. "It's to enable you to inflict suffering without a bad conscience, and therefore it is a bad thing." On the other hand, he added, "I think sin is something that it is positively good to punish, such as murder, not only because you want to prevent murder, but because the murderer deserves to suffer." Other observations concerning sin:

• Question: What kind of sins are the greatest?
Answer: Adultery, fornication, murder, theft, swearing, witchcraft, sedition, heresies, or any the like.

–John Bunyan,
"Instructions for the Ignorant" (1675)

• Sin is not hurtful because it is forbidden, but it is forbidden because it is hurtful.

–Benjamin Franklin

• The different religions have never overlooked the part played by the sense of guilt in civilization. What is more, they come forward with a claim . . . to save mankind [sic] from this sense of guilt, which they call sin.

–Sigmund Freud

• That which others call sin is experiment for us.

–Ralph Waldo Emerson

• He said he was against it.

–Attributed to President Calvin Coolidge,
when asked what was said by a minister
who preached about sin.

• The worst sin towards our fellow creatures is not to have them, but to be indifferent to them: that's the essence of inhumanity.

–George Bernard Shaw

• Wickedness is a myth invented by good people to account for the curious attractiveness of others.

–Oscar Wilde

• All the things I really like to do are either immoral, illegal, or fattening.

–Alexander Woollcott

• All sins are attempts to fill voids.

–Simone Weil

• Sin has always been an ugly word, but it has been made so over the last half-century. It has been made not only ugly, but passé. People are no longer sinful: they are only immature or underprivileged or frightened, or, more particularly, sick.

–Phyllis McGinley

• The biggest sin is sitting on your ass.

–Florynce Kennedy

In the 1990s, Satan continued to bedevil. Islamic fundamentalists referred to America as "the great Satan." Religionist Pat Robertson asserted that feminism "encourages women to leave their husbands, kill their children, practice witchcraft" and, worse, become lesbians. Hindus saw the devil in Muslims. Muslims saw the devil in Jews. African nationalists saw Satan in Nordic blondes. And some secular humanists, nonplused that the political as well as religious center was seemingly moving more to the right and conservatism, extrapolated that "the Devil must've made 'em do it." (See the entry for S. Levin concerning sinosis and the entry for fornication, in which Bertrand Russell explains how Christians differ in the way they deal with the "sin" of fornication. Also see entries for mortal sin and for venial sin.) {CE; Lee Eisler, *The Quotable Bertrand Russell*; ER}

SIN, EXAMPLES OF

• The Presbyterian Church (U.S.A.) voted not to change its constitution in order to allow practicing homosexuals to be ordained as clergy members.

• A small group of Orthodox rabbis declared that the Reform and Conservative movements were "not Judaism," urging Jews to stay away from those synagogues because their rabbis were allowing people to drive on the Sabbath.

• A Baptist church in Berryville, Arkansas, closed its sole day care center because it encouraged women to work when God wanted them at home.

• An Orthodox rabbinic board in New York City ruled that women's prayer groups violated Jewish tradition inasmuch as they allowed women to read the Torah publicly.

• Orthodox fundamentalist mullahs in Bangladesh called for the death of the gynecologist and poet Taslima Nasrin because she allegedly blasphemed the Qur'an.

• The State of Michigan warned Dr. Jack Kevorkian who since 1990 had attended forty-five suicides who or whose families had requested his assistance, to stop helping people hopelessly ill to commit suicide.

• Marshall Herff Applewhite convinced thirty-eight Heavens Gate followers in California that a sleek spaceship was trailing in the wake of the Hale-Bopp comet and that if they swallowed barbituates and vodka or smothered themselves with plastic bags the 39 of them (of the 18 men, one-third had been castrated to enforce adherence to a celibate lifestyle) would be taken by God into Heaven. In their pockets were rolls of quarters and United States $5. bills.

SINA, IBN (AVICENNA): See entry for Avicenna.

Sinclair, Upton (1879–1968)

Sinclair is presently known as a novelist, but future generations may consider him more as a Utopian whose hundred or so books included well-known historical figures as fictional characters. His eleven-volume Lanny Budd series, *World's End* (1940–1953), is more a political commentary than a literary achievement, and how future critics will accept his work is debatable.

Highly critical of Christianity, he has held that correcting organized religion is preferable to abolishing it. In *Profits of Religion* (1918), he rankled many with his view that religion is a capitalist tool, that it teaches the poor to accept the fact that God has allotted them their positions in life. In one work, *They Call Me Carpenter* (1922), he describes the dream a rich man has upon meeting the Christ. Theodore Dreiser was unhappy with the speculation that Sinclair had used him as his model for the fictional infidel being portrayed. Although Sinclair rejected his youthful Episcopalianism, he never rejected his faith in socialism, with the novel serving as a device to express his liberal views. The work which received the most critical acclaim was *The Jungle* (1906), in which through the character of Jurgis Rudkus he indicts the inhumanistic and immoral conduct of meat-packing officials toward their own workers, and his memorably vivid descriptions of what was wrong with the industry ("There were things that went into the sausage in comparison with which a poisoned rat was a tidbit.") led to governmental reform in the food inspection laws. Sinclair's liberal stands included opposing prostitution, alcohol, and erotic materials. Although he lost the California race as Democratic candidate for governor of California in 1934, he went on to write the Pulitzer Prize-winning work, *Dragon's Teeth* (1942).

Critical of the Church, he wrote, "Various Catholic societies . . . in every city and town in America, are pushing and plotting to get Catholics upon library boards, so that the public may not have a chance to read scientific books; to get Catholics into the public schools and on school boards, so that children may not hear about Galileo, Bruno, and Ferrer; to have Catholics in control of police and on magistrates' benches, so that priests who are caught in brothels may not be exposed or punished."

Asked if he was a theist or a humanist, he wrote the present author concerning humanism,

> Answering your statement that my views on theism are difficult to find, I refer you to my book called *What God Means To Me* (1935). No doubt you will find the material you desire there, and you have my permission to quote from the book anything which may be of use to you in compiling your article.

In short, Sinclair was against Christianity's anti-scientific thrusts, its fostering notions of class, and its outlook on women, but basically he was a spiritualist. The book tells of his meeting, when seventeen, a Unitarian clergyman "who informed me that he had several times met and talked with ghosts." The book which "came nearest to swaying my mind toward the spiritist idea is Sir Oliver Lodge's *Raymond*," and Sinclair declares he had "communications" with Jack London, who told him things no medium could have known. His wife, said Sinclair, once attended a séance and heard Oliver Wendell Holmes "speaking with a very decided New York accent." Concluded Sinclair, "We have a choice of two courses. We can say that life is a chaos, and that we are the sport of blind forces, and take ourselves out of it forthwith. Or we can listen to the inner voice which tells us that there must be a plan, even though we cannot understand it. I have chosen the latter course." As noted by McCabe, in Sinclair's later years "he took up Spiritualism and wrote *What God Means to Me.*" {CE; FUS; JM; RAT; RE; TRI; TYD; WAS, 20 February 1951}

Sinclaire, Frederick (1881–1954)

Sinclaire was an Australian Unitarian, socialist, and theistic humanist. An admirer of the works of George Bernard Shaw, he saw religion not as a supernatural force but as an inherent part of mankind's nature. In 1907 he was appointed minister of the Melbourne Unitarian Church, resigning four years later to become co-editor with Marie Pitt of the *Socialist.* In 1916 he formed the Free Religious Fellowship, editing their *Fellowship.* "Rationalism," he said in 1920, "is like nitrogen, a necessary ingredient of the air we breathe, in itself not poisonous but simply innutritious. The cure for rationalism is not anti-rationalism . . . but post-rationalism." In New Zealand, he became professor of English at Canterbury College, returned to the Church of England, but still retained his liberal beliefs. {SWW}

Sindona, Michele (20th Century)

Sindona is author of *St. Peter's Banker* (1983), which relates the scandal at the Pope's own bank in the Vatican and includes his own involvement.

Sinfield, Peter (20th Century)

Sinfield, who writes lyrics for King Crimson's first albums, is a non-theist. Two of his titles which contain inflammatory lyrics for theists are "In the Court of the Crimson King" and "In the Wake of Poseidon." {Fredrik Bendz on the Internet}

Singer, Charles (20th Century)

A freethinker, Singer wrote *The Christian Failure* (1943). {GS}

Singer, Irving (1925–)

Singer is a philosophy educator, a Santayana scholar, and a naturalistic humanist. He has taught at Cornell University, the University of Michigan, Johns Hopkins University, and M.I.T. (since 1969). He wrote *Santayana's Aesthetics* (1957); *The Nature of Love: Plato to Luther* (1966); *The Goals of Human Sexuality* (1973); *Mozart and Beethoven* (1977); *Meaning in Life: The Creation of Value* (1992); and *The Pursuit of Love* (1994). *The Harmony of Nature and Spirit* (1998) details Singer's aesthetic naturalism and his search for a happiness that involves feeling good in our life and *about* our life. {*Free Inquiry*, Winter 1998-1999}

Singer, Peter (1946-)

In *Rethinking Life and Death: The Collapse of Our Traditional Ethics* (1995), Singer finds the Judeo-Christian teaching—that life is "sacred"—has lost its validity, that decisions concerning euthanasia are better decided on the basis of the patients' "ethically relevant characteristics." For example, is life of any value to those who are handicapped with Downs disease, or are permanently comatose, or are enduring intense pain because of cancer? If judged case by case, it is possible that abortion, choosing not to treat handicapped children, and voluntary euthanasia are morally acceptable. Adults not constrained by past conventions have every right, he holds, to hasten a painful death. As for children, he suggests an arbitrary twenty-eight days of life before decisions are made by parents as to whether or not to allow hopeless cases to have their life mercifully terminated. This skirts the problem others have as to when a fetus can be aborted, and Singer recommends the same for fellow animals, such as a farmer's cattle or others' pets. Specifically, he would not feed Downs syndrome infants, arguing that they do not have "genuine" consciousness.

He includes examples of "commandments," the Old Commandments (OC) and what he terms the New Commandments (NC); e.g.,

> OC 1: Treat all human life as of equal worth.
> NC 1: Recognise that the worth of human life varies.
>
> OC 2: Never intentionally take innocent human life.
> NC 2: Take responsibility for the consequences of your actions.
>
> OC 3: Never take your own life and always try to prevent others taking theirs.
> NC 3: Respect a person's desire to live or die.
>
> OC 4: Be fruitful and multiply.
> NC 4: Bring children into the world only if they are wanted.
>
> OC 5: Treat all human life as always more precious than any non-human life.
> NC 5: Do not discriminate on the basis of species.

As might be expected, his views have been hotly challenged. When he was announced as joining the Princeton University faculty's bioethics department, *The New York Times* (10 April 1999) headlined the story, "Princeton's Choice of a Euthanasia Backer Causes a Stir."

Interviewed in Sweden by Staffan Gunnarson, Singer when asked if he considers himself a humanist, responded, "Well, not in any limited and traditional 'Jewish' or 'Christian' sense of the word, that's for sure. From that point of view I am not a humanist. I would rather consider myself to be a utilitarian, so far." He said he is an atheist, a person who thinks parents have the right to end the life of newborn children who are really and ill and will only endure a life of pain and despair, and favors self-determined euthanasia. He has supported the proposed new laws on euthanasia in Northern Australia. {*The Freethinker*, August 1997; *International Humanist News*, December 1997}

Singh, Buta (20th Century)

Singh spoke at the Atheist Centre's 50th Anniversary International Conference in 1980.

Singh, Hajom Kissor (19th Century)

Singh in 1887 founded the Indian Council of Unitarian Churches. A tribal Khasi, he objected to the mass converstion to Christianity of so many of his tribal sisters and brothers midway through the 19th century. By forming his own church, he emphasized the teachings of Jesus but also those of the Buddha, the Sikh prophets, and the Hindu and Islamic scriptures. His church also borrowed elements of the indigenous tribal faith, that of Seng Khasi. (See entries for Indian Council of Unitarian Churches and for Unitarians in India.)

Singh, Jai Prithvi Bahadur (1877–1940)

Singh was the Nepalese founder and president of the Humanist Club in Banglore, South India. He was the eldest son of Bikram Bahadur Singh and Rudra Kumari Devi (daughter of the first Rana Prime Minister Jung Bahadur Rana). In 1889 when then Rana Prime Minister Bir Shumsher forced his father to abdicate his power of Bajhangi Raja, he was coronated as the Raja of Bajhang. In 1894 he married fourteen-year-old Khageshori Devi, daughter of Rana Prime Minister Chandra Shumshere Rana. From 1902 to 1905 he became Counselor General at Calcutta, after which he returned to Kathmandu with a hand press in order to print badly needed textbooks in the Nepali language.

In 1907 he published *A History of Japan*, which described how the sovereign emperor (Mikado) was kept in virtual imprisonment and rendered powerless by the autocratic rule of Shoguns. When Chandra Shumshere Rana, his father-in-law, read the book, he felt threatened that the book was an indication of some kind of conspiracy against the autocratic Rana family rule. They and he differed openly, and the resultant rift widened considerably.

In 1911 he published *Prakrit vyakaran* (Nepali Grammar), a useful educational work. In 1913 he published *Tatto Prashansha*, a book on humans and humanity.

From 1907 to 1913 he was chief of Court (Bharadari Shabha) and, because of the major differences of opinion with the Rana rules, he opted to return to Bahjang. In 1916 he handed his crown to his father and journeyed to Nainital, India, during which time he wrote the three-volume *Philosophy of Humanism* to propagate his idea of world peace and world brotherhood.

In 1927, traveling in disguise as a Burmese, he reached England with a passport from the French rule of Pandechhori. He stayed six months, then returned to Banglore, where at Chetty Road Banglore he constructed the Humanist Club and published three books on humanism, initiated the publication of *Humanist Magazine*, and wrote *Shanti ko Jhanda* (Flag of Peace).

The first phase of his life was devoted to his struggle against Rana oligarchy. As early as 1905 he hurled a bombshell against the Rana regime by writing *Sichya Darpan*, a three-volume work in which he became noted as a political cartoonist of the period following World War I. Using stories, fables, and parables, he talked about freedom in diverse forms: freedom from arbitrary power, freedom of speech, freedom of movement, and the freedom to realize one's own talent. Following World War I, Singh went into voluntary exile in Banglore, devoting the rest of his life to the cause of humanism.

Following are the tenets of Jai Pritnvi's philosophy:

- Instead of entering into unhealthy competition and dogmatic contradictions, humans should direct their behavior toward a path of reconciliation so that security, privileges, and prosperity can be insured through mutual understanding.
- The general public needs an organization through which it can interact, exchange ideas, and solve common problems.
- If the doctrine of self-security is based on humanitarian grounds, the path leading to a peaceful society will automatically open.
- Whatever is done to destroy human civilization is, lamentably, a symbol of animalistic instinct.
- Humanism is a philosophic outlook which human beings, creatures who are distinct from other animals, choose to observe as a duty and not as a religion.

Jai Prithvi died in Jaya Bhawan, India, but his influence upon Nepalese philosophers continues to be a major one. (See entry for Nepal Humanists.) {HNS2}

Singh, Min Bahadur (20th Century)

Singh is President of Research Academica for Humanism & Jaya Prithvi Bdr. Singh in Nepal. (See entry for Nepal Humanists.)

Singletary, Mary Jo (20th Century)

Singletary is president of the Alliance of Humanist, Atheist, and Ethical Culture Organizations of Los Angeles County, California. She also heads the Humanist Association of Los Angeles. In 1994 she spoke at the Alliance's 14th annual conference, which was held aboard the *Queen Mary*.

Sinha, V. K. (20th Century)

Sinha, of the Indian Secular Society, has written in the Indian *Secularist*, which he edits, that he favors euthanasia. The Right to Life, he holds, recognizes the individual's total possession of his own life—a life to make or mar; a life to achieve his highest potential or a life merely to eke out animal existence. A person is free to be a poet or an humble artisan. The rights *belong* to him simply because he is human.

Speaking at a 1995 conference of humanists in India, Sinha predicted that "The BJP, which is a communal party, with its saffron brigade comprising the RSS, the Hindu Vishwas Parishad, the Bajrang Dal, and a host of other Hindu fundamentalist groups might capture, if not political power at the center, at least the power to determine the social and political agenda in the coming decade. . . . It is the fundamentalism and nationalism which the saffron brigade presents that contemporary India faces its greatest threat and challenge. . . . This poses the gravest challenge to the humanists and secularists in India."

Sinha is author of *Secularism in India* (1966). {*New Humanist*, February 1996}

Sinnott, Nigel Hugh (1944–)

Sinnott, who was born in England of an Anglican father and a right-wing, agnostic mother, is an Australian atheist, freethinker, research historian, editor, and writer. At the age of ten, he has written, he "decided that Christianity was not only false, but nasty to boot." Two of Lord Macaulay's poems—"Naseby" and "Horatius"—led him to become a convinced republican and militant atheist. In 1963 he joined Oxford University's Humanist Group, the Ethical Union, and the Rationalist Press Association. In 1972–1973 he became full-time editor of the *Freethinker*. Migrating to Australia in 1976, he was the founder member and secretary of the Secular Society of Victoria. His publications include *Charles Bradlaugh and Ireland* (1971); *Joseph Symes, "The Flower of Atheism"* (1977); *Matilda, Agnes, and Stella Symes* (1978). Sinnott also edited *Joseph Skurrie's Freethought Reminiscences* (1977). He has contributed to *The Rationalist News* (Sydney); *New Zealand Rationalist and Humanist* (Auckland); and the *Victorian Humanist* (Melbourne).

In 1999, in a legal battle against the Alexandra Primary School, Victoria, he won a battle to scrap the Loyal Declaration that was worded, "I love God and my country. I will honour the flag. I will serve the Qeen, and cheerfully obey my parents, teachers and the laws." The new wording, which his ten-year-old daughter Miriam will now use: "As a young Australian, I promise to obey the laws of my country, and respect the rights of people through my words and actions. I will try to make my home, school and community a better place for all." {*The Freethinker*, May 1999; FUK; SWW}

Siqueiros, David Alfaro (1896–1974)

Siqueiros is a Mexican muralist who, according to Lamont, "concentrated on Humanist themes." One of the principal figures in 20th-century Mexican mural painting, Siqueiros was expelled from the United States for his revolutionary activities. One of his major works, at the *Hotel de México*, is "March of Humanity." Siqueiros was both a communist and a humanist. {CL}

SIREN

• Siren, n. One of several musical prodigies famous for a vain attempt to dissuade Odysseus from a life on the ocean wave. Figuratively, any lady of splendid promise, dissembled purpose, and disappointing performance.

–Ambrose Bierce
The Devil's Dictionary

SISYPHUS

In Greek mythology, Sisyphus was the son of Aeolus and founder and king of Corinth. Renowned for his cunning, he was said even to have outwitted Death. However, for his disrespect to Zeus he was condemned to eternal punishment in Tartarus. There he eternally pushed a heavy rock to the top of a steep hill, where it would roll down again. "The Myth of Sisyphus," by Camus, is an essay based on the legend. (See entry for Tartarus.) {CE}

Sitting Bull (c. 1831–1890)

Sitting Bull, the Sioux leader in the battle of the Little Bighorn, was a pagan who was feared by the whites who had forced Indians under his command to be settled on a reservation. His actual name was Tatanka Iyotake. During the battle with George Armstrong Custer and his men, Sitting Bull's forces in 1876 defeated and killed his enemies. This became a Pyrrhic victory, for the shock of Custer's defeat spurred Washington to wage "total war" on the Sioux. Sitting Bull then escaped to Canada but returned in 1881 on a promise of a pardon. In 1885 he appeared in Buffalo Bill's Wild West Show, selling his autograph to gentlemen for $1 to $5 and to ladies, free. But when he encouraged the Sioux not to sell their lands and advocated a ghost dance religion, he was arrested by an Indian policeman who, during a struggle, accidentally killed him. The Indian policeman, who was immediately killed by outraged spectators, was given a Christian burial with military honors. Sitting Bull was interred in a pauper's grave.

"I wish it to be remembered," Sitting Bull had said when giving himself up to a representative of the U.S. Army, "that I was the last man of my tribe to surrender my rifle."

A symbolic victim of American brutality and exploitation, Sitting Bull had been a holy man to his people. For the tribal goddess, White Buffalo Woman, he performed the sun dance. With skewers, he had pierced his chest and back, dancing suspended in the air until the flesh tore loose, all the while staring into the sun and praying. "The life of white men is slavery," he observed. "They are prisoners in towns or farms. Look at me. See if I am poor, or my people either. . . . The whites may get me at last, as you say, but I will have good times till then." Another Indian chief, reports Robert M. Utley in *The Lance and the Shield: The Life and Times of Sitting Bull* (1993), said, "They made us many promises, more than I can remember, but they never kept but one: they promised to take our land, and they took it." A relative in 1953 stole Sitting Bull's bones from the North Dakota pauper's grave, retrieving them for burial in South Dakota.

SIX DEGREES OF SEPARATION

The popular belief is that anyone on earth can be linked to anyone else by a chain of only six other people, the link being called "six degrees of separation." Playwright John Guare dramatized the view in a 1993 play of the same name.

Mathematicians have shown that any large set of linked, dynamic components—people, electric power stations, brain cells, etc.—can be transformed into a small world by introducing short cuts between a few components. Relatively few short cuts can make big changes in a network, linking clusters of people, power stations, or brain cells together in unexpected ways. For example, a person who knows Secretary of State Madeline K. Albright will be connected to everyone she knows, including kings and queens. However, if a person knows that his neighbor's daughter-in-law was Ms. Albright's college roommate, the person would be connected to the Queen of England by three degrees of separation.

Practical applications of the concept include the idea that—using regular networks, small-world networks, and random networks—it takes few short cuts between nodes and clusters to turn a big world into a small world. However, adding more short cuts does not necessarily improve network efficiency. Short cuts can make networks more efficient, as in the case of improving the efficiency of cell phone networks by deliberately introducing a few random connections between nodes, or phones. Short cuts can also have negative effects, as when human populations that are isolated experience disease epidemics that are localized but jet travel makes it possible for diseases to spread rapidly and exponentially.

Poet Allen Ginsberg, illustrating the concept, claimed five degrees of separation with poet Walt Whitman. Ginsberg said he had had sex with Neal Cassady, who had had sex with Arthur Gavin, who had had sex with Edward Carpenter, who had had sex with Whitman. {Sandra Blakeslee, "Mathematicians Prove That It's A Small World," *The New York Times*, 16 June 1998; *Lavender Lists* (1990)}

Sjoberg, Walter (19th Century)

Sjoberg, a Finn, took part in founding the Utilistiska Samfundet. During the imprisonment of Mr. Lennstrand, Sjoberg gave bold lectures on his behalf at Stockholm. {BDF}

Sjöö, Monica (20th Century)

With Barbara Mor, Sjöö wrote *The Great Cosmic Mother* (1991).

SKEPTIC

A monthly, *Skeptic* is at PO Box 475, Manchester M60 1TH, United Kingdom.

SKEPTIC

Skeptic (2761 North Marengo Avenue, PO Box 338, Altadena, California 91001) is a quarterly published by the Skeptics Society. Michael Shermer, assistant professor of the history of science at Occidental College and author of *Why People Believe Weird Things: Pseudoscience, Superstition, and Other Confusions of Our Time* (1997), is publisher and editor-in-chief. E-mail: <skepticmag@aol.com>. On the Internet: <http://www.skeptic.com/>.

SKEPTIC'S DICTIONARY

Robert T. Carroll is webmaster for materials about UFOs, the paranormal, and skepticism. On the Web: <http://dcn.davis.ca.us/~btcarroll/skeptic/dictcont.html>

SKEPTICAL BRIEFS

A bi-monthly, *Skeptical Briefs* is at PO Box 703, Buffalo, NY 14226-0703.

SKEPTICAL INQUIRER

Skeptical Inquirer is a bi-monthly published by the Committee for the Scientific Investigation of Claims of the Paranormal (3965

Rensch Road, Amherst, New York 14228). Paul Kurtz heads the committee and Kendrick Frazier, the editor, is at 944 Deer Drive NE, Albuquerque, New Mexico 87122. Noted members of the editorial board include Martin Gardner, Philip J. Klass, and Joe Nickel.

E-mail: <skeptinq@aol.com>. On the Web: <http://www.csicop.org>.

SKEPTICAL REVIEW

Skeptical Review (PO Box 617, Canton, Illinois 61520) is a quarterly edited by Farrell Till, a highly respected Biblical scholar who as a non-believer patiently demolishes the positions of any believers who dare to take him on. E-mail: <errancy@infidels.org>.

SKEPTICISM

Democritus, the first skeptic, held that sense perception is not a certain guide to objective reality. The Sophists were early skeptics, as was Protagoras, who taught the relativity of knowledge, and Gorgias, whose extreme skepticism held that either nothing can be known or, if anything were known, it could not be communicated. Pyrrho held a similar extreme view of skepticism. Arcesilaus, however, taught that probable knowledge, not certitude, which is impossible, is attainable. Other skeptics have been Michel de Montaigne, Pierre Charron, Blaise Pascal, René Descartes, Pierre Bayle, David Hume, and Immanuel Kant. F. H. Bradley held that skepticism means "to become aware of and to doubt all preconceptions." Of these, Montaigne and Bayle, along with Joseph Glanvil in England, combined skepticism with a devout theism. Both the supporters and some of the opponents of religion have held that skepticism rests on faith rather than reason.

Non-believers are attracted to skepticism as well as to Kantian agnosticism, for the scientific method demands that all things assumed as facts must be questioned. Since the time of Descartes, critics in religion and morals have tended to depict skepticism as a form of negative dogmatism, as seeking actually to deny the existence of anything whose nature is in doubt.

Academic skepticism, which is associated with the Academy of Carneades, held that although the same evidence is always compatible with two contrary conclusions, some beliefs are more reasonable than others and we can act upon the balance of probabilities.

Some believers point to "holy" people's ability to walk on fire. However, skeptics, quick to point out the physics behind firewalking, explain the conductivity and capacity of heat. A hand placed into a 450° oven to remove a cake, for example, does not get burned, but a hand placed onto a metal pan will sizzle inasmuch as metal has a high heat capacity and conducts heat rapidly. Coals in a fire are more like cake than the metal pan. A show-off intent upon being a faker, however, needs to move as quickly as a fakir if he does not want to be burned.

A major journal which has an international audience is *Skeptical Inquirer*, published by the Committee for the Scientific Investigation of Claims of the Paranormal (Box 703, Buffalo, NY 14226). The committee has subcommittees to investigate astrology, paranormal health claims, unidentified flying objects (UFOs), and parapsychology.

Another is *Skeptic*, which is devoted to the investigation and promotion of science and rational skepticism and is published by the Skeptics Society, 2761 North Marengo Avenue, Altadena, California 91001. (See entries for Edgar Sheffield Brightman and for Ghosts. For a history and the values of skepticism to philosophy, see Richard H. Popkin's article in the *Encyclopedia of Philosophy*, Vol. 7.) {CE; DCL; ER; OEL}

SKEPTICS CORNER

Louis W. Cable has a web site, Skeptics Corner, devoted to refuting biblical claims: <http://www.inu.net/skeptics>.

SKEPTICS SOCIETY

The Skeptics Society is on the Web: <http://www.skeptic.com/>.

SKEPTICS, OUTSTANDING

Skeptical Inquirer (January-February 2000) listed the following as the outstanding skeptics of the 20th century: James Alcock; Isaac Asimov; Robert A. Baker; Stephen Barrett; Bart Bok; Samuel Clemens; Richard Dawkins; Albert Einstein; Richard Feynman; Kendrick Frazier; Martin Gardner; Stephen Jay Gould; Harry Houdini; Ray Hyman; Philip J. Klass; Paul Kurtz; H. L. Mencken; Joe Nickell; Oscar Pfungst; Karl Popper; James Randi; Bertrand Russell; Carl Sagan; and Michael Shermer. Also: Milburne Christopher (1914-1984); Joseph Jastrow (1863-1944); and D. H. Rawcliffe.

Skerry, James Humphrey (c. 1899–1971)

Skerry in 1925 was the first treasurer of the Rationalist Association of Australia LTD., a post he kept until his death. {SWW}

Skiles, Frank and **Marie Skiles** (20th Century)

The Skileses published *Slant Press*, a newsletter for empiricists, secular humanists, freethinkers, agnostics, and atheists. (See entry for Montana Freethinkers.) {FD}

SKIN

Without it, our sweat glands could not excrete waste products and our body could not cool when it over-heats. Skin is the flexible tissue that encloses the body of vertebrate animals and, in humans and other mammals, serves vital protective and metabolic functions.

Of the many unscientific tales about skin, *Genesis* is one of the worst and most misleading. Literalists believe that Noah, after the deluge, divided the world among his three sons. Japheth received Europe, Shem got Asia, and Ham was given Africa. Ham got the worst of the property for two reasons: first, he had accidentally seen his father's nakedness when he walked into a tent; and second, he had disobeyed Noah's order that on the ark everyone was supposed to be sexually continent—Ham, however, with the aid of a magic demon had slept with his wife, and the punishment was that Ham and all his offspring were given a black skin. The blackness of some people's skin, in short, is a symbol of Ham's having broken a taboo about seeing naked skin, according to the author or authors of *Genesis*.

In 1991 in the Tyrolean Alps of northern Italy, a mummified body was found in a melting glacier. Called the Iceman's body, it is the oldest known human-flesh remains. *The New York Times* science reporter John Noble Wilford (17 February 1999) has described the autopsies which showed that the Iceman was probably herding sheep or was on a solitary journey, that he was no more than forty years old and in poor health, that his teeth were worn to nubs from chewing dried meat, working leather, or both. Possibly as the result of living in a shelter with an open hearth, his lungs were as black as a smoker's. His body was tattooed close to or on the classic acupuncture points for treatment of pain from arthritis of the spine, hips, knees, and ankles. The two walnut-size lumps of a tree fungus that he possessed could, if ingested, have killed certain parasitic bacteria, thus acting as a natural laxative and antibiotic. Inasmuch as the Iceman suffered from a parasitic worm, the fungus may have been his remedy for the acute stomach and intestinal pain he must have suffered on the last day of a hard life.

Stuffed derma (the Greek word for skin)—a beef casing that includes seasoned mixture of matzo meal or flour, onion, and suet, prepared by boiling, then roasting—is a delicacy both to dermatologists (medical physicians concerned with the physiology and pathology of the skin) as well as to sausage-eating non-dermatologists. (See entry for Skin.) {CE}

Skinner, B(urrhus) F(rederic) (1904–1990)

A famed behaviorist and professor of psychology at Harvard University, Skinner wrote *The Behavior of Organisms* (1938), *Walden Two* (1961), and *About Behaviorism* (1974).

Known for his "Skinner box," an experimental chamber with doors, switches, and a dispenser of food pellets, he observed the behavior of rats and, using reward techniques, applied his findings to human learning. His imagined utopian community, Walden Two, infuriated counterculturists of the 1960s, and his *Beyond Freedom and Dignity* (1971) rankled many with its conclusion that freedom and dignity are illusions. However, two small communities based upon Walden II—Twin Oaks in Virginia and Los Horcones in Mexico–still survive. Further, his concept of programmed instruction continues to affect educational theories and methods, particularly in the United States. Critics of a form of psychotherapy which developed from Skinner's views complain that behavior modification treats symptoms rather than causes.

In 1972, Skinner was elected an honorary associate of the British Rationalist Association. Also, he received the Humanist of the Year award from the American Humanist Association. Skinner signed Humanist Manifesto II. {CE; HM2; HNS2; PK; SHD}

Skinner, Clarence Russell (1881–1949)

Skinner, a professor at Tufts College and a Universalist minister, opposed both world wars. He was dean of Crane Theological School (1933–1945) and is generally considered as being the most important 20th-century Universalist leader. He moved the denomination toward a more political and "this-worldly" understanding of the term Universalist. For him it is not enough simply to be in the world—it is also necessary to judge the world, ethically and religiously.

With Alfred S. Cole, Skinner wrote *Hell's Ramparts Fell* (1941), a biography of John Murray. Charles A. Howe has edited *Clarence R. Skinner, Prophet of a New Universalism* (1999). {U; U&U; UU}

Skinner, Ebenezer (1830–1892)

Skinner was a freethinker, bookseller, secularist, and spiritualist. In the early 1880s, he was president of the Liberal Association of New South Wales, an organization initiated by a spiritualist group aiming to attract both religious and skeptical members. An enthusiast in building the Sydney Lyceum, he was compiler of *The Secularists' Guide*. Skinner's daughter married secularist William Whitehouse Collins. {FUK; SWW}

Skinner, William (19th Century)

Skinner, of Kirkcaldy, Scotland, was a deist, the author of *Thoughts on Superstition, or An Attempt to Discover Truth* (1822). He also is credited with *Jehovah Unveiled, or the God of the Jews* (1819), which Carlile published. {BDF}

Skolimowski, Henryk (20th Century)
Skolimowski wrote *Ecological Humanism* (1976).

Skou, Jens Christian (1918–)

Skou, a biophysics educator in Denmark, was co-recipient in 1997 of the Nobel Prize for Chemistry. A member of the Danish Royal Academy of Scientists, Skou signed Humanist Manifesto 2000. E-mail: <des@mil.aau.dle>.

Skoyles, John R. (20th Century)

Skoyles wrote "A Mind Virus Writes to Richard Dawkins" for *The Freethinker* (January 1997).

Skurrie, Joseph (1858–1949)

Skurrie was a secularist, freethinker, rationalist, advocate of Esperanto, a teetotaller, and vegetarian. After joining the Australian Secular Association in Bendigo in 1880, he became its corresponding secretary to Joseph Symes's *Liberator*. Skurrie was caretaker of the Hall of Science, then joined the re-formed Rationalist Society of Australia. {SWW}

Slack, Samuel Benjamin (Born 1859)

Slack, a philologist, taught classics and comparative philology at McGill University in Montreal. For the Rationalist Press Association, he translated Dr. van den Bergh van Eysinga's *Radical Views About the New Testament* (1912), with an introduction in which he expressed his own rationalism. {RAT}

Slaten, A. Wakefield (20th Century)

Slaten is a Unitarian who wrote *The Appeal of Fundamentalism* (1925) and *What If the World Went Atheist?* (1928). In 1929 after editing "The Humanist Pulpit" for *The New Humanist*, he was succeeded by Edwin H. Wilson. {EW; GS}

Slater, Humphrey (20th Century)

Slater wrote a little-known novel, *Heretics*, in which he shows a resemblance between the 12th- century Children's Crusade and the 20th-century Spanish Civil War. Of particular interest is his view that, because so many parents were killed during the Crusades, society had trouble dealing with all the homeless orphans who became delinquent. How best to resolve the problem? Ship them out to kill the Moslems, for the sake of Christianity!

Slater, John G. (20th Century)

Slater, in *Bertrand Russell* (1994), quotes Russell's definitive answer about immortality: "I believe that when I die I shall rot, and nothing of my ego will survive." Slater found that Russell saw much that was good in Christianity, particularly the central place of "love" in Christian teaching. He considered "worship" and "acquiescence" of value but not if interpreted as involving supernaturalism.

Slater, Thomas (1820–1900)

Slater was an English lecturer, for many years an advocate of secularism and cooperation. He was on the town council of Bury and lived at Leicester. The circuit he was given by the National Secular Society was Lancashire, Yorkshire, the Midlands, and Tyneside, and he became one of the popular speakers in the north of England. Slater had charge of the Secularist Bookstore at Leicester at the time of his death. {BDF; RAT; RSR}

Slattery, J. R. (20th Century)
Slattery wrote *State Grants and Church Graft* (c. 1915). {GS}

SLAVERY

> • Some slaves told me a sure way to keep the dogs from ketching you. They said if you put red pepper and turpentine in your shoes, they can't run you, 'cause they can't scent you.
>
> –Jean-Claude Baker in *Josephine*,
> quoting John Crawford in *Bullwhip Days*
> that Southern whites hunted runaway slaves with dogs

"Slavery" to most Americans is a reference to the South, the Civil War, and the fact that John Rolfe in 1619 had written that "a dutchman of war…sold us twenty Negars."

But Herodotus had described how Aesop, a legendary Greek fabulist, was a slave who lived in Samos and was eventually set free by his master. Yale University's David Brian Davis among others has pointed out that Portugal was importing slaves from sub-Saharan Africa in the 1440s. African kings and merchants from the Senegambia region had sold large numbers of slaves to Portuguese, Spanish, Italian, Dutch, English, French, Swedish, Danish, German, American, Cuban, and Brazilian traders, and representatives of the various religions—Muslims, Catholics, Protestants, Jews, New Christians, even Moravians and for a time Quakers—did not object.

From the mid-16th until the 19th century, Europeans shipped as many as 12,000,000 African slaves, purchased from their African captors, across the Atlantic. Arab slavers took millions more to the Middle East. Serfdom was abolished by the tsar of Russia in 1861.

As to why slavery succeeded, Hugh Thomas's *The Slave Trade: The Story of the Atlantic Slave Trade, 1440-1870* (1998) and Robin Blackburn's *The Making of New World Slavery: From the Baroque to the Modern, 1492-1800* (1998) document that a major reason was greed. The late African American scholar Nathan Huggins illustrated this when he wrote

The racial wrong was lost on African merchants, who saw themselves as selling people other than their own. The distinctions of tribe were more real to them than race, a concept that was yet to be refined by nineteenth- and twentieth-century Western rationalists. The most famous of the former slave-trading houses in Senegal was on Gorée Island. Visitors can see where millions passed through after being branded like cattle, with each European company having its distinctive mark. "The value of a woman," according to the seventy-four year-old guide Joseph Ndiaye, "was fixed according to the fullness of her breasts. Men were weighed to insure that they met the minimum requirement of 120 pounds. After being weighed, the men were appraised by their age and origin, with certain ethnic groups prized for their hardiness or as supposedly prolific breeders. The Yoruba, for example, were prized as 'stallions.' " Although in 1996 *Le Monde* in Paris cited a French Jesuit's asserting that "only 200 to 500 slaves a year" were sold in Gorée, the Senegalese Government and scholars countered with archives from the French port of Nantes that showed more than 103,000 slaves had been traded in that one port alone between 1763 and 1775. The first slaves were taken from Gorée in 1536, and the trade continued at least until 1848.

Except for the brotherhood-of-man-under-the-fatherhood-of-God idea, slavery as a practice was not denounced by Jesus nor Paul nor any Father of the Church, although slavery was common in the Roman world (and in one frontier-war the Romans took 100,000 captives). The Church did not condemn slavery until the abolitionist sentiment of recent times, and St. Augustine expressly defended slavery, states McCabe, "as a divinely ordered social arrangement, and there is nothing in the writings of the other Fathers to suggest that he differed from them." Augustine even wrote that there is "no crime in the eyes of God," although he was not writing specifically about slavery. In the last centuries of the Republic, slaves probably were twice as numerous as free workers. One estimate had it that the ratio was thirty to one. Zeno included slaves in his principle that all men were born equal, and Epicurus was "conspicuous among Greek philosophers for his kindness to slaves, according to Lecky. Epicurus, in fact, welcomed slaves to his table.

Slavery was justified by the Bible and was good for blacks, said a first-term Republican from Jasper, Alabama, in a 1996 speech prepared for a Senate debate over his proposal to fly the Confederate battle flag atop the state's Capitol. *Leviticus 25:44*, he quoted, says, "You may acquire male and female slaves from the pagan nations that are around you." Furthermore, *I Timothy 61* states that slaves should "regard their own masters as worthy of all honor." Continuing, Alabama State Senator Charles Davidson said, "The incidence of abuse, rape, broken homes, and murder are one hundred times greater, today, in the housing projects than they ever were on the slave plantations in the Old South. . . . The truth is that nowhere on the face of the earth, in all of time, were servants better treated or better loved than they were in the Old South by white, black, Hispanic, and Indian slave owners."

McCabe's *Rationalist Encyclopedia* contains a thorough discussion of slavery, one that is extraordinarily caustic about the Church's role. "The Slave Trade and the Jews," by David Brion Davis in *The New York Review of Books* (22 December 1994), is a thoroughly documented study of the subject. Davis writes that black slavery was taken for granted by Catholics, Muslims, Lutherans, Huguenots, Calvinists, Anglicans, and Jews alike. He adds, "The participants in the Atlantic slave system included Arabs, Berbers, scores of African ethnic groups, Italians, Portuguese, Spaniards, Dutch, Jews, Germans, Swedes, French, English, Danes, white Americans, Native Americans, and even thousands of New World blacks who had been emancipated or were descended from freed slaves but who then became slaveholding farmers or planters themselves."

Historian Ira Berlin, in *Many Thousands Gone: The First Two Centuries of Slavery in North America* (1998), details four distinct regional types of slavery—the type in the North (the mid-Atlantic and New England colonies or states); the Chesapeake (Virginia and Maryland); the Carolina low country; and the lower Mississippi valley (principally Louisiana). The earliest people of African origin arrived before the 17th century in English North America and were not from traditional African societies. In the 17th century those who arrived often had Spanish or Portuguese surnames and had been exposed to Christianity. In the 18th century the "plantation generations" usually came from societies in the African interior. Between 1803 and 1808 some 35,000 arrived. It was north of the Carolinas, Berlin wrote, that Americans' tradition of classifying people with any known African ancestray as "black" first began. (David Brion Davis, "A Big Business," *The New York Review of Books*, 11 June 1998; *The Economist*, 31 December 1999; Howard French, *The New York Times*, 6 March 1998; George M. Fredrickson, "Of Human Bondage," *The New York Times Book Review*, 4 October 1998) {RE}

Sleeper, John F. (19th Century)

Sleeper, a freethinker, wrote *The Mythologic Christ* (1881). {GS}

Slenker, Elizabeth "Elmina" Drake (1827–1908)

Slenker was daughter of a Quaker whose congregation in La Grange, New York, frowned upon freethinking. She wrote essays critical of the Bible in the *Boston Intelligencer* and wrote four novels with freethinking overtones. With Lillian and Moses Harman, she worked on a free-love journal, *Lucifer, the Light-Bearer*, which advocated using contraceptive devices, for which she developed a sex survey, anticipating the Kinsey Reports. Agents of Anthony Comstock's Society for the Suppression of Vice arrested her, and in a trial Slenker refused to swear on the Bible. Exonerated, she continued her efforts to disperse information concerning sexual education. From 1892 to 1893, she edited from Snowville, Virginia, *Little Freethinker*. {BDF; EU, William F. Ryan; PUT; WWS}

Sloan, John (1871–1951)

Sloan, who was in the forefront of the American realist tradition in painting, was a naturalistic humanist. Among his works are "McSorley's "Bar" and "Wake of the Ferry." He is also known for his nudes. Sloan's painting owes its distinction to a natural interest in human beings, whose life he portrayed with a directness often verging on satire. He was equally gifted as an etcher. {CL}

Sloan, Richard P. (20th Century)

Sloan wrote a lead article in *Lancet*, "Religion, Spirituality, and Medicine," in which he cautioned physicians not to prescribe religion as medicine. He is an associate professor in the Department of Psychiatry at the College of Physicians and Surgeons, Columbia University. He is also chief of the Department of Behavioral Medicine at the New York State Psychiatric Institute and Director of the Behavioral Medicine Program at Columbia Presbyteran Medical Center in New York.

Sloan was a featured speaker in San Antonio at the 1999 national Convention of the Freedom From Religion Foundation.

SLOVAK HUMANISTS

The Prometheus Society, which is an associated member of the International Humanist and Ethical Union (IHEU), publishes *Prometheus–Spravodai Spolocnosti Prometheus* in Slovak, with English summaries quarterly, at Pavovicova 14, 82 1 08 Bratislava, Slovakia.

In a 1995 Berlin conference arranged by the IHEU, Alexander Rehak told of the 1990 founding of the Prometheus Society, which cooperates with the World Union of Freethinkers. He detailed the problems of unemployment, heavy taxation, decline in living standards, growth of crime, drug use, and development of a mafia, all of which contribute to the difficulty of developing humanism in Slovakia. The influence of Catholicism is increasing, he stated, but Slovak humanists continue to campaign for separation of church and state and for an open and tolerant society. J. Celko and A. Rehak are activists in the Slovakian humanist movement. {Ladislav Hubenák, "Secular Humanism in Slovakia," *New Humanist*, December 1995}

Smart, John Jamieson Carswell (1920–)

Smart, son of the Astronomer Royal in England, came to Australia in 1950 as a practicing Christian. Upon studying philosophy, however, he came to reject religion. An atheist and a philosopher, he is known for his espousal of the identity theory of mind: that mental processes are identical to physical processes in the brain. He developed the thesis, in *Philosophy of Scientific Realism* (1963) that the theories of science are the best account that we can have of the nature of reality and the entities that constitute it. A number of other Australian philosophers, including David Armstrong, support the view. After his professorship of philosophy at the University of Adelaide he was professor of philosophy at the Australian National University. A defender of materialism, Smart also wrote *Outline of a System of Utilitarian Ethics* (1961), *Between Science and Philosophy* (1968), *Ethics, Persuasion, and Truth* (1984), *Metaphysics and Morality* (1987), *Our Place in the Universe* (1989), and *Atheism and Theism* (1996).

In 1996, he was elected a Humanist Laureate by the Council for Secular Humanism's International Academy of Humanism. He is a contributing editor on *Philo* and a signer of Humanist Manifesto 2000. {CA; SWW}

Smeal, Eleanor (20th Century)

Smeal, a past president of the National Organization for Women and co-founder and president of the Feminist Majority, was awarded the 1994 Freethought Heroine Award and gave the keynote speech at the 17th annual Freedom From Religious Foundation convention in Madison, Wisconsin. In 1993 she was chosen as "the fourth most influential woman in the United States." Smeal wrote *Why and How Women Will Elect the Next President* (1984).

Smetana, Augustin (1814–1851)

Smetana taught philosophy at the University of Prague but was deposed because of his liberal views. He then severed his connection with the Catholic Church in 1850 and became one of the leading Bohemian freethinkers. {PUT; RAT}

Smiles, Samuel (1812–1904)

Smiles, a freethinker and an individualist, wrote *Self-Help* (1859). {TRI}

Smith, Adam (1723–1790)

Smith, the eminent Scottish economist who became known as the prophet of modern capitalism, while at Oxford was reprimanded for reading David Hume's allegedly atheistic "Treatise of Human Nature." His own "The Theory of Moral Sentiments" (1759) became known for its extensive and lengthy argument which utilized three of his favorite words: sympathy, duty, and propriety. David Garrick, the actor and Smith's fellow club member, called Smith's conversation "flabby" (although Smith's biographer, Ian Simpson Ross, in *The Life of Adam Smith* (1995), ascribes the remark to Oliver Goldsmith). The critic Peter Ackroyd has written that Smith's voice was harsh, that he was easily embarrassed, that he was prone to stammer. He dictated to an amanuensis, because he could wield a pen only with great difficulty and "his own handwriting remained clumsy, large, and almost childish."

Smith traveled on the Continent from 1764 to 1766 as tutor to the Duke of Buccleuch. While in France he met some of the Physiocrats and began to write *An Inquiry into the Nature and Causes of the Wealth of Nations*, which was finally published in 1776. Led by the rationalist current of the century and influenced by Hume and others, he came to believe that in a laissez-faire economy the impulse of self-interest would bring about the public welfare. His pragmatism, as well as the leaven of ethical content and social insight in his thought, differentiates him from the rigidity of David Ricardo and the school of early 19th-century utilitarianism. His *Essays on Philosophical Subjects* (1795) appeared posthumously. In 1751, as Professor of Moral Philosophy in Glasgow University, he upset the orthodox by abandoning the Sunday class on Christian Evidences, and he petitioned the Senatus to be allowed to be relieved of the duty of opening his class with prayer. When permission was not given, word got out that the compulsory prayers were "thought to savour strongly of natural religion." Smith was well-founded in rationalism before he met Voltaire and other French freethinkers, and his *Theory of Moral Sentiments* (1759) contained a positive hostility to certain ecclesiastical forms of theistic optimism.

Smith's *Wealth of Nations*, states Robertson, "is so completely naturalistic that only the habit of taking the Christian religion for granted could make men miss seeing that its account of the conditions of the rise of new cults applied to that in its origin no less than to the rise of any of its sects. As a whole, the argument might form part of Gibbon's fifteenth chapter. And even allowing for the slowness of the average believer to see the application of a general sociological law to his own system, there must be inferred a great change in the intellectual climate of Scottish life before we can account for Smith's general popularity at home as well as abroad after his handling of 'enthusiasm and superstition' in the *Wealth of Nations*. The fact stands out that the two most eminent thinkers in Scotland in the latter half of the eighteenth century [Hume and Smith] were non-Christians, and that their most intellectual associates were in general sympathy with them." According to McCabe, Smith "was cautious about expressing his Deism, and shortly before he died he had sixteen volumes of his manuscripts burned."

In the 20th Century, particularly with the fall of communism, Smith's laissez-faire views have been misappropriated by some. Nobel laureate James Buchanan, a conservative economist at George Mason University, has written that Smith "was certainly not an extreme advocate of laissez faire." Journalist Sylvia Nasar adds that, far from being a conservative, Smith was a philosopher who inspired French revolutionaries, American suffragettes, and Japanese political reformers. He had the fundamental view that charity alone, while essential, cannot suffice to create prosperity: "It is not from the benevolence of the butcher, the brewer, or the baker that we can expect our dinner, but from their regard to their own interest." He was a person who thumbed his nose not only at the church but also at university and empire. His "invisible hand," often misinterpreted as implying divine approval of greed, was a reference to the fact that self-interest, not charitable impulses, motivated butchers, brewers and bakers to feed society. Every individual, he concluded, is "led by an invisible hand to . . . without intending it, without knowing it, advance the interest of society."

Ian Ross in *The Life of Adam Smith* (1995) tells how Smith claimed he had been kidnapped by gypsies at the age of three, a story entirely untrue. Ross also tells how Smith was visited by a certain noble lady "as he was going to breakfast, and falling into discourse, Mr. Smith took a piece of bread and butter, which, after he had rolled it round and round, he put into the teapot and pour'd water upon it: some time after he poured it into a cup, and when he had tasted it, he said it was the worst tea he had ever met with." Samuel Johnson, who disliked Smith's skepticism, called him a dull dog. In Hume's words, Smith was affected by "indolence and love of solitude." Smith's mother, who lived into her nineties and was a person in his words who "loved me more than any other person ever did or ever will love me," was the only woman in his life. Smith died six years after his mother's death of "chronic obstruction" of the bowels. {CE; JMR; JMRH; RAT; RE; *The Economist*, 11 November 1995; TRI; TYD}

Smith, A. D. Howell (20th Century)

Smith, a freethinker, wrote *In Search of the Real Bible* (1943). {GS}

Smith, Alfred E. (20th Century)

In 1954, Smith, a marketing consultatnt, was a counselor for the

Humanist Fellowship of Boston, a group affiliated with the American Humanist Association.

Smith, Arthur H. (1845–1932)

Smith, in *Chinese Characteristics* (1892), wrote, "There never was on this earth a body of educated and cultured men so thoroughly agnostic and atheistic as the mass of Confucian scholars." {TYD}

Smith, Carol (20th Century)

Smith, a member in Milwaukee of Atheists and Agnostics of Wisconsin, has written for the group's newsletter, *Humanist Quest*, and for *Secular Nation*. A regional director of the Council for Secular Humanism, she edits "Humanist Quest" on the Internet.

E-mail: <csmith@omnifest.uwm.edu>. On the Web: <humanist1@juno.com>.

Smith, Charles (1887–1964)

Smith from 1926 to 1964 edited the *Truth Seeker*, a rationalist journal in New York City. He is one of the foremost American atheist leaders of the century. With W. L. Oliphant he authored the *Debate on Atheism*, a debate in the Shawnee, Oklahoma, Church of Christ (1929). Although Smith wrote extensively, little has been written about him. Gordon Stein, however, has compiled many stories about Smith's having gone from Harvard to Vladivostok to Little Rock. In Arkansas, when he was found guilty of distributing obscene, slanderous, or scurrilous literature, he insisted upon working off the $25 fine by serving time in jail at $1 per day—he then commenced a hunger strike and was hospitalized. When the case was dismissed, he again opened his bookstore and again was found guilty, this time being sentenced to ninety days in jail. Smith's intent was to "nullify the anti-atheist laws of this country," and Arkansas suffered from publicity in newspapers which painted it as some sort of primitive backwater. In 1925 he and Freeman Hopwood founded the American Association for the Advancement of Atheism (the 4A's), which soon had over 3000 members and chapters on twenty college campuses. The 4A's conducted an Ingersoll Forum and brought suit to stop such things as the employment of chaplains in Congress and the reading of the Ten Commandments in schools. In 1930 he purchased the *Truth Seeker*, which in the 1950s was converted into a small monthly. Smith had an antipathy to Jews and non-whites which (perhaps because of the influence of his assistant, Woolsey Teller) became increasingly apparent in the journal. "In a sense," Stein has written of the famed libertarian, "Smith was born at the wrong time in history. He would have done much better if he had lived as an adult during the last half of the 19th century, when freethought was in its Golden Age."

Negative about the subject of humanism, Smith wrote as follows:

> That is Humanism: an all-over-the-lot gush-out that hopes to cure the world's ills by a flood of sentimentalism. There is only one kind of "atheist plus" or "atheist minus"; it depends on whether he believes in full steam ahead for atheism or in rumbling along at slow-freight speed. This is an age of specialization, and the atheist, as an atheist, is a specialist, with one objective in mind: the smashing of the God superstition.
>
> What he may do apart from this, in matters of social interest, is a matter of individual taste. The atheist can be just as interested in art, music, architecture, literature, drama, finer human relations, public health, new housing, and the making of a better noodle soup as the most enthusiastic "Humanist," but he does not have to become a cultist to do it, nor splatter his "humanitarianism" onto public billboards.
>
> It is precisely this sentimental rhapsodizing that causes my distaste for Humanism, which, apart from its desire to do good, is burdened by wishy-washy methods and an old-maid's outlook.

Smith's Manhattan office was a dark, seemingly disorganized clutter of books, magazines, and papers. Just before his death from a heart attack, he responded to a request, after the present author's visit, for an updating of his views on humanism:

> *Sensism*, to be published about the end of next month (1956), may contain usable material [about atheistic humanism].

In that book, he restated his lifelong acceptance of the logic of and need for atheism. {EU, Gordon Stein; WAS, 26 March 1956}

Smith, Colin (20th Century)

Smith, a journalist, was a leader in 1910 of the Rationalist Association of New South Wales in Australia.

Smith, David (20th Century)

Smith, while a student at Pennsylvania State University, was one of the founding members of Campus Freethought Alliance. {*International Humanist News*, December 1996}

Smith, Edward Garstin (20th Century)

Smith wrote *The Life and Reminiscences of Robert G. Ingersoll* (1904). {GS}

Smith, Francis Barrymore (1932–)

Smith, a professor of history at the Australian National University, wrote a study, "Religion and Freethought in Melbourne, 1870–1890," along with other research articles on freethought and secularism. {FUK}

Smith, Frank (1907–)

An attorney now retired as a professor at George Washington University, Smith is author of *Robert G. Ingersoll, A Life* (1989), the only biography of Ingersoll which is in print. He has written for *Truth Seeker* and *Free Inquiry*.

Smith, George Augustus (Born 1861)

Smith, a freethinker and member of the North London Ethical Society, wrote "A Humanist Religion" (1920) and *Little Essays in Religion* (1926). From 1917 to 1923 he edited the society's publication, *The Humanist*. {GS; RAT}

Smith, George H. (1949–)

Smith is the author of *Atheism: The Case Against God* (1979) and is president of Signature Books. In the work, he holds that the belief in God is irrational to the point of absurdity and that this irrationality, when manifested in specific religions such as Christianity, is quite harmful. "Belief in God is irrational to the point of absurdity," he declared, "and . . . this irrationality, when manifested in specific religions such as Christianity, is extremely harmful."

Smith is on the Council for Secular Humanism's Committee for the Scientific Examination of Religion. He also is author of *Atheism, Ayn Rand, and Other Heresies* (1991). {CA; E; *Free Inquiry*, Spring, 1981}

Smith, Gerritt (1797–1874)

Smith was an American reformer who was graduated by Hamilton College. Elected to Congress in 1850, he served one session. Though of a wealthy slave-holding family, he largely devoted his fortune to the anti-slavery cause, perhaps spending over £8,000,000. Smith is thought to have aided John Brown in planning the Harper's Ferry raid. In religion, originally a Presbyterian, Smith came to give up all dogmas and wrote the deistic *Religion of Reason* (1864) and *Nature the Base of a Free Theology* (1867). McCabe states that although Smith dissented from all the churches, he tried to establish an independent church, a sort of Theistic Ethical Society, and preached for it. {BDF; CE; JM; RAT; RE}

Smith, Glenn (Died 1999)

Smith, who served in World War II and was a steam locomotive engineer in the Rocky Mountains, was a member of the Freedom From Religion Foundation's Denver chapter. He was a plaintiff and witness in a lawsuit to have the Ten Commandments monument removed from the Colorado State Capitol grounds. His objecting to the Ten Commandments was partly based on his having some Native American ancestors.

Smith, Goldwin (1823–1910)

From 1858 to 1866 Smith was Regius professor of modern history at Oxford. He had conveyed to America a message of British sympathy with the north in 1864, and been warmly received. When his father committed suicide in 1867, Smith migrated to the United States and was appointed honorary professor of English constitutional history at Cornell. The corrupt public life of the United States drove him in 1871 to Canada, where he lived for the rest of his life. Smith's rationalist views are found in *Guesses at the Riddle of Existence* (1897), *Lines of Religious Inquiry* (1904), and *No Refuge but in Truth* (1908). In the latter book he entirely rejected the Christian creed, while pleading for its ideals. He left open the question of a future life, and he accepted "some moral power" but thought it "impossible that we should ever have direct proof through human observation and reasoning of the existence of Deity." {RAT}

Smith, Goldwin (1823–1910)

Smith was an English educator, historian, and journalist. While a student at Oxford, he helped execute reforms at the university and in 1858 became professor of modern history there. Smith became known for his ardently democratic, strongly anti-imperialistic, and antimilitaristic outlook. In 1868, "driven to America by a domestic tragedy" according to McCabe, Smith became a professor of English literature and constitutional history at Cornell University. In *No Refuge But the Truth*, Smith rejects Christianity, is skeptical about a future life, and thinks it "impossible that we should ever have direct proof through human observation and reasoning of the existence of deity." {CE; JM}

Smith, Grafton Elliot [Sir] (1871–1937)

An Australian by birth, Smith came to England and became professor of anatomy at London University (1919–1936). He is said to have been so thorough that he examined 20,000 bodies in Egypt. His *Evolution of Man* (1924) is materialistic. An agnostic, Smith was an Honorary Associate of the Rationalist Press Association. {JM; RE}

Smith, Harold D. (20th Century)

A freethinker, Smith wrote *A Criticism of Christian Dogma* (1964). {GS}

Smith, Harry Clark (1887–1975)

Smith, an Iowa grain dealer, played third base for the Portland farm team of Chicago Cubs in the 1910s and had a .400 batting average. During the winters, he was employed to oversee snowbound grain elevators in Saskatchewan. Wounded in the Battle of Verdun while fighting in World War I with the 33rd Infantry Division, Smith was hospitalized at the Buckingham Palace barracks and received the Purple Heart medal. When Queen Mary visited the American soldiers and inquired where he had come from, she was surprised at his mention of Canada and said, "Why, then, you're one of *my* boys!" Smith's father, Spencer, had indeed been born in Aylmer, Ontario, Canada, and Smith had lived and worked grain elevators in several Canadian provinces. Again wounded by a German plane which swooped down over the trenches, Smith later received a second Purple Heart.

The founder of the first American Legion chapter in Iowa, Smith was secretary of the Masonic Lodge in Minburn, a town of 328. In the 1930s or 1940s he showed a booklet concerning the Essenes, possibly one obtained through Masonic Lodge channels, to his son, Warren Allen Smith. Although the large number of Dead Sea Scrolls were not discovered until 1947, and it was not until the 1950s that Edmund Wilson's and Duncan Howlett's books were published about the small Jewish religious order that developed in the 2nd century B.C.E., Smith was not the only person who considered the possibility that Jesus may have been an Essene or was influenced by Essenes.

Smith was a nominal Methodist, but his son in retrospect thinks his father was basically a deistic Mason. A stickler for accuracy, Smith would have been infuriarted to know that Iowa's Greene County Clerk would one day list his middle name as Carl on the death certificate.

Ruth Marion Miles Smith (1891-1975), his wife, was a South Dakota equestrienne who fell in love with the baseball player. It was her second marriage—in 1921 she was one of the first divorcées in a state which had only entered the union in 1889. The daughter of a successful homesteader, she was a nominal Methodist, but she could not explain who John or Charles Wesley were and had no idea whatsoever how the concept of trinitarianism came about. When a Christian minister solemnly told her that she would not be with her son in Heaven because he had become a Unitarian, she for the first time questioned what religion was all about. For her, the Order of Eastern Star was a kind of religion, particularly because, at the auction bridge games members played while socializing, she was able to serve her popular popcorn balls with the secret ingredient she would reveal to no one: vinegar. {WAS}

Smith, Henry Dorr (20th Century)

Smith, a freethinker, wrote "Thoughts—Read and Digest Them" (19–?). {GS}

Smith, Homer W. (20th Century)

Smith's *Man and His Gods* (1952) is a masterful study in freethought.

Smith, I. B. (19th Century)

A freethinker, Smith wrote *The Speculative Dictionary* (1835). {GS}

Smith, Isaac (19th Century)

In the 1830s, Smith was president of the United Moral and Philosophical Society in England. {GS}

Smith, Jack Clifford (1916–1996)

Smith, a journalist and author, was a reporter for the Bakersfield *Californian*, the Honolulu *Advertiser*, the Los Angeles *Daily News*, the Los Angeles *Herald-Express*, and the Los Angeles *Daily News*. A newspaper columnist, he wrote books including *Three Coins in the Birdbath* (1965); *Smith on Wry* (1970), and *Alive in La La Land* (1989).

According to Atheist Celebrities on the internet, Smith was a non-believer.

Smith, John Maynard: See entry for John Maynard Smith.

Smith, Joseph (1805-1844)

The American Mormon leader who founded the Church of Jesus Christ of the Latter-Day Saints, Joseph Smith, said that in 1827 he found golden tablets God had sent to him. In 1829 upon translating the tablets, he wrote *The Book of Mormon*. In his short life, he took thirty-three wives, including a mother and a daughter, the widow of his brother, and two sisters. Eleven were between 14 and 20 years of age, nine were 21 to 30, eight were in his own peer group (31 to 40), two were 41 to 50, and three were 51 or over. Counting Emma, his first wife, he may have had an additional eight wives. After his death, almost all of the wives married again, many having already been in secular marriages—thus, in addition to polygamy (plural wives) the early Mormons practiced polyandry (plural husbands). According to Todd Compton's *In Sacred Loneliness: The Plural Wives of Joseph Smith* (1998), the wives experienced depression, despair, anxiety, helplessness, abandonment, and anger by fulfilling "their sacred duty." (See entry for Church of Jesus Christ of Latter-Day Saints.) {Vern L. Bullough, "What God Has Joined," *Free Inquiry*, Summer 1998}

Smith, Karl (20th Century)

Smith is Secretary of the Thomas Paine Pennsylvania Memorial Committee (Box 242, Pocopson, PA 19366).

Smith, Katie Kehm (1868–1895)
Smith, born in Indiana, moved to Iowa and became a prominent freethought lecturer when sixteen. When she moved to Oregon in 1893, she and her husband organized the First Secular Church of Portland. Three to four hundred attended regularly, and she became secretary of the Oregon State Secular Union. {PUT}

Smith, Kay Nolte (1932–1993)
Smith was an actor, teacher, atheist, and award-winning novelist. She and her husband ran a summer theater in Michigan, where they performed at dinner theaters and co-produced Ayn Rand's "Penthouse Legend" (known as "Night of January 16"). She wrote *Watcher* (1980), a novel which won the Edgar Allen Poe award, followed by *Mindspell* (1983), *Country of the Heart* (1988), and *Tale of the Wind* (1991). In 1983 she spoke to the Freedom From Religion Foundation convention in Peoria, Illinois. {WWS}

Smith, Kenneth J. (20th Century)
A leader of the Ethical Culture Society in Philadelphia, Smith signed Humanist Manifesto II. {HM2; EU, Howard B. Radest}

Smith, L. Windsor (20th Century)
In Little Falls, New York, from 1833 to 1834, Smith published *Mohawk Liberal.* {FUS}

Smith, Lee (20th Century)
A freethinker, Smith wrote "The Truth Shall Make You Mad" (c. 1960). {GS}

Smith, Lila (20th Century)
Smith is on the Executive Board of the Humanist Society of Metropolitan New York.

Smith, Lillian (1897–1966)
Author of *Strange Fruit* (1944), Smith depicted the love of a white boy for a black girl, an unusual topic for its time. A social critic and a social worker in George, the Florida-born novelist supported the use of violence as a means to its ends. Her *Killers of the Dream* (1949) included the following:

> Belief in Some One's right to punish you is the fate of all children in Judaic-Christian culture. But nowhere else, perhaps, have the rich seedbeds of Western homes found such a growing climate for guilt as is produced in the South by the combination of a warm moist evangelism and racial segregation.
>
> {TYD}

Smith, Michael (1932-)
A Nobel Prize winner in Chemistry in 1993, Smith has achievements which include research in nucleic acid and nucletide chemistry and biochemistry using in-vitro mutagenesis gene expression. English-born, he lives in Vancouver.

In an autobiographical sketch, Smith said, "My only prizes from the Sunday School were 'for attendance,' so I presume my atheism, which developed when I left home to attend university, although latent, was discernible." {CA}

Smith, Morton (1915–1991)
Smith, a professor emeritus of ancient history at Columbia University, was for many years a member of the Council for Democratic and Secular Humanism's Committee for the Scientific Examination of Religion. In 1958 he discovered a previously unknown fragment of the *Gospel of Mark,* and in 1973 his *The Secret Gospel* theorized that early Christian groups owed some of their appeal to the magical rituals which played an important part, as well as their licentiousness. His *Jesus the Magician* (1978) developed the theory that some of Jesus's charisma is attributable to his ability to use "magic." With R. Joseph Hoffmann, Smith has edited *What the Bible Really Says.*

Smith, Noel W. (20th Century)
A professor of psychology at the State University of New York at Plattsburgh, Smith specializes in the history of psychology and current theoretical systems of psychology. He is author of *An Analysis of Ice Age Art: Its Psychology and Belief System* (1992) and *Greek and Interbehavioral Psychology* (1993).

Smith, Orlando J. (1842–1908)
Smith, a freethinker, wrote *A Short View of Great Questions* (1899) and *The Agreement Between Science and Religion* (1906). {GS}

Smith, Peter R. (20th Century)
Smith was born in London and studied nuclear engineering at the University of London. In 1982, he became a consulting engineer at Niagara Falls in Canada and has worked for the Polysar Rubber Corporation since 1987. From 1991–1993, Smith was the first Vice President of the Humanist Association of Canada (HAC), and in 1993 he became President.

Smith is a writer and researcher for Ontario Skeptics and is a member of the United Kingdom's National Secular Society as well as of the Rationalist Press Association. In 1994 at the Toronto conference of the Coalition for Secular Humanism, Atheism, and Freethought (CSHAFT), Smith was one of the leaders.

Smith, Preservèd (1880–1941)
Smith, a famed Harvard, Williams, Amherst, and Cornell University historian, once wrote a book on theophagy (god-eating), leading quite a few individuals to research the origins of the Christian communion service, which involves symbolically drinking the blood and eating the flesh of God. That 1922 work was entitled *A Short History of Christian Theophagy.*

Among his comments about religion are the following:

> There can be no doubt that the Bible . . . became a stumbling-block in the path of progress, scientific, social, and even moral. It was quoted against Copernicus as it was against Darwin.
>
> The common assumption, hardly disputed even now, that the moral influence of the Bible has been wholly good, and that all that is needed to improve our society is to "spread the gospel," is not borne out by a candid study of history.

Smith, known as an expert on Erasmus, was an editor of the *Journal of Modern Medicine* and of the *American Historical Review* (1936–1941). He was the author of *The Life and Letters of Martin Luther* (1911); *The Age of the Reformation* (1920); and *Erasmus—A Study of His Life, Ideals, and Place In History* (1923).

Preservèd Smith was the father of humanist editor and historian Priscilla Robertson. {CE; TYD}

Smith, Quentin (1952–)
Smith, a supporter of Internet Infidels, is professor of philosophy at Western Michigan University. He has published five books, including *Theism, Atheism, and Big Bang Cosmology* (1993), which he coauthored with William Lane Craig.

In 1996 at the Atheist Alliance convention in Minneapolis, Minnesota, he addressed the group. Smith holds that "[t]he claim that the beginning of the universe has a cause conflicts with current scientific theory," concluding that "scientific cosmology is not only *not* supported by any theistic theory, it is actually logically inconsistent with theism." For *Philo,* of which he is a contributing editor,

Smith wrote "Why Stephen Hawking's Cosmology Precludes a Creator" (Spring-Summer 1998). {*Free Inquiry*, Spring 1998}

Smith, Robert (20th Century)

A recording artist with the band called The Cure, Smith stated during a press conference in 1992, "I don't believe in God. I wish I did." {CA}

Smith, Robin (20th Century)

Smith, who lives in Northumberland, England, participated in the 1996 Humanist World Congress in Mexico City. His interests include assisting individuals with physical disabilities.

Smith, Samantha (1972–1985)

When Smith as a youngster asked Soviet Premier Yuri Andropov if the USSR and USA were going to get into a nuclear war, he replied to her letter by inviting her to visit Moscow. She then became an American celebrity, turning attention to the need for the two nations to improve international relations. After her early death on a foggy Maine night when a small commuter plane crashed, killing everyone on board, Smith was depicted on a commemorative postage stamp. The Soviets named an asteroid after her. Samantha had attended Unitarian Universalist churches in Houston and Augusta. {EG; UU}

Smith, Thomas Southwood (1788–1861)

A nonconformist minister who abandoned Christianity and took up medicine, Smith became prominent in medical and social reform. He was Bentham's physician and, when he dissected Bentham's body (as directed in his will in the interest of science), Smith said that he shared Bentham's atheistic humanitarianism. {RAT; RE}

Smith, Thomas Vernor (1890–1964)

Smith wrote *The Democratic Way of Life* (1926), *Beyond Conscience* (1934), *Creative Skeptics* (1934), and *The Ethics of Compromise* (1959). {EW}

Smith, Warren Allen (1921–):

Smith, a roué and sybarite currently living in New York City's Greenwich Village, was Methodist Church pianist in his home town of Minburn, Iowa (population 328). When a teenager, he loudly disputed the existence of the Holy Ghost with visiting Methodist Bishop Oxnam. The discussion had taken place at a church supper where, after the bishop had just given a homily about miracles, everyone was shocked upon seeing ripples atop the bishop's bowl of oyster stew. The hushed speculation was that the oysters were somehow alive and were . . . *miraculously* . . . swimming. When it was determined that, no, the disturbance had been caused by Smith's pumping air through a rubber palpitator hidden under the tablecloth, the teenager was not so miraculously removed from the speaker's table, to the bishop's obvious relief.

Upon leaving home for college, Smith left the dour Methodist group and experienced, in succession, nihilism, agnosticism, deism, Emersonianism, pantheism, transcendentalism, Unitarian humanism of the John H. Dietrich-Curtis W. Reese vintage, freethought, rationalism, naturalistic humanism, and humanistic naturalism.

Drafted into the Army and wearing identifying "dog tags" which listed his religion as "None," Acting First Sergeant Smith led his company onto Omaha Beach in 1944, experienced being an atheist in a foxhole (with an absentee ballot he voted for Norman Thomas of the Socialist Party), and was chief clerk in Headquarters Oise of the Adjutant General's office in the Little Red Schoolhouse in Reims, General Eisenhower's headquarters, in which Nazi General Alfred Jodl eventually signed the surrender.

Upon returning home unwounded, Smith used the "G.I. Bill of Rights"—a government payment for furthering soldiers' education—to study philosophy with logician Charner Perry and metaphysician Charles Hartshorne at the University of Chicago. At the University of Northern Iowa, he majored in English and in 1948 founded the first Humanist Club on any college campus. For the Des Moines Unitarians in the 1940s, he wrote "Song of the Pantheist," an atonal selection which was performed by their choir and organist.

Hitchhiking from Iowa to New York City in 1949, he became a graduate student at Columbia University, studying with Corliss Lamont, George Counts, Paul Tillich, and Allen Walker Read, among others. The present study is partly an extension of his research with Lionel Trilling, sponsor of his M. A. thesis and chairman at that time of the English Department. At Columbia, Smith founded a second Humanist Club and secured John Dewey as the first dues-paying ($1.) member.

In addition to teaching high school English in New York City and New Canaan, Connecticut, he founded with Fernando Vargas a major Manhattan independent recording studio (Variety Sound Corporation, 1961–1990), working with such showbiz figures as Harold Prince, Robert Whitehead, Arthur Miller, John Guare, and Tito Puente.

He was book review editor of *The Humanist* during the editorships of Edwin Wilson and Priscilla Robertson; wrote a syndicated column, "Manhattan Scene," in West Indian and Caribbean newspapers; and was on the board of directors of the American Humanist Association (voting in 1957 for Margaret Sanger to become Humanist of the Year).

Smith, who is an editorial associate for *Free Inquiry* and has written for *The American Rationalist*, *Gay and Lesbian Humanist* (United Kingdom), *The Freethinker* (England), *Humanist in Canada*, *New Humanist* (London), and *Skeptical Inquirer*, is continuously seen in the company of Allen Windsor, with whose pen he has written widely.

In 1989, upon the death of Vargas, his companion of forty years, Smith arranged a secular humanist memorial at their recording studio, playing Vargas's own recording of Liza Minnelli's first demonstration record as well as music by Marvin Hamlisch, Paul Simon, Barry Manilow, David Amram, Celia Cruz, and other notables whom Vargas had recorded. Vargas was the first member of the Secular Humanist Society of New York, which was initially formed and which first met in the recording studio. Smith was the group's president and edited its newsletter, *Pique*. Upon his own death, Smith has directed that his ashes be comingled with some of Vargas's that he saved and are to be buried at the Smith family plot in Waukee, Iowa.

In 1994, Smith helped arrange the founding in San José, Costa Rica, of *Asociación Iberoamericana Ético Humanista* (ASIBEHU), a Spanish-speaking humanist group for Central and South America which is on the net at <http://idt.net/~wasm/asibehu>.

Smith signed Humanist Manifesto II as well as Humanist Manifesto 2000 (for which he suggested part of the wording in Part VII, "Society should not deny homosexuals, bisexuals, or transgendered and transsexuals equal rights"); is a member of the Black Hawk County (Iowa) Unitarian congregation, which he finds inconvenient to attend; of the Rationalist Press Association in England; the Hume Society; has been a director of the Bertrand Russell Society since 1967; was a founding member of the Voltaire Society of America, a founding member and treasurer of Stonewall Riot Veterans; and has headed Mensa's oldest interest group, the M[ensa] Investment Club (1967 to date).

In 1991 after purchasing a Macintosh computer with a font

called "symbol," he was the first to end correspondence with the salutation "humanist♥ically."

In 1998, after years of Taslima Nasrin's hiding in Sweden as well as elsewhere in Europe, and upon her return to Bangladesh despite the fatwa on her head, Smith was a key person in publicizing her plight. Their friendship began when they were introduced at a conference of humanists in Mexico—"I tell friends I found her hiding in a Mexican cave, for that is where the restaurant was"—and he visited her after she was forced to flee for asylum in Sweden, following which she hid with him for a time in New York City.

In 1999 he finally finished the present project—*Who's Who in Hell*—that he had started five decades earlier. The phrase which he had used to describe his outlook had been "Unitarian humanist," but as the result of his extensive research he now describes his outlook as that of a "humanistic naturalist."

Smith's home page on the World Wide Web is autobiographical: <http://idt.net/~wasm>. His e-mail address: <wasm@idt.net>. (See entries for John Cowley, Martin L. Grant, Greenwich Village Humanist Club, Humanist Club, Humanistic Naturalism, Horace Kallen, *Pique*, Augustus Reccord, Margaret Sanger, Jun Sczesnoczkawasm, Lionel Trilling, Fernando Vargas, and Allen Windsor.) {CL; FD; HM2; HNS; LEE}

Smith, Warren Sylvester (1919–)

Smith is the author of a scholarly book, *The London Heretics, 1870–1914* (1968), which contains highly original research concerning non-Christians and non-theists.

Smith, Wilford B. (1884–1939)

"I was born bare-footed in a thorny world with a tin spoon in my teeth and a bottle of paregoric close by," Smith wrote. "I was born in a log house, chained with mud, built at the brink of an alkali pond, where the bumblebee bumbed and the woodpeckers pecked and the straddle bugs straddled around, where the sage hen sang her complaint to the moon and the whippoorwill called to its mate thru the gloom, where the briars grew hard by the door and the centipede crawled on the floor; I slept to the trill of the nightingale and awoke at dawn as the tarantula tickled me under the chin with his hairy legs."

After being admitted to the bar in 1905, Smith started *Plain Talk*, a newspaper which was suppressed three times and, finally, "thousands of copies were burned by order of the Chief of Police." In Dallas he began a monthly, *The Pitchfork*, which was satirical in nature. Ana ardent foe of Prohibition, he staged a mock funeral for John Barleycorn when the nation went "dry." He attacked a Baptist preacher, J. Frank Norris, for his anti-Semitism and anti-Catholicism. Although he remained a believer, he was greatly influenced by freethought, especially in its attacks on puritan repression. {*Freethought History #15*, 1995}

Smith, William Benjamin (1850–1934)

After teaching mathematics or physics at various universities, Smith taught philosophy at Tulane. He wrote *Der vorchristliche Jesus* (1906) and *Ecce Deus* (1912), in the latter of which he denied the historicity of Jesus. {RAT; RE}

Smith, William Henry (1808–1872)

Smith wrote chiefly for *Blackwood's Magazine*, although he completed some plays and poems and novels. Smith had discarded orthodoxy in his early years, was a friend of Mill, and admired Comte. {RAT}

Smith, William Robertson (1846–1894)

Smith was deposed from his chair at the Free Church College of Aberdeen, and from the ministry, because of articles he wrote for the 1881 *Encyclopaedia Britannica*. He then taught Arabic at Cambridge. Smith wrote *Prophets of Israel* (1882) and *The Religion of the Semites* (1889), showing that he rejected supernaturalism but was a theist. {RAT}

Smoker, Barbara (20th Century)

Smoker, a "cradle Catholic," is author of a British Rationalist Association pamphlet, "Humanism." In the late 1960s she was editor of the South Place Ethical Society's magazine. A Vice President of the Gay and Lesbian Humanist Association (GALHA) and a president of the National Secular Society for over twenty years until she was defeated by Daniel O'Hara for the office in 1996, she is a vigorous proponent of liberal and militant causes. She is an honorary associate of the New Zealand Association of Rationalists and Humanists.

Smoker has officiated at more than four hundred secular humanist funerals. Many know her as the publisher of "anti-Xmas" greeting cards, known as Heretic Cards. She wrote *Good God!* (1977), a collection of satirical verse. {FUK; WWS}

Smolin, Lee (20th Century)

A physicist and cosmologist, Smolin in *The Life of the Cosmos* argues that universes have the capacity to "reproduce," just as organisms do. In *Lingua Franca* (July 1997), Smolin was asked about the metaphysical implications of his research. He replied, "As a friend of mine says, the whole show of the universe is so extraordinary that the absence of God is God enough." (See entry for Cosmology.) {CA}

Smyth, Brettena Bridgetena (1842–1898)

A lapsed Roman Catholic, Smyth was an Australian feminist, family planner, and secularist. One of the early campaigners for the Australian Women's Suffrage Society, she favored birth control, which was a radical proposal in the 1880s. She wrote *Diseases Incidental to Women* (1895) and a book on birth control, *The Limitation of Offspring.* {SWW}

SNAKE WORSHIP

Snakes have played a role in many religions, adored as a regenerative power by some, and by others a god of evil, as a god of good, as Christ (by the Gnostics), as a phallic deity, as a solar deity, and as a god of death. The snake also has served as a symbol of Satan and many deities, including Apollo and the Egyptian god Ra. *The Columbia Encyclopedia* details the extent to which the snake has been considered divine in Ancient Greece, in Buddhism, in Siam, and elsewhere. David L. Kimbrough, in *Taking Up Serpents: Snake Handlers of Eastern Kentucky* (1995), has detailed what he learned in more than three hundred Holiness churches in the Appalachian area. {CE; Joe Nickell, "Snake Handling," *Free Inquiry*, Spring 1996}

Snedeker, Caroline Dale (20th Century)

Snedeker wrote *The Town of the Fearless* (1931). {GS}

Snell, Henry [of Plumstead] (1865–1945)

A British statesman, Snell was a poorly-educated peasant boy who rose to a high position in the political world, on the Labor side. For some years he was chairman of the London County Council and Deputy Leader for his party in the House of Lords. In 1898 he was appointed lecturer to the English Union of Ethical Societies, and in 1905 general secretary of the Union. An agnostic from youth, Snell eventually became President of the Rationalist Press Association. {FUK; JM; RAT; RE}

Snider, Kellie (20th Century)

Snider, a self-described "recovering Fundamentalist," has spoken about "The Trauma of Dogma" to the North Texas Church of Freethought. {Freethought Observer, November-December 1996}

Snitzer, Herb (20th Century)

Snitzer, a professional photographer, is on the board of directors of the Humanist Association: St. Petersburg (HASP). In their newsletter, "Arts and Issues" (July 1996), he wrote that art has a grand and noble history "too often ignored and certainly not understood." He added in 1995 that humanists must recognized that art "is one of the foundations upon which we know that we are a very special species, similar to but so different form other life forms and that we as artists have a responsibility to continue making art because it is a wonderful thing to do. We also have a special responsibility to those who will inhabit this planet in 2095, and through our art (and science) those distant relatives will know us and their own world more deeply, lovingly, and intelligently."

Snoilsky, Karl Johan Gustav (1841–1903)

Count Snoilsky was a Swedish poet who displayed his freethought in works published under the name of "Sventröst." He translated Goethe's ballads into Swedish and followed the German poet's pantheistic philosophy. {BDF; RAT; RE}

Snowden, James Keighley (20th Century)

Snowden, a freethinker, wrote *Myth and Legend in the Bible* (1915). {GS}

Snyder, Carl (1869–1946)

Snyder, a writer on science, specialized in the popular presentation of science in the press and in books which had a wide circulation. In *New Conceptions of Science* (1903), Snyder wrote that "the influence of the Christian Church was evil, incomparably evil." {JM; RAT; RE}

Snyder, Eric (20th Century)

Snyder has been president of the University of Minnesota Atheists and Humanists (UMAH). He edited their newsletter, *The Heretic*, which commenced in 1994 and in 1995 he edits their *Minnesota Atheists*.

Snyder, Louis Leo (1907–)

Snyder, a German-born historian, was foreign correspondent from Germany of the Paris edition of the *New York Herald-Tribune* (1928–1931). He taught at New York's City College and the University of Cologne. Among his many books are *The Age of Reason* (1955), *The Dreyfus Affair* (1971), and *Historical Guide to World War II* (1982). {GS}

Sobczak, A. H. (20th Century)

Sobczak, the editor of *Fade Away and Radiate*, a bi-monthly publication of opinion and science fiction, is a freethinker who writes for *Truth Seeker*.

SOCIAL CONTRACT

A major work of Jean-Jacques Rousseau, *The Social Contract* (1762) states that governmental organization should be based on the general will of a society and should conform to the nature of human beings. The majority in a government, he held, had a right to banish resistant minorities. {DCL}

SOCIALISM

Socialism has been defined as any of various economic and political theories advocating collective or governmental ownership and administration of the means of production and distribution of goods. Many adherents call it a humanistic outlook in political science. Nicolas Walter (*New Humanist*, September 1996) has categorized some of the socialists who are theists:

> Keir Hardie, Lansbury, Clement Attlee, Stafford Cripps, Harold Wilson, Smith

and listedsocialists who are not theists:

> Ramsay MacDonald, Harold Laski, Hugh Gaitskell, Aneurin Bevan, Michael Foot, Neil Kinnock

SOCIETY AGAINST RELIGION

Society Against Religion (PO Box 76, Commack, NY 11725) is "a national organization dedicated to creating an open forum of discussion in order to educate the populace to the dangers of religion and hold religion itself answerable to its crimes against humanity," according to its founder and president Vincent Bruzzese. Its board members include Maire Caruso, Scott Cziepl, and Adam Turner. E-mail: <nogod1@ol.com>.

SOCIETY FOR HUMANISM AND INDEPENDENT ETHICS

The Society for Humanism and Independent Ethics (SHIE) was established in Poland in 1991. The group opposes anti-democratic and anti-pluralistic activities; the subordination of government policies to any ideology; nationalism, racism, and all forms of discrimination; threats to the use of reason and science; and restrictions on human rights. The group cooperates in publishing and distributing a journal, *Bez Dogmatu* (Without a Dogma). The headquarters is in Warsaw, but branches are found in other Polish cities, according to Jan Wolenski, a professor in the Institute of Philosophy at Jagiellonian University in Kraków.

SOCIETY FOR HUMANISTIC JUDAISM

The Society for Humanistic Judaism (28611 West Twelve Mile Road, Farmington Hills, Michigan 48334) was established in 1969 to create a humanistic alternative to Jewish life. It sponsors the journal *Humanistic Judaism* and the newsletter *Humanorah*. The 1997 officers were Rick Naimark, President; Rabbi Sherwin T. Wine, Rabbinic Advisor; M. Bonnie Cousens, Executive Director; Stacie Fine, Community development Director; Yehuda Bauer and Albert Memmi, Honorary Presidents of the International Federation; and Yaakov Malkin and Rabbi Sherwin T. Wine, deans of the International Institute. The Society is affiliated with the International Federation of Secular Humanistic Jews. Vern Bullough has said the Society's members observe many of the Jewish traditions and customs but are atheists. They hold that humanism, even secular humanism, is tainted with Christianity, and they want to keep a Jewish cultural identity.

"My own experience with [a] secular humanist Jewish organization [the Vancouver Peretz Institute]" is that "Jewish secularism shows no interest in promoting humanism—at least not in British Columbia." Expressing this view Herb Fears, past president of the British Columbia Humanist Association, added that the Institute's president, Sol Jackman, never worked with his organization to join in a humanist alliance. Chicago's Sherwin Wine, asked at the Institute about the matter of co-operation between humanist groups, was evasive. And Fears concluded, "It would seem that the secular Jews who adopt the humanist nomenclature are, by their isolationism, merely subscribing to the conceit of the 'chosen ones' held by their religious counterparts. Not exactly a productive way of achieving common goals considering how few we secularists are, methinks." On the Web: <http://www.shj.org/>. (See entry for Sherwin T. Wine.) {*Humanist in Canada*, Spring 1998; *International Humanist News*, December 1997}

SOCIETY FOR LOGIC AND REASON

The Society for Logic and Reason is at Oregon State University in Corvallis. Daisy Peel is its President. On the Web:
<http://osu.orst.edu/groups/slr>.

SOCIETY OF EVANGELICAL AGNOSTICS

In the early 1980s, the Society of Evangelical Agnostics (SEA) was formed and gained around twelve hundred members. Bill Young in *12 Years at SEA* described the group, which was dissolved in 1987.

SOCIETY OF FRIENDS: See entry for Quakers.

SOCIETY OF HUMANIST PHILOSOPHERS

The Society of Humanist Philosophers publishes *Philo*, a magazine for analyzing humanist ethics, naturalism, and arguments for and against theism.

Lewis Vaughan is its Executive Editor. On the Web: <http://www.secularhumanism.org".

SOCIETY OF SEPARATIONISTS: See entry for Madalyn Murray O'Hair.

SOCINIANS

Socinians were adherents of a sixteenth-century Italian sect of humanists which held unitarian views, including a denial of the divinity of Jesus. They were influenced by Servetus's criticisms of the Trinity. Forced to flee the Inquisition they first sought refuge in Switzerland. Those who survived persecution took shelter in a tolerant Poland, where their views of doctrinal reform found acceptance in the Reformed Church of Poland (1565). From a center at Raków (Racovia), they maintained a press that sent books and emissaries throughout western Europe. The *Racovian Catechism* (1605) was a compilation of doctrines which had no little influence on doctrinal thinking among Protestants. It based its teachings strictly on Scripture and adhered to the Apostles' rather than the Nicene and Athanasian creeds. Socinians taught non-resistance, refused to partake in war, and would not hold serfs.

In 1638 when the Raków center was broken up, the school abolished, and their press destroyed, members found themselves harshly suppressed and in 1658 the whole sect was banished on pain of death. Those who chose not to conform to the Catholic Church went into exile, some to Transylvania and some to East Prussia and Holland. They influenced the Dutch by their liberalizing views and by the middle of the eighteenth century lost their separate identity, having become absorbed in the general religious life of the country. Their influence was long felt in the growth of rationalistic views. Through their contact in Holland with Dissenters from England or liberal Anglicans, their views were transplanted into England, where they became the most important single source of Unitarianism,, according to Earl M. Wilbur, once the President of the Pacific Unitarian School for the Ministry in Berkeley, California. {ER}

Socinus, Faustus (Sozzini, Fausto) (1539–1604)

"Jesus saved men not by dying for them, but by setting an example for them to follow," wrote Socinus, leader of the Polish Socinian or Unitarian movement. He arrived in Poland in 1579, and under his leadership Kraków became an intellectual center of religious liberalism. Socinus, who had left the Roman Catholic Church because he denied the Trinity, knew that anti-trinitarianism had occurred as early as 1546 in Poland.

In 1585, the first official Unitarian press, Rakow, began. Socinus traveled over half of Europe teaching his creed, and he was bitterly persecuted everywhere. In 1591, a mob destroyed the Socinian Church in Kraków, and by 1638 the movement had been seriously damaged because of severe Roman Catholic persecution. By 1658, the Polish Diet banished Socinians. {BDF; CE; EU, Paul H. Beattie; JM; RE; U}

Socinus, Laelius (or **Sozzini, Lelio**) (1525–1562)

Laelius, the uncle of Faustus Socinus, was an Italian religious reformer. Escaping the Inquisition, and attracted by the writings of Martin Luther, he moved to the Swiss cantons and became good friends with Heinrich Bullinger and John Calvin. When the anti-trinitarian Servetus was burned in 1553, however, Socinus became an anti-trinitarian also and developed a friendship with Bernardino Ochino, who had been vicar general of the Capuchins but who had turned to belief in justification by faith alone, becoming an independent Protestant. In 1598, he fled from Kraków when an enraged mob of Christians tried to kill him.

Socinus's writings, left to his nephew Faustus, became the basis for the anti-trinitarian religious movement known as Socinianism. {CE; JM; RE; U}

Socolow, A. Walter (1907–1994)

Socolow, a lay leader in the Jewish Reconstructionist movement, was a founder of the Reconstructionist Rabbinical College in Wyncote, Pennsylvania. He had been president of the Board of Jewish Education of Greater New York (1968–1971) and president of the Society for the Advancement of Judaism (1949–1952). Reconstructionism redefines Judaism not only as a religion but also as a civilization that includes language, customs, and culture. (See entry for Reconstructionism.)

Socrates (469?–399 B.C.E.)

One of the ancient humanists whom today's secular humanists often cite as a forerunner of today's humanism, Socrates used a dialogue or dialectic that required students to question the implications of their answers. Virtue, he said, is knowledge of one's true self. Upon being tried for religious heresies and corrupting the morals of youth, he endured a martyr-death because he would not recant and believed that "the unexamined life is not worth living." His confession that he knew nothing but the fact of his own ignorance continues to inspire many skeptics. There is the story that he was so involved with helping his fellow citizens seek wisdom that he neglected his own affairs (changing his undergarments)—whether or not it is true, it does make one of the wisest men of all time understandably "human."

According to Robertson, Socrates started all inquiries from a position of professed ignorance, thereby repudiating all dogmatics. Although he had no real faith in the current religion, he never explicitly dissented. Tales abound that an example of "Socratic love" was his own love for Alcibiades, the general who was said to have knocked the penises off many statues but who was so powerful that he could not be punished for such.

Sophisticates who check on people's competence by inquiring if they have read any of Socrates's work know very well that he left no writings, that most of what we know about him came from the writings of his most famous pupil, Plato, who may not have been an objective reporter. Whether Plato intends "Socrates" in his dialogues "to be merely the mouthpiece of his own opinions" is unknown, Bertrand Russell has written. In addition to being a philosopher, Plato was an imaginative writer of great genius and charm and Russell has questions about Plato's being an objective historian. But Plato was at the trial of Socrates, and the main facts are not in doubt, says Russell: "The prosecution was based upon the charge that 'Socrates is an evildoer and a curious person, searching into things under the earth and above the heavens, and making the worse appear the better cause, and teaching all this to others.' The real ground of hostility to him was, almost certainly, that he was supposed to be connected with the aristocratic party; most of his pupils belonged to this faction, and some, in positions of power, had proved themselves very pernicious. But this ground could not be made evident on account of the amnesty. He was found guilty by the majority, and it was then open to him, by Athenian law, to propose some lesser penalty than death. The judges had to choose, if they found the accused guilty, between the penalty demands by the prosecution and that suggested by the defense. It was therefore in the interest of Socrates to suggest a substantial penalty, which the court might have accepted as adequate. He, however, proposed a fine of thirty *minae*, for which some of his friends (including Plato) were willing to go surety. This was so small a punishment that the court was annoyed, and condemned him to death by a larger majority than that which had found him guilty. Undoubtedly he foresaw this result. It is clear that he had no wish to avoid the death penalty by concessions which might seem to acknowledge his guilt." According to Bury, the real reason the judges found Socrates guilty was that he needed to be punished for his association, through Pericles and his group, with the cultured anti-democrats.

Upon being condemned, Socrates bathed to avoid "giving the women the trouble of washing me when I am dead." Surrounded by his students and friends, he asked his friend Crito to bring the glass of poison which he had been sentenced to drink. Crito, hesitating, suggested that there was really no hurry, that there was plenty of time. To which Socrates responded, "I believe that I should gain nothing by drinking the poison a little later—I should only make myself ridiculous in my own eyes if I clung to life and hugged it when it had no more to offer. Come, do as I say and don't make difficulties." Whereupon he drank it down with no sign of revulsion, then reprimanded those who were crying. "Calm yourselves and be brave." As related by Plato and paraphrased by Slater and Solomita, "When he began to feel numb he lay down and the coldness spread from his legs upward. When it reached his heart, he'd been told, he would die. He covered himself in a sheet from head to toe. Just before the end he pulled the sheet from his face and said, 'Crito, we ought to offer a cock to Asclepius. See to it and don't forget.' Asclepius was the god of healing. The offering was Socrates's gesture of thanks for being cured of life."

As is the case with his teacher Socrates, Plato is not really a humanist in the contemporary meaning of that word, but humanistic elements are seen in both of their philosophies. McCabe says of Socrates that he "must, however, be classed as a great freethinker inasmuch as he rejected the current religion and urged men to reason out the problems of life. On this pretext he was condemned to death, but the real ground was political." (See selection by I. G. Kidd on Socrates in the *Encyclopedia of Philosophy*, Vol. 7.) {CE; CL; Lee Eisler, *The Quotable Bertrand Russell*; ER; JM; JMR; JMRH; PUT; RE; TYD; TYD}

SOCRATES

An associate member organization of the International Humanist and Ethical Union (IHEU), Socrates is the foundation for professorships in humanist studies. It is at Nieuwegracht 69A, 3512 LG Utrecht, Netherlands.

Soddy, Frederick (1877–1956)

Soddy, an English chemist, worked under Lord Rutherford at McGill University and with Sir William Ramsay at the University of London. He taught at the University of Glasgow, the University of Aberdeen, and at Oxford. His special research was in radioactivity. With others he discovered a relationship between radioactive elements and the parent compound, which led to his theory of isotopes. For this work he won the 1921 Nobel Prize in Chemistry. An advocate of technocracy and of the social credit movement, Soddy wrote several books setting forth his political and economic views. In *Science and Life* (1920), Soddy wrote that "the ancient creeds are working an infinitude of harm in the world" and called upon everyone to disown them. Although vaguely theistic, Soddy held that the universe is eternal, not created, and "the task of controlling it is man's, not God's." (See entry for Elenchus, Socrates's method of refutation.) {JM; RE; TRI}

Söderberg, Hjalmar (1869–1941)

Söderberg, a Swedish novelist, was a non-theist. (See entry for Scandinavian Unbelievers.)

Södergran, Edith (1892–1923)

Södergran, a Swedo-Finnish poet, conveyed a Nietzschean, anti-Christian view of life in *Septemberlyran* (September's Lyre, 1918) and *Rosenaltaret* (The Rose Altar, 1919). *Landet som icke är* (The Country That Is Not There, 1925) was published posthumously, and the collection of poetry reveals in its title her view of any afterlife. {EU, Faith Ingwersen}

SODOMY

The term "sodomy" is an antiquated euphemism which in *Genesis* 19:1 referrs to the alleged inhospitality of the biblical inhabitants in Sodom. In the Hebrew bible, Sodom and Gomorrah were two cities said to have been destroyed by God. Religionists and the U.S. Supreme Court find that sodomy is criminal, defining it as performing oral sex, receiving oral, or indulging in anal intercourse. The term was coined by a Christian reformer and zealous hermit, Peter Damian, during the eleventh century.

"Sodomy is a custom in all of Tuscany," Bernardino of Siena lamented in the 1420s. Michael Rocke, in *Forbidden Friendships: Homosexuality and Male Culture in Renaissance Florence* (1996), found that a special magistracy—the *Ufficiali di Notte*, or Officers of the Night—found that in Florence some 17,000 people were incriminated at least once and nearly 3000 were convicted of sodomy in the 1400s, this in a city of only 40,000 people.

In Florence, however, no subculture of homosexuals existed, such as was found in the Molly-houses of 18th-century England where sex for effeminate adult males centered, or as is found today worldwide. Mary McCarthy in *The Stones of Florence* wrote, "In the Florentine *quattrocento*, the well-turned, sturdy male leg and buttock cased in the tight hose of the day is always painted with a flourish; this leg is seen from all angles, in profile, in demi-profile, full on, and perhaps most often, from the rear or slightly turned, so that the beauty of the calf can be shown."

In the sixteenth and seventeenth centuries, Geneva, Switzerland, put to death twenty-eight men convicted of homosexual acts. Holland executed sixty in 1730-1731. The British hanged 105 between 1703 and 1829. At one time all fifty states, Puerto Rico, and the District of Columbia forbade anal sex as well as fellatio and cunninlingus: lawmakers usually cited *Leviticus* (which book also contains an injunction to establish slavery). In the 1960s, two men risked being jailed if they were caught dancing in a public place. Often this led to psychiatric examination, possible incarceration in a mental hospital, and publishing of their names in the local newspapers.

Mark D. Jordan, in *The Invention of Sodomy in Christian Theology* (1997), wrote, "To invent sodomy was to invent a pure essence of the erotic without a connection to reproduction. It was to isolate the erotic in its pure state, where it could be described in frightening colors and condemned without concession. 'Sodomy' is a name not for a kind of human behavior, but for a failure of theologians. 'Sodomy' is the nervous refusal of theologians to understand how pleasure can survive the preaching of the Gospel." Jordan, a professor in the Medieval Institute, University of Notre Dame, has written essays on medieval medicine, ancient rhetoric, gay film, and the paradoxes of histories of philosophy."

Christian theology must abandon its past condemnation of sodomy as a capital crime, according to Mark D. Jordan, a professor in the Medieval Institute at Indiana's University of Notre Dame. His *The Invention of Sodomy in Christian Theology* (1997) not only declares that he is gay but also that to be openly gay and a practicing Catholic need not be a paradox.

In 1999, Florida has a law in which "any unnatural and lascivious act"—from oral sex to toe sucking, apparently—can result in sixty days in jail, although mothers breast-feeding are exempt. Oral-genital contact in Michigan carries a penalty of up to fifteen years' hard time in jail. In Massachusetts, an "abominable and detestable crime against nature, either with mankind or with a beast, shall be punished by imprisonment in the state prison for not more than twenty years." In five states—Arkansas, Oklahoma, Missouri, Kansas, and Texas—gays and lesbians are exclusively targeted. In Texas in 1999 a bill was introduced in the state legislature to prohibit the state from placing children in adoptive or foster homes if those homes are the likely sites of "deviate sexual intercourse," which includes oral, anal, or "object-assisted acts," presumably involving everything from dildos to cigars.

Oral sex (both giving and receiving) is illegal in twenty states for heterosexuals and twenty-seven states for homosexuals, according to Peter Mc Williams's *Ain't Nobody's Business If You Do*. What usually is not clear in the public press, when an individual is accused of sodomy, is whether receiving or giving oral sex, or anal sex, is involved. (See entries for bugger and fucking. Also, for a discussion of the distaste for, as well as the popularity of, sodomy—as discussed in the Bible, in Colonial America, and elsewhere—see *Queering the Renaissance* [1994], edited by Jonathan Goldberg.) {Debbie Nathan, "Sodomy for the Masses," *The Nation*, 19 April 1999}

Soeters, G. C. (20th Century)

A Dutch humanist leader, Soeters has written for *Free Inquiry*. {*Free Inquiry*, Winter, 1986-1987}

Sohl, Jerry (20th Century)

Sohl, who has been a metropolitan newspaper editor, music critic, and drama critic, is a charter member of the Science Fiction and Fantasy Writers of America. He was a staff writer for and wrote the first segment of the "Star Trek" television series. Also, he wrote for "Alfred Hitchcock Presents" and "The New Breed" in addition to writing for "The Twilight Zone," "G. E. Theater," "Naked City," "The Outer Limits," and "The Invaders." Sohl is a life member of Writers Guild of America, West, Inc., the Authors Guild, and Authors League of America.

A Unitarian, he has written books which have been printed in seventeen foreign languages. His titles include *The Spun Sugar Hole*, *The Lemon Eaters*, *The Resurrection of Frank Borchard*, *Costigan's Needle*, *The Altered Ego*, *Point Ultimate*, and *The Transcendent Man*. Television segments of his have been shown in all countries where television is broadcast. For 20th Century Fox he wrote "Twelve Hours to Kill," and for American International he wrote one of Boris Karloff's last films, "Die, Monster, Die."

E-mail: <76232.2761@compuserve.com>.

Sohlman, Per August Ferdinand (1824–1874)

Sohlman was a Swedish publicist who edited the *Aftonbladet* of Stockholm in 1857. Sohlman was a distinguished Liberal politician. {BDF}

Sokolov, Alexej (20th Century)

In 1996, Sokolov along with Professor L. Yakovleva organized a Centre for Inquiry in Russia. The centre monitors activities of clerical groups and paranormal phenomena.

He has named difficulties for the humanist movement in Russia: (a) the impoverishment of the people, the decrease of the middle class, the concern for one's daily bread reduce the concern about culture; (b) the indifference to the fate of the secular culture of the plutocratic state, because an egotistical and short-sighted oligarchy in power cannot derive the short-term benefits from it; and (3) the spread of ideology and values in society that emphasize above all profit and commercial success also make an unfavorable atmosphere for the development of secular culture. Sokolov is a philosopher at Moscow State University. in Russia. {International Humanist News, *November 1996*}

Solarin, Tai (1922–1994)

Solarin was a social critic who wrote for the *Guardian* and *Punch* in Nigeria. Once sacked as a headmaster of a boys' school for refusing to march the students to church on Sunday and to start the day with hymns and prayers, he founded in 1956 the Mayflower School, which is fully residential and has several thousand students, 800 of whom are girls. Upon his and his wife's retirement, Mayflower continued to run as a secular school, the only one in Nigeria which teaches neither the Christian nor the Muslim religion. He became chairman of the People's Bank of Nigeria.

An atheist, Solarin wrote *Towards Nigeria's Moral Self-Government* (1959). Just before his death, Solarin said of his junior school, "It is special because of its secularity. We go all out to tackle the problems of life instead of spending several hours of the week explaining the significance of the deity. We have been able to debunk the conservative idea that morality is only realized from the menu of religion. We have been visited by no end of employers who openly declare they would opt for our finished products any time as compared with the products of religious schools. They are convinced our graduates work harder. And we know that, too. Our products are more sure of themselves. They are more ready to take risks. Education in self-reliance has positive results."

Solarin has said that Robert Green Ingersoll was a major influence upon his thinking, that "he gave me the courage to stand on my feet and declare my stand on issues where for years I was too afraid to air my doubts. He tore off the dingy curtains across my mind's eye, and let me stand, unafraid, to wend my way through life."

As for philosophy, Solarin said, "Humanism and atheism develop in the mind of man, not for a special breed of *Homo sapiens*, but for humanity, just as the wheel has been invented, not for whatever race invented it, but for humans everywhere. Whatever are branded 'un-African,' 'for the Aryan races' are epithets for cheating." {*Free Inquiry*, Spring, 1992 and Winter 1993}

Solbrig, Otto Thomas (20th Century)

In 1998, Argentine-born Solbrig, the Bussey Professor of Biology at Harvard University, was awarded the International Prize for Biology at a Tokyo ceremony attended by the emperor and empress of Japan. The prize, considered the most prestigious in the field, was for his work on the biology of biodiversity. He is a member of the First Unitarian Universalist Church of Harvard, Massachusetts, where he serves as the chair of the social responsibility committee. (*World*, March-April 1999)

Solheim, Rolf (20th Century)

Solheim, who is Ceremonies Secretary of the Norwegian Human Etisk-Forbund, has developed a flexible guideline for humanist funeral counseling. At the 1995 European Humanist Federation/European Humanist Professionals meeting in Oslo, he conducted a workshop on the topic.

SOLIPSISM

In philosophy, solipsism is the theory that the self is the only thing that can be known and verified, that the self is the only reality and that the only person existing in the universe is one's self.

Were we, Flew has pointed out, to concede (following Descartes, Locke, and others) "that the immediate objects of sense experience are mind-dependent (ideas, impressions, sense data, etc.), it is indeed questionable whether we can argue validly to the existence or nature of a mind-independent external world. Modern critics have, however, challenged this initial premise as misuse of terms; similarly objections have been raised against the use of 'I' which eliminates its normal contrasts. And Wittgenstein's private language argument, if valid, in effect makes solipsism incompatible with our having a language to express it." {AF}

Solomon, Abraham (20th Century)

Solomon was instrumental in the formation of the Rationalist Youth League in Bombay in 1934. When he signed Humanist Manifesto II, Solomon was coordinator of the Indian Secular Society. To the Norwegian editor of *Human-Etisk*, Levi Fragell, Solomon told of his high praise for the family planning project being carried out in India by Dr. Indumati Parikh. But, he added, "Mother Teresa has been a disaster for India." Although Dr. Parikh remained discreetly quiet on the subject, her associates nodded they were entirely in agreement. Solomon is President of the Indian Secular Society and has drafted "A Declaration of Human Values."

In 1998 at the congress of the International Humanist and Ethical Union held in Mumbai, Solomon was presented with a distinguished service award and was noted as having founded the IHEU Endowment Fund. He told the congress of having heard someone advise years ago that "one who is born must die, so why not die for a good cause," to which he decided that "one who is born must live, so why not live for a good cause." {HM2; International Humanist News, *December 1998*}

Solomon, Anita (Mrs. Herbert E. Solomon): See entry for Anita Weschler.

Solomon, Carol (20th Century)

An ethical humanist, Solomon attended the 1996 international conference of humanists in Mexico City. Her e-mail: <rsolomon@hcfa.gov>.

Solomon, Herbert E. (1902–1995)

Solomon, a freethinker, was a financial analyst in New York City. He was a fiercely independent thinker, one whose mental acuity always led him to be quietly amused by the claims of believers.

Solomon, Robert C. (20th Century)

Solomon is author of *Entertaining Ideas: Popular Philosophical Essays, 1970–1990* (1992) and *A Passion for Wisdom* (1997). "Philosophy, I have always believed," he writes in the preface, "is one of the most enjoyable activities in the world, comparable to food and sex in both its urgency and intensity." A humanist as well as a humorist, he includes such observations as the following:

> Illiteracy is an established part of American life—not just the obvious tragic illiteracy of those who cannot read at all, but of the more subtle tragic illiteracy of those who can read quite well and read all the time—sports-page headlines, the front page of the *National Enquirer* at the checkout stand, food-can labels, billboards, and an occasional *People* magazine photo option. But they don't read books. Or any article that requires a turn of the page (as in, "cont'd, p. xxx.").

Solomon, Ronald (20th Century)

Solomon is an ethical humanist who attended the 1996 international conference of humanists in Mexico City. Solomon's e-mail: <rsolomon@hcfa.gov>.

Solon (c. 639–559 B.C.E.)

Although Solon, the eminent Athenian statesman, lawgiver, and reformer, is not included by many freethought scholars, he is included in a listing by Stanley Charles W. Stokes of Australia. At a time of social stress in Athens, Solon was elected the chief Archon in 594 and he achieved humanistic goals in granting liberty to the Athenian citizens. The assembly was now opened to all freemen, the propertied classes became represented by a Council of Four Hundred, and Solon prepared the agenda for a popular assembly.

Although Solon endured much opposition, his reforms became the basis of the Athenian state and his introduction of a more humane law code replaced the prior code of Draco. {CE; "The Rational Calendar and Compendium," PO Box 189, Geebung, Queensland, 4034, Australia}

Soloviev, Vladimir Sergievitch (1853–1900)

A Russian philosopher who taught at Moscow and St. Petersburg, Soloviev was deposed for demanding the abolition of the death penalty at a time when the Tsar was using it liberally. In his *Crisis of Western Philosophy*, he followed Hegel. In his French work, *La Russie et l'église universelle* (1889), Soloviev was believed by some to have discarded all supernaturalism.

However, Alexei Gostev has called him a Christian believer, a philosopher of religion who helped turn Russian philosophical thought from positivism and naturalism to idealism and mysticism. (WAS, interview with Alexei Gostev, 1998) {RAT}

Somerby, Charles Pomeroy (19th Century)

Somerby was an American publisher who issued many freethought books. He was business manager of the *Truthseeker*. {BDF; FUS}

Somerset, Edward Adolphus (1804–1885)

Somerset, the 12th Duke of Saint Maur, was educated at Eton and Oxford. He sat as M.P. for Totnes in 1834–1835 and was Lord of the Treasury from 1835 to 1839. After being First Lord of the Admiralty, 1859–1866, Somerset startled the aristocratic world by a trenchant attack, *Christian Theology and Modern Scepticism* (1872), on orthodoxy. He also wrote on mathematics, monarchy, and democracy. {BDF}

Somerville, John (1905–1994)

Somerville, a philosopher and peace advocate, wrote books and plays on peace themes. During the years of the "cold war," he founded the International Philosophers for the Prevention of Nuclear Omnicide.

Somerville, Mary (1780–1872)

Somerville was a British educationist, the daughter of Admiral Sir W. G. Fairfax. The discovery of Neptune was ultimately based upon observations of hers, and she also won several gold medals for her work in geography. Somerville was an anti-ecclesiastical theist who never went to church and was once "publicly censured by name from the pulpit of York Cathedral."

One of the chief women's university colleges in Britain, Somerville Hall, bears her name, and there is a Somerville Scholarship at Oxford. In her *Personal Recollections* (1873), Somerville wrote that she was once "publicly censured by name from the pulpit of York Cathedral," and she said she had rejected Christianity early in life. {JM; PUT; RAT; RE; TRI; WWS}

Sommerfeld, Ernest (20th Century)

Sommerfeld, a former Unitarian minister, has been a leader at the Westchester Ethical Culture Society in New York.

Sommerhof, Gerd (20th Century)

A theoretical biologist and cognitive scientist, Sommerhof is a member of Trinity College, Cambridge. He founded and chairs the Cambridge University Humanist Workshop. Somerhof wrote *Life Brain and Consciousness* (1990).

Sommers, Christina Hoff (20th Century)

Sommers, an associate professor of philosophy at Clark University and the W. H. Brady Fellow at the American Enterprise Institute, is author of numerous articles on ethics, feminist philosophy, and moral education. For *Free Inquiry* (Winter 1997-1998), she wrote, "Where Have All the Good Deeds Gone?"

Sone, Robert (20th Century)

Sone was a signer of Humanist Manifesto II. {HM2}

Sonne, Niels Henry (20th Century)

Sonne, in *Liberal Kentucky* (1939), tells of the spread of deism in Kentucky. He traces the conflict between liberal and Calvinist forces, especially at Lexington's Transylvania University. {FUS; *Freethought History #14*, 1995}

Sontag, Susan (1933-)

Sontag, the critic and "new intellectual," may or may not have gone on record concerning her non-theism, but she wrote, "Religion is probably, after sex, the second oldest resource which human beings have available to them for blowing away their minds."

Sontarck, John (20th Century)

Sontarck, with Anne Nicol Gaylor and Annie Laurie Gaylor, founded the Freedom From Religion Foundation. (See entry for Freedom From Religion Foundation.)

SOORYAGATHA

A Malayalam monthly of the Kerala Rationalist Association, *Sooryagatha* is at P.B. 3517, T. D. Road, Kochi, Kerala 682 035, India.

Soos, Wolfgang (20th Century)

Soos is chairman of the Austrian freethinker group, *Freidenkerbund Österreichs*. (See entry for Austrian Freethinkers.)

Soper, Kate (20th Century)

Soper wrote *Humanism and Anti-Humanism* (1986).

SOPHISTS

Originally itinerant teachers who were paid for their lectures, the Greek Sophists in the 5th century B.C.E. taught the art of successful living. Protagoras was an early Sophist, and those who followed became known for their adroit, subtle, and allegedly often specious reasoning. Today, a sophist is one more interested in winning arguments through crafty rhetoric than in pursuing truth.

Sophists would contrast the law and convention with nature's eternal universally binding morality. According to Flew, this was "identified with some sort of hedonism (as by Antiphon) or 'the right of the stronger' (as by Callicies in Plato's *Gorgias* and Thrasymachus in the *Republic*). The contrast was to provide a basis for Cynic critiques of society, eventually finding a certain resolution in the Stoic concept of 'natural law.' " (See the *Encyclopedia of Philosophy*, Vol. 7.) {CE; DCL; AF; RE}

Sophocles (c 496–406 B.C.E.)

In his *Antigone* (c. 441 B.C.E.)., Sophocles states, "Many are the wonders of the world / And none so wonderful as Man." Lamont calls Sophocles a forerunner of contemporary naturalistic humanists. Robertson, however, states that although Sophocles dramatized the cruel consequences of Greek religion, he "never made any sign of being delivered from the ordinary Greek conceptions of deity, or gave any help to wise thought." Still, whereas Aeschylus emphasized the gods, the struggles of the gods, and destiny, "it is with man that Sophocles is concerned." His *Ajax, Oedipus and King* (c. 429 B.C.E.), and *Electra* represent the epitome of classical Greek drama. {CE; CL; JMR; JMRH; TYD}

Sorce, Carol (20th Century)

Sorce is vice president of the Humanists of New Jersey.

Sorel, Albert (1842–1906)

Sorel was a French historian and sociologist. In 1876 he became general secretary to the President of the Senate. His historical and political works (chiefly *L'Europe et la révolution française*, 8 volumes, 1885–1891), were numerous; and his *Châte de la Royauté* (2 volumes, 1885–1887) was crowned by the Academy. Sorel became a member of the French Academy and the Academy of Moral and Political Sciences. {RAT}

Sorel, Edward (1929–)

Sorel is a noted artist whose cartoons are familiar to readers of *The Nation*, *The New Yorker*, *American Heritage*, and *The Atlantic*. In 1988 he received the Page One award of the Newspaper Guild of New York for best editorial cartoon in magazines. His satiric drawings are noted for their wit and timeliness.

A free-lance artist since 1956, Sorel is author-illustrator of *Making the World Safe for Hypocrisy* (1972) and illustrator of *Gwendolyn the Miracle Hen* (1963), *Superpen* (1978), *The Zillionaire's Daughter* (1990), *Fine Encounters* (1994), and *Unauthorized Portraits* (1997). At the 1997 Freedom From Religion Foundation convention in Tampa, Florida, Sorel was one of the featured speakers. (See entry for George W. Lucas Jr.)

Sorley, William Ritchie (Born 1855)

Sorley taught philosophy at London University, Cardiff, Aberdeen, and Cambridge. He is a Fellow of the British Academy. Sorley edited Adamson's works (2 volumes, 1903) and wrote a number of volumes on philosophy, including *The Ethics of Naturalism* (1885). He rejected "revealed religion" in the *Hibbert Journal* (April, 1913). {RAT}

Soros, George (1930-)

Soros, a fund management executive who became one of the world's richest men, was born in Budapest. His prosperous Jewish parents arranged his escape from the Nazis by having him pose as the godson of a non-Jew. According to Celebrity Atheists online, Soros now is a non-believer.

In 1956 he came to the United States, where he became an arbitrage trader for F. M. Mayer (1956-1959), an analyst for Wertheim & Co. (1959-1963), vice president of Arnold and S. Bleichroeder (1963-1973), and CEO and CFO of Soros Fund Management (1973 to date). One of his funds, the Quantum Fund, grew rapidly as the result of daring speculations, and in 1979 a network of Soros Foundations, mainly in Eastern Europe, was established to advance opportunities in education and business. Soros reportedly gave, then lost, an estimated two billion dollars to Russia following the fall of the Soviet Union, in order to prop up its economy. {CA}

Sorrentino, Roger (1930-)

A retired New York teacher and a visiting teacher at Beijing Language and Culture University as well as Yan Shan University, Sorrentino found at the age of fifty-four that "my Roman Catholic faith totally collapsed." It took three years of psychological counseling to recover. Reading *Skeptical Inquirer* was a help. Sorrentino, knowing now that there is no afterlife, has left "a written declaration abjuring any deathbed confession or reconciliation I might make. I shall ask my sisters to give it after my cremation to the priest who attended me." {*Pique*, November 1998}

Sorvino, Mira (1968-)

Sorvino in 1995 won a Best Supporting Actress Oscar for her role in Woody Allen's "Mighty Aphrodite." In *GQ* (August 1997), she told an interviewer

> When you are a Christian, your law is laid out for you in codified form. You can have some kind of debate about this or that, but basically you're supposed to accept God's will. There is no argument about whether there is a definitive right and wrong. And once you know this law, nobody else can be right unless they agree with you. And so you wind up with, "You are wrong. You are mistaken. You are sinning. You are in error." I find that extremely restrictive and impossible. . . . Think, just think, about how every last man and woman and child of the Pharisees was killed for their blasphemy and their infidelity when their greatest crime was they were mistaken. So they believe in the wrong God—they should be killed for this? Is this justice? Is it?
>
> [When the interviewer challenged her]: No, this is not what a fair God would do. And why does it not say anywhere in the Bible that slavery is wrong? It only says that you should treat your slaves well. Well, I don't care if you treat them well. How is it possible that it is not immoral to own another person? Why isn't that one of the Ten Commandments? "Thou shalt not own another person." You want to sit here and tell me that fornication is worse than owning someone?

{CA}

SOS

The Secular Organizations for Sobriety (SOS), also called Save Our Selves, was founded in 1986 in North Hollywood, California, by Jim Christopher. It is an alternative to Alcoholics Anonymous (AA). Unlike AA and other support groups, SOS takes a strictly secular approach, emphasizing that each individual must draw upon his or her own resources to deal with the problems of addiction. The SOS support groups are flexible and accommodate family members and friends of alcoholics and addicts, compulsive overeaters, and those addicted to drugs other than alcohol. No appeal to a "higher power" is made, because addiction is held to be a physical rather than a "spiritual" problem, and most of its members are uninterested in organized religions. SOS (5521 Grosvenor, Los Angeles, California 90066) is sponsored and supported by the Council for Secular Humanism. Over 1000 groups have been formed worldwide. On the Web: <www.secularhumanism.org/sos/>.

A similar humanistic organization, Rationalist Recovery Organization. is at <rational.org/recovery/index.html>.

SOS INTERNATIONAL NEWSLETTER

SOS International Newsletter, a quarterly of the Secular Organization for Sobriety, is at PO Box 5, Amherst, New York 14215-0005. E-mail: <sosla@loop.com>.

SOTERIOLOGY (CREATIONISM

Soteriology, with roots in the Greek *soteria*, or deliverance, is a term to designate the traditional branch of Christian theology devoted to the doctrine of salvation. Soteriologists posit the following: (a) souls exist; (b) humans have [or are] souls; (c) souls survive corporeal death; and (d) at death, souls go to Heaven or Hell. Anthropologist Richard A. Fox of the University of South Dakota finds that "most Christians rely on faith in Christ for salvation, embracing the Bible as a moral and spiritual aid, not as a scientific document. Not so the peculiar soteriologists—'creationists' as they are called. They insist on a fifth requirement for salvation: you must accept scripture literally as the inerrant word of the Bible-deity." Fox and other secular humanists have objected strongly to a CBS television airing of "The Incredible Discovery of Noah's Ark," an independently produced program purchased by and shown by CBS television 20 February 1993. "CBS should have known better," he complains, adding that anthropologists and archaeologists were disregarded and soteriologists were featured. The telecast purported that archaeologists had conclusive proof that Noah's ark still is atop Mount Ararat in Turkey, as claimed in *Genesis*. A hoax was involved, however, for an actor had purposely charred a piece of fresh pinewood, soaking it in various substances to make it appear ancient, then gave it to producers and claimed he had found it on Mount Ararat. The actor later reenacted his performance on television, except that fewer saw the hoax revealed than saw the original program. "Carbon-14 testing would have revealed immediately that the wood was a modern forgery," said Gerald A. Larue, a noted biblical scholar and secular humanist. "But the fundamentalists who produced 'Discovery' do not believe in the accuracy of Carbon-14 research," he added, so the phony "relic" was accepted and presented to millions of viewers as a genuine piece of Noah's Ark. {ER; *Free Inquiry*, Summer 1993}

Soukup, Ottakar (20th Century)

Soukup wrote *Essays in Cartoons* (c. 1960?). {GS}

SOUL

> Heaven, Hell, Paradise, where's your soul to go?
> Into Heaven, into Hell, just like so.
>
> (Song from a children's game)

"Soul," in light of the Verification Principle, is unverifiable and is considered meaningless by freethinkers except as a poetic abstraction. Believers in reincarnation speak of the unverifiable transmigration of souls. The Stoics taught the doctrine of *logos*, or world-reason, with the soul being an offshoot of fine material substance like warm air. And they introduced the word *pneuma*, something like a pervasive spirit or principle which possessed a meaning more than soul or *psyche*.

Non-believers appreciate the symbolism of Psyche, the princess who was so beautiful that Eros, god of love, pursued her. For many Westerners, including Descartes (who denied there was an animal soul but located man's soul in the pineal body), soul is synonymous with mind. Others, including Kant, say the soul is undefinable but see it as a useful element in a system of ethics. William James, citing that undefinability, postulated ethical systems based upon a humanistic conception of man's nature. Many non-believers, who do not use the word, do use Freudian terms, terms which also are unverifiable: psyche, id, ego, superego, libido. Dr. David E. H. Jones of the University of Newcastle-upon Tyne, better known by his pen name Daedalus, has wittily proposed applying advanced laboratory techniques to measure the soul and put theological ideas to a quantitative test. He suggests that by attaching piezoelectric transducers, inertial-navigation acceler- ometers, and other instruments to a dying person, it should be possible to measure the direction, velocity, and spin of the soul as it leaves the body, causing the body to recoil slightly. "Traditional theology is silent on the spin of the soul," Daedalus writes, "though it may predict that the soul of a sinner would depart downward and might weigh less than that of a righteous believer." His tongue-in-cheek proposal was greeted with merriment by many. However, Dr. Brian D. Josephson, co-winner of the 1973 Nobel Prize in Physics and an outspoken believer in spiritualism, wrote to *Nature*, "Any scientific study of religion should take account of the fact that a central theme of religion (pathological variants excluded) is the attempt to maximize human 'goodness.' I speculate that religious practices have in part a genetic basis, involving genes linked to the potential for goodness." (See entries for Francis Crick and Spirit.) {CE; ER; RE}

SOUL OR MIND

> Neither the soul nor the mind can serve as a term in the causal explanation of anything unless it is interpreted as the word for a substance. If "having a soul" is defined as equivalent to "being alive," or "having a first-class mind" as being able to perform at that level, then the soul or mind cannot be said to produce the phenomena; and to say that this has a soul or that has a first-class mind is just another slightly more picturesque way of expressing (and therefore cannot explain) the facts that this is alive or that that displays high academic ability. (You cannot explain why it is the case that *p* simply by reiterating that *p*!) If, on the other hand, "having a soul" or "having a first-class mind" are understood as referring to the possession and presence of entities that, although presumably incorporeal, are nevertheless in the present sense substantial, then it does at least make sense both to say that these entities might survive the dissolution of the bodies to which they are temporarily attached and to suggest that various important phenomena are to be attributed to their activity.

As for Aristotle's above account of the soul in *De Anima*, Flew concludes it is "just nonsensical to suggest that this might survive the death and dissolution of its body." (Freethinkers generally speak of "consciousness," not "soul." See entry for Consciousness.) {AF}

Soury, Auguste Jules (1842–1906)

Soury was a French philosopher who became librarian in 1865 at the *Bibliotèque Nationale*. In *Jesus and the Gospels* (1878), he maintained that Jesus had an unbalanced mind.

His *Studies of Psychology* (1879) indicated a new direction in his freethought. Among his many books are *A Breviary of the History of Materialism* (1880), in which he confessed his Agnosticism; *Naturalist Theories of the World and of Life in Antiquity* (1880); and *Natural Philosophy* (1882). {BDF; RAT; RE}

SOUTH AFRICAN FREETHOUGHT

South African freethinkers are discussed in *Freethought in the United Kingdom and the Commonwealth*, by Gordon Stein.

In 1997, a South African Freethinkers' Homepage, <http://www.eec.co.za/free> was launched by John van Zelst, whose e-mail is <eec@eastcoast.co.za>.

The University of South Africa humanists are at: <http://www.secularhumanism.org/cfa/orgs.html>

SOUTH AFRICAN UNITARIANS

In 1867 the Rev. Faure of the Dutch Reformed Church, who had absorbed liberal views while studying for the ministry in the Netherlands, was rejected upon returning home and established an independent congregation. After his retirement, the congregation was served by a succession of ministers from Britain and the United States.

The Johannesburg Unitarian Fellowship was formed in 1956 and has been served by Cilliers de Wet as lay minister since 1995.

The Durban Fellowship is served by the Rev. Graham Brayshaw, formerly a Presbyterian minister.

The newly established Pietermaritzburg Fellowship (1996) is led by Professor Martin Prozesky of the Department of Religious Studies at the University of Natal and author of *A New Guide to the Debate About God*.

The Somerset West Fellowship was formed in 1985 and was served by the Cape Town minister, the late Rev. Robert C. Steyn.

On the Web: <http://www.uua.org/icuu/icuu-africa.html#South Africa>.

SOUTH AMERICAN FREETHOUGHT, HUMANISM

South American freethinkers have an organization, *Asociación Iberoamericana Ético Humanista* (ASIBEHU). On the World Wide Web: <http://idt.net/~wasm/asibehu>. (See entry for *Asociación Iberoamericana Ético Humanista*.)

SOUTH ASIAN HUMANIST NETWORK

The South Asian Humanist Network (SAHN) includes groups in that geographical area. Included is the Bihar Buddhiwadi Samaj. (See entry for Southeast Asian Humanist Network.)

SOUTH AUSTRALIAN HUMANIST POST

A monthly of the Humanist Society of South Australia, *South Australian Humanist Post* is at GPO Box 177, Adelaide 5001, Australia; e-mail <rmc@adelaide.on.net>.

SOUTH CAROLINA HUMANISTS

• American Humanist Association, Mid-Atlantic Region (AHA), A-140, 1 College Row, Brevard, North Carolina 28712. O. Andrews Ferguson is coordinator.

• College of Charleston Humanists are at <http://www.secularhumanism.org/cfa/orgs.html>.

• Monkey's Uncle, 109 Burwood Drive, Simpsonville, South Carolina 29681. Ed Babinski is the contact.

• Secular Humanists of Greenville, Suite 168, Box 3000, Taylors, South Carolina 29687. Jacques Benbassat is the contact.

• Secular Humanists of the Low Country (ASHS), PO Box 32256, Charleston, South Carolina 29417; (803) 577-0637. David Peterson is a contact. E-mail: <sechumlo@mail.serve.com>. Web: <www.serve.com/sechumlo/>.

• Secular Humanists of the South Carolina Midlands, PO Box 5123, Columbia, SC 29250; (803) 731-9378. David Kennison is a contact. E-mail: <neoabs@scsn.net>

• Skeptical Humanists at the Grand Strand, 1414 Twelve Oaks Drive, Pawleys Island, South Carolina 29585; (843) 237-7262

• Upstate South Carolina Secular Humanists (ASHS), Suite 168, Box 3000, Taylors, South Carolina 29687. Contacts are Lee Deitz and Jacques Benbassat. E-mail: <leeingvl@aol.com>. On theWeb: <http://home.earthlink.net/~joannmooney/humanism.html>.

• Winthrop University's Atheist Students Assn. is at <http://www.secularhumanism.org/cfa/orgs.html>.

SOUTH DAKOTA HUMANISTS, FREETHINKERS

• Bernie Schatz is American Humanist Association coordinator of the northern region of the United States.

• The Humanist Association of South Dakota, 815 Beta Place, Sioux Falls, South Dakota 57106. Mary Groethe is contact member.

• South Dakota School of Mines and Technology's Tech Freethought Society is found on the Web: <http://www.secularhumanism.org/cfa/orgs.html>. (See entry for Minnesota Atheists, Humanists)

SOUTH DAKOTA SCHOOL OF MINES AND TECHNOLOGY

The Tech Freethought Society of the South Dakota School of Mines and Technology is on the Web: <http://www.secularhumanism.org/cfa/orgs.html>.

SOUTH PLACE ETHICAL SOCIETY

South Place Ethical Society (Bradlaugh House, 47 Theobald's Road, London WC1X 8SP; telephone 0171 831 7723) is the oldest freethought organization in Britain, having evolved from a radical religious congregation formed in East London in 1793. It meets in Conway Hall, Red Lion Square, Holborn, London WC 1.

It began as a Christian congregation in February 1793. The first sermons were entitled "The Three Woe Trumpets; of which the First & Second are already past; and the Third is now begun; under which the Seven Vials of the Wrath of God are to be Poured Out Upon the World. Being the Substance of two Discourses, from *Revelations* xi, 14, 15, 16, 176, 18, delivered at the Chapel in Parliament Court, Artillery Street, Bishopsgate Street, on February 3 & 24, 1793."

Ethanan Winchester, an American Baptist preacher who had converted to Universalism in 1781 and come to England in 1787, was the first minister. He was followed by William Vidler, an English Baptist preacher who was converted to Universalism in 1792, and then by William Johnson Fox, a Congregationalist preacher who was converted to Unitarianism in 1811. Fox led the Society for 35 years. It was Moncure Conway who in his twenty years as leader took the society from theism to humanism. Stanton Coit followed, persuading it to become an Ethical Society, and later leaders have been J. A. Hobson, J. M. Robertson, Joseph McCabe, Cecil Delisle Burns, C. E. M. Joad, Barbara Smoker, Harry Knight, and Peter Cadogan.

In 1897 it ceased to have a minister, and from 1899 it had a panel of appointed lecturers. South Place slowly abandoned religious forms, from prayers in the 1860s to secular humans in the 1960s, and in 1980 it acquired the status of a non-religious charity. (See "Freethought Congregations, South Place and Others" in *London Heretics*, by Warren Sylvester Smith.)

Southack, Theodore L Jr. (20th Century)

Southack in 1954 was Vice President and a member of the board of directors of the Humanist Fellowship of Boston, a group affiliated with the American Humanist Association.

SOUTHEAST ASIA HUMANIST NETWORK

Some of the humanist and ethical organizations in India have formed a Southeast Asia Humanist Network which is allied with the International Humanist and Ethical Union.

Southern, Terry (1924–1995)

A noted entertainer, Southern wrote a variety of works: novels (*Flesh and Filigree*, 1958; *The Magic Christian* (1959); *Blue Movie* (1970); an anthology (*Writers in Revolt*, with Alex Trocchi, 1960); short stories (*Red Dirt Marijuana and Other Tastes*, 1967); and screenplays ("Dr. Strangelove," with Stanley Kubrick, 1963); "The Loved One" with Christopher Isherwood, 1964); "The Cincinnati Kid," with Ring Lardner Jr., 1965); "Easy Rider," 1968). His first writing was in the 1950s for *Paris Review*.

At his memorial in the Unitarian Church of All Souls in New York City, Peter Matthiessen lamented the passing of Southern, whom he dubbed a "delicious eccentric." George Plimpton spoke lovingly of the "rumpled, soft-spoken, and rather owlish" Southern who had a tendency to freeload. Mindful of the 1960s, David Amram played twin flutes out of either side of his mouth, and Larry Rivers played "Boulevard of Broken Dreams" on his saxophone.

The memorial was noted for its laughter, particularly when actor Rip Torn told a story about Southern's last hospital stay. A nurse, he said, shook him and inquired, "Mr. Southern, do you know where you are? Do you know where you are?" Southern opened his eyes. "Yes, my dear," he told the inquiring nurse, "I'm afraid I do."

SOUTHERN BAPTIST CONVENTION

The Southern Baptist Convention, organized in 1845, is at 901 Commerce Street (Suite 750), Nashville, Tennessee 37203. It has around 40,500 churches and 15,600,000 members.

SOUTHERN ILLINOIS UNIVERSITY AT CARBONDALE

Humanists and freethinkers at Southern Illinois University at Carbondale are on the Web:
<http://www.secularhumanism.org/cfa/orgs.html>.

Southwell, Charles (1814–1860)

A maverick British freethought leader, Southwell was a publisher responsible for reviving the wave of blasphemy prosecutions that occurred during the early 1840s. His publishing *The Oracle of Reason* is credited with moving the freethought movement into a more open and defiant atheistic phrase. For one article, on "The Jew Book," he was tried for blasphemy and was sentenced to a year in prison and a fine of one hundred pounds.

According to Berman, Southwell took over the championship of atheism from Richard Carlile, "who had moved away from atheism in the 1830s to a confused form of mystical theism." Berman makes the point that Southwell and Holyoake "claimed only to disbelieve in God, because there was no sufficient reason for belief. They did not, as they put it, directly deny there is a God."

He was an editor of *Oracle of Reason* (1841–1843), *Lancashire Beacon* (1842), and *Investigator* (1843). In Auckland, New Zealand, he edited *Auckland Examiner* (1857–1860). Although recorded as a stage performer and an orator of considerable capacity and endurance, Southwell developed a reputation that was largely defined by his work as a publisher. His placement among the founders of rationalist freethought and activities in Australasia is more firmly based on his earlier reputation in England rather than what he achieved later. {BDF; EU, Gordon Stein; FUK; HAB; RAT; SWW; TRI; VI}

Souverain, N. (17th Century)

Souverain was a French author of *Platonism Unveiled* (1700), a posthumous work. He had been a minister of Poitou and was deposed on account of his opinions. {BDF}

Souza, Armand de (20th Century)

A Sri Lankan freethinker, Souza wrote *The Credentials of Christianity Examined by the East* (1909). {GS}

SOVIET ATHEISM: See entry for Daniel Peris.

Sower or Sauer, Christopher (1693–1758)

The German-born Sower migrated to Pennsylvania in 1724 and, after having a medical practice and farming, established a press in Germantown. Here, with the assistance of George de Benneville in 1743, he produced the first Bible in America translated into German. In it, Sower used large type to emphasize the universal character of religion. A Universalist Quaker, he was joined in his business by his son Christopher Jr. (1721–1784), who became a deacon of the German Baptist Brethren, popularly called Dunkers (also called Dunkards or Tunkers), from the German *tunken*, to dip. {CE}

Sowerby, John (1924–)

Sowerby, a freethinker, was secretary of the League Against Cruel Sports in England. {GS}

Soyinka, Wole (Adkinwande Oluwole Soyinka) (1934–)

• With the blood-soaked banner of religious fanaticism billowing across the skies as one prominent legacy of this millennium, Martin Luther's famous theses against religious absolutism struck me early as a strong candidate for the best idea of the last thousand years. By progressive association, so did the microprocessor and its implications—the liberalization of access to knowledge, and a quantum boost for the transmission of ideas. There is, however, a nobler idea that has spread by its own power in this millennium and that has now begun to flourish: the idea that certain fundamental rights are inherent to all humanity.

Thus spake Soyinka, who was awarded the Nobel Prize for Literature in 1986. He wrote such works as *Lion and the Jewel* (1963); *The Interpreters* (1965); *La danse de la foret* (1971); *Les gens des marais* (1971); *Collected Plays* (1973); *Myth, Literature, and the African World* (1976); and *Mandela's Earth and Other Poems* (1988).

He founded a national theatre, which is now called Orisun Theatre. When he dropped a stage production of Orwell's "Animal Farm," critics attacked him as being a crypto-Marxist. Other critics, however, complain that he is not radical enough. To counter his critics, Soyinka in 1994 published *Art, Dialogue, and Outrage*, a volume which updates one published in 1988. In it, he states that Islam is not an African religion and reminds readers of "the unspeakable cruelties perpetrated on African humanity in the name of Islamic conversion." Michael Gorra, of Smith College, feels the "Outrage" of the title is well chosen, for Soyinka "excoriates African intellectuals for both their reliance on 'Western intellectual caucuses' and their 'self-abnegating posture before . . . Eastern Communism.'. . . Yet just when one thinks he might be ready to embrace the banner of African authenticity, Mr. Soyinka repudiates that idea as well, as a 'rag' behind which too many authoritarian regimes have tried to hide." Gorra notes that although Soyinka's parents were Christian, the Yoruban writer himself takes the Yoruba god Ogun, the deity of creativity and destruction alike, as his patron."

In 1991, Adewale Maja-Pearce wrote *Who's Afraid of Wole Soyinka? Essays on Censorship*, detailing how Soyinka was considered a threat by Nigerian military leaders. Although regarded as a hero by millions of Nigerians, certain leaders of the establishment disliked him for having issued a "call for the abolition of the theocratic ideal in all forms of government."

In the 1960s, he backed what many thought was the wrong side in his country's civil war, for which he had to spend two years in prison, much of which was in solitary confinement. Soyinka also has written,

> As a state instrument of internal control, and even in the conduct of foreign policies (including terrorism), it is possible to suggest that religious fanaticism has once again attained prime position as the most implacable enemy of the basic rights of humanity. . . . I have one abiding religion: human liberty.

"I have nothing but contempt for religions that kill in the name of piety," Soyinka wrote in "Why I Am a Secular Humanist."

During the 1990s when Soyinka was critical of the military government in Nigeria, he complained that votes in a June 1993 presidential election had not accurately been counted. As a result, his passport was seized and the government refused to let him attend a human rights conference in Sweden.

He then fled in 1994, calling for an international effort to isolate the military government of General Sani Abacha. Charged in absentia with treason, he supported Ken Saro-Wiwa, a human rights activist who upon General Abacha's orders was executed. Upon Abacha's death in 1998, Soyinka again called upon the military to step aside and allow Ken Wiwa, son of the executed Nigerian dissident, to become president. In 1998, ever the activist, he announced the creation of a truth tribunal to expose human rights abuses by Nigeria's military government.

"He's a humanist, he's a radical, and he's always been fearless," Dudley Thompson, the former Jamaican Ambassador to Nigeria, has said of Soyinka. Thompson resigned his post in 1995 after seeing a man set afire by a mob on the streets of Lagos.

In *The Open Sore of a Continent: A Personal Narrative of the Nigerian Crisis* (1995), he summarizes his views about the Abacha regime, which he feels is "yet another circus of political mutants and opportunists" and "back-alley abortionists" of democracy. And he laments that Nigeria has become a "tightly sealed can within cans, within cans of worms." His most important thesis, however, is that "ethical maps" rather than geographical ones are better for determining national boundaries. As the world becomes more transnational, he declares, nations will of necessity need to be politically progressive in order to withstand the pressures from global corporatism, racial and ethnic squabbles, and a population explosion in which fewer resources will be fought over by more and more human beings.

In 1999, now a member of the Emory University faculty in Georgia, Soyinka addressed the American Academy of Arts and Letters in New York City at its 101st annual ceremonial. In his Blashfield Address, "Liberty Hall and the House of Correction," he discussed changes in the English language, remarking about "political correct" objections to words such as *human*, *mankind*, and *history*—*hero*, he noted, was named after Hero, a female, again without regard to gender. In his indictment of our culture for its compromising truth in light of the proliferation of euphemisms and jargon, he remarked that in our quest to become politically correct we risk losing reality. (*Free Inquiry*, Fall 1997). (See the article about Soyinka by Ketu H. Katrak of the University of Massachusetts in *The Johns Hopkins Guide to Literary Theory & Criticism* [1994].) {*The New York Times*, 1 May 1997}

Spaink, Pierre François (Born 1862)

Spaink was a Dutch physician who studied in Amsterdam and wrote for a time on *De Dageraad*, using the pen names "A. Th Eist" [sic] and "F.R.S." Spaink translated Romanes' *Scientific Evidences of Organic Evolution*. {BDF}

SPANISH ACADEMY

In 1713, ***La Real Academia Española*** was founded in Spain. Like the French Academy, the Spanish Academy serves as an authority concerning what is and is not "correct" in the language. The motto of the forty-six member group states that the academy "cleanses, fixes, and adds splendor" to the language of Spanish that is spoken by an estimated four hundred million, protecting it from debasing infiltrators. Nine out of ten who speak Spanish now live outside Spain. "It's wonderful that our language, which is so dispersed, has kept a single set of spelling rules," the academy's director Victor Garcia de la Concha told reporter Marlise Simons. Unlike Hindi and Arabic, also widely spoken languages, spelling is universal and based upon phonetics. English spelling, he lamented, is not uniform; however, some Anglicisms have been accepted: *mitin* (meeting), fûtbol (football), and *guisqui* (whisky). Although the academy has branches in most Latin American countries, they are subordinate to Madrid. {*The New York Times*, 23 June 1999}

SPANISH HUMANISM

Robertson has detailed the problems of freethinkers in Spain, including the paralysis wrought by the combined tyranny of Church and Crown, incarnate in the Inquisition. During the dominion of Philip II there are said to have been 58 archbishops, 684 bishops, 11,400 abbeys, 23,000 religious fraternities, 46,000 monasteries, 13,500 nunneries, 312,000 secular priests, 400,000 monks, 200,000 friars and other ecclesiastics. Spain had 9,088 monasteries. Robertson states, "In the opening years of the seventeenth century (1610–1612), under Philip III, on the score that the great Armada had failed because heretics were tolerated at home, it was decided to expel the whole race; and now a million Moriscoes, among the most industrious inhabitants of Spain, were driven the way of the Jews." The dramatic literature was "notably unintellectual, dealing endlessly in plot and adventure, but yielding no great study of character, and certainly doing nothing to further ethics. Calderon was a thorough fanatic, and became a priest; Lope de Vega found solace under bereavement in zealously performing the duties of an Inquisitor; and was so utterly swayed by the atrocious creed of persecution which was blighting Spain that he joined in the general exultation over the expulsion of the Moriscoes." Even Cervantes was affected by the iron wall of Catholic orthodoxy, Robertson states.

"Humanism" does not translate well into contemporary Spanish, for there is a Humanist Party and the political overtones clash. But in Spain a movement exists which shares many of the ideals of the International Humanist and Ethical Union: The *Ateneos* (The Atheneums). According to *International Humanist News* (July 1993), "The Ateneos were founded in the nineteenth century, stimulated by classical Athens and devoted to humanist values and freethought. Indeed, the Spanish Republic was inspired by the Ateneo, and Spain's leadership, including many presidents and prime ministers, have come from the Ateneo." Dr. Cesar Navarro de Francisco is a former president of the Ateneo of Madrid, which was built in 1884 and contains a library, lecture halls, and a cafeteria, all open to students and the general public.

Spaniards who signed Humanist Manifesto 2000 included José M. R. Delgado and Alberto Hidalgo Tuñon. (See entries for classical humanism and Cervantes. Also, consult the *Encyclopedia of Philosophy*.)

SPANISH INQUISITION: See Erna Paris's *The End of Days: A Story of Tolerance, Tyranny and the Expulsion of the Jews from Spain* (1995). Paris describes the politics of the Inquisition and its psychology of terror.

SPANISH PHILOSOPHY: See the *Encyclopedia of Philosophy*.

SPANISH UNITARIANS

Contact for the New Age Universalist Movement, which was started in 1992, is Jaume de Marcos, c/o Pare Rodes, 11, 24, 08208 Sabadell, Spain. E-mail: <jmarcos@lix.intercom.es>.

SPANISH-AMERICAN HUMANISM

In 1994, an organization was founded in Costa Rica for Spanish-speaking humanists: *Asociación Iberoamericana Ético Humanista* (ASIBEHU, PO Box 374-2050, San Pedro, Costa Rica). Participants from Argentina to Mexico, as well as from Puerto Rico and the Dominican Republic to Cuba, were invited to join. The association's first president was Alexander Cox Alvarado.

Sparks, Jared (1789–1866)

Sparks, an eminent historian and educator, was pastor of a Unitarian church in Baltimore (1819–1823). He founded and edited (1821–1822) the *Unitarian Miscellany* and was chaplain of the U.S. House of Representatives (1821–1823). Sparks bought and edited the *North American Review* (1824–1830) and founded and edited (1830) *The American Almanac and Repository of Useful Knowledge*. From 1849 to 1853, he was president of Harvard University. His historical works were about the diplomatic correspondence of the American revolution and the lives of Gouverneur Morris, George Washington, and Benjamin Franklin. He edited the twenty-five-volume *Library of American Biography* (1834–1848). {CE; FUS; U}

SPARTA

Sparta was settled by Dorian Greeks who invaded around 1100 B.C.E. and who were culturally and linguistically distinct from the Greek world. It reached its pinnacle in the 6th century B.C.E.

Jacob Burckhardt's *The Greeks and Greek Civilization* (1998) praises the Spartans for their military excellence. He describes Alcibiades's dislike of democracy. (See entry for Athens.)

Spaventa, Bertrando (1817–1888)

Spaventa was an Italian philosopher who, starting in 1861, was professor of philosophy at Naples. Spaventa wrote upon the philosophy of Kant, Gioberti, Spinoza, Hegel, and others. {BDF; RAT}

Spear, Charles (1801–1863)

Spear, a Universalist minister, was a noted prison reformer during the 19th century. {U}

Specht, Karl August (Born 1845)

Specht, a German writer, was for many years editor of *Menschenthum* at Gotha. He wrote *Brain and Soul, Theology and Science,* and *A Popular History of The World's Development*. Dr. Specht was a leading member of the German Freethinkers' Union. {BDF; PUT}

SPECIES

> As a result of natural selection, species—or more precisely, the organisms composing species—generally perform brilliantly in the niche to which they are specialized. There are probably 10 million or more species alive on earth. Which are the best at filling their niches? All are, I guess. Consider this Zenlike question: Can a bird fly better than a fish can swim? Live species are by definition all successes, because the losers are extinct, having fallen victim to nature's equivalent of the Foreign Legion command, March or die.

Edward O. Wilson, after expressing the above, was asked which of the species is most abundant ("There are more *E. coli* and other intestinal bacteria in your colon at this moment than there are human beings who have ever lived."); the longest lived (Homo sapiens as a species is less than 1/100th as old as ancient forms); the most likely to survive ("Without doubt, bacteria and allied organisms known as archaea win again, especially the species that use photosynthesis or inorganic chemicals to grow and reproduce."); the most social (ants, termites, honeybees); most intelligent (humans); most powerful (humans, except that we humans must learn to wisely manage the environment, "an enterprise for which we have so far shown little dedication or talent"). {*The New York Times Magazine*, 18 April 1999}

SPELLING

Although spelling allegedly is not a problem for students of Spanish, it is for students of English. George Bernard Shaw had ideas for resolving the problem. In his final will, he left the bulk of his sizable fortune for the development of a British alphabet having forty letters. The request was contested and a legal compromise was accepted: with only a £500 prize being offered in a competition to select a letter design; the four winners who split the award were also asked to continue their studies in the search for a replacement to Dr. Samuel Johnson's alphabet.

Samuel Clemens also had some tongue-in-cheek ideas about the spelling of English words:

> For example, in Year 1 that useless letter "c" would be dropped to be replaced either by "k" or "s," and likewise "x" would no longer be part of the alphabet. The only kase in which "c" would be retained would be the "ch" formation, which will be dealt with later.
>
> Year 1 might reform "w" spelling, so that "which" and "one" would take the same konsonant, wile Yar 3 might well abolish "y,"

> replasing it with "i" and Iear 4 might fiks the "g/j" anomali wonse and for all.
>
> Jenerally, then, the improvement would kontinue iear bai iear with Iear 5 doing awai with useless double konsonants, and Iears 6-12 or so modifaiing vowlz and the rimeining voist and unvoist konsonants. Bai Iear 15 or sou, it wud fainali bi posibl tu meik ius ov thi ridandant letez "c," "y," and "x"—bai now jast a memori in the maindz ov ould doderez—tu riplais "ch," "sh," and "th" rispektivli.
>
> Fainali, xen, aafte sam 20 iers ov orxogrefkl riform, wi wud hev a lojikl, kohirnt speling in ius xrewawt xe Ingliy-spikingwerld.

Others, however, point to the romance of tracing words to their various sources. How else, they reason, would we know that the Taino Indians gave the word *hamaca* to the Spanish, or *hammock* in English. The Taino and Carib Indians in the West Indies (not tribes dining on missionaries, for example) also gave us our word for *cannibal.* English, unlike many other tongues, has borrowed words from all other languages. Linguists as well as philosophers delight in studying the origins of such words, concentrating particularly on their spelling for clues as to their past meanings. (See entry for Allen Walker Read.) {PA}

Spencer, Anna Carpenter Garlin (1851–1931)

A Unitarian, Spencer was the first woman ordained in Rhode Island. However, she associated with Unitarian, Universalist, and Ethical Culture congregations and, rather than considering herself a "member," identified with the broder "free religion" of the Free Religious Association. An important social philosopher, she was a professor of sociology and ethics at Meadville Theological School. After marrying the Rev. William H. Spencer in 1878 and becoming ordained in 1891, she held a pastorate in Providence, Rhode Island. Later, she was an Ethical Culture Leader from 1904 to 1913 in New York, then moved on in feminist protest to teaching. Her *Woman's Share in Social Culture* (1913) advocates not only equality for women in the masculine world but also the evolution of new ethical and social positions based on women's perspectives and insights. She also wrote *The Family and Its Members* (1922). Spencer was a founder of thE National Association for the Advancement of Colored People.

One of her popularly sung hymns included

> Hail the hero workers
> of the might past (present and future)

and concluded

> Hail ye, then, all workers,
> Of all lands and time,
> One brave band of heroes
> With one task sublime!

Spencer was the anthropologist who suspected an antomist—not Sir Arthur Conan Doyle—was behind the 1912 hoax involving the Piltdown Man. *Piltdown, a Scientific Forgery* (1990), established that the scientist with the most to gain from the Piltdown discovery was Sir Arthur Keith. He allegedly provided the technical expertise and possibly the bones, which were stained to look prehistoric, and Charles Dawson then planted them in the gravel pit where he then led others, including Dr. Pierre Teilhard de Chardin, on fossil hunts. When the fraud was discovered in 1953, numerous explanations were given, but it was Spencer's work and that of Dr. Ian Langham in Australia which solved the mystery. (See entries for Ethical Culture, CE, and Piltdown Man.) {*The New York Times*, 3 June 1999)

Spencer, Herbert (1820–1903)

An agnostic before Thomas H. Huxley originated the word, Spencer did not believe there is sufficient evidence either to prove or to disprove the existence of God and immortality. He coined the phrase "survival of the fittest" and is credited with establishing sociology as a discipline.

His parents were originally Methodists, but at an early age Spencer showed an inclination to think for himself concerning theological matters. His philosophic and religious beliefs are not easily labeled, for his philosophy was distinct from that of the various movements. He was a philosopher who offered the Victorians both metaphysical and moral certainty, and an explanation of the place of religion in a scientific world. His *Introduction to Society* (1873), in the chapter on "The Theological Bias," contained his First Principles, a mordant attack on the Christian creed. The Rationalist Press Association (RPA) was chosen to publish his *Education* (1861).

One of Spencer's prayers included the following: "O Lord, you know that I do not believe in you as you are described in the Bible and believed in by the Church. You know that I do not believe the Bible as the word of God. If it be true, as affirmed, that you created the universe, it follows that you have created all that is in it. You have created evil as well as good, the devil as well as the angels, hell as well as heaven. If you have made men at all, you made them as they are. If they are good, it is because you have made them so; if they are wicked, it is equally your work. If you are omnipotent and universal, as you are said to be, there can be no evil or wicked deed that is not the result of characters and conditions which you have created. If there is a hell and men are to be burned, it is because you have wished it to be so. It has pleased you to make them evil and wretched. You are not, then, good, nor do you love your creatures." Five or so minutes later, he concludes, "I can only be thankful that I am not cowardly enough to fear nor weak enough to worship so horrible a creature as you, the God of the Church. Amen."

In *Facts and Comments*, written the year before his death, he denies emphatically the common Christian assertion that Freethinkers "occupy themselves exclusively with material interests." But he finds no ground whatever for belief in a future life, which is a superstition handed down from the savage. As there is no evidence of the existence of consciousness apart from brain, Spencer wrote, "we seem obliged to relinquish the thought that consciousness continued after physical organization has become inactive."

Spencer "passed peacefully away" on 8 December 1903, and his remains were cremated at Golder's Green. On September 16 he wrote to John Morley stating that he contemplated the end "as not far off—an end to which I look forward with satisfaction"—and that he had "interdicted any such ceremony as is performed over the bodies or ashes of those who adhere to the current creed." (See Jack Kaminsky's article on Spencer in the *Encyclopedia of Philosophy*, Vol. 7.) {BDF; CE; CL; ER; EU, Mark Francis; FUK; HNS2; JM; JMR; JMRH; PUT; RAT; TRI; TYD}

Spender, Stephen Harold [Sir] (1909–1995)

Spender, an English poet and critic, was son of E. H. Spender, a liberal journalist on whose mother's side he was partly "of German-Jewish descent." During the Spanish Civil War he did propaganda work in Spain for the Republican side. With Cyril Connolly he co-edited *Horizon* (1939–1941) and *Encounter* (1956–1966), the latter of which was paid for secretly and to his embarrassment by the United States Counter Intelligence Agency. Spender's essay in *The God That Failed* told of his relationship with the Communist Party. In the diaries of George Orwell, the creator of Big Brother speculated that Spender was a "sentimental sympathiser" of the Party and "very unreliable," "easily influenced, "with a "tendency towards homosexuality." Virginia Woolf, whom he admired, once called him "rattle-headed."

Spender characterized his father as a "Puritan Decadent" who taught him that the human body "is a nameless horror of nameless desires which isolate him within a world of his own." In The Temple (1929; published 1988), he tells how he liberated himself of such nonsense. It was W. H. Auden, his teacher, who told him that "guilt and inhibition stood between oneself and the satisfaction of one's needs," and in 1933 he began a stormy homosexual relationship with Tony Hyndman. Suddenly in 1936, after being engaged for only three weeks, Spender married Inez Pearn, whom he divorced in 1939, then married Natasha Litvin, with whom he had two children. Spender told Francis Bacon he was "Christian; at least in believing, we must help each other." (See entry for Francis Bacon.) {CE; David Leeming, *Stephen Spender*; OEL}

SPERM

Sperm, the male gamete or reproductive cell, is every adolescent boy's mystery when first it appears. Instead of urine, a white substance is found exiting the penis, and some children who have not been educated on the subject fear they are somehow defective and in rare cases consider committing suicide. Some become aware only after having a "wet dream," or involuntary ejaculation of the semen while one is asleep.

Corresponding to the female ovum in organisms that reproduce sexually, sperm in higher animals is produced in the male's testis. Smaller than the ovum and consisting primarily of a head, its nucleus bears the hereditary material of the male parent. A slender whiplike process (flagellum) provides the motility necessary for fertilization in a fluid medium.

A California woman in 1999 gave birth to a girl using sperm retrieved from her dead husband, raising ethical questions over whether a man must give his consent to be a father. The sperm was retrieved thirty hours after the man's death and was then frozen for fifteen months before use. Some medical ethics experts argue that the procedure should not become a standard medical service. Others argue that it is an issue of reproductive freedom that society has no right to prevent. (CE) {*The New York Times*, 27 March 1999}

Spetter, Matthew Ies (20th Century)

When he signed Humanist Manifesto II, Spetter was chairman of the department of ethics of the Ethical Culture Schools. He has since 1955 led the Riverdale-Yonkers Society for Ethical Culture, and he has represented the American Ethical Union on the board of the International Humanist and Ethical Union (IHEU), of which was a founding member. From 1953 to 1955, he led the Brooklyn Ethical Culture group. At the Eighth World Congress of the IHEU held in Hannover (1982), at the Ninth held in Oslo (1986), and also at the Tenth held in Buffalo (1988), he addressed the groups. Spetter is a Leader of the Society for Ethical Culture in New York City and one of the IHEU's representatives to the United Nations.

A Dutch humanist, he has related that the 1957 gala dinner of the British Ethical Union in the House of Commons was arranged by Lord Snell. As guests arrived, they were loudly announced by name. Some of the Americans were so impressed by hearing their names trumpeted out at the House of Commons that they passed *twice* through the wide opened doors. (See entry for Ethical Culture.) {CL; HM2}

Spicer, Richard (20th Century)

Spicer is honorary secretary of the Association of Irish Humanists and is secretary of the Irish Campaign to Separate Church and State. He is author of *The Humanist Philosophy, With an Irish Guide to Non-Religious Ceremonies* (1997). At the Eleventh International Humanist and Ethical Union (IHEU) World Congress held in Brussels (1990), Spicer addressed the group. He signed Humanist Manifesto 2000. {"Irish Democracy Continues Its Advance," *Free Inquiry*, Spring 1996; and *New Humanist*, February 1996}

Spiegelstein, Max (20th Century)

With Robert F. Bartley, freethinker Spiegelstein wrote *Paul, the Saint Who Ain't* (1980). {GS}

Spiller, Gustav (20th Century)

Spiller wrote *The Mind and Man* (1902) and was editor of *Generation of Religious Progress* (1916). {FUK; GS}

Spinner, Michel (20th Century)

Spinner is one of the IHEU's representatives to UNESCO, Paris.

SPINO

A Dutch publication published five times per year by Jonge Humanisten, *Spino* is at Langeviele 39, 4331 LR, Middelburg, The Netherlands.

Spinoza, Baruch (or **Benedict de**) (1632–1677)

A Dutch philosopher, Spinoza was the son of one of the Sephardic Jewish fugitives from Spain who had settled in the Netherlands to escape the Inquisition. Developing an independent mind at an early age, he broke from the teachings of his family and teachers and, after many vain admonitions, was excommunicated. Foote described the experience: "His anathema was pronounced in the Synagogue on July 27, 1656. It was a frightful formula, cursing him by day and night, waking and sleeping, sitting and standing, and prohibiting every Jew from holding any communication with him, or approaching him within a distance of four cubits. Of course it involved his exile from home, and soon afterwards he narrowly escaped a fanatic's dagger."

Spinoza, wrote James Martineau after reading a Dutch pastor's description, "was of middle height and slenderly built; with regular features, a broad and high forehead, large dark, lustrous eyes, full dark eyebrows, and long curling hair of the same hue. His character was worthy of his intellect. He made no enemies except by his opinions. Even bitter opponents could not but own that he was singularly blameless and exacting, kindly and disinterested. Children, young men, servants, all who stood to him in any relation of dependence, seem to have felt the charm of his affability and sweetness of temper."

According to McCabe, Spinoza "is the best-known of Pantheists, holding that God and Nature, mind and matter, are one reality. His system differs from Monism in the fact that he insisted that this reality is God and the object of religious feeling." According to H. James Birx, Spinoza's pantheism represented a daring transitional stage in philosophy between earlier theism and modern atheism.

During the French Revolution, Maréchal cited Spinoza as being only a "possible" atheist. It was, at any rate, not politically expedient to be identified as his friend, such was his notoriety as an atheist. The Israeli philosopher, Ryarmiyahu Yovel, in his *Spinoza and Other Heretics* (1989), considers Spinoza to have been "the first secular Jew," for he was the one who took the initial steps necessary to lead to the eventual secularization of Jewish life. For him, secularism was an alternative to theism. In his *Theological-Political Treatise* (1677), he writes, "Philosophy has no end in view save truth; faith looks for nothing but obedience and piety."

Robertson points out that Spinoza's teacher, Van den Ende, was a scientific materialist, hostile to all religion, and it was while under his influence that Spinoza was excommunicated by his father's synagogue. . . . Still more profound, probably, was the effect of the posthumous *Ethica* (1677), which he had been prevented from publishing in his lifetime. In it, he not only propounded in parts an absolute pantheism but also definitely grounded ethics in human nature. Prof. E. E. Powell in his *Spinoza and Religion* (1906) equates that "absolute pantheism" with atheism, agreeing with Martineau that Spinoza has no valid ground for retaining the word "God." Powell states that "the right name for Spinoza's philosophy is Atheistic Monism." The bi-centenary of his death was celebrated with an address by M. Rénan.

At the time of his death, Spinoza lodged with a poor Dutch family at the Hague. They regarded him with veneration and gave him every attention. But he had a delicate constitution and became emaciated. On 20 February 1677, he sent for a medical friend, Dr. Meyer, from Amsterdam. Martineau hints that inasmuch as the hosts were at church and Spinoza died alone with his physician that the two may have arranged to carry out a method of euthanasia. However, he wrote, "There is no tittle of evidence" for such a thing. Neither, as

Colerus found, is there evidence that Spinoza had cried out several times in dying, "Oh God, have mercy on me, a miserable sinner!" Dr. Meyer was the only person with Spinoza when he died, so it would have been impossible for any scandalmongers to have heard Spinoza's last words. (See the article by Alasdair MacIntyre on Spinoza in the *Encyclopedia of Philosophy*, Vol. 7.) {BDF; CE; CR; ER; EU, John L. McKenney; FO; FUK; HNS2; ILP; JM; JMR; JMRH; PUT; RAT; RE; TRI; TYD}

SPIRIT

Sir Arthur Keith, the British anatomist and author of *Human Embryology and Morphology* (1902, 6th edition), wrote concerning spirit: "Medical men can find no grounds for believing that the brain is a dual organ—a compound of substance and of spirit. Every fact known to them compels the inference that mind, spirit, soul are the manifestations of the living brain, just as flame is the manifest spirit of a burning candle. At the moment of extinction, both flame and spirit cease to have separate existence."

SPIRITISM

Some spiritists, such as mediums who interpret a person with an aura which may appear small to lay individuals as meaning that he will not live long, are involved in clairvoyance or telepathy, trance speaking, apparitions, levitation, automatic writing, and poltergeistic, and ectoplasmic activities. Skeptics have been unable to document the validity of any such claims. Non-believers are highly amused by such nonsense. (For an estimate of the number of spiritists, see entry for Hell.)

SPIRITUALISM: See entry for Science and Non-Science.

SPIRITUALITY

> • "Spirit" comes from the Latin word "to breathe." What we breathe is air, which is certainly matter, however, thin. Despite usage to the contrary, there is no necessary implication in the word "spiritual" that we are talking of anything other than matter (including the matter of which the brain is made), or anything outside the realm of science. On occasion, I will feel free to use the word. Science is not only compatible with spirituality; it is a profound source of spirituality.
>
> —**Carl Sagan**, *The Demon-Haunted World*

> • Believers in supernaturalism are incapable of experiencing spirituality the way a scientist can when he sequences genes, views distant galaxies, or looks into the eyes of a betta, a burmese cat, a bluebird, or a newborn babe.
>
> —**Fernando Vargas**

"In the world in which I was raised," Antony Flew has written, the word 'spiritual' was pretty well synonymous with the word 'religious'; and, since that was long before the mass immigration into Europe of adherents of non-Christian religions, 'religious' was in practice equivalent to 'Christian.' For me, therefore, talk about spiritual life was talk about worshipping and praying to the Mosaic God of Judaism and Christianity. Since ceasing, in my middle teens, to believe in the existence of that God, I have in consequence simply not had, at any rate in that understanding, any spiritual life at all." In *The New Humanist* (May 1995), Flew gives typically humanistic views about "spirit," "spirited," "spiritual," and "spirituality." (For discussions of "modern spiritualities" by Margaret Chatterjee, Paul Kurtz, Justin Meggit, Joseph E. Barnhart, R. Joseph Hoffman, Harry Stopes-Roe, James Penney, Ian Coton, Bernard Farr, H. James Birx, and Lawrence Brown, see *New Humanist* [May 1995].)

Spitteler, Carl Friedrich George (1845–1924)

A Swiss poet who won the 1919 Nobel Prize in Literature, Spitteler used the pseudonym Carl Felix Tandem. His chief works were the epics *Prometheus and Epimetheus* (1881) and *Olympischer Frühling* (Olympian Spring), the latter a complex allegory of the necessity for ethics in the modern world. Biographer W. Raith, spoke of Spitteler's "thoroughgoing hostility to Church and priesthood *and* quotes his saying that the clergy ought to be put upon "a diet of locusts and wild honey with cold-water sauce." He referred to "the long-buried gods" and elsewhere said that "the gods are sick to death." {RE}

Spitzer, Hugo (Born 1854)

Spitzer, an Austrian philosopher, taught at Gratz University and was one of the earliest advocates of Darwinism in Austria, writing *Beiträge zur Descendenztheorie* (1885). He distinguished himself in tracing aesthetic evolution, proclaimed himself a "pupil of Haeckel," and spoke highly of *The Riddle of the Universe*. He thought the only philosophers who ought to attack it are those who embrace a "childish Dualism" or who want "not the clearing-up, but the further obscuring and complicating, of the great problems of existence." {RAT}

Spitzer, Lyman Jr. (1914-)

Spitzer is an astronomer whose specialties include research on interstellar matter, space astronomy, stellar dynamics, broadening of spectral lines, conductivity of ionized gases, and controlled release of thermonuclear energy.

He is author the monograph "Physics of Fully Ionized Gases" (1956, revised 1962); "Diffuse Matter in Space" (1968); "Physical Processes in the Interstellar Medium" (1978); "Searching Between the Stars" (1982); "Dynamical Evolution of Globular Clusters" (1987); and "Dreams, Stars in the Sea" (1946). The recipient of numerous astronomical awards and honors, Spitzer is a Unitarian.

Spock, Benjamin McLane (1903–1998)

"You know more than you think you do," pediatrician and author Spock wrote in *The Common Sense Book of Baby and Child Care* (1946). The work is said to have sold more copies that any other original title ever published in the United States. 'Don't be afraid to trust your common sense," he wrote. "What good mothers and fathers instinctively feel like doing for their babies is usually best." Such a view differed radically from that found in the 1928 book, *Psychological Care of Infant and Chil,* by Dr. John B. Watson. "Never, never kiss your child," Watson had warned. "Never hold it in your lap. Never rock its carriage." His break with authority, Dr. Spock said in 1972, gave "practical application" to the ideas of Sigmund Freud and John Dewey. "John Dewey and Freud said that kids don't have to be disciplined into adulthood but can direct themselves toward adulthood by following their own will."

In 1968 he was named the Humanist of the Year by the American Humanist Association. In *The Humanist* January-February 1968 issue, he was quoted:

> The nation that brings up its children with the idea that all they have to be concerned about is their future well-being and their own success in life is headed for trouble. We must bring up our children with a strong sense of service to their community, to their country, and to their world. This education has to start way back in the family.

That same year he was tried and convicted for having counseled draft evasion during the United States involvement in Vietnam. On appeal, the conviction was overturned. In 1972, he was the pacifist People's Party presidential candidate. Dr. Spock has been termed "the American physician everyone knows." According to biographer Thomas Maier, Spock was a product of too little love from his parents, flirted wildly with his female patients, gave little consideration to his first wife's dependence on the antidepressant Miltown, and seldom touched, hugged, or kissed his own sons. Dr. Spock's entry in *Who's Who*:

> In pediatric practice I was trying, with difficulty, to reconcile concepts gained in psychoanalytic training with what mothers told me about their children. After ten years of that I was able to write *Baby and Child Care*, which, in turn, brought invitations to research and teaching jobs. To save children from radiation I became a public supporter of a test ban treaty and co-chairman of the National Committee for a Sane Nuclear Policy (SANE) in 1962 which led, eventually to full-time opposition to the Vietnam war, conviction for conspiracy, conversion to socialism.

{CE; E; HNS2; Eric Pace, *The New York Times*, 17 March 1998}

Spong, John Shelby [Bishop] (1931–)

A controversial Episcopal bishop, author of *Rescuing the Bible From Fundamentalism: A Bishop Rethinks the Meaning of Scripture* (1991), Spong holds that St. Paul, the first great teacher of Christianity, was a "self-loathing and repressed gay male." His *Born of a Woman: A Bishop Rethinks the Birth of Jesus* (1992) suggests that Mary, whom he describes as being far from a virgin, was "a sexually violated teen-age girl." By holding Mary up as a virgin, he holds, women have been hurt. Her humanity is lessened, and this becomes a weapon against women. "Someone known as the Virgin Mother," he writes, "cannot be presented with credibility to contemporary men or women as an ideal woman." In *Resurrection: Myth or Reality* (1994), he argued that the details of Jesus's life and his crucifixion are not historical but, instead, derive from the Jewish tradition of Midrash. Spong suggested, according to critic James A. Cox, that the physical bodily resurrection of Jesus was not originally part of the Christian Easter claim; that the Resurrection actually occurred in Galilee, not in Jerusalem; that the phrase "on the third day" does not refer to chronological time; that the story of Jesus's burial and the account of the empty tomb are late-developing Christian legends; that the Jerusalem account of Easter was created from the Jewish Festival of Tabernacles (or Sukkot); that the triumphant journey of Palm Sunday was undertaken not by Jesus but by Peter well after the crucifixion. Bishop William Wantland of the Diocese of Eau Claire, Wisconsin, has called his fellow bishop "anti-Christian." Asked by Bruce Bawer for a *New York Times* article 28 May 1996) about Spong, Bishop Wantland replied, "I'm sure you're aware of his presentation at Foundry United Methodist Church in Washington a few months ago. He said the Ten Commandments are immoral, he said that Joseph, the foster father of Our Lord, and Judas Iscariot weren't real people, he's denied incarnation, virgin birth, resurrection." Spong's *Why Christianity Must Change or Die: A Bishop Speaks to Believers in Exile, A New Reformation of the Church's Faith and Practice* (1998) further attacks the idea that the monotheistic god is other than a human invention. Freethinkers have been known to place bets on how long Spong will remain in the theistic camp and when he will formally exchange his clerical collar for the non-theists' sports shirt. {TYD}

Spooner, Lysander (1808–1887)

Spooner was an American writer whose first pamphlet was *Deist's Reply to the Alleged Supernatural Evidences of Christianity* (1836). Spooner published works against slavery and was in favor of individualism. Called a "libertarian pietist," he had a strong belief in individual rights and in harming no one. {BDF}

SPONTANEOUS HUMAN COMBUSTION

"There is not any scientific evidence whatsoever that any person ever spontaneously combusted, and no scientifically known means by which it could happen," Joe Nickell claims. He is a senior research fellow of the Committee for the Scientific Investigation of Claims of the Paranormal.

In the 19th century, temperance movement leaders promoted the idea that the body could spontaneously ignite. Charles Dickens in *Bleak House* had a drunkard burned in such a manner. But according to Nickell, "Why these people burn like this must be examined on a case-by-case basis. Just as with freak auto accidents, not all burning deaths, even unusual ones, happen in one way." {*The New York Times*, 26 May 1998}

SPORTS

• A hit, a very palpable hit!

–William Shakespeare,
Hamlet

• Because it's there.

–G. H. L. Mallory,
explaining why he wanted to climb Mt. Everest

• Europeans definitely do not mix sports and religion. They even keep their sports apart from nationalism. . . . Until a couple of decades ago, the sports field in the United States was one arena in which religion played no part. Sadly, those days are gone, and the trend is toward more of a sports/religion mix with little or no opposition from athletes. The media have become willing collaborators in solidifying the new alliance.

–**Jeff Archer**, Editor,
The Alternative

• Serious sport has nothing to do with fair play. It is bound up with hatred, jealousy, boastfulness, disregard of all rules and sadistic pleasure in witnessing violence: in other words, it is war minus the shooting.

–George Orwell

• God absolutely could not play basketball, tennis, or soccer. Because He is omnipresent, He would always be out of established bounds.

–Anonymous

• When I watched the World Cup last summer and saw the supporters of the various national teams waving their country's flag and singing patriotic songs, I understood that the Europeans had finally found a substitute for war.

–Paul Auster

Sporus: Sporus was Nero's boy "bride." (See entry for Alexander Pope.)

Sprading, Charles T (20th Century)

An atheist, Sprading wrote *What Freethinkers Affirm* (19–?) and *The Science of Materialism* (1942) and *Liberty and the Great Libertarians* (1972). {GS}

Sprague, H. (20th Century)

In 1957, Sprague was Secretary of the United Secularists of America in Clifton, New Jersey.

Spuhler, Andrée (20th Century)

Spuhler is a Secular Humanist Mentor of the Council for Secular Humanism. She was President and founder of Freethinkers, Inc., a Winter Park, Florida, group that disbanded in 1996 after years of activities in the Orlando, Florida, area. {FD}

SRI LANKAN FREETHINKERS

Freethought in the United Kingdom and the Commonwealth, by Gordon Stein, discusses Sri Lankan freethought, which dates to the Sri Lankan Rationalist Association in the 1950s. (See entries for Arthur C. Clarke, Royston Ellis, and Buddha's Tooth. Also, see entry for Tissa Balasuriya, a Sri Lankan Catholic priest excommunicated in 1996 for heresy.)

SRI LANKAN UNITARIANS

Walter Jayewardene is the Director-Secretary General of the Unitarian Universalist Association of Sri Lanka (UUSL, 61/3 Old Road, Nawala, Rajagiriya, Sri Lanka). Although wounded in 1996 by a Tamil bomb attack, he has led his group to establish a business making and selling silver chalice jewelry.

Sumanasiri Hullugalle, who is secretary to the Ministry of Labor and Vocational Training in Sri Lanka, is President of the UUSL.

There are seven main branches of Unitarians with a total membership of around five hundred. Because the island is multi-ethnic, members are Sinhalese, Tamils, Muslims, Eurasian, and Malays. The UUSL was founded in 1992. (See entry for Walter Jayewardene.)

Srikanth, Gautam (20th Century)

Srikanth, while a student at Christopher Newport University in Virginia, was one of the founders of Campus Freethought Alliance. {*International Humanist News*, December 1996}

St.: See Saint and Sainte.

Staaf, Karl (19th Century)

Staff, who was a prime minister of Sweden, was a non-theist. (See entry for Scandinavian Unbelievers.)

Stacpoole, Henry de Vere (1863–1931)

A novelist and ship's doctor, of Irish ancestry, Stacpoole wrote a best-selling romance, *The Blue Lagoon* (1908), the story of two cousins marooned on a tropical island at the age of eight. They grow up, mature, produce a baby, and eventually are swept away by accident across their lagoon to the ocean and the oblivion of "the never-wake berries" which they providentially carry with them in their dinghy. Stacpoole had studied Carlyle and German philosophy, then the French stylists. He translated from the Italian, Spanish, French, German, and Swedish. In 1916, he wrote a *Life of François Villon* and translated Villon's work. {RAT}

Staël-Holstein, Anne Louise Germaine de [Baroness] (1766–1817)

A French-Swiss woman of letters, whose full name was Anne Louise Germaine Necker, Staël was born in Paris and early absorbed the intellectual and political atmosphere of her mother's salon. Her father was the French Minister of Finance. Early on in life she shed her Protestantism and became a Voltairean. In 1786 she married Baron Staël-Holstein, a Swedish diplomat. Although moderately sympathizing with the French Revolution, she left France in 1792, returning to Paris under the Directory. After separating amicably from her husband, she became intimately associated with Benjamin Constant. In 1803 because of her opposition to Bonaparte, she was exiled from Paris and retired to her estate at Coppet, on the Lake of Geneva.

She wrote *Delphine* (1802) and *De la littérature considérée dans ses rapports avec les institutions sociales* (1800), a study of the influence of social conditions on literature. Copies of her principal work, *De L'Allemagne* (1810), the result of a tour through Germany, were destroyed in Paris by order of Napoleon, who resented the book as an invidious comparison between German and French culture and mores.

Threatened by Napoleon's police, Mme. de Staël fled to Russia and England, later returning to Switzerland. John Quincy Adams, when an ambassador in Paris, knew her and described her to his mother: "She spoke much about the preservation of religion, in which, she gave me to understand, she did not herself believe." {JM; RAT; RE; WWS}

Stafford, Russell Henry L: See entry for Theism.

Stahl, Harold: See entry for Eldon Scholl.

Stalker, Bill (20th Century)

Stalker is Treasurer of Free Inquirers of Northeastern Ohio.

Stalin, Joseph Vissarionovich (1879–1953)

The Georgian cobbler's son (who was named Ioseb Dzhugashvili) moved from being a seminarian to becoming leader of the Communist Party and one of the internationally best-known atheists. Accepting the view in Karl Marx's *Critique of Hegel's Philosophy of Right* that "Religion . . . is the opium of the people," Stalin (a pseudonym meaning "man of steel") ruled as dictator of the state without the need for any sanction from the church. Early on, Stalin became the darling of much of the international intelligentsia (McCabe in 1940 wrote that "it is now generally agreed that he is one of the greatest statesmen in Europe and a distinguished strategist"), but his rule was marked by a paranoia that led to periods of terror, and he has become a symbol of a ruthless dictator without real feelings for the uplifting of mankind.

A story current in the 1940s had it that Roosevelt, Churchill, and Stalin were breakfasting at Teheran. Roosevelt mentioned his odd dream last night, that God had appointed him head of the United Nations. Churchill piped up that, indeed, that was a coincidence, that he, too, had dreamed God had appointed him Premier of the United Nations. Stalin, still a bit groggy from a sleepless night, retorted, "I had a dream last night, too, but I don't remember appointing anyone to anything."

Scholars are still estimating the enormous numbers of people who were killed because of Stalin's ruthlessness, illustrating that, although he was an unbeliever, Stalin was by no stretch of the imagination a humanist. {CE; JM; RE}

Stallard, H. H. (20th Century)

Stallard in 1928 wrote *The Debunkers*. {GS}

Stallman, Richard (20th Century)

Stallman at the 1996 Humanist World Congress held in Mexico City spoke about education and global humanism for the cyber-age. His e-mail is <rms@gnu.ai.mit.edu> and homepage is <http://www.gnu.org/people/rms.html>.

Stallone, Sylvester (1946–)

Stallone is an entertainer cited by Paul Edwards in *Reincarnation* as being a believer in reincarnation. "Stallone thinks he may have been a monkey in Guatemala," Edwards noted jocularly about the Hollywood star, "something I find entirely credible."

Stamm, August Theodor (19th Century)

Stamm was a German humanist who wrote *The Religion of Action* (1866). After the events of 1848, Stamm went to England, then to America. {BDF}

Stamos, David N. (20th Century)

Stamos is author of "A Stumper for Theists Revisited" in *American Rationalist*, November-December, 1990.

Standley, Albert (Deceased)

Stanley was a member of the National Secular Society, South Place Ethical Society, and the Fabian Society. An annual Albert Standley lecture, organized by the South London Republican Forum, is arranged to honor his contribution to Republicanism and other progressive causes. The 1999 speaker was Terry Liddle. (*The Freethinker*, April 1999)

Standring, George (1855–1924)

Standring was an English lecturer and writer. For some years he was chorister at a Ritualistic Church, but he discarded theology after independent inquiry in 1873. He then became honorary secretary of the National Secular Society, started *Republican Chronicle* (1875), which afterwards was called *The Republican*, and still later *The Radical* (1888). Standring was contributor to the *National Reformer*, *Freethinker*, *Progress*, and other publications.

His older brother, **Sam Standring Jr.** (born 1853), was also a freethinker. Their father, **Sam Standring Sr.**, was what was later to be called an "agnostic." Their mother was a Wesleyan who had brought the boys up as Wesleyans. George, who was highly critical of G. W. Foote, formed the Freethought Federation in 1896. In his later years, George devoted himself to the Fabian Society and the Malthusian League rather than the National Secular Society. Standring wrote *An Atheist At Church* (1894). {BDF; FUK; PUT; RAT; RSR; TRI}

Stanfield, Marion Baar (Died 1967)

In 1949, Stanfield created a fund of art scholarships for Unitarian artists of the "conservative New England Type." A resident of Westport, Connecticut, she included in her will a stringent gender requirement: To qualify, art students had to be female. That stipulation has since been overturned in court and her stipulations about the recipients' Unitarian faith is now "interpreted loosely." Since 1977, more than one hundred art scholarships (generally ranging from $1,000 to $3,000 a year) have been presented. {Susanne Skubik, "The Stanfield Art Scholarships," *World*, November-December 1994}

Stanford, Leland [Governor; Senator] (1824-1893)

A Unitarian, Stanford was Governor of California from 1861 to 1863 and was U. S. Senator from 1885 to 1893. A capitalist who was one of the four founders of Central Pacific Railroad and was President of Southern Pacific Railroad from 1885 to 1890. He founded Stanford University with an endowment in memory of his son, Leland Stanford Jr.

Stanford, S. (20th Century)

Stanford is on the editorial committee of New Zealand's *Rationalist and Humanist*.

Stanhope, Hester Lucy [Lady] (1776–1839)

Stanhope, the daughter of Earl Stanhope and grand-daughter of Lord Chatham, was the niece of William Pitt. Reared in a freethinking atmosphere, she kept house for Pitt in his later years. Then, disgusted with the hypocrisy of English religious life, she went to live in the Near East. Adopting Eastern male dress and a religion that was a composite of Christianity and Islam, she settled among the Druses of the Lebanon Mountains in an abandoned convent that she rebuilt and fortified. The indigenous population regarded her as a prophetess as, in time, she came to regard herself. Stanhope incited them to resist an Egyptian invasion (1831) of Syria. According to McCabe, Lady Lucy "scorned Christianity and was a woman of great ability and character." {JM; RAT; RE}

Stanley, F. Lloyd (19th Century)

Stanley was the American author of *An Outline of the Future Religion of the World*, a deistic work in which he criticized preceding religions. {BDF}

Stanosz, Barbara (20th Century)

Stanosz, a professor of philosophy in Poland who specializes in logic, has been active in supporting a Polish humanist magazine, *Bez Dogmatu*. In an interview (*International Humanist News*, June 1995), Stanosz was concerned that democracy is in danger in her country. In 1996, she was a participant not only in the Polish Humanist Conference on European Integration in Utrecht but also in the Humanist World Congress held in Mexico City. She signed Humanist Manifesto 2000. (See entries for Polish humanism and for the Society for Humanism and Independent Ethics.) {*Free Inquiry*, Winter 1996-1997}

Stansbury, Hubert (20th Century)

A freethinker, Stansbury wrote *In Quest of Truth* (1913). {GS}

Stansfield, James [Sir] (1820–1898)

Stansfield, a warm friend of Holyoake, supported Secularist societies and was a lawyer who contributed generously to reform movements. He entered Parliament and became Under-Secretary of State for India, Financial Secretary of the Treasury, and President of the Local Government Board. {RAT; RE}

Stanton, Elizabeth Cady (1815–1902)

"The Bible and the Church have been the greatest stumbling blocks in the way of women's emancipation," Stanton once wrote. "The religious superstition of women perpetuate their bondage more than all other adverse influences." A leader of the woman suffrage movement, she with several others called the first woman's rights convention in the United States in 1848 at Seneca Falls, New York. With Susan B. Anthony as publisher, she and Parker Pillsbury edited (1868–1870) the *Revolution*, a magazine of militant feminism. With Anthony and Matilda Joslyn Gage, Stanton compiled the first three volumes of *History of Woman Suffrage* (1881–1886). Feminists, however, point to Stanton's daring work with a small committee in 1895 on *The Women's Bible*. At that time, few women dared to involve themselves in a scholarly commentary on the entire Bible. Of her group's work, Stanton wrote, "The Old Testament makes woman a mere afterthought in creation; the author of evil; cursed in her maternity; a subject in marriage; and all female life, animal and human, unclean. The Church in all ages has taught these doctrines and acted on them, claiming divine authority therefor. . . . This idea of woman's subordination is reiterated times without number, from *Genesis* to *Revelation*; and this is the basis of all church action." In 1898, Stanton wrote *Eighty Years and More: Reminiscences 1815–1897*.

In a life of William Lloyd Garrison, Stanton is described at a public meeting as having said, "In the darkness and gloom of a false theology I was slowly sawing off the chains of my spirit-bondage when, for the first time, I met Garrison in London. A few bold strokes from the hammer of his truth, and I was free!"

Carol A. Newsom and Sharon H. Ringe, in their editing of *The Women's Bible Commentary* (1992), mention that Stanton edited an expurgated version of the Bible for women in 1895. Women are particularly sensitive about passages such as *Exodus* 22:18 (a warrant for witch burning); *I Corinthians* 14 (Paul's outburst against women speaking in church); *Nahum* 3:5 (in which the Lord of Hosts threatens to lift the women's skirts over their faces to reveal their nakedness); *I Timothy* 2:12 (instructing women to be silent and let only men to do the teaching); *Genesis* (in which Eve is the woman-as-evil temptress); and, as described in *Friend Journal* (January 1993) by Chuck Fager, the *Commentary* points up "the repeated images, beginning with Hosea, and including Isaiah, Jeremiah, Ezekiel, Nahum and others, portraying God's relationship to Israel and humans in general as a marriage. Here God is the steadfast, long-suffering (but all-powerful) husband, and Israel / humankind a chronically adulterous, promiscuous whore of a spouse. The female sinner is repeatedly punished by the righteously angry Divine Husband, through the most gruesome violence imaginable: exposure, multiple rapes, the murder of her children, dismemberment, cannibalism, etc." Some of the forty-one contributors to the study, faced by the near-total androcentricity of the biblical text, were "tempted to toss the entire cultural tradition it epitomizes aside and start over" but decided to examine it, as did Stanton, "from a consciously female perspective, if only to resist its negative impact on them." {BDF; JM; PUT; RE; TRI; TYD; WWS}

Stanton, Luke (1960–1993)

Stanton, a native of Trinidad who moved to New York City, was a secular humanist who died of AIDS. A member of AASH, he had helped advise others who were HIV-positive, and he owned a New York City hairdressing shop.

At his memorial, which was attended by several hundred, "A Letter From Luke" was distributed which contained not only the Council for Secular Humanism's "Affirmations of Humanism" but also stated the following:

> I was raised Roman Catholic and spent the greater part of my teenage years trying to come to terms with the hypocrisies and contradictions of Catholic dogma. The realization that my sexual orientation was homosexual and the church's adamantly homophobic position of opposing all issues that pertain to the Gay and Lesbian community finally solidified my feelings about Catholicism—this religion was not for me. I spent some time thinking about and exploring other forms of worship and spirituality and just wasn't convinced with their doctrines, either. I began to realize that I was very much a skeptic and held all religious dogma, including all the New

Age free form spirituality, at bay. I kept saying to myself, 'they can't seriously believe that people are gonna go for this stuff?' But, yes, people do go for that stuff and sometimes with zest and vigor. This was something that I had to come to terms with. Even though I did not believe in supreme beings, deities, spirits, saints, goblins, and the hereafter, there are many people who do and it was important to me that I respected their feelings on these issues. So it became apparent that I, an atheist, could live among the masses who were believers with little or no problems.

In my late twenties I became interested in a philosophy called "Secular Humanism." I read a few books about it, subscribed to some publications about Humanism, and even discovered that the Unitarian Church and the Ethical Culture Society were outstanding examples of humanistic organizations. The tenets of humanism were exactly how I felt about life on planet Earth as it pertained to Luke Stanton. It gave me quite a bit of joy discovering this facet of my life and today I am very pleased to call myself a "Secular Humanist." Well, anyway, if anybody knows anything about humanism—it's about the farthest thing from Catholicism that you can find.

Stanton instructed his companion, Michael Stanton—the two had agreed to take the same final name—that he wished to be cremated and have a niche in an outdoor mausoleum at Trinity Church Cemetery in Upper Manhattan. He further requested that Aaron Copeland's "Fanfare for the Common Man" be played.

Stap, A. (19th Century)

Stap wrote *Historic Studies on the Origins of Christianity* (1864) and *The Immaculate Conception.* {BDF}

Stapledon, Olaf (20th Century)

Stapledon's *Beyond the Isms* (1942) called for a synthesis of religion and materialism.

Stapp, Owill V. (20th Century)

Stapp wrote "Why the Doctor Will Not 'Condesund' " (1913). {GS}

STAR DUST AND STARS

"Look, a beautiful shooting star!"

"Beautiful, my dear, yes; but stars do not shoot! You just saw a meteor that fell into Earth's atmosphere!"

According to scientists, stars are self-luminous bodies consisting of a mass of gas that is held together by its own gravity. Their energy is generated by nuclear reactions in the interior that are balanced by the outflow of energy to the surface, and the inward-directed gravitational forces are balanced by the outward directed gas and radiation pressure.

According to humanists, and in the words of Ann and Jane Taylor from their *Rhymes for the Nursery* (1806),

Twinkle, twinkle, little star,
How I wonder what you are,
Up above the world so high,
Like a diamond in the sky.

What neither the scientists nor the humanists are sure about is what "star dust" is. In 1999 NASA sent an unmanned craft to rendezvous with a comet for the purpose of collecting some of its microscopic particles in order to test this interstellar dust. If successful, the mission will be the first ever to retrieve extraterrestrial material from beyond the Earth's Moon.

Starbuck, Edwin Dilles (1866–1947)

Starbuck taught philosophy at Iowa State University. His rationalistic views are found in his *Psychology of Religion* (1899) and *The Forward Look in Philosophy* (1913). Holding a vague pantheism, Starbuck made "no distinction between divine and human beings." {RAT; RE}

Starcke, Carl Nicolay (1858–1926)

Starcke was a teacher of philosophy in the University of Copenhagen. A decided disciple on Feuerbach, on whom he published a dissertation in 1883, Starcke wrote critical surveys of the views of Lubbock, Maine, McLennan, and Feuerbach. {BDF}

Stark, Rodney (20th Century)

Stark, a sociologist, wrote *The Rise of Christianity*, in which he tries to explain the success of Christianity. In *A Theory of Religion*, Stark and collaborator William Bainbridge wrote, "Neither of us is religious, as that term is conventionally understood and as we use it in this book. Neither of us belongs to a religious organization, and neither of us believes in the supernatural." {CA; E}

Starkes, George (20th Century)

An African American, Starkes is a writer and atheist activist from Tampa, Florida. He is an admirer of the works of Robert G. Ingersoll, who he believes should inspire contemporaries by his freethinking activism.

Starkey, David (20th Century)

Starkey, a historian and broadcaster, became an Honorary Associate of the Rationalist Press Association in 1995. He has written *Wishes and Fears* (1988), *British Privateering Enterprise in the Eighteenth Century* (1990), *Henry VIII: A European Court in England* (1991), *Koan Americana* (1991), *and Reign of Henry VIII: Personalities and Politicians* (1992). In 1996, Starkey gave the 70th Conway Memorial Lecture at Conway Hall in London.

He has been described as "the rudest man in Britain" and "the thinking man's Alf Garnett." In *The Sunday Telegraph*, he was reported as saying, "My first boyfriend called himself a High Church atheist. I remember going with him to a church with altars crammed with statues and crosses; four Knights of Malta with purple socks. I'd like to have taken a sledgehammer to it all." Starkey was formerly chairman of the Gay Tory group, Torche.

Starkey has written of his past and his views:

As usual, origins say much, if not all. I was born into a Quaker family in the 1940s. The secret of Quakerism's extraordinary fertility in so many areas—from science and the arts to business—is that Quakers are marginal but self-confidently so. And my family was marginal even within the minority. The Quaker Meeting in Kendal was high bourgeois, prosperous and dominated by old, local families; my parents were working class, poor and "off-comers" into this standoffish little town.

Personal traits added to this sense of not quite belonging. I was born pretty badly crippled. Brilliant surgery corrected the problem almost completely. But for much of my boyhood I had to wear surgical boots. And I was soon aware that I was different sexually. I did not yet have a name for it. But this was the early intimation of my homosexuality.

All this could have led to mere chippiness. I was saved by two things. The first was the confidence instilled into me by my mother. The second was that I was academically very successful—so much so that, in the 1960s, becoming an academic seemed the obvious choice of career.

I became an historian, I suppose, because history was the subject that best answered to my sense of being both outsider and insider. My most important work is on the Tudor Court. Choosing this topic was another act of dissent. The orthodoxy was that Tudor England was becoming a modern bureaucratic state; to me it was obvious that it was a personal monarchy. There were intrinsic reasons as well: the history of royal Courts is doubly satisfying. It shows high politics at its most brutal. This is universal. But it also deals in a set of values radically different from our own: aristocracy, hierarchy, magnificence.

This is where my academic history connects with my role as a media antimoralist on Radio 4's The Moral Maze and Talk radio, where I have my own show on Sunday mornings. For the relativism of values and morality is, it seems to me, not a debatable philosophical position but a demonstrable historical fact. And this, in turn, is the intellectual basis of my atheism. Values are a changeable human construct; they are not the immutable gift of an eternal God. But nor are they a necessary deduction from the Laws of Nature. This is why for me atheism is necessarily individualistic, not socialistic. The world is something we have to make sense of. We start with both the help and the hindrance of inherited traditions. But finally the meaning we give to our lives is our own.

Humanism is simply the best way of arbitrating between these individual perceptions.

{*The Freethinker* November 1997; *New Humanist*, March 1998}

Starkey, Marion: The American Library Association's *Banned Books* (1998) cites Starkey's *The Tall Man From Boston* as often being banned because it "would lead children to believe ideas contrary to the teachings of the Bible." (See entry for Banned Books.)

Starosta, Miroslav (20th Century)

Starosta is chairperson of the Czech Unitarian Association. (See entry for Czech Unitarian Association.)

Starr, Lillian (20th Century)

Starr is on the editorial board of *The Truth Seeker*, a San Diego, California, freethinkers' magazine.

Starr, Mark (1894–1985)

Starr, an American Federation of Labor union leader, was educational director in New York City of the International Ladies' Garment Workers' Union. With Harold U. Faulkner, he wrote *Labor in America* (1944). He also was chairman of the Esperanto Information Center and, in 1965, the United Nations representative of *Universala Esperanto-Asocoo*.

On the subject of humanism, he wrote the present author:

Bearing in mind all the semantic weakness that persists in the use of words, I think my closest association is with #7, "naturalistic humanism." While not forgetting how dark and deep are the passions from which all men and women yet suffer, I still have faith that human beings can become progressively the masters of their fate. The basis for that hope is the record of past progress as shown by history. Because of the circumstances of my upbringing where I saw the class struggle operating in actual life, I became interested in the Marxian theories as, of course, clearly distinguished from the totalitarian applications of a minor part of them concerned with the "dictatorship of the proletariat." It is indeed fascinating to see how men's ideas and morals and ethics are the sublimations and rationalizations of their economic needs. The way in which men, as members of social groups, make their living can be correlated with their beliefs in a very illuminating way. There is, of course, no automatic reaction between economics and ideas. Outstanding individuals can be the exceptional cases who raise themselves above their social environment. The way itself by which men get their living depends upon a mass of geographic, climatic, cultural, and economic factors which are all in process of continual change.

I think my humanism is less individualist than that of some of my colleagues. I think we must develop a *group* ethic in order to make any application of public enterprise operate satisfactorily. What happened in Nazi Germany and in Soviet Russia shows that collectivism can be applied at the expense of the liberty and integrity of the individual. The importance of the healthy, happy human being as the end product of any effective society has been impressed upon our minds by such experiences. In pessimistic moments we wish that there were some Universal Intelligence upon which one could rely to solve all our problems. Even the acceptance of any kind of humanist principles does not make unnecessary the hard, tough job of applying those principles to specific instances. The acceptance of any dogma or faith in some anthropomorphic omniscient force seems to me to be an understandable demonstration of human weakness and the natural desire for explanation and solution of things which still have to be understood and overcome. I am constantly amazed at the wonder and the immensity of the Universe and the power of thinking man (as a conscious part of that universe) to use his mind to generalize the One out of the Many. Also the slow evolution, which has achieved in man its highest and articulate expression, awakens reverence and a sense of responsibility to aid in future progress.

These are the premises of my humanism which has relations to other forms but cannot be encompassed by any simple label. Here is the challenge and the response to further progress without mystic and supernatural connotations. Here, I hope, is the basis for all men and women of good will, irrespective of their individual beliefs and theologies, to find a basis for cooperation in helping men to improve the world and simultaneously themselves.

Starr, a signer of Humanist Manifesto II, was a member of the New York City humanist group, writing in *The Humanist Newsletter* (Summer 1953),

I feel that the humanist should participate in politics, and it would be surprising if he did not cooperate with the most progressive group available in his locality. My own view is that the humanist should be led by logic and facts to advocate social planning plus the Bill of Rights. In the fight for civil liberties, he cannot take a back seat. My guess would be that, at the present moment, most humanists would feel close to the position of the Americans for Democratic Action generally, and in New York State to that of the Liberal Party.

{HM2; HNS; WAS, 18 April 1956}

STARGAZER

Stargazer, *Star Walker*, and *Sunrise Journal* are at PO Box 4153, Salem, Oregon 97302. E-mail: <lloydk@teleport.com>.

STATE UNIVERSITY OF NEW YORK, ALBANY

Humanists at the Albany branch of the State University of New York are on the Web: <www.secularhumanism.org/cfa/orgs.html>.

STATE UNIVERSITY OF NEW YORK, BUFFALO

Humanists at the Buffalo branch of the State University of New York are on the Web: <www.secularhumanism.org/cfa/orgs.html>.

Statham, Francis Reginal (19th Century)

Statham wrote *Rational Theology* (1872). {GS}

Statius, Publius Papinius (c. 40–c. 96 CE)

A Latin poet and a favorite of Emperor Domitian, Statius was much esteemed both in his time and through the Middle Ages.

He agreed with Petronius that it was fear first made gods in the world, and his ranking of Domitian with the gods made its truth no less pointed. {CE; JMR; JMRH; TYD}

Stauffer, James (20th Century)

Stauffer is active with the South Bay Secular Humanists. (See entry for California Atheists, Humanists.) {FD}

Stavrum, Lorentz (20th Century)

Stavrum is President of the Norwegian Humanist Association.

Stcherbatsky, Th. (20th Century)

In India, Stcherbatsky wrote *History of Materialism in India* (19–?). {GS}

Stebbing, Susan (1885–1943)

Stebbing was a philosopher who criticized Eddington and was, according to Colin McCall, "a model of clarity and demolition. In his day, Eddington made "picturesque" pronouncements which are amusing today but were eagerly devoured by the religiously inclined then. Stebbing's logical and linguistic analysis are commendable, McCall stated. {*Freethinker*, June 1996}

Stebbing, T. (20th Century)

Stebbing, a freethinker, has written, "The Christian God knew before He created man that man would sin, and so He condemned the human race to Hell and endless suffering. What dreadful demon could rival such a Creator?"

Stebbins, Horatio (1821–1902)

Although it was Starr King who established a Unitarian presence on the West Coast, it was Thomas Lamb Eliot and Horatio Stebbins who maintained that presence through their steady leadership of the San Francisco and Portland churches. He wrote *Prayers* (1903).

Criticized at the outbreak of the Civil War for what some of his congregation thought was a too-blatant expression of patriotism and politics in the pulpit, Stebbins replied: "I have great respect for the people, and it gives me pain to come in collision with their convictions; but there is one man whose respect I must have, and his name is Stebbins." {U&U}

Stec, Michael (20th Century)

On the Web, Stec sells books of interest to atheists: <http://members.tripod.com/~mstec/atheism.html>.

Stecher, Carl (20th Century)

Stecher is a former Woodrow Wilson Fellow and a professor of English at Salem State College in Salem, Massachusetts. In "Looking for God in All the Wrong Places" (*The Humanist*, May-June 1998), he tends toward using the Christians' terminology but finds that in his own search for God he has settled more for "a God freed from the barbarism of ancient origins, a God who does not need editing or sanitizing or rationalizing. Perhaps we can have a God who embodies only our highest ideals."

Stedman, D. B. (19th Century)

Stedman, a freethinker, wrote "Why I Am Not a Christian" (189–?). {GS}

Steeg, F. W. (20th Century)

Steeg wrote *Babylon the Great* (1913). {GS}

Steegman, A. T(heodore) (1936–)

A professor of anthropology at State University of New York in Buffalo, Steegman is on the Council for Secular Humanism's Committee for the Scientific Examination of Religion. In 1983 Steegman wrote *Boreal Forest Adaptations.*

Steenhaut, O. (20th Century)

At the International Humanist and Ethical Union's (IHEU's) Second Moral Education Conference held in Brussels (1985), Prof. Steenhaut of Belgium addressed the group.

Stefanoni, Luigi (Born 1842)

Stefanoni was an Italian writer and publicist. His first romance, *The Spanish in Italy,* was suppressed by the Austrians. Joining Garibaldi's volunteers, Stefanoni contributed to *Unita Italiana*. In 1866 in Milan he founded the Society of Freethinkers and its organ, *Il Libero Pensiero*. Stefanoni wrote *A Critical History of Superstition*, compiled a philosophical dictionary (1873–1875), and translated Büchner's *Force and Matter*. {BDF; RAT}

Stefansson, Vilhjalmur (1879–1962)

A Canadian-born U.S. explorer of the Arctic Circle (1913–1918), Stefansson became curator of the Stefansson collection of polar material at the Baker Library, Dartmouth College, and author of *My Life with the Eskimo* (1913).

Encyclopedist Sherman Wakefield wrote the present writer (29 August 1956), "In connection with your Humanist questionnaire to prominent people, I wonder if you ever sent one to Dr. Vilhjalmur Stefansson, the Arctic explorer. His address is Dept. of Northern Studies, Dartmouth College, Hanover, New Hampshire. He attends a Unitarian church in Hanover, but he may be more than an orthodox Unitarian. I met him several years ago at a party, and he told me then he had studied Comparative Religions at Harvard under Moore. Several weeks ago I sent him an old copy of *The Arbitrator* in which I quoted from Peary and an Eskimo to the effect that Eskimos have no religion but they had all the virtues. I have been surprised that he did not acknowledge its receipt and wonder if he was shocked. Without mentioning my name, I wish you would send him your questionnaire (if you have not already done so) and let me know his answer."

Stefansson in 1954 had written,

> I have not read Corliss Lamont's *Humanism As A Philosophy*, but he and I have conversed in that field and I suppose us to be in general agreement, at least enough so that we might both be tagged [naturalistic] humanists. I have read others of his.

On the subject of religion he has written:

> The Stone Age people had a religion by which they believed themselves able to control their environment, but it was neither a religion of hope nor of fear. There was no permanent future life; there was nothing resembling heaven or hell. The spirits were powerful but they were not in themselves good or evil, though they might do the good or evil bidding of people who controlled them. . . .They had as much desire to live as any of us but less fear of dying than most of us. . . . These people who lived were to all appearances so much happier than any other group I have ever known. . . . The chief factor in the happiness of the Stone Age Eskimos was they were living according to the golden rule. . . . The successful man stood above his fellows in nothing but their good opinion. . . . Your importance in the community depended on your judgment, your ability, and your character, but notably upon your unselfishness and kindness.
>
> {CE; CL; RAT; WAS, 5 October 1954}

Steffens, (Joseph) Lincoln (1866–1936)

An American author, known as a Muckraker, Steffens turned out articles exposing municipal corruption. He wrote *The Shame of the Cities* (1904) and *Upbuilders* (1909), but it was his autobiography in 1931 which particularly described his era. Among his observations:

> • Why is it that the less intelligence people have, the more spiritual they are? They seem to fill all the vacant, ignorant spaces in their heads with soul. Which explains how it is that the less knowledge they have, the more religion.
>
> {TYD}

Steiger, Rod (1925-)

Steiger, a well-known actor, has appeared in numerous movies and plays. In 1967 he won an Academy Award for "In the Heat of the Night."

He occasionally is asked to give speeches on the kosher dinner circuit, for he has played Jewish characters in such films as "The Pawnbroker" and "The Chosen." However, according to Tim Boxer's *Jewish Celebrity Anecdotes*, Steiger is an agnostic whose parents were Lutheran. {CA}

Stein, Anita (20th Century)

Stein was in the Birmingham project that was organized by the American Ethical Union's Commission on Race and Equality. {EU, Howard B. Radest}

Stein, Gertrude (1874–1946)

Philosophic naturalists like to quote Stein's observation, "There ain't no answer. There ain't going to be any answer. There never has been an answer. That's the answer." They do not, however, share her attraction to saints, as shown in her and her companion Alice B. Toklas's *Lucy Church Amiably* (1930).

Lansing Warren in a 1934 interview with Stein related one of her controversial, opinionated, and ironic viewpoints: "I say that Hitler ought to have the peace prize because he is removing all elements of contest and of struggle from Germany. By driving out the Jews and the democratic and left elements, he is driving out everything that conduces to activity. That means peace." Her critics accused her of supporting Marshal Henri Pétain and his armistice with Germany, which embroiled her with the general public as much as did her open lesbianism.

The author of "Rose is a rose is a rose" was praised for her creative work, however, by such as the composer John Cage and the Living Theater's Julian Beck and Judith Malina. {GL; Seymour I. Toll, "A Loopy Genius," *The New York Times*, 9 February 1997; TYD}

Stein, Gordon (1941–1996)

Stein was one of the most extensive researchers on the topic of unbelief.

For humanist and rationalist publications, he wrote in excess of six hundred book reviews. He was associated with such journals as *The American Rationalist*, *Free Inquiry*, and *The Truth Seeker*. Also, he was an officer of the Freedom from Religion Foundation, a Secular Humanist Mentor of the Council for Secular Humanism, and that group's director of the Center for Inquiry libraries. Dr. Stein wrote a number of basic, exhaustive, and definitive references on freethought topics. In 1981, he wrote *Freethought in the United Kingdom*. In 1980, he edited *An Anthology of Atheism and Rationalism*. In 1987, he edited *A Second Anthology of Atheism and Rationalism*. In 1990, he wrote the scholarly *God Pro and Con: A Bibliography of Atheism*.

In 1993 he wrote not only the *Encyclopedia of Hoaxes* but also *The Sorcerer of Kings: The Case of Daniel Dunglas Home and William Crookes*, which describes the rise in spiritualism, or survival of the spirit after death, that began in the 1840s in upstate New York; he details how the "phenomena" of spiritualism was produced. In 1994 at the Toronto conference of the Coalition for Secular Humanism, Atheism, and Freethought (CSHAFT), Stein spoke on "What Is the Good Life? A Humanist Perspective." His consummate achievement was the editing of *The Encyclopedia of Unbelief* (1985).

Just before his death from cancer, Stein's editing of *The Encyclopedia of the Paranormal* (1996), a comprehensive and major collection, was published. The work examined "a wide range of claims, claimants, phenomena, and beliefs, from the certifiably false to the intriguingly possible, and all stops between," according to Jerome Clark. Wendy M. Grossman, founder of the United Kingdom's *The Skeptic*, praised the work highly as "an ambitious and difficult project." Contributors included Geoffrey Dean, Arthur Mather, Ivan W. Kelly, Joe Nickell, Ray Human, Terence Hines, Paul Kurtz, and other experts. Carl Sagan wrote the foreword.

Nicolas Walter, in *The Independent* (6 September 1996), described Stein as "a leading activist in the English-speaking freethought movement," one who "will be missed as a key figure in a growing movement." Walter also wrote, "Stein was an unusual personality among Americans and humanists, being rather introverted and taciturn, but he was a loyal colleague and a stimulating if abrasive conversationalist. He was a severe critic of work by other people, yet sensitive to criticism by others. " Stein, he noted, had "helped to found the best paper in the American free-thought movement, *Free Inquiry*," and became "a considerable scholar in a movement which contains many considerable scholars."

Some 8,000 of Stein's books were contributed to the Center for Inquiry Libraries. They represent important works on atheism, Bible criticism, the historicity of Jesus, freethought history, spiritualism, the occult, and parapsychology. {EU, Anne N. Gaylor and Eldon Scholt; FUK; FUS; SHD}

Stein, Robert M. (20th Century)

When he signed Humanist Manifesto II, Stein was co-chairman, Public Affairs Committee, American Ethical Union. Stein in 1990 wrote *Urban Alternatives: Public and Private Markets in the Provision of Local Services*. {HM2}

Stein, Stuart (20th Century)

Stein, when he signed Humanist Manifesto II, was a member of the board of directors of the American Ethical Union. {HM2}

Steinbart, Gotthelf Samuel (1738–1809)

A German rationalist, Steinbart was brought up in a pietist school but upon reading Voltaire became a freethinker. In 1874 he became professor of philosophy at Frankfurt-on-the-Oder and wrote *A System of Pure Philosophy* (1878). {BDF}

Steinbeck, John (1902–1968)

Steinbeck is the Pulitzer- nd Nobel Prize-winning novelist of *The Grapes of Wrath*, *Of Mice and Men*, and *East of Eden*. Asked his views about humanism, he wrote the present author:

> Forgive me for not answering your letter. I have been working very hard. Too hard indeed for self-scrutiny. My approach to philosophy is usually on tiptoe ready to run like hell at the first growl. Frankly, I haven't the slightest idea what my approach is or even whether I have one. I think my favorite evaluation is one wherein a very erudite man proved beyond doubt with parallel quotations that my whole body of thinking was stolen from an eighteenth-century Frenchman of whom I had never heard. I can't help further. Working on a long and difficult book. These [post]cards are designed to break me of a vicious habit of writing letters.

That "long and difficult book" was *East of Eden* (1952), in which Adam Trask considers naming his children Cain and Abel, because his Chinese servant had interpreted the Biblical story to show that although God exiled Cain to the land east of Eden, He had said to him, "if thou doest well . . . thou mayest rule over sin." Instead, Adam names them Caleb and Aron.

Also humanistic is his *Of Mice and Men* (1937), which is capable of drawing tears from some highschoolers who are assigned to read the work and who find in the 1990s an understanding of the poor and homeless which may have not been quite so evident to their parents. "Guys like us," says George to his fellow itinerant worker with the feeble intellect, "are the loneliest guys in the world. They got no family. They don't belong no place." What they have, however, is each other and human warmth. Called misogynistic by some, the short work was inspired by a person Steinbeck had worked alongside, one who did not kill a girl but who did kill a ranch foreman by sticking a pitchfork right through his stomach. Steinbeck's empathy for hobos, drifters, field hands, and the destitute is unique.

Humanists also enjoy reading his *Grapes of Wrath* (1939; a Japanese edition mis-titles the work *Angry Raisins*), especially noticing Steinbeck's outlook concerning the social scene. Casy the preacher (with the symbolic initials J. C.) is a "homely" humanist capable of offering prayers of the humanist variety. "Ma," one of the most memorable characters in American fiction, knows that her Joad family faces starvation, but she valiantly cries out, "We ain' gonna die out. People is goin' on—changin' a little, maybe, but goin' right on." The novel's final scene, which is shocking in its realism, has been said to be *the* most inspiring to be found in any humanistic work of fiction.

The Unitarian minister, L. M. Birkhead, head of Friends of Democracy, wrote Steinbeck apologetically on 2 May 1940, "There is very widespread propaganda, particularly among the extreme reactionary religionists of the country, that you are Jewish and that *Grapes of Wrath* is Jewish propaganda."

A few days later, Steinbeck responded,

> I am answering your letter with a good deal of sadness. I am sad for a time when one must know a man's race before his work can be approved or disapproved. . . . It happens that I am not Jewish and have no Jewish blood.

He then added, "I find that I do not experience any pride that it is so."

George Orwell, the creator of Big Brother, described Steinbeck in his diaries as a "spurious writer, pseudo-naif."

To his personal physician, Dr. Kenny Fox, Steinbeck wrote the following toward the end of his life:

> Now finally, I am not religious so that I have no apprehension of a

hereafter, either a hope or reward or a fear of punishment. It is not a matter of belief. It is what I feel to be true from my experience, observation, and simple tissue feeling.

His final estate was about $4.35 million in 1990 dollars. Following Steinbeck's wishes, and in spite of his non-theism, his funeral was performed according to the rites of the Church of England. Actor Henry Fonda read from Petrarch's sonnets to Laura. (See entry for George Orwell.) {WAS, 24 April 1951}

Steinberger, Jack (1921-)

A physicist who won the Nobel Laureate in 1988, Steinberger came to the United States in 1935. He taught at Columbia University (1950-1968) and currently is with the European Organization for Nuclear Research in Geneve, Switzerland. Steinberger signed Humanist Manifesto 2000.

Steinem, Gloria (1936–)

Steinem, an American journalist and noted feminist, declared, "By the year 2000 we will, I hope, raise our children to believe in human potential, not God." She also observed, "We are discovering, with the very helpful tutelage of the religious right, the ways in which organized religion is very often politics made sacred. Religion decrees the proper structure here on Earth by placing it in heaven, so to speak, and sanctifying it.…It's an incredible con job when you think of it, to believe something now in exchange for life after death. Even corporations with all their reward systems don't try to make it posthumous." When Pope John Paul II visited New York City in 1995, Steinem told a crowd, including humanist activists Dennis Middlebrooks and Warren Allen Smith,

> We will live to see the day that St. Patrick's Cathedral is a child-care center and the Pope is no longer a disgrace to the skirt that he has on.
>
> {HNS2; *The Humanist*, July-August 1998; TYD}

Steiner, Franklin (Born 1872)

Steiner was born in Des Moines, Iowa, of Lutheran parents, but he rejected Christianity upon carefully reading the Bible. In 1924, he co-founded Chicago's American Rationalist Association. Steiner wrote *Infidels and Charity* (1893) and *Religion and Roguery* (1924). In a 1936 work first published as a Haldeman-Julius Blue Book, *The Religious Beliefs of Our Presidents from Washington to F.D.R.*, he made it known that President Washington did *not* kneel when he attended church. Four Presidents (Harrison, Johnson, Grant, Hayes) were not members of any church. Four were Unitarians (John as well as John Quincy Adams, Fillmore, Taft).

Garfield, he noted, was our only "preacher President," one who came out of the Disciples of Christ ("Campbellites"); although he at first opposed Darwinian concepts of the earth's age, he came around to more liberal views. When Blaine eulogized Garfield, he said that among his friends were the names of "a pious Catholic priest and of an honest, high-minded and generous-hearted Freethinker." {*Freethought History* #17, 1996}

Steiner, Robert (20th Century)

Steiner, the chairman of the Occult Committee, Society of American Magicians, is on the Council for Secular Humanism's Faith-Healing Investigation Project. Steiner wrote *The Truth Shall Make You Free* (1980).

Steiner, Rudolf (1861–1925)

Steiner, once an occultist and theosophist, developed a German school of "anthroposophy" which dealt with knowledge produced by the spiritual side of man. (See entry for Anthroposophy.)

Steinmetz, Charles Proteus (1865–1923)

An electrical engineer, Steinmetz discovered the law of hysteresis and developed a process that led to the making of lightning rods. He participated in and preached at the First Unitarian Society of Schenectady, but he never actually joined the church. In *American Freeman* (1941) he was quoted as saying, "In the realm of science, all attempts to find any evidence of supernatural beings, of metaphysical conceptions, as God, immortality, infinity, etc., thus have failed, and if we are honest, we must confess that in science there exists no God, no immortality, no soul or mind as distinct from the body." Steinmetz wrote *The Place of Religion in Modern Scientific Civilization* (1922). {CE; TYD; U; UU}

Steinmetz, Sebald Rudolph (1862-1940)

Steinmetz taught sociology and ethnology at Leyden University. His long residence in the Dutch East Indies made him the chief authority in Holland on political geography and ethnology as well as an authority on comparative religion. In *Social Papers* (1906), Steinmetz wrote, "Religion was very rarely, if ever, a progressive way-making power. . . . In higher culture I think religion is a very dangerous help to living, for it makes us forget the realities of life for imaginary gratifications." {RAT; RE}

Steinthal, Hajjim (1823–1899)

A German philologist, Steinthal wrote works on language and mythology. From 1852 to 1855 he studied Chinese at Paris, and in 1863 he was appointed professor of general philology at Berlin. With Lazarus, he was joint editor of the *Zeitschrift für Völkerpsychologie und Sprachwissenschaft*. His rationalist views are best seen in his *Allgemeine Ethik* (1885) and *Zu Bibel und Religionsphilosophie* (1890). {BDF; RAT}

Steller, Johann (17th Century)

Steller was an advocate at Leipzig. He published a heretical work, *Pilatus Liberatoris Jesu Subsidio Defensus* (1674). {BDF}

Stendhal (Marie-Henri Beyle) (1783–1842)

Stendhal was an art historian, a musicologist, journalist, biographer, and diarist. But his fame is based on his having written two of the world's greatest novels, *The Red and the Black* (1831) and *The Charterhouse of Parma* (1839). His acute character analysis shows up in a hero which possesses a personal moral code along with an ambitious and passionate pursuit of happiness. The Vatican prohibited reading *Omnes fabulae amatoriae* in 1828 and again in 1864. His *De_l'amour* (1822) was a psychological analysis of love, one that predated Sigmund Freud by several decades and is a notable work. *The Red and the Black* uses red to symbolize liberalism and the army; the black symbolizes a reactionary clergy. The story of Julian Sorel, who shoots his mistress and eventually is guillotined, is played out as if life is a chessboard in which some win and some lose. When Louis Philippe appointed Stendhal to the consulate at Trieste, Metternich objected to Stendhal's liberalism and in 1833 he was shifted to a post in Civitavecchia. During a three-year leave of absence, he wrote *The Charterhouse of Parma*, which many consider his best work. Its hero, Fabrizio del Dongo, shares with Julian Sorel a special egoism which Stendhal calls "Beylism." Both derive great energy from passion, have their own moral code, and pursue happiness in the form of love and power.

"All religions are founded on the fear of the many and the cleverness of the few," he observed.

Balzac esteemed him highly. Edith Wharton considered Stendhal her favorite novelist and liked to cite his epigram, which he had told Prosper Merimee, "The one thing that excuses God is that he does not exist." (*Ce qui excuse Dieu, c'est qu'il n'existe pas.*")

While on leave from the consulate, Stendhal died in Paris after suffering from a stroke. Although he was born in Grenoble, France, his tombstone in Montmartre is inscribed, "Arrigo Beyle, Milanese." {CE; ILP; JMR; RE; TYD}

Stenerson, Douglas C. (20th Century)
Stenerson is author of *H. L. Mencken: Iconoclast from Baltimore* (1975). {GS}

Stenger, Victor (1935–)

A professor of physics and astronomy at the University of Hawaii, Stenger is a secular humanist. In *Free Inquiry* (Winter 1992-1993), he wrote that data from the Cosmic Background Explorer (COBE) satellite "made the first observation of temperature fluctuations in the cosmic microwave background. Overly enthusiastic statements on the significance of the experiment from several of the scientists interviewed prompted the media to interpret the COBE results as an unprecedented verification of the biblical view of creation. Consequently, an important scientific result was so grossly misrepresented to the public as to turn its actual meaning on its head." But the data provides no evidence for the creator which believers are seeking and, in fact, "make the existence of a creator that much more unlikely." Stenger concludes that "those who look to science to bolster their faith in the fantasies of a creator and an invisible world of the spirit won't find it in the ripples of the big bang or any other scientific observation." He wrote *Not by Design: The Origin of the Universe* (1988) and *Physics and Psychics, the Search for a World Beyond the Senses* (1990).

In *The Unconscious Quantum: Metaphysics in Modern Physics and Cosmology* (1995), he argues that the materialist stance does justice to explaining both quantum phenomena and mental activity. He finds no need to resort to holistic cosmology, idealistic ontology, or outmoded theology. Stenger, who signed Humanist Manifesto 2000, is president of Humanists of Hawaii. (See entry for Hawaii Humanists. Also, see Stenger's article about New Age Physics in *Free Inquiry*, Summer 1996.) {FD}

Stephans, Hildegard (20th Century)
Stephans gave the Thomas Paine Collection of Richard Gimbel to the Library of the American Philosophical Society in 1976. {FUK}

Stephen, James Fitzjames [Sir] (1829–1894)

Stephen, the brother of Leslie Stephen, was a baronet, a judge, a professor of law, and author of many books on law. *A General View of Criminal Law* (1863) exposed certain legal anomalies. His most famous book is *History of the Criminal Law of England* (1883). Like his brother, according to Joseph McCabe, Stephen entirely abandoned his belief in the orthodox dogmas. He was counsel for the Rev. Rowland Williams when tried for heresy for writing in *Essays and Reviews*, and Stephen's speech was reprinted in 1862. Of his brother, Sir Leslie wrote that he had "entirely abandoned his belief in the orthodox dogmas." {BDF; JM; RAT; RE}

Stephen, Leslie [Sir] (1832–1904)

The first serious critic of the novel, Sir Leslie was editor of the monumental *Dictionary of National Biography*. Although ordained a minister in 1859, he took up a study of philosophy which led him to relinquish his holy orders. In an 1865 journal entry he wrote, "I now believe in nothing, to put it shortly; but I do not the less believe in morality." Defending his agnosticism, he wrote *Essays on Free Thinking and Plain Speaking* (1873), in which he details how he reached a point when the Christian viewpoint of life, which he had accepted on faith, simply collapsed and fell away into unreality. Stephen was an expert on English thought in the 18th century and was a well-known, fearless mountaineer. Virginia Woolf was his youngest daughter by his second wife. In his house, wrote Miranda Seymour in *Ottoline Morrell: Life on the Grand Scale* (1993), the subject of God was not to be discussed. Ever. His *History of English Thought in the Eighteenth Century* (1876) dealt with the deistic movement. His final work was *An Agnostic's Apology* (1904).

Stephen was an honorary associate of the Rationalist Press Association (RPA), and his signature appeared on the RPA's initial financial appeals for £1,000.

Sir Leslie died of a painless cancer and retained to the last his complete disbelief in all forms of religion. {BDF; CE; FUK; JM; RAT; RE; TRI; TYD}

Stephens, Alfred George (1865–1933)

Stephens was a secularist, writer, and literary critic. In 1891 he was leader of the radical *Boomerang* in Brisbane.

In J. F. Archibald's *Bulletin* his literary column known as "The Red Page" selected and encouraged promising authors. In a 1904 book, *The Red Pagan*, his anti-clerical freethinking was evident in the following: "Thought and speech and writing should be as free as the winds. . . . There is no opinion so sacred that it ought not to be ridiculed and opposed. If it be rooted in truth it will triumph over ridicule and opposition; if it be rooted in falsehood, let it perish quickly." {SWW}

Stephens, Samuel Eugene (20th Century)
Stephens wrote *The Philosophy of the Great Unconscious* (1908). {GS}

Stephens, Zela (19th Century)
Stephens was the author of *Orthodox Prayer* (1896). {GS}

Stephensen, Percy Reginald (1901–1965)

"Inky" Stephensen was an Australian rationalist, publisher, and author. A Rhodes Scholar, he managed two publishing companies in England, then returned to Sydney where he issued the *Australian Mercury* and in the mid-1930s produced *The Publicist* with rationalist William J. Miles. The latter became a pro-fascist Australia First movement, and although Stephensen is said by Ray Dahlitz to have been one of the best creative writers to explore the potential of a native Australian culture, the publication did not help the cause of rationalism nor the development of Australian freethought. {SWW}

Stephenson, George (1781–1848)

An English engineer, Stephenson invented the first locomotive. He has been said to have been a Unitarian, although Elizabeth Gillis does not list him as having joined a specific church. {UU}

Stepsay, David (20th Century)

Stepsay is treasurer of Atheists United, which publishes a monthly newsletter in Sherman Oaks, California.

Sterling, John (1806–1844)

Sterling was a minister of the Church of England who became a skeptic and turned to literature. Just before his death, Sterling wrote to Carlyle, who later wrote his biography, "I tread the common road into the great darkness without any thought of fear and very much of hope. Certainty, indeed, I have none." Sterling did not believe in a personal God. {RAT; RE}

Stern, Howard Allan (1954–)

Stern, a much-publicized radio disc jockey and television show host, wrote *Private Parts* (1993). In 1994, he arranged to be the Libertarian candidate for New York State Governor. Many of his views are delivered tongue-in-cheek, as in his response to a New York *Daily News* poll in 1997 which asked if he believed in God, "I actually believe in a God who looks like Leon Russell and acts like Rosie O'Donnell." At another time, "I believe in God—I'm afraid not to." Some say that on his radio show he said, "I definitely believe in God and I thank him for me being alive." However, when Camille Paglia interviewed him in the *Advocate* to promote his book, *Miss America*, she asked how he felt about religion and politics. "I'm sickened," he responded, "by all religions. Religion has divided people. I don't think there's any difference between the Pope wearing a large hat and parading around with a smoking purse and an African painting his face white and praying to a rock." {CA; E; *Daily News*, 19 January 1997}

Stern, J. (19th Century)

Stern, whose father was a rabbi in Liederstetten, went to the Talmud High school, studied the Kabbalah, and researched Spinoza. A convert to Spinoza's views, Stern wrote *Old and New Faith Among the Jews* (1878), which was attacked by the orthodox Jews. In *Women in the Talmud* (1879), he pleaded for mixed marriages. Stern translated Spinoza into German. {BDF}

Stern, Madeleine B. (1912–)

Stern wrote *The Pantarch: A Biography of Stephen Pearl Andrews* (1968). {*Freethought History #15*, 1995}

Stern, Richard (20th Century)

Triangulo Rosa, a "pink triangle" association commenced with the help of individuals from ASIBEHU in Costa Rica, was founded with money which Stern rounded up. He has been instrumental in working with Guillermo Murillo, director of the group that counsels HIV-positives and people with AIDS in Costa Rica. In 1998, because of problems within the group, the two founded *Asociación Agua Buena Pro Defense de Los Derechos Humanos y Minorias* (The Agua Buena Human Rights Association, Apartado 366-2200, Coronado, Costa Rica).

"AIDS in the Developing World: Where Is Your Anger?" (*Free Inquiry*, Fall 1999) pleads for activists to pressure Americans, for "about one and a half yards of a Stealth Bomber," to donate the stockpiled medications that sit in pharmaceutical factories throughout the developing world. Stern's e-mail: <rastern@sol.racsa.co.cr>.

Stevens, Charles E. (20th Century)

The Charles E. Stevens American Atheist Library and Archives Inc. was formed by Madalyn Murray O'Hair after Stevens became a donor to her various causes.

Stevens, Don (20th Century)

Stevens is a professional comic in San Francisco, California. He has entertained at numerous secular humanist events.

Stevens, Edward A. (Born 1846)

Stevens, of Chicago, was secretary of the American Secular Union. He wrote *God in the State* and contributed to American freethought journals. {BDF; PUT}

Stevens, Fritz (20th Century)

Stevens is Executive Director of Free Inquiry-West in Los Angeles, California, and a regional director of the Council for Secular Humanism. He has lamented that the Thomas Paine Coffeehouse, a community center managed by Tim Groya and gathering place for local freethinkers, had been vandalized in August 1997. Eggs had been flung at the storefront and an anonymous phone caller had warned that "heretics must heed the word of God." Stevens also lamented that the local television stations and the *San Diego Union* did not report upon the vandalism.

Stevens, Halsey R. (19th Century)

Stevens, a freethinker, wrote *Faith and Reason* (1879). {GS}

Stevens, Phillips Jr. (20th Century)

An anthropologist on the staff of the State University of New York at Buffalo, Stevens wrote "Dealing with Religious Beliefs: Some Suggestions from Anthropology" on *Free Inquiry* (Winter 1995-1996). Religion, he noted, "is a deeply rooted and powerful cultural system, interrelated with other institutions in culture. Certain forms of supernatural beliefs, such as magic, operate according to universally similar principles of cognitive reasoning that are, in fact, not irrational; moreover, religious beliefs answer some questions that science cannot answer, such as 'Why me?' and "Why just then?' " He also has written, "Children, Witches, Demons, and Cultural Reality" in *Free Inquiry* (Spring 1997).

Stevens, Wallace (1879–1955)

Stevens, the Pulitzer Prize-winning poet, author of *Man With the Blue Guitar* (1937), was Vice President of the Hartford Accident and Indemnity Company, Hartford, Connecticut. Asked in 1951 for his views on humanism, Stevens wrote the present author, "I am afraid that I am allergic to pigeonholes. Some one of these days I shall look at all this, which is of the greatest interest to me, but I just cannot do it now." He died in 1955.

In a 1902 journal entry, when he was twenty-two, he wrote,

> An old argument with me is that the true religious force in the world is not the church but the world itself.

In his obscure but meditative poem, "*Esthétique du Mal*," Stevens remarks that without Satan we are "shaken realists" who no longer have the old supernatural explanations. He hoped to find in a realism purged of the supernatural "the imagination's new beginning":

> Natives of poverty, children of malheur,
> The gaiety of language is our seigneur.

Such a new and imaginative apprehension of evil as illustrated in poetry, he held, would give us the needed resource against the natural evil of life, what critic Frank Kermode has called "against the unhappiness to which we are born, in a world called poor because the old consolations and remedies are no longer valid. A further resource is love, itself allied to language: 'phrases/Compounded of dear relation, spoken twice,/Once by the lips, once by the services/Of central sense. . . .' "

Stevens's wife, Elsie Kachel Moll, posed as the model for the iconic head on the Mercury dime (1916-1945), so called because Miss Liberty wears an anomalous winged headdress atop her icy female profile. She also posed for the full-length Miss Liberty on the fifty-cent piece; and posed for the Standing Liberty quarter (1916-1930), whose figure was criticized for showing too much naked flesh and was more heavily draped in the second year of its issue. {John Updike, *The New Yorker*, 26 April-3 May 1999; WAS, 26 March 1951}

Stevenson, Adlai Ewing (1900–1965)

Stevenson, a Governor of Illinois and a Unitarian, was an eminent spokesman for internationalism and liberal reform, but he was unsuccessful as the Democratic presidential candidate in 1952 and 1956. His grandfather had been Vice-President under President Grover Cleveland. Called Adlai by most, he was said to have felt that he inherited his Democratic politics from his father's side of the family and his Unitarian religion from his mother's. Few in his time were so witty, and Stevenson was likened to Abraham Lincoln, also from Illinois. A reader once wrote to Eleanor Roosevelt, "I know Adlai Stevenson and other important people have belonged to the Unitarian Church, but to me a Christian religion that does not admit the divinity of Christ just isn't a religion. It's certainly not much of a test of your faith, is it?" To which the President's wife responded in *McCalls*,

> I have always had a great respect for Unitarians. My husband's mother was brought up a Unitarian and later became an Episcopalian, but there never was any question that she was a good Christian; and most of the Unitarians I have known have been extremely good Christians. The Trinity is not essential, evidently, to leading a Christian life, nor does its denial seem to detract from the reverence in which Christ is held.

Wags and gossips still discuss the meaning of *Washington Post* owner Katharine Graham's autobiography, on page 378 of which she says that Stevenson left his tie and glasses in her room the night before he dropped dead on the street in London. {CE; EG; U; UU}

Stevenson, Ian (1918–)

Stevenson is the prominent psychiatrist cited by Paul Edwards in *Reincarnation* as actually believing in reincarnation. Edwards found his views "sincere but deluded."

Stevenson, Robert Louis (1850–1894)

Stevenson, the Scottish novelist, poet, and essayist, was the son of Thomas Stevenson, joint-engineer to the Board of Northern Lighthouses. A sickly child, he was unable to follow his father's strenuous profession and although he studied law and was admitted advocate in 1875, Stevenson was fascinated by Edinburgh low life and cultivated a Bohemian life style. In 1875 he met the author of "Invictus," William Ernest Henley, who was hospitalized after having a foot amputated, and the two collaborated on several plays, none of which had much success.

Another friend was Charles Baxter, with whom he drank in pubs and grimy dives frequented by sailors. Baxter, "the only person I ever knew who could *advise*," was the one to whom he confided about his problems at home. His father's Scots Presbyterian theology was fanatical and did not allow any disagreeing with his viewpoint. This led Stevenson to write Baxter,

> The thunderbolt has fallen with a vengeance now. You know the aspect of a house in which somebody is still waiting burial—the quiet step—the hushed voices and rare conversation—the religious literature that holds a temporary monopoly—the grim, wretched faces; all is here reproduced in this family circle in honour of my (what is it?) atheism or blasphemy. On Friday night after leaving you, in the course of conversation, my father put me one or two questions as to beliefs, which I candidly answered. I really hate all lying so much now...but if I had foreseen the real Hell of everything since, I think I should have lied as I have done so often before. . . . I do not think I am thus justly to be called a "orrible atheist" and I confess I cannot exactly swallow my father's purpose of praying down continuous afflictions on my head.

To escape such comments from his father as "You have rendered my whole life a failure," and from his mother as "This is the heaviest affliction that has ever befallen me," Stevenson left on a visit to his cousin Maud Babington. She was married to a clergyman in Suffolk, and Stevenson's letters at this time indicate that he fell in love with Frances Sitwell, who was estranged from her husband and had recently lost her older son. To her he confided about the rift with his parents as well as his moods, his fears, his thoughts about writing. Much of his life was spent traveling in search of health, for he suffered from a chronic bronchial condition (possible tuberculosis).

In France in 1876 he met his future wife, the American Mrs. Fanny Osbourne, whom he married after her divorce in 1880. She was ten years his senior and cared for him through many bouts of serious illness. His first full-length work of fiction, *Treasure Island* (1883) brought him fame, which increased with *The Strange Case of Dr. Jekyll and Mr. Hyde* (1886), and *Kidnapped* (1886). Although he returned to Europe, settling at Bournemouth for three years, he then set out with his family entourage for the South Seas. He settled in Samoa at Vailima, where he temporarily regained his health and gained a reputation as "Tusitala," or the story teller. While working on unfinished masterpieces, *Weir of Hermiston* (published 1896) and *St. Ives* (published 1897), Stevenson died from a brain hemorrhage.

His biographers, A. Johnston and F. Watt, both reported that Stevenson was an agnostic until his death, although he had prayers said at his house daily on account of a pious mother. "I am religious in my own way," Stevenson once wrote, "but I am hardly brave enough to interpose a theory of my own between life and death. Here both our creeds and our philosophies seem to me to fail." In 1994, the first two volumes of *The Letters of Robert Louis Stevenson* were published. The 2,800 letters in eight volumes included one love letter that referred to what was an admission of physically unrequited passion and included, "I believe in you as others believe in the Bible."

Tusitala, the teller of tales, was how Stevenson was called by Samoans, who seldom used his given name. He had lived in a sprawling, two-story villa at Valima. Some 1,500 feet above, on the summit of Mount Vaea, Stevenson's body lies in a cement-block tomb which is topped by a plinth. A bronze plaque on one side bears the words "The Tomb of Tusitala" and a biblical passage. On the other side, a bronze plaque is inscribed with the words of Stevenson's "Requiem":

> Under the wide and starry sky,
> Dig the grave and let me lie.
> Glad did I live and gladly die,
> And I laid me down with a will.
>
> This be the verse you grave for me:
> *Here he lies where he longed to be;*
> *Home is the sailor, home from sea,*
> *And the hunter home from the hill.*

{CE; JM; RAT; RE}

Stevenson, T. J. (20th Century)

Stevenson wrote *Reason: A Million Dollars in Cash for a Devil* (1946). {GS}

Steward, Ann and Mike (20th Century)

The Stewards edited *Comfort Women in Comfort History* (1993). The work of short biographies emphasizes community and church activities. {*Freethought History #15*, 1995}

Stewart, A. G. (20th Century)

Stewart, an industrial radiologist, is a freethinker and a poet who built a house "with my own hands." His "Jeffersonian Democracy" was printed in *Freethought History* (#21, 1997).

Stewart, Al (20th Century)

Stewart, a recording artist, has two gold albums ("Past Present and Future" and "Modern Times") and two platinum albums ("Year of the Cat" and "Time Passages").

Had compulsory school prayers left him with any religious belief?" an interviewer asked from *Rock 'n Reel* (Issue 22, 1995). "No, absolutely no," Stewart responded. "I'm actually of the opinion that idealism in any form is to be avoided at all costs, just because I see what happens when idealists get hold of almost anything. . . . The Bolsheviks were all idealists originally, well Stalin probably wasn't, but they made a hell of a mess of the Soviet Union. Intellectuals are also very dangerous, especially intellectuals with a chip on their shoulder."

Asked following a performance in Philadelphia if he was Catholic, Stewart responded that he was an agnostic. {CA}

Stewart, Chauncey (19th Century)

Stewart wrote *The Usefulness of Prayer* (c. 1890). {GS}

Stewart, D. J. (20th Century)

In 1990, Dr. Stewart was elected an honorary associate of the Rationalist Press Association (RPA). He has written,

> I joined the RPA when I was at university, reading Philosophy and Psychology, but my first close contact with it was when I submitted a winning entry in the F.C.C. Watts Essay Competition. The set topic was "rationalism as a positive philosophy" and I wrote: Continued success in destroying old beliefs together with a shirking

of the problems which the destruction raises for many people could give rise to a situation worse than that which the RPA set out to improve.

Perhaps rationalists should be thankful that they are likely to become ineffective before they can become dangerous. They have indeed bombed with precision, but can they rebuild?' The positive philosophy I advocated was that there is no area of problems in which scientific thinking is not competent—in which one cannot or must not use it. The practical role I recommended to the RPA was to be educational as well as militant, predicting that, without this constructive side, all sorts of irrational beliefs would rush in to fill the vacuum. In the event, this was much too optimistic: today we have, not only a flood of new superstitions, but repaired versions of all the old ones, and some not seen since medieval times.

Some years later, I developed the same theme, of how unceasing logico-empirical probing in all things is the essence of rationalism, and provides a guide to behaviour as well as to belief, at the 1971 RPA Conference.

In the meantime, I had become Secretary of a local humanist group, helped to found another, and then gone on to other roles, including Chairman of the University Humanist Federation, Chairman of the British Humanist Association, Chairman of the RPA, and Associate Editor of the *Journal of Moral Education*. Experience in these helped to confirm my view, that the only sort of humanism worth having is one based on scientific rationalism, and that, if you do not educate positively in a scientific way of thinking and living, people will regard what you offer as shallow and limited, and may be tempted to look elsewhere. Seeing the rationalist and humanist organisations as they are today, my main feeling is one of sadness at opportunities they have missed.

It would not have been possible for me to devote so much time to voluntary work for these organisations if my professional career had not been conceptually related: at first at university in lecturing in psychology, and then directing post-graduate and post-doctoral research—chiefly of projects connected with management, government, and design—combined with consultancy and writing. The part of my own research that pleases me most has been the development of an augmented mechanistic theory of purpose and directiveness, one application of which is to give an improved formal basis for rationalism.

{*New Humanist*, February 1995}

Stewart, John (1750–1822)

Commonly called "Walking Stewart," he walked through India, Africa, and America. Stewart was a materialist. {BDF}

Stewart, M. A. (1937–)

In England, Stewart is a corresponding member of The Hume Society, a group engaged in scholarly activity concerning David Hume. He is author of *The Kirk and the Infidel* (1995) and *Hume and Hume's Connexions* (1995).

Stewart, Rod (1933–1994)

Stewart at the time of his death was district executive of the Pacific Northwest District of the Unitarian Universalist Association. A chartered accountant, he helped found the district's leadership school, which became a model for similar schools in the Americas and the United Kingdom.

Stiebing, William H. (20th Century)

Stiebing in 1984 wrote *Ancient Astronauts, Cosmic Collision, and Other Popular Theories About Man's Past*. A skeptic and a freethinker, he then wrote *Out of the Desert? Archaeology and the Exodus/Conquest Narratives*, a summary of archaeological findings. His research found that facts do not support the biblical accounts of the exodus and later wars of conquest.

Stifler, James Madison (20th Century)

Stifler wrote *The Religion of Benjamin Franklin* (1925). {GS}

Still, James (20th Century)

Still is secretary of Internet Infidels. E-mail: <jims@infidels.org>.

Stiller, Richard (20th Century)

Stiller wrote *Commune on the Frontier: The Story of Frances Wright* (1972). {FUS}

Stilpo (fl. 307 B.C.E.)

Stilpo of Megara, of the school of Euclides, is said to have been hailed before the Areopagus for the offense of saying that the Pheidian statue of Athênê was "not a God." Although he was clearly an unbeliever, he shrewdly admitted with the jest that, true, she was not a god . . . but a goddess . . . whereupon he was exiled. {JMR; JMRH; TYD}

Stipe, Michael (1960–)

Stipe is a musician who has received numerous major awards, including gold and platinum records. In 1983 "Murmur" became a gold record and won the Rolling Stone Critics Poll for Best Album of the year. In 1992 he was the recipient of the MTV Video Music Video of the Year Award and was the Rolling Stone Male Vocalist of the Year. In 1994 he received a Breakthrough Video Award for "Everybody Hurts."

"I don't believe in God," he told *Cornerstone*, "but [The Reverend] Howard [Finster, a folk painter whose work graces album covers] has given me respect for people that do." {CA; E}

Stirner, Max (1806–1856)

A freethinker, Stirner rejected all religion. For him, morality is a belief, too. Religion continues through morality. Although they are believed in, ethical commandments cannot be proved. He loved man because love made him happy and seemed natural to him. The order of society, he felt, needs founding on the interdependence of its members. The individual in society remains dependent on society, nature, and its laws. But Stirner wondered how Feuerbach could hope to turn people away from God if he let them keep the idea of the divine, so he ridiculed Feuerbach's humanism. *The Ego and His Own* (1845) is a criticism of Feuerbach's conceptual system. Some find that his line of thinking has been a source of 20th-century existentialism. {EU, 223, 289, Dale Riepe, Karl Becker}

Stites, Tom (20th Century)

Stites is Editor-in-Chief of *World*, the journal of the Unitarian Universalist Association.

Stitt, M. (19th Century)

Stitt was a grocer in Crook, England. A secularist, he was known for issuing a placard appealing to his friends in Wolsingham, Willington, Tow Lane, and other districts to meet at his house to form a Crook Secular Society. He exemplifies how the initiative for starting freethought groups often rest with a single individual. {RSR}

Stocker, Barbara (20th Century)

Stocker is president of the Rationalist Society of St. Louis, Missouri, and a regional director of the Council for Secular Humanism. In 1994 in Rochester, New York, she appeared on a program, "Elizabeth Cady Stanton Meets Susan B. Anthony," in which she played the role of Stanton. The meeting was a commemoration by the Robert Green Ingersoll Committee of Ingersoll's work on behalf of women's equality. In the November 1994 election, she ran for a seat in the Missouri House of Representatives from the 100th District. Her observations upon attending the Non-Governmental Organizations (NGO) World Conference on Women in Beijing in 1994 include the view that "very few of the women at the conference seem to recognize the fundamental role that religion plays in patriarchies and the degradation of women." She lamented that many were ready to embrace "New Age" ideas or return to ancient goddess religions in an attempt to circumvent patriarchy. Muslim women, she found, "were intent on explaining that their religion was 'misunderstood' and that they were very happy with their freely chosen lot." Stocker added, "It is still difficult for me to believe that a woman wrapped up in heavy black cloth in 90-degree heat is 'liberated.' "

Stocker, who is on the board of directors of the Freedom From Religion Foundation, participated in the 1996 Humanist World Congress in Mexico City. Her e-mail: <rsslbarb@aol.com>. {Viewpoints," *Free Inquiry*, Winter 1995-1996}

Stöcker, Helene (1869–1943)

Stöcker, a German writer who graduated in philosophy, wrote on child-welfare and ethical and social questions in *Nietzsche und die Frauen, Die Liebe und die Frauen*, etc.). She was a member of the Goethe Society and the Progressive Women's League, and she was President of the Society for the Protection of Mothers. A Monist, she was a great admirer of Haeckel. {RAT}

STOCKPORT (England) SECULARISTS

For information, write Carl Pinel, 85 Hall Street, Offerton, Stockport SK1 4DE; telephone 0161 480 0732.

Stockton, Eric (1924–)

Stockton was the founding editor of *Scottish Humanist* and continued until 1995. He has written, "We owe it largely to the feminists that personal autonomy has become a live ethical issue. The feminist claim is that men have explicitly, and tacitly, imposed upon women the status of non-autonomous objects—sexually, reproductively, domestically *usable chattels*." Just as women have been objects in the sense that they are not seen as human ends but as men's means to this or that male-determined end, Stockton reasons, so people in the medical world often use terminally-ill people just to show how "pro-life" they are—instead of allowing the voluntary aspect of voluntary euthanasia, they "keep the old banger on the road somehow!" "The truly freethinking person," stated Stockton, "is an autonomous person neither intruding upon others nor being intruded upon by them."

"I am glad I am not a theist because," Stockton has also written, "if I were, I would have to fight Christianity tooth-and-nail. As it is, I am an atheist and, to me, one bent faith is much like another, even if Christianity is, in some ways, the worst of them. But in any case one ought to love the Christians while hating the Christianity, ought one not?" Stockton, who lives in Orkney, publishes a freethought journal, *Lady Godiva*.

On the Web:<http://www.shetland-news.co.uk/godiva/godiva.html>. His e-mail: <stockton.sanday.orkney@zetnet.co.uk>. {*The Freethinker*, June 1994; September 1995}

Stockton, Richard (20th Century)

Stockton is a playwright, the author of *A Plot on Robert Ingersoll*.

Stockwell, C. T. (19th Century)

Stockwell is author of *The Evolution of Immortality* (1887). {FUS}

Stockwell, Wallace (20th Century)

Stockwell wrote *A Shield Has Two Sides* (c. 1946). {GS}

Stoddard, George D. (1897–1981)

A naturalistic humanist, Stoddard was President of the University of Illinois. When ousted, he gave two reasons for his discord with university trustees: (a) that isolationists in the Illinois legislature regarded his active role in the formation of UNESCO as "only one step from communism," and (b) that animosity against him existed among some Roman Catholic legislators because his book, *The Meaning of Intelligence*, had been termed "godless" in 1945 by the then Roman Catholic Bishop of Springfield.

During the 1950s, he was critical of a drug called Krebiozen, about which he wrote a controversial book dedicated to another eminent humanist, Anton J. Carlson. Stoddard, who commenced his professional career as a psychologist, was a Unitarian. {HNS}

Stoddard, Lothrop (20th Century)

An American, Stoddard wrote *Scientific Humanism* (1926).

Stoessinger, John George (20th Century)

Author of *The Refugee and the World Community* (1956), Stoessinger was a lecturer in government at M.I.T., a professor of government at the Babson Institute, and an associate professor of political science at Hunter College. In 1962 he wrote *Why Nations Go To War*.

STOICISM

Zeno of Citium around 300 B.C.E. founded the school of philosophy known as Stoicism, having been influenced by Socratic ideals and by the thought of Heraclitus, Aristotle, and Plato. The Stoics held that wise men should not be affected by or show passion or feeling. All reality, they held, is material, but it is shaped by a universal working force (which some call God) that pervades everything. By putting aside passion, unjust thoughts, and indulgence, and by performing one's duty with the right disposition, one can live consistently with nature, thereby achieving true freedom. Romans who were Stoics included Cicero, Seneca, Epictetus, and Marcus Aurelius.

A prime concern of the Stoics was ethics. Right behavior had to be grounded on a general understanding of the universe. Their "Physics" taught that everything was material, the universe being a continuum. Thought was an ethereal form of matter which had the power to shape and control its grosser forms. Given the name of Providence, it functioned as a World-Soul or immanent God. Man's soul was said to be a part of the World-Soul, which made all human beings brothers, and the ethereal element in Man—his Reason—was in harmony with the purposes of Providence. To be virtuous consisted, therefore, in following Reason undeterred by pain, pleasure, desire, or fear, emotions that belong to a lower level of existence. By extolling Providence, the brotherhood of men, and the need to curb natural desires, Stoicism had some things in common with Christianity. The Stoic viewpoint enjoyed a revival at the time of the Renaissance, and it has been said that Stoicism was the effective religion of the Victorian public schools. (See the entry for ancient humanism. Also see Philip P. Hallie's article on stoicism in the *Encyclopedia of Philosophy*, Vol. 8.) {CE; OEL; RE}

Stojanovic, Svetozar (20th Century)

A Humanist Laureate in the Council for Secular Humanism's International Academy of Humanism, Stojanovic was elected in recognition of his defense of human rights and democracy. A professor of philosophy at the University of Belgrade, he signed Humanist Manifesto II and is a contributing editor on *Free Inquiry* and *Philo*. At the Tenth International Humanist and Ethical Union (IHEU) held in Buffalo (1988), Stojanovic addressed the group. In 1973, Stojanovic wrote *Between Ideals and Reality: A Critique of Socialism and Its Future*. In 1988, he wrote *Perestroika: From Marxism and Bolshevism to Gorbachev* (1988). With Paul Kurtz, Stojanovic co-wrote *Revolution and Tolerance*.

In an interview with Paul Kurtz (*Free Inquiry*, Summer 1996), Stojanovic told of his early days as a Marxist humanist, of being repressed by the Tito regime, of his difficulties on the faculty of the University of Belgrade, and of his now calling himself a "social-eco-democrat, because I put in the center of my concerns global ecological problems in the widest possible sense of the world, including the concern for sheer survival of humankind." Although Karl Marx is dead, he noted, "What is *not* dead in Karl Marx is his critical insights into alienation and reification phenomena, ideology, the economic dimension of social classes, capitalism. There is no way to avoid recognizing that Marx was pretty successful in his critical but not in his constructivist approach, and that radical conclusions ought to be drawn from that. For instance, I do not buy his rejection of a market economy."

As for whether the wars in Yugoslavia are religious in origin, Stojanovic explained, "In my opinion, there is no doubt that our conflicts are fratricidal, inter-national, and inter-religious civil wars. . . . Serbs, Croats, and Muslims are of the same ethnic stock. These three nationalities, all South-Slavs, speaking one language (Serbo-Croatian) are divided by religion and history. You first have a division between Christians (Serbs and Croats) and Muslims (former Christians, Serbs, or Croats, who converted to Islam during the Turkish rule). And the second division is within Christianity, between Catholics (Croats) and Orthodox Christians (Serbs). In other words, the basic constituting and defining characteristic of these three main nationalities in the former Yugoslavia is religion."

"We have to build," Stojanovic continued, "to build a 'quasi-religion' of humanity, or at least to poeticize the existence of humankind. Admiration, thrill, amazement, awe—that is how astronauts describe the spectacle of Earth and us on it when they are temporarily separated from it and can view it from space. Unfortunately, the most radical positive humanist utopia is increasingly going to be the survival of humankind and the most radical negative utopia the self-annihilation of humankind. This is humanism and post-humanism at once."

At the time of the NATO bombing of Serbia in 1999, Stojanovic complained that "The whole world is shocked by the plight of ethnic Albanian refugees but at the same time overlooks tens of thousands of Serbs and other minorities fleeing from Kosovo to the other parts of Serbia and to Montenegro." He was critical of the part played by the United States. Stojanovic signed Humanist Manifesto 2000. {*Free Inquiry*, Summer 1996 and 1999; HM2; SHD}

Stoker, Bram (Abraham) (1847–1912)

Stoker is internationally known for his *Dracula* (1897). *Dracul* is Romanian for Devil, which partly explains why mystics and religionists are interested in Prince Vlad Tepes, known to the peasants of Wallachia and Transylvania as the impaler of up to 20,000 human beings. Vlad impaled live victims upon stakes at a time when Turks and Romanians were battling, but he impaled, boiled, decapitated, scalped, skinned, and generally maimed anyone who offended him, even fellow Transylvanians.

Stoker was born in Dublin. In 1878 he started a twenty-seven year stint as secretary and touring manager for Sir Henry Irving (John Henry Broadribb), who was manager of the Lyceum Theatre. In 1906, Stoker wrote the two-volume *Personal Reminiscences of Henry Irving*. Barbara Belford, in a 1996 biography, found it difficult to discover details of Stoker's life. A six-foot two-inch Irishman with a red beard, he suffered from some mysterious illness that made him unable to stand upright until he was seven. He married Florence Balcombe, and they had one son. He liked Walt Whitman's work and was fascinated by Tennyson's long canine teeth—"the vampire's forks." Lady (Speranza) Wilde's son and her son, Oscar, were friends. Mark Twain asked him to represent his plays. Stoker may have died of syphilis, although Belford thinks not. {Margot Peters, "The Boss From Hell," *The New York Times*, 7 April 1996}

Stokes, Anson Phelps (20th Century)

Stokes, with Leo Pfeffer, wrote *Church and State in the United States*. {FUS}

Stokes, Geoffrey (1940–1995)

Stokes was a *Village Voice* (New York City) and *Boston Globe* columnist and feature writer. Once a director of a New York City drug treatment program, he also was deputy commissioner of the city's environmental protection agency. He wrote books on rock music, baseball, and food, leading some to call him the "house polymath" inasmuch as he was capable of writing on so many subjects. His "A Parent Comes Out" is about a teacher whose son informed her he was gay. At Woodstock, Vermont, Stokes served on the North Universalist Chapel Society board.

Stokes, Stanley Charles W. (20th Century)

An Australian, Stokes has compiled "The Rational Calendar and Compendium" (Box 189, Geebung, Queensland, 4034 Australia). The work lists not only freethinkers going back to Imhotep and Ptahhotep but also includes them on a "new era" calendar which combines Esperanto and rationality. Noting that 1995 is 5756 in the Jewish calendar, 2539 in the Buddhist, 1917 in the Saka, and 1363 in the Muslim, he suggests that everyone call it 19 of *Mondo Erao*, the World Era in Esperanto, thereby celebrating *antau lego*, "before the law in 1976." Included are birthdays or names of several hundred individuals whose names were gleaned from standard freethought books.

Stoll, James Lewis (1936–1994)

Stoll was a gay rights pioneer. In 1965 he joined Martin Luther King's call to religious leaders to join the civil rights march from Selma to Montgomery, Alabama, in memory of murdered civil rights workers, including Jim Reeb, a Unitarian minister. In 1969, Stoll became the first Unitarian clergy person to declare his homosexuality. In 1993, he was president of the San Francisco chapter of the American Civil Liberties Union.

Stoller, B. B. (20th Century)

In the 1950s, Stoller from Minnesota was a director of the American Humanist Association.

Stone, Irving (1903–1989)

Stone, whose original name was Irving Tennenbaum, was an editor and an author of best-selling books. In 1937, he edited *Dear Theo*, the autobiography of Vincent Van Gogh. Stone wrote *Lust for Life* (1934), about Van Gogh; *Sailor on Horseback* (1938), about Jack London; *Clarence Darrow for the Defense* (1941); *Adversary in the House* (1947), about Eugene V. Debs; *Love Is Eternal* (1954), about Mary Todd Lincoln; *The Agony and the Ecstasy* (1961); *I, Michelangelo, Sculptor* (1962); *Passions of the Mind* (1971), about Sigmund Freud); *The Greek Treasure* (1975); and *The Origin* (1980), about Darwin. {GS}

Stone, Lucy (1818–1893)

A leader in the American feminist movement, Stone founded and edited *Women's Journal*, the official organ of the National American Woman Suffrage Association. She was called Mrs. Stone, although actually she was married to Henry Brown Blackwell, brother of famed physician Elizabeth Blackwell. It was her way of protecting against the unequal laws which applied at that time to married women. Lucy Stone believed that all should vote, that no adult should be denied the vote, a position not held by Susan B. Anthony and Elizabeth Cady Stanton, who opposed giving black men the vote unless white women also were allowed to vote. This difference led to a break in their working together.

"Christianity," she wrote, "that musty old theology, which already has its grave clothes on, and is about to be buried. . . . A wall of Bible, brimstone, church, and corruption has hitherto hemmed women into nothingness." After Stone's death, the journal was continued by her daughter, Alice Stone Blackwell, and in 1921 the Lucy Stone League was formed to continue its namesake's efforts to fight for women's rights. "Lucy," wrote Alice Stone Blackwell in *Lucy Stone*, "had become a Unitarian through listening to Professor Finney's lectures on God." {CE; EG; Lois K. Porter, "Lucy Stone: Woman of Firsts," *Free Inquiry*, Winter 1996-1997); YD; U; UU}

Stone, Merlin (20th Century)

Stone is author of *When God Was A Woman* (1976).

Stone, Oliver (1946–)

Stone, a director and screenwriter, was awarded the American Humanist Association's Arts Award in 1996. Stone has directed such Academy Award-winning movies as "Midnight Express" (1978) and "Platoon" (1986). His works interpreting presidents John F. Kennedy and Richard Nixon received mixed reviews.

Stone, Peter (1971–)

Stone, a graduate student studying political science at the University of Rochester, is a member of the Bertrand Russell Society.

Asked about humanism, he wrote the present author:

> I do not believe in any form of supernatural existence. I have no reason to believe there is an afterlife and, therefore, I don't. My practical attitude is that of Woody Allen's father in "Hannah and Her Sisters." When confronted by his son's desire to know what happened after death, his response was, "When I'm dead, I'm dead. . . . I'll worry about it then."

Politically, Stone admits to being something of an anarchist. Philosophically, he adds, "I'm definitely an agnostic. For all practical purposes, however, I'm an atheist. Without any evidence of the existence of God or the supernatural, I must for practical purposes assume there is no God or supernatural realm of which to speak." {WAS, 27 August 1996}

Stone, Robert (20th Century)

Stone is a past president of *The Jewish Humanist*.

Stone, William (19th Century)

Stone wrote *The Story of the Garden of Eden* (1873). {GS}

Stones, N. L. (20th Century)

Stones, who has called himself/herself "a gender dysphoric," is aware that most have not heard of the phrase, which describes a syndrome in which people suffer from gender identity conflict/distress. More recognize the word "transsexual." Stones then offers further definitions: "Under the umbrellas of gender dysphoria are found 'primary' and 'secondary' transsexuals (TSs), transgenderists (TGs), and transvestites (TVs). Hermaphrodites are a separate category, since they have a definite intersex medical condition at birth. TSs and TGs can be celibate or heterosexual, or their sexual orientation may be homosexual or bisexual. TVs are normally heterosexual men, who although they cross-dress are content with their sex of birth."

Stone, who was born biologically female, adds that as a primary TS "I felt 'male' from a very early age (4 or 5). Although I have now been living as a 'man' for 20 years, I am still trying to decide how androgynous I am and whether I'm bisexual in a platonic sense (since I am celibate, but can be attracted to both sexes). I'm having to accept that my gender identity is on a continually moving spectrum. As society confuses us, I find I confuse myself."

In Samoa, a "fa'afafine" is a son brought up as a daughter. In India there are 1.2 million "Hyjpas," who are male transsexuals. Among North American Indians a "Wintke" is a "two-souls person, a gender-crosser and mysterious spirit-person who has the gift of prophecy." Stones suggests that a breaking down of gender barriers might be advantageous to society. {*New Humanist*, June 1996}

STONEWALL RIOT

Early in the morning of 28 June 1969, a routine police raid on the Stonewall Bar at 53 Christopher Street in New York City turned into a riot. When police arrived at about 3 a.m., they ordered customers to leave, began arresting employees, and started to remove several "homo's" and "drag queens." Such incidents had been routine, but this morning the customers as well as those outside unexpectedly began chanting "Pigs!" at the police, and they fought back. The police barricaded themselves inside until rescued by other officers. For the next several evenings, further disturbances took place—the incidents have been referred to as the Stonewall Rebellion or the Stonewall Riot, the event that sparked the contemporary lesbian and gay movement which spread nationally as well as internationally.

Four secular humanists known to have been present—names associated with one of the major human rights fights of the century—later became officers or friends of the Stonewall Riot Veterans group: Howard Cruse, Martin Duberman, Warren Allen Smith, and Randy Wicker. (See entry for Homosexuality.) {AA}

Stong, Phil (1899–1957)

Stong, the Iowa author of *State Fair* (1932), was a journalist and Hollywood scenarist. Asked to comment on humanism, Stong responded to the present author:

> I've never gone deeply enough into any of the various definitions of "humanism" to be able to make any intelligent or instructive comment on the subject. When I read any of these tenuous expositions, they remind me (a) of the blind men and the elephant and (b) that I'd better have a glass of beer and get to bed. I don't see how you distinguish between the humanism of More and that of Dewey or of Aristophanes or Lackland or Chaucer or Bunyan or Saintsbury or Taine. The boys that practice it seem to me tremendously more effective than the ones who preach it from the varied pulpits.
>
> {WAS, 13 February 1951}

Stopes-Roe, Harry (1924–)

A senior lecturer in science studies, University of Birmingham, Stopes-Roe is the former president of the British Humanist Association and is on the board of directors of the Rationalist Press Association. In Buffalo, at the 1988 Congress of the International Humanist and Ethical Union Congress, he proposed that humanism should be considered a "life stance." He suggests that the question whether humanism is a philosophy, a culture, an academic discipline, or a religion is best resolved by considering it a life stance. His proposal is to avoid dividing humanists into two camps according to how they respond to the word "religion." The new term, he holds, incorporates the idea and ideal of religion but opens it out so that it is not discriminatory. Thus, a life stance "is theistic or naturalistic according to whether it sees 'that which is of ultimate importance' in terms of God; or something naturalistic. It is fundamental that a god-religion—or simply 'religion' as these people would say—is precisely a theistic life stance. The two terms are synonymous, each carrying the same depth of meaning. 'Life stance' has latent in it all the power of 'religion' (in the sense 'god-religion'); this power is realised (as the god-religious would say) on the acknowledgment of God." He adds, "I hope that even those who are most antipathetic to creeds and dogmas will concur in my suggestion that sentient beings, with their enjoyments and sufferings, and moral sensibilities, are of ultimate importance to Humanists."

Nicolas Walter (*New Humanist*, December, 1988) gives ten specific arguments against the use of "life stance." For example, he questions whether humanism is a stance, adding it is not necessarily about life. Most humanists, he holds, do not see humanism and religion as two equal and opposite entities—most see humanism as a rejection of all (not just some) of the essential features of religion. It is the "religious humanists" who see humanism as an actual form of religion. In short, states Walter, "life stance" is of little use and probably will do more harm than good to whatever it is that we do all have in common. In a response (*New Humanist*, December, 1988), Stopes-Roe says Walter misunderstands the issues and his basic attitude is anti-rational. He does admit, however, that one genuine difficulty is that "life stance" is difficult to translate into French.

At the Tenth International Humanist and Ethical Union (IHEU) World Congress held in Buffalo (1988), Stopes-Roe addressed the group. In 1994 at the conference of the Coalition for Secular Humanism, Atheism, and Freethought (CSHAFT), he spoke on "Humanism and Ethics." In 1995 at the International and Humanist Ethical Union's meeting in India, he spoke about the tradition of humanism from the ancient Greeks to the Enlightenment and the current day, emphasizing the importance of David Hume and the British empirical tradition.

Stopes-Roe, who signed Humanist Manifesto 2000, is a Vice

President of the Gay and Lesbian Humanist Association (GALHA). In 1996 he was a participant at the Humanist World Congress held in Mexico City. {*New Humanist*, February 1996; SHD}

Stoppard, Tom (1937–)

Stoppard, a dramatist born in Czechoslovakia but who moved with his parents to Singapore when two, left school at the age of seventeen and worked as a journalist. His given name was Tomas Straussler, but when his widowed mother remarried he took his stepfather's name. Stoppard is the author of *Rosencrantz and Guildenstern Are Dead* (1966), *The Real Thing* (1982), and *Hapgood* (1988). His writing is notable for its intellectual word-play. *Arcadia* (1995), for example, starts with a thirteen-year-old's asking her tutor, "Septimus, what is carnal embrace?" To which Septimus responds, "Carnal embrace is the practice of throwing one's arms around a side of beef." "Carnal" does indeed mean sensual, and who could overlook the phallus which is implied. Stoppard's work is full of such verbal pyrotechnics, and he long has been fascinated with linguistic philosophy, particularly as found in the writings of Wittgenstein, G. E. Moore, and A. J. Ayer. His telecast, "Professional Foul" (1977), portrays an English philosopher and English football team in Prague, during which the G. E. Moore-like professor is caught between the abstractions of his own discipline and the realities of a regime which stifles free intellectual exchange. As Anne Barton of Cambridge University has pointed out, "when various philosophical journals sniped at his account of Wittgenstein and British logical positivism as incorporated in *Jumpers*, he was able to take comfort from the fact that no less a figure than A. J. Ayer instantly rose to his defense." *Jumpers* (1972) has as its central character a professor of moral philosophy, George Moore, who like G. E. Moore teaches about intuitionist ethics.

Stoppard's parodies of academic philosophy have made him a favorite among theatergoers. {CE; OEL}

Storm, Carl A. (20th Century)

Storm, a liberal minister, has been a member of the American Humanist Association. {HNS}

Storer, Morris R. (20th Century)

Storer was editor of *Humanist Ethics* (1980). {GS}

Storey, David (1965-1999)

Storey obtained a degree at York in 1985, trained as a civil service accountant in Coventry, then became a registered nurse in the field of mental handicap. While at York, he stood for the Student Union Presidency on a gay platform and came in a respectable third. He favored vegetarianism and was concerned about gay rights, women's rights, and racial equality. When he died of a chronic stomach problem, a Humanist funeral ceremony was conducted by John Hemsley, parts of which had been arranged by Storey himself. *[Gay and Lesbian Humanist, Autumn 1999]*

Storr, Anthony (20th Century)

A British psychiatrist, Storr in *Human Destructiveness* (1991) wrote, "What chiefly concerns and alarms many of us are the problems arising from religious fanaticism. As long as large numbers of militant enthusiasts are persuaded that they alone have access to the truth, and that the rest of us are infidels, we remain under threat. Lord Acton's famous phrase about power can be used of another danger. Dogma tends to corrupt, and absolute dogma corrupts absolutely." {TYD}

Story, Joseph (1779–1845)

Story, an Associate Justice of the US Supreme Court, was the youngest person to be appointed to the court. Writing to William Williams (17 February 1823), Story stated, "[I am] a decided Unitarian." {U; UU}

Stosch, Friedrich Wilhelm (1646–1704)

Stosch, also called Johann Friedrich Stoss, published *Concordia rationis et fidel* (1692), which was rigorously suppressed. Anyone possessing the work was threatened with a penalty of five hundred thalers. Lange classed Stosch with German Spinozists, saying, "Stosch curtly denies not only the immateriality but also the immortality of the soul." {BDF; RAT}

Stout, Alan Ker (1900–1983)

Stout, an Australian humanist and philosopher, was born in England and educated at Edinburgh and Oxford. From 1939 to 1965 he was professor of Moral and Political Philosophy at the University of Sydney. He edited the *Australian Journal of Philosophy* and contributed "Morality Without Religion" to *A Humanist View* (1969). A member of the New South Wales Humanist Society, he was a foundation member and president of the Council for Civil Liberties, New South Wales, from 1963 to 1967. Stout also was chairman of the Prison Reform Council. {SWW}

Stout, George Frederick (Born 1860)

Stout, a philosopher who taught at Aberdeen University, Oxford, London, and St. Andrews, was editor of *Mind* starting in 1891. He was admitted to the British Academy in 1903. His chief works are *Analytic Psychology* (1896) and *Manual of Psychology* (1899). {RAT}

Stout, Robert [Sir] [Chief Justice] (1844–1930)

Stout, one of New Zealand's leading public figures of the late 19th and early 20th centuries, had few rivals as regards the range of his contributions to public life. He played a prominent role in the Dunedin Free Thought Association, where he encouraged large numbers to ask questions, demand proof, reject dogma, and take nothing for granted. He was closely associated with the Unitarian church and frequently spoke at their meetings. In Dunedin, he edited *Echo* in the 1860s to 1880s. Stout in 1884 was President of New Zealand's Freethought Federal Union. The 1887 New Zealand census showed 3,925 Freethinkers, with a further 189 Secularists, 105 Atheists, 207 Agnostics, 83 Deists and Theists, 11 Materialists, and 668 of no religion. In 1899 he was appointed Chief Justice. Throughout his life, Sir Robert remained a freethinker and agnostic, and he was an Honorary Associate of the Rationalist Press Association. According to Royle, "Stout was to New Zealand what Ingersoll was to the United States and Bradlaugh to Britain." {BDF; EU, D. A. Hamer; FUK; JM; RAT; RE; SWW; TRI}

Stowe, Emily Jennings (1831–1903)

A Canadian leader for women's rights, Dr. Stowe founded Canada's first woman suffrage society. She was a member of the Second Unitarian Church in Toronto. {U; UU}

Strachey, (Giles) Lytton (1880–1932)

An eminent biographer and essayist, Strachey was the eleventh child of a father who had served for more than thirty years in India as a public administrator. Following an unhappy and sickly childhood, he attended Trinity College, Cambridge, and became a friend of G. E. Moore, John Maynard Keynes, and Leonard Woolf. Becoming a prominent member of the Bloomsbury group, he spent the last sixteen years of his life in a *ménage à trois* with the painter Dora Carrington and her husband, Ralph Partridge.

In 1918 his *Eminent Victorians* received critical acclaim, and he became noted for his satiric edge, his wit, and his iconoclasm. Strachey was interested in the humanities, not in organized religion, and his homosexuality was well-known among his contemporaries. Strachey is credited with writing biography, not necessarily with respect for the individual but with "warts and all," as shown in his *Queen Victoria.*

Lasting love proved elusive for Strachey, according to Lee Arnold of the Historical Society of Pennsylvania. "He did, however, have one person totally devoted to him, the painter Dora Carrington," Arnold has written. "Carrington knew Strachey was gay but was still hopelessly in love with him—even to the exclusion of several well-meaning suitors. She committed suicide after Strachey's death from cancer in 1932."

When, as a conscientious objector in World War I, he was asked what he would do if a foreign soldier was found trying to rape his own sister, the sharp-tongued Strachey replied dryly, "Do my best to get between them." {AA; GL; OEL}

Straczynski, J. Michael (20th Century)

Straczynski is a producer, author, and script writer, a creative force behind the science fiction television series "Babylon 5."

While online (3 November 1994), he commented, "Speaking as an atheist, if there is to be a Church of J. Michael Straczynski, then I must become its first apostate and refuse to believe in myself (adding further insecurity to my life), and nail a whole bunch of theses to the front door on the way out." {CA; E}

Strahan, Ronald (1922–)

Strahan is an Australian humanist, zoologist, historian of science, author, and editor. A youthful chorister in an Anglican church, he became an agnostic by age eleven, an atheist by age fourteen. From 1967 to 1974, he was a zoo director. Strahan is an active proponent of the materialist interpretation of evolutionary theory and a strong opponent of "creation science" in radio broadcasts, public lectures, and contributions to symposia. He has articles in *A Humanist View* (1969) and wrote *Confronting Creationism: Defending Darwin* (1987). {SWW}

Strahler, Arthur N. (1918–)

Strahler, a professor of geology at Columbia University, is a secular humanist who has written for *Free Inquiry*. In 1972 he wrote *Modern Physical Geography* and, in 1987, *Science and Earth History.* {*Free Inquiry*, Summer, 1991}

Strain, Daniel T. (20th Century)

"The lack of an absolute authoritative source for morality," Strain wrote in the Houston, Texas, newsletter, *HSH News* (January 1999), "means that we may not ever know for certain what the 'best' behaviors are, but we *can* make rational arguments in support of, or in opposition to, various behaviors. We can come to general consensus on the more clear issues."

Straker, Jean (20th Century)

Straker was a secularist who, in 1966, had some of his artistic nude photos seized in England for what he claimed was in contravention of Article 10 of the European Convention on Human Rights and Articles 19 and 27 of the Universal Declaration of Human Rights. As a result, Straker founded Freedom of Vision.

Strange, Thomas Lumsden (Died 1884)

Long, at first an Evangelical Christian, became one of the Plymouth Brethren, then became a weak theist, always an earnest advocate of practical piety in life and conduct. When a judge, he once sentenced a Brahmin to death, seeking to bring the prisoner "to Jesus." At the gallows, however, the person "proclaimed his trust to be in Rama and not in Christ," which set Judge Strange to thinking. He then investigated Christianity's claims, writing *The Bible, Is It the Word of God?* (1871), *The Development of Creation on the Earth* (1874), and *The Legends of the Old Testament* (1874). Strange was a friend of T. Scott and General Forlong. McCabe labels him a theistic rationalist. {BDF; RAT; RE}

Stranneby, Ebron (20th Century)

Stranneby is the chairperson of Human-Etiska Forbunder I Sverige. Her group publishes *Human-Etik*. (See entry for Swedish Secularism.) {FD}

Stratton, Richard F. (20th Century)

Stratton, a non-believer, writes for *The American Rationalist.*

Straub, Gerard Thomas (20th Century)

Straub, a former producer of "The 700 Club," is author of *Salvation For Sale: An Insider's View of Pat Robertson's Ministry* (1986). {HNS2}

Straus, Nathan (20th Century)

"A Forgotten Founding Father" by Straus appeared in Joseph Lewis's magazine, *Age of Reason* (June 1959).

Strauss, Bernice (1924–1996)

Strauss, a World War II veteran who worked as a medical lab technician for the Women's Army Corps, was one of the family members which founded Marial Whippets, a successful whippet kennel in Wisconsin. She had long been interested in and raced as a hobby the small, greyhound-like dogs.

Strauss, David Friedrich (1808–1874)

When he wrote *The Life of Jesus, Critically Examined* (1835), Strauss was dismissed from a theological teaching post at the University of Tübingen in Germany because, along with other things, he rejected the Biblical miracles, and his work had applied the "myth theory" to the life of Jesus, treated the Gospel narrative like any other historical work, and denied all supernatural elements in the Gospels. The work excited as much discussion as Renan's later work. Littré translated it into French, and George Eliot translated it into English (1844). The Zürich government in 1839 appointed him professor of church history, but it was obliged to repeal the decision because of a storm of Christian indignation. In 1870 Strauss published *Voltaire*, and In his final work, *The Old Faith and the New* (1872), Strauss declared he was no longer a Christian nor did he believe in immortality nor a personal God. Specifically, he wrote, "If we would speak as honest, upright men, we must acknowledge we are no longer Christians." Famed novelist George Eliot made the first translation of his *Life of Jesus* in 1846. McCabe wrote, "The fact is generally suppressed that [Strauss] had a faithful disciple and friend in the German Empress," a reference to Victoria, the Empress of Germany and eldest daughter of Queen Victoria. The Empress, daughter of the prim and pious Queen Victoria, was a freethinker.

Strauss died of cancer of the stomach. Of his illness his biographer, Edward Zeller, wrote: "But in these very sufferings the mental greatness and moral strength of the sufferer proclaimed their most glorious victory. He was fully aware of his condition. With unshaken firmness he adhered to the convictions which be had openly acknowledged in his last work (*The Old Faith and the New*), and he never for a moment repented having written them. But with these convictions he met death with such repose and with such unclouded serenity of mind, that it was impossible to leave his sick room without the impression of a moral sanctity which we all the more surely receive from greatness of soul and mastery of mind over matter, the stronger are the hindrances in the surmounting of which it is manifested."

Strauss left directions for his funeral. He expressly forbade all participation of the Church in the ceremony, but on the day of his interment a sum of money was to be given to the poor. "On February 10

(1874) therefore," Zeller reported, "he was buried without ringing of bells or the presence of a clergyman, but in the most suitable manner, and amid the lively sympathy of all, far and near." (See entry for Princess Maud Mary Alice.) {BDF; CE; CL; ER; EU, G. A. Wells; JM; JMR; JMRH; RAT; RE}

Strauss, Leo (1899–1973)

Strauss, who moved from Germany to Paris in 1932, moved then to London, settling eventually as a teacher at the University of Chicago. There, according to historian Michael Oakeshott (1901–1990), Strauss developed a systematic political doctrine based on the history of philosophy from Socrates to Nietzsche. His views became popular with American conservatives. He wrote, "A just political order must be grounded in immutable demands of natural right. Nature, however, is inherently unequal. The capacity to discover truth is restricted to a few, and to endure it exhibited by scarcely more. The best regime will therefore reflect differences in human excellence, and be led by an appropriate elite. But although the highest virtue is philosophical contemplation of truth, this does not mean (contrary to a superficial reading of *The Republic*) that a just city will be ruled by philosophers. For philosophy gazes without faltering, not only at the necessary conditions of political order, discomfiting as these may be to demotic prejudice, but at the far more terrible realities of cosmic disorder: the absence of any divine authority, the delusion of any common morality, the transience of the earth and its species." To Strauss, philosophers should teach the "leisured gentlemen" to rule, which made him popular at the National Security Council during the time of President Ronald Reagan and later by Vice President Dan Quayle. Both Reagan and Quayle, political conservatives were Christians. Strauss was an atheist.

Strauss, Richard (1864–1949)

Strauss, the German composer and conductor, began composing when he was six years old. His "Symphony in D Minor" (1880) was performed when he was but a teenager. He wrote romantic symphonic poems. "Death and Transfiguration *(1889),* "Till Eulenspiegel's Merry Pranks" (1895), and "Thus Spake Zarathustra" (1895) are evocative and richly orchestrated. His dramatic operas include "Salomé" (1905) and, with librettos by Hofmannsthal, "Electra" (1909), "Der Rosenkavalier" (1911), and "Ariadne auf Naxos" (1912).

A close student of philosophy, Strauss expressed his convictions in the symphonic poem based upon Nietzsche's work, *Also Sprach Zarathustra*, which the clergy angrily denounced. Alex Ross, calling him in *The New Yorker* (20 December 1999) the "the composer of the century," added, "He did not believe in God, and he saw no spiritual dimension in his art." {JM; RAT; RE; TYD}

Strayer, James (1935–)

Strayer, a retired biology instructor who taught thirty-four years, is a member of the Board of Atheists of Florida. His father was an atheist, his brother is an atheist, he is a second generation atheist, and his two sons are atheists. Strayer leads the Florida East Coast Freethinkers. He spoke on the subject "Evolution of Structure and Function" at the 1999 convention of Humanists of Florida. {*Humanists of the Palm Beaches Newsletter*, October 1997}

Streams, Michael L. (20th Century)

Streams, a physician and civil rights activist in Century City, California, is an Advisory Board Member of African Americans for Humanism.

STREE SWETCHA

A monthly publication of the Telugu Women's Liberation group, *Stree Swetcha* is at 9 MIGH, Mehdipatnam, Hyderabad 500 028, India.

Streedhar, Katharine (20th Century)

Streedhar is director for the Unitarian Universalists of the Holdeen India Program, which distributes trust income that has been designated for use in India. Money is allotted for social justice, maternity, child welfare, education, and migration expenses.

Streiker, Lowell D. (20th Century)

A counselor and therapist in California, Streiker is a secular humanist who has written for *Free Inquiry*. His books include *The Jesus Trip* (1971), *The Gospel Time Bomb: Ultrafundamentalism and the Future of America* (1984); and *Mind-Bending: Brainwashing, Cults, and Deprogramming in the 80s* (1984). {*Free Inquiry*, Spring, 1984}

Streminger, Gerhard (1952–)

Streminger's biography of Hume, *David Hume: Sein Leben und sein Werk* (1995), received critical acclaim in Germany.

Strindberg, Johan August (1849–1912)

Strindberg was a major Swedish playwright, historian, writer of stories, and poet, one whose work combined psychology and literary naturalism. He has been termed the greatest master of the Swedish language. Known for having led a tumultuous life, with three disastrous marriages, he suffered from a persecution mania.

Mäster Olof (1872–1878) was about God but, rather than perpetuating Christianity, was basically an exploration of the inhuman nature of idealism. Men meet their fate, not because of God: They meet their fate because of the result of human instinct and cultural ideologies. *The Father* (1887) was misogynistic, seeing man as being victimized by woman in a war between the sexes. *The Red Room* satirized Swedish hypocrisy and injustice. *Married* (2 vols., 1884–1885), which derogated women and denounced the practices of conventional religion, was confiscated by the authorities because of its content. *Miss Julie* (1888) told of an upper-class woman seduced by an insensitive chauffeur. Like *Creditors* (1889), it showed the influence of Zola and Nietzsche. From 1894 to 1896, influenced by Swedenborg, he experienced an "inferno crisis," exploring the occult and believing he was being persecuted by other-worldly creatures, which he depicted in *Inferno* (1897). After marrying the actress Harriet Bosse in 1901 but parting in 1904, he lost, as in his two previous marriages, custody of his offspring.

Strindberg then experimented with visual effects as well as other aspects of dramatic form, becoming internationally known for expressionist dream sequences and symbols that were combined with religious mysticism. *A Dream Play* (1902), *To Damascus* (1898–1904), and *The Ghost Sonata* (1907) illustrated this new experimentation, all showing man's discordant existence along with varying degrees of pessimism. *Gustav Vasa* (1899) was a historical drama, and *The Great Highway* (1909) was a symbolic study of his own life.

In 1884, after being a leader in the Rationalist group of young followers of Edvard Brandes, he was driven abroad but, when he returned to face a charge of ridiculing the Eucharist, he was found not guilty. *Son of a Servant* (1886) is Strindberg's bitter autobiography. The Swedish Academy never inducted him, but his works influenced Sean O'Casey and Eugene O'Neill. According to critic Robert William McKay, Strindberg was an atheist during most of his life "but he had a mental breakdown, lost his virility, and drifted into mysticism." However, Strindberg despite his interest in

Swedenborgianism, never returned to the church. {BDF; CE; EU, Faith Ingwersen; JM; JMR; RE}

STRING THEORY

In physics the string, or superstring, is a reference to the study of an elementary particle in a theory of space-time incorporating supersymmetry. The hypothetical particle consists of a short one-dimensional string that exists in ten dimensions. Although it has never been proved experimentally, the theory rests on a simple premise which has been described by Jennifer Senior (*New York*, 1 February 1999): "that the smallest building blocks of the universe—muons, photons, gluons, and all those other particles that sound like Santa's reindeer—are generated by the vibrations of tiny, quivering loops of string. The whole universe is made up of them, *tied up* with them, if you prefer, as if the cosmos were a shimmering aeolian harp."

Columbia University's Brian Greene described the theory in *The Elegant* Universe: Superstrings, Hidden Dimensions, and the Quest for the Ultimate Theory (1999). One of the leading exponents, Senior found, Greene is working to reconcile two previously incompatible tenets of contemporary physics,

> the theory of general relativity (which describes the behavior of very large things, like the steady outward streaming of the galaxies) and quantum mechanics (which describes very small things, like the flighty path of an electron). The former supposes that space is gently curving; the latter implies that space is jittery and unpredictable. String theory modifies Einstein's theory in just such a way that these two conceptions of space are brought into alignment . . . . Space [it is postulated] only seems like space *to us*. And time . . . only feels like time *to us*. But if human beings were smaller, they'd see that space and time were merely the perceivable facets of a much more nuanced series of organizing principles—the same way that crude patterns are the only thing one sees, at first, when thumbing through the pages of a Magic Eye book. "So if we were born not 20 inches long, but 10-to-the-minus-33 inches long–that's a billionth of a trillionth of a trillionth of an inch—then we would know what those organizing principles were," says Greene. "They would be of second nature to us, just like time and space."

Skeptics of string theory include Sheldon Glashow, a Nobel Prize-winning particle physicist at Harvard. One objection physicists have is that until recently five different string theories are competing to describe the same world. Greene, however, showed that the five are simply different views of a single underlying theory. Despite the skeptics, Steven Weinberg, a Nobel-laureate physicist at the University of Texas, has written that "I still think string theory is the only game in town."

Stromer, Hjalmar (1849–1887)

Stromer was a Swedish astronomer who published not only works on astronomy but also wrote *Confessions of a Freethinker*. {BDF}

Strong, Charles (1844–1942)

Strong was an Australian clergyman and social reformer. Born in Scotland of a Presbyterian clerical family, he rejected Calvinist scholasticism and adopted a liberal theology. After being threatened by the Presbytery for a libel for heresy, he helped found the Australasian Church in 1885. Charles Strong was its first minister. Known as "Melbourne's high priest of ethical religion," Strong taught that Christianity was more endangered by theological obscurantism than critical historical investigation, and that failure to love one's neighbor was more serious than doctrinal doubt. {SWW}

Strossen, Nadine (1950–)

Strossen, who is president of the American Civil Liberties Union, is a law educator and human rights activist. A Harvard graduate, she was named in 1986 one of the ten outstanding young Americans by the Jaycees International.

In *Defending Pornography: Free Speech, Sex, and the Fight for Women's Rights* (1995), she holds that free speech and thought are essential to achieving the needed equality of the sexes. Differing with those militant feminists who see free speech as the enemy and who try to purge all forms of speech and expression of "degrading" elements, Strossen counters that a censorship movement such as Feminists Against Pornography would lead to a dead end, that without free speech progress toward the eventual equality of the sexes is impossible. Those feminists who argue for censorship, therefore, are the arch reactionaries who never wanted equality for women in any case.

Strossen has been cited by many freethinkers as being one of the most eloquent spokespersons on behalf of human rights.

Strothman, Wendy J. (20th Century)

Strothman, who had been vice president of the Unitarian Universalist Association and director of Beacon Press since 1983, left in 1995 to become vice president and publisher of adult trade and reference books at Houghton Mifflin Company. Beacon Press, she has noted, is the second oldest independent publisher—Houghton Mifflin is the oldest.

Strozzi, Piero (1500–1558)

Strozzi, who was of a noble Florentine family, became an Italian general in the service of France. Intended for the Church, he chose to abandon religion for a military career and around the year of 1555 was created marshal of France by Henry II. Being injured at the siege of Thionville, he was exhorted by the Duc de Guise to think of Jesus. But Strozzi calmly declared himself an atheist. {BDF}

STRUCTURALISTS

Structuralism in philosophy is a method, not a distinct philosophy, of analyzing phenomena. It is chiefly characterized by contrasting the elemental structures of the phenomena in a system of binary opposition—for example, good/evil; internal/external; universal/particular; transcendental/empirical. Structuralists include Althuser, Barthes, Foucault, Lacan, and Lévi-Strauss. Post-structuralists reject such binary opposites.

In linguistics, structuralism is best described in terms of its irreducible structural units in morphology and phonology. {AF}

Struve, Gustav von (1805–1870)

Struve was a German reformer, son of a Russian State-Councilor. He studied law in Germany and edited the *Mannheimer Journal*. Several times, he was jailed for taking an active part in the attempt to set up a republic in Baden. When it failed, he fled to Switzerland. Venturing back in 1849, he was condemned to five and one-half years in prison. Republicans released him, but they again failed, and Struve migrated to America where he wrote his most important work, *Allgemeine Weltgeschichte* (9 volumes, 1853–1860). His rationalist views are given in this and in his *Pflanzenkost* (1869). After fighting in the American Civil War, he returned to Germany in 1868. {RAT}

Stuart, Carole (1941-)

Stuart wrote *Why Was I Adopted*; *To Turn You On*; *39 Sex Fantasies for Women; Why Am I Going to the Hospital?* (with Claire Ciliotta); *I'll Never Be Fat Again*; and *How to Lose 5 Pounds Fast*. A resident of New Jersey, Stuart is publisher of Barricade Books in New York City.

She has gone on record as being, like her husband Lyle Stuart, a non-believer. {WAS, numerous conversations]

Stuart, Gilbert (1755–1828)

Stuart, an eminent American artist, has been said to have been a Unitarian, although he is not included by Elizabeth Gillis as having been a member of a specific church. He is noted for his portraits of George Washington, the best-known of which is found on the United States $1 bill. {CE; UU}

Stuart, Lyle (1922-)

When a young man, Stuart wrote a country song, "Someone

Left That Golden Gate Open," that was recorded by Grand Ole Opry star Red Foley. An atheist, he nevertheless wrote "Go to Church on Sunday Morning" for retailer and philanthropist J. C. Penney. Stuart was once a reporter for International News Service (1945) and *Variety* (1945-1946), editor of *Music Business* (1946-1948), founder of *Exposé* (1951), publisher of *The Independent* (1951-1975), business manager of *MAD* (1952-1954), and president of Citadel Press (1970-1989). Since 1990 he has been President of Barricade Books.

Never one to shun taboo subjects or controversial books, he has published *The Anarchist Cookbook*, Ferdinand Lundberg's *The Rich and the Super-Rich*, *Running Scared* (an exposé of Steve Wynn as "emperor" of Nevada), *The Sensuous Woman*, *The Sensuous Man*, *The Marriage Art*, and *Where Did I Come From?*, a book for youngsters about sex. He is author of *God Wears A Bowtie* (1949); *The Secret Life of Walter Winchell* (1953, a time when the gossip columnist was most powerful); *Mary Louise* (1970); *Casino Gambling for the Winner* (1978); *Lyle Stuart on Baccarat* (1983, revised 1997); and *Winning at Casino Gambling* (1995).

Known as a skilled casino gambler, he once entered two baccarat tournaments in Atlantic City, winning first place both at Bally's Grand and the Taj Mahal for a total of $245,000.

In 1999 on Radio WEVD's Alan Colmes's talk show, Stuart livened the discussion by saying,

> There is no god. There are no gods. There is no life before conception, and there is no life after death. Religion thrives on ignorance, fear, superstition, and ignorance.

Callers immediately telephoned their objections, but Colmes has no taboos on his show and, according to Stuart, "is one of the few sound liberal voices still on any major radio station." {WAS, numerous conversations}

Stuck, Franz Ritter von (1863–1928)

A German painter, von Stuck was a professor at the Munich Academy of Plastic Arts. He was a member of the *Société Internationale de Peinture et de Sculpture,* and the Berlin, Munich, Dresden, Milan, Antwerp, and other academies. Von Stuck, an outspoken supporter of Haeckel, was one of the founders of the Monist League. {RAT}

STUDENT FREETHINKERS: See entry for Campus Freethought Alliance. A list of student freethought organizations is found on the Web at <http://www.infidels.org/org/student.html>.

STUDY GROUP OF THE HISTORY OF WESTERN HUMANISM

A Chinese group with associate membership in the International Humanist and Ethical Union (IHEU) is the Study Group of the History of Western Humanism, the Library of Chinese, Political College of Young, Beijing, China.

STUDY OF RELIGION IN POLITICS

For a study of religion in politics, see the Web: <http://www.isrp.org/>.

Stuhr, Christian (20th Century)

Stuhr, a writer and teacher in Swift Current, Saskatchewan, has written humanistic articles in *Humanist in Canada*.

Sturoc, William C. (Born 1822)

By the age of sixteen, Scottish-born Sturoc had read Volney, Voltaire, d'Holbach, and others. In 1846 he migrated to Canada, then moved to New Hampshire where he became a lawyer. An agnostic, Sturoc attended the International Congress of Freethinkers at Chicago in 1893 and was one of the vice-presidents of the American Secular Union. {PUT}

Styer, Timothy M. (20th Century)

In 1996, Styer was awarded the Rudi Gelsey Social Justice Award by the Unitarian Universalist Church of the Restoration in Philadelphia, Pennsylvania, which was celebrating its 175th anniversary. During the 1960s, Gelsey, then minister of the church, led a campaign against "blockbusting," a real estate practice that involves scaring white residents into selling their houses because people of color are moving into the area.

Styron, William (1925–)

Styron's novel, *The Confessions of Nat Turner* (1967), won a Pulitzer Prize in 1968. But after the work's initial praise, many African American intellectuals objected to the novel's recreation of the 1831 slave rebellion in Virginia, claiming as a white man he was unable to depict a black man's experiences. This despite his statement that blacks had "a constant hold on my boyhood" and "black experience motivated much of my writing." One defender, Henry Louis Gates Jr., remarked, "He set himself up as a sacrificial victim, and I believe he knew it. A black hero as gay? Of course, he knew it." Gates deliberately did not include Styron in his *Dictionary of Global Culture* (1997).

His first novel, *Lie Down in Darkness* (1951), also received great critical praise. Other of his works are *Sophie's Choice* (1968); a play called *In the Clap Shack* (1972); and *Darkness Visible: A Memoir of Madness* (1990), a description of his bout with clinical depression. Styron is a member of the American Academy of Arts and Letters and of *Académie Goncourt.*

In "A Case of the Great Pox," Styron describes the news that a nineteen-year-old U.S. Marine received from his physician. That news was that he had syphilis, which had been detected by a medical Kahn test "was so high it had gone off the chart." It was a time when the very word *syphilis* was taboo, was uttered sotto voce, if at all, and if cited at all was called a "social disease" or a "vice disease." Styron explained further: "But it was the doctrine of original sin, falling upon both Catholics and backslid Presbyterians like me, that made the sufferers of syphilis pay a special price in moral blame unknown to those who acquired other diseases. . . . [S]yphilis, in a puritanical culture [had] a peculiar aura of degradation. As Susan Sontag has shown in "Illness as Metaphor," her study of the mythology of disease, all the major illnesses have prompted a moralistic and punitive response, and have given rise to entire theoretical systems based on phony psychologizing. The bubonic plague implied widespread moral pollution; tuberculosis was the product of thwarted passion and blighted hopes, or sprang from 'defective vitality, or vitality misspent'; out of emotional frustration or repression of feeling has come the curse of cancer, whose victims are also often demonically possessed." In a secular age, Styron related, "gags were appropriate for an inexplicable calamity that in olden times was regarded as divine retribution. Previous centuries had seen people calling on God for help, and God had not answered." The physician, he now detected, had had a "personal fixation" about the disease all along. He was "supposed to be free of such proscriptive attitudes, but there are always some who are as easily bent as anyone else by religion or ideology. Klotz (the physician) was one of these . . . a doctor who hated not the disease but its victims . . . . Klotz was obviously the inheritor of a tradition with a firm root in Southern Christian fundamentalism." When it transpired that Styron had had Vincent's disease, not syphilis, and that it was easily cleared up by old-fashioned applications of gentian violet.

Styron revealed in "A Case of the Great Pox" that his stepmother, "an observant Christian, curiously illiberal for an Episcopalian," considered his own skepticism and fealty to Camus "diabolical." He thought her a prig. Meanwhile, she disapproved of hearing that he had a fealty to Camus' "*Le Mythe de Sisyphe*," which he had read "laboriously but with happiness in French at Duke."

Among Styron's literary admirers are Peter Matthiessen, Carlos Fuentes, and Arthur Miller. Asked which writer he wishes he could have been and of what book, Styron chose the historian C. Vann Woordward for his *The Burden of Southern History*: "[I]t is so mageristerial in its understanding of the spirit and the traditions of the South and the way they evolved that it's really kind of a work of almost perfect authority." {*Free Inquiry*, Winter 1995-1996; Mary B. W. Tabor, *The New York Tims*, 7 November 1998}

Styvesant, Peter (c. 1610–1672)

When Styvesant, the Dutch director-general of the North American colony of New Netherlands (1647–1664), battled the Spanish in the Caribbean in 1644, he suffered a badly mangled leg and was rushed to Curaçao for medical treatment. The shattered limb was amputated and accorded a Christian burial with full military honors. Twenty-eight years later, the rest of the body of the harsh, autocratic ruler who was intolerant of religious dissenters, was buried. {PA}

Suard, Jean Baptiste Antoine (1734–1817)

Suard was a French writer. He became a devoted friend of Baron d'Holbach and of Garat. He also corresponded with Hume and Walpole. Working as the censor of theatres, Suard wrote *Miscellanies of Literature* and other works related to the humanities. {BDF}

Suarez, John M. (20th Century)

Suarez, a physician, spoke in 1997 on "The Radical Religious Right—Beyond Stealth" at the 20th Anniversary convention of the Freedom from Religion Foundation. He is a member of the Outreach Committee at the Center for Inquiry West.

Subbamma, Malladi (20th Century)

Subbamma [original name in Telugu: **Mahila Abhyudaya Samstha**], who wrote *Women and Social Reforms* (1994), is editor of *Stree Swetchcha* in Hyderabad, India and head of the Institute for the Advancement of Women. She is the wife of M. V. Ramamurthy, and both are active in the Indian Rationalist Association.

Subbamma is one of the few humanist-feminist activists in India, working in many developmental activities for the empowerment of women. Specifically, she is concerned about the following subjects:

- the anti-women agenda which is apparent in Muslim countries, as exemplified by an Afghani Mujahideen's statement that it is time to send women "back to the bag."
- sati, a custom in which childless widows allow themselves to be burned along with their dead husbands because of tremendous social pressure and the veneration shown toward a person who commits sati. In the period 1815–1825, at least 8,142 widows burned themselves. The practice was abolished by the English government at the instance of Raja Rarn Mohan Roy.
- kanyasulkam, a custom designed to enable the parents to sell away in marriage their daughters to the person offering the highest amount of money, whatever his age, the result of which was an increase of widows.
- dowry, a universally practiced system by which the prospective groom is willing to marry only that girl whose parents pay the highest amount in dowry and also tender valuable gifts. The default in paying a dowry either in full or in part has often resulted in what is called dowry deaths or bridge burnings. In 1985, at least 989 were reported. In 1987, the figure increased to 1,793.

(See entry for G. Vijayam.)

Subedi, Ganga Prasad (20th Century)

Subedi from Nepal was a participant in 1996 at the Mexico City humanist congress. He signed Humanist Manifesto 2000.

SUCCESS

- There is an old motto that runs, "If at first you don't succeed, try, try again." This is nonsense. It ought to read, "If at first you don't succeed, quit, quit at once."

–Stephen Leacock

- Moderation is a fatal thing. Nothing succeeds like excess.

–Oscar Wilde

- It is not enough to succeed; others must fail.

–Gore Vidal

Sudermann, Herman (1857–1928)

Sudermann was a German dramatist and novelist. His play, *Die Ehre* (1889), was one of the first successes of the burgeoning German naturalist movement. One of his finest dramas is *Fritzchen*, which portrays the harshness of the Prussian officer code. *Heimat* (1893; tr. *Magda*, 1896) was a vehicle for Sarah Bernhardt and for Mrs. Patrick Campbell. His novels bare the crudity and immorality of the Prussian aristocracy and the corruption of Berlin society. With Haeckel, Sudermann helped found the Monist League, openly expressing his agnosticism. {CE; JM; RAT; RE}

Sue, Marie Joseph (1804–1857)

Sue, called Eugène, was a French novelist. He wrote many romances, including *The Mysteries of Paris* and *The Wandering Jew* (1842–1845). In 1850 he was elected deputy and sat at the extreme left, then was exiled by the coup d'état. Sue was a declared freethinker. {BDF; RAT; RE}

Suffocation (20th Century)

According to Celebrity Atheists, the recording artists known as Suffocation are non-theists. {E}

Sühl, Klaus (20th Century)

Sühl, who is president of the *Humanistischer Verband Deutschlands*, spoke at the 1993 Congress of the European Humanist Federation (EHF), at which he said that following the fall of the Berlin wall many had naively dreamed of a unified Europe and a peaceful world. "There is no likelihood of former Eastern Germany being converted back to Christianity," adding that "the humanist movement faces new tasks in this situation." Sühl also is Treasurer General of the European Humanist Federation. He wrote *Auf dem weg Mach Europa* (1994).

Suhl, Yuri (19th Century)

Suhl in 1889 wrote "A Defense of Atheism." In a posthumous printing, his *Ernestine L. Rose and the Battle for Human Rights* (1959) was published.

Suhre, Richard (1911-   )

In 1994 in a North Carolina county courtroom, Suhre challenged the district court's right to place the Ten Commandments in a courtroom. He said he was "repulsed" by the marble tablets hanging in the Haywood County courtroom in his hometown of Waynesville.

"They have the laws of Moses prominently displayed where they have the laws of North Carolina adjudicated," he complained, "and they do not mesh. I see the state is promoting a religion." The county has spent well over $133,000 to maintain the tablets, and a three-judge panel of the 4th U.S. Circuit Court of Appeals agreed in 1998 to hear the case. {*Freethought Today*, September 1998}

SUICIDE

- The thought of suicide is a great consolation; with its help you can get through many a bad night.

–Friedrich Nietzsche

- There are many who dare not kill themselves for fear of what the neighbors will say.

–Cyril Connolly

• There is only one truly philosophical problem, and that is suicide.
—**Albert Camus**

• Suicide kills two people. That's what it's for!
—**Arthur Miller**
a point made in "After the Fall" that most suicides have a devastating impact on family and friends

"Suicide is against Roman law," says a character in the Broadway musical, "A Funny Thing Happened on the Way to the Forum. "The penalty is death."

Socrates is a major example of a pre-Christian suicide. Recent suicides have been photographer Diane Arbus, actress Judy Garland, writer Abbie Hoffman, camera inventor George Eastman, Secretary of Defense James Forrestal, novelist Ernest Hemingway, musicians Jimi Hendrix and Kurt Cobain, writer Primo Levi, novelist Jack London, actress Marilyn Monroe, musician Jim Morris, writer Sylvia Plath, painter Jackson Pollack, painter Mark Rothko, composer Robert Schumann, poet Ann Sexton, painter Vincent Van Gogh, and author Virginia Woolf.

Taking one's own life, according to some Christians, is condemned—unqualifiedly—as an offense against God's will, grace, and judgment. Although harakiri (disembowelment) and seppuku (a more polite Japanese term for suicide by disembowelment) have been recommended by some non-Christians under certain circumstances, Christian theologians generally consider suicide reprehensible legally, morally, and religiously. Judaism and Islam also expressly proscribe the act.

Unitarian Universalists and others of more liberal religious groups often approve "living wills," in which individuals condone the refusal of life-sustaining treatment in the event they are hopelessly ill; and of "health care proxies," which appoint friends to make treatment decisions on their behalf in the event they are rationally unable to do so. Charles Francis Potter, the Unitarian minister who in 1929 founded and led the First Humanist Society in New York, was founder in 1938 of the Euthanasia Society of America. **Euthanasia** is the practice for reasons of mercy of permitting the death of a hopelessly sick or injured individual (a person, or an animal), in a relatively painless way.

In 1994, Judge Barbara Rothstein of the United States District Court in Seattle ruled that the Constitution guarantees people not only the right to terminate pregnancies without Government interference but also the right to end their own lives. By striking down a 140-year-old Washington State ban on assisted suicide, she said the law violated the 14th Amendment clause against state infringement of individual liberty. This, coupled with a Michigan jury's acquitting Dr. Jack Kevorkian of charges that he had violated that state's law against helping people kill themselves, has encouraged various humanistic groups that euthanasia may eventually be legalized with appropriate and specific restrictions.

In 1995, Peter Singer discussed the subject in *Rethinking Life and Death*. So did Herbert Hendin in *Suicide in America*. Singer argues that euthanasia should be allowed if the person suffers from the absence or irreversible loss of cortical capacity. He also argues that assisted suicide should be legal—as both have been in the Netherlands since November 1993—to those unimpaired cortically but who have a painful, irreversible disease and plead for the right to die. Hendin, a psychiatrist, might better be treated for their depressive condition and states that many who are counseled then become grateful that they have additional time to live. Singer approves of Dr. Jack Kevorkian's efforts, whereas Hendin does not.

In 1996, the Episcopal Diocese of Newark ruled that committing suicide is morally acceptable for the terminally ill. "Nowhere in the Bible does it say that there is a value to suffering simply for the sake of suffering," said the Rev. Lawrence Falkowski of West Orange, New Jersey. Bishop John Shelby Spong, the leader of the 40,000-member diocese and an advocate of assisted suicide, agreed, saying the time has come for religious faiths to "redefine what life means."

Dennis Rodman, the professional basketball player sometimes seen sporting feminine articles of clothing and yellow hair, takes a positive stand on suicide. Once when he was terribly depressed and had a gun in his hand, ready to end his life, he used logic to determine the causes of his unhappiness—when young he had been called a sissy; when in his 30s and having become wealthy, people only wanted his money: he had become the person others wanted him to be. So he killed his outer self. He became what he really was, and this included a well-publicized liaison with the actress-singer Madonna and book-signings of his work, *Bad As I Want To Be* (1996), during which he appeared in drag (but insisted he is not gay or bisexual), all made possible by the "suicide" of his outer or other self. Rodman's frank confessions to such a wide audience resulted in much discussion by individuals recognizing that they, also, should not allow arbitrary mores to keep them from being their true self.

Kay Redfield Jamison's *Night Falls Fast* (1999) estimates that every seventeen minutes someone in the United States commits suicide, that it ranks third among causes of death for young people and second for college students. More young people died of suicide in 1995 than of AIDS, cancer, stroke, pneumonia, influenza, birth defects, and heart disease combined. The World Health Organization reported that in 1998 suicide was the cause of almost 2% of deaths worldwide and is increasing—thus, more are dying from suicide than from war or homicide. (See entry for Ralph Mero of Compassion for Dying and for Derek Humphry, who describes successful means which individuals have used in order to commit suicide when their terminal illness brings them unbearable pain. Also, see the article by Glanville Williams which includes Anthony Flew's views in favor of euthanasia in the *Encyclopedia of Philosophy*, Vol. 7.)

Sullivan, Andrew (20th Century)

Sullivan, the gay editor of *The New Republic*, spoke on "The Gay Catholic Paradox" at Notre Dame University in 1995. Asked how he can be openly gay and Catholic, he responded, "I am openly gay *because* I am Catholic." His church, he explained, had taught him to witness to the truth and to love one another. What he has trouble understanding is why his church insists on the dignity of the homosexual person and the blamelessness of homosexuality in itself but teaches that "if this blameless condition was acted upon, it would be always and everywhere evil." Meanwhile, an unresolved debate at Notre Dame continued as to whether the Catholic institution should give official status to the organization of gay and lesbian students which had arranged his visit.

In *Virtually Normal: An Argument About Homosexuality* (1995), Sullivan tackles the Biblical condemnation by St. Paul of those who "change the natural use into that which is against nature." This Sullivan reads as meaning that homosexuals do not "change the natural use" in their sexual act—thus, it is not they who are being condemned. "What Paul is describing here is heterosexuals engaging, against *their* own nature, in homosexual behavior." {Peter Steinfels, *The New York Times*, 18 February 1995)

Sullivan, Claudia (20th Century)

Sullivan is Secretary of the Arizona Secular Humanists, PO Box 3738, Scottsdale, Arizona 85271.

Sullivan, J. (19th Century)

Sullivan wrote *Search for Deity*, an inquiry as to the origin of the conception of God (1859). {BDF}

Sullivan, Marilyn and **Michael Sullivan** (20th Century)

The Sullivans were founding directors of the North Texas Church of Freethought (NTCOF), a fellowship of unbelievers which commenced in 1995. Their mail address: PO Box 111894, Carrollton, Texas 76011.

Sullivan, Walter Seagar Jr. (1918–1996)

Sullivan, a science reporter and editor for *The New York Times*, was noted for his articles that took him from pole to pole and ranged from the seabed to the shifting continents. In the 1960s, he told of the marvels of galaxies, explaining in clear prose what readers found understandable for the first time. He became known for his knowledge of science and his skill in making it comprehendable. Sullivan visited Antarctica seven times, and a thirty-mile mountain chain there is named the Sullivan Range in his honor. Among his published works are *White Land of Adventure* (1957), about the Arctic; *Assault on the Unknown* (1961); and *Continents in Motion* (1974). He was editor of *America's Race for the Moon* (1962). Sullivan, a naturalist in philosophy, was a Unitarian.

Sullivan William Laurence (1872–1935)

A chief advocate of Christian theism in 20th-century Unitarianism, Sullivan once had been a Catholic priest and a professor of theology. But Pope Pius X's 1907 encyclical condemning modernism turned him to the writings of James Martineau and in 1911 he became a Unitarian. He scornfully rejected the Humanist movement, seeing Humanists as atheists or agnostics who were unwilling to accept that designation, styling themselves Humanist to preserve their respectability in a church that historically had been Christian. In his own time, however, Unitarianism dropped its Christian label. {U&U}

Sully, James (1842–1923)

Sully taught psychology at London University College. He was a declared agnostic. {RAT; RE}

Sully-Prudhomme, René François Armand (1839–1907)

Sully-Prudhomme was a French poet associated with the Parnassians. His major works are two long philosophical poems, *La Justice* (1878) and *Le Bonheur* (1889, *Happiness*). They treat abstract, humanitarian themes. His prose, *Que sais-je?* (1896, *What Do I Know?*) was awarded the first Nobel Prize in literature, in 1901. In 1882, Sully-Prudhomme had become a member of the French Academy. His poems were of a pessimistic cast, described by Wheeler as being "full of the delicacy of philosophic suggestion." According to McCabe, Sully-Prudhomme "declared his skepticism in a preface to his first volume of poems but he was a freethinker of the very rare type that wants to believe in religion and cannot. He came to believe at the most in a sort of pantheistic halo of the moral universe which he called 'the divine.' " {BDF; JM; RAT; RE}

Sulzberger, Arthur ["Punch"] Ochs Jr. (1951-)

The editor of *The New York Times* is an agnostic.

After studying at Tufts and Harvard, Sulzberger worked as a reporter for *The Raleigh* (North Carolina) *Times*, a correspondent in London for the Associated Press (1976-1978), and then a series of jobs on the newspaper that was founded by his grandfather in 1896.

Lazarus Ochsenhorn, a prosperous diamond merchant and Talmudic scholar in Bavaria, emigrated to America in 1845 to escape the oppressive laws that restricted Jewish marriages and professions, according to a seven-year study of the noted journalistic family by Susan E. Tifft and Alex S. Jones (*The New Yorker* 19 April 1999). His son Julius (1858-1935) shortened the name to Ochs; married Iphigenia Miriam Wise, daughter of the Rabbi Isaac Mayer Wise who was instrumental in the formation of the Union of American Hebrew Congregations and of Hebrew Union College, and is generally considered the founder of Reform Judaism in America; and used the Wise connection to his advantage to acquire the failing New-York *Times* by forming a new company, the New York Times Company. William Randolph Hearst attacked Ochs as an "oily little commercial gentleman with . . . obsequiously curved shoulders" who took orders from Jewish banker August Belmont and passed them along to his editor. Ochs, however, was so rattled by this Shylock-like portrait of himself that he bent over backwards to downplay any Jewish slant to stories in the newspaper. Upon his death, his son-in-law, Arthur Hays Sulzberger, who had been acting as the effective publisher for two years, became controlling owner of the *Times*.

Arthur Ochs Sulzberger, like his father-in-law, "was skittish about showcasing Jewish talent in the paper," Tifft and Jones found in their research. Called "Punch" by his family members, he rejected the idea that Jews were members of a "race" and vehemently opposed the use of collective phrases such as "the Jewish people"; instead, he instructed editors to use "people of the Jewish faith," or simply "Jews"—expressions that he felt subtly conveyed the notion that being Jewish "was something one could freely choose, like being a Methodist or a Presbyterian." His daughter Judy told the two researchers, "Deep down, my father probably would just as soon not have been Jewish." Like his father, he became a strong opponent of Zionism, suggesting that as an alternative to a Jewish Palestine a "great state" carved out of several nations in the Holy Land should be created, one that would "welcome all who wish to come," Jews and non-Jews alike." He was attacked for being a "self-hating Jew" and a "Jewish Bourbon." As the result of the attacks, he became an anti-Zionist. He also became what is called an "assimilated Jew," marrying outside the Jewish heritage. He remained editor from 1963 to 1992, at which time his son, Arthur Jr., became editor.

Arthur Jr.'s mother, Barbara Grant, was not Jewish. Shortly after her divorce from "Punch" in 1956, she became an Episcopalian. Arthur Jr. and his sister Karen were confirmed at Manhattan's St. James Episcopal Church, and although Arthur ("Pinch") read books about Judaism and erratically attended Jewish services he told Tifft and Jones that in London as an Associated Press reporter during the 1970s he held a Passover seder in his flat. His grandmother Iphigene, who happened to be in Britain, came as an honored—and somewhat nonplussed—guest. "I consider myself Jewish. No one else would, but I do," Arthur Jr. told an oral historian for the American Jewish Committee several years later.

The Trust (2000), by Susan Tifft and Alex Jones, includes the gossip that in the 1950s Sulzberger fathered an illegitimate child with a widowed reporter and that in the 1980s then-executive editor Abe Rosenthal had an affair with "a young *Times* secretary" whom he later promoted "to an executive position."

In 1994, two years after Sulzberger became publisher, Tifft and Jones asked him to describe his personal faith. His freethinking became clearly evident in his unhesitant reply:

> I have the *Times*. That's my religion. That's what I believe in, and it's a hell of a thing to hold on to.

Sumberg, Chris (20th Century)

Sumberg's "Living Humanism" appears in *The Humanist*. A free-lance writer, he was born in Boston and now lives in Nashville, Tennessee.

Summa Theologica

The *Summa Theologica*, in which Thomas Aquinas treats the whole of theology by careful analysis of arguments, contains his five ways of attempting to prove that there is a God.

Summers, John H. (20th Century)

Summers, a graduate student in American History at the University of Rochester, wrote in *Free Inquiry* (Spring 1998) the media should take seriously the notion that they should engage, not pander to, their audiences. "A healthy democracy demands journalistic integrity and intelligence," he wrote. "Alas, as things currently stand, tough ideas in the wastelands of Gannett and Times-Mirror are too often fugitives: rarely sighted, never captured. We deserve better."

Sumner, Charles (1811–1874)

An American statesman, Sumner was quite vocal against slavery and openly criticized Abraham Lincoln. He supported the impeachment of President Andrew Johnson and opposed President Ulysses Grant's project for the acquisition of Santo Domingo. In one speech to the Senate, Sumner made personal attack on Senator Butler of South Carolina. Later, Congressman Preston Brooks, a relative of Butler, attacked Sumner as he sat at his Senate desk. The injury was so serious that it took over three years before Sumner could resume all his duties in the Senate. Such occurrences were typical of the emotions which eventually led to the War Between the States. According to McCabe, Sumner was "a non-Christian theist" who once wrote a letter in which he rejected the supernatural theory of Christ, saying, "I am without religious feeling." He believed in God, he said, but he "rarely thought about him or prayed." Sumner's funeral was at King's Chapel in Boston, where he and his family had worshiped as Unitarians for many years and where the funeral service was held by the Rev. Henry W. Foote, according to his biographer, Walter Shotwell. {CE; EG; JM;RAT; RE; TYD; U; UU}

SUN

Mythologies throughout the world have included Sun myths. Sun symbols have been found in Neolithic deposits, which implies that sun worship was the earliest form of religion. The Sun, however, may have been more directed toward the elaborate calendars of ancient peoples and the simple calculations of the most primitive tribes on the course of the sun. In the Babylonian and Mayan civilizations, the study of the Sun's movements correlated with that of moon and stars, leading to the science of astronomy and aiding the development of mathematics.

Sun worship reached its highest development in Egypt, Mexico, and Japan, according to Maynard L. Cassady, then chairman of the department of religion at the University of Rochester. In Egypt, the pyramids were probably associated with Sun-worship. The Sun god Ra persists throughout Egyptian ancient history. In the 13th century B.C.E., Ikhnaton established a monotheistic religion of high ethical character, centering about the Sun god Aton, represented by a disk with rays extended as beneficent hands. Solar worship spread to Greece and into Western Europe. In Mexico, the Mayans pictured the Sun god as a jaguar. In Japan, the royal house was believed to stem from the Sun goddess Amaterasu and to have maintained an unbroken line for at least twenty-six centuries.

"Where it is the duty to worship the sun," John Morley once quipped, "it is pretty sure to be a crime to examine the laws of heat."

During a 1994 solar eclipse, Aymara or Quechua Indians in Bolivia lit fires on hillsides to warm the Earth for the brief period when the Sun could not. According to Aymara tradition, an eclipse means the Sun is sick and near death. In Andean mythology, a puma devours the Sun, a belief reflected in stone engravings that date to pre-Colombian times. To prevent the Sun's death, the puma is frightened away by the screams of children and of animals beaten with sticks.

Just as the Earth moves around the Sun, the Sun revolves around the center of the Milky Way. One revolution—traveling a distance that is about ten billion times the distance between the Sun and the Earth—takes 250,000,000 Earth years. Even as the Sun moves around in the Milky Way, the Earth moves with the Sun, revolving around it. The entire solar system zips by at 155 miles per second. Also, the Sun rotates on its own axis. The Earth rotates about thirty times—thirty days—during the time it takes Sun to complete one rotation.

Rationalists are intrigued by eclipses but not by the mythology which has accompanied them. A total solar eclipse can have particular scientific importance, providing information about the motions of the moon and about the surface phenomena of the sun and permitting tests of Albert Einstein's general theory of relativity. {CE; ER}

SUNDAY

• Sunday: A day given over by Americans to wishing they were dead and in heaven, and that their neighbors were dead and in hell.

–H. L. Mencken

SUNDAY SCHOOL

• A Sunday School is a prison in which children do penance for the evil conscience of their parents.

–H. L. Mencken

Sun Yat-sen (1866–1925)

Sun Yat-sen, also known as Sun Wen or Sun Zhong Shan, was a Chinese physician, a revolutionary leader of the 1920s who is said by Corliss Lamont to have been a naturalistic humanist. Sun was influenced by the writings of Karl Marx. In 1905 he organized in Japan a revolutionary league based upon the Three People's Principles (nationalism, democracy, and the people's livelihood). After a revolution in China, he was elected (1911) provisional president of the Chinese republic, then becoming director of the party or Kuomintang. {CE; CL}

Sunderland, Jabez Thomas (1842–1936)

Sunderland was a leading participant in the theological controversy which took place in the Western Unitarian Conference (WUC) in the 1880s and was known as the "Western Issue." In it, he played a conservative role. He also publicized to Unitarians and others the injustice of the colonization of India. Following a visit to India, he supported the Indian nationalist movement and strengthened ties between American Unitarianism and India. His *India in Bondage* (1928) was suppressed in India. In one of his sermons, he stated, "The rejection of the doctrine of the Trinity by Channing was the solemn revolt of what was deepest and holiest in the moral nature of man against the conception of an immoral God, against a God who could do so unspeakably unjust, so morally monstrous a thing as to create a human race of sentient beings and of his own will elect one part to be happy forever, and the other part with no fault of their own, and with nothing they could do to prevent it, to writhe in endless torment."

A Biblical scholar, Sunderland wrote the following: "There is no use trying to evade it; the Bible contains errors of many kinds. It contains incredible stories, as for example those of the talking serpent, the speaking ass, and Jonah living three days in the fish. It contains historic inaccuracies, as the statement in *Luke* that the governor of Syria at the time of the birth of Jesus was Cyrenius (Quirinus), when in fact it was Quintus Sentius Saturnius. It contains contradictions, as when in connection with David's numbering of Israel we are told in one place that it was the devil and in another that it was the Lord that tempted him to do the numbering. It contains exaggerations, as when the statement is made that Jeroboam, the king of only about one-half of little Palestine (the whole of Palestine was smaller than New Hampshire) went into a certain battle with 800,000 picked men, and of that number 500,000 died, a number twice as large as the combined armies of North and South at the battle of Gettysburg. It contains contradictions of science, as when we are told of the creation of the world in six days. It contains cruel, unjust and immoral teachings, as in the imprecatory *Psalms* (CIX and CXXXVII); the injunction to establish slavery (*Leviticus* XXV: 44-46); the permission to sell bad meat to strangers (*Deuteronomy,* XIV: 21); and the command, 'Thou shalt not suffer a witch to live.' It contains morally degrading representations of God, as in *Exodus* VII: 13 and XI: 10, where we are told that God hardened Pharaoh's heart that he should not let the children of Israel go, and then punished him severely for not letting them go; and in *Joshua* X: 28-42, where the leader of the Israelites is commanded of God to murder innocent women and helpless babes." {U&U}

Sunderland, La Roy (1803–1885)

Sunderland, an American author and orator, started as a Methodist preacher prominent in the temperance and anti-slavery movements. Leaving the church and calling it a great bulwark of slavery, Sunderland for the forty years preceding his death then opposed Christianity. He wrote many works against slavery and Pathetism (which term he did not define), including *Book of Human Nature* (1853) and *Ideology* (3 volumes, 1886–1889). {BDF}

Suner y Capderila (19th Century)

Suner y Capderila was a Spanish physician who became deputy to the Cortes in 1829 and was noted for his discourses against Catholicism. {BDF}

SUNRISE JOURNAL

Sunrise Journal ,*Stargazer*, and *Star Walker*, are children's publications edited by Lloyd Kumley (POB 4153, Salem Oregon 97302).

They are for children up to eight years, from eight to twelve years, and from twelve to sixteen years, respectively. {FD}

Supek, Ivan (20th Century)

Supek, from Yugoslavia, addressed the Fourth International Humanist and Ethical Union World Congress held in Paris (1966). In *Drame* (1971), Supek writes about Serbo-Croatian drama.

SUPERMAN

Friedrich Nietzsche, in *Thus Spake Zarathustra*, describes the *Übermensch*, which has been translated as Superman, or Overman, and is the single goal of all human striving, for which people must be willing to sacrifice all. It is doubtful that Nietzsche thought of the Overman as an individual person but, rather, as an ideal superior man who forgoes transient pleasure, exercises creative power, lives at a level of experience beyond standards of good and evil, and is the goal of human evolution.

Some have suggested that the comic book character of Superman is a freethinker and a secular humanist. He is devoted to helping mankind, and he has no connection with organized religion. (See the material on Superman by Paul Edwards in *The Encyclopedia of Philosophy*.)

SUPERNATURALISM

> • There used to be fairies, goblins, trolls, pooks, gnomes, snow maidens, munchkins, sylphs and hobbits who seized and transported us to other dimensions, where time got funny. There used to be saints, Christian or Sufic and variously possessed by Clouds of Unknowing, Uncreated Light, ecstasy and automatic writing. There have always been freaks—Wild Men and Missing Links, wolf boys and zombies, witches and geeks.
>
> –John Leonard, {*Nation*, 15-22 May 1998}

Supernaturalism, unlike naturalism, is a belief in forces which transcend the laws of nature and relate to God or a god, demigod, spirit, devil, or some such other-worldly or invisible agent, such as a ghost or spirit. Judaism and Christianity are built upon a belief in a supernatural creator, God, although apologists following attacks by the rationalists have argued that God is above nature and therefore is not supernatural.

Supernaturalism also has its supporters in Asia, from Filipino healing techniques to Chinese card-reading to Japanese ghosts. *Fen shui* is (wind and water) is a practice followed in China, Hong Kong, and Singapore, as well as Japan and Vietnam, in which a practitioner will recommend the most favorable conditions for any venture. For example, suggestions include placement of office buildings and the arrangement of desks, doors, and other items in business. To have good *feng shui* a building should face the water and be flanked by mountains. It should not block the view of the mountain spirits. Thus, many Hong Kong office buildings have see-through lobbies. Similarly, elevators are often placed on a diagonal to the front of a building to prevent its own good spirits from escaping. The American architect, I. M. Pei, is said to have designed bad *fen shui* with his Bank of China building in Hong Kong, for it has sharp angles. The Bank of China, however, opened on the luckiest day of the century: 8/8/88 (8 August 1988).

In Japan, the Sony Corporation has had a four-member "esper" (extrasensory perception and excitation research) laboratory which studied such phenomena as telepathy and ki. Ki is said to be the fundamental life force. Yoichiro Sako, a Tokyo University engineering graduate, heads the ki lab and has reported, "Our ultimate goal is to discover the mind or consciousness that all humanity, and the whole of creation, must possess—to pursue the spirit or soul that exists in our universe."

P. V. Narashimba Rao, the seventy-four-year-old Prime Minister of India, had in 1995 a "spiritual adviser" by the name of Chandraswamy, a forty-six-year-old faith healer, self-professed psychic, and rags-to-riches millionaire. Chandraswamy has been called by *The Indian Express* "Rao's Rasputin," a "controversial godman," and a person with "enormous, extra-constitutional clout in the higher echelons of power and public life." Mr. Rao has a strong belief in the supernatural, and in India it is not considered unusual for politicians, industrialists, entertainers, and others prominent in public life to take a Hindu holy man into their entourage. When over one thousand swamis, sadhus, yogis, and gurus justified their support of Chandraswamy by protesting in New Delhi, many were said to be unsure of what they were protesting, but one man replied, "I am accompanying the brothers to attain nirvana." Saeed Naqvi, a columnist for *The Pioneer*, responded, "It may seem like so much humbug to those inclined toward agnosticism, but irrational faith is a fact of life in India. What we do in our private lives with the Chandraswamis is our business, but it is the transgression of superstition into public life that is unseemly."

"Belief in the supernatural," wrote Ernest Renan in the 1800s, "is the shame of civilization." The tenaciousness of supernaturalism in being accepted by hoi polloi is legendary. In the United States, Nancy Reagan reportedly relied on the occult, using an astrologer for advice to influence the schedule of her husband, Ronald Reagan, when he was President. Major newspapers carry daily astrological tables. Psychic hotlines in the 1990s were the rage on television and the World Wide Web. (See entries for Amulets and Superstition.) {*The New York Times*, "Indian Premier's Swami Has a Run of Bad Karma," 21 September 1995}

SUPERSTITION

Superstition is an irrational belief or practice resulting from ignorance or fear of the unknown. Carol Orsag has listed the seven most common superstitions in the United States:

> • sneezing—When God made man, the Judeo-Christian story goes, He "breathed into his nostrils the breath of life." Roman citizens feared sneezing when a plague hit their city during the reign of Pope Gregory the Great. Maybe it was the devil which could enter a person during that unguarded moment of sneezing? After all, some did die from sneezing. Ergo, "God bless you" if said in the person's presence seemed to keep the person from dying. The *Gesundheits* and God-bless-you's annoy many non-believers and rationalists who are aware that the explosive, spasmodic and involuntary action results mainly from an irritation of the nasal mucous membrane.
>
> • getting out of bed on the "wrong" side—The Romans thought the left side to be the "evil one." Citizens entered a friend's home with the right foot forward. At times, a "footman" was hired to insure proper entry of all guests. The English word *sinister* (meaning wicked or evil) is derived from the Latin word meaning "left side."
>
> • breaking a mirror—before mirrors, humans saw their "other side" by looking into lakes and pools. If the image was distorted, it was a mark of impending disaster. An "unbreakable" metal mirror of the early Egyptians and Greeks was valued because of its magical property of having no distortions. After glass mirrors were introduced, the Romans tagged the broken mirror a sign of bad luck which would last seven years, seven because that was the number of years the Romans believed humans are rejuvenated and become, in effect, a new person.
>
> • spilling salt—salt once was rare and costly, and it was an economic waste to spill any. It was mixed into the foods used in the religious ceremonies of both the Greeks and Romans. In da Vinci's painting of the "Last Supper," Judas is shown having accidentally spilled salt onto the table.
>
> • walking under ladders—a ladder which leans against a wall makes a triangle, and this signifies the Holy Trinity. Ergo, to cross into the sacred enclosed area is to weaken the powers of the gods and unleash the powers of evil spirits.
>
> • encountering a black cat—Egyptians worshiped the cat and punished anyone who dared to kill one. In the Middle Ages, however, the black cat was linked to witches and Satan. Inasmuch as a witch was thought to be able to transform herself into a cat, a cat who crossed one's path must be a witch in disguise.
>
> • opening an umbrella indoors—as early as the 11th century B.C.E., umbrellas were used in the East by the political and religious hierarchy, not only as a protective measure against the hot sun rays but also to ward off any spirits who might do them harm. Because of the umbrella's sacred relationship to the sun, it is wrong to open it in the shade.
>
> • three vital good luck charms to protect one—(a) When Adam and

Eve were evicted from the Garden, Eve snatched a *four-leaf clover* as a remembrance of her days in Paradise; (b) when St. Dunstan, a blacksmith, encountered the Devil who asked to be "shoed," St. Dunstan tied him up, inflicted pain until the Devil screamed for murder, and let him loose only when he promised never to enter a home protected by a *horseshoe*; also, the reason witches rode broomsticks was that they were deathly afraid of horses, so a *horseshoe* provided protection; also, a *horseshoe*'s crescent-shaped size like a moon is a sign of prosperity; and because a rabbit is so clever, speedy, and meets with other rabbits on moonlit evenings, carrying a *rabbit's foot* became a sign of good fortune and the hind feet became a treasured amulet.

• nine rules of superstitious etiquette—(1) Eve and Adam were tempted on Friday; the biblical Flood began on Friday; Jesus died on Friday; thirteen men were at the Last Supper; Greek philosophers and mathematicians scorned thirteen as an "unperfect" number; in Norse mythology, there were twelve gods present when Loki, spirit of evil and dissension, stormed a banquet hall, making him the thirteenth guest, and killed Balder, hero and most revered of all the gods; ergo, take no risks or attempt any new enterprise on Friday the Thirteenth; (2) Do not hang a horseshoe with its prongs pointed upward, or the good luck will "run out"; (3) Do not light three cigarettes with one match, three being usually a lucky number but it represents the Holy Trinity and one should be careful of its use; (4) Wear clothing inside and out, for it is an excellent disguise to keep Death from recognizing you and singling you out as a victim; (5) Do not get married in May, the month Romans honored their dead and an unlucky time for lovers; (6) Do knock on wood three times after mentioning good luck, for Jesus died on a wooden cross; (7) Do not cross knives on the dinner table, for that would symbolize the crossing of daggers and swords in dueling matches and could bring on arguments; (8) Do enter and exit from the same door when visiting a friend's house; also, if you leave for a time, then return, sit down outside the door and count to ten before your second entrance; and (9) Do not trip before you start out a new day; if you do, turn around three times and say, "I turn myself three times about and thus I put bad luck to rout."

Noted individuals have been superstitious or commented about the subject:

• Shakespeare wrote, "For many men that stumble at the threshold / Are well foretold that danger lurks therein."

• Mary Queen of Scots was said (by some) to have had her fortune told by a deck of cards before her death and was dealt a hand full of spades.

• Samuel Johnson never entered a house with his left foot first because it "brought down evil on the inmates."

• Samuel Pepys wrote, "Now I am at a loss to know whether it be my hare's foot which is my preservative against wind, for I never had a fit of collique since I wore it."

• Napoleon Bonaparte suffered from ailurophobia (fear of cats) and the number thirteen (triskaidekaphobia).

• Charles Stewart Parnell never signed a legislative bill that contained thirteen clauses, not until one was added or subtracted.

• Thomas Henry Huxley told his son, Leonard, "The most remarkable achievement of the Jew was to impose on Europe for eighteen centuries his own superstitions."

• Cornelius Vanderbilt had the legs of his bed placed in dishes of salt to ward off attacks from evil spirits.

• Al Jolson always wore old clothes to open a new show.

• Adolf Hitler favored the number seven (planned major military battles on the seventh of the month) and had the Nazi swastika designed to resemble an ancient Buddhist symbol representing, among other things, the wheel of life.

• Winston Churchill petted black cats to *obtain* good luck.

• President Harry S. Truman displayed a horseshoe over the door of his office in the White House.

• Somerset Maugham had the "evil eye" symbol carved into his fireplace mantel and had it stamped on his stationery and books.

"Have we lost our common sense?" *Le Matin* headlined a front-page story in Dakar, Senegal in 1997. At issue was a story about lynch mobs that had burned and beaten to death suspected sorcerers with powers to cause a man's penis to vanish or shrink with a mere handshake. *Le Soleil* in Niger reported similar cases, saying that five had been killed by mobs. Scores of people died in similar bouts of hysteria in Ghana and the Ivory Coast. Meanwhile, police in West African cities tried to assure the public that allegations of vanishing penises are baseless and often are started by thieves who profit from the ensuing panic.

The United States Social Security Administration has ruled that anyone assigned a number that includes the biblical mark of the Antichrist—666—can request a different number. "Christians are supposed to refuse the mark of the beast," a mother complained to the *Orange County register* in California, and the father added, "I'm not a religious fanatic. The number is as offensive to me as if an African American were given a KKK on his card or a Jewish person had to have a swastika."

Astute "business" people—for example, psychics, fortune tellers, occultists, spiritualists—can make considerable amounts of money playing on people's superstitions. Two practitioners of *feng shui*—the Chinese art of arranging the environment "harmoniously"–charged the real estate development firm Kaufman and Broad $6,000 to perform a four-hour "seven-star blessing" to cleanse the area—which previously had been a Native American burial site—of "negative" or "stagnant" energies. "So if nothing dreadful happens there, like in the movie *Poltergeist*, joked science writer Robert Sheaffer, "it'll be proof that the *feng shui* was successful." (See Eric Maple, *Superstition and the Superstitious* and Julie Forsyth Batchelor and Claudia De Lys, *Superstitious? Here's Why!*) {CE; PA, *Playboy*, March 1997; *Skeptical Inquirer*, March-April 1999}

Suplee, Zelda (20th Century)
Suplee was on the advisory board in 1972 of the Humanist Society of Greater New York.

SUPREME COURT OF THE UNITED STATES
In 1999, the eight of the twelve members of the U.S. Supreme Court were known to be members of the following religious denominations:

Roman Catholic
Anthony Kennedy, Antonin Scalia, Clarence Thomas
Protestant
Sandra Day O'Connor (Episcopalian); David Souter (Episcopalian); John Paul Stevens (no denomination given)
Jewish:
Stephen Breyer; Ruth Bader Ginsburg
Humanist:
None

Suri, Surindar S. (20th Century)
When he reviewed books for The Humanist in the 1950s, Suri was a member of the sociology department at the University of California in Berkeley. In 1974 Suri wrote Politics and Society in India (1974). Upon returning to India, he worked to establish a college at Bangalore based on humanistic principles blended with Indian philosophy. {HNS}

SURVIVAL OF THE FITTEST: See the entry for Herbert Spencer.

SURVIVAL OF THE LUCKIEST: See the entry for Stephen Jay Gould.

Suryanarayana, A. (20th Century)
In 1971, Suryanarayana and Jyothi Sankar founded for the Indian Rationalist a monthly, *Free Thought*. His wife, Ms. Vasundhara, has also been an active member of the Indian rationalist movement. {FUK}

Susanne, Charles (20th Century)
Dr. Susanne, Director of the Centre for Bioethics at the Free University in Brussels, spoke at the Humanist World Congress in 1990. Enormous developments have taken place in genetics since DNA's structure was discovered forty years ago. Biologists were accused of playing God. Now, however, "they can do better than

God. They can reduce congenital diseases." The human application of genetic research is enormous, and he feels humanists must look seriously at all its ramifications, formulating appropriate guidelines.

Susterich, Edward (20th Century)
Susterich, from Wisconsin, is on the board of directors of the Freedom From Religion Foundation.

Susterich, Maria (20th Century)
Susterich, from Wisconsin, is on the board of directors of the Freedom From Religion Foundation.

Sutherland, Alexander (1852–1902)
Sutherland was taken from Glasgow by his father to Australia in 1864, where he eventually purchased Carlton College. He was a prolific writer and able teacher. His *Victoria and its Metropolis* (1888) is a history of Victoria. Sutherland's rationalist views are the main inspiration for *The Origin and Growth of the Moral Instinct* (2 volumes, 1898). For eight years he was secretary of the Royal Society of Victoria. {RAT}

Suttner, Bertha (Gräfin Kinsky) [Baroness] (1843–1914)
An Austrian baroness, Suttner is known chiefly as an ardent pacifist. Her pacifist novel, *Die Waffen nieder* (1889, tr. *Lay Down Your Arms*), had a great social impact. Through her subsequent friendship with Alfred Nobel, she influenced him to establish the Nobel Prizes. She was the first woman awarded the Nobel Peace Prize, in 1905. In her *Memoirs*, Suttner tells that in early years she rejected all religious beliefs. Later, she took up Spencer, Darwin, and Haeckel, adopting a vague pantheistic creed which is similar to Spencer's agnosticism. {CE; JM; RAT; RE}

Sutton, Henry S. (19th Century)
Sutton was the anonymous author of *Quinquenergia, or Proposals for a New Practical Theology* and *Letters From a Father to a Son on Revealed Religion*. {BDF}

SUTTON (England) HUMANIST GROUP
The Sutton Humanist Group (IHEU) is at 29 Fairview Road, Sutton, Surrey SMI 4PD, United Kingdom; or telephone 0181 642 4577. {FD}

Sveen, Barbro (20th Century)
A Norwegian humanist, Sveen attended in 1996 the international conference of humanists in Mexico City. A new law in Norway, she laments, has made it compulsory for children to attend some religious education. She is editor of the HEF magazine. E-mail: <sveen@human.no> and <fri.tanke@human.no>.

Svendsen, Borre (20th Century)
A Norwegian humanist, Svendsen participated in 1996 at the international conference of humanists in Mexico City. Borre's e-mail: <umoe@sn.no>.

Svensson, Gunnar (1951–)
Svensson, a computer consultant in Sweden, is a secularist and non-theist.

Svuták, Ivan (20th Century)
Sviták, an author in Czechoslovakia, called himself a humanist.

Swableses, Margaret Ann (1869–1963)
Swableses was a freethinker and an activist in Australia. A pioneer of the Victoria Socialist movement with Tom Mann in 1905, she was a colleague of Scott Bennett and Bernard O'Dowd. Swableses requested that upon her death that her body be cremated and there be no religious service. The eulogy address by Sir John V. Barry quoted from writings by Robert G. Ingersoll. {SWW}

Swaminathan (20th Century)
Swaminathan the Magician accompanied Abraham T. Kovoor, President of the Ceylon Rationalist Association, on a tour of India in order to advance the cause of rationalism. He and hypnotist P. K. Narayan in the 1970s exposed with their magic and hypnotism shows the tricks of Satya Sai Baba, educating the audience as to how suggestion sways devotees into getting into trances. With their speeches, they exhorted the audience to cultivate a critical outlook and a scientific spirit. {Chirala, India, *Rationalist Essays*, 1993}

Swan, Frederick W. (1903–c. 1975)
Swan was an Australian atheist, rationalist, and architect. An early secretary of the Rationalist Society of South Australia, he became in 1970 president of the new Atheist Society of Australia. Later, he was active in Tasmania in promoting secular matters. {SWW}

Swancara, Frank (20th Century)
A freethinker, Swancara wrote *Bad By Products of Religion* (1947) and *Religion and Crime* (1947). {FUS}

Swamy, Dalip S. (20th Century)
Swamy, a Delhi academic, presented a paper, "Globalization, Nation State and Human Rights Movement, at the World Humanist Congress at Mumbai in January 1999. {*The Radical Humanist*, June 1999}

SWEARING
• Swearing includes

> making profane oaths or cursing, drawing upon religious terms; i.e., "God damn you!"; "For Chrisake!"; "Jesus bloody fucking Christ on a crutch!"; "You Jesus freak!"; "Jew the person down [on his price]!"; "She's a JAP [Jewish American princess]"; "the yin and yang dynamic"; "buddha sticks [herbal marijuana]; "Hymie-town [New York City]"; "priest bait [young boys]"; "and may Matthew, Mark, Luke, and John all shit on your mother's bones."

and

> making solemn declarations which invoke a deity or make some solemn vow: In United States courts, witnesses are required to swear on the Judeo-Christian Bible before testifying, swearing to tell the truth, the whole truth, and nothing but the truth "so help me God." Those who find this medieval, however, are allowed to "affirm" they will tell the truth. Lawyers Roger Cossack and Greta Van Susteren, who appear often on television programs, have noticed that "Witnesses can put their hand on the Bible and swear to tell the truth, or simply raise their hand and 'avow' to tell the truth. Both are promises to testify truthfully. We have seen witnesses promise just about every deity that they will testify truthfully—and five minutes later lie through their teeth."

"Bad" or "foul" swearing presents a problem to rationalists. It is considered illogical for freethinkers to imitate the various religious examples, for how could a non-existent God damn anyone. And it is not "politically correct" to use some of the other swear words. For example, "bitch" is rightfully frowned upon by feminists, who cite it as a proper noun to describe the female dog. "Asshole" is understandably frowned upon by sodomists, who might cite it as an erotic source of pleasure. "Fuck" is certainly frowned upon by all with a happy sex life and who would not, not even to an enemy, suggest that copulation is an unpleasant experience.

A 1970s musical group, the Sex Pistols, gained much notoriety by their use of vulgate swear words. As soon as these musicians appeared with their singer Johnny Rotten on radio or television and were asked by their host to say something, they eagerly complied, leaving station managers and networks with outcries from some of their listeners as well as complaints from their advertisers. In the 1990s, however, "realistic" scenes on television or in movies become box office hits. Martin Clunes, a British sit-com star, has suggested that by 2006 "the dreaded F-word" will be thought acceptable even in programs for children, adding, "It's *only* a word!" Many agree, but they pity the rebellious today, young or old, who find it almost impossible to say anything in order to shock. {*The Economist*, 22 June 1996; *USA Weekend*, 26-28 April 1996}

Swedenborg, Emanuel (1688–1772)

Swedenborg the scientist was a mystic known for "his odd mixture of scripturalism and innovating dogmatism." Of the Adam and Eve myth, he wrote, "For who can suppose that the creation of the world could have been as there described?" He reportedly disliked hearing trinitarian sermons and for many years avoided going to church. But after professing that he understood spirituality because "heaven was opened" to him in 1745 (his having received the true sense of the Scriptures from the Lord Himself), Swedenborg inaugurated the New Church and, although he may not have intended to establish a new sect, Swedenborgianism developed. An eighteen-volume edition of Swedenborg's writings was published between 1901 and 1916. Some followers believe a few individuals can see auras over other people's heads, indicating (depending upon the aura's color) the number of past existences the people have had. One follower, Gustavus III, an ardent admirer of Voltaire, was said to have died "with the fortitude and resignation of a Christian" on the occasion of his having been assassinated. Robertson, however, states the King "was indeed flighty and changeable, and after growing up a Voltairean was turned into a credulous mystic, the dupe of pseudo-Swedenborgian charlatans; but there is small sign of religious earnestness in his fashion of making his dying confession." Robert Frost, asked Abbott religion, replied that his mother had been attracted to Swedenborgianism, avoiding any other answer to the question. The sect is exceedingly small in numbers today, but it appeals to numbers of mystics. Upon his death, Swedenborg was buried in London in 1772. In 1908, however, the body was removed to the cathedral in Uppsala, Sweden. Outside are striking mounds in which early Vikings were buried. {CE; ER; JMR; JMRH; RE}

SWEDENBORGIAN CHURCH

The Swedenborgian Church, organized in 1792 in the United States, is at 48 Sargent St., Newton, Massachusetts 02158.

SWEDISH HUMANISM AND SECULARISM

Finngeir Hiorth, the Norwegian scholar, has written *Secularism in Sweden* (1994), the fullest history to date of humanism in Sweden. He estimated that twenty-eight percent of the Swedes in 1994 are secularists but that only eight hundred are members of the Swedish Human-Etiska Forbundet i Sverige, or Humanist-Ethical Association. In 1995, Mikael Goransson was elected its presiding officer. Its bimonthly publication is *Human-Etik*, Box 108, S-649 23 Hallsberg.

In 1996, Sweden voted to denationalize its Lutheran Evangelical Church, one of the world's oldest remaining state churches. The king no longer had to be a Lutheran, and the long union of church and state started its planned end. Since 1593, all Swedes have had to belong to the Lutheran Church. Since the 1850s, however, they were no longer forced to be baptized, and in 1951 they could legally quit the church and stop paying it 1.1% of their annual income in taxes. Commencing in the year 2000, the church, rather than the state, will appoint bishops.

Botulf-bladet, a quarterly of HEF-Västeras, is at Torsgatan 47, 1 tr., 113 37 Stockholm, Sweden. The journal's e-mail: <christiaan.vos@vasteras.mail.telia.com>.

The E-mail address for *Fri Tanke* is <gunnar.staldal@stockholm.mail.telia.com>.

Fritänkeren (Freethinker), a Swedish quarterly, is at Torsgatan 47, 1 tr., 113 37 Stockholm, Sweden *Humanisten*, the humanist magazine, is available from Box 5048, S402 21 Göteborg, Sweden. E-mail: <mikael.goransson@migor.se>.

Human-Etiska Forbundet i Sverige, which is an associate member of the International Humanist and Ethical Union, is at Box 5048, 402 21, Göteborg, Sweden.

The Swedish Humanist and Ethical Association on the Web is at <http://hem.passagen.se/humanist>.

Fredrik Bendz, the Swedish webmaster for humanism, is online with "The Page of Reason" at <http://www.update.uu.se/~fbendz>. (See entries for Fredrik Bendz, Mikael Göransson, Per Christian Jersild, Scandinavian Unbelievers, and Herbert Tingsten.)

SWEDISH-AMERICAN FREETHOUGHT

Swedish-American freethinkers are described in Gordon Stein's *Freethought in the United States.*

Sweet, Nick (20th Century)

Sweet is an English poet and novelist. He has reviewed Camus' *The First Man* in *New Humanist* (February 1996). Also, he has written about Raymond Carver, an American short story writer; and about the respective worth of literature and working for the poor, with special reference to Sartre and Vargas Llosa. {*New Humanist*, June 1996, November 1997}

Sweet, William Warren (20th Century)

Sweet wrote *Religion in Colonial America* (1942). {GS}

Swenson, May (1917–1989)

Swenson, a poet and member of the American Academy of Arts and Letters, wrote *In Other Words, New Poems* (1987). She was a frequent contributor to *The New Yorker*. Of humanism she wrote in 1989 to the present author:

> I subscribe to Secular Humanism. Thank you for taking notice of the opinions of women, which I think, was not the case in the questionnaire some 40 years ago.

Swenson, a lesbian, was an honorary member of the Secular Humanist Society of New York. {GL; WAS, 4 February 1989}

Swerdlow, Lanny (20th Century)

Swerdlow is president of Portland's Center for Rational Thought. He wrote, "Atheists Arise! We Too Can Be Warm and Fuzzy" in *Secular Nation*(April-June, 1999). (See entry for Oregon Rationalists, Humanists.) {FD}

Swift, Graham (20th Century)

Peter Faulkner, reviewing Swift's *Last Orders* (1996), found it the most interesting of his novels since *Waterland*. "Swift's view of life," Faulkner states, "is that of a kind of stoic humanist who respects those who make whatever they can out of the small changes that life gives them (or us). And he leaves us with the question of how far humanism might hope or help to give shape and commitment to lives that in our present culture so manifestly lack it." {*New Humanist*, June 1996}

Swift, Jonathan (1667–1745)

Swift, the English author of *Gulliver's Travels*, was ordained an Anglican priest and in 1695 was given the small prebend of Kilroot in Ireland. Unable to make a success there, he returned to England. His *A Tale of a Tub* (1696, published 1704) was a satire on religious excesses which was intended to divert Hobbes's *Leviathan* and the wits of the age from picking holes in the weak sides of religion and government. His series of pamphlets, *Argument Against Abolishing Christianity* (1708), was followed by *Letter Concerning the Sacramental Test*, an attack on the Irish Presbyterians which made him unpopular with the Whigs. In 1713 Swift became dean of St. Patrick's, all the while writing many political works and spending the final thirty years of his life there.

Nearly all his works were published anonymously. Only one, *Gulliver's Travels*, resulted in a payment (£200). Despite its author's never having traveled abroad, the work described Lemuel Gulliver's travels to Lilliput, a land inhabited by tiny people who diminutive size renders all their pompous activities absurd. He then goes to Brobdingnag, a land populated by giants who are amused when Gulliver tells them about the glories of England. Then on to Laputa and Lagado, peopled by quack philosophers and scientists. Then to the land of the Houhnhnms, where horses behave with reason and men, called Yahoos, behave as beasts. The work was a ruthless satire of human follies.

Swift attacked Bishop Burnet in his *A Preface to the B–p of S–r–m's Introduction* (1713). His *Mr. C–ns's Discourse on Free Thinking, Put into Plain English, By Way of Abstract, For Use of the Poor* (1713) was a satire on Anthony Collins, the leading freethinker of the day. His pamphlet, *A Modest Proposal* (1729) satirically suggests that children of the poor be sold as food for the tables of the rich: "a most delicious, nourishing and wholesome food, whether stewed, baked or boiled."

Victoria Glendinning's biography, *Jonathan Swift* (1998), discusses Swift's love life, tells the nature of his meeting and his relationship with the eight-year-old Esther Johnson (whom he called Stella) as well as with Vanessa (Hester Vanhomrigh), and speculates that Swift possibly married Stella in some kind of garden ceremony. Gossip was that perhaps he was gay, for no union appears to have occurred—however, at that time up to 20% of the aristocracy never married. Glendinning found possibly another reason: Stella could have been the daughter of Sir William Temple and Temple's sister, Martha Giffard; and Swift just possibly could have been the son of Temple's father, Sir John Temple.

Swift spent a third of his income on charities and saved another third to found St. Patrick's Hospital for Imbeciles (opened 1757). Toward the end of his life Swift suffered the decay of his faculties, because of Ménière's disease, leading to gossip that he was insane. Swift is buried in St. Patrick's, Dublin, with the following epitaph: ubi *saeva indignatio ulterius cor lacerare nequit*. {CE; OEL; TYD}

Swift, Lindsay (19th Century)

Swift wrote *Brook Farm, Its Members, Scholars, and Visitors* (1901). {FUS}

Swift, Morrison Isaac (Born 1856)

Swift, a freethinker, wrote *The Evil Religion Does* (1927). {GS}

Swift, W. Frank (1901–1933)

Swift was a signer of Humanist Manifesto I in 1933. A British-Canadian Unitarian in training for Ethical leadership in St. Louis, New York, and Boston, he unfortunately died in an automobile accident, according to James F. Hornback, "as a good Samaritan on icy roads." (See entry for Ethical Culture.) {EW; HM1}

Swinburne, Algernon Charles (1837–1909)

The London-born Swinburne was brought up piously, but before his twenty-first year he had abandoned all belief in Christianity.

Swinburne's *Poems and Ballads* (1866) were attacked for their pagan sentiments and sensuality, and this English Victorian poet was an iconoclast in virtually all he undertook. His *Atalanta in Calydon* (1865) denounced "the supreme evil, God," a phrase which disturbed, among others, Christina Rossetti. The book's aggressive hedonism and skepticism was liked by generations of younger readers. His contempt for theism also repudiates the asceticism of Christianity, in keeping with his being a nominal Unitarian. "Hertha" he described as one of his "mystic atheistic democratic anthropologic" poems that contained "the most in it of my deliberate thought and personal feeling or faith." In *Songs Before Sunrise* (1871), Swinburne glorifies freethought and republicanism.

McCabe wrote of Swinburne: "Like Shelley he became an atheist and a republican at Oxford and, although he somehow blended his hatred of tyrants—he openly rejoiced when Orsini tried to assassinate Napoleon III and wrote magnificent poems in praise of European rebels—with High Toryism in domestic politics, he never wavered. In some of his *Poems and Ballads* he is very contemptuous of Christianity and its ascetic rules."

For his last thirty years he was in poor health and was cared for by a friend of Rossetti, Theodore Watts-Dunston, who in 1879 possibly saved Swinburne's life by weaning him from alcohol and from friends who had encouraged him to drink. Swinburne continued to write for thirty years, as a result. The story is told in *The Alyson Almanac* (1989) that when he was living alone with a monkey on the Isle of Wight Swinburne invited a person home and, "once there, began making advances on the young man. The monkey, overcome with jealousy, attacked his guest, who ran away." Upon his death in 1909, to quote his lines on the death of Edward Trelawny, Swinburne was "moored at last on the stormless shore." His complete works, in twenty volumes, were edited by Edmund Gosse and T. J. Wise.

He died peacefully. Up to the last he chatted with his friends, and his illness was brief and almost painless. Swinburne was buried in the cemetery at Bonchurch "in the midst of the graves of his family." His will directed that there should be no religious ceremony at his funeral; however, his executor, Watts-Dunton, allowed the rector of Bonchurch to read part of the Church of England burial service, and to offer some pious reflections of his own. Several of those present cried "Shame!" {BDF; CE; CL; EU, Terry L. Meyers; *Freethinker*, 25 April 251909; GL; JM; JMR; PUT; RAT; RE; TRI; TYD}

Swinburne, Richard (20th Century)

Swinburne has been described by Paul Edwards in *God and the Philosophers* as "one of the most influential Christian philosophers in the Anglo-Saxon world." He developed a new formulation for the existence of God, emphasizing that "[t]he orderliness of the universe is a very striking fact about the universe," then holding that the universe "might so naturally have been chaotic, but it is not—it is very orderly." Thus, "If there is no explanation in terms of the action of God," this orderliness must be one of "coincidence." Because "the order of the world" is "very improbable *a priori*," Swinburne concludes that it is evidence for the existence of God. According to Edwards, such an argument is logically and philosophically invalid. {*Free Inquiry*, Winter 1998-1999}

Swindler, Adrian C. (20th Century)

Swindler, in *The Trinity: An Absurdity Borrowed from Paganism*, wrote, "At first, Christianity did not hold to the Trinity doctrine. That doctrine developed slowly and did not become officially a creedal fact until C.E. 325."

Swinny, Shapland Hugh (Born 1857)

Starting in 1901, Swinny was President of the London Positivist Society. In 1904 he became President of the English Positivist Committee. In 1905, he edited the *Positivist Review*. Swinny was a member of the Council of the Sociological Society, which he chaired from 1907 to 1909. His chief work is a *History of Ireland* (1890). {RAT; TRI}

SWITZERLAND FREETHINKERS, HUMANISTS

The following Swiss groups and magazines are humanistic:

- *Frei Denker* is published by *Freidenker Vereinigung Der Schweiz* (IHEU), Postfach 14, 8545 Rickenbach, Switzerland.
- *Le Libre Penseur* (The Freethinker), a quarterly of *Association Suisse des Libres Penseurs*, Case Postale 131, CH-1000 Lausanne-17, Switzerland
- World Union of Freethinkers, Postfach 6207, 3001 Bern, Switzerland.

Swiss signers of Humanist Manifesto 2000 were Diana Brown and Roy W. Brown.

{FD}

SWITZERLAND UNITARIANS

Unitarians in Geneva or Bern can be contacted by telephoning (41) 31-352 3721 or (41) 52-232-0051.

Swomley, John M. (20th Century)

Swomley, an emeritus professor of social ethics at St. Paul School of Theology in Kansas City, Missouri, is president of Americans for Religious Liberty. He has written for *The Humanist* (USA) and in 1998 was named the American Humanist Association's Humanist Distinguished Service Awardee.

Swope, Herbert Bayard (1882–1958)

In 1917, Swope, a journalist and policy consultant, won a Pulitzer Prize for being the best newspaper reporter. In the 1950s, he was on the advisory board of Charles Francis Potter's First Humanist Society of New York.

SYCHOPHANT

- Sychophant, n. One who approaches Greatness on his belly so that he may not be commanded to turn and be kicked. He is sometimes an editor.

–Ambrose Bierce
The Devil's Dictionary

Syers, Edgar (20th Century)

Syers, after being a lieutenant in the Middlesex Regiment, was a member of the Compton Comedy Company. He has written for various freethought magazines and was a director of the Rationalist Press Association. {RAT}

SYLLOGISM

- Syllogism, n. A logical formula consisting of a major and a minor assumption and an inconsequent. e.g.,

Major Premise: Sixty men can do a piece of work sixty times as quickly as one man.
Minor Premise: One man can dig a posthole in sixty seconds; therefore—
Conclusion: Sixty men can dig a posthole in one second.

This may be called the syllogism arithmetical, in which, by combining logic and mathematics, we obtain a double certainty and are twice blessed.

–Ambrose Bierce
The Devil's Dictionary

Sylvester, Arnold E. (20th Century)

Sylvester has been a president of the American Ethical Union, and he was a signer of Humanist Manifesto II. {HM2; EU, Howard B. Radest}

SYMBOLIC LOGIC or MATHEMATICAL LOGIC

Symbolic logic is a formalized system of deductive logic which employs abstract symbols for the various aspects of natural language. In the mid-19th century, Augustus De Morgan and George Boole developed the study, and it was further developed by W. S. Jevons, C. S. Peirce, Ernst Schröder, Gottlob Frege, Giuseppe Peano, Bertrand Russell, Alfred North Whitehead, David Hilbert, and others.

Negation, conjunction, and alternation: these are the basic connectives. The *negation* of a statement is false if the original statement is true and true if the original statement is false—negation corresponds to "it is not the case that," or simply "not" in ordinary language. The *conjunction* of two statements is true only if both are true; it is false in all other instances—conjunction corresponds to "and" in ordinary language. The *alternation,* or disjunction, of two statements is false only if both are false and is true in all other instances—alternation corresponds to the nonexclusive sense of "or" in ordinary language, as opposed to the exclusive "either . . . or . . . but not both." (Texts which go into detail are David Hilbert and Wilhelm Ackermann's *Principles of Mathematical Logic* (1950); and two books by W. V. Quine: *Mathematical Logic* (1968) and *Methods of Logic* [3rd Edition, 1972].) {CE}

SYMBOLS

A symbol is something that represents something else. Scales often are the symbol of justice; the scepter, royal power; a thistle, Scotland; ichthus, Christianity. A scepter, symbolic of a god's or a human's authority, is often a phallic symbol. A lily is associated with purity, innocence, resurrection, chastity, the Virgin Mary, and Easter.

Freethought organizations are more apt to utilize a logo, which is short for logogram. (See entry for Ichthus.)

Syme, David (1827–1908)

Syme was a Scottish rationalist, social reformer, and newspaper proprietor. Rejecting Calvinism, he proclaimed that the doctrine of original sin, of predestination, and of the arbitrary salvation of the elect were all abhorrent to his sense of justice. Upon visiting Germany in 1848, he became more interested in Hegelianism than in theology. After he and his brother Ebenezer migrated to Australia in 1852, they purchased *The Age*, which helped play a dominant role in setting examples for civic discussion and social dissertation. McCabe writes of Syme, "In several works on religion he rejects Christianity and calls himself a pantheist, though his biographer says that 'his religion was humanity.' " {JM; RAT; RE; SWW}

Symes, Agnes Taylor (1866?–1935)

Symes, formerly Wilson, was an early Australian secularist. The second wife of Joseph Symes, she helped in the printing and publishing of his tracks as well as Charles Knowlton's birth control pamphlet, "Fruits of Philosophy." {SWW}

Symes, Joseph (1841–1906)

A Scottish-Australian freethinker and publisher, Symes became vice president of the National Secular Society and helped launch the *Freethinker* in London, with George William Foote as its first editor. Originally, Symes had been a Methodist circuit preacher. But, doubting orthodoxy, he resigned in 1872 and preached his first open freethought lecture at Newcastle in 1876. He made major contributions to secularism on two continents, and his views on sex have been said to have been a century ahead of their time. From 1882 to 1884, Symes and Thomas Walker were lecturers for the Australasian Secular Association. In 1883 he established *The Liberator*. From 1884 to 1904, Symes edited the weekly Melbourne publication, *Liberator*. He has been called one of the most effective freethought journalists. His militant atheism and propagandist style did not endear him to all secularists, but his ability, sincerity, and sense of purpose place him in the top bracket of secular achievers. He wrote for the *Freethinker* "My Twenty Years' Fight for Freethought in Australia," and other of his works included "Christianity Essentially a Persecuting Religion" and "The Christ of the New Testament not Historic but Dramatic."

Symes returned to England in 1906, dying December 29 of the same year. The conclusion of a series of articles, "They Are Coming Round," appeared in the *Freethinker* of December 30. He was lucid within a few days of his death. Shortly before his last illness, which came very suddenly, he spoke to Foote, with some feeling of pride, of the way in which he was standing the English winter. "A few days afterwards he was very ill," Foote reported, "but he refused to have a doctor until Christmas night." {BDF; EU, Nigel H. Sinnott; FO; FUK; RAT; RE; RSR; SWW}

Symes, Stella Bradlaugh (1894–1935)

Symes was an Australian secularist, gynecologist, and venereologist. The only child of Joseph and Agnes Symes, she chose the field of medicine. In 1935 when a fire destroyed their house, she died from burns after unsuccessfully trying to save her mother. {SWW}

Symonds, Carol (20th Century)

A marriage counselor, Symonds signed Humanist Manifesto II. {HM2}

Symonds, Emerson (20th Century)

Symonds, when he signed Humanist Manifesto II, was a director of the Sensory Awareness Center. {HM2}

Symonds, John Addington (1840–1893)

Symonds was an English poet and author, the son of an eminent physician. Because he suffered from tuberculosis, he spent much of his life in Italy and Switzerland. In his work, Symonds scoffed at the idea that the Renaissance artists owed their excellence to religious inspiration. Symonds's largest work was *Renaissance in Italy* (1875–1886, 7 volumes), but he wrote volumes on Jonson, Sidney, Shelley, Whitman, and Michelangelo. In addition he translated the autobiography of Cellini and much Greek and Italian poetry. Among his wide circle of literary friends were Lear, Swinburne, Stephen, and Stevenson.

Although his father had taught him that the love of men was evil, Symonds became infatuated with one choirboy after another while a fellow at Magdalen College, and he suffered several nervous breakdowns. In Switzerland, where he moved, he found that homosexuality was not a crime and one could admire the human body more openly than in England. Symonds was much attracted by the Hellenism of the Renaissance, and both his prose and poetry show his concept of Platonic love and his admiration for male beauty. Although he married in 1864, he acknowledged his homosexuality and campaigned, discreetly, for legal reform and more outspoken recognition of homosexuality as being a congenital condition. After siring four daughters, he arrived at a liberal understanding with his wife which allowed him the asexual freedom he craved.

"We maintain," he wrote as a homosexual, "that we have the right to exist after the fashion which nature made us. And if we cannot alter your laws, we shall go on breaking them. You may condemn us to infamy, exile, prison—as you formerly burned witches. You may degrade our emotional instincts and drive us into vice and misery. But you will not eradicate inverted sexuality."

He also wrote in his *Memoirs* (1890), "I can also defend, on what appears to me sufficient grounds, a large amount of promiscuity. In the very nature of the sexual contract between two males there inheres an element of instability. No children come of the connection. There can be no marriage ceremonies, no marriage settlements, no married life in common. Therefore, the parties are free, and the sexual flower of comradeship may spring afresh for each of them wherever favourable soil is found."

H. D. Brown, one of his biographers, wrote that Symonds rejected not only Christianity but also any belief in a future life. {BDF; CE; GL; JM; RAT; RE; TRI}

Symons, Arthur (1865–1945)

Symons is a poet and dramatist who said he did not reject Christianity because "it had never taken hold of me." He was a leader of the Symbolists in England and interpreted French decadent poetry to the English through translations. Symons edited *Savoy* (1896) until a period of insanity, which he described in his *Confessions* (1930) and which incapacitated him from 1908 to 1910.

His chief critical work is *The Symbolist Movement in Literature* (1899). In *Spiritual Adventures* (1905), Symons wrote that as a boy the prayers in church "made me ashamed as if I were unconsciously helping to repeat absurdities to God." {CE; RAT; RE; TRI}

SYNCRETISM

In philosophy or religion, syncretism is the reconciliation or fusion of differing systems of belief.

For example, Umberto Eco, in mentioning "the Black Rome" in a novel, referred to the mixing in Brazil of Roman Catholicism and Candomblé. St. George, for instance, is also called Ogum, the god of war and of metals. Cardinal Lucas Moreira Neves in 1987 found the trend toward fusion of the two religions harmful, adding, "I am going to continue combating syncretism." Such practices were understandable when slaves were forced to abandon African beliefs, he said, but "now, with total freedom of religion in Brazil, everyone must follow their own faith, without mixtures."

The Rev. Pierre Mathon illustrated his being in agreement, celebrating a "Mass of repudiation" of religious practices that he described as "demonic." (See entry for Candomblé.) {Larry Rohter, *The New York Times*, 10 January 2000}

SYNECHISM: See entry for Charles Sanders Peirce.

Synge, (Edmond) J(ohn) M(iddleton) (1871–1909)

Synge, the Irish poet and dramatist born of Protestant parents, was an important figure in the Irish Literary Renaissance. His first play, *In the Shadow of the Glen* (1903), was a grim one-act peasant comedy, in which an elderly husband feigns death to test his wife's fidelity. *Riders to the Sea* (1904) is an elegiac tragedy in which an elderly mother stoically anticipates "a great rest" after the death of the last of her six sons. His most controversial play was *The Playboy of the Western World* (1907), because it created a furor of resentment among Irish patriots stung by Synge's spoof of heroic ideals and nationalism. David Tribe labels Synge an outright freethinker, pointing to his anti-clerical *The Tinker's Wedding*. However, Synge is not known ever to have professed being a non-theist.

From 1897 on, Synge suffered from Hodgkin's disease, and his last play, *Deirdre of the Sorrows*, was completed while he was dying. Yeats said of Synge, "He was but the more hated because he gave his country what it needed, an unmoved mind," and described him in "In Memory of Major Gregory" as one who had come

Towards nightfall upon certain set apart
In a most desolate stony place,
Towards nightfall upon a race
Passionate and simple like his heart.

{CE; OEL}

Syphers, John (19th Century)

Syphers, a freethinker, wrote *Gods and God-Houses* (189–?) and *The Devil's Due Bills, or Give the Devil His Due* (c. 1890?). {GS}

SYPHILIS

A most dangerous venereal disease, syphilis is probably ancient in origin although evidence exists that it may have been transported to Europe by Columbus's returning crew members. It is almost always transmitted by sexual contact, but one can be infected through an open wound or lesion that could permit the organisms to enter a body. It can also occur through infected blood or plasma and from an infected mother to her fetus.

Pandarus's farewell speech from the epilogue of Shakespeare's *Troilus and Cressida* includes the line, "Neapolitan bone-rot," Neapolitan being the period slang for syphilis.

Measure for Measure includes references to infectious sores and madness due to the disease, as do *A Comedy of Errors*, *King Lear*, and *Romeo and Juliet*. {*A&U*, June 1999; CE}

SYRIAN HUMANISTS: See entry for Sadik Al Azm of the University of Damascus, who signed Humanist Manifesto 2000.

Sytsma, Curt (20th Century)

In every age, the bigot's rage
requires another focus,
Another devil's forced on stage
by hatred's hocus-pocus.
The devil used to be the Jew
and then it was the witches;
And then it was the Negroes who
Were digging in the ditches.
The devil once was colored pink
And labeled Communistic;
Now, all at once, in just a blink
The devil's humanistic.

{*The Utah Humanist*, January 1998}

Szabo, Arpad (1934–)

The Rev. Szabo is Vice President of the International Council of Unitarians and Universalists. He was secretary of the Romanian Bishopric in Chuj from 1958 to 1965 and from 1965 to 1976 the minister of the Chuj Unitarian Church. From 1977 to 1978, Szabo studied at Meadville/Lombard Theological School in Chicago.

An estimated 80,000 Romanians are Unitarian Universalists. (See entry for Romanian Unitarians.)

Szalanski, Andrea (20th Century)

Szalanski is the managing editor of *Free Inquiry*. She is a Secular Humanist Mentor of the Council for Secular Humanism.

Szasz, Thomas (1920–)

A professor of psychiatry at the State University of New York Medical School, the Hungarian born Dr. Szasz (pronounced: sass) was named 1973 Humanist of the Year by the American Humanist Association. Szasz is a Humanist Laureate in the Council for Secular Humanism's International Academy of Humanism and is a contributing editor on *Free Inquiry*.

He has written *Psychiatric Justice* (1965); *The Insanity Plea and the Insanity Verdict* (1974), which argues that the insanity plea should be abolished; *Cruel Compassion* (1994); and *Our Right to Drugs* (1996). With Milton Friedman, he wrote *On Liberty and Drugs* (1992).

Szasz has been criticized negatively by many whereas others credit him with having done more than most in alerting the American public about the potential dangers of an excessively psychiatrized society. "In a free society," Szasz claims in one of his controversial views, "a person must have the right to injure or kill himself." He also holds that "the poor need jobs and money, not psychoanalysis." {HNS2}

Szilard, Leo (1898–1964)

A Hungarian-born American nuclear physicist and biophysicist, Szilard with Enrico Fermi developed the first self-sustained nuclear reactor based on uranium fission. Although he was one of the first to realize the military possibilities of his discoveries, he actively protested nuclear warfare and supported the use of nuclear energy only for peaceful purposes. In 1960 he was named Humanist of the Year by the American Humanist Association. In *Second Thoughts About Atomic Power: Report of the Committee on Social and Political Implications* (1945), Szilard wrote, "If no efficient international agreement is achieved, the race for nuclear armaments will be on in earnest not later than the morning after our first demonstration of the existence of nuclear weapons. . . . The best possible atmosphere for the achievement of an international agreement could be achieved if America could say to the rest of the world, 'You see what sort of weapon we had but did not use.' " {CE; HNS2}

Szimhart, Joseph P. (20th Century)

Szimhart is a specialist in controversial new religions, therapies, and cults. He has worked as a consultant to help groups and individuals to understand or reevaluate participation in questionable behaviors and beliefs. Szimhart writes for *Skeptical Inquirer*.

Szykowny, Rick (20th Century)

Szykowny was an executive editor as well as an interim co-editor of *The Humanist*. In 1994 he wrote a searing attack on the journal's publisher, the American Humanist Association (AHA):

> Let's face it: Organized humanism in the United States doesn't have anything near the resources or the political clout wielded by the religious right; nor is it attracting significant numbers of young people, working-class people, people of color, or women to its ranks.

The AHA president, Michael Werner, berated Szykowny and tried to get co-editor Gerry O'Sullivan to intervene. When O'Sullivan declined, citing editorial autonomy, Werner dismissed him. The honorary AHA president, Kurt Vonnegut Jr., immediately pulled his name from the magazine's editorial advisory board and reportedly said he was looking into resigning his honorary presidency, also, noting that "to have an organization is, in a sense, antihumanist." Following the disruption, Szykowny in the November-December 1994 issue of *The Humanist* was listed as "Associate Editor/Permissions" but is no longer with them.

Tabash, Edward (20th Century)

Tabash spoke on the need for tolerance among atheists at their First Annual Atheist Alliance Conference in 1994 in California. A Beverly Hills, California lawyer, he is the chairman of the Outreach Committee of the Council for Secular Humanism for the Los Angeles area. Tabash has served on the board of directors of the California Abortion and Reproductive Rights Action League. Also, he is a trustee of Americans United for Separation of Church and State. {"Why I Support President Clinton," *Free Inquiry*, Spring 1996}

Taber, Henry Morehouse (Born 1825)

Taber, who was born in Westport, Connecticut, engaged in the cotton business in New York City. He married a Presbyterian clergyman's daughter and attended church with her "for the pleasure of her company" up until the time she died, at which time he stopped. Taber wrote *Faith or Fast* (1897). Highly esteemed by Robert Ingersoll, Taber ordered that there be no religious services and that his body be cremated. Like so many, he was a churchman in name only. {PUT}

Tabler, Barbara M. (1916–1996)

A founding member of the Freethought Society of Greater Philadelphia, Tabler signed Humanist Manifesto II. She was noted for singing freethought songs at humanist conferences. {HM2; HNS2}

Tabler, Ward (20th Century)

Tabler, who has taught at Starr King School, signed Humanist Manifesto II. He is on the editorial board of *The Humanist*. {HM2}

TABOO: See entry for Animism.

TABULA RASA

John Locke believed that a child's mind is a *tabula rasa*, Latin for "blank state." We start life, he explained, with a mind that is new, fresh, unmarked, uninfluenced. {DCL}

Tacitus (Cornelius Tacitus) (c. 55–c. 117)

Tacitus, the Roman historian, was known for his high moral tone as well as his criticism of contemporary Rome. His observation of the Jews was that they, unlike members of other religions, refused to bow to polytheism on certain occasions, as if their views were exclusive. As a result, he viewed Judaism negatively. In addition, he wrote in *Thebaid*, "Christianity is a pestilent superstition."

Tadema, Lawrence Alma [Sir] (1836–1912)

Tadema became an Associate of the Royal Academy in 1876 and a full Academician in 1879. His first notable picture, "Clothilde at the Tomb of Her Grandchildren," was exhibited in 1858, and for years he was devoted to historical subjects. He also painted scenes of Greek and Roman life. Tadema was knighted in 1899 and received the Order of Merit in 1905. He was an agnostic. {RAT}

Taft, William Howard [President; Chief Justice of the Supreme Court] (1857–1930)

Taft, the 27th United States President, also served as Chief Justice from 1921 to 1930. He defeated William Jennings Bryan in 1908 and became Theodore Roosevelt's successor. Taft once wrote: "If a man can be a Christian only when he believes in the literal truth of the creed as it is recited in the orthodox evangelical churches, then we Unitarians are not Christians. A Unitarian believes that Jesus founded a new religion and a new religious philosophy on the love of God for man, and of men for one another, and for God, and taught it by his life and practice, with such Heaven-given sincerity, sweetness, simplicity, and all-compelling force that it lived after him in the souls of men, and became the basis for a civilization struggling toward the highest ideals. Unitarians, however, do not find the evidence of the truth of many traditions which have attached themselves to the life and history of Jesus to be strong enough to overcome the presumption against supernatural intervention in the order of nature. They feel the life of Jesus as a man to be more helpful to them as a religious inspiration, than if he is to be regarded as God in human form." Had he made the letter public, he would most certainly have hurt his chances in politics.

When offered the presidency of Yale University, he had declined, saying all previous presidents had been Congregationalists and "I do not believe in the divinity of Christ, and there are many other of the postulates of the orthodox creed to which I cannot subscribe." Although doubters have stated the 332-pound Taft changed his mind, he is quoted in Henry F. Pringle's *The Life and Times of William Howard Taft* (1939) as saying, "I am a Unitarian. I believe in God." {CE; TYD; U; UU}

Tagore, Rabindranath [Sir] (1861–1941)

Tagore, a Bengali poet and guru who wrote the national anthem of India, was a Unitarian. He was the author of more than fifty dramas, one hundred books of verse, forty volumes of novels and other fiction, much of which denounced nationalism and violence. In *Sadhanaq: The Realization of Life* (1913) Tagore emphasized philosophic sentiments in keeping with sacred Hindu writing. Writing in Bengali, he translated his work into English. Tagore traveled widely, liked the West's ability to industrialize but deprecated what he said was its lack of spirituality. In 1913, he received a Nobel Prize in Literature, especially for *Gitanjali* (1912), his collection of poetry. According to McCabe, Tagore had rejected both Christianity and all forms of the Hindu religion, and his biographer, H. D. Brownshows that he had no belief in any future life. McCabe calls Tagore an atheist, the Unitarians claim he was a Unitarian, and some say he was a Unitarian atheist, a category not uncommon among Unitarians. The Tagore Center in Urbana, Illinois, holds annual festivals in Tagore's honor. When Tagore visited Urbana in 1912, he addressed the Unitarian congregation and returned several times to lecture. (For a discussion of Tagore's differences with Gandhi, for whom he had popularized the descriptive term "Mahatma," or great soul, see Amartya Sen's "Tagore and His India," *The New York Review of Books*, 27 June 1997.) {CE; HNS2; JM; RE; U; UU}

Tailliandier, René Gaspard Ernest (1817–1879)

Tailliandier, the French writer commonly known as "Saint René," taught at Strasbourg, Montpelier, and the Sorbonne. He belonged to the Republican anti-clerical party and became general secretary to the Minister of Education at the Revolution of 1870. He was admitted to the Legion of Honour in 1870 and to the French Academy in 1873. Tailliandier translated into French the correspondence of Goethe and Schiller. His views are given in his *Histoire et philosophie religieuse* (1860). {RAT}

Taine, Hippolyte Adolphe (1828–1893)

Taine, the French critic and historian, was the typical French rationalist of his time according to Robertson. However, he was in his latter years a reactionary on political grounds. For 20 years, he was a professor of aesthetics and art history at the *École des Beaux-Arts*. His *French Philosophers of the Nineteenth Century* (1856) sharply criticized the spiritualist and religious school. In 1878 Taine was elected to the French Academy, much to the regret of the clergy, which had tried for years to keep him out. But his *History of English Literature* (1864), *Origins of Contemporary France* (1876–1894, 6 volumes), and other works gave him worldwide acclaim, and he was recognized, along with Renan, as "one of the intellectual guides of the generation which formed between 1860 and 1890," according to the *Grande Encyclopédie*. Taine's socio-historical method of analysis had considerable influence on philosophy, aesthetics, literary criticism, and the social sciences. Boutmy, a biographer, showed that, although Taine became conservative in politics, he remained an agnostic to the end. {BDF; JM; JMR; JMRH; RAT; RE}

Tai-tsung [Emperor] (600–650)

Tai-tsung, a Chinese emperor of the T'ang dynasty, was described by McCabe:

> His name was Shih-min but he was named Tai-tsung (Great Ancestor) after his death and lives as such in Chinese history. The missionary expert on China, Dr. Giles, says that his was "a reign of unrivalled brilliance and glory," and the historian of China, D. Boulger, says, "No ruler of any country had had sounder claims to be entitled Great." He had in a quarter of a century done more for China than any other emperor and raised it to a wonderful height while Europe was in semi-barbarism; but you will find your encyclopedias and history books full of Europe at the time and rarely mentioning Tai-tsung. His character was very high and his ideas, especially in the treatment of crime and in toleration, beyond anything in 1,500 years of Christian history.

McCabe added that "the three really great monarchs of the Christian Era are Hadrian, Tai-tsung, and Abd-er-Rahman III, all atheists." {JM}

Talandier, Alfred (Born 1828)

Talandier was a French publicist who, after entering the bar, became a socialist and took part in the revolution of 1848. He became professor at the *Lycée* in 1870 but in 1874 was deprived of his chain. Elected on the Municipal Council of Paris, he later was chosen deputy and was re-elected in 1881. In 1883 Talandier published a *Popular Rabelais* and also wrote on freethought topics. {BDF; RAT}

Talbert, E. L. (20th Century)

A member of the sociology department in the 1950s at the University of Cincinnati, Talbert was an associate editor of *The Humanist*. Asked in the 1950s who he considered were the top exponents of humanist viewpoints, he named E. A. Burtt and H. J. Muller. {HNS; WAS, 26 December 1954}

Talbot, Kate (20th Century)

An American humanist, Talbot attended in 1996 the international conference of humanists in Mexico City. Her e-mail: <ktalbot@earthlink.net>.

Talleyrand-Périgard, Maurice de Maurice de [Prince] (1754–1838)

Talleyrand was a French statesman and diplomat. Born into the high nobility, he was early destined for the Roman Catholic Church because of a childhood accident that left him partially lame. Despite his notorious impiety, King Louis XIV made him bishop of Autun (1789). As a representative of the clergy in the States-General of 1789, he sided with the revolutionists. He then proposed the appropriation of church property by the state, endorsed the civil constitution of the clergy, and was excommunicated in 1791 after having consecrated two "constitutional" bishops. Talleyrand supported the French Revolution at first, but, after the fall of the monarchy, fled to England in 1792 and then to the United States in 1794. Returning to France in 1796, he became foreign minister under the Directory (1797–1799) and Napoleon I (1799–1807). However, Napoleon tended to ignore Talleyrand's cautious advice. After Napoleon's defeat, Talleyrand persuaded the allies in 1814 to restore the Bourbon monarchy and represented France at the Congress of Vienna in 1815. Later, he served Louis Philippe as ambassador to London. Although often labeled an opportunist, Talleyrand consistently aimed at peace and stability for Europe as a whole. According to McCabe, Talleyrand was an atheist "and went, rather cynically, through a form of reconciliation with the Church in his last year solely, and expressly, to ensure that he should have a funeral undisturbed by the new Catholic mob." {JM; RAT; RE; TYD}

Tallien, Jean Lambert (1767–1820)

Tallien was a journalist who became a leading member of the Paris Commune and saved many from cruel treatment. He was one of the corps of savants whom Napoleon took to Egypt, but after the fall of the Emperor Tallien refused to be reconciled with the throne and the Church. {RAT; RE}

TALMUD

An Aramaic word, *Talmud* means learning and is a compilation of Jewish oral law. Its *Mishna*, written in Hebrew, contains the oral law and the *Gemera*, in Aramaic, is a commentary on and supplement to the *Mishna*. Written from around 200 to 500, it contains hairsplitting arguments. For example and as explained by Nat Hentoff, "A rabbi in the Talmud tells the story of a roofer who took his clothes off while on the job because it was hot. Below, in the courtyard, also feeling the heat, a woman also removed her clothes. A gust of wind caused the roofer to lose his footing. He fell, landed on top of the woman, and through the force of his descent, his penis accidentally entered her. The result, however brief, was sexual intercourse." Because the roofer did not fall with the intent of landing on the woman in order to have sex with her and because he had no control over where he was going to land, the man was not liable. But when Jesus in the Sermon on the Mount said that "Anyone who so much as looks with lust on a woman has already committed adultery with that woman," it follows that if you think about doing the act you have therefore done it. {*Village Voice*, 26 July 1994}

Tamassia, Arrigo (Born 1849)

Tamassia, an Italian physician, was professor of legal medicine at Padua University and editor of the *Rivista di Medicina Legale*. Tamassia supported Ardigó in his effort to eliminate, as he said, "all tyranny, all corruption, and all villainies." {RAT}

Tambureno, Anthony (20th Century)

Tambureno won the Humanist Association of Canada's 1998 essay contest for young writers. The Mississauga, Ontario, resident laments that "the job of the media is selling consumers to advertisers, not informing the public. {*Humanist in Canada*, Autumn 1998}

Tamlyn, John (19th Century)

Tamlyn wrote *The Dream Heaven of Our Fathers, and the Heaven That Is to Be* (c. 1885). {GS}

Tampieri, Susana Elisa (1934–)

In the late 1950s and 1960s, Tampieri was an active leader of the humanist movement in Córdoba, Argentina. A leading personality in university circles, she engaged in the democratic revolution in 1955 that pulled down the Perón regime. She was a leader of the Pro-Democracy Revolution in Paraguay (1957-1958).

Tampieri has written twenty-six plays, two novels, three works of poetry, and many essays. Her work depicts the situation of women and the middle class in the changing moral world of the past half-century. Tampieri was the first president of the Argentine Humanist Society. {WAS, conversation July 1999 with Hugo Estrella.}

Tan, Cheng Imm (20thCentury)

The Maylaysian daughter to devout Buddhist parents, Tan attended Catholic school for twelve years. She found the two different religious outlooks had in common a certain ethics: do good, reap good fruits; do evil, reap evil fruits; every action has a result; if you harm yourself or others, you will be punished in this life or the next. Reincarnation, however, seemed like Catholic Hell. Although she found Buddhism legalistic and lacking in warmth, Catholicism offered a loving, forgiving God. But Catholicism taught that females were sinful, had no willpower, and her feminism took precedence.

After entering Harvard's Master of Divinity program, Tan became active with Arise, a program that proposes to empower all immigrant and refugee women. Frustrated with a Christian dualism that condemned women and the earth as base, she returned to her ancestral Buddhism in 1986. Now a Unitarian Universalist minister, she holds that "[l]ife is uncontrolled. You must receive it with openness and compassion and acceptance. Accept that injustice is happening—and then work against it. . . . You do what you can do, but you can't get attached to your results. If you're attached to your results, well, that will lead to your suffering." {*World*, November-December 1998}

Tanase, Al (20th Century)

Tanase, from Romania, addressed the Second European Conference of the International Humanist and Ethical Union (IHEU) held in Hannover (1968).

TANDEM PROJECT

The Tandem Project is a non-sectarian, nonprofit international human rights organization founded in 1985 to promote, implement, and monitor the 1981 United Nations Declaration on the Elimination of All Forms of Intolerance and Discrimination Based on Religion or Belief. (See entry for Michael Roan.)

Tangherlini, Frank R. (20th Century)

"Catholic Girl and Atheist" (1947) was written by Tangherlini, a freethinker. {GS}

Tango, David (20th Century)

Tango, an activist-atheist in Costa Mesa, California, writes for *Secular Nation*. E-mail: <tango@deltanet.com>.

Tanner, James (c. 1817–1870)

Tanner was the son of Kentuckian John Tanner, who had been captured by Indians when seven or eight years of age. His father, brought up by the Chippewas, married an Indian woman, as did his son James. Seeking money for farming implements needed by the Indians, James journeyed to Boston and talked with officials of the American Unitarian Association, who were helpful. Tanner is considered the first missionary in the territory that became North Dakota. He sided wholly with the Indians in their complaints that they were being defrauded of moneys legally owed them. {EG}

TANTALUS

A son of Zeus in Greek mythology and the father of Pelops and Niobe, Tantalus was a legendary king of Lydia who got into so much trouble that he was condemned by the gods to suffer eternally at Tartarus. One legend has it that he had divulged divine secrets and stolen the gods' sacred food. Another told that he had murdered Pelops and served his body to the gods to test their omniscience. As punishment, Tantalus was hanged from the bough of a fruit tree over a pool of water (although another version had him standing up to his neck in that pool). When he bent to drink, the water would recede. When he reached for a fruit, the wind would blow it from his reach. The word *tantalize* is convenient to describe one's frustration in being exposed to something desirable, yet not being able to have it. {CE}

TAOISM: See entry for Daoism

Tapp, Robert B. (20th Century)

Tapp, a professor emeritus of humanities, religious studies, and South Asian studies at the University of Minnesota, is dean of the Humanist Institute in New York City. He signed Humanist Manifesto 2000. {*The Humanist*, January-February 1998}

Tappan, Caroline Sturgis (1819-1868)

A transcendentalist and a Unitarian, Tappan was a poet and a children's author. Her sister was Ellen Sturgis Hooper.

TARAKBODH

Tarakbodh (Rationalist), is a bi-monthly in Punjabi of the Tarksheel Society Bharat. It is at B-XI-413, Ram Bagh Road, Barnala-148 101, Punjab, India.

Tarde, Gabriel (1843–1904)

Tarde was a French sociologist whose criminological and sociological works were widely recognized. He was appointed head of the statistical department at the Ministry of Justice and professor at the *Collège de France*. He is known for his theory of imitation in sociology—that a few individuals initiate changes, and the majority imitate them. In 1900, Tarde was admitted to the Academy of Moral and Political Sciences. {RAT}

TARKJYOTY

Tarkjyoty, a rationalist monthly in Hindi of the Rationalist Society of Haryana, is at G. H. S. Badsikri, The. & Distt. Kaithal, Haryana 136 027, India.

Tarkunde, V(ithal) M(ahadev) (1912–)

A retired Supreme Court judge and chairman of the Indian Radical Humanist Association, Tarkunde is a Humanist Laureate in the Council for Secular Humanism's International Academy of Humanism. He signed Humanist Manifesto II. In 1952, he was on the first Board of Directors of the International Humanist and Ethical Union (IHEU). In 1976, he was elected an honorary associate of the British Rationalist Press Association. In Amsterdam at the Sixth International Humanist and Ethical Union (IHEU) World Congress (1974), he addressed the group, as he did also at the Seventh held in London (1978). In 1978, he received that group's Humanist Award for defending the values of democracy. *For Freedom* in 1984 commemorated his seventy-fifth birthday. In 1983 he wrote *Radical Humanism.* Tarkunde is a contributing editor to *Free Inquiry* and, in his eighties, is editor emeritus of Mumbai's *Radical Humanist.* Indian humanists regard him both as a theoretician and as an activist on behalf of humanism. He has written,

> I believe in a country of mass poverty and ignorance, like India, humanism must take a radical form. It must be concerned with developing a movement aimed at spreading the humanist-democratic values of freedom, rationalism, and secular morality among the people so that they can take the necessary initiatives for the elimination of poverty and removal of mass ignorance.

Speaking in 1995 at a conference of humanists in India, Tarkunde said, "In many post-colonial countries, democracy was replaced by dictatorial regimes and democracy almost disappeared from India in 1975 when Mrs. Gandhi took emergency powers. At present, Indian democracy is being threatened from a different direction. A Hindu chauvinist party (the BJP) which also claims to be ardently nationalistic, has a chance of coming to power in New Delhi. A party which combines religious chauvinism with aggressive nationalism is likely to establish a Fascist regime of an Indian variety." To resist this, he called upon Indian humanists to provide a democracy of the people, "not of political parties which represent them" as in Western Europe and America. "The State should consist," he continued, "of a network of local republics which may be called People's Committees, that as much power as is possible should be invested in the primary People's

Committee, that power which is required to be exercised at higher levels of government should be in the hands of persons who are the real representatives of the people and who are subject to their control and recall and that Parliament should be the apex of such People's Committees and intermediate centres of power."

In 1996, Levi Fragell interviewed Tarkunde in India. As to the conflicts between humanism and religion, Tarkunde saw no danger, stating, "I believe that we are so strongly committed to rationalism that contact between us and religious humanists is likely to augment their rationalism without affecting ours."

In 1998 at the International Humanist and Ethical Union's congress in Mumbai, Justice Tarkunde was cited as the "father of modern humanism and human rights in India." In an address, he lamented that of India's population of 900+ million one-third live below the povery line and 60% of women and 40% of men are illiterate. Tarkunde signed Humanist Manifesto 2000. (See entry for G. Vijayam.)
{FUK; HM2; HNS2; *New Humanist*, February 1996; SHD}

Tarozzi, Giuseppe (1831–1907)

Tarozzi, an Italian philosopher, taught at Palermo University and was a positivist. He scorned not only orthodox theology but also the whole "modern delirium of pseudo-idealism." He wrote *Lezioni di filosofia* (2 volumes, 1896–1897) and *La coltura intellettuale contemporanea* (1897). {RAT}

TARTARUS

In Greek mythology, Tartarus was the lowest region of the underworld, a place where wicked individuals such as Sisyphus, Tantalus, and Ixion were sent as punishment. It was presided over by Hades. The concept is believed to be far older than that of the concept of Hell.

Tarter, Jill (20th Century)

Tarter, who holds the Bernard M. Oliver Chair of the SETI Institute, signed Humanist Manifesto 2000.

Tatchell, Peter (20th Century)

Following a peaceful protest during the Archbishop of Canterbury's 1998 Easter sermons at Canterbury Cathedral, Tatchell—a gay rights campaigner—was arrested and charged with "indecent behaviour in a church," specifically that of interrupting services in violation of Section 2 of the Ecclesiastical Courts Jurisdiction Act of 1860. Tatchell countered that his protest "highlighted the perverted moral priorities of many Christians. They are more offended, apparently, by a brief peaceful protest in a church than by [the Archbishop's] opposition to lesbian and gay human rights. The real indecency was not our peaceful protest but the fact that the Archbishop of Canterbury says that gay people are not entitled to equality and fair treatment under the law." The National Secular Society and others immediately called for changes in that archaic law.

Saying he once was a Baptist Sunday school teacher, he continued that

> I gave up my religious faith for a number of reasons. Firstly, I was very distressed by the way in which the Church, or some of the churches, was endorsing the barbarism of capital punishment and the genocidal war being waged by Australia and the United States in Vietnam. I was also very angry at the way in which they were taking aboriginal kids away from their parents and opposing aboriginal land rights. And then, of course, when I realised I was gay, I felt furious that my love and commitment to another man could be treated (a) as a sin and (b) as a criminal offence endorsed by the Church.

Pressed further, Tatchell said, "The Church of England is an oppressive, homophobic institution. I think that any lesbian or gay person who is a part of that Church, unless they are overtly, actively campaigning to change things, they are a part of the problem. . . . And I've got to say that the Bible is to lesbian and gay people what *Mein Kampf* is to Jews. {*The Freethinker*, October 1998; *Gay and Lesbian Humanist*, Winter 1998}

Tate, Allen (1899–1979)

Tate was the Tennessee-born writer of metaphysical poetry, editor of *Fugitive* (1922–1925) and of *Sewanee Review* (1944–1946). He taught English at the University of Minnesota. Asked about humanism, Tate responded to the present author:

> I have written two essays on the general subject, or at least touching it, and I should think that my views could be partly derived from them: first, "Humanism and Naturalism" in *Reactionary Essays* (Scribner, 1936), and "The Hovering Fly" in *On The Limits of Poetry* (Swallow-Morrow, 1948). A third essay, in the latter volume and entitled "Techniques of Fiction," touches upon literary aspects of naturalism.
>
> It is difficult to make a short statement on the literary value of naturalistic humanism that could have much value; it would be merely *ad hoc*, without supporting argument. In general, I should say, humanism cannot maintain itself as naturalism; for man, if he is to remain human, must have access to truths of which unaided he is not capable. The great literary "naturalists," Flaubert and Joyce, were overtly anti-Christian; but the configuration of meaning in both is supra-rational. I need not allude to Joyce's idea of "epiphanies," or to the Christian allegory implicit in *Un Coeur Simple*, to say nothing of the death-scene of Emma Bovary. This is a very large subject. I may add that there has been a great deal of misunderstanding of literary naturalism in our time, as it comes to us from Flaubert, James, and Joyce. These men embodied the symbol in the natural object, and thus returned to the kind of symbolism that Dante gives us, rather than the symbolism of Bunyan, which is superimposed upon the natural order of experience. The naturalism represented by the influence of Zola seems to me to have come to a dead-end.
>
> {WAS, 16 February 1951}

Taubert, A. (19th Century)

Taubert was the maiden name of Dr. Karl Hartmann's first wife. She wrote *The Pessimists and Their Opponents* (1866). {BDF}

Taubert, Kenneth F. Sr. (20th Century)

Taubert is a contributor to *Freethought Today*, which is published by the Freedom From Religion Foundation, of which he is a member of the board of directors. Also, he is treasurer of that group's Executive Council.

Taule, Ferdinand (19th Century)

Taule was a physician born in Strasbourg. He wrote *Notions on the Nature and Properties of Organised Matter* (1866). {BDF}

Taurellus, Nicolaus (1547–1606)

Taurellus was a German physician and philosopher. Wheeler reports that "for daring to think for himself, and asking how the Aristotelian doctrine of the eternity of the world could be reconciled with the dogma of creation, he was stigmatised as an atheist." He wrote many works in Latin, including *Philosophiae Triumphans* (1573). Dr. Taurellus died of the plague in 1606. {BDF}

Tavris, Carol (20th Century)

Tavris, a psychologist and author, is on the executive council of the Committee for the Scientific Investigation of Claims of the Paranormal, which publishes *Skeptical Inquirer*. She wrote *Psychology in Perspective* (1997).

Tawiah, Hope N. (20th Century)

At the Tenth International Humanist and Ethical Union (IHEU) World Congress held in Buffalo (1988), Tawiah, who is chairman of the Rational Centre in Accra, Ghana, addressed the group. In Pokuasi, a village near the capital of Accra, Tawiah has gathered a group of followers in what he calls the Rational Centre of Ghana, the motto of which is "Down with Superstition." The chief of the village, Nii Otto Kwame II, considers himself a rationalist and has given land for the center. (See entry for Rational Centre.)

TAXES AND RELIGIOUS ORGANIZATIONS

In the United States, churches that are 501(c)(3) organizations cannot involve themselves in partisan political campaigns. Contributors to churches are allowed certain tax deductions if the church remains out of politics.

The Unitarian Universalist Fellowship of Anchorage is unique inasmuch as it voluntarily makes an annual check to the city of Anchorage for "payment in lieu of taxes" (PILOT). Art Curtis, the group's minister, said, "There is no reason why churches should be exempt from municipal services. It is only fair." PILOT, which is the brainchild of Stanley J. Erickson, was first instituted in 1968. {*World*, March-April 1999}

Taylor, Alan John Percivale (1906–1990)

In 1986, Taylor was elected an honorary associate of the Rationalist Press Association. A historian and journalist, he wrote *Beaverbrook* (1972), about Baron William Maxwell Aitken Beaverbrook. He also has written over thirty books, including *Struggle for Mastery in Europe 1848–1918* (1954), *Trouble Makers* (1957), *English History 1914–1945* (1965), *The Last of Old Europe* (1976), *How Wars Begin* (1979), and *A Personal History* (1983). One work, which aroused passionate hostility, was his *Origins of the Second World War* (1983), in which he suggested that historical events are often shaped by accident. His biography, *A Personal History*, was published in 1983. A biography by Adam Sisman, *A. J. P. Taylor* (1993), describes his tangled personal life and mentions his early abandonment of nonconformist Christianity and adoption of militant atheism.

Taylor, Carol (20th Century)

Taylor, a Los Angeles psychologist and author, signed Humanist Manifesto 2000.

Taylor, David (20th Century)

Taylor is author of *Was Jesus the Essene Teacher of Righteousness?* (1990).

Taylor, E. G. (19th Century)

Taylor, a freethinker, wrote *Shall Thought Be Fettered in England?* (1895). {GS}

Taylor, G. H. (Died c. 1957)

Taylor wrote *Can Materialism Explain Mind* (1950). His "Chronology of British Secularism" is found in *An Anthology of Atheism and Rationalism* (1980), edited by Gordon Stein. {FUK}

Taylor, George (20th Century)

Taylor is Vice President for Membership of the Secular Humanist Association of San Antonio, Texas.

Taylor, Harold (1914–1993)

Dr. Taylor was president of Sarah Lawrence College from 1949 to 1959. When he took office at the age of thirty, he was the nation's youngest college president. A critic of traditional educational practices, he said, "What is wrong with a great deal of higher education in America is that it is simply boring." To counteract this he became a leading proponent of change. As a result, the college became nationally known as the one which gave no grades or report cards. Classes were few and small in size. Independent study by students was evaluated by close consultation with professors. During his presidency, Taylor defended academic freedom against McCarthyism, and he pressed for racial integration at the school, which had been predominantly white.

Taylor's *On Education and Freedom* was reviewed for *The Humanist* by William Clark Trow of the University of Michigan, who described the Canadian-born educator as having written "with the literary flare of the past but with an observant eye on the present." Trow quotes Taylor: "But what John Dewey suggested throughout the whole of his life was not that we give up reading any serious book of any period of history, but that we read such books in order to help with the matter of testing our ideas in action." Trow agreed with Taylor that the humanities departments often assume they teach values whereas the students learn facts in the other departments, which Taylor reasons is nonsense.

In addition to signing Humanist Manifesto II, Taylor was on the editorial board of *The Humanist*. {HM2; HNS}

Taylor, Harriet (19th Century)

Taylor, along with Eliza Flower, Sarah Flower, and Harriet Martineau, was one of the 19th-century freethought activists known as "Ladies of South Place," a reference to the South Place Ethical Society. {*Freethought History #9*, 1994}

Taylor, Helen (1831–1907)

In 1851 Taylor's mother married J. S. Mill. Upon her death seven years later, Miss Taylor devoted herself to the care of her stepfather and was esteemed by him. She co-operated with him in writing his *Subjection of Women* (1869). After Mill's death, she lived mainly in London, where she edited Buckle's works (1872) and Mill's *Autobiography* (1873) and *Essays on Religion* (1874). Taylor was a humanitarian who worked for the abolition of school-fees and the provision of free food and boots for the children of the poorer workers. She worked also for land nationalization and the enfranchisement of women. {RAT; WWS}

Taylor, James (20th Century)

Taylor, a singer-songwriter, when interviewed by Bill Flanagon in *Rolling Stone* (July 10-24, 1997), was asked how an unbeliever could make sense of life.

"Well, I find myself with a strong spiritual need," Taylor responded. "And, certainly, it's acknowledged as an important part of recovery from addiction. Yet, it's hard for me to find an actual handle for it. I'm not saying that it's not helpful to think of having a real handle on the universe, your own personal point of attachment. But . . . I think it's crazy. It's an insanity that keeps us sane. You might call a lot of these songs 'spirituals for agnostics.' "

Asked if not having faith in a personal god makes it harder to stick with a 12-step recovery program, Taylor said, "Twelve-step programs say an interesting thing: Either you have a god, or you are God and you don't want the job." (See entry for Secular Organization for Sobriety.) {CA}

Taylor, Joan Kennedy (20th Century)

Taylor wrote *Reclaiming the Mainstream: Individualist Feminism Rediscovered* and "In Support of the Right To Choose" (*Free Inquiry*, Summer 1996). She is national coordinator of the Association of Libertarian Feminists and is on the board of directors of Feminists for Free Expression. Taylor wrote *Women's Issues* (1993).

Taylor, Karyn (20th Century)

Taylor, who hosts "Common Ground," an online environmental forum on Women's WIRE in San Francisco, has written for *The Humanist*.

Taylor, Keith R. (20th Century)

Taylor wrote "Beliefs of a Nonbeliever" in *Atheist Nation* (July-August 1998). He noted that "God doesn't seem to mind fornication if one kills the victim afterwards. I think it says so in that book of his."

Taylor, Norman (20th Century)

Taylor, of the Atheist Foundation of Australia, spoke in 1996 at the fourth World Atheist Conference held in Vijayawada, India. He called for an end to the religious brainwashing of children and urged standing up to the fear used to quiet potential critics of religion.

Taylor, Richard (1919–)

Taylor, a professor emeritus of philosophy at Union College and the University of Rochester, is a Humanist Laureate in the Council for Secular Humanism's International Academy of Humanism. He is a member of the Society of Friends and, in addition, is a contributing editor of *Free Inquiry*. Among his books are *Good and Evil* (1970), *Having Love Affairs* (1982), *Ethics, Faith, and Reason* (1985), *Reflective Wisdom* (1989), and *Restoring Pride: The Lost Virtue of Our Age* (1996). Taylor, who taught many years at Brown University, is author of "Joseph Fletcher's Situation Ethics, Once Again." At the Tenth International Humanist and Ethical Union (IHEU) World Congress held in Buffalo (1988), Taylor, who is known as a leading exponent of the philosophy of Schopenhauer, addressed the gathering.

"Taylor is a peculiar humanist," Paul B. Cliteur has observed. "He combines his humanist stance with adherence to what he calls a kind of 'theism.'" He has a belief in God that "springs from an awareness of the profound mystery of nature and of life." But he adheres to no church, affirms no creed, and abominates organized religious practice. Taylor is "a fideist with decided pantheistic proclivities," according to Jack Donnelly, who thinks his religiosity is "rather idiosyncratic."

Taylor signed Humanist Manifesto 2000 but added, "There is much that I do not agree with in this document, but I do accept the overall thesis." (*Free Inquiry*, Fall 1995; *Philo*, Fall-Winter 1998).

Taylor, Robert (1784–1844)

An English clergyman who converted to unbelief, Taylor became a deist which, in 1818, was considered by many to be a crime worse than murder. In 1827 he was arrested for blasphemy, and during the year spent in Oakham jail he wrote two books: *Syntagma of the Evidences of the Christian Religion* (1828) and *The Diegesis: Being A Discovery of the Origin, Evidence, and Early History of Christianity, Never Yet Before or Elsewhere So Fully and Faithfully Set Forth* (1829). His friend Richard Carlile published both. After his release from jail, he and Carlile went on "an infidel mission" about the country. In 1833, he edited a London publication, *Philalethian*. When Carlile published Taylor's weekly lectures as *The Devil's Pulpit*, Taylor against was charged with blasphemy and was sentences to two years in Horsemonger Lane jail. In jail, he was badly treated but, upon being released, married a wealthy woman. He then moved to France, became a surgeon and never again published another word about unbelief. {BDF; EU, Gordon Stein; FUS; FUK; PUT; RAT; RE; VI; TRI}

Taylor, Thomas (1758–1835)

Taylor, known as "The Platonist," devoted his life to the propagation of the Platonic philosophy. He translated the works of Plato, Aristotle, Porphyry, five books of Polotinus, six books of Proclus, Gamblichus on the Mysteries, Arguments of Celsus taken from Origin, Arguments of Julian against the Christians, Orations of Julian, and more. So thorough a pagan was Taylor, it was alleged, that he once sacrificed a bull to Zeus. {BDF; RAT; RE}

Taylor, W. (19th Century)

In 1883, Taylor edited *Freedom* in Brisbane, Australia. {FUK}

Taylor, Warren (1903–1992)

In the 1950s when he was on the staff at Antioch College, Taylor was an associate editor of *The Humanist*. He wrote *Poetry in English* (1970).

Taylor, William (1765–1836)

Taylor was an English acquaintance of Southey who translated from the German, notably Lessing's *Nathan the Wise*. He also wrote a *Survey of German Poetry* and *English Synonyms* (1830). In his *Who Was the Father of Jesus Christ?* (1810), Taylor argues that it was Zacharias and that Jesus was an illegitimate son of Mary. {BDF; RE}

Tchaikovsky, Peter Ilyich (1840–1893)

Tchaikovsky (also spelled Tschaikovsky and Chaikovsky), the Russian composer, was a towering figure in Russian music and one of the most popular composers in history. His father was a mining inspector who arranged for his son to study music, and at the age of twenty-one Tchaikovsky entered the St. Petersburg Conservatory, where he studied composition with Anton Rubinstein. An annuity from a wealthy patroness, Mme. von Meck, allowed him for years to devote himself to music, and it is not clear why she terminated her friendship and support without apparent reason. His music, richly orchestrated, is melodious, intensely emotional, and often melancholy. Among his works are his last three symphonies; the fantasy "Romeo and Juliet" (1869); the ballets "Swan Lake" (1876), "The Sleeping Beauty" (1889), and "The Nutcracker" (1892); the "Piano Concerto in B Flat Minor" (1875); and the "Violin Concerto in D" (1878). His operas include "Eugene Onegin" (1879) and "The Queen of Spades" (1890). His influence was great not only during the Soviet era but also in England, the United States, and elsewhere.

Tchaikovsky was known for his high-strung temperament. He also was known for his homosexuality. In 1876 in a letter to his brother he wrote that "I am aware that my inclinations are the greatest and most unconquerable obstacle to happiness; I must fight my nature with all my strength. I shall do everything possible to marry this year." The following year, in fact, he did marry. But their union was doomed and his wife, frustrated by his lack of interest in her, finally took another lover and, later, was institutionalized.

His many affairs included one with his student, Vladimir Shilovsky, and with his nephew, Vladimir Davidov, whose nickname was Bobyk and to whom he dedicated his famous "Pathétique Symphony." "Bob will finally drive me simply crazy with his indescribable fascination," Tchaikovsky wrote in his diary about his teenaged nephew. "I begin to crave Bob and get lonely without him. . . . Frightful how I love him!" Frightful also, complain contemporary homosexuals, that the Church had so brainwashed him that he felt he had to fight his nature and that he was driven to such despair. And then there was fifteen-year-old Eduard Zak, who came to Moscow to study acting but killed himself instead. Fourteen years later Tchaikovsky wrote in his diary, "How amazingly clearly I remember him, the sound of his voice, his movements, but especially the extraordinarily wonderful expression on his face. It seems to me that I have never loved anyone so strongly as him."

His brother edited his letters, which appear to show an interest in theism. When the Kirov Opera Chorus performed his music in New York City, the 1998 program notes noted that neither Tchaikovsky nor Rachmaninoff "expressed anything approaching religious fervor," suggesting that "exhaustion, not spirituality, provided the impetus" for Tchaikovsky's "Liturgy." Vladmir Morosan, writing in *Musica Russica*, however, averred, "By all evidence, faith and religion played an important role throughout his life."

According to McCabe, Tchaikovsky "seems in the end to have become an atheist after reading Flaubert's letters. 'I have,' he said, 'found some astonishing answers to my questions about God and religion in this little book.' He was unconscious when his brother summoned a priest," McCabe says, "to smear him with the sacrament."

Although *The New Grove Dictionary of Music and Musicians* chooses to repeat a Soviet-era rumor that Tchaikovsky poisoned himself at the behest of a "court of honor" of former law-school classmates who were scandalized by his homosexuality, Alex Ross in *The New Yorker* (30 November 1998) wrote that such a "penny-dreadful version" may have satisfied some but is untrue. Alexander Poznansky's *Tchaikovsky's Last Days* refutes the tale that the composer duplicated the symptoms of cholera. Further, he had no free time during his St. Petersburg visit to have seen such schoolfellows—the day after he allegedly took poison, he wrote a letter inquiring about possible dates for a trip to Odessa. Meanwhile, four physicians gave cholera as the cause of Tchaikovsky's death.

Not only did he not contract cholera deliberately, he had no fatal obsession for a young nephew, as Klaus Mann claimed in a 1935 novel, *Pathetic Symphony*. The musicicologist Richard Taruskin has noted that in the wake of the Oscar Wilde trial critics began to describe the composer as "pathological" and "hysterical," suggesting that his manly Beethovenian forms were weak and effeminate. Nonsense, Ross retorts, for the composer was not neurotic nor hysterical in the least. As Poznansky showed, Tchaikovsky was a proud, aristocratic, libidinous person who, despite a disastrous marriage and "various silly flings with peasant boys," at the end of his life had an inspiring electricity in his mind and his creative works. {*The Advocate*, 19 August 1997; CE; JM; RAT; RE; TRI; TYD}

Tchekov, Anton Pavlovich: See entry for Chekhov.

TEACHING

• On the subject of teaching: If you see a turtle atop a fence, you know it didn't get there on its own.

—Anonymous

"I never thought of myself as a teacher," a retired English department chairman from New Canaan High School in Connecticut has observed. "Students were not assigned to me in order that I, the fountain of all knowledge, could have them memorize textbooks. Nor was I a know-it-all professor, one who would require that they take notes about whatever ideas I might profess, then be tested to make sure they had been awake. Rather, I preferred the role of a mentor, a guide, a counselor, a friend. The classroom was a laboratory, not a room for grade-grubbing. Examinations, yes, included tests over factual material: 'When did Sophocles and Shakespeare write, who came first, and what did they write?' But the examinations also included the pragmatic: 'Antigone or Hamlet—which says the most to you at this time in your life, and why? Your essay will be read with attention to how well you communicate your ideas.'"

As to how one best prepares to be a teacher, the person responded, "Others might point to John Dewey's books or to education classes, but my approach has simply been to imitate those few teachers who managed to inspire me over the years."

Tead, Ordway (1891–1973)

A naturalist and a humanist, Tead in the 1950s was an editor of social and economic books for Harper & Brothers. While on the Columbia University staff, he wrote, "Toward the Knowledge of Man, an Unorthodox Approach to College Studies," for *Main Currents*. Basically, he liked Paul Valéry's "fecundity of opposites," or the value one receives when probing the reasons why others hold opposite views. On the one hand, he found merits in the arguments of the various either-or groups: absolutism or relativism; objectivity or commitment; authority or freedom; egoism or altruism; the state and other large corporate organizations or the individual; the secular or the sacred. On the college level, he finds that studies need to identify and clarify the elements of this inevitable problem of world conflict among plural value systems. He asks if the public schools and colleges are "godless" in some detrimental way. He asks what is the nature of the sacred, and is there in our thought too sharp and rigid a dualism. He asks if scientific humanism is enough or if the sacred helps by giving height and depth and universality of meaning to the human career. The secular humanist view, he laments, can be too imperious, too apt to overlook the basic values inherent in the religious quests. For him, "a religious way of life" includes creativity, flux, permanency, aloneness, dependency, tranquility, orderliness, community and fraternal love, beauty, meditation, value, restoration (or redemption), freedom, and an innate imperative. As did the Hindu philosopher Sarvepalli Radhakrishnan, whose *Recovery of Faith* (1955) he liked, Tead attempted to reconcile the either-or camps of thinkers, finding much in religion to be admired but finding much in secular humanism also to be admired. In 1969, Tead wrote *Instincts in Industry*. {WAS, 23 January 1957}

Teagle, Jeffrey J. (20th Century)

Teagle heads the General Assembly of Unitarian and Free Christian Churches (1-6 Essex Street, Strand, London, WC2R 3HV, England). (See entry for General Assembly of Unitarian and Free Christian Churches.)

Tedder, Henry Richard (Born 1850)

Tedder in 1873 and 1874 was librarian to Lord Acton. He then became librarian to the Athenaeum Club. In addition to organizing the First International Conference of Librarians, he became President of that body. Besides many contributions to the *Dictionary of National Biography*, the *Encyclopedia Britannica*, and other volumes, he edited the continuation of Herbert Spencer's *Descriptive Sociology*. Tedder is a member of the Rationalist Press Association. {RAT}

Tee, Bob (20th Century)

Tee in Britain is active with the Leeds and District Humanist Group.

Teeple, Howard Meade (1911–)

Teeple, author of *How Did Christianity Really Begin* (1992), is interested in the historical-archeological approach to Christian origins. A former fundamentalist, he has written *Historical Approach to the Bible* (1982) and *The Noah's Ark Nonsense* (1978).

TEESIDE (England) HUMANISTS

For information, write J. Cole, 94 High Street, Norton, Stockton-on-Tees, telephone 01642 559418; or telephone R. Wood at 01740 650861.

Teimourian, Hazhir (20th Century)

Teimourian, a journalist and broadcaster, specizlises in the Middle East. In Birmingham, England, at the centenary conference of the Rationalist Press Association in 1999, Teimourian spoke on "Fundamentalism in the Next Century." He signed Humanist Manifesto 2000.

Tela, Josephus: See the entry for Joseph Webbe.

Telesio, Bernardino (1509–1590)

Telesio, born of a noble Italian family, was a philosopher known for his optical discoveries and for his new opinions in philosophy. He wrote *On the Nature of Things According to Proper Principles* (1565), opposing the Aristotelian doctrine in physics and employing mathematical principles to explain nature. Telesio's works were placed on the *Index* but were published in Venice despite complains by the clergy. {BDF}

Telle, Reinier (1578–1618)

Telle, or Regnerus Vitellius, was a Dutch humanist who translated Servetus's *On the Errors of the Trinity* (1620). {BDF}

Teller (20th Century)

Teller, of the comedy team of Penn and Teller, in addition to being a magician is an accomplished musician. Asked by Chris

Carter, creator of "The X-Files," if he believed in God, Teller as well as Penn replied no. "Do any scientists believe in God?" they were asked. "None of the important ones," they humorously responded.

However, he was quoted in the New England Skeptics Society newsletter (Summer 1998) as saying, "Atheists do look for answers to existence itself. They just don't make them up." Asked if even the most hardened atheist doesn't have to believe, Teller answered, "I might qualify as the most hardened atheist, and I have not the slightest need to believe in stuff that is not in some way verifiable. I believe in art, mind you. I don't believe that art is supernatural. I think that beauty and humor are wonderful things, and quite important to us—in fact, one of the major distinguishing features between us and some of the lesser species. My mother, who is eighty-nine now, says, 'Oh, you know, I see these old people going to church, and I really envy them. It must be so consoling for them to be able to believe in that stuff. [Laughs] I think she genuinely envies people who are suckers in the sense that there are some things that might be a little easier to confront. It's not going to change her point of view, because it doesn't make any sense to her. It seems like non-sense. And it is!" [Laughs]

In the team act, Penn is the verbal one, Teller the one who comically does not speak but plays piano expertly.

On the Web: <www.theness.com/teller.html>. (See entry for Penn Jillette.) {E}

Teller, Woolsey (20th Century)

Taller, once an associate editor of *The Truth Seeker*, wrote, "How can men whose diet is intellectual sawdust and who can't tell us the size of a feather or an angel's wing, or the length of Lucifer's tail, expect to enlighten us on such matters as burning forever hereafter, or whether men should be sprinkled or dunked?"

During World War II, he wrote, "In a poll taken by the Armed Forces Radio Service, our men under arms are not at all partial to religious music. Popular music registered 38.3%; comedy-variety, 25%; and light concern music, 10.8%. Religious music trailed the list, with the insignificant showing of 2.5%." . . . As for family values, he noted that "Religious 'morals' are concerned not with justice and everyday decency, but with whether a man should eat pork or not, whether he should eat meat on Friday, or whether, after brawling in a tavern or seducing a minor, he can get forgiveness by a priest." Woolsey wrote *The Atheism of Astronomy* (1938) and *Essays of an Atheist* (1945). {FUS}

Temple, William [Sir] (1628–1699)

A famed English diplomat, Temple wrote an essay, "Of Ancient and Modern Learning" (1690), which precipitated a famous "ancients versus moderns" controversy, leading Swift to write *The Battle of the Books* (1697). Temple was just one of several eminent public men who were accused of being deists. Bishop Burnet has a description in which he writes, "He had a true judgment in affairs, and very good principles with relation to government, but in nothing else. He seemed to think that things are as they were from all eternity; at least he thought religion was only for the mob. He was a great admirer of the sect of Confucius in China, who were atheists themselves, but left religion to the rabble." The praise of Confucius is the note of deism; and Burnet rightly held that no orthodox Christian in those days would sound it, observes Robertson. {JMR; JMRH; RAT; RE}

TEMPLE UNIVERSITY HUMANISTS

In Pennsylvania, Temple University humanists are found on the Worldwide Web at <www.secularhumanism.org/cfa/orgs.html>.

Templeton Prize for Progress in Religion

If the ultimate measure of success is money, wrote Malcolm W. Browne, religion is gaining on science. The Nobel Prizes in the sciences (which in 1998 came to $978,000 each) have been exceeded by the Templeton Prize for Progress in Religion, which in 1999 was $1,240,000. (See entry for John Templeton.) {*The New York Times*, 18 May 1999}

Templeton, Charles (20th Century)

Templeton, for two decades one of North America's most successful preachers, described in *Free Inquiry* (Winter 1997-1998) how although the Billy Graham of Canada he left the faith. He has been Executive Managing Editor of the *Toronto Star*, editor-in-Chief of *Maclean's*, and director of news and public affairs for the CTI television network. Templeton has written twelve books, hosted Canadian and American telecasts, and broadcast daily radio program, "Dialogue," with Pierre Berton for eighteen years. He wrote *Farewell to God: My Reasons for Rejecting the Christian Faith* (1996). {CA}

Templeton, Chris (20th Century)

Templeton, an experienced radio and television producer in England, has suggested to the British Humanist Association and the Rationalist Press Association that they should create humanist material to be sold to radio and television stations. He aims "to explore and advance humanist approaches to thinking and living" and believes such programs "will promote the ideals of free inquiry, social cooperation, individual responsibility, and freedom from authoritarian and supernatural beliefs." The first series he has planned has the title, "Living Without Religion."

In a December 1995 *New Humanist* interview, he outlined his plans for Humanist Horizons, a production company to make radio and television programs relating to humanism.

For his Human Horizons production company, Templeton produced a radio version of Ms. Ad de Bont's *Mirad*, a work about the Bosnian war by the Dutch dramatist. On the Web: <human-horizons@easynet.co.uk>. {*New Humanist*, August 1997}

Templeton, John [Sir] (1912–)

Templeton is the British-born investment counsellor whose foundation gives the largest monetary award, the Templeton Prize for Progress in Religion. In 1973, the first recipient was Mother Teresa, founder of the Missionaries of Charity. In 1996 the prize went to Bill Bright, head of Campus Crusade for Christ. In 1997 the $1.21-million prize was given to Pandurang Shastri Athavale, a seventy-six-year-old from Bombay who preaches *swadhyaya* (a Sanskrit word for self-study), which he says leads people to cultivate greater self-respect and love for others by believing that God dwells in everyone.

TEMPTATION

I love the girls who don't.
I love the girls who do;
But best, the girls who say, "I don't . . .
But maybe just for you."

—Willard R. Espy (1911-1999)

• Lead me not into temptation. . . .
I can find the way myself.

—Rita Mae Brown

TEN COMMANDMENTS

The Ten Commandments, as freethinkers are aware, flew in out of the sky. The Code of Hammurabi, however, can be seen at the Louvre and is an eight-foot pillar of black diorite, discovered at Susa, Iran, in 1901 by J. V. Scheil. Hammurabi was the sixth king of the first Babylonian dynasty, ruling the entire area between the Tigris and Euphrates rivers and composing the Code in the fortieth year of his reign, approximately 1910 BCE. According to the Code, woman was the equal of man. Forty-four sections provided justice and a minimum wage to workers of all classes. Priests had no privileges and were mentioned only as citizens. Any point-by-point comparison of the latter half of the Commandments with the Code, according to David L. Kent, "shows clearly how crude, vague, and ethically inadequate the Jahvist edition is." For example:

Moses: Thou shalt not kill.

Hammurabi: If a man strikes the daughter of a man and causes her to lose the fruit of her womb, he shall pay 10 shekels of silver. If a surgeon causes a man's death . . . they shall cut off his forehand. If a man strikes a man in an affray, and if he dies of the striking, he may swear, "Surely I did not strike wittingly" and pay 1/2 maneh of silver.

> Moses: Neither shall thou commit adultery.
>
> Hammurabi: If a married lady is caught lying with another man, if her husband wishes to let his wife live, the king shall let his servant live. If a man has taken himself off and there is not means for food in his house, his wife may enter another man's house; that woman shall suffer no punishment. If a woman hates her husband and states, "Thou shalt not have me," her history shall be determined in her district and, if she has kept herself chaste and has no fault, while her husband is given to going about out of doors and so has greatly belittled her, that woman shall suffer no punishment; she may take her dowry and go to her father's house.

The commandments, which serve as a basis of Mosaic Law, were allegedly given by God to Moses on Mount Sinai. Robert Korn is one of many who are not impressed by the ten, finding "the average modern high school student could write a better set of commandments than these from the Bible. . . . It seems strange that a set of commandments that condemns someone who draws pictures, works on Saturday, or covets a neighbor's ox would neglect to find fault with the drug addicted, bigoted, child molesting rapist, arsonist, and torturer."

Nicholas Tate, chief executive of a British group, the School Curriculum and Assessment Authority, called in 1995 for the development of a modern, secular Ten Commandments. So few are familiar with the old set, he reasoned, and a new set might include "punctuality," "patience," and "a sense of fair play."

Cullen Murphy, writing in *The Atlantic Monthly* (November 1996), suggested the Day of Judgment might then change to the Day of Assessment if Tate's idea was carried out. Murphy found some cynics suggested adding "Thou shalt not get caught" and "Thou shalt not get involved," whereas others questioned why the need for ten, rather than seven. As for seven, why not revise the Seven Deadly Sins as well, he added.

Religious fundamentalists with backers in the American Congress demanded in 1999 that the Ten Commandments be posted in all public schools. One Manhattan wag liked the idea: "Condemn those who place engraved statuary in their cathedrals or draw images, who work on Saturday, and who covet their neighbor's ox," he reasoned, adding that "These are far more important than condemning the bigots, the absolutists, the drug pushers, the child molesters, the arsonists, the torturers, and the homophobes."

The Catholic author Hillaire Belloc facetiously suggested, concerning the Ten Commandments, "Candidates should not attempt more than six of these." {*Secular Nation*, October-December 1998}

Tendys, John (20th Century)

Tendys, in New South Wales, was succeeded as editor of *Humanist Viewpoints* by Affie Adagio. E-mail: <jtendys@triode.net.au>. (See entry for Australian Humanists.)

TENGRI

In an early Mongolian religion, Tengri was god of the sky. {LEE}

TENNESSEE HUMANISTS

Tennessee has the following groups:

• American Humanist Association, Mid-Atlantic Region (AHA), A-140, 1 College Row, Brevard, North Carolina 28712. O. Andrews Ferguson is coordinator.

• Humanist Association of Middle Tennessee (AHA), POB 24970, Nashville, Tennessee 37202. Edward Morris is the contact. Bill Conte at 8070, Regency Drive, Nashville, Tennessee, is at (615) 646-6245. E-mail: <fcvs53a@prodigy.com>.

• Rationalists of East Tennessee (ASHS), 2123 Stonybrook Road, Louisville, TN 37777. E-mail: <ledker@aol.com> and <reality@kornet.org>. Web: <www.korrnet.org/reality/>

• University of Tennessee at Martin's Humanists: <www.secularhumanism.org/cfa/orgs.html>.

Tenney, Daniel Kent (20th Century)

Tenney, a freethinker, wrote "Jehovah Interviewed, or Orthodoxy From Headquarters" (1901). {GS}

Tennyson, Alfred Tennyson [1st Baron] (1809-1892)

The first Lord Tennyson, and the most famous English poet of the Victorian age, was a profound spokesman for the ideas and values of his times. He once wrote, "It is inconceivable that the whole universe was merely created for us who live in this third-rate planet of a third-rate son."

He was the son of an intelligent but unstable clergyman in Lincolnshire. In 1850, Tennyson became poet laureate, and in 1853 he was made a peer. He had not married until 1850, the stated reason for the delay being his poverty that was caused by the disinheritance of the Somersby Tennysons in favor of his socially ambitious uncle Charles Tennyson. R. B. Martin, however, suggested in *Tennyson: The Unquiet Heart* (1980) that Alfred feared the "black blood" of the Tennysons, a notoriously melancholic and unstable family, and suspected that he, like his father, suffered from epilepsy.

Although expressions of love between men and androgynous characters are found in his early poetry, Tennyson was heterosexual, had many unrequited romantic attachments to women during his twenties and thirties, and in his forties married Emily Sellwood, with whom he later had two children. "In Memoriam," written for his beloved friend Henry Hallam portrays a chaste male love. So does his "Mort d'Arthur" (1842), in which the great medieval king is attended by a loving attendant Sir Bedivere, in whose arms he dies. Also, so does "The Holy Grail" (1869), in which King Arthur meets a "beautiful" Sir Galahad and in which Sir Percivale fails to find the Grail but does not fall into the clutches of the monk with whom he ends, one who tries unsuccessfully, in the words of the University of California's Donald E. Hall, "to elicit an admission of love from Percivale."

Tennyson was a member of the Metaphysical Society, at which one of his long poems on pantheism was delivered. McCabe wrote that Tennyson was severely condemned by British freethinkers for his *Promise of May* and his use of theistic language, leading preachers to quote him as an orthodox Christian. "But there is ample evidence," adds McCabe, "that he was a pantheist and skeptical about a future life. Allingham who knew him well so testifies in his *Diary*, and his son reluctantly confirms this in his biography of his father. Dr. Jowett says the same, and the cautious trimmer Masterman, who wrote a book on his religion, has to admit it. Tennyson received the 'communion' shortly before he died, but his son admits that he protested that he did not take in the Church sense, and a few days later he said of the pantheist Giordano Bruno, 'His view of God is in some ways mine.' Bruno, of course, had been burned at the stake for heresy."

Tennyson was buried in Westminster Abbey, and a biography by his son Hallam appeared in 1897. (See entry for Joseph Warren Beach.) {GL; JM; RAT; TYD}

Tenuta, Judy (20th Century)

Tenuta, the author of *The Power of Judyism* (1991), is a satirist whose comic television performances put one into a joyous Spike Jones mood.

> As you know [she has explained], I was not born. I am the Eternal Goddess, the Aphrodite of the Accordion. Once, at the dawn of time (before Nintendo), I sprouted from the left nostril of Toadra, Goddess of the Horny Water Lily. My father, Blowhard, God of Boxer Shorts, just stood there like a troglodyte on wheels and chanted, "Right on time, slime," as I popped out of my mom's pulchri-

tudinous proboscis into a patch of petunias. Thus I was christened "The Petite Flower."

The Petite Flower then finds that "all men are begging to pollinate me." Calling herself "a major cult figurine," she says she is a Saint ("I have the power to bleed from my hands and talk to small animals, especially critics.") who thinks of the Pope as a "guy in a dress."

Recalling her early years when laughing was not allowed in the living room, "We had to wait until Sunday mass, when the priest asked for money. Right, Pop, I really have a quarter for your Cadillac. I was so religious that at the dinner table every Easter I'd shout, 'Jesus rose from the dead, have a chocolate egg.' Then of course I had to go to confession; of course I would confess things I did not do, because I would listen to other trolls and their sins sounded a lot better."

She parodies writers of advice columns, and she undermines our preoccupation with fatness, thinness, God, respectability, the suburbs, celebrities, food, and sex. When the U. S. Navy started fretting about gays aboard ships, she quipped, "Like there would be a Navy without them!"

Tenuta is a freethinker with an unforgettable sense of humor. {Fred Whitehead, *Freethought History* #22, 1997}

TERATOLOGY

Thomas Jefferson's view, that it is self-evident that all men are created equal, is inspiring to secular humanists and teratologists, who interpret Jefferson to mean that all are equal under the law. Teratology is the study of biological malformations. Teratologists do not think in terms of "physical imperfections" or "mistakes of nature." Rather, the teratologist observes *very special people* such as the following:

• Chang and Eng, "the original Siamese twins joined at the chest for life," who married sisters, set up separate homes, and fathered twenty-two children between them;

• Myrtle Corbin, who had two lower bodies, bore three children with one and two with the other;

• John Merrick, the so-called "Elephant Man" whose neurofibromatosis caused tumors to grow around the nerves under his skin and in his bones and who was dragged from town to town and from fair to fair as if a strange beast in a cage . . . but who once was visited by Queen Alexandra—then Princess of Wales—who sat by his chair and talked to him as to a person she was glad to see;

• Grace Gilbert, one of many bearded ladies who were shunned by the general population and forced to make a living by being exhibited at circuses;

• Frieda Pushnick, who although born without arms and legs was able to type and sew;

• Francesco Lentini, who used his third leg for soccer;

• Johnny Eck, the legless runner (on his hands) who said, "To ask me if I'm sorry I have no legs is like asking an Eskimo if he's sorry he never tasted an artichoke";

• Charles Tripp, who had no hands but used his feet as hands;

• Eli Bowen, who had no legs but had feet;

• The Tocci brothers, who were two down to the sixth rib but only one person with two legs below;

• Tom Thumb, whom President Abraham Lincoln knew as the smallest human of that time and who at his death of a stroke was three feet four inches tall and weighed seventy pounds;

• Luciz Aarate, the Mexican-born woman who was under twenty inches tall and weighed but five pounds;

• Robert Wadlow, a giant who was 8' 11.1" tall;

• Jean Libbera, who had a miniature twin called Jacques that grew out of his body;

• Carl Unthan, the armless fiddler who perfored in Vienna with Johann Strauss conducting.

All the above were termed "freaks" by hoi polloi. Humanists, however, consider *natural*—specimens of nature—any so-called oddities of any of the various organisms in plant or human life. We all are humans, whether we are giants, dwarfs, midgets, hairy, legless, having two penises, having two vaginas, having no eyes or three eyes, having one breast or three breasts, having three legs or four legs, having green eyes, being homosexual or bisexual, being left-handed or right-handed, being large- or thin-lipped, having red hair, etc. We are all humans whether or not we lack such variations and, instead, more closely resemble individuals featured in commercial advertising, dramatic productions, and movies. (See entries for Exceptional People and for Frederick Drimmer, Very *Special People, the Struggles, Loves, and Triumphs of Human Oddities*, (1973) and Leslie Fiedler, *Freaks* [1993].)

Terence (Publius Terentius Afer) (c. 175 or 195–c. 159 B.C.E.)

Terence, the Roman writer of comedies, penned the famous humanistic saying, "I am a man, and nothing that concerns mankind do I deem a matter of indifference to me." {CE}

Teresa (Mother) (1910–1997)

Agnes Goxha Bojaxhiu, the Albanian known in Catholic circles as Mother Teresa, won the Nobel Peace Prize in 1979. She is one of the Church's most vocal exponents of the total ban on artificial methods of birth control. At the age of eighty-three in Calcutta, she videotaped a message to a Catholic conference in Omaha, Nebraska, on the twenty-fifth anniversary of the church's order banning artificial birth control: "The same selfishness that wants to prevent the child by contraception will grow until it wants to kill the child already conceived. We must fight selfishness with a true, generous, and sacrificing love." Asked by the conservative Catholic Malcolm Muggeridge if "you wouldn't agree with people who say there are too many children in India?" Mother Teresa responded, "I do not agree because God always provides. He provides for the flowers and the birds for everything in the world He has created. And those little children are his life. There can never be enough."

Christopher Hitchens, in *Vanity Fair* (February 1995), is an American who writes mercilessly and negatively about the "presumable virgin," Mother Teresa: "If M.T.'s such an innocent, how come her political timing is so thoroughly consistent and always ends up supporting either the fundamentalists or the status quo—if she's so unworldly, how come she knows men such as (publisher Robert) Maxwell and (Charles) Keating [who was found guilty of improper financial dealings during a Lincoln Savings & Loan scandal]? If she's so darn modest, why does she claim the divine warrant? If she's so sweet and tender, why did she say that no family using contraception should be allowed to adopt a child? If she's so nonideological, why did she say that the Inquisition was right and Galileo was wrong?"

Hitchens added that when Dr. Robin Fox, the editor of *The Lancet* visited her Home for the Dying in Calcutta, he found that "patients admitted to the home are not being properly investigated or treated and that those in pain are being denied powerful analgesics." The sign on the morgue reads, in English, "I AM ON MY WAY TO HEAVEN." Dr. Fox wrote of his visits: "There are doctors who call in from tie to time but usually the sisters and volunteers (some of whom have medical knowledge) make decisions as best they can. I saw a young man who had been admitted in poor shape with high fever, and the drugs prescribed had been tetracycline and paracetamol. Later, a visiting doctor diagnosed probably malaria and substituted chloroquine. Could not someone have looked at a blood film? Investigations, I was told, are seldom permitted. . . . Mother Teresa prefers providence to planning; her rules are designed to prevent any drift towards materialism. . . . I was disturbed to learn that the formulary includes no strong analgesics." Her hostel for homeless men with HIV follows her philosophy of penance through suffering—the men were not allowed to watch the Olympics (xbecause they were making their "Lenten sacrifice"), nor could they smoke, drink, or have visits from close friends.

Other critics, Arthur C. Clarke included, have complained that she helps to exacerbate the world's overpopulation problem, particularly, in all places, India. Indumati Parikh, for example, has called her "a disaster for India." Similarly, law clerk Debasis Bhattachariya in Calcutta, where she worked with the poor and received the Nobel Prize committee's attention, has said, "We believe that Mother Teresa is not at all any better than all the other godmen and godwomen, because she helps to place a more kindly mask on the overall exploitation in our society." Furthermore, Indian freethinkers entirely disapprove of her recognizing India's caste system, even tacitly.

In April 1966, Mother Teresa told *Ladies' Home Journal* that Princess Diana would be better off when free of her marriage, adding, "It is good that it is over. Nobody was happy anyhow," a statement which Christopher Hitchens says supports his view that he consoles "the rich and powerful, allowing them all manner of indulgence, while preaching obedience and resignation to the poor." Further, Hitchens points out that Mother Teresa makes no real effort at medical or social relief, "and that her mission is religious and propagandistic and includes surreptitious baptism of unbelievers."

To some, in short, Mother Teresa can do no wrong. To others, she is a prime example of wrong. (See entries for Bill Baird and Christopher Hitchens. The entry for Susan Shields describes the nun's "house of illusions." For a review of the Hitchens book by Barbara Smoker, see *New Humanist*, February 1996. Anne Sebba's *Mother Teresa: Beyond the Image* is reviewed by Charlotte Franklin in *New Humanist* December 1997.) {CE; *The New York Review of Books,* 19 December 1996}

Terry, William Henry (1836–1913)

Terry, a London-born freethinker, Unitarian, bookseller, clairvoyant, herbalist, and spiritualist, arrived in Melbourne, Australia, in 1853. In 1857, he discovered spiritualism and was editor from 1870 to 1905 of *The Harbinger of Light*, a publication described as a monthly journal devoted to "zoistic science," freethought, spiritualism, and "the harmonial philosophy." A bookshop he started served as headquarters for the Victorian Association of Spiritualists, whose platform was used for activities by the early freethinkers. Spiritualism at that time was considered the first stepping stone away from Christian orthodoxy. Terry, who was known as the "Father of Australian Spiritualism," also was a fellow of the Theosophical Society in Australia. {SWW}

Terzian, Yervant (20th Century)

Terzian, who is David C. Duncan Professor in the Physical Sciences at Cornell University, signed Humanist Manifesto 2000.

Tessler, Albert Denis (1900–1996)

Tessler, a pianist, composer, and humanist, died at the age of ninety-six.

Testa, Giacinto (19th Century)

Testa was an Italian author who wrote *Storia di Gesù di Nazareth* (1870), a curious work maintaining that Jesus was the son of Giuseppe Pandera, a Calabrian of Brindisi. {BDF}

TESTAMENT

"Testify," "testimony," "intestate" have a common origin in *testis*, the diminutive *testiculus* referring to one's testicles. During the time of the Roman Empire, a man at court covered himself by folding his hand on his testicles, his most prized possession, and literally swore to tell the truth.

TESTICLE

> • When Voltaire was asked why no woman has ever written a tolerable tragedy, "Ah (said the Patriarch), the composition of a tragedy requires testicles."
>
> —Letter from **Lord Byron** to **John Murray**, 2 April 1817

A testicle is a testis, the reproductive gland in the male vertebrate. Testicles contained within the scrotum are the sperm-secreting organs described in English as far back as 1425, then in reference to their unusual swelling during some sickness. Justamond in 1785 erroneously wrote that "It is very certain and has often been observed that the Hottentot men have but one testicle. According to Rudolph Bell in *How To Do It* (1999), Renaissance Italian wives were advised to tie up one of a husband's testicles before having intercourse, the best time for balling being early in the day.

Some contemporary female freethinkers have been heard, slightly gesticulating as they whispered, that male freethinkers of their acquaintance do far too much testiculating, too little anything else. "All balls!" the males could respond after 1931, when the interjection meaning "nonsense" was held by a non-puritanical court to be non-obscene.

TETRAGRAMMATON

For reasons of reverence, Jews found ineffable, or not to be uttered, the name of the god of Israel. Jehovah originally was pronounced Yahweh (Jahve). When first the vowels were inserted into the Hebrew Bible in the 7th century, the vowels of the "*a*D*o*N*a*Y," or "Lord," were written with the consonants YHWH. This word was to be substituted when reading aloud. As a result, a transliteration of the resulting hybrid, according to R. B. Y. Scott, who taught at the United Theological College in Montreal, Canada, "first came into use in the 14th century through the failure of Christian scholars to recognize the origin and purpose of the vocalization; it has now acquired by usage independent standing in English." Those four letters, YHWH, are called a tetragrammaton, and the name is never supposed to be pronounced save with the vowels of Adonai or Elohim. {ER}

TEUTHOLOGY

Architeuthis, the giant squid, is one of more than fifty thousand species in the phylum Mollusca. Early legends of the kraken and the sea serpent have been described in Jules Verne's *Twenty Thousand Leagues Under the Sea*. A squid expert—a teuthologist—knows that the creature lives only in the deep ocean where it is icily cold and dark. It does not rise to the surface unless it is dying or already dead.

Richard Ellis's *The Search for the Giant Squid* (1998) illustrates the fascination of teuthology. Although the largest Architeuthis can grow to a known length of sixty feet, little is known about this animal, one of the largest on Earth. Ellis found it has eyes as big as dinner plates, is without eyelids, and if eaten tastes like household cleaner because it contains so much ammonium chloride. In a humanistic overture to this fellow animal, Ellis asks that we "envision the giant squid lurking almost invisibly in the blackness of the depths, its amazing eyes able to pick out the tiniest light or movement, its muscular tentacles shooting out to capture its unsuspecting prey."

TEUTONIC GODS: See the entry for Germanic Religion.

TEXAS HUMANISTS, FREETHINKERS, ATHEISTS

Texas has the following groups:

• American Atheist Newsletter is no longer coming from Austin, Texas. Ellen Johnson in 1997 did revive the publication. However, some groups, such as the Atheist Community of Austin, refused to affiliate, citing as their concerns the American Atheist's corporate structure's lack of democracy, its financial secrecy, its future direction, and an alleged lack of real benefits from affiliation. Johnson's newsletter, however, continued to portray Madalyn O'Hair as an atheist heroine and cited the need for continuing the organization. American Atheists Inc. has since moved to Box 5733, Parsippany, New Jerseey 07054-6733. On the Web: <www.atheists.org/>.

• American Humanist Association, Mid South Region (AHA) A-J2, 1301 Richmond Avenue, Houston, Texas 77006. Steven Schafersman is the contact. E-mail: <frankprahl@earthlink.net>.

• Atheist Community of Austin's e-mail: <tankgirl@swbell.net>. On the Web: <http://www.atheist-community.org>. In November 1998, the group voted against affiliation with American Atheists, Inc.

• Atheist Experience is a Sunday 9 a.m. call-in show on Austin public access TV.

• Atheist Network (Atheist Alliance), POB 130898, Houston, Texas 77219. Gipson Arnold is its president (713) 686-6310.

• Atheists and Freethinkers United, 1730 Clydesdale, Louisville, Texas 75267. Gene Geirman is its president.

• Corpus Christi freethinkers can be contacted by e-mailing Brian Meyer <bmmagic@earthlink.net> or Kathy Risinger at <steigener@aol.com>.

• Dallas/Ft. Worth Metroplex Secular Humanists, 3616 Bryce Ave. (26-B), Fort Worth, TX 76107 (817) 737-8190

• Dial a Gay Atheist: (713) 880-4242

• Dial-the-Atheist in Austin: (512) 458-5731

• Ethical Culture Fellowship of Austin can be contacted at (512) 306-1111, <ccfa@usa.net>, and <http://www.main.org/cc>.

• Freethinkers Association of Central Texas (ASHS), PO Box 160881, San Antonio, TX 78280; (210) 491-6829. Contacts: Blake Olson, Don Lawrence at:
<blakeo@flash.net> and <lawdon99@earthlink.net>.
On the Web: <http://www.geocities.com/Athens/Forum/8317>.

• Freethought Forum is an 11:00 Tuesday morning program on San Antonio public access TV.

• Houstonians for Secular Humanism, PO Box 925872, Houston, TX 77292 (713) 864-0363. Daniel Strain's e-mail:
<dts2000@flash.net>. On the Web: <http://www.flash.net/~dts2000>.

• Human Concerns Center (AHA), 7481 Daingerfield, Dallas, Texas 75227. H. Bruce Hunter is the contact.

• Humanist Association of Montgomery County, 224 Dawns Edge, Montgomery, Texas 77356. Phone (409) 447-4745. Ralph D. Davis is President.

• Humanists Involved in Greater Houston (HIGH)(AHA), POB

5888, Pasadena, Texas 77508.

• Humanists of Austin (AHA), POB 4721, Austin, Texas 78765. Steve Bratteng is the contact.

• Humanists of Greater Dallas, 7417 Alto Caro Drive, Dallas, Texas 75248; phone (214) 980-7706. Dick Nelson is a contact member.

• Humanists of Houston (AHA), 8423 Burwood Park Drive, Spring, Texas 77379. Kyle Nagel is the contact. (713) 479-6829. Robert Finch, a contact at 211 Lombardy Drive, Sugar Land, Texas 77478. Phone (713) 491-1608. E-mail: <frankprahl@earthlink.net>.

• Lufkin Area Freethinkers and humanists can contact Lou Cable at <skeptic@inu.net> or <http://www.inu.net/skeptic>.

• Metropolex Atheists, Arlington, Texas. Contact Colin Sewards at (817) 473-8213.

• North Texas Church of Freethought, Dallas-Fort Worth, Texas (817) 461-2145. E-mail: <church@freethought.org>. On the Web: <http://church.freethought.org>.

• Post-Christian Support Group. E-mail: <postxian@aol.com> and <JCnot4me@aol.com>

• Secular Humanist Association of San Antonio (ASHS), POB 160881, San Antonio, Texas 78280. Jimmie Barnes is the President. The newsletter is *The Alternative Approach.*

• Texas A&M Atheists and Agnostics are on the Web: <http://atheist.tamu.edu/~aasg>.

• *The Texas Atheist,* edited by Howard Thompson, is on the Web at <http://gofreemind@aol.com>.

• Texas Hill Country Freethinkers. Contact is Julie Fisher at (210) 354-3311. E-mail: <txfreethinker@geocities.com>.

• University of Houston humanists are on the Web: <www.secularhumanism.org/cfa/orgs.html>.

• University of Texas at Austin humanists are at: <www.secularhumanism.org/cfa/orgs.html>.

• University Skeptics Society in Austin is on the Web: <www.utexas.edu/students/skeptics>.

Thackeray, William Makepeace (1811–1863)

Thackeray, the Calcutta-born English novelist, was a brilliant satirist. He left Trinity College, Cambridge, without taking a degree, because he lost some of his inheritance through gambling. During the winter of 1830–1831 he visited Weimar, where he met Goethe. By 1833 virtually all his inherited money had been lost, probably in the collapse of the Indian agency-houses. Thackeray lived in Paris from 1834 until 1837, making a meager living from journalism. There, in 1836, he married Isabella Shawe, who three years later became hopelessly insane. She was cared for by a family in Essex and survived her husband by thirty years. Thackeray sent his two young daughters to be raised by his parents in Paris, then lived the life of a clubman in London and worked to support his family. As a contributor to *Punch,* he often parodied the false romantic sentiment pervading the fiction of his day. His eldest daughter, Lady Anne Ritchie, was also an author. His younger daughter Harriet married Sir Leslie Stephen, an ordained minister who became an agnostic. Thackeray frequently wrote against the use of tobacco, including in his fiction such lines as, "Cigars introduced with the coffee, do, if anything can, make us forget the absence of the other sex." In 1841, Thackeray wrote *Comic Tales and Sketches,* followed in 1848 by the popular *Book of Snobs* and, the work which led him to become known as a major English novelist, the satirical *Vanity Fair.* (That work, inspired by a phrase from John Bunyon's *Pilgrim's Progress,* he had originally been titled *The Novel Without a Hero: Pen and Pencil Sketches of English Society*). According to McCabe, Tennyson was a theist but was skeptical about a future life. "About my future state I don't know," he was quoted as saying in Melville's *Life of Thackeray.* In *The Letters of Dr. J. Brown,* there is a letter in which Thackeray says that he has listened to a preacher "on the evangelical dodge" and he adds, "Ah, what rubbish." Melville states that Thackeray "formed no very definite creed." (See entry for Joseph Warren Beach.) {CE; JM; RAT; RE}

Thaer, Albrecht Daniel (1752–1828)

Thaer was a German agriculturist who is said to have inspired Lessing's work on *The Education of the Human Race.* {BDF}

Thales (c. 636–c. 546 B.C.E.)

The first recorded Western philosopher, Thales reputedly founded the Milesian school of philosophy in Ionia, a Greek province on the Aegean coast of what is now Turkey. Although little is known about his teachings, he is said to have concerned himself with the "nature of things," with understanding the elements and origins of the physical world. Denying the approaches used by mythology in explaining the physical world, he taught that nature is composed of one basic stuff, which he thought to be water.

It is not his answer but his approach which is significant. He is believed to have introduced geometry into Greece as well as to have predicted an eclipse of the sun in 585 B.C.E. By predicting an eclipse, Thales thus contributed to the idea that the heavens are separate from the gods. McCabe calls Thales "the first freethinker in history."

Plato's *Theaetetus* tells this tale:

> It seems that while Thales was engaged in studying the stars and gazing upwards he fell into a cistern; whereupon he was jeered at (they say) by a witty and attractive serving-wench from Thrace for being so eager to know what was happening in the sky that he did not see what was under his nose.

Matt Cherry has observed that Thales was undeterred by the jeers of saucy serving-wenches and that several younger colleagues of Thales continued his study into the "nature of things." Chief among these first philosophers were the Ionian Greeks Anaximander, Anaximenes, and Xenophanes. {CE; JM; TYD}

Thandeka (20th Century)

An African American and a Unitarian theologian, Thandeka works with various Unitarian Universalist societies on subjects relating to race. In "A Conversation on Race and Class" (*World,* July-August 1998), she said she is writing a book on "race, money, and God."

THANKSGIVING DAY: See entry for Blamesgiving Day.

Thaxter, Celia (Laighton) (1835–1894)

Thaxter lived in New Hampshire where her father was a lighthouse keeper on the Isles of Shoals. She depicted the various moods of the sea in such of her works as *Poems* (1872), *Drift-Weed* (1879), and *Idyls and Pastorals* (1886). Thaxter's family ran a hotel, and she became a favorite of visiting artists and authors such as Thoreau, Lowell, and Whittier. Thaxter was a Unitarian. {EG}

Thayer, Dorothea (20th Century)

Thayer was secretary-treasurer of the New York City Humanists when Warren Allen Smith founded the group and led it until 1953. She then continued when Ingersoll's granddaughter, Eva Ingersoll Wakefield, succeeded to the post. Thayer never missed a meeting, joyfully greeted such speakers as Erich Fromm and George Axtelle, and helped considerably to give the group a feeling of togetherness and purpose. A person with little money to spare, she contributed heavily to humanist causes both in time and resources.

Thayer, Sylvanus (1785–1872)

Founder of the U.S. Military Academy, Thayer was its superintendent from 1817 to 1833. He was a Unitarian. {U; UU}

Thayer, Thomas Baldwin (1812–1886)

Thayer's *Theology of Universalism* (1862) has been called "the most thorough and systematic treatment of Universalist theology before the Civil War." He edited *Universalist Quarterly* from 1884 to 1886. One of the intellectual leaders of mid-19th-century Universalism, he also wrote *The Origin and History of the Doctrine of Endless Punishment* (1855). {U&U}

Thayer, V(ivian) T(row) (1886–1979)

Thayer, a director of Ethical Culture Schools (1928–1947), was trusted by Felix Adler although Thayer was a Deweyite and Adler disliked Dewey. He signed both Humanist Manifesto I and II. A progressive educator, he wrote *Religion in Public Education* (1943) and *Formative Ideas in American Education* (1965). In 1964 he was named Pioneer Humanist of the Year by the American Humanist Association. In 1969, he was recipient of the John Dewey Society award for distinguished lifetime service to education. (See entry for Ethical Culture.) {EU, Howard B. Radest; FUS; HM1; HM2; HNS}

THE FIRST NATIONAL CHURCH OF THE EXQUISITE PANIC, INC.: See the entry for dadaist Robert Delford Brown.

THE GREATEST STORY EVER SOLD

The cover of *Thee Freethinker* (May 1998) was entitled "The Greatest Story Ever Sold," a take-off on religionists' reference to the Bible and implying the adeptness of its early marketing.

The Residents (20th Century)

The Residents are a 26-year-old band whose members' identities have never been divulged. In photographs and performances, they appear with giant, veiny eyeballs on their heads, crowned with top hats.

The San Francisco-based group has dealt with everything from fascism to Elvis Presley, but its "Wormwood" (1999) specifically mocks religion. In their appearances they sometimes sing, to the tune of "There's No Business Like Show Business," a song, "God business is our business!" Other songs emphasize the Bible's cruelty to women, as in the *Genesis* story of Dinah, whose marriage causes her brothers-in-law to kill all the men and enslave all the women of her town. Or about God's brutality: ordering Abraham to kill his son, rejecting Cain's offering of grain, transforming Lot's wife into a pillar of salt. Their female singer (Jephthah) intones, "I'm gonna die with no tears in my eyes, 'cause God digs my daddy!" The performance might end with a disorderly version of "That Old Time Religion," the words including, "It was good for making millions/selling platitudes to pilgrims." The group typefies an end-of-the-century freedom to attack what previously had been called blasphemy. {Ben Ratliff, *The New York Times*, 7 April 1999}

The The (20th Century)

In 1979 The The was formed by then seventeen-year-old Matt Johnson. During an online chat session in 1995, a participant observed that the song "I Saw the Light" is a long distance from "I Ain't Never Been to Church or Believed in Jesus Christ" and asked if Johnson's religious feelings had changed. Replied Johnson, "I'm a born-again agnostic!" {CA; E}

THE UNITARIAN

The Unitarian is a monthly publication of the British Unitarians. (See entry for General Assembly of Unitarian and Free Christian Churches.)

THEISM

- Polytheism—ancient man's invention
- Monotheism—14th Century BCE retro-invention
- Theism—successful Middle Ages commercial idea
- Zerotheism—21st Century outlook

—**Jun Sczesnoczkawasm**

Theism in philosophy and religion is the belief in a personal God. Atheism is its denial. Unlike pantheism, theism refuses to identify God and the universe. Unlike deism, theism rejects the insistence on the purely transcendent nature of God, holding that God is at once immanent and transcendent. William of Ockham at the end of the Middle Ages denied God's existence could be proved solely by reason. Those who agreed have been Kant, the Barthians, existentialists, and empiricists who reject the possibility of metaphysics in any form. However, some philosophers and theologians remain theists, including Étienne Gilson, Jacques Maritain, E. L. Mascall, and A. M. Farrer. Robert Coles, an essayist and psychiatrist, wrote of his own "spiritual" quest in *The Secular Mind* (1999), an example of a scientist who is interested in the sacred but not that of the contemporary right in the United States.

Numbers of American authors are theists: Protestants, such as Toni Morrison and John Updike; Jews such as Saul Bellow and Isaac Bashevis Singer; Catholics such as G. K. Chesterton and Seamus Justin Heaney. Popular writer Stephen King on "60 Minutes" (2 August 1998) mentioned his belief "in a personal God."

Asked about humanism, the following authors responded to the present author:

- Faith Baldwin: My belief is simple. It is in God and His spirit in mankind. It is in man and his struggle. It is in the Golden Rule and in the valor of men, however ignoble their shortcomings. {WAS, 11 February 1951}

- Paul de Kruif: Humanism connotes to me only what can be read in *St. Matthew*, 5, verses 38 to 48. Forgive me if this is old-fashioned. I know it will leave agnostics and eggheads cold. What it teaches is an ideal, not attainable, but worth striving for. If one so strives, then in my book one is a humanist. {WAS, 1 November 1956}

- Alan Dowling: I am looking forward to neo-supernaturalistic humanism with intense eagerness. {WAS, 28 February 1951}

- Lynn Harold Hough: My book, *Christian Humanism and the Modern World*, best answers the question. In a general way, I belong with Babbitt and More (see my book, *Great Humanists*). Louis Mercier's *American Humanism and the New Age* deals with my position. My books, *The Christian Criticism of Life* and *The Meaning of Human Experience* were Religious Book of the Month Club selections. . . . My book, *The Meaning of Human Experience*, remains the fullest statement of my position. {WAS, 21 August 1956}

- Keith Scott Latourette: I am not entirely clear as to what reply to give, for I am not sure that I belong under any classification of humanism. If I fall under any one of the seven categories in your scheme, it would be under the fourth, namely theistic humanism. Obviously I am a Christian and a Protestant and have a deep concern for human values. I believe profoundly that with the help of God as He has revealed Himself in Christ, individual men can become what Saint Paul describes as "heirs of God, joint heirs with Jesus Christ," that such are what the New Testament calls "the light of the world" and "the salt of the earth," and that through them many of the chronic ills that beset mankind and indeed the animal creation can be mitigated and some of them removed. I do not expect a perfect society in history. That must wait for a stage beyond the boundaries of time and place. But we do have the high privilege of working toward a society that is better than what we have now. {WAS, 18 April 1956}

- Denise Levertov: Theistic humanism would probably come closest to my position, though I don't think or speak of myself *as* a theistic humanist. We human being are far too self-important in any case. {WAS, 15 May 1989}

- Jacques Maritain: (commenting on his new book): (Integral humanism), considering man in the integrality of his natural and his supernatural being and setting no limits *a priori* or the descent of divinity into man, can also be called Humanism of the Incarnation.

- E. L. Mayo: When it comes to cold prose, I suspect that most poets have difficulty in stating their philosophic views. It is notorious, of course, among poets like Coleridge and Santayana, who have also written philosophy, that their philosophy is often at odds with their poems; and I suspect that the principle works the other way, i.e., from poetry to philosophy. I know where I began. In the twenties I thought of myself as a disciple of Irving Babbitt and Paul Elmer More. I am not a Harvard man, but I have attended lectures by both men and am still deeply impressed by their courage and learning, courage especially, for it took plenty of it to stem as they did the whole tide of scientific and literary opinion of the twenties. At the time, in 1925, I wrote an early poem dedicated to Babbitt; not a very good one, I'm afraid, but it reflects my admiration of the man along with a certain skepticism about the "Inner Chec"' or "*frein vital*" which he made the cornerstone of his humanist philosophy. I suspected then as I suspect now that the Inner Check was simply Irving Babbitt himself, slightly disguised in Buddhistic trappings. T. S. Eliot, also at one time one of Babbitt's disciples, has expressed much the same view in a well-known essay.

For Irving Babbitt

Now salamander-like you thread the flame
Of Tophet with a certain decent poise,
And several friends of ours are also here
And exchange salutation. We are come
For many reasons, but a single end:
This Chastening. The newly damned
Are prone to shriek among the bluer flames.
You scorn such things as not aristocratic,
And that is well—you will go far. And now
Come, let us visit Irving in his cave.
Strange snorts, and grunts, and very heavy breathing

Are to be heard there, but of all the Hells
In Torment his is coolest. We'll discuss
The Inner Check, a thermal hardening process
For turning lava into sterner stuff
And many other better things than death.

Perhaps you have noted how the adjective "human" has undergone a sea-change in ordinary American colloquial speech, has become, in fact, a noun, the use of which somehow puts the speaker outside the biological phylum he is discussing. "Humans"—not human beings—collect in bargain basements, pack the subways, have their opinions tested by the Gallup Poll. It is a symptom no doubt; I cannot quite say of what, but I suspect that as the concept 'human' has gradually changed in contemporary metaphysics and philosophy—in Dewey's, for example—it has lost something that we used to call "spiritual values"—notions I mean that tied it up with traditional Christianity with its fixed beliefs in Original Sin, equality before God, and the rest. Insensibly, such associations as these have come to be replaced with new ones drawn from biology, economics, etc. In a word, humanity's conception of itself seems to be changing, and the "new" man is a biologico-political unit; that, as far as I can tell, is what a "human," as opposed to a human being, really is. Now, since this is a development uncongenial to me, I look about me for some means of changing it. As William Blake said, "We become what we contemplate," and if we contemplate ourselves as biologico-political mechanisms that is what we will become.

The only solution of the difficulty, it seems to me, is first to recognize that there *is* a difficulty and a serious one. The next is to face the fact that humanism, as a *historical* movement (whether in China with Confucius, in India with Buddha, or in Europe with Erasmus) has never existed as an independent system of thought but rather as a corrective and criticism of an already existent body of thought religious in nature. If not exactly a parasite, humanism has at any rate become a symbiote; and it is hard to think of it as existing as a complete philosophy in its own right. It is as though for man to remain human he must take into account factors as much beyond ordinary humanity as he himself is beyond the water-spider. Nietzsche, who was, after all, the son of a Lutheran clergyman, was quite right, I think, in maintaining that in essence man is a *bridge* between something less and something greater than his ordinary self. Religion heightens man's inner tension; humanism relaxes it; so we need both. But with a secular and naturalistic humanism alone, I doubt whether we can succeed in remaining fully human. Rather, to use a word popular with the science-fictioneers, we shall become "humanoids," creatures that look like men until they are subjected to a closer examination.

Yes, as you no doubt by this time suspect, so far as I am a humanist at all (it has always been an ambition of mine, at any rate, to *become* human), I am a theistic humanist along with William Blake, Soren Kierkegaard, and Simone Weil. {WAS, 3 August 1954}

• Howard A. Murphy: In general, I would say that my position corresponds most closely to the theistic humanism exemplified by Maritain, Niebuhr, and Tillich. Actually, my position is most clearly stated by Raynor Johnson's new book, *The Imprisoned Splendor*, which I consider one of the clearest and best statements of the place of ESP and mysticism in life. {WAS, 18 August 1954}

• Reinhold Niebuhr: I suppose it is right to put my thought in the category of "theistic humanism." {WAS, 24 March 1949}

• J. B. Priestley: My wife (Jacquetta Hawkes, the pre-historian) and I find your categories of humanism puzzling. Men like Eliot and Niebuhr do not seem to us humanists at all. Both of us reject, for varying reasons, Huxley's scientific humanism. But we do not accept Christianity. We might be described as religious persons without a religion. In this we probably follow Jung. In your categories I come closest to "theistic humanism," believing as I do that Man should not regard himself as a sort of end product and that higher levels of being exist (symbolised in the Unconscious by the archetype of deity, the "numinous," while being sceptical in my attitude towards the theologians, who talk about God as if they had been to college with him. I do not pretend to be a philosopher and am certainly no mystic, but would if necessary side with the mystics against the "scientific humanists." I have just been correcting the proofs of a little piece called "Pigs at Sea" for the September number of *Encounter*, in which I deal humorously with these various views. I hope you will see it. Of contemporary thinkers Jung, whom we know, has had the greatest influence upon my wife and me. {WAS, 26 July 1954}

• Dorothy L. Sayers: . . . Other people might reasonably include me in the category of theistic humanism; but I do not call myself a "Theistic Humanist." I call myself a Christian. . . . *All* Christians are "humanists," in the sense that they believe the individual human person to be infinitely precious in the sight of God. *No* Christian is a "humanist" insofar as that excludes belief in God. {WAS, 5 April 1956}

• Paul Scherer: The humanism that stems from the perversion of man's place in the universe brought about by the Renaissance and the Enlightenment finds no welcome to my mind. Lynn Harold Hough, whom you may know, calls himself a Christian humanist; with that I have some measure of sympathy. Harry Overstreet's statement [See entry herein.] seems to me utterly self-contradictory. If nature includes more than any of our systems of knowledge have ever included or now include, how can the only way of knowing be through the natural processes of the mind? And what if man were incapable of knowing himself apart from his relationship to God? You can see that the only contribution I should feel called on to make would be in the nature of an explosion. {WAS, 1 May 1956}

• Karl Shapiro: I believe in God, the Constitution, and poetry, in that order. What kind of Humanist does that make me? Thomas Jefferson said, "I am of a sect by myself, as far as I know." John Milton, a man of God, despised every and all churches. Both would have believed in the Constitution in my sense. And poetry too, it goes without saying. This is neither Secular nor Theological nor Humanistic, I think. {WAS, 22 February 1989}

• Russell Henry Stafford: By contrast with secularism or positivism or scientism, so widely the temper of our time—the doctrine that there is no God, nor any future that makes any difference—this other way of seeing life is what I like to call humanism: Christian humanism. Humanism, on the tongues of people who know history, does not mean the same thing as secularism. For hundreds of years it has meant a concentration of interest and effort upon the life of man in this world; because this world is where we are, and only fools will day-dream of what lies beyond while there is so much to do right now. But we are to do it by the light that comes to our souls from beyond, as light comes to our bodies from sun and moon and stars. . . . Jesus was the first Christian humanist. There is never a taint of otherworldliness in his teaching, save for faint echoes of popular folklore which he twisted for his own purpose, so that it was easy to see through. He takes the life to come for granted; "If it were not so, I would have told you," says he, as if that depressing news would be astonishing indeed to any sensible person. Then he goes on to tell and show us how to live where we are now as God's children, and not donkeys or hyenas of a larger growth. {WAS, 1 May 1956}

• Richard Wilbur: I've been a student of the humanities, and I know that my view of human capacities for greatness and corruption has been shaped in part by Renaissance art and letters. I also adhere to a religious position which is not scornful of this life or of humanity. You might there, I should think, admit me as a humanist to as many as three of your categories. It seems to me that we should not despair of any word—"democracy," for example—merely because it has various and conflicting meanings. Yet it is good to be alert to words which are in a temporary state of confusion—words such as 'experimental,' which is often applied at present to the most imitative and repetitive of our artists. Your enquiry makes it plain that "humanist," if it is to be currently useful, must be employed in clear contexts which enforce the intended sense. . . . I don't think much of atheism, because it is foolish to be sure of a non-existence. I think agnosticism an honorable state of mind. As for me, I am a theist; I know at all times that God exists and is good. Beyond that, my beliefs come and go. {WAS, 9 February 1989 and 1 December 1994}

Meanwhile, some theologians, such as Emory University's Thomas J. J. Altizer, were changing the usual meaning of theism. In 1965 he said, "We must recognize that the death of God is a historical event: God has died in our time, in our history, in our existence." However, J. C. A. Gaskin, in *Varieties of Unbelief From Epicurus to Sartre* (1989), defined theism as being "[b]elief in a single God who created and sustains the ordered universe and who also knows about and cares about each individual human being (Jews, Christians, and Muslims are all, in this sense, theists)." (For a discussion of theism, see the article by H. P. Owen in the *Encyclopedia of Philosophy*, Vol. 8; See John Updike's *The Future of Faith: Confessions of a Churchgoer*, *The New Yorker*, 29 November 1999) {CE; RE; TYD}

THEISTIC HUMANISM

The "Back to Aristotle" trend in the 1930s developed into a "Back to God" movement as well. When the former designation lost favor as a battle cry some individuals still remained who continued the second slogan, one which ordinarily has commanded respect throughout the ages and one which appeared to have a better chance of surviving.

Catholic support of neo-humanism gave that movement a substantial though temporary shot-in-the-arm, but when Catholic periodicals such as *Thought*, *Commonweal*, *America*, and the organ of the Knights of Columbus withdrew their support; and when *Bookman* and *Saturday Review of Literature* no longer showed interest, the attempted revival of classical humanism died along with its main founders. More than any other, it was Jacques Maritain who shaped Catholic thought toward humanism. At first, he was counted by neo-humanists as being within their fold. But by 1936 upon publication of *l'Humanisme Integral* it became evident that he was going to solve the Catholic dilemma over humanism by founding a separate branch of philosophy and giving it his own trademark. Speaking of it, he said, "Such a humanism, considering man in the integrality of his natural and his supernatural being and setting no limits *a priori* on the descent of divinity into man, can also be called Humanism of the Incarnation." His views were contested by many, including M. C. Otto, Roy Wood Sellars, Harold A. Larrabee, and Blodwen Davies in *New Humanist* (and later in *The Humanist*), a magazine which served as the pivoting point around which opposition to supernaturalistic, and defense of naturalistic, humanism revolved. Maritain was criticized as being anti-pragmatic, anti-naturalistic, pro-Kierkegaard, pro-Barth, and neo-Thomistic. In 1945, as pointed out in *Educational Principles of American Humanism* by J. T. Foudy, many Catholics accepted Maritain's views if they were interested in the subject of humanism. However, a few might be "common sense humanists" with Babbitt and Foerster; or "metaphysical humanists" with Hutchins and Adler; or "religious humanists" with Paul Elmer More, to repeat the terms Foudy used.

Protestants were not so united in their views. A. J. B. Balfour, as early as 1915, had warned that humanism without theism was inadvisable and, if effected, would lose more than half its value. Although most Protestants agreed, they did not agree upon how to achieve this. One of the most vociferous proponents of Protestant theistic humanism was Lynn Harold Hough, the former dean of Drew Theological Seminary. Just as materialism robs man of his dignity, he preached, so do some theologies. "God does not want to speak to man flat on his face," he wrote. "He wants man to stand erect and on his own feet." In the main, theistic humanism emphasizes human values and denies the *complete* impotence of man to work out his own salvation. Without vigorous self-effort, it is reasoned, man can never expect to achieve this salvation. But man's efforts toward that end are not entirely without support, for the good and wise God who created man is working with him all the time. Though not wholly this-worldly, the theistic humanist places little stress upon the future life. *Humanism, Another Battle Line* (1931), a symposium of ten authors edited by W. P. King, served as one of the best rallying points around which Protestant theistic humanism could group its forces. The several authors expressed deep concern over the advances being made by naturalistic humanism and summarized their views: "Our present battle is with materialism in the realm of philosophy and science; Humanism, which is religion without God; and behaviorism, which is psychology without a soul."

A constructively critical approach came in 1937 when Charles Hartshorne, a University of Chicago professor and the biographer of Alfred North Whitehead, wrote *Beyond Humanism*. He outlined the new trend toward humanism, suggesting that it was insufficient and that its proponents should go from their present positions to a type of theistic humanism which he believed could be called either "theistic naturalism" or "naturalistic theism." Hartshorne, known for his mystical profundity, received some support from those theists who could comprehend what he had written.

That which the Catholic and Protestant humanist hold in common is an adherence to Christianity, an insistence upon human values and upon man's capability of working out his salvation with his God, and a concern over the growing forces of non-theistic philosophies. Yet, other than scattered books and articles on the subject, no united action has been taken and theistic humanism as a movement has little present support. Mostly, it is confined to seminary conversation, articles of description in church magazines, and serious discussions in theological treatises. Although Paul Tillich's theistic existentialism was also a kind of theistic humanism, other theologians seldom use such terminology. {ER}

THEO- AND THE-

The roots of *theo* and *the* are Latin and Greek and mean "god" or "God." Over the centuries theists and religious institutions have developed theological studies that have invented such as the following, which are of little empirical value to secular humanists:

THEODICY

Theodicy is a theological coinage to describe "the defense of God's goodness and omnipotence in view of the existence of evil." If bad things occur, God may have done to illustrate His mysterious ways. Secular humanists find that such thinking borders on idiocy.

THEODY

A theody is a religious hymn that praises God. It is not to be confused with *threnody*, which is both a lamentation for the dead and, in animals, the rare sound made for example by a mother if any of her offspring are dying.

THEOLOGIAN

"I have only a small flickering light to guide me in the darkness of a thick forest," wrote Denis Diderot. "Up comes a theologian and blows it out."

THEOLOGICAL

"Theological," according to one of the New York City editors of *Pique*, "not only sounds like, but *is*, illogical."

THEOLOGOUMENON

If a theological statement or concept is an individual opinion rather than authoritative doctrine, it is a theologoumenon.

THEOLOGY

In Christianity, theology is the systematic study of the nature of God and His relationship with man and with the world. Judaism, which holds that God is unknowable, is not inclined toward theology. Non-believers are more apt to consider it a study leading to a huge bureaucratic expense which church officials justify through pointing out that they are fine-tuning religion by making relevant to the ordinary man-on-the-street such studies as homiletics, apologetics, polemics, metaphysics, theopneustia, religious ontology, religious epistemology, religious cosmogonies, dogmatics, etc. How else would parishioners know about grace, revelation, salvation, sacraments, immanence, symbolics, exegesis, tetragrammatoms, etc., which are so important to a person in understanding "why" he needs religion. One theologian who was a student of Cardinal Newman, Frederick W. Faber (1814–1863), inexplicably explained in his *Spiritual Conferences*, "Religious talk is a very feast to self-deceit." Another, Archdeacon Frederic William Farrar (1831–1903) of Westminster Cathedral, observed, and it is unknown whether he was pleased or displeased, "Science has had to struggle for life against the fury of theological dogmatists, but in every instance the dogmatists have been ignominiously defeated." For Baron d'Holbach, in *The System of Nature* (1770), "Theology is but the ignorance of natural causes reduced to a system." (See entry for *Bullshitus Episcopalis*.) {CE; ER; TYD}

THEOMACHIST

A theomachist resists God, the gods, and divine will. From a semantic viewpoint, *theomachist* is a snarl word, one with negative overtones.

THEOMANIA

Theomania consists of a religious madness in which the patient believes that he or she is actually the Deity or is inspired by the Deity. Psychiatrists find that theomaniacs are difficult to treat.

THEOMANCY

Individuals who can divine the future by the way oracles respond practice theomancy.

THEONOMY

Theonomy, a word based upon the Greek for "God's law," was described by an authoritative theonomist in *The Scotsman* (12 May 1997):

Theonomy applies to drunkards and gluttons and children who are violent towards their parents. This wouldn't apply to younger children. The parents would give testimony to civil magistrates and the child would be put to death on the basis of that. I would stress that it would be an absolute last resort applied to children who ignored repeated attempts at discipline.

Teaching "that murderers, homosexuals, people who have had premarital sex and even teenagers who are abusive to their parents should all be stoned to death," the group believes that capital punishment is necessary in order to deter people from certain crimes. According to *The Scotsman*, the Free Church of Scotland general Assembly Committee on Public Questions, Religion, and Morals has warned that the Church could be fertile soil for Theonomy because of the common strict theological stance of the two sects. {*The Freethinker*, June 1997}

THEOPHAGY

Theophagy is eating the god: *theos*, god; *phagein*, to eat.

The religious practice can be traced to the eating of a sacred animal in order to secure *mana*, or the god in the form of an animal. Mystery religions encouraged theophagy, and the practice is carried over into Christian practice where it is known as sacramental meal, or communion. H. R. Willoughby wrote about the subject in *Pagan Regeneration* (1929), as did Preservèd Smith in *A Short History of Christian Theophagy* (1922). In 1994, a representative sample of American Catholics was asked which statement came closest to "what you believe takes place at mass." According to the New York Times/CBS poll, only one out of three chose "the bread and wine are changed into Christ's body and blood." More than sixty percent preferred "the bread and wine are symbolic reminders of Christ." Even among theophagists going to mass regularly, more said that "symbolic reminder" came closest to their belief. Since ancient times, however, the church has taught that the bread and wine offered at mass during the sacrament of holy communion are mysteriously changed into the actual body and blood of Christ, in keeping with Jesus's words at the Last Supper. {ER}

THEOPHILANTHROPIST

A theophilanthropist (an adorer of God and of Mankind) was a member of a deistic society established in Paris during the period of the Directory aiming to institute, in place of Christianity, which had been officially abolished, a new religion of theophilanthropism affirming a deistic belief in the existence of God, in the immortality of the soul, and in virtue. After being suppressed in 1801 by Napoléon, the group members often became Freemasons.

THEOPHOBIA

Theophobia is a dread of the wrath of God, a phobia of which God is the object.

THEORY OF RELATIVITY: See entries for Albert Einstein and for String Theory.

THEOSOPHY

• Theosophy, n. An ancient faith having all the certitude of religion and all the mystery of science. The modern Theosophist holds, with the Buddhists, that we live an incalculable number of times on this earth, in as many as several bodies, because one life is not long enough for our complete spiritual development; that is, a single lifetime does not suffice for us to become as wise and good as we choose to wish to become. To be absolutely wise and good—that is perfection; and the Theosophist is so keen-sighted as to have observed that everything desirous of improvement eventually attains perfection. Less competent observers are disposed to except cats, which seem neither wiser nor better than they were last year. The greatest and fattest of recent Theosophists was the late Madame Blavatsky, who had no cat.

—**Ambrose Bierce**
The Devil's Dictionary

Theosophy as interpreted by Madame Helena Petrovna Blavatsky followed Buddhist and Brahmanic theories concerning pantheistic evolution and reincarnation. Individuals properly trained to interpret auras (symbolized by artists as an arc over a person's or a holy person's head) and other mystical symbols. Madame Blavatsky's books were accused of being fraudulent. She countered that Master Koot Hoomi, an invisible spirit which had dictated letters to her, had indeed copied a passage verbatim from a speech by Henry Kiddle, another American medium. Her followers believed she could create supernatural miracles. At the 1922 Australian Convention of Theosophists, Charles Leadbeater was accused of ventriloquism as well as pederasty, and his colleague, James Wedgwood, was seen to have visited no fewer than eighteen public lavatories in two hours. Wedgwood explained to police that he was searching for a friend he had known in a previous life.

In addition to William Butler Yeats, Vice President Henry Wallace became intrigued by Blavatsky's theosophy. Wallace was introduced to the doctrines by Yeats's friend George

W. Russell ("AE"), who was a firm believer in what he called "an order of reality which can be contacted by people who have certain types of perception.

"A direct line of descent," claims Frederick Crews, "connects Theosophy to an array of ludicrous and generally harmless New Age practices that now surround us, from astrology, crystal gazing, homeopathy, and pyramid power to Wicca nature worship, prophecy, channeling, past-life regression, goddess theology, belief in extraterrestrial visitation, and obeisance to self-designed gurus and ascended masters." Crews adds, "Although one can agree with Carl Sagan's contention, in his recent book *The Demon-Haunted World* (1996), that such fads reflect a popular revolt against science and a lamentable resurgence of superstition, it would be perverse to mention them in the same breath with Nazi ideology." (See entries for William Emmette Coleman, Helena Petrovna Blavatsky, and Annie Besant.) {Frederick Crews, "The Consolation of Theosophy," *The New York Review of Books*, 19 Sep and 3 Oct 1996; ER; RE; Peter Washington, *Madame Blavatsky's Baboon: A History of the Mystics, Mediums, and Misfits Who Brought Spiritualism to America*}

Theobold, Erwin (20th Century)

Theobold was an instructor at Pasadena City College in California when he signed Humanist Manifesto II. {HM2}

Theodoric the Great (c. 454–526)

Theodoric was King of the Ostrogoths, and the end of his reign was clouded by a quarrel with his subjects and Pope John I over the edicts of Emperor Justin I against Arianism and by his hasty execution of Boethius. An Arian himself, Theodoric was impartial in religious matters. {CE; RE}

Theodorus (c. 312 B.C.E.)

David Berman cites Theodorus along with Diagoras and Epicurus as being atheists. However, Thomas Wise in *A Confutation of the Reason and Philosophy of Atheism* denies that they atheistic. Berman makes the better argument, suggesting that "Wise wishes to conflate absolute and plain speculative atheism so as to suggest the impossibility of the latter as well as the former, and thereby eliminate Diagoras, Theodorus, etc. from the class of dangerous atheistic precedents. Thus as the passage proceeds the qualifiers 'absolute' and 'speculative' drop out, leaving the more general 'Atheists': the suggestion is that there have never been atheists in *any* respectable sense of the term." Meanwhile, according to Robertson, Diogenes Laërtius said that Theodorus was nicknamed "the God," implying an emphasis upon "the." When threatened with crucifixion, Theodorus reportedly said it mattered little whether he rotted in the ground or in the air. {BDF; JMR; JMRH; TYD}

Theophile de Viau (1590–1626)

Theophile was a French satiric poet. For the alleged publication of *Le Parnasse Satyriques*, he was accused of atheism, condemned to death, and burned in effigy. He fled and was received by the Duc de Montmorency at Chantilly, where he died. {BDF; RAT}

THERALI

A Malayalam monthly, *Therali* is at 779, Pocket 5, Mayur Vihar-1, New Delhi 110 091, India.

THERMOPYLAE

In ancient times a narrow mountain pass, Thermopylae, was used as an entrance into Greece from the north. In 480 BCE, Leonidas with his Spartans and their allies lost a heroic battle here to the Persians under Xerxes. In 279 BCE at the pass, the Greeks held back the Gauls under Brennus, who ultimately broke through. In 191 BCE, Antiochus III of Syria was defeated there by the Romans.

Steven Pressfield's novel, *Gates of Fire* (1998), tells the story of how the Persians and their allies defeated the Spartans in a battle "that saved democracy."

Thibaudeau, Antoine Claire [Count] (1765–1854)

Thibaudeau, a French historian, was a lawyer who joined the revolutionaries and, after the death of Robespierre, became President of the Council of Five Hundred. Napoleon made him a count, but he was exiled by the royalists, returning after the Revolution of 1830 to devote himself to writing. His chief work was *Histoire generale de Napoléon Bonaparte* (1827–1828, 3 volumes). {RE}

Thiebaud, Wayne (1920–)

An artist who is a member of the American Academy of Arts and Letters, Thiebaud wrote the present author about humanism:

> It seems to me that painting is somewhat anti-categorical by its "nature." So naturalistic (or aesthetic) humanism is closest to my easel and my life.

His works include "Watermelon Slices" (1961), which has thick paint slopped on as if with a mop; "Yo-Yos" (1962–1963); "Window Cakes" (1963); "French Pastries" (1963); and "Kneeling Woman" (1964). Following his first one-man show in Manhattan in 1962, Thiebaud has exhibited throughout the nation.

Critic Michael Kimmelman has written, "Not precisely Pop, his choices of gum ball machines and window displays as subjects for paintings, not to say the sumptuous and eye-popping way he depicts them, make him an uneasy ally of sober Realists like William Bailey. He's obviously not a Photo-Realist, despite his precision in rendering objects, because his handling of paint is so opulent and sensuous and is so much about paint as a physical and expressive medium." Kimmelman adds that Thiebaud "doesn't fit easily into any of the usual slots, which means he's on the periphery, an odd man out. That is an artistic niche in itself." In 1994, Thiebaud was honored at the White House and awarded a National Medal of Arts. {WAS, 24 August 1992}

Thiers, Adolphe [President] (1797–1877)

Thiers, a French statesman, journalist, and historian, was one of a group of writers that attacked the reactionary government of King Charles X. His *History of the French Revolution* (1823–1827, 10 volumes) illustrated his moderate liberal views. Thiers held ministerial posts under Louis Philippe, whose candidacy as king of the French he had promoted. As minister of the interior, he brutally suppressed in 1834 the workers' insurrection in Paris and Lyons. In 1836, he became premier, but his projected intervention against the Carlists in Spain caused his dismissal. After the February Revolution of 1848, Thiers opposed the Second Empire of Napoleon III, and he headed the provisional government after France's defeat in the Franco-Prussian War. Thiers crushed the Commune of Paris and was president (1871–1873) of the republic. Contemporary historians criticize his historical works as being superficial and inaccurate. Although many Frenchmen returned to the Church, politically, after the Commune, Thiers remained an agnostic all his life. {CE; JM; RAT; RE; TRI}

THING-IN-ITSELF

Kant had the philosophic notion of a thing-in-itself. A thing-in-itself is an object as it would appear to us if we did not have to approach it under the conditions of space and time. {DCL}

Thilly, Frank (Born 1865)

Thilly taught philosophy at Cornell, Missouri University, and Princeton. He edited the University of Missouri *Studies* (1901–1904) and was associate editor of the *International Journal of Ethics*. In 1917 Thilly, a rationalist, was President of the American Association of University Professors. {RAT}

THINKING

• Many people would rather die than think; in fact, most do.

—**Bertrand Russell**

Thiong'o, Ngugi wa: See entry for Ngugi.

THIRTY YEARS WAR (1618-1648)

As many as ten million people died in the general European war, the Thirty Years War, fought mainly in Germany over territorial, dynastic, and religious issues. German Protestant princes and foreign powers (France, Sweden, Denmark, England, the United Provinces) fought against Ferdinand II and the power of the Holy Roman Empire as represented by the Hapsburgs, who were allied with the Catholic princes.

"Compromise was impossible," wrote Fareed Zakaria of *Foreign Affairs*. "Either the Pope was Christ's vicar on earth or he wasn't. Protestants were heretics or heroes. You couldn't split the difference." The big losers were the Hapsburgs of Austria and the Catholics. The Peace of Westphalia "ended the idea that Europe was a single Christian empire, governed spiritually by the Pope and temporally by the Holy Roman Emperor. The treaty also gingerly extended the idea of religious tolerance." {*The New York Times Magazine*, 18 April 1999}

Thoenes, Piet (Died 1995)

At the Sixth International Humanist and Ethical Union (IHEU) World Congress held in Amsterdam (1974), Prof. Thoenes of the Netherlands addressed the group. A retired professor of sociology, he has said, "Humanism is both a philosophy and a lifestyle. . . . We must maintain an equilibrium between the philosophical (as represented by Jaap Van Praag) and the practical (represented by Rob Tielman). Equilibrium between individuality and the collective is also important." In 1969, he wrote of utopias in *Utopie en ratio*, and in 1971 he wrote *Sociologie in Europe*. From 1975 to 1978, he was co-chairman of the International Humanist and Ethical Union.

According to Howard Radest, Thoenes "remained a socialist even when socialism became unpopular and the 'free-market' became everyone's solution to the world's problems. A kindly sceptics, he was never a dogmatist and had little use for either sloppy thinking or ideological rigidity. . . . I can recall his never-failing good humour particularly when board meetings—as board meetings often do—were more like bored meetings. He would lean over and whisper some bit of nonsense to me and I, in turn, could stop being as 'serious' as the 'chairman' is supposed to be. At the same time, Piet was a very serious social scientist, social critic, and humanist as indeed his research and numerous publications on community and social organisation demonstrate." {*International Humanist News*, October 1995}

Thomas, Antoine Léonard (1732–1785)

In 1756 Thomas, a writer, published *Réflexions philosophiques et littéraires sur le poême de la Religion Naturelle de Voltaire*, a criticism of Voltaire. But by 1762 Thomas was a thorough rationalist, as shown in his *Éloge de Descartes* (1765), a work crowned by the Academy but attacked by the clergy. His *Éloge de Marc Aurèle*, which he read at the Academy in 1770, was forbidden publication until l775. Thomas's collected works were published in four volumes in 1775. {RAT}

Thomas, Art (1908–)

Thomas is a somewhat typical small-town American non-believer. He and his father, a physician, were atheists "but not the 'Village Atheists' " that would startle their fellow townspeople. Just as his father liked the works of Thomas Paine, his son subscribed to the *American Freeman* and built a library of about six hundred of E. Haldeman-Julius's Little Blue Books. He subscribed to Joseph Lewis's *Common Sense*, later called *The Age of Reason*, and to *Progressive World*, the latter being a publication of the United Secularists of America.

In Oregon, Thomas has helped launch The Center for Rational Thought, an atheist community center. "Generally," Thomas told *Freethought History* (#23, 1997), "I don't like to be labelled, although I am comfortable as a freethinker to call myself an Atheist." His heroes include Confucius, Voltaire, Paine, Jefferson, Darrow, Haldeman-Julius, Joseph McCabe, Noam Chomsky, and Gore Vidal. Despite his age, he occasionally pickets or leaflets. In short, Thomas is a typical American non-believer. {*Freethought History*, #23, 1997}

Thomas, Hugh (20th Century)

Thomas is a psychologist in industry and is the secretary of the Bristol Humanist Group. In "Last Word," he noted that it is difficult to answer why so many people become interested in organized religions. He holds that young minds turn to objects—people, ideas, habits, vices, political or religious ideologies—which become the subject of fixations which continue to influence them thereafter. Once a Catholic, always a Catholic, as the saying goes. "Our job as Rationalists and Humanists," he suggested, "is to try to change people's beliefs and inbred attitudes." {*The Freethinker*, September 1995}

Thomas, John (1926–1996)

Thomas was acting president of the Humanist Association of Canada (1977–1978). In 1947 he came from Wales to Canada with Baptist Bible training, then taught philosophy at McMaster University after questioning fundamentalist aspects of his religion. His popular undergraduate course, Moral Issues, examined abortion, euthanasia, and organized religions. As resident ethicist at Chedoke-McMaster Hospital, Thomas championed the patient's right to make choices about treatment. {*Humanist in Canada*, Spring 1997)

Thomas, Keith [Sir] (1933–)

Thomas has been President of the British Academy since 1993 and the President of Corpus Christi College, Oxford, since 1986. A historian, he wrote *Religion and the Decline of Magic* (1971) and *Man and the Natural World* (1982). With Donald Pennington, he edited *Puritans and Revolutionaries* (1978). He was named Knight Bachelor in 1988. Sir Keith is a member of the Council for Secular Humanism's Academy of Humanism.

Thomas, Norman (Mattoon) (1884–1968)

Thomas in 1911 was a Presbyterian minister, one who opposed World War I in 1918 and remained a pacifist for the rest of his life. In 1931 he demitted, withdrawing from the ministry. He led the Socialist party in 1926 and was its candidate for president in 1928, 1932, 1936, 1940, 1944, and 1948. Thomas was a founder of the American Civil Liberties Union (ACLU), and from 1921 to 1922 he was editor of *The Nation*. With Paul Blanshard, he wrote *What's the Matter with New York?* (1932). Although coming from a Protestant background, Thomas attended New York's Community Church (Unitarian), and he shared Paul Blanshard's criticism of Catholicism and organized religious groups within Protestantism. {CE}

Thomas, Philip (20th Century)

Thomas wrote *A Religion of This World* (1913). {GS}

Thomasius, Christian (1655–1728)

In *De jure principis circa haereticos* (1697) and other words, Thomasius separated theology from philosophy, and belief from knowledge. Along with Christian Wolff, he developed a "neologism," or new term, which opened the way for successive biblical critics. Robertson commented that in philosophy Thomasius was "an unsystematic pantheist [who] taught, after Plutarch, Bayle, and Bacon, that 'superstition is worse than atheism'; but his great practical service to German civilization, over and above his furthering of the native speech, was his vigorous polemic against prosecutions for heresy, trials for witchcraft, and the use of torture, all of which he did more than any other German to discredit, though judicial torture subsisted for another half-century." {CE; EU, Volker Dürr; JMR; JMRH}

THOMISM

The philosophy of Thomas Aquinas, called thomism, underwent a revival starting in the middle of the nineteenth century. The thomistic approach teaches that philosophy and theology are separate, one seeking truth through reason, the other through revelation, but their conclusions support each other. Theologians teach student theologues are taught the relation between "efficacious grace" and "free will" as "a free determination of the will accomplished by virtue of a divine physical premotion." {DCL}

Thompson, Claude W. (20th Century)

Thompson, an assistant dean of Sir George Williams College at Montreal, in the 1950s, was an active naturalistic humanist who believed that the job of the modern humanist is to establish a philosophy suitable for present-day living. For *The Humanist* in the 1950s, he wrote a review of Will Durant's *The Reformation.* {HNS}

Thompson, Daniel Greenleaf (1850–1897)

An American author, Thompson wrote *The Problem of Evil* (1887) and *The Religious Sentiments*, among other works. Thompson was President of the Nineteenth Century Club, and he was an agnostic. {BDF; JM; RAT}

Thompson, Donald (20th Century)

Thompson, whose outspoken commitment to civil liberties in and around Jackson, Mississippi, resulted in his receiving multiple gunshot wounds in the 1960s, typifies the Unitarian Universalist minister's concern for social justice.

Thompson, Donald Claude (20th Century)

In 1952 for his M. S. degree at the University of Wisconsin, Thompson wrote about Robert G. Ingersoll and the freethought press. {GS}

Thompson, Donald Kingsley (1908–1989)

Thompson was an Australian humanist, administrator, and flying instructor. From the age of ten he questioned religion, finding himself in adult life to be an atheist. A pilot and flying instructor during World War II, he was the co-founder and administrator of motor sport in Australia. A sub-editor at *The Herald*, Thompson was known as a Renaissance man with erudite literary skills and an engaging blend of seasoned and contemporary attitudes. When eighty, he wrote, "Some men, when they die after busy, toilsome successful lives, leave a great treasure stock of scrip and securities, of acres or factories or the goodwill of large undertakings." To this Thompson added, "I hope that none of you will depart today without the knowledge that part of my treasure is banked in your hearts." {SWW}

Thompson, Dorothy B. (20th Century)

Thompson, an atheist and poet who wrote *Blasphemous Satire and Other Reflections on Life*, was brought up in the Methodist and Baptist churches, always hating the hymn that says "such a worm as I." When the Baptist preacher she married was abusive, she divorced him. Living in Bandon, Oregon, she has been a teacher for twenty-three years and is associate editor of *Freethought Perspective.* Typical of her parodies of "favorite hymns" are the following:

CROCK OF AGES
Crock of Ages, not for me,
I'm too smart to swallow thee.
You're just bunk, you can't atone,
Christian nutes, leave me alone.
Crock of Ages, what a lie.
We live once, and then we die!

AMAZING FAITH
Amazing faith, repulsive sound,
Devoid of harmony.
Once long deceived my brain I found.
Now I'm untied and free.
I spent a lot of years in fear.
Guilt was my middle name.
But now I've dumped my church career,
I'm one old happy dame!

(See entry for Frank Tiefenbach.) {African Americans for Humanism *Examiner*, Fall 1998; *Freethought History*, #25/1998}

Thompson, Edward (20th Century)

With Stuart Hall, Thompson edited two journals of "socialist humanism," *New Reasoner* and *Universities and Left Review*.

Thompson, Henry [Sir] (1820–1904)

A British surgeon, Thompson painted well enough to exhibit in the London Academy and the Paris Salon. Also, he published two novels. In a 1902 booklet, "The Unknown God," according to McCabe, "he rejected all beliefs except the 'great power' (impersonal) which many scientific men vaguely invoke." To Edward Clodd, who criticized him in a friendly way, Sir Henry said, "I am agnostic to the backbone." {JM; RAT; RE; TRI}

Thompson, Howard (20th Century)

Thompson edits *The Texas Atheist*, a Web magazine found at <http://gofreemind@aol.com>.

Thompson, Patricia (20th Century)

Thompson is the daughter of Vladimir Mayakovsky, the celebrated poet of the Russian Revolution. Secretly brought up as a daughter by her mother's husband, an Englishman named George Jones, she has refused to be called "illegitimate." Incensed in 1992 when *Variety Fair* referred to Mayakovsky's having had an illegitimate daughter with a Russian-American woman, Thompson of Lehman College retorted, "I am his *natural* or *biological* daughter. I am also a feminist, and we are moving away from those kinds of pejorative, patriarchal terms." She has made reference to Pope Alexander VI, allegedly the father of ten illegitimate children by four mistresses, whose daughter Lucrezia Borgia inspired Victor Hugo's drama and Donizetti's opera. Thompson disapproves of the negative connotations of "bastard," as did humanist writer Miriam Allen deFord, who compiled a list of "famous bastards," in which Jesus was included as one whom the father did not recognize as his own.

Thompson, Sheila (20th Century)

Thompson wrote "Misogyny Is the Sweetest Story Ever Told" (1979). {GS}

Thompson, William (1785–1833)

Thompson, a native of Cork, was a disciple of Bentham and wrote *The Distribution of Weatlh* (1824), *An Appeal for Women* (1825), and *Labor Reward* (1827). Adopting Bentham's and Robert Owen's atheistic and humanitarian views, Thompson worked to help the poor peasants by introducing cooperation. His 1824 *Distribution of Wealth* pre-dated similar views by Karl Marx, for he stated that all wealth ought to go to the producer. A freethinker, he wrote for the *Co-operative Magazine*. Thompson's writing on behalf of the rights of women stirred many. In his personal life, Thompson was said by McCabe to have been "very strict and ascetic," a teetotaller and vegetarian. {BDF; JM; RAT; RE; TRI}

Thomson, Ann (20th Century)

Thomson wrote *Materialism and Society in the Mid-Nineteenth Century* (1981), which was about Julian La Mettrie. {GS}

Thomson, Charles Otto (Born 1833)

Thomson was a Swedish-born captain. At Eskilstuna he started a Utilitarian Society in 1888, of which he became president. He supported Lennstrand in his freethought work in Sweden, translated articles by Ingersoll and Foote, and lectured on behalf of the movement. {BDF; RAT}

Thomson, James (1834–1882)

A Scottish poet and essayist, Thomson wrote *The City of Dreadful Night* (1880; republished 1993), a darkly pessimistic poem said by some to be the most powerful pessimistic poem in the English language. It was a favorite of Gordon Stein, and excerpts from it were read at Stein's memorial service.

Robertson described him as the ill-starred but finely gifted author who, though he celebrated the liberating power of unbelief, was a despairing unbeliever. Thomson's sense is that there is nothing to live for in a world without God. For a time, he lodged with and was a friend of Charles Bradlaugh. Thomson died an alcoholic derelict at the age of forty-eight. {BDF; CE; EU, Victor N. Paananen; JM; JMR; RAT; RE}

Thomson, Virgil (1896–1989)

Thomson, an eminent American organist, composer, and critic, wrote two operas: *Four Saints in Three Acts* (1928) and *The Mother of Us All* (1947), with librettos by Gertrude Stein. From 1940 to 1954, he was the noted music critic of *The New York Herald Tribune.*

Anthony Tommasini's *Virgil Thomson: Composer on the Aisle* (1997) relates the composer's varied musical successes. Included are details of the composer's various loves as well as his lack of interest in the Christian theology believed in by his family and the small Missouri community in which he had grown up. At one point, in fact, Thomson had dissected a collection of Baptist hymns and had found closeted erotic feelings throughout. God, he found, interested believers less than Jesus, "the perfect, though very human 'lover of my soul.' " This love-is-the-theme message led to hymnal exhortations to "taste his delights" and "Resist Him no more!" H. L. Mencken, himself a non-believer, failed to be convinced, however, that closeted erotic feelings are to be found everywhere in church hymns.

At Kansas City Polytechnic Institute Thomson founded the Pansophists, writing in its publication, *Pans*, that the club aimed to emulate the Sophists of Greece, who "disputed for the sake of dispute, and who discussed merely for the pleasure of talking well." When accused of heading an artificial, narrow, elitist, and undemocratic group, Thomson pleaded guilty: "Any attempt to unite distinct classes of minds is necessarily artificial. . . . Humanism itself is narrow." As for the club's and its members' being different, "Conventionality is its own punishment," he retorted, Wilde-like.

Thomson lifted fragments of ideas from Schopenhauer (his view of the world as a constant conflict of individual wills resulting in frustration and pain), said Tommasini, and from Nietzsche (his contemptuous rejection of Christian "slave morality" in favor of a "will to power"). When the club publicized Edgar Lee Masters's *Spoon River Anthology* and the campus heard of the poetry's tales of abortion, lust, lesbian relationships, hypocrisy of small-town neighborliness, and corruption of civic officials, Thomson had to appear before a disciplinary committee which threatened him with expulsion.

Thomson had tried peyote once during his junior college days in Kansas City. His supplier had been Dr. Frederick Madison Smith, whose grandfather had founded the Mormon religion and who became head of the church. Smith described his peyote "highs" to Thomson, with their "characteristic excitation to feats of endurance and to colored visions," then supplied him with "five bumpy little buttons, less than an inch across and hard as wood" obtained from Texas Indians. Although the Mormons had prohibitions against alcohol and drugs, as head of the church Smith reasoned that peyote was a natural substance, not a drug, an ancient means to tap one's inner powers. He had observed native American Indians who ate the drug in pellet form and had seen others, Catholic converts, who made from it a tea for communion. Smith's Ph. D. dissertation, subsequently a book, was *The Higher Powers of Man* (1918), an examination of ecstatic states, a phenomenon that some men and, likely, that Jesus had experienced.

After further study at Harvard, Thomson became one of America's best music critics, a master of the organ, and a composer with an international standing.

Flamboyantly homosexual, Thomson when ninety showed a new secretary around his Hotel Chelsea apartment on 23rd Street in New York, telling him,

> This is what you do if you show up and I'm dead. Don't call a doctor; it will be too late. Call the lawyer. He knows what to do. Then call the locksmith to come change the locks. Then call AP, UPI, and *The New York Times*—the culture desk, *not* the obit boys.

Thomson also wanted to make sure his final memorial would be a memorable one and requested that it be held in Manhattan's biggest cathedral. Asked if he wanted to be buried or cremated, Thomson told his friend Dick Flender, "Cremated. Easier to ship."

Thomson's memorial was held per his instructions at New York City's largest church, which he termed "St. John's the Too-Too Divine." Despite his wish that absolutely no words be spoken, the minister successfully insisted that he say something at the very beginning. Tommasini's biography makes it clear that Thomson was not into organized religion but, however, did not go on record any further concerning his freethinking. Although he was not a card-bearing secular humanist and had written church music, Thomson had said, wryly, "I just didn't take to salvation."

Thorburn, James Alexander (1924–)

Thorburn, the son of parents who were nominal Christians, was a Scottish-born socialist who was active in the Socialist Party of Great Britain. He moved to New Zealand in 1953 and to Australia in 1955. Thorburn, who was proprietor of the Pocket Bookshop in Sydney from 1959 to 1979, was a member of the Rationalist Association of New South Wales and was an early member of the North South Wales Humanist Society. {SWW}

Thoreau, Henry David (1817–1862)

Thoreau's philosophy of life combined diverse strains, and his heritage—French, Scottish, Quaker, Puritan—was similarly mixed. Carlos Baker described Thoreau as having a nose that "resembled the beak of a predatory bird" and arms "thickly matted with fur, like the pelt of an animal." On the one hand, Thoreau called himself "a mystic, a transcendentalist, and a natural philosopher to boot." On the other, he was a quasi-Unitarian, Emerson's disciple, and a non-joining individualist who, unlike some of his Unitarian acquaintances, said, "If I knew for a certainty that a man was coming to my house with the conscious design of doing me good, I should run for my life." He was fond of quoting the line of Ennius, "I say that there are gods but they care not what men do."

Thoreau's building a cabin for $28.12 1/2 near Walden Pond (1845–1847) resulted in his most famous work, *Walden* (1854). When he went to Walden, his brother John had recently died. The two had previously run a private school, one of whose students was Bronson Alcott's daughter, Louisa May. Unlike other transcendentalists, who retreated to Brook Farm to make cooperative plans, Thoreau according to James D. Hart chose the naked simplicity of life where he could "subdue and cultivate a few cubic feet of flesh," chew the cud of his thoughts, and get to the very core of the universe by living deep and sucking out all the "marrow of life." His desire was "so to love wisdom as to live according to its dictates, a life of simplicity, independence, magnanimity, and trust . . . to solve some of the problems of life, not only theoretically, but practically. When he was imprisoned a day for refusing to pay a poll tax to the government that supported the Mexican War, which he considered merely a land-grabbing scheme of the Southern slaveholders, he was met by Emerson's "Henry, what are you doing in there?" to which he replied, "Ralph, what are you doing out there!"

In his "Civil Disobedience," Thoreau (pronounced THOR-o by his relatives, although pronounced differently by most academics) expresses his belief in passive resistance, a means of protest which later is said to have inspired Gandhi, Martin Luther King, John F. Kennedy, Nelson Mandela, Tolstoy, and untold others. Although he enjoyed the scientific view of nature, he also was a transcendentalist who longed for the wideness of heaven more than the limits of the microscope. He contributed to their journal, *The Dial.* Active in the anti-slavery movement, he at the time when he met Walt Whitman was beginning to be weakened by tuberculosis. Despite becoming an invalid, he worked on a long, unpublished ethnological study of American Indians and edited his journals for publication. Robertson has categorized Thoreau as being a more stringent thinker than Emerson, calling him "either a pantheist or a Lucretian theist, standing aloof from all churches."

Bradbury P. Dean, the editor of the Thoreau Society Bulletin, has combined newly found and organized Thoreau writings which include "Dispersion of Seeds" with other writings of natural history, entitling his editing *Faith in a Seed* (1993). Commenting upon the book, Professor of American Literature Robert D. Richardson Jr. of Wesleyan University has remarked that "the new book tells us that Thoreau is a pioneering scientist as well as a humanist." Instead of being characterized merely as an eccentric who fished in Walden Pond, lived off nuts and berries, and had little human contact, Thoreau is being described as one who participated in the Underground Railroad, sheltering escaping slaves in his family's house. In addition, he was an abolitionist, an early advocate of civil disobedience, and one of the first American writers to believe that knowledge comes from knowing the links between the humanities and nature. "Though I do not believe that a plant will spring up where no seed has been," said Thoreau, one of the nation's first ecologists, "I have great faith in a seed. Convince me that you have a seed there, and I am prepared to expect wonders."

One "seed" of life which caught his fancy was a rare and remarkable fungus, which in *Walden* he describes:

> The whole height [is] six and three-quarters inches. It may be divided into three parts, pilcus, stem, and base—or scrotum, for it is a perfect phallus. One of those fungi named *impudicus*, I think. In all respects [it is] a most disgusting object, yet very suggestive. It was as offensive to the eye as to the scent, the cap rapidly melting and defiling what it couched with a fetid, olivaceous, semiliquid matter. In an hour or two the plant scented the whole house wherever placed, so that it could not be endured. I was afraid to sleep in my chamber where it had lain until the room had been well ventilated. It smelled like a dead rat in the ceiling, in all the ceilings of the house. Pray, what was Nature thinking of when she made this? She almost puts herself on a level with those who draw in privies.

This was not Thoreau's only interest in the phallus, claims Martin Greif, who states that Thoreau meditated on the higher meaning of male friendship in his notebooks, fell in and out of love with his male acquaintances, and never married. Thoreau's only proposal of marriage, to Ellen Sewell, had been rejected because her father, a Unitarian minister, found Thoreau a rabble-rouser with his antislavery and freethinking ideas. "People talk about Bible miracles because there is no miracle in their lives," he would tell them. "Cease to gnaw that crust. There is ripe fruit over your head."

In 1840 Thoreau proposed to Ellen Sewall, who rejected the offer, and he never married. Critic Marylynne Diggs has noted that it is uncertain if Thoreau was a "repressed" homosexual or if he was asexual. Two men Thoreau found attractive, however, were Tom Fowler, his guide on a trip to the Maine woods; and Alek Therien, a Canadian woodchopper who visited him at Walden Pond. Nowhere in his writing does he refer to women. As Diggs points out, "But his *Journals*, his essay 'Chastity and Sensuality,' and the long discourse on 'Friendship' in *A Week* are prolific expressions of the beauty, and the agony, of love between men."

Thoreau's final day was spent in Concord, surrounded by family and friends. Slater and Solomita have described the scene, in which Thoreau is dying of tuberculosis:

> "Never spent an hour with more satisfaction. Never saw a man dying with so much pleasure and peace," noted Thoreau's former jailer, the tax collector Sam Staples, after a visit. Thoreau was writing, editing, and revising ("You know it is the fashion to leave an estate behind you," he said), despite the fact that to do so was an exhausting, nearly impossible chore for him. Thoreau was aware the end was near; when reminded of this he was invariably good-humored. "It is better some things should end," he told one comforter. During a visit the Quaker abolitionist Parker Pillsbury mused, "You seem so near the brink of the dark river that I almost wonder how the opposite shore may appear to you." Thoreau replied, "My friend, one world at a time." When his Calvinist Aunt Louisa asked him if he had made his peace with God, Thoreau protested, "I never knew that we had quarreled." Concord was enjoying a beautiful spring in 1862, the morning of May 6 being no exception. Thoreau's room was filled with flowers, fruits of the season, game, sweetmeats, and get-well messages—the gifts of friends, villagers and even strangers who knew he was ill. Thoreau was deeply touched by these attentions, knowing nature was being brought to him because he could not go into nature. At eight o'clock, as Thoreau lay tossing and turning in this room he murmured his last words—"Moose . . . Indian."

After his death, selections from his journals were edited by his friend, Harrison G. O. Blake. Thoreau's funeral took place at First Parish (Unitarian), at the behest of Emerson, who delivered the funeral oration. Thoreau is buried at Authors' Ridge, Sleepy Hollow Cemetery, Concord, Massachusetts. His gravestone is a small granite marker on the Thoreau family plot, inscribed only with his first name. {Carlos Baker, *Emerson Among the Eccentrics*; CE; CL; EG; FUS; HNS2; JM; JMR; RAT; RE; TYD; U; UU}

Thoren, Lloyd H. (20th Century)

Thoren, who founded Dial-an-Atheist and was instrumental in maintaining the American Atheist Museum in Petersburg, Indiana, has received the Pioneer Atheist Award from American Atheists, Inc.

Thorild, Thomas (1759–1808)

Thorild, or Thoren, was a Swedish writer. In 1786 he wrote *Common Sense on Liberty*, with a view of extending the liberty of the press. He was a partisan of the French Revolution, and for a political work he was imprisoned and exiled. Thorild also wrote a *Sermon of Sermons*, attacking the clergy and maintaining the rights of women. {BDF; RAT}

Thorne, Tony (20th Century)

Thorne is an activist supporter of the Pink Triangle Trust in England. {*Gay and Lesbian Humanist*, Winter 1998}

Thorpe, Robert (Born 1818)

Thorpe, a Pittsburgh, Pennsylvania, lawyer, became an abolitionist and personally knew President Lincoln as a lawyer long before the war. After the war, he wrote that he wanted to devote himself strictly to legal business but "the encroachments of the church on the rights of the people have become so great and unjust that I feel it necessary to go again upon the war-path." {PUT}

Thorvaldsen, Albert Bertel (1770–1844)

Thorvaldsen (also, Thorwaldsen) was a Danish sculptor who, going to Rome in 1797, shared with Canova the leadership of the neo-classicists. His adherence to Greek art is seen in his "Jason" (1802–1803), which is rendered with respect for antique prototypes. In 1819 he designed the "Lion of Lucerne," a memorial to the Swiss Guard, and his historical portrait sculptures include "Conradin, Last of the Hohenstaufen." In Copenhagen, the Thorvaldsen Museum has a large collection of his work. The son of an Iceland wood-carver, Thorvaldsen did much work based on religious themes, including a statue of Pope Pius VII. According to McCabe, "His pious biographer Thiele admits, almost with tears, that [Thorvaldsen] rejected Christianity, and in fact he had from youth a passion for ancient Greece and Rome, but in his time there was not much money in classical art." Asked how he could produce such beautiful religious statues, Thorvaldsen replied, "Neither do I believe in the gods of the Greeks, but for all that I can represent them." {CE; JM; RE}

THOTH

In mythology, Thoth was the Egyptian god of wisdom, learning, and the moon.

THE THOUGHT

The Thought is a bi-monthly journal of the Philosophers Guild (PO Box 10760, Glendale, Arizona 85318). Edited by Ronald C. Tobin, it discusses monopolistic capitalism, individual collectivity, and freethought subjects.

Threlkeld, Simon (20th Century)

Threlkeld is a Toronto lawyer who thinks "juries" should select many of the decision-makers now selected by the government. Such a change, he has described in "Democratizing Public Institutions," would represent a major advance for democracy. {*Humanist in Canada*, Spring 1997}

Threlfall, Violet Dorothy (1898–1993)

Threlfall was an Australian humanist, teacher, scholar, and Esperantist. She was a lecturer in English literature at Claremont and Graylands colleges, and she studied at the Sorbonne and in Germany. A founding member of the Humanist Society of Western Australia, Threlfall campaigned for peace studies in Australian schools, saw Esperanto as an agent of peace, translated from the original Esperanto, and published *Longing for Peace* (the story of a Nagasaki victim) and *Private Life of Gandhi.* {SWW}

Thresh, William Henry (Born 1868)

Convinced that "Christianity is opposed to progress," Thresh opened a school (Ruskin House) along rationalist lines in 1903 at Southend-on-Sea for the education of children. He was Principal until, in 1916, the abnormal conditions set up by the War compelled him to close it. The school was commended to rationalists in the *Literary Guide* and *Freethinker*. {RAT}

Thressell, Robert (20th Century)

Thressell is a New Zealand freethinker.

Thrower, James (20th Century)

Thrower is the Scottish author of *A Short History of Western Atheism* (1971); *The Alternative Tradition: Religion and Rejection of Religion in the Ancient World* (1980); and *Western Atheism, A Short History*, 2000). In the latter work, the University of Aberdeen professor takes up atheism in classical antiquity, then western atheism to the 17th century, then modern atheism up to the present. He holds that unbelief rose significantly in Western Europe as a result of the clash in the Middle Ages between the powerful force of faith and the limits it placed on reason. Both John Stuart Mill and his godson, Bertrand Russell, are termed humanists.

Angelo Juffras, noting in 1985 that Thrower believed that "the rejection of a religious understanding of the world, and of life" is *not* a modern phenonomenon but that a consistently held naturalistic view of the world was evident in the ancient world, editorialized: "It may be that Thrower's position will prove to the correct as more evidence is found. As yet, however, his views are not sufficiently backed by evidence." {Angelo Juffras, EU}

Thucydides (c. 460–c. 400 B.C.E.)

Thucydides, the Greek historian of Athens, was a general and a student of politics. His one work, which made him the greatest of ancient historians, is a *History of the Peloponnesian War* to 411 B.C.E. He was unable to prevent the surrender of Amphipolis to the Spartan commander Brasidas, being exiled until the end of the war. But during his exile he had the opportunity to observe both the Athenians and the Spartans, and from his observations and firsthand information he created a new style of historical writing. His work contains the eloquent funeral oration by Pericles, and he adeptly describes the plague which beset Greece at that time and which he lived through. William T. Bluhm, in the *Encyclopedia of Philosophy*, Vol. 8, states that the writings of Thucydides build self-consciously "on a clearly defined philosophical position, an antimetaphysical naturalism and positivism which he probably learned from the practices of Hippocratic medicine and from the Sophists."

Why still read Thucydides? Bertrand Russell answers: "Thucydides, the second of the great historians, has a smaller theme than that of Herodotus, but treats it with more art and also with a more careful regard for accuracy. His subject is the conflict of Athens and Sparta in the Peloponnesian War. His history, as Cornford has pointed out, is modeled on Greek tragedy: Athens, his own beloved city, which was finally defeated, is like the typical hero, driven by Fate and overweening pride to a disastrous but not inglorious end. His writing is severe, and confined strictly to what is relevant; there are no gossipy digressions, and there is little that is amusing. But there is a presentation, full of epic grandeur, of the spectacle of men driven by destiny into folly, choosing wrongly over and over again when a right choice would have brought victory, becoming wicked through exasperation; and falling at last into irretrievable ruin. The theme is one that appealed to the Greek mind. A great impersonal Power, called indifferently Fate or Justice or Necessity, ruled the world, and was superior to the gods. Whatever person or country or thing overstepped the ordained boundaries, suffered the punishment of pride. This was the real religion of the Greeks, and Thucydides in his history magnificently illustrated it." {Lee Eisler, *The Quotable Bertrand Russell*}

Thulié, Jean Baptiste Henri (Born 1832)

Thulié was a French physician and anthropologist. In 1856 he founded a journal, *Realism*, and in 1866 he published a work on *Madness and the Law*. In *La Pensée Nouvelle*, he defended the view of Büchner. Thulié was a President of the Paris Municipal Council. {BDF; RAT}

Thurber, James (1894–1961)

Thurber, a principal contributor of cartoons to *The New Yorker*, was known to his inner circle as a freethinker and joyful humanist, one with a deep psychological insights into man's foibles and man's obsessive interest in supernaturalism. Half-blinded when only seven when his brother struck him with a toy boy and arrow, he spent a life wearing glasses that eventually were "as thick as binoculars." In this respect, he resembled James Joyce, whose *Finnegans Wake* he enjoyed hearing his secretary read aloud. When he drove, ". . . flecks of dust and streaks of bug blood on the windshield look to me often like old admirals in uniform, or crippled apple women, or the front ends of barges and I whirl out of their way, thus going into ditches and fields and up on front lawns, endangering the life of authentic admirals and apple women who may be out on the roads for a breath of air before retiring." Harrison Kinney in *James Thurber: His Life and Times*

(1996) related that, for Thurber, undoing a woman's girdle "is likely to lead to a grave and determined effort, in which the gentleman goes about the process much as if he were trying to fix a gasoline engine." Kinney speculated that the handicap led Thurber to dislike himself and others who are dependent, leading to his drawing of women as daisy-plucking airheads or emasculating harridans. What he took comfort from, particularly, was his dog.

Thurber wrote, "For some curious reason Man has always assumed that his is the highest form of life in the universe. . . . The survival of almost any species of social animal, no matter how low, has been shown to be dependent on Group Cooperation, which is itself a product of instinct. 'Group struggles to the death between animals of the same species, such as occur in human warfare, can hardly be found among non-human animals,' says W. C. Allee in his extremely interesting *The Social Life of Animals*. One has but to observe a community of beavers at work in a stream to understand the loss in sagacity, balance, cooperation, competence, and purpose which Man has suffered since he rose up on his hind legs. . . . It is surely permissible to hazard the guess that somewhere beyond Betelgeuse there may be a race of men whose intelligence makes ours seem like the works of an old-fashioned music box. The Earth, it seems to me, may well be the Siberia, or the Perth Amboy, of the inhabited planets of the Universe."

In 1950 he tackled anti-communist hysteria:

> The Thing can blacken a man at a distance of 10,000 miles, by using one or another of its many stings: the thundering charge, the sweeping generalization, the bold assumption, the mysterious record, the secret testimony, the overheard insinuation, the patriotic gesture, the enormous lie, the fearful warning. . . . Do not attempt to take the Thing single-handed. It is armed and dangerous and, what is worse, it has a lot of friends.

With E. B. White, Thurber wrote a satire concerning psychoanalysis, *Is Sex Necessary?* (1929). His other works include *The Male Animal* (1940), *The Thurber Carnival* (1945), and *Credos and Curios* (1962). His later career was hampered by a growing blindness, and by 1953 he was almost totally blind. A fellow cartoonist, Stuart E. Hample, said when Thurber spoke he looked directly at people through his thick, magnifying lenses, leading many to be unaware that he was blind. Hample found him unpretentious and anecdotal, once relating how an American woman in Paris told him she had read translations of his stories and thought they were funnier in French. His response, illustrating that his humor extended to words as well as cartoons, was to agree, adding, "They tend to lose something in the original."

According to biographer Harrison Kinney, "Thurber had never allowed his probing, restless mind to settle on any single theological insurance policy concerning the possibilities of the hereafter. He remained agnostic and probably about where he was, philosophically, in 1927, when he was 34 years old and the best part of his life was ahead of him." Once, however, when writing about his brother's dog, Muggs, Thurber implied that he was curious as to whether the afterlife might be "lovelier and more happy, than this life."

Thurber died of a blood clot in his lung. A Methodist minister read some brief prayers, and Thurber's cremains were placed in a bronze urn. {CE}

Thurman, Uma Karuna (1970–)

Thurman, an actress, was an Academy Award nominee for Best Supporting Actress in "Pulp Fiction" (1994). She has appeared in such other films as "Kiss Daddy Good Night" (1987), "Dangerous Liaisons" (1988), and "A Month by the Lake" (1995). On television, she appeared in the movie "Robin Hood" (1991).

In a brief autobiography in *Cosmopolitan* (November 1995), she listed "Religion: Agnostic (Buddhism if must choose)." Her father, she explained, was the first American to be ordained as a Buddhist monk and now "he teaches Indo-Tibetan studies at Columbia University and is regarded as this country's foremost authority on Buddhism. When the Dalai Lama comes to America, it's my father who is his host. When asked if I consider myself Buddhist, the answer is, Not really. But it's more my religion than any other because I was brought up with it in an intellectual and spiritual environment. I don't practice or preach it, however. But Buddhism has had a major effect on who I am and how I think about the world. What I have learned is that I like all religions, but only parts of them." {CA; E}

Thurtle, Ernest (1884–1954)

Thurtle was the general secretary of the Rationalist Press Association (RPA) from 1932 to 1940 and was chairman in 1941. He wrote *The Fellowship of Reason* (1938). {FUK; TRI}

THUS SPAKE ZARATHUSTRA

In *Thus Spake Zarathustra*, Nietzsche put forth the idea of the Superman, or Overman. (See entry for Nietzsche.)

Thwaites, William (20th Century)

Thwaites, a biology professor at San Diego State University, was honored in 1995 by the American Humanist Association for his valiant defense of biology against biblical creationism.

Tichenor, Henry (20th Century)

Tichenor, a leading forethought figure, wrote *The Life and Exploits of Jehovah* (1915). {GS}

Ticknor, George (1791–1871)

A professor of language and literature at Harvard, Ticknor wrote a significant survey of Hispanic literature. Ticknor's Unitarian minister was William Ellery Channing. Upon his death, Ticknor's extensive library of Spanish and Portuguese books were donated to the Boston Public Library. {CE; EG; U; UU}

Tieck, Johann Ludwig (1773–1853)

Tieck, a personal friend of Goethe and Schiller, was a rationalist who joined the romantic movement in opposition to the Aufklärung. He was a medievalist in his artistic nature but a thinker on the lines of heterodoxy in the eighteenth century. Tieck was one of the early German enthusiasts for Shakespeare, and he edited Schlegel's translation of Shakespeare (9 volumes, 1825–1833). From 1825 onward, Tieck composed pieces for the Dresden Court Theatre. {RAT}

Tiefenbach, Frank (Died 1993)

A Czech attorney, Tiefenbach refused when the Nazi invaders required professionals to sign a document that they agreed with Hitler. As a result, he was forced to work with the underground.

Following the war he and his wife for fifty-five years, **Mila Tiefenbach**, worked with the British Red Cross to help survivors of a Belsen concentration camp. Mrs. Tiefenbach, an atheist, is a member of the Freedom From Religion Foundation in Oregon. She has written for *Freethought Perspective* (April 1999). {Dorothy B. Thompson, "A Czechoslovakian WWII Story," *Freethought Perspective*, May 1998}

Tiele, Cornelis Petrus (1830–1902)

A Dutch scholar, Tiele though brought up in the Church wrote works with freethought overtones. He edited the poems of Genestet together with an account of his life, wrote articles on comparative religion, and published *Outlines of the History of Religion* (1888), and *Comparative History of the Egyptian and Mesopotamian Religions* (1882). He was a theist, but he felt that the creeds have "fallen far below the level of the science and philosophy, the knowledge of the world, and the civilization of a later age." {RAT}

Tielman, Robert A. P. (1946–)

Tielman, a professor of sociology at the University of Utrecht, is vice-president of the European Humanist Federation. At the International Humanist and Ethical Union's (IHEU's) Second Moral Education Conference held in Brussels (1985), and at the Tenth held in Buffalo (1988), Tielman addressed the groups. In 1998 he resigned as President of the International Humanist and Ethical Union (IHEU).

In 1982, he wrote *Homosessualiteit in Nederland* and, in 1991, *Bisexuality and HIV / AIDS: A Global Perspective.* In 1994 at the Toronto conference of the Coalition for Secular Humanism, Atheism, and Freethought (CSHAFT), he spoke on "International Humanism in the 21st Century," mentioning a census which shows that currently 55% are non-religious in the Netherlands, that 25% are humanists, and that 40,000 children voluntarily have enrolled in humanist education courses. Tielman is chairman of the board for Dutch public schools, is a member of the Dutch mental health board, and is a Dutch representative to the WHO.

For his being President of the Dutch Humanist League from 1977-1987, Dr. Tielman received a knighthood.

A contributing editor to *Free Inquiry,* Tielman is a Humanist Laureate in the Council for Secular Humanism's International Academy of Humanism. Also, he is a Vice President of the Gay and Lesbian Humanist Association (GALHA).

In 1995 he spoke in Delphi, Greece, at the first International Multidisciplinary Conference on Human Behaviour and the Meaning of Modern Humanism. Also in 1995, at the IHEU meeting in India, he noted that there is still discrimination in Europe against atheists and humanists. Also, there is a struggle to create a secular European Union, but the Vatican is working for a Christian union. The Vatican, he holds, should be a church, not a state.

In 1996 Tielman was a participant in the 1996 Humanist World Congress held in Mexico City. "[The] close ties between humanism and the homosexual rights movement can be explained by the fact that they both accept the principle of human self-determination," he wrote in "Homosexual Rights: Why Humanism Cares" (*Free Inquiry,* Fall 1997). The article tells of his and his companion's being gay foster parents for twenty-five years. He signed Humanist Manifesto 2000. Tielman's e-mail: <r.tielman@aps.NL>. On the Web: <http://www.aps.NL/>. {HNS2; *New Humanist,* February 1996; *International Humanist News,* December 1998}

Tiernan, Robert (20th Century)

Tiernan, a Denver attorney for the Freedom From Religion Foundation (FFRF), spoke at that group's 1994 convention in Madison, Wisconsin. He has defended the Foundation's challenge of a Ten Commandments monument on the Denver Capitol grounds, and he has represented the group in a challenge of the motto "In God We Trust" on U.S. currency. Tiernan practiced law for twenty-five years in Washington, D.C., before moving to Denver. He is on the board of directors of the Freedom From Religion Foundation.

Tiffin, Lee (1906–)

Tiffin, in *Creationism's Upside-Down Pyramid* (1994), relates how science refutes fundamentalism.

Tiger, Lionel (1937–)

Tiger, a Canadian social scientist, is a fellow of the Great Britain Anthropology Institute and of the American Sociology Association for the Study of Evolution. He is author of *Men In Groups* (1969) and, with Robin Fox, *The Imperial Animal* (1971). With Joseph Schepher, he wrote *Women in the Kubbutz* (1975) and *Optimism: The Biology of Hope and the Pursuit of Pleasure.* Tiger is known for the "pleasure principle" and studies on male bonding. A member of the Humanist Association of Canada, Tiger signed Humanist Manifesto 2000.

Till, Farrell (20th Century)

Till is editor of *The Skeptical Review* (PO Box 717, Canton, Illinois). A Biblical scholar, he writes also for *The Secular Humanist Bulletin* and *American Rationalist.* He debates in person and in writing individuals who are Biblical inerrantists. In 1994, he spoke on "From Bible Thumper to Atheist" at the Freedom From Religion Foundation (FFRF) conference in Madison, Wisconsin. Till was once an ordained Church of Christ minister and he has taught English at Spoon River College in Illinois. E-mail: <jftill@midwest.net>.

Tillich, Paul Johannes (1886–1965)

Tillich, a German-born American philosopher and theologian, embraced the concept of the "Protestant Principle" and aimed at correlating questions arising out of the human condition and the divine answers drawn from the symbolism of Christian revelation. He taught at Union Theological Seminary in New York City, at Harvard University, and the University of Chicago.

As pointed out by Paul Edwards in *God and the Philosophers,* Tillich in his *Systematic Theology* disagrees with a traditional theism that "has made God a heavenly, completely perfect person who resides above the world and mankind." Against such a highest person, Tillich agrees, "the protest of atheism is correct." Tillich repeatedly pours scorn on what he terms "monoarchic monotheism" and the theology of the "cosmic-policeman." Edwards holds that Tillich's reconstruction of belief in God "is consistent with a thoroughgoing atheism. "God" does not now stand "for a reality transcending the natural world but for a certain feature of certain human beings. If human beings disappeared from the world, so would *God* in this sense of the word." The philosopher W. V. Quine was once told by Tillich that he was not an atheist since logic and philosophy were objects of his ultimate concern, to which Quine replied, "I protest against conversion by definition."

At Union Theological Seminary, asked by the present author during a course on existentialism if he would make clear his objections to naturalistic humanism, Tillich replied that he was a Christian humanist, that he therefore was a believer, and that he felt naturalism was not the solution to the human condition. {CE}

Tillier, Claude (1801–1844)

A French writer born of poor parents, Tillier served as a conscript, wrote some telling pamphlets directed against tyranny and superstition, and completed a romance, *My Uncle Benjamin.* His works were edited by F. Pyat. {BDF}

Tillotson, John (1630–1694)

Tillotson, an English prelate and the Archbishop of Canterbury, was chaplain to Charles II and was admitted to the special favor of William and Mary. According to Anthony Collins, Archbishop Tillotson was the one "whom all English free-thinkers own as their head. Inasmuch as T. H. Huxley once called Collins a "Goliath of freethinking," Tillotson was one of the more liberal Protestant thinkers of his day.

Tilney, Frederick (1875–1938)

Tilney, a neurologist, was on the advisory board of Charles Francis Potter's First Humanist Society of New York.

TIME

Theoretically, were we able to travel to some point light-years from Earth and have a spy satellite—something with advanced photoreconnaissance capable of reading the washing instructions on a black silk chemisette from 22,300 miles in geosynchronous orbit—we could actually observe ourselves in the past.

But until we can outrace light, until we can set up our hyperresolution telescope on some planetoid fifteen, twenty, thirty light-years from Earth and—by dint of its optical wizardry—watch our youth unfold, we must make do with our memories, our diaries and notebooks, our videotapes, microcassettes, floppy disks, our photo albums, our evocative souvenirs and bric-a-brack—all the various and sundry madeleines we use to goad our hippocampi into reverse-scan.

Mark Leyner, preface to *The Tetherballs of Bougainville* (1998)

Archbishop Ussher in 1654 dated the creation as having been in 4004 B.C.E. Rosalind, in *As You Like It*, described the world as "almost 6,000 years old."

"The French Revolution's calendar, adopted in 1792, had months that were each 30 days long (with a five- or six-day end-of-year festival), three 10-day weeks a month, and days divided into 10 hours. Each of the hours was divided into 100 minutes, and each of the minutes was divided into 100 seconds. Watches and clocks from the era survive," Jay M. Pasachoff, a professor of astronomy at Williams College, has reported.

As the World Wide Web expanded toward the end of the century, interest increased in some similar such decimal system for marking time. One plan, that breaks the day into 1,000 units each equivalent to 86.4 seconds, was offered. Thus 3 p.m. on a 24-hour clock would be the equivalent in universal time of "@625":

Midnight	@000	Noon	@500
01:00	@041	13:00	@541
02:00	@083	14:00	@583
03:00	@125	15:00	@625
04:00	@166	16:00	@666
05:00	@208	17:00	@708
06:00	@250	18:00	@750
07:00	@291	19:00	@791
08:00	@333	20:00	@833
09:00	@375	21:00	@875
10:00	@416	22:00	@916
11:00	@458	23:00	@958
		24:00	@000

Critics of such a new global Internet time, or decimal "milliday," point out that Greenwich Mean Time (GMT) already works. Watches easily display local times anywhere on earth. The offset from GMT can be contained in any E-mail message's header. (See entry for Time.) [On the Net: <http://www.universal-time.org/index.htm>; Kenneth J. Kahn, Albert S. Kirsch, and Jay M. Pasachoff, *The New York Times*, 11 March 1999]

Timofeyev, Victor (20th Century)

At the Tenth International Humanist and Ethical Union (IHEU) World Congress held in Buffalo (1988), Timofeyev of the USSR addressed the group.

Timon of Phlius (c. 320–c. 230 B.C.E.)

The chief disciple of Pyrrho, Timon was a skeptical philosopher who denied that possibility of certain knowledge. If one can learn to suspend judgment and be indifferent to externals, he taught, one can achieve peace of mind. Little is left of his writings, but his importance lies in his having continued Pyrrho's philosophy of skepticism. Bertrand Russell (*History of Philosophy*, 1945) cites two of Timon's statements: "The phenomenon is always valid" and "That honey *is* sweet I refuse to assert; that it appears sweet, I fully grant." He then observes, "A modern Skeptic would point out that the phenomenon merely *occurs*, and is not either valid or invalid; what is valid or invalid must be a statement, and no statement can be so closely linked to the phenomenon as to be incapable of falsehood. For the same reason, he would say that the statement 'honey appears sweet' is only highly probable, not absolutely certain." Hume, Russell states, similarly maintained "that something which had never been observed—atoms, for instance—could not be validly inferred; but when two *phenomena* had been frequently observed together, one could be inferred from the other." {CE}

Tindal, Matthew (1657–1733)

An English deist writer who had converted to Roman Catholicism, then became a freethinker, Tindal wrote *Christianity as Old as Creation: or, the Gospel, a Republication of the Religion of Nature*, which often is described as "the deist's Bible." Some consider he was an atheist, not a deist, and on his deathbed he uttered blasphemies "scarce fit to be repeated," according to a witness, and "as proud of dying hard as ever he was to be reputed a Top Free Thinker." From Robertson's viewpoint, Tindal believed "that the idea of a good God involved that of a simple, perfect, and universal religion, which must always have existed among mankind, and must have essentially consisted in moral conduct. Christianity, insofar as it is true, must therefore be a statement of this primordial religion; and moral reason must be the test, not tradition or Scripture." Like Collins, Tindal wrote anonymously and so escaped prosecution. The second part of a book he had been written was, upon his death, deliberately destroyed by Bishop Gibson, into whose hands it came. In 1736 Tindal and Shaftesbury are described by an orthodox apologist as the "two oracles of deism." Although Tindal wrote a second volume of *Christianity as Old as the Creation* (1730), of which Voltaire made some use, upon his death the manuscript was destroyed by order of Gibson, Bishop of London. {BDF; CE; EU, David Berman; FUK; JM; JMR; JMRH; RAT; RE}

Tingsten, Herbert (1896–1973)

Tingsten was a Swedish expert in political science. A publicist and professor at the University of Stockholm from 1935–1946, he was editor of *Dagens Nyheter* from 1946–1960. Because of his sharpness in logic, personal engagement, and polemic brilliance, according to Fredrik Bendz, Tingsten reached a unique position in the Swedish press. His efforts, for example, led to the removal of mandatory school prayers from public schools.

Tippett, Michael (Kemp) [Sir] (1905–1998)

Tippett, a composer and the artistic director of the Bath Festival, was Director of Music of Morley College, London, from 1940 to 1951. His father was a liberal and a rationalist, his mother a suffragette who went to prison, was a novelist, and was a member of the Labour Party. At school he rejected religion and stopped accompanying the school hymns. In his autobiography he wrote that he and his father "both had this feeling that we had come to the end of a world that was god-centered."

During the Second World War he was imprisoned for his failure to comply with some of the conditions laid down for conscientious objectors. He remained a leading figure in the Peace Pledge Union throughout his life.

As for his homosexuality, he wrote in his autobiography, "I accepted it without reservation as something instinctive and therefore natural." One of his musical compositions is a love song Achilles addresses to Patroclus.

Jim Herrick, in *Gay & Lesbian Humanist* (Spring, 1998), described Tippett as an outstanding Humanist in his concern for justice, for the individual, for the future. "He put into his music all his vigour, humanity, imagination, and exuberance. Many may find his work difficult, but the difficulty lessens as it becomes more familiar—and it is worth it, to experience the sound and insight of an extraordinary twentieth-century Humanist." {*New Humanist*, March 1998}

Tippitt, Jason (20th Century)

Tippitt, while a student at the University of Tennessee at Martin, was one of the founding members of Campus Freethought Alliance. {*International Humanist News*, December 1996}

Tishler, H. (20th Century)

In 1959 for his M.A. thesis at Columbia University, Tishler wrote about Robert Ingersoll.

Tisserand, François Félix (1845–1896)

In 1869, Tisserand was professor of astronomy at the Sorbonne. In 1873 he became director of the observatory and professor of astronomy at Toulouse University. In 1874 he went to Japan, and in 1882 to Martinique, to observe for French science the transit of Venus. Tisserand edited the *Bulletin Astronomique*. His *Traité de mécanique célese* (4 volumes, 1888–1896) was well received, and his *Leçons de cosmographie* (1895) and other manuals were of high academic value. {RAT}

Tissot, Pierre François (1768–1854)

During the Revolution, Tissot volunteered for the Vendean War (against the Catholic Royalists). In 1810 he became assistant professor of Latin poetry at the *Collège de France*. He translated Vergil's *Bucolics* (1800) and in 1813 was appointed professor. The Bourbons deposed him, but the Revolution of 1830 restored his position. Tissot founded the *Pilote* in 1823, but the clergy suppressed it. In 1833, he was admitted to the French Academy for his *Études sur Virgile*, but his most important work was *Histoire complète de la révolution Française* (6 volumes, 1833–1836). Tissot was staunchly anti-clerical and Bonapartist. {RAT}

TITHE

A tithe is one-tenth of one's annual income or produce, a sum suggested by some religious groups and based upon Biblical tales for raising money to pay expenses. The tithe could be paid as dues to the priests and the Levites.

Freethinkers in leadership positions jocularly state they also would happily accept one-tenth of people's annual incomes "for services rendered." (See entry for Pledges.) {ER}

Tittle, Peg (20th Century)

Tittle, who teaches at Nipissing University, North Bay, Ontario, has written "Rational Bases of Identity: Toward Cultural Anarchy" for *Humanist in Canada* (Autumn 1996). She is on that journal's editorial committee and has written "The Humanist View of Animal Rights" for *The New Zealand Rationalist and Humanist* (Winter 1998). {*New Humanist*, September 1999}

Tizard, Catherine [Dame] (20th Century)

Tizard, the former mayor of Auckland and Governor-General of New Zealand, is an honorary associate of the New Zealand Association of Rationalists and Humanists.

Tobin, Ronald C. (20th Century)

Tobin edits *The Thought*, a bi-monthly journal of the Philosophers Guild (PO Box 10760, Glendale, Arizona 85318).

Tocco, Felice (1845–1911)

An Italian philosopher and anthropologist, Tocco taught philosophy at the University of Pisa. He wrote in the *Rivista Bolognese* on Leopardi and on positivism in the *Rivista Contemporanea*. Tocco's books include *A. Bain's Theory of Sensation* (1872); *Thoughts on the History of Philosophy* (1877); *The Heresy of the Middle Ages* (1884); and *Giordano Bruno* (1886). {BDF; RAT}

Tocqueville, Alexis de (1805–1859)

An astute French social philosopher, de Tocqueville was briefly foreign minister after the Revolution of 1848. When he visited the United States, he wrote a classic work about his findings, *Democracy in America* (2 volumes, 1835), in which he predicted that America's ideas about social equality and political democracy would one day replace Europe's aristocratic institutions. He also observed that "From time to time strange sects arise that endeavor to strike out extraordinary paths to eternal happiness. Religious insanity is very common in the United States." {CE}

Todd, Amanda (Died 1997)

Todd, the administrator of the British Humanist Association, committed suicide in 1997. Her friends were asked to make any donations to the Voluntary Euthanasia Society in London.

Tóibin, Colm (1955–)

An Irish novelist and writer of travel books, Tóibin was born in Enniscorthy. When a friend mentioned that he had lost his faith, Tóibin realized, at the age of fourteen, that "I had always known that the interest all around me in security, money, power, and status was greater than any love of God or belief in his mercy." Religion, he felt early in his life, "was consolation, like listening to music after a long day's work; it was pure theatre, it was a way of holding people together." In *The Sign of the Cross: Travels in Catholic Europe* (1995), he went to university ("I knew no one who believed"), moving on to Barcelona. "I did not think about Catholicism again for some years," he mentions, adding, "It did not cost me a thought." Of the book, critic Paul Elie remarked, "When he was a boy, Tóibin's Catholicism consisted of watching Catholics stick out their tongues for the communion wafer; now he is a man, and he is free to stand aside and stick his tongue out at them." Tóibin described his travels to various places: the climb u Croagh Patrick in Ireland, the pilgrimage of St. James in Spain, the trip to the site of the Medjugorje visitations in Croatia. At Lourdes, he decided to "take the waters," baths believed to cure the sick, and wondered if bathing suits would be provided. No, he found out, he had to strip to the underwear. "I wondered if I was wearing underpants, and when I realised that I was, I panicked once more, wondering if they were clean." After dropping his drawers and having a handler wrap a towel around him while holding him down in the waters, he came up shaking and quickly put his underwear on (but backwards, with the fly in the rear). The handler kindly interceded: "He . . . suggested that I come back and do it right. There was all the time in the world," he said, then held up the towel as a shield in order that Tóibin could put his pants on the right way around. Such, he found, is "the twilit world of half-medieval Catholicism." {"Smells and Bells," *The New Republic*, 11 December 1995}

TOILET PAPER

• People in many of the poorer parts of the world use only the right hand for eating. And for good reason: the left hand is reserved for wiping while at the toilet.

—Anonymous

• Queen Victoria lived before the advent of sewers, when raw sewage was thrown directly into rivers. Visiting Cambridge University in 1843, Her Majesty asked the master of Trinity College as they walked along the banks of the Cam why pieces of paper were floating down the river. With great tact and very little hesitation, the diplomatic master responded, "Those, Ma'am, are notices that bathing is forbidden." {*Playboy*, September 1996}

TOILET ETIQUETTE OF THE GODS: See entry for Gipson Arnold.

TOILETS

Conservative religious fundamentalists, ordinarily, are averse to saying *toilet* aloud. It is often described as "the necessary room" or "the little boys' [or girls'] room." The word has come to describe a disgusting, squalid, or depressing place. "A place to wash my hands," however, can result in being shown just that. Euphemisms for the toilet include powder room, bathroom, ladies' room, men's room, lavatory, restroom, comfort station, and watercloset (WC). Usually avoided are terms such as shithouses, johns, heads, cans, slop pails, outhouses, privies, chamberpots. In Europe, the socially acceptable euphemism, of unknown origin, is loo. Similarly, freethinkers are apt to choose a euphemism rather than ask for directions to the can.

Comedian George Carlin always speculated as to why we "take" a shit when what we mean is that we "leave" it. "Make your deposits now," Army sergeants used to advise if no toilet facilities would be available for a period of time.

Two who literally died "on the throne," as the toilet stool is sometimes called, were singers Judy Garland and Elvis Presley. Presley's medical examiner wrote that Presley "underwent his terminal event while on the commode."

In the vulgate, individuals can be expected to inquire where they can take a shit, crap, or piss. Studies are not readily available as to preferred terms of hoi polloi during past centuries. Biblical scholars avoid the subject altogether. (See entry for Allen Walker Read.)

Toland, John (1660–1722)

Toland, an Irish-born deist and one of the first to call himself a Freethinker, tried in his *Christianity not Mysterious* (1696) to reconcile the scriptural claims of Christianity with the epistemology of John Locke. The work was "presented" by the Grand Jury of Middlesex and condemned by the Lower House of Convocation. It also was burned in Ireland in 1697, and one member of the Irish House of Commons moved "that Mr. Toland himself should be burnt." His *Life of Milton* (1698), which, mentioning *Eikon Basilike*, referred to the "suppositious pieces under the name of Christ, his apostles, and other great persons." For this he was denounced by Dr. Blackhall before Parliament. He replied with *Amytor*, in which he gives a catalogue of such pieces. Toland was the first to use the term "pantheism," and in 1720 his most exotic work, *Pantheisticon*, was published, containing a liturgy that was taken to be a burlesque of the Christian liturgy. His pantheism is generally considered to be closer to that of Giordano Bruno than to that of Benedict Spinoza. *Deists* (1718) and the *Pantheisticon* (1720), "opened new windows." Robertson considers Toland "a thorough deist until he became pantheist," saying a certain amount of evasion was forced upon him because of the Blasphemy Law of 1697. Jonathan Swift described Toland as "the great Oracle of the anti-Christians."

For some years before his death, Toland lived in obscure lodgings with a carpenter at Putney. His health was broken, and his circumstances were poor. His last illness was painful, but he bore it with fortitude. According to one of his most intimate friends, Toland looked earnestly at those in the room a few minutes before breathing his last, and on being asked if he wanted anything, he answered, "I want nothing but death." His biographer, Des Maizeaux, said that "he looked upon death without the least perturbation of mind, bidding farewell to those that were about him, and telling them he was going to sleep." Wheeler added that Toland "died with the calmness of a philosopher, at Putney. Lange praises him highly." {Tony Akkermans, *The Freethinker*, June 1997; BDF; CE; EU, David Berman; FO; FUK; JM; JMR; JMRH; Sean Kearney, "John Toland: Father of Secular Philosophy, *New Humanist*, November 1997; RAT; RE}

TOLERANCE

Bertrand Russell Speaks His Mind (1969) gives Russell's definition of tolerance: "Toleration of opinion, if it's really full-blown, consists in not punishing any kind of opinion as long as it doesn't issue in some kind of criminal act." Lord Russell explains: "The first really tolerant state was Holland. All the leading intellects of the seventeenth century at some period of their lives had to take refuge in Holland, and if there hadn't been Holland, they'd have been wiped out. The English were no better than other people at that time. There was a parliamentary investigation which decided that Hobbes was very, very wicked, and it was decreed that no work by Hobbes was to be published in England. And it wasn't, for a long, long time." Russell believed that "the true test of a lover of freedom comes only in relation to things that he dislikes. To tolerate what you like is easy. It is toleration of what you dislike that characterizes the liberal attitude."

Russell realizes there are limits to tolerance. For example, "If there were no law against murder, we should all have to go armed and avoid solitude and be perpetually on the watch. Many liberties which we now take for granted would disappear. It is, therefore, in the interests of liberty to curtail the liberty of would-be murders," and here he includes states, concluding that "if a civilized way of life is to continue, it will be necessary to arrive at a method of preventing aggressive war."

Russell also recognizes that where any large group is basically out of sympathy with the rest of the citizens of the State, "democracy is apt to become unworkable, except by a use of force, which will produce great discontent in the subordinate group, and a harsh temper in the dominant group." As examples, he cites the situation of Jews in a country where popular sentiment is strongly anti-Semitic, of Muslims in India, of Hindus in Pakistan. Then, he writes in *Fact and Fiction* (1961), "Democracy in such cases can only be successful if there is a diffused sentiment of tolerance."

"Humanists cannot limit their battle for tolerance," French astronomer Jean-Claude Pecker has written, "to the rather narrow views of the religiously minded preachers. We have to speak for a *positive kind of tolerance*, a tolerance that considers, on equal footing, men and women throughout the world over as having the same right to be confident in their beliefs, and the same freedom to express them, without any exclusion. In no case should the color of skin, social origin, language, religion or beliefs, philosophical attitude, nationality, sex, etc., be the cause of any discrimination in any field of the human activity." As to whether we should tolerate everything, Pecker responded, "As Locke considers the Catholics intolerable, as Saint Paul found intolerable those who refused the true God, there are several behaviors that we do not tolerate either. Where is the line? All that is criminal is of course intolerable. All the preaching for the superiority of any doctrine in that it can lead to intolerable actions is intolerable. Xenophobia, Nazism, fundamentalism, etc., are intolerable."

On the subject, Paul Kurtz has written, "What libertarian humanists insist upon as part of the private sphere are inner thoughts and conscience, religious belief or unbelief, control over one's own body, sexual preference between consenting adults, abortion, reproductive freedom, euthanasia, the right to die with dignity, artistic expression , and so on. . . . In a free society where racists abound, where a drug culture runs rampant (I am in favor of the decriminalization of drugs), where promiscuity, violence in the media, and wasted lives are everywhere in evidence, humanists need to defend moral excellence, noble deeds, and qualitative standards. . . . We have an obligation to encourage the finest cultural expressions, intellectual, aesthetic, and moral appreciation." As for tolerance regarding ethnicity, Kurtz added, "You cannot find a defense of human rights in the Bible or the Koran. They have emerged only with the democratic and humanist revolutions of the modern era. Included in this are the rights of the child. . . . Humanists need to defend tolerance provided it is accompanied by moral responsibility, which should be achieved by education rather than legislation. Similarly, we need to encourage the development of a humanist culture in which no ethnic, racial, or religious pockets exist and in which we reach a new planetary culture."

To test one's tolerance, humanists discuss such matters as to whether certain customs should be "tolerated"; e.g.,

- In Maine, a refugee from Afghanistan was seen kissing the penis of his baby boy, a traditional expression of love by this father.
- In Seattle, a hospital invented a harmless female circumcision procedure to satisfy conservative Somali parents wanting to keep an African practice alive in their community.
- In India, some widows are immolated.
- In many Muslim countries, removal of the female clitoris at a minimum is practiced as well as male circumcision.
- In Cambodia, hot objects are pressed on a child's forehead or back in a practice called "coining" that is meant to cure various maladies but leaves welts.
- In Afghanistan, a wronged family may demand the death penalty and carry it out themselves with official blessing.
- In Madhya Pradesh State in India, marriages of seven-year-olds occur.

• Rastifarians use marijuana in their religious ceremonies.

Inasmuch as many immigrants have moved into countries in which legal systems do not permit certain acts, more and more law schools have taken an interest in religion and the different customs of other cultures. While some may want judgment-free considerations of immigrants' practices and traditional rituals in the countries they come from, others from those same countries beg to be admitted in order to escape from tribal rites in the name of human rights. {Barbara Crossette, *The New York Times*, 6 March 1999; Lee Eisler, *The Quotable Bertrand Russell*; *Free Inquiry*, Winter 1995-1996}

TOLERATION

• Toleration is not the *opposite* of intoleration, but the *counterfeit* of it. Both are despotisms.

—**Thomas Paine**

Tollemache, Lionel Arthur (Born 1838)

Tollemache was the son of Baron Tollemache, a friend of C. Austin, of whom he wrote. He had many articles in *Fortnightly Review* and published *Safe Studies* (1884), *Recollections of Pallison* (1885), and *Mr. Romanes's Catechism* (1887). {BDF; RAT}

Toller, Ernst (1893–1939)

A German dramatist and poet of the expressionist school, Toller was imprisoned (1919–1924) for participating in the Communist Bavarian revolution. He wrote many works of social protest, including *Die Maschinen-stürmer* (1922, The Machine-Wreckers), based on the Luddite riots in England. A non-theist, he wrote an autobiography, *Eine Jugend in Deutschland* (1933). {CE}

Tolley, Howard Jr. (20th Century)

Tolley has worked as a senior law clerk in the U. S. Court of Appeals for the Sixth Circuit, as a professor at Wilberforce University, and as a U. S. Peace Corps volunteer in Nigeria. He formerly was president in Ohio of the Yellow Springs Unitarian fellowship and now is on the board of directors of the Unitarian Universalist Service Committee.

Tolson, Melvin B. (1898–1966)

An African American columnist for the now defunct *Washington Tribune*, Tolson according to Norm Allen Jr. was a rationalist. In 1947 he was appointed poet laureate of Liberia by Liberian President V. S. Tubman, and in 1954 he was awarded the Order of the Star of Africa by Liberian Ambassador Simpson. {AAH}

Tolstoy, Leo (Lev Nikolayevitch Tolstoi) [Count] (1828–1910)

Tolstoy, a major Russian novelist and philosopher, wished for a "rationalized" Christianity. Like characters in his novels, he struggled between belief and unbelief. He liked much of what he read about William Ellery Channing and the Brahmo-Somaj movement in India. He particularly liked a pioneering work on nonviolence, *Christian Non-Resistance*, by Adin Ballou, a Universalist minister, whom he described as being one of America's greatest writers. But when he satirized the Orthodox church in his *Resurrection* (1889–1899), he was excommunicated. He remained, however, a Christian of sorts whose relations with his God, thought Maxim Gorki, were "very suspicious: they sometimes remind me of the relation of two bears in one den." McCabe labeled him "a mystic theist" who enjoyed flogging "the Churches."

Tolstoy was a brawny man who, at the time of his marriage when he was thirty-four, had lost most of his teeth. He married Sofya Andreyevna Behrs, daughter of the chief court physician of Czar Alexander II. Tolstoy's mother-in-law, who with her family of three daughters lived in the Kremlin, was only two years older than he. His young bride, the middle child of the three, had been mesmerized since childhood by the writer, and Tolstoy was enamored of the young bride who was said to have had *du chien*, a "bite" that combined stylishness and sex appeal. Following a custom of the Czar and others at that time to exchange the reading of each other's diaries, Tolstoy required as a condition of marriage that Sofya, whom he called Sonya, agree that the two should read each other's diaries in order that they might never conceal secrets from each other. She agreed. Before the wedding, therefore, he read her chaste and meditative entries. However, she was shocked to learn about his past gambling, drunken orgies, whoring even at the age of fourteen, homosexual longings, venereal diseases, and an affair with a peasant woman, Axinya, who lived nearby with their illegitimate son. Just the same, she consented.

According to historian William L. Shirer's *Love and Hatred* (1994), the two lived in Yasnaya Polyana for most of the next forty-eight years, during which time he gained world-wide fame, she had sixteen pregnancies, and she had thirteen childbirths. Only eight of the offspring survived into adulthood, all such details dutifully noted in their diaries.

Sonya, a devout, traditional Orthodox Christian, wrote that she had not particularly enjoyed making love to her husband almost nightly when she was not expecting a child. After her fifties when she was beyond child-bearing, however, she noted that she rather enjoyed sex. Although theirs was a stormy relationship filled with strife, she faithfully researched for her husband, made translations, and copied his difficult-to-read handwriting into legible script. Meanwhile, twenty-two years into their marriage Sonya read in her husband's diary that "[s]he will remain a millstone around my neck . . . until I die." Still, he assigned her all copyrights from his writings, and she acted as his literary agent and publisher, notes critic Francine du Plessix Gray.

When Tolstoy began to change his philosophy, saying he was a sinner, rejecting the Church, repudiating private property, and declaring he would no longer write "artistic" novels, Sonya at first declared the renunciation of worldly goods was a publicity ploy. Although Tolstoy was denouncing marriage and family and sex, the diaries show he continued to lust for his wife into his seventies and eighties. Sonya had become pregnant for the tenth time, in fact, the year he began to preach marital chastity.

The new villain on the scene, his biographers explain, was Vladimir Chertkov. Although not exactly a charlatan, Shirer writes, Chertkov cast a spell over Tolstoy in order to try to get control of the diaries and take the manuscripts away from Sonya. She considered Chertkov an intruder, writing to him, " (My husband's) diaries are the holy of holies of his life, and consequently of mine with him." She accused him of trying to take from her "all I have lived by for forty-eight years." Getting no support from Alexandra (Sasha), their youngest surviving child, and unable to get her husband away from Chertkov, she wrote, "Falling for men was more in his line as a boy! And now he is absolutely at that man's beck and call." Her jealousy became so blinding, according to Leigh W. Rutledge, that she threatened to kill Chertkov, left the house, and was found "babbling incoherently and lying face-down in some wet grass on the estate." Although she had thought the two men were writing love letters and were confiding secrets as they walked together in the woods, Chertkov said they had only been conversing and exchanging letters on the terms of Tolstoy's will, which left sole control of Tolstoy's manuscripts to Chertkov. Sonya later was successful in getting that will revoked, following her husband's death.

Meanwhile, Sonya brandished part of a diary entry Tolstoy had written six decades earlier, when he was twenty-three: "I have never been in love with a woman," the entry read, "but I have quite often fallen in love with a man. . . . I feel in love with a man before I knew what pederasty was. . . . Beauty has always been a powerful factor in my attractions; there is D—, for example. I shall never forget the night we left Pirogovo together, when, wrapped up in my blanket, I wanted to devour him with kisses and weep. Sexual desire was not totally absent, but it was impossible to say what role it played."

To a friend, Tolstoy complained, "Tell her (Sonya), that if she's trying to kill me, she'll soon succeed." Tolstoy did leave, writing to her that "My position in this house is becoming—has already become—intolerable." Although she threatened suicide if he did not return, he refused. With a doctor friend and Sasha, he set out in search of some peace. In a railroad junction town, Astapovo, Tolstoy developed pneumonia, a fact reported in the newspaper. This resulted in crowds of journalists eager to record and even make photojournalistic movies of the dying author. Tolstoy, who had thought that by leaving home he could meditate further on the Meaning of Life, now found himself at the center of unwanted attention. An emissary from the Holy Synod arrived to receive, unsuccessfully, his repentance and return to the Church. Chertkov and Sasha found themselves part of the media circus. Sonya, kept from her husband for fear he would die of anger upon seeing her, was only allowed in to his bedside after he had lost consciousness. In his last three hours of life, she whispered prayers over the still excommunicated Tolstoy. Upon her husband's death, Chertkov, also, departed from her life.

Until her own death, ten years later in 1919, Sonya Tolstoy walked daily to her husband's burial site near their home, which after the Russian Revolution was turned into a government farm. Lenin decreed that she was to be allowed to remain there for the rest of her life. (See entry for James Wood, who states, "Tolstoy, for instance, could not be called a Christian in any proper use of the word, but is always banging on about God and Christ.") {CE; JM; RAT; TYD}

Tomashevich, George Vid (1927–)

Tomashevich, a professor emeritus of anthropology at Buffalo State University College, signed the Secular Humanist Declaration in 1980. In 1981, he wrote *Aging in America and Other Cultures*. Originally, Tomashevich was from Montenegro. {SHD}

Tomavic, Victor (20th Century)

Tomavic is professor emeritus of sociology at Brock University, St. Catherines, Ontario, Canada, and adjunct professor of sociology at the State University of New York at Buffalo. He spoke at the 1994 humanist conference in San José, Costa Rica.

Tombaugh, Clyde William (1906-)

Tombaugh is an educator and astronomer. He was associated with White Sands Proving Grounds, Las Cruces, New Mexico, starting in 1946; was chief optical measurement section of the Ballistics Laboratories in 1948; was chief of the research and evaluation branch planning department of the Flight Determination division from 1948 to 1953, among his many positions. He taught astronomy at New Mexico State University.

Tombaugh is credited with having discovered Pluto in 1930. He was a Unitarian.

TOMBSTONES: See entry for Death and Tombstones.

Tomkyns, Martin: See entry for Joshua Toulmin.

Tommasi, Salvatore (19th Century)

An Italian evolutionist, Tommasi wrote *Evolution, Science, and*

Naturalism (1877). He also wrote a pamphlet in 1882 in commemoration of Darwin. {BDF}

Tompkins, Henry (20th Century)

Tompkins was a noted British positivist and non-theist.

Tompkins, Jerry R. (20th Century)

Tompkins edited *D-Day at Dayton: Reflections on the Scopes Trial* (1965). {FUS}

Tompson, Marian Leonard (20th Century)

Tompson was given the 1999 A. D. Black Award of the Ethical Humanist Society for her pioneering work in educating mothers, physicians, and the public about breasteeding. She is the founder and for twenty-four years was president of La Leche League International. On the Web: <http://lalecheleague.org>.

Tone, Theobald Wolfe (1763–1798)

An Irish patriot, Tone founded the Society of United Irishmen in 1791. He related to the French revolutionists and in 1796 induced the French Directory to send an expedition against England. Tone, eventually taken prisoner, committed suicide in prison before his execution could be carried out. In 1826, his son edited his father's journals and an autobiography, which confirm that Tone was a deist. According to McCabe, that fact is suppressed in Eire, where Tone remained a popular idol. {BDF; JM; RAT; RE}

TONGUES, SPEAKING IN

Glossolalia, or speaking in tongues, is defined as the ecstatic utterances usually of unintelligible sounds made by individuals in a state of religious excitement. Various Pentecostal groups cite for authority the *Acts of the Apostles 2:4*. Paul in *1 Corinthians* 12 and 14 encouraged the practice. In *Acts*, however, the use of the gift produces speech in other human languages as a kind of reversal of the confusion of tongues produced at the Tower of Babel. Some American Negro sects that are pentecostal in character call the emotional automata "tongue talking." Others suggest it is a sign of demonic possession. Meanwhile, polyglottal freethinkers are known for speaking intelligble sounds. (See Martin Gardner, "Klingon and Other Artificial Languages," *Skeptical Inquirer*, July-August 1995.) {CE}

Tonkin, Don (20th Century)

Tonkin has written for the *South Australian Humanist Post*, and he is in favor of Australia's devising legislation concerning euthanasia which will allow a physician to give a lethal dose to a patient in great pain and with absolutely no chance of recovery.

Tönnies, Ferdinand (Born 1855)

A German sociologist who held a modified version of Schopenhauer's theory of reality, Tönnies called his outlook "Critical Voluntarism." For him, will is the ultimate reality, and all sound knowledge is rationalistic and empirical. He wrote several works, including *Gemeinschaft und Gesellschaft* (1887) and *Das Wesen der Soziologie* (1907). Tönnies supported the German Monist League and wrote in *Das Monistische Jahrhundert*. {RAT}

Tonne, Herbert A. (1902–1998)

When he signed Humanist Manifesto II, Tonne was on the editorial board of the *Journal of Business Education*. He was active in the American Humanist Association and in humanist circles in the New Jersey and New York areas. Tonne, who was a professor of business education at New York University and the State University of New York at Albany, wrote a number of texts on education: (with P. S. Lomax), *Problems of Teaching Economics* (1932); (with M. H. Tonne) *Social-Business Subjects in the Secondary Schools* (1932); *Consumer Education in the Schools* (1941); (with L. L. Jones and R. G. Price) *Functions of Business* (1941); *A Realistic Philosophy of Education* (1942); (with E. L. Popham and M. H. Freeman), *Methods of Teaching Business Subjects* (1957); (with S. I. Simon and E. C. McGill), *Business Principles: Organization and Management* (1958); (4th and 5th editions with L. C. Nanassy), *Principles of Business Education* (1947, 1954, 1961, 1967, 1973); and (with L. C. Nanassy and D. R. Malsbury) *Principles and Trends in Business Education* (1977). He also wrote *Looking Ahead to 2084 (*1974); *The Human Dilemma: Finding Meaning in Life* (1980); *Scribblings of a Concerned Secular Humanist* (1988); and "Why Are There So Few Humanists?"

Tonne was an articulate secular humanist who knew many influential humanist leaders and, in turn, influenced many. (See entry for Humanist Manifestos. Also see "Religious Belief in America: A New Poll," *Free Inquiry*, Summer 1996, which he commissioned. Among other facts, the study showed that over 88% of Americans believe in a personal God who can answer prayer; that only 8.2% believe God is an invention of the human mind; that 88% believe an atheist is anyone who does not believe in the existence of a superior being who created and rules the universe; that 93.2% believe miracles are performed today by the power of God; and that 80.3% believe in life after death, as contrasted with 26.1% among people who consider themselves very non-religious. Tonne found the Goldhaber Research Associations poll's findings, which he funded, surprising. Do people just ignore or disbelieve what they read and hear? he wondered. {HM2}

Tooke, John Horne (1736–1812)

Tooke was an English radical politician and philologist. Born John Horne, he adopted the name Tooke in 1782 after being designated heir to the estate of a rich friend, William Tooke. In 1760 he became an Anglican priest but soon abandoned his clerical duties for politics. In 1771, he founded the Constitutional Society to promote parliamentary reform and support for the American colonists. Fined and imprisoned in 1778, he was later tried for treason but was acquitted. In 1801 he was elected to Parliament, but in the same year the government passed an act specifically directed against him which disqualified clergy from sitting in the House of Commons. McCabe reports that when Tooke "threw off his cassock," he said that he had had "the infectious hand of a bishop waved over him." McCabe labeled Tooke a Deist. Philologists have complained that Tooke's speculative etymologies delayed for decades the introduction of the new and sounder philology from the Continent. Tooke left instructions (which were disregarded) that he was to be buried in his garden at Purley and the only speaker was to be his atheist friend Sir F. Burdett. {CE; JM; RAT; RE}

Tool (20th Century)

The recording artists known as Tool include the following in liner notes for their album "Aenima":

> This sort of behavior is left to the psychotic, dogmatic, fundamentalist believers you see on T.V. every day letting off bombs and killing people in the name of God. Beliefs are dangerous. Beliefs allow the mind to stop functioning. A non-functioning mind is clinically dead. *Believe* in nothing.

{CA; E}

Toomey, Samuel (Born 1830)

At first a blacksmith, Toomey became a carriage maker and invented various improvements on carriages. In 1868, he invented what was then widely known as Toomey's method of constructing bent-rim wheels. He wrote of religion, "My father and mother belonged to the old German Lutheran church, but I was taken away from home so very young that I got little religious instruction from them, but I mainly fell into the hands of the same class of people, so I had to go to church. In this way I grew up, and being a natural abolitionist from my youth up, I joined the United Brethren church when eighteen years of age but never could fully believe the Bible stories. At the same time I became a reader of the *Antislavery Bugle* published in Salem, Ohio. Salem was at that time the headquarters for those then known as Broad-gangers, or Infidels. Such reading brought about thinking and investigation, and, as you know, investigation brings Infidelity. So for the last thirty years I did my own thinking, reading such books as any unbiased man should read; and, of course, as with the great Darwin, it ended in Agnosticism, and very strongly in Atheism." {PUT}

Toon, Nicholas (20th Century)

For *The Freethinker* (October 1997), Toon wrote "Fallacious Arguments for God." "Freewill is an illusion," he stated. "There are no absolute standards of right and wrong; we make our own morality."

Topazio, Virgil W. (20th Century)

When he reviewed books on Diderot and Sterne for *The Humanist* in the 1950s, Topazio taught French at the University of Rochester.

Topinard, Paul (19th Century)

Topinard was a French anthropologist and physician. He edited the *Revue d'Anthropologie*, the standard work on that subject published in the Library of Contemporary Science. In *Science and Faith* (1899), he did not, he said, want "a grain of mysticism" in life. {BDF; RAT}

Topp, Arthur Manning (1844–1916)

Topp was an Australian secularist, journalist, and editor. Son of an English wool importer, he emigrated to Melbourne, Australia, in 1858 and, with H. G. Turner, launched the *Melbourne Review*. Topp was an admirer of Herbert Spencer's analysis of religious belief and philosophy. In 1867 he was an Australian leader in the Eclectic Association of Victoria, some of whose members joined the Secular Society. {SWW}

TORAH

The Torah (which in Hebrew means *law*) is the law on which Judaism is founded. It is contained in the first five books of the Bible (*Genesis, Exodus, Leviticus, Numbers, Deuteronomy*). Torah can also refer to the entire body of Jewish law and wisdom, including what is contained in oral tradition. {DCL}

Torcaso, Roy R. (20th Century)

Torcaso was a notary public from Wheaton, Maryland, whose commission was withheld because he refused to take an oath declaring belief in God. The Supreme Court ruled against the provision of the Maryland Constitution which stated, "No religious test ought ever to be required as a qualification for any office of profit or trust in this state, other than a declaration of belief in the existence of God." Corliss Lamont has written that "in delivering the unanimous opinion of the Court that this statute was unconstitutional under the First Amendment, Justice Hugo L. Black observed in a footnote: 'Among religions in this country which do not teach what would generally be considered a belief in the existence of God are Buddhism, Taoism, Ethical Culture, Secular Humanism and others.' " Justice Black's observation upsets those secular humanists who consider themselves part of a philosophic movement, not a religion. Torcaso is on the Board of Directors of the American Humanist Association and of the Freedom From Religion Foundation. (See entry for Hugo L. Black and the 1995 ruling by the Ninth Circuit Court of Appeals which ruled that secular humanism is *not* a religion.) {CL; FD}

Torquemada, Tomás de (1420–1498)

Señor de Torquemada was the highly efficient Spanish Inquisitor-General who sent misbelievers, for example Jews, as well as non-believers to their deaths. In addition to being Queen Isabella's and King Ferdinand V's confessor, he is credited "with having burned over ten thousand persons in his eighteen years of office as Grand Inquisitor, besides torturing many thousands. Close upon a hundred thousand more were terrified into submission; and a further six thousand burned in effigy in their absence or after death." He punished crypto-Jews, apostates, witches, and spiritual offenders. Even the *Catholic Encyclopedia* admits some 2000 were executed and vast other numbers were punished. He encouraged the expulsion of the Jews in 1492 and, ironically, was of Jewish descent. In 1571, Cardinal Alonso Manrique of Seville compiled a work which thoroughly details the Inquisition's work: *Compilacion de las instrucciones del oficio de la Santa Inquisicion, hechas por el muy reverendo Señor Fray Tomas de Torquemada . . . E por los otros reverendissimos señores Inquisidores Generales, que despues sucedieron*. The work was republished for Diego Diaz de la Carrera in 1667 and again in 1747 for Francisco Perez de Prado y Cuesta. In a 1992 movie, "Christopher Columbus: The Discovery," Marlon Brando had a bit part in which he played the part of Spain's most notorious inquisitor. Comedian Mel Brooks, in a song, "The Inquisition," noted that his prisoners couldn't "torquemada (talk him out of) anything." {CE; JMR; JMRH}

Torrey, Jesse Jr. (19th Century)

In Poughkeepsie, New York, in 1835, Torrey edited *Herald of Reason & Common Sense*. {FIS}

Torrey, Norman L. (1894–1980)

A professor of French at Columbia University, Torrey was author of *Spirit of Voltaire* (1938) and co-editor with Otis Fellows of *Diderot Studies* (1953). Active in New York City humanist circles, Torrey wrote to the present author about humanism:

> I was a student of Irving Babbitt but reacted against his brand, becoming a naturalistic humanist. My idea of humanism is a development of my special interest in French literature and history of ideas. A clear notion of the growth of humanism can be found in the Preliminary Discourse (1750) of the first great Encyclopedia, edited by Diderot and d'Alembert. The spirit of the enterprise was modeled after Alexander Pope's couplet, "Know thyself. Presume not God to scan; / The proper study of mankind is Man." In the Preliminary Discourse, d'Alembert explains the French Enlightenment, represented by Montesquieu, Voltaire, Diderot, and Rousseau, as the natural fulfillment of the Renaissance, which he understood as the rebirth of pagan philosophy and culture. The first step in this return, after the Dark Ages, to the wisdom of the Greeks and the Romans was of necessity the thorough understanding of the languages of those peoples.
>
> The sixteenth century Humanists (with a capital H), were a group of scholars, composers of grammars and dictionaries, jealous pedants whose unsavory reputation as wranglers was compensated for by the genuine contribution they made to the comprehension of such authors as Cicero, Lucian, and Lucretius. The full development of this pagan culture took place two centuries later. D'Alembert connects it with the "light of reason" and the rise of the scientific spirit, but cannot yet use the word humanist in its modern sense. The appeal to humanity, however, and to the inalienable rights of man, becomes more and more frequent both in France and America; for example in our Declaration of Independence. In Montesquieu's plea to the Spanish Inquisitors, he urges them, since they have shown that they cannot be Christians, to at least be men.
>
> Voltaire likewise reminded man of his essential dignity and righted many an injustice in the name of humanity. With an assist from Jefferson, the century was fittingly summed up in the Declaration of the Rights of Man and of the Citizen, one of the great humanist documents of all time. It has taken another two centuries for the word humanist to recapture its fundamental historical meaning. There is every indication that the present decade of the twentieth century is witnessing this victory.

Dr. Torrey was an active member of secular humanist groups in New York City. For the *Encyclopedia of Philosophy*, Vol. 8, he wrote the selection on Voltaire. {FUK; HNS; WAS, 24 April 1956}

TORTURE

The *Rationalist Encyclopedia* details forms of torture in Ancient China, in Babylonia, and particularly in the Dark Ages. During the Norman Conquest, McCabe points out, kings and nobles devised and inflicted the most horrible torture on Anglo-Saxons or any—even clerics, monks, and nuns—who were suspected of having concealed money or treasure. During the Age of Chivalry (1100–1400), the knights, nobles, and even princes and "noble" ladies (who often led their own bandit troops) wrought fiendish tortures, sometimes with their own hands, on travelers, priests, monks, nuns, and others believed to have hidden treasure. Not to be outshone, pious abbots castrated monks for irregularities as early as the year 600. Cutting or burning out the eyes was an even more common practice. Chopping off hands or feet or ears, and cutting out tongues or piercing them with a hot iron, were equally common. Also, cheaters of the King were boiled in oil. Molten lead was poured over offenders, people were "broken on the wheel" or nearly torn asunder on the rack; the bones of the lower leg were broken with the "Spanish Boots," and the thumbs with thumbscrews; weights were hung from the genitals; water dripped from a height onto the stomach; the feet were washed with salt water and goats were brought to lick the soles; intense hunger and thirst were inflicted; men were hung up for hours by the wrists or (sometimes in the case of nuns) smeared naked with honey and spread in the sun to attract insects; hot boiled eggs were fixed under the armpits of men or to the breasts of women; legs were wrapped tight in calf-skin and boiling oil poured over; hands or feet were burned off; string was tied tight round the head; nails were torn out and teeth broken; the flesh was torn with red-hot pincers.

Voltaire's *Treatise on Toleration* states that Protestants were broken on the wheel as late as 1762. However, the French Revolution resulted in abolishing the official use of torture in all countries which its armies conquered. With the fall of Napoleon, torture resumed by the joint authorities of the State and the Catholic Church. Rationalists of the 17th and 18th centuries (Montaigne, Bayle, Voltaire, Montesquieu, Beccaria, and others) stirred the conscience of Europe against using the kinds of torture which the Church had used for more than a thousand years. But torture continued to be used, as pointed out in McCabe's *Papacy in Politics Today* (1937). (See entry for George E. Macdonald. Also, see McCabe's *Rationalist Encyclopedia* for a thorough discussion of torture.) {RE}

TOTEM: See entry for animism.

Toth, Arpad (20th Century)

Toth is active with the Humanist Association of New Hampshire-Vermont. A retired Commander of the United States Navy, he chose as his New Hampshire license plate ATIEST. (See entry for New Hampshire Humanists.) {FD; *Freethought Today*, October 1996}

Toth, Judith (20th Century)

Toth in the 1980s joined Ethical Leadership after intensive training. She has served several years as executive secretary and an organizational trainer in the Washington Society, and in 1985 continued her leadership in Baltimore. (See entry for Ethical Culture.)

Toulmin, George Hoggart (18th Century)

Toulmin wrote *The Antiquity and Duration of the World* (1785). A physician, he also wrote *The Eternity of the Universe* (1789). Dr. Toulmin was born in Wolverhampton, England. {BDF}

Toulmin, Joshua (18th Century)

A Unitarian "antipaedobaptist," or one who opposed infant baptism, Toulmin was a one-time Anglican vicar who wrote lives of Socinus (1777) and Biddle (1797). His sermon on "The Injustice of Classing Unitarians with Deists and Infidels" (1797) was termed inconvenient, and the effigy of Paine was burned before his door and his windows were broken. His businesses of schoolkeeping and bookselling had to be given up. Robertson mentions that it was a time when the Unitarians were doing a considerable amount of freethinking, and among these authors were E. Evanson, Martin Tomkyns, Isaac Watts the hymnist ("Joy to the World"; "O God, Our Help in Ages Past"), and Joseph Priestley. {JMR; JMRH}

Toulmin, Stephen Edelston (1922–)

Toulmin is a London-born humanities educator who teaches at the University of Southern California in Los Angeles. He wrote *The Place of Reason in Ethics* (1949); *Wittgenstein's Vienna* (with A. Jankik, 1973); *The Return to Cosmology* (1982); and *Cosmopolis* (with J. Goodfield, 1989). He has contributed numerous scientific articles to professional journals and has revived an interest in ethical casuistry.

In 1994 in Utrecht at the University of Humanist Studies, he spoke at a conference entitled "Embarrassment of Identities: Humanism and the Future of Europe." In discussing "Are Nation States Obsolescent?" he responded in the affirmative. Among other factors, Dr. Toulmin suggests that the growth of human population and the evolution of society have reached a point, ecologically speaking, at which attempts to preserve the system of Nation States will be *maladaptive*. How to move into a different, multiethnic, and transnational future, however, is not clear. {*New Humanist*, May 1994}

Touré, Ahmed Sékou [President] (1922–1984)

Touré was President of the Republic of Guinea (1958–1984) and founder of the Rassemblement Démocratique Africain. He led Guinea out of the French Community (1958) and, at the time of his death, was seeking the position as chairman of the Organization of African Unity. A Marxist, he called his philosophic outlook "a new humanism." {CE}

Tourin, Jack (20th Century)

When he signed Humanist Manifesto II, Tourin was president of the American Ethical Union. {HM2}

Toy, Anne (20th Century)

Toy is a leader in England of the Humanist Speakers Network.

Toynbee, Polly (1946–)

Columnist for *The Guardian* and broadcaster Polly Toynbee spoke at Conway Hall in 1995 at the first joint annual dinner of Secular and Humanist organizations. The great-granddaughter of Gilbert Murray, Toynbee lamented the fact that "just as conventional religions are on the wane, so a New Wave of nonsense is rising up to engulf us. Cults, superstitions, astrology, numerology, every kind of *ism* and *ology* seems to gain an astonishing tolerance and credulity these days in the most surprising paces. As people turn away from the church, all too often they turn towards things that are even worse. Anything goes these days, in the way of belief."

"What I find even odder," she continued, "is that the beleaguered conventional religions are responding by drawing closer together. Ecumenicism is everywhere. The Methodists want to join the Church of England. Many Protestants even want to get into bed with the Pope, if only he were willing to use contraception. Multi-faith worship is all the thing. The Jews who killed Christ are being forgiven by Christians who have been killing them in pogroms for generations. Sikhs and Hindus are welcomed by Christians keen on cultural diversity. Religious leaders everywhere are coming together across ancient divides in an attempt to protect their interests collectively."

But what this shows non-believers, she explained, "is that they don't really believe, either. After all, if you believe that Jesus Christ is the one and only son of God, sent to earth with a unique message; if you believe the secret of your particular religion had been revealed to you exclusively and that it is your duty to go out and proselytise the rest of the world, how can you suddenly decide that somebody else's religion is just as valid as yours, just as worthy of respect, understanding, and so on?" In short, "If one God and one Prophet is as good as another, if wearing a turban and a dagger is just as good as putting a wafer on your tongue, then it's all exposed as the nonsense that it really is." {*The Freethinker*, June 1995}

Tracy, Antoine Louis Claude Destutt de [Count] (1754–1836)

Tracy was a Field-Marshall during the French Revolution. During the Terror he studied science and philosophy and was a friend of Cabanis and Condorcet. His principal work, *Elements d'Idéologie* (1817–1818, 4 volumes) is materialistic and regards theology as "a part of zoology." Jefferson, a friend and admirer, translated the work into English. In his later years, Tracy enjoyed the company of Voltaire, who read to him. {RAT; RE}

Tracy, César Victor Charles Destutt d' [Marquis] (1781–1864)

Tracy, the son of Count Antoine Tracy, served in all of Napoleon's campaigns. In 1822 he was sent to Parliament, where he sat on the anti-clerical left with Lafayette's son, who married his sister. In Parliament, he worked for the abolition of slavery and the death penalty, the freedom of education, the suppression of the hereditary peerage, and other reforms. Although made Minister of Marine by Louis Napoleon, Tracy protested against the coup d'état and retired to the study of scientific agriculture, on which he wrote several works. {RAT}

Tracy, Henry C. (20th Century)

An American, Tracy wrote *Towards the Open* (1927), a work about scientific humanism.

TRAGEDY

• Tragedy is a form of drama exciting the emotions of pity and fear. Its action should be single and complete, presenting a reversal of fortune, involving persons renowned and of superior attainments, and it should be written in poetry embellished with every kind of artistic expression.

—Aristotle

• The tragedy of life is not so much what men suffer but rather what they miss.

—**Thomas Carlyle**

• There are two tragedies in life: one is to lose your heart's desire, the other is to gain it.

—**George Bernard Shaw**

Journalists and others constantly confuse tragedy with pathos (a quality, as of an experience or a work of art, that arouses feelings of pity, sympathy, tenderness, or sorrow) and comedy (a dramatic work that is light and often humorous or satirical in tone and that usually contains a happy resolution of the thematic conflict).

A headline, 200 KILLED IN TRAGIC CRASH, will need to be accompanied by a story that indicates what the pilot chose to do that he should not have done, perhaps aiming the stricken plane at a busy shopping center instead of an open space. A headline, PATHETIC LADY STARVES, needs to be accompanied by a story that indicates why the person chose to deprive herself of food.

Traherne, Thomas: See entry for Ganymede.

Traiger, Saul (20th Century)

Traiger, a professor of philosophy, is secretary-treasurer of The Hume Society, a group engaged in scholarly activity concerning David Hume.

Traill, Ralph Cuthbert (1905–1991)

Traill was an Australian rationalist, humanist, and scientist. In 1963 he was vice principal of the Royal Melbourne Institute of Technology. During the McCarthyism of the 1950s, he found it expedient to use the pseudonyms John Arcot for his musical compositions and Ross Tracy for his poetry, one a play on his initials, the other a play on his name. He was president and a life member of the Rationalist Society of Australia, and from 1965 to 1973 he was vice president of the Humanist Society of Victoria. {SWW}

Traina, Tommaso (19th Century)

Traina was an Italian jurist, the author of a work on *The Ethics of Herbert Spencer* (1881). {BDF}

TRANSACTIONAL ANALYSIS: See entry for Mary Bancroft Boulton, one of the practitioners of this form of group therapy.

TRANSACTIONALISM: See entry for Arthur F. Bentley.

TRANSCENDENTALISM

Transcendentalism as a literary and philosophic movement flourished in New England from the 1830s to the 1860s, partly as a reaction against the orthodoxy of Calvinism and the rationalism of the Unitarian Church. Its strongest influence came from Kantian idealism, and evidence of its eclecticism is found in its owing much to Platonic and Oriental influences, relying on intuition, and being optimistic regarding human nature. Kant in his *Critique of Practical Reason* (1788) had declared, "I call all knowledge *transcendental* which is concerned, not with objects, but with our mode of knowing objects so far as this is possible *a priori*." Other German philosophers—Fichte, Herder, Jacobi, Schleiermacher, Schelling—emphasized mysticism and practical action as an expression of the will. In England, Carlyle, Coleridge, and Wordsworth were influential in developing the philosophy, which was never rigorously systematic. In the United States, Louisa Mae Alcott, Margaret Fuller, Emerson, and Thoreau were representative of the literary movement. Emerson's *Nature* (1836) and *The American Scholar* (1837) expressed his transcendental ideas, as did such of his poems as "Self-Reliance," "The Over-Soul," and "The Rhodora." Thoreau's *Walden* (1854) was indicative of his transcendentalism. Whereas in the previous century deists had emphasized the possibilities of science, transcendentalists were citing Plato, Polotinus, Confucius, the Muhammadan Sufis, the writers of the Upanishads and the Bhagavad-Gita, the Buddhists, the eclectic idealist Victor Cousin, the Hebrew and Greek scriptural authors, Thomas à Kempis, Pascal, and Swedenborg.

Bronson Alcott in 1843 started a Fruitlands commune in 1843 which centered around his bizarre and quixotic experiments with food and sexuality—e.g., cold showers, sexual abstinence, and a diet confined to grain and fruit. Lacking Ripley's organizational gifts, he failed to build any lasting structure.

Sometimes the transcendentalists met at Emerson's home in Concord, and those intellectuals (in what became known as the Transcendental Club) included Emerson, Alcott, J. F. Clarke, the younger W. E. Channing, Theodore Parker, Margaret Fuller, George Ripley, Orestes Augustus Brownson, Jones Very, C. P. Cranch, Charles Follen, W. H. Channing, and Convers Francis.

Brook Farm, from 1841 to 1847, was a cooperative community near West Roxbury, Massachusetts, which the Transcendental Club formed and about which Nathaniel Hawthorne wrote in *The Blithedale Romance*. Its members were supposed to share in the work and the educational and social advantages, but the experiment did not long survive after the burning of its uncompleted central building. Brook Farm was mainly an outgrowth of Unitarianism, for many of its members had left that church and were now advocates of philosophic transcendentalism.

The movement's literary magazine was a quarterly, *The Dial*, first edited by Margaret Fuller and later by Emerson. It was attacked by the press and was considered obscure by the general public. Although transcendentalism was basically monist and held to the unity of the world and God and the immanence of God in the world, its very spirit permitted contradiction. As pointed out by James D. Hart, "Because of this indwelling of divinity, everything in the world is a microcosm containing within itself all the laws and meaning of existence. Likewise, the soul of each individual is identical with the soul of the world, and latently contains all that the world contains. Man may fulfill his divine potentialities either through a rapt mystical state, in which the divine is infused into the human, or through coming into contact with the truth, beauty, and goodness embodied in nature and originating in the Over-Soul. Thus occurs the doctrine of correspondence between the tangible world and the human mind, and the identity of moral and physical laws. Through belief in the divine authority of the soul's intuitions and impulses, based on this identification of the individual soul with God, there developed the doctrine of self-reliance and individualism, the disregard of external authority, tradition, and logical demonstration, and the absolute optimism of the movement." {Carlos Baker, *Emerson Among the Eccentrics: A Group Portrait* (1996); CE; Richard Francis, *Transcendental Utopias: Individual and Community at Brook Farm, Fruitlands, and Walden* (1997); ER; RE; *World*, November-December 1997}

TRANSFERENCE

Transference is a Freudian term to represent the process by which emotions and desires originally associated with a person are unconsciously shifted to another person, often an analyst. Paul Edwards has given the illustration of a girl who had been in his class, one who thought that as the professor he was a figure of authority like the father she did not like. She therefore chose to sit in the very back row of a large room although told to move up closer in order that she could hear.

TRANSGENDER: See entries for N. L. Stones and Transsexuality.

TRANSMIGRATION OF SOULS: See entry for reincarnation.

TRANSPARENT EYEBALL: See entry for Christopher Pearse Cranch, who drew Emerson as a "transparent eyeball."

TRANSSEXUALITY

To wear clothing of the opposite sex is to be a transvestite. However, to identify *mainly* with the opposite sex, or particularly to have undergone a sex change, is to be a transsexual. Transgendered individuals are those who have chosen to have a sex-change but have not completed the surgery.

Although transsexual feelings have been written about over the centuries, only since the 1930s have physicians developed the surgical skills to perform sex-change operations. In the late 1950s a celebrated case of genital reconstruction for Christine Jorgenson in Denmark led transsexuals to use the language of core gender identity in their demand to be operated upon. Neither transvestites nor transsexuals are necessarily homosexuals. Nan Alamilla Boyd's "Bodies in Motion: Lesbian and Transsexual Histories" in Martin Duberman's editing of *A Queer World* (1997) details examples of the controversial operations.

Following are two 1999 descriptions by theists, the first by an American, the second by an Indian, that were found on the World Wide Web:

> In 1993 I was part of a movement of transsexuals to discover who we were—the medical model of "a woman trapped in a man's body" was unsatisfying. It simply wasn't a good explanation, and it put us in the role of victim. This model placed psychiatrists and doctors in the position of playing God with our lives, and so we were looking for other ways of understanding ourselves, ones that gave more dignity and agency to our experience. I had been reading an anthropologist's report about a religious sect called the Hijras in N. India. I travelled to India to meet these folks, and was impressed with the community, so I ultimately joined it. Now I split my time between the US and India.

> I was born as one who was neither man nor woman. When someone comes to know that they are neither a man nor a woman, we pray to the Goddess that she will protect us, for we have no protection in society. We give up our useless organ and in this way dedicate our lives to her, and she takes us up into her protection and gives us some power. We take up women's clothing and live as *brahmacharis* with our guru. We have no contact with our families, and live together, calling one another sister or mother. When we die our property must go back to our community, for we own nothing ourselves. When a woman gives birth, we go to that place and sing and dance to celebrate. Our coming is considered very auspicious. We live on the alms we are given at this time, and at the time of marriage.

"Humanist Manifesto 2000," Part VII, states the humanist view that because all humans are members of the planetary community such individuals should not be discriminated against:

> Gender discrimination should not be permitted. Women have a right to be treated equally with men. Discrimination in job opportunity, education, or cultural activities is insupportable. Society should not deny homosexuals, bisexuals, or transgendered and transsexuals equal rights.

{See entries for Deborah Hartin and N. L. Stones.}

TRANSUBSTANTIATION

According to the traditional teaching of the Catholic Church, the way in which Jesus becomes present in the Sacrament of Communion is through transubstantiation. This is done with bread and wine consumed by worshipers in communion, but the bread and wine is in "appearance," not in "substance." In substance, the bread and wine become the body and blood of Jesus when a priest, acting on Jesus's behalf, speaks the words, "This is my body" and "This is my blood" over them. (See entries for cannibalism and theophagy.) {DCL}

TRANSVESTISM: See entries for Cross-Dressing and for N. L. Stones.

TRANSYLVANIAN UNITARIANS

Prince John Sigismund in the mid-16th century proclaimed Unitarianism the official religion of Transylvania. According to Andrei Codrescu, a regular commentator on National Public Radio and a native of Transylvania, the prince convened the first debate on religions in 1566 in the town of Alba Iulia, known as Gyulafehérvár in Hungarian. Francis David, who had been a Lutheran and a Calvinist before developing the doctrines of Unitarianism, convinced the prince by convening the heads of all the churches, then asking them what they would do if they were made official. The Catholic replied he would insure the complete triumph of Catholicism by persecuting all others. The Lutheran and the Calvinist had basically the same idea. The Unitarian said he would tolerate all the faiths, and the prince preferred his way. "There is only one Father for whom and by whom is everything. . . . Outside of this God there is no other God, neither three, neither four, neither in substance, neither in persons, because the Scripture nowhere teaches anything about a triple God." David also held that Jesus was a man, the son of God certainly, but not God. Transylvania, said Codrescu, became the freest, most tolerant region of Europe for a brief but significant time. In 1571 Unitarianism reached the peak of its popularity, with almost 500 congregations. After Prince Sigismund died, intolerance, which was more the norm, seized the day again. The Calvinists condemned Unitarianism and imprisoned Francis David. He died in prison in 1579.

Codrescu's criticism of the group is that "it has no other nationalities—no Romanians, Germans, Gypsies, or Jews. Their attitude toward women also leaves quite a bit to be desired." Some hold that Codrescu had an anti-Hungarian bias. Further, according to Richard Beal of the Louisville, Kentucky, Unitarians, during the Holocaust, "Not all Jews were deported to death camps because, with the blessing of the Unitarian bishop, Jews [and Gypsies] were listed as members of Unitarian churches." Beal also disagrees with Codrescu about women, replying that the Unitarians are "the only church training women for its ministry. [While] there is a great deal to be done to improve women's rights," Unitarian women are among those "helping to do that." Beal, while visiting the various churches, found that men and women sit on different sides of the church, that the members of the one hundred twenty Unitarian churches speak Hungarian and are considered a minority church in Romania. The Rev. Donald Harrington, retired senior minister of the Community Church of New York, and his Hungarian wife, Aniko, moved in 1991 to Transylvania, where they both preach and work with various Unitarian groups. (See entry for Unitarianism.) {*The World*., July-August 1995}

Trapp, Jacob (1899–1992)

Trapp, who was raised as a member of the Christian Reformed Church, was charged with heresy and was excommunicated by them when he was only nineteen years old. He was then recruited for the Unitarian ministry by Earl Morse Wilbur and was ordained in 1929 as an assistant minister at the Berkeley church, after which he was minister of the First Unitarian Church of Salt Lake City from 1930 to 1941. In 1945, he was called to succeed A. Powell Davies at the Unitarian Church in Summit, New Jersey. A prolific writer, Trapp gathered his sermons, essays, and lectures into *Return to the Springs* (1987), his meditations in *In Stillness Renewal*, and his thoughts about secularity and world religion in *The Light of a Thousand Suns: Mystery, Awe, and Renewal in Religion* (1973).

Travis, Henry (1807–1884)

Travis, whose interests included the socialistic aspect of co-operation, became a friend and the literary executor to Robert Owen. During 1851–1853 he edited *Robert Owen's Journal*. He also wrote *Free Will and Law*, among other books, and contributed to the *National Reformer*. {BDF; RAT}

Treadway, Oswell (20th Century)

In 1952, Treadway was secretary of the American Humanist Association.

Treby, Ivor C. (20th Century)

Treby wrote *Translations from the Human* (1998), a collection of poetry that at times is openly gay and strongly anti-religious. Witty, as for example describing the priest found in the "submissionary position," he thinks that at the end there will be "no self, no Heaven, no Hell, no gain, no loss." "In the end, in his own image/man created God," Treby concludes. {Jim Herrick, *Gay and Lesbian Humanist*, Winter 1998}

Tree, Herbert Beerbohm [Sir] (1853–1917)

Tree was an English actor-manager whose original name was

Herbert Draper Beerbohm. He was a half brother of Max Beerbohm, the essayist, caricaturist, and parodist. Tree married the actress Helen Maud Holt (1863–1937), who became his leading lady. His greatest distinction as manager was his staging of Shakespeare at the Haymarket theater (1887–1897) and at Her Majesty's Theatre, which he built and opened in 1897. In his *Thoughts and Afterthoughts* (1913), Tree expressed his freethought. All sects will die, he predicted, and only "a religion of humanity" will be left. Of Shakespeare, he wrote, "His wide spirit will outlive the mere letter of narrow doctrines, and his winged words, vibrant with the music of the larger religion of humanity, will go wilting down the ages while dogmas die and creeds crumble in the dust!" {JM; RAT; RE}

Treilhard, Jean Baptiste [Count] (1747–1810)

Treilhard was a lawyer who accepted the Revolution and pressed the Assembly for the secularization of the Church and the burial of Voltaire in the Pantheon. He held many important offices and was a key person in the drafting of the Code Civil. Treilhard was a Voltairean deist. {RAT; RE}

Trelawny, Edward John (1792–1881)

Trelawny became an intimate in Italy with Shelley, was at Livorno when he drowned, and not only recovered but also helped cremate Shelley in August 1822. Legend has it that during the cremation he reached in and retrieved Shelley's heart, although it has been speculated he might have grabbed the liver from the flames. Trelawny accompanied Byron on his Greek expedition, serving with him in the Greek War of Independence and marrying a daughter of a Greek chief. Trelawny wrote a party autobiographical novel, *Adventures of a Younger Son* (1831), and *Records of Shelley, Byron, and the Author* (1878). Upon his death, he was cremated at Gotha, his ashes being afterwards placed beside those of Shelley. He once had told Carpenter, in *My Days and Dreams*, that Shelley "couldn't have been the poet he was if he had not been an atheist." Trelawny was a vehement pagan who despised the creeds and conventions of society. Swinburne called him "world-wide liberty's lifelong lover." (See entry for Shelley.) {BDF; JM; RAT; RE}

Trelawny, John Salisbury [Sir] (1816–1885)

As chairman of the committee on Church Rates, Trelawny issued a report which was full of thrusts at the Church, which he detested. He translated *The First Two Books of Lucretius* (1842) and was a supporter of Holyoake. {RAT}

Trench, Frederic Herbert (1865–1923)

Trench from 1909 to 1911 was artistic director of the Haymarket Theatre. Although his own plays had little success, a poem entitled "Apollo and the Seaman" (1907) received favorable notice. It tells of a debate between Apollo and a seaman who discuss the sinking of a great ship, *Lost Immortality*, and the future of the soul. His work contained anti-Christian sentiment. In his *New Poems* (1907), Trench vigorously rejects Christianity and says of Jesus in his "Stanzas to Tolstoi,"

> The Man upraised on the Judaean crag
> Captains for us the war with death no more.
> His kingdom hangs as hangs the tattered flag
> Over the tomb of a great knight of yore.
>
> {JM; RAT; RE}

Trenchard, John (1699–1723)

Trenchard was an English deist and political writer. He once was the Commissioner of Forfeited Estates in Ireland. In conjunction with Gordon, he wrote *Cato's Letters* on civil and religious liberty, and he conducted *The Independent Whig*. Trenchard sat in the House of Commons as M.P. for Taunton. Although he wrote *The Natural History of Superstition* (1709), *La Contagion Sacree*, attributed to him, is by d'Holbach. {BDF; RAT; RE}

Trent, Barbara (20th Century)

In 1992 Trent won the Academy Award for Best Documentary for "The Panama Deception." Other of her award-winning productions include "Destination Nicaragua," "Bus to Topanga," and "Coverup: Behind the Iran-Contra Affair." Known for being a grass-roots organizer and social activist, she has been a three-time target of FBI counterintelligence operations. Trent has written that

> Democracy is dependent on a free press, but ours is being strangled by corporate and government interests. . . . The videomaker has the potential to blast a hole through that corporate image of reality.
>
> {*The Humanist*, January-February 1998}

Trent, Theodora Dolores (20th Century)

Trent has been on the Board of Directors of the American Humanist Association (AHA). She is AHA coordinator for New York, Pennsylvania, and New Jersey. (See entry for New York Atheists, Freethinkers, Humanists.) {FD}

Trenwith, William Arthur (1846–1925)

Trenworth was the second son of a convict parent in Tasmania, but he became a militant leader of the Labor movement in Australia. In 1897, he became the only Labor member elected to the Australasian Federal Convention. On his death, commentators noted that he once had refused to pledge himself to a party or platform and that he had fallen out with the Bootmaker's Union. His obituaries decried the apostasy of his earlier achievement, deeming the avowed rationalist to be "unwept, unhonoured, and unsung." {SWW}

Trevelyan, Arthur (1802–1878)

Trevelyan was a Scottish landowner who was prominent in the progressive movement in Britain. He worked on the *Reasoner* and *National Reformer*. Trevelyan published *The Insanity of Mankind* (1850) and numerous tracts. In 1844, he wrote to Holyoake, "I will thank you to propose me as a member of your atheistical society." The historian, George Macaulay Trevelyan, was of a different family but also was a freethinker. At one time, Arthur Trevelyan was vice-president of the National Secular Society. {BDF; JM; RAT; RE; VI}

Trevelyan, George Macaulay (1876–1962)

In 1958 when Bertrand Russell was its president, the distinguished historian Trevelyan was an honorary associate of the Rationalist Press Association. A master of the so-called "literary" school of historical writing, he held that historians should be imaginatively speculative when they wrote rather than historically "scientific." V. H. Galbraith described him as being "probably the most widely read historian in the world: perhaps in the history of the world." A. N. Wilson, reviewing *G. M. Trevelyan, A Life in History* by David Cannadine (1993), has described the Trevelyan family as being high-minded patricians "who wished to extend the values of their class and kind throughout the world. They genuinely believed that after the limitation of religious and monarchical tyranny in the 17th century, and the passing of the Great Reform Bill in 1832, which spelled the end of the ancien régime in Britain, civilized values and liberalism, in the best sense of the word, would make the world a better place. Religion, if not eliminated altogether, was diluted to the point of near nonexistence." Cannadine notes that Trevelyan came from Northumbrian gentry, never needed to earn a living, and lived so frugally that once, upon delivering a honeymoon present to the rooms of John Elliott, he was mistaken by the cleaner for a tramp.

When Trevelyan married Janet Penrose Ward, daughter of the novelist Mrs. Humphry Ward, Trevelyan's mother described the "very high-toned and 'ethical' " ceremony, "all allusions to the Deity being qualified by the words 'If thou existest.' " To this, Wilson adds, "In later life, Trevelyan relaxed his agnosticism somewhat, saying 'I am a flying buttress of the Church; I support it, but from the outside.' " {CE; JM; RAT; RE; TRI}

Trezza, Gaetano (Born 1828)

Trezza, an Italian writer, was brought up and ordained a priest known for his eloquent sermons. Study, however, led him to resign , he published *Confessions of a Sceptic* (1878), and became professor of literature at the Institute of High Studies in Florence. To the first number of the *Revue Internationale* (1883), Trezza contributed *Les Dieux s'en Vont*. He also wrote *Religion and Religions* (1884). His study of Lucretius enjoyed several editions because of its popularity. {BDF}

TRIANGULO ROSA

Triangulo Rosa, a "pink triangle" association commenced by ASIBEHU in Costa Rica, was founded with money from the International Humanist and Ethical Union (IHEU). Richard Stern was instrumental in its working with HIV-positives and people with AIDS under the direction of Guillermo Murillo. In 1998, because of problems within the association, the two founded *Asociación Agua Buena Pro Defensa de Los Derechos Humanos y Minorias* (The Agua Buena Human Rights Association).

Tribe, David (1931–)

Tribe is an Australian-born secularist and polymath writer. From 1955 to 1972, chiefly in England, he was a freelance journalist, author, poet, editor, critic, lecturer, Hyde Park orator, and public relations consultant. He was an executive of the United Kingdom National Council for Civil Liberties (1961–1972), chairman of Humanist Group Action (1961–1964), and the first and only Australian president of the National Secular Society (1968–1972). He edited *Freethinker* (1966), returned to Australia in 1972, and has been a philosopher of freethought in relation to education ethics, law reform, and libertarianism. He is an honorary associate of the New Zealand Association of Rationalists and Humanists.

Reminiscing about the 1960s, Tribe has recalled that remarkable progress was achieved so far as reforms involving "abortion, censorship, contraception, suicide, adoption, penology, feminism, sex education, and voluntary euthanasia." Tribe is author of *Why We Are Here?* (1965); *100 Years of Free Thought* (1967), in which he takes up Owenism, Chartism, Holyoake, secularism, Paine, and international movements; *Nucleoethics: Ethics in Modern Society* (1972); and *The Rise of the Mediocracy* (1976). He has written on the subject of religion for *The Raven*, an anarchist quarterly. In 1995, Tribe became an Honorary Associate of the Rationalist Press Association. {FUK; PK; SWW}

Tribonian (Died 545?)

A Roman jurist, Tribonian under the command of Justinian I directed the compilation of the *Corpus Juris Civilis*. Much of it is believed to have been authored by Tribonian. According to McCabe, "The code of law which is attributed to the Christian emperor Justinian was mainly compiled (as Dean Milman admits in his *History of Latin Christianity*) by this skeptical jurist who held high office in his court." Milman wrote that there is "no sign of Christianity" in the work, and he favored the tradition that Tribonian was an atheist, as the Greek Suidas says in his *Lexicon*. Gibbon said of Tribonian that "his genius embraced all the knowledge and business of his age." {CE; JM}

TRICKERY

• Fool me once, shame on you. Fool me twice, shame on me.

—Anonymous

Tridon, Edme Marie Gustave (1841–1871)

Tridon was a French publicist who, although educated with a doctorate of law, never practiced. In 1864 he published in *Le Journal des Ecoles* his study of revolutionary history, *Les Hébertistes*. In 1865, he founded with Blanqui and others *Le Candide*, the precursor of *La Libre Pensée* (1866), in both of which the doctrines of materialism were expounded. In 1865 he was a delegate to the International Students Congress at Liége. His speech was furiously denounced by Bishop Dupanloup. Tridon received more than two years in prison for articles in the two journals, and in Ste. Pelagie he contracted the malady which killed him. While in prison he wrote the greater part of his work, *Du Molochisme Juif*, a philosophical study of the Jewish religion. After 1870 he founded *La Patrie en Danger* and in 1871 was elected deputy to the Bordeaux Assembly. After voting against the declaration of peace, however, he resigned, becoming a member of the Paris Commune. Upon his death, Tridon received what Wheeler has described as "the most splendid Freethinker's funeral witnessed in Belgium." {BDF}

Trilling, Lionel (1905–1975)

Known as the "intellectuals' intellectual," Trilling was an eminent critic who wrote *The Liberal Imagination* (1950) and *The Opposing Self* (1955). His work not only contained literary criticism and scholarship but also included his views on political and psychological subjects. Trilling was known at the time as "the first Jew" to gain a permanent position in Columbia University's English department. He also was known as one of the New York Intellectuals (Edmund Wilson, Alfred Kazin, Philip Rahv, Irving Howe, Daniel Bell) who helped make the *Partisan Review*, according to historian Richard Hofstadter, the "house organ of the American intellectual community."

Isaiah Berlin, however, said that in comparison with the critic Edmund Wilson, he preferred Wilson: "Trilling was like other critics, just intelligent sentences. But in Wilson's case the writing was filled with some kind of personal content. That's why one would read him."

When in the late 1940s Trilling, the present author's department chairman, was shown the very earliest material in the present work, including a letter from Thomas Mann and a bibliography detailing works about humanism, he jocularly noted,

> Your seven categories have led me to understand that I must never use the word humanism again!

He added that he felt akin to the position of the naturalistic humanists but disliked all labels. Asked about his own lecturing to the class and calling Emerson a transcendentalist, Trilling smiled and speculated that one day lecturers might label him (Trilling) a naturalistic humanist. However, when asked specifically if humanism had a connection with Judaism, Trilling not only showed little interest in the subject but also did not go care to be quoted, partly confirming some of his critics' views that he was "insufficiently Jewish." During one conversation, when asked if a person could be a "partial atheist" or a "partial Jew," Trilling smiled as if the query was meant as a rhetorical question.

In one of his classes in American literature at Columbia University, Trilling remarked that "in the 19th century the religion of most of the great writers, unlike Poe whose religion was alcoholism, was Unitarianism." Asked if he was a "partial Unitarian," Trilling again smiled without responding, but the implication was there: He may have had Hebrew ancestors, but he was not theologically or linguistically a Jew, although he was known as such, and, further, that he was not much interested in organized religion or supernaturalism. His interest was in how religion did or did not affect individual authors, such as E. M. Forster or Matthew Arnold, neither of whom was a Jew.

His son James, an independent art historian who specializes in the history of ornament, feels that his father was blinded by his love of Freud and psychoanalysis, so much so that he overlooked his own problem, that of attention deficit disorder. Writing in *The American Scholar* (April 1999), James Trilling told not only of his father's neurological condition but also of his mother's "panic disorder with agoraphobia, which made her an emotional cripple for many years." Tourette's syndrome ran in the family, and the son added that "the most insidious culprit in my family" is attention deficit disorder, "the inability to maintain a productive level of concentration ('focus') through the normal range of daily activities." The son also challenges his father's literary judgment: "During his entire career as an interpreter of literature, I doubt my father ever solved a problem, in the sense of marshaling evidence to prove or disprove a theory. On the contrary, he built his career on the mistrust of certainties and was rarely content with a simple answer when a complex one could be found. . . . Of all 'simple' solutions he mistrusted happiness the most. The idea of living happily ever after must have seemed almost crass to him. Certainly it left him all dressed up with no place to go."

Lionel's wife, Diana Trilling, in *The Marriage of Diana and Lionel Trilling* (1993), tended to confirm his lack of interest in religion. She wrote that "as far back as anyone knew, the family name had always been Trilling," that he had not fabricated his name to disguise any Jewish origins, and that he was as indifferently religious as were his parents. She added that, like her husband, she grew up in a largely secular home and, like him, "had the childhood of an American who happened to be a Jew, not that of a Jew who happened to be an American": her husband might well have inquired if she meant Jew or Hebrew. The poet Richard Howard, who visited her often during her later years, said she once remarked, "Seventeen years have now passed since Lionel's death, and hour by hour, minute by minute I still listen for a clock which no longer ticks." {See the article on Trilling by William M. Chace of Wesleyan University in *The Johns Hopkins Guide to Literary Theory & Criticism*. Lewis M. Dabney's interview with Isaiah Berlin is in *The New York Times Book Review*, 29 November 1998; Sarah Boxer, "A Son's Simple Diagnosis of His Father's Complexities," is in *The New York Times*, 25 April 1999}

Trimpey, Jack and **Lois** (20th Century)

The Trimpeys founded the Rational Recovery Systems. He is author of *The Small Book* and edits the *Journal of Rational Recovery* (Box 800, Lotus, California 95651). {FD; HNS2}

TRINIDAD FREETHOUGHT

In the 1890s, the National Secular Society had a branch in Trinidad. For a discussion of freethought in Trinidad, see *Freethought in the United Kingdom and the Commonwealth* by Gordon Stein. (See entries for Edgar Maresse-Smith and Emanuel dos Santos.)

TRINITARIAN

• The Trinitarian believes a virgin to be the mother of a son who is her maker.

—Roger Bacon

TRINITY

> We firmly believe and confess without reservation that there is only one true God, eternal, infinite (*immensus*) and unchangeable, incomprehensible, almighty, and ineffable, the Father and the Son and the Holy Spirit; three persons indeed, but one essence, substance or nature entirely simple.

The above is the official dogma from the *Cathechism of the Catholic Church* (1994).

A key aspect of Trinitarian Christianity is the view that God is one in being (or substance), power, and majesty, but subsists eternally in three co-equal, perfect persons or hypostases, to which are appropriate respectively the individual names Father, Son or Word (*Logos*), and Holy Spirit. The doctrine is accepted as a dogma by all Catholic and Eastern Orthodox Christians and by the principal Protestant Churches. In 382 of the Christian Era, the doctrine was formally adopted in a synodical letter of a council held in Constantinople. In 1993, a Roman Catholic priest, the Reverend William Larkin, instead of saying God the Father, Son, and Holy Spirit, said, "God our Creator, through Jesus the Christ in the power of the Holy Spirit," believing such a wording was more sensitive to women believers. However, Auxiliary Bishop John P. Boles of the Archdiocese of Boston immediately wrote to Father Larkin's order, the Paulist Fathers, declaring that any baptisms performed using such terminology were invalidated.

Non-believers have been known to refer to the Trinity as Big Daddy, Sonny Boy, and The Bird. Also, the Big Three, Daddy-O, J.C., and Spook. Thomas Jefferson believed in the Trinity: Francis Bacon, Isaac Newton, and John Locke. (See entries for Holy Ghost and for Origen.) {ER}

Trinius, J. A. (1722–1784)

Trinius was a compiler of the four-volume *Freydenker Lexicon* (1759–1765). The work covered deist literature in all languages up to 1765. {FUK; GS}

Trinkaus, Charles (1911-1999)

Trinkaus was a leading scholar of the Renaissance, one who in the 1940s and 1950s "launched the wonderful flowering of Renaissance historical scholarship in North America," according to John O'Malley, president of the Renaissance Society of America. *In Our Image and Likeness: Humanity and Divinity in Italian Humanist Thought* (1970), a two-volume work, re-evaluated the religious aspects of the Italian Renaissance. He also wrote *Adversity's Noblemen: The Italian Humanists on Happiness* (1940), which criticized past academic views of Renaissance humanism. *Collected Works of Erasmus: Controversies* (1999) examined Erasmus and the 16th-century religious conflict between humanism and the Reformation.

Trinkaus taught at Sarah Lawrence College from 1936 until 1970, then spent twelve years teaching at the University of Michigan. He was a past president of the Renaissance Society of America and a member of the American Academy of Arts and Sciences.

Tripp, Edward Howard (Died 1953)

In 1998 the Rationalist Press Association Ltd. received a legacy of £166,000 from the residuary estate of Dr. Tripp, who died in 1953.

Trollope, Anthony (1815–1882): See entries for Marriage and Frances Wright.

Trombly, Dennis (20th Century)

Trombly, a student at the University of Michigan-Flint, is a freethinker. In 1997 he started to form a group, Atheist and Freethinkers Organization (AFO), at his university.

Trotsky, Leon (1879–1940)

Trotsky, the noted Russian Communist revolutionary and atheist, was a principal figure in the establishment of the Union of Socialist Soviet Republics. Born Lev Davidovich Bronstein of Jewish parents, he became attracted as early as 1896 to Marxism. Imprisoned, he theorized that Russia could combine a bourgeois and a socialist revolution which could serve as a proletarian model for the world. Trotsky was one of the organizers of the October Revolution, which brought the Bolsheviks to power. In 1917 he became the people's commissar for foreign affairs under Lenin. In 1918 he became commissar of war. Trotsky clashed both with Lenin and Stalin and, following Lenin's death in 1924, was dismissed by Stalin, who by this time headed the Communist Party. In 1929, upon being ordered to leave the USSR, Trotsky fled to the Princes' (Prinkipo) Islands near Istanbul, Turkey, then to France, then Norway. In 1936, 1937, and 1938 Trotsky was charged with heading a plot against Stalin, and Trotsky now fled with his family to America (where he is rumored to have acted as an extra in silent films) and to Mexico City.

An unrepentant freethinker, he observed about organized religions and individuals' outlooks that

> Today, not only in peasant homes but also in the city sky-scrapers, there lives alongside the twentieth century the tenth or thirteenth. A hundred million people use electricity and still believe in the magic power of signs and exorcisms. . . . What inexhaustible reserves they possess of darkness, ignorance, and savagery!

In 1940, Trotsky was working on a full-scale "antibiography" called *Stalin*, in which he would detail Stalin's crimes and his methods of falsifying history. That same year, on 20 August 1940, while feeding his pet rabbits, Trotsky was approached by a nervous twenty-six-year-old visitor, Ramón Mercader, who asked him to read an original article. The two retired to Trotsky's study, where Trotsky sat at his desk and began to read. Mercader, standing to the left and blocking an alarm button which could have summoned a dozen armed guards, later confessed, "I put my raincoat on the table on purpose so that I could take out the ice ax which I had in the pocket. . . . I took the *piolet* out of my raincoat, took it in my fist, and, closing my eyes, I gave Trotsky a tremendous blow on the head. . . . The man screamed in such a way that I will never forget it as long as I live. His scream was Aaaaaaa! . . . very long, infinitely long, and it still seems to me as if that scream were piercing my brain. . . ." The three-inch hole in the skull led to Trotsky's death twenty-six hours later. Jaime Ramón Mercader del Rio Hernandez (alias Jacques Mornard and Frank Jackson) was the son of an undistinguished middle-class Barcelona businessman. His mother, a Cuban who developed into an ardent Stalinist, had fought in the Spanish Civil War and allegedly became the mistress of the Soviet secret police general who later organized the conspiracy to kill Trotsky. Mercader was severely beaten, arrested, tried, convicted of murder, and spent twenty years in prison before being released in 1960, at which time he fled to Czechoslovakia.

Years before, John Dewey chaired a famous simulated "trial" that cleared Trotsky of all the charges hurled at him during the Moscow purges. George Bernard Shaw, describing Trotsky's brilliance in slaughtering his opponents by the pen, not by the sword, observed, "When he cuts off his opponent's head, he holds it up to show that there are no brains in it." (See entry for Jean van Heijenoort.) {CE; Christopher Hitchens, *Vanity Fair*, February 1999; PA}

Trow, William Clark (Born 1894)

Trow, professor of educational psychology at the University of Michigan at Ann Arbor, was author of *Religious Development of Adolescents* and editor of *The Journal of Educational Psychology*. He wrote the present author concerning his humanism:

> If Humanism means anything at all, it means, in my opinion, the acceptance of the same intelligent attitude toward human nature that we have toward inanimate nature. The evidence from astronomy has banished the myths of the earth-centered universe, and that from the physical and biological sciences has largely freed us from animistic and supernaturalistic interpretations of natural events. Similarly the evidence from the behavioral sciences is beginning to reveal the intricacies of human behavior and interaction, and the nature and sources of beliefs, convictions, and conscience. Many of the dogmas of an earlier day have come to be recognized as systematic delusions, often with strong institutional backing, and their fallacies and inconsistencies noted. Just as it was difficult for many to abandon the friendly little universe with God and the angels floating among the nearby clouds as represented in Renaissance art, so it will be difficult for many to abandon the idea that God is whispering in their ears and the devil in the ears of their rivals.
>
> But Humanism, for an increasing number of people, is making it unnecessary to resort to tortured logic, and is freeing them from primitive, irrational tabus so that they can study facts and their consequences impartially. There is doubt about "truth" that leads deductively to conflicting conclusions or to the condemnation or destruction of men, women, and children, either in this life or in any other.
>
> I look to Naturalistic Humanism to spearhead the attack on present day superstition, and to seek out and gradually to institutionalize human values, freeing the spirit of mankind from thralldom to past errors and opening the way to new heights of accomplishment and happiness.

{WAS, 19 July 1957}

Trübner, Nicolas (Born 1817)

Trübner was a German-born publisher who, after serving with Longman and Co., set up his own business. He distinguished himself by publishing works on freethought, religions, philosophy, and Oriental literature. Trübner's house was a meeting place of culture, and he received the orders of the Crown of Prussia, the Ernestine Branch of Saxony, the Francis Joseph of Austria, the St. Olaf of Norway, the Lion of Aähringen, and the White Elephant of Siam. {BDF; RAT}

Truelove, Edward (1809–1899)

An English publisher, Truelove early in life embraced the views of Robert Owen and for years was secretary of the John Street Institution. Truelove published Voltaire's *Philosophical Dictionary*, Paine's complete works, d'Holbach's *System of Nature*, and Taylor's *Syntagma* and *Diegesis*. In 1858 he was prosecuted for publishing a pamphlet on *Tyrannicide* by W. E. Adams, but the prosecution was abandoned. In 1878 he was, after two trials, sentenced to four months in prison for publishing R. D. Owen's *Moral Physiology*. Upon his release Truelove was presented with a testimonial and a purse of two hundred sovereigns. {BDF; FUK; PUT; RAT; RE}

Truett, Bob (20th Century)

Truett wrote *The Apostle Frankenstein,* in which he develops his opinion as to what motivated Paul to concoct his story of a supernatural deity. For thirty years, Truett was director of the Birmingham, Alabama, Zoo. He edits *Along the Way*, an educational magazine published by the Church of the Natural Way (PO Box 97, Vandiver, Alabama 35176).

Trumbull, Matthew M. (Born 1826)

An American general but a native of London, Trumbull at the age of twenty went to America, served in the army in Mexico and afterwards in the Civil War, and then by Ulysses S. Grant was made the Collector of Revenue for Iowa. After holding that office for eight years, he then visited England before traveling to Chicago, where he exerted himself on behalf of a fair trial for the anarchists. Wheeler lists Trumbull as being a freethinker. {BDF; RAT}

TRUTH

• Truth is relative. What is true for some is not true for others. Nonbelievers search for truths, not Truth. The only Truth is that everything changes . . . even Truth.

—Heraclitus (c. 553–475 B.C.E.)

• "Nothing is easier than self-deceit, for what each man wishes, that he also believes to be true.

—Demosthenes (384–322 B.C.E.)

• "What is truth?" said a jesting Pilate, and did not wait for a reply.

—Anatole France

• The most formidable weapon against errors of every kind is reason. I have never used any other and I trust I never shall.

—Thomas Paine

• To kill an error is as good a service as, and sometimes better than, the establishing of a new truth or fact.

—Charles Darwin

• Truth is so precious we should use it sparingly.

—Oscar Wilde

• Truth, in matters of religion, is simply the opinion that has survived.

—Oscar Wilde

• One thing is not necessarily true because a man dies for it.

—Oscar Wilde

• The truth cannot be asserted without denouncing the falsehood.
—Leslie Stephens

• If you are out to describe the truth, leave elegance to the tailor.
—Albert Einstein

• Until the tide goes out you don't know who's swimming naked.
—Warren Buffet

Truth, philosopher Max Hocutt has observed, is not synonymous with knowledge and belief. "Knowledge consists of truths that are known, but since there are truths that are not known, truth cannot be identified with knowledge." Thus, he continues, " 'Truth' is what has been called true, presumably because it is believed to be true; but what is believed may not be true, and what is true may not be believed." Further, although truth may be relative to belief because all facts are interpretations, all interpretations "are not facts; instead, some interpretations are false." And as to whether belief in objective truth implies dogmatism, Hocutt states that "only those who believe that there is such a thing as the objective truth can admit that they might not know what it is. These truisms matter politically, because the doctrine that there is no truth, just equally good competing beliefs, has always been the great enemy of reason and the great excuse for arbitrary power." {*Reason*, January 1996}

In 1928, Bertrand Russell wrote in *Sceptical Essays*, "In the State of New York, it was till lately illegal to teach that Communism is good; in Soviet Russia, it is illegal to teach that Communism is bad. No doubt one of these opinions is true and one is false, but no one knows which. Either New York or Soviet Russia was teaching truth and proscribing falsehood, but neither was teaching truthfully, because each was representing a doubtful proposition as certain." The solution, Lord Russell held, is to allow the freedom to find facts without being threatened with penalties for doing so. "Truth," he added, "is for the gods; from our human point of view it is an ideal toward which we can approximate, but which we cannot hope to reach. Education should fit us for the nearest possible approach to truth, and to do this it must teach truthfulness. Truthfulness, as I mean it, is the habit of forming our opinions on the evidence, and holding them with that degree of conviction which the evidence warrants. The degree will always fall short of complete certainty, and therefore we must always be ready to admit new evidence against previous beliefs." The scientist, he noted, states his result along with the "probable error." "But who ever heard of a theologian or a politician stating the probable error of his dogmas, or even admitting that any error is conceivable. That is because in science, where we approach nearest to real knowledge, a man can safely rely on the strength of his case, whereas, where nothing is known, blatant assertion and hypnotism are the usual ways of causing others to share our beliefs. If the fundamentalists thought they had a good case against evolution, they would not make the teaching of it illegal." {*The Economist*, 25 September 1999; Lee Eisler, *The Quotable Bertrand Russell*}

TRUTH SEEKER

The Truth Seeker, A Journal of Independent Thought (PO Box 2872, San Diego, California 92112) is called the "World's Oldest Freethought Publication—Since 1873." It is a continuation of the publication first printed by D. M. Bennett.

Over the years, as pointed out by Fred Whitehead, "the journal has passed through numerous intellectual migrations, including racism, anti-Semitism, etc. Now, under the editorship of William B. Lindley, it has largely been given into the hands of New Age fringe belief systems." Whitehead adds, "I wonder if anyone at the *Truth Seeker* ponder[s] on what Bennett himself would think of the magazine today."

Tschirn, Gustav (Born 1865)

Although in his youth he had been religious and was training for the Church, Tschirn read Haeckel and anthropological works and turned to rationalism. In 1889 he was in charge of the Free Religious Community (a sort of Ethical Society) at Breslau. In 1892 he founded and edited *Geistesfreiheit.* Tschirn was a President of the German Union of Freethinkers. In 1906 he was prosecuted, and received a month in prison, for a moderate rationalist pamphlet. He recounted his experiences and told his creed in *Was Wir Ernst Haeckel Verdanken.* {RAT}

Tschirnhausen, Walthier Ehrenfried (1651–1708)

A German count, Tschirnhausen was a friend of Leibniz and Wolff. In philosophy, he was a follower of Spinoza's general outlook. {BDF}

Tubino, Francisco Maria (1833–1888)

A Spanish positivist, Tubino took part in Garibaldi's campaign in Sicily. He contributed to the *Rivista Europea.* {BDF}

Tucker, Abraham (1705–1774)

A wealthy provincial, Tucker took up the study of philosophy, followed Locke, and became a deist. He wrote, under the pseudonym of Edward Search, *Freewill, Foreknowledge, and Fate* (1763), eight years after which he became blind. {RAT; RE}

Tucker, Benjamin Ricketson (1854–1939)

Tucker was an American writer born in Dartmouth, Massachusetts. In Boston, he edited *Liberty.* Tucker adopted the views of Herbert Spencer in philosophy and of Proudhon in politics and economics. He translated works of Proudhon and Bakunin and wrote a rationalist book, *Instead of a Book* (1893), *State-Socialism and Anarchism* (1899), and other works. {BDF; RAT}

Tucker, Cynthia Grant (20th Century)

A Unitarian, Tucker is author of a group biography of pioneering female Unitarian and Universalist ministers, *Prophetic Sisterhood: Liberal Women Ministers of the Frontier, 1880–1930* (1994).

Tucker, Helen (1904–)

In 1994, Tucker was given the Mark DeWolfe Social Action Award from the Unitarian Congregation of South Peel, Ontario. She had founded the international peace group, the Voice of Women, in 1960 and worked for many years with other peace and United Nations group. Then 90 at the time of the award, Tucker described her philosophy as "One people, one planet, one flag." {*World*, May-June 1995}

Tucker, Nicholas (20th Century)

Tucker, an educationist, was a friend of Edward Blishen and, at a secular funeral, described his friend as a "humanist" who was "an advertisement for the human race, which is something all humanists should aspire to be." {*New Humanist*, December 1996}

Tucker, Scott (20th Century)

Tucker has written as a radical socialist in publications ranging from *Drummer* to *The Humanist.* A 1996 pamphlet called "Fighting Words: An Open Letter to Queers and Radicals" gave his views about being a sadist-masochist activist and a person with AIDS. "I would really like to see a socialist democracy," he told an interviewer. "To talk that way at this point in the United States is considered cloud-cuckooland. Queers should be a little more sophisticated because to talk about a public gay culture was once considered cloud-cuckooland. We were resigned to having nooks and crannies that were subject to police raids."

Tucker is author of *The Queer Question: Essays on Desire and Democracy* (1997) and, although he draws on academic sources from Michel Foucault to Jeffrey Weeks, decries the tendency of intellectuals to theorize rather than find tangible, practical solutions. An artist and a founding member of the Philadelphia chapter of ACT UP, Tucker lives with his lover of over twenty years, *Contested Closets* author Larry Gross. {*New York Blade News*, 9 January 1998}

Tuckerman, Joseph (1778–1840)

Under the leadership of William Ellery Channing and Henry Ware Jr., Unitarians in the early 1820s began to take measures to address the growing problem of poverty in Boston. Tuckerman was called to be the first full-time minister-at-large in Boston, and he entered upon the difficult task not only of addressing the needs of the poor but also of educating the sometimes obtuse Unitarian clergy and laity about the nature of urban poverty. In 1830, Tuckerman wrote *An Essay on the Wages Paid to Females For Their Labor*. He founded the Benevolent Societies of Boston, a council of social agencies, in 1834. {U; U&U; EG}

Tuckett, Ivor (Born 1873)

Tuckett, a physiologist brought up in the Society of Friends but who became "a convinced agnostic," wrote a critical study of Spiritualism, *The Evidence for the Supernatural* (1911). In 1920 he gave the Conway Memorial Lecture, *Mysticism and the Way Out*) {RAT}

Tufts, James Hayden (1862–1942)

Tufts was co-writer with John Dewey of the humanistic and naturalistic study, *Ethics* (1908, 1922). He was editor of the *International Journal of Ethics* (1914–1930) and President of the American Philosophical Association (1914). In 1992, James Campbell edited Tufts' *Selected Writings*. {CL}

Tunnecliffe, Thomas (1869–1948)

Tunnecliffe was an Australian rationalist, politician, and bootmaker. A delegate to the International Socialist Congress in Sydney in 1888, he wrote regularly for *Ross's Magazine*. Tunnecliffe was a member from 1921 to 1947 of the Victorian Legislative Assembly.

Tuñon Hidalgo, Alberto (20th Century)

Prof. Hidalgo is president of the *Sociedad Asturiana de Filosofia* in Oviedo, Spain. He is a Humanist Laureate in the Council for Secular Humanism's International Academy of Humanism. In Spain, because *humanism* carries a connotation of a current political party, humanists are more apt to organize *Ateneos*, or Atheneums, rather than humanist chapters. Hidaglo in 1993 spoke in Madrid on the subject, "Liberal Humanism and the Spirit of Our *Ateneos*." In 1995, he spoke to the Spanish Association of Rational Humanism and the Ateneo of Madrid on the subject, "*Entre relativismo y fundamentalismo*." Hidalgo signed Humanist Manifesto 2000.

Turati, Filippo (1857–1932)

Turati was an Italian lawyer and writer, the Provincial Councilor at Milan. He adopted socialism and edited the *Critica Sociale* (1891–1903), the chief organ of his views. Turati was a rationalist. {RAT}

Turbiglio, Sebastiano (Born 1842)

Turbiglio was an Italian philosopher. He wrote *Spinoza and the Transformation of His Thoughts*. {BDF}

Turchin, Valentin (20th Century)

A Soviet dissident, Turchin is a computer scientist at City College of the City University of New York. He is one of the signers of the Secular Humanist Declaration of 1980. {SHD}

Turgenev, Ivan (1818–1883)

Turgenev was a Tsarist Russian whose writings "showed distinct Humanist leanings," according to Corliss Lamont. Hugh McLean also states that Turgenev is "the typical unbeliever of modern times, much influenced in his philosophical thinking by Arthur Schopenhauer." Robertson terms Turgenev "the Sophocles of the modern novel." An enthusiastic advocate of the westernization of Russia, Turgenev attacked serfdom in *A Sporsman's Sketches* (1852), a work which is said to have led Alexander II to emancipate the serfs.

His masterpiece is *Fathers and Sons* (1861), in which he depicts the differences between generations. One character, Bazarov, is an unforgettable nihilist, philosophizing that everything is so bad the only way to bring about progress is to destroy all that is, then rebuild. The novel of nihilism was so severely criticized by the Establishment that Turgenev remained outside Russia, continuing a passionate, lifelong love affair with Pauline Viardot-Garcia, a French singer. Pavlovsky says of Turgenev in his *Souvenirs* that he "was a freethinker and detested the apparatus of religion very heartily." {BDF; CE; CL; EU, Hugh McLean; JM; JMR; RAT; RE; TRI; TYD}

Turgot, Anne Robert Jacques (1727–1781)

A famed French economist, Turgot advocated free trade and was a disciple of the physiocrats. "No bankruptcy, no increase in taxes, no borrowing, but economy" was his motto, and as comptroller general of finances, he introduced such reforms as abolishing some sinecures and monopolies. In his youth, he trained for the Church, but when he adopted deistic views he decided that he "could not bear to wear a mask all his life." Turgot antagonized the clergy because he favored toleration of the Protestants.

Because his opponents were so numerous, and included Marie Antoinette, he retired to a life of scientific, historical, and literary study. One of the Encyclopedists, he was a freethinker and deist. {CE; JM; JMR; JMRH; RAT; RE}

TURIN SHROUD

The Cathedral of San Giovanni in Turin, Italy, has an urn containing a shroud. Believers have held that the shroud was the one in which the body of Jesus was wrapped after his crucifixion. Many traveled from all around the world in order to be in the presence of the cloth, and photographs were widely disseminated for the general public. However, in 1988 the shroud was given radiocarbon tests by three independent laboratories, who found the material dated only to the period from 1200 to 1400. Fundamentalists challenged the findings, refusing to believe the shroud is a fake. Others claim Leonardo did the faking, using his own image as the face, an ironic twist inasmuch as he was a non-believer. Still others claim that would have been impossible, for the shroud dates to the late 1300s before Leonardo's time.

A fireman, breaking through four layers of bullet-proof glass to rescue the shroud when the Guarini chapel was gutted by fire in 1997, was able to save. Remarked the Archbishop of Turin, Cardinal Giovanni Saldarini, "It is intact. It is a miracle!" ("A miracle that God gutted the chapel?" freethinkers might well respond.) Meanwhile, the Cathedral enjoys a profitable tourist trade. An estimated three million lined up to view the shroud in 1998, when it was displayed publically for the first time in twenty years.

In *Judgment Day for the Shroud of Turin* (1999), Walter McCrone, a scientist trained in chemistry, microanalysis, materials analysis, painting authentication, and chemical microscopy, gives a complete account of his findings. In 1974 he had been asked by the Catholic Church to submit a proposal for the study of the shroud, and after studying 32 samples he concluded that the shroud dated only back to 1325, that it could not possibly have been Jesus's. In 1999, however, another study appeared to contradict radiocarbon dating tests that in 1988 concluded the shroud was likely a medieval forgery. Avinoam Danin, a botanist at the Hebrew University in Jerusalem, told attendees at the 16th International Botanical Congress in St. Louis, Missouri, that the 1988 analysis was performed on a small corner of the cloth whereas a new one involved the whole shroud. He concluded that the cloth's origin placed it in or near Jerusalem before the eighth century. Alan D. Whanger, of the Duke University Medical Center, countered that the tested sample came from a water-stained, scorched edge of the shroud, that carbon could have been added to the cloth, and that living fungi and bacteria that had been found possibly had contaminated the sample.

A creation by freethinker Joe Nickell, seen in Buffalo, New York, has been not nearly so profitable: a shroud of Bing Crosby. (See Lynn Picknett and Clive Prince, *In Whose Image? The Truth Behind the Centuries-Long Conspiracy of Silence* [1994].) {*The Freethinker*, June 1997}

TURKISH SECULARISM: See "Secularization in Turkey" by Ioanna Kuçuradi, *Free Inquiry*, Winter 1995-1996. Also see the entries for Oruc Aruoba and Aziz Nesin.

Turkot, Andy (Deceased 1996)

Turkot was treasurer of Humanists of the San Joaquin Valley in California. At his memorial service, the Unitarian minister Stephanie Nichols in a humanistic service emphasized that Andy lives on in the genes and minds of the lives he left behind.

Turmel, Joseph (1859–1943)

Turmel wrote *The Second Epistle to the Corinthians, etc.* (1927). {GS}

Turnbridge, William (19th Century)

Turnbridge wrote *A Report of the Proceedings in the Mock Trial of William Turnbridge, for the Publication of a Book Called "Palmer's Principles of Nature," as an Alleged Blasphemous Libel Upon the Christian Religion* (1833). {GS}

Turner, Adam (20th Century)

Turner is on the board of directors of Society Against Religion.

Turner, Alice K. (20th Century)

Turner is author of *The History of Hell* (1993), which focuses on the concept of Hell as depicted by artists and writers throughout the years.

Turner, Ben [Sir] (1863–1942)

Turner, an alderman and mayor of Batley, was chairman in 1911 of the Labour Party. David Tribe includes him in *Victorian Heretics*. {TRI}

Turner, Christy (20th Century)

"I was baptized without being consulted. Presbyterian. I hated it so much it turned me quickly to Darwin," Turner, an Arizona State University professor, told Douglas Preston (*The New Yorker*, 30 November 1998).

Turner is the physical anthropologist who is best known for work he has done on dental morphology—the shapes of human teeth. In recent years, looking at teeth while tracing the various waves of human migration from Asia to America, he has achieved notoriety for his view that a great civilization in the Southwest, the Hopi, was cannibalistic. Some time in the late 1600s Hopi villagers of Awatovi, who had largely converted to Christianity under the influence of Spanish friars, set out to purge witchcraft and after murdering those considered to be witches they ate parts of them.

The Hopi have objected to such a crude slur about their ancestors, but Turner identified many Anasazi sites believed to represent "charnel deposits"—heaps of cannibalized remains. With his wife, Jacqueline, Turner described his conclusions in *Man Corn: Cannibalism and Violence in the Prehistoric American Southwest* (1998).

Turner, E. L. Dwight (20th Century)

Turner, a freethinker, was a member of the American Humanist Association. {HNS}

Turner, Henry Gyles (1831–1920)

Turner was a Unitarian, banker, liberal, and historian who, although born in London, emigrated to Melbourne in 1854 upon receiving an appointment in the Bank of Australasia. A writer, he contributed to journals in Victoria and projected the *Melbourne Review*, of which he was an editor and a contributor. Turner, a Spencerian individualist, was the founder, leading contributor, and first President from 1868 to 1870 of the Eclectic Association. He was instrumental in having Moncure Conway lecture in Australia, although the humanistic lectures by the South Place Ethical Society's leader were broken up by "singing Salvationists." A determined opponent to ecclesiastical harassment, Turner supported George Higinbotham and Charles Strong in the 1883 Scots Church conflict and was on the committee of the anti-Sabbatarian Sunday Liberation Society. {SWW}

Turner, James (20th Century)

Turner wrote *Without God, Without Creed* (1985), a study of the origins of unbelief in the United States.

Turner, Joel (20th Century)

Turner is vice-president of Free Inquirers of Northeastern Ohio, PO Box 2379, Akron, Ohio 44309.

Turner, Joseph Mallard William (1775–1851)

Turner, a major English landscape painter, completed works which conveyed a romantic vision of the magnificence of nature as well as the violence of elements. He painted storms at sea, fires, snow, wind, floods, avalanches. Turner, who received almost no general education and was the son of a London barber, at the age of fourteen had already become a student at the Royal Academy of Arts and at sixteen had exhibited there. Although he encountered criticism as his style became increasingly free, he was defended by Sir Thomas Lawrence and the youthful Ruskin. Turner left a fortune of $700,000 to found a home for needy artists, and he left more than 19,000 watercolors, drawings, and oils to the nation. Ruskin, his executor, said Turner was "an infidel," and P. G. Hamerton primly reported in a biography that Turner "did not profess to be a member of any visible Church." In plain English, McCabe added, "he was a thoroughgoing freethinker who despised religion." {CE; JM; RAT; RE}

Turner, M. M. (19th Century)

Turner wrote *The Bible God, Bible Teachings, and Selections from the Writings of Scientists* (1899). {GS}

Turner, Martha (1839–1915)

A Unitarian and feminist, Turner was one of the pioneers of the Australian Woman's Movement. The sister of Henry Gyles Turner, she was congregation's third regular minister and became the first female minister of any church in Australia. A conservative, Turner was critical of the humanist evaluation of Christ, and her sermons were described as academic in style as well as quite devoid of religious fervor. {SWW}

Turner, Matthew (Died 1788 or 1789)

The first avowedly atheistic book published in Britain was Turner's *Answer To Priestley* (1782). Because so many had been claiming there could be no such individual as an atheist, Turner wrote, "As to the question whether there is such an existent Being as an atheist, to put that out of all manner of doubt, I do declare upon my honour that I am one. Be it therefore for the future remembered, that in London in the kingdom of England, in the year of our Lord one thousand seven hundred and eighty-one, a man publicly declared himself to be an atheist." To which Samuel Badcock retorted, "He swears to the truth of it. But what doth he swear by? Whom doth he appeal to? not to God: for he believes there in none. And as he thinks he can swear by nothing better, he swears by his HONOUR!" Playing it safe, Turner, a chemist who had popularized the use of ether for medical purposes, wrote the work under the feigned name of William Hammon. {FUK; HAB; RAT; RE}

Turner, Muriel Winifred [Baroness of Camden] (1927–)

In 1989 Baroness Turner was elected an honorary associate of the Rationalist Press Association. Commencing in 1988, Turner became the principal opposition Spokesman on Employment. She is a vice-president of the British Humanist Association and a member of the Parliamentary Humanist Group.

She has written, "I grew up on a London County Council housing estate in South East London. My father was an active Labour supporter—a skilled manual worker who was sceptical of all religions, but my mother was a Roman Catholic who had attended a convent school. Children of such 'mixed' marriages were expected to be raised as Roman Catholics, and my early recollections are of a home with a predominantly Catholic atmosphere. My father, however, would not allow his children to be sent to Catholic schools, so we attended the excellent LCC schools of the time. My father was a great admirer of Herbert Morrison—then Leader of the LCC (this was just before the Second World War). Herbert Morrison probably did more of practical value for working-class people in London than any other Labour Leader, before or since. Standards in housing and education were generally acknowledge to be a very high indeed."

"The Jesuits," she continued, "are alleged to have claimed that if they had charge of a child up to the age of seven, he or she would be won over for life. This did not happen to me. By the time I had reached my mid-teens, I had begun to question basic religious assumptions. Much of these seemed to be based on cruelty and fear—on retribution and revenge—and I soon abandoned all religious belief." She then turned away from the Labour attachment of her father and, to his concern and regret, joined the Young Communist League. At the end of the war, she realized "there is a religious dimension to Communism—it is a belief system which demands the faithful adherence of its supporters. It does claim to provide answers to everything. And of course it punishes its heretics severely." Although she does not regret her youthful decisions and beliefs, "the revelations of the Khrushchev era were therefore devastating." In 1957, she rejoined the Labour Party.

"I have long since abandoned the search for an all-embracing philosophy," Baroness Turner of Camden has written, "and am content, pragmatically, to do the best I can. I am proud to call myself a Humanist and to be an Honorary Associate. At the same time, I recognise that for many people, life is so sad—and in many instances, tragic—that the 'crutch' of religious belief is necessary for them. If the world were a better and more caring place, perhaps the search for rigid systems of belief would cease." {*New Humanist*, May 1995}

Turner, Robert (1931-1999)

Turner was an Australian who taught in England, the United States and Australia. A committed humanist, he was a fighter for gay rights. {*Gay and Lesbian Humanist*, Summer 1999}

Turner, Ted Robert Edward (1938–)

Founder of CNN Television, an international business that importantly changed the nature of news reportage, Turner is a humanist who majored in the classics at Brown University. In 1980 he launched Cable News Network (CNN) and took an interest in planetary survival. In 1985 he founded the Better World Society, to develop television documentaries dealing with the global crises confronting humanity.

He received the 1987 Distinguished Peace Leadership Award of the Nuclear Age Peace Foundation. In his acceptance speech when awarded the 1990 Humanist of the Year Award by the American Humanist Association, Turner stated,

> Though the danger of nuclear war has receded greatly, I'm not going to really feel comfortable until all nuclear weapons and other weapons of mass destruction are destroyed by mutual agreement. I certainly can't believe that we wonderful human beings should keep killing and torturing and maiming each other as we have throughout the past centuries.

In 1997 he pledged $1 billion to the United Nations to aid refugees and children, clear land mines, and fight disease.

Turner is one of the leading freethinkers to speak out boldly against supernaturalism. He has described Christianity as "a religion for losers." At a 1999 speech to the National Family Planning and Reproductive Health Association in Washington, he chided Pope John Paul, saying, "Welcome to the 20th Century" and advising him to "get with it" on the subjects of abortion and artificial contraception. Asked what he would say if he actually were to meet the Pope, Turner mused that he would probably respond with ethnic humor, something like (and he pointed to his foot), "Ever seen a Polish mine detector?" The Ten Commandments, he continued, are "a little out of date. If you're only going to have ten rules, I don't know if [prohibiting] adultery should be one of them."

Turner is married to actress Jane Fonda, daughter of Henry Fonda who is known for being politically active in anti-nuclear and feminist peace movements. {*The Humanist*, January-February 1991} {CA; E; HNS2; New York *Daily News*, 18 February 1999}

Turner, William (18th Century)

Turner was a surgeon of Liverpool who, under the name of William Hammon, published an *Answer to Dr. Priestley's Letters to a Philosophical Unbeliever* (1782). In it, he avows himself an atheist. {BDF}

Turpin, François Henri (1709–1799)

Turpin, a professor of philosophy who was a friend of Helvétius, translated into French E. W. Montague's *History of Government in the Ancient Republics* (1769) and wrote *La France illustrée, ou le Plutarque Français* (5 volumes, 1777–1790). {RAT}

Turnipseed, Thomas (20th Century)

Turnipseed is a South Carolina Unitarian Universalist who once served as George Wallace's national campaign manager. He presently is board president of the Center for Democratic Renewal, an Atlanta-based civil rights group.

Tussman, Joseph (20th Century)

Tussman edited *The Supreme Court on Church and State* (1962). {FUS}

Tutankhamen: See entry for Ikhnaton.

Tuthill, Charles A.H. (19th Century)

Tuthill wrote *The Origin and Development of Christian Dogma* (1889). {BDF}

Tuttle, Hudson (19th Century)

Tuttle, a freethinker, wrote *Career of Religious Ideas, Their Ultimate, the Religion of Science* (1878). {GS}

Tuuk, Titia, Van der (Born 1854)

Tuuk, a Dutch lady, was converted to freethought by reading Dekker (whose pseudonym was Multatuli). She became one of the editors of *De Dageraad*. {BDF}

Tvind

Although touted as a humanistic and charitable organization which began in Denmark, Tvind (or "Humana" in English-speaking countries) was found by a Swedish government report in 1992 to have given only 2% of money raised by the organization to recipients in Third World countries. Almost 80% went for the salaries of project leaders and to train "solidarity" workers. {*The Guardian* (UK), 8 July 1993; Lotte Lund, "Mysterious Organization Behind LLCD," *Dagbladet Politiken* (Copenhagen), 22 Sep 1991}

Twain, Mark: See entry for Samuel Clemens.

TWELVE-STEP PROGRAMS: See entries for Jim Christopher, Rational Recovery Self-Help Network, Secular Organization for Sobriety, and James Taylor.

Twesten, Karl (1820–1870)

A German publicist and writer, Twesten became a magistrate in Berlin and one of the founders of the National Liberal Party. He wrote on the religious, political, and social ideas of Asiatics and Egyptians (1872). {BDF}

Tweyongyere, Silver (20th Century)

Tweyongyere and M. J. Collins founded the Humanist

Friendship Association in Kampala, Uganda, in 1994. {*International Humanist News*, December 1998}

Twomey, Sean (20th Century)

Twomey in 1995 was President of the Humanists of North Jersey, a regional chapter of the American Humanist Association and which group publishes *News and Views*.

Tyerman, John (1820?–1880?)

Tyerman, who had once been an Anglican clergyman, was an Australian freethinker and spiritualist lecturer who toured Australia and New Zealand. At an 1883 Freethought Conference in Melbourne, Tyerman discussed contemporary "spiritualism," which included investigation into "zoistic science, freethought, and the harmonial philosophy." It was a time when freethought and spiritualism were linked, and he was editor from 1873 to 1874 of the Melbourne weekly, *Progressive Spiritualist and Freethought Advocate*. {SWW}

Tyler, Alice Felt (20th Century)

Tyler wrote *Freedom's Fermant* (1944). {FUS}

Tylor, Edward Burnet [Sir] (1832–1917)

Tylor was an English anthropologist who devoted himself to the study of the races of mankind and is said to have been the first living authority upon the subject. He wrote *Anahuac, or Mexico and the Mexicans* (1861); *Researches into the Early History of Mankind* (1865); *Primitive Culture* (1871), researches into the development of mythology, philosophy, religion, art, and customs. In his work he traces religion to animism, the belief in spirits. Tylor also wrote *Anthropology* and contributed to the *Encyclopaedia Britannica*. He became President of the Anthropological Society. McCabe has commented that Tylor "is now best-known for his theory of the origin of religion: Animism, which held the field for half a century and is still widely accepted in a modified form. It plainly destroys the whole supernatural theory of religion but, like Frazer and others, Tylor was very unwilling to tell his own creed. It was hardly necessary." {BDF; JM; RAT; RE; TRI}

Tyndale, William (c. 1495–1536)

Theists, not just atheists, were also burned as heretics. Tyndale (also, Tindal) was the English biblical translator and a Protestant martyr. After he translated the Scriptures into the vernacular (c. 1522), disputes with the clergy led him to move to Hamburg, where he visited Martin Luther, began printing the New Testament in Cologne, was interrupted by an injunction, had the edition completed at Worms, found the English bishops denounced and suppressed the work, and was forced to live in concealment because Cardinal Wolsey had ordered him seized in Worms. His work was suppressed in England (1526), but he continued translating the Scriptures and writing tracts which defended the English Reformation. Tyndale became a follower of Ulrich Zwingli, irked Sir Thomas More for defending the Reformation, and by condemning the divorce of Henry VIII angered the king. In 1535 he was seized (1535) in Antwerp upon Cardinal Wolsey's order and imprisoned at Vilvorde Castle. Tried, he was condemned for heresy, was tied to the stake, was strangled, and was then burned. His last words (supposedly) were, "Lord, open the king of England's eyes." {CE}

Tyndall, John (1820–1893)

Tyndall, an Irish scientist, succeeded Michael Faraday as professor of natural philosophy at the Royal Institution in 1867. In 1856 he had studied in Switzerland with Professor Huxley, and they wrote a joint work on glaciers. His philosophical writings are reprinted in a two-volume work, *Fragments of Science* (1881), and show him to be a naturalist and an agnostic. He contributed in 1866 to the *Fortnightly Review*, notably an article on miracles and special providence. In 1874, when he was appointed President of the British Association, Tyndall, according to McCabe, made his address "so pointedly materialistic that it roused a storm throughout Britain." {BDF; JM; RAT; RE; TYD}

TYNESIDE HUMANIST SOCIETY

The Tyneside Humanist Society (IHEU) is at 58 Garmondsay Road, West Cornforth County, Durham, United Kingdom.

Tyson, John Harrison (19th Century)

Tyson, a musician, used the *Secular Chronicle* in 1875 to float the idea of a "Secular Church," making available to freethinkers "the glories of harmony" and he heritage of the poets. It was proposed that a secular libretto be written for "The Messiah." At a Stalybridge lecture in 1876, Mozart's "*Gloria In Excelsis Deo*" was performed, its words changed. Tyson urged fellow freethinkers to compete with the churches in attractiveness, and C. A. Watts later expressed a general sentiment that singing would attract more women and children to the meetings. Alice Bradlaugh, in fact, played the piano before a morning lecture at the Hall of Science in 1869. {RSR}

Tyson, Orin (20th Century)

"Spike" Tyson was the office manager and live-in caretaker of the Madalyn Murray O'Hair home in Texas. Asked in 1997 what happened to Madalyn and asked if the O'Hairs who had disappeared are dead, the Vietnam veteran said, "It's easy to hide bodies. I'm not gonna pray for 'em, that's for sure." (See entry for Madalyn Murray O'Hair.) {*Vanity Fair*, March 1997}

Tyssot de Patot, Symon (Born 1655)

A professor of mathematics at Deventer, Tyssot de Patot wrote *Voyages et Avantures de Jacques Massé* (1710), which was published in Amsterdam. It was a romance, written under the pen name of "Jacques Massé," in which a traveler discovers a strange land inhabited by surprisingly rational people. It along with a similar work, *Histoire de Calejava* by Claude Gilbert (1700), was immediately suppressed. The Tyssot book puts into the mouths of priests of the imaginary land such mordant arguments against the idea of a resurrection, the story of the fall, and other Christian ideas, that there could be small question of the author's deism, Robertson notes. As to why the book was allowed, he adds, "For the moment the Government was occupied over an insensate renewal of the old persecution of Protestants, promulgating in 1715 a decree that all who died after refusing the sacraments should be refused burial, and that their goods should be confiscated. The edict seems to have been in large measure disregarded." {BDF; CE; JMR; JMRH; RAT}

Tzanetakos, Christos (20th Century)

Tzanetakos is president of the Atheist Alliance. At the 1994 Toronto conference of the Coalition for Secular Humanism, Atheism, and Freethought (CSHAFT), Tzanetakos spoke on the need for nonreligious ceremonies. E-mail: <athalflc@aol.com>.

At that meeting, Tom Flynn, seeing Tzanetakos sitting next to Jesús Antonio Puertas Fuertes from Spain, supplied the wittiest introduction of the event. He approached and introduced them by pointing and saying, "Jesús, Christos!" {FD}

Ubaldini, Ottavio: See entry for Epicurus.

Uberti, Farinita Degli: See entry for Epicurus.

Ubiquitous Perpetuity God

In 1996, a San Rafael, California, sixty-eight-year old man who had come to the United States from Cuba was convicted of indecent exposure and was sentenced to nine months in jail. He had changed his name to Ubiquitous Perpetuity God and exposed himself to women, he swore, so they "could see him and have some type of awareness of God."

Wolf Roder, commenting upon the man, who had been convicted eighteen times for similar acts since 1978, said, "Well, it's better than murdering all the Canaanites." (See entry for God, Ubiquitous.)

Uchtman, Vern (20th Century)

Uchtman is Secretary of the Cincinnati, Ohio, Free Inquiry Group. In *Free Inquiry* (Winter 1996-1997), he wrote "Camp Quest '96," describing the creation and inauguration of the first summer camp for children of secular humanist families.

UCOS NIEUWSBRIEF (Belgium)

UCOS Nieuwsbrief, a Dutch quarterly, *Universitair Centrum voor Ontwikkelingssamenwerking*-Humanist Development Cooperation, is at Pleinlaan 2Y, 1050 Brussels, Belgium. E-mail: <lawauter@vub.ac.BE>.

Ueberweg, Friedrich (1826–1871)

A German philosopher, Ueberweg studied at Göttingen and Berlin and became professor of philosophy at Königsberg. His chief work is *A History of Philosophy*. Lange cites Czolbe as saying of Ueberweg, "He was in every way distinctly an Atheist and Materialist." McCabe finds that judgment "too strong, as he recognized a sort of impersonal purpose in the universe." {BDF; JM; RAT; RE}

Ufomadu, Charles (20th Century)

Ufomadu is Chairman of the Humanist Friendship Centre of Imo State in Nigeria. (See entry for Nigerian Humanists.) {FD}

UGANDA, HUMANISTS IN

M. J. Collins, of the K. Executive Club of Humanists, is at POB 3092, Kampala, Uganda. (See entry for Silver Tweyongyere.)

Ssekitooleko Deogratias heads the Uganda Humanist Association (UHASSO) at PO Box 4427, Kampala, Uganda.

UGLINESS

• Ugliness, n. A gift of the gods to certain women, entailing virtue without humility.

—**Ambrose Bierce**
The Devil's Dictionary

• I was so ugly when I was born that the doctor slapped my mother.

—Henny Youngman,
American comic

• Give me an ugly man, someone no one else will want when we walk in a room of people.

—Anonymous

• It is the plain women who know about love; the beautiful women are too busy being fascinating.

—**Katharine Hepburn**

Uhland, Johann Ludwig (1787–1862)

Uhland, a German poet, was leader of the Swabian group. His lyrics and ballads, written when he was a youth, made him one of the most popular German poets of the romantic period. "The Minstrel's Curse," "The Good Comrade," and "Taillefer" are noted for their polished style. He also wrote songs of the fatherland (*Vaterländische Gedichte*) and an unsuccessful drama, *Ludwig der Bayer* (1819), which contains some of his best verse. When he became professor of literature at Tubingen, he was forced to resign on account of his free-thinking and radical views. {CE; JM; RAT; RE}

Uhlich, Johann Jacob Marcus Lebericht (1799–1872)

A German religious reformer, Uhlich studied at Halle and became a preacher. But because of his rationalist views he was suspended in 1847, whereupon he founded the Free Congregation at Magdeburg. Uhlich wrote numerous brochures defending his opinions, and he wrote *Religion of Common Sense*. {BDF; RAT}

Ukpaby, Ernest N. (20th Century)

When he signed Humanist Manifesto II, Ukpaby was a dean of the University of Nigeria. He is author of *American Education, A Critical Analysis of Its Possible Implications for Nigerian Education* (1956). {HM2}

UKRAINIAN HUMANISTS AND UNITARIANS

Jean and Dick Rodes head a Unitarian group, Friends of Russia and the Ukraine (5250 Patriot Lane, Columbia, MD 21045).

Ule, Otto (1820–1876)

Ule was a German scientific writer who studied at Halle and Berlin. In 1852 he started a journal, *Die Natur*, and wrote many works popularizing science. {BDF}

Ulpianus, Domitius (Wrote c. 211–222)

A jurist, one of the great Stoic lawyers of the classic period of Roman law, Ulpianus worked under Alexander Serverus and was his chief advisor. The originals of his work have been lost, but citations from him form about one-third of Justinian's *Digest* and are in accordance with the "Law of Nature." Ulpianus was murdered by the soldiers for his having curtailed their vicious privileges. {RE}

Ulrici, Hermann (1806–1884)

A German philosopher, Ulrici was professor at Halle from 1834 until his death. A free thinker, he held that the soul was an "etheric fluid" but immortal. He called himself a pantheist. According to McCabe, Ulrici's view of the unity or identity of God and the world hardly differed from that of other pantheists. He was nominally (ethically) Christian, but Ulrici said that he accepted the title only on condition that he believed what he could prove and understand. {JM; RAT}

ULSTER HUMANIST ASSOCIATION

For information about the Ulster Humanist Association, write Brian McClinton, 25 Riverside Drive, Lisburn BT27 4HE, United Kingdom. E-mail: <alan.watson1@virgin.net>.

ULTRAISM

Ultraismo was a Spanish movement, its pioneer being Guillermo de Torre, a poet and critic. It was, according to Martin Seymour-Smith, "a somewhat violent version of expression: the image and the metaphor were elevated above the 'story' and above rhetoric or ornament; man was no more than a small part of the universe, not its centre (as implied in nineteenth-century novels)." Jorge Luis Borges was an ultaist, then rejected ultraism although retaining its anti-realism. {WWTCL}

Ulvskog, Marita (20th Century)

For several years Ulvskog edited *Arbetet*, the Social Democrat newspaper. She became the last "church minister" of the Swedish government before the separation of church and state in 2000. In articles in various newspapers, she has written that she does not believe in God. {E-mail, Fredrik Bendz, 29 Nov 99}

UNANIMISM: See entry for Jules Romains.

Unamuno y Jugo, Miguel (1864–1936)

An existentialist, Unamuno based his philosophy upon a faith in faith itself. His *The Tragic Sense of Life in Men and Nations* (1913) was added to the Vatican's list of prohibited reading in 1957, along with his *La Agonia del Cristianismo* (1925). Most theistic systems posit God first and immortality second. Unamuno's equation demands that God *should* exist because we desperately want immortality. His aim included waking Spaniards up to understand that if they searched carefully they would find that the problem of God was not neatly wrapped up. Anxiety, he stressed, has a vital role in driving humans to fulfill the most they can in life. {CE; ER; EU, John Devlin; ILP, additus, 15 December 1961}

UNBAPTISM

Many who have been baptized are asking that they be "unbaptized." In France, for example, as a protest at the Pope's visit in 1996, hundreds of French Roman Catholics asked that their names be removed from church baptism registers. A Montpellier-based group, *Vivre au Présent* (Living in the Present) produced pre-printed cards that stated, "I would be grateful if you would amend the baptism register as follows:

> *Renounced his/her baptism in writing on (date). My philosophical beliefs no longer correspond with those of the people who, in good faith, considered that I should be baptised.*

In other countries, similar requests have been reported. (See entry for Debaptism.) {*The Freethinker*, October 1996}

UNBELIEF

According to J. C. A. Gaskin, in *Varieties of Unbelief from Epicurus to Sartre* (1989), unbelief is at least

> (a) lack of belief in any supernatural agents and, by implication,
> (b) lack of belief in miracles,
> and often, but not connected with (a) and (b) only contingently,
> (c) lack of belief in personal survival after death.

{See entries for Atheistic Humanism and Nullifidian.}

UNBELIEVING JEW: See entry for Harold Bloom.

Underdown, James D. (20th Century)

A stand-up comic, scuba diver, tandem parachuter, and actor, Underdown is a Freedom From Religion Foundation member who has written "Mixing Religion and Humor" in *Freethought Today* (May 1998).

Underwood, Benjamin Franklin (1839–1914)

An American author, materialist, and freethinker, Underwood likened his atheism to that of Charles Bradlaugh. In 1887, he served for a short time as editor and manager of *Open Court*, a freethought journal in Chicago. Open Court has continued as a publisher ever since. In 1888 he edited the *Illustrated Graphic News*. An excellent debater who drew on Thomas Henry Huxley's writings, Underwood once took on Asa Gray, a protégé of Darwin who professed theism and adherence to the Nicene Creed. With F. E. Abbot, he edited *Index*, a freethought publication from Toledo, Ohio, and Bolston, Massachusetts, that was published from 1870 to 1886. Infidels, he wrote, "have been among the most indefatigable workers in every reform." {BDF; EU, William F. Ryan; FUS; RAT; WWS}

Underwood, Sara A. (19th Century)

Underwood, sister of Benjamin Underwood, wrote *Heroines of Freethought* (1876), including in the preface,

> The word Freethinker in times past has implied a censure of the person so designated, and especially if the one so called chanced to be a woman. But, in spite of this fact, here and there in the history of Freethought has appeared a woman strong enough of heart and brain to understand and accept Liberal truths, and brave enough to avow publicly her faith in the 'belief of the unbelievers.' Among these courageous souls we find the names of some of the most brilliant lights of feminine literature. The Orthodox world could not well afford to reject their valuable contributions to the pleasure and well-being of society, but in accepting them did so with an ungracious protest against the religious conclusions of these daring Thinkers.

The book offers a biography of eleven freethinking women: Madame Roland, Mary Wollstonecraft Godwin, Mary W. Godwin Shelley, George Sand, Harriet Martineau, Frances Wright D'Arusmont, Emma Martin, Margaret Reynolds Chapplesmith, Ernestine L. Rose, Frances Power Cobbe, and George Eliot, some of whom were deists. {WWS}

Underwood, Reginald (20th Century)

Underwood, a British author, is a freethinker, according to David Tribe. He wrote *Bachelor's Hall* (1975), a work about homosexuality. {TRI}

UNFALSIFIABLE

That which is falsifiable can be shown to be false; e.g., The only state capitol building in Iowa is in Des Moines.

That which is unfalsifiable cannot be shown to be false; e.g., God is one meter tall; Satan is a fallen angel; humans have a soul.

Ungar, Frederick (Born 1898)

Ungar, an Austrian-born publishing executive who came to the United States in 1929, was a member of the Ethical Society of North Westchester. He wrote *Goethe's World View* (1963) and with Lina Maniero edited *The Encyclopedia of World Literature in the 20th Century, Vol. 4* (1975).

UNIE VRIJZINNIGE VERENIGINGEN

The Flemish-speaking equivalent of Belgium's *Centre d'Action Laïque* (CAL) is *Unie Vrijzinnige Verenigingen*, which coordinates the activities of about thirty Flemish-speaking humanist groups. In 1998, the UVV applied for membership in the International Humanist and Ethical Union. (See entry for Belgian Humanists.)

UNIFICATION CHURCH: See entry for Sun Myung Moon.

UNIFORMITARIANISM

Biblical explanations shackled geology until two Scottish geologists, James Hutton in his *Theory of the Earth* (1785, 1795) and John Playfair in his *Illustrations of the Huttonian Theory* (1802), challenged what were known as the "catastrophists." Catastrophism was expounded by the German geologist, Abraham Gottlob Werner and the French naturalist, G. L. Cuvier, who held that changes in the earth's crust were brought about in the past in ways which cannot be observed today. The uniformitarians, on the contrary, held that geologic phenomena can be explained as the result of existing forces which have operated uniformly from the origin of the earth to the present time.

For the catastrophists, Noah's flood was a supernatural event. Sir Charles Lyell, however, blamed terrestrial forces which had acted over millions of years, forces like earthquakes and sea level changes. The implication was that there was no such thing as Noah's flood. The conflict did for geologists what Darwinism did for biologists. It led to the hypothesis that South America was once joined to Africa, that the land was separated by plate tectonics which moved the continents over eons.

Uniformitarianism, as explained by journalist Nicholas Wade (*The New York Times* 28 May 1995), "teaches that the earth accreted some 4.6 billion years ago and, after a brief bombardment from remaining bits of solar-system debris, has been independent from outside influences ever since. " "A majority of geologists throughout the English-speaking world," wrote Ursula B. Marvin of the Harvard-Smithsonian Center for Astrophysics in 1990, "still regard themselves as uniformitarians, the intellectual heirs of Hutton and Lyell."

However, Wade adds, Luis Alvarez and others claim that the mass extinction of species 65 million years ago was caused by a large impact, probably the huge buried crater on the Yucatán Peninsula. Now that the Apollo astronauts have determined that the moon's craters were caused by impacts, not volcanoes, and almost two hundred crater impact sites have been found on Earth, astronomers have also found that Earth is embedded in a swirl of asteroids and comets, many of which objects will eventually hit Earth. An asteroid or comet about one mile in diameter would suffice to derange the world's climate and agriculture, and the dust that would be caused could block the sunlight for over two months. The conflict between catastrophists and uniformitarians continues.

UNION OF ETHICAL SOCIETIES

The Union of Ethical Societies became the Ethical Union in 1920 and the British Humanist Association in 1967. It had been formed in 1896. {Nicolas Walter, *New Humanist*, February 1996}

UNION OF FREETHINKERS OF FINLAND

The Union of Freethinkers of Finland is at Siltasaarenkatu 15 C 65, 00530 Helsinki, Finland.

UNION OF ITALIAN RATIONALISTS

The Union of Italian Rationalists, Atheists, and Agnostics is c/o Lega Per l'Ambiente, Via Cornaro 1A, 35128 Padova, Italy.

UNION RADICAL-HUMANISTE LUXEMBOURGE-OISE

Union Radical-Humaniste Luxembourgeoise is at 39 Rue de Hollerich, 1741 Luxembourg, Grand Duchy of Luxembourg.

UNION RATIONALISTE

Union Rationaliste is at 14 Rue de l'Ecole Polytechnique, 75005, Paris, France.

UNITARIAN CHRISTIANS

"The Unitarian establishment, mostly in the East, called itself Unitarian Christian," Edwin H. Wilson, himself a Unitarian minister, has written. "Dissenters were represented by the Western Unitarian Conference. In the late nineteenth-century, a controversy ensued (known as the 'Issue of the West') over whether there would be a Unitarian creed to exclude non-theists and other post-Christian dissenters," which Charles Lyttle described in *Freedom Moves West* (1952). "The Western Unitarian Conference stood steadfastly opposed to creeds. For example, William Channing Gannett, a minister at St. Paul, reportedly stated that he wanted the basis of fellowship in his church to be so broad that even the well-meaning atheist would be welcome."

Although "Christ" by definition would appear to be a non-Unitarian concept, many Unitarian Universalists have considered themselves Christians during different time periods, including the present. Inasmuch as the various Unitarian Universalist groups are independent, their General Assembly is an association and has no statutory power over the individual congregations. As such, the groups' theology ranges from noticeably christocentric through all sorts of humanism to neo-paganism. {EW}

UNITARIAN CHURCH OF THE LARGER FELLOWSHIP (CLF)

The Unitarian Church of the Larger Fellowship is a Boston-based group that communicates with its far-flung members—who do not live near any organized Unitarian group or who are unable to attend any services—largely by mail and telephone. In 1998 CLF had an estimated 2,600 members. {*World*, May-June 1998}

UNITARIAN HUMANISTS

Individual Unitarian Universalists are requested to define their own religious-philosophic outlook rather than accept a doctrinal viewpoint developed by Unitarian leaders. As a result, great varieties of viewpoints are found in all Unitarian congregations. "Are you a UU theist or a UU humanist?" members have been known to ask each other, and the statistical estimates usually suggest that theists were in the majority during the first part of the century but that the humanists are in the latter part.

As for "God," contemporary Unitarian humanists will likely not use the 18th century "Supreme Architect" or the 19th century "Oversoul" terms. Many, in fact, are averse to using the word whatsoever. Or, if the term is used, it will be used much as is the term Jove, a historic allusion (or, as some say, illusion).

Kurt Vonnegut Jr., who has headed the American Humanist Association, is a Unitarian. The number of Unitarians who say they are atheists or agnostics or freethinkers or secular humanists are found in far greater numbers than individual Unitarians may suspect. Often these Unitarians are also members of the Freedom From Religion Foundation, the American Rationalist Association, the American Humanist Association, or of the Council for Secular Humanism.

Large numbers of Unitarian humanists, in short, are non-theistic and more apt to be atheists than agnostics. A 1989 UUA Commission on Appraisal showed that about three-fourths of Unitarians are humanists. An informal poll at the 1997 General Assembly, according to Edd Doerr, confirmed such a figure.

Jone Johnson, a Unitarian and a third generation humanist, has written her views:

> While the term "humanism" may not have been used until the late 1910s or the 1920s, the sentiments were around a lot earlier. Some Unitarian ministers were preaching positively about agnosticism as early as the 1870s. . . .
>
> The combination that we tend to call humanism with Unitarian Universalism—skepticism, disbelief, or de-emphasis on concepts of deity, plus emphasis on the worthiness of human beings (as opposed to the basic sinfulness of them), plus emphasis on human individual ethical responsibility (as opposed to divine intervention or a set of divinely-given ethical rules), plus emphasis on this life on earth as "all and enough"—were around well before the twentieth century.
>
> Certainly science and its discoveries were part of what produced the new emphasis and views. Another key change was the related and earlier movement to analyze the bible with the same views one analyzed literature, making easy faith in the miracles impossible for many. The Transcendentalist fascination with nature, the discovery and beginnings of in-depth study of other world religions (especially Asian), the German philosophical skepticisms of Hume, Spinoza, and especially Kant, the freethought and social reform traditions of the nineteenth century: these are all our precursors and in a solid sense "causes." The Christian humanism of the Renaissance, which focused on this world and humanity, on classical Greek and Roman philosophy and literature as having important insights to supplement and illuminate the Christian worldview: all these trends are, of course, interrelated: dare I say interdependent.
>
> Darwin and the general acceptance of naturalistic evolution is, though, perhaps the greatest "root" of modern naturalistic humanism, within the Unitarian Universalist Association and outside of it. After Darwin, it was far more difficult to reconcile the way the world as we know it works and the way the Christian and other religious scriptures teach that the world began. In this sense, humanism *is* the enemy of fundamentalist Christianity—our ideas threaten the very foundations of their world view, which has God as responsible for solving ultimate problems, the Bible as needing to the literally true, and humans so pitiful that we cannot understand that anything on this earth in nature that seems to contradict the Scriptures, must be our failure to understand and not a failure of God's truth.

{Jone Johnson on the Web 16 Apr 1999; *World*, March-April 1998}

UNITARIAN SERVICE COMMITTEE: See entry for Lotta Hitschmanova, its director for thirty-five years. (See entry for Unitarian Universalist Service Committee.)

UNITARIAN THEISTS

Early Unitarians were theists who believed in God but not in the theologians' supernatural inventions: the Holy Ghost, the Christ.

Over the centuries, some Unitarians and particularly many Universalists have chosen to call themselves theists. A typical example is the Reverend Harvey Swanson, an outspoken opponent of humanism. He set forth his criticism of "humanism without God" in early issues of *The New Humanist*. Edwin H. Wilson tells the story that when laymen in Swanson's Lancaster, Pennsylvania, church once invited him to speak on humanism, he did "while a mighty-voiced and indignant Swanson, speaking before another group on the other side of a folding door, all but drowned me out with his stentorian thunder." (See entry for Unitarian Christians.) {EW}

UNITARIAN UNIVERSALIST ASSOCIATION

The Unitarian Universalist Association, 25 Beacon Street, Boston, Massachusetts 02108, is a cooperating organization of the International Humanist and Ethical Union. The Unitarian Church organized in the 1790s and today has an estimated 215,000 members. On the World Wide Web: <http://uua.org/>. (See entry for Unitarianism.)

UNITARIAN UNIVERSALIST MERGER

In 1961 at the time of the merger between the Unitarians and Universalists, there were 42,858 Universalists in 289 churches and 9 fellowships; and there were 106,759 Unitarians in 361 churches and 245 fellowships. (See Charles Howe's *The Larger Faith*.)

UNITARIAN UNIVERSALIST SERVICE COMMITTEE

Much like the Quaker Service Committee, the Unitarian Universalist Service Committee (130 Prospect Street, Cambridge, Massachusetts 02139) promotes international social justice through public policy advocacy and support of local development initiatives.

UNITARIANISM

• Unitarian, n. One who denies the divinity of a Trinitarian.

—**Ambrose Bierce**
The Devil's Dictionary

Unitarianism is "the doctrinal system characterized chiefly by belief in the unipersonality of God and the normal humanity of Jesus, as contrasted with the Trinity and the eternal deity of Christ," explained Earl Wilbur, when he was the President of Pacific Unitarian School for the Ministry in Berkeley, California.

Arius (c. 250–336) and his followers, the Arians, thought of God as a unity and Jesus as a human prophet, which is a premise also of Unitarianism. The earliest anti-Trinitarian book was **Martin Cellarius**'s *On the Works of God* (1527), followed by *On the Errors of the Trinity* (1531) by **Michael Servetus**. Servetus was burned at the stake in 1553 for his anti-trinitarian views. Unitarianism took form in 1568, almost simultaneously with **Faustus Socinus**'s Socinianism in Poland, though independently of it, when a group split off from the Reformed Church in Transylvania, where in the 1560s **Francis David** had laid foundations for the Unitarian Church there and where the Prince and many of the nobility gave it legal standing as one of the four "received religions." **King John Sigismund of Transylvania** is the only Unitarian king in history, and in 1568 he proclaimed the earliest edict of complete religious toleration. Although oppressed by later Calvinists and Catholics, the Transylvanian Unitarians have continued and consist mostly of Szekler and Magyar free farmers. The English and Transylvanian Unitarians did not discover each other until 1821, although in 1550 the Church of the Strangers (which was Socinian in influence) had been established in London.

In England, where many in the 16th century were imprisoned or put to death for their "Arianism," **John Biddle** in the 17th century founded English Unitarianism and his followers increased in numbers during the time of the "Trinitarian Controversy." In 1774, **Theophilus Lindsey** gave up his living and in London opened the first Unitarian chapel. **Joseph Priestley**, **Thomas Belsham**, and others advanced the cause, which emphasizes the humanity, not the divinity, of Jesus. In the mid-19th century, **James Martineau** led Unitarianism as a religion of reason.

In the United States, **Joseph Priestley** and later **William Ellery Channing** advanced the unitarian view that the deity exists only in one person. This help promote a positive Christianity which treated Jesus as a human. Many Congregational churches became Unitarian, hastened by **Henry Ware**'s being chosen in 1805 as Hollis Professor of Divinity at Harvard University. In 1825, both the British Unitarian Association and the American Unitarian Association were formed. According to Wilbur, "The Unitarian polity is pure Congregationalism; and church extension is managed by the American Unitarian Association in regional departments."

In Canada, the first recorded meeting was in Montreal in 1832. In the 1840s, churches were established in Halifax and Toronto. In 1891, an Icelandic-speaking Unitarian Church was organized in Winnipeg. In 1962, a French language fellowship, *Cercle Unitaire de Langue Française*, was founded in Montreal.

A number of Unitarian ministers, starting with **John H. Dietrich** and including **Curtis Reese**, developed a "religious humanism," and in the 1990s a large percentage of Unitarians admit to being either religious, agnostic, atheistic, or secular humanists.

In 1961, the American Unitarian Association and the Universalist Church of America merged, becoming the Unitarian Universalist Association.

The "church," often called a "society," is congregational, and neither ministers nor members are required to profess any particular doctrine. They have adopted no creed. According to James Luther Adams, the philosopher Alfred North Whitehead had the best definition of Unitarianism: "belief in up to one God."

In the 20th Century, some Unitarian congregations became involved in new theistic-style movements such as New Age and Wiccan Paganism, holding that the intentional exploration of theological diversity is desirable and a sign of growth. Three branches of Unitarian Universalist thinking became evident: Christian, Pagan, and Humanist. Some congregations also investigated feminism, naturalistic theism, and Kwanzaa, but none showed any interest in returning to revealed religion.

The alternative to welcoming diversity, many claimed in letters and articles in *World* (November-December 1996), is to be "univocal," thinking their particular brand of Unitarian Universalism is preferable to the other kinds. Meanwhile, a minister in any congregation finds some members who object to the lighting of candles while still other members object that God is not named. If the strength of Unitarian Universalism is its diversity, it also follows that theoretical diversity is quite different from practical diversity, that it is a problem for any Unitarian Universalist leaders to advance new ideas as well as keep a broad perspective and balance the various views in a congregation. (See entries for American Unitarian Association, Carl Bihldorf, *Unitarios Universalistas de Habla Hispana*; Pelagius; and Transylvanian Unitarians.) {CE; ER}

UNITARIANISM DEFINED

Unitarians do not just believe anything they want. A typical response to that accusation is one by the Rev. Rod Debs of the Unitarian-Universalist Society of Blackhawk County, Iowa. He describes his society's mission:

> • . . . to be an accepting and supportive community that nurtures spiritual, emotional, and intellectual explorations, articulates ethical values, and encourages actions based on personal beliefs. This community is a voice for religious diversity, human tolerance, improvement of the human condition, and preservation of our environment.
>
> • We do not require belief in a creed or theology, yet we are not free of responsibility. We are a "covenant" community, promising to one another to be an accepting, supportive, and nurturing community. In expression of our covenant responsibilities to one another, one can observe certain beliefs commonly held among us:
>
> • UUs believe in being honest: Are we Christian? Such labels are not what's really important to religious faith. Honesty is most important, and respect for each person's honest faith journey whether Christian, Jewish, Muslim, humanist, Buddhist, pagan, uncommitted or whether shaped by all these. . . .
>
> • UUs believe reality is an awesome gift: Many names are used to grasp the wonder of reality, like "god," but none is sufficient. Reality can be seen (as a strong arm of "our Father" lifting us up and providing for our needs; as a universal master, "The Lord" demanding compliance and dealing out sure discipline; as a vulnerable infant in our care, the Baby Jesus; as a loyal brother, Jesus willingly sacrificing his life; as the sacrifice and resurrection of Christ in plant and animal cycles, the seasons of harvest dying to feed us and spring renewal; as a lover, intimate and sensually embracing us as earth, air, fire, and water; as "Mother-God," life-giving, nurturing, healing, and receiving us to its bosom in death. But all are insufficient names for reality's giftedness.
>
> • UUs believe truth and meaning are revealed in many sources still unfolding: sources besides sacred texts—poetry, children's books, newspapers, the scientific method, intuition, and nature. No single source has a monopoly on truth or meaning.
>
> • UUs believe that relationships of kindness and mutual participation save us from social evil. Do we believe in an afterlife of individual heaven or hell? UUs believe there is a place at life's welcome table for

every living being, now and here. Life's giftedness is bestowed on all without distinction. At the end of life, death also comes as a gift in the process of cyclical renewal, blessed relief, and peace.

• UUs believe that every person and all of life is worthy of respect: Nothing in nature nor any being is all good or bad. . . .

• UUs are not trapped into saying that we do not believe this or that. Our beliefs commonly involve an honest faith journey; awe at the gift of reality; attentiveness to many sources of truth and meaning; commitment to relationships of community, kindness, and justice; and respect for all in the web of interdependent existence.

UNITARIANS AND HUMANISTS WHO HOMESCHOOL

Unitarians and humanists who educate their children outside an institutional setting publish a bimonthly newsletter obtainable from Mary Marsh, 2892 Cedar Ave., Lummi Island, Washington 98262; and have a homepage: <HUUH-L-request@uua.org>.

UNITARIANS AND ROBERT G. INGERSOLL

In 1892 at a Unitarian club dinner, Robert G. Ingersoll said the following:

> The Unitarian Church has done more than any other church—and maybe more than all other churches—to substitute character for creed, and to say that a man should be judged by his spirit; by the climax of his heart; by the autumn of his generosity; by the spring of his hope, that he should be judged by what he does; by the influence that he exerts, rather than by the mythology he may believe. . . .
>
> I want to thank the Unitarian Church for what it has done; and I want to thank the Universalist Church, too. They at least believe in a God who is a gentleman; and that is much more than was ever done by an orthodox church.

UNITARIANS IN INDIA

"Return to Meghalaya," by John Hewerdine (*World*, March-April 1999), describes an estimated eight thousand Unitarians in the Khasi and Jaintia Hills of northeast India. Hewerdine is a British Unitarian and professor of photography. Although geography makes them Indians, the tribal people of the region, which is about 350 miles northeast of Calcutta, prefer to manage their own affairs, following one of their slogans, "Tribal by Blood, Indians by Accident."

Hajom Kissor Singh was the tribal Khasi who, objecting to the Christian missionaries and their orthodox messages, founded the Unitarian Church, one which taught the teachings of Jesus but also those of the Buddha, the Sikh prophets, and the Hindu and Islamic scriptures. His church also borrowed elements of the indigenous tribal faith: Seng Khasi. Today a total of thirty-five churches and fellowships are associated, and their emphasis is theistic.

UNITARIANS, AMERICAN

- Historically the nation's most liberal religious body, the Unitarian Universalist Association in 1999 announced that for the first time women outnumber men among its active clergy members, making up 51% of the total, up from fewer than 3% in 1968.
- The total of Unitarian Universalist (UU) congregations in the United States and Canada in 1995: 1,026
- The average congregation membership: 145
- The number of UU congregations with more than 1000 members: 3
- The percentage of all church members who have changed denominations: 40%
- Total expenditures of all UU congregations in 1994–1995: $110,700,000.
- Total number of UU ministers in fellowship, including retirees and associate fellowships: 1,273
- Percentage of active UU ministers over the age of 40: 86%
- Number of registered UU ministerial students and candidates: 524
- Number enrolled at UU seminaries: 106
- Increase since 1991 in persons of color among UU ministerial candidates: 1300%
- Median compensation (salary and housing) for UU parish ministers: $33,100
- Average compensation for ministers in the Reformed Church in America: $43,000
- Average compensation for ministers in the Episcopal Church: $44,721
- Percentage of women in the UU ministry: 51%
- Where to find more about Unitarians on the Internet: <http://www.uua.org/>

A 1998 survey of more than 8,000 Unitarian Universalists found that when asked what best described their "theological perspective," results were as follows:

48.1%	Humanist
19.0	Earth-Nature Centered
13.0	Theist
9.5	Christian
6.7	Mystic

(*World*, Sep-Oct 1995; *World*, May-June 1998}

UNITARIANS, EUROPEAN

European Unitarian Universalists can be contacted by writing EUU, c/o Hertz, Fryden-lundsvej 49, DK-2950 Vedbeer, Denmark. E-mail: <ghertz@nordita.dk>. Their fax and telephone is (45) 42-89-4184. (Also, see listings in the various countries.)

UNITARIANS, FAMOUS WOMEN: On the Web: <http://www.geocities.com/~bread_n_roses/>.

UNITARIANS, LATIN-AMERICAN

Ruth Alatorre, the Rev. Alma Nieves, Julio Noboa, the Rev. Patricia Jimenez, and the Rev. José Ballester are leaders of LUUNA (Latino/Latina Unitarian Universalist Networking Association). {*World*, July-August 1998}

UNITARIANS, NOTED

A website on the World Wide Web has been formed which identifies noted Unitarians and Universalists if

• they were raised Unitarian, Universalist, or Unitarian Universalist, and/or

• at some time regularly attended or joined a Unitarian, Universalist, or Unitarian Universalist church or society, and/or

• at some time identified themselves as Unitarian, Universalist, or Unitarian Universalist in theology or membership.

The page is maintained by Jone Johnson, and its links and lists are by Sue Bennett, Dan Hotchkiss, Lorella Thomas, Steve Champion, and Jim Mason. It is at <http://www.pbat.com/famousuus/>.

UNITARIANS, SPANISH-SPEAKING, ONLINE

Spanish-speaking Unitarians who are online and who publish *Luuna Luz* are headed by Lawrence Peers. E-mail: <lpeers@uua.com>.

In Spain Unitarians have a homepage: <members.tripod.com/~jdemarcos/uuesp.htm>.

Also, Spanish-speaking Unitarians who are ethical humanists or secular humanists are on the Web: <http://idt.net/~wasm/asibehu>.

UNITARIANS, TRAINING OF MINISTERS

"My judgment is that the most erudite pastors come from the Harvard and Union seminaries, the least from Meadville/Lombard and Starr King," wrote J. Gaston, a classical musician and a Unitarian. (See entry for J. Gaston.) {WAS, 16 July 1997}

UNITARIANS, UNITED KINGDOM

Contact for United Kingdom Unitarians is Matthew Smith, Essex Hall, 1-6 Essex Street, Strand, London WC2R, 3HY, England. Unitarians in Britain are on the World Wide Web: <http://www.unitarian.org.uk>.

UNITARIOS UNIVERSALISTAS DE HABLA HISPANA: See "A Spanish-Language Ministry" by David Reich in *World*, July-August 1995. A San José, California, Unitarian Universalist church with Spanish-speaking members led by Ervin Barrios is described. Barrios can be reached at (408) 254-7799. He is one of the steering committee members of *Luuna Luz*.

UNITARISCHE BLATTER FUR GANZHEITLICHE RELIGION UND KULTUR: See entry for German Unitarians.

UNITED CHURCH OF CHRIST

A Reformed church, the United Church of Christ, organized in 1957, is at 700 Prospect Avenue, Cleveland, Ohio 44115.

UNITED KINGDOM, FREETHOUGHT AND HUMANIST GROUPS

Following are groups and publications in the United Kingdom—up-to-date lists are published in bi-monthly issues of *The Freethinker*:

- Birmingham Humanist Group: phone Tova Jones 0121 4544692
- Blackpool & Fylde Humanist Group: phone D. Baxter at 01253 726112
- Brighton & Hove Humanist Group, Joan Wimble, Flat 5, 67 St. Aubryns, Hove BN3 2TL; tel 01273 733215
- Bristol Humanists: Margaret Dearnley on 0117 9049490
- Bromley Humanists: D. Elvin on 0181 777 1680
- Chiltern Humanists: phone 01296 623730
- Cornwall Humanists: B. Mercer, "Amber", Short Cross Road, Mount Hawke, Truro TR 4 8EA; tel 01209 890690
- Cotswold Humanists: Philip Howell, 2 Cleevelands Close, Cheltenham GL50 4PZ; tel 01242 528743
- Coventry and Warwickshire Humanists: phone 01926 858450
- Devon Humanists: Christine Lavery, 5 Prospect Garden, off Blackboy Road, Exeter; tel 01392 56600
- Ealing Humanists: Derek Hill 0181 422 4956 or Charles Rudd 0181 904 6599
- Edinburgh Group: 2 Saville Terrace, Edinburgh EH 9 3AD; tel 0131 667 8389
- *Ethical Record*, a monthly, at Bradlaugh House, 47 Theobald's Road, London, WC1X 8SP, United Kingdom
- Ealing Humanists: Derek Hill 0181 422 4956 or Charles Rudd 0181 904 6599
- *Freethinker*, Bradlaugh House, 47 Theobald's Road, London WC1X 8SP. The magazine's e-mail:<iduke@compuserve.com>. On the Web: <http://www.freethinker.co.uk>
- *Gay and Lesbian Humanist*, a quarterly, 34 Spring Lane, Kenilworth, CV8 2HG; tel 01926 858450
- Glasgow Group: Alan Henness, 138 Lumley St., Grangemouth FK3 8 BL; tel 01324 485152
- Hampstead Humanist Society: N. I. Barnes, 10 Stevenson House, Boundary Road, London NW 8 OHP
- Harrow Humanist Society: tel 0181 863 2977
- Havering & District Humanist Society: J. Condon at 01708 473597 or J. Baker at 01708 458925
- *Humanism Scotland*, a quarterly, 11A Strathkiness High Road, St Andrews, Fife, KY16 9UA
- *Humanist News*, bi-monthly, Bradlaugh House, 47 Theobald's Road, London, WC1X 8SP
- Humanist Society of Scotland: Secretary George Rodger, 17 Howburn Place, Aberdeen AB 1 2XT; tel 01224 573034; convener Robin Wood, 37 Inchmurrin Drive, Kilmarnock, Ayshire at tel 01563 526710
- *Humanity's* e-mail address: <robert@humanism.org.uk>.
- Kent Humanists: M. Rogers, 2 Lyndhurst Road, Broadstairs CT10 1DD; tel 01843 864506
- Lancashire Humanist Alliance: Steve Johnson, PO Box 111, Blackburn BB1 8GD
- Leeds & District Humanist Group: Robert Tee on 0113 2577009
- Leicester Secular Society: Secular Hall, 75 Humberstone Gate, Leicester LE 1 1W; tel 0116 2622250 or 0116 241 4060
- Lewisham Humanist Group: Denis Cobell on 0181 690 4645; Unitarian Meeting House, 41 Bromley Road, Catford, London SE6
- Manchester Humanist Group: Arthur Chappell is the contact and can be telephoned: 0161 681 7607; E-mail and Web addresses: <arthurchappell@clara.net>; <www.arthurchappell.clara.net/contents.htm>.
- Musical Heathens: Karl Heath on 01203 673306
- *New Humanist*, a quarterly, Bradlaugh House, 47 Theobald's Road, London, WC1X 8SP <jim.rpa@humanism.org.uk>.
- *North-East Humanist Newsletter*, a quarterly, 36 Partridge Close, Washington, Tyne and Wear, NE 38 OES <owen.dumpleton@mfl.org>
- North East Humanists (Teesside Group): J. Cole 01642 559418 or R Wood 01740 650861
- North London Humanist Group: Anne Toy on 0181 360 1828
- Norwich Humanist Group: Vincent G. Chainey, Le Chene, 4 Mill St., Bradenham, Thetford IP25 7PN; tel 01362 820982
- Sheffield Humanist Society: Gordon Sinclair on 01226 743070 or Bill McIlroy on 0114 2509127
- *The Skeptic*, monthly, 29 Barnstone Street, Hexthorpe, Doncaster, South Yorkshire, DN4 OET
- Somerset and South Somerset Humanists: Wendy Sturgess on 01458 274456
- Stockport Secular Group: Carl Pinel, 85 Hall St., Offerton, Stockport SK1 4DE; on 0161 480 0732
- Sutton Humanist Group: on 0181 642 4577
- *The Ulster Humanist*, monthly, Brian Clinton, 25 Riverside Drive, Lisburn, BT27 4HE; on 01846 677264
- West Glamorgan Humanist Group; Julie Norris, 3 Maple Grove, Uplands, Swansea SA2 OJY; on 01792 206108 or 01792 296375
- West Kent Secular Humanist Group: Ian Peters on 01892 890485 or Chris Ponsford on 01892 862855

For a discussion of freethought in the United Kingdom, see Gordon Stein's *Freethought in the United Kingdom and the Commonwealth* (1981).

UNITED KINGDOM UNITARIANS

Unitarians in the United Kingdom are on the Web: <http://www.unitarian.org.uk>.

UNITED METHDOST CHURCH

The United Methodist Church, organized in 1968, is at PO Box 320, Nashville, Tennessee 37202. Its membership of over 8,400,000 make it the largest of the Methodist organizations.

UNITED STATES OF AMERICA: See the entries for Thomas Paine and for Usonia.

UNITED STATES OF AMERICA, A CHRISTIAN

To A. N. Wilson's op-ed article in *The New York Times* (8 June 1999), fearing an evangelical theocracy in the United States and an overall political flocking to the religious right, David Blankenhorn—president of the Institute for American Values—replied, "His attempt to read God out of the American founding is especially paradoxical, since our Declaration of Independence, with its revolutionary assertion that human rights derive from the 'Creator' rather than from the government, and the document's 'firm Reliance on the Protection of divine Providence,' specifically concerned the pretensions of the authorities in England."

Disagreeing, Joseph Chuman retorted, "The embrace by a growing number of American politicians of the values of ultraconservative religion would cause the Founding Fathers to turn in their graves and should be viewed by the rest of us with alarm." {*The New York Times*, 12 June 1999}

UNITED SECULARISTS OF AMERICA: See entries for H. Sprague and Sherman Wakefield.

UNITED WORLD ATHEISTS: See entry for Madalyn Murray O'Hair.

UNITIES

Aristotle decreed in his *Poetics* that a drama should have but one plot and it should take place in a single day and be confined to a single locale. Those three requirements are called *unities*. French neoclassicists and others imitated the three. However, from the time the three unities were put forward, playwrights regularly disregarded them. {DCL}

UNIVERSAL DECLARATION OF HUMAN RIGHTS (UDHR)

A major humanistic document, one that states in writing that everyone's misery matters to everyone else, is the Universal Declaration of Human Rights (UDHR), which was adopted 10 December 1948 by the United Nations. It has been signed by every UN government, and most have since incorporated in their various human-rights treaties the requirement to treat their *own* citizens with decency.

King Hammurabi in 1740 B. C. E. had codified laws against unfair trials, torture, and slavery, but on 10 December 1948 the member states of the United Nations adopted the far-reaching and revolutionary document, one that rates the adjective "sacred" to non-believers and freethinkers everywhere.

Eleanor Roosevelt, the chair of the Commission on Human Rights, presented the Universal Declaration of Human Rights to the General Assembly, which enacted it 10 December 1948. She then observed,

> We stand today at the threshold of a great event both in the life of the United Nations and in the life of mankind. This declaration may well become the international Magna Carta for all men everywhere. We hope its proclamation by the General Assembly will be an event comparable to the proclamation in 1789 [of the French Declaration of the Rights of Man], the adoption of the Bill of Rights by the people of the United States, and the adoption of comparable declarations at different times in other countries.

Although for years a French human-rights activist, René Cassin, was publicly regarded as the author and even received a Nobel Peace Prize in 1968, researchers later unearthed papers at McGill University showing that John Peter Humphrey, a Canadian, had written the original draft of the ideas contained in the Declaration.

UNIVERSALISM

> • Universalist, n. One who foregoes the advantage of a Hell for persons of another faith.
>
> —**Ambrose Bierce**
> *The Devil's Dictionary*

Universalism, according to Clarence Prouty Shedd of the Yale University Divinity School in New Haven, Connecticut, "centers about the belief that all men will finally be saved. This doctrine is of ancient origin and has existed among many of the schools of Christianity. There are Biblical passages in both the Old and New Testaments which are interpreted as furnishing Scriptural authority for the belief. Such men as Alexandrinus, Origen (who in 225 CE advocated universal salvation—in 553, Emperor Justinian got the Council of Constantinople to declare Origen's universalism a heresy), Diodorus, Theodore of Mopsuestia, and others laid the foundation for the system. They taught that punishment was remedial, that the nature of God was love, and that the Divine mercy could not be satisfied with partial salvation or everlasting punishment."

In the 6th century, the universalist doctrine was considered heretical and was neglected during the Middle Ages. In the 14th century, an English reform movement, the Lollards, maintained a belief in universal salvation. **Samuel Gorton**, a pioneer of Christian Universalism, was driven out of Massachusetts in 1637 for his political and religious radicalism. In 1684, **Joseph Gatchell** had his tongue pierced with a hot iron for stating that "All men should be saved." In the 18th century, **John Relly** of London preached universalism, and **John Murray** brought it to America in 1770. **Christopher Sower**, a Universalist Quaker, with **George de Benneville** printed the first Bible in America translated into German—it produced in heavier type those passages which supported the universal character of religion. The earliest systematic account of Universalism was **Hosea Ballou**'s T*reatise of the Atonement* (1805). Whereas Murray had espoused a Universalism of the Calvinistic type, Ballou was a powerful force in moving the denomination in a different direction. Ballou's doctrine of "Christ's subordination to the Father" gave the group a position similar to that of Unitarianism.

Universalists in 1935 in a Washington Avowal of Faith affirmed "the universal fatherhood of God; the spiritual authority and leadership of Jesus Christ, His son; the trustworthiness of the Bible as containing a revelation from God; the certainty of just retribution for sin; and the final harmony of all souls with God." In 1961, however, the Universalist Church of America at 16 Beacon Street in Boston merged with the American Unitarian Association at 25 Beacon Street in Boston, and the new church is known as the Unitarian Universalist.

Individual Universalists started the California Institute of Technology and Bradley University. But the Universalist denomination founded five institutions of higher institution: Tufts in Medford, Massachusetts, and St. Lawrence University in Canton, New York, were founded in the 1850s and still retain their original names. Also founded in the 1850s was Lombard University (now the Meadville/Lombard Theological School). The two others, both founded in 1872, no longer exist: Smithson College of Muncie, Indiana, was in operation only two years; and Buchtel College of Akron, Ohio, is now the liberal arts branch of the state-supported University of Akron.

Universalists, celebrating their 200 years in America in 1993, pointed to the following:

- The largest church of Universalist heritage is the 900-member Universalist Church in Minneapolis. In West Hartford, Connecticut, a 500-member church exists.
- The first book published in America which proposed a unitarian theology was Hosea Ballou's *A Treatise on Atonement* (1805).
- The first African American Universalist was Gloster Dalton, a charter member of the Independent Christian Church of Gloucester, Massachusetts, the first Universalist congregation in North America.
- The first national women's organization of an American denomination was The Universalist Women's Centenary Association, founded in 1869.
- The site of Sojourner Truth's famous "Ain't I A Woman?" speech, delivered in 1851, was the First Universalist Church of Akron, Ohio.
- The first woman to preach from a Universalist pulpit was Maria Cook, in 1811.
- The first woman fully licensed as a minister was Universalist Lydia A. Jenkins.
- The first woman in Canada to be officially recognized as a preacher was Mary Ann Church, who, though not ordained, was listed in *The Universalist Register* (1838).
- The first Native North American ordained as a Universalist

minister was Native Canadian George Moses, in 1871.
• The first prison reform newspaper was *The Prisoner's Friend*, edited by Universalist minister Charles Spear.
• The oldest surviving Universalist church in Canada is at Halifax, Nova Scotia.
• The only Universalist cathedral ever built, the Fourth Universalist Society in New York City, was designed by William Stuart Potter. In the mid-19th century, the Rev. Edwin Chapin preached to as many as 2,000 people here on Sundays. (In 1997, the membership was down to around 100.) The stained glass is Tiffany, Henry Steinway personally designed the piano, and Mrs. Andrew Carnegie, a member of the congregation, donated the organ. Circus magnate Phineas Taylor Barnum was a member.

"Universalism is misconstrued as some sort of sponge that welcomes everything," the Rev. Scott Alexander has said. But actually it is a faith of "high expectations," he added, drawing upon ethical values and spiritual expressions shared among other faiths: "Universalism embraces these different perspectives and instinctively looks for the common good."

A large number of present Unitarian Universalists consider themselves religious, agnostic, atheist, or secular humanists. Many, however, call themselves theists, and some of the services incorporate Buddhist as well as neo-pagan Celtic or Wiccan elements (See entries for Anna Flemming, typical of an early female Universalist minister in the Midwest, and Jim Morrison. For Robert G. Ingersoll's view of Universalists, see entry for Unitarians and Robert G. Ingersoll.) {CE; ER}

UNIVERSALIST HERALD

In 1997, the *Universalist Herald* (c/o Lewis Graphics, Route 4, Box 16, Elkton, Virginia 22827) celebrated its 150th anniversary. Its editor is the Rev. John C. Morgan, 142 Hanover Street, Northumberland, Pennsylvania 17857. E-mail: <jmorgan900@aol.com>.

UNIVERSALIST THEISTS

In England, the Rev. John Clifford in 1997 described himself as follows:

> Theologically, I am a Universalist Theist with both unitarian and christian sympathies. In Britain the Universalists largely joined forces with the Unitarians in the late 18th century and adopted the Unitarian label being pushed by Joseph Priestley as a rallying flag for disparate religious liberals. Consequently, the Universalist label as originally used pretty well died out. Current institutional usage in Britain is focused on a Bristol-based group of Universalist Quakers.

UNIVERSE

• The universe is a big place, perhaps the biggest.

—Kilgore Trout
(**Kurt Vonnegut Jr.**)

• Two forces rule the universe: light and gravity.

—Simone Weil

• We are an impossibility in an impossible universe.

—**Ray Bradbury**

• My theology, briefly, is that the universe was dictated but not signed.

—Christopher Morley

• I'm astounded by people who want to "know" the universe when it's hard enough to find your way around Chinatown.

—**Woody Allen**

As to how old our universe is, no definitive answer is available. Astronomers seek to come up with a consensus on the universe's age, but they remain separated by billions of years. One group holds that the universe is from nine to twelve billion years old, whereas another estimates it is from eleven to fifteen billion years of age. By measuring the rate of expansion and the distance between objects, astronomers believe they can then determine how long it has been since the initial Big Bang, but it is clear that no absolute number will be ascertainable or even desirable.

Meanwhile, scientists in 1997 made a startling observation: that the universe has an "up" and a "down." Previously, it had been held that space is uniform, that it is the same in all directions, with no north and south or up and down. That tenet was challenged in 1997 by physicists at the University of Rochester and the University of Kansas, who concluded after analyzing radio waves from 160 distant galaxies that the radiations rotate as they move through space, in a subtle corkscrew pattern unlike anything observed before. This could mean that there is an "up" and a "down" in the universe, but which is which remains purely arbitrary.

The new view meant that scientists would now need to reconsider the concept that the Big Bang, the theorized moment of cosmic origin, was completely symmetric. If the universe in which people live was asymmetric at creation, it raises the possibility of the simultaneous creation of another universe with an opposite twist. Astrophysicists will obviously need to test this new information thoroughly before any conclusions can be accepted.

In May 1999, after eight years of measurements by the Hubble Space Telescope, astronomers estimated that the universe has been expanding for at least twelve billion years since its theorized explosive creation in the Big Bang. Depending on the density of cosmic matter and the possible existence of a mysterious form of vacuum energy, John Noble Wilford reported, the age of the universe could be closer to 13.5 billion or even 15 billion years. According to Dr. Neta A. Bahcall of Princeton University, there is the possibility "that some cosmic dark energy exists that opposes the self-attraction of matter and causes the expansion of the universe to accelerate." If so, the universe could keep on expanding, almost to the point of vanishing. In such a case, the University of Chicago's Michael S. Turner extrapolates that "the universe will become a bleaker and bleaker place" and as the galaxies speed away from one another and the stars grow dimmer, "in 400 to 500 billion years, we're only going to be able to see a few neighboring galaxies." (See entry for Neutrino, the elusive particle which in 1998 was found to have mass.) {John Noble Wilford, *The New York Times*, 18 April 1997, and 26 May 1999}

UNIVERSITEIT VOOR HUMANISTEIK

Universiteit Voor Humanisteik (IHEU) is at POB 797, 3500 AT Utrecht, Netherlands. It is a university for humanist studies. On the Web: <http://home.pi.net/~pderkx/hmlwv.html>.

UNIVERSITIES AND COLLEGES

Colleges and universities arose in the 12th and 13th centuries to train individuals in the professions of law, theology, and medicine. Salerno (9th Century) and Montpellier (13th Century) specialized in medicine. Bologna (1088) specialized in law, Paris (12th Century) in theology. The oldest universities in the New World, both founded in 1551, are Mexico University and San Marcos of Lima.

Although many required religious tests, by 1900 many universities were secularized in administration and curriculum. Religious tests in England were largely eliminated by an act of Parliament in 1871. (For a wry comment about how some teachers live in "ivy towers," see the entry for Professorial Acadamese. For information about freethinking clubs at universities and colleges, see entry for Campus Freethought Alliance.)

UNIVERSITY ACADAMESE: See entry for Professional Acadamese, a style of writing.

UNIVERSITY CENTRE FOR DEVELOPMENT COOPERATION (IHEU)

A specialist member of the International Humanist and Ethical Union is the University Centre for Development Cooperation, Pleinlaan 2, Gebouwy, 1050 Brussels, Belgium.

UNIVERSITY CHAPTERS OF HUMANISTS

The following university chapters of humanists and freethinkers — which grew rapidly during 1999—are on the Web. For an updated list: <www.secularhumanism.org/cfa/orgs.html>.

• Auckland University
• Brock University
• Christopher Newport University
• Cornell University
• Duke University

- Florida International University
- Florida State University
- Harvard University
- Johns Hopkins University
- Marshall University
- McGill University
- Michigan Technological University
- Millersville University
- New York University
- Ohio State University
- Oklahoma State University
- Oregon State University
- Pennsylvania State University
- Princeton University
- Queens University
- Radford University
- San Diego State University
- Southern Illinois University, Carbondale
- State University of New York at Albany
- State University of New York at Buffalo
- Temple University
- University of Alabama at Birmingham
- University of British Columbia
- University of California, Irvine
- University of California, Santa Cruz
- University of Chicago
- University of Colorado at Boulder
- University of Colorado at Colorado Springs
- University of Florida
- University of Guelph
- University of Houston
- University of Louisville
- University of Maryland at College Park
- University of Michigan, Flint
- University of Minnesota at Twin Cities
- University of Missouri, Kansas City
- University of Oregon
- University of Puget Sound
- University of Regina
- University of South Africa
- University of South Alabama
- University of Tennessee at Martin
- University of Texas at Austin
- University of Virginia
- University of Waterloo
- University of Wisconsin, Madison
- University of Wisconsin, Milwaukee
- Virginia Polytechnic Institute and State U
- Washington University in St. Louis
- Western Michigan University
- Western Washington University
- Winthrop University
- Yale University

UNIVERSITY OF SOUTH AFRICA

University of South Africa humanists on the Web: <http://www.secularhumanism.org/cfa/orgs.html>.

UNIVERSITY OF VIRGINIA

When Thomas Jefferson helped create the University of Virginia in 1819, he demanded that the public school be free from sectarian control, going so far as to insist that the institution have no chaplain, no chapel and no courses in theology. At that time, universities were owned and operated by religious groups. Students were required to attend church services as well as take courses in religion, and ministers frequently served on university boards or as school presidents. In deference to the principle of church-state separations, however, Jefferson's University of Virginia would have none of those features. (See entry for Thomas Jefferson.) {Rob Boston, *Church & State*, February 1995}

UNIVERSITY OF WATERLOO

The University of Waterloo Freethinkers are at <http://www.secularhumanism.org/cfa/orgs.html>.

Unna, Paul (1850–1929)

A German anatomist, Unna worked with Haeckel's Monist Association, frequently writing for its journal. Unna was a surgeon whose specialty was skin diseases. In the memorial volume to commemorate Haeckel's eightieth birthday, Unna thanked Haeckel for his "spiritual emancipation" and talked contemptuously about "the men of darkness round the throne and the altar." {JM; RAT}

UPANISHADS

The Upanishads are a group of writings sacred in Hinduism concerning the relations of humans, God, and the universe. {DCL}

Updike, John (1932–)

Updike, in his novels, short stories, and poetry, depicts "American, Protestant, small-town, middle-class" life. Sometimes referred to as "the sexy WASP," for he does not avoid the erotic, Updike is a major figure at *The New Yorker* and the American Academy of Arts and Letters. *Rabbit, Run* (1960) is one of his best-known works. In his criticism, he often downplays fellow authors' non-belief and he makes no secret of his Christian beliefs. (See entry for Theism.) {"The Future of Faith, Confessions of a Churchgoer," *The New Yorker*, 29 November 1999}

Upham, Frederick P. (c. 1850–1920?)

Upham, originally an American born in Rhode Island, emigrated to Australia and became an anarchist. Along with David and William Andrade, he formed the Melbourne Anarchist Club in 1886, and in 1887 he took a stand against his former secularism "Secularism has outlived its usefulness. Our hope does not lie in Secularism, which is crystallised and conservative, but in Anarchy which is based on rebellion against authority. Anarchy is a revolt. It means ultimately . . . breaking the power of the majority politically and morally. It cries an end to reform and strikes for revolution. It calls upon men and women to free themselves, instead of remaining the slaves of Secularism or any other orthodox system." The following year, Joseph Symes called a showdown meeting, and two rival factions emerged. The anti-Symes Australasian Secular Society took the original Association's books, documents, and funds, while the pro-Symes Australasian Secular Association retained the rented Hall of Science and the *Liberator*. {SWW}

Upreti, Gopi (20th Century)

Upreti is executive director of Nepal's National Academy for Environment, Population, and Development and President of the Humanist Association of Nepal. He was a participant in the 1996 Humanist World Congress held in Mexico City, at which he lamented that what has taken nature a billion years to make is now being destroyed in but a year. Maintaining the eco-system's health needs to be a humanistic priority, he holds, and the scarcity of natural resources needs to be met on a reappointed basis in which the gap between rich and poor are narrowed radically.

He signed Humanist Manifesto 2000. Upreti's e-mail addresses: <naecan@casnov.attmail.com> and <naecan@vishnu.ccsl.com.np>.

URANTIA BOOK

The *Urantia Book*, published in 1955 under the direction of cult leader Dr. William Sadler, is the largest work ever said to have been channeled by superbeings through human contactees. It contains facts not found in the gospels, including a detailed biography of Jesus Christ. In *Urantia, the Great Cult Mystery* (1995), Martin Gardner outlines how Urantian cultists believe that they also receive messages from the celestials who are preparing Urantia (the cult's name for Earth) and how they have developed a mind-set that becomes impossible to alter regardless of how strong the evidence is against those beliefs.

Urban, Jerzy (1934?–)

Urban, the editor of *Nie* (No), a weekly Polish newspaper, has been described by journalist Jane Perlez as one who "represents all that Poland's anti-Communists love to hate. He was, after all, the manipulative Government spokesman during martial law. In his reinvention as a publisher, he decorates his devastating words with pornographic drawings of Lech Walesa, the Pope, and parish priests."

Urban has been given suspended prison sentences for violating a 1983 law protecting state secrets, and in 1990 he wrote a memoir based on dirty tales about political opponents in the Solidarity movement. His newspaper offers prizes to readers who provide "true" stories about infidelities of local priests and outlandish spending by the Roman Catholic Church. "He mercilessly attacked former President Lech Walesa," Perlez has described, "and derided what he saw as Mr. Walesa's prudish family life. By Polish standards, *Nie* is outrageous." So much so that it has a reported circulation of 780,000. Meanwhile, Urban is said to be enjoying his job of being "editor in mischief," and visitors to his office sit in a chair that directly faces a painting of a banana peeled to reveal a penis. (See entry for Polish Humanism.) {Jane Perlez, "Warsaw Journal," *The New York Times*, 27 February 1996}

Urken, Maddy (20th Century)

In 1999 Urken was elected President of Humanists of North Jersey, which is affiliated with the American Humanist Association.

Usher, Andrew (20th Century)

Usher, a member of the House of Usher whose family five or seven generations ago built a ship and sailed to Australia, is a Unitarian and a student at London University for a Ph. D. in mathematics. He does not believe the family is related to Bishop Ussher of 4000 B.C.E. fame nor to Poe's Roderick Usher. Nor does he have any idea what it was that inspired Poe.

His uncle, **David Usher**, a Unitarian minister in Peterborough, New Hampshire, is President of the Executive Committee of the International Council of Unitarians and Universalists. His father, **Geoff Usher**, is Unitarian minister at Upper Chapel, Sheffield, the United Kingdom, one involved with the Unitarian Peace Fellowship and the secretary of the International Council of Unitarians and Universalists.

Andrew has written to the present author about his views:

> I describe myself simply as "Unitarian," although "agnostic Unitarian atheist" might be more accurate. I have not ruled out the existence of some sort of deity, but neither have I seen anything to convince me of it. However, if I tried to be more specific I would end up contradicting myself and putting myself in boxes which I don't belong in and which I don't think should exist anyway.
>
> {WAS, 22 October 1996}

USONIA

Usonia (as in the **US Of North America**) was Samuel Butler's acronymic name for the United States which had its capitol in Washington, District of Columbia. Architect Frank Lloyd Wright from the 1930s through the 1950s called his affordable homes "Usonian houses." The non-ambiguous word may eventually become widely accepted, particularly because of complaints by individuals in the United States of Mexico and by Canadians, Costa Ricans, Uruguayans, and other Americans.

Ussher (or Usher), James (1581–1686)

An Anglo-Irish prelate, Ussher was chancellor of St. Patrick's Cathedral in 1605. In 1620 or 1621 he became bishop of Meath and, in 1625, the archbishop of Annagh. A believer in the Divine Right of Kings, Bishop Ussher wrote *Annales Veteris et Novi Testamenti*, which was published in the 1650s. In that two-volume work, he figured out the genesis, deducing from Biblical sources that the creation was at 4004 B.C.E. For some time, his dating was used in the King James Version of the Bible. Specifically, he alleged that God created the world at 9 a.m. (some say noon) on October 23rd. It is believed he referred to Greenwich mean time, and the date was widely accepted in the Christian world up until the 19th Century.

In keeping with Ussher's research, the 6000th birthday party of Earth, on 23 October 1996, was celebrated by secular humanists at the Buffalo, New York, Center for Inquiry. Anthropologist H. James Birx dressed up as himself, Tim Madigan dressed up as Noah, and biology professor Clyde Herreid dressed up as Darwin for a jocular press meeting.

Nicolas Walter has taken issue with Stephen Jay Gould's *Questioning the Millennium*, which states that "Ussher set the moment of creation that would live in both infamy and memory—4004 BC (at noon on October 23." But Walter, quoting from a copy in the British Library, found that Ussher had stated,

> In the beginning God created Heaven and Earth . . . which beginning of time (according to our Chronology) occurred at the beginning of that night which preceded the 23rd day of October in 4004 BC.

That is, at dusk on October 22, writes Walter. What was created at midday on October 23 was light, thereby correcting Gould. {CE; ER}

USSHER, GEOLOGY AND HISTORY ACCORDING TO

On the assumption that Bishop Ussher was, indeed, correct in his calculations, according to freethinkers, the following corrections to all standard reference books needs to be made:

4004 B.C.E.	Earth is molten. Adam and Eve invent asbestos waders.
3554 B.C.E.	Persistent lava incinerates Noah's Ark.
3264 B.C.E.	Methuselah notices passage of geological time.
2444 B.C.E.	Breathable atmosphere develops. First sermon preached.
1704 B.C.E.	Charshumash the Hittite bitten by first vertebrate. Lawyers emerge from the slime.
1024 B.C.E.	Goliath stepped on by irate Barosaurus. David takes credit.
794 B.C.E.	Jonah swallowed by Carcharus megalodon.
454 B.C.E.	Marble deposits form in Greece. Parthenon erected.
0	Nothing much happened, there being no such year.
31 C.E.	Miracle of the loaves and Ichthyosaurs.
70	Paul undergoes identity crisis on the road to Damascus and writes Epistle to the Cephalopods.
49	Snakes evolve and are driven out of Ireland.
1215	Magna Carta is eaten by Velociraptor.
1324	Gunpowder introduced. Dinosaurs hunted to extinction.
1384	Dante Alighieri describes Earth's coremantle boundary.
1484	Leonardo da Vinci designs Archaeopteryx.
1588	Spanish Armada frustrated by the continuing absence of the English Channel.
1636	Earliest primates appear. Harvard founded.
1664	Archbishop Ussher deduces the last four digits of the age of the earth.
1754	Gibbons evolve and write "Decline and Fall of the Roman Empire."
1835	Charles Darwin, after being attacked by a giant Ratite in the Galapagos Islands, switches from Darwinism to Neptunism.
1846	Ape evolution confirmed by birth of a son to Lady and Bishop Wilberforce (whom Huxley defeated in evolution debates).
1914	Holy Roman Empire wins World War I.
1961	Rachel Carson links DDT to Glyptodonts's decline.
1993	"Jurassic Park" grosses $357M. Secular humanists agree with its message, that it is mad to use technology to control nature.
1997	"The Lost World" lays dinosaur egg. UCs (unidentified compsognathi) cited throughout the Bible Belt.
3001	Arthur C. Clarke will be resurrected.

{WAS, with apologies to Russell Seitz, *Earth*, February 1996}

Ustinov, Peter [Sir] (1921)

In a 1995 interview, Warren Allen Smith wrote the following: "Upon first meeting Sir Peter Ustinov, the Goodwill Ambassador-at-Large for UNICEF and president of the World Federalist Movement, one hears the voice of 'Peter and the Wolf.' One feels the presence of Beethoven (from his stage performance in Beethoven's 'Tenth'); of Carabosse (from the play, *The Love of Four Colonels*); of the General (from the film and play, 'Romanoff and Juliet'); and of Nero (from his film role in 'Quo Vadis')."

"Surprisingly, Ustinov, who amusingly responds 'Your Excellency' when addressed as 'Sir Peter,' comes across as friendly, witty, ready to imitate the facial expressions of François Mitterand, eloquent when discussing the world's children, and sincere when lamenting intolerance, bigotry, flag-waving, self-importance, idleness, and superstition. He is not intimidating, yet this is the man who has worked with Jack Paar, Steve Allen, Pavarotti, Herbert von Karajan, André Kostelanetz, David Niven, Yvonne de Carlo, Maggie Smith, Helen Hayes, Bette Davis, Nick Nolte, and John Gielgud. And the man who, in 1990, was knighted by Queen Elizabeth II."

The English actor, director, playwright, screenwriter, novelist, and raconteur has acted in more than fifty films in addition to acting in, producing, or directing many of his plays. He received Emmy Awards for his performance in "Barefoot in Athens" and "Omnibus," and in 1979 he received the award for Best Actor from the Variety Club of Great Britain.

Asked if his father, a liberal Lutheran and a journalist, was closer to Greek or Judeo-Christian thinking, Ustinov replied, "Oh, the Greeks! He was absolutely unpracticing in his belief. In point of fact, it was *his* father who was so religious. His mother, and I remember her vividly because she was half Ethiopian, held religion very close, and for her the Crucifixion happened yesterday. I sat on her knee in my pajamas and had to listen to the history of the Crucifixion as though it had been brought in from Pittsburgh, and she used to cry copiously and my pajama tops were wet from her tears."

Smith then asked, "In the 1930s, we humanists were alarmed about the growth in the world's population. Then there were 2 billion humans. In 1970 there were 3.7 billion. Now there are almost 6 billion. Sir Peter," Smith asked with a straight face, "*why* did you allow this to happen?" Ustinov stammered, humorously, then with theatrical embarrassment responded, "Well, yes, I didn't take the precautions, I know, I know." He then lambasted the Pope for his stand on population control and the use of condoms but praised the Chinese for their admittedly Draconian methods to limit their births. "I'm depressed that once children are born they're so often neglected. And what is life then, something that is lived in third gear or only in first gear? Our responsibility should be with children, not merely with embryos."

Ustinov, who holds that humanists are united by our doubts, has been on the Advisory Panel of the British Humanist Association. In 1993 the Council for Secular Humanism elected him as a Humanist Laureate in the International Academy of Humanism. Ustinov's autobiography is entitled *Dear Me* (1977). His collection of newspaper articles from *The European* is *Ustinov Still At Large* (1995). In one article, he wrote, "If the world should blow itself up, the last audible voice would be that of an expert saying it can't be done." {CE; TYD; WAS, *Free Inquiry*, Summer 1995}

UTAH ATHEISTS, HUMANISTS

Utah has the following groups:

• American Atheists, Utah Chapter, POB 11622, Salt Lake City, Utah. Chris Allen is its director. (801) 531-7987. E-mail: <callen@atheists.org>

• Secular Humanists of the Great Basin, 10271 S. 1300 E. PMB 190, Sandy, UT 84094

• *The Utah Humanist*, PO Box 900212, Sandy, Utah 84090, is a publication of Humanists of Utah. Wayne Wilson is the editor.

• Humanists of Utah (AHA), PO Box 900212, Sandy, Utah 84090; phone (801) 273-7144. Florien J. Wineriter is President, and Wayne Wilson is a general contact. Webmaster is David Egan Evans.

E-mail: <wilson@utw.com> On the Web: <http://www.humanistsofutah.org/>.

UTILITARIANISM

In ethics, utilitarianism is a theory that the rightness or wrongness of an action is determined by the goodness or badness of its consequences. Specifically, it is a theory that the aim of action is best when it encourages the largest possible balance of pleasure over pain or encourages the greatest happiness of the greatest number. Jeremy Bentham measured happiness by the intensity, duration, certainty, propinquity, fecundity, purity, and extent of pleasures. John Stuart Mill and Herbert Spencer developed the theory, but G. E. Moore in his *Principia Ethica* (1903) rejected the traditional equating of good with pleasure. Meanwhile, James MacKaye in *Americanized Socialism* (1918) gave the theory a socialized slant, claiming that collectivism is the best approach in promoting universal happiness. J. J. C. Smart has written about the subject in *Utilitarianism: For and Against* (1973). (See J. J. C. Smart's discussion of utilitarianism in the *Encyclopedia of Philosophy*, Vol. 8.) {CE; ER}

UTOPIA

Sir Thomas More wrote, in *Utopia* (1516), about an imaginary, ideal society free of poverty and suffering. By extension, a **utopia**, which in Greek means "no place," is an ideal state. Erasmus supervised the printing. The form may have been suggested by the narrative of the voyages of Vespucci, printed in 1507. In More's utopia, communism is the general law, a national system of education is extended to men and women alike, and the freest toleration of religion is recognized. Other utopias: Plato's *Republic*; Bacon's *New Atlantis*; Harrington's *The Commonwealth of Oceana*; Morris's *News from Nowhere*; Bellamy's *Looking Backward*. Satirical utopias include the following: Swift's *Gulliver's Travels* and Samuel Butler's *Erewhon*, which reveals its purpose when the word is spelled backwards. The opposite of a utopia is **dystopia** (a bad place), and examples include Huxley's *Brave New World*, Zamyatin's *We*, and Orwell's *Nineteen Eight-four*. Many works of science fiction use the utopian and dystopian forms. {OEL}

UUA

UUA is an abbreviation for the Unitarian Universalist Association. (See entries for Unitarianism and for Universalism.)

Uyttebrouck, André (20th Century)

At the Eleventh International Humanist and Ethical Union (IHEU) World Congress held in Brussels (1990), Prof. Uyttebrouck of Belgium addressed the group. In 1975, he wrote *Le Gouvernement du duche de Brabant au bas Moyen Age (13551430)*.

Uzunoglu, Kazim (20th Century)

An authority on Mustafa Kemal Atatürk, Uzunoglu is a secular humanist in Turkey. {*Free Inquiry*, Fall, 1991}

V FOR VICTORY SIGN: See entry for its originator, Sir John Alexander Hammerton.

Vacherot, Étienne (18091897)

Vacherot was a French writer. In 1839 he replaced Victor Cousin in the chair of philosophy at the Sorbonne. For his free opinions as expressed in his *Critical History of the School of Alexandria*, he was crowned by the Institute. But he was attacked by the clergy so effectively that he lost his position. He also was sentenced to a year in prison for writing a republican work. Afterwards, he wrote *Essays of Critical Philosophy* (1864) and *La Religion* (1869). In spite of his radical reputation, Vacherot was admitted to the Academy of Moral and Political Science, and he held high office under the Third Republic. He explained that when he spoke of God, he meant only "the ideal of perfection in the mind of man." {BDF; JM; RAT; RE}

Vacquerie, Auguste (18191895)

A French writer, Vacquerie wrote many dramas and novels and was director of *Le Rappel.* When Victor Hugo founded the *Événement*, Vacquerie was an able member of the staff until it was suppressed at the coup d'état of 1851 and the group was scattered. Vacquerie voluntarily accompanied Hugo in exile, although he continued to produce plays at the Paris theatres. His rationalist views are best seen in his long philosophical poem, *Futura* (1890). {BDF; RAT}

VACUUM

Theoretically, a vacuum is space without matter in it. However, a perfect vacuum has never been obtained. In ancient times, it was widely held that "nature abhors a vacuum," but Galileo and the Italian physicist Evangelista Torricelli demonstrated the essential fallacy of that viewpoint. Torricelli created a nearly perfect vacuum in his mercury barometer. (Asked in a high school examination what a vacuum is, one student wrote, "A vacuum is a large empty space where the Pope lives.") {CE; *The Secular Humanist Bulletin*, Summer 1996}

Vahanian, Gabriel (1927)

Vahanian is the author of *Wait Without Idols* (1964) and *The Death of God* (1962). In the latter, he declared, "We live in a post-Christian era because Christianity has sunk into religiosity." {GS; TYD}

Vaihinger, Hans (1852–1933)

People act "as if" the real is what they assume it to be, Vaihinger held, or at least it was his view that we cannot actually know what reality is. Unable to know, we construct systems of thought which make us feel good, and we then assume that what actuality is agrees with this constructed system.

The Philosophy of "As If" (1911, translated into English in 1924), by the German philosopher, was an important work that advocated the notion of "useful fictions."

It followed his *Kant—ein Metaphysiker?* (1899). Vaihinger taught philosophy at Halle, where he was known as one of the great Kant scholars, an explicit atheist, and a follower of Schopenhauer. {CE}

Vaillant, Denis d'Alais (17th Century)

Vaillant was a French writer of the seventeenth century who became both soldier and lawyer. He wrote *Histoire des Severambes* (1677), imaginary travels in which he introduced free opinions and satirized Christianity. {BDF}

VAISHWIK MANAVVAD (Cosmopolitan Humanism)

A Gujarati monthly, *Vaishwik Manavvad* is at IRHA, 4 Sanmitra Society, Jivraj Park Area, Opp. Malav Talav, Ahmedabad 380 051, India.

Valdar, Stewart (20th Century)

Valdar, writing in *The Freethinker* (January 1996), holds that after sixty years of reading about Jesus he finds that the best source has been Chapman Cohen, particularly his over half-century old pamphlet, "Did Jesus Christ Exist?"

In "The Crucifixion That Never Was," Valdar notes that the Christian symbol of the cross actually was a hieroglyph used more than seven thousand years ago and is associated with the *ankh*, the symbol of life, the Chinese character for Earth which also was used by the Assyrians to represent the sky god, Anu. {*The Freethinker*, April 1996}

Vale, Gilbert (1788–1866)

An Anglo-American freethinker, Vale settled in New York in the 1820s and expounded his version of rational religion and rational republicanism with clarity and vigor. Although never an outright unbeliever, he wrote *Fanaticism: Its Source and Influence* (1835) to warn individuals about coming under the influence of deluded religious figures.

He published *A Life of Paine* (1841), which contained materials about and poetry of Thomas Paine, including *A Catalogue of Persecuted Infidels* (c. 1845). Vale raised money for a monument at Paine's grave site and for the sixty-acre Paine farm in New Rochelle, New York, which he envisioned as a home for elderly, indigent freethinkers. From 1836 to 1846, he edited from New York a monthly *Beacon*. Vale died in Brooklyn.

Of him, Appleton's *Encyclopedia of American Biography* wrote, "Mr. Vale was a Freethinker, and all his writings are arguments for his peculiar tenets." {EU, Roderick S. French; BDF; FUK; FUS; JM; RAT; RE}

Valéry, Paul (1871–1945)

Valéry, a French poet, wrote in *Tel quel I* (1943) "That which has been believed by everyone, always and everywhere, has every chance of being false." {TYD}

Valk, T. A. F. van der (19th Century)

Valk was a Dutch freethinker who, after having been a missionary in Java, changed his opinions and wrote in *De Dageraad* between 1860 and 1870, using the pen name of "Thomas." {BDF}

Valla, Lorenzo (1406–1457)

One of the leading humanists of the Renaissance, Valla when twenty-six wrote *De Voluptate et Vero Bono*, a vindication of Epicurus at a time when "Epicurean" connoted freethinker. That dialogue, in three books, analyzed pleasure and offered a humanist condemnation of scholasticism and monastic asceticism. Because of its aggressive tone, it was received with hostility by the Church. In *De libero arbitrio*, he demonstrated that theological disputes over divine prescience and human free will could never be resolved. In a pioneering work of criticism. Valla proved that the long suspect Donation of Constantine was a forgery, because the Latin text was written four centuries after Constantine's death. When he impugned the authenticity of the Apostles' Creed and challenged many of the translations in the Vulgate, he was summoned before the Inquisition at Naples and was condemned to be burned, at which point he found reconciliation with the papacy and spent the rest of his days in Latin scholarship, not visionary reformation. Valla's investigations into the textual errors in the Vulgate spurred Erasmus to undertake the study of the Greek New Testament. {BDF; CE; JM; JMR; JMRH}

Valle, Michael S. (20th Century)

Valle, when a student at the University of Illinois in Chicago and the University of Minnesota, was one of the founding members of Campus Freethought Alliance. {*International Humanist News*, December 1996}

Vallée, Geoffrey (1556–1574)

At the age of sixteen, Vallée had written a freethinking treatise, *La Béatitude des Chrétiens, ou le fléau de la foy*, which was a discussion between a Huguenot, a Catholic, a *libertin*, an Anabaptist, and an atheist. Charged with being an atheist himself, Vallée, a man of good family in Orléans, was not only hanged at the Place de Gréve in Paris but the eighteen-year-old also was burned. {BDF; JMR; JMRH}

Valliss, Rudolph (19th Century)

Valliss was a German author. He wrote *The Natural History of Gods* (1875, *The Eternity of the World* (1875), and *Catechism of Human Duty* (1876), among other works. {BDF}

VALUES

Religious groups often teach exactly the values which should be discouraged, rather than encouraged, in our public life, according to Isaac Kramnick and R. Laurence Moore in *The American Prospect*.

For example, most evangelicals, both black and white, are said to agree that "churches should express views on social and political matters," Kramnick and Moore add. "In its more authoritarian forms, religion punishes questioning and rewards gullibility. . . . Faith denies facts, and that is not always a virtue. . . . Government can help make people comfortable, ensuring access to health care, housing, education, and the workplace," they continue, "but government cannot make people good."

Nicholas Tate, writing in the London *Times*, produced a list of good values: honesty; respect for others; politeness; a sense of fair play; forgiveness; punctuality; non-violent behaviour; patience; faithfulness; and self-discipline.

The British Humanist Association, in a leaflet, "Education for Living," suggested that pupils should have a commitment to: taking responsibility for their own actions; honesty and the open-minded pursuit of truth; fairness and justice; respecting the knowledge and experience of others; mutual understanding and co-operation between people of different backgrounds and beliefs; recognising that situations and relationships are rarely ideal , and have to be "worked at"; contributing to, rather than detracting from, the welfare of life on earth.

To those who hold that Western in contrast with non-Western values consists of toleration, respect for individual liberty, and brotherly love, Bertrand Russell replies, "I am afraid this view is grossly unhistorical. If we compare Europe with other continents, it is marked out as the persecuting continent. Persecution only ceased after long and bitter experience of its futility; it continued as long as either Protestants or Catholics had any hope of exterminating the opposite party. The European record in this respect is far blacker than that of the Mohammedans, the Indians, or the Chinese. No, if the West can claim superiority in anything, it is not in moral values but in science and scientific technique." What Lord Russell personally valued most were knowledge, art, instinctive happiness, and relations of friendship or affection. (See entry for Family Values, in which Jesus's statements show he was against such.) {Lee Eisler, *The Quotable Bertrand Russell*}

Vámbéry, Armin (1832–1913)

Vámbéry, a Hungarian-Jewish philologist, knew a dozen languages before he was out of his teens, and he was tutor to the sons of a Turkish prince. At one point, he nearly got to Mecca in the guise of a pilgrim. His Turkish-German dictionary became a standard. In his autobiography, *The Story of My Struggles* (1904), Vámbéry tells that he was an agnostic and considered that "religion offers but little security against moral deterioration, and it is not seemly for the 20th Century to take example by the customs and doings of savages." As to the religious solution of cosmic problems, he added, "One grain of common sense is worth a bushel of theories." {JM; RE}

Vambery, Renate (20th Century)

Vambery, when she signed Humanist Manifesto II, was associated with the Ethical Society of St. Louis. {HM2}

VAMPIRES

The University of British Columbia's David Dolphin speculated in 1985 that vampirism is related to an illness known as porphyria, one in which the skin becomes sensitive to sunlight. Sufferers—King George III of England may have been a victim—tend to avoid the sun, their teeth appear to be larger because their gums have retracted, and their urine is red "which might, in a convoluted way, have led to the notion of drinking blood," states *The Economist* (31 October 1998).

However, a Spanish neurologist, Juan Gomez-Alonso, thinks the vampire legend is inspired by rabies. Insomnia, an aversion to mirrors and strong smells, and an increased sex drive are symptoms of rabies, and rabies is transmitted by biting. Also rabies is the explanation for lycanthropy—the apparent tendency of some people to turn into wolves from time to time. Lycanthropy is transmitted by a wolf's bite.

In his *Philosophic Dictionary*, Voltaire discusses many topics. One topic was vampires, and he wrote nineteen paragraphs, including the following material, which reveals his wit and wisdom:

> What! is it in our eighteenth century that vampires exist? Is it after the reigns of Locke, Shaftesbury, Trenchard, and Collins? Is it under those of D'Alembert, Diderot, St. Lambert, and Duclos, that we believe in vampires, and that the reverend father Dom Calmet, benedictine priest of the congregation of St. Vannes and St. Hidulphe, abbé of Senon,—an abbey of a hundred thousand livres a year, in the neighborhood of two other abbeys of the same revenue,—has printed and reprinted the history of vampires, with the approbation of the Sorbonne, signed Marcilli?
>
> These vampires were corpses, who went out of their graves at night to suck the blood of the living, either at their throats or stomachs, after which they returned to their cemeteries. The persons so sucked waned, grew pale, and fell into consumptions; while the sucking corpses grew fat, got rosy, and enjoyed an excellent appetite. It was in Poland, Hungary, Silesia, Moravia, Austria, and Lorraine, that the dead made this good cheer. We never heard speak of vampires in London, nor even at Paris. I confess, that in both these cities there were stock-jobbers, brokers, and men of business, who sucked the blood of the people in broad day-light; but they were not dead, though corrupted. These true suckers lived not in cemeteries, but in very agreeable palaces.
>
> Who would believe that we derive the idea of vampires from Greece? Not from the Greece of Alexander, Aristotle, Plato, Epicurus, and Demosthenes; but from christian Greece, unfortunately schismatic.
>
> For a long time, christians of the Greek rite have imagined that the bodies of christians of the Latin church, buried in Greece, do not decay, because they are excommunicated. This is precisely the contrary idea to that of we christians of the Latin church, who believe that corpses which do not corrupt are marked with the seal of eternal beatitude. So much so, indeed, that when we have paid a hundred thousand crowns to Rome, to give them a saint's brevet, we adore them with the worship of "dulia."
>
> The Greeks are persuaded that these dead are sorcerers; they call them *broucolacas*, or *vroucolacas*, according as they pronounce the second letter of the alphabet. The Greek corpses go into houses to suck the blood of little children, to eat the supper of fathers and mothers, drink their wine, and break all the furniture. They can only be put to rights by burning them when they are caught. But the precaution must be taken of not putting them into the fire until after their hearts are torn out, which must be burned separately.
>
> The celebrated Tournefort, sent into the Levant by Louis XIV, as well as so many other virtuosos, was witness of all the acts attributed to one of these *broucolacas*, and to this ceremony.
>
> After slander, nothing is communicated more promptly than superstition, fanaticism, sorcery, and tales of those raised from the dead. There were *broucolacas* in Wallachia, Moldavia, and some among the Polanders, who are of the Romish church. This supersti-

> tion being absent, they acquired it, and it went through all the east of Germany. Nothing was spoken of but vampires from 1730 to 1735; they were laid in wait for, their hearts torn out and burned. They resembled the ancient martyrs—the more they were burned, the more they abounded.

Voltaire then cites stories of vampires in the Jewish *Letters of D'Argens*, "whom the jesuit authors of the journal of Trevoux have accused of believing nothing." He states that the theologians of Lorraine, of Moravia, and Hungary "related all that St. Augustine, St. Ambrose, and so many other saints, had most unintelligibly said on the living and the dead." People may have believed that the dead drank and ate, since in so many ancient nations food was placed on their tombs, adding their difficulty must have been to know whether it was the soul or the body of the dead which ate. They decided, apparently, that it was both. The kings of Persia the first who caused themselves to be served with viands after their death, he notes, adding, "Almost all the kings of the present day imitate them, but they are the monks who eat their dinner and supper, and drink their wine. Thus, properly speaking, kings are not vampires: the true vampires are the monks, who eat at the expense of both kings and people."

"It is true," Voltaire continues, "that St. Stanislaus, who had bought a considerable estate from a Polish gentleman, and not paid him for it, being brought before king Boleslas, by his heirs, raised up the gentleman; but this was solely to get quittance. It is not said that he gave a single glass of wine to the seller, who returned to the other world without having eaten or drunk. They afterwards treated of the grand question, whether a vampire could be absolved who died excommunicated, which comes more to the point." Voltaire, admitting that he was certainly no expert in theology, observed that "I would willingly be for absolution, because in all doubtful affairs we should take the mildest part."

Voltaire, still amused, concluded by observing that a great part of Europe has been "infested with vampires for five or six years, and that there are now no more; that we have had convulsionaries in France for twenty years, and that we have them no longer; that we have had demoniacs for seventeen hundred years, but have them no longer; that the dead have been raised ever since the days of Hippolytus, but that they are raised no longer; and lastly, that we have had jesuits in Spain, Portugal, France, and the two Sicilies, but we have them no longer."

"No longer?" literalists ask. {VOL}

Van Beber, Ruth (1925–)

Van Beber's freethinking views have been described in *Freethought Today* (June-July 1996).

Vanbergen, Pierre (20th Century)

Vanbergen is the chairman of the Belgian *Ligue de l'Enseignment* as well as the President of the European Teachers' Association. He addressed the 1994 symposium of humanist associations in Brussels. {*International Humanist News*, March 1994}

Van Bergen, Scott (20th Century)

A freethinker, Van Bergen won a Freedom From Religion Foundation award for writing of his experiences in keeping prayer out of public schools. {*Freethought Today*, October 1996)

van Brakel, Ernst (20th Century)

At UNESCO, van Brakel represented the International Humanist and Ethical Union (IHEU), an organization which gained status on the Non-Governmental Organization (NGO) within the UN.

Van Cauberg, Adolphe (Died 1886)

Van Cauberg was a Belgian advocate. He was one of the founders and the president of the International Federation of Freethinkers. {BDF}

Vance, Edith Maurice (Born 1860)

Vance in 1877 was a Sunday school teacher who visited the Hall of Science and prayed for the conversion of Mrs. Besant. But then she herself became an atheist and a follower of Bradlaugh. Revolting against parental bigotry, Vance left home and toured the provinces with a theatrical company. In 1878 she joined the National Secular Society, becoming London branch Secretary and Vice-President in 1887. She later became General Secretary. As representative of the National League of the Blind, for she had become sightless, Vance was in 1919 elected Poor Law Guardian and Borough Councilor of St. Paneras in London. {RAT}

Vance, Thomas L. (20th Century)

Vance, a freethinker, wrote *Yahweh—A God of Blood and Fire* (1924). {GS}

Van Coesant, Marcel (20th Century)

Van Coesant is a member of the board of the Netherlands Humanist Broadcasting Foundation. He was a participant in the 1996 Humanist World Congress in Mexico City and is the media secretariat for the International Humanist and Ethical Union. His e-mail: <mvan.coesant@net.hcc.NL>.

Vanderlaan, Eldred C. (20th Century)

Vanderlaan is a lecturer who signed both Humanist Manifesto I and II. He once wrote to the present author concerning humanism:

> After one pastorate in the Dutch Reformed Church at Kinderhook, New York, I decided I wanted to be a theological professor rather than a pastor. I took some work at Union Theological Seminary in church history, also some work in Marburg, Germany, and in 1924 got a Th. D. from Union—which is now comical, for how can a man be a Doctor of Theology after he has lost his theology! Then I got located in Berkeley in a combined post as Professor in the Pacific Unitarian School (now Starr King School) and minister of the Berkeley Unitarian Church. The school had a financial crisis owing to embezzlement by the Treasurer of the Board, and my position was abolished. For a few years I continued in the church. I imagined I was a darn good preacher, but I lacked other qualifications for making a church prosper. Thanks to the generosity of my wife, I then went to Stanford and acquired a teaching credential, spending 20 years as a high school teacher. A few years ago I reached retirement age. My wife died soon after, and I am living in our house alone, taking my meals out. Some time during this last period, Ed Wilson got me on the staff of *The Humanist* . . . .
>
> I found in Saul Padover's big volume, *The Complete Jefferson*, that Dr. Benjamin Rush reported to Jefferson around February 1, 1799, that on the occasion of Washington's leaving office a group of clergy sent him an Address containing some wording designed to make him declare once and for all whether he was a Christian. Dr. Rush then said, "The old fox was too clever for them. He answered every point in their address but left this matter untouched." Jefferson then comments: "I know that Gouverneur Morris, who pretended to be in his secrets and believed himself to be so, has often told me that General Washington believed no more of that system (Orthodox Christianity) than he himself did."

In the mid-1950s, Vanderlaan was a consulting and contributing editor for *The Humanist*. He wrote *Fundamentalism vs. Modernism* (1925). {HM1; HM2; HNS; WAS, 4 November 1958}

Vanderpuye, Franz (20th Century)

A member of the Rational Centre of Accra, Ghana, Vanderpuye has written extensively on the need to develop humanism on the African continent. In Norm Allen Jr.'s book, *African-American Humanism*, Vanderpuye discusses problems Ghana educators have in the field of sex education. "Shhh! Who Is Talking About Sex?" states that in public the word "sex" is shunned and avoided in Ghana, leading to distorted information which peers transmit to each other. Because of political turmoil in Ghana, Vanderpuye has sought sanctuary in the Netherlands. E-mail: <vanpee@ighmail.com>. {AAH}

van der Schaaf, W. (20th Century)

At the International Humanist and Ethical Union's (IHEU's) International Peace Conference in Zutphen (1983), van der Schaaf of the Netherlands addressed the group.

Van der Spuy, Manie (20th Century)

Van der Spuy is a professor of psychiatry at McMaster University in Hamilton, Ontario. Also, he is Director of Psychology at the Chedoke-McMaster Hospital. His "The Anatomy of Ideology" was printed in *Humanist in Canada* (Summer 1997).

Vandervelde, Émile (1866–1938)

Vandervelde, a Belgian statesman and socialist leader, entered parliament in 1894 and served in many cabinets, notably as minister of justice (1918–1921), foreign minister (1925–1927), and vice premier and minister of public health (1936–1937). When Belgium recognized the Franco government during the Spanish civil war, Vandervelde resigned in protest. He played a leading role in the Second, or Socialist, International (1889–1914), serving as the first president of the International Socialist Bureau. McCabe labeled Vandervelde "an atheist and zealous humanitarian." {CE; JM}

van der Wal, L. (20th Century)

In 1952, van der Wal was on the first Board of Directors of the International Humanist and Ethical Union (IHEU). He addressed the organization's First International Congress in Amsterdam (1952).

Van der Weyde, William M. (20th Century)

Van der Weyde wrote *Life of Thomas Paine* (1925). {FUK; FUS}

Van Deventer, Betty (20th Century)

A freethinker, Van Deventer wrote *Why Preachers Go Wrong* (19–?) {GS}

van Dijk, Pieter (20th Century)

Dr. van Dijk, professor of the Law of International Organisations at the University of Utrecht, was interim successor following Dr. I. Samkalden as the International Humanist and Ethical Union's Human Rights Commissioner. Prof. Jan Glastra van Loon succeeded him.

Van Doren, Carl (Clinton) (1885–1950)

Van Doren, a Columbia University professor, was a Pulitzer Prize winning author for his biography of Benjamin Franklin (1938). He also wrote a biography of Thomas Paine (1925) and one of Sinclair Lewis (1933). He was literary editor of *The Nation* (1919–1922) and *Century Magazine* (1922–1925), managing editor of *The Cambridge History of American Literature* (1917–1922), and editor of the Literary Guild (1926–1934). His autobiography, *Three Worlds* (1936), described his illustrious achievements. In *Why I Am An Unbeliever*, Van Doren wrote, "The race of men, while sheep in credulity, are wolves for conformity." {TYD}

Van Doren, Mark (1894–1972)

Van Doren, poet, critic, a staff member of *The Nation* (1924–1928), and author with his brother Carl Van Doren of *American and British Literature Since 1890*, taught English at Columbia University. He was a Pulitzer prize-winner for *Collected Poems* (1929). Asked by the present author about humanism, he responded,

> I don't recognize any of those [seven categories of humanism that you sent] as containing me. One may, but I'd rather have somebody else say which one—and then, perhaps, disagree with him.

In his class, Twentieth Century British literature at Columbia University, Van Doren professed to be in tune with naturalistic humanism, but with his own special qualifying reservations. {WAS, 3 March 1951}

van Doren, Wim (20th Century)

A professor of philosophy at Delft University of Technology in Holland, van Doren is a secular humanist.

Van Dyk, Gen (20th Century)

A Dutch humanist, Van Dyk in 1996 participated in the international conference of ethical humanists in Mexico City. His e-mail: <hu@euronet.NL>.

Van Eck, Stephen (20th Century)

Van Eck, a Pennsylvanian from Rushville who has written for *The Skeptical Review* (January-February 1997) and *Freethought Perspective* (April 1999), holds that Jesus's birth in Bethlehem "is almost certainly a fictional element." He adds that skeptics have the job of distinguishing fact from fiction "in the man from Galilee." In "The Naked Truth: Freeing the Mind and Body with Naturism" (*Secular Nation*, April-June 1998) he described nudism, adding that "freeing your mind is incomplete until you've freed your body. If you have body hangups, this is a problem in your mind, but it can be remedied with a little resolve and effort, and it's an enjoyable process to boot. If you still have clothes on by this point, shame on you!" Van Eck heads what he calls "Wet Water Ministries." (See entry for Wet Water Ministries.)

Van Gogh, Vincent (1853–1890)

The Dutch postimpressionist painter, Van Gogh, produced most of his work, according to the *Columbia Encyclopedia*, "in 29 months of frenzied activity interspersed with epileptoid seizures and despair that finally ended in suicide."

During a six-week companionship with painter Paul Gauguin, Van Gogh threw a glass of absinthe in Gauguin's face. The next day he attacked him with an open razor in his hand. In an ensuing argument, Van Gogh ran back into the house they shared and, watching himself in a mirror, hacked off part of his left ear, wrapped the part in a scarf, and took it to the local brothel, where he gave it to a girl who had preferred Gauguin to himself. The prostitute, expecting it to be a present, opened the package and, upon finding the blood-covered object inside, fainted.

Van Gogh's mental health then deteriorated rapidly, and two years later he committed suicide by shooting himself, dying two days later in the arms of his brother, Theo.

In his letters to his brother, who supported him through years of poverty and unsold pictures, Van Gogh showed a sense of humor, such as, upon arriving in Arles, noting "the priest in his surplice, who resembles a dangerous rhinoceros." The letters show the painter's once having had a bout of religious fervor during which his sister described him as "groggy with piety." (See *The Letters of Vincent Van Gogh*, 1996.) {CE; PA}

van Heijenoort, Jean (1912–1986)

When eighteen, van Heijenoort arrived on a state scholarship in Paris, the son of an humble Dutch restaurant worker. Besides his major studies in mathematics and philosophy, according to Anita Burdman Feferman's *Politics, Logic, and Love: The Life of Jean van Heijenoort* (1993), "he had taken chemistry and physics, seven years of Latin, four of Greek, four of German, as well as French history, literature, and language. Independently, he had read widely, and he had even taught himself Russian, because he had a vague notion that, one day soon, he might go to the Soviet Union for a visit." In 1932, van Heijenoort sailed to Prinkipo Island, where for seven years he served as fellow atheist Leon Trotsky's additional bodyguard and amanuensis. Totally devoted to the man hunted by Stalin's agents, van Heijenoort sided with Trotsky and served as his translator, secretary, and courier. In Mexico, when Trotsky and Diego Rivera began their acrimonious disputes, van Heijenoort tended to favor the painter. Upon divorcing his distant French wife and marrying Loretta (Bunny) Guyer, a New Yorker, van Heijenoort was sent in 1939 to New York to try to reconcile factions among the North American Trotskyites. Upon Trotsky's assassination the following year, van Heijenoort lamented that he might have saved Trotsky's life had he stayed in Mexico, that with his native French he could have detected the fake accent of the assassin, Ramón Mercader.

van Heijenoort obtained his Ph. D. in New York University's mathematics department, carefully disguising his past. He then taught at Brandeis, wrote forty-three reviews in *The Journal of Symbolic Logic*, and for the *Encyclopedia of Philosophy* wrote an analysis of Bertrand Russell's famous paradox of 1901. His classic work is *From Frege to Gödel: A Source Book in Mathematical Logic, 1879–1931* (1967). Meanwhile, New York Trotskyites began exposing his past and accusing him of treason. At the same time, rumors spread that he had obtained U.S. citizenship because the F.B.I. had helped him. A consultant to the Trotsky Archive at the Harvard College Library, van Heijenoort in his move from dialectical materialism questioned, according to critic George Steiner, whether a Trotskyite victory over Stalin "would have guaranteed a humane regime for the Soviet Union."

In 1969 van Heijenoort married Anne-Marie Zamora in Mexico City, then divorced her, remarrying her in 1984. In 1986, his unbalanced wife shot three 3.8-caliber bullets into the head of her sleeping husband, then fired one into her own mouth. (See entry for Leon Trotsky.)

Van Howe, Annette (20th Century)

In 1996, Van Howe received the Humanist Heroine of the Feminist Caucus award, given for her "lifetime dedication to women's education, history, and rights." A Unitarian, she has headed the Voice for Choice in Florida and participated in the 3rd Annual Atheist Alliance Convention.

Van Hyatt, P. (20th Century)

Van Hyatt, a freethinker, wrote "Christ, A Myth" (19–?). {GS}

Vanini, Giulio Cesare (1585–1619)

Lucilio Vanini, an Italian freethinking priest and alleged believer in witchcraft, tried to break with the dogmas of scholasticism and the authority of Aristotle. He denied the current views on immortality, knew that the world could not have been created out of nothing, and said Jesus was not divine. As a result, Lucilio—who gave himself the name Julius Caesar—was driven from one country to another, preaching such views in France, England, Holland, and Germany. Vanini published a pantheistic work in Latin, *On the Admirable Secrets of Nature, the Queen and Goddess of Mortals*, which was condemned by the Sorbonne and burned, forcing him to flee to Toulouse in 1617. Four of his books made the Vatican's *Index Librorum Prohibitorum.* An attempt was made to force him to beg God, the king, and the judicial body for pardon, but he insisted he believed neither in God nor in the devil. During the French Revolution, Maréchal cited Vanini as being one of the greatest atheists of all time. Robertson, however, writes, "He was in fact a deist with the inevitable leaning of the philosophic theist to pantheism; and whatever he may have said to arouse priestly hatred at Toulouse, he was rather less of an atheist than Spinoza or Bruno or John Scotus." In Paris, he reportedly had fifty thousand followers.

The Church brought him to trial, he was convicted at Toulouse by the voices of the majority. At the trial, he protested his belief in God and defended the existence of Deity with the flimsiest arguments, so flimsy, noted Foote, that one can easily suspect he was pouring irony on the judges. They found him guilty, ordered that his tongue be cut out, then that he burned alive. It is said that, afterwards, he confessed, took the communion, and declared himself ready to subscribe to the Church tenets. However, the sentence was carried out on the same day, February 9, 1619. Drawn on a hurdle, in his shirt, with a placard on his shoulders inscribed "Atheist and Blasphemer of the name of God," he cried out in Italian that he rejoiced to die like a philosopher. "Jesus facing death sweated with fear," he said. "I die undaunted." Or, as described by President Gramond, author of *History of France Under Louis XIII*, "I saw him in the tumbril as they led him to execution, mocking the Cordelier who had been sent to exhort him to repentance, and insulting our Savior by these impious words, 'He sweated with fear and weakness, and I die undaunted.' "

Before burning him, his Christian benefactors did tear out his tongue by the roots, although he was said to have been so obstinate they had to use pincers. One Christian historian found humorous the victim's long cry of agony. Vanini then was strangled, his body was burned in Toulouse, and the ashes of the thirty-four-year-old person described as the Antichrist, the disciple of Satan, were scattered to the wind. {BDF; CE; EU, Giovanni Papuli; ILP; JM; JMR; JMRH; RAT; RE}

van Loon, Hendrik Willem (1882–1944)

An eminent historian and biographer, van Loon wrote *The Story of Mankind* (1921), *The Story of the Bible* (1923) for children, and *Tolerance* (1925). His *Liberation of Mankind, The Story of Man's Struggle for the Right To Think* (1926) is a classic study of rationalism. At the outbreak of the Russian Revolution in 1905, he was an Associated Press correspondent. In 1914, at the outbreak of the European war, he was an Associated Press correspondent in Belgium. In New York City, he was a member of All Soul's Church (Unitarian).

In 1938, van Loon wrote:

> Instinct . . . taught me at a very early age, to beware of those citizens who went around with blueprints of The Truth in their pockets. I am all for truth. But The Truth, in the Pauline sense of the word, is as little to my liking as cyanide of potassium. For not only is it apt to be equally fatal, but, unlike cyanide of potassium, there are no legal restrictions upon its sale and distribution. Indeed, it is given away for nothing at all to even the meekest of applicants. . . . I greatly prefer Socrates to Moses. . . . I have never been an admirer of either the tyrant or the dictator; and Moses in his personal aspirations and his public fulminations was much too much like Adolf Hitler or Benito Mussolini to be admitted to my private Pantheon of those who were true prophets. "What think you of the Christ?" I think everything of him. I unqualifiedly accept him as one of the greatest of my gay [*sic*] philosophers. But I have always experienced great difficulties in getting at him because his figure was completely obscured by the dark shadow of that Paul of Tarsus who in his Pharisaic self-righteousness and arrogance had undertaken to explain him to the rest of the world as he thought he ought to be explained. The simple, lovable carpenter of Nazareth, so beautifully and sublimely unconscious of the practical world around him, so bravely fighting his lonely battle against those forces of malice and evil and greed which turn our lovely planet into a perpetual vale of tears—yet, he is a teacher whom I would most happily follow unto the ends of the earth. But not if Paul the tentmaker has to be one of our companions. For that brash individual would forever be pushing his unwelcome self between us, and instead of letting me listen to the Master, he would volunteer to explain what the Master really intended to say (even before he had said it) until in despair I would either have pushed him aside (in which case he would have called me a dirty Nazi or something equally unpleasant) or I would have been obliged to bid these wanderers farewell and strike out for myself—as indeed, I have been obliged to do. . . . I know that it (the earth) was started by some force outside of myself but, having humbly accepted that fact, I refuse to waste my energies on a futile quest (which will never lead me anywhere anyway). I prefer to concentrate my powers upon that which it is within my reach to do: to make this world with its tremendous, with its incredible potentialities, for beauty and happiness—a place in which every man, woman, and child will be truly able to say, "We are grateful that we are alive, for life indeed is good!" {CE; U; UU}

van Loon, Jan Glastra (20th Century)

Prof. van Loon succeeded Pieter van Dijk as the International

Humanist and Ethical Union's Human Rights Commissioner, or ombudsman. He is the former president of the Dutch Humanist League, the former Secretary of State of the Ministry of Justice, the former President of the Democratic Party, and a member of the Senate and Professor of law at the University of Amsterdam. van Loon is committed to international human rights.

Individuals who have cases of interest are invited to submit them to the Commissioner for Human Rights (Plompetorengracht 19, 3512 CB, Utrecht, Holland). At the Tenth International Humanist and Ethical Union (IHEU) World Congress held in Buffalo (1988), van Loon addressed the group.

VAN MENS TOT MENS

A Dutch monthly publication of *Humanitas*, *Van Mens tot Mens* is at Postbus 71, 1000 AB Amsterdam, The Netherlands. E-mail: <info@lb.humanitas.nl>.

Vannerus, Allen (1862–1946)

Vannerus, a Swedish non-theist, wrote *Atheism Versus Theism*. (See entry for Scandinavian Unbelievers.)

van Noordwijk, Jacobus (20th Century)

A medical pharmacologist in the Netherlands, van Noordwijk is a rationalist who has written for *New Humanist*.

van Noordwijk-Van Veen, Johanna C. (20th Century)

With her husband Jacobus, Mrs. van Noordwijk-Van Veen is a rationalist who has written for *New Humanist*. She is a former chairman of the Netherlands National Council for the Environment.

Van Nostrand, Walter (20th Century)

A freethinker, Van Nostrand wrote *A Freethinker in the Holy Land* (1930). {GS}

Vannucci, Atto (1810–1883)

Vannucci entered the Roman priesthood and was for some years professor of literature at the ecclesiastical college of Prato. A student of Latin literature, he published commentaries on Tacitus, Sallust, Catullus, and other ancient Roman writers. The increasing demand for reform in the Papal States aroused his enthusiasm and, after a fruitless period as a liberal Catholic, he adopted a definite attitude of hostility to the Papacy and quit the Church. In 1848 he became the Tuscan ambassador to the Roman Republic. At the restoration of the Papacy, Vannucci fled to Switzerland and then to France, where he began his chief work, *La Storia dell' Italia antica* (4 volumes, 1884). Returning to Italy in 1854, he collaborated on the *Archivio Storico Italiano* and the *Rivista di Firenze*, becoming the editor of the latter. In 1859 he was elected Deputy, later becoming a Senator. Vannucci was admitted to the *Accademia dei Lincei*. His *Martiri della libertá Italiana* (2 volumes, 1887) is an account of the struggle with the Papacy. {RAT}

van Oosten, Aad (20th Century)

At the 1992 Congress of the International Humanist and Ethical Union (IHEU), van Oosten, who has been secretary and managing director of *Humanitas*, addressed the group on "Tolerance and Social Assistance."

van Paassen, Pierre (1895-1968)

A novelist and a Unitarian minister who was born in Gorcum (Gorinchem), Holland, van Paassen was a religious humanist. In *That Day Alone* (1941), he wrote, "Half of our misery and weakness derives from the fact that we have broken with the soil and that we have allowed the roots that bound us to the earth to rot. We have become detached from the earth, we have abandoned her. And a man who abandons nature has begun to abandon himself." Van Paassen's *Earth Could Be Fair* satirizes the ridiculous aspects of Calvinistic and Catholic religious orthodoxy. It exposes racial hatred, colonial greed, and the harmful belief in the inherent badness of man. In 1949 van Paassen wrote Why *Jesus Died*, pointing out that the trial of Jesus before the Sanhedrin as depicted in the Bible is "pure fabrication, causing its utter rejection as unhistorical and untrue by a long and impressive line of savants from Reimarus and Strauss to Loisy, Guignebert, and Eysinga." In 1960, he turned his attention on the Dominican religious reformer who had attacked the moral laxity of his time: *A Crown of Fire, the Life and Times of Girolamo Savonarola*. Savonarola, who had called for a reformation of the scandalously corrupt court of Pope Alexander VI, ignored the pope's order to stop preaching. Found guilty of being a false prophet, Savonarola was finally executed in 1498. {U}

van Praag, Jaap P. (1911–)

Van Praag, a professor of philosophy at Utrecht, was the first chairman of the International Humanist and Ethical Union (IHEU). The World Union of Freethinkers had been founded in 1880, and the International Ethical Union followed in 1896. According to van Praag, after the Dutch *Humanistish Verbond* was founded, Harold Blackham, J. Hutton Hynd, and he spoke in 1947 about the possibility of closer international cooperation. So, with the help of Julian Huxley, and despite some differences inasmuch as Humanism was the favored word in the United States but the Ethical Culture group was opposed to using the term, it was decided to embrace both notions. As a result, the International Humanist and Ethical Union (IHEU) was formed in 1952. When he signed Humanist Manifesto II, van Praag presided over the International Humanist and Ethical Union. He read papers at the First International Congress of the IHEU in Amsterdam (1952), at the Third Congress in Oslo (1962), at the Fifth in Boston (1970), at the 6th in Amsterdam (1974), and at the Seventh held in London (1978). In 1978, he received a special award "for 25 years of devoted service to IHEU." {HM2; HNS2; PK; TRI}

Van Rompaey, Wim (20th Century)

A Belgian humanist, Van Rompaey participated in the 1996 international conference of humanists in Mexico City. His e-mail: <wim.vanrompaey@lichtpunt.be>.

Van Ryswyck, Hermann (Died 1512)

The Inquisitors accused Van Ryswyck, a Dutch priest, in 1502. As described by Robertson, Van Ryswyck declared "with his own mouth and with sane mind" that the world is eternal, and was not created as was alleged by "the fool Moses," that there is no hell, and no future life; that Christ, whose whole career was flatly contrary to human welfare and reason, was not the son of Omnipotent God but a fool, a dreamer, and a seducer of ignorant men, of whom untold numbers had been slain on account of him and his absurd evangel; that Moses had not physically received the law from God; and that "our" faith was shown to be fabulous by its fatuous Scripture, fictitious Bible, and crazy Gospel. "The most learned Aristotle and his commentator Averroës," he declared, "were nearest the truth." Never one for understatement, Van Ryswyck added, "I was born a Christian, but am no longer one: they are the chief fools." Sentenced in 1502 to perpetual imprisonment, he was given a second chance ten years later. But he remained unbroken, refusing to recant. Therefore, the unrepentant heretic was told by the inquisitor, "*Nimis infelix quidam*," whereupon the same day Van Ryswyck was burned to death. {JMR}

Van Vloten, Johannes (1818–1883)

Van Vloten was one of the foremost freethought authors of Holland. Deposed for his views that theological schools should reconcile religion with science, he became a writer. Van Vloten wrote *De Levensbode* and *Life of Spinoza*. {PUT}

Van Zelst, J. (20th Century)

In 1997, van Zelst launched a South African Freethinkers' page. His e-mail addresses are <eec@eastcoast.co.za> and <members.wbs.net/homepages/k/a/p/kaptein.html>.

VAPAA AJATTELIJA

A Finnish freethought publication, *Vapaa Ajattelija* is at Neljäs linja 1, Helsinki, Finland; <http://personal.eunet.fi/pp.val/>.

Vapereau, Louis Gustave (Born 1819)

Vapereau was a French man of letters. In 1841 he became the secretary of Victor Cousin. He collaborated on the *Dictionnaire des Sciences Philosophiques* and the *Liberté de Penser*, but he is best known for his *Dictionnaire Universel des Contemporains*. In 1870 he was nominated prefect of Cantal, but because of violent attacks by clericals he was suspended in 1873 and resumed his literary labors, compiling *A Universal Dictionary of Writers* (1876) and *Elements of the History of French Literature* (1883–1885). {BDF; RAT}

Varela, Félix (1787–1853)

Varela, although a priest, and José Luz y Caballero attacked scholasticism, promoted liberal principles, and introduced the rationalist philosophy that would enrich the intellectual life of Cubans. {EU}

Vargas Llosa, Mario (1936–)

A Peruvian novelist and Anti-Marxist politician, Vargas Llosa in 1990 unsuccessfully ran for the presidency. His works emphasize the ugly and grotesque, and he delves into the minds of his characters, overcoming barriers of both time and space. His fiction paints a portrait of Peruvian society that is both severe and tender. His novels include *The Time of the Hero* (1962; tr. 1966), *The Green House* (1966, tr. 1968), *Conversation in the Cathedral* (1969, tr. 1975), *The Real Life of Alejandro Mayta* (1984, tr. 1986), and *The War of the End of the World* (1981, tr. 1982). Vargas Llosa also wrote *The Perpetual Orgy: Flaubert and Madame Bovary* (1975, tr. 1986), *Writer's Reality* (tr. 1991), and *Death in the Andes* (1996).

Although his doctoral dissertation had been about Gabriel Garcia Márquez, he came to disagree with Garcia Márquez's support of Fidel Castro, and the two one night got into an argument in a Mexico City theater. Vargas Llosa punched Garcia Márquez, and the novelist returned the punch, writing later that it was "something that one hardly ever gets to do to the subject of one's doctoral dissertation."

Vargas Llosa is a non-theist who, in 1995, was elected a Humanist Laureate in the Council for Secular Humanism's International Humanist Academy. {CE}

Vargas Z., Luis (20th Century)

A Mexican, Vargas was moderator of a panel that discussed humanism and the arts at the 1996 Humanist World Congress held in Mexico City.

Vargas Zamora, Fernando Rodolfo de Jesus (1928–1989)

Raised a Catholic, Vargas renounced Catholicism when as a teenager he left Costa Rica. The co-founder of Variety Recording Studio in New York City, Vargas was a significant figure in show business from the late 1950s until his death in 1989.

Corliss Lamont came early one morning to his 103rd Street Manhattan apartment to speak with Vargas's roommate. Finding Vargas in red pajamas, he said, "Oh, your roommate rooms with the Devil?" It was Vargas's first introduction both to a Columbia University professor and to a bona fide naturalistic humanist. On another occasion he attended Charles Francis Potter's humanist "church," laughing at the lecture on the joys of sex. But astronomy, not religion or academic philosophy, was his major diversion. A nominal member of the Bertrand Russell Society, he was only mildly interested in the various philosophers. For its founding meeting in 1989, he allowed the New York Chapter of Secular Humanists to meet in his recording studio and became its first member.

To have lived a great life, no matter how long, is life's purpose, he believed. To that end he mastered acetate disks, using his own inventive modification of a Scully lathe and being one of the few in the Greater New York Area who could operate such a machine; recorded Broadway plays, working with Arthur Miller, Paddy Chayevsky, Robert Whitehead, Hal Prince, David Amram; worked with internationally known songwriters and performers (he recorded Liza Minnelli's first demo record, at which Marvin Hamlisch was accompanist); worked with songwriter Jerry Bock on "Fiorello" and "Fiddler on the Roof"; completed master acetates for Sun Ra, arguing over wine with him about mysticism; and was well-known among a who's who of Broadway and Latino musicians and artists. Vargas produced a collector's LP of "Costa Rica's Caruso," *Manuel Salazar*; sang "I-gotta-be-me"; and fearlessly ventured on life's less-traveled roads.

Vargas, who died six months after being diagnosed with having Kaposi's sarcoma in the lungs, was resigned to his condition and spent much of his final and painful weeks studying the latest developments in astronomy.

A portion of his cremains were scattered in the Hell's Kitchen and Times Square neighborhoods of New York City, where he had spent most of his life. Another portion was saved to be mixed with the cremains of his companion of forty years, Warren Allen Smith. The bulk was returned to Costa Rica, where his cremains are buried in the family tomb next to his father (Elias) and mother (Elena) at San José's Central Cemetery. The homepage of Spanish-speaking ethical humanists, a memorial, is at <http://idt.net/~wasm/asibehu>. In his honor, an AIDS support group was formed in Costa Rica. (See entries for José Figueres, Secular Humanist Society of New York, and Warren Allen Smith.)

Varisco, Bernardo (1850–1933)

Varisco, an Italian philosopher, was a critical idealist or neo-Kantian, as shown in his *Scienza e Opinioni* (1901) and *Le mie opinione* (1903). Varisco departed from Kant's personal theism and was a pantheist, rejecting the idea of personal immortality. {RAT}

Varnhagen von Ense, Karl August Ludwig Philipp (1785–1858)

Varnhagen von Ense was a German author who studied medicine and philosophy, entered the Austrian and Russian armies, and served in the Prussian diplomatic service. He was an intimate friend of Alex. von Humboldt and shared his freethinking opinions. In his *Diary*, Varnhagen von Ense vividly depicts the men and events of his time. {BDF; RAT}

Vasileff, Nick D. (20th Century)

When Vasileff signed Humanist Manifesto II, he was associated with the St. Louis Ethical Society. {HM2}

Vassin, Vladimir (20th Century)

Vassin, in Canada, signed Humanist Manifesto 2000.

Vasudevan, K. (20th Century)

Vasudevan is a National Council Member of the Indian Rationalist Association.

VATICAN CITY (The Holy See)

"The Vatican should be a church, not a state," Rob Tielman of the Netherlands has stated. Freethinkers are in general agreement. Even by its unusual standards of membership, the United Nations has only two entities that are nonmember states with permanent observer status: Switzerland and the Vatican.

The Holy See's status became official in 1964 when Pope Paul VI appointed its first UN envoy.

Catholics for a Free Choice, leading a coalition of more than seventy nongovernmental organizations from around the world, similarly challenges the Vatican's Non-Member State Permanent Observer status at the United Nations. As noted by Katha Pollitt in *The Nation* 19 April 1999),

> Because of the superficial resemblance of Vatican City to an independent city-state, the Catholic Church is the only one among thousands of religions to enjoy an official designation that gives it voting rights at some conferences and agency meetings, which it has used to block, [regarding] contraception, sex education, and AIDS prevention. Why should one religion—that is, the all-male hierarchy, not the laypeople, who increasingly differ with the Pope on such issues—be able to impose its views on people who don't believe in it?

Frances Kissling, president of Catholics for a Free Choice, agrees:

> Why should an entity that is in essence 100 square acres of office space and tourist attractions . . . with a citizenry that excludes women and children have a place at the table where governments set policies affecting the very survival of women and children?

VATICAN RAG: See entry for Tom Lehrer.

VATICAN, GONE WITH THE WIND IN THE

Gone With the Wind in the Vatican (1999) created a furore upon publication, for it documented intrigue, homosexuality, and corruption within the Vatican bureaucracy. Infuriated Roman Catholic Church officials were red-faced upon finding that one of the book's two authors has remained anonymous and the other, the Rev. Luigi Marinelli, a priest who had worked in the Vatican's Congregation of Eastern Churches, was ordered by a letter in Latin to *ne damna graviore forte provocentur* (to prevent further serious damage by stopping any new printing runs and to remove the offending book from stores).

But Father Marinelli had no authority to do this. Besides, he insisted, "the book does not question the sanctity of Jesus Christ, the Eucharist, or the Catholic Church. It just points out that the Vatican is made up of men who, like me, are flawed." No dissolute priests or scheming cardinals are identified by name. However, anecdotes include one about a priest who tried to smuggle a suitcase full of cash in Switzerland, and one was about a priest who had engaged in homosexual acts and was reassigned and promoted to sweep the scandal under the rug.

Father Marinelli, who was seventy-two at the time of the book's publishing, compared his present persecution by the Vatican to that of Savanarola, the reformer who was burned at the stake, and Padre Pio, the mystic friar who was investigated by the church many times before he was beatified in 1999. {Alessandra Stanley, T*he New York Times*, 17 July 1999}

Vatke, Johann Karl Wilhelm (1806–1882)

After teaching theology in Berlin, Vatke was appointed extraordinary professor at Berlin University although his rationalist views excited hostility from the orthodox theologians. His *Religion des Alten Testaments nach den kanonischen Büchern entwickelt* (1835) was one of the foundations of the science of Biblical criticism. His *Menschliche Freiheit* (1841) is Hegelian in philosophy. Although said to have been a Protestant, Vatke wrote to Strauss: "Are we Christians?" and replied that neither is a Christian in the customary or the primitive-Christian sense. "Have we any religion?" he asked, answering that he believed in Hegel's Absolute. {RAT}

Vaughan, Henry Halford (1811–1885)

Vaughan, a British historian, was for some years a professor of modern history at Oxford University. In one of Benjamin Jowett's letters, the Oxford leader confides that Vaughan's opinions go far beyond his own and have to be concealed at Oxford. Vaughan wrote a work, *Man's Moral Nature*, which gave his views, but he was persuaded to destroy the manuscript. {JM; RAT; RE}

Vaughan, Percy (Died 1917)

A London barrister, Vaughan upon reading rationalist literature became an agnostic. For some years he was a Director of the Rationalist Press Association, and he was associate editor of "The Inquirers' Library." Vaughan fought in World War I in the Anti-Aircraft Corps, and soon after returning to the front, after an illness, he was instantaneously killed. {RAT}

Vaughn, Erin (20th Century)

Vaughan, while a student at Cornell University in 1998, signed the Campus Freethought Alliance's "Bill of Rights for Unbelievers."

Vaughn, Lewis (1950-)

In 1997, Vaughn was named executive editor of *Free Inquiry*, of which in 1999 he became editor. He also is executive editor of *The Scientific Review of Alternative Medicine* and *Philo*, a philosophical journal. With co-author Theodore Schick Jr., Vaughn wrote two college textbooks, *How to Think About Weird Things* and *Doing Philosophy: An Introduction Through Thought Experiments*. He signed Humanist Manifesto 2000. E-mail: <fivaughn@aol.com>.

Vauvenargues, Luc de Clapier [Marquis] (1715–1770)

Vauvenargues, a Marquis, was a French moralist. At eighteen he entered the army, leaving the service with ruined health in 1743. In 1746 he wrote *An Introduction to the Knowledge of the Human Mind, Followed by Reflections and Maxims*, which was praised by his friend Voltaire as "one of the best I know for the formation of character." Although his work was only mildly deistic, it was rigorously suppressed and not reprinted until about 1770. McCabe, discussing Vauvenargues, remarked, "He was a Deist, of great promise, but cut off prematurely." {BDF; JM; RAT; RE}

Väyrynen, Gunn (20th Century)

Väyrynen is chairperson of the Finnish Humanist Union. In "The Humanist Movement in Finland" (*International Humanist News*, October 1995), she wrote a concise history of humanism. (See entry for Finnish Freethinkers, Humanists.)

Veblen, Thorstein (1857–1929)

Whitehead and Muhrer have described the economist Veblen as being openly agnostic, one who compared the publicizing of religion to the techniques of "modern" salesmanship. An intellectual vagabond who taught for a while, then got forced out and moved on, he applied for a position teaching science at St. Olaf College in Minnesota. Although his brother was a trustee, Veblen was found deficient in his religious beliefs and a bad influence. He also taught at the University of Missouri, which dismissed him. He called the college "a woodpecker hole in a rotten stump."

Henry Steele Commager described Veblen as follows: "His rebellion went so deep that it confounded even dissenters; his heresies were so profane that they baffled orthodoxy and heterodoxy alike."

In 1973, John Kenneth Galbraith wrote an introduction for Veblen's internationally provocative *Theory of the Leisure Class* (1899).

Veblen's studies helped lay the foundations for the school of institutional economics.

Of Veblen, Wesley C. Mitchell has said, "No other such emancipator of the mind from the subtle tyranny of circumstance has been known in social science, and no other such enlarger of the realm of inquiry. . . . He was like a visitor from another world."

Veblen was a pioneer in describing the role of technicians in modern society, describing a basic conflict between the processes of technology for "industry" (which tend toward maximum efficiency of production) and those of "business" (which, in his view, restrict output and manipulate prices to maximize profit. Although his views were not widely acclaimed during his lifetime, they have since become profoundly influential. {CE; *Freethought History #12*, 1994}

VEDA

In Hinduism, Veda is a reference to any of the oldest Hindu sacred texts. They were composed in Sanskrit and gathered into four collections.

VEDANTA

Vedanta, which means "the end of the Veda," is one of the six classical systems of Indian philosophy. It refers both to the teaching of the Upanishads, the last section of the Veda scriptures, and to the knowledge of its ultimate meaning. Well-known modern Vedantists include Sarvepalli Radhakrishnan, Swami Vivekananda, and Aurobindo Ghose (Sri Aurobindo). (For a negative critique, see the entry for V. R. Narla.) {CE; ER}

Vediner, David (20th Century)

Vediner holds the facetious title of "High Exalted Lord of Publicity" for Oregon State University's Society for Logic and Reason in Corvallis. His e-mail: <vedinerd@ucs.orst.edu>.

Veeramani, K. (20th Century)

Veeramani leads a socio-political and atheistic movement in Tamil Nadu in southern India. It is called the Self Respect Movement. He heads the Periyar Rationalist organization, which focuses on achieving social equality for members of the lower castes and women. At the fourth World Atheist Conference in 1996, he gave the welcoming address, declaring, "The oncoming century will be definitely a century of fast-growing science which will result in the triumph of atheism and equality. The atheists have ample scope and prospects for the furtherance of activities and betterment of society. Every atheist today is a potential liberator of a section of humanity from the shackles of injustice, inequality, superstition, maladjustment with fellow-beings, wastage of money, time and energy, and lack of reasoning power and freedom of expression." (See entries for Self Respect Movement and for World Atheist Conference.) {FD; *New Humanist*, February 1996 and April 1996}

VEGETARIANISM

• I have always eaten animal flesh with somewhat guilty conscience.

—**Albert Einstein**
The Quotable Einstein

• "Corpse-food was on the way out even in your time." Anderson explained. "Raising animals to—ugh—eat them became economically impossible. I don't know how many acres of land it took to feed one cow, but at least ten humans could survive on the plants it produced. And probably a hundred, with hydroponic techniques. But what finished the whole horrible business was not economics but disease. It started first with cattle, then spread to other food animals—a kind of virus, I believe, that affected the brain, and caused a particularly nasty death. Although a cure was eventually found, it was too late to turn back the clock—and anyway, synthetic foods were now far cheaper, and you could get them in any flavor you liked."

—**Arthur C. Clarke**
3001 (1997)

• Ethical vegetarians feel that it is morally wrong to kill animals to eat when one can live a healthy life without doing so. . . .In *Genesis*, we are told that God gave man [dominion over the fish, fowl, cattle and every creeping thing]. It was denied that animals had souls or felt suffering. Despite this belief, in the Middle Ages cats, pigs, cows, and sheep were tried for such crimes as stubbornness, damage to property, lack of respect, etc. They were punished by hanging, flogging, and whipping. Religions, as far as I know, no longer punish animals, but neither do they condemn cruelty to them. Humanists, however, regard animals, including fish and invetebrates, as being capable of feeling, and there is plenty of physicological evidence that this is. . . . I would suggest that humanists follow these guidelines: (1) We should avoid all pain to animals and the use of products requiring animals to suffer; (2) When animals have been used for medical research, experiments should be designed to minimize the number of animals to be used and to avoid the animals' suffering; and (3) Where there is a choice of animals to be used, one should choose those lower in evolution in preference to the higher.

—**Harold Hillman**
{*Free Inquiry*, Fall 1998}

Veil, Simone [President, European Parliament] (1927–)

Veil, a French woman who was the former President of the European Parliament, is a Humanist Laureate in the Council for Secular Humanism's International Academy of Humanism. With Prof. Launay and Dr. Soule, she co-wrote *Les donnees psycho-sociologiques de l'adoption* (1969). In 1974, Veil was Minister of Health in France, also being responsible for Social Security. She has been chairman of the Information Board on Nuclear Power (1977).

Veitch, John (1829–1894)

Although his parents wanted him to study theology, Veitch abandoned Christianity and wrote, "With all [Shelley's] blasphemy and denunciation of Deity and Christianity, I immensely prefer him to all the whining evangelicals I ever heard or read of." In 1856 he was appointed assistant to Sir W. Hamilton in the chair of logic and metaphysics at Edinburgh University, and he became in 1860 professor of logic, rhetoric, and metaphysics at St. Andrews. In 1864 he moved to Glasgow, becoming professor of logic and rhetoric. Veitch wrote a number of philosophical works, a *History and Poetry of the Scottish Border* (2 volumes, 1893), and several small volumes of verse. He was a theist of the sentimental Wordsworth school, but far less definite in his natural theology than Wordsworth. "I know no theory of the relation of the infinite to the finite which is not merely a wandering in cloud-land," he wrote in his *Essays in Philosophy* (published 1895). {RAT}

Veld, Joris in 't (Born 1895)

At the Second International Humanist and Ethical Union Congress in London (1957), Dr. Veld from the Netherlands addressed the group. One of his works on politics and government is *Ons staatsbestuur in een stroomversnelling* (1945).

Velthuysen, Lambert (1622–1685)

Velthuysen was a Dutch physician who in Latin wrote many works on theology and philosophy. *De Officio Pastorum* and *De Idolatria et Superstition* resulted in charges, but he was let off in 1668 with a fine. {BDF}

Vena, Andrew (20th Century)

An atheist activist, Vena has commissioned pamphlets for publishing by the American Atheist Press. He has placed some of the 35,000 pamphlets of eleven different titles on car windshields, in his personal mail, and enclosed others in postage-paid business return envelopes that he receives in his "junk mail." Vena considers himself a missionary . . . of atheism.

Venetianer, Moritz (19th Century)

Venetianer was a German pantheist, the author of *Der Allgeist* (1874) and a work on *Schopenhauer as a Scholastic*. {BDF}

VENIAL SINS

Venial sins, according to Roman Catholic theology, are not so serious as mortal sins. A venial sin is done without deliberate intent and thus does not estrange the soul from the grace of God. Putting salt in a disliked parson's sugar bowl would be a venial sin; putting arsenic would be a mortal sin. Chaucer in *The Canterbury Tales* depicts venial sins, often quite humorously, as when in "The Miller's Tale" a lover who expects to kiss a married lady's lips is blindfolded and kisses her "nether-eye" (anus).

Venkatadri, Ravipudi (20th Century)

In India, Venkatadri edits *Hetuvadi*. He signed Humanist Manifesto 2000.

Venkateswarareddi (20th Century)

Venkateswarareddi is editor in India of a freethought journal, *Misimi*.

Ventura, Jesse [Governor] (1951—)

A professional wrestler and former Navy SEAL who became Minnesota's governor, Ventura was a member of an American third party movement, the Reform Party, which at the end of the century vied with businessman Ross Perot for its leadership.

In a *Playboy* interview (November 1999), the professional athlete well-known for his dramatic television wrestling, blamed organized religion for the unpopularity of legalized prostitution, which he feels should be debated by legislatures and which he personally favors. He also said,

> • Organized religion is a sham and a crutch for weak-minded people who need strength in numbers. It tells people to go out and stick their noses in other people's business.

He added, however, that although he did not need organized religion, which is for the "weak-minded," he did not fault those who do.

Vera, Augusto (1813–1885)

Vera was trained in law, but he deserted it for archaeology, which he studied in Paris. Under Victor Cousin's influence, he was appointed professor of philosophy in a French provincial college. A friend of Thiers and Vacherot, he left France at the coup d'état of 1851, returning to his native Italy in 1860. He received the chair of philosophy at Naples University and was throughout in sympathy with the anti-Papal movement. In philosophy he was a follower of Hegel, and Hegel translated some of Vera's writings into German. One of the most eminent Italian philosophers of the century, he wrote *Philosophie de la nature* (3 volumes, 1863–1865). {RAT}

Vera, Ernesto (20th Century)

Vera, a Cuban, spoke about current problems of the media at the 1996 Humanist World Congress held in Mexico City.

Verb, Hal (20th Century)

Verb is president of the Atheists of San Francisco Region. (See entry for California Atheists, Humanists.)

Vercruysse, Jeroom (20th Century)

Vercruysse wrote *Bibliographie Descriptive des Écrits du Baron d'Holbach* (1971), the first full biography of France's most outspoken atheist. He wrote *Voltaire et la Hollande* (1966). {GS}

Verdi, Giuseppe (1813–1901)

Verdi, the foremost composer of Italian opera, may have been interested in Nebuchadnezzar (in 1841 his third opera was *Nabucodonosor*), the First Crusade (*I Lambardi alla prima Crociata*), Manzoni (*Requiem*, written in 1874); and Shakespeare (*Macbeth* in 1847, *Otello* in 1867, *Falstaff* in 1893). But in one of the best examples of grand opera, *Don Carlos*, Verdi exuded an obvious dislike for the institutional Roman Catholic Church. As detailed in *Verdi* (1993), a biography by Mary Jane Phillips-Matz, Verdi had an affair in the 1870s with a soprano, one that was callously conducted in front of his heart-broken second wife, whom belatedly he had married. Also, when twenty-one he fought for the position in Busseto of *maestro di cappella* and organist. The Church, however, objected to hiring a theatrical composer. Whereupon fistfights resulted between partisans, and Verdi thereafter expressed a strong anticlericalism. He mockingly called one of his pet dogs Pretin (Little Priest). And he boasted that as a youth he had cursed a priest with death by lightning, an event that somehow took place some time later. In 1861 Verdi served as a representative to the first Italian parliament.

According to McCabe, F. T. Garibaldi showed in his biography that Verdi expressly ordered in his will that he should be buried "without any part of the customary formulae." He was a man of generous character. In 1898 he gave 2,000,000 lire to the city of Milan to build a home for aged and inform musicians. Upon his death in Milan, an estimated 300,000 mourners turned out, but the Church continued to claim him although Verdi was one of the many apostates from the Roman faith who were employed to compose music for its services.

In its coverage of Verdi's "Macbeth," *New York City Opera* (September 1997) wrote

> Of all the level-headed, down-to-earth, and unshakably practical men who ever earned a living composing music, Giuseppe Verdi stands at the very top of the class. He loved clarity and hated obfuscation; he made fun of anything that suggested the supernatural, superstition, spiritualism, and seances. Everything in his world had to be examined in the light of day, or in bright sunshine, for he was a model rationalist. In a letter to a friend, Verdi's wife Giuseppina Strepponi wrote that he was an atheist. She then crossed that word out, and over it she wrote, "not much of a believer."

{CE; JM; RAT; RE; TRI; TYD}

Vereshchagin, Vassili Vasilyevich (1842–1904)

Vereshchagin was a Russian painter, soldier, atheist, and traveler. He is best known for his military pictures, which portrayed war in all its horror and brutality. He also is known for his studies of Turkistan and Asian life. Most of his works are collected in the Tretyakov Gallery in Moscow. During an explosion of the flagship *Petropavlovsk* in the Russo-Japanese War, Vereshchagin was killed while seeking battle material.

The realistic and anti-religious conceptions of his "Holy Family" and "Resurrection" were the cause of their being withdrawn, by order of the archbishop, from the Vienna Exhibition (1885). In his autobiographical sketches (1887), Vereschagin unequivocally rejected Christianity and deplored the widespread hypocrisy, especially in England, of professing to believe it. {BDF; JM; RAT; RE}

Vergil [or Virgil], Polydore (70–19 B.C.E.)

Vergil (the spelling Virgil is not found earlier than the 5th century) became part of the literary circle in Rome that was patronized by Maecenas and Augustus. His *Ecologues*, or *Bucolics* (37 B.C.E.) idealized rural life much in the manner of his Greek predecessor Theocritus. He then wrote *Georgics* (40 B.C.E.), seeking as had the Greek Hesiod before him to interpret the joy of farm life. For the rest of his life he worked on *Aeneid*, a national epic, which honored Rome and foretold the prosperity to come.

Vergil's pastoral poems were not merely a literary convention, the University of Nebraska's Louis Crompton has noted. Vergil was born on a farm near Mantua and throughout life struck his contemporaries as being shy, awkward, and countrified. Although of sturdy build, he suffered from poor health and was often ill from headaches and hemorrhaging lungs. His lack of aggressiveness and modesty earned him a nickname, "the Virgin." When the *Commentary* of Donatus characterized Vergil as "inclined to passions for boys," it was considered unusual for a Latin biographer to also name the boys, Cebes and Alexander, two of his students. Vergil's Corydon eclogue, a poem in which shepherds converse, is considered the most famous poem on male love in Latin literature. Vergil never married but owned a slave named Alexander, with whom he fell in love.

Dante, Marlowe, Byron, and Jeremy Bentham are but three of Vergil's admirers. Dante, who apparently knew the Donatian biography, made Vergil his guide through Hell and Purgatory. Crompton comments, "[A]nd the unusual courtesy he shows to sodomites in both domains may stem partly from his knowledge of his mentor's tastes. Nevertheless, an unamiable medieval legend (traceable to the thirteenth century) held that all sodomites had died at the moment of Christ's birth, and some ecclesiastics who were confused about the date of Virgil's death maintained that he too had died in the holocaust."

As creator of one of the greatest long poems in world literature, Vergil is not believed to have been actively involved in any religion. His epitaph, which might have been written by the poet himself, is

> *Mantua me genuit, Calabri* rapuere, tenet nunc
> *Parthenope; cecini pascua rura duces.*
>
> Mantua was my birthplace; I died in Calabria;
> And now I rest at Parthenope. I sang of pastures, farms, and leaders.

{CE; GL}

Vergniaud, Pierre Victurnien (1759–1793)

Vergniaud was a French Girondist orator who once said, "Reason thinks. Religion dreams." Elected to the Legislative Assembly in 1791, he also became President of the Convention. At the trial of the King he voted for the appeal to the people but, when that was rejected, later voted for death. With Gensonné and Guadet, he opposed the sanguinary measures of Robespierre and, being beaten in the struggle, was executed with the Girondins. He had prepared to take poison but, inasmuch as there was an insufficient amount for his comrades, he chose to suffer with them. {BDF; RAT}

Verhaegen, Pierre Théodore (1800–1860)

A lawyer, Freemason, and freethinker, Verhaegen was a prominent supporter of the 1830 revolution which led to the establishment of the independent kingdom of Belgium. Verhaegen also was one of the founders of the anti-clerical Free University of Brussels. {RAT; TRI}

Verhaeren, Émile (1855–1916)

Verhaeren was a Belgian poet and critic, a Fleming who wrote in French. His passion for social reform was accompanied by a disgust with mankind, as in the naturalistic verse of *Les Flamandes* (1883); in pessimism over the growth of urban industrialization, as in *Les Villages illusoires* and *Les Villes tentaculaires* (both 1895); and finally in optimistic glorification of the energy of man, as in the lyrical *Les Forces tumultueuses* (1902) and *La Multiple Splendeur* (1906). Verhaeren, the son of a devout and wealthy Catholic, had studied with Maeterlinck and had shed his faith for agnosticism. His freethought is found particularly in his poems, for example in "The Monk," in which he tells the monks, "You alone survive of the Christian world that is dead." In his later years, Verhaeren became more mystic but never returned to the Church. {JM; RAT; RE}

Verhoeven, Paul (1938-)

A film director, Verhoeven was born in the Netherlands. He directed such films as "*Wat Zien Ik*?", "Turkish Delight" (1973; "The Fourth Man" (1983); "Robocop" (1987); and "Showgirls" (1995).

"The Fourth Man," he said, "has to do with my vision of religion. In my opinion, Christianity is nothing more than one of many interpretations of reality, neither more nor less. Ideally, it would be nice to believe that there is a God somewhere out there, but it looks to me as if the whole Christian religion is a major symptom of schizophrenia in half the world's population: civilizations scrambling to rationalize their chaotic existence. Subsequently, Christianity has a tendency to look like magic or the occult. And I liked that ambiguity, because I wanted my audience to take something home with them. I wanted them to wonder about what religion really is. Remember, that Christianity is a religion grounded in one of the most violent acts of murder, the crucifixion. Otherwise, religion wouldn't have had any kind of impact." {CA}

VERIFIABILITY, or VERIFICATION PRINCIPLE

Logical positivists hold that the verification principle enables one to distinguish between meaningful and meaningless statements as well as between meaningful and meaningless questions. A statement is meaningful only if it is at least in principle verifiable or testable in experience. If it is not, then it must be condemned as meaningless, or nonsense. A statement is testable in practice if humans can actually subject it to a test here and now. To say a statement is testable in principle is to say we can describe what a test of it would be like, whether or not we can carry out the test. It is evident that if a statement is testable in practice it also is testable in principle, but the converse does not hold.

According to the **verification principle**, a statement does not need to be testable in practice in order to be meaningful, but it must be testable in principle. A requirement for the meaningfulness of a factual statement is its susceptibility to the possibility of being either theoretically or actually proved true or false by reference to empirical facts. Meanwhile, according to the **confirmability theory** the meaningfulness of a factual statement depends upon the statement's reducibility of its descriptive predicates to a set of observation predicates.

Bertrand Russell has given the example that 4000 miles down to the center of Earth one can find iron—although it may be unlikely that any actual test is possible, it does follow that, if through some mining operation a hole could be cut and a camera could record iron deposits 4000 miles down, the question as to the evidence of iron in the center of the earth is meaningful when the verification principle is applied. As to whether fate exists, or if karma is a true doctrine, or if eating is an absolute, or if God has four eyes, the verification principle reveals the *meaninglessness* of such ideas inasmuch as no tests can be made to verify them. (See some negative criticism of verificationism in the entry for Isaiah Berlin. For discussions of the principle by R. W. Ashby, see *Encyclopedia of Philosophy*, Vol. 8; and by Ernest LePore of Rutgers University in *The Cambridge Dictionary of Philosophy*.)

Verigan, Vitaly (20th Century)

Verigan is associated with a Moscow Unitarian group at A/J 667, OTD/Sv 5, Zhukovske, Moskow, OBL Russia 140160.

Verity, Walter (20th Century)

An Illinoian, Verity once was a director of the American Humanist Association.

Verlag, Angelika Lenz (20th Century)

Verlag publishes *Kristall* (Fasaneweg 8, W-3057 Neustadt 1, Germany). {FD}

Verlet, Henri (19th Century)

Verlet was the French founder and editor of *La Libre Pensée* (1871) and author of a pamphlet, "Atheism and the Supreme Being." {BDF}

Verliere, Alfred (19th Century)

A French author, Verliere wrote *Guide du Libre-Penseur* (1869), and he collaborated with *La Libre Pensée* and *Rationaliste*. To Bishop Dupanloup's *Atheism et Peril Social*, he replied with *Deisme et Peril Social*, for which he was condemned to several months' imprisonment. {BDF}

Verma, Ramswaroop: See entry for Ramendra.

Vermeer, Jan (or Johannes) (1632–1675)

Vermeer was a Dutch genre and landscape painter, one who is ranked among the greatest Dutch masters and the foremost of all colorists. Nicolas Walter has observed that although it is true that Vermeer was a Christian, indeed a Catholic convert, "yet his religious paintings are his weakest and his masterpieces are scenes of ordinary people (probably his wife and daughters) doing ordinary things—to my mind better representations of humanism in art than anything produced by the Italian Renaissance." {*New Humanist*, June 1996}

Vermersch, Eugène (18th Century)

Vermersch was a French journalist who took part in the Commune and wrote on many radical journals. {BDF}

VERMONT HUMANISTS

Arpad Toth and Valerie White are contacts for the Humanist

Association of New Hampshire-Vermont, POB 23, Keene, New Hampshire 03431. B. J. Nelson is secretary-treasurer of the group. {FD}

Vernes, Maurice (19th Century)

A French biblical critic, Vernes published *Melanges de Critique Religieuse* and translated works by several freethinkers. For many years, Vernes had been a Protestant minister who led the Liberal Christians in France and edited their magazine. The orthodox protested when he was appointed professor of Protestant theology at Paris University. Vernes issued volumes on the lines of the Higher Criticism, and he collaborated in translating the Bible into French. In 1904 he became Vice-President of the French National Association of Freethinkers and, McCabe reports, "sent a rousing message to the International Freethought Congress at Rome." {BDF; JM; RAT}

Vernet, Émile Jean Horace (1789–1863)

Vernet, who came from a French family of painters, was one of the most famous military painters of the 19th Century. He is known for his decorations of the Constantine Room at Versailles and his "Defense of the Barrier at Clichy," which is in the Louvre. His father, Antoine Charles Horace Vernet (1758–1835), was also an atheist, and Émile sustained the anti-clerical tradition. He won and became director of the French Academy at Rome, was Commander of the Legion of Honor, and was a Grand Medallist. {JM; RAT}

Vernial, Paul (19th Century)

Vernial was a French physician and member of the Anthropological Society of Paris. He wrote *On the Origin of Man* (1881). {BDF}

Vernon, Thomas S. (1914–)

A professor of philosophy at the University of Arkansas, Vernon is a secular humanist who has written for *Free Inquiry* and *American Rationalist*. He is author of *Untimely Discourses* (1986), *The Age of Unreason* (1987), and *The Complete Secularist* (1994). Once a Baptist minister, Vernon became unhappy about the "charlatanism and boobery" of our age and had the intellectual courage to reject Protestantism. "Today we are witnessing such a resurgence of religious bigotry," he lamented in *Great Infidels* (1989), "that one cannot help wondering how long it will be before 'equal time' in our schools is demanded for geocentrism and flat-earthism as well as for creationism." {*Free Inquiry*, Winter, 1984-1985; *Freethought History* #10, 1994; TYD}

Véron, Eugène (1825–1889)

Véron was a French writer and publicist. He founded *La France Républicaine* at Lyons. In his later years he was General Inspector of Museums and editor of *L'art* in Paris. His agnostic views are seen in his *Progrès intellectuel dans l'humanité* (1862), *La morale* (1884), and *Histoire naturelle des religions* (2 volumes, 1885). Véron was an aesthetician of wide repute.

Verwey, Bellicent (20th Century)

Verwey, who was born in Richmond, Virginia, in her words "to an alcoholic father and a delusional poetess of a mother," has published a poem, "An Atheist's Faith," in *Atheist Nation* (July-August 1998).

Verworn, Max (1863–1921)

A German physiologist, a colleague and close friend of Haeckel at Jena, Verworn rose to the first rank in his science. His *General Physiology* became a standard work throughout Europe. Verworn openly professed agnosticism, especially in his *Science and Philosophy*, and he contributed to a work commemorating Haeckel's eightieth birthday. {JM; RAT; RE}

VESAK

Vesak is a Buddhist holiday that honors Gautama's birth, enlightenment, and death.

Very, Jones (1813–1880)

Very, upon graduating from Harvard in 1836, tutored Greek there while studying at the Divinity School. He began having poetic visions of the Holy Ghost and claimed that the poetry he was writing was being communicated to him through mystical visions. According to Bronson Alcott, Very was "diswitted in the contemplation of the holiness of Divinity." Carlos Baker considered him "a newborn bard of the Holy Ghost." Emerson liked Very's poetry, but the Harvard faculty questioned Very's sanity and Very was committed to an asylum for the insane. Although a friend of the Transcendentalists, Very became such a mystic that he believed in the absolute surrender of the will to God. Upon leaving the asylum, and without a degree in divinity, he temporarily held pastorates in Maine and Massachusetts but for his last four decades was a recluse who lived with his sister. J. F. Clarke edited Very's *Poems and Essays* (1866), which contained some six hundred poems.

A mild Unitarian, he was clearly a theist. {Carlos Baker, *Emerson Among the Eccentrics*; CE; U}

Vesalius, Andreas (1514–1564)

A Flemish anatomist, Vesalius made many discoveries by dissecting human cadavers. His work overturned many of the doctrines held by the second-century anatomist Galen and caused much criticism from other anatomists who objected to his stealing the bodies of criminals from the gallows. He countered that it was the only way, in light of the Church's teachings, to obtain cadavers. His work was revolutionary inasmuch as he was among the first to dissect cadavers. This allowed him to show that Galen's anatomy was simply an attempt to apply animal structure to the human body, that it was not based on any direct knowledge of human anatomy. Chased from country to country, he left Padua to become physician to Emperor Charles V and to his son Philip II of Spain. McCabe writes, "There is a grossly inaccurate account of him in the Catholic Dr. Walsh's *Popes and Science*—the account in White's *Warfare of Science with Theology* is perfectly correct—and the very just appreciation of him by the Vice-President of the Anatomical Society of Great Britain in the *Encyclopedia Britannica* has been expunged from the last (Catholic-revised) edition, though he was one of the greatest scientists of the Middle Ages."

In 1563, Vesalius made a pilgrimage to Jerusalem and, on the return voyage, died in Greece. Throughout his life he incurred the hostility of the clergy, and he died carrying out a sentence of the Spanish Inquisition, which had sought to burn him at the stake. The Emperor saved him, but on condition that he make a pilgrimage to Jerusalem. The hardships of a shipwreck hastened the end of Vesalius's broken life. {CE; JM; RE}

VESPERS

According to Claude Bernard, the Sunday evening service in Catholic churches known as Vespers is "the servant girls' opera." (See entry for Claude Bernard.)

Vetter, George B. (20th Century)

Vetter wrote "Personality and Group Factors in the Making of Atheists," which was published by the *Journal of Abnormal and Social Psychology* (1932). In his *Magic and Religion* (1973), he declared that "Supernaturalism is, in its social functions and consequences, a dangerous opiate. And, what is perhaps even worse, it discourages objective attempts at intelligent social trial-and-error, planning, and even research, and undermines man's faith in his own resources." {FUS}

Via, Arnold (20th Century)

Via was an officer of American Atheists and was one of the last to see Madalyn O'Hair, who visited him in Grottoes, Virginia, in mid-August 1995 just before she disappeared with son Jon and granddaughter Robin. To journalist David Van Biema, Via said that during working hours "they didn't bother one another unless they wanted to get into another's throats," in which case screaming fights ensued. However, they dined together and lived together, "three peas in a pod. . . . Jon had no girlfriend, and Robin had no boyfriend, and Madalyn was too far gone to have anything." Madalyn seemed healthy, he said of their last visit, despite her chronic medical problems. {*Time*, 10 February 1997}

Viardot, Louis (1800–1883)

A French writer, Viardot founded the *Revue Independante* with George Sand and Pierre Leroux. He made translations from the Russian. In addition to many works on art Viardot, wrote *The Jesuits* (1857) and *Apology of an Unbeliever* (1869), which was republished as *Libre Examen* (1871). {BDF; RAT}

Viau, Théophile de (1590–1626)

A poet and an atheist, Viau was persecuted for alleged libertinism. When in 1622 for political reasons Théophile converted to Catholicism, Father Garasse accused him of leading a band of atheists, calling him the king of libertines. Convicted in 1623, he was condemned to the stake but was only burned in effigy. Théophile was then banished forever from France, as was the Jesuit father Voisin, one of his chief adversaries. Although he was generally acknowledged to have been a homosexual, according to Kathleen Collins-Clark of the University of Michigan, "all of his intimate relationships remain largely a matter of inference drawn from his highly personal poetry. His contemporary Tallement des Réaux refers to Jacques la Valée as Théophile's widow, thus indicating that their physical relationship was common knowledge at the time."

Viau wrote the tragedy, *Pyramé et Thisbe* (1621). The poems which he contributed to *La Parnasse satyrique* were considered obscene. His credo, "Follow Nature's law," takes on added resonance, Collins-Clark notes, "when natural inclination leads the lover outside relationships condoned by the Church." {*Free Inquiry*, Fall, 1991; GL}

Vick, Lesley (1944–)

Vick is an Australian rationalist and humanist. In 1977 she became secretary of the Rationalist Society of Victoria, and in 1982 she was appointed to the Board of Directors of the Rationalist Association of Australia Ltd. When she became president of the Rationalist Society of Australia in 1987, her presidential address was published as a booklet, "The Role of Rationalism Today." {SWW}

Vickery, Alice Drysdale (19th Century)

Drysdale was honorary president of the Neo-Malthusian league, which Margaret Sanger credits as having inspired her birth control efforts.

Vico, Giovanni Battista (1668–1744)

Vico, who is among the great freethinkers in philosophy, is a forerunner of cultural anthropology, or ethnology. His *Principles of a New Science* (1725), according to Robertson, "on the whole excels Montesquieu's *Spirit of Laws*." Although his vocabulary used the words ordinarily associated with faith, he "grappled with the science of human development in an essentially secular and scientific spirit." He posits "Deity and Providence, but proceeds nevertheless to study the laws of civilization inductively from its phenomena. He permanently obscured his case, indeed, by insisting on putting it theologically, and condemning Grotius and others for separating the idea of law from that of religion. Only in a pantheistic sense has Vico's formula any validity; and he never avows a pantheistic view, refusing even to go with Grotius in allowing that Hebrew law was akin to that of other nations. But a rationalistic view, had he put it, would have been barred. The wonder is, in the circumstances, not that he makes so much parade of religion, but that he could venture to undermine so vitally its pretensions, especially after he had found it prudent to renounce the project of annotating the great work of Grotius, *De Jure Belli et Pacis*, on the score that (as he puts it in his Autobiography) a good Catholic must not endorse a heretic." But his method of writing history was systematic, far in advance of his time and not fully recognized until the nineteenth century. He taught that history is the account of the birth and development of human societies and their institutions—others had written that it was the development of God's will. In short, he taught that history is a valid object of human knowledge because man himself created history, that the historian can never be a prophet. To manage such in the Catholic world of 1720 was difficult, and when his motives were questioned he is said to have had "a tendency to hedge." Benedetto Croce, in *The Philosophy of Giambattista Vico* (1913), writes that Vico is fundamentally at one with the Naturalists: "Like them, in constructing his science of human society, he excludes with Grotius all idea of God, and with Pufendorf considers man as without help or attention from God, excluding him, that is, from revealed religion and its God." Upon his death, Vico was carried to his house, the stairway of which was too narrow so the coffin had to be lowered through a window. Fellow professors tried to save his remains from the indignity of Christian burial. But, after being carried without ceremony to the church of the Oratarian priests, the body remained with them and remains with them to this day. {BDF; CE; JM; RAT}

Victor, Jeffrey S. (20th Century)

Victor, a professor of sociology at Jamestown Community College, is author of *Satanic Panic* (1993), which won the 1994 H. L. Mencken Award for best book from the Free Press Association. Victor finds that a Satanism scare has penetrated our society but that objective investigators find no evidence to support the allegations that Satanist cults are responsible for conspiracies to enslave, abuse, molest, and kill children. Victor find that the claims of a Satanist conspiracy are a social phenomenon, and his book provides guidelines for investigating their false claims.

Victor, Viggo Floria (20th Century)

In 1934 for his M.A. thesis at Northwestern University in Illinois, Victor wrote about Robert G. Ingersoll's use of history and literary materials. {FUS}

Victoria, (Adelaide) (Mary) (Louisa), [Empress] (1840-1901)

Victoria, Empress of Germany, was the eldest daughter of Victoria of England and the mother of the Kaiser. In 1858 she married the German crown prince (later Emperor Frederick III). Upon her husband's death, she was often called Empress Frederick. A dogmatic English liberal, she was bitterly hostile to the imperial chancellor Otto von Bismarck but was unable to make her dislike effective. McCabe noted that "it is interesting that the two daughters, Victoria and Alice, of the very prim and pious Queen Victoria of England were freethinkers of the advanced type, probably agnostics." He added, "Even the cautious *Dictionary of National Biography*, which generally conceals heresies, says of Victoria that although she retained her attachment to the Church of England her religion was undogmatic and she 'sympathized with the broad views of Strauss, Renan, Schopenhauer, and Huxley.' " Prince von Buelow, who knew both princesses well, wrote in his *Memoirs* that "the Grand Duchess Alice was as liberal in politics and especially in religion as her sister the Crown Princess," that Victoria was "an out and out Rationalist of the temper of Herbert Spencer and John Stuart Mill." Reportedly, Victoria was a sincere patroness of culture who detested her son, the Kaiser, and Prussian ideas. In fact, she is quoted by Prince von Buelow as having said, "My son will be the ruin of Germany." {CE; JM; RE}

VICTORIAN HUMANIST

An Australian publication, *Victorian Humanist* is at GPO Box 1555 P, Melburne, Victoria 3001, Australia.

E-mail: <leeman@connexus.apana.org.au>.

Vidal, Gore (1925–)

Vidal's original name was Eugene Luther Gore Vidal, the first two being his father's names. Although his forte is history, he is better known as a novelist whose *Myra Breckenridge* (1968) was turned into a movie that starred Mae West, among other novels. Vidal, also a playwright and critic, shocked the public in 1948 when *The City and the Pillar* was published, its main character being a homosexual.

Known for being highly acerbic, Vidal for example said of Aleksandr Solzhenitsyn, "He is a bad novelist and a fool. The combination usually makes for great popularity in the United States." Of Ronald Reagan: "A triumph of the embalmer's art." Of Truman Capote: "Truman Capote has made lying an art. A *minor* art." Upon hearing about Capote's death: "Good career move." Of fame: "Never miss a chance to have sex or appear on television." Of America: "The civilization whose absence drove Henry James to Europe." Of theology: "Once people get hung up on theology, they've lost sanity forever. More people have been killed in the name of Jesus Christ than any other name in the history of the world." He is not so well-known for a first-rate essay, "Pink Triangle and Yellow Star" (1976).

In 1992, the gospel according to Gore Vidal was entitled *Live From Golgotha*, a Vidalian satire as blasphemous as anything Salman Rushdie might imagine. It describes an NBC camera crew that somehow is able to break the time barrier and photograph Jesus's crucifixion, live from Calvary. The well-endowed bishop of Ephesus, the heterosexual Timothy, who is represented as having once been an acolyte and "love toy" of St. Paul, is the storyteller whose relationship with Paul is revealed. This leaves the telecasters certain the show will boost NBC's fall ratings. "I'm really interested now," Vidal stated in 1992, "in trying to destroy monotheism in the United States. That is the source of all the problems." The novel was both praised and panned by Robert Gorham Davis in *Free Inquiry* (Spring, 1993): "Vidal can make his alter ego, the rascally slangy Timothy (with 'the largest dick in our part of Asia Minor'), a charming though unlikely narrator. But Vidal's satire on television moguls is too trite and predictable to teach us anything, and his travesty of early Christianity so outrageously broad as to be irrelevant to those holding present-day Christian beliefs and unilluminating to those who have already rejected them."

The Essential Gore Vidal (1998), the title implying one really should read *everything* by the author, is an anthology edited by Fred Kaplan, one that spans five decades of his work. Kaplan's *Gore Vidal: A Biography* (1999) contained few new facts about his subject. Kaplan cites Vidal's affair with Anaïs Nin and mentions his being a regular customer at a Times Square gay hangout, the Astor Bar.

The Smithsonian Institution: A Novel (1999) includes a what-if plot; for example, what if key historical events had happened differently; e.g., if Mr. Lincoln had been rescued at Ford's Theater, if there had been no Adolf Hitler on the scene in 1939; if Franklin Roosevelt had had only the Japanese to fight in the 1940s.

A revealing work, *Sexually Speaking* (1999), suggests that George Washington had a homosexual side, that a touch of Norman Mailer's feminism is apparent, and that Eleanor Roosevelt had sapphic tendencies.

The autobiograpy, *Palimpsest* (1995), remains one of his best works. It describes the major love of his life, a school-friend Jimmy Trimble, who was killed on Iwo Jima in 1945. He tells of his father's fame as a football star, his success in aviation, and his having three testicles; relates stories about his grandfather, Senator Thomas P. Gore of Oklahoma; writes of his mother's alcoholism and his decision when thirty-two to cut all ties with her; gossips about VIPs in Washington, D.C., including sexual references about President Kennedy; has stories about Truman Capote, Tennessee Williams, Princess Margaret, Christopher Isherwood, and numerous others.

Christopher Hitchens has made a shrewd observation about the wide variety in Vidal's work, that his achievements as a writer

> . . . can recur to a favored subject many times without repeating himself. Three Vidalian commitments seem to undergird what he writes on any topic. The first is the curse of monotheism: enemy of pleasure and foe of rational inquiry. The second is the blight of sexual stereotyping. (He insists that *acts*, not persons, are homo- or heterosexual.) The third is the awful temptation of America to meddling and blundering overseas: imperialism, to give it the right name.

In 1954 he wrote the present author concerning humanism:

> I have put most of my attitudes into *The Judgment of Paris* (1952; revised, 1965), a comedy, and *Messiah* (1954; revised, 1965), a tragedy. I can think of no one label which particularly fits me, though some odd ones have got applied along the way! I should say, though, right off, that I am not interested in any of the theologies I have ever heard of, despite the indubitable charm of the divers sacred books of this world. I do not see any law to the universe though I am perfectly prepared to entertain the idea that one exists. Though I am no mathematician, I am reasonably confident that Einstein's Unified Field Theory will prove inconclusive, to say the least. The origin of the universe is a fact *not* in the mind of man. Therefore, I doubt if it can be discovered at the far end of a syllogism, much less an equation. "We are all dullards in divinity; we know nothing," as Anaxandrides put it. I have always thought the game of first causes amusing but pointless. The origin of the universe is mystery and its fate is a mystery. We know it is in a state of flux. We know it is changing. That is all we know, or are ever apt to know. In one short century we have discarded so many 'undying' truths that I suspect soon we will be able, a few of us at least, to get along without absolutes, other than those expedient ones we use to regulate society.
>
> I suppose I am closer to Lucretius and the Atomists than to any of the Christian divines or their philosophic antagonists in the last century, writers amongst whose works I have sniffed like a curious but not a hungry dog. I do not, very simply, believe. I have attitudes, opinions, and I observe but that is all. I attempt, through literature, to make order in the moral, the human sphere (and only in the human scale do our actions matter—the stars are inattentive, I suspect). I reject the idea, even semantically, of the supernatural because all is natural. We call supernatural only those events which are inexplicable or, worse, inconvenient. In human affairs, political affairs, I am continually at sea. Sometimes I incline toward benevolent tyranny, other times toward oligarchy in the Platonistic sense. I have even thought an enlightened Republic might work, but since I have never had the experience of living under any one of these governments I shall probably never know what I think.
>
> Finally, *au fond*, I have a sense of reality which prevents me from being either optimistic or gloomy. I can imagine vividly all the millennia when this world was uninhabited by men and I can imagine, with equal equanimity, a cold, dusty planet on which the race of man

has long since perished, his entire history a brief instant in creation, his works and days all gone at least in that spiraling bright flux we call the universe. This sense of eternity (there is no better word), of unhuman duration makes it possible for me to live without too much agony in an unreasoning civilization where men seldom contain for long the predatory life force within which exists only by the displacement, the assimilation of other life. We are cancers: the body we prey on is the earth . . . and one another. The most one can do, that *I* can do, is to arrange my better daydreams so that they may prove communicable to others, decorating their solitude, relieving my own. I take pleasure in writing, and in the act indulge myself in a double vision hard to explain to others: realizing poignantly on the one hand that I and my race are nothing in eternity and yet aware, at the precise same moment, that, to me at least, literature, art together matter more than anything else, save kindness. The dogmatic, needless to say, cannot entertain two conflicting realities at the same time in their pursuit of certainty and its devilish accomplice power. I am more modest, less ambitious. I *know* we shall not endure. But the present is all time . . . and enough.

Vidal also went on record concerning religion:

> I regard monotheism as the greatest disaster ever to befall the human race. I see no good in Judaism, Christianity, or Islam—god people, yes, but any religion based on a single, well, frenzied, and virulent god, is not as useful to the human race as, say, Confucianism, which is not a religion but an ethical and educational system.

Elected to the American Academy of Arts and Letters, Vidal declined, stating, "Thanks, but I already belong to the Diners Club." In 1999, to the surprise of many, he accepted membership in the Academy but was not present on the date of the awards.

In 1995, after leaving unanswered many offers to become listed as Humanist Laureate in the International Academy of Humanism, he was approached by the present writer, whom he had never before seen. "Mr. Vidal," he was told in a dour voice, and brusquely, "you and I are in love with the same man!" Conversation in the vicinity hushed. A publisher's representative approached. The novelist was taken aback, looking quizzically ahead and wondering what was about to transpire. After a studied pause, during which I looked somewhat stonily into his eyes, I relaxed. "The man? Lucretius."

"Oh," he laughed uproariously, "and Tiberius and Apuleius, too?"

The amused Vidal then accepted an envelope containing a copy of *Free Inquiry* along with a stamped, self-addressed envelope with a typed statement, "I agree to be listed as a Humanist Laureate," under which was a "Yes" and a line for him to sign his name. In the mail two days later was the envelope, in which, indeed, was the signed agreement. {CA; CE; E; GL; Christopher Hitchens, *The New York Review of Books*, 22 April 1999; TYD; WAS, 25 August 1954; WAS 12 October 1995.}

VIDUTHALAI

A Tamil rationalist daily, *Viduthalai* is at 50, E. V. K. Sampath Salai, Chennai (Madras) 600 007, India.

Vidyasagar, Isvar Chandra (19th Century)

According to Sibnarayan Ray of City College, Calcutta University, Vidyasagarwas one of the outstanding secular humanists in India of the 19th century. However, his work has not been translated from Bengali into English. (See also the entries for Nehru and Sibnarayan Ray.)

Vigeland, Gustav (1869–1943)

Vigeland is a Norwegian sculptor whose nude figures in Oslo's Frogner Park, according to Corliss Lamont, symbolize "the life and aspirations of man." The park contains tree groups, reliefs, thirty-six large granite groups in twelve rows radiating from a column more than fifty-five feet tall, containing 121 figures in gray granite. Vigeland is author of *The Condition of Man*. {CE; CL}

Vigeland, Kari (20th Century)

Vigeland is a Norwegian humanist leader who is Secretary-General of the Norwegian Humanist Association (HEF). Also, she has been a Board member and co-president of the International Humanist and Ethical Union from 1983 to 1987. A professor of psychology at the University of Oslo, Vigeland has described the humanist movements in Norway, Denmark, Sweden, Finland, and Iceland in "The Norwegian Humanist Movement and Its Emphasis on Non-Theistic Ceremonies." She is co-chair of the International Humanist and Ethical Union (IHEU).

Vigny, Alfred Victor Comte de (1797–1863)

A French poet, novelist, and dramatist, Vigny was one of the foremost romantics. He expressed a philosophy of stoical pessimism, stressing the lonely struggle of the individual in a hostile universe. Unlike the other romantics, Vigny did not emphasize personal emotion; instead, he presented his ideas through general symbols with dramatic force. Although his reputation temporarily was dimmed by that of Hugo and Lamartine, it was revived by the time of Baudelaire. Vigny was known for professing a sort of sentimental Christianity in his early works, but according to McCabe in his later work "he is completely atheistic." {CE; JM; RE}

Vijayam, G. (20th Century)

Dr. Vijayam is executive director of the Atheist Centre in Vijayawada, India. Article 51A(h) of India's Constitution states that it is the fundamental duty of every citizen "to promote scientific temper, spirit of enquiry, reform and humanism." The Indian humanism is based on compassion, fellow-feeling, and on rendering timely help to the needy. For example, Indumati Parikh's "Stree Hitakarini" works in the slums of Bombay. Malladi Subbamma renders assistance to women in distress. Hemalata Lavanam works among the jogins. V. M. Tarkunde strives for civil liberties. Dr. Samaram leads a crusade for sex education and for dispelling superstitions. India's humanist pioneers were Periyar, E. V. Ramaswamy, M. N. Roy, Gora, and A. T. Kovoor. In *The Atheist* (India, August 1991), Vijayam wrote an article, "Charles Bradlaugh: Ardent Champion of Atheism and Secularism." Vijayam was a participant in the 1996 Humanist World Congress held in Mexico City.

Vikin, Joe (1933–)

Vikin, formerly a professor of chemistry at Corning Community College, is a trainer at the Center for Diversity Training (PO Box 515, Corning, NY 14830). A freethinker, he was a member of the NY Society for Ethical Culture when he lived in Brooklyn. When he moved upstate, he joined the Unitarian Universalist Fellowship of Big Flats. He is the author of "Diversity, Trust and Tolerance" and "Diversity: A Poetic Celebration," both used by the Center in their training. He also wrote "Herstory: A Sampling from 1421 to 1775" and "Biblical Stories: Throw the Water Out, Keep the Baby." Born in Colombia, Vikin had a grandmother of the Quimbaya tribe and other ancestors who were Basques. He has been in the United States since 1954. (WAS, interview by Internet.)

VILAGOSSOAG (Light)

A Hungarian publication, *Vilagossoag* is at H-1054 Budapest, Szenese Street 10, Hungary.

Villard, Oswald Garrison (1872–1949)

Villard was on the advisory board of Charles Francis Potter's First Humanist Society of New York. A journalist, he wrote *Memoirs of a Liberal Editor* (1939) and in 1943 a biography of John Brown. As the editor of *Nation*, Villard made it a leading liberal journal. When in 1940 the magazine became non-pacifist, he severed all connections. {CE}

Villari, Pasquale (1826–1917)

An Italian historian and statesman, Villari fought against the Papal troops in the Revolution of 1848, served in the legislative chamber (1867–1882), and was minister of education (1889–1892). He wrote works on Savonarola, Machiavelli, Dante, Cavour, Galileo, and Garibaldi. McCabe wrote of Villari that "after the liberation of Italy from the Popes, he attained the highest honors in the state (Minister of Education, etc.) and the academic world. He does not conceal his freethinking in his preface to Negri's *Julian the Apostate*." {CE; JM; RAT; RE}

Vincent, Henry (1813–1878)

Vincent was a reformer who, at the age of eleven, had to earn his living as an apprentice to a printer. As he matured, he was active in the early reform movement and threw himself into the Chartist agitation. Molesworth said of Vincent that he was "the Demosthenes" of the movement. In 1839 Vincent was condemned, though plainly innocent, to a year in prison, and he was so vilely treated that Lord Brougham protested in the House. A body of 20,000 armed miners tried to release him. In 1840 Vincent again suffered a year's vile treatment in prison, after which he moved to Bath and edited the *Vindicator*. He made successful lecture tours in America. Although he never joined any denomination, Vincent gave lay sermons at services of the Society of Friends. He was married in a Registry Office and was a theistic "Free Christian." {RAT}

Vincent, Tom (20th Century)

Vincent is President of the Arizona Secular Humanists. On the Web: <http://getnet.com/ ~huey/ash.html>.

Vinson, John (20th Century)

Vinson, lawyer for Madalyn Murray O'Hair, declared bankruptcy after working for, and then falling out with, O'Hair. "She treated the organization as her own charity," he complained. "The money would come in and it would all just basically go to the same place," one of her companies. {*Vanity Fair*, March 1997}

Virchow, Rudolf (1821–1902)

Virchow was a German pathologist, a founder of cellular pathology. He became director of the Pathological Institute in Berlin in 1856. Virchow contributed to nearly every branch of medical science as well as to anthropology, and he introduced sanitary reforms in Berlin. He was a member of the Prussian lower house and later of the Reichstag (1880–1893). Also, he was a leader of the liberal Progressive party opposed to Bismarck. In 1847, Virchow founded the *Archiv für pathologische Anatomie und Physiologie und für klinische Medizin*. Although Virchow's scientific views were advanced, he opposed Haeckel in regard to absolute teaching of evolution. For some years he led the Freethinking Liberals in the Reichstag, especially in the attacks on Catholics. Virchow thought that Darwinism led to Socialism, leading Darwin to write Haeckel, "Virchow's conduct is shameful, and I hope he will some day feel the shame." However, contemporary freethinkers often cite Virchow as one of their inspirations. {BDF; CE; JM; RAT; RE}

Viret, Pierre (17th Century?)

Viret was the first to use "Deist" to describe those who believe in God but not in the divinity of Jesus. He was a Swiss Protestant. {FUS}

Virgil: See entry for Vergil.

VIRGIN BIRTH

Egyptians have believed that their queens were impregnated by the gods, and the Japanese have believed that the first emperor was born of a goddess—a part of the collusion of kings and priests in order to sustain the power of both. Diogenes Laertius in his *Life of Plato* wrote that the Greek philosopher's nephew, Speusippus, claimed that Plato's mother conceived him by a god, and later Buddhist literature says the same of Gautama's mother. Plutarch gave and defended the legend of Plato.

Justin in the second century appealed to the pagans to see the reasonableness of the Christian belief that Mary conceived Jesus by a miracle, without male contact, in light of their own belief in the divine impregnation of Leda, Semele, Danae, and others by Zeus. When in the early 1920s the bishops of the Protestant Episcopal Church of America tried to enforce the belief in the Virgin Birth, the professors of their chief theological school (Cambridge) issued a work, *Creeds and Loyalties* (1923), in which they pointed out that the legend was a late interpolation in the New Testament, and to be rejected. This interpretation is confirmed by several reference in the Gospels to the "brothers" of Jesus, and the apologetic reply that this means "cousins" is strained and arbitrary, according to McCabe. Modernists are said to reject Virgin Birth although Catholics, Baptists, Methodists, and others strictly adhered to it up to the 1940s.

Meanwhile, secular humanists, upon hearing about virgin births, suspect sexual cover-ups. (See entry for William Provine.) {RE}

VIRGIN MARY: See entry for the Great Mother Goddess.

Virgin Mary, the Holy: See entry for Chris Ofili, an African whose painting "The Holy Virgin Mary" is collaged with lumps of elephant dung and close-up photographs of female genitalia. Shown in Berlin and London to throngs, it faced trouble in New York City when Mayor Rudy Giuliani—a Catholic—found it "offensive" and threatned to evict the museum in which it was shown.

VIRGIN MARY SHRINES

Shrines to the Virgin Mary are ubiquitous around the world. Mary is often depicted with baby and halo, and the shrines are found not only on but also off church property. Some are placed in the countryside, and others are featured in art museums.

"La Adolorida de Bucay" at the Guayaquil Municipal Museum in Ecuador appears at first glance to show a sad Virgin Mary, her hands folded, and the words (translated, "The Afflicted One of Bucay") in the background. Upon closer inspection, however, one notices that the virgin, her heart pierced with miniature swords, holds a knife in one of her crossed hands, a dismembered penis in the other. The work is framed by condoms and an urn of plastic feces. This "virgin" is Lorena Bobbitt, who angrily had cut her husband John Wayne Bobbitt's penis off to the delight of the international media, which featured the story about the dysfunctional married couple during the 1990s. The work won artist Hernán Zúñiga second prize in Ecuador's annual art show, "Salón de Julio."

VIRGINIA FREETHINKERS, HUMANISTS

Virginia has the following groups:

• American Humanist Association, Mid-Atlantic Region (AHA), 3708 Brightview Street, Wheaton, Maryland 20902. Roy R. Torcaso is coordinator for the District of Columbia, Delaware, Maryland, and Virginia.

• Central Virginia Secular Humanists (ASHS; chapter of WASH), PO Box 184, Ivy, VA 22945 (804) 979-2508. E-mail: <cvsh@rlc.net>.

• Humanists in the Jefferson Tradition (AHA), R-4, Box 411, Bassett, Virginia 24055. Preston Page is the president.

• Northern Virginia Secular Humanists (ASHS; chapter of WASH), 6400 Lyric Lane, Falls Church, VA 22044 (703) 256-4192. E-mail: <secularhumanists@hotmail.com>. On the Web: <http://www.noves.org/> and <http://www.jjnet.com/jjtalks>.

• Radford University humanists and freethinkers: <www.secularhumanism.org/cfa/orgs.html>.

• Richmond Area Free-Thinkers (RAFT) (ASHS, a chapter of WASH, c/o Kim Carlton, PO Box 3916, Richmond, VA 23235; (804) 560-0055 or (804) 560-6903. E-mail: <freethinkers@hotmail.com>.

• *Savant of Virginia*, POB 911, Rocky Mount, Virginia 24151. Abram B. Carter edits the publication for members who were in the (now formally dissolved) Society of Evangelical Agnostics and for a wide range of independent thinkers.

• Secular Humanists of Roanoke, 180 Bailey Blvd., Hardy, Virginia 24101; (540) 890-3957. E-mail: <NurXand@aol.com>.

• University of Virginia's Atheist-Freethought Alliance is on the Web at <www.secularhumanism.org/cfa/orgs.html>.

• Virginia Polytechnic Institute and State University's freethinkers are on the Web at <www.secularhumanism.org/cfa/orgs.html>.

• Virtual Ethical Society has a homepage at <www.aeu.org>.

• Washington Area Secular Humanists (WASH), PO Box 15319, Washington, DC 20003; (202) 298-0921. E-mail: <secularhumanists@hotmail.com>. Web: <www.wash.org>.

VIRGINITY

• Virginity is like a bubble. It lasts until it meets up with a prick.

"The Mystery of Irma Vepp"
a 1984 play by Charles Ludlam and Everett Quinton

A 1966 *Playboy* survey of 10,000 people in fifteen countries found that the average age for loss of virginity in the United States was 16.2 years. The global average for loss of virginity was 17.6 years.

VIRGINS

Elizabeth Bailey, sixty-four, became the first officially consecrated virgin in almost 900 years when the Vatican revived a holy rite in 1970, one which had encouraged life-long vows of chastity among lay people. The tradition had ended in Britain in the 3rd century and was phased out entirely by the Church during the 10th century.

Although the virgins have no official network or organization within the Church, according to the news agency Reuters, more than twenty-five countries have reinstituted the ancient rite in which virgins pledge themselves as servants of God. Freethinkers are aghast at such a cruel practice. (See entry for Virgin Mary.) {*NY Daily News*, 20 May 1997}

Virolleaud, Charles (1879–1968)

Virolleaud, a freethinker, wrote *The Legend of Christ* (1908). {GS}

VIRTUAL ETHICAL SOCIETY: See entry for Jone Johnson.

VIRUSES, RELIGIOUS

Religion is a virus of the mind, Richard Dawkins posits in *Viruses of the Mind, the 1992 Voltaire Lecture.* If it were judged by criteria best adapted to selecting true beliefs and beneficial behavior, religion would not be accepted, he holds. In the future, tests might be devised to show that religious viruses, like other self-replicators, are harmful to their hosts. In *Free Inquiry* (Summer 1993), the cover of which has the heading IS RELIGION A FORM OF INSANITY?, Dawkins develops his argument: "It is no wonder that child brains are gullible, open to almost any suggestion, vulnerable to subversion, easy prey to Moonies (followers of the Korean religious leader Sun Myung Moon, who was convicted in 1982 of brainwashing converts and of various illegal activities), scientologists, and nuns. Like immune-deficient patients, children are wide open to mental infections that adults might brush off without effort." (See entry for Richard Dawkins.)

Vischer, Friedrich Theodor (1807–1887)

Vischer was a German art critic. Educated for the Church, he became a minister, then renounced theology and became professor at Zürich. In 1844, because of his *Jahbücher der Gegenwart*, Vischer was accused of blasphemy for his freethinking opinions, and he was suspended for two years. Vischer wrote *Aesthetic*, concerning the science of the beautiful. {BDF; RAT}

VISHNU

In Hinduism, Vishnu is known as the Preserver. He has appeared as Krishna and as the Buddha, according to Hindus. {DCL}

Vispo, Adolfo (20th Century)

Vispo, an Argentinean, is a member of the Ibero-American Commission, a group of humanist leaders in Spanish-speaking countries.

Visscher, Maurice Bolkes (Born 1901)

Dr. Visscher, a physician and professor emeritus of the University of Minnesota, signed Humanist Manifesto II. He wrote *Chemistry and Medicine* (1940) and *Humanistic Perspectives in Medical Ethics* (1972). In 1952, he was a director of the American Humanist Association. {HNS}

Visser, H. (20th Century)

A Dutch humanist, Visser spoke at the first International Multidisciplinary Conference on Human Behaviour and the Meaning of Modern Humanism. The conference was held in 1995 in Delphi, Greece.

Vitale, A. (20th Century)

An Italian, Vitale addressed the Fourth International Humanist and Ethical Union World Congress held in Paris (1966).

Vitry, Guarin de (19th Century)

A French author, Vitry wrote *Rapid Examination of Christian Dogma*, which he addressed to the Council of 1869. {BDF}

Vitzthum, Richard C. (1936–)

Vitzthum wrote *Materialism: An Affirmative History and Definition* (1995), a short but thorough history of materialism. He has chapters on Lucretius's *On the Nature of Things*, d'Holbach's *The System of Nature*, and Büchner's *Force and Matter*. In the present century, Vitzthum discusses the speculations about materialism by C. D. Broad, Roy Wood Sellars, Gilbert Ryle, D. M. Armstrong, John J. C. Smart, John R. Searle, and others. In a critique, Gordon Stein wrote that Vitzthum's study is far better than that on materialism by F. A. Lange. {*The American Rationalist*, March-April 1996}

Viviani, René Raphael (1863–1925)

Viviani was Minister of Labor under Clemenceau, and he secured the opening of the legal profession to women in France and other reforms. In his first speech as Minister, he created a sensation by saying that we have "slain the religious chimera" and "extinguished stars in the firmament which will never shine again." Viviani was an agnostic. {RAT; RE}

Vizetelly, Henry (1820–1894)

With his brother, Vizetelly started the *Pictorial Times* in London. In 1865 he went to Paris as correspondent of the *Illustrated London News*, remaining there until 1880. Vizetelly issued translations of Zola in 1884, and in 1888 he was fined £100 for publishing *The Soil.* In the following year, he courageously republished the whole of Zola's novels and was condemned to three months in prison. He described his life experiences in *Glances Back Through Seventy Years* (1893). Vizetelly had no more regard for religion than did Zola. {RAT}

Vizzuet, Juan A. (20th Century)

Vizzuet, a Mexican, spoke on new forms of production and the diffusion of art at the 1996 Humanist World Conference held in Mexico City.

Vladár, Leo V. (20th Century)

Vladár, from Czechoslovakia, addressed the Third International Humanist and Ethical Union World Congress held in Oslo (1962).

Vloten, Johannes van (1818–1883)

Vloten was a Dutch author who studied theology at Leiden, receiving his Doctorate of Divinity degree in 1843. He then devoted himself to literature, translating Shakespeare, editing Spinoza, and writing a life of Spinoza. Vloten edited *De Levensbode* (1865). {BDF; RAT}

Voas, David (20th Century)

Voas is author of *The Bad News Bible: The New Testament* (1995), in which he aims to make the least-read best-seller readable. He points out that studying the work can be an alarming experience. Jesus, for example, does not live up to his Good Shepherd reputation. And the promise of heaven comes from Paul, whose views on sex, women, and the family do little for his credibility. Voas is professor in the division of mathematics, science, and technology at New Mexico State University.

VOCABULARY: See entry for Language.

VOCAL

VOCAL is an abbreviation for Victims of Clergy Abuse Linkup, Inc. (See the entry for Jeanne Miller, its founder.)

Voelkel, Titus (Born 1841)

A German lecturer and writer who was born in Prussian Poland, Voelkel was a *sprecher* of freethought associations and an editor of *Neues Freireligioses Sonntags-Blatt* at Magdenburg. He was prosecuted several times in 1888 for blasphemy and each time was acquitted. At the Paris Congress of Freethinkers in 1889, Voelkel represented several German societies. {BDF; PUT; RAT}

Vogel, Catherine (Died 1539)

Vogel, a Polish noblewoman, was accused of being a heretic, and the Church set her ablaze along with others of her time who questioned religious doctrines. {U}

Vogel, Johann (17th Century)

A propagandist who in 1649 wrote *Meditationes emblematicae de restaurata pace Germaniae* in Nuremberg, Vogel was a practicing Socinian prior to his forced recantation.

Voglet, Prosper (Born 1825)

A Belgian singer, Voelkel was blinded through his baptism by a Catholic priest and, in consequence, earned his living as a street singer. His compositions are anti-religious, and many appeared in *La Tribune du Peuple*, which he edited. {BDF}

Vogt, Carl (1817–1895)

Vogt, the son of a distinguished naturalist, was a German scientist, a geologist, a physiologist, an atheist, and a scientific materialist. Finngeir Hiorth has compared Vogt with Karl Marx, "but it is clear that Vogt's anarchism and laissez-faire ideology were quite different from Marx's ideas. Vogt spoke of 'false prophets' without thinking of Marx. But eventually his words applied to authoritarian Marxism." (*New Humanist*, February 1994). In fact, he came to dislike Marx, and the hatred was mutual. Vogt at one time worked as an assistant for Louis Agassiz in Neuchâtel, met anarchists such as Michael Bakunin and Pierre Joseph Proudhon in Paris, and wrote books on physiology and science. According to Hiorth, Vogt came to denounce the middle class, religion, and all forms of government, and he called for the establishment of anarchy. He attacked Rudolph Wagner as a superstitious scientist who still believed in a Creator. Vogt's importance, Hiorth writes, is that he "influenced the philosophical pattern of 'scientific' or physicalistic materialism, as different from historical and dialectical materialism. In this way Vogt played an important role in the rise of atheism and materialism in Germany. He once referred to Christmas as "the festival which brought the hypocrisy of humility into the world." In addition Vogt's activity as a political radical is of great interest." Vogt's lectures on *Man, His Position in Creation and in the History of the Earth* (1863) endorsed Darwinism. He contributed to the leading freethought journals of Germany and Switzerland. {BDF; HNS2; JM; RAT; RE; TRI}

VOICE OF REASON

A quarterly, *Voice of Reason* is at PO Box 6656, Silver Spring, Maryland.

Voisin, Marcel (20th Century)

Voisin, a professor of philosophy, is a Belgian who has written *Vivre La Laïcite* (Experiencing Humanism). For him, it is not enough "merely to suppress the reference to a divinity or the supernatural," for moral teaching must build up alternate ideas. These include relativity of values; systematic doubt; concern about search for evidence; a constant endeavor to conquer rationality; an optimistic vision of man inspired by the thought "If pleasure is easy, happiness has to be taught"; promotion of a responsible citizenship and active civic duties; a special care about justice; self-awareness and curiosity about the world around us; and dialogue with others, generosity, and humor.

Volkmar, Gustav (1809–1893)

Volkmar was a Swiss critic. Among his many rationalist works are *The Gospel of Marcion* (1852), *Justin Martyr* (1853), *The Origin of the Gospels* (1866), and *Jesus and the First Christian Ages* (1882). {BDF; RAT}

Volney, Constantin François de Chasseboeuf de [Comte] (1757–1820)

A French scholar, Volney wrote *Méditation sur les révolutions des empires* (1791), popularizing religious skepticism. His work was influential both in England and in the United States, where he spent some time. His freethinking books were translated widely and stimulated much controversy because of their deistic attacks on Christianity. A friend of d'Holbach, Count Volney was a wealthy landlord who wrote and spoke for the division of landed property. During the Terror, he was imprisoned for ten months. When Napoleon asked him to become a colleague in the consulship, Volney declined. Volney also wrote *A History of Samuel* (1819), which sometimes is wrongly ascribed to Voltaire, and *The Law of Nature*.

A religious tract alleged that during a storm, Volney became cowardly and threw himself on the ship's deck and cried, "Oh, my God, my God!" When one of the passengers inquired, "There is a God, then, Monsieur Volney?, he responded, "Oh, yes, there is, there is. Lord save me!" But, when the vessel arrived in port, the story continued, Volney "returned to his atheistical sentiments." The fictional story appeared in *Tract Magazine* (July 1832) and in the eighth volume of the *Evangelical Magazine*.

Adolphe Bossange, in a notice prefixed to an 1838 edition of his works, gave the following account of Volney's last hours: "His health, which had always been delicate, became languid, and soon he felt his end was approaching. It was worthy of his life. He dictated his will with the utmost calmness, and not abandoning at the last moment the idea which had never ceased to occupy his mind during twenty-five years and doubtless fearing that his labors would be brought to a cessation by his death, he devoted the sum of 24,000 francs to founding an annual prize for the best essay on the philosophical study of languages." Three days prior, when Volney spoke to his doctor, he said, "I know the custom of your profession, but I wish you not to play on my imagination like that of other patients. I do not fear death. Tell me frankly what you think of my condition, for I have arrangements to make." When the physician appeared to hesitate, Volney said, "I know enough. Let them bring a notary." Abbé Migne, in the *Catholic Dictionary*, wrote, "It appears that in his last moments he refused the consolations of religion." {BDF; CE; FO; FUK; JM; JMR; JMRH; RAT; RE}

Voltaire, François-Marie Arouet de (1694–1778)

One of the most beloved of writers named by other humanists, Voltaire is a towering genius in intellectual and literary history. A skeptic and deist, he has the distinction of having merited thirty specific works on the Vatican's index of prohibited reading. Son of the Paris notary Arouet—Voltaire is a later pen-name—he was educated by the Jesuits, who found that early on he distinguished himself by his wit.

Among his witty Gallic morsels: "England has 42 religions and only 2 sauces." Of martyrs, he wrote, "We can only burst into laughter at all the humbug we are told about martyrs. . . . Can it be seriously repeated, that the Romans condemned seven virgins, each seventy years old, to pass through the hands of all the young men of the city of Ancyra—those Romans who punished the Vestals with death for the least gallantry?"

Today he is best known for his *Candide* (1759; the word comes from the Latin for "glowing with innocence"), in which he satirizes Leibniz's philosophy of optimism. "Let us cultivate our garden," he concludes in common sense fashion instead of advising that we should spend our lives speculating about unanswerable questions.

Voltaire opposed atheism as well as materialism, reportedly saying of Helvétius and Holbach, although some claim it is a false quotation, that "if God did not exist, he would have to be invented." He smiled, however, that "atheism is the vice of a few intelligent people." He thought Christianity was ideal for chambermaids and tailors but thought deism was best for the elite. He had learned about deism as a boy, for his godfather, a priest, is said to have taught him at the age of three a poem by J. B. Rousseau (not Jean Jacques Rousseau). That was a poem in which Moses and religious revelations in general are derided as being fraudulent. Voltaire's anticlericalism was such that he called the Jews "an ignorant and barbarous people, who have long united the most sordid avarice with the most detestable superstition." In "For and Against," Voltaire wrote, "I am not a Christian." He also wrote

> I tried to believe in God, but I confess to you that God meant nothing in my life, and that in my secret heart I too felt a void where my childhood faith had been. But probably this feeling belonds only to invidual in transition. The grandchildren of these pessimists will frolic in the freedom of their lives, and have more happiness than poor Christians darkened with fear of Hell.

This he confirmed in a letter to Frederick the Great:

> Christianity is the most ridiculous, the most absurd, and bloody religion that has ever infected the world.

For a satirical pamphlet on the death of Louis XIV Voltaire was sent to the Bastille for a year (1716) and, afterwards, was committed again for a quarrel with the Chevalier de Rohan—he threatened to duel his footmen, having been assaulted by them. On his liberation Voltaire went to England at the invitation of Lord Bolingbroke, where he became acquainted with the English freethinkers. He spent most of his life in exile for the right of free speech, moving to Prussia and, from 1758 until his death, on the border of Switzerland in the event he had to flee. "During all this time," McCabe wrote, "most of the chief bishops and archbishops lived in open license and luxury, and their modern successors profess to be shocked at the wicked Voltaire!"

According to Wheeler, Voltaire dedicated *Mahomet* to the Pope, "who was unable to see that its shafts were aimed at the pretences of the church." Wheeler adds that in 1750 Voltaire accepted Frederick II's invitation to reside at his court, "but he could not help laughing at the great king's poetry." Wheeler holds that Voltaire "did more than any other man of his century to abolish torture and other relics of barbarism, and to give just notions of history. To the last he continued to wage war against intolerance and superstition," using more than one hundred thirty different pen-names.

Parton's *Life of Voltaire* (Vol. II) tells of the following insight into Voltaire's personality: While the great philosopher was living at Ferney in 1768, he gave a curious exhibition of that profane sportiveness which was a strong element in his character. On Easter Sunday he took his Secretary Wagniere with him to commune at the village church, and also "to lecture a little those scoundrels who steal continually." Apprised of Voltaire's sermon on theft, the Bishop of Anneci rebuked him, and finally "forbade every curate, priest, and monk of his diocese to confess, absolve, or give the communion to the seigneur of Ferney, without his express orders, under pain of interdiction." With a wicked light in his eyes, Voltaire said he would commune in spite of the Bishop; nay, that the ceremony should be gone through in his chamber. Then ensued an exquisite comedy. Feigning a deadly sickness, Voltaire took to his bed. The surgeon, who found his pulse was excellent, was bamboozled into certifying that he was in danger of death. Then the priest was summoned to administer the last consolation. The poor devil at first objected, but Voltaire threatened him with legal proceedings for refusing to bring the sacrament to a dying man, who had never been excommunicated. This was accompanied with a grave declaration that M. de Voltaire "had never ceased to respect and to practice the Catholic religion." Eventually the priest came "half dead with fear." Voltaire demanded absolution at once, but the Capuchin pulled out of his pocket a profession of faith, drawn up by the Bishop, which Voltaire was required to sign. Then the comedy deepened. Voltaire kept demanding absolution, and the distracted priest kept presenting the document for his signature. At last the Lord of Ferney had his way. The priest gave him the wafer, and Voltaire declared, "Having God in my mouth," that he forgave his enemies. As soon as he left the room, Voltaire leapt briskly out of bed, where a minute before he seemed unable to move. "I have had a little trouble," he said to Wagniere, "with this comical genius of a Capuchin; but that was only for amusement, and to accomplish a good purpose. Let us take a turn in the garden. I told you I would be confessed and commune in my bed, in spite of M. Biord."

His *Mahomet* remains controversial. In 1994, when it was proposed to stage the play in Geneva, representatives of rival Islamic cultural centers denounced the threatened "blasphemy," and vague threats were made as to what might befall the actors, the directors, even the theatre-goers. In 1742 when the play had first been staged, an austere Catholic movement based at the Abbey of Port-Royal was similarly successful in stopping the production.

A profound and philosophic discussion of Voltaire's achievements is found in *Encyclopedia of Unbelief*, in which Paul Edwards discusses how Voltaire covered the problem of evil, the argument from design, mortality, and miracles. What, Voltaire was asked, would he say if he saw the sun stop, if all the dead came back to life, and if all mountains fell into the ocean at the same time. "I would turn Manichean," replied Voltaire. "I would say that there is one principle that unmakes what the other principle has made."

More than any of the other Founding fathers, Thomas Jefferson admired Voltaire. He had begun to read Voltaire during his student days at the College of William and Mary. While America's envoy to France, he acquired a complete set of Voltaire's works and also shipped a copy of Voltaire's memoirs back to James Madison in America. At Monticello Jefferson showed off a plaster bust of Voltaire made by the French sculptor Houdon and an inkwell bearing the likeness of the French philosophe, said to have been given him by Lafayette during his farewell tour to America in 1824.

Michael Foot (*New Humanist*, December 1988) states that, if virtue consists of doing good and if loving mankind with a passion constitutes being a saint, then Voltaire is one. He quotes Voltaire's witty description of a true saint, Professor Zapata, of the University of Salamanca: "He isolated truth from falsehood and separated religion from fanaticism. He taught and practised virtue. He was gentle, benevolent, modest; and was roasted at Valladolid in the year of grace, 1631." His criticism was not merely directed against Christianity, for his *Mahomet* (1742) dealt with the fanaticism of Islam. In his *Selected Works*, Voltaire apparently glimpsed into his own future when he wrote, "The man who says to men, 'Believe as I do, or God will damn you,' will presently say, 'Believe as I do, or I shall kill you.' "

"Animals have these advantages over man," Voltaire wrote in 1769. "They never hear the clock strike, they die without any idea of death; they have no theologians to instruct them, their last moments are not disturbed by unwelcome and unpleasant ceremonies, their funerals cost them nothing, and no one starts lawsuits over their wills."

A translation in English of Voltaire's *Philosophic Dictionary* is not in print, but a two-volume work in 1856 was advertised as the first American stereotyped edition. Under the A's, Voltaire included such as the following: Abraham, Adam, Adultery, Angels, Apocrypha, Apostate, Apostle, Ararat, Arianism, Aristotle, Army, Armies, Arts and Fine Arts, Ass, Astrology, Astronomy, Atoms, Avbarice, Augustine, Austerities, Authors, Authority. Under "Religion" in the dictionary, Voltaire starts as follows:

> The Epicureans, who had no religion, recommended retirement from public affairs, study, and concord. The sect was a society of friends, for friendship was their principal dogma.

He then says, while contemplating nature,

> when one of those genii who fill the spaces between worlds came down to me in order to reveal some of God's works. . . . [The genie took him to a desolate spot to show him] the 23,000 Jews who danced before a calf, together with the 24,000 who were slain while ravishing Midianitish women. . . . "Here," said the spirit," are the 12 millions of Americans, slain in their own country for not having been baptised . . . etc.

Voltaire, in *Micromégas*, wrote about "aliens from outer space" visiting earth. They came from Saturn and from a planet in the solar system of the star Sirius, sometimes traveling by comet, sometimes by light waves. Unlike humans, with their five or six senses, the Sirian had a thousand senses although the poor Saturnian had only seventy-two. Presumably, the expression, "aliens from outer space," was first used by Voltaire. The work contains jibes at the Jesuits, the sage who believes "God does everything for me," and other philosophical or religious outlooks. As noted by Jim Herrick, the work approves "the Lockean who thinks humans must rely on their senses for knowledge, must revere the eternal power, and be content to believe 'that more things are possible than we like to think.' "

Interesting fabrications have occurred concerning Voltaire's death. One is that in his last illness Voltaire sent for Dr. Tronchin. When the Doctor came, he found Voltaire in the greatest agony, exclaiming with the utmost horror, "I am abandoned by God and man." He then supposedly said, "Doctor, I will give you half of what I am worth, if you will give me six months' life." The doctor answered, "Sir, you cannot live six weeks." Voltaire replied, "Then I shall go to hell, and you will go with me!" and soon after expired.

Carlyle, the historian, relates the following: "Two days before that mournful death, M. l'Abbé Mignot, his nephew, went to seek the Curé of St. Sulpice and the Abbé Gautier, and brought them into his uncle's sick room; who, on being informed that the Abbé Gautier was there, 'Ah, well!' said be, 'give him my compliments and my thanks.' The Abbé spoke some words to him, exhorting him to patience. The Curé of St. Sulpice then came forward, having announced himself, and asked of M. de Voltaire, elevating his voice, if he acknowledged the divinity of our Lord Jesus Christ? The sick man pushed one of his hands against the Curé's *calotte* (coif), shoving him back, and cried, turning abruptly to the other side, 'Let me die in peace (*Laissez-moi mourir en paix*).' The Curé seemingly considered his person soiled, and his coif dishonored, by the touch of the philosopher. He made the sicknurse give him a little brushing, and then went out with the Abbé Gautier."

However, the *Columbia Encyclopedia* has a different account:

> In 1778, his 84th year, Voltaire attended the first performance of his tragedy, *Irène*, in Paris. His journey and his reception were a triumph and apotheosis, but the emotion was too much for him and he died of uremia in Paris soon afterward. In order to obtain Christian burial he signed a partial retraction of his writings. This was considered insufficient by the church, but he refused to sign a more general retraction. To a friend he gave the following written declaration, "I die adoring God, loving my friends, not hating my enemies, and detesting persecution."

"Contrary to Catholic libels," wrote McCabe, "he died peacefully (at 27 Rue des Sts.-Pères, near 1 Quai Voltaire), and he courteously declined to see the priest who wanted to be present."

Richard Holmes described the end as follows:

> Voltaire was exhausted, and in the privacy of his bedroom spitting blood. He died in much pain on May 30, 1778. He had received a Jesuit priest in his dying hours, whom he seems to have teased, as in the old days: on being urged to renounce the devil, Voltaire gently replied, "This is no time for making new enemies." But to the relief of Enlightenment Europe, he refused to renounce any of his works.

An abbot secretly conveyed Voltaire's corpse to an abbey in Champagne, where he was buried in 'unholy ground' but given Christian burial. His remains were brought back to Paris during the Revolution in 1791 and buried in the Panthéon.

Carlyle's description was as follows:

> He expired about a quarter past eleven at night, with the most perfect tranquillity, after having suffered the cruelest pains in consequence of those fatal drugs, which his own imprudence, and especially that of the persons who should have looked to it, made him swallow. Ten minutes before his last breath he took the hand of Morand, his valet-de-chambre, who was, watching him; pressed it, and said, "*Adieu, mon cher Morand, je me meurs* (Adieu, my dear Morand, I am gone)." These are the last words uttered by M. de Voltaire.

Sir Charles Morgan published further details, using extracts from a letter by Dr. Burard who, as assistant physician, was with Voltaire in his last moments:

> I feel happy in being able, while paying homage to truth, to destroy the effects of the lying stories which have been told respecting the last moments of M. de Voltaire. I was, by office, one of those who were appointed to watch the whole progress of his illness, with M. M. Tronchin, Lorry, and Try, his medical attendants. I never left him for an instant during his last moments, and I can certify that we invariably observed in him the same strength of character, though his disease was necessarily attended with horrible pain. (Here follow the details of his case.) We positively forbade him to speak in order to prevent the increase of a spitting of blood, with which he was attacked; still he continued to communicate with us by means of little cards, on which he wrote his questions; we replied to him verbally, and if he was not satisfied, he always made his observations to us in writing. He therefore retained his faculties up to the last moment, and the fooleries which have been attributed to him are deserving of the greatest contempt. It could not even be said that such or such person had related any circumstance of his death as being witness to it; for at the last, admission to his chamber was forbidden to any person. Those who came to obtain intelligence respecting the patient, waited in the saloon, and other apartments at hand. The proposition, therefore, which has been put in the mouth of Marshal Richelieu is as unfounded as the rest.

Further proof that Voltaire made no recantation, according to Foote, lies in the fact that the Bishop of Troyes sent a peremptory dispatch to the Prior of Scellieres, which lay in his diocese, forbidding him to inter the heretic's remains. The dispatch, however, arrived too late, and Voltaire's ashes remained there until 1791, when they were removed to Paris and placed in the Pantheon, by order of the National Assembly. Foote insists that Voltaire made no recantation and refused to utter or sign a confession of faith. With the connivance of his nephew, in fact, he tricked the Church into granting him a decent burial, not choosing to be flung into a ditch or buried like a dog. His heresy was never seriously questioned at the time, and the clergy actually clamored for the expulsion of the Prior, who had allowed his body to be interred in a church vault. Another slander appears to emanate from the Abbé Barruel, who was so well informed about Voltaire that he called him "the dying Atheist," when, as was well known at the time, he was a Deist.

In the 1860s when Voltaire's tomb was opened in the 1860s, Voltaire was no longer there. Fanatics had pillaged his grave, throwing the remains onto a rubbish heap. His brain, kept in a jar and sold at auction to an unknown buyer, remains somewhere. His heart, bequeathed by the third marquis de Villette to the bishop of Orléans, who sold it to Napoleon III, who gave it to the National Library in Paris, remains in the National Library in Paris. (See entry for Intellecutals. Also see Norman L. Torrey's article on Voltaire in the *Encyclopedia of Philosophy*, Vol. 8. For samples of Voltaire's wit and wisdom, see the entry for Vampires in the present work. Also, see Richard Holmes, "Voltaire's Grin," *The New York Review of Books*, 30 November 1995—the extensive article includes Voltaire's writing about priests of every denomination who "rise from an incestuous bed, manufacure a hundred versions of God, then eat and drink God, then piss and shit God.") {CB; CE; CL; ER; EU, Paul Edwards; FO; FUK; HNS2; LP; JMR; JMRH; PA; RAT; RE; TRI; TSV; TYD}

VOLTAIRE SOCIETY

A Board of Directors composed of four governs the Voltaire Society of America: George W. Gowen, chairman; James W. Reid, president; Garry Agpar, secretary-treasurer; and Katrina de Carbonnel. On the Web: <http://humanities.uchicago.edu/homes/VSA>. By e-mail one can receive information about the newsletter: <garryapgar@aol.com>.

VOLTAIRE'S HOME AT FERNEY

The French government in 1998 was close to purchasing Voltaire's home at Ferney and turning it into a *Centre culturel de rencontres* to be known as *L'Auberge de l'Europe*. The title comes from Voltaire who liked to refer to himself as *l'aubergiste de l'Europe* (the innkeeper of Europe) because of the numerous visitors he received at Ferney over the years.

The Centre, which will be set up on Voltaire's former estate, is seen as having essentially three roles: (1) as a museum devoted to Voltaire's life and work; (2) as a focus of artistic creation, notably in the realm of the theater; and (3) as a center for the defense of human rights and of writers, like a Salman Rushdie, who are victims of persecution. Concurrently, there are plans at Ferney for a *Centre international d'étude du XVIIIe siècle*. {Voltaire Society of America Newsletter, April 1998. For information, e-mail: <garryapgar@aol.com>.}

von Behrens, Dierk (1938–)

Von Behrens arrived in Australia from Jaffa, Palestine, in 1951. He was founding secretary of the Humanist Society of South Australia (1962) and later was President of the Humanist Society of Canberra. In 1976 he initiated the first bibliography of humanism for the National Library. His interests include voluntary euthanasia, pro-choice, social justice, and participative democracy. {SWW}

von Braun, Wilhelm (19th Century)

A Swedish poet, von Braun carried on an anti-Biblical warfare in his work, according to Robertson. {JMR}

von Frankenberg, Gerhard (20th Century)

Representing Germany, von Frankenberg addressed the First International Congress on Humanism and Ethical Culture in Amsterdam (1952). At the 1968 Second European Conference (1968) in Hannover, von Frankenberg presided.

von Schiller: See entry for Johann Schiller

von Sydow, Max (Carl Adolph von Sydow) (1929–)

Von Sydow, the Swedish-born actor, is said "to look like God," or at least the one many Scandinavians envision. In the words of one Scandinavian Lutheran on the Internet, Von Sydow is tall, gaunt, and has white hair, pale skin, grey eyes. "In dark clothes, he stands on a lone, cold, wind-swept cliff, under a grey sky, gazing out over an empty grey sea. He has all the existential anxiety of ancient Odin. He knows he's not the God we'd like him to be, that God does not exist, but he is too proud to waste words explaining himself or apologizing. It makes him rather sad that we think God should be something else, but he's resigned himself to the situation."

Von Sydow acted at Malmo Stadsteater (1955–1960) and Stockholm's Dramaten. Ingmar Bergman movies he has played in are "The Seventh Insight" (1956), "The Face" (1958), "As In A Mirror" (1961), and "The Shame" (1968). He also was in "The Man From Nazareth" (1965), "The Exorcist" (1973), and "Flash Gordon" (1980).

During the filming of the "Exorcist," Von Sydow had troubles with his lines. His director, William Friedkin, said, "I threw the script on the bed, grabbed him, and said 'What the fuck is wrong?' He said, 'I don't believe in God, and I don't believe in this,' I said, 'But Max, you played Christ in 'The Greatest Story Ever Told.' He said, 'Yes. But I played him as a man.' " {CA; Thomas D. Clagett, *William Friedkin: Films of Aberration, Obsession, and Reality*, 1990; E}

Vonnegut, Bernard (1914–1997)

Vonnegut was a physicist, one of two researchers who first figured out how to wring more raindrops from cloud cover for croplands below. He taught atmospheric sciences at the State University of New York at Albany. During the 1940s, when his colleague Vincent J. Schaefer found that a tiny grain of dry ice produced millions of ice crystals when dropped into a cloud of water droplets below the freezing point, Vonnegut established that silver iodide got better results in nucleating clouds than did dry ice.

About his brother, the novelist Kurt Vonnegut wrote

> There is original virtue as well as original sin. My late brother, Bernard Vonnegut, whom I loved, had original virtue. He was a Ph. D. physical chemist out of M.I.T., famous for discovering that silver-iodide particles can make it snow or rain sometimes. From birth to death, Bernard was merrily appreciative of all the physical universe was doing, and was always generous and amiable, although somewhat absent-minded, no matter what was going on in the human sphere....
>
> When he died of cancer at the age of 82 last April, a widower for 25 years with five sons, he had become, arguably, the world's outstanding theoretician about thunderstorms.
>
> And, as I have said, Bernard was kind and reasonable. He was funny, often verging on hilarious, because devising and carrying out experiments was for him so terrifically amusing. It was almost as though, man and boy, he were playing jokes on Mother Nature, putting salt in her sugar bowl, say, to make her reveal a previously unsuspected facet of her personality.

Following Vonnegut's death from cancer, a private non-religious service was held. Peter, one of his five sons, has confirmed that his father was not a member of any organized faith. {*The New York Times*, 27 April 1997; *The New York Times Magazine*, 4 January 1998; Peter Vonnegut to WAS, 28 Apr 1997}

Vonnegut, Clemens (19th Century)

Vonnegut wrote *A Proposed Guide for Instruction in Morals from the Standpoint of a Freethinker* (published 1900). {FUS}

Vonnegut, Kurt Jr. (1922–)

Vonnegut, a fourth generation German-American, has said, "For at least four generations my family has been proudly skeptical of organized religion." His father designed a Unitarian chapel, and Vonnegut is a nominal Unitarian.

Once described by Graham Greene as "one of the best living American writers," Vonnegut writes wry, whimsical, and satirical works about organized religion and the horrors of contemporary life. His *Slaughterhouse Five* (1969) appealed to collegiates, although some have complained that he shows the lack of humanity which his works advocate. Pollution of the environment, dehumanization, mass death: All rate his disapproval as he evaluates this latter half of the century, despairing of the human condition. Martin Seymour-Smith, however, criticizes his work, saying its black pessimism, guiltily convoluted irony, and black humor tend to rob his work of lucidity. Others have objected to such of Vonnegut's statements as, "Say what you will about the sweet miracle of unquestioning faith, I consider a capacity for it terrifying and absolutely vile."

In *Slaughterhouse Five*, Vonnegut wrote, "During World War II, while I was serving with the Third Army in Germany, I removed a belt buckle from the uniform of a dead German soldier. The lettering on the buckle read *Gott Mit Uns* (God Is With Us)." "So it goes," he often comments about the human condition in which we find ourselves.

Cat's Cradle (1963) has Deweyan overtones of pragmatism, and many of his short stories also show humanistic touches. Its character, Bokonon, rejects the New Testament message of "Render unto Caesar the things which are Caesar's" to "Pay no attention to Caesar. Caesar doesn't have the slightest idea of what is going on." Bokonon, like a guru-figure, is humorous, anarchistic, pleasant, humanistic, and skeptical. To him, only man is sacred. Well-meaning lies help humanity more than absolute truths, he holds. What is sacred is not the beautiful sunrises, sunsets, and other delights of nature: What is sacred in Bokononism is man. Just man.

In 1969, J. Michael Crichton who had then received fame for his *Andromeda Strain* and since has become known for his *Jurassic Park*, wrote in *New Republic* (26 April 1969):

> A Vonnegut book is not cute or precious. It is literally awful, for Vonnegut is one of the few writers able to lift the lid of the garbage can, and dispassionately examine the contents. . . . The ultimate difficulty with Vonnegut is precisely this: that he refuses to say who is wrong. The simplest way . . . is to say that everything is wrong but the author. Any number of writers have done it, with good success. But Vonnegut refuses. He ascribes no blame, sets no penalties. His commentary on the assassination of Robert Kennedy and Martin Luther King is the same as his comment on all other deaths: "So it goes," he says and nothing more.

His work also includes *Player Piano* (1951) and *Deadeye Dick* (1982). Life, Vonnegut appears to say in his writings that some term "wacko stories," is a series of errors, orchestrated by a few mighty technocrats whose power is leading humanity into the ridiculousness of these our times. He neatly brings the message, but he implies, "Don't shoot the messenger." So it goes!

In a 1994 concert, the Magic Circle Opera Repertory Ensemble performed a Vonnegut poem, of which critic Bernard Holland wrote the following: "After intermission came Edgar David Grana's choral setting of 'Stones, Time and Elements,' a 'Humanist Requiem' in poetry written by Kurt Vonnegut Jr. What Mr. Grana's curious jumble of music does most egregiously is render Mr. Vonnegut helpless. Through the maze of overlapping musical styles, rhythms, meters and instrumental colors words rarely penetrated. All the musical gestures are familiar but are rearranged in new contexts. Post-modernism is meant to thrive on nonsense but here drowns under its weight." So it goes!

Whereas the 19th century boasted large numbers of Unitarians who were writers, Vonnegut is one of the few contemporary Unitarian authors. Asked why, he once said contemporary Unitarianism appears not to be so intellectually appealing in our time as it was in Emerson's and Coleridge's era. His *Fates Worse Than Death: An Autobiographical Collage of the 1980s* (1991) confirmed this, for he wrote, "I am an atheist (or at best a Unitarian who winds up in churches quite a lot)."

In 1992, Vonnegut was named Humanist of the Year by the American Humanist Association (AHA), of which he had become Honorary President and was on the editorial board of *The Humanist*. He is a Humanist Laureate in the Council for Secular Humanism's International Academy of Humanism and in 1993 accepted an honorary membership in the Secular Humanist Society of New York.

In 1994, when AHA President Michael Werner battled with the two co-editors of *The Humanist*, both cited editorial autonomy and left. This led Vonnegut to pull his name from the magazine's editorial advisory board. In doing so, he accused the AHA of being "highly politicized," adding that he might also resign his honorary presidency. He did not, however.

Timequake (1997) included the following:

> I am Honorary President of the American Humanist Association, whose headquarters in Amherst, New York, I have never seen. I succeeded the late author and biochemist Dr. Isaac Asimov in that functionless capacity. That we have an organization, a boring business, is to let others know we are numerous. We would prefer to live our lives as humanists and not talk about it or think amore about it than we think about breathing.
>
> Are we enemies of members of organized religions? No. My great war buddy Bernard V. O'Hare, now dead, lost his faith as a Roman Catholic during World War Two. I didn't like that. I thought that was too much to lose.

I had never had faith like that, because I had been raised by interesting and moral people who, like Thomas Jefferson and Benjamin Franklin, were nonetheless skeptics about what preachers said was going on. But I knew Bernie had lost something important and honorable. Again, I did not like that, did not like it because I liked *him* so much.

I spoke at a Humanist Association memorial service for Dr. Asimov a few years back. I said, "Isaac is up in Heaven now." That was the funniest thing I could have said to an audience of humanists. I rolled them in the aisles. . . . When I myself am dead, God forbid, I hope some wag will say about me, "He's up in Heaven now."

. . . The German philosopher Friedrich Wilhelm Nietzsche, who had syphilis, said that only a person of deep faith could afford the luxury of religious skepticism. Humanists, by and large educated, comfortably middle-class persons with rewarding lives like mine, find rapture enough in secular knowledge and hope. Most people can't.

Voltaire, French author of *Candide*, and therefore the humanists' Abraham, concealed his contempt for the hierarchy of the Roman Catholic Church from his less educated, simpler-minded, and more frightened employees, because he knew what a stabilizer their religion was for them.

{CA; CE; E; HNS2; *The Village Voice*, 6 Sep 1994; TYD; U}

Voo, G. W. van der (Born 1806)

A Dutch writer, Voo for more than half a century was a schoolmaster and teacher of the French language at Rotterdam. He contributed articles to *De Dageraad*. {BDF}

VOODOO

Vodoun or V*audou*, commonly called voodoo, refers to the Vodoun religious beliefs and practices which are West African in origin (In Ouidah, Benin, the center of the Vodoun religion, it is called *vodoun*) and are found in Haiti, where *Voudou* is found for example in the village of Soukre. Mixed with Catholicism and West Indian influences, voodoo is based upon an animistic belief in *Gran Met* (God), *Guine* (ancestral Africa, particularly the area of Dahomey, now called Benin), and *loa* (spirits). The African spirits have been identified with certain Christian saints among practitioners who claim also to be Catholics. *Houngans* (sorcerers) are believed to be able to use for evil purposes a zombi or zombie (a person raised from the grave)—such an individual appears to resemble the so-called "walking dead" (and the term is also used to describe drugged individuals who appear not to be in command of their faculties). However, such necromancy, or appeal to the spirits of the dead to reveal the future or influence the course of events, is claimed to be of a positive nature by its adherents. Outsiders, however, have the picture of a group of worshipers who speak of *hounsies*, who bite into a chicken's neck as they dance to haunting drum beats, who stick pins in dolls in order to bring unhappiness to its enemies, and so forth. In the various voodooistic services, ecstatic trances and magical practices can be involved.

Related movements are Candomblé, a voodooistic religion found in Brazil; Santeria, which is found in Cuba and in which Yoruba deities are identified with Roman Catholic saints; Wanga or Ouanga, sorcery or witchcraft with Angolan overtones; and Obeah, which is found throughout the West Indies, the Guianas, and the southeastern United States, in which sorcery and magic ritual are used. Non-believers rarely observe authentic services "back in the bush," although the present writer has gotten blood on his pants after a dancing worshiper bit into a live chicken's neck, then veered backwards as if in a trance, knocking the accompanying musicians off a small Haitian stage.

Journalist Howard W. French has written extensively about Voodoo. In 1996 in Benin, he met Daagbo Hounon Houna, the Supreme Chief of the Grand Council of the Vodoun Religion of Benin, whose followers think of him as their Pope and throw themselves at his feet and kiss the sand before him. Vodoun, the leader laments, has been vilified like few other religions. "When the first Europeans walked on our soil, "Mr. Houna said, speaking in his native Fon language through a translator, "they began calling us fetishists. That was the first of many efforts by whites to introduce their beliefs and destroy our culture." He explained that there is one god, Mawu, but countless names for this supreme deity's manifestations—spirits like Gu, Legba, Damballa, and Hevioso. Vodoun, he added, has nothing to do with the common Western perception of sticking pins in dolls to persecute real or imagined enemies. "There are women who cannot conceive children, men who cannot find work, and elders who cannot find peace. Vodoun restores hope. It protects our land and brings the cool breeze." French wrote, "To the charge that their ancestor [Viceroy Don Francisco Felix de Souza, a Brazilian who allegedly came to Ouidah in 1754 to run a Portuguese slaving fort) was a principal actor in the deportation of many thousands of slaves, today's de Souzas portray the first Viceroy as something of a humanist. 'Our ancestor traded in slaves, but it isn't fair just to stop there,' said Marcellin Norberto de Souza, son of the sixth Viceroy, whose white mustache and hair offsetting his dark sin are characteristic of the deSouza clan. 'He was in fact a very generous man living in what you might call a barbarous time.' " This, it was noted, was uttered at the very site where 1,500,000 million "pieces of ebony" were shipped off to the Western hemisphere. (See entries for Candomblé and Santeria. Christianity, to some, is "the white man's voodoo.") {CE; Howard W. French, *The New York Times*, 10 March 1996}

VOODOO, WHITE MAN'S AND WHITE WOMAN'S : See entry for Christianity.

Vosmaer, Carel (1826–1888)

Vosmaer was a Dutch writer who edited the *Tydstroom* (1858–1859) and *Spectator* (1860–1873). Vosmaer also wrote works on Dutch art and other subjects. {BDF}

Voss, Anna (20th Century)

Voss is one of the counsels for *Secular Nation*, the International Atheist Alliance magazine. She holds that religion "is greatly to blame for women being raised as tame, frightened, and passive individuals," and she disagrees with the good religious people who use the phrase "passed away." "When I die," she says, "tell people that I *died*. Anything else is worse than euphemism." "Away" is an undesirable concept in relation to dying, she reasons, for we are taught to throw things "away." In 1996, she and her husband Howard Kreisner were reportedly in the process of an amicable divorce. Voss resigned as President of San Diego's Atheist Coalition upon moving to Los Angeles. {*Secular Nation*, Fall 1995}

Voss, Carl Hermann (20th Century)

Voss wrote *Rabbi and Minister: The Friendship of Stephen S. Wise and John Haynes Holmes* (1980). {EW}

Voss, Johann Heinrich (1751–1826)

Voss, a German poet and philologist, studied for the Church at Göttingen but became a rationalist and turned to philology. He was editor of the *Musenalmanach* and in 1781 published a translation of Homer's *Odyssey*. He then translated into German Vergil's *Bucolics*, the *Iliad*, Horace, Theocritus, Tibullus, Aristophanes, and others. He rendered into German thirteen of Shakespeare's plays (1818–1829). In 1805 he was appointed professor of classical philology at Heidelberg University. When his personal friend, Count von Stolberg, joined the Roman Church, Voss severely attacked him. {RAT}

Voss, William J. (1921–1997)

Voss, a Life Member of the Freeedom From Religion Foundation, was founder and president of Voss Industries, Inc., a company which pioneered the design and application of V-band couplings for industrial, defense, and aerospace applications. Robert Ingersoll was one of his favorite authors, and he was active in humanist chapters. {*Freethought Today*, November 1997}

Vostrovsky, Jaroslav (Born 1836)

Born in Bohemia, Vostrovsky traveled in Europe and went to America in 1864. He engaged in business enterprises in Nebraska, Iowa, and California. Vostrovsky contributed in the Bohemian language to liberal journals and was vice-president of the California State Liberal Union. {PUT}

Voysey, Charles (Born 1828)

Voysey was an English non-Christian theist, a vicar at Healaugh, Yorkshire (1864–1871) who was deprived of his position in 1871 for heresy in sermons published in *The Sting and the Stone*. (See "Freethought Congregations: South Place and Others" in *Victorian Heretics*, by Warren Sylvester Smith.) {BDF; FUK; RAT; WSS}

Vredenburg, Charles Edwin (19th Century)

Vredenburg wrote *The Case Against the Church* (1876). {GS}

Vukadinovic, Radovan (20th Century)

A professor in Croatia, Vukadinovic is a signer of Humanist Manifesto 2000.

Vuletic, Mark (20th Century)

Vuletic, a graduate student of philosophy at the University of Illinois at Chicago, is an atheist who wrote "The Moral Foundations of Atheism and Christianity" in *The Free Mind* (February 1996). E-mail: <mvuletic@infidels.org>.

VULGARITY

- Vulgarity is the garlic in the salad of taste.

—Cyril Connolly

Vulpian, Edme Felix Alfred (1826–1887)

A French physician, Vulpian wrote several medical works. Upon being appointed lecturer at the School of Medicine in 1869, he was violently opposed because of his atheism. Vulpian was afterwards elected to the Academy of Sciences. {BDF; RAT}

Vye, Mel (20th Century)

Vye is President of Free Inquirers of Northeastern Ohio. {FINO, 1 January 1998}

Waaldijk, Kees (20th Century)

A member of the Gay & Lesbian Humanist Association in England, Waaldijk lectures in law at the University of Leiden.

Wachtelaer, Claude (20th Century)

Dr. Wachtelaer is secretary-general of the European Humanist Federation. On the International Humanist and Ethical Union (IHEU) Board, he represents Belgium's *Centre d'Action Laïque.* Wachtelaer is author of "Secularism, Humanism and Freethought in Belgium and France," in the *International Humanist* (July 1992). The article describes the difficulties Belgium has had throughout the 19th and 20th centuries. Clericals and anticlericals, Catholics and free thinkers, all have fought over the question of free schools, civil burials, Church-controlled education, and the rights of the *Grand Orient de Belgique* (a Masonic organization, which is open to deists, agnostics, and atheists). The Flemish counterpart of the *Centre d'Action Laïque* is the *Unie Vrijzinnige Verenigingen*, and both receive public funds from the Belgian Department of Cults. He was a participant in 1996 at the Polish Humanist Conference on European Integration held in Utrecht. E-mail: <cwachtelaer@arcadis.be>.

Wächtershäuser, Günter (20th Century): See entry for Genesis.

Waddell, John Henry (20th Century)

Waddell, a sculptor, is active in the First Unitarian Universalist Church of Phoenix, Arizona, on whose grounds stand one of his works, "That Which Might Have Been, Birmingham 1963." The bronze sculpture memorializes the four girls killed in the 1963 bombing of the Sixteenth Street Baptist Church in Birmingham, Alabama. He wrote *The Beauty of Individual Differences* (1985). {*World*, November-December 1994}

Waddell, W. A. (20th Century)

In 1939, Waddell was President in Canada of Regina's Rationalist Club. {FUK}

Waddington, C. H. (1905–)

Waddington, a biologist, was a non-theist. He is listed in *Victorian Infidels*. {TRI}

Waddington, Samuel (Born 1844)

Although Waddington followed Pusey in his earlier years and intended to enter the Church, "more Rationalistic impulses prevailed," wrote R. le Gallienne, in the introduction to Waddington's poems. After becoming private secretary to Lord Balfour of Burleigh, Waddington then became secretary to Thomas Burt. He compiled *English Sonnets by Living Writers* (1881) and wrote *Arthur Hugh Clough* (1883) and *Sonnets and Other Verses* (1884). In many of his poems, Waddington expresses his agnosticism in regard to any future life. {RAT}

Wade, Benjamin (20th Century)

Wade, president of Thinking Skills in Maynard, Massachusetts, and a member of the Humanist Association of Massachusetts, spoke on "Critical Thinking: A Paradigm for Education in the Age of Cybernetics" at the 1996 Humanist World Congress held in Mexico City. He teaches critical thinking courses throughout the United States.

Wade, Robert (19th Century)

Wade, originally of England, moved to Troy, New York, where he was a supporter of Freethought and wrote columns in *The Truth Seeker* and *Investigator*. {PUT}

Wagner, Phil (20th Century)

Wagner edits a literary magazine, *The Iconoclast* (1675 Amazon Road, Mohegan Lake, NY 10547).

Wagner, Wilhelm Richard (1813–1883)

Wagner is the German composer whose operas represent the fullest musical and theatrical expression of German romanticism. Instead of using the sharply differentiated recitative and aria, he used a continuous flow of melody, calling his operas "music-dramas" to signify their fusion of text and music. Wagner's operas include *Rienzi* (1838–1840), *The Flying Dutchman* (1841), *Tannhäuser* (1843–1844), and *Lohengrin* (1846–1848).

A participant in the Revolution of 1848, Wagner fled to Dresden. Aided by Liszt, he escaped to Switzerland where he stayed for ten years. His *Der Ring des Nibelungen* (1852–1874) is a tetralogy that embodies his aesthetic principles, and in 1872 Wagner moved to Bayreuth, Bavaria, where he completed the Ring cycle and built a theater. His later compositions include *Tristan und Isolde* (1857–1859) and *Parsifal* (1877–1882), called a sacred festival drama.

Many authors claim that Wagner was anti-Semitic. W. H. Auden described him as "an absolute shit." James Wood in *The New Republic* (29 July 1996) compared Wagner's with T. S. Eliot's anti-Semitism:

> Eliot's eccentric praise of the Jewish poet [Isaac Rosenberg] is consistent with his larger deprecations. "That a Jew can do this!" registers the surprise of the anti-Semite. What is it to write like a Jew? Richard Wagner explains: "The Jew speaks the language of the country in which he has lived from generation to generation, but always speaks it as a foreigner." A Jew cannot compose German music; when he purports to do so, he deceives. The Jewish composer could only compose music as a Jew by drawing on the "ceremonial music" of the synagogue service, a "nonsensical gurgling, yodelling and cackling."
>
> These "rhythms . . . dominate his musical imagination": they are irresistible. So while the talented Jewish composer is disqualified by his race from composing German music, he is disqualified by his talent from composing Jewish music. Rosenberg was luckier. He was able, by "almost a miracle," to write in English "like a Jew." The difference between Eliot's anti-Semitism and Wagner's is defined, on this point, by the possibility of this "miracle."

The composer's fifty-one-year-old great-grandson Gottfried Wagner, who has written an autobiography, *Twilight of the Wagners*, was interviewed by Alex Ross (*The New Yorker*, 10 August 1998), who observed,

> It's a strange kind of autobiography—a quarrel with an ancestor who has been dead since 1883. Gottfried, a musicologist who wrote his dissertation on Kurt Weill, views his great-grandfather as a prophet of Nazism and as an unambiguously political composer. He attacks his grandmother Winifred for befriending Hitler, and he attacks his own father—Wolfgang, the current director of the Wagner festival in Bayreuth—for concealing the family's dismal history. He writes that the festival and the city at large have been infiltrated by neo-Nazi elements, with skinheads demonstrating nearby in sympathy. He writes that James Levine and Daniel Barenboim are hypocrites for conducting in Bayreuth in spite of their Jewishness. As a result of his agitations, he is no longer welcome at the festival. . . . Gottfried is not clin-

ically insane, as one Wagnerite has suggested, but he is plainly in the grip of an obsession.

Gottfried, however, holds that Wagner

> • allowed Hermann Levi, a Jew, to conduct the premiere of "Parsifal" for no other reason than that King Ludwig II of Bavaria, who was supporting Wagner and paying for the premiere, ordered him to. The King, who liked Jews, brought enormous pressure on Wagner. Wagner fought till the last moment and treated Levi sadistically, ordering him to convert. Levi refused.
> • did not sign the anti-Semitic petition of 1881, not because he wished to protect the civil rights of Jews, but because the petition was insufficiently restrictive to Jews. By 1880, Wagner was contemplating ridding Germany of Jews entirely. How this was to be accomplished, Wagner left to a future generation.
> • portrayed all his major characters in depth, including his "Jewish villains." The fact that Wagner was capable of creating multi-dimensional figures does not make him less of a Jew-hater or less of a revolutionary german chauvinist. His portraits of the Germanic gods sometimes show them as being venal, selfish and stupid, and capable of being deceived by the dwarfish [translation: Jewish], hairy and clever Jewish types. Wagner was an artist—an evil artist.

Contemporary Jews appear divided about Wagner: one group holds that Israel needs to lift its ban on performances of Wagner's music in public halls and outdoor venues. Another group holds that the ban should remain.

Wagner was a follower of Schopenhauer, who is often termed "the philosopher of pessimism" and one of the first of avowed atheists. (Ironically, Schopenhauer did not care for Wagner's music.)

Of Wagner, McCabe wrote:

> All admit that he was an atheist and radical—he took part in the revolution of 1848—in the first part of his life but when he produced *Parsifal* in 1882 Nietzsche (who had once been his greatest admirer) and others charged him with having lapsed into mysticism. It is clear that he was then in a romantic and more or less mystic mood, but all experts admit that he never returned to the Christian faith. The chief writer on his religious ideas, Otto Hartwich, says: "Wagner was a Christian in a large sense, though not a man of the Church. He had little taste for the other-worldly speculations of dogmatic theology and none at all in the Church's pressure on faith and conscience." In other words he began to admire what he believed to be the Christian ethic–hence the bitterness of Nietzsche who thought it the worst feature of Christianity—and no more.
>
> The British musical critic and freethinker Ernest Newman, who has a work on Wagner, reminds us that by the age of fifty all his greatest work had been done (while he was an atheist) and his intellectual powers were now less vigorous though his art was still great.

{CE; BDF; JM; RAT; RE; TRI; TYD; Gottfried Wagner, *The New York Times*, 22 November 1998}

Wahba, Mourad (20th Century)

A professor of education at the University of Ain Shams in Cairo, Egypt, Wahba is a Humanist Laureate in the Council for Secular Humanism's International Academy of Humanism. In 1994 his essay, "Peace and Progress," was included in *Challenges to the Enlightenment, Essays in Defense of Reason and Science*. Prof. Wahba is chairman of the Afro-Asian Philosophy Association.

In 1996 he participated in the Humanist World Congress held in Mexico City. Creativity, he holds, is the antidote of dogmatism. If the cyber-age leads to a Second Enlightenment, either Ortega y Gasset's "mass man" will be involved or civilization as we know it will change for the worse. He signed Humanist Manifesto 2000. {*International Humanist News*, December 1996}

WAHHABISM: See entry for Islamic Fundamentalism.

Waisbrooker, Lois (1826–1909)

When Moses Harman, editor of the anarchist weekly, *Lucifer the Light-Bearer*, was having trouble because of his having published obscene literature, he asked Waisbrooker to co-edit while he went to jail. According to *Freethought on the American Frontier* by Whitehead and Muhrer, she quoted a section of a U.S. Department of Agriculture book on diseases of the horse, comparing it to a passage from one of the objectionable letters Harman had published and gotten in trouble over. The post office confiscated the entire issue, the dispute coming to be known as the Horse Penis Affair. Just before her death, she published "The Curse of Christian Morality."

Freethinker Ezra Heywood, upon first seeing her in 1875, wrote that Waisbrooker "seemed to be a Roman Sibyl, Scott's Meg Merrilies, enacted by Charlotte Cushman, Margaret Fuller, and Sojourner Truth rolled into one. . . . She rose, went up the aisle, mounted the platform, and the tall, angular, weird, quaint kind of a she Abraham Lincoln was introduced to the audiences as 'Lois Waisbrooker.' "

"Until you let go of God," Waisbrooker wrote in "The Curse of Goddism," "and take hold of yourselves, of the innate powers of your own beings, there is no hope for you. . . . Stop praying and go to work." {WWS}

Wait, Margie (20th Century)

Wait is Colorado State Director of American Atheists, Inc. E-mail: <mdwait@atheists.org>.

Waite, Charles Burling Lame (1824–1895)

Waite, an American judge, was appointed by President Abraham Lincoln to the Supreme Court of Utah. In 1881, Waite issued his *History of the Christian Religion*, a rationalistic work which is negatively critical of the evangelical narratives. Waite became president of the Philosophical Society and the Secular Union of Chicago. He assisted in the formation of the Historical Society of Washington, D.C., of which President Garfield, then a congressman, was a member. A strong fighter for woman suffrage, Waite became president of the American Secular Union. {BDF; FUS; JM; PUT; RAT; RE}

Waite, Lucy (20th Century)

Waite in 1923 issued the *Freethought Year Book*.

Waitz, Theodor (1821–1864)

Waitz was a German psychologist and anthropologist who taught at Marburg. He edited Aristotle's *Organon* (2 volumes, 1844) and wrote works on psychology at a time when he was a Herbartian. He developed along more empirical lines and became an authority on anthropology. Waitz's mature views are found in his *Anthropologie der Naturv Uolker* (4 volumes, 1859–1864). {RAT}

Wakefield, Eva Ingersoll (1891–1970)

The granddaughter of Robert Ingersoll, an atheist who called herself a naturalistic humanist, Mrs. Wakefield succeeded Warren Allen Smith in 1954 as president of the New York City Humanists, which then affiliated with the American Humanist Association. As was her husband Sherman, Wakefield supported liberal causes and was outspoken as a freethinker. In 1959, she edited the work of her famous grandfather, whose letters she previously had edited.

Typical of her activism, Wakefield took part in a 1953 "squabble" over a New York City Health and Welfare Council decision, observing,

> I am happy to report that the fight waged by the Planned Parenthood Federation's Committee of Mothers' Health Centers for reinstatement on the Health and Welfare Council of New York City, has finally been successful. A majority of the Board of the Council

> has recently voted to admit the Planned Parenthood agency to membership. In consequence, the fifty-three Roman Catholic agencies have resigned from the Council. This controversy is merely another in the endless series of controversies pointing up the vast and irreconcilable differences between this mighty totalitarian institution, the Roman Catholic Church, and the liberal religious and secular institutions and principles that form the substance and spirit of the democratic way of life.
>
> Roman Catholicism, no less than Soviet Communism, is seeking world domination, through political and social, as well as religious, channels. It infiltrates every governmental, economic, and social agency, and works unceasingly in every direct and devious manner to achieve its objective of total control of the minds and destinies of mankind everywhere. Humanists must be alerted to this Catholic menace, and must come out of their intellectual cloisters into the heat and turmoil of the market place of ideas, and take up the challenge uncompromisingly and courageously that this totalitarian church has presented to us.

When she wrote Mayor Elect Robert F. Wagner Jr., a Catholic, on behalf of the New York Humanists for his views on the separation of church and state, she received his response:

> In connection therewith, I wish to advise you that I am fully in accord with the constitutional problem (doctrine?) of separation of church and state and I am opposed to using public funds for the support of private and parochial schools. I deeply appreciate your writing to me about this matter.

Wakefield was humiliated late in life, fleeced out of a sizable amount of money in a Gypsy *bajour*, but to all who knew her she was a generous, wise, kind, and stately person. Her interests included world federalism, euthanasia, Indian affairs, civil liberties, and the separation of church and state. (See entry for K. M. Whitten.) {FUS; HNS; *The Humanist Newsletter*, November-December 1953; WAS, numerous conversations}

Wakefield, Edward (1774–1854)

Wakefield, whose father had been a Quaker but became a rationalist, was brought up as a rationalist. His son, Edward Gibbon Wakefield, also was a rationalist. {RAT; RE}

Wakefield, Edward Gibbon (1796–1862)

Wakefield was a standard authority on colonization and had much to do with the founding of the colonies of South Australia and New Zealand. He served as advisor to Lord Durham in Canada and later as Acting Governor of New Zealand. His biographer, R. Garnett, quoted Lord Lyttelton as saying that Wakefield is "the man in these days beyond comparison of the most genius and the widest influence in the great science of colonization." Garnett adds, "His sympathies were by no means ecclesiastical: His creed appears to have been a masculine Theism." {RAT; RE}

Wakefield, Gilbert (1756–1801)

For a time Wakefield was classical professor at Hackney seminary, but, finding the creed impossible, he took to literature. His translations of Latin and Greek classics, including one on Lucretius (1796–1799, 3 volumes) gave him "a distinct position in the history of English scholarship," according to the *Dictionary of National Biography*. Because he once wrote an attack on Paine, Wakefield is sometimes described as a Christian. However, according to McCabe, Wakefield "was not even a Unitarian. In 1798 he was sent to prison for two years for a criticism of the Bishop of Llandaff. He never went to church, but was a simple Theist of high character and idealism." {RAT; RE}

Wakefield, Homer (20th Century)

Dr. Wakefield, writing under the pseudonym of Prescott Locke, wrote a freethought novel, *The Conversion of Hamilton Wheeler* (1917).

Wakefield, Sherman D. (1894–1971)

Wakefield was an encyclopedist, atheist, and naturalistic humanist, the husband of Eva Ingersoll Wakefield and grandson-in-law of Robert G. Ingersoll. He wrote extensively about Lincoln's lack of religion and other topics related to rationalism. Although not a charismatic speaker, he was a consummate correspondent and collector. Finding *The Humanist* tame for his tastes, Wakefield edited a humanistic journal, *Progressive World*, for the United Secularists of America. Wakefield wrote "Theodore Roosevelt and Robert G. Ingersoll as Revealed in Their Letters" (1969). Like his wife, Wakefield was active in New York City humanist activities, becoming a member of the local chapter's executive committee in 1953. (See entries for Viljamur Stefansson and for K. M. Whitten.) {CL; HNS; HNS2; *The Humanist Newsletter*, November-December 1953; TRI; WAS, numerous conversations}

Wakeman, Thaddeus Burr (1834–1913)

Wakeman was an American lawyer and positivist. In New York, he was one of the editors of *Man* (1878–1884) and was president of the New York Liberal Club. Wakeman was an editor of *Torch of Reason* (1896–1903, a newspaper of Liberal University) and *Liberal Review* (1904–1906). McCabe wrote of Wakeman, "He called himself a Positivist, but broadly, he was an agnostic, a great admirer of Haeckel (who loathed Positivism), and an aggressive freethinker." {FUS; JM; PUT; RAT; RE}

Wakerlin, George E. (20th Century)

A physiologist at the University of Illinois College of Medicine, Dr. Wakerlin like his friend Anton J. Carlson was a naturalistic humanist.

Walcott, Derek (Alton) (1930–)

An Antillean dramatist, poet, and 1992 Nobel Prize winner, Walcott was born in St. Lucia and has taught at Boston University, Columbia, and Harvard. An honorary member of the American Academy of Arts and Letters, he is known for such dramas as "A Branch on the Blue Nile" (1986) and poetry such as *Collected Poems* (1986). Much of his work describes the West Indian conflict between its local culture and that of Europe's, "the choice of home or exile, self-realisation or spiritual betrayal of one's country."

His epic poem, *Omeros* (1990), sounds based upon Ancient Greek literature, but Achille is the "main man" and son of an African slave; Patroclus becomes a crippled Philoctetes whose wound fails to heal but whose cure marks the end of the war; Hector is not killed by Achille but dies as the result of his own recklessness. If the gods brought order to Homer's world, in Walcott's poem all of us who are exiles return to a home which has so changed we no longer remember it. {OEL}

Walckenaer, Charles Athanase [Baron] (1771–1852)

A French writer, Walckenaer during the Revolution emigrated to Scotland, returning in 1816 and becoming one of the Mayors of Paris. He wrote several novels, the lives of Lafontaine (1820) and Mme. de Sévigné (5 volumes, (1842–1852), and *Histoire de la vie et des poésies d'Horace* (1 volumes, 1840). The Baron did not abandon the Voltaireanism of pre-Revolution days, and his rationalist showed in his various works. {RAT}

WALDO, H. H.: See Raube Marks.

WALES, HUMANISM AND RATIONALISM IN

Richard Paterson cites Zephaniah Williams as the pioneer freethinker of Wales. Humanist groups include the following:

- Cardiff: Richard Paterson, Fir Tree Cottage, Royal Oak, Machen, Newport NP 8SN (01633) 441044.
- Humanist Society of Mid-Wales: Thalia Campbell, Glangors, Ynyslas, Borth SY24 5JU (01970) 871360.

- North Wales Humanist Group: Zonia Bowen, 6 Stad Glandwr, Caeathro, Caernarfon LL55 2SG (01286) 673488.
- West Glamorgan Humanist Group: Julie Norris, 3 Maple Grove, Uplands, Swansea SA2 OJY (01792) 206108.

In Wales, an estimated twenty-five Unitarian congregations are found mainly in the south, and services are in Welsh. These congregations, according to John Clifford, are in the Black Spot, named as such by 19th century Methodist revivalist missionaries who made little headway in the area because of the Unitarian influence. The average size of the congregations is around fifty, their leaning being toward theism of the liberal Christian type.

(See entry for Zephaniah Williams.)

Wales, Hubert (20th Century)

Wales wrote *The Rationalist* (1917). {GS}

Walferdin, François Hippolyte (1795–1880)

Walferdin, who was a friend of Arago, contributed with him to the enlargement of science and was decorated in 1844 with the Legion of Honor. He published an edition of the works of Diderot (1857) and left the bust of that philosopher to the Louvre. Among the new instruments he invented were a new thermometer, a hyp-sothermometer, and the hydrobarometer. {BDF; RAT}

Walinski, Joe (20th Century)

In 1999 Walinski was elected Vice President of the Humanists of North Jersey, which is affiliated with the American Humanist Association.

WALKAWAY

WalkAway was a newsletter for ex-fundamentalists. Now defunct, it was published by Skipp Porteous.

Walker, Albert C. (20th Century)

Walker is active in the Humanist Fellowship of the First Unitarian Society of San Francisco (AHA). (See entry for California Atheists, Humanists.) {FD}

Walker, Alice (1944-)

Walker, an African American novelist and poet, received the Pulitzer Prize for her 1982 work that focused on women and their struggle for racial and sexual equality, *The Color Purple. The Third Life of Grange Copeland* (1970) described a kind of emotional slavery that spanned three generations.

In 1997 Walker was named Humanist of the Year by the American Humanist Association.

Walker, Barbara G. (1930–)

Walker was named 1993 Humanist Heroine by the American Humanist Association. She is author of *The Skeptical Feminist* and *The Woman's Encyclopedia of Myths and Secrets* (1983), the latter of which is often banned, according to the American Library Association's *Banned Books* (1998), because the book "is of no benefit to anyone."

An atheist, she finds "the archetypical Goddess image" to be of psychological importance to women, calls fortune-telling "just a parlor trick," and delights in debunking New Age assertions about crystals. "Our culture," she has written, "has been deeply penetrated by the notion that 'man' . . . not woman . . . is created in the image of god. This notion persists, despite the likelihood that the creation goes in the other direction: that god is a human projection of the image of man." (See entry for Banned Books.) {WWS}

Walker, Dwayne (20th Century)

Walker, a Long Beach, California, freethinker, is director of a movie, "Waco, Bible Madness" and supplier of various freethought videos. On the Web: <http://www.netcom.com/~wilsie/biblemadness.html>.

Walker, E. (19th Century)

A native of Worcester, England, Walker was an Owenite who wrote *Is the Bible True?* and *What Is Blasphemy?* (1843). {BDF}

Walker, Edwin C. (Born 1849)

Walker, of Valley Falls, Kansas, was editor of *Lucifer* and *Fair Play*. At first a Universalist, he later became a writer for *The Truth Seeker* and "a radical of the radicals," according to Putnam. Walker held that the great danger threatening liberty in America was the machinations of the Protestant organizations; that the Catholics are dangerous only as the Protestants prepare the way for them. {BDF; FUK; PUT}

Walker, Ernest (Born 1870)

A composer, Walker edited the *Musical Gazette* and wrote a number of works on music. He made his profession of Rationalism in an article in the *Almanacco del Coenoblum* (1913) and was for years a member of the Rationalist Press Association. {RAT; RE}

Walker, Imogene B. (20th Century)

Walker wrote *James Thomson: A Critical Study* (1950). {GS}

Walker, James (1794–1874)

One of the early defenders of the liberal theology in the 19th century, Walker took an active role in the formation of the American Unitarian Association in 1825. His tolerance of mind allowed several of the Transcendentalists to publish their works in the *Christian Examiner*, and he added the intuitionist doctrine of the Transcendentalists to his own "Common-Sense philosophy" which he had learned from the Scottish thinkers Thomas Reid and Dugald Stewart. {U&U}

Walker, Jeff (20th Century)

Walker is a freelance Toronto writer who wrote the two-hour Canadian Broadcasting Corporation "Ideas" radio documentary on Ayn Rand, which aired in 1992. Rand's followers, he notes, consider her *Atlas* "not just the greatest novel of all time but the greatest human achievement of all time," much greater than that of Plato, Shakespeare, Galileo, Mozart, Einstein, etc. His evaluation: "To paraphrase Voltaire: 'Every sensible man, every honorable man, must hold the Randian sect in horror.' "

Walker, John (1759–1830)

Walker began life in a blacksmith's shop, became an engraver, then a teacher, and at the age of thirty-five took up the study of medicine, becoming admitted to the Royal College of Physicians. An ardent humanitarian, he admired the Quaker religion. The Friends, however, declined to receive him inasmuch as he was a well-known Deist and a friend of Paine. {RAT; RE}

Walker, Joseph (20th Century)

Walker, a prominent Boston attorney, was a signer of Humanist Manifesto I. Edwin H. Wilson in *The Genesis of a Humanist Manifesto* (1995) has described Walker's connection with that document. He had been a Republican candidate for governor of Massachusetts and, for two years, Speaker of the House of Representatives. In 1932, with the encouragement of John Dietrich, Walker published *Humanism As A Way of Life*.

"I signed the Humanist Manifesto," Walker wrote, "because I am in general accord with the statements therein contained. If men are to discover a satisfactory way of life they must face squarely the facts of life. Realistic thinking must take the place of wishful thinking. Men may wish to believe in a personal God, like the Christian God. Men may wish to believe in a future life; but the question is, not what men wish to believe but rather what, with intellectual honesty, they can believe." {EW; HM1}

Walker, Kenneth C. (20th Century)

A liberal minister in Illinois, Walker once was a director of the American Humanist Association. {HNS}

Walker, Stanley (1898–1962)

A Texan who once was city editor of New York's *Daily News*, Walker in 1933 wrote *The Night Club Era*, an earthy picture of New York City. In the 1950s he reviewed for *The Humanist* David W. Maurer's *Whiz Mob, A Correlation of the Technical Argot of Pickpockets With Their Behavior Pattern.*

He included among his memories that almost forty years ago old Frank Notfleet, who appears in "The Big Con" and in Va Cise's excellent account of the Blonger account of the Blonger mob of Denver, "came to see me in New York while on the trail of the men who had robbed him. I got two moderately honest detectives to help and we went up to the Ansonia Coffee Shop and nabbed Joe Furey, one of the mob of con men. Joe later died in bad shape, after a prison term. Norfleet, though of course he must have had a streak of larceny in him, was the damnedest one-man nemesis I ever heard of. He put everybody in jail, often at great personal risk. He scared hell out of me when I first met him. I was having breakfast and he threw two big 45s on the table by way of introduction. . . . I used to know the wonderful Detective Dan Champion in New York and heard much from him. Also, former Commissioner Mulrooney once told me a strange tale—of the worst woman he had ever known. She trained her children to be pickpockets, using a tailor's dummy as a model, and thwacking the little nippers briskly with a switch for their clumsiness."

Walker was both dis- and un-interested in religion. As a journalist, he reported disinterestedly. As an individual, he was a freethinker who openly expressed his naturalistic humanism. Walker wrote *The Story of the Dominican Republic and Its People*. Also, he wrote *Dewey: An American of This Century*.

In 1995, Walker's *City Editor* (1934) was cited by *The New York Times* as one of *the* best books ever to have been written about New York City.

The book was described as follows: "Some of these wornout gaffers [city editors] pass their old age boring helpless listeners with tales of how good they were in the days when there were giants in journalism. Others putter around in gardens, and the great stories of yesterday, which once were so urgently important and so exciting with life, now seem dim and pale. The memory of the throbbing office—the incessant ringing of the telephones, the daily attempts to keep the office boys awake, the clean inky smell of the fresh editions just off the press, the practical jokes on the office half-wit, the cruse for some cause which at the time was like another Holy War, the parade of freaks and fakers and mountebanks, the complaints and libel suits, the reporters who got drunk and couldn't write their stories, the campaign to get a $5 a week raise for a deserving reporter with a wife and too many children, the pictures with the wrong captions, the tense speed of election night, the patient drive to instill a few sensible don'ts into the heads of the young men—all grow indistinct and without meaning." {WAS, 6 May 1957 and 26 April 1958}

Walker, Thomas (1858–1932)

Walker, an Englishman, migrated to Canada in the 1870s, then to Australia in 1877, where in 1881 he became editor of *Reflector*. He was a secularist, lecturer, editor, parliamentarian, journalist, newspaper proprietor, farmer, lawyer, and legislator who as a precocious child had been a Wesleyan preacher. His first spiritualist lecture in Melbourne was delivered in a trance said to be under the "control" of Giordano Bruno. Splitting with the spiritualists in 1882, Walker became a materialist, founding the Australasian Secular Association with himself as salaried president and lecturer. Convicted in 1885 for exhibiting obscene pictures while advocating birth control, he conducted his own appeal and won. A controversial freethinker, he was president of the West Australian Rationalist Association in 1916. As Attorney-General in Western Australia, then Minister for Education and finally Speaker, Walker successfully placed a number of secular reforms on the statute books. {FUK; SWW}

Walker, William C. (20th Century)

Walker is a Pennsylvanian who has written for *Freethought Today*. He is a member of the Freedom from Religion Foundation.

Wallace, Alfred Russel (1823–1913)

Wallace, doing scientific research in the Malay archipelago, sent Charles Darwin an 1858 manuscript, "On the Tendencies of Varieties to Part from the Original Type." Wallace's concept of evolution was so like that of Darwin's that he asked his fellow English naturalist to look it over and show it to other scientists. Darwin was troubled by the work's similarity to his own thinking, remarking, "I would far rather burn my whole book than that Wallace or any other man should think that I behaved in a paltry spirit." A compromise was reached, one in which a short abstract of Darwin's theory was read at the Linnaean Society, along with Wallace's manuscript. Both had been influenced by the works of Malthus and Lyell, but Wallace's specialty was biogeography, shown in his *The Geographical Distribution of Animals* (1876). That work postulated a dividing line, which is still called Wallace's Line, between Asian and Australian fau na in the Malay Archipelago.

When Darwin's *Origin of Species* was published in 1859, Wallace remarked, "The one great result which I claim for my paper of 1858 is that it compelled Darwin to write and publish his *Origin of Species* without further delay." As reported in the *Encyclopedia Britannica* (1911), Wallace was "in no way connected with Christianity, for he had long before given up all belief in revealed religion."

"Unfortunately," wrote McCabe, "Wallace allowed himself to be duped by a fraudulent and impudent Spiritualist medium and the works of his later years were pathetic. He refused to admit the evolution of the mind. But he never returned to the Christian Church." McCabe adds that most of Wallace's distinctions were awarded on the ground that he was the co-discoverer with Darwin of Natural Selection, whereas "in point of fact there was nothing like equal merit, and he owed his recognition to Darwin's modesty and generosity. For Darwin, it was the outcome of twenty years of research; in the case of Wallace, a sudden and rather superficial guess."

Michael Shermer, in *Skeptic* (Vol. 3, No. 1 and 2, 1995), goes into detail as to how Wallace, the co-discoverer of natural selection, came to believe in the supernatural, which he calls a lesson on the limitations of science. Gordon Stein has written in *The American Rationalist* that Wallace was anything but a freethinker, that he "was as credulous a believer as there ever was." {CE; JM; RE; TDY}

Wallace, Graham (1858–1932)

Wallace, a freethinker, was a Fabian Society member who believed in education and reform rather than agitation and revolution. {TRI}

Wallace, Henry (1888-1965): See entry for George Orwell, who thought the former Vice President of the United States and Editor in Chief of *New Republic* somewhat of a fellow Communist Party traveler, one who had an unofficial connection with the Progressive Citizens of America.

Wallace, William (1844–1897)

A Scottish philosopher, Wallace taught moral philosophy at Oxford and was a Hegelian theist. He translated Hegel's *Logic* and *Phenomenology of the Mind*. In his *Lectures and Essays on Natural Theology* (published 1898), Wallace rejects supernaturalism and the belief in personal immortality. {RAT; RE}

Wallach, Judith D. (20th Century)

Wallach, President of the Society for Ethical Culture, is an activist in New York City. She is on the Board of Governors of the Humanist Institute.

Wallach, Sylvan (20th Century)

Wallach is editor of the New York Society for Ethical Culture's newsletter.

Wallin, Robert (19th Century)

In the *Boston Investigator*, a freethought newspaper, Wallin made a call in 1857 for an organizational meeting to set up an Infidel Association of the United States. {FUS}

Walling, Frank M. (20th Century)

In the mid-1950s, Walling was an editorial assistant on *The Humanist.*

Wallwork, Daniel (1824–1909)

Wallwork was a chartist and freethinker. Although he had been a Sunday School teacher and a church member in his native England, he discarded the religious convictions of his youth in 1853 and became a belligerent and outspoken atheist. In 1857, denying the truth of the Bible, he insisted as a witness in Court that he be allowed to affirm, rather than testify on oath. In 1865, two years after emigrating to Australia, he was secretary of the Newcastle Secular Society, now believed to be the first Freethought Society in Australia.

A prolific writer on the subject of temperance, he also was a prime mover and claimed to be the originator of the eight hour day system in New South Wales. {SWW; RSR}

Wally, Stefan (20th Century)

An Austrian member of the *Freidenkerbund Oesterreichs*, Wally was a participant in 1996 of the Mexico City congress of humanists. E-mail: <swally@fc.alpin.or.at>.

Walpole, Horatop (Horace) [4th Earl of Orford] (1717–1797)

Walpole was the youngest son of Sir Robert Walpole. He toured the Continent with his friend Thomas Gray from 1739 to 1741, when the two quarreled and parted. An admirer of the medieval, he built a pseudo-Gothic (showpiece castle at Strawberry Hill, near Twickenham, and in 1757 started a press there, publishing Gray's Pindaric odes and his own works. "A Gothic church," he made it clear, "or a convent fills one with romantic dreams—but for the mysterious, the church in the abstract, it is a jargon that means nothing, or a great deal too much, and I reject it and its apostles."

Walpole and Thomas Gray, the most popular poet of the century, went on the "Grand Tour" after Cambridge University, during which they had a falling out that lasted for years. According to George E. Haggerty of the University of California, "Walpole shared Gray's devotion to other men, and though he is as little likely to have actually had sexual experiences with men, he did love several in his long life, for a great portion of it devoting himself to one cousin, Henry Conway."

Walpole's reputation rests on more than three thousand letters written from 1732 to1797—he was the most famous letter-writer of his age—that give an invaluable picture of Georgian England and speak of his freethought. Walpole's *Castle of Otranto* (1765) anticipated the literary movement of romanticism. Almost singlehandedly, Haggerty has written, the work instituted the Gothic novel vogue.

McCabe wrote that Walpole was one of the most brilliant authors of the Deistic school and was skeptical about immortality. In a letter to a clergyman in 1783, Walpole ridiculed the Christian heaven, or "the absurd idea of the beatified sitting on golden thrones and chanting eternal allelujahs to golden harps." (See the Earl of Orford's caustic comment about Christianity in the entry for Joseph Addison.) {CE; GL; JM; RE; TYD}

Walpole, Robert [1st Earl of Orford] [Sir] (1676–1745)

Walpole was a noted British statesman. In 1702 he took the seat in Parliament for King's Lynn, from which he was regular returned thereafter. In 1708 he became secretary of war, and his successful handling of the financial wreckage known as the South Sea Bubble led to his appointment in 1721 as first lord of the treasury and chancellor of the exchequer. A Whig, he shared power with Viscount Townshend until 1730. Enjoying the confidence of George I and George II, he mollifed the largely Tory gentry by reducing the land tax. In foreign affairs he favored friendship with France but was drawn into a war with Spain. Because of military reverses, he was forced to resign in 1742. Walpole usually is described as the first prime minister.

A. C. Ewald referred to Walpole's "genial paganism." McCabe has written of Walpole that "he was cynical and not over-scrupulous in promoting his own affairs—political life was at the time thoroughly corrupt—and promoted his bastards to bishoprics, but folk must have smiled when he described himself in the House of Commons as 'a sincere member of the Church of England.' He went beyond the Deism that was then prevalent at court (the queen being a serious skeptic), and it is fairly clear that he was an atheist. The English translation of Bayle's freethinking dictionary was dedicated to him, and the letter dedicating it spoke blandly of 'the blind zeal and stupidity cleaving to superstition."

When Queen Caroline was dying, and there was a discussion as to whether the Archbishop should minister to her, Sir Robert said, "Let this farce be played; the Archbishop will act it very well. . . . It will do the Queen no hurt, no more than any good." {CE; JM; RAT}

Walser, George Henry (1834–1910)

After reading some of Robert Ingersoll's works, Walser, a state legislator and attorney in Ohio, started a small group of agnostics known as "The Sacred Brotherhood." He also founded a town in Missouri—Liberal—which contained a Freethought University but had no priest, church, chapel, or drinking saloon. That town achieved notoriety because a fire-and-brimstone Methodist minister built a church nearby and accused Walser and the 300 townspeople of being heathens, whereupon Walser built a quarter-mile fence through the middle of town, to keep out the Christians. The story is related, along with some of his poetry, in Whitehead and Muhrer's *Freethought on the American Frontier* (1992). From 1881 to 1889 in Liberal, Ohio, he edited *Liberal.* {BDF; FUS}

Walsh, Anthony (20th Century)

Walsh, while a student at the University of Missouri in Kansas City, was one of the founders of Campus Freethought Alliance. {*International Humanist News*, December 1996}

Walsh, J. (20th Century)

An English writer who once was a head teacher and a contributor to the *Literary Guide*, Walsh in looking at modern physics finds no evidence that the universe had a beginning.

"It is legitimate," he reasons, "to consider the universe after the explosion not as a newly-created entity but as merely a change of form. So those who seek an absolute beginning must range further back than the Big Bang and ascertain where the fireball came from in the first place. Such a search introduces the possibility commonly found in cosmological speculation, that the dense fireball may be the result of a preceding big crunch itself preceded by a previous Big Bang and consequent expansion. And, in fact, it renders feasible the possibility of a whole series of such events ad infinitum."

The task for rationalists, he adds, is for the inquirer, "if he can detach himself from the universe as he experiences it, to see it as an unconscious though changing assembly of matter. Then to realise that into one tiny and possibly insignificant part of its immensity circumstances have caused something called life to arise. And that life, in the course of its evolution, has thrown up a creature which has developed consciousness and self-consciousness." {*New Humanist*, February 1994}

Walsh, Jill Paton (20th Century)

Walsh's novel, *Knowledge of Angels* (1994), received considerable attention in England, partly because many British publishers rejected it. The author imported copies of the American edition and published it herself in England, where it was short-listed for the Booker Prize. The fable about belief in God is a double story set in an Mediterranean island in the 15th century. A wild girl who has lived with wolves and cannot talk is captured and confined with the expectation that once she learns English she will show an intuitive knowledge of God.

Meanwhile, a man from another island who has been shipwrecked and is found to have no belief in God is interrogated by a theologian to see whether he can be converted by reason. Walsh is a lapsed Catholic writer. {*New Humanist*, November 1994}

Walsh, Walter (Born 1857)

Walsh was a theistic preacher who succeeded Voysey. He was Vice-President of the Universal Peace Union and described himself as "a non-Christian Theist," or "Leader of the Free Religious Movement in London." {RAT}

Walter, Annika (20th Century)

Walter, a German Olympic silver medalist in diving, told in a television interview after her success that she is an atheist. The reporter, Dieter Kurten, promptly asked, "What does atheism mean to you?" to which Walter hesitated for a moment, then replied, "I haven't been educated to believe in God." {CA; E}

Walter, Edward (20th Century)

Walter is a contributor of material to *The American Rationalist.*

Walter, Nicolas (20th Century)

Walter was an editor of the *New Humanist*, a well-known British freethought activist, and head of the Rationalist Press Association from 1975 to the end of 1999. In *Blasphemy in Britain* (1977) and *Blasphemy Ancient and Modern* (1990), he argued that the legal dodo of blasphemous libel was not dead in England, that it was reprieved from extinction by Mary Whitehouse, who in 1977 successfully prosecuted *Gay News* for its publication of James Kirkup's homo-erotic poem, "The Love That Dares To Speak Its Name."

In 1980, Walter signed the Secular Humanist Declaration.

He argued, when opponents spoke of "the right not to be offended," that a world without offense would be a world without speech. Walter wrote from the viewpoint of the blasphemers rather than of the religions they offended or the laws they transgressed, his concentration being Britain although he referred to the United States as well as other countries. "In 1940," he illustrated, "A. R. Woodhall was sentenced to a month's imprisonment in Jersey for making a passport photograph resemble Christ on the Cross, but after protest he was released by the Home Secretary after a fortnight." Similarly, he cited other cases, supplying representative selections of literary texts and allowing the reader to judge their content.

As for Harry Stopes-Roe's suggestion that humanism is a "life stance," Walter disagreed (in *New Humanist*, December, 1988), explaining that, for most, humanism is not a stance and it is not necessarily about life. "It is not in any significant way analogous with religion. Most who call themselves humanists, in fact, see humanism as a rejection of all (not just some) of the essential features of religion; but the people who call themselves religious humanists see humanism as an actual form of religion."

A statement of Walter's outlook is found in "There is War Between Religion and Humanism" (*The Freethinker*, January 1996), in which he states the three most important elements of Humanism:

- that all the factors, interests, criteria of any situation are always subordinated to human factors, interests, criteria;
- there is no spirit or mind or principle or force or power or pattern behind the universe, no point to it other than what we give it;
- the rejection of authority.

Because of the wide gap between religion and Humanism, there may be a truce between them, but never peace. Of his outlook, Walter has written: "My own Humanism is a pretty minimal one. It involves neither religion nor ritual; I am not a religious or ritualistic animal. It is entirely sane; my right-brain is fully occupied with art, music and literature, and humour. It is not a 'life-stance' or 'eupraxophy'; I have no more need for secular than for sacred nonsense. It avoids such terms as 'spirit' and 'worship,' however defined; I have no need for alien vocabulary. It perceives nothing as ultimately important; as A. J. Balfour said, nothing matters very much, and most things don't matter at all."

He continued: "I agree with Freud that religion is a neurosis; but so is psychoanalysis. I agree with the Marquis de Sade that nature is hostile to us. I agree with Matthias Claudius that 'man is not at home in the world.' I agree with Max Stirner that there is no such thing as 'Man,' only me and others like me. We should exorcise all the spectres which have haunted us, from God to Humanism itself. I am atheist about God, and agnostic about most other things in the same category. Questions about the value of existence or the meaning of life have no value or meaning. There are no categorical imperatives or fundamental principles. The ultimate reality is that there is no ultimate reality. The golden rule is that there are no golden rules. Here I may not share much common ground with some other Humanists, but I can speak for many others."

Typical of his understanding of philosophic naturalism, Nicolas in "Oh, God!" laments in a book review how "so many seemingly intelligent people can talk about such obvious nonsense (as supernaturalism and religion), and that such poor treatment of such important subjects can be produced by a leading journalist, a leading philosopher, and a leading scientist (Russell Stannard, author of *Science and Wonders*), and circulated by leading periodicals, publishers (Faber & Faber), and broadcasting organisations." However, he noted, "The encouraging thing is that most people—including most scientists and philosophers—remain unaffected by such stuff and get on with their lives without worrying about where they came from or where they are going or what, if anything, it all means."

Walter is probably the only freethinker in decades who has written about *ditheism*, noting that Paul Johnson's *The Quest for God* fails to discuss "*a* god of some kind but *the* God of Judaism, Christianity and Islam, not pantheism or deism or ditheism or polytheism but strict monotheism."

The grandson of S. K. Ratcliffe, Walter has long been on the board of directors of the Rationalist Press Association—he attended only one of four meetings in 1998, however.

In December 1999, he wrote in *New Humanist*: "This is my farewell to arms. I am at the same time retiring from the Rationalist Press Association and moving out of London, leaving the organisations I have belonged to and dropping the periodicals I have subscribed to, and saying goodbye to my native city and to many of my friends and all of my enemies."

Explaining that he had been a professional humanist for too long and "it is time to take my leave of all this," he looked forward to becoming "an amateur human being again." He added that he was sorting papers which have accumulated and which he would give to the South Place Ethical Society library at Conway Hall. He also had thousands of letters to be kept somewhere: "Future archaeologists will wonder at the papyraceous layer deposited by our civilisation, and I am afraid I have contributed more than my fair share to it." (See entry for Humanisms. Also, see Walter's article, "Are Humanists Human?", *New Humanist*, November 1989; "Oh Hell! Christians Deny Christianity Again," in *The Freethinker*, February 1996; and "Oh, God!" *The Freethinker*, May 1996. A capsule summary of Walter's philosophic outlook is contained in the entry under Humanisms. In 1996, mailed a draft of the present book plus $75 for return postage along with an inquiry about the possibility of acceptance for publishing by the Rationalist Press Association, Walter never got around to making suggestions for changes, nor did he return the manuscript and cash—his *Humanism: What's in the Word* [1997] covers some similar material. Edward Royle has reviewed the work favorably, but Harry Stopes-Roe has taken issue with some of its contents (*New Humanist* [December 1997]. Walter has written a history of the RPA, found in issues #2 and #4 of *New Humanist* [1999]). {FUK; SHD}

Walter, W. Grey (Died 1977)

Walter, the father of Nicolas Walter, was an atheist. But upon his death, his college arranged a funeral that was dominated by the liturgy of the Book of Common Prayer. "Here is yet another reminder," Nicolas Walter has written, "that unbelievers should make sure that whatever rituals mark their deaths should not contradict their known beliefs during their lives." {*New Humanist*, November 1997}

Walters, Kerry S. (20th Century)

In his *The American Deists: Voices of Reason and Dissent in the Early Republic* (1992), Walters points out that in America the first reaction against orthodox Christianity was the philosophic movement of deism. Benjamin Franklin, Thomas Jefferson, Tom Paine, Elihu Palmer, Ethan Allen, Philip Freneau, and Constantin Volney wrote voluminously on the subject. Walters underlines the point that deism was a direct precursor of American freethought.

Walther, Eric (20th Century)

Walther, a professor at Long Island University in New York, is knowledgeable not only about philosophy but also about communication. A member of Freethinking Activist Non-believing New Yorkers (FANNY), he took part in a 1999 remembrance of Robert Green Ingersoll which was held at one of Ingersoll's former residences, the Gramercy Hotel in Manhattan. Walther long as been active in humanist and freethought circles.

Walther, Jeff (20th Century)

Walther edits *Green Light*, the newsletter of the International Naturalist Church. (See entry for International Naturalist Church.)

Walther, Johannes (Born 1860)

From 1886 to 1906 Walter was a private teacher at Jena University. In 1906 he was appointed Haeckel Professor of Geology, after which he taught paleontology at Halle University and became director of the Royal Geological Institute. Walther was a pupil of Haeckel and holds that, in importance, Haeckel must be named after Goethe and Humboldt. Walter is a thorough and outspoken Monist. {RAT}

Walton, Don (Died 1999)

Walton, a member in Oxford of the Gay and Lesbian Humanist Association, met Bernard Conolly, an editorial executive on the *Daily Mail* in the 1950s, and their partnership lasted forty years. Conolly became deputy editor of the *Oxford Mail*. When he knew in the last few weeks that he was dying, Walton set to work recording the music he wanted to be played at his Humanist funeral ceremony. {*G&L Humanist*, Winter 1999-2000}

Walwyn, William (1600–1681)

Walwyn, a grandson of a Bishop of Hereford, was a writer, described by Edwards in his *Gangraena* as "a seeker, a dangerous man." Walwyn attacked all the sects and professed to "seek" truth apart from them. Although respecting the Bible, he was imprisoned in the Tower on political charges and was accused of communism and atheism. The government charged that he had urged people to read Plutarch and Cicero on Sundays instead of going to church. Walwyn replied in his *Fountain of Slander Discovered* (1649). {RAT}

Walz, Frederick (20th Century)

Walz wrote *New vs. Old: The Guilt of Organized "Religions" in the Decline and Fall of the United States of America* (1971). {GS}

Wang, Ch'ung (Chong) (c. 27-c 100)

"One of the greatest men of his nation in any age" was the description of Wang given by science historian Joseph Needham. Wang was a monistic naturalist with ideas similar to those of Lucretius. A teacher and minor official, he wrote about politics, morality, and how to prolong life. *Lun Heng* (Critical Essays, written c. 82-83) fills 750 pages in an English translation.

Wang's outlook was that of the "hatred of fictions and falsehoods." He rejected all the supernatural assumptions of Chinese metaphysics and physics, not the natural ones. He denied the existence of divinity, saw *ying* and *yan* as natural substances, heaven and earth as natural elements. Fate he saw as an impersonal necessity, not a personal reward or punishment. Earthquakes, floods, thunder, lightning were natural events not the work of something supernatural.

Nicholas Walter has further summarized Wang's views:

> He believes in the reliability of astrology and physiognomy and the significance of dreams and omens, but for scientific rather than magical reasons. He believes in spirits but not as dangerous beings, in portents but not in the power of prayer or ritual. All living things are born and die, and meanwhile struggle for existence. We are animals, living on the earth as lice live on us. The death of a person is like the extinction of a fire, and both the soul and the body are physical entities which come and return to universal existence. He repudiates reverence for the past, and although he cites the Confucian masters he criticises them. His moral doctrine is a modified and moderate version of Confucianism: do as you would be done by, within reason and following common sense. His position was a combination of scepticism and naturalism, materialism and secularism, rationalism and empiricism, which was as rare in China as elsewhere. Yet this attitude never quite faded, and such thinkers continued to appear—especially in the Neo-Confucian tradition—until the 18th century and the beginning of Western influence.
>
> {*New Humanist*, October 1998}

WANTED/NURTURED CHILDREN

Wanted/Nurtured Children is a monthly published by the American Humanist Association, PO Box 1001, San Jacinto, California 92581.

WAR

Although the Early Church had no concern with social or collective problems and before the year 300 opposed military service, chiefly because it involved a profession of paganism, from the time of Constantine onward the opposition relented. For a thousand years after the fall of Rome there was no Christian pacifism. Popes Gregory VII and Innocent III ordered wars as freely as most princes did, and the Papacy had its own army, often led by cardinals and sometimes by the Popes themselves, down to the middle of the nineteenth century. The Church further held that war upon infidels and heretics was holy work, and that war upon any prince they excommunicated was more than just. They blessed the banners of any prince, for example William the Conqueror, who promised them docility. In his introduction to the translation of Kant's *Perpetual Peace*, Campbell Smith wrote that the Church, instead of denouncing war, made it worse than ever. The Church of Rome, he said, was "in some respects a more warlike institution than the states of Greece and Rome" and "the history of the Middle Ages came nearer to a realization of the idea of perpetual war than was possible in ancient times." At the time of the Reformation, Erasmus the humanist and Grotius the Protestant spoke out against war, and during the 18th century a French priest, St. Pierre, published his *Project of Peace*, which was received with general disdain. But inasmuch as neither the Catholic nor Protestant church supported these individual utterances, they had little or no significance so far as the growth of a world-feeling against war is concerned.

That world-feeling against war commenced during the age of skepticism that opened with Rousseau, Voltaire, and the Encyclopedists. Kant, whose *Perpetual Peace* (1795) was the first direct attack, stood apart from the Churches. Bentham the atheist, author of the phrase "International Law," organized a humanitarian campaign in England. The atheist Robert Owen took up the challenge. The Quakers were encouraged to join. In 1816, the first Peace Society was founded in London. No Church gave the weight of its support, for, in McCabe's words, "it was still the fashion to sneer at infidels as a few eccentric individuals." McCabe makes the case that of twenty-six major individuals who have attacked war in principle and worked for the substitution of arbitration, thirteen were Rationalists, three were avowed Christians, and ten were, to him, of unknown attitude.

In 1994, Steve Karr in the *Secular Humanist Bulletin* listed religion-inspired violence then current around the world in these countries: Afghanistan; Algeria; Azerbaijan; Bosnia; Burma; Croatia; Egypt; Ethiopia; Lebanon; Northern Ireland; India; Iran; Iraq; Israel; Serbia; Sri Lanka; Somalia; Sudan; Tibet; United States.

Although even the most optimistic of individuals do not envisage a future which will ever be devoid of war, Christopher Logue in the following sample from *Selected Poems* (1996) thinks poetry through satire and humor has the potential for changing things:

> When I was serving my country
> a staff-sergeant said:
> There's dozens of ways, but if everything fails,
> put your head on her shoulder
> your prick in her hand,
> and cry.

The French comic, Fernand Reynaud, had an unforgettable definition of wars, that they are fought by people who do not know each other on behalf of those who do know each other but don't fight. A coincidental and satirical view, by novelist Joseph Heller in *Closing Time* (1994), is that "People with force have a right to do anything we can't stop them from doing." (See entry for Pacifism.) {*The Economist*, 13 July 1996; RE}

Warbasse, James Peter (1866–1957)

A world leader in the cooperative movement, Warbasse was a surgeon who switched his interests and devoted full time to the cooperative movement, which was based on mutual aid in the conduct of economic enterprises and on a social theory that finds expression in these enterprises. During the Spanish-American War, he was a surgeon. In 1892, he set up the first laboratory of surgical pathology and bacteriology in America, at Methodist Hospital. He wrote *Surgical Treatment* (3 volumes, 1919), *What is Cooperation?* (1927), and *Peace Through Cooperation* (1949).

In 1955, he was named Humanist of the Year by the American Humanist Association, of which he was a member. {CL; HNS; HNS2}

Ward, Charles (20th Century)

Ward writes for *The Freethinker* in England. In "Caring, Co-Operation, Clarity" (March 1994), he holds that humanists need not imitate the old-fashioned custom favored by religious bodies, of listing aims, beliefs, and modes of behavior in rigid phraseology with which they clearly expect all recruits to agree. Instead, he suggests humanists are beyond such.

Ward, looking into the future, also warns that the last thing needed on our voyage into the new millennium is the Ten Commandments, which he finds of negative value and a "museum piece." {*The Freethinker*, May 1996}

Ward, H. Percy (20th Century)

In Bradford, England, Ward edited *Secularist* in 1902.

Ward, Lester Frank (1841–1911)

Ward was an American sociologist and paleontologist. One of the first and most important of American sociologists, he developed a theory of planned progress, called telesis, whereby man, through education and development of intellect, could direct social evolution. According to William F. Ryan, Ward "was one of the first theorists to state that the female sex had preceded the male on this planet, and that women were in several ways superior to men, especially in prehistoric times." Ward, an agnostic, viewed Christianity as a calamity. From Washington, DC, he edited *Iconoclast* (1870–1871). His *Applied Sociology* (1906) had a wide audience.

Ward was wounded during the Civil War, after which he became librarian of the United States Bureau of Statistics and later curator of botany and fossil plants in the national museum. (See entry for Emily Cape.) {BDF; CE; CL; EU, William F. Ryan; FUS; JM; RAT; RE; TYD}

Ward, Mary Augusta (1851–1920)

The granddaughter of Thomas Arnold, Mary Augusta Arnold married Thomas Humphrey Ward, an editor of the Oxford *Spectator*, in 1872. She made her reputation as a novelist with *Robert Elsmere* (1888), a story which defended an ethical rather than a mystical interpretation of the Bible. Christians saw it as a description of a hero's lapse into unbelief, but others found that the hero's commitment to the welfare of other human beings shows that, after Christianity's supernatural elements are gone, the former Christians can be inspiring people. Ward translated *Amiel's Journal*. {CE}

Ward, Percy (20th Century)

Ward, a former Wesleyan, was a co-founder in 1924 of Chicago's American Rationalist Association. Previously, he had been secretary of the British Secular League in Yorkshire, England. Ward wrote *What I Believe and Why* (1915) and *Atheism and Americana in the Public Schools* (1919). {FUK; FUS; RSR}

Ward, Robert (1917–)

A composer who is a member of the American Academy of Arts and Letters, Ward wrote the present author concerning humanism: "Both Theistic Humanism and Naturalistic Humanism would be included in my set of beliefs and my view of 'humanism.' Aspects of all the other definitions have been considered in arriving at my conclusion." {WAS, 13 July 1992}

Ware, Henry (1764–1845)

Ware's election as Hollis Professor of Divinity in 1803 was one of the earliest public manifestations of the growing split between Calvinists and liberals in New England, and the opposition voiced to his election by the Calvinists constituted the first phase of the Unitarian controversy. He was minister of the First Parish in Hingham, Massachusetts, and he taught at Harvard until 1840, founding the divinity school. His son, Henry, took a leading role among the next generation of liberals. {FUS; U&U}

Ware, Henry, Jr. (1794–1843)

A pastor of Boston's Second Unitarian Church (1817–1830), Ware left the church in the hands of his young colleague, Ralph Waldo Emerson.

Despite poor health, he became a professor in the Harvard divinity school (1830–1842), where he argued that the aim of religion is the cultivation of the ability to give "your heart a permanent bias toward God," this despite the denomination's reputation of being a church of rational rather than pietistic religion. {U; U&U}

Waring, E. Graham (20th Century)

Waring edited *Deism and Natural Religion* (1967). {FUK; GS}

Waring, John A. (1914–1997)

Waring was a researcher who was an authority on the social impact of technological development. He retired in 1978 from Fort Belvoir as editor of *Defense Systems Management Review*. Afterwards, he was research director for a report of the Mahler Institute on nuclear radiation hazards. Waring was a member of the Washington (D.C.) Area Secular Humanists. {*Washington Post*, 15 June 1997}

Warm, Anna (1946-)

A seasoned teacher of high school literature and writing in Fairfield County, Connecticut, Warm has written, "I became an atheist in Methodist Sunday School when, one day, I looked around and said to myself, incredulously, 'These kids are buying this?' Also, I hated the Welch's grape juice communions." {WAS, 21 April 1999}

Warner, Sylvia Townsend (1893–1978)

Warner, an English novelist and poet, began working as one of the editors of *Tudor Church Music* (10 volumes, 1922–1929), and her interest in music continued for the rest of her life. In her twenties, she wrote *The Espalier* (1925), a book of poetry followed by *Whether A Dove or A Seagull* (1933), the latter written in collaboration with her companion of forty years, Valentine Ackland. Warner was an admirer of such poets as Thomas Hardy and George Crabbe.

Her fiction, which reveals her freethought, included *Lolly Willowes* (1926), about a maiden aunt who realizes her vocation as a witch, and *Mr. Fortune's Maggot* (1927), about the visit of an ex-clerk missionary to a remote South Sea island of Fanua, where he makes only one doubtful convert, then loses his own faith out of love for the islanders. Her *Letters* (1982) and her diaries (1996) tell of an intense feminism, an interest in "Uncle Joe" Stalin and communism (*Summer Will Show*, a 1936 novel, ends with the heroines sitting down and reading "The Communist Manifesto"), and her love for Ackland. As pointed out by Claire Tomalin, "In her published work, Townsend Warner did not proclaim her lesbianism, following in the tradition of kindred British women writers like Mansfield, Woolf and Sackville-West, all of whom tiptoed discreetly around this fascinating but dangerous subject. There was good reason for caution, since writings that edged too close to homosexual themes had brought both D. H. Lawrence and Radclyffe Hall to the law courts and led to the banning of their work."

After the war, during which her and Ackland's home was destroyed by a bomb dropped by a German warplane, the two spent the remainder of their lives at Frome Vauchurch, Dorset. Warner was shocked when Ackland converted to Roman Catholicism near the end of her life. As a result, according to *I'll Stand By You, Selected Letters of Sylvia Townsend Warner and Valentine Ackland* (1999), she had to put up with the sight of rosaries and prayer books around the house.

Warner wrote numerous stories for *The New Yorker*, "potboilers," she sometimes called them. Patricia Juliana Smith of the University of Connecticut claims that "lesbian and feminist critics are increasingly recognizing [Warner] as an important lesbian voice of the early twentieth century." {GL; OEL; Claire Tomalin, "Burning Happiness," *The New York Times*, 18 February 1996}

Warnock, Mary (20th Century)

Warnock's *Women Philosophers* (1996) lists, among other women philosophers, the following: Anne Conway (1631–1679); Mary Wollstonecraft (1759–1797); Harriet Martineau (1802–1876); Victoria Lady Welby (1837–1912); Mary Whiton Calkins (1863–1930); Susan Stebbing (1885–1943); Hannah Arendt (1906–1975); Simone de Beauvoir (1908–1986); and Iris Murdoch (1919–). Her *Intelligent Person's Guide to Ethics* (1998, according to Colin McCall, is "an intelligent person's guide to ethics" by "a very wise woman." {Colin McCall, *The Freethinker*, June 1996 and November-December 1998}

Warrag, Ibn Al (1928-)

In *The Radical Humanist* (June 1999, as adopted from *New Humanist*), Warrag related the story of Anwar Shaikh, an ex-Muslim who became a liberal humanist. (See entry for Anwar Shaikh)

Warraq, Ibn [pseudonym] (20th Century)

Warraq is a pseudonym for a former Muslim said to be "a lecturer in cultural studies at a Western university." In "Islamic Intolerance" (*Free Inquiry*, Summer 1993), he detailed why Muslims are intolerant of Christians, Jews, Hindus, Bahais, and Buddhists, concluding that "even Islam's staunchest supporters will testify to the uneasy and precarious position of non-Muslims in the Muslim states of today—the Copts of Egypt, the Jews in Syria, the Christians, and Hindus in Pakistan."

Why I Am Not A Muslim (1995) discusses the totalitarian nature of Islam and its law, Islamic colonialism, how Islam treats heretics and freethinkers, the status of women, the undemocratic pressures applied by Islamic immigrants in the West, and its taboos (wine, pork, and homosexuality). G. A. Wells, professor of German at the University of London, has praised the book not only for being "courageous" but also for scrutinizing the fundamental tenets of Islam so uncompromisingly.

Religion, Warraq finds, "is largely a reshuffling of ideas of a yesterday, and to this Islam is no exception. It has taken a great deal from both Jewish and Christian traditions, but I doubt whether many Christians are aware of in what strange guise Christianity figures in the Koran. According to Sura 4, Jesus was not crucified: the Jews 'Killed him not, they did not crucify him, but it was made to appear that way to them.' This strikes at the heart of what is now established as Christian doctrine. If there was no atoning death, there is no redemption, through such a death."

What is in the Qur'an about Christianity, Warraq claims and Wells notes, derives from heretical sects. Writes QWarraq, "The Qur'an looks more authentic than the Gospels, in that its author works no miracles and makes no claim to divinity. . . . Also, there are so many variant readings that it is misleading to speak of the Koran: The definitive text still had not been achieved as late as the ninth century."

Islam never really encouraged science, if by science is meant "disinterested inquiry," according to Warraq. What Islam means by "knowledge" is religious knowledge, for all other knowledge is dangerous to the faith. Whatever real science occurred under Islam occurred despite, not because, the religion. Further, he holds, the Muslim world has been indebted from the beginning to the Greeks and is indebted now to science for understanding its own intellectual and cultural history.

He concludes that he is "convinced that despite all the shortcomings of Western liberal democracy, it is far preferable to the authoritarian, mind-numbing certitudes of Islamic theocracy." Few other works have dared touch such subjects, and like Salmon Rushdie Warraq is afraid to reveal his exact whereabouts for fear of being assassinated.

He did, however, participate in the 1996 Mexico City conference of humanists, and he is an honorary associate of the New Zealand Association of Rationalists and Humanists. In Mexico, he said that fundamentalists fear the humanities and history more than science, for they relativize human outlooks. Many humanists are to be found of Muslim origin, but one should see himself or herself as, for example, an Egyptian, not as an Egyptian Moslem or an Egyptian humanist. He looked forward to the time when the humanist movement will be as well known as Amnesty International. Warraq has written,

> My close family members identify themselves as Muslim: some more orthodox, others less. My earliest memories are of my circumcision and my first day at Koranic school—psychoanalysts may make what they wish of that. Even before I could read or write the national language I learned to read the Koran in Arabic without understanding a word of it—a common experience for thousands of Muslim children.
>
> As soon as I was able to think for myself, I discarded all the religious dogmas that had been foisted on me. I now consider myself a secular humanist who believes that all religions are sick men's dreams, false—demonstrably false—and pernicious.

The Origins of the Qur'an: Classic Essays in Islam's Holy Book (1998) is a controversial work which undermines the traditional account of the origin of the Qur'an and of the role of the Prophet in its formation. Muslim history is a fantasy, Warraq wrote, and Muslim "revelation" is actually a human, not a divine, construction.

Warraq, a signer of Humanist Manifesto 2000 and one of the members of the IHEU's Committee on Religious Extremism and Rational Inquiry, is Executive Director of the International Society for Islamic Secularization (ISIS, PO Box 229, Buffalo, NY 14215).

The group's e-mail address: <info@secularislam.org>. On the Web: <http://www.secularislam.org>. (See "Standing Up to Scrutinize Islam," *Free Inquiry*, Winter 1995-1996.) {WAS, numerous conversations}

Warren, Barbara (20th Century)

Warren, a Seattle-area lawyer and a member of Seattle's University Unitarian Church, is executive director of the Unitarian Universalist Affordable Housing Corporation (UUAHC).

Warren, Josiah (1798–1874)

An American reformer, Warren took an active part in Robert Owen's communistic experiment at New Harmony, Indiana (1825–1826). His own ideas were illustrated when he established in Cincinnati a "time store." Warren's outlook is found in his *True Civilisation*. {BDF; RAT}

Warren, Sidney (20th Century)

Warren was an American freethinker. Historian Allan Nevins wrote the foreword to his *American Freethought 1860–1914* (1943). {FUS}

WARS OF RELIGION

The Wars of Religion (1562–1598) spread throughout France following the Saint Bartholomew's Day Massacre (1572) in Paris. (See entry for Saint Bartholomew's Day Massacre.) {CE}

Warwick, Frances Evelyn (Countess of) (1861–1938)

Warwick, who was the daughter of Colonel Maynard the wife of the Earl of Warwick, became known for her Socialist views. She disliked the name "philanthropist," but she was generous in helping many institutions. In the *Hibbert Journal* (July, 1917), Warwick called for "a religion of humanity" without theology, ritual, or priests, and she pronounced the Church of England "bankrupt." She was, however, a theist. {RAT; RE}

Washburn, Cadwallader Colden [Governor] (1818–1882)

A Unitarian, Washburn was active in politics and founded the Gold Medal flour company. He was Governor of Wisconsin from 1867 to 1871 and again from 1872 to 1874. {U}

Washburn, Elihu (Benjamin) (1816–1887)

Washburn, a diplomat and American politician, was the U.S. Representative from Illinois (1853–1869) and became known as a radical Republican who insisted upon limiting expenses. President Ulysses S. Grant appointed Washburne Secretary of State but, feeling unqualified, he resigned within two weeks to become minister to France (1869–1877). A Unitarian, he wrote *Israel, Elihu, and Cadwallader Washburn* (1925). {CE; U}

Washburn, Israel (1813–1883)

A Maine Universalist, Washburn had four sons out of seven who served in the United States Congress. One, Representative Israel Washburn Jr., called the meeting of an anti-slavery political party which resulted in the Republican Party, according to David Johnson, minister of First Parish in Brookline, Massachusetts.

Washburn, Lemuel K. (Born 1846)

Washburn was an American lecturer and writer. Ordained in Ipswich as a Unitarian in 1870, he popularized the work of Parker, Emerson, and others rather than the Bible. In Minneapolis, he organized the first Freethought Society in Minnesota. Washburn was editor of the *Boston Investigator*, and he wrote *Cosmian Hymn Book* (1888) and *Is the Bible Worth Reading?* (1911). {BDF; PUT; RAT}

Washington, Corey (20th Century)

At the University of Washington in 1995, Washington debated the existence of God with Christian apologist Dr. William Lane Craig.

Washington, an atheist-agnostic philosopher, discussed abstract objects, the cosmological argument, the anthropic principle, objective moral values, the resurrection, religious experience, and the problem of evil. He is a supporter of Internet Infidels.

Washington, David M. (20th Century)

An artist living in Chicago, Illinois, Washington is an Advisory Board Member of African Americans for Humanism.

Washington, George [President] (1732–1799)

"There is no doubt that George Washington, a rather indifferent member of the Episcopal Church, and John Adams, second President of the United States and sympathetic to Unitarianism, were strongly influenced by Deism, both through their colleagues and as a result of the general intellectual atmosphere," wrote Corliss Lamont.

Washington was a member of the Masonic Lodge, which is open to individuals of all religions and uses a ritual that utilizes deistic terminology. Masonic practice is to use a deistic term such as "Supreme Architect" instead of God or Allah, and although Masons are required to believe in a "greater power" than themselves, they are allowed to define that power as they see fit. Washington consistently abstained from any public mention of the Christian religion. In his valedictory letter to the governors of the States on resigning his commission, Robertson points out, he did speak of the " 'benign influence of the Christian religion'—the common tone of the American deists of that day."

Richard Brookhiser, in *Founding Father: Rediscovering George Washington* (1995), also mentions that the Anglican Church, the Bible, Freemasonry, the theater, and farming were important to Washington. But his familiarity with the Scriptures was limited to a few quotations which were clichés expressed by others around him, such as "every man under his vine and under his fig tree." The Bible and Freemasonry may have been important to him, but Washington's mind was not that of an intellectual so much as it was a mind of practicality. Like Cincinnatus, he was devoted to farming.

As pointed out by Michael S. Medved, "One of the most seriously misleading of the Washington legends is the story of the pious general kneeling in prayer in the snow at Valley Forge. Not only is there no evidence to support this tale but also Washington was notorious in his parish church for refusing to kneel at any of the customary moments in the Episcopal service. As his minister declared disapprovingly after the President's death, 'Washington was a Deist.' Although Martha was a devout churchwoman, George never shared her enthusiasm. On communion Sundays he always walked out before taking the Eucharist, leaving Martha to participate in the service alone."

In short, the first United States President was not interested in promised heavenly treasures in the hereafter. Even Jefferson had difficulty getting Washington to go on record concerning organized religion.

Of Washington, McCabe wrote: "Clerical writers are naturally unwilling to admit that he was a freethinker—a non-Christian theist—but, while the evidence of faith which they allege is of the flimsiest description there is ample and solid proof of his heresy. Jefferson says that Morris, who was intimate with Washington, 'often told me that General Washington believed no more of that system (Christianity) than he himself did.' He quotes a chaplain to Congress who said that when the clergy presented an address to the President at his retirement, they pointed out that in his acknowledgment he had not said a word that identified him with Christianity, and in a further reply 'the old fox' evaded that point. In a sermon delivered at Albany and reported in the *Daily Advertiser* (Oct. 29, 1831), one of the chief ministers of the city said that 'among all our Presidents from Washington downward not one was a professor of religion,' which gives us the clerical tradition on the question. It is true that while he was President he attended the Episcopal church, but the rector, Dr. Abercrombie, told this preacher, Dr. Wilson (who says it in the same sermon), that Washington always left before the communion and when the rector pointed this out ceased to attend any service that was followed by communion. It is admitted that he did not send for or have a clergyman in his last hours; and the statement that he asked his family to leave the room and let him 'spend his last hour with his Maker' shows only that he believed in God, which nobody ever disputed. Some apologists give us the prayer he said when he was 'alone with God,' who must have let them into the secret. It cannot be disputed that he said in his will: 'It is my express desire that my corpse may be interred in a private manner, without parade or funeral oration.' Against all this the chief champion of the angels, Jared Sparks, who edited Washington's writings nearly forty years after the death, urges such matters as that Washington wrote a hymn when he was a boy of thirteen; that (being a Deist) he often spoke of 'the Author of the Universe;' that a granddaughter, who was still a child when Washington died, said he prayed every day in private (which Washington's adopted daughter questioned and was, in any case, consistent with deism); and that once or twice he spoke favorably of the Christian religion. The man is obviously a religious twister. He ignores decisive evidence in the very letters he edited—as when Washington speaks of 'the professors of Christianity' or Bishop White says that he never saw him kneel at prayer or heard him speak about religion—and most of the evidence given above. The evidence on both sides is given in Franklin Steiner's *The Religious Beliefs of Our Presidents* (Haldeman-Julius, 1936) and Remsburg's *Six Historic Americans*."

For some patriots, Washington has himself become somewhat deified. But the man who personally surveyed the future boundaries of Washington, D.C., and who personally signed every passport issued during his presidency was once joked about by Nathaniel Hawthorne. The novelist, seeing a statue of the half-clad Washington which was erected in the Capitol Rotunda in the 1840s, remarked, "Did anybody ever see Washington naked? It is inconceivable. He has no nakedness, but I imagine was born with his clothes on and his hair powdered, and made a stately bow on his first appearance in the world."

Although known as "the father of his country," Washington sired no children and allegedly showed little interest in women. "As a young unmarried man," states the *Alyson Almanac*,

> . . . he told friends that there was only one woman that he would ever consider marrying and that she was already married to his friend George William Fairfax. He did eventually marry Martha Dandridge Custis after being persuaded that it was unseemly for a public figure to remain unmarried. Nevertheless, his closest attachments were always to men, particular Alexander Hamilton. Throughout the Revolution, Hamilton served as Washington's aide-de-camp, personal secretary, and closest companion. During Washington's term of office, Treasury Secretary Hamilton was the guiding force of the administration and was the author of Washington's Farewell Address. Due to the fact that Hamilton also had a history of intense friendships with men, there has been speculation—but no hard evidence—that the relationship went further than that.

Scandalmongers of his time, however, said Washington illegitimately fathered dozens of children and alleged, without documentation, that Alexander Hamilton was one such; some implied, on the contrary, that Hamilton was his secret love. Others said he did not smile because his wooden false teeth hurt—according to Ben Swanson, executive director of the National Museum of Dentistry, Washington had dentures that were made of ivory, sometimes even of human tooth enamel, but not wood. They were hinged together with gold springs and caused considerable pain.

When he died of quinsy, or acute laryngitis, Washington owned 33,000 acres of land in Virginia, Kentucky, Maryland, New York, and the Northwest Territory. He had 640 sheep, 329 cows, horses, and mules. He also owned hundreds of slaves. His will stated,

> Upon the decease of my wife, it is my Will & desire that all Slaves which I hold in *my own right*, shall receive their freedom. . . . And whereas among those who will receive freedom according to this devise, there may be some, who from old age or bodily infirmities, and others who on account of their infancy, that will be unable to support themselves; it is my Will and desire that all . . . shall be com-

fortably cloathed & fed by my heirs while they live. . . . And I do expressly forbid the Sale, or transportation out of the said Commonwealth of Virginia, of any Slave I may died possessed of, under any pretence whosoever. . . . And to my Mulatto man William (calling himself William Lee) I give immediate freedom; or if he should prefer it (on account of the accidents which have befallen him, and which have rendered him incapable of walking or any active employment) to remain in the situation he now is. . . . This I give him as a testimony of my sense of his attachment to me, and for his faithful services during the Revolutionary war.

At the time of his death, he had been bled heavily for four times and given gargles of molasses, vinegar, and butter. On his throat was placed a preparation, a blister of cantharides, made from dried beetles. On his deathbed, he uttered no words of a religious nature nor did he ask for a clergyman. "I die so hard," he said, "but I am not afraid to go. I feel myself going. I thank you for your attention, but I pray you to take no more trouble about me. Let me go off quietly. I cannot last long." (See also the entry for E. C. Vanderlaan, who confirms Washington's lack of interest in religion; and for Gouverneur Morris, who told Thomas Jefferson that Washington believed no more of Christianity than he himself did. Paul Boller's *George Washington and Religion* discusses the topic, also.) {AA; CE; CL; FUS; HNS2; JM; JMR; JMRH; PA; RAT; RE; TRI; TYD}

WASHINGTON ATHEISTS, HUMANISTS

• Atheist League of Washington (Atheist Alliance), POB 1785, Seattle, Washington 98111.

• *Free Mind*, a bi-monthly, 4116 Candlewood Dr. S.E., Lacey, Washington 98503-4422

• Humanist Association of Palouse Area (AHA), A-9, 600 Crestview SW, Pullman, Washington 99163. Tyre Newton is the contact.

• Humanists of North Puget Sound, PO Box 405, La Conner, Washington 98257; phone (360) 466-4513. E-mail: <apptwo@halcyon.com>. Harry App is President.

• Humanist Society of South Puget Sound (AHA–Bette Chambers is the contact. Phone (360) 491-8671), 4116 Candlewood Drive SE, Lacey, Washington 98503.

• Spokane, Washington, Freedom from Religion Chapter, PO Box 436, Greenacres, WA 99016. Contact: <hhforester@aol.com>

• University of Puget Sound Humanists are at: <http://www.secularhumanism.org/cfa/orgs.html>.

• Western Washington University's Atheists, Heathens, and Agnostics on the Web:: <www.secularhumanism.org/cfa/orgs.html>.

WASHINGTON, D.C., HUMANISTS

The District of Columbia has the Washington Area Secular Humanists (ASHS), POB 15319, Washington, DC 20003; (202) 298-0921. Ken Marsalek is the contact for the Maryland and District of Columbia chapters. E-mail: <wash@poboxes.com>. On the Web: <http://www.wam.umd.edu/~kaugust/asatext/wash.html>.

Wason, C. R. (20th Century)

Wason writes for the English *Freethinker*. "Modern Jews claim that they have a right to rule Palestine because this right was given by a promise made to their ancestor Abraham," he has stated. But the curious conclusion of history, he finds, is that the Palestine Arabs have the best claim to be the "Children of Abraham" inasmuch "as the original population of Israel has occupied the country since the days of Moses, though it has been diluted by successive invasions." Wason holds that the Jews have every right to be proud of their noble tradition of democracy and learning, which was given to them by Moses, but not "if they rob and oppress the legitimate population and justify this by the fraudulent claim that this was promised to them by a fictitious Jehovah." {*The Freethinker*, July 1994}

WASP

"WASP" refers to White Anglo-Saxon Protestants. The term usually has negative connotations. Inasmuch as the "W" is redundant, many shorten the expression to ASP. E(dward) Digby Baltzell (1912–1996), a sociologist, wrote *The Protestant Establishment: Aristocracy and Caste in America* (1964), a work credited with being the inspiration for "WASP," although Baltzell was not pleased at the prospect of being remembered for but a single word. His sociological concern was that the American elite maintained barriers against minorities and was often racially prejudiced against talented outsiders.

Surprisingly, Baltzell admired Al Capone, whom he called "one of the organizing geniuses of his generation." Capone had made his money exploiting the market created by prohibition (a law passed by traditional Protestants largely to curb the drinking habits of the ethnic masses). Capone, said Baltzell, simply had followed in the tradition of the American dream of the self-made man and was not much different from the self-made Protestant "robber barons" of an earlier era. {*The Economist*, 31 August 1996}

Wasserman, Yoel (20th Century)

Wasserman, a Coloradoan who is fluent in Hebrew, is one of many who term the Septuagint translation of the Bible "a bad one." He claims that "the only reason its existence is in any way seemingly relevant in modern theology is because most early Christians did not know Hebrew but *did* know Greek. Otherwise, it would be nothing more than another old document. The language of the Jews was Hebrew, not Greek, and the language of the Old Testament was Hebrew, not Greek. That's just the way it is." {*The Skeptical Review*, January/February 1997}

Wassil-Grimm, Claudette (20th Century)

A Unitarian, Wassil-Grimm is author of *Diagnosis for Disaster: The Devastating Truth About False Memory Syndrome and Its Impact on Accusers and Families* (1995) and *The Twelve-Step Journal* (1996). She debunks the idea that people repress memories of abuse, retrieving them only years afterwards. Those memories, she holds, are often false but are encouraged by therapists. Her work quotes many "retractors," people who once believed they had remembered sexual abuse but have since come to doubt such memories.

WATER

Water, the most familiar and abundant liquid on earth, is the essential ingredient of life. If non-believers were forced to name something that is "sacred," they would name water, without which life as we know it would be an impossibility. In 1994, when a radiotelescope found water 200 million light-years ago in Markarian 1, the constellation of Pisces the fish, non-believers speculated that water may be present throughout the universe. "If this stuff is out there," said Jack Welch at the American Astronomical Society's national meeting, "then there is a good chance that there are living beings elsewhere. . . . The presence of water makes for the likelihood of life emerging in a number of places." The water in Markarian 1 is contained in clouds that are rotating at thousands of miles an hour around the center of the galaxy, where a black hole could exist. (See entry for Air.)

Waterman, William R. (20th Century)

Waterman wrote *Frances Wright* (1924). {GS}

Waters, Ann (20th Century)

Waters, who works on the *Fitchburg Star* in Wisconsin, is President of the International Internet Leathercrafters Guild of Chicago. At the 1998 Midwest Horse Fair in Madison, Wisconsin, she displayed work that included three-dimensional leather portraits of horses. Waters is a freethinker whose journalistic stories have been critical of organized religion. E-mail: <clearh20s@aol.com>.

Waters, Brianna (20th Century)

In 1995 Waters and Ali Aliabadi founded the Atheist Students Association (ASA) at the University of Maryland in College Park. The two also were founding members of Campus Freethought Alliance. {*International Humanist News*, December 1996}

Waters, Nathaniel Ramsey (19th Century)

Waters was the American author of *Rome v. Reason* (1888). {BDF}

Watkin, Frances (20th Century)

Watkin in Britain is active with the Oxford Humanists.

Watkins, Bert (20th Century)

Watkins has been editor of *The Shreveport Humanist Bulletin*. E-mail: <wwatkins40@aol.com>.

Watkins, Steve (20th Century)

A novelist who teaches at Mary Washington College in Fredericksburg, Virginia, Watkins wrote *The Black O*. The work describes how Shoney's, a billion-dollar chain with restaurants in thirty-five states, ended up paying out $132.5 million, most of it to nearly 21,000 former employees. The title comes from one of the company's bizarre hiring practices: manager were instructed to blacken the *o* in *Shoney's* on job applications as a secret code indicating the applicant was African American. A Unitarian, he left the United Methodist church because "I didn't believe what they believed and couldn't pretend otherwise." {*World*, July-August 1998}

Watson, Alan (20th Century)

Watson is an activist in Ireland of the Ulster Humanist Association. His e-mail: <alan.watson1@virgin.net>.

Watson, Geoffrey (20th Century)

Watson, a psychologist, was Principal Lecturer at King Alfred's College, Winchester, England. In "Life—A Meaning and a Morality" (*New Humanist*, December 1997), he argues that it is possible to give meaning to our lives at the same time creating moral values ourselves.

Watson, Goodwin (1899?–1976)

When he signed Humanist Manifesto II, Watson was an association coordinator of Union Graduate School. He was on the editorial board of the *Journal of Social Psychology*. {HM2}

Watson, James (1799–1874)

Watson was known as one of the bravest heroes in the struggle for a free press in England. During the prosecution of Carlile and his shopmen in 1822, Watson volunteered to come from London to Leeds. For selling a deist book, Palmer's *Principles of Nature*, Watson, a British freethought publisher, was convicted of blasphemous libel in 1823 and sentenced to one year in Cold Bath Fields prison. More a deist than an atheist, he took part in Robert Owen's agitation for universal suffrage, and he was active in trade-union matters and in the struggle for an unstamped press. He was one of Richard Carlile's shopmen, and took his share of imprisonment when the Government tried to suppress Thomas Paine's *Age of Reason* and several other Freethought publications. His forte was as a publisher, and he issued many anti-Christian works in cheap editions by Paine, Mirabeau, Palmer, d'Holbach, Frances Wright, Shelley, Haslam, Holyoake, Volney, and others.

W. J. Linton, a biographer, reported that Watson died at the age of seventy-five, "passing away in his sleep, without a struggle, without a sigh." {BDF; EU, Joel H. Wiener; FO; FUK; RAT; RE; VI; TRI; Nicholas Walter, *New Humanist*, September 1999}

Watson, James Dewey (1928-)

A 1962 Nobel Prize for Physiology or Medicine winner, along with Francis Crick and Maurice Wilkins, Watson is a Chicago-born geneticist. He became professor of biology at Harvard in 1961 and in 1994 President of the Cold Spring Harbor Laboratory at Long Island, New York.

Interviewed in 1996 for a BBC film, Watson said:

> I don't think we're for anything, we're just products of evolution. You can say, "Gee, your life must be pretty bleak if you don't think there's a purpose," but I'm anticipating a good lunch. [Asked if he knew many religious scientists]: Virtually none. Occasionally I meet them, and I'm a bit embarrassed [laugh], because I can't believe that anyone accepts truth by revelation.

{CA}

Watson, John (20th Century)

Watson is a director of William Sinclair Holdings and is chairman of Sinclair McGill (Scotland) Ltd. He is an activist member of the Humanist Society of Scotland.

Watson, Paul (20th Century)

Watson is an environmentalist and agnostic. In 1995, Heather Ramsay asked him whether he had any personal relationship with a spiritual being. He said he was not spiritual at all. She then asked where he got his morality from, his sense of purpose, and he said,

> I have an understanding of who and what I am, which is a part of the earth. So that's what I identify with, is the planet as a whole. We come out of the earth and go back into the earth. What gives me great joy is knowing that everything around . . . is a part of my body. Almost all theological thought is anthropocentric, and I just cannot buy into the anthropocentric ideology. Basically we're a bunch of conceited apes.

As for the importance of man to protect his environment, Watson said, "To be responsible for an extinction [of a species] is to commit blasphemy against the divine. It is the greatest of all possible crimes, more evil than murder, more appalling than genocide, more monstrous than even the apparent unlimited perversities of the human mind. To be responsible for the complete and utter destruction of a unique and sacred life form is arrogance that seethes with evil, for the very opposite of evil is live. It is no accident that these two words spell out each other in reverse." {CA; E}

Watson, Thomas (19th Century)

Watson wrote *The Mystagogue* (1847). {BDF}

Watson, William [Sir] (1858–1935)

An English poet, Watson wrote *Wordsworth's Grave* (1890), followed by a meditative elegy on Tennyson, *Lachrymae Musarum* (1892). His agnosticism is shown in such of his poems as "The Unknown God" and "The Hope of the World." God to him was "the mystery we make darker with a name," and, according to McCabe, Watson scorned the "God for ever hearkening unto his self-appointed laud" of his Churches. Watson was knighted in 1917 for his distinction as a poet. {CE; JM}

Watt, Fergus (20th Century)

Watt, the Executive Director of the World Federalists of Canada, wrote "Why Does the UN Need a Criminal Court" for *Humanist in Canada* (Summer 1998). "The impunity enjoyed by Pol Pot and other architects of this century's worst massacres," he wrote, "underscores the urgent need for a global judicial body."

Watt, James (1736–1819)

The Scottish inventor of an improved steam engine, Watt coined the term "horsepower." The unit of electrical power, watt, is named for him. His new type of engine, upon which Matthew Boulton helped, was vastly more efficient than that of Thomas Newcomen, whose crude machine had been invented sixty years earlier. Watt's steam engine had a separate condensing chamber, and parts of the engine were insulated. When James Boswell came to inspect the invention, Boulton told him, "I sell here, Sir, what all the world desires to have: *Power*!" Not perpetual power, of course: Watt, a Deist who never attended any church, believed that to be an impossibility. {CE; JM; RAT; RE; TYD}

Watters, Wendell W. (20th Century)

A professor emeritus of psychiatry at McMaster University (Hamilton, Ontario), Watters is a secular humanist who has written for *Free Inquiry* and for *Humanist in Canada*. At the Tenth International Humanist and Ethical Union (IHEU) World Congress held in Buffalo (1988), and at the Eleventh held in Brussels (1990), Watters addressed the groups. In *Deadly Doctrine: Health, Illness, and Christian God-Talk* (1992), Watters, who is a physician, disbelieves that Christianity brings contentment, physical and emotional health, spiritual (psychological) healing, and personal well-being. On the contrary, he holds that many aspects of Christian doctrine—for example, beliefs about sin, sex, personal sacrifice, pleasure and guilt, self-esteem, and the like—actually damage lives and predispose believers to ill-health by creating a world of artificial contrasts (God and the Devil, sin and salvation, flesh and the spirit) designed to encourage dependency, self-effacement, denial, ignorance, intolerance, and alienation. Further, the addictive power of Christian beliefs frequently results in antisocial behavior, poor psychological development, sexual dysfunctioning, depression, anxiety, low self-image, and even schizophrenia. Watters has written, "People who are no longer religious are more able to be honest with themselves and with others, about how they feel, whatever that feeling is."

During World War II, Watters was a bomber navigator and flew with the Royal Canadian Air Force (RCAF) in Burma. {*Free Inquiry*, Winter, 1989-1990}

Wattleton, Faye (1943–)

A President of the Planned Parenthood Federation of America, Wattleton was named Humanist of the Year in 1986 by the American Humanist Association. In 1981 she wrote *How To Talk With Your Child About Sexuality*. {HNS2}

Watts, Charles (1836–1906)

An English freethought writer-publisher, the son of a Wesleyan minister, Watts in 1899 founded the Rationalist Press Association (RPA) and gave forty years of his life to the freethought movement. The RPA published its first best-seller, Joseph McCabe's translation of Ernst Haeckel's *The Riddle of the Universe*. Hundreds of thousands of cheaply printed freethought books followed. In 1894 he had started *Watts's Literary Guide*, which in 1894 became *The Literary Guide* and more recently *The Humanist* (1956) and *New Humanist* (1972). The initial appeal of the Rationalist Press Association for £1000 bore the signatures of such Honorary Associates as Leslie Stephen (author and father of Virginia Woolf), Émile Zola, and Ernst Haeckel. Other Honorary Associates have included Arnold Bennett, the novelist; G. J. Trevelyan (the historian); Albert Einstein; Somerset Maugham; Sigmund Freud; and A. J. Ayer. Watts started the *Secular Review* with G. W. Foote and, afterwards, *Secular Thought* of Toronto. He wrote a portion of *The Freethinker's Text Book* and has published *Christianity: Its Origin, Nature and Influence*; *The Teachings of Secularism Compared with Orthodox Christianity*, and other brochures. Andrew Carnegie, who wrote about Watts's life, described him as a deist who never went to church.

A sample of his writing:

> About six thousand years ago an all-wise, all-powerful, and beneficent God made man and woman, and placed them in a position surrounded by temptations it was impossible for them to withstand. For instance, he implanted within them desires, which as God, he must have known would produce their downfall. He next caused a tree to bear fruit that was adapted to harmonize with the very desires which he had previously imparted to his children. God, all-good, then created a serpent of the worst possible kind, in order that it might be successful in tempting Eve to partake of the fruit. God commanded Adam and Eve not to eat of this fruit, under the penalty of death, knowing at the same time that they would eat of it, and that they would not die. The serpent is allowed to succeed in his plan of temptation, and then God curses the ground for yielding the tree which he himself had caused to grow; further, the almighty Being dooms both man and woman to lives of pain and sorrow, and assures them that their posterity shall feel the terrible effects of their having done what was impossible, under the circumstances, for them to avoid.
>
> Although at first God pronounced his creative work to be "very good," it proved to be quite the opposite. So bad did the human family become that God determined to bring a flood upon the earth and wash every member, one household excepted, out of existence. This 'water-cure' was not, however, sufficient to correct the 'divine' errors, for the people grew worse than ever.
>
> God now decided upon another plan, namely to send his son—who was as old as himself, and, therefore, not his son—to die, but who was invested with immortality and could not die, to atone for sins that had never been committed by people who were not then born, and who could not, therefore, have been guilty of any sin. As a conclusion to the whole scheme, this all-merciful God prepared a hell, containing material fire of brimstone, to burn the unmaterial souls of all persons who should fail to believe the truth, justice, and necessity of this jumble of cruelty and absurdity.

The death in 1870 of his first wife, Mary Ann, at the age of thirty-one was followed closely by the deaths of two of their sons, leaving one son, Charles who in 1877 began sharing his father's life and work. Watts's second wife was Kate. In 1881 the *Radical* described Watts in hostile fashion as "thick-set, black, podgy, round-headed, goggle-eyed."

Others were more generous, writing that "His trunk is square and well-built, and in his walk there is something of quiet and careless dignity. Although his frame is adipose rather than muscular, it has a fine, free outline, and is far from flaccid. He meets you, he recognises you. With a frank and jovial, but somewhat noisy and stagey *bonhommie*, he shakes you by the hand repeatedly, addressing you 'My friend.' He uses this expression indiscriminately to everybody he knows, for it does not seem to have occurred to the genial and kindly man that anybody who knows him can be less than his 'friend.' " Royle adds, "Watts was, in fact, just short of greatness in everything: without the ruthlessness of Bradlaugh, the culture of Besant, or the style of Ross and Foote, he was *par excellence* the ordinary man's leader—effective but limited; a little dull, a little plodding, and, as Ross recognised, 'deficient in originality of conception and boldness of generalisation.' " {BDF; EU, Gordon Stein; FUK; FUS; RAT; RE; RSR; TRI; VI; WSS}

Watts, Charles Albert (1858–1946)

Watts, the son of Charles Watts, started as a compositor. At the death of Austin Holyoake in 1876, Charles Watts acquired the business, which in 1882 passed to Charles. In 1885 he inaugurated *The Literary Guide* and, later, *The Agnostic Annual* (now *The Rationalist Annual*).

His children, **Frederick C. C. Watts** and **Gladys Watts**, began working with their father as soon as their scholastic career was over. Frederick became chairman and managing director both of the Rationalist Press Association and C. A. Watts & Co., Ltd., as well as editor of *The Literary Guide* and *The Rationalist Annual.* Gladys Watts (who became Mrs. Dixon) became secretary and a director of C. A. Watts & Co., Ltd.

The fourth generation of the family is represented by the two daughters of F. C. C. Watts, **Doreen** and **Marion**. A thorough description of Watts has been written by Nicolas Walter for *Rationalist Review 8* (Spring 1996). {BDF; FUK; PUT; RAT; RE; VI; TRI}

Watts, George Frederic (1817–1904)

Watts, an English painter and sculptor, studied at the Royal Academy and in Italy, where he developed an enthusiasm for Renaissance painting and Greek sculpture. His works are found in London's Tate Gallery, London's National Portrait Gallery, New York's Metropolitan Museum, and elsewhere. Twice offered a baronetcy for his distinction in art, he refused. His paintings were symbolic and "of an ethical tendency, but they were humanist not Christian," observed McCabe. The orthodox Mrs. Barrington, his biographer, admitted his freethought in the usual diplomatic language: "No formalities of any Church appealed personally to Watts's feelings," and "he did not feel so definitely the sense of the reality of the spiritual life." McCabe adds, "In honest English, he was an Agnostic." {JM; RAT; RE}

Watts, Isaac (1674–1748)

Watts, a deist and hymnist, wrote "Joy to the World" and "O God, Our Help In Ages Past," a fact which trinitarians find difficult to justify. He wrote *The Christian Doctrine of the Trinity*, which was attacked in two works by Martin Tomkyns, leading Robertson to remark that "the result seems to have been an unsettlement of the orthodoxy of the hymn-writer. There is express testimony from Dr. Lardner, a very trustworthy witness, that Watts in his latter years, 'before he was seized with an imbecility of his faculties,' was substantially a Unitarian." John Murray, the Universalist, has told about hearing that upon Watts's death some friends had discovered among his papers a defense of universal salvation, which they had burned in order to prevent any injuring of his other works' credit. {CE; JMR; JMRH}

Watts, John (1818–1887)

A reformer, Watts was the son of a weaver and was partly paralyzed as a child. He became assistant secretary and librarian at the Mechanics' Institution (1831–1838), setting up a business in 1838 but giving it up in order to become an Owenite lecturer. Watts was an important influence in the establishment of the first Free Library at Manchester, and he fought for the repeal of the "taxes on knowledge." A promoter of the People's Provident Assurance Society, he drafted the Life Assurance Act of 1870. An active leader in various humanitarian groups, Watts was a rationalist. {RAT}

Watts, John (1834–1866)

Watts, the brother of Charles Watts, was the son of a Wesleyan preacher and was converted to freethought by his brother Charles. Watts became sub-editor of the *Reasoner* and for a time edited the *National Reformer.* He also edited, in collaboration with Charles Bradlaugh, *Half Hours With Freethinkers* and published pamphlets such as "Logic and Philosophy of Atheism," "Origin of Man," "Is Man Immortal?" "The Devil," and "Who Were the Writers of the New Testament?" At the time of his death, Dr. George Sexton published the following in *National Reformer*: "At about half past seven in the evening he breathed his last, so gently that although I had one of his hands in mine, and his brother the other in his, the moment of his death passed almost unobserved by either of us. No groan, no sigh, no pang indicated his departure. He died as a candle goes out when burned to the socket." {BDF; FUK; RAT; VI; TRI}

Watts, Kate (19th Century)

Watts, an actress and well-known British freethinker, expressed the classic radical position, according to Royle, who added, "In a series of articles on 'The Education and Position of Women' in the *Secular Review* in 1879, Watts saw the educated woman not only as an asset in the home and to her husband, but also as a person in her own right, capable of earning her own living, marrying at leisure, or if need by not marrying at all without having to fear the alternative of the life of a spinster in a sweatshop." Watts's greatest rival was Annie Besant. {PUT; RSR; WWS}

Watts-Dunton, Walter Theodore (1832–1914)

For years the leading critic on the *Athenaeum*, Watts published several volumes of poems and wrote a novel, *Aylwin* (1898). Swinburne lived in his house for thirty years and, although he offended many by giving the rebel-poet a Christian burial, Watts-Dunton himself was a Rationalist. (See entry for Swinburne.) {RAT; RE; TRI}

Watts [of Lewes] (19th Century)

Watts of Lewes, Sussex, was author of *Yahoo* (1833), a satire in verse, and *The Great Dragon Cast Out.* {BDF}

Wayne, Gordon (20th Century)

Wayne in "A Rational Perspective on Religion" in *Humanist in Canada* (Spring 1999) suggests that if the Creator had the power and the inclination to communicate with prophets in millennia long gone, and in light of improvements in communication since that time, is it not reasonable to expect that an all-powerful entity would utilize the extant multimedia systems to reveal the cosmic secrets to all people simultaneously? A thoughtful Creator would give the media sufficient advance notice, then demand prime time coverage.

WEB

The internet contains several sites concerning agnosticism, atheism, freethought, humanism, and rationalism; for example:

- The American Humanist Association:
  <http://www.humanism.net>
- The American Rationalist:
  <http://www.infidels.org/org/ar>.
- Council for Secular Humanism:
  <http://www.secularhumanism.org>
- Freedom From Religion Foundation:
  <http://www.ffrf.org>
- Humanist Net
  <http://humanist.net>
- The Secular Web:
  Volunteers run this United States-based non-profit organization
  <http://www.infidels.org>

Webb, Beatrice (1858–1943)

A follower of Herbert Spencer and a freethinker, Webb was prominent in the Fabian Society. Born into a wealthy and well-connected family, she was interested in both the theoretical and practical aspects of social reform, political economy, and sociology, concerns were shared by her husband, Sidney Webb (1859–1947), whom she married in 1892.

The two appear in H. G. Wells's novel, *The New Machiavelli* (1911), as the Baileys, "two active self-centred people, excessively devoted to the public service . . . the most formidable and distinguished couple conceivable." {OEL; TRI}

Webb, Benjamin (19th Century)

Webb, with W. W. Baker, published *The Delaware Free Press* (1830–1833). {FUS}

Webb, David (20th Century)

Webb is honorary director of the National Campaign for the Reform of the Obscene Publications Acts (NCROPA) in England. He writes for *The Freethinker*.

Webb, George (20th Century)

Webb is author of *The Evolution Controversy in America* (1994), in which he describes objections to evolution not only by religionists but also by some scientists.

Webb, Jack (1920–1982)

Webb, a radio, TV producer, writer, director, and actor, had a character, Joe Friday, who coined the phrase that sums up the rationalists' position: "Just the facts, ma'am."

Webb, Sidney (1859–1947)

Webb, who was influenced first by J. S. Mill, was prominent in the Fabian Society, as was his wife Beatrice Webb. Both were freethinkers. {TRI}

Webbe, Joseph (19th Century)

Webbe, whose Latinized name was Josephus Tela, edited the *Philosophical Library* (1818), which contained the life and morals of Confucius, Epicurus, Isoscrates, Mahomet, and others. Cushing cites Webbe as an American writer, a grand master of Freemasons in America, but Wheeler believes that was a different individual, Joseph Webb. {BDF}

Webber, Harold W. (20th Century)

A Groton, Massachusetts, scientist, Webber supported Priscilla Robertson when she was editor of *The Humanist* and also wrote book reviews for the magazine in the 1950s.

Webber, Zacharias (Died 1679)

A Dutch painter, Webber wrote heretical works such as *On the Temptation of Christ* and *The Seduction of Adam and Eve*. He defended Bekker and, under the pen name J. Adolphs, wrote *The True Origin, Continuance and Destruction of Satan*. {BDF}

Weber, Karl Julius (1767–1832)

Weber was a German author who studied French philosophy while in Switzerland and found it suited his satirical turn of mind. He wrote a history of *Monkery* (1818–1820); *Letters of Germans Travelling in Germany* (1826–1828); and *Demokritos, or the Posthumous Papers of a Laughing Philosopher* (1832–1836). {BDF; RAT}

Weber, W. (20th Century)

Weber, a freethinker during the early part of the century, wrote *What Does Life Mean to You?* (190–?). {GS}

Webster, Daniel (1782–1852)

An orator, attorney, and champion of conservative economic policies, Webster ran for President and served as Secretary of State. "When you came to Boston, you went to the Unitarian Church and now they speak of you as a Unitarian," Webster's biographer Peter Harvey relates. "I am not a Unitarian," Webster replied. I should be regarded as perhaps rather liberal in my views. . . . When I came to Boston, many of my friends went to Brattle Street Church. . . . Then the divisions were not so marked as now." According to Harvey, Webster also attended Congregational and Episcopal churches.

Webster's legalistic mind persisted to the end, as evidenced by his informing his physician, "Doctor, you have carried me through the night. I think you will get me through today. I shall die tonight." Biographer George Ticknor Curtis wrote that the doctor answered, "You are right, sir." When Mrs. Webster cried hysterically at the bedside, Webster said, "My dear wife, when you and I were married at the Bowling Green we knew that we must one day part."

That evening, October 23rd, he tried to stay awake, not to avoid death but because he wanted to experience the event he knew was about to happen. "Am I alive, or am I dead?" he inquired, having dozed off. A little after midnight, he struggled to see where he was, then stated, "I still live!" Three hours later, apparently believing in an afterlife, he died. His funeral was conducted at his home by a Congregational minister from Marshfield. {CE; EG; TYD}

Webster, John (c. 1580–c. 1625)

An English dramatist, Webster observed, "Religion, oh, how it is commedled with policy! The first bloodshed in the world happened about religion." {TYD}

Webster, Richard (20th Century)

Webster is author of *A Brief History of Blasphemy* (1990).

Wechsler, Joseph R. (20th Century)

Wechsler has written articles critical of organized religion in *American Rationalist,* including "The Biological Aspect of Religion" (October 1992) and "Behold a New Religion!" (October 1994).

Wedderburn, Robert (19th Century)

Wedderburn wrote *The Address of Rev. R. Wedderburn to the Court of King's Bench at Westminster* (1820). {GS}

Wedgwood, Josiah (1730–1795)

An English potter, Wedgwood founded Wedgwood pottery in England. He was a member of the Unitarian Chapel at Newcastle-under-Lyme in England. {CE; U; UU}

Weeks, Caleb (19th Century)

Weeks, a freethinker, wrote *My Religious Life Experience* (1893). {GS}

Weeks, Daphne Edith (1905–)

Weeks, whose family were practicing Presbyterians, is an Australian teacher and humanist. In 1960 she founded the Australian Humanist Movement after placing an advertisement in the London *Humanist* seeking other Australians who might be interested. She remained its secretary from 1960 to 1975. {SWW}

Weeks, William George (1909–1975)

Weeks, whose family were Congregationalists, was an Australian teacher and humanist. He chaired the first meeting in 1960 of the

Sydney Humanist Group, which that year changed its name to the New South Wales Humanist Society. Weeks remained chairman and committee member until 1975. {SWW}

WEGE OHNE DOGMA

A German freethought publication, *Wege ohne Dogma* is at Freirelogopse Verlagsbuchandlung, L 10.4-6, 68161 Mannheim, Germany

Weidhorn, Manfred (1931–)

Weidhorn has written scholarly articles for *The American Rationalist.* He is author of *Sword and Pen; A Survey of the Writings of Sir Winston Churchill* (1974).

Weightman, John (20th Century)

Weightman is a rationalist who has written for England's *New Humanist.* Most contemporary believers or half-believers, he finds, "are not really interested in the literal truth of Christianity. They accept the Bible story more or less consciously as a psychological shield against raw existential awareness. If the need for such a shield is a recurrent feature in some individuals, no amount of argument will eliminate it, and indeed there may even be favourable things to be said about Christianity as a therapeutic sado-masochistic fantasy, so long as it remains non-aggressive." Granting but regretting this, Weightman adds that total humanists "are still a long way from knowing whether total humanism is a possibility for mankind in general."

Weil, André (1906-1998)

Weil, the eminent mathematician, was a precocious child who taught himself Greek before he was twelve years old, was fluent in Latin, and could declaim speeches from Corneille and Racine. As a teenager he became interested in philosophy but, upon receiving what he thought was an inflated grade on an examination, decided that "a subject in which one could do so well while barely knowing what one was talking about was hardly worthy of respect."

His 1928 thesis at the University of Paris solved a problem concerning elliptic curves that had been posed by the mathematician and philosopher Henri Poincaré.

Weil (pronounced VAY) was known as an ill-tempered, impossible character who, avoiding the French draft—he believed he had the duty not to be slaughtered as his country's young scientific élite had been in World War I—went to Finland and was returned to be imprisoned by the French for six months. During the confusion that followed the German invasion of France, Weil obtained an American visa. In his autobiographical *Souvenirs d'apprentissage* he described how President Franklin Roosevelt had sent him to France expressly to try to save French intellectuals.

A former professor at the Institute for Advanced Study in Princeton, New Jersey, he won in 1994 the equivalent of the Nobel Prize, which is not awarded in mathematics, when he received the Kyoto Prize in Basic Science from the Inamori Foundation of Kyoto, Japan. The award honored the part of his work known as "the Weil conjectures," which provided the principles for modern algebraic geometry. The patterns of numbers he discovered are now applied, for example, in writing almost-unbreakable secret codes and in enhancing the accurate transmission of computer data.

One of the founders of an influential Bourbaki group of French mathematicians, which rebelled against the French establishment, Weil and only his close friends knew that the group was named after an imaginary Russian general from an invented land of Poldavia. At his death, the only honor listed in his official biography at the Institute simply said, "Member, Poldavian Academy of Science and Letters.

He is believed to have been a non-theist, one not interested in religion or mysticism the way his younger sister, Simone, was. His obituary (*The Economist*, 22 August 1998) pointed out that he "took particular pride in the way he solved 'a problem of combinatories concerning marriage rules in a tribe of Australian aborigines' for Claude Lévi-Strauss. This achievement at least would have made his sister proud. Simone identified with downtrodden people everywhere, and starved herself to death in England in 1943 to express her solidarity with the suffering of her compatriots after the French Resistance refused to parachute her into occupied France." {Ford Burkhart, *The New York Times*, 10 August 1998}

Weil, Simone (1909–1943)

Weil, a French philosopher and mystic, was deprived of her *lycée* teaching job because of her "Jewish race." However, according to Alfred Kazin, she "coupled Pascal with Racine in demonstrating her cultural reverence as a French patriot. She hotly denied the Jewish roots of Christianity, to the wonder of Catholic friends impatient to see her in the Church; saw the Jews as the 'impure element' that kept her out. She liked to recite the Lord's Prayer in Greek, but made nothing of Jesus' praying to Our Father and in the Gospels reiterating 'My Father, Our Father.' She called herself a Christian, and in her extraordinary notebooks described herself as a tormented pilgrim coming close to the Church but never able to join it."

In 1940, although originally Jewish, she became a practicing Roman Catholic, believing that Christ on the Cross was a bridge between God and man. However, Kazin concludes after reading her *First and Last Notebooks* (1970), "In the ghastly trial of humanity that was Hitler's war, she, too, would have been obliterated if her posthumously published notebooks had not revealed her, in all her excess, as a genius of the spiritual life. Representing nothing and no one but herself, she was no more with the Church than she was with the Jews. As William Blake said, 'Organized religion: an impossibility.' Like so many homeless believers before her, she was speaking as 'the Alone to the Alone.' " (See entry for André Weil.) {CE; Alfred Kazin, "A Genius of the Spiritual Life," *The New York Review of Books* (18 April 1996)}

Weinburg, Arthur (20th Century)

Weinburg wrote *Attorney for the Damned* (1967), about Clarence Darrow. {GS}

Weinberg, Steven (1933–)

In *Dreams of a Final Theory: The Search for the Fundamental Laws of Nature* (1992), Weinberg illustrates as he did in *The First Three Minutes* (1977) that he is an author worthy of being called one of the world's leading theoretical physicists. Weinberg finds no place for God, or for a reconciliation between science and religion. "The more we refine our understanding of God to make the concept plausible," he wrote, "the more it seems pointless."

For him, science has demystified to the point where the "retreat of religion from the ground occupied by science is almost complete." Further, he holds that "though we shall find beauty in the final laws of nature, we will find no special status for life or intelligence." Weinberg attacks the religious conservatives for standing in the way of scientific inquiry, but also he criticizes religious liberals for reducing theology to vacuousness in attempting to reconcile religion with science.

In *The New York Review of Books* (12 June 1997), Weinberg made some salient points:

> The Milky Way is not something out there, far from us—rather, we are in it. It is our galaxy: a flat disk of about a hundred billion stars, almost a hundred thousand light years across, within which our own solar system is orbiting, two thirds of the way out from the center. What we see in the sky as the Milky Way is the combined light of the many stars that are in our line of sight when we look out along the plane of the disk, almost all of them too far away to be seen separately. Staring at the Milky way and not being able to make out individual stars in it gave me a chilling sense of how big it is, and I found myself holding on tightly to the arms of my lawn chair. . . .
>
> Here is the account that is now accepted by almost all working cosmologists. About 10 to 15 billion years ago, the contents of the universe were so crowded together that there could be no galaxies or stars or even atoms or atomic nuclei. There were only particles of matter and antimatter and light, uniformly filling all space. No defi-

nite starting temperature is known, but our calculations tell us that the contents of the universe must once have had a temperature of at least a thousand trillion degrees centigrade. At such temperatures, particles of matter and antimatter were continually converting into light, and being created again from light.

Meanwhile, the particles were also rapidly rushing apart, just as the galaxies are now. This expansion caused a fast cooling of the particles, in the same way that a refrigerator is cooled by the expansion of the freon gas in its coils. After a few seconds, the temperature of the matter, antimatter, and light had dropped to about ten billion degrees. Light no longer had enough energy to turn into matter and antimatter. Almost all matter and antimatter particles annihilated each other, but (for reasons that are somewhat mysterious) there was a slight excess of matter particles—electrons, protons, and neutrons—which could find no antimatter particles to annihilate them, and they therefore survived this great extinction. After three more minutes of expansion the leftover matter became cold enough (about a billion degrees) for protons and neutrons to bind together into the nuclei of the lightest elements: hydrogen, helium, and lithium. . . .

No one is certain what happened before the big bang, or even if the question has any meaning. When they thought about it at all, most physicists and astronomers supposed until recently that the universe started in an instant of infinite temperature and density at which time itself began, so that questions about what happened before the big bang are meaningless, like questions about what happens at temperatures below absolute zero. Some theologians welcome this view, presumably because it bears a resemblance to scriptural accounts of creation. Moses Maimonides taught that "the foundation of our faith is the belief that God created the Universe from nothing; that time did not exist previously, but was created. . . ." Saint Augustine thought the same.

But opinions among cosmologists have been shifting lately, toward a more complicated and far-reaching picture of the origin of the universe. (He then reviewed books by Timothy Ferris, Alan H. Guth, and Martin Reese, all three of which he said "give clear introductions to the standard big-bang theory and to the physical theories used by cosmologists.")

In Washington, D.C., in a 1999 debate with John Polkinghorne that was held in the same National Museum of Natural History auditorium as a famous 1920 debate on the size of the universe between Harlow Shapley and Heber Curtis, Weinberg deplored any science-and-religion trend—it "could help to give religion a kind of legitimacy it shouldn't have."

"With or without religion," he said, "you would have good people doing good things and evil people doing evil things. But for good people to do evil things, that takes religion."

In 1979 Weinberg shared the Nobel Prize in Physics with Abdus Salam and Lee Glashow. In 1996, he was elected a Humanist Laureate in the Council for Secular Humanism's International Academy of Humanism. In 1999, for his plain speaking by public figures on the subject of religion, he was presented with the "Emperor Has No Clothes" statuette by the Freedom From Religion Foundation.

As to his predictions about what will be the physicists' "wave of the future," Weinberg cited Brian Greene's projections about the "string theory" as being "the only game in town." (See entry for Christian de Duve.) {CA; CE; E; *New York*, 1 February 1999; Carey Goldberg, *The New York Times*, 20 April 1999}

Weiner, Neal O. (20th Century)

In *The Harmony of the Soul: Mental Health and Moral Virtue Reconsidered* (1993), Weiner details a humanistic and naturalistic basis for ethics.

Weinstein, Jacob J. (1902–1974)

Weinstein was a signer of Humanist Manifesto I. A rabbi, he advised students at Columbia University in 1932 and 1933. {HM1}

Weinstein, Steven (20th Century)

"It is very hard to realize that this all is just a tiny part of an overwhelmingly hostile universe. It is even harder to realize that this present universe has evolved from an unspeakably unfamiliar early condition, and faces a future extinction of endless cold or intolerable heat. The more the universe seems comprehensible, the more it also seems pointless," wrote Weinstein in *The First Three Minutes* (1977).

Weis, May H. (20th Century)

Weis was a UN representative for the International Humanist and Ethical Union when she signed Humanist Manifesto II. {HM2}

Weismann, August (1834–1914)

Weismann, a German biologist, is known as the originator of the germ-plasm theory of heredity. His doctrine, formerly called Weismannism, stresses the unbroken continuity of the germ plasm and the nonheritability of acquired characteristics. His works include *The Germ-Plasm* (1892) and a series of essays translated into English as *Essays Upon Heredity and Kindred Biological Problems* (1891–1892). According to McCabe, "Although Weismann was an agnostic and materialist—the Unitarian and bigoted Sir Arthur Thompson deliberately altered several materialistic passages in translating his principal work into English—he wrote nothing on religion." {CE; JM; RAT; RE}

Weiss, John (1818–1879

With O. B. Frothingham, Weiss worked to found the Free Religious Association. His acerbity combined with wit resulted in the observation that "Time was that when the brain was out a man would die, but now they make a Unitarian minister out of him." Frothingham called Weiss "eminently religious," but his faith was "purely natural, scientific . . . unorthodox to the last degree." Weiss looked to Theodore Parker as a leader, and his biography of Parker (1863) is a monument to the man who Weiss believed had "conscience and humanity enough to feed a generation." {U&U}

Weitling, Wilhelm (1808–1871)

A German social democrat, Weitling was leader of "Der Bund der Gerechten," the League of the Just. In Zürich, he published *The Gospel of Poor Sinners* and wrote *Humanity, As It Is and As It Should Be*. Weitling emigrated to America, where he died in 1871. {BDF; RAT}

Welby, Victoria [Lady] (1837–1912)

Lady Welby is described in *Women Philosophers* (1996) as "a thoroughly independent thinker" whose long correspondence with C. S. Peirce "contributed to the development of pragmatism as a kind of systematic epistemology." Undeniably, the freethinking Lady Welby wrote, "obscurity or confusion in language, if it does not betray the same defect in thought, at least tends to create it." {*Freethinker*, June 1996}

Welch, Brett (20th Century)

Welch is a co-director of ATVOP, the Atheist TV Outreach Project.

Weld, Madeline (20th Century)

Weld wrote "How Does Canada Determine Its Population Policies?" and "Our Native Land" for *Humanist in Canada* (Summers 1997 and 1998).

Wellhausen, Julius (1844–1918)

Wellhausen was a German critic who had studied theology at Göttingen and then became professor in Griefswald, Halle, and Marburg. Wellhausen is recognized for his documentary hypothesis that sought to account for both the composition of the Penateuch (*Genesis-Deuteronomy*) and for the evolution and history of Judaism. He is also known for his *Prolegomena to the History of Israel* (1883) and his contributions to the *Encyclopaedia Britannica*. Although he remained a theist, his great work in the naturalistic criticism of the Bible at the end of the 19th century, which helped considerably in understanding the hows and the whys of that book. {BDF; CE; JM; RAT; RE}

Wellman, Greydon (20th Century)

Wellman is president of the Humanist Community of the Peninsula (AHA). (See entry for California Atheists, Humanists.) {FD}

Wellman, Robert J. (20th Century)

When he signed Humanist Manifesto II, Wellman was a humanist chaplain at the C.W. Post Center of Long Island University. {HM2}

Wells, George Albert (1926–)

An emeritus professor of German at the University of London, Wells is a Humanist Laureate in the Council for Secular Humanism's International Academy of Humanism. In 1989, he was elected an honorary associate of the British Rationalist Press Association. His *Religious Postures: Essays on Modern Christian Apologists and Religious Problems* (1988) attempts to demolish notions of biblical inerrancy. Wells cites inconsistent passages of scripture, shows the historical impossibilities, and suggests why apologists persist. He discusses Kant's fantastic view of mind, the Jehovah's Witnesses, and Paul Tillich, lamenting the continuance of biblical inerrantism. He also is negatively critical of Julian Huxley's brand of religious humanism. Wells is on the Council for Secular Humanism's Committee for the Scientific Examination of Religion. He has been a director as well as Chairman of the Rationalist Press Association.

Among his other books are *The Historical Evidence for Jesus* (1982); *Did Jesus Exist?* (1986); and *Belief and Make-Believe: Critical Reflections on the Sources of Credulity* (1992), in which he acknowledges the impact on his thinking of F. R. H. Englefield, one of his teachers—Jesus never existed, Wells holds, and religion is a form of make-believe.

What's In A Name? Reflections on Language, Magic, and Religion (1993) is a major work by a humanist linguist. His 1994 essay, "The Difficulties of Today's Religious Apologists," was included in *Challenges to the Enlightenment, Essays in Defense of Reason and Science*. In 1996 he wrote *The Jesus Legend*, noting that Christians argue the man *must* have existed because reports of his exploits spread quickly after his reported demise, that therefore they *must* be based on actual events. Such an argument Wells solidly refutes. In 1999, the Rationalist Press Association published his booklet, "The Origin of Language."

Wells, H(erbert) G(eorge) (1866–1946)

Wells was an author, historian, and social thinker who "strenuously championed during most of his career all of the main Humanist ethical and social goals," according to Corliss Lamont. A Unitarian, he also was an associate of the Fabian Society with George Bernard Shaw. Wells wrote the highly successful *Invisible Man* (1897) and *The War of the Worlds* (1898).

He is said to have had a number of unusual sex affairs and is known to have had a child with Rebecca West. After one night of sex in 1924 with Margaret Sanger, for instance, he wrote her, "Wonderful! Unforgettable!", to which she responded that he was "a sort of naughty boy-man," one who while at a conference would whisper ribald things in her ear that she feared were being heard over the PA system. *Intimate Lives of Famous People* reports that once when depressed he wrote to his wife Rebecca, "I can't—in my present state anyhow—bank on religion. God has no thighs and no life. When one calls to him in the silence of the night he doesn't turn over and say, 'What is the trouble, Dear?'"

Outline of History (1920) listed Jesus as a non-supernatural human being:

> Jesus was a penniless teacher who wandered about the dusty sun-bit country of Judea, living upon casual gifts of food; yet he is always represented clean, combed, and sleek, in spotless raiment, erect, and with something motionless about him as though he was gliding through the air. This alone has made him unreal and incredible to many people who cannot distinguish the core of the story from the ornamental and unwise additions of the unintelligently devout.

In *Crux Ansata* (1899), he tells how the church "stands for everything most hostile to the mental emancipation and stimulation of mankind" and details why he believes so. In the 1930s, and as head of the International Association of Poets, Playwrights, Editors, Essayists, and Novelists (PEN), Wells interviewed Stalin and Roosevelt because of his concern over the dangerous divisions between state and private capitalism. Wells's influence on his contemporaries, particularly on the younger generation, was pervasive and permanent. His more than one hundred books significantly helped to shape the thinking of the 20th century, especially in the matters of popularizing science and liberalizing sexual mores. Those in the cognoscenti know that Wells had an excellent foundation in zoology, having studied at the London Royal College of Science as a youth. They knew, also that it was Wells who invented the term "atomic bomb" in his 1914 novel, *The World Set Free*. Leo Szilard has said that the work was his inspiration for having come up with the process that led to the Manhattan Project. Wells also predicted the advent of tanks ("land ironclads"), aerial warfare, and an eventual Japanese attack on the United States.

In his autobiography, Wells told of visiting the Portsmouth Roman Catholic Cathedral and hearing a sermon about Hell:

> I realised as if for the first time, the menace of these queer shaven men in lace and petticoats who had been intoning, responding, and going through ritual gestures at me. I realised something dreadful about them. They were thrusting an incredible and ugly lie upon the world and the world was making no such resistance as I was disposed to make to this enthronement of cruelty. Either I had to come into this immense luminous coop and submit, or I had to declare the Catholic Church, the core and substance of Christendom with all its divines, sages, saints, and martyrs, with successive thousands of believers, age after age, wrong." From that moment on, he found, "I found my doubt of his essential integrity, and the shadow of contempt it cast, spreading out from him to the whole Church and religion of which he with his wild spoutings about the agonies of Hell, had become the symbol. I felt ashamed to be sitting there in such a bath of credulity.

Wells was an honorary associate of the Rationalist Press Association, which published his *First and Last Things* (1908). {CE; CL; EU, Warren Sylvester Smith; *Freethinker*, July 1996; JM; RAT; RE; TRI; TYD}

WELSH FREETHOUGHT AND RATIONALISM: See entry for Wales.

Welsh, Elizabeth (20th Century)

At the 1994 Toronto conference of the Coalition for Secular Humanism, Atheism, and Freethought (CSHAFT), Welsh spoke at a workshop for young adults on "What Is the Good Life?" Welsh is in the Continuing Education Department of Brock University.

Welsh, Elliott (20th Century)

Welsh, a secular humanist, is a contributing editor of *Freethought Today*.

Welsh, Patrick (1924–1996)

Welsh was assistant director of the Tampa Bay chapter of the Atheist Alliance. An artist and sculptor, he was a mechanical and civil engineer.

Wendt, Gerald L(ouis) (1891–1973)

An expert on nuclear industry and its uses in peace, Wendt was a leading Ethical Culturist and member of the American Humanist Association. Of humanism, he wrote to the present author:

> Humanism connotes to me a sense of fellowship, if not of brotherhood, with every human being; a sense of responsibility for the genetic inheritance of man as the highest product of evolution, and for its best use in man's creative functions; awareness of man's ignorance of his environment, of his own nature, and of the possibilities of human society; a conviction that he can increase his understanding and thus improve all three by the use of his intelligence in research; a willingness to consider any hypothesis, recognized as such, concerning the vast, pervading and surrounding unknown, but freedom from any mythical, mystical, or authoritarian dicta concerning it; a fervor to bring the best that man has achieved within the reach of all men through education; and a faith that future generations will use improved understanding to accelerate the processes of psychic and social evolution, and to solve the mysteries amid which we, in this infancy of the human race, must live.
>
> Certainly, of the seven categories, I fit only into the seventh, naturalistic or scientific humanism. I cannot answer for others, though they must be legion. Perhaps it will do to mention Jean Rostand and Julian Huxley. I deplore the use of the same word to cover both the first three and the last four categories. The first three are literary classifications, not philosophical. Aristotle may have been a member of one of the last four categories, but he was not a devotee of Aristotle and not a "classical humanist." Present devotees of Aristotle, Montaigne, or Babbitt are *literary* devotees, or devotees of the literature of humanity. "The proper study of mankind is man" is a literary, not a scientific or philosophic statement. In general, the first three categories are literary, the last four philosophical.

From 1938 to 1940, Dr. Wendt was director of science and education at the New York World's Fair that opened in 1939. He was science editor of *Time* from 1942 to 1945 and then editorial director of *Science Illustrated* until becoming head of UNESCO's division of teaching and dissemination in the department of natural science at its Paris headquarters, from 1950 to 1954.

From 1959 to 1964, Wendt edited *The Humanist*, and he was chairman of the North American Commission of the International Humanist and Ethical Union from 1965 to 1968. At the Fourth International Humanist and Ethical Union World Congress held in Paris (1966), Dr. Wendt addressed the group.

Among his books were *Atomic Energy and the Hydrogen Bomb* (1951), *You and the Atom* (1956), and *The Prospects of Nuclear Power and Technology* (1957). {EU, Howard B. Radest; HM2; HNS; HNS2; WAS, 1 May 1956}

Wendte, Charles William (1844–1931)

Son of German immigrants, Wendte met Theodore Parker because his mother gave him language lessons. He later met Starr King in California. Choosing after graduating from Harvard's Divinity School in 1869 to be a Unitarian missionary, Wendte became an important force in the establishment of Unitarianism on the West Coast and was a leader in Unitarian efforts to establish cooperation with religious liberals throughout the world. As described by Samuel A. Eliot, Wendte "combined German diligence, California optimism, and New England idealism." {U&U; WSS}

Wentz, Wendell (20th Century)

Wentz is a Missouri freethinker who has written for *Freethought History*.

Werbe, Peter (20th Century)

Werbe, a freethinker, has written for *Freethought Today* about church/state issues in Michigan.

Werkmeister, William Henry (Born 1901)

In his *A History of Philosophical Ideas in America* (1953), Werkmeister wrote, "The strength of humanism lies in its criticism of, and opposition to, the absolutism of a barren idealistic-theological tradition and in its staunch assertion of human freedom and creativity. In this opposition, it allies itself with modern science wherever such an alliance is possible; and out of such alliance the conception of a 'scientific humanism' has arisen." Werkmeister wrote *Kant and Critique* (published 1993).

Werner, Michael W. (20th Century)

Werner was President of the American Humanist Association's Board of Directors until 1995, at which time Ed Doerr replaced him. In 1994, in a flare-up with *The Humanist*'s co-editors, Rick Szykowny and Gerry O'Sullivan, Szykowny resigned after a "prolonged and vociferous argument" with Werner. When O'Sullivan was ordered by Werner to intervene, O'Sullivan refused, citing editorial autonomy. Werner then fired O'Sullivan.

James Ledbetter in *The Village Voice* (6 September 1994) noted that "the 53-year-old magazine's internecine battle caught the ear of America's best-known humanist (and honorary AHA president) Kurt Vonnegut. Since O'Sullivan's departure, Vonnegut pulled his name from the mag's editorial advisory board (which also includes Betty Friedan and Walter Mondale's brother Lester). Although he's had no oversight of the magazine, Vonnegut told me he 'approved of the editorials in *The Humanist*,' and described AHA as 'highly politicized,' " adding that he was considering resigning as its honorary president. He remains, however, the honorary president. Previous AHA boards had similar battles over editorial autonomy, resulting in the removal of Paul Kurtz and Priscilla Robertson. Werner's e-mail: <mwwerner@aol.com>. {FD}

Wernig, Erich (1927–)

With Joachim Kahl, Wernig of Köln wrote *Freidenker, Geschishte und Gegenuart* (1981), a study of freethought in Germany.

Weschler, Anita (1903–)

Weschler, a sculptor, is known for her representational statues and groups. She studied at the Parsons School of Design and graduated from the National Academy of Design. She also studied with Albert Laessle at the Pennsylvania Academy of Fine Arts and with William Zorach at the Art Students League. One of her life-size works, "The Humanist" (1955), received national notice when a photograph in *Look* showed the statue being carried on the back of the diminutive sculptor, a feat made possible because it was the first such to be made out of lightweight, unbreakable glass fibers and plastic resins. It depicts a man of ambiguous race, two arms outstretched, one for giving, one for receiving. *The Humanist* (#6, 1956) described the work and Weschler's artistic philosophy. Her sculpture includes multi-figure groups, single figures, portraits, constructions, collages, and stone collages. She has used such media as bronze, aluminum, cast stone, stone, durastone (hydrocal), wood, plastic, plaster, terra cotta, and fiber glass. Her paintings include "organic abstractions" (synthetic glazes on panels), "translucencies" (plastic resins, abstractions backlighted in shadow box frames); and "linear abstractions" (works on paper).

Her work is in the public collections of the Whitney Museum in New York City; Yale University in New Haven, Connecticut; Brandeis University; Wichita State Museum; and a variety of other United States as well as foreign collections, both private and public. Her sculpture has been commissioned by the United States Treasury Department, and various portraits were commissioned by the U.S. Post Office in Elkin, North Carolina. Ten life-size portrait heads in bronze are in the Institute for Achievement of Human Potential, Philadelphia, Pennsylvania. She has had forty one-person shows nationwide. Weschler has been a delegate to the US Committee of the International Association of Art, on the board of directors of the Sculptors' Guild, and on the executive committee of the Federation of Modern Painters and Sculptors. She is the author of a book of poems, *Nightshade*, the recipient of many awards including the Audubon Artists Medal of Honor, and is a fellow of the MacDowell Colony and Yaddo. Weschler, who since her youth has considered herself an atheist and a deist. She is an honorary member of the Secular Humanist Society of New York. Her husband, Herbert Solomon, also was a freethinker.

Her "The Humanist," a life-size statue, was donated in 1995 by Warren Allen Smith to the Council for Secular Humanism, at the time of the dedication of the Center for Inquiry building in Amherst, New York. Visitors have said it is noteworthy for its texture and symbolism.

"A statue," Weschler often declared, "should be touched," an outlook frowned upon by gallery and museum guards. Shown a photo of Nobel Prize-winning biochemist Herbert Hauptman speaking at the Center for Inquiry's dedication ceremony while, just behind, someone had placed a hat atop "The Humanist," Weschler laughed appreciatingly. {WAS, numerous conversations}

Wescott, Glenway (20th Century)

Wescott, a member of the American Academy of Arts and Letters, kept a frank homosexual journal from 1937 until the 1950s. He described relationships with lovers and fellow homosexual artists, including Monroe Wheeler, George Platt Lynes, and Paul Cadmus. The work was not published until 1990, under the title *Continual Lessons*. Alfred Kinsey once interviewed as well as filmed him and his lover Wheeler, finding that at the point of orgasm Wescott was so violent that he "jackknifed" off the bed.

Asked in the 1970s his views about naturalistic humanism, Wescott responded that his generation had lived through a period of fear about openly discussing religion as well as sex. He said, however, that belief was not a subject he cared to discuss, that finesse in writing articularte prose had always been his interest. (See entry for Alfred Kinsey.) {WAS, interviews at several of the annual ceremonials of the American Academy of Arts and Letters.}

Wesker, Arnold (1932–)

Wesker, an English playwright born of Jewish immigrant parents, at various times has been a carpenter's mate, a seed sorter, and a pastry cook. He wrote a trilogy (*Chicken Soup with Barley*, 1958; *Roots*, 1959; *I'm Talking About Jerusalem*, 1960) about a family of Jewish Communist intellectuals, and the socialist point of view he used came to be known as "kitchen sink drama." His socialism is reflected in other plays, notably *The Kitchen* (1961), *Chips With Everything* (1962), and *The Four Seasons* (1969). *The Old Ones* (1972) describes the enforced isolation of the elderly. *The Merchant* (1977) treats the story of Shylock in a manner that constitutes an attack on anti-Semitism. His *Caritas* (1981) shows the spiritual anguish of a 14th-century anchoress, a person who lived in seclusion for religious reasons, then realized she had mistaken her vocation. In *The Merchant* (1977), Wesker treats the Shylock story in a manner that constitutes an attack on anti-Semitism. In 1991 two world premieres took place: an opera based on *Caritas* for which he wrote the libretto, music by Robert Saxton; and his fifth play for one woman, *The Mistress*, was premiered in Rome. The following year saw two more premieres: *Three Women Talking in Chicago* and his sixth play for one woman *Letter to a Daughter* in Seoul. His autobiography is entitled *As Much As I Dare* (1994). In 1995, Wesker became an Honorary Associate of the Rationalist Press Association. {OEL; TRI}

West, Cornel Ronald (1953–)

West, a noted African American intellectual, wrote *The American Evasion of Philosophy*, using "evasion" as a term of praise. In 1977 he became an assistant professor of philosophy at Union Theological Seminary in New York City. He also has taught at the Yale Divinity School. Marx and Emerson, West has held, herald self-realization and promote democracy. Marx is even more important after the collapse of communism in the Soviet Union and Eastern Europe than it was before. World War II was a major setback for anti-imperialist struggles in black America. Malcolm X moved "toward a more informed humanist position just prior to his assassination." And "the classical Marxist critique of religion is not an a priori rejection of religion." Speaking to fellow blacks, West wrote in 1988, "The relative unity and strength of our capitalist foes requires that we must come together if our struggle is to win!" For him, the Black Panthers were "the leading black lumpenproletarian revolutionary party in the sixties," and the black middle class is described as collaborators with the market, creatures of "conspicuous consumption and hedonistic indulgence."

Critic Leon Wieseltier in "The Unreal World of Cornel West" (*The New Republic*, 6 March 1995), notes that West describes himself as a "prophetic pragmatist, by which he means a Christian who believes in the gospel according to John Dewey, for whom there are no stable and lasting essences, no self and no world except the self and the world that we created, no invisible reality at the end of visible reality, no expression of the human spirit that refers to anything more than its experience." West, he adds, "is not a philosopher, he is a cobbler of philosophies; and so he reports the pragmatist and historicist tidings and proceeds to the manufacture of what he needs." When West concludes, "To put it bluntly, I do hope that the historicist turn in philosophy of religion enriches the prophetic Christian tradition and enables us to work more diligently for a better world." But, Wieseltier counters, West will be disappointed because "[T]he Christian tradition will not be enriched by a faith for which God is not real. Before what, exactly, does the postmodernist bow his head? For the anti-essentialist, what kingdom is at hand? Rorty claims that the abolition of transcendence is necessary for liberalism, but West claims that the abolition of transcendence is necessary for religion. He does not see that his position is a dire contraction. 'Prophetic pragmatism' is not rich and revolutionary; it is indulgent and impossible. He can have the prophets or he can have the pragmatists, he can have truth or he can have truths, but he cannot have both. (It was Pilate who spoke in the voice of the pragmatist.)"

Noting that Wieseltier feels West's work is "almost completely worthless," Columbia Professor Andrew Delbanco in *The New York Times Book Review (16 April 1995)* disagrees, writing, "Mr. West is still trying to transmit the American progressive tradition as it comes down from Emerson through William James and John Dewey to Richard Rorty, when deriding those thinkers has been fashionable."

West, Don (20th Century)

A Southern freethinker, West wrote *In a Land of Plenty: A Don West Reader* (1982). A radical minister from north Georgia, he wrote about the freedom-loving culture of Southern mountain folk. His home and extensive library were burned out by the Ku Klux Klan. {*Freethought History #14*, 1995}

West, Emory Scott (20th Century)

West, a freethinker, wrote *Impeachment of the Bible* (1923). {GS}

West, Dame Rebecca (1892–1983)

West is the adopted name of **Cecil Isabel Fairfield**, a pseudonym she chose from a character in Ibsen. She was the daughter of Charles Fairfield, of Anglo-Irish descent, who was known for his witty defense of extreme individualism in debates with Herbert Spencer and George Bernard Shaw.

A writer of psychological novels, West is best known for a historical study of Yugoslavia, *Black Lamb and Grey Falcon* (1942) and an insightful look at traitors and spies, *The New Meaning of Treason* (1964). She has written:

> I have no faith in the sense of comforting beliefs which persuade me that all my troubles are blessings in disguise. . . . Creeds pretend to explain the total universe in terms comprehensible to the human intellect, and that pretension seems to me bound to be invalid. I feel this as strongly about the non-Christian and anti-Christian creeds as about the Christian creeds, insofar as they make the statement, which seems to me the lie of lies, that seeks to cut down the growing tree of life before it has borne fruit, "All is now known." But I have faith in process. . . . I find an ultimate value in the efforts of human beings

> to do more than merely exist, to choose and analyze their experiences and by the findings of that analysis help themselves to further experiences which are of a more pleasurable kind. . . . The fear that pleasure is an unreliable standard because the common man will identify pleasure with debauchery has two sources, neither of which is discreditable. . . .
>
> The belief that all higher life is governed by the idea of renunciation poisons our moral life by engendering vanity and egotism. . . . I do not believe people are cruel because they are greedy; I am sure they invent greed as a pretext for cruelty. I am as sure that the sexual caprice which makes people desert still loving mates or thrust their attentions on those who are offended by them has not its origin in the pure sexual instinct, but is a use made of it by cruelty, seeking an instrument. . . . If we do not live for pleasure we will soon find ourselves living for pain. . . . I can imagine no better news than to hear that there had emerged from the South American forest or the Australian desert specimens of a new species which would, by reason of some new organ or adaptation of an organ, be able to dominate man as man has dominated the other animals.

Although her reputation tended to lessen because of her reportage and journalism, today's feminists and others have re-assessed her strong and unconventional heroines as well as her fine craftsmanship. They also note that she had an affair with historian H. G. Wells. {CE; OEL}

West, Mae (1892–1980)

West was born Mary Jane West to an unhappy German mother and a drunken prizefighter father, Emily Wortis Leider wrote in *Becoming Mae West* (1997). She had lovers at the age of thirteen, went steady with a vaudeville pianist and singer when fifteen, then professed to have remained chaste until her marriage to Frank Wallace when she was seventeen, a marriage she later denied had ever happened.

An unparalleled mistress of the double-entendre, she was a Brooklyn-born film actress who took a comic approach to hedonism, religion, and sex.

"To err is human . . . but it feels divine," she ethicized. "Is that a gun in your pocket, or are you just glad to see me?" she epistemologized. "I like a man what takes his time," she aestheticized. And "Some men are all right in their place—if they only knew the right places!" she moralized.

West was always depicted as being surrounded by men. In one scene, for example, would be a muscular type male at whose groin area she would gaze, following which she would remark that he appeared to be a new face in town. In "Diamond Lil," her memorable line was, "Come up some time and (pause) see me." Another variation of the line was, "Whyncha come up some time and see me?" Another often quoted Westism was made to her black maid, "Beulah, peel me a grape."

In 1926 at Daly's Theater in New York City, at which religious lectures and Biblical movies had previously been shown, she starred in "Sex," a play she wrote and produced. The place was soon raided, and she spent ten days in jail for "corrupting the morals of youth." The following year she wrote but did not appear in "Drag," which was successful in Paterson, New Jersey, but she never brought it to New York. The play led to rumors that she really was a man, a transvestite, but she wrote:

> I have a double-thyroid, ya know. . . . It means I have twice as much sexual vitality. That sort of thing runs in the family. My father was a boxer and my mother was famed far and near for her hourglass figure—she was New York's top corset model at one time. And one of my grandmothers had three breasts.

As for homosexuals, she disliked lesbians. Gay men were perverts, victims of a tragic disease that needed to be treated like cancer, Leider claims. He also said that as a teenager West devised sexually suggestive acts based on ideas picked up from belly dancers such as Little Egypt.

In 1930 she wrote *The Constant Sinner*, a novel about a white woman who worked in Harlem, took a black lover who was a prizefighter and ex-pimp, but she denied having had liaisons with her chauffeur-boxer Chalky Wright or with any other black men.

On Broadway, appearing as Catherine the Great, she penned the material for Catherine to ask of her male hairdresser, "And what do you want me to give you for Christmas?", followed by his fey response, "One of your discarded lovers, your highness," or lines to that effect. In another production, West offered a plan to insure that whoever passed the plate at church services could not pocket the money: Choose parishioners with one arm. According to legend, novelist Frank O'Hara claimed that by her demeanor and pronouncements West was the inventor of "small-town faggot psychology." Humorists enjoy pointing to other of her one-liners:

- When a woman goes wrong, men go right after her.
- Marriage is a great institution—but I'm not ready for an institution.
- Give a man a free hand, and he'll try to put it all over you.
- I wrote the story myself. It's all about a girl who lost her reputation and never missed it.
- Between the two evils I always pick the one I haven't tried before.
- It's better to be looked over than to be overlooked.
- I was in a tight spot, but I managed to wriggle out of it.
- It's not the men in my life that count—it's the life in my men.
- A man has more character in his face at forty than at twenty—he has suffered longer.
- I like a man who's good, but not too good. or the good die young, and I hate a dead one.
- When I'm good I'm very good, but when I'm bad, I'm better.
- (Hatcheck girl): Goodness, what lovely diamonds!
  (Miss West): Goodness had nothing to do with it, dearie.

At the age of seventy-seven, by her count, West made what some critics termed a "creepy" appearance in Gore Vidal's movie, "Myra Breckenridge," six decades after her start on Broadway in burlesque: a rococo figure in curls, feather bow, and Cheshire-cat face. Returning from the set to her beach home in Santa Monica, West was surrounded with murals of naked men who had golden phalluses and disembodied testicles.

Philosophers weary of analyzing ratiocinative processes have been known to consult her *The Wit and Wisdom of Mae West* (1967) and *Goodness Had Nothing to Do With It* (1959). However, the little educated performer was not known for her intellectual profundity and was, in fact, intrigued by occult matters. She enjoyed attending Catholic mass with a friend, never quite comprehending why the Church disapproved of her. {CE; Emily Wortis Leider, *Becoming Mae West*, 1997

West, Robert Nelson (1929–)

West was the second President of the Unitarian Universalist Association. He presided from 1969 to 1977. {U}

WEST GLAMORGAN HUMANIST GROUP (England)

The West Glamorgan Humanist Group's contact is Julie Norris, 3 Maple Grove, Uplands, Swansea SA2 OJY

WEST VIRGINIA HUMANISTS

Larry Reyka, POB 3208, Columbus, Ohio 43210, is the coordinator of the north central region of the AHA. West Virginian humanists interested in meetings in their area consult him. {FD}

Westbrook, Richard Brodhead (1820–1899)

Westbrook was an American author who first was a Methodist preacher, then a Presbyterian, and in 1888 was elected President of the American Secular Union. Westbrook wrote *The Bible: Whence And What?* (1882) and *Man: Whence and Whither?* (188–?). {BDF; FUS}

Westcott, Thompson (19th Century)

Westcott, a freethinker, wrote the *Life of John Fitch, Inventor of the Steamboat* (1878). {FUS}

Westerkamp, José (20th Century)

Westerkamp, an Argentinean, is a member of the Ibero-American Commission, a group of humanist leaders in Spanish-speaking countries.

Westerman, W. B. (19th Century)

Westerman from 1856 to 1868 was an active co-operator on *De Dageraad*, the Dutch freethought publication. {BDF}

Westermarck, Edward Alexander (1862–1939)

A Finnish anthropologist and founder of Finnish sociology, Westermarck started a student association, Prometheus, in 1905. As its president he supported the fight against religions and churches. A professor of philosophy at London University and a professor of sociology at Helsinki University, Westermarck wrote *The History of Human Marriage* (1891), *Ethical Relativity* (1932), and *Christianity and Morals* (1929). Why, he wondered, did Jesus not forbid his disciples to use weapons? Why did Christianity recognize the right to make war? Why did St. Peter and St. Paul approve of slavery? Why did Abraham have slaves? "Abolitionists of slavery," he noted, "were the name by which atheists were known . . . because only through slavery—the Christians said—could the Negroes enjoy the blessings of Christianity and civilization."

A world traveler, he also wrote *Belief in Morocco* (2 volumes, 1926) and *Marriage Ceremonies in Morocco* (1914). In *The Origin and Development of Moral Ideas* (1906), he delves into why "sodomy" is thought to be disgusting. After looking at ethnography, he contends that as "people emancipated themselves from theological doctrines," they regard homosexuality with "somewhat greater leniency." McCabe has written that, from personal knowledge, Westermarck was an atheist. He also was an honorary associate of the British Rationalist Association. {CE; GL; JM; RAT; RE; TRI}

WESTERN AUSTRALIA—HUMANIST NEWS

Western Australia—Humanist News is at GPO Box T1799, Perth 6001, Western Australia.

WESTERN CIVILIZATION, WESTERN WORLD

Asked about Western Civilization, Mohandas K. Gandhi was quoted as replying, "It would be a good idea."

"The Western world," explained the poet Patricia Storace, "is called the Western world because it descends from the western Roman Empire, while Greece belonged to the eastern Roman Empire of Byzantium." (For a critique, see entries for Afrocentrism and for Greek Civilization.)

Westlake, John (1828–1913)

Westlake, a jurist, was professor of international law at Cambridge from 1888 to 1908. He was a rationalist who, from 1900 to 1906, was one of the members for the United Kingdom of the International Court of Arbitration set up by the Hague Conference. He was Honorary President of the Institute of International Law. Although there is no biography and Westlake never wrote on religion, his fellow jurists stated that he had "a reverent faith in reason." {RAT; RE}

WESTMINSTER ABBEY

Westminster Abbey is a national shrine in London. Nearly every English king and queen since William I has been crowned there, and it is the burial place of eighteen monarchs. In addition, England's most notable statesmen and distinguished subjects have been given burial in the Abbey since the 14th century. In the Poets' Corner in the south transept rest the tombs of Chaucer, Browning, Tennyson, and other great English poets.

Although one would expect all who are buried there were members of the Church of England, Foote smiled that somehow freethinkers are buried there. He named as early examples Ephraim Chambers, Sir Charles Lyell, Charles Darwin, and George Grote.

Weston, Paul D. (20th Century)

When he signed Humanist Manifesto II, Weston was a leader of the Ethical Culture Society of Bergen County. {HM2}

Weston, S(amuel) Burns (1855–1936)

Weston was the father of metaphysician Charles Hartshorne, and he was one of Felix Adler's colleagues. He was a victim of a Unitarian "heresy" trial for not preaching the "Unitarian Christianity" specified in the bequest supporting his Unitarian church in Leicester, Massachusetts, so he became Adler's founding Ethical Culture Leader in Philadelphia (1885).

In 1887, he founded a settlement house in Philadelphia. {EU, Howard B. Radest; RAT}

Westra, P. (Born 1851)

Westra was a Dutch freethinker, secretary of the Dutch Freethought Society, *De Dageraad*. {BDF}

Westwood, Arnold (20th Century)

Westwood, when minister of the Westport, Connecticut, Unitarian Society, was a liberal who evidenced his comprehension of theism, humanism, and Unitarian history.

WET WATER MINISTRIES

A person-to-person outreach to "poor benighted Christians," Wet Water Ministries (RR1, Box 63, Rushville, Pennsylvania 18839) is dedicated to undermining religious delusions. Stephen Van Eck edits its newsletter.

Wettstein, Hermann (Born 1840)

Wettstein was born in Barmen, Elberfeld, Germany, but migrated with his parents to America in 1848. A jeweler, he was a freethinker in Wisconsin and Illinois. Wettstein wrote *The Teleo-Mechanics of Nature* (1911). {GS; PUT; RAT}

Wettstein, Otto (Born 1838)

Wettstein was a German-American materialist who contributed to the *Freethinkers' Magazine*, *The Ironclad Age*, and other journals. He was a treasurer of the National Secular Union. Wettstein wrote *The Suicide of Christianity* (c. 1900). {BDF; GS; PUT; RAT}

We'wha (1849-1896)

One of the most famous Native American berdaches, We'wha was a member of the Zuni nation. To the anthropologist Matilda Coxe Stevenson, he recited numerous myths, one concerning the supernatural two-spirit Ko'lhamana (*ko*, supernatural + *lhamana*, "berdache"). By using traditional tribal literature, according to Will Roscoe, author of *The Zuni Man-Woman*, We'wha constructed and expressed his gay identiy as a two-spirit.

WHALE: See entry for Animal.

Whale, George (1849–1925)

Once the Mayor of Woolwich, Whale was a lawyer who wrote works on the history of London. He was a founder of the Omar Khayyam and the Pepys clubs. An agnostic, Whale was Chairman of the Rationalist Press Association (1922–1925). {FUK; RAT; RE}

Whale, James (1896–1957)

Whale was a magazine cartoonist who was imprisoned by the Germans during World War I. He is best remembered as the film director in the 1930s of a quartet of horror classics: "Frankenstein," "The Bride of Frankenstein," "The Old Dark House," and "The Invisible Man."

He depicted Frankenstein as a helpless outcast, one much nobler than so many of those with whom he came into contact. For the role of the doctor's creation, Whale chose his friend Boris Karloff.

Openly gay and a lover of Hollywood producer David Lewis, Whale was known as an eccentric in an industry more comfortable with compromise and predictability. After a bitter artistic dispute with Universal Studios, Whale retired. He attempted a comeback in 1949 but, suffering a series of debilitating strokes, committed suicide in 1957 by drowning in his swimming pool. Whale was a non-theist. {AA}

Whatley, George B. (1921-)

A physician and a Life Member of the Freedom From Religion Foundation (FFRF), Whatley was raised in poverty in Alabama, put himself through medical school, practiced for thirty years, and retired in 1985. In "Scientific Medicine vs. Theology" (*Freethought Today*, April 1999), he laments that "Through ignorance, superstition, and reliance on the bible as the 'word of God,' the Church opposed all scientific endeavors, including medicine." In 1999 he was awarded FFRF's first "Freethought Medal of Honor." Willa Mae Whatley, his late wife, is the person after whom the Freedom From Religion Foundation auditorium at Lake Hypatia is named.

Whedon, Joss (20th Century)

Whedon is a producer, director, and scriptwriter. He created "Buffy the Vampire Slayer," telling a Web group that redemption, hope, purpose, and Santa are all important to him, whether or not he might believe in an afterlife or some universal structure . . . but added, however, "I'm an atheist." {CA}

Wheeler, Daniel E. (20th Century)

Wheeler edited the ten-volume *Life and Writings of Thomas Paine* (1915). {GS}

Wheeler, Joseph Mazzini (1850–1898)

A British scholar of unbelief, Wheeler was a prolific writer and reader. He converted from Christianity by reading Newman, Mill, Darwin, and Spencer, among others. His *Biographical Dictionary of Freethinkers* (1899) has been called by J. M. Robertson the nearest approach "to a general historic treatment" of atheism and freethought, along with Maréchal's *Dictionnaire des Athèes*. Wheeler was responsible for the publishing of David Hume's *Essay on Miracles* and a work known as *The Jewish Life of Christ*, also called the *Sepher Toldroth Jeshu*. According to Gordon Stein, Jews carefully concealed the latter book from Christians because of its plot. The work depicted Jesus as a bastard son of a Jewish soldier, Ben Pandera (son of the panther). Jesus becomes a magician of the conjuror variety, stealing the magic name of God (the Tetragrammaton) from a temple and using it to achieve recognition from the general population. Wheeler's last work was *Footsteps of the Past* (1895). He contributed to all the freethought publications of his day.

Describing himself, Wheeler once wrote that he was "a willing drudge in the cause he loves, and hopes to empty many an inkstand in the service of Freethought." When he wrote his own obituary, he attributed his atheism to having read Newman, Mill, Darwin, and Spencer. Others saw him as a person suffering from nervous diathesis, one prone to mental breakdowns with outbursts of uncontrollable mania. Confined for a time to an asylum, Wheeler recovered with the help of Foote and Wheeler's wife, but eventually he had a final breakdown in 1898. A gentle, honest scholar, he was respected by many, including the secretary of the Christian Evidence Society, who was moved upon his death to send a letter of condolence. {BDF; EU, Gordon Stein; FUK; FUS; JMR; JMRH; PUT; RAT; RE; RSR; TRI; WSS}

Wheelright, Farley (20th Century)

Wheelright was a member of the American Humanist Association's board of directors.

Wheless, Joseph (Born 1868)

Wheless, an attorney and associate of the atheist Joseph Lewis, is author of *Is It God's Word?* (1926) and *Forgery in Christianity* (1930). His work exposes textual inconsistencies, contradictions, discrepancies, anachronisms, forgeries, and mythical content in the Holy Bible. {FUS}

Whicher, George F. (1889–1954)

Whicher, a freethinker, wrote *The Transcendentalist Revolt Against Materialism* (1949). {FUS}

Whims, Davilyn (20th Century)

Whims is treasurer and membership chairperson of Humanists of Palm Beaches in Florida.

Whistler, James Abbott McNeill (1834–1903)

Whistler, whose mother became one of the best-known Americans upon his having painter her, was an eminent American painter, etcher, wit, and eccentric. The painting of his mother was fancifully called "Arrangement in Gray and Black." To advertise and defend his credo of art for art's sake Whistler resorted to elaborate exhibits, lectures, polemics, and more than one lawsuit. He sued Ruskin in 1878 for writing that Whistler asked "two hundred guineas for flinging a pot of paint in the public's face." He won the argument in court but payment of the court costs left him bankrupt. When first he studied art in Paris, he shed all religious beliefs. Armstrong describes in his *Reminiscences* with what gusto Whistler used to sing blasphemous songs and ridicule the Bible. Few painters of the time were so rich in international honors. {CE; JM; RAT; RE; TRI; TYD}

Whiston, William (1667–1752)

Whiston was an English clergyman and mathematician who, in 1701, became deputy to Sir Isaac Newton and whom he succeeded (1703) as Lucasian professor of mathematics at Cambridge. Whiston aroused opposition by proclaiming his opinion that the faith of the early Christian centuries was Arian. As a result, he was dismissed from the university in 1710 for heresy. He propounded his Arian views in *Primitive Christianity Revised* (5 volumes, 1711–1712). Whiston's translation of Josephus has been many times reprinted. {CE; FUK; TRI}

Whitaker, Thomas R. (20th Century)

A professor of English at Oberlin in the 1950s, Whitaker reviewed books for *The Humanist*. Also, he published articles Yeats and on the poetry of Robert Herrick and Ralph Waldo Emerson, comparing the conflict between Christianity and a variety of pantheism in their thought. In 1977 he wrote *Fields of Play in Modern Drama*, in 1983 *Tom Stoppard*, and in 1989 *William Carlos Williams*.

White, Andrew D(ickson) (1832–1918)

White's *A History of the Warfare of Science with Theology in Christendom* (2 volumes, 1896), according to Corliss Lamont, "proved of signal service to the documentation of Humanism by showing that the theologians had fought practically every forward step in scientific investigation since the founding of Christianity, much to the detriment of religion as well as of science." White had been the first president of the American Historical Association and also was the first president of Cornell University (1867–1885), which he largely endowed with funds for a land-grant college. Prior to being at Cornell, White had been a history teacher at the University of Michigan, where he had developed the idea of a university detached from all sects and parties and free to pursue truth without deference to dogma. Ezra Cornell had been a fellow senator in the New York State Senate and had helped him with financial aid.

White, who was gay, also wrote *Studies in General History and in the History of Civilization* (1885), and he was chairman of the

American delegation to the First Hague Conference in 1899. He also is known for having persuaded Andrew Carnegie to build the Palace of Justice to house the Hague Tribunal. {BDF; CE; CL; FUS; Stephen Jay Gould, *Rocks of Ages*; JM; RAT; RE; TRI}

White, Edward A. (20th Century)

White wrote *Science and Religion in American Thought* (1952). {GS}

White, James H. (20th Century)

White has been an activist member of the American Humanist Association. {HNS}

White, John (c. 1860–1920?)

White was an Australian freethinker and anarchist. In Melbourne, he was fined in 1892 for distributing a manifesto, "Anarchy, the Principles of Revolutionary Communist Anarchism," without the correct printer imprint.

Insisting in court that he be allowed to read the manifesto, the magistrate cleared the court to insure that outsiders would not hear him. {SWW}

White, John (20th Century)

A former teacher, White is secretary of the British Humanist Association's education committee.

White, Maria (Lowell) (19th Century): See entry for Maria White Lowell.

White, Micah (1982-)

White, upon moving from the liberal environment of Columbia, Maryland, to the fundamentalist Christian environment of Grand Blanc, Michigan, started an Atheist Club in his junior year of high school. Despite objections by the school administration, he successfully and with the help of Americans United for Separation of Church and States was able to found the group.

"Burn in Hell" messages were received, but over forty students attended the first meeting. "Becoming my school's number one enemy didn't take a single insult, a single disruption in class, or a single disciplinary action. Instead it took seven simple words: 'I want to start an Atheist Club,' " he lamented.

"Atheists Under Siege," published as an op-ed article in *The New York Times* (21 June 1999), argues against prayer in schools, concluding that it makes for ugly social divisions.

White is president of the Young Freethinkers Alliance. {*Secular Humanist Bulletin*, Spring 1999}

White, Michael James Denham (1910–1983)

White was a world leader in the field of evolutionary genetics. Educated privately at University College in London, he visited Australia in 1953 as a refugee from McCarthyism. In 1959 in Melbourne he was appointed professor of zoology, and in 1962 he became an Australian citizen. White was active in Australian rationalist organizations. {SWW}

White, Oliver (19th Century)

White was vice president of the United Moral and Philosophical Society for the Diffusion of Useful Knowledge in the 1830s. {GS}

White, Paul Dudley (1886–1973)

A physician and authority on heart disease, White taught at Harvard Medical School, treated President Dwight Eisenhower, and served with the Unitarian Service Committee in France and Italy. He was an active member of the First Unitarian Church in Belmont, Massachusetts, as was his wife. {UU}

White, Valerie (20th Century)

White, an attorney and author of *Protect Your Interests in Family Court*, spoke at the 1995 Atheist Alliance Convention in North Hollywood, California. She is a senior editor of *The Humanist*, is Vice-President and on the American Humanist Association's board of directors, and is a regular columnist for the Secular Organization for Sobriety (SOS) newsletter. White wrote *Choosing Your Children's Books* (1991). Her e-mail: <vw@jacks.place.mit.edu>. (See entry for Vermont Humanists.) {FD}

White, William (20th Century)

White is an American humanist who retired in Costa Rica. He participated in the 1996 Humanist World Congress held in Mexico City.

White, William Allen (1868–1944)

White, editor of the Kansas *Emporia Gazette*, has written, "For who is to tell you the truth? . . . No one. You must search it out yourself! The Department of War will not tell you. Certainly the Church isn't going to tell you the truth. . . .Search in all the obscure places . . . not the established high towers and cathedrals for the answers." The spokesman for those with a grass roots political opinion, he wrote mainly on political subjects. His autobiography won the 1946 Pulitzer Prize.

White, William Hale (1830–1913)

White, a writer who used the pen name "Mark Rutherford," became a clerk in the Admiralty and rose to the position of Assistant Director of Contracts. In his leisure, he attracted much attention by his *Autobiography of Mark Rutherford, Dissenting Minister* (1881), which was followed by *Mark Rutherford's Deliverance* (1885) and *The Revolution in Tanner's Lane* (1887). They formed a prolonged autobiography in the form of fiction. The character, Rutherford, attends a Dissenting college, becomes a minister, is beset both by theological doubts and by distress at the narrowness and hypocrisy of his colleagues and congregations, and becomes an easy prey to melancholy. He gradually loses his faith, becoming as disillusioned by the Unitarians as he was by his own church. The work is an account of the progress of 19th Century doubt. White's work shows an interest in Wordsworthian pantheism. White translated Spinoza's *Ethics* (1883), then returned to a non-Christian theism and to his love of the Bible. He added, however, the change "has not solved any of the great problems which disturbed my peace." His own life was overshadowed by the prolonged illness of his wife, who died in 1891, and whose patient suffering he began to see as "salvation through Crucifixion." {OEL; RAT}

Whitehead, Alfred North (1861–1947)

Whitehead, who taught mathematics at the University of London (1911–1924) and philosophy at Harvard University (after 1924), wrote *Principia Mathematica* (3 volumes, 1910–1913) with Bertrand Russell. Like Russell, Whitehead was critical of organized religion: "The greatest disaster in the history of the human race has been Christian theology," he wrote. But unlike Russell, Whitehead was a metaphysician whose "philosophy of organism" concerned a view that what we experience consists of processes of becoming. God, he held, is interdependent with the world and, in fact, develops from it. Lovejoy called his system "the most large-minded synthesis since Hegel," adding that it recalled views of Alexander, Bergson, Lloyd Morgan, and Peirce. God, Whitehead believed, receives enrichment from the world process, thereby being in a sense temporal. Some have exaggerated that only Russell understood Whitehead's mathematics and only Charles Hartshorne understood his metaphysics. Whitehead had a wry sense of humor, once defining Unitarianism, according to James Luther Adams, as a "belief in up to one God."

Whitehead and his wife lived an eventful life. Bertrand Russell apparently fell in love with Whitehead's wife while writing the *Principia Mathematica*. Meanwhile, Whitehead's affair with Christiana Morgan has been documented by Morgan's Jungian biographer, Claire Douglas, in *Translate This Darkness* (1993). Under Carl Jung's guidance, Morgan had "plumbed the depth of her unconscious" and had contributed to the early development of psychoanalysis.

Morgan, who was married to William Morgan and who became a celebrated psychologist, had an affair not only with Whitehead but also with writer Lewis Mumford, with Chaim Weizmann before he became Israel's first President, and with Harry Murray, head of Harvard's Psychological Clinic.

Twenty years after the eighty-six-year-old Whitehead had died, the seventy-year-old Morgan, drunken, depressed, and with Murray's love turned to loathing, drowned herself in 1967 in the sea off St. John in the Caribbean. {CE; ER; TYD}

Whitehead, Fred (20th Century)

Whitehead, who with Verle Muhrer edited *Freethought on the Frontier* (1992), is on the administrative staff of the University of Kansas School of Medicine. For several decades he has collected scarce materials on American cultural history, especially concerning labor, radicalism, and intellectual controversy, and has published extensively on these subjects. His *Freethought History* is a well-documented publication about the heritage of freethought. Included are articles and photographs about authors as well as freethought memorabilia. (*Freethought History*, Box 5224, Kansas City, Kansas 66119 $10/year, quarterly)

Whitehead, George (20th Century)

Whitehead, a freethinker, wrote *Gods, Devils, and Man* (1928) and *The Case Against Theism* (1930s). {FUK; GS}

Whitehorn, Katherine (20th Century)

Whitehorn, a British journalist, declared, "Why do born-again people so often make you wish they'd never been born the first time?" {TYD}

Whitenack, Oscar O. (20th Century)

A freethinker, Whitenack wrote *Theological Delusions of the Clergy and the Futility of Guessing and Drifting* (c. 1910?). {GS}

Whitford, O'Dillon B. (19th Century)

Whitford, a freethinker, wrote *Origin of the Christian Bible* (1888). He also wrote *Christianity, A Reward for Crime* (190–?). {GS}

Whiting, John (1917–1963)

Whiting, an English playwright, wrote works which, at first ill-received, marked a historic break from the prevailing vogue for drawing-room comedy. He wrote *A Penny for a Song* (1956), *Saint's Day* (1951), and *The Gates of Summer* (1956), which all showed his talent. But he did not achieve success until he adapted Aldous Huxley's *The Devils of Loudon* as *The Devils* (1961), a play which deals with a case of hysterical demonic possession in a French nunnery. Tribe calls Whiting an avowed freethinker. {OEL; TRI}

Whitman, Walt (1819–1892)

Whitman is *a*, if not *the*, major American poet. "Although by no means free of supernaturalist illusions," Corliss Lamont has written, Whitman sang of the robust pleasures of the whole man, body and soul, and heartily disbelieved in all asceticisms." As a youth he met his father's friend, Elias Hicks of Hicksville, New York, leader of a liberal branch of Friends somewhat similar to the Unitarians in their non-trinitarianism. Sometimes mystical, sometimes transcendental, the Good G(r)ay Poet liked Robert Ingersoll so much he requested that Ingersoll speak at his funeral. Wrote Whitman in "By Blue Ontario's Shore": "Piety and conformity to them that like, / Peace, obesity, allegiance, to them that like . . . / I am he who walks the States with a barb'd tongue, questioning every one I meet, / Who are you that wanted only to be told what you knew before?' / Who are you that wanted only a book to join you in the nonsense?" His free verse, use of "barbaric yawp," baring his soul (saying he was bisexual, although there is little evidence of his feminine interest), his poetic belief in democracy, and his belief in fairness for all have inspired many, repelled others.

"But for opera, I could never have written *Leaves of Grass,*" he once remarked. Whitman read Paine, Homer, Shakespeare, Coleridge, Dickens, Scott, and the Bible. He worked for Martin van Buren's presidential campaign in 1840 and from 1846 to 1848 edited the *Brooklyn Daily Eagle*, from which he was fired because, according to the management, "He is too indolent to kick a musketo." His interests were universal, his dynamism great, his advocacy of abolitionism and the "free-soil" movement vehement. Whitman's love of peace and his distaste of war—he served as an unofficial nurse for Northern as well as Southern soldiers in army hospitals—is evidenced in "Reconciliation":

> Beautiful that war and all its deeds of carnage must in time be utterly lost,
> That the hands of the sisters Death and Night incessantly softly wash again, and ever again, this soil'd world;
>
> For my enemy is dead, a man as divine as myself is dead,
> I look where he lies white-faced and still in the coffin—I draw near,
> Bend down and touch lightly with my lips the white face in the coffin.

When the English poet and sexologist, John Addington Symonds, inquired in a letter if Whitman was a homosexual, Whitman hotly denied any such tendencies. But Whitman's verses leave little doubt. In the "Calamus" section of *Leaves of Grass* (1847 was the earliest edition, and revisions were made until 1892), he deals with the "institution of the dear love of comrades." (In 1841 when he was in his early 20s, Whitman suffered the disgrace of being tarred and feathered and ridden out of Southold, Long Island, on a rail for an alleged act of sodomy.) In "When I Heard At the Close of Day," he describes his truly happiest moment as being when "the one I loved most lay sleeping by me under the same cover in the cool night. . . . And his arm lay lightly around my breast—and that night I was happy." Also, a revealing selection about sexual ecstasy exists in which Whitman uses the word "God," later replacing it with "hugging and loving bedfellow:

> I am satisfied . . . . I see, dance, laugh, sing;
> As God comes a loving bedfellow
> and sleeps at my side all
> night and close on the peep of the day,
> And leaves for me baskets covered with
> white towels bulging
> the house with their plenty,
> Shall I postpone my acceptation and
> realization and scream at my eyes,
> That they turn from gazing
> after and down the road,
> And forthwith cipher and
> show me to a cent,
> Exactly the contents of
> one, and exactly the
> contents of two,
> and which is ahead?

Whitman's most intimate friend was a trolley-car conductor, Peter Doyle, and in their 1868 to 1880 correspondence Whitman expressed intense feelings for Doyle, closing with such phrases as "Many, many loving kisses to you." Doyle, interestingly, had been in the audience the night President Lincoln, about whom Whitman wrote "O Captain, My Captain," was assassinated. When fifty-seven, Whitman gave eighteen-year-old Harry Stafford a ring, then posed with him in a formal photographic portrait (which is in the collection of Jonathan Ned Katz).

In *Walt Whitman's America* (1995), David S. Reynolds points out how acceptable up to the 1890s was the "eroticized language of same-sex affection," at which time in 1890 the word "homosexual" came to be used. "But who cares?" about Whitman's homosexuality, Alfred

Kazin has written. "The important thing about Whitman's sexuality was his affirmation of sex as the basic life force and the effect this had on his living, breathing, propulsive style." That style Whitman continued, even though Emerson suggested that the sexual poems be removed from later editions of *Leaves of Grass*.

"Whoever degrades another degrades me," he wrote, "and whatever is done or said returns at last to me." During the Civil War, according to the Universalist National Memorial Church in Washington, D.C., he and Clara Barton worshiped there. Whitman in 1873 had a paralytic stroke and lingered for twenty years in poverty. Stricken with paralysis in his old age, he retired to Camden, New Jersey, where he lived with the family of a Unitarian physician. As noted in his "Sister Death," he did not believe in immortality. (See entru for Elias Hicks. Paul Berman in *The New Yorker* [12 June 1995] delineates Whitman's link to Brooklyn. Also see entry for Alfred Kazin) {BDF; CE; CL; EU, William F. Ryan; GL; HNS2; JM; JMR; RAT; RE; TRI; TYD}

Whitney, Willis R. (20th Century)

A scientist, Whitney was a member of the American Humanist Association. {HNS}

Whittaker, Thomas (1856–1935)

Whittaker was assistant editor of and frequently contributor to *Mind* (1885–1891). He wrote *The Neo-Platonists* (1901), *The Origins of Christianity* (1904), and with Bain edited Crooms Robertson's *Philosophical Remains* (1894). Whittaker was a director of the Rationalist Press Association. {RAT; RE}

Whittemore, Thomas (1800–1861)

The most prominent publicist and popularizer of Universalism in the early 19th century, Whittemore edited *Trumpet and Universalist Magazine* (1828–1861). It was the chief Universalist periodical in the pre-Civil War era and one of the most widely circulated of any Boston religious periodicals. He fought against the Massachusetts tradition of tax support for the Standing Order churches, and in theology he defended Ballou's ultra-Universalism against the Restorationists. Whittemore wrote *The Modern History of Universalism, From the Era of the Reformation to the Present Time* (1830). {U; U&U}

Whitten, K. M. (20th Century)

Whitten was president of the Friendship Liberal League in Philadelphia that published the rationalist and freethought journal, *The Liberal,* from 1947 to around 1970. The group in 1956 dedicated a Thomas Paine Center, which was enthusiastically supported by Eva Ingersoll Wakefield and Sherman D. Wakefield.

Whitworth, T. (19th Century)

Whitworth wrote *An Apology for Deism* (1820). {GS}

Whyte, Adam Gowans (Born 1875)

A writer, Whyte was sub-editor of the *Glasgow Weekly Citizen,* the editor of *Electrical Industries,* and the author of several novels. Also, he wrote *The Religion of the Open Mind* (1913) and *The Natural History of Evil* (1920). Whyte was one of the original directors of the Rationalist Press Association. He is author of *The Story of the Rationalist Press Association* (1949), in which he wrote,

> *Humanism,* which is still used occasionally as a mild synonym for Rationalism, suffers from vagueness which permits too wide a variety of interpretations.

{FUK; RAT; RE; TRI}

WICCA

Wicca (*wicca,* necromancer) is a pagan nature religion with roots in pre-Christian western Europe. In the present century it has been revived, particularly in the United States and Great Britain. Calling themselves benevolent witches, Wiccans honor masculine and/or feminine divinities and practice magic and folk traditions which involve healing and the mystical development of the self. Many freethinking Unitarians are not happy at being associated with the Wiccan groups that have made inroads into some UU groups. (See entries for Pagan and Witchcraft.)

Wichern, Calvin (20th Century)

Wichern is President of Atheists of Northern Colorado. E-mail: <cwichern@aol.com>.

WICKEDNESS

• I prefer the wicked rather than the foolish. The wicked sometimes rest.

—Alexander Dumas père

• Wickedness is a myth invented by good people to account for the curious attractiveness of others.

—Oscar Wilde

Wicker, Randolfe (Randy) (20th Century)

Wicker, an "Atheist on Call" according to his business cards, has actively led a New York City AIDS Atheist Ministry. The owner of a Greenwich Village lamp store, he was a key member of a campaign to expose and replace the Christopher Street Festival Committee, which in the early 1990s had run the "festival" part of an annual Gay Pride Day celebration but which he accused of being a profiteering venture. The group was selling $25 plaques honoring those who had died of AIDS, and the church received a percentage of the profits.

"I've always been political," he told a *Village Voice* reporter (2 July 1996). "I was one of the first openly gay media spokespeople, way back when I was in the Mattachine Society. I was on the radio in 1962." Once a member of the Secular Humanist Society of New York and of AASH (a support group for agnostics, atheists, and secular humanists who were HIV-positive), Wicker nursed a number of people with AIDS and housed them up until their deaths. With Kay Tobin, Wicker wrote *The Gay Crusaders* (1972).

Wicker has been an activist upon behalf of Stonewall Bar veterans, appearing in a movie which documented the 1969 uprising by homosexuals at that Greenwich Village site.

The New York Times Magazine (25 May 1997) featured him for his having founded CRUF, Cloning Rights United Front. He was quoted as saying, "I've already contacted a scientist rumored to be developing human cloning technology. My decision to clone myself should not be the Government's business, or Cardinal O'Connor's, any more than a woman's decision to have an abortion is. Cloning is hugely significant. It's part of the reproductive rights of every human being." Additionally, he said of cloning that heterosexual reproduction is now obsolete, a fact which pleased him but raised other freethinkers' eyebrows. E-mail: <rwicker@gateway.net>. (See entry for Larry Gutenburg.)

Wicks, Ben (20th Century)

Wicks, a Canadian cartoonist, is a non-theist.

Wicks, Frank S. C. (20th Century)

Wicks was a signer of Humanist Manifesto I. {FUS; HM1}

Wicksell, Anna B. (1862–1928)

Wicksell, a Swedish pacifist, was a member of a League of Nations committee. (See entry for Scandinavian Unbelievers.)

Wicksell, Knut (1851–1926)

Wicksell was a Swedish author and lecturer. He wrote brochures on population, emigration, and prostitution. Under the name Tante

Malin, he wrote a satirical work on Bible stories. During the Paris Conference in 1889, Wicksell represented Sweden. He joined the Freethought Federation of Sweden in 1890. Wicksell followed Lennstrand as editor of the *Freethinker* and *Think for Yourself!* (See entry for Scandinavian Unbelievers.) {BDF; PUT; RAT}

Widdicombe, T. C. (20th Century)
Widdicombe wrote "Science Versus Religion" (19–?). {GS}

Wiedenfeld, Esther (20th Century)
Wiedenfeld edited *Lasting Faith* (1991), a well-documented history of the Lutheran Church in Comfort, Texas. {*Freethought History #15,* 1995}

Wieland, Christopher Martin (1733–1813)

One of the foremost German men of letters of his time, Wieland became a deist of the school of Shaftesbury. A poet and novelist, he wrote in a style typical of the German rococo: elegant, satiric, often playful. John Quincy Adams translated his *Oberon* (1780, translated in 1799), and Wieland had translated Shakespeare, thereby helping pave the way for future literary developments in Germany. He edited *Teutsche Merkur* (1773–1810), an influential literary journal in which he wrote on the free use of reason in matters of faith. He read the British deists as well as the French encyclopedists and was a deist without any belief in future life. Wieland was called the Voltaire of German, and his translations of Shakespeare helped to pave the way for future literary developments in Germany, such as those of Goethe and Schiller. Wieland's last words were said to have been, "To be or not to be." {BDF; CE; JM; JMR; JMRH; RE}

Wieman, Henry Nelson (1884–1975)

A professor emeritus of philosophy and religion at the University of Chicago, Wieman is said by Lamont to have produced "a new concept of Deity every time he puts pen to paper." One such definition of his theological outlook, which involved "creative interchange," was that "God is that interaction between individuals, groups, and ages which generates and promotes the greatest possible mutuality of good." Among his books are *Religious Experiences and Scientific Method* (1926) and *The Source of Human Good* (1964). A Unitarian who represented the furthest extreme of Christian modernism, he was critical of 20th Century supernaturalism and neo-orthodoxy because both excluded science as a tool and both denied religious responsibility. He found Tillich's work and Barth's neo-orthodoxy pernicious because of their stress on a theism that transcended human reason. He held that ultimate reality does not consist of levels or orders of disconnected atomic agents of beings but, rather, of the "organic process of events and their qualities." Wieman signed Humanist Manifesto II. {CL; HM2; U}

Wiemhoff, Henry (Died 1995)

Wiemhoff was an active member in the Unitarian Universalist Buddhist Fellowship and in the UUS for Socialism. A gay activist, he was a member of the New York Fourth Universalist Church.

Wiener: See Weiner, Neil O.

Wiener, Christian (19th Century)

Wiener was the German author of a materialistic work on the *Elements of Natural Laws* (1863). {BDF}

Wiener, Norbert (1894–1964)
Wiener, the American mathematician, is best known for his theory of cybernetics, the comparative study of control and communication in humans and machines. He wrote *God and Golem Inc.* (1966). {GS}

Wierdu, Kwasi (20th Century)

A professor of philosophy at the University of South Florida, Wierdu has written in the Norm Allen Jr. volume about "Morality and Religion in Akan Thought."

The Akan group is found in Ghana, the Ivory Coast, and parts of Togo. They hold, basically, that even were there no belief in God there would still be rules of good conduct so "it follows also and *a fortiori* that morality, as a set of rules of good conduct, is for the Akan, logically independent of the minor 'deities.' " He finds "it is pleasing to me that the Akan moral outlook is thus logically independent of religion, for it means that the ethics of our culture can survive the withering away of the belief in God, a belief for which I know no good arguments." {AAH}

Wiessner, Alexander (19th Century)

Wiessner was a German writer, author of an examination of spiritualism (1875). {BDF}

WIFE, HOW TO OBTAIN A

The Separationist (December 1996) suggested fifteen Biblical ways to acquire a wife:

1. Find an attractive prisoner of war, bring her home, shave her head, trim her nails, and give her new clothes.
Deuteronomy 21:11-13
2. Find a prostitute and marry her.
Hosea 1:1-3
3. Find a man with seven daughters and impress him by watering his flock.
Exodus 2:16-21
4. Purchase a piece of property and get a woman as part of the deal.
Ruth 4:5-10
5. Go to a party and hide. When the women come out to dance, grab one and carry her off to be your wife.
Judges 21:19-25
6. Have God create a wife for you while you sleep. Note: This will cost you.
Genesis 2:19-24
7. Agree to work seven years in exchange for a woman's hand in marriage. Get tricked into marrying the wrong woman. Then work another seven years for the woman you wanted to marry in the first place. Total: 14 years.
Genesis 29:15-30
8. Cut 200 foreskins off your future father-in-law's enemies and get his daughter for a wife.
Samuel 18:27
9. Even if no one is out there, wander around a bit and you'll definitely find someone. It's all relative, of course.
Genesis 4:16-17
10. Become the emperor of a huge nation and hold a beauty contest.
Esther 2:3-4
11. When you see someone you like, go home and tell your parents to get her for you.
Judges 14:1-3
12. Kill any husband and take his wife . . . but prepare to lose four sons, however.
2 Samuel 11
13. Wait for your brother to die. Take his widow. It's not just a good idea—it's the law.
Ruth–Onana and Boaz;
also described in *Deuteronomy* and *Leviticus*
14. Don't be so picky. Make up for quality with quantity.
1 *Kings* 119-123
15. A wife? Not!
I Corinthians 7:32-35

Wigand, Otto Friedrich (1795–1870)

A German publisher, Wigand established himself in Leipzig, where he issued the works of Ruge, Bauer, Feuerbach, Scherr, and other freethinkers. He also was a powerful orator and for some years was a member of the Prussian Diet. {BDF; RAT}

Wiggam, Albert Edward (1871–1957)

Wiggam was on the advisory board of Charles Francis Potter's First Humanist Society of New York. An author and lecturer, Wiggam wrote a newspaper column, "Let's Explore Your Mind." He also wrote *The Next Age of Man* (1927) and *The Marks of an Educated Man* (1930).

Wightman, Edward (Died 1612)

Wightman was an English anti-Trinitarian, a martyr of Burton-on-Trent. He was burned at Lichfield 11 April 1612, allegedly the last person burned for heresy in England. (See entry for Heretics.) {BDF}

Wihl, Ludwig (1807–1882)

Wihl was a German poet, whose work depicted his freethought. {BDF}

Wijetunga, Chandranie (20th Century)

Wijetunga, the Assistant Director of Ministry of Finance in Sri Lanka, is a Unitarian as are her two children and her husband Walter Jayewardene, the Director-Secretary General of the Unitarian Universalist Association of Sri Lanka.

Wilbrandt, Adolf (1837–1911)

A German author, Wilbrandt wrote about Heinrich von Kleist and Friedrich Hölderlin, the poet of pantheism. He also published novels and plays, one of which was *Giordano Bruno* (1874). His rationalism is chiefly found in a novel, *Geister und Menschen* (1864) and *Hölderlin, der Dichter des Pantheismus* (1870). {RAT}

Wilbur, Earl Morse (1866–1956)

The most prominent modern student of the history of Unitarianism in Europe, Wilbur described the historical development of Socinian and Unitarian theology. He was a President of the Pacific Unitarian School for the Ministry in Berkeley, California. Wilbur wrote *Our Unitarian History* (1925) and later a two-volume *History of Unitarianism* (1945; 1952). {FUS; U&U}

Wilbur, Richard: See entry for Theism.

Wilcox, Ella Wheeler (1850–1919)

Wilcox, a poet, hovered in her views between pantheism and theism, as shown in her *New Thought Common Sense*. She rejected orthodox Christianity, saying, "I am neither a Roman Catholic nor a Protestant. . . . (I believe in) the Divinity which dwells in us." Her popular sentimental poetry had a favorable influence in breaking the crust of orthodoxy, and her *Poems of Passion* (1883) sold 60,000 copies in two years. Freethinkers like her four-line poem, "The World's Need":

> So many Gods, so many creeds,
> So many paths that wind and wind,
> When just the art of being kind
> Is all this sad world needs.

{JM; RAT; RE; TRI; TYD; WWS}

Wild, George John (19th Century)

Wild, a freethinker, wrote *Sacerdotalism* (c. 1873). {GS}

Wilde, Oscar (1854–1900)

Swinburne wrote of Oscar Wilde, "It was for sinners such as this / Hell was created bottomless." Wilde, in his characteristic style, wrote, "The public is wonderfully tolerant." An aesthete, Wilde glorified beauty for itself alone, influenced as he was by Pater and Ruskin. This resulted, however, in his being satirized in *Punch* and in Gilbert and Sullivan's operetta, "Patience." Sensual indulgence and moral indifference are featured in his *The Picture of Dorian Gray* (1891). Generally considered to be his best work is *The Importance of Being Earnest* (1895), which contains such examples of his wit as . . .

- It is very vulgar to talk like a dentist when one isn't a dentist. It produces a false impression.
- The truth is rarely pure, and never simple.
- To lose one parent, Mr. Worthing, may be regarded as a misfortune; to lose both looks like carelessness.
- All women become like their mothers. That is their tragedy. No man does. That's his.
- I hope you have not been leading a double life, pretending to be wicked and being really good all the time. That would be hypocrisy.

Elsewhere,

- I couldn't help it. I can resist anything except temptation.
- There is no sin except stupidity.
- We are all in the gutter, but some of us are looking at the stars.
- (A cynic is) a man who knows the price of everything and the value of nothing.
- There is no such thing as a moral or an immoral book. Books are well written, or badly written.
- There is only one thing in the world worse than being talked about, and that is not being talked about.
- A man cannot be too careful in the choice of his enemies.
- The English country gentleman galloping after a fox—the unspeakable in full pursuit of the uneatable.
- A thing is not necessarily true because a man dies for it.
- He hasn't a single redeeming vice.
- He is old enough to know worse
- Nothing is so dangerous as being too modern; one is apt to grow old-fashioned quite suddenly.
- Conscience and cowardice are really the same things; conscience is the trade-name of the firm.
- Work is the curse of the drinking classes.
- The only way to get rid of a temptation is to yield to it.
- To love oneself is the beginning of a lifelong romance.
- (While imprisoned) If this is the way the Queen treats her convicts, she doesn't deserve to have any.
- (At the New York Custom House) I have nothing to declare except my genius.

In 1884 Wilde married Constance Lloyd, and they had two boys, Cyril and Vyvyan. "When I married, my wife was a beautiful girl, white and slim as a lily," Wilde wrote Frank Harris, but "[i]n a year or so all the flowerlike grace had vanished; she became heavy, shapeless, deformed." By 1887 he had had a "same sex" romance with Robbie Ross, and in 1891 he took up with Lord Alfred (Bosie) Douglas, one of the Marquis of Queensberry's two homosexual sons. Critic Adam Gopnik (*The New Yorker*, 18 May 1998) and others believe that the Marquis, who codified the rules of boxing, seemed to think his son and Wilde were "playing at buggers" in order to *épater* the bourgeoisie, for he left a card at Wilde's club inscribed "For Oscar Wilde posing Somdomite" (sic). Surprisingly and self-destructively, Wilde commenced a libel case against Queensberry, knowing that Bosie hated his father and desiring to see him humiliated. The noted case, however, resulted in Wilde's being asked about his involvement with "rent boys," leading to his observation that sex with the young and Victorian poor was like "feasting with panthers," which according to Gopnik "might be how the boys would have described it, too."

The trial was scandalous and included Wilde's reference to "the Love that dare not speak its name." The opposing counsel, Edward Carson, made a strong case, and to the surprise of many Wilde was found guilty and unmercifully jailed. "An argument has been made," wrote Gopnik, "that Queensberry got the government to go on with the prosecution of Wilde after the libel suit was dropped by threatening, in effect, to blackmail the Prime Minister, Lord Rosebery, who was said to have had an affair with another of Queensberry's sons."

After spending two years in jail for homosexual "offenses," unprepared for the suffering which this involved, Wilde at last was released and escorted by two prison officials to a train station. "At the sight of a budding bush at the station," Gopnik observed, "[Wilde] opened his arms and cried, 'Oh beautiful world! Oh, beautiful world!' Knowing that only one prisoner would say such a thing, one of the warders turned to him, chiding, 'Now Mr. Wilde, you mustn't give yourself away like that.'"

Freed, Wilde found his former friends had left him. One of the few who did not, journalist W. T. Stead who had exposed child prostitution in London, wrote, "If all the persons guilty of Oscar Wilde's offenses were to be clapped into jail, there would be a very surprising exodus from Eton and Harrow, Rugby and Winchester (England's famous schools). Moving to France, Wilde suffered the recurring ear trouble he had had in prison, and surgery was performed. In the hospital, he regaled his close friends Reggie Turner and Robert Ross while sipping iced champagne and saying, "I am dying as I've lived: beyond my means." Advised by his friends not to stop consuming so much alcohol, Wilde congratulated them: "You are qualifying for a doctor. When you can refuse bread to the hungry, and drink to the thirsty, you may apply for your Diploma." But when he developed a cold, his ear condition worsened and, depressed, he told Turner and Ross that the night before he had dreamed he was "supping with the dead." Their response delighted him: "My dear Oscar, you must have been the life and soul of the party."

(Oscar's mother, Speranza Wilde, was a friend of the mother of Djuna Barnes, Zadel, who once introduced her to Eleanor Marx, Karl's daughter. What transpired among these unlikely three, according to Phillip Herring's *Djuna: The Life and Work of Djuna Barnes* (1995), is not known. Zadel Barnes was sent in 1880 by the American journal, *McCall's*, as a correspondent in London, and interviewing the famous writer's mother was a journalistic goal.)

According to biographers H. Montgomery Hyde and Hesketh Pearson, Wilde contracted cerebral meningitis, an acute brain inflammation, and on November 30th, 1900, after being baptized into the Catholic Church, he died. As to why he made such a decision, and why the Church agreed, there are unanswered questions. Most of his life, he had been a non-believer who was aware of the hypocrisy of church officials, particularly in regards to their morality. Gopnik suggests it was because of his "insistence on seeing his own suffering in Christian terms," that Wilde the Catholic was in denial. "His Catholicism has become as much an embarrassment to his admirers as his homosexuality used to be. But there is a sense in which his Christianity, like Auden's years later, was conceived not in opposition to his homosexuality but as a reflection on it, and it ennobles the most exasperating thing about his last years: his reconciliation with Alfred Douglas, long after it should have been clear to him—indeed, he had announced that it was clear to him—that Bosie had been poison. ('He once played dice with his father for my life and lost,' Wilde had said once.)"

Speaking of death, Wilde once remarked to his lifelong friend Robert Ross: "When the Last Trumpet sounds, and we are couched in our porphyry tombs, I shall turn and whisper to you, 'Robbie, Robbie, let us pretend we do not hear it.' " It likely is not the case that on his deathbed he opened his eyes and murmured, "Either that wallpaper goes or I do." But he did say, "I am dying beyond my means."

When he died in Paris with syphilis at the age of forty-six, he was laid to rest in the unfashionable Bagneaux cemetery outside Paris, after which ten years later an English woman later provided money to remove the remains to the more elegant Pére Lachaise in eastern Paris. Upon that exhumation, however, the English funeral director Harold Nicholson described what became a fiasco: "On the previous night the sextons had dug up the grave, leaving the coffin exposed with two ropes underneath it. The soil had been placed on each side of the grave and, since it had been raining during the night, the sextons thought it wise to put three tombstones on the top of the earth so as to hold it down. There were many official representatives and journalists present at Bagneaux cemetery, and as they pressed forward to gaze into the grave one of the heavy stones became dislodged and fell upon the coffin, splitting the lid open. For a few seconds the face of Wilde could be seen, peaceful and white. Then the earth followed and in a few seconds his face was obliterated by mud."

Wilde, after this brief reappearance, was then transferred to another coffin, and in 1914 some of his admirers unveiled an Epstein statue suggested by Wilde's poem, "The Sphinx." However, the fig leaf along with the figure's private parts beneath the leaf were hacked away by someone, and the severed testicles reportedly now serve as paperweights in the cemetery conservator's office. Meanwhile, in 1995 a stained-glass window in his memory was installed in the Poets' Corner of London's Westminster Abbey. {CB; CE; GL; TYD}

Wilder, Gene (1935-)

Wilder is an actor, director, and writer. He received a 1967 Academy Award nomination for "The Producers); received a 1974 Academy Award nomination for his co-writing of "Young Frankenstein"; and appeared in numerous Broadway plays and films. In 1968 he campaigned for Eugene McCarthy, Allard Lowenstein, and Paul O'Dwyer.

Asked in 1998 on Bravo, a US-based cable television network, what heaven is, he responded in agnostic fashion that he wasn't even sure that heaven exists, then added they everyday life can be thought of as heaven. {CA}

Wildes, Harry Emerson (Born 1890)

Wildes wrote *Lonely Midas, the Story of Stephen Girard.*

Wile, Ira Solomon (20th Century)

Wile was on the advisory board of Charles Francis Potter's First Humanist Society of New York. He wrote *The Sex Life of the Unmarried Adult* (1987).

Wilhelmi, Hedwig Henrich (19th Century)

A German lecturer, Wilhelmi wrote *Vortrage*, a work published in Milwaukee, Wisconsin, in 1889. She attended the Paris Freethought Congress of 1889. {BDF}

Wilkenson, Jemima (1752–1829)

The daughter of a Quaker farmer in Rhode Island, Wilkenson "died" when she was twenty. Before her family could bury her, however, she rose as a reincarnation of Christ. She then was sent on a divine mission to found the Church and prepare the Chosen Few for the Second Coming, scheduled to occur, she claimed, in her lifetime. When she died the second time, members in keeping with her instructions did not bury her but, instead, waited anxiously for her to rise once again. When her body merely decomposed, the faith of many of the Universal Friends declined. By 1874, the last of the believers had died. {LEE}

Wilkes, Eliza Tupper (1844–1917)

Wilkes was one of the first women to be ordained as a Universalist minister. She was the first female to preach in the Dakota territory and, in 1886, founded the Church of All Souls, Unitarian, in Sioux Falls, South Dakota. Wilkes was active in the campaigns for temperance and women's suffrage. {*World*, Mar-Apr 1997}

Wilkes, John (1727–1797)

Wilkes was an English politician and journalist. He entered Parliament in 1757, and while Lord Mayor of London he was recognized by the King as one of the best the city had ever had. Wilkes was the idol of many workers, but the public hangman burned some of his writings. In his periodical, *North Briton*, Wilkes attacked George III in one issue, going so far as to criticize the speech from the throne. He was immediately arrested, but Chief Justice Charles Pratt ruled that the general warrant which had been issued did not specify who was to be arrested and was therefore illegal. The government then secured Wilkes's expulsion on the grounds of seditious libel and obscenity—Wilkes had issued an obscene parody of Alexander Pope's *Essay on Man*. Upon being released from prison, he was greeted by large group of supporters. According to McCabe, "the clergy were shocked and the young bloods delighted at his vices, frivolities, and irreligion." Although repeatedly reelected, he was not allowed to take his seat, despite being supported by Edmund Burke, until 1774., the year he became Lord Mayor of London. McCabe quotes a biographer, Bleackly, who "reluctantly admits that Wilkes once said that the word 'religion' would be as incongruous on his lips as the word 'liberty' on the lips of Dr. Johnson." Although termed a demagogue by some, he is remembered as an atheist and a champion of freedom of the press and the rights of the electorate. {CE; JM; RAT; RE; TRI}

Wilkins, Leslie T. (20th Century)

Wilkins, a writer, editor, and consultant, was Dean of the School of Criminology, University of California at Berkeley (1966—1969) and from 1979 to 1980 was visiting professor at Simon Fraser University in Canada. For the English *Freethinker* (April 1994), he reassessed drug controls and concluded that marijuana "is almost universally accepted as a medically-desirable treatment in some illnesses" and should "forthwith and without question be made available on medical prescription without constraint as to the ailment for which it may be prescribed."

Wilkinson, Christopher (Born 1803)

Wilkinson wrote with Squire Farrah *An Examination of Dr. Godwin's Arguments for the Existence of God* (1853). {BDF}

Wilkinson, Pat (20th Century)

Wilkinson is the state director of Arizona for American Atheists, Inc. E-mail: <pwilkinson@atheists.org>.

WILL TO BELIEVE

Under certain specified conditions, William James wrote in his 1897 article, "The Will to Believe," we have a right to let our passional nature decide which of two alternative hypotheses to adopt. As summarized by the University of Edinburgh's T. L. S. Sprigge, "These are that the matter cannot be settled on intellectual grounds, and that the choice between them is *living* (we find each credible), *forced* (we must act in the light of one or the other), and *momentous* (really important). Examples are the choice between theism and atheism or free will and determinism." {OCP}

Willans, Angela (20th Century)

Willans is a Vice President of the Gay and Lesbian Humanist Association. (GALHA). She is author of *Breakaway: Family Conflict and the Teenage Girl* (1977).

Willard, Emma (1787–1870)

An American educator who was a pioneer in women's education, Mrs. John Willard was invited by Gov. Clinton to start a school in Waterford, Connecticut, but when financial help did not follow she opened the Troy Female Seminary in 1821, which offered education to women and jobs to teachers and which later was renamed in her honor. She was a freethinker. {CE}

Willard, Frances Elizabeth (1829–1898)

President of the Woman's Christian Temperance Union, Willard was an activist upon behalf of women's suffrage. Her autobiography is *Glimpses of Fifty Years* (1889). {CE; UU}

Willdigg, Ronald (20th Century)

Willdigg is on the Executive Board of New York City's Corliss Lamont Chapter of the American Humanist Association.

Wille, Bruno (Born 1860)

A prominent German Freethinker, Wille edited *Der Freidenker* and was president of the Free Religious Society of Berlin. A follower of Darwin and Haeckel, Wille was a member of the Freethought Federation of Germany and upon several occasions was fined and imprisoned for his attacks on the government and church. {PUT; RAT}

William of Occam (or Ockham) (c. 1285–c. 1349)

Robertson calls William of Occam the most rationalistic of medieval philosophers. William, an English Franciscan who taught at Paris, had been a pupil of the Realist Duns Scotus, but William became the renewer of nominalism, which is the specifically rationalistic as opposed to the religious mode of metaphysics. Occam had such a strong anti-clerical bias that he had to flee France to Bavaria for protection from the clergy. Pope John XXII (or XXI) directed his prosecution, and in 1328 Occam was imprisoned in the papal palace at Avignon. Also imprisoned there was Marsiglio of Padua, the author of *Defensor Pacis* (1324), "the greatest and most original political treatise of the Middle Ages." The two escaped to Bavaria, where William supported the Holy Roman Emperor Louis IV in his struggle with Pope John. It is believed William died in the "black plague" which swept Europe in the 14th century.

The *Columbia Encyclopedia* explains that Occam "denied the existence of universals except in men's minds and in language. An empiricist, Occam disputed the self-evidence of principles of Aristotelian logic (such as the final cause) and of Christian theology (such as the existence of God). For this reason Occam severely restricted the province of philosophy in order to safeguard theology, denying the competence of reason in matters of faith." He is remembered for his use of the principle of parsimony, "Occam's razor": "What can be done with fewer [assumptions] is done in vain with more."

One of Occam's pupils was Buridan, rector of the University of Paris (fl. 1340) and famous for the Buridan's Ass story (about the hungry animal standing between two haystacks that, unable to make up his mind from which of the two to sup, died of starvation). Robertson notes that "it appears to be broadly true that Occam had at Paris an unbroken line of successors down to the Reformation." In 1376, the distinguished university's freethought was evidenced by a startling list of 219 theses, under cover of the doctrine of two-fold truth. In them, the students (a) "denied the Trinity, the divinity of Jesus, the resurrection, and the immortality of the soul; (b) affirmed the eternity of matter and the uselessness of prayer, but also posited the principles of astrology; (c) argued that the higher powers of the soul are incapable of sin, and that voluntary sexual intercourse between the unmarried is not sinful; and (d) suggested that there are fables and falsehoods in the gospels as in other books." The students were strongly scolded, but the element of the perseverance of the spirit of reason by youth in those times of darkness is memorable. {CE; JMR,; JMRH}

Williams, B. W. (20th Century)

Williams, a freethinker, wrote *The Joke of Christianizing China* (1927). {GS}

Williams, Barry (20th Century)

Williams is president of the Australian Skeptics.

Williams, C. (20th Century)

Informed that the 1953 *Humanist Newsletter* in New York City had fewer than one hundred subscribers, Williams wrote,

> In the whole of New York City? For about two years, Smith, I've watched you knock yourself out organizing meetings and publicizing humanism. Get smart—utilize your efforts more wisely, in ADA or some similar organization. Let these N.Y. bitches wake up after the hierarchy and McCarthy have taken over. Don't you know that New Yorkers are the most conservative of animals; take a look at N.Y. Unitarians if you think local liberals are ready for humanism. . . . If three others match me, I'll send $50 to wipe out your deficit, though. But what you really need is about $500 to buy a mimeograph and pursue humanism in a big way.

Williams, Charles Hanbury [Sir] (1708–1759)

Williams was Paymaster to the Marine Forces (1739–1742) and Lord Lieutenant of Herefordshire (1742–1747). When he became Envoy-Extraordinary to Berlin, Williams became an intimate friend of Voltaire. Known in skeptical circles at Holland House as "the Atheist," Williams shocked many when the *Quarterly* in 1822 published his "horrible blasphemies." Williams died by his own hand and was buried in Westminster Abbey. {RAT; RE}

Williams, Daniel Hale (1858–1931)

Williams is said to have become a successful physician, partly because there were so few black doctors at the time. One of his friends, Jenkin Lloyd Jones, was a Unitarian minister, and although Williams did not attend services regularly he considered himself a Unitarian, too. He attended Chicago Medical College and became a physician. He found, however, that often he needed to operate on patients in their own homes, because they did not have the funds to go into a hospital. So Williams arranged for such a place to be built, a place for training black women to be nurses and to give black medical students a chance to get experience under competent supervision. In 1893 when James Cornish, a young black, was brought into Provident Hospital, there were no X-ray machines, no way to determine how deeply a stab wound had gone. Because Cornish continue to get worse, Dr. Williams with other physicians watching made a deep decision, found an important artery had been damaged and the heart itself had sustained a tiny cut from the stabbing incident. As a result of his experimental surgery on the dying patient, who recovered, "Dr. Dan" is cited as having been the first surgeon to perform successful heart surgery. {CE; EG}

Williams, Dar (20th Century)

Williams, a folk recording artist, was asked on Audio Chat (22 Jan 1998) what an alleged "existential crisis" was that happened to him when he was sixteen that he blamed for his creativity and sharp sense of humor. Williams replied, "I decided there was no God. So I had to [muddle] my way out alone." [CA]

Williams, David (1738–1816)

A Welsh deist, Williams, after publishing two volumes of *Sermons on Religious Hypocrisy* (1774), gave up his post as a dissenting preacher. In conjunction with Benjamin Franklin and other freethinkers, Williams opened a short-lived deistic chapel in Margaret Street, Cavendish Square, London (1776), where there was used a "Liturgy on the Universal Principles of Religion and Morality." The only creed he professed was, in his own words, the deistic, not theistic, "I believe in God. Amen." {BDF; FUK; JMR; JMRH; RAT; RE}

Williams, David (20th Century)

Williams has written for the English *New Humanist*. Criticizing Francis Crick's *The Astonishing Hypothesis*, Williams regrets that Crick "misses an important point by ignoring or playing down the contributions made by philosophers and other wordsmiths of this century in the exploration of ideas about brains and what they do." He cites Gilbert Ryle's *The Concept of Mind*, which came out four years before the DNA discovery. In 1995, he edited *A Celebration of Humanism and Freethought*, a collection of quotations, short pieces, poetry, and other comments on thought, philosophy, and the human condition.

Williams, David Allen (1939–)

Williams, a writer from Utah and a world-traveler, is author of *A Celebration of Humanism and Freethought* (1995), which contains poetry, prose, and steel engravings which celebrate humanism.

Williams, David Rhys (Born 1890)

When Williams signed Humanist Manifesto I, he was leader of the First Unitarian Church in Rochester. In correspondence with Bragg and Wilson, however, he took exception to point three of the manifesto, which deals with body-soul dualism. Although he signed, he later renounced the humanist position, attacking its nontheism. {CL; EW; FUS; HM1; HNS}

Williams, F. R. J. [O.B.E] (20th Century)

Williams, an officer of the Order of the British Empire, wrote *Science and a Global Ethic*. He considers different types of societies and their potentiality for approaching a global ethic, in particular contrasting the open, civil society with the autocratic (sometimes theocratic) closed society. {"Creating a Global Ethic," *New Humanist*, December 1995}

Williams, Gardner (20th Century)

Williams, a professor of philosophy at the University of Toledo, is author of *Humanistic Ethics* (1951). {CL; HNS; PK}

Williams, George (1914–)

A church historian, Williams in a 1949 work on Frederic Henry Hedge noted that a "spiritual ambivalence of Unitarianism constitutes one of the most remarkable features of our body." This he summed up in the simultaneous existence of a "broad-*churchly* tradition" and a dissenting sectarianism. "Unitarianism will do well to preserve both the broad conserving churchmanship of the former and the latter's intense spirit of prophetic dissent." He favored connecting Unitarian Universalism to the worldwide history of the Christian church. He is author of *American Universalism: A Bicentennial Historical Essay* (1983). {U&U}

Williams, Glanville (1911–)

Williams, a jurist and freethinker, was described by David Tribe as a "champion" of every cause that might raise legal eyebrows." He was president of the Abortion Law Reform Association and committee member of the Homosexual Law Reform Society. {TRI}

Williams, Gwyn A. (19th Century)

Williams wrote *Rowland Detrosier, A Working-Class Infidel, 1800–1834* (1956). {GS}

Williams, H. W. (20th Century)

In *The True Wilderness* (1965), Williams wrote, "All fanaticism is a strategy to prevent doubt from becoming conscious." {TYD}

Williams, Hayward A. (20th Century)

Williams wrote *Fifty Years to Atheism* (1966). {FUS}

Williams, Lorrie (20th Century)

A native of Winnipeg, Manitoba, Williams was named Humanist Heroine in 1999 by the American Humanist Association. She founded and is the president of the Canadian Harambee Education Society, has instructed teachers in Ethiopia and Thailand with Project Overseas, and has served as a workshop facilitator with the British Columbia Teachers' Federation. E-mail: <lorriew@home.com>. {*The Humanist*, March-April 1999; *Humanist in Canada*, Autumn 1999}

Williams, Paulette: See entry for Ntozake Shange.

Williams, Robert L. (20th Century)

Williams, a college teacher interested in researching Thomas Paine, has written for *Truth Seeker*.

Williams, Robyn (1944—)

Williams, who was born in England, arrived in Australia in 1972 and is a humanist, scientist, journalist, and broadcaster. In 1975 he produced the ABC "Science Show," then "Ockham's Razor," and many other radio and television documentaries. Williams is president of the Australian Museum Trust and Chairman of Committee for the Future. He is author of *Best of the Science Show* (1983) and *Uncertainty Principle* (1989). Williams has been awarded the United Nations Peace Prize five times, the Order of Australia (AM) in 1988, the Australian Skeptics Journalist of the Year award in 1989, and the Humanist of the Year award in 1993. {SWW}

Williams, Roger (c. 1602–1683)

The founder of Rhode Island, Williams left Massachusetts to escape religious persecution by the Puritans. An advocate of religious freedom, he was one of the architects of the principle of separation of church and state, a belief he held not out of liberalism but out of his profound religious conservatism. He held that Puritans who are "saved" should not worship with the "unregenerate," those who did not hold his strict Puritanism. Knowing that all family members would not be among the godly, he reasoned that it is wrong to pray with one's children or even one's spouse. For Williams, wrote Lew Petterson in *The New York Times* (29 June 1992), the state did not have the power to say you can pray nor that you cannot pray, for both are equally destructive if one believes in the right to worship as one pleases. Petterson extrapolates that Williams would have said "Amen" to the 1992 ruling in *Lee v. Weisman* which reaffirms the ban on school prayer. Williams is known for having, during the time he was Governor of Rhode Island from 1654 to 1657, protecting the Quakers, while dissenting strongly from their creed. {CE; ER; RAT}

Williams, Thomas (18th Century)

Williams wrote *Speeches of the Honorable Thomas Erskine, in the Court of King's Bench, On the Trial of the King vs. Thomas Williams for Publishing* The Age of Reason (1797). {GS}

Williams, Thomas Lanier (Tennessee) (1911–1983)

Williams, one of America's foremost playwrights, was born on Palm Sunday, "a kind of righteous pagan, who, like Shannon, the defrocked priest in 'The Night of the Iguana' (1961), saw himself as 'a man of God, on vacation,' " critic John Lahr has written. Williams was raised by his beloved grandfather the Reverend Walter Dakin, of whom Williams wrote, "My grandfather was very, very High Church (Episcopal). He was Higher than the Pope." At the age of sixteen, Williams had a religious brainstorm in which he thought "the grace of God touched me," and his 1943 diary contains the prayer, "Help me, dear God, to find what I need." An image of the Virgin Mary was by his bedside and Williams converted "only for one day" to Catholicism in 1969, a time when he was having severe personal problems. "I wanted to have my goodness back" was the reason Williams gave for converting, encouraged by his brother, a convert. But Christianity never really consoled Williams, although it tempted him with its ideas about salvation and the glory of self-sacrifice. Particularly in "Sweet Bird of Youth," Lahr holds, Williams dreamed of salvation. His character, Chance, says, "Something's got to mean something." The story concerns an aging movie star whose kept young man is castrated by the father of the girl he deserted. The castration is a kind of leap of faith, Lahr writes, an explanation of Williams's own longing to reclaim his belief.

Williams's outlook is found in *The Glass Menagerie* (1945), a partly autobiographical work that immortalized his sister, Rose, who like its character Laura "is like a piece of her own glass collection, too exquisitely fragile to move from the shelf." Rose (1919–1996) was a schizophrenic who underwent a prefrontal lobotomy and was institutionalized until her death. *A Streetcar Named Desire* (1947—winner of a Pulitzer Prize) further details his outlook and is known for the hypersensitive and lonely Blanche DuBois who exits saying, "Whoever you are, I have always depended on the kindness of strangers." His outlook is further shown in *Cat On A Hot Tin Roof* (1955—winner of a Pulitzer Prize), in which characters live by a full emotional involvement in life rather than shrinking from or denying it, despite the terrible violence they encounter; and *Memoirs* (1975), in which he candidly discusses his career, his love affairs, his homosexual one-night stands, his thoughts.

When Hollywood mogul Jack Warner at dinner one night asked Frank Merlo (1922–1963), "And what do *you* do, young man?" Merlo responded, "I *sleep* with Mr. Williams." Williams made no secret of the fact, writing that when Merlo died, "I went to pieces. I retreated into a shell. For nine months, I wouldn't speak to a living soul. I just clammed up. I wouldn't answer the telephone and I wouldn't leave the house."

Tallulah Bankhead, over drinks, once told him, "You and I are the only constantly 'high' Episcopalians I know." Lyle Leverich in *Tom* (1995) quotes a journalist to whom Williams said, "Of course, God exists. I don't understand how. But He exists. How can there be a creation without a Creator? Still, I don't think there is an afterlife. At least I'm afraid there isn't." He echoed that thought in his little-known 1980 work, "Something Cloudy, Something Clear," in which a character representing him says, looking up at the sky, "Life is all—it's just one time. It finally seems to all occur at one time."

Williams did not wish to be cremated or buried in the family plot, writing in *Memoirs* that he wanted his body sewn up in a clean white sack and dropped as close as possible to the area at sea where Hart Crane committed suicide. He specifically did not want to be buried in the family plot in St. Louis, where he once had been locked up in a psychiatric ward. As his biographer Lyle Leverich has pointed out, "Unfortunately, he failed to make this a provision in his will, or his attorney failed to include it." Tennessee's brother Dakin made the decision to have his brother buried in St. Louis, saying, "When I arrived in New York on February 26th, my brother's body was already placed in a very handsome 'orthodox Jewish' casket. The decision to bury him had previously been made by trustees Maria St. Just and attorney John Eastman. The funeral director, Frank Campbell, took me aside and said, 'We are planning to ship the remains to Waynesville, Ohio, to be buried alongside his grandparents.' I then selected St. Louis, where visitors could come to pay their respects, rather than inaccessible Waynesville."

The open casket at the Campbell funeral parlor displayed a shaved face, but it was Tennessee and not Dakin who had shaved the beard shortly before he died. One viewer scarcely recognized the body lying with an object on the breast, an icon temporarily placed by Maria St. Just. Tennessee was said to have had suffered a lifelong dread of confinement, and to be enclosed in a coffin anywhere, not just St. Louis, was what he had never wanted. However, his remains were placed into a large "Orthodox Jewish" casket, the funeral was held in an ornate Byzantine cathedral, and over twelve hundred attended the final rites. "Lamentably," says Leverich, "he left the final decision to others." {CE; John Lahr, "Fugitive Mind," *The New Yorker*, 18 July 1994; GL; Lyle Leverich letter to WAS, 3 June 1991; OCAL; TRI; TYD}

Williams, Thomas Rhondda (20th Century)

Williams wrote *The Working Faith of a Liberal Theologian* (1914). {GS}

Williams, William Carlos (1883–1963)

The first decisively pragmatic poet of America, Williams is said to have delivered babies by day (he was a New Jersey physician) and poems by night (sometimes vice versa). He won a posthumous Pulitzer Prize for his *Pictures From Brueghel* (1963), a collection of poems, and he is the author of *Paterson* (1946–1958), a book in five parts (which was written party, and ironically, after he had suffered a series of strokes; he was unable to write a sixth part). By describing life in an American city, Williams voiced his feelings as to a poet's duty. This meant for him writing about what he could see, touch, and be certain of—coming in late, doing his rounds, watching his wife do chores, parking the car, looking at a wheelbarrow or at flowers or birds. Wallace Stevens thought Williams's work was too casual, and Martin Seymour-Smith says his poetic achievement is but a minor one. Others, however, consider him to be one of the most important and original American poets of the century. Still others have praised his witty play, "Many Loves" (1940), about a playwright loved by his leading lady as well as by a rich homosexual patron. The work was one of the first to portray realistic homosexual and lesbian relationships on Broadway.

He wrote the present author concerning humanism:

> There is no good to be got in my pondering the question as between a "theistic humanism" or a "humanistic humanism" for more than a passing moment. Atheism is laughable as a positive belief. The death of every man is for him the end; knowing nothing about it, I am forced by common observation to believe it. I can't say positively that this is so; I can only say that since all data in the case are withheld from me, I find myself absolutely unconcerned.
>
> As a physician I do not find any basis for believing in the supernatural. I live side by side with men who believe in the miracles of Christ and, though they are my friends, we never discuss our beliefs together. I am not interested in their beliefs. Nor am I interested in the existentialists, whose more or less complex beliefs are of no more importance to me than the demonstrations of Descartes.
>
> The brain is a complex mechanism and the fascination for man in becoming involved in its complexities has always intrigued me. This is a necessity for the development of our mechanistic sciences including the theories of Dr. Freud, but it has nothing to do with the beginning and the course and the death of a man. Since I can't exclude what I do not know and can't at the same time believe in it, I am forced to spend my time on earth with other occupations.
>
> Laughter at the fools does not completely fill my days, though it occupies many of my idle moments—accompanied by tolerant tears as befits a man of my predilections.
>
> I was bred a Unitarian, but whether I transect the cone of my preferences nearer or farther from the light has become, as I grow older, indifferent to me. There is much that is attractive in polytheism to the artist—the poet, that is—when he contemplates the spectrum.
>
> All that is left to me, being forced back from any knowledge except the report of the senses, is a humanistic naturalism, lit by the lightnings which play about the minds of saints and sinners.

Dr. Williams was a member of the Rutherford Unitarian Church in New Jersey, which his parents had helped to found. {CE; TYD; UU; WAS, 25 March 1956}

Williams, William Mattieu (1820–1892)

At the age of fourteen, Williams was apprenticed to a mathematical and optical instrument maker, and having inherited a little money attended Edinburgh College for two years. He spent two years in a walking tour over Europe, earning his living as an artisan. Later, he became headmaster of the Birkbeck School but found the clergy were hostile inasmuch as they had been criticized in his *Who Should Teach Christianity to Children?* (1853). Williams, a rationalist, was a successful chemist, one who was zealous for popular education. {RAT}

Williams, Zephaniah (1775–1854)

A pioneer freethinker of Wales, Williams was a Chartist. In 1995, Ron Davies MP, Labour's Shadow Secretary of State, described Williams as "one whose name deserves to be remembered by all who value freedom of thought."

A master collier, Williams was born in Monmouthshire and was prominent in the National Union of the Working Classes. A leader in agitating for the Six Point Charter, he led an 1839 march on Newport during which at least twelve Chartists were shot and killed by soldiers garrisoned in the Westgate Hotel. Captured later, he was tried and sentenced to be hanged. The death sentence was changed, but he endured floggings, hard labor, and news that his wife had been told he was dead. In 1854, he received a conditional pardon, joined his wife and daughter, and died in 1874 "full of years and prosperity."

Rationalism and freethought were at the bedrock of his principles and activities, according to Richard Paterson (*The Freethinker*, December 1995). He considered Christ "to have been simply a good man who, had he been living in that time and place, would have had his house pulled down by the 'friends of order.' " Paterson added, "It was said, however, that Williams kept at the Royal Oak a large portrait of Christ crucified, with the caption, 'The Man who Stole the Ass.'"

A vocal enemy of hypocrisy, Williams made a special plea for rationalism: "I would advise all men to take nothing upon trust, but all upon trial; whether in politics, religion, ethics, or any thing else: to sit down with a determined resolution; to examine closely; and to be directed by that which reason most approves."

Williamson, Audrey (20th Century)

Williamson wrote *Thomas Paine, His Life, Work, and Times* (1973). {FUK; GS}

Williamson, Clarence Charles (1877–1965)

Williamson was graduated in 1907 from Columbia University, where his doctoral dissertation was *The Finances of Cleveland*. For a time, he was chairman of the department of economics at Bryn Mawr College, then accepted the job of heading the economics and sociology division of a new library building to be opened in New York City at Fifth Avenue and 42nd Street. In 1921, he left library work to become the director of the information service of the Rockefeller Foundation. The culmination of his professional career was being named in 1926 as director of Columbia University Libraries and of the University's School of Library Service, remaining until his retirement in 1943. Working under President Nicholas Murray Butler, he developed what has come to be known as Butler Library, a major research center. At the time of his retirement, the Columbia libraries, with 1,844,600 volumes, ranked third behind the collections at Harvard and Yale.

The French government named Williamson the "Chevalier of the

Legion of Honor" for his work toward the publication of the catalog of the *Bibliothèque Nationale*. Williamson's major book was *Training for Library Service*, but with Alice Jewett he edited the first edition of *Who's Who in Library Service* (1933).

In the 1960s, a retiree living in Greenwich, Connecticut, Williamson often drove to nearby New Canaan to chat about naturalistic humanism with *The Humanist's* book review editor. His knowledge of ancient and Renaissance humanism was superlative (and he insisted that VERGIL [not Virgil] be inscribed in stone on the front of the Butler Library). Williamson was a student of philosophers from ancient Greece to the present; he had known and admired John Dewey, but the final years of his life found him particularly interested in what young philosophers were thinking and writing, especially the philosophic naturalists.

Williamson, W. H. (20th Century)
Williamson wrote *Thinker or Believer?* (1928). {GS}

Willis, Annie B. (1893–1977)

Willis, a Unitarian Universalist, was director of the Jordan Neighborhood House and principal of the Jordan School, a Universalist institution in Virginia which emphasized character-building, self-discipline, and self esteem for its African Americans students. (See "Black Universalist Centennial," *The World*, January/February 1995.)

Willis, Bruce Walter (1955-)

An actor-singer who was born in the Federal Republic of Germany and came to the United States in 1957, Willis is married to Demi Moore. He has appeared in numerous off-Broadway productions (e.g, "Heaven and Earth," 1977); television film (e.g., "Trackdown"); and feature films (e.g., "Prince of the City," 1981; "The Verdict," 1982; "Blind Date," 1987; "Sunset," 1988; "Die Hard," 1988, "In Country," 1989, for which he received the 1990 Golden Globe nomination); "Die Hard 2"; "Bonfire of the Vanities," 1990; and "Billy Bathgate," 1991. He has appeared on the television series "Miami Vice," received an Emmy award in 1987, and appeared in numerous commercials. On the subject of religion, Willis has said:

> Organized religions in general, in my opinion, are dying forms. They were all very important when we didn't know why the sun moved, why weather changed, why hurricanes occurred, or volcanoes happened. Modern religion is the end trail of modern mythology. But there are people who interpret the Bible literally. *Literally*! I choose not to believe that's the way.
>
> {CA; John Mahony, *New York Post*, 15 June 1998}

Willis, Edward Henry [Baron] (1918–1992)

Lord Willis, a playwright, was elected an honorary associate of the Rationalist Press Association in 1966. In 1990, he moved an amendment to the Broadcasting Bill, proposing that "in addition to Christianity, the religious programmes shall, from time to time, cover the other great religions of the world and include, in a balanced way, the viewpoint of agnosticism and humanism." Then he gave a statement of his position:

> Let me be quite honest with the Committee. I happen to be an atheist. I am not an agnostic. An agnostic is simply a shame-faced atheist. I am a total non-believer. I do not apologise to the Committee for that. I was brought up as a primitive Methodist. I do not think they exist any more. If one sat in chapel on a cushion that was a great sin. I lost my faith when I was about 14. I went to the bottom of the garden and said, "If there is a God, please lift that dustbin lid. Let that dustbin lid rise and that will prove him to me." I am sure that we have all done that at some time or another. Of course God ignored me and the dustbin lid did not rise. More seriously, my faith was lost in the Holocaust during the Second World War. I could not believe that a God could exist who would allow such things to happen or who would allow man to allow such things to happen. Later in Cambodia I could not believe that a God could exist who could allow these things to happen. How could one square the idea of God with that horrible slaughter.
>
> Neither could I believe in a selective God. When my father was dying of cancer, a neighbour of mine also had a relative who was dying of cancer. She said, "We prayed and prayed to God to save our father," and in fact he survived. My father died. I did not pray; perhaps that was my sin. But I could not believe that God could be so selective. Why should he pick one person out and say, "You will be saved," and pick another out and say, "You will not be saved"?
>
> I am simply indicating my position to the Committee. It does not mean that I do not have moral standards or do not live by moral standards. It does not mean that I have not brought my children up by moral standards. I believe deeply in the Ten Commandments and what they preach. Above all, I believe in the first draft of the American Declaration of Independence, which states that all men are created equal, and by virtue of that all men are entitled to life, liberty, and the pursuit of happiness. I believe in all those things. I am trying to make the point that there are hundreds of thousands of people, if not millions, who believe exactly as I do. They would not call themselves Christians—some of them might but they do not go to church—but they have the same moral standards that I have. I would not steal my neighbour's wife or his ox or anything else and there are millions of people the same as me. I want their views to be represented on television.

Some of the resultant reactions by the Earl of Halsbury, Lord Dormand, Earl Ferrers, and Lord Houghton are cited in *New Humanist* (October 1990). Halsbury said, "Post-war immigration has given rise to hospitality and to tolerance for the faiths of others, but do not let us call ourselves a multi-faith culture. We are a Christian culture, and, on any assessment of it by pollster methods, anything from 75 to 85 per cent of this country confesses the Christian religion. . . . Agnosticism is not a viewpoint; it is a lack of viewpoint and was coined by Thomas Henry Huxley in order to avoid answering the question, 'Do you believe in God?' Humanism means all things to all men. . . . I cannot believe that anything as variegated as man can be the measure of anything as though he were a standard yard or the standard metre." Halsbury was supported by the Bishop of Southwark: "Humanism and agnosticism are not religions. It has to be said, and it would be unkind not to say this, that considerable irritation is sometimes caused by using religious slots in programming for programmes which appear to have no religious content whatever in the usual sense of the word."

Lord Houghton supported Lord Willis's amendment, stating, "If we are to have freedom of discussion about religion and broadcasting of a wider kind, we must get rid of the law of blasphemy." Speaking for the Government, Earl Ferrers emphasized that humanism and agnosticism were not religious and it would create confusion to include them in religious broadcasting. He then opposed The Earl of Halsbury's amendment, and the amendment was defeated by 34 votes to 24.

"Ted" Willis's best-known TV series, *Dixon of Dock Green*, lasted twenty-five years. He wrote two volumes of autobiography: *Whatever Happened to Tom Mix* (1970) and *Evening All: Fifty Years Over a Hot Typewriter* (1991).

Willis, Robert (1799–1878)

A physician and writer, Willis became librarian to the College of Surgeons in London. Besides many medical works, he wrote a *Life of Spinoza* (1870) and *Servetus and Calvin* (1877). Other of his works are *The Pentateuch and Book of Joshua in the Face of the Science and Moral*

Senses of Our Age and *A Dialogue by Way of Catechism*. Willis followed Spinoza's pantheism as he indicated in his life of the master. {BDF; RAT}

Willis, W. L. (19th Century)

Willis wrote *Remodeling the Government Bible Defense of the Saloon and Liquor Business* (1894). {GS}

Willis, William (1830–1894)

Willis was an Australian bookseller and secularist. Migrating to Australia from England in 1885, he became in 1886 President of the Australasian Secular Association of New South Wales. Also in 1886, he purchased E. B. Skinner's Sydney Bookshop. {SWW}

Williscroft, Robert G. (20th Century)

Williscroft is a freethinker who writes for *Truth Seeker*. He has lived at the South Pole, and he has wide experience in management, editing and publishing, computer applications, and undersea engineering.

WILLPOWER

• Free will and determinism are like a game of cards: the hand that is dealt you is determinism; the way you play your hand is free will.

—Norman Cousins

WILLS: See entry for Last Will and Testament.

Willson, Jane Wynne (20th Century)

Willson, former chair of the British Humanist Association and one of the directors of the Rationalist Press Association, is author of *Funerals Without God, A Practical Guide to Non-Religious Funerals* (1991) and *Parenting Without God: Experiences of a Humanist Mother* (1997). She is Vice-President of the International Humanist and Ethical Union (IHEU). At the 1994 Toronto conference of the Coalition for Secular Humanism, Atheism, and Freethought (CSHAFT), Willson stated that humanism needs to be accessible, not just a movement for philosophers. Humanists need to present a united front in giving the message of humanism. She is of the view that humanists should omit "secular" and other qualifying adjectives: "Let's all just be Humanists!" The Norwegians, she finds, are succeeding in increasing their numbers whereas in Britain although one-third of the population is said to be sympathetic to Humanism there are only five or so thousand humanists there. "We Humanists need to attack the non-joiner syndrome," she explained, for it is important to make Humanism influential throughout society. "The only immortality for humanists," she points out, "lies in the memories of those who knew us and any influence we have left behind. So it is doubly important for us to remember and to celebrate in an honest and appropriate way." Willson in 1996 gave the Narsingh Narain Keynote Address, "The Role of Alternative Ceremonies in Transforming Societies," at the World Atheist Conference held in India. Also in 1996, she was a participant in the Humanist World Conference held in Mexico City. She signed Humanist Manifesto 2000. E-mail: <janewynnew@aol.com>. (See her article, "Humanist Celebrations," in *Free Inquiry*, Winter 1995-1996.) {*New Humanist*, February 1996}

Wilmot, John (1647–1680)

Wilmot, the Earl of Rochester, was a poet and a wit. On the one hand, he "believed neither in God nor Jesus Christ." But on his deathbed, he reportedly said, "I think I can never sufficiently admire the goodness of practices, by which I have hitherto lived without Hope, and without God in the world." Such sentiment differed remarkably from his previous stands.

However, Berman, calling him an "apostate free-thinker," concludes that Rochester "was not only an atheist but an avowed atheist who associated with other avowed atheists, such as Fanshaw. But the oral and second-hand nature of his surviving statements preclude a conclusive judgment." {CE; HAB}

Wilmut, Ian (20th Century)

Nature (27 February 1997) featured the news that Ian Wilmut and his colleagues at the Roslin Institute near Edinburgh, Scotland, had cloned their first sheep back in 1995, using the cells of an embryo rather than an adult. After a twenty-five-year odyssey that led to the electrifying accomplishment, they had succeeded in cloning the first mammal from the tissue of an adult animal. Dolly, they named the cloned sheep in July 1996. Scientists around the world took note that it now was clear that the cloning of an adult mammal is possible.

Wilmut, called a meek and affable researcher who lives in a village where sheep outnumber people, was said to earn the equivalent of $60,000-a-year as a government employee and will not stand to earn more than $25,000 in royalties if the breakthrough is commercial successful. "I give everything away," he told the media. "I want to understand things."

The father of three, Wilmut in 1971 went to Darwin College at Cambridge, receiving his doctoral degree two years later after submitting a thesis on freezing of boar semen.

Sheepishly admitting that he scarcely reads science fiction, Wilmut added to reporters that his wife is an elder in the Church of Scotland but that he "does not have a belief in God." {CA; Michael Specter with Gina Kolata, *The New York Times*, 3 March 1997}

Wilson, Agnes (19th Century)

Wilson, the wife of Joseph Symes, was the Australian publisher known as A. T. Wilson, having founded the firm in 1890.

Wilson, Andrew (1852–1912)

A Scottish physician and lecturer, Wilson was a university lecturer in zoology and comparative anatomy. In *What is Religion?* (1884), Wilson showed he was a Spencerian Agnostic who rejected "the petty conceptions which theologies in their anthropomorphism have devised." {RE}

Wilson, A(ndrew) N(orman) (1950–)

Wilson, a novelist, journalist, and biographer (of Milton, Belloc, Tolstoy, C. S. Lewis), is a provocative writer.

In 1991 he wrote *Against Religion: Why We Should Live Without It.* In 1992, he wrote *Jesus*, in which he finds it impossible "to believe that a first-century Galilean holy man . . . believed himself to be the Second Person of the Trinity. It was such an inherently improbable thing for a monotheistic Jew to believe. Nor . . . could I find the smallest evidence that Jesus had ever entertained such beliefs."

In *How Can We Know?* (1985), Wilson had been something of an apologist for Christianity. Now, he contends that Jesus never saw himself as anyone except someone to cleanse the old law-ridden Judaism, never wanted any following among non-Jews, never thought of himself as anything but a Jew. Wilson's "Against Religion" was a pamphlet in which he described a trek from being religious to his present agnostic, anti-religious stance. Religion, he held, is "to live happily, to deal mercifully, to act justly in all things."

We cannot, *New Humanist* has said of his outlook, hope for organized religion to die out. In face of frightening threats from religious people we should remember that "it is a definition of cowardice it is felt that we should feel frightened of saying boo to a goose: The Pope is a very powerful goose. The Ayatollah Khomeini is an even greater goose. Mrs. Whitehouse is a minor goose. The Reverend Tony Higton and Ian Paisley are noisy little ganders. Boo, boo, boo to them all."

Wilson's ability to gain publicity is well-known. In a newspaper column, he described Robert Runcie, then the Archbishop of Canterbury, as "a nasty tenth-rate figure," whom he also referred to as Agatha Runcieballs. A. J. Ayer he craftily described in *The Healing Art* as an academic drone who "liked good-looking women so long as they listened to his monologues without interruption."

Although once a convert to Catholicism, Wilson according to *The New York Times* editor James Atlas was thought to be anti-clerical and intended by *Jesus* to provoke:

> He argues, among other things, that Jesus was probably born in Nazareth instead of Bethlehem; that few if any of the mythic events surrounding his life—the Virgin Birth, the Last Supper, the Annunciation—could have happened the way they've been represented in religious mythology over the past 2,000 years, and probably never happened at all; and that Christianity as it has evolved since the death of Christ bears virtually no resemblance to his teachings. Indeed, Christianity's main achievement, Wilson contends, is the deadly legacy of anti-Semitism' that culminated in the Holocaust. If Jesus had foreseen "the whole of Christian history," he writes on the last page, "he would have exclaimed with Job: 'Why died I not from the womb? Why did I not give up the ghost when I came out of the belly?' "

God's Funeral (1999) declared that humankind, "which had worshiped God or the Gods time out of mind, from the era of the cave men until the French Revolution, went crazy and thew off God" during the late 19th century. Hume, he noted, brought into question the very notion of Causation (and the image of a Designer behind the Universe), while Gibbon's *Decline and Fall of the Roman Empire* made it difficult to admire many of the church's greatest saints and popes, exposing them as "morally absurd." He pointed out that Ivy Compton-Burnett's novels uniformly made the point that religion had had its day; Swinburne liberated us from "the sexual constraints and intellectual absurdities (as they saw things) of Christianity"; and Samuel Butler's work had as themes the "dismissal of Christianity and hatred of family life."

Wilson's conclusion, wrote *The New York Times* critic Michiko Kakutani (2 July 1999), is that "that 'the God-idea' was not wrenched from human consciousness with the ease that so many late Victorians predicted. Kakutani noted Wilson's view that the Christian ethical ideal would retain immense potency in the 20th century and that women and men—as disparate as the Rev. Dr. Martin Luther King Jr., Simone Weil, Dietrich Bonhoeffer and Pierre Tielhard de Chardin—would decide to 'ignore the death of God in the 19th century' and put their trust in One who said, "I was dead, and see, I am alive for evermore." ' " {Jim Herrick in *New Humanist* September 1999 wrote that *God's Funeral* "witnesses the wake of the deity but gives the impression that he would prefer to be at the resurrection. . . . There is much to fascinate in Wilson's intelligent book. But I think if he starts by saying 'Goodbye' to God, by the end he is ready to say 'Hello' again"; Timothy Madigan has observed that Wilson, once an Anglican-turned-atheist, had now become an anti-atheist and that *God's Funeral* showed him to be "a mushy liberal Catholic"; RAT; A. N. Wilson, "The Flesh Made Word," *New Humanist*, December 1996}

Wilson, Angus (Frank) (Johnstone) (1913–1991)

A novelist who described English middle-class life in *The Wrong Set* (1949) and *Setting the World on Fire* (1980), Wilson had a vision of life which is far from optimistic. Peter Faulkner, in *New Humanist* (September, 1991), stated that "the recent death of Angus Wilson has deprived humanism of one of its most committed and deviously eloquent voices." Faulkner also has written that "although the majority of contemporary British authors write with generally humanistic rather than religious assumptions, few have associated themselves directly with the humanist movement. E. M. Forster and Angus Wilson are exceptions to this."

Wilson in 1972 wrote, concerning his *As If By Magic*, "My theme is always *humanistic*. . . . Life today is junglelike. . . . It is inhuman in its materialism. Almost everybody in the book . . . seeks a short cut answer to a long term (eternal?) complex human problem. The 'magics' they offer are many and fashionable. . . . All are deceptions, substitutes for the hard job of using reason and industry and intuition and compassion to solve even a little bit of the muddle with humaneness and awe for the natural world and the complexity of human being." This and other details about Wilson are found in Margaret Drabble's *Angus Wilson: A Biography* (1995). {CE; *New Humanist*, August 1995}

Wilson, Colin Henry (1931–)

Wilson, an English writer, has in more than eighty books exhorted humankind to expand its powers and realize its full potential. In *The Outsider* (1956), he described an individual who realizes that life is futile, that society conceals this unpleasant truth. Wilson has shown a considerable interest in the occult and mysticism, although David Tribe lists him as a freethinker. Wilson helped popularize a version of existentialism in Britain. {TRI}

Wilson, David Alex (1864–1930)

Although called to the Scottish Bar, Wilson entered the Indian Service in Burma and served the full term of office as a judge. Returning to Scotland in 1912, he devoted himself to research and wrote a leading biography of Carlyle (1912–1929, 6 volumes). In earlier works he professed belief in an "eternal unchanging Spirit of the Universe," but in later years he was an agnostic. {RAT; RE}

Wilson, Dawn (20th Century)

Wilson is associated with the Atheist League of the State of Washington. (See entry for Washington Atheists, Humanists.) {FD}

Wilson, Edmund (1895–1972)

A, if not *the*, foremost American social and literary critic of the century, Wilson, primarily as a journalist, explored the conditions which have shaped literary ideas. He studied symbolism in *Axel's Castle* (1931), a work he called "Asshole's Cactus" in his letters; compared writers' critical views of one another in *The Shock of Recognition* (1943); investigated European revolutionary traditions in *To the Finland Station* (1940); analyzed Freudian and Marxist views in *The Wound and the Bow* (1941); wrote *Memoirs of Hecate County* (1949), which many librarians at the time put on side shelves because of its alleged obscenities. For a model he used Frances, a Ukrainian whom he once had met after buying tickets at a dance hall on New York's 14th Street, then danced and rubbed up against her. The memoirs depicted a character named Anna, for whom cunnilingus left her "weak with pleasure" and who enjoyed the ecstasy of having "her little mouth under the moist kisses of my mouth and my finger on her little moist cunt rubbing its most sensitive spot." (He failed to mention that the real-life Frances gave Wilson not only self-satisfaction but also a case of gonorrhea.)

He criticized religionists in *The Scrolls from the Dead Sea* (1955). The latter book when printed in *The New Yorker* brought the news that a small Jewish religious order, called the Essenes, emphasized the philosophy of love and that Jesus assented to and preached their ideas, the implication being that the ideas were not original with Jesus, who was thought to be a non-supernatural man with an admittedly charismatic personality. In 1956, Wilson wrote *A Piece of My Mind*, which expressed many of the provocative ideas which led many to call him the most important social and literary critic of his century. *Patriotic Gore* (1962) was a study of major and minor writers of the period as well as of the war's roots in the national psyche and the futility of war. For Wilson, just as sea slugs stupidly and blindly devour other sea slugs, Lincoln, Bismark, and Lenin were sea-slug-like imperialists who devoured their neighbors–Lincoln, he lamented to many Southerners' delight, devoured the South. Irrational forces are everywhere, Wilson thought, and the intelligent person's problem is to recognize that, as Lincoln illustrated, reason can often be powerless. The viewpoint piqued many.

Wilson, once married to the Catholic-born author, Mary McCarthy, encouraged her well-known non-belief in God, for he had been an outspoken atheist since youth. McCarthy in her *Intellectual Memories, New York 1936–1938* (1992), describes him as being "short, stout, middle-aged, breathy . . . with popping reddish-brown eyes and fresh pink skin." At one point she says she might have married him because "I may have felt a kind of friendship for the poor minotaur in his maze, so sadly dependent on the yearly sacrifice of maidens." At another she says, "I agreed to marry him as my punishment for having gone to bed with him." At yet another point, "I could not accept the fact that I had slept with this fat, puffing man for no reason, simply because I was drunk. . . . Marrying him, though against my inclinations, *made* it make sense. There is something faintly Kantian here. But I did not know Kant then. Maybe I was a natural Kantian." But although she has said "I never loved Wilson," she stayed married to him for seven tempestuous years and had a child by him. Wilson's first sexual experience had been with Edna St. Vincent Millay, who was not interested in repeating the episode, whom he described in the epilogue to *The Shores of Light* as well as in his first novel, *I Thought of Daisy*.

Scholars revel in talking about Wilson's eccentricities. He quibbled about absolutely everything. He once drew a mustache on his passport photo, explaining it was a poor picture. Observing Alfred Kazin working on galley proofs for a review of one of Wilson's books, Wilson grabbed the paper and started rewriting the evaluation. His high-pitched voice took many off guard, particularly when he spoke with a little gasp, and he detested giving the very few lectures he ever did agree to give. When some British publishers threw a party in his honor, Wilson retired to a corner and said to Kazin, "Let's get away from these Limeys." His *Memoirs of Hecate County* (1949) was deemed so pornographic librarians kept it behind their counters.

Although he was an Anglophobe, Wilson was (in the words of Harvard Professor Daniel Aaron) "drenched" in English literature and an expert on all of its literary aspects. Women and booze were constantly on his mind. He did not approve of America's getting into World War II, saying the Jews had already been killed so why endanger any American lives. Many of his other outlooks were considered shocking by his friends. His interest in butterflies along with his clinical observations about sex led some to observe that Wilson was a naturalist in the zoo of his own life. They added that the zoo was well equipped, pointing to *The Forties*, a work in which he described Elena, soon to be his wife number four, as follows: "Her white bosom with the pink just above it looked like a delicious ice-cream brick with strawberry against vanilla." Although he had wanted to marry Anaïs Nin, she showed no interest, nor had an English woman who, instead, married Arthur Koestler.

"Although his work on the Dead Sea Scrolls brought him into contact with intelligent Jesuits," John Updike in *The New Yorker* (29 November 1993) has observed, "[Wilson] stopped reading a book by Father Martin D'Arcy with the remark 'I can't enter into the point of view of someone who talks about this love between God and the human race.' He sat Wilfrid Sheed down at a party and complained that 'I couldn't even understand the idea about Christ: sent down by the Father to suffer and redeem the human race. If you believe this, you will be forgiven. What sense does this make? [Wilson] commented on the moon landing, 'Heaven and God are not up there,' and marvelled that 'we have not yet completely sloughed off the absurdities of those old theologies . . . that have been hanging around our lives for thousands of years.'" To poet Allen Tate, Wilson wrote, "You are wrong, and have always been wrong, in thinking I am in any sense a Christian. Christianity seems to me the worst imposture of any of the religions I know of."

Wilson's interest in Judaism may have started when he found his grandfather's Bible in Hebrew along with a Hebrew dictionary, according to Mark Krupnick of the University of Chicago's School of Divinity. This challenge to out-do his grandfather led him to study Hebrew, and Krupnick suggests that when Wilson was no longer intrigued by communism or Freud, he continued his interest in Judaism by research the Dead Sea Scrolls, that he thought of himself as a "kind of Jew," or at least he incorporated some of Judaism into his "ego ideal."

As a result, and because of his balanced critiques, many Jewish authors looked to Wilson as if he were some kind of Yankee messiah. Marx, Wilson had felt, was a Jewish moralist but a kind of non-Jewish Jew whose emphasis was not on religion but on social philosophy.

Although on the printed page Wilson may have appeared forbidding, two of his friends—Daniel Aaron, author of *Writers on the Left*, and historian Arthur Schlesinger Jr.—found him delightful: a good listener, particularly when trivia was described that he did not know about; and a splendid conversationalist, particularly when he was interested in the topic. Aaron has said that upon returning from researching the Dead Sea Scrolls, Wilson took a shower, then regaled him for an extended period with news of what he had found, all the while standing in his shorts. Schlesinger has said that Wilson greatly enjoyed New York City's dynamism, even impulsively choosing to go to a Broadway play in the middle of a first act. Others have described Wilson as an agreeable man who, like Emerson, dearly loved to deal in ideas and who kept a notebook in order to "Boswellize" himself. Elizabeth Hardwick's main complaint was that Wilson kept a journal and wrote about his visit in her Boston home. Beware of entertaining individuals who keep journals, she has joked.

When Wilson received the National Medal for Literature and the American Academy of Arts and Sciences gave him an award, he wrote in his summer 1966 journal: "These awards I am getting make me rather nervous. They mean that I am an O.K. character like Thornton Wilder. When I think about how stupid old frauds like Herbert Hoover and John F. Dulles get buildings and things named after them, without people's seriously protesting or considering it inappropriate, I realize that an accepted reputation can be derived from no real merit whatever."

When Arthur Schlesinger Jr. asked Wilson if he was willing to go to the White House to accept a Presidential medal, Wilson answered in the affirmative but only if the President was aware he was writing a diatribe against the Internal Revenue Service, with which he was having a long battle. Although the Internal Revenue Service vociferously objected to giving any such honor to Wilson, the President disagreed, saying the medal was not for Wilson's mathematical accuracy or honesty but for his skill in writing.

His criticisms were known for being provocative. For example, he called the Qur'an "unreadable" (and continued to call the religion Mohammadenism). Part 2 of Goethe's *Faust* he found lacking all "sense of form." "Hiroshima, Mon Amour," the film, he found boring and annoying. W. H. Auden's wrinkled face, he observed, looked "like some kind of technical map." Truman Capote, he said upon meeting him, "seemed to me a not unpleasant little monster, like a fetus with a big head." He had many negative views of Bennett Cerf, Roger W. Straus, the publisher, has reported. Wilson also enjoyed reporting gossip. In *The Last Journal 1960–1972* (1993), he said that Tennessee Williams had once asked Jacqueline Kennedy her analysis of the Warren Commission Report. Also, that Robert Frost, although in Rio de Janeiro at a time when William Faulkner was attending a literary congress, avoided sharing the spotlight with Faulkner. Wilson denied, however, ever having punched a business executive's wife in the nose when she asked, "You wrote "Finlandia," didn't you?" Rather, he said he had replied, "No: that was written by a Finn."

Wilson was not a joiner. He never became a Unitarian, but he enjoyed playfully criticizing the Unitarians, many of whom—like himself—were "old American patriots" with whom he sided and who stood in contrast to the less intellectually inclined who were members of other churches.

Neither did he ever join the Communist Party, although he flirted with communism in 1932; upon investigation, however, he argued that Americans should take communism away from the Communists because he disliked what he saw when he visited Russia. Although he had become interested in socialism through the writings of H. G. Wells and George Bernard Shaw, Wilson scoffed at wording such as "the toiling masses" and the "dictatorship of the proletariat." But Wilson found politics only a side issue and, as others have noted, he often jumped to conclusions and was not a student nor an evangelist.

In 1995, the 100th anniversary of Wilson's birth, Jeffrey Meyers published *Edmund Wilson: A Biography*. Jason Epstein, critiquing the Meyers volume, called it a squalid work in which Meyers describes Wilson as "an irascible erotomaniac, short, stout, and red-faced, whose chronic irritability is relieved mainly by alcohol. Meyers concedes that Wilson was his country's foremost literary critic, even though he often overpraised the work of women he had seduced or wanted to seduce and underestimated the work of Robert Frost, whom he disliked personally, as well as that of Wallace Stevens, while largely ignoring American writers who came of age after World War II." Epstein, the Executive Vice-President of Random House, noted that Wilson in an essay once depicted Abraham Lincoln "as a rationalist disciple of Darwin for whom God does not exist but later professes to be an instrument of God's will or even God's spokesman. Wilson sees not a spiritual but a political or, more precisely, a rhetorical conversion reflecting the greater intensity of the occasion." Wilson is depicted as "a man of the last century, a Darwinian who believed that nature, including his own nature, could be understood by distinguishing its components and identifying their logical connections. "His criticism," Epstein continues (*The New York Review of Books*, 8 June 1995), "was essentially journalistic and reflected the same conviction: that if he arranged the components of a work of literature, including the author's intentions, in a coherent, critical narrative, the various meanings implicit in the work would become clear or at least clearer."

Wilson exasperated individuals who wrote to him. He responded to the present author's three requests with the following check marks on printed cards:

Edmund Wilson regrets that it is impossible for him without compensation to

x read manuscripts
contribute to books or periodicals
do editorial work
judge literary contests
deliver lectures
address meetings
make after-dinner speeches
broadcast

Under any circumstances to

x contribute to or take part in symposiums
take part in chain-poems or other collection compositions
contribute manuscripts for sales
donate copies of his books to libraries
autograph copies of his books to libraries
supply personal information about himself
supply photographs of himself
allow his name to be used on letter-heads
receive unknown persons who have no apparent business with him.

For Wilson, the irrational components of actual life or of a literary work were themselves data to be fitted rationally into the narrative account." Wilson is said to have disliked Frost and also T. S. Eliot, except that when he met them he changed his mind somewhat. Although he had thought of Eliot as "too Episcopalian," he was impressed favorably upon learning that Eliot was cuddly and loving with his new bride, Valerie. Contemporary critics, Epstein argues, do well to turn to Wilson as the master of literary criticism.

Wilson's final years were physically uncomfortable for him, for as he complained in his autumn 1967 journal: "Monotony of my life and its limitations: I wake up first about 4 and read for a couple of hours. I look up from time to time and gauge how near morning is by the blue of dawn outside the window. Then I go to sleep again and have an unpleasant dream, from which I wake feeling rather worse than I had at 4 o'clock. I sit on the edge of the bed for a while and stare at my bare feet. . . . I then go to my bathroom and sit on the toilet, reading Jules Renard's journal or something, which helps me to face the rest: getting the yellow good off my tongue with a washcloth or towel, hawking up blood-embrowned phlegm, perfunctorily brushing my largely artificial teeth. (After supper) I read or play more solitaire or am so muggy and sleepy that I go to bed and take a Nembutal or a whisky and go right to sleep. . . ." Just the same, Epstein has observed, toward the end of his life when he was having trouble breathing Wilson was still involved with two love affairs.

At the age of seventy-seven, with his daughter Rosalind present, Wilson died in his easy chair while his nurse, Elizabeth Stabb, administered oxygen to him. His wife's tombstone inscription contains Greek, but his own contains Hebrew. (See entry for Mary McCarthy, his third wife, who tells of her reasons for marrying Wilson. Also, see the article on Wilson by Louis Menand of the City University of New York in *The Johns Hopkins Guide to Literary Theory & Criticism* [1994].) {CE; OEL; conversations with Alfred Kazin, 12 April 1995; Daniel Aaron and Arthur Schlesinger, 19 April 1995, and with Lewis Dabney, Jason Epstein, Elizabeth Hardwick, Mary Meigs, and Rogert W. Straus Jr., 24 May 1995}

Wilson, E(dward) O(sborne) (1929–)

Wilson, who was the undersized only child of Southern Baptist parents who divorced when he was seven years old, had a father who drank, gambled, and was a peripatetic accountant. The father, who changed "his job and location of his home every year or two," took him and a second wife to a variety of places before committing suicide in 1951 at the age of forty-eight. In *Naturalist* (1994), Wilson describes having started his formal education at the age of seven in a military boarding school, then going to a succession of fourteen schools in and out of Alabama, at that time known as one of the most racist and segregated parts of America. Wilson suffered from impaired hearing and, while fishing and having the spine of a pinfish pierce the pupil of his right eye, became virtually blind in that eye.

Admittedly poor at mathematics and memorization, he compensated by collecting lizards, snakes, butterflies, cave insects, bats, and ants. At sixteen, he became intent upon studying Alabama ants, and his zeal eventually led him to become a Junior Fellow of Harvard's Society of Fellows as well as a science researcher in Malaysia, Indonesia, and elsewhere. In 1994 with Bert Holldobbler, he wrote *Journey to the Ants: A Story of Scientific Exploration*, which was an updating of the definitive 1990 reference book on myrmecology which won them a 1991 Pulitzer Prize. (Fellow humanist Julian Huxley also was a leading authority on ants.)

Wilson admits that he finds the theists' appeal of supernaturalistic religion understandable:

> On religion I lean toward deism but consider its proof largely a problem in astrophysics. . . . [T]he existence of a biological God, one who directs organic evolution and intervenes in human affairs [as envisioned by theism] is increasingly contravened by biology and the brain sciences. . . . Religions are analogous to superorganisms. They have a life cycle. They are born, they grow, they compete, they reproduce, and, in the fullness of time, most die.

A professor emeritus of Harvard University, and a leading proponent of sociobiology, Wilson spends part of his time defending the controversial views he expressed in *Sociobiology: The New Synthesis* (1977), views which concern the genetic factors in human behavior. Among other works, he wrote *Insect Societies* (1971), *Of Human Nature* (1978), *Biophilia* (1984), *The Diversity of Life* (1992), and an essay, "Scientific Humanism and Religion," in *Challenges to the Enlightenment, Essays in Defense of Reason and Science* (1994). *Naturalist* revives the controversy caused by the 1977 work on sociobiology. In 1978, for example, during a speech at the annual meeting of the American Association for the Advancement of Science, he was assaulted for his views. Anti-sociobiologists actually seized the dais and dumped a pitcher of ice water on his head, chanting, "Wilson, you're all wet!" To which Wilson later observed, the episode "may be the only occasion in recent American history on which a scientist was physically attacked, however, mildly, simply for the expression of an idea," adding "I had been blind-sided by the attack."

In *Naturalist*, Wilson wrote that

> Human beings inherit a propensity to acquire behavior and social structures, a propensity that is shared by enough people to be called human nature. Although people have free will and the choice to turn in many directions, the channels of their psychological development are nevertheless—however much we might wish otherwise—cut more deeply by the genes in certain directions than in others.

He added,

> History did not begin 10,000 years ago in the villages of Antolia and Jordan. It spans the two million years of the life of the genus Homo. Deep history—by which I mean biological history—made us what we are, no less than culture.

His emphasis is that the architecture and physiology of the brain both evolve together, that the brain is like a vast road map of interconnecting nerve cells and that the brain learns in patterns determined by one's genes.

In a provocative article, "Back From Chaos" (*The Atlantic Monthly*, March 1998), Wilson detailed his views about how the Enlightenment thinkers knew a lot about everything whereas today's specialists know a lot about a little. Although postmodernists doubt that we can know anything at all, he claims that we *can* know what we need to know and that we will discover underlying all forms of knowledge a fundamental unity. He focuses on the ideas of Bacon, Descartes, Newton, and Condorcet, explains the attraction of deism and the weaknesses of postmodernism, then introduces the idea of "consilience":

> The ongoing fragmentation of knowledge and the resulting chaos in philosophy are not reflections of the real world but artifacts of scholarship. The key to unification is consilience. I prefer this word to "coherence," because its rarity has preserved its precision, whereas "coherence" has several possible meanings. William Whewell, in his 1840 synthesis *The Philosophy of the Inductive Sciences*, was the first to speak of consilience—literally a "jumping together" of knowledge as a result of the linking of facts and fact-based theory across disciplines to create a common groundwork of explanation. He wrote, "The Consilience of Inductions takes place when an Induction, obtained from one class of facts, coincides with an Induction, obtained from another different class. This Consilience is a test of the truth of the Theory in which it occurs."
>
> Consilience can be established or refuted only by methods developed in the natural sciences—in an effort, I hasten to add, not led by scientists, or frozen in mathematical abstraction, but consistent with the habits of thought that have worked so well in exploring the material universe. . . .
>
> If contemporary scholars work to encourage the consilience of knowledge, I believe, the enterprises of culture will eventually devolve into science—by which I mean the natural sciences—and the humanities, particularly the creative arts. These domains will continue to be the two great branches of learning in the twenty-first century.

A way exists out of the chaos of all the information we have at hand, he says. It involves understanding that a balanced perspective cannot be acquired by studying disciplines in pieces but, rather, "the consilience among them must be pursued." What has been achieved in the natural sciences needs, in short, to be extended to the humanities and the social sciences.

Wilson argues that an empiricist ethic is needed, mindful as he is that because of the divorce between ethics and empirical knowledge, ethicists contend that one cannot go from "is" to "ought":

> Moral reasoning will either remain centered in idioms of theology and philosophy, where it is now, or it will shift toward science-based material analysis. . . . Because the success of an ethical code depends on how wisely it interprets the moral sentiments, those who frame it should know how the brain works, and how the mind develops. The success of ethics also depends on the accurate prediction of the consequence of particular actions as opposed to others, especially in cases of moral ambiguity.

Such an ethic, Peter B. Denison has noted, must be based on science, inowledge of our biology and brain functioning, and also an understanding of evolution.

Wilson, whose love of life led him to coin the word *biophilia*, is a Humanist Laureate in the Council for Secular Humanism's International Academy of Humanism, a member of the Humanist Association of Massachusetts, and a signer of Humanist Manifesto 2000. (For Richard Rorty's critique of Wilson's ideas, see entry for Consilience.) {CA; CE}

Wilson, Edwin H(enry) (1898–1993)

Wilson was raised in Concord, Massachusetts, where he attended the First Parish Church, a Unitarian fellowship. His mother introduced him to Unitarianism, but his father had no use for the church. "The people," said the father, "worship God Almighty half the time and Ralph Waldo Emerson the other." After serving in World War I, Wilson attended Meadville Theological School, graduating in 1926 with a doctorate degree, after which he studied at the Sorbonne in Paris. In 1928, he was the Unitarian minister in Dayton, Ohio, later having pulpits in Schenectady, New York; Chicago, Illinois; Yellow Springs, Ohio; Salt Lake City, Utah; and Cocoa Beach, Florida. Early in his ministry, he composed "Where Is Our Holy Church?"

A Unitarian minister, Wilson in 1929 became a regular contributor to *The New Humanist*, a mimeographed newsletter published in

Chicago by the Humanist Fellowship. The following year, he managed the publication. In 1936, *The New Humanist* ceased because of lack of funds, so using his own funds he commenced a modest *Humanist Bulletin* which, in 1941, was succeeded by *The Humanist*, which is still being published. He edited the journal for sixteen years (1941 to 1956) and was interim editor from 1963 to 1964. In addition to editing and contributing to *The Humanist*, he was one of the founders of the American Humanist Association (AHA) in 1941 and served as its executive director from 1949 to 1970, then becoming its official historian. In 1952 he participated in the founding and named of the International Humanist and Ethical Union (IHEU). Wilson was one of several editors of *The Humanist* who would be "eased out" of his job, Herbert A. Tonne has observed, by the AHA board of directors.

In 1933, Wilson was the guiding force behind the formulation of Humanist Manifesto I. That document, signed by thirty-four liberal humanists, defined and enunciated the philosophical and religious principles that they considered to be fundamental. It was committed to reason, science, and democracy, and many of the signers were Unitarian clergymen. The document emphasized the view that human beings determine the moral principles which govern their lives. Wilson gathered leading thinkers of the time into a group which rallied behind the philosophy variously termed religious, scientific, or naturalistic humanism. They criticized religious dogmatism, called for universal education, advocated more participatory democracy, and declared that nationalism and war were obsolete. Further, they affirmed euthanasia as well as the right of women to choose abortion and the right to birth control.

In 1941 he moved from Chicago to the Unitarian pulpit at Schenectady, New York, for a five-year war-time ministry. Corliss Lamont and Max Otto encouraged him to resume publication of *The New Humanist*, now as editor and under a new title, *The Humanist*. By 1952 the magazine circulation had grown and its sponsor was changed from the Humanist Press Association to the American Humanist Association (AHA). Writing of the controversy at that time, Wilson explained,

> Because various philosophic points of view emerge religiously and ethically as humanism, there came a time in the 1940s when there was a rather vigorous complaint that the editorial policy of *The Humanist* was too pragmatic in its orientation. (This was the position of philosopher Arthur Murphy who chose to drop out.) Roy Wood Sellars was a critical realist and therefore, in epistemology, anti-Dewey. Eventually there was also a rather sharp conflict between the logical positivists, as represented by Charles Morris, John Dewey, and Arthur Bentley, and conflict between Bertrand Russell and John Dewey.

Wilson was able to keep the group together and in 1953 published a symposium about the original manifesto, asking a number of people what they would change now that twenty years had passed. Sellars called humanism a religion, "the next great religion," and he suggested what could be the next big push. In *The Genesis of a Humanist Manifesto* (1995), Wilson collected further critiques, calling them "The Symposium: Part I" from J.A.C. Fagginer Auer; E. Burdette Backus; Harry Elmer Barnes; L. M. Birkhead; Edwin Arthur Burtt; Ernest Caldecott; A. J. Carlson; Frank H. Hankins; A. Eustace Haydon; Llewellyn Jones; Robert Morss Lovett; Harold P. Marley; Lester Mondale; Charles Francis Potter; J. H. Randall Jr.; Curtis W. Reese; Oliver L. Reiser; Clinton Lee Scott;V. T. Thayer; E. C. Vanderlaan; Jacob J. Weinstein; and David Rhys Williams.

Later, in "The Symposium: Part II," he published further critiques from Van Meter Ames; Fred G. Bratton; Albert C. Dieffenbach; John H. Dietrich; Corliss Lamont; Harold A. Larrabee; Alfred McClung Lee; Francis Meyers; Lloyd Morain; Arthur E. Morgan; Herbert J. Muller; Harold Scott; Mark Starr; Gerald Wendt; and Gardner Williams. Wilson was expert in collecting humanistic comments, and *The Humanist* in the 1950s was noted for its intellectual content and a growing reputation among a large variety of philosophers.

Wilson in 1956 wrote these views concerning humanism:

> Humanism appears wherever thinkers or doers meet the problems of man and life in terms of the scientific world view rather than of the pre-scientific world view. Today's Humanism shares with all Humanisms—including the Christian Humanism of the Renaissance—a central concern for the good life for men here and now. Humanism is always this-worldly and regards life this side of the grave as the locus of fulfillment and moral achievement. But today's Humanism more clearly yields to man a place of dignity in his own right. It does not need theological sanctions. It refuses to rob man to pay theology. It is itself a new synthesis, naturalistic rather than supernaturalistic, unitary rather than bifurcated. The old vertical dualisms of body and mind, spirit and matter disappear in Naturalistic Humanism. Humanists claim that man's unique rationality emerges from his sub-rational animal past. Naturalistic humanists see the spiritual as an emergent quality of the material. Nature is relatively predictable; right and wrong are relative to a human nature that is much the same in all cultures and times. Man lives in relation to a relatively more stable universe. All is part of one web of relationships to which man belongs, yet in which he has achieved a grandeur of his own. In our own day man has developed his rationality to the point at which scientific method and cooperative skills exist in sufficient potential to enable him to place control of the major obstacles to planetary control of his own destiny within his reach. But there remains the stirring of the will to do so, the growth of that confidence and vision that makes it possible.
>
> Humanism, as an organized movement slowly growing around the world, must accept the moral responsibility of the Humanist idea—the idea that all men are one and that potentially they have what it will take to end war and create a significant common life for a qualitatively produced race. Their task is to articulate the implications for man's common destiny, of the new knowledge that is science and the promise of the method that is scientific method.

A long-time editor of *The Humanist*, he remained for years on its editorial board despite having been eased out of the editorship. In 1979, the American Humanist Association named him Humanist of the Year. At the age of over ninety, he helped form an active humanist group in Salt Lake City, Utah.

Wilson was in demand at dinners to say grace, and he was always pleased to accept:

> Oh, God, for as much as without Thee
> We would be unable to doubt Thee,
> Give us power by Thy grace
> To convince the whole race
> It knows nothing whatever about Thee.

Whereupon those present responded with loud and boisterous amens.

Wilson wrote "A New Synthesis: Among the Intellectuals" (*The New Humanist*, January 1930); "A New Synthesis: The Development of Method in Cooperative Problem Solving" (*The New Humanist*, February 1930); "A New Synthesis: The Organization of Knowledge" (*The New Humanist*, March 1930); "A New Synthesis: Integrating Science" (*The New Humanist*, April 1930); "A New Synthesis: Adult Education, England" (*The New Humanist* , May 1930); "A New Synthesis: Adult Education, the United States," *The New Humanist* (June 1930); and "The Origins of Modern Humanism," *The Humanist* (January-February 1991).

Three years after his death, in a work edited by Teresa Maciocha, Wilson's *The Genesis of a Humanist Manifesto* (1995) was published.

It contains candid descriptions of the various individuals involved in the writing of the Manifesto and clarifies who specifically contributed what, who failed to sign the drafts and why, and who even twenty years later were still its supporters as well as who remained its critics. The work, which contains much new information, is surprisingly gentle in its treatment of some individuals who are known to have irked Wilson tremendously. (See entry for American Humanist Association. Also see a critique of Wilson's humanism by Herbert A. Tonne in *Free Inquiry*, Fall 1996.) {CL; EW; FUS; HM1; HM2; HNS; HNS2; PK; WAS, 3 November 1956, and numerous conversations.}

Wilson, Georgia H. (20th Century)

A retired member of Brooklyn College's political science department, Wilson signed Humanist Manifesto II. {HM2}

Wilson, H. H. (20th Century)

A book reviewer for *The Humanist* in the 1950s, Wilson taught at Princeton.

Wilson, H. Van Rensselaer (20th Century)

When Wilson signed Humanist Manifesto II, he was professor emeritus of philosophy at Brooklyn College. He is on the editorial advisory board of *Religious Humanism,* the quarterly published by the Fellowship of Religious Humanists. {HM2}

Wilson, John (19th Century)

An Irish author, Wilson wrote *Thoughts on Science, Theology, and Ethics* (1885). {BDF}

Wilson, J. B. (20th Century)

Wilson wrote a *Funeral Oration Giving An Exposition of the Principles of Agnosticism and Freethought* (c. 1906). In 1899, he became a medical doctor and worked for three years in the slums of Cincinnati. At different times, he was president of the American Secular Union and of the American Freethought Association. {Cincinnati, Ohio, *Fig Leaves*, May 1995; GS}

Wilson, Jim (20th Century)

Wilson is editor in Georgia of the Atlanta Freethought Society's newsletter, *Atlanta Freethought News*. E-mail: <jkwilson@cris.com>.

Wilson, John Bowie (1820–1883)

Wilson was a Scottish-born freethinker and radical politician who migrated to Australia twice, first in 1840 and again in 1854. Opposed to his father's religion, Wilson developed a lifelong interest in spiritualism and freethought. Entering New South Wales Legislative Assembly in 1859, he became a radical opponent of State Aid to Religion. In 1861, he moved to have the Church and school lands be declared as waste lands to insure that any money raised from them would go into consolidated revenue. Wilson was one of the founders in 1882 of the Liberal Association of New South Wales, an attempt to fuse religious and atheist freethought groups into "one party of progress." He was buried without religious rites in the Unitarian section of the Rookwood cemetery, and his friend and associate Charles Bright gave the panegyric. {SWW}

Wilson, J. M. (20th Century)

Wilson wrote *Religion, A Primitive Fable* (1959). {GS}

Wilson, Roland (Died 1919)

A jurist, Wilson was a reader in Indian law at the University of Cambridge and author of numerous legal works. In later years, he concerned himself much with religion and, according to McCabe, ended as an agnostic. In an article a few weeks before he died, he wrote in the *Hibbert Journal* that for thirty years he had followed Francis Newman, the theistic brother of the Cardinal, but "I have of late felt myself less and less able to affirm with any confidence the existence of any supreme mind behind the visible universe." Even if there were such a thing, said Sir Roland Knynet of Delhi, men must ignore it in practice and follow human ideals. {JM; RAT; RE}

Wilson, Sloan (1920–)

Wilson wrote *The Man in the Gray Flannel Suit* (1955), in which the hero is commended for being a corporate cog but one who has a nice home and family to come home to. Corporations might be evil to some, who possibly prefer going "on the road" in the 1950s with Jack Kerouac and "the beat generation." But to Wilson, who was on the school board of the benchmark school of New Canaan, Connecticut, was asked his views on humanism. He responded to the present author:

> I can't imagine why anyone would be interested in my thoughts on this subject, but I guess I'm a convert to Naturalistic Humanism, with certain qualifications. I don't reject any and all forms of supernaturalism. Although I can't accept a dogma, and do set up as a supreme value the long-range welfare of all humanity, I am at heart a sort of optimistic mystic. The only standard of morality I understand is the ultimate effect of any action on the welfare of all humanity, but I don't see how one can avoid admitting there must be a higher power. Certainly the mind tells us that. My heart goes on to assert that it must, despite all evidence to the contrary, be an ultimately benign power. One must belief that, I think, to achieve any real serenity in the face of death and the other trials we all face. This is what "humanism" connotes to me. I think that probably Tolstoy and other Russian writers of his general period influenced me, as well as most of the good contemporary American and British writers. Perhaps I simply read what I believe into their work. I don't have any other comments pro or con the other concepts of humanism, except to say that any philosophy which tends to set man against man, such as Communism and the more rigid sectarian beliefs, can scarcely qualify as "humanism" to me.
>
> The heart of humanism, I think, is the hands-off attitude toward any human action which does not hurt other human beings. I cannot imagine a true believer in humanism trying to convince another man that his faith is wrong, or enlisting men in an army to force "humanism" down the throats of others. The philosophy I've worked out for myself is really very simple: within his power, a man should try to do all he can to help all other men; he should, within his power, avoid any action which would hurt anyone; and he must have faith that even when he has not the strength to behave properly himself or to withstand the evil actions of others, he is still a small part of an overall design that has purpose, justice, and charity.
>
> {WAS, 7 May 1956}

Wilson, Thomas (19th Century)

Wilson, a Scot, wrote "Priestly Systems Repugnant to Christian Principles" (1851). {GS}

Wilson, William E. (20th Century)

Wilson wrote *The Angel and the Serpent, the Story of New Harmony* (1946). {GS}

Wilson, Woodrow [President] (1856–1924)

Writing to an academic in 1922, Wilson stated, "May it not suffice for me to say . . . that of course I do believe in organic evolution. It surprises me that at this late date such questions should be raised." His uncle, Prof. James Woodrow, had been fired by Presbyterian Theological Seminary in South Carolina in 1884 for defending evolution. {TYD}

Wiltsee, Herbert (20th Century)

In 1941 for his Ph. D. dissertation at the University of Chicago, Wiltsee wrote "Robert G. Ingersoll, A Study in Religious Liberalism." {FUS}

Wiltshire, Thomas (20th Century)

Wiltshire wrote "The Ultimate Authority in Matters of Faith" (1976). {GS}

Wimble, Joan (20th Century)

Wimble in Britain is secretary of the Brighton and Hove Humanist Group.

Winans, R. (19th Century)

Winans was a freethinker who wrote "Extracts From 'One Religion': Many Creeds" (1871) and *Modern Scepticism* (1873). {GS}

Winchester, Elhanan (1751–1797)

When as a Baptist minister in 1781 Winchester proclaimed "universal salvation," he was ousted from his church and took a large portion of the congregation with him to form a Universalist society in Philadelphia. Because God was all-powerful, he reasoned, and because God was benevolent, the eventual restoration of all souls was assured. In 1787 he took his Universalist ideas to England and had his asthmatic condition not worsened he might well have come to rival John Murray as the leader of his denomination. {FUK; U; U&U}

Winckler, Hugo (1863–1913)

A German orientalist, Winckler was appointed professor of oriental languages and history at Berlin University in 1904. He had written *Geshichte Babyloniens und Assyriens* (1892) and translated into German the Hammurabi Code (*Gesetze Hammurabis*, 1904). His rationalist views are freely expressed in *Alttestamentliche Untersuchungen* (1892) and *Geschichte Israels* (1898). {RAT}

Windelband, Wilhelm: See entry for Hominism.

Winkler, Kenneth (20th Century)

Winkler, of Wellesley College, is a 1997 Hume Conference Director of The Hume Society, a group engaged in scholarly activity concerning David Hume.

Windeyer, William Charles (1834–1897)

Windeyer was an Australian social reformer, jurist, and parliamentarian. Judge of the New South Wales Supreme Court, 1879–1896, he delivered a seminal judgment in the William Whitehouse Collins case. Collins, who had been convicted for selling Annie Besant's *Law of Population* advocating birth control, had appealed to the Supreme Court to have his conviction set aside. Windeyer's judgment effectively put an end to almost all prosecutions for selling or publishing books on birth control. {SWW}

Windship, Charles W. (19th Century)

Windship was a freethinker who wrote *Discourse on Religion and Doctrines* (1829). {GS}

Windsor, Allen (1921–)

In 1994, Windsor was a contributing editor for the short-lived *QWER Quarterly*, a publication of North America's Lesbian and Gay Secular Humanists.

To conceal his gender, nationality, and identity, Windsor, ever the practical joker, writes for a variety of publications under pseudonyms—G. Hovah, Rev. DooDoo, Jesús Ethelbert Plaisir, W. Allen Smith, Jun Sczesnoczkawasm. Although accused of it, he denies being related to any of several queens, including Elizabeth II.

Following is one of his erotic poems:

Ratiocination From On High

They believe omniscience is My given.
Still, they fail to comprehend the joy with which,
as his Tommasso jealously looked on,
I goaded Michelangelo
to shape the thighs and grasp the balls,
his chisel with a tender movement carving love.

What if they knew
that I—original Original, hermaphrodite—
am not alone but, like Jove, burn with joy
not for his Ganymede but for my own adored,
my David, my angelic one-of-all!

They, I know, look heavenward,
yet will not know of Heaven
'til they feel the warmth of phalli 'neath the skin,
of tongues entwined,
the very acts they foolishly call sin.

In *One* (July 1958), an early American homosexual journal, he wrote, "If One Needs Religion":

> One's viscera has more to do with his religion than most realize. There are other factors which determine one's religion, of course—geography, environmental conditioning, family influence, etc. But basically if one's biological makeup leads him to be the cool, reflective, and intellectual type like Adlai Stevenson, there is every chance that he will be a Unitarian rather than a Jehovah's Witness. And if he is a searcher for order, absolutes, and *the* truth like Bing Crosby, there is every chance that he will be a Catholic rather than a Congregationalist. Were God Himself to declare, in the morning newspaper, that a particular religion or a certain bible were the only *true* one—say the Buddhist Order of Circumcised Vegetarians—can you imagine the nervous breakdowns which would be experienced by Cardinal Spellman, Nehru, Eisenhower, Sartre, Elvis Presley, or Jane Russell in abandoning their old religion in order to please God?

His conclusion was that most homosexuals, if happy with their present religion, should probably make no changes. But any who are uncomfortable feeling like second-class humans in the various organized religions, he continued, might well look into groups such as the Friends, the Ethical Culturists, the Universalists, and the Unitarians. Specifically, he recommended an alternative: the philosophic outlook of naturalistic humanism as described in *The Humanist* and in the writings of H. L. Mencken, Robert Ingersoll, and Bertrand Russell.

Wine, Sherwin T. [Rabbi] (1928–)

Rabbi Wine, an atheist, founded the Society for Humanistic Judaism. He celebrates traditional Jewish holidays, has founded temples, and conducts "religious" services although they are non-theistic and naturalistic. He is generally regarded as a religious rather than a secular humanist, but he signed Humanist Manifesto II and, in 1980, the Secular Humanist Declaration. He wrote *Judaism Beyond God* (1985) and *Staying Sane in a Crazy World*, the latter a reference to Alcoholics Anonymous: "One of the signs of personal strength is that we take blame for what we do wrong. The other sign is that we take credit for what we do right. We do not alienate our power by assigning it to someone else. . . . Strong people are comfortable in recognizing their own power . . . nor do they call their power 'a higher power.'"

Rabbi Wine has written articles in *Free Inquiry* and was one of the principal founders of Americans for Religious Liberty. Wine is the Founding Chairman of The Humanist Institute. Since 1977, he has edited the quarterly *Humanistic Judaism*.

Wine's take on God is one that he describes as ignosticism, by which he means he regards the question of God's existence to be meaningless—it has no verifiable consequences. From this, he concludes that people can and should live without reference to such a supernatural being. (See entries for the International Federation of Secular Humanistic Jews and for *The Jewish Humanist*. For a negative critique, see Society for Humanistic Judaism.) {E; FD; HM2; HNS2; SHD}

Winell, Marlene (20th Century)

Winell is author of *Leaving the Fold* (1993), which describes how a missionary's daughter became a freethinking psychologist. Her *A Guide for Former Fundamentalists and Others Leaving Their Religion* (1994) investigates the dangers of religious indoctrination and outlines what therapists and victims can do to reclaim their lives in order to have a healthier outlook on life. She lives in Brisbane, Australia, and is involved with art and film-making. {*Secular Nation*, Fall 1994}

Wineriter, Florien J. (20th Century)

Wineriter, an activist with the Salt Lake City, Utah, humanists, is on the Board of Directors and is treasurer of the American Humanist Association. Winewriter's e-mail: <jdht30a@prodigy.com>.

Winetrout, Kenneth (1912–)

A book reviewer for *The Humanist* in the 1950s, Winetrout was head of the education department at American International College in Massachusetts. In 1974, he wrote *Arnold Toynbee, the Ecumenical Vision*.

Wing, Joseph (c. 1840–1910?)

In Australia, Wing edited *The Spiritual Inquirer* (1874 to 1875) and *The Reformer* (1880 to 1883), both spiritualist and freethought journals. {FUK; SWW}

Wingrove, Nigel (20th Century)

Wingrove's 1996 film, "Visions of Ecstasy," depicted St. Teresa of Avila having a sexual fantasy about a nun and an imagined erotic relationship with Jesus. {*New Humanist*, December 1996}

Winslow, Moses (18th Century)

Winslow was one of the "coterie of infidels." (See entry for North Carolina Freethinkers.)

Winsor, Doreen (20th Century)

Winsor has been on the editorial committee of *Humanist in Canada*.

Winsor, Ellen (20th Century)

The pseudonymous Ellen Winsor writes for *Freethinker*. Her articles include "The Case of Robert Ferguson," "The *Freethinker* Fire of 1886," and "The National Secular Society Almanack, 1870–1904."

Winsor, Mary (20th Century)

Winsor has been a member of the American Humanist Association. {HNS}

Winspear, William Robert (1861–1944)

Winspear was an Australian freethinker, publisher, and socialist. In 1877 he launched the *Radical*, the nation's first regularly produced socialist journal. Moving away from the Labor Party, he used his journalistic and poetic efforts to expose the hypocrisy of established religion and political practices.

Following are some of his irreverent versions:

Of Christ's Sermon on the Mount:
- Blessed are the cruel in spirit: for theirs are the kingdoms of men.

Of the Ten Commandments of Capitalism:
- I, the Capitalist, am the Lord thy God. Thou shalt have no other gods before me.

Of a Christian hymn:
- Praise Gold from which all blessings flow—of all your gods praise it the most.

During Australia's first conscription campaign in 1916, Winspear's poem, "The Blood Vote," was forceful propaganda against compulsory militarism.

Winston, George R. (20th Century)

Winston wrote *John Fiske* (1972). {GS}

Winter, Alice Ames (1865-1944)

Winter, a Unitarian and a Woman's Club leader, was an author. Her mother was Fanny Baker Ames.

Wintermute, Carol (20th Century)

Wintermute is a director and a former secretary of the American Humanist Association. Also, she is on the Board of Governors of The Humanist Institute. {HNS2}

Wintermute, Harry (20th Century)

Wintermute, who wrote "Christianity or Natural Law?" (19—?), was described by Gordon Stein as being a freethinker. {GS}

Wiredu, Kwasi (20th Century)

Wiredu, a professor of philosophy at the Unviersity of South Florida, is an Advisory Board Member of African Americans for Humanism.

Wirmarsius, Henrik (18th Century)

Wirmarsius is the Dutch author of *Den Ingebeelde Chaos* (1710). {BDF}

Wirtz, Raoul (20th Century)

A Dutch humanist, Wirtz participated in the 1996 the international conference of humanists in Mexico City. E-mail: <hr@euronet.nl>.

WISCONSIN HUMANISTS

- Atheists and Agnostics of Wisconsin, PO Box 290, Madison, Wisconsin 53701 (608) 233-7239; E-mail: <mbr@execpc.com> and on the Web: <http://www.cs.wisc.edu/~krisna/aaw/>
- Freethought Society of Wisconsin, 8816 W. Greenfield Ave., West Allis, Wisconsin 53214. (414) 771-0743. E-mail: <fsw@teamwork.com/fsw/>. Glenn Curry, President, is at <gcurry@inc.net>. Web: <http://www.teamworkweb.com/ftsm/>.
- *Humanist Quest*, 3402 North 40th St., Milwaukee, WI 53216. Contact is Wendell Harris.
- Humanist Quest of Milwaukee, 3458 North Newhall, Milwaukee, Wisconsin 53211; phone (414) 964-5585. Ted Scher is President. Carol Lee Smith, the e-mail contact, is at <human@csd.uwm.edu>.
- Milwaukee Area Unbelievers, 1908 East Edgewood, Shorewood, Wisconsin 53211; telephone (414) 964-5271
- Milwaukee Freethought Society(ASHS), PO Box 13204, Milwaukee, WI 53213; (414) 771-0743. Carol Smith can be e-mailed at <csmith@omnifest.uwm.edu>. Another contact is at <ftsm@rocketmail.com>. On the Web: <http://www.teamwork-web.com/ftsm/>.
- North East Wisconsin Humanists, PO Box 8114, Green Bay, WI 54308 (920) 866-9707.

- Secular Humanists of Madison, Wisconsin, 5322 Fairway Drive, Madison, WI 53711; (608) 274-2152. E-mail: cmdejoie@facstaff.wisc.edu>.
- Bernie Schatz is American Humanist Association coordinator of the northern region of the United States
- University of Wisconin at Madison Atheists and Agnostics are on the Web at <http://www.secularhumanism.org/cfa/orgs.html>.
- University of Wisconsin at Milwaukee humanists are on the Web at <http://www.secularhumanism.org/cfa/orgs.html>.

(See entry for Minnesota Atheists, Humanists.) {FD}

WISDOM

"Too soon old; too late smart," a Buffalo-Rochester editor has observed.

Wisdom can be defined as accumulated philosophic or scientific learning. Believers hold that wisdom is found in the teachings of the ancient wise men. Non-believers point to numerous examples of the lack of wisdom in, for example, biblical writings and look instead to contemporary research. Sir William Osler (1849-1919), the most brilliant and influential teacher of medicine in Canada, illustrated his own wisdom when he wrote, "The philosophies of one age have become the absurdities of the next, and the foolishness of yesterday has become the wisdom of tomorrow."

Bertrand Russell in *Fact and Fiction* (1961) wrote of wisdom, "It is a word concerned partly with knowledge and partly with feeling. It should denote a certain intimate union of knowledge with apprehension of human destiny and the purposes of life. It requires a certain breadth of vision, which is hardly possible without considerable knowledge. But it demands, also, a breadth of feeling, a certain kind of universality of sympathy. I think that higher education should do what is possible towards promoting not only knowledge but wisdom. I do not think that this is easy; and I do not think that the aim should be too conscious, for, if it is, it becomes stereotyped and priggish. It should be something existing almost unconsciously in the teacher and conveyed almost unintentionally to the pupil. I agree with Plato in thinking that this is the greatest thing that education can do." (See the essay on wisdom by Brand Blanshard in the *Encyclopedia of Philosophy*, Vol. 8.) {Lee Eisler, *The Quotable Bertrand Russell*}

WISE MEN

The anecdote is told about Earl Shaftesbury that when overheard by a scrubwoman remarking that "All wise men have the same religion," she eagerly inquired what this religion of all wise men was.

"Wise men," he reportedly responded, "never tell." (See entry for Anthony Ashley Cooper Shaftesbury.)

Wise, Herbert A. (20th Century)

Wise, who has been a member of the American Humanist Association, is a naturalistic humanist. {HNS}

Wise, John Richard de Capel (1831–1890)

An authority on birds and natural history, Wise also was an authority on Shakespeare. Wise was an agnostic who was a friend of George Henry Lewes and George Eliot. {RE}

Wise, Thomas E. (19th Century)

An African American, Wise was minister of the First Universalist Church of Norfolk, Virginia, and of St. Paul's Universalist Church of Suffolk, Virginia, in the 1890s. (See "Black Universalist Centennial," *The World*, January/February 1995.)

Wiseman, Richard (20th Century)

Wiseman, a professor of psychology at the University of Hertfordshire, England, wrote "Participatory Science and the Mass Media for *Free Inquiry* (Fall 1998).

Wislicensus, Gustav Adolf (1803–1885)

Wislicensus was a German rationalist who, after studying theology at Halle, became suspended as a minister because of his *Letter or Spirit* (1845). He then founded the Free Congregation. For writing *The Bible in the Light of Modern Culture*, he was sentenced in 1853 to two years in prison. After serving his sentence, he went to America, lecturing in Boston and New York. Wislicensus's chief work was *The Bible for Thinking Readers* (1863). {RAT}

Wisotsky, Morris (20th Century)

In 1972, Wisotsky was on the advisory board of the Humanist Society of Greater New York.

WISSELKRANT

A Dutch quarterly magazine for humanist activists, *WisselKrant* is at Postbus 75490, 1070-AL Amsterdam, The Netherlands; <HV@euronet.NL>.

WIT

• The humorous story is American, the comic story is English, the witty story is French.

—**Mark Twain**

• An example of old words now bereft of meaning but still is use [is] "*to wit*," where the [early meaning of the] word—*wit*, as a verb meaning "know"—has been lost.

—William Safire

WITCH-CHILDREN: See entry for Hans Sebald.

WITCHCRAFT

• Witch, n. (1) An ugly and repulsive old woman, in a wicked league with the devil. (2) A beautiful and attractive young woman, in wickedness a league beyond the devil.

—**Ambrose Bierce**
The Devil's Dictionary

Naturalists are amused by, but not convinced by, various supernaturalists' claims of being able to use black magic, sorcery, enchantment, Satanism, and other occult arts, either for good or for bad. During the Spanish Inquisition, as many as one hundred alleged witches were burned in a day. Pope Gregory IX had established the Inquisition in 1233 to root out witches, heretics, and other of Satan's helpers. Two centuries later, Pope Innocent VIII commissioned a guide, *The Malleus Maleficarum* (1484), which was written by prominent inquisitors in heresy-riddle Germany to stop those thought to be destroying the clerical and political orders. For example,

• We excommunicate all followers, protectors, defenders, and patrons of [accused witches]. . . . When any such has been so sentenced and has scorned to recant his heresy . . . he shall be considered an outlaw.

• Concerning witches who copulate with devils. . . . What else is woman but a foe to friendship, an unescapable punishment, a necessary evil, a natural temptation, a desirable calamity, a domestic danger, a delectable detriment, an evil of nature, painted with fair colors! . . . They have slippery tongues, and are unable to conceal from their fellow-women those things which by the evil arts they know.

• What, then, is to be thought of witches who . . . sometimes collect male organs in great numbers, as many as 20 or 30 members, and put them in a bird's nest, or shut them up in a box . . . as has been seen by many and is a matter of common report? . . . For a certain man tells that, when he had lost his member, he approached a known witch to ask her to restore it to him. She told the afflicted man to climb a certain tree, and that he might take which he liked out of a nest in which there were several members. And when he tried to take a big one, the witch said: You must not take that one, adding, because it belonged to a parish priest.

• Soothsayers and diviners . . . whose art involves some worship of or subjection to devils, and who by essay of divination predict the future or something of that nature which manifestly savours of heresy are . . . liable to the Inquisitional Court.

In 1692, twenty persons were executed as witches in Salem, Massachusetts. Of approximately 350 who were accused of witchcraft in colonial New England from 1620 to 1725, an estimated 78% were women, many of whom according to *The Gay Almanac*(1996) were thought to be lesbians.

More than any other heresy—for the Catholic church considered witchcraft heretical—medieval and Renaissance witchcraft has provoked a wide variety of incompatible explanations. It was not a reinterpretation of the teachings of Jesus, a new formulation of church doctrine, or a reform movement within Christianity. An enormous literature has grown concerning the subject and its relation to religion. Included are books by Montague Summers, *The History of Witchcraft and Demonology* (1926); R. H. Robbins, *The Encyclopedia of Witchcraft and Demonology* (1959); and L. L. Martello, *Witchcraft* (1973). Sprenger estimated that Christians put 9,000,000 witches to death, although it is not clear how he determined that figure.

In the present century, witchcraft continues, mainly to cloak an ulterior motive—an unforgiven grievance, a bad debt, sheer jealousy—which includes drumming up business for witch doctors. In South Africa at a time when the votes in the first free elections were being counted in a town with the self-effacing name, Nobody, a mob accosted Sinna Mankwane in front of her home. They pinioned her arms with three gasoline-splashed tires, forced her husband, Johannes, to set fire to his wife, and made the couple's son and daughter watch as she burned alive. A few days later, they returned, doused Johannes with gasoline, and set him aflame inside his house. The two children were similarly killed. Their crime? They were accused of casting a lethal spell on a neighbor. Journalists estimated up to one hundred had been put to death as witches in 1994 in one area alone.

The usual technique is to use gasoline filled tires—a "necklace"—and it is a practice used in Haiti and elsewhere, sometimes to get rid of political enemies.

"In the old days, the victim of the witch would go and hire a *nyanga*, a witch doctor, to reverse the spell," said Abram Maharala in South Africa. "Everyone knows you cannot smell out a witch. Only a *nyanga* can do that." He added to a journalist that he suspects one of his two wives turned his village against him, and he fled to safety. Observed Piet Magnate, a grandfather banished from the village of ga-Kolopo under suspicion of calling down the lightning that killed a young girl, "There has been witchcraft form time immemorial. But witches were never necklaced until recently."

Proof that witches existed, Andrea Dworkin jocularly pointed out in 1987, was that the witches "have sex with men while they sleep; they use a man against his will, especially at night when he is asleep and helpless. He ejaculates proof that, by magic, a woman came to him in the night and did something to or with his penis." Those who were touched obviously were ignorant about male "wet dreams."

"Witchcraft springs out of the notion that any misfortune—a death, or an accident—is caused by something," a South African policeman observed in Motonawabaloi. "They just don't believe in accidents," he added of the Genda, Sotho, and Shangaan tribes. The Venda believe in *zwivhuya*, the idea that only a certain amount of material and spiritual goods are available. Thus, if anyone has more than another, it is the result of witchcraft: success cannot be earned. As a result, those named and killed as witches often are prosperous with large numbers of cattle, or had worked in the cities and earned a pension for their old age. "Jealousy is probably the most common motivation for the killing of witches, regardless of gender, Anthony Minnaar has written in *To Live in Fear: Witchburning and Medicine Murder in Venda* (1995). Although hundreds of suspects are killed, another 200,000 or so traditional "healers" practice witchcraft. They are consulted for advice before taking a long journey, for protection from physical danger or evil spirits, or even by white businessmen with many black employees who seek to obtain protection for their company from theft. Victor Ralushai, an anthropologist who heads a South African witchcraft commission, stated, "We hope that, with better education, we'll at least live in a society where people aren't killed because of their beliefs." In 1996, a witch trial was held in Maine. The board of the National Spiritualist Association of Churches held a closed-door trial of Ms. Valerie Van Winkle. Accused by a former Northport, Maine, town clerk of declaring herself a witch, hissing, and threatening to hex the official, she was convicted not only of calling herself a witch but also of breaking church bylaws in the way she managed a spiritualist summer camp. Ms. Van Winkle, however, insisted she has never maintained she is a witch. The camp has meetings three weeknights and twice on Sundays. The services include hymns, healings, a lecture or sermon, and messages from beyond. "Message services" occur in which a medium communicates a message from the spirit world to each of about fifteen people, who pay $8. per person. The Rev. Brenda Wittich is President of the National Spiritualist Association of Churches.

Claviceps purpurea, a fungus, has been implicated in witchcraft. *Claviceps* is a natural source of LSD, a hallucinogen, which grows as a parasite on rye. When eaten, the "trip" that is produced by eating infected rye is called ergotism. In Salem, where rye was widely cultivated, it is possible that the fungus was connected with the unusual behavior alleged by the religionists looking for Satanists. Another hallucinogenic drug is *muscarine*, the active ingredient of the fly agarics—the red and white toadstools illustrated in books of fairy tales. Even a small amount of fly agaric could enable a diner to talk with the gnomes that inhabit the toadstools, or perhaps, to fly. (See entries for Pagan, Halloween, and Wicca. Also, see "The Science of Hallowe'en," *The Economist*, 31 October 1998; and "Witchcraft in South Africa," *The Economist*, 9 Dec 1995) {CE, EH; ER; *The New York Times*, 1 May 1996; Joe Sharkey, *The New York Times*, 24 January 1999}

Witkin, Jerome (1939–)

An artist who has taught at Syracuse University since 1971, Witkin is a Unitarian. According to the *San Francisco Chronicle*, Witkin has resuscitated "the tradition of European narrative painting presumed dead by twentieth-century modernism. . . . More than any other painter working today, except perhaps Lucian Freud, Witkin recapitulates, at the level of fine detail, the emergence form traditional structures of modern painting's distinct expressive freedom." Among his works: "Benny La Terre," which confronts AIDS; "A Jesus for Our Time," a five-panel work portraying the career of an evangelist who believes he is called upon to heal the world and eventually winds up drunk in a hotel room; and "Terminal," an expressionless Jewish man who stares out from a railroad car on his way to a death camp. Witkin has described himself as "a religious painter but not a religious person." {Neil Miller, "The Paintings of Jerome Witkin," *World*, November-December 1994}

Wittgenstein, Ludwig (Josef Johan) (1889–1951)

Wittgenstein is a major philosopher, an Austrian who had been secretary for Bertrand Russell and whose *Principles of Mathematics* (1903) had greatly influenced him. Wittgenstein differed from other logical positivists in that he allowed for a metaphysics.

Although he did not believe in God or any metaphysical system, he is said by Paul Edwards to have had a strong mystical streak in him, that "Emotionally he was much closer to such gloomy Christian believers as Blaise Pascal and Sören Kierkegaard than to the thinkers of the Enlightenment revered by the Vienna Circle."

His work greatly influenced the Vienna Circle of logical positivists. "A proposition," Wittgenstein held, "is a picture of reality. A proposition is a model of reality as we think it to be." Language, thought, and the world are inter-related. Language can posit things which do not exist (which is where metaphysics comes in). Sentences, which can be formulated to state nonsense, can still result in philosophical insights.

An unworldly man, Wittgenstein was the son of a millionaire steel industrialist and the sister of Margaret Stonborough, both individuals of culture and conviction. His sister had helped to arrange Freud's escape to England in 1938, and his father (Karl) took his violin with him on business trips and counted Brahms, Mahler, and Bruno Walter among his house guests. Wittgenstein attended Cambridge. While in England for aeronautical research, he designed a jet engine, concentrating on propellers—the mathematics needed for such led him to the foundations of mathematics, followed by his meeting Bertrand Russell. Although it was said that Russell could not make a cup of tea, Wittgenstein could and did build a house. The young Austrian also lived to hear Russell admit that much of his and Alfred North Whitehead's *Principia Mathematica* was in error, made so because in *Logico-Philosophicus* and *Philosophical Investigations* Wittgenstein had in somewhat revolutionary fashion had demonstrated that logical truths are merely tautologous.

Bertrand Russell thought that Wittgenstein somewhat resembled Pascal, the mathematician of genius who "abandoned mathematics for piety," and Tolstoy, who "sacrificed his genius as a writer to a kind of bogus humility which made him prefer peasants to educated men and *Uncle Tom's Cabin* to all other works of fiction." Russell admired *Tractatus* "but not his later work, which seemed to me to involve an abnegation of his own best talent very similar to those of Pascal and Tolstoy." He was aware that Wittgenstein's followers set forth a number of arguments against his views but remarked, "I have been unable, in spite of serious efforts, to see any validity in their criticisms of me."

Further supporting his view, Russell wrote, "There had been two views about empirical statements: one, that they were justified by some relation to facts; the other, that they were justified by conformity to syntactical rules. But the adherents of Wittgenstein's *Philosophical Investigations* do not bother with any kind of justification, and thus secure for language an untrammeled freedom which it has never hitherto enjoyed. The desire to understand the world is, they think, an outdated folly. This is my most fundamental point of disagreement with them."

Wittgenstein gave away his fortune to his siblings, refused to wear a tie, furnished his rooms with deckchairs, whistled entire concertos, played a clarinet, and wolfed down cream doughnuts while watching John Wayne films, *The Economist* reported. "Are you thinking about logic or your sins?" Bertrand Russell once asked him as Wittgenstein paced for hours up and down his room in agitated silence, like a wild beast. "Both," he replied to Russell, then continued his pacing.

Wittgenstein and Karl Popper differed greatly in their outlooks. Popper thought scientific theories can be proved false but cannot be proved true, that genuine philosophical problems exist; Wittgenstein, on the other hand, argued that puzzles caused by language's imprecision exist, not genuine philosophical problems, that the puzzles could be "dissolved" through a better understanding of language. In 1937 at Cambridge,

Wittgenstein succeeded G. E. Moore in the chair of philosophy, retiring in 1947.

In World War II, he worked in hospitals. He was, however, himself often ill and, upon finding in 1949 that he had cancer, remarked that he was not concerned, that he had "*no*" wish to live on.

Describing his impact, *The Economist* (17 April 1993) wrote: "Monty Python hymned his beer-drinking abilities in a memorable verse. *Harper's & Queen* has dubbed him the 'Elvis of philosophy.' He has been made the hero of a detective story ('Philosophical Investigations') and the subject of many memoirs (including one by the man who delivered peat to his cottage). Poems have been written about him, paintings inspired by him, and, so rumour has it, a West End musical is soon to be devoted to him. Now Derek Jarman has made him the subject of a startlingly cliché-ridden film." The 1993 movie starred Karl Johnson as Wittgenstein, Michael Gough as Bertrand Russell, John Quentin as John Maynard Keynes, and Tilda Swinton as Lady Ottoline Morrell. In one scene, Jarman has the dying philosopher tell economist John Maynard Keynes (with whom he had once shared a lover), "I'd quite like to have composed a philosophical work that consisted only of jokes." Asked by Keynes why he had not, Jarman has Wittgenstein reply, in words that define the clever philosopher's thinking rather than serve as mere fact, "Sadly, I had no sense of humor."

How Wittgenstein influenced and changed the history of philosophy is detailed by P. M. S. Hacker in *Wittgenstein's Place in Twentieth Century Analytic Philosophy* (1996). Described are the origins of analytic philosophy, Wittgenstein's achievements in the *Tractatus*, the impact of that work on the Vienna Circle, Cambridge and Oxford during the inter-war years, the achievement of his *Philosophical Investigations*, his impact on post-war philosophy, post-positivism in the United States, and the decline in analytical philosophy. John Shosky of American University evaluates the Hacker book as being a consummate study of Wittgenstein, one that is better than other similar works by Anscombe, Malcolm, Pitcher, Hintikka, Fogelin, Kripke, Pears, and Genova.

Paul Wijdeveld's *Ludwig Wittgenstein, Architect* (1994) describes Kundmanngasse, a house in Vienna which he designed and built for his sister, Margaret, and which now is the Bulgarian Cultural Institute. Though not an architect, Wittgenstein rethought and refined preliminary plans made by Paul Engelman, an architect. "Ludwig," wrote his sister, "designed every window and door, every window lock and radiator, with as much care and attention to detail as if they were precision instruments." Critic Adele Freedman has written, "(Wittgenstein) allowed no baseboards, mouldings, exotic woods, carpets, curtains, built-ins, or chandeliers. Walls and ceilings are finished in fine white plaster; floor slabs are of lustrous artificial stone called xylolite; doors and windows are greyish green painted steel; lighting is courtesy of naked lightbulbs. Rhythm and proportion were all, necessitating craftsmanship of the utmost precision. Wittgenstein's final act before handing the house over for occupancy was to have the ceiling of the salon pulled down and rebuilt three centimetres higher. 'Nothing was unimportant,' wrote (his sister) Hermine, 'except time and money.' "

In 1973, Stanford scholar W. W. Bartley III published *Wittgenstein*, which included several pages concerning Wittgenstein's homosexuality. Many knew that Wittgenstein cruised Vienna looking for "rough young men [who] were ready to cater to him sexually," that later he lived with a lover in England. But others denied the accusation, and some launched a writing campaign to have Bartley "drummed out" of the international academic community. Upon Wittgenstein's death in 1951, his executor complained about revealing aspects of Wittgenstein's personal life: "There are certain stories which it would be foul to relate or tell about somebody even if they were true."

In 1975, Wittgenstein's posthumous writings, *Philosophical Remarks*, were edited by Rush Rhees. (See entries for Logical Atomism and Jacques Bouveresse; also, see Norman Malcolm on Wittgenstein in the *Encyclopedia of Philosophy*, Vol. 8; and an essay on Wittgenstein by Jules David Law of Northwestern University in *The Johns Hopkins Guide to Literary Theory & Criticism* [1994].) {CE; EU, Paul Edwards; Lee Eisler, *The Quotable Bertrand Russell*; Sarah Lyall, *The New York Times*, 21 March 1998; John Shosky, *The Bertrand Russell Society Quarterly*, November 1997; TRI}

Wittichius, Jacobus (1671–1739)

A Dutch Spinozist, Wittichius wrote *On the Nature of God* (1711). {BDF}

Wixon, Susan Helen (1847–1912)

Author of the first freethought children's book, *Summer Days At Onset* (1887), Wixon was a Universalist, later writing the children's corner of *Truth Seeker*, the atheist weekly. Also, she wrote extensively on the subject of women's rights, including what in her time was considered radical, *Sunday Observance, How to Spend Sunday* (1883). Wixon was a schoolteacher and a member of the board of education of Fall River, Massachusetts. Her *The Story Hour* (1885) was described as the "only illustrated Freethinkers' children's story-book in the world." {EU, William F. Ryan; BDF; PUT; RAT; WWS}

WIZARD OF OZ

There are four characters in *The Wizard of Oz* in search of secular humanistic qualities: the Scarecrow wants a brain (reason, rationality). The Tin Woodsman wants a heart (compassion and integrity). The Cowardly Lion wants courage (reality). And Dorothy wants to get back home (security, peace). The Wizard or Supreme Being is revealed to be a quasi-theological no-such-thing. The four obtain what they want by using their own strengths and sharing them with each other for a life of quality. (See entry for L. Frank Baum.) {Quoted from the *Secular Humanistic Jewish Newsletter* by the Humanists of North Jersey *News & Views* 11 December 1999}

Wodehouse, P(elham) G(renville) [Sir] (1881–1975)

Wodehouse was a British-born American humorist, novelist, lyricist, playwright, columnist, and critic. His mother was the daughter of a clergyman, his father a British judge in Hong Kong. Until the age of four, he lived with his parents in Hong Kong, then was cared for by various aunts in England. He established himself as one of the most widely read humorists, writing for *Strand Magazine*, *Punch*, and others.

Of the more than 120 volumes which he wrote, the first novel to include characters Bertie Wooster, a "stage dude," and Jeeves, his imperturbable valet who rescues him at every turn, was *Thank You, Jeeves* (1934). The two characters, however, had been introduced earlier in his short stories, a collection of which was *The Man With Two Left Feet* (1917).

During World War II he was captured by the Germans at Le Touquet on the French Riviera and was interned in upper Silesia, where he wrote *Money in the Bank* (1942), about a bumbling nobleman who converts his fortune into diamonds, then forgets where he stashed them. When a CBS representative talked him into giving some talks by shortwave radio in June-July 1941, Wodehouse, a political innocent, agreed and made light of his experiences and the war. In Britain, his reputation plummeted as a result, despite support from Malcolm Muggeridge, George Orwell, and Evelyn Waugh, who reasoned the remarks were innocuous.

Had he returned to England after the war, according to British intelligence papers released in September 1999, Wodehouse might have faced charges of treason. Evidence was provided that showed he had received payments and favors from the Germans. However,

Norman Murphy of the P. G. Wodehouse Society, disagreed, arguing that payments from the German Embassy were either royalties or maintenance "because the Germans didn't want their world-famous prisoner to die in their hands. It is as likely that Wodehouse performed treacherous acts as it is for the sun not to rise tomorrow," he retorted.

On Long Island, New York, Wodehouse settled on a ten-acre estate and became a U.S. citizen in 1955. Oxford gave him an honorary doctorate of letters degree in 1959. "Plum," as his family called him, was a tall freckled man who liked television soap operas and was a non-theist uninterested in deep religious matters. {*The New York Times*, 18 September 1999; OEL}

Wolenski, Jan (20th Century)

At a 1996 Polish Humanist Conference on European Integration, Wolenski spoke about humanism and rationalism, both historically and philosophically. Humanism, he said, was founded on the concepts of Cicero, who proposed education as a means of cultivating the liberal arts. The word *humanism*, he said, is both descriptive and evaluative.

Wolf, Rolland (20th Century)

Wolf, in *What Is the Bible?*, wrote, "The Bible is simply inadequate as a textbook for people living in so altered a world as our own. All things considered, it is a very limited asset, a vastly overrated guidebook for the good life. It requires too much explanation, revision and cutting, to make it practical. We are beguiled by its poetry and overawed by its claims to authority. We have given it more credit for moral insight than it deserves. The biblical tradition has become a chain upon the ankle."

Wolf, William (20th Century)

Wolf was vice-president of the Friendship Liberal League in Philadelphia, which published the rationalist and freethought journal, *The Liberal*, from 1947 to around 1970.

Wolf, William J. (20th Century)
Wolf wrote *The Religion of Abraham Lincoln* (1963). {FUS}

Wolfe, Bertram D. (1896–1977)

When he signed Humanist Manifesto II, Wolfe was associated with the Hoover Institution on War, Revolution and Peace. He wrote *Diego Rivera: His Life and Times* (1939), *Three Who Made A Revolution* (1948), and *Strange Communists I Have Known* (1965). {HM2}

Wolfe, Gregory (20th Century)
Wolfe's *The New Religious Humanists: A Reader* (1997) "is not about the mainstream religious humanism found in the Unitarian Universalist, Ethical Culture, and Humanistic Judaism movements and congregations," according to Edd Doerr. {*The Humanist*, May-June 1998}

WOLFENDEN REPORT

A remarkable and humanistic document, the Wolfenden Report was published in 1957 by the British government. The report was issued by a group headed by Baron John Frederick Wolfenden, a librarian and educator, author in 1932 of *The Approach to Philosophy* and a member of the Departmental Committee on Homosexual Offences and Prostitution from 1954 to 1957. The report recommended the legalization of homosexual acts between consenting adults:

> There must be a realm of private morality and immorality which is, in brief and crude terms, not the law's business.

Most of the report's recommendations were implemented by 1967, and the British Medical Association endorsed it. The Catholic Church, although emphasizing that homosexuality is a sin, did recommend decriminalizing homosexuality.

However, after a nationwide debate ensued, the House of Commons defeated by a two-to-one margin the proposal to adopt the report's recommendations. In the United States, homosexuals were classified as security risks during this time.

Vern Bullough was commissioned by then *Humanist* book review editor Warren Allen Smith to write a critique for the magazine. Bullough has marked the review as the beginning point of his becoming an historian of homosexuality. {AA}

Wolff or Wolf, Christian von (1679–1754)

Called *the* German thinker of his age, the foremost German representative of rationalism, Wolff was one of the first to use German rather than Latin, and he systematized and popularized the doctrines of Leibniz. His philosophic view of apparent fatalism aroused the Pietists to secure his banishment, but later he returned to become Halle's university chancellor. His major work is *Vernünftige Gedanken von Gott, der Welt, und der Seele der Menschen* (Rational Thoughts on God, the World, and the Soul of Humankind) (1719). He promoted a rationalistic temper in his works, and Voltaire is said to have been pleased by the dictum that men ought to be just "even though they had the misfortune to be atheists." Wolff's warm praise for the ethics of Confucius was thought by many to be a disparaging of Christianity, but basically he was inviting all thinkers to be clear and precise in their thinking. Along with fellow "neologist" Christian Thomasius, Wolff opened the way for the biblical criticism of their successors. {CE; EU, Volker Dürr; JMR; JMRH}

Wolfgang, Otto (Born 1898)
Wolfgang was a staff member of the National Council for Civil Liberties. {TRI}

Wolfson, Theresa (Born 1897)
With A. J. G. Perkins, Wolfson wrote *Frances Wright: Free Engineer* (1939). {GS}

Wollaston, William (1660–1724)

Wollaston was a philosopher who was a master of Birmingham School in England. At the age of twenty-eight he inherited money and retired from teaching as well as abandoned clerical work. He made a thorough study of philosophy and religion and was regarded as "an infidel." Unfortunately, before he died he burned all the manuscripts he had written except that of a work entitled *The Religion of Nature Delineated*, which was published (1724) after his death. It sold ten thousand copies in a few years. Wollaston ignores Christianity as only a discreet deist would ignore it in those days. The speculations about man's future state, which he regarded as only probable, entirely excluded the Christian idea of Hell. At the most he concluded that the wicked will be "really unhappy" after death. {RAT}

Wollastone, William Hyde (1766–1828)

An English scientist and physician, Wollastone discovered in 1802 the dark lines (Fraunhofer lines) in the solar spectrum. He invented the reflecting goniometer (an instrument by which the angles of crystals are measured). And he discovered the elements palladium (1803) and rhodium (1804). After establishment of the equivalence of galvanic and frictional electricity, Wollaston created an endowment with the Wollaston medal to be awarded annually by London's Geological Society. Wollastonite, a mineral named in his honor, is a mineral compound of calcium, silicon, and oxygen. {CE; FUK; FUS; JM}

Wollny, F. (19th Century)

Wollny was the German author of *Principles of Psychology* (1887). In the preface of the book, he notes that he is an atheist. {BDF}

Wollpert, Frederick (20th Century)
Wollpert wrote *A Man Amongst Men* (1901). {GS}

Wollstonecraft, Mary (Godwin) (1759–1797)

An English writer who was once called "a hyena in petticoats" by a male who denigrated her feminism, Wollstonecraft wrote *Vindication of the Rights of Women* (1792), the first great feminist document. She lived in Paris with Gilbert Imlay during much of the

French Revolution, but they did not marry and she relished being his wife "in everything save the sanction of the law." When, however, he tired "of what to him was only a bit of romance," she twice attempted suicide, once succeeding so far in her design as to throw herself in the Thames, being rescued in a state of insensibility. Imlay pretended to take her and their daughter (Frances) back, but she found after he sent her on a business trip to Scandinavia that he had left for America with some new love. In 1797 after having lived with William Godwin for some time, she married him, fearful of the legal rights of their unborn baby. "Their short marital experience was, apparently, one of unclouded happiness," Underwood reports, and Wollstonecraft died while giving birth to Mary Godwin, who later became the wife of Percy Bysshe Shelley.

Underwood cites Wollstonecraft as a heroine of freethought. When in 1785 she journeyed to Portugal to be with her dying friend, Frances Blood, she became indignant upon Blood's death that Portugal would not allow her friend, a Protestant, to be buried in consecrated ground. Successfully arranging to "steal her friend a grave," she experienced her first defiance of the "powers that be." She then challenged Edmund Burke for his "Reflections on the French Revolution," saying it contained perfidy to his previously enunciated principles. Whereupon she wrote, *A Vindication of the Rights of Man*, which introduced her to fame and helped place her among the celebrities of that period. She followed with a companion work on the rights of women, which Underwood describes as "a passionate defense of the true dignity, and an eloquent plea for the fitter education, of woman; a work coming directly from her heart, and sanctioned by the deliberate reasoning of her brain." She "is almost masculinely severe and contemptuous in her estimate of her own sex, attacking with sarcasm and pitying scorn its attempts to hold men's hearts in bondage by sensual attraction, rather than by superior excellence of morals or high intellectual attainments."

According to Underwood, "Mary's religious opinions, like many other things in regard to her, have been misrepresented. She has been called a Materialist, and Atheist; she was neither of these, though a Freethinker. She was a Deist: a devout and reverential believer in the existence of an all-wise and all-loving God." As proof, she cites Wollstonecraft's *A Vindication of the Rights of Women*, in which she "found it impossible to accept the dogmas of the churches as true, and yet in unison with the idea of an all-pervading, all-wise, and all-creative Power, such as she believed God to be, she could not narrow *her* God within the church limits, so, rather than loose her hold of her high conception, she let go the churches and their narrow creeds, but held fast, with all the deep ardor and breadth of her nature, to the unknowable, but all-sufficient God."

Elizabeth Larson, in an extensive article in *Free Inquiry* (Spring 1992) tells of Wollstonecraft's fight for women's rights and how, in 1788, she wrote the first lesbian novel, *Mary, A Fiction*, based upon her real-life passion for Fanny Blood, an emotion which Mary's husband once described as "so fervent (that it) constituted the ruling passion in her mind."

She died several days after giving birth to a daughter, the future Mary Shelley. Wollstonecraft is buried in the Godwin family plot at St. Peter's Church in Bournemouth, England. The tombstone cites her as author of *A Vindication of the Rights of Women*. Adjacent is the tomb of her daughter, Mary (who is buried with Shelley's liver, or possibly his heart).

Underwood has described the scene prior to the entombment:

> The orthodox preacher who officiated in the church to which this graveyard belongs objected seriously to having the bodies of such notorious heretics interred within its sacred precincts, but the present Lady Shelley, wife of Sir Percy, evidently a woman of determination and spirit, as well as an enthusiastic admirer of the noble dead whom she wishes thus to pay honor to, made up her mind that the bodies should be buried there; and, says Mr. Conway, my authority for this statement, one day actually came from Christchurch in her carriage, following a hearse which bore the bodies. She sat in her carriage before the locked iron gates, and expressed her resolution to sit there until the bodies were admitted for burial.
>
> The rector, dreading perhaps the scandal which would be caused, yielded; the gravedigger did his work with haste; and by night, without any ceremonial, the bodies were let down into their graves. When afterward the baronet and his lady wished to place over the graves a marble slab, the rector again protested, on account of the inscription, which said that Mary Wollstonecraft was the author of *A Vindication of the Rights of Woman*.
>
> Lady Shelley asked him rather pointedly if he had ever read Mary Wollstonecraft's book; and he having said he had not, she said he had better read it and state his objections afterward. So she sent him the volume, and he read it. He then said he could not find fault with it, and so the inscription went on.

(See the entry for Percy Bysshe Shelley. Also see an article on Wollstonecraft by Esther H. Schor of Princeton University in *The Johns Hopkins Guide to Literary Theory & Criticism* (1994). Schor writes, "Wollstonecraft's admonition to women to 'effect a revolution in female manners' and to 'labour by reforming themselves to reform the world' remains the manifesto of modern feminism.")
{CE; FUK; JM; PA; RAT; RE; SAU; TRI; TYD; U; WWS}

Wolpert, Lewis (1929–)

Wolpert, a professor of anatomy at University College, London, was named an Honorary Associate of the Rationalist Press Association in 1993. He is an honorary associate of the New Zealand Association of Rationalists and Humanists and the author of *Malignant Sadness: the Anatomy of Depression*. In *New Humanist* (June 1996), he wrote:

> My family in South Africa, where I was born (1929), was more Jewish than religious. I had a traditional Bar-Mitzvah and continued to study Hebrew through matriculation. All my friends at the University of the Witwatersand were, not surprisingly, involved in Anti-apartheid activities—they were left-wing liberals and communists. After becoming a civil engineer, I worked as the assistant to the Building Research Institute, hitch-hiked up Africa, and worked for Water Planning in Israel, and took a Diploma in soil mechanics at Imperial College, London. The Nuffield Foundation, to whom I am eternally grateful, gave me a scholarship to convert to biology and I did a Ph. D. at King's College on the mechanics of cell division.
>
> Since then I have concentrated on the problem of pattern formation (*Triumph of the Embryo*). I became involved in the media early on and was Bronowski's biological advisor for his Insight series, gave the 1986 Christmas lectures and have done numerous radio interviews (*A Passion for Science*, with A. Richards). I am proud of *The Unnatural Nature of Science* and am best-known for my article in *The Guardian* on my recent clinical depression. Presently I am Chairman of the Committee on the Public Understanding of Science and Professor of Biology as Applied to Medicine at University College.

In Birmingham, England, at the centenary conference of the Rationalist Press Association in 1999, he spoke on "Belief and the Unbelievable."

Wolpert signed Humanist Manifesto 2000 but added that "I am not supportive of an international parliament—it is unrealistic. Not enough attention is given to helping those with genetic disabilities and those affected by environmental disasters. Not enough attention is given to removing the stigma from mental illness. Not enough attention is given to the importance of openness in the applications of science and medical treatments. Telling the truth as best one knows it is paramount. Nevertheless I wish to sign the Manifesto."

Wolsch, Lois and Robert (20th Century)

The Wolsches are active with the Humanist Friendship Center of Western Connecticut and the Thomas Jefferson Society of Freethinkers. He is the author of *Poetic Composition Through the Grades* (1970), *From Speaking to Writing to Reading* (1982, and *Literacy Assured* (1996). (See entry for Connecticut Atheists, Humanists.) {FD}

WOMAN: See entries for Female and for Wife, How To Obtain A

WOMEN

Sir Arthur C. Clarke tells a favorite joke of his, one that "will be appreciated by at least half the race":

Question: What is the correct name for the useless piece of skin at the end of the penis?
Answer: A man.

WOMEN IN POLITICS

Swedish women have more than 40% of the seats in Parliament, putting them atop gender-equality ranks in legislatures around the world, according to the Inter-Parliamentary Union in Geneva at the end of 1999. The United States is 43rd when ranked by the House of Representatives, the larger chamber of Congress, with women in only 13.3 % of the seats. {*The New York Times*, 24 December 1999}

Wonner, Monique (20th Century)

Wonner is one of the International Humanist and Ethical Union's representatives to UNESCO in Paris.

Wood, Charles Erskine Scott (1884–1919)

Wood, after an army career in the West became an Oregon lawyer and published his first poetry in *A Masque of Love* (1904). A dialogue in *The* (1852–1944) *Poet in the Desert* protests against social injustice and champions humanitarian ideals. Wood is best known for *Heavenly Discourse* (1927), a series of forty dialogues written during World War I for *The Masses*, although few were published before the magazine was suppressed. He satirized the folly and inhumanity of war, as well as other manifestations of meanness, irreligion, economic inequality, sentimental art, Puritanism, political abuses, and persecutions. The humorous conversations take place in Heaven among God, Satan, Jesus, and such angels or temporary visitors as Rabelais, Voltaire, Paine, Clemens, Jefferson, Carry Nation, Bryan, Billy Sunday, Ingersoll, Joan of Arc, Anthony Comstock, and Charles Evans Hughes. A second collection of *Earthly Discourse* was published in 1937. {GS; OAL}

Wood, Forrest (1937–)

Wood, a professor history, is the freethinking author of *The Arrogance of Faith: Christianity and Race in America From the Colonial Era to the Twentieth Century* (1990). In 1986 he wrote *Whiteheadian Thought as a Basis for a Philosophy of Religion* (1986).

Wood, Henry Joseph [Sir] (1869–1944)

Wood was a popular concert-conductor in England. He conducted at a number of the annual musical festivals in British cathedrals but, according to McCabe, was an atheist. Sir Henry was an honorary associate of the Rationalist Press Association. Arthur Jacobs, in *Henry J. Wood: Maker of the Proms* (1994), wrote, "On matters outside music he made hardly any display of his opinions. There is one striking exception. In June 1906 he enrolled as a member of the Rationalist Press Association, at that time the principal outlet for intellectual opposition to the claims of religion—a mode of thought now more generally known as humanism. In 1937 the RPA would elect Wood an Honorary Associate." Writing about "an all too familiar irony," Nicolas Walter observed that "[Wood's] funeral was held in Hitchin parish church and his ashes were buried at St. Sepulchre's church in Holborn, London, where a memorial window was later installed and where annual services are still held in his memory. Like George Eliot, he was denied a place in Westminster Abbey not because of his unorthodox views about religion but because of his unorthodox attitude to sex, living with someone he wasn't married to!" {JM; RAT; RE; TRI}

Wood, James B. (20th Century)

Wood, a critic who has written for *The New Republic*, wrote *Religion and the State: Essays in Honor of Leo Pfeffer*.

He has told of his interest in authors' philosophic outlooks:

> In literature, it is often very difficult to determine what people believe: Tolstoy, for instance, could not be called a Christian in any proper use of the word, but is always banging on about God and Christ. Melville is tough. Using the word "theist" to mean a belief would say that Melville *was* a theist. But he was not a Christian theist. I think he was tormented by the *impossibility* of God, and equally tormented by a sense that he could not relinquish this idea of God. There is nothing in his early development like George Eliot's clear awareness, at 22, that she did not believe in a supernatural God. Melville, I think, *did* believe—and *hated* God for existing. This is my own reading.
>
> I was brought up in the Church of England in a strongly evangelical English household. I am strongly non-theistic, with a slight Melvillean urge to attack the Biblical God, or the idea of the Biblical God. But I do not believe that we were created by a God, nor that a creating God exists. I think that we are a miraculous and tragic accident—though even to say such a thing is terrifying. This is always my test, when confronted by "new religionists"—do you believe that you were created by a force that you are willing to call "God"? On this test, *very*, *very* few people are non-theists; though most people *act* as if they were.

In *The Broken Estate: Essays on Literature and Belief* (1999), Wood described his conversion from the "charismatic" evangelicalism of his childhood to his present embrace of atheism: "Life-under-God seems a pointlessness posing as a purpose . . . life-without-God seems to me also a pointlessness posing as a purpose (jobs, family, sex and so on—all the usual distractions)."

For Wood, belief must include the freedom *not* to believe: "The gentle *request* to believe is what makes literature so moving. Fiction moves *in the shadow of doubt*, knows itself to be a true lie. . . ." The title refers to Christianity's losing its claim to divine truth, and literature's attempt to fill in that which was lost. With literature, one can accept fictional truths; however, this does not imply belief, for "one can always close the book, go outside, and kick a stone."

Wood: not the typical non-theist! {*The Economist*, 13 March 1999; WAS, 5 August 1997}

Wood, John (19th Century)

A freethinker, in the 1830s Wood was vice president of the United and Moral Philosophical Society for the Diffusion of Useful Knowledge. {FUS}

Wood, Keith Porteous (1948–)

"Small clouds of white smoke have floated over Bradlaugh House," Peter Brearey described as the National Secular Society convened and voted to make Wood its General Secretary in place of Terry Mullins, who had held the post since 1979. He is a Fellow of the

Chartered Association of Certified Accountants who spent twenty-five years in senior managerial and professional roles covering administration, accounting, legal, and company secretarial issues.

Wood has been active in the Humanist Forum, is auditor of the Gay and Lesbian Humanist Association, is a Life Member of both the British Humanist Association and the Voluntary Euthanasia Society, and belongs to the Rationalist Press Association.

Wood has campaigned for (a) pensions equality, with attention to the significant financial discrimination suffered by unmarried partners over pension issues compared with those who are married; (b) the West Highland Line, a campaign that was successful in saving the Euston to Fort William sleeper service; (c) sex education in schools, with attention to removing parents' right of withdrawal of children from sex education classes, increasing awareness of the significantly higher teenage suicide rate for lesbians and gays, and replacing with constructive ones the pejorative references in sex education guidelines to homosexuality.

Wood has worked with Stonewall and other groups to reduce the age of homosexual consent from 21 to 18, and he has backed campaigns for the removal of criminal sanction on homosexual activity in the Merchant Navy and the Armed Forces. An opponent of the teaching of religion in schools, he has written for *The Freethinker* and has been described as "a radical campaigner in a business suit" by that journal. E-mail: <kpw@secularism.org.uk>. (*The Freethinker*, June 1996)

Wood, Raymond (20th Century)

Wood in Britain is active with the Tyneside Humanist Group.

Wood, Robin (20th Century)

In Kilmarnock, Ayrshire, Scotland, Wood is Secretary of the Scottish Humanist Council. When the Girl Guides movement in the United Kingdom found that her daughter was a humanist and therefore could not promise to do her duty to "God, Queen, and Country," she was dismissed. Ironically, where the daughter was training to be a leader had to disband soon thereafter because of a lack of leaders.

Wood, an admirer of Robert Burns and Robert G. Ingersoll, writes for *Humanism Scotland*.

Woodbridge, Frederick J(ames) E(ugene) (1867–1940)

Philosophic naturalism took place mainly in the United States where, according to Corliss Lamont, "its strongest and most influential school developed at Columbia University under the original inspiration of original inspiration of Professors John Dewey and Frederick J. E. Woodbridge."

Woodbridge was editor of *Archives of Philosophy* and the *Journal of Philosophy, Psychology, and Scientific Methods*. Among his many books are *The Purpose of History* (1916) and *The Realm of Mind* (1926). In *An Essay on Nature* (1940), he wrote, "Nature is the domain in which both knowledge and happiness are pursued." Work by Woodbridge in included in *American Philosophic Naturalism in the Twentieth Century* (1994). {CE; CL}

Wooden, W. Frederick (20th Century)

Wooden is the senior minister in New York of Brooklyn's First Unitarian Church.

Woodhall, A. R. (20th Century)

Woodhall, according to Nicolas Walter's *Blasphemy Ancient and Modern*), was sentenced in 1940 to a month's imprisonment in Jersey for making a passport photograph resemble Christ on the Cross. After a protest, however, he was released by the Home Secretary. {*Freethought History #13*, 1995}

Woodman, Jean (20th Century

Woodman was an administrator of the British Humanist Association. She helped to lead all the national humanist organizations into a single Humanist Centre.

Woodress, James (20th Century)

Woodress wrote *A Yankee's Odyssey, the Life of Joel Barlow* (1958). {GS}

Woodrow, James E. (20th Century)

When he signed Humanist Manifesto II, Woodrow was executive director of Asgard Enterprises, Inc. {HM2}

Woods, Brian (20th Century)

A British televisiondocumentary maker and member of Rosslyn Hill Unitarian Chapel in London, Woods in 1999 won the Robert F. Kennedy Journalism Award. With his co-producer Kate Blewett, he won the first prize in the International Television Broadcast category for a documentary, "Innocents Lost," which exposes the exploitation of children in eight different countries, ranging from domestic child slavery in Togo to abuse of disabled children in Greece to the participation of young girls in sex tourism in Costa Rica. {*World*, July-August 1999}

Woods, Leonard (1774–1854)

Woods was a freethinker who wrote *The Province of Reason in Matters of Religion* (1830). {GS}

Woodward, William (20th Century)

Woodward, a freethinker, wrote *Thomas Paine, America's Godfather* (1945). {FUS}

Woodworth, Fred (20th Century)

Woodworth is author of a pamphlet, "The Atheist Cult" (available from Atheist Coalition, POB 4786, San Diego, CA 92164), in which he alleges that Madalyn Murray O'Hair was "ego-mad" and once tried to have him jailed. {Fred Whitehead, *Freethought History* #22, 1997}

Woolcock, Peter George (1945–)

Woolcock, who was raised in a family of Jehovah's Witnesses, left his religion after reading Will Durant's *The Story of Philosophy* and the poetry of Shelley and Swinburne. He is a professor of philosophy and education at the University of South Australia. Woolcock is co-author of *Dissent in Paradise: The Religious Controversy in South Australia* and has been President of the Humanist Society of South Australia (1973–1977), editor of the *Australian Humanist*, and President of the Skeptics in South Australia since its inauguration in 1984. Most recently he has written *Secular Humanism—Ethics Without Religion* (1989), sometimes called "The Little Red Book." {SWW}

Wooley, Celia Parker (1848-1919)

A Unitarian minister and member of the Free Religious Association, Wooley was an activist upon behalf of social reform.

Wooley, Milton (Died 1885)

Wooley was the American author of *Science of the Bible* (1877), *The Career of Jesus Christ* (1877), and a pamphlet on the name of God. {BDF}

Woolf, Leonard Sidney (1880–1969)

An author, Fabian, and social reformer, Woolf was the second son of a Jewish barrister who died in 1892. Much influenced by G. E. Moore while at Cambridge, he entered the colonial service and in

1904 went to Ceylon, which was to form the background for his first novel, *The Village in the Jungle* (1913). It was a study of the difficulties and dangers of rural life, threatened by superstition, drought, disease, and the encroaching jungle. Woolf married Virginia Stephen (1912), and their home became known as the gathering place for a circle of artists, critics, and writers known as the Bloomsbury Group. He wrote his second and last novel, *The Wise Virgins* (1914). In 1917, Woolf and his wife founded the Hogarth Press. Woolf was literary editor of the *Nation* (1923–1930) and wrote on the co-operative movement, the League of Nations, and international affairs. The five volumes of his autobiography, written after his wife's death, reached a wide audience. They included *Sowing* (1960), *Growing* (1961), *Beginning Again* (1964), *Downhill All the Way* (1967), and *The Journey not the Arrival Matters* (1969). Woolf was a freethinker. {CE; OEL;TRI}

Woolf, Virginia (Stephen) (1882–1941)

Woolf, daughter of Sir Leslie Stephen, was an innovator whose novels included *Jacob's Room* (1922), *Mrs. Dalloway* (1925), *To the Lighthouse* (1917), *Orlando* (1928), and *A Room of One's Own* (1929), the latter being a classic of the feminist movement. Her love-life has been the subject of much speculation. When five, her half brother Gerald and George Duckworth examined her private parts, according to Quentin Bell, her nephew. Even when she was a teenager, George would come to her bedroom and paw her. Disagreeing with others, Bell insists in *Bloomsbury Recalled* (1996) that George never raped, just pawed. George, in fact, was said to have been a virgin when he married. Bell's father, Clive, is said to have flirted with Woolf, two years before Bell was born in 1910. Many speculate as to why Virginia would marry the "penniless Jew" Leonard Woolf, for generally she did not like Jews. But after marrying Woolf, a writer on economics, the two set up Hogarth Press in 1917 and their home became a gathering place for what came to be called the Bloomsbury Group, a large number of whom professed atheism or were rationalists, as was she. Rather than emphasize plot or characterization, Woolf described a character's consciousness and feelings. She became a leader in utilizing the stream of consciousness method. Meanwhile, it was Leonard Woolf who asked Bell to write about Virginia, who then divulged her painful secrets.

Woolf is known for having had a lesbian affair with Ethel Smyth, to whom she once wrote concerning her intense interest in reading as a means "of transcending the self," "Sometimes I think heaven must be one continuous unexhausted reading." But her greatest love in life, wrote Martin Greif, was Vita Sackville-West, the wife of Sir Harold Nicolson, a poet who was a member of the Bloomsbury Group. Mrs. Sackville-West, she said, made her feel like "a real woman" for the first time, although there is no documentation whatsoever that the two ever had any physical intimacy. Many at the time believed that they did. For her she wrote what some consider is the longest love poem in the English language: *Orlando*, in which the main character starts out as a man and becomes a woman. (In a 1993 movie, Orlando starts as a woman and becomes a man.) A 1995 biography by James King, *Virginia Woolf*, after telling of her menstrual problems, her attacks of diarrhea, and her sexual frigidity, hypothesizes that Woolf never received the attention from her mother that she so badly wanted and that Sackville-West was thought of as a substitute mother. In a Freudian interpretation, King argues that having been molested as a young girl by her half-brother, Woolf mistrusted men, and that the early deaths of her half-sister, Stella, and her older brother, Thoby, resulted in her being obsessed with the subject of death. King states that Woolf flirted with Clive Bell, her sister Vanessa's husband, and speculates that she had an incestuous relationship with Vanessa herself. However, by the time of her last book, *Between the Acts* (1941), Woolf is said to have felt deeply alienated from Leonard, Vanessa, and Vita, and that the affair with Vita had long since wound down.

In a June 1926 letter to her sister, Vanessa Bell asked, "But do you really like going to bed with women?" Woolf responded: "Women alone stir my imagination. . . . Vita (Sackville-West) is now arriving to spend two nights alone with me. . . . I say no more; as you are bored by Vita, bored by love, bored by me, and everything to do with me. . . . Still, the June nights are long and warm; the roses flowering; and the garden full of lust and bees, mingling in the asparagus beds." Meanwhile, Camille Paglia, for one, discounts any such gossip that Woolf was lesbian.

Her periods of depression have been well documented, by Dr. Kay Redfield Jamison in *Touched With Fire: Manic Depressive Illness and the Artistic Temperament* (1993). Shortly before her death, she wrote her husband Leonard Woolf, a critic and writer on economics, on 28 March 1941: "I don't think two people could have been happier than we have been." But, as described by biographer Quentin Bell, she also wrote Leonard, "I feel I am going mad again. I feel we can't go through another of those terrible times . . . . Everything has gone from me but the certainty of your goodness. I can't go on spoiling your life any longer."

Then, mindful of her previous mental breakdowns in 1895 and 1915, and after finishing *Between the Acts* (1941), she took her walking stick, crossed the meadows to the River Ouse, put a heavy stone into her coat pocket, walked into the river, and drowned. Remarked King,

> She carefully chose the time and circumstances of her death, very much in the manner of an artist imposing her will upon life. Her decision was deeply courageous: although she would not be able to write about death, she would actually face the experience itself.

Edward Albee's three-act 1962 play, "Who's Afraid of Virginia Woolf?" was not about her but, rather, described a middle-aged professor and his wife who torture each other verbally. This has been said to be Albee's illustration of our need to "try to claw our way into compassion." Virginia Woolf experienced that need, also.

"I read the *Book of Job* last night—I don't think God comes well out of it," Woolf wrote in one of her criticisms of organized religion. (See an article by Queen's University's Susan Dick in *The Johns Hopkins Guide to Literary Theory & Criticism* (1994); and Hermione Lee, *Virginia Woolf* [1997].) {CE; GL; OEL; TRI; TYD}

Woolley, Celia Parker (1848–1918)

Woolley worked with Jenkin Lloyd Jones as a member of his All Souls Church and worked with his periodical *Unity* from the middle 1880s on. Her interest in racial justice led her to found the Frederick Douglass Center in South Chicago. She was important both for her work in social reform and her presence as a woman in the Unitarian ministry. {U&U}

Woolley, Milton (19th Century)

A freethinker, Wooley wrote *The Career of Jesus Christ* (1877) and *Hebrew Mythology* (1888). {GS}

Woolner, Thomas (1825–1892)

Woolner, a British sculptor, exhibited his first work when he was seventeen. Three years later he had a work admitted by the Royal Academy. He joined the pre-Raphaelites and moved in a circle of brilliant artists, but he made so little money that he left to make a fortune in the Australian goldfields. Failing this, he returned to England and became one of the most distinguished sculptors of the time. Like so many other great artists, McCabe noted, Woolner did church work but was no churchman. He was a freethinker like his friends Rossetti, Ford Madox Brown, and George Holyoake. {JM; RAT; RE}

Woolnough, James (1915–1992)

Woolnough was an Australian humanist and medical practitioner. From 1964 on, he edited *Viewpoints* for the Humanist Society of New South Wales. In 1966, he was joint editor of the *Australian Humanist.* One of the authors of *Sex for Modern Teenagers* (1969), a radical book for its time, he listed four-letter words and added their explanation, had a chapter on the choices facing an unmarried mother, and provided a descriptive view of coitus. A foundation and committee member of the Voluntary Euthanasia Society and the Abortion Law Repeal Society, he was invited by the Auckland Medical Aid Trust to go to New Zealand, where he was the operating doctor at that nation's first abortion clinic. Accused of performing illegal abortions, he was acquitted. In 1982 he co-produced a booklet on *Humanist Funerals*. In 1990, Woolnough received the Ray Carr Award for outstanding service to humanism in New Zealand. {SWW}

Woolston, Thomas (1669–1731)

Woolston was an English parson who was deprived of his fellowship at Cambridge University for writing heresy, so he set out to found a new Christian sect. From his studies of ecclesiastical history, he determined that miracles were incredible and that all the supernatural stories of the New Testament must be regarded as figurative. For this, he was prosecuted on a charge of blasphemy and profaneness. In 1705 he published *The Old Apology for the Truth of the Christian Religion Against the Jews and Gentiles Revived.* In it, the historicity of Moses practically disappeared, and he interpreted Moses as a "type" of Christ and the Israelites as a "type" of the Christian Church. Between 1727 and 1730, he wrote six *Discourses on the Miracles of Our Saviour*, in which he ridiculed the absurdities of what so many believed as literal truth and dedicated the work to six bishops. In these the Church was assailed in homely language and her doctrines mercilessly ridiculed. A fresh prosecution for blasphemy was commenced by the bishops, and the Attorney-General declared the work to be the most blasphemous that ever was published in any ages whatever. Woolston defended himself but was found guilty, sentenced to one year's imprisonment, and fined £100. Being too poor to pay the fine, he was detained permanently in the King's Bench Prison. Voltaire said that 30,000 copies of his *Discourses* had been sold, while sixty pamphlets were written in opposition. Woolston's style was to jest, and he swayed many of the light-hearted when his cause called for the winning-over of the earnest. To him, the Old Testament was only allegorical. In 1729 he was tried for blasphemy and sentenced to a year in prison and a fine of £100. Inasmuch as he had no money—he had given away his money paying the fines imposed upon his publishers—he was relegated to the Debtors' Prison and remained there until he died. Woolston called himself a Christian, but he was a quasi-deist who rejected the miracles of the Gospels, including the resurrection and the virgin birth. William H. Trapnell in *Thomas Woolston: Madman & Deist?* (1994) states that although Woolston was never formally associated with the deists, they considered him one of them.

The *Daily Courant* (29 January 1733) carried the following story: "On Saturday night, about nine o'clock, died Mr. Woolston, author of the 'Discourses on our Savior's Miracles,' in the sixty-sixth year of his age. About five minutes before he died he uttered these words: 'This is a struggle which all men must go through, and which I bear not only with patience but willingness.' Upon which be closed his eyes, and shut his lips, with a seeming design to compose his face with decency, without the help of a friend's hand, and then he expired. 'Without the help of a friend's hand!' Helpless and friendless, pent in a prison cell, the brave old man faced Death in solitary grandeur." {EU, E. Graham Waring; FO; FUK; FUS; JM; JMR; JMRH; RAT; RE; TYD}

Wooton, Barbara [Baroness of Abinger] (1897–1988)

Lord McGregor of Durris, at Wootton's memorial service, spoke of her having written that in her early twenties she had "discarded the religion in which I had been brought up, and adopted an attitude which could equally well be described as agnostic or atheistical." Her agnosticism was, she said, "more outspoken than is usual even among many of those who share the same fundamental philosophy." Instead of swearing the oath, she affirmed it. She did not attend church. She was a professor of social studies at the University of London. An honorary associate of the Rationalist Press Association, and President from 1970 to 1973, she amicably resigned, saying her views on abortion were different from those of many in the humanist movement.

Wootton also was associated with the British Humanist Association and the National Secular Society. In 1952, she addressed the First International Congress on Humanism and Ethical Culture in Amsterdam. In 1965, she introduced into the House of Lords a bill which led to the abolition of the death penalty. In 1976, she introduced an Incurable Patients Bill, which might have legalized a limited form of voluntary euthanasia but failed to gain a second reading. Wootton was one of the first women appointed a British life peer. Her many books include *Crime and the Criminal Law: Reflection of a Criminal Magistrate and Social Scientist.*

Wootton was named a Humanist Laureate in the Council for Secular Humanism's International Academy of Humanism and in 1980 signed the Secular Humanist Declaration. The baroness's secular humanist funeral ceremony took place at Golden Green Crematorium in 1988. {FUK; SHD}

Wootton, David (20th Century)

Wootton is co-editor with Michael Hunter of *Atheism From the Reformation to the Enlightenment* (1992). The period covered, from about 1500 to 1780, has previously not been covered in as great detail. For example, the chapter on "Unbelief and Atheism in Italy, 1500–1700" is said by Gordon Stein to be relevant and confirms that atheism has had an unbroken tradition since ancient times.

WORD

In the beginning, according to humanistic lexiphanes, was the word. Humanists like to research not only a word's meaning but also its genesis:

- abcedarian
  a novice, tyro
- agelast
  someone who never laughs
- aristophren
  someone of superior intelligence
- asyndeton
  omission of the conjunctions that ordinarily coordinate words or clauses, as in "I came, I saw, I conquered"
- Augean stable
  a staggering accumulation of corruption and filth
- autotonsorialist
  Christopher Corbett's coinage for a person who looks as if he cuts his own hair
- badaud, numquid, polypragmon, quidnunc, yenta
  all words to describe foolish, meddling gossip
- bel-esprit
  a person of refined intellect and graceful wit

- bibliobibuli
  an H. L. Mencken proposal for "people who read too much"
- borborygmi
  rumbling sounds made by the movement of gas in the intestine, heard often by freethinkers at speakers' tables
- bubo
  an inflammatory swelling of a lymph node, especially in the groin that is due to the absorption of infective material (as in gonorrhea, syphilis, or the plague)
- coprophilia
  use of feces or filth for sexual excitement; in man, coprophagy, or eating of dung, is related to insanity but in many insects, birds, and other animals it is normal behavior
- chronophobe
  one who dreads the passing of time
- derriere-garde
  those not in the avant-garde; those who are unoriginal, unproductive, uncreative
- dysphemism
  the opposite of euphemism
- dystopia
  the opposite of utopia
- epicene
  having characteristics typical of the other sex
- esprit escalier
  having an idea just after it is untimely to express it; e.g., As the judge began to state his ruling, it occurred to me I had forgotten to supply an important fact
- evitable
  avoidable; "Even unhistorical events are evitable," said Sidney Hook
- gallimaufry
  a hodgepodge, jumble; e.g., a unique gallimaufry of contestants
- glabrous
  having a smooth even surface, free of roughness,
- heliolaters
  worshipers of the sun, including scantily clad sun-bathers
- hoi polloi
  [= the many, in Greek; "the" hoi polloi is redundant]
  ordinary people, the masses; slang: the élite or people of wealth
- hominist
  someone who advocates equal rights for men
  (proposed by G. B. Shaw)
- horripilation
  a bristling of the hair; gooseflesh
- ipsedixist
  a person given to dogmatic assertions
- lexiphanes
  word show-offs who exude lexiphanicism
- lickdish, or smellfeast
  a person who drops in uninvited at mealtime
- macrologist
  an infernally dull conversationalist
- oligophrenia
  mental deficiency; feeblemindedness
- philodox
  someone in love with his or her own opinions
- pleonasm
  iteration or repetition in speaking or in writing by using more words than are necessary to denote mere sense (e.g., the man he said)
- retromingent
  an animal such as a cat that urinates backward
- scrutable
  capable of being deciphered
- solipsism
  the epistemological theory that the self can know nothing but its own modifications and states; a metaphysical theory that all real entities are modifications and states of the self
- steatopygia
  an unusually large development of fat on the buttocks, especially of Hottentot females; a sign of beauty to some Hottentot males
- theomicrist
  someone who mocks God
- theophagy [*the-*, god + *-phagy-*, eating of]
  the sacramental eating of a god; "the body and the blood" at communion—a popular practice among cannibals and Christians
- theophilanthropist
  member of a deistic society established in Paris during the peri od of the Directory aiming to institute in place of Christianity, which had been officially abolished, a new religion affirming belief in the existence of God, in the immortality of the soul, and in virtue
- vinciple
  capable of being overcome
- Zyp
  (See entry herein for Zyp.)

{Charles Harrington Elster, "Naming Names," *The New York Times*, 4 August 1996}

Wordsworth, William (1770–1850)

Wordsworth is known for his love of nature, and as one of the "Lake Poets" he introduced romanticism into England. Not so well known was that in 1791 the twenty-one-year-old went to France where Annette Vallon, the daughter of a surgeon and whom he never married, bore him a daughter, Caroline. Also in the 1790s, he acted as a low-level British spy. Imbued with the spirit of the French Revolution, however, he returned to England unable to return to France because of the Reign of Terror.

Why he switched from radical rebel to counter-revolutionary agent will probably never be known for sure, a point detailed in a 1998 biography, *The Hidden Wordsworth*, by Kenneth Johnston. *Wordsworth and the Victorians* (1998) by Stephen Gill supplied evidence concerning the Wordsworth family's failure to cover up many controversial parts of the poet's life.

Although Mrs. Humphrey Ward disapproved of the private lives of Coleridge, Shelley, Byron, and even Keats, she wrote of Wordsworth that he was "a *respectable* genius." Wordsworth's son, William Jr., felt the rumor of his father's having sired Caroline was scurrilous "gossip." They lived at a time during which such matters were considered "no laughing matter," as critic Anne Barton has observed. Not until 1916, in George Harper's two-volume biography of Wordsworth did Harper admit to having suppressed certain facts as found in Henry Crabb Robinson's diaries Robinson had written that Caroline had called Wordsworth "father" when they met years later in Paris.

Wordsworth settled in Dorsetshire with his sister Dorothy (1771–1855), a fellow writer who shared his life and his poetic vision. In 1799 the two moved to the Lake District of England, staying there for the rest of their lives. As best he could, he helped support Annette and their daughter Caroline, finally in 1835 settling a sum of money on them. In 1802, he married Mary Hutchinson, and the couple had five children.

A close friend of Samuel Taylor Coleridge, who had been a Unitarian minister, Wordsworth similarly had an intense interest in David Hartley's empiricist philosophy. With Coleridge, Wordsworth wrote *Lyrical Ballads* (1798), a landmark in the history of English Romanticism and using the language of ordinary people in poetry. Included was Wordsworth's "Tintern Abbey," in which he stated his faith in the restorative and associative power of nature, all the while recognizing the philosophic pleasures of maturity informed by "the still, sad music of humanity." The work became a manifesto of romanticism for other poets.

For a time he became estranged from Coleridge, and in his later years he became far more conservative in his views. In 1843 Wordsworth succeeded Robert Southey as poet laureate.

Byron and Shelley mocked Wordsworth as being "simple" and "dull." Keats distrusted his "egotistical sublime." Hazlitt and Browning deplored him as "the lost leader," one who had abandoned his early radicalism. Robert Browning was displeased that Wordsworth had betrayed his youthful ideas, and one Victorian satirist dubbed him "an old half-witted sheep." However, Matthew Arnold and John Stuart Mill venerated him for his work which, in an age of doubt, emphasized the transcendent in nature and the good in man.

DeQuincey in 1835 wrote of Wordsworth, "Up to 1820 the name of Wordsworth was trampled underfoot; from 1820 to 1830 it was militant; from 1830 to 1835 it has been triumphant." Bertrand Russell summarized his view: "In his youth, Wordsworth sympathized with the French Revolution, went to France, wrote good poetry and had a natural daughter. Then he became good, abandoned his daughter, adopted correct principles, and wrote bad poetry." Wordsworth was both a literary and a philosophic naturalist, one whose religion was bound up with his appreciation of Nature. (See Joseph Warren Beach's comments on the British poet.) {Anne Barton, *The New York Review of Books*, 14 January 1999; CE; *The Economist*, 29 August 1998; HNS2; OEL; TYD}

WORLD

World, the journal of the Unitarian Universalist Association, began publishing in its current magazine format in 1987. But it descends from a long line of Unitarian and Universalist publications going back almost two centuries: *Universalist Magazine* was founded in 1819, and the Unitarian *Christian Register* in 1821.

World is at 25 Beacon Street, Boston, Massachusetts 02108. E-mail: <world@uua.org>. On the Web: <www.uua.org/world>. Its staff in 1999 included the following:

Editor-in-Chief: Tom Stites
Editor: David Reich
Executive Editor: Amy Hoffman
Contributing Editor: Warren R. Ross
Production Editor: Hanna Bordas
Editorial Assistant: Angela Clarke
Art Director: Joe Polevy
Advertising Manager: Myha Nguyen
Circulation Manager: Irene Greene

WORLD ATHEIST CONFERENCE

The fourth World Atheist Conference was held January 4th to 6th, 1996, at the Atheist Center in Vijayawada, India.

Jointly sponsored by India's Atheist Center and by the Periyar Rationalist organization, it featured addresses by Lavanam (of India's Atheist Center), K. Veeramani (leader of the Periyar Rationalists), Sir Hermann Bondi (President of the British Humanist Association), Norman Taylor (of the Atheist Foundation of Australia), Patricia Mendoza (representing the Mexican Ethical Rationalist Association), Jim Herrick (British editor of *International Humanist News*), Dr. Joseph Gerstine and Jerry Rauser (American atheists), Levi Fragell (of Norway's humanist group), Marie Castle (co-chair of the Minnesota Atheists), and others. {*Secular Nation*, November-December 1996}

WORLD HUMANIST DAY (June 21st)

World Humanist Day was first celebrated in the 1980s by humanists in Belgium. It currently is June 21st.

WORLD RELIGIONS READER

Ian S. Markham, editor of an educational text, *A World Religions Reader*, begins the book with Secular Humanism, including readings from Charles Darwin, Karl Marx, Sigmund Freud, Emile Durkheim, Bertrand Russell, Richard Dawkins, A. N. Wilson, Fay Weldon, Mary Daly, and Michael Goulder. He starts with John Lennon's song "Imagine," one of the best-known humanist tests.

WORLD UNION OF DEISTS

The World Union of Deists has a bi-monthly publication, *Think!* (Box 47026, St. Petersburg, Florida 33743). On the Web: <www.deism.com/>.

WORLD UNION OF FREETHINKERS

The World Union of Freethinkers, coordinated by Jean Kaech, is at PF 6207, 3001 Bern, Switzerland. In 1998 they met in Luxembourg.

WORLD WIDE WEB: See entry for Cyberspace. Also see entry for the Unitarian who was its brainchild: Tim Berners-Lee.

Worrell, Donald (20th Century)

Worrell, from Alabama, is on the board of directors of the Freedom From Religion Foundation.

Worsfold, Robert (20th Century)

Worsfold has been active in New Jersey humanist circles and is a Unitarian. He was a president of Estée Lauder International Inc., the Executive Vice President of Estée Lauder Inc., and a member of the board of directors of Johns Hopkins University.

In 1995, Worsfold, a practical as well as a theoretical humanist, became one of the directors of the Council for Secular Humanism.

WORSHIP

• Justice is the only worship.
Love is the only priest.
Ignorance is the only slavery.
Happiness is the only good.
The time to be happy is now,
The place to be happy is here,
The way to be happy is to make others so.

—**Robert Green Ingersoll** (1833–1899)

• Worship, n. Homo Creator's testimony to the sound construction and fine finish of Deus Creatus. A popular form of abjection, having an element of pride.

—**Ambrose Bierce** (1842–1914)

• Worship the Lord in the beauty of holiness.

—*Psalms* XXX:2

• O unbelievers, I will not worship that which ye worship; nor will ye worship that which I worship. . . . Ye have your religion, and I my religion.

—The Qur'an, Chapter 109

• Where it is a duty to worship the sun, it is pretty sure to be a crime to examine the laws of heat.

—**John Morley** (1838–1923)

WORTHING (England) HUMANISTS

For information, telephone Mike Sargent on 01903 239823.

Wortman, Fred P. (20th Century)

An atheist, Wortman wrote "Christian Principles," an atheistic work.

Wright, Austin (20th Century)

Wright is author of *Disciples* (1997), a novel with freethought overtones. The work, about a small religious cult in New Hampshire, is about how members think about sex, love, belief, and discipleship. Its leader-minister actually convinces his followers he is God. Wright taught English at the University of Cincinnati from 1962 until 1993, when he retired. {*Fig Leaves*, March 1998}

Wright, Bruce (McMarion) [Judge] (1918–)

An outspoken critic of racism in the U.S. criminal justice and political system, Wright was a New York Supreme Court justice (1982-1994). He wrote *Black Robes, White Justice* (1998), about his experiences as a judge. *Love Hangs Upon an Empty Door* (1999) is a collection of his poems and contains the message, "The law has not civilized America. Poetry might."

Because of his policy of setting low bail where he deemed it appropriate, he was derisively called "Turn 'Em Loose Bruce" by some journalists. Son of a West Indian (Montserrat) agnostic father and an Irish Catholic mother, Wright has described his Catholic background and education in Peter Occhiogrosso's *Once A Catholic* (1987). In it he relates that when Cardinal Spellman was informed Wright was an intellectual and a poet, the two met and Wright concluded that "Spellman was a lousy poet, by the way—wrote like somebody in the fourth grade." Wright came to find that religion and superstition were one and, as a lawyer, he demanded evidence for the existence of a Holy Ghost or God and found none. As for the afterlife, he suggests that at his memorial service the Duke Ellington tune played by Randy Weston be aired: "Do nothing till you hear from me." As for being an altar boy, he humorously advised kids to be careful because "you know what happens when you renounce sex and take to whiskey and things like that: chasing lads."

Wright was one of the most outspoken African American humanists of his time. "Whites," he once stated, "almost have a chemical reaction when they see a black face and assign to that face a place. White judges don't fraternize with us. What they know about us is what they get from novels, the silver screen, or servants in their own homes."

He admitted to liking radicals, saying, "I have always made fun of well-behaved blacks who I think should be radicals in this country. There's a lot to be radical about. If we're going to consider ourselves Americans, we should be able to aspire to anything every other American has. That does not mean keeping your mouth shut."

One of the few good things he has to say about religion is, as he put it, "What's the black bishop's name in Harlem? Emerson Moore—he knows how to kiss the proper ass. Where did the pope stop when he came to Harlem? Emerson Moore's church. . . . "

Wright has been married five times and is the father of a daughter and five sons, one born when he was in his seventies. On Father's Day in 1996, Keith told the *Daily News* that when six he and his twelve-year-old brother Geoffrey (now an Assemblyman in Harlem) had been five minutes late to meet their father, and he left them. Penniless and stranded on Wall Street, the brothers walked in the snow from lower Manhattan to their home on 138th Street in Harlem. "It took us a long time to get home," said Keith, 41. "My mother hit the roof when she found out Daddy left us. From that day on, I've tried my best to be on time."

In 1975 the New York Ethical Culture Society gave him their 1975 Humanist Award, of which award he has said "I'm really proudest." Wright, who in retirement became a visiting professor at Cooper Union, wrote the following poem:

Some orthodox wear a yarmulke,
Some Christians sport a cross:
I wonder who, among all the gods,
Is absolutely boss.

{AAH; CA; E}

Wright, Cedric (20th Century)

Wright, author of *The Words of the Earth*, wrote for *Humanist World Digest, A Quarterly of Liberal Religion* in the 1950s.

Wright, Charles Conrad (1917–)

The leading historian of American Unitarianism, Wright has led a movement in the reinterpretation of Unitarian history that has influenced both American historians and literary scholars. He has stressed the indigenous origins of the American Unitarian movement, locating them in the Arminian theology of 18th-century New England. Those liberals who called themselves Arminians did so "not because they were directly influenced by Jacobus Arminius (1560–1609), the Dutch Remonstrant, but because their reaction to Calvinism was similar to his," Wright wrote in his *The Beginnings of Unitarianism in America* (1955). Thus it was in the reaction to the Puritan Calvinism of the New England churches that liberal Christianity took shape. At issue was their rejection of the doctrine of original sin, a "supernatural rationalism" that stressed the need for both human reason and biblical revelation, and an Arian Christology that rejected the doctrine of the Trinity in orthodox Calvinism. He also wrote *The Liberal Christians* (1979), *Three Prophets of Religious Liberalism: Channing, Emerson, Parker* (1986), and *A Sesquicentennial History of American Unitarianism* (1975). {U&U}

Wright, Chauncy (1830–1875)

Wright was a mathematician who greatly influenced the pragmatists. After publishing a series of papers, he was appointed corresponding secretary of the American Academy of Arts and Sciences and made an instructor at Harvard. Wright is known as one of the ablest champions of Herbert Spencer and Darwin in America. {JM; RAT}

Wright, Elizur (1804–1885)

Robert Ingersoll described Wright as "one of the Titans who attacked the monsters, the gods, of his time." A graduate of Yale (1826), Wright became secretary of the Anti-Slavery Society, editor of the *Abolitionist*, President of the National Liberal League, contributor to the *Boston Investigator* and the *Freethinkers Magazine*, and an aggressive atheist. Wright was an expert on life insurance and was instrumental in compelling insurance companies to hold reserve funds to be applied against policies, and he has been called "the father of life insurance" because of his development of actuarial tabulations. Lawrence B. Goodheart wrote his biography, *Abolitionist, Actuary, Atheist: Elizur Wright and the Reform Impulse* (1990). At Wright's funeral, Ingersoll delivered the oration. {CE; FUS; JM; PUT; RAT; RE}

Wright, Frances [d'Arusmont] (1795–1858)

A Scottish-American women's rights and freethought lecturer, Wright when eighteen years of age wrote about Epicureanism in *A Few Days in Athens* (1822)—Walt Whitman wrote of this radical deist novel, "I kept it about me for years." In 1825 she published *A Plan for the Gradual Abolition of Slavery in the United States Without Danger of Loss to the Citizens of the South.* With Robert Owen she co-edited *New Harmony Gazette*, which changed its name to the *Free Enquirer*. With Owen, she had founded in 1825 the publishing concern of Wright & Owen. Wright bought 2000 acres near Memphis,

Tennessee, peopling it with slave families she had purchased and redeemed, calling it Nashoba. The experiment of helping thirty or forty slaves proved a failure, so "Fanny" as she became known gave her slaves freedom, sending them to Hayti, where they were placed under the protection of the President and were given an amount of money in order to begin a life of freedom. Afterwards, she took editorial charge of the Owenses' New Harmony *Gazette*, changing its name to *Free Enquirer*. Later, she assisted in the founding of the *Boston Investigator*.

Although she did not live to see the emancipation of black slaves and better education for women, her courage in defying the conventions about female propriety in order to speak on behalf of both was recognized in later years. Susan B. Anthony and Elizabeth Cady Stanton, who also came to believe that the clergy were responsible for restricting women to a narrow sphere of home and church, lauded Wright as the first woman to lecture in public on behalf of women. Frances Trollope, the English author, was a friend and supporter, writing that she had accompanied her to an 1830 lecture in Philadelphia at which a bodyguard of Quaker ladies dressed in the peculiar costume of that sect applauded her strong anti-slavery stand. Mrs. Trollope, the mother of novelist Anthony Trollope, after attending one of "Fanny" Wright's lectures in Cincinnati, commented:

> That a lady of fortune, family, and education, whose youth had been passed in the most refined circles of private life, should present herself as a public lecturer, would naturally create surprise anywhere. But in America, where women are guarded by a sevenfold shield of habitual insignificance, it caused an effect that can hardly be described. I shared the surprise but not the wonder.

The clergy, however, called her the "high priestess of Beelzebub," "infidel," and "dog," whereas General Lafayette called her "daughter."

In 1838, according to Underwood, Wright "took what seems to have proved a most disastrous step for her happiness, in marrying her old-time friend, M. Phiquepal d'Arusmont, whose acquaintance she first formed at New Harmony, where he was a teacher of some new system of education, and of whom in her fragmentary autobiography she speaks in the most enthusiastic and laudatory manner. How long they lived happily together I do not know, but they did so at least until 1844." Elizabeth Oakes Smith quoted Mrs. d'Arusmont's lawyer as saying she had been treated in an ungenerous and unmanly way and tried to wrest her property from her. The marriage was dissolved in 1845.

"Halfhours with Freethinkers" contains an account of Wright's death: "Madame d'Arusmont died suddenly in Cincinnati, on Tuesday, December 14, 1852. She had been for some time unwell, in consequence of a fall upon the ice, the previous winter, which broke her thigh, and probably hastened her decease, but the immediate cause of her death was the rupture of a blood-vessel. She was aware of her situation, knew when she was dying, and met her last hour with perfect composure."

Wright is buried in the Cincinnati Spring Grove Cemetery. In 1997, in a joint venture by Freedrom From Religion Foundation, the American Humanist Association Feminist Cause, and the Free Inquiry Group of Cincinnati, the cemetery monument was cleaned with fine sand and treated to retard future deterioration. Whereas formerly it appeared dark, after 150 years of exposure to the weather its white marble stands out. {BDF; EU; Fred Whitehead, "An Expedition to Ohio," *Freethought History*, #23, 1997, is a thorough article about Cincinnati's Freethought heritage; FUS; JM; Phyllis Palmer, *Free Inquiry*, Fall, 1990; RE; SAU; TRI; RAT; VI; WWS}

Wright, Frank Lloyd (1867–1959)

Wright was the son of a Unitarian minister who left his wife and children when Frank was a teenager. The father was never again seen. His mother was of the Welsh Lloyd-Jones clan and attended Unitarian services which were held in Welsh. Garry Wills of Northwestern University has written that "The Welsh relative who had greater influence on Wright than anyone but his mother was the liberal Unitarian preacher, Jenkin Lloyd Jones, Wright's 'Uncle Jenk,' who became a surrogate father to him after his own father's defection. Jones was one of Addams's principal allies, a regular presence at Hull House. Wright met her at his uncle's dinner table, and was frequently at Hull House himself, where his mother and first wife did volunteer work. He gave one of his most important early lectures there, in 1901, pleading with Morrisites like Ellen Starr not to reject machinery in their regard for handmade arts and crafts. (Wright wrote of William Morris that he) did the best in his time for art and will live in history as the great sociologist, together with Ruskin the great moralist: significant fact worth thinking about, that the two great reformers of modern times professed the artist."

Wright studied engineering at the University of Wisconsin but left as a sophomore to obtain a drafting job with the skyscraper builder, Louis Sullivan, around the time of the 1893 Chicago World's Fair—Wright was booted out of the firm for moonlighting. He then commenced his own "organic architecture" business, which led to "Prairie style" buildings in Iowa, Illinois, and elsewhere in the Midwest. Wright was radically innovative both as to structure and aesthetics, and his work has been imitated widely around the world. An unrealized project was his proposed mile-high skyscraper ("The Illinois") for Chicago. *A Testament* (1957) and an autobiography (revised 1943) contain his personal ideas on architecture and philosophy. Of the 800 buildings he designed, roughly half were built. In Madison, Wisconsin, the Unitarian church he built became one he joined as its 696th member. His career had actually begun with his uncle's construction of a Unitarian chapel, one to which, almost a century later, Wright returned in order to build his own tomb.

Unconventional in his personal life, Wright proclaimed that it was more honorable to be open and have a mistress than to have secret affairs. In 1910 Wright abandoned the first of his three wives, Catherine Tobin, for the wife of a client, Mamah Borthwick Cheney. But because Catherine would not give him a divorce, he built in Spring Green, Wisconsin, a home of "organic architecture" called Taliesin (Welsh for "shining brow"), in which he and Mamah lived, unmarried. When a disgruntled West Indian butler-handyman impulsively set fire to the building, possibly because asked to leave, Mamah, her two children, and four neighbors were chopped to death with the servant's ax as they attempted to escape the fire. Mamah's skull was split.

"In his grief," Ken Burns wrote (*Vanity Fair*, November 1998), "Wright refused to let the undertaker touch the body of the woman he had loved. Instead, he had his own carpenters fashion a simple wooden box for her. There was no formal funeral either. The coffin was placed on a plain farm wagon, covered with flowers, and drawn by horses. Wright's son John and two cousins helped him bury her in the little cemetery behind his mother's family chapel. "I wanted to fill the grave myself,' Wright remembered. 'No monument yet marks the spot where she was buried. . . . Why mark the spot where desolation ended and began?' " Today, however, a small stone resting against a tree marks Mamah Cheney's grave.

Wright then rebuilt Taliesin as a memorial, installing another mistress, Miriam Noel, a sculptor who wore a monocle and who had fallen in love with his photograph. When Catherine thirteen years after their initial separation granted him a divorce, he and Miriam wed but five months later ended the "luckless love affair." At the age of fifty-seven, Wright then fathered a child with twenty-six-year-old Olga Milanoff Hinzenberg (Olgivanna Lazovich), a Montenegrin dancer. Miriam sued Wright but was unable to abort the affair, once even trying to move back into Taliesin and forcing Olgivanna into temporary hiding. After their daughter Iovanna was born in 1925 and Wright finally secured a divorce from Miriam, he and Olgivanna wed in 1928 and the two were devoted to each other for Wright's final three decades.

Biographer Meryle Secrest states that Wright had the religious impulse, yes, but *he* was the god he wanted to be worshiped. He was outraged by Ayn Rand's portrayal of him in *The Fountainhead*—one of Rand's secretaries, however, is said to have claimed that she had another famous architect in mind. Secrest believes that Wright lied through his teeth half the time. This Wright was said to have justified, for after all he was an *artist*! That he was, as evidenced by the Imperial Hotel in Tokyo (which survived an earthquake that killed 150,000), the Guggenheim Museum in New York City, and the numerous distinctively designed contemporary homes constructed throughout the nation. Soulless modern architecture he despised, leading many to describe his hedonistically designed structures as spiritually humanistic.

Wright's collective writings cite the individuals who had most influenced him. Included were Pythagoras, Aristophanes, Socrates, Lao-tze, Gautama, Jesus, Shakespeare, Goethe, Milton, Voltaire, Cervantes, Carlyle, Nietzsche, Tolstoy, Thoreau, Melville, Thorstein Veblen. And the man, Louis Sullivan, whose firm once had fired him. He also approved of Samuel Butler's acronymic name for the United States: Usonia. From the 1930s through the 1950s, dozens of his affordable Usonian houses were built all around the country. They were sleek, stretched-out ranch-style structures which helped define the suburban style that later came to be called "contemporary."

"I hated him, of course," said the noted architect Philip Johnson, "but that's only normal when a man is so great. It's a combination of hatred, envy, contempt, and misunderstanding. All of which gets mixed up with his genius. . . . Trying to find the genius of a man like that, who you realize is a genius when you're talking to him, and more of a genius as you get to know his work, is one of those things that probably doesn't go into words."

Wright's 800 or so works included a variety of constructions: churches, banks, businesses, a filling station, a synagogue, an art museum, a hotel, skyscrapers, resorts, a European-style beer garden, houses for the wealthy as well as Usonian structures that cost only $5,500. Unfortunately, many complained, his flat-roofed buildings often leaked water during a rainstorm.

In 1959 when the Guggenheim Museum (which some have derisively called "the washing machine by the park") was being finished, Wright's eyesight had begun to fail. That spring when his wife, Kitty, died, his son David waited a day before informing him. "Why didn't you tell me as soon you knew?" Wright wept. "Why should I have bothered?" his son answered. "You never gave a goddamn for her when she was alive." It was not long afterwards that Wright had surgery to remove an intestinal obstruction, and although the operation was successful the ninety-one-year-old died quietly in his sleep.

His coffin was loaded onto a pickup truck, and his architectural family drove for twenty-eight hours to Wisconsin where, just as Mamah had been, he was carried on a flower-strewn farm wagon and buried at the Unity Chapel Cemetery in Spring Green, Wisconsin. The gravestone is a narrow triangular building stone that is surrounded by a circle of wildflowers, and it is inscribed with name and vital dates. A Unitarian clergyman read Emerson's "Whoso would be a man must be a nonconformist. . . . Nothing is at last sacred but the integrity of your own mind."

In 1995, after fifty-seven years of false starts, political sabotage, and dashed hopes, Madison, Wisconsin, construction workers started building the Monona Terrace Convention Center. Wright originally had unveiled the plan in 1938 and revised it in the 1950s, but businessmen who despise his politics and complained about the building's costs successfully delayed its start. He had the reputation of being a habitual deadbeat who bounced checks and dodged bill collectors, but in making the announcement that finally the civic complex was to be realized George Nelson, a broadcasting executive and head of the development commission, observed, "The money that the city will make off of this—in the economy and the jobs created—will be enough to pay every bill that Frank Lloyd Wright stiffed people for many times over. People said he never paid his debts. He's paying them now."

When Olgivanna died in 1985 and her ashes were placed at Taliesin West, her followers secretly exhumed the body of her husband in Wisconsin, had it cremated, and had the ashes transported to Arizona. So despite his having been buried in Wisconsin, Wright's body was "grave-robbed" to his son David's and others' outrage. To this day the remains rest near Olgivanna's in a garden wall.

Wright, in addition to creating numerous architectural works, wrote his *Autobiography* (1932, revised 1943) and *A Testament* (1957). "I believe in God," he wrote, "only I spell it Nature." His widow reportedly was heavy into mysticism.

His granddaughter, Elizabeth Wright Ingraham, in a postscript to John Lloyd Wright's *My Father Who Is On Earth* (1994), explained that the absence of a memorial service following her father's (John's) death "was consistent with a desire—inherited from his father—to keep the emphasis on the living; and, if he cared little for other details of what happened after he had departed, such as legacies, that too was an attitude he inherited." Her father was an accomplished architect, a noted toy manufacturer, and an active member of his community. {CE; PA; TYD; U; UU}

Wright, Henry Clarke (1797–1870)

Wright was an American reformer, a conspicuous anti-slavery orator and a friend of Ernestine Rose and Lucretia Mott. He wrote *The Living, Present, and the Dead Past.* {BDF}

Wright, J. A. (19th Century)

Wright wrote "Was President Garfield Providentially Removed by the Assassin, Guiteau, or Do Liberals Fear to Die?" (1882?). {GS}

Wright, John (20th Century)

Wright, of the University of Windsor, is on the Executive Committee of The Hume Society, a group engaged in scholarly activity concerning David Hume.

Wright, Larry M. (20th Century)

Wright is author of *Jesus the Pagan Sun God* (1996), a restatement of the myth theory: that the Jesus of the Christian Church is not an historical character, being based upon ancient solar mythology. It shows how the developing Christian church adapted and adopted numerous

"Pagan" customs, rituals and traditions for its own ends—in particular the ancient legend of the dying and resurrected savior god.

Wright, a freethinker and member of the National Secular Society, is a lecturer and teaches sociology, philosophy, and comparative religion. {*The Freethinker*, June 1996}

Wright, Michael (1818–1881)

An Owenite, Wright early in life settled in Manchester, meeting George Jacob Holyoake and accepting the social teaching and rationalism of Robert Owen. For a time he lived on one of the Owenite farm colonies in Cambridgeshire. In 1857 he settled at Leicester. He and Josiah Gimson and others founded the Leicester Secular Society, afterwards building the Leicester Secular Hall (1881). {RAT}

Wright, Richard (1908–1960)

Born on a Mississippi plantation, the African American novelist Richard Wright came to be as estranged from God as he was by the oppressive religious practices of his Seventh-Day Adventist grandmother, according to Michel Fabre. "On the whole," Fabre adds, "he is a humanist whose values are not created by a transcendental entity but by the common workings of mankind. Wright makes no difference between religion and superstition in his short stories, "Superstition" and "Man, God Ain't Like That." He was mainly a rationalist, one who in *Blueprint for Negro Writing*, stated, "I abhor the very notion of mysticism."

In 1932 Wright joined the Communist party, later leaving it in disillusionment.

His work deals mainly with Southern racial problems, and *Native Son* (1942), which is an example of literary naturalism, tells of the victimized Negro fighting against the complicated political and social conditions of Chicago in the 1930s. Fabre states that "American naturalism, both as a philosophy and as a literary technique in the line of Dreiser and James Farrell, provided (Wright) only with a starting point; then either, as we suggested, a larger definition of naturalism must be given—if it is to encompass the many facets of Wright's writing—or it must be recognized that he often overstepped its boundaries," for he also included the fanciful, the mysterious, the irrational. {AAH, Michel Fabre; CE; TYD}

Wright, Robert (20th Century)

Wright is the freethinking author of *The Moral Animal* (1994) and *Nonzero, the Logic of Human Destiny* (2000). His outlook, rather than on revelation, is based on evolution.

Wright, Roy Douglas (1907–1990)

"Pansy" Wright, a Tasmanian, was an atheist, iconoclast, maverick freethinker, freethinker, professor of physiology, and university chancellor. He taught physiology at the University of Melbourne, and he was a founder of the Australian National University, the Peter MacCallum Cancer Institute, and the Florey Institute of Experimental Medicine.

Wright was known as a person willing to rock the boat, often and hard, "to keep the passengers awake." His interpretation of nonconformity was linked to the ancient principle that the liberty of the individual is above reproach. He identified with the minority in many unpopular causes of social injustice, often to the distaste of the conservative establishment. {SWW}

Wright, Susannah (19th Century)

Wright was one of Carlile's shopwomen. For selling pamphlets by Carlile, she was tried in 1822 and, according to Wheeler, made a good defense. {BDF}

Wright, Theodore (19th Century)

Wright wrote the "Address at the Opening of the New Hall of the Leicester Secular Society" (1881). {GS}

Wright, Thomas (19th Century)

Wright shocked his contemporaries with a book on phallic worship, *The Worship of the Generative Powers During the Middle Ages of Western Europe* (1866). In it, he includes some of the practices incident to membership in certain orders and societies and represents, according to Ashley Montagu in *Sexual Symbolism* (1957), a continuation of the work of Richard Payne Knight.

When Wright's work was published in the Age of Victoria, it was immediately withdrawn because of complaints by puritan authorities.

WRINKLES

Wrinkles are, by far, more apt to concern freethinkers than worry about any hereafter. Dr. Larry Meyer, a dermatologist and geriatrician at the University of Utah Health Sciences Center in Salt Lake City, has advised that to avoid wrinkles in old age one should avoid smoking, stay out of the sun, routinely use hats and sunscreens, and use a moisturizer that will hold water in the dermis and plump it up.

An exception so far as smoking is Jeanne Calment of Arles, France, considered the world's oldest human until her death in 1997 at the age of 122. She saw Vincent Van Gogh when she was twelve or thirteen, remarking that he was "very ugly, ungracious, impolite, sick—I forgive him, they called him loco." Treated by the French as "the doyenne of humanity," she for much of her life ate more than two pounds of chocolate a week, treated her skin with olive oil, rode a bicycle until she was 100, and only quit smoking five years before her death.

Of her many bons mots, Calmen when asked about wrinkles responded,

> I've never had but one wrinkle.
> And I'm sitting on it.

Writer, Clement (end of 16th Century)

Writer, appropriately, was a writer. He started as a master tailor in London, a Presbyterian who left the church about 1638, a person whose heresy turned into atheism. Not only did he reject the authority of the Bible, the doctrines of the church, and the immortality of the soul, but also he was aggressively outspoken at a time when it was dangerous to do so.

Jus Divinum Presbyterii, an anti-clerical work of his with an ironical title, has been lost, but reference was made to it in Richard Baxter's *Unreasonableness of Infidelity*. {RAT}

Wrybisz, Andrzej (20th Century)

Wyrbisz, president of the Polish Association for Humanism and Independent Ethics, is a professor of history. At the 1993 Congress of the European Humanist Federation in Berlin, he stated that communism was never accepted wholeheartedly in Poland, even by those who profited from it. In Poland, he said, there was a hatred of everything non-Polish. Minority groups were supported then, but he regretted that they are not supported now.

Wünsch, Christian Ernest (Born 1744)

A German physician and freethinker, Wünsch was professor of mathematics and physics in Frankfort on the Oder (1828). Wünsch has been labeled by McCabe as being "half a heretic", or a moderate rationalist. {BDF}

WUFT: The letters refer to the World Union of Freethinkers.

Wundt, Wilhelm Max (1832–1920)

Wundt was a German scientist, the son of a clergyman. A freethinker, he wrote *Principles of Physiological Psychology* (1874); *A Manual of Human Physiology, Logic* (1883); *Essays* (1885); and *Ethik* (1886).

According to McCabe, Wundt was "one of the leading workers in the gradual shift of psychology from its old metaphysical character to that of a positive science. At Leipzig, where he taught, he founded an Institute of Experimental Psychology, which was the forerunner of the psychological laboratories of our time. He had been trained in physiology, and he carried its empirical method into psychology (and was followed by William James in America). This compelled him to reject the idea that the mind is a spiritual and immortal entity, and he admitted God only as a 'divine world-ground' or little more than a symbol of the unity of the universe. He was one of the founders also of folk psychology and probably the greatest psychologist of his time." {BDF; JM; RAT; RE}

Wurtz, Charles Adolph (1817–1884)

A French chemist, Wurtz was noted for his research in organic chemistry. He discovered methyl and ethyl amines (1849), glycol (1856), and aldol condensation (1872). He developed (1855) a method of synthesizing hydrocarbons by treating alkyl halides with sodium (called the Wurtz reaction), and this was adapted by the German chemist Rudolf Fittig to the preparation of mixed aliphatic and aromatic hydrocarbons (called the Wurtz-Fittig reaction). Wurtz also invented a bulbed fractioning column known as the Wurtz column. He wrote in support of the atomic theory and on medical and biological chemistry, and one of his works is the *Dictionaire de chimie pure et appliquée* (1868–1878, 3 volumes).

The Third Republic made him a Life-Senator, and Wurtz took his seat amongst the anti-clericals. {JM; RAT}

Wyclif, John (c. 1328–1384)

Wyclif (also spelled Wycliffe and Wickliffe) was an English reformer who taught theology and philosophy at Oxford University. He believed in the doctrine that Christ is man's only overlord, that power should depend on a state of grace. This made him a champion of the people against the abuses of the church. Such views led him to be condemned as a heretic in 1380 and again in 1382, and his followers were persecuted. In 1428, forty-four years after his death, his bones were dug up, burned, and his ashes were thrown into the River Swift to stamp out his "unsavory" memory.

Wyeth, N(ewell) C(onverse) (1882–1945)

A major painter, Wyeth once gave his "Parables of Jesus" to the Wilmington Unitarian Society, of which he was a member. It shows Christ with an aura, a baby on his lap. Wyeth's son, Andrew, was raised in the church, but none of the Wyeth family currently is a Unitarian. {U}

Wylie, Philip (1902–1971)

Wylie, the author of *Generation of Vipers* (1942), was asked about humanism and responded to the present author:

> None of the definitions of 'humanism" supplies, in my view, any acceptable semantic for my philosophical position. The word "humanism" leaves too little room, at one end of the evolutionary scale, for the fact of our relation to and derivation from other animals; it is, so to speak, too "precious," biologically. At the other end, it leaves no adequate room for the conjectural possibility of other, non-human forms of awareness in the universe. Exponents of the various "humanisms"—furthermore—have corroded the term with old mythologies, supernaturalism, sentimentality, fatuity.
>
> I regard humanity as an incident—however important to you, to me, to us—in space and time and evolution—and feel this broader view will better serve to make us wiser, nobler, more humble and more honest, more aware of our ignorance and limitations—more eager to improve on them—than any further terms which lead almost automatically to a further doting upon ourselves, unexamined, insufficiently, examined, or examined by prior and arbitrary rules, creed, faiths, and the like. If my attitude needs a name, a brand, and a slogan, doubtless I shall think of adequate ones in due course. Meanwhile, the above indicates, without characterizing, what it is I believe.
>
> {WAS, 24 August 1954}

Wynne Willson, Jane: See entry for Jane Wynne Willson.

Wyrouboff, Grigorio Nicolaievich [Count] (Born 1842)

Wyrouboff was a Russian positivist who established with Littré the *Revue de Philosophie Positive*. Also with Littré, Wyrouboff edited the review from 1867 to 1883. In Paris, Wyrouboff abandoned the Orthodox Church for the Church of Humanity, but he thought more of the negative or atheistic side of positivism than the ceremonial. The count wrote on positivism and also on physics and chemistry. In 1904 he was appointed professor of the history of science at the College de France. {BDF; JM; RAT}

Xanthopoulos, John (20th Century)

A writer, editor, and scholar at Florida Atlantic University in Boca Raton, Florida, Xanthopoulos spoke at the 1995 Atheist Alliance Convention in North Hollywood, California, and at the 1997 convention in Florida. He is author of *Equity and Empowerment of Women* and has written for *Secular Nation* and is chairman of the board of Atheists of Florida (PO Box 130753, Tampa, Florida 33681-0753).

Xenophanes (c. 570 B.C.E.–c. 480 B.C.E.)

Xenophanes of Colophon, unlike Homer and Hesiod, did not portray the gods anthropomorphically. Nietzsche, as pointed out by H. J. Blackham in *New Humanist* (January 1990), contrasted "the healthy Greek popular idea of lusty human gods, decried by Xenophanes, with the pathological Judaeo-Christian slavish obedience to their idea of an Almighty. The idea of Xenophanes is neither the one nor the other, and can be assimilated to the Socinian or Deist disbelief in orthodox Christian dogmas." Xenophanes' outlook was somewhat pantheistic, if not entirely unbelieving, in his elegies and poetry. He was a satirist who preached the importance of understanding virtue. His contemporaries, Robertson writes, likely called Xenophanes an atheist more than anything else, for his references to any god was not physically or mentally anthropomorphic. "Mortals," he wrote, "suppose that the Gods are born, and wear man's clothing, and have voice and body. But if cattle or lions had hands, so as to paint with their hands and make works of art as men do, they would paint their Gods and give them bodies like their own—horses like horses, cattle like cattle. . . . Ethiopians make their Gods black and snub-nosed; the Thracians say theirs have reddish hair and blue eyes; so also they conceive the spirits of the Gods to be like themselves." Like Epicurus, Xenophanes absolutely rejected all divination and also held the unpopular view that the Greeks erred by worshiping athletes extravagantly. {BDF; CE; ER; HNS2; JMR; TYD}

Xiao, Xuehui (1950?–)

In 1995, the International Humanist and Ethical Union started an international campaign against the Chinese government, charging it with persecuting Dr. Xiao, a humanist philosopher in Sichuan province. She had led the pro-democracy movement in Sichuan in 1989, causing a nationwide controversy by rejecting the official Marxist doctrine that morality is determined by economics. She argued that individuals must take responsibility for their own actions, wrote Matt Cherry in *The Freethinker* (June 1995). As a result, she was imprisoned and regularly beaten, worsening her serious kidney and liver problems. International pressure forced her release after nineteen months, but then she was deprived of her teaching post and continued to be harassed.

"Like Sakharov," stated IHEU Co-President Jane Wynne Willson, "Xiao Xuehui is a leading thinker who has the great courage to make a stand for her principles, no matter what the personal cost."

Ximenes, Augustin Louis (1726–1817)

A French marquis, Ximenes was an intimate friend of Voltaire, was a freethinker, and wrote several plays. McCabe reports that Ximenes and Voltaire had some kind of quarrel and states "it is suspected that in the quarrel with Rousseau the works written against him professedly by Ximenes were really written by Voltaire." Ximenes had joined with Voltaire against Rousseau's optimistic deism. {BDF; JM; RAT; RE}

XTC (20th Century)

The recording artists known as XTC, according to Celebrity Atheists, are non-theists. Those in the cognoscenti are aware of the title's sounding like Ecstasy, a drug. {E}

Yablon, Irving J. (1921–)

Yablon has been a generous supporter of freethought, atheist, and humanist causes. He appeared in a televised American Atheist Forum with Madalyn Murray O'Hair and Jon G. Murray which was shown in one hundred twenty cities. Yablon was one of the original members of the Secular Humanist Society of New York City, and he is a member of the Freedom from Religion Foundation. "It's amazing how many non-believers are present in our society," Yablon has written. "Most of them are bound to family, career, neighbors, tenure, and discretion. By presenting myself as a living, day-by-day, godless person, I pin-prick the protective bubble these people hide. As an atheist in Alcoholics Anonymous, with a record of over three decades of continuous sobriety, I talk about atheism in a light atmosphere and with jokes and laughter perhaps I encourage a few to emerge."

When the Pope arrived in Missouri in 1999, Yablon joined freethinkers there who picketed his visit. (WAS, numerous discussions)

Yaciw, Brent (20th Century)

Yaciw, a contributor to *The Freethought Observer.*, was a participant at the 3rd Annual Atheist Alliance Convention.

Yadava, R. S. (20th Century)

Professor Yadava was president of the Indian Rationalist Association from 1958 to 1965.

YAHWEH: See entry for God.

Yakovleva, L. (20th Century)

Yakovleva and A. Sokolov have organized a Centre for Inquiry in Russia. Its task is to monitor the activities of clerical groups and paranormal phenomena.

Yallop, David A. (20th Century)

Yallop's *In God's Name* (1984) makes an investigation into the murder of Pope John Paul I. He speculates as to whether or not it was "an inside job." Quentin Crisp, among many others, has suggested such a possibility.

Yaroslavski, Emel'Yan Mikhailovich (20th Century)

Yaroslavski, whose real name was Miney Izrailevich Gubel'man, was the son of a Jewish deportee whose father had been banished to Siberia for trying to evade military service. Yaroslavski, as a leading figure among the older Bolsheviks and head of the All-Union Society of Exiles and Former Political Convicts, worked his way up to being elected in 1939 to the USSR Academy of Sciences and being awarded the Order of Lenin and the State Prize. He was the chief antireligious propagandist following the Bolshevik Revolution of 1917. He felt that religion "poisons the brain" and produces an "incorrect" and "mutilated" understanding of the world and human relationships. Religion is harmful because it sanctions slavery and is an obstacle to social progress and the creation of a more rational and better world. "Religion," he wrote in *Religion in the USSR* (1932), "acts as a bandage over the eyes of man, preventing him from seeing the world as it is. It is our task to tear off this bandage and to teach the masses of workers and peasants to see things correctly, to understand what does exist and what does not, so as to be able to rebuild this world to fit the needs of the workers and peasants. We must, therefore, convince the masses that Communism and religion cannot go together, that it is not possible to be a Communist and at the same time believe in devils or gods, in heavenly creatures, in the Virgin Mary, in the saints, in pious princes and princesses, bishops, and landowners, who have been canonized by the priests." His life is best summarized by Fédor Dostoyevski's remark that only in Russia could atheism become a kind of religion. Yaroslavski wrote *Religion in the USSR* (1932). {EU, Rolf H. W. Theen}

Yarros, Victor S. (20th Century)

Yarros is author of *My Eleven Years With Clarence Darrow* (1939). With Darrow, he had written *Prohibition Mania* (1927). In the 1950s Yarros was an editorial associate on *Humanist World Digest, A Quarterly of Liberal Religion.*

Yarwood, Vaughan (20th Century)

Yarwood, in "God's Work: Does Business Need Religion?" (*New Zealand Rationalist*, April 1994), observes the "The United States, a nation seemingly bewitched by off-the-wall ideas," has business leaders interested in offering such personal growth experiences as stress reduction and creativity enhancement, a "New Age without the glazed eyes." He details other instances from the time of the ancient Chinese to the contemporary New Zealanders in which business and religion have been mixed. "Even straight-laced corporates these days are beginning meetings with karakia when Maori are present," he notes. "A surprising number of companies invoke Him," Yarwood quotes Alan Farnham in *Fortune.* "Cleaning colossus Service Master, for example, spurring its employees to vacuum major pet hair out of the carpets, manages to invoke—in its values statement and in annual reports—not just God, but Christ and Mother Theresa too." However, as Yarwood notes, "A church may excommunicate an occasional heretic, but it doesn't impose layoffs on the congregation." {*New Zealand Rationalist*, April 1994}

YAZIDI

The Yazidis have been described as devil worshipers. (See entry for Satan.)

Yearsley, Percival Macleod (1867–1951)

Yearsley, a freethinker, wrote *The Story of the Bible* (1922). He was an aural surgeon, an otologist, and Chairman of the Medical Publications Committee of the National Bureau for the Welfare of the Deaf. He translated Forel's *Sensations des insectes.* Yearsley was a member of the Rationalist Press Association. {GS; RAT}

Yeats, William Butler (1865–1939)

The greatest lyric poet that Ireland has produced and one of the major figures of 20th-Century literature, Yeats was the acknowledged leader of the Irish Literary Renaissance. Son of a painter, William studied painting but turned instead to writing. He was fascinated by the legends of Ireland and by the occult, and he fostered Irish nationalism with his writing about Maud Gonne, an Irish patriot for whom he had a hopeless passion. In 1898 with Lady Augusta Gregory, George Moore, and Edward Martyn, Yeats founded the Irish Literary Theatre in Dublin, their first production being his own "The Countess Cathleen" (1899). in 1917 Yeats married Georglie Hyde-Lees, and his interest in occultism was encouraged by his wife's power of automatic writing. Her "communicators" ultimately provided him with the system of symbolism described in *A Vision* (1925) Yeats was intrigued by Madame Blavatsky's understanding of symbolism, and the story has been told by William York Tindall and others that Yeats once placed a rose in a closed bottle that somehow was devoid of any air on the inside. At a time thought to be occultly opportune and while the full moon was shining, he pointed the bottle upwards toward the moon and expected to see the rose's "soul" rise to the heavens. The experiment did not work the first time, and he made several other unsuccessful efforts which always ended "in a vacuum." Yeats was interested not only in psychical research and the occult but also in the philosophy of G. E. Moore. In 1923 Yeats, who was known for spending so much time with spiritualists, mediums, and bogus wizards, won the Nobel Prize for Literature.

McCabe points out that, so far as organized religion was concerned, Yeats was not a Catholic. In his youth he had been friends with freethinkers like Morris, Huxley, and Symons, at which time he did not conceal his skepticism. *Ideas of Good and Evil* (1903) speaks of a "divine love in sexual passions," stating that "the great passions are angels of God," which is not a Christian viewpoint. He had a vague belief in a "supersensible world" and wrote about mystical events, but, according to Joseph McCabe, basically he was critical of the Catholicism in which he had been born. In addition, he was repelled by Protestantism's concern for material success.

Upon his death in the south of France, he was buried there, but in 1948 his body was brought back to Ireland and interred in a little Protestant cemetery at Drumcliffe in Sligo, where much of his childhood had been spent. The epitaph came from "Under Ben Bulben" in his *Last Poems*:

> Cast a cold eye
> On life, on death.
> Horseman, pass by!

{CE; JM; OEL; RE; TYD}

Yelanich, Stephen (20th Century)

Yelanich is an activist with the Humanist Community of Pittsburgh (AHA). (See entry for Pennsylvania Humanists.) {FD}

Yel'tsin, Boris Nikolayevich (1931–)

When Peter Jennings of ABC News (6 Sep 1991) asked Gorbachev and Yel'tsin about their religious views, Gorbachev responded that he is an atheist. Yel'tsin said he personally is superstitious and sometimes goes to church services "because during the service there's a kind of internal feeling of moral cleansing, as it were." (See entry for Gorbachev.)

Ye'or, Bat (20th Century)

Bat Ye'or is author of *The Decline of Eastern Christianity Under Islam: From Jihad to Dhimmitude, 7th to 20th Century* (1996). According to Tariq Ismail, the "daughter of the Nile" is finally getting the recognition that she richly deserves. Her book openly criticizes Islam and explodes the myth of absolute Islamic tolerance of non-Muslims. {*New Humanist*, December 1996}

Yesenin-Volpin, Alexander S. (20th Century)

A mathematician, Yesenin-Volpin signed Humanist Manifesto II. {HM2}

Yeulett, David (20th Century)

In Greenwich, England, Yeulett has gone on record concerning his views about Darwinism:

EVOLUTION:	People out of monkeys.
RELIGION :	Monkeys out of people.

(*The Freethinker*, June 1995)

Yevtushenko, Yevgeny Aleksandrovich (1933–)

Yevtushenko is the Russian poet whose "Babi Yar" (1961) and "The Heirs of Stalin" (1962) exposed what he considered wrong in Soviet society. Decrying the lack of freedom among Soviet creative artists, he helped organize opposition to Soviet policies by announcing in 1985 that such artists demanded a free and open literature, not one dictated by Kremlin leaders. A friend of international writers, including Norman Cousins, Yevtushenko became known as the angry young man of Soviet poetry. In 1993, Boris N. Yeltsin, awarding the 6' 3" Siberian the honorary Order of People's Friendship, sent a congratulatory message saying that poets during the period of the post-Stalinist thaw had "played an immense role in the cultural and spiritual emancipation and awakening of people in Russia. Profound gratitude to you for your courage and unflinching devotion to the ideals of democracy and humanism, which you upheld in the most dramatic days of our history." Yevtushenko reportedly is a freethinker and an atheist.

YHWH: See entry for God.

YIDDISH-AMERICAN FREETHOUGHT PUBLICA-TIONS

Gordon Stein, in *Freethought in the United States*, describes numbers of Yiddish-American freethought publications.

YIN AND YANG

Two symbols, yin and yang, are found in the humanistic and rationalistic system of Confucianism and are always contrasting but complementary. Yin denotes the feminine passive principle in nature that in Chinese cosmology is exhibited in darkness, cold, or wetness. Yang is the masculine active principle in nature that in Chinese cosmology is exhibited in light, heat, or dryness. Yin and yang combine to produce all that comes to be. {ER}

Yóer, Bat (20th Century)

Bat Yóer is a specialist on Dhimmis, the non-Muslims in Muslims countries. She resides in Switzerland but frequently visits the United States.

YOGA

Yoga, in Hinduism, is a set of mental and physical exercises aimed at producing spiritual enlightenment. Those exercises often are self-taught. {DCL}

Yokie, Gary (20th Century)

Yokie wrote "Frank Zappa: A Tribute" (*Secular Nation*, Fall 1994). (See entry for Frank Zappa.)

Yoltan, John (20th Century)

Yoltan is a corresponding member of The Hume Society, a group engaged in scholarly activity concerning David Hume.

Yong-shen, Lei (20th Century)

Yong-shen, a professor at the Chinese Political College of the Young in Beijing, heads its discussion group on humanism.

York, James L. (Born 1830)

An American blacksmith who became a Methodist minister, then a Unitarian, and finally a freethought advocate, York for many years was a member of the California legislature. He lectured widely about freethought not only in the United States but also in Australia. York wrote *Freethought Lectures and Poems* (1888). {BDF; FUS}

Yorke, J. F. (19th Century)

Yorke was the English author of *Notes on Evolution and Christianity* (1882). {BDF}

Yost, Frank H. (20th Century)

Yost, with Alvin York, wrote *Separation of Church and State in the United States* (1948). {GS}

Youmans, Edward Livingstone (1821–1887)

An American scientist, Youmans although partially blind was an exceptional student who became a physician. He popularized Herbert Spencer, planned the "International Scientific Series," and in 1872 established the *Popular Science Monthly*, in which he wrote many articles. His brother, Dr. W. J. Youmans, studied under Huxley in England, adopted his views, and collaborated on the *Popular Science Monthly*. {BDF; JM; RAT; RE}

Youmans, William Jay (1838–1901)

Youmans, the brother of Edward Youmans, was an American editor who studied in England under Huxley, then practiced medicine in Minnesota. He joined his brother in editing *Popular Science Monthly*. Youmans edited the American edition of Huxley's *Lessons in Elementary Physiology* (1867). {RAT}

YOUNG FREETHINKERS ALLIANCE (YFA): See entries for Micah White and Youthful Humanists, Freethinkers. On the Web: <www.secularhumanism.org/ashs/>.

Young, Andrew Jackson Jr. (1932–)

Young, a Congregational minister, noted civil rights activist, and former mayor, ambassador, and congressman, was awarded in 1997 the Frederic Melcher Book Award for *An Easy Burden: The Civil Rights Movement and the Transformation of America* (1996). The General Assembly of the Unitarian Universalist Association voted it "the most significant contribution to religious liberalism during the past calendar year."

Young, Ann (1942–)

Young, born in the United Kingdom and a third-generation freethinker, arrived in Australia in 1953. In 1969 she joined the Humanist Society of New South Wales. In 1986 she initiated the Australia-wide Funeral Information Network. A humanist, teacher, and dancer, she wrote the humanists' submission for the New South Wales religious education syllabus, some items of which were incorporated in the final draft. From 1991 to 1993, Young presided over the New South Wales Humanist Society. {SWW}

Young, Frederick Rowland (19th Century)

Young, who was attracted by Holyoake's views, became a Unitarian minister in 1855. {GS}

Young, John Zachary (1907—1997)

In 1952, Young was elected an honorary associate of the Rationalist Press Association. An anatomist, he wrote *The Life of Vertebrates* (1951); *Programs of the Brain* (1978); and *Philosophy and the Brain* (1987). His ancestry includes long Quaker associations: Thomas Young, F.R.S., the physicist who first formulated the wave theory of light and also translated the Rosetta Stone; his great-great grandfather Eliot Howard, F.R.S., who discovered how to free quinine from toxic substances and so opened Africa to travelers; and his father, Luke Howard, F.R.S., a meteorologist who named the clouds Cumulus, Nimbus, and Cirrus. A cousin, Henry Eliot Howard, was a naturalist who established the function of territory and birdsong. Young, who taught zoology at Magdalen, taught anatomy and developed his interest in the nervous system of animals at University College, London, until his retirement in 1973.

"I was brought up as an Anglo-Catholic," Young has written, "and Bishop Gore was my godfather. I remained a believer until I was about twenty and then revolted because of the obvious incompatibility of belief in spirits with scientific knowledge. I still think that religion does more harm than good and is one of the main causes of human strife. Yet religion is a comfort to many people and humanists must look for other ways of giving them equal help with their lives." {*New Humanist*, February 1996}

Young, [Lord of Darlington] (1932–)

In 1986, Baron Young was elected an honorary associate of the Rationalist Press Association.

Young, Owen D. (1879–1962)

An industrialist and lawyer, Young founded the Radio Corporation of America (RCA). In 1924, with Charles G. Dawes, he was a U.S. representative at the reparations conference following World War I. In 1929, his formulation, called the Young Plan, made reparations a financial, rather than a purely political, matter. He was a member of the Universalist National Memorial Church in Washington, D.C., which has "The Owen D. Young Peace Tower" in his honor. {CE; U; UU}

Young, Perry Deane (20th Century)

Young is author of *God's Bullies: Power Politics and Religious Tyranny* (1982) and *Lesbians and Gays and Sports* (1995).

Young, Richard (20th Century)

Young is on the editorial committee of *Humanist in Canada.*

Young, Thomas: See entry for Ethan Allen.

Young Jr., Whitney M(oore) (1921–1971)

A United States civil rights leader, Young was Executive Director of the National Urban League from 1961 to 1971. He was one of the leading civil rights activists of the 1960s. Young was a member of the White Plains Community Church (Unitarian) in White Plains, New York. Many of his specific proposals were incorporated into President Lyndon B. Johnson's antipoverty programs in the mid-1960s. He wrote *To Be Equal* (1964) and *Beyond Racism* (1969).

A 1998 biography, *Militant Mediator* by Dennis C. Dickerson, challenged the black militant view that Young was an "Oreo cookie" who favored corporate chieftains rather than his own people. Young, he found, depended upon corporations and the government for funds to support the Urban League's services. He condemned Stokely Carmichael's "black power" fights and, yes, may have "failed to maintain the delicate balance between acceptability to powerful whites and credibility with grass-roots blacks." But his was a patriotic message of self-help, and he was widely respected for his efforts to improve interracial cooperation. {U; UU}

Young, William Henry (20th Century)

Founder of the Society of Evangelical Agnostics, Young is a secular humanist who writes for *Free Inquiry*. He has been instrumental, with the Cedar Springs Library in Auberry, California, of editing the newsletter of the San Joaquin Valley Humanists and maintaining a collection of freethought materials, including over forty newsletters from freethought organizations. (See entry for California Atheists, Humanists.) { FD; FI, Summer, 1985}

Younghusband, Francis Edward [Sir] (1863–1942)

Younghusband, a British explorer, was born in India and in 1886 explored Manchuria. The following year he journeyed from China to India, crossing the Gobi desert and the Mustagh Pass of the Karakorum range. In 1904, he was sent with a military expedition into Tibet, where he forced a treaty upon the Dalai Lama, opening Tibet to Western trade. Later he surveyed the Brahmaputra and Sutlej rivers and the upper reaches of the Indus. Three times he tried and failed to scale Mt. Everest. McCabe reported that Younghusband had strong religious sentiments, "but his views about doctrine are decidedly freethinking. In an article pleading for the reform of religion in the *Hibbert Journal* and in his books he wishes to see public worship maintained—he detests aggressive rationalism—but his 'God' is 'not a separate personal Being wholly outside men' but 'what results from the Mutual Influence of all men and all the component parts of the universe." Younghusband rejected all creeds and formularies. {CE; JM; RAT}

Yourcenar, Marguérite [Marguerite Antoinette Jeanne Marie Ghislaine Cleenewerck de Crayencour] (1903–1987)

Yourcenar (an anagram of her birth name) was the first female "immortal" admitted to the French academy (1981) since its founding in 1635. The Belgian-born writer also was elected (1969) to the Royal Belgian Academy. In 1939 when she came to the United States to be with Grace Frick, an American college professor who remained her lifelong collaborator and translator until her death in 1979, Yourcenar ended up exiled by the outbreak of World War II. The two moved to Hartford, Connecticut, where Frick found a job, then moved permanently into a house they nicknamed *"Petit Plaisance"* at Mount Desert Island, off the coast of Maine.

Yourcenar, who was not attracted to organized religion, wrote in French and adapted classical humanism to contemporary concerns, gaining a wide readership. Her *Memoirs of Hadrian* (1951) recounts Hadrian's life in the first person. She also wrote *Oriental Stories* (1938), *Coup de Grace* (1939), *Alexis* (1968), and a work about Ms. Frick, *Two Lives and a Dream* (1982).

"Her frequent use of transgressive eroticism, expressed through 'in extremis' characters and situations, underscores certain similarities to Colette, Marguerite Duras, and Violette Leduc," Wisconsin journalist Jacob Stockinger has observed, adding that she "dwelled in history, to be sure, but she also resided in her own age." {CE; GL}

YOUTHFUL HUMANISTS, FREETHINKERS

High school humanists or freethinkers on the Web: <http://www.secularhumanism.org/cfa/orgs.html>. (See entry for Young Freethinkers Alliance.)

YOUTHSPEAK

YouthSpeak is a British organization for British lesbians and gay men under the age of twenty-five. The group opposes the demand by churches to be exempted from the provisions of the Human Rights Bill. On the Web: <http://www.youthspeak.org.uk>.

YUGOSLAVIAN HUMANISM, ATHEISM

Two who signed Humanist Manifesto 2000 were Jovan Babic, chair, Faculty of Philosophy, University of Belgrade; and Svetozar Stojanovic, professor and president, Institute of Philosophy, University of Belgrade.

Although it no longer is active, a Yugoslav group, the Humanist and Ethical Section of the Yugoslav Association of Philosophy, was once operated by Dr. Vogislav Kostunica at N Fronta 45, 11000 Belgrade, Yugoslavia.

A Yugoslavian atheist homepage is on the Web: <http://SOLAIR.Eunet.yu/~milane/msesbook.html>. Its webmaster is Milan Elesin. (See the entry for Svetozar Stojanovic. Also, see the discussion of Yugoslav philosophy by Mihailo Markovic in the *Encyclopedia of Philosophy, Vol. 8*.)

YUKTHI REKHA

A Malayalam monthly, *Yukthi Rekha* is at 115 Hill Gardens, Thrissur - 14, Kerala, India.

YUKTHI VICHARAM

A Malayalam monthly, *Yukthi Vicharam* is at Kuttipuzha Nagar, Thrissur District, Kerala State 680 004, India.

Zaborowski Moindrin, Sigismond (Born 1851)

Zaborowski was a French scientific writer, author of *The Antiquity of Man* (1874); *Pre-historic Man* (1878); *Origin of Languages* (1879); *The Great Apes* (1881); and *Scientific Curiosities* (1883). {BDF}

ZAIREAN HUMANISTS

An associate member of the IHEU is Humanism and Solidarity, BP 15849, Kinshasa, Zaire.

Zakarov, Alice Olive (1929–)

Zakarov is an Australian humanist, teacher, and senator. From 1983, she was Labor Senator for Victoria. As a teacher, she was involved in educational counseling and establishing human relations courses, including units on sex education. In 1986, Zakarov received the Humanist of the Year award. {SWW}

Zaluba, Jim (20th Century)

Zaluba founded the Free Inquiry Network (Council for Secular Humanism) and has widely distributed its newsletter, *Ideas*, which contains a directory and a calendar of events for freethought and humanism activities in the greater Chicago area. E-mail: <Jimzaluba@sprintmail.com>. On the Web: <http://www.freeinquirynetwork.com>. {FD}

Zambrini, Francesco (1810–1887)

Zambrini was an Italian writer who wrote extensively about literature. He was a freethinker. {BDF}

Zamecki, Joe (20th Century)

"Diversity is one of our nation's greatest attributes. Let's keep it that way," Zamecki wrote in *The Village Voice* (10 August 1999). He was complaining that a right-wing religious leader, Paul Weyrich, was being hypocritical regarding non-Christians in the military. Weyrich's attitudes, Zemecki wrote, "illustrate why minority religions deserve to be given legitimate status. And I would add that atheists deserve no less acceptance. It's equally shocking to see their rights being trampled in the name of 'religious liberty.'" Zamecki is a member of Union County Atheists in Elizabeth, New Jersey.

Zamenhof, Ludwig L. (19th Century)

Zamenhof, a Polish oculist, was creator of Esperanto, which he believed would make communication easier between speakers of different languages. Zamenhof is termed a freethinker by the Australian writer Stanley Charles W. Stokes, an unbeliever by Nicolas Walter. (See entry for Homaranismo.)

Zanardelli, Giuseppe [Premier] (1826–1903)

Zanardelli was elected to the Italian Parliament in 1859 and sat among the members on the left. A liberal and a democrat, he helped improve relations with France during his premiership (1901–1903). A new penal code he helped author was passed in 1890 and remained in force until 1931. Zanardelli served as Minister of Public Works, Minister of the Interior, and Minister of Justice (1881–1883, 1887–1891). In 1894, 1896, and 1898 he was President of the Camera. In face of violent Papal hostility, he worked to pass a measure of divorce; but his health failed and he retired in 1903. {CE; RAT}

Zangwill, Israel (1864–1926)

An English author, Zangwill became a journalist and founded *Ariel*, a humorous paper. He wrote *Children of the Ghetto* (1892), which later was dramatized and performed in England and America. A prominent Zionist, he wrote *The Principle of Nationalities* (1917). One of his plays, *The Next Religion* (1912), was so explicit in its freethought that he could not get it licensed. After that, he was reticent about his views. {CE; JM; RAT; RE; TRI}

Zappa, Frank (1940–1993)

Zappa, a musician, vocalist, and composer not only of popular but also of highly structured serious music, came to prominence in the 1960s with his Mothers of Invention band. Known for challenging the dominant culture as well as the counterculture, the group used guest musicians, colorful props, and improvisational dialogue. "200 Motel" was a semi-autobiographical movie and gave his account of the rock scene in American music. In the 1980s he became known for his sarcastic aim at the religious right and for championing the First Amendment. "Anybody who claims that the Road to Righteousness is mapped out in some book (or pamphlet) he's waving around is an asshole (at least) or (more likely) a fanatic, in the clinical sense of the word," he exclaimed.

A lapsed Catholic, he said, "Anybody who wants religion is welcome to it, as far as I'm concerned—I support your right to enjoy it. However, I would appreciate it if you exhibited more respect for the rights of those people who do not wish to share your dogma, rapture, or necrodestination.

"Zappa Volume One" and "Zappa Volume Two" were performed by the London Symphony Orchestra. Pierre Boulez conducted Zappa's "The Perfect Stranger." Germany's Ensemble Modern performed his "The Yellow Shark." He won a Grammy Award for "Jazz From Hell," an album of instrumentals written and performed on the state-of-the-art Synclavier computer synthesizer. When the Communist system began to collapse, Zappa traveled to Eastern Europe, befriending Czech president Vaclav Havel and serving as an unofficial American envoy for trade and culture. Despite his acceptance in serious music institutions, Zappa is usually thought of as "the Wild Man of Rock." Zappa particularly appealed to those who felt "I just don't fit in," for he responded with the comforting sentiment "Who cares?" He once sold a photo of himself on the toilet and labeled it, "Phi Zappa Crappa."

Upon his death, Zappa's family announced that "Composer Frank Zappa has left for his final tour." {Gary Yokie, "A Tribute," *Secular Nation*, Fall 1994}

Zaprianov, Iordan (20th Century)

Zaprianov spoke at a 1995 Berlin conference arranged by the International Humanist and Ethical Union (IHEU), reporting that although no humanist organization currently existed in Bulgaria he thinks a silent majority of non-believers exists and he is interested in creating a Bulgarian association of humanists.

Zarathustra: See entry for Zoroaster.

Zarco, Francisco (1829–1869)

A Mexican journalist, Zarco edited *El Siglo XIX* and *La Ilustracion*, in which he used the pen name of "Fortun." Elected to Congress in 1855, Zarco was imprisoned by reactionaries in 1860.

Juarez made him Secretary of State and President of Council. Zarco was a friend of Heinrich Christoph von Gagern. {BDF; RAT}

Zarkov (20th Century)
Zarkov is part of a pair of writers, Gracie and Zarkov, who write for *Mondo 2000*. Their *Notes From Underground: A Gracie and Zarkov Reader* is a personal reference book for psychedelic drugs.

Discussing Trence McKenna's views in Douglass Rushkoff's *Cyberia*, Zarkov wrote, "A drug is a tool, like a microscope, a telescope, or a radio. Is it some godlike metaphysical entity? Where I part company with Terence is where he talks about the drug as a metaphysical entity which looks, smells, tastes, and acts like God. I don't believe in God." {CA; E}

Zarlenga, Peter (20th Century)
Zarlenga wrote *Immortal Light of Genius* (1979). {GS}

Zarse. Harry (20th Century)
Zarse, from Indiana, is on the board of the Freedom From Religion Foundation.

Zarse, Lucy (20th Century)
Zarse, from Indiana, is on the board of the Freedom From Religion Foundation.

Zayed, Martin (20th Century)
Zayed, an activist humanist in Canada, signed Humanist Manifesto 2000.

ZDRAVYI SMYSL (Common Sense)
A quarterly of the Russian Humanist Society, *Zdravyi Smysl*, is at 119899 Moscow Vorobjovi Gory, Moscow University, Philosophy Department, Moscow, Russia.

Zdrubek, F. B. (19th Century)
In Czech, Zdrubek edited from Chicago a freethought publication called *Svornost* (1875).

Zea, Leopoldo (1912–)
Zea is author of *Positivism in Mexico* (1974).

Zebi, Sabbatai (1626–1676)
Zebi is illustrative of a false Messiah. He was born in Smyrna, Turkey. Waiting for God to send him a bride, he found Sarah, a Polish prostitute who had long maintained that she was destined to marry the Messiah. When Zebi's wanton sexual activity and erratic behavior drew fire from Muslim authorities, he was exiled to a remote Albanian seaport where he died on the day of Atonement, in 1676. {LEE}

Zecchitella, Joseph (20th Century)
Zecchitella, an agnostic, wrote "A Discussion Among Two Friends and a Minister" (1979). {GS}

Zedd, Nick (20th Century)
Zedd is an artist, writer, actor, and director known for his underground filmmaking. In an interview with Alexander Laurence in *Querty Arts*, Zedd said,

> It's great that Christianity is falling apart. I'm surprised that so many born-again Christians are invading Manhattan. These are people who claim to be creative but mentally they are not too creative, especially if they believe in God. I don't believe in God. I'm an atheist. I think that religion is really stupid. It's a sign of weakness.

Is secular humanism a step in the right direction, then?

> Yes. That means that man is the center of one's universe, instead of a higher authority or an unseen humanoid deity.

And is it necessary to have some belief system?

> No. Belief is not necessary. You live your life and you do things. God is not a necessary concept either. God is dead. I thought people knew this. Nietzsche pointed this out. . . . Anyone with a brain who reads Nietzsche will see the truth.

{CA}

Zedong, Mao: See entry for Mao.

Zeid, Nasr Abu (20th Century)
Zeid, an Egyptian Muslim academic, outraged fundamentalists because of his writings on the Qur'an. Condemned a non-believer, he was instructed by a religious court to separate from his wife. Mr. and Mrs. Zeid, however, fled to The Netherlands after taking part in a 1994 Council for Secular Humanism-sponsored conference in Cairo.

Zeilstra, Anne (20th Century)
Zeilstra is associated with the Humanists of Utah (AHA). (See entry for Utah Atheists, Humanists.) {FD}

ZEITGEIST
Zeitgeist is German for "time-spirit," which is a general, moral, intellectual, and cultural climate of an era. For example, the Zeitgeist of England in the Victorian Period included a belief in industrial progress. {DCL}

Zeller, Eduard (1814–1908)
Zeller was a German critic who, although he studied theology at Tübingen and Berlin, gave up theology for philosophy. He did, in fact, lose a job as a professor of theology because of his skepticism. In philosophy, he maintained that he was a liberal Christian, but upon making a profound study of Greek thinkers he became an agnostic, as shown by his three-volume *Philosophy of the Greeks*. Zeller wrote a memoir of D. F. Strauss, his close friend, in 1874, and he is noted for having written *Outlines of the History of Greek Philosophy* (1883) and *Frederick the Great as a Philosopher* (1886). {BDF; JM; RE}

Zellner, William W. (20th Century)
Zellner is president of the Association for the Scientific Study of Religion. In Oklahoma, he is a professor of sociology at East Central University." His *Countercultures, a Sociological Analysis* (1995) studies American cults. Zellner has written for *Freethought Today*.

Zemel, Joe (20th Century)
Zemel is an editor of *The Greater Philadelphia Story*, newsletter of The Freethought Society of Greater Philadelphia (FSGP).

ZEN and ZEN KOANS
Zen is an approach to religion, arising from Buddhism. It seeks religious enlightenment by meditation, in which there is no consciousness of self. Deliberately irrational statements are sometimes used in Zen to jar persons into realizing the limits of the common uses of the intellect. A Zen koan is a riddle in the form of a paradox, and it is used in meditation to gain intuitive knowledge (rather than knowledge which can be documented). "What does one think of while sitting?," a monk asked Yueh-shan. "One thinks of not-thinking," the Master replied. "But how does one think of not-thinking?" the monk asked. "Replied the Master, "Without thinking."

- A Zen koan
  "What is the sound of one hand clapping?

- A typical secular humanist response:
  "Castanets."

{DCL}

Zeno of Elea (c. 490–c. 430 B.C.E.)
Zeno of Elea was a philosopher of the Eleatic school along with Melissos of Samos and Parmenides. Zeno supported Parmenides by demonstrating that it is logically impossible to have motion and multiplicity. Aristotle claimed that Zeno was the first to employ the dialectical method. If, Zeno held, a whole consists of parts, then each part is divisible into units and each of these is divisible ad infinitum.

His argument against motion was that whatever moves can never come to the end of a line, for first it must cover half the line, then half of what remains, and so on ad infinitum. Through logical reasoning, then, he dramatized the errors of commonplace notions concerning time and space. Using a specific example: An arrow can never reach its target, because the distance it must travel can be divided into an infinite number of sub-distances, and therefore the arrow must take an infinite amount of time to arrive at its destination.

In the 18th century, the paradox was resolved with the recognition that an infinite number of terms could have a finite sum: 1 + 1/2 + 1/4 + 1/8 + 1/16 etc. = Z. {CE; AF; JM; JMR; JMRH; OCP; RE; TYD}

Zeppetello, Philip (20th Century)

A freethinker in Syracuse, New York, Zeppetello has described in "A Son's Gift: Dying With Dignity" (*Free Inquiry*, Summer 1999) how his aging and ill father escaped an undignified death of "assisted living" with its diapers, pills, pablum, and sad loss of self, choosing euthanasia instead.

Zerffi, George Gustavus (1821–1892)

Zerffi wrote *The Origin and the Abstract and Concrete Nature of the Devil* (1874). His *Spontaneous Dissolution of Ancient Creeds* (1876) is agnostic and strongly worded. {GS; RAT}

Zerritsch, Veronika (1741–1754)

Zerritsch, a girl of only thirteen, was executed for witchcraft in Bavaria. When Joe Vikin read about this while researching the Inquisition, he was moved to tears and wrote the following in her memory:

You had not begun to live yet;
your womanhood was still to blossom,
your bosom was at a budding stage,
your monthly flow had not begun to stain your legs.

Your sexual needs had not awakened
when your life was cut short
after they kindled
dry wood under your feet.

Your execution ordained
by clerics who feared women,
hated beauty, envied youth,
mistrusted laughter:

Those men were made eunuchs
by their beliefs, destroyers of
what they could not possess.

Veronika, your memory will live,
while decent humanity will
curse the men who caused your death.

Zerwick, James (20th Century)

Zerwick, from Wisconsin, is on the board of directors of the Freedom From Religion Foundation.

Zetkin, Klara (1857–1933)

A German Communist leader and feminist, Zetkin was a founder and theoretician of the Socialist woman's movement. She established the party's paper for women, *Gleichheit*, editing it until 1916. In 1919 she was a chief founder of the German Communist party and from 1920 to 1932 was a Communist member of the Reichstag. Her *Reminiscences of Lenin* was translated into English in 1929. An atheist, Zetkin is not known to have written extensively about religion. {CE}

Zeuch, William E. (20th Century)

Dr. Zeuch has contributed articles to *The American Rationalist*. In the 1950s he was an editorial associate for *Humanist World Digest, A Quarterly of Liberal Religion*.

ZEUS: See entry for God. Zeus, unlike the Judeo-Christian God, enjoyed wine, women, men, and song. A wag has suggested that Hispanic fathers, instead of naming their sons Jesús, could name their children Zeus, then be heard to beckon, "Hey, Zeus!"

Zeyed, Marvin (20th Century)

Zeyed, a distinguished Arab philosopher, is Chairperson of the International Society for Islamic Secularization (ISIS, PO Box 229, Buffalo, NY 14215).

Ziegler, Heinrich Ernst (Born 1858)

A German embryologist, Ziegler was a professor at Freiburg and Jena. He edited the *Zoologisches Wörterbuch* (1907–1908). Also, he wrote *Lehrbuch der vergleichenden Entwickelungsgeschichte der niederen Wirbelthiere* (1902), and *Die Vererbungslehre in der Biologie* (1905). Ziegler was one of the founders of the German Monist Association. {RAT}

Ziegler, Theobald (Born 1846)

A German educationist, Ziegler taught in the Schönthal Theological Seminary for a time, then quit the clerical world and became a professor of pedagogy at Strasbourg University. In 1899–1900 he became Rector of that university. His rationalism finds expression in his *David Friedrich Strauss* (2 volumes, 1908). {RAT}

Ziehen, Georg Theodor (Born 1862)

Ziehen was a German pathologist, an authority on the anatomy, physiology, and pathology of the nervous system. He edited *Zeitschrift für Psychologie und Physiologie der Sinne*. His technical works show him to be a materialist. {RAT}

Zijde, Karel van der (Born 1838)

Zijde was a Dutch writer, a teacher at Rotterdam who under the pen name of M. F. ten Gergen wrote *The Devil's Burial* (1874). {BDF}

Zimmerman, Brett (20th Century)

Zimmerman is an instructor of English and Humanities at York University in Toronto. He has published *Herman Melville: Stargazer* (1998) and articles in magazines and scholarly Canadian, American, and British journals. {*Humanist in Canada*, Winter 1999-2000}

Zimmerman, Marvin (20th Century)

A professor emeritus of philosophy at the State University of New York at Buffalo, Zimmerman is author of *Contemporary Problems of Democracy* (1972). He_signed both the Humanist Manifesto II and the Secular Humanist Declaration. He has been chairman of the New York City chapter of the American Humanist Association. {HM2; PK; SHD}

Zimmern, Helen (1846–1895)

Although born in Hamburg, Germany, Zimmern became a naturalized English citizen. She wrote lives of Schopenhauer and Lessing as well as a paraphrase of Firdusi's *Shah Nahmeh*. {BDF; JM; RAT; RE}

Zindler, Frank (20th Century)

Zindler, an atheist leader in Columbus, Ohio, has been a professor of biology and geology. A debate he had with John P. Koster is published under the title of *Does God Exist?: A Debate* (1990). Zindler, an ex-Lutheran minister and a supporter of Internet Infidels, hosts a Channel 21 American Atheist TV Forum in Columbis, Ohio. (See entry for Ohio Atheists, Humanists.) {FD}

ZIONISM

• . . . the only good Zioinist is a dead Zionist . . . . we must take a lesson from Hitler.
—Stokely Carmichael (Kwame Ture, 1941-1998), former Black Panther and coiner of "black power"

Zionism is the "movement for the return of the Jews to the Promised Land, i.e., Palestine," according to Louis Lipsky, who once was an editor of *The New Palestine* and Vice President of the Zionist Organization of America. The dispersion of the Jews was considered only a temporary incident, Israel being punished "for its sins." But Jews believed a time would come when God would forgive them and bring them back to the Promised Land, at which time the Messiah would, according to the *Jewish Encyclopedia*, "gather the children of Israel around him and march to Jerusalem; and then after overcoming the hostile powers establish the Temple and set up his own dominion."

Theodor Herzl in 1907 convened the first World Zionist Congress. Under Chaim Weizmann, the movement was helped by the 1917 Balfour Declaration that promised Jews a national homeland in Palestine. After World War II, Zionism divided between followers of individuals such opponents as David Ben-Gurion and Menachem Begin. When the state of Israel was created in 1948, the World Zionist Congress was separated from the Israeli government. Zionists today assist immigration to Israel and encourage cultural and educational activities in Israel as well as elsewhere.

A historian of American Judaism, Murray Polner, has described the American Council for Judaism as being opposed to Zionism. Set up in 1942, it acted to combat the founding of a Jewish state in what was then Palestine. "The Council comprised wealthy, acculturated, Reform German Jews," Polner declared. Its organization of 14,000 members was accused of being "indifferent if not hostile to Jews who had lived through the Holocaust and had nowhere to go." Rabbi Elmer Berger, the Council's executive vice president from 1943 to 1967, was noted for being a foe of Zionism as well as of Israel. {CE; ER}

ZIPPERS

"Peeling your girlfriend (or your boyfriend) is the work of a moment."

That description by Alison Lurie, author of *The Language of Clothes*, identifies the clothes fastener invented by Whitcomb L. Judson in 1893, perfected by Gideon Sundback in 1917, and named by B. F. Goodrich Company, which put zippers on galoshes in the 1920s.

"When you're talking about zippers, you're already talking about sex." Not only are these under-appreciated humanistic devices efficient but also they make taking clothes on, or off, pragmatically speedy.

Zoethout, C. M. (20th Century)

In 1995, Zoehout, a Dutch humanist, spoke in Delphi, Greece, at the first International Multidisciplinary Conference on Human Behaviour and the Meaning of Modern Humanism.

Zola, Émile Édouard Charles Antoine (1840–1902)

Zola is the leading exemplar of literary naturalism, which utilized the methods of science to depict life as it really is. Many objected to the sordid details of his work, but his response was that he wished to present humans as they exist, not as the romanticists wish they would exist. Alcoholism, disease, and degeneracy are shown in *Les Rougon-Macquart* (1871–1893). Lower-class life is shown in *L'Assommoir* (The Dram-Shop) (1877), *Nana* (1880), and *Germinal* (1885), the latter a "proletarian" novel of life in a coal-mining area. In 1886, he was quoted as saying, "We have stopped believing in God, but not in our own immortality." A noted anti-Catholic, Zola was added to the Vatican's index of prohibited reading from 1894, for he was on record as believing that civilization will not attain to its perfection until the last stone from the last church falls on the last priest. When the clericals accused him of simply making money out of "immoral books," according to McCabe Zola retorted by exposing the hypocrisy of the Church in a trio of novels on Lourdes, Rome, and ecclesiastical Paris. Because of his part in the Dreyfus Affair, writing an article, "*J'accuse*" (1898) in *L'Aurore*, he fled to England until an amnesty was arranged for his return to France. His publisher was imprisoned in 1888. Inasmuch as Zola had previously been thought to live only for his art, his surprising championing of the Dreyfus Affair, Henry James wrote, was "the act of a man with arrears of personal history to make up . . . treating itself at last to a luxury of experience." Zola, after the massacre of the Commune during which the regular army gunned down an estimated twenty thousand men and women in the streets of Paris, served as a nonpartisan journalist. In 1892, however, in the closing chapters of *La Débâcle*, he described the streets of unburied corpses and portrayed a fictitious Communard dying in the arms of a former comrade against the background of a Paris consumed in flames.

Zola was an honorary associate of the British Rationalist Press Association, and their initial appeals for £1,000 carried his signature. Although a candidate twenty-four times, he never made the French Academy, which considered him a writer of pornography. Inhaling fumes from a blocked fireplace chimney which had a defective flue, he was asphyxiated by carbon monoxide fumes in his sleep and died in 1902. This was four years before Dreyfus was rehabilitated.

Zola's remains were removed in 1908 to the *Panthéon*. On the centennial in 1998 of the publication of his *J'accuse*, France's Prime Minister Lionel Jospin and others went to the Panthéon and saluted Zola's having come to the defense of the Jewish captain in the French Army who had unjustly been convicted of treason in 1894. "Truth is on the march, and nothing can stop it," Zola had written in his manifesto. "History proved him right," Mr. Jospin said at the ceremony. (See a biography, *Zola, A Life*, by Frederick Brown [1995].) {BDF; CE; CL; ILP; JM; RAT; TRI; TYD}

ZOMBI OR ZOMBIE

In the Bantu language of Mbundu or Kimbundu, a *zombi* is a ghost, a departed spirit. Caribbean French and English Creole vocabularies describe a zombi as being related to a snake god. In voodoo, a zombi has a supernatural power or spell that can enter into and bring a corpse back to life. In West Africa, Haiti, and the southern United States a zombi is avoided at all costs. With the advent of large numbers of drug addicts, individuals who are so addicted appear to be walking corpses, "living dead." In spiritualists' descriptions, zombies are therefore "without soul."

Physicians, however, sometimes trace the zombie-like condition to puffer fish, which have a toxin used to make the prized but dangerous Japanese dish *fugu*. Such a toxin makes a person go into a death-like trance—to revive the person, a potion is administered that has been made from the seeds of a hallucinogenic plant known as the zombie cucumber. {*The Economist*, 31 October 1998}

Zoroaster (c. 628–c. 551 B.C.E.)

Zoroaster, ancient Persian religious teacher and prophet, is derived from the Greek form of Zarathustra (or Zarathustra), his Persian name. Ancient Persia's *Avesta* or the *Zend Avesta* describes Zoroaster's monotheistic god, Ahura Mazdah (also Ormadzd, or Ormuzd, supreme knowledge). In his time, Zoroaster taught that Mazdah headed the good spirits. He was assisted by six deities, the Amesha Spentas, who were as follows: Vohu Manah (good thought); Asha Vahista (highest righteousness); Khshathra Vairya (divine kingdom); Spenta Amaiti (pious devotion); Haurvatat (salvation); and Ameretat (immortality). The six eventually became archangelic.

Their opposite was Ahriman, who led the evil spirits known as daevas, or divs. Zoroastrianism describes the war between these two supernatural forces. Upon an individual's death, he crosses the Chinvato Peretav (bridge of the separator), which spans a kind of Hell. If the bridge narrows, he has been adjudged a reprobate and falls to perdition; if, however, the bridge widens, he enters the realm of light. Saoshyant, the savior, will one day appear, the dead will rise to be rewarded or punished, and the good will reign eternally—this concept has proven so popular that much of it has been "borrowed" by other religions.

Until the 6th Century B.C.E., Mithra (called Mitra in India) was a minor Zoroastrian figure, but by the 5th Century .B.C.E. Mithra was the principal Persian deity, the good of light and wisdom and associated with the sun. In the 2nd Century of the Christian Era, Mithraism was popular with the Roman legions, inasmuch as he was an ideal fighter and comrade.

Zoroastrianism's main aspect was that of describing the struggle between good and bad forces. The Good God was not omnipotent, so if the ideal world was to be won it would be necessary that all creatures help. Devotees were given hope of blessed immortality, and rituals such as the sacred banquet and baptism eventually were adopted by other religions. By the 3rd Century of the Christian Era, it was superseded mainly by Christianity which by this time, remarkably, had similar theological ideas. (See Ninian Smart's entry on Zoroaster in the *Encyclopedia of Philosophy*, Vol. 8. For an estimate of the number of Zoroastrians worldwide, see the entry for Hell.) {CE; ER}

Zorrilla, Manuel Ruiz (Born 1834)

A Spanish statesman, Zorrilla was prosecuted for having written a brochure against the neo-Catholics. In 1870 he became President of the Cortes but later was exiled for his Republicanism. {BDF; RAT; RE}

ZUCCHETTO

When a strong wind reportedly "blew away the Pope's zucchetto" in 1999 while he was in Slovenia, some freethinkers mistakenly assumed a variety of squash had flown off his head. *Zucca*, a gourd, is related to the Late Latin *cucatia*. A zucchetto, however, is a Catholic skullcap worn by clerics. Depending upon its color, the zucchetto signifies the wearer's rank. Jesus, who did not wear one, is theistically unrankable.

Zucker, Frances Hancock (Died 1999)

Zucker was a member of the Freethought Society of Greater Philadelphia, which in 1998 gave her its "Sweetheart of the Year" Award. This was in recognition of the work she had completed in placing freethought books on library shelves and for gathering grant information.

Zucker, Louis C. (20th Century)

A professor of English at the University of Utah in the 1950s, Zucker was a naturalistic humanist.

Zucker, Sydney A. (20th Century)

Zucker was an editor of *Progressive World*.

Zueblin, Charles (Born 1866)

In 1891 Zueblin founded the North Western University Settlement, and in the following year he was appointed secretary of the Chicago Society for University Extension. He taught sociology at Chicago University and edited the *Twentieth Century Magazine* (1911–1912). His rationalism is given in his *Religion of a Democrat* (1908). {RAT}

Zúñiga, Hernán (20th Century)

Zúñiga in 1994 won second prize in Ecuador for what appears to be a shrine to the Virgin Mary but, upon closer inspection, is of Lorena Bobbitt holding the dismembered penis of her husband, a scene which titillated large numbers of feminists and others in the 1990s. Church officials were both startled and angered by his artistic creation. (See entry for Virgin Mary Shrines.)

Zuppetta, Luigi (Born 1810)

Zuppetta was an Italian patriot and jurist. After studying at Naples, he took part in the democratic movement of 1848, was exiled, and returned in 1860 to become professor of penal law at the University of Pavia. {BDF; RAT}

Zweig, Stefan (1881–1942)

Zweig was an Austrian biographer, poet, and novelist. He wrote biographies of Marie Antoinette, ´rasmus, Mary Queen of Scots, Magellan, Balzac, and ◊erlaine. His autobiography, published posthumously in 1943, was entitled *The World of Yesterday*. Under National Socialism Zweig went into exile in England. In 1941 he and his second wife went to Brazil, where they committed suicide.

Zwicker, Barry (20th Century)

A Canadian journalist, formerly with the *Globe and Mail*, *Toronto Star*, and *Detroit News*, Zwicker is Vision TV's regular media critic. A humanist, he has written for *Humanist in Canada* (Winter 1998-1999).

Zwicker, Daniel (1612–1678)

In 1653, the States of Holland forbade the publication of all Unitarian books and all Socinian worship. But when the Unitarian physician Zwicker, according to Robertson, "found his own country (Danzig) too hot to hold him, hold him, he came to Holland 'for security and convenience.' He was able to publish at Amsterdam in 1658 his Latin *Irenicum Irenicorum*, where he lays down three principles for the settlement of Christian difficulties, the first being "he universal reason of mankind,' while Scripture and tradition hold only the second and third places. His book is a remarkable investigation of the rise of the doctrines of the *Logos* and the Trinity, which he traced to polytheism, making out that the first Christians, whom he identified with the Nazarenes, regarded Jesus as a man." Surprisingly, Zwicker escaped serious persecution and died peacefully in Amsterdam. {JMR; JMRH}

Zwinge, Randall: See entry for James Randi.

Zyp

Zyp is an as-yet-unborn-deity. S(h)e will be the husband as well as the wife of Aag. The two are scheduled to be metaphysically worshiped commencing at 00:01, 1 January 2001, after their creation by immaculate abiogenesis.

In keeping with 1990s political correctness, each will have male as well as female sexual organs—like yin and yang, each will complement, not predominate, the other.

Around 1845, Baron Karl von Reichenbach discovered a new force which he named Od. That force, he explained, is only apparent to sensitive humans, whom he called *sensitives*. Od, a coinage to honor the Norse Odin, is behind such otherwise unexplained natural phenomena, he felt, as hypnotism, faith healing, and water dowsing.

In an attempt to explicate, it should be pointed out that the baron is not categorically behind the quiddity of Aag and Zyp: he only exemplifies—in words only a learnèd Ivy League metaphysician could write—"how some individuals are easily attracted to the possibility that such a quasi-panentheistic quid pro quo will come about through a miracle-like cosmic stridulation, that as certain as aglets and octothorpes exist there in truth *is* something spiritual 'out there' which will, some day, become evident and result in all numbers of I-told-you-so's."

Aag and Zyp are expected formally to announce at the very moment the 21st century commences that Od had been their inspiration, that Od not only exists, for real, but also was the Original Original, that all *sensitives* including God and all believers in supernaturalism and/or life after death are therefore, thereunto, thereabouts, and thereinafter to be referred to as "one of the Od"—analogous to the expressions "one of the Christians," "one of the Jews," "one of the Hindus," et cetera.

A sci-fi writer, who will insist on anonymity, is rumored already writing a script to satirize religion in general, superstition in particular, and humankind's most ignoble century: the 20th. The film—which a Hollywood executive will turn into the greatest boxoffice hit to date and which one British philosopher will predict will bring an end to organized religions as freethinkers now know them—will be entitled "The Od Ones." (See entries for Immaculate Abiogenesis and William Jensen.)

AN AFTERWORD

The present work's listings illustrate the great diversity of human personality, action, and accomplishment. Not overlooked are the sexual peccadilloes of men and women, for freethinkers are well aware of life's pleasures (its heavens) as well as its miseries (its hells).

Shakespeare—William Shakspere, or whoever wrote the works—is but one example of a humanist who did not sterilize the subject of life's pleasures, illustrating as he did how amusing, erotic, compassionate, and inspiring sexual and intellectual relations are, or can be, during our challenging adventure as Earthlings. Voltaire is another inspiration, the first modern intellectual who refused to recognize as off-limits almost any subject that positively or negatively intrigued him.

Inasmuch as fundamentalists so often claim that "deathbed conversions" have occurred for non-believers, the listings herein—a "Burke's Peerage" of nonbelievers—have frequently included biographers' descriptions of individuals' final moments. Included are those who, although they may have lived or died as non-believers, may for a part of their lives have been believers; or, as in the cases of Oscar Wilde or Kay Boyle, converted to Catholicism during the final hours of their life.

What have I concluded after years of listening to people with a free mind and after reading their views?

- There are no people *in* Hell. There never have been any people *in* Hell.
- Hell is solely an idea . . . the the idea has gotten in people, and it makes their life a hell.
- We make our heaven now.
- We make our hell now.
- There is no physical Heaven nor any physical Hell . . . although by our actions we achieve a pleasurable heaven now or make of our lives a hell.
- Believers look forward to a Heaven that is the joyful abode of the blessed dead. Such an outlook appears to give them solace. I, however, am well aware that I will *die* when I die.
- So "Where do we go when we die?" I am asked in light of people's lack of agreement on such an important topic? This actually is a meaningless question, unless the questioner is asking for a coroner's detailed report. The rational question (which those dour souls should be asking) is, "What concrete evidence is there concerning life after death?" Or, better, "Where should we be going now that we are alive?"
- For the rationalist, any answer has nothing to do with "belief" but, rather, involves verifiable facts. For those who do lazily "believe" what is unverifiable, the present work will not be helpful. It is not aimed at those who aspire to be believers rather than inquirers. The distinction, as pointed out by Steve Allen, is that rationalists do not believe that 2 + 2 = 4. They know it. To believe is to aver that one does not know, that the person simply believes or takes on faith. As for the "believers," one can only paraphrase Grinnell College anthropologist John Whittaker: Trying to squelch "belief" is like stamping on a rubber spider: It was never real. It simply can't be killed.

Bibliography and Symbols Used

The following works are here acknowledged as having been particularly useful. The symbol on the left refers to bibliographical references {shown in curly brackets, or braces} which are found following the listings of individuals and subjects. All authors' names have been boldfaced, although elsewhere in the book only freethinkers have been. An alphabetical listing of the symbols is found toward the opening pages of the book.

<u>**Symbol**</u>	<u>**Author and Work**</u>
ACK	**Ackerman, Diane**. *A Natural History of Love* (New York: Random House, 1994) Love has many forms and faces, explains Ackerman, a staff writer for *The New Yorker*. "Love is the great intangible," her book commences, whereupon she discusses the historical, cultural, religious, and biological roots of love from a feminine, humanistic viewpoint.
AAH	**Allen, Norman R. Jr.**, ed. *African-American Humanism, An Anthology* (Buffalo, New York: Prometheus Books, 1991) Allen, an editorial associate at *Free Inquiry*, has surveyed contemporary African-American humanists and freethinkers, who are included herein.
AA	*Alyson Almanac* (Boston: Alyson Publications, Inc., 1989) The *Alyson Almanac* is a source for finding the various sexual proclivities ordinarily omitted in the past by most reference books.
--	*American Heritage Dictionary of the English Language* (Boston: Houghton Mifflin Co., 1992) Both this dictionary and *Webster's Third New International Dictionary* have been used throughout for definitions of words. Neither lists "secular humanism."
DGC	**Appiah, Kwame Anthony** and **Henry Louis Gates Jr.**, *The Dictionary of Global Culture* (New York: Alfred A. Knopf, 1997) Whereas E. D. Hirsch Jr. and his fellow editors in their *Dictionary of Cultural Literacy* had emphasized terms common in Western culture, Appiah and Gates emphasize the achievement of the non-Western world. By the year 2000, they note, half the world's people will be Asian and one-eighth will be African. A majority will be non-Christian. Of the world's twenty largest cities, none will be in Europe nor in the United States. Appiah is professor of philosophy and of Afro-American studies at Harvard, and Gates is professor of humanities and chair of the department of Afro-American Studies at Harvard. *The Economist* (15 March 1997) echoes the present writer's view: "The omissions are peculiar. V. S. Naipaul is not listed, either as a British or as a Trinidadian author. Nor, among African writers, are Nadine Gordimer, Doris Lessing and J. M. Coetzee. There are entries for lots of West African people–Mossi, Bambara, Baulé (whose culture, we are told, "is re-emerging")–but none for Caucasian tribes such as Georgians, Abkhaz, Mingrelians. The Watutsi do not make it, either as perpetrators or as victims of genocide–or as the originators of a one-time American dance craze. . . . As a canon-buster, then, this book is a bit of a failure. Perhaps Messrs. Appiah and Gates were too busy to find time for the lexicographer's harmless drudgery. Their non-delivery of what they promised is a let-down for them, their university and–what matters more–their students."
HAB	**Berman, David.** *A History of Atheism in Britain, From Hobbes to Russell* (London and New York: Routledge, 1988) Dr. Berman, a senior lecturer in philosophy at Trinity College of the University of Dublin, explains how atheism was repressed, denied, and suppressed, but how at the surprisingly late date of 1782 covert atheists such as Collins, Hume, and Turner appeared.
FD	**Briars, David.** "Freethinker's Directory" (Privately printed. Route 1, B-45, Craftsbury, Vermont 05826) Briars in 1993 issued a second edition of a work that presumably lists all a-theist, freethought, and non-goddist organizations. The work has been liberally quoted herein. Inasmuch as the various chapters that are cited have frequent elections, the officers listed likely have changed since 1993.
EH	**Clifton, Charles S.** *Encyclopedia of Heresies and Heretics* (Santa Barbara, California: ABC-CLIO, 1992) Clifton, a contributing editor of *Gnosis: A Journal of the Western Inner Traditions*, includes in his listings an extensive bibliography.
CE	*Columbia Encyclopedia, 5th Edition, 1993; Concise Columbia Encyclopedia, 2nd Edition, 1989; Columbia Encyclopedia,* 1975 (New York: Columbia University Press, 1935, 1993) This scholarly tome, edited in 1975 by William H. Harris and Judith S. Levey, is quoted throughout the present study. The concise edition's, as well as the 1993 edition's, editors have been Barbara A. Chernow and George A. Vallasi. Of the various reference sources, *Columbia Encyclopedia* is an outstanding one.
SWW	**Dahlitz, Ray**. *Secular Who's Who, A Biographical Collection of Australasian Humanists, Rationalists, Secularists, and Freethinkers* (GPO Box 1555, Melbourne, Victoria, 3001, Australia, 1993) Here is a remarkable compendium of significant Australasians in the last 150 years of their secular history. It contains more than 60 photographs, 200 biographies, 300 organizations, and 2000 references.

DCL *Dictionary of Cultural Literacy*, E. D. Hirsch Jr., Joseph F. Kett, and James Trefil, eds. (Boston: Houghton Mifflin Company, 1993)

A compilation of commonly used terms, the work as the title denotes is a listing of words and phrases generally known by educated individuals.

EP **Edwards, Paul**, ed. *Encyclopedia of Philosophy* (NY: Macmillan, 1967)

This definitive four-volume survey of the entire subject of philosophy is invaluable in any study of various philosophic topics. Featured are articles by some of the most revered names in philosophy. The editor is a major philosopher as well as teacher.

IM **Edwards, Paul**, ed. *Immortality* (New York: Macmillan Publishing Company, 1992)

The selections herein concern not only the subject of immortality but also the mind-body problem and the nature of personal identity.

PE **Edwards, Paul**. *Reincarnation: A Critical Examination* (Amherst, New York: Prometheus Books, 1996)

A first, the work critiques reincarnation and concludes that empirical and conceptual objections to reincarnation and karma are so strong that the ideas are sheer nonsense. Edwards is thorough and witty, even riotously funny, and he is pleased if he is described as having an "irrepressible Voltairean sense of humor."

QBR **Eisler, Lee**. *The Quotable Bertrand Russell* (Amherst, New York: Prometheus Books, 1993)

When Lord Russell died in 1970 at the age of 98, he had written eighty-nine books, numerous articles, as well as countless newspaper and magazine stories. Also, he had given many interviews. The late Lee Eisler's reader-friendly volume makes it easy to locate Russell's views on a variety of subjects.

E **Esau, Reed,** editor of a World Wide Web page listing "Celebrity Atheists, Agnostics, and Other Non-Theists." On the Web: <http://www.infidels.org:80/infidels>.

Reed edits an offbeat collection of notable individuals who have been public about their lack of belief in deities. He provides documentation and states that the following homepages are a collaborative effort. E-mail: <reed.esau@pobox.com> .

ER **Ferm, Vergilius**, ed., *Encyclopedia of Religion* (New York: Philosophical Library, 1945)

Working with 190 collaborators, Ferm compiled thousands of facts concerning religion and religionists in the 1940s.

PGA **Fitts, Dudley**. *Poems From The Greek Anthology* (New York: New Directions, 1941)

Mr. Fitts's rendering into English of poems from the Greek, or Palatine, anthology first appeared in a volume published in 1938.

AF **Flew, Antony**. *A Dictionary of Philosophy*, Revised Second Edition (New York: St. Martin's Press, 1984)

Antony Flew, emeritus professor of philosophy at the University of Reading and professor of philosophy at York University in Ontario, has been editorial consultant of the revised second edition. A concise dictionary of philosophic terms and a handbook for the general reader, the work has contributions by thirty-three specialists and was edited by Jennifer Speake.

FO **Foote, George William**. *Infidel Death-Beds* (New York: Truth Seeker Press, 1892)

Truth Seeker Press published the 1886 version with some additions by A. D. McLaren. The work concentrates mostly upon freethinkers' final moments.

FI *Free Inquiry*. a quarterly published by the Council for Secular Humanism Inc. (Box 664, Buffalo, New York 14226)

Editor-in-Chief Paul Kurtz has been described as the leading exponent of the philosophy of secular humanism, which he calls eupraxophy. The magazine includes editorials, interviews, articles, book reviews, and news about current developments in philosophy. The Council for Secular Humanism sponsors many organizations, including the following: African Americans for Humanism; Committee for the Scientific Examination of Religion (CSER); Inquiry Media Productions; Institute for Inquiry; International Development Committee; James Madison Memorial Committee; Robert G. Ingersoll Memorial Committee; Secular Organization for Sobriety (SOS); Secular Humanist Aid and Relief Effort (SHARE); and Society of Humanist Philosophers.

In addition, it sponsors the Alliance of Secular Humanist Societies (ASHS), a network of regional groups in several dozen United States and ten Canadian cities. Also, it has established The International Academy of Humanism, which consists of eminent members from nations around the world. Included herein are listings of many of the authors of articles in *Free Inquiry*.

VU **Gaskin, J. C. A.**, ed., *Varieties of Unbelief: From Epicurus to Sartre* (New York: Macmillan, 1988)

This collection exhibits in historical sequence the main *ideas* that have challenged the claims of supernatural religions. The author is a Fellow of Trinity College in Dublin, Ireland.

WWS **Gaylor, Annie Laurie**, ed. *Women Without Superstition: "No Gods—No Masters"* (Madison, Wisconsin: Freedom From Religion Foundation)

Gaylor has edited the collected writings of women freethinkers of the nineteenth and twentieth centuries. Anyone wishing more information about eminent women in the freethought movement will find the present work most helpful.

EG **Gillis, Elizabeth**. *People Like Us, Stories About Unitarian Universalists*, volumes 1 (1988) and 2 (1991), (72 Peterborough Street, Apt 35, Boston, MA 02215)

Gillis is a scholar interested in verifying Unitarian and Universalist memberships. She is of the opinion, which she wrote in the Unitarian publication, *World* (September-October, 1992), that some who allegedly were members "dabbled in many denominations" and may not have considered themselves 100% Unitarians.

JHG **Groden, Michael** and **Martin Kreiswirth**. *The Johns Hopkins Guide to Literary Theory and Criticism*, (Baltimore, Maryland: Johns Hopkins University Press, 1994)

A valuable resource book, the guide includes more than two hundred alphabetically arranged entries on critics and theorists, critical schools and movements, and the critical and theoretical innovations of specific countries and historical periods.

OCAL **Hart, James D**. *The Oxford Companion to American Literature* (New York: Oxford University Press, 1965; 1983)

This source is a standard but old reference concerning American authors and their works.

TYD **Haught**, **James A.** *2000 Years of Disbelief, Famous People with the Courage to Doubt* (Amherst, New York: Prometheus Books, 1996)

Haught, editor of the *Charleston Gazette*, wrote this anthology in which are listed noted disbelievers from the ancient to contemporary times. In addition to citing individuals who will be found listed in the present work, Haught includes a chapter on "Troubled Believers," in which he cites Vice President Albert Gore Jr. and others. Some of these so-called "troubled" believers have been included in the present work.

HM1 "Humanist Manifesto I" (which first appeared in *The New Humanist*, May-June 1933, Vol. VI, No. 3) (Buffalo, New York: Prometheus Books, 1973)

Individuals who signed this 1933 document are listed in the present work.

HM2 "Humanist Manifesto II" (which first appeared in *The Humanist*, September-October 1973, Vol. XXXIII, No. 5) (Buffalo, New York: Prometheus Books, 1973)

Individuals who signed this 1973 document are listed in the present work.

ILP *Index Librorum Prohibitorum* (Typis Polyglottis Vaticanis: 1948, 1961) (Imprimatur: Fr. Alfonsus C. De Romanis, Ep. Porphyreonen, Vic. Gen. Civitatis Vaticanae)

The index, which lasted from 1559 to 1966, includes in its long list of writers such names as Balzac, Cervantes, De Beauvoir, De Unamuno, Descartes, Gide, Hugo, Kazantzakis, Moravia, Pascal, Sartre, and Stendhal. It is a definitive work not only of those works which believers *must* not read but also of those writers who achieved the distinction of being prohibited. Of the 508 pages of authors and books prohibited, only a sampling is included herein. For example:

Abauzit, Firmin. v. *Réflexious impartiales sur les évangiles.*

Abbadie, Jacques. *Traité de la vérité de la religion chrétienne*. Decr. 5 iul, 1695.

_____ *Traité de la divinité de notre seigneur Jésus-Christ. Decr. 15 maii 1702.*

Abominationes papatus, seu invicta demonstratio papam romanum esse no Domini 1666, excuso Londini 1665, Decr. 22 sept. 1692. v. Romae ruina finalis.

Acton, Lord. *Zur Geschichte des vaticanischen Concils. Decr. S. Off, 20 sept. 1871*

Browsers, even those who are polyglots, will find few works and names which they will recognize in the volume's 508 mausoleum-like pages. For example, twenty-seven works by Ioannes Launoius (Launoy) were banned from 1662 to 1704, including such off-putting titles as *Véritable tradition de l'Église sur la prédestination et la grâce* and *Explicata ecclesiae traditio circa canonem "Omnis utriusque sexus."*

ISL *Intimate Sex Lives of Famous People*, edited by Irving Wallace, Amy Wallace, David Wallechinsky, and Sylvia Wallace (New York: Delacorte Press, 1981)

Unlike most prudish biographical references, this volume highlights the humanity of individuals by citing their physical problems, their loves, their human strengths, their weaknesses.

PK **Kurtz, Paul**, ed. *The Humanist Alternative: Some Definitions of Humanism* (Buffalo, New York: Prometheus Books, 1973)

Dr. Kurtz, a leading exponent of the philosophy of secular humanism, has written a variety of books about *eupraxophy* (*Toward A New Enlightenment* [1994] and *Living Without Religion* [1994] are two). The present work contains definitions of humanism by thirty different individuals, including Edwin H. Wilson, David Tribe, Sidney Hook, Gora, Algernon D. Black, Herbert W. Schneider, Antony Flew, B. F. Skinner, and others.

CL **Lamont, Corliss**. *The Philosophy of Humanism*, 6th Edition (New York: Frederick Ungar Publishing Co., 1986)

Dr. Lamont once taught a course about naturalistic humanism at Columbia University. This book commenced as its text. In 1948, the present author was in that course's first class.

UU **Lange, Fred E. Jr**. "Famous Unitarians / Universalists" PO Box 274, Garwood, New Jersey 07027, 1987)

Unitarians and Universalists are outside the Judeo-Christian groupings and many of the congregations have members as well as ministers who are religious humanists (who often choose to use terms common to other churches) or secular humanists (who are basically interested in philosophy, the humanities, and the sciences rather than in religion). The Unitarians and Universalists whom Lange describes are listed in the present work. Rather than distinguish between the two groups, Unitarian is ordinarily used throughout. A considerable number of contemporary Unitarian Universalists are humanists.

LEE **Leedom, Tim C.** ed., *The Book Your Church Doesn't Want You To Read* (Dubuque, Iowa: Kendall-Hunt Publishing Company, 1993)

Leedom was an administrative aide to both the Governor and Lt. Governor of Hawaii. He then worked seven years in the Hawaii State Legislature.

This book is an anthology of freethought viewpoints; however, it could have used a careful fact-checker.

CA **Lippard, Jim**, "Celebrity Atheist List" on the Web: <www.primenet.com/~lippard/atheist.celebs/>

Lippard is webmaster for an Internet page, "Celebrity Atheist List." He emphasizes that all his listings are provided by online readers, that there is no intent to misrepresent any person's beliefs or lack thereof, and that any errors will be corrected when brought to the editor's attention. His compilation of such information not only is evidence of the newly found worth of the World Wide Web but also has been important in supplying many of the details found herein.

JM **McCabe, Joseph**. *A Biographical Dictionary of Ancient, Medieval, and Modern Freethinkers* (Girard, Kansas: Haldeman-Julius Publications, 1945)

Complaining that Wheeler, John M. Robertson, and others "have too readily admitted liberal members of organized religions," McCabe proposed narrowing his list. He noted that "all the thinkers during seven centuries of ancient Greece except Plato and Pythagoras rejected the idea of spirit or a personal God and immortality. So did nearly all the writers of ancient Rome. At the other end of the scale it is hardly necessary to record that such men as Haldeman-Julius, McCabe, Bertrand Russell, Joseph Lewis, etc., are atheists." He also noted that Prof. James Leuba has twice shown, "from their own private assurances, that three-fourths of the 500 leading men of science and history in America 'disbelieve' in God, and that is the dictionary definition of atheism." His list is on the Web: <http://www.infidels.org/library/historical/joseph_mccabe/dictionary.html>.

RAT **McCabe, Joseph.** *Biographical Dictionary of Modern Rationalists* (London: Watts, 1920)

Written in 1920 when he was in his forties, the book is a study of modern rationalists up until the 1910s. The word "rationalist" first appeared in English letters about the middle of the seventeenth century, he states, denoting a sect of people who follow "what their reason dictates to them in Church or State." Somewhat earlier, Bacon applied the term "Rationals" to the philosophers who sought to attain truth by deductions from the first principles which reason was supposed to perceive rather than by induction from the observed facts of nature. "In neither sense," McCabe writes, did the term pass into general currency at the time; but in the course of the nineteenth century it was adopted as the most fitting name for those who uphold what is vaguely called the supremacy of reason in the discovery and establishment of truth."

RE **McCabe, Joseph**. *A Rationalist Encyclopedia: A Book of Reference on Religion, Philosophy, Ethics, and Science* (London: Watts & Co., 1950)

"The distinctive feature of this book," states the foreword, "is that it challenges the widespread conviction that all that is most precious in our civilization has been derived from Christianity." In over 600 pages, with alphabetical listings, McCabe names and describes the legends without their halo. It should be noted that many now consider parts of the work obsolete because it contains errors (such as inclusion of the Piltdown Man as being authentic, which fooled many at that time, including Sir Arthur Keith).

HNS **Morain, Lloyd** and **Mary Morain**. *Humanism as the Next Step, An Introduction for Liberal Protestants, Catholics, and Jews* (Boston, Massachusetts: Beacon Press, 1954)

Lloyd Morain—once president of the American Humanist Association—and his wife, Mary—once a director of the International Humanist and Ethical Union—wrote this book to describe the new and humanistic "Fourth Faith."

HNS2 **Morain, Lloyd** and **Mary Morain**. *Humanism as the Next Step* (Amherst, New York: Humanist Press, 1998

The work is a second edition, one that contains many personal reminiscences. However, its Appendix One, "The Background of Modern Humanism," unfortunately is an admixture of names and terms. Typical of its prose: "Philo Judaeus, living at the time of Christ, developed Hellenistic Jewish philosophy." Furthermore, the Morains, leaders of the American Humanist Association, refer to the Christ and the Buddha rather than to Jesus and Gautama, as one would expect humanists to do. Appendix Two, by Frederick Edwords, is an edited version of an article entitled "The Humanist Philosophy in Perspective." The index is disappointingly incomplete.

WRF **Nass, Herbert E.** *Wills of the Rich and Famous* (New York: Warner Books. 1991)

A will sometimes reveals an individual's paramount interests or last-minute changes of mind.

OAL *Oxford Companion to American Literature, 4th Edition* (New York: Oxford University Press. 1965)

Editor James D. Hart arranges authors and subjects alphabetically and the entries are generous with details.

OEL *Oxford Companion to English Literature, 5th Edition* (New York: Oxford University Press. 1985)

Editor Margaret Drabble has up-dated Sir Paul Harvey's 1932 compilation of biographies and facts concerning English literature.

OCP *Oxford Companion to Philosophy* (New York: Oxford University Press, 1995)

The work is a particularly important reference book. A total of 249 contributors, including Dr. Paul Edwards, have provided several thousand alphabetically arranged entries. The editor was Ted Honderich.

PUT **Putnam, Samuel P.** *400 Years of Freethought* (New York: The Truth Seeker Company, 1894)

Putnam includes many photos and artistic likenesses of eminent freethinkers from the time of Columbus, Vasco de Gama, and Magellan to leaders.

JMRH **Robertson, John M.** *A History of Freethought, Ancient and Modern to the Period of the French Revolution*

(London: Watts & Co., 1936)

This is an updating of the two-volume *Short History of Freethought, Ancient and Modern*. It is a major work, a triumph of research and readable prose.

JMR **Robertson, John M.** *A Short History of Freethought, Ancient and Modern* (London: Watts & Co., 1915)

In his two-volume work issued for the Rationalist Press Association, Robertson compiled a phenomenal number of facts concerning freethought. Polytheists, he revealed, once called the early Christians "atheists" because they did not agree with the image-adoring polytheists. "Infidels" referred then chiefly to Jews and pagans. "Deism" and "naturalism" came into use about the middle of the 16th century. In scholarly fashion, Robertson details the ramifications of freethought. According to Gordon Stein in the *Encyclopedia of Unbelief*, Robertson wrote 115 or more books and "had perhaps the greatest knowledge of freethought of any freethinker who has ever lived."

U&U **Robinson, David**. *The Unitarians and the Universalists* Westport, Connecticut: Greenwood Press, 1985)

The work lists major Unitarians and Universalists. As for a definition of Unitarianism, James Luther Adams cites the philosopher Alfred North Whitehead: "Unitarianism is belief in up to one God." In 1962, Pope John XXIII told Dana McLean Greeley, "The Unitarians are the people who made a religion of all our heresies."

— *Routledge Encyclopedia of Philosophy*. Edward Craig, General Editor. (New York: Routledge, 1998)

This mammoth survey of the history of philosophy cost $2,495. upon publication, has ten volumes, and is 8,680 pages in length. It was published in 1998 at a time when the present author's work was just being finished. No references thereunto are included.

RSR **Royle, Edward**. *Radicals, Secularist and Republicans: Popular Freethought in Britain, 1866–1915* (Totowa, New Jersey: Rowman and Littlefield, 1980)

Secularists in the England of the period covered held that the evils of contemporary society were attributable to the baneful effects of religion and their aim was to discredit Christianity and those social institutions which depended upon it. They were republicans in a country increasingly devoted to its Queen. They were atheists in a society which, outwardly at least, was profoundly religious. Their hero was Thomas Paine.

VI **Royle, Edward**. *Victorian Infidels* (Totowa, New Jersey, Rowman and Littlefield, 1974)

The work describes the origins of the British secularist movement, 1791 to 1866.

HWP **Russell, Bertrand**. *A History of Western Philosophy* (New York: Simon & Schuster, 1945)

Lord Russell was the renowned logical atomist, mathematician, and humanist. His thinking has greatly influenced the rationalist and humanist movements.

SHD *Secular Humanist Declaration*, 1980 (Reprinted from *Free Inquiry*, Vol. 1, #1, Winter, 1980, and available from Prometheus Books, 59 John Glenn Drive, Amherst, New York 14228.)

Drafted by Paul Kurtz, the declaration is endorsed by fifty-eight prominent scholars and writers from Canada, France, Great Britain, India, Israel, Norway, the United States of America, and the former country of Yugoslavia.

WWTCL **Seymour-Smith, Martin**. *Who's Who in Twentieth Century Literature* (New York: McGraw Hill, 1976)

The reference is a standard 1970s study of world literature.

ESDM **Slater, Scott**, and **Alec Solomita**. *Exits, Stories of Dying Moments and Parting Words* (New York: E. P. Dutton, 1980)

The volume is a collection of individuals' purported last words before dying. Non-believers are not known for their last-minute or deathbed confessions of faith, although believers have widely spread the erroneous view that in their dying moments most non-believers "find God."

WAS **Smith, Warren Allen**. *Humanists on Humanism*

An as yet unpublished manuscript, *Humanists on Humanism* contains correspondence from individuals who were informed by the author that *seven* humanisms appeared in the current literature of the 1950s. These seven humanisms were described and defined as follows:

• 1 **humanism**—to the lexicographer, a term denoting devotion to human interests as well as one referring to the study of the humanities;
• 2 **ancient humanism**—to the historiographer, a term pertaining to the collective philosophies of such as Aristotle, Democritus, Epicurus, Lucretius, Pericles, Protagoras, and Socrates;
• 3 **classical humanism**—to the educator, a term referring to the ancient humanist views brought back into vogue during the Renaissance by such as Bacon, Boccaccio, Erasmus, Montaigne, More, and Petrarch;
• 4 **theistic humanism**—to the seminarian, a term including both Christian existentialists and those modern theologians who insist upon human values, upon man's capability of working out his salvation with his God, all within the framework of a supernaturalistic philosophy;
• 5 **atheistic humanism**—to the Continental critic, a term describing the philosophy of French playwright and novelist Jean-Paul Sartre and others;
• 6 **communistic humanism**—to the political scientist, a term signifying the philosophic beliefs of some Marxists–for example, Cuba's Fidel Castro; Raya Dunayevskaya, former secretary to Leon Trotsky, averred that Karl Marx was a thoroughgoing naturalist who at first had called his outlook "a new humanism."
• 7 **naturalistic (or scientific) humanism**–to philosophers, an eclectic set of beliefs born of the modern scientific age and centered upon a faith in, or an assumption of, the supreme value and self-improvability of human personality (in the 1970s to 1990s, usually

called "secular humanism" or, by a few, "humanistic naturalism").

Individuals were then asked to comment on any or all of the seven humanisms. Their replies are followed by brackets showing the date they replied, from 1948 on. Some were simply asked to go on record as to whether they are theists or non-theists.

WSS **Smith, Warren Sylvester**. *The London Heretics, 1870–1914* (New York: Dodd, Mead, & Co., 1968)

Smith, in addition to listing heretics of the period, includes periodicals of the secularist movement, 1845–1914. He also discusses the non-Christians as well as the new Christians of the 1910–1914 period.

EU **Stein, Gordon**, ed., *Encyclopedia of Unbelief* with a Foreword by Paul Edwards (Buffalo, New York: Prometheus Books, 1985)

Biographies of prominent individuals associated with freethought, agnosticism, atheism, humanism, skepticism, and unbelief are included in this work, which contains several hundred articles by a variety of experts. No other work goes into such depth, and it is an ideal resource for further research on the subject of unbelief, particularly in its treatment of unbelief in the ancient world, in various countries, in literature, in all aspects of philosophy. As a caveat, it should be noted that a major British rationalist in 1994 described the work as "unreliable," that, for example, it confused Charles and Charles Albert Watts and contained other mistaken details concerning English entries.

FUK **Stein, Gordon**. *Freethought in the United Kingdom and the Commonwealth, A Descriptive Bibliography* (Westport, Connecticut: Greenwood Press, and London, England, 1981)

The work includes the Rise of Deism (1614–1760); the National Secular Society to 1860; the Bradlaugh/Besant/Foote Era; and Freethought After Foote (1915–1981). Included are bibliographic entries concerning Australia, Canada, India, New Zealand, etc.

FUS **Stein, Gordon** and **Marshall G. Brown**. *Freethought in the United States* (Westport, Connecticut. Greenwood Press, and London, England, 1978)

The work refers to the rise and decline of deism, popular freethought, the Golden Age of Freethought, and Freethought in the 20th Century.

GS **Stein, Gordon**. *God Pro and Con* (New York: Garland Publishing, 1990)

A short work by the late Gordon Stein, it contains a thorough bibliography of atheism.

GL **Summers, Claude J., ed**. *The Gay and Lesbian Literary Heritage* (New York: Henry Holt and Co., 1995)

The extensive work is a reader's companion to the writers and their works, from antiquity to the present. Many gay writers formerly have been overlooked as being non-theists.

TRI **Tribe, David**. *100 Years of Freethought* (London: Elek Books Limited, 1967)

"Freethought has no beginning and no end," Tribe commences. He then mentions some early dates:

1825	Early unitarianism
1833	Mexican secularism
1848	German free-religious movement
1854	Organized Positivism
1856	New Zealand rationalism
1862	Australian secularism
1864	Belgian *Ligue de l'Enseignement*
1869	Italian anti-clericalism
1871	Voysey's theistic church
1873	U. S. freethought (based on the *Truth Seeker*, "now regrettably aiding racism")
1876	American Ethical Culture
1881	Dutch *Dageraad* (Dawn) as a national movement
1883	Argentinean secularism
1887	Austrian secularism

SAU **Underwood, Sara A**. *Heroines of Freethought* (New York: Charles P. Somerby, 1876)

"To-day we stand at the opening of a grand vista of civil and religious liberty," Underwood prefaced her book in 1876. She concentrated on eleven freethinkers: Madame Roland (Marie Jeanne Phlipon), Mary Wollstonecraft Godwin, George Sand, Harriet Martineau, Frances Wright D'Arusmont, Emma Martin, Margaret Chappellsmith, Ernestine L. Rose, Frances Power Cobbe, and George Eliot.

U "Unitarian Universalist Religious Education Calendar, 1992" (Unitarian Universalist Association, 25 Beacon Street, Boston, MA 02108)

The calendar lists "individuals who were historically connected with the Universalist or Unitarian movements, or with the merged denomination."

TSV **Vernon, Thomas S**. *Great Infidels* (m & m Press, PO Box 338, Fayetteville, Arkansas 72702, 1989)

Dr. Thomas S. Vernon is Emeritus Professor of Philosophy at the University of Arkansas and author of *Unheavenly Discourses* and *The Age of Unreason.*

PROFESSIONAL INDEX

Following is a sampling of some of the professions of individuals mentioned herein, people who were, or are, or are thought to be freethinkers rather than believers in tenets of some organized religion or cult.

Caveat: Transcendentalists are listed along with atheists, deists along with rationalists, religious humanists along with naturalistic humanists—however, no two freethinkers think alike, or should:

Actors, Actresses, Comedians, Entertainers, or Individuals Associated with Films and Drama

Anarchists

Anatomist

Anesthetists, Euthanasianists

Anthropologists

Arab Caliph

Arab Philosopher

Arab Physician

Arabian Pantheists

Abu Bakr Ibn Al-Tufail (Died 1185)\

Around-the-world Sailor

Autissier, Isabelle (20th Century)

Architects

Bulfinch, Charles (1763—1844)
Fuller, Buckminister (1895—1983)
Pelli, Cesar (1926—)
Wright, Frank Lloyd (1867—1959)

Artists, Art Historians, Painters, Sculptors

Alma-Tadema, Laurence (1836—1912)
Avery, Milton Clark (1893—1965)
Barr, Alfred Hamilton (1902—1981)
Bonheur, Marie Rosalie (1822—1899)
Brown, Ford Madox (1821-1893)
Cadmus, Paul (1904—1999)
Collier, John (1850—1934)
Currier, Nathaniel (1813—1888)
Delacroix, Eugène (1798—1863)
Freud, Lucian (1922—)
Hogarth, William (1697—1764)
Holyoke, George (19th Century)
Kahlo, Frida (1907—1954)
Kollwitz, Käthe Schmidt (1867-1945)
Matisse, Henri (1869—1954)
Morris, William (1834—1896)
Orozco, José (1883-1949)
Picasso, Pablo Ruiz y (1881—1973)
Rivera, Diego (1886—1957)
Rodin, Auguste (1840—1917)
Rossetti, Dante Gabriel (1828—1882)
Rowland, Anne (20th Century)
Sloan, John (1871—1951)
Sorel, Edward (1929—)
St. Gaudens, Augustus (1848—1907)
Tadema, Lawrence (1836-1912)
Thiebaud, Wayne (1920—)
Thorvaldsen, Albert Bertel (1770—1844)
Turner, Joseph (1775-1851)
Watts, George (1674-1748)
Weschler, Anita (1903—)
Whistler, James Abbott (1834—1903)
Witkin, Jerome (1939-)
Woolner, Thomas (1825-1892)
Wyeth, N. C. (1882—1945)

Astronaut, strophysicist, Space Agency Executive

Bonnet, R. M. (20th Century)
Gagarin, Yuri (1934—1968)
Jastrow, Robert (1925—)

Astronomers

Abell, George, O(gden) (1927—1983)
Anaximandros (610—547 B.C.E.)
Aristarchus of Samos (c. 310—230 B.C.E.)
Darwin, George Howard (1845—1912)
Dommanget, Jean (20th Century)
Efremov, Yuri N. (20th Century)
Eratosthenes (c. 275—195 B.C.E.)
Hale, Alan (20th Century)
Halley, Edmund (1656—1742)
Hoyle, Fred (1915—)
Hubble, Edwin Powell (1889—1953)
La Grange, Joseph (1736-1813)
Lalande, Joseph (1732-1807)
Pecker, Jean-Claude (20th Century)
Sagan, Carl (1934—1996)
Schatzman, Evry (20th Century)
Shapley, Harlow (1885—1972)

Athlete

Owens, Jesse (1913—1980)

Authors

About, Edmond François (1826—1885)
Adamic, Louis (1899—1951)
Alger, Horatio Jr. (1832—1899)
Alvarez, A(lfred) (1929-)
Arnould, Arthur (1833—1895)
Atwood, Margaret (1939—)
Aury, Dominique (1908—1998)
Baggeson, Jens Immanuel (1764—1826)
Barlow, Joel (1754—1812)
Beach, Joseph Warren (1880—1957)
Bennett, Arnold (1867—1931)
Bierce, Ambrose (1842—1914?)
Blixen, (Baroness) Karen (1885—1962)
Boccaccio, Giovanni (1313—1375)
Bojer, Johan (1872—1952)
Bowles, Paul (1910—1999)
Brooks, Van Wyck (1886-1963)
Burgess, Anthony (1917—1993)
Butler, Samuel (1835—1902)
Cabell, James Branch (1879—1958)
Camus, Albert (1913—1960)
Cargill, Oscar (1898—1971)
Carlyle, Thomas (1795—1881)
Carson, Rachel (1907-1964)
Channing, William Ellery (1780—1842)
Chekhov, Anton Pavlovich (1860—1904)
Cleland, John (1709—1789)
Clemens, Samuel (1835—1910)
Coleridge, Samuel Taylor (1772—1834)
Connolly, Cyril Vernon (1903-1974)
Conrad, Joseph (1857—1924)
Cousins, Norman (1915—1990)
Crisp, Quentin (1908—)
Cyrano de Bergerac, Savinien (1619—1655)
Daudet, Alphonse (1840—1897)
Defoe, Daniel (1660?—1731)
deFord, Miriam Allen (1888—1975)
Dickens, Charles (1812—1870)
Dreiser, Theodore (1871—1945)
Du Maurier, George Louis (1834—1896)
Dumas, Alexandre fils (1824—1895)
Durang, Christopher (1949—)
Eliot, George (1819—1880)
Ellis, Royston (1941—)
Emerson, Ralph Waldo (1803—1882)
Farrell, James T(homas) (1904—1979)
Faulkner, William (1897—1962)
Ficke, Arthur Davison (1883—1945)
Fielding, Henry (1707—1754)
Fisher, Dorothy Canfield (1879—1958)
FitzGerald, Edward (1809—1883)
Fitzgerald, F(rancis) Scott (1896—1940)
Forster, E(dward) M(organ) (1879—1970)

Fowles, John (1926-)
France, Anatole (1844—1924)
French, Marilyn (1929—)
Fuller, Margaret (1810—1850)
Gaddis, William (1922-1998)
Gale, Zona (1874—1939)
Galsworthy, John (1867—1933)
García Lorca, Federico (1898—1936)
Gautier, Théophile (1811—1872)
Glasgow, Ellen (1873—1945)
Goethe, Johann Wolfgang von (1749—1832)
Goldsmith, Oliver (1730?—1774)
Goncourt, Edmond Louis (1822—1896)
Goncourt, Jules Alfred Huot (1830—1870)
Gorky, Maxim (1868—1936)
Hahn, Emily (1905—1997)
Hansberry, Lorraine (1930—1965)
Harte, Bret (1836—1902)
Hawthorne, Nathaniel (1804—1864)
Hazlitt, William (1778—1830)
Hearn, Lafcadio (1850—1904)
Hearst, James (1900—1983)
Hellman, Lillian (1905—1984)
Hentoff, Nathan Irving (1925—)
Hicks, Granville (1901—1982)
Higginson, Thomas W. (1823—1911)
Hoffer, Eric (1902—1983)
Holmes, Oliver Wendell Jr. (1841—1935)
Housman, A(lfred) E(dward) (1859—1936)
Howells, William Dean (1837—1920)
Hughes, Langston (1902—1967)
Hughes, Rupert (1872—1956)
Hugo, Victor Marie (1802—1885)
Hurston, Zora Neale (1891—1960)
Huxley, Aldous (1894—1963)
Ibsen, Henrik (1828—1906)
Jonas, Carl (1913—1976)
Joyce, James (1882—1941)
Kafka, Franz (1883—1924)
Kesey, Ken (1935-)
Kinsella, William Patrick (1935-)
Koestler, Arthur (1905—1983)
Konrád, György (1933—)
Kramer, Larry (1935-
Krutch, Joseph Wood (1893—1970)
Kushner, Tony (20th Century)
Lamb, Charles (1775—1834)
Lardner, Ring Wilmer Jr. (1915—)
Lawrence, D(avid) H(erbert) (1885—1930)
Lermontov, Mikhail (1814—1840)
Lessing, Doris May (1919—)
Lewis, Joseph (1889—1968)
Lewis, Sinclair (1885—1951)
Lin Yutang (1895—1976)
London, Jack (1876—1916)
Longfellow, Henry W. (1807—1882)
Lovett, Robert Morss (1870—1956)
.**Lovecraft, H. P.** (1890-1937)
Ludwig, Emil (1881-1948)
MacLeish, Archibald (1892—1982)
Malraux, André (1901—1976)
Mann, Thomas (1875—1955)
Maréchal, Pierre Sylvain (1750—1803)
Marquand, John (Phillips) (1893—1960)
Martineau, Harriet (1802—1876)
Masters, Edgar Lee (1869—1950)
Maugham, Somerset (1874—1965)
Maupassant, Guy de (1850—1893)
McCabe, Joseph (Martin) (1867—1955)
McCarthy, Mary (1912—1989)
Melville, Herman (1819—1891)
Meredith, George (1829—1909)
Mérimée, Prosper (1803—1870)
Michener, James (1907—1997)
Millay, Edna St. Vincent (1892—1950)
Miller, Arthur (1915—)
Milne, A. A. (1882—1956)
Mitford, Jessica (1917—1996)
Molière, Jean Baptiste (1622—1673)
Monette, Paul (1945—1995)
Monravia (Pincherle) Alberto (1907—1990)
Moore, George Augustus (1852—1933)
Moravia, Alberto (1907—)
Morris, William (1834-1896)
Muller, Herbert J. (1905—)
Murdoch, (Jean) Iris (1919—1999)
Naipul, V. S. (1932-)
Nin, Anaïs (1903—1977)
Nott, Kathleen (1910—1995)
Oates, Joyce Carol (1938-)
O'Brien, Conor Cruise (1917-)
O'Casey, Sean (1880—1964)
O'Hair, Madalyn Murray (1919—1996?)
O'Hara, Frank (1926-1966)
O'Neill, Eugene Gladstone (1888—1953)
Oates, Joyce Carol (1938—)
Paglia, Camille (1947—)
Perez Galdós, Benito (1843-1920)
Peyrefitte, Roger (1907-)
Phillips, Julia Miller (1944-)
Phillpotts, Eden (1862-1960)
Pinter, Harold (1930-)
Pobo, Kenneth (1954-)
Poe, Edgar Allan (1809—1849)
Pollitt, Katha (1949—)
Potter, Dennis (1935-1994)
Potter, (Helen) Beatrix (1866-1943)
Potter, Charles Francis (1885—1962)
Proust, Marcel (1871—1922)
Pushkin, Aleksandr (1799—1837)
Rand, Ayn (1905—1982)
Reid, Alastair (1926—)
Renan, Joseph Ernest (1823—1892)
Rhodes, Cecil John (1853—1902)
Richter, Johann Paul (1763—1825)
Rolland, Romain (1866—1944)
Romains, Jules (1885—1972)
Rostand, Edmond (1868-1918)
Rousseau, Jean Jacques (1712-1778)
Royall, Anne Newport (1769-1854)
Rudnick, Paul (20th Century)
Rushdie, (Ahmed) Salman (1947—)
Rusk, Ralph (1888—1962)
Sade, Donatien, Comte de (1740—1814)
Sand, George (1804—1876)
Sandburg, Carl (1878—1967)
Sardou, Victorien (1831-1908)
Sarton, May (1912-1995)
Schiller, Johann (1759-1805)
Scopes, John T(homas) (20th Century)

Sedgwick, Eve Kosofsky (20th Century)
Self, Will (1961—)
Serling, Rod (1924-1975)
Servetus, Michael (1511—1553)
Shaw, George Bernard (1856-1950)
Shawn, William (1907-1992)
Shelley, Mary Wollstonecraft (1797—1851)
Shelley, Percy Bysshe (1792—1822)
Silone, Ignazio (1900—1978)
Southern, Terry (1924—1995)
Steffens, (Joseph) Lincoln (1866—1936)
Steinbeck, John (1902—1968)
Stendhal (Marie-Henri Beyle) (1783—1842)
Stevenson, Robert Louis (1850—1894)
Stoppard, Tom (1937-)
Strindberg, Johan August (1849-1912)
Styron, William (1925—)
Sully-Prudhomme, René (1839-1907)
Swenson, May (1917-1989)
Swinburne, Algernon (1837-1909)
Symonds, John Addington (1840-1893)
Taine, Hippolyte (1828-1893)
Thoreau, Henry David (1817—1862)
Trilling, Lionel (1905—1975)
Trotsky, Leon (1879—1940)
Turgenev, Ivan (1818—1883)
Van Doren, Carl (1885—1950)
van Paassen, Pierre (Born 1895)
Vargas Llosa, Mario (1936—)
Vidal, Gore (1925—)
Voltaire, François-Marie (1694—1778)
Vonnegut, Kurt Jr. (1922—)
Walker, Alice (1944—)
Walpole, Horace (1717-1797)
Wheeler, Joseph Mazzini (1850—1898)
Whitman, Walt (1819—1892)
Wieland, Christopher (1733-1813)
Williams, William Carlos (1883-1963)
Wilson, A(ndrew) N(orman) (1950—)
Wilson, Angus (1913—1991)
.**Wilson, Colin** (1931-)
Wilson, Sloan (1920—)
Wodehouse, P. G. (1881-1975)
Wollstonecraft, Mary (Godwin) (1759—1797)
Woolf, Virginia (1882—1941)
Yourcenar, Marguérite (1903—1987)
Zola, Émile Édouard (1840—1902)
Zweig, Stefan (1881—1942)

Biographers

Arvin, Newton (1900—1963)
Hellman, Lillian (1905-1984)
Huxley, Leonard (1860—1933)
Ludwig, Emil (1881—1948)
Nevins, Allan (1890-1971)
Sandburg, Carl (1878-1967)
Strachey, Lytton (1880—1932)

Biologists, Botanists, Chemists, Scientists

Armstrong, Henry Edward (1848—1937)
Bartram, John (1699—1777)
Berthelot, Pierre (1827—1907)
Berthollet, Claude Louis (1748—1822)
Bhargava, P. M. (20th Century)
Blakemore, Colin (1944—)
Burbank, Luther (1849—1926)
Carson, Rachel (1907—1964)
Cavendish, Henry (1731—1810)
Chaptal, Jean Antoine (1756—1832)
Commoner, Barry (1917—)
Darwin, Francis (1848—1925)
Delgado, José M. R. (20th Century)
Hooker, Joseph Dalton (1817—1911)
Huxley, Julian Sorrell (1887—1975)
Huxley, Thomas Henry (1825—1895)
Klein, Georg (20th Century)
Priestley, Joseph (1733—1804)
Riddle, Oscar (1877—1968)
Salk, Jonas (1914-1995)
Wilson, E. O. (1929—)

Business Executives, Bankers, Financiers, Manufacturers

Baker, George Fisher (1840—1931)
Buffett, Warren Edward (1930—)
Eaton, Cyrus (1883—1979)
Gates, William Henry (1955—)
Goldsmith, James (1933—1997)
Khosla, Vinod (20th Century)
Loeb, John Langeloth (1902—1996)
Piech, Ferdinand (1937-)
Pinkham, Lydia (1819—1883)
Pullman, George (1831-1897)
Soros, George (1930-)
Turner, Ted (1938—)
Young, Owen D. (1879—1962)

Cartoonists

Addis, Don (20th Century)
Busiek, Kurt (20th Century)
Cervone, Ed (20th Century)
Feiffer, Jules (1929-)
Groening, Matthew (1954-)
McFarlane, Todd (20th Century)
Pekar, Harvey (20th Century)
Rall, Ted (20th Century)
Sorel, Edward (1929-)
Thurber, James (1894—1961)
Whale, James (1896-1957)

Circus owner

Barnum, Phineas Taylor (1810—1891)

Civil libertarians, civil rights leaders and activists

Baldwin, Roger Nash (1884—1981)
Bonner, Elena (1922—)
Du Bois, W. E. B. (1868—1963)
Forman, James (1928—)
Robertson, Priscilla Smith (1910—1989)
Rustin, Bayard (1910—1987)
Sanger, Margaret (1879-1966)
Young Jr., Whitney M. (1921—1971)

Columnists

Adams, Phillip (1939—)
Faulkner, Charles W. (20th Century)
Teimourian, Hazhir (20th Century)

Computer Experts

Berniers-Lee, Tim (1956—)
Gates, William Henry (1955—)

Nelson, Ted (1938?-)

Cooking Expert

Farmer, Fannie (1857—1915)

Criminologists

Andrieux, Louis (Born 1840)
Beccaria, Cesare Bonesana (1738—1794)
Bertillon, Alphonse (1853—1914)

Critics

Blanshard, Paul (1892—1980)
Brooks, Van Wyck (1886—1963)
Geismar, Maxwell (1909—1979)
Howe, Irving (1920—1993)
Jones, Llewellyn (1884-1961)
Pater, Walter (1839—1894)
Ruskin, John (1819—1900)
Simon, John Ivan (1925—)
Sainte-Beuve, Charles (1804-1869)
Stephen, Leslie (1832-1904)
Taine, Hippolyte (1828-1893)
Wilson, Edmund (1895—1972)

Dancers

Baryshnikov, Mikhail (1948—)
Duncan, Isadora (1878-1927)
Nureyev, Rudolf (1938-1993)

Ecologist

Bookchin, Murray (1921—)

Economists

Bastiat, Frédéric (1801—1850)
Chase, Stuart (1888—1985)
Dupont de Nemours, Pierre (1739—1817)
Galbraith, John Kenneth (1908—)
Hazlitt, Henry (1894—1993)
Heilbroner, Robert Louis (1919—)
Myrdal, Gunnar (1898—1987)
Smith, Adam (1723—1790)
Veblen, Thorstein (1857—1929)

Educators

Agassiz, Elizabeth Cabot (1822—1907)
Barnard, Henry (1811—1900)
Davis, Robert Gorham (1908—1998)
Dewey, John (1859—1952)
Dix, Dorothea Lynde (1802—1887)
Eliot, Charles William (1834—1926)
Hopkins, Mark (1801—1887)
Kilpatrick, William Heard (1871—1965)
Mann, Horace (1796—1859)
Morgan, Arthur E. (1878—1975)
Neill, A. S. (1883—1973)
Norton, Charles Eliot (1827—1908)
Pestalozzi, Johann Heinrich (1746—1827)
Pitkin, Royce S. (20th Century)
Quincy, Josiah (1772-1864)
Stoddard, George (1897-1981)
Taylor, Harold (1914—1993)

Egyptologist

Mariette, François Auguste (1821—1881)

Embryologist

Albini, Giuseppe (1863—1933)

Encyclopedists

d'Alembert, Jean le Rond (1717—1783)
d'Holbach, Paul Henri Thiry (1723—1789)
Diderot, Denis (1713—1784)
Montesquieu, Charles Louis (1689—1755)
Quesnay, François (1694—1774)
Turgot, Anne Robert Jacques (1727—1781)
Rousseau, Jean Jacques (1712-1778)
Voltaire, François-Marie (1694—1778)

Engineer
MacCready, Paul B. (1925—)

Ethnologist

Achelis, Thomas (1850—1909)

Evolutionist

Darwin, Charles Robert (1809—1882)

Explorers

Arnesen, Liv (20th Century)
.**Bougainville, Louis de** (1729—1811)
Burton, Richard Francis (1821—1890)
Hillary, Edmund Percival (1919-)
Magellan, Ferdinand (c. 1480—1521)
Stefansson, Vilhjalmur (1879—1962)

Feminists

Anthony, Susan Brownell (1820—1906)
Ehrenreich, Barbara (1941—)
Friedan, Betty Naomi (1921—)
Howe, Julia Ward (1819—1910)
Nasrin, Taslima (1962—)

Geologists

Lyell, Charles (1797—1875)
Murchison, Roderick Impey (1792—1871)

Historians

Amari, Michele (1806—1889)
Aulard, François Victor (1849—1928)
Barnes, Harry Elmer (1888—1968)
Bulwer-Lytton, Edward (1803—1873)
Burkhardt, Jakob (1818-1897)
Commager, Henry Steele (1902—1998)
Duberman, Martin (1930—)
Gibbon, Edward (1737—1794)
Haydon, A. Eustace (1880—1975)
Hecataeus (c. 500 B.C.E.)
Herodotus (484?—425? B.C.E.)
Maréchal, Pierre Sylvain (1750-1803)
Michelet, Jules (1798—1874)
Muzzey, David Saville (1870—1965)
Nevins, Allan (1890-1971)
Parkman, Francis (1823—1893)
Passmore, John Arthur (1914—)
Persons, Stow (1913-)
Renan, Joseph Ernest (1823-1892)
Rogers, Joel Augustus (1883-1966)
Rowse, A. L. (1903-1997)

Schlesinger Jr., Arthur M. (1917—)
. **Ste. Croix, Geoffrey de** (1910-2000)
Tacitus (c. 55-c. 177)
Thucydides (c. 460—c. 400 B.C.E.)
Trevelyn, George (1876-1962)
Thomas, Keith (1933-)
van Loon, Hendrik Willem (1882—1944)
Villari, Pasquale (1826-1917)
Wells, H(erbert) G(eorge) (1866—1946)
White, Andrew D. (1832-1918)
Wilbur, Earl Morse (1866—1956)
Wright, Charles Conrad (1917-)

Humorists

Adams, Douglas (1952-)
Allen, Steve (1921—)
Cobb, Irvin S(hrewsbury) (1876—1944)
Wodehouse, P. G. (1881—1975)

Inventors

Bell, Alexander Graham (1847—1922)
Cooper, Peter (1791—1883)
Edison, Thomas Alva (1847—1931)
Maxim, Hiram Stevens (1840—1916)
Montgolfier, Joseph Michel (1740—1810)
Pullman, George (1831—1897)
Watt, James (1736—1819)

Journalists

Baker, Russell Wayne (1925—)
Chancellor, John (1927—1996)
Cockburn, Alexander (20th Century)
Dahlitz, Ray (1926—)
Dana, Charles Anderson (1819—1897)
Davis, Elmer (1890—1958)
Ellerbee, Linda (1944—)
Freneau, Philip (1752—1832)
Gaines, William M. (1922; deceased)
Gora (Goparaju Rama-chandra Rao) (1902—1975)
Haught, James (20th Century)
Herrick, James (20th Century)
Ivins, Molly (1944—)
Kaminer, Wendy (20th Century)
King, Larry (Larry Zeiger) (1933—)
Kinsley, Michael (1951—)
Lerner, Max(well) (Allen) (1902—1992)
Lippmann, Walter (1889—1974)
Mencken, Henry (Louis) (1880—1956)
Pozner, Vladimir (20th Century)
Reed, John (1887—1920)
Rooney, Andrew (Andy) (1919—)
Ross, Harold W. (1892-1951)
Savage, Dan (20th Century)
Stanosz, Barbara (20th Century)
Sullivan, Walter Seagar Jr. (1918—1996)
Sulzberger, Arthur Ochs Jr. (1951-)
Swope, Herbert Bayard (1882-1958)
Walker, Stanley (1898-1962)
White, William Allen (1868-1944)

Jurists and lawyers

Ahrens, Heinrich (1808—1874)
Barry, John Vincent William (1903—1969)
Castillo Rojas, Marco (20th Century)
Costikyan, Edward Nazar (1924—)
Darrow, Clarence (1857—1938)
Ingersoll, (Colonel) Robert G. (1833—1899)
Kawamura, Matasuke (20th Century)
Marshall, John (1755—1835)
Rao, Avula Sambasiva (20th Century)
Rood, Max (20th Century)
Samkalden, I. (20th Century)
Stout, Robert(1844-1930)
Taft, William Howard (1857—1930)
Tarkunde, V. M. (1912—)
Wright, Bruce (1918-)

Labor Union Organizers

Randolph, A. Philip (1889-1979)
Starr, David (1894-1995)

Lexicographers

Larousse, Pierre Athanase (1817—1875)
Read, Allen Walker (1906—)

Librarian

Williamson, Clarence Charles (1877—1965)

Linguist

Chomsky, Avram Noam (1928—)

Magicians

Jillette, Penn Fraser (1955—)
Randi, James (1928—)
Teller (20th Century)

Mathematicians

Bondi, Hermann (1919—)
Fourier, Jean Baptiste (1768—1830)
Hypatia of Alexandria (355?—415)
Jeans, James Hopwood (1887—1946)
Omar Khayyám (Born 18 May 1048)
Poincaré, Jules Henry (1854—1912)
Weil, André (1906-1988)

Musicians

Bartok, Bela (1881—1945);
Beethoven, Ludwig van (1770—1827);
Berlioz, Louis Hector (1803—1869);
Bizet, Georges (1838—1875)
Boulez, Pierre (1925—)
Boult, Adrian Cedric (1899—1983)
Brahms, Johannes (1833—1897
Britten, Benjamin (1913—1976)
Callen, Michael (1954—1993)
Currie, Justin (20th Century)
Debussy, Claude (1862—1918)
Diamond, David (1915—)
Gil, Gilberto (1942—)
Grieg, Edvard Hagerup (1843—1907)
Harrison, Lou (1917—)
Haydn, Franz Joseph (1732—1809)
Hill, Joe (1879—1915)
Joel, William Martin (Billy) (1929—)
Lehrer, Thomas Andrew (1928—)
Lennon, John (1940—1980)
Longfellow, Samuel (1819—1892)
Mahler, Gustav (1860—1911)
Manilow, Barry (1946)
Mascagni, Pietro (1863-1945)

Massenet, Jules Emile (1842—1912)
Menuhin, Yehudi (1916—)
Morrison, Jim (1943—1971)
Mozart, Wolfgang Amadeus (1756—1791)
Newman, Randy (1943—)
Ozawa, Seiji (1935-)
Paganini, Niccolo (1782-1840)
Partridge, Andy (20th Century)
Pierpont, James Lord (1822-1893)
Rampal, Jean-Pierre Louis (1922—)
The Residents (20th Century)
Rimsky-Korsakov, Nicolai (1844—1908)
Robeson, Paul (1898—1976)
Rorem, Ned (1923—)
Saint-Saëns, Camille (1835—1921)
Schumann, Robert Alexander (1810-1856)
Seeger, Pete (1919—)
Stewart, Al (20th Century)
Stipe, Michael (1960-)
Strauss, Richard (1864-1949)
Thomson, Virgil (1896—1989)
Tippett, Michael (Kemp) (1905—1998)
Verdi, Giuseppe (1813—1901)
Wagner, Richard (1813-1883)
Watts, Isaac (1674—1748)
Wood, Henry Joseph (1869-1944)
Zappa, Frank (1940—1993)

Naturalists

Burroughs, John (1827—1921)
Humboldt, Friedrich Heinrich (1769—1859)
Lamarck, Jean Baptiste (1744—1829)

Nobel Prize Winners

Angell, Norman (1872?—1967)
Arnoldson, Klas Pontus (1844—1916)
Arrhenius, Svante August (1859—1927)
Baulieu, Etienne (20th Century)
Beckett, Samuel (1906—1989)
Benaceraff, Baruj (1920—)
Bjørnson, Bjørnstjerne (1832—1910)
Boyd Orr, John Boyd Orr (1880—1971)
Boyer, Paul D. (20th Century)
Camus, Albert (1913—1960)
Carducci, Giosuè (1835—1907)
Crick, Francis Harry (1916—)
Curie, Marie (1867—1934)
De Duve, Christian René (1917—)
Faulkner, William (1897—1962)
Fischer, Edmond H. (1920—)
Fo, Dario (1926—)
Gell-Mann, Murray (1929—)
Hauptman, Herbert Aaron (1917—)
Hemingway, Ernest (1898—1961)
Kroto, Harold W. (1939—)
Lagerlof, Selma (1858-1940)
Lagerkvist, Pär Fabian (1891—1974)
Laveran, Charles (1845-1922)
Lehn, Jean-Marie (1939—)
Lewis, Sinclair (1885-1951)
Lwoff, André Michel (1902—1994)
Maeterlinck, Maurice (1862—1949)
Mahfouz, Naguid (1911-)
Mann, Thomas (1875—1955)
Molina, Mario (1943—)
Mommsen, Theodor (1817-1903)
Monod, Jacques (1910—1976)
Muller, Hermann Joseph (1890—1967)
Murad, Ferid (1936—)
Myrdal, Gunnar (1898—1987)
Nansen, Fridtjof (1861-1930)
O'Neill, Eugene (1888-1953)
Ossietzky, Carl von (1889-1938)
Pauling, Linus Paul (1901—1994)
Pavlov, Ivan Petrovich (1849—1936)
Paz, Octavio (1914—1998)
Pontoppidan, Henrik (1857-1929)
Quidde, Ludwig (1858-1929)
Richet, Charles (1850-1935)
Ross, Ronald (1857-1932)
Russell, Bertrand (1872—1970)
Sakharov, Andrei D. (1921—1989)
Saramago, José (1922-)
Schrödinger, Erwin (1887-1961)
Schweitzer, Albert (1875—1965)
Shaw, George Bernard (1856-1950)
Sherrington, Charles Scott (1857-1952)
Skou, Jens C. (1918—)
Smith, Michael (1932-)
Soyinka, Wole (1934—)
Steinbeck, John (1902—1968)
Steinberger, Jack (1921-)
Szilard, Leo (1898-1964)
Tagore, Rabindranath (1861-1941)
Watson, James Dewey (1928-)
Weinberg, Steven (1933—)

Paleontologists

Gould, Stephen Jay (1941—)
Halstead, Beverly (1933—1991)
Piero, Angela (1928—)

Patriot

Revere, Paul (1735—1818)

Pediatrician

Spock, Benjamin McLane (1903—1998)

Philanthropists

Baillie, George (1784—1873)
Carnegie, Andrew (1835—1919)
Cornell, Ezra (1807-1874)
Girard, Stephen (1750—1831)

Philosophers

Abbagnano, Nicola (1901—)
Adamson, Robert (1852—1902)
Adickes, Erich (1866—1928)
Adler, Felix (1851—1933)
Aenesidemus (1st Century B.C.E.)
Ames, Van Meter (Born 1898)
Ammonius (3rd Century)
Anaxagoras (c. 500—428 B.C.E.)
Anaximenes (c. 548 B.C.E.)
Arcesilaus (c. 315—241 B.C.E.)
Aristippus (c. 435 B.C.E.—360 B.C.E.)
Ayer, Alfred J. (1910—1989)
Bahrdt, Carl Friedrich (1741—1792)

Beauvoir, Simone de (1908—1986)
Bentham, Jeremy (1748—1832)
Bentley, Arthur F. (1870—1957)
Berlin, Isaiah (1909—1997)
Blanshard, Brand (1892—1987)
Blount, Henry (1602—1682)
Boas, George (1891—1980)
Brownell, Baker (1887—1965)
Bruno, Giordano (1548—1600)
Büchner, Friedrich Karl (1824—1899)
Bunge, Mario Augusto (1919—)
Burtt, Edwin Arthur (1892—1983)
Carnap, Rudolf (1891—1970)
Carneades (c. 213 —129 B.C.E.)
Cleanthes (c. 331—232 B.C.E.)
Clitomachus (Fl. 129 B.C.E.)
Cohen, Morris R. (1880—1947)
Comte, Auguste (1798—1857)
Condillac, Étienne Bonnot de (1715—1780)
Condorcet, Marie Jean (1743—1794)
Congreve, Richard (1818—1899)
Croce, Benedetto (1866—1952)
Danto, Arthur C(oleman) (1924—)
Democritus (c. 460— 370 B.C.E.)
Dennett, Daniel Clement (1942—)
Diogenes (412—323 B.C.E.?)
Dunham, Barrows (1905-1995)
Durant, Ariel (1898—1981)
Durant, Will (1885—1981)
Edman, Irwin (1896—1954)
Edwards, Paul (1923—)
Empedocles (c. 495— 435 B.C.E.)
Engels, Friedrich (1820—1895)
Epictetus (c. 50—138)
Epicurus (341—270 B.C.E.)
Euripides (c. 480-405 B.C.E.)
Feuerbach, Friedrich (1806—1880)
Fichte, Johann Gottlieb (1762—1814)
Flew, Antony (1923—)
Fourier, François Marie (1772—1837)
Franklin, Benjamin (1706—1790)
Gautama, Siddhartha (The Buddha) (c. 566—483 B. C. E)
Geiger, George Raymond (1903-1998)
Gora, Saraswati (1912—)
Grünbaum, Adolf (1923—)
Hartshorne, Charles (1897)
Hippo (5th Century B.C.E.)
Hobbes, Thomas (1588—1679)
Hook, Sidney (1902—1989)
Hume, David (1711—1776)
Jaspers, Karl (1883—1969)
Kallen, Horace (1892—1974)
Kaufmann, Walter (1918—1991)
Kongfu-zi [Confucius] [Kong Fuzi] (c. 571—479 B.C.E.)
La Mettrie, Julien Offray de (1709—1751)
Lamont, Corliss (1902—1995)
Lange, Friedrich Albert (1828—1875)
Lao-zi (Lao-tzu) (Born c. 604 B.C.E.)
Larrabee, Harold A. (1894—1979)
Lavanam, Hemalata (20th Century)
Lessing, Gotthold Ephraim (1729—1781)
Leucippus (5th Century B.C.E.)
Lovejoy, Arthur Oncken (1873—1962)
Lucretius (c. 96—c. 55 B.C.E.)
Madigan, Tim (1962-)
Marx, Karl (1818—1883)
Mead, George Herbert (1863—1931)
Meng-zi (Mencius; Meng Tzu) (371?—288? B.C.E.)
Mill, John Stuart (1806—1873)
Montesquieu, Charles Louis (1689—1755)
Nagel, Ernest (1901—1985)
Otto, Max (1876—1968)
Overstreet, Harry Allen (1875—1970)
Parmenides (500 B.C.E.)
Philodemus (1st Century B.C.E.)
Popper, Karl Raimund (1902—1994)
Posidonius (c. 125—51 B.C.E.)
Protagoras (c 481—411 B.C.E.)
Ptah-Hotep (2nd or 3rd Century B.C.E.?)
Pyrrho of Elis (c. 360 —c. 170 B.C.E.)
Quine, Willard Van Orman (1908—)
Randall Jr., John Herman (1899—1980)
Ratner, Joseph (1901?—1979)
Ratner, Sidney (1908—1996)
Reiser, Oliver L. (1895—1974)
Romanell, Patrick (1912—)
Rorty, Richard (1931—)
Rousseau, Jean Jacques (1712—1778)
Roy, M(anabendra) N(ath) (1887—1954)
Russell, Bertrand (1872—1970)
Ryan, Alan (1940—)
Santayana, George (1863—1952)
Sartre, Jean-Paul (1905—1980)
Schelling, Friedrich von (1775—1854)
Schneider, Herbert W. (1892—1984)
Schopenhauer, Arthur (1788—1860)
Schweitzer, Albert (1875—1965)
Searle, John R. (1932-)
Sellars, Roy Wood (1880—1973)
Singer, Peter (1946-)
Spencer, Herbert (1820—1903)
Spinoza, Baruch (1632—1677)
Thales (c. 636—c. 546 B.C.E.)
Wieman, Henry Nelson (1884-1975)
Wittgenstein, Ludwig (1889—1951)
Woodbridge, Frederick J. E. (1867-1940)
Xenophanes (c. 570 B.C.E.—c. 480 B.C.E.)
Zeno of Elea (c. 490—c. 430 B.C.E.)

Photographers, Photojournalists

Avedon, Richard (1923—)
Bachrach, Fabian (20th Century)
Bourke-White, Margaret (1904—1971)
Cartier-Bresson, Henri (1908—)
Salgadáo, Sebastiao (20th Century)

Physicians

Abano, Petrus de (1250—1320)
Allbutt, Thomas Clifford (1826—1925)
Darwin, Erasmus (1731—1802)
Godwin, William (1756—1836)
Hippocrates (c. 460—c. 370 B.C.E.)
Holmes, Oliver Wendell Sr. (1809—1894)
Kevorkian, Murad (Jack) (1928—)
LaMettrie, Julien (1709-1751)
Rhoads, Corneilius P. (20th Century)
Rush, Benjamin (1745—1813)
Salk, Jonas Edward (1914—1995)
Spock, Benjamin (1903-1998)
White, Paul Dudley (1856-1973)

Williams, Daniel Hale (1858-1931)
Williams, William Carlos (1883-1963)
Yearsley, Percival (1867-1951)

Physicists

Archelaos (5th Century B.C.E.)
Battelli, Angelo (Born 1862)
Compton, Arthur Holly (1892—1962)
Einstein, Albert (1879—1955)
Hawking, Stephen (1942—)
Infeld, Leopold (1898—1968)
Mach, Ernest von (1838-1916)
Planck, Max (1858—1947)
Sakharov, Andrei D. (1921—1989)

Physiologist

Hogben, Lancelot (1895-1975)

Playwrights

Aristophanes (c. 448—388 B.C.E.)
Beckett, Samuel (1906—1989)
Brecht, Bertold (1898—1956)
Brieux, Eugene (1858—1938)
Büchner, Georg (1813—1837)
Euripides (c. 480—405 B.C.E.)
Fierstein, Harvey (1954—)
Marlowe, Christopher (1564—1593)
Pinter, Harold (1930—)
Pirandello, Luigi (1867—1936)
Rostand, Edmond (1868—1918)
Rudnick, Paul (20th Century)
Shaw, George Bernard (1856—1950)
Stoppard, Tom (1937—)
Strindberg, Johan August (1849—1912)

Poets

Abu'l-ala-al-Ma'aari (Abu al-Ala al-Maarri) (973—1057)
Aiken, Conrad (1889—1973)
Allingham, William (1824—1889)
Appleman, Philip (1926—)
Asklepiades (Ancient Greece)
Bryant, William Cullen (1794—1878)
Burns, Robert (1759—1796)
Butler, Samuel (1612—1680)
Bynner, Witter (1881—1968)
Byron, George Gordon (1788—1824)
Ciardi, John (1916—1986)
Creeley, Robert (1926—)
Cummings, Edward Estlin (1894—1962)
Dickinson, Emily (1830—1886)
Epicharmus (Died c. 450 B.C.E.)
Ferlinghetti, Lawrence (1913—)
Holmes, John (Albert) (1904—1962)
Horace (65—8 B.C.E.)
Jeffers, Robinson (1887—1962)
Keats, John (1795—1821)
Lowell, Amy (1874—1925)
Lowell, Robert (1917—1977)
Lucilius, Gaius (c 180—102 B.C.E.?)
Markham, Edwin (1852—1940)
O'Hara, Frank (1926—1966)
Ovid (43 B.C.E.—18 C.E.)
Sarton, May (1912—1995)
Swenson, May (1917—1989)
Swinburne, Algernon Charles (1837—1909)
Tagore, Rabindranath (1861—1941)
Tennyson, Alfred Tennyson (1809-1892)
Williams, William Carlos (1883—1963)
Wordsworth, William (1770—1850)
Yevtushenko, Yevgeny (1933—)

Psychiatrists, psychoanalysts

Andhazi, Federico (1964—)
Asimov, Janet (20th Century)
Chisholm, Brock (1896—1971)
Freud, Sigmund (1856—1939)
Fromm, Erich (1900—1980)
Jones, Ernest (1879—1958)
Menninger, Karl A. (1893—1990)
Reich, Wilhelm (1897—1957)

Psychologists

Ardila, Ruben (1942—)
Ellis, Albert (1913—)
Skinner, B. F. (1904—1990)

Publishers

Flynt, Larry (20th Century)
Goldstein, Al (1935—)
Guccione, Robert (1930—)
Haldeman-Julius, Emanuel (1889—1951)
Hefner, Hugh M. (1926—)
Holyoake, Austin (1827—1874)
Hubbard, Elbert (1856—1915)
Saginian, Armen A. (20th Century)
Stuart, Carole (1941-)
Stuart, Lyle (1922-)
Watts, Charles (1836—1906)
Watts, Charles Albert (1858—1946)

Rapper

Anthony, Brenda (20th Century)

Red Cross Founder

Barton, Clara (1821—1912)

Reformers, Abolitionists, Women's Rights Crusaders

Baird, Bill (1932—)
Carlile, Richard (1790—1843)
Douglass, Frederick (1817—1895)
Garrison, William Lloyd (1805—1879)
Morgentaler, Henry (1923—)
Owen, Robert (1771—1858)
Nasrin, Taslima (1962-)
Phillips, Wendell (1811—1884)
Sanger, Margaret (1879—1966)
Shaw, Robert Gould (1837-1863)
Stanton, Elizabeth Cady (1815—1902)
Stowe, Emily Jennings (1831-1903)
Wollstonecraft, Mary (1759-1797)
Woolf, Leonard (1880-1969)
Wright, Elizur (1804-1885)
Wright, Frances (1795-1858)

Revolutionaries

Bakunin, Mikhail (1814—1876)
Bolívar, Simón (1783—1830)
Danton, Georges Jacques (1759—1794)
Lenin (1870—1924)

Marat, Jean Paul (1743—1793)
Paine, Thomas (1737—1809)
Roy, M. N. (1887-1954)

Satirists

Aretino, Pietro (1492—1556)
Aristophanes (448-388 B.C.E.)
Boileau-Despréaux, Nicolas (1636-1711)
Butler, Samuel (1835-1902)
Byron, George Gordon (1788-1824)
Clemens, Samuel (1835-1910)
Dickens, Charles (1812-1870)
Fielding, Henry (1707-1754)
Hogarth, William (1697-1764)
Holmes, Oliver Wendell (1841-1935)
Horace (65-8 B.C.E.)
Huxley, Aldous (1894-1963)
Lewis, Sinclair (1885-1951)
Lowell, James Russell (1819-1891)
Mencken, H. L. (1880-1956)
Petronius Arbiter, Gaius (c. 27—66)
Saint-Évremond, Charles (1613?-1703)
Shaw, George Bernard (1856-1950)
Thurber, James (1894-1961)
Voltaire, François-Marie Arouet de (1694-1778)

Scholars, Academicians

Allegro, John (1923—1988)
Amicis, Edmonde de (1846—1908)
Arago, Dominique François (1786—1853)
Crick, Bernard (1919—)
Pliny the Elder (c. 23—79 CE)
Porphyry (c. 242—c. 305)
Volney, Constantin (1757—1820)

Science Fiction Producers and Writers

Asimov, Isaac (1920—1992)
Bradbury, Ray (Douglas) (1920—)
Clarke, Arthur C. (1917—)
Ellison, Harlan Jay (1934)
Heinlein, Robert A. (1907—1988)
Roddenberry, Eugene Wesley (1921—1991)
Sohl, Jerry (20th Century)
Straczynski, J. Michael (20th Century)

Scientists

Aristarchus of Samothrace (c. 217—145 B.C.E.)
Ado-Dwanka, Niitse Akufo Awuku (20th Century)
Bronowski, Jacob (1908—1974)
Carlson, Anton J. (1875-1956)
Curie, Pierre (1859—1906)
Gay-Lussac, Joseph Louis (1778—1850)
Givishvili, Givi (20th Century)
Haldane, J. B. S. (1892—1964)
Lamarck, Jean (1744-1829)
Latimer, Lewis H. (1848-1928)
Laubeuf, Maxine (Born 1864)
Laveran, Charles (1845-1922)
Levi-Montalcini, Rita (1909-)
Newton, Isaac (1642—1727)
Pasteur, Louis (1822—1895)
Levi-Montalcini, Rita (1909-)
Sakharov, Andrei D. (1921—1989)
Steinmetz, Charles Proteus (1865—1923)
Szilard, Leo (1898—1964)
Wilmot, Ian (20th Century)

Sexologists

Kinsey, Alfred (1854—1956)
Pomeroy, Wardell Baxter (1913—)

Sociologists

Durkheim, Émile (1858—1917)
Tielman, Robert A. P. (1946—)

Soldiers and Seamen

Allen, Ethan (1738—1789)
Garibaldi, Guiseppe (1807—1882)
Lafayette, Marie Jean Paul (1757—1834)
Lawrence, Thomas Edward (1888—1935)
Lebed, Alexander Ivanovich (1950-)
Lee, Charles (1731—1782)
Perry, (Admiral) William J. (1927—)
Raleigh or **Ralegh, Walter** (1554?—1618)
Shaw, Robert Gould (1837—1863)
Sherman, William Tecumseh (1820—1891)

Statesmen, Stateswomen

Abd-er-Rahman III (891-961)
Adams, Charles Francis (1807—1886)
Adams, John (1735—1826)
Adams, John Quincy (1767—1848)
Alfonso X (1223—1284)
Allende Gossens, Salvador (1908—1973)
Aloni, Shulamit (20h Century)
Amberley, John Russell (1843—1876)
Amenhotep III (14th Century B.C.E.)
Aranda, Pedro Pablo (1718—1799)
Argenson, Marc (1696—1764)
Armellini, Carlo (1777—1863)
Arriaga. Manoel, José d' (1839—1917)
Avila Camacho, Manuel (20th Century)
Azaña Díaz, Manuel (1880—1940)
Baccelli, Guido (1832—1916)
Balmaceda, José (1840-1891)
Barrow, R(uth) Nita (1916—1995)
Benes, Eduard (1884—1948)
Bevan, Aneurin (1897—1960)
Bolivar, Simón (1783-1830)
Bonaparte, Napoléon (1822—1891)
Braga, Teófilo (Born 1843)
Brandt, Willy (1913—1992)
Briand, Aristide (1862—1932)
Burgers, Thomas Francis (1834-1881)
Burr, Aaron (1756—1836)
Caesar, (Caius) Julius (102?—44 B.C.E.)
Calhoun, John Caldwell (1782—1850)
Casimir-Périer, Jean Paul (1847—1907)
Castro, Fidel (1926—)
Catherine II (The Great) (1729—1796)
Chamberlain, Arthur Neville (1869—1940)
Clemenceau, Georges (1841—1929)
Cosic, Dobrica (20th Century)
Cranston, Alan (1914—)
Critias (c. 460—403 B.C.E.)
Deng Xiaoping (1904—1997)
Deschanel, Paul (Born 1856)
Diaz, Porfirio (1830—1915)

Djilas, Milovan (1911—1995)
Dubcek, Alexander A. (1921—1992)
Faure, François Felix (1841—1899)
Figueres Ferrer, José (1906—1990)
Fillmore, Millard (1800—1874)
Frederick II (1194—1250)
Frederick II (The Great) (1712—1786)
Gaitskell, Hugh Todd Naylor (1906—1963)
Gallatin, Albert (1761—1849)
Gambetta, Léon Michel (1838—1882)
Gorbachev, Mikhail S. (1931—)
Gore, Thomas Pryor (1870—1949)
Grévy, François Paul Jules (1813—1891)
Hadrian (76—138)
Hamlin, Hannibal (1809—1891)
Hancock, John (1737—1793)
Hayden, William (1933-)
Herriot, Édouard (1872—1957)
Ikhnaton (or Akhenaton) (Died c. 1354 B.C.E.)
Jefferson, Thomas (1743—1826)
Joseph II (1741—1790)
Jospin, Lionel (1937—)
Kinnock, Neil (1942—)
Kwasniewska, Aleksander (1954—)
La Follette, Robert (1855—1925)
Lamb, William (1779-1848)
Lamm, Richard (1935-)
Laski, Harold J. (1891—1950)
Lincoln, Abraham (1809—1865)
Madison, James (1751—1826)
Manfred [King of Sicily] (1232—1266)
Mao Zedong (1893—1976)
Marcus Aurelius (121—180)
Masaryk, Tomás Garrigue (1850—1937)
Millerand, Alexandre (1859—1943)
Mirabeau, Honoré Gabriel (1749—1791)
Molteno, John (1814-1886)
Moreley, John (1838-1923)
Morris, Gouverneur (1752-1816)
Obregón, Álvaro (1880-1928)
Nehru, Jawaharlal (1889—1964)
Pericles (c. 495—429 B.C.E.)
Pitt, William (1759—1806)
Pitt, William (1708—1778)
Plumer, William (1759-1850)
Poincaré, Raymond (1860—1934)
Ptolemy II (c. 308—246 B.C.E.)
Restrapo, Antonio José (1855-1933)
Rhodes, Cecil John (1853-1902)
Richardson, Eliot (1920-)
Rivadavia, Bernardino (1780-1845)
Robinson, Svend (20th Century)
Rush, Benjamin (1745-1813)
St. John, Henry (1678-1751)
Salmeron y Alonso, Nicolas (1838-1881)
Santa Maria, Domingo (1838-1881)
Sarmiento, Domingo (1811-1888)
Senghor, Léopold Sédar (1906—)
Sigismund, John (16th Century)
Sitting Bull (1831-1890)
Stalin, Joseph Vissarionovich (1879—1953)
Stanford, Leland (1824-1893)
Stevenson, Adlai Ewing (1900—1965)
Sumner, Charles (1811-1874)
Sun Yat-sen (1866—1925)
Tai-tsung (600—650)
Talleyrand-Périgard, Maurice de (1754—1838)
Veil, Simone (1927—)
Ventura, Jesse (1951—)
Victoria (1840-1901)
Walpole, Robert (1676—1745)
Washington, George (1732—1799)
Temple, William (1628-1699)
Thiers, Adolphe (1797-1897)
Washburn, Cadwallader (1815-1892)
Zanardell, Guiseppe (1826-1903)

Television Producer

Lear, Norman (1922—)

Undertaker

Antill, W. J. (19th Century)

Zoologists

Dawkins, Richard (1941—)
Mayr, Ernst (1904-)
Morris, Desmond (20th Century)

Special thanks

to the following six
who are still alive after my long undertaking (*)
. . . and in memory of the others

John S. Arents *

whose initial criticism of drafts of this work, when it was only a few hundred pages, has been invaluable.

Andrew de Masi

an ex-Catholic who was a Jesuit-trained father and who at the most difficult time of his life–while suffering the ravages of AIDS–helped considerably in the present editing. Andrew, a noted harpsichordist, had been a proud atheist since 1965. In September 1993 at the age of forty-six, he died of an extremely painful case of Kaposi's sarcoma and AIDS-connected lymphoma of the brain. At St. Vincent's Hospital in New York City, he spent his final days joyfully complaining about the Catholic pillows, the Catholic sheets, the Catholic food, the Catholic nurses, the Catholic priests who arrived daily to offer their sympathy, etc. Andrew was a great believer in empathy, and he had traveled from Catholicism to Nestorianism to Madalyn Murray O'Hair's atheism, reveling all the while in iconoclasm, hedonism, and sensualism.

Robert DePasquale *

who introduced me to J. M. Robertson's *Short History of Freethought* and advised me to beware of thieves in priestly robes.

James Duncan

who, to my high school class of thirteen in Minburn, Iowa (population 328), may have taught us nothing directly about philosophy, in which he had majored, nor the Ancient Greeks. But he taught me every sport in the decathlon and convinced me I was not Olympic material nor would I ever become the Chicago Cubs farm team player my father had been;

Paul Edwards *

who was unaware that Allen Windsor, the student #189922 auditing his survey of philosophy course at New School for Social Research in 1993, was the present author.

Charles Hartshorne

who, at the University of Chicago, helped me discern I would never become a metaphysician;

James F. Hornback *

for his memories about the Ethical Culture Society and the American Humanist Association;

Corliss Lamont

who gave me an "A" in his 1948 course on Naturalistic Humanism at Columbia University, although I was undeserving;

Tim Madigan *

one of the few secular humanists who volunteered suggestions for entries and, despite preparing for his Ph. D. examinations, literally read over a thousand pages of the present work in its draft stage;

Thomas Mann

who, in my very first request for information from noted individuals, responded with his ideas about humanism;

Augustus Reccord

who, when I was in the Army at Fort Knox, gave a sermon in Louisville, Kentucky, on "Good Men in Hell," convincing me I didn't want to end up in Heaven with all those fellow Methodists. No, he suggested, going to Hell with God's frozen (make that "unchosen") people, the Unitarians, would be much more stimulating. As a result, he helped lead me to the present work's conclusion. After surviving history's largest battle—the Normandy invasion during World War II when I led my company onto Omaha Beach—I wrote Dr. Reccord my regards "from an atheist in a foxhole."

Priscilla Robertson

who, combining history with philosophy with naturalism with love, was a major influence upon my thinking. Unlike many of the academic philosophers, Priscilla found naturalistic humanism in music or poetry or drama or painting or sculpture as well as in aesthetics or logic or metaphysics or ethics or epistemology or her children. The first intellectual to spent hours with me, she was a loving human being above all.

Gordon Stein

who suggested the importance of McCabe, Putnam, J. M. Robertson, and Underwood, and whose *Encyclopedia of Unbelief* has been a reference source although one in need of further development;

Paul Tillich

who allowed me to audit his course at Union Theological Seminary and helped me confirm that I was no theist, no existentialist, and no theologian;

Lionel Trilling

who, as my advisor at Columbia University, allowed me to research the word "humanism"; and who, when I found seven humanisms, jocularly observed, "Your seven categories have led me to understand that I must never use the word humanism again!"

Fernando Vargas

who distracted me needfully;

Fred Whitehead *

for his scholarly notes, which were an important part of the present study.

• • •

And particularly, thanks to the dozens of busy individuals noted herein who took the time to respond to my persistent letters.

To the Reader

• In this first edition, appropriate individuals have likely been omitted, for which apologies are hereby extended.

• Or some have been included who should not have been, in which case apologies are also hereby extended and corrections will be made if so requested . . . particularly if the individuals aspire to Heaven and *absolutely* do not want their record on Earth to be misunderstood by the mythical St. Peter & Co.

• Or birth and death dates have not been included. Or other pertinent material is not given.

• Readers are kindly solicited to forward suggestions, *with documentation*, of corrections and/or additions for inclusion or exclusion in a future edition. Send to Warren Allen Smith, c/o Barricade Books, 150 Fifth Avenue, New York, New York 10011, United States of America.